2019
Harris
Pennsylvania
Industrial Directory

MERGENT
Exclusive Provider of
Dun & Bradstreet Library Solutions

dun & bradstreet

HOOVERS™

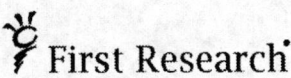
First Research·

HARRIS
INFOSOURCE™

Published June 2019 next update June 2020

Publisher

Mergent Inc.
444 Madison Ave
New York, NY 10022

©Mergent Inc All Rights Reserved
2019 Mergent Business Press
ISSN 1080-2614
ISBN 978-1-64141-226-1

TABLE OF CONTENTS

SUMMARY OF CONTENTS

Number of Companies.. 20,838

Number of Decision Makers................................... 41,444

Minimum Number of Employees 3

EXPLANATORY NOTES

How to Cross-Reference in This Directory

Sequential Entry Numbers. Each establishment in the Geographic Section is numbered sequentially (G-0000). The number assigned to each establishment is referred to as its "entry number." To make cross-referencing easier, each listing in the Geographic, SIC, Alphabetic and Product Sections includes the establishment's entry number. To facilitate locating an entry in the Geographic Section, the entry numbers for the first listing on the left page and the last listing on the right page are printed at the top of the page next to the city name.

Analysis

Every effort has been made to contact all firms to verify their information. The one exception to this rule is the annual sales figure, which is considered by many companies to be confidential information. Therefore, estimated sales have been calculated by multiplying the nationwide average sales per employee for the firm's major SIC/NAICS code by the firm's number of employees. Nationwide averages for sales per employee by SIC/NAICS codes are provided by the U.S. Department of Commerce and are updated annually. All sales—sales (est)—have been estimated by this method. The exceptions are parent companies (PA), division headquarters (DH) and headquarter locations (HQ) which may include an actual corporate sales figure—sales (corporate-wide) if available.

Types of Companies

Descriptive and statistical data are included for companies in the entire state. These comprise manufacturers, machine shops, fabricators, assemblers and printers. Also identified are corporate offices in the state.

Employment Data

The employment figure shown in the Geographic Section includes male and female employees and embraces all levels of the company: administrative, clerical, sales and maintenance. This figure is for the facility listed and does not include other plants or offices. It should be recognized that these figures represent an approximate year-round average. These employment figures are broken into codes A through G and used in the Product and SIC Sections to further help you in qualifying a company. Be sure to check the footnotes on the bottom of pages for the code breakdowns.

Standard Industrial Classification (SIC)

The Standard Industrial Classification (SIC) system used in this directory was developed by the federal government for use in classifying establishments by the type of activity they are engaged in. The SIC classifications used in this directory are from the 1987 edition published by the U.S. Government's Office of Management and Budget. The SIC system separates all activities into broad industrial divisions (e.g., manufacturing, mining, retail trade). It further subdivides each division. The range of manufacturing industry classes extends from two-digit codes (major industry group) to four-digit codes (product).

For example:

Industry Breakdown	Code	Industry, Product, etc.
*Major industry group	20	Food and kindred products
Industry group	203	Canned and frozen foods
*Industry	2033	Fruits and vegetables, etc.

*Classifications used in this directory

Only two-digit and four-digit codes are used in this directory.

Arrangement

1. The **Geographic Section** contains complete in-depth corporate data. This section is sorted by cities listed in alphabetical order and companies listed alphabetically within each city. A County/City Index for referencing cities within counties precedes this section.

IMPORTANT NOTICE: It is a violation of both federal and state law to transmit an unsolicited advertisement to a facsimile machine. Any user of this product that violates such laws may be subject to civil and criminal penalties, which may exceed $500 for each transmission of an unsolicited facsimile. Mergent Inc. provides fax numbers for lawful purposes only and expressly forbids the use of these numbers in any unlawful manner.

2. The **Standard Industrial Classification (SIC) Section** lists companies under approximately 500 four-digit SIC codes. An alphabetical and a numerical index precedes this section. A company can be listed under several codes. The codes are in numerical order with companies listed alphabetically under each code.

3. The **Alphabetic Section** lists all companies with their full physical or mailing addresses and telephone number.

4. The **Product Section** lists companies under unique Harris categories. An index preceding this section lists all product categories in alphabetical order. Companies can be listed under several categories.

USER'S GUIDE TO LISTINGS

GEOGRAPHIC SECTION

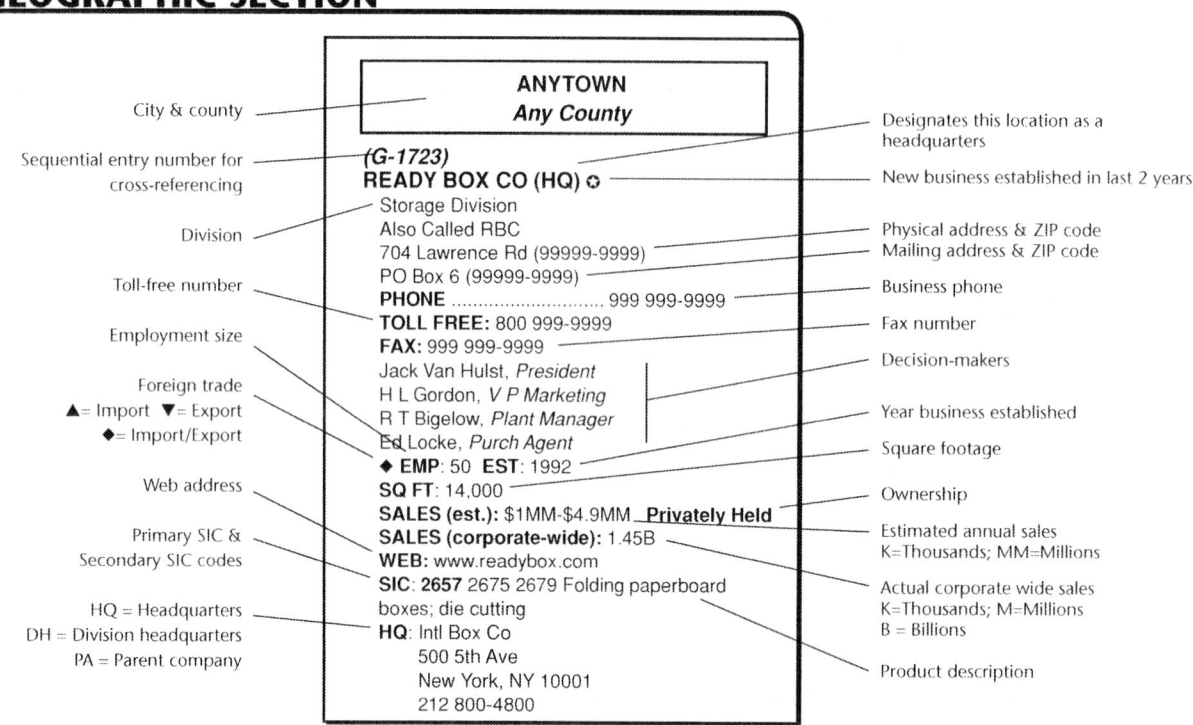

City & county

Sequential entry number for cross-referencing

Division

Toll-free number

Employment size

Foreign trade
▲= Import ▼= Export
◆= Import/Export

Web address

Primary SIC & Secondary SIC codes

HQ = Headquarters
DH = Division headquarters
PA = Parent company

ANYTOWN
Any County

(G-1723)
READY BOX CO (HQ) ✿
Storage Division
Also Called RBC
704 Lawrence Rd (99999-9999)
PO Box 6 (99999-9999)
PHONE 999 999-9999
TOLL FREE: 800 999-9999
FAX: 999 999-9999
Jack Van Hulst, *President*
H L Gordon, *V P Marketing*
R T Bigelow, *Plant Manager*
Ed Locke, *Purch Agent*
◆ **EMP**: 50 **EST**: 1992
SQ FT: 14,000
SALES (est.): $1MM-$4.9MM **Privately Held**
SALES (corporate-wide): 1.45B
WEB: www.readybox.com
SIC: **2657** 2675 2679 Folding paperboard
boxes; die cutting
HQ: Intl Box Co
500 5th Ave
New York, NY 10001
212 800-4800

Designates this location as a headquarters

New business established in last 2 years

Physical address & ZIP code
Mailing address & ZIP code

Business phone

Fax number

Decision-makers

Year business established

Square footage

Ownership

Estimated annual sales
K=Thousands; MM=Millions

Actual corporate wide sales
K=Thousands; M=Millions
B = Billions

Product description

SIC SECTION

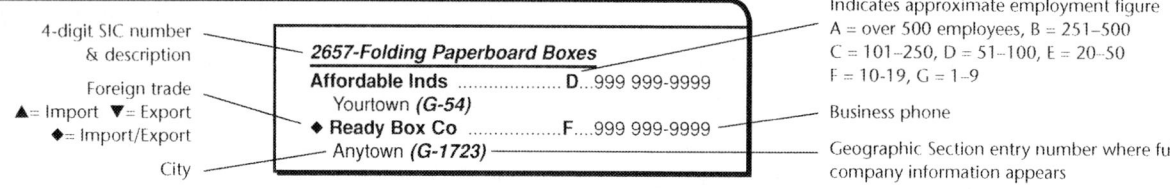

4-digit SIC number & description

Foreign trade
▲= Import ▼= Export
◆= Import/Export

City

2657-Folding Paperboard Boxes
Affordable Inds .... D...999 999-9999
Yourtown *(G-54)*
◆ **Ready Box Co** .... F....999 999-9999
Anytown *(G-1723)*

Indicates approximate employment figure
A = over 500 employees, B = 251–500
C = 101–250, D = 51–100, E = 20–50
F = 10-19, G = 1–9

Business phone

Geographic Section entry number where full company information appears

ALPHABETIC SECTION

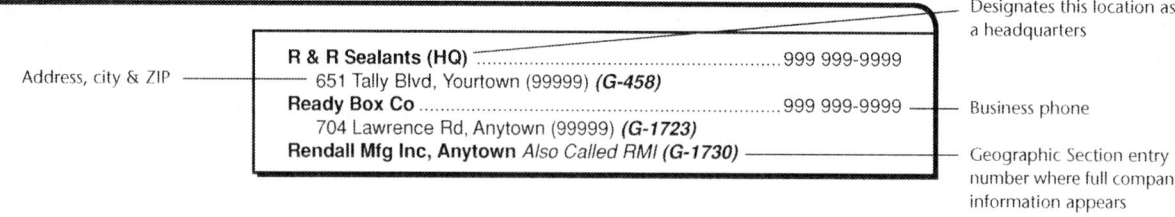

Address, city & ZIP

R & R Sealants (HQ) 999 999-9999
651 Tally Blvd, Yourtown (99999) *(G-458)*
Ready Box Co 999 999-9999
704 Lawrence Rd, Anytown (99999) *(G-1723)*
Rendall Mfg Inc, Anytown *Also Called RMI (G-1730)*

Designates this location as a headquarters

Business phone

Geographic Section entry number where full company information appears

PRODUCT SECTION

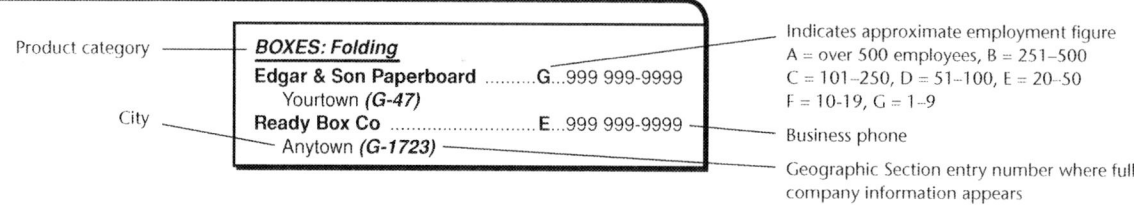

Product category

City

BOXES: Folding
Edgar & Son Paperboard ....G...999 999-9999
Yourtown *(G-47)*
Ready Box Co ....E...999 999-9999
Anytown *(G-1723)*

Indicates approximate employment figure
A = over 500 employees, B = 251–500
C = 101–250, D = 51–100, E = 20–50
F = 10-19, G = 1–9

Business phone

Geographic Section entry number where full company information appears

GEOGRAPHIC SECTION

Companies sorted by city in alphabetical order

In-depth company data listed

STANDARD INDUSTRIAL CLASSIFICATIONS

Alphabetical index of classifcation descriptions

Numerical index of classifcation descriptions

Companies sorted by SIC product groupings

ALPHABETIC SECTION

Company listings in alphabetical order

PRODUCT INDEX

Product categories listed in alphabetical order

PRODUCT SECTION

Companies sorted by product and manufacturing service classifications

GEOGRAPHIC

SIC

ALPHABETIC

PRDT INDEX

PRODUCT

Pennsylvania
County Map

COUNTY/CITY CROSS-REFERENCE INDEX

Adams

	ENTRY #
Abbottstown	(G-3)
Aspers	(G-741)
Bendersville	(G-1138)
Biglerville	(G-1661)
East Berlin	(G-4519)
Fairfield	(G-5765)
Gardners	(G-6259)
Gettysburg	(G-6281)
Littlestown	(G-10062)
Mc Sherrystown	(G-10649)
New Oxford	(G-12401)
Orrtanna	(G-13036)
Peach Glen	(G-13205)
York Springs	(G-20763)

Allegheny

	ENTRY #
Allison Park	(G-445)
Aspinwall	(G-746)
Bethel Park	(G-1399)
Blawnox	(G-1762)
Brackenridge	(G-1936)
Braddock	(G-1942)
Bradfordwoods	(G-1998)
Bridgeville	(G-2049)
Buena Vista	(G-2340)
Bunola	(G-2343)
Carnegie	(G-2763)
Cheswick	(G-3100)
Clairton	(G-3146)
Coraopolis	(G-3651)
Creighton	(G-3879)
Crescent	(G-3886)
Cuddy	(G-3940)
Dravosburg	(G-4350)
Duquesne	(G-4494)
East Liberty	(G-4579)
East Mc Keesport	(G-4582)
East Pittsburgh	(G-4594)
Elizabeth	(G-4855)
Gibsonia	(G-6323)
Glassport	(G-6410)
Glenshaw	(G-6477)
Glenwillard	(G-6546)
Greenock	(G-6644)
Harwick	(G-7257)
Hazelwood	(G-7446)
Homestead	(G-7683)
Imperial	(G-8056)
Indianola	(G-8135)
Jefferson Hills	(G-8273)
Leetsdale	(G-9676)
Library	(G-9953)
Mc Kees Rocks	(G-10596)
Mc Keesport	(G-10642)
Mckees Rocks	(G-10660)
McKeesport	(G-10662)
McKnight	(G-10688)
Millvale	(G-11223)
Monroeville	(G-11322)
Moon Township	(G-11480)
Morgan	(G-11517)
Munhall	(G-11844)
Natrona Heights	(G-11933)
North Versailles	(G-12771)
Oakdale	(G-12887)
Oakmont	(G-12913)
Pittsburgh	(G-14623)
Presto	(G-16104)
Rankin	(G-16305)
Russellton	(G-16883)
Sewickley	(G-17383)
Sharpsburg	(G-17467)
South Park	(G-17781)
Springdale	(G-17897)
Swissvale	(G-18191)
Tarentum	(G-18238)
Turtle Creek	(G-18558)
Verona	(G-18745)
Wall	(G-18779)
Warrendale	(G-19067)
West Elizabeth	(G-19692)
West Homestead	(G-19719)
West Mifflin	(G-19734)
West View	(G-19773)
Wexford	(G-19786)
White Oak	(G-19853)
Wilkinsburg	(G-19981)
Wilmerding	(G-20158)

Armstrong

	ENTRY #
Adrian	(G-29)
Cowansville	(G-3795)
Dayton	(G-4034)
Ford City	(G-6041)
Freeport	(G-6199)
Kittanning	(G-8753)
Leechburg	(G-9641)
North Apollo	(G-12726)
Parker	(G-13165)
Rural Valley	(G-16876)
Schenley	(G-17136)
Seminole	(G-17363)
Spring Church	(G-17854)
Worthington	(G-20226)
Yatesboro	(G-20348)

Beaver

	ENTRY #
Aliquippa	(G-65)
Ambridge	(G-605)
Baden	(G-869)
Beaver	(G-977)
Beaver Falls	(G-996)
Clinton	(G-3261)
Conway	(G-3619)
Darlington	(G-4025)
Fombell	(G-6029)
Freedom	(G-6189)
Georgetown	(G-6274)
Hookstown	(G-7769)
Industry	(G-8136)
Koppel	(G-8813)
Midland	(G-11087)
Monaca	(G-11279)
New Brighton	(G-12031)
New Galilee	(G-12220)
Rochester	(G-16781)
Shippingport	(G-17567)
West Bridgewater	(G-19491)

Bedford

	ENTRY #
Alum Bank	(G-559)
Bedford	(G-1039)
Breezewood	(G-2003)
Clearville	(G-3238)
Everett	(G-5566)
Hyndman	(G-8048)
Imler	(G-8054)
Manns Choice	(G-10408)
New Enterprise	(G-12194)
Saxton	(G-17099)
Schellsburg	(G-17132)

Berks

	ENTRY #
Bally	(G-898)
Barto	(G-941)
Bechtelsville	(G-1030)
Bernville	(G-1295)
Bethel	(G-1392)
Birdsboro	(G-1686)
Blandon	(G-1752)
Boyertown	(G-1892)
Centerport	(G-2832)
Dauberville	(G-4032)
Douglassville	(G-4166)
Fleetwood	(G-5967)
Hamburg	(G-6837)
Hereford	(G-7568)
Kempton	(G-8489)
Kutztown	(G-8836)
Leesport	(G-9657)
Lenhartsville	(G-9756)
Limekiln	(G-9968)
Mertztown	(G-11000)
Mohnton	(G-11260)
Mohrsville	(G-11273)
Morgantown	(G-11518)
Mount Aetna	(G-11605)
New Berlinville	(G-12024)
Oley	(G-12978)
Pine Forge	(G-14587)
Reading	(G-16307)
Reading Station	(G-16573)
Robesonia	(G-16772)
Shillington	(G-17503)
Shoemakersville	(G-17570)
Strausstown	(G-18099)
Temple	(G-18326)
Topton	(G-18409)
Virginville	(G-18770)
Wernersville	(G-19483)
West Reading	(G-19764)
Womelsdorf	(G-20205)
Wyomissing	(G-20286)

Blair

	ENTRY #
Altoona	(G-468)
Bellwood	(G-1137)
Claysburg	(G-3201)
Curryville	(G-3945)
Duncansville	(G-4449)
East Freedom	(G-4559)
Hollidaysburg	(G-7642)
Martinsburg	(G-10518)
Roaring Spring	(G-16761)
Tipton	(G-18374)
Tyrone	(G-18575)
Williamsburg	(G-19982)

Bradford

	ENTRY #
Athens	(G-810)
Canton	(G-2662)
Gillett	(G-6380)
Le Raysville	(G-9543)
Milan	(G-11146)
Monroeton	(G-11320)
New Albany	(G-12012)
Rome	(G-16796)
Sayre	(G-17109)
Stevensville	(G-18059)
Towanda	(G-18421)
Troy	(G-18517)
Ulster	(G-18597)
Wyalusing	(G-20245)
Wysox	(G-20290)

Bucks

	ENTRY #
Bedminster	(G-1080)
Bensalem	(G-1140)
Blooming Glen	(G-1765)
Bristol	(G-2102)
Buckingham	(G-2338)
Chalfont	(G-2862)
Croydon	(G-3909)
Danboro	(G-3991)
Doylestown	(G-4266)
Dublin	(G-4430)
Durham	(G-4502)
Erwinna	(G-5538)
Fairless Hills	(G-5771)
Feasterville Trevose	(G-5880)
Ferndale	(G-5950)
Furlong	(G-6231)
Holicong	(G-7638)
Holland	(G-7639)
Ivyland	(G-8205)
Jamison	(G-8242)
Kintnersville	(G-8727)
Lahaska	(G-8885)
Langhorne	(G-9271)
Levittown	(G-9810)
Line Lexington	(G-9976)
Mechanicsville	(G-10911)
Morrisville	(G-11550)
New Britain	(G-12045)
New Hope	(G-12297)
Newtown	(G-12493)
Ottsville	(G-13058)
Penndel	(G-13238)
Penns Park	(G-13243)
Perkasie	(G-13265)
Pipersville	(G-14610)
Plumsteadville	(G-15806)
Point Pleasant	(G-15887)
Quakertown	(G-16167)
Revere	(G-16653)
Richboro	(G-16672)
Richlandtown	(G-16690)
Riegelsville	(G-16743)
Rushland	(G-16879)
Sellersville	(G-17339)
Silverdale	(G-17591)
Southampton	(G-17795)
Springtown	(G-17926)
Trevose	(G-18485)
Trumbauersville	(G-18529)
Upper Black Eddy	(G-18655)
Warminster	(G-18814)
Warrington	(G-19104)
Washington Crossing	(G-19252)
Wycombe	(G-20260)
Yardley	(G-20292)

Butler

	ENTRY #
Boyers	(G-1889)
Bruin	(G-2314)
Butler	(G-2370)
Cabot	(G-2452)
Callery	(G-2466)
Chicora	(G-3125)
Connoquenessing	(G-3513)
Cranberry Township	(G-3798)
East Butler	(G-4530)
Evans City	(G-5555)
Fenelton	(G-5944)
Harmony	(G-7066)
Harrisville	(G-7252)
Karns City	(G-8480)
Lyndora	(G-10136)
Mars	(G-10485)
Petrolia	(G-13305)
Portersville	(G-15923)
Prospect	(G-16111)
Renfrew	(G-16638)
Sarver	(G-17064)
Saxonburg	(G-17081)
Seven Fields	(G-17374)
Slippery Rock	(G-17617)
Valencia	(G-18697)
West Sunbury	(G-19769)
Zelienople	(G-20787)

Cambria

	ENTRY #
Barnesboro	(G-937)
Carrolltown	(G-2807)
Colver	(G-3453)
Cresson	(G-3897)
Ebensburg	(G-4778)
Elton	(G-4960)
Fallentimber	(G-5851)
Flinton	(G-5983)
Gallitzin	(G-6245)
Hastings	(G-7260)
Johnstown	(G-8349)
Loretto	(G-10102)
Mineral Point	(G-11252)
Nanty Glo	(G-11905)
Nicktown	(G-12618)
Northern Cambria	(G-12863)
Patton	(G-13187)
Portage	(G-15917)
Saint Benedict	(G-16936)
Saint Michael	(G-17032)
Salix	(G-17047)
South Fork	(G-17772)
Summerhill	(G-18154)
Twin Rocks	(G-18572)
Vintondale	(G-18769)

Cameron

	ENTRY #
Driftwood	(G-4377)
Emporium	(G-5048)

Carbon

	ENTRY #
Albrightsville	(G-48)

	ENTRY#
Beaver Meadows	(G-1017)
Jim Thorpe	(G-8337)
Lansford	(G-9447)
Lehighton	(G-9708)
Nesquehoning	(G-12003)
Palmerton	(G-13099)
Parryville	(G-13186)
Summit Hill	(G-18159)
Weatherly	(G-19453)
Weissport	(G-19461)

Centre
Aaronsburg	(G-1)
Bellefonte	(G-1091)
Blanchard	(G-1750)
Boalsburg	(G-1863)
Centre Hall	(G-2840)
Clarence	(G-3161)
Coburn	(G-3333)
Howard	(G-7885)
Julian	(G-8455)
Milesburg	(G-11151)
Millheim	(G-11217)
Mingoville	(G-11256)
Moshannon	(G-11604)
Pennsylvania Furnace (G-13263)	
Philipsburg	(G-14507)
Pleasant Gap	(G-15791)
Port Matilda	(G-15901)
Rebersburg	(G-16577)
Snow Shoe	(G-17669)
Spring Mills	(G-17884)
State College	(G-17939)
University Park	(G-18651)

Chester
Atglen	(G-799)
Avondale	(G-848)
Berwyn	(G-1351)
Brandamore	(G-2001)
Chester Springs	(G-3070)
Coatesville	(G-3284)
Cochranville	(G-3354)
Devault	(G-4110)
Devon	(G-4113)
Downingtown	(G-4208)
Elverson	(G-4961)
Exton	(G-5633)
Glenmoore	(G-6463)
Honey Brook	(G-7734)
Kelton	(G-8488)
Kennett Square	(G-8500)
Kimberton	(G-8573)
Landenberg	(G-9246)
Lincoln University	(G-9973)
Malvern	(G-10176)
Modena	(G-11258)
Nottingham	(G-12881)
Oxford	(G-13070)
Paoli	(G-13134)
Parker Ford	(G-13168)
Parkesburg	(G-13171)
Phoenixville	(G-14527)
Pomeroy	(G-15890)
Pottstown	(G-15941)
Sadsburyville	(G-16904)
Saint Peters	(G-17033)
Spring City	(G-17856)
Thorndale	(G-18353)
Toughkenamon	(G-18417)

	ENTRY#
Unionville	(G-18647)
Valley Forge	(G-18707)
West Chester	(G-19492)
West Grove	(G-19698)
Worcester	(G-20222)

Clarion
Callensburg	(G-2465)
Clarion	(G-3172)
East Brady	(G-4527)
Fairmount City	(G-5808)
Foxburg	(G-6101)
Hawthorn	(G-7443)
Knox	(G-8809)
Leeper	(G-9655)
Marble	(G-10433)
Mayport	(G-10546)
New Bethlehem	(G-12025)
Rimersburg	(G-16749)
Shippenville	(G-17556)
Sligo	(G-17615)
Strattanville	(G-18097)
Tylersburg	(G-18573)

Clearfield
Bigler	(G-1658)
Burnside	(G-2363)
Clearfield	(G-3210)
Coalport	(G-3283)
Curwensville	(G-3946)
Drifting	(G-4374)
Du Bois	(G-4385)
Frenchville	(G-6217)
Glen Hope	(G-6426)
Grampian	(G-6571)
Grassflat	(G-6577)
Houtzdale	(G-7883)
Hyde	(G-8047)
Karthaus	(G-8483)
Kylertown	(G-8865)
Lanse	(G-9446)
Luthersburg	(G-10120)
Madera	(G-10162)
Mahaffey	(G-10170)
Morrisdale	(G-11547)
Olanta	(G-12960)
Osceola Mills	(G-13055)
Penfield	(G-13221)
West Decatur	(G-19687)
Woodland	(G-20211)

Clinton
Avis	(G-838)
Beech Creek	(G-1081)
Castanea	(G-2811)
Lock Haven	(G-10081)
Loganton	(G-10094)
Mackeyville	(G-10137)
Mc Elhattan	(G-10585)
Mill Hall	(G-11170)
North Bend	(G-12727)
Renovo	(G-16649)
Salona	(G-17049)
Woolrich	(G-20220)

Columbia
Benton	(G-1277)
Berwick	(G-1307)
Bloomsburg	(G-1766)
Catawissa	(G-2818)
Mifflinville	(G-11145)
Millville	(G-11224)

	ENTRY#
Orangeville	(G-13005)
Stillwater	(G-18062)

Crawford
Adamsville	(G-25)
Atlantic	(G-814)
Cambridge Springs	(G-2473)
Centerville	(G-2833)
Cochranton	(G-3334)
Conneaut Lake	(G-3470)
Conneautville	(G-3483)
Guys Mills	(G-6808)
Harmonsburg	(G-7064)
Linesville	(G-9978)
Meadville	(G-10693)
Saegertown	(G-16907)
Spartansburg	(G-17847)
Springboro	(G-17894)
Titusville	(G-18375)
Townville	(G-18444)
Venango	(G-18740)

Cumberland
Boiling Springs	(G-1872)
Camp Hill	(G-2485)
Carlisle	(G-2688)
Enola	(G-5080)
Lemoyne	(G-9740)
Mechanicsburg	(G-10815)
Mount Holly Springs	(G-11631)
New Cumberland	(G-12180)
New Kingstown	(G-12394)
Newburg	(G-12474)
Newville	(G-12600)
Shippensburg	(G-17515)
Shiremanstown	(G-17568)
Walnut Bottom	(G-18788)

Dauphin
Elizabethville	(G-4892)
Grantville	(G-6574)
Gratz	(G-6578)
Halifax	(G-6824)
Harrisburg	(G-7077)
Hershey	(G-7603)
Highspire	(G-7632)
Hummelstown	(G-7901)
Lykens	(G-10129)
Middletown	(G-11047)
Millersburg	(G-11186)
Pillow	(G-14586)
Steelton	(G-18044)
Wiconisco	(G-19895)
Williamstown	(G-20103)

Delaware
Aldan	(G-59)
Aston	(G-747)
Boothwyn	(G-1875)
Brookhaven	(G-2241)
Broomall	(G-2277)
Bryn Mawr	(G-2315)
Chadds Ford	(G-2847)
Chester	(G-3037)
Chester Township	(G-3088)
Chesterbrook	(G-3089)
Clifton Heights	(G-3250)
Collingdale	(G-3402)
Concordville	(G-3456)
Crum Lynne	(G-3935)
Darby	(G-4017)
Drexel Hill	(G-4360)

	ENTRY#
Eddystone	(G-4798)
Edgemont	(G-4807)
Essington	(G-5541)
Folcroft	(G-5998)
Folsom	(G-6022)
Garnet Valley	(G-6264)
Glen Mills	(G-6428)
Glenolden	(G-6471)
Havertown	(G-7416)
Holmes	(G-7661)
Lansdowne	(G-9429)
Lenni	(G-9761)
Linwood	(G-9989)
Lower Merion	(G-10109)
Marcus Hook	(G-10437)
Media	(G-10913)
Morton	(G-11589)
Newtown Square	(G-12565)
Norwood	(G-12880)
Philadelphia	(G-13313)
Primos	(G-16106)
Prospect Park	(G-16114)
Radnor	(G-16285)
Ridley Park	(G-16733)
Rose Valley	(G-16818)
Secane	(G-17316)
Sharon Hill	(G-17452)
Springfield	(G-17906)
Swarthmore	(G-18185)
Thornton	(G-18355)
Trainer	(G-18462)
Upper Chichester	(G-18656)
Upper Darby	(G-18677)
Villanova	(G-18765)
Wallingford	(G-18780)
Wayne	(G-19290)
Woodlyn	(G-20216)
Yeadon	(G-20350)

Elk
Brockport	(G-2220)
Johnsonburg	(G-8343)
Kersey	(G-8553)
Ridgway	(G-16691)
Saint Marys	(G-16943)
Weedville	(G-19458)
Wilcox	(G-19897)

Erie
Albion	(G-40)
Corry	(G-3741)
Cranesville	(G-3867)
East Springfield	(G-4599)
Edinboro	(G-4808)
Erie	(G-5161)
Fairview	(G-5809)
Girard	(G-6383)
Harborcreek	(G-7008)
Lake City	(G-8897)
Mc Kean	(G-10591)
North East	(G-12729)
Union City	(G-18605)
Waterford	(G-19259)
Wattsburg	(G-19282)
West Springfield	(G-19766)

Fayette
Allison	(G-444)
Belle Vernon	(G-1085)
Brier Hill	(G-2101)
Brownsville	(G-2310)
Chalk Hill	(G-2895)

	ENTRY#
Connellsville	(G-3489)
Dawson	(G-4033)
Dunbar	(G-4439)
East Millsboro	(G-4583)
Everson	(G-5580)
Fairbank	(G-5764)
Farmington	(G-5860)
Fayette City	(G-5875)
Grindstone	(G-6779)
Hopwood	(G-7776)
Lemont Furnace	(G-9732)
Markleysburg	(G-10479)
Masontown	(G-10535)
Mc Clellandtown	(G-10555)
Mill Run	(G-11185)
Mount Braddock	(G-11616)
New Salem	(G-12445)
Normalville	(G-12623)
Ohiopyle	(G-12939)
Perryopolis	(G-13303)
Point Marion	(G-15886)
Republic	(G-16652)
Rostraver Township	(G-16825)
Smithfield	(G-17641)
Smock	(G-17665)
Star Junction	(G-17938)
Uniontown	(G-18614)
Vanderbilt	(G-18719)
Waltersburg	(G-18795)
White	(G-19844)

Forest
Cooksburg	(G-3620)
Endeavor	(G-5078)
Marienville	(G-10457)
Tionesta	(G-18369)

Franklin
Amberson	(G-565)
Blue Ridge Summit	(G-1859)
Chambersburg	(G-2896)
Doylesburg	(G-4265)
Dry Run	(G-4384)
Fannettsburg	(G-5857)
Fayetteville	(G-5876)
Fort Loudon	(G-6057)
Greencastle	(G-6595)
Lemasters	(G-9731)
Marion	(G-10470)
Mercersburg	(G-10981)
Mont Alto	(G-11365)
Orrstown	(G-13032)
Roxbury	(G-16838)
Saint Thomas	(G-17036)
Scotland	(G-17182)
Shady Grove	(G-17420)
Waynesboro	(G-19393)
Zullinger	(G-20838)

Fulton
Crystal Spring	(G-3938)
Mc Connellsburg	(G-10562)
Needmore	(G-11996)
Warfordsburg	(G-18810)

Greene
Aleppo	(G-61)
Brave	(G-2002)
Carmichaels	(G-2754)
Dilliner	(G-4125)
Greensboro	(G-6646)
Holbrook	(G-7637)

	ENTRY #		ENTRY #		ENTRY #		ENTRY #		ENTRY #
Jefferson	(G-8269)	**Lackawanna**		Mount Joy	(G-11644)	Zionsville	(G-20835)	Rew	(G-16654)
Mount Morris	(G-11677)	Archbald	(G-686)	Mountville	(G-11789)	**Luzerne**		Rixford	(G-16759)
New Freeport	(G-12218)	Blakely	(G-1746)	Narvon	(G-11915)	Ashley	(G-739)	Smethport	(G-17632)
Rices Landing	(G-16669)	Carbondale	(G-2669)	New Holland	(G-12224)	Avoca	(G-839)	Turtlepoint	(G-18571)
Rogersville	(G-16795)	Childs	(G-3131)	New Providence	(G-12433)	Dallas	(G-3958)	**Mercer**	
Sycamore	(G-18201)	Chinchilla	(G-3132)	Paradise	(G-13152)	Drifton	(G-4376)	Carlton	(G-2753)
Waynesburg	(G-19433)	Clarks Green	(G-3189)	Peach Bottom	(G-13195)	Drums	(G-4380)	Clark	(G-3188)
Wind Ridge	(G-20176)	Clarks Summit	(G-3190)	Quarryville	(G-16262)	Dupont	(G-4489)	Farrell	(G-5865)
Huntingdon		Covington Township	(G-3793)	Reamstown	(G-16574)	Duryea	(G-4503)	Fredonia	(G-6179)
Alexandria	(G-62)	Dalton	(G-3987)	Reinholds	(G-16630)	Edwardsville	(G-4823)	Greenville	(G-6736)
Blairs Mills	(G-1711)	Dickson City	(G-4119)	Rheems	(G-16668)	Exeter	(G-5581)	Grove City	(G-6780)
Hesston	(G-7627)	Dickson Cty	(G-4123)	Ronks	(G-16802)	Forty Fort	(G-6098)	Hadley	(G-6816)
Huntingdon	(G-7936)	Dunmore	(G-4467)	Salunga	(G-17054)	Freeland	(G-6194)	Hermitage	(G-7571)
James Creek	(G-8234)	Elmhurst Township	(G-4957)	Silver Spring	(G-17590)	Glen Lyon	(G-6427)	Jackson Center	(G-8225)
Mapleton Depot	(G-10431)	Eynon	(G-5754)	Smoketown	(G-17668)	Hanover Township	(G-6978)	Jamestown	(G-8235)
Mill Creek	(G-11169)	Fleetville	(G-5966)	Stevens	(G-18050)	Harding	(G-7010)	Mercer	(G-10958)
Mount Union	(G-11739)	Greenfield Township	(G-6643)	Strasburg	(G-18090)	Harveys Lake	(G-7256)	Sandy Lake	(G-17059)
Neelyton	(G-11997)	Jermyn	(G-8305)	Talmage	(G-18206)	Hazle Township	(G-7447)	Sharon	(G-17430)
Orbisonia	(G-13006)	Jessup	(G-8326)	Terre Hill	(G-18339)	Hazleton	(G-7491)	Sharpsville	(G-17469)
Shade Gap	(G-17416)	La Plume	(G-8869)	Washington Boro	(G-19250)	Hughestown	(G-7893)	Stoneboro	(G-18068)
Shirleysburg	(G-17569)	Madison Township	(G-10168)	Willow Street	(G-20151)	Hunlock Creek	(G-7931)	Transfer	(G-18465)
Three Springs	(G-18356)	Mayfield	(G-10541)	**Lawrence**		Kingston	(G-8711)	West Middlesex	(G-19721)
Warriors Mark	(G-19142)	Moosic	(G-11501)	Bessemer	(G-1390)	Lattimer Mines	(G-9530)	Wheatland	(G-19834)
Indiana		Moscow	(G-11596)	Edinburg	(G-4822)	Luzerne	(G-10124)	**Mifflin**	
Armagh	(G-723)	Old Forge	(G-12962)	Ellwood City	(G-4923)	Mountain Top	(G-11750)	Allensville	(G-106)
Blairsville	(G-1712)	Olyphant	(G-12983)	Enon Valley	(G-5087)	Nanticoke	(G-11899)	Belleville	(G-1125)
Cherry Tree	(G-3031)	Peckville	(G-13206)	Hillsville	(G-7636)	Nescopeck	(G-12000)	Burnham	(G-2359)
Clarksburg	(G-3199)	Ransom	(G-16306)	New Castle	(G-12051)	Pittston	(G-15740)	Lewistown	(G-9924)
Clymer	(G-3269)	Roaring Brook Twp	(G-16760)	New Wilmington	(G-12464)	Plains	(G-15785)	Mc Clure	(G-10557)
Commodore	(G-3455)	S Abingtn Twp	(G-16888)	Pulaski	(G-16123)	Plymouth	(G-15815)	Mc Veytown	(G-10653)
Creekside	(G-3874)	Scott Township	(G-17183)	Volant	(G-18771)	Shavertown	(G-17478)	Milroy	(G-11228)
Glen Campbell	(G-6423)	Scranton	(G-17204)	Wampum	(G-18796)	Shickshinny	(G-17502)	Reedsville	(G-16620)
Heilwood	(G-7548)	Simpson	(G-17592)	West Pittsburg	(G-19752)	Sugar Notch	(G-18149)	Yeagertown	(G-20357)
Home	(G-7668)	Sprng Brk Twp	(G-17932)	**Lebanon**		Sugarloaf	(G-18152)	**Monroe**	
Homer City	(G-7670)	Taylor	(G-18258)	Annville	(G-641)	Sweet Valley	(G-18187)	Bartonsville	(G-946)
Indiana	(G-8079)	Throop	(G-18357)	Campbelltown	(G-2529)	Swoyersville	(G-18194)	Blakeslee	(G-1748)
Lucernemines	(G-10117)	Waverly	(G-19285)	Cleona	(G-3244)	Wapwallopen	(G-18807)	Brodheadsville	(G-2237)
Marion Center	(G-10472)	**Lancaster**		Cornwall	(G-3737)	West Hazleton	(G-19706)	Canadensis	(G-2530)
Northpoint	(G-12864)	Adamstown	(G-19)	Fredericksburg	(G-6172)	West Pittston	(G-19753)	Cresco	(G-3890)
Penn Run	(G-13228)	Akron	(G-33)	Jonestown	(G-8449)	West Wyoming	(G-19775)	Delaware Water Gap	(G-4042)
Rochester Mills	(G-16790)	Bainbridge	(G-871)	Lebanon	(G-9544)	White Haven	(G-19846)	East Stroudsburg	(G-4601)
Rossiter	(G-16823)	Bird In Hand	(G-1668)	Myerstown	(G-11872)	Wilkes Barre	(G-19902)	Effort	(G-4825)
Saltsburg	(G-17050)	Blue Ball	(G-1811)	Newmanstown	(G-12477)	Wyoming	(G-20274)	Gilbert	(G-6361)
Shelocta	(G-17484)	Bowmansville	(G-1886)	Ono	(G-13004)	Yatesville	(G-20349)	Henryville	(G-7565)
Smicksburg	(G-17638)	Brownstown	(G-2307)	Palmyra	(G-13115)	**Lycoming**		Kresgeville	(G-8820)
Jefferson		Christiana	(G-3133)	Richland	(G-16683)	Cogan Station	(G-3358)	Kunkletown	(G-8832)
Big Run	(G-1656)	Columbia	(G-3427)	Schaefferstown	(G-17128)	Hughesville	(G-7895)	Mount Pocono	(G-11733)
Brockway	(G-2223)	Conestoga	(G-3461)	**Lehigh**		Jersey Shore	(G-8310)	Mountainhome	(G-11785)
Brookville	(G-2248)	Denver	(G-4065)	Alburtis	(G-49)	Lairdsville	(G-8886)	Pocono Lake	(G-15880)
Coolspring	(G-3621)	Drumore	(G-4378)	Allentown	(G-109)	Montgomery	(G-11367)	Pocono Pines	(G-15881)
Falls Creek	(G-5853)	East Earl	(G-4537)	Breinigsville	(G-2004)	Montoursville	(G-11428)	Pocono Summit	(G-15885)
Hamilton	(G-6858)	East Petersburg	(G-4586)	Catasauqua	(G-2812)	Muncy	(G-11805)	Reeders	(G-16619)
Punxsutawney	(G-16127)	Elizabethtown	(G-4865)	Center Valley	(G-2823)	Pennsdale	(G-13262)	Saylorsburg	(G-17103)
Reynoldsville	(G-16655)	Elm	(G-4956)	Coopersburg	(G-3623)	Picture Rocks	(G-14585)	Sciota	(G-17181)
Ringgold	(G-16751)	Ephrata	(G-5089)	Coplay	(G-3638)	South Williamsport	(G-17789)	Stroudsburg	(G-18101)
Stump Creek	(G-18143)	Gap	(G-6248)	East Texas	(G-4639)	Trout Run	(G-18512)	Swiftwater	(G-18188)
Summerville	(G-18156)	Gordonville	(G-6548)	Emmaus	(G-5017)	Unityville	(G-18650)	Tannersville	(G-18234)
Sykesville	(G-18202)	Holtwood	(G-7667)	Fogelsville	(G-5991)	Williamsport	(G-19983)	Tobyhanna	(G-18406)
Valier	(G-18706)	Intercourse	(G-8137)	Germansville	(G-6278)	**Mckean**		**Montgomery**	
Juniata		Kinzers	(G-8731)	Laurys Station	(G-9532)	Bradford	(G-1953)	Abington	(G-9)
East Waterford	(G-4640)	Kirkwood	(G-8744)	Macungie	(G-10138)	Duke Center	(G-4438)	Ambler	(G-566)
Honey Grove	(G-7768)	Lampeter	(G-8917)	Neffs	(G-11998)	Eldred	(G-4852)	Arcola	(G-697)
Mc Alisterville	(G-10548)	Lancaster	(G-8918)	New Tripoli	(G-12453)	Gifford	(G-6360)	Ardmore	(G-699)
Mifflin	(G-11091)	Landisville	(G-9258)	Orefield	(G-13008)	Hazel Hurst	(G-7445)	Audubon	(G-822)
Mifflintown	(G-11107)	Leola	(G-9764)	Schnecksville	(G-17137)	Kane	(G-8458)	Bala Cynwyd	(G-872)
Port Royal	(G-15909)	Lititz	(G-9992)	Slatington	(G-17604)	Lewis Run	(G-9871)	Blue Ball	(G-1812)
Richfield	(G-16679)	Manheim	(G-10366)	Trexlertown	(G-18510)	Ludlow	(G-10118)	Bridgeport	(G-2034)
Thompsontown	(G-18347)	Marietta	(G-10460)	Wescosville	(G-19488)	Mount Jewett	(G-11642)	Cheltenham	(G-3027)
		Millersville	(G-11209)	Whitehall	(G-19860)	Port Allegany	(G-15891)		

	ENTRY #
Collegeville	(G-3365)
Colmar	(G-3411)
Conshohocken	(G-3514)
Creamery	(G-3873)
Dresher	(G-4352)
Eagleville	(G-4512)
East Greenville	(G-4565)
East Norriton	(G-4584)
Elkins Park	(G-4900)
Flourtown	(G-5984)
Fort Washington	(G-6061)
Franconia	(G-6110)
Frederick	(G-6171)
Gilbertsville	(G-6370)
Gladwyne	(G-6407)
Glenside	(G-6503)
Green Lane	(G-6586)
Gwynedd Valley	(G-6815)
Harleysville	(G-7011)
Hatboro	(G-7264)
Hatfield	(G-7312)
Haverford	(G-7407)
Horsham	(G-7778)
Huntingdon Valley	(G-7959)
Jenkintown	(G-8281)
King of Prussia	(G-8575)
Kulpsville	(G-8823)
Lafayette Hill	(G-8877)
Lansdale	(G-9338)
Limerick	(G-9969)
Linfield	(G-9987)
Mainland	(G-10175)
Maple Glen	(G-10429)
Merion Station	(G-10996)
Montgomeryville	(G-11382)
Narberth	(G-11907)
Norristown	(G-12626)
North Wales	(G-12784)
Oaks	(G-12930)
Oreland	(G-13017)
Palm	(G-13094)
Penn Valley	(G-13232)
Pennsburg	(G-13244)
Perkiomenville	(G-13299)
Plymouth Meeting	(G-15826)
Pottstown	(G-15959)
Red Hill	(G-16580)
Rockledge	(G-16791)
Royersford	(G-16839)
Rydal	(G-16885)
Sanatoga	(G-17058)
Sassamansville	(G-17080)
Schwenksville	(G-17172)
Skippack	(G-17594)
Souderton	(G-17719)
Spring House	(G-17881)
Stowe	(G-18072)
Telford	(G-18266)
Trappe	(G-18466)
Tylersport	(G-18574)
Upper Gwynedd	(G-18695)
West Conshohocken	(G-19684)
West Point	(G-19758)
Willow Grove	(G-20105)
Worcester	(G-20223)
Wyncote	(G-20261)
Wynnewood	(G-20267)
Zieglerville	(G-20831)

Montour

Danville	(G-3996)

Northampton

	ENTRY #
Bangor	(G-908)
Bath	(G-949)
Bethlehem	(G-1441)
Danielsville	(G-3994)
Easton	(G-4643)
Fountain Hill	(G-6100)
Freemansburg	(G-6197)
Hellertown	(G-7553)
Lehigh Valley	(G-9707)
Martins Creek	(G-10517)
Mount Bethel	(G-11606)
Nazareth	(G-11951)
Northampton	(G-12841)
Palmer	(G-13098)
Pen Argyl	(G-13210)
Portland	(G-15938)
Roseto	(G-16819)
Stockertown	(G-18063)
Tatamy	(G-18256)
Treichlers	(G-18476)
Walnutport	(G-18790)
Wind Gap	(G-20164)

Northumberland

Coal Township	(G-3279)
Dalmatia	(G-3984)
Dewart	(G-4118)
Dornsife	(G-4165)
Elysburg	(G-4971)
Herndon	(G-7597)
Kulpmont	(G-8821)
Milton	(G-11232)
Montandon	(G-11366)
Mount Carmel	(G-11622)
Northumberland	(G-12865)
Paxinos	(G-13190)
Riverside	(G-16757)
Shamokin	(G-17423)
Sunbury	(G-18162)
Turbotville	(G-18554)
Watsontown	(G-19273)

Perry

Blain	(G-1710)
Duncannon	(G-4444)
Elliottsburg	(G-4918)
Ickesburg	(G-8052)
Landisburg	(G-9256)
Liverpool	(G-10077)
Loysville	(G-10114)
Marysville	(G-10531)
Millerstown	(G-11204)
New Bloomfield	(G-12029)
Newport	(G-12486)
Shermans Dale	(G-17500)

Philadelphia

Phila	(G-13309)
Philadelphia	(G-13317)

Pike

Bushkill	(G-2364)
Dingmans Ferry	(G-4142)
Greeley	(G-6583)
Greentown	(G-6732)
Hawley	(G-7434)
Lackawaxen	(G-8876)
Matamoras	(G-10539)
Milford	(G-11153)
Shohola	(G-17578)
Tafton	(G-18205)

Tamiment	(G-18232)

Potter

Austin	(G-833)
Coudersport	(G-3780)
Galeton	(G-6238)
Genesee	(G-6271)
Mills	(G-11222)
Roulette	(G-16833)
Shinglehouse	(G-17504)
Ulysses	(G-18600)

Schuylkill

Andreas	(G-640)
Ashland	(G-725)
Auburn	(G-815)
Barnesville	(G-940)
Cressona	(G-3903)
Frackville	(G-6102)
Gilberton	(G-6365)
Girardville	(G-6405)
Gordon	(G-6547)
Hegins	(G-7539)
Kelayres	(G-8487)
Klingerstown	(G-8805)
Mahanoy City	(G-10173)
McAdoo	(G-10655)
Middleport	(G-11045)
Minersville	(G-11253)
New Philadelphia	(G-12432)
New Ringgold	(G-12437)
Orwigsburg	(G-13038)
Pine Grove	(G-14589)
Pitman	(G-14621)
Port Carbon	(G-15897)
Pottsville	(G-16072)
Ringtown	(G-16752)
Saint Clair	(G-16937)
Schuylkill Haven	(G-17145)
Shenandoah	(G-17492)
Sheppton	(G-17499)
Spring Glen	(G-17873)
Summit Station	(G-18161)
Tamaqua	(G-18208)
Tower City	(G-18438)
Tremont	(G-18478)
Valley View	(G-18716)

Snyder

Beaver Springs	(G-1019)
Beavertown	(G-1025)
Freeburg	(G-6188)
Hummels Wharf	(G-7900)
Kreamer	(G-8817)
Middleburg	(G-11021)
Mount Pleasant Mills	(G-11724)
Port Trevorton	(G-15911)
Selinsgrove	(G-17320)
Shamokin Dam	(G-17428)

Somerset

Addison	(G-27)
Berlin	(G-1283)
Boswell	(G-1881)
Cairnbrook	(G-2463)
Central City	(G-2838)
Confluence	(G-3463)
Friedens	(G-6219)
Hollsopple	(G-7656)
Hooversville	(G-7770)
Meyersdale	(G-11008)
Rockwood	(G-16792)

	ENTRY #
Salisbury	(G-17044)
Somerset	(G-17672)
Springs	(G-17925)
Stoystown	(G-18074)
West Salisbury	(G-19765)
Windber	(G-20177)

Sullivan

Dushore	(G-4508)
Forksville	(G-6056)
Hillsgrove	(G-7635)
Muncy Valley	(G-11843)

Susquehanna

Clifford	(G-3246)
Clifford Township	(G-3247)
Forest City	(G-6053)
Friendsville	(G-6229)
Great Bend	(G-6581)
Hallstead	(G-6832)
Hop Bottom	(G-7772)
Kingsley	(G-8702)
Montrose	(G-11459)
New Milford	(G-12395)
South Gibson	(G-17779)
Springville	(G-17928)
Susquehanna	(G-18178)
Thompson	(G-18346)
Vandling	(G-18739)

Tioga

Blossburg	(G-1807)
Covington	(G-3791)
Elkland	(G-4916)
Gaines	(G-6236)
Knoxville	(G-8812)
Lawrenceville	(G-9541)
Liberty	(G-9951)
Mansfield	(G-10412)
Middlebury Center	(G-11043)
Millerton	(G-11214)
Morris	(G-11544)
Morris Run	(G-11546)
Tioga	(G-18363)
Wellsboro	(G-19462)
Westfield	(G-19776)

Union

Allenwood	(G-441)
Lewisburg	(G-9896)
Mifflinburg	(G-11092)
Millmont	(G-11219)
New Berlin	(G-12021)
New Columbia	(G-12173)
Winfield	(G-20198)

Venango

Cooperstown	(G-3637)
Cranberry	(G-3797)
Emlenton	(G-5004)
Franklin	(G-6112)
Kennerdell	(G-8497)
Oil City	(G-12940)
Pleasantville	(G-15797)
Polk	(G-15889)
Reno	(G-16645)
Rouseville	(G-16835)
Seneca	(G-17364)
Utica	(G-18696)

Warren

Clarendon	(G-3166)
Garland	(G-6263)

	ENTRY #
Grand Valley	(G-6573)
Irvine	(G-8139)
Pittsfield	(G-15738)
Russell	(G-16880)
Sheffield	(G-17482)
Sugar Grove	(G-18144)
Sugargrove	(G-18150)
Warren	(G-19007)
Youngsville	(G-20769)

Washington

Allenport	(G-104)
Avella	(G-834)
Bentleyville	(G-1273)
Bulger	(G-2342)
Burgettstown	(G-2344)
California	(G-2464)
Canonsburg	(G-2531)
Cecil	(G-2821)
Charleroi	(G-3004)
Claysville	(G-3209)
Coal Center	(G-3275)
Cokeburg	(G-3364)
Daisytown	(G-3957)
Donora	(G-4144)
Eighty Four	(G-4830)
Finleyville	(G-5951)
Fredericktown	(G-6178)
Hickory	(G-7628)
Houston	(G-7867)
Langeloth	(G-9270)
Lawrence	(G-9533)
Marianna	(G-10456)
Mc Donald	(G-10572)
Mc Murray	(G-10643)
Meadow Lands	(G-10689)
Midway	(G-11090)
Monongahela	(G-11303)
New Eagle	(G-12193)
Prosperity	(G-16122)
Roscoe	(G-16817)
Scenery Hill	(G-17124)
Slovan	(G-17630)
Venetia	(G-18741)
Washington	(G-19143)
West Alexander	(G-19490)
Westland	(G-19782)

Wayne

Beach Lake	(G-974)
Bethany	(G-1391)
Clifton Twp	(G-3260)
Covington Township	(G-3794)
Damascus	(G-3989)
Equinunk	(G-5159)
Gouldsboro	(G-6567)
Hawley	(G-7442)
Honesdale	(G-7699)
Jefferson Township	(G-8278)
Lake Ariel	(G-8887)
Lakeville	(G-8913)
Lakewood	(G-8915)
Newfoundland	(G-12476)
Preston Park	(G-16105)
Prompton	(G-16109)
South Canaan	(G-17769)
South Sterling	(G-17787)
Sterling	(G-18048)
Waymart	(G-19286)

Westmoreland

Acme	(G-15)

	ENTRY #		ENTRY #		ENTRY #		ENTRY #		ENTRY #
Adamsburg	(G-18)	Laughlintown	(G-9531)	Scottdale	(G-17189)	Nicholson	(G-12612)	Manchester	(G-10354)
Alverton	(G-564)	Ligonier	(G-9956)	Seward	(G-17381)	Noxen	(G-12886)	Mount Wolf	(G-11747)
Apollo	(G-662)	Lower Burrell	(G-10105)	Smithton	(G-17658)	Tunkhannock	(G-18533)	New Freedom	(G-12200)
Ardara	(G-698)	Loyalhanna	(G-10110)	Stahlstown	(G-17935)	**York**		New Park	(G-12429)
Avonmore	(G-862)	Madison	(G-10165)	Sutersville	(G-18184)	Airville	(G-32)	Red Lion	(G-16586)
Bradenville	(G-1952)	Manor	(G-10409)	Trafford	(G-18450)	Brogue	(G-2239)	Rossville	(G-16824)
Calumet	(G-2472)	Monessen	(G-11296)	Vandergrift	(G-18721)	Codorus	(G-3357)	Seven Valleys	(G-17377)
Champion	(G-3003)	Mount Pleasant	(G-11685)	Webster	(G-19456)	Dallastown	(G-3970)	Shrewsbury	(G-17581)
Delmont	(G-4046)	Murrysville	(G-11845)	Wendel	(G-19480)	Delta	(G-4062)	Spring Grove	(G-17875)
Derry	(G-4099)	New Alexandria	(G-12017)	West Newton	(G-19748)	Dillsburg	(G-4126)	Stewartstown	(G-18060)
Export	(G-5587)	New Derry	(G-12191)	Westmoreland City	(G-19783)	Dover	(G-4183)	Thomasville	(G-18341)
Forbes Road	(G-6040)	New Florence	(G-12196)	Whitney	(G-19894)	Emigsville	(G-4983)	Wellsville	(G-19476)
Greensburg	(G-6647)	New Kensington	(G-12320)	Youngwood	(G-20776)	Etters	(G-5547)	Windsor	(G-20195)
Harrison City	(G-7249)	New Stanton	(G-12447)	Yukon	(G-20784)	Felton	(G-5940)	Wrightsville	(G-20235)
Herminie	(G-7569)	North Huntingdon	(G-12767)	**Wyoming**		Glen Rock	(G-6449)	Yoe	(G-20358)
Hunker	(G-7928)	Norvelt	(G-12878)	Factoryville	(G-5756)	Glenville	(G-6545)	York	(G-20361)
Irwin	(G-8141)	Penn	(G-13226)	Falls	(G-5852)	Hanover	(G-6859)	York Haven	(G-20756)
Jeannette	(G-8247)	Pleasant Unity	(G-15796)	Laceyville	(G-8870)	Hellam	(G-7549)		
Jones Mills	(G-8448)	Rillton	(G-16746)	Lake Winola	(G-8912)	Jacobus	(G-8230)		
Larimer	(G-9451)	Ruffs Dale	(G-16870)	Mehoopany	(G-10957)	Lewisberry	(G-9879)		
Latrobe	(G-9452)	Salina	(G-17043)	Meshoppen	(G-11005)	Loganville	(G-10101)		

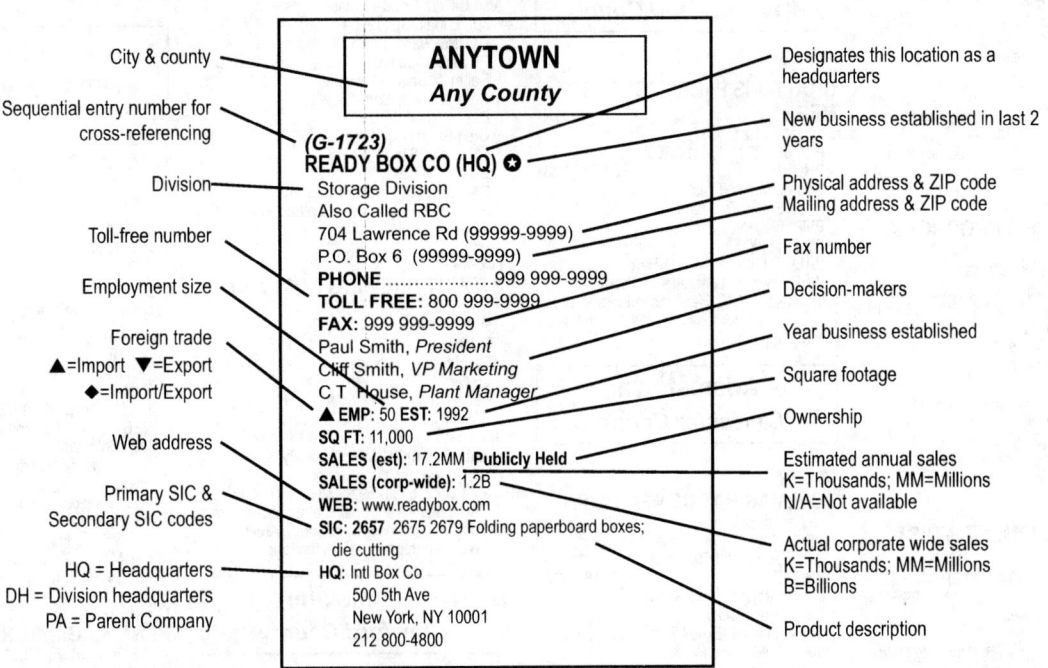

City & county → **ANYTOWN** *Any County* ← Designates this location as a headquarters

Sequential entry number for cross-referencing → **(G-1723)**

New business established in last 2 years

READY BOX CO (HQ) ✿

Division → Storage Division
Also Called RBC

Physical address & ZIP code → 704 Lawrence Rd (99999-9999)
Mailing address & ZIP code → P.O. Box 6 (99999-9999)

Toll-free number → **PHONE** 999 999-9999
TOLL FREE: 800 999-9999 ← Fax number

Employment size → **FAX:** 999 999-9999
Paul Smith, *President* ← Decision-makers

Foreign trade
▲=Import ▼=Export
◆=Import/Export → Cliff Smith, *VP Marketing*
C T House, *Plant Manager*
▲ **EMP:** 50 **EST:** 1992 ← Year business established

SQ FT: 11,000 ← Square footage

Web address → **SALES (est):** 17.2MM **Publicly Held** ← Ownership

Primary SIC &
Secondary SIC codes → **SALES (corp-wide):** 1.2B
WEB: www.readybox.com

Estimated annual sales
K=Thousands; MM=Millions
N/A=Not available

SIC: 2657 2675 2679 Folding paperboard boxes; die cutting

HQ = Headquarters
DH = Division headquarters
PA = Parent Company → **HQ:** Intl Box Co
500 5th Ave
New York, NY 10001
212 800-4800

Actual corporate wide sales
K=Thousands; MM=Millions
B=Billions

Product description

See footnotes for symbols and codes identification.
• This section is in alphabetical order by city.
• Companies are sorted alphabetically under their respective cities.
• To locate cities within a county refer to the County/City Cross Reference Index.

IMPORTANT NOTICE: It is a violation of both federal and state law to transmit an unsolicited advertisement to a facsimile machine. Any user of this product that violates such laws may be subject to civil and criminal penalties which may exceed $500 for each transmission of an unsolicited facsimile. Harris InfoSource provides fax numbers for lawful purposes only and expressly forbids the use of these numbers in any unlawful manner.

G E O G R A P H I C

Aaronsburg
Centre County

(G-1)
POORMANS WLDG FABRICATION INC
168 Kramer Rd (16820-9303)
PHONE..................................814 349-5893
Roger Poorman, *President*
David Poorman, *Vice Pres*
EMP: 14
SQ FT: 9,000
SALES (est): 3.1MM **Privately Held**
SIC: 3441 3312 3365 Fabricated structural metal; stainless steel; aluminum foundries

(G-2)
PRICE C L LUMBER LLC (PA)
Also Called: Price CL Lumber Mill
319 Tattletown Rd (16820-8902)
PHONE..................................814 349-5505
Clarence Price, *Mng Member*
Betty Price,
EMP: 13
SALES: 900K **Privately Held**
SIC: 2421 5031 Cants, resawed (lumber); lumber: rough, dressed & finished

Abbottstown
Adams County

(G-3)
ABBOTTSTOWN INDUSTRIES INC
420 W Fleet St (17301-8812)
PHONE..................................717 259-8715
James Lewis, *President*
Dan Althoff, *President*
John Teel, *Treasurer*
Tammy Althoff, *Admin Sec*
EMP: 37
SQ FT: 30,000
SALES (est): 6.3MM **Privately Held**
WEB: www.abbind.com
SIC: 3544 7692 Special dies & tools; welding repair

(G-4)
G & S FOODS INC (PA)
101 Sutton Rd (17301-9704)
PHONE..................................717 259-5323
Dale C Spahr, *President*
Steven G Garvick, *Corp Secy*
EMP: 47
SQ FT: 20,000
SALES (est): 17.5MM **Privately Held**
SIC: 7389 2096 5149 5145 Packaging & labeling services; potato chips & similar snacks; specialty food items; snack foods

(G-5)
OMNIA LLC
301 Pleasant St (17301-9586)
PHONE..................................717 259-1633
▲ **EMP:** 4

SALES (est): 504.4K **Privately Held**
SIC: 3821 Incubators, laboratory

(G-6)
OSSPRAY INC
301 Pleasant St (17301-9586)
PHONE..................................866 238-9902
Jacqueline Walker, *CEO*
Gary Debruin,
EMP: 6
SALES: 80K **Privately Held**
SIC: 3843 Dental equipment & supplies

(G-7)
TASTYSNACK QUALITY FOODS INC
105 Sutton Rd (17301-9704)
PHONE..................................717 259-6961
Dale Spahr, *President*
Dale C Spahr, *President*
Steven G Garvick, *Vice Pres*
Woodrow Stoddard, *CFO*
EMP: 25
SQ FT: 25,000
SALES (est): 4.2MM **Privately Held**
SIC: 5145 2096 Candy; cheese curls & puffs

(G-8)
TEL TIN
45 Cherry Ln (17301-9066)
PHONE..................................717 259-9004
Cynthia Linebaugh, *Principal*
EMP: 3
SALES (est): 247.8K **Privately Held**
SIC: 3356 Tin

Abington
Montgomery County

(G-9)
ABILITY SYSTEMS CORPORATION
1422 Arnold Ave (19001-1695)
PHONE..................................215 657-4338
Arthur C Volta, *President*
EMP: 3
SALES: 250K **Privately Held**
WEB: www.abilitysystems.com
SIC: 3679 7371 Electronic circuits; computer software systems analysis & design, custom

(G-10)
CUSTOM CRAFT CABINETS
1274 Thomson Rd (19001-3015)
PHONE..................................215 886-6105
EMP: 5
SQ FT: 8,000
SALES: 320K **Privately Held**
SIC: 2542 Mfg Cabinets Store Fixtures & Candy Racks

(G-11)
ELEVATED SIGN SOLUTIONS LLC
1377 Reservoir Ave (19001-1622)
PHONE..................................267 374-4758
John Kulak, *Principal*
EMP: 5
SALES (est): 303.9K **Privately Held**
SIC: 3993 Signs & advertising specialties

(G-12)
FAST BY FERRACCI INC
1372 Edgewood Ave (19001-2308)
PHONE..................................215 657-1276
Eraldo Ferracci, *President*
Lawrence Ferracci, *Vice Pres*
▲ EMP: 10
SQ FT: 17,000
SALES (est): 1.9MM Privately Held
WEB: www.ferracci.com
SIC: 5013 3751 Motorcycle parts; motorcycles & related parts

(G-13)
PENN SCIENTIFIC PRODUCTS CO (PA)
1000 Old York Rd (19001-4512)
P.O. Box 162, Buckingham (18912-0162)
PHONE..................................888 238-6710
Beverly Karnell, *CEO*
William Furrelle, *COO*
EMP: 11 EST: 1949
SQ FT: 3,000
SALES (est): 1.4MM Privately Held
WEB: www.pennscientific.com
SIC: 3291 3545 3425 Diamond powder; machine tool accessories; saw blades & handsaws

(G-14)
READING EQUIPMENT & DIST LLC
1704 Rockwell Rd (19001-1721)
PHONE..................................717 445-6746
Norm Zeigler, *President*
EMP: 38
SALES (corp-wide): 1.2B Privately Held
WEB: www.readingequipment.com
SIC: 5013 7538 3713 7692 Truck parts & accessories; general truck repair; truck bodies & parts; welding repair
HQ: Reading Equipment & Distribution, Llc
1363 Bowmansville Rd
Bowmansville PA 17507
717 445-6746

Acme
Westmoreland County

(G-15)
BROWN TIMBER AND LAND CO INC
2573 Rte 31 (15610)
P.O. Box 127 (15610-0127)
PHONE..................................724 547-7777
Neil Brown, *President*
EMP: 13
SQ FT: 2,000
SALES (est): 2MM Privately Held
SIC: 2421 2426 Sawmills & planing mills, general; hardwood dimension & flooring mills

(G-16)
BROWN TOOL & DIE INC
130 Redwood Rd (15610-1304)
PHONE..................................724 547-3366
Dan L Brown, *President*
EMP: 4 EST: 1994
SALES: 450K Privately Held
SIC: 3312 Tool & die steel

(G-17)
TWENTY FIRST CENTURY TOOL CO
176 County Line Rd (15610-1022)
PHONE..................................724 423-5357
Dennis Shinsky, *Owner*
EMP: 4
SALES: 435K Privately Held
SIC: 3599 Machine shop, jobbing & repair

Adamsburg
Westmoreland County

(G-18)
GRATTONS FABRICATING & MFG
198 Main St (15611)
P.O. Box 388 (15611-0388)
PHONE..................................724 527-5681
George Matus, *President*
Janet Smith, *Treasurer*
EMP: 6
SQ FT: 5,000
SALES: 650K Privately Held
WEB: www.grattonfabricating.com
SIC: 3443 3549 Heat exchangers, condensers & components; coilers (metalworking machines)

Adamstown
Lancaster County

(G-19)
BOLLMAN HAT COMPANY (PA)
Also Called: Betmar
110 E Main St (19501-5009)
P.O. Box 517 (19501-0517)
PHONE..................................717 484-4361
Donald Rongione, *President*
Dave Huber, *COO*
Chris Fitterling, *Exec VP*
Mark Craley, *Vice Pres*
Charlotte Dyslin, *Vice Pres*
▲ EMP: 300
SQ FT: 500,000
SALES (est): 291.8MM Privately Held
WEB: www.bollmanhats.com
SIC: 2353 5136 Hats: cloth, straw & felt; hats, men's & boys'

(G-20)
BOLLMAN INDUSTRIES INC (HQ)
Also Called: Bollman Industries-San Angelo
110 E Main St (19501-5009)
PHONE..................................717 484-4361
Don Rongione, *Ch of Bd*
Gary Craley, *Vice Pres*
Curtis Glass, *Sales & Mktg St*
Rich Bainbridge, *Info Tech Dir*
Chris Fitterling, *Admin Sec*
EMP: 165
SALES (corp-wide): 291.8MM Privately Held
WEB: www.baileyhats.com
SIC: 2299 2353 5632 5136 Scouring: wool, mohair & similar fibers; harvest hats, straw; apparel accessories; caps, men's & boys'
PA: Bollman Hat Company
110 E Main St
Adamstown PA 19501
717 484-4361

(G-21)
ENSINGER PRINTING SERVICE
50 W Main St (19501-5000)
P.O. Box 26 (19501-0026)
PHONE..................................717 484-4451
Kent Lesher, *Owner*
EMP: 6
SQ FT: 4,500
SALES: 582K Privately Held
SIC: 2752 Commercial printing, offset

(G-22)
HALLER ENERGY SERVICES LLC
Also Called: Sauder Fuel
1976 Bowmansville Rd (19501)
P.O. Box 518 (19501-0518)
PHONE..................................717 721-9560
Matther Sauder, *Mng Member*
EMP: 12
SALES (est): 1.7MM Privately Held
SIC: 2869 2911 Fuels; diesel fuels; kerosene

(G-23)
RALPH GOOD INC (PA)
Also Called: Good's Potato Chips
306 E Main St (19501-5006)
P.O. Box 924 (19501-0924)
PHONE..................................717 484-4884
Ralph W Good, *President*
Carol A Good, *Corp Secy*
Duane Good, *Vice Pres*
Greg Good, *Vice Pres*
EMP: 43 EST: 1940
SQ FT: 12,000
SALES (est): 4.6MM Privately Held
SIC: 2096 Potato chips & other potato-based snacks

(G-24)
STOUDT BREWING COMPANY
Rr 272 Box 880 (19501)
P.O. Box 880 (19501-0880)
PHONE..................................717 484-4386
Carol Stoudt, *President*
Edward D Stoudt, *Vice Pres*
Kevin Romer, *Sales Staff*
▲ EMP: 50
SQ FT: 20,000
SALES (est): 8.2MM Privately Held
WEB: www.stoudtsbeer.com
SIC: 2082 5181 5921 5812 Beer (alcoholic beverage); beer & other fermented malt liquors; beer (packaged); American restaurant; banquet hall facilities

---

Adamsville
Crawford County

(G-25)
EDMUND BURKE INC
Also Called: Salem Hardwood, Inc.
2880 State Highway 18 (16110-1516)
PHONE..................................724 932-5200
William Marc Reese, *President*
Marygrace L Reese, *Vice Pres*
Carie Haworth, *Admin Sec*
EMP: 10
SALES: 2.3MM Privately Held
SIC: 2411 5031 Logging; lumber, plywood & millwork

(G-26)
PENN-SYLVAN INTERNATIONAL INC
Also Called: Salem Hardwood
2880 State Highway 18 (16110-1516)
PHONE..................................724 932-5200
Marc Reese, *President*
EMP: 6 Privately Held
WEB: www.salemhardwood.com
SIC: 2421 Lumber: rough, sawed or planed
PA: Penn-Sylvan International, Inc.
43647 Fairview Rd
Spartansburg PA 16434

Addison
Somerset County

(G-27)
JUERGENSEN DEFENSE CORPORATION
1448 Polk Hill Rd (15411-2018)
PHONE..................................814 395-9509
Kevin Juergensen, *President*
Eric Hilty, *CTO*
EMP: 5
SALES: 1,000K Privately Held
WEB: www.electricfilm.com
SIC: 3679 Electronic circuits

(G-28)
PRECISION PALLETS & LUMBER INC
3593 Listonburg Rd (15411-2122)
P.O. Box 51 (15411-0051)
PHONE..................................814 395-5351
Harry Whetsell, *President*
Gary E Rugg, *Shareholder*
EMP: 18
SQ FT: 20,000

SALES (est): 2.5MM Privately Held
SIC: 2448 2421 Pallets, wood; lumber: rough, sawed or planed

Adrian
Armstrong County

(G-29)
GRAYCO CONTROLS LLC
719 Tarrtown Rd (16210-1219)
PHONE..................................724 545-2300
EMP: 3
SALES (est): 303.8K Privately Held
SIC: 1311 Natural gas production

(G-30)
GROWMARK FS LLC
656 Tarrtown Rd (16210-1218)
PHONE..................................724 543-1101
Paul Masula, *Manager*
EMP: 20
SALES (corp-wide): 7.2B Privately Held
WEB: www.growmarkfs.com
SIC: 2874 2875 5191 2873 Phosphatic fertilizers; fertilizers, mixing only; pesticides; seeds: field, garden & flower; nitrogen solutions (fertilizer)
HQ: Growmark Fs, Llc
308 Ne Front St
Milford DE 19963
302 422-3002

(G-31)
PENN MAG INCORPORATED
719 Tarrtown Rd (16210-1219)
PHONE..................................724 545-2300
Anil G Bhadsavle, *President*
▼ EMP: 17
SALES (est): 2.5MM Privately Held
SIC: 3295 Minerals, ground or treated

Airville
York County

(G-32)
SUNNYBURN WELDING
Also Called: (FORMERLY : J K LAPP INDUSTRIES)
32 W Telegraph Rd (17302-9135)
PHONE..................................717 862-3878
Joseph Lapp, *Owner*
Marie Lapp, *Manager*
EMP: 6
SQ FT: 4,000
SALES (est): 260K Privately Held
SIC: 7692 3531 Automotive welding; scrapers (construction machinery)

Akron
Lancaster County

(G-33)
BERKLEY PRODUCTS COMPANY
405 S 7th St A (17501-1466)
PHONE..................................717 859-1104
Thomas R Henry, *President*
EMP: 10 EST: 1949
SQ FT: 48,000
SALES (est): 2MM Privately Held
SIC: 2851 2842 Paints & paint additives; enamels; lacquer: bases, dopes, thinner; specialty cleaning, polishes & sanitation goods

(G-34)
BIBLE VISUALS INTERNATIONAL
650 Main St (17501-1312)
P.O. Box 153 (17501-0153)
PHONE..................................717 859-1131
Melody Mayer, *Bookkeeper*
Thomas Luttmann, *Director*
EMP: 4
SQ FT: 4,000

SALES: 238.8K **Privately Held**
WEB: www.biblevisuals.org
SIC: 2731 8661 Books: publishing only; religious organizations

(G-35)
HOMESTEAD CUSTOM CABINETRY
120 S 11th St (17501-1510)
PHONE..............................717 859-8788
Randall Esch, *President*
EMP: 22
SQ FT: 22,000
SALES: 3.2MM **Privately Held**
WEB:
www.homesteadcustomcabinetry.com
SIC: 2434 Wood kitchen cabinets

(G-36)
MARTINS PRETZEL BAKERY
1229 Diamond St (17501-1634)
PHONE..............................717 859-1272
Clarence B Martin, *Owner*
EMP: 40
SQ FT: 2,400
SALES (est): 3.3MM **Privately Held**
WEB: www.martinspretzelspa.com
SIC: 2052 5461 Pretzels; pretzels

(G-37)
RICKS CUSTOM WOOD DESIGN INC
10 Lauber Rd (17501-1457)
PHONE..............................717 627-2701
Rick L Fisher, *President*
Michael Knauer, *General Mgr*
EMP: 14
SQ FT: 10,600
SALES (est): 1.5MM **Privately Held**
SIC: 2511 Wood household furniture

(G-38)
ROSENBERGER N AMER AKRON LLC
309 Colonial Dr (17501-1210)
PHONE..............................717 859-8900
Andreas Ruzic, *CEO*
Kyle Hofmann, *Engineer*
Jim Devere, *Sales Staff*
Pete Robinson, *Sales Staff*
Maria Mitton, *Marketing Staff*
▲ **EMP:** 155
SQ FT: 55,000
SALES (est): 42MM
SALES (corp-wide): 16.9MM **Privately Held**
WEB: www.rosenbergerna.com
SIC: 3678 Electronic connectors
PA: Rosenberger Usa, Corp.
1100 Prof Dr Ste 100
Plano TX 75074
717 859-6013

(G-39)
WINDGLO MANUFACTURING CO
1 Lauber Rd (17501-1456)
PHONE..............................717 859-2932
EMP: 3
SALES (est): 69K **Privately Held**
SIC: 2841 Mfg Soap/Other Detergents

Albion
Erie County

(G-40)
ALTMAN MANUFACTURING INC
54 Umburn Dr (16401-1323)
PHONE..............................814 756-5254
William H Altman, *President*
Scott A Altman, *Admin Sec*
EMP: 10
SALES (est): 1.8MM **Privately Held**
WEB: www.altman-aluminum.com
SIC: 3365 Aluminum foundries

(G-41)
CORNWELL QUALITY TOOLS COMPANY
14800 W Cherry Hill Rd (16401-7828)
PHONE..............................814 756-5484
Kevin Watson, *Manager*
EMP: 5

SQ FT: 9,062
SALES (corp-wide): 173.8MM **Privately Held**
WEB: www.cornwelltools.com
SIC: 5085 3423 Industrial supplies; mechanics' hand tools
PA: The Cornwell Quality Tools Company
667 Seville Rd
Wadsworth OH 44281
330 336-3506

(G-42)
DAVID COPELAND
Also Called: Copeland Lumber
10140 S Akerley Rd (16401-9742)
PHONE..............................814 756-3250
David Copeland, *Owner*
EMP: 6
SQ FT: 4,500
SALES: 1.2MM **Privately Held**
SIC: 2421 Lumber: rough, sawed or planed

(G-43)
DOUG HERHOLD
Also Called: D & J Welding
9901 Route 6n (16401-8621)
PHONE..............................814 756-5141
Doug Herhold, *Owner*
EMP: 4
SALES: 300K **Privately Held**
SIC: 7692 Welding repair

(G-44)
GLASS MOLDERS POTTRY PLSTC
8751 Crossingville Rd (16401-8905)
PHONE..............................814 756-4042
Elaine Kimmy, *Admin Sec*
EMP: 71
SALES (corp-wide): 14MM **Privately Held**
WEB: www.gmpiu.org
SIC: 3089 Plastic containers, except foam
PA: Glass, Molders, Pottery, Plastics & Allied Workers International Union
608 E Baltimore Pike
Media PA 19063
610 565-5051

(G-45)
JET TOOL COMPANY INC
Also Called: Jet Tool and Die
25 Euclid St (16401-1234)
PHONE..............................814 756-3169
Gary Richardson, *President*
Eileen Richardson, *Vice Pres*
EMP: 7
SALES (est): 494.9K **Privately Held**
SIC: 3494 3599 Valves & pipe fittings; machine shop, jobbing & repair

(G-46)
LESKO ENTERPRISES INC
21 Euclid St (16401-1252)
P.O. Box 71 (16401-0071)
PHONE..............................814 756-4030
John Lesko, *President*
Steven Lesko, *Vice Pres*
Eugene Lesko, *Treasurer*
Dorothy Lesko, *Admin Sec*
EMP: 105
SQ FT: 65,000
SALES (est): 18.7MM **Privately Held**
WEB: www.leskoenterprises.com
SIC: 3089 7692 2789 2752 Injection molding of plastics; welding repair; bookbinding & related work; commercial printing, lithographic; automotive & apparel trimmings

(G-47)
THORNTON INDUSTRIES INC
14200 Route 226 (16401-7806)
PHONE..............................814 756-3578
William Thornton Jr, *President*
EMP: 16
SQ FT: 6,500
SALES (est): 2.7MM **Privately Held**
WEB: www.thorind.com
SIC: 3599 Machine shop, jobbing & repair

Albrightsville
Carbon County

(G-48)
D&D CIGAR & CIGARETTE EMPORIUM
2591 State Route 903 # 4 (18210-3760)
PHONE..............................570 722-4665
Peter Dillon, *President*
EMP: 4
SALES (est): 360.2K **Privately Held**
SIC: 3999 Cigarette & cigar products & accessories

Alburtis
Lehigh County

(G-49)
ACME CRYOGENICS INC
7662 Church St (18011-9502)
PHONE..............................610 966-4488
Sean Farrell, *Mfg Dir*
Steve Leonard, *Sales Staff*
Bob Elliot, *Manager*
EMP: 43
SALES (corp-wide): 39.6MM **Privately Held**
WEB: www.acmecryo.com
SIC: 3559 3498 3599 Cryogenic machinery, industrial; piping systems for pulp paper & chemical industries; machine shop, jobbing & repair
PA: Acme Cryogenics, Inc.
2801 Mitchell Ave
Allentown PA 18103
610 966-4488

(G-50)
AMITY MACHINE CORPORATION
3750 Chestnut Rd (18011-9580)
P.O. Box 451 (18011-0451)
PHONE..............................610 966-3115
Edward O Selwyn Jr, *President*
▲ **EMP:** 24
SQ FT: 25,000
SALES (est): 4.5MM
SALES (corp-wide): 10.8MM **Privately Held**
WEB: www.amitymachine.com
SIC: 3599 Machine shop, jobbing & repair
PA: Amity Industries, Inc.
491 Old Swede Rd
Douglassville PA 19518
610 385-6075

(G-51)
COOPER TIRE & RUBBER COMPANY
8000 Quarry Rd Ste B (18011-9599)
PHONE..............................610 967-0860
Steve Miller, *General Mgr*
EMP: 30
SALES (corp-wide): 2.8B **Publicly Held**
WEB: www.coopertire.com
SIC: 3011 Tires & inner tubes
PA: Cooper Tire & Rubber Company Inc
701 Lima Ave
Findlay OH 45840
419 423-1321

(G-52)
JNB SCREEN PRINTING INC
Also Called: J N B Screen Printing
699 Huffs Church Rd (18011-2228)
PHONE..............................610 845-7680
Newton Longacre, *President*
John Gheer, *Vice Pres*
Jason Longacre, *Admin Sec*
EMP: 3
SALES (est): 190K **Privately Held**
SIC: 2752 Commercial printing, lithographic

(G-53)
JOHNSTONE SUPPLY
Also Called: Johnson Contrls Authorized Dlr
8000 Quarry Rd Ste A (18011-9599)
PHONE..............................610 967-9900
R Jansen, *President*
EMP: 4

SALES (est): 582.3K **Privately Held**
SIC: 7694 5722 5063 5075 Electric motor repair; air conditioning room units, self-contained; electrical supplies; warm air heating & air conditioning

(G-54)
K C STOVES & FIREPLACES INC
120 N Main St (18011-9505)
PHONE..............................610 966-3556
Kevin Oldt, *President*
EMP: 8
SQ FT: 2,000
SALES (est): 2.5MM **Privately Held**
WEB: www.kcstovesandfireplaces.com
SIC: 3585 Heating equipment, complete

(G-55)
LADISCH CORPORATION INC
292 Baldy Hill Rd (18011-2202)
PHONE..............................267 313-4189
Thomas Ladisch, *Owner*
EMP: 8
SQ FT: 2,000
SALES (est): 1.3MM **Privately Held**
SIC: 3559 Pharmaceutical machinery

(G-56)
LUTRON ELECTRONICS CO INC
8240 Spring Creek Rd (18011-9507)
PHONE..............................610 282-6617
EMP: 99
SALES (corp-wide): 673.9MM **Privately Held**
SIC: 3625 Control equipment, electric
PA: Lutron Electronics Co., Inc.
7200 Suter Rd
Coopersburg PA 18036
610 282-3800

(G-57)
MILLWOOD INC
8018 Quarry Rd (18011-9529)
PHONE..............................610 421-6230
EMP: 153 **Privately Held**
SIC: 3565 Packaging machinery
PA: Millwood, Inc.
3708 International Blvd
Vienna OH 44473

(G-58)
VICTAULIC COMPANY OF AMERICA
8023 Quarry Rd (18011-9532)
PHONE..............................610 966-3966
Gene Miller, *Branch Mgr*
Laura Fell, *Executive*
EMP: 150
SQ FT: 92,617
SALES (corp-wide): 746.3MM **Privately Held**
SIC: 3559 3317 3312 Foundry, smelting, refining & similar machinery; steel pipe & tubes; blast furnaces & steel mills
PA: Victaulic Company
4901 Kesslersville Rd
Easton PA 18040
610 559-3300

Aldan
Delaware County

(G-59)
FOAM FAIR INDUSTRIES INC
Also Called: F F I
3 Merion Ter (19018-3034)
P.O. Box 99, Broomall (19008-0099)
PHONE..............................610 622-4665
Alan I Memmo, *President*
Marcel Talbot, *Principal*
▲ **EMP:** 40 EST: 1970
SQ FT: 50,000
SALES (est): 5.2MM **Privately Held**
WEB: www.foamfairindustries.com
SIC: 3086 Packaging & shipping materials, foamed plastic

(G-60)
RODDY PRODUCTS
3 Merion Ter (19018-3034)
PHONE..............................610 623-7040
EMP: 4

SALES (est): 329.7K **Privately Held**
SIC: 2621 Packaging paper

Aleppo
Greene County

(G-61)
MOUNTAIN ENERGY INC
1593 Aleppo Rd (15310)
PHONE..................724 428-5200
Kevin Concord, *Vice Pres*
Dwight Dunton III, *Shareholder*
Marcus Dunton, *Shareholder*
EMP: 12 **EST:** 1995
SQ FT: 2,400
SALES (est): 803.7K **Privately Held**
SIC: 1311 Natural gas production

Alexandria
Huntingdon County

(G-62)
ACCUBAR ENGINEERING & RORCO
Woolverton Way (16611)
PHONE..................814 669-9005
George Rohrbaugh, *Owner*
EMP: 3
SALES (est): 157.1K **Privately Held**
WEB: www.accubar.com
SIC: 3949 Targets, archery & rifle shooting; arrows, archery

(G-63)
DAVID KARR
Also Called: Windy Hill Furniture
6425 Barree Rd (16611-3047)
PHONE..................814 669-4406
David Karr, *Owner*
EMP: 6 **EST:** 1995
SQ FT: 7,200
SALES (est): 703.3K **Privately Held**
WEB: www.windyhillfurniture.com
SIC: 2511 5712 Wood household furniture; furniture stores

(G-64)
TITAN CO2 INC
5559 William Penn Hwy (16611-2808)
PHONE..................814 669-4544
Ralph Keller, *President*
EMP: 6 **EST:** 2008
SQ FT: 10,000
SALES (est): 940K **Privately Held**
SIC: 3443 Cryogenic tanks, for liquids & gases

Aliquippa
Beaver County

(G-65)
AMERICAN PRECISION POWDER
1296 Airport Rd (15001-4315)
PHONE..................724 788-1691
James M Verostek,
▲ **EMP:** 5
SALES (est): 718.1K **Privately Held**
WEB: www.appowdercoating.com
SIC: 3479 Coating of metals & formed products

(G-66)
ARDEX L P (HQ)
Also Called: Ardex Engineered Cements
400 Ardex Park Dr Ste 1 (15001-8420)
PHONE..................724 203-5000
Jesse David, *President*
Stephen Bass, *Purchasing*
Lori P Angelo, *Treasurer*
Rhonda West, *Human Res Mgr*
Nick Dandrea, *Marketing Staff*
◆ **EMP:** 115
SALES: 46.8MM
SALES (corp-wide): 1.6MM **Privately Held**
WEB: www.ardex.com
SIC: 3241 Cement, hydraulic

PA: Ardex Anlagen Gmbh
Friedrich-Ebert-Str. 45
Witten 58453
230 266-40

(G-67)
B X S BASS INC
2256 Brodhead Rd (15001-4688)
PHONE..................724 378-8697
Bernard Fiumara, *President*
Anette Fiumara, *Admin Sec*
EMP: 3
SALES (est): 221.3K **Privately Held**
SIC: 3931 5736 Musical instruments, electric & electronic; musical instrument stores

(G-68)
BEAVER VALLEY SLAG INC
6010 Woodlawn Rd (15001-2461)
PHONE..................724 378-8888
Roxsan Bettes Albanes, *CEO*
Bob McAllistar, *CFO*
Matthew Dean, *Sales Mgr*
▲ **EMP:** 17
SALES (est): 3.7MM **Privately Held**
WEB: www.bvslag.com
SIC: 3295 Slag, crushed or ground

(G-69)
BOULEVARD SPORTS
1503 Kennedy Blvd (15001-2622)
PHONE..................724 378-9191
John Feher, *Principal*
EMP: 3
SALES (est): 223.5K **Privately Held**
SIC: 2759 5099 5941 Screen printing; signs, except electric; sporting goods & bicycle shops

(G-70)
BRIGHTON MACHINE COMPANY INC
1306 Airport Rd (15001-4394)
PHONE..................724 378-0960
Joseph Downie, *President*
Jacqueline Downie, *Treasurer*
EMP: 16
SQ FT: 30,000
SALES (est): 2.5MM **Privately Held**
SIC: 3599 7692 3541 Machine shop, jobbing & repair; welding repair; machine tools, metal cutting type

(G-71)
CRONIMET CORPORATION (DH)
1 Pilarsky Way (15001-5421)
PHONE..................724 375-5004
Guenter Pilersky, *Ch of Bd*
Frank Santoro, *President*
Robert Santoro, *Vice Pres*
Kevin Covell, *Treasurer*
David Porco, *Admin Sec*
◆ **EMP:** 65
SQ FT: 4,500
SALES (est): 96.7MM
SALES (corp-wide): 2.5B **Privately Held**
WEB: www.cronimet.com
SIC: 5093 5051 3312 Ferrous metal scrap & waste; iron & steel (ferrous) products; blast furnaces & steel mills
HQ: Cronimet Ferroleg. Gmbh
Sudbeckenstr. 22
Karlsruhe 76189
721 952-250

(G-72)
CULVER INDUSTRIES INC
1000 Industrial Blvd # 400 (15001-4862)
PHONE..................724 857-5770
Thomas McKnight, *President*
Oliver Lengthorn, *Sales Staff*
▼ **EMP:** 11
SALES (est): 911.6K **Privately Held**
SIC: 3231 5023 Decorated glassware: chipped, engraved, etched, etc.; glassware; kitchen tools & utensils

(G-73)
DOBISH SIGNS & DISPLAY INC
3182 Green Garden Rd (15001-1019)
PHONE..................724 375-3943
Michael Dobish, *President*
Russel Dobish, *Vice Pres*
Ryan Dobish, *Office Admin*
EMP: 6

SQ FT: 5,000
SALES: 500K **Privately Held**
SIC: 3993 Signs & advertising specialties

(G-74)
DOREN INC PARKWAY
2321 Todd Rd (15001-8407)
PHONE..................724 375-6637
Joe Masciantonio, *Principal*
EMP: 5
SALES (est): 562.6K **Privately Held**
SIC: 3272 Building materials, except block or brick: concrete

(G-75)
FIVE POINTS PET SUPPLY LLC
2061 Brodhead Rd (15001-4962)
PHONE..................724 857-6000
Richard Bell, *Owner*
EMP: 3
SALES (est): 234.6K **Privately Held**
SIC: 3999 Pet supplies

(G-76)
HERITAGE BOX CO
3204 Industrial Dr (15001-1216)
PHONE..................724 728-0200
James S Mudron, *Owner*
EMP: 5 **EST:** 1973
SQ FT: 6,000
SALES (est): 320K **Privately Held**
SIC: 2441 Boxes, wood

(G-77)
K&C MACHINE INC
310 Steel St (15001-5416)
PHONE..................724 375-3633
William Campbell, *President*
EMP: 3
SALES (est): 358K **Privately Held**
SIC: 3599 Machine shop, jobbing & repair

(G-78)
KENNEDY BEVERAGE LLC
1523 Kennedy Blvd (15001-2619)
PHONE..................724 302-0123
Gloria Krotec, *Bd of Directors*
EMP: 6
SALES (est): 352.2K **Privately Held**
SIC: 2082 Beer (alcoholic beverage)

(G-79)
KROSS CABINETS
2313 W Main St (15001-2821)
PHONE..................724 375-7504
Dan Kross, *Principal*
EMP: 4
SALES (est): 444.4K **Privately Held**
SIC: 2434 Wood kitchen cabinets

(G-80)
LEHIGH CEMENT COMPANY LLC
100 Woodlawn Rd (15001-5404)
PHONE..................724 378-2232
Mike Pusack, *Manager*
EMP: 3
SALES (corp-wide): 20.6B **Privately Held**
WEB: www.lehighcement.com
SIC: 3273 Ready-mixed concrete
HQ: Lehigh Cement Company Llc
300 E John Carpenter Fwy
Irving TX 75062
877 534-4442

(G-81)
M & R WOODWORKS INC
412 Chapel Rd Apt C (15001-1695)
PHONE..................724 378-7677
Ronald Stillwagon, *President*
Marty Gussenhofen, *Vice Pres*
EMP: 5
SALES: 500K **Privately Held**
SIC: 2431 5211 2499 Millwork; millwork & lumber; decorative wood & woodwork

(G-82)
MACS DONUT SHOP INC (PA)
2698 Brodhead Rd (15001-2768)
P.O. Box 1172 (15001-6172)
PHONE..................724 375-6776
James Mc Kittrick, *President*
Twila Mc Kittrick, *Vice Pres*
EMP: 28
SQ FT: 3,500

SALES (est): 3.1MM **Privately Held**
SIC: 5461 5149 2051 Doughnuts; bakery products; bread, cake & related products

(G-83)
MED-FAST PHARMACY LP (PA)
2003 Sheffield Rd (15001-2799)
PHONE..................866 979-7378
Doug Kaleugher, *Partner*
EMP: 6
SALES (est): 1.9MM **Privately Held**
SIC: 2834 Adrenal pharmaceutical preparations

(G-84)
METALWERKS INC
401 Steel St (15001-5497)
PHONE..................724 378-9020
Edward Demailo, *President*
EMP: 30
SALES (est): 2MM **Privately Held**
SIC: 3444 Sheet metalwork

(G-85)
MICROLITE CORPORATION
2315 Mill St (15001-2228)
PHONE..................724 375-6711
D Thomas Podnar, *President*
Lois Podnar, *Admin Sec*
EMP: 7
SQ FT: 5,400
SALES (est): 818.3K **Privately Held**
WEB: www.backupedge.com
SIC: 7372 5045 Utility computer software; computer peripheral equipment

(G-86)
MODERNE GLASS COMPANY INC (PA)
1000 Industrial Blvd (15001-4871)
PHONE..................724 857-5700
Thomas J McKnight, *President*
Kris Fredericks, *President*
Paul Kofalt, *President*
Brian Miller, *General Mgr*
Joe Snyder, *General Mgr*
◆ **EMP:** 138 **EST:** 1967
SQ FT: 86,000
SALES (est): 38.6MM **Privately Held**
WEB: www.glassamerica.com
SIC: 3231 Decorated glassware: chipped, engraved, etched, etc.

(G-87)
NATIONAL SIGNS INC
2003 Sheffield Rd (15001-2758)
PHONE..................724 375-3083
Douglas Kaleugar, *President*
Diane Kaleugar, *Vice Pres*
EMP: 9
SALES (est): 1MM **Privately Held**
SIC: 3993 Signs & advertising specialties

(G-88)
PHOENIX BRONZE RESOURCES LLC
100 Steel St (15001-5402)
PHONE..................724 857-2225
William Bonomo, *Owner*
EMP: 6
SALES (est): 1.1MM **Privately Held**
SIC: 3366 Bronze foundry

(G-89)
PRECISION KIDD STEEL CO INC (PA)
1 Quality Way (15001-2459)
PHONE..................724 695-2216
Nicolo Vergani, *President*
Nirav Amin, *Vice Pres*
Joel Ruckert, *QC Mgr*
Dom Lea, *CFO*
Susan Henderson, *Treasurer*
▲ **EMP:** 48
SQ FT: 94,300
SALES: 24.4MM **Privately Held**
WEB: www.precisionkidd.com
SIC: 3316 3315 3312 Cold finishing of steel shapes; steel wire & related products; blast furnaces & steel mills

(G-90)
PROCEQ USA INC (DH)
117 Corporation Dr (15001-4859)
PHONE..................724 512-0330

▲ = Import ▼=Export
◆ =Import/Export

Robert Shaffer, *President*
Robert D Shaffer, *President*
Thomas Ott, *Sls & Mktg Exec*
EMP: 2
SQ FT: 2,000
SALES: 3MM **Privately Held**
WEB: www.procequsa.com
SIC: 3829 Measuring & controlling devices
HQ: Proceq Ag
Ringstrasse 2
Schwerzenbach ZH 8603
433 553-800

(G-91)
SARDELLO INC
Also Called: Sardello's
1000 Corporation Dr (15001-4867)
PHONE..................................724 375-4101
Ray Sardello, *CEO*
David Sardello, *President*
Marc Opalka, *Sales Executive*
Della Junker, *Manager*
Lisa Golonka, *Info Tech Mgr*
▲ **EMP:** 65 **EST:** 1932
SALES (est): 30.3MM **Privately Held**
WEB: www.sardello.com
SIC: 5088 3743 Railroad equipment &
supplies; railroad equipment

(G-92)
SCOTT SMITH G
2116 Sheffield Rd (15001-2732)
PHONE..................................724 378-2880
Scott G Smith, *Owner*
EMP: 3
SALES (est): 247.9K **Privately Held**
SIC: 3851 Frames & parts, eyeglass &
spectacle

(G-93)
SELECTRODE INDUSTRIES INC
100 Commerce Way (15001-4880)
PHONE..................................724 378-6351
Randi Rankin, *Production*
Rich Oliveri, *Branch Mgr*
EMP: 25
SALES (est): 7.3MM
SALES (corp-wide): 21.6MM **Privately
Held**
SIC: 3356 3496 Nonferrous rolling & draw-
ing; miscellaneous fabricated wire prod-
ucts
PA: Selectrode Industries, Inc.
230 Broadway
Huntington Station NY 11746
631 547-5470

(G-94)
SHASTA INC (HQ)
300 Steel St (15001-5416)
PHONE..................................724 378-8280
John Shutey Sr, *Ch of Bd*
John Shutey Jr, *President*
Martin Ragan, *Vice Pres*
EMP: 31
SQ FT: 150,000
SALES (est): 8.7MM
SALES (corp-wide): 975.7MM **Publicly
Held**
WEB: www.shasta.com
SIC: 3599 8742 Machine shop, jobbing &
repair; industrial consultant
PA: National Beverage Corp.
8100 Sw 10th St Ste 4000
Plantation FL 33324
954 581-0922

(G-95)
**SHASTA HOLDINGS COMPANY
(PA)**
300 Steel St (15001-5416)
PHONE..................................724 378-8280
John Shutey Jr, *President*
Tina Oros, *Office Mgr*
EMP: 140
SQ FT: 150,000
SALES (est): 14.2MM **Privately Held**
SIC: 3599 8742 Grinding castings for the
trade; industrial consultant

(G-96)
**SIMPSON TECHNICAL SALES
INC**
212 University Dr (15001-1645)
PHONE..................................724 375-7133
David B Simpson, *CEO*

Leona Simpson, *Corp Secy*
EMP: 5
SQ FT: 3,000
SALES: 500K **Privately Held**
SIC: 3599 Machine shop, jobbing & repair

(G-97)
**SPECIAL ELECTRIC MOTOR
COMPANY**
148 Davidson Ln (15001-5778)
PHONE..................................724 378-4200
Ben Koda, *President*
Linda Koda, *Corp Secy*
EMP: 7
SALES (est): 1.2MM **Privately Held**
SIC: 7694 Electric motor repair

(G-98)
**UNITED STATES GYPSUM
COMPANY**
1 Woodlawn Rd (15001-5400)
PHONE..................................724 857-4300
John Kibler, *Foreman/Supr*
Pedro Menedez, *Branch Mgr*
EMP: 100
SALES (corp-wide): 3.3B **Publicly Held**
WEB: www.usg.com
SIC: 3275 Gypsum products
HQ: United States Gypsum Company
550 W Adams St Ste 1300
Chicago IL 60661
312 606-4000

(G-99)
VALVES INC
1291 Airport Rd (15001-4314)
P.O. Box 1186 (15001-0986)
PHONE..................................724 378-0600
George Wilson, *President*
Curtis Woods, *Vice Pres*
Amy Woods, *Treasurer*
Susan Wilson, *Admin Sec*
EMP: 18 **EST:** 1962
SQ FT: 20,000
SALES (est): 2.9MM **Privately Held**
WEB: www.valvesinc.com
SIC: 7699 5085 3494 Valve repair, indus-
trial; industrial supplies; valves & pipe fit-
tings

(G-100)
**VERSATEX BUILDING
PRODUCTS LLC**
400 Steel St (15001-5420)
PHONE..................................724 857-1111
John Pace, *President*
Evan Kaffenes, *Vice Pres*
Jared Krehnovi, *Production*
Josh Pace, *Engineer*
Matt Rossi, *Regl Sales Mgr*
▲ **EMP:** 70
SQ FT: 55,000
SALES (est): 18.3MM
SALES (corp-wide): 958.4MM **Publicly
Held**
WEB: www.wolftec.com
SIC: 3089 Plastic hardware & building
products
HQ: Cpg International Llc
1330 W Fulton St Ste 350
Chicago IL 60607
570 558-8000

(G-101)
VINOMIS LABORATORIES LLC
841 23rd St Ste 2 (15001-2784)
PHONE..................................877 484-6664
Barry Yarkoni,
EMP: 5
SALES (est): 139.9K **Privately Held**
SIC: 2023 Dietary supplements, dairy &
non-dairy based

(G-102)
**VISTA MANUFACTURING INC
(PA)**
1201 State Route 18 (15001-5998)
PHONE..................................724 495-6860
Barbara A McGaffic, *President*
EMP: 5
SQ FT: 14,000
SALES (est): 1MM **Privately Held**
SIC: 3599 Machine shop, jobbing & repair

(G-103)
WW HENRY COMPANY LP (DH)
400 Ardex Park Dr (15001-8420)
PHONE..................................704 203-5000
Stephan Liozu, *Partner*
Lori Pietsch Angelo, *Partner*
Dieter Gundlach, *Partner*
▲ **EMP:** 20 **EST:** 2003
SALES (est): 40.5MM
SALES (corp-wide): 1.6MM **Privately
Held**
WEB: www.wwhenry.com
SIC: 2891 Adhesives
HQ: Ardex, L. P.
400 Ardex Park Dr Ste 1
Aliquippa PA 15001
724 203-5000

Allenport
Washington County

(G-104)
**CAPSTONE ENERGY SERVICES
LLC (PA)**
1 Wheeling Pittsburgh Dr (15412)
PHONE..................................724 326-0190
Louis Ruscitto, *CEO*
Gentry Williams, *President*
Michelle Herron, *CFO*
EMP: 250 **EST:** 2014
SQ FT: 1,500
SALES: 30MM **Privately Held**
SIC: 1389 Servicing oil & gas wells; pipe
testing, oil field service

(G-105)
**T & T PRTG T & SYMBOL T
PRINTI**
1875 Main St (15412)
PHONE..................................724 938-9495
Teri Mitchell, *Principal*
EMP: 3 **EST:** 2010
SALES (est): 273.4K **Privately Held**
SIC: 2752 Commercial printing, litho-
graphic

Allensville
Mifflin County

(G-106)
**ALLENSVILLE PLANING MILL
INC (PA)**
108 E Main St (17002-9750)
P.O. Box 177 (17002-0177)
PHONE..................................717 483-6386
Robert P Meai, *President*
Joseph M Westover, *Vice Pres*
Mark R Bechtel, *Treasurer*
Linda M Frehn, *Treasurer*
Rick Carson, *Manager*
EMP: 150
SQ FT: 63,000
SALES (est): 47.3MM **Privately Held**
WEB: www.apm-inc.net
SIC: 5211 2439 Millwork & lumber; home
centers; trusses, wooden roof

(G-107)
BIG VALLEY HARDWOOD
12794 Fawn Ln (17002-9529)
PHONE..................................717 483-6440
Joseph Peachy, *Owner*
EMP: 11
SQ FT: 10,000
SALES: 2MM **Privately Held**
SIC: 2421 Sawmills & planing mills, gen-
eral

(G-108)
J M WOOD PRODUCTS
Hc 61 (17002)
PHONE..................................717 483-6700
David Zook, *Owner*
EMP: 10
SALES (est): 760.2K **Privately Held**
SIC: 2426 Lumber, hardwood dimension

Allentown
Lehigh County

(G-109)
13 BIG BEARS INC
Also Called: Signs By Tomorrow
5925 Tilghman St Ste 400 (18104-8101)
PHONE..................................610 437-6123
Steve Cunic, *President*
EMP: 4
SALES (est): 39K **Privately Held**
SIC: 3993 Signs & advertising specialties

(G-110)
**639 E CONGRESS REALTY
CORP**
639 E Congress St (18109-3202)
PHONE..................................610 434-5195
James C Apgar, *President*
EMP: 10
SALES (est): 485K **Privately Held**
SIC: 1382 Oil & gas exploration services

(G-111)
A L BAZZINI CO INC (PA)
1035 Mill Rd (18106-3101)
PHONE..................................610 366-1606
Rocco Damato, *President*
James Strong Jr, *Corp Secy*
Eric Currivan, *Shareholder*
Joanne Marino, *Shareholder*
Herman Oveidia, *Shareholder*
◆ **EMP:** 27 **EST:** 1969
SALES (est): 59.4MM **Privately Held**
WEB: www.bazzininuts.com
SIC: 5149 2068 3423 5145 Fruits, dried;
salted & roasted nuts & seeds; dehy-
drated fruits, vegetables, soups; nuts,
salted or roasted

(G-112)
A SCHULMAN INC
6355 Farm Bureau Rd (18106-9253)
PHONE..................................610 398-5900
Eric Parsons, *Owner*
EMP: 3
SALES (est): 294.4K **Privately Held**
SIC: 2821 Plastics materials & resins

(G-113)
ABE ALARM SERVICE
1014 N Quebec St (18109-1607)
P.O. Box 90007 (18109-0007)
PHONE..................................484 664-7304
Hal Long, *Principal*
Mark Withers, *Sales Staff*
EMP: 3 **EST:** 2008
SALES (est): 187.5K **Privately Held**
SIC: 7382 5063 3699 Burglar alarm main-
tenance & monitoring; electric alarms &
signaling equipment; high-energy particle
physics equipment

(G-114)
ACME CRYOGENICS INC (PA)
2801 Mitchell Ave (18103-7111)
P.O. Box 445 (18105-0445)
PHONE..................................610 966-4488
John Michael Brown, *President*
Eileen Brotzman, *Buyer*
Tony Delong, *Engrg Mgr*
Bob Bennet, *Engineer*
Ardyth Schaffer, *Senior Engr*
▲ **EMP:** 55 **EST:** 1976
SQ FT: 32,000
SALES (est): 39.6MM **Privately Held**
WEB: www.acmecryo.com
SIC: 3559 3498 3599 3494 Cryogenic
machinery, industrial; piping systems for
pulp paper & chemical industries; ma-
chine shop, jobbing & repair; valves &
pipe fittings

(G-115)
ADCOMM INC
2626 W Washington St (18104-3871)
PHONE..................................610 820-8565
Richard D Mikitz, *President*
Leo V Morrison Jr, *Admin Sec*
EMP: 14 **EST:** 1968
SQ FT: 14,000

GEOGRAPHIC

SALES (est): 1.3MM **Privately Held**
SIC: 7336 2752 7311 2791 Graphic arts & related design; commercial printing, offset; advertising agencies; typesetting

(G-116)
ADHESIVES SPECIALISTS INC
Also Called: As
739 Roble Rd (18109-9141)
PHONE....................610 266-8910
Steven Russo, *President*
Virginia Kingsnorth, *Vice Pres*
Michael Patterson, *Opers Staff*
Laurett Elfand, *Manager*
▲ EMP: 35
SQ FT: 50,000
SALES (est): 12.5MM **Privately Held**
WEB: www.adhesivesspecialists.com
SIC: 2891 Adhesives

(G-117)
AETNA FELT CORP
Also Called: Weppco
2401 W Emaus Ave (18103-7234)
PHONE....................610 791-0900
James F Weppler, *President*
Peg Donmoyer, *Traffic Mgr*
Janet Dodgen, *Admin Sec*
▲ EMP: 55
SQ FT: 93,000
SALES (est): 9.4MM **Privately Held**
WEB: www.aetnafelt.com
SIC: 2299 Felts & felt products

(G-118)
AGERE SYSTEMS INC
1110 American Pkwy Ne (18109-9117)
PHONE....................610 712-1000
Richard L Clemmer, *CEO*
John Gamble Jr, *Vice Pres*
Peter Kelly, *CFO*
Hanjo Van Houwelingen, *Manager*
▲ EMP: 1500
SALES (est): 169.4MM
SALES (corp-wide): 20.8B **Publicly Held**
WEB: www.agere.com
SIC: 3674 Microcircuits, integrated (semiconductor)
HQ: Lsi Corporation
    1320 Ridder Park Dr
    San Jose CA 95131
    408 433-8000

(G-119)
AIR PRODUCTS AND CHEMICALS INC (PA)
7201 Hamilton Blvd (18195-9642)
PHONE....................610 481-4911
Seifollah Ghasemi, *Ch of Bd*
Sean D Major, *Exec VP*
Corning F Painter, *Exec VP*
Samir Serhan, *Exec VP*
Victoria Brifo, *Senior VP*
◆ EMP: 3800 EST: 1940
SALES: 8.9B **Publicly Held**
WEB: www.airproducts.com
SIC: 2842 2891 3569 2813 Ammonia, household; adhesives; gas producers, generators & other gas related equipment; gas separators (machinery); separators for steam, gas, vapor or air (machinery); oxygen, compressed or liquefied

(G-120)
AIR PRODUCTS AND CHEMICALS INC
7331 William Ave (18106-9325)
PHONE....................610 395-2101
Dave Hoover, *Branch Mgr*
EMP: 25
SALES (corp-wide): 8.9B **Publicly Held**
SIC: 2813 Industrial gases
PA: Air Products And Chemicals, Inc.
    7201 Hamilton Blvd
    Allentown PA 18195
    610 481-4911

(G-121)
AIR PRODUCTS AND CHEMICALS INC
645 Hamilton St (18101-2109)
PHONE....................610 481-2057
EMP: 5

SALES (corp-wide): 8.9B **Publicly Held**
SIC: 2813 Industrial gases
PA: Air Products And Chemicals, Inc.
    7201 Hamilton Blvd
    Allentown PA 18195
    610 481-4911

(G-122)
AIR PRODUCTS AND CHEMICALS INC
1919 Vultee St (18103-4744)
PHONE....................610 481-3706
David Fritts, *Manager*
EMP: 100
SQ FT: 32,708
SALES (corp-wide): 8.9B **Publicly Held**
WEB: www.airproducts.com
SIC: 2813 Industrial gases
PA: Air Products And Chemicals, Inc.
    7201 Hamilton Blvd
    Allentown PA 18195
    610 481-4911

(G-123)
AIR PRODUCTS LLC
7201 Hamilton Blvd (18195-9642)
PHONE....................610 481-4911
Laurie Stewart, *President*
George Bitto, *Vice Pres*
Jeffry Byrne, *Vice Pres*
William Hammarstrom, *Vice Pres*
Paul Huck, *Vice Pres*
EMP: 192
SALES (est): 203.8K
SALES (corp-wide): 8.9B **Publicly Held**
SIC: 2813 Industrial gases
HQ: Air Products Helium, Inc.
    15139 County Road 9
    Gruver TX 79040

(G-124)
ALL TECH-D OUT LLC
1155 Union Blvd (18109-1556)
PHONE....................610 814-0888
Jason Gutierrez, *Owner*
EMP: 13 EST: 2011
SALES: 500K **Privately Held**
SIC: 7378 3661 5946 Computer & data processing equipment repair/maintenance; PBX equipment, manual or automatic; cameras

(G-125)
ALLEGRA PRINT IMAGING
Also Called: Insty-Prints
435 Allentown Dr (18109-9121)
PHONE....................610 882-2229
Gary Chowansky, *President*
Carol Chowansky,
EMP: 9
SQ FT: 6,000
SALES (est): 1.4MM **Privately Held**
SIC: 2752 7334 Commercial printing, offset; photocopying & duplicating services

(G-126)
ALLENTECH INC
6350 Hedgewood Dr # 100 (18106-9257)
PHONE....................484 664-7887
Douglas Leh, *President*
Mike Knapik, *Engineer*
Kevin Hancharik, *Treasurer*
Terry Wise, *Executive*
Brandon Troxell, *Admin Sec*
◆ EMP: 85
SQ FT: 42,000
SALES (est): 22.4MM **Privately Held**
WEB: www.allentech.com
SIC: 3444 Sheet metalwork

(G-127)
ALLENTOWN AUTO ELECTRIC LLC
527 N Madison St (18102-2130)
PHONE....................610 432-2888
David Matos, *Mng Member*
EMP: 4
SALES (est): 106.9K **Privately Held**
SIC: 3699 Electrical work

(G-128)
ALLENTOWN LIMB & BRACE INC
1808 W Allen St (18104-5025)
PHONE....................610 437-2254

Henry Schondorfer, *President*
EMP: 5 EST: 1971
SALES (est): 680.3K **Privately Held**
SIC: 3842 Limbs, artificial; braces, orthopedic; orthopedic appliances

(G-129)
ALLENTOWN OPTICAL CORP
525 Business Park Ln (18109-9115)
P.O. Box 25003, Lehigh Valley (18002-5003)
PHONE....................610 433-5269
Michael Gassler, *President*
Leroy Hausrath, *Admin Sec*
▲ EMP: 30
SALES (est): 3.4MM **Privately Held**
WEB: www.allentownoptical.com
SIC: 5048 3851 3827 Ophthalmic goods; lens grinding, except prescription: ophthalmic; optical instruments & lenses

(G-130)
AMCOR RIGID PLASTICS USA INC
Also Called: Amcor Rigid Plas - Allentown
6974 Schantz Rd (18106-9399)
PHONE....................610 871-9000
Michael Warhola, *Principal*
▲ EMP: 29
SALES (est): 172.3MM **Privately Held**
SIC: 3089 Blow molded finished plastic products; plastic containers, except foam
HQ: Amcor Packaging (Usa), Inc.
    2801 Sw 149th Ave Fl 3
    Miramar FL 33027
    714 562-6000

(G-131)
AMCOR RIGID PLASTICS USA LLC
Also Called: Schmalbch-Lubeca Plastic Cntrs
6974 Schantz Rd Ste C (18106-9399)
PHONE....................610 871-9035
Craig Psass, *Manager*
EMP: 190 **Privately Held**
WEB: www.slpcamericas.com
SIC: 3089 Plastic containers, except foam
HQ: Amcor Rigid Plastics Usa, Llc
    935 Technology Dr Ste 100
    Ann Arbor MI 48108

(G-132)
AMERICAN ARCHITECTURAL METAL M
575 Business Park Ln (18109-9115)
PHONE....................610 432-9787
Sahar Atiyeh, *President*
George Atiyeh Jr, *Vice Pres*
EMP: 12
SQ FT: 10,000
SALES: 2.5MM **Privately Held**
WEB: www.americanarch.com
SIC: 3444 Metal roofing & roof drainage equipment

(G-133)
AMERICAN ATELIER INC
Also Called: A A I
2132 Downyflake Ln (18103-4725)
PHONE....................610 439-4040
David Goodman, *President*
Donald Goodman, *President*
Jim Decamp, *Vice Pres*
Kyle Henning, *Purchasing*
Jim Banko, *CFO*
▲ EMP: 175
SQ FT: 100,000
SALES (est): 25.2MM **Privately Held**
WEB: www.americanatelierinc.com
SIC: 2511 2531 2521 2512 Wood household furniture; blackboards, wood; wood office furniture; chairs: upholstered on wood frames

(G-134)
AMERICAN DENTAL SUPPLY INC
Also Called: ADS
1075 N Gilmore St (18109-3210)
PHONE....................484 223-3940
Ricky Hochhauser, *President*
Leslie Hochhauser, *Vice Pres*
▲ EMP: 10
SQ FT: 10,000

SALES (est): 1.8MM **Privately Held**
WEB: www.americandentalinc.com
SIC: 3843 Dental materials

(G-135)
AMERICAN HYDRAULIC MFG
109 Roble Rd (18103)
PHONE....................610 264-8542
James Schlegel, *President*
EMP: 5
SQ FT: 9,500
SALES (est): 569.4K **Privately Held**
SIC: 3594 3593 7699 Pumps, hydraulic power transfer; fluid power cylinders, hydraulic or pneumatic; hydraulic equipment repair

(G-136)
AMERICAN PHARMACEUTICAL
4825 W Tilghman St (18104-9374)
PHONE....................610 366-9000
Yasin Khan, *Principal*
EMP: 6
SALES (est): 624K **Privately Held**
SIC: 2834 Pharmaceutical preparations

(G-137)
ANTHONY HAUZE
Also Called: T Gear
391 Auburn St Ste A (18103-3355)
PHONE....................610 432-3533
Anthony Hauze, *President*
EMP: 3
SQ FT: 2,000
SALES (est): 355K **Privately Held**
SIC: 2339 Women's & misses' athletic clothing & sportswear; sportswear, women's

(G-138)
ANTONES AT THE MARK INC
1801 S 12th St Ste 5 (18103-2927)
PHONE....................610 798-9218
Frank Costantino, *President*
Tony Costantino, *Vice Pres*
EMP: 5
SQ FT: 10,000
SALES: 500K **Privately Held**
SIC: 5722 2434 Kitchens, complete (sinks, cabinets, etc.); wood kitchen cabinets

(G-139)
ANVIL FORGE & HAMMER IR WORKS
6337 Airport Rd (18109-9002)
PHONE....................610 837-9951
Kenneth Di Menichi, *President*
Nancy Di Menichi, *Treasurer*
Richard Di Menichi, *Manager*
EMP: 4 EST: 1955
SALES (est): 200K **Privately Held**
SIC: 3542 3446 Machine tools, metal forming type; railings, prefabricated metal

(G-140)
APEX APPAREL INC
Also Called: Summit Apparel
1801 S 12th St Ste 4 (18103-2927)
PHONE....................610 432-8007
Emanuel Mayeri, *CEO*
▲ EMP: 80
SQ FT: 4,000
SALES (est): 7MM **Privately Held**
SIC: 2253 T-shirts & tops, knit

(G-141)
APPLIED SEPARATIONS INC
Also Called: Asi Holding
930 Hamilton St Ste 4 (18101-1194)
P.O. Box 20032, Lehigh Valley (18002-0032)
PHONE....................610 770-0900
Rolf Schlake, *President*
Martin J Fetner, *Vice Pres*
Alfred C Kaziunis, *Vice Pres*
Jerry Soltes, *Senior Engr*
Lisa Williams, *Admin Asst*
▲ EMP: 30
SQ FT: 37,000
SALES (est): 6.5MM **Privately Held**
WEB: www.appliedseparations.com
SIC: 3826 3829 3821 Analytical instruments; measuring & controlling devices; laboratory apparatus & furniture

▲ = Import ▼=Export
◆ =Import/Export

G
E
O
G
R
A
P
H
I
C

(G-142)
ARAI HELMET AMERICAS INC
Also Called: Arai Technical Services
7020 Snowdrift Rd (18106-9274)
PHONE.................................610 366-7220
Roger B Weston, *President*
Brian Weston, *Vice Pres*
▲ EMP: 5
SALES (est): 529.2K **Privately Held**
SIC: 3469 Helmets, steel

(G-143)
ARTMAN AND ARTMAN INC
Also Called: Trinity Manufacturing Tech
1137 N Godfrey St Unit 2 (18109-3503)
PHONE.................................610 821-3970
James Artman, *President*
Tammy Artman, *Corp Secy*
EMP: 10
SALES (est): 1.3MM **Privately Held**
WEB: www.artman.net
SIC: 3599 Machine shop, jobbing & repair

(G-144)
ASGCO (PA)
302 W Gordon St (18102-3135)
PHONE.................................610 821-0216
Scott Unger, *Exec Dir*
▲ EMP: 4
SALES (est): 1.5MM **Privately Held**
SIC: 3535 Conveyors & conveying equip-
ment

(G-145)
ATIYEH PRINTING INC
1002 W Tilghman St (18102-2227)
PHONE.................................610 439-8978
Raymond Atiyeh, *President*
Elie Atiyeh, *Vice Pres*
Lynette Atiyeh, *Treasurer*
EMP: 4
SQ FT: 5,400
SALES: 300K **Privately Held**
WEB: www.atiyehprinting.com
SIC: 2759 Screen printing

(G-146)
**BASF CONSTRUCTION CHEM
LLC**
7234 Penn Dr (18106-9310)
PHONE.................................610 391-0633
Carl Griffin, *Manager*
EMP: 8
SQ FT: 20,000
SALES (corp-wide): 71.7B **Privately Held**
WEB: www.basf-admixtures.com
SIC: 2899 Concrete curing & hardening
compounds
HQ: Master Builders, Llc
23700 Chagrin Blvd
Beachwood OH 44122
216 831-5500

(G-147)
BAZZINI HOLDINGS LLC
1035 Mill Rd (18106-3101)
PHONE.................................610 366-1606
Richard Toltzis, *COO*
Kevin Thornton, *CFO*
Rocco Damato, *Mng Member*
▲ EMP: 250 EST: 2005
SQ FT: 200,000
SALES: 76MM **Privately Held**
SIC: 2068 2064 Salted & roasted nuts &
seeds; candy & other confectionery prod-
ucts

(G-148)
BEHR PROCESS CORPORATION
7529 Morris Ct Ste 500 (18106-9226)
PHONE.................................610 391-1085
Jeffrey D Filley, *Branch Mgr*
EMP: 153
SALES (corp-wide): 8.3B **Publicly Held**
WEB: www.behr.com
SIC: 5198 2851 Paints; paints & allied
products
HQ: Behr Process Corporation
1801 E Saint Andrew Pl
Santa Ana CA 92705

(G-149)
BELLETIERI SAUCES INC (PA)
1207 Chew St (18102-3751)
PHONE.................................610 433-4334

Louis Belletieri, *President*
EMP: 4
SALES (est): 456.5K **Privately Held**
SIC: 2035 5812 Seasonings & sauces, ex-
cept tomato & dry; eating places

(G-150)
BETHLEHEM ALUMINUM INC
270 E Hamilton St (18109-2548)
PHONE.................................610 432-4541
Robert M Burdette, *President*
Bonnie Burdette, *Admin Sec*
EMP: 13 EST: 1955
SQ FT: 25,500
SALES (est): 2.8MM **Privately Held**
WEB: www.bethlehemaluminum.com
SIC: 5051 3441 3446 Aluminum bars,
rods, ingots, sheets, pipes, plates, etc.;
fabricated structural metal; architectural
metalwork

(G-151)
BIO MED SCIENCES INC
7584 Morris Ct Ste 218 (18106-9250)
PHONE.................................610 530-3193
Mark E Dillon, *CEO*
EMP: 14
SQ FT: 16,000
SALES (est): 2.3MM **Privately Held**
WEB: www.biomedsciences.com
SIC: 8731 3841 Medical research, com-
mercial; surgical & medical instruments

(G-152)
**BIOSCIENCE MANAGEMENT
INC**
2201 Hangar Pl Ste 200 (18109-9342)
PHONE.................................484 245-5232
Thomas Zitrides, *President*
Don Egner, *General Mgr*
▼ EMP: 10
SQ FT: 12,000
SALES (est): 2.1MM **Privately Held**
WEB: www.bioscienceinc.com
SIC: 2836 3826 Biological products, ex-
cept diagnostic; analytical instruments

(G-153)
BITARS SPORTSWEAR
207 W Tilghman St (18102-2516)
PHONE.................................610 435-4923
Michael Bitar, *Owner*
EMP: 5
SALES (est): 152.4K **Privately Held**
SIC: 2329 2339 Men's & boys' sportswear
& athletic clothing; sportswear, women's

(G-154)
BLACK & DECKER (US) INC
Also Called: Sws Vidmarlista
11 Grammes Rd (18103-4760)
PHONE.................................610 797-6600
EMP: 678
SALES (corp-wide): 13.9B **Publicly Held**
SIC: 3699 Security devices
HQ: Black & Decker (U.S.) Inc.
1000 Stanley Dr
New Britain CT 06053
860 225-5111

(G-155)
BLUE STEEL DISTILLERY
321 S Carlisle St (18109-2801)
PHONE.................................610 820-7116
EMP: 3
SALES (est): 142.8K **Privately Held**
SIC: 2085 Distilled & blended liquors

(G-156)
BOAS SURGICAL INC (PA)
3050 Hamilton Blvd # 220 (18103-3691)
PHONE.................................484 895-3451
Jeffrey P Fussner, *President*
EMP: 34
SQ FT: 13,000
SALES (est): 6.8MM **Privately Held**
WEB: www.boassurgical.com
SIC: 5999 3842 Orthopedic & prosthesis
applications; prosthetic appliances

(G-157)
BOMBOY INC
1621 E Race St (18109-9569)
PHONE.................................610 266-1553
Paula Bomboy, *President*
Kevin Downey, *Plant Mgr*

Dan Barr, *Project Mgr*
EMP: 15
SQ FT: 22,000
SALES (est): 3.5MM **Privately Held**
WEB: www.bomboy.com
SIC: 2441 2673 Cases, wood; bags: plas-
tic, laminated & coated

(G-158)
**BRADLEY PULVERIZER
COMPANY (PA)**
123 S 3rd St (18102-4909)
PHONE.................................610 432-2101
Dames D Fronheiser, *President*
James Fronheiser, *President*
David I Fronheiser, *Vice Pres*
Kevin Perl, *Prdtn Mgr*
Keith Wetzel, *Purchasing*
◆ EMP: 18
SQ FT: 30,000
SALES (est): 6.5MM **Privately Held**
WEB: www.bradleypulv.com
SIC: 3532 Pulverizers (stationary), stone

(G-159)
C J APPAREL INC
747 Pittston St Ste 3 (18103-3255)
PHONE.................................610 432-8265
Nguyet Nguyen, *President*
Paul Reid, *Vice Pres*
EMP: 45
SQ FT: 65,000
SALES (est): 4.4MM **Privately Held**
WEB: www.cjapparel.com
SIC: 2231 Apparel & outerwear broadwo-
ven fabrics

(G-160)
C LESLIE SMITH INC
Also Called: Smith, C Leslie
3100 W Tilghman St (18104-4266)
PHONE.................................610 439-8833
Charles Leslie Smith, *President*
Tom Jones, *Vice Pres*
EMP: 23
SQ FT: 4,000
SALES (est): 2.4MM **Privately Held**
SIC: 3911 5944 5947 Jewelry, precious
metal; jewelry, precious stones & precious
metals; gift shop

(G-161)
**CARD PRSNLZATION
SOLUTIONS LLC (PA)**
Also Called: C P S
7520 Morris Ct Ste 100 (18106-9236)
PHONE.................................610 231-1860
Jim Cooney, *COO*
Rob Schasteen, *Vice Pres*
Ethan Stehman, *Vice Pres*
Tom Marchak, *Project Mgr*
Tim Johnson, *Prdtn Mgr*
EMP: 100 EST: 1998
SQ FT: 20,000
SALES (est): 25.8MM **Privately Held**
WEB: www.crdpersol.com
SIC: 2752 Commercial printing, litho-
graphic

(G-162)
**CARIBBEAN ELITE MAGAZINE
INC**
448 N 17th St (18104-5015)
PHONE.................................718 702-0161
Keyonee Hill, *President*
EMP: 4
SALES (est): 99.8K **Privately Held**
SIC: 2731 Books: publishing only

(G-163)
CARPENTER CO
57 Olin Way (18106-9368)
PHONE.................................610 366-5110
David Bailey, *Manager*
▲ EMP: 4 EST: 2012
SALES (est): 566.1K **Privately Held**
SIC: 3086 Insulation or cushioning mate-
rial, foamed plastic

(G-164)
CARPENTER CO
1100 Mill Rd (18106-3124)
PHONE.................................610 366-8349
EMP: 3 EST: 2013

SALES (est): 200K **Privately Held**
SIC: 3086 Mfg Plastic Foam Products

(G-165)
CAST PAC INC
206 Cascade Dr (18109-9579)
PHONE.................................610 264-8131
Donald Caldwell, *President*
EMP: 46
SALES (est): 4.1MM **Privately Held**
WEB: www.castdiv.com
SIC: 7389 3441 Packaging & labeling
services; fabricated structural metal

(G-166)
CELLULAR CONCRETE LLC
Also Called: Aerix Industries
7020 Snowdrift Rd (18106-9395)
PHONE.................................610 398-7833
Rich Palladino,
EMP: 10
SALES (est): 1.3MM **Privately Held**
SIC: 5169 3531 3272 Concrete additives;
construction machinery; concrete prod-
ucts

(G-167)
**CENCO GRINDING
CORPORATION**
411 Business Park Ln (18109-9120)
PHONE.................................610 434-5740
Michael Meade, *CEO*
Steve Zimmerman, *President*
EMP: 4
SQ FT: 3,200
SALES (est): 709.6K **Privately Held**
WEB: www.drillblanks.com
SIC: 3545 Machine tool accessories

(G-168)
CHEMEX INC (PA)
327 Burrell Blvd (18104-9523)
P.O. Box B, Trexlertown (18087-0886)
PHONE.................................610 398-6200
Barry S Melnick, *President*
Jan Melnick, *Vice Pres*
▼ EMP: 2
SALES (est): 18.3MM **Privately Held**
SIC: 5162 5169 3084 4953 Plastics ma-
terials; chemicals & allied products; plas-
tics pipe; recycling, waste materials

(G-169)
**CHERRYDALE FUNDRAISING
LLC**
1035 Mill Rd (18106-3101)
PHONE.................................610 366-1606
Nellie Mahabir,
EMP: 5
SALES (est): 222K **Privately Held**
SIC: 2066 Chocolate

(G-170)
CISCO SYSTEMS INC
7540 Windsor Dr (18195-1015)
PHONE.................................610 336-8500
John T Chambers, *CEO*
Mark Webster, *Sales Staff*
EMP: 656
SALES (corp-wide): 48B **Publicly Held**
SIC: 3577 Data conversion equipment,
media-to-media: computer
PA: Cisco Systems, Inc.
170 W Tasman Dr
San Jose CA 95134
408 526-4000

(G-171)
CLARKE SYSTEM
1857 W Walnut St (18104-6701)
PHONE.................................610 434-9889
Fax: 610 434-9868
EMP: 25 EST: 2010
SALES (est): 1.7MM **Privately Held**
SIC: 3993 Mfg Signs/Advertising Special-
ties

(G-172)
COCA-COLA COMPANY
7551 Schantz Rd (18106-9009)
PHONE.................................610 530-3900
Jan Jenkins, *Principal*
EMP: 250

SALES (corp-wide): 35.4B **Publicly Held**
WEB: www.cocacola.com
SIC: **2087** 2086 2033 2037 Concentrates, drink; syrups, drink; fruit drinks (less than 100% juice): packaged in cans, etc.; soft drinks: packaged in cans, bottles, etc.; fruit juices: fresh; fruit juice concentrates, frozen
PA: The Coca-Cola Company
　1 Coca Cola Plz Nw
　Atlanta GA 30313
　404 676-2121

(G-173)
COMMERCIAL COLOR INC
6330 Farm Bureau Rd Frnt (18106-9584)
PHONE..................................610 391-7444
Paul R Weis Jr, *President*
EMP: 4
SQ FT: 5,000
SALES (est): 476K **Privately Held**
WEB: www.commercialcolor.com
SIC: **2759** Poster & decal printing & engraving

(G-174)
CONESTOGA CO INC
323 Sumner Ave (18102-1856)
P.O. Box 405, Bethlehem (18016-0405)
PHONE..................................610 866-0777
Ercole Spinosa, *President*
EMP: 8
SQ FT: 2,000
SALES (est): 945.1K **Privately Held**
WEB: www.bigbangcannons.com
SIC: **3944** 5945 Games, toys & children's vehicles; hobby, toy & game shops

(G-175)
CONFLUENSE LLC
7277 William Ave Unit 300 (18106-9198)
P.O. Box 113, Furlong (18925-0113)
PHONE..................................215 530-6461
Stephen Benner, *President*
EMP: 3
SALES (est): 179.9K **Privately Held**
SIC: **3291** Scouring abrasive materials

(G-176)
CONNECTIVE TSSUE GENE TSTS LLC
6575 Snowdrift Rd 106 (18106-9353)
PHONE..................................484 244-2900
Kerry K Brown, *Associate Dir*
Leena Alakokko,
EMP: 17
SALES (est): 3MM **Privately Held**
WEB: www.ctgt.net
SIC: **2869** Laboratory chemicals, organic

(G-177)
CONTINENTAL AUTO SYSTEMS INC
Trading & Aftermarket Div
6755 Snowdrift Rd (18106-9353)
PHONE..................................610 289-1390
Mark Pnakovich, *Project Mgr*
Ken Coll, *QC Mgr*
Juvenal Herrera, *Engineer*
Jason Linville, *Engineer*
Derek Whiting, *Engineer*
EMP: 20
SALES (corp-wide): 50.8B **Privately Held**
SIC: **4225** 5084 3714 General warehousing & storage; fuel injection systems; fuel pumps, motor vehicle
HQ: Continental Automotive Systems, Inc.
　1 Continental Dr
　Auburn Hills MI 48326
　248 393-5300

(G-178)
CONTINENTAL CORPORATION
6755 Snowdrift Rd (18106-9353)
PHONE..................................610 289-0488
Martin Sb Okekearu, *President*
Mark Gunderson, *President*
Mark Hall, *Regional Mgr*
James Bayley, *Vice Pres*
Peter Huizinga, *Vice Pres*
EMP: 4
SALES (est): 607.9K
SALES (corp-wide): 50.8B **Privately Held**
SIC: **3714** Motor vehicle brake systems & parts

HQ: Continental Automotive Systems, Inc.
　1 Continental Dr
　Auburn Hills MI 48326
　248 393-5300

(G-179)
CONTOUR SEATS INC
6530 Chapmans Rd (18106-9200)
PHONE..................................610 395-5144
Carl A Gross Jr, *President*
EMP: 7 EST: 1999
SQ FT: 6,800
SALES (est): 1MM **Privately Held**
WEB: www.contourseats.com
SIC: **2531** Stadium seating

(G-180)
CORBY INDUSTRIES INC
812 N Gilmore St (18109-1812)
P.O. Box 4307, Bethlehem (18018-0307)
PHONE..................................610 433-1412
Glenn M Matz, *CEO*
Timothy W Corby, *Exec VP*
Kathleen S Matz, *Vice Pres*
EMP: 5
SQ FT: 4,000
SALES (est): 896.3K **Privately Held**
WEB: www.corby.com
SIC: **3625** Control circuit devices, magnet & solid state

(G-181)
CORETECH INTERNATIONAL INC
1237 Sesqui St (18103-5679)
PHONE..................................908 454-7999
Lauren Green, *Principal*
EMP: 10 EST: 2009
SALES (est): 1.8MM **Privately Held**
SIC: **3541** Machine tools, metal cutting type

(G-182)
CORPORATE IMAGES COMPANY
1434 W Union St (18102-4474)
PHONE..................................610 439-7961
Deck Meginnis, *President*
EMP: 3
SALES (est): 234K **Privately Held**
SIC: **2759** Screen printing

(G-183)
CRAFCO INC
1680 E Race St (18109-9580)
PHONE..................................610 264-7541
William Alesick, *Branch Mgr*
Rich Mitchell, *Executive*
EMP: 8
SQ FT: 30,970
SALES (corp-wide): 1B **Privately Held**
WEB: www.crafco.com
SIC: **2951** Asphalt & asphaltic paving mixtures (not from refineries)
HQ: Crafco, Inc.
　6165 W Detroit St
　Chandler AZ 85226
　602 276-0406

(G-184)
CRAVE CUPCAKES BY TAMARA LLC
4209 Windsor Dr (18104-4405)
PHONE..................................610 417-4909
EMP: 4
SALES (est): 215.2K **Privately Held**
SIC: **2051** Bread, cake & related products

(G-185)
CREATIVE GRAPHICS INC
6620 Grant Way (18106-9316)
PHONE..................................610 973-8300
Joseph Cunningham, *President*
EMP: 40
SQ FT: 12,000
SALES (est): 1.8MM **Privately Held**
WEB: www.bookpub.com
SIC: **7336** 2791 Graphic arts & related design; typesetting

(G-186)
CRESPO & DIAZ INDUSTRIES LLC
850 N 5th St (18102-1762)
PHONE..................................484 895-7139
Crespo Ercides, *Principal*

EMP: 3
SALES (est): 215.5K **Privately Held**
SIC: **3999** Manufacturing industries

(G-187)
CROWN FOOD CARTS INCORPORATED
527 Sumner Ct (18102-1765)
PHONE..................................610 628-9612
Robert Scifo, *CEO*
EMP: 6
SQ FT: 25,000
SALES: 500K **Privately Held**
SIC: **3589** 3537 Commercial cooking & foodwarming equipment; lift trucks, industrial: fork, platform, straddle, etc.

(G-188)
CRYOGENIC GAS TECHNOLOGIES INC
Also Called: Cryo Technologies
241 N Cedar Crest Blvd (18104-4603)
PHONE..................................610 530-7288
Richard Hessinger, *President*
Gerry N Gottier, *Vice Pres*
James McCleery, *Engineer*
Richard Brichta, *Shareholder*
Karen Renninger, *Shareholder*
▲ EMP: 20
SALES (est): 4.7MM **Privately Held**
WEB: www.cryotechnologies.com
SIC: **3559** Cryogenic machinery, industrial

(G-189)
CURIO ELECTRICAL MOTOR REPR SP
825 S 5th St (18103-3307)
PHONE..................................610 432-9923
Daniel M Nasatka Jr, *Owner*
EMP: 3
SQ FT: 1,250
SALES: 320K **Privately Held**
SIC: **7694** Electric motor repair; rewinding services

(G-190)
CUTTS GROUP LLC
847 Dorset Rd (18104-3330)
PHONE..................................610 366-9620
Allyn Cutts, *President*
Diane Cutts, *Admin Sec*
EMP: 10
SALES (est): 642.6K **Privately Held**
WEB: www.cuttsgroup.com
SIC: **2741** 7941 Miscellaneous publishing; sports promotion

(G-191)
DAVEN SHARPE MACHINE PRODUCTS
817 N Gilmore St (18109-1811)
PHONE..................................610 821-4022
Steven Lewellin, *President*
EMP: 6
SQ FT: 5,000
SALES (est): 540K **Privately Held**
WEB: www.daven-sharpe.com
SIC: **3599** Machine shop, jobbing & repair

(G-192)
DAVID WALTERS
Also Called: Dave's Counter Tops
136 W Linden St (18101-1945)
PHONE..................................610 435-5433
David Walters, *Owner*
EMP: 3
SQ FT: 4,000
SALES: 250K **Privately Held**
SIC: **2541** Table or counter tops, plastic laminated

(G-193)
DAYTON SUPERIOR CORPORATION
7130 Ambassador Dr (18106-9254)
PHONE..................................610 366-3890
Jeff Brunel, *Manager*
EMP: 19 **Publicly Held**
WEB: www.daytonsuperior.com
SIC: **3429** Builders' hardware
HQ: Dayton Superior Corporation
　1125 Byers Rd
　Miamisburg OH 45342
　937 866-0711

(G-194)
DIRECT MAIL SERVICE & PRESS
Also Called: DMS
313 Sumner Ave (18102-1898)
PHONE..................................610 432-4538
Tim Spinosa, *President*
David J Spinosa, *Corp Secy*
EMP: 15
SQ FT: 25,000
SALES (est): 2MM **Privately Held**
WEB: www.directdms.com
SIC: **7331** 2752 Mailing service; commercial printing, lithographic

(G-195)
DOMENIC STANGHERLIN
Also Called: Line Tool Co
943 Kurtz St (18102-1427)
PHONE..................................610 434-5624
Domenic Stangherlin, *Owner*
EMP: 6 EST: 1954
SQ FT: 13,500
SALES (est): 578.8K **Privately Held**
WEB: www.linetool.net
SIC: **3625** Positioning controls, electric

(G-196)
DRONETTI UPHOLSTERY INC
415 Auburn St (18103-3317)
PHONE..................................610 435-2957
Joseph Dronetti, *President*
Michael J Dronetti, *Vice Pres*
Claire Dronetti, *Treasurer*
EMP: 4
SQ FT: 6,000
SALES: 200K **Privately Held**
SIC: **2512** 7641 Upholstered household furniture; reupholstery

(G-197)
DT DAVIS ENTERPRISES LTD
Also Called: Hovertech International
4482 Innovation Way (18109-9404)
PHONE..................................610 694-9600
David Davis, *President*
Jerome Smith, *COO*
Susan Pavelko, *QC Mgr*
Jason Davis, *Manager*
Kent Wilson, *Director*
▲ EMP: 4
SQ FT: 67,000
SALES (est): 919.8K **Privately Held**
SIC: **3842** Surgical appliances & supplies

(G-198)
DW SERVICES LLC
1874 Catasauqua Rd # 335 (18109-3128)
PHONE..................................484 241-8915
Dan Sobey,
EMP: 3
SALES (est): 72.9K **Privately Held**
SIC: **1799** 7349 3589 2842 Cleaning new buildings after construction; window cleaning; high pressure cleaning equipment; window cleaning preparations

(G-199)
E SCHNEIDER & SONS INC
616-656 Sumner Ave (18102)
PHONE..................................610 435-3527
John Schneider, *President*
Kristy Friend, *Sales Staff*
EMP: 24
SQ FT: 4,800
SALES (est): 6.5MM **Privately Held**
SIC: **5093** 3341 Ferrous metal scrap & waste; secondary nonferrous metals

(G-200)
EASTERN EXTERIOR WALL
645 Hamilton St Ste 300 (18101-2191)
PHONE..................................610 868-5522
Charles Marcon, *Principal*
Robert Rider, *COO*
EMP: 91
SALES (corp-wide): 172.4MM **Privately Held**
SIC: **2452** Panels & sections, prefabricated, wood
HQ: Wall Eastern Exterior Systems Inc
　645 Hamilton St Ste 300
　Allentown PA 18101
　610 868-5522

2019 Harris Pennsylvania
Manufacturers Directory
▲ = Import ▼=Export
◆ =Import/Export

(G-201)
EASTERN SURFACES INC
601 S 10th St (18103-3689)
PHONE.............................610 266-3121
Brian Rocca, *President*
Charles E Martin, *Vice Pres*
Eileen Flanagan, *Accounts Mgr*
Joan Reese, *Accounts Mgr*
Karen Kuranda, *Sales Staff*
▲ EMP: 85
SALES (est): 15.7MM **Privately Held**
SIC: 3281 1799 Altars, cut stone; counter top installation

(G-202)
ECOTECH INC
999 Postal Rd Ste 100 (18109-9338)
PHONE.............................610 954-8480
Justin Lawyer, *President*
Christopher Clough, *Vice Pres*
Patrick Clasen, *Treasurer*
Tim Marks, *Admin Sec*
EMP: 87 **Privately Held**
SIC: 6719 3561 4941 3646 Investment holding companies, except banks; pumps & pumping equipment; water supply; commercial indusl & institutional electric lighting fixtures; electric lamps

(G-203)
ECOTECH MARINE LLC
999 Postal Rd Ste 100 (18109-9338)
PHONE.............................610 954-8480
Rosemary Serfass, *Buyer*
Mark Lindenmoyer, *Electrical Engi*
Sabrina Weinholtz, *Accounting Mgr*
Jay Sperandio, *Sales Dir*
Eric Brennan, *Sales Staff*
▲ EMP: 13
SALES (est): 5.2MM **Privately Held**
SIC: 3561 Pumps & pumping equipment

(G-204)
EGYPT STAR INC (PA)
608 N Front St (18102-5125)
PHONE.............................610 434-8516
Esther Erdessy, *Owner*
Beth Sipos, *Principal*
Steven Zdrofcoff, *Vice Pres*
EMP: 34 EST: 1938
SQ FT: 7,000
SALES (est): 3.2MM **Privately Held**
SIC: 2051 5461 2052 Bakery products, partially cooked (except frozen); rolls, bread type: fresh or frozen; pastries, e.g. danish: except frozen; bakeries; cookies & crackers

(G-205)
EL TORERO SPANISH NEWSPAPER
505 N 7th St (18102-2801)
P.O. Box 4311 (18105-4311)
PHONE.............................610 435-6608
Ricardo Montero, *Owner*
EMP: 4 EST: 2002
SALES (est): 173.6K **Privately Held**
SIC: 2711 Newspapers, publishing & printing

(G-206)
ENERSYS DELAWARE INC
7055 Ambassador Dr (18106-9285)
PHONE.............................484 244-4150
Richard W Zuidema, *Manager*
EMP: 9
SALES (corp-wide): 2.5B **Publicly Held**
SIC: 5063 3691 Electrical apparatus & equipment; lead acid batteries (storage batteries)
HQ: Enersys Delaware Inc.
2366 Bernville Rd
Reading PA 19605

(G-207)
ESILICON CORPORATION
1605 N Cedar Crest Blvd # 615 (18104-2351)
PHONE.............................610 439-6800
Thomas Baker, *Branch Mgr*
EMP: 4
SALES (corp-wide): 59.1MM **Privately Held**
SIC: 3674 Semiconductors & related devices

PA: Esilicon Corporation
2130 Gold St Ste 100
Alviso CA 95002
408 635-6300

(G-208)
EVONIK CORPORATION
Also Called: Performance Materials Division
7201 Hamilton Blvd (18195-9642)
P.O. Box 25760, Lehigh Valley (18002-5760)
PHONE.............................800 345-3148
EMP: 5
SALES (corp-wide): 2.4B **Privately Held**
SIC: 2851 Paints & allied products
HQ: Evonik Corporation
299 Jefferson Rd
Parsippany NJ 07054
973 929-8000

(G-209)
EXPRESS BUSINESS CENTER INC
5539 Stonecroft Ln (18106-9177)
PHONE.............................610 366-1970
Murtaza Jaffer, *President*
EMP: 7 EST: 2009
SALES (est): 442.1K **Privately Held**
SIC: 2759 Commercial printing

(G-210)
EXTREMITY IMAGING PARTNERS
3131 College Heights Blvd # 400 (18104-4876)
PHONE.............................610 432-1055
Rene Montgomery, *Branch Mgr*
EMP: 4
SALES (est): 194.3K **Privately Held**
SIC: 3826 Magnetic resonance imaging apparatus

(G-211)
F & R CARGO EXPRESS LLC
716 W Liberty St (18102-2857)
PHONE.............................610 351-9200
Marc Berson, *President*
EMP: 4
SALES (est): 456.7K **Privately Held**
SIC: 3537 Containers (metal), air cargo

(G-212)
FIGHTERS QUARTERS
725 N 15th St (18102-1220)
PHONE.............................334 657-4128
Esli Gonzalez, *Principal*
EMP: 3
SALES (est): 161.5K **Privately Held**
SIC: 3131 Mfg Footwear Cut Stock

(G-213)
FILMTECH CORP
Also Called: Filmtech Group Sgma Plas Group
2121 31st St Sw (18103-7006)
PHONE.............................610 709-9999
Ralph A Jiorle Sr, *Vice Pres*
Mark Jordan, *Sales Mgr*
Matt June, *Info Tech Mgr*
▲ EMP: 75
SALES (est): 18MM **Privately Held**
SIC: 3081 Polyethylene film
HQ: Omega Plastics Corp.
Page & Schuyler Ave Ste 5
Lyndhurst NJ 07071
201 507-9100

(G-214)
FITZPATRICK CONTAINER COMPANY
6923 Schantz Rd (18106-9273)
P.O. Box 1338, North Wales (19454-0338)
PHONE.............................215 699-3515
Thomas J Shallow Sr, *President*
Thomas J Shallow, *President*
John B Lynch III, *Vice Pres*
John Hayes, *Treasurer*
EMP: 50
SQ FT: 86,000
SALES (est): 15.4MM **Privately Held**
WEB: www.fitzbox.com
SIC: 2653 Boxes, corrugated: made from purchased materials

(G-215)
FLAVORPROS LLC
Also Called: Flavor Pros
737 N 13th St (18102-1259)
PHONE.............................610 435-4300
Richard Brach, *EMP*: 10
SALES (est): 1.4MM **Privately Held**
SIC: 2099 2095 Tea blending; roasted coffee

(G-216)
FLEXLINK SYSTEMS INC (DH)
6580 Snowdrift Rd Ste 200 (18106-9331)
PHONE.............................610 973-8200
Dave Clark, *President*
Armando Gonzalez, *General Mgr*
Brian Cannon, *Vice Pres*
Mike Hilsey, *Vice Pres*
Magnus Lindblad, *Project Mgr*
▲ EMP: 63
SQ FT: 75,000
SALES (est): 33.5MM **Privately Held**
WEB: www.flexlinksystems.com
SIC: 3535 Conveyors & conveying equipment
HQ: Flexlink Ab
Byfogdegatan 11
Goteborg 415 0
313 373-110

(G-217)
FOOTERS INC
335 N 7th St (18102-3211)
PHONE.............................610 437-2233
Craig E Pursel, *President*
EMP: 5
SQ FT: 5,000
SALES (est): 532.4K **Privately Held**
WEB: www.footers.com
SIC: 2329 2339 7336 Men's & boys' athletic uniforms; uniforms, athletic: women's, misses' & juniors'; silk screen design

(G-218)
FRAGRANCE MANUFACTURING INC
Also Called: F M I
100 Cascade Dr (18109-9527)
PHONE.............................610 266-7580
Kevin H Rhodes, *President*
Jennifer Bellesfield, *Project Mgr*
Paul Lara, *Prdtn Mgr*
Sheryl Rhoder, *Sales Staff*
Linda Cascario, *Manager*
▲ EMP: 37
SQ FT: 52,000
SALES (est): 13.3MM **Privately Held**
WEB: www.fragrancemfg.com
SIC: 2869 5149 2899 Perfumes, flavorings & food additives; flavourings & fragrances; chemical preparations

(G-219)
FRESH TOFU INC
1101 Harrison St (18103-3132)
PHONE.............................610 433-4711
Gary Abramowitz, *President*
Mark Amey, *Opers Mgr*
EMP: 20
SQ FT: 18,000
SALES (est): 2.5MM **Privately Held**
WEB: www.freshtofu.com
SIC: 2099 Tofu, except frozen desserts

(G-220)
FRITZSCHE ORGAN CO INC
505 E Emmaus Ave (18103-5917)
PHONE.............................610 797-2510
Stephen Emery, *President*
EMP: 6 EST: 1931
SQ FT: 7,500
SALES (est): 441.1K **Privately Held**
SIC: 3931 Pipes, organ

(G-221)
G H LAINEZ MANUFACTURING INC
314 N 12th St (18102-2714)
PHONE.............................610 776-0778
George Lainez, *President*
EMP: 11
SQ FT: 10,000

SALES (est): 840K **Privately Held**
SIC: 2326 2339 Men's & boys' work clothing; sportswear, women's; women's & misses' athletic clothing & sportswear

(G-222)
GALOMB INC
523 N 22nd St (18104-4305)
PHONE.............................610 434-3283
David E Galomb, *President*
EMP: 4
SQ FT: 1,500
SALES: 1.1MM **Privately Held**
SIC: 3089 3999 5162 Injection molding of plastics; barber & beauty shop equipment; plastics resins

(G-223)
GANNONS GOURMET
526 N Saint Cloud St (18104-5041)
PHONE.............................610 439-8949
Irene Gannon, *Owner*
EMP: 10
SALES (est): 598.6K **Privately Held**
SIC: 2051 Bread, cake & related products

(G-224)
GATECO INC
Also Called: Gateway Industrial Services
805 Harrison St (18103-3189)
PHONE.............................610 433-2100
Larry McEnroe, *CEO*
James E Weedling, *Treasurer*
EMP: 15 EST: 1994
SQ FT: 44,000
SALES (est): 2.5MM **Privately Held**
WEB: www.gatewayis.com
SIC: 3441 Fabricated structural metal

(G-225)
GEMANIAS JEANS COLLECTION INC
625 N 7th St (18102-1671)
PHONE.............................610 776-1777
Miguel Rodriguezflores, *President*
EMP: 6
SALES (est): 455.2K **Privately Held**
SIC: 2253 Pants, slacks or trousers, knit

(G-226)
GENERAL ELECTRIC COMPANY
404 Union Blvd (18109-3228)
PHONE.............................610 770-1881
EMP: 3
SALES (corp-wide): 121.6B **Publicly Held**
SIC: 3721 Research & development on aircraft by the manufacturer
PA: General Electric Company
41 Farnsworth St
Boston MA 02210
617 443-3000

(G-227)
GENUS LIFESCIENCES INC
Also Called: L V T
514 N 12th St (18102-2756)
PHONE.............................610 782-9780
Jeff Moshal, *CEO*
Michael Libman, *COO*
Larry Dalesandro, *CFO*
EMP: 102
SQ FT: 30,000
SALES (est): 18.1MM **Privately Held**
SIC: 2834 Pharmaceutical preparations

(G-228)
GENX SUSTAINABLE SOLUTIONS INC
1275 Glenlivet Dr Ste 100 (18106-3107)
PHONE.............................484 244-7016
Michael Tucker, *CEO*
Robert Hughes, *COO*
Sumner Douglas, *CFO*
Dave Mueller, *Shareholder*
Paul Mueller, *Shareholder*
EMP: 3
SQ FT: 100
SALES (est): 231.8K **Privately Held**
SIC: 3511 Hydraulic turbine generator set units, complete

(G-229)
GEO SPECIALTY CHEMICALS INC
2409 N Cedar Crest Blvd (18104-9733)
PHONE..................................610 433-6331
Michael Weber, *QC Dir*
Kurt Fritzinger, *Human Res Mgr*
Robert Zacker, *Manager*
Ron Hachey, *Manager*
Steve Kern, *Maintence Staff*
EMP: 85
SQ FT: 2,400 **Privately Held**
WEB: www.geosc.com
SIC: 2819 Industrial inorganic chemicals
PA: Geo Specialty Chemicals, Inc.
　401 S Earl Ave Ste 3
　Lafayette IN 47904

(G-230)
GERALD S STILLMAN
Also Called: Tee & Gee Pallets
3440 Lehigh St (18103-7001)
PHONE..................................610 377-7650
Gerald S Stillman, *Owner*
EMP: 7 EST: 2000
SALES (est): 399.3K **Privately Held**
SIC: 2448 Wood pallets & skids

(G-231)
GERHART SYSTEMS & CONTRLS CORP (PA)
754 Roble Rd Ste 140 (18109-9132)
PHONE..................................610 264-2800
Anthony Cattell, *President*
Mark Walker, *Purch Mgr*
Steven Braithwaite, *Director*
Andrew Cattell, *Director*
Stuart Cattell, *Director*
EMP: 18 EST: 1997
SALES (est): 2.9MM **Privately Held**
SIC: 3829 Measuring & controlling devices

(G-232)
GILLESPIE PRINTING INC
709 Roble Rd Unit 1 (18109-9500)
PHONE..................................610 264-1863
David Hebig, *President*
Julie M Hebig, *Vice Pres*
EMP: 17 EST: 1954
SALES (est): 2.3MM **Privately Held**
WEB: www.gillespieprinting.com
SIC: 2791 2752 2759 Typesetting; commercial printing, lithographic; letterpress printing

(G-233)
GLEN-GERY CORPORATION
Also Called: Glen Gery Brick Setter
1960 Weaversville Rd (18109-9328)
PHONE..................................484 240-4000
Amy Neyer, *Branch Mgr*
EMP: 6
SALES (corp-wide): 571K **Privately Held**
SIC: 3251 Brick & structural clay tile
HQ: Glen-Gery Corporation
　1166 Spring St
　Reading PA 19610
　610 374-4011

(G-234)
GLOBAL ENVIRONMENTAL TECH (PA)
Also Called: G E T
1001 S 10th St 1003 (18103)
PHONE..................................610 821-4901
Primo Acernese, *President*
EMP: 5
SQ FT: 500
SALES (est): 529.4K **Privately Held**
WEB: www.getwater.com
SIC: 3589 Water treatment equipment, industrial

(G-235)
GLOROY INC
Also Called: Royal Graphics
2001 Hamilton St (18104-6401)
PHONE..................................610 435-7800
Royal Peiffer, *President*
EMP: 4
SQ FT: 1,100
SALES (est): 451K **Privately Held**
SIC: 2752 Commercial printing, offset

(G-236)
GREAT NORTHERN CORPORATION
Laminations East
Westpark Buss Ctr Ii 7220 (18106)
PHONE..................................610 706-0910
Terry Rupell, *Executive*
EMP: 35
SALES (corp-wide): 431.7MM **Privately Held**
SIC: 2672 2671 2631 Coated & laminated paper; packaging paper & plastics film, coated & laminated; paperboard mills
PA: Great Northern Corporation
　395 Stroebe Rd
　Appleton WI 54914
　920 739-3671

(G-237)
GREAT NORTHERN FOAM
2571 Mitchell Ave (18103-6609)
PHONE..................................610 791-3356
Thomas Higgins, *Owner*
EMP: 40
SQ FT: 1,500
SALES (est): 3.8MM **Privately Held**
SIC: 3086 2273 Plastics foam products; carpets & rugs

(G-238)
GROTTO
2203 Union Blvd (18109-1637)
PHONE..................................610 570-9060
James I Richie, *Principal*
EMP: 4
SALES (est): 333.8K **Privately Held**
SIC: 2819 Mfg Industrial Inorganic Chemicals

(G-239)
GTS ENTERPRISES INC
Also Called: Chem and Lube
1801 S 12th St Ste 7 (18103-2927)
PHONE..................................610 798-9922
George Sipp, *President*
John Eder, *Controller*
◆ EMP: 20
SALES (est): 4.5MM **Privately Held**
WEB: www.chemandlube.com
SIC: 2992 Oils & greases, blending & compounding

(G-240)
HAJOCA CORPORATION
1801 Union Blvd Ste 104 (18109-1672)
P.O. Box 830 (18105-0830)
PHONE..................................610 432-0551
Matt Gdowik, *Branch Mgr*
EMP: 7
SALES (corp-wide): 2.4B **Privately Held**
WEB: www.hajoca.com
SIC: 3494 5999 Valves & pipe fittings; plumbing & heating supplies
PA: Hajoca Corporation
　2001 Joshua Rd
　Lafayette Hill PA 19444
　610 649-1430

(G-241)
HANG XING FA INC
911 W Linden St 921 (18101)
PHONE..................................646 250-7175
Yi-Hang LI, *President*
EMP: 4
SALES (est): 428.7K **Privately Held**
SIC: 3582 Commercial laundry equipment

(G-242)
HANOVER PAPER BOX COMPANY INC
1122 Hamilton St (18101-1068)
PHONE..................................215 432-5033
William R Grovatt, *President*
EMP: 4
SALES (est): 213.2K **Privately Held**
SIC: 2652 Setup paperboard boxes

(G-243)
HANSON AGGREGATES PA LLC (DH)
Also Called: Lehigh Masonry Cement
7660 Imperial Way (18195-1016)
PHONE..................................610 366-4626
Daniel M Harrington, *CEO*
Sterling Thomas, *Info Tech Mgr*
EMP: 31 EST: 1900
SQ FT: 20,000
SALES (est): 750.2MM
SALES (corp-wide): 20.6B **Privately Held**
WEB: www.hrico.com
SIC: 1422 1442 1429 2951 Limestones, ground; common sand mining; grits mining (crushed stone); concrete, bituminous

(G-244)
HANSON LEHIGH INC
7660 Imperial Way Ste 200 (18195-1016)
PHONE..................................610 366-4600
Richard Manning, *CEO*
Michael Reylander, *Comp Lab Dir*
Eric Lin, *Administration*
EMP: 3
SALES (est): 620.2K **Privately Held**
SIC: 3273 Ready-mixed concrete

(G-245)
HERR FOODS INCORPORATED
6810 Tilghman St (18106-9346)
PHONE..................................610 395-6200
Toll Free:................................888　-
Rebecca McCormick, *Senior VP*
Jim Mitchell, *Manager*
EMP: 27
SALES (corp-wide): 436.1MM **Privately Held**
WEB: www.herrs.com
SIC: 2096 5145 Potato chips & similar snacks; potato chips
PA: Herr Foods Incorporated
　20 Herr Dr
　Nottingham PA 19362
　610 932-9330

(G-246)
HOMESTEAD VALVE MFG CO
160 W Walnut St (18102-4915)
PHONE..................................610 770-1100
Scott Warmkessel, *Principal*
EMP: 3
SALES (est): 81.1K **Privately Held**
SIC: 3999 Manufacturing industries

(G-247)
HOTWASH
2069 28th St Sw (18103-7084)
PHONE..................................610 351-2119
Gary Huntington, *Owner*
EMP: 10
SALES (est): 1.2MM **Privately Held**
SIC: 3589 7542 Car washing machinery; washing & polishing, automotive

(G-248)
HP HOOD LLC
Rosenberger's Dairies
711 N Brick St (18102-1900)
PHONE..................................215 855-9074
Joseph Cervantes, *Branch Mgr*
EMP: 260
SALES (est): 2.1B **Privately Held**
WEB: www.hphood.com
SIC: 2026 2033 Milk processing (pasteurizing, homogenizing, bottling); fruit juices: packaged in cans, jars, etc.
PA: Hp Hood Llc
　6 Kimball Ln Ste 400
　Lynnfield MA 01940
　617 887-8441

(G-249)
ICE RIVER SPRINGS USA INC
734 Roble Rd (18109-9110)
PHONE..................................828 391-6900
EMP: 12
SALES (corp-wide): 143.3MM **Privately Held**
SIC: 2086 Water, pasteurized: packaged in cans, bottles, etc.
HQ: Ice River Springs Usa, Inc.
　100 Ceramic Tile Dr
　Morganton NC 28655

(G-250)
ICO POLYMERS NORTH AMERICA INC
6355 Farm Bureau Rd (18106-9253)
PHONE..................................610 398-5900
Andrean Horton, *Principal*
EMP: 124
SALES (corp-wide): 34.5B **Privately Held**
SIC: 2821 Molding compounds, plastics

HQ: Ico Polymers North America, Inc.
　24624 Interstate 45
　Spring TX 77386
　832 663-3131

(G-251)
ICREATE AUTOMATION INC
964 Marcon Blvd Ste 120 (18109-9361)
PHONE..................................610 443-1758
Kiet Ly, *President*
Imad Azar, *COO*
EMP: 12
SQ FT: 5,000
SALES (est): 2MM **Privately Held**
SIC: 5084 3625 8742 Industrial machinery & equipment; industrial controls: push button, selector switches, pilot; automation & robotics consultant

(G-252)
IMAGING FX INC
Also Called: Minuteman Press
1801 W Tilghman St (18104-4115)
PHONE..................................484 223-3311
Ray Reichardt, *President*
Colleen Reichardt, *Vice Pres*
EMP: 6
SQ FT: 5,300
SALES (est): 659.6K **Privately Held**
SIC: 2752 Commercial printing, lithographic

(G-253)
IMF PRINTING LLC (PA)
840 W Linden St (18101-1232)
PHONE..................................844 463-2726
Shirley Layer, *Mng Member*
EMP: 5
SALES: 26K **Privately Held**
SIC: 2752 7389 Commercial printing, lithographic;

(G-254)
IMMUNOTEK BIO CENTERS LLC
1587 Lehigh St (18103-3813)
PHONE..................................484 408-6376
Renee Collins, *Manager*
EMP: 20
SALES (corp-wide): 27MM **Privately Held**
SIC: 2836 Blood derivatives
PA: Immunotek Bio Centers, L.L.C.
　5750 Johnston St Ste 302
　Lafayette LA 70503
　337 500-1175

(G-255)
IMPERIAL COUNTER TOP COMPANY
211 W Turner St 213 (18101-1824)
PHONE..................................610 435-4803
Eve Wolfer, *Owner*
Rich Wolfer, *Co-Owner*
EMP: 8
SQ FT: 2,800
SALES (est): 897.2K **Privately Held**
SIC: 2541 Table or counter tops, plastic laminated; counter & sink tops

(G-256)
INDUSTRYBUILT SOFTWARE LTD
1275 Glenlivet Dr Ste 100 (18106-3107)
PHONE..................................866 788-1086
David Pilz, *CEO*
Glen Richardson, *CFO*
Dan Oughton, *CTO*
EMP: 23
SALES (est): 203.6K
SALES (corp-wide): 619.5MM **Privately Held**
SIC: 7372 Prepackaged software
PA: Aptean, Inc.
　4325 Alexander Dr Ste 100
　Alpharetta GA 30022
　770 351-9600

(G-257)
INFINEON TECH AMERICAS CORP
1110 American Pkwy Ne (18109-9117)
PHONE..................................408 503-2655
Sans Bangler, *Manager*
EMP: 20

▲ = Import ▼=Export
◆ =Import/Export

SALES (corp-wide): 8.7B **Privately Held**
WEB: www.infineon.com
SIC: 3674 Semiconductors & related devices
HQ: Infineon Technologies Americas Corp.
  101 N Pacific Coast Hwy
  El Segundo CA 90245
  310 726-8000

(G-258)
INFINEON TECH AMERICAS CORP
1110 American Pkwy Ne (18109-9117)
PHONE..............................610 712-7100
Klaus Gohlke, *Branch Mgr*
EMP: 230
SALES (corp-wide): 8.7B **Privately Held**
WEB: www.infineon-ncs.com
SIC: 3679 3674 Quartz crystals, for electronic application; microwave components; transistors
HQ: Infineon Technologies Americas Corp.
  101 N Pacific Coast Hwy
  El Segundo CA 90245
  310 726-8000

(G-259)
INFINERA CORPORATION
7584 Morris Ct (18106-9250)
PHONE..............................408 572-5200
Tom Fallon, *CEO*
EMP: 8
SALES (corp-wide): 943.3MM **Publicly Held**
SIC: 3669 3827 Intercommunication systems, electric; optical instruments & lenses
PA: Infinera Corporation
  140 Caspian Ct
  Sunnyvale CA 94089
  408 572-5200

(G-260)
INFINERA CORPORATION
7360 Windsor Dr (18106-9318)
PHONE..............................484 866-4600
Jeff Matlack, *Prdtn Mgr*
Dave Coult, *Manager*
EMP: 9
SALES (corp-wide): 943.3MM **Publicly Held**
SIC: 3674 Semiconductors & related devices
PA: Infinera Corporation
  140 Caspian Ct
  Sunnyvale CA 94089
  408 572-5200

(G-261)
INNOVATIVE EXHIBIT PRODUCTIONS
841 N Fenwick St (18109-1846)
PHONE..............................610 770-9833
Leonard Pedone, *President*
EMP: 3 EST: 2000
SALES (est): 236.6K **Privately Held**
SIC: 3999 Preparation of slides & exhibits

(G-262)
INSULATION CORPORATION AMERICA
Also Called: I C A
2571 Mitchell Ave (18103-6690)
PHONE..............................610 791-4200
Cynthia Masiko, *President*
William J Dean, *Vice Pres*
Sandra L Posocco, *Treasurer*
▲ EMP: 35
SALES (est): 7.2MM **Privately Held**
WEB: www.insulationcorp.com
SIC: 3086 Insulation or cushioning material, foamed plastic
PA: Northern Lehigh Erectors Corp
  2571 Mitchell Ave
  Allentown PA 18103
  610 791-4200

(G-263)
INTEL CORPORATION
1110 American Pkwy Ne F100
(18109-9117)
PHONE..............................908 894-6035
EMP: 6
SALES (corp-wide): 70.8B **Publicly Held**
SIC: 3577 Computer peripheral equipment

PA: Intel Corporation
  2200 Mission College Blvd
  Santa Clara CA 95054
  408 765-8080

(G-264)
INTEL NETWORK SYSTEMS INC
1110 American Pkwy Ne (18109-9117)
PHONE..............................610 973-5566
Chitra Gautham, *Engineer*
Heather EBY, *Manager*
Debra Timer, *Executive Asst*
EMP: 11
SALES (corp-wide): 70.8B **Publicly Held**
SIC: 3577 Computer peripheral equipment
HQ: Intel Network Systems Inc
  77 Reed Rd
  Hudson MA 01749
  978 553-4000

(G-265)
INTER TECH SUPPLIES INC
802 E Fairmont St (18103-3373)
PHONE..............................610 435-1333
Robert Robbins, *President*
▲ EMP: 11
SALES (est): 2.3MM **Privately Held**
WEB: www.inter-techsupplies.com
SIC: 3053 Gaskets & sealing devices

(G-266)
ISING LLC
3140b W Tilghman St # 190 (18104-4222)
PHONE..............................610 216-2644
Brian Levine,
EMP: 3
SQ FT: 1,200
SALES (est): 148.6K **Privately Held**
SIC: 2051 Bread, cake & related products

(G-267)
J R PETERS INC
6656 Grant Way (18106-9316)
PHONE..............................610 395-7104
John R Peters, *President*
Louise Henrich, *Purch Agent*
William McEvoy, *Manager*
◆ EMP: 27
SALES (est): 6.5MM **Privately Held**
WEB: www.jrpeters.com
SIC: 2875 8734 Fertilizers, mixing only; testing laboratories

(G-268)
JEFF ENTERPRISES INC
Also Called: Fastsigns
700 N 13th St (18102-1200)
PHONE..............................610 434-7353
Kevin Wenck, *President*
Jeff Wenk, *President*
EMP: 10
SALES (est): 893.5K **Privately Held**
WEB: www.jeffenterprises.com
SIC: 3993 Signs & advertising specialties

(G-269)
JOHN JOST JR INC
Also Called: Jost Iron Works
4344 Hamilton Blvd (18103-6015)
PHONE..............................610 395-5461
Alfred Jost, *President*
EMP: 4 EST: 1957
SQ FT: 6,000
SALES (est): 643.3K **Privately Held**
SIC: 3446 7692 3441 Architectural metalwork; welding repair; fabricated structural metal

(G-270)
JOHNSON CONTROLS
6330 Hedgewood Dr Ste 250 (18106-9215)
PHONE..............................610 398-7260
Richard Dumbach, *Branch Mgr*
John Kurzeja, *Supervisor*
EMP: 75 **Privately Held**
WEB: www.simplexgrinnell.com
SIC: 3669 Security systems services
HQ: Johnson Controls Fire Protection Lp
  6600 Congress Ave
  Boca Raton FL 33487
  561 988-7200

(G-271)
JOSH EARLY CANDIES INC (PA)
4640 W Tilghman St (18104-3210)
PHONE..............................610 395-4321

Barry Dobil Sr, *President*
Lisa Medero, *Vice Pres*
Marcy Dobil, *Admin Sec*
EMP: 15 EST: 1953
SQ FT: 10,000
SALES (est): 1.5MM **Privately Held**
WEB: www.joshearlycandies.com
SIC: 2064 5441 5947 Candy & other confectionery products; candy; gift shop; novelties

(G-272)
JULABO USA INC
884 Marcon Blvd (18109-9558)
PHONE..............................610 231-0250
Ralph Juchheim, *President*
Zachary Adams, *Opers Mgr*
Tony Fristick, *CFO*
Julie McGee, *Human Res Mgr*
Lisa Sprenger, *Accounts Mgr*
◆ EMP: 40
SQ FT: 15,000
SALES (est): 11.1MM **Privately Held**
WEB: www.julabo.com
SIC: 3822 3823 Temperature controls, automatic; temperature instruments: industrial process type

(G-273)
JULABO WEST INC
754 Roble Rd Ste 180 (18109-9135)
PHONE..............................610 231-0250
Ralph Juchheim, *President*
Zachary Adams, *Manager*
EMP: 12
SALES (est): 890K **Privately Held**
SIC: 3829 Thermometers & temperature sensors

(G-274)
JUST KIDSTUFF INC
Also Called: Kidstuff Coupon Books
6520 Stonegate Dr Ste 160 (18106-9227)
PHONE..............................610 336-9200
Heidi Schiffman, *President*
EMP: 55
SALES (est): 4.9MM **Privately Held**
SIC: 2741 Miscellaneous publishing

(G-275)
K HEEPS INC
721 N 17th St (18104-4103)
PHONE..............................610 434-4312
EMP: 3
SALES (est): 172.8K **Privately Held**
SIC: 2011 Meat packing plants

(G-276)
K MATKEM OF MORRISVILLE LP (HQ)
6612 Snowdrift Rd (18106-9352)
PHONE..............................215 428-3664
Dick Bus, *Partner*
EMP: 5
SALES (est): 812.7K
SALES (corp-wide): 48MM **Privately Held**
SIC: 3479 Etching & engraving
PA: Atas International, Inc.
  6612 Snowdrift Rd
  Allentown PA 18106
  610 395-8445

(G-277)
K&L SERVICES
215 N 8th St (18102-4012)
PHONE..............................610 349-1358
Jeffrey M McGinley, *President*
EMP: 6
SALES: 300K **Privately Held**
SIC: 3629 1731 Electronic generation equipment; general electrical contractor

(G-278)
K12SYSTEMS INC
Also Called: Sapphire Software
7540 Windsor Dr Ste 314 (18195-1015)
PHONE..............................610 366-9540
Brenda Shahpari, *President*
Chucky Knutson, *Info Tech Dir*
Bill Prehl, *Info Tech Dir*
Jamie Howe, *Director*
EMP: 14
SALES (est): 1.4MM **Privately Held**
WEB: www.k12system.com
SIC: 7372 Application computer software

(G-279)
KALAMATA FARMS LLC
1330 S Race St (18103-3466)
PHONE..............................570 972-1021
Ilias Intzes, *Managing Dir*
▲ EMP: 13
SALES (est): 968.7K **Privately Held**
SIC: 2079 Olive oil

(G-280)
KAYLIN MFG CO
1701 Union Blvd Ste 201 (18109-1697)
PHONE..............................610 820-6224
Fax: 610 820-7015
EMP: 12
SALES (est): 1.1MM **Privately Held**
SIC: 2321 Mfg Men's/Boy's Furnishings

(G-281)
KFW AUTOMATION INC
795 Roble Rd Unit 3 (18109-9147)
P.O. Box 90067 (18109-0067)
PHONE..............................610 266-5731
Joseph Keane, *President*
Donato Farole, *Vice Pres*
Jenn LI, *Purchasing*
Glenn Nester, *Associate*
EMP: 8
SALES (est): 1MM **Privately Held**
WEB: www.kfwa.com
SIC: 3599 7389 Custom machinery; design, commercial & industrial

(G-282)
KILIMANJARO DISTILLERY
995 Postal Rd (18109-9530)
PHONE..............................484 661-2488
EMP: 3
SALES (est): 194K **Privately Held**
SIC: 2085 Distilled & blended liquors

(G-283)
KING COATINGS LLC
Also Called: King Strength Mfg.
929 N 9th St (18102-1407)
PHONE..............................610 435-1212
John Karpyn, *Mng Member*
Jaryd Karpyn,
EMP: 3
SQ FT: 8,500
SALES: 200K **Privately Held**
SIC: 3479 Coating of metals & formed products

(G-284)
KING PUBLICATIONS
126 N 37th St (18104-5106)
PHONE..............................610 395-4074
Richard Stough, *Owner*
EMP: 3
SALES: 20K **Privately Held**
WEB: www.kingpublications.com
SIC: 2741 Misc Publishing

(G-285)
KNOLL INC
7132 Daniels Dr (18106-9216)
PHONE..............................484 224-3760
Stephen Sandre, *Branch Mgr*
EMP: 56 **Publicly Held**
SIC: 2521 Panel systems & partitions (free-standing), office: wood
PA: Knoll, Inc.
  1235 Water St
  East Greenville PA 18041

(G-286)
KUTZTOWN PUBLISHING CO INC
7036 Snowdrift Rd Ste 110 (18106-9582)
PHONE..............................610 683-7341
EMP: 3
SALES (est): 45.4K **Privately Held**
SIC: 2741 Miscellaneous publishing

(G-287)
KUTZTOWN PUBLISHING COMPANY
7036 Snowdrift Rd Ste 110 (18106-9582)
PHONE..............................610 683-7341
Stephen J Esser, *Ch of Bd*
David K Esser, *President*
Robert P Gottlund, *Principal*
EMP: 45 EST: 1916
SQ FT: 40,000

SALES (est): 8.5MM **Privately Held**
WEB: www.kutztownpbl.com
SIC: **2752** Commercial printing, offset

(G-288)
KW PLASTICS
Also Called: Kw Container
7529 Morris Ct (18106-9226)
PHONE..................................334 566-1563
Kenny Campbell, *Partner*
EMP: 20
SALES (corp-wide): 70.7MM **Privately Held**
WEB: www.kwplastics.com
SIC: **3081** 3089 Polypropylene film & sheet; molding primary plastic
PA: Kw Plastics
279 Pike County Lake Rd
Troy AL 36079
334 566-1563

(G-289)
L B G MACHINE INC
744 E Highland St (18109-3255)
PHONE..................................610 770-2550
Eugene R Heisner Jr, *President*
Jody Snyder, *Manager*
EMP: 10
SQ FT: 7,000
SALES (est): 1.8MM **Privately Held**
SIC: **3599** Machine shop, jobbing & repair

(G-290)
LA CRONICA NEWSPAPER
34 N 12th St (18101-1030)
PHONE..................................484 357-2903
William Asayag, *Principal*
EMP: 3
SALES (est): 126.6K **Privately Held**
SIC: **2711** Newspapers

(G-291)
LAMMS MACHINE INC
3216 Berger St (18103-7087)
PHONE..................................610 797-2023
Jeffrey A Lamm, *President*
Darrell Longenberger, *Senior VP*
Eric Lamm, *VP Sales*
Christine Wexler, *Office Mgr*
Jane L Lamm, *Admin Sec*
▲ EMP: 25 EST: 1965
SQ FT: 30,000
SALES (est): 4.7MM **Privately Held**
WEB: www.lamms.com
SIC: **3599** 3544 Machine shop, jobbing & repair; special dies, tools, jigs & fixtures

(G-292)
LEHIGH CEMENT COMPANY LLC
7660 Imperial Way Ste 400 (18195-1016)
PHONE..................................610 366-4600
EMP: 4
SALES (corp-wide): 20.6B **Privately Held**
SIC: **3273** Ready-mixed concrete
HQ: Lehigh Cement Company Llc
300 E John Carpenter Fwy
Irving TX 75062
877 534-4442

(G-293)
LEHIGH ELECTRIC PRODUCTS CO
6265 Hamilton Blvd # 106 (18106-9760)
PHONE..................................610 395-3386
Lloyd Jones, *President*
Stanley Kapral, *Prdtn Mgr*
Herman Dehaan, *Project Engr*
Linda St Hilaire, *Manager*
John Mehltretter, *Admin Asst*
EMP: 30
SALES (est): 5.4MM **Privately Held**
WEB: www.lehighdim.com
SIC: **3648** 5065 Stage lighting equipment; sound equipment, electronic

(G-294)
LIBERTY BELL BOTTLING CO INC
Also Called: Liberty Bell Beverages
718 N 13th St (18102-1200)
PHONE..................................610 820-6020
Lee Goldstein, *President*
EMP: 5

SALES (est): 655.8K **Privately Held**
SIC: **5921** 5499 3585 Beer (packaged); soft drinks; soda fountain & beverage dispensing equipment & parts

(G-295)
LIFEAIRE SYSTEMS LLC
1275 Glenlivet Dr Ste 100 (18106-3107)
PHONE..................................484 224-3042
Katy Worrilow, *CEO*
Kathryn Worrilow, *Principal*
Philip Coburn, *COO*
Christy Sutton, *Exec VP*
Pam Palmer, *Bookkeeper*
EMP: 5
SQ FT: 800
SALES: 1MM **Privately Held**
SIC: **3564** Air cleaning systems

(G-296)
LINDA K WOODWARD INC
2310 26th St Sw (18103-6604)
PHONE..................................610 791-3694
Linda Woodward, *Principal*
EMP: 4
SALES (est): 236.2K **Privately Held**
SIC: **2082** Malt beverages

(G-297)
LINDNER WOOD TECHNOLOGY INC
1411 W Linden St (18102-4226)
PHONE..................................610 820-8310
Terrence Lindner, *President*
EMP: 16
SALES (est): 1MM **Privately Held**
SIC: **2421** Building & structural materials, wood

(G-298)
LLOYD JONES
Also Called: Jones, L H & Associates
6265 Hamilton Blvd (18106-9688)
PHONE..................................610 395-3386
Lloyd Jones, *President*
Demitry Herman, *Engineer*
EMP: 30
SALES (est): 2.7MM **Privately Held**
SIC: **3648** Lighting equipment

(G-299)
LLS GRAPHICS
632 N 8th St (18102-2342)
PHONE..................................610 435-9055
Don Newhart, *Owner*
EMP: 4
SQ FT: 2,250
SALES: 130K **Privately Held**
SIC: **2752** Commercial printing, offset

(G-300)
LONERGAN PUMP SYSTEMS INC
127 N Lumber St (18102-4062)
PHONE..................................610 770-2050
Chris Lonergan, *CEO*
EMP: 6
SALES (est): 1.1MM **Privately Held**
WEB: www.lonerganpump.com
SIC: **3561** Pumps & pumping equipment

(G-301)
LOUIS P CANUSO INC
7522 Morris Ct Ste 1 (18106-9700)
PHONE..................................610 366-7914
Fenton Harpster, *Branch Mgr*
EMP: 10
SALES: 1.3MM
SALES (corp-wide): 39.7MM **Privately Held**
SIC: **3321** Water pipe, cast iron
PA: Louis P. Canuso, Inc.
401 Crown Point Rd
West Deptford NJ 08086
856 845-2700

(G-302)
LUTRON ELECTRONICS CO INC
6540 Stonegate Dr (18106-9239)
PHONE..................................610 282-6268
Mike Sweeney, *Opers Staff*
Plazarte Enrique, *Branch Mgr*
EMP: 12

SALES (corp-wide): 673.9MM **Privately Held**
WEB: www.lutron.com
SIC: **3625** Control equipment, electric
PA: Lutron Electronics Co., Inc.
7200 Suter Rd
Coopersburg PA 18036
610 282-3800

(G-303)
LYNAR CORPORATION
6837 Patterson Ct (18106-9338)
PHONE..................................610 395-3155
P Aaron Lesko, *President*
Chad Lesko, *Vice Pres*
Kevin Lesko, *Vice Pres*
EMP: 15 EST: 1978
SALES (est): 3.1MM **Privately Held**
WEB: www.lynar.com
SIC: **3599** Machine shop, jobbing & repair

(G-304)
MACK DEFENSE LLC
7310 Tilghman St Ste 600 (18106-9039)
PHONE..................................484 387-5911
David Hartzell, *President*
Stephen Zink, *President*
Stefano Chmielewski, *Principal*
Paul Hollowell, *Principal*
Charles Mahan, *Principal*
◆ EMP: 25
SALES (est): 6.3MM
SALES (corp-wide): 39.6B **Privately Held**
SIC: **3711** 5012 Trucks, noncommercial; motor vehicles & car bodies
HQ: Mack Trucks, Inc.
7900 National Service Rd
Greensboro NC 27409
336 291-9001

(G-305)
MACSON COMPANY (PA)
Also Called: Mac Kitchens
2500 Schoenersville Rd (18109-9510)
PHONE..................................610 264-7733
Douglas Mac George Sr, *Owner*
EMP: 3
SQ FT: 2,000
SALES: 400K **Privately Held**
WEB: www.mackitchens.com
SIC: **2541** 3281 3088 2434 Cabinets, except refrigerated: show, display, etc.: wood; counters or counter display cases, wood; cut stone & stone products; plastics plumbing fixtures; wood kitchen cabinets

(G-306)
MANCOR-PA INC
160 Olin Way (18106-9370)
PHONE..................................610 398-2300
Art Church, *Ch of Bd*
Dale Harper, *COO*
Poul Hansen, *Admin Sec*
◆ EMP: 72
SQ FT: 110,000
SALES (est): 36.4MM
SALES (corp-wide): 156.6MM **Privately Held**
SIC: **3714** Motor vehicle body components & frame
PA: Mancor Canada Inc
2485 Speers Rd
Oakville ON L6L 2
905 827-3737

(G-307)
MARCON & BOYER INC (PA)
Also Called: Duggan and Marcon
645 Hamilton St Ste 300 (18101-2191)
PHONE..................................610 866-5959
L Charles Marcon, *President*
Michael Carroll, *Superintendent*
Joe Taschner, *Superintendent*
Kenneth H Kline Jr, *Corp Secy*
Frank B Boyer, *Senior VP*
EMP: 100
SQ FT: 28,000
SALES (est): 172.4MM **Privately Held**
SIC: **3448** 1742 1743 1799 Panels for prefabricated metal buildings; drywall; tile installation, ceramic; fireproofing buildings

(G-308)
MARK-A-HYDRANT LLC
2863 Edgemont Dr (18103-5407)
PHONE..................................888 399-5532
Joshua J Guttman,
Josh Guttman,
EMP: 5
SALES (est): 491.5K **Privately Held**
SIC: **3231** Reflector glass beads, for highway signs or reflectors

(G-309)
MARTIN FABRICATING INC
601 S 10th St (18103-3689)
PHONE..................................610 435-5700
Charles E Martin, *President*
EMP: 22
SQ FT: 15,000
SALES (est): 2.5MM **Privately Held**
SIC: **2421** 1521 Building & structural materials, wood; general remodeling, single-family houses

(G-310)
MATTHEWAS AUTO SUPPLIES
2336 S 12th St (18103-5604)
PHONE..................................610 797-3729
Regina Mc Whinney, *Principal*
EMP: 4 EST: 2009
SALES (est): 365.1K **Privately Held**
SIC: **3714** Motor vehicle parts & accessories

(G-311)
MAZAK CORPORATION
1275 Glenlivet Dr Ste 145 (18106-3117)
PHONE..................................610 481-0850
Joseph Menzak, *Branch Mgr*
EMP: 3
SALES (corp-wide): 941.2MM **Privately Held**
SIC: **3541** Numerically controlled metal cutting machine tools
HQ: Mazak Corporation
8025 Production Dr
Florence KY 41042
859 342-1700

(G-312)
MCGIVERN BINDERY INC
747 Pittston St Ste 2 (18103-3255)
PHONE..................................610 770-9611
Michael Mc Givern, *President*
EMP: 10
SALES (est): 580K **Privately Held**
SIC: **2789** Bookbinding & related work

(G-313)
MECHANICAL SERVICE CO INC
Also Called: Msci
710 N Jefferson St (18102-1325)
PHONE..................................610 351-1655
George S Hudimac Jr, *President*
Patricia Hudimac, *Admin Sec*
▲ EMP: 10 EST: 1925
SQ FT: 20,000
SALES (est): 206.5K **Privately Held**
WEB: www.msicorp.com
SIC: **3599** 3842 3586 Machine shop, jobbing & repair; surgical appliances & supplies; measuring & dispensing pumps

(G-314)
MEDICO INTERNATIONAL INC
440 Allentown Dr (18109-9122)
P.O. Box 3092, Palmer (18043-3092)
PHONE..................................610 253-7009
Leslie Anderson, *President*
Kristin Verrastro, *Accounts Mgr*
▲ EMP: 17
SQ FT: 1,000
SALES (est): 1.9MM **Privately Held**
WEB: www.medicointernational.com
SIC: **2211** Bandages, gauzes & surgical fabrics, cotton

(G-315)
MICHELMAN STEEL ENTPS LLC
6338 Farm Bureau Rd (18106-9223)
PHONE..................................610 395-3472
Eric Michelman, *General Mgr*
Gizella Milne, *Manager*
EMP: 17 EST: 2011
SALES (est): 4MM **Privately Held**
SIC: **3411** Metal cans

▲ = Import ▼=Export
◆ =Import/Export

GEOGRAPHIC

(G-316)
MICROSEMI STOR SOLUTIONS INC
3500 Winchester Rd # 400 (18104-2263)
PHONE..........................610 289-5200
Tom Snodgrass, *Branch Mgr*
EMP: 40
SALES (corp-wide): 3.9B **Publicly Held**
SIC: 3674 Integrated circuits, semiconductor networks, etc.
HQ: Microsemi Storage Solutions, Inc.
1380 Bordeaux Dr
Sunnyvale CA 94089
408 239-8000

(G-317)
MMSCC-2 LLC
Also Called: Mmscc2
515 Hamilton St Ste 200 (18101-1537)
PHONE..........................610 266-8990
Joseph V Topper Jr,
EMP: 13
SALES (est): 2MM **Privately Held**
SIC: 1311 Crude petroleum & natural gas production

(G-318)
MOBILE MINI INC
1960 Weaversville Rd (18109-9328)
PHONE..........................484 540-9072
EMP: 20
SALES (corp-wide): 593.2MM **Publicly Held**
SIC: 3448 Buildings, portable: prefabricated metal
PA: Mobile Mini, Inc.
4646 E Van Buren St # 400
Phoenix AZ 85008
480 894-6311

(G-319)
MONA LISA FASHIONS
Also Called: Monalisa Fashions
650 E Green St (18109-1822)
PHONE..........................610 770-0806
Nagib Najm, *Owner*
EMP: 5
SQ FT: 14,794
SALES (est): 99.8K **Privately Held**
WEB: www.monalisamfg.com
SIC: 2331 2337 Women's & misses' blouses & shirts; pantsuits: women's, misses' & juniors'

(G-320)
MONARCH PRECAST CONCRETE CORP
425 N Dauphin St (18109-2199)
PHONE..........................610 435-6746
Paul Stein Jr, *President*
John Stein, *Executive*
EMP: 45 **EST:** 1949
SQ FT: 22,000
SALES (est): 8.2MM **Privately Held**
WEB: www.haroldgay.com
SIC: 3272 3561 Septic tanks, concrete; manhole covers or frames, concrete; covers, catch basin: concrete; pumps & pumping equipment

(G-321)
MORGAN ADVANCED CERAMICS INC
7331 William Ave (18106-9312)
PHONE..........................610 366-7100
Rick Newsome, *Facilities Mgr*
John Stang, *Branch Mgr*
EMP: 25
SALES (corp-wide): 1.3B **Privately Held**
WEB: www.morganelectroceramics.com
SIC: 3251 Brick & structural clay tile
HQ: Morgan Advanced Ceramics, Inc
2425 Whipple Rd
Hayward CA 94544

(G-322)
MORNING CALL LLC (HQ)
Also Called: Upper Bucks Publishing Company
101 N 6th St (18101-1480)
P.O. Box 1260 (18105-1260)
PHONE..........................610 820-6500
Robert York, *Chief*
Christine Campbell, *Marketing Mgr*
Rita Fritz, *Marketing Mgr*
Jessica Fisher, *Manager*
Kristine Meichtry, *Executive Asst*
EMP: 800 **EST:** 1905
SQ FT: 370,000
SALES (est): 201.2MM
SALES (corp-wide): 1B **Publicly Held**
WEB: www.mcall.com
SIC: 2752 2711 Commercial printing, lithographic; newspapers, publishing & printing
PA: Tribune Publishing Company
160 N Stetson Ave
Chicago IL 60601
312 222-9100

(G-323)
MULLER MARTINI MAILROOM (HQ)
4444 Innovation Way (18109-9404)
PHONE..........................610 266-7000
Rudolf Mller, *Ch of Bd*
Amrish Thaker, *President*
Charles A Spierto, *Treasurer*
▲ **EMP:** 200
SQ FT: 85,000
SALES (est): 51.2MM **Privately Held**
SIC: 3555 3535 Printing trades machinery; conveyors & conveying equipment
PA: Grapha-Holding Ag
Sonnenbergstrasse 13
Hergiswil NW
416 326-868

(G-324)
NACCI PRINTING INC
1327 N 18th St (18104-3147)
PHONE..........................610 434-1224
Frank Nacci, *President*
Becky Yorgey, *Engineer*
Carole Nacci, *Treasurer*
Kenny Bretz, *Sales Mgr*
EMP: 22
SQ FT: 10,000
SALES (est): 4.6MM **Privately Held**
WEB: www.nacciprinting.com
SIC: 2752 Commercial printing, offset

(G-325)
NAURA AKRION INC (DH)
6330 Hedgewood Dr Ste 150 (18106-9268)
PHONE..........................610 391-9200
Michael Ioannou, *President*
William Whittle, *CFO*
Ismail Kashkoush, *CTO*
EMP: 75
SQ FT: 39,200
SALES: 30MM
SALES (corp-wide): 335.4MM **Privately Held**
SIC: 3559 Semiconductor manufacturing machinery
HQ: Beijing Naura Microelectronics Equipment Co., Ltd.
No.8, Wenchang Ave., Economic And Technological Development Zone
Beijing 10017
105 784-6789

(G-326)
NE FIBERS LLC
Also Called: Fiberamerica
7072 Snowdrift Rd (18106-9274)
PHONE..........................610 366-8600
Varun Bedi,
Gabriel Wood,
EMP: 38
SALES (est): 9.4MM **Privately Held**
SIC: 2823 Cellulosic manmade fibers
HQ: Us Greenfiber, Llc
5500 77 Center Dr Ste 100
Charlotte NC 28217

(G-327)
NEON TRADING
1324 Sherman St Rear (18109-1799)
PHONE..........................610 530-2988
EMP: 5
SALES (est): 389K **Privately Held**
SIC: 3993 Neon signs

(G-328)
NESTLE PURINA PETCARE COMPANY
2050 Pope Rd (18104-9308)
PHONE..........................610 398-4667
Ed Banyo, *Branch Mgr*
EMP: 83
SALES (corp-wide): 90.8B **Privately Held**
WEB: www.purina.com
SIC: 2047 3999 2048 3411 Cat food; pet supplies; dry pet food (except dog & cat); metal cans
HQ: Nestle Purina Petcare Company
1 Checkerboard Sq
Saint Louis MO 63164
314 982-1000

(G-329)
NESTLE PURINA PETCARE COMPANY
Also Called: Friskies Pet Care Factory
2050 Pope Rd (18104-9308)
PHONE..........................610 395-3301
Rich Jarecke, *Branch Mgr*
EMP: 200
SQ FT: 1,600
SALES (corp-wide): 90.8B **Privately Held**
WEB: www.purina.com
SIC: 2047 Dog & cat food
HQ: Nestle Purina Petcare Company
1 Checkerboard Sq
Saint Louis MO 63164
314 982-1000

(G-330)
NEW ENTERPRISE STONE LIME INC
Also Called: Berks Products
5050 Crackersport Rd (18104-9345)
PHONE..........................610 374-5131
Fax: 610 481-9174
EMP: 25
SQ FT: 7,358
SALES (corp-wide): 651.9MM **Privately Held**
SIC: 3273 Mfg Ready-Mixed Concrete
PA: New Enterprise Stone & Lime Co., Inc.
3912 Brumbaugh Rd
New Enterprise PA 16664
814 224-6883

(G-331)
NEW VISION LENS LAB LLC
1918 W Tilghman St (18104-4345)
PHONE..........................610 351-7376
Manuel Santos, *Principal*
Ally Santos,
EMP: 3 **EST:** 2009
SALES (est): 307.3K **Privately Held**
SIC: 3851 Ophthalmic goods

(G-332)
NICK-OF-TIME TEXTILES LTD
1701 Union Blvd Ste 301 (18109-1697)
PHONE..........................610 395-4641
Harris Malkovsky, *President*
Marc Malkovsky, *Principal*
EMP: 8
SQ FT: 20,000
SALES (est): 1.3MM **Privately Held**
SIC: 5131 3496 Knit fabrics; fabrics, woven wire

(G-333)
NIGHT VISION DEVICES INC
542 Kemmerer Ln (18104-9339)
P.O. Box 3415 (18106-0415)
PHONE..........................610 395-9743
William Grube, *President*
EMP: 10
SQ FT: 3,400
SALES (est): 1.6MM **Privately Held**
WEB: www.nvdepot.com
SIC: 3812 Search & navigation equipment

(G-334)
NIKON PRECISION INC
1544 Hamilton St Ste 205 (18102-4364)
PHONE..........................610 439-6203
Bill Cole, *Director*
EMP: 4
SALES (corp-wide): 6.7B **Privately Held**
SIC: 3826 Electrolytic conductivity instruments
HQ: Nikon Precision Inc.
1399 Shoreway Rd
Belmont CA 94002
650 508-4674

(G-335)
NORTHERN LEHIGH ERECTORS CORP (PA)
2571 Mitchell Ave (18103-6609)
PHONE..........................610 791-4200
Thomas F Higgins, *Chairman*
Lawrence Dotter, *Assistant VP*
EMP: 25
SQ FT: 30,000
SALES (est): 7.2MM **Privately Held**
SIC: 2821 Polystyrene resins

(G-336)
NU-CHEM CORP
Also Called: Nuchem
747 N Fenwick St (18109-1879)
PHONE..........................610 770-2000
Le Roi Yaffey, *President*
EMP: 10
SQ FT: 25,000
SALES (est): 1.8MM **Privately Held**
SIC: 2869 3823 2842 Fuels; industrial instrmnts msrmnt display/control process variable; specialty cleaning, polishes & sanitation goods

(G-337)
OIL PROCESS SYSTEMS INC
Also Called: Allentown Scientific Assoc
602 Tacoma St (18109-8103)
PHONE..........................610 437-4618
Bernard Friedman, *President*
EMP: 40
SQ FT: 30,000
SALES (est): 7.9MM **Privately Held**
WEB: www.miroil.com
SIC: 3569 3533 Filters, general line: industrial; oil & gas field machinery

(G-338)
OLDCASTLE APG NORTHEAST INC
1960 Weaversville Rd (18109-9328)
P.O. Box 20065, Lehigh Valley (18002-0065)
PHONE..........................484 240-2176
Glen Cline, *General Mgr*
EMP: 12
SALES (corp-wide): 29.7B **Privately Held**
SIC: 3271 Blocks, concrete or cinder: standard
HQ: Oldcastle Apg Northeast, Inc.
13555 Wellington Cntr Cir
Gainesville VA 20155
703 365-7070

(G-339)
OLSON TECHNOLOGIES INC (PA)
160 W Walnut St (18102-4915)
PHONE..........................610 770-1100
James E Olson, *President*
Erik J Olson, *Vice Pres*
Peter Farkas, *CFO*
Cindi Miller, *Human Res Dir*
▲ **EMP:** 41
SQ FT: 100,000
SALES (est): 4.1MM **Privately Held**
WEB: www.asphaltvalves.com
SIC: 3491 Industrial valves

(G-340)
ORAM TRANSPORT CO INC
238 Peach St (18102-3891)
PHONE..........................702 559-4067
Jason Cunningham, *Ch of Bd*
EMP: 10
SALES (est): 411.2K **Privately Held**
SIC: 3537 Trucks, tractors, loaders, carriers & similar equipment

(G-341)
ORANGE PRODUCTS INC (PA)
1929 Vultee St (18103-4744)
PHONE..........................610 791-9711
Paul Sachdev, *President*
Jeff Welker, *Natl Sales Mgr*
◆ **EMP:** 60
SQ FT: 60,000
SALES (est): 18.5MM **Privately Held**
SIC: 3089 3944 Plastic processing; games, toys & children's vehicles

(G-342)
PACKAGING CORPORATION AMERICA
Also Called: Pca/Northeast Area
7451 Cetronia Rd (18106-9123)
PHONE.................................610 366-6501
Jeff Maynard, *QC Mgr*
EMP: 5
SALES (corp-wide): 7B **Publicly Held**
SIC: **2653** Boxes, corrugated: made from purchased materials
PA: Packaging Corporation Of America
1 N Field Ct
Lake Forest IL 60045
847 482-3000

(G-343)
PACKAGING CORPORATION AMERICA
Also Called: Pca/Trexlertown 388
7451 Cetronia Rd (18106-9123)
PHONE.................................610 366-6500
Rebecca Orth, *Plant Mgr*
Ray Cruz, *Engineer*
Bruce Ellsberry, *Controller*
Vince Peluso, *Manager*
EMP: 150
SQ FT: 146,022
SALES (corp-wide): 7B **Publicly Held**
WEB: www.packagingcorp.com
SIC: **2653** Boxes, corrugated: made from purchased materials
PA: Packaging Corporation Of America
1 N Field Ct
Lake Forest IL 60045
847 482-3000

(G-344)
PARKLAND BINDERY INC
2232 Walbert Ave (18104-1439)
PHONE.................................610 433-6153
Henry R Haas Jr, *President*
Marion Haas, *Corp Secy*
Eric Haas, *Shareholder*
EMP: 7
SQ FT: 3,000
SALES: 350K **Privately Held**
WEB: www.totalmail.com
SIC: **2752** 2759 2789 Commercial printing, offset; letterpress printing; pamphlets, binding

(G-345)
PEN PAL LLC
1045 Webster Ave (18103-5342)
PHONE.................................917 882-1441
Tyson Daniels,
Daniel Grudovich,
EMP: 3 EST: 2011
SALES (est): 209K **Privately Held**
SIC: **3951** Penholders & parts

(G-346)
PENCOR SERVICES INC
Also Called: East Penn Publishing Co
1633 N 26th St Ste 102 (18104-1805)
PHONE.................................610 740-0944
Josephine Jackson, *Manager*
EMP: 20
SALES (corp-wide): 108.7MM **Privately Held**
WEB: www.pennspeak.com
SIC: **2711** Newspapers, publishing & printing
PA: Pencor Services, Inc.
613 3rd Street Palmerton
Palmerton PA 18071
610 826-2115

(G-347)
PENN BLIND MANUFACTURING INC
1301 Union Blvd (18109-1572)
PHONE.................................610 770-1700
Sanders J Mishkin, *Manager*
EMP: 14
SQ FT: 3,200
SALES (est): 1.8MM **Privately Held**
WEB: www.pennblinds.com
SIC: **2591** 5023 Window blinds; shade, curtain & drapery hardware; venetian blinds; vertical blinds; window covering parts & accessories

(G-348)
PENN FOAM CORPORATION
2625 Mitchell Ave (18103-6610)
PHONE.................................610 797-7500
Sandra Fromknecht, *President*
David Quinn, *Vice Pres*
Leo F Quinn III, *Vice Pres*
Leo Quinn, *Vice Pres*
Christy Ernst, *Plant Mgr*
▲ EMP: 60
SQ FT: 90,000
SALES (est): 15.3MM **Privately Held**
WEB: www.pennfoam.com
SIC: **3069** 5712 2821 Foam rubber; furniture stores; plastics materials & resins

(G-349)
PENN STATE PAPER & BOX CO INC
Also Called: Miller Wholesale Paper Co Div
323 Sumner Ave (18102-1856)
P.O. Box 1906 (18105-1906)
PHONE.................................610 433-7468
Ercole Spinosa, *President*
Tim Spinosa, *Vice Pres*
David Spinosa, *Treasurer*
Bud Grimshaw, *Sales Staff*
Patricia Spinosa, *Shareholder*
EMP: 23 EST: 1946
SQ FT: 35,000
SALES (est): 4.7MM **Privately Held**
WEB: www.pennstatepaper.com
SIC: **2675** 5113 Die-cut paper & board; bags, paper & disposable plastic

(G-350)
PHOENIX FORGING COMPANY INC
Also Called: Phoenix Hotform
7550 Walker Way (18106-3100)
PHONE.................................610 530-8249
Steve Bottcher, *Manager*
EMP: 9
SALES (corp-wide): 11.5MM **Privately Held**
SIC: **3462** 3599 Iron & steel forgings; fan forges
PA: Phoenix Forging Company, Inc.
800 Front St
Catasauqua PA 18032
610 264-2861

(G-351)
PHYSICAL GRAFFI-TEES
1951 W Tilghman St (18104-4344)
PHONE.................................610 439-3344
Stephen Toth, *Owner*
EMP: 7 EST: 1996
SALES: 850K **Privately Held**
WEB: www.physicalgraffitees.com
SIC: **2395** 7532 5199 Embroidery & art needlework; body shop, automotive; advertising specialties

(G-352)
PIGNUTS INC
Also Called: Sealmaster
6853 Ruppsville Rd (18106-9272)
PHONE.................................610 530-8788
Darryl Stein, *President*
EMP: 8
SALES (est): 1.8MM **Privately Held**
WEB: www.sealmasterallentown.com
SIC: **2951** Asphalt paving mixtures & blocks

(G-353)
PPT RESEARCH INC
515 Business Park Ln (18109-9115)
PHONE.................................610 434-0103
Dr Chip Ward, *President*
Jodi Bear-Bernecker, *CFO*
▲ EMP: 3
SQ FT: 55,000
SALES (est): 357.5K **Privately Held**
SIC: **3291** Abrasive products

(G-354)
PRAXAIR INC
7355 William Ave Ste 200 (18106-9336)
PHONE.................................610 530-3885
Scott Kaltrider, *Branch Mgr*
EMP: 20 **Privately Held**
SIC: **2813** Industrial gases

HQ: Praxair, Inc.
10 Riverview Dr
Danbury CT 06810
203 837-2000

(G-355)
PRAXAIR DIST MID-ATLANTIC LLC
Also Called: GTS-Welco
5275 Tilghman St (18104-9378)
PHONE.................................610 398-2211
Bryan Gentry, *Mng Member*
Susan Amoroso, *Manager*
Michael A Masha,
▲ EMP: 600
SALES (est): 69.4MM **Privately Held**
SIC: **4925** 3548 Gas production and/or distribution; welding apparatus
HQ: Welco-Cgi Gas Technologies Llc
425 Avenue P
Newark NJ 07105
973 589-8795

(G-356)
PRAXAIR DISTRIBUTION INC
5275 Tilghman St (18104-9378)
PHONE.................................610 398-2211
Gail Greaves, *Human Resources*
Bryan Gentry, *Branch Mgr*
EMP: 600 **Privately Held**
SIC: **4925** 3548 Gas production and/or distribution; welding apparatus
HQ: Praxair Distribution, Inc.
10 Riverview Dr
Danbury CT 06810
203 837-2000

(G-357)
PRECISE GRAPHIX LLC
2310 26th St Sw (18103-6604)
PHONE.................................610 965-9400
Keith Lyden,
Dee Lyden,
EMP: 20
SALES (est): 4.6MM **Privately Held**
WEB: www.precisegraphix.com
SIC: **7336** 2522 Graphic arts & related design; office cabinets & filing drawers: except wood

(G-358)
PRECISION ROLL GRINDERS INC (PA)
6356 Chapmans Rd (18106-9261)
PHONE.................................610 395-6966
James Manley, *President*
George Schildge, *Chairman*
Thomas Pecuch, *Treasurer*
Victor Schmidt, *Human Res Mgr*
Robert Snyder, *Human Res Mgr*
▲ EMP: 67
SQ FT: 70,000
SALES (est): 26.4MM **Privately Held**
WEB: www.precisionrollgrinders.com
SIC: **3471** 7389 3449 Polishing, metals or formed products; grinding, precision: commercial or industrial; custom roll formed products

(G-359)
PRIMAXX INC
Also Called: Spts Technologies
7377 William Ave Unit 800 (18106-9324)
PHONE.................................610 336-0314
Paul Hammond, *President*
Frank Gioia, *Vice Pres*
Bob Garbarino, *Engineer*
Steve Di Rugrius, *CFO*
Paul Mumbauer, *Manager*
EMP: 17 EST: 1998
SQ FT: 15,000
SALES (est): 4.1MM
SALES (corp-wide): 900.8MM **Privately Held**
WEB: www.primaxxinc.com
SIC: **3559** Semiconductor manufacturing machinery
HQ: Spts Technologies, Inc.
1150 Ringwood Ct
San Jose CA 95131

(G-360)
PRINTFORCE INC
2361 Sunshine Rd (18103-4706)
PHONE.................................610 797-6455
Andrew L Brahm, *President*

Patricia L Little, *Vice Pres*
Margaret A Brahm, *Admin Sec*
EMP: 9
SQ FT: 10,000
SALES (est): 1.8MM **Privately Held**
SIC: **5112** 2752 7334 Business forms; commercial printing, offset; photocopying & duplicating services

(G-361)
PROFI VISION INC
1150 Glenlivet Dr Ste C41 (18106-3119)
PHONE.................................610 530-2025
Thomas Jankowski, *Principal*
EMP: 7
SALES (est): 1MM **Privately Held**
SIC: **3699** Security control equipment & systems

(G-362)
PROTECTIVE PACKAGING CORP
6813b Ruppsville Rd (18106-9360)
PHONE.................................610 398-2229
Karen Tremain, *President*
EMP: 4
SQ FT: 16,000
SALES (est): 553.4K **Privately Held**
WEB: www.protectivepackaging.com
SIC: **3086** Packaging & shipping materials, foamed plastic

(G-363)
PSMLV INC
Also Called: Penn Sheet Metal
18106 Schantz Rd (18104)
P.O. Box 3535 (18106-0535)
PHONE.................................610 395-8214
Craig A Townsend, *President*
Craig Townsend, *CFO*
EMP: 13
SQ FT: 14,000
SALES (est): 3.2MM **Privately Held**
WEB: www.pennsheetmetal.com
SIC: **3444** Sheet metal specialties, not stamped

(G-364)
R & D AMERICAS BEST PACKAGING
737 N 13th St (18102-1259)
PHONE.................................610 435-4300
Charlene Brach, *Principal*
EMP: 3 EST: 2007
SALES (est): 130.7K **Privately Held**
SIC: **5411** 2621 Grocery stores; wrapping & packaging papers

(G-365)
R & D ASSEMBLY INC
1660 E Race St (18109-9565)
PHONE.................................610 770-0700
James Russell, *President*
Mark Yaeger, *Vice Pres*
EMP: 5
SALES (est): 516.4K **Privately Held**
SIC: **3674** Semiconductors & related devices

(G-366)
R C PAPER COMPANY
374 Auburn St (18103-3316)
PHONE.................................610 821-9610
Mark Klein, *Principal*
EMP: 3
SALES (est): 280K **Privately Held**
SIC: **2621** Paper mills

(G-367)
R S QUALITY PRODUCTS INC
719 Roboe Rd Ste 103 (18109)
P.O. Box 90130 (18109-0130)
PHONE.................................610 266-1916
Adam Serfas, *President*
◆ EMP: 6
SQ FT: 5,400
SALES (est): 2.6MM **Privately Held**
WEB: www.rsquality.com
SIC: **5085** 3991 Brushes, industrial; brushes, household or industrial

(G-368)
R&D CIRCUITS INC
1660 E Race St (18109-9565)
PHONE.................................610 443-2299

▲ = Import ▼=Export
◆ =Import/Export

Russell James, *Principal*
Douglas Martin, *Buyer*
EMP: 9 **EST:** 2013
SALES (est): 879.3K **Privately Held**
SIC: 3674 Semiconductors & related devices

(G-369)
R&D SOCKETS INC
Also Called: R&D Interconnect Solutions
1660 E Race St Unit B (18109-9565)
PHONE..............................610 443-2299
James Russell, *President*
Scott Evans, *Principal*
Joseph Falsetti, *Principal*
Adrian Ironside, *Principal*
Rodney Ames, *Engineer*
EMP: 8
SALES (est): 1MM **Privately Held**
SIC: 3672 Circuit boards, television & radio printed

(G-370)
RAMSAY MACHINE DEVELOPMENT
4017 Hampshire Ct (18104-3336)
PHONE..............................610 395-4764
John L Ramsay, *President*
EMP: 12 **EST:** 1925
SQ FT: 6,500
SALES (est): 1.5MM **Privately Held**
WEB: www.ramsaymade.com
SIC: 3599 5063 Custom machinery; motors, electric

(G-371)
RANDALL PUBLICATIONS
6047 Adams Ln (18109-9000)
PHONE..............................610 871-1427
EMP: 4
SALES (corp-wide): 2.5MM **Privately Held**
SIC: 2851 Shellac (protective coating)
PA: Randall Publications
      1840 Jarvis Ave
      Elk Grove Village IL 60007
      847 437-6604

(G-372)
REDNERS MARKETS INC
Also Called: Redner's Warehouse Market 85
1201 Airport Rd (18109-3308)
PHONE..............................610 776-2726
Jeff Treichler, *Branch Mgr*
EMP: 100
SALES (corp-wide): 838.7MM **Privately Held**
WEB: www.rednersmarkets.com
SIC: 5411 2051 Supermarkets, chain; bread, cake & related products
PA: Redner's Markets, Inc.
      3 Quarry Rd
      Reading PA 19605
      610 926-3700

(G-373)
REGO PRECISION MACHINE LLC
671 E Allen St (18109-2035)
PHONE..............................610 434-1582
Garrett L Rego, *Principal*
EMP: 7
SALES (est): 1MM **Privately Held**
SIC: 3599 Machine shop, jobbing & repair

(G-374)
RICH REENIE INC
1434 W Union St (18102-4474)
PHONE..............................610 439-7962
Richard McGinnis Sr, *CEO*
Richard McGinnis Jr, *President*
▲ **EMP:** 12
SQ FT: 27,000
SALES (est): 1.3MM **Privately Held**
WEB: www.reenierich.com
SIC: 2339 Sportswear, women's

(G-375)
RICHARDS AND DANIELSON LLC
737 N 13th St (18102-1259)
PHONE..............................610 435-4300
Charlene Brach, *Agent*
EMP: 12

SALES (est): 531K **Privately Held**
SIC: 2087 Flavoring extracts & syrups

(G-376)
ROBERTS MANUFACTURING LLC
Also Called: Core Covers
1801 Union Blvd Ste E (18109-1672)
PHONE..............................855 763-7450
Robert Ghelerter, *President*
Jerry Greer, *Principal*
EMP: 15
SALES (est): 3.8MM **Privately Held**
SIC: 5092 5945 3429 Arts & crafts equipment & supplies; hobby & craft supplies; keys, locks & related hardware

(G-377)
RODALE INC
Also Called: Rodale Press Distribution Ctr
6461 Snowdrift Rd (18106-9514)
PHONE..............................610 398-2255
EMP: 50
SQ FT: 100,000
SALES (corp-wide): 374.8MM **Privately Held**
SIC: 2721 2731 Whol Book Store
PA: Rodale Inc.
      400 S 10th St
      Emmaus PA 18015

(G-378)
ROKAT MACHINE
351 Star Rd (18106-9029)
PHONE..............................610 432-1830
Roy Klucsarics, *President*
EMP: 3
SALES (est): 428.5K **Privately Held**
SIC: 3599 Machine shop, jobbing & repair

(G-379)
ROSEYS CREATIONS INC
1466 Hampton Rd (18104-2018)
PHONE..............................610 704-8591
Robert Levine, *CEO*
Cindy Levine, *Vice Pres*
EMP: 5
SALES (est): 1.5MM **Privately Held**
WEB: www.myboysbaking.com
SIC: 2339 Sportswear, women's

(G-380)
RR DONNELLEY & SONS COMPANY
Also Called: R R Donnelley
7108 Daniels Dr (18106-9216)
PHONE..............................610 391-8825
Ray Young, *Manager*
EMP: 36
SALES (corp-wide): 6.8B **Publicly Held**
WEB: www.moore.com
SIC: 2761 Manifold business forms
PA: R. R. Donnelley & Sons Company
      35 W Wacker Dr Ste 3650
      Chicago IL 60601
      312 326-8000

(G-381)
RR ENTERPRISES INC
Also Called: Vue-More Manufacturing
1885 Weaversville Rd (18109-9427)
PHONE..............................610 266-9600
Rich Remetta, *Owner*
▲ **EMP:** 5
SQ FT: 11,400
SALES: 750K **Privately Held**
SIC: 3621 Motors, electric

(G-382)
SANI-BRANDS INC
Also Called: Defence Sport
1636 N Cedar Crest Blvd (18104-2318)
PHONE..............................610 841-1599
Albert Dolceamore, *President*
Mary S Dolceamore, *Admin Sec*
EMP: 3
SALES (est): 445.3K **Privately Held**
SIC: 2833 Medicinal chemicals

(G-383)
SAPPI NORTH AMERICA INC
Also Called: Sappi Fine Paper North America
1340 Hickory Ln (18106-9350)
PHONE..............................610 398-8400
Greg Nichols, *Branch Mgr*

EMP: 60
SALES (corp-wide): 5.3B **Privately Held**
SIC: 2679 4225 Paper products, converted; general warehousing & storage
HQ: Sappi North America, Inc.
      255 State St Fl 4
      Boston MA 02109
      617 423-7300

(G-384)
SARAH LYNN SPORTSWEAR INC
Also Called: Sarah Lynn Fashions
707 N 4th St Fl 2 (18102-1963)
PHONE..............................610 770-1702
Richard Koury, *President*
Dale Hart, *Plant Mgr*
Kim Kollar, *QC Mgr*
▲ **EMP:** 40
SALES (est): 3.3MM **Privately Held**
WEB: www.slsportswear.com
SIC: 2331 Blouses, women's & juniors': made from purchased material; shirts, women's & juniors': made from purchased materials; T-shirts & tops, women's: made from purchased materials

(G-385)
SCENTS KRAFTS & STITCHES
1071 Hill Dr (18103-6112)
PHONE..............................610 770-0204
EMP: 3
SALES (est): 164.2K **Privately Held**
SIC: 2022 Mfg Cheese

(G-386)
SCHRANTZ INDUS ELECTRICIANS
13 W Tilghman St (18102-5128)
PHONE..............................610 435-8255
Edward J Schrantz, *President*
Helen Schrantz, *Vice Pres*
EMP: 5 **EST:** 1973
SALES (est): 486.7K **Privately Held**
SIC: 1731 3613 General electrical contractor; control panels, electric

(G-387)
SCRIBE INC
7540 Windsor Dr Ste 200b (18195-1011)
PHONE..............................215 336-5095
David Rech, *President*
EMP: 11 **Privately Held**
SIC: 2731 Book publishing
PA: Scribe Inc.
      842 S 2nd St
      Philadelphia PA 19147

(G-388)
SHEPHERD GOOD WORK SERVICES
Also Called: Good Shepherd Thrift Store
1901 Lehigh St (18103-4731)
PHONE..............................610 776-8353
Carol Jones, *Vice Pres*
EMP: 225
SQ FT: 30,000
SALES: 4.1MM **Privately Held**
SIC: 8331 3699 2672 Sheltered workshop; electrical equipment & supplies; coated & laminated paper

(G-389)
SHIFT4 PAYMENTS LLC (HQ)
Also Called: Harbortouch
2202 N Irving St (18109-9554)
PHONE..............................800 201-0461
Jared Isaacman, *CEO*
Phil Crofton, *Exec VP*
Michael Ward, *Exec VP*
Joe Messina, *Vice Pres*
Steve Skrzenski, *Opers Mgr*
EMP: 96
SALES (est): 23.3MM
SALES (corp-wide): 95.2MM **Privately Held**
SIC: 7389 7372 Credit card service; financial services; business oriented computer software
PA: Searchlight Capital Partners, L.P.
      745 5th Ave Fl 27
      New York NY 10151
      212 293-3730

(G-390)
SIGN DESIGN ASSOCIATES INC
510 S Fawn St (18103-3397)
PHONE..............................610 791-9301
Dennis Wirth, *President*
EMP: 5
SQ FT: 3,000
SALES (est): 403.4K **Privately Held**
WEB: www.signdesignassoc.com
SIC: 3993 Signs, not made in custom sign painting shops

(G-391)
SIGNLINE LLC
Also Called: Ilkem Marble and Granite
997 Postal Rd (18109-9337)
PHONE..............................610 973-3600
Ersan Cundar,
Ersan Dundar,
▲ **EMP:** 6
SALES (est): 506K **Privately Held**
SIC: 1423 Crushed & broken granite

(G-392)
SILBERINE MANUFACTURING
4905 W Tilghman St (18104-9130)
PHONE..............................570 668-8361
EMP: 8
SALES (est): 1.5MM **Privately Held**
SIC: 3999 Manufacturing industries

(G-393)
SILVER CHARM CLOTHING COMPANY
930 N 4th St (18102-1869)
PHONE..............................484 274-6796
Steve Schuster, *Owner*
EMP: 2
SQ FT: 18,000
SALES: 2MM **Privately Held**
SIC: 3161 Clothing & apparel carrying cases

(G-394)
SKAFFL LLC
4283 Elm Dr (18103-6105)
PHONE..............................484 809-9351
Rita Chesterton, *CEO*
Michael Hanssen, *COO*
EMP: 3 **EST:** 2012
SALES (est): 180.8K **Privately Held**
SIC: 7372 Application computer software

(G-395)
SKF USA INC
Flex Link Systems
6580 Snowdrift Rd Ste 200 (18106-9331)
PHONE..............................610 954-7000
Otto Wieber, *Vice Pres*
Sue A Mazzei, *Marketing Mgr*
Bo Ljunggren, *Branch Mgr*
Noel Pfeiffer, *Manager*
EMP: 12
SALES (corp-wide): 9.2B **Privately Held**
SIC: 3535 3053 Conveyors & conveying equipment; gaskets, packing & sealing devices
HQ: Skf Usa Inc.
      890 Forty Foot Rd
      Lansdale PA 19446
      267 436-6000

(G-396)
SOLAR TECHNOLOGY INC
Also Called: Agile Displays
7620 Cetronia Rd (18106-9293)
PHONE..............................610 391-8600
Eric Zerphy, *President*
Sabrina Zerphy, *Vice Pres*
Gerald Fillman, *Opers Staff*
Andrew Chellel, *Engineer*
Louise Laba, *Asst Controller*
▼ **EMP:** 100
SQ FT: 64,000
SALES (est): 43.8MM **Privately Held**
WEB: www.solartech-online.com
SIC: 3669 3993 Traffic signals, electric; signs & advertising specialties

(G-397)
SOVEREIGN STEEL MFG LLC
2027 S 12th St Bldg 507 (18103-4719)
PHONE..............................610 797-2800
EMP: 7 **EST:** 2014

SALES (est): 566.7K **Privately Held**
SIC: 3999 Atomizers, toiletry

(G-398)
SPECTRUM AUTOMATED INC
701 E Congress St (18109-3204)
PHONE..................................610 433-7755
Scott Bickley, *President*
Kimberly Krasley, *Vice Pres*
EMP: 8
SQ FT: 6,500
SALES: 975K **Privately Held**
SIC: 3451 Screw machine products

(G-399)
SPRUNG INSTANT STRUCTURES INC
5000 W Tilghman St # 155 (18104-9101)
PHONE..................................610 391-9553
Glenn Harsmann, *Manager*
EMP: 6
SALES (corp-wide): 19.2MM **Privately Held**
SIC: 2394 Tents: made from purchased materials
HQ: Sprung Instant Structures, Inc.
5711 W Dannon Way
West Jordan UT 84081
801 280-1555

(G-400)
STANLEY INDUSTRIAL & AUTO LLC
Also Called: Vidmar
11 Grammes Rd (18103-4760)
PHONE..................................800 523-9462
Jim Cannon, *President*
Dan White, *Vice Pres*
William Arnold, *Engineer*
Betsy Solt, *Info Tech Mgr*
EMP: 220
SALES (corp-wide): 13.9B **Publicly Held**
WEB: www.stanleyworks.com
SIC: 3699 Security devices
HQ: Stanley Industrial & Automotive, Llc
505 N Cleveland Ave
Westerville OH 43082
614 755-7000

(G-401)
STANLEY STORAGE SYSTEMS INC
11 Grammes Rd (18103-4760)
P.O. Box 1151 (18105-1151)
PHONE..................................610 797-6600
John Kleinoder, *Principal*
Ed Roma, *Opers Mgr*
Ruth Meckes, *Purchasing*
▲ **EMP:** 8
SALES (est): 800.2K **Privately Held**
SIC: 2522 1799 Office cabinets & filing drawers: except wood; office furniture installation

(G-402)
STANLEY VIDMAR (HQ)
11 Grammes Rd (18103-4776)
PHONE..................................610 797-6600
Peter Lariviere, *President*
John Alfieri, *Vice Pres*
Ryan Stauffer, *Finance Mgr*
Jill Wheeler, *Marketing Staff*
Tom Pinchuk, *Director*
▲ **EMP:** 50
SALES (est): 60K
SALES (corp-wide): 13.9B **Publicly Held**
SIC: 3699 Door opening & closing devices, electrical
PA: Stanley Black & Decker, Inc.
1000 Stanley Dr
New Britain CT 06053
860 225-5111

(G-403)
STEEL FITNESS PREMIER LLC
250 Cetronia Rd Ste 100 (18104-9124)
PHONE..................................610 973-1500
Thomas Senstermacher, *Mng Member*
EMP: 30 **EST:** 2012
SALES (est): 1.6MM **Privately Held**
SIC: 8099 7991 3634 Nutrition services; athletic club & gymnasiums, membership; massage machines, electric, except for beauty/barber shops

(G-404)
SUMITOMO SHI CRYGNICS AMER INC (HQ)
1833 Vultee St (18103-4742)
PHONE..................................610 791-6700
David Dedman, *President*
Isamu Dekiya, *Exec VP*
Robert Deo Bil, *Vice Pres*
Dekiya Isamu, *Vice Pres*
Craig Fry, *Facilities Mgr*
▲ **EMP:** 60
SQ FT: 56,500
SALES (est): 24MM
SALES (corp-wide): 7.4B **Privately Held**
WEB: www.shicryogenics.com
SIC: 3559 7699 Cryogenic machinery, industrial; industrial equipment services
PA: Sumitomo Heavy Industries, Ltd.
2-1-1, Osaki
Shinagawa-Ku TKY 141-0
367 372-000

(G-405)
SUSAN REABUCK
2848 Klein St (18103-7450)
PHONE..................................610 797-7014
EMP: 4
SALES (est): 250.1K **Privately Held**
SIC: 3161 Mfg Luggage

(G-406)
SYLRAY MANUFACTURING LLC
639 E Allen St (18109-2035)
P.O. Box 325, Orwigsburg (17961-0325)
PHONE..................................570 640-0689
EMP: 3
SALES (est): 158.1K **Privately Held**
SIC: 3999 Manufacturing industries

(G-407)
TAMA MFG CO INC (PA)
100 Cascade Dr A (18109-9527)
PHONE..................................610 231-3100
Mark Fogelman, *President*
Tama Fogelman, *Corp Secy*
Ruth Green, *Vice Pres*
▲ **EMP:** 285 **EST:** 1946
SQ FT: 95,000
SALES (est): 16.1MM **Privately Held**
WEB: www.tamamfg.com
SIC: 2339 2337 Slacks: women's, misses' & juniors'; skirts, separate: women's, misses' & juniors'

(G-408)
TERRA GROUP CORP
735 Pittston St (18103-3256)
PHONE..................................610 821-7003
Primo L Acernese, *President*
EMP: 33
SQ FT: 128,000
SALES (est): 4.1MM **Privately Held**
SIC: 5999 3589 Water purification equipment; water treatment equipment, industrial

(G-409)
THYSSENKRUPP ELEVATOR CORP
5925 Tilghman St Ste 100 (18104-9160)
PHONE..................................610 366-0161
Mark Decocinis, *Manager*
EMP: 35
SALES (corp-wide): 39.8B **Privately Held**
WEB: www.tyssenkrupp.com
SIC: 5084 7699 3534 1796 Elevators; elevators: inspection, service & repair; elevators & moving stairways; installing building equipment
HQ: Thyssenkrupp Elevator Corporation
11605 Haynes Bridge Rd # 650
Alpharetta GA 30009
678 319-3240

(G-410)
TIMOTHY A MUSSER & CO INC
213 N 14th St (18102-4988)
PHONE..................................610 433-6380
Timothy A Musser, *President*
Joseph Nirschel, *Treasurer*
EMP: 3
SQ FT: 1,000
SALES (est): 324.7K **Privately Held**
SIC: 1389 Detection & analysis service, gas

(G-411)
TRE GRAPHICS ETC INC
5012 Med Ctr Cir Ste 3 (18106)
PHONE..................................610 821-8508
Edward Howe, *President*
Richard Long, *Vice Pres*
EMP: 6 **EST:** 1978
SQ FT: 3,600
SALES (est): 979.9K **Privately Held**
WEB: www.tregraphics.com
SIC: 2752 Commercial printing, offset

(G-412)
TRI CITY MARBLE INC
4724 Springside Ct (18104-9488)
PHONE..................................610 481-0177
George Conly, *President*
EMP: 30
SQ FT: 18,000
SALES (est): 3.2MM **Privately Held**
WEB: www.tricitymarble.com
SIC: 3281 Table tops, marble; bathroom fixtures, cut stone; household articles, except furniture: cut stone

(G-413)
TRI-CITY MARBLE LLC
4724 Springside Ct (18104-9488)
PHONE..................................610 481-0177
John Angelella, *Mng Member*
EMP: 10
SALES (est): 1MM **Privately Held**
SIC: 3281 5211 Table tops, marble; bathroom fixtures, cut stone; household articles, except furniture: cut stone; concrete & cinder block

(G-414)
TRI-DIM FILTER CORPORATION
7036 Snowdrift Rd (18106-9407)
PHONE..................................610 481-9926
John C Stanley, *CEO*
EMP: 11
SALES (corp-wide): 4.5B **Privately Held**
SIC: 3569 Filters
HQ: Tri-Dim Filter Corporation
93 Industrial Dr
Louisa VA 23093
540 967-2600

(G-415)
TUSCAN/LEHIGH DAIRIES INC
711 N Brick St (18102-1900)
PHONE..................................610 434-9666
Peter Kurecian, *Branch Mgr*
EMP: 18 **Publicly Held**
SIC: 2026 Fermented & cultured milk products
HQ: Tuscan/Lehigh Dairies, Inc.
117 Cumberland Blvd
Burlington NJ 08016
570 385-1884

(G-416)
U R I COMPRESSORS INC (PA)
405 Allentown Dr Unit A (18109-9144)
PHONE..................................484 223-3265
Bruce Reich, *President*
EMP: 4 **EST:** 1975
SQ FT: 24,000
SALES (est): 832.1K **Privately Held**
SIC: 3585 Compressors for refrigeration & air conditioning equipment

(G-417)
UNICAST COMPANY
1653 Hausman Rd (18104-9257)
PHONE..................................610 366-8836
Louis Monaco, *CEO*
EMP: 4
SALES (est): 414.5K **Privately Held**
SIC: 3321 Gray iron castings

(G-418)
UNITED ENRGY PLUS TRMINALS LLC
2 N 9th St (18101-1139)
PHONE..................................610 774-5151
Jerry Aunet, *General Mgr*
EMP: 25
SALES (est): 4MM
SALES (corp-wide): 2.5B **Privately Held**
SIC: 4911 4924 2869 ; ; natural gas distribution; fuels

PA: Red Apple Group, Inc.
800 3rd Ave Fl 5
New York NY 10022
212 956-5803

(G-419)
VALCO INVESTMENT CORPORATION
Also Called: MI Products
404 Union Blvd (18109-3228)
PHONE..................................610 770-1881
Steven Goldthwaite, *President*
Duval Goldthwaite, *Vice Pres*
EMP: 40
SQ FT: 38,287
SALES (est): 7.1MM **Privately Held**
WEB: www.outlookserver.net
SIC: 3599 Machine shop, jobbing & repair

(G-420)
VALLEY EXTRUSIONS LLC
795 Roble Rd Unit 1 (18109-9147)
PHONE..................................610 266-8550
Robert Carrier, *President*
John Lenti, *Project Mgr*
Chris Presler, *Engineer*
EMP: 50
SALES (est): 10.2MM **Privately Held**
SIC: 3089 Extruded finished plastic products

(G-421)
VALUMAX INTERNATIONAL INC
848 Hausman Rd (18104-9391)
PHONE..................................610 336-0101
Janice Jia, *President*
◆ **EMP:** 14
SALES (est): 223K **Privately Held**
SIC: 2389 Disposable garments & accessories

(G-422)
VANGUARD MANUFACTURING INC
Also Called: Consolidated Container
6831 Ruppsville Rd (18106-9360)
PHONE..................................610 481-0655
Richard Meyersburg, *President*
Rick Meyersburg, *Sales Staff*
Noelle Laroza, *Manager*
▲ **EMP:** 19
SALES (est): 3MM **Privately Held**
SIC: 3089 Plastic containers, except foam

(G-423)
VERSUM MATERIALS US LLC
1919 Vultee St (18103-4744)
PHONE..................................610 481-3946
John Ivankovits, *Director*
EMP: 11
SALES (corp-wide): 1.1B **Publicly Held**
SIC: 2842 2891 3559 Specialty cleaning preparations; adhesives; gas producers, generators & other gas related equipment; gas separators (machinery); separators for steam, gas, vapor or air (machinery)
HQ: Versum Materials Us, Llc
8555 S River Pkwy
Tempe AZ 85284
602 282-1000

(G-424)
VITRA INC
7528 Walker Way Ste 200 (18106-3100)
PHONE..................................610 391-9780
Alan Severance, *Manager*
EMP: 33
SALES (corp-wide): 166.7MM **Privately Held**
SIC: 2522 2521 Chairs, office: padded or plain, except wood; wood office furniture
HQ: Vitra, Inc.
10 Gansevoort St
New York NY 10014
212 463-5700

(G-425)
VITRA RETAIL INC
Also Called: Visplay, Inc.
7528 Walker Way (18106-3100)
PHONE..................................610 366-1658
Jessica Hicks, *CEO*
EMP: 8

▲ = Import ▼=Export
◆ =Import/Export

SALES (est): 2MM
SALES (corp-wide): 166.7MM **Privately Held**
SIC: 5046 2542 Store fixtures & display equipment; garment racks: except wood
HQ: Vitra Retail Systems Gmbh
Charles-Eames-Str. 2
Weil Am Rhein 79576
762 170-20

(G-426)
VORTEQ COIL FINISHERS LLC
2233 26th St Sw (18103-6601)
PHONE..................................610 797-5200
Jim Dockey, *Branch Mgr*
EMP: 55
SALES (corp-wide): 37.7MM **Privately Held**
SIC: 3479 Coating of metals & formed products
PA: Vorteq Coil Finishers, Llc
930 Armour Rd
Oconomowoc WI 53066
262 567-1112

(G-427)
W B MASON CO INC
966 Postal Rd 100 (18109-9506)
PHONE..................................888 926-2766
EMP: 60
SALES (corp-wide): 773MM **Privately Held**
SIC: 5943 5712 2752 Office forms & supplies; office furniture; commercial printing, lithographic
PA: W. B. Mason Co., Inc.
59 Center St
Brockton MA 02301
781 794-8800

(G-428)
WACKER CHEMICAL CORPORATION
6870 Tilghman St (18106-9346)
PHONE..................................610 336-2700
Patrick De Wolf, *Managing Dir*
Keith Hansen, *Business Mgr*
Lan Huang, *Business Mgr*
Alois Riedl, *Vice Pres*
Alex Lee, *Technical Mgr*
EMP: 100
SALES (corp-wide): 5.8B **Privately Held**
WEB: www.wackerchemicalcorporation.com
SIC: 2869 5169 Silicones; industrial chemicals
HQ: Wacker Chemical Corporation
3301 Sutton Rd
Adrian MI 49221
517 264-8500

(G-429)
WAGNER & SONS MACHINE SHOP
420 Business Park Ln (18109-9119)
PHONE..................................610 434-6640
Tim Wagner, *President*
Maryjane Wagne, *President*
EMP: 6 EST: 1979
SQ FT: 6,000
SALES: 1MM **Privately Held**
WEB: www.wagnersons.com
SIC: 3599 7539 Machine shop, jobbing & repair; machine shop, automotive

(G-430)
WEIDENHAMMER SYSTEMS CORP
951 Marcon Blvd (18109-9370)
PHONE..................................610 317-4000
John Weidenhammer, *President*
EMP: 50
SALES (corp-wide): 40MM **Privately Held**
SIC: 7372 Prepackaged software
PA: Weidenhammer Systems Corp
935 Berkshire Blvd
Reading PA 19610
610 378-1149

(G-431)
WENZ CO INC
1928 Hamilton St (18104-6442)
P.O. Box 112, Breinigsville (18031-0112)
PHONE..................................610 434-6157

Daniel F Kainz, *Principal*
EMP: 5
SALES (est): 249.9K **Privately Held**
SIC: 3281 Monuments, cut stone (not finishing or lettering only)

(G-432)
WENZCO SUPPLIES
1928 Hamilton St (18104-6442)
PHONE..................................610 434-6157
Earl Binder, *President*
William Binder, *Admin Sec*
▲ EMP: 12 EST: 1847
SQ FT: 18,000
SALES: 1MM **Privately Held**
SIC: 3281 3272 Tombstones, cut stone (not finishing or lettering only); monuments, cut stone (not finishing or lettering only); granite, cut & shaped; marble, building: cut & shaped; art marble, concrete

(G-433)
WESTWOOD PRECISION LLC
1530 E Race St (18109-9592)
PHONE..................................610 264-7020
Steve Szabo, *Mng Member*
Paul Sagun,
EMP: 4
SALES: 500K **Privately Held**
SIC: 3469 Metal stampings

(G-434)
WILD BIRDS UNLIMITED
4251 W Tilghman St (18104-4429)
PHONE..................................610 366-1725
Patricia M Varner, *Owner*
EMP: 7
SALES (est): 485.8K **Privately Held**
SIC: 5999 2048 Pets & pet supplies; bird food, prepared

(G-435)
WILLIAMSIGNS
6346 Farm Bureau Rd (18106-9223)
PHONE..................................610 530-0300
Norman Williamson, *Owner*
EMP: 3 EST: 1992
SQ FT: 4,100
SALES (est): 190K **Privately Held**
SIC: 2759 Screen printing

(G-436)
WIN-HOLT EQUIPMENT CORP
7028 Snowdrift Rd (18106-9274)
PHONE..................................516 222-0335
Greg Clark, *Manager*
EMP: 129
SALES (corp-wide): 83.1MM **Privately Held**
SIC: 3499 3556 3537 Machine bases, metal; food products machinery; industrial trucks & tractors
PA: Win-Holt Equipment Corp.
20 Crossways Park Dr N # 205
Woodbury NY 11797
516 222-0335

(G-437)
WINDKITS LLC
7346 Penn Dr Unit 2 (18106-9310)
PHONE..................................610 530-5704
Eric Schwartz, *Mng Member*
▲ EMP: 29 EST: 2008
SALES (est): 8.1MM **Privately Held**
SIC: 3511 Turbines & turbine generator sets

(G-438)
WORLDWIDE TURBINE LLC
350 Union Blvd (18109-3500)
PHONE..................................610 821-9500
Vince Abate,
▲ EMP: 39
SALES (est): 2.8MM **Privately Held**
WEB: www.worldwidewindturbines.com
SIC: 3511 Turbines & turbine generator sets

(G-439)
YEAGERS FIELD
Also Called: Honeywell Authorized Dealer
1431 W Green St (18102-1233)
PHONE..................................610 434-1516
Jim Yeagers, *Owner*
EMP: 3

SALES (est): 204.3K **Privately Held**
SIC: 3433 Heaters, swimming pool: oil or gas

(G-440)
ZIPPERCORD LLC
1801 S 12th St (18103-2927)
PHONE..................................610 797-6564
Kenneth C Jonas, *President*
Jenn Young, *Office Mgr*
Terri Farrell, *Manager*
▲ EMP: 18
SQ FT: 32,000
SALES (est): 4.3MM **Privately Held**
WEB: www.zippercord.com
SIC: 2298 Twine, cord & cordage

Allenwood
Union County

(G-441)
EMANUEL K FISHER
1065 Bob Drick Rd (17810-9477)
PHONE..................................570 547-2599
Emanuel K Fisher, *Principal*
EMP: 6
SALES (est): 491.1K **Privately Held**
SIC: 2411 Logging

(G-442)
PURITY CANDY CO (PA)
18047 Us Route 15 (17810-9141)
PHONE..................................570 538-9502
Margaret Burfeint, *President*
John D Burfeint, *Vice Pres*
EMP: 12 EST: 1880
SALES (est): 1.2MM **Privately Held**
WEB: www.puritycandy.com
SIC: 2064 5441 2099 2066 Candy & other confectionery products; candy; food preparations; chocolate & cocoa products

(G-443)
WHITE DEER WOODWORKING
16150 S State Route 44 (17810-9421)
PHONE..................................570 547-1664
Ben Fisher, *Principal*
EMP: 4
SALES (est): 383K **Privately Held**
SIC: 2431 Millwork

Allison
Fayette County

(G-444)
ACF GROUP LLC
Also Called: Allison Custom Fabrication
120 Mine St (15413-9704)
PHONE..................................724 364-7027
Donald Croftcheck, *Mng Member*
Scott Croftcheck,
EMP: 40
SQ FT: 60,000
SALES (est): 9.1MM
SALES (corp-wide): 855.1MM **Privately Held**
SIC: 3441 7699 3444 Fabricated structural metal; industrial equipment services; sheet metalwork
HQ: Fenner Dunlop Americas, Llc
1000 Omega Dr Ste 1400
Pittsburgh PA 15205

Allison Park
Allegheny County

(G-445)
ADVANCED CNSTR ROBOTICS INC (PA)
3812 William Flynn Hwy (15101-3660)
PHONE..................................412 756-3360
EMP: 3
SALES (est): 1.5MM **Privately Held**
SIC: 3531 Construction machinery

(G-446)
ALLISON PARK GROUP INC
Also Called: Apg
4055 Alpha Dr (15101-2961)
PHONE..................................412 487-8211
Christopher McGeary, *President*
Richard Schubert, *Design Engr*
EMP: 7
SALES (est): 1.2MM **Privately Held**
SIC: 3861 7389 Cameras & related equipment; design services

(G-447)
ANDERSON INC
4715 William Flynn Hwy (15101-2412)
PHONE..................................412 486-2211
James Anderson, *President*
EMP: 18
SQ FT: 5,000
SALES (est): 2MM **Privately Held**
SIC: 3799 5015 Automobile trailer chassis; automotive parts & supplies, used

(G-448)
CREATIVE CHEMICAL CO
4609 Woodlake Dr (15101-1015)
PHONE..................................724 443-5010
Dave Hoburg, *President*
EMP: 4
SALES (est): 308.1K **Privately Held**
WEB: www.creative-supply.net
SIC: 2869 2899 High purity grade chemicals, organic; chemical preparations

(G-449)
DAVIS & DAVIS GOURMET FOODS
3614 William Flynn Hwy (15101-3722)
PHONE..................................412 487-7770
Ken Davis, *Owner*
EMP: 6
SALES: 500K **Privately Held**
WEB: www.davisanddavisonline.com
SIC: 5149 2099 Specialty food items; food preparations

(G-450)
EASY USE AIR TOOLS INC
Also Called: Super Sonic Air Knife
3876 William Flynn Hwy (15101-3607)
PHONE..................................412 486-2270
Thomas F Hursen, *President*
EMP: 3
SQ FT: 1,200
SALES: 220K **Privately Held**
SIC: 3421 Knife blades & blanks

(G-451)
GLENSHAW DISTRIBUTORS INC
3114 William Flynn Hwy # 101 (15101-3840)
PHONE..................................412 753-0231
Kenneth R Rogg, *President*
Cindi Ankney, *Business Mgr*
EMP: 21
SQ FT: 22,000
SALES: 1.7MM **Privately Held**
SIC: 2499 Decorative wood & woodwork

(G-452)
GSM HOLD CO
Also Called: W.C. Weil Company
3812 William Flynn Hwy # 2 (15101-3660)
P.O. Box 199 (15101-0199)
PHONE..................................412 487-7140
Greg Madia, *President*
Danny Lusk, *Sales Staff*
EMP: 5 EST: 1988
SALES: 2.8MM
SALES (corp-wide): 4.9MM **Privately Held**
WEB: www.wcweil.com
SIC: 5084 3589 Pumps & pumping equipment; water treatment equipment, industrial
PA: Pumpman Holdings, Llc
600 Madison Ave
New York NY 10022
626 939-0300

(G-453)
INDUSTRIAL LEARNING SYSTEMS
4244 Yarmouth Dr (15101-1568)
PHONE..................................412 512-8257

Rajeev Kutty, *CEO*
EMP: 3
SALES: 100K **Privately Held**
WEB: www.ilsystems.net
SIC: 3823 Industrial instrmnts msrmnt display/control process variable

(G-454)
JMA GROUP
Also Called: Minuteman Press
4790 W Flynn Hwy 27 (15101)
PHONE..........................724 444-0004
Herb Briar, *Owner*
EMP: 6
SALES (est): 610.6K **Privately Held**
WEB: www.minutemanap.com
SIC: 2752 Commercial printing, lithographic

(G-455)
KERRY COMPANY INC
3003 Wildwood Sample Rd (15101)
P.O. Box 51 (15101-0051)
PHONE..........................412 486-3388
John B Keegan, *President*
Agnes Keegan, *Vice Pres*
C Eugene Boyle, *Controller*
EMP: 18
SQ FT: 12,000
SALES (est): 4.9MM **Privately Held**
WEB: www.kerryactuator.com
SIC: 3593 5084 Fluid power cylinders & actuators; industrial machinery & equipment

(G-456)
LONGWALL MINING SERVICES INC
9862 Old Kummer Rd (15101)
PHONE..........................724 816-7871
John M Whitfield, *President*
EMP: 6 **EST:** 2009
SALES (est): 267.5K **Privately Held**
SIC: 1241 Coal mining services

(G-457)
PAPER EXCHANGE INC
2504 College Park Rd (15101-4105)
PHONE..........................412 325-7075
Dan Prunzik, *President*
EMP: 16
SQ FT: 500
SALES (est): 3.4MM **Privately Held**
WEB: www.thepaperexchange.org
SIC: 2679 Paper products, converted

(G-458)
PITTSBURGH ELC MTR REPR INC
Also Called: Pittsburgh Electric Mtr & Repr
4790 William Flynn Hwy # 24 (15101-2459)
P.O. Box 129 (15101-0129)
PHONE..........................724 443-2333
David Ujazdowski, *CEO*
EMP: 6
SALES (est): 901.6K **Privately Held**
SIC: 7694 5999 Electric motor repair; motors, electric

(G-459)
PPG INDUSTRIES INC
Also Called: P P G Coatings & Resins R & D
4325 Rosanna Dr (15101-1423)
P.O. Box 360175m, Pittsburgh (15251-0001)
PHONE..........................412 487-4500
Roger Scriven, *Manager*
EMP: 24
SALES (corp-wide): 15.3B **Publicly Held**
WEB: www.ppg.com
SIC: 2851 2891 8731 Paints & allied products; adhesives; commercial physical research
PA: Ppg Industries, Inc.
    1 Ppg Pl
    Pittsburgh PA 15272
    412 434-3131

(G-460)
PULSEMETRICS LLC
3911 Ash Dr (15101-3144)
PHONE..........................412 656-5776
Santosh Ananthraman, *CEO*
Edwin Fabiszak, *Managing Prtnr*
Yen Chin, *COO*
EMP: 9

SALES (est): 445.6K **Privately Held**
WEB: www.pulsemetrics.com
SIC: 7371 7372 7373 8733 Computer software development & applications; prepackaged software; computer integrated systems design; noncommercial research organizations

(G-461)
RECATHCO LLC
2855 Oxford Blvd (15101-2452)
PHONE..........................412 487-1482
Stephen Brushey,
▼ **EMP:** 12
SQ FT: 4,000
SALES: 650K **Privately Held**
SIC: 3841 Catheters

(G-462)
SERVO REPAIR INTERNATIONAL
3812 William Flynn Hwy # 7 (15101-3611)
PHONE..........................412 492-8116
Gary L Cummings, *President*
Andrew T Suity, *Treasurer*
Robert Renda, *Manager*
Andrew Suity, *Info Tech Mgr*
Stephen Suity, *Info Tech Mgr*
EMP: 15
SQ FT: 8,500
SALES (est): 2.4MM **Privately Held**
WEB: www.servorep.com
SIC: 3621 Servomotors, electric

(G-463)
STEVENS WOODWORKS
4437 Birchwood Ln (15101-1346)
PHONE..........................412 487-4408
Carl G Stevens, *President*
EMP: 3
SALES: 100K **Privately Held**
SIC: 2431 Millwork

(G-464)
TERRA ESSENTIAL SCENTS SY
4361 William Flynn Hwy (15101-1434)
PHONE..........................412 213-3600
Carin Consentacis, *Owner*
EMP: 3
SALES (est): 292.5K **Privately Held**
SIC: 3999 5999 Candles; candle shops

(G-465)
TYBOT LLC
3812 William Flynn Hwy (15101-3660)
PHONE..........................412 756-3360
Jeremy Serock, *Mng Member*
EMP: 7
SALES (est): 305.4K
SALES (corp-wide): 1.5MM **Privately Held**
SIC: 3531 Construction machinery
PA: Advanced Construction Robotics, Inc.
    3812 William Flynn Hwy
    Allison Park PA 15101
    412 756-3360

(G-466)
VWR SCIENTIFIC INC
3830 Mount Royal Blvd (15101-3511)
PHONE..........................412 487-1983
Charles M Wittmer, *Principal*
EMP: 6
SALES (est): 495K **Privately Held**
SIC: 3821 Laboratory apparatus & furniture

(G-467)
WEST SIGNS INC
Also Called: Sign-A-Rama
3130 Westwind Dr (15101-1141)
PHONE..........................724 443-5588
Liza West, *President*
EMP: 3
SALES: 200K **Privately Held**
SIC: 3993 Signs & advertising specialties

Altoona
Blair County

(G-468)
A+ PRINTING INC
Also Called: A Plus Printing
2415 13th Ave (16601-2105)
PHONE..........................814 942-4257

Michael A Colledge, *President*
Miriam K Colledge, *Corp Secy*
Miriam Colledge, *Admin Sec*
EMP: 7
SQ FT: 7,400
SALES (est): 713.8K **Privately Held**
SIC: 2752 Commercial printing, offset

(G-469)
ALLEGHENY CUT STONE CO
911 9th Ave (16602)
PHONE..........................814 943-4157
Anthony G Fiore, *Owner*
EMP: 3
SALES: 250K **Privately Held**
SIC: 3281 5999 Marble, building: cut & shaped; monuments, finished to custom order

(G-470)
ALPHA ASSEMBLY SOLUTIONS INC
Also Called: Alpha Advanced Materials
4100 6th Ave (16602-1523)
PHONE..........................814 946-1611
EMP: 106
SALES (corp-wide): 1.9B **Publicly Held**
WEB: www.alphametals.com
SIC: 3356 3357 3341 3339 Solder: wire, bar, acid core, & rosin core; nonferrous wiredrawing & insulating; secondary nonferrous metals; primary nonferrous metals; blast furnaces & steel mills; mineral wool
HQ: Alpha Assembly Solutions Inc.
    300 Atrium Dr Fl 3
    Somerset NJ 08873
    908 791-3000

(G-471)
ALTOONA MIRROR
301 Cayuga Ave (16602-4323)
P.O. Box 2008 (16603-2008)
PHONE..........................814 946-7506
Ed Kruger, *President*
Linda Gracey, *Editor*
Neil Rudel, *Editor*
Susan Gerwert, *Credit Staff*
Peter Berzonsky, *Human Res Mgr*
EMP: 100
SALES (est): 8.3MM **Privately Held**
WEB: www.altoonamirror.com
SIC: 2711 Newspapers, publishing & printing

(G-472)
ALTOONA NEON SIGN SERVICE
809 S 10th St (16602-6367)
PHONE..........................814 942-7488
Brad Evans, *Owner*
Tom Bennett, *Production*
Scott Bowers, *Graphic Designe*
▲ **EMP:** 9
SQ FT: 12,000
SALES (est): 939.9K **Privately Held**
WEB: www.altoonaneon.com
SIC: 7629 3993 Electrical repair shops; neon signs; electric signs

(G-473)
ALTOONA SOFT WATER COMPANY
Also Called: Crystal Pure Bottled Water
445 Logan Blvd Lakemont (16602)
PHONE..........................814 943-2768
Michael Washko, *President*
Craig Castel, *Sales Staff*
EMP: 10
SQ FT: 7,000
SALES (est): 1.1MM **Privately Held**
SIC: 7389 1781 2086 Water softener service; water well servicing; pasteurized & mineral waters, bottled & canned

(G-474)
AMERICAN PATCH AND PIN
1503 Bell Ave (16602-4603)
PHONE..........................814 935-4289
Gary Hunter, *Principal*
EMP: 3
SALES (est): 222.1K **Privately Held**
SIC: 3452 Pins

(G-475)
AUTO CARE
1022 Old Mill Run Rd (16601-7625)
PHONE..........................814 943-8155
Timothy Bracken, *Principal*
EMP: 3 **EST:** 2008
SALES (est): 228.5K **Privately Held**
SIC: 7539 3542 Electrical services; brakes, metal forming

(G-476)
BETTER BATTER GLUTEN FREE FLUR
1885 E Pleasant Vly Blvd (16602-7514)
PHONE..........................814 946-0958
Naomi Poe, *CEO*
Allen Fuller, *Opers Mgr*
EMP: 6
SQ FT: 5,500
SALES: 704K **Privately Held**
SIC: 2052 Bakery products, dry

(G-477)
BIMBO BAKERIES USA INC
Also Called: Stroehmann Bakeries
116 Stroehman Dr (16601-9422)
PHONE..........................814 941-1102
Tom Lundgren, *Manager*
EMP: 12 **Privately Held**
SIC: 2051 Bakery: wholesale or wholesale/retail combined
HQ: Bimbo Bakeries Usa, Inc
    255 Business Center Dr # 200
    Horsham PA 19044
    215 347-5500

(G-478)
BIRDS EYE FOODS INC
Also Called: Snyder of Berlin
307 4th Ave Ste 1 (16602-2709)
PHONE..........................814 942-6031
Dick Doug, *Branch Mgr*
EMP: 15
SALES (corp-wide): 7.9B **Publicly Held**
WEB: www.agrilinkfoods.com
SIC: 2037 2096 Vegetables, quick frozen & cold pack, excl. potato products; potato chips & other potato-based snacks; corn chips & other corn-based snacks; tortilla chips; cheese curls & puffs
HQ: Birds Eye Foods, Inc.
    121 Woodcrest Rd
    Cherry Hill NJ 08003
    585 383-1850

(G-479)
BLAIR COMPANIES
259 Lakemont Park Blvd (16602-5945)
P.O. Box 2566 (16603-2566)
PHONE..........................814 949-8280
Scott Rizzo, *Vice Pres*
Kathy Wagner, *Branch Mgr*
EMP: 67
SALES (corp-wide): 80.7MM **Privately Held**
WEB: www.blairsign.com
SIC: 3993 Electric signs
PA: Blair Companies
    5107 Kissell Ave
    Altoona PA 16601
    814 949-8287

(G-480)
BLAIR COMPANIES (PA)
Also Called: Blair Sign Company
5107 Kissell Ave (16601-1050)
P.O. Box 2566 (16603-2566)
PHONE..........................814 949-8287
Vince Iapalucci, *President*
Phillip Devorris, *Principal*
Joe Deleo, *Vice Pres*
Donald Devorris, *Vice Pres*
Janice Anderson, *Project Mgr*
◆ **EMP:** 219
SQ FT: 140,000
SALES (est): 80.7MM **Privately Held**
WEB: www.blairsign.com
SIC: 3993 Electric signs

(G-481)
BLAIR COMPOSITES LLC
259 Lakemont Park Blvd (16602-5945)
PHONE..........................423 638-5847
Mike Carlton, *CEO*
▲ **EMP:** 50

▲ = Import ▼ =Export
◆ =Import/Export

SALES (est): 11.2MM **Privately Held**
SIC: 3229 Glass fiber products

(G-482)
BLAIR FIXTURES & MILLWORK INC
4100 Industrial Park Dr (16602-1736)
P.O. Box 2566 (16603-2566)
PHONE..............................814 940-1913
Philip Devorris, *President*
Donald Devorris, *Chairman*
Kathy Wagner, *Treasurer*
Jacqueline Moore, *Admin Sec*
▲ EMP: 25
SQ FT: 40,000
SALES (est): 7.2MM **Privately Held**
SIC: 3496 2599 Grocery carts, made from purchased wire; factory furniture & fixtures

(G-483)
BOYER CANDY COMPANY INC
821 17th St (16601-2074)
PHONE..............................814 944-9401
Anthony Fortione, *CEO*
Debra Forgione, *Mktg Dir*
EMP: 70
SQ FT: 130,000
SALES: 4MM **Privately Held**
WEB: www.boyercandies.com
SIC: 2064 Candy bars, including chocolate covered bars; chocolate candy, except solid chocolate

(G-484)
BRINIC DONUTS INC
Also Called: Dunkin' Donuts
3132 Pleasant Valley Blvd (16602-4309)
PHONE..............................814 944-5242
Terry Breinich, *President*
Vicki Breinich, *Admin Sec*
EMP: 20
SALES (est): 818.4K **Privately Held**
SIC: 5461 2051 Doughnuts; doughnuts, except frozen

(G-485)
BRYCE SAYLOR & SONS INC
4235 6th Ave (16602-1596)
PHONE..............................814 942-2288
Gregory Saylor, *President*
Barry Saylor, *Corp Secy*
Tracy Saylor, *Vice Pres*
EMP: 12 EST: 1961
SQ FT: 5,000
SALES (est): 2.2MM **Privately Held**
WEB: www.rechargewebdesign.com
SIC: 7353 3441 Cranes & aerial lift equipment, rental or leasing; fabricated structural metal

(G-486)
CARPENTER CO
2337 E Pleasant Vly Blvd (16601-8965)
PHONE..............................814 944-8612
Scott Schultz, *Branch Mgr*
EMP: 110
SALES (corp-wide): 2B **Privately Held**
WEB: www.carpenter.com
SIC: 3086 1311 2869 2823 Insulation or cushioning material, foamed plastic; carpet & rug cushions, foamed plastic; padding, foamed plastic; crude petroleum & natural gas; industrial organic chemicals; cellulosic manmade fibers; household furnishings; carpets & rugs
PA: Carpenter Co.
5016 Monument Ave
Richmond VA 23230
804 359-0800

(G-487)
CASSIDYS BREW ZOO
3415 Pleasant Valley Blvd # 48 (16602-4321)
PHONE..............................814 946-2739
Rick Vee, *President*
David Cassidy, *Admin Sec*
EMP: 7
SALES (est): 800.7K **Privately Held**
WEB: www.brewzoo.com
SIC: 2086 5921 Bottled & canned soft drinks; beer (packaged)

(G-488)
CENTRAL BLAIR ELECTRIC CO
259 Lakemont Park Blvd (16602-5945)
P.O. Box 2566 (16603-2566)
PHONE..............................814 949-8280
Donald Devorris, *President*
Kathy Wagner, *Vice Pres*
EMP: 15
SQ FT: 6,000
SALES: 300K **Privately Held**
SIC: 7699 3599 Engine repair & replacement, non-automotive; machine shop, jobbing & repair

(G-489)
CENTRAL PENNSYLVANIA
301 Cayuga Ave (16602-4323)
P.O. Box 2008 (16603-2008)
PHONE..............................814 946-7411
Ed Kruger, *Administration*
EMP: 3
SALES (est): 76.2K **Privately Held**
SIC: 2711 Newspapers

(G-490)
CHARLES CRACCIOLO STL MET YARD
1813 Old 6th Avenue Rd (16601)
PHONE..............................814 944-4051
Charles B Caracciolo, *President*
EMP: 25
SQ FT: 1,400
SALES (est): 4.2MM **Privately Held**
SIC: 5093 3444 Ferrous metal scrap & waste; sheet metalwork

(G-491)
CHARLIES TREE SERVICE
611 N 6th Ave (16601-6001)
PHONE..............................814 943-1131
Travis Deyarmin, *Owner*
Mark Lindeck, *Co-Owner*
EMP: 3
SALES (est): 188K **Privately Held**
SIC: 1629 2411 0783 Land clearing contractor; logging; ornamental shrub & tree services

(G-492)
CHERYL HEWITT
Also Called: We Love Wood
1321 Jefferson Ave (16602-6022)
PHONE..............................814 943-7222
Cheryl Hewitt, *Owner*
EMP: 3
SALES (est): 119.7K **Privately Held**
WEB: www.welovewood.com
SIC: 2499 Carved & turned wood

(G-493)
COLOR SCAN LLC
2000 7th Ave (16602-2240)
PHONE..............................814 949-2032
Sara Masci, *Owner*
Bryan Melius, *Sls & Mktg Exec*
EMP: 3
SQ FT: 12,000
SALES (est): 237.3K **Privately Held**
WEB: www.colorscn.com
SIC: 2796 7336 Color separations for printing; commercial art & graphic design

(G-494)
COOKIE GRAMS
919 Logan Blvd (16602-4025)
PHONE..............................814 942-4220
Terry Adams, *Owner*
Eydie Adams, *Co-Owner*
EMP: 3 EST: 2007
SALES (est): 245.6K **Privately Held**
SIC: 2052 Cookies

(G-495)
CROGAN INC
Also Called: Press Box Printing
2109 9th Ave (16602-2210)
PHONE..............................814 944-3057
David Hogan, *CEO*
Michael Cree, *President*
EMP: 9
SALES (est): 1.1MM **Privately Held**
SIC: 2759 Promotional printing

(G-496)
D L DRAVIS & ASSOCIATES INC (PA)
Also Called: Copy Rite
711 N 9th Ave (16601)
PHONE..............................814 943-6155
David Dravis, *President*
Lisa Noel, *Marketing Staff*
EMP: 5
SALES (est): 1.6MM **Privately Held**
SIC: 6411 2752 7334 Insurance adjusters; commercial printing, lithographic; photocopying & duplicating services

(G-497)
D L DRAVIS & ASSOCIATES INC
1904 Union Ave (16601-2028)
PHONE..............................814 944-5880
David Dravis, *Branch Mgr*
EMP: 5
SALES (corp-wide): 1.6MM **Privately Held**
SIC: 6411 2752 7334 Insurance adjusters; commercial printing, lithographic; photocopying & duplicating services
PA: D L Dravis & Associates Inc
711 N 9th Ave
Altoona PA 16601
814 943-6155

(G-498)
DEFFIBAUGH BUTCHER SUPPLY
Also Called: Deffibaugh James W Butcher Sup
1200 N 6th Ave (16601-6204)
PHONE..............................814 944-1297
James W Deffibaugh, *Owner*
EMP: 3
SALES (est): 320K **Privately Held**
SIC: 5085 3421 5046 Knives, industrial; table & food cutlery, including butchers'; restaurant equipment & supplies

(G-499)
EAST SIDE CONCRETE SUPPLY CO (PA)
114 Old Mill Run Rd (16601-7616)
PHONE..............................814 944-8175
Marianne Drenning, *President*
Emmor Boslet, *Treasurer*
EMP: 10 EST: 1946
SQ FT: 14,000
SALES (est): 950.8K **Privately Held**
WEB: www.eastsideconcrete.com
SIC: 3273 5211 Ready-mixed concrete; cement

(G-500)
EASY TO USE BIG BOOKS
Also Called: Easytousebigbooks.com
301 Cayuga Ave (16602-4323)
P.O. Box 1433 (16603-1433)
PHONE..............................814 946-7442
Dawn Stair, *Prdtn Mgr*
Julia Glunt, *Accounts Exec*
Edward Kruger, *Manager*
Sherri Holmberg,
EMP: 75
SALES (est): 3.8MM **Privately Held**
SIC: 2741 Telephone & other directory publishing

(G-501)
ELECTRIC MOTOR & SUPPLY INC
1000 50th St (16601-1014)
P.O. Box 152 (16603-0152)
PHONE..............................814 946-0401
Patrick Illig II, *President*
Sandra Illig, *Corp Secy*
Robert Whitaker, *Engineer*
Lonny Lallemand, *Manager*
EMP: 29
SQ FT: 70,000
SALES (est): 6.9MM **Privately Held**
WEB: www.electricmotorandsupply.com
SIC: 7694 5063 Electric motor repair; motor controls, starters & relays: electric; motors, electric; power transmission equipment, electric

(G-502)
EYE CATCHER GRAPHICS INC
Also Called: Eye Catchers
2513 6th Ave (16602-2129)
PHONE..............................814 946-4080
D Barger, *President*
Tg Foor, *Vice Pres*
EMP: 3 EST: 1991
SALES (est): 182.3K **Privately Held**
SIC: 3993 Signs & advertising specialties

(G-503)
EZ TO USE DIRECTORIES INC (PA)
1811 Valley View Blvd (16602-6042)
PHONE..............................814 949-7100
Betty Holmes Reilly, *President*
Ronnie G Reilly, *Vice Pres*
David Reilly, *Treasurer*
James O Courtney, *Admin Sec*
EMP: 20 EST: 1997
SALES (est): 1.3MM **Privately Held**
SIC: 2741 Directories, telephone: publishing & printing

(G-504)
FABCO INC (HQ)
1128 9th Ave (16602-2535)
PHONE..............................814 944-1631
Shirley A Pechter, *President*
Richard S Pechter, *Vice Pres*
George Mansfield, *Manager*
EMP: 7
SQ FT: 500
SALES (est): 2.4MM
SALES (corp-wide): 29.1MM **Privately Held**
WEB: www.altoonapipeandsteel.com
SIC: 3499 Bank chests, metal
PA: Pechter, Inc.
1128 9th Ave
Altoona PA 16602
814 944-1631

(G-505)
FABCO INC
Also Called: Altoona Pipe & Steel
2111 Beale Ave Rear (16601-2010)
P.O. Box 112 (16603-0112)
PHONE..............................814 944-1631
George Mansfield, *Manager*
EMP: 13
SALES (corp-wide): 29.1MM **Privately Held**
WEB: www.altoonapipeandsteel.com
SIC: 3441 Fabricated structural metal
HQ: Fabco Inc.
1128 9th Ave
Altoona PA 16602
814 944-1631

(G-506)
FEDERAL WHITE CEMENT
154 Woods Ln (16601-9400)
P.O. Box 69, Bellwood (16617-0069)
PHONE..............................814 946-8950
Monica Schultes, *Branch Mgr*
EMP: 4
SALES (corp-wide): 17.9MM **Privately Held**
WEB: www.federalwhite.com
SIC: 3241 Cement, hydraulic
PA: Federal White Cement Ltd
355151 35th Line
Embro ON N0J 1
519 485-5410

(G-507)
FORSHT CONCRETE PDTS CO INC
616 Grandview Rd (16601)
PHONE..............................814 944-1617
Marjorie Forsht, *President*
Margery Forsht, *President*
William Forsht, *Admin Sec*
EMP: 6 EST: 1946
SQ FT: 8,500
SALES: 350K **Privately Held**
SIC: 3272 5211 5087 5051 Burial vaults, concrete or precast terrazzo; septic tanks, concrete; steps, prefabricated concrete; masonry materials & supplies; concrete burial vaults & boxes; pipe & tubing, steel; septic system construction

G
E
O
G
R
A
P
H
I
C

(G-508)
GALLIKER DAIRY COMPANY
Also Called: Altoona Division
819 9th Ave (16602-2531)
PHONE................................814 944-8193
Louis G Galliker, *Branch Mgr*
EMP: 14
SALES (corp-wide): 105.3MM **Privately Held**
WEB: www.gallikers.com
SIC: 2026 Fluid milk
PA: Galliker Dairy Company
　143 Donald Ln
　Johnstown PA 15904
　814 266-8702

(G-509)
GARDNER DENVER HOLDINGS INC
150 Enterprise Campus Dr (16601-8978)
PHONE................................814 742-9600
EMP: 14
SALES (corp-wide): 2.6B **Publicly Held**
SIC: 3564 Blowers & fans
HQ: Gardner Denver Investments, Inc.
　222 E Erie St Ste 500
　Milwaukee WI 53202
　217 222-5400

(G-510)
GENERAL CABLE INDUSTRIES INC
Altoona, PA Plant
3101 Pleasant Valley Blvd (16602-4308)
PHONE................................814 944-5002
Jack Lawless, *Manager*
EMP: 250
SQ FT: 200,000
SALES (corp-wide): 1.3B **Privately Held**
WEB: www.generalcable.com
SIC: 3357 Nonferrous wiredrawing & insulating
HQ: General Cable Industries, Inc.
　4 Tesseneer Dr
　Highland Heights KY 41076

(G-511)
GOGREENAPU LLC
1052 Neil Run Rd (16601)
PHONE................................814 943-9948
Harry Benjamin, *Mng Member*
Harry K Benjamin, *Mng Member*
EMP: 5
SALES (est): 271K **Privately Held**
SIC: 3728 Research & dev by manuf., aircraft parts & auxiliary equip

(G-512)
HENDERSONS PRINTING INC (PA)
Also Called: Times Tribune Co
Green Ave & Ninth St 9th (16601)
PHONE................................814 944-0855
R Thomas Henderson, *Ch of Bd*
Dorothy M Henderson, *Vice Pres*
Leona Gebhart, *Controller*
EMP: 20
SQ FT: 42,000
SALES (est): 9.2MM **Privately Held**
SIC: 2752 7389 Commercial printing, offset; packaging & labeling services

(G-513)
HESFORD KEYSTONE PRINTING CO
221 Parrish St (16602-5853)
PHONE................................814 942-2911
Larry Hesford, *President*
Sharon Hesford, *Vice Pres*
EMP: 3
SQ FT: 1,800
SALES: 220K **Privately Held**
SIC: 2759 2752 Commercial printing; commercial printing, lithographic

(G-514)
HILLTOP TOWER LEASING INC
400 Highland Ave (16602-2800)
PHONE................................814 942-1888
David Kephart, *President*
EMP: 20
SALES (est): 1.6MM **Privately Held**
SIC: 3663 Transmitter-receivers, radio

(G-515)
IMAGE SIGNS INC
1720 Margaret Ave B (16601-2020)
PHONE................................814 946-4663
Valentine Zavilanski, *President*
Susanne Zavilanski, *Corp Secy*
EMP: 6
SQ FT: 10,000
SALES (est): 876.5K **Privately Held**
WEB: www.imagesigns.com
SIC: 3993 Neon signs

(G-516)
IMMUNOTEK BIO CENTERS LLC
5901 6th Ave (16602-1114)
PHONE................................814 283-6421
Henna Khan, *Manager*
EMP: 21
SALES (corp-wide): 27MM **Privately Held**
SIC: 2836 Blood derivatives
PA: Immunotek Bio Centers, L.L.C.
　5750 Johnston St Ste 302
　Lafayette LA 70503
　337 500-1175

(G-517)
INTEGRITAS INC
1331 12th Ave (16601-3340)
PHONE................................814 941-7006
Ed Stroupe, *Manager*
EMP: 4
SALES (corp-wide): 2.4B **Publicly Held**
WEB: www.integritas.com
SIC: 3822 Hydronic controls
HQ: Integritas, Inc.
　40 24th St Fl 5
　Pittsburgh PA 15222

(G-518)
ITI INMATE TELEPHONE INC
5000 6th Ave Ste 1 (16602-1445)
PHONE................................814 944-0405
Anthony Bambocci, *President*
James Faith, *Vice Pres*
David Perove, *Shareholder*
EMP: 93
SALES (est): 5.9MM **Privately Held**
WEB: www.inmatetelephone.com
SIC: 1731 3661 Telephone & telephone equipment installation; telephone & telegraph apparatus

(G-519)
JUNIATA FABRICS INC
1301 Broadway (16601-5314)
P.O. Box 1806 (16603-1806)
PHONE................................814 944-9381
Terry Wray, *President*
David A Detwiler, *Vice Pres*
Joseph M Wyland, *Treasurer*
EMP: 13
SALES (est): 2.2MM **Privately Held**
WEB: www.juniatafabrics.com
SIC: 2221 2241 2211 Broadwoven fabric mills, manmade; narrow fabric mills; broadwoven fabric mills, cotton

(G-520)
KEYSTONE CASEWORK INC
2101 Beale Ave (16601-2010)
PHONE................................814 941-7250
EMP: 25
SQ FT: 27,000
SALES (est): 2.1MM **Privately Held**
SIC: 2541 2439 Mfg Wood & Laminated Wooden Display Fixtures

(G-521)
LAWRUK MACHINE & TOOL CO INC
302 E 6th Ave (16602-7027)
P.O. Box 1825 (16603-1825)
PHONE................................814 943-6136
Michael Frederick, *President*
Sheila Frederick, *Corp Secy*
Romona Lawruk, *Treasurer*
Barbara Lawruk, *Admin Sec*
EMP: 32 EST: 1966
SQ FT: 13,760
SALES (est): 5.5MM **Privately Held**
SIC: 3599 Machine shop, jobbing & repair

(G-522)
LOYAL GAMING REWARDS LLC
139 Stadium Dr (16601-9421)
PHONE................................814 822-2008
Scott A Orolin, *President*
EMP: 6
SALES (est): 755.1K **Privately Held**
SIC: 3944 Bingo boards (games)

(G-523)
M C TOOL & DIE INC
3387 Colonel Drake Hwy (16601-7522)
PHONE................................814 944-8654
EMP: 6
SQ FT: 9,500
SALES (est): 759.3K **Privately Held**
SIC: 3544 Mfg Dies/Tools/Jigs/Fixtures

(G-524)
MARTIN AMR LLC
3709 Beale Ave (16601-1317)
PHONE................................908 313-2459
Martin Blendulf,
EMP: 5 EST: 2017
SALES (est): 150.7K **Privately Held**
SIC: 3999 Manufacturing industries

(G-525)
MCCABES CUSTOM LEATHER
125 Byron Ave (16602-4173)
PHONE................................814 414-1442
EMP: 3 EST: 2011
SALES (est): 256.5K **Privately Held**
SIC: 3199 Leather goods

(G-526)
MCMULLENS FURNITURE STORE
601 N 2nd St (16601-5805)
PHONE................................814 942-1202
Edward Miller, *President*
James Shannon, *Shareholder*
Ann Wiley, *Admin Sec*
EMP: 4
SQ FT: 7,000
SALES (est): 707.3K **Privately Held**
SIC: 5712 2515 Mattresses; bedsprings, assembled

(G-527)
MILLER ELECTRIC SERVICE & SUP
2701 Washington Ave (16601-2641)
PHONE................................814 942-9943
William Miller, *Owner*
EMP: 12 EST: 1970
SQ FT: 21,000
SALES (est): 1.2MM **Privately Held**
WEB: www.millerbilt.net
SIC: 1731 5063 7694 General electrical contractor; electrical supplies; electric motor repair

(G-528)
MODERN CABINET AND CNSTR CO
110 Frankstown Rd (16602-4145)
PHONE................................814 942-1000
Calvin M Detwiler, *Ch of Bd*
Daniel Detwiler, *President*
Sherry Wise, *Admin Sec*
EMP: 13 EST: 1940
SQ FT: 11,500
SALES (est): 1.8MM **Privately Held**
SIC: 2426 5712 Hardwood dimension & flooring mills; cabinet work, custom

(G-529)
MOUNTAIN SIDE SUPPLY LLC
400 E Pleasant Vly Blvd (16602-5515)
PHONE................................814 201-2525
Tayler Atkin, *Manager*
EMP: 3 EST: 2015
SALES (est): 232.4K **Privately Held**
SIC: 3272 Building materials, except block or brick; concrete

(G-530)
NEW LOOK UNIFORM & EMBROIDERY
800 S 20th St (16602-4541)
PHONE................................814 944-5515
Kimberly McEldowney, *President*
James R Hollenbach, *President*
Sherry Hollenbach, *Corp Secy*
Pamela Schuh, *Vice Pres*
EMP: 10
SQ FT: 4,500
SALES (est): 1.5MM **Privately Held**
SIC: 5199 5699 2395 7336 Advertising specialties; uniforms; embroidery products, except schiffli machine; silk screen design

(G-531)
NORFOLK SOUTHERN CORPORATION
200 N 4th Ave (16601-6702)
PHONE................................814 949-1551
Lynn Ramsey, *General Mgr*
William Roberts, *Foreman/Supr*
EMP: 43
SALES (corp-wide): 11.4B **Publicly Held**
WEB: www.nscorp.com
SIC: 4011 3743 Railroads, line-haul operating; railroad equipment
PA: Norfolk Southern Corporation
　3 Commercial Pl Ste 1a
　Norfolk VA 23510
　757 629-2680

(G-532)
OAK SPRING WINERY INCORPORATED (PA)
2401 E Pleasant Vly Blvd (16601-8967)
PHONE................................814 946-3799
Silvia H Scharff, *President*
John J Scharff, *Corp Secy*
EMP: 9
SQ FT: 8,000
SALES (est): 871.7K **Privately Held**
WEB: www.oakspringwinery.com
SIC: 2084 5921 Wines; wine

(G-533)
ODELLICK BAKING LLC
4209 5th Ave (16602-1520)
PHONE................................814 515-1337
EMP: 4
SALES (est): 160.8K **Privately Held**
SIC: 2051 Bread, cake & related products

(G-534)
OGDEN DIRECTORIES PA INC
301 Cayuga Ave (16602-4323)
PHONE................................814 946-7404
Ogden G Nutting, *President*
Edward Kruger, *General Mgr*
Duane D Wittman, *Treasurer*
EMP: 200
SALES: 45MM **Privately Held**
WEB: www.ogdendirectories.com
SIC: 2741 Telephone & other directory publishing
HQ: Ogden Directories, Inc.
　1500 Main St
　Wheeling WV 26003

(G-535)
OGDEN NEWSPAPERS INC
Also Called: Altoona Mirror
301 Cayuga Ave (16602-4323)
P.O. Box 2008 (16603-2008)
PHONE................................814 946-7411
Ray Eckenrode, *Manager*
EMP: 200 **Privately Held**
SIC: 2711 Newspapers: publishing only, not printed on site
HQ: The Ogden Newspapers Inc
　1500 Main St
　Wheeling WV 26003
　304 233-0100

(G-536)
PA OUTDOOR TIMES
301 Cayuga Ave (16602-4323)
P.O. Box 2008 (16603-2008)
PHONE................................814 946-7400
EMP: 4
SALES (est): 223.2K
SALES (corp-wide): 683.9MM **Privately Held**
SIC: 2741 5941 Misc Publishing Ret Sporting Goods/Bicycles
PA: The Ogden Newspapers Inc
　1500 Main St
　Wheeling WV 26003
　304 233-0100

(G-537)
PENN PUBLIC TRUCK & EQUIPMENT
Also Called: Penn Public Services
714 11th St (16602-2536)
PHONE..................................814 944-5314
Michael Ventere, *Owner*
EMP: 16
SALES (est): 1.4MM **Privately Held**
SIC: 7538 3599 General truck repair; machine shop, jobbing & repair

(G-538)
PRESS BOX PRINTING
2109 9th Ave (16602-2217)
PHONE..................................814 944-3057
Mike Cree, *Partner*
David Hogan, *Partner*
Cheyenne Lee, *Graphic Designe*
EMP: 8
SQ FT: 5,000
SALES (est): 1.4MM **Privately Held**
SIC: 2752 2759 Commercial printing, offset; commercial printing

(G-539)
PRO ACTIVE SPORTS INC
5910 California Ave (16602-1010)
PHONE..................................814 943-4651
Douglas Rhodes, *President*
EMP: 9
SALES (est): 1.2MM **Privately Held**
SIC: 2759 Advertising literature: printing; screen printing

(G-540)
R C PRINT SPECIALIST
Also Called: R C'S Print Specialists
810 S 12th St (16602-6246)
PHONE..................................814 942-1204
Randy Campbell, *Owner*
Louise Campbell, *Co-Owner*
EMP: 3
SQ FT: 2,000
SALES (est): 262.4K **Privately Held**
SIC: 2759 Screen printing

(G-541)
RAVINE INC
610 7th St (16602-2629)
PHONE..................................814 946-5006
James M Moschella, *President*
EMP: 15
SALES (est): 1.4MM **Privately Held**
SIC: 2395 2759 2396 Embroidery & art needlework; screen printing; printing & embossing on plastics fabric articles

(G-542)
REAL ESTATE BOOK SOUTH CENT
206 6th Ave (16602-2734)
PHONE..................................814 943-8110
Carol Decker, *Partner*
Tim Brown, *Partner*
EMP: 3
SALES (est): 149.3K **Privately Held**
SIC: 2741 Miscellaneous publishing

(G-543)
REED MICRO AUTOMATION INC
3900 Industrial Park Dr # 6 (16602-1732)
PHONE..................................814 941-0225
Herbert Reed, *President*
EMP: 9
SQ FT: 5,700
SALES (est): 818.6K **Privately Held**
WEB: www.reed-micro.com
SIC: 3672 7371 Printed circuit boards; custom computer programming services

(G-544)
ROBERT JOHN ENTERPRISES INC (PA)
Also Called: Allegheny Orthtics Prosthetics
3500 6th Ave (16602-1814)
PHONE..................................814 944-0187
John Roberts Jr, *President*
Mark Hinton, *Director*
EMP: 12
SQ FT: 5,000
SALES (est): 1.3MM **Privately Held**
WEB: www.alleghenyoandp.com
SIC: 3842 5999 Prosthetic appliances; orthopedic & prosthesis applications

(G-545)
RPM NITTANY PRINTING
Also Called: R P M Nittany Printing Service
404 27th Ave (16601-3637)
P.O. Box 1862 (16603-1862)
PHONE..................................814 941-7775
Robert Mastos, *Owner*
EMP: 3
SALES (est): 188.6K **Privately Held**
SIC: 2761 Manifold business forms

(G-546)
SAMFAM INC
Also Called: Embroidery Just For You
3614 6th Ave (16602-1709)
PHONE..................................814 941-1915
Michelle Samson, *CEO*
Micheal Samson, *Vice Pres*
EMP: 4
SQ FT: 1,800
SALES (est): 398.3K **Privately Held**
WEB: www.embroideryjustforyou.com
SIC: 2395 Embroidery & art needlework

(G-547)
SEVEN D TRUSS LP (PA)
3229 Pleasant Valley Blvd (16602-4435)
PHONE..................................814 317-4077
Bruno De Gol Jr, *Partner*
David De Gol, *Partner*
Dennis De Gol, *Partner*
Donald A De Gol Sr, *Partner*
EMP: 50
SQ FT: 12,000
SALES (est): 2.8MM **Privately Held**
SIC: 2439 Trusses, wooden roof

(G-548)
SEYMORE BROS INC
4221 6th Ave (16602-1598)
P.O. Box 805, Duncansville (16635-0805)
PHONE..................................814 944-2074
Toll Free:..................................888 -
Timothy Seymore, *President*
Gregory Seymore, *Corp Secy*
Jeff Seymore, *Vice Pres*
EMP: 22 EST: 1917
SQ FT: 15,000
SALES (est): 3MM **Privately Held**
WEB: www.seymorebros.com
SIC: 3271 Blocks, concrete or cinder: standard

(G-549)
SIGNATURE DOOR INC
401 Priority St (16602-7066)
PHONE..................................814 949-2770
Hilde Lewkowitz, *President*
Bernd Lewkowitz, *Corp Secy*
Dennis Nixon Sr, *Vice Pres*
EMP: 75
SQ FT: 15,000
SALES (est): 10.2MM **Privately Held**
WEB: www.signaturedoor.com
SIC: 3231 2431 Products of purchased glass; doors, wood; doors & door parts & trim, wood

(G-550)
SYNTHEX ORGANICS LLC
4601 Cortland Ave (16601-1268)
P.O. Box 98, Duncansville (16635-0098)
PHONE..................................814 941-8375
Mike Stoltz, *CEO*
Thomas Stoltz, *CEO*
EMP: 3
SALES (est): 656.4K **Privately Held**
SIC: 2869 Industrial organic chemicals

(G-551)
THERMAL INDUSTRIES INC
810 S 12th St (16602-6246)
PHONE..................................814 944-4534
EMP: 6
SALES (corp-wide): 1.2B **Privately Held**
SIC: 3442 5211 5023 Mfg Metal Doors/Sash/Trim Ret Lumber/Building Materials Whol Homefurnishings
HQ: Thermal Industries, Inc.
3700 Haney Ct
Murrysville PA 15668
724 325-6100

(G-552)
THOMPSON MACHINE COMPANY INC
1128 N 4th Ave (16601-6127)
PHONE..................................814 941-4982
Agnes Thompson, *Principal*
Tracey McDermitt, *Corp Secy*
Tim Drenning, *Vice Pres*
William Lightner, *Vice Pres*
EMP: 50
SQ FT: 12,000
SALES (est): 7.2MM **Privately Held**
SIC: 3599 3441 Machine shop, jobbing & repair; fabricated structural metal

(G-553)
UNION ROOFING AND SHTMTL CO
Also Called: Union Roofing & Sheet Metal
430 7th Ave (16602)
PHONE..................................814 946-0824
Joseph H Orr Jr, *President*
Joseph H Orr III, *Treasurer*
EMP: 25
SQ FT: 10,000
SALES (est): 1MM **Privately Held**
SIC: 1761 3444 Roofing contractor; sheet metalwork; sheet metalwork

(G-554)
UNION TANK CAR COMPANY
Chestnut Ave And Sixth St (16601)
PHONE..................................814 944-4523
Dave Gildea, *Manager*
EMP: 100
SALES (corp-wide): 225.3B **Publicly Held**
WEB: www.utlx.com
SIC: 3743 Railroad equipment
HQ: Union Tank Car Company
175 W Jackson Blvd # 2100
Chicago IL 60604
312 431-3111

(G-555)
W B MASON CO INC
1640 E Pleasant Valley Bl (16602-7369)
PHONE..................................888 926-2766
EMP: 40
SALES (corp-wide): 773MM **Privately Held**
SIC: 5943 5712 2752 Writing supplies; cabinets, except custom made: kitchen; commercial printing, lithographic
PA: W. B. Mason Co., Inc.
59 Center St
Brockton MA 02301
781 794-8800

(G-556)
W S LEE & SONS LP
3000 7th Ave (16602-1965)
P.O. Box 1631 (16603-1631)
PHONE..................................814 317-5010
Robert Lee, *President*
EMP: 3
SALES (est): 332.4K **Privately Held**
SIC: 2395 Embroidery & art needlework

(G-557)
WARNERS INNVTIVE SOLUTIONS INC
1304 11th Ave (16601-3302)
PHONE..................................814 201-2429
▲ EMP: 10
SALES (est): 920K **Privately Held**
SIC: 3643 8999 Mfg Conductive Wiring Devices Services-Misc

(G-558)
WICK COPY CENTER
503 E Plank Rd (16602-4114)
PHONE..................................814 942-8040
Lois Wick, *Owner*
EMP: 3
SALES (est): 331.7K **Privately Held**
SIC: 7334 2759 Blueprinting service; commercial printing

Alum Bank
Bedford County

(G-559)
CPK MANUFACTURING LLC (DH)
Also Called: Kenway Composites
214 Industrial Ln (15521-8304)
PHONE..................................814 839-4186
Shane Weyant, *President*
Ian Kopp, *Principal*
Persis Fungaroli, *Treasurer*
EMP: 4
SALES (est): 16.5MM
SALES (corp-wide): 773.1MM **Privately Held**
SIC: 3089 Hardware, plastic
HQ: Creative Pultrusions, Inc.
214 Industrial Ln
Alum Bank PA 15521
814 839-4186

(G-560)
CREATIVE PULTRUSIONS INC (HQ)
214 Industrial Ln (15521-8304)
PHONE..................................814 839-4186
Shane E Weyant, *President*
Melissa Miller, *Controller*
Persis S Fungaroli, *Finance Dir*
◆ EMP: 142 EST: 1973
SQ FT: 160,000
SALES: 30.2MM
SALES (corp-wide): 773.1MM **Privately Held**
SIC: 2821 Plastics materials & resins
PA: Hill & Smith Holdings Plc
Westhaven House
Solihull W MIDLANDS B90 4
121 704-7430

(G-561)
GEPHARTS FURNITURE
199 Dorchester Rd (15521-8545)
PHONE..................................814 276-3357
Glen Gephart, *Owner*
EMP: 3
SALES: 60K **Privately Held**
SIC: 2599 Factory furniture & fixtures

(G-562)
MISSION CRITICAL SOLUTIONS LLC
271 Industrial Ln (15521-8306)
PHONE..................................814 839-2078
Bob McGowan, *CEO*
George Bohrer, *President*
◆ EMP: 45
SQ FT: 55,000
SALES (est): 19.1MM **Privately Held**
SIC: 3799 All terrain vehicles (ATV)

(G-563)
YONISH DISPOSAL COMPANY
300 Mountain Rd (15521-8802)
PHONE..................................814 839-4797
Daryl Yonish, *Principal*
EMP: 5
SALES (est): 474.9K **Privately Held**
SIC: 3089 Garbage containers, plastic

Alverton
Westmoreland County

(G-564)
GRANDVIEW MANUFACTURING CO
2391 State Route 981 (15612-1002)
PHONE..................................724 887-0631
Michael Tomasello, *President*
Colleen Tomasello, *Corp Secy*
EMP: 3 EST: 1997
SQ FT: 6,000
SALES (est): 477.5K **Privately Held**
WEB: www.grandviewmfg.com
SIC: 3599 Machine shop, jobbing & repair

Amberson
Franklin County

(G-565)
SOCIETY OF GOOD SHEPHERD
22012 Indian Spring Trl (17210-9601)
P.O. Box 122 (17210-0122)
PHONE..................................717 349-7033
David Bercot, *President*
Andre Bercot, *General Mgr*
EMP: 3
SALES: 123.6K **Privately Held**
SIC: 8661 2711 8699 Lutheran Church; newspapers: publishing only, not printed on site; charitable organization

Ambler
Montgomery County

(G-566)
ALLFLEX PACKAGING PRODUCTS INC (PA)
Also Called: Shell Containers Inc PA
100 Race St (19002-4421)
PHONE..................................215 542-9200
Joel B Cohen, *President*
Marilyn Gerhardt, *Bookkeeper*
Kristine Koelzer, *Sales Staff*
EMP: 15 **EST:** 1967
SQ FT: 3,000
SALES (est): 5.8MM **Privately Held**
WEB: www.allflex.com
SIC: 2679 Cardboard: pasted, laminated, lined, or surface coated

(G-567)
ARMSTRONG SUPPLY CO
22 Schiavone Dr (19002-5007)
PHONE..................................215 643-0310
John S Armstrong, *Owner*
EMP: 3
SALES (est): 262.6K **Privately Held**
SIC: 2732 5044 Book printing; office equipment

(G-568)
AURORA OPTICS INC
7 E Skippack Pike Ste 202 (19002-5310)
PHONE..................................215 646-0690
Laurence N Wesson, *President*
Federico Cabato, *Principal*
Nellie L Cabato, *Vice Pres*
Simon Bush, *Research*
Korina Orden, *Marketing Staff*
EMP: 5
SQ FT: 4,000
SALES (est): 650K **Privately Held**
WEB: www.aurora-instruments.com
SIC: 8731 3661 Commercial research laboratory; fiber optics communications equipment

(G-569)
BALFOUR SALES COMPANY
2 Balfour Cir (19002-3102)
PHONE..................................215 542-9745
Wally Swiger, *Partner*
Susanne Swiger, *Partner*
EMP: 3 **EST:** 1995
SQ FT: 2,000
SALES (est): 248.3K **Privately Held**
SIC: 2752 Commercial printing, offset

(G-570)
BINARY RESEARCH INC
809 N Bethlehem Pike B (19002-2534)
PHONE..................................215 233-3200
Somers K Butcher, *President*
Robert Foley, *Shareholder*
EMP: 25
SQ FT: 7,000
SALES (est): 4.2MM **Privately Held**
WEB: www.binaryresearch.com
SIC: 3695 5045 7378 Computer software tape & disks: blank, rigid & floppy; computer software; computer maintenance & repair

(G-571)
BRADFORD WHITE CORPORATION (PA)
725 Talamore Dr (19002-1873)
PHONE..................................215 641-9400
A Robert Carnevale, *Ch of Bd*
Nicholas Giuffre, *President*
Michael Deluca, *Vice Pres*
◆ **EMP:** 57
SQ FT: 22,000
SALES (est): 224.5MM **Privately Held**
WEB: www.bradfordwhite.com
SIC: 1711 3433 Plumbing, heating, air-conditioning contractors; heating equipment, except electric

(G-572)
BURNT CIRCUIT INC
321 Norristown Rd Ste 210 (19002-2793)
PHONE..................................215 913-6594
Steven Pottash, *President*
EMP: 8
SALES: 1.3MM **Privately Held**
SIC: 3651 Household audio & video equipment

(G-573)
CHROMATAN CORPORATION
727 Norristown Rd Bldg 3 (19002)
PHONE..................................617 529-0784
Oleg Shinkazh, *President*
EMP: 10
SALES (est): 59.2K **Privately Held**
SIC: 2834 Pharmaceutical preparations

(G-574)
CONSHOHOCKEN STEEL PDTS INC
301 Randolph Ave (19002-5617)
PHONE..................................215 283-9222
Mohammed S David, *President*
Shelly Brown, *Sales Staff*
EMP: 25
SQ FT: 205,000
SALES (est): 3.5MM **Privately Held**
SIC: 7692 3441 Welding repair; fabricated structural metal

(G-575)
DIGITAL PLAZA LLC
Also Called: Digital Plaza Direct
741 Tennis Ave (19002-2729)
PHONE..................................267 515-8000
Jay Scott Aemisegger, *President*
Yuki Aemisegger, *Vice Pres*
EMP: 10
SQ FT: 10,000
SALES (est): 1.5MM **Privately Held**
WEB: www.digitalplazadirect.com
SIC: 5731 7373 3677 5043 Radio, television & electronic stores; value-added resellers, computer systems; transformers power supply, electronic type; photographic cameras, projectors, equipment & supplies; modems, monitors, terminals & disk drives: computers

(G-576)
DYNACELL LIFE SCIENCES LLC
19 Hendricks St (19002-4405)
P.O. Box 213, Spring House (19477-0213)
PHONE..................................215 813-8775
Ramon J Garcia PHD, *Managing Prtnr*
Ramon J Garcia, *Managing Prtnr*
Ramon Garcia, *Managing Prtnr*
Heather McKay, *CFO*
EMP: 10
SQ FT: 250
SALES (est): 875.5K **Privately Held**
WEB: www.dynacellsciences.com
SIC: 2296 Cord & fabric for reinforcing fuel cells

(G-577)
DYNAMIC PRINTING INC
852 Burgdorf Dr (19002-2321)
PHONE..................................215 793-9453
Larry Wilks, *President*
EMP: 5
SQ FT: 3,000
SALES: 606K **Privately Held**
SIC: 2893 2752 Letterpress or offset ink; billheads, lithographed

(G-578)
E & E BUILDING GROUP LP
1104 N Bethlehem Pike (19002-1418)
PHONE..................................215 453-5124
Joe Ernst, *Principal*
EMP: 13
SALES (est): 2.7MM **Privately Held**
SIC: 3553 Woodworking machinery

(G-579)
GEO SPECIALTY CHEMICALS INC
300 Brookside Ave (19002-3436)
PHONE..................................215 773-9280
Thomas Longstaff, *VP Opers*
Caroline Mulvey, *Cust Mgr*
Joseph Wohr, *Manager*
Bill Mahoney, *Manager*
Joyce N Nevaril, *Supervisor*
EMP: 35
SQ FT: 20,000 **Privately Held**
WEB: www.geosc.com
SIC: 2869 2821 Industrial organic chemicals; plastics materials & resins
PA: Geo Specialty Chemicals, Inc.
401 S Earl Ave Ste 3
Lafayette IN 47904

(G-580)
GRECO INTERNATIONAL INC (PA)
Also Called: Greco Apparel
921a N Bethlehem Pike # 2 (19002-1309)
PHONE..................................215 628-2557
Joseph Greco, *President*
▲ **EMP:** 10 **EST:** 1951
SQ FT: 1,200
SALES (est): 1.1MM **Privately Held**
WEB: www.grecoapparel.com
SIC: 5651 2337 Family clothing stores; women's & misses' capes & jackets

(G-581)
HISTAND BROTHERS INC
114 Poplar St (19002-4744)
P.O. Box 4, Doylestown (18901-0004)
PHONE..................................215 348-4121
Robert C Grater, *President*
Linda Connor, *Treasurer*
EMP: 12 **EST:** 1872
SQ FT: 14,000
SALES (est): 1MM **Privately Held**
WEB: www.histandbros.com
SIC: 1761 3444 5033 Roofing contractor; sheet metal specialties, not stamped; roofing, asphalt & sheet metal

(G-582)
JAAK HOLDINGS LLC
Also Called: Minuteman Press
12 E Butler Ave Ste 119 (19002-4500)
PHONE..................................267 462-4092
EMP: 4 **EST:** 2016
SALES (est): 111.6K **Privately Held**
SIC: 2752 Commercial printing, offset

(G-583)
JNA MATERIALS LLC
254 S Main St (19002-4806)
P.O. Box 179 (19002-0179)
PHONE..................................215 233-0121
David Caddick Jr, *Principal*
EMP: 7 **EST:** 2010
SALES (est): 1MM **Privately Held**
SIC: 3272 Concrete products

(G-584)
K & L OPERATING CO
Also Called: A B C Insert Co
155 N Ridge Ave (19002-4518)
PHONE..................................215 646-0760
Bill Lamb, *Mng Member*
Mark Koenig,
EMP: 9 **EST:** 1958
SQ FT: 22,000
SALES (est): 1.8MM **Privately Held**
WEB: www.abcinsert.com
SIC: 2657 Folding paperboard boxes

(G-585)
K M B INC
822 Bell Ln (19002-3304)
P.O. Box 314 (19002-0314)
PHONE..................................215 643-7999
Diane M Kelly, *President*

Robert A Kelly, *Vice Pres*
EMP: 2
SALES: 3MM **Privately Held**
SIC: 8741 2541 Construction management; cabinets, lockers & shelving

(G-586)
KAPPA PUBLISHING GROUP INC
Kappa Publishing Group Div
7002 W Butler Pike # 100 (19002-5107)
P.O. Box 750, Fort Washington (19034-0750)
PHONE..................................215 643-6385
Nick Karabots, *Owner*
EMP: 50
SALES (corp-wide): 15.3MM **Privately Held**
WEB: www.kappapublishinggroup.com
SIC: 2721 Magazines: publishing only, not printed on site
PA: Kappa Publishing Group, Inc.
6198 Butler Pike Ste 200
Blue Bell PA 19422
215 643-6385

(G-587)
KAPPA PUBLISHING GROUP INC
Quinn Publishing Div
7002 W Butler Pike # 100 (19002-5107)
P.O. Box 750, Fort Washington (19034-0750)
PHONE..................................215 643-6385
Nick Karabots, *Chairman*
EMP: 50
SALES (corp-wide): 15.3MM **Privately Held**
WEB: www.kappapublishinggroup.com
SIC: 2721 Magazines: publishing only, not printed on site
PA: Kappa Publishing Group, Inc.
6198 Butler Pike Ste 200
Blue Bell PA 19422
215 643-6385

(G-588)
KAPPA PUBLISHING GROUP INC
Magazine Editorial Svcs Div
7002 W Butler Pike # 100 (19002-5107)
P.O. Box 750, Fort Washington (19034-0750)
PHONE..................................215 643-6385
Bill Maimwaring, *Manager*
EMP: 70
SALES (corp-wide): 15.3MM **Privately Held**
WEB: www.kappapublishinggroup.com
SIC: 2721 Magazines: publishing only, not printed on site
PA: Kappa Publishing Group, Inc.
6198 Butler Pike Ste 200
Blue Bell PA 19422
215 643-6385

(G-589)
KOREA WEEK INC
273 Woodcock Ln (19002-5415)
PHONE..................................215 782-8883
Hee Lee Kyung, *President*
▲ **EMP:** 3
SALES (est): 194.6K **Privately Held**
SIC: 2731 Books: publishing & printing

(G-590)
MICROMED LLC
224 S Maple St (19002)
PHONE..................................480 236-4705
David Baker,
EMP: 3
SALES: 700K **Privately Held**
SIC: 3841 Surgical & medical instruments

(G-591)
MOBERG RESEARCH INC
224 S Maple Way (19002-5528)
PHONE..................................215 283-0860
Richard Moberg, *President*
Andrea Pearson, *Info Tech Mgr*
Matthew Ramsey, *Sr Software Eng*
EMP: 11
SQ FT: 4,000

▲ = Import ▼=Export
◆ =Import/Export

SALES (est): 1.8MM **Privately Held**
WEB: www.neuromonitoring.com
SIC: 8748 8733 3845 3842 Systems analysis & engineering consulting services; research institute; electromedical equipment; surgical appliances & supplies

(G-592)
MONOMER-POLYMER AND DAJAC LABS
340 Mathers Rd (19002-3420)
PHONE..............................215 364-1155
Stephen Bell, *Principal*
EMP: 9
SALES (est): 593.7K **Privately Held**
SIC: 2819 Industrial inorganic chemicals

(G-593)
NET REACH TECHNOLOGIES LLC
Also Called: Netreach
124 S Maple Way Ste 210 (19002-5527)
PHONE..............................215 283-2300
William Bast, *President*
Heidi Merscher, *Corp Secy*
Will Bast, *COO*
Stephen Bouikidis, *Vice Pres*
Nancy Parsons, *Project Mgr*
EMP: 15
SALES (est): 1.2MM **Privately Held**
SIC: 7372 7371 Application computer software; computer software systems analysis & design, custom

(G-594)
NEW THERMO-SERV LTD
Also Called: Gessner Products
241 N Main St (19002-4224)
PHONE..............................215 646-7667
EMP: 70
SALES (corp-wide): 39.5MM **Privately Held**
SIC: 3089 Injection molding of plastics; plastic processing
PA: Ntl-Brands, Ltd.
3901 Pipestone Rd
Dallas TX 75212
214 631-0307

(G-595)
ON SEMICONDUCTOR CORP
768 N Bethlehem Pike # 301 (19002-2657)
PHONE..............................602 244-6600
Tom Tsergas, *President*
Jim McGough, *Principal*
William Schromm, *Exec VP*
Sonny Cave, *Vice Pres*
Bill Hall, *Vice Pres*
EMP: 23 **EST:** 2011
SALES (est): 1.8MM **Privately Held**
SIC: 3674 Semiconductors & related devices

(G-596)
ON SEMICONDUCTOR CORPORATION
768 N Bethlehem Pike (19002-2657)
PHONE..............................215 654-9700
Lisa Merrill, *Buyer*
James Miller, *QC Dir*
Jeffrey Witt, *Engineer*
Christine King, *Branch Mgr*
EMP: 23
SALES (corp-wide): 5.8B **Publicly Held**
WEB: www.amis.com
SIC: 3674 Semiconductors & related devices
PA: On Semiconductor Corporation
5005 E Mcdowell Rd
Phoenix AZ 85008
602 244-6600

(G-597)
PENTAVISION LLC
321 Norristown Rd Ste 150 (19002-2755)
PHONE..............................215 628-6550
Thomas Wilson, *President*
Mark Durrick, *Vice Pres*
Doug Parry, *Vice Pres*
Robert Verna, *Vice Pres*
Roger Zimmer, *Vice Pres*
EMP: 37
SQ FT: 5,700
SALES (est): 4.9MM **Privately Held**
SIC: 2721 Magazines: publishing & printing

(G-598)
PHOTOSONIX MEDICAL INC
23 Brookline Ct (19002-1904)
PHONE..............................215 641-4909
Mark Schafer, *President*
EMP: 3
SALES (est): 264.5K **Privately Held**
SIC: 3845 Electromedical equipment

(G-599)
PRESTO PACKAGING INC
155 N Ridge Ave (19002-4518)
PHONE..............................215 646-7514
Jeff Dlugosz, *President*
EMP: 3 **Privately Held**
WEB: www.prestopackaging.com
SIC: 3086 3547 3544 2671 Packaging & shipping materials, foamed plastic; rolling mill machinery; special dies, tools, jigs & fixtures; packaging paper & plastics film, coated & laminated
PA: Presto Packaging, Inc
1795 Keystone Dr
Hatfield PA 19440

(G-600)
PROCESS TECHNOLOGY OF PA
25 Tennis Ave (19002-4216)
PHONE..............................215 628-2222
K W Wang, *President*
Suzie Wang, *Corp Secy*
EMP: 10 **EST:** 1981
SQ FT: 2,000
SALES (est): 1.1MM **Privately Held**
WEB: www.medzilla.com
SIC: 3494 Valves & pipe fittings

(G-601)
RAVAGO AMERICAS LLC
Also Called: Entec Polymers
554 Ellington Ct (19002-1863)
PHONE..............................215 591-9641
Tom Angelus, *Owner*
EMP: 3
SALES (corp-wide): 1.4MM **Privately Held**
SIC: 2821 Plastics materials & resins
HQ: Ravago Americas Llc
1900 Summit Tower Blvd
Orlando FL 32810
407 875-9595

(G-602)
SNYDER PRINTING & PROMOTIONAL
714 N Bethlehem Pike # 201 (19002-2655)
PHONE..............................215 358-3178
John Snyder, *Principal*
EMP: 6
SALES (est): 283K **Privately Held**
SIC: 2759 Commercial printing

(G-603)
STAR SURPLUS ONE
1164 Limekiln Pike (19002-1136)
PHONE..............................215 654-9237
Carman Miroddi, *Principal*
EMP: 3
SALES (est): 332.7K **Privately Held**
SIC: 3531 Automobile wrecker hoists

(G-604)
VINTAGE COLOR GRAPHICS INC
1218 Joseph Rd (19002-1509)
PHONE..............................215 646-6589
Glen Gaertner, *President*
Mark Gaertner, *Vice Pres*
EMP: 5
SQ FT: 6,000
SALES: 778.2K **Privately Held**
WEB: www.vintagecolor.com
SIC: 2759 Commercial printing

Ambridge
Beaver County

(G-605)
ADVANCED ALLOY DVSION/NMC CORP
2305 Duss Ave (15003)
PHONE..............................724 266-8770

Joseph Anscher, *President*
EMP: 10
SALES (est): 1.7MM **Privately Held**
SIC: 3089 Molding primary plastic

(G-606)
ADVANCED PROCESSES INC
2097 Duss Ave (15003-1832)
PHONE..............................724 266-7274
Fax: 724 266-8274
▼ **EMP:** 15
SQ FT: 9,000
SALES (est): 4.7MM **Privately Held**
SIC: 4953 3532 Refuse System Mfg Mining Machinery

(G-607)
ALLEGHENY ASPHALT SERVICES LLC
921 Pine St (15003-1732)
PHONE..............................724 732-6637
Debroah Eonta, *CEO*
EMP: 4
SALES (est): 207.1K **Privately Held**
SIC: 2951 Paving mixtures; asphalt & asphaltic paving mixtures (not from refineries); road materials, bituminous (not from refineries)

(G-608)
ALLEGHENY PETROLEUM PDTS CO
2911 Duss Ave Ste 3 (15003-1476)
PHONE..............................724 266-3247
James Kudis, *President*
Ray Cudis, *Manager*
EMP: 9
SALES (corp-wide): 102MM **Privately Held**
WEB: www.oils.com
SIC: 2992 Lubricating oils & greases
PA: Allegheny Petroleum Products Co
999 Airbrake Ave
Wilmerding PA 15148
412 829-1990

(G-609)
ANDRITZ HERR-VOSS STAMCO INC
2970 Duss Ave (15003-1400)
PHONE..............................724 251-8745
Mark Martin, *Manager*
Joan Leo, *Executive*
EMP: 20
SALES (corp-wide): 6.9B **Privately Held**
WEB: www.gen-world.com
SIC: 3541 Machine tools, metal cutting type
HQ: Andritz Herr-Voss Stamco, Inc.
130 Main St
Callery PA 16024
724 538-3180

(G-610)
BAKER HGHES OLFLD OPRTIONS INC
100 Industry Dr (15003-2532)
PHONE..............................724 266-4725
Martin Craighead, *CEO*
EMP: 4
SALES (est): 464.3K **Privately Held**
SIC: 3533 Oil & gas field machinery

(G-611)
BETTER LIVING CENTER LLC
607 Merchant St (15003-2466)
PHONE..............................724 266-3750
Anthony Zimbo,
Greg Paul,
EMP: 5
SQ FT: 10,000
SALES: 390K **Privately Held**
SIC: 1799 3651 1731 Central vacuum cleaning system installation; home entertainment equipment, electronic; electrical work

(G-612)
CENTRIA INC
Also Called: Hh Robertsons Flooring
500 Perth Dr (15003-4213)
PHONE..............................724 251-2300
EMP: 13

SALES (corp-wide): 2B **Publicly Held**
SIC: 3479 3471 Etching & engraving; finishing, metals or formed products
HQ: Centria, Inc.
1005 Beaver Grade Rd # 2
Moon Township PA 15108
412 299-8000

(G-613)
CREEKSIDE SPRINGS LLC (PA)
667 Merchant St (15003-2466)
PHONE..............................724 266-9000
James Sas, *CEO*
EMP: 25
SQ FT: 26,000
SALES: 15MM **Privately Held**
WEB: www.creeksidesprings.com
SIC: 2086 Water, pasteurized: packaged in cans, bottles, etc.

(G-614)
CREEKSIDE SPRINGS LLC
667 Merchant St (15003-2466)
PHONE..............................724 266-9000
James J Sas,
EMP: 25
SALES (corp-wide): 15MM **Privately Held**
WEB: www.creeksidesprings.com
SIC: 2086 Water, pasteurized: packaged in cans, bottles, etc.
PA: Creekside Springs, Llc
667 Merchant St
Ambridge PA 15003
724 266-9000

(G-615)
DESIGN DYNAMICS INC
Also Called: Pittsburgh Poster
2920 Duss Ave (15003-1431)
P.O. Box 55 (15003-0055)
PHONE..............................724 266-4826
John J Provich Jr, *President*
Linda Davis, *Corp Secy*
EMP: 19
SQ FT: 30,000
SALES: 1.5MM **Privately Held**
SIC: 2759 7948 Posters, including billboards: printing; motor vehicle racing & drivers

(G-616)
ECONOMY INDUSTRIAL CORPORATION
2097 Duss Ave 2 (15003-1832)
PHONE..............................724 266-5720
Thomas R Allen Jr, *President*
Jack A Donovan, *Engineer*
Paulette Schleiter, *Admin Sec*
▼ **EMP:** 4 **EST:** 1976
SQ FT: 90,000
SALES (est): 897.6K **Privately Held**
WEB: www.economyindustrial.com
SIC: 3559 Foundry machinery & equipment

(G-617)
ECONOMY TOOLING CORP PA
1703 Ridge Road Ext (15003-1126)
PHONE..............................724 266-4546
Suzanne Kubick, *CEO*
Mark Kubick, *President*
EMP: 7 **EST:** 1967
SQ FT: 10,500
SALES: 242K **Privately Held**
SIC: 3312 Tool & die steel

(G-618)
HANNON COMPANY
Also Called: Hannon Electric
2940 Duss Ave (15003-1400)
PHONE..............................724 266-2712
Michael McAllister, *Branch Mgr*
Nate Harper, *Manager*
EMP: 8
SALES (corp-wide): 25.8MM **Privately Held**
WEB: www.hanco.com
SIC: 3621 3825 5084 Motors, electric; test equipment for electronic & electrical circuits; transformers, portable: instrument; industrial machinery & equipment
PA: The Hannon Company
1605 Waynesburg Dr Se
Canton OH 44707
330 456-4728

(G-619)
HUSSEY PERFORMANCE LLC
2601 Duss Ave (15003-1426)
PHONE..................................724 318-8292
David Allen, *Principal*
EMP: 3
SALES (est): 338.2K **Privately Held**
SIC: 7539 3053 Automotive repair shops; gaskets, all materials

(G-620)
IPSCO KOPPEL TUBULARS LLC
Also Called: Koppel Steel
2225 Duss Ave (15003)
P.O. Box 410 (15003-0410)
PHONE..................................724 266-8830
Michael Hvostal, *Engineer*
Frank Corona, *Manager*
EMP: 320
SALES (corp-wide): 355.8K **Privately Held**
SIC: 3312 3317 Bars, iron: made in steel mills; steel pipe & tubes
HQ: Ipsco Koppel Tubulars, L.L.C.
6403 6th Ave
Koppel PA 16136
724 847-6389

(G-621)
IPSCO TUBULARS INC
2300 Duss Ave (15003-1857)
PHONE...........................:........724 251-2539
Mike Panceri, *Principal*
Mike Coley, *Supervisor*
EMP: 6
SALES (corp-wide): 355.8K **Privately Held**
SIC: 3498 Fabricated pipe & fittings
HQ: Ipsco Tubulars Inc.
10120 Houston Oaks Dr
Houston TX 77064

(G-622)
JOBCO MFG & STL FABRICATION
800 Keystone Rd (15003-1474)
PHONE..................................724 266-3210
Debra Goulding,
EMP: 6 EST: 2007
SALES (est): 1MM **Privately Held**
SIC: 7692 Welding repair

(G-623)
K & B OUTFITTERS INC
Also Called: Signature Flags
514 Merchant St (15003-2463)
PHONE..................................724 266-1133
Mark A Somma, *President*
Kevin Morrison, *Corp Secy*
EMP: 20
SQ FT: 3,000
SALES (est): 1.9MM **Privately Held**
SIC: 2399 Banners, pennants & flags

(G-624)
K & C MACHINE
3086 Sylvan Rd (15003-1333)
PHONE..................................724 266-1737
William Campbell, *Owner*
EMP: 3
SALES (est): 342.3K **Privately Held**
SIC: 3599 Machine shop, jobbing & repair

(G-625)
LED TUBE USA
1693 Merchant St (15003-2261)
PHONE..................................724 650-0691
Heidi Anderson, *Principal*
EMP: 3
SALES (est): 200K **Privately Held**
SIC: 5063 3646 3641 Light bulbs & related supplies; fluorescent lighting fixtures, commercial; tubes, electric light

(G-626)
METAL USA PLATES AND SHAPES
81 Century Dr (15003-2543)
PHONE..................................724 266-1283
Ken Thomas, *Principal*
EMP: 70
SALES (corp-wide): 11.5B **Publicly Held**
SIC: 3441 Fabricated structural metal

HQ: Metals Usa Plates And Shapes, Inc.
50 Cabot Blvd E
Langhorne PA 19047
267 580-2100

(G-627)
MICROSONIC INC (PA)
2960 Duss Ave (15003-1400)
P.O. Box 184 (15003-0184)
PHONE..................................724 266-2031
Monika Major, *President*
Mitch Soman, *General Mgr*
▲ EMP: 42 EST: 1964
SQ FT: 3,400
SALES (est): 4.8MM **Privately Held**
WEB: www.earmolds.com
SIC: 3089 Plastic processing

(G-628)
MUNROE INCORPORATED
12 Century Dr (15003-2541)
PHONE..................................412 231-0600
EMP: 5
SALES (est): 497K **Privately Held**
SIC: 3443 Fabricated plate work (boiler shop)

(G-629)
MZP KILN SERVICES INC
328 14th St (15003-2211)
PHONE..................................724 318-8653
EMP: 5
SALES (est): 343.1K **Privately Held**
SIC: 3559 Kilns

(G-630)
NATIONAL MOLDING LLC
2305 Duss Ave Bldg 4 (15003)
PHONE..................................724 266-8770
Richard Bruckner, *Branch Mgr*
EMP: 35 **Privately Held**
SIC: 3089 Thermoformed finished plastic products
PA: National Molding, Llc
14420 Nw 60th Ave
Miami Lakes FL 33014

(G-631)
PRECISION LASER AND INSTR INC (PA)
85 11th St (15003-2305)
PHONE..................................724 266-1600
Howard Creese, *CEO*
Rod Creese, *President*
Mark Maximovich, *Vice Pres*
Eric Benjamin, *Purch Mgr*
Robert Barth, *Treasurer*
EMP: 30 EST: 1989
SALES (est): 6.1MM **Privately Held**
WEB: www.laserinst.com
SIC: 3829 Measuring & controlling devices

(G-632)
S & S FASTENERS INC
2501a Duss Ave (15003-1424)
PHONE..................................724 251-9288
Chris Villella, *President*
Kimberly Villella, *Vice Pres*
EMP: 3
SQ FT: 2,500
SALES: 450K **Privately Held**
SIC: 3452 5085 Bolts, metal; fasteners, industrial: nuts, bolts, screws, etc.

(G-633)
SAFRAN BROTHERS INC
Also Called: Ambridge Shop N Save
2910 Duss Ave (15003-1431)
PHONE..................................724 266-9758
Phil Safran, *President*
Philip Safran, *Executive*
EMP: 50
SQ FT: 32,000
SALES (est): 7.1MM **Privately Held**
SIC: 5411 2051 5812 Supermarkets, independent; delicatessens; bread, cake & related products; eating places

(G-634)
SIPPEL CO INC
Also Called: Sippel Steel Fab
101 Port Ambridge Dr (15003-2544)
PHONE..................................724 266-9800
Al Wilson, *Principal*
EMP: 90

SALES (corp-wide): 65.9MM **Privately Held**
SIC: 3449 Bars, concrete reinforcing: fabricated steel
PA: Sippel Co., Inc.
21 Century Dr
Ambridge PA 15003
724 266-9800

(G-635)
SIPPEL CO INC (PA)
Also Called: Sippel Steel Fab
21 Century Dr (15003-2543)
PHONE..................................724 266-9800
Robert John Sippel, *President*
David J Sippel, *Vice Pres*
Al Wilson, *Plant Mgr*
Nick Gann, *Project Mgr*
Zach Shue, *Project Mgr*
EMP: 30
SQ FT: 16,000
SALES: 65.9MM **Privately Held**
WEB: www.sippelsteelfab.com
SIC: 3441 Building components, structural steel

(G-636)
SUKUP STEEL STRUCTURES LLC
360 14th St (15003-3202)
PHONE..................................724 266-6484
Jerry Carr,
EMP: 114
SALES: 10MM
SALES (corp-wide): 196MM **Privately Held**
SIC: 3448 Prefabricated metal buildings
PA: Sukup Manufacturing Co.
1555 255th St
Sheffield IA 50475
641 892-4222

(G-637)
W V FABRICATING & WELDING INC
2197 Duss Ave (15003-1800)
PHONE..................................724 266-3000
Steven P Woods, *President*
EMP: 8
SALES (est): 700K **Privately Held**
SIC: 7692 Welding repair

(G-638)
WATCHWORD WORLDWIDE
Also Called: Bible Channel, The
1001 Merchant St (15003-2381)
PHONE..................................814 366-2770
James Fitzgerale, *President*
EMP: 5
SALES (est): 69.4K **Privately Held**
SIC: 8661 7372 Churches, temples & shrines; application computer software

(G-639)
WILLIAM COTTAGE
Also Called: Bill's Woodworking & Rmdlg
311 Creese St (15003-2243)
PHONE..................................724 266-2961
William Cottage, *Owner*
EMP: 4
SQ FT: 3,760
SALES (est): 220K **Privately Held**
SIC: 2541 1521 5031 2499 Cabinets, except refrigerated: show, display, etc.: wood; general remodeling, single-family houses; kitchen cabinets; decorative wood & woodwork; wood office furniture; wood household furniture

Andreas
Schuylkill County

(G-640)
REBS PALLET CO INC
645 Pine Hill Rd (18211-3137)
PHONE..................................570 386-5516
Alan Kistler, *President*
Jeanne Kistler, *Corp Secy*
EMP: 6 EST: 1975
SALES: 300K **Privately Held**
SIC: 2448 Skids, wood

Annville
Lebanon County

(G-641)
ADAMS VINTNER LLC
30 E Main St (17003-1411)
PHONE..................................717 685-1336
Matthew Shirk, *Principal*
EMP: 7 EST: 2014
SALES (est): 434K **Privately Held**
SIC: 2084 Wines

(G-642)
ANNVILLE SHOULDER STRAP CO
400 W Sheridan Ave (17003-1798)
PHONE..................................717 867-4831
EMP: 20
SQ FT: 12,000
SALES (est): 2.1MM **Privately Held**
SIC: 2259 2396 Fabric Converters & Mfg Shoulder Straps For Women's Undergarments

(G-643)
BLUESCOPE BUILDINGS N AMER INC
400 N Weaber St (17003-1103)
PHONE..................................717 867-4651
A W Stephenson, *Branch Mgr*
EMP: 87 **Privately Held**
SIC: 3448 Prefabricated metal buildings
HQ: Bluescope Buildings North America, Inc.
1540 Genessee St
Kansas City MO 64102

(G-644)
CARMEUSE LIME INC
Also Called: Carmeuse Lime-Annville
3 Clear Spring Rd (17003-9054)
PHONE..................................717 867-4441
Ken Kauffman, *Branch Mgr*
EMP: 7 **Privately Held**
SIC: 1422 3274 Crushed & broken limestone; lime
HQ: Carmeuse Lime, Inc.
11 Stanwix St Fl 21
Pittsburgh PA 15222
412 995-5500

(G-645)
COLONIAL CRAFT KITCHENS INC (PA)
344 W Main St (17003-1327)
PHONE..................................717 867-1145
Jerome L Hoffsmith, *President*
EMP: 4
SQ FT: 3,500
SALES (est): 1.1MM **Privately Held**
WEB: www.colonialcraftkitchens.com
SIC: 2434 5211 Wood kitchen cabinets; lumber & other building materials

(G-646)
CUSTOM DIE SERVICES INC
409 Ono Rd (17003-8449)
PHONE..................................717 867-5400
Barry Borrell, *President*
Ahn Priest, *Corp Secy*
EMP: 14
SQ FT: 10,000
SALES (est): 1.7MM **Privately Held**
SIC: 3544 Special dies & tools

(G-647)
EAGLE GRAPHICS INC
150 N Moyer St (17003-1600)
PHONE..................................717 867-5576
Ed Jocham, *CEO*
Mark Jocham, *President*
Robert Jocham, *Chairman*
Patrick Sheehan, *Purch Mgr*
Andrew Jocham, *VP Sales*
◆ EMP: 55
SQ FT: 35,000
SALES (est): 11.6MM **Privately Held**
WEB: www.eaglegraphic.com
SIC: 2752 Commercial printing, lithographic

▲ = Import ▼=Export
◆ =Import/Export

(G-648)
FSM TOOLS (PA)
255 N Ulrich St (17003-1537)
PHONE....................................717 867-5359
Frank T Hackett, *Owner*
Jim Mueller, *Manager*
▼ EMP: 5
SQ FT: 3,300
SALES (est): 1.1MM **Privately Held**
SIC: 5084 3546 Machine tools & accessories; power-driven handtools

(G-649)
GLENN SHUTTER
387 Palmyra Bellegrove Rd (17003-9101)
PHONE....................................717 867-2589
Glenn Shutter, *Principal*
EMP: 3
SALES (est): 168K **Privately Held**
SIC: 3442 Shutters, door or window: metal

(G-650)
H&K GROUP INC
Also Called: Lebanon Materials
155 Syner Rd (17003-9154)
PHONE....................................717 867-0701
Ron Chick, *General Mgr*
EMP: 5
SALES (corp-wide): 71.6MM **Privately Held**
WEB: www.hkgroup.com
SIC: 2951 Asphalt paving mixtures & blocks
PA: H&K Group, Inc.
2052 Lucon Rd
Skippack PA 19474
610 584-8500

(G-651)
KEY DIES INC
22 Landings Dr (17003-8879)
PHONE....................................717 838-5200
Ralph Moyer, *President*
EMP: 27
SALES (est): 4.4MM **Privately Held**
WEB: www.keydies.com
SIC: 3544 Dies & die holders for metal cutting, forming, die casting; special dies & tools

(G-652)
LAUDERMILCH MEATS INC
724 W Main St (17003-9046)
P.O. Box 154 (17003-0154)
PHONE....................................717 867-1251
Dennis Laudermilch, *President*
Lee Laudermilch, *President*
EMP: 80
SQ FT: 5,000
SALES (est): 5.1MM **Privately Held**
SIC: 5421 2013 2011 Meat markets, including freezer provisioners; sausages & other prepared meats; meat packing plants

(G-653)
LIGHTS WELDING INC
2628 Brandt Rd (17003-8860)
PHONE....................................717 838-3931
Earl W Light, *President*
James S Blouch, *Treasurer*
Kathryn Light, *Admin Sec*
EMP: 17
SQ FT: 17,800
SALES: 6.9MM **Privately Held**
SIC: 7692 Welding repair

(G-654)
MISTER BOBBIN EMBROIDERY INC
1525 N State Route 934 (17003-8925)
PHONE....................................717 838-5841
Dave Weaver, *President*
Darrell Eckert, *Vice Pres*
EMP: 15
SQ FT: 9,500
SALES (est): 2MM **Privately Held**
SIC: 2395 Embroidery & art needlework

(G-655)
OLDCASTLE MATERIALS INC
1 Clear Spring Rd (17003-9054)
PHONE....................................717 898-2278
EMP: 3

SALES (corp-wide): 29.7B **Privately Held**
SIC: 3273 Ready-mixed concrete
HQ: Oldcastle Materials, Inc.
900 Ashwood Pkwy Ste 700
Atlanta GA 30338

(G-656)
PENNSY SUPPLY INC
1 Clear Spring Rd (17003-9054)
PHONE....................................717 867-5925
Robert Olsen, *Branch Mgr*
EMP: 11
SALES (corp-wide): 29.7B **Privately Held**
SIC: 2951 Asphalt & asphaltic paving mixtures (not from refineries); coal tar paving materials (not from refineries)
HQ: Pennsy Supply, Inc.
1001 Paxton St
Harrisburg PA 17104
717 233-4511

(G-657)
R E M AUTOMOTIVE PARTS INC
20 Landings Dr (17003-8879)
PHONE....................................717 838-4242
Ralph Moyer, *President*
Doug Moyer, *Vice Pres*
EMP: 12
SQ FT: 15,000
SALES (est): 2.4MM **Privately Held**
SIC: 3714 Motor vehicle parts & accessories

(G-658)
ROBERT MRVEL PLASTIC MULCH LLC
2425 Horseshoe Pike (17003-8859)
PHONE....................................717 838-0976
Michael Marvel, *Principal*
◆ EMP: 14
SALES (est): 2.2MM **Privately Held**
SIC: 3081 5162 Unsupported plastics film & sheet; plastics film

(G-659)
SUNWORKS ETC LLC
2612 Brandt Rd (17003-8860)
PHONE....................................717 473-3743
Barbara Sunderlin, *Principal*
David Leas,
EMP: 5 EST: 2010
SALES (est): 489.4K **Privately Held**
SIC: 2541 Counter & sink tops

(G-660)
TAYLORMAID CUSTOM CABINETRY
87 Crooked Rd (17003-8519)
PHONE....................................717 865-6598
Scott L Albert, *Owner*
EMP: 4
SALES (est): 210K **Privately Held**
SIC: 2434 Wood kitchen cabinets

(G-661)
TVC COMMUNICATIONS LLC (DH)
800 Airport Rd (17003-9002)
PHONE....................................717 838-3790
James R Manari, *CEO*
Steve Quinn, *President*
Jan Dewinter, *Business Mgr*
David Lee, *Business Mgr*
Matt Hartman, *Vice Pres*
◆ EMP: 50
SQ FT: 38,000
SALES (est): 138.9MM **Publicly Held**
WEB: www.tvcinc.com
SIC: 3663 2298 Radio & TV communications equipment; cable, fiber

---

Apollo
Westmoreland County

(G-662)
ARTMAN EQUIPMENT COMPANY INC
Also Called: Kubota Equipment
854 State Route 380 (15613-1904)
PHONE....................................724 337-3700
Robert Artman Jr, *President*
Robert E Artman Jr, *President*

Kurk Michaels, *Treasurer*
EMP: 10
SQ FT: 22,000
SALES: 2.5MM **Privately Held**
SIC: 5083 5082 7692 3531 Agricultural machinery & equipment; excavating machinery & equipment; welding repair; buckets, excavating: clamshell, concrete, dragline, etc.

(G-663)
BARON CREST ENERGY COMPANY
601 1st Street Ext (15613-8962)
PHONE....................................724 478-1121
Frank Garufi, *President*
Francesca Garufi, *Vice Pres*
EMP: 7 EST: 1963
SQ FT: 2,500
SALES (est): 550K **Privately Held**
SIC: 1381 1389 Drilling oil & gas wells; oil & gas wells: building, repairing & dismantling

(G-664)
BITTINGER DRILLING CO
104 Spring Dr (15613-9720)
PHONE....................................724 727-3822
Leland Bittinger, *Owner*
EMP: 4
SALES (est): 343.7K **Privately Held**
SIC: 1381 Drilling oil & gas wells

(G-665)
BLOKSBERG INC
Also Called: Flagship By Bloksberg
4203 State Route 66 # 101 (15613-1533)
PHONE....................................724 727-9925
Lasse Syzersen, *President*
EMP: 10
SALES (est): 784K **Privately Held**
SIC: 7372 Business oriented computer software

(G-666)
BLUPANDA LLC
1719 Coulter Rd (15613-8972)
PHONE....................................724 494-2077
R Craig Coulter, *Principal*
Ralph Gross, *Officer*
EMP: 5 EST: 2009
SALES (est): 355.9K **Privately Held**
SIC: 7372 Application computer software

(G-667)
CE READY MIX
185 N Washington Rd (15613-9603)
P.O. Box 314 (15613-0314)
PHONE....................................724 727-3331
Jeff Cable, *Owner*
EMP: 20
SALES (est): 3.7MM **Privately Held**
SIC: 1311 3273 Natural gas production; ready-mixed concrete
PA: Cable Enterprises, Inc.
2876 State Route 286
Saltsburg PA 15681

(G-668)
CHARLES SMITH
Also Called: Charles S Smith McHning Draftg
305 Woodland Rd (15613-8210)
PHONE....................................724 727-3455
Charles Smith, *Owner*
EMP: 3 EST: 2000
SALES (est): 239.4K **Privately Held**
SIC: 3549 Metalworking machinery

(G-669)
CHILD EVNGELISM FELLOWSHIP INC
Findley St (15613)
P.O. Box 322 (15613-0322)
PHONE....................................724 339-4825
EMP: 41
SALES (corp-wide): 24.4MM **Privately Held**
SIC: 2752 Commercial printing, lithographic
PA: Child Evangelism Fellowship Incorporated
17482 Highway M
Warrenton MO 63383
636 456-4321

(G-670)
CLIFTON CUSTOM FURN & DESIGN
Also Called: Ccf Industries
4716 State Route 66 (15613-1404)
PHONE....................................724 727-2045
Kenneth J Clifton, *President*
Dale Clifton, *Corp Secy*
Tamara Clifton, *Vice Pres*
Tammy Clifton, *Vice Pres*
EMP: 15
SQ FT: 6,000
SALES: 1.4MM **Privately Held**
WEB: www.ccfdrawers.com
SIC: 2511 Wood household furniture

(G-671)
CNC SPECIALTIES MFG INC
760 Pine Run Rd (15613-8301)
PHONE....................................724 727-5680
Brian D Woodhall, *President*
Michele Angelini, *Admin Sec*
EMP: 25
SQ FT: 35,000
SALES (est): 5MM **Privately Held**
WEB: www.cncspecialtiesmfg.com
SIC: 3599 3471 Machine shop, jobbing & repair; plating & polishing

(G-672)
COAL CENTRIFUGE SERVICE
700 Old State Rd (15613-9701)
PHONE....................................724 478-4205
Howard Jackson, *Owner*
EMP: 7
SALES (est): 1.2MM **Privately Held**
SIC: 3569 Centrifuges, industrial

(G-673)
COMPOSIDIE INC (PA)
Also Called: EDM Services
1295 Route 380 (15613-1913)
PHONE....................................724 845-8602
L Ted Wohlin, *President*
▲ EMP: 170 EST: 1972
SQ FT: 18,500
SALES (est): 60.5MM **Privately Held**
WEB: www.composidie.com
SIC: 3544 3471 3469 3473 Die sets for metal stamping (presses); plating & polishing; metal stampings; etching on metals; drilling machine tools (metal cutting); extruding machines (machine tools), metal

(G-674)
D & M PRECISION MFG INC
718 Pine Run Rd (15613-8301)
P.O. Box 27, Vandergrift (15690-0027)
PHONE....................................724 727-3039
Michele Seaholm, *President*
Douglas Seaholm, *Vice Pres*
EMP: 4
SQ FT: 5,500
SALES: 150K **Privately Held**
SIC: 3369 Castings, except die-castings, precision

(G-675)
GEORGE L WILSON & CO INC A
156 N Washington Rd (15613-9607)
PHONE....................................412 321-3217
Mark Schaffer, *Manager*
EMP: 3
SALES (corp-wide): 18.6MM **Privately Held**
WEB: www.georgelwilson.com
SIC: 5082 3444 General construction machinery & equipment; concrete forms, sheet metal
PA: George L. Wilson & Co., Inc. A Close Corporation
220 E General Robinson St
Pittsburgh PA 15212
412 321-3217

(G-676)
H W NICHOLSON WLDG & MFG INC
3899 State Route 66 (15613-1525)
PHONE....................................724 727-3461
Nancy Coking, *President*
Eleanor Nicholson, *Principal*
EMP: 35 EST: 1961
SQ FT: 23,000

SALES (est): 6.2MM **Privately Held**
SIC: **3599** 3441 Machine shop, jobbing & repair; fabricated structural metal

(G-677)
IRWIN CONCRETE CO
185 N Washington Rd (15613-9603)
PHONE.................................724 863-1848
Joseph A Laspina, *Owner*
EMP: 10 EST: 1971
SQ FT: 3,000
SALES (est): 1MM **Privately Held**
SIC: **3273** Ready-mixed concrete

(G-678)
J K TOOL INC
321 N Washington Rd (15613-9639)
PHONE.................................724 727-2490
Celesta Kiebler, *President*
Hudson Rock, *General Mgr*
James Kevin, *Vice Pres*
Jim Clinger, *Plant Mgr*
EMP: 40
SQ FT: 29,000
SALES (est): 6.7MM **Privately Held**
SIC: **3544** Mfg Dies/Tools/Jigs/Fixtures

(G-679)
JIT GLOBAL ENTERPRISES LLC
Also Called: Rearick Tooling Inc/Jit
2025 Shady Plain Rd (15613-8976)
PHONE.................................724 478-1135
Sam Rearick, *Mng Member*
Joyce Rearick,
EMP: 30
SQ FT: 35,000
SALES (est): 4.1MM
SALES (corp-wide): 7MM **Privately Held**
WEB: www.jitprototyping.com
SIC: **3544** Special dies, tools, jigs & fixtures
PA: Rearick Tooling, Inc.
 2025 Shady Plain Rd
 Apollo PA 15613
 724 478-1135

(G-680)
KERR LIGHT MANUFACTURING LLC
761 Old State Rd (15613-9701)
PHONE.................................724 309-6598
Patricia D Kerr, *Principal*
EMP: 3
SALES (est): 192.9K **Privately Held**
SIC: **3999** Manufacturing industries

(G-681)
LAUREL INDUSTRIAL FABRIC ENTPS (PA)
Also Called: Laurel Awning Company
1573 Hancock Ave (15613-8404)
PHONE.................................724 567-5689
A C Schmieler, *President*
Kelly Schmieler, *Treasurer*
EMP: 22
SALES (est): 2.8MM **Privately Held**
SIC: **2394** Awnings, fabric: made from purchased materials

(G-682)
LUBE SYSTEMS COMPANY
416 Utopia Rd (15613-9637)
PHONE.................................724 335-4050
Frank Farine, *Principal*
EMP: 5
SALES (est): 655.2K **Privately Held**
WEB: www.lubesystemsco.com
SIC: **7549** 3569 Lubrication service, automotive; lubricating equipment

(G-683)
MARIETTA CLOSSON
Also Called: Closson Press
257 Delilah St (15613-1933)
PHONE.................................724 337-4482
Marietta Closson, *Owner*
EMP: 4
SALES: 450K **Privately Held**
WEB: www.clossonpress.com
SIC: **2741** Catalogs: publishing & printing

(G-684)
PREPTECH INC (PA)
4412 State Route 66 (15613-2015)
PHONE.................................724 727-3439

Barbara Arnold, *President*
John H Munjack, *Vice Pres*
John M Munjack, *Engineer*
▲ EMP: 2
SQ FT: 250
SALES: 1MM **Privately Held**
WEB: www.preptech.com
SIC: **1481** Nonmetallic mineral services

(G-685)
SJM MANUFACTURING INC
119 Florida Ave Bldg 1 (15613-9705)
PHONE.................................724 478-5580
Steven Monte, *President*
EMP: 5
SQ FT: 3,000
SALES: 500K **Privately Held**
SIC: **3465** Body parts, automobile: stamped metal

Archbald
Lackawanna County

(G-686)
CABLE ASSOCIATES INC
1 Export Ln (18403-1957)
P.O. Box 116 (18403-0116)
PHONE.................................570 876-4565
James P Rogan, *President*
Brian Pember, *Corp Secy*
Timothy Graff, *Mfg Staff*
Ryan Rogan, *Associate*
EMP: 35
SQ FT: 10,000
SALES: 6.2MM **Privately Held**
WEB: www.cableassociates.com
SIC: **3357** Fiber optic cable (insulated)

(G-687)
INNOCOR FOAM TECH - ACP INC
103 Power Blvd (18403-2012)
PHONE.................................570 876-4544
EMP: 7
SALES (corp-wide): 209.9MM **Privately Held**
SIC: **3069** Bathmats, rubber
HQ: Innocor Foam Technologies - Acp, Inc.
 200 Schulz Dr Ste 2
 Red Bank NJ 07701
 732 945-6222

(G-688)
INNOCOR FOAM TECH - ACP INC
103 Power Blvd (18403-2012)
PHONE.................................570 876-4544
Carol S Eicher, *CEO*
EMP: 7
SALES (est): 538.5K **Privately Held**
SIC: **3086** Plastics foam products

(G-689)
L & G MANUFACTURING
100 S Main St Frnt (18403-1792)
PHONE.................................570 876-1550
Louis Giordano, *President*
EMP: 6
SQ FT: 15,000
SALES (est): 571.2K **Privately Held**
SIC: **2325** Trousers, dress (separate): men's, youths' & boys'

(G-690)
LAMINATIONS INC
101 Power Blvd (18403-2012)
PHONE.................................570 876-8199
Jim Gavigan, *CFO*
Michael Lynch, *Treasurer*
▲ EMP: 150 EST: 1953
SQ FT: 135,000
SALES (est): 4.2MM
SALES (corp-wide): 464.7MM **Privately Held**
WEB: www.laminations.com
SIC: **3081** 2821 3083 3089 Plastic film & sheet; thermosetting materials; laminated plastic sheets; plastic containers, except foam; molding primary plastic
HQ: Simona America Inc.
 101 Power Blvd
 Archbald PA 18403
 570 579-1300

(G-691)
LOCKHEED MARTIN CORPORATION
459 Kennedy Dr (18403-1598)
PHONE.................................570 876-2132
Matthew Beylo, *Safety Dir*
Sean Wolfe, *Safety Dir*
John Kemp, *Opers Mgr*
John Kamp, *Opers Mgr*
James Palucci, *Purch Agent*
EMP: 500 **Publicly Held**
WEB: www.lockheedmartin.com
SIC: **3671** 3761 3489 3483 Transmittal, industrial & special purpose electron tubes; guided missiles & space vehicles; ordnance & accessories; ammunition, except for small arms
PA: Lockheed Martin Corporation
 6801 Rockledge Dr
 Bethesda MD 20817

(G-692)
LUCCIS BAKERY
171 S Main St (18403-1734)
PHONE.................................570 876-3830
Robert J Lucci, *Owner*
EMP: 10
SQ FT: 5,000
SALES (est): 685.4K **Privately Held**
SIC: **2051** Bread, cake & related products

(G-693)
MTL HOLDINGS INC
Also Called: Santana Lamination
101 Power Blvd (18403-2012)
PHONE.................................570 343-7921
Michael Lynch, *President*
Jim Gavigan, *CFO*
▼ EMP: 115
SQ FT: 135,000
SALES (est): 11.1MM **Privately Held**
SIC: **3089** Flat panels, plastic

(G-694)
SIMONA AMERICA INC (HQ)
101 Power Blvd (18403-2012)
PHONE.................................570 579-1300
Michael Schmitz, *CEO*
John Ploskonka, *Exec VP*
Adam Mellen, *Vice Pres*
William Minogue, *Vice Pres*
Bill Minogue, *Opers Staff*
▲ EMP: 65
SQ FT: 100,000
SALES (est): 56.5MM
SALES (corp-wide): 464.7MM **Privately Held**
WEB: www.simona-america.com
SIC: **3081** Unsupported plastics film & sheet
PA: Simona Ag
 Teichweg 16
 Kirn 55606
 675 214-0

(G-695)
SOFTWARE ENGINEERING ASSOC
Also Called: Tr Technology Solutions
1 Export Ln (18403-1957)
P.O. Box 116 (18403-0116)
PHONE.................................570 803-0535
Thomas G Speicher, *President*
John Birrane, *Purch Agent*
Eric Tallman, *Sr Software Eng*
EMP: 12
SALES (est): 845.8K **Privately Held**
WEB: www.sea-incorporated.com
SIC: **7372** 7371 5734 Prepackaged software; computer software systems analysis & design, custom; computer software writing services; computer software development & applications; computer software development; personal computers

(G-696)
T-R ASSOCIATES INC
1 Export Ln (18403-1957)
P.O. Box 116 (18403-0116)
PHONE.................................570 876-4067
Thomas G Speicher, *President*
Brian Pember, *Vice Pres*
Tom Pratico, *Vice Pres*
Joanne Speicher, *Vice Pres*
Allison Morgan, *Export Mgr*

EMP: 30
SQ FT: 31,000
SALES (est): 7.8MM **Privately Held**
SIC: **5063** 3571 Wiring devices; electronic computers

Arcola
Montgomery County

(G-697)
ASPHALT PRESS INDUSTRIES
3513 Arcola Rd (19420)
P.O. Box 10, Oaks (19456-0010)
PHONE.................................610 489-7283
John Adams, *Owner*
Barbara Adams, *Manager*
EMP: 3
SALES (est): 151K **Privately Held**
WEB: www.asphaltpress.com
SIC: **2741** 5032 Miscellaneous publishing; paving materials

Ardara
Westmoreland County

(G-698)
ARDARA TECHNOLOGIES LP
12941 State Route 993 (15615-1013)
P.O. Box 73 (15615-0073)
PHONE.................................724 863-0418
Randall Pedder, *Partner*
Chris Taormina, *Research*
EMP: 10
SALES (est): 930K **Privately Held**
SIC: **3826** Analytical instruments

Ardmore
Montgomery County

(G-699)
ACME NEWSPAPERS INC (HQ)
Also Called: News of Delaware County
311 W Lancaster Ave (19003)
PHONE.................................610 642-4300
Robert Jelenic, *CEO*
EMP: 135 EST: 1936
SQ FT: 20,000
SALES (est): 7.2MM
SALES (corp-wide): 661.2MM **Privately Held**
SIC: **2711** Newspapers, publishing & printing
PA: Journal Register Company
 5 Hanover Sq Fl 25
 New York NY 10004
 212 257-7212

(G-700)
AMERICAN TRENCH LLC
7 E Lancaster Ave Ste 220 (19003-2318)
PHONE.................................215 360-3493
EMP: 3 EST: 2011
SALES (est): 140.7K **Privately Held**
SIC: **2211** 2329 Apparel & outerwear fabrics, cotton; men's & boys' leather, wool & down-filled outerwear

(G-701)
ATHENS REPRODUCTION
19 W Athens Ave (19003-1391)
PHONE.................................610 649-5761
Augustus R Tooke, *Owner*
EMP: 5
SQ FT: 5,000
SALES (est): 538.5K **Privately Held**
SIC: **2752** 7334 2791 Commercial printing, offset; photocopying & duplicating services; typesetting

(G-702)
BAILEY & IZETT INC
2538 Haverford Rd (19003-2621)
PHONE.................................610 642-1887
George G Izett, *President*
Dorothy G Izett, *Treasurer*
EMP: 6 EST: 1941
SQ FT: 7,500

▲ = Import ▼=Export
◆ =Import/Export

SALES: 200K **Privately Held**
WEB: www.izettgolf.com
SIC: **5941** 3949 Golf goods & equipment;
golf equipment

(G-703)
BUSINESS PLANNING INC
63 W Lancaster Ave Ste 1 (19003-1413)
P.O. Box 506 (19003-0506)
PHONE.................................610 649-0550
Arthur Menko, *President*
EMP: 3
SALES (est): 182.8K **Privately Held**
SIC: **7372** 7375 7379 Prepackaged soft-
ware; data base information retrieval;
computer related consulting services

(G-704)
C W E INC
315 E County Line Rd (19003-2709)
PHONE.................................610 642-7719
Charles Ward III, *President*
Doreen Ward, *Treasurer*
EMP: 6
SQ FT: 3,500
SALES: 1MM **Privately Held**
WEB: www.cwe-inc.com
SIC: **3845** Electromedical apparatus

(G-705)
CALCONIX INC
Also Called: Time Zone
821 Aubrey Ave Ste B (19003-2040)
PHONE.................................610 642-5921
Paul Smith, *Ch of Bd*
Christopher Smith, *President*
▲ EMP: 15
SQ FT: 15,000
SALES (est): 2.9MM **Privately Held**
WEB: www.timezoneus.com
SIC: **3873** Watches, clocks, watchcases &
parts

(G-706)
CYRUS-XP INC
9 Rittenhouse Pl (19003-2209)
P.O. Box 393, Wynnewood (19096-0393)
PHONE.................................610 986-8408
Ashwin Koleth, *CEO*
Jenny Koleth,
EMP: 20 EST: 2001
SQ FT: 2,000
SALES (est): 1.1MM **Privately Held**
WEB: www.cyrusxp.com
SIC: **7379** 8742 7372 Computer related
maintenance services; computer related
consulting services; business consultant;
application computer software; business
oriented computer software

(G-707)
DEIN-VERBIT ASSOCIATES INC
Also Called: Samuel Deans Associates
337 E County Line Rd (19003-2709)
P.O. Box 894 (19003-0894)
PHONE.................................610 649-9674
EMP: 11
SQ FT: 2,000
SALES: 3MM **Privately Held**
SIC: **3579** 5046 5094 5063 Mfg Office
Machines Whol Commercial Equip Whol
Jewelry/Precs Stone Whol Electrical
Equip

(G-708)
HAYDEN PRINTING CO
206 E Lancaster Ave (19003-3210)
PHONE.................................610 642-2105
Thomas C Hayden Jr, *Owner*
Mary McKee,
EMP: 13
SQ FT: 4,000
SALES: 800K **Privately Held**
WEB: www.haydenprinting.com
SIC: **2752** Commercial printing, offset

(G-709)
**INTERNATIONAL WATCH
MAGAZINE**
Also Called: Fine Life Media
65 Saint James Pl (19003-2407)
PHONE.................................484 417-2122
Jim Bugden, *President*
EMP: 16

SALES (est): 1.3MM **Privately Held**
WEB: www.finelifemedia.com
SIC: **2741** Miscellaneous publishing

(G-710)
KAAST MACHINE TOOLS INC
194 Midfield Rd (19003-3213)
PHONE.................................224 216-8886
Angus Catterson, *President*
◆ EMP: 6
SQ FT: 5,000
SALES: 12MM **Privately Held**
SIC: **3542** 3541 Machine tools, metal
forming type; machine tools, metal cutting
type; drilling machine tools (metal cut-
ting); numerically controlled metal cutting
machine tools

(G-711)
KANE COMMUNICATIONS INC
Also Called: K C I
10 E Athens Ave Ste 208 (19003-2115)
PHONE.................................610 645-6940
Scott C Borowsky, *President*
EMP: 13 EST: 1977
SQ FT: 5,000
SALES: 5MM **Privately Held**
WEB: www.kanec.com
SIC: **2721** Trade journals: publishing only,
not printed on site

(G-712)
MARULA OIL HOLDINGS LLC
Also Called: Marula Pure Beauty Oil
40 E Montgomery Ave (19003-2421)
PHONE.................................310 559-8600
Jay Lucas, *Senior Partner*
Ashton A Kaidi, *Mng Member*
EMP: 6
SALES (est): 378.3K **Privately Held**
SIC: **2844** 5122 Cosmetic preparations;
cosmetics, perfumes & hair products

(G-713)
**PHILADELPHIA SKATING CLUB
A**
Also Called: ARDMORE ICE SKATING RINK
220 Holland Ave (19003-1214)
PHONE.................................610 642-8700
Charlotte Martin, *President*
Cathy Rahab, *Vice Pres*
Michael Farrell, *Treasurer*
Carolyn Rhodes, *Admin Sec*
EMP: 15
SALES: 935.3K **Privately Held**
WEB: www.pschs.org
SIC: **3949** 7999 Ice skates, parts & acces-
sories; skating instruction, ice or roller

(G-714)
RAND 2339 HAVERFORD LP
50 Hood Rd (19003-3114)
PHONE.................................215 620-6993
EMP: 3 EST: 2009
SALES (est): 170K **Privately Held**
SIC: **3131** Mfg Footwear Cut Stock

(G-715)
RGL DISTRIBUTORS LLC
Also Called: Regal Sales and Marketing
2517 Huntingdon Ln (19003-1607)
PHONE.................................610 207-9000
Ron Landy, *Mng Member*
▲ EMP: 3
SALES: 800K **Privately Held**
SIC: **2844** 5122 7389 Toilet preparations;
drugs, proprietaries & sundries;

(G-716)
SIGNS BY TOMORROW USA INC
130 E Lancaster Ave Rear (19003-3209)
PHONE.................................484 592-0404
David Friedenburg, *President*
EMP: 6
SALES (est): 618.6K **Privately Held**
SIC: **3993** Signs & advertising specialties

(G-717)
SOLARIAN US
2617 Saint Davids Ln (19003-1708)
PHONE.................................610 550-6350
Renee Pearlman, *Owner*
EMP: 3
SALES: 95K **Privately Held**
SIC: **3441** 7389 Tower sections, radio &
television transmission;

(G-718)
STONE BREAKER LLC
10 E Athens Ave Ste 209 (19003-2115)
PHONE.................................312 203-5632
Tom Welch, *Vice Pres*
Heath Mathias, *Software Dev*
EMP: 7
SQ FT: 1,500
SALES (est): 500K **Privately Held**
SIC: **2381** Fabric dress & work gloves

(G-719)
SUGAR MAGNOLIA INC
637 Loraine St (19003-2629)
PHONE.................................610 649-9462
Mark Lord, *President*
EMP: 3
SALES (est): 96.3K **Privately Held**
SIC: **2024** 2097 5143 Ice cream & frozen
desserts; manufactured ice; ice cream &
ices

(G-720)
**SUPERIOR TRANSPARENT
NOISE**
220 Golfview Rd (19003-1002)
PHONE.................................610 715-1969
Robert Rex, *President*
EMP: 4
SQ FT: 4,700
SALES (est): 161.4K **Privately Held**
SIC: **3089** Casting of plastic

(G-721)
TAPP TECHNOLOGY LLC
Also Called: Tapptek
120-124 E Lancaster Ave (19003)
PHONE.................................800 288-3184
Jamie Robinson, *CEO*
Joe Callahan,
EMP: 3
SQ FT: 2,500
SALES: 250K **Privately Held**
SIC: **3993** 7379 Electric signs;

(G-722)
WAVE SWIMMER INC
116 E Athens Ave (19003-2803)
PHONE.................................215 367-3778
Andrew Bender, *President*
EMP: 5 EST: 2017
SALES (est): 150.7K **Privately Held**
SIC: **3999** Manufacturing industries

Armagh
Indiana County

(G-723)
BELLAIRE CORPORATION
196 Grange Hall Rd (15920)
P.O. Box 245 (15920-0245)
PHONE.................................814 446-5631
EMP: 4
SALES (corp-wide): 104.7MM **Publicly
Held**
SIC: **1241** Coal mining services
HQ: Bellaire Corporation
14785 Preston Rd Ste 1100
Dallas TX 75254
972 448-5400

(G-724)
**LEHIGH ANTHRACITE COAL
LLC**
224 Grange Hall Rd (15920)
PHONE.................................814 446-6700
EMP: 3
SALES (est): 103.4K **Privately Held**
SIC: **1221** Coal preparation plant, bitumi-
nous or lignite

Ashland
Schuylkill County

(G-725)
**ALEX COLOR COMPANY INC
(PA)**
17th & Market St (17921)
PHONE.................................570 875-3300
Joseph J Alex, *President*

EMP: 5 EST: 1977
SQ FT: 12,000
SALES (est): 838.4K **Privately Held**
WEB: www.alexcolor.com
SIC: **2869** 2865 Industrial organic chemi-
cals; color pigments, organic

(G-726)
ALEX COLOR COMPANY INC
1638 Market St (17921-1131)
PHONE.................................570 875-3300
Joseph Alex, *Owner*
EMP: 6
SALES (corp-wide): 838.4K **Privately
Held**
WEB: www.alexcolor.com
SIC: **2869** Industrial organic chemicals
PA: Alex Color Company, Inc.
17th & Market St
Ashland PA 17921
570 875-3300

(G-727)
**ASHLAND FOUNDRY & MCH
WORK LLC**
500 E Centre St (17921-2018)
PHONE.................................570 875-6100
Michael Bargani, *President*
Sharrel Hebert, *Vice Pres*
EMP: 164
SALES (est): 45.1MM **Privately Held**
SIC: **3599** 3365 3312 Machine shop, job-
bing & repair; aluminum foundries; blast
furnaces & steel mills; bars, iron: made in
steel mills

(G-728)
CAROL FETTEROLF
Also Called: Karel Construction
26 Rolling Meadows Rd (17921-9266)
PHONE.................................570 875-2026
Carol Fetterolf, *Owner*
EMP: 6
SALES (est): 707.9K **Privately Held**
SIC: **1231** Strip mining, anthracite

(G-729)
CREATIVE PRINTING CO
430 S Hoffman Blvd (17921-1912)
PHONE.................................570 875-1811
Richard L Singmaster, *President*
Bernice Singmaster, *Corp Secy*
EMP: 5 EST: 1970
SALES (est): 410K **Privately Held**
SIC: **2759** 2752 2741 Letterpress printing;
commercial printing, offset; shopping
news: publishing & printing

(G-730)
GOULDS PUMPS LLC
500 E Centre St (17921-2015)
PHONE.................................570 875-2660
Buddy Morris, *Marketing Staff*
Gerald Wetzel, *Manager*
Juma Abdiroglu, *Supervisor*
EMP: 140
SALES (corp-wide): 2.7B **Publicly Held**
WEB: www.gouldspumps.com
SIC: **3561** Industrial pumps & parts
HQ: Goulds Pumps Llc
240 Fall St
Seneca Falls NY 13148
315 568-2811

(G-731)
HANCOCK COMPANY
Also Called: Gitman Bros
2309 Chestnut St (17921-1054)
PHONE.................................570 875-3100
John Minahan, *President*
▲ EMP: 8
SQ FT: 20,000
SALES (est): 2.1MM
SALES (corp-wide): 631.4MM **Privately
Held**
WEB: www.gitmanco.com
SIC: **2321** Men's & boys' furnishings
PA: Tom James Company
263 Seaboard Ln
Franklin TN 37067
615 771-1122

(G-732)
JO MI PALLET CO INC
615 Market St (17921-1333)
PHONE.................................570 875-3540

GEOGRAPHIC

John Polcovich, *President*
John Mick Polcovich, *President*
EMP: 9 **EST:** 1972
SQ FT: 15,000
SALES: 2.2MM **Privately Held**
SIC: 2448 Pallets, wood

(G-733)
KENNEDY CONCRETE INC
570 Dutchtown Rd (17921-9306)
P.O. Box 327, Gordon (17936-0327)
PHONE....................................570 875-2780
Al Kennedy Jr, *President*
Al Kennedy III, *Vice Pres*
EMP: 10
SQ FT: 1,200
SALES (est): 1MM **Privately Held**
WEB: www.kennedyconcreteproducts.com
SIC: 3272 Concrete products, precast

(G-734)
LINDENMUTH SAW MILL
Taylorsville Rd (17921)
PHONE....................................570 875-3546
Walter R Lindenmuth, *Owner*
EMP: 8 **EST:** 1965
SQ FT: 2,500
SALES (est): 737.3K **Privately Held**
SIC: 2421 4212 Sawmills & planing mills,
general; local trucking, without storage

(G-735)
OAKS WELDING LLC
50 Dutchtown Rd (17921-9429)
PHONE....................................570 527-7328
Gregory Oakill, *Owner*
EMP: 4
SQ FT: 5,500
SALES (est): 155.7K **Privately Held**
SIC: 3548 Electrodes, electric welding

(G-736)
SCHUYLKILL COAL
PROCESSING
Duhctown Ex 116off Rte901 (17921)
P.O. Box 134 (17921-0134)
PHONE....................................570 875-3123
Walter N Lindenmuth, *President*
EMP: 5
SALES (est): 480K **Privately Held**
SIC: 1221 Bituminous coal & lignite loading
& preparation

(G-737)
TOM JAMES COMPANY
2309 Chestnut St (17921-1054)
PHONE....................................570 875-3100
John Ryan, *Vice Pres*
EMP: 25
SALES (corp-wide): 631.4MM **Privately
Held**
WEB: www.englishamericanco.com
SIC: 2311 Suits, men's & boys': made from
purchased materials
PA: Tom James Company
263 Seaboard Ln
Franklin TN 37067
615 771-1122

(G-738)
TRI-STATE ENVELOPE
CORPORATION (PA)
20th Market St (17921)
PHONE....................................570 875-0433
John Swensen, *President*
Frank De Carlo, *Vice Pres*
Bob Earls, *Vice Pres*
Anthony Aulenti, *CFO*
Joel W Orgler, *Treasurer*
EMP: 330 **EST:** 1966
SQ FT: 150,000
SALES (est): 154.4MM **Privately Held**
WEB: www.tristateenvelope.com
SIC: 2677 Envelopes

Ashley
Luzerne County

(G-739)
CRAIGJILL INC
Also Called: Daron Northeast
36 Hazleton St (18706-2818)
PHONE....................................570 803-0234

Craig Daron, *President*
James Kiesling, *Corp Secy*
Dave Lewis, *Sales Mgr*
EMP: 40 **EST:** 1924
SQ FT: 1,500
SALES (est): 6.9MM **Privately Held**
SIC: 3271 Blocks, concrete or cinder: stan-
dard

(G-740)
THEPAPERFRAMERCOM
75 Mary St (18706-1622)
PHONE....................................570 239-1444
Larry Peterson, *Principal*
EMP: 4
SALES (est): 212K **Privately Held**
SIC: 2711 Newspapers

Aspers
Adams County

(G-741)
KEURIG DR PEPPER INC
45 Aspers North Rd (17304-9486)
PHONE....................................717 677-7121
Tom Leedy, *Manager*
EMP: 100 **Publicly Held**
SIC: 2086 Soft drinks: packaged in cans,
bottles, etc.
PA: Keurig Dr Pepper Inc.
53 South Ave
Burlington MA 01803

(G-742)
KEYSTONE FUR DRESSING INC
1495 Carlisle Rd (17304-9708)
P.O. Box 243 (17304-0243)
PHONE....................................717 677-4553
Michael Showers, *President*
Angie Taylor, *General Mgr*
EMP: 7
SALES (est): 1.3MM **Privately Held**
SIC: 3111 Hides: tanning, currying & finish-
ing

(G-743)
MOTTS LLP
Also Called: Dr Pepper's Snapple Drink
45 Aspers North Rd (17304-9486)
P.O. Box 68 (17304-0068)
PHONE....................................717 677-7121
Brian Group, *Branch Mgr*
EMP: 280 **Publicly Held**
WEB: www.maunalai.com
SIC: 5046 2033 Commercial equipment;
canned fruits & specialties
HQ: Mott's Llp
55 Hunter Ln
Elmsford NY 10523
972 673-8088

(G-744)
PREMIER MAGNESIA LLC
1305 Center Mills Rd (17304-9464)
PHONE....................................717 677-7313
EMP: 14
SALES (corp-wide): 60.2MM **Privately
Held**
SIC: 3295 Minerals, ground or treated
PA: Premier Magnesia, Llc
1275 Drummers Ln Ste 102
Wayne PA 19087
610 828-6929

(G-745)
ROBISONS CABINET STUDIO
33 Prospect St (17304)
PHONE....................................717 677-9828
Bruce M Robison, *Owner*
EMP: 3
SALES (est): 160K **Privately Held**
SIC: 2521 Cabinets, office: wood

Aspinwall
Allegheny County

(G-746)
M & M CREATIVE LAMINATES
INC
4 5th St (15215-2131)
PHONE....................................412 781-4700
Derik Morrow, *President*
EMP: 8
SQ FT: 16,000
SALES (est): 1.2MM **Privately Held**
SIC: 2541 5023 2511 Counter & sink
tops; table or counter tops, plastic lami-
nated; cabinets, lockers & shelving;
kitchenware; wood household furniture

Aston
Delaware County

(G-747)
3 PRIME LLC
2 New Rd Ste 300 (19014-1038)
PHONE....................................610 459-3468
David Eyler, *Vice Pres*
EMP: 4
SQ FT: 2,000
SALES (est): 347.6K **Privately Held**
SIC: 2869 Laboratory chemicals, organic

(G-748)
3M COMPANY
50 Milton Dr (19014-2217)
PHONE....................................610 497-7032
EMP: 14
SALES (corp-wide): 31.6B **Publicly Held**
SIC: 2821 Plastics materials & resins
PA: 3m Company
3m Center
Saint Paul MN 55144
651 733-1110

(G-749)
AELLA INDUSTRIES
CORPORATION
45 Milton Dr (19014-2217)
PHONE....................................610 399-9086
Kristine Fisher, *President*
Joseph Burke, *Vice Pres*
Christine Burke, *Treasurer*
EMP: 3
SALES (est): 199.1K **Privately Held**
SIC: 3444 Ducts, sheet metal

(G-750)
AMACOIL INC
2100 Bridgewater Rd (19014-2133)
P.O. Box 2228 (19014-0228)
PHONE....................................610 485-8300
Humberto Zavaleta, *President*
Bob Eisele, *Marketing Mgr*
Ed Miles, *Info Tech Mgr*
Caesar Crognale, *Admin Sec*
EMP: 20
SQ FT: 15,000
SALES (est): 7.3MM **Privately Held**
WEB: www.amacoil.com
SIC: 5084 3599 Hydraulic systems equip-
ment & supplies; custom machinery

(G-751)
AMERICAN SUN INC
50 Mcdonald Blvd (19014-3202)
PHONE....................................610 497-2210
Nick Sotiropoulos, *President*
EMP: 11
SQ FT: 26,000
SALES (est): 1.3MM **Privately Held**
WEB: www.americansun.net
SIC: 3728 Aircraft parts & equipment

(G-752)
BIMBO BAKERIES USA INC
Also Called: Maier's Bakery
75 Mcdonald Blvd (19014-3202)
PHONE....................................800 635-1685
Nelson Cousins, *Manager*
EMP: 50 **Privately Held**

SIC: 2051 5149 Bread, all types (white,
wheat, rye, etc): fresh or frozen; groceries
& related products
HQ: Bimbo Bakeries Usa, Inc
255 Business Center Dr # 200
Horsham PA 19044
215 347-5500

(G-753)
BRANDYWINE FUEL INC
16 Crozerville Rd (19014-1432)
P.O. Box 147, Chester Heights (19017-
0147)
PHONE....................................484 574-8274
EMP: 3 **EST:** 2013
SALES (est): 210K **Privately Held**
SIC: 2869 Fuels

(G-754)
CHOICE CLEANGEAR LLC
369 Turner Industrial Way (19014-3014)
PHONE....................................610 497-9756
Charles M Lillie, *President*
EMP: 4
SALES (est): 320K **Privately Held**
SIC: 5699 3842 5091 Sports apparel;
clothing, fire resistant & protective;
firearms, sporting

(G-755)
CHOICE MARKETING INC
369 Turner Industrial Way (19014-3014)
P.O. Box 4040, Media (19063-7040)
PHONE....................................610 494-1270
Charles Lillie, *President*
Karen M Lillie, *Treasurer*
Vince Sculli, *Sales Staff*
EMP: 28
SQ FT: 6,000
SALES (est): 6.2MM **Privately Held**
WEB: www.choicemarketing.net
SIC: 7331 7389 2759 Direct mail advertis-
ing services; fund raising organizations;
card printing & engraving, except greeting

(G-756)
CONNER PRINTING INC
2977 Dutton Mill Rd (19014-2842)
PHONE....................................610 494-2222
Alan B Conner, *President*
EMP: 9
SQ FT: 6,500
SALES (est): 2MM **Privately Held**
WEB: www.connerprinting.com
SIC: 2752 Commercial printing, offset;
photo-offset printing

(G-757)
CONTAINER RESEARCH
CORPORATION (PA)
Also Called: CRC
2 New Rd Ste 1 (19014-1038)
P.O. Box 159, Glen Riddle Lima (19037-
0159)
PHONE....................................610 459-2160
Stanley E Rines Jr, *President*
Stanley E Rines, *Vice Pres*
Chris Handago, *Design Engr*
Kathy Gallagher, *Mktg Coord*
William E Swan, *Admin Sec*
▲ **EMP:** 120
SQ FT: 150,000
SALES (est): 42.1MM **Privately Held**
WEB: www.crc-flex.com
SIC: 3412 3441 Metal barrels, drums &
pails; fabricated structural metal

(G-758)
DEL VAL FLAG PHILADELPHIA
SP
407 Virginia Ln (19014-2022)
PHONE....................................610 235-7179
Audrey Golder, *Principal*
EMP: 5 **EST:** 2007
SALES (est): 550.6K **Privately Held**
SIC: 2399 Fabricated textile products

(G-759)
DYNEON LLC
50 Milton Dr (19014-2217)
PHONE....................................610 497-8899
Jim Abate, *Branch Mgr*
EMP: 51

▲ = Import ▼=Export
◆ =Import/Export

SALES (corp-wide): 32.7B **Publicly Held**
WEB: www.dyneon.com
SIC: 2899 3089 3087 Chemical prepara-
tions; plastic containers, except foam;
custom compound purchased resins
HQ: Dyneon Llc
6744 33rd St N
Oakdale MN 55128

(G-760)
EASTERN INDUSTRIAL PDTS INC
Also Called: Smith-Koch Co
830 Tryens Rd (19014-1533)
PHONE..................................610 459-1212
Henry Peck, *President*
James Kealy, *Vice Pres*
Valerie H Koch, *Treasurer*
Ann L Koch, *Admin Sec*
▲ EMP: 23
SQ FT: 27,000
SALES (est): 6.5MM
SALES (corp-wide): 66.3MM **Privately Held**
WEB: www.smith-koch.com
SIC: 3561 5084 7699 3594 Pumps & pumping equipment; pumps & pumping equipment; industrial machinery & equipment repair; fluid power pumps & motors
PA: Geiger Pump And Equipment Company
8924 Yellow Brick Rd
Baltimore MD 21237
410 682-2660

(G-761)
EGR VENTURES INC
Also Called: P S A
1 Crozerville Rd (19014-1431)
PHONE..................................610 358-0500
Edward G Robson, *President*
Regina Robson, *Admin Sec*
EMP: 20
SQ FT: 11,000
SALES (est): 3.7MM **Privately Held**
SIC: 8711 3625 Electrical or electronic engineering; electric controls & control accessories, industrial

(G-762)
ELECTROVUE LLC
Also Called: Electromenu
200 Turner Industrial Way (19014-3015)
PHONE..................................855 226-4430
Mark Evans, *President*
Ray Brown, *Vice Pres*
EMP: 5 EST: 2015
SALES (est): 557.6K **Privately Held**
SIC: 3571 Computers, digital, analog or hybrid

(G-763)
FLEXTRON INDUSTRIES INC
720 Mount Rd (19014-1105)
PHONE..................................610 459-4600
William E Swan, *President*
Stanley E Rines, *Corp Secy*
▲ EMP: 15 EST: 1957
SQ FT: 50,000
SALES (est): 2.3MM **Privately Held**
WEB: www.flextronindustries.com
SIC: 3053 3086 2621 3714 Packing, rubber; packing, metallic; packaging & shipping materials, foamed plastic; packaging paper; motor vehicle parts & accessories; corrugated & solid fiber boxes; carpets & rugs

(G-764)
FOCUS ONE PROMOTIONS INC
340 Turner Industrial Way (19014-3014)
PHONE..................................610 459-7781
Max Messinger, *President*
EMP: 5
SALES (est): 521.6K **Privately Held**
SIC: 2759 Calendars: printing

(G-765)
FOLSOM TOOL & MOLD CORP
12 Mount Pleasant Rd (19014-1408)
PHONE..................................610 358-5030
Pete Crognale, *President*
Paul Silva, *Prdtn Mgr*
Ed Follett, *Purch Agent*
Debra Miles, *Treasurer*
EMP: 50
SQ FT: 10,000

SALES (est): 9.9MM **Privately Held**
WEB: www.folsomtool.com
SIC: 3599 Machine shop, jobbing & repair

(G-766)
FXI INC
Also Called: Foamex
120 Concord Rd (19014-2909)
PHONE..................................610 245-2800
David Welsh, *Branch Mgr*
EMP: 180 **Privately Held**
SIC: 3086 Plastics foam products
HQ: Fxi, Inc.
1400 N Providence Rd # 2000
Media PA 19063

(G-767)
GENERAL CIVIL COMPANY INC
56a Concord Rd (19014-2902)
P.O. Box 72592, Thorndale (19372-0592)
PHONE..................................484 571-1998
George Detore, *Principal*
Carol Detore, *CFO*
Lawrence McLaughlin, *Admin Sec*
EMP: 10
SALES (est): 740K **Privately Held**
SIC: 8744 1389 1799 1741 ; oil & gas wells: building, repairing & dismantling; building site preparation; concrete block masonry laying; plumbing, heating, air-conditioning contractors; industrial buildings, new construction

(G-768)
GIESLER ENGINEERING INC
2881 Mount Rd (19014-1179)
PHONE..................................800 428-8616
Greg R Giesler, *President*
EMP: 9 EST: 1948
SALES (est): 721.6K **Privately Held**
SIC: 3599 5571 Machine & other job shop work; motorcycle dealers

(G-769)
I & I SLING INC (PA)
205 Bridgewater Rd (19014-2135)
P.O. Box 2423 (19014-0423)
PHONE..................................800 874-3539
Scott St Germain, *President*
Robert Capone, *Treasurer*
◆ EMP: 35
SQ FT: 80,000
SALES (est): 16.9MM **Privately Held**
WEB: www.iandisling.com
SIC: 2298 3496 Wire rope centers; slings, rope; slings, lifting: made from purchased wire

(G-770)
JOSEPH F MARIANI CONTRS INC
10 Mount Pleasant Rd (19014-1408)
PHONE..................................610 358-9746
Joseph Mariani Jr, *President*
EMP: 15
SALES (est): 2MM **Privately Held**
SIC: 1389 Excavating slush pits & cellars

(G-771)
KGC ENTERPRISES INC (PA)
Also Called: Kc Signs Co
142 Conchester Hwy (19014-3415)
PHONE..................................610 497-0111
William Clark, *President*
EMP: 45
SQ FT: 20,000
SALES (est): 6.9MM **Privately Held**
SIC: 1799 3993 Sign installation & maintenance; signs & advertising specialties

(G-772)
L & L SPECIAL FURNACE CO INC
20 Kent Rd (19014-1494)
P.O. Box 2129 (19014-0129)
PHONE..................................610 459-9216
Gregory D Lewicki, *President*
Stephen J Lewicki, *Corp Secy*
▲ EMP: 18
SQ FT: 13,000
SALES (est): 5.2MM **Privately Held**
WEB: www.hotfurnace.com
SIC: 3567 Industrial furnaces & ovens

(G-773)
MAGUIRE PRODUCTS INC (PA)
11 Crozerville Rd (19014-1431)
P.O. Box 2056 (19014-0056)
PHONE..................................610 459-4300
Stephen Maguire, *President*
Stephen B Maguire, *Vice Pres*
Steven Maguire Jr, *Vice Pres*
Eric Maguire, *Plant Mgr*
Jamie Kulp, *Prdtn Mgr*
◆ EMP: 35
SQ FT: 3,637
SALES (est): 12.7MM **Privately Held**
WEB: www.maguire.com
SIC: 3824 3823 3586 3561 Integrating & totalizing meters for gas & liquids; industrial instrmnts msrmnt display/control process variable; measuring & dispensing pumps; pumps & pumping equipment; construction machinery; fabricated plate work (boiler shop)

(G-774)
MAJESTY MARBLE AND GRANITE INC
2939 Dutton Mill Rd (19014-2842)
P.O. Box 561, Cape May NJ (08204-0561)
PHONE..................................610 859-8181
Fax: 610 859-8558
▲ EMP: 20
SQ FT: 17,000
SALES (est): 3.5MM **Privately Held**
SIC: 3281 5032 Mfg Cut Stone/Products Whol Brick/Stone Material

(G-775)
MCGEE INDUSTRIES INC
Also Called: McLube
9 Crozerville Rd (19014-1499)
P.O. Box 2425 (19014-0425)
PHONE..................................610 459-1890
Edward L McClatchy Jr, *President*
Constance J McClatchy, *Chairman*
Wendy I McClatchy, *Corp Secy*
Karen Lancianese, *Purchasing*
Ron Rosenberg, *Mktg Dir*
▲ EMP: 20
SQ FT: 10,000
SALES (est): 8MM **Privately Held**
WEB: www.mclube.com
SIC: 2899 Chemical preparations

(G-776)
MICRONIC
210 Bridgewater Rd Ste 3 (19014-2142)
PHONE..................................484 480-3372
Jim Mortimer, *Principal*
▲ EMP: 8
SALES (est): 1.1MM **Privately Held**
SIC: 3841 Surgical & medical instruments

(G-777)
MICRONIC AMERICA LLC
210 Bridgewater Rd Ste 3 (19014-2142)
PHONE..................................484 483-8075
EMP: 3
SALES (est): 123.9K **Privately Held**
SIC: 2655 Tubes, for chemical or electrical uses: paper or fiber

(G-778)
MICRONIC MANUFACTURINGUSA LLC
210 Bridgewater Rd Ste 3 (19014-2142)
PHONE..................................484 483-8075
Jackson Hyde, *Mng Member*
EMP: 10 EST: 2016
SALES (est): 127.7K **Privately Held**
SIC: 3011 Tires & inner tubes

(G-779)
MULCH WORKS RECYCLING INC
22 Mount Pleasant Rd (19014-1408)
P.O. Box 3800 Mount Rd (19014)
PHONE..................................888 214-4628
Albert F Quercetti, *President*
Andrew Quercetti, *Vice Pres*
EMP: 14
SALES (est): 1.9MM **Privately Held**
SIC: 4953 7389 2875 Recycling, waste materials; tombstone engraving; compost

(G-780)
NALCO WTR PRTRTMENT SLTONS LLC
2 New Rd (19014-1038)
PHONE..................................610 358-0717
EMP: 39
SALES (corp-wide): 14.6B **Publicly Held**
SIC: 3589 5074 Water treatment equipment, industrial; water purification equipment
HQ: Nalco Water Pretreatment Solutions, Llc
1601 W Diehl Rd
Naperville IL 60563
708 754-2550

(G-781)
NEW WAY MACHINE COMPONENTS INC
Also Called: New Way Air Bearings
50 Mcdonald Blvd (19014-3202)
PHONE..................................610 494-6700
Nicholas R Hackett, *CEO*
Drew Devitt, *Chairman*
Nickolaos Sotiropoulos, *Treasurer*
Rick Pollick, *Director*
Brooke Richards, *Executive Asst*
▼ EMP: 40
SQ FT: 40,000
SALES (est): 13.3MM **Privately Held**
WEB: www.newwaymachine.com
SIC: 3339 Antifriction bearing metals, lead-base

(G-782)
OLDCO EP INC
15 Milton Dr (19014-2217)
PHONE..................................484 768-1000
Frank Flectcher, *Branch Mgr*
EMP: 4
SALES (corp-wide): 8.3B **Publicly Held**
SIC: 3949 5999 Swimming pools, except plastic; swimming pools, above ground
HQ: Oldco Ep, Inc.
1601 Dutton Mill Rd
Aston PA 19014
888 314-9356

(G-783)
OLDCO EP INC (HQ)
1601 Dutton Mill Rd (19014-2831)
PHONE..................................888 314-9356
James Murdock, *President*
David Biles, *COO*
Dan Harshbarger, *CFO*
▼ EMP: 7
SQ FT: 16,000
SALES (est): 11.1MM
SALES (corp-wide): 8.3B **Publicly Held**
WEB: www.endlesspools.com
SIC: 3949 5999 Swimming pools, except plastic; swimming pools, above ground
PA: Masco Corporation
17450 College Pkwy
Livonia MI 48152
313 274-7400

(G-784)
OLYMPIC TOOL & MACHINE CORP
2100 Bridgewater Rd (19014-2133)
P.O. Box 2069 (19014-0069)
PHONE..................................610 494-1600
Humberto Zavaleta, *CEO*
Walter C Goldstein, *Ch of Bd*
Caesar Crognale, *COO*
Ches Crognale, *President*
Andrew Ray, *Prdtn Mgr*
EMP: 71
SQ FT: 75,000
SALES (est): 25MM **Privately Held**
WEB: www.olymtool.com
SIC: 3728 3599 Aircraft parts & equipment; machine shop, jobbing & repair

(G-785)
PENN ASSURANCE SOFTWARE LLC
32 Venuti Dr (19014-3611)
PHONE..................................610 996-6124
Paul Soscia, *Mng Member*
EMP: 15
SALES: 1MM **Privately Held**
SIC: 7372 Application computer software

GEOGRAPHIC

(G-786)
PHILADELPHIA ELECTRICAL EQP CO
Also Called: Peeco
14 Mount Pleasant Rd (19014-1408)
P.O. Box 1480, West Chester (19380-0032)
PHONE..................................484 840-0860
Robert G Guarini, *President*
▼ EMP: 13
SQ FT: 26,500
SALES (est): 4.6MM **Privately Held**
WEB: www.peecoenergy.com
SIC: 3612 5063 Transformers, except electric; transformers & transmission equipment

(G-787)
PHONETICS INC
Also Called: Sensaphone
901 Tryens Rd (19014-1522)
PHONE..................................610 558-2700
Laura Trout, *General Mgr*
Debbie Hargy, *Vice Pres*
Dat Bui, *Prdtn Mgr*
Dave Breisacher, *Engineer*
David Defusco, *Engineer*
EMP: 43
SQ FT: 20,000
SALES (est): 11.2MM **Privately Held**
SIC: 3822 Auto controls regulating residntl & coml environmt & applncs

(G-788)
PRODUCTION SYSTEMS AUTOMTN LLC (PA)
1 Crozerville Rd (19014-1431)
PHONE..................................610 358-0500
Michael H McHale, *CEO*
Nathaniel Storch, *CFO*
EMP: 12
SALES: 2.3MM **Privately Held**
SIC: 3535 Robotic conveyors

(G-789)
PYROPURE INC
Also Called: Pyromet
5 Commerce Dr (19014-3201)
PHONE..................................610 497-1743
C Scott Smith, *CEO*
Tony Dangelo, *Vice Pres*
Kimberly Flicker, *Controller*
Tony D'Angelo, *VP Sales*
Toni Seitz, *Executive*
▲ EMP: 28
SQ FT: 21,000
SALES (est): 8.5MM **Privately Held**
SIC: 3339 Precious metals; silver refining (primary)

(G-790)
RIEKER ELECTRONICS INC
34 Mount Pleasant Rd (19014)
PHONE..................................610 500-2000
Vida Denigan, *President*
Edward P Denigan, *Vice Pres*
Cindy Quinley, *Admin Sec*
EMP: 45 EST: 1917
SQ FT: 20,000
SALES: 3MM **Privately Held**
SIC: 3823 Level & bulk measuring instruments, industrial process

(G-791)
RIEKER INSTRUMENT COMPANY INC
34 Mount Pleasant Rd (19014)
PHONE..................................610 500-2000
Edward P Denigan, *President*
Cyndy Williams, *General Mgr*
Vida Denigan, *Vice Pres*
Joann Coates, *Executive*
Glenn Wiseman, *Technician*
▲ EMP: 47 EST: 1917
SQ FT: 20,000
SALES (est): 10.6MM **Privately Held**
WEB: www.riekerinc.com
SIC: 3829 Aircraft & motor vehicle measurement equipment

(G-792)
RIVERDALE GLOBAL LLC
11 Crozerville Rd (19014-1431)
PHONE..................................610 358-2900
Paul Maguire, *President*

Charles Irish, *Vice Pres*
George Herman, *Treasurer*
Pilar Jimenez, *Cust Mgr*
EMP: 6
SQ FT: 3,000
SALES: 1MM **Privately Held**
SIC: 2821 Plastics materials & resins

(G-793)
SHARON MCGUIGAN INC
Also Called: Wellington's Best Foods
35 Mount Pleasant Rd (19014-1407)
PHONE..................................610 361-8100
Sharon McGuigan, *President*
Joseph McGuigan, *Corp Secy*
EMP: 22
SALES (est): 3.3MM **Privately Held**
SIC: 2011 2015 Meat packing plants; poultry, processed: fresh

(G-794)
SUN VALLEY FILM WASH INC
5 Commerce Dr (19014-3201)
PHONE..................................610 497-1743
C Scott Smith, *President*
Elaine Frieberg, *Shareholder*
Paul Frieberg, *Shareholder*
Lon Rudnitsky, *Shareholder*
Laurieann Smith, *Shareholder*
EMP: 8 EST: 1998
SQ FT: 6,000
SALES (est): 208.2K **Privately Held**
SIC: 7349 3861 Cleaning service, industrial or commercial; washers, photographic print & film

(G-795)
UPS STORE 6410
4920 Pennell Rd (19014-1867)
PHONE..................................484 816-0252
John Nachman, *Principal*
Kathleen C Nachman, *Principal*
EMP: 5
SALES: 225K **Privately Held**
SIC: 7389 2759 Mailbox rental & related service; commercial printing

(G-796)
VSI METER SERVICES INC
2900 Dutton Mill Rd 200 (19014-2842)
PHONE..................................484 482-2480
Gregory W Holman, *President*
Joseph P Dwyer, *Corp Secy*
George E Graham, *Vice Pres*
EMP: 5
SALES (est): 600K **Privately Held**
SIC: 3612 Electronic meter transformers

(G-797)
WEEDS INC (PA)
250 Bodley Rd (19014-1412)
PHONE..................................610 358-9430
Brian Oneill, *President*
Ken Lynch, *General Mgr*
Walter Kenneth Lynch, *Vice Pres*
Drew Oneill, *Vice Pres*
Melissa Drennon, *Office Mgr*
EMP: 37
SQ FT: 16,200
SALES: 5.2MM **Privately Held**
WEB: www.weedsinc.com
SIC: 0711 3523 Weed control services before planting; weeding machines, agricultural

(G-798)
WESTROCK CP LLC
100 Mcdonald Blvd (19014-3202)
PHONE..................................610 485-8700
Thomas Licht, *General Mgr*
EMP: 200
SALES (corp-wide): 16.2B **Publicly Held**
WEB: www.smurfit-stone.com
SIC: 2653 Boxes, corrugated: made from purchased materials
HQ: Westrock Cp, Llc
1000 Abernathy Rd
Atlanta GA 30328

Atglen
Chester County

(G-799)
ACTION MANUFACTURING COMPANY
500 Bailey Crossroads Rd (19310-1623)
PHONE..................................610 593-1800
Randy Aukamp, *Manager*
EMP: 90
SQ FT: 600
SALES (corp-wide): 85.5MM **Privately Held**
SIC: 3613 3823 2892 3489 Switchgear & switchboard apparatus; industrial instrmnts msrmnt display/control process variable; explosives; ordnance & accessories; detonators for ammunition over 30 mm.
PA: Action Manufacturing Company Inc
190 Rittenhouse Cir
Bristol PA 19007
267 540-4041

(G-800)
ERNST HOFFMANN INC
806 Valley Ave (19310-9420)
PHONE..................................610 593-2280
Ernst Hoffmann, *President*
▲ EMP: 8
SQ FT: 12,000
SALES (est): 500K **Privately Held**
WEB: www.hoffmanndiamonds.com
SIC: 7699 3545 Knife, saw & tool sharpening & repair; diamond cutting tools for turning, boring, burnishing, etc.

(G-801)
JOSEPH PIAZZA
Also Called: Viper Holsters
398 Bryson Rd (19310-9679)
P.O. Box 188 (19310-0188)
PHONE..................................610 593-3053
Joseph Piazza, *Owner*
Anne Piazza, *Principal*
EMP: 3
SALES (est): 121.7K **Privately Held**
SIC: 3083 Thermosetting laminates: rods, tubes, plates & sheet

(G-802)
ORGANIC UNLIMITED INC
120 Liberty St (19310)
P.O. Box 238 (19310-0238)
PHONE..................................610 593-2995
Roger E Grimes Jr, *CEO*
Eric Weidman, *General Mgr*
Kenneth R Rice, *Vice Pres*
▲ EMP: 6
SALES (est): 828.3K **Privately Held**
WEB: www.organicunlimited.com
SIC: 2048 5999 Prepared feeds; feed & farm supply

(G-803)
QG LLC
Also Called: Worldcolor Atglen
4581 Lower Valley Rd (19310-1766)
PHONE..................................414 208-2700
Steve Eggleston, *Branch Mgr*
EMP: 234
SALES (corp-wide): 4.1B **Publicly Held**
WEB: www.qwdys.com
SIC: 2754 2752 Commercial printing, gravure; commercial printing, lithographic
HQ: Qg, Llc
N61w23044 Harrys Way
Sussex WI 53089

(G-804)
QG PRINTING II CORP
4581 Lower Valley Rd (19310-1766)
PHONE..................................610 593-1445
EMP: 519
SALES (corp-wide): 4.1B **Publicly Held**
SIC: 2752 Lithographic Commercial Printing
HQ: Qg Printing Ii Corp.
N61w23044 Harrys Way
Sussex WI 53089

(G-805)
ROLLER DERBY SKATE CORP
Also Called: Tour Skate Company
401 Zion Hill Rd (19310-1701)
P.O. Box 170 (19310-0170)
PHONE..................................610 593-6931
Ed Seltzer, *Manager*
EMP: 20
SQ FT: 4,608
SALES (est): 1.8MM
SALES (corp-wide): 15.7MM **Privately Held**
WEB: www.rollerderbyskates.com
SIC: 3949 5091 Ice skates, parts & accessories; athletic goods
PA: Roller Derby Skate Corp.
311 W Edwards St
Litchfield IL 62056
217 324-3961

(G-806)
SCHIFFER PUBLISHING LTD
4880 Lower Valley Rd (19310-1768)
PHONE..................................610 593-1777
Peter Schiffer, *President*
Nancy N Schiffer, *Corp Secy*
▲ EMP: 38
SALES (est): 4.5MM **Privately Held**
SIC: 2741 Miscellaneous publishing

(G-807)
SELLARS NONWOVENS
808 Valley Ave (19310-9420)
P.O. Box 270 (19310-0270)
PHONE..................................610 593-5145
Thomas Fellars, *President*
Jim Rygalski, *Manager*
EMP: 20
SQ FT: 35,000
SALES (est): 3.8MM
SALES (corp-wide): 36.3MM **Privately Held**
WEB: www.sellarswipers.com
SIC: 2297 Nonwoven fabrics
PA: Sellars Absorbent Materials, Inc.
6565 N 60th St
Milwaukee WI 53223
414 353-5650

(G-808)
STOLTZFUS STRUCTURES
5075 Lower Valley Rd (19310-1769)
PHONE..................................610 593-7700
Gideon Zook, *Partner*
John Yoder, *Partner*
David Zook, *Partner*
Jonathan Zook, *Partner*
EMP: 10
SQ FT: 40,000
SALES (est): 2MM **Privately Held**
WEB: www.mysheds.net
SIC: 2452 Prefabricated buildings, wood

(G-809)
SUMMERS & ZIMS INC
Also Called: HONEYWELL AUTHORIZED DEALER
403 Valley Ave (19310-1402)
P.O. Box 220 (19310-0220)
PHONE..................................610 593-2420
Joseph L Zimmerman, *President*
G Lee Summers, *Vice Pres*
Jere L Zimmerman, *Vice Pres*
EMP: 35
SALES: 5.5MM **Privately Held**
WEB: www.sumzim.com
SIC: 1711 3444 Refrigeration contractor; plumbing contractors; warm air heating & air conditioning contractor; sheet metalwork

---

Athens
Bradford County

(G-810)
BRIAN KINGSLEY
514 Round Top Rd (18810-9692)
PHONE..................................570 888-8668
Brian Kingsley, *Principal*
EMP: 3 EST: 2011
SALES (est): 246.7K **Privately Held**
SIC: 2411 Logging

(G-811)
GUTIERREZ MACHINE CORPORATION
1069 Front St (18810-9471)
P.O. Box 71 (18810-0071)
PHONE..................................570 888-6088
George M Gutierrez, *President*
EMP: 12
SQ FT: 12,000
SALES (est): 800K **Privately Held**
WEB:
www.gutierrezmachinecorporation.com
SIC: 3599 Machine shop, jobbing & repair

(G-812)
MASCO CABINETRY LLC
217 Lamoka Rd (18810)
P.O. Box 158, Sayre (18840-0158)
PHONE..................................570 882-8565
Robert Hawthorne, *Branch Mgr*
EMP: 266
SALES (corp-wide): 8.3B **Publicly Held**
SIC: 2431 Doors, wood
HQ: Masco Cabinetry Llc
4600 Arrowhead Dr
Ann Arbor MI 48105
734 205-4600

(G-813)
WHEELER TOOL CO
215 Wheelock Ave (18810-1208)
PHONE..................................570 888-2275
Robert Wheeler, *Owner*
James Schultz, *Technology*
EMP: 5 EST: 1960
SQ FT: 4,000
SALES: 350K **Privately Held**
WEB: www.wheelertool.com
SIC: 3545 3546 Drilling machine attachments & accessories; power-driven hand-tools

Atlantic
Crawford County

(G-814)
TRUMCO INC
3324 Mcmaster Rd (16111-1030)
PHONE..................................814 382-7767
William R Merrifield, *President*
James F Bertin, *Treasurer*
EMP: 35
SQ FT: 20,000
SALES (est): 3.9MM **Privately Held**
SIC: 2411 2421 Timber, cut at logging camp; sawmills & planing mills, general

Auburn
Schuylkill County

(G-815)
CHAR-MARK INC
3084 Fair Rd (17922-9069)
PHONE..................................570 754-7310
Mark L Schropp, *President*
Charles H Fix, *Admin Sec*
EMP: 4
SALES: 200K **Privately Held**
WEB: www.usdiners.com
SIC: 3544 7389 Special dies & tools; grinding, precision: commercial or industrial

(G-816)
IFM EFECTOR INC
2007 Running Deer Dr (17922-9338)
PHONE..................................610 524-2000
EMP: 74
SALES (corp-wide): 1B **Privately Held**
SIC: 3679 Electronic switches
HQ: Ifm Efector Inc.
1100 Atwater Dr
Malvern PA 19355
800 441-8246

(G-817)
JOHN F KRAFT
1489 Bearcat Cv (17922-9260)
PHONE..................................570 516-1092
John F Kraft, *Principal*

EMP: 3
SALES (est): 186.7K **Privately Held**
SIC: 2022 Mfg Cheese

(G-818)
LONG TROUT ENTERPRISES INC
84 Fork Mountain Rd (17922-8735)
PHONE..................................570 366-6443
Harold T Leibensperger, *President*
EMP: 4
SALES (est): 146.6K **Privately Held**
SIC: 2084 Wines, brandy & brandy spirits

(G-819)
NOVA PRECISION CASTING CORP
12 Hickory Dr (17922-9777)
PHONE..................................570 366-2679
Richard Boyd, *Principal*
Patrick Gehringer, *Vice Pres*
Scot Boyd, *Sales Mgr*
Ron St Clair, *Shareholder*
▲ EMP: 20 EST: 1971
SQ FT: 17,000
SALES: 3MM **Privately Held**
WEB: www.novaprecisioncasting.com
SIC: 3324 3369 Commercial investment castings, ferrous; nonferrous foundries

(G-820)
OMNOVA SOLUTIONS INC
Also Called: Reneer Films
95 Hickory Dr (17922-9625)
PHONE..................................570 366-1051
Randy Marvel, *Plant Mgr*
Linda Maberry, *Master*
EMP: 275
SALES (corp-wide): 769.8MM **Publicly Held**
WEB: www.omnova.com
SIC: 3089 3081 Synthetic resin finished products; unsupported plastics film & sheet
PA: Omnova Solutions Inc.
25435 Harvard Rd
Beachwood OH 44122
216 682-7000

(G-821)
PORTER AO CO
Rr 2 (17922)
PHONE..................................570 366-1387
Allen Porter, *Owner*
EMP: 5
SALES (est): 240K **Privately Held**
SIC: 3599 Machine shop, jobbing & repair

Audubon
Montgomery County

(G-822)
AIROS MEDICAL INC
2501 Monroe Blvd Ste 1200 (19403-2422)
PHONE..................................866 991-6956
Gerald Makoid, *CEO*
EMP: 4
SALES (est): 149.2K **Privately Held**
SIC: 3841 Surgical & medical instruments

(G-823)
ALMAC PHARMA SERVICES LLC
2661 Audubon Rd (19403-2413)
PHONE..................................610 666-9500
Graeme McBurney, *President*
Colin Hayburn, *Admin Sec*
▲ EMP: 101
SQ FT: 4,462
SALES: 567MM
SALES (corp-wide): 69.2K **Privately Held**
SIC: 2834 Druggists' preparations (pharmaceuticals)
HQ: Almac Group Incorporated
25 Fretz Rd
Souderton PA 18964

(G-824)
CSP TECHNOLOGIES INC
2570 Blvd Of The Gen 215 (19403)
PHONE..................................610 635-1202
Peter Segona, *Manager*
EMP: 5

SALES (corp-wide): 114.6MM **Privately Held**
SIC: 3089 Blister or bubble formed packaging, plastic
HQ: Csp Technologies, Inc.
1031 Riverfront Ctr
Amsterdam NY 12010
518 627-0051

(G-825)
FRANK DADDARIO WDWRKNG
1633 Sheridan Ln (19403-3336)
PHONE..................................610 476-3414
Frank Daddario, *Principal*
EMP: 5
SALES (est): 450.5K **Privately Held**
SIC: 2431 Millwork

(G-826)
GLOBUS MEDICAL INC (PA)
2560 Gen Armistead Ave (19403-5214)
PHONE..................................610 930-1800
David M Demski, *CEO*
David C Paul, *Ch of Bd*
Anthony L Williams, *President*
A Brett Murphy, *Exec VP*
Eric Schwartz, *Vice Pres*
EMP: 375
SALES: 712.9MM **Publicly Held**
WEB: www.globusmedical.com
SIC: 3841 Surgical & medical instruments

(G-827)
HIGH AVLBLITY STOR SYSTEMS INC
Also Called: H. A. Storage Systems
820 Adams Ave Ste 200 (19403-2328)
PHONE..................................610 254-5090
Greg Robertson, *President*
EMP: 22
SALES (est): 3.2MM **Privately Held**
SIC: 3572 Computer auxiliary storage units
PA: High Availability Storage Systems, Inc.
11479 Valley View Rd
Eden Prairie MN 55344

(G-828)
JOHNSON CONTROLS INC
950 Forge Ave (19403-2305)
PHONE..................................800 877-9675
EMP: 5 **Privately Held**
SIC: 2531 Seats, automobile
HQ: Johnson Controls, Inc.
5757 N Green Bay Ave
Milwaukee WI 53209
414 524-1200

(G-829)
LOCKHEED MARTIN CORPORATION
900 Forge Ave (19403-2305)
P.O. Box 61511, King of Prussia (19406-0911)
PHONE..................................610 354-7782
Stan Sloane, *Vice Pres*
EMP: 50 **Publicly Held**
WEB: www.lockheedmartin.com
SIC: 3812 Search & navigation equipment
PA: Lockheed Martin Corporation
6801 Rockledge Dr
Bethesda MD 20817

(G-830)
MATTHEY JOHNSON INC
900 Forge Ave (19403-2305)
PHONE..................................484 320-2223
EMP: 127
SALES (corp-wide): 19.7B **Privately Held**
SIC: 3341 3339 Platinum group metals, smelting & refining (secondary); platinum group metal refining (primary)
HQ: Matthey Johnson Inc
435 Devon Park Dr Ste 600
Wayne PA 19087
610 971-3000

(G-831)
VALERIO COFFEE ROASTERS INC
2675 Eisenhower Ave (19403-2316)
PHONE..................................610 676-0034
Anthony Valerio, *President*
Angela C Henchel, *Director*
Joseph P Valerio Jr, *Director*
▲ EMP: 8 EST: 2001

SQ FT: 8,000
SALES: 977.6K **Privately Held**
WEB: www.cafeexcellence.com
SIC: 2095 Coffee roasting (except by wholesale grocers)

(G-832)
YORK INTERNATIONAL CORPORATION
950 Forge Ave Unit 110 (19403-2305)
PHONE..................................414 524-1200
EMP: 27 **Privately Held**
SIC: 3585 Refrigeration & heating equipment
HQ: York International Corporation
631 S Richland Ave
York PA 17403
717 771-7890

Austin
Potter County

(G-833)
EMPORIUM SPECIALTIES COMPANY
94 Foster St (16720-1336)
P.O. Box 65 (16720-0065)
PHONE..................................814 647-8661
Marvin Deupree, *President*
Meredith Deupree, *Admin Sec*
EMP: 50 EST: 1947
SQ FT: 60,000
SALES (est): 2.2MM **Privately Held**
WEB: www.empspec.com
SIC: 3541 3469 3714 3433 Machine tools, metal cutting type; metal stampings; clutches, motor vehicle; burners, furnaces, boilers & stokers; wrenches, hand tools; friction material, made from powdered metal

Avella
Washington County

(G-834)
C & J METALS
25 Penny Ln (15312-2393)
PHONE..................................562 634-3101
Gregory Tarolli, *President*
Jason Torolli, *Vice Pres*
EMP: 10
SQ FT: 10,000
SALES (est): 1.4MM **Privately Held**
WEB: www.candjmetals.com
SIC: 3469 5046 Kitchen fixtures & equipment: metal, except cast aluminum; restaurant equipment & supplies

(G-835)
DELLOVADE FABRICATORS INC
18 Seneca Pl (15312-2459)
P.O. Box D (15312-0803)
PHONE..................................615 370-7000
Fred Dellovade, *President*
EMP: 10
SALES (corp-wide): 950.8K **Privately Held**
SIC: 3315 Welded steel wire fabric
PA: Dellovade Fabricators, Inc.
108 Cavasina Dr
Canonsburg PA 15317
724 873-8190

(G-836)
G & D ERECTORS INC
1552 Avella Rd (15312-3307)
PHONE..................................724 587-0590
Stephanie Gordon, *President*
Bob Amic, *Controller*
Elizabeth Beckus, *Office Mgr*
Jeff Gordon, *Manager*
EMP: 30
SQ FT: 1,000
SALES (est): 2.6MM **Privately Held**
SIC: 1761 1791 3448 Roofing, siding & sheet metal work; structural steel erection; prefabricated metal buildings

GEOGRAPHIC

(G-837)
N J K LETTERING
928 Old Ridge Rd (15312-2624)
PHONE..............................724 356-2583
Norma J Kelso, *Owner*
EMP: 4
SALES (est): 156.9K **Privately Held**
SIC: 2395 Embroidery products, except
schiffli machine

Avis
Clinton County

(G-838)
SUZANNES CHOCLAT &
CONFECTIONS
Rr 150 (17721)
PHONE..............................570 753-8545
Victoria Ward, *President*
James Ward Jr, *Vice Pres*
Robert Charles Ward, *Treasurer*
Tammy Sue Ward, *Admin Sec*
EMP: 4
SQ FT: 1,600
SALES (est): 241.4K **Privately Held**
SIC: 2066 2064 5411 Chocolate; candy &
other confectionery products; co-opera-
tive food stores; delicatessens

Avoca
Luzerne County

(G-839)
AMERICAN SPORTS APPAREL
INC
914 Hope St (18641-1716)
PHONE..............................570 357-8155
Salim Reza, *Principal*
EMP: 99
SALES (est): 6MM **Privately Held**
SIC: 2254 Knit underwear mills

(G-840)
AVIATION TECHNOLOGIES INC
Also Called: Publiccharters.com
201 Hanger Rd Ste 2 (18641-2229)
PHONE..............................570 457-4147
James Gallagher, *President*
Chaunce Phebus, *Opers Mgr*
Mike Gallagher, *CFO*
Joe Stahurski, *Controller*
Vince Colarusso, *Maintence Staff*
EMP: 6
SQ FT: 480
SALES: 5.6MM **Privately Held**
WEB: www.justaplanebroker.com
SIC: 7359 4522 2759 4512 Aircraft
rental; flying charter service; schedules;
transportation; printing; air transportation,
scheduled; jet fuels

(G-841)
CJ PACKAGING INC
590 Rocky Glen Rd (18641-9508)
PHONE..............................570 209-7836
Robert Tocki, *President*
EMP: 6
SALES (est): 966K **Privately Held**
SIC: 2673 3081 Plastic & pliofilm bags;
polyethylene film

(G-842)
CJC CONTRACT PACKAGING
INC
590 Rocky Glen Rd (18641-9508)
PHONE..............................570 209-7836
Robert Tocki, *President*
▲ EMP: 5
SQ FT: 40,000
SALES (est): 731.3K **Privately Held**
SIC: 2671 3081 3089 3643 Plastic film,
coated or laminated for packaging; ther-
moplastic coated paper for packaging;
plastic film & sheet; blister or bubble
formed packaging, plastic; current-carry-
ing wiring devices; bags: plastic, lami-
nated & coated

(G-843)
GALAXY MFG COMPANY INC
Also Called: Galaxy Brushes
500 Gleason Dr (18641-9541)
PHONE..............................570 457-5199
Douglas Batzel, *President*
Lee Batzel, *Vice Pres*
Joe Bone, *Opers Mgr*
▲ EMP: 10
SQ FT: 56,000
SALES: 800K **Privately Held**
WEB: www.galaxybrushes.com
SIC: 3624 Brushes & brush stock contacts,
electric

(G-844)
HUDSON ANTHRACITE INC
641 Main St (18641-1583)
PHONE..............................570 655-4151
Gail Popple, *President*
William Chase, *Admin Sec*
EMP: 12
SQ FT: 500
SALES (est): 841.3K **Privately Held**
SIC: 1231 Anthracite mining

(G-845)
MESKO GLASS AND MIRROR
CO INC
100 Glendale Rd (18641-9518)
PHONE..............................570 457-1700
George Mesko, *Manager*
EMP: 55
SALES (corp-wide): 26.1MM **Privately**
Held
WEB: www.mesko.com
SIC: 1542 3231 3211 1793 Commercial
& office building contractors; products of
purchased glass; flat glass; glass & glaz-
ing work
PA: Mesko Glass And Mirror Co Inc.
801 Wyoming Ave
Scranton PA 18509
570 346-0777

(G-846)
MIA PRODUCTS COMPANY (HQ)
4 Rocky Glen Rd (18641-9537)
PHONE..............................570 457-7431
Gerald Shreiber, *President*
▲ EMP: 25
SALES (est): 14.4MM
SALES (corp-wide): 1B **Publicly Held**
SIC: 2024 Ices, flavored (frozen dessert)
PA: J & J Snack Foods Corp.
6000 Central Hwy
Pennsauken NJ 08109
856 665-9533

(G-847)
PENNSY SUPPLY INC
7 Regulators Ln Ste 4 (18641-1692)
PHONE..............................570 471-7358
EMP: 3
SALES (corp-wide): 29.7B **Privately Held**
SIC: 3273 Ready-mixed concrete
HQ: Pennsy Supply, Inc.
1001 Paxton St
Harrisburg PA 17104
717 233-4511

Avondale
Chester County

(G-848)
ANHOLT TECHNOLOGIES INC
(PA)
Also Called: Qfix
440 Church Rd (19311-9786)
PHONE..............................610 268-2758
Daniel Coppens, *President*
▲ EMP: 12
SALES (est): 2.7MM **Privately Held**
WEB: www.anholt.com
SIC: 2821 3083 3089 3728 Plastics ma-
terials & resins; laminated plastics plate &
sheet; plastic containers, except foam;
aircraft parts & equipment; X-ray appara-
tus & tubes; engineering services

(G-849)
AVONDALE MACHINE
PRODUCTS INC
1304 Glen Willow Rd (19311-9526)
P.O. Box 208 (19311-0208)
PHONE..............................610 268-2121
Eleanor Willard, *President*
Robert A Willard, *Corp Secy*
Jeffrey L Willard, *Vice Pres*
EMP: 6
SQ FT: 10,000
SALES (est): 774.8K **Privately Held**
SIC: 3599 Machine shop, jobbing & repair

(G-850)
E I DU PONT DE NEMOURS & CO
Also Called: Dupont
Chestnut Run Plz (19311)
PHONE..............................302 996-7165
Sherry Morgan, *Principal*
EMP: 5
SALES (corp-wide): 85.9B **Publicly Held**
WEB: www.dupont.com
SIC: 2819 Industrial inorganic chemicals
HQ: E. I. Du Pont De Nemours And Com-
pany
974 Centre Rd
Wilmington DE 19805
302 774-1000

(G-851)
EDGECRAFT CORPORATION
Also Called: Chef'schoice
825 Southwood Rd (19311-9765)
PHONE..............................610 268-0500
Samuel Weiner, *President*
Angelo D'Agostino, *Warehouse Mgr*
Joshua Rhody, *Warehouse Mgr*
Terry McFarlane, *Senior Buyer*
George Jensen, *Engineer*
▲ EMP: 150
SQ FT: 40,000
SALES (est): 33.7MM
SALES (corp-wide): 200MM **Privately**
Held
WEB: www.edgecraft.com
SIC: 3634 Electric household cooking ap-
pliances
PA: Greenfield World Trade, Inc.
3355 Entp Ave Ste 160
Fort Lauderdale FL 33331
954 202-7419

(G-852)
EDLON INC (DH)
150 Pomeroy Ave (19311-1504)
P.O. Box 667 (19311-0667)
PHONE..............................610 268-3101
Gary L Brewer, *President*
Christopher N Hix, *Vice Pres*
Kevin I Brown, *Vice Pres*
Linn S Harson, *Admin Sec*
▲ EMP: 65
SQ FT: 60,000
SALES (est): 21.7MM
SALES (corp-wide): 8.4B **Publicly Held**
WEB: www.edlon.com
SIC: 2821 3568 3443 3441 Polytetrafluo-
roethylene resins (teflon); power trans-
mission equipment; fabricated plate work
(boiler shop); fabricated structural metal
HQ: Robbins & Myers, Inc.
10586 N Highway 75
Willis TX 77378
936 890-1064

(G-853)
HILLENDALE PEAT MOSS INC
519 Hillendale Rd (19311-9778)
P.O. Box 677, Kennett Square (19348-
0677)
PHONE..............................610 444-5591
Augustine Carozzo, *President*
Christopher Lafferty, *General Mgr*
EMP: 5
SQ FT: 1,800
SALES (est): 738.3K **Privately Held**
SIC: 2873 Plant foods, mixed: from plants
making nitrog. fertilizers

(G-854)
LAUREL VALLEY SOILS
705 Penn Green Rd (19311)
P.O. Box 70, Landenberg (19350-0070)
PHONE..............................610 268-5555
Valley Farm Laurel, *Principal*

▲ EMP: 3
SALES (est): 179.8K **Privately Held**
SIC: 2875 Compost

(G-855)
NAAMANS CREEK CO INC
353 Indian Run Rd (19311-9360)
PHONE..............................610 268-3833
EMP: 3
SALES (est): 310.6K **Privately Held**
SIC: 5999 3993 Ret Misc Merchandise
Mfg Signs/Advertising Specialties

(G-856)
PANNELL MFG CORP
1780 Baltimore Pike (19311-9793)
PHONE..............................610 268-2012
Robert T Pannell, *President*
Denise A Pannell, *Corp Secy*
▼ EMP: 7 EST: 1950
SQ FT: 19,200
SALES (est): 1.2MM **Privately Held**
SIC: 7692 3523 Welding repair; fertilizing
machinery, farm

(G-857)
PHENOMENEX
341 Indian Run Rd (19311-9360)
PHONE..............................484 680-0678
EMP: 3
SALES (est): 157.8K **Privately Held**
SIC: 3826 Analytical instruments

(G-858)
RALSTON SHOP INC
Old Rte 1 And Rte 41 (19311)
PHONE..............................610 268-3829
Frederick Ralston, *President*
Diane Ralston, *Treasurer*
EMP: 13
SQ FT: 10,000
SALES (est): 1.6MM **Privately Held**
SIC: 2431 2541 Millwork; wood partitions
& fixtures

(G-859)
SCHUIBBEO HOLDINGS INC
568 Baltimore Pike (19311-9558)
PHONE..............................610 268-2825
Andy Mattrick, *President*
EMP: 9
SALES (est): 656.3K **Privately Held**
SIC: 2512 Upholstered household furniture

(G-860)
SCOTTS COMPANY LLC
944 Newark Rd (19311-1133)
PHONE..............................610 268-3006
JP Miller, *Plant Mgr*
Jim Gleason, *Branch Mgr*
EMP: 40
SQ FT: 10,000
SALES (corp-wide): 2.6B **Publicly Held**
WEB: www.scottscompany.com
SIC: 2875 Fertilizers, mixing only
HQ: The Scotts Company Llc
14111 Scottslawn Rd
Marysville OH 43040
937 644-0011

(G-861)
THOMSON CANDIES
201 Pennsylvania Ave (19311-1200)
P.O. Box 70 (19311-0070)
PHONE..............................610 268-8337
Mabel Thomson, *Owner*
EMP: 3 EST: 1964
SALES (est): 93.5K **Privately Held**
SIC: 2064 5441 Candy & other confec-
tionery products; candy

Avonmore
Westmoreland County

(G-862)
AKERS NATIONAL ROLL
COMPANY (DH)
Also Called: Union Electric Akers
400 Railroad Ave (15618-9700)
PHONE..............................724 697-4533
Thomas P Adams, *President*
Hongyi Liu, *General Mgr*
John S Cicala Jr, *Vice Pres*

▲ = Import ▼=Export
◆ =Import/Export

Lewis Prenni, *Vice Pres*
Christopher Schiano, *CTO*
◆ **EMP:** 250
SQ FT: 320,000
SALES (est): 52.5MM
SALES (corp-wide): 419.4MM **Publicly Held**
WEB: www.akersrolls.com
SIC: 3325 Steel foundries
HQ: Union Electric Steel Corporation
726 Bell Ave Ste 101
Carnegie PA 15106
412 429-7655

(G-863)
CANTERBERY INDUSTRIES LLC
435 Allshouse Rd (15618-1199)
P.O. Box 522 (15518-0522)
PHONE..................................724 697-4231
Dwayne Smith, *Mng Member*
EMP: 4
SALES (est): 828.7K **Privately Held**
SIC: 3625 5065 Industrial electrical relays & switches; electronic parts & equipment

(G-864)
ENCLOSURE DIRECT CORP
4097 State Route 819 (15618-1106)
PHONE..................................724 697-5191
Dwayne Altman, *President*
EMP: 20
SALES (est): 609.8K **Privately Held**
SIC: 3444 Sheet metalwork

(G-865)
HILLTOP WOODSHOP INC
1269 School Rd (15618-1020)
PHONE..................................724 697-4506
Douglas P Ukish, *President*
EMP: 8
SQ FT: 3,000
SALES (est): 357.7K **Privately Held**
WEB: www.hilltopwoodshop.com
SIC: 2541 2434 Store fixtures, wood; wood kitchen cabinets; vanities, bathroom: wood

(G-866)
OUTLAW PERFORMANCE INC
136 Nelson Rd (15618-1151)
PHONE..................................724 697-4876
Barbara Davison, *President*
John Davison, *Treasurer*
EMP: 26
SQ FT: 90,000
SALES: 1.5MM **Privately Held**
SIC: 3711 5531 3452 3441 Automobile bodies, passenger car, not including engine, etc.; chassis, motor vehicle; automotive parts; automotive accessories; bolts, nuts, rivets & washers; fabricated structural metal

(G-867)
REYNOLDS MANUFACTURING CO INC
621 Railroad Ave (15618-1600)
PHONE..................................724 697-4522
Debra A Stevenson, *CEO*
Brett A Stevenson, *CFO*
Spencer A Stevenson, *Director*
▲ **EMP:** 10 **EST:** 1947
SQ FT: 105,000
SALES: 500K **Privately Held**
SIC: 3443 3441 Vessels, process or storage (from boiler shops): metal plate; building components, structural steel

(G-868)
ROLLS TECHNOLOGY INC
400 Railroad Ave (15618-9700)
PHONE..................................724 697-4533
Thomas Adams, *President*
Bengt Nillson, *Chairman*
Ronald Frank, *Admin Sec*
◆ **EMP:** 350
SQ FT: 320,000
SALES (est): 31.2MM
SALES (corp-wide): 419.4MM **Publicly Held**
SIC: 3321 Rolling mill rolls, cast iron
HQ: Akers Ab
Bruksallen 4
Akers Styckebruk 647 5
159 321-00

Baden
Beaver County

(G-869)
ANDERSONS CANDIES INC
1010 W State St (15005-1338)
PHONE..................................724 869-3018
Goldie Anderson, *President*
Mary Candice Anderson, *Treasurer*
Pamela M Anderson, *Admin Sec*
EMP: 33 **EST:** 1916
SQ FT: 30,000
SALES (est): 2MM **Privately Held**
WEB: www.andersonscandies.com
SIC: 2064 5441 2066 Candy & other confectionery products; candy; chocolate & cocoa products

(G-870)
CHUCKS SALSA
917 3rd St (15005-1406)
PHONE..................................724 513-5708
Chad Seamon, *Principal*
EMP: 3 **EST:** 2012
SALES (est): 154.9K **Privately Held**
SIC: 2099 Food preparations

Bainbridge
Lancaster County

(G-871)
A & R NISSLEY INC (PA)
Also Called: Nissley Vineyards
140 Vintage Dr (17502-9357)
PHONE..................................717 426-3514
Judith W Nissley, *President*
John R Nissley, *Vice Pres*
Joyce W Nissley, *Treasurer*
Joyce Nissley, *Treasurer*
Mary Lee Nissley, *Asst Treas*
EMP: 36
SQ FT: 7,500
SALES (est): 5.4MM **Privately Held**
SIC: 2084 0172 Wines; grapes

Bala Cynwyd
Montgomery County

(G-872)
ACT INC
29 Bala Ave Ste 114 (19004-3206)
PHONE..................................484 562-0063
Joseph H Ball, *President*
EMP: 6
SALES (est): 330.7K **Privately Held**
SIC: 2721 Periodicals

(G-873)
BISIL NORTH AMERICA INC
111 Presidential Blvd # 246 (19004-1008)
PHONE..................................610 747-0340
Manoj Sinha, *CEO*
EMP: 5
SALES (est): 489.4K **Privately Held**
SIC: 7372 Business oriented computer software

(G-874)
C PUROLITE CORPORATION
150 Monument Rd Ste 202 (19004-1725)
PHONE..................................610 668-9090
Stefan Brodie, *President*
Don Brodie, *Vice Pres*
James F Downey, *CFO*
EMP: 810
SQ FT: 12,000
SALES (est): 73.7MM **Privately Held**
SIC: 2821 Plastics materials & resins

(G-875)
CHEMROCK CORPORATION (DH)
225 E City Ave (19004-1704)
PHONE..................................610 667-6640
Raymond G Perelman, *CEO*
Whitney H Waugh, *Vice Pres*
Mike Cull, *Treasurer*
▼ **EMP:** 15 **EST:** 1963

SALES (est): 4.9MM **Privately Held**
SIC: 3677 3296 3295 Filtration devices, electronic; insulation: rock wool, slag & silica minerals; perlite, aggregate or expanded

(G-876)
COVENANT GROUP OF CHINA INC
2 Bala Plz Ste 300 (19004-1512)
PHONE..................................610 660-7828
Kenneth Wong, *President*
Justin D Csik, *CFO*
EMP: 77
SALES: 7.1MM **Privately Held**
SIC: 3699 Security control equipment & systems

(G-877)
DESIGN OPTIONS HOLDINGS LLC
273 Montgomery Ave # 204 (19004-2808)
PHONE..................................610 667-8180
Alan Robins,
EMP: 20
SQ FT: 12,000
SALES: 12MM **Privately Held**
WEB: www.designoptions.com
SIC: 2522 Office furniture, except wood

(G-878)
EAST ASSOCIATES INC
Also Called: E Y Productions
11 Union Ave Fl 1 (19004-3343)
P.O. Box 2581 (19004-6581)
PHONE..................................610 667-3980
Harry Conry, *President*
Eileen Conry, *Vice Pres*
EMP: 8
SALES (est): 633.5K **Privately Held**
WEB: www.eyproductions.com
SIC: 7374 2752 Data processing service; commercial printing, offset

(G-879)
GRC HOLDING INC (HQ)
1 Bala Ave Ste 310 (19004-3210)
PHONE..................................610 667-6640
Raymond G Perelman, *President*
EMP: 8
SQ FT: 7,000
SALES (est): 57.9MM **Privately Held**
SIC: 3255 1741 1499 Firebrick, clay; castable refractories, clay; foundry refractories, clay; refractory or acid brick masonry; diatomaceous earth mining; perlite mining

(G-880)
HLC INDUSTRIES INC
4 E Montgomery Ave (19004-3300)
PHONE..................................610 668-9112
Emanuel Landau, *President*
Elaine Landau, *Admin Sec*
EMP: 11 **EST:** 1916
SQ FT: 10,000
SALES (est): 3.7MM **Privately Held**
WEB: www.hlcindustries.com
SIC: 2261 Finishing plants, cotton

(G-881)
J MARGULIS INC
50 Belmont Ave Apt 803 (19004-2429)
PHONE..................................215 739-9100
Seymour Margulis, *President*
EMP: 7 **EST:** 1951
SQ FT: 12,000
SALES: 380K **Privately Held**
SIC: 3993 Signs & advertising specialties

(G-882)
JACK PRESSMAN
Also Called: Minuteman Press
301 Montgomery Ave (19004-2815)
PHONE..................................610 668-8847
Jack Pressman, *Owner*
EMP: 5
SQ FT: 1,000
SALES: 600K **Privately Held**
WEB: www.mmpbala.com
SIC: 2752 Commercial printing, lithographic

(G-883)
JO-AN INC
Also Called: JOHN ANTHONY JEWELERS
133 Montgomery Ave (19004-2828)
PHONE..................................610 664-8777
John Anthony Jr, *President*
John A Mizi, *Vice Pres*
Rita Mizii, *Vice Pres*
EMP: 7
SQ FT: 4,500
SALES: 342.3K **Privately Held**
WEB: www.johnanthonyjewelers.com
SIC: 5944 3911 7631 Jewelry, precious stones & precious metals; pearl jewelry, natural or cultured; jewelry repair services

(G-884)
MAIN LINE CENTER FOR SKIN SURG
191 Presidential Blvd (19004-1207)
PHONE..................................610 664-1414
Tatyana Humphreys, *President*
EMP: 8 **EST:** 2006
SALES (est): 145K **Privately Held**
SIC: 2834 8011 Dermatologicals; medical centers

(G-885)
MEDTRONIC MONITORING INC
111 Presidential Blvd # 102 (19004-1009)
PHONE..................................610 257-3640
EMP: 5 **EST:** 2015
SALES (est): 126.9K **Privately Held**
SIC: 3845 Mfg Electromedical Equipment

(G-886)
MICRO OSCILLATOR INC
118 Cornell Rd (19004-2146)
PHONE..................................610 617-8682
Fred A Mirow, *President*
Micheal Hershwitz, *COO*
EMP: 3
SQ FT: 350
SALES (est): 221.1K **Privately Held**
WEB: www.micro-oscillator.com
SIC: 3679 5065 Oscillators; electronic parts & equipment

(G-887)
NEW MAINSTREAM PRESS INC
167 Old Belmont Ave 200 (19004-1934)
PHONE..................................610 617-8800
Yi Qian Tsao, *President*
Tingting Wan, *Administration*
EMP: 9
SALES (est): 708.8K **Privately Held**
SIC: 2741 Miscellaneous publishing

(G-888)
PAPERWORKS INDUSTRIES INC (HQ)
40 Monument Rd Ste 200 (19004-1735)
PHONE..................................215 984-7000
C Anderson Bolton, *CEO*
Tom Garland, *President*
Adam Jones, *General Mgr*
Chris K Wetherford, *General Mgr*
Lonnie Rosenfeld, *Vice Pres*
◆ **EMP:** 180
SQ FT: 5,050
SALES (est): 524MM
SALES (corp-wide): 11.9B **Privately Held**
SIC: 2653 Boxes, corrugated: made from purchased materials
PA: Sun Capital Partners, Inc.
5200 Town Center Cir # 600
Boca Raton FL 33486
561 962-3400

(G-889)
PUROLITE CORPORATION (PA)
150 Monument Rd Ste 202 (19004-1725)
PHONE..................................610 668-9090
Stefan Brodie, *President*
Don Brodie, *Vice Pres*
James F Downey, *CFO*
◆ **EMP:** 130
SQ FT: 12,000
SALES (est): 312MM **Privately Held**
WEB: www.puroliteusa.com
SIC: 2821 Plastics materials & resins

G E O G R A P H I C

(G-890)
READING REFRACTORIES COMPANY
Also Called: Snyder Contractors
1 Bala Ave Ste 310 (19004-3210)
PHONE.................................610 375-4422
Barry Katz, *President*
EMP: 11
SQ FT: 55,000
SALES (est): 1.6MM **Privately Held**
SIC: 1741 5085 3297 Refractory or acid brick masonry; refractory material; non-clay refractories
HQ: Grc Holding, Inc
　1 Bala Ave Ste 310
　Bala Cynwyd PA 19004

(G-891)
RIGHTERS ASSOCIAT FERRY
600 Righters Ferry Rd (19004-1303)
PHONE.................................610 667-6767
EMP: 4
SALES (est): 284.3K **Privately Held**
SIC: 2653 Corrugated & solid fiber boxes

(G-892)
SLEEP SPECIALISTS LLC
Also Called: 2z Medical
150 Monument Rd (19004-1702)
PHONE.................................610 304-6408
Sila Yesiloy, *Exec VP*
Joseph Crocetti, *Med Doctor*
EMP: 5
SALES: 160K **Privately Held**
SIC: 3841 Surgical & medical instruments

(G-893)
SPECIALTY VERMICULITE CORP (HQ)
1 Bala Ave Ste 310 (19004-3210)
PHONE.................................610 660-8840
Raymond Perelman, *President*
Derek Cusack, *Senior VP*
EMP: 70
SALES (est): 26.3MM
SALES (corp-wide): 34.9MM **Privately Held**
SIC: 1499 Vermiculite mining
PA: Dicalite Management Group, Inc.
　1 Bala Ave Ste 310
　Bala Cynwyd PA 19004
　610 660-8808

(G-894)
TECHNOLOGY DATA EXCHANGE INC
Also Called: OEM Technology News
721 Yale Rd (19004-2115)
P.O. Box 2570 (19004-6570)
PHONE.................................610 668-4717
George Pachter, *President*
EMP: 4
SQ FT: 10,000
SALES (est): 336.9K **Privately Held**
WEB: www.oemtechnology.com
SIC: 2721 8611 Magazines: publishing only, not printed on site; business associations

(G-895)
VALLEY PRESS INC
5 E Montgomery Ave Ste 3 (19004-2398)
PHONE.................................610 664-7770
Aloysius J Mc Carthy Jr, *President*
Ann C Mc Carthy, *Corp Secy*
EMP: 20 EST: 1954
SALES (est): 3.7MM **Privately Held**
WEB: www.valleypressinc.com
SIC: 2752 Commercial printing, offset

(G-896)
WATCH U WANT INC
166 E Levering Mill Rd # 100 (19004-2664)
PHONE.................................954 961-1445
Oj Whatley, *CEO*
Shannon Beck, *President*
EMP: 6
SALES (est): 1MM **Privately Held**
SIC: 3873 5094 Watches & parts, except crystals & jewels; watches & parts

(G-897)
ZIPF ASSOCIATES INC
25 Bala Ave Ste 201 (19004-3215)
P.O. Box 2431 (19004-6431)
PHONE.................................610 667-1717
Mark Zipf, *President*
Stacy Fink, *Software Dev*
EMP: 6
SALES (est): 688.4K **Privately Held**
SIC: 3534 Elevators & moving stairways

Bally
Berks County

(G-898)
BALLY BLOCK COMPANY (DH)
30 S 7th St (19503-9665)
P.O. Box 188 (19503-0188)
PHONE.................................610 845-7511
James P Reichart, *President*
John J Dau, *Chairman*
Ann D Conway, *Vice Pres*
Carol L Beadencup, *Treasurer*
Carol Beadencup, *CIO*
EMP: 62 EST: 1913
SQ FT: 143,300
SALES: 7.9MM
SALES (corp-wide): 14.8MM **Privately Held**
SIC: 2499 Kitchen, bathroom & household ware: wood
HQ: Bally Holding Company Of Delaware
　3411 Silverside Rd 108wb
　Wilmington DE 19810
　610 845-7511

(G-899)
BALLY HOLDING COMPANY PA (PA)
Also Called: Bally Block Co
30 S 7th St (19503-9665)
P.O. Box 188 (19503-0188)
PHONE.................................610 845-7511
John J Dau, *Ch of Bd*
James P Reichart, *President*
Ann D Conway, *Vice Pres*
EMP: 9
SQ FT: 143,300
SALES (est): 14.8MM **Privately Held**
SIC: 2499 Kitchen, bathroom & household ware: wood

(G-900)
BALLY RIBBON MILLS (PA)
23 N 7th St (19503-9638)
PHONE.................................610 845-2211
Raymond G Harries, *President*
Herbert Harries, *General Mgr*
Robert Costello, *Vice Pres*
Herbert D Harries III, *Vice Pres*
Ray Harries, *Vice Pres*
▲ **EMP:** 170
SQ FT: 130,000
SALES (est): 73.9MM **Privately Held**
WEB: www.ballyribbon.com
SIC: 2241 Manmade fiber narrow woven fabrics; fabric tapes; webbing, woven; ribbons

(G-901)
BALLY RIBBON MILLS
23 N 7th St (19503-9638)
P.O. Box D (19503-1004)
PHONE.................................610 845-2211
EMP: 50
SALES (corp-wide): 73.9MM **Privately Held**
WEB: www.ballyribbon.com
SIC: 2241 Narrow fabric mills
PA: Bally Ribbon Mills
　23 N 7th St
　Bally PA 19503
　610 845-2211

(G-902)
BALLY RIBBON MILLS
24 N 7th St (19503-9638)
PHONE.................................610 845-2211
Herbert D Harris III, *Branch Mgr*
EMP: 50

SALES (corp-wide): 73.9MM **Privately Held**
WEB: www.ballyribbon.com
SIC: 2241 Manmade fiber narrow woven fabrics; fabric tapes; webbing, woven; ribbons
PA: Bally Ribbon Mills
　23 N 7th St
　Bally PA 19503
　610 845-2211

(G-903)
GREAT AMERICAN WEAVING CORP
20 N Front St Ste 3 (19503-9605)
PHONE.................................610 845-9200
Michael McAllister, *President*
EMP: 12
SQ FT: 12,000
SALES (est): 3.2MM **Privately Held**
WEB: www.greatamericanweaving.com
SIC: 5131 2299 Textiles, woven; narrow woven fabrics: linen, jute, hemp & ramie

(G-904)
HUNSINGER PLASTICS
20 N Front St (19503-9605)
PHONE.................................610 845-9111
Anthony J Madison, *President*
EMP: 4
SALES (est): 334.9K **Privately Held**
SIC: 3089 Plastic processing

(G-905)
P E H INC
20 N Front St (19503-9605)
PHONE.................................610 845-9111
Anthony J Madison, *President*
Annette Madison, *Shareholder*
EMP: 10 EST: 1972
SQ FT: 24,000
SALES (est): 940K **Privately Held**
WEB: www.hunsinger.com
SIC: 3089 Plastic hardware & building products

(G-906)
PB HEAT LLC (HQ)
131 S Church St (19503-9672)
P.O. Box 280 (19503-0280)
PHONE.................................610 845-6100
Doug Shuff, *President*
Pete Morgan, *Exec VP*
Gary Hainley, *Vice Pres*
Barry Walsh, *Vice Pres*
Dave Fuller, *Controller*
▲ **EMP:** 47
SQ FT: 35,000
SALES (est): 8.3MM
SALES (corp-wide): 1.8B **Privately Held**
SIC: 3443 Autoclaves, industrial
PA: Noritz Corporation
　93, Edomachi, Chuo-Ku
　Kobe HYO 650-0
　783 913-361

(G-907)
TANCREDI MACHINING INC
20 N Front St Ste 9 (19503-9605)
P.O. Box 165 (19503-0165)
PHONE.................................215 679-8985
Dave Tancredi, *President*
EMP: 3
SQ FT: 4,000
SALES (est): 156.6K **Privately Held**
WEB: www.tancredimachining.com
SIC: 3599 Machine shop, jobbing & repair

Bangor
Northampton County

(G-908)
BIOSPECTRA INC
100 Majestic Way (18013-2860)
PHONE.................................610 599-3400
Richard Mutchler, *President*
EMP: 35 **Privately Held**
SIC: 2836 Biological products, except diagnostic
PA: Biospectra, Inc.
　1474 Rockdale Ln
　Stroudsburg PA 18360

(G-909)
CAPOZZOLO BROTHERS
1342 Ridge Rd (18013-5425)
PHONE.................................610 588-7702
Charles Capozzollo, *Partner*
John Capozzollo, *Partner*
James Capozzollo, *Partner*
EMP: 3
SALES (est): 268.7K **Privately Held**
WEB: www.capozzoloslate.com
SIC: 1429 0241 Slate, crushed & broken-quarrying; dairy farms

(G-910)
CRAIG R WICKETT
190 Washington Blvd (18013-2742)
PHONE.................................610 599-6882
Craig R Wickett, *Principal*
EMP: 3
SALES (est): 241.1K **Privately Held**
SIC: 2851 Removers & cleaners

(G-911)
D GILLETTE INDUS SVCS INC
46 N Main St (18013-1913)
PHONE.................................610 588-4939
D Gillette-Spencer, *President*
Dorothea Gillette-Spencer, *President*
EMP: 10
SQ FT: 7,000
SALES (est): 1MM **Privately Held**
SIC: 3599 Machine shop, jobbing & repair

(G-912)
DESHLERS MACHINE INC (PA)
120 N Main St (18013-1937)
PHONE.................................610 588-5622
David Deshler, *President*
Pauline Deshler, *Corp Secy*
EMP: 9 EST: 1930
SQ FT: 1,500
SALES (est): 1.7MM **Privately Held**
SIC: 3599 1711 Machine shop, jobbing & repair; mechanical contractor

(G-913)
FIVE STAR ASSOCIATES INC
1 Blue Valley Dr (18013-1501)
PHONE.................................610 588-7426
Scott Phelan, *President*
Eileen Phelan, *Vice Pres*
EMP: 10 EST: 2000
SQ FT: 4,500
SALES (est): 1.2MM **Privately Held**
WEB: www.fivestarassoc.com
SIC: 3699 8711 Electronic training devices; engineering services

(G-914)
FRANKLIN HILL VINEYARDS INC (PA)
7833 Franklin Hill Rd (18013-4039)
PHONE.................................610 588-8708
Elaine Tivinski, *President*
EMP: 2
SALES (est): 1.7MM **Privately Held**
WEB: www.franklinhillvineyards.com
SIC: 2084 0762 Wines; vineyard management & maintenance services

(G-915)
GENERAL MEDICAL MFG LLC
519 Pennsylvania Ave (18013-1841)
PHONE.................................610 599-0961
Christine Shirley, *Manager*
Heinz Bayer,
EMP: 6 EST: 2006
SALES (est): 1MM **Privately Held**
SIC: 2392 Dishcloths, nonwoven textile: made from purchased materials

(G-916)
HOPE UNIFORM CO INC
Also Called: Hope Uniform & Security Pdts
201 Roseto Ave (18013-1407)
PHONE.................................908 496-4899
Gus Belverio, *President*
Fred Belverio, *Treasurer*
EMP: 25
SQ FT: 2,500

SALES (est): 3.1MM **Privately Held**
WEB: www.hopeuniform.com
SIC: **2311** 2326 Policemen's uniforms: made from purchased materials; firemen's uniforms: made from purchased materials; men's & boys' work clothing

(G-917)
K & C MACHINING COMPANY INC
2132 Lake Minsi Dr (18013-5410)
PHONE..................................610 588-6749
Randy Nystrand, *President*
EMP: 12
SALES: 1MM **Privately Held**
SIC: **3599** Machine shop, jobbing & repair

(G-918)
KAISER MULCH
6 Flicksville Rd (18013-2706)
PHONE..................................610 588-8111
Donald Kaiser, *Owner*
Donald Keyser, *Vice Pres*
EMP: 3
SQ FT: 7,200
SALES (est): 180K **Privately Held**
SIC: **2499** Mulch, wood & bark

(G-919)
KB SYSTEMS INC
90 Jacktown Rd (18013-9504)
P.O. Box 229 (18013-0229)
PHONE..................................610 588-7788
Mark Rosenberg, *CEO*
Ken Johnson, *President*
▲ EMP: 53
SQ FT: 18,000
SALES: 10MM **Privately Held**
SIC: **3556** Bakery machinery; flour mill machinery

(G-920)
KIEFER PALLET
9766 N Delaware Dr (18013-4412)
PHONE..................................610 599-0971
Tammy Kiefer, *Principal*
EMP: 8
SALES (est): 1MM **Privately Held**
SIC: **2448** Pallets, wood

(G-921)
MERRY MAID INC
25 W Messinger Street Ext (18013-2046)
P.O. Box 228 (18013-0228)
PHONE..................................800 360-3836
Marilyn Rettaliata, *President*
Stephen Rettaliata, *Treasurer*
EMP: 20
SQ FT: 50,000
SALES (est): 543.4K **Privately Held**
WEB: www.specialeventsonline.com
SIC: **7349** 7299 2339 Maid services, contract or fee basis; party planning service; women's & misses' outerwear

(G-922)
MERRY MAID NOVELTIES
25 W Messinger Street Ext (18013-2046)
P.O. Box 228 (18013-0228)
PHONE..................................610 599-4104
Michael Ruggiero, *Partner*
Maria C Ruggiero, *Partner*
EMP: 10
SQ FT: 50,000
SALES (est): 840K **Privately Held**
SIC: **2253** 6512 Knit outerwear mills; commercial & industrial building operation

(G-923)
OWENS MONUMENTAL COMPANY
245 S 1st St (18013-2617)
PHONE..................................610 588-3370
T Keith Jones, *President*
Brian Jones, *Vice Pres*
EMP: 5 EST: 1934
SQ FT: 1,200
SALES (est): 500K **Privately Held**
SIC: **3281** Monuments, cut stone (not finishing or lettering only); tombstones, cut stone (not finishing or lettering only)

(G-924)
PERFORMNCE CTNGS INTL LABS LLC
Also Called: PCI Labs
600 Murray St (18013-2800)
PHONE..................................610 588-7900
Colleen Heiser, *Office Mgr*
George E Drazinaki, *Mng Member*
EMP: 15 EST: 2010
SQ FT: 25,000
SALES: 2MM **Privately Held**
WEB: www.pcoatingsintl.com
SIC: **2295** Resin or plastic coated fabrics

(G-925)
RASLEY ENTERPRISE
905 Lower South Main St (18013-2833)
PHONE..................................610 588-9520
Brian Rasley, *Owner*
EMP: 3 EST: 1992
SALES (est): 345.3K **Privately Held**
SIC: **3599** Machine shop, jobbing & repair

(G-926)
REPUBLIC LENS CO INC
1683 Valley View Dr (18013-6101)
PHONE..................................610 588-7867
William Lurie, *President*
EMP: 10 EST: 1939
SQ FT: 12,500
SALES: 1MM **Privately Held**
SIC: **3827** Optical instruments & apparatus

(G-927)
SLATE BELT WOODWORKERS INC
729 1/2 S Main St (18013-2829)
PHONE..................................610 588-1922
Ronald Erney Sr, *President*
Nancy M Erney, *Treasurer*
EMP: 5
SQ FT: 8,000
SALES (est): 843.8K **Privately Held**
SIC: **2431** Staircases, stairs & railings; moldings & baseboards, ornamental & trim; doors & door parts & trim, wood

(G-928)
SMITHS WILBERT VAULT COMPANY (PA)
Also Called: Bangor Concrete
8 Wildon Dr (18013-5250)
P.O. Box 9 (18013-0009)
PHONE..................................610 588-5259
Larry Bruen, *President*
Randy L Sandt, *Vice Pres*
Michael Herkalo, *Plant Mgr*
Marsha Bruen, *Treasurer*
Lisa E Sandt, *Admin Sec*
EMP: 28 EST: 1951
SALES (est): 3.8MM **Privately Held**
WEB: www.smithwilbert.com
SIC: **3272** 5087 3995 Burial vaults, concrete or precast terrazzo; caskets; burial caskets

(G-929)
SMITHS WILBERT VAULT COMPANY
Also Called: Smith Wilbert Vault Co
882 Lower South Main St (18013-2856)
P.O. Box 9 (18013-0009)
PHONE..................................610 588-5259
Randy Sandt, *Manager*
EMP: 14
SALES (corp-wide): 3.8MM **Privately Held**
WEB: www.smithwilbert.com
SIC: **3499** Safes & vaults, metal
PA: Wilbert Smith's Vault Company
8 Wildon Dr
Bangor PA 18013
610 588-5259

(G-930)
STATE OF ARC WLDG & FABG LLC (PA)
800 Rutt Rd (18013-9649)
PHONE..................................610 216-6862
Michael Baird,
EMP: 5
SQ FT: 5,000

SALES: 580K **Privately Held**
SIC: **3599** 3441 7692 Machine shop, jobbing & repair; fabricated structural metal; welding repair

(G-931)
TOLINO VINEYARDS LLC (PA)
Also Called: Tolino Vineyards Bangor
280 Mount Pleasant Rd (18013-9244)
PHONE..................................610 588-9463
Liz Tolino, *Social Dir*
Carl Tolino,
EMP: 3
SALES (est): 305.8K **Privately Held**
SIC: **2084** Wines

(G-932)
VAN VARICK INC
530 S Main St (18013-2810)
PHONE..................................610 588-9997
Pat Van Varick, *President*
Kendra Van Varick, *Admin Sec*
EMP: 6
SQ FT: 8,900
SALES: 1MM **Privately Held**
SIC: **3449** Miscellaneous metalwork

(G-933)
VICOR TECHNOLOGIES INC
399 Autumn Dr (18013-5543)
PHONE..................................570 897-5797
James E Skinner PHD, *Ch of Bd*
Gary A Schwartz, *CTO*
Daniel N Weiss MD Facc, *Officer*
EMP: 16
SALES (est): 189K **Privately Held**
WEB: www.vicortech.com
SIC: **3841** Surgical And Medical Instruments & Apparatus

(G-934)
WINDJAMMER CORPORATION INC (PA)
525 N Main St (18013-1989)
PHONE..................................610 588-0626
Anthony J Capozzolo, *President*
Michele J Taylor, *Corp Secy*
Joseph H Capozzolo, *Vice Pres*
EMP: 15
SQ FT: 24,000
SALES (est): 7.7MM **Privately Held**
SIC: **2329** Windbreakers: men's, youths' & boys'; athletic (warmup, sweat & jogging) suits: men's & boys'

(G-935)
WINDJAMMER CORPORATION INC
Also Called: Universal
Quarry Rd (18013)
PHONE..................................610 588-0626
Anthony Capozzolo, *Owner*
EMP: 20
SALES (corp-wide): 7.7MM **Privately Held**
SIC: **2329** 2321 2325 5136 Windbreakers: men's, youths' & boys'; athletic (warmup, sweat & jogging) suits: men's & boys'; sport shirts, men's & boys': from purchased materials; shorts (outerwear): men's, youths' & boys'; sportswear, men's & boys'; hats, men's & boys'
PA: Windjammer Corporation, Inc.
525 N Main St
Bangor PA 18013
610 588-0626

(G-936)
WINDJAMMER CORPORATION INC
519 Pnnsylvnia Ave Fl 1 Flr 1 (18013)
PHONE..................................610 588-2137
John Cannavo, *Manager*
EMP: 3
SALES (corp-wide): 7.7MM **Privately Held**
SIC: **2329** 2321 2325 5136 Windbreakers: men's, youths' & boys'; athletic (warmup, sweat & jogging) suits: men's & boys'; sport shirts, men's & boys': from purchased materials; shorts (outerwear): men's, youths' & boys'; sportswear, men's & boys'; hats, men's & boys'

PA: Windjammer Corporation, Inc.
525 N Main St
Bangor PA 18013
610 588-0626

Barnesboro
Cambria County

(G-937)
AFCO ENERGY PRODUCTION CO INC
857 Cameron Bottom Rd (15714)
P.O. Box 538, Indiana (15701-0538)
PHONE..................................724 463-3350
James Carino, *President*
Laura Carino, *Manager*
EMP: 3
SQ FT: 40,000
SALES (est): 244.7K **Privately Held**
SIC: **1311** Crude petroleum & natural gas

(G-938)
BUTERBAUGH BROS LAND & TIMBER
835 Shawna Rd Ste 2 (15714-8605)
P.O. Box 245, Cherry Tree (15724-0245)
PHONE..................................814 948-9510
William Buterbaugh, *President*
Cindy Sensabaugh, *Treasurer*
EMP: 3 EST: 1920
SQ FT: 1,000
SALES (est): 299.6K **Privately Held**
SIC: **2421** Lumber: rough, sawed or planed

(G-939)
D L ENTERPRISE INC
333 Main St (15714-7506)
PHONE..................................814 948-6060
Dallas Leamer, *President*
EMP: 4
SALES: 200K **Privately Held**
SIC: **1241** Coal mining services

Barnesville
Schuylkill County

(G-940)
ROLAND LYNAGH ASSOCIATES LLC
Also Called: TNT
830 Barnesville Dr (18214-2016)
P.O. Box 68 (18214-0068)
PHONE..................................570 467-2528
James Haddad, *Editor*
Adrienne Haddad, *Mng Member*
EMP: 8
SALES (est): 1.1MM **Privately Held**
WEB: www.truckntrailer.com
SIC: **2721** Trade journals: publishing only, not printed on site

---

Barto
Berks County

(G-941)
CWI INC
Also Called: C W I
1827 County Line Rd (19504-8713)
PHONE..................................610 652-2211
Keith Menser, *President*
Gregory Scott, *Vice Pres*
EMP: 36
SALES (est): 10.4MM **Privately Held**
SIC: **3531** 4789 Railroad related equipment; railroad maintenance & repair services

(G-942)
EXCEL-PRO
11 Mountain Rd (19504-8954)
PHONE..................................610 845-9752
Jane Benning, *President*
EMP: 3 EST: 2001
SALES: 300K **Privately Held**
SIC: **3679** 7539 Harness assemblies for electronic use: wire or cable; electrical services

GEOGRAPHIC

(G-943)
GRAPHIC PRINT SOLUTIONS L
1892 County Line Rd (19504-8714)
P.O. Box 116 (19504-0116)
PHONE...................................610 845-0280
W T Lees, *CEO*
EMP: 3 **EST:** 1999
SALES (est): 432K **Privately Held**
WEB: www.graphicprintsolutionsltd.com
SIC: 2752 Commercial printing, offset

(G-944)
JACK MURRAY DESIGN
20 Birch Dr (19504-9120)
PHONE...................................610 845-9154
Jack Murray, *Owner*
EMP: 3
SQ FT: 1,456
SALES (est): 261K **Privately Held**
SIC: 3993 Signs & advertising specialties

(G-945)
LONGACRES MODERN DAIRY INC
1445 Rte 100 (19504)
PHONE...................................610 845-7551
Daniel T Longacre, *President*
Timothy Longacre, *Partner*
Newton T Longacre, *Vice Pres*
Kathryn Longacre, *Executive*
Kathryn T Longacre, *Admin Sec*
EMP: 20 **EST:** 1920
SQ FT: 14,000
SALES (est): 2.9MM **Privately Held**
WEB: www.longacresicecream.com
SIC: 2026 Milk processing (pasteurizing, homogenizing, bottling)

Bartonsville
Monroe County

(G-946)
HOWANITZ ASSOCIATES INC
Also Called: American Candle
3414 Route 611 (18321-7814)
PHONE...................................570 629-3388
Stephen E Howanitz, *Owner*
Patty Howanitz, *Admin Sec*
▼ **EMP:** 45
SQ FT: 100,000
SALES (est): 4MM **Privately Held**
WEB: www.american-candle.com
SIC: 3999 5999 5947 Candles; candle shops; gift shop

(G-947)
JD PRODUCT SOLUTIONS LLC
Also Called: Jd's Carribean Spice
3115 Route 611 (18321)
PHONE...................................570 234-9421
Jean Dennis, *Mng Member*
EMP: 4
SQ FT: 1,050
SALES (est): 2MM **Privately Held**
SIC: 5047 3556 Hospital equipment & supplies; dehydrating equipment, food processing

(G-948)
POCONO HYDRPONIC SOLUTIONS LLC
3280 Route 611 (18321-7826)
PHONE...................................570 730-4544
Jerry Napolitano, *Mng Member*
EMP: 3 **EST:** 2010
SALES (est): 201.1K **Privately Held**
SIC: 3999 Hydroponic equipment

Bath
Northampton County

(G-949)
ADVANCED MACHINE SYSTEMS INC
Also Called: Wheel Collision Center
7286 Penn Dr (18014-8512)
PHONE...................................610 837-8677
Daryl L Robbins, *President*
George J Herschman, *Vice Pres*
Joanne Kratochvil, *Office Mgr*

▼ **EMP:** 17
SQ FT: 4,500
SALES (est): 2.1MM **Privately Held**
WEB: www.wheelcollision.com
SIC: 7699 3565 Wheel & caster repair; packaging machinery

(G-950)
AMERICAN TOOL MFG LLC
280 Smith Rd (18014-9500)
PHONE...................................610 837-8573
John Vallance, *Mng Member*
William Vallance,
▲ **EMP:** 5
SQ FT: 12,000
SALES: 750K **Privately Held**
SIC: 3569 Filters

(G-951)
ASSOCIATED FASTENERS INC
6854 Chrisphalt Dr (18014-8503)
PHONE...................................610 837-9200
David M Lack, *President*
Tom Dieter, *Vice Pres*
Deborah D Lack, *Vice Pres*
EMP: 12
SQ FT: 14,000
SALES (est): 6.7MM **Privately Held**
WEB: www.associatedfasteners.com
SIC: 5072 3452 Miscellaneous fasteners; bolts, nuts, rivets & washers

(G-952)
BLUE MOUNTAIN WOODWORKING
2413 Community Dr (18014-8840)
PHONE...................................610 746-2588
Richard Knecht, *President*
Deborah Knecht, *Corp Secy*
EMP: 23
SQ FT: 16,000
SALES (est): 2.8MM **Privately Held**
SIC: 2434 Wood kitchen cabinets

(G-953)
C & G PALLET COMPANY INC
1000 Deemer Rd (18014-9761)
PHONE...................................610 759-5625
Devatt Christopher, *President*
EMP: 3 **EST:** 2010
SALES (est): 200.1K **Privately Held**
SIC: 2448 Pallets, wood

(G-954)
COMMERCIAL METAL POLISHING
369 Moorestown Dr (18014-9708)
PHONE...................................610 837-0267
Herb Schmoyer, *President*
Diane Schmoyer, *CFO*
EMP: 10
SQ FT: 10,000
SALES: 1MM **Privately Held**
SIC: 3541 3471 3479 Grinding machines, metalworking; polishing, metals or formed products; painting of metal products

(G-955)
COPIERS INC
102 W Northampton St Frnt (18014-1147)
PHONE...................................610 837-7400
Stephen Nikles, *President*
EMP: 5
SALES (est): 543K **Privately Held**
WEB: www.copiersinc.com
SIC: 7334 5045 3577 Photocopying & duplicating services; computers; printers, computer

(G-956)
CORBAN CORPORATION
Also Called: Encor Coatings
Rr 248 (18014)
PHONE...................................610 837-9700
Edward G Gleason, *CEO*
EMP: 85
SQ FT: 100,000
SALES (est): 11.9MM **Privately Held**
SIC: 2851 Epoxy coatings

(G-957)
EFFORT ENTERPRISES INC
6982 Chrisphalt Dr (18014-8505)
PHONE...................................610 837-7003
Hamburg Charles, *President*

EMP: 4
SQ FT: 5,000
SALES (est): 430.2K **Privately Held**
SIC: 3543 3544 Industrial patterns; special dies, tools, jigs & fixtures

(G-958)
EFFORT FOUNDRY INC
6980 Chrisphalt Dr (18014-8505)
P.O. Box 158 (18014-0158)
PHONE...................................610 837-1837
William C Easterly, *President*
Charles D Hamburg, *Treasurer*
Jane Cory, *Admin Sec*
EMP: 75
SQ FT: 34,000
SALES (est): 23.2MM **Privately Held**
WEB: www.effortfoundry.com
SIC: 3325 Steel foundries

(G-959)
FLEXIBLE COMPENSATORS INC
Also Called: Flex Com
6864 Chrisphalt Dr (18014-8503)
PHONE...................................610 837-3812
James T Wall, *President*
EMP: 15
SQ FT: 10,000
SALES (est): 3.1MM **Privately Held**
WEB: www.flexcomonline.com
SIC: 3494 Expansion joints pipe

(G-960)
HUNLOCK SAND & GRAVEL COMPANY
2437 Southmoore Dr (18014-9293)
PHONE...................................570 256-3036
Judith A Rampp, *President*
EMP: 16
SQ FT: 6,000
SALES (est): 1.6MM **Privately Held**
SIC: 1442 3273 Sand mining; ready-mixed concrete

(G-961)
KEY INGREDIENT MARKET LLC
7289 Park Dr (18014-8854)
PHONE...................................484 281-3900
EMP: 5
SALES (est): 455.4K **Privately Held**
SIC: 2022 Cheese spreads, dips, pastes & other cheese products

(G-962)
KEYSTONE CEMENT COMPANY
6507 N Bath Blvd (18014)
P.O. Box A (18014-0058)
PHONE...................................610 837-1881
Jose A Llontop, *President*
Robert K Aichele, *Vice Pres*
William Biddix, *Vice Pres*
Gerry Geier, *Vice Pres*
John Von Tress, *Vice Pres*
▲ **EMP:** 121 **EST:** 1926
SQ FT: 6,000
SALES (est): 30.8MM **Privately Held**
WEB: www.keystone-cement.com
SIC: 3241 Portland cement; masonry cement
HQ: Giant Cement Holding, Inc.
  396 W Greens Rd Ste 300
  Houston TX 77067

(G-963)
L & M FABRICATION AND MCH INC
6814 Chrisphalt Dr (18014-8503)
P.O. Box 124 (18014-0124)
PHONE...................................610 837-1848
Bruce Lack, *President*
Robert M Cesanek Jr, *General Mgr*
Keith Ashner, *Vice Pres*
Tracey Vanderstad, *Purch Mgr*
Donald Willauer, *Engineer*
EMP: 80 **EST:** 1967
SQ FT: 50,000
SALES (est): 30.8MM **Privately Held**
WEB: www.lmfab.com
SIC: 3443 3444 3441 Industrial vessels, tanks & containers; heat exchangers, condensers & components; boiler & boiler shop work; liners/lining; sheet metalwork; building components, structural steel

(G-964)
LEHIGH GASKET INC
7709 Beth Bath Pike (18014-8972)
P.O. Box 20006, Lehigh Valley (18002-0006)
PHONE...................................610 837-1818
Robert Dressler, *President*
▲ **EMP:** 15 **EST:** 1983
SALES (est): 1.8MM **Privately Held**
SIC: 3053 Gaskets, all materials

(G-965)
LINCOLN TEXTILE PDTS CO INC
Also Called: Kensington Home Fashions
900 Conroy Pl (18014)
PHONE...................................484 281-3999
Michael A Mitch, *President*
Kenneth Anderson, *Chairman*
Phil Anderson, *Vice Pres*
▲ **EMP:** 100 **EST:** 1946
SQ FT: 90,000
SALES (est): 17.4MM **Privately Held**
WEB: www.lincolntextile.com
SIC: 2392 2391 Bedspreads & bed sets: made from purchased materials; comforters & quilts: made from purchased materials; blankets, comforters & beddings; curtains, window: made from purchased materials; draperies, plastic & textile: from purchased materials

(G-966)
MC IRON WORKS INC
Also Called: Michalman Cancelliere Ir Works
7230 Beth Tach Pike (18014)
P.O. Box 20431, Lehigh Valley (18002-0431)
PHONE...................................610 837-9444
EMP: 80
SALES (est): 20.9K **Privately Held**
SIC: 3441 Structural Metal Fabrication

(G-967)
MICHELMN-CNCLLERE IRNWORKS INC
Also Called: Mc Ironworks
7230 Beth Bath Pike (18014)
PHONE...................................610 837-9914
John Cancelliere, *CEO*
Lionel Michelman, *Vice Pres*
Donald C Smith, *Treasurer*
EMP: 110
SQ FT: 110,000
SALES (est): 27.4MM **Privately Held**
WEB: www.mcironworks.com
SIC: 3441 Fabricated structural metal

(G-968)
PENLIN FABRICATORS LLC
335 Moorestown Dr (18014-9766)
PHONE...................................610 837-6667
EMP: 3
SALES (est): 400.5K **Privately Held**
SIC: 2295 Coated fabrics, not rubberized

(G-969)
STARRHOCK SILICONES INC
6854b Chrisphalt Dr (18014-8503)
P.O. Box 97 (18014-0097)
PHONE...................................610 837-4883
Jeffrey A Miner, *President*
EMP: 15
SALES (est): 860K **Privately Held**
SIC: 3069 Rubber hardware

(G-970)
STAVER HYDRAULICS CO INC
Also Called: Lehigh Gasket
7709 Beth Bath Pike (18014-8972)
P.O. Box 20006, Lehigh Valley (18002-0006)
PHONE...................................610 837-1818
Robert Dressler, *President*
EMP: 8
SALES (corp-wide): 12.1MM **Privately Held**
WEB: www.staverhydraulics.com
SIC: 3053 3494 3429 Gaskets, all materials; valves & pipe fittings; manufactured hardware (general)
PA: Staver Hydraulics Co., Inc.
  2371 Elmira St
  Sayre PA 18840
  570 888-5829

▲ = Import ▼ =Export
◆ =Import/Export

(G-971)
SUNS MANUFACTURING INC (PA)
8318 Airport Rd (18014-9088)
PHONE..................................610 837-0798
Kathy Diodoardo, *President*
Roberto Diodoardo, *Vice Pres*
EMP: 30
SALES (est): 3MM **Privately Held**
SIC: 2326 Men's & boys' work clothing

(G-972)
T/A REBORN PALLETS
428 Grouse Dr (18014-9133)
PHONE..................................484 841-3085
Edward Mathis, *CEO*
EMP: 3
SALES (est): 131.9K **Privately Held**
SIC: 2448 Pallets, wood

(G-973)
WORKTASK MEDIA INC
7511 Richard Ln (18014-8910)
PHONE..................................610 762-9014
Joseph Angelitis, *CEO*
Mike Rinkunas, *Vice Pres*
Lisa Ann Angeltis, *Admin Sec*
EMP: 4
SALES: 60K **Privately Held**
SIC: 7372 Educational computer software

Beach Lake
Wayne County

(G-974)
LB WOODWORKING LLC
621 River Rd (18405-4043)
PHONE..................................570 729-0000
Larry Braverman, *Principal*
EMP: 4 **EST:** 2009
SALES (est): 240K **Privately Held**
SIC: 2431 Millwork

(G-975)
MARK CASE LOGGING
108 Logger Rd (18405-8424)
PHONE..................................570 729-8856
Mark R Case, *Principal*
EMP: 3 **EST:** 2012
SALES (est): 172.7K **Privately Held**
SIC: 2411 Logging camps & contractors

(G-976)
W J REINING & SONS INC
Also Called: Reining Force Products
1257 Beach Lake Hwy (18405-3015)
P.O. Box 277 (18405-0277)
PHONE..................................570 729-7325
David Reining, *President*
EMP: 12
SALES (est): 2.2MM **Privately Held**
SIC: 2421 Lumber: rough, sawed or planed

Beaver
Beaver County

(G-977)
ADVANTECH US INC
333 4th St (15009-2309)
PHONE..................................412 706-5400
Whitten E Little, *President*
Blake Brocato, *Vice Pres*
Scott Lauer, *Vice Pres*
◆ **EMP:** 20
SQ FT: 10,000
SALES (est): 3.1MM **Privately Held**
SIC: 2396 Printing & embossing on plastics fabric articles

(G-978)
B WS PIZZA
4790 Tuscarawas Rd (15009-9102)
PHONE..................................724 495-2898
Barbara Worell, *Owner*
EMP: 6
SALES (est): 250K **Privately Held**
SIC: 2038 Pizza, frozen

(G-979)
BEAVER NEWSPAPERS INC
Also Called: Ellwood City Ledger
400 Fair Ave (15009-1958)
PHONE..................................724 775-3200
Mark Contreras, *President*
Michael White, *Treasurer*
Wesley Ellis, *Admin Sec*
EMP: 325
SQ FT: 45,000
SALES (est): 48.9MM
SALES (corp-wide): 1.5B **Publicly Held**
WEB: www.timesonline.com
SIC: 2711 Newspapers, publishing & printing
PA: New Media Investment Group Inc.
1345 Avenue Of The Americ
New York NY 10105
212 479-3160

(G-980)
EATON CORPORATION
1 Tuscarawas Rd (15009-1720)
PHONE..................................724 773-1231
Mike Flannery, *Electrical Engi*
William Schmidt, *Manager*
Deborah Mort, *Fellow*
EMP: 400 **Privately Held**
WEB: www.eaton.com
SIC: 3613 3823 3643 3625 Switchgear & switchboard apparatus; industrial instrmnts msrmnt display/control process variable; current-carrying wiring devices; relays & industrial controls; transformers, except electric
HQ: Eaton Corporation
1000 Eaton Blvd
Cleveland OH 44122
440 523-5000

(G-981)
ESMARK EXCALIBUR LLC
Also Called: Excalbur Mch Fbrction - Vnport
658 State Ave (15009-9501)
PHONE..................................724 371-3059
John Kelman, *Branch Mgr*
EMP: 37
SALES (corp-wide): 249.1MM **Privately Held**
SIC: 3441 Fabricated structural metal
HQ: Esmark Excalibur, Llc
9723 Us Highway 322
Conneaut Lake PA 16316

(G-982)
GOLD BUG EXCHANGE
474 3rd St (15009-2227)
PHONE..................................724 770-9008
Tim Snyder, *Managing Prtnr*
EMP: 3 **EST:** 2012
SALES (est): 396.1K **Privately Held**
SIC: 5094 3339 Precious metals; precious metals

(G-983)
HAMILTON AWNING CO
488 Buffalo St (15009-2004)
PHONE..................................724 774-7644
David Mulcahy, *Owner*
EMP: 12
SQ FT: 6,400
SALES (est): 858K **Privately Held**
SIC: 2394 5999 2591 2393 Awnings, fabric: made from purchased materials; canvas products; drapery hardware & blinds & shades; textile bags; curtains & draperies

(G-984)
IDLEWOOD INDUSTRIES INC
17 Georgetown Ln (15009-1719)
PHONE..................................724 624-1499
Edwin Kwiat, *President*
EMP: 8
SALES (est): 710K **Privately Held**
SIC: 3999 Barber & beauty shop equipment

(G-985)
INTERSTATE CHEMICAL CO INC
725 Riverside Dr (15009-3058)
PHONE..................................724 774-1669
Bill Karks, *Manager*
EMP: 4

SALES (corp-wide): 338.6MM **Privately Held**
WEB: www.interstatechemical.com
SIC: 5169 2819 Industrial chemicals; industrial inorganic chemicals
PA: Interstate Chemical Company, Inc.
2797 Freedland Rd
Hermitage PA 16148
724 981-3771

(G-986)
KRETCHMAR BAKERY INC
664 3rd St (15009-2116)
PHONE..................................724 774-2324
Henry Kretchmar Jr, *Owner*
Mary Lea Kretchmar, *Corp Secy*
Desiree Kretchmar, *Manager*
EMP: 30
SQ FT: 4,000
SALES (est): 1.3MM **Privately Held**
WEB: www.kbakery.com
SIC: 5461 2052 2051 Cakes; cookies & crackers; bread, cake & related products

(G-987)
MSF MANAGEMENT LLC
685 State Ave (15009-9502)
PHONE..................................724 371-3059
Ken Tamburrino,
▲ **EMP:** 45 **EST:** 2008
SQ FT: 65,000
SALES (est): 4.5MM
SALES (corp-wide): 70.7B **Privately Held**
WEB: www.kma-usa.com
SIC: 8711 3443 Engineering services; annealing boxes, pots, or covers
HQ: Marubeni America Corporation
375 Lexington Ave
New York NY 10017
212 450-0100

(G-988)
NEO-SOLUTIONS INC
1340 Brighton Rd (15009-9238)
P.O. Box 26 (15009-0026)
PHONE..................................724 728-7360
Gerald W Groff, *President*
James Carlson, *Vice Pres*
Sherry Neal, *Personnel*
Jim Herceg, *Sales Mgr*
Tom Croup, *Sales Staff*
EMP: 27
SALES (est): 7.5MM **Privately Held**
WEB: www.neosolutionsinc.com
SIC: 2843 2869 2819 Surface active agents; emulsifiers, except food & pharmaceutical; industrial organic chemicals; aluminum sulfate

(G-989)
PHILLY ORIGINALS
478 3rd St (15009-2227)
PHONE..................................724 728-3011
Mitch Green, *President*
EMP: 7
SALES (est): 380K **Privately Held**
SIC: 2051 Cakes, bakery: except frozen

(G-990)
ROMANS PRECISION MACHINING
327 S Walnut Ln (15009-1700)
PHONE..................................724 774-6444
Al Roman, *President*
Bill Gaguzis, *Supervisor*
EMP: 8
SQ FT: 3,000
SALES (est): 589.3K **Privately Held**
SIC: 3599 Machine shop, jobbing & repair

(G-991)
ROPRO DESIGN INC
530 Bradys Ridge Rd (15009-9210)
PHONE..................................724 630-1976
Raymond Russell, *CEO*
Ray Russell, *Principal*
Russell Dryer, *Education*
◆ **EMP:** 3
SALES: 214K **Privately Held**
WEB: www.roprodesign.com
SIC: 3535 Robotic conveyors

(G-992)
T HELBLING LLC
119 Highlandwood Dr (15009-9092)
PHONE..................................724 601-9819

Thomas Helbling, *Mng Member*
EMP: 6
SALES: 6.5MM **Privately Held**
SIC: 3255 3363 3317 1771 Clay refractories; aluminum die-castings; steel pipe & tubes; concrete pumping

(G-993)
TRI-STATE RIVER PRODUCTS INC
334 Insurance St (15009-2126)
PHONE..................................724 775-2221
Thomas J Bryan III, *President*
▲ **EMP:** 10
SALES (est): 1.1MM
SALES (corp-wide): 17.5MM **Privately Held**
SIC: 1442 Construction sand & gravel
PA: Frank Bryan, Inc.
1263 Chartiers Ave
Mc Kees Rocks PA 15136
412 331-1630

(G-994)
TWO RIVERS OLIVES OIL COMPANY
428 3rd St (15009-2227)
PHONE..................................724 775-2748
EMP: 3
SALES (est): 91.3K **Privately Held**
SIC: 2079 Olive oil

(G-995)
WEEKEND DIRECTIONAL SERVICES
22 Georgetown Ln A (15009-1719)
PHONE..................................800 494-4954
Charles Castleforte, *President*
EMP: 66 **EST:** 1999
SQ FT: 5,000
SALES (est): 1MM **Privately Held**
SIC: 3993 Letters for signs, metal

Beaver Falls
Beaver County

(G-996)
AL KACZMARCZYK
Also Called: American Machining Fabrication
3185 Bennetts Run Rd (15010-5270)
PHONE..................................724 775-1366
Al Kaczmarczyk, *Owner*
EMP: 9
SQ FT: 6,800
SALES (est): 1MM **Privately Held**
SIC: 3599 3441 Machine shop, jobbing & repair; fabricated structural metal

(G-997)
BRIGHTON STEEL INC
Also Called: Brighton Electric Stl Cast Co
2900 7th Avenue Ext (15010-3703)
PHONE..................................724 846-7377
William I Snyder, *CEO*
John Barch, *Controller*
EMP: 20 **EST:** 2000
SALES (est): 2.6MM **Privately Held**
SIC: 3325 Alloy steel castings, except investment

(G-998)
CHIPPEWA TWP SEWAGE PLANT
701 Constitution Blvd (15010-1749)
PHONE..................................724 846-3820
Clair Young, *Manager*
EMP: 6
SALES (est): 590K **Privately Held**
SIC: 3589 Sewage & water treatment equipment

(G-999)
GESCO INC
Also Called: Grinding Engineering & Svcs Co
711 4th St (15010-4726)
PHONE..................................724 846-8700
John T Jasko, *President*
James Rimmel, *Vice Pres*
Jennifer Chinchilla, *CPA*
Shelly Gleason, *Admin Asst*
Michael Chinchilla, *Administration*
EMP: 15

GEOGRAPHIC

SQ FT: 17,000
SALES (est): 2MM **Privately Held**
WEB: www.gescoinc.net
SIC: 7389 3545 8711 3351 Grinding, precision: commercial or industrial; shear knives; consulting engineer; copper rolling & drawing

(G-1000)
INGENUWARE LTD
1610 6th Ave (15010-4007)
PHONE....................................724 843-3140
Robert Ryniak, *Partner*
EMP: 3
SALES (est): 165.2K **Privately Held**
WEB: www.ryniak.net
SIC: 7372 Prepackaged software

(G-1001)
IZZO EMBROIDERY & SCREEN PRTG
517 2nd Ave E (15010-4807)
PHONE....................................724 843-2334
Walter Izzo, *President*
Jodi McGaffick, *Principal*
EMP: 10
SALES: 390K **Privately Held**
WEB: www.izzoemb.com
SIC: 2759 Screen printing

(G-1002)
J A MITCH PRINTING & COPY CTR
Also Called: Ink Star
2243 Darlington Rd (15010-1364)
PHONE....................................724 847-2940
Richard Fudurich, *Owner*
EMP: 4 EST: 1973
SALES (est): 53.4K **Privately Held**
SIC: 2752 2721 Commercial printing, offset; magazines: publishing only, not printed on site

(G-1003)
KENSON PLASTICS INC
2835 Darlington Rd (15010-1027)
PHONE....................................724 776-6820
David Oleary, *President*
Christopher B Oleary, *Vice Pres*
David J Oleary, *VP Sales*
Elizabeth A Gahagan, *Admin Sec*
EMP: 22
SALES (est): 6.7MM **Privately Held**
WEB: www.kensonplastics.com
SIC: 3089 Injection molding of plastics; plastic processing

(G-1004)
MCDANEL ADVNCED CRMIC TECH LLC
510 9th Ave (15010-4700)
PHONE....................................724 843-8300
Mike Ingram, *CEO*
John Dodsworth, *Vice Pres*
W Lori Hoskisson, *VP Mfg*
Mark Hall, *Senior Engr*
Stefanie Cindric, *Human Res Mgr*
▲ EMP: 119 EST: 1919
SQ FT: 100,000
SALES (est): 21MM **Privately Held**
SIC: 3299 Sand lime products

(G-1005)
MINUTEMAN PRESS
920 7th Ave (15010-4542)
PHONE....................................724 846-9740
Jim Burke, *Owner*
EMP: 4
SQ FT: 3,200
SALES (est): 531.6K **Privately Held**
SIC: 2752 2791 2789 Commercial printing, offset; typesetting; bookbinding & related work

(G-1006)
MORGAN BROTHERS COMPANY
1401 10th Ave (15010-4100)
P.O. Box 208 (15010-0208)
PHONE....................................724 843-7485
Jeff Androlia, *President*
Joel Morris, *Corp Secy*
Adam Crepp, *Vice Pres*
EMP: 12
SQ FT: 85,000

SALES: 2.5MM **Privately Held**
WEB: www.morganbrothersonline.com
SIC: 3449 5172 Miscellaneous metalwork; petroleum products

(G-1007)
PRO ACTION INC (PA)
Also Called: Pro-Action Suspension
3611 8th Ave (15010-3430)
PHONE....................................724 846-9055
George Quay, *President*
Julie Quay, *Corp Secy*
Dj Korzen, *Vice Pres*
Wendy Robords, *Director*
Jean Keeney, *Receptionist*
EMP: 10 EST: 1977
SALES (est): 1.2MM **Privately Held**
WEB: www.proaction.biz
SIC: 3751 7699 5571 Motorcycles & related parts; motorcycle repair service; motorcycle parts & accessories

(G-1008)
PTC ALLIANCE CORP
Also Called: Beaver Falls Tubular Products
4400 W 3rd Ave (15010)
PHONE....................................724 847-7137
Peter Whiting, *President*
Joshua Marrara, *Human Res Mgr*
Chuck Mancuso, *Director*
EMP: 51
SALES (est): 2.8MM **Privately Held**
SIC: 3317 Tubing, mechanical or hypodermic sizes: cold drawn stainless

(G-1009)
PTC GROUP HOLDINGS CORP
4400 W 3rd Ave (15010)
PHONE....................................724 847-7137
Bill Bradley, *Branch Mgr*
EMP: 51 **Privately Held**
SIC: 3317 Tubing, mechanical or hypodermic sizes: cold drawn stainless
PA: Ptc Group Holdings Corp.
6051 Wallace Road Ext # 2
Wexford PA 15090

(G-1010)
RACERESQ INC
Also Called: Fire Station Resources Center
1001 15th St (15010-4114)
P.O. Box 18 (15010-0018)
PHONE....................................724 891-3473
Patrick Moore, *President*
Cynthia Moore, *Vice Pres*
EMP: 9
SQ FT: 112,000
SALES (est): 1.5MM **Privately Held**
SIC: 3569 5088 7699 Firefighting apparatus & related equipment; transportation equipment & supplies; industrial machinery & equipment repair

(G-1011)
SENSIBLE ORGANICS INC
3740 W 4th Ave (15010-1904)
PHONE....................................724 891-4560
Rob Robillard, *President*
Nir Liberboim, *Admin Sec*
EMP: 26
SQ FT: 40,000
SALES: 8MM **Privately Held**
SIC: 2841 2844 Soap & other detergents; face creams or lotions; shampoos, rinses, conditioners: hair; deodorants, personal

(G-1012)
SME SALES AND SERVICE INC
328 Aley Hill Rd (15010-5727)
PHONE....................................724 384-1159
Douglas Kost, *President*
▲ EMP: 138
SQ FT: 4,200
SALES: 11.2MM **Privately Held**
WEB: www.smesalesservice.com
SIC: 3547 Rolling mill machinery

(G-1013)
SPINAL ACOUSTICS LLC
1104 Darlington Rd (15010-2829)
PHONE....................................724 846-3600
Kelly J Allen, *President*
EMP: 5
SALES: 500K **Privately Held**
SIC: 3841 Surgical & medical instruments

(G-1014)
STANDARD STEEL SPECIALTY CO
Also Called: SSS
100 Jamison St (15010)
PHONE....................................724 846-7600
Rober E Conley, *President*
Robert Conley, *President*
Jack G Armstrong, *Principal*
Thomas G Armstrong, *Principal*
C R Moore, *Principal*
▲ EMP: 60
SQ FT: 100,000
SALES (est): 14.2MM **Privately Held**
WEB: www.stdsteel.com
SIC: 3446 3493 3429 Railings, bannisters, guards, etc.: made from metal pipe; hot wound springs, except wire; coiled flat springs; metal fasteners

(G-1015)
TOOKAN SCREENING & DESIGN INC
Also Called: Tookan Graphics & Screen Prtg
2305 6th Ave (15010-3741)
PHONE....................................724 846-2264
Paul Cooper, *President*
Tina Cooper, *Corp Secy*
Eric Cooper, *Vice Pres*
EMP: 4
SQ FT: 3,500
SALES: 350K **Privately Held**
SIC: 2759 Screen printing

(G-1016)
WALKER FABRICATING
712 7th St (15010-4533)
P.O. Box 328 (15010-0328)
PHONE....................................724 847-5111
Timothy Walker, *Owner*
EMP: 3
SQ FT: 4,000
SALES (est): 200K **Privately Held**
SIC: 3441 Fabricated structural metal

Beaver Meadows
Carbon County

(G-1017)
RMB SPECIALTEES LLC
85 Broad St (18216)
P.O. Box 45 (18216-0045)
PHONE....................................570 578-8258
EMP: 4
SALES (est): 273.6K **Privately Held**
SIC: 2759 Screen printing

(G-1018)
ROSSI EXCAVATING COMPANY
10 Centtown Rd (18216-7005)
PHONE....................................570 455-9607
Leonard A Rossi, *Partner*
John Avillian, *Partner*
EMP: 4
SALES (est): 540K **Privately Held**
SIC: 1231 1794 Strip mining, anthracite; excavation work

Beaver Springs
Snyder County

(G-1019)
MIDDLECREEK PALLET
13274 Route 235 (17812-9233)
PHONE....................................570 658-7667
Ken Hassinger, *Owner*
EMP: 4
SALES (est): 302K **Privately Held**
SIC: 2448 Pallets, wood

(G-1020)
PEACHEY-YODER LP
Also Called: Weaver Bros Pallets
3782 Sawmill Rd (17812-9111)
PHONE....................................570 658-8371
Marvin Peachey, *Partner*
Ken Yoder, *Partner*
EMP: 15 EST: 2011
SALES (est): 2.4MM **Privately Held**
SIC: 2448 Pallets, wood

(G-1021)
REMMEY PALLET CO
3685 Sawmill Rd (17812-9110)
PHONE....................................570 658-7575
Donald B Remmey Jr, *President*
EMP: 28
SQ FT: 11,040
SALES (est): 3.9MM **Privately Held**
SIC: 2448 Pallets, wood

(G-1022)
SETHS AUTO MACHINE SHOP
19362 Route 522 (17812-9435)
PHONE....................................570 658-2886
Sethrick C Grenoble, *Owner*
EMP: 3 EST: 2014
SALES (est): 257.6K **Privately Held**
SIC: 3599 Machine shop, jobbing & repair

(G-1023)
SHADE LUMBER COMPANY INC
3627 Sawmill Rd (17812-9110)
PHONE....................................570 658-2425
Peter Berry, *President*
Debra Berry, *Treasurer*
EMP: 20
SALES (est): 3.1MM **Privately Held**
SIC: 2448 Pallets, wood

(G-1024)
SUN PRECAST COMPANY
4051 Ridge Rd (17812-9466)
PHONE....................................570 658-8000
Joseph A Schmadel, *President*
Angela L Hockenbrock, *Vice Pres*
Michele D Wetzel, *Treasurer*
EMP: 30
SQ FT: 25,000
SALES (est): 3.7MM **Privately Held**
WEB: www.sunprecast.com
SIC: 3272 Cast stone, concrete

Beavertown
Snyder County

(G-1025)
CONESTOGA WOOD SPC CORP
441 W Market St (17813-9795)
P.O. Box 158 (17813-0158)
PHONE....................................570 658-9663
Robin Long, *Human Res Mgr*
Tom Tingrich, *Branch Mgr*
Bill Sedlis, *Analyst*
EMP: 150
SALES (corp-wide): 213MM **Privately Held**
WEB: www.conestogawood.com
SIC: 2521 2426 Panel systems & partitions (free-standing), office: wood; hardwood dimension & flooring mills
PA: Conestoga Wood Specialties Corporation
245 Reading Rd
East Earl PA 17519
717 445-6701

(G-1026)
GRA-TER INDUSTRIES INC
131 S Orange St (17813-9767)
P.O. Box 81 (17813-0081)
PHONE....................................570 658-7652
Terry Hummell, *President*
EMP: 6
SQ FT: 14,000
SALES (est): 753.9K **Privately Held**
SIC: 3713 Truck tops

(G-1027)
MECKLEYS LIMESTONE PDTS INC
2401 Quarry Rd (17813)
PHONE....................................570 837-5228
Lavern Smeltz, *Manager*
EMP: 3
SALES (est): 142.7K
SALES (corp-wide): 13.7MM **Privately Held**
WEB: www.meckleys.com
SIC: 1422 1771 Limestones, ground; blacktop (asphalt) work

PA: Meckley's Limestone Products, Inc.
1543 State Route 225
Herndon PA 17830
570 758-3011

(G-1028)
TOP NOTCH CNC MACHINING INC
543 W Market St Ste 2 (17813-9601)
P.O. Box 355 (17813-0355)
PHONE..................................570 658-3725
Todd Reich, *President*
Towdb Reich, *President*
EMP: 15 **EST:** 2001
SQ FT: 7,500
SALES (est): 532.4K **Privately Held**
SIC: 3541 Machine tools, metal cutting type

(G-1029)
USA EMBROIDERY & SILKSCRE
317 W Mulberry Aly (17813-9534)
PHONE..................................570 837-7700
Robin Barrett, *Principal*
EMP: 4
SALES (est): 276.7K **Privately Held**
WEB: www.usaembroideryonline.com
SIC: 2395 Embroidery products, except schiffli machine

Bechtelsville
Berks County

(G-1030)
CAMPBELL MANUFACTURING INC (DH)
Also Called: Monoflex
127 E Spring St (19505-9153)
P.O. Box 207 (19505-0207)
PHONE..................................610 367-2107
Emery W Davis, *Ch of Bd*
Robert Benson, *Plant Mgr*
Julie Harris, *Purch Agent*
Ryan Kohler, *Buyer*
John Cooper, *Treasurer*
▼ **EMP:** 70 **EST:** 1977
SQ FT: 82,000
SALES (est): 17.8MM
SALES (corp-wide): 52.3MM **Privately Held**
WEB: www.monoflex.net
SIC: 3823 3494 3561 3589 Water quality monitoring & control systems; pipe fittings; well adapters; pumps, domestic: water or sump; sewage & water treatment equipment; water filters & softeners, household type; fabricated pipe & fittings; manufactured hardware (general)

(G-1031)
CAMPBELL MANUFACTURING LLC (HQ)
127 E Spring St (19505-9153)
P.O. Box 207 (19505-0207)
PHONE..................................610 367-2107
Donna Wheller, *Vice Pres*
Debbie Schur, *CFO*
Emery Davis,
◆ **EMP:** 48
SQ FT: 82,000
SALES (est): 43.4MM
SALES (corp-wide): 52.3MM **Privately Held**
WEB: www.campbellmfg.com
SIC: 3561 Pumps & pumping equipment
PA: Baker Manufacturing Company, Llc
133 Enterprise St
Evansville WI 53536
608 882-5100

(G-1032)
EVERYTHING POSTAL INC
Also Called: Everything Prtg & Shipg Ctr
828a N Route 100 (19505-9200)
PHONE..................................610 367-7444
Lee R Levengood, *President*
EMP: 4
SQ FT: 1,150
SALES (est): 640K **Privately Held**
WEB: www.everythingpostal.com
SIC: 7389 7331 2621 Mailing & messenger services; direct mail advertising services; printing paper

(G-1033)
MOORHOUSE STAIR
2009 Weisstown Rd (19505-9781)
PHONE..................................610 367-9275
Frank Moorhouse, *Owner*
EMP: 3 **EST:** 1992
SQ FT: 3,500
SALES (est): 331.2K **Privately Held**
SIC: 2431 Staircases & stairs, wood

(G-1034)
PERFORMANCE METALS INC
650 N Route 100 (19505-9229)
PHONE..................................610 369-3060
Henry C Leipert Jr, *CEO*
Raymond Schratz, *Shareholder*
Martin E Wigg, *Admin Sec*
▲ **EMP:** 72
SQ FT: 40,000
SALES (est): 8.9MM **Privately Held**
SIC: 3365 Aluminum foundries

(G-1035)
POINTER HILL PETS INC
Also Called: Pointer Hill Pet Products
625 Hoffmansville Rd # 1 (19505-9502)
PHONE..................................610 754-7830
James Kreitz, *Owner*
EMP: 6 **EST:** 1981
SALES (est): 390K **Privately Held**
SIC: 3496 3999 Cages, wire; smokers, bee (beekeepers' supplies)

(G-1036)
SCICAST INTERNATIONAL INC
Also Called: Performance Metals
650 N Route 100 (19505-9229)
PHONE..................................610 369-3060
Henry Leipert, *CEO*
Scott Soeder, *Facilities Mgr*
Audrey Turczynski, *Controller*
Steven Calamia, *Accounting Mgr*
Rae Reinhard, *Human Resources*
▲ **EMP:** 41
SQ FT: 34,000
SALES (est): 10.9MM **Privately Held**
SIC: 3363 3364 Aluminum die-castings; zinc & zinc-base alloy die-castings

(G-1037)
SEVENTY-THREE MFG CO INC
136 Stauffer Rd (19505-9012)
PHONE..................................610 845-7823
Richard Croyle, *President*
Michael Croyle, *Natl Sales Mgr*
Evelyn Croyle, *Admin Sec*
EMP: 20
SQ FT: 40,000
SALES (est): 3.6MM **Privately Held**
WEB: www.rotacyl.com
SIC: 3823 3492 3625 3586 Industrial instrmnts msrmnt display/control process variable; control valves, fluid power: hydraulic & pneumatic; actuators, industrial; measuring & dispensing pumps; rotary type meters

(G-1038)
WORLD VIDEO SALES CO INC
Also Called: Microimage Video Systems
625 Hoffmansville Rd # 4 (19505-9501)
P.O. Box 331, Boyertown (19512-0331)
PHONE..................................610 754-6800
John Taylor, *President*
Jayne Swavely, *Principal*
EMP: 4
SQ FT: 4,000
SALES (est): 700K **Privately Held**
WEB: www.mivs.com
SIC: 3841 3829 3823 3663 Surgical & medical instruments; measuring & controlling devices; industrial instrmnts msrmnt display/control process variable; radio & TV communications equipment; household audio & video equipment; computer peripheral equipment

Bedford
Bedford County

(G-1039)
ACCRA MACHINE SHOP INC
554 N Thomas St (15522-1166)
PHONE..................................814 623-8009
John S Wracher, *President*
Jeff Wracher, *Treasurer*
Carolyn Wracher, *Admin Sec*
EMP: 4
SALES (est): 200K **Privately Held**
SIC: 3599 Machine shop, jobbing & repair

(G-1040)
BEDFORD FARM BUREAU COOP ASSN (PA)
102 Industrial Ave (15522-1032)
PHONE..................................814 623-6194
Doug Smith, *President*
Jim Shade, *General Mgr*
James Shade, *General Mgr*
Richard Emerick, *Vice Pres*
Denise Sollenberger, *Controller*
EMP: 15
SQ FT: 10,000
SALES (est): 3.7MM **Privately Held**
WEB: www.indianapropane.com
SIC: 2875 5191 2048 Fertilizers, mixing only; farm supplies; livestock feeds

(G-1041)
BEDFORD FOREST PRODUCTS INC
205 Barclay St (15522-1807)
PHONE..................................814 977-3712
Thomas L Mereen, *President*
▼ **EMP:** 3
SALES (est): 472.4K **Privately Held**
SIC: 2411 Mine timbers, hewn; pulpwood contractors engaged in cutting

(G-1042)
BEDFORD GAZETTE LLC
424 W Penn St (15522-1230)
PHONE..................................814 623-1151
George Sample, *Owner*
Sherri Growden, *Adv Dir*
Joseph Beegle, *Manager*
Elizabeth Coyle, *Assoc Editor*
EMP: 50 **EST:** 1805
SQ FT: 6,000
SALES (est): 2.3MM **Privately Held**
WEB: www.bedfordgazette.com
SIC: 2711 2752 Newspapers, publishing & printing; commercial printing, lithographic

(G-1043)
BEDFORD PALLETS
5425 Business 220 (15522-7640)
PHONE..................................814 623-1521
William Popovich, *President*
EMP: 16
SQ FT: 25,000
SALES (est): 2.4MM **Privately Held**
SIC: 2448 Pallets, wood

(G-1044)
BEDFORD REINFORCED PLAS INC (PA)
Also Called: B.R.p
1 Corporate Dr Ste 106 (15522-7983)
PHONE..................................814 623-8125
Melvin Stahl, *CEO*
Brian Stahl, *President*
Carin Stahl, *Corp Secy*
Allen Stahl, *Vice Pres*
Troy Ickes, *Project Mgr*
◆ **EMP:** 80 **EST:** 1974
SQ FT: 40,000
SALES (est): 23.2MM **Privately Held**
WEB: www.bedfordplastics.com
SIC: 3089 3993 3496 3446 Reinforcing mesh, plastic; signs & advertising specialties; miscellaneous fabricated wire products; architectural metalwork; blast furnaces & steel mills

(G-1045)
CARSON BOXING LLC
797 Sloans Hollow Rd (15522-7242)
PHONE..................................814 839-2768
Stephen R Carson, *Principal*
Sophia Carson, *Mng Member*
EMP: 4 **EST:** 2013
SALES (est): 219.8K **Privately Held**
SIC: 3949 Gloves, sport & athletic: boxing, handball, etc.

(G-1046)
CELL-CON INC
8468 Us Route 220 (15522-6205)
PHONE..................................814 623-7057
Joel Cunard, *Vice Pres*
Dixie Tew, *Plant Mgr*
EMP: 28
SALES (corp-wide): 10.4MM **Privately Held**
WEB: www.cell-con.com
SIC: 3691 Storage batteries
PA: Cell-Con, Inc.
305 Commerce Dr Ste 300
Exton PA 19341
800 771-7139

(G-1047)
COVER LUMBER CO
108 Sawmill Ln (15522-5657)
PHONE..................................814 750-2006
EMP: 4
SALES: 100K **Privately Held**
SIC: 2421 Sawmill

(G-1048)
CYCLING SPORTS GROUP INC (HQ)
Also Called: Cannondale Sports Group
16 Trowbridge Dr (15522)
PHONE..................................203 749-7000
Ron Lombardi, *CFO*
David Budd, *Director*
Robert Silvis, *Admin Sec*
◆ **EMP:** 70
SQ FT: 32,500
SALES (est): 171.8MM
SALES (corp-wide): 2.5B **Privately Held**
SIC: 3751 2329 Bicycles & related parts; men's & boys' sportswear & athletic clothing; athletic (warmup, sweat & jogging) suits: men's & boys'
PA: Industries Dorel Inc, Les
1255 Av Greene Bureau 300
Westmount QC H3Z 2
514 934-3034

(G-1049)
DIXIE S YOUNG CLEANING
317 N Richard St (15522-1020)
PHONE..................................814 623-3015
Dixie Young, *Owner*
EMP: 4
SALES (est): 222.7K **Privately Held**
SIC: 2842 Specialty cleaning preparations

(G-1050)
FRITZ LOGGING
620 S Richard St (15522-1847)
PHONE..................................814 623-6011
Russell E Fritz Jr, *Owner*
EMP: 5
SALES (est): 497.8K **Privately Held**
SIC: 2411 Logging camps & contractors

(G-1051)
GALLIKER DAIRY COMPANY
Also Called: Bedford Depot
170 Transport St (15522-7730)
PHONE..................................814 623-8597
Louis G Galliker, *Branch Mgr*
EMP: 3
SALES (corp-wide): 105.3MM **Privately Held**
WEB: www.gallikers.com
SIC: 2026 Buttermilk, cultured
PA: Galliker Dairy Company
143 Donald Ln
Johnstown PA 15904
814 266-8702

(G-1052)
GARY JAMES DESIGNS
3759 Business 220 Ste 205 (15522-1180)
PHONE..................................814 623-2477
Gary Young, *Owner*
EMP: 3
SALES (est): 148.4K **Privately Held**
SIC: 2759 Screen printing

G E O G R A P H I C

(G-1053)
GREEN GARDEN INC
1088 Greengarden Ln (15522)
PHONE..................................814 623-2735
Anita Ketcham, *Corp Secy*
Dara Beutman, *Vice Pres*
Jane Francis, *Vice Pres*
EMP: 50
SQ FT: 55,000
SALES (est): 9.1MM **Privately Held**
WEB: www.greengardeninc.com
SIC: 3432 Lawn hose nozzles & sprinklers

(G-1054)
HUNTS PROMOTIONS
782 W Pitt St (15522-6556)
PHONE..................................814 623-2751
Vernon D Hunt, *Owner*
EMP: 3
SALES (est): 190K **Privately Held**
SIC: 2396 7336 Screen printing on fabric
   articles; commercial art & graphic design

(G-1055)
JLG INDUSTRIES INC
450 Sunnyside Rd (15522-8601)
P.O. Box 676 (15522-0676)
PHONE..................................814 623-2156
Eugene Swope, *Manager*
EMP: 13
SALES (corp-wide): 6.8B **Publicly Held**
WEB: www.jlg.com
SIC: 3536 3537 3531 Hoists, cranes &
   monorails; industrial trucks & tractors;
   construction machinery
HQ: Jlg Industries, Inc.
   1 J L G Dr
   Mc Connellsburg PA 17233
   717 485-5161

(G-1056)
JLG INDUSTRIES INC
441 Weber Ln (15522-7717)
PHONE..................................814 623-0045
Julie Stroup, *Principal*
EMP: 125
SALES (corp-wide): 6.8B **Publicly Held**
WEB: www.jlg.com
SIC: 3531 3536 Cranes; hoists, cranes &
   monorails
HQ: Jlg Industries, Inc.
   1 J L G Dr
   Mc Connellsburg PA 17233
   717 485-5161

(G-1057)
KENNAMETAL INC
442 Chalybeate Rd (15522-8637)
PHONE..................................814 623-2711
Danny Slack, *Engineer*
Chad Swope, *Engineer*
Anita Callihan, *Human Res Mgr*
David R Settimio, *Branch Mgr*
Robert Lewicki, *Manager*
EMP: 188
SALES (corp-wide): 2.3B **Publicly Held**
WEB: www.kennametal.com
SIC: 3545 Cutting tools for machine tools
PA: Kennametal Inc.
   600 Grant St Ste 5100
   Pittsburgh PA 15219
   412 248-8000

(G-1058)
KENNAMETAL INC
550 Sunnyside Rd (15522-8666)
PHONE..................................814 624-2406
Bob Lewicki, *Branch Mgr*
EMP: 126
SALES (corp-wide): 2.3B **Publicly Held**
SIC: 3545 Machine tool accessories
PA: Kennametal Inc.
   600 Grant St Ste 5100
   Pittsburgh PA 15219
   412 248-8000

(G-1059)
KENNAMETAL INC
442 Chalybeate Rd (15522-8637)
PHONE..................................276 646-0080
EMP: 140
SALES (corp-wide): 2.1B **Publicly Held**
SIC: 3545 3532 3613 3531 Mfg Machine
   Tool Access Mfg Mining Machinery Mfg
   Switchgear/Boards Mfg Construction
   Mach

PA: Kennametal Inc.
   600 Grant St Ste 5100
   Pittsburgh PA 15219
   412 248-8200

(G-1060)
L B FOSTER COMPANY
Also Called: Fabricated Products
202 Weber Ln (15522-7711)
PHONE..................................814 623-6101
Julian Pedrazzani, *Plant Mgr*
Scott Wilhelm, *Human Res Mgr*
Beth Kotsenas, *Sales Staff*
Mark Maxwell, *Manager*
EMP: 45
SALES (corp-wide): 626.9MM **Publicly
Held**
WEB: www.lbfoster.com
SIC: 3441 3446 3444 3272 Fabricated
   structural metal; architectural metalwork;
   sheet metalwork; concrete products
PA: L. B. Foster Company
   415 Holiday Dr Ste 1
   Pittsburgh PA 15220
   412 928-3400

(G-1061)
LANE ENTERPRISES INC
Also Called: Lane Metal Products
682 Quaker Valley Rd (15522)
P.O. Box 164 (15522-0164)
PHONE..................................814 623-1191
Doc Miller, *Principal*
Larry Whitsel, *Principal*
Thomas Mickle, *Branch Mgr*
EMP: 45
SALES (corp-wide): 70.5MM **Privately
Held**
WEB: www.lanepipe.com
SIC: 3444 Culverts, sheet metal
PA: Lane Enterprises, Inc.
   3905 Hartzdale Dr Ste 514
   Camp Hill PA 17011
   717 761-8175

(G-1062)
LEISTER MACHINE
1170 Dogwood Rd (15522-6823)
PHONE..................................814 623-5992
John Leister, *Owner*
EMP: 3
SALES (est): 253.8K **Privately Held**
SIC: 3599 Machine shop, jobbing & repair

(G-1063)
MARTZ CHASSIS INC
646 Imlertown Rd (15522-8425)
P.O. Box 538 (15522-0538)
PHONE..................................814 623-9501
Gary L Martz, *President*
EMP: 8 EST: 1970
SALES (est): 600K **Privately Held**
WEB: www.martzchassis.com
SIC: 3711 Automobile assembly, including
   specialty automobiles

(G-1064)
**MDL MANUFACTURING INDS
INC (PA)**
15 Commerce Ct (15522-7943)
PHONE..................................814 623-0888
M Douglas Lingsch, *President*
EMP: 50
SQ FT: 54,000
SALES: 6.2MM **Privately Held**
WEB: www.mdlmanufacturing.com
SIC: 3444 3599 1799 Sheet metalwork;
   machine shop, jobbing & repair; welding
   on site

(G-1065)
**MOBILE WASH POWER WASH
INC**
124 Finland Rd (15522-3722)
PHONE..................................814 327-3820
Thomas Brusko, *President*
EMP: 3
SALES: 400K **Privately Held**
SIC: 3589 1799 High pressure cleaning
   equipment; cleaning building exteriors

(G-1066)
NELSON WRAP DISPENSER INC
2406 Younts Rd (15522-8186)
PHONE..................................814 623-1317
Nelson Pharo, *President*

EMP: 4
SALES (est): 617.6K **Privately Held**
SIC: 3565 Packing & wrapping machinery

(G-1067)
OILFIELD LLC
Also Called: Oilfield Supply Company
264 Reynoldsdale Rd (15522-7401)
PHONE..................................814 623-8125
Bradley Wise, *Principal*
Glenn Smith,
EMP: 4
SALES (est): 184.8K **Privately Held**
SIC: 3082 Unsupported plastics profile
   shapes

(G-1068)
OLD BEDFORD VILLAGE INC
220 Sawblade Rd (15522-7702)
PHONE..................................814 623-1156
Bonnie Miller, *Treasurer*
Roger Kirwin, *Director*
EMP: 4
SALES: 350K **Privately Held**
WEB: www.oldbedfordvillage.com
SIC: 7999 5945 3944 Tourist attractions,
   amusement park concessions & rides;
   arts & crafts supplies; craft & hobby kits &
   sets

(G-1069)
**P/S PRINTING & COPY
SERVICES**
133 Mann St Ste 3 (15522-1033)
PHONE..................................814 623-7033
Richard Naugle, *Partner*
Greg Naugle, *Partner*
EMP: 8
SQ FT: 3,000
SALES (est): 1.3MM **Privately Held**
WEB: www.psprinting.us
SIC: 2752 Commercial printing, offset

(G-1070)
PASER INC
1804 Fleegle Rd (15522-7215)
PHONE..................................814 623-7221
Roger E Christiana, *President*
EMP: 8
SALES (est): 703.9K **Privately Held**
SIC: 2448 Wood pallets & skids

(G-1071)
POMPS TIRE SERVICE INC
550 Sunnyside Rd Ste 201 (15522-8666)
PHONE..................................814 623-6764
Dave Smith, *Manager*
EMP: 10
SALES (corp-wide): 669.5MM **Privately
Held**
WEB: www.pompstire.com
SIC: 3011 Industrial tires, pneumatic
PA: Pomp's Tire Service, Inc.
   1123 Cedar St
   Green Bay WI 54301
   920 435-8301

(G-1072)
RECOIL INC
170 Transport St (15522-7730)
PHONE..................................814 623-3921
Mark Way, *Manager*
EMP: 4 **Privately Held**
SIC: 2992 Re-refining lubricating oils &
   greases
PA: Recoil, Inc.
   280 N East St
   York PA

(G-1073)
**REVOLTNARY ELCTRNIC
DESIGN LLC**
Also Called: Red
7127 Lincoln Hwy (15522-6654)
PHONE..................................814 977-9546
Josh Brown, *CEO*
EMP: 6
SALES: 55K **Privately Held**
SIC: 2844 2899 Perfumes & colognes;
   cosmetic preparations; essential oils

(G-1074)
**REX HEAT TREAT -LANSDALE
INC**
7 Corporate Dr (15522-7946)
PHONE..................................814 623-1701
John Rex, *Principal*
Doug Gerber, *Manager*
EMP: 30
SALES (corp-wide): 20.9MM **Privately
Held**
WEB: www.rexheattreat.com
SIC: 3398 Metal heat treating
PA: Rex Heat Treat -Lansdale, Inc.
   951 W 8th St
   Lansdale PA 19446
   215 855-1131

(G-1075)
ROCKLAND INC
Also Called: Rockland Manufacturing Com-
pany
152 Weber Ln (15522-7782)
P.O. Box 5 (15522-0005)
PHONE..................................814 623-1115
Samuel J Pratt, *President*
Anne E Pratt, *Corp Secy*
Dan Shaffer, *COO*
Daniel D Shaffer III, *Vice Pres*
Bob Glessner, *Maint Spvr*
◆ EMP: 255 EST: 1947
SQ FT: 40,000
SALES (est): 156.3MM **Privately Held**
WEB: www.loaderattachments.com
SIC: 3531 Construction machinery attach-
   ments; blades for graders, scrapers, doz-
   ers & snow plows; plows: construction,
   excavating & grading

(G-1076)
SHAWNEE STRUCTURES
6231 Lincoln Hwy (15522-6968)
PHONE..................................814 623-8212
Aaron Martin, *Owner*
Seth Stoltzfus, *Marketing Staff*
EMP: 7
SQ FT: 15,000
SALES: 1MM **Privately Held**
WEB: www.shawneestructures.com
SIC: 2452 Prefabricated wood buildings

(G-1077)
STRUCTURAL FIBERGLASS INC
4766 Business 220 (15522-7747)
P.O. Box 615 (15522-0615)
PHONE..................................814 623-0458
Garry Goss, *President*
Peggy Goss, *Vice Pres*
EMP: 10
SQ FT: 9,500
SALES (est): 1.9MM **Privately Held**
WEB: www.structuralfiberglass.com
SIC: 3089 3446 3441 Plastic hardware &
   building products; architectural metal-
   work; fabricated structural metal

(G-1078)
TMC CANDIES LLC
Also Called: Bedford Candies
106 E Pitt St (15522-1317)
PHONE..................................814 623-1545
Tammy Wiley, *Mng Member*
Celeste Millward
Edward Millward,
EMP: 5
SALES (est): 467.7K **Privately Held**
SIC: 3999 5441 Candles; candy

(G-1079)
**WAKEFOOSE OFFICE SUPPLY &
PRTG**
240 W Penn St (15522-1226)
PHONE..................................814 623-5742
Henry Wakefoose, *Owner*
EMP: 4
SQ FT: 2,000
SALES (est): 395.3K **Privately Held**
SIC: 5943 2752 3953 2791 Office forms
   & supplies; commercial printing, offset;
   embossing seals & hand stamps; typeset-
   ting; commercial printing

▲ = Import ▼ =Export
◆ =Import/Export

Bedminster
Bucks County

(G-1080)
FIRST STATE SHEET METAL INC
3 Appletree Ln (18910)
PHONE.....................215 766-9510
John Marrinucci, *President*
EMP: 2
SALES (est): 4MM **Privately Held**
SIC: 3444 Sheet metalwork

Beech Creek
Clinton County

(G-1081)
APPALACHIAN DRILLING SVCS INC
105 Industrial Park Rd (16822-7220)
PHONE.....................570 907-0136
Seth Martin, *President*
Trent Muthler, *Vice Pres*
EMP: 12 EST: 2011
SQ FT: 42,700
SALES: 5MM **Privately Held**
SIC: 1389 Gas field services; oil field services

(G-1082)
GLOSSNERS CONCRETE INC
515 Laurel Run Rd (16822-7903)
PHONE.....................570 962-2564
Jess Glossner, *President*
EMP: 10
SALES (est): 1.5MM **Privately Held**
SIC: 3273 Ready-mixed concrete

(G-1083)
TRUCK LITE CO INC
107 Industrial Park Rd (16822-7220)
PHONE.....................716 664-3519
EMP: 3
SALES (est): 128.6K **Privately Held**
SIC: 3647 Vehicular lighting equipment

(G-1084)
YOUR BUILDING CENTERS INC
Keystone Truss & Manufacturing
109 Industrial Park Rd (16822-7220)
PHONE.....................570 962-2129
Tim Leupold, *Branch Mgr*
EMP: 50
SALES (corp-wide): 96.9MM **Privately Held**
SIC: 2439 Structural wood members
PA: Your Building Centers, Inc.
   2607 Beale Ave
   Altoona PA 16601
   814 944-5098

Belle Vernon
Fayette County

(G-1085)
CUMMINS INC
483 Rehoboth Rd (15012-3832)
PHONE.....................724 798-4511
EMP: 9
SALES (corp-wide): 23.7B **Publicly Held**
SIC: 3519 Internal combustion engines
PA: Cummins Inc.
   500 Jackson St
   Columbus IN 47201
   812 377-5000

(G-1086)
ELLISON INDUSTRIAL CONTRLS LLC
19 State St (15012-1015)
PHONE.....................724 483-0251
Maureen A Ellison, *Mng Member*
H Kent Ellison, *Mng Member*
EMP: 6
SQ FT: 2,750

SALES: 965K **Privately Held**
WEB: www.ellisonic.com
SIC: 3625 3613 3823 Relays & industrial controls; switchgear & switchboard apparatus; industrial instrmnts msrmnt display/control process variable

(G-1087)
SOLAR POWER SOLUTIONS LLC
13 Airport Rd (15012)
PHONE.....................724 379-2002
Lawrence Stern, *Chairman*
▲ **EMP:** 4
SALES (est): 322.9K **Privately Held**
SIC: 3674 Solar cells

(G-1088)
TMS INTERNATIONAL LLC
891 Mills Ln (15012-4565)
PHONE.....................724 929-4515
EMP: 10
SALES (corp-wide): 216.9MM **Privately Held**
SIC: 5032 3295 Whol Brick/Stone Material Mfg Minerals-Ground/Treated
HQ: Tms International Group Llc
   12 Monongahela Ave
   Glassport PA 15045
   412 678-6141

(G-1089)
USNR LLC
Twilight Industries
212 State St Ste 1 (15012-1152)
PHONE.....................724 929-8405
Fax: 724 929-7688
EMP: 12
SQ FT: 3,574
SALES (corp-wide): 316.7MM **Privately Held**
SIC: 1221 0851 Bituminous Coal/Lignite Surface Mining Forestry Services
PA: Usnr, Llc
   1981 Schurman Way
   Woodland WA 98674
   360 225-8267

(G-1090)
USNR LLC
212 State St (15012-1152)
P.O. Box 256 (15012-0256)
PHONE.....................724 929-8405
EMP: 3
SALES (corp-wide): 316.4MM **Privately Held**
SIC: 2821 Mfg Plastic Materials/Resins
PA: Usnr, Llc
   1981 Schurman Way
   Woodland WA 98674
   360 225-8267

Bellefonte
Centre County

(G-1091)
ACTUATED MEDICAL INC
310 Rolling Ridge Dr (16823-8445)
PHONE.....................814 355-0003
Maureen L Mulvihill, *President*
Paul L Frankhouser, *Director*
EMP: 19
SQ FT: 4,000
SALES (est): 3.4MM **Privately Held**
WEB: www.actuatedmedical.com
SIC: 8731 3841 Medical research, commercial; surgical & medical instruments

(G-1092)
APACHE TURBINES
531 Saint Paul Cir (16823-8415)
PHONE.....................814 880-0053
Edmond D Pope, *Principal*
EMP: 5
SALES (est): 230K **Privately Held**
SIC: 3511 Turbines & turbine generator sets

(G-1093)
BEAVERTOWN BLOCK CO INC
121 N Harrison Rd (16823-3318)
P.O. Box 337, Middleburg (17842-0337)
PHONE.....................814 359-2771

Doug Steiner, *Manager*
EMP: 30
SALES (corp-wide): 10.5MM **Privately Held**
WEB: www.beavertownblock.com
SIC: 3271 5211 3272 Blocks, concrete or cinder: standard; brick; concrete products, precast
PA: Beavertown Block Co., Inc.
   3612 Paxtonville Rd
   Middleburg PA
   570 837-1744

(G-1094)
BOLTON METAL PRODUCTS CO INC
2042 Axemann Rd 300 (16823-8142)
PHONE.....................814 355-6217
EMP: 9
SALES (est): 421K **Privately Held**
SIC: 3341 Secondary nonferrous metals

(G-1095)
BUTLER MACHINE INC
236 S Potter St (16823-1313)
PHONE.....................814 355-5605
Shawn E Butler, *President*
Donald Clontz, *Office Mgr*
EMP: 6
SQ FT: 500
SALES: 700K **Privately Held**
SIC: 3599 7692 Machine shop, jobbing & repair; welding repair

(G-1096)
CUSTOM STONE INTERIORS INC
360 Rolling Ridge Dr (16823-8136)
PHONE.....................814 548-0120
John Waltz, *President*
Jeremy Everhart, *Vice Pres*
Eric Bliesmer, *Sales Staff*
EMP: 9
SALES: 810K **Privately Held**
SIC: 3281 5211 Cut stone & stone products; counter tops

(G-1097)
GRAYMONT INC (HQ)
375 Graymont Rd (16823-6869)
PHONE.....................814 353-4613
William Dodge, *President*
Randy Pletcher, *Vice Pres*
Martin Turecky, *Plant Mgr*
Rick Fisher, *Materials Mgr*
Terry Spooner, *Sales Mgr*
▼ **EMP:** 60
SQ FT: 2,500
SALES (est): 36.1MM
SALES (corp-wide): 171.4MM **Privately Held**
WEB: www.graymont.com
SIC: 3274 1422 Agricultural lime; hydrated lime; quicklime; limestones, ground; agricultural limestone, ground
PA: Graymont Inc
   301 S 700 E 3950
   Salt Lake City UT 84102
   801 262-3942

(G-1098)
GRAYMONT INC
Also Called: Bellefonte Lime Co Quarry
980 E College Ave (16823)
PHONE.....................814 359-2313
Thomas Elsner, *Plant Supt*
Rick Fisher, *Materials Mgr*
Tim Bruss, *Facilities Mgr*
Charlie Mitchell, *Maint Spvr*
Tyson Sweat, *Opers Staff*
EMP: 12
SALES (corp-wide): 171.4MM **Privately Held**
WEB: www.graymont.com
SIC: 1411 Limestone & marble dimension stone
HQ: Graymont Inc.
   375 Graymont Rd
   Bellefonte PA 16823
   814 353-4613

(G-1099)
GRAYMONT INC
375 Graymont Rd (16823-6869)
P.O. Box 448 (16823-0448)
PHONE.....................814 357-4500

Paul Gori, *CEO*
Sue Catherman, *Purch Mgr*
Shawn Stedman, *Human Res Dir*
Becky Richards, *Administration*
EMP: 15
SALES (corp-wide): 171.4MM **Privately Held**
WEB: www.graymont.com
SIC: 1422 Lime rock, ground
HQ: Graymont Inc.
   375 Graymont Rd
   Bellefonte PA 16823
   814 353-4613

(G-1100)
GROFF TRACTOR & EQUIPMENT LLC
210 Rolling Ridge Dr (16823-8444)
PHONE.....................814 353-8400
Greg Grimes, *Manager*
EMP: 10
SALES (corp-wide): 83MM **Privately Held**
WEB: www.grofftractor.com
SIC: 5082 3531 General construction machinery & equipment; backhoes, tractors, cranes, plows & similar equipment
PA: Groff Tractor & Equipment, Llc
   6779 Carlisle Pike
   Mechanicsburg PA 17050
   717 766-7671

(G-1101)
GROVE PRINTING INC
152 Raspberry Ln (16823-7019)
PHONE.....................814 355-2197
Howard Grove Jr, *Owner*
Debra Green, *Info Tech Dir*
EMP: 8
SQ FT: 4,000
SALES (est): 1.1MM **Privately Held**
SIC: 2752 Commercial printing, offset

(G-1102)
GROWMARK FS LLC
552 Feidler Rd (16823-7556)
PHONE.....................814 359-2725
Greg Connor, *Manager*
EMP: 9
SALES (corp-wide): 7.2B **Privately Held**
WEB: www.growmarkfs.com
SIC: 2875 2873 2874 5191 Fertilizers, mixing only; nitrogenous fertilizers; nitrogen solutions (fertilizer); phosphatic fertilizers; pesticides; seeds: field, garden & flower
HQ: Growmark Fs, Llc
   308 Ne Front St
   Milford DE 19963
   302 422-3002

(G-1103)
HANSON AGGREGATES PA LLC
1394 Forest Ave (16823-9364)
PHONE.....................814 355-4226
Barry Davis, *Superintendent*
EMP: 21
SALES (corp-wide): 20.6B **Privately Held**
SIC: 1429 1422 Slate, crushed & broken-quarrying; limestones, ground
HQ: Hanson Aggregates Pennsylvania, Llc
   7660 Imperial Way
   Allentown PA 18195
   610 366-4626

(G-1104)
HC HOODCO INC
649 E Rolling Ridge Dr (16823-8135)
PHONE.....................814 355-4003
Sandra Hood, *President*
David Gallagher, *Project Mgr*
Vincent Hood, *Project Mgr*
Thomas K Hood, *Treasurer*
EMP: 19
SQ FT: 19,000
SALES (est): 4.3MM
SALES (corp-wide): 217.4MM **Privately Held**
WEB: www.thedoorpeople.com
SIC: 1541 3442 5072 1751 Renovation, remodeling & repairs: industrial buildings; metal doors, sash & trim; window & door frames; builders' hardware; window & door (prefabricated) installation; glass & glazing work

PA: The Cook & Boardman Group Llc
3916 Westpoint Blvd
Winston Salem NC 27103
336 768-8872

(G-1105)
HOMESCAPERS
421 Valentine Hill Rd (16823-2840)
P.O. Box 249, Lemont (16851-0249)
PHONE..............................814 353-0507
Mark Modaffare, *Principal*
EMP: 5
SALES (est): 288.8K **Privately Held**
SIC: 1389 Construction, repair & dismantling services

(G-1106)
JOE GROW INC
442 E Linn St (16823-1708)
PHONE..............................814 355-2878
Mike Theuer, *President*
EMP: 10
SQ FT: 3,000
SALES (est): 869.6K **Privately Held**
SIC: 2875 5261 Fertilizers, mixing only; fertilizer

(G-1107)
LECO CORPORATION
Also Called: Tem Pres Division
1150 Blanchard St (16823-8618)
PHONE..............................814 355-7903
Charles Gates, *Opers-Prdtn-Mfg*
Michael Herold, *Sales Associate*
EMP: 32
SALES (corp-wide): 192MM **Privately Held**
WEB: www.pier33.com
SIC: 3821 4493 3826 3825 Laboratory apparatus, except heating & measuring; chemical laboratory apparatus; boat yards, storage & incidental repair; marine basins; analytical instruments; instruments to measure electricity; industrial instrmnts msrmnt display/control process variable; porcelain electrical supplies
PA: Leco Corporation
3000 Lakeview Ave
Saint Joseph MI 49085
269 983-5531

(G-1108)
MID-STATE AWNING INC
113 Musser Ln (16823-9163)
PHONE..............................814 355-8979
Terry Phillips, *President*
EMP: 6
SQ FT: 7,200
SALES (est): 560.7K **Privately Held**
SIC: 1799 1521 2394 Awning installation; patio & deck construction & repair; awnings, fabric: made from purchased materials

(G-1109)
NANOHORIZONS INC
270 Rolling Ridge Dr (16823-8420)
PHONE..............................814 355-4700
David A Woodle, *CEO*
Daniel Hayes, *President*
Robert Burlinson, *Bd of Directors*
EMP: 20
SQ FT: 3,000
SALES (est): 4.4MM **Privately Held**
SIC: 5169 2899 Chemical additives; acid resist for etching

(G-1110)
PATRICK MC COOL (PA)
Also Called: P A M P
136 S Harrison Rd (16823-3320)
PHONE..............................814 359-2447
Patrick Mc Cool, *Owner*
EMP: 10
SQ FT: 6,000
SALES (est): 999.5K **Privately Held**
WEB: www.pamp.com
SIC: 2752 2759 Commercial printing, offset; screen printing

(G-1111)
PENN FUEL GAS INCORPORATED
109 Rishel Hill Rd (16823-8141)
PHONE..............................814 353-0404
Shirl Dillon, *Principal*

EMP: 3 **EST:** 2008
SALES (est): 173.2K **Privately Held**
SIC: 2869 Fuels

(G-1112)
PIEZO KINETICS INC (DH)
660 E Rolling Ridge Dr (16823-8135)
PHONE..............................814 355-1593
J Michael Goodson, *President*
Karl Fazler, *CFO*
Joseph K Frye, *Treasurer*
Brian E Henry, *Admin Sec*
▲ **EMP:** 48
SQ FT: 22,000
SALES (est): 7.4MM
SALES (corp-wide): 45.4MM **Privately Held**
WEB: www.piezo-kinetics.com
SIC: 3679 Electronic circuits; piezoelectric crystals; crystals & crystal assemblies, radio; transducers, electrical
HQ: Crest Ultrasonics Corp.
18 Graphics Dr
Ewing NJ 08628
609 883-4000

(G-1113)
QMAC-QUALITY MACHINING INC
622 E Rolling Ridge Dr (16823-8135)
PHONE..............................814 548-2000
Nicholas P Koleno, *President*
John Kernan, *Supervisor*
Kenneth Lyle, *Info Tech Mgr*
Doris Bickle, *Admin Sec*
Tammy Koleno, *Admin Sec*
EMP: 59
SQ FT: 40,000
SALES: 5MM **Privately Held**
SIC: 3599 Machine shop, jobbing & repair

(G-1114)
RICHARD MEYERS
Also Called: Acura-Cut
270 Commerce St (16823-7423)
PHONE..............................814 359-4340
Richard Meyers, *Owner*
EMP: 10
SQ FT: 3,600
SALES (est): 1MM **Privately Held**
SIC: 3599 Machine shop, jobbing & repair

(G-1115)
RIGHTNOUR MACHINING
229 Hale Ln (16823)
PHONE..............................814 383-4176
EMP: 13
SALES (est): 2.2MM **Privately Held**
SIC: 3599 Mfg Industrial Machinery

(G-1116)
ROBINSON VACUUM TANKS INC
306 Runville Rd (16823-4714)
PHONE..............................814 355-4474
Wade J Robbins, *President*
Sherry Robbins, *Vice Pres*
EMP: 5
SALES (est): 1.3MM **Privately Held**
SIC: 5012 3537 5084 Trucks, commercial; industrial trucks & tractors; trucks, industrial

(G-1117)
SCOTT R MIX
112 Richmond Rd (16823-7129)
PHONE..............................570 220-5887
Scott R Mix, *Principal*
EMP: 3
SALES (est): 250.5K **Privately Held**
SIC: 3273 Ready-mixed concrete

(G-1118)
SILCOTEK CORP
225 Penntech Dr (16823-7461)
PHONE..............................814 353-1778
EMP: 32 **EST:** 2008
SALES (est): 4.4MM **Privately Held**
SIC: 3399 Mfg Primary Metal Products

(G-1119)
SPICER WLDG & FABRICATION INC
123 Spicer Ln (16823-7033)
PHONE..............................814 355-7046

David Spicer, *President*
Kathy M Spicer, *Corp Secy*
EMP: 4
SALES (est): 267.8K **Privately Held**
SIC: 7692 Welding repair

(G-1120)
THERMO FISHER SCIENTIFIC INC
320 Rolling Ridge Dr (16823-8445)
PHONE..............................814 353-2300
Rich Leathers, *Branch Mgr*
EMP: 34
SALES (corp-wide): 24.3B **Publicly Held**
WEB: www.thermo.com
SIC: 3826 Analytical instruments
PA: Thermo Fisher Scientific Inc.
168 3rd Ave
Waltham MA 02451
781 622-1000

(G-1121)
THERMO HYPERSIL-KEYSTONE LLC
Also Called: Thermo Electron
320 Rolling Ridge Dr (16823-8438)
PHONE..............................814 353-2300
Richie Leathers, *Mng Member*
▲ **EMP:** 50
SQ FT: 25,000
SALES (est): 8.5MM
SALES (corp-wide): 24.3B **Publicly Held**
WEB: www.thermo.com
SIC: 3826 3821 Chromatographic equipment, laboratory type; laboratory apparatus & furniture
PA: Thermo Fisher Scientific Inc.
168 3rd Ave
Waltham MA 02451
781 622-1000

(G-1122)
THOMAS TIMBERLAND ENTERPRISES
244 Breons Ln (16823-7444)
PHONE..............................814 359-2890
Richard D Thomas, *President*
EMP: 6 **EST:** 1973
SQ FT: 1,200
SALES (est): 4MM **Privately Held**
SIC: 2411 2421 1629 2426 Logging camps & contractors; pulpwood contractors engaged in cutting; sawmills & planing mills, general; land clearing contractor; hardwood dimension & flooring mills

(G-1123)
TOPSMAL DAIRY LLC
2289 Jacksonville Rd (16823-9340)
PHONE..............................814 880-3724
Thomas Gardner, *Mng Member*
Laura Gardner, *Mng Member*
Sarah Gardner, *Admin Asst*
EMP: 9
SALES: 135K **Privately Held**
SIC: 0241 2026 2013 Milk production; farmers' cheese; head cheese from purchased meat products

(G-1124)
WASH N GRIND LLC
366 Aspen Ridge Way (16823-6527)
PHONE..............................814 383-4707
Ronald Ritter, *Principal*
EMP: 3
SALES (est): 194K **Privately Held**
SIC: 3599 Grinding castings for the trade

Belleville
Mifflin County

(G-1125)
B V PALLETS
2451 W Back Mountain Rd (17004-8953)
PHONE..............................717 935-5740
Samuel R Peachey, *Partner*
Samuel S Peachey, *Partner*
EMP: 12
SQ FT: 1,600
SALES: 2MM **Privately Held**
SIC: 2448 Pallets, wood & wood with metal

(G-1126)
BARRVILLE LUMBER
52 Cherry Tree Ln (17004-8591)
PHONE..............................717 667-9600
Deana B Yoder, *Partner*
Sam Yoder, *Partner*
EMP: 9
SALES (est): 1.5MM **Privately Held**
SIC: 2448 Pallets, wood

(G-1127)
BIG VALLEY CABINETS
80 Rockville Rd (17004-8922)
PHONE..............................717 935-2788
Donald E Mathews Jr, *Owner*
EMP: 5
SQ FT: 3,200
SALES (est): 583.9K **Privately Held**
SIC: 2541 5031 Cabinets, except refrigerated: show, display, etc.: wood; kitchen cabinets

(G-1128)
BIG VALLEY CONCRETE
2649 Front Mountain Rd (17004-8809)
PHONE..............................717 483-6538
Dale Yoder, *Owner*
EMP: 5
SALES (est): 972K **Privately Held**
WEB: www.bigvalleyconcrete.com
SIC: 3273 Ready-mixed concrete

(G-1129)
CHEMGRO FERTILIZER CO INC
Union Mill Division
316 Applehouse Rd (17004-8628)
PHONE..............................717 935-2185
Donald Hartzler, *Opers-Prdtn-Mfg*
Don Hartzler, *Consultant*
EMP: 15
SALES (corp-wide): 26.9MM **Privately Held**
WEB: www.chemgro.com
SIC: 2873 2879 5191 Nitrogenous fertilizers; pesticides, agricultural or household; fertilizers & agricultural chemicals
PA: Chemgro Fertilizer Co., Inc.
1550 State St
East Petersburg PA 17520
717 560-1174

(G-1130)
DAVID M BYLER
Also Called: Kish Lumber Co
157 Sawmill Rd (17004-8527)
PHONE..............................717 667-6157
David M Byler, *Owner*
EMP: 10
SALES (est): 866.3K **Privately Held**
SIC: 2421 5031 Specialty sawmill products; lumber, plywood & millwork

(G-1131)
DONSCO INC
Also Called: Bellville Foundry
4381 Front Mountain Rd (17004-8848)
PHONE..............................717 252-1561
Charles Cutshall, *Branch Mgr*
EMP: 120
SALES (est): 13.8MM
SALES (corp-wide): 191.5MM **Privately Held**
WEB: www.donsco.com
SIC: 3321 Gray iron castings
PA: Donsco, Inc.
124 N Front St
Wrightsville PA 17368
717 252-1561

(G-1132)
J R YOUNG
76 S Penn St (17004-8600)
P.O. Box 20 (17004-0020)
PHONE..............................717 935-2919
Jeff Young, *President*
EMP: 3
SQ FT: 6,200
SALES (est): 389.3K **Privately Held**
SIC: 7699 7692 3531 Aircraft & heavy equipment repair services; welding equipment repair; welding repair; construction machinery; excavators: cable, clamshell, crane, derrick, dragline, etc.

(G-1133)
MOUNTAINSIDE WOOD PRODUCTS
3559 Front Mountain Rd (17004-8854)
PHONE..................................717 935-5753
Jonathan Zook, *Partner*
Leon Zook, *Partner*
Sarah King, *Admin Sec*
EMP: 17
SQ FT: 4,500
SALES: 1.8MM **Privately Held**
WEB:
www.mountainsidewoodproducts.com
SIC: 2434 Wood kitchen cabinets

(G-1134)
PEACHEYS SAWMILL INC
122 Sunnyside Ln (17004-9162)
PHONE..................................717 483-6336
Jonas Peachey, *President*
Sally Peachey, *Vice Pres*
EMP: 10
SALES (est): 1.1MM **Privately Held**
SIC: 2421 Sawmills & planing mills, general

(G-1135)
ZOOKS PALLETS INC
10 State St (17004-8602)
PHONE..................................717 935-5030
Mark C Zook, *President*
EMP: 4
SALES (est): 324.5K **Privately Held**
SIC: 2448 Pallets, wood

(G-1136)
ZOOKS PALLETS LLC
149 Sawmill Rd (17004-8527)
PHONE..................................717 667-9077
Mark C Zook, *Mng Member*
EMP: 10
SALES (est): 1.5MM **Privately Held**
SIC: 2448 Pallets, wood

Bellwood
Blair County

(G-1137)
EDMISTON SIGNS
809 N 6th St (16617-1003)
PHONE..................................814 742-8930
Frank Edmiston, *Owner*
Sue Edmiston, *Co-Owner*
EMP: 4
SQ FT: 3,600
SALES: 300K **Privately Held**
WEB: www.edmistonsigns.com
SIC: 5999 5084 3993 Awnings; cranes, industrial; neon signs

Bendersville
Adams County

(G-1138)
BENDERSVILLE WOOD CRAFTS
182 Park St (17306)
P.O. Box 64 (17306-0064)
PHONE..................................717 677-6458
Loyd Shelleman, *Partner*
EMP: 3
SALES (est): 260K **Privately Held**
WEB: www.bendersvillewoodcrafts.com
SIC: 2541 Wood partitions & fixtures

(G-1139)
KIME CIDER MILL
171 Church St (17306)
P.O. Box 419 (17306-0419)
PHONE..................................717 677-7539
Ricky Kime, *Managing Prtnr*
Randy Kime, *Partner*
EMP: 10
SQ FT: 4,000
SALES (est): 1.5MM **Privately Held**
WEB: www.kimescidermill.com
SIC: 2099 2033 0175 Cider, nonalcoholic; preserves, including imitation: in cans, jars, etc.; fruits: packaged in cans, jars, etc.; apple orchard

Bensalem
Bucks County

(G-1140)
3D PRINTING AND COPY CTR INC
Also Called: 3 D Printing & Digital Imaging
1296 Adams Rd 150 (19020-3977)
PHONE..................................215 968-7900
William F Quinn, *President*
EMP: 10
SQ FT: 3,000
SALES (est): 1.9MM **Privately Held**
WEB: www.3d-printing.com
SIC: 2752 7334 Commercial printing, offset; photocopying & duplicating services

(G-1141)
A OLEK & SON INC
Also Called: Olek Belts
443 Mill Rd (19020-6338)
PHONE..................................215 638-4550
John A Olek Jr, *President*
▲ EMP: 10 EST: 1917
SQ FT: 1,500
SALES (est): 1.2MM **Privately Held**
SIC: 2211 Canvas; cotton broad woven goods; laundry fabrics, cotton

(G-1142)
ABSOLUTE PALLET INC
550 State Rd Ste B (19020-8702)
PHONE..................................215 331-4510
David Senss, *President*
William Senss, *Manager*
EMP: 5 EST: 2006
SALES (est): 825K **Privately Held**
SIC: 1542 2448 Commercial & office building contractors; pallets, wood & wood with metal

(G-1143)
ADEMCO INC
Also Called: ADI Global Distribution
358 Dunksferry Rd (19020-6543)
PHONE..................................215 244-6377
Rob Amadio, *Manager*
EMP: 5
SALES (corp-wide): 4.8B **Publicly Held**
WEB: www.adilink.com
SIC: 5063 3669 Electrical apparatus & equipment; emergency alarms
HQ: Ademco Inc.
1985 Douglas Dr N
Golden Valley MN 55422
800 468-1502

(G-1144)
ADVANCED LUBRICATION SPC INC (PA)
Also Called: Advanced Lubrication Spc
420 Imperial Ct (19020-7327)
PHONE..................................215 244-2114
Greg T Julian, *President*
Gary Julian, *Chairman*
Joe Fitzmier, *Vice Pres*
Bob Mack, *Vice Pres*
Dave Parish, *Plant Mgr*
◆ EMP: 46
SQ FT: 115,000
SALES (est): 73.1MM **Privately Held**
WEB: www.advancedlubes.com
SIC: 5172 2899 2992 5531 Lubricating oils & greases; chemical preparations; lubricating oils & greases; lubricating oils; cutting oils, blending: made from purchased materials; transmission fluid: made from purchased materials; automotive & home supply stores

(G-1145)
AFAB INDUSTRIAL SERVICES INC
Also Called: Novelty Concepts
350 Camer Dr (19020-7302)
PHONE..................................215 245-1280
Everett L Farr, *President*
▲ EMP: 31
SALES (est): 7MM **Privately Held**
SIC: 2819 2821 Chemicals, high purity: refined from technical grade; chemicals, reagent grade: refined from technical grade; plastics materials & resins

(G-1146)
AKAS TEX LLC
Also Called: Akas Textiles & Lamination
1360 Adams Rd (19020-3913)
PHONE..................................215 244-2589
Sid Sharma, *Mng Member*
EMP: 10 EST: 2014
SALES (est): 3MM **Privately Held**
SIC: 2211 2221 2295 Upholstery fabrics, cotton; manmade & synthetic broadwoven fabrics; laminating of fabrics

(G-1147)
ALCO FUEL INC
2803 Bristol Pike (19020-5362)
PHONE..................................215 638-4800
EMP: 4 EST: 2009
SALES (est): 192.4K **Privately Held**
SIC: 2869 Fuels

(G-1148)
AMERICAN ACCESSORIES INC
1355 Adams Rd (19020-3912)
PHONE..................................215 639-8000
Allan Ford, *President*
EMP: 45
SALES (corp-wide): 18.5MM **Privately Held**
SIC: 3172 3161 Checkbook covers; attache cases
PA: American Accessories, Inc.
11100 Hope St
Cypress CA 90630
949 240-1418

(G-1149)
ASSOCIATED MACHINE SERVICE (PA)
6560 Senator Ln (19020-1960)
PHONE..................................215 335-1940
Harvey Berkowitz, *President*
EMP: 8 EST: 1978
SQ FT: 8,300
SALES (est): 250K **Privately Held**
SIC: 7694 Motor repair services

(G-1150)
ASTRAZENECA PHARMACEUTICALS LP
3600 Marshall Ln (19020-5914)
PHONE..................................215 501-1739
EMP: 3
SALES (est): 154.9K **Privately Held**
SIC: 2834 Pharmaceutical preparations

(G-1151)
ATLANTIC SHELVING SYSTEMS LLC
480 State Rd Ste D (19020-7829)
PHONE..................................215 245-1310
Michael Domanico, *CEO*
EMP: 6
SALES: 1,000K **Privately Held**
SIC: 2541 Wood partitions & fixtures

(G-1152)
AVEX ELECTRONICS CORP
1683 Winchester Rd (19020-4541)
P.O. Box 1026 (19020-5026)
PHONE..................................215 245-4848
Michael Hasness, *President*
Richard Hasness, *VP Prdtn*
Ron Alcott, *Controller*
▲ EMP: 20 EST: 1976
SQ FT: 8,500
SALES (est): 3.1MM **Privately Held**
WEB: www.avexelectronics.com
SIC: 3691 3825 3679 Storage batteries; measuring instruments & meters, electric; oscillographs & oscilloscopes; harness assemblies for electronic use: wire or cable

(G-1153)
B & J MACHINE INC
309 Camer Dr Unit 3 (19020-7323)
PHONE..................................215 639-8800
William O'Brien Jr, *President*
James O'Brien, *Vice Pres*
EMP: 8
SQ FT: 5,000
SALES: 700K **Privately Held**
SIC: 3599 Machine shop, jobbing & repair

(G-1154)
BCMI AD CONCEPTS INC
Also Called: Promedia Publishing
3412 Progress Dr Ste C (19020-5817)
PHONE..................................215 354-3000
Robert Smylie, *Publisher*
EMP: 42
SQ FT: 7,500
SALES (est): 8MM
SALES (corp-wide): 807.2MM **Publicly Held**
WEB: www.mcclatchy.com
SIC: 2711 Newspapers, publishing & printing
PA: The Mcclatchy Company
2100 Q St
Sacramento CA 95816
916 321-1844

(G-1155)
BEDSIDE HARP LLC
4802 Neshaminy Blvd Ste 9 (19020-1041)
PHONE..................................215 752-7599
Sharon Brown, *President*
Edie Elkan, *Sales Executive*
Leslie Stickley, *Associate Dir*
EMP: 10
SALES (est): 928.1K **Privately Held**
WEB: www.bedsideharp.com
SIC: 3931 Harpsichords

(G-1156)
BENSALEM METAL INC
2424 State Rd Ste 3 (19020-7300)
PHONE..................................215 526-3355
Yury Kozhan, *President*
EMP: 5
SQ FT: 6,000
SALES (est): 214.9K **Privately Held**
SIC: 3444 Sheet metalwork

(G-1157)
BESS MANUFACTURING COMPANY
156 Dunksferry Rd (19020-6531)
PHONE..................................215 447-1032
David Ashe, *Ch of Bd*
W Thomas Klenert, *President*
▲ EMP: 5 EST: 1938
SQ FT: 40,000
SALES: 19.3MM **Privately Held**
SIC: 2392 Scarves: table, dresser, etc., from purchased materials; tablecloths: made from purchased materials

(G-1158)
BLUE STAR BASKETBALL
1950 Street Rd Ste 104 (19020-3749)
P.O. Box 530 (19020-0530)
PHONE..................................215 638-7060
Mike Flynn, *Owner*
EMP: 3 EST: 1978
SALES (est): 306.6K **Privately Held**
WEB: www.bluestarbb.com
SIC: 7941 2721 Basketball club; periodicals

(G-1159)
BONNIT BRUSH LLC
3161 State Rd (19020-6545)
PHONE..................................215 355-4115
Robert Brentari, *Principal*
▲ EMP: 3
SALES (est): 270K **Privately Held**
SIC: 2851 Paintbrush cleaners

(G-1160)
BRADLEY GRAPHIC SOLUTIONS INC
Also Called: Bradley Business Forms
941 Mill Rd (19020-6342)
PHONE..................................215 638-8771
Robert M Bradley, *President*
William Frey, *Treasurer*
Brian Bradley, *Admin Sec*
EMP: 45
SALES (est): 9.1MM **Privately Held**
WEB: www.bradleygraphics.net
SIC: 2752 Commercial printing, offset

(G-1161)
BRENNER AEROSTRUCTURES LLC
Also Called: Atlas Group The
450 Winks Ln 3 (19020-5932)
PHONE.................................215 638-3884
John Brenner, *President*
Jonathan Jecen, *Opers Mgr*
Gus Kokolis, *Parts Mgr*
Bob Baltzer, *QC Mgr*
Kathleen Brenner, *CFO*
EMP: 50
SALES (est): 9.7MM **Privately Held**
WEB: www.brenneraero.com
SIC: 3728 Airframe assemblies, except for
guided missiles
HQ: Aerostructures Acquisition Llc
18008 N Black Canyon Hwy
Phoenix AZ 85053

(G-1162)
BUCKS COUNTY FUEL LLC
890 Jordan Dr (19020-4075)
PHONE.................................215 245-0807
John Leary, *Principal*
EMP: 5
SALES (est): 376.7K **Privately Held**
SIC: 2869 Fuels

(G-1163)
C A SPALDING COMPANY
4529 Adams Cir (19020-3927)
PHONE.................................267 550-9000
Javier Kuehnle, *President*
G Wesley Kuehnle, *President*
George Kuehnle, *Vice Pres*
EMP: 30 EST: 1932
SQ FT: 37,000
SALES (est): 6.3MM **Privately Held**
WEB: www.caspalding.com
SIC: 3544 3444 7692 Special dies, tools,
jigs & fixtures; sheet metalwork; welding
repair

(G-1164)
C E CONOVER & CO INC
Also Called: Reliable Rubber Products Co
4106 Blanche Rd (19020-4430)
P.O. Box 157 (19020-0157)
PHONE.................................215 639-6666
J Bruce Hamilton, *CEO*
James A Ennis, *President*
Lisa A Loffredo, *CFO*
EMP: 37 EST: 1947
SQ FT: 18,000
SALES (est): 7MM **Privately Held**
WEB: www.conoverseals.com
SIC: 3053 3061 Gaskets, all materials;
gaskets & sealing devices; packing mate-
rials; mechanical rubber goods

(G-1165)
CAS PACK CORPORATION
1750b Woodhaven Dr (19020-7108)
PHONE.................................215 254-7225
David Clewell, *President*
Jesse Smith, *Vice Pres*
W Russell Smith, *Treasurer*
▼ **EMP:** 22 EST: 1966
SQ FT: 45,000
SALES (est): 9.1MM **Privately Held**
WEB: www.caspack.com
SIC: 2653 2671 2672 Boxes, corrugated:
made from purchased materials; packag-
ing paper & plastics film, coated & lami-
nated; coated & laminated paper

(G-1166)
CERAMIC SERVICES INC
1060 Park Ave (19020-4652)
PHONE.................................215 245-4040
Cameron G Harman Jr, *President*
Samuel J Trublood, *Admin Sec*
EMP: 5
SQ FT: 750
SALES (est): 480K **Privately Held**
WEB: www.kilnman.com
SIC: 3567 Ceramic kilns & furnaces

(G-1167)
CGM INCORPORATED
1445 Ford Rd (19020-4503)
PHONE.................................215 638-4400
Fred Geary, *President*
Joseph Giulli, *Vice Pres*
◆ **EMP:** 20

SQ FT: 47,000
SALES (est): 5.4MM **Privately Held**
WEB: www.cgmbuildingproducts.com
SIC: 3272 Concrete products

(G-1168)
CHARLES SCHILLINGER CO INC
1329 Ford Rd (19020-4501)
P.O. Box 718 (19020-0718)
PHONE.................................215 638-7200
John McGeever, *President*
▲ **EMP:** 25 EST: 1921
SQ FT: 40,000
SALES (est): 5.9MM **Privately Held**
WEB: www.charlesschillinger.com
SIC: 3469 Spinning metal for the trade

(G-1169)
CNI INC
Also Called: C. N. I.
1683b Winchester Rd (19020-4541)
PHONE.................................215 244-9650
Maria Ryan, *President*
David Comitale, *Vice Pres*
Bernadette Goldsmith, *Vice Pres*
Glenn Dibernardo, *Accounts Exec*
Michael Comitale, *Executive*
▲ **EMP:** 35
SQ FT: 35,000
SALES (est): 6.8MM **Privately Held**
WEB: www.comitalenational.com
SIC: 3585 Air conditioning equipment,
complete

(G-1170)
COLA INTERNATIONAL LLC
433 Brister Rd (19020-1649)
PHONE.................................267 977-6700
EMP: 3
SALES (est): 154.4K **Privately Held**
SIC: 2086 Soft drinks: packaged in cans,
bottles, etc.

(G-1171)
COLFAB INDUSTRIES LLC
2522 State Rd Ste A (19020-7346)
PHONE.................................215 768-2135
Gregory Mason, *Mng Member*
EMP: 20
SQ FT: 70,000
SALES (est): 3MM **Privately Held**
SIC: 3442 Sash, door or window: metal

(G-1172)
COMPASS SIGN CO LLC (PA)
1505 Ford Rd (19020-4505)
PHONE.................................215 639-6777
Milly Dube, *Controller*
Phillip Doerle,
EMP: 25
SQ FT: 10,000
SALES (est): 4.2MM **Privately Held**
WEB: www.compass-sign.net
SIC: 3993 Signs, not made in custom sign
painting shops

(G-1173)
COREN METAL INC
600 Center Ave (19020-6507)
PHONE.................................215 244-4260
Douglas Beck, *President*
Irene Beck, *CFO*
EMP: 20
SQ FT: 25,000
SALES (est): 1.1MM **Privately Held**
SIC: 3444 Sheet metalwork

(G-1174)
COREN METALCRAFTS COMPANY
600 Center Ave (19020-6507)
P.O. Box 1005 (19020-5005)
PHONE.................................215 244-0532
Mark Berenato, *President*
EMP: 12 EST: 1997
SQ FT: 22,000
SALES (est): 1.9MM **Privately Held**
SIC: 3444 Sheet metal specialties, not
stamped

(G-1175)
CREATIVE ARCHITECTURAL METALS
1642 Woodhaven Dr (19020-7106)
PHONE.................................215 638-1650

James Mee, *President*
Thomas Kanuck, *Vice Pres*
Patricia Kanuck, *Treasurer*
Barbara Mee, *Admin Sec*
EMP: 21
SQ FT: 12,000
SALES: 2MM **Privately Held**
SIC: 3446 Architectural metalwork

(G-1176)
CUMMINS - ALLISON CORP
3260 Tillman Dr (19020-2029)
PHONE.................................215 245-8436
J Thomas Timmins, *Principal*
EMP: 7
SALES (corp-wide): 383.8MM **Privately
Held**
SIC: 5084 3519 Machine tools & metal-
working machinery; internal combustion
engines
PA: Cummins - Allison Corp.
852 Feehanville Dr
Mount Prospect IL 60056
847 759-6403

(G-1177)
CURTISS LABORATORIES INC
2510 State Rd (19020-7312)
PHONE.................................215 245-8833
David Sloviter, *President*
Sandra Masicantonio, *Admin Sec*
◆ **EMP:** 9 EST: 1963
SQ FT: 12,000
SALES (est): 1.5MM **Privately Held**
WEB: www.curtisslabs.com
SIC: 2819 Chemicals, reagent grade: re-
fined from technical grade

(G-1178)
CUSTOM MANUFACTURING CORP
2542 State Rd (19020-7312)
PHONE.................................215 638-3888
Nicholas J Pucci, *President*
Marguerite Pucci, *Corp Secy*
EMP: 45 EST: 1957
SQ FT: 49,000
SALES (est): 10.1MM **Privately Held**
WEB: www.custommfgcorp.com
SIC: 3334 3444 Primary aluminum; sheet
metalwork

(G-1179)
DANIEL C TANNEY INC
3268 Clive Ave (19020-6509)
P.O. Box 272 (19020-0272)
PHONE.................................215 639-3131
Daniel C Tanney, *Ch of Bd*
Michael R Tanney, *President*
James A Tanney Jr, *Vice Pres*
Theresa R Murray, *Treasurer*
Jeanne T Hughes, *Admin Sec*
EMP: 65
SQ FT: 40,000
SALES (est): 13.1MM **Privately Held**
WEB: www.dctanney.com
SIC: 3499 3441 3914 3444 Boxes for
packing & shipping, metal; fabricated
structural metal; silverware & plated ware;
sheet metalwork

(G-1180)
DBEX TEK LLC
1105 William Penn Dr (19020-4376)
PHONE.................................267 566-0354
Jonathan Norman-Finkel,
EMP: 4
SALES (est): 195.4K **Privately Held**
SIC: 2834 Chlorination tablets & kits (water
purification)

(G-1181)
DELAWARE VALLEY SHIPPERS INC
Also Called: Delaware Valley Shippers Inc
3685 Marshall Ln (19020-5913)
PHONE.................................215 633-1535
Mark Kraeuter, *President*
William Boothby, *Vice Pres*
EMP: 19
SQ FT: 9,387
SALES (est): 4.8MM
SALES (corp-wide): 15MM **Privately
Held**
SIC: 3715 Truck trailers

PA: Combined Express, Inc.
3685 Marshall Ln
Bensalem PA 19020
215 633-1535

(G-1182)
DELAWARE VALLEY SHIPPING & PAC
Also Called: Delaware Valley Packg Group
1425 Wells Dr (19020-4469)
P.O. Box 96 (19020-0096)
PHONE.................................215 638-8900
Stephen J Kiszely, *CEO*
Stephen T Kiszely, *President*
Thomas Di Paolo, *Corp Secy*
Tom Dipaolo, *CFO*
John Kelly, *Controller*
EMP: 29
SQ FT: 30,000
SALES (est): 8.9MM **Privately Held**
WEB: www.dvpg.com
SIC: 2675 Die-cut paper & board

(G-1183)
DRAKE REFRIGERATION INC
2900 Samuel Dr (19020-7306)
PHONE.................................215 638-5515
Michael Coyle, *President*
John H Reilly III, *Vice Pres*
James J Meiler, *Vice Pres*
Nicholas V Hope, *Vice Pres*
Carmen D Carosella, *Admin Sec*
▲ **EMP:** 15
SQ FT: 120,000
SALES (est): 4.4MM **Privately Held**
WEB: www.drakechillers.com
SIC: 3585 3569 Refrigeration & heating
equipment; heaters, swimming pool: elec-
tric

(G-1184)
E K L MACHINE INC
500 Mill Rd (19020-6301)
PHONE.................................215 639-0150
Edward Lydon, *President*
EMP: 29
SQ FT: 28,000
SALES (est): 5.1MM **Privately Held**
SIC: 3599 7692 Machine shop, jobbing &
repair; welding repair

(G-1185)
EBERHARTS CSTM EMBRODIERY INC
3448 Progress Dr Ste E (19020-5813)
PHONE.................................215 639-9530
Richard A Eberhart Jr, *President*
EMP: 6
SQ FT: 1,800
SALES (est): 579K **Privately Held**
SIC: 2395 Embroidery products, except
schiffli machine; embroidery & art needle-
work

(G-1186)
EDDINGTON THREAD MFG CO INC (PA)
3222 Knights Rd (19020-2825)
P.O. Box 446 (19020-0446)
PHONE.................................215 639-8900
Massoud Matinfar, *CEO*
Michele C Leckerman, *Corp Secy*
Linda Liebman, *Vice Pres*
S James Lovenstein, *VP Mfg*
EMP: 50 EST: 1946
SQ FT: 56,000
SALES (est): 33.4MM **Privately Held**
WEB: www.edthread.com
SIC: 2284 2298 Sewing thread; twine,
cord & cordage

(G-1187)
ELECTRONIC TOOL & DIE WORKS
Also Called: TI Lighting Co
3156 Tucker Rd (19020)
PHONE.................................215 639-0730
Herbert Tucker, *President*
Frederick Tucker, *Vice Pres*
EMP: 9 EST: 1922
SQ FT: 8,574
SALES (est): 699.4K **Privately Held**
SIC: 3544 3469 Special dies & tools; jigs
& fixtures; metal stampings

(G-1188)
ELECTRONICS INSTRS & OPTICS (PA)
Pennsylvania Wicker Ave (19020)
PHONE..................................215 245-6300
Frank Richards, *President*
EMP: 48
SALES (est): 4.3MM **Privately Held**
SIC: 3443 3444 Fabricated plate work (boiler shop); sheet metalwork

(G-1189)
EMERSON ELECTRIC CO
855 Dunksferry Rd A (19020-6515)
PHONE..................................215 638-8904
Bernadette Michaels, *Manager*
EMP: 4
SALES (corp-wide): 17.4B **Publicly Held**
WEB: www.gotoemerson.com
SIC: 3823 Industrial instrmnts msrmnt display/control process variable
PA: Emerson Electric Co.
8000 West Florissant Ave
Saint Louis MO 63136
314 553-2000

(G-1190)
ENSINGER PENN FIBRE INC (DH)
2434 Bristol Rd (19020-6002)
PHONE..................................215 702-9551
Rick Phillips, *President*
Robert Racchini, *Corp Secy*
Lisa Hignutt, *Sales Staff*
EMP: 70
SALES (est): 15.6MM
SALES (corp-wide): 434.6MM **Privately Held**
WEB: www.pennfibre.com
SIC: 3053 3081 3452 3083 Gaskets, all materials; unsupported plastics film & sheet; bolts, nuts, rivets & washers; laminated plastics plate & sheet; unsupported plastics profile shapes
HQ: Ensinger Industries, Inc.
365 Meadowlands Blvd
Washington PA 15301
724 746-6050

(G-1191)
ERNST TIMING SCREW COMPANY
1534 Bridgewater Rd (19020-4508)
PHONE..................................215 639-1438
Suzanne Cannon, *President*
Ted Cannon, *Technology*
Lee Cannon, *Executive*
EMP: 21 **EST:** 1957
SQ FT: 12,000
SALES: 1.2MM **Privately Held**
WEB: www.ernsttiming.com
SIC: 3451 3625 Screw machine products; relays & industrial controls

(G-1192)
EVOQUA WATER TECHNOLOGIES LLC
258 Dunksferry Rd (19020-6540)
PHONE..................................215 638-7700
Carole Klingerman, *Manager*
EMP: 40
SALES (corp-wide): 1.3B **Publicly Held**
SIC: 3823 Water quality monitoring & control systems
HQ: Evoqua Water Technologies Llc
210 6th Ave Ste 3300
Pittsburgh PA 15222
724 772-0044

(G-1193)
FAMILY FOOD PRODUCTS INC
Also Called: Arnold's Meats
1271 Ford Rd (19020-4529)
PHONE..................................215 633-1515
Sheldon Dosik, *President*
EMP: 80
SALES (est): 10.6MM **Privately Held**
SIC: 2013 Sausages & other prepared meats

(G-1194)
FENCOR GRAPHICS INC
1505 Ford Rd (19020-4505)
PHONE..................................215 745-2266
Fax: 215 745-8402

EMP: 39
SQ FT: 18,000
SALES (est): 4.4MM **Privately Held**
SIC: 2752 Lithographic Commercial Printing

(G-1195)
FLAGSTAFF INDUSTRIES CORP (PA)
364 Dunksferry Rd (19020-6543)
PHONE..................................215 638-9662
Sheila Pollack, *President*
Ronald Turiak, *Corp Secy*
Lee Pollack, *Vice Pres*
Valerie I Pollack, *Vice Pres*
◆ **EMP:** 232
SQ FT: 6,350
SALES (est): 21.6MM **Privately Held**
WEB: www.flagstaffuniforms.com
SIC: 2311 2337 Men's & boys' uniforms; uniforms, except athletic: women's, misses' & juniors'

(G-1196)
FLEX RIG INC
Also Called: Flextron Systems
1935 Juniper Ln (19020-4436)
PHONE..................................215 638-5743
EMP: 19
SQ FT: 10,000
SALES: 1MM **Privately Held**
SIC: 3672 Mfg Electronic Printed Circuits

(G-1197)
FORMS GRAPHICS LLC
Also Called: Printing
1296 Adams Rd Ste 3 (19020-3977)
PHONE..................................215 639-3504
William R Coulter, *President*
EMP: 10 **EST:** 2012
SQ FT: 2,000
SALES: 650K **Privately Held**
SIC: 2759 Business forms: printing

(G-1198)
FRANKS ICE SERVICE LLC
3566 Hulmeville Rd (19020-4312)
P.O. Box 454 (19020-0454)
PHONE..................................215 741-2026
Frank Glass, *Mng Member*
EMP: 3
SALES (est): 190K **Privately Held**
SIC: 3299 5812 Architectural sculptures: gypsum, clay, papier mache, etc.; caterers

(G-1199)
FREDERICK WOHLGEMUTH INC
Also Called: Burns & Wohlgemuth
3901 Bristol Pike (19020-5924)
PHONE..................................215 638-9672
George Wohlgemuth, *President*
Robert C Emberger, *Corp Secy*
Frederick G Wohlgemuth, *Vice Pres*
EMP: 30 **EST:** 1946
SQ FT: 40,000
SALES: 2MM **Privately Held**
WEB: www.bwwoodcrafters.com
SIC: 2541 3543 Store fixtures, wood; industrial patterns

(G-1200)
FRP DOOR CONCEPTS INC
Also Called: Frp Architectural Doors
2424 State Rd Ste 8 (19020-7300)
PHONE..................................215 604-1545
Nick Santoro, *President*
Nicholas Irwin, *Vice Pres*
Larry McCanney, *Vice Pres*
Joe Piascik, *Vice Pres*
EMP: 8
SQ FT: 15,000
SALES: 200K **Privately Held**
SIC: 2431 Door frames, wood

(G-1201)
G M C INC
Also Called: Cgm
1445 Ford Rd (19020-4503)
PHONE..................................215 638-4400
Peter Terreri, *Managing Prtnr*
Patrick Mullins, *Managing Prtnr*
Vince Serratore, *Managing Prtnr*
Lisa Terreri, *Controller*
EMP: 40

SALES (est): 3.2MM **Privately Held**
SIC: 3241 Natural cement

(G-1202)
GALERON CONSULTING LLC
507 Windsor Ct Apt B3 (19020-7078)
PHONE..................................267 293-9230
France Guerrier, *CEO*
EMP: 25
SALES: 191K **Privately Held**
SIC: 8748 2741 2731 7371 Publishing consultant; miscellaneous publishing; book publishing; computer software development & applications; real estate investors, except property operators; financial consultant

(G-1203)
GENERAL METAL COMPANY INC
1286 Adams Rd (19020-3923)
PHONE..................................215 638-3242
Michael Tuszl, *President*
John Tuszl Sr, *Chairman*
Susan Knecht, *Treasurer*
Caroline Tuszl, *Admin Sec*
EMP: 40
SQ FT: 25,000
SALES (est): 9.5MM **Privately Held**
WEB: www.generalmetal.com
SIC: 3444 3577 2542 Sheet metal specialties, not stamped; computer peripheral equipment; partitions & fixtures, except wood

(G-1204)
GILL POWDER COATING INC
1384 Byberry Rd (19020-3972)
PHONE..................................215 639-5486
Andrew Gill Jr, *President*
EMP: 20 **EST:** 1951
SQ FT: 40,000
SALES (est): 2.9MM **Privately Held**
WEB: www.gillpowder.com
SIC: 3479 Coating of metals & formed products

(G-1205)
GIORDANO INCORPORATED
Also Called: Dial Machine Co
840 Mill Rd (19020-6331)
PHONE..................................215 632-3470
Michael J Giordano, *President*
John Giordano, *Vice Pres*
EMP: 15 **EST:** 1965
SQ FT: 10,000
SALES (est): 2.3MM **Privately Held**
SIC: 3599 3451 Machine shop, jobbing & repair; screw machine products

(G-1206)
GRAHAM PAINING CO
1501 Auburn Dr (19020-4470)
PHONE..................................215 447-8552
EMP: 3 **EST:** 2012
SALES (est): 162.8K **Privately Held**
SIC: 2435 Hardwood veneer & plywood

(G-1207)
GYROTRON TECHNOLOGY INC
Also Called: Gti
3412 Progress Dr (19020-5817)
PHONE..................................215 244-4740
Vlad Sklyarevich, *President*
Michael Shevelev, *Technology*
Jerome M Balsam, *Admin Sec*
EMP: 4
SQ FT: 8,000
SALES (est): 80.7K **Privately Held**
WEB: www.gyrotrontech.com
SIC: 3567 3443 Heating units & devices, industrial: electric; autoclaves, industrial

(G-1208)
H R SALES INC
Also Called: H R Clutches
3977 Bristol Pike Ste 1 (19020-5996)
PHONE..................................215 639-7150
Joseph Lalli, *President*
Jospeh Lalli Jr, *Admin Sec*
EMP: 7
SQ FT: 7,000
SALES (est): 949K **Privately Held**
SIC: 3714 Clutches, motor vehicle

(G-1209)
HERBAL EXTRACTS PLUS
350 Camer Dr (19020-7302)
PHONE..................................215 245-5055
EMP: 3
SALES (est): 318.6K **Privately Held**
SIC: 2836 Extracts

(G-1210)
HERFF JONES LLC
654 Street Rd (19020-7321)
PHONE..................................215 638-2490
Abe Orlick, *Branch Mgr*
EMP: 10
SALES (corp-wide): 1.1B **Privately Held**
WEB: www.herffjones.com
SIC: 3911 Rings, finger: precious metal
HQ: Herff Jones, Llc
4501 W 62nd St
Indianapolis IN 46268
800 419-5462

(G-1211)
JADEITE FOODS LLC
3684 Marshall Ln (19020-5914)
PHONE..................................267 522-8193
Xiao Yan Huang, *Mng Member*
▲ **EMP:** 7
SQ FT: 64,000
SALES (est): 781.2K **Privately Held**
SIC: 2099 Tofu, except frozen desserts

(G-1212)
JANZER CORPORATION
Also Called: Parthenon
5898 Tibby Rd (19020-1122)
PHONE..................................215 757-1168
Todd Janzer, *President*
EMP: 5
SQ FT: 30,000
SALES: 1.2MM **Privately Held**
WEB: www.janzer.com
SIC: 3446 Architectural metalwork

(G-1213)
JERRY LISTER CUSTOM UPHOLSTERI (PA)
Also Called: Lister Uphlstring Win Fashions
2075 Byberry Rd Ste 108 (19020-3859)
PHONE..................................215 639-3880
Dennis Lister, *President*
EMP: 6
SQ FT: 6,200
SALES (est): 1.8MM **Privately Held**
SIC: 2512 7641 2591 Upholstered household furniture; reupholstery; window blinds

(G-1214)
JOSEPH H TEES & SON INC
1450 Bridgewater Rd (19020-4431)
PHONE..................................215 638-3368
Robin Dickson, *President*
Jeffrey Dickson, *Vice Pres*
Russell G Tees, *Vice Pres*
EMP: 7 **EST:** 1934
SQ FT: 10,000
SALES (est): 1.1MM **Privately Held**
SIC: 2752 2759 Commercial printing, offset; letterpress printing

(G-1215)
KIMRE INC
501 Cambria Ave # 108112 (19020-7213)
PHONE..................................305 233-4249
EMP: 3 **EST:** 2014
SALES (est): 233.6K **Privately Held**
SIC: 2819 Industrial inorganic chemicals

(G-1216)
KLOECKNER METALS CORPORATION
555 State Rd (19021)
P.O. Box 6055, Philadelphia (19114-0655)
PHONE..................................215 245-3300
Michael Hoffman, *CEO*
Russ Delaney Jr, *Vice Pres*
EMP: 1100
SALES (corp-wide): 7.7B **Privately Held**
WEB: www.macsteelusa.com
SIC: 3317 3316 3312 Steel pipe & tubes; cold finishing of steel shapes; blast furnaces & steel mills

GEOGRAPHIC

HQ: Kloeckner Metals Corporation
500 Colonial Center Pkwy # 500
Roswell GA 30076

(G-1217)
KYRON NAVAL ARCHITECTURE
Also Called: Kyron International
111 Royal Mews (19020-8713)
PHONE...................................516 304-1769
Robert Cook, *Vice Pres*
EMP: 5
SALES (est): 131.4K **Privately Held**
SIC: 8711 3764 3761 8748 Consulting
engineer; guided missile & space vehicle
engines, research & devel.; guided mis-
siles & space vehicles, research & devel-
opment; industrial development planning

(G-1218)
LAMINATED MATERIALS CORP
Also Called: Lmc-Plasticsource
625 Winks Ln (19020-5922)
PHONE...................................215 425-4100
Joseph Coughlin, *President*
James Alexander, *CFO*
Daniel Coughlin, *Treasurer*
▲ EMP: 40
SQ FT: 44,000
SALES (est): 8.3MM **Privately Held**
WEB: www.lmcplastics.com
SIC: 3089 5162 Injection molded finished
plastic products; plastics products

(G-1219)
LARSON-JUHL US LLC
1574 Bridgewater Rd (19020-4508)
PHONE...................................215 638-5940
George Walmsley, *Branch Mgr*
EMP: 7
SALES (corp-wide): 225.3B **Publicly
Held**
SIC: 5023 2499 Frames & framing, picture
& mirror; picture frame molding, finished
HQ: Larson-Juhl Us Llc
3900 Steve Reynolds Blvd
Norcross GA 30093
770 279-5200

(G-1220)
**LEXICON INTERNATIONAL
CORP**
Also Called: VSC Services Division
1400 Adams Rd Ste A (19020-3965)
PHONE...................................215 639-8220
Marvin Stabler, *President*
EMP: 49
SALES (est): 2.6MM **Privately Held**
SIC: 3661 3577 3571 5045 Telephones &
telephone apparatus; computer peripheral
equipment; electronic computers; comput-
ers, peripherals & software; catalog &
mail-order houses

(G-1221)
LINEAR TECHNOLOGY LLC
3220 Tillman Dr Ste 120 (19020-2028)
PHONE...................................215 638-9667
EMP: 13
SALES (corp-wide): 5.1B **Publicly Held**
SIC: 3674 Mfg Semiconductors/Related
Devices
HQ: Linear Technology Llc
1630 Mccarthy Blvd
Milpitas CA 95035
408 432-1900

(G-1222)
LOUISVILLE LADDER INC
855 Dunksferry Rd (19020-6515)
PHONE...................................215 638-8904
Patricia Wells, *Branch Mgr*
EMP: 8
SALES (corp-wide): 173.9MM **Privately
Held**
SIC: 3499 Fire- or burglary-resistive prod-
ucts
PA: Louisville Ladder Inc.
7765 National Tpke # 190
Louisville KY 40214
502 636-2811

(G-1223)
**MAXIMUM GRAPHICS
CORPORATION**
1408 Ford Rd (19020-4504)
PHONE...................................215 639-6700

Thomas Kane, *President*
Michael Kane, *Vice Pres*
Rosemary Kane, *Admin Sec*
EMP: 12
SQ FT: 6,800
SALES (est): 2MM **Privately Held**
WEB: www.maximumgraphics.net
SIC: 2752 Commercial printing, offset

(G-1224)
MEDIHILL INC
3466 Progress Dr Ste 111 (19020-5814)
PHONE...................................215 464-7016
Michael Smetov, *CEO*
▲ EMP: 3
SALES (est): 485.1K **Privately Held**
SIC: 5047 8082 3845 Medical equipment
& supplies; patient monitoring equipment;
home health care services; patient moni-
toring apparatus

(G-1225)
MEDIMMUNE LLC
3600 Marshall Ln (19020-5914)
PHONE...................................215 501-1300
William C Bertrand Jr, *Exec VP*
Dawn Valentine, *Branch Mgr*
Dwight Rivera, *Manager*
Sandrina Phipps, *Associate*
EMP: 275
SALES (corp-wide): 22.4B **Privately Held**
SIC: 2836 Vaccines
HQ: Medimmune, Llc
1 Medimmune Way
Gaithersburg MD 20878
301 398-0000

(G-1226)
**MEN OF STEEL ENTERPRISES
LLC**
Also Called: Independent Fbrc
555 State Rd 101 (19020-7704)
PHONE...................................609 871-2000
Robert Vogelbacher, *Mng Member*
EMP: 25
SALES (est): 4.2MM **Privately Held**
SIC: 3449 Bars, concrete reinforcing: fabri-
cated steel

(G-1227)
MERCURY SYSTEMS INC
2182 Lillian Dr (19020-2972)
P.O. Box 625 (19020-0625)
PHONE...................................215 245-0546
Eugene H Curran, *President*
Thomas Walsh, *Principal*
Cathy Marino, *Materials Mgr*
Gary Fisher, *Engineer*
EMP: 6
SQ FT: 13,000
SALES (est): 1.1MM **Privately Held**
SIC: 3669 Emergency alarms

(G-1228)
**NATIONAL RFRGN & AC PDTS
INC (PA)**
Also Called: National Refrigeration Pdts
539 Dunksferry Rd (19020-5908)
PHONE...................................215 244-1400
John H Reilly, *CEO*
Brian Kelly, *President*
Nicholas V Hope, *Vice Pres*
Amanda Smith, *Mfg Mgr*
Jeff Bauman, *Engineer*
▲ EMP: 50
SQ FT: 85,000
SALES (est): 77MM **Privately Held**
WEB: www.nationalcomfortproducts.com
SIC: 3585 5075 Refrigeration equipment,
complete; air conditioning equipment,
complete; warm air heating & air condi-
tioning

(G-1229)
**NATIONAL TOWELETTE
COMPANY**
Also Called: NTC
1726 Woodhaven Dr (19020-7108)
PHONE...................................215 245-7300
Timothy Brock, *President*
Mark Pennink, *Vice Pres*
Bev Keating-Veczko, *Office Mgr*
Simons Edward, *Admin Sec*
▲ EMP: 40
SQ FT: 67,000

SALES (est): 11.8MM **Privately Held**
SIC: 2844 5084 Towelettes, premoistened;
safety equipment

(G-1230)
NESHAMINY VALLEY MILLWORK
773 American Dr (19020-7342)
PHONE...................................215 604-0251
Shawn Cannon, *Owner*
Don Waysz, *Project Mgr*
EMP: 10
SALES (est): 1.3MM **Privately Held**
SIC: 2431 Millwork

(G-1231)
NORTHEAST FOODS INC
Also Called: Bake Rite Rolls
2945 Samuel Dr (19020-7305)
PHONE...................................215 638-2400
Richard Tommy, *Branch Mgr*
EMP: 150
SQ FT: 20,000
SALES (corp-wide): 335.5MM **Privately
Held**
SIC: 2051 Buns, bread type: fresh or
frozen
PA: Northeast Foods, Inc.
601 S Caroline St
Baltimore MD 21231
410 276-7254

(G-1232)
**NORTHSTERN PRECISION PDTS
CORP**
Also Called: Ne
2230 Pennsylvania Ave (19020-7226)
P.O. Box 928 (19020-0928)
PHONE...................................215 245-6300
Frank Richards, *President*
Sue McGuigan, *Admin Sec*
EMP: 43
SALES (est): 8.5MM
SALES (corp-wide): 4.3MM **Privately
Held**
WEB: www.neprecision.com
SIC: 3444 Sheet metalwork
PA: Electronics Instruments & Optics Inc
Pennsylvania Wicker Ave
Bensalem PA 19020
215 245-6300

(G-1233)
NOVELTY CONCEPTS INC
Also Called: Si Novelties
350 Camer Dr (19020-7302)
P.O. Box 1025, Langhorne (19047-6025)
PHONE...................................215 245-5570
Everett Farr, *President*
▲ EMP: 6
SALES (est): 710K **Privately Held**
SIC: 3089 Plastic containers, except foam

(G-1234)
NYTEF PLASTICS LTD
633 Dunksferry Rd (19020-5909)
PHONE...................................215 244-6950
Ashoo Saigal, *Ch of Bd*
French Morton R III, *President*
John C French, *Vice Pres*
▲ EMP: 1
SALES (est): 5.8MM
SALES (corp-wide): 67.9MM **Privately
Held**
SIC: 3089 Plastic processing
PA: Polymer Industries, Llc
10526 Highway 40
Henagar AL 35978
256 657-6291

(G-1235)
OFFICELOGIC INC
2452 Williamson Ct (19020-2227)
P.O. Box 1590 (19020-5590)
PHONE...................................215 752-3069
Stephan Sherman, *Principal*
EMP: 5
SALES (est): 323.9K **Privately Held**
SIC: 2599 Restaurant furniture, wood or
metal

(G-1236)
OLDSKOOL PRODUXIONS INC
2100 Bristol Pike (19020-5200)
PHONE...................................215 638-4804
Mike Mallon, *President*
Lou Mallon, *Corp Secy*

John Mallon, *Vice Pres*
EMP: 6
SQ FT: 1,600
SALES: 400K **Privately Held**
WEB: www.oldskoolproduxions.com
SIC: 2759 Screen printing

(G-1237)
PAK-IT DISPLAYS INC
1324 Adams Rd (19020-3913)
P.O. Box 607 (19020-0607)
PHONE...................................215 638-7510
Bruce Blatt, *President*
Raymond F Blatt, *Corp Secy*
David H Blatt, *Vice Pres*
Bob Mainart, *Vice Pres*
Dave Conover, *Project Mgr*
▲ EMP: 30 EST: 1961
SQ FT: 52,000
SALES (est): 4.8MM **Privately Held**
WEB: www.pak-it.com
SIC: 3993 Displays & cutouts, window &
lobby

(G-1238)
PEI/GENESIS INC
651 Winks Ln (19020-5934)
PHONE...................................215 638-1645
EMP: 6
SALES (corp-wide): 325.8MM **Privately
Held**
SIC: 3678 3677 Mfg Electronic Connec-
tors Mfg Electronic Coils/Transformers
PA: Pei/Genesis, Inc.
2180 Hornig Rd Ste 2
Philadelphia PA 19116
215 464-1410

(G-1239)
PELSEAL TECHNOLOGIES LLC
3161 State Rd Ste G (19020-6545)
PHONE...................................215 245-0581
EMP: 10
SALES (est): 1.3MM **Privately Held**
SIC: 2891 Mfg Fluoroelastomer Adhesives
Sealants And Coatings

(G-1240)
PENDANTS SYSTEMS MFG CO
Also Called: Pendant Systems
1670 Winchester Rd (19020-4540)
P.O. Box 371 (19020-0371)
PHONE...................................215 638-8552
Michael Lenherr, *President*
Kimberly Lenherr, *Vice Pres*
Jessie Lenherr, *Executive Asst*
▲ EMP: 14
SQ FT: 12,000
SALES (est): 3MM **Privately Held**
WEB: www.pendantsystems.com
SIC: 3646 Commercial indusl & institu-
tional electric lighting fixtures

(G-1241)
PENN FIBRE INC
2434 Bristol Rd (19020-6002)
P.O. Box 160, Greenwood DE (19950-
0160)
PHONE...................................800 662-7366
EMP: 4
SALES (est): 220.6K **Privately Held**
SIC: 3089 3999 Plastic processing; atom-
izers, toiletry

(G-1242)
PENN FIBRE & SPECIALTY CO
2434 Bristol Rd (19020-6002)
PHONE...................................215 702-9551
Mike Gahrig, *Principal*
EMP: 3
SALES (est): 211.8K **Privately Held**
SIC: 3081 Unsupported plastics film &
sheet

(G-1243)
PICKELL ENTERPRISES INC
Also Called: Parent Metal Products
1345 Bridgewater Rd (19020-4553)
PHONE...................................215 244-7800
Edward B Pickell, *President*
Gary B Pickell, *Admin Sec*
EMP: 23
SALES (est): 3.9MM **Privately Held**
WEB: www.parentmetal.com
SIC: 2522 Office furniture, except wood

▲ = Import ▼=Export
◆ =Import/Export

(G-1244)
PROFILE SHOP INC (PA)
Also Called: Profile Shop, The
3300 Tillman Dr Ste 101 (19020-2071)
PHONE..................................215 633-3461
Diane Gesualdi, *President*
Heather McClure, *Vice Pres*
EMP: 13
SQ FT: 200
SALES (est): 1.7MM **Privately Held**
WEB: www.theprofileshop.com
SIC: 3842 Prosthetic appliances

(G-1245)
PROMOTIONAL PRINTING ASSOC
2025 State Rd (19020-7230)
PHONE..................................215 639-1662
Frank R Bertolino, *President*
EMP: 6 EST: 1960
SQ FT: 5,400
SALES (est): 743.5K **Privately Held**
SIC: 2752 Commercial printing, offset

(G-1246)
QUARTZ TUBING INC
2273 New York Ave (19020-7266)
PHONE..................................215 638-0909
John Stein, *President*
EMP: 14
SQ FT: 6,000
SALES (est): 1.6MM **Privately Held**
WEB: www.quartztubing.com
SIC: 3567 5074 Heating units & devices, industrial: electric; heating equipment & panels, solar

(G-1247)
R J REYNOLDS TOBACCO COMPANY
3580 Progress Dr Ste B2 (19020-5800)
PHONE..................................215 244-9071
EMP: 7
SALES (corp-wide): 26.8B **Privately Held**
SIC: 2111 Mfg Cigarettes
HQ: R. J. Reynolds Tobacco Company
401 N Main St
Winston Salem NC 27101
336 741-5000

(G-1248)
RANSOME IDEALEASE LLC
2975 Galloway Rd (19020-2327)
PHONE..................................215 639-4300
April Ale, *President*
EMP: 3
SALES (est): 119.9K **Privately Held**
SIC: 3519 Marine engines

(G-1249)
SAMUEL GROSSI & SONS INC
2526 State Rd (19020-7312)
PHONE..................................215 638-4470
Robert Grossi, *President*
John M Grossi, *Vice Pres*
Joseph Beck, *Safety Mgr*
Nicole Anselmo, *Purch Dir*
Chuck Discher, *Marketing Mgr*
EMP: 75 EST: 1946
SQ FT: 260,000
SALES (est): 23.1MM **Privately Held**
WEB: www.grossisteel.com
SIC: 3312 3441 Structural shapes & pilings, steel; fabricated structural metal

(G-1250)
SANDVIK MINING AND CNSTR
777 American Dr (19020-7342)
PHONE..................................215 245-0280
Gary Hughes, *President*
▲ EMP: 3
SALES (est): 491.8K **Privately Held**
SIC: 3532 Drills, core

(G-1251)
SAPA EXTRUSIONS INC
335 Camer Dr (19020-7352)
PHONE..................................870 235-2609
EMP: 5
SALES (est): 632K **Privately Held**
SIC: 3354 Aluminum extruded products

(G-1252)
SCHRAGE BOX & DESIGN INC
2511 State Rd (19020-7311)
PHONE..................................215 604-0800
Robert Schrage, *CEO*
Mary Anne Schrage, *Corp Secy*
EMP: 17
SQ FT: 19,995
SALES (est): 4.2MM **Privately Held**
WEB: www.schragebox.com
SIC: 2653 Boxes, corrugated: made from purchased materials

(G-1253)
SIGMAPHARM LABORATORIES LLC
3375 Progress Dr (19020-5801)
PHONE..................................215 352-6655
Ishari Piya, *President*
Spiridon Spireas PHD, *Chairman*
Lokanath Lenka, *Vice Pres*
Basil Theofanopoulos, *Vice Pres*
Doug Van Pelt, *Vice Pres*
▲ EMP: 120
SQ FT: 60,000
SALES: 40MM **Privately Held**
SIC: 2834 Tablets, pharmaceutical

(G-1254)
SOFT PRETZELS FRANCHISE SYSTEM (PA)
1525 Ford Rd (19020-4505)
PHONE..................................215 338-4606
Dan Dizio, *President*
Len Lehman, *Vice Pres*
Victoria Santillo, *Human Resources*
Frank Weiss, *Senior Mgr*
EMP: 6
SALES (est): 1.5MM **Privately Held**
SIC: 2051 Bakery: wholesale or wholesale/retail combined

(G-1255)
SPALDING AUTOMOTIVE INC (PA)
4529 Adams Cir (19020-3927)
PHONE..................................215 638-3334
Javier Kuehnle, *President*
G Wesley Kuehnle Jr, *Vice Pres*
Andrew Horn CPA, *CFO*
▲ EMP: 39
SQ FT: 37,000
SALES (est): 12.4MM **Privately Held**
WEB: www.spaldingautomotive.com
SIC: 3714 Motor vehicle parts & accessories

(G-1256)
SPECTRIM BUILDING PRODUCTS LLC
3433 Marshall Ln (19020-5910)
P.O. Box 826 (19020-0826)
PHONE..................................267 223-1030
Mike Andersen, *Senior VP*
Rick Berju, *Vice Pres*
Michael Conway, *Vice Pres*
Jeanette Walker, *Project Mgr*
Dennis Kubach, *Mng Member*
▲ EMP: 12
SALES (est): 1.3MM **Privately Held**
WEB: www.spectrimbp.com
SIC: 2431 Millwork

(G-1257)
SUPERIOR TOOL AND DIE CO
3170 Tucker Rd (19020-2821)
P.O. Box 340 (19020-0340)
PHONE..................................215 638-1904
Herbert J Tucker, *Vice Pres*
EMP: 10 EST: 1940
SQ FT: 8,000
SALES (est): 1.2MM **Privately Held**
WEB: www.tuckerind.com
SIC: 3544 Special dies & tools

(G-1258)
SVT INC
Also Called: Video Tech
350 Camer Dr (19020-7302)
P.O. Box 1025, Langhorne (19047-6025)
PHONE..................................215 245-5055
Melvin Metzker, *CEO*
Everett Farr, *President*
EMP: 11

SALES (est): 1MM **Privately Held**
SIC: 3069 2842 Medical & laboratory rubber sundries & related products; cleaning or polishing preparations

(G-1259)
TC MILLWORK INC
3433 Marshall Ln (19020-5910)
P.O. Box 826 (19020-0826)
PHONE..................................215 245-4210
Dennis Kubach, *President*
Arthur Kubach, *Vice Pres*
◆ EMP: 120
SQ FT: 420,000
SALES (est): 31.1MM **Privately Held**
SIC: 2522 2431 Office furniture, except wood; millwork

(G-1260)
THERMTREND INC
480 State Rd Ste B (19020-7829)
PHONE..................................215 752-0711
Kaz Kozlowski, *President*
EMP: 3
SQ FT: 2,000
SALES: 500K **Privately Held**
SIC: 3567 Calcining kilns

(G-1261)
TOTAL PLASTICS RESOURCES LLC
Also Called: Northeast Plastics Supply
633 Dunksferry Rd (19020-5909)
PHONE..................................215 637-2221
Erwin Edelson, *Branch Mgr*
EMP: 35
SALES (corp-wide): 869.1MM **Privately Held**
SIC: 3083 5162 Thermoplastic laminates: rods, tubes, plates & sheet; plastics sheets & rods
HQ: Total Plastics Resources Llc
2810 N Burdick St Ste A
Kalamazoo MI 49004
269 344-0009

(G-1262)
TRANSPARENT PROTECTION SYST
633 Dunksferry Rd (19020-5909)
PHONE..................................215 638-0800
Morton French, *President*
EMP: 20
SQ FT: 33,000
SALES (est): 2.3MM
SALES (corp-wide): 30.6MM **Privately Held**
WEB: www.transparentprotection.com
SIC: 3081 Plastic film & sheet
PA: Nytef Group, Inc.
25 Wann Cir
Pisgah AL 35765
256 657-5197

(G-1263)
TRI-STATE CONTAINER CORP
1440 Bridgewater Rd (19020-4431)
PHONE..................................215 638-1311
Allen Friedman, *President*
Elizabeth Stanton, *Principal*
Dan Forster, *Sales Staff*
EMP: 50 EST: 1958
SQ FT: 61,000
SALES (est): 13.4MM **Privately Held**
SIC: 2653 Boxes, corrugated: made from purchased materials

(G-1264)
TRISTAR LIGHTING COMPANY
1349 Ford Rd (19020-4501)
PHONE..................................215 245-3400
Dariush Zarrinnia, *CEO*
EMP: 48
SQ FT: 50,000
SALES (est): 6MM **Privately Held**
WEB: www.tristarlighting.com
SIC: 3646 Fluorescent lighting fixtures, commercial

(G-1265)
TUCKER INDUSTRIES INCORPORATED
3170 Tucker Rd (19020-2821)
P.O. Box 340 (19020-0340)
PHONE..................................215 638-1900

Herbert Tucker, *President*
Frank A Tucker, *Vice Pres*
Ed Felmey, *Opers Mgr*
Sam Diaz, *Technology*
Michael Tucker, *Admin Sec*
EMP: 80 EST: 1973
SQ FT: 50,000
SALES (est): 19.4MM **Privately Held**
WEB: www.toolsanddies.com
SIC: 3469 Stamping metal for the trade

(G-1266)
TUDOR DESIGN
2205 Lillian Dr (19020-2973)
P.O. Box 124 (19020-0124)
PHONE..................................215 638-3366
Walter Tudor, *Owner*
EMP: 3
SALES: 200K **Privately Held**
SIC: 3672 7389 Printed circuit boards; drafting service, except temporary help

(G-1267)
VIBROPLATING INC
353 Camer Dr (19020-7351)
PHONE..................................215 638-4413
Jeff Clark, *President*
▼ EMP: 5
SQ FT: 6,700
SALES (est): 724.8K **Privately Held**
WEB: www.vibroplating.com
SIC: 3471 Plating of metals or formed products

(G-1268)
WALNUT INDUSTRIES INC
Also Called: Ty-Gard 2000
1356 Adams Rd (19020-3913)
P.O. Box 624 (19020-0624)
PHONE..................................215 638-7847
David Blatt, *President*
Mitchell Spector, *COO*
Raymond Blatt, *Treasurer*
Cathy Burnett,
◆ EMP: 20 EST: 1961
SQ FT: 30,000
SALES (est): 8.4MM **Privately Held**
WEB: www.walnutind.com
SIC: 3524 Loaders (garden tractor equipment)

(G-1269)
WARNERS CANDIES
3518 Bristol Pike (19020-4641)
PHONE..................................215 639-1615
George Knauth, *Owner*
EMP: 5
SQ FT: 3,000
SALES (est): 372.5K **Privately Held**
SIC: 2064 5441 Candy & other confectionery products; candy

(G-1270)
WCR INC
4080 Blanche Rd (19020-4430)
PHONE..................................215 447-8152
Scot Biernat, *Sales Staff*
Mary Haselbarth, *Sales Staff*
Andrea Lane, *Sales Staff*
Edward Aring, *Manager*
EMP: 7
SALES (est): 729.6K
SALES (corp-wide): 39.9MM **Privately Held**
SIC: 3443 Fabricated plate work (boiler shop)
PA: Wcr Inc
2377 Commerce Center Blvd B
Fairborn OH 45324
937 223-0703

(G-1271)
WELLSPRING WIRELESS INC
Also Called: H2o Degree
3580 Progress Dr Ste L (19020-5818)
PHONE..................................215 788-8485
Richard Whiffen, *CEO*
Donald Millstein, *President*
Susan Epstein, *Controller*
EMP: 11
SQ FT: 3,500
SALES (est): 3MM **Privately Held**
SIC: 3824 Water meters

(G-1272)
WHITE TROPHY CO INC
Also Called: White The
2248 Bristol Pike (19020-5210)
PHONE..................215 638-9134
Susan White, *President*
Phyllis White, *Corp Secy*
EMP: 6
SQ FT: 3,400
SALES: 500K **Privately Held**
SIC: 3993 3914 Signs & advertising specialties; trophies, pewter

---

Bentleyville
Washington County

(G-1273)
PENN PRINT & GRAPHICS
200 Main St (15314-1531)
PHONE..................724 239-5849
Ronald Moyer, *Owner*
EMP: 4
SALES (est): 230K **Privately Held**
WEB: www.pennprint.com
SIC: 2752 2759 Commercial printing, offset; screen printing

(G-1274)
R & D RACEWAY INC
1054 State Route 917 (15314-1959)
PHONE..................724 258-8754
Randy W Powell, *Principal*
EMP: 4
SALES (est): 200.7K **Privately Held**
SIC: 3644 Raceways

(G-1275)
RAINBOW GRAPHICS INC
105 Dolson St (15314-1039)
PHONE..................724 228-3007
Robert Johnson, *President*
EMP: 4
SQ FT: 3,000
SALES: 400K **Privately Held**
SIC: 2752 2791 2759 Commercial printing, offset; typesetting; commercial printing

(G-1276)
TRAFFIC CONTROL EQP & SUPS CO
979 State Route 917 (15314-1978)
P.O. Box 18348, West Mifflin (15236-0348)
PHONE..................412 882-2012
Walter Brunner, *President*
Lois Brunner, *Treasurer*
EMP: 4
SALES (est): 785.9K **Privately Held**
SIC: 3669 Transportation signaling devices

Benton
Columbia County

(G-1277)
BENTON FOUNDRY INC
5297 State Route 487 (17814-7641)
PHONE..................570 925-6711
Jeffrey B Hall, *President*
Thomas S Brown, *Corp Secy*
Chad Davis, *Engineer*
Edward Gill, *Engineer*
Alan Wertz, *Engineer*
EMP: 250
SQ FT: 240,000
SALES (est): 75.8MM **Privately Held**
WEB: www.bentonfoundry.com
SIC: 3321 Gray iron castings; ductile iron castings

(G-1278)
CHARLES SHAVINGS INC
500 Sawmill Rd (17814-8234)
PHONE..................570 458-4945
Randy B Charles, *Principal*
EMP: 9
SALES (est): 814.3K **Privately Held**
SIC: 2421 Lumber: rough, sawed or planed

(G-1279)
FRITZ TASTEE CREME
372 Distillery Hill Rd (17814-8167)
PHONE..................570 925-2404
EMP: 3 EST: 2010
SALES (est): 176.2K **Privately Held**
SIC: 2024 Ice cream, bulk

(G-1280)
GAMMA IRRADIATOR SERVICE LLC
337 Distillery Hill Rd (17814-8167)
PHONE..................570 925-5681
Doyle T Stout, *Mng Member*
EMP: 5
SQ FT: 2,400
SALES: 350K **Privately Held**
SIC: 3844 8734 7699 Calibration & certification; scientific equipment repair service

(G-1281)
RADO ENTERPRISES INC
4441 Red Rock Rd (17814-7606)
PHONE..................570 759-0303
David Zeitler, *President*
Sabrina Hunsinger, *Admin Sec*
EMP: 40
SQ FT: 5,106
SALES (est): 5.6MM
SALES (corp-wide): 62MM **Publicly Held**
WEB: www.radoenterprises.com
SIC: 1711 3444 Mechanical contractor; ducts, sheet metal
PA: Moro Corporation
994 Old Eagle School Rd # 1000
Wayne PA 19087
484 367-0300

(G-1282)
SCHALOW VISUAL CONCEPTS INC
347 Hurley St (17814)
P.O. Box 269 (17814-0269)
PHONE..................570 336-2714
James Remley, *President*
Jeffrey Remley, *Admin Sec*
EMP: 8
SQ FT: 1,000
SALES: 50K **Privately Held**
SIC: 2531 1542 5049 School furniture; school building construction; school supplies

---

Berlin
Somerset County

(G-1283)
BINGMAN PACKING CO
165 5th Ave (15530)
PHONE..................814 267-3413
Robert Bingman Jr, *Owner*
EMP: 9
SALES (est): 533.1K **Privately Held**
SIC: 2011 Meat packing plants

(G-1284)
BIRDS EYE FOODS INC
Also Called: Snyder Potato Chips
1313 Stadium St (15530-1446)
PHONE..................814 267-4641
Bobby Thompson, *Principal*
Jerry Barker, *Manager*
EMP: 200
SQ FT: 58,000
SALES (corp-wide): 7.9B **Publicly Held**
WEB: www.agrilinkfoods.com
SIC: 2037 2096 Vegetables, quick frozen & cold pack, excl. potato products; potato chips & other potato-based snacks; corn chips & other corn-based snacks; tortilla chips; cheese curls & puffs
HQ: Birds Eye Foods, Inc.
121 Woodcrest Ave
Cherry Hill NJ 08003
585 383-1850

(G-1285)
BIRDS EYE FOODS LLC
Also Called: Snyder of Berlin
1313 Stadium St (15530-1446)
PHONE..................814 267-4641
Daniel Leonardi, *President*
EMP: 320

SALES (est): 30.7MM
SALES (corp-wide): 7.9B **Publicly Held**
SIC: 2096 Potato chips & other potato-based snacks; corn chips & other corn-based snacks; tortilla chips; cheese curls & puffs
HQ: Pinnacle Foods Inc.
399 Jefferson Rd
Parsippany NJ 07054
973 541-6620

(G-1286)
BROAD ST CMNTY NEWSPAPERS INC
16 Haines Ave (15530)
PHONE..................215 354-3135
Ed McCartney, *Director*
EMP: 4
SALES (est): 190K **Privately Held**
SIC: 2711 Newspapers

(G-1287)
CENTER ROCK INC (PA)
Also Called: C R I
118 Schrock Dr (15530-7118)
P.O. Box 307 (15530-0307)
PHONE..................814 267-7100
Brandon Fisher, *President*
Dale Miller, *Prdtn Mgr*
Frank Funa, *Materials Mgr*
Peggy Pletcher, *Buyer*
Lori Ling, *Human Res Mgr*
▲ EMP: 5
SALES (est): 15.9MM **Privately Held**
SIC: 3532 Drills & drilling equipment, mining (except oil & gas)

(G-1288)
GRAY SPACE DEFENSE ❂
1461 Salco Rd (15530-6017)
PHONE..................814 475-2749
Justin Herman, *Principal*
EMP: 3 EST: 2018
SALES (est): 155K **Privately Held**
SIC: 3812 Defense systems & equipment

(G-1289)
KNEPPCO EQUIPMENT LLC
465 Log House Rd (15530-9544)
PHONE..................814 483-0108
Mark Knepper, *Principal*
EMP: 3 EST: 2016
SALES (est): 101.5K **Privately Held**
SIC: 3523 Farm machinery & equipment

(G-1290)
LUBEDEALERCOM
417 Yonai Rd (15530-8735)
P.O. Box 303 (15530-0303)
PHONE..................814 521-9625
EMP: 6
SALES (est): 230K **Privately Held**
SIC: 2992 Mfg Lubricating Oils/Greases

(G-1291)
MOUNTAINEER MINING CORPORATION
1010 Garrett Shortcut Rd (15530-6807)
PHONE..................814 445-5806
Robert George Koval, *CEO*
EMP: 7 EST: 1996
SALES (est): 1.1MM **Privately Held**
SIC: 1011 Iron ore beneficiating

(G-1292)
R FRITZ ENTERPRISES INC
326 Vanyo Rd (15530-8310)
PHONE..................814 267-4204
Roy Fritz Jr, *President*
EMP: 5
SALES (est): 660K **Privately Held**
WEB: www.rfei.net
SIC: 5734 7378 7372 5941 Computer & software stores; computer maintenance & repair; prepackaged software; firearms

(G-1293)
VARCHETTIS FURNITURE
163 Fochtman Rd (15530-5132)
PHONE..................814 733-4318
Sam Varchetti, *Owner*
EMP: 3
SALES: 200K **Privately Held**
SIC: 2511 Wood household furniture

(G-1294)
ZUBEK INC
173 House Coal Rd (15530-8823)
P.O. Box 5, Cairnbrook (15924-0005)
PHONE..................814 443-4441
Betty Zubek, *President*
Bonita Jarvas, *Principal*
Bob Zubek, *Corp Secy*
William Zubek, *Vice Pres*
Edward P Zubek, *Treasurer*
EMP: 9 EST: 1977
SQ FT: 300
SALES (est): 774.1K **Privately Held**
WEB: www.zube.com
SIC: 1221 Strip mining, bituminous

Bernville
Berks County

(G-1295)
ADVANCED SKIN TECHNOLOGIES INC (PA)
Also Called: A S T
7143 Bernville Rd (19506-8624)
P.O. Box 579 (19506-0579)
PHONE..................610 488-7643
Steven M Pugliese, *President*
EMP: 8
SQ FT: 8,000
SALES (est): 1.3MM **Privately Held**
SIC: 2841 2844 2899 Soap & other detergents; face creams or lotions; acids

(G-1296)
APPLE FOX
5715 Mount Pleasant Rd (19506-8208)
PHONE..................484 388-0011
EMP: 3 EST: 2008
SALES (est): 287.4K **Privately Held**
SIC: 3571 Mfg Electronic Computers

(G-1297)
AURAL HARMONICS
91 Miller Rd (19506-8106)
P.O. Box B, Strausstown (19559-0106)
PHONE..................610 488-0232
John Stephens, *Owner*
EMP: 10
SALES (est): 478.2K **Privately Held**
SIC: 3674 8731 Semiconductors & related devices; commercial physical research

(G-1298)
EAST CAST EROSION BLANKETS LLC (PA)
443 Bricker Rd (19506-8712)
PHONE..................610 488-8496
Rickey Geissler, *President*
John G Smith, *Vice Pres*
◆ EMP: 10
SQ FT: 1,568
SALES (est): 3MM **Privately Held**
WEB: www.erosionblankets.com
SIC: 2211 Blankets & blanketings, cotton

(G-1299)
GLORAY IF LLC
Also Called: Central Park West
104 Jefferson Ct (19506-9461)
PHONE..................610 921-3300
Ivan Gordon,
Arnold Bernsteen,
Dee Rothenberger,
▲ EMP: 10
SQ FT: 13,000
SALES: 3MM **Privately Held**
SIC: 5632 5699 2253 Knitwear, women's; knit dresses, made to order; knit outerwear mills

(G-1300)
HAWKEYE-JENSEN INC
203 Oak Ln (19506-9406)
PHONE..................610 488-8500
Wendy Pugliese, *Officer*
EMP: 35
SALES (est): 6.5MM **Privately Held**
SIC: 2844 Face creams or lotions

(G-1301)
MAINSTREAM INDUSTRIES
7340 Bernville Rd (19506-8620)
PHONE..................................610 488-1148
Jean Finer, *Principal*
EMP: 7
SALES (est): 753.9K **Privately Held**
SIC: 3669 Transportation signaling devices

(G-1302)
MOYERS SAWMILL COMPANY
361 Pearl Rd (19506-8978)
PHONE..................................610 488-1462
Nancy Kieffer, *Managing Prtnr*
Nancy Kieffer, *Managing Prtnr*
Mary Hagg, *Partner*
EMP: 6
SALES: 200K **Privately Held**
SIC: 2421 Custom sawmill

(G-1303)
POLYMER DIV OF WYOMISSING SPC
231 E 2nd St (19506-9206)
P.O. Box 334 (19506-0334)
PHONE..................................610 488-0981
Dave Gehr, *President*
David Gehr, *President*
Joseph Bisconti, *Vice Pres*
Jordan Leahy, *Admin Sec*
EMP: 6
SQ FT: 5,000
SALES: 630K **Privately Held**
SIC: 3089 Injection molding of plastics

(G-1304)
RDY GUTTERS PLUS LLC
60 Paddock Dr (19506-9111)
PHONE..................................610 488-5666
EMP: 3
SALES (est): 249.7K **Privately Held**
SIC: 1761 3444 5031 5211 Gutter & downspout contractor; siding contractor; gutters, sheet metal; doors & windows; siding

(G-1305)
SABOLD DESIGN INC
242 Grandview Rd (19506-9417)
PHONE..................................610 401-4086
Bret Sabold, *President*
EMP: 6
SALES (est): 175.4K **Privately Held**
SIC: 3999 8711 Manufacturing industries; engineering services

(G-1306)
VERTIRACK MANUFACTURING CO
74 Pleasant Dr (19506-9309)
PHONE..................................484 971-7341
William Stoppi, *President*
▼ EMP: 5
SQ FT: 14,000
SALES (est): 482.3K **Privately Held**
SIC: 2542 Racks, merchandise display or storage: except wood

Berwick
Columbia County

(G-1307)
ACURLITE STRL SKYLIGHTS INC
1017 N Vine St (18603-2025)
P.O. Box 5 (18603-0005)
PHONE..................................570 759-6882
Ron Palombo, *President*
Donna Palombo, *Principal*
Keith Mazzie, *Engineer*
Tom Kozak, *Director*
Gary Roth, *Director*
▼ EMP: 20
SQ FT: 26,500
SALES (est): 5MM **Privately Held**
WEB: www.acurlite.com
SIC: 3444 Sheet metalwork

(G-1308)
BEACH MACHINE INC
61 Hosicks Rd (18603-6302)
PHONE..................................570 752-7786

Fax: 570 752-7835
EMP: 5
SQ FT: 6,000
SALES: 250K **Privately Held**
SIC: 3599 Machine Shop

(G-1309)
BERRY GLOBAL INC
910 E 7th St (18603-3430)
PHONE..................................570 759-6240
Les Schramm, *Manager*
EMP: 360
SQ FT: 20,000 **Publicly Held**
WEB: www.6sens.com
SIC: 3089 3081 Bottle caps, molded plastic; unsupported plastics film & sheet
HQ: Berry Global, Inc.
101 Oakley St
Evansville IN 47710
812 424-2904

(G-1310)
BERWICK MACHINE LLC
705 Maple St Unit 1 (18603-3034)
PHONE..................................570 759-1888
Karl Jan Johnson, *Mng Member*
EMP: 8
SQ FT: 5,000
SALES (est): 649.2K **Privately Held**
SIC: 3599 Machine shop, jobbing & repair

(G-1311)
BERWICK OFFRAY LLC (HQ)
Also Called: Berwick Industries
2015 W Front St (18603-4102)
P.O. Box 428 (18603-0428)
PHONE..................................570 752-5934
Christopher J Munyan, *CEO*
◆ EMP: 277 EST: 1999
SQ FT: 12,500
SALES (est): 56.6MM
SALES (corp-wide): 361.9MM **Publicly Held**
WEB: www.berwickindustries.com
SIC: 3089 3081 2396 Extruded finished plastic products; polypropylene film & sheet; automotive & apparel trimmings
PA: Css Industries, Inc.
450 Plymouth Rd Ste 300
Plymouth Meeting PA 19462
610 729-3959

(G-1312)
BERWICK OFFRAY LLC
Ninth St & Bombay Ln (18603)
PHONE..................................570 752-5934
Rudy Singh, *Branch Mgr*
EMP: 600
SALES (corp-wide): 361.9MM **Publicly Held**
WEB: www.berwickindustries.com
SIC: 3089 3081 2396 Extruded finished plastic products; polypropylene film & sheet; automotive & apparel trimmings
HQ: Berwick Offray Llc
2015 W Front St
Berwick PA 18603
570 752-5934

(G-1313)
BERWICK OFFRAY LLC
1414 Susquehanna Ave (18603-4327)
PHONE..................................570 752-5934
Jack Farber, *Ch of Bd*
EMP: 6
SALES (corp-wide): 361.9MM **Publicly Held**
WEB: www.berwickindustries.com
SIC: 3089 Extruded finished plastic products
HQ: Berwick Offray Llc
2015 W Front St
Berwick PA 18603
570 752-5934

(G-1314)
BLACK ROCK MANUFACTURING CO
Also Called: Leisure Line Stove Co
R620 Broad St (18603)
PHONE..................................570 752-1811
Matthaus Atkinson, *President*
David Donnora, *Vice Pres*
Hope Fogarty, *Treasurer*
Amy Donnora, *Admin Sec*
EMP: 6

SQ FT: 4,000
SALES (est): 1.3MM **Privately Held**
SIC: 3433 Burners, furnaces, boilers & stokers; stoves, wood & coal burning

(G-1315)
BUDDY BUTLERS INC
1665 Spring Garden Ave (18603-2502)
PHONE..................................570 759-0550
Frederick Broyan, *President*
◆ EMP: 8
SQ FT: 4,000
SALES (est): 1.2MM **Privately Held**
WEB: www.butlersbuddy.com
SIC: 3534 Dumbwaiters

(G-1316)
CASTEK INC
23 River Rd (18603-6721)
P.O. Box 129 (18603-0129)
PHONE..................................570 759-3540
Tony Krisanda, *Branch Mgr*
EMP: 17
SALES (est): 4MM
SALES (corp-wide): 7.4MM **Privately Held**
WEB: www.castek.net
SIC: 3272 5211 Concrete products, precast; masonry materials & supplies
HQ: Castek, Inc.
20 Jones St
New Rochelle NY 10801

(G-1317)
CHEETAH CHASSIS CORPORATION (PA)
Also Called: Cheetha
3rd & Oak Sts (18603)
P.O. Box 388 (18603-0388)
PHONE..................................570 752-2708
Frank Katz, *President*
Dave Koval, *Purchasing*
Sharon Schmick, *Info Tech Dir*
▲ EMP: 141
SQ FT: 100,000
SALES (est): 40.6MM **Privately Held**
WEB: www.cheetahc.com
SIC: 3711 5531 3537 Chassis, motor vehicle; truck equipment & parts; industrial trucks & tractors

(G-1318)
COLUMBIA INDUSTRIES INC
930 Back Rd (18603-1146)
PHONE..................................570 520-4048
Charles Klatt, *Enginr/R&D Mgr*
EMP: 30
SALES (corp-wide): 18.9MM **Privately Held**
SIC: 3713 3563 Truck bodies (motor vehicles); air & gas compressors
PA: Columbia Industries Inc
567 Commerce St
Franklin Lakes NJ 07417
201 337-7332

(G-1319)
CONSOLIDATED CONTAINER CO LLC
910 Back Rd (18603-1146)
PHONE..................................570 759-0823
Bryan Statskey, *Manager*
EMP: 120
SALES (corp-wide): 14B **Publicly Held**
WEB: www.cccllc.com
SIC: 2656 2655 3085 Sanitary food containers; fiber cans, drums & containers; plastics bottles
HQ: Consolidated Container Company, Llc
2500 Windy Ridge Pkwy Se # 1400
Atlanta GA 30339
678 742-4600

(G-1320)
CPO 2 INC
Also Called: Rotech
1437 Fairview Ave (18603-2608)
PHONE..................................570 759-1233
EMP: 4
SALES (corp-wide): 412.5MM **Privately Held**
SIC: 3845 Mfg Electromedical Equipment
HQ: Cpo 2, Inc.
3600 Vineland Rd Ste 114
Orlando FL
407 822-4600

(G-1321)
CRISPIN VALVE LLC
600 Fowler Ave (18603-3307)
PHONE..................................570 752-4524
Darren Crispin, *Mng Member*
▲ EMP: 6
SALES (est): 2.2MM **Privately Held**
SIC: 3491 Industrial valves

(G-1322)
DALOS BAKERY INC
1201 Freas Ave (18603-1611)
PHONE..................................570 752-4519
Donato A Dalo Sr, *President*
Donato A Dalo Jr, *Vice Pres*
Anthony Dalo, *Treasurer*
Nicholas Dalo, *Admin Sec*
Paul Dalo, *Admin Sec*
EMP: 25
SQ FT: 1,400
SALES (est): 3MM **Privately Held**
SIC: 2051 5149 5461 2099 Bakery: wholesale or wholesale/retail combined; bakery products; bakeries; food preparations; cookies & crackers

(G-1323)
DELTA MECHANICAL INC
Also Called: Delta Fabricating
325 S Eaton St (18603-4232)
PHONE..................................570 752-5511
Gregory D Iacovoni, *President*
Thomas I Iacavoni, *Vice Pres*
Sean Bennie, *Sales Mgr*
Marie L Iacavoni, *Admin Sec*
EMP: 10
SQ FT: 23,400
SALES (est): 1.9MM **Privately Held**
SIC: 3443 Fabricated plate work (boiler shop)

(G-1324)
EMS CLOTHING & NOVELTY INC
764 Knob Mountain Rd (18603-5853)
PHONE..................................570 752-2896
Neil Young, *President*
Jack Young, *Vice Pres*
EMP: 3
SQ FT: 1,716
SALES (est): 309.7K **Privately Held**
SIC: 2253 5961 T-shirts & tops, knit; women's apparel, mail order; clothing, mail order (except women's)

(G-1325)
G & B SPECIALTIES INC
535 W 3rd St (18603-2937)
P.O. Box 305 (18603-0305)
PHONE..................................570 752-5901
John Mensinger, *President*
Ralph Pollock, *Vice Pres*
Tom Madigan, *Admin Sec*
◆ EMP: 165
SQ FT: 25,000
SALES (est): 30MM
SALES (corp-wide): 4.3B **Publicly Held**
WEB: www.gandbspecialties.com
SIC: 3599 3462 Machine shop, jobbing & repair; railroad, construction & mining forgings
PA: Westinghouse Air Brake Technologies Corporation
1001 Airbrake Ave
Wilmerding PA 15148
412 825-1000

(G-1326)
GREAT AMERICAN PRINTER INC
525 E 2nd St (18603-4901)
PHONE..................................570 752-7341
Marilyn J Zlobik, *President*
EMP: 6 EST: 1924
SQ FT: 5,500
SALES (est): 668.7K **Privately Held**
SIC: 2732 2721 2752 Textbooks: printing & binding, not publishing; magazines: publishing & printing; circulars, lithographed

(G-1327)
GTF CORPORATION
Also Called: B J Sales Co Div
103 Blair St 111 (18603-3501)
PHONE..................................717 752-3631
George T Forese, *President*
Barbara J Forese, *Treasurer*

EMP: 22 **EST:** 1950
SQ FT: 20,000
SALES (est): 1.6MM **Privately Held**
SIC: 3599 Machine shop, jobbing & repair

(G-1328)
HAMPSHIRE PAPER COMPANY
2015 W Front St (18603-4102)
P.O. Box 428 (18603-0428)
PHONE..............................570 759-7245
Christopher Munyan, *CEO*
EMP: 5
SALES (est): 532K **Privately Held**
SIC: 2679 Converted paper products

(G-1329)
JAMES J TUZZI JR
Also Called: Tuzzi Bakery
504 Washington St (18603-2818)
PHONE..............................570 752-2704
James J Tuzzi Jr, *Owner*
EMP: 45
SQ FT: 15,000
SALES (est): 1.4MM **Privately Held**
SIC: 5461 5149 2099 2051 Bakeries;
   bakery products; food preparations;
   bread, cake & related products

(G-1330)
K- FLO BUTTERFLY
600 Fowler Ave (18603-3307)
PHONE..............................570 752-4524
Darren Crispen, *Owner*
▲ **EMP:** 5
SALES (est): 330K **Privately Held**
SIC: 3491 Valves, automatic control

(G-1331)
K-FAB INC
1408 N Vine St (18603-1218)
P.O. Box 345 (18603-0345)
PHONE..............................570 759-8411
Martin F Koch, *President*
Doreen A Koch, *Vice Pres*
Martin Koch, *CFO*
Martin N Koch, *Treasurer*
Gary Slusser, *Manager*
▲ **EMP:** 85
SQ FT: 24,000
SALES (est): 27.3MM **Privately Held**
WEB: www.kfabinc.com
SIC: 3544 3599 Special dies & tools; ma-
   chine shop, jobbing & repair

(G-1332)
**LEGGETT & PLATT
INCORPORATED**
Also Called: Leggett & Platt 0383
515 Salem Blvd (18603-6459)
PHONE..............................570 542-4171
Mike Mitchell, *COO*
Teresa Kasarda, *Manager*
EMP: 90
SALES (corp-wide): 4.2B **Publicly Held**
WEB: www.leggett.com
SIC: 2515 Mattresses & bedsprings
PA: Leggett & Platt, Incorporated
   1 Leggett Rd
   Carthage MO 64836
   417 358-8131

(G-1333)
LION RIBBON COMPANY LLC
2015 W Front St (18603-4102)
PHONE..............................570 752-5934
Christopher J Munyan, *Mng Member*
EMP: 4
SALES (est): 177K
SALES (corp-wide): 361.9MM **Publicly
Held**
SIC: 3081 Polypropylene film & sheet
HQ: Berwick Offray Llc
   2015 W Front St
   Berwick PA 18603
   570 752-5934

(G-1334)
MALATESTA ENTERPRISES
201 E 2nd St (18603-4803)
PHONE..............................570 752-2516
Fred Malatesta, *President*
EMP: 10
SALES (est): 473.6K **Privately Held**
SIC: 3999 Military insignia

(G-1335)
**MONTGOMERY LABORATORIES
INC**
355 Bowers Rd (18603-6529)
PHONE..............................570 752-7712
Paul Magini, *President*
EMP: 10 **EST:** 2001
SALES (est): 1,000K **Privately Held**
SIC: 2834 Pharmaceutical preparations

(G-1336)
**MOREY GENERAL
CONTRACTING**
Also Called: American Log Homes
20 Maplewood Rd (18603-5629)
PHONE..............................570 759-2021
William Morey, *Owner*
EMP: 3
SALES (est): 310K **Privately Held**
SIC: 1521 1531 2452 New construction,
   single-family houses; speculative builder,
   single-family houses; log cabins, prefabri-
   cated, wood

(G-1337)
**MULTIPLEX MANUFACTURING
CO**
Also Called: Crispin Valve
600 Fowler Ave (18603-3307)
P.O. Box 427 (18603-0427)
PHONE..............................570 752-4524
Bill Crispin, *CEO*
Darren Crispin, *President*
Jarrod Yenne, *Regl Sales Mgr*
▲ **EMP:** 45 **EST:** 1905
SQ FT: 25,000
SALES (est): 12.2MM **Privately Held**
WEB: www.crispinvalve.com
SIC: 3491 3494 Pressure valves & regula-
   tors, industrial; valves & pipe fittings

(G-1338)
**NATIONAL FILM CONVERTING
INC**
106 W 11th St (18603-2006)
P.O. Box 1152 (18603-6152)
PHONE..............................800 422-6651
Christian Krupsha, *President*
EMP: 16
SQ FT: 35,000
SALES (est): 4.5MM **Privately Held**
SIC: 2759 Bags, plastic: printing

(G-1339)
**PATRIOT METAL PRODUCTS
INC**
Also Called: Pmp
1005 N Vine St (18603-2026)
PHONE..............................570 759-3634
Martin F Koch, *President*
Chris Garman, *Principal*
Duane M Koch, *Vice Pres*
EMP: 25
SALES (est): 6.6MM **Privately Held**
WEB: www.patriotmetalproducts.com
SIC: 3339 3479 Zinc refining (primary), in-
   cluding slabs & dust; coating of metals &
   formed products

(G-1340)
PENFORD CAROLINA LLC
920 E 7th St (18603)
PHONE..............................570 218-4321
Ryan Jones, *Principal*
Larry Krisanits, *Maint Spvr*
EMP: 20 **EST:** 2012
SALES (est): 2.9MM
SALES (corp-wide): 5.8B **Publicly Held**
SIC: 2046 Wet corn milling
HQ: Penford Corporation
   345 Inverness Dr S # 200
   Englewood CO 80112
   303 649-1900

(G-1341)
PENNSYLVANIA ALUMINUM
Also Called: Polyports
2637 W Front St (18603-4113)
PHONE..............................570 752-2666
Michael Zenzel, *Owner*
EMP: 4
SQ FT: 6,000

SALES (est): 530.6K **Privately Held**
SIC: 3444 3448 Awnings, sheet metal;
   carports: prefabricated metal

(G-1342)
RIVERVIEW BLOCK INC
Also Called: Berwick Concrete & Aggergate
1507 Salem Blvd (18603-6914)
PHONE..............................570 752-7191
Randall R Rinehimer, *President*
EMP: 9 **EST:** 1946
SQ FT: 7,200
SALES (est): 960K **Privately Held**
SIC: 3271 Blocks, concrete or cinder: stan-
   dard

(G-1343)
SHOWTEX LOGISTICS LLC
404 E 10th St (18603-3225)
PHONE..............................570 218-0054
Jeff Diehl Showtex, *Mng Member*
Gail Mowery, *Software Dev*
EMP: 25
SALES (est): 2MM **Privately Held**
SIC: 2399 Emblems, badges & insignia

(G-1344)
**SPECIALTY ROLLER AND MCH
INC**
233 Columbia Ave (18603-2002)
PHONE..............................570 759-1278
Harry T Davies, *President*
Tom Van Why, *General Mgr*
Gene Urban, *QA Dir*
EMP: 10
SQ FT: 8,500
SALES (est): 1.6MM **Privately Held**
WEB: www.specialtyroller.com
SIC: 3069 Platens, except printers': solid
   or covered rubber

(G-1345)
STONEMAK ENTERPRISES INC
5 Glennwood St (18603-5644)
PHONE..............................570 752-3209
Christina Force, *President*
Fred Malatesta, *Vice Pres*
EMP: 8
SQ FT: 2,000
SALES (est): 369.9K **Privately Held**
SIC: 2311 Vests: made from purchased
   materials

(G-1346)
TECHNISERV INC
351 S Eaton St (18603-4232)
PHONE..............................570 759-2315
Paul Heaps Sr, *CEO*
Paul Heaps II, *President*
Michael S Smith, *Vice Pres*
Tuck Talanca, *Project Engr*
Arden Oliver, *Design Engr*
▲ **EMP:** 55
SQ FT: 59,000
SALES (est): 12MM **Privately Held**
WEB: www.techniservinc.com
SIC: 2834 8711 Adrenal pharmaceutical
   preparations; engineering services

(G-1347)
WISE FOODS INC (HQ)
228 Rasely St (18603-4533)
PHONE..............................888 759-4401
Jolie Weber, *CEO*
Ken Krakosky, *Controller*
Jaime Miguel Sanchez Fernandez, *Admin
Sec*
James Farmer, *Asst Sec*
◆ **EMP:** 850
SALES (est): 297.9MM **Privately Held**
SIC: 2096 Potato chips & similar snacks

(G-1348)
**WISE FOODS EMPLOYEES
CHRTBLE E**
228 Rasely St (18603-4533)
PHONE..............................570 759-4095
B Hippenstiel, *General Mgr*
Blake Hippenstiel, *Plant Mgr*
EMP: 4
SALES: 18.9K **Privately Held**
SIC: 2096 Potato chips & similar snacks

(G-1349)
YEAGER WIRE WORKS INC
620 Broad St (18603-1418)
PHONE..............................570 752-2769
David W Ungemach, *President*
EMP: 4 **EST:** 1947
SQ FT: 20,000
SALES: 250K **Privately Held**
SIC: 3444 3496 Sheet metal specialties,
   not stamped; miscellaneous fabricated
   wire products

(G-1350)
ZENZEL III MICHAEL
2637 W Front St (18603-4113)
PHONE..............................570 752-2666
Michael Zenzel III, *Owner*
EMP: 5
SALES (est): 349.2K **Privately Held**
SIC: 3449 Miscellaneous metalwork

Berwyn
Chester County

(G-1351)
AMETEK INC (PA)
1100 Cassatt Rd (19312-1177)
PHONE..............................610 647-2121
David A Zapico, *Ch of Bd*
Tony J Ciampitti, *President*
John W Hardin, *President*
Timothy N Jones, *President*
Thomas C Marecic, *President*
◆ **EMP:** 90 **EST:** 1930
SQ FT: 43,000
SALES: 4.8B **Publicly Held**
SIC: 3823 3824 3825 3621 Industrial in-
   strmnts msrmnt display/control process
   variable; temperature instruments: indus-
   trial process type; pressure gauges, dial &
   digital; controllers for process variables,
   all types; vehicle instruments; tachometer,
   centrifugal; engine electrical test equipment; motors, electric

(G-1352)
AMETEK EMG HOLDINGS INC
1100 Cassatt Rd (19312-1177)
PHONE..............................610 647-2121
EMP: 3 **EST:** 2014
SALES (est): 136.3K
SALES (corp-wide): 4.8B **Publicly Held**
SIC: 3621 Motors & generators
PA: Ametek, Inc.
   1100 Cassatt Rd
   Berwyn PA 19312
   610 647-2121

(G-1353)
AMETEK EUROPE LLC
1100 Cassatt Rd (19312-1177)
PHONE..............................610 647-2121
Edwin Marr, *Opers Dir*
Steven Berger, *Buyer*
EMP: 3
SALES (est): 9.5MM **Privately Held**
SIC: 3679 Electronic components
PA: Ametek Holdings B.V.
   Onbekend Nederlands Adre
   Onbekend

(G-1354)
**BRYN MAWR SHOWER DOOR
INC**
579 Lancaster Ave (19312-1678)
PHONE..............................610 647-0357
Douglas Kirscher, *President*
EMP: 9 **EST:** 1978
SALES (est): 511.2K **Privately Held**
SIC: 3211 Window glass, clear & colored

(G-1355)
CAPTEK INC
Also Called: Science Products
1043 Lancaster Ave (19312-1242)
P.O. Box 144, Southeastern (19399-0144)
PHONE..............................610 296-2111
Lenore M Benham, *President*
Kathleen Manzo, *Corp Secy*
EMP: 5 **EST:** 1954
SQ FT: 3,000

▲ = Import ▼=Export
◆ =Import/Export

SALES (est): 877.7K **Privately Held**
WEB: www.captek.com
SIC: 3827 5961 Magnifying instruments, optical; catalog & mail-order houses

(G-1356)
COMPLEXA INC
1055 Westlakes Dr Ste 200 (19312-2422)
PHONE..................................412 727-8727
Francisco D Salva, *President*
David Sinkway, *Admin Sec*
EMP: 8
SQ FT: 5,000
SALES (est): 84.5K **Privately Held**
SIC: 8733 2834 Medical research; pharmaceutical preparations

(G-1357)
COOPER WILBERT VAULT CO INC
1052 Waterloo Rd (19312-2233)
PHONE..................................610 842-7782
EMP: 3
SALES (est): 146.9K **Privately Held**
SIC: 3272 Burial vaults, concrete or precast terrazzo

(G-1358)
CRYSTAL ENGINEERING CORP
1100 Cassatt Rd (19312-1177)
PHONE..................................610 647-2121
EMP: 3 EST: 2014
SALES (est): 169.1K
SALES (corp-wide): 4.8B **Publicly Held**
SIC: 3621 Motors & generators
PA: Ametek, Inc.
1100 Cassatt Rd
Berwyn PA 19312
610 647-2121

(G-1359)
CURRENT THERAPEUTICS INC
477 Howellville Rd (19312-1010)
PHONE..................................610 644-5995
EMP: 5
SQ FT: 2,000
SALES (est): 1MM **Privately Held**
SIC: 2721 Medical Publications

(G-1360)
DERMAVANCE PHARMACEUTICALS INC
1055 Westlakes Dr (19312-2422)
PHONE..................................610 727-3935
Keith Greathouse, *President*
EMP: 12
SALES (est): 930.1K **Privately Held**
SIC: 2834 Pharmaceutical preparations

(G-1361)
FIRE 1ST DEFENSE INC
451 Cassatt Rd (19312-1329)
PHONE..................................610 296-7576
Brian Weller, *President*
Richard Jacobson, *Vice Pres*
EMP: 3
SQ FT: 1,500
SALES (est): 210K **Privately Held**
WEB: www.fire1stdefense.com
SIC: 3999 Fire extinguishers, portable

(G-1362)
FLUID INTELLIGENCE LLC
641 Llewelyn Rd (19312-2012)
P.O. Box 191 (19312-0191)
PHONE..................................610 405-2698
Kevin Goldstein, *Mng Member*
EMP: 3
SALES (est): 100K **Privately Held**
SIC: 8711 3699 3492 Electrical or electronic engineering; security control equipment & systems; control valves, fluid power: hydraulic & pneumatic

(G-1363)
FORMULA PHARMACEUTICALS INC
1055 Westlakes Dr Ste 300 (19312-2410)
PHONE..................................610 727-4172
Wolfgang Oster, *Ch of Bd*
Maurits Geerlings, *President*
Steven Feder, *General Mgr*
Daniel D Von Hoff, *Chairman*
Eric Steager, *Senior VP*
EMP: 7

SALES (est): 1.1MM **Privately Held**
SIC: 2834 Pharmaceutical preparations

(G-1364)
GOURMAIL INC (PA)
Also Called: Jyoti Natural Foods
816 Newtown Rd (19312-2200)
PHONE..................................610 522-2650
Vijai Gupta, *CEO*
Jyoti Gupta, *President*
Sunil Manchandra, *Business Mgr*
Gupta V P, *Vice Pres*
▲ **EMP:** 2
SQ FT: 54,000
SALES (est): 2.9MM **Privately Held**
WEB: www.jyotifoods.com
SIC: 2099 5411 Food preparations; supermarkets

(G-1365)
IMAGE MAKERS ART INC
Also Called: Renaissance Art Gallery
62 Central Ave Apt A (19312-1785)
PHONE..................................610 722-5807
John Sozanski, *President*
EMP: 6
SQ FT: 1,900
SALES (est): 422.4K **Privately Held**
WEB: www.imagemakersart.com
SIC: 2741 Art copy: publishing only, not printed on site

(G-1366)
ITF PHARMA INC (PA)
850 Cassatt Rd Ste 350 (19312-2701)
PHONE..................................484 328-4964
Dennis Willson, *CEO*
Peter Cook, *COO*
Mercedes Alexander, *Vice Pres*
Brent Cowgill, *Vice Pres*
Jim Smith, *Vice Pres*
EMP: 4 EST: 2015
SALES (est): 20MM **Privately Held**
SIC: 2834 Pharmaceutical preparations

(G-1367)
JUSTI GROUP INC (PA)
804 Old Lancaster Rd (19312-1220)
PHONE..................................484 318-7158
Henry M Justi, *President*
Helen Wheeler, *Vice Pres*
Steve Morrison, *Officer*
Karla Wagner, *Analyst*
EMP: 28
SQ FT: 61,000
SALES (est): 20.3MM **Privately Held**
WEB: www.justigroup.com
SIC: 2899 Chemical preparations

(G-1368)
MEDIA HIGHWAY
Also Called: Pyramed Health Systems
850 Cassatt Rd Ste 350 (19312-2701)
PHONE..................................610 647-2255
Eric Wolgamott, *Owner*
Connie Cox, *Human Resources*
EMP: 16
SQ FT: 2,000
SALES (est): 1.7MM **Privately Held**
WEB: www.media-highway.com
SIC: 7372 Application computer software

(G-1369)
MORRIS PRINT MANAGEMENT
632 Contention Ln (19312-1430)
PHONE..................................610 408-8922
Chad Morris, *President*
EMP: 3
SALES: 1MM **Privately Held**
WEB: www.morrisprintmanagement.com
SIC: 7336 2759 Commercial art & graphic design; commercial printing

(G-1370)
PELLA CORPORATION
Also Called: Pella Window Door
555 Lancaster Ave Ste B (19312-1680)
PHONE..................................610 648-0922
Rick Balabon, *Branch Mgr*
EMP: 7
SALES (corp-wide): 1.8B **Privately Held**
SIC: 2431 3442 Windows, wood; window & door frames

PA: Pella Corporation
102 Main St
Pella IA 50219
641 621-1000

(G-1371)
PELLA CORPORATION
Also Called: Pella Window Door
555 Lancaster Ave Ste B (19312-1680)
PHONE..................................610 648-0922
EMP: 316
SALES (corp-wide): 1.8B **Privately Held**
SIC: 2431 Windows, wood
PA: Pella Corporation
102 Main St
Pella IA 50219
641 621-1000

(G-1372)
PELLA CORPORATION
Also Called: Pella Window Door
555 Lancaster Ave Ste B (19312-1680)
PHONE..................................610 648-0922
EMP: 316
SALES (corp-wide): 1.8B **Privately Held**
SIC: 2431 Windows, wood
PA: Pella Corporation
102 Main St
Pella IA 50219
641 621-1000

(G-1373)
RESUN MODSPACE INC
1200 W Swedesford Rd (19312-1172)
PHONE..................................610 232-1200
Charles R Paquin, *CEO*
EMP: 12 EST: 2007
SALES (est): 1.3MM
SALES (corp-wide): 243.6MM **Privately Held**
SIC: 2542 Partitions & fixtures, except wood
PA: Modular Space Corporation
1200 W Swedesford Rd Fl 2
Berwyn PA 19312
610 232-1200

(G-1374)
ROLLED STEEL PRODUCTS CORP PA
511 Old Lancaster Rd # 9 (19312-1671)
P.O. Box 645 (19312-0645)
PHONE..................................610 647-6264
Edward H Caterson Jr, *President*
Ed Caterson, *Manager*
EMP: 3
SQ FT: 450
SALES: 600K **Privately Held**
WEB: www.rolledsteelproducts.com
SIC: 5051 3312 Steel; tubing, metal; hot-rolled iron & steel products

(G-1375)
SELF-POWERED LIGHTING INC (PA)
31 Waterloo Ave (19312-1730)
P.O. Box 657 (19312-0657)
PHONE..................................484 595-9130
William E Lynch Jr, *President*
EMP: 3
SALES (est): 281.6K **Privately Held**
WEB: www.self-powered.com
SIC: 3646 Commercial indusl & institutional electric lighting fixtures

(G-1376)
TE CONNECTIVITY CORPORATION (DH)
1050 Westlakes Dr (19312-2400)
P.O. Box 3608, Harrisburg (17105-3608)
PHONE..................................610 893-9800
Tom Lynch, *President*
Christine Voelz-Dexter, *Principal*
John Jenkins, *Exec VP*
Robert N Shaddock, *Exec VP*
Luke Whitebread, *Vice Pres*
▲ **EMP:** 200 EST: 1941
SQ FT: 100,000
SALES (est): 20.6B
SALES (corp-wide): 13.1B **Privately Held**
WEB: www.raychem.com
SIC: 3678 3643 Electronic connectors; current-carrying wiring devices; connectors & terminals for electrical devices

HQ: Te Connectivity Inc.
601 13th St Nw Ste 850s
Washington DC 20005
202 471-3400

(G-1377)
TE CONNECTIVITY FOUNDATION
1050 Westlakes Dr (19312-2400)
PHONE..................................717 810-2987
EMP: 36
SALES: 1.9MM **Privately Held**
SIC: 3679 Electronic crystals

(G-1378)
TRINSEO LLC (HQ)
1000 Chesterbrook Blvd # 300
(19312-1084)
PHONE..................................610 240-3200
Christopher D Pappas, *President*
Martin Pugh, *COO*
Angelo Chaclas, *Exec VP*
Marilyn Horner, *Exec VP*
Jeff Denton, *Vice Pres*
◆ **EMP:** 150
SALES (est): 752.2MM **Publicly Held**
WEB: www.styron.com
SIC: 2821 Plastics materials & resins

(G-1379)
TRINSEO MATERIALS FINANCE INC
1000 Chesterbrook Blvd (19312-1084)
PHONE..................................610 240-3200
EMP: 147 EST: 2015
SALES (est): 97.7K **Publicly Held**
SIC: 2821 Plastics materials & resins
PA: Trinseo S.A.
1000 Chesterbrook Blvd
Berwyn PA 19312

(G-1380)
TRINSEO S A (PA)
1000 Chesterbrook Blvd (19312-1084)
PHONE..................................610 240-3200
Stephen M Zide, *Ch of Bd*
Christopher D Pappas, *President*
Martin Pugh, *COO*
E Jeffery Denton, *Senior VP*
Marilyn N Horner, *Senior VP*
EMP: 25
SALES: 4.6B **Publicly Held**
SIC: 2821 Plastics materials & resins

(G-1381)
TRIUMPH AEROSPACE SYSTEMS GRP (HQ)
899 Cassatt Rd Ste 210 (19312-1190)
PHONE..................................610 251-1000
Richard C III, *Principal*
Chris Solomon, *Info Tech Mgr*
Mark Lillis, *Director*
EMP: 30
SALES (est): 188MM **Publicly Held**
SIC: 3728 Aircraft assemblies, subassemblies & parts

(G-1382)
TRIUMPH AVIATIONS INC
899 Cassatt Rd Ste 210 (19312-1190)
PHONE..................................610 251-1000
Dan Crowley, *President*
Brad Garrow, *Engineer*
William Nostadt, *VP Bus Dvlpt*
Pamela Penn, *Human Resources*
Dan Rose, *Director*
EMP: 6
SALES (est): 698.5K **Publicly Held**
WEB: www.triumphgrp.com
SIC: 3728 Aircraft assemblies, subassemblies & parts
PA: Triumph Group, Inc.
899 Cassatt Rd Ste 210
Berwyn PA 19312

(G-1383)
TRIUMPH GROUP INC (PA)
899 Cassatt Rd Ste 210 (19312-1190)
PHONE..................................610 251-1000
Ralph E Eberhart, *Ch of Bd*
Daniel J Crowley, *President*
Michael R Abram, *Exec VP*
Thomas K Holzthum, *Exec VP*
William Kircher, *Exec VP*
◆ **EMP:** 174
SQ FT: 22,000

SALES: 3.2B **Publicly Held**
WEB: www.triumphgrp.com
SIC: 3728 3724 3812 Aircraft body & wing
assemblies & parts; aircraft engines & engine parts; aircraft control instruments

(G-1384)
TRIUMPH GROUP ACQUISITION
CORP (HQ)
899 Cassatt Rd Ste 210 (19312-1190)
PHONE...................................610 251-1000
Thomas Powers, *Principal*
Laura Akana, *Counsel*
Doug Riley, *Vice Pres*
Bill Wherry, *Vice Pres*
John B Wright, *Vice Pres*
EMP: 7
SALES (est): 2.7MM **Publicly Held**
WEB: www.triumphgrp.com
SIC: 3728 Aircraft parts & equipment

(G-1385)
TRIUMPH GROUP HOLDINGS -
MEXIC (PA)
899 Cassatt Rd Ste 210 (19312-1190)
PHONE...................................610 251-1000
EMP: 88 EST: 2015
SALES (est): 16MM **Privately Held**
SIC: 3728 Aircraft parts & equipment

(G-1386)
TRIUMPH GROUP OPERATIONS
INC (HQ)
899 Cassatt Rd Ste 210 (19312-1190)
PHONE...................................610 251-1000
Tony Johnson, *President*
Richard M Eisenstaedt, *Vice Pres*
Barry Startz, *Purchasing*
John R Bartholdson, *Treasurer*
Kevin E Kindig, *Controller*
◆ EMP: 19
SQ FT: 10,000
SALES (est): 69.5MM **Publicly Held**
WEB: www.triumphairrepair.com
SIC: 5051 3479 3724 Steel; galvanizing
of iron, steel or end-formed products; air-
craft engines & engine parts

(G-1387)
TRIUMPH INSULATION
SYSTEMS LLC
899 Cassatt Rd Ste 210 (19312-1190)
PHONE...................................610 251-1000
EMP: 4 EST: 2015
SALES (est): 239.4K **Publicly Held**
SIC: 3728 Aircraft body & wing assemblies
& parts
PA: Triumph Group, Inc.
899 Cassatt Rd Ste 210
Berwyn PA 19312

(G-1388)
TRIUMPH STRUCTURES - E
TEXAS
899 Cassatt Rd Ste 210 (19312-1190)
PHONE...................................610 251-1000
Tina Barasha, *Director*
EMP: 1001
SALES (est): 24.6MM **Privately Held**
SIC: 3728 Aircraft parts & equipment

(G-1389)
TYCO ELEC LATIN AMER
HOLDG LLC (DH)
1050 Westlakes Dr (19312-2400)
PHONE...................................610 893-9800
EMP: 5
SALES (est): 512K
SALES (corp-wide): 13.1B **Privately Held**
SIC: 3643 Current-carrying wiring devices
HQ: Tyco Electronics (Schweiz) Holding Ii
Gmbh
Rheinstrasse 20
Schaffhausen SH 8200
526 336-600

Bessemer
Lawrence County

(G-1390)
CREATIVE LABWORKS INC
203 W Poland Ave (16112-2529)
P.O. Box 146, New Wilmington (16142-
0146)
PHONE...................................724 667-4093
Kristen Jordan, *President*
Kristen L Jordan, *President*
EMP: 5
SALES: 280K **Privately Held**
SIC: 3999 8742 7311 Education aids, de-
vices & supplies; marketing consulting
services; advertising consultant

Bethany
Wayne County

(G-1391)
UPPER DELAWARE VALLEY ID
54 Miller Dr (18431-5934)
PHONE...................................570 251-8040
EMP: 3
SALES (est): 226.5K **Privately Held**
SIC: 3131 Mfg Footwear Cut Stock

Bethel
Berks County

(G-1392)
ASSEMBLIES OF YAHWEH
Also Called: Obadiah School
190 Frantz Rd (19507-9798)
P.O. Box C (19507-0198)
PHONE...................................717 933-4518
Jacob O Meyer, *Pastor*
Jacob Meyer, *Director*
EMP: 17
SQ FT: 6,450
SALES (est): 594K **Privately Held**
WEB: www.assembliesofyahweh.com
SIC: 8661 4832 2731 8299 Churches,
temples & shrines; radio broadcasting
stations; pamphlets: publishing only, not
printed on site; religious school

(G-1393)
BLUE MOUNTAIN METAL
FINISHING
137 Kline Rd (19507-9609)
PHONE...................................717 933-1643
Luther Mathias, *Owner*
EMP: 4
SALES (est): 434.7K **Privately Held**
SIC: 3471 Finishing, metals or formed
products

(G-1394)
CONCRETE SAFETY SYSTEMS
LLC
Also Called: C S S
9190 Old Rte 22 (19507)
PHONE...................................717 933-4107
Rashad Baig, *General Mgr*
Kelly Yoder, *Human Res Mgr*
Joe Brubaker, *Manager*
Danny Silvano, *Manager*
M Amir Ulislam,
EMP: 45
SQ FT: 30,000
SALES (est): 8.4MM **Privately Held**
WEB: www.concretesafety.com
SIC: 3272 Concrete products, precast

(G-1395)
JAYS RAILING & FABRICATION
CO
9630 Old Rte 22 (19507)
PHONE...................................717 933-9244
Jason Mumma, *President*
Jeremy Mumma, *Vice Pres*
EMP: 6
SQ FT: 6,000

SALES (est): 1MM **Privately Held**
SIC: 3446 Railings, bannisters, guards,
etc.: made from metal pipe

(G-1396)
LEFEVER LOGGING
147 Fort Henry Rd (19507-9507)
PHONE...................................717 587-7889
EMP: 3
SALES (est): 98.8K **Privately Held**
SIC: 2411 Logging

(G-1397)
PENN JERSEY FARMS INC
162 Talbert Rd (19507)
P.O. Box 220, Bernville (19506-0220)
PHONE...................................610 488-7003
Judy Stafford, *President*
Jackie Heflich, *Vice Pres*
EMP: 9
SQ FT: 1,750
SALES (est): 448.4K **Privately Held**
SIC: 0291 2875 4953 Livestock farm,
general; compost; refuse systems

(G-1398)
R & J LOGGING INC
300 Schneck St (19507-9591)
PHONE...................................717 933-5646
Richard Powell, *President*
EMP: 5
SALES (est): 516.8K **Privately Held**
SIC: 2411 Logging camps & contractors

Bethel Park
Allegheny County

(G-1399)
ABE CUSTOM METAL
PRODUCTS
3500 Maplevue Dr (15102-1422)
PHONE...................................412 298-0200
Merry Carol, *President*
Larry Ott, *Vice Pres*
EMP: 4
SALES: 500K **Privately Held**
SIC: 3541 Pointing & burring machines

(G-1400)
ACTION WIRELESS NETWORK
3540 Maplevue Dr (15102-1422)
PHONE...................................412 292-1712
Maryam Emamzadeh, *Principal*
EMP: 5
SALES (est): 449K **Privately Held**
SIC: 7372 Prepackaged software

(G-1401)
AL MAY MANUFACTURING
JEWELERS
2309 Casswell Dr (15102-1912)
PHONE...................................412 391-8736
Dorothy May, *Partner*
EMP: 5
SALES (est): 330K **Privately Held**
SIC: 3911 Jewelry, precious metal

(G-1402)
AMERI-SURCE SPECIALTY PDTS
INC
5372 Enterprise Blvd (15102-2685)
PHONE...................................412 831-9400
Ajay Goel, *President*
Birender Saini, *Vice Pres*
◆ EMP: 28
SALES (est): 15MM **Privately Held**
SIC: 5085 3624 3569 Abrasives; elec-
trodes, thermal & electrolytic uses: car-
bon, graphite; filters

(G-1403)
APPROVED INFO DESTRUCTION
INC
3946 Mimosa Dr (15102-3516)
PHONE...................................412 722-8124
Ronald D Lenneman Jr, *Principal*
EMP: 3 EST: 2008
SALES (est): 324K **Privately Held**
SIC: 3559 Tire shredding machinery

(G-1404)
ARKWOOD PRODUCTS INC
5309 Enterprise Blvd (15102-2531)
P.O. Box 126 (15102-0126)
PHONE...................................412 835-8730
Albert Cuneo, *President*
EMP: 3
SALES (est): 217.1K **Privately Held**
WEB: www.arkwoodproducts.com
SIC: 2759 5943 Card printing & engraving,
except greeting; office forms & supplies

(G-1405)
ASR INSTRUMENTS INC
5547 Saddlebrook Dr (15102-4509)
PHONE...................................412 833-7577
Abdul Rauf, *President*
EMP: 10
SALES: 500K **Privately Held**
WEB: www.asrinstruments.com
SIC: 3825 Analog-digital converters, elec-
tronic instrumentation type

(G-1406)
BETHEL MACHINE &
MANUFACTURING
3050 Industrial Blvd (15102-2538)
P.O. Box 550 (15102-0550)
PHONE...................................412 833-5522
Lawrence Sakowitz, *President*
Jeff Lalley, *Vice Pres*
EMP: 12
SQ FT: 17,000
SALES (est): 2MM **Privately Held**
WEB: www.bethelmachine.net
SIC: 3599 Machine shop, jobbing & repair

(G-1407)
BOEH TOOL & DIE CO INC
1098 Highfield Rd (15102-1024)
PHONE...................................412 833-8707
Francis J Boeh, *President*
Wilberta M Boeh, *Corp Secy*
Robert F Boeh, *Vice Pres*
EMP: 5
SQ FT: 4,500
SALES (est): 370K **Privately Held**
SIC: 3599 Machine shop, jobbing & repair

(G-1408)
CAR CLEEN SYSTEMS INC
1000 Transit Blvd (15102-2556)
PHONE...................................717 795-8995
Ernest R Dalessandro, *President*
Marjorie A Dalessandro, *Treasurer*
Craig S Dalessandro, *Admin Sec*
EMP: 10
SQ FT: 7,400
SALES (est): 1.5MM **Privately Held**
SIC: 2842 5013 5087 Specialty cleaning,
polishes & sanitation goods; automotive
supplies; service establishment equip-
ment

(G-1409)
CARBON CAPTURE SCIENTIFIC
LLC
2940 Industrial Blvd (15102-2536)
P.O. Box 188, South Park (15129-0188)
PHONE...................................412 854-6713
Shiaoguo Chen, *General Mgr*
EMP: 7
SALES (est): 1MM **Privately Held**
SIC: 2813 Industrial gases

(G-1410)
CENTRAL ROAD LLC
4607 Lib Rd Ste 220-303 (15102)
PHONE...................................888 319-7778
Jurabek Begmatov,
EMP: 3
SALES (est): 174.6K **Privately Held**
SIC: 3537 Trucks, tractors, loaders, carri-
ers & similar equipment

(G-1411)
DIE-QUIP CORPORATION
5360 Enterprise Blvd (15102-2532)
PHONE...................................412 833-1662
Thomas Maxwell Jr, *President*
EMP: 10
SQ FT: 9,800
SALES (est): 1.5MM **Privately Held**
WEB: www.diequip.com
SIC: 3542 Die casting machines

▲ = Import ▼=Export
◆ =Import/Export

(G-1412)
DIGITAL DYNAMICS AUDIO INC
3383 Industrial Blvd # 5 (15102-2590)
PHONE..................................412 434-1630
Thomas J Kikta Jr, *President*
Francisco Rodriguez, *Vice Pres*
M Agnes Kikta, *Treasurer*
Thomas J Kikta Sr, *Admin Sec*
EMP: 4
SQ FT: 2,500
SALES (est): 260K **Privately Held**
WEB: www.4ddai.com
SIC: 3652 Pre-recorded records & tapes

(G-1413)
DUKANE RADIATOR INC
1029 Transit Blvd (15102-2555)
PHONE..................................412 233-3300
Thomas A Stoner, *President*
Nikki Stoner, *Treasurer*
EMP: 3
SQ FT: 2,518
SALES (est): 518.5K **Privately Held**
SIC: 7539 3714 3444 Radiator repair shop, automotive; radiators & radiator shells & cores, motor vehicle; sheet metalwork

(G-1414)
FRANCHISE BSNESS OPPORTUNITIES
1155 Greenbriar Rd (15102-2615)
PHONE..................................412 831-2522
William Griser, *Owner*
EMP: 6
SALES (est): 750K **Privately Held**
WEB: www.key4money.com
SIC: 2741 Miscellaneous publishing

(G-1415)
GENERAL MANUFACTURING CO
3249 Industrial Blvd # 2 (15102-2690)
P.O. Box 115 (15102-0115)
PHONE..................................412 833-4300
Lynn Fastuca, *President*
EMP: 15
SQ FT: 13,000
SALES (est): 4.8MM **Privately Held**
SIC: 5072 3599 Miscellaneous fasteners; machine shop, jobbing & repair

(G-1416)
HUNTER SALES CORPORATION
3338 Industrial Blvd (15102-2544)
P.O. Box 234 (15102-0234)
PHONE..................................412 341-2444
R Russell Hunter, *President*
Gregory Hunter, *Corp Secy*
William H Hunter, *Vice Pres*
EMP: 12 **EST:** 1959
SQ FT: 15,000
SALES (est): 2.4MM **Privately Held**
WEB: www.huntersalescorp.com
SIC: 3053 5085 Gaskets & sealing devices; industrial supplies

(G-1417)
INFORMATION MKTG GROUP INC
1000 Transit Blvd 1 (15102-2556)
PHONE..................................508 626-8682
Dennis W Cardiff, *President*
Frank M Piso, *Treasurer*
Jeremiah O'Connor, *Clerk*
EMP: 13
SQ FT: 3,600
SALES (est): 1.4MM **Privately Held**
WEB: www.imgsoftware.com
SIC: 7372 Business oriented computer software

(G-1418)
INSTRUMENTATION INDUSTRIES INC
Also Called: Advantage Tool & Die-Div
2990 Industrial Blvd (15102-2536)
PHONE..................................412 854-1133
Edward C Horey Jr, *President*
Edward J Horey, *Vice Pres*
Sherry Dear, *Purch Agent*
Rita Rigas, *Manager*
Brenda Blasinsky, *Technical Staff*
▼ **EMP:** 27
SQ FT: 15,000

SALES: 3.1MM **Privately Held**
WEB: www.iiioem.com
SIC: 3841 3842 Inhalation therapy equipment; surgical appliances & supplies

(G-1419)
JM DAUGHERTY INDUSTRIES LLC
3003 S Park Rd (15102-1639)
PHONE..................................412 835-2135
Jeffrey P Daugherty, *President*
EMP: 3
SALES (est): 237.5K **Privately Held**
SIC: 3259 1711 Sewer pipe or fittings, clay; plumbing contractors

(G-1420)
JMD ERSION CTRL INSTLLTONS INC
5401 Progress Blvd (15102-2517)
PHONE..................................412 833-7100
Herbert E Forse Jr, *President*
EMP: 4
SALES (est): 462.6K **Privately Held**
SIC: 2299 Narrow woven fabrics: linen, jute, hemp & ramie

(G-1421)
JOHNSTON-MOREHOUSE-DICKEY CO (PA)
Also Called: Jmd Company
5401 Progress Blvd (15102-2517)
P.O. Box 173 (15102-0173)
PHONE..................................412 833-7100
Herbert E Forse Jr, *Ch of Bd*
Mark Forse, *President*
Scot Forse, *Vice Pres*
Scott Forse, *Sales Mgr*
Bill Vechter, *Sales Staff*
▲ **EMP:** 41
SQ FT: 28,000
SALES (est): 33.8MM **Privately Held**
SIC: 2299 3089 5039 Narrow woven fabrics: linen, jute, hemp & ramie; plastic hardware & building products; netting, plastic; soil erosion control fabrics

(G-1422)
KIEFER COAL AND SUPPLY CO
5088 W Library Ave (15102-2732)
PHONE..................................412 835-7900
Russ Smith, *President*
Jane Smith, *Admin Sec*
EMP: 8
SQ FT: 4,000
SALES (est): 1.3MM **Privately Held**
SIC: 5032 3273 Concrete & cinder building products; ready-mixed concrete

(G-1423)
M & R ELECTRIC INC
2025 Milford Dr (15102-2102)
PHONE..................................412 831-6101
Gretchen Oswald, *President*
Scott Stanley, *Vice Pres*
William Miller, *Treasurer*
EMP: 48
SQ FT: 30,000
SALES (est): 3.3MM **Privately Held**
SIC: 1731 7694 Electrical work; electric motor repair

(G-1424)
MEINERT HOLDINGS INC
Also Called: BCT
5309 Enterprise Blvd (15102-2531)
P.O. Box 667 (15102-0667)
PHONE..................................412 835-2727
Melissa Meinert, *President*
Paul Meinert, *Corp Secy*
Mathew Meinert, *Manager*
EMP: 16
SQ FT: 6,500
SALES (est): 3MM **Privately Held**
WEB: www.larita.com
SIC: 2752 Commercial printing, lithographic

(G-1425)
MENDEL STEEL & ORNA IR CO
3017 S Park Rd (15102-1639)
PHONE..................................412 341-7778
Joan Mendel, *Ch of Bd*
Eric Mendel, *Vice Pres*
EMP: 18

SQ FT: 12,000
SALES (est): 3.9MM **Privately Held**
SIC: 3446 Architectural metalwork

(G-1426)
METAL TECH MACHINE COMPANY
1065 Grandview Farms Dr (15102-3777)
PHONE..................................412 833-3239
William Layman, *President*
Ron Nowak, *Corp Secy*
EMP: 4
SQ FT: 2,500
SALES (est): 489.7K **Privately Held**
WEB: www.metalpass.com
SIC: 3599 Machine shop, jobbing & repair

(G-1427)
MULLIGAN MINING INC
5945 Pudding Stone Ln (15102-3335)
PHONE..................................412 831-1787
Sean Taylor, *President*
EMP: 9
SALES (est): 701.5K **Privately Held**
SIC: 1241 Coal mining services

(G-1428)
POST GAZETTE
2892 Oneill Dr (15102-2664)
PHONE..................................412 854-9722
Jeff T Greer, *Principal*
EMP: 3
SALES (est): 162.6K **Privately Held**
SIC: 2711 Newspapers

(G-1429)
PROSOFT TECHNOLOGIES INC (DH)
Also Called: Prosoft Harris School Solution
2000 Oxford Dr Ste 610 (15102-1838)
PHONE..................................412 835-6217
Scott A Anderson, *President*
EMP: 17
SQ FT: 14,000
SALES (est): 3.6MM
SALES (corp-wide): 2.4B **Privately Held**
WEB: www.prosofttech.com
SIC: 7371 7372 Custom computer programming services; prepackaged software
HQ: N. Harris Computer Corporation
1 Antares Dr Suite 400
Nepean ON K2E 8
613 226-5511

(G-1430)
RACO INTERNATIONAL LP
3350 Industrial Blvd (15102-2544)
PHONE..................................412 835-5744
Reinhard Wilke, *Partner*
Induland LLC, *Partner*
Ken McGough, *VP Prdtn*
Steve Becze, *Purch Agent*
John A Piaggesi, *Controller*
EMP: 15
SQ FT: 12,000
SALES (est): 4.7MM **Privately Held**
SIC: 5084 3699 Engines & parts, diesel; electrical equipment & supplies

(G-1431)
RUCK ENGINEERING INC
1246 Plantation Dr (15102-3539)
PHONE..................................412 835-2408
EMP: 6
SALES (est): 440K **Privately Held**
SIC: 7389 3599 3993 Custom Design & Mfg Of Specialty Machines And Animated Displays

(G-1432)
SALMEN TECH CO INC
533 N St (15102-3726)
PHONE..................................412 854-1822
Kenneth L Salmen Jr, *President*
Mary Jo Salmen, *CFO*
EMP: 3
SALES (est): 3MM **Privately Held**
WEB: www.salmentech.com
SIC: 3569 5063 Firefighting apparatus; fire alarm systems

(G-1433)
SCHEIRER MACHINE COMPANY INC
2857 Tischler Rd (15102-3836)
PHONE..................................412 833-6500
Marlene B Scheirer, *President*
Eric Scheirer, *Vice Pres*
EMP: 21
SALES (est): 4.1MM **Privately Held**
WEB: www.scheirer.com
SIC: 3532 3549 Flotation machinery (mining machinery); metalworking machinery

(G-1434)
STEEL CITY CONTROLS INC
3672 Maplevue Dr (15102-1459)
PHONE..................................412 851-8566
EMP: 3
SALES (est): 320.1K **Privately Held**
SIC: 3625 Motor controls & accessories

(G-1435)
STEEL SHIELD TECHNOLOGIES INC
3351 Industrial Blvd (15102-2543)
PHONE..................................412 479-0024
George Fennel, *President*
Mark Pushnick, *Vice Pres*
Robert I Ferraro, *Treasurer*
EMP: 5
SQ FT: 5,400
SALES (est): 853.1K **Privately Held**
SIC: 3714 Lubrication systems & parts, motor vehicle

(G-1436)
TURNINGS BY EDRIC
240 Graeser Ave (15102-1716)
PHONE..................................412 833-5127
Edric Florence, *Owner*
EMP: 4
SALES: 30K **Privately Held**
SIC: 2499 Carved & turned wood

(G-1437)
WASTE RECOVERY DESIGNED PDTS
2936 Industrial Blvd (15102-2536)
PHONE..................................724 926-5713
Frank Bonidie, *President*
Joseph Bonidie, *Treasurer*
EMP: 5
SQ FT: 9,600
SALES (est): 342.6K **Privately Held**
WEB: www.wrdpinc.com
SIC: 3585 Parts for heating, cooling & refrigerating equipment

(G-1438)
WEGCO WELDING INC
3180 Industrial Blvd # 2 (15102-2540)
PHONE..................................412 833-7020
Walter E Gregg, *President*
EMP: 8
SQ FT: 13,000
SALES (est): 1.6MM **Privately Held**
SIC: 3441 7692 Building components, structural steel; welding repair

(G-1439)
WESTER BURLAP BAG & SUPPLY CO
3446 S Park Rd (15102-1124)
PHONE..................................412 835-4314
Walter Araneicka, *President*
Florence Poxon, *Vice Pres*
EMP: 5 **EST:** 1959
SQ FT: 15,000
SALES (est): 1MM **Privately Held**
SIC: 5085 2393 2673 Packing, industrial; bags & containers, except sleeping bags: textile; bags: plastic, laminated & coated

(G-1440)
ZYLUX AMERICA INC (HQ)
225 Library Rd Pmb 500 500 Pmb (15102)
PHONE..................................412 221-5530
Herman Lu, *CEO*
Wyatt Briant, *President*
Sophia Young, *Vice Pres*
Terri Pollino, *Sales Staff*
▲ **EMP:** 3
SQ FT: 3,912

SALES (est): 807K
SALES (corp-wide): 15.2MM **Privately Held**
WEB: www.zyluxacoustic.com
SIC: 3651 Speaker systems
PA: Zylux Acoustic Corporation
2, 3, 3f, 3f-1, No. 22, Lane 35, Jihu Rd.
Taipei City TAP 11491
226 587-878

Bethlehem
Northampton County

(G-1441)
ABARTA INC
2150 Industrial Dr (18017-2136)
PHONE......................610 807-5319
Joe Brake, *Vice Pres*
Deborah L Chinsoon, *MIS Mgr*
EMP: 3
SALES (est): 82.6K **Privately Held**
SIC: 2086 Soft drinks: packaged in cans, bottles, etc.

(G-1442)
ABEC INC (PA)
Also Called: Stainless Technolgy
3998 Schelden Cir (18017-8936)
PHONE......................610 882-1541
Scott Pickering, *CEO*
John D Wilson, *Chairman*
Gary Bender, *CFO*
Fay Young, *Accountant*
Debbie Benbenek, *Sales Staff*
◆ **EMP:** 175 **EST:** 1974
SQ FT: 125,000
SALES (est): 76.3MM **Privately Held**
WEB: www.abec.com
SIC: 3556 8711 Food products machinery; engineering services

(G-1443)
ACTIVE DATA INC
Also Called: Active Data Exchange
190 Brodhead Rd Ste 300 (18017-8617)
PHONE......................610 997-8100
Susan Yee, *CEO*
David Yanoshik, *Vice Pres*
Tina Fritzinger, *Human Res Mgr*
Jonathan Ozimek, *Sales Executive*
EMP: 20
SQ FT: 5,000
SALES (est): 3.4MM **Privately Held**
WEB: www.activedatax.com
SIC: 7372 Publishers' computer software

(G-1444)
ADAMS OUTDOOR ADVG LTD PARTNR
Adams Outdoor of Lehigh Valley
2176 Avenue C (18017-2120)
PHONE......................610 266-9461
Todd Kohn, *Manager*
EMP: 33
SQ FT: 12,500
SALES (est): 4.2MM
SALES (corp-wide): 49.1MM **Privately Held**
WEB: www.adamsoutdoor.com
SIC: 7312 3993 Billboard advertising; signs & advertising specialties
PA: Adams Outdoor Advertising Limited Partnership
500 Colonial Center Pkwy
Roswell GA 30076
770 333-0399

(G-1445)
AIR PRODUCTS AND CHEMICALS INC
1025 E Market St (18017-7017)
PHONE......................610 317-8706
Randy Sobotka, *Branch Mgr*
EMP: 20
SALES (corp-wide): 8.9B **Publicly Held**
WEB: www.airproducts.com
SIC: 2813 5084 Industrial gases; welding machinery & equipment
PA: Air Products And Chemicals, Inc.
7201 Hamilton Blvd
Allentown PA 18195
610 481-4911

(G-1446)
AIR PRODUCTS AND CHEMICALS INC
1011 E Market St (18017-7017)
PHONE......................610 317-8715
Joseph Martelliti, *Manager*
EMP: 23
SALES (corp-wide): 8.9B **Publicly Held**
WEB: www.airproducts.com
SIC: 2813 2869 Oxygen, compressed or liquefied; amines, acids, salts, esters
PA: Air Products And Chemicals, Inc.
7201 Hamilton Blvd
Allentown PA 18195
610 481-4911

(G-1447)
ALBARELL ELECTRIC INC
Also Called: Albarell Electric Mtr Repr Sp
1005c W Lehigh St (18018-5146)
P.O. Box 799 (18016-0799)
PHONE......................610 691-7030
Jess Garguilo, *Manager*
EMP: 8
SQ FT: 5,000
SALES (corp-wide): 36.6MM **Privately Held**
WEB: www.albarell.com
SIC: 7694 Electric motor repair; rewinding stators
PA: Albarell Electric, Inc.
901 W Lehigh St Unit 1
Bethlehem PA 18018
610 691-8606

(G-1448)
ALPHA PACKAGING NORTH EAST INC
2115 Spillman Dr (18015)
PHONE......................610 974-9001
David Spence, *President*
Dan Creston, *COO*
Gary Seeman, *CFO*
EMP: 62
SALES: 20MM **Privately Held**
SIC: 3085 Plastics bottles
HQ: Alpha Plastics Inc.
1555 Page Industrial Blvd
Saint Louis MO 63132
314 427-4300

(G-1449)
ALPLA INC
2120 Spillman Dr (18015)
PHONE......................770 914-1407
Christopher Gross, *Branch Mgr*
EMP: 21 **Privately Held**
SIC: 3085 Plastics bottles
HQ: Alpla Inc.
289 Highway 155 S
Mcdonough GA 30253
713 671-2600

(G-1450)
APOLLO METALS LTD
Also Called: Apollo Metals, Ltd.
1001 14th Ave (18018-2207)
PHONE......................610 867-5826
Remco Blaauw, *President*
William E Flederbach, *Vice Pres*
Mark Lesnett, *Sales Staff*
Patty Mohney, *Director*
▲ **EMP:** 50 **EST:** 1915
SQ FT: 150,000
SALES (est): 7.8MM
SALES (corp-wide): 9.2B **Privately Held**
WEB: www.apollometals.com
SIC: 3471 Electroplating of metals or formed products
HQ: Tata Steel Europe Limited
30 Millbank
London SW1P
207 975-8382

(G-1451)
APPRISE SOFTWARE INC (PA)
3101 Emrick Blvd Ste 301 (18020-8057)
PHONE......................610 991-3600
Jeff Broadhurst, *President*
Steven Yuan, *General Mgr*
Dana Lindsey, *Business Mgr*
Kevin Ryer, *Vice Pres*
Steve Spagnolo, *CFO*
EMP: 43
SQ FT: 16,000

SALES (est): 29.5MM **Privately Held**
WEB: www.apprise.com
SIC: 7372 Business oriented computer software

(G-1452)
ARCHER DOUBLE DS PRODUCT
3215 Bingen Rd (18015-5708)
PHONE......................610 838-1121
Brian Deiter, *Principal*
EMP: 3
SALES (est): 248.7K **Privately Held**
SIC: 3949 Sporting & athletic goods

(G-1453)
ARTSKILLS INC
3935 Rabold Cir S (18020-8988)
PHONE......................610 253-6663
Steven B Golden, *President*
Bradford Demsky, *President*
Michele Demsky, *President*
Marilyn B Golden, *Corp Secy*
▲ **EMP:** 40
SQ FT: 17,874
SALES (est): 8.9MM **Privately Held**
WEB: www.artskills.com
SIC: 3944 8742 Craft & hobby kits & sets; marketing consulting services

(G-1454)
B BRAUN MEDICAL INC (DH)
824 12th Ave (18018-3524)
P.O. Box 4027 (18018-0027)
PHONE......................610 691-5400
Caroll H Neubauer, *Ch of Bd*
Wes Cetnarowski MD, *Chairman*
Frank Katona, *COO*
Cathy L Codrea, *Senior VP*
Joe Grispo Jr, *Senior VP*
◆ **EMP:** 600 **EST:** 1957
SQ FT: 107,000
SALES (est): 1B **Privately Held**
SIC: 3841 Surgical & medical instruments; catheters
HQ: B. Braun Of America Inc.
824 12th Ave
Bethlehem PA 18018
610 691-5400

(G-1455)
B BRAUN OF AMERICA INC (DH)
824 12th Ave (18018-3524)
P.O. Box 4027 (18018-0027)
PHONE......................610 691-5400
Caroll H Neubauer, *Ch of Bd*
Gina Moore, *Sales Staff*
Leigh Nickens, *Manager*
Inge Schimmer, *Manager*
Charles Dinardo, *Admin Sec*
EMP: 1
SALES (est): 1.3B **Privately Held**
SIC: 6719 3841 Investment holding companies, except banks; surgical & medical instruments
HQ: B. Braun Nordamerika Verwaltungs-ges. Mbh
Carl-Braun-Str. 1
Melsungen
566 171-0

(G-1456)
BACKDOOR BAKERSHOP
92 E Broad St (18018-5917)
PHONE......................610 625-0987
Lehman Gail, *Principal*
EMP: 4
SALES (est): 289.8K **Privately Held**
SIC: 2051 Bakery: wholesale or whole-sale/retail combined

(G-1457)
BARRY CALLEBAUT USA LLC
4863 Hanoverville Rd (18020-9480)
PHONE......................312 496-7305
EMP: 4 **EST:** 2017
SALES (est): 200.1K **Privately Held**
SIC: 2066 Chocolate & cocoa products

(G-1458)
BATTERY ZONE (PA)
902 4th Ave Ste 200 (18018-3702)
P.O. Box 6435, Bridgewater NJ (08807-0435)
PHONE......................800 371-5033
James Sapp, *President*
Terri Sapp, *Vice Pres*

▲ **EMP:** 15
SQ FT: 2,600
SALES (est): 2.6MM **Privately Held**
WEB: www.batteryzone.com
SIC: 3691 3692 3699 5063 Batteries, rechargeable; nickel cadmium storage batteries; primary batteries, dry & wet; appliance cords for household electrical equipment; storage batteries, industrial

(G-1459)
BENCHMARK GROUP MEDIA INC
Also Called: Lehigh Valley Magazine
65 E Elizabeth Ave # 307 (18018-6518)
PHONE......................610 691-8833
Richard J Royer, *Vice Pres*
Sherry Slabinski, *Marketing Staff*
EMP: 8
SALES (est): 884.7K **Privately Held**
WEB: www.lehighvalleymagazine.com
SIC: 2721 Magazines: publishing only, not printed on site

(G-1460)
BETHLEHEM APPARATUS CO INC
935 Bethlehem Dr (18017-7021)
PHONE......................610 882-2611
Robert Schlegel, *General Mgr*
EMP: 4
SALES (corp-wide): 20MM **Privately Held**
WEB: www.bethlehemapparatus.com
SIC: 2819 3559 Mercury, redistilled; glass making machinery: blowing, molding, forming, etc.
PA: Bethlehem Apparatus Company, Inc.
890 Front St
Hellertown PA 18055
610 838-7034

(G-1461)
BETHLEHEM APPARATUS CO INC
Also Called: Warehouse
890 Front St (18017)
PHONE......................610 838-7034
Bruce Lawrence, *President*
EMP: 20
SALES (corp-wide): 20MM **Privately Held**
WEB: www.bethlehemapparatus.com
SIC: 2819 3559 Mercury, redistilled; glass making machinery: blowing, molding, forming, etc.
PA: Bethlehem Apparatus Company, Inc.
890 Front St
Hellertown PA 18055
610 838-7034

(G-1462)
BETHLEHEM PRE-CAST INC
Also Called: Plant
835 E North St (18017-7023)
P.O. Box 247 (18016-0247)
PHONE......................610 691-1336
Thomas Engelman, *President*
EMP: 4
SALES (est): 405.4K
SALES (corp-wide): 8.9MM **Privately Held**
WEB: www.bethlehemprecast.com
SIC: 3272 Concrete products, precast
PA: Bethlehem Pre-Cast Inc.
4702 Indian Creek Rd
Macungie PA 18062
610 967-5531

(G-1463)
BETHLEHEM WASTE WATER
144 Shimersville Rd (18015-9528)
PHONE......................610 865-7169
Jack Lawrence, *Superintendent*
Richard Mann, *Technician*
EMP: 36
SALES (est): 4MM **Privately Held**
SIC: 3823 Water quality monitoring & control systems

(G-1464)
BG JEWELRY
2189 Rovaldi Ave (18015-4711)
PHONE......................610 691-0687
Barry L Gebhart, *Owner*

▲ = Import ▼=Export
◆ =Import/Export

Sandra Gebhart, *Co-Owner*
EMP: 3
SALES: 60K **Privately Held**
SIC: 3961 5945 Costume jewelry; arts & crafts supplies

(G-1465)
BIKE USA INC
2811 Brodhead Rd Ste 1 (18020-8941)
PHONE..............................610 868-7652
Ssu-Liu Liu, *President*
Marc Weiner, *Vice Pres*
Scott M Abraham, *Treasurer*
Kai-CHI Su Liu, *Admin Sec*
▲ **EMP:** 8
SQ FT: 7,200
SALES (est): 1.2MM **Privately Held**
WEB: www.bikeusainc.com
SIC: 3949 Exercise equipment

(G-1466)
BIMBO BAKERIES USA INC
Also Called: Stroehmann Maiers Bakeries
2415 Brodhead Rd (18020-8905)
PHONE..............................610 865-7402
George Volandt, *Manager*
EMP: 70 **Privately Held**
SIC: 2051 5149 Bakery: wholesale or wholesale/retail combined; groceries & related products
HQ: Bimbo Bakeries Usa, Inc
255 Business Center Dr # 200
Horsham PA 19044
215 347-5500

(G-1467)
BITRONICS LLC
261 Brodhead Rd Ste 100 (18017-8698)
PHONE..............................610 997-5100
Aubrey Zey,
Ron Gullickson,
Novatech LLC,
Volker Oakey,
EMP: 35
SQ FT: 25,000
SALES (est): 10.8MM
SALES (corp-wide): 44.6MM **Privately Held**
WEB: www.novatech-llc.com
SIC: 3825 Electrical power measuring equipment
PA: Novatech, L.L.C.
1720 Molasses Way
Quakertown PA 18951
484 812-6000

(G-1468)
BLUE TORO TECHNOLOGIES LLC
4431 Wagner Dr (18020-8804)
PHONE..............................610 428-0891
Brandon Paulus, *CEO*
EMP: 4 **EST:** 2013
SALES (est): 236.3K **Privately Held**
SIC: 7389 3571 ; mainframe computers

(G-1469)
BONN PLACE BREWING INC
310 Taylor St (18015)
PHONE..............................845 325-6748
Samuele Masotto, *President*
EMP: 6
SALES (est): 364.1K **Privately Held**
SIC: 2082 Beer (alcoholic beverage)

(G-1470)
BOSCH REXROTH CORPORATION
2315 City Line Rd (18017-2131)
P.O. Box 25407, Lehigh Valley (18002-5407)
PHONE..............................610 694-8300
George Stasko, *Safety Mgr*
Gopal Patel, *Senior Buyer*
Manfred Hahn, *Branch Mgr*
Andreas Hassold, *Senior Mgr*
Daniel Green, *Technical Staff*
EMP: 600
SALES (corp-wide): 301.8MM **Privately Held**
WEB: www.us.rexroth.com
SIC: 3795 3594 Tanks & tank components; fluid power pumps & motors

HQ: Bosch Rexroth Corporation
14001 S Lakes Dr
Charlotte NC 28273
704 583-4338

(G-1471)
BOSCH REXROTH CORPORATION
2655 Brodhead Rd Ste 150 (18020-8961)
PHONE..............................610 694-8300
Manfred Hahn, *Plant Mgr*
EMP: 600
SALES (corp-wide): 301.8MM **Privately Held**
SIC: 3594 Pumps, hydraulic power transfer
HQ: Bosch Rexroth Corporation
14001 S Lakes Dr
Charlotte NC 28273
704 583-4338

(G-1472)
BOWE BELL + HOWELL POSTAL SYST
2625 Brodhead Rd (18020-8966)
PHONE..............................610 317-4300
EMP: 14
SALES (corp-wide): 17.6MM **Privately Held**
SIC: 3579 Mfg Office Machines
PA: Bowe Bell + Howell Postal Systems Company
760 S Wolf Rd
Wheeling IL 27713
847 675-7600

(G-1473)
BREEZY RIDGE INSTRUMENTS LTD
3644 Route 378 Unit B (18015-5448)
PHONE..............................610 691-3302
Mary Faith Rhoads- Lewis, *Principal*
Mary Rhoads, *Treasurer*
John Pearse, *Accountant*
EMP: 6
SQ FT: 2,100
SALES (est): 614.2K **Privately Held**
WEB: www.jpstrings.com
SIC: 3931 Guitars & parts, electric & non-electric

(G-1474)
BRONKHORST USA INC
57 S Commerce Way (18017-8968)
PHONE..............................610 866-6750
Teus Bruggeman, *Principal*
Ben Brussen, *Principal*
Wybren Jouwsma, *Principal*
EMP: 5
SALES (est): 1.3MM **Privately Held**
SIC: 3823 Industrial instrmnts msrmnt display/control process variable

(G-1475)
BSG CUSTOM DESIGNS LLC
826 Monocacy St (18018-3844)
PHONE..............................610 867-7361
Annette Klien,
EMP: 9
SALES: 1MM **Privately Held**
SIC: 2759 2395 Screen printing; embroidery & art needlework

(G-1476)
BUZZI UNICEM USA INC (DH)
100 Brodhead Rd Ste 230 (18017-8935)
PHONE..............................610 882-5000
Dave Nepereny, *Ch of Bd*
Massimo Toso, *President*
Nancy L Krial, *Vice Pres*
▲ **EMP:** 43
SALES (est): 474.5MM
SALES (corp-wide): 287.7MM **Privately Held**
SIC: 3241 Portland cement

(G-1477)
C G S ENTERPRISES INC
Also Called: Henderson Industries
3864 Courtney St Ste 220 (18017-8987)
PHONE..............................610 758-9263
David Simmons, *President*
Richard Hand, *Manager*
EMP: 15
SQ FT: 10,000

SALES (est): 2.3MM **Privately Held**
WEB: www.cgsenterprises.com
SIC: 3469 Machine parts, stamped or pressed metal

(G-1478)
CAMERON SUPPLY CORPORATION
Also Called: Liberty Atlantic
1850 W Market St (18018-4500)
PHONE..............................610 866-9632
Robert Cameron, *President*
Thelma K Cameron, *Corp Secy*
EMP: 11
SQ FT: 10,000
SALES (est): 1.5MM **Privately Held**
SIC: 2087 7359 Beverage bases; equipment rental & leasing

(G-1479)
CANDELA CORPORATION
2550 Brodhead Rd Ste 300 (18020-8922)
PHONE..............................610 861-8772
Bill Baas, *Branch Mgr*
EMP: 4
SALES (corp-wide): 24.8MM **Privately Held**
SIC: 3645 5063 Residential lighting fixtures; lighting fixtures
PA: Candela Corporation
14420 Myford Rd Ste 100
Irvine CA 92606
714 662-4900

(G-1480)
CARL R HARRY
Also Called: Bethlehem Ice Service
1521 Linden St (18017-4706)
PHONE..............................610 865-7104
Carl R Harry, *Owner*
EMP: 3 **EST:** 1950
SQ FT: 1,800
SALES (est): 221.3K **Privately Held**
SIC: 2097 Manufactured ice

(G-1481)
CERA-MET LLC
2175 Avenue C (18017-2182)
PHONE..............................610 266-0270
Henri M Fine, *President*
Marc Riquelme, *General Mgr*
Paul Krawiec, *Engineer*
Maria Schwartz, *Controller*
Ken Claypool, *Technology*
▲ **EMP:** 120
SQ FT: 50,000
SALES (est): 27MM **Privately Held**
SIC: 3365 Aerospace castings, aluminum; aluminum & aluminum-based alloy castings

(G-1482)
CEWA TECHNOLOGIES INC
384 Kevin Dr (18017-2461)
PHONE..............................484 695-5489
William Van Geertruyden, *CEO*
EMP: 3
SALES (est): 147.2K **Privately Held**
SIC: 3599 Industrial machinery

(G-1483)
CHRISTMAS CITY PRINTING CO INC
861 14th Ave (18018-2244)
PHONE..............................610 868-5844
Glen Allan, *Ch of Bd*
Paul Sicinski, *President*
Christopher Sicinski, *Vice Pres*
James Herr, *Treasurer*
James Bucchin, *Sales Executive*
EMP: 36
SQ FT: 8,000
SALES (est): 7.1MM **Privately Held**
WEB: www.xmascity.com
SIC: 2752 2791 2789 2759 Commercial printing, offset; typesetting; bookbinding & related work; commercial printing

(G-1484)
CHRISTMAS CITY SPIRITS LLC
564 Main St (18018)
PHONE..............................484 893-0590
Michael Santanasto, *Manager*
EMP: 7
SALES (est): 550.5K **Privately Held**
SIC: 3556 Distillery machinery

(G-1485)
CLEOGEO INC
21 E 3rd St (18015-1303)
PHONE..............................610 868-7200
Cleo Smith, *President*
EMP: 4
SALES (est): 314.8K **Privately Held**
SIC: 1044 Silver bullion production

(G-1486)
COCA-COLA BTLG OF LEHIGH VLY
2150 Industrial Dr (18017-2176)
PHONE..............................610 866-8020
Charlie Bitzer, *President*
Joe Brake, *Vice Pres*
Joseph Brake, *Vice Pres*
Ash Abdellatif, *Supervisor*
Jeanette Cruz, *Supervisor*
EMP: 140
SQ FT: 100,000
SALES (est): 31.2MM
SALES (corp-wide): 361.4MM **Privately Held**
SIC: 2086 Soft drinks: packaged in cans, bottles, etc.
HQ: Wilmington Trust Sp Services
1105 N Market St Ste 1300
Wilmington DE 19801
302 427-7650

(G-1487)
COORDINATED HEALTH SYSTEMS (PA)
2775 Schoenersville Rd (18017-7394)
PHONE..............................610 861-8080
Jason Buck, *District Mgr*
Allison Yenchik, *Project Mgr*
Maria Donato, *Purch Mgr*
Nicole Protzman, *Research*
Michael Busch, *Surgeon*
EMP: 200
SALES (est): 54.1MM **Privately Held**
SIC: 8011 3841 Orthopedic physician; surgical & medical instruments

(G-1488)
CORTAPE NE INC
Also Called: Tapeworks
2285 Avenue A (18017-2107)
PHONE..............................610 997-7900
Randall Emmons, *President*
Richard Chambers, *Treasurer*
▲ **EMP:** 10
SQ FT: 5,000
SALES (est): 2.2MM **Privately Held**
WEB: www.tape-works.com
SIC: 2672 Tape, pressure sensitive: made from purchased materials

(G-1489)
CRAYOLA LLC
3025 Commerce Center Blvd (18015-9547)
PHONE..............................610 814-7681
EMP: 464
SALES (corp-wide): 3.3B **Privately Held**
SIC: 3952 Lead pencils & art goods
HQ: Crayola Llc
1100 Church Ln
Easton PA 18040
610 253-6272

(G-1490)
CRYOSTAR USA
5897 Colony Dr (18017-9349)
PHONE..............................484 281-3261
Daniel Meyer, *Principal*
Mark Van Eps, *Senior Buyer*
Frangois Le Scraigne, *Marketing Staff*
Jose Moreno, *Manager*
EMP: 5 **EST:** 2010
SALES (est): 801.5K **Privately Held**
SIC: 3679 Cryogenic cooling devices for infrared detectors, masers

(G-1491)
CTS BULK TERMINALS
4677 Hanoverville Rd (18020-9410)
PHONE..............................610 759-8330
Tom Brown, *Principal*
EMP: 3 **EST:** 2007
SALES (est): 337.4K **Privately Held**
SIC: 5032 3271 Cement; concrete block & brick

(G-1492)
CUMMINGS GROUP INC
Also Called: Cowboy Magic
2020 Highland Ave (18020-8963)
PHONE..................................714 237-1140
Jim Cummings, *President*
Charlotte Cummings, *Vice Pres*
EMP: 6
SALES: 2MM **Privately Held**
WEB: www.cowboymagic.com
SIC: 3999 Pet supplies

(G-1493)
CURTISS-WRIGHT ELECTRO-
Curtiss Wrght Engnred Pump Div
1185 Feather Way (18015-9404)
PHONE..................................610 997-6400
Greg Hempsling, *Manager*
EMP: 84
SALES (corp-wide): 2.4B **Publicly Held**
SIC: 3561 Industrial pumps & parts
HQ: Curtiss-Wright Electro-Mechanical Cor-
poration
1000 Wright Way
Cheswick PA 15024
724 275-5000

(G-1494)
CYBEL LLC
1195 Pennsylvania Ave (18018-2026)
PHONE..................................610 691-7012
Kyle Heckler, *Mng Member*
EMP: 4
SALES (est): 580.2K **Privately Held**
SIC: 3827 Optical instruments & lenses

(G-1495)
D & A EMERGENCY EQUIPMENT
INC
1655 Jeter Ave (18015-2423)
PHONE..................................610 691-6847
Dean A Harper, *President*
EMP: 6
SQ FT: 3,600
SALES: 1MM **Privately Held**
SIC: 3569 5999 Firefighting apparatus &
related equipment; police supply stores

(G-1496)
DIGESTIVE CARE INC
1120 Win Dr (18017-7059)
PHONE..................................610 882-5950
Tibor Sipos, *President*
Steve Berens, *President*
Robin Lapadula, *Administration*
▼ EMP: 25
SALES (est): 5.7MM **Privately Held**
WEB: www.digestivecare.com
SIC: 2834 Pharmaceutical preparations

(G-1497)
DIGITAL PRESS INC
90 S Commerce Way Ste 340
(18017-8611)
PHONE..................................610 758-9680
Willard Edinger, *President*
Ellie Stein, *Admin Sec*
Chang Ye Edinger, *Administration*
EMP: 5
SQ FT: 4,000
SALES (est): 1MM **Privately Held**
WEB: www.digitalpressusa.com
SIC: 3599 5084 Machine & other job shop
work; industrial machinery & equipment

(G-1498)
DONNA KARAN COMPANY LLC
77 Sands Blvd (18015-7705)
PHONE..................................610 625-4410
Laurie Engleman, *Branch Mgr*
EMP: 157
SALES (corp-wide): 3B **Publicly Held**
SIC: 2335 Women's, juniors' & misses'
dresses
HQ: The Donna Karan Company Llc
240 W 40th St
New York NY 10018
212 789-1500

(G-1499)
DYETS INC
Also Called: 2508 Easton Ave
2508 Easton Ave (18017-5014)
PHONE..................................610 868-7701
Donald H Yowell, *President*

Shawn P McGee, *Vice Pres*
Shawn McGee, *Vice Pres*
Lisa Wagner, *Treasurer*
Warren Smith, *Manager*
EMP: 8
SALES: 150K **Privately Held**
SIC: 2048 Prepared feeds

(G-1500)
EAST PENN TRUCK EQUIPMENT
INC
1100 Win Dr (18017-7059)
PHONE..................................610 694-9234
John H Oberly III, *President*
Casey Smith, *Vice Pres*
Amy Persing, *Office Mgr*
EMP: 8
SQ FT: 22,600
SALES: 14MM **Privately Held**
WEB: www.eastpenntrucks.com
SIC: 5531 5511 3713 Automotive parts;
automobiles, new & used; truck & bus
bodies

(G-1501)
ELEMENT ID INC
520 Evans St (18015-1915)
PHONE..................................610 419-8822
Jack Romaine, *CEO*
EMP: 12
SALES (est): 1.3MM **Privately Held**
SIC: 3679 5065 Recording & playback ap-
paratus, including phonograph; telephone
& telegraphic equipment

(G-1502)
ELEMENT ROOFING LLC
1909 Aripine Ave (18018-1413)
PHONE..................................610 737-0641
EMP: 3 EST: 2016
SALES (est): 81.8K **Privately Held**
SIC: 2819 Mfg Industrial Inorganic Chemi-
cals

(G-1503)
ELLIOTT PRINTING SERVICES
LLC
3000 Portage Rd (18020-1325)
PHONE..................................610 614-1500
Kenneth Kelly,
EMP: 10
SQ FT: 1,500
SALES (est): 1.5MM **Privately Held**
WEB: www.eliprint.com
SIC: 2759 Screen printing

(G-1504)
ESSROC CEMENT
5 Highland Ave (18017-8967)
PHONE..................................610 882-2498
EMP: 7
SALES (est): 146.8K **Privately Held**
SIC: 5032 3241 Stucco; cement, hydraulic

(G-1505)
EUTHANEX CORPORATION
Also Called: E-Z Systems
944 14th Ave Unit 1 (18018-2209)
P.O. Box 3544, Palmer (18043-3544)
PHONE..................................610 559-0159
Les Anderson, *President*
David Anderson, *Sales Staff*
Steve Miller, *Sales Executive*
▲ EMP: 10
SALES (est): 940K **Privately Held**
WEB: www.euthanex.com
SIC: 3821 Laboratory apparatus & furniture

(G-1506)
FACCHIANO IRONWORKS INC
1762 Acker Ave (18015-3804)
PHONE..................................610 865-1503
Gary Facchiano, *President*
John Facchiano, *Vice Pres*
Edna Facchiano, *Treasurer*
Patricia Facchiano, *Admin Sec*
EMP: 3 EST: 1959
SQ FT: 3,875
SALES (est): 450K **Privately Held**
SIC: 3446 7692 7699 Grillwork, ornamen-
tal metal; gratings, tread: fabricated
metal; welding repair; construction equip-
ment repair

(G-1507)
FEDCHEM LLC
275 Keystone Dr (18020-9464)
PHONE..................................610 837-1808
William Sickenberger, *Branch Mgr*
Joe David, *Administration*
EMP: 14
SALES (corp-wide): 25.5MM **Privately**
Held
WEB: www.fedchemproducts.com
SIC: 2819 Industrial inorganic chemicals
HQ: Fedchem, L.L.C.
275 Keystone Dr
Bethlehem PA 18020
610 837-1808

(G-1508)
FEDCHEM LLC (HQ)
275 Keystone Dr (18020-9464)
PHONE..................................610 837-1808
William Sickenberger, *Branch Mgr*
John Outcalt Jr, *Mng Member*
◆ EMP: 4
SALES (est): 5MM
SALES (corp-wide): 25.5MM **Privately**
Held
WEB: www.fedchemproducts.com
SIC: 2819 Industrial inorganic chemicals
PA: Federal Process Corporation
4520 Richmond Rd
Cleveland OH 44128
216 464-6440

(G-1509)
FLAGSTONE SMALL BUS
VLTONS LLC
714 Leibert St (18018-5111)
PHONE..................................484 515-2621
Ernest Nemeth, *Principal*
EMP: 3 EST: 2008
SALES (est): 184.6K **Privately Held**
SIC: 3281 Flagstones

(G-1510)
FLEXICON CORPORATION (PA)
2400 Emrick Blvd (18020-8006)
PHONE..................................610 814-2400
David R Gill, *President*
William S Gill, *Principal*
▲ EMP: 128 EST: 1974
SQ FT: 90,000
SALES (est): 29.1MM **Privately Held**
SIC: 3535 Conveyors & conveying equip-
ment

(G-1511)
FLOWSERVE CORPORATION
1480 Valley Center Pkwy (18017-2264)
PHONE..................................908 859-7408
Gene Mills, *Vice Pres*
EMP: 15
SALES (corp-wide): 3.8B **Publicly Held**
SIC: 3561 Pumps & pumping equipment
PA: Flowserve Corporation
5215 N Oconnor Blvd Connor
Irving TX 75039
972 443-6500

(G-1512)
FLS US HOLDINGS INC (DH)
2040 Avenue C (18017-2118)
PHONE..................................610 264-6011
Thomas Schulz, *Principal*
Kyle Kyle Aulenbach, *Engineer*
◆ EMP: 19
SQ FT: 265,000
SALES (est): 105.4MM
SALES (corp-wide): 2.8B **Privately Held**
WEB: www.flsmidth.com
SIC: 3559 3554 3549 3532 Cement mak-
ing machinery; paper industries machin-
ery; metalworking machinery; crushing,
pulverizing & screening equipment; con-
veyors & conveying equipment
HQ: Flsmidth A/S
Vigerslev Alle 77
Valby 2500
361 810-00

(G-1513)
FLSMIDTH INC
Air Pollution Ctrl Sls - USA
2040 Avenue C (18017-2118)
PHONE..................................610 264-6101
Dan Nemith, *Branch Mgr*
EMP: 600

SALES (corp-wide): 2.8B **Privately Held**
SIC: 8711 3564 Engineering services;
blowers & fans
HQ: Flsmidth Inc.
2040 Avenue C
Bethlehem PA 18017
610 264-6011

(G-1514)
FLURER MACHINE AND TOOL
Also Called: Flurer Machine & Tool
294 Nazareth Pike (18020-9626)
PHONE..................................610 759-6114
Douglas L Flurer, *Owner*
EMP: 4
SQ FT: 13,786
SALES (est): 350K **Privately Held**
SIC: 3599 7692 Machine shop, jobbing &
repair; welding repair

(G-1515)
FOLLETT LLC
157 N Commerce Way (18017-8933)
PHONE..................................800 523-9361
EMP: 9
SALES (corp-wide): 2.7B **Publicly Held**
SIC: 3585 Ice boxes, industrial
HQ: Follett Llc
801 Church Ln
Easton PA 18040
610 252-7301

(G-1516)
FOULK EQUIPMENT LEASING
INC
Also Called: Foulk Warehousing
1235 Easton Rd (18015-5912)
PHONE..................................610 838-2260
Allen Foulk, *President*
Bonita Foulk, *Admin Sec*
EMP: 9
SALES: 2MM **Privately Held**
SIC: 4226 2421 Special warehousing &
storage; lumber: rough, sawed or planed

(G-1517)
FOUR WINDS CONCRETE INC
(PA)
925 Harvard Ave (18015-9545)
PHONE..................................610 865-1788
Sherri Lee Casilio, *President*
Brian Casilio, *Principal*
Joseph Casilio, *Principal*
Frank Casilio, *Vice Pres*
EMP: 20
SQ FT: 2,000
SALES (est): 5.1MM **Privately Held**
WEB: www.4windsconcrete.com
SIC: 3273 5211 Ready-mixed concrete;
sand & gravel

(G-1518)
FRANK CASILIO AND SONS INC
(PA)
Also Called: Casilio Concrete
1035 Mauch Chunk Rd (18018-6622)
P.O. Box 1036 (18016-1036)
PHONE..................................610 867-5886
John F Casilio, *President*
Maria Medei, *Vice Pres*
EMP: 15
SQ FT: 3,000
SALES (est): 7.5MM **Privately Held**
WEB: www.casilioconcrete.com
SIC: 5211 3273 Sand & gravel; ready-
mixed concrete

(G-1519)
FRANKLIN HILL VINEYARDS INC
597 Main St Fl 2 (18018-5810)
PHONE..................................610 332-9463
Elaine Pivinski, *Branch Mgr*
EMP: 6
SALES (est): 487.3K
SALES (corp-wide): 1.7MM **Privately**
Held
SIC: 2084 Wines
PA: Franklin Hill Vineyards Inc
7833 Franklin Hill Rd
Bangor PA 18013
610 588-8708

(G-1520)
FRESHPET INC
Also Called: Fresh Pet
176 N Commerce Way (18017-8614)
PHONE..............................610 997-7192
Richard Thompson, *CEO*
Ed Gengaro, *Warehouse Mgr*
EMP: 15
SALES (corp-wide): 193.2MM **Publicly Held**
SIC: 2047 Dog & cat food
PA: Freshpet, Inc.
400 Plaza Dr Fl 1
Secaucus NJ 07094
201 520-4000

(G-1521)
G & L DESIGNS
Also Called: Sign Factory
4406 Easton Ave Unit 1 (18020-9339)
PHONE..............................610 868-1381
Gary Gower Jr, *Partner*
Joe Harvalla, *Manager*
EMP: 4
SQ FT: 1,600
SALES (est): 333.1K **Privately Held**
SIC: 3993 Signs & advertising specialties

(G-1522)
GAP STAMPING LLC
3717 Lyndon St (18020)
PHONE..............................610 759-7820
Gurjeet Panesar,
▲ **EMP:** 5
SQ FT: 20,000
SALES (est): 610.7K **Privately Held**
SIC: 3469 Metal stampings

(G-1523)
GARDNER CRYOGENICS INC
2136 City Line Rd (18017-2152)
PHONE..............................610 264-4523
Eric Schnable, *President*
▼ **EMP:** 150 **EST:** 1988
SALES (est): 15.2MM
SALES (corp-wide): 8.9B **Publicly Held**
SIC: 3443 Fabricated plate work (boiler shop)
PA: Air Products And Chemicals, Inc.
7201 Hamilton Blvd
Allentown PA 18195
610 481-4911

(G-1524)
GARMENT DIMENSIONS INC
1760 Wyndham Ter (18015-5836)
PHONE..............................610 838-0484
William R Haller, *President*
EMP: 2
SALES (est): 183.1K **Privately Held**
SIC: 3829 Measuring & controlling devices

(G-1525)
GENERAL FOUNDRY LLC
2350 Spring Valley Rd (18015-9045)
PHONE..............................610 997-8660
Edmund G Riccio,
EMP: 2
SQ FT: 1,100
SALES (est): 2MM **Privately Held**
WEB: www.generalfoundry.com
SIC: 3321 Gray iron castings; ductile iron castings

(G-1526)
GOW-MAC INSTRUMENT CO (PA)
277 Brodhead Rd (18017-8600)
PHONE..............................610 954-9000
Jeffrey B Lawson, *CEO*
Robert I Mathieu, *Treasurer*
Phyllis Mathieu, *Admin Sec*
EMP: 40 **EST:** 1993
SQ FT: 26,000
SALES (est): 10.3MM **Privately Held**
WEB: www.gow-mac.com
SIC: 3826 3823 Analytical instruments; industrial instrmnts msrmnt display/control process variable

(G-1527)
H & Z AUTO LLC
2450 Catasauqua Rd (18018-1008)
PHONE..............................610 419-8012
EMP: 3 **EST:** 2015

SALES (est): 41.2K **Privately Held**
SIC: 7539 7694 7549 Automotive repair shops; motor repair services; high performance auto repair & service

(G-1528)
HAMMERTEK CORPORATION
2400 Emrick Blvd (18020-8006)
PHONE..............................717 898-7665
Larry Hess, *President*
Charles Williston, *Natl Sales Mgr*
Miaja Marek, *Manager*
EMP: 50
SQ FT: 2,000
SALES (est): 10.2MM **Privately Held**
WEB: www.hammertek.com
SIC: 3535 Conveyors & conveying equipment

(G-1529)
HARRIS REBAR ATLANTIC INC
1700 Riverside Dr Unit 1 (18015-1277)
PHONE..............................610 882-1401
Les Wodard, *President*
Zuzelle Martin, *Sales Staff*
Joe Charnick, *Manager*
Angela Kramer, *Asst Office Mgr*
Mario Trinidad, *Info Tech Mgr*
▲ **EMP:** 80
SQ FT: 100,000
SALES (est): 13.4MM
SALES (corp-wide): 25B **Publicly Held**
WEB: www.harrissteel.com
SIC: 3449 1791 3441 Fabricated bar joists & concrete reinforcing bars; concrete reinforcement, placing of; fabricated structural metal
HQ: Harris Steel Group Inc
318 Arvin Ave
Stoney Creek ON L8E 2
905 662-0611

(G-1530)
HEALY GLASS ARTISTRY LLC
3930 Bigal Ct (18020-7846)
PHONE..............................484 241-0989
William Healy, *President*
Nichole Healy, *Vice Pres*
EMP: 5 **EST:** 2009
SALES (est): 310K **Privately Held**
SIC: 7699 3479 China & glass repair; etching & engraving

(G-1531)
HILLSIDE EQUITY INC
535 Wood St Unit 437 (18016-6417)
PHONE..............................484 707-9012
Jared Moyer, *CEO*
EMP: 3
SALES (est): 177.6K **Privately Held**
SIC: 3625 7389 Electric controls & control accessories, industrial;

(G-1532)
HOWMET ALUMINUM CASTING INC
Also Called: Cera-Met
2175 Avenue C (18017-2119)
PHONE..............................610 266-0270
Bill Rossi, *General Mgr*
EMP: 160
SALES (corp-wide): 14B **Publicly Held**
SIC: 3544 3324 Special dies, tools, jigs & fixtures; steel investment foundries
HQ: Howmet Aluminum Casting, Inc.
1600 Harvard Ave
Newburgh Heights OH 44105
216 641-4340

(G-1533)
HYDAC CORP
2280 City Line Rd (18017-2146)
P.O. Box 22050, Lehigh Valley (18002-2050)
PHONE..............................610 266-0100
Joel Daub, *Division Mgr*
Eric Ramseyer, *Division Mgr*
Matthias Mueller, *General Mgr*
Randall Symes, *General Mgr*
Mark Haake, *Area Mgr*
▲ **EMP:** 20
SQ FT: 25,000

SALES (est): 5.3MM
SALES (corp-wide): 216.7MM **Privately Held**
WEB: www.hydac.com
SIC: 3593 3594 3443 Fluid power cylinders & actuators; fluid power pumps & motors; fabricated plate work (boiler shop)
PA: H Y D A C Technology Gmbh
Industriestr.
Sulzbach 66280
689 750-901

(G-1534)
HYDAC TECHNOLOGY CORP (HQ)
2260 Cy Line Rd Ste 2280 (18017)
P.O. Box 22050, Lehigh Valley (18002-2050)
PHONE..............................205 520-1220
Matthias Mueller, *President*
Eric Ringholm, *General Mgr*
Werner Dieter, *Chairman*
Ilek Ozsoy, *Vice Pres*
Kate Wood, *Vice Pres*
▲ **EMP:** 250
SQ FT: 150,000
SALES (est): 138MM
SALES (corp-wide): 216.7MM **Privately Held**
WEB: www.hydacusa.com
SIC: 3492 Fluid power valves & hose fittings
PA: H Y D A C Technology Gmbh
Industriestr.
Sulzbach 66280
689 750-901

(G-1535)
HYDAC TECHNOLOGY CORP
2204 Avenue C (18017-2122)
PHONE..............................610 266-3143
EMP: 3
SALES (corp-wide): 216.7MM **Privately Held**
SIC: 2869 3593 Hydraulic fluids, synthetic base; fluid power cylinders, hydraulic or pneumatic
HQ: Hydac Technology Corp.
2260 Cy Line Rd Ste 2280
Bethlehem PA 18017
205 520-1220

(G-1536)
HYGRADE ACQUISITION CORP (PA)
1990 Highland Ave (18020-9083)
PHONE..............................610 866-2441
I Douglas Sherman, *CEO*
Vincent A Pagano, *Ch of Bd*
EMP: 70
SALES (est): 17.4MM **Privately Held**
SIC: 3354 3356 3316 Aluminum pipe & tube; nonferrous rolling & drawing; cold finishing of steel shapes

(G-1537)
HYGRADE COMPONENTS
1990 Highland Ave (18020-9083)
PHONE..............................610 866-2441
Vincent A Pagano, *Ch of Bd*
Douglas Sherman, *Vice Ch Bd*
▲ **EMP:** 100
SALES (est): 6.4MM **Privately Held**
SIC: 3272 Concrete window & door components, sills & frames

(G-1538)
HYGRADE MTAL MOULDING MFG CORP (HQ)
Also Called: Hygrade Components
1990 Highland Ave (18020-9083)
PHONE..............................610 866-2441
Vincent A Pagano, *Ch of Bd*
Randy Meyers, *Plant Mgr*
Jeff Goldstein, *Sales Mgr*
I Douglas Sherman, *Admin Sec*
▲ **EMP:** 50
SQ FT: 50,000
SALES (est): 17.4MM **Privately Held**
SIC: 3354 3356 3316 Aluminum pipe & tube; nonferrous rolling & drawing; cold finishing of steel shapes

(G-1539)
INGERSOLL-RAND CO
1495 Valley Center Pkwy # 200 (18017-2342)
PHONE..............................610 882-8800
Jim Lindstrom, *Principal*
EMP: 7
SALES (est): 704.8K **Privately Held**
SIC: 3131 Rands

(G-1540)
IQE INC
119 Technology Dr (18015-1327)
PHONE..............................610 861-6930
Andrew Nelson, *President*
Alex Ceruzzi, *Vice Pres*
Stephen Gergar, *Vice Pres*
Daily Hill, *Vice Pres*
Kevin Schild, *Facilities Mgr*
▲ **EMP:** 100
SQ FT: 50,000
SALES (est): 31.5MM
SALES (corp-wide): 204.1MM **Privately Held**
WEB: www.iqep.com
SIC: 3674 Wafers (semiconductor devices)
PA: Iqe Plc
Pascal Close
Cardiff S GLAM CF3 0
292 083-9400

(G-1541)
IQE RF LLC
119 Technology Dr (18015-1327)
PHONE..............................732 271-5990
Alex Ceruzzi, *Mng Member*
William Kurtz,
◆ **EMP:** 71
SALES (est): 12.2MM
SALES (corp-wide): 204.1MM **Privately Held**
SIC: 3679 Electronic circuits
PA: Iqe Plc
Pascal Close
Cardiff S GLAM CF3 0
292 083-9400

(G-1542)
IQE USA INC
119 Technology Dr (18015-1327)
PHONE..............................610 861-6930
EMP: 99 **EST:** 2015
SALES (est): 4.1MM **Privately Held**
SIC: 3679 Electronic circuits

(G-1543)
J & L PRECISION MACHINE CO INC
102 N Commerce Way (18017-8932)
PHONE..............................610 691-8411
John J Lack, *President*
Jay Najpauer, *Manager*
EMP: 30
SQ FT: 40,000
SALES (est): 6MM **Privately Held**
WEB: www.jandlprecisionmachine.com
SIC: 3599 Machine shop, jobbing & repair

(G-1544)
JAMES JESSE & CO INC
Also Called: Jesse James Beads
950 Jennings St Unit 1b (18017-7080)
PHONE..............................610 419-9880
Jesse M James, *President*
Karen B James, *President*
▲ **EMP:** 50
SALES (est): 14MM **Privately Held**
SIC: 5094 3695 3999 5131 Beads; magnetic disks & drums; beads, unassembled; buttons

(G-1545)
JENKINS MACHINE INC
5901 Colony Dr (18017-9348)
PHONE..............................610 837-6723
Michael Jenkins, *President*
EMP: 30
SQ FT: 10,000
SALES (est): 2MM **Privately Held**
SIC: 3599 Machine shop, jobbing & repair

GEOGRAPHIC

(G-1546)
JOHNNIE LUSTIGS HOTDOGS LLC
835 N New St (18018-2743)
PHONE..................................484 661-8333
John Lustig, *Principal*
EMP: 3 **EST:** 2015
SALES (est): 121.6K **Privately Held**
SIC: 2099 Emulsifiers, food

(G-1547)
JOSHI BHARKATKUMAR
Also Called: Nuts About Ice Cream
1124 Linden St Frnt (18018-2956)
PHONE..................................610 861-7733
Bharatkumer Joshi, *Owner*
EMP: 12
SQ FT: 7,504
SALES (est): 328.4K **Privately Held**
WEB: www.nutsabouticecream.com
SIC: 5812 2024 5143 Ice cream stands or dairy bars; ice cream & frozen desserts; ice cream & ices

(G-1548)
JUST BORN INC (PA)
Also Called: Just Born Quality Confections
1300 Stefko Blvd (18017-6672)
PHONE..................................610 867-7568
Ross J Born, *CEO*
Kevin McElvain, *President*
David Yale, *President*
David N Shaffer, *Principal*
Carol Saeger, *Editor*
◆ **EMP:** 480 **EST:** 1923
SQ FT: 412,000
SALES (est): 170.4MM **Privately Held**
WEB: www.justborn.com
SIC: 2064 Candy & other confectionery products

(G-1549)
KEURIG DR PEPPER INC
2172 City Line Rd (18017-2128)
PHONE..................................610 264-5151
Durante Rich, *Principal*
EMP: 170 **Publicly Held**
SIC: 2086 Soft drinks: packaged in cans, bottles, etc.
PA: Keurig Dr Pepper Inc.
53 South Ave
Burlington MA 01803

(G-1550)
KEYSTONE AUTOMOTIVE INDS INC
3658 Route 378 (18015-5434)
PHONE..................................610 866-0313
Doug Hurley, *Manager*
Tony Kilpatrick, *Executive*
EMP: 70
SALES (corp-wide): 11.8B **Publicly Held**
WEB: www.kool-vue.com
SIC: 5013 3714 Automotive supplies & parts; wheels, motor vehicle
HQ: Keystone Automotive Industries, Inc.
5846 Crossings Blvd
Antioch TN 37013
615 781-5200

(G-1551)
KEYSTONE FABRICATING INC
1220 Win Dr (18017-7061)
PHONE..................................610 868-0900
Beverly Vogt, *President*
Mark A Bumbulsky Sr, *Vice Pres*
Dale Lifer, *Vice Pres*
Chris G Greener, *Plant Supt*
Sharon A Transue, *Director*
EMP: 43
SQ FT: 28,500
SALES (est): 8.1MM **Privately Held**
SIC: 3444 Sheet metal specialties, not stamped

(G-1552)
KGB USA INC (HQ)
Also Called: Infonxx
3864 Courtney St Ste 411 (18017-8987)
PHONE..................................610 997-1000
David Cautin, *CEO*
Robert Pines, *Chairman*
EMP: 78

SALES (est): 13.8MM **Privately Held**
SIC: 2741 Telephone & other directory publishing

(G-1553)
KOLLER CONCRETE INC
900 Marshall St (18017-7035)
PHONE..................................610 865-5034
Dale R Koller, *President*
Carolyn Koller, *Admin Sec*
EMP: 40 **EST:** 1986
SQ FT: 5,000
SALES (est): 6.3MM **Privately Held**
SIC: 3273 Ready-mixed concrete

(G-1554)
KUNSMAN AGGREGATES
1080 Win Dr (18017-7063)
PHONE..................................610 882-1455
Tom Kunsman, *Owner*
EMP: 8
SALES (est): 1.1MM **Privately Held**
SIC: 2952 Asphalt felts & coatings

(G-1555)
KWIK KERB OF VALLEY
4980 Long Dr (18020-8866)
PHONE..................................610 419-8854
Jerry Niccum, *Principal*
EMP: 3
SALES (est): 210K **Privately Held**
SIC: 3281 Curbing, paving & walkway stone

(G-1556)
LEE HIGH VALLEY BAKERS LLC (PA)
Also Called: Lusitania Bakery
957 Minsi Trail St (18018-4416)
PHONE..................................610 868-2392
Manuel Teixeira,
Roger Sobreiro,
EMP: 15 **EST:** 1986
SQ FT: 10,000
SALES (est): 2.5MM **Privately Held**
SIC: 2051 Bread, all types (white, wheat, rye, etc): fresh or frozen; rolls, bread type: fresh or frozen

(G-1557)
LEHIGH HEAVY FORGE CORPORATION
275 Emery St (18015-1984)
PHONE..................................610 332-8100
Charles R Novelli, *President*
Christopher J Coholich, *Vice Pres*
Allan Robertson, *Vice Pres*
Desiree Bauer, *Purchasing*
Jennifer Boardman, *Project Engr*
◆ **EMP:** 165
SQ FT: 871,465
SALES (est): 46MM
SALES (corp-wide): 574.3MM **Privately Held**
WEB: www.lhforge.com
SIC: 3312 Blast furnaces & steel mills
HQ: Whemco Inc.
5 Hot Metal St Ste 300
Pittsburgh PA 15203
412 390-2700

(G-1558)
LEHIGH VALLEY PLASTICS INC
187 N Commerce Way (18017-8933)
PHONE..................................484 893-5500
Gretchen Mohan, *General Mgr*
Tom Prochilo, *Controller*
Kimberly Anders, *Human Res Mgr*
Kurt Imdorf, *CTO*
EMP: 90 **EST:** 1978
SQ FT: 70,000
SALES (est): 21.6MM
SALES (corp-wide): 300MM **Privately Held**
WEB: www.lehighvalleyplastics.com
SIC: 3083 2821 3082 Laminated plastics plate & sheet; plastics materials & resins; rods, unsupported plastic; tubes, unsupported plastic
PA: Port Plastics, Inc.
5800 Campus Circle Dr E 150a
Irving TX 75063
469 299-7000

(G-1559)
LEHIGH VALLEY PRINTING LLC (PA)
1314 Lorain Ave (18018-2443)
PHONE..................................610 905-5686
William Delorenzo, *Mng Member*
EMP: 3
SALES (est): 401.6K **Privately Held**
SIC: 2759 Screen printing

(G-1560)
LENOX CORPORATION
77 Sands Blvd Ste 223 (18015-7707)
PHONE..................................610 954-7590
EMP: 4 **Privately Held**
SIC: 3229 Tableware, glass or glass ceramic
PA: Lenox Corporation
1414 Radcliffe St Fl 1
Bristol PA 19007

(G-1561)
LIGHTBOX INC
Also Called: Ecotech
532 E 4th St (18015-1804)
PHONE..................................610 954-8480
Justin Lawyer, *President*
Patrick Clasen, *Treasurer*
Jay Sperandio, *Sales Staff*
Tim Marks, *Admin Sec*
◆ **EMP:** 40
SALES (est): 5.5MM **Privately Held**
SIC: 3641 Electric lamps

(G-1562)
LOUIS FLISZAR
Also Called: Alpine Sales and Distribution
3721 Amherst Ct (18020-1357)
PHONE..................................610 865-6494
Louis Fliszar, *Owner*
EMP: 5
SALES (est): 242.3K **Privately Held**
SIC: 3949 Winter sports equipment

(G-1563)
M A HANNA COLOR
2513 Highland Ave (18020-8942)
PHONE..................................610 317-3300
William Fedoriw, *Principal*
EMP: 11
SALES (est): 1MM **Privately Held**
SIC: 3559 Sewing machines & attachments, industrial

(G-1564)
MACHEREY-NAGEL INC
2850 Emrick Blvd (18020-8014)
PHONE..................................484 821-0984
Carolin Wagner, *President*
Achim Leitzke, *Vice Pres*
▲ **EMP:** 10
SQ FT: 4,700
SALES: 7.1MM
SALES (corp-wide): 501K **Privately Held**
WEB: www.mn-net.com
SIC: 2819 Chromates & bichromates
HQ: Macherey-Nagel Gmbh & Co. Kg
Neumann-Neander-Str. 6-8
Duren 52355
242 196-90

(G-1565)
MALEK HAM
151 W 4th St (18015-1605)
PHONE..................................610 691-7600
Ham Malek, *Owner*
EMP: 5
SALES (est): 272.3K **Privately Held**
SIC: 3999 5047 Wheelchair lifts; medical & hospital equipment

(G-1566)
MEDEAST POST-OP & SURGICAL INC
2591 Baglyos Cir Ste C43 (18020-8058)
PHONE..................................888 629-2030
John Blaskovich, *President*
John Krier, *COO*
EMP: 3
SALES (est): 227.3K **Privately Held**
SIC: 3842 Surgical appliances & supplies

(G-1567)
MENASHA PACKAGING COMPANY LLC
4000 Miller Cir N (18020-8600)
PHONE..................................630 236-4925
EMP: 151
SALES (corp-wide): 1.7B **Privately Held**
SIC: 2653 Boxes, corrugated: made from purchased materials
HQ: Menasha Packaging Company, Llc
1645 Bergstrom Rd
Neenah WI 54956
920 751-1000

(G-1568)
MERRIGAN CORPORATION
Also Called: National Woodwork Mfg
950 Jennings St Unit 3 (18017-7080)
PHONE..................................610 317-6300
Christine Merrigan, *President*
Donald Merrigan, *Treasurer*
EMP: 18
SALES (est): 2.1MM **Privately Held**
SIC: 2541 2431 Cabinets, lockers & shelving; millwork

(G-1569)
MESSER LLC
Boc Gases Division
1011 E Market St (18017-7017)
PHONE..................................610 317-8500
Tim Lynn, *Opers-Prdtn-Mfg*
EMP: 4
SALES (corp-wide): 1.4B **Privately Held**
SIC: 2813 Oxygen, compressed or liquefied; acetylene
HQ: Messer Llc
200 Somerset Corporate
Bridgewater NJ 08807
908 464-8100

(G-1570)
MESSER LLC
5897 Colony Dr (18017-9349)
PHONE..................................484 281-3261
Mark Sutton, *Manager*
EMP: 10
SALES (corp-wide): 1.4B **Privately Held**
SIC: 3443 Cryogenic tanks, for liquids & gases
HQ: Messer Llc
200 Somerset Corporate
Bridgewater NJ 08807
908 464-8100

(G-1571)
MICOR INC
824 12th Ave (18018-3524)
PHONE..................................412 487-1113
Stephen Brushey, *President*
EMP: 46
SQ FT: 12,000
SALES (est): 5.8MM **Privately Held**
SIC: 3089 Injection molding of plastics

(G-1572)
MICRO TOOL COMPANY
284 Brodhead Rd (18017-8937)
PHONE..................................610 882-3740
William Krisovitch, *CEO*
David Krisovitch, *President*
Elizabeth A Krisovith, *Corp Secy*
Jim Krisovitch, *Vice Pres*
Shon Rowen, *Vice Pres*
EMP: 58 **EST:** 1965
SQ FT: 30,000
SALES (est): 11.8MM **Privately Held**
WEB: www.microtool.com
SIC: 3599 Machine shop, jobbing & repair

(G-1573)
MIDWEST MATERIAL INDS INC (DH)
100 Brodhead Rd Ste 230 (18017-8935)
PHONE..................................610 882-5000
Massimo Toso, *CEO*
Nancy Krial, *CFO*
EMP: 3
SALES (est): 33MM
SALES (corp-wide): 287.7MM **Privately Held**
SIC: 3273 3251 3241 Ready-mixed concrete; brick clay: common face, glazed, vitrified or hollow; portland cement

(G-1574)
MINTEQ INTERNATIONAL INC
(HQ)
35 Highland Ave (18017-9482)
PHONE..................................724 794-3000
Joseph C Muscari, *Ch of Bd*
Han Schut, *Managing Dir*
Johannes Schut, *Vice Pres*
Brian J Seelig, *Vice Pres*
Douglas Dietrick, *CFO*
▲ EMP: 650
SQ FT: 42,000
SALES (est): 908MM **Publicly Held**
WEB: www.minteq.com
SIC: 3297 Nonclay refractories

(G-1575)
MORNING CALL INC
515 Main St Unit 1 (18018-5846)
PHONE..................................610 861-3600
Colleen Payler, *Manager*
EMP: 35
SALES (corp-wide): 1B **Publicly Held**
WEB: www.mcall.com
SIC: 2711 2731 2721 Newspapers; book
publishing; periodicals
HQ: The Morning Call Llc
101 N 6th St
Allentown PA 18101
610 820-6500

(G-1576)
MYERS POWER PRODUCTS INC
Also Called: Myers/Abacus
44 S Commerce Way (18017-8915)
PHONE..................................610 868-3500
B Steigerwald, *Branch Mgr*
EMP: 65
SALES (corp-wide): 196MM **Privately
Held**
WEB: www.myerspower.com
SIC: 3629 3612 Inverters, nonrotating:
electrical; generator voltage regulators
PA: Myers Power Products, Inc.
2950 E Philadelphia St
Ontario CA 91761
909 923-1800

(G-1577)
**NATIONAL ASSN CLLGES
EMPLOYERS**
Also Called: NACE
62 Highland Ave (18017-9481)
PHONE..................................610 868-1421
R Samuel Ratcliffe, *President*
Marilyn Mackes, *Exec Dir*
Marilyn F Mackes, *Exec Dir*
Eileen Lewis, *Surgery Dir*
EMP: 31
SQ FT: 11,000
SALES: 6.2MM **Privately Held**
SIC: 8621 7361 2741 2721 Education &
teacher association; employment agen-
cies; miscellaneous publishing; periodi-
cals

(G-1578)
**NATIONAL MAGNETICS GROUP
INC (PA)**
Also Called: Magneticsgroup
1210 Win Dr (18017-7061)
PHONE..................................610 867-7600
Paul B Oberbeck, *President*
James Lohr, *Vice Pres*
Abby Oberbeck, *Vice Pres*
Ashim Samanta, *Engineer*
Mark Northrup, *VP Sales*
▲ EMP: 50 EST: 1940
SQ FT: 80,000
SALES (est): 26.6MM **Privately Held**
WEB: www.magneticsgroup.com
SIC: 3264 Ferrite & ferrite parts; magnets,
permanent: ceramic or ferrite

(G-1579)
**NATIONAL MAGNETICS GROUP
INC**
Ceramic Powders
1210 Win Dr (18017-7061)
PHONE..................................610 867-7600
EMP: 5
SALES (corp-wide): 26.6MM **Privately
Held**
SIC: 2819 Tungsten carbide powder, ex-
cept abrasive or metallurgical

PA: National Magnetics Group, Inc.
1210 Win Dr
Bethlehem PA 18017
610 867-7600

(G-1580)
**NATIONAL MAGNETICS GROUP
INC**
Ferronics
1210 Win Dr (18017-7061)
PHONE..................................610 867-7600
EMP: 10
SALES (corp-wide): 26.6MM **Privately
Held**
SIC: 3264 Ferrite & ferrite parts
PA: National Magnetics Group, Inc.
1210 Win Dr
Bethlehem PA 18017
610 867-7600

(G-1581)
**NATIONAL MAGNETICS GROUP
INC**
Ceramic Magnetics
1210 Win Dr (18017-7061)
PHONE..................................610 867-7600
EMP: 30
SQ FT: 80,000
SALES (corp-wide): 26.6MM **Privately
Held**
SIC: 3264 Ferrite & ferrite parts
PA: National Magnetics Group, Inc.
1210 Win Dr
Bethlehem PA 18017
610 867-7600

(G-1582)
**NATIONAL MAGNETICS GROUP
INC**
TCI Ceramics
1210 Win Dr (18017-7061)
PHONE..................................610 867-6003
EMP: 90
SALES (corp-wide): 26.6MM **Privately
Held**
SIC: 3679 Microwave components
PA: National Magnetics Group, Inc.
1210 Win Dr
Bethlehem PA 18017
610 867-7600

(G-1583)
NATIONAL PLASTICS
212 E Broad St (18018-6207)
PHONE..................................610 252-6172
Munish Suri, *Owner*
EMP: 8
SALES (est): 1.6MM **Privately Held**
SIC: 2821 Plastics materials & resins

(G-1584)
NEWLY WEDS FOODS INC
Also Called: Continental Seasoning
23 S Commerce Way (18017-8916)
PHONE..................................610 758-9100
Tom Caffrey, *Principal*
Stu Trestrail, *Executive*
EMP: 161
SALES (corp-wide): 116.5MM **Privately
Held**
SIC: 2099 Seasonings & spices
PA: Newly Weds Foods, Inc.
4140 W Fullerton Ave
Chicago IL 60639
773 489-7000

(G-1585)
OAK HILL CONTROLS LLC
22 S Commerce Way Ste 9 (18017-8965)
PHONE..................................610 758-9500
Gail Meyers, *Sales Staff*
Scott Larrison, *Branch Mgr*
EMP: 11 **Privately Held**
SIC: 3495 3613 Wire springs; control pan-
els, electric
PA: Oak Hill Controls Llc
3433 Oak Hill Rd
Emmaus PA 18049

(G-1586)
**OH LITTLE TOWN CUPCAKES
LLC**
1731 W Market St (18018-6444)
PHONE..................................484 353-9709
Sahar Simmons, *Principal*

EMP: 4
SALES (est): 85.1K **Privately Held**
SIC: 2051 Bread, cake & related products

(G-1587)
**OPINIONMETER
INTERNATIONAL LTD**
44 E Broad St Fl 1 (18018-5946)
PHONE..................................888 676-3837
Morgan Strickland, *Principal*
Nick Supures, *Director*
EMP: 40
SALES (est): 1.3MM **Privately Held**
SIC: 7372 Application computer software

(G-1588)
**ORASURE TECHNOLOGIES INC
(PA)**
220 E 1st St (18015-1360)
PHONE..................................610 882-1820
Stephen S Tang, *Ch of Bd*
Douglas A Michels, *President*
Anthony Zezzo II, *Exec VP*
Jack E Jerrett, *Senior VP*
Michael Reed, *Senior VP*
EMP: 277
SQ FT: 48,000
SALES: 181.7MM **Publicly Held**
WEB: www.orasure.com
SIC: 2835 3841 In vitro diagnostics; surgi-
cal & medical instruments

(G-1589)
ORASURE TECHNOLOGIES INC
150 Webster St (18015-1338)
PHONE..................................610 882-1820
Stacy Urbany, *Accountant*
David Oxley, *Branch Mgr*
Michael Brannon, *Manager*
Dean Fritch, *Manager*
Todd Reinert, *Network Analyst*
EMP: 40
SALES (corp-wide): 181.7MM **Publicly
Held**
WEB: www.orasure.com
SIC: 2835 8731 In vitro & in vivo diagnos-
tic substances; agricultural research
PA: Orasure Technologies, Inc.
220 E 1st St
Bethlehem PA 18015
610 882-1820

(G-1590)
ORASURE TECHNOLOGIES INC
1745 Eaton Ave (18018-1769)
PHONE..................................610 882-1820
Mike Formica, *Vice Pres*
Jennifer Stringer, *Purch Mgr*
EMP: 40
SQ FT: 29,492
SALES (corp-wide): 181.7MM **Publicly
Held**
WEB: www.orasure.com
SIC: 2835 In vitro & in vivo diagnostic sub-
stances
PA: Orasure Technologies, Inc.
220 E 1st St
Bethlehem PA 18015
610 882-1820

(G-1591)
PARTICLE SCIENCES INC
3894 Courtney St (18017-8920)
PHONE..................................610 861-4701
Mark Mitchnick, *CEO*
Robert W Lee, *President*
Karen Bossert, *VP Opers*
EMP: 43
SQ FT: 15,000
SALES: 12.3MM
SALES (corp-wide): 225.3B **Publicly
Held**
WEB: www.particlesciences.com
SIC: 2834 Pharmaceutical preparations
HQ: The Lubrizol Corporation
29400 Lakeland Blvd
Wickliffe OH 44092
440 943-4200

(G-1592)
PAVLISH BEVERAGE CO INC
Also Called: Pavlish Ice Company
2800 Easton Ave (18017-4204)
PHONE..................................610 866-7722
Berry Pavlish, *President*
EMP: 7 EST: 1968

SQ FT: 5,000
SALES (est): 960.5K **Privately Held**
WEB: www.pavlishbev.com
SIC: 5921 2086 5999 Beer (packaged);
bottled & canned soft drinks; ice

(G-1593)
PENN JERSEY ADVANCE INC
Also Called: Express-Times, The
531 Main St (18018-5837)
PHONE..................................610 258-7171
Denise L Smith, *President*
Jennifer Watson, *Branch Mgr*
EMP: 5 **Privately Held**
SIC: 2711 Newspapers
PA: Penn Jersey Advance Inc.
18 Centre Sq
Easton PA 18042

(G-1594)
**PENNSYLVANIA PERLITE CORP
YORK (PA)**
1428 Mauch Chunk Rd (18018-2338)
PHONE..................................610 868-0992
Jose Abud, *President*
EMP: 5
SALES: 2.7MM **Privately Held**
WEB: www.pennperlite.com
SIC: 3297 3295 Nonclay refractories; min-
erals, ground or treated

(G-1595)
PHILIP J STOFANAK INC
176 Nazareth Pike (18020-9456)
PHONE..................................610 759-9311
Philip J Stofanak Jr, *President*
Mark Stofanak, *Vice Pres*
Michael Stofanak, *Vice Pres*
Kathleen F Wilhelm, *Treasurer*
Linda S Audenried, *Admin Sec*
EMP: 50 EST: 1951
SQ FT: 40,000
SALES (est): 6.9MM **Privately Held**
WEB: www.stofanak.com
SIC: 2434 5712 Wood kitchen cabinets;
cabinet work, custom

(G-1596)
PHOENIX TUBE CO INC
1185 Win Dr (18017-7060)
PHONE..................................610 865-5337
Anthony Reale, *President*
Barbara Reale, *Corp Secy*
Mark Lorrah, *Maint Spvr*
Bob Fucito, *Sales Executive*
Ralph Dimaria, *Executive*
▲ EMP: 105
SQ FT: 108,000
SALES (est): 72.3MM **Privately Held**
WEB: www.phoenixtube.com
SIC: 3317 Steel pipe & tubes

(G-1597)
PIKEWOOD INC
Also Called: Minuteman Press
123 E Broad St (18018-6219)
PHONE..................................610 974-8000
Dorothy K Woodyatt, *President*
L Richard Woodyatt, *Vice Pres*
Woodyatt Richard, *Treasurer*
David Pike, *VP Persnl*
David A Pike Jr, *Admin Sec*
EMP: 13
SQ FT: 10,000
SALES (est): 2.6MM **Privately Held**
WEB: www.pikewood.com
SIC: 2752 7334 4783 2791 Commercial
printing, offset; photocopying & duplicat-
ing services; packing goods for shipping;
typesetting; bookbinding & related work

(G-1598)
**PIRAMAL CRITICAL CARE INC
(HQ)**
3950 Schelden Cir (18017-8936)
P.O. Box 21170, Lehigh Valley (18002-
1170)
PHONE..................................800 414-1901
Vivek Sharma, *Ch of Bd*
William G Burns, *President*
Kirk Kamsler, *Vice Pres*
Karen Sonnhalter, *Vice Pres*
Steve Braun, *VP Sls/Mktg*
▲ EMP: 30

SALES (est): 16MM **Privately Held**
WEB: www.minrad.com
SIC: 2834 3841 Drugs acting on the central nervous system & sense organs; surgical & medical instruments

(G-1599)
PIRAMAL CRITICAL CARE INC
Also Called: Piramal Healthcare
3950 Schelden Cir (18017-8936)
P.O. Box 21170, Lehigh Valley (18002-1170)
PHONE.....................................610 974-9760
Michael Tomaine, *Mfg Mgr*
Michael Teague, *Manager*
EMP: 60 **Privately Held**
SIC: 3841 Surgical instruments & apparatus
HQ: Piramal Critical Care, Inc.
　　3950 Schelden Cir
　　Bethlehem PA 18017
　　800 414-1901

(G-1600)
PIRAMAL HEALTHCARE INC (PA)
3950 Schelden Cir (18017-8936)
PHONE.....................................610 974-9760
Mahesh Sane, *Treasurer*
Lillian Deruosi, *Sales Staff*
Ryan Guray, *Manager*
Cindy Herring, *Manager*
Laura Fecher, *Director*
EMP: 2
SALES (est): 25.1MM **Privately Held**
SIC: 2834 6719 Pharmaceutical preparations; personal holding companies, except banks

(G-1601)
POLVAC CORP
2442 Emrick Blvd (18020-8006)
PHONE.....................................610 625-1505
Marek G Ringwelski, *Principal*
Marek Ringwelski, *Vice Pres*
EMP: 6 EST: 2009
SALES (est): 681.1K **Privately Held**
SIC: 3563 Vacuum (air extraction) systems, industrial

(G-1602)
POLYONE CORPORATION
2513 Highland Ave (18020-8942)
PHONE.....................................610 317-3300
Joe Sirianny, *Manager*
EMP: 10 **Publicly Held**
WEB: www.polyone.com
SIC: 2821 Plastics materials & resins
PA: Polyone Corporation
　　33587 Walker Rd
　　Avon Lake OH 44012

(G-1603)
PRAXAIR INC
145 Shimersville Rd (18015-9544)
PHONE.....................................610 691-2474
Cindi Teets, *Export Mgr*
Carol Millroy, *Manager*
EMP: 131 **Privately Held**
SIC: 2813 Industrial gases
HQ: Praxair, Inc.
　　10 Riverview Dr
　　Danbury CT 06810
　　203 837-2000

(G-1604)
PRESS-ENTERPRISE INC
Also Called: Eastern Pennsylvania Bus Jurnl
65 E Elizabeth Ave # 700 (18018-6518)
PHONE.....................................610 807-9619
Brandon Eyerly, *Manager*
EMP: 13
SALES (corp-wide): 25MM **Privately Held**
WEB: www.perealestate.com
SIC: 2711 Commercial printing & newspaper publishing combined
PA: Press-Enterprise, Inc.
　　3185 Lackawanna Ave
　　Bloomsburg PA 17815
　　570 784-2121

(G-1605)
PRESTIGE GIFT BOX SYSTEMS
16 S Commerce Way (18017-8915)
PHONE.....................................610 865-6768

EMP: 18
SQ FT: 52,000
SALES (est): 2MM
SALES (corp-wide): 1.9B **Publicly Held**
SIC: 2657 Mfg Boxes
HQ: Deluxe Enterprise Operations, Llc
　　3680 Victoria St N
　　Saint Paul MN 55126

(G-1606)
QUIET CORE INC
1440 Schoenersville Rd (18018-1929)
PHONE.....................................610 694-9190
Thomas Calwonsen, *President*
EMP: 10
SQ FT: 32,000
SALES (est): 1.3MM **Privately Held**
WEB: www.quietcore.com
SIC: 3296 Fiberglass insulation; acoustical board & tile, mineral wool

(G-1607)
RC CEMENT CO INC
100 Brodhead Rd Ste 230 (18017-8935)
PHONE.....................................610 866-4400
David A Nepereny, *Principal*
EMP: 7
SALES (est): 445K **Privately Held**
SIC: 1499 Gypsum & calcite mining

(G-1608)
RC LONESTAR INC (HQ)
Also Called: Buzzi Unicem USA
100 Brodhead Rd Ste 230 (18017-8935)
PHONE.....................................610 882-5000
Massimo Toso, *President*
Thomas Marnell, *Senior VP*
Daniel Nugent, *Senior VP*
Fabio Rizzi, *Senior VP*
John White, *Senior VP*
▲ EMP: 70
SALES (est): 839.9MM
SALES (corp-wide): 287.7MM **Privately Held**
WEB: www.buzziunicemusa.com
SIC: 3241 Portland cement
PA: Buzzi Unicem Spa
　　Via Luigi Buzzi 6
　　Casale Monferrato AL 15033
　　014 241-6111

(G-1609)
REDCO FOODS INC (HQ)
1 Hansen Is (18017)
P.O. Box 1027, Little Falls NY (13365-1027)
PHONE.....................................800 556-6674
Gordon Boggis, *CEO*
Glen Mucica, *CFO*
▲ EMP: 5
SALES (est): 13MM
SALES (corp-wide): 272.4MM **Privately Held**
WEB: www.greentea.com
SIC: 2393 Tea bags, fabric: made from purchased materials
PA: Teekanne Holding Gmbh
　　Kevelaerer Str. 21-23
　　Dusseldorf 40549
　　211 508-50

(G-1610)
REYNOLDS & REYNOLDS ELEC INC
2501 Baglyos Cir (18020-8027)
P.O. Box 1710 (18016-1710)
PHONE.....................................484 221-6381
W John Reinartz, *President*
EMP: 12
SQ FT: 25,000
SALES (est): 2.4MM **Privately Held**
WEB: www.reynoldselectronics.com
SIC: 3699 Security control equipment & systems

(G-1611)
RIGHT REASON TECHNOLOGIES LLC
3864 Adler Pl Ste 200 (18017-8102)
P.O. Box 1330, Brodheadsville (18322-1330)
PHONE.....................................484 898-1967
Dominick Meglio, *Principal*
EMP: 4 EST: 2010

SALES (est): 574.4K **Privately Held**
SIC: 3699 Teaching machines & aids, electronic

(G-1612)
ROBERT BOSCH LLC
2315 City Line Rd (18017-2131)
PHONE.....................................610 694-8200
Daniel McPeek, *Principal*
Aaron Fry, *Project Mgr*
EMP: 441
SALES (corp-wide): 301.8MM **Privately Held**
SIC: 3714 Motor vehicle parts & accessories
HQ: Robert Bosch Llc
　　2800 S 25th Ave
　　Broadview IL 60155
　　248 876-1000

(G-1613)
ROCKET CLOUD INC
116 Research Dr (18015-4731)
PHONE.....................................484 948-0327
Zeiad Hussein, *Risk Mgmt Dir*
EMP: 5
SALES (est): 117.2K **Privately Held**
SIC: 7372 Business oriented computer software

(G-1614)
SAINT LUKES HOSP BETHLEHEM PA
Also Called: St Lukes Hsptl St Lukes
4379 Easton Ave Ste 103 (18020-1483)
PHONE.....................................610 954-3531
Alfred Hokenson Etal, *Owner*
EMP: 5
SALES (corp-wide): 1.1B **Privately Held**
SIC: 2835 In vitro & in vivo diagnostic substances
HQ: Saint Luke's Hospital Of Bethlehem, Pennsylvania
　　801 Ostrum St
　　Bethlehem PA 18015
　　484 526-4000

(G-1615)
SALADAX BIOMEDICAL INC
116 Research Dr (18015-4731)
PHONE.....................................610 419-6731
Kevin M Harter, *President*
Gregory C Critchfield, *Chairman*
Mark D Myslinski, *Officer*
EMP: 25
SALES (est): 5.2MM **Privately Held**
WEB: www.saladax.com
SIC: 2835 In vitro diagnostics

(G-1616)
SEAL SCIENCE INC
Also Called: Seal Science East
1160 Win Dr (18017-7059)
PHONE.....................................610 868-2800
David Miles, *Manager*
EMP: 10
SALES (est): 1.2MM
SALES (corp-wide): 10.8MM **Privately Held**
WEB: www.sealscience.com
SIC: 3053 Gaskets, all materials
PA: Seal Science, Inc.
　　17131 Daimler St
　　Irvine CA 92614
　　949 253-3130

(G-1617)
SHELLY ENTERPRISES -US LBM LLC
Also Called: Shelly & Son Fenstermacher Div
6410 Airport Rd (18017-9345)
PHONE.....................................610 432-4511
Bill Blieler, *Manager*
EMP: 35
SALES (corp-wide): 2B **Privately Held**
WEB: www.shellys.cc
SIC: 5211 2431 2439 Lumber products; millwork; trusses, except roof: laminated lumber; trusses, wooden roof
HQ: Shelly Enterprises -Us Lbm, Llc
　　3110 Old State Rd
　　Telford PA 18969
　　215 723-5108

(G-1618)
SIGNATURE STRUCTURES LLC
312 E Broad St (18018-6343)
PHONE.....................................610 882-9030
Rennie Turner, *Vice Pres*
Susan Hoover, *Controller*
John Dufal, *Mng Member*
Melvin Nelson, *Director*
EMP: 4
SALES (est): 1MM **Privately Held**
SIC: 3448 Buildings, portable: prefabricated metal

(G-1619)
SING-OUT CORPORATION
Also Called: Sing Out Magazine
360 16th Ave (18018-4602)
P.O. Box 5460 (18015-0460)
PHONE.....................................610 865-5366
Mark D Moss, *Exec Dir*
EMP: 5
SALES (est): 123K **Privately Held**
WEB: www.singout.org
SIC: 2721 2731 8732 Magazines: publishing only, not printed on site; book music: publishing only, not printed on site; educational research

(G-1620)
SMOYER L M BRASS PRODUCTS INC
Also Called: LMS Stampings
1209 W Lehigh St (18018-4830)
PHONE.....................................610 867-5011
Dodge L Whipple Jr, *President*
Velma S Whipple, *Corp Secy*
Sam Charnegie, *Project Engr*
EMP: 4
SQ FT: 10,000
SALES (est): 759.8K **Privately Held**
WEB: www.lmsstampings.com
SIC: 3366 3365 3469 Brass foundry; bronze foundry; machinery castings: brass; aluminum foundries; machinery castings, aluminum; metal stampings

(G-1621)
SOCIAL STILL LLC
530 E 3rd St (18015-1314)
PHONE.....................................610 625-4585
Adam Flatt, *Mng Member*
EMP: 20
SALES (est): 1.8MM **Privately Held**
SIC: 2085 5812 Distilled & blended liquors; American restaurant

(G-1622)
SOLTECH SOLUTIONS LLC
520 Evans St 4 (18015-1915)
PHONE.....................................484 821-1001
Paul Hodges, *CEO*
Michael Planer,
EMP: 3
SQ FT: 250
SALES (est): 161.4K **Privately Held**
SIC: 3645 Residential lighting fixtures

(G-1623)
SPECIALTY MEASUREMENTS INC
Also Called: SMI Incorprated
2420 Emrick Blvd (18020-8006)
PHONE.....................................908 534-1500
Mary Ann Kulawiec, *President*
Gary Bubb, *Vice Pres*
Gary E Bubb, *Vice Pres*
Jennifer McGonigle, *Purch Mgr*
Brian Dilley, *Manager*
EMP: 10 EST: 1982
SALES: 3MM **Privately Held**
SIC: 3559 2833 5084 Pharmaceutical machinery; medicinals & botanicals; industrial machinery & equipment

(G-1624)
SPECIALTY MINERALS INC
1 Highland Ave (18017-9482)
PHONE.....................................860 824-5435
T Masimime, *Senior VP*
Marianne Barbaz, *Project Mgr*
Jim Cummins, *Manager*
EMP: 400 **Publicly Held**
WEB: www.specialtyminerals.com
SIC: 2819 Industrial inorganic chemicals

HQ: Specialty Minerals Inc.
622 3rd Ave Fl 38
New York NY 10017
212 878-1800

(G-1625)
SPECIALTY MINERALS INC
9 Highland Ave (18017-9482)
PHONE..........................610 861-3400
Nikhil Trivedi, *Vice Pres*
EMP: 350
SQ FT: 38,330 **Publicly Held**
WEB: www.specialtyminerals.com
SIC: 2819 Industrial inorganic chemicals
HQ: Specialty Minerals Inc.
622 3rd Ave Fl 38
New York NY 10017
212 878-1800

(G-1626)
SPECIALTY MINERALS INC
Also Called: Minerals Technologies
5 Highland Ave (18017-8967)
PHONE..........................212 878-1800
Paul R Saueracker, *Branch Mgr*
EMP: 200 **Publicly Held**
WEB: www.specialtyminerals.com
SIC: 5032 2819 Brick, stone & related material; industrial inorganic chemicals
HQ: Specialty Minerals Inc.
622 3rd Ave Fl 38
New York NY 10017
212 878-1800

(G-1627)
SPRAY-TEK INC
3010 Avenue B (18017-2114)
PHONE..........................610 814-2922
Iliya Spasov, *Manager*
EMP: 20
SQ FT: 32,600
SALES (corp-wide): 15.9MM **Privately Held**
SIC: 3563 Air & gas compressors
PA: Spray-Tek Inc
344 Cedar Ave
Middlesex NJ 08846
732 469-0050

(G-1628)
SPX HEAT TRANSFER LLC
95 Highland Ave Ste 210 (18017-9435)
PHONE..........................610 250-1146
Manuel Espinel, *Project Mgr*
Rusty Lewis, *Purch Mgr*
Brent Jones, *Branch Mgr*
EMP: 39
SALES (corp-wide): 1.5B **Publicly Held**
WEB: www.yuba.com
SIC: 3443 Condensers, steam
HQ: Spx Heat Transfer Llc
2121 N 161st East Ave
Tulsa OK 74116
918 234-6000

(G-1629)
STILTZ INC
57 S Commerce Way Ste 300
(18017-8964)
PHONE..........................610 443-2282
Mark Blomfield, *President*
EMP: 5
SALES (est): 1.7MM **Privately Held**
SIC: 5084 3534 Elevators; elevators & equipment

(G-1630)
STRAHMAN INDUSTRIES INC
2801 Baglyos Cir (18020-8033)
PHONE..........................484 893-5080
Jack Roessner III, *Ch of Bd*
Franz Hubert, *Treasurer*
Cora Strahman, *Admin Sec*
EMP: 124
SQ FT: 50,000
SALES (est): 12.7MM **Privately Held**
SIC: 3491 Industrial valves

(G-1631)
STRAHMAN VALVES INC (PA)
2801 Baglyos Cir (18020-8033)
PHONE..........................877 787-2462
August F Percoco, *President*
Kevin Carroll, *Vice Pres*
William Doll, *Opers Staff*
Robert Mayers, *Purch Mgr*

Daina Spruill, *Research*
▲ EMP: 94 EST: 1921
SQ FT: 50,000
SALES: 12MM **Privately Held**
WEB: www.strahmanvalves.com
SIC: 3494 5085 Valves & pipe fittings; hose, belting & packing

(G-1632)
STRAIGHT ARROW PRODUCTS INC (PA)
2020 Highland Ave (18020-8963)
P.O. Box 20350, Lehigh Valley (18002-0350)
PHONE..........................610 882-9606
Devon Katzev, *President*
Terry Miller, *Vice Pres*
Edward Lubinsky, *Plant Mgr*
Amy Rodriguez, *Production*
Larry Novack, *Research*
▼ EMP: 85
SQ FT: 35,550
SALES (est): 29.6MM **Privately Held**
WEB: www.straightarrowinc.com
SIC: 2844 Shampoos, rinses, conditioners: hair

(G-1633)
STRAIGHT ARROW PRODUCTS INC
2655 Brodhead Rd (18020-8957)
PHONE..........................610 882-9606
Devon Katzev, *Branch Mgr*
EMP: 5
SALES (est): 597K
SALES (corp-wide): 29.6MM **Privately Held**
SIC: 2841 Soap & other detergents
PA: Straight Arrow Products, Inc.
2020 Highland Ave
Bethlehem PA 18020
610 882-9606

(G-1634)
SUPERIOR QUARTZ PRODUCTS INC
Also Called: Sqp
2701 Baglyos Cir (18020-8031)
PHONE..........................610 317-3450
Dennis A Losco, *CEO*
Jack Sabo, *Principal*
Jeffrey W Losco, *Vice Pres*
Jeffry W Losco, *Vice Pres*
Sandy Greco, *Sales Staff*
▲ EMP: 51
SQ FT: 62,000
SALES (est): 14.2MM **Privately Held**
WEB: www.sqpuv.com
SIC: 3641 Electric lamps

(G-1635)
SUPERMEDIA LLC
252 Brodhead Rd Ste 300 (18017-8944)
PHONE..........................610 317-5500
Robert Sax, *Branch Mgr*
EMP: 254
SALES (corp-wide): 1.8B **Privately Held**
SIC: 2741 Directories, telephone: publishing only, not printed on site
HQ: Supermedia Llc
2200 W Airfield Dr
Dfw Airport TX 75261
972 453-7000

(G-1636)
SYN APPAREL LLC (PA)
Also Called: Peerless Printery
18 W 3rd St (18015-1222)
PHONE..........................484 821-3664
Layne Gehris, *Prdtn Mgr*
Lori Shuey,
EMP: 3
SALES: 300K **Privately Held**
SIC: 2759 2284 Screen printing; embroidery thread

(G-1637)
T & P BAGELS INC
Also Called: Tom's Bagel Cafe'
2910 Easton Ave Unit 10 (18017-4282)
P.O. Box 3382 (18017-0382)
PHONE..........................610 867-8695
Thomas Haidopoulous, *President*
EMP: 4

SALES (est): 268.4K **Privately Held**
SIC: 2051 5461 Bagels, fresh or frozen; bagels

(G-1638)
TEXAS INSTRS LEHIGH VLY INC
116 Research Dr (18015-4731)
PHONE..........................610 849-5100
EMP: 3 EST: 2017
SALES (est): 141.9K
SALES (corp-wide): 13.3B **Publicly Held**
SIC: 3674 Mfg Semiconductors/Related Devices
PA: Texas Instruments Incorporated
12500 Ti Blvd
Dallas TX 75243
214 479-3773

(G-1639)
TEXAS INSTRUMENTS INCORPORATED
116 Research Dr (18015-4731)
PHONE..........................610 849-5100
Mark Granahan, *Branch Mgr*
Chris Kocon, *Technology*
EMP: 50
SALES (corp-wide): 15.7B **Publicly Held**
WEB: www.ti.com
SIC: 3674 Semiconductor circuit networks
PA: Texas Instruments Incorporated
12500 Ti Blvd
Dallas TX 75243
214 479-3773

(G-1640)
TRAK CERAMICS INC
1210 Win Dr (18017-7061)
PHONE..........................610 867-7600
Paul A Oberbeck, *President*
Amal Chatterjee, *Vice Pres*
Tyke Negas, *Vice Pres*
EMP: 24 EST: 1972
SQ FT: 40,000
SALES (est): 2MM
SALES (corp-wide): 26.6MM **Privately Held**
WEB: www.tciceramics.com
SIC: 3679 Microwave components
PA: National Magnetics Group, Inc.
1210 Win Dr
Bethlehem PA 18017
610 867-7600

(G-1641)
TREXLER INDUSTRIES INC
95 Southland Dr (18017-8926)
PHONE..........................610 974-9800
Gene D Trexle, *President*
EMP: 30
SQ FT: 24,000
SALES (est): 5.2MM **Privately Held**
WEB: www.trexlerindustries.com
SIC: 3444 3699 Sheet metal specialties, not stamped; machine guards, sheet metal; laser systems & equipment

(G-1642)
TRIPLE W ENTERPRISES INC
Also Called: Warren's Honda
1230 Illicks Mill Rd (18017-3654)
PHONE..........................610 865-0071
Warren W Wilson, *President*
Cheryl Wilson, *Admin Sec*
EMP: 4
SQ FT: 4,900
SALES: 300K **Privately Held**
WEB: www.triplewenterprises.com
SIC: 3568 5261 Power transmission equipment; lawn & garden equipment

(G-1643)
TROFI IDONI SPECIALTY BAKING
421 Central Blvd (18018-4554)
PHONE..........................484 892-0876
EMP: 4
SALES (est): 164.3K **Privately Held**
SIC: 2051 Bread, cake & related products

(G-1644)
TYBER MEDICAL LLC
Also Called: Unified Orthopedics
83 S Commerce Way Ste 310
(18017-8934)
PHONE..........................303 717-5060
Jeff Tyber, *CEO*

Gary Thomas, *COO*
Wesley Johnson, *Exec VP*
EMP: 12
SALES (est): 1.8MM **Privately Held**
SIC: 3841 Surgical & medical instruments

(G-1645)
TYT LLC
177 Mikron Rd Ste 1 (18020-9353)
PHONE..........................800 511-2009
Frank Shue, *Branch Mgr*
EMP: 30
SALES (corp-wide): 2B **Publicly Held**
SIC: 2752 Commercial printing, offset
HQ: T.Y.T. Llc
2861 Mandela Pkwy
Oakland CA 94608

(G-1646)
UCG GEORGIA LLC
3001 Emrick Blvd Ste 320 (18020-8041)
PHONE..........................610 515-8589
Samuel D Piazza Sr, *President*
EMP: 5
SALES (est): 229.7K
SALES (corp-wide): 10.7MM **Privately Held**
SIC: 2813 Industrial gases
HQ: Ucg Georgia, Llc
1050 Booth Rd
Warner Robins GA 31088
610 515-8589

(G-1647)
UNGERER INDUSTRIES INC
Also Called: Ungerer & Company
110 N Commerce Way (18017-8932)
PHONE..........................610 868-7266
Don Rives, *Manager*
EMP: 70
SALES (corp-wide): 103.1MM **Privately Held**
WEB: www.ungererandcompany.com
SIC: 2899 2869 2844 2087 Essential oils; industrial organic chemicals; toilet preparations; flavoring extracts & syrups
PA: Ungerer Industries, Inc.
4 Ungerer Way
Lincoln Park NJ 07035
973 628-0600

(G-1648)
US SPECIALTY FORMULATIONS LLC
116 Research Dr (18015-4731)
PHONE..........................610 849-5030
Kyle Flanigan, *Info Tech Mgr*
Garry Morefield,
EMP: 10 EST: 2013
SQ FT: 2,000
SALES: 2MM **Privately Held**
SIC: 5122 2834 Pharmaceuticals; pharmaceutical preparations; intravenous solutions

(G-1649)
VALCO
Also Called: Valco Tool Co
1410 Stonewood Dr (18017-3527)
PHONE..........................610 691-3205
Karen Scheltzer, *Owner*
EMP: 30
SQ FT: 1,200
SALES (est): 3.1MM **Privately Held**
SIC: 3829 5084 Measuring & controlling devices; measuring & testing equipment, electrical

(G-1650)
VALLOS BAKERY LLC
Also Called: Vallos Baking Company
1800 Broadway (18015-3802)
PHONE..........................610 866-1012
Tina Hanuschak, *Principal*
Scott Hanuschak, *Principal*
EMP: 20 EST: 1935
SQ FT: 8,000
SALES (est): 2.1MM **Privately Held**
SIC: 2051 Bakery: wholesale or whole-sale/retail combined; bread, all types (white, wheat, rye, etc): fresh or frozen; rolls, bread type: fresh or frozen

(G-1651)
VERSALIFT EAST LLC (HQ)
2706 Brodhead Rd (18020-9411)
PHONE..............................610 866-1400
Keith Joseph, *President*
Jay Jeffrey, *Vice Pres*
David Post, *Treasurer*
Kevin Kurtz, *Regl Sales Mgr*
Peggy Yehl, *Technology*
EMP: 117
SQ FT: 56,000
SALES (est): 115.5MM
SALES (corp-wide): 138.7MM **Privately Held**
WEB: www.versalifteast.com
SIC: 3711 Automobile assembly, including specialty automobiles
PA: Time Manufacturing Company
7601 Imperial Dr
Waco TX 76712
254 399-2100

(G-1652)
VIZINEX LLC
Also Called: Vizinex Rfid
6343 Winside Dr (18017-9350)
PHONE..............................215 529-9440
Ken Horton, *CEO*
Sandra Garby, *President*
Philip Koppenhofer, *Vice Pres*
Robert Oberle, *Vice Pres*
EMP: 8
SQ FT: 3,800
SALES (est): 1.4MM **Privately Held**
SIC: 3679 3825 Electronic circuits; radio frequency measuring equipment

(G-1653)
WARREN CONTROLS INC
2600 Emrick Blvd (18020-8010)
PHONE..............................610 317-0800
C Alan Trent, *Ch of Bd*
Elizabeth Ewell, *President*
Jeanette Trent, *Corp Secy*
Raymond Yaros Jr, *Vice Pres*
Thomas Dolan, *VP Sales*
▲ **EMP:** 57 **EST:** 2002
SQ FT: 26,000
SALES (est): 14.4MM **Privately Held**
WEB: www.warrencontrols.com
SIC: 3491 3822 Automatic regulating & control valves; auto controls regulating residntl & coml environmt & applncs

(G-1654)
WEIR WELDING COMPANY INC
1745 Eaton Ave Ste 2 (18018-1797)
PHONE..............................610 974-8140
Jim O'Reilly, *Branch Mgr*
Anthony Liparini, *Manager*
Cyndy Gardner, *Admin Sec*
EMP: 55
SALES (corp-wide): 16MM **Privately Held**
SIC: 3441 Fabricated structural metal
PA: Weir Welding Company Inc.
316 12th St
Carlstadt NJ 07072
201 939-2284

(G-1655)
WELDSHIP INDUSTRIES INC (PA)
225 W 2nd St Unit 2 (18015-1274)
P.O. Box 5423 (18015-0423)
PHONE..............................610 861-7330
Robert Arcieri, *President*
Robert F Arcieri, *President*
Paul Horrigan, *Vice Pres*
William E Angus, *Admin Sec*
◆ **EMP:** 12
SQ FT: 8,000
SALES (est): 3.2MM **Privately Held**
WEB: www.weldship.com
SIC: 3537 5085 7513 7519 Industrial trucks & tractors; ink, printers'; truck leasing, without drivers; utility trailer rental

---

Big Run
Jefferson County

(G-1656)
KENDALLS KREATIONS
223 W Main St (15715)
P.O. Box 166 (15715-0166)
PHONE..............................814 427-2517
Kirby Kendall, *Owner*
EMP: 7
SALES (est): 739.2K **Privately Held**
SIC: 2752 Commercial printing, lithographic

(G-1657)
STANDARD PENNANT COMPANY INC
109 Main St (15715)
P.O. Box 415 (15715-0415)
PHONE..............................814 427-2066
James H Casaday, *President*
Jim Casaday, *CFO*
EMP: 20 **EST:** 1920
SQ FT: 15,000
SALES (est): 2.2MM **Privately Held**
SIC: 2759 2399 Screen printing; pennants; banners, made from fabric

---

Bigler
Clearfield County

(G-1658)
EAST COAST CONTROL SYSTEMS
Main St (16825)
P.O. Box 486 (16825-0486)
PHONE..............................814 857-5420
Jonathan L Frantz, *President*
Marcia J Frantz, *Vice Pres*
EMP: 5
SQ FT: 4,500
SALES (est): 627.9K **Privately Held**
WEB: www.eastcoastcontrol.com
SIC: 3625 8711 Positioning controls, electric; engineering services

(G-1659)
FUEL & SAVE INC
Rr 879 (16825)
P.O. Box 365 (16825-0365)
PHONE..............................814 857-5356
Donna Lucas, *Principal*
EMP: 3
SALES (est): 223.7K **Privately Held**
SIC: 2869 Fuels

(G-1660)
GLEN-GERY CORPORATION
24 Pine Top Rd (16825)
PHONE..............................814 857-7688
Joe Francemore, *Opers-Prdtn-Mfg*
EMP: 78
SALES (corp-wide): 1.2MM **Privately Held**
WEB: www.glengerybrick.com
SIC: 3251 3255 Brick clay: common face, glazed, vitrified or hollow; clay refractories
HQ: Glen-Gery Corporation
1166 Spring St
Reading PA 19610
610 374-4011

Biglerville
Adams County

(G-1661)
CHEP (USA) INC
Also Called: Pallet Outlet
3177 Biglerville Rd (17307-9499)
PHONE..............................717 778-4279
Brian Grihur, *General Mgr*
Kevin Mitchell, *General Mgr*
EMP: 90 **Privately Held**
WEB: www.ifcosystems.com
SIC: 2448 Pallets, wood

HQ: Chep (U.S.A.) Inc.
5897 Windward Pkwy
Alpharetta GA 30005

(G-1662)
GVM INC (PA)
374 Heidlersburg Rd (17307-9256)
P.O. Box 358 (17307-0358)
PHONE..............................717 677-6197
Mark Anderson, *President*
Tom Bair, *Vice Pres*
Ron Weigle, *Production*
Mark McClintock, *Sales Staff*
▲ **EMP:** 80
SQ FT: 50,000
SALES (est): 29MM **Privately Held**
SIC: 3953 3523 Marking devices; fertilizing machinery, farm

(G-1663)
HAUSER ESTATE INC
Also Called: Hauser Estate Winery, The
410 Cashtown Rd (17307-9528)
PHONE..............................717 334-4888
Jonathan Apatrong, *President*
EMP: 55 **Privately Held**
SIC: 2084 Wines
PA: Hauser Estate, Inc.
28 W Middle St
Gettysburg PA 17325

(G-1664)
INTERNATIONAL PAPER COMPANY
136 E York St (17307-9425)
PHONE..............................717 677-8121
Kathy Culp, *Human Res Dir*
Casey Cellny, *Branch Mgr*
EMP: 92
SALES (corp-wide): 23.3B **Publicly Held**
WEB: www.tin.com
SIC: 2653 Boxes, corrugated: made from purchased materials
PA: International Paper Company
6400 Poplar Ave
Memphis TN 38197
901 419-9000

(G-1665)
KLINGLER FAMILY SAWMILL
875 Narrows Rd (17307-9547)
PHONE..............................717 677-4957
Francis Klingler, *Owner*
Terry Klingler, *Admin Sec*
EMP: 6
SALES (est): 601.6K **Privately Held**
SIC: 2411 2421 Logging camps & contractors; sawmills & planing mills, general

(G-1666)
KNOUSE FOODS COOPERATIVE INC
53 E Hanover St (17307-9421)
P.O. Box 807 (17307-0807)
PHONE..............................717 677-9115
Cy Korper, *Manager*
EMP: 160
SALES (corp-wide): 281.7MM **Privately Held**
SIC: 2033 2099 2087 Fruits: packaged in cans, jars, etc.; fruit juices: packaged in cans, jars, etc.; jellies, edible, including imitation: in cans, jars, etc.; food preparations; flavoring extracts & syrups
PA: Knouse Foods Cooperative, Inc.
800 Pach Glen Idaville Rd
Peach Glen PA 17375
717 677-8181

(G-1667)
MORITZ MACHINE & REPAIRS LLC
211 E York St (17307-9494)
P.O. Box 638 (17307-0638)
PHONE..............................717 677-6838
Gary L Moritz, *Mng Member*
Aliene Moritz,
EMP: 6
SQ FT: 1,300
SALES (est): 878.4K **Privately Held**
SIC: 3599 7699 7692 Machine shop, jobbing & repair; welding equipment repair; welding repair

---

Bird In Hand
Lancaster County

(G-1668)
AMES REESE INC
2575 Old Phladelphia Pike (17505-9797)
P.O. Box 413 (17505-0413)
PHONE..............................717 393-1591
Cesar Molins, *President*
Henry Trebel, *President*
Peter Alexich, *Vice Pres*
Enrique Trabel, *Vice Pres*
Henry Trebal, *Vice Pres*
▲ **EMP:** 45 **EST:** 1996
SQ FT: 24,000
SALES (est): 10.6MM
SALES (corp-wide): 2.7MM **Privately Held**
WEB: www.amesreese.com
SIC: 3499 Friction material, made from powdered metal
HQ: Ames Group Sintering S.A.
Carretera Laurea Miro 388
Sant Feliu De Llobregat 08980
936 855-111

(G-1669)
B & B STRUCTURES
568 Gibbons Rd (17505-9786)
PHONE..............................717 656-0783
Sam Blank, *Partner*
Edric Blank, *Partner*
EMP: 8
SQ FT: 9,000
SALES (est): 1.5MM **Privately Held**
SIC: 2452 Prefabricated buildings, wood

(G-1670)
BULLGATER LIMITED
159 Glenbrook Rd (17505-9748)
PHONE..............................717 606-5414
John Leaman, *CEO*
Nancy Leaman, *President*
EMP: 5 **EST:** 2014
SQ FT: 500
SALES (est): 255.2K **Privately Held**
SIC: 3524 Lawn & garden equipment

(G-1671)
CARRIAGE MACHINE SHOP LLC
250 Maple Ave (17505-9703)
PHONE..............................717 397-4079
Christian Stoltzfus,
Ephraim Elam,
Stephen Stoltzfus,
EMP: 18
SQ FT: 13,000
SALES (est): 3.1MM **Privately Held**
SIC: 3799 3441 Carriages, horse drawn; fabricated structural metal

(G-1672)
CUSTOM DOORCRAFT LLC
2902 Miller Ln (17505-9740)
PHONE..............................717 768-7613
John Stoltzfus,
▲ **EMP:** 10
SALES (est): 1MM **Privately Held**
SIC: 2431 Millwork

(G-1673)
DAVID S STOLTZSUS
Also Called: Victorian Backyard
2441 Stumptown Rd (17505-9775)
PHONE..............................717 556-0462
David S Stoltzsus, *Owner*
David S Stoltzfus, *Treasurer*
EMP: 4 **EST:** 1997
SQ FT: 100
SALES (est): 450K **Privately Held**
SIC: 2452 Prefabricated wood buildings

(G-1674)
FISHER S HAND MADE QUILTS
2713a Old Phila Pike (17505)
P.O. Box 286 (17505-0286)
PHONE..............................717 392-5440
Ellen Parmer, *Owner*
EMP: 3

▲ = Import ▼=Export
◆ =Import/Export

SALES (est): 223.1K **Privately Held**
SIC: **2221** 5949 5947 Comforters & quilts, manmade fiber & silk; quilting materials & supplies; gift shop

(G-1675)
GIDEON B STOLTZFUS
2613 Stumptown Rd (17505-9779)
PHONE...................717 656-4903
Gideon Stoltzfus, *Principal*
EMP: 5 EST: 2009
SALES (est): 738.2K **Privately Held**
SIC: **3565** Bottling & canning machinery

(G-1676)
GREGORY TROYER
Also Called: Great Signs
2688 Old Phladelphia Pike (17505-9600)
PHONE...................717 393-0233
Gregory Troyer, *Principal*
EMP: 4
SQ FT: 2,700
SALES (est): 234.2K **Privately Held**
SIC: **2759** 5099 7532 Embossing on paper; signs, except electric; truck painting & lettering

(G-1677)
KOUNTRY KUSTOM KITCHENS
338 N Ronks Rd (17505-9711)
PHONE...................717 768-3091
Emanuel R Fisher Jr, *Partner*
Steven Fisher, *Partner*
EMP: 3
SALES (est): 326.4K **Privately Held**
SIC: **2434** Wood kitchen cabinets

(G-1678)
LANCASTER CABINET COMPANY LLC
584 Gibbons Rd (17505-9786)
PHONE...................717 556-8420
David Allgyer,
EMP: 8 EST: 2014
SALES (est): 983K **Privately Held**
SIC: **2434** Wood kitchen cabinets

(G-1679)
LANCO MANUFACTURING COMPANY
2740 Stumptown Rd (17505-9781)
PHONE...................717 556-4143
Sam Stoltzfoos, *President*
EMP: 5
SALES (est): 1.1MM **Privately Held**
SIC: **3531** Rakes, land clearing: mechanical

(G-1680)
SHROCK FABRICATION
229 Maple Ave (17505-9705)
PHONE...................717 397-9500
Stanley Shrock, *Owner*
Mike Wilder, *Marketing Staff*
Tony Wivell, *Manager*
EMP: 5 EST: 2001
SALES (est): 661.6K **Privately Held**
WEB: www.shrockfab.com
SIC: **3441** Fabricated structural metal

(G-1681)
SMUCKER MANAGEMENT CORPORATION
Also Called: Bird In Hand Bakery
2715 Old Phladelphia Pike (17505-9707)
P.O. Box 402 (17505-0402)
PHONE...................717 768-1501
James Chudnovsky, *Manager*
EMP: 5
SALES (corp-wide): 5.9MM **Privately Held**
SIC: **5461** 2051 Bakeries; bread, cake & related products
PA: Smucker Management Corporation
2727 Old Phladelphia Pike
Bird In Hand PA
717 768-8272

(G-1682)
STOLTZFUS EPHRAM
Also Called: Monterey Shop
339 Monterey Rd (17505-9746)
PHONE...................717 656-0513
Ephram Stoltzfus, *Owner*
EMP: 6

SALES (est): 402.7K **Privately Held**
SIC: **1751** 2452 Garage door, installation or erection; prefabricated buildings, wood

(G-1683)
VAL PRODUCTS INC (HQ)
2599 Old Phladelphia Pike (17505-9797)
P.O. Box 8, New Holland (17557-0008)
PHONE...................717 392-3978
Joseph A Wetzel, *President*
Frederick Steudler Jr, *Vice Pres*
Richard S Steudler, *Vice Pres*
John J Shields, *Treasurer*
Joan M Stonesifer, *Admin Sec*
◆ EMP: 75
SQ FT: 25,000
SALES (est): 32.9MM
SALES (corp-wide): 72.5MM **Privately Held**
WEB: www.valproducts.com
SIC: **3523** Farm machinery & equipment
PA: Valco Companies, Inc.
2710 Division Hwy
New Holland PA 17557
717 354-4586

(G-1684)
VALLORBS JEWEL COMPANY
2599 Old Phladelphia Pike (17505-9797)
P.O. Box 958, Lancaster (17608-0958)
PHONE...................717 392-3978
Jeanette Steudler, *President*
Frederick W Steudler Jr, *Vice Pres*
Richard Steudler, *Vice Pres*
Joan Stonesifer, *Admin Sec*
EMP: 160 EST: 1934
SQ FT: 40,000
SALES (est): 24.7MM
SALES (corp-wide): 72.5MM **Privately Held**
SIC: **3451** 3568 3541 3471 Screw machine products; power transmission equipment; machine tools, metal cutting type; plating & polishing; copper foundries
PA: Valco Companies, Inc.
2710 Division Hwy
New Holland PA 17557
717 354-4586

(G-1685)
WEAVERTOWN COACH SHOP
3007 Old Phladelphia Pike (17505-9724)
PHONE...................717 768-3299
Jacob King, *Partner*
Sylvia King, *Partner*
EMP: 9 EST: 1970
SQ FT: 2,000
SALES (est): 882.2K **Privately Held**
SIC: **7699** 3799 Horse drawn vehicle repair; carriages, horse drawn

---

Birdsboro
Berks County

(G-1686)
ARKEMA INC
Also Called: Birdsboro Plant
1112 Lincoln Rd (19508-1804)
PHONE...................610 582-1551
Darrell Roberts, *Plant Mgr*
Cory Mulcahy, *Production*
Gary Hall, *Engineer*
Barry Oakley, *Engineer*
Elaine Hawkins, *Office Mgr*
EMP: 140
SALES (corp-wide): 77.8MM **Privately Held**
SIC: **2819** Hydrocyanic acid
HQ: Arkema Inc.
900 First Ave
King Of Prussia PA 19406
610 205-7000

(G-1687)
ATOCHEM INTL INC/POLYMERS DIV
1112 Lincoln Rd (19508-1804)
PHONE...................610 582-1551
EMP: 3
SALES (est): 290.2K **Privately Held**
SIC: **2821** Plastics materials & resins

(G-1688)
BEACON CONTAINER CORPORATION (PA)
Also Called: Beacon Container Corp PA
700 W 1st St (19508-2128)
PHONE...................610 582-2222
Steven Walter, *President*
Jerome K Grossman, *President*
John Kauffman, *General Mgr*
Mark Hunter, *Opers Staff*
Tom Rowley, *Accounts Mgr*
EMP: 120 EST: 1955
SQ FT: 140,000
SALES (est): 23.6MM **Privately Held**
WEB: www.beaconcontainer.com
SIC: **2653** Boxes, corrugated: made from purchased materials

(G-1689)
BIRDSBORO EXTRUSIONS LLC
1 Industrial Dr (19508)
P.O. Box 99 (19508-0099)
PHONE...................610 582-0400
Chris Witthout, *Manager*
▲ EMP: 3
SALES (est): 605.6K **Privately Held**
WEB: www.birdsboroextrusions.com
SIC: **3331** 4513 Primary copper; air courier services

(G-1690)
BIRDSBORO KOSHER FARMS CORP
1100 Lincoln Rd (19508-1804)
PHONE...................610 404-0001
Issy Perlmutter, *CEO*
Sara Cruz, *Office Mgr*
EMP: 235 EST: 2012
SQ FT: 15,000
SALES (est): 43.8MM **Privately Held**
SIC: **2015** Poultry slaughtering & processing

(G-1691)
CAST-RITE METAL COMPANY
101 Fairview Chapel Rd (19508-8801)
P.O. Box 367 (19508-0367)
PHONE...................610 582-1300
Christopher R Degruchy, *President*
Joseph Wesolowski, *President*
Robert R Martz, *Corp Secy*
Brian I Kelley, *Vice Pres*
EMP: 28
SQ FT: 4,000
SALES (est): 6.8MM **Privately Held**
WEB: www.castritemetal.com
SIC: **3365** Aluminum & aluminum-based alloy castings

(G-1692)
COUNTRY ADDITIONS INC
420 Beacon St (19508-2014)
PHONE...................610 404-2062
Vincent Sugila, *President*
EMP: 4
SALES (est): 384.9K **Privately Held**
SIC: **2511** Wood household furniture

(G-1693)
DYER QUARRY INC
1275 Rock Hollow Rd (19508-7900)
P.O. Box 188 (19508-0188)
PHONE...................610 582-6010
James J Anderson, *President*
Bill Hedl, *Info Tech Dir*
EMP: 35
SALES (est): 11.6MM **Privately Held**
SIC: **5032** 1429 3312 3281 Stone, crushed or broken; grits mining (crushed stone); blast furnaces & steel mills; cut stone & stone products

(G-1694)
EMPOREUM PLASTICS CORPORATION
1522 Golf Course Rd (19508-7964)
P.O. Box 523, Douglassville (19518-0523)
PHONE...................610 698-6347
Andrew Fallis, *CEO*
Bradley Liskey, *President*
Daniel White, *Vice Pres*
Ryan Phillips, *Admin Sec*
EMP: 4
SALES (est): 300.7K **Privately Held**
SIC: **3089** Molding primary plastic

(G-1695)
F M BROWNS SONS INCORPORATED
127 S Furnace St (19508-2340)
P.O. Box 67 (19508-0067)
PHONE...................610 582-2741
Frank Brown, *President*
EMP: 40
SQ FT: 24,000
SALES (corp-wide): 57.1MM **Privately Held**
WEB: www.fmbrown.com
SIC: **2048** 5191 5153 Livestock feeds; feed; seeds: field, garden & flower; grains
PA: F M Brown's Sons Incorporated
205 Woodrow Ave
Reading PA 19608
800 334-8816

(G-1696)
FRENCH CREEK OFFSET INC
127 N Mill St (19508-2042)
PHONE...................610 582-3241
Jeffrey Little, *President*
EMP: 5
SALES (est): 410K **Privately Held**
SIC: **2752** Commercial printing, offset

(G-1697)
GRANT MFG & ALLOYING INC (PA)
200c N Furnace St (19508-2062)
P.O. Box 69 (19508-0069)
PHONE...................610 404-1380
Daniel C Craige, *President*
Kenneth W Thompson, *Vice Pres*
EMP: 8
SQ FT: 20,000
SALES (est): 1.3MM **Privately Held**
WEB: www.grantmfg.com
SIC: **3341** Secondary nonferrous metals

(G-1698)
HARNERS AUTO BODY INC
422e524 Ben Franklin Hwy (19508)
PHONE...................610 385-3825
Joseph Harner, *Branch Mgr*
EMP: 7
SALES (corp-wide): 695.7K **Privately Held**
SIC: **3711** 3713 7532 Automobile bodies, passenger car, not including engine, etc.; truck & bus bodies; top & body repair & paint shops
PA: Harner's Auto Body Inc
524 Ben Franklin Hwy E
Birdsboro PA 19508
610 582-9880

(G-1699)
HSK MANUFACTURING INC
200 N Furnace St Ste J (19508-2062)
P.O. Box 43 (19508-0043)
PHONE...................610 404-1940
Randall Kriscky, *President*
Pete Haines, *President*
EMP: 6
SQ FT: 3,400
SALES: 290K **Privately Held**
SIC: **3599** Machine shop, jobbing & repair

(G-1700)
ICP INDUSTRIES LLC
Also Called: Minusnine Technologies
200 N Furnace St (19508-2062)
PHONE...................888 672-2123
EMP: 20
SALES (corp-wide): 140.9MM **Privately Held**
SIC: **3479** Coating of metals & formed products
HQ: Icp Industries Llc
100 Business Park Ave
San Antonio TX 78204

(G-1701)
KER CUSTOM MOLDERS INC
5 Riga Ln (19508-1303)
PHONE...................610 582-0967
Edward Salaneck, *President*
Donald M Hurley, *Vice Pres*
Kurt H Kohler, *Treasurer*
Shelby Gaul, *Admin Sec*
EMP: 34
SQ FT: 10,700

SALES (est): 11MM **Privately Held**
SIC: 3089 Injection molding of plastics

(G-1702)
KW INC
Also Called: Kennedy Tool & Die
325 W Main St (19508-1909)
PHONE..................................610 582-8735
William S Kennedy Jr, *President*
Joel H Wilson, *Vice Pres*
Brian Fuoco, *Sales Staff*
Carole Miller, *Manager*
Daniel Tschudy, *Manager*
EMP: 40 EST: 1959
SQ FT: 16,000
SALES (est): 9.8MM **Privately Held**
WEB: www.ktdmold.com
SIC: 3544 Forms (molds), for foundry &
plastics working machinery

(G-1703)
PICKAR BROTHERS INC
5 Riga Ln (19508-1303)
PHONE..................................610 582-0967
Harold J Pickar Jr, *President*
Joanne Pickar, *Corp Secy*
Harold J Pickar Sr, *Vice Pres*
Robert Yanos, *Vice Pres*
EMP: 21 EST: 1955
SQ FT: 20,000
SALES (est): 2.3MM **Privately Held**
SIC: 3089 3544 3312 Injection molding of
plastics; industrial molds; tool & die steel

(G-1704)
REITNOUER INC
Also Called: Reitnouer Trailers
5 E Point Dr (19508-8151)
P.O. Box 13069, Reading (19612-3069)
PHONE..................................610 929-4856
Miles A Reitnouer, *President*
Tom Donkin, *President*
Mitzi Reitnouer, *Corp Secy*
Jason Reitnouer, *Vice Pres*
▼ EMP: 50
SQ FT: 50,000
SALES (est): 35.7MM **Privately Held**
WEB: www.reitnouer-trailers.com
SIC: 3715 3537 3354 Trailer bodies; in-
dustrial trucks & tractors; aluminum ex-
truded products

(G-1705)
RIDGEWOOD WINERY
2039 Philadelphia Ave (19508-8152)
PHONE..................................484 509-0100
William Smith, *Owner*
EMP: 3
SALES (est): 118.1K **Privately Held**
SIC: 2084 Wines

(G-1706)
SPARTON AYDIN LLC (DH)
Also Called: Aydin Displays
1 Riga Ln (19508-1303)
PHONE..................................610 404-7400
Ruth Ramplin, *Senior Buyer*
Jeffrey Bennett, *Engineer*
Keith Cariani, *Manager*
EMP: 100
SQ FT: 45,000
SALES: 25MM
SALES (corp-wide): 52.3MM **Privately
Held**
SIC: 3571 Electronic computers
HQ: Sparton Corporation
425 N Martingale Rd
Schaumburg IL 60173
847 762-5800

(G-1707)
VAN INDUSTRIES INC
2 Industrial Dr (19508-1901)
P.O. Box 31 (19508-0031)
PHONE..................................610 582-1118
Doug Van Tiggelen, *President*
Charles Leiendecker, *Buyer*
Kris Keller, *Engineer*
Carrie M Moore, *Manager*
EMP: 48
SQ FT: 12,000
SALES (est): 16.1MM **Privately Held**
WEB: www.vanindustries.com
SIC: 3443 Weldments

(G-1708)
VISION CUSTOM TOOLING INC
5 Riga Ln (19508-1303)
PHONE..................................610 582-1640
Robert F Benning, *CEO*
Edward Salaneck Jr, *President*
Lorraine Salaneck, *Treasurer*
EMP: 15
SQ FT: 10,250
SALES (est): 2.8MM **Privately Held**
SIC: 3089 Injection molded finished plastic
products; injection molding of plastics

(G-1709)
**WUNSCH TECHNOLOGIES
CORP**
Also Called: W T
471 Fairview Chapel Rd (19508-8823)
PHONE..................................610 207-0628
Ronald J Wunsch Jr, *President*
Rachel Biltz, *Office Mgr*
Marvin Coldren, *Manager*
Don Geddio, *Executive*
EMP: 20 EST: 2007
SQ FT: 7,400
SALES: 1MM **Privately Held**
SIC: 3679 Antennas, receiving

Blain
Perry County

(G-1710)
CONOCO WOODWORKING
99 Gideon Ln (17006-6300)
PHONE..................................717 536-3948
EMP: 4
SALES: 450K **Privately Held**
SIC: 2431 Mfg Millwork

Blairs Mills
Huntingdon County

(G-1711)
JOHN W BURDGE
20577 Van Buren Rd (17213-9335)
PHONE..................................814 259-3901
John W Burdge, *Principal*
EMP: 3
SALES (est): 156.7K **Privately Held**
SIC: 2411 Logging

Blairsville
Indiana County

(G-1712)
**A C MILLER CONCRETE PDTS
INC**
9558 Route 22 (15717-4125)
P.O. Box 93 (15717-0093)
PHONE..................................724 459-5950
Alan Conrad, *COO*
Michael Buchan, *VP Opers*
Peg Mazei, *Purch Agent*
James Reitnour, *QC Mgr*
Dave Gautreau, *Sales Mgr*
EMP: 65
SALES (corp-wide): 22MM **Privately
Held**
WEB: www.acmiller.com
SIC: 3272 5211 3442 Concrete products,
precast; masonry materials & supplies;
metal doors, sash & trim
PA: A. C. Miller Concrete Products, Inc.
31 E Bridge St
Spring City PA 19475
610 948-4600

(G-1713)
APPLERIDGE STONE INTL INC
1094 Old William Penn Hwy (15717-7865)
PHONE..................................724 459-9511
William Ostach, *President*
Margaret Ostach, *Vice Pres*
EMP: 20
SQ FT: 14,000
SALES (est): 3.6MM **Privately Held**
SIC: 3272 Concrete products, precast

(G-1714)
BALCO INC
Also Called: Irwin Car and Equipment
400 Serell Dr (15717)
PHONE..................................724 459-6814
Fax: 724 459-0793
▲ EMP: 10
SQ FT: 12,000
SALES (est): 1.6MM **Privately Held**
SIC: 3532 5945 Mfg Mining Machinery Ret
Hobbies/Toys/Games

(G-1715)
**BENTLEY DEVELOPMENT CO
INC (PA)**
101 Serrell Dr (15717-1177)
P.O. Box 338 (15717-0338)
PHONE..................................724 459-5775
William J Stefan Jr, *President*
EMP: 15
SQ FT: 10,000
SALES (est): 14.7MM **Privately Held**
SIC: 1629 7353 1221 Earthmoving con-
tractor; heavy construction equipment
rental; coal preparation plant, bituminous
or lignite

(G-1716)
BLACK LICK STAKE PLANT
Also Called: Sunoco
1610 Cornell Rd (15717-8018)
P.O. Box 495 (15717-0495)
PHONE..................................724 459-7670
Cristie Campbell, *Owner*
EMP: 4
SALES: 100K **Privately Held**
SIC: 5541 2499 Filling stations, gasoline;
surveyors' stakes, wood

(G-1717)
**BLAIRSVILLE WILBERT BURIAL
VLT (PA)**
Also Called: Lavale Wilbert Vault Division
6 Decker St (15717-1225)
PHONE..................................724 459-9677
J De Wayne Dills, *President*
Margaret B Dills, *Treasurer*
EMP: 25 EST: 1924
SQ FT: 50,000
SALES: 5MM **Privately Held**
SIC: 3272 7261 Burial vaults, concrete or
precast terrazzo; funeral service & crema-
tories

(G-1718)
CARBIDE METALS INC
176 Cherry St (15717-4358)
P.O. Box 7924, New Castle (16107-7924)
PHONE..................................724 459-6355
Dennis Gennaro, *President*
EMP: 15 EST: 1934
SQ FT: 100,000
SALES (est): 1.4MM **Privately Held**
WEB: www.carbidemetal.com
SIC: 3291 3545 3544 3366 Tungsten
carbide abrasive; machine tool acces-
sories; special dies, tools, jigs & fixtures;
copper foundries

(G-1719)
CLARK METAL PRODUCTS CO
100 Serrell Dr (15717-1150)
P.O. Box 600 (15717-0600)
PHONE..................................724 459-7550
Dave Clark Sr, *CEO*
David A Clark, *President*
David Clark Jr, *Exec VP*
Dave Kemerer, *Director*
Paul Labuda, *Director*
EMP: 114
SQ FT: 68,000
SALES (est): 33.3MM **Privately Held**
WEB: www.clark-metal.com
SIC: 3444 3471 3613 3469 Sheet metal
specialties, not stamped; finishing, metals
or formed products; switchgear & switch-
board apparatus; metal stampings

(G-1720)
ERIE BOLT CORPORATION
Also Called: Ebc
1325 Liberty St (15717)
PHONE..................................814 456-4287
Harry Brown, *President*
Ken Caratelli, *President*

Charles Roundtree, *Vice Pres*
Dennis Kendziora, *Opers Mgr*
Don Perry, *Opers Staff*
EMP: 65
SQ FT: 49,000
SALES (est): 11.1MM
SALES (corp-wide): 3.4B **Privately Held**
WEB: www.ebcind.com
SIC: 3462 3452 Iron & steel forgings;
bolts, metal
HQ: Doncasters Inc.
835 Poquonnock Rd
Groton CT 06340

(G-1721)
**H & W GLOBAL INDUSTRIES
INC**
414 Innovation Dr (15717-8096)
PHONE..................................724 459-5316
Jean-Pierre Habets, *President*
Sandra K Habets, *Vice Pres*
Chantal L Townsend, *Admin Sec*
EMP: 26
SQ FT: 47,400
SALES (est): 3.6MM **Privately Held**
SIC: 3479 Etching & engraving; coating of
metals & formed products

(G-1722)
HANSON AGGREGATES LLC
311 Quarry Rd (15717)
PHONE..................................724 459-6031
Roger Melville, *Manager*
EMP: 40
SALES (corp-wide): 20.6B **Privately Held**
SIC: 3281 Stone, quarrying & processing
of own stone products
HQ: Hanson Aggregates Llc
8505 Freport Pkwy Ste 500
Irving TX 75063
469 417-1200

(G-1723)
HARTER PRECISION
Hwy 982 & Rte 22 Rt 22 (15717)
PHONE..................................724 459-5060
William Harter, *Owner*
EMP: 4
SQ FT: 8,000
SALES (est): 367.1K **Privately Held**
SIC: 3469 3312 3452 Metal stampings;
tool & die steel; bolts, nuts, rivets & wash-
ers

(G-1724)
HMS INDUSTRIES INC
1256 Route 22 Hwy W (15717-7906)
PHONE..................................724 459-5090
John A Hornock, *President*
Peggy Hornock, *Treasurer*
EMP: 20 EST: 1977
SQ FT: 44,000
SALES (est): 4.3MM **Privately Held**
WEB: www.hmsindustries.com
SIC: 3541 3469 3546 3465 Machine tool
replacement & repair parts, metal cutting
types; stamping metal for the trade; spe-
cial dies, tools, jigs & fixtures; automotive
stampings; fabricated structural metal

(G-1725)
**INDUSTRIAL PACKAGING
SUPPLIES**
285 Westinghouse Rd (15717-4133)
PHONE..................................724 459-8299
Richard Rause, *Owner*
Dolores Rause, *Finance*
EMP: 9
SQ FT: 30,000
SALES (est): 2.9MM **Privately Held**
WEB: www.indpkgsup.com
SIC: 5085 5113 2631 Packing, industrial;
industrial & personal service paper; pa-
perboard mills

(G-1726)
**INTERNATIONAL CONVEYOR
RBR LLC**
72 Industrial Park Rd (15717-8545)
PHONE..................................724 343-4225
Larry Jones, *President*
Bill Machak, *Vice Pres*
Cary Octavio, *Vice Pres*
EMP: 4

▲ = Import ▼=Export
◆ =Import/Export

SALES (est): 378.8K **Privately Held**
SIC: 3496 Conveyor belts

(G-1727)
JOHNS CUSTOM LEATHER
523 S Liberty St (15717-1512)
PHONE..............................724 459-6802
John R Stumpf, *Owner*
EMP: 9
SQ FT: 3,000
SALES: 300K **Privately Held**
SIC: 3949 5941 Sporting & athletic goods;
sporting goods & bicycle shops

(G-1728)
K H CONTROLS INC
75 Innovation Dr (15717-8098)
PHONE..............................724 459-7474
Kevin Huczko, *President*
Roger Huczko, *Admin Sec*
▲ EMP: 75
SQ FT: 32,500
SALES (est): 12MM **Privately Held**
WEB: www.khcontrols.com
SIC: 3629 Power conversion units, a.c. to
d.c.: static-electric

(G-1729)
KARADON CORPORATION
4125 Route 22 Hwy E (15717-7416)
PHONE..............................724 676-5790
James L Kovalcik, *President*
Donna Kovalcik, *Corp Secy*
Daniel Kovalcik, *Vice Pres*
EMP: 10 EST: 1970
SQ FT: 10,000
SALES (est): 1.3MM **Privately Held**
WEB: www.karadoncorp.com
SIC: 8711 3544 3547 Machine tool de-
sign; special dies & tools; forms (molds),
for foundry & plastics working machinery;
rolling mill machinery

(G-1730)
KEYSTONE FUELS LLC
175 Cornell Rd Ste 1 (15717-8076)
PHONE..............................724 357-1710
Valerie Marsico,
EMP: 8 EST: 2012
SALES (est): 629.4K **Privately Held**
SIC: 2869 Fuels

(G-1731)
LAUREL PRINTING (PA)
Also Called: Laurel Printing & Copy
48 W Market St (15717-1328)
PHONE..............................724 459-7554
Alton Weeks, *Owner*
EMP: 7
SQ FT: 1,450
SALES (est): 50C.1K **Privately Held**
SIC: 2752 Commercial printing, offset

(G-1732)
LAUREL VALLEY METALS LLC
4200 Route 22 Hwy E (15717-7421)
P.O. Box 116 (15717-0116)
PHONE..............................724 990-8189
Thomas Leyland, *President*
Mark Eichenlaub,
EMP: 2
SALES: 1MM **Privately Held**
SIC: 3312 Stainless steel

(G-1733)
M D CLINE METAL FABG INC
832 Penn View Rd (15717-6649)
PHONE..............................724 459-8968
Thelma Cline, *President*
Jeffrey Cline, *Vice Pres*
David Cline Jr, *Treasurer*
EMP: 6
SQ FT: 30,000
SALES (est): 2MM **Privately Held**
WEB: www.microserve.net
SIC: 5051 3599 3499 Sheets, metal; cus-
tom machinery; machine bases, metal

(G-1734)
**MCFADDEN MACHINE & MFG
CO**
160 Hill Rd (15717-5917)
PHONE..............................724 459-9278
Robert Hlusko, *President*
Barry Jamison, *Vice Pres*
Dave Urchek, *Vice Pres*

EMP: 20 EST: 1965
SQ FT: 23,000
SALES (est): 4.5MM **Privately Held**
WEB: www.mcfadden.com
SIC: 3569 3599 Assembly machines, non-
metalworking; machine shop, jobbing &
repair

(G-1735)
**NATIONAL CENTER FOR DEF
(PA)**
486 Cornell Rd Ste 2 (15717-8007)
PHONE..............................724 539-8811
Ralph Resnick, *President*
Brian Schmidt, *Project Engr*
EMP: 33
SQ FT: 7,914
SALES: 29.6MM **Privately Held**
SIC: 8711 2752 Engineering services; pro-
motional printing, lithographic

(G-1736)
PENN MACHINE COMPANY
310 Innovation Dr (15717-8094)
PHONE..............................724 459-0302
Scott Cole, *Branch Mgr*
EMP: 14
SALES (corp-wide): 225.3B **Publicly
Held**
WEB: www.pmcgearbox.com
SIC: 3599 Machine shop, jobbing & repair
HQ: Penn Machine Company
106 Station St
Johnstown PA 15905

(G-1737)
**PRECISION WIRE PRODUCTS
INC**
207 E Brown St (15717-1110)
P.O. Box 103 (15717-0103)
PHONE..............................724 459-5601
James Pryce, *President*
Glenn Pryce, *Shareholder*
Eleanor Pryce, *Admin Sec*
EMP: 20
SQ FT: 33,000
SALES (est): 3.7MM **Privately Held**
WEB: www.precisionwire.net
SIC: 3496 Cages, wire

(G-1738)
PREFORM SPECIALTIES INC
176 Cherry St (15717-4358)
PHONE..............................724 459-0808
Dennis Gennaro, *CEO*
Joseph A Walsh, *President*
Richard Natale, *Treasurer*
Erika Mitchell, *Sales Staff*
EMP: 21
SQ FT: 6,000
SALES (est): 3MM **Privately Held**
WEB: www.psicmi.com
SIC: 3545 Cutting tools for machine tools

(G-1739)
QUALITY STAMPING
9177 Route 22 (15717-4054)
PHONE..............................724 459-5060
Bill Harter, *Owner*
EMP: 7
SALES (est): 877.8K **Privately Held**
SIC: 3465 Automotive stampings

(G-1740)
**RON ANTHONY WOOD
PRODUCTS INC**
9488 Route 22 (15717-4126)
P.O. Box 420 (15717-0420)
PHONE..............................724 459-7620
Ronald Anthony, *President*
EMP: 12
SALES (est): 1.9MM **Privately Held**
SIC: 2441 Boxes, wood

(G-1741)
SIGBET MANUFACTURING
3994 Chestnut Ridge Rd (15717-7520)
PHONE..............................724 459-7920
Robert T Sigafoes, *Owner*
EMP: 3
SQ FT: 4,800
SALES: 350K **Privately Held**
SIC: 3544 3599 Special dies, tools, jigs &
fixtures; machine shop, jobbing & repair

(G-1742)
**SPECIALTY BAR PRODUCTS
COMPANY (DH)**
200 Martha St (15717-1412)
P.O. Box 127 (15717-0127)
PHONE..............................724 459-0544
Brian K Murray, *President*
Ken Caratelli, *President*
David Bubar, *Vice Pres*
Rick Ward, *Project Mgr*
Dave Robert, *Engineer*
▲ EMP: 175
SQ FT: 87,500
SALES (est): 44.8MM
SALES (corp-wide): 3.4B **Privately Held**
WEB: www.specialty-bar.com
SIC: 3499 3452 3398 Shims, metal; bolts,
nuts, rivets & washers; metal heat treating
HQ: Fastentech, Inc.
8500 Normandale Lake Blvd
Minneapolis MN 55437
952 921-2090

(G-1743)
TECHNIPFMC US HOLDINGS INC
451 Innovation Dr (15717-8096)
PHONE..............................724 459-7350
EMP: 15
SALES (corp-wide): 15B **Privately Held**
SIC: 3533 Oil & gas field machinery
HQ: Fmc Technologies, Inc.
11740 Katy Fwy Energy Tow
Houston TX 77079
281 591-4000

(G-1744)
WATERLOO WOODCRAFT
4474 Route 217 Hwy N (15717-5612)
PHONE..............................724 221-0438
Todd Halteman, *Principal*
EMP: 4
SALES (est): 327.1K **Privately Held**
SIC: 2434 Wood kitchen cabinets

(G-1745)
WILBERT VAULT CO
100 N East Ln (15717-1226)
PHONE..............................724 459-8400
J Dewayne Dills, *Principal*
EMP: 3
SALES (est): 266.9K **Privately Held**
SIC: 3272 Burial vaults, concrete or pre-
cast terrazzo

Blakely

Lackawanna County

(G-1746)
CAPRA COLLINA VINEYARD INC
1971 Scranton Carbondale (18447-7006)
PHONE..............................570 489-0489
Kevin Betti, *Principal*
EMP: 4
SALES (est): 252.3K **Privately Held**
SIC: 2084 Wines

(G-1747)
FALCON PROPANE LLC
1630 Main St (18447-1367)
PHONE..............................570 207-1711
Charles Passeri, *President*
EMP: 3
SALES (est): 169.2K **Privately Held**
SIC: 1321 Propane (natural) production

Blakeslee

Monroe County

(G-1748)
LIQUID FENCE CO INC (DH)
5683 Route 115 (18610-7973)
PHONE..............................570 722-8165
Edward P Abraham, *President*
Eddie Abraham, *President*
Rosemary L Kaskie, *Treasurer*
Rocky Alleshouse, *Controller*
▲ EMP: 28
SQ FT: 24,000

SALES (est): 5.1MM
SALES (corp-wide): 3.1B **Publicly Held**
WEB: www.liquidfence.com
SIC: 2879 5191 Insecticides & pesticides;
pesticides
HQ: United Industries Corporation
1 Rider Trail Plaza Dr # 300
Earth City MO 63045
608 275-3340

(G-1749)
**POCONO TRANSCRETE
INCORPORATED (PA)**
179 Burger Rd (18610-7705)
PHONE..............................570 646-2662
Robert J Chaya, *President*
Mike Smith, *QC Mgr*
EMP: 35
SQ FT: 1,500
SALES (est): 5.2MM **Privately Held**
SIC: 3273 Ready-mixed concrete

Blanchard

Centre County

(G-1750)
VALLEY ENTERPRISE CONT INC
111 Eagleville Rd (16826)
P.O. Box 230 (16826-0230)
PHONE..............................570 962-2194
Aquilla Floltzfus, *President*
EMP: 10
SQ FT: 53,000
SALES (est): 454.3K **Privately Held**
SIC: 3443 Dumpsters, garbage; hoppers,
metal plate

(G-1751)
VALLEY ENTERPRISE CONT LLC
111 Eagleville Rd (16826)
P.O. Box 230 (16826-0230)
PHONE..............................570 962-2194
Aquilla Floltzfus, *President*
EMP: 10
SALES (est): 1.8MM **Privately Held**
SIC: 3443 Dumpsters, garbage; hoppers,
metal plate

Blandon

Berks County

(G-1752)
**CAN CORPORATION AMERICA
INC (PA)**
Also Called: C C
326 June Ave (19510-9566)
PHONE..............................610 926-3044
Ronald Moreau, *President*
Thomas R Moreau, *President*
Peter F Giorgi, *Vice Pres*
David Fryer, *Treasurer*
Philip M Impink, *Treasurer*
▲ EMP: 174
SQ FT: 150,000
SALES (est): 53.8MM **Privately Held**
SIC: 3411 Metal cans

(G-1753)
**EXCELSIOR BLOWER SYSTEMS
INC (PA)**
331 June Ave (19510-9550)
P.O. Box 15126, Reading (19612-5126)
PHONE..............................610 921-9558
William G Montgomery, *President*
Gene Franckowiak, *Vice Pres*
Gene Frankowiak, *Vice Pres*
Helen Montgomery, *Accountant*
Matt Manwiller, *Marketing Staff*
▲ EMP: 17
SQ FT: 16,000
SALES (est): 6.6MM **Privately Held**
WEB: www.excelsiorblower.com
SIC: 3564 Blowers & fans

(G-1754)
GLAXOSMITHKLINE LLC
345 W Walnut Tree Dr (19510-9624)
PHONE..............................610 223-9089
EMP: 26

G
E
O
G
R
A
P
H
I
C

SALES (corp-wide): 39.8B **Privately Held**
SIC: 2834 Pharmaceutical preparations
HQ: Glaxosmithkline Llc
5 Crescent Dr
Philadelphia PA 19112
215 751-4000

(G-1755)
ISIMAC MACHINE COMPANY INC (PA)
Excelsr Indl Park June Av (19510)
P.O. Box 259 (19510-0259)
PHONE..................................610 926-6400
Edward C Graeff, *President*
Jeff Graeff, *General Mgr*
Brian T Graeff, *Treasurer*
Jeffrey S Graeff, *Admin Sec*
EMP: 40
SQ FT: 38,000
SALES (est): 8.1MM **Privately Held**
WEB: www.prizer-painter.com
SIC: 3599 Machine shop, jobbing & repair

(G-1756)
ISIMAC MACHINE COMPANY INC
June Ave (19510)
P.O. Box 259 (19510-0259)
PHONE..................................610 926-6400
Jeffrey Graeff, *General Mgr*
EMP: 40
SQ FT: 15,000
SALES (corp-wide): 8.1MM **Privately Held**
WEB: www.isimac.com
SIC: 3599 Machine shop, jobbing & repair
PA: Isimac Machine Company, Inc.
Excelsr Indl Park June Av
Blandon PA 19510
610 926-6400

(G-1757)
PRIZER-PAINTER STOVE WORKS INC
Also Called: Blue Star Cooking
328 June Ave (19510)
PHONE..................................610 376-7479
Michael Trapp, *President*
Jeffrey Bilger, *Vice Pres*
Zach Kuhn, *Project Mgr*
Doug Edmondson, *Production*
Brian Mehle, *Manager*
▲ EMP: 50 EST: 1880
SQ FT: 80,000
SALES (est): 20.1MM **Privately Held**
WEB: www.prizer-painter.com
SIC: 3469 3444 6512 Porcelain enameled products & utensils; sheet metalwork; commercial & industrial building operation

(G-1758)
R & D PALLETT CO
Breazy Ind Park Rr 73 (19510)
P.O. Box 137 (19510-0137)
PHONE..................................610 944-9484
Rod Hannahoe, *Owner*
EMP: 6
SQ FT: 2,000
SALES (est): 541.9K **Privately Held**
SIC: 2448 Pallets, wood

(G-1759)
SHUBANDIT LLC
133 Penrose Ave (19510-9577)
PHONE..................................610 916-8313
EMP: 4
SALES (est): 291.8K **Privately Held**
SIC: 3949 Sporting & athletic goods

(G-1760)
STEVE DAY
Also Called: Petrified Forest
663 Gulden Rd (19510-9520)
PHONE..................................610 916-1317
Steve Day, *Owner*
EMP: 3
SALES: 100K **Privately Held**
WEB: www.petrified-forest.com
SIC: 3269 Pottery products

(G-1761)
TEMPLE ALUMINUM FOUNDRY INC
1145 Park Rd (19510-9561)
PHONE..................................610 926-2125

James W Schoellkops Jr, *CEO*
Eric F Schoellkopf Sr, *President*
Vicki Row, *Corp Secy*
EMP: 25 EST: 1952
SQ FT: 30,000
SALES (est): 4.4MM **Privately Held**
WEB: www.templealuminumfoundry.com
SIC: 3366 Copper foundries

Blawnox
Allegheny County

(G-1762)
ALLEGHENY RUBBER STAMP INC
Also Called: Allegheny Marking Products
122 4th St (15238-3233)
PHONE..................................412 826-8662
Patricia Staudt, *President*
EMP: 8
SALES (est): 985.5K **Privately Held**
WEB: www.alleghenymarking.com
SIC: 3953 5999 3999 Embossing seals & hand stamps; rubber stamps; buttons: Red Cross, union, identification

(G-1763)
CHASE CORPORATION
Also Called: Chase Specialty Coatings
128 1st St (15238-3223)
PHONE..................................800 245-3209
Gregg A Pelagio, *Principal*
Rick Specht, *Research*
EMP: 15
SALES (corp-wide): 252.5MM **Publicly Held**
SIC: 3644 Insulators & insulation materials, electrical
PA: Chase Corporation
295 University Ave
Westwood MA 02090
781 332-0700

(G-1764)
JNB INDUSTRIAL SUPPLY INC
114 Riverview Ave (15238-2735)
PHONE..................................412 455-5170
Mark Lombardi, *Principal*
Michael Lombardi, *Principal*
Nicholas Lombardi, *Principal*
William Lombardi, *Principal*
Janet Lombardi, *Co-Owner*
EMP: 5
SALES (est): 428.6K **Privately Held**
SIC: 3052 5072 3569 5084 Rubber & plastics hose & beltings; miscellaneous fasteners; lubrication equipment, industrial; water pumps (industrial)

Blooming Glen
Bucks County

(G-1765)
ROGER S WRIGHT FURNITURE LTD
911 S Perkasie Rd (18911)
P.O. Box 362 (18911-0362)
PHONE..................................215 257-5700
Roger Wright, *President*
EMP: 6
SALES (est): 824.7K **Privately Held**
WEB: www.rswfurniture.com
SIC: 3429 5712 Furniture builders' & other household hardware; furniture stores

---

Bloomsburg
Columbia County

(G-1766)
ALASKA COMPANY INC
Also Called: Alaska Stove
3162 Columbia Blvd (17815-8889)
PHONE..................................570 387-0260
Charles Gorchowski, *Owner*
EMP: 10

SALES (est): 520K **Privately Held**
WEB: www.alaskastove.com
SIC: 3631 3433 Electric ranges, domestic; heating equipment, except electric

(G-1767)
ALASKA STOKER STOVE INC
3162 Columbia Blvd (17815-8889)
PHONE..................................570 387-0260
Charles Gorchowski, *Owner*
EMP: 9
SALES (est): 338.5K **Privately Held**
SIC: 3444 Stove boards, sheet metal

(G-1768)
ALUMAX LLC
Also Called: Amerimax Building Products
851 Railroad St (17815-2400)
PHONE..................................570 784-7481
Claire Yoder, *Manager*
EMP: 30
SALES (corp-wide): 14B **Publicly Held**
SIC: 3353 3444 Flat rolled shapes, aluminum; sheet metalwork
HQ: Alumax Llc
201 Isabella St
Pittsburgh PA 15212
412 553-4545

(G-1769)
AMERICAN CYCLE FABRICATION
7175 Columbia Blvd Apt 1 (17815-8643)
PHONE..................................570 752-8715
Paul Freebus, *President*
Barbara Msith, *Manager*
◆ EMP: 4
SALES: 500K **Privately Held**
WEB: www.americancyclefab.com
SIC: 7699 3714 Motorcycle repair service; motor vehicle parts & accessories

(G-1770)
ARDAGH METAL PACKAGING USA INC
6670 Lowe St (17815-8613)
PHONE..................................570 389-5563
George Morris, *Manager*
EMP: 200
SALES (corp-wide): 242.1K **Privately Held**
WEB: www.impresspkg.com
SIC: 3411 Metal cans
HQ: Ardagh Metal Packaging Usa Inc.
600 N Bell Ave
Carnegie PA 15106

(G-1771)
AUTONEUM NORTH AMERICA INC
480 W 5th St (17815-1563)
PHONE..................................570 784-4100
Patrick Torbit, *Branch Mgr*
EMP: 590
SALES (corp-wide): 2.2B **Privately Held**
SIC: 3714 Motor vehicle parts & accessories
HQ: Autoneum North America, Inc.
29293 Haggerty Rd
Novi MI 48377
248 848-0100

(G-1772)
BIG HEART PET BRANDS
Also Called: Del Monte Foods
6650 Lowe St (17815-8613)
PHONE..................................570 389-7650
Giannie Cieless, *President*
EMP: 115
SALES (corp-wide): 7.3B **Publicly Held**
SIC: 2047 Dog food
HQ: Big Heart Pet Brands, Inc.
1 Maritime Plz Fl 2
San Francisco CA 94111
415 247-3000

(G-1773)
BIG HEART PET BRANDS
Star-Kist
6670 Lowe St (17815-8613)
PHONE..................................570 784-8200
Luke Livingston, *Opers Mgr*
Giannie Cieless, *Controller*
James Green, *Controller*
Nate Van Berkum, *Human Res Mgr*

Paul Hackett, *Branch Mgr*
EMP: 115
SALES (corp-wide): 7.3B **Publicly Held**
SIC: 2047 Dog food; cat food
HQ: Big Heart Pet Brands, Inc.
1 Maritime Plz Fl 2
San Francisco CA 94111
415 247-3000

(G-1774)
BIRDS PRINTING
622 East St (17815-2344)
PHONE..................................570 784-8136
Dennis L Bird, *Owner*
EMP: 6 EST: 1969
SQ FT: 1,200
SALES (est): 350K **Privately Held**
SIC: 2752 2759 Commercial printing, offset; letterpress printing

(G-1775)
BLOOMSBURG CARPET INDS INC (PA)
Also Called: Silver Creek
4999 Columbia Blvd (17815-8854)
PHONE..................................800 233-8773
Thomas Habib, *President*
Adam Bowman, *CFO*
Martin J Bowman, *Treasurer*
Patty Fink, *Controller*
Raymond P Habib, *Admin Sec*
◆ EMP: 200
SQ FT: 225,000
SALES (est): 50MM **Privately Held**
WEB: Www.bloomsburGcarpet.com
SIC: 2273 Carpets, hand & machine made

(G-1776)
COMMERCIAL STAINLESS INC
955 Patterson Dr (17815-2927)
PHONE..................................570 387-8980
Bryan Wawroski, *President*
Brian Wawroski, *President*
Brian W Wawroski, *Manager*
Fred Clark, *Shareholder*
EMP: 35
SQ FT: 21,000
SALES (est): 3.7MM **Privately Held**
SIC: 3444 5046 Restaurant sheet metalwork; sheet metal specialties, not stamped; commercial cooking & food service equipment

(G-1777)
CUSTOM FAB CO INC
1439 Millville Rd Ste 1 (17815-8524)
PHONE..................................570 784-0874
Eileen Breisch, *President*
EMP: 10
SALES (est): 820K **Privately Held**
SIC: 3589 Commercial cooking & food-warming equipment; cooking equipment, commercial

(G-1778)
DENNIS ALBERTSON LLC
Also Called: Conner Printing Co
1180 Old Berwick Rd (17815-2914)
PHONE..................................570 784-1677
Dennis Albertson, *Owner*
EMP: 6 EST: 2008
SALES (est): 591.3K **Privately Held**
SIC: 2752 Business forms, lithographed

(G-1779)
DYCO INC
50 Naus Way (17815-8784)
PHONE..................................800 545-3926
Peter Yohe, *President*
Dan Bierdziewski, *Vice Pres*
John Wittman, *Opers Mgr*
Brian Boone, *Purch Mgr*
Michael Slodysko, *Engineer*
◆ EMP: 70
SQ FT: 38,000
SALES (est): 16.5MM **Privately Held**
WEB: www.dyco-inc.com
SIC: 3535 3565 Conveyors & conveying equipment; packaging machinery; bottling machinery: filling, capping, labeling

(G-1780)
EDWIN JOHNSON & SONS
Also Called: Johnson, Edwin & Sons Saw Mill
575 Eyersgrove Rd (17815-6638)
PHONE..................................570 458-4488

Edward Johnson, *Partner*
Reginald Johnson, *Partner*
EMP: 5
SALES (est): 606.4K **Privately Held**
SIC: 2421 Sawmills & planing mills, general

(G-1781)
ESSENTIAL WATER TECHNOLOGIES
150 E 9th St 246-1 (17815-2708)
PHONE..................................570 317-2583
Day Williams, *CEO*
EMP: 10 **EST:** 1997
SALES (est): 980.9K **Privately Held**
SIC: 3589 Water treatment equipment, industrial

(G-1782)
FOAM FABRICATORS INC
17 Industrial Dr (17815-8758)
PHONE..................................570 752-7110
Dan McCracken, *Manager*
EMP: 50 **Publicly Held**
WEB: www.foamfabricators.com
SIC: 2899 4953 3086 Foam charge mixtures; recycling, waste materials; plastics foam products
HQ: Foam Fabricators, Inc.
      8722 E San Alberto Dr # 200
      Scottsdale AZ 85258
      480 607-7330

(G-1783)
FROMM ELC SUP CORP RDING PENNA
1877 Columbia Blvd (17815-3081)
PHONE..................................570 387-9711
Tammie Kipp, *Branch Mgr*
EMP: 6
SALES (corp-wide): 172.5MM **Privately Held**
SIC: 5063 3699 Electrical supplies; electrical equipment & supplies
PA: Fromm Electric Supply Corp. Of Reading, Penna.
      2101 Centre Ave Ste 4
      Reading PA 19605
      610 374-4441

(G-1784)
HANSON AGGREGATES PA LLC
800 Paper Mill Rd (17815-8830)
PHONE..................................570 784-1640
Dale Slusser, *Manager*
Bill Bressler, *Manager*
EMP: 15
SQ FT: 2,100
SALES (corp-wide): 20.6B **Privately Held**
SIC: 1442 Gravel mining; common sand mining; construction sand mining
HQ: Hanson Aggregates Pennsylvania, Llc
      7660 Imperial Way
      Allentown PA 18195
      610 366-4626

(G-1785)
HANSON AGGREGATES PA LLC
Rural Dr 4 Rte 42 N (17815)
PHONE..................................570 784-2888
Jack Roadmal, *Manager*
EMP: 20
SALES (corp-wide): 20.6B **Privately Held**
SIC: 1442 Gravel mining
HQ: Hanson Aggregates Pennsylvania, Llc
      7660 Imperial Way
      Allentown PA 18195
      610 366-4626

(G-1786)
HANSON AGGRGATES SOUTHEAST INC
Rr 4 (17815)
PHONE..................................570 784-2888
Jack Roadarmeo, *Manager*
EMP: 5
SALES (corp-wide): 20.6B **Privately Held**
SIC: 1429 Grits mining (crushed stone)
HQ: Hanson Aggregates Southeast, Inc.
      3237 Satellite Blvd # 210
      Duluth GA 30096
      770 491-2777

(G-1787)
KAWNEER COMPANY INC
500 E 12th St (17815-3900)
P.O. Box 629 (17815-0629)
PHONE..................................570 784-8000
John Collins, *Branch Mgr*
EMP: 350
SQ FT: 2,184
SALES (corp-wide): 14B **Publicly Held**
WEB: www.kawneer.com
SIC: 3446 3442 Architectural metalwork; metal doors, sash & trim
HQ: Kawneer Company, Inc.
      555 Guthridge Ct
      Norcross GA 30092
      770 449-5555

(G-1788)
LYCO I LLC
147 W 4th St (17815-1758)
PHONE..................................570 784-0903
Richard Truslowe,
Jon Difucci,
Jeffrey Dunne,
EMP: 4
SALES (est): 330K **Privately Held**
SIC: 2869 Industrial organic chemicals

(G-1789)
MAINVILLE AG SERVICES INC
360 Main-Mifflin Rd (17815-6753)
PHONE..................................570 784-6922
William D Gallick, *President*
EMP: 5
SALES (est): 823.8K **Privately Held**
SIC: 2875 Fertilizers, mixing only

(G-1790)
MILCO INDUSTRIES INC (PA)
550 E 5th St (17815-2300)
P.O. Box 568 (17815-0568)
PHONE..................................570 784-0400
Norman Belmonte, *Chairman*
Randy Weirman, *Vice Pres*
Anthony J Peluso, *CFO*
Renee Rine, *Human Res Mgr*
Pamela Teichman, *Manager*
◆ **EMP:** 200
SQ FT: 156,000
SALES (est): 54.9MM **Privately Held**
SIC: 2341 2258 2339 2384 Nightgowns & negligees: women's & children's; tricot fabrics; women's & misses' outerwear; maternity clothing; robes & dressing gowns; finishing plants, manmade fiber & silk fabrics

(G-1791)
NEXARC INC
76 Guys Ln (17815-9565)
PHONE..................................570 458-6990
Rick Laubach, *President*
EMP: 1
SQ FT: 500
SALES: 1.2MM **Privately Held**
WEB: www.nexarc.us
SIC: 3356 3548 3312 Nickel & nickel alloy: rolling, drawing or extruding; electrodes, electric welding; plate, steel; stainless steel

(G-1792)
ON FUEL
711 Market St (17815-2628)
PHONE..................................570 784-5320
Vijay Patel, *Principal*
EMP: 4
SALES (est): 489.4K **Privately Held**
SIC: 2869 Fuels

(G-1793)
PEYTY CONSTRUCTION
741 Poplar St B (17815-2871)
PHONE..................................570 764-5995
EMP: 4 **EST:** 2015
SALES (est): 95.8K **Privately Held**
SIC: 2431 1521 Millwork; single-family housing construction

(G-1794)
PRESS-ENTERPRISE INC
3185 Lackawanna Ave (17815-3398)
PHONE..................................570 752-3645
Don Whipmeier, *Manager*
EMP: 8
SQ FT: 660

SALES (corp-wide): 25MM **Privately Held**
WEB: www.perealestate.com
SIC: 2711 Newspapers: publishing only, not printed on site
PA: Press-Enterprise, Inc.
      3185 Lackawanna Ave
      Bloomsburg PA 17815
      570 784-2121

(G-1795)
PRESS-ENTERPRISE INC (PA)
Also Called: Press Enterprise Coml Prtg Div
3185 Lackawanna Ave (17815-3398)
PHONE..................................570 784-2121
Paul R Eyerly III, *Ch of Bd*
Paul R Eyerly IV, *President*
Linda Dancho, *Editor*
Brooke Michael, *Editor*
Bill Bason, *Prdtn Mgr*
EMP: 230
SQ FT: 55,000
SALES: 25MM **Privately Held**
WEB: www.perealestate.com
SIC: 2711 Commercial printing & newspaper publishing combined

(G-1796)
PRINT SHOP INC
3820 Old Berwick Rd (17815-3407)
P.O. Box 563 (17815-0563)
PHONE..................................570 784-4020
Ron Lee, *President*
EMP: 3
SALES (est): 193.4K **Privately Held**
SIC: 2759 2396 Screen printing; screen printing on fabric articles

(G-1797)
PURPLE COW WINERY
281 Welliversville Rd (17815-7233)
PHONE..................................570 854-6969
Hemsarth Andrew, *Principal*
EMP: 4
SALES (est): 210.6K **Privately Held**
SIC: 2084 Wines

(G-1798)
ROBERT G DENT HEATING & AC
Also Called: Rgb Duct Cleaning
1140 Main St (17815-8948)
PHONE..................................570 784-6721
Terry L Dent, *President*
John Dent, *Corp Secy*
EMP: 12 **EST:** 1955
SQ FT: 14,000
SALES: 1.4MM **Privately Held**
SIC: 1711 3444 7349 Warm air heating & air conditioning contractor; ventilation & duct work contractor; heating systems repair & maintenance; sheet metalwork; air duct cleaning

(G-1799)
RON LEE INC
4065 Old Berwick Rd (17815-3410)
P.O. Box 435 (17815-0435)
PHONE..................................570 784-6020
Ron Lee, *President*
EMP: 18
SQ FT: 10,000
SALES (est): 1.4MM **Privately Held**
WEB: www.ronleeinc.com
SIC: 2396 8748 Printing & embossing on plastics fabric articles; business consulting

(G-1800)
S & B FOUNDRY CO
3825 Columbia Blvd (17815-8895)
PHONE..................................570 784-2047
George T Forese, *President*
EMP: 30
SQ FT: 60,000
SALES: 1.3MM **Privately Held**
SIC: 3321 Gray iron castings

(G-1801)
SEKISUI POLYMR INNOVATIONS LLC (DH)
Also Called: Sekisui SPI
6685 Lowe St (17815-8613)
PHONE..................................570 387-6997
Martin Wondergem, *President*
Mike Angell, *Plant Mgr*
Dave Hebda, *Plant Mgr*

Liane Klobe, *Opers Mgr*
Shawn Ayers, *Mfg Mgr*
◆ **EMP:** 275
SQ FT: 10,000
SALES (est): 125.5MM
SALES (corp-wide): 10.3B **Privately Held**
WEB: www.kydex.com
SIC: 2821 Plastics materials & resins
HQ: Sekisui America Corporation
      333 Meadowlands Pkwy
      Secaucus NJ 07094
      201 423-7960

(G-1802)
SUSQUEHANNA FISHING MAG LLC
13 York Rd (17815-8448)
PHONE..................................570 441-4606
John K Oast, *Principal*
EMP: 3 **EST:** 2009
SALES (est): 136.8K **Privately Held**
SIC: 2721 Magazines: publishing only, not printed on site

(G-1803)
TAR HUNT CUSTOM RIFLES INC
101 Dogtown Rd (17815-7544)
PHONE..................................570 784-6368
Randy Fritz, *President*
▲ **EMP:** 3
SALES (est): 250K **Privately Held**
WEB: www.tarhunt.com
SIC: 3841 3484 Rifles for propelling hypodermics into animals; guns (firearms) or gun parts, 30 mm. & below

(G-1804)
TRINITY HIGHWAY RENTALS INC
900 Patterson Dr (17815-2927)
PHONE..................................570 380-2856
Steve Hayes, *Principal*
Will Burney, *Senior VP*
Theresa Delucca, *Controller*
EMP: 6
SALES (est): 1.2MM **Privately Held**
SIC: 3499 Barricades, metal

(G-1805)
ULTRA-POLY CORPORATION
480 W 5th St (17815-1563)
PHONE..................................570 784-1586
Alan Lafiura, *President*
EMP: 4
SALES (est): 419.4K
SALES (corp-wide): 12.4MM **Privately Held**
SIC: 2821 Plastics materials & resins
PA: Ultra-Poly Corporation
      102 Demi Rd
      Portland PA 18351
      570 897-7500

(G-1806)
VERIZON COMMUNICATIONS INC
Also Called: Bell Atlantic
5 W 3rd St (17815-1706)
PHONE..................................570 387-3840
Ann Marie Durako, *Branch Mgr*
EMP: 113
SALES (corp-wide): 130.8B **Publicly Held**
WEB: www.verizon.com
SIC: 4813 4812 2741 8721 Data telephone communications; local telephone communications; voice telephone communications; cellular telephone services; directories, telephone: publishing only, not printed on site; billing & bookkeeping service; computer integrated systems design
PA: Verizon Communications Inc.
      1095 Ave Of The Americas
      New York NY 10036
      212 395-1000

G E O G R A P H I C

Blossburg
Tioga County

(G-1807)
HANSON AGGREGATES PA LLC
Blossburg Mtns Rr 15 (16912)
PHONE..................................570 324-2514
Scott Hubler, *District Mgr*
EMP: 10
SALES (corp-wide): 20.6B **Privately Held**
SIC: 1442 3281 Gravel mining; building
stone products
HQ: Hanson Aggregates Pennsylvania, Llc
7660 Imperial Way
Allentown PA 18195
610 366-4626

(G-1808)
RNS SERVICES INC (HQ)
7 Riverside Plz (16912-1137)
P.O. Box 38 (16912-0038)
PHONE..................................570 638-3322
Neil Hedrick, *President*
James Martin, *Exec VP*
Richard Taylor, *Vice Pres*
Patricia Warren, *Admin Sec*
EMP: 9
SQ FT: 1,000
SALES (est): 775.1K
SALES (corp-wide): 206.6MM **Privately Held**
SIC: 1231 Recovery of anthracite from
culm banks
PA: Robindale Energy Services Inc
1 Lloyd Ave Fl 2
Latrobe PA 15650
814 446-6700

(G-1809)
SEALS OF BLOSSBURG
Also Called: Hill's Creek Truss Co
329 N Williamson Rd (16912-1212)
PHONE..................................570 638-2161
Joseph Searfoss Jr, *Owner*
EMP: 5
SQ FT: 4,500
SALES (est): 589.1K **Privately Held**
SIC: 5211 2439 Millwork & lumber;
trusses, wooden roof

(G-1810)
WARD MANUFACTURING LLC
(DH)
117 Gulick St (16912-1001)
P.O. Box 9 (16912-0009)
PHONE..................................570 638-2131
Eiji Nakano, *CEO*
Ike Campbell, *Vice Pres*
Matt Hirst, *Plant Mgr*
Greg West, *Plant Mgr*
Ken Keller, *Maint Spvr*
▲ EMP: 211
SQ FT: 425,000
SALES (est): 159.9MM
SALES (corp-wide): 87.9B **Privately Held**
WEB: www.wardmfg.com
SIC: 3321 3322 3498 Cast iron pipe & fit-
tings; ductile iron castings; malleable iron
foundries; fabricated pipe & fittings
HQ: Hitachi Metals America, Ltd.
2 Manhattanville Rd # 301
Purchase NY 10577
914 694-9200

Blue Ball
Lancaster County

(G-1811)
M H EBY INC (PA)
Also Called: Mh EBY Trailers
1194 Main St (17506)
P.O. Box 127 (17506-0127)
PHONE..................................800 292-4752
Mennoh EBY Jr, *President*
N Travis EBY, *President*
Nicholas A EBY, *Vice Pres*
Karen L EBY, *Admin Sec*
◆ EMP: 130

SALES: 100MM **Privately Held**
WEB: www.mheby.com
SIC: 3713 5012 Truck bodies (motor vehi-
cles); trailers for trucks, new & used

Blue Bell
Montgomery County

(G-1812)
ADACONN
538 Township Line Rd (19422-2719)
PHONE..................................215 643-1900
Dave Albrecht, *Principal*
EMP: 20
SALES (est): 394.6K **Privately Held**
WEB: www.adaconn.com
SIC: 3511 Turbines & turbine generator
sets

(G-1813)
AXION LLC
610 Sentry Pkwy Ste 220 (19422-2314)
PHONE..................................484 243-6127
EMP: 3 EST: 2015
SALES (est): 223.2K **Privately Held**
SIC: 2421 Railroad ties, sawed

(G-1814)
BANES AND MAYER INC
6198 Butler Pike Ste 225 (19422-2600)
P.O. Box 717, Ambler (19002-0717)
PHONE..................................215 641-1750
Lester R Mayer Jr, *President*
Thomas N Mayer, *Corp Secy*
Lester R Mayer III, *Vice Pres*
EMP: 5 EST: 1913
SQ FT: 1,015
SALES (est): 67.5K **Privately Held**
SIC: 2752 Lithographing on metal

(G-1815)
BAXANO SURGICAL INC (PA)
1301 Skippack Pike Ste 7a (19422-1254)
PHONE..................................919 800-0020
Paul Laviolette, *Ch of Bd*
Ken Reali, *President*
Stephen D Ainsworth, *Vice Pres*
Greg Welsh, *Vice Pres*
Timothy M Shannon, *CFO*
EMP: 21
SQ FT: 12,750
SALES: 18.5MM **Privately Held**
WEB: www.trans1.com
SIC: 3841 Medical instruments & equip-
ment, blood & bone work

(G-1816)
BLACK BOX CORPORATION
540 Township Line Rd (19422-2719)
PHONE..................................215 274-1044
Bruce Logeman, *Engineer*
Ron Iski, *Manager*
EMP: 5
SALES (corp-wide): 1.8MM **Privately Held**
SIC: 3577 Computer peripheral equipment
HQ: Black Box Corporation
1000 Park Dr
Lawrence PA 15055
724 746-5500

(G-1817)
BLUE BELL PRINT SOLUTIONS
1018 Hickory Dr (19422-1519)
PHONE..................................215 591-3903
Toby Brackin, *Owner*
EMP: 3
SALES (est): 176.2K **Privately Held**
SIC: 2752 Commercial printing, offset

(G-1818)
BTI OF AMERICA LLC
Also Called: Bti of North America
1730 Walton Rd Ste 110 (19422-2301)
PHONE..................................215 646-4067
Christine Louise Battilana, *Mng Member*
Christine Battilana, *Mng Member*
▲ EMP: 4
SQ FT: 12,000
SALES (est): 972K **Privately Held**
SIC: 3843 Dental equipment

(G-1819)
C&D INTRNTNAL INV HOLDINGS
INC (HQ)
1400 Union Meeting Rd (19422-1952)
PHONE..................................215 619-2700
Jeffrey Graes PHD, *President*
EMP: 6
SALES (est): 2.5MM
SALES (corp-wide): 680.2MM **Privately
Held**
SIC: 3629 Battery chargers, rectifying or
nonrotating
PA: C&D Technologies, Inc.
1400 Union Meeting Rd # 110
Blue Bell PA 19422
215 619-2700

(G-1820)
C&D TECHNOLOGIES INC (PA)
1400 Union Meeting Rd # 110
(19422-1952)
PHONE..................................215 619-2700
Armand F Lauzon Jr, *President*
Oscar Ayala, *General Mgr*
Justin Hu, *Vice Pres*
Roger Keirn, *Plant Mgr*
Joe Desutter, *Mfg Mgr*
◆ EMP: 120
SQ FT: 48,000
SALES (est): 680.2MM **Privately Held**
WEB: www.cdtechno.com
SIC: 3691 3613 3692 3674 Lead acid
batteries (storage batteries); panel & dis-
tribution boards & other related appara-
tus; primary batteries, dry & wet;
semiconductors & related devices; recti-
fier transformers

(G-1821)
COMMUNICATION GRAPHICS
INC
1787 Sentry Pkwy W # 240 (19422-2239)
PHONE..................................215 646-2225
Douglas M Webster, *President*
Joseph E Grande, *Vice Pres*
EMP: 10
SQ FT: 1,200
SALES (est): 1.2MM **Privately Held**
WEB: www.comgraphics.com
SIC: 2752 Commercial printing, offset

(G-1822)
COMMUNICATION SVCS &
SUPPORT
Also Called: CSS
850 Pnllyn Blue Bell Pike (19422-1648)
PHONE..................................215 540-5888
Frank Cymbala, *President*
EMP: 3
SQ FT: 3,000
SALES (est): 325.1K **Privately Held**
SIC: 2752 Commercial printing, offset

(G-1823)
COMPUTERTALK ASSOCIATES
INC
Also Called: Computer Talk Associates
492 Norristown Rd Ste 160 (19422-2339)
PHONE..................................610 825-7686
William A Lockwood III, *President*
Tony Molinaro, *Principal*
Margaret L Lockwood, *Vice Pres*
EMP: 4
SQ FT: 1,500
SALES (est): 417K **Privately Held**
WEB: www.computertalk.com
SIC: 2721 7379 Magazines: publishing
only, not printed on site; computer related
consulting services

(G-1824)
CRAFTEX MILLS INC
PENNSYLVANIA
Also Called: Craftex By Victor
450 Sentry Pkwy E (19422-2319)
PHONE..................................610 941-1212
Robert M Blum, *President*
Robert J Proske, *CFO*
▲ EMP: 40 EST: 1903
SQ FT: 13,200

SALES (est): 5.3MM **Privately Held**
WEB: www.craftex.com
SIC: 2211 2231 2221 Cotton broad
woven goods; wool broadwoven fabrics;
nylon broadwoven fabrics; polyester
broadwoven fabrics

(G-1825)
DAHILL BOTTLING COMPANY
INC
135 Belle Cir (19422-1438)
PHONE..................................215 699-6432
David E Hillhouse, *Principal*
EMP: 5
SALES (est): 274.1K **Privately Held**
SIC: 2086 Bottled & canned soft drinks

(G-1826)
DAWN EVENING INC
1410 Cortez Rd (19422-3670)
PHONE..................................610 272-0518
George A Shal, *President*
EMP: 4 EST: 1992
SALES (est): 201.1K **Privately Held**
WEB: www.eveningdawn.com
SIC: 2731 Book music: publishing only, not
printed on site

(G-1827)
DOCTOR IN THE HOUSE INC
1515 Dekalb Pike Ste 204 (19422-3367)
PHONE..................................610 277-1998
Scott M Fried, *President*
▲ EMP: 6
SALES (est): 378.8K **Privately Held**
SIC: 3841 Surgical & medical instruments

(G-1828)
E W YOST CO
340 N Wales Rd (19422-1324)
PHONE..................................215 699-4868
Edward W Yost, *President*
Patrick Yost, *Vice Pres*
Keith Bauer, *Purch Dir*
EMP: 11
SQ FT: 10,000
SALES (est): 2.2MM **Privately Held**
SIC: 3489 Ordnance & accessories

(G-1829)
FIBERLINK COMMUNICATIONS
CORP (HQ)
1787 Sentry Pkwy W # 200 (19422-2213)
PHONE..................................215 664-1600
James Sheward, *CEO*
Chris Clark, *President*
Steve Hammond, *President*
Christopher Clark, *COO*
Mark Parin, *CFO*
EMP: 140
SQ FT: 38,593
SALES (est): 52.2MM
SALES (corp-wide): 79.5B **Publicly Held**
WEB: www.fiberlink.com
SIC: 7372 Prepackaged software
PA: International Business Machines Cor-
poration
1 New Orchard Rd Ste 1 # 1
Armonk NY 10504
914 499-1900

(G-1830)
GKLD CORP (PA)
794 Pnllyn Blue Bell Pike (19422-1669)
PHONE..................................215 643-6950
Gus Monastero, *President*
Donald Fields, *Vice Pres*
Keith Harper, *CFO*
Louis Monastero, *Treasurer*
EMP: 8
SQ FT: 43,000
SALES (est): 5.8MM **Privately Held**
WEB: www.polyphaseinstrument.com
SIC: 3677 Transformers power supply,
electronic type; filtration devices, elec-
tronic

(G-1831)
GS FUEL INC
1399 Skippack Pike (19422-1248)
PHONE..................................484 751-5414
EMP: 3
SALES (est): 158.8K **Privately Held**
SIC: 2869 Fuels

(G-1832)
H & M NET WORKS
3 Valley Sq Ste 200 (19422-2718)
PHONE..................................484 344-2161
Mark Lehman, *Vice Pres*
EMP: 10 EST: 2013
SALES (est): 1.5MM **Privately Held**
SIC: 3674 Integrated circuits, semiconductor networks, etc.

(G-1833)
HERB & LOUS LLC
1710 Walton Rd Ste 207 (19422-2304)
PHONE..................................267 626-7913
EMP: 6
SALES (est): 121.5K **Privately Held**
SIC: 2026 Eggnog, fresh: non-alcoholic

(G-1834)
HIGHWAY MATERIALS INC
T.D.P.S. Materials
3870 N 2nd St (19422)
PHONE..................................215 225-7020
Anthony Paul, *Branch Mgr*
EMP: 6
SALES (corp-wide): 10.1MM **Privately Held**
SIC: 2951 Road materials, bituminous (not from refineries)
PA: Highway Materials, Inc.
   409 Stenton Ave
   Flourtown PA 19031
   610 832-8000

(G-1835)
INSERTA PRODUCTS INC
534 Township Line Rd (19422-2710)
PHONE..................................215 643-0192
David Albrecht, *President*
EMP: 20
SQ FT: 20,000
SALES (est): 1.3MM **Privately Held**
WEB: www.inserta.com
SIC: 3599 5084 Machine shop, jobbing & repair; industrial machinery & equipment

(G-1836)
INTEGRTED PRODUCTIVITY SYSTEMS
Also Called: Ipsi
1037 Hickory Dr (19422-1518)
P.O. Box 97 (19422-0097)
PHONE..................................215 646-1374
Joe McAluney, *President*
Joseph McAulney, *President*
William Barnhart, *Vice Pres*
EMP: 4
SQ FT: 1,000
SALES (est): 1MM **Privately Held**
WEB: www.ipsiscan.com
SIC: 3695 3577 Computer software tape & disks: blank, rigid & floppy; optical scanning devices

(G-1837)
JOSEPH NEDOREZOV (PA)
Also Called: Welding Technologies
1365 Horseshoe Dr (19422-1857)
PHONE..................................610 278-9325
Joseph Nedorezov, *Owner*
EMP: 5
SALES (est): 456.5K **Privately Held**
WEB: www.weldingnet.com
SIC: 3548 8748 Welding apparatus; business consulting

(G-1838)
JPA PRINTING
1716 Glenn Ln (19422)
PHONE..................................610 270-8855
Joseph Cummings, *Partner*
EMP: 3
SALES (est): 158.7K **Privately Held**
SIC: 2752 Commercial printing, lithographic

(G-1839)
KAPPA BOOKS PUBLISHERS LLC
6198 Butler Pike Ste 200 (19422-2606)
PHONE..................................215 643-6385
Nicholas G Karabots, *Ch of Bd*
Despina McNultey, *President*
EMP: 4
SQ FT: 500

SALES (est): 300K **Privately Held**
SIC: 2721 Magazines: publishing only, not printed on site

(G-1840)
KAPPA GRAPHICS L P
Also Called: Kappa Books
6198 Butler Pike Ste 200 (19422-2606)
PHONE..................................215 542-2800
Nick Karabots, *Manager*
EMP: 12
SALES (est): 1.2MM **Privately Held**
SIC: 2732 Books: printing only
PA: Kappa Graphics, L. P.
   50 Rock St
   Hughestown PA 18640

(G-1841)
KAPPA MAP GROUP LLC (HQ)
6198 Butler Pike (19422-2600)
PHONE..................................215 643-5800
Scott Horner,
Tom Breslin,
EMP: 2
SALES (est): 10.5MM
SALES (corp-wide): 149.5MM **Privately Held**
SIC: 2741 Maps: publishing only, not printed on site
PA: Kappa Media Group, Inc.
   40 Skippack Pike
   Fort Washington PA 19034
   215 643-5800

(G-1842)
KAPPA PUBLISHING GROUP INC (PA)
6198 Butler Pike Ste 200 (19422-2606)
P.O. Box 750, Fort Washington (19034-0750)
PHONE..................................215 643-6385
Nick Karabots, *Ch of Bd*
Dames Hindley, *Vice Pres*
Despina McNulty, *Vice Pres*
Bill Siebert, *CFO*
William Mainwaring, *Treasurer*
EMP: 71
SQ FT: 24,000
SALES (est): 15.3MM **Privately Held**
WEB: www.kappapublishinggroup.com
SIC: 2721 2741 2759 Magazines: publishing only, not printed on site; miscellaneous publishing; publication printing

(G-1843)
KAPPA PUBLISHING GROUP INC
Jbh Publishing Div
6198 Butler Pike Ste 200 (19422-2606)
P.O. Box 750, Fort Washington (19034-0750)
PHONE..................................215 643-6385
Nick Karabots, *Ch of Bd*
EMP: 50
SALES (corp-wide): 15.3MM **Privately Held**
WEB: www.kappapublishinggroup.com
SIC: 2721 Magazines: publishing only, not printed on site
PA: Kappa Publishing Group, Inc.
   6198 Butler Pike Ste 200
   Blue Bell PA 19422
   215 643-6385

(G-1844)
LINDE ENGINEERING N AMER INC
Selas Linde North America
5 Sentry Pkwy E Ste 300 (19422-2312)
PHONE..................................610 834-0300
Andreas Seliger, *General Mgr*
John Oakley, *Engineer*
Jared Remster, *Engineer*
Paul Van Helmond, *Engineer*
Matthew Christopher, *Manager*
EMP: 40
SALES (corp-wide): 1.4B **Privately Held**
SIC: 3567 Industrial furnaces & ovens
HQ: Linde Engineering North America Inc.
   12140 Wickchester Ln
   Houston TX 77079
   918 477-1200

(G-1845)
LOCUS PHARMACEUTICALS INC (PA)
512 Township Line Rd (19422-2700)
PHONE..................................215 358-2000
Jamie Freedman, *President*
Robert Dickey IV, *CFO*
Donald W Kufe, *Oncology*
Daniel D Von Hoff, *Oncology*
EMP: 65
SALES (est): 3.5MM **Privately Held**
WEB: www.locuspharma.com
SIC: 2834 Pills, pharmaceutical

(G-1846)
MAM SOFTWARE INC
512 Township Line Rd # 220 (19422-2700)
PHONE..................................610 336-9045
Brian Callahan, *President*
Brian Allibon, *President*
Dan Klinge, *Engineer*
Brian Schobel, *Controller*
John Nehez, *Natl Sales Mgr*
EMP: 52
SALES (est): 7.6MM
SALES (corp-wide): 22.7MM **Privately Held**
SIC: 7372 Prepackaged software
PA: Mam Software Limited
   15 Duncan Close
   Northampton NORTHANTS NN3 6
   160 449-4001

(G-1847)
MERCK SHARP & DOHME CORP
10 Sentry Pkwy (19422-2331)
PHONE..................................484 344-2493
Christine Furtek, *Branch Mgr*
Randolph Leinhauser, *Director*
EMP: 500
SALES (corp-wide): 42.2B **Publicly Held**
SIC: 2834 Pharmaceutical preparations
HQ: Merck Sharp & Dohme Corp.
   2000 Galloping Hill Rd
   Kenilworth NJ 07033
   908 740-4000

(G-1848)
MID-ATLNTIC BLDG SOLUTIONS LLC
650 Sentry Pkwy Ste 1 (19422-2318)
PHONE..................................484 532-7269
Bob Falasco, *Mng Member*
EMP: 4
SQ FT: 2,000
SALES (est): 499.3K **Privately Held**
SIC: 3589 Commercial cleaning equipment

(G-1849)
MOLD 911 LLC
635 Wyndrise Dr (19422-2902)
PHONE..................................267 312-1432
EMP: 3
SALES (est): 226.1K **Privately Held**
SIC: 3544 Industrial molds

(G-1850)
NOVATIVE DESIGNS INC
275 Norristown Rd (19422-2805)
PHONE..................................215 794-3380
Darryl E Berlinger, *President*
▲ **EMP:** 4
SQ FT: 5,500
SALES (est): 616.3K **Privately Held**
WEB: www.novativedesigns.com
SIC: 3546 Power-driven handtools

(G-1851)
NOVUS X-RAY LLC (HQ)
726 Boehms Church Rd (19422-1719)
PHONE..................................215 962-3171
David Diprato, *CEO*
Michael J McGraw, *CFO*
EMP: 10
SQ FT: 6,800
SALES (est): 2.4MM **Publicly Held**
SIC: 3844 X-ray apparatus & tubes

(G-1852)
SIEMENS INDUSTRY INC
1450 Union Meeting Rd (19422-1920)
PHONE..................................215 654-8040
Eric Lamb, *Project Mgr*
Dave Stephenson, *Opers Spvr*
Ryan Barth, *Finance*

Mark Nicholson, *Accounts Exec*
Peter Tubolino, *Manager*
EMP: 80
SALES (corp-wide): 95B **Privately Held**
WEB: www.sibt.com
SIC: 3822 7382 1711 Auto controls regulating residntl & coml environmt & applncs; security systems services; plumbing, heating, air-conditioning contractors
HQ: Siemens Industry, Inc.
   1000 Deerfield Pkwy
   Buffalo Grove IL 60089
   800 743-6367

(G-1853)
SUNBELT DRILLING SERVICES INC
651 E Township Line Rd # 1345 (19422-5115)
PHONE..................................215 764-9544
Justin Godell, *CEO*
Walter Rusinski, *COO*
Romeo Cosica, *Admin Sec*
EMP: 13
SQ FT: 1,300
SALES: 125K **Privately Held**
SIC: 1623 1389 8711 Water, sewer & utility lines; building oil & gas well foundations on site; construction & civil engineering

(G-1854)
SWEETZELS FOODS LLC
1166 Dekalb Pike (19422-1844)
P.O. Box 549 (19422-0549)
PHONE..................................610 278-8700
Robert Borzillo, *President*
EMP: 4
SALES (est): 475.3K **Privately Held**
SIC: 2052 Cookies

(G-1855)
TASTY FRIES INC
Also Called: (DEVELOPMENT STAGE COMPANY)
650 Sentry Pkwy Ste 1 (19422-2318)
PHONE..................................610 941-2109
Edward C Kelly, *President*
Leonard J Klarich, *Admin Sec*
EMP: 4
SQ FT: 1,400
SALES (est): 178.9K **Privately Held**
WEB: www.tastyfries.com
SIC: 5812 3581 Eating Place Mfg Vending Machines

(G-1856)
VIRAL GENOMIX INC
Also Called: Vgx Pharmaceuticals
450 Sentry Pkwy E (19422-2319)
PHONE..................................267 440-4200
Joseph Kim, *President*
Ernest E Shin, *COO*
Young K Park, *Vice Pres*
Kevin W Rassas, *Vice Pres*
Jo White, *Chief Mktg Ofcr*
EMP: 12
SALES (est): 1.6MM **Privately Held**
WEB: www.viralgenomix.com
SIC: 2834 Druggists' preparations (pharmaceuticals)

(G-1857)
WEIDENHAMMER SYSTEMS CORP
1787 Sentry Pkwy W 305 (19422-2239)
PHONE..................................610 687-0037
Rick Finley, *General Mgr*
Jody Pillard, *Accounts Mgr*
Tom Gorley, *Manager*
Robert Campling, *Technology*
Paul Roche, *Programmer Anys*
EMP: 20
SALES (corp-wide): 40MM **Privately Held**
WEB: www.hammer.net
SIC: 7372 7379 Prepackaged software;
PA: Weidenhammer Systems Corp
   935 Berkshire Blvd
   Reading PA 19610
   610 378-1149

GEOGRAPHIC

(G-1858)
YELLOW PAGES GROUP LLC
Also Called: Your Community Phonebook
1 Sentry Pkwy E Ste 7000 (19422-2310)
PHONE..................................610 825-7720
EMP: 24
SALES (est): 3.4MM **Privately Held**
SIC: 2741 Misc Publishing

Blue Ridge Summit
Franklin County

(G-1859)
ROWMAN & LITTLEFIELD PUBLISH
15200 Nbn Way (17214-9735)
P.O. Box 190 (17214-0190)
PHONE..................................717 794-3800
Robert Marsh, *COO*
EMP: 400
SALES (corp-wide): 293.8MM **Privately Held**
SIC: 2731 Books: publishing only
PA: The Rowman & Littlefield Publishing Group Inc
4501 Forbes Blvd Ste 200
Lanham MD 20706
301 459-3366

(G-1860)
ROWMAN & LITTLEFIELD PUBLS INC
15200 Nbn Way (17214-9735)
PHONE..................................717 794-3800
Melissa Kay, *Branch Mgr*
EMP: 11
SALES (corp-wide): 293.8MM **Privately Held**
WEB: www.rlpgbooks.com
SIC: 2731 Textbooks: publishing only, not printed on site
HQ: Rowman & Littlefield Publishers, Inc.
4501 Forbes Blvd Ste 200
Lanham MD 20706
301 459-3366

(G-1861)
SPECIALTY GRANULES INC
Also Called: Isp Minerals
1455 Old Waynesboro Rd (17214)
PHONE..................................717 794-2184
Michael Shelbert, *Manager*
EMP: 120
SALES (corp-wide): 86.2MM **Privately Held**
WEB: www.ispcorp.com
SIC: 3295 Roofing granules
PA: Specialty Granules Llc
13424 Pa Ave Ste 303
Hagerstown MD 21742
301 733-4000

(G-1862)
STACKPOLE INC
Also Called: Wildfowl Carving & Collecting
15200 Nbn Way (17214-9735)
PHONE..................................717 796-0411
M David Detweiler, *President*
Anne Lodge-Smith, *Vice Pres*
▲ EMP: 40 EST: 1932
SQ FT: 26,000
SALES (est): 4.8MM **Privately Held**
SIC: 2731 Books: publishing & printing

Boalsburg
Centre County

(G-1863)
ABL ENGINEERING
227 W Main St (16827-1350)
PHONE..................................814 364-1333
EMP: 3
SALES (est): 168.5K **Privately Held**
SIC: 3825 Mfg Electrical Measuring Instruments

(G-1864)
BLUE SPIN LLC
1120 Kay St (16827-1630)
PHONE..................................814 863-4630

Corey Cochrane, *Mng Member*
Patrick Lenahan,
EMP: 3
SALES (est): 153.1K **Privately Held**
SIC: 3821 Physics laboratory apparatus

(G-1865)
COLONIAL PRESS LLC
500 Torrey Ln (16827-1547)
PHONE..................................814 466-3380
Glenn Dry, *Mng Member*
Chris Dry,
Stephanie Dry,
EMP: 9
SQ FT: 3,000
SALES: 1.1MM **Privately Held**
SIC: 2752 Commercial printing, lithographic

(G-1866)
CPI LOCUS MICROWAVE INC
176 Technology Dr Ste 200 (16827-1758)
PHONE..................................814 466-6275
Robert Fickett, *President*
Scott Smithmyer, *Engineer*
EMP: 27
SALES (est): 4MM **Privately Held**
WEB: www.locusmicrowave.com
SIC: 3663 Microwave communication equipment
HQ: Communications & Power Industries Llc
607 Hansen Way
Palo Alto CA 94304

(G-1867)
HANSON AGGREGATES PA LLC
850 Boalsburg Rd (16827-1001)
PHONE..................................814 466-5101
David Rider, *Manager*
EMP: 19
SALES (corp-wide): 20.6B **Privately Held**
SIC: 1442 1422 Common sand mining; crushed & broken limestone
HQ: Hanson Aggregates Pennsylvania, Llc
7660 Imperial Way
Allentown PA 18195
610 366-4626

(G-1868)
PRB MFG REPRESENTATIVES
436 Bailey Ln (16827-1315)
PHONE..................................814 466-2161
EMP: 3 EST: 2010
SALES (est): 140K **Privately Held**
SIC: 3999 Mfg Misc Products

(G-1869)
SENSOR NETWORKS INC
176 Technology Dr Ste 500 (16827-1759)
PHONE..................................814 466-7207
James Barshinger, *President*
Jeffrey Anderson, *General Mgr*
Bruce Pellegrino, *Director*
EMP: 20 EST: 2014
SQ FT: 1,800
SALES: 5MM **Privately Held**
SIC: 3829 3699 Ultrasonic testing equipment; generators, ultrasonic

(G-1870)
SENSOR NETWORKS INC
171 Technology Dr Ste 500 (16827-1683)
PHONE..................................814 441-2476
Bruce Pellegrino, *Ch of Bd*
James Barshinger, *President*
Jeffrey Anderson, *Vice Pres*
Tim Ray, *Admin Sec*
EMP: 4 EST: 2016
SQ FT: 1,800
SALES (est): 197K **Privately Held**
SIC: 3829 Ultrasonic testing equipment

(G-1871)
SENSOR NETWORKS CORPORATION
171 Technology Dr Ste 500 (16827-1683)
PHONE..................................717 466-7207
Bruce Pellegrino, *Ch of Bd*
James Barshinger, *President*
EMP: 5 EST: 2014
SALES (est): 319.1K **Privately Held**
SIC: 3829 Measuring & controlling devices

Boiling Springs
Cumberland County

(G-1872)
CHIMNEYS VIOLIN SHOP
614 Lerew Rd Fl 2 (17007-9500)
PHONE..................................717 258-3203
Edward C Campbell, *Partner*
Mary Campbell, *Partner*
EMP: 4
SQ FT: 3,600
SALES (est): 506.7K **Privately Held**
WEB: www.thechimneysviolinshop.com
SIC: 3931 5736 Violins & parts; musical instrument stores

(G-1873)
COLUCCI AND CO
200 S Ridge Rd (17007-9562)
PHONE..................................717 243-5562
Melissa Colucci, *Principal*
EMP: 3
SALES (est): 449.5K **Privately Held**
SIC: 3911 Jewelry mountings & trimmings

(G-1874)
KEYSTONE COATING LLC
419 Glenn Ave (17007-9528)
PHONE..................................717 440-5922
Alex Daniel, *Principal*
EMP: 3 EST: 2017
SALES (est): 140.6K **Privately Held**
SIC: 3471 Plating & polishing

Boothwyn
Delaware County

(G-1875)
ALLOY SURFACES COMPANY INC
151 Garnet Mine Rd (19060)
PHONE..................................610 558-7100
Elaine Soltani, *Principal*
EMP: 50
SALES (corp-wide): 734.6MM **Privately Held**
SIC: 3489 Ordnance & accessories
HQ: Alloy Surfaces Company, Inc.
121 N Commerce Dr
Chester PA 19014
610 497-7979

(G-1876)
BRENDAN G STOVER PRINTING
1460 Garnet Mine Rd (19060-2112)
PHONE..................................610 459-2851
Brendan G Stover, *Owner*
EMP: 3
SALES: 250K **Privately Held**
SIC: 2752 Commercial printing, offset

(G-1877)
EATON CORPORATION
7 Chelsea Pkwy Ste 700 (19061-1300)
PHONE..................................610 497-6100
Brigid Falasca, *Sales Engr*
Jerry Nuernebreger, *Manager*
EMP: 40 **Privately Held**
WEB: www.eaton.com
SIC: 5063 3613 Electrical apparatus & equipment; switchgear & switchboard apparatus
HQ: Eaton Corporation
1000 Eaton Blvd
Cleveland OH 44122
440 523-5000

(G-1878)
LIGHTNING GAMING INC (PA)
23 Creek Cir Ste 400 (19061-3151)
PHONE..................................610 494-5534
Brian Haveson, *Ch of Bd*
Christopher Strano, *President*
Adam Parkes, *Art Dir*
EMP: 16
SQ FT: 11,566
SALES: 5.6MM **Privately Held**
SIC: 3999 Coin-operated amusement machines, slot machines

(G-1879)
MCKINLEY BLACKSMITH LIMITED
2011 Foulk Rd (19060-1317)
PHONE..................................610 459-2730
James McKinley Sr, *President*
James W Mc Kinley Jr, *Treasurer*
EMP: 4
SQ FT: 3,200
SALES (est): 372.9K **Privately Held**
SIC: 7692 3441 Welding repair; fabricated structural metal

(G-1880)
QUOTIENT SCIENCES - PHILA
3 Chelsea Pkwy Ste 305 (19061-1341)
PHONE..................................610 485-4270
Mark Egerton, *President*
Nutan Gangrade, *Managing Dir*
Bethanne Lee, *Business Mgr*
Naga A Palivela, *Research*
Gordon Cameron, *Admin Sec*
EMP: 125
SQ FT: 43,000
SALES (est): 53.7MM
SALES (corp-wide): 466.7K **Privately Held**
WEB: www.qspharma.com
SIC: 2834 Pharmaceutical preparations
HQ: Quotient Sciences Limited
Mere Way
Nottingham NOTTS NG11

Boswell
Somerset County

(G-1881)
BOSWELL LUMBER COMPANY
4904 Penn Ave (15531-4004)
PHONE..................................814 629-5625
Dennis Neri, *President*
Douglas Damico, *Vice Pres*
EMP: 22 EST: 1909
SQ FT: 32,000
SALES: 2MM **Privately Held**
WEB: www.shorttreeproducts.com
SIC: 2431 2426 2421 Millwork; hardwood dimension & flooring mills; sawmills & planing mills, general

(G-1882)
HERITAGE WOOD PRODUCTS LLC
216 Pelesky Rd (15531-2704)
PHONE..................................814 629-9265
John D Pelesky,
EMP: 3 EST: 2007
SALES: 120K **Privately Held**
SIC: 2426 Hardwood dimension & flooring mills

(G-1883)
HORNER LUMBER COMPANY
764 N Fork Dam Rd (15531-1823)
PHONE..................................814 629-5861
Harvey Horner Jr, *Partner*
Kenneth Horner Sr, *Partner*
EMP: 5
SALES (est): 467.6K **Privately Held**
SIC: 2421 5211 Sawmills & planing mills, general; planing mill products & lumber

(G-1884)
LAUREL RIDGE RESAWING
561 N Fork Dam Rd (15531-1820)
PHONE..................................814 629-5026
EMP: 3
SALES (est): 201.8K **Privately Held**
SIC: 2653 Mfg Corrugated/Solid Fiber Boxes

(G-1885)
TOTAL MOBILITY SERVICES INC (PA)
4785 Penn Ave (15531-4000)
P.O. Box 7 (15531-0007)
PHONE..................................814 629-9935
Raymond D Dallape Jr, *President*
EMP: 7
SQ FT: 12,500

▲ = Import ▼=Export
◆ =Import/Export

SALES (est): 1MM Privately Held
WEB: www.totalmobilityservices.com
SIC: 7532 3999 7539 7538 Van conversion; wheelchair lifts; trailer repair; recreational vehicle repairs; recreational vehicle parts & accessories; automotive accessories

Bowmansville
Lancaster County

(G-1886)
ALPHA ADVERTISING & MKTG LLC
1268 Reading Rd (17507)
P.O. Box 407 (17507-0407)
PHONE...................................717 445-4200
EMP: 4
SALES: 450K Privately Held
SIC: 8742 2759 3999 Management Consulting Services Commercial Printing Mfg Misc Products

(G-1887)
HARTINGS BAKERY INC
Also Called: Country Maid Bakery Foods
1212 Reading Rd Rr 625 (17507)
PHONE...................................717 445-5644
Jere Heft, *President*
Jocelyn Heft, *Chairman*
Thomas Lesher, *Vice Pres*
William Burkhart, *Treasurer*
Susan Burkhart, *Admin Sec*
EMP: 32 **EST:** 1940
SQ FT: 8,000
SALES (est): 4.2MM Privately Held
WEB: www.hartingscountrymaidbky.com
SIC: 2051 Bakery products, partially cooked (except frozen); pies, bakery: except frozen; cakes, bakery: except frozen; rolls, sweet: except frozen

(G-1888)
UNCLE HENRYS PRETZEL BAKERY
Also Called: Uncle Henrys Handmade Pretzels
1550 Bowmansville Rd (17507)
P.O. Box 219 (17507-0219)
PHONE...................................717 445-4698
A Timothy Martin, *Owner*
EMP: 35
SQ FT: 6,000
SALES (est): 3.1MM Privately Held
WEB: www.unclehenry.com
SIC: 2052 2099 Pretzels; food preparations

Boyers
Butler County

(G-1889)
LOUIS EMMEL CO
821 Branchton Rd (16020-1201)
PHONE...................................412 859-6781
Ronald Koller, *Owner*
EMP: 5
SALES (est): 330K Privately Held
SIC: 3446 Ornamental metalwork

(G-1890)
SONY MUSIC HOLDINGS INC
1137 Branchton Rd (16016-0001)
PHONE...................................724 794-8500
Strauss Zelnick, *President*
EMP: 40
SALES (corp-wide): 80.1B Privately Held
WEB: www.bmgentertainment.com
SIC: 3652 4226 Pre-recorded records & tapes; special warehousing & storage
HQ: Sony Music Holdings Inc.
    25 Madison Ave Fl 26
    New York NY 10010
    212 833-8000

(G-1891)
TALL OAK ENERGY INC
317 W Tall Oak Ln (16020-2214)
PHONE...................................724 636-0621
Mark Alexander, *CEO*

Rebel Alexander, *Co-Owner*
EMP: 4
SALES (est): 126.7K Privately Held
SIC: 1311 Crude petroleum & natural gas

Boyertown
Berks County

(G-1892)
A W MERCER INC
104 Industrial Dr (19512)
PHONE...................................610 367-8460
Jack Meade, *President*
James F Meade, *President*
John Meade, *President*
Thomas A Meade Sr, *Vice Pres*
Marty Erb, *Production*
EMP: 130
SQ FT: 63,400
SALES (est): 30MM
SALES (corp-wide): 60.3MM Privately Held
WEB: www.awmercer.com
SIC: 3444 3644 3469 3433 Sheet metalwork; noncurrent-carrying wiring services; metal stampings; heating equipment, except electric; partitions & fixtures, except wood
PA: Vari Corporation
    155 Route 61 S
    Schuylkill Haven PA 17972
    570 385-0731

(G-1893)
ADVANCED TECHNICAL PEDDLER INC
Also Called: Atp Associates
112 Edgewood Rd (19512-8173)
PHONE...................................610 689-4017
Peter P Iannelli, *President*
EMP: 4
SALES (est): 325.1K Privately Held
SIC: 7379 1711 3822 Computer related consulting services; plumbing, heating, air-conditioning contractors; hydronic pressure or temperature controls

(G-1894)
ADVANCED THERMAL HYDRONICS
Also Called: Hydrotherm
203 W Spring St (19512-1099)
P.O. Box 443, New Berlinville (19545-0443)
PHONE...................................610 473-1036
Rick Riggs, *President*
Terry Essig, *Plant Mgr*
EMP: 14 **EST:** 2007
SALES (est): 2.6MM Privately Held
SIC: 3443 5074 Boiler & boiler shop work; boilers, power (industrial)

(G-1895)
ALBRIGHT PAPER & BOX CORP
198 Popodickon Dr (19512-2041)
PHONE...................................484 524-8424
Gary Gross, *President*
Ruth Gross, *Corp Secy*
EMP: 5
SQ FT: 14,000
SALES (est): 660.8K Privately Held
SIC: 2652 5113 Filing boxes, paperboard: made from purchased materials; boxes & containers

(G-1896)
ALLOY DESIGN INC
320 Old State Rd (19512-9078)
PHONE...................................610 369-9265
William W Stone, *CEO*
Wendy Stevens, *Vice Pres*
EMP: 3
SALES: 500K Privately Held
WEB: www.wendystevens.com
SIC: 3441 Fabricated structural metal

(G-1897)
APEX FABRICATION & DESIGN INC
7938 Boyertown Pike (19512-8144)
PHONE...................................610 689-5880
Jim Smith, *CEO*
Steve Mohler, *Project Mgr*
Amanda James, *Office Mgr*

EMP: 42
SALES (est): 9.5MM Privately Held
SIC: 3441 Fabricated structural metal

(G-1898)
BERK INTERNATIONAL LLC
Also Called: Berk Wiper Converting & Packg
400 E 2nd St (19512-1603)
PHONE...................................610 369-0600
Larry Berk, *CEO*
Jill Blatstein, *General Mgr*
Joe Rhodes, *Accounts Exec*
Jeff Berk,
◆ **EMP:** 100
SQ FT: 170,000
SALES (est): 33.1MM Privately Held
SIC: 2676 Towels, paper: made from purchased paper

(G-1899)
BOYERTOWN FOUNDRY COMPANY
9th St & Rothermel Dr (19512)
P.O. Box 443, New Berlinville (19545-0443)
PHONE...................................610 473-1000
Richard Riggs, *President*
Stephen M Shea, *Vice Pres*
Steven F Olearcek, *Admin Sec*
▲ **EMP:** 147 **EST:** 1998
SQ FT: 2,069
SALES (est): 24.1MM
SALES (corp-wide): 669.8MM Privately Held
SIC: 3433 Boilers, low-pressure heating: steam or hot water
PA: Mestek, Inc.
    260 N Elm St
    Westfield MA 01085
    413 568-9571

(G-1900)
BOYERTOWN FURNACE COMPANY
156 Holly Rd (19512)
P.O. Box 100 (19512-0100)
PHONE...................................610 369-1450
Thomas A Meade Sr, *President*
Thomas Meade Sr, *President*
James F Meade, *Corp Secy*
EMP: 27
SQ FT: 46,000
SALES (est): 5.5MM Privately Held
WEB: www.boyertownfurnace.com
SIC: 3567 3433 Metal melting furnaces, industrial: fuel-fired; heating equipment, except electric

(G-1901)
BOYERTOWN LABEL CO
1252 Montgomery Ave (19512-8439)
PHONE...................................800 260-4934
Steven George, *Owner*
EMP: 5
SQ FT: 2,000
SALES (est): 460K Privately Held
WEB: www.label6.com
SIC: 2672 Labels (unprinted), gummed: made from purchased materials

(G-1902)
C S GARBER & SONS INC
7928 Boyertown Pike (19512-8144)
PHONE...................................610 367-2861
Dennis H Stoudt, *President*
Eric G Hafer, *Corp Secy*
George A Parke, *Vice Pres*
Elaine Marmer, *Office Mgr*
EMP: 40 **EST:** 1929
SQ FT: 1,320
SALES (est): 7.3MM Privately Held
SIC: 1481 1781 7699 5999 Mine & quarry services, nonmetallic minerals; water well drilling; pumps & pumping equipment repair; water purification equipment

(G-1903)
CAMPBELL FITTINGS INC (PA)
301 S Washington St (19512-1533)
P.O. Box 417 (19512-0417)
PHONE...................................610 367-6916
Thomas J Paff, *President*
Joe McGlynn, *Exec VP*
Gene Wentzel, *Opers Mgr*
Jarid Miller, *Production*
Randi Kremer, *Engineer*

▲ **EMP:** 35 **EST:** 1945
SQ FT: 150,000
SALES (est): 19.8MM Privately Held
WEB: www.campbellfittings.com
SIC: 3494 Pipe fittings; couplings, except pressure & soil pipe

(G-1904)
CONSTRUCTION ON SITE WELDING
945 N Reading Ave (19512-8950)
PHONE...................................610 367-1895
Kim Halterman, *Owner*
EMP: 3
SALES: 178K Privately Held
SIC: 7692 Welding repair

(G-1905)
COOPERS
813 S Reading Ave Bldg C (19512-2060)
PHONE...................................610 369-8992
William Cooper, *Owner*
Dawn Cooper, *Co-Owner*
EMP: 8
SALES (est): 959.7K Privately Held
SIC: 3444 1721 Bins, prefabricated sheet metal; painting & paper hanging

(G-1906)
DICES CREATIVE CAKES
30 N Reading Ave (19512-1038)
PHONE...................................610 367-0107
Mary Dice, *Owner*
EMP: 3
SALES (est): 107K Privately Held
SIC: 5461 2053 Cakes; cakes, bakery: frozen

(G-1907)
DRUG PLASTICS AND GLASS CO (HQ)
1 Bottle Dr (19512-8623)
P.O. Box 797 (19512-0797)
PHONE...................................610 367-5000
Frederick N Biesecker II, *CEO*
Suzanne K Biesecker, *Corp Secy*
Lissa Longacre, *Vice Pres*
Fred Miller, *Vice Pres*
Joseph Asterino, *VP Finance*
EMP: 6
SQ FT: 39,000
SALES (est): 11.8MM
SALES (corp-wide): 166.9MM Privately Held
SIC: 3089 Caps, plastic
PA: Drug Plastics And Glass Company, Inc.
    1 Bottle Dr
    Boyertown PA 19512
    610 367-5000

(G-1908)
DRUG PLASTICS CLOSURES INC (HQ)
850 Montgomery Ave (19512-9637)
P.O. Box 608 (19512-0608)
PHONE...................................610 367-5000
Frederick N Biesecker, *CEO*
Suzanne K Biesecker, *Corp Secy*
Frederick N Biesecker II, *Vice Pres*
Frederick T Miller, *Vice Pres*
Gregory Spushen, *Vice Pres*
▼ **EMP:** 62 **EST:** 1980
SALES (est): 25.2MM
SALES (corp-wide): 166.9MM Privately Held
SIC: 3089 Caps, plastic
PA: Drug Plastics And Glass Company, Inc.
    1 Bottle Dr
    Boyertown PA 19512
    610 367-5000

(G-1909)
E&M WHOLESALE FOODS
105 Fortress Dr (19512-8698)
PHONE...................................610 367-2299
Lori Erb, *Partner*
Jeff Erb, *Partner*
Barbara Moyer, *Partner*
EMP: 12
SQ FT: 2,000
SALES: 500K Privately Held
SIC: 2099 5142 Potatoes, peeled for the trade; packaged frozen goods

(G-1910)
EHST CUSTOM KITCHENS INC
1 Sweinhart Rd (19512)
PHONE....................610 367-2074
Dennis Weller, *President*
Gerald Ehst, *Vice Pres*
EMP: 13 EST: 1961
SQ FT: 14,860
SALES (est): 980K **Privately Held**
SIC: 2434 1751 5722 Wood kitchen cabinets; cabinet building & installation; electric household appliances, major

(G-1911)
FRACCARO INDUSTRIES INC
1032 N Reading Ave (19512-8967)
PHONE....................610 367-2777
Yolanda Fraccaro, *President*
Gustavo Fraccaro, *Treasurer*
Patricia Fraccaro, *Admin Sec*
EMP: 25 EST: 1972
SQ FT: 20,000
SALES (est): 4.6MM **Privately Held**
WEB: www.fraccaro-industries.com
SIC: 3599 Machine shop, jobbing & repair

(G-1912)
GLOBAL ADVANCED METALS USA INC
Also Called: Boyertown Plant
1223 County Line Rd (19512)
PHONE....................610 367-2181
Mark Lackey, *Manager*
EMP: 76
SALES (est): 26.5MM
SALES (corp-wide): 24.2MM **Privately Held**
SIC: 3339 Primary nonferrous metals
PA: Global Advanced Metals Usa, Inc.
    100 Worcester St Ste 200
    Wellesley Hills MA 02481
    781 996-7300

(G-1913)
GRABER LETTERIN INC
58 School House Rd (19512-7925)
PHONE....................610 369-1112
Jeff Graber, *President*
Evan Alena, *Production*
Cheryl Graber, *Treasurer*
Carl Krott, *Graphic Designe*
EMP: 8
SALES (est): 939.8K **Privately Held**
WEB: www.graberletterin.com
SIC: 7532 3993 Truck painting & lettering; signs & advertising specialties

(G-1914)
GREG KLINE
Also Called: Kline Construction
217 Old State Rd (19512-9062)
PHONE....................610 367-4060
Greg Kline, *Owner*
Jessica Kline, *Co-Owner*
EMP: 5
SALES: 330K **Privately Held**
SIC: 2452 1521 Log cabins, prefabricated, wood; new construction, single-family houses

(G-1915)
GREYSTONE QUARRIES INC
329 Oysterdale Rd (19512-8360)
PHONE....................610 987-8055
Gary Weller, *President*
EMP: 9 EST: 2002
SALES (est): 474.4K **Privately Held**
WEB: www.greystonequarries.com
SIC: 1422 Crushed & broken limestone

(G-1916)
HOT OFF PRESS INC
200 N Washington St (19512-1115)
PHONE....................610 473-5700
Kenneth Webb, *President*
Patricia L Webb, *Vice Pres*
Bernice Zeccardi, *Sales Staff*
EMP: 12
SQ FT: 22,000
SALES (est): 1.3MM **Privately Held**
WEB: www.hotp.net
SIC: 2675 2759 Die-cut paper & board; embossing on paper

(G-1917)
INNOVATIVE MACHINING TECH INC
1090 N Reading Ave (19512-8967)
PHONE....................610 473-5600
Joseph Lomanto, *President*
Stephanie Lomanto, *Vice Pres*
EMP: 3
SALES (est): 276.8K **Privately Held**
SIC: 3599 Machine shop, jobbing & repair

(G-1918)
INNOVATIVE MACHINING TECH INC
8 Rowell Rd (19512-8923)
PHONE....................610 473-5600
Joe Lomanto, *President*
Joseph Lomanto, *Vice Pres*
Kim Keefer, *Info Tech Mgr*
EMP: 30
SQ FT: 25,000
SALES (est): 4.7MM **Privately Held**
SIC: 3599 7692 Machine shop, jobbing & repair; welding repair

(G-1919)
J C H ASSOCIATES INC
2204 Farmington Ave (19512-8464)
PHONE....................610 367-5000
Robert Naso, *Principal*
EMP: 3 EST: 2010
SALES (est): 175.1K **Privately Held**
SIC: 3613 Switchgear & switchboard apparatus

(G-1920)
JUDSON A SMITH COMPANY
857-863 Sweinhart Rd (19512)
P.O. Box 563 (19512-0563)
PHONE....................610 367-2021
Peter Frost, *CEO*
Russ Moser, *Division Mgr*
Ron Kulp, *Purch Mgr*
Anita Lloyd, *Purch Agent*
Mark Bonnes, *Design Engr*
▲ EMP: 125
SQ FT: 60,000
SALES (est): 47.2MM
SALES (corp-wide): 86.7MM **Privately Held**
WEB: www.judsonsmith.com
SIC: 3498 Tube fabricating (contract bending & shaping)
PA: Atw Companies, Inc.
    125 Metro Center Blvd # 3001
    Warwick RI 02886
    401 244-1002

(G-1921)
KEYSTONE FIRE CO APPARATUS
240 N Walnut St (19512-1025)
P.O. Box 158 (19512-0158)
PHONE....................610 587-3859
George Conrad, *President*
EMP: 14 EST: 2009
SALES (est): 1.3MM **Privately Held**
SIC: 3669 Fire alarm apparatus, electric

(G-1922)
KING COILS MANUFACTURING INC
201 Water St (19512-8602)
PHONE....................484 645-4054
Bryan S Doudna, *President*
EMP: 3 EST: 2009
SALES (est): 237.6K **Privately Held**
SIC: 3999 Manufacturing industries

(G-1923)
KORSAK GLASS & ALUMINUM INC
809 Hill Church Rd (19512-8379)
PHONE....................610 987-9888
Timothy P Korsak, *President*
Margaret Korsak, *Vice Pres*
EMP: 5
SALES (est): 510K **Privately Held**
SIC: 3172 5051 Cases, glasses; window & door (prefabricated) installation; aluminum bars, rods, ingots, sheets, pipes, plates, etc.

(G-1924)
PREMIER APPLIED COATINGS INC
Also Called: P A C
326 S Franklin St (19512-1532)
P.O. Box 606 (19512-0606)
PHONE....................610 367-2635
Ricky L Watt, *President*
Jeff Pinder, *Opers Staff*
Bill Lindsay, *Sales Staff*
Rick Slegel, *Supervisor*
Ellen Watt, *Admin Asst*
EMP: 12
SQ FT: 16,000
SALES (est): 1.5MM **Privately Held**
SIC: 3479 Coating of metals & formed products

(G-1925)
RALPH GOOD INC
Also Called: Good's Distribution Center
860 Sweinhart Rd (19512-8204)
PHONE....................610 367-2253
Phil Weller, *Sales Mgr*
Duane Good, *Manager*
EMP: 15
SQ FT: 9,999
SALES (est): 1MM
SALES (corp-wide): 4.6MM **Privately Held**
SIC: 2096 Potato chips & similar snacks
PA: Ralph Good, Inc.
    306 E Main St
    Adamstown PA 19501
    717 484-4884

(G-1926)
ROLLING ROCK BLDG STONE INC
40 Rolling Rock Rd (19512-8394)
PHONE....................610 987-6226
Gary Lee Weller, *President*
Betty M Weller, *Principal*
Lucille Grampp, *Corp Secy*
Kimberly R Weller, *Corp Secy*
Debra Shabrach, *Vice Pres*
▲ EMP: 72
SQ FT: 60,800
SALES (est): 10.5MM **Privately Held**
WEB: www.rollrock.com
SIC: 3281 Building stone products

(G-1927)
ROYER QUALITY CASTINGS INC
380 S Reading Ave (19512-1812)
PHONE....................610 367-1390
David A Royer, *President*
Hope Royer, *Corp Secy*
Armond Royer, *Vice Pres*
EMP: 8 EST: 1951
SQ FT: 8,000
SALES (est): 1.4MM **Privately Held**
SIC: 3365 3369 Aluminum & aluminum-based alloy castings; nonferrous foundries

(G-1928)
SCHWENK CUSTOM MACHINING INC
7a Rowell Rd (19512-8933)
P.O. Box 561 (19512-0561)
PHONE....................610 367-1777
Fax: 610 369-1177
EMP: 8
SQ FT: 20,000
SALES (est): 830K **Privately Held**
SIC: 3542 Mfg Metal Parts Machinery & Refractory Parts & Operates Commercial Property

(G-1929)
SELF-SEAL CONT CORP DEL VLY
Also Called: Med-Pak Division
315 329 E 2nd St (19512)
P.O. Box 431 (19512-0431)
PHONE....................610 275-2300
John McCormick, *President*
Brian McCormick, *Vice Pres*
Patricia McCormick, *Manager*
Jacqueline McCormick, *Admin Sec*
EMP: 5

SALES: 200K **Privately Held**
WEB: www.selfsealtubes.com
SIC: 2655 Tubes, mailing: made from purchased paper fiber; containers, liquid tight fiber: from purchased material

(G-1930)
SUN AND SHADE INC
704 E 4th St Ste 4 (19512-2120)
PHONE....................610 409-0366
Richard Harmon, *President*
Wayne Wolfe, *Vice Pres*
EMP: 4 EST: 2008
SALES: 200K **Privately Held**
SIC: 3993 Signs, not made in custom sign painting shops

(G-1931)
TAYLOR-BACKES INC
0 2nd And Washington St (19512)
PHONE....................610 367-4600
William Dexter, *President*
EMP: 5
SALES (est): 512.2K **Privately Held**
SIC: 3229 Vases, glass

(G-1932)
TRM EMERGENCY VEHICLES LLC
41 Spring Rd (19512-8155)
PHONE....................610 689-0702
Robert W Jackson,
EMP: 5 EST: 2000
SALES: 397K **Privately Held**
SIC: 5731 3647 7389 Radios, two-way, citizens' band, weather, short-wave, etc.; motor vehicle lighting equipment;

(G-1933)
TROTTER INDUSTRIES
30 S Jefferson St (19512-1613)
PHONE....................610 369-9473
Christian D Trotter, *President*
Heather McNeill, *Manager*
EMP: 10
SALES (est): 1MM **Privately Held**
SIC: 3999 Manufacturing industries

(G-1934)
UNICAST COMPANY
241 N Washington St (19512-1114)
PHONE....................610 366-8836
Tim Zeh, *CEO*
Daniel M Schultz, *President*
Joe Maynard, *Vice Pres*
Matthew Mull, *Vice Pres*
Shankar Subramanian, *Vice Pres*
▲ EMP: 67 EST: 1981
SQ FT: 110,000
SALES (est): 17.5MM **Privately Held**
WEB: www.unicastco.com
SIC: 3321 Gray iron castings

(G-1935)
WATSON MCDANIEL COMPANY
813 S Reading Ave Bldg 6 (19512-2060)
PHONE....................610 367-7191
Bob Hickey, *Manager*
EMP: 3 **Privately Held**
WEB: www.watsonmcdaniel.com
SIC: 3491 3561 Industrial valves; pumps & pumping equipment
HQ: Watson Mcdaniel Company
    428 Jones Blvd
    Pottstown PA 19464
    610 495-5131

Brackenridge
Allegheny County

(G-1936)
AII ACQUISITION LLC
100 River Rd (15014-1537)
PHONE....................724 226-5947
Deborah L Calderazzo, *Principal*
EMP: 3 **Publicly Held**
SIC: 3312 Stainless steel
HQ: Aii Acquisition, Llc
    1000 Six Ppg Pl
    Pittsburgh PA 15222
    412 394-2800

▲ = Import ▼=Export
◆ =Import/Export

(G-1937)
ALLEGHENY LUDLUM LLC
Also Called: ATI Allegheny Ludlum
100 River Rd (15014-1537)
PHONE.................................724 226-5000
Robert P Bozzone, *President*
Thomas Foucault, *Division Mgr*
John Craver, *General Mgr*
Harry R Wagner, *Vice Pres*
Harry Wagner, *Vice Pres*
EMP: 60 **Publicly Held**
WEB: www.alleghenyludlum.com
SIC: 3312 Stainless steel
HQ: Allegheny Ludlum, Llc
1000 Six Ppg Pl
Pittsburgh PA 15222
412 394-2800

(G-1938)
DEANGELIS CARBIDE TOOLING INC
1047 1st Ave (15014-1530)
PHONE.................................724 224-7280
Raymond Q Deangelis, *Principal*
EMP: 3
SALES (est): 195K **Privately Held**
SIC: 2819 Carbides

(G-1939)
FLABEG AUTOMOTIVE US CORP
851 3rd Ave (15014-1445)
P.O. Box 71, Naugatuck CT (06770-0071)
PHONE.................................724 224-1800
Charly Johnson, *President*
Terry Stryjewski, *QC Mgr*
Donna Andrew, *Human Res Mgr*
▲ EMP: 37 EST: 1990
SALES (est): 4.4MM **Privately Held**
SIC: 3231 Mirrors, truck & automobile:
made from purchased glass
HQ: Flabeg Us Holding Inc.
1000 Church St
Naugatuck CT 06770

(G-1940)
PANDALAI COATINGS COMPANY INC
837 6th Ave (15014-1040)
PHONE.................................724 224-5600
Bhanumathi Pansalai, *CEO*
Gopi Panasali, *President*
EMP: 5
SQ FT: 750
SALES (est): 574.8K **Privately Held**
WEB: www.pandalaicoatings.org
SIC: 5231 2851 Ret Paint/Glass/Wallpaper Mfg Paints/Allied Products

(G-1941)
TFC LLC
851 3rd Ave (15014-1445)
P.O. Box 121 (15014-0121)
PHONE.................................412 979-1670
Charles Johnson,
EMP: 4 EST: 2012
SALES (est): 249K **Privately Held**
SIC: 3231 Scientific & technical glassware:
from purchased glass

Braddock
Allegheny County

(G-1942)
A-BOSS OPTICIANS (PA)
634 Braddock Ave (15104-1810)
PHONE.................................412 271-4424
Albert J Boss, *Owner*
EMP: 6 EST: 1965
SALES (est): 626.5K **Privately Held**
SIC: 3851 5995 Lens grinding, except prescription: ophthalmic; eyeglasses, prescription

(G-1943)
CONWAY-PHILLIPS HOLDING LLC
Also Called: Phillips Tank & Structure
13a Talbot Ave (15104-1113)
PHONE.................................412 315-7963
Leonard Phillips, *President*
Jeffrey Sassic, *Vice Pres*
Chris Johnson, *Project Mgr*

Matt Bache, *Buyer*
Carl Lovejoy, *Buyer*
EMP: 50
SQ FT: 2,500
SALES (est): 18MM **Privately Held**
SIC: 1791 1721 3443 8711 Storage tanks, metal: erection; industrial painting; standpipes; tanks, standard or custom fabricated: metal plate; professional engineer

(G-1944)
GRAY WLDG FABRICATION SVCS INC
19 Talbot Ave (15104-1475)
PHONE.................................412 271-6900
Barbara I Gray, *President*
Bernard W Gray Jr, *Vice Pres*
Desiree Corbett, *Administration*
EMP: 20
SALES (est): 5.6MM **Privately Held**
WEB: www.graywelding.com
SIC: 3441 Fabricated structural metal

(G-1945)
INK DIVISION LLC
218 Braddock Ave (15104-1432)
PHONE.................................412 381-1104
Jason Lott, *Mng Member*
Robert Eliot,
EMP: 6
SALES (est): 500K **Privately Held**
SIC: 2893 Printing ink

(G-1946)
MAVERICK STEEL COMPANY LLC
98 Antisbury St (15104-1186)
PHONE.................................412 271-1620
Sam Eakin, *President*
EMP: 80
SQ FT: 80,000
SALES (est): 6.3MM **Privately Held**
SIC: 3441 Fabricated structural metal

(G-1947)
MESSER LLC
1000 Washington Ave (15104-2012)
PHONE.................................412 351-4580
Jim Sherwin, *Branch Mgr*
EMP: 10
SALES (corp-wide): 1.4B **Privately Held**
SIC: 2813 Nitrogen; oxygen, compressed or liquefied
HQ: Messer Llc
200 Somerset Corporate
Bridgewater NJ 08807
908 464-8100

(G-1948)
TMS INTERNATIONAL LLC
1300 Braddock Ave (15104-1743)
PHONE.................................412 271-4430
Randy White, *Branch Mgr*
EMP: 6 **Privately Held**
SIC: 3312 Blast furnaces & steel mills
HQ: Tms International, Llc
12 Monongahela Ave
Glassport PA 15045
412 678-6141

(G-1949)
TRAU & LOEVNER INC
Also Called: TRAU & LOEVNER OPERATING CO
838 Braddock Ave (15104-1715)
PHONE.................................412 361-7700
Steve Loevner, *President*
▲ EMP: 72 EST: 1897
SQ FT: 52,000
SALES (est): 14MM **Privately Held**
WEB: www.trau-loevner.com
SIC: 2321 2331 Men's & boys' sports & polo shirts; T-shirts & tops, women's: made from purchased materials

(G-1950)
UNITED STATES STEEL CORP
Also Called: U. S. Steel
1300 Braddock Ave (15104-1743)
PHONE.................................412 273-7000
Renny Blakemore, *Manager*
EMP: 60
SALES (corp-wide): 14.1B **Publicly Held**
SIC: 3312 5051 Blast furnaces & steel mills; metals service centers & offices

PA: United States Steel Corp
600 Grant St Ste 468
Pittsburgh PA 15219
412 433-1121

(G-1951)
W & K STEEL LLC
98 Antisbury St (15104-1186)
PHONE.................................412 271-0540
Edward C Wilhelm, *Mng Member*
EMP: 30
SALES (est): 6.8MM **Privately Held**
SIC: 3441 Fabricated structural metal

Bradenville
Westmoreland County

(G-1952)
TECH SHEET METAL COMPANY INC
133 Center St (15620-1006)
PHONE.................................724 539-3763
Marilyn Sabota, *President*
EMP: 12
SALES (est): 2.2MM **Privately Held**
SIC: 3444 Sheet metalwork

Bradford
Mckean County

(G-1953)
AAA NAIL
115 Main St (16701-2054)
PHONE.................................814 362-2863
Nick Ngo, *Owner*
EMP: 4
SALES (est): 285.4K **Privately Held**
SIC: 2844 Manicure preparations

(G-1954)
ALLEGHENY STORE FIXTURES INC
Also Called: Allegheny Trico
57 Holley Ave (16701-1810)
P.O. Box 215 (16701-0215)
PHONE.................................814 362-6805
Darcy Difazio, *CEO*
Steven Difazio, *President*
John Haid, *Vice Pres*
Ryan Williamson, *Vice Pres*
Michael Rychcik, *Treasurer*
▲ EMP: 40
SQ FT: 55,000
SALES (est): 8.9MM **Privately Held**
WEB: www.allstorefix.com
SIC: 2541 2542 5046 Store & office display cases & fixtures; fixtures: display, office or store: except wood; store fixtures

(G-1955)
AMERICAN REFINING GROUP INC
77 N Kendall Ave (16701-1726)
PHONE.................................814 368-1378
Janine Schoenecker, *President*
John Robinson, *President*
Richard Smith, *President*
EMP: 300
SALES (corp-wide): 194.1MM **Privately Held**
WEB: www.amref.com
SIC: 2911 5171 5172 Petroleum refining; petroleum bulk stations & terminals; lubricating oils & greases
PA: American Refining Group, Inc.
77 N Kendall Ave
Bradford PA 16701
814 368-1200

(G-1956)
B & T CONTRACTORS INC
612 S Kendall Ave (16701-3629)
P.O. Box 795 (16701-0795)
PHONE.................................814 368-7199
Susan Teribery, *President*
Kevin Teribery, *Vice Pres*
Ed Stover, *Sales Staff*
Matthew Teribery, *Business Dir*
EMP: 135
SQ FT: 7,000

SALES (est): 6.4MM **Privately Held**
WEB: www.btcontractors.com
SIC: 7349 2851 Janitorial service, contract basis; epoxy coatings; polyurethane coatings

(G-1957)
BDH OIL INC
580 Interstate Pkwy (16701-2921)
PHONE.................................814 362-5447
EMP: 7
SALES (est): 750K **Privately Held**
SIC: 1311 Oil And Gas Production

(G-1958)
BRADFORD FOREST INC
444 High St (16701-3735)
PHONE.................................570 835-5000
Mark Conolly, *President*
Steve Bukowski, *General Mgr*
Mary J Sandy, *Human Res Mgr*
Fredrik Sturesson, *Sales Mgr*
Peggy Leonard, *Accounts Mgr*
EMP: 30
SALES (est): 2.3MM **Privately Held**
WEB: www.bradfordforest.com
SIC: 2421 Lumber: rough, sawed or planed

(G-1959)
BRADFORD JOURNAL MINER
Also Called: McKean County Miner
69 Garlock Holw (16701-3420)
P.O. Box 17 (16701-0017)
PHONE.................................814 465-3468
Grant Nichols, *Partner*
Debi Nichols, *Partner*
EMP: 7
SQ FT: 1,000
SALES (est): 346.8K **Privately Held**
SIC: 2711 Newspapers, publishing & printing

(G-1960)
BRADFORD PUBLISHING COMPANY (HQ)
Also Called: Bradford Publications Inc
43 Main St (16701-2019)
P.O. Box 365 (16701-0365)
PHONE.................................814 368-3173
John Satterwhite, *President*
EMP: 56 EST: 1887
SALES (est): 10.9MM **Privately Held**
WEB: www.oleantimesherald.com
SIC: 2711 Newspapers, publishing & printing

(G-1961)
CLINE OIL INC
1 Longfellow Ave (16701-1715)
PHONE.................................814 368-5395
Willard M Cline, *President*
Joyce Cline, *Manager*
EMP: 6
SALES: 500K **Privately Held**
SIC: 1311 Crude petroleum production

(G-1962)
CONTROL CHIEF CORPORATION
200 Williams St (16701-1411)
P.O. Box 141 (16701-0141)
PHONE.................................814 362-6811
Douglas Bell, *President*
Jake Bryner, *Vice Pres*
David Dedionisio, *Vice Pres*
David Higgs, *Vice Pres*
Brian Landries, *Vice Pres*
EMP: 49
SQ FT: 20,000
SALES: 3.5MM
SALES (corp-wide): 7.1MM **Privately Held**
SIC: 3625 Relays & industrial controls
PA: Control Chief Holdings, Inc.
200 Williams St
Bradford PA 16701
814 362-6811

(G-1963)
CONTROL CHIEF HOLDINGS INC (PA)
200 Williams St (16701-1411)
PHONE.................................814 362-6811
Douglas S Bell, *Ch of Bd*
Mike Carapellatti, *Engineer*

GEOGRAPHIC

Mark A George, *Treasurer*
David I Cohen, *Admin Sec*
EMP: 98 **EST:** 1968
SQ FT: 20,000
SALES: 7.1MM **Privately Held**
SIC: 3625 Relays & industrial controls

(G-1964)
DALLAS - MORRIS DRILLING INC (PA)
29 Morris Ln (16701-4843)
PHONE..................................814 362-6493
Thomas I Morris Jr, *President*
David E Morris, *Treasurer*
Steven C Morris, *Admin Sec*
EMP: 55 **EST:** 1979
SALES (est): 23.5MM **Privately Held**
WEB: www.dallas-morris.com
SIC: 1381 Directional drilling oil & gas wells

(G-1965)
DALLAS - MORRIS DRILLING INC
103 S Kendall Ave (16701-6001)
PHONE..................................814 362-6493
Fax: 724 463-0118
EMP: 20
SALES (corp-wide): 21.3MM **Privately Held**
SIC: 1381 Oil/Gas Well Drilling
PA: Dallas - Morris Drilling, Inc.
29 Morris Ln
Bradford PA 16701
814 362-6493

(G-1966)
DANZER LUMBER NORTH AMER INC
444 High St (16701-3735)
PHONE..................................814 368-3701
Gregory Lottes, *President*
Mike Mitchell, *Sales Staff*
Mary Jo Sandy, *Manager*
◆ **EMP:** 200
SALES: 52MM **Privately Held**
SIC: 2426 Hardwood dimension & flooring mills

(G-1967)
DRESSER LLC
Dresser Pipeline Solutions
41 Fisher Ave (16701-1649)
PHONE..................................814 362-9200
Larry Shattenberg, *Mfg Staff*
Joe Tarszowicz, *Branch Mgr*
EMP: 200
SQ FT: 5,356
SALES (corp-wide): 22.8B **Publicly Held**
WEB: www.dresser.com
SIC: 3498 3494 Fabricated pipe & fittings; valves & pipe fittings
HQ: Dresser, Llc
1333 Corporate Dr Ste 300
Irving TX 75038

(G-1968)
FAULT LINE OIL CORPORATION (PA)
Also Called: Medina Wells Servicing Limited
652 Derrick Rd (16701-3400)
PHONE..................................814 368-5901
Dale Fox, *President*
Lynne Humphrey, *Manager*
EMP: 6
SALES (est): 559.4K **Privately Held**
SIC: 1382 Oil & gas exploration services

(G-1969)
GEORGIA-PACIFIC LLC
1 Owens Way (16701-3750)
PHONE..................................814 368-8700
Roger Williams, *Branch Mgr*
Denny Harrold, *Maintence Staff*
Douglas Smith, *Maintence Staff*
Kristen Parsons, *Assistant*
EMP: 111
SALES (corp-wide): 42.4B **Privately Held**
WEB: www.gp.com
SIC: 2653 5113 3412 Boxes, corrugated: made from purchased materials; corrugated & solid fiber boxes; metal barrels, drums & pails

HQ: Georgia-Pacific Llc
133 Peachtree St Nw
Atlanta GA 30303
404 652-4000

(G-1970)
GRAHAM PACKAGING COMPANY LP
105 Bolivar Dr (16701-3128)
PHONE..................................814 362-3861
Dustin Craig, *Plant Mgr*
Robert Plante, *Plant Mgr*
Virginia Allen, *Buyer*
Brian Bailey, *Buyer*
Jerry Crump, *Buyer*
EMP: 81
SALES (corp-wide): 1MM **Privately Held**
WEB: www.grahampackaging.com
SIC: 3089 Plastic containers, except foam
HQ: Graham Packaging Company, L.P.
700 Indian Springs Dr # 100
Lancaster PA 17601
717 849-8500

(G-1971)
HANGER PRSTHETCS & ORTHO INC
Also Called: Hanger Clinic
900 Chestnut Street Ext (16701-2298)
PHONE..................................814 368-3702
EMP: 4
SALES (corp-wide): 1B **Publicly Held**
SIC: 3842 Limbs, artificial
HQ: Hanger Prosthetics & Orthotics, Inc.
10910 Domain Dr Ste 300
Austin TX 78758
512 777-3800

(G-1972)
HEMLOCK OIL & GAS CO INC
83 Rutherford Run (16701-3752)
PHONE..................................814 368-6261
Jeffery Krieg, *President*
EMP: 7
SALES (est): 788.9K **Privately Held**
SIC: 1381 Drilling oil & gas wells

(G-1973)
HOUNDS & HUNTING PUBLISHING
Also Called: H & H Print Shop
554 Bolivar Dr (16701-3143)
P.O. Box 231, Lexington IN (47138-0231)
PHONE..................................812 820-1588
Robert Slike Jr, *President*
Arthur Slike, *Corp Secy*
EMP: 6 **EST:** 1903
SQ FT: 2,400
SALES (est): 619.6K **Privately Held**
WEB: www.houndsandhunting.com
SIC: 2721 Magazines: publishing & printing

(G-1974)
JARRETT MACHINE CO (PA)
1061 Lafferty Ln (16701-4707)
P.O. Box 436 (16701-0436)
PHONE..................................814 362-2755
Harry M Jarrett, *Ch of Bd*
Fred Gainer, *President*
Robert M Jarrett, *President*
John P Jarrett, *Vice Pres*
Harold Wright, *Director*
EMP: 35
SQ FT: 10,000
SALES (est): 4.7MM **Privately Held**
SIC: 3599 Machine shop, jobbing & repair

(G-1975)
JARRETT MACHINE CO
20 Roberts St (16701-2147)
P.O. Box 436 (16701-0436)
PHONE..................................814 362-2755
Bob Skaggs, *President*
EMP: 15
SALES (corp-wide): 4.7MM **Privately Held**
SIC: 3599 Machine shop, jobbing & repair
PA: Jarrett Machine Co
1061 Lafferty Ln
Bradford PA 16701
814 362-2755

(G-1976)
KERYGMA INC
Also Called: Kerygma Program
20 Russell Blvd E (16701-3247)
PHONE..................................412 344-6062
David G Ferguson, *President*
EMP: 3
SQ FT: 2,000
SALES (est): 316.8K **Privately Held**
WEB: www.kerygma.com
SIC: 2731 Books: publishing only

(G-1977)
KEYSTONE WIRELINE INC (PA)
344 High St (16701-3733)
PHONE..................................814 362-0230
Richard Carpenter, *President*
Brad Carpenter, *Principal*
Patricia Carpenter, *Principal*
Patrick Corsiglia, *Principal*
David O'Liner, *Principal*
EMP: 4
SQ FT: 1,000
SALES: 1MM **Privately Held**
SIC: 1382 Oil & gas exploration services

(G-1978)
LABELCOM
400 Chestnut Street Ext (16701-2288)
PHONE..................................814 362-3252
Denise Strouse, *Partner*
Randy Bittinger, *Partner*
EMP: 6
SQ FT: 3,500
SALES (est): 1.4MM **Privately Held**
WEB: www.labeldotcom.com
SIC: 2679 2671 Labels, paper: made from purchased material; packaging paper & plastics film, coated & laminated

(G-1979)
LABELPACK AUTOMATION INC (PA)
20 Russell Blvd Bldg E (16701-3247)
PHONE..................................814 362-1528
David G Ferguson, *President*
Marsha Thomas, *General Mgr*
Jane E Luzzi, *Vice Pres*
Olindo Eger, *Engineer*
David Taylor, *Design Engr*
EMP: 25
SQ FT: 3,000
SALES (est): 7.4MM **Privately Held**
WEB: www.lpautomation.com
SIC: 7373 3565 Systems integration services; labeling machines, industrial

(G-1980)
LUMINITE PRODUCTS CORPORATION
148 Commerce Dr (16701-4736)
PHONE..................................814 817-1420
Richard F Songer, *CEO*
John Vosburg III, *Vice Pres*
EMP: 60 **EST:** 1926
SQ FT: 35,000
SALES (est): 8.4MM **Privately Held**
WEB: www.luminite.com
SIC: 2759 Textile printing rolls: engraving

(G-1981)
MICALE FABRICATORS INC
85 Forman St (16701)
PHONE..................................814 368-7133
Jeff Piscarella, *President*
EMP: 5
SALES (est): 712.4K **Privately Held**
SIC: 3441 Fabricated structural metal

(G-1982)
MINARD RUN OIL COMPANY (PA)
609 South Ave (16701-3977)
P.O. Box 18 (16701-0018)
PHONE..................................814 362-3531
Meridith Fesenmyer, *President*
Frederick W Fesenmyer, *Chairman*
EMP: 61 **EST:** 1875
SQ FT: 8,000
SALES: 13.4MM **Privately Held**
WEB: www.minardrunoil.com
SIC: 1381 1389 Directional drilling oil & gas wells; well plugging & abandoning, oil & gas

(G-1983)
MINARD RUN OIL COMPANY
Music Mtn (16701)
P.O. Box 18 (16701-0018)
PHONE..................................814 368-4931
EMP: 5
SALES (corp-wide): 13.4MM **Privately Held**
SIC: 1311 Crude Petroleum/Natural Gas Production
PA: Minard Run Oil Company
609 South Ave
Bradford PA 16701
814 362-3531

(G-1984)
MS WHEELCHAIR PA PROGRAM
18 Woodlawn Ave (16701-3256)
PHONE..................................814 331-1722
Megan M Abrams, *President*
EMP: 3
SALES: 22.6K **Privately Held**
SIC: 3842 Wheelchairs

(G-1985)
NATURAL OIL & GAS CORP
5 Fairway Dr (16701-4104)
PHONE..................................814 362-6890
John H Reetz Jr, *President*
EMP: 6
SQ FT: 3,500
SALES (est): 895.9K **Privately Held**
SIC: 1382 Oil & gas exploration services

(G-1986)
PEPPERELL BRAIDING COMPANY INC
548 High St (16701-3737)
P.O. Box 527 (16701-0527)
PHONE..................................814 368-4454
Amado Cota-Robles, *Manager*
EMP: 65
SQ FT: 88,000
SALES (corp-wide): 13.5MM **Privately Held**
WEB: www.pepperell.com
SIC: 2821 Plastics materials & resins
PA: Pepperell Braiding Company, Inc.
22 Lowell St
Pepperell MA 01463
978 433-2133

(G-1987)
PRECISION FBRCTION CONTRLS INC
195 Chestnut St (16701-2255)
P.O. Box 934, Sheffield (16347-0934)
PHONE..................................814 368-7320
Robert J Stewart, *President*
Vicki Button, *Vice Pres*
EMP: 37
SQ FT: 45,000
SALES (est): 5.8MM **Privately Held**
WEB: www.pfc-inc.com
SIC: 3643 Contacts, electrical

(G-1988)
QUAKER BOY INC
Also Called: Game Call
20 Russell Blvd (16701-3247)
PHONE..................................814 362-7073
John Kelly, *Branch Mgr*
EMP: 15
SALES (corp-wide): 5.4MM **Privately Held**
WEB: www.quakerboy.com
SIC: 3949 5961 5941 Game calls; hunting equipment; mail order house; hunting equipment
PA: Quaker Boy, Inc.
5455 Webster Rd
Orchard Park NY 14141
716 662-3979

(G-1989)
RANGE RESOURCES
80 Hillside Ave (16701-2153)
PHONE..................................570 858-1200
EMP: 3
SALES (est): 48.4K **Privately Held**
SIC: 4924 1382 Natural gas distribution; oil & gas exploration services

▲ = Import ▼=Export
◆ =Import/Export

(G-1990)
RJB WELL SERVICES INC
557 Interstate Pkwy (16701-2922)
PHONE..............................814 368-9570
R James Barnes, *President*
Jane Barnes, *Corp Secy*
EMP: 15
SALES (est): 2.7MM **Privately Held**
SIC: 1382 1389 Oil & gas exploration
services; oil field services

(G-1991)
SCOTT NEILLY
Also Called: Neilly, S W Air Notching
350 Minard Run Rd (16701-3708)
P.O. Box 414 (16701-0414)
PHONE..............................814 362-4443
Scott Neilly, *Owner*
EMP: 7
SQ FT: 8,500
SALES (est): 1.1MM **Privately Held**
SIC: 1389 Oil Field Services

(G-1992)
STATE LINE SUPPLY COMPANY
1333 E Main St (16701-3257)
PHONE..............................814 362-7433
Robert Douglas, *President*
David Zuckerman, *Owner*
Tom Vinciquera, *Sales Associate*
EMP: 11 **EST:** 1900
SQ FT: 33,000
SALES (est): 3.3MM **Privately Held**
WEB: www.statelinesupply.com
SIC: 3317 Boiler tubes (wrought)

(G-1993)
SUBWAY
48 Davis St (16701-2016)
PHONE..............................814 368-2576
EMP: 10
SALES (est): 223.7K **Privately Held**
SIC: 5812 2099 Eating Place Mfg Food
Preparations

(G-1994)
**TOP LINE PROCESS
EQUIPMENT**
Valley Hunt Dr (16701)
PHONE..............................814 362-4626
Thomas R Bromeley, *Ch of Bd*
Robert L Leslie, *President*
Robert L Christjohn, *Vice Pres*
Staci Frantz, *Vice Pres*
John T Mc Candless, *Vice Pres*
▼ **EMP:** 90
SQ FT: 28,000
SALES (est): 14.2MM **Privately Held**
SIC: 3556 Mfg Stainless Steel Food Prod-
ucts Machinery

(G-1995)
WERZALIT OF AMERICA INC
40 Holley Ave (16701-1899)
PHONE..............................814 362-3881
Guenter Hegemann, *Ch of Bd*
Anthony M Manning, *President*
Hermann Henke, *Vice Pres*
Christopher G Hauser, *Admin Sec*
◆ **EMP:** 51
SQ FT: 120,000
SALES (est): 8MM
SALES (corp-wide): 69.4MM **Privately
Held**
WEB: www.werzalit-usa.com
SIC: 2426 3995 2511 2421 Furniture
stock & parts, hardwood; burial caskets;
wood household furniture; sawmills &
planing mills, general; commercial print-
ing; architectural services
PA: Werzalit Gmbh + Co. Kg Indus-
triebeteiligungen
Gronauer Str. 70
Oberstenfeld 71720
706 250-0

(G-1996)
WOODLINE PRODUCTIONS INC
317 W Corydon St (16701-3909)
PHONE..............................814 362-5397
John Costik, *President*
Sally Costik, *Vice Pres*
EMP: 5
SQ FT: 5,700
SALES (est): 272K **Privately Held**
SIC: 2499 Spars, wood

(G-1997)
ZIPCORP INC (PA)
Also Called: Zippo Manufacturing Company
33 Barbour St (16701-1973)
PHONE..............................814 368-2700
Gregory W Booth, *Principal*
George B Duke, *Vice Pres*
Charles J Duke, *Admin Sec*
EMP: 494
SQ FT: 73,200
SALES (est): 181.7MM **Privately Held**
WEB: www.zipcorp.com
SIC: 3999 5172 Cigarette lighters, except
precious metal; petroleum products

Bradfordwoods
Allegheny County

(G-1998)
INNOVATE SOFTWARE INC
106 Forest Rd (15015-1202)
PHONE..............................724 935-1790
William Claire, *President*
EMP: 5
SALES (est): 269.6K **Privately Held**
SIC: 7372 8748 Prepackaged software;
business consulting

(G-1999)
SKI HAUS LLC
Also Called: Patio Concepts
716 Woodland Rd (15015-1328)
PHONE..............................412 760-7547
Robert Drescher, *Mng Member*
▲ **EMP:** 9
SQ FT: 10,000
SALES (est): 872.6K **Privately Held**
SIC: 2329 Ski & snow clothing: men's &
boys'

(G-2000)
**VAUGHENS PRICE PUBG CO
INC**
809 Oak Rd (15015-1209)
PHONE..............................412 367-5100
Donald M Lammers, *President*
EMP: 4
SALES (est): 241.6K
SALES (corp-wide): 430K **Privately Held**
WEB: www.vaughens.net
SIC: 2741 Miscellaneous publishing
PA: Vaughen's Price Publishing Co., Inc.
9400 Mcknight Rd Ste 203
Pittsburgh PA 15237
412 367-5100

Brandamore
Chester County

(G-2001)
CONTROL ELECTRONICS INC
148 Brandamore Rd (19316)
P.O. Box 330 (19316-0330)
PHONE..............................610 942-3190
Eugene Traband, *President*
Kathleen M Traband, *Vice Pres*
EMP: 8
SQ FT: 2,000
SALES (est): 1MM **Privately Held**
WEB: www.controlelectronics.com
SIC: 3823 Industrial instrmnts msrmnt dis-
play/control process variable

Brave
Greene County

(G-2002)
**CERRO FABRICATED
PRODUCTS LLC**
County Rd (15316)
PHONE..............................724 451-8202
Sam Insana, *Manager*
EMP: 5
SALES (corp-wide): 225.3B **Publicly
Held**
WEB: www.cerrofabricated.com
SIC: 3351 Copper rolling & drawing

HQ: Cerro Fabricated Products Llc
300 Triangle Dr
Weyers Cave VA 24486
540 208-1606

Breezewood
Bedford County

(G-2003)
KEREX INC
1106 S Breezewood Rd (15533-8914)
P.O. Box 255 (15533-0255)
PHONE..............................814 735-3838
Rex D Bennett, *President*
Kerry Richards, *Corp Secy*
EMP: 29
SQ FT: 8,100
SALES (est): 5.5MM **Privately Held**
WEB: www.kerex.com
SIC: 5031 2421 Lumber, plywood & mill-
work; sawmills & planing mills, general

Breinigsville
Lehigh County

(G-2004)
AESCULAP BIOLOGICS LLC
9999 Hamilton Blvd (18031-9300)
PHONE..............................610 984-9000
Chuck Dinardo, *President*
Keith Moser, *Finance Dir*
Janie Nye, *Sales Associate*
Larry Kiefer, *Manager*
EMP: 25 **EST:** 2011
SQ FT: 10,000
SALES (est): 2.2MM **Privately Held**
SIC: 3841 Surgical & medical instruments

(G-2005)
**AESCULAP IMPLANT SYSTEMS
LLC**
9999 Hamilton Blvd # 120 (18031-9300)
PHONE..............................610 984-9404
Paul Weaver, *Branch Mgr*
EMP: 8 **Privately Held**
SIC: 3841 Surgical & medical instruments
HQ: Aesculap Implant Systems, Llc
3773 Corp Pkwy Ste 200
Center Valley PA 18034
610 984-9000

(G-2006)
ALLENTOWN PLASTICS INC
405 Nestle Way (18031-1500)
PHONE..............................610 391-8383
William Estes, *Principal*
Timothy Brasher, *Principal*
Henry Carter, *Principal*
EMP: 25
SALES (est): 2.2MM
SALES (corp-wide): 14B **Publicly Held**
WEB: www.cccllc.com
SIC: 3089 Plastic containers, except foam
HQ: Consolidated Container Company, Llc
2500 Windy Ridge Pkwy Se # 1400
Atlanta GA 30339
678 742-4600

(G-2007)
**AMERICAN CRAFT BREWERY
LLC**
7880 Penn Dr (18031-1508)
PHONE..............................610 391-4700
Sal Tortora, *Branch Mgr*
EMP: 400 **Publicly Held**
SIC: 2082 Beer (alcoholic beverage); ale
(alcoholic beverage)
HQ: American Craft Brewery Llc
1 Design Center Pl # 850
Boston MA 02210
617 368-5000

(G-2008)
**AMERICAN TACK & HDWR CO
INC (HQ)**
Also Called: Amertac
250 Boulder Dr (18031-1528)
PHONE..............................610 336-1330
Charles Peifer, *CEO*
John Cooper, *President*

Joel Weinberg, *President*
Salvatore Mirra, *CFO*
Chris Kokkinakis, *Controller*
▲ **EMP:** 49
SQ FT: 20,000
SALES (est): 29.7MM **Privately Held**
SIC: 5072 3648 Hardware; decorative
area lighting fixtures

(G-2009)
B BRAUN MEDICAL INC
200 Boulder Dr Ste 1 (18031-1532)
PHONE..............................610 336-9595
Donna Reiser, *Sales Staff*
Bob McFadden, *Manager*
EMP: 1300 **Privately Held**
SIC: 3841 Catheters
HQ: B. Braun Medical Inc.
824 12th Ave
Bethlehem PA 18018
610 691-5400

(G-2010)
BIMBO BAKERIES USA INC
150 Boulder Dr (18031-1838)
PHONE..............................610 391-7490
EMP: 53 **Privately Held**
SIC: 2051 Bakery: wholesale or whole-
sale/retail combined
HQ: Bimbo Bakeries Usa, Inc
255 Business Center Dr # 200
Horsham PA 19044
215 347-5500

(G-2011)
BOSTON BEER COMPANY INC
7880 Penn Dr (18031-1508)
PHONE..............................610 395-1885
EMP: 213 **Publicly Held**
SIC: 2082 Malt beverages
PA: The Boston Beer Company Inc
1 Design Center Pl # 850
Boston MA 02210

(G-2012)
**CLOVER HILL ENTERPRISES
INC (PA)**
Also Called: Clover Hill Vineyards & Winery
9850 Newtown Rd (18031-1808)
PHONE..............................610 395-2468
John Skrip, *President*
EMP: 30
SALES (est): 3.4MM **Privately Held**
WEB: www.cloverhillwinery.com
SIC: 2084 Wines

(G-2013)
CYOPTICS INC (DH)
Also Called: Broadcom Limited
9999 Hamilton Blvd # 250 (18031-9301)
PHONE..............................484 397-2000
Ed J Coringrato Jr, *CEO*
Joseph P Keska, *Vice Pres*
Daniel Sutryn, *Engineer*
Jamie Zuk, *Engineer*
Warren Barratt, *CFO*
▼ **EMP:** 270
SQ FT: 117,000
SALES (est): 114.9MM
SALES (corp-wide): 20.8B **Publicly Held**
WEB: www.cyoptics.com
SIC: 3827 Optical instruments & lenses
HQ: Avago Technologies Wireless (U.S.A.)
Manufacturing Llc
4380 Ziegler Rd
Fort Collins CO 80525
970 288-2575

(G-2014)
EARL WENZ INC
9038 Breinigsville Rd (18031-1207)
P.O. Box 209 (18031-0209)
PHONE..............................610 395-2331
Bill Wenz, *President*
EMP: 10
SQ FT: 3,000
SALES (est): 1.4MM **Privately Held**
SIC: 3281 1542 Tombstones, cut stone
(not finishing or lettering only); mau-
soleum construction

GEOGRAPHIC

(G-2015)
FIBER OPTIC MARKETPLACE LLC
Also Called: Fiberoptic.com
9999 Hamilton Blvd # 220 (18031-9301)
PHONE.....................................610 973-6000
Brad Morehouse, *Vice Pres*
Chris Labonge,
EMP: 10
SQ FT: 6,345
SALES (est): 2.1MM **Privately Held**
SIC: 3357 Nonferrous wiredrawing & insulating

(G-2016)
FIBEROPTICSCOM INC
1 Tek Park (18031)
PHONE.....................................610 973-6000
Christopher L Labonge, *President*
▲ EMP: 25
SALES: 10MM **Privately Held**
SIC: 3357 Fiber optic cable (insulated)

(G-2017)
GODSHALL WOODCRAFT
10022 Allison Dr (18031-1941)
PHONE.....................................610 530-9386
Dean Godshall, *Principal*
EMP: 3
SALES (est): 243K **Privately Held**
SIC: 2511 Wood household furniture

(G-2018)
GREAT EASTERN SEATING CO
416 Arrowhead Ln (18031-1417)
PHONE.....................................610 366-8132
Kirk Jacobson, *Owner*
EMP: 4
SALES (est): 374.7K **Privately Held**
SIC: 2531 Stadium seating

(G-2019)
JOHNSTONE SUPPLY INC
200 Boulder Dr Ste 200 # 200 (18031-1532)
PHONE.....................................484 765-1160
Mark Harmon, *Principal*
EMP: 36
SALES (corp-wide): 1.2B **Privately Held**
SIC: 3585 5075 5251 5722 Heating equipment, complete; warm air heating equipment & supplies; hardware; electric household appliances, major
PA: Johnstone Supply, Inc.
11632 Ne Ainsworth Cir
Portland OR 97220
503 256-3663

(G-2020)
NESTLE USA INC
555 Nestle Way (18031-1518)
PHONE.....................................610 391-7900
Robert Schult, *Principal*
EMP: 139
SALES (corp-wide): 90.8B **Privately Held**
WEB: www.nestleusa.com
SIC: 2023 Evaporated milk
HQ: Nestle Usa, Inc.
1812 N Moore St
Rosslyn VA 22209
818 549-6000

(G-2021)
NESTLE WATERS
305 Nestle Way (18031-1422)
PHONE.....................................484 221-0876
EMP: 34
SALES (est): 6.1MM **Privately Held**
SIC: 2086 Bottled & canned soft drinks

(G-2022)
OCEAN SPRAY CRANBERRIES INC
Also Called: Nestle Ocean Spray Alliance
151 Boulder Dr (18031-1850)
PHONE.....................................609 298-0905
Tim Haggerty, *Manager*
EMP: 300
SALES (corp-wide): 1.6B **Privately Held**
WEB: www.oceanspraycrantastics.com
SIC: 2033 Canned fruits & specialties
PA: Ocean Spray Cranberries, Inc.
1 Ocean Spray Dr
Middleboro MA 02349
508 946-1000

(G-2023)
OCEAN SPRAY CRANBERRIES INC
151 Boulder Dr (18031-1850)
PHONE.....................................508 946-1000
Ibrahim Shillo, *Engineer*
Christina Khoo, *Director*
Aileen Pla, *Administration*
EMP: 39
SALES (corp-wide): 1.6B **Privately Held**
SIC: 2037 2033 Fruit juice concentrates, frozen; preserves, including imitation: in cans, jars, etc.
PA: Ocean Spray Cranberries, Inc.
1 Ocean Spray Dr
Middleboro MA 02349
508 946-1000

(G-2024)
PREMISE MAID CANDIES INC
10860 Hamilton Blvd (18031-1731)
PHONE.....................................610 395-3221
Joseph Damiano, *President*
Michael Damiano, *Treasurer*
Lorraine Barebo, *Sales Staff*
William Damiano, *Shareholder*
Lorraine Damiano-Barebo, *Admin Sec*
EMP: 20
SQ FT: 4,000
SALES (est): 2.6MM **Privately Held**
SIC: 2066 2024 Chocolate candy, solid; ice cream & ice milk

(G-2025)
R R DONNELLEY & SONS COMPANY
Also Called: Moore Wallace North America
700 Nestle Way Ste 200 (18031-1522)
PHONE.....................................610 391-3900
Alice Wimmer, *Opers-Prdtn-Mfg*
EMP: 55
SQ FT: 31,000
SALES (corp-wide): 6.8B **Publicly Held**
WEB: www.rrdonnelley.com
SIC: 2754 Commercial printing, gravure
PA: R. R. Donnelley & Sons Company
35 W Wacker Dr Ste 3650
Chicago IL 60601
312 326-8000

(G-2026)
R R DONNELLEY & SONS COMPANY
Also Called: R R Donnelley
700 Nestle Way Ste 200 (18031-1522)
PHONE.....................................610 391-0203
R Donnelly, *Branch Mgr*
EMP: 146
SALES (corp-wide): 6.8B **Publicly Held**
WEB: www.rrdonnelley.com
SIC: 2759 Commercial printing
PA: R. R. Donnelley & Sons Company
35 W Wacker Dr Ste 3650
Chicago IL 60601
312 326-8000

(G-2027)
SILGAN CONTAINERS CORPORATION
8201 Industrial Blvd (18031-1241)
PHONE.....................................484 223-3189
John Robbins, *Branch Mgr*
EMP: 9
SALES (corp-wide): 4.4B **Publicly Held**
SIC: 3411 Metal cans
HQ: Silgan Containers Corporation
21600 Oxnard St Ste 1600
Woodland Hills CA 91367
818 348-3700

(G-2028)
TRINITY GLASS INTL INC
Feather River Door Company
8014 Industrial Blvd # 200 (18031-1225)
PHONE.....................................610 395-2030
Nick Turn, *Manager*
EMP: 90 **Privately Held**
WEB: www.trinityglassinternational.com
SIC: 5211 3442 Doors, storm: wood or metal; metal doors, sash & trim
PA: Trinity Glass International, Inc.
33615 1st Way S Ste A
Federal Way WA 98003

(G-2029)
TRITON SERVICES INC
Also Called: Electron Technology Division
9999 Hamilton Blvd # 350 (18031-9313)
PHONE.....................................484 851-3883
Steven Black, *President*
Paul Jones, *Vice Pres*
Cecil Fenchtel, *Vice Pres*
Dave Stidle, *Vice Pres*
Vance Valencia, *Vice Pres*
EMP: 6 **Privately Held**
SIC: 3671 Electron tubes, industrial
PA: Triton Services, Inc.
222 Severn Ave Ste 100
Annapolis MD 21403

(G-2030)
VYNECREST LLC
172 Arrowhead Ln (18031-1462)
PHONE.....................................610 398-7525
John Landis, *Managing Prtnr*
Dominic Strohlein, *Partner*
EMP: 10
SALES (est): 608.9K **Privately Held**
SIC: 2084 Wine cellars, bonded: engaged in blending wines

(G-2031)
VYNECREST LLC
Also Called: Vynecrest Winery
172 Arrowhead Ln (18031-1462)
PHONE.....................................610 398-7525
Janice W Landis,
John G Landis,
Sam Landis,
EMP: 4
SQ FT: 5,000
SALES (est): 390K **Privately Held**
WEB: www.vynecrest.com
SIC: 2084 Wines

(G-2032)
WESTPORT AXLE
Also Called: Westport Allentown
650 Boulder Dr Ste 100a (18031-1536)
PHONE.....................................610 366-2900
Alex Vanleyen, *President*
Rena Sharpe, *Vice Pres*
▲ EMP: 500
SQ FT: 500,000
SALES (est): 82.1MM **Privately Held**
SIC: 3714 Motor vehicle parts & accessories

(G-2033)
ZEP INC
Also Called: Zep Manufacturing
860 Nestle Way Ste 200 (18031-1669)
PHONE.....................................610 295-1360
George Martin, *Branch Mgr*
EMP: 131
SALES (corp-wide): 1B **Privately Held**
SIC: 2841 2879 2842 5169 Scouring compounds; detergents, synthetic organic or inorganic alkaline; pesticides, agricultural or household; degreasing solvent; sanitation preparations; chemicals & allied products
HQ: Zep Inc.
3330 Cumberland Blvd Se # 700
Atlanta GA 30339
877 428-9937

Bridgeport
Montgomery County

(G-2034)
DECKMAN ELECTRIC INC
49 W Front St (19405-1022)
PHONE.....................................610 272-6944
Charlie Deckman Jr, *President*
Mark Deckman, *Admin Sec*
EMP: 5
SQ FT: 6,000
SALES (est): 1.1MM **Privately Held**
SIC: 5063 7694 7699 Motors, electric; electric motor repair; printing trades machinery & equipment repair

(G-2035)
E C T INC (PA)
401 E 4th St Ste 20 (19405-1815)
PHONE.....................................610 239-5120
Bruce Tassone, *President*
▲ EMP: 9
SQ FT: 10,000
SALES (est): 1.4MM **Privately Held**
WEB: www.ectinc.net
SIC: 3511 Gas turbines, mechanical drive

(G-2036)
FREAS GLASS WORKS INC
401 E 4th St Ste 8f (19405-1815)
PHONE.....................................610 825-0430
Mark J Renda, *President*
▲ EMP: 19
SALES (est): 2.4MM **Privately Held**
SIC: 3823 Industrial instrmnts msrmnt display/control process variable

(G-2037)
G WB EUROPEAN TREASURES
401 E 4th St Ste 12a (19405-1822)
PHONE.....................................610 275-4395
Marta Bolt, *Owner*
▲ EMP: 3
SALES (est): 115.1K **Privately Held**
SIC: 3281 Cut stone & stone products

(G-2038)
JO SUZY DONUTS
49 E 4th St (19405-1419)
PHONE.....................................610 279-1350
Betty Davis, *Owner*
Lynn Barkmeyer, *Partner*
Ray Barkmeyer, *Partner*
EMP: 5
SALES (est): 242K **Privately Held**
SIC: 2051 Doughnuts, except frozen

(G-2039)
MENDIT CHEMICAL INC
401 E 4th St Ste 20 (19405-1815)
PHONE.....................................610 239-5120
Bruce Tassone, *President*
EMP: 12
SQ FT: 10,000
SALES (est): 1.4MM **Privately Held**
SIC: 3589 High pressure cleaning equipment

(G-2040)
MILLI-SWITCH MANUFACTURING CO
61 E 4th St Ste 2 (19405-1465)
PHONE.....................................610 270-9222
Michael Salmons, *President*
EMP: 3
SALES (est): 368.2K **Privately Held**
SIC: 3643 Electric switches

(G-2041)
NORSTONE INCORPORATED
Also Called: S.E. Firestone Associates
315 E 4th St (19405-1808)
PHONE.....................................484 684-6986
Daniyel Firestone, *President*
Norma Firestone, *Treasurer*
Amanda Williamson, *Sales Staff*
▲ EMP: 6
SQ FT: 1,500
SALES (est): 4.2MM **Privately Held**
WEB: www.norstoneinc.com
SIC: 5084 3291 3443 2851 Industrial machinery & equipment; abrasive products; industrial vessels, tanks & containers; paints & allied products; cyclo rubbers, natural; mining machinery & equipment, except petroleum

(G-2042)
ORLOTRONICS CORPORATION
401 E 4th St Ste 4 (19405-1822)
PHONE.....................................610 239-8200
Stephen Shankin, *Principal*
Marjorie Shankin, *Corp Secy*
Robert Shankin, *Vice Pres*
Lynn Aversano, *Controller*
EMP: 28
SQ FT: 20,000
SALES (est): 5.5MM **Privately Held**
WEB: www.orlotronics.com
SIC: 3489 3669 3648 3612 Ordnance & accessories; intercommunication systems, electric; visual communication systems; lighting equipment; airport lighting fixtures: runway approach, taxi or ramp; airport lighting transformers; household cooking & kitchen utensils, metal

(G-2043)
PAUL DOWNS CABINET MAKERS INC
401 E 4th St Ste 4 (19405-1822)
PHONE..................................610 239-0142
Paul Downs, *President*
Nathan Rossman, *Design Engr*
Kemper Ryan, *Sales Mgr*
EMP: 12
SALES: 2.5MM **Privately Held**
WEB: www.custom-conference-tables.com
SIC: 2521 Wood office furniture

(G-2044)
PRINTERS PARTS STORE INC
21 Depot St (19405-1427)
PHONE..................................610 279-6660
Mike Capizzi, *CEO*
EMP: 11
SALES (est): 855.3K **Privately Held**
WEB: www.ppspa.com
SIC: 5734 2752 Printers & plotters: computers; commercial printing, offset

(G-2045)
SEAQUAY ARCHTCTURAL MLLWK CORP
55 E Front St Ste C221 (19405-1453)
P.O. Box 437, Eagleville (19408-0437)
PHONE..................................610 279-1201
Larry Knowles, *President*
Carmela Knowles, *Vice Pres*
EMP: 15
SQ FT: 10,090
SALES (est): 2MM **Privately Held**
SIC: 2431 5211 Windows & window parts & trim, wood; millwork & lumber

(G-2046)
SHERMAN & GOSWEILER INC
401 E 4th St Ste 8e (19405-1815)
PHONE..................................610 270-0825
Dick Gosweiler, *President*
Charles Sherman, *Vice Pres*
Janet Freitick, *Office Mgr*
EMP: 8 EST: 1976
SQ FT: 10,800
SALES (est): 1MM **Privately Held**
WEB: www.shergos.com
SIC: 2434 Wood kitchen cabinets

(G-2047)
TUBE METHODS INC
416 Depot St (19405-1408)
PHONE..................................610 279-7700
Gary J Johnson, *President*
Kathleen Mazei, *Traffic Mgr*
Bruce Johnson, *Human Res Mgr*
Anna Profrock, *Receptionist*
▲ EMP: 120
SQ FT: 60,000
SALES (est): 60.3MM **Privately Held**
WEB: www.tubemethods.com
SIC: 3317 Tubes, seamless steel

(G-2048)
VETERINARY TAG SUPPLY CO INC
Also Called: Specialty Trading Co
401 E 4th St Ste 2 (19405-1822)
P.O. Box 9, Gladwyne (19035-0009)
PHONE..................................610 649-1550
Ricky J Pasternack, *President*
Barry J Pasternack, *Vice Pres*
▲ EMP: 5 EST: 1975
SQ FT: 3,800
SALES (est): 630K **Privately Held**
SIC: 5999 3469 Pet supplies; metal stampings

Bridgeville
Allegheny County

(G-2049)
A LINK PRTG & PROMOTIONS LLC
3189 Washington Pike (15017-1432)
PHONE..................................412 220-0290
Jacqueline E Maher,
EMP: 7
SQ FT: 3,500

SALES (est): 607.7K **Privately Held**
WEB: www.alinkprinting.com
SIC: 2752 7331 7389 Commercial printing, offset; direct mail advertising services; printers' services: folding, collating

(G-2050)
ACCELIGHT NETWORKS INC
70 Abele Rd (15017-3470)
PHONE..................................412 220-2102
James R Fultz, *President*
EMP: 54
SALES (est): 4MM **Privately Held**
SIC: 3625 Industrial electrical relays & switches

(G-2051)
ACCION LABS US INC (PA)
1225 Wash Pike Ste 401 (15017-2844)
PHONE..................................724 260-5139
Kinesh Doshi, *CEO*
Anand Raja, *President*
Derek Schwartz, *Business Mgr*
Tony Kernan, *Senior VP*
Pramod Patil, *Senior VP*
EMP: 35
SALES (est): 7.3MM **Privately Held**
SIC: 7371 7372 Software programming applications; business oriented computer software

(G-2052)
ACHIEVA
Also Called: Parkway Industries
360 Commercial St (15017-2347)
PHONE..................................412 221-6609
Rob Cene, *Manager*
EMP: 57
SALES (corp-wide): 5.5MM **Privately Held**
SIC: 8322 8331 2448 2441 Social service center; job training & vocational rehabilitation services; wood pallets & skids; nailed wood boxes & shook
HQ: Achieva
711 Bingham St
Pittsburgh PA 15203
412 995-5000

(G-2053)
ALPINE ELECTRIC
1273 Washington Pike (15017-2803)
PHONE..................................412 257-4827
John Deklewa, *Owner*
EMP: 4
SALES (est): 467.6K **Privately Held**
SIC: 3699 Electrical work

(G-2054)
AUSTRALTEK LLC
800 Old Pond Rd Ste 706k (15017-3415)
PHONE..................................412 257-2377
Federico Ahualli,
EMP: 3
SQ FT: 200
SALES (est): 426.8K **Privately Held**
SIC: 8711 3441 Electrical or electronic engineering; building components, structural steel

(G-2055)
BLUEPHONE
625 Elm St (15017-2117)
PHONE..................................412 337-1965
Joshua Bryant, *Principal*
EMP: 3
SALES: 20K **Privately Held**
WEB: www.bryantweb.com
SIC: 3661 Telephone & telegraph apparatus

(G-2056)
BRIGHTLINE LP
580 Mayer St Ste 7 (15017-2700)
PHONE..................................412 206-0106
Samuel Cercone, *Managing Prtnr*
Sam Cercone, *Managing Prtnr*
Kathy Katz, *Managing Prtnr*
Ryan Cercone, *Prdtn Mgr*
Nona Stein, *Purchasing*
▲ EMP: 18
SQ FT: 24,000
SALES (est): 3.8MM **Privately Held**
WEB: www.brightlines.com
SIC: 3645 Residential lighting fixtures

(G-2057)
COLUSSY ENTERPRISES INC
Also Called: Flawless Lawncare
336 Station St Ste 2 (15017-1853)
PHONE..................................412 221-4750
Chris Colussy, *President*
EMP: 4 EST: 2010
SALES (est): 447.2K **Privately Held**
SIC: 3271 Blocks, concrete: landscape or retaining wall

(G-2058)
CUSTOM STEEL PRODUCTS INC (PA)
98 Vanadium Rd Ste 12 (15017-3003)
PHONE..................................412 215-9923
Walter T Cielecy, *President*
Leonard Schuetz, *Corp Secy*
John Snyder, *Vice Pres*
EMP: 5
SQ FT: 3,000
SALES (est): 1.2MM **Privately Held**
SIC: 3441 Fabricated structural metal

(G-2059)
E R SHAW INC
Also Called: Small Arms Manufacturing Co.
5312 Thoms Run Rd (15017-2830)
PHONE..................................412 212-4343
Carl Behling, *President*
Chris Murray, *Sales Executive*
EMP: 40
SQ FT: 20,000
SALES (est): 7.4MM **Privately Held**
WEB: www.ershawbarrels.com
SIC: 5961 3484 Ret Mail-Order House Mfg Small Arms

(G-2060)
EASTERN OIL CORPORATION
98 Vanadium Rd Ste 3 (15017-3079)
PHONE..................................412 221-2911
Tom Fowler, *President*
Tara Zaharoff, *President*
EMP: 8
SQ FT: 9,000
SALES (est): 876.9K **Privately Held**
SIC: 3999 Candles

(G-2061)
EVANS COMMERCIAL SERVICES LLC
2000 Fortune Ct (15017-3529)
PHONE..................................412 573-9442
Michael Evans,
Tracy Evans,
EMP: 15
SALES (est): 10K **Privately Held**
SIC: 3621 3612 8748 Power generators; power & distribution transformers; auto-transformers, electric (power transformers); reactor transformers; systems analysis & engineering consulting services

(G-2062)
EVEREST SOFTWARE LP
Also Called: Sherpa Software Partners
456 Washington Ave Ste 2 (15017-2368)
PHONE..................................412 206-0005
Kevin Ogrodnik, *Partner*
EMP: 20
SQ FT: 6,000
SALES (est): 2MM **Privately Held**
SIC: 7372 Prepackaged software

(G-2063)
F M P HEALTHCARE PRODUCTS
1018 Ryeland Ct (15017-1117)
PHONE..................................800 611-7776
Jeffery Forman, *CEO*
Ed Paugh, *President*
Brian Forman, *Vice Pres*
EMP: 4
SALES (est): 340K **Privately Held**
SIC: 2676 5047 Cleansing tissues: made from purchased paper; medical & hospital equipment

(G-2064)
FLOWSERVE CORPORATION
1885 Mayview Rd (15017-1518)
PHONE..................................412 257-4600
Chuck Kursen, *General Mgr*
John Mucka, *Accounting Mgr*

Charles Kruzan, *Manager*
EMP: 80
SALES (corp-wide): 3.8B **Publicly Held**
SIC: 3561 Industrial pumps & parts
PA: Flowserve Corporation
5215 N Oconnor Blvd Connor
Irving TX 75039
972 443-6500

(G-2065)
G B WELL SERVICE
533 Wshington Ave Ste 200 (15017)
PHONE..................................412 221-3102
Paul Rankin, *Principal*
EMP: 8
SALES (est): 520K **Privately Held**
SIC: 1389 Pumping of oil & gas wells

(G-2066)
GIFFIN INTERIOR & FIXTURE INC
500 Scotti Dr (15017-2938)
PHONE..................................412 221-1166
Gordon Giffin, *President*
Deborah Giffin, *Admin Sec*
EMP: 150
SQ FT: 95,000
SALES (est): 30.2MM **Privately Held**
WEB: www.giffininterior.com
SIC: 2541 1542 2511 Store & office display cases & fixtures; commercial & office building, new construction; wood household furniture

(G-2067)
HALL FOODS INC
3249 Washington Pike (15017-1461)
PHONE..................................412 257-9877
Loretta Hall, *Principal*
EMP: 3
SALES (est): 96K **Privately Held**
SIC: 2099 Food preparations

(G-2068)
HENNECKE INC
Also Called: Hennecke USA
1000 Energy Dr (15017-2562)
P.O. Box 617, Lawrence (15055-0617)
PHONE..................................724 271-3686
Alois Schmid, *President*
▲ EMP: 69
SALES (est): 18.8MM
SALES (corp-wide): 18.6K **Privately Held**
SIC: 3569 Assembly machines, non-metalworking
PA: Hen Group Gmbh & Co. Kg
Theatinerstr. 7
Munchen
892 919-640

(G-2069)
INDUSTRIAL COMPOSITES INC
373 Carol Ave (15017-2374)
PHONE..................................412 221-2662
Mark E Mihalyi, *Treasurer*
Raymond E Reagle, *Admin Sec*
EMP: 6
SQ FT: 4,000
SALES (est): 740K **Privately Held**
WEB: www.industrial-composites.com
SIC: 3535 5084 3312 Unit handling conveying systems; conveyor systems; blast furnaces & steel mills

(G-2070)
INTERFORM CORPORATION (HQ)
Also Called: Interform Solutions
1901 Mayview Rd (15017-1583)
P.O. Box A (15017-0206)
PHONE..................................412 221-7321
Ronald H Scott, *President*
James Rhodes, *Vice Pres*
E Romutis, *Treasurer*
Helen R Kennedy, *Sales Staff*
Darlene Sabo, *Sales Staff*
EMP: 185 EST: 1964
SQ FT: 120,000

GEOGRAPHIC

SALES (est): 64.1MM **Publicly Held**
WEB: www.interformsolutions.com
SIC: 5112 2761 2791 7331 Manifold business forms; computer forms, manifold or continuous; continuous forms, office & business; fanfold forms; strip forms (manifold business forms); typesetting; direct mail advertising services; commercial printing; commercial printing, lithographic

(G-2071)
ITALIAN MUTUAL BENEFIT SOCIETY
Also Called: Bridgeville Italian Club
414 Market St (15017)
PHONE.............................412 221-0751
Elio Dreon, *President*
John Franjione, *Corp Secy*
Paul Campbell, *Vice Pres*
EMP: 9
SALES: 82.1K **Privately Held**
SIC: 3412 Metal barrels, drums & pails

(G-2072)
J H R INC
533 Wshington Ave Ste 200 (15017)
PHONE.............................412 221-1617
Paul B Rankin Jr, *President*
Faye Rankin, *Admin Sec*
EMP: 3
SALES (est): 569.3K **Privately Held**
SIC: 6512 6513 1381 Commercial & industrial building operation; apartment building operators; drilling oil & gas wells

(G-2073)
JANKENSTEPH INC
1597 Wash Pike Ste A38 (15017-2876)
PHONE.............................412 446-2777
Greg Glass, *President*
EMP: 7
SALES (est): 476.3K **Privately Held**
SIC: 4783 2759 Packing goods for shipping; commercial printing

(G-2074)
JEM GRAPHICS LLC
Also Called: A-Link Printing & Promotions
3189 Washington Pike (15017-1432)
PHONE.............................412 220-0290
Jacqueline Maher,
EMP: 9
SALES (est): 449.4K **Privately Held**
SIC: 7336 7331 2752 7334 Commercial art & graphic design; direct mail advertising services; offset & photolithographic printing; photocopying & duplicating services

(G-2075)
JEX MANUFACTURING INC
648 Chestnut St (15017-2116)
PHONE.............................412 292-5516
Jesse Exlar, *President*
EMP: 7
SALES (est): 829.1K **Privately Held**
SIC: 3599 Machine shop, jobbing & repair

(G-2076)
KLOSTERMAN BAKING CO
98 Vanadium Rd Ste 2 (15017-3003)
PHONE.............................412 564-1023
EMP: 5
SALES (corp-wide): 207.2MM **Privately Held**
SIC: 2051 Bread, cake & related products
PA: Klosterman Baking Co.
4760 Paddock Rd
Cincinnati OH 45229
513 242-5667

(G-2077)
LIMESTONE PRODUCTS & SUPPLY CO
260 Millers Run Rd (15017-1328)
P.O. Box 403 (15017-0403)
PHONE.............................412 221-5120
Fax: 412 221-2336
EMP: 7
SQ FT: 5,000
SALES (est): 860K **Privately Held**
SIC: 5032 3273 Whol Brick/Stone Material Mfg Ready-Mixed Concrete

(G-2078)
MERCER LIME COMPANY (DH)
50 Abele Rd Ste 1006 (15017-3442)
PHONE.............................412 220-0316
Edward Solomon III, *President*
R Campolong, *Treasurer*
H Y Gutnickk, *Admin Sec*
EMP: 4 EST: 1946
SQ FT: 2,500
SALES (est): 16.8MM
SALES (corp-wide): 361MM **Privately Held**
WEB: www.mercerlime.com
SIC: 3274 Building lime
HQ: Mississippi Lime Company
3870 S Lindbergh Blvd # 200
Saint Louis MO 63127
314 543-6300

(G-2079)
MOBILE MINI INC
981 Steen Rd (15017-2843)
PHONE.............................412 220-4477
Charles Guest, *Branch Mgr*
EMP: 20
SALES (corp-wide): 593.2MM **Publicly Held**
WEB: www.mobilemini.com
SIC: 3448 Buildings, portable: prefabricated metal
PA: Mobile Mini, Inc.
4646 E Van Buren St # 400
Phoenix AZ 85008
480 894-6311

(G-2080)
MULTISCOPE DCMENT SLUTIONS INC
300 Bursca Dr Ste 307 (15017-1448)
PHONE.............................724 743-1083
Michael McCay, *CEO*
EMP: 45
SALES (est): 1MM **Privately Held**
SIC: 2759 Commercial printing

(G-2081)
NETHERCRAFT INCORPORATED
580 Mayer St (15017-2700)
PHONE.............................248 224-1963
Tomak Baksik, *President*
EMP: 4
SALES: 250K **Privately Held**
SIC: 3089 Plastic processing

(G-2082)
NORTH JCKSON SPECIALTY STL LLC (HQ)
Also Called: Universal Stainless
600 Mayer St (15017-2705)
PHONE.............................412 257-7600
Dennis Oats, *CEO*
Charlie Chambers, *Facilities Mgr*
Keith Galbraith, *Engineer*
Kris Janocfko, *Human Res Mgr*
Shawna Locke, *Sales Staff*
EMP: 41
SALES (est): 13.1MM **Publicly Held**
SIC: 3312 Stainless steel

(G-2083)
NORTH JCKSON SPECIALTY STL LLC
600 Mayer St (15017-2705)
PHONE.............................412 257-7600
EMP: 175
SALES (est): 14.1MM **Privately Held**
SIC: 3315 Mfg Steel Wire/Related Products

(G-2084)
PAT LANDGRAF
Also Called: PC Workshop
260 Millers Run Rd Ste 1 (15017-1328)
PHONE.............................412 221-0347
Pat Landgraf, *Owner*
EMP: 3
SQ FT: 500
SALES: 150K **Privately Held**
SIC: 7377 7371 7372 Computer rental & leasing; computer software writers, freelance; business oriented computer software

(G-2085)
PATI PETITE BUTTER COOKIES INC
Also Called: Pati Petite Cookies
1785 Mayview Rd (15017-1516)
PHONE.............................412 221-4033
Keith R Graham, *President*
Bruce L Graham, *Vice Pres*
William P Graham, *Treasurer*
Cathy Bockstoce, *Manager*
EMP: 25 EST: 1964
SQ FT: 45,000
SALES (est): 4.9MM **Privately Held**
SIC: 2052 Cookies

(G-2086)
PITTSBURGH POWDER COAT L
621 Mclaughlin Run Rd (15017-2511)
PHONE.............................724 348-8434
EMP: 4
SALES (est): 448K **Privately Held**
SIC: 2851 Paints & allied products

(G-2087)
ROADSIDE PRODUCTS INC
124 Hickory Heights Dr (15017-1076)
PHONE.............................412 220-9694
John Cosco, *President*
Katie Cosco, *Vice Pres*
Charlie Goetz, *CFO*
EMP: 10
SALES: 500K **Privately Held**
SIC: 2033 Barbecue sauce: packaged in cans, jars, etc.

(G-2088)
SCHWEBEL BAKING COMPANY
111 Southpointe Dr (15017-1235)
PHONE.............................412 257-6067
Scott Baumgardner, *Manager*
EMP: 34
SALES (corp-wide): 170MM **Privately Held**
WEB: www.schwebels.com
SIC: 2051 Bread, cake & related products
PA: Schwebel Baking Company
965 E Midlothian Blvd
Youngstown OH 44502
330 783-2860

(G-2089)
SILHOL BUILDERS SUPPLY CO INC
100 Union St (15017-2420)
PHONE.............................412 221-7400
Richard Teodori, *President*
June Chase, *Admin Sec*
EMP: 32
SQ FT: 50,000
SALES (est): 7.7MM **Privately Held**
SIC: 5031 3273 5211 Lumber: rough, dressed & finished; plywood; doors; ready-mixed concrete; planing mill products & lumber; doors, storm: wood or metal

(G-2090)
SMITH & NEPHEW INC
300 Bursca Dr Ste 308 (15017-1448)
PHONE.............................412 914-1190
Kavya Suresh, *Project Mgr*
Eric Trier, *Branch Mgr*
Lindsay Russell, *Manager*
EMP: 50
SALES (corp-wide): 4.7B **Privately Held**
SIC: 3842 Prosthetic appliances
HQ: Smith & Nephew, Inc.
1450 E Brooks Rd
Memphis TN 38116
901 396-2121

(G-2091)
ST CLAIR PRECAST CONCRETE INC
601 4th Ave (15017-1309)
PHONE.............................412 221-2577
James K Kaucic, *President*
John Kaucic Jr, *Corp Secy*
EMP: 4
SQ FT: 1,200
SALES (est): 475.3K **Privately Held**
SIC: 3272 Concrete products, precast

(G-2092)
SUBURBAN PUMP AND MCH CO INC
98 Vanadium Rd Bldg B (15017-3061)
PHONE.............................412 221-2823
Frank Stuckwish, *President*
Linda Stuckwish, *Corp Secy*
EMP: 9
SQ FT: 18,500
SALES (est): 1.4MM **Privately Held**
SIC: 7699 3599 Pumps & pumping equipment repair; machine shop, jobbing & repair

(G-2093)
TARPON ENERGY SERVICES LLC
1901 Mayview Rd Ste 10 (15017-1583)
PHONE.............................570 547-0442
Mike Voegtle, *Manager*
EMP: 99
SALES (est): 3.5MM **Privately Held**
SIC: 1731 1389 Electrical work; construction, repair & dismantling services

(G-2094)
THESPIDERFRIENDS COM LLC
434 Pine Valley Dr (15017-3436)
PHONE.............................412 257-2346
Katherine Drinkhall,
EMP: 3
SALES (est): 81.1K **Privately Held**
SIC: 2731 Book publishing

(G-2095)
THYSSNKRUPP INDUS SLUTIONS USA
1370 Washington Pike (15017-2862)
PHONE.............................412 257-8277
Lorriane Race, *Branch Mgr*
EMP: 100
SQ FT: 20,000
SALES (corp-wide): 39.8B **Privately Held**
SIC: 7699 1011 3559 1389 Miscellaneous building item repair services; iron ore mining; kilns; cement; gas compressing (natural gas) at the fields
HQ: Thyssenkrupp Industrial Solutions (Usa), Inc
6400 S Fiddlers Green Cir
Greenwood Village CO 80111

(G-2096)
TMS INTERNATIONAL LLC
600 Mayer St (15017-2705)
P.O. Box 204 (15017-0204)
PHONE.............................412 257-1083
EMP: 5 **Privately Held**
SIC: 3479 Metal Coating And Allied Services, Nsk

(G-2097)
UNIVERSAL STAINLESS & ALLOY (PA)
600 Mayer St (15017-2790)
PHONE.............................412 257-7600
Dennis M Oates, *Ch of Bd*
Paul McGrath, *VP Admin*
Paul A McGrath, *Vice Pres*
Graham McIntosh, *Vice Pres*
Lee Burkett, *Plant Mgr*
▲ EMP: 277
SQ FT: 760,000
SALES: 255.9MM **Publicly Held**
SIC: 3312 Blast furnaces & steel mills; tool & die steel; stainless steel

(G-2098)
VANADIUM ENTERPRISES CORP (PA)
Also Called: Vanadium Group
100 Emerson Ln Ste 1513 (15017-3484)
PHONE.............................412 206-2990
Matthew D Schneider, *President*
Robert Bartolacci, *Corp Secy*
EMP: 35
SQ FT: 3,500
SALES (est): 54.6MM **Privately Held**
WEB: www.vanadium.com
SIC: 5075 7372 Warm air heating & air conditioning; prepackaged software

(G-2099)
WINN-MARION BARBER LLC
200 Old Pond Rd Ste 106 (15017-1269)
PHONE...................................412 319-7392
Gary Fuller, *Manager*
EMP: 4
SALES (corp-wide): 44MM **Privately Held**
SIC: 7699 1389 Industrial machinery & equipment repair; oil & gas wells: building, repairing & dismantling
PA: Winn-Marion Barber, Llc
7084 S Revere Pkwy Unit A
Centennial CO 80112
303 778-6767

(G-2100)
Z & F USA
700 Old Pond Rd Ste 606 (15017-1274)
PHONE...................................412 257-8575
Dirk Langer, *CEO*
Christoph Froehlich, *President*
Eric Dejans, *Treasurer*
EMP: 4
SALES (est): 846.3K
SALES (corp-wide): 29.5MM **Privately Held**
WEB: www.zf-usa.com
SIC: 3315 Wire & fabricated wire products
PA: Zoller & Frohlich Gmbh
Simoniusstr. 22
Wangen Im Allgau 88239
752 293-080

Brier Hill
Fayette County

(G-2101)
SANDVIK INC
Also Called: Sandvik Mining and Tunneling
6701 National Pike (15415)
PHONE...................................724 246-2901
Ralph Oberdorfer, *Branch Mgr*
EMP: 50
SALES (corp-wide): 10.7B **Privately Held**
SIC: 3532 Mining machinery
HQ: Sandvik, Inc.
17-02 Nevins Rd
Fair Lawn NJ 07410
201 794-5000

Bristol
Bucks County

(G-2102)
ABTEC INCORPORATED
2570 Pearl Buck Rd (19007-6809)
PHONE...................................215 788-0950
William S Sinclair, *President*
Janice Chuch, *Human Res Dir*
Janine McCormick, *Sales Executive*
EMP: 100
SQ FT: 22,500
SALES (est): 14.5MM **Privately Held**
WEB: www.abtecinc.com
SIC: 3089 Injection molding of plastics
PA: Aries Electronics, Inc.
2609 Bartram Rd
Bristol PA
215 781-9956

(G-2103)
**ACTION MANUFACTURING
COMPANY (PA)**
190 Rittenhouse Cir (19007-1618)
PHONE...................................267 540-4041
Sean Gibbs, *President*
Francis Mattia, *Vice Pres*
Arthur Mattia Jr, *Treasurer*
▼ EMP: 267
SQ FT: 122,000
SALES (est): 85.5MM **Privately Held**
SIC: 3489 2892 3483 Ordnance & accessories; explosives; ammunition components

(G-2104)
**ADVENT DESIGN
CORPORATION**
Also Called: API
925 Canal St Ste 1301 (19007-3999)
PHONE...................................215 781-0500
William Leroy Chesterson, *CEO*
Thomas Lawton, *President*
Debbie Chesterson, *COO*
Frank Garcia, *Admin Sec*
▲ EMP: 112
SQ FT: 150,000
SALES: 15.6MM **Privately Held**
WEB: www.adventdesign.com
SIC: 3569 7389 3826 3825 Robots, assembly line: industrial & commercial; design services; laser scientific & engineering instruments; instruments to measure electricity; consulting engineer

(G-2105)
AMERICA HEARS INC (PA)
806 Beaver St (19007-3825)
PHONE...................................215 785-5437
Henry Smith Jr, *Ch of Bd*
David Wright, *President*
Heidi Sharpe, *Vice Pres*
EMP: 16
SALES (est): 4.9MM **Privately Held**
WEB: www.americahears.com
SIC: 3842 5047 5999 Hearing aids; hearing aids; hearing aids

(G-2106)
**AMI ENTERTAINMENT
NETWORK INC (HQ)**
Also Called: Merit Entertainment
925 Canal St (19007-3931)
PHONE...................................215 826-1400
Peter Feuer, *President*
Garth Gadberry, *Engineer*
▲ EMP: 30
SQ FT: 45,000
SALES (est): 15.4MM
SALES (corp-wide): 4B **Privately Held**
WEB: www.meritind.com
SIC: 3999 Coin-operated amusement machines
PA: The Gores Group Llc
9800 Wilshire Blvd
Beverly Hills CA 90212
310 209-3010

(G-2107)
ANJU SYLOGENT LLC
1414 Radcliffe St Ste 115 (19007-5433)
PHONE...................................215 504-7000
EMP: 15
SALES (corp-wide): 3MM **Privately Held**
SIC: 7372 Prepackaged software
HQ: Anju Sylogent, Llc
251 W 19th St
New York NY 10011
480 326-2358

(G-2108)
**ARC RMEDIATION SPECIALISTS
INC**
258 Main St (19007-6115)
PHONE...................................386 405-6760
Alex Chester, *President*
Patricia Chester, *Vice Pres*
EMP: 12 EST: 2010
SQ FT: 3,500
SALES (est): 138.5K **Privately Held**
SIC: 8999 3842 4959 8748 Earth science services; personal safety equipment; environmental cleanup services; safety training service; ; safety inspection service

(G-2109)
ARKEMA INC
Also Called: Bristol Plant
100 Route 413 (19007-3605)
PHONE...................................215 826-2600
Linda Fitzsimmons, *Purch Agent*
Robert Loose, *Engineer*
Scott Tatro, *Manager*
Susan Pirollo, *Manager*
Patrick Webb, *Technical Staff*
EMP: 120

SALES (corp-wide): 77.8MM **Privately Held**
SIC: 2812 2819 2869 2891 Chlorine, compressed or liquefied; industrial inorganic chemicals; industrial organic chemicals; adhesives & sealants; metal treating compounds; lubricating oils & greases
HQ: Arkema Inc.
900 First Ave
King Of Prussia PA 19406
610 205-7000

(G-2110)
ASTATECH INC (PA)
2525 Pearl Buck Rd (19007-6807)
PHONE...................................215 785-3197
Rona Yang, *President*
Xueliang Liu, *QC Dir*
Xiao Qiu, *Research*
◆ EMP: 22
SQ FT: 4,500
SALES: 13MM **Privately Held**
WEB: www.astatechinc.com
SIC: 2899 2869 Chemical preparations; laboratory chemicals, organic

(G-2111)
**ATLANTIC CONCRETE
PRODUCTS INC (PA)**
8900 Old Route 13 (19007)
PHONE...................................215 945-5600
Joseph A Westhoff, *President*
Eric Ditcher, *Vice Pres*
Scott Ditcher, *Treasurer*
Jerry Donahue, *Human Res Mgr*
Gerald Donahue, *Sales Mgr*
▲ EMP: 90
SQ FT: 9,000
SALES (est): 26.9MM **Privately Held**
WEB: www.atlanticconcrete.com
SIC: 3272 Concrete products, precast

(G-2112)
**ATLANTIC PRECAST
CONCRETE**
8900 Old Route 13 (19007)
PHONE...................................215 945-5600
Eric A Ditcher, *President*
Scott A Ditcher, *Vice Pres*
Joseph A Westhoff, *Treasurer*
John C Westhoff, *Admin Sec*
EMP: 97
SALES (est): 18.2MM
SALES (corp-wide): 26.7MM **Privately Held**
SIC: 3272 Concrete products
PA: Atlantic Precast Industries Inc
8900 Old Rte 13
Bristol PA 19007
215 945-5600

(G-2113)
**ATLANTIC PRECAST
INDUSTRIES (PA)**
Also Called: Atlantic Precast Concrete
8900 Old Rte 13 (19007)
PHONE...................................215 945-5600
Eric Ditcher, *President*
Jerry Donahue, *Principal*
Barry Sullivan, *Principal*
Joseph Westhoff Jr, *Corp Secy*
EMP: 200
SQ FT: 13,312
SALES (est): 26.7MM **Privately Held**
SIC: 3272 5999 Liquid catch basins, tanks & covers: concrete; concrete products, pre-cast

(G-2114)
AUTHORIZED EARMOLD LABS
806 Beaver St (19007-3825)
PHONE...................................215 788-0330
Henry Smith, *President*
EMP: 65
SQ FT: 10,000
SALES (est): 5.7MM **Privately Held**
SIC: 3842 Hearing aids

(G-2115)
AUTO TOPS INC (PA)
320 Howell St (19007-3526)
PHONE...................................215 785-3310
Vaughn D Williams, *President*
Sharon Principato, *Office Mgr*
EMP: 17 EST: 1977

SQ FT: 4,500
SALES (est): 2.2MM **Privately Held**
WEB: www.autotopsinc.com
SIC: 3714 Tops, motor vehicle

(G-2116)
BARNES GROUP INC
Associated Spring Raymond
1900 Frost Rd Ste 101 (19007-1519)
PHONE...................................215 785-4466
Stewart Stumpo, *Branch Mgr*
EMP: 4
SALES (corp-wide): 1.5B **Publicly Held**
WEB: www.barnesgroupinc.com
SIC: 5072 3495 Hardware; wire springs
PA: Barnes Group Inc.
123 Main St
Bristol CT 06010
860 583-7070

(G-2117)
BAY SALES LLC
113 Fillmore St (19007-5409)
PHONE...................................215 331-6466
Michael Roseman, *President*
Allen Smith, *Vice Pres*
◆ EMP: 5
SALES (est): 4.8MM **Privately Held**
SIC: 2678 5112 Stationery products; stationery & office supplies

(G-2118)
**BIOPLAST MANUFACTURING
LLC**
128 Wharton Rd (19007-1622)
PHONE...................................609 807-3070
Christopher Conway, *Mng Member*
Brian Conway,
EMP: 42 EST: 2008
SQ FT: 15,000
SALES: 3.5MM **Privately Held**
SIC: 3841 Surgical & medical instruments

(G-2119)
BLENDCO SYSTEMS LLC (HQ)
1 Pearl Buck Ct (19007-6812)
PHONE...................................215 785-3147
Brent McCurdy, *President*
Dan Fulton, *Regional Mgr*
Steve Harper, *Mfg Staff*
Brent Anderson, *Manager*
Wes Osborne,
EMP: 25
SQ FT: 25,000
SALES (est): 2.7MM **Privately Held**
WEB: www.blendco.com
SIC: 2841 Detergents, synthetic organic or inorganic alkaline

(G-2120)
BONSAL AMERICAN INC
1214 Hayes Blvd (19007-2913)
PHONE...................................215 785-1290
Gary Barlow, *Manager*
EMP: 15
SQ FT: 23,400
SALES (corp-wide): 29.7B **Privately Held**
WEB: www.bonsalamerican.com
SIC: 3272 Concrete products
HQ: Bonsal American, Inc.
625 Griffith Rd Ste 100
Charlotte NC 28217
704 525-1621

(G-2121)
**BUCKS COUNTY OFF SVCS &
PRTG**
Also Called: Snyder Graphics
2297 Seabird Dr (19007-5220)
P.O. Box 316, Fairless Hills (19030-0316)
PHONE...................................215 295-7060
Patricia Snyder, *President*
EMP: 4
SQ FT: 1,000
SALES: 220K **Privately Held**
SIC: 2752 Commercial printing, offset

(G-2122)
**BURNELLS WELDING
CORPORATION**
1231 Hayes Blvd (19007-2904)
PHONE...................................215 757-2896
Charles Burnell, *President*
Michael Burnell, *Treasurer*
Marie Burnell, *Admin Sec*

GEOGRAPHIC

EMP: 5
SALES: 260.8K **Privately Held**
SIC: 7692 Welding repair

(G-2123)
CARDOLITE CORPORATION (PA)
140 Wharton Rd (19007-1622)
PHONE..................................609 436-0902
Anthony Stonis, *President*
Timothy Stonis, *President*
Tom Claessen, *Business Mgr*
Angel Soto, *Vice Pres*
Shannon Donohue, *Purchasing*
◆ **EMP:** 50
SALES (est): 11.7MM **Privately Held**
WEB: www.cardolite.com
SIC: 3479 3499 2891 Coating of metals &
formed products; friction material, made
from powdered metal; adhesives

(G-2124)
CERAMIC ART COMPANY INC
Also Called: Lenox Collections
1414 Radcliffe St Fl 2 (19007-5413)
PHONE..................................952 944-5600
EMP: 711
SALES (est): 25.8MM **Privately Held**
SIC: 3229 3262 5719 5948 Mfg
Pressed/Blown Glass Mfg Vetreous China
Tblwr Ret Misc Homefurnishings Ret Lug-
gage/Leather Good
PA: Cac Group Inc.
6436 City West Pkwy
Eden Prairie MN

(G-2125)
CHINA LENOX INCORPORATED
1414 Radcliffe St (19007-5413)
PHONE..................................267 525-7800
Stephen Garrell, *Prgrmr*
Tom Johnson, *Director*
EMP: 1500 **EST:** 2007
SALES (est): 79.7MM **Privately Held**
SIC: 3263 Semivitreous table & kitchen-
ware

(G-2126)
CLARENCE J VENNE LLC
7900 N Radcliffe St Ste 4 (19007-5900)
PHONE..................................215 547-7110
Jeffrey Fischer, *President*
Franceen Kopena, *Accounting Mgr*
▲ **EMP:** 53 **EST:** 1964
SQ FT: 39,000
SALES (est): 11.3MM **Privately Held**
WEB: www.daboink.com
SIC: 3951 Markers, soft tip (felt, fabric,
plastic, etc.)

(G-2127)
CO-AX VALVES INC
1518 Grundy Ln (19007-1521)
PHONE..................................215 757-3725
Andreas Wurst, *President*
Theresa Glover,
EMP: 11 **EST:** 1965
SQ FT: 11,000
SALES (est): 2.2MM **Privately Held**
WEB: www.coaxvalves.com
SIC: 3491 Industrial valves

(G-2128)
CONE GUYS LTD
925 Canal St Ste 3210 (19007-3947)
PHONE..................................215 781-6996
Michael D Williamson, *President*
Allison Borenstein, *Shareholder*
EMP: 10
SQ FT: 3,000
SALES: 500K **Privately Held**
SIC: 2052 Cones, ice cream

(G-2129)
CUMMINS INC
2727 Ford Rd (19007-6805)
PHONE..................................215 785-6005
EMP: 3
SALES (corp-wide): 23.7B **Publicly Held**
SIC: 5084 3519 Engines, gasoline; inter-
nal combustion engines
PA: Cummins Inc.
500 Jackson St
Columbus IN 47201
812 377-5000

(G-2130)
CUSTOM BUILT PRODUCTS INC
760 Oxford Ave (19007-6012)
PHONE..................................215 946-9555
Allan Payne, *President*
David Payne, *Vice Pres*
EMP: 10
SQ FT: 5,000
SALES (est): 1.7MM **Privately Held**
SIC: 3499 Metal household articles

(G-2131)
DIE URGLAAWISCH SIPPSCHAFT
1817 Benson Pl (19007-4203)
PHONE..................................215 499-1323
Robert Lusch, *Principal*
EMP: 4
SALES: 35.1K **Privately Held**
SIC: 3544 Special dies & tools

(G-2132)
DOW CHEMICAL COMPANY
200 Route 413 (19007-3606)
PHONE..................................215 785-8000
Mark Mummert, *Branch Mgr*
EMP: 130
SALES (corp-wide): 85.9B **Publicly Held**
WEB: www.rohmhaas.com
SIC: 2851 Paints & allied products
HQ: The Dow Chemical Company
2211 H H Dow Way
Midland MI 48642
989 636-1000

(G-2133)
DOW CHEMICAL COMPANY
310 Grge Pttrson Dr 100 (19007)
PHONE..................................215 785-7000
EMP: 100
SALES (corp-wide): 62.4B **Publicly Held**
SIC: 2819 2821 Mfg Industrial Inorganic
Chemicals Mfg Plastic Materials/Resins
HQ: The Dow Chemical Company
25500 Whitesell St
Hayward CA 94545
510 786-0100

(G-2134)
DUNMORE CORPORATION (DH)
145 Wharton Rd (19007-1621)
PHONE..................................215 781-8895
Matthew T Sullivan, *President*
Jeff Blake, *President*
Neil Gillespie, *President*
Diana Dunbar, *General Mgr*
Edward Mitchell, *General Mgr*
◆ **EMP:** 90
SQ FT: 60,000
SALES (est): 41.2MM **Privately Held**
WEB: www.dunmore.com
SIC: 3081 Unsupported plastics film &
sheet
HQ: Api Group Plc
Second Avenue
Stockport SK12
162 585-8700

(G-2135)
DUNMORE INTERNATIONAL CORP (PA)
145 Wharton Rd (19007-1621)
PHONE..................................215 781-8895
Matthew T Sullivan, *President*
Mary Sullivan, *CFO*
EMP: 4
SQ FT: 60,000
SALES (est): 7.6MM **Privately Held**
SIC: 3081 Unsupported plastics film &
sheet

(G-2136)
EAST COAST SIGN ADVG CO INC
Also Called: Icon Identity Solutions
5058 Rte 13 N (19007)
PHONE..................................888 724-0380
Greg Goulette, *CEO*
EMP: 134
SALES (est): 14.3MM **Privately Held**
SIC: 3993 1799 Signs, not made in cus-
tom sign painting shops; neon signs; sign
installation & maintenance

(G-2137)
EASTERN RAIL SYSTEMS INC
2014 Ford Rd Ste G (19007-6743)
PHONE..................................215 826-9980
James Gunnerson, *President*
Richard Heraty, *Vice Pres*
EMP: 3
SQ FT: 4,200
SALES: 700K **Privately Held**
WEB: www.easternrail.com
SIC: 3841 Surgical & medical instruments

(G-2138)
ELECTRIC METERING CORP USA
202 William Leigh Dr (19007-6307)
PHONE..................................215 949-1900
Steven Torsivia, *President*
Rita Perez, *Vice Pres*
▲ **EMP:** 60
SQ FT: 25,000
SALES (est): 9.1MM **Privately Held**
WEB: www.electricmeteringcorp.com
SIC: 3825 Measuring instruments & me-
ters, electric; watt-hour meters, electrical;
meters, power factor & phase angle;
transformers, portable: instrument

(G-2139)
ELECTRONIC IMAGING SVCS INC
Also Called: Vestcom Retail Solutions
1501 Grundy Ln (19007-1506)
PHONE..................................215 785-2284
EMP: 8 **Privately Held**
SIC: 8742 2759 Mgmt Consulting Svcs
Commercial Printing
HQ: Electronic Imaging Services, Inc.
2800 Cantrell Rd Ste 400
Little Rock AR 72202
501 663-0100

(G-2140)
ELF ATOCHEM
100 Route 413 (19007-3605)
PHONE..................................215 826-2600
EMP: 3
SALES (est): 427.6K **Privately Held**
SIC: 2869 Mfg Industrial Organic Chemi-
cals

(G-2141)
ENPRO INDUSTRIES INC
Also Called: France Compressor Products
107 William Leigh Dr (19007-6313)
PHONE..................................215 946-0845
Gregg Reichard, *Manager*
EMP: 7
SALES (corp-wide): 1.5B **Publicly Held**
WEB: www.enproindustries.com
SIC: 3053 3519 3089 Gaskets & sealing
devices; engines, diesel & semi-diesel or
dual-fuel; marine engines; gasoline en-
gines; bearings, plastic
PA: Enpro Industries, Inc.
5605 Carnegie Blvd # 500
Charlotte NC 28209
704 731-1500

(G-2142)
ESTEE LAUDER COMPANIES INC
300 Crossing Dr (19007-1509)
PHONE..................................215 826-4247
WEI Xie, *Plant Engr*
Stephanie Ehredt, *Branch Mgr*
EMP: 504 **Publicly Held**
SIC: 2844 Toilet preparations
PA: The Estee Lauder Companies Inc
767 5th Ave Fl 1
New York NY 10153

(G-2143)
F C YOUNG & CO INC
Also Called: Youngcraft
400 Howell St (19007-3525)
PHONE..................................215 788-9226
Kevin Long, *President*
F C Young, *President*
Kevin Young, *President*
Dorothy T Young, *Admin Sec*
◆ **EMP:** 125
SQ FT: 33,000

SALES (est): 16.6MM **Privately Held**
SIC: 3999 5199 Tinsel; Christmas novelties

(G-2144)
FERAG INC
190 Rittenhouse Cir (19007-1618)
PHONE..................................215 788-0892
Walter Wild, *Vice Pres*
Roger Honegger, *Vice Pres*
EMP: 65
SQ FT: 126,000
SALES (est): 6.3MM **Privately Held**
WEB: www.ferag-americas.com
SIC: 3555 3554 3537 3535 Printing
trades machinery; paper industries ma-
chinery; industrial trucks & tractors; con-
veyors & conveying equipment

(G-2145)
FIBER PRODUCTIONS II INC
2705 Old Rodgers Rd (19007-1734)
PHONE..................................267 546-7025
George T Berry II, *President*
EMP: 3
SQ FT: 7,000
SALES: 500K **Privately Held**
SIC: 3544 Industrial molds

(G-2146)
GENERAL DOORS CORPORATION (PA)
1 Monroe St (19007-5408)
P.O. Box 205 (19007-0205)
PHONE..................................215 788-9277
George P Cain, *Ch of Bd*
George P Cain Sr, *Ch of Bd*
William I Cain, *Vice Pres*
EMP: 55
SQ FT: 91,000
SALES (est): 12.3MM **Privately Held**
WEB: www.general-doors.com
SIC: 2431 Doors & door parts & trim,
wood; garage doors, overhead: wood

(G-2147)
GENTELL INC
2701 Bartram Rd (19007-6810)
P.O. Box 490, Langhorne (19047-0490)
PHONE..................................215 788-2700
David Navazio, *Vice Pres*
Glenn Paul, *Vice Pres*
Mike Morris, *Prdtn Mgr*
▲ **EMP:** 82
SQ FT: 40,000
SALES: 16MM **Privately Held**
SIC: 2834 2844 Ointments; mouthwashes;
shampoos, rinses, conditioners: hair

(G-2148)
GESUALDI PRINTING
2225 Farragut Ave (19007-4440)
PHONE..................................215 785-3960
Matt Gesualdi, *Owner*
Donna Gray, *Office Mgr*
EMP: 3
SQ FT: 1,500
SALES: 200K **Privately Held**
SIC: 3993 2752 Signs & advertising spe-
cialties; commercial printing, lithographic

(G-2149)
GOODSON HOLDING COMPANY
Also Called: Intercounty Newspaper Group
2100 Frost Rd (19007-1517)
PHONE..................................215 370-6069
Fax: 215 785-0809
▲ **EMP:** 125 **EST:** 1869
SQ FT: 5,000
SALES (est): 6.6MM
SALES (corp-wide): 894.1MM **Privately
Held**
SIC: 2711 Newspapers-Publishing/Printing
PA: Journal Register Company
5 Hanover Sq Fl 25
New York NY 10004
212 257-7212

(G-2150)
GRASSROOTS UNWIRED INC
10 Canal St Ste 235 (19007-3943)
PHONE..................................215 788-1210
Sarah Bacon, *Director*
EMP: 6 **EST:** 2014
SALES (est): 971.2K **Privately Held**
SIC: 3315 Steel wire & related products

(G-2151)
HARMONY LL PLASTICS INC
100 Main St Ste 2c (19007-6108)
PHONE.............................215 943-8888
Denny Liu, *President*
EMP: 7
SALES: 1.9MM **Privately Held**
SIC: 2673 Plastic bags: made from purchased materials

(G-2152)
HEARING LAB TECHNOLOGY LLC
806 Beaver St (19007-3825)
PHONE.............................215 785-5437
EMP: 696 **Privately Held**
SIC: 3842 Hearing aids
PA: Hearing Lab Technology, Llc
14301 F A A Blvd
Fort Worth TX 76155

(G-2153)
HOLO IMAGE TECHNOLOGY INC
Also Called: Hit
101 William Leigh Dr (19007-6313)
PHONE.............................215 946-2190
Tom Chiang, *President*
▲ EMP: 6
SQ FT: 2,400
SALES (est): 18.9K **Privately Held**
WEB: www.holoimagetechnology.com
SIC: 3826 Laser scientific & engineering instruments

(G-2154)
IMA NORTH AMERICA INC
211 Sinclair Rd (19007-1500)
PHONE.............................215 826-8500
Donna Polcino, *Principal*
Paul E Egee, *Vice Pres*
Shawn Gallagher, *Accounts Mgr*
EMP: 7
SALES (est): 100.1K **Privately Held**
SIC: 7372 Prepackaged software

(G-2155)
IMAC SYSTEMS INC
90 Main St (19007-6117)
P.O. Box 1605, Tullytown (19007-7605)
PHONE.............................215 946-2200
Donald E Kohart, *President*
Nicholas P Kohart, *Vice Pres*
Andre Nel, *Engineer*
Julie Loftus, *Accounting Mgr*
Laszlo Kocsis, *Sales Staff*
▲ EMP: 45 EST: 1979
SQ FT: 30,000
SALES: 9MM **Privately Held**
WEB: www.imacsystems.com
SIC: 3829 5084 Measuring & controlling devices; instruments & control equipment; measuring & testing equipment, electrical; meters, consumption registering; recording instruments & accessories

(G-2156)
JAMES D MORRISSEY INC
1200 Veterans Hwy (19007-2525)
PHONE.............................267 554-7946
James D Morrissey, *Principal*
EMP: 3 EST: 2014
SALES (est): 165K **Privately Held**
SIC: 3273 Ready-mixed concrete

(G-2157)
L3 TECHNOLOGIES INC
Also Called: L3 Telemetry & Rf Products
1515 Grundy Ln (19007-1506)
P.O. Box 729 (19007-0729)
PHONE.............................267 545-7000
Burt Smith, *Branch Mgr*
EMP: 180
SALES (corp-wide): 10.2B **Publicly Held**
SIC: 3663 3669 3679 3769 Telemetering equipment, electronic; receiver-transmitter units (transceiver); amplifiers, RF power & IF; signaling apparatus, electric; intercommunication systems, electric; microwave components; guided missile & space vehicle parts & auxiliary equipment; aircraft control systems, electronic

PA: L3 Technologies, Inc.
600 3rd Ave Fl 34
New York NY 10016
212 697-1111

(G-2158)
LED LIVING TECHNOLOGIES INC
211 Sinclair Rd Ste 100 (19007-1500)
PHONE.............................215 633-1558
Oliver Szeto, *CEO*
Norman Simms, *Vice Pres*
Jasmin Molina, *Executive*
EMP: 50
SQ FT: 40,000
SALES (est): 8.4MM **Privately Held**
SIC: 3645 8731 5063 Residential lighting fixtures; commercial physical research; lighting fixtures

(G-2159)
LENOX CORPORATION (PA)
Also Called: Dansk
1414 Radcliffe St Fl 1 (19007-5418)
P.O. Box 735 (19007-0735)
PHONE.............................267 525-7800
Mads Ryder, *CEO*
Lester Gribetz, *President*
Barry Bramley, *Chairman*
Jerome Ciszewskiis, *COO*
Brian Gowen, *COO*
▲ EMP: 13
SALES (est): 314.8MM **Privately Held**
SIC: 3229 3161 5719 5948 Tableware, glass or glass ceramic; luggage; briefcases; traveling bags; china; glassware; luggage & leather goods stores

(G-2160)
LIMB TECHNOLOGIES INC (PA)
Also Called: LTI Orthotic Prosthetic Center
2925 Veterans Hwy (19007-1605)
PHONE.............................215 781-8454
Frank Sosky, *President*
EMP: 14
SQ FT: 5,000
SALES (est): 2.2MM **Privately Held**
SIC: 3842 Limbs, artificial; prosthetic appliances

(G-2161)
LITTLE SHEET METAL INC
413 River Rd Bldg 90-1 (19007)
P.O. Box 16 (19007-0016)
PHONE.............................215 946-9970
Scott Little, *President*
Kim Kebert, *Manager*
EMP: 11
SQ FT: 12,000
SALES (est): 3MM **Privately Held**
SIC: 3444 Ducts, sheet metal

(G-2162)
LUCISANO BROS INC
665 River Rd Ste 1 (19007-6111)
PHONE.............................215 945-2700
David Lucisano, *President*
EMP: 21 EST: 1946
SQ FT: 11,000
SALES: 3MM **Privately Held**
SIC: 3271 5211 Blocks, concrete or cinder: standard; lumber & other building materials

(G-2163)
LYNN ELECTRONICS CORP
Also Called: Keystone Wire and Cable
171 Rittenhouse Cir (19007-1617)
PHONE.............................215 826-9600
Steve Schmiceinger, *Manager*
EMP: 20
SALES (corp-wide): 20MM **Privately Held**
WEB: www.lynnelec.com
SIC: 3679 3643 Electronic circuits; current-carrying wiring devices
PA: Lynn Electronics Corp.
154 Railroad Dr
Ivyland PA 18974
215 355-8200

(G-2164)
MARO ELECTRONICS INC
1246 Hayes Blvd (19007-2913)
PHONE.............................215 788-7919
Joseph L Marozzi, *President*

EMP: 23 EST: 1982
SQ FT: 6,000
SALES (est): 3.7MM **Privately Held**
SIC: 3679 3699 Electronic circuits; electrical equipment & supplies

(G-2165)
MEDARBOR LLC
Also Called: Medarbor Pharma
200 Rittenhouse Cir 5e (19007-1625)
PHONE.............................732 887-6111
Chuck McCue, *Office Mgr*
Sowon Yoon, *Pharmacist*
Miroslav Kesic, *Mng Member*
Arthur Jewell, *Manager*
EMP: 8
SALES (est): 6.8MM **Privately Held**
SIC: 5122 2834 Pharmaceuticals; ointments

(G-2166)
METAL FINISHING CORPORATION
2979 State Rd (19007)
P.O. Box 1441 (19007-8441)
PHONE.............................215 788-9246
Thomas E Calkins, *President*
Frederic H Calkins Jr, *Shareholder*
EMP: 5
SALES: 275K **Privately Held**
SIC: 3599 Machine shop, jobbing & repair

(G-2167)
METAPHASE TECHNOLOGIES INC
Also Called: Metaphase Lighting
211 Sinclair Rd Ste 100k (19007-1500)
PHONE.............................215 639-8699
Oliver Szeto, *President*
Susan Johansen, *Purch Mgr*
EMP: 50
SQ FT: 40,000
SALES (est): 14.4MM **Privately Held**
WEB: www.metaphase-tech.com
SIC: 3827 Optical elements & assemblies, except ophthalmic

(G-2168)
MIL-DEL CORPORATION (PA)
Also Called: General Doors
1 Monroe St (19007-5408)
P.O. Box 205 (19007-0205)
PHONE.............................215 788-9277
George P Cain, *President*
William Cain, *Corp Secy*
EMP: 2 EST: 1940
SQ FT: 2,000
SALES (est): 1.3MM **Privately Held**
SIC: 2431 Panel work, wood

(G-2169)
MONACH ASSOCIATES INC (PA)
Also Called: Cir-Q-Tek
2210 E Farragut Ave (19007-4403)
PHONE.............................888 849-0149
William Monach Sr, *CEO*
Richard Monach, *President*
Carlotta I Monach, *Vice Pres*
Dorothy Latimer, *Project Mgr*
Bill Monach Jr, *Opers Mgr*
▲ EMP: 7 EST: 1982
SQ FT: 3,000
SALES (est): 5MM **Privately Held**
WEB: www.cir-q-tek.com
SIC: 3672 Printed circuit boards

(G-2170)
MRI FLEXIBLE PACKAGING COMPANY
181 Rittenhouse Cir (19007-1617)
PHONE.............................800 448-8183
Mike Speeney III, *Partner*
EMP: 38
SALES (corp-wide): 757.8MM **Privately Held**
SIC: 2759 Commercial printing
HQ: Mri Flexible Packaging Company
181 Rittenhouse Cir
Bristol PA 19007

(G-2171)
MRI FLEXIBLE PACKAGING COMPANY (DH)
181 Rittenhouse Cir (19007-1617)
PHONE.............................215 860-7676

Mike Speeney III, *Mng Member*
▲ EMP: 40
SQ FT: 24,000
SALES (est): 19.2MM
SALES (corp-wide): 757.8MM **Privately Held**
WEB: www.mriflex.com
SIC: 2759 Bags, plastic: printing; labels & seals: printing
HQ: C. P. Converters, Inc.
15 Grumbacher Rd
York PA 17406
717 764-1193

(G-2172)
NORTHEAST INDUS BATTERIES INC
2300 David Dr Ste 6 (19007-2042)
PHONE.............................215 788-8000
Robert B Lee, *President*
EMP: 31
SQ FT: 26,000
SALES (est): 5.4MM **Privately Held**
WEB: www.northeastbatteries.com
SIC: 3691 5531 3629 5046 Storage batteries; automobile air conditioning equipment, sale, installation; battery chargers, rectifying or nonrotating; shelving, commercial & industrial; industrial machinery & equipment

(G-2173)
NORTHTEC LLC
150 Rittenhouse Cir (19007-1618)
PHONE.............................215 781-2731
Leonard Lauder, *Principal*
EMP: 10
SALES (est): 1.5MM **Privately Held**
SIC: 2844 7389 Cosmetic preparations; cosmetic kits, assembling & packaging
PA: Northtec Llc
411 Sinclair Rd
Bristol PA 19007

(G-2174)
NORTHTEC LLC (PA)
411 Sinclair Rd (19007-1525)
PHONE.............................215 781-1600
Leonard A Lauder, *Principal*
Saul H Magram, *Principal*
Carlos Quintero, *Manager*
Lori Santoli, *Director*
EMP: 20
SALES (est): 5.2MM **Privately Held**
WEB: www.northland.ac.nz
SIC: 2844 7389 Cosmetic preparations; cosmetic kits, assembling & packaging

(G-2175)
NOSCO INC
1504 Grundy Ln (19007-1521)
PHONE.............................215 788-1105
EMP: 6
SALES (corp-wide): 322.3MM **Privately Held**
SIC: 2752 Commercial printing, lithographic
HQ: Nosco, Inc
2199 N Delany Rd
Gurnee IL 60031
847 336-4200

(G-2176)
NPC ACQUISITION INC (DH)
Also Called: Art Kraft
100 Main St (19007-6108)
PHONE.............................215 946-2000
Dennis D Mehiel, *President*
Randy Poisson, *CFO*
EMP: 131
SQ FT: 138,000
SALES (est): 13.9MM
SALES (corp-wide): 3.3B **Publicly Held**
SIC: 2653 Corrugated boxes, partitions, display items, sheets & pad
HQ: Kapstone Container Corporation
1601 Blairs Ferry Rd Ne
Cedar Rapids IA 52402
319 393-3610

(G-2177)
OTOTECH INC
Also Called: Oto Tech
806 Beaver St (19007-3825)
PHONE.............................215 781-7987
Henry Smith, *CEO*

Heidi Sharpe, *Vice Pres*
Henry Smtih Jr, *Vice Pres*
EMP: 66
SQ FT: 7,268
SALES (est): 8.9MM **Privately Held**
SIC: 3842 Hearing aids

(G-2178)
P K B INC
570 Otter St (19007-3616)
PHONE..................................215 826-1988
EMP: 6
SALES (est): 44.4K **Privately Held**
SIC: 7692 Welding repair

(G-2179)
PADC 1 (DH)
411 Sinclair Rd (19007-1525)
PHONE..................................215 781-1600
Leonard A Lauder, *CEO*
Robert J Aquilina, *Treasurer*
▲ **EMP:** 200
SQ FT: 69,000
SALES (est): 35.1MM **Publicly Held**
SIC: 2844 Toilet preparations
HQ: Estee Lauder Inc.
767 5th Ave Fl 1
New York NY 10153
212 572-4200

(G-2180)
PENN STEEL FABRICATION INC
805 N Wilson Ave Ste 206 (19007-4529)
PHONE..................................267 878-0705
Muhammad A Afridi, *President*
Aftab H Siddiqui, *Vice Pres*
EMP: 23
SALES: 2.1MM **Privately Held**
SIC: 3441 Building components, structural
steel

(G-2181)
PHILADELPHIA SAFETY DEVICES
10 Canal St Ste 205 (19007-3916)
PHONE..................................215 245-7554
John B Hamblin, *President*
Ralph Murphy, *Vice Pres*
EMP: 3
SQ FT: 750
SALES (est): 330.1K **Privately Held**
WEB: www.philasafetydevices.com
SIC: 3442 Metal doors, sash & trim

(G-2182)
PINNACLE CLIMATE TECH INC
1602 William Leigh Dr (19007-6317)
PHONE..................................215 891-8460
EMP: 6
SALES (est): 960.2K
SALES (corp-wide): 45.9MM **Privately
Held**
SIC: 3567 Industrial furnaces & ovens
PA: Pinnacle Climate Technologies, Inc.
1660 13th Ave Ne
Sauk Rapids MN 56379
320 257-9535

(G-2183)
PINNACLE PRODUCTS INTL INC
1602 William Leigh Dr (19007-6317)
PHONE..................................215 302-1417
▲ **EMP:** 12
SALES (est): 2.1MM **Privately Held**
SIC: 3585 Mfg Refrigeration/Heating
Equipment

(G-2184)
POLICE SHIELD CORP
323 Otter St (19007-3611)
PHONE..................................215 788-3489
David J Armitage, *President*
EMP: 21
SALES (est): 1.6MM **Privately Held**
SIC: 2731 2741 Book publishing; miscella-
neous publishing

(G-2185)
POLY-TEC PRODUCTS INC
Also Called: A-Lok Products
697 Main St (19007-6303)
P.O. Box 1647, Tullytown (19007-7647)
PHONE..................................215 547-3366
Jim Westhoff, *President*
Tammy McNamara, *Treasurer*
EMP: 14

SQ FT: 18,000
SALES (est): 2.3MM **Privately Held**
WEB: www.ammoclip.com
SIC: 3053 Gaskets & sealing devices

(G-2186)
PREMIER BRNDS GROUP HLDNGS LLC
Jones New York
180 Rittenhouse Cir (19007-1618)
PHONE..................................212 835-3672
Frank Lech, *Branch Mgr*
EMP: 22
SALES (corp-wide): 2.3B **Privately Held**
WEB: www.jny.com
SIC: 2339 3999 2389 Women's & misses'
accessories; atomizers, toiletry; men's
miscellaneous accessories
HQ: Premier Brands Group Holdings Llc
1441 Broadway
New York NY 10018
212 785-4000

(G-2187)
PREMIER BRNDS GROUP HLDNGS LLC
Gloria Vanderbilt
180 Rittenhouse Cir (19007-1618)
PHONE..................................215 785-4000
Jack Gross, *Manager*
EMP: 8
SALES (corp-wide): 2.3B **Privately Held**
SIC: 2337 Women's & misses' suits &
coats
HQ: Premier Brands Group Holdings Llc
1441 Broadway
New York NY 10018
212 785-4000

(G-2188)
PREMIER BRNDS GROUP HLDNGS LLC
Also Called: (JAG)
180 Rittenhouse Cir (19007-1618)
PHONE..................................212 642-3860
EMP: 12
SALES (corp-wide): 2.3B **Privately Held**
SIC: 2337 Women's & misses' suits &
coats
HQ: Premier Brands Group Holdings Llc
1441 Broadway
New York NY 10018
212 785-4000

(G-2189)
PULSER LLC
Also Called: Pulse Ruggedized Solutions
2 Pearl Buck Ct (19007-6812)
PHONE..................................215 781-6400
◆ **EMP:** 50
SALES (est): 1.8MM **Privately Held**
SIC: 3679 Mfg Electronic Components

(G-2190)
PULSER LLC
Also Called: Pulse Ruggedized Solutions
311 Sinclair Rd (19007-1524)
PHONE..................................215 781-6400
Mark Twaalfhoven, *CEO*
Ryan Neder, *CFO*
EMP: 50
SQ FT: 25,139
SALES (est): 7MM **Privately Held**
SIC: 3679 Pulse forming networks

(G-2191)
QUADAX VALVES INC
1518 Grundy Ln (19007-1521)
PHONE..................................713 429-5458
Bryan Harris, *Principal*
▲ **EMP:** 13 EST: 2011
SALES (est): 1.8MM **Privately Held**
SIC: 3491 Boiler gauge cocks

(G-2192)
R & D MACHINE CONTROLS INC (PA)
806 Branagan Dr (19007)
PHONE..................................267 205-5976
Wayne Deblasio, *President*
Jodi Deblasio, *Manager*
EMP: 4
SQ FT: 2,800

SALES (est): 647.3K **Privately Held**
SIC: 3613 1731 Panelboards & distribution boards, electric; general electrical
contractor

(G-2193)
REECE LIGHTING & PROD LLC
245 Radcliffe St Fl 2 (19007-5017)
PHONE..................................215 460-8560
EMP: 3 EST: 2014
SALES (est): 173.8K **Privately Held**
SIC: 3646 Mfg Commercial Lighting Fix-
tures

(G-2194)
REINERT & SONS INC
5800 Elwood Ave Ste A (19007-3409)
PHONE..................................215 781-8311
Donald Reinert, *President*
EMP: 18
SQ FT: 20,000
SALES (est): 1.4MM **Privately Held**
SIC: 5031 2431 Millwork; doors & door
parts & trim, wood

(G-2195)
ROBERN INC
Also Called: Pl Bath Products
701 N Wilson Ave (19007-4517)
PHONE..................................215 826-0280
Steven Bissel, *President*
Rachael Turner, *CFO*
▲ **EMP:** 100
SQ FT: 10,000
SALES (est): 27.9MM
SALES (corp-wide): 7.9B **Privately Held**
WEB: www.robern.com
SIC: 2514 3446 Medicine cabinets & vani-
ties: metal; railings, prefabricated metal
PA: Kohler Co.
444 Highland Dr
Kohler WI 53044
920 457-4441

(G-2196)
S G FRANTZ CO INC
Also Called: FERRO FILTER
1507 Branagan Dr (19007-6314)
P.O. Box 1138, Trenton NJ (08606-1138)
PHONE..................................215 943-2930
Jens Dahl, *President*
Stephen Fortunak, *Vice Pres*
Anne Fortunak, *Admin Sec*
EMP: 6 EST: 1935
SQ FT: 8,400
SALES: 1.1MM **Privately Held**
WEB: www.sgfrantz.com
SIC: 3569 Separators for steam, gas,
vapor or air (machinery)

(G-2197)
SEKO DOSING SYSTEMS CORP
913 William Leigh Dr (19007-6312)
PHONE..................................215 945-0125
William Decristofano, *General Mgr*
Patrizia Esposito, *Purch Mgr*
Stephen Dufort, *Regl Sales Mgr*
Angela Felver, *Manager*
Dave Hunter, *Technical Staff*
▲ **EMP:** 3
SALES (est): 545.6K **Privately Held**
WEB: www.sekousa.com
SIC: 3594 Pumps, hydraulic power transfer

(G-2198)
SMITH AUTO SERVICE
3112 Hilltop Ave (19007-6708)
PHONE..................................215 788-2401
Elwyn H Smith Jr, *Owner*
EMP: 3
SQ FT: 1,281
SALES: 100K **Privately Held**
SIC: 3714 7549 Exhaust systems & parts,
motor vehicle; towing service, automotive

(G-2199)
SOLVAY USA INC
Also Called: Center For RES & Tech Bristol
350 George Patterson Dr (19007-3624)
PHONE..................................215 781-6001
John Cherkauskas, *Vice Pres*
EMP: 100
SALES (corp-wide): 10MM **Privately
Held**
WEB: www.food.us.rhodia.com
SIC: 2819 Industrial inorganic chemicals

HQ: Solvay Usa Inc.
504 Carnegie Ctr
Princeton NJ 08540
609 860-4000

(G-2200)
SONCO WORLDWIDE INC
Also Called: Sonco Fence
805 N Wilson Ave Ste 205 (19007-4529)
PHONE..................................215 337-9651
Bob Long, *President*
EMP: 10
SALES (corp-wide): 60.3MM **Privately
Held**
WEB: www.soncoww.com
SIC: 5211 3315 Fencing; steel wire & re-
lated products
PA: Sonco Worldwide, Inc.
6500 Ammendale Rd
Beltsville MD 20705
240 487-2490

(G-2201)
SPECIALTY TANK & WLDG CO INC
7900 N Rdcliffe St Ste 11 (19007)
PHONE..................................215 949-2939
John Riccio, *President*
EMP: 31
SQ FT: 24,000
SALES (est): 3.6MM **Privately Held**
SIC: 3443 1623 4959 Tanks, lined: metal
plate; pipe laying construction; environ-
mental cleanup services

(G-2202)
SUNSHINE PLASTICS INC
100 Main St Unit 2 (19007-6108)
P.O. Box 1628, Tullytown (19007-7628)
PHONE..................................215 943-8888
Cheung WEI Yeung, *President*
EMP: 10
SQ FT: 28,000
SALES: 80K **Privately Held**
SIC: 2673 Plastic bags: made from pur-
chased materials

(G-2203)
T S BEH TRUCKING SERVICES
230 Buckley St (19007-3718)
PHONE..................................267 918-0493
Tonia S Beh, *Principal*
James N Jackson, *Principal*
EMP: 4 EST: 2010
SALES (est): 374.5K **Privately Held**
SIC: 3537 Industrial trucks & tractors

(G-2204)
TECOMET INC
Also Called: Hd Surgical
1507 Clyde Waite Dr Ste 2 (19007-2916)
PHONE..................................215 826-8250
EMP: 10
SALES (corp-wide): 784.1MM **Privately
Held**
SIC: 3841 Surgical & medical instruments
PA: Tecomet Inc.
115 Eames St
Wilmington MA 01887
978 642-2400

(G-2205)
TELSTAR NORTH AMERICA INC
1504 Grundy Ln (19007-1521)
PHONE..................................215 826-0770
Paul Stewart, *President*
Paul Valerio, *General Mgr*
Mazedul Islam, *Technical Staff*
Jochen Dick, *Officer*
▲ **EMP:** 900
SALES (est): 115.1MM
SALES (corp-wide): 2.4B **Privately Held**
SIC: 3565 Packaging machinery
HQ: Azbil Telstar Sl.
Avenida Font I Sague ((Parc Cientific I
Tecnologic Orbital 40))
Terrassa 08227
937 361-600

(G-2206)
THRESHER PHARMACEUTICALS
1200 Veterans Hwy Ste 827 (19007-2525)
PHONE..................................215 826-0227
Theodore Strowhouer, *Principal*
EMP: 6

▲ = Import ▼=Export
◆ =Import/Export

SALES (est): 616.6K **Privately Held**
SIC: 2834 5122 Pharmaceutical preparations; pharmaceuticals

(G-2207)
TMS PRECISION MACHINING INC
5 Fox Dr Bldg Jc5 Jc (19007)
P.O. Box 1681, Tullytown (19007-7681)
PHONE..............................215 547-6070
Antonio Silva, *President*
Maria Silva, *Vice Pres*
EMP: 3
SQ FT: 4,300
SALES (est): 363K **Privately Held**
SIC: 3541 Machine tool replacement & repair parts, metal cutting types

(G-2208)
TOAD-ALLY SNAX INC
1410 Farragut Ave (19007-5403)
PHONE..............................215 788-7500
Darlette Jenkins, *President*
Paula Ribeiro, *Office Mgr*
EMP: 30
SQ FT: 80,000
SALES (est): 9.6MM **Privately Held**
SIC: 2064 Candy & other confectionery products

(G-2209)
TORYTOWN SCULPTURE
701 Canal St (19007-3950)
PHONE..............................215 458-8092
EMP: 3
SALES (est): 220K **Privately Held**
SIC: 3089 Molding primary plastic

(G-2210)
TRIDENT PLASTICS INC
Also Called: Trident Engineering Plastics
7900 N Radcliffe St Ste 7 (19007-5900)
PHONE..............................215 946-3999
Ronald Cadic, *President*
Bill Marmer, *Sales Staff*
Dean Cadic, *Manager*
EMP: 7
SALES (corp-wide): 14MM **Privately Held**
WEB: www.tridentplastics.com
SIC: 3089 4225 Plastic containers, except foam; general warehousing & storage
PA: Trident Plastics, Inc.
1029 Pulinski Rd
Warminster PA 18974
215 443-7147

(G-2211)
TRIPLE D SCREEN PRINTING
2854 Veterans Hwy (19007-1604)
PHONE..............................215 788-4877
Daniel J Tettlow, *President*
EMP: 25
SQ FT: 4,500
SALES (est): 2.3MM **Privately Held**
SIC: 2396 Screen printing on fabric articles

(G-2212)
UCT INC
2500 Pearl Buck Rd (19007-6811)
PHONE..............................215 781-9255
EMP: 3
SALES (est): 356.2K **Privately Held**
SIC: 3826 Analytical instruments

(G-2213)
UCT INC (PA)
2731 Bartram Rd (19007-6810)
PHONE..............................215 781-9255
Michael Telepchak, *CEO*
Stephanie Magrann, *President*
Wayne King, *Research*
Jerry Taylor, *Plant Engr*
Philip Spraker, *Sales Mgr*
EMP: 38
SQ FT: 24,000
SALES (est): 17.1MM **Privately Held**
WEB: www.unitedchem.com
SIC: 2819 2869 Industrial inorganic chemicals; industrial organic chemicals

(G-2214)
UCT LLC
2731 Bartram Rd (19007-6810)
PHONE..............................215 781-9255
Jeff Hackett, *Principal*

Michael Telechak,
EMP: 30
SQ FT: 12,000
SALES: 10MM
SALES (corp-wide): 17.1MM **Privately Held**
SIC: 2869 Laboratory chemicals, organic
PA: Uct, Inc.
2731 Bartram Rd
Bristol PA 19007
215 781-9255

(G-2215)
VIRTUS PHARMACEUTICALS LLC
310 George Patterson Dr (19007-3634)
PHONE..............................267 938-4850
Vivek Desai, *Manager*
EMP: 20
SALES (corp-wide): 9.7MM **Privately Held**
SIC: 2834 Pharmaceutical preparations
HQ: Virtus Pharmaceuticals, Llc
2050 Cabot Blvd W Ste 200
Langhorne PA 19047
267 938-4850

(G-2216)
WAKINS FOOD CORPORATION
218 Us Highway 13 Rear (19007-3517)
PHONE..............................215 785-3420
George Wakin, *President*
EMP: 3
SQ FT: 2,400
SALES: 1MM **Privately Held**
SIC: 2038 Frozen specialties

(G-2217)
WICKED COOL TOYS HOLDINGS LLC (PA)
10 Canal St Ste 327 (19007-3900)
PHONE..............................267 536-9186
Michael Rinzler,
▲ **EMP:** 22
SQ FT: 2,500
SALES (est): 3.9MM **Privately Held**
SIC: 3944 Games, toys & children's vehicles

(G-2218)
WOUND CARE CONCEPTS INC
2701 Bartram Rd (19007-6810)
P.O. Box 490, Langhorne (19047-0490)
PHONE..............................215 788-2700
Fredric Brotz, *President*
EMP: 25
SALES (est): 4.4MM **Privately Held**
SIC: 2841 Soap & other detergents

(G-2219)
YORKSHIRE LEAD GLASS COMPANY
7128 N Radcliffe St (19007-5821)
PHONE..............................215 694-2727
Florence Cantiello, *President*
▲ **EMP:** 12
SALES (est): 596.6K **Privately Held**
SIC: 3231 Products of purchased glass

Brockport
Elk County

(G-2220)
BROCKPORT GLASS COMPONENTS LLC
6185 Route 219 (15823-1827)
PHONE..............................814 265-1479
James Geer, *Mng Member*
Kevin Grecco,
EMP: 3
SALES (est): 170.8K **Privately Held**
SIC: 3559 Glass making machinery: blowing, molding, forming, etc.

(G-2221)
J I T TOOL & DIE INC
7294 Route 219 (15823-2504)
PHONE..............................814 265-0257
Robert Beimel, *President*
Bonnie Beimel, *Corp Secy*
EMP: 43
SQ FT: 5,000

SALES (est): 6MM **Privately Held**
WEB: www.jittoolanddie.com
SIC: 3544 3599 Dies & die holders for metal cutting, forming, die casting; machine & other job shop work

(G-2222)
OWENS-ILLINOIS INC
Also Called: Owens Brockway Glass
3831 Route 219 (15823-3811)
PHONE..............................814 261-5200
Al Stroucken, *Ch of Bd*
Hayes Gary, *Sales Staff*
EMP: 350
SALES (corp-wide): 6.8B **Publicly Held**
SIC: 3221 Glass containers
PA: Owens-Illinois, Inc.
1 Michael Owens Way
Perrysburg OH 43551
567 336-5000

Brockway
Jefferson County

(G-2223)
BROCKWAY SINTERED TECHNOLOGY (HQ)
1228 Main St (15824-1634)
PHONE..............................814 265-8090
Peter Varischetti, *President*
EMP: 5
SALES (est): 11.5MM **Privately Held**
SIC: 3399 Powder, metal

(G-2224)
EASTERN ENVIRONMENTAL INDS LLC
4456 Route 219 (15824-4604)
P.O. Box 486, Mifflinville (18631-4486)
PHONE..............................814 371-2221
Mark Kile, *President*
Gregory Slusser, *Vice Pres*
EMP: 48
SQ FT: 1,200
SALES (est): 12.9MM **Privately Held**
SIC: 1381 Drilling oil & gas wells

(G-2225)
FALLS CREEK POWDERED METALS
82 Industrial Park Dr (15824-1240)
P.O. Box 239 (15824-0239)
PHONE..............................814 265-8771
Hamid Alattas, *President*
EMP: 15
SQ FT: 30,000
SALES (est): 1.5MM **Privately Held**
WEB: www.fallscreekpm.com
SIC: 3399 Powder, metal

(G-2226)
FREMER MOULDING INC
22 Sawmill Dr (15824-6856)
PHONE..............................814 265-0671
Ander Fremer, *President*
Kathleen Fremer, *President*
Katleen Fremer, *Vice Pres*
Michael Fremer, *Treasurer*
Andrew Fremer, *Shareholder*
EMP: 15
SQ FT: 11,400
SALES (est): 2.1MM **Privately Held**
SIC: 2431 Hardwood dimension & flooring mills

(G-2227)
GUY CODER
Also Called: Coder's Print Shop of Brockway
1701 Bond St (15824-1705)
PHONE..............................814 265-0519
Guy Coder, *Owner*
EMP: 3
SQ FT: 5,400
SALES: 100K **Privately Held**
SIC: 2752 2791 2789 2672 Commercial printing, offset; typesetting; bookbinding & related work; coated & laminated paper

(G-2228)
MOORE WELDING
1790 Sugar Hill Rd (15824-6244)
PHONE..............................814 328-2399
Tom Moore, *Owner*

EMP: 7
SQ FT: 10,000
SALES (est): 100K **Privately Held**
SIC: 7692 Welding repair

(G-2229)
OWENS-BROCKWAY GLASS CONT INC
Cherry St (15824)
PHONE..............................814 261-6284
EMP: 111
SALES (corp-wide): 6.8B **Publicly Held**
SIC: 3221 Mfg Glass Containers
HQ: Owens-Brockway Glass Container Inc.
1 Michael Owens Way
Perrysburg OH 43551
567 336-8449

(G-2230)
PHOENIX SINTERED METALS LLC
921 Clark St (15824-1644)
PHONE..............................814 268-3455
Peter Varischetti, *President*
Steve Leuschel, *COO*
Andy Canter, *Vice Pres*
Frank Varishetti, *Vice Pres*
Steven Varischetti, *Treasurer*
EMP: 44
SQ FT: 72,000
SALES (est): 11.3MM **Privately Held**
SIC: 3399 Powder, metal
HQ: Brockway Sintered Technology Inc
1228 Main St
Brockway PA 15824
814 265-8090

(G-2231)
PROCHEMTECH INTERNATIONAL INC (PA)
51 Pro Chem Tech Dr (15824-7323)
P.O. Box 214 (15824-0214)
PHONE..............................814 265-0959
Kathy Keister, *CEO*
Timothy Keister, *President*
Patrick H Gill, *General Mgr*
Jim Sleigh, *Vice Pres*
EMP: 21
SQ FT: 27,000
SALES (est): 5.4MM **Privately Held**
WEB: www.prochemtech.com
SIC: 2899 Water treating compounds

(G-2232)
PROSHORT STAMPING SERVICES INC
6025 Route 219 (15824-4621)
PHONE..............................814 371-9633
J Thomas Stafford Jr, *President*
EMP: 9
SQ FT: 15,000
SALES (est): 1.4MM **Privately Held**
WEB: www.proshort.com
SIC: 3444 Sheet metalwork

(G-2233)
RECLAMATION INC
1915 Fermantown Rd (15824-6143)
PHONE..............................814 265-2564
Joseph P Fremer Jr, *President*
EMP: 15 **EST:** 1966
SALES (est): 2.9MM **Privately Held**
SIC: 1221 Bituminous coal & lignite-surface mining

(G-2234)
SUFFOLK MCHY & PWR TL CORP
Rr 219 Box N (15824)
PHONE..............................631 289-7153
Arthur F Gschwind Sr, *President*
EMP: 6
SALES (corp-wide): 1.2MM **Privately Held**
WEB: www.timberwolf1.com
SIC: 3425 Saw blades & handsaws
PA: Suffolk Machinery & Power Tool Corporation
12 Waverly Ave
Patchogue NY 11772
631 289-7153

(G-2235)
SUPERIOR ENERGY RESOURCES LLC
Also Called: Superior Hose & Fittings
2691 Route 219 (15824-7329)
PHONE...............................814 265-1080
Peter Varischetti, *Principal*
EMP: 3 **Privately Held**
SIC: 1389 3492 3533 Gas field services; hose & tube fittings & assemblies, hydraulic/pneumatic; oil & gas drilling rigs & equipment
HQ: Superior Energy Resources, Llc
   2691 Route 219
   Brockway PA 15824
   814 265-1080

(G-2236)
SUPERIOR ENERGY RESOURCES LLC (HQ)
Also Called: Superior Hose & Fittings
2691 Route 219 (15824-7329)
PHONE...............................814 265-1080
Peter Varischetti,
▲ **EMP:** 25
SALES (est): 5.5MM **Privately Held**
SIC: 1389 3533 3492 Gas field services; oil & gas drilling rigs & equipment; hose & tube fittings & assemblies, hydraulic/pneumatic

Brodheadsville
Monroe County

(G-2237)
OLEUM EXPLORATION LLC
108 Switzgabel Dr (18322-7121)
PHONE...............................855 912-6200
Salvatore Cheho, *President*
Mark Goffredo, *Vice Pres*
Mark Reese, *Vice Pres*
Scott Slater,
EMP: 16
SQ FT: 10,000
SALES: 200K **Privately Held**
SIC: 1382 Oil & gas exploration services

(G-2238)
ROGUE AUDIO INC
545 Jenna Dr (18322)
PHONE...............................570 992-9901
Mark Obrien, *President*
Phillip Koch, *Vice Pres*
EMP: 8
SQ FT: 5,000
SALES: 2MM **Privately Held**
SIC: 3651 Audio electronic systems

Brogue
York County

(G-2239)
R & C FOLTZ LLC
Also Called: Hill Woodworks
2270 Delta Rd (17309-9102)
P.O. Box 88 (17309-0088)
PHONE...............................717 927-9771
Christine Foltz, *Mng Member*
Royce Foltz,
EMP: 15
SQ FT: 15,000
SALES: 300K **Privately Held**
SIC: 2431 Millwork

(G-2240)
RIVER SUPPLY INC
2555 Delta Rd (17309-9107)
PHONE...............................717 927-1555
Joseph Nolan, *President*
Timothy Bratton, *Vice Pres*
EMP: 20 **EST:** 2013
SALES: 1MM **Privately Held**
SIC: 3443 1761 Metal parts; architectural sheet metal work

Brookhaven
Delaware County

(G-2241)
A TRU DIVA LLC
224 E Avon Rd (19015-3308)
PHONE...............................888 400-1034
Della Beaver,
EMP: 1 **EST:** 2009
SALES: 4.3MM **Privately Held**
SIC: 5139 3171 5621 8748 Shoes; handbags, women's; boutiques; business consulting

(G-2242)
ACE CONTROLS & INSTRUMENTATION
601 Upland Ave Ste 219 (19015-2467)
PHONE...............................610 876-2000
Susan McCrossan, *President*
John McCrossan, *Vice Pres*
Erik Taylor, *Sales Mgr*
Brian Lewis, *Contractor*
EMP: 9
SQ FT: 29,000
SALES (est): 1.8MM **Privately Held**
WEB: www.ace-controls.com
SIC: 3823 Industrial instrmnts msrmnt display/control process variable

(G-2243)
CHESTER MULTI COPY INC
Also Called: Multi-Copy Printing
4007 Edgmont Ave (19015-2302)
PHONE...............................610 876-1285
Willis Wissler III, *President*
Wiliam Wissler, *Treasurer*
EMP: 3
SQ FT: 1,600
SALES: 245K **Privately Held**
SIC: 2752 Commercial printing, offset; photo-offset printing

(G-2244)
ENDEAVOUR SKY INC
3719 Arlington Ave (19015-2201)
PHONE...............................610 872-5694
John D Massaro, *President*
EMP: 3
SALES: 105K **Privately Held**
SIC: 3999 Manufacturing industries

(G-2245)
HERTZ MACHINE & FABRICATION
3751 Clearwater Ln (19015-2602)
PHONE...............................610 874-7848
Dave Hertz, *Owner*
EMP: 3
SALES (est): 260.2K **Privately Held**
SIC: 3599 Machine shop, jobbing & repair

(G-2246)
MAC MACHINE LLC
Also Called: Mac Hydraulics
4901 Chester Creek Rd (19015-1520)
PHONE...............................610 583-3055
Mike Maccready,
EMP: 10
SALES (est): 1.1MM **Privately Held**
WEB: www.macmachine.net
SIC: 3599 7699 Custom machinery; hydraulic equipment repair

(G-2247)
REBEL INDIAN SMOKE SHOP
4101 Edgmont Ave (19015-2313)
PHONE...............................610 499-1711
Lisa Massaro, *Owner*
EMP: 4 **EST:** 2015
SALES (est): 331.1K **Privately Held**
SIC: 3634 2111 2121 Cigar lighters, electric; cigarettes; cigars

Brookville
Jefferson County

(G-2248)
BERRY GLOBAL INC
2890 Maplevale Rd (15825-2318)
PHONE...............................814 849-4234
Frank Brown, *Principal*
EMP: 31 **Publicly Held**
SIC: 3089 3081 Plastic containers, except foam; cups, plastic, except foam; bottle caps, molded plastic; caps, plastic; unsupported plastics film & sheet
HQ: Berry Global, Inc.
   101 Oakley St
   Evansville IN 47710
   812 424-2904

(G-2249)
BEVERAGE AIR
1082 Route 28 (15825-7200)
PHONE...............................814 849-2022
Ray Frerich, *Principal*
Calvin Lapier, *Opers Mgr*
Bill Zellner, *Engineer*
Ryan Ricker, *Regl Sales Mgr*
◆ **EMP:** 16
SALES (est): 3.8MM **Privately Held**
SIC: 3585 Refrigeration & heating equipment

(G-2250)
BEVERAGE-AIR CORPORATION
Progress St (15825)
PHONE...............................814 849-7336
Ken Doverspike, *Design Engr*
Ray Frerich, *Branch Mgr*
EMP: 250
SQ FT: 8,000
SALES (est): 5.3MM **Privately Held**
SIC: 3585 3556 Cold drink dispensing equipment (not coin-operated); food products machinery
HQ: Beverage-Air Corporation
   3779 Champion Blvd
   Winston Salem NC 27105

(G-2251)
BPREX PLASTIC PACKAGING INC
Maplevale Rd (15825)
PHONE...............................814 849-4240
E A Grzeda, *Branch Mgr*
EMP: 170 **Publicly Held**
SIC: 3089 Closures, plastic
HQ: Bprex Plastic Packaging Inc.
   1 Seagate
   Toledo OH 43604

(G-2252)
BROOKVILLE EQUIPMENT CORP
Also Called: Brookville Mining Equipment
175 Evans St (15825-9411)
PHONE...............................814 849-2000
Dalph McNeil, *CEO*
Andy Cable, *Vice Pres*
Larry Conrad, *Vice Pres*
Brent McNeil, *Vice Pres*
Ron Smith, *Project Mgr*
▲ **EMP:** 150 **EST:** 1920
SQ FT: 100,000
SALES: 66.9MM **Privately Held**
WEB: www.bmec.com
SIC: 3743 Locomotives & parts

(G-2253)
BROOKVILLE GLOVE MFG CO INC (PA)
98 Service Center Rd B (15825-7176)
PHONE...............................814 849-7324
Elizabeth Breene, *Ch of Bd*
Charles Breene, *President*
EMP: 45
SQ FT: 57,000
SALES (est): 22MM **Privately Held**
WEB: www.brookvilleglove.com
SIC: 2381 5136 Gloves, work: woven or knit, made from purchased materials; gloves, men's & boys'

(G-2254)
BROOKVILLE LOCOMOTIVE INC
175 Evans St (15825-9411)
P.O. Box 130 (15825-0130)
PHONE...............................814 849-2000
Dalph McNeil, *President*
Stan Bailey, *Controller*
Sheila Hockman, *Human Res Dir*
EMP: 145 **EST:** 1918
SQ FT: 72,000
SALES (est): 17.3MM **Privately Held**
WEB: www.brookvilleequipment.com
SIC: 3532 3743 3531 3537 Mining machinery; railroad equipment; construction machinery; industrial trucks & tractors

(G-2255)
BROWNLEE LUMBER INC
2652 Hzen Rchardsville Rd (15825-7616)
PHONE...............................814 328-2991
Charles Brownlee, *President*
Dan Brownlee, *Exec VP*
▼ **EMP:** 30
SALES (est): 5.3MM **Privately Held**
WEB: www.brownleelumber.com
SIC: 2426 5031 2439 Lumber, hardwood dimension; lumber, plywood & millwork; structural wood members

(G-2256)
BUCK KOOLA INC
494 Service Center Rd (15825-7175)
PHONE...............................814 849-9695
EMP: 4
SALES (est): 360.5K **Privately Held**
SIC: 3949 Sporting & athletic goods

(G-2257)
BUFFS ICE CREAM
1 Mabon St (15825-1410)
PHONE...............................814 849-8335
Clifford Buffington, *Owner*
Milly Buffington, *Owner*
EMP: 4
SQ FT: 2,640
SALES (est): 172.3K **Privately Held**
SIC: 2024 5812 Ice cream & frozen desserts; ice cream stands or dairy bars

(G-2258)
BWP HARDWOODS INC
12942 Route 322 (15825-6946)
PHONE...............................814 849-7331
Matthew Gutchess, *President*
Terry Stodkdale, *President*
Greta Notto, *Bookkeeper*
Blake Gilmore, *Supervisor*
Lee Stitzinger, *Admin Sec*
EMP: 63
SALES (est): 10.3MM **Privately Held**
WEB: www.bwphardwoods.com
SIC: 2421 Lumber: rough, sawed or planed; sawdust, shavings & wood chips

(G-2259)
DAN SMITH CANDIES INC (PA)
77 Barnett St (15825-1264)
PHONE...............................814 849-8221
Lennea Darrin, *President*
Frank Decker, *Vice Pres*
EMP: 15 **EST:** 1948
SQ FT: 2,400
SALES (est): 2.3MM **Privately Held**
WEB: www.dansmithcandies.com
SIC: 2064 Chocolate candy, except solid chocolate

(G-2260)
DARTONYA MANUFACTURING INC
243 Dartonya Ln (15825-2741)
PHONE...............................814 849-3240
Charles A Shaffer, *President*
Judith Shaffer, *Admin Sec*
EMP: 8
SQ FT: 6,000
SALES (est): 1.8MM **Privately Held**
WEB: www.pcaindustries.com
SIC: 3559 Rubber working machinery, including tires

▲ = Import ▼=Export
◆ =Import/Export

(G-2261)
GEORGE I REITZ & SONS INC (PA)
Also Called: Brookville Tanks
17214 Route 36 (15825-4640)
PHONE..................................814 849-2308
Alan L Reitz, *President*
Greg Waggett, *Engineer*
John Lechene, *Accounts Mgr*
Brian Reitz, *Admin Sec*
EMP: 40 EST: 1944
SQ FT: 38,000
SALES (est): 22.8MM **Privately Held**
WEB: www.gireitz.com
SIC: 5084 3443 7692 3714 Pumps & pumping equipment; tanks, standard or custom fabricated: metal plate; welding repair; motor vehicle parts & accessories; sheet metalwork; fabricated structural metal

(G-2262)
ISHMAN PLASTIC & WOOD CUTTING
67 S White St (15825-2427)
PHONE..................................814 849-9961
Andrew Ishman, *President*
EMP: 7
SQ FT: 7,500
SALES (est): 126.2K **Privately Held**
SIC: 3089 2441 Molding primary plastic; shipping cases, wood: nailed or lock corner

(G-2263)
MATSON INDUSTRIES INC (PA)
132 Main St (15825-1213)
PHONE..................................814 849-5334
Paul D Sorek, *President*
Len Domenick, *Corp Secy*
Becky Matson, *Exec VP*
Barbara Conti, *Vice Pres*
Richard G Conti, *Vice Pres*
EMP: 20
SQ FT: 2,400
SALES: 38MM **Privately Held**
SIC: 2421 Sawmills & planing mills, general

(G-2264)
MATSON LUMBER COMPANY (HQ)
Also Called: Matson Wood Products
132 Main St (15825-1213)
PHONE..................................814 849-5334
Robert Matson, *President*
Richard Conti, *President*
Jean Mehrten, *Corp Secy*
Barbara Conti, *Vice Pres*
Becky Matson, *Vice Pres*
◆ EMP: 15 EST: 1952
SQ FT: 2,400
SALES (est): 15.3MM
SALES (corp-wide): 38MM **Privately Held**
WEB: www.bwpbats.com
SIC: 2421 Lumber: rough, sawed or planed
PA: Matson Industries, Inc.
132 Main St
Brookville PA 15825
814 849-5334

(G-2265)
MILLER WELDING AND MACHINE CO (PA)
Also Called: Miller Fabrication Solutions
111 2nd St (15825-2033)
P.O. Box G (15825-0607)
PHONE..................................814 849-3061
David K Miller, *CEO*
Pamela G Lindermuth, *President*
Eric D Miller, *President*
Bradley R Miller, *Senior VP*
Jeffrey C Miller, *Vice Pres*
▲ EMP: 168 EST: 1963
SQ FT: 200,000
SALES (est): 33.4MM **Privately Held**
WEB: www.millerwelding.com
SIC: 7692 3599 3444 Welding repair; machine shop, jobbing & repair; sheet metalwork

(G-2266)
MPC LIQUIDATION INC
Also Called: Jeffersonian Democrats
301 Main St (15825-1204)
P.O. Box 498 (15825-0498)
PHONE..................................814 849-6737
Debbie Bonavita, *Manager*
EMP: 9 **Privately Held**
SIC: 2711 Newspapers

(G-2267)
OWENS-BROCKWAY GLASS CONT INC
1082 Route 28 (15825-7200)
PHONE..................................814 849-4265
Lenny Siscus, *Controller*
EMP: 6
SALES (corp-wide): 6.8B **Publicly Held**
SIC: 3221 Glass containers
HQ: Owens-Brockway Glass Container Inc.
1 Michael Owens Way
Perrysburg OH 43551
567 336-8449

(G-2268)
PCS FERGUSON INC
1191 Route 36 (15825-4735)
PHONE..................................412 264-6000
David Bahlgren, *Branch Mgr*
EMP: 7
SALES (corp-wide): 1.2B **Publicly Held**
SIC: 3533 Oil field machinery & equipment
HQ: Pcs Ferguson, Inc.
3771 Eureka Way
Frederick CO 80516
720 407-3550

(G-2269)
PENN SEPARATOR CORP
5 S Pickering St (15825-1429)
P.O. Box 340 (15825-0340)
PHONE..................................814 849-7328
Steve Mc Neil, *President*
Jean Dush, *Controller*
▼ EMP: 20 EST: 1962
SQ FT: 24,000
SALES (est): 4.3MM **Privately Held**
WEB: www.pennseparator.com
SIC: 3443 Boiler & boiler shop work

(G-2270)
RICKY E SHAFFER
873 Jim Town Rd (15825-4013)
PHONE..................................814 328-2318
Ricky Shaffer, *Principal*
EMP: 6
SALES (est): 605.6K **Privately Held**
SIC: 2411 Logging

(G-2271)
SCHLUMBERGER TECHNOLOGY CORP
147 Industrial Park Rd (15825-7201)
PHONE..................................814 220-1900
Chris McGinnis, *General Mgr*
EMP: 202 **Publicly Held**
SIC: 1382 1389 3825 3824 Geophysical exploration, oil & gas field; geological exploration, oil & gas field; well logging; cementing oil & gas well casings; pumping of oil & gas wells; oil field services; measuring instruments & meters, electric; meters: electric, pocket, portable, panelboard, etc.; controls, revolution & timing instruments; counters, revolution
HQ: Schlumberger Technology Corp
100 Gillingham Ln
Sugar Land TX 77478
281 285-8500

(G-2272)
STANTON DYNAMICS INC
11575 Route 36 (15825-9207)
PHONE..................................814 849-6255
Scott Dinger, *President*
Maria Dinger, *Admin Sec*
▲ EMP: 18
SQ FT: 4,000
SALES: 4MM **Privately Held**
WEB: www.stantondynamics.com
SIC: 3715 3496 3799 Truck trailers; miscellaneous fabricated wire products; trailers & trailer equipment

(G-2273)
TIOGA PUBLISHING COMPANY
Also Called: Courier-Express
301 Main St (15825-1204)
PHONE..................................814 849-6737
Randy Bartley, *Principal*
EMP: 6 **Privately Held**
SIC: 2711 Newspapers: publishing only, not printed on site
HQ: Tioga Publishing Company
25 East Ave Frnt Ste
Wellsboro PA 16901

(G-2274)
TRACK TRAIL SEARCH RESCUE INC
26 Cherry St (15825-1054)
P.O. Box 205 (15825-0205)
PHONE..................................814 715-5608
Elaine Parker, *Admin Sec*
EMP: 6
SALES (est): 442.4K **Privately Held**
SIC: 3812 Search & navigation equipment

(G-2275)
WAGNER TARPS INC
244 Indl Park Rd (15825)
PHONE..................................814 849-3422
Merle Wagner, *President*
Sheri Wonderling, *Corp Secy*
EMP: 6
SQ FT: 5,000
SALES (est): 785.8K **Privately Held**
SIC: 2394 Tarpaulins, fabric: made from purchased materials

(G-2276)
WHITE-BROOK INC
1 Sylvania St (15825-1424)
PHONE..................................814 849-8441
Thomas E Dinger, *President*
David S Dinger, *Corp Secy*
Michael E Dinger, *Vice Pres*
EMP: 23
SQ FT: 20,000
SALES (est): 3.8MM **Privately Held**
WEB: www.white-brook.com
SIC: 3599 Machine shop, jobbing & repair

Broomall
Delaware County

(G-2277)
ACTION SCREEN PRINTING INC
650 Park Way Frnt Frnt (19008-4218)
PHONE..................................610 359-1777
Ralph Di Giovanni, *President*
James Di Giovanni, *Corp Secy*
Jeffrey Di Giovanni, *Vice Pres*
Chris Woodall, *Opers Staff*
EMP: 15 EST: 1974
SQ FT: 24,000
SALES: 900K **Privately Held**
WEB: www.actionscreenprinting.com
SIC: 7336 2752 Silk screen design; commercial printing, lithographic

(G-2278)
AMPERE ELECTRIC CO
210 1st Ave (19008-2301)
PHONE..................................215 426-5356
EMP: 5
SQ FT: 2,000
SALES: 200K **Privately Held**
SIC: 5063 7694 Whol Electrical Equipment Armature Rewinding

(G-2279)
AVIVA TECHNOLOGY INC
511 Abbott Dr Fl 2 (19008-4305)
P.O. Box 2020, Upper Darby (19082-0520)
PHONE..................................610 228-4689
Jeyaraj Raja, *President*
EMP: 3
SQ FT: 300
SALES: 1MM **Privately Held**
SIC: 3429 3053 1761 3313 Metal fasteners; packing, metallic; sheet metalwork; electrometallurgical products; bellows, industrial: metal

(G-2280)
B & E SPORTSWEAR LP
1005 Sussex Blvd Ste 9 (19008-4011)
PHONE..................................610 328-9266
William McDevitt Jr, *General Ptnr*
EMP: 10
SALES (est): 1.4MM **Privately Held**
WEB: www.besportswear.com
SIC: 2759 Screen printing

(G-2281)
BRADLEY COMMUNICATIONS CORP
Also Called: Radio-TV Interview Report
390 Reed Rd Fl 1 (19008-4008)
P.O. Box 360 (19008-0360)
PHONE..................................484 477-4220
William T Harrison, *President*
John Gay, *Editor*
EMP: 25
SQ FT: 4,000
SALES (est): 1.9MM **Privately Held**
SIC: 2721 2741 Magazines: publishing only, not printed on site; miscellaneous publishing

(G-2282)
CHRISTOPHER GANS
Also Called: Nicholas Smith Trains
2343 W Chester Pike (19008-2519)
PHONE..................................610 353-8585
Christopher Gans, *Owner*
EMP: 4
SQ FT: 20,000
SALES (est): 475.6K **Privately Held**
WEB: www.nstoys.com
SIC: 3944 5945 Trains & equipment, toy: electric & mechanical; hobby, toy & game shops

(G-2283)
CLOSET SPACE
2610 Oriole Rd (19008-2237)
PHONE..................................610 359-0583
EMP: 4
SALES (est): 302.4K **Privately Held**
SIC: 2673 Mfg Bags-Plastic/Coated Paper

(G-2284)
CUMMINS - ALLISON CORP
630 Park Way Frnt 1a (19008-4209)
PHONE..................................610 355-1400
Robert Katiz, *Principal*
Doug Mennie, *Principal*
Jim Mentzer, *Principal*
Joe Pangrely, *Principal*
Doug Raterman, *Principal*
EMP: 13
SALES (corp-wide): 383.8MM **Privately Held**
WEB: www.gsb.com
SIC: 5046 3519 Commercial equipment; internal combustion engines
PA: Cummins - Allison Corp.
852 Feehanville Dr
Mount Prospect IL 60056
847 759-6403

(G-2285)
DAVIDSONS FABRICATING INC
511 Abbott Dr (19008-4305)
P.O. Box 381 (19008-0381)
PHONE..................................610 544-9750
James D Davidson Jr, *President*
Colleen Hurst, *General Mgr*
Kathy Koci, *Administration*
EMP: 25
SQ FT: 16,000
SALES: 4.5MM **Privately Held**
WEB: www.davidsonfab.com
SIC: 3444 Sheet metal specialties, not stamped

(G-2286)
DOOLEY GASKET AND SEAL INC
Also Called: Jim E Dooley
838 Sussex Blvd (19008-4324)
P.O. Box 127 (19008-0127)
PHONE..................................610 328-2720
James E Dooley, *President*
Stephen Abbot, *Vice Pres*
Elisabeth Ebert, *CFO*
Kate Dooley, *Manager*
Jacqueline Dooley, *Admin Sec*

▲ EMP: 25
SQ FT: 30,000
SALES (est): 12.7MM **Privately Held**
WEB: www.dooleygaskets.com
SIC: 5085 3053 Gaskets; gaskets & sealing devices

(G-2287)
DRUMMOND SCIENTIFIC COMPANY
500 Parkway (19008-4293)
P.O. Box 700 (19008-0700)
PHONE...................................610 353-0200
Michael Drummo, *President*
Lawrence Picci, *Vice Pres*
Jack Walker, *CFO*
Joseph Drummon, *Admin Sec*
▲ EMP: 100 EST: 1964
SQ FT: 65,000
SALES (est): 23.5MM **Privately Held**
WEB: www.drummondsci.com
SIC: 3821 3586 3231 3229 Laboratory equipment: fume hoods, distillation racks, etc.; measuring & dispensing pumps; products of purchased glass; pressed & blown glass

(G-2288)
EDMAR ABRASIVE COMPANY
1107 Sussex Blvd (19008-4013)
P.O. Box 217 (19008-0217)
PHONE...................................610 544-4900
Mario V Mascioli, *CEO*
Thomas Mascioli, *President*
Shirley Garrison, *Purch Agent*
David Charlton, *Marketing Staff*
▲ EMP: 15 EST: 1953
SQ FT: 12,225
SALES (est): 1.7MM **Privately Held**
WEB: www.edmarabrasive.com
SIC: 3291 Wheels, abrasive

(G-2289)
ICON MARKETING LLC
Also Called: Paulson Brands
2215 Anthony Ave Fl 3 (19008-3031)
PHONE...................................610 356-4050
Paul L Quintavalla, *Mng Member*
Paul J Quintavalla,
EMP: 2
SALES: 6.4MM **Privately Held**
SIC: 2038 8748 8742 Ethnic foods, frozen; business consulting; sales (including sales management) consultant

(G-2290)
INCYTE CORPORATION
109 Diane Dr (19008-2636)
PHONE...................................302 498-6700
EMP: 78
SALES (corp-wide): 1.8B **Publicly Held**
SIC: 2834 Pharmaceutical preparations
PA: Incyte Corporation
1801 Augustine Cut Off
Wilmington DE 19803
302 498-6700

(G-2291)
KEYS WHOLESALE DISTRIBUTORS
417 Lyndhurst Dr (19008-4111)
PHONE...................................610 626-4787
William Kline, *President*
Darcey Kline, *Vice Pres*
EMP: 9
SQ FT: 3,500
SALES (est): 1.1MM **Privately Held**
SIC: 3429 Keys & key blanks

(G-2292)
KINESIS SOFTWARE LLC
Also Called: 1st Choice Athlete
2600 Andrew Rd (19008-1609)
PHONE...................................610 353-4150
EMP: 5
SALES (est): 261K **Privately Held**
SIC: 7372 Prepackaged software

(G-2293)
LANSDOWNE ICE & COAL CO INC
Also Called: J Halligan and Son
610 Park Way Ste A (19008-4207)
PHONE...................................610 353-6500
Delores Halligan, *President*

EMP: 30 EST: 1960
SALES (est): 2.8MM **Privately Held**
SIC: 5983 2097 Fuel oil dealers; manufactured ice

(G-2294)
LOGO DEPOT INC
Also Called: Logo Wearhouse
627 Park Way (19008-4206)
PHONE...................................610 543-3890
Chris Borromeo, *President*
Bob Handschuh, *Sales Staff*
EMP: 4
SALES (est): 577.7K **Privately Held**
WEB: www.logowearhouse.com
SIC: 2759 Screen printing

(G-2295)
MARDINLY ENTERPRISES LLC
701 Park Way Ste 2 (19008-4213)
PHONE...................................610 544-9490
Frank Morgan, *Office Mgr*
David Mardinly,
EMP: 20
SQ FT: 1,000
SALES (est): 3.4MM **Privately Held**
SIC: 3599 7538 Machine shop, jobbing & repair; general automotive repair shops

(G-2296)
MARTINO FUEL
122 Beechtree Dr (19008-1729)
PHONE...................................484 802-2183
Stephen Martino, *Principal*
EMP: 5
SALES (est): 644.2K **Privately Held**
SIC: 2869 Fuels

(G-2297)
MASON CREST PUBLISHERS INC (PA)
450 Park Way Ste 206 (19008-4202)
PHONE...................................610 543-6200
Dan Hilfe, *President*
Diana Daniels, *Controller*
Linda McGee, *Sales Executive*
EMP: 6
SALES (est): 654K **Privately Held**
WEB: www.masoncrest.com
SIC: 2731 Books: publishing & printing

(G-2298)
MILLIKEN NONWOVENS LLC (HQ)
370 Reed Rd Ste 200 (19008-4018)
PHONE...................................610 544-7117
Jeffrey Shapiro, *CEO*
Steven Derman, *President*
Joseph Ruffo, *Senior VP*
Larry Wright, *VP Mfg*
▲ EMP: 6
SQ FT: 2,860
SALES (est): 17.5MM
SALES (corp-wide): 3.2B **Privately Held**
WEB: www.kasbarnational.com
SIC: 2299 2395 Batts & batting: cotton mill waste & related material; quilted fabrics or cloth
PA: Milliken & Company
920 Milliken Rd
Spartanburg SC 29303
864 503-2020

(G-2299)
MOBILE VIDEO CORPORATION
501 Abbott Dr Ste 4 (19008-4320)
PHONE...................................215 863-1072
John McKenzie,
EMP: 16
SALES (est): 496.8K **Privately Held**
SIC: 7373 3861 Systems software development services; systems engineering, computer related; microfilm equipment: cameras, projectors, readers, etc.

(G-2300)
PEGASUS PRINT & COPY CENTERS
2501 W Chester Pike (19008-2343)
PHONE...................................610 356-8787
Harry R Bowen, *President*
EMP: 4
SALES (est): 551.2K **Privately Held**
WEB: www.pegasusprint.net
SIC: 2752 Commercial printing, offset

(G-2301)
PEPPERIDGE FARM INCORPORATED
Also Called: Pepperidge Farm Thrift Store
2058 Sproul Rd (19008-2725)
PHONE...................................610 356-0553
Ellen Friemmell, *Manager*
EMP: 4
SALES (corp-wide): 8.6B **Publicly Held**
WEB: www.pepperidgefarm.com
SIC: 5145 2052 2099 2053 Snack foods; cookies; bread crumbs, not made in bakeries; frozen bakery products, except bread
HQ: Pepperidge Farm, Incorporated
595 Westport Ave
Norwalk CT 06851
203 846-7000

(G-2302)
PHOENIX AVS LLC
501 Abbott Dr Side E (19008-4320)
PHONE...................................610 910-6251
Nathan Geller, *Principal*
Sean Quigley, *Principal*
EMP: 4
SALES (est): 182.3K **Privately Held**
SIC: 3651 5999 Household audio & video equipment; audio-visual equipment & supplies

(G-2303)
TECHNICAL APPLICATIONS INC
610 Park Way Ste B (19008-4207)
PHONE...................................610 353-0722
William E Mc Breen, *President*
Robert Sammons, *Treasurer*
EMP: 8
SQ FT: 3,750
SALES (est): 1.4MM **Privately Held**
SIC: 3625 Relays & industrial controls

(G-2304)
VARITRONICS INC
620 Park Way Ste 4 (19008-4291)
P.O. Box 268 (19008-0268)
PHONE...................................610 356-3995
Alan Abrams, *President*
EMP: 15 EST: 1970
SQ FT: 6,000
SALES (est): 2.6MM **Privately Held**
WEB: www.varitronics.com
SIC: 3841 Ophthalmic instruments & apparatus

(G-2305)
WAYNE PRODUCTS INC
Also Called: Electra-Kool Division
888 Sussex Blvd Ste 3 (19008-4314)
PHONE...................................800 255-5665
Don Ware, *President*
▲ EMP: 10
SQ FT: 9,000
SALES (est): 2MM **Privately Held**
WEB: www.wayneproducts.com
SIC: 3569 3585 3564 Filters; refrigeration & heating equipment; blowers & fans

(G-2306)
XA FISHING INC
88 Cherry Hill Ln (19008-1507)
PHONE...................................610 356-0340
Joseph Bobrowski, *President*
EMP: 4
SQ FT: 2,000
SALES (est): 354.4K **Privately Held**
SIC: 5091 3949 7389 Fishing tackle; fishing tackle, general; design services

Brownstown
Lancaster County

(G-2307)
DUREX COVERINGS INC (PA)
53 Industrial Dr (17508-5070)
P.O. Box 639 (17508-0639)
PHONE...................................717 626-8566
Bruce R Bucher, *President*
Kevin Dicarlo, *Vice Pres*
Dean Bucher, *Admin Sec*
EMP: 30
SQ FT: 7,500

SALES (est): 7.1MM **Privately Held**
WEB: www.durexcoverings.com
SIC: 1799 1771 2273 Coating of concrete structures with plastic; flooring contractor; floor coverings: paper, grass, reed, coir, sisal, jute, etc.

(G-2308)
KRIEG DIETER
Also Called: Farmshine
3 W Main St (17508-5095)
P.O. Box 219 (17508-0219)
PHONE...................................717 656-8050
Dieter Krieg, *Owner*
Ashley Denlinger, *Admin Sec*
EMP: 5
SALES: 780K **Privately Held**
SIC: 2711 Newspapers: publishing only, not printed on site

(G-2309)
STEFFY PRINTING INC
103 Zooks Mill Rd (17508-5066)
P.O. Box 457 (17508-0457)
PHONE...................................717 859-5040
Donald Steffy, *President*
EMP: 8
SQ FT: 5,000
SALES (est): 1.2MM **Privately Held**
SIC: 2752 Business forms, lithographed

Brownsville
Fayette County

(G-2310)
BUGSTUFF
709 Jefferson Ave (15417-2316)
PHONE...................................724 785-7000
Jack Rymarchyk, *Owner*
EMP: 4
SQ FT: 10,000
SALES (est): 374.8K **Privately Held**
WEB: www.bugstuff.com
SIC: 3442 5013 5531 3714 Metal doors, sash & trim; automotive supplies & parts; automotive parts; motor vehicle parts & accessories; motor vehicles & car bodies

(G-2311)
DELEX CO
116 Blaine Rd (15417-9314)
PHONE...................................724 938-2366
Gary Gorecki, *President*
EMP: 3
SALES: 70K **Privately Held**
SIC: 2511 Wood household furniture

(G-2312)
HEARTLAND FABRICATION LLC
1800 Paul Thomas Blvd (15417-1555)
PHONE...................................724 785-2575
Brian Mueller, *Mng Member*
Ted Stilgenbauer, *Mng Member*
EMP: 200
SQ FT: 1,873,080
SALES (est): 54.6MM **Privately Held**
WEB: www.brownsvillemarine.com
SIC: 3731 Barges, building & repairing

(G-2313)
NOVOTNY MICHEAL
Also Called: Express Optical Laboratories
18 Bridge St (15417-1600)
P.O. Box 92 (15417-0092)
PHONE...................................724 785-2160
Michael Novotny, *Owner*
EMP: 18 EST: 1980
SQ FT: 10,000
SALES (est): 1.5MM **Privately Held**
WEB: www.expresseol.com
SIC: 3851 5812 3229 Eyeglasses, lenses & frames; restaurant, family: independent; pressed & blown glass

▲ = Import ▼=Export
◆ =Import/Export

Bruin
Butler County

(G-2314)
FAWNWOOD ENERGY INC (PA)
105 Daubenspeck Rd (16022)
P.O. Box 157 (16022-0157)
PHONE....................................724 753-2416
Jerry Macurak, *President*
EMP: 4
SQ FT: 600
SALES (est): 706.1K **Privately Held**
SIC: 1389 Gas field services; oil field services; pumping of oil & gas wells; roustabout service

Bryn Mawr
Delaware County

(G-2315)
BALDT INC
400 S Roberts Rd (19010-1136)
PHONE....................................610 447-5200
Glenn Suplee, *President*
EMP: 35
SQ FT: 88,000
SALES (est): 4.9MM **Privately Held**
WEB: www.baldt.com
SIC: 3429 3462 Marine hardware; iron & steel forgings

(G-2316)
BODYX LLC
22 N Bryn Mawr Ave (19010-3304)
PHONE....................................610 519-9999
EMP: 4
SALES (est): 74.1K **Privately Held**
SIC: 7991 7372 Physical fitness facilities; application computer software

(G-2317)
BRYN MAWR EQUIPMENT FIN INC
Also Called: Equipment Finance Advisor
801 W Lancaster Ave (19010-3305)
PHONE....................................610 581-4996
Frank Leto, *President*
Alison J Eichert, *COO*
Michael W Harrington, *CFO*
Patrick M Killeen, *Officer*
EMP: 13
SALES (est): 2.8MM
SALES (corp-wide): 188.6MM **Privately Held**
SIC: 7372 Publishers' computer software
HQ: Bryn Mawr Trust Company
801 W Lancaster Ave
Bryn Mawr PA 19010
610 581-4819

(G-2318)
CFM DESIGNS INC
Also Called: Augostinos
840 W Lancaster Ave (19010-3224)
PHONE....................................610 520-7777
Frank Augustino, *President*
EMP: 5
SALES (est): 74.7K **Privately Held**
SIC: 2335 Women's, juniors' & misses' dresses

(G-2319)
DAVID K HART CO
9 Meadowood Rd (19010-1022)
PHONE....................................610 527-0388
James Riley, *President*
EMP: 7
SALES (est): 951.5K **Privately Held**
WEB: www.die-cut.com
SIC: 3555 Printing trades machinery

(G-2320)
DOONER VENTURES LLC
Also Called: Ivvi Media
301 Highland Ln (19010-3710)
PHONE....................................610 420-1100
Brian Dooner,
EMP: 5 **EST:** 2012
SALES (est): 280.7K **Privately Held**
SIC: 2731 7389 Book publishing;

(G-2321)
DUCHESNAY USA INC
919 Conestoga Rd 1-203 (19010-1352)
PHONE....................................484 380-2641
Dean Hopkins, *General Mgr*
EMP: 7 **EST:** 2012
SALES (est): 1.5MM **Privately Held**
SIC: 2834 Pills, pharmaceutical
HQ: Duchesnay Inc
950 Boul Michele-Bohec
Blainville QC J7C 5
450 433-7734

(G-2322)
ENTERPRISE CLOUDWORKS CORP
1022 E Lancaster Ave (19010-1449)
PHONE....................................215 395-6311
Christopher Gali, *CEO*
EMP: 35 **EST:** 2011
SALES (est): 1.4MM **Privately Held**
SIC: 7372 Application computer software

(G-2323)
EXECUTIVE DISTRIBUTORS INTL
Also Called: Edi-USA
400 Morris Ave (19010-2922)
PHONE....................................610 608-1664
Christopher Sfedu, *Director*
EMP: 5
SQ FT: 4,000
SALES (est): 177.6K **Privately Held**
SIC: 2299 Textile goods

(G-2324)
HLS THERAPEUTICS (USA) INC
919 Conestoga Rd 3-310 (19010-1365)
PHONE....................................844 457-8900
Gregory Gubitz, *CEO*
Bill Wells, *Ch of Bd*
Gilber Godin, *COO*
Gilbert Godin, *COO*
Jason Gross, *Vice Pres*
EMP: 10
SALES (est): 922.3K **Privately Held**
SIC: 2834 7389 Proprietary drug products;

(G-2325)
HYDROCOIL POWER INC
1164 Saint Andrews Rd (19010-1951)
PHONE....................................610 745-1990
Jonathan B Rosefsky, *President*
Richard Deluca, *President*
▼ **EMP:** 3 **EST:** 2006
SALES (est): 210.9K **Privately Held**
SIC: 3511 Turbines & turbine generator sets

(G-2326)
INDUSTRIAL VISION SYSTEMS INC
436 Morris Ave (19010-2922)
PHONE....................................215 393-5300
Walter Macilvain, *Partner*
Jim Aman, *Partner*
William Haller, *Partner*
EMP: 4
SALES (est): 312.3K **Privately Held**
SIC: 3999 Manufacturing industries

(G-2327)
JAMES B CARTY JR MD
Bryn Mawr Medical (19010)
PHONE....................................610 527-0897
James B Carty, *Branch Mgr*
EMP: 3
SALES (corp-wide): 1.2MM **Privately Held**
SIC: 3827 Optical instruments & apparatus
PA: James B Carty Jr Md
830 Old Lancaster Rd # 100
Bryn Mawr PA 19010
610 527-1133

(G-2328)
K T & CO
Also Called: K.T. Originals
841 1/2 W Lancaster Ave (19010-3337)
PHONE....................................610 520-0221
Helen Texada, *Owner*
EMP: 4 **EST:** 1977

SALES (est): 218.5K **Privately Held**
WEB: www.ktandcompany.com
SIC: 2519 5719 Household furniture, except wood or metal: upholstered; wicker, rattan or reed home furnishings

(G-2329)
MEDUNIK USA INC
919 Conestoga Rd (19010-1352)
PHONE....................................484 380-2641
Dean Hopkins, *General Mgr*
EMP: 15 **EST:** 2016
SALES (est): 58.2K **Privately Held**
SIC: 2834 Tablets, pharmaceutical

(G-2330)
MOLLOY ASSOCIATES INC
919 Conestoga Rd 3-213 (19010-1354)
PHONE....................................610 293-1300
Gerald F Parrotto, *President*
Rita Garwood, *Finance*
Frank Battista, *Marketing Staff*
Patricia Mc Devitt, *Admin Sec*
EMP: 20
SQ FT: 5,000
SALES (est): 1.3MM **Privately Held**
WEB: www.monitordaily.com
SIC: 7361 2711 Executive placement; newspapers: publishing only, not printed on site

(G-2331)
NEWMAN WINE & SPIRITS GP LLC
1079 Baron Dr (19010-1836)
PHONE....................................610 476-3964
Jonathan H Newman, *CEO*
EMP: 3 **EST:** 2007
SALES (est): 109.6K **Privately Held**
SIC: 5182 2084 Bottling wines & liquors; wines, brandy & brandy spirits

(G-2332)
NOBLEMEDICAL LLC
Also Called: Noblemd
364 Thornbrook Ave (19010-1660)
PHONE....................................917 750-9605
Todd Johnson, *Mng Member*
EMP: 5
SALES (est): 387.9K **Privately Held**
SIC: 7372 7373 8733 8732 Business oriented computer software; educational computer software; systems software development services; medical research; educational research

(G-2333)
SAMUEL YELLIN METALWORKERS CO
721 Moore Ave (19010-2208)
P.O. Box 148 (19010-0148)
PHONE....................................610 527-2334
Clare L Yellin, *President*
EMP: 5 **EST:** 1909
SALES (est): 354K **Privately Held**
WEB: www.samuelyellin.com
SIC: 3446 Grillwork, ornamental metal; gates, ornamental metal; fences or posts, ornamental iron or steel

(G-2334)
STARLITE INDUSTRIES INC
Also Called: Starliteindustries
1111 E Lancaster Ave # 2 (19010-2724)
P.O. Box 990 (19010-0990)
PHONE....................................610 527-1300
Jay Rosenbluth, *President*
Jay Rowe, *Marketing Staff*
EMP: 35
SQ FT: 25,000
SALES (est): 6.5MM **Privately Held**
WEB: www.starliteindustries.com
SIC: 3545 5085 Wheel turning equipment; diamond point or other; industrial supplies

(G-2335)
TURNER WHITE CMMUNICATIONS INC
339 Millbank Rd (19010-2929)
PHONE....................................610 975-4541
Bruce M White, *President*
Barbara T White, *Exec VP*
EMP: 15
SQ FT: 4,500

SALES (est): 1.5MM **Privately Held**
WEB: www.turner-white.com
SIC: 2721 Periodicals: publishing only; magazines: publishing only, not printed on site

(G-2336)
UNDERCOVERALLS INC
Also Called: Mac Carty & Sons
815 E Railroad Ave (19010-3829)
PHONE....................................610 519-0858
Linda Radabaugh, *President*
Richard Radabaugh, *Corp Secy*
EMP: 10
SALES (est): 695.7K **Privately Held**
SIC: 2394 7216 Awnings, fabric: made from purchased materials; canvas awnings & canopies; cleaning & dyeing, except rugs

(G-2337)
XEROTHERA INC
763 Applegate Ln (19010-1116)
PHONE....................................610 525-9916
Edwin H Ruzinsky, *Principal*
Sanjib Bhattacharyya, *Principal*
EMP: 5
SALES (est): 193K **Privately Held**
SIC: 3842 Implants, surgical

Buckingham
Bucks County

(G-2338)
BUCKINGHAM VALLEY VINEYARDS
1521 Rte 413 (18912)
P.O. Box 371 (18912-0371)
PHONE....................................215 794-7188
Gerald Forest, *Partner*
Jon Forest, *Partner*
Kathleen Forest, *Partner*
Kevin Forest, *Partner*
EMP: 5
SQ FT: 13,500
SALES (est): 319.8K **Privately Held**
WEB: www.pawine.com
SIC: 0172 2084 Grapes; wine cellars, bonded: engaged in blending wines

(G-2339)
BUCKS COUNTY HERALD
5667 York Rd (18912)
P.O. Box 685, Lahaska (18931-0685)
PHONE....................................215 794-1096
Joseph Wingert, *President*
EMP: 20
SALES (est): 1.2MM **Privately Held**
WEB: www.buckscountyherald.com
SIC: 2711 Commercial printing & newspaper publishing combined; newspapers, publishing & printing

Buena Vista
Allegheny County

(G-2340)
BASIC CARBIDE CORPORATION
900 Blythedale Rd (15018)
P.O. Box 525 (15018-0525)
PHONE....................................412 751-3774
Michael Shelton, *Manager*
EMP: 100
SALES (corp-wide): 19.2MM **Privately Held**
WEB: www.basiccarbide.com
SIC: 3291 2819 Tungsten carbide abrasive; carbides
PA: Basic Carbide Corporation
900 Main St
Irwin PA 15642
724 446-1630

(G-2341)
DAUGHERTY TOOL AND DIE INC
325 Industry Rd (15018-9712)
PHONE....................................412 754-0200
Timothy E Beringer, *President*
David Beringer, *Admin Sec*

G E O G R A P H I C

D Mitchell, *Maintence Staff*
EMP: 75
SQ FT: 37,000
SALES (est): 9.9MM **Privately Held**
WEB: www.daughertytool.com
SIC: 3542 3544 Pressing machines; special dies, tools, jigs & fixtures

Bulger
Washington County

(G-2342)
C & M AGGREGATE COMPANY INC
76 Station St (15019-2017)
PHONE..................724 796-3821
EMP: 22
SALES (est): 1.6MM **Privately Held**
SIC: 1442 1422 1221 Construction Sand/Gravel Crushed/Broken Limestone Bituminous Coal/Lignite Surface Mining

Bunola
Allegheny County

(G-2343)
DYER INDUSTRIES INC
Also Called: Prototype Precision
2013 Church Hollow Rd (15020)
P.O. Box 207 (15020-0207)
PHONE..................724 258-3400
Glenn Dyer, *President*
Margaret Dyer, *Corp Secy*
EMP: 17
SQ FT: 4,400
SALES (est): 3.8MM **Privately Held**
WEB: www.dyerind.com
SIC: 3312 3599 3544 Tool & die steel; machine shop, jobbing & repair; special dies, tools, jigs & fixtures

Burgettstown
Washington County

(G-2344)
CUSTOM HYDRAULICS INC
38 Steubenville Pike (15021-8529)
PHONE..................724 729-3170
Robert A Dalfol, *President*
Don Leonhart, *Vice Pres*
Bill Devault, *Purchasing*
EMP: 10
SQ FT: 8,000
SALES (est): 1.5MM **Privately Held**
SIC: 3492 3599 Fluid power valves & hose fittings; custom machinery

(G-2345)
DEDICATED CUSTOMS INC
Also Called: DCI
327 Meadow Rd (15021-2336)
PHONE..................724 678-6609
Matthew Smiley, *President*
EMP: 5 EST: 2014
SALES (est): 244.1K **Privately Held**
SIC: 1791 3443 3444 3498 Iron work, structural; pile shells, metal plate; sheet metalwork; fabricated pipe & fittings; machine & other job shop work

(G-2346)
DUERR PACKAGING COMPANY INC (PA)
892 Steubenville Pike (15021-9510)
PHONE..................724 947-1234
Samuel Duerr III, *President*
Lorraine Duerr, *Corp Secy*
David Duerr, *Vice Pres*
EMP: 60 EST: 1953
SALES (est): 9MM **Privately Held**
WEB: www.duerrpack.com
SIC: 3086 Packaging & shipping materials, foamed plastic

(G-2347)
HORMANN FLEXON LLC
117 Starpointe Blvd (15021-9506)
PHONE..................724 385-9150

Jay Ambrosini, *Parts Mgr*
Alice M Permigiani, *Mktg Dir*
Patrick G Boyle, *Mng Member*
▲ **EMP:** 26
SQ FT: 80,000
SALES (est): 4.8MM
SALES (corp-wide): 426.2MM **Privately Held**
WEB: www.flexoninc.com
SIC: 3442 Metal doors
HQ: Iwis Antriebssysteme Gmbh
Essener Str. 23
Wilnsdorf 57234
273 986-0

(G-2348)
LANXESS CORPORATION
8 Morgan Rd (15021-9503)
PHONE..................412 809-4735
Charlie Freeman, *Plant Mgr*
EMP: 27
SALES (corp-wide): 8.2B **Privately Held**
SIC: 2869 2821 2822 2816 Industrial organic chemicals; plastics materials & resins; synthetic rubber; inorganic pigments
HQ: Lanxess Corporation
111 Ridc Park West Dr
Pittsburgh PA 15275
800 526-9377

(G-2349)
MAXWELL WELDING AND MCH INC
11 Starck Dr (15021-9594)
PHONE..................724 729-3160
Gary Maxwell, *President*
▲ **EMP:** 48
SQ FT: 60,600
SALES (est): 9.7MM **Privately Held**
SIC: 3441 7692 3599 1799 Fabricated structural metal; welding repair; machine shop, jobbing & repair; welding on site

(G-2350)
MILLER PLASTIC PRODUCTS INC
24 Todd Dr (15021-9505)
PHONE..................724 947-5000
Donald Miller, *President*
Margaret Miller, *Corp Secy*
Melvin Krek, *VP Sales*
Stacy Eichner, *Administration*
EMP: 17 EST: 1973
SQ FT: 19,500
SALES (est): 3.7MM **Privately Held**
WEB: www.millerplastics.com
SIC: 3089 3084 Cases, plastic; plastic & fiberglass tanks; plastics pipe

(G-2351)
MULTIFAB & MACHINE INC
Also Called: Mmi
670 Steubenville Pike (15021-2211)
P.O. Box 465, Hickory (15340-0465)
PHONE..................724 947-7700
Beverly Adams-Hoover, *President*
Michael Hoover, *Vice Pres*
EMP: 19
SQ FT: 11,000
SALES (est): 3.5MM **Privately Held**
WEB: www.mmifab.com
SIC: 3441 Fabricated structural metal

(G-2352)
NATIONAL OILWELL VARCO INC
Also Called: T-3
1132 Route 18 (15021-8535)
PHONE..................724 947-4581
EMP: 13
SALES (corp-wide): 20B **Publicly Held**
SIC: 3533 Mfg Oil/Gas Field Machinery
PA: National Oilwell Varco, Inc.
7909 Parkwood Circle Dr
Houston TX 77036
713 346-7500

(G-2353)
RC CONCRETE INC
N Of Burgettstown Rr 18 (15021)
P.O. Box 288 (15021-0288)
PHONE..................724 947-9005
Rita Creps, *President*
Richard Creps, *Vice Pres*

EMP: 3
SALES (est): 395.7K **Privately Held**
SIC: 3273 Ready-mixed concrete

(G-2354)
ROBERT WIRTH
Also Called: Wood Craft
60 Center Ave (15021-1115)
PHONE..................724 947-3615
Robert Wirth, *Owner*
EMP: 4 EST: 1970
SALES (est): 240.7K **Privately Held**
SIC: 2499 Decorative wood & woodwork

(G-2355)
SUTHERLAND LUMBER CO
Also Called: Sutherland Hardwoods
1664 Langeloth Rd (15021)
PHONE..................724 947-3388
William M Sutherland, *Owner*
EMP: 20 EST: 1907
SALES (est): 2.4MM **Privately Held**
WEB: www.sutherlandhwd.com
SIC: 2448 5031 2491 Pallets, wood; pallets, wood; flooring, treated wood block

(G-2356)
TEMCO INDUSTRIES INC
670 Steubenville Pike (15021-2211)
PHONE..................412 831-5620
Andrew Mitch, *President*
EMP: 3
SALES (est): 157.2K **Privately Held**
SIC: 3999 Manufacturing industries

(G-2357)
THREE RIVERS GAMMA SERVICE
1132 Route 18 Ste A (15021-8635)
PHONE..................724 947-9020
Shawn Miller, *CEO*
EMP: 4
SALES: 375K **Privately Held**
SIC: 7692 Welding repair

(G-2358)
UNION ELECTRIC STEEL CORP
Also Called: Union Electric Drive
31 Union Electric Rd (15021-2121)
P.O. Box 151 (15021-0151)
PHONE..................724 947-9595
Craig Mauro, *Plant Mgr*
Joe Durinsky, *Branch Mgr*
EMP: 100
SALES (corp-wide): 419.4MM **Publicly Held**
WEB: www.uniones.com
SIC: 3325 3312 3462 Rolling mill rolls, cast steel; blast furnaces & steel mills; iron & steel forgings
HQ: Union Electric Steel Corporation
726 Bell Ave Ste 101
Carnegie PA 15106
412 429-7655

Burnham
Mifflin County

(G-2359)
CENTRAL PA WILBERT VAULT
201 6th Ave (17009-1403)
P.O. Box 43 (17009-0043)
PHONE..................717 248-3777
Jim Schnure, *Vice Pres*
Fred Zimmerman, *Manager*
EMP: 5
SALES (est): 178K **Privately Held**
SIC: 3272 Burial vaults, concrete or precast terrazzo

(G-2360)
FREEDOM WELDING
816 E Freedom Ave (17009-1311)
PHONE..................717 437-0943
Andy Mateer, *Principal*
EMP: 9
SALES (est): 94.9K **Privately Held**
SIC: 7692 Welding repair

(G-2361)
SEMLER ENTERPRISES INC
Also Called: Kish Printing
20 Windmill Hl Ste 2 (17009-1837)
PHONE..................717 242-0322
David Semler, *President*
Kay E Semler, *Treasurer*
Kay Semler, *Admin Sec*
EMP: 7
SQ FT: 1,700
SALES (est): 1MM **Privately Held**
WEB: www.kishprinting.com
SIC: 2752 7334 Commercial printing, offset; blueprinting service

(G-2362)
STANDARD STEEL LLC (DH)
500 N Walnut St (17009-1644)
PHONE..................717 242-4615
Daniel J Condon, *CEO*
Yukinori Akimoto, *President*
John M Hilton, *COO*
Takashi Fujimura, *Senior VP*
Alan M Majewski, *Vice Pres*
▲ **EMP:** 277
SALES (est): 128.4MM
SALES (corp-wide): 53.2B **Privately Held**
WEB: www.trimarancapital.com
SIC: 3312 3462 Wheels, locomotive & car: iron & steel; railroad wheels, axles, frogs or other equipment: forged
HQ: Nippon Steel & Sumitomo Metal U.S.A., Inc.
1251 Ave Of The Ave Fl 23 Flr 23
New York NY 10020
212 486-7150

Burnside
Clearfield County

(G-2363)
RORABAUGH LUMBER CO
Rr 219 Box 321 (15721)
PHONE..................814 845-2277
Robert Rorabaugh, *Partner*
Daniel Rorabaugh, *Partner*
Roger Rorabaugh, *Partner*
EMP: 15
SQ FT: 60,000
SALES: 2.1MM **Privately Held**
SIC: 2421 Lumber: rough, sawed or planed; kiln drying of lumber

Bushkill
Pike County

(G-2364)
BUSHKILL TOOL COMPANY INC
5063 Milford Rd (18324)
PHONE..................570 588-7000
Thomas Haelsig, *President*
EMP: 7
SQ FT: 2,600
SALES (est): 1.1MM **Privately Held**
SIC: 3599 Machine shop, jobbing & repair

(G-2365)
FABRICATED PRODUCTS
Milford Rd (18324)
PHONE..................570 588-1794
Tom Meizanis Sr, *Partner*
Eileen Meizanis, *Partner*
Tom Meizanis Jr, *Partner*
EMP: 3
SQ FT: 1,736
SALES: 170K **Privately Held**
SIC: 2295 3444 Coated fabrics, not rubberized; sheet metalwork

(G-2366)
LIONS WORLD MEDIA LLC
1498 Pine Rdg (18324)
PHONE..................917 645-7590
Maleche Stewart, *President*
Towon Stewart, *President*
EMP: 15
SALES (est): 280.6K **Privately Held**
SIC: 7819 3861 7812 Film processing, editing & titling: motion picture; motion picture film; television film production

(G-2367)
NEW HOPE INDUSTRIES LLC
206 Welford Ct (18324-8786)
PHONE..................................570 994-6391
Michael Austin,
Kathleen Marcel,
EMP: 4
SALES (est): 125.1K **Privately Held**
SIC: 3999 Manufacturing industries

(G-2368)
OPEN SOLUTION
631 Saw Creek Est (18324)
PHONE..................................646 696-8686
Peter Kinev, *Principal*
EMP: 3
SALES: 100K **Privately Held**
SIC: 7372 Prepackaged software

(G-2369)
SKYDIVE STORE INC
354 Brentwood Dr (18324-7808)
PHONE..................................856 629-4600
Art Sherry, *President*
Kathy Sherry, *Vice Pres*
EMP: 4
SALES (est): 281.4K **Privately Held**
WEB: www.vantagemarketing.com
SIC: 5941 2399 Specialty sport supplies;
parachutes

Butler
Butler County

(G-2370)
A D SWARTZLANDER & SONS
399 Keck Rd (16002-1050)
PHONE..................................724 282-2706
Alfred Swartzlander, *Partner*
EMP: 5
SQ FT: 3,000
SALES (est): 1MM **Privately Held**
SIC: 3273 Ready-mixed concrete

(G-2371)
AGR INTERNATIONAL INC
Also Called: American Glass Research
603 Evans City Rd (16001-8704)
PHONE..................................724 482-2164
Henry M Dimmick Jr, *Principal*
EMP: 20
SALES (corp-wide): 26.2MM **Privately Held**
WEB: www.agrintl.com
SIC: 3829 Testing equipment: abrasion,
shearing strength, etc.
PA: Agr International, Inc.
615 Whitestown Rd
Butler PA 16001
724 482-2163

(G-2372)
AGRIUM ADVANCED TECH US INC
121 Pflugh Rd (16001-8301)
PHONE..................................724 865-9180
Jack Cairns, *Branch Mgr*
EMP: 9
SALES (corp-wide): 8.8B **Privately Held**
SIC: 2873 Nitrogenous fertilizers
HQ: Agrium Advanced Technologies (U.S.)
Inc.
2915 Rocky Mountain Ave # 400
Loveland CO 80538

(G-2373)
AK STEEL CORPORATION
210 Pittsburgh Rd (16001-3825)
P.O. Box 832 (16003-0832)
PHONE..................................724 284-2854
Scott Ashworth, *QC Mgr*
Wade Wright, *Branch Mgr*
Jeff Renwick, *Manager*
Geoff Rule, *Manager*
Chris Silverio, *Manager*
EMP: 550 **Publicly Held**
WEB: www.ketnar.org
SIC: 3312 Stainless steel
HQ: Ak Steel Corporation
9227 Centre Pointe Dr
West Chester OH 45069
513 425-4200

(G-2374)
AMERIKOHL MINING INC (PA)
202 Sunset Dr (16001-1396)
PHONE..................................724 282-2339
John M Stilley, *President*
Gerard Baroffio, *Vice Pres*
Jerry Baroffio, *Vice Pres*
Todd M Fiedor, *Vice Pres*
Scott Kroh, *Vice Pres*
EMP: 100
SQ FT: 5,000
SALES: 28.4MM **Privately Held**
WEB: www.amerikohl.com
SIC: 1221 5052 Strip mining, bituminous;
coal

(G-2375)
APPLIED TEST SYSTEMS LLC
154 Eastbrook Ln (16002-1024)
PHONE..................................724 283-1212
Floyd Ganassi, *President*
Michael A Asti, *President*
David L Fair, *Vice Pres*
David Fair, *Vice Pres*
Roger Yohe, *Buyer*
◆ EMP: 46 EST: 2009
SQ FT: 40,000
SALES (est): 13.1MM **Privately Held**
WEB: www.atspa.com
SIC: 3826 3567 3829 3825 Analytical in-
struments; electrical furnaces, ovens &
heating devices, exc. induction; measur-
ing & controlling devices; instruments to
measure electricity; laboratory apparatus
& furniture; heating equipment, except
electric

(G-2376)
BARNES P S P INC
355 Unionville Rd (16001-8544)
P.O. Box 189 (16003-0189)
PHONE..................................724 287-6711
Barbara Barnes, *President*
Candee Barnes, *Manager*
EMP: 7 EST: 1974
SQ FT: 1,900
SALES (est): 1.1MM **Privately Held**
WEB: www.barnespsp.com
SIC: 3011 Tire sundries or tire repair mate-
rials, rubber

(G-2377)
BELLEVILLE INTERNATIONAL LLC
330 E Cunningham St (16001-6021)
PHONE..................................724 431-0444
Don Smetanick, *President*
Emily Fennell, *General Mgr*
Mike Floyd, *Purch Mgr*
Aaron Martz, *Engineer*
Chrissy McGregor, *Accountant*
EMP: 27
SALES (est): 6.3MM **Privately Held**
SIC: 3452 Spring washers, metal

(G-2378)
BENNETT FLOORING LLC
465 Pittsburgh Rd (16002-7655)
PHONE..................................724 586-9350
Alan Offstein, *Mng Member*
EMP: 20
SALES (est): 1.8MM **Privately Held**
SIC: 2426 Flooring, hardwood

(G-2379)
BIOFAB PRODUCTS INC
140 Eastbrook Ln (16002-1024)
PHONE..................................724 283-4801
John L Murphy, *President*
Ronald Kaplan, *Treasurer*
Michael Holtz, *Admin Sec*
Melissa Snyder, *Admin Sec*
EMP: 25
SQ FT: 30,000
SALES (est): 7.5MM **Privately Held**
SIC: 3441 3444 3443 Fabricated struc-
tural metal; sheet metalwork; fabricated
plate work (boiler shop)

(G-2380)
BIOPTECHS INC
3560 Beck Rd (16002-9259)
PHONE..................................724 282-7145
Daniel Focht, *President*
Karla Clark, *Vice Pres*
Margie Focht, *CFO*

EMP: 14
SQ FT: 7,000
SALES (est): 2.8MM **Privately Held**
WEB: www.bioptechs.com
SIC: 3827 Microscopes, except electron,
proton & corneal

(G-2381)
BLASTMASTER SURFACE RESTORATIO
314 Broad St (16001-5310)
PHONE..................................724 282-7669
Jason Brewer, *Principal*
EMP: 4
SALES (est): 400.7K **Privately Held**
SIC: 3479 Painting of metal products

(G-2382)
BMC LIQUIDATION COMPANY
Also Called: Bear Metallurgical
679 E Butler Rd (16002-9127)
PHONE..................................724 431-2800
Huseyin Ayman, *Vice Pres*
Janice Pakozdi, *Treasurer*
Ozgur Yilmaz, *Admin Sec*
EMP: 26
SQ FT: 100,000
SALES: 8.7MM
SALES (corp-wide): 5.4MM **Privately Held**
WEB: www.bearmet.com
SIC: 3313 Ferromolybdenum; ferrovana-
dium
HQ: Evergreen Metallurgical Llc
679 E Butler Rd
Butler PA 16002
724 431-2800

(G-2383)
BRACKETT MACHINE CO INC
152 North Rd (16001-0274)
PHONE..................................724 287-5804
William Brackett, *President*
Francis Brackett, *Corp Secy*
EMP: 3
SQ FT: 3,000
SALES (est): 529.4K **Privately Held**
SIC: 3599 Machine shop, jobbing & repair

(G-2384)
BUTLER CIRCULATION CALLS
114 W Diamond St (16001-5747)
PHONE..................................724 282-1859
Vernon L Wise Jr, *President*
EMP: 3
SALES (est): 118.6K **Privately Held**
SIC: 2711 Newspapers, publishing & print-
ing

(G-2385)
BUTLER COLOR PRESS INC
119 Bonnie Dr (16002-8503)
P.O. Box 31 (16003-0031)
PHONE..................................724 283-9132
Vernon L Wise III, *President*
John L Wise III, *Corp Secy*
Ray Sielski, *Vice Pres*
Vernon L Wise Jr, *Vice Pres*
Bruce Ziegler, *Vice Pres*
▲ EMP: 115
SQ FT: 110,000
SALES (est): 27.9MM **Privately Held**
WEB: www.butlercp.com
SIC: 2752 Color lithography

(G-2386)
BUTLER TECHNOLOGIES INC
231 W Wayne St (16001-5858)
PHONE..................................724 283-6656
Nadine M Tripodi, *President*
Tristan Tripodi, *General Mgr*
Christine Ring, *Corp Secy*
Mark Bachman, *Prdtn Mgr*
Lesley Bachman, *Purchasing*
EMP: 62
SQ FT: 6,000
SALES (est): 11.4MM **Privately Held**
WEB: www.butlertechnologies.com
SIC: 3613 2672 3577 Switches, electric
power except snap, push button, etc.;
panel & distribution boards & other re-
lated apparatus; adhesive papers, labels
or tapes: from purchased material;
graphic displays, except graphic terminals

(G-2387)
BWI EAGLE INC
105 Bonnie Dr (16002-8503)
PHONE..................................724 283-4681
David Festog, *President*
▲ EMP: 15
SQ FT: 10,000
SALES (est): 2.1MM **Privately Held**
WEB: www.bwieagle.com
SIC: 3625 Switches, electronic applica-
tions; industrial controls: push button, se-
lector switches, pilot

(G-2388)
CHICK MACHINE COMPANY LLC
118 Chick Ln (16002-9014)
PHONE..................................724 352-3330
Robert Petrini, *President*
Ron Harkless, *Foreman/Supr*
Eric Strobel, *Foreman/Supr*
Norma Harkless, *Manager*
Michael Lynn, *Information Mgr*
EMP: 46
SALES (est): 7.1MM **Privately Held**
SIC: 3599 Machine shop, jobbing & repair

(G-2389)
CLASSIC INK USA LLC
556 S Benbrook Rd (16001-1774)
PHONE..................................724 482-1727
Brian K Ellenberger, *Principal*
EMP: 3
SALES (est): 327.2K **Privately Held**
SIC: 2759 Screen printing

(G-2390)
COMMONWEALTH UTILITY EQP INC
Also Called: Cueco
129 Pillow St (16001-5619)
P.O. Box 1503 (16003-1503)
PHONE..................................724 283-8400
Susan Closkey, *President*
Anthony F Closkey, *Corp Secy*
Cynthia Closkey, *Vice Pres*
Kathleen Wayne, *Vice Pres*
EMP: 45
SQ FT: 20,000
SALES: 5MM **Privately Held**
WEB: www.cueco.com
SIC: 3713 3537 Truck cabs for motor vehi-
cles; industrial trucks & tractors

(G-2391)
CREATIVE CERAMICS
606 New Castle Rd (16001-8656)
PHONE..................................724 504-4318
Lynne Lloyd, *Principal*
EMP: 3
SALES (est): 198.3K **Privately Held**
SIC: 3269 Pottery products

(G-2392)
DANIEL LEO OLESNEVICH
Also Called: Olesnevich Fabg & Trck Repr
120 Equine Ln (16002-9018)
PHONE..................................724 352-3160
Daniel Leo Olesnevich, *Owner*
EMP: 4
SQ FT: 4,900
SALES (est): 366K **Privately Held**
SIC: 3715 Truck trailer chassis

(G-2393)
DECTILE HARKUS CONSTRUCTION
195 Kriess Rd (16001-8706)
PHONE..................................724 789-7125
EMP: 21 EST: 1969
SQ FT: 2,016
SALES (est): 775.9K **Privately Held**
SIC: 3272 1542 3251 2952 Mfg Concrete
Products Nonresidential Cnstn Mfg
Brick/Structrl Tile Mfg Asphalt Felt/Coat-
ing

(G-2394)
DELP FAMILY POWDER COATINGS
692 Glenwood Way (16001-8422)
PHONE..................................724 287-3200
Clyde Delp, *President*
Brent Delp, *Principal*
Walter Delp, *Vice Pres*

EMP: 8
SQ FT: 10,000
SALES (est): 1MM **Privately Held**
SIC: 3479 Coating of metals & formed products

(G-2395)
DONUT CONNECTION
330 Center Ave (16001-7042)
PHONE..................................724 282-6214
Karen Stockburger, *Partner*
Jerry Stockburger, *Partner*
EMP: 10
SQ FT: 1,400
SALES (est): 360K **Privately Held**
SIC: 5461 2051 Doughnuts; doughnuts, except frozen

(G-2396)
DUBROOK INC
303 Bantam Ave (16001-5695)
P.O. Box 68 (16003-0068)
PHONE..................................724 283-3111
Mike Perdew, *Plant Mgr*
Jeff Wilson, *Purchasing*
Norm Lindsey, *Sales Staff*
EMP: 28
SALES (corp-wide): 9.1MM **Privately Held**
WEB: www.dubrook.com
SIC: 3273 Ready-mixed concrete
PA: Dubrook, Inc.
40 Hoover Ave
Du Bois PA 15801
814 371-3113

(G-2397)
EAGLE PRINTERY INC
107 Bonnie Dr (16002-8503)
P.O. Box 550 (16003-0550)
PHONE..................................724 287-0754
Karen Wise, *President*
EMP: 18
SQ FT: 10,000
SALES (est): 2.5MM **Privately Held**
WEB: www.eagleprintery.com
SIC: 2759 2752 Screen printing; commercial printing, lithographic

(G-2398)
EAGLE PRINTING COMPANY (PA)
Also Called: Butler Eagle
114 W Diamond St (16001-5747)
P.O. Box 271 (16003-0271)
PHONE..................................724 282-8000
Vernon L Wise III, *President*
Joel Christy, *President*
Beth Koop, *Editor*
John L Wise Jr, *Vice Pres*
John L Wise III, *Vice Pres*
EMP: 65 EST: 1869
SQ FT: 60,000
SALES (est): 25.4MM **Privately Held**
SIC: 2711 2752 Newspapers, publishing & printing; commercial printing, lithographic

(G-2399)
ERVIN INDUSTRIES INC
Also Called: Ervin Amasteel Division
681 E Butler Rd (16002-9197)
PHONE..................................724 282-1060
Donald Gerhart, *Manager*
EMP: 74
SALES (corp-wide): 200MM **Privately Held**
WEB: www.ervinindustries.com
SIC: 3291 Coated abrasive products
PA: Ervin Industries, Inc.
3893 Research Park Dr
Ann Arbor MI 48108
734 769-4600

(G-2400)
EVERGREEN METALLURGICAL LLC (DH)
Also Called: Bear Metallurgical
679 E Butler Rd (16002-9127)
PHONE..................................724 431-2800
Dr Alp Malazgirt, *President*
EMP: 7
SALES (est): 12MM
SALES (corp-wide): 5.4MM **Privately Held**
SIC: 3313 Ferromolybdenum

HQ: Yilmaden Holding Anonim Sirketi
Bingol Karayolu 55.Km
Elazig
212 290-3080

(G-2401)
FILMTRONICS INC
675 Saxonburg Rd (16002-0957)
P.O. Box 1521 (16003-1521)
PHONE..................................724 352-3790
Neal M Christensen, *President*
Duane Burtner, *Vice Pres*
Seth Burtner, *Sales Executive*
Howie Huellen, *Manager*
EMP: 22 EST: 1971
SQ FT: 5,000
SALES (est): 6.8MM **Privately Held**
WEB: www.filmtronics.com
SIC: 3674 2869 2819 Semiconductor circuit networks; industrial organic chemicals; industrial inorganic chemicals

(G-2402)
FOUR WHEELING FOR LESS LLC
762 Route 422 E (16002-9224)
PHONE..................................724 287-7852
Steve Hartle,
William Mitch,
EMP: 7
SALES (est): 495.3K **Privately Held**
SIC: 3799 Recreational vehicles; all terrain vehicles (ATV)

(G-2403)
GCL INC
685 Glenwood Way (16001-8425)
PHONE..................................724 282-2221
George Gibson, *Manager*
EMP: 18
SALES (est): 2.6MM
SALES (corp-wide): 4.8MM **Privately Held**
WEB: www.cambergroup.com
SIC: 3469 Stamping metal for the trade
PA: Gcl, Inc.
2559 Brandt School Rd # 201
Wexford PA 15090
724 933-7260

(G-2404)
HANGER PRSTHETCS & ORTHO INC
108 Evans Rd (16001-1970)
PHONE..................................724 285-1284
Michael Virostek, *QC Mgr*
EMP: 3
SALES (corp-wide): 1B **Publicly Held**
SIC: 3842 Prosthetic appliances
HQ: Hanger Prosthetics & Orthotics, Inc.
10910 Domain Dr Ste 300
Austin TX 78758
512 777-3800

(G-2405)
HARSCO CORPORATION
Rr 8 Box S (16001)
P.O. Box 198, Lyndora (16045-0198)
PHONE..................................724 287-4791
Roy Brick, *Manager*
EMP: 36
SALES (corp-wide): 1.6B **Publicly Held**
WEB: www.hmwest.com
SIC: 5031 3312 3295 Millwork; blast furnaces & steel mills; minerals, ground or treated
PA: Harsco Corporation
350 Poplar Church Rd
Camp Hill PA 17011
717 763-7064

(G-2406)
HOTLINEGLASS-USA LLC
295 Delwood Rd (16001-2065)
P.O. Box 469 (16003-0469)
PHONE..................................800 634-9252
Kent Hurtley, *Mng Member*
Ladonna Young,
EMP: 8 EST: 2010
SALES (est): 199.1K **Privately Held**
SIC: 2392 Mattress pads

(G-2407)
IBIS TEK INC (HQ)
912 Pittsburgh Rd (16002-8913)
PHONE..................................724 431-3000

Vince Nardy, *CEO*
Ronald Zulick, *Technology*
▲ EMP: 90 EST: 2016
SALES (est): 23MM **Privately Held**
SIC: 3711 Military motor vehicle assembly
PA: Ibis Tek Holdings, Inc.
912 Pittsburgh Rd
Butler PA 16002
724 431-3000

(G-2408)
IBIS TEK APPAREL LLC
912 Pittsburgh Rd (16002-8913)
PHONE..................................724 586-2179
Stacy Flick, *General Mgr*
Rachel Berglund, *Vice Pres*
Jim Helms, *Vice Pres*
Bill Rosemeyer, *Vice Pres*
Bryan Dehart, *Prdtn Mgr*
EMP: 45
SALES (est): 4.3MM **Privately Held**
WEB: www.ibistekapparel.com
SIC: 5699 2395 Ret Misc Apparel/Accessories Pleating/Stitching Services

(G-2409)
IBIS TEK HOLDINGS INC (PA)
912 Pittsburgh Rd (16002-8913)
PHONE..................................724 431-3000
Vince Nardy, *CEO*
EMP: 3
SALES (est): 23MM **Privately Held**
SIC: 3711 6719 Motor vehicles & car bodies; investment holding companies, except banks

(G-2410)
INK VAULT
310 Center Ave (16001-7042)
PHONE..................................724 355-8616
EMP: 3
SALES (est): 110.5K **Privately Held**
SIC: 3272 Burial vaults, concrete or precast terrazzo

(G-2411)
ISM ENTERPRISES INC
629 E Butler Rd (16002-9127)
PHONE..................................800 378-3430
Farhad Geranmayeh, *President*
▲ EMP: 7
SALES (est): 40.6K **Privately Held**
SIC: 3315 Steel wire & related products

(G-2412)
JAMES F GEIBEL
Also Called: Key Septic Tank Company
416 Chicora Rd (16001-2304)
PHONE..................................724 287-1964
James F Geibel, *President*
EMP: 7
SQ FT: 7,800
SALES (est): 849.4K **Privately Held**
SIC: 3272 5074 Septic tanks, concrete; pipes & fittings, plastic; plumbing fittings & supplies

(G-2413)
JOHN A ROMEO & ASSOCIATES INC
Also Called: Jara
890 Pittsburgh Rd Ste 7 (16002-8958)
PHONE..................................724 586-6961
Pam Romeo, *President*
John A Romeo, *Vice Pres*
John Romeo, *Marketing Mgr*
EMP: 19
SQ FT: 4,000
SALES (est): 3.9MM **Privately Held**
SIC: 3699 Electrical equipment & supplies

(G-2414)
JOHN R NOVAK & SON INC
Also Called: On The Edge
107 E Quarry St (16001-7007)
PHONE..................................724 285-6802
John R Novak III, *President*
EMP: 8
SALES (est): 920K **Privately Held**
SIC: 3444 Sheet metalwork

(G-2415)
JSP INTERNATIONAL LLC
150 Eastbrook Ln (16002-1024)
PHONE..................................724 477-5100
Zachary Estrin, *Vice Pres*

Bill Rodgers, *Purch Mgr*
Phyllis Deal, *Buyer*
Joe Gamble, *QC Mgr*
Tyler Campbell, *Engineer*
EMP: 200
SALES (corp-wide): 5.9B **Privately Held**
SIC: 2821 Polypropylene resins
HQ: Jsp International Llc
1285 Drummers Ln Ste 301
Wayne PA 19087
610 651-8600

(G-2416)
KEYSTONE CRYSTAL CORPORATION
140 Green Manor Dr (16002-3654)
PHONE..................................724 282-1506
James Hawkey, *Ch of Bd*
Carl R Hawkey, *President*
Michael Traficante, *Treasurer*
Caroline T Hawkey, *Admin Sec*
EMP: 5
SQ FT: 5,000
SALES (est): 801.8K **Privately Held**
SIC: 3679 Crystals & crystal assemblies, radio

(G-2417)
KEYSTONE RIDGE DESIGNS INC
670 Mercer Rd (16001-1840)
PHONE..................................724 284-1213
Carl A Slear, *President*
Nancy L Slear, *Corp Secy*
Arthur Slear, *Vice Pres*
Heather A Starcher, *Vice Pres*
David W Starcher, *Natl Sales Mgr*
EMP: 40
SQ FT: 20,000
SALES (est): 8.1MM **Privately Held**
WEB: www.keystoneridgedesigns.com
SIC: 2531 Picnic tables or benches, park

(G-2418)
LADMAC SERVICES
205 Freeport Rd (16002-3603)
PHONE..................................724 679-8047
Linda Mc Millin, *Owner*
EMP: 3
SALES (est): 160K **Privately Held**
SIC: 3714 5712 Motor vehicle body components & frame; cabinet work, custom

(G-2419)
LARRY J EPPS
Also Called: Epps Manufacturing
507 Dodds Rd (16002-8816)
PHONE..................................724 712-1156
Larry J Epps, *Owner*
EMP: 3
SALES (est): 238.3K **Privately Held**
WEB: www.esmgroupinc.com
SIC: 3443 Fabricated plate work (boiler shop)

(G-2420)
LEMOS LABS LLC
329 Pillow St (16001-5623)
PHONE..................................724 519-2936
Alexander Keffalas,
EMP: 3
SALES (est): 563.6K **Privately Held**
SIC: 3826 Environmental testing equipment

(G-2421)
MARK IM COM
115 N Main St (16001-4902)
PHONE..................................724 282-0997
Mary Schnur, *Principal*
EMP: 4
SALES (est): 237.9K **Privately Held**
SIC: 2395 Embroidery products, except schiffli machine

(G-2422)
MECHLING ASSOCIATES INC
Also Called: Mechling Bookbindery
124 Evans Rd (16001-1970)
PHONE..................................724 287-2120
Allen R Mechling, *President*
Marla K Mechling, *Vice Pres*
EMP: 13
SQ FT: 10,000

SALES: 677K **Privately Held**
WEB: www.mechlingbooks.com
SIC: **2789** 5942 Binding only: books, pamphlets, magazines, etc.; book stores

(G-2423)
MICHALSKI REFRIGERATION INC
Also Called: Icy Ice Co
368 Dinnerbell Rd (16002-8864)
PHONE.................................724 352-1666
Chester P Michalski, *President*
EMP: 3
SQ FT: 5,700
SALES (est): 350.8K **Privately Held**
SIC: **1711** 2097 5046 Refrigeration contractor; manufactured ice; restaurant equipment & supplies

(G-2424)
MICRO MINIATURE MANUFACTURING
506 Pittsburgh Rd (16002-7658)
PHONE.................................724 481-1033
Joseph T Stritzinger, *Principal*
EMP: 4
SALES (est): 398.5K **Privately Held**
SIC: **3549** Draw benches

(G-2425)
MURDICK AUTO PARTS & RACG SUPS
576 Evans City Rd (16001-8794)
PHONE.................................724 482-2177
Ira E Murdick, *Owner*
EMP: 5 EST: 1969
SQ FT: 3,900
SALES: 300K **Privately Held**
SIC: **5531** 5013 3599 7513 Automotive parts; automotive supplies & parts; machine shop, jobbing & repair; truck rental & leasing, no drivers

(G-2426)
NORTH AMERICAN STL & WIRE INC
629 E Butler Rd (16002-9127)
PHONE.................................724 431-0626
Maroune Farah, *President*
Greg Staresinic, *Principal*
Stephen Gauci, *Chairman*
EMP: 36
SALES (est): 9MM **Privately Held**
SIC: **3496** Miscellaneous fabricated wire products

(G-2427)
NORTH AMERICAN WIRE LLC
629 E Butler Rd (16002-9127)
PHONE.................................724 431-0626
Luigi Sorichetti,
EMP: 5
SALES (est): 470K **Privately Held**
SIC: **3496** Miscellaneous fabricated wire products

(G-2428)
OESTERLINGS CONCRETE CO INC
690 Glenwood Way (16001-8422)
PHONE.................................724 282-8556
Robert Oesterling Jr, *President*
Janet M Oesterling, *Corp Secy*
EMP: 5
SQ FT: 2,000
SALES (est): 1MM **Privately Held**
SIC: **5032** 3271 Concrete mixtures; concrete block & brick

(G-2429)
OESTERLINGS SNDBLST & PNTG INC
Also Called: Oesterlings Sndblst & Pntg
686 Glenwood Way (16001-8422)
PHONE.................................724 282-1391
Owen Oesterling, *President*
Lori Smead, *Opers Mgr*
Tamara Oesterling, *Admin Sec*
EMP: 22 EST: 1972
SALES (est): 2.3MM **Privately Held**
SIC: **1799** 1721 3471 Sandblasting of building exteriors; commercial painting; plating & polishing

(G-2430)
ON THE EDGE MFG INC
107 E Quarry St (16001-7007)
PHONE.................................724 285-6802
John Novak, *President*
EMP: 12
SALES (est): 329.6K **Privately Held**
SIC: **3999** Manufacturing industries

(G-2431)
PARC PRODUCTIONS
112 Hollywood Dr Ste 202 (16001-5697)
PHONE.................................724 283-3300
Phil Rosebauer, *Principal*
EMP: 7
SALES (est): 203.7K **Privately Held**
SIC: **8322** 8331 2759 2752 Individual & family services; job training & vocational rehabilitation services; commercial printing; commercial printing, lithographic

(G-2432)
PATRIOT EXPLORATION CORP
202 Sunset Dr (16001-1334)
PHONE.................................724 282-2339
John M Stilley, *President*
EMP: 5
SALES (est): 265.1K **Privately Held**
SIC: **1381** Directional drilling oil & gas wells

(G-2433)
PHOENIX METALS OF PA INC
308 Mitchell Hill Rd (16002-9182)
P.O. Box 1628 (16003-1628)
PHONE.................................724 282-0679
Michael Himchak, *President*
Robert Hoehn, *General Mgr*
Sophia Himchak, *Treasurer*
Marsha Himchak, *Admin Sec*
EMP: 10
SQ FT: 10,000
SALES (est): 1.5MM **Privately Held**
SIC: **3341** Secondary nonferrous metals

(G-2434)
PJR PRINTING INC
Also Called: Sir Speedy
229 S Main St (16001-5908)
PHONE.................................724 283-2666
Peter Richdale, *President*
Joellen Richdale, *Corp Secy*
EMP: 8
SQ FT: 2,000
SALES (est): 455.5K **Privately Held**
SIC: **2752** 7334 Commercial printing, offset; photocopying & duplicating services

(G-2435)
PRIME TURBINES LLC
485 Airport Rd (16001-7633)
PHONE.................................724 586-0124
Charles Praniewicz, *Branch Mgr*
EMP: 6
SALES (corp-wide): 697.2MM **Publicly Held**
SIC: **3724** Aircraft engines & engine parts
HQ: Prime Turbines Llc
1615 Diplomat Dr Ste 120
Carrollton TX 75006
972 406-2100

(G-2436)
QOL MEDS
112 Hillvue Dr (16001-3426)
PHONE.................................724 602-0532
EMP: 4
SALES (est): 375.6K **Privately Held**
SIC: **5912** 5122 2834 Drug stores & proprietary stores; pharmaceuticals; pharmaceutical preparations

(G-2437)
RECLAMATION BREWING COMPANY
221 S Main St (16001-5908)
PHONE.................................724 282-0831
John A Smith,
EMP: 12
SALES (est): 438.8K **Privately Held**
SIC: **2082** 5813 Beer (alcoholic beverage); beer garden (drinking places)

(G-2438)
REFRACTORY MACHINING SERVICES
610 E Butler Rd (16002-9128)
PHONE.................................724 285-7674
James Fry, *President*
▲ EMP: 13
SALES (est): 1.6MM **Privately Held**
SIC: **3599** 1459 Machine shop, jobbing & repair; brucite mining

(G-2439)
RIVER CITY VENOM
225 Kilgallen Rd (16002-8921)
PHONE.................................724 316-5886
EMP: 3 EST: 2016
SALES: 81.6K **Privately Held**
SIC: **2836** Venoms

(G-2440)
SCRAPBOOK STATION
168 Point Plz (16001-2572)
PHONE.................................724 287-4311
James Shepard, *Owner*
EMP: 7
SQ FT: 6,650
SALES: 650K **Privately Held**
SIC: **2782** Scrapbooks

(G-2441)
SIGNS BY RICK INC
217 Freeport Rd (16002-3603)
PHONE.................................724 287-3887
Mark Davanzati, *President*
EMP: 4
SALES (est): 471.3K **Privately Held**
SIC: **3993** Electric signs

(G-2442)
SOUTHERN STRETCH FORMING &
300 Mitchell Hill Rd (16002-9182)
PHONE.................................724 256-8474
Sam Thompson, *Branch Mgr*
EMP: 3 **Privately Held**
SIC: **3441** Fabricated structural metal
PA: Southern Stretch Forming & Fabrication, Inc.
9070 Teasley Ln
Denton TX 76210

(G-2443)
SPECIALTY ICE
229 Cecelia St Rear (16001-5111)
PHONE.................................724 283-7000
Todd Frederick, *Owner*
EMP: 3
SALES (est): 166K **Privately Held**
SIC: **2024** Ices, flavored (frozen dessert)

(G-2444)
STADIUM SOLUTIONS INC
108 Elliott Dr (16001-1118)
PHONE.................................724 287-5330
Mark Klopfer, *CEO*
Cory Roenigk, *Treasurer*
EMP: 13
SALES (est): 1.7MM **Privately Held**
SIC: **2531** Stadium seating

(G-2445)
SWEEPER CITY INC
156 Point Plz (16001-2570)
PHONE.................................724 283-0859
William Eisenman, *President*
EMP: 4
SQ FT: 5,000
SALES (est): 899.2K **Privately Held**
SIC: **2842** 7629 Sweeping compounds, oil or water absorbent, clay or sawdust; shoe polish or cleaner; vacuum cleaner repair

(G-2446)
TOMPKINS MANUFACTURING CO
190 Oak Ridge Dr (16002-3940)
PHONE.................................724 287-4927
Frederick D Tompkins, *Principal*
EMP: 3
SALES (est): 154.8K **Privately Held**
SIC: **3999** Manufacturing industries

(G-2447)
VERNON PRINTING INC
Also Called: Minuteman Press
112 Hollywood Dr Ste 103 (16001-5691)
PHONE.................................724 283-9242
Dan Vernon, *President*
Shirley Vernon, *Treasurer*
EMP: 11
SQ FT: 1,500
SALES (est): 1.5MM **Privately Held**
SIC: **2752** 2759 Commercial printing, offset; commercial printing

(G-2448)
WIEST ASPHALT PRODUCTS AND PAV
310 Mitchell Hill Rd (16002-9182)
PHONE.................................724 282-6913
Joseph C Wiest, *President*
Scott Wiest, *Vice Pres*
Robert C Wiest, *Treasurer*
EMP: 19 EST: 1969
SQ FT: 3,500
SALES (est): 2MM **Privately Held**
SIC: **1771** 2951 Blacktop (asphalt) work; asphalt & asphaltic paving mixtures (not from refineries)

(G-2449)
WISE BUSINESS FORMS INC
150 Kriess Rd (16001-8754)
PHONE.................................724 789-0010
Greg Stiros, *Branch Mgr*
EMP: 100
SALES (corp-wide): 139.3MM **Privately Held**
WEB: www.form-1.com
SIC: **2761** 2782 2759 Manifold business forms; blankbooks & looseleaf binders; commercial printing
PA: Wise Business Forms Incorporated
555 Mcfarland 400 Dr
Alpharetta GA 30004
770 442-1060

(G-2450)
WISE MACHINE CO INC
244 S Cliff St (16001-6093)
PHONE.................................724 287-2705
Robert H Garrard, *Principal*
Floyd Barnhart, *Engineer*
Linda Desmond, *CFO*
▲ EMP: 43 EST: 1911
SQ FT: 57,000
SALES (est): 9.3MM **Privately Held**
WEB: www.wisemachine.com
SIC: **3559** 8711 7699 3568 Foundry machinery & equipment; engineering services; industrial equipment services; power transmission equipment

(G-2451)
WIST ENTERPRISES INC
Also Called: Butler Winding
201 Pillow St (16001-5621)
P.O. Box 111, Gowanda NY (14070-0111)
PHONE.................................724 283-7230
Dennis Wist, *President*
Jay Smith, *Vice Pres*
Kevin Angert, *Purchasing*
EMP: 12
SQ FT: 4,080
SALES (est): 794.7K **Privately Held**
WEB: www.butlerwinding.com
SIC: **3677** Transformers power supply, electronic type

Cabot
Butler County

(G-2452)
ARMSTRONG CEMENT & SUPPLY CORP
100 Clearfield Rd (16023-9521)
PHONE.................................724 352-9401
Dennis C Snyder, *President*
Charles H Snyder Jr, *Chairman*
Paul J Benec, *Vice Pres*
Richard L Smith, *Vice Pres*
David E Snyder, *Treasurer*
EMP: 60
SQ FT: 6,000

G
E
O
G
R
A
P
H
I
C

SALES (est): 11.1MM
SALES (corp-wide): 790.5MM **Privately Held**
WEB: www.armstrongcement.com
SIC: 3241 Portland cement
PA: Snyder Associated Companies, Inc.
1 Glade Park Dr
Kittanning PA 16201
724 548-8101

(G-2453)
BUTLER STONECRAFT INC
772 N Pike Rd (16023-2224)
PHONE..................................724 352-3520
James Miller, *President*
EMP: 5
SALES (est): 564.3K **Privately Held**
WEB: www.butlerstonecraft.com
SIC: 3281 Cut stone & stone products

(G-2454)
DAVID B LYTLE PRODUCTS INC
920 N Pike Rd (16023-2028)
P.O. Box 8 (16023-0008)
PHONE..................................724 352-3322
David B Lytle, *President*
Ronald Bowser, *Vice Pres*
▲ EMP: 7
SQ FT: 6,000
SALES (est): 240.6K **Privately Held**
WEB: www.magneticframes.com
SIC: 3499 Picture frames, metal

(G-2455)
DMAND ENERGY
901 N Pike Rd (16023-2029)
PHONE..................................970 201-4976
EMP: 10
SQ FT: 2,600
SALES (est): 498.5K **Privately Held**
SIC: 1389 Oil/Gas Field Services

(G-2456)
ENI USA R & M CO INC
539 Marwood Rd (16023-9526)
PHONE..................................724 352-4451
Joe Krisky, *Vice Pres*
EMP: 30
SQ FT: 30,000
SALES (corp-wide): 34.1B **Privately Held**
WEB: www.americanagip.com
SIC: 2992 5172 Lubricating oils &
greases; petroleum products
HQ: Eni Usa R&M Co. Inc.
485 Madison Ave Fl 6
New York NY 10022
646 264-2100

(G-2457)
FRANK FERRIS INDUSTRIES INC
(PA)
Also Called: Mitchell & Westerman
901 N Pike Rd (16023-2029)
P.O. Box 266, Cuddy (15031-0266)
PHONE..................................724 352-9477
Francis P Ferris, *President*
Christine C Ferris, *Admin Sec*
EMP: 4
SALES (est): 2.4MM **Privately Held**
WEB: www.frankferris.com
SIC: 5113 2448 Industrial & personal serv-
ice paper; pallets, wood

(G-2458)
MARWOOD MACHINE COMPANY
INC
557 Marwood Rd (16023-9526)
PHONE..................................724 352-2646
Donald Crimbchin, *President*
Frank J Crimbchin, *Admin Sec*
EMP: 6 EST: 1978
SQ FT: 16,000
SALES: 350K **Privately Held**
WEB: www.marwoodmachine.com
SIC: 3599 Machine shop, jobbing & repair

(G-2459)
MC KRUIT MEAT PACKING
Also Called: McKruit Hide & Glove
1011 Bear Creek Rd (16023-9716)
PHONE..................................724 352-2988
Daniel McKruit, *Owner*
EMP: 3
SQ FT: 600
SALES (est): 212.8K **Privately Held**
SIC: 2011 Meat packing plants

(G-2460)
PENN UNITED TECHNOLOGIES
INC (PA)
Also Called: American Carbide Tooling Div
799 N Pike Rd (16023-2297)
P.O. Box 399, Saxonburg (16056-0399)
PHONE..................................724 352-1507
William A Jones, *President*
Karen Craig, *General Mgr*
Esther Locke, *Editor*
Barry C Barton, *Exec VP*
Jerry R Purcell, *Exec VP*
▼ EMP: 596
SALES (est): 147.3MM **Privately Held**
WEB: www.pennunited.com
SIC: 3544 2819 Special dies & tools; in-
dustrial inorganic chemicals

(G-2461)
WINFIELD LIME & STONE CO
INC (PA)
340 Fisher Rd (16023-2106)
PHONE..................................724 352-3596
Robert M Weleski, *Vice Pres*
Richard F Weleski, *Treasurer*
EMP: 14 EST: 1954
SQ FT: 1,500
SALES (est): 1.6MM **Privately Held**
SIC: 1422 4212 Crushed & broken lime-
stone; local trucking, without storage

(G-2462)
WINFIELD WINERY LLC
1026 Winfield Rd (16023-3104)
PHONE..................................724 352-9589
John Ricchiuto,
John A Ricchuito,
EMP: 4
SALES (est): 400K **Privately Held**
SIC: 2084 7389 Wines;

Cairnbrook
Somerset County

(G-2463)
NEW ENTERPRISE STONE LIME
INC
417 Sandplant Rd (15924-8423)
PHONE..................................814 754-4921
Stacy Calhoun, *Manager*
EMP: 23
SALES (corp-wide): 651.9MM **Privately
Held**
WEB: www.nesl.com
SIC: 1422 Crushed & broken limestone
PA: New Enterprise Stone & Lime Co., Inc.
3912 Brumbaugh Rd
New Enterprise PA 16664
814 224-6883

California
Washington County

(G-2464)
PENNATRONICS CORPORATION
75 Technology Dr (15419)
P.O. Box 638 (15419-0638)
PHONE..................................724 938-1800
Ralph Andy, *President*
Keith James, *Vice Pres*
James Dillinger, *Production*
Mark Emerson, *Production*
Rose Keffer, *Production*
EMP: 100
SQ FT: 45,000
SALES (est): 31.5MM **Privately Held**
WEB: www.pennatronics.com
SIC: 3678 3672 Electronic connectors;
printed circuit boards

Callensburg
Clarion County

(G-2465)
RANDY LARKIN
Also Called: Crudeaco
217 Main St (16213)
P.O. Box 58 (16213-0058)
PHONE..................................814 358-2508
Randy Larkin, *Owner*
EMP: 4
SALES (est): 200K **Privately Held**
SIC: 1389 Well plugging & abandoning, oil
& gas

Callery
Butler County

(G-2466)
ANDRITZ HERR-VOSS STAMCO
INC (DH)
130 Main St (16024)
P.O. Box Ab (16024-0178)
PHONE..................................724 538-3180
Kip Mostowy, *CEO*
Larry Scott, *Vice Pres*
Gregory Santillo, *Engineer*
Bill Wolf, *Engineer*
Kate Davidson, *Chief Mktg Ofcr*
▲ EMP: 165
SALES (est): 78.9MM
SALES (corp-wide): 6.9B **Privately Held**
WEB: www.herr-vossstamco.com
SIC: 3559 Metal finishing equipment for
plating, etc.
HQ: Andritz (Usa) Inc.
5405 Windward Pkwy # 100
Alpharetta GA 30004
770 640-2500

(G-2467)
BYRNES AND KIEFER COMPANY
(PA)
Also Called: B and K Manufacturing
131 Kline Ave (16024)
PHONE..................................724 538-5200
E G Byrnes, *President*
Thomas Byrnes, *Vice Pres*
J J Thier, *Treasurer*
EMP: 25
SQ FT: 55,000
SALES: 23MM **Privately Held**
SIC: 2865 2087 5149 2064 Food dyes or
colors, synthetic; beverage bases, con-
centrates, syrups, powders & mixes; bak-
ery products; candy & other confectionery
products; bread & bread type roll mixes:
from purchased flour

(G-2468)
BYRNES AND KIEFER COMPANY
Also Called: Chefmaster East Division
131 Kline Ave (16024)
P.O. Box L (16024-0176)
PHONE..................................724 538-5200
Don Yoest, *Manager*
EMP: 30
SALES (corp-wide): 23MM **Privately
Held**
SIC: 2087 Extracts, flavoring
PA: Byrnes And Kiefer Company
131 Kline Ave
Callery PA 16024
724 538-5200

(G-2469)
GENESIS WORLDWIDE II INC
130 Main St (16024)
P.O. Box Ab (16024-0178)
PHONE..................................724 538-3180
Kip Mostowy, *President*
Randy Mickey, *General Mgr*
Randy Saputo, *CFO*
James McKenna, *VP Sales*
◆ EMP: 291
SQ FT: 125,000

SALES (est): 46.7MM
SALES (corp-wide): 6.9B **Privately Held**
WEB: www.gen-world.com
SIC: 3541 Machine tools, metal cutting
type
HQ: Andritz (Usa) Inc.
5405 Windward Pkwy # 100
Alpharetta GA 30004
770 640-2500

(G-2470)
PLANT GROWERS WORKSHOP
INC
106 Center St Bldg 3 (16024)
PHONE..................................724 473-1079
Edward J Stumm, *President*
Peter J Stumm, *Vice Pres*
▲ EMP: 7
SALES (est): 1MM **Privately Held**
SIC: 3646 Commercial indusl & institu-
tional electric lighting fixtures

(G-2471)
WM S LONG INC
127 Breakneck St (16024)
PHONE..................................724 538-3775
William S Long Jr, *President*
EMP: 7
SQ FT: 3,000
SALES (est): 987.5K **Privately Held**
WEB: www.wslonginc.com
SIC: 3272 Manhole covers or frames, con-
crete

Calumet
Westmoreland County

(G-2472)
J RUSSEL TOOLING CO
Poplar St (15621)
PHONE..................................724 423-2766
James Russell Hill, *Owner*
EMP: 9
SQ FT: 2,800
SALES: 300K **Privately Held**
SIC: 3599 7692 Machine shop, jobbing &
repair; welding repair

Cambridge Springs
Crawford County

(G-2473)
A A ROBBINS INC
Also Called: Robbins Concrete Block Mfg
260 Railroad St (16403-1072)
P.O. Box 261 (16403-0261)
PHONE..................................814 398-4607
Dennis Robbins, *President*
Betsy Ross, *Admin Sec*
EMP: 13
SQ FT: 2,700
SALES (est): 1.6MM **Privately Held**
WEB: www.aarobbins.com
SIC: 3271 5211 Blocks, concrete or cin-
der: standard; lumber & other building
materials

(G-2474)
B H B INDUSTRIES
116 Railroad St (16403-1060)
PHONE..................................814 398-8011
Steven Hills, *Partner*
Lawrence Coblentz, *Partner*
Harold Hills, *Partner*
EMP: 5 EST: 1970
SQ FT: 5,000
SALES: 200K **Privately Held**
SIC: 3086 Plastics foam products

(G-2475)
CAMPBELL STUDIOS INC (PA)
146 Railroad St (16403-1060)
PHONE..................................814 398-2148
Jane A Campbell, *President*
William H Campbell, *Vice Pres*
EMP: 45 EST: 1996
SQ FT: 20,000
SALES (est): 4.6MM **Privately Held**
WEB: www.campbellpottery.com
SIC: 3269 Stoneware pottery products

(G-2476)
CUSSEWAGO TRUSS LLC
23416 Middle Rd (16403-1946)
PHONE..............................814 763-3229
Larry Otto,
EMP: 20
SQ FT: 23,000
SALES (est): 1.1MM **Privately Held**
SIC: 2439 Trusses, wooden roof

(G-2477)
DONLEE TOOL CORP
21 North St (16403-3330)
P.O. Box 233 (16403-0233)
PHONE..............................814 398-8215
Donald Rodgers, *President*
Jeffrey Rodgers, *Vice Pres*
Kevin Rodgers, *Treasurer*
EMP: 18 **EST:** 1973
SQ FT: 3,600
SALES (est): 2.9MM **Privately Held**
WEB: www.donleetool.com
SIC: 3544 Dies, steel rule; special dies &
tools

(G-2478)
KALEIDAS MACHINING INC
24195 State Highway 99 (16403-3109)
PHONE..............................814 398-4337
Matthew Kaleida, *President*
EMP: 5
SQ FT: 5,400
SALES (est): 600K **Privately Held**
SIC: 3541 Screw machines, automatic

(G-2479)
KDL INDUSTRIES
27360 Zilhaver Rd (16403-4266)
PHONE..............................814 398-1555
Kevin Le Suer, *Owner*
EMP: 3 **EST:** 1984
SQ FT: 3,100
SALES (est): 160K **Privately Held**
WEB: www.kdlindustries.net
SIC: 3451 Screw machine products

(G-2480)
**KRAFT AND JUTE
INCORPORATED**
273 S Main St (16403-1156)
PHONE..............................814 969-8121
Jessica Lewis, *Principal*
Heather Simitoski, *Graphic Designe*
EMP: 6
SALES (est): 489.2K **Privately Held**
SIC: 2022 Mfg Cheese

(G-2481)
LORD CORPORATION
124 Grant St (16403-1014)
PHONE..............................814 398-4641
Rick McNeel, *CEO*
EMP: 99
SQ FT: 125,000
SALES (corp-wide): 1B **Privately Held**
WEB: www.lordcorp.com
SIC: 3069 3829 3651 3568 Hard rubber
& molded rubber products; measuring &
controlling devices; household audio &
video equipment; power transmission
equipment
PA: Lord Corporation
111 Lord Dr
Cary NC 27511
919 468-5979

(G-2482)
MARTINS STARTER SERVICE
27749 Oregon Corners Rd (16403-6719)
PHONE..............................814 398-2496
Anthony Martin, *Partner*
Conrad Martin, *Partner*
Joseph Martin, *Partner*
Jerry Martin, *General Ptnr*
EMP: 4
SALES: 180K **Privately Held**
SIC: 3694 Automotive electrical equipment

(G-2483)
**MEADVILLE FORGING
COMPANY LP**
440 Mcclellan St (16403-1002)
PHONE..............................814 398-2203
Gary Klink, *Principal*
EMP: 74

SQ FT: 30,000
SALES (corp-wide): 98.2MM **Privately
Held**
WEB: www.meadvillepa.com
SIC: 3462 Iron & steel forgings
HQ: Meadville Forging Company, L.P.
15309 Baldwin Street Ext
Meadville PA 16335
814 332-8200

(G-2484)
**NEW ENTERPRISE STONE LIME
INC**
Also Called: Protection Services
14341 Route 19 Ste 2 (16403-9123)
PHONE..............................814 796-1413
EMP: 36
SALES (corp-wide): 651.9MM **Privately
Held**
WEB: www.nesl.com
SIC: 1422 Crushed & broken limestone
PA: New Enterprise Stone & Lime Co., Inc.
3912 Brumbaugh Rd
New Enterprise PA 16664
814 224-6883

Camp Hill
Cumberland County

(G-2485)
ADM MILLING CO
811 Spangler Rd (17011-5823)
P.O. Box 3100 (17011-3100)
PHONE..............................717 737-0529
Erett Lowe, *Manager*
EMP: 30
SALES (corp-wide): 64.3B **Publicly Held**
WEB: www.admmilling.com
SIC: 2041 Grain mills (except rice)
HQ: Adm Milling Co.
8000 W 110th St Ste 300
Overland Park KS 66210
913 491-9400

(G-2486)
**AMERICAN SOC FOR DEAF
CHILDREN**
3820 Hartzdale Dr (17011-7809)
PHONE..............................717 909-5577
Natalie Long, *President*
EMP: 4
SALES (est): 116.1K **Privately Held**
WEB: www.deafchildren.org
SIC: 8399 8641 2721 Advocacy group;
social service information exchange; civic
social & fraternal associations; maga-
zines: publishing only, not printed on site

(G-2487)
AMES COMPANIES INC
465 Railroad Ave (17011-5611)
PHONE..............................717 737-1500
Dave Randolph, *Branch Mgr*
EMP: 61
SALES (corp-wide): 1.5B **Publicly Held**
WEB: www.ames.com
SIC: 3423 Garden & farm tools, including
shovels
HQ: The Ames Companies Inc
465 Railroad Ave
Camp Hill PA 17011
717 737-1500

(G-2488)
AMES COMPANIES INC (DH)
465 Railroad Ave (17011-5611)
P.O. Box 8859 (17001-8859)
PHONE..............................717 737-1500
Michael A Sarrica, *President*
Dean Cross, *Plant Mgr*
Mark Schrage, *Plant Mgr*
Bill Wolf, *Opers Staff*
Richard Green, *Mfg Staff*
◆ **EMP:** 412
SQ FT: 400,000
SALES (est): 404MM
SALES (corp-wide): 1.5B **Publicly Held**
WEB: www.ames.com
SIC: 3423 3799 3524 Garden & farm
tools, including shovels; shovels, spades
(hand tools); wheelbarrows; lawn & gar-
den equipment

(G-2489)
AMSTED RAIL COMPANY INC
3420 Simpson Ferry Rd (17011-6410)
PHONE..............................717 761-3690
John Fetterolf, *Branch Mgr*
EMP: 100
SALES (corp-wide): 2.4B **Privately Held**
SIC: 3743 Railroad equipment
HQ: Amsted Rail Company, Inc.
311 S Wacker Dr Ste 5300
Chicago IL 60606

(G-2490)
APPLE FASTENERS INC
2850 Appleton St Ste A (17011-8036)
P.O. Box 310, Dover (17315-0310)
PHONE..............................717 761-8962
William D Often, *President*
Dave Often, *Principal*
◆ **EMP:** 26
SALES (est): 4.2MM **Privately Held**
SIC: 2591 Shade pulls, window

(G-2491)
**ARCHER-DANIELS-MIDLAND
COMPANY**
Also Called: ADM
2000 Hummel Ave (17011-5944)
PHONE..............................717 761-5200
Tim Minnich, *Branch Mgr*
EMP: 20
SALES (corp-wide): 64.3B **Publicly Held**
SIC: 2041 Flour & other grain mill products
PA: Archer-Daniels-Midland Company
77 W Wacker Dr Ste 4600
Chicago IL 60601
312 634-8100

(G-2492)
**ATLAS ROOFING
CORPORATION**
817 Spangler Rd (17011-5823)
PHONE..............................717 760-5460
Paul Roberts, *Vice Pres*
Steve Acker, *Transptn Dir*
Robin Flake, *Human Res Mgr*
Yesenia Guardado, *Accounts Exec*
Charles Paulk, *Sales Staff*
EMP: 50 **Privately Held**
WEB: www.atlasroofing.com
SIC: 3086 2952 Insulation or cushioning
material, foamed plastic; asphalt felts &
coatings
HQ: Atlas Roofing Corporation
802 Highway 19 N Ste 190
Meridian MS 39307
601 484-8900

(G-2493)
**BROTHER AND SISTER FD SVC
INC**
811 Spangler Rd (17011-5823)
PHONE..............................717 558-0108
Aziz Sahovic, *President*
Vedad Sahovic, *Vice Pres*
▲ **EMP:** 9
SQ FT: 33,180
SALES (est): 1.7MM **Privately Held**
SIC: 2013 Sausages & other prepared
meats

(G-2494)
**CAROL VINCK WINDOW
CREATION**
4401 Carlisle Pike Ste J (17011-4136)
PHONE..............................717 730-0303
Carol Vinck, *Owner*
EMP: 8
SALES (est): 440K **Privately Held**
SIC: 2591 Drapery hardware & blinds &
shades

(G-2495)
**EMERGING COMPUTER
TECHNOLOGIES**
3518 Hawthorne Dr (17011-2720)
PHONE..............................717 761-4027
Mary Dennis, *Owner*
EMP: 4 **EST:** 1994
SALES: 230K **Privately Held**
SIC: 7372 Operating systems computer
software

(G-2496)
ENVIRODYNE SYSTEMS INC
75 Zimmerman Dr (17011-6822)
PHONE..............................717 763-0500
Laurence T Sheker, *President*
Catherine M Sheker, *Corp Secy*
Eric Bushey, *Vice Pres*
Roy Shanafelter, *Info Tech Mgr*
◆ **EMP:** 48
SQ FT: 10,000
SALES (est): 10.1MM **Privately Held**
WEB: www.envirodynesystems.com
SIC: 3589 5084 8731 Water treatment
equipment, industrial; sewage treatment
equipment; industrial machinery & equip-
ment; commercial physical research

(G-2497)
FERDIC INC (PA)
Also Called: Dickinson's FDA Review
165 S 32nd St (17011-5102)
P.O. Box 28 (17001-0028)
PHONE..............................717 731-1426
James G Dickinson, *President*
Sheila Dickinson, *Vice Pres*
David McFarland, *Vice Pres*
EMP: 9
SALES (est): 713.4K **Privately Held**
WEB: www.fdaweb.com
SIC: 2721 Magazines: publishing only, not
printed on site

(G-2498)
GRINDERS ON GO
3605 Kohler Pl (17011-2700)
PHONE..............................717 712-0977
Cherry Distefno, *Owner*
EMP: 3
SALES (est): 133K **Privately Held**
SIC: 2099 Ready-to-eat meals, salads &
sandwiches

(G-2499)
**HANGER PRSTHETCS & ORTHO
INC**
Also Called: Teufles
3514 Trindle Rd (17011-4444)
PHONE..............................717 731-8181
Robert Teufel, *Branch Mgr*
EMP: 7
SALES (corp-wide): 1B **Publicly Held**
SIC: 3842 Surgical appliances & supplies
HQ: Hanger Prosthetics & Orthotics, Inc.
10910 Domain Dr Ste 300
Austin TX 78758
512 777-3800

(G-2500)
HEMPT BROS INC (PA)
205 Creek Rd (17011-7499)
P.O. Box 278 (17001-0278)
PHONE..............................717 774-2911
Max J Hempt, *President*
Heath Sands, *Superintendent*
Gerald L Hempt, *Corp Secy*
Joseph R Nokovich, *Vice Pres*
Lance Leber, *Materials Mgr*
EMP: 91 **EST:** 1925
SQ FT: 8,500
SALES (est): 88.9MM **Privately Held**
SIC: 1611 2951 3273 1442
Highway/Street Cnstn Mfg Ready-Mixed
Concrete Mfg Asphalt Mixtr/Blocks Con-
struction Sand/Gravel

(G-2501)
HIGHWAY MANOR BREWING
2238 Gettysburg Rd (17011-7301)
PHONE..............................717 743-0613
EMP: 4 **EST:** 2017
SALES (est): 190.7K **Privately Held**
SIC: 2082 Beer (alcoholic beverage)

(G-2502)
KONHAUS FARMS INC
Also Called: Konhaus Print & Marketing
3544 Gettysburg Rd (17011-6801)
PHONE..............................717 731-9456
Melissa Konhaus, *President*
Paul Konhaus, *Vice Pres*
EMP: 8
SQ FT: 1,750
SALES (est): 1.2MM **Privately Held**
WEB: www.transamericaprint.com
SIC: 2752 Commercial printing, offset

(G-2503)
LANE ENTERPRISES INC (PA)
3905 Hartzdale Dr Ste 514 (17011-7837)
PHONE..............................717 761-8175
Thomas J Wonsiewicz, *President*
Patrick X Collings, *President*
Marlin J Cathers, *Vice Pres*
Jerry A Saylor, *Vice Pres*
Richard A Walter, *Vice Pres*
▼ EMP: 15 EST: 1934
SQ FT: 1,000
SALES (est): 70.5MM **Privately Held**
WEB: www.lanepipe.com
SIC: 3479 3444 Coating of metals &
formed products; pipe, sheet metal

(G-2504)
MCKENZIE SPORTS PRODUCTS LLC
460 Sterling St Ste 3 (17011-5701)
PHONE..............................717 731-9920
David Sachs, *Principal*
EMP: 116
SALES (corp-wide): 99.9MM **Privately Held**
SIC: 3949 Sporting & athletic goods
PA: Mckenzie Sports Products, Llc
1910 Saint Luke Church Rd
Salisbury NC 28146
704 279-7985

(G-2505)
MIRADA ENERGY INC
3920 Market St (17011-4202)
PHONE..............................717 730-9412
Mark Rodak, *President*
Dan McCormick, *Vice Pres*
EMP: 20
SALES: 6MM **Privately Held**
SIC: 1241 Bituminous coal mining services, contract basis

(G-2506)
NESTLE PIZZA COMPANY INC
Also Called: Kraft Foods
1177 Shoreham Rd (17011-6136)
PHONE..............................717 737-7268
Michele Sabitsky, *Branch Mgr*
EMP: 15
SALES (corp-wide): 90.8B **Privately Held**
SIC: 2038 Pizza, frozen
HQ: Nestle Pizza Company, Inc.
1 Kraft Ct
Glenview IL 60025
847 646-2000

(G-2507)
OLIFANT USA INC
3507 Market St Ste 102 (17011-4310)
PHONE..............................916 996-6207
Jack McKenzie, *President*
▲ EMP: 4
SALES (est): 177.7K **Privately Held**
SIC: 2085 Vodka (alcoholic beverage)

(G-2508)
OVEN INDUSTRIES INC
434 Railroad Ave (17011-5601)
P.O. Box 290, Mechanicsburg (17055-0290)
PHONE..............................717 766-0721
Michael D Carlini, *President*
Kerry Krafthefer, *Vice Pres*
David Sellers, *Engineer*
▲ EMP: 30
SQ FT: 12,500
SALES (est): 10.1MM **Privately Held**
WEB: www.ovenind.com
SIC: 3822 3625 Temperature controls, automatic; relays & industrial controls

(G-2509)
PA MINING PROFESSIONAL
704 Lisburn Rd (17011-7490)
PHONE..............................717 761-4646
Eric Flicker, *Principal*
EMP: 3
SALES (est): 127.6K **Privately Held**
SIC: 1241 Coal mining exploration & test boring

(G-2510)
PENNSYLVANIA MOTOR TRUCK ASSN
Also Called: PMTA
910 Linda Ln (17011-6401)
PHONE..............................717 761-7122
James W Runk, *President*
EMP: 8 EST: 1928
SQ FT: 3,000
SALES: 1.1MM **Privately Held**
WEB: www.pmta.org
SIC: 8611 2721 Trade associations; periodicals

(G-2511)
PURINA ANIMAL NUTRITION LLC
475 Saint Johns Church Rd (17011-5755)
P.O. Box 248 (17001-0248)
PHONE..............................717 737-4581
John T Zerbe, *Branch Mgr*
EMP: 70
SQ FT: 80,128
SALES (corp-wide): 10.4B **Privately Held**
WEB: www.landolakesidd.com
SIC: 2048 Prepared feeds
HQ: Purina Animal Nutrition Llc
100 Danforth Dr
Gray Summit MO 63039

(G-2512)
PURINA MILLS LLC
475 Saint Johns Church Rd (17011-5755)
P.O. Box 248 (17001-0248)
PHONE..............................717 737-4581
John Zerbe, *Vice Pres*
EMP: 10
SALES (corp-wide): 10.4B **Privately Held**
SIC: 2048 Prepared feeds
HQ: Purina Mills, Llc
555 Maryvle Univ Dr 200
Saint Louis MO 63141

(G-2513)
R T GRIM CO
3925 Trindle Rd (17011-4216)
PHONE..............................717 761-4113
Robert R Grim, *President*
Jack Wenrich, *Supervisor*
Suzanne Grim, *Admin Sec*
EMP: 41 EST: 1928
SQ FT: 41,000
SALES (est): 7.9MM **Privately Held**
WEB: www.rtgelectronics.com
SIC: 3694 7622 Automotive electrical equipment; radio repair shop; television repair shop

(G-2514)
RAM INDUSTRIAL SERVICES LLC
2850 Appleton St Ste D (17011-8036)
PHONE..............................717 232-4414
Paul Gnall, *Manager*
EMP: 50
SALES (corp-wide): 242.5MM **Privately Held**
SIC: 7694 Electric motor repair
PA: Ram Industrial Services, Llc
2850 Appleton St Ste D
Camp Hill PA 17011
717 737-7810

(G-2515)
REMILUX LLC
Also Called: Remington Lamp Company
2500 Gettysburg Rd # 101 (17011-7228)
PHONE..............................717 737-7120
Douglas A Scott,
▲ EMP: 7
SQ FT: 17,000
SALES (est): 1.4MM **Privately Held**
SIC: 3645 Lamp & light shades

(G-2516)
ROYALTON PRESS INC
351 Martingale Dr (17011-8314)
PHONE..............................610 929-4040
Louis M Malamud, *President*
Sara Malamud, *Treasurer*
EMP: 3 EST: 1931
SQ FT: 1,700
SALES: 250K **Privately Held**
SIC: 2752 2759 Commercial printing, offset; letterpress printing

(G-2517)
SABA HOLDING COMPANY INC
2001 State Rd (17011-5927)
P.O. Box 134 (17001-0134)
PHONE..............................717 737-3431
R E Jordan, *Branch Mgr*
EMP: 3
SALES (corp-wide): 39.6B **Privately Held**
SIC: 3531 Construction machinery
HQ: Saba Holding Company, Llc
312 Volvo Way
Shippensburg PA 17257
717 532-9181

(G-2518)
SILK SCREEN PRINTERS
3814 Seneca Ave (17011-6813)
PHONE..............................717 761-1121
EMP: 8
SALES (est): 519.4K **Privately Held**
SIC: 2759 Commercial Printing

(G-2519)
SUNSET TEES
2236 Gettysburg Rd Ste 2 (17011-7328)
PHONE..............................717 737-9919
Tamela Warner, *Owner*
EMP: 3
SQ FT: 1,200
SALES (est): 191.3K **Privately Held**
SIC: 2396 Screen printing on fabric articles

(G-2520)
TATA AMERICA INTL CORP
50 Utley Dr Ste 100 (17011-8031)
PHONE..............................717 737-4737
EMP: 70
SALES (corp-wide): 10.3B **Privately Held**
SIC: 7372 Prepackaged Software Services
HQ: Tata America International Corporation
101 Park Ave Rm 2603
New York NY 10178
212 557-8038

(G-2521)
UTILITY SERVICE GROUP INC
1304 Slate Hill Rd (17011-8013)
P.O. Box 3143, Shiremanstown (17011-3143)
PHONE..............................717 737-6092
Herbert S Schlagman, *President*
James P Straub, *President*
Charles Lightcap, *Project Mgr*
Victor Howard, *Info Tech Mgr*
EMP: 30
SALES (est): 5.2MM **Privately Held**
SIC: 3272 5983 Concrete stuctural support & building material; fuel oil dealers

(G-2522)
VANTAGE FOODS PA LP
2700 Yetter Ct (17011-4909)
PHONE..............................717 691-4728
Leonal Kilgore, *President*
EMP: 41
SQ FT: 140,000 **Privately Held**
SIC: 2013 Prepared beef products from purchased beef
HQ: Vantage Foods Inc
4000 4 St Se Suite 225
Calgary AB T2G 2
403 215-2820

(G-2523)
WARRELL CORPORATION (PA)
Also Called: Pennsylvania Dutch Candies
1250 Slate Hill Rd (17011-8011)
PHONE..............................717 761-5440
Lincoln A Warrell, *Ch of Bd*
Scott Lutz, *Business Mgr*
Daniel Margherio, *Business Mgr*
Richard Warrell, *Exec VP*
Robert Bard, *Vice Pres*
▲ EMP: 265 EST: 1965
SQ FT: 200,000
SALES: 65.3MM **Privately Held**
WEB: www.padutchcandies.com
SIC: 2066 2064 Chocolate candy, solid; candy & other confectionery products

(G-2524)
WEATHER SHIELD MFG INC
1401 Slate Hill Rd (17011-8018)
PHONE..............................717 761-7131
Bev James, *Branch Mgr*
EMP: 453
SALES (corp-wide): 490.5MM **Privately Held**
WEB: www.weathershield.com
SIC: 3442 2431 Storm doors or windows, metal; window frames, wood; doors, wood
PA: Weather Shield Mfg., Inc.
1 Weathershield Plz
Medford WI 54451
715 748-2100

(G-2525)
WESTERBROOK CUSTOM MADE DRAP
Also Called: Draperies Plus
4 Amherst Dr (17011-7703)
P.O. Box 541, New Cumberland (17070-0541)
PHONE..............................717 737-8185
Robert J Smith, *President*
EMP: 4
SALES (est): 350K **Privately Held**
SIC: 2391 5023 Draperies, plastic & textile: from purchased materials; vertical blinds

(G-2526)
WORLD ENERGY HARRISBURG LLC
2850 Appleton St Ste E (17011-8036)
PHONE..............................717 412-0374
Gene Gebolys, *Owner*
EMP: 19
SALES (est): 450K **Privately Held**
SIC: 2911 Diesel fuels

(G-2527)
ZOLL
2001 Clarendon St (17011-3828)
PHONE..............................717 761-1842
EMP: 3
SALES (est): 226.9K **Privately Held**
SIC: 3845 Electromedical equipment

(G-2528)
ZUR LTD
Also Called: Echurchdepot
75 Utley Dr (17011-8000)
PHONE..............................717 761-7044
Kenneth R Paton, *President*
Ken Paton, *President*
Doug Waardenburg, *CFO*
▲ EMP: 45
SALES (est): 1.6MM **Privately Held**
WEB: www.christiancampus.com
SIC: 5942 2731 5192 Book stores; book publishing; books, periodicals & newspapers

---

Campbelltown
Lebanon County

(G-2529)
BLOSE PRINTING
2709 Horseshoe Pike (17010)
P.O. Box 32 (17010-0032)
PHONE..............................717 838-9129
Ronald Blose, *Owner*
EMP: 3
SQ FT: 2,800
SALES: 250K **Privately Held**
SIC: 2752 Commercial printing, offset

Canadensis
Monroe County

(G-2530)
HYDROSOURCE
Rr 390 (18325)
P.O. Box 81 (18325-0081)
PHONE..............................570 676-8500
G D Hooke, *Owner*
EMP: 15 EST: 2000
SALES (est): 1.5MM **Privately Held**
WEB: www.hydrosource.com
SIC: 3732 Jet skis

▲ = Import ▼=Export
◆ =Import/Export

GEOGRAPHIC

Canonsburg
Washington County

(G-2531)
A STUCKI COMPANY
Hankison Division
1000 Philadelphia St (15317-1700)
PHONE..................724 746-4240
A Stucki, *Chairman*
EMP: 50
SALES (corp-wide): 26.7MM **Privately Held**
WEB: www.stucki.com
SIC: 3567 5084 Driers & redriers, industrial process; industrial machinery & equipment
PA: A. Stucki Company
360 Wright Brothers Dr
Coraopolis PA 15108
412 424-0560

(G-2532)
ACCUTREX PRODUCTS INC (PA)
112 Southpointe Blvd (15317-9559)
PHONE..................724 746-4300
Martin P Beichner Jr, *President*
Bob Tomayko, *General Mgr*
Natalie Wooldridge, *General Mgr*
Samuel R Bruckner, *Vice Pres*
John Buchanan, *Plant Mgr*
◆ EMP: 150
SQ FT: 93,000
SALES (est): 43.9MM **Privately Held**
WEB: www.accutrex.com
SIC: 3053 3441 3469 3452 Gaskets, all materials; fabricated structural metal; stamping metal for the trade; machine parts, stamped or pressed metal; bolts, nuts, rivets & washers

(G-2533)
AES DRILLING FLUIDS LLC
4 Grandview Cir (15317-6507)
PHONE..................724 743-2934
EMP: 24
SALES (corp-wide): 806.7MM **Privately Held**
SIC: 1381 Drilling oil & gas wells
HQ: Aes Drilling Fluids Llc
11767 Katy Fwy Ste 230
Houston TX 77079
888 556-4533

(G-2534)
AL LORENZI LUMBER CO INC (PA)
Also Called: Do It Best
3928 Washington Rd (15317-2592)
PHONE..................724 222-6100
Vincent A Lorenzi, *President*
Vince Lorenzi, *Principal*
David Alderson, *Vice Pres*
Valeria Lorenzi, *Treasurer*
Karen Unger, *Admin Sec*
▲ EMP: 60 EST: 1975
SQ FT: 30,000
SALES (est): 21.6MM **Privately Held**
SIC: 5031 2431 5211 5072 Building materials, exterior; doors & windows; lumber: rough, dressed & finished; millwork; home centers; hardware; hardware

(G-2535)
AL TEDESCHI
Also Called: Art Works
805 S Central Ave (15317-1420)
PHONE..................724 746-3755
Al Tedeschi, *Owner*
EMP: 3
SALES (est): 213.3K **Privately Held**
SIC: 3993 2759 2396 Signs & advertising specialties; screen printing; automotive & apparel trimmings

(G-2536)
ALL-CLAD HOLDINGS INC
424 Morganza Rd (15317-5716)
PHONE..................724 745-8300
Jose Deoliveria, *CEO*
Matthew Trigona, *Mfg Staff*
Cheryl McFarland, *Marketing Staff*
McGowan Ken, *Research Analys*

▲ EMP: 5
SALES (est): 724.7K
SALES (corp-wide): 355.8K **Privately Held**
WEB: www.krups.com
SIC: 3469 Utensils, household: metal, except cast
HQ: Groupe Seb Usa
5 Woodhollow Rd Fl 2
Parsippany NJ 07054

(G-2537)
ALL-CLAD METALCRAFTERS LLC (DH)
Also Called: Emerilware
424 Morganza Rd (15317-5716)
PHONE..................724 745-8300
Dan Taylor, *COO*
Ragan Neil, *Production*
Thomas Beaufils, *Controller*
Gary La Spisa, *Finance Dir*
Heidi Mariak, *Marketing Staff*
▲ EMP: 70
SQ FT: 100,000
SALES (est): 27.8MM
SALES (corp-wide): 355.8K **Privately Held**
WEB: www.all-clad.com
SIC: 3354 3331 3469 3316 Aluminum extruded products; primary copper; utensils, household: metal, except cast; sheet, steel, cold-rolled: from purchased hot-rolled
HQ: Groupe Seb Holdings, Inc.
1105 N Market St Ste 1142
Wilmington DE 19801
973 736-0300

(G-2538)
ALL-CLAD METALCRAFTERS LLC
424 Morganza Rd (15317-5716)
PHONE..................724 745-8300
Marc Navarre, *CEO*
EMP: 3
SALES (corp-wide): 355.8K **Privately Held**
WEB: www.all-clad.com
SIC: 3469 3471 Utensils, household: metal, except cast; plating & polishing
HQ: All-Clad Metalcrafters, L.L.C.
424 Morganza Rd
Canonsburg PA 15317
724 745-8300

(G-2539)
AMERICAN PETROLEUM PARTNERS
Also Called: App
380 Sthpinte Blvd Ste 120 (15317)
PHONE..................844 835-5277
Varun Mishra, *President*
Mark Butta, *Vice Pres*
Collin King, *Vice Pres*
Braulio Silva, *Vice Pres*
EMP: 5
SALES (est): 832.4K **Privately Held**
SIC: 5172 1311 1382 Petroleum products; natural gas liquids production; geological exploration, oil & gas field

(G-2540)
ANDRITZ INC (DH)
500 Technology Dr (15317-9584)
PHONE..................724 597-7801
Timothy J Ryan, *President*
Christopher Keays, *Vice Pres*
Jay Miele, *Vice Pres*
Robert Ward, *Vice Pres*
John E Morphis, *Treasurer*
▲ EMP: 243 EST: 1992
SQ FT: 24,000
SALES (est): 161.5MM
SALES (corp-wide): 6.9B **Privately Held**
SIC: 3554 8711 7389 Pulp mill machinery; industrial engineers; design, commercial & industrial
HQ: Andritz (Usa) Inc.
5405 Windward Pkwy # 100
Alpharetta GA 30004
770 640-2500

(G-2541)
ANSYS INC (PA)
2600 Ansys Dr (15317-0404)
PHONE..................884 462-6797
James E Cashman III, *Ch of Bd*
Ajei S Gopal, *President*
Richard Mahoney, *Senior VP*
Janet Lee, *Vice Pres*
Eldon Staggs, *Engrg Mgr*
EMP: 148
SQ FT: 186,000
SALES: 1.2B **Publicly Held**
WEB: www.ansys.com
SIC: 7372 Application computer software

(G-2542)
AQUADOR
3855 Washington Rd (15317-2959)
PHONE..................724 942-1525
EMP: 3 EST: 1991
SALES (est): 130K **Privately Held**
SIC: 3423 Mfg Hand/Edge Tools

(G-2543)
AQUATECH INTERNATIONAL LLC (PA)
Also Called: Aqua Group
1 Four Coins Dr (15317-1776)
PHONE..................724 746-5300
Venkatesh Sharma, *President*
C Ravi, *Exec VP*
Devesh Sharma, *Vice Pres*
M Rama Subba RAO, *CFO*
Larry Millar, *Marketing Mgr*
◆ EMP: 220
SQ FT: 31,000
SALES (est): 211MM **Privately Held**
WEB: www.aquatech.com
SIC: 3589 Water treatment equipment, industrial

(G-2544)
AQUATECH INTL SLS CORP
1 Four Coins Dr (15317-1776)
PHONE..................724 746-5300
Anthony Williams, *Project Mgr*
Kedar Maslekar, *Engineer*
Vince Senatore, *Personnel*
Rick Hansen, *Manager*
Lisa Schollaert, *Manager*
EMP: 7
SALES (est): 170.3K **Privately Held**
SIC: 3589 Water treatment equipment, industrial

(G-2545)
AUMA ACTUATORS INC (HQ)
100 Southpointe Blvd (15317-9559)
PHONE..................724 743-2862
Samuel A Bennardo, *President*
Henrik Newerla, *Managing Dir*
Matthias Dinse, *Chairman*
Matthew Thiel, *Exec VP*
Mark Bujalski, *Project Mgr*
◆ EMP: 119
SQ FT: 82,000
SALES (est): 34.6MM
SALES (corp-wide): 427.5MM **Privately Held**
WEB: www.auma-usa.com
SIC: 3593 3625 Fluid power cylinders, hydraulic or pneumatic; relays & industrial controls
PA: Auma Riester Gmbh & Co. Kg
Aumastr. 1
Mullheim 79379
763 180-90

(G-2546)
AUMA ACTUATORS INC
100 Southpointe Blvd (15317-9559)
PHONE..................714 247-1250
Bob Knoles, *Branch Mgr*
EMP: 5
SALES (corp-wide): 427.5MM **Privately Held**
WEB: www.auma-usa.com
SIC: 3625 3593 Actuators, industrial; fluid power cylinders & actuators
HQ: Auma Actuators, Inc.
100 Southpointe Blvd
Canonsburg PA 15317
724 743-2862

(G-2547)
BAILEY ENGINEERS INC (PA)
125 Technology Dr Ste 205 (15317-9557)
PHONE..................724 745-6200
Richard A Barcelona, *Ch of Bd*
Emil Galis, *Exec VP*
Jack Barcelona, *Vice Pres*
William J Miller, *Admin Sec*
EMP: 40
SQ FT: 45,000
SALES (est): 3.2MM **Privately Held**
SIC: 3547 Rolling mill machinery

(G-2548)
BAILEY OXIDES LLC (PA)
125 Technology Dr (15317-9541)
PHONE..................724 745-9500
Richard A Barcelona Sr, *President*
Jack Barcelona,
EMP: 4
SQ FT: 47,000
SALES (est): 5.6MM **Privately Held**
WEB: www.baileypvs.com
SIC: 8731 2816 Industrial laboratory, except testing; iron oxide pigments (ochers, siennas, umbers)

(G-2549)
BALTEC CORPORATION
121 Hillpointe Dr Ste 900 (15317-7544)
PHONE..................724 873-5757
Fritz Boesch, *Ch of Bd*
Ralph E Hardt, *President*
Charles A Rupprecht, *President*
Dennis M Lytle, *Vice Pres*
Claire M Tintori, *Treasurer*
EMP: 30
SALES (est): 12.7MM
SALES (corp-wide): 3.3B **Privately Held**
WEB: www.baltecorporation.com
SIC: 5084 3542 Metalworking tools (such as drills, taps, dies, files); riveting machines
PA: Baltec Maschinenbau Ag
Obermattstrasse 65
PfAffikon ZH 8330
449 531-333

(G-2550)
BPL GLOBAL LLC
Also Called: Connected Energy
2400 Ansys Dr Ste 102 (15317-0403)
PHONE..................724 933-7700
Mark Rupnick, *CEO*
Geraldo Guimaraes, *Director*
Joseph W Craver,
EMP: 12
SALES: 15.8MM
SALES (corp-wide): 6.4B **Publicly Held**
WEB: www.bplglobal.net
SIC: 1731 7372 Communications specialization; prepackaged software
HQ: Qualitrol Company Llc
1385 Fairport Rd
Fairport NY 14450
586 643-3717

(G-2551)
BRODYS FURNITURE INC
111 W Pike St (15317-1379)
PHONE..................724 745-4630
EMP: 3
SALES (est): 61.6K **Privately Held**
SIC: 2511 Wood household furniture

(G-2552)
BRYMONE INC
Also Called: Bryan Management
125 Technology Dr Ste 105 (15317-9557)
PHONE..................724 746-4004
Richard Bryan, *President*
Virginia Bryan, *Corp Secy*
EMP: 5
SQ FT: 600
SALES: 3MM **Privately Held**
SIC: 1311 Crude petroleum & natural gas

(G-2553)
BUCHANAN MINING COMPANY LLC
1000 Consol Energy Dr (15317-6506)
PHONE..................724 485-4000
Nicholas J Deluliis, *CEO*
James A Brock, *President*
Luann Datesh, *Vice Pres*
William D Gillenwater, *Vice Pres*

James C Grech, *Vice Pres*
EMP: 11
SALES (est): 1.1MM
SALES (corp-wide): 1.4B **Publicly Held**
SIC: 1221 Bituminous coal surface mining
HQ: Consol Mining Holding Company Llc
1000 Consol Energy Dr
Canonsburg PA 15317
724 485-4000

(G-2554)
C L WARD FAMILY
1100 Ashwood Dr Ste 1101 (15317-4981)
PHONE..................................724 743-5903
Scott Ward, *Principal*
EMP: 11
SALES (est): 1.6MM **Privately Held**
SIC: 3499 Fabricated metal products

(G-2555)
C&J WELL SERVICES INC
380 Southpointe Blvd # 210 (15317-8561)
PHONE..................................724 746-2467
EMP: 27 **Privately Held**
SIC: 1389 Surveying wells; servicing oil &
gas wells
HQ: C&J Well Services, Inc.
3990 Rogerdale Rd
Houston TX 77042
713 325-6000

(G-2556)
CANNON TOOL COMPANY
Also Called: Aero Tool & Supply Division
165 Valley Rd (15317-1298)
PHONE..................................724 745-1070
Charles R Benedict Jr, *President*
Kristine Benedict, *Manager*
EMP: 12
SQ FT: 20,800
SALES (est): 1MM **Privately Held**
SIC: 3599 7692 3544 Machine shop, job-
bing & repair; welding repair; special dies,
tools, jigs & fixtures

(G-2557)
CAPPELLI INDUSTRIES INC
218 Mcclelland Rd (15317-2233)
PHONE..................................724 745-6766
Raymond Cappelli, *Principal*
EMP: 3
SALES (est): 330.2K **Privately Held**
SIC: 3999 Manufacturing industries

(G-2558)
CENTRAL OHIO COAL COMPANY (HQ)
1000 Consol Energy Dr (15317-6506)
PHONE..................................740 338-3100
Jay Brett Harvey, *President*
William Lyons, *CFO*
EMP: 250
SALES (est): 22.7MM
SALES (corp-wide): 4.8B **Publicly Held**
SIC: 1221 Bituminous coal surface mining
PA: Murray Energy Corporation
46226 National Rd
Saint Clairsville OH 43950
740 338-3100

(G-2559)
CNX GAS COMPANY LLC (HQ)
1000 Consol Energy Dr (15317-6506)
PHONE..................................724 485-4000
Richard L Toothman, *President*
Daniel Zajdel, *Principal*
EMP: 1
SALES (est): 6MM **Publicly Held**
SIC: 1311 Natural gas production

(G-2560)
CNX GAS CORPORATION (HQ)
1000 Consol Energy Dr (15317-6506)
PHONE..................................724 485-4000
Nicholas J Deiuliis, *President*
Robert P King, *Exec VP*
J Michael Onifer, *Senior VP*
Ronald I Campanelli, *Vice Pres*
Richard L Toothman, *Vice Pres*
EMP: 55
SALES (est): 328MM **Publicly Held**
SIC: 1311 Natural gas production

(G-2561)
CNX LAND LLC
1000 Consol Energy Dr (15317-6506)
PHONE..................................724 485-4000
EMP: 120
SALES (est): 90.1K **Publicly Held**
SIC: 1311 Crude petroleum & natural gas
PA: Cnx Resources Corporation
1000 Consol Energy Dr
Canonsburg PA 15317

(G-2562)
CNX RESOURCES CORPORATION (PA)
1000 Consol Energy Dr (15317-6506)
PHONE..................................724 485-4000
William N Thorndike Jr, *Ch of Bd*
Nicholas J Deiuliis, *President*
James McCaffrey, *Vice Pres*
Donald Rush, *CFO*
Dale Leefers, *Director*
EMP: 400
SALES: 1.7B **Publicly Held**
WEB: www.consolenergy.com
SIC: 1311 4924 Natural gas production;
natural gas distribution

(G-2563)
COBB & DABALDO PRINTING CO
110 Bremen Ln (15317-3163)
PHONE..................................724 942-0544
Ronald J Cobb, *President*
Thomas Dabaldo, *Vice Pres*
EMP: 3
SQ FT: 3,000
SALES: 500K **Privately Held**
SIC: 2759 Commercial printing

(G-2564)
COMMERCIAL PRECAST
116 Cancilla Dr (15317-1828)
PHONE..................................724 873-0708
EMP: 3
SALES (est): 254.1K **Privately Held**
SIC: 3272 Concrete products

(G-2565)
COMTECH INDUSTRIES INC
1301 Ashwood Dr (15317)
PHONE..................................724 884-0101
Dean Grose, *President*
Jeff Ryan, *Exec VP*
Nicki Tennant, *Buyer*
Lindsay Kusturiss, *Accountant*
Tom Mathison, *Manager*
EMP: 50
SQ FT: 10,000
SALES (est): 14MM **Privately Held**
SIC: 3589 Water treatment equipment, in-
dustrial

(G-2566)
CONSOL AMONATE MINING CO LLC
1000 Consol Energy Dr (15317-6506)
PHONE..................................724 485-4000
Nicholas J Deluliis, *CEO*
James A Brock, *President*
Luann Datesh, *Vice Pres*
James C Grech, *Vice Pres*
Stephen W Johnson, *Vice Pres*
EMP: 4
SALES (est): 249.5K
SALES (corp-wide): 1.4B **Publicly Held**
SIC: 1221 Auger mining, bituminous
HQ: Consol Mining Holding Company Llc
1000 Consol Energy Dr
Canonsburg PA 15317
724 485-4000

(G-2567)
CONSOL COAL RESOURCES LP
1000 Consol Energy Dr (15317-6506)
PHONE..................................724 485-3300
James A Brock, *CEO*
Consol Coal Resources GP LLC, *General
Ptnr*
David M Khani, *CFO*
Lorraine L Ritter, *CFO*
Tom Prokop, *Info Tech Dir*
EMP: 1600 **EST:** 1967

SALES: 351.9MM
SALES (corp-wide): 1.4B **Publicly Held**
SIC: 1222 Bituminous coal-underground
mining
PA: Consol Energy Inc.
1000 Consol Energy Dr
Canonsburg PA 15317
724 485-3300

(G-2568)
CONSOL ENERGY INC (PA)
1000 Consol Energy Dr (15317-6506)
PHONE..................................724 485-3300
James A Brock, *President*
James McCaffrey, *Senior VP*
Cody Rogers, *Foreman/Supr*
Danny Caldwell, *Production*
David M Khani, *CFO*
EMP: 13
SALES: 1.4B **Publicly Held**
SIC: 1222 1221 Bituminous coal-under-
ground mining; bituminous coal & lignite-
surface mining

(G-2569)
CONSOL ENERGY INC
1000 Consol Energy Dr (15317-6506)
PHONE..................................412 854-6600
Steve Winberg, *Vice Pres*
EMP: 32 **Publicly Held**
SIC: 1221 Bituminous coal & lignite-sur-
face mining
PA: Cnx Resources Corporation
1000 Consol Energy Dr
Canonsburg PA 15317

(G-2570)
CONSOL MINING COMPANY LLC
1000 Consol Energy Dr (15317-6506)
PHONE..................................724 485-4000
Nicholas J Deiulis, *CEO*
James A Brock, *President*
Luann Datesh, *Vice Pres*
William D Gillenwater, *Vice Pres*
Stephen W Johnson, *Vice Pres*
EMP: 10
SALES (est): 859.9K
SALES (corp-wide): 1.4B **Publicly Held**
SIC: 1221 Bituminous coal & lignite-sur-
face mining
HQ: Consol Mining Holding Company Llc
1000 Consol Energy Dr
Canonsburg PA 15317
724 485-4000

(G-2571)
CONSOL PA COAL CO LLC
1000 Consol Energy Dr (15317-6506)
PHONE..................................724 485-4000
James A Brock, *CEO*
John Rothka, *Controller*
EMP: 1200
SALES (corp-wide): 1.4B **Publicly Held**
WEB: www.consolenergy.com
SIC: 1311 1222 Natural gas production;
bituminous coal-underground mining
PA: Consol Energy Inc.
1000 Consol Energy Dr
Canonsburg PA 15317
724 485-3300

(G-2572)
CONSOLIDATION COAL COMPANY (HQ)
1000 Consol Energy Dr (15317-6506)
PHONE..................................740 338-3100
Bart I Hyita, *President*
Loius Barlettai Jr, *Vice Pres*
John Reilly, *Treasurer*
Luanne Datesh, *Admin Sec*
▲ **EMP:** 1 **EST:** 1965
SQ FT: 150,000
SALES (est): 2.2B
SALES (corp-wide): 4.8B **Publicly Held**
SIC: 1221 Bituminous coal surface mining
PA: Murray Energy Corporation
46226 National Rd
Saint Clairsville OH 43950
740 338-3100

(G-2573)
COOPER POWER SYSTEMS LLC
122 Bethany Dr (15317-2910)
PHONE..................................636 394-2877
Neal E Roth, *Director*

EMP: 3 **Privately Held**
WEB: www.cooperpower.com
SIC: 3612 Power transformers, electric
HQ: Cooper Power Systems, Llc
2300 Badger Dr
Waukesha WI 53188
262 896-2400

(G-2574)
CORSA COAL CORP
4600 J Barry Ct Ste 220 (15317)
PHONE..................................724 754-0028
George G Dethlefsen, *CEO*
Fred Cushmore, *Vice Pres*
Kenneth J Lund, *Vice Pres*
Matthew Schicke, *Ch Credit Ofcr*
EMP: 8 **EST:** 2017
SALES (est): 117K **Privately Held**
SIC: 1221 Bituminous coal & lignite-sur-
face mining

(G-2575)
CUSTOM NUCLEAR FABRICATION LLC
Also Called: Custom Nuclear Fabrication CNF
50 Curry Ave (15317-1743)
PHONE..................................724 271-3006
EMP: 7
SALES (est): 261.4K **Privately Held**
SIC: 3999 8999 Mfg Misc Products Serv-
ices-Misc

(G-2576)
DALE PROPERTY SERVICES PENN LP
1000 Town Center Way # 325
(15317-5834)
PHONE..................................724 705-0444
Larry Dale, *Partner*
EMP: 9 **EST:** 2009
SALES (est): 969.1K **Privately Held**
SIC: 1382 Oil & gas exploration services

(G-2577)
DIGITAL CONCEPTS INC
8 Grandview Cir (15317-8533)
PHONE..................................724 745-4000
Mary Ellen Fetchko, *Ch of Bd*
Dale W Roddy, *President*
Daniel L Knepper, *Senior VP*
EMP: 17
SALES (est): 1.7MM **Privately Held**
WEB: www.digiconinc.com
SIC: 7372 Application computer software

(G-2578)
DISCOVERY OIL GAS LLC
125 Technology Dr Ste 105 (15317-9557)
PHONE..................................724 746-4004
Richard Bryan, *President*
EMP: 3
SALES (est): 364.6K **Privately Held**
SIC: 1382 Oil & gas exploration services

(G-2579)
DONALDSON SUPPLY & EQP CO
40 Murdock St (15317-1310)
PHONE..................................724 745-5250
Bob Kemp, *President*
John Kemp, *Vice Pres*
EMP: 13
SQ FT: 10,000
SALES (est): 2.3MM **Privately Held**
SIC: 3273 5032 Ready-mixed concrete;
sand, construction; stone, crushed or bro-
ken; concrete mixtures

(G-2580)
EDGEMARC ENERGY HOLDINGS LLC (PA)
1800 Main St Ste 220 (15317-5860)
PHONE..................................724 749-8466
Alice Rump, *Office Mgr*
Brian McCurrie, *Mng Member*
Callum Streeter,
EMP: 45
SQ FT: 5,000
SALES: 116MM **Privately Held**
SIC: 1381 Drilling oil & gas wells

(G-2581)
EIGHTY-FOUR MINING COMPANY (HQ)
1000 Consol Energy Dr (15317-6506)
PHONE..................................740 338-3100

▲ = Import ▼=Export
◆ =Import/Export

Bart Hyita, *President*
Daniel S Cangilla, *Treasurer*
Alexander Reyes, *Admin Sec*
EMP: 1
SQ FT: 18,000
SALES (est): 28.2MM
SALES (corp-wide): 4.8B **Publicly Held**
SIC: 1222 Bituminous coal-underground mining
PA: Murray Energy Corporation
46226 National Rd
Saint Clairsville OH 43950
740 338-3100

(G-2582)
EM ENERGY EMPLOYER LLC
601 Technology Dr Ste 300 (15317-9523)
PHONE..................................412 564-1300
Michael Tapp, *CFO*
EMP: 26
SALES (est): 1.8MM
SALES (corp-wide): 116MM **Privately Held**
SIC: 4924 1311 Natural gas distribution; natural gas production
PA: Edgemarc Energy Holdings, Llc
1800 Main St Ste 220
Canonsburg PA 15317
724 749-8466

(G-2583)
EM ENERGY PENNSYLVANIA LLC
1800 Main St Ste 220 (15317-5860)
PHONE..................................412 564-1300
Michael Tapp, *CFO*
Callum Streeter, *Mng Member*
EMP: 43
SALES (est): 99.7K
SALES (corp-wide): 116MM **Privately Held**
SIC: 1311 4924 Natural gas production; natural gas distribution
PA: Edgemarc Energy Holdings, Llc
1800 Main St Ste 220
Canonsburg PA 15317
724 749-8466

(G-2584)
EMPIRE ENERGY E&P LLC (PA)
380 Sthpinte Blvd Ste 130 (15317)
PHONE..................................724 483-2070
Bill Waller, *President*
Robert Kramer, *Vice Pres*
EMP: 23
SALES (est): 13.2MM **Privately Held**
SIC: 1381 Drilling oil & gas wells

(G-2585)
ENERFLEX ENERGY SYSTEMS INC
106 Springfield Dr (15317-5626)
PHONE..................................724 627-0751
Chris Piehl, *Manager*
EMP: 20
SALES (corp-wide): 1.2B **Privately Held**
SIC: 3585 Refrigeration & heating equipment
HQ: Enerflex Energy Systems Inc.
10815 Telge Rd
Houston TX 77095
281 345-9300

(G-2586)
EOG RESOURCES INC
400 Sthpinte Blvd Ste 300 (15317)
PHONE..................................724 745-9063
Gary Smith, *Manager*
EMP: 25
SALES (corp-wide): 17.2B **Publicly Held**
WEB: www.eogresources.com
SIC: 1311 Crude petroleum production; natural gas production
PA: Eog Resources, Inc.
1111 Bagby Sky Lbby 2
Houston TX 77002
713 651-7000

(G-2587)
EQT RE LLC (HQ)
2200 Rice Dr (15317-1001)
PHONE..................................274 271-7200
David Porges, *CEO*
Joshua Eicher, *Production*
EMP: 3 EST: 2017

SALES (est): 103.1MM
SALES (corp-wide): 4.5B **Publicly Held**
SIC: 1311 Crude petroleum & natural gas
PA: Eqt Corporation
625 Liberty Ave Ste 1700
Pittsburgh PA 15222
412 553-5700

(G-2588)
FIRED UP
4151 Washington Rd (15317-2522)
PHONE..................................724 941-0302
Tina Imgrund, *Owner*
EMP: 3 EST: 2000
SALES (est): 165.5K **Privately Held**
WEB: www.firedupwithus.com
SIC: 3269 5947 Art & ornamental ware, pottery; gift shop

(G-2589)
FTS INTERNATIONAL LLC
6000 Town Center Blvd (15317-5841)
PHONE..................................724 873-1021
EMP: 3
SALES (est): 47.6K **Privately Held**
SIC: 7699 5983 1382 Repair Services, Nec, Nsk

(G-2590)
FYDA FRGHTLINER PITTSBURGH INC
Also Called: Fyda Energy Solutions
20 Fyda Dr (15317-1466)
PHONE..................................724 514-2055
Timothy J Fyda, *Principal*
Robert Bodkin, *Principal*
Tim Fyda, *Vice Pres*
Patricia Depaola, *Admin Sec*
EMP: 65
SALES (est): 22.6MM **Privately Held**
SIC: 5012 3519 Trucks, commercial; engines, diesel & semi-diesel or dual-fuel

(G-2591)
GANTREX INC
6000 Town Center Blvd # 240 (15317-5841)
PHONE..................................412 347-0300
Art Avlon, *President*
Lal Agwani, *General Mgr*
Mark Veydt, *General Mgr*
Dan Muren, *Manager*
EMP: 10
SALES (est): 1.8MM
SALES (corp-wide): 223.6MM **Privately Held**
SIC: 3536 Cranes, industrial plant
HQ: Cavotec Group Holdings N.V.
Pompmolenlaan 13 C
Woerden 3447
348 460-160

(G-2592)
GANTREX CRANE RAIL I INSTALLAT
6000 Town Center Blvd (15317-5841)
PHONE..................................412 655-1400
Jean F Meaza, *President*
Mark Veydt, *Vice Pres*
Steve Hope, *Purchasing*
David Guest, *Treasurer*
Charlie Bowers, *Admin Sec*
EMP: 4
SALES (est): 596.8K **Privately Held**
SIC: 3531 Crane carriers

(G-2593)
GE-HITACHI NUCLEAR ENERGY
Also Called: Geh
50 Curry Ave (15317-1743)
PHONE..................................724 743-0270
EMP: 184
SALES (corp-wide): 122B **Publicly Held**
SIC: 3312 Mfg Custom Fabrication Of Stainless And Alloy Steel Components
HQ: Ge-Hitachi Nuclear Energy America Llc
3901 Castle Hayne Rd
Wilmington NC 28401

(G-2594)
HAHN UNIVERSAL
163 Orchard Dr (15317-3331)
PHONE..................................724 941-6444
W Hahn Smith, *Owner*
EMP: 3
SQ FT: 2,800

SALES (est): 120K **Privately Held**
SIC: 2298 2891 Binder & baler twine; adhesives & sealants

(G-2595)
HEETER PRINTING COMPANY INC
Also Called: Heeter Direct
441 Technology Dr (15317-9583)
PHONE..................................724 746-8900
Scott Heeter, *President*
Tom Boyle, *Vice Pres*
Chris Connors, *Vice Pres*
Timothy Thomas, *Vice Pres*
Kirk Schlecker, *VP Opers*
EMP: 90 EST: 1962
SQ FT: 30,200
SALES (est): 43.5MM **Privately Held**
WEB: www.heeterprinting.com
SIC: 2752 Commercial printing, offset

(G-2596)
HESLIN-STEEL FAB INC
7 Four Coins Dr (15317-1751)
P.O. Box 248 (15317-0248)
PHONE..................................724 745-8282
John J Heslin, *President*
EMP: 8
SQ FT: 9,750
SALES (est): 1.2MM **Privately Held**
SIC: 3441 3599 Fabricated structural metal; machine shop, jobbing & repair

(G-2597)
INTEGRTED ASSEMBLY SYSTEMS INC (PA)
Also Called: I A S
3 Four Coins Dr Ste 400 (15317-1778)
P.O. Box 1288 (15317-4288)
PHONE..................................724 746-6532
James C Dudiak, *President*
EMP: 25
SALES (est): 5.1MM **Privately Held**
SIC: 3679 Electronic circuits

(G-2598)
KEYSTONE COAL MINING CORP
1000 Consol Energy Dr (15317-6506)
PHONE..................................740 338-3100
Bart Hyita, *President*
Alexander Reyes, *Vice Pres*
Daniel S Cangilla, *Treasurer*
Luann Datesh, *Admin Sec*
EMP: 425
SQ FT: 76,309
SALES (est): 20.2MM
SALES (corp-wide): 4.8B **Publicly Held**
SIC: 1221 Bituminous coal surface mining
PA: Murray Energy Corporation
46226 National Rd
Saint Clairsville OH 43950
740 338-3100

(G-2599)
LAUREL RUN MINING COMPANY LLC
1000 Consol Energy Dr (15317-6506)
PHONE..................................412 831-4000
EMP: 72
SALES (est): 3.4MM
SALES (corp-wide): 1.4B **Publicly Held**
SIC: 1222 Bituminous Coal-Underground Mining
PA: Consol Energy Inc.
1000 Consol Energy Dr
Canonsburg PA 15317
724 465-4000

(G-2600)
M S S I INC
264 Valley Brook Rd (15317-3256)
PHONE..................................412 771-5533
Douglas Scott Carter, *President*
Joel Hammer, *Vice Pres*
Steven Wake, *Treasurer*
Marinko Milos, *Admin Sec*
EMP: 20
SQ FT: 65,000
SALES (est): 2.3MM **Privately Held**
SIC: 3297 3255 5085 Nonclay refractories; clay refractories; refractory material

(G-2601)
MASTERS INK CORPORATION
617 Giffin Ave Ste A (15317-2034)
PHONE..................................724 745-1122
Stephen Moskal, *President*
EMP: 3
SALES (est): 220K **Privately Held**
WEB: www.mastersink.com
SIC: 2752 Commercial printing, offset

(G-2602)
MCELROY COAL COMPANY (HQ)
1000 Consol Energy Dr (15317-6506)
PHONE..................................724 485-4000
P B Lilly, *President*
J N Magro, *Vice Pres*
EMP: 11
SQ FT: 150,000
SALES (est): 41.1MM
SALES (corp-wide): 4.8B **Publicly Held**
SIC: 1221 Bituminous coal surface mining
PA: Murray Energy Corporation
46226 National Rd
Saint Clairsville OH 43950
740 338-3100

(G-2603)
MI SWACO
4600 Jbarry Ct Ste 200 (15317-5854)
PHONE..................................724 820-3306
EMP: 8 EST: 2010
SALES (est): 609.6K **Privately Held**
SIC: 1389 Oil/Gas Field Services

(G-2604)
MLRE LLC
1500 Corporate Dr Ste 400 (15317-8574)
PHONE..................................724 514-1800
Robert J Coury, *Principal*
EMP: 4
SALES (est): 316.7K
SALES (corp-wide): 204.1K **Privately Held**
WEB: www.mylan.com
SIC: 2834 Tranquilizers or mental drug preparations
HQ: Mylan Inc
1000 Mylan Blvd
Canonsburg PA 15317
724 514-1800

(G-2605)
MONG FABRICATION & MACHINE
112 Acme Rd (15317-4905)
PHONE..................................724 745-8370
Carl D Miller Jr, *President*
Eileen M Miller, *Corp Secy*
EMP: 5
SQ FT: 4,500
SALES (est): 609.2K **Privately Held**
SIC: 3441 3599 Fabricated structural metal; machine shop, jobbing & repair

(G-2606)
MULTISCOPE INCORPORATED
Also Called: Multiscope Dgital Offset Print
135 Technology Dr Ste 402 (15317-9549)
PHONE..................................724 743-1083
Michael McCay, *President*
Patricia Bornder, *CFO*
Lana Oneill, *Admin Sec*
EMP: 45
SQ FT: 7,500
SALES (est): 7.1MM **Privately Held**
WEB: www.multiscopedigital.com
SIC: 2752 2741 7334 Commercial printing, offset; miscellaneous publishing; photocopying & duplicating services

(G-2607)
MYLAN INC (HQ)
1000 Mylan Blvd (15317-5853)
PHONE..................................724 514-1800
Heather Bresch, *CEO*
Robert J Coury, *Ch of Bd*
Rodney L Piatt, *Vice Ch Bd*
Rajiv Malik, *President*
Daniel C Rizzo Jr, *Principal*
▲ **EMP:** 8

SALES (est): 7.4B
SALES (corp-wide): 204.1K **Privately Held**
WEB: www.mylan.com
SIC: 2834 Druggists' preparations (pharmaceuticals); analgesics; antibiotics, packaged; tranquilizers or mental drug preparations

(G-2608)
MYLAN PHARMACEUTICALS INC
1000 Mylan Blvd (15317-5853)
PHONE................................724 514-1800
Anthony Mauro, *President*
David Kennedy, *Vice Pres*
EMP: 25
SALES (est): 3.5MM **Privately Held**
SIC: 2834 Pharmaceutical preparations

(G-2609)
NABCO INC (PA)
1001 Corporate Dr Ste 205 (15317-6505)
PHONE................................724 746-9617
Frank Tobin, *CEO*
Kim King, *Engineer*
William Presutti, *Accountant*
Charles Gibson, *Director*
Tiffany Novotney, *Director*
EMP: 6
SQ FT: 10,000
SALES (est): 3.8MM **Privately Held**
WEB: www.nabcoinc.com
SIC: 3441 Fabricated structural metal

(G-2610)
NABCO SYSTEMS LLC
171 Hillpointe Dr Ste 303 (15317-9554)
P.O. Box 753, Washington (15301-0753)
PHONE................................724 746-9617
William Preesutti, *CFO*
EMP: 20
SALES (est): 967.1K **Privately Held**
SIC: 3443 Tanks for tank trucks, metal plate; tanks, lined: metal plate; tanks, standard or custom fabricated: metal plate; vessels, process or storage (from boiler shops): metal plate

(G-2611)
NATIONAL OILWELL VARCO INC
T-3
100 Alpha Dr (15317-8701)
PHONE................................724 745-6005
EMP: 15
SALES (corp-wide): 8.4B **Publicly Held**
SIC: 3533 Oil & gas field machinery
PA: National Oilwell Varco, Inc.
7909 Parkwood Circle Dr
Houston TX 77036
713 346-7500

(G-2612)
NATIONAL RUBBER CORPORATION
367 Morganza Rd (15317-5717)
PHONE................................412 831-6100
Perry Monpara, *President*
◆ EMP: 16
SQ FT: 55,000
SALES: 3MM **Privately Held**
WEB: www.nationalrubber.com
SIC: 3069 Rubber floor coverings, mats & wallcoverings

(G-2613)
NETGEAR INC
107 Scenery Cir (15317-2739)
PHONE................................724 941-5748
EMP: 3
SALES (est): 144.8K **Privately Held**
SIC: 3661 Modems

(G-2614)
OBSERVER PUBLISHING COMPANY
Also Called: ADS By Phone
395 Valley Brook Rd (15317-3379)
PHONE................................724 941-7725
Karina Kowalccyk, *Manager*
EMP: 30

SALES (corp-wide): 28.7MM **Privately Held**
WEB: www.observer-reporter.com
SIC: 7311 2711 Advertising agencies; newspapers
PA: Observer Publishing Company
122 S Main St
Washington PA 15301
724 222-2200

(G-2615)
OIL STATES ENERGY SERVICES LLC
255 Johnson Rd (15317-4934)
PHONE................................724 746-1168
Jerred Smith, *Manager*
EMP: 7
SALES (corp-wide): 1B **Publicly Held**
SIC: 3533 5082 Oil field machinery & equipment; oil field equipment
HQ: Oil States Energy Services, L.L.C.
333 Clay St Ste 2100
Houston TX 77002
713 425-2400

(G-2616)
P D PLASTICS
609 E Mcmurray Rd (15317-3419)
PHONE................................724 941-3930
James J Doty, *Owner*
EMP: 5 EST: 1978
SALES (est): 450.8K **Privately Held**
SIC: 3827 Optical instruments & lenses

(G-2617)
PBS COALS INC (HQ)
4600 J Barry Ct Ste 220 (15317)
P.O. Box 260, Friedens (15541-0260)
PHONE................................814 443-4668
Lynn Shanks, *President*
Peter J Vuljanic, *Exec VP*
Dmitry Goryachev, *CFO*
▼ EMP: 30
SALES (est): 212.5MM
SALES (corp-wide): 96.9MM **Privately Held**
WEB: www.pbscoals.com
SIC: 1221 Strip mining, bituminous

(G-2618)
PENNSYLVANIA TRANS TECH INC (PA)
30 Curry Ave Ste 2 (15317-1786)
PHONE................................724 873-2100
Ravi Rahangdale, *President*
Shashi Rahangdale, *Vice Pres*
Robert Moore, *Engineer*
Paul Stritzinger, *Engineer*
Adyasha Agrawal, *Design Engr*
▲ EMP: 325
SQ FT: 43,000
SALES (est): 68MM **Privately Held**
WEB: www.patransformer.com
SIC: 3612 3677 5063 Distribution transformers, electric; power transformers, electric; electronic coils, transformers & other inductors; electrical apparatus & equipment

(G-2619)
PITTSBURGH SHED COMPANY INC
2544 Washington Rd (15317-5224)
PHONE................................724 745-4422
Joe Campenella, *President*
EMP: 4
SQ FT: 43,000
SALES: 1.5MM
SALES (corp-wide): 5.5MM **Privately Held**
WEB: www.floridashed.com
SIC: 2511 2452 2431 Lawn furniture: wood; prefabricated buildings, wood; garage doors, overhead: wood
PA: Florida Shed Company, Inc.
6425 Ulmerton Rd Unit A1
Largo FL 33771
727 524-9191

(G-2620)
PRIMETALS TECHNOLOGIES USA LLC
501 Technology Dr (15317-7535)
PHONE................................724 514-8500
Mike McGuire, *Vice Pres*

John Lorenz, *Branch Mgr*
EMP: 120
SALES (corp-wide): 38.5B **Privately Held**
WEB: www.sea.siemens.com
SIC: 3312 Blast furnaces & steel mills
HQ: Primetals Technologies Usa Llc
5895 Windward Pkwy Fl 2
Alpharetta GA 30005
770 740-3800

(G-2621)
PRO-SLTONS FOR CHROPRACTIC INC
370 Sthpinte Blvd Ste 100 (15317)
PHONE................................724 942-4284
Maurice Pisciottano, *President*
Edward Bishop, *Vice Pres*
EMP: 50
SALES (est): 10.7MM **Privately Held**
WEB: www.pro-adjuster.us
SIC: 3845 Electromedical equipment

(G-2622)
RAKOCZY INDUSTRIES INC
125 W Pike St Ste 3 (15317-1315)
P.O. Box 146 (15317-0146)
PHONE................................412 389-3123
John M Rakoczy, *Principal*
EMP: 8
SALES (est): 671.7K **Privately Held**
SIC: 3999 Manufacturing industries

(G-2623)
RANDY GEORGE WDWKG CSTM SIGNS
227 Smithfield St (15317-1701)
PHONE................................724 514-7201
Randy George, *Principal*
EMP: 3
SALES (est): 331.2K **Privately Held**
SIC: 2431 Millwork

(G-2624)
RANGE RSURCES - APPALACHIA LLC (HQ)
3000 Town Center Blvd (15317-5839)
PHONE................................724 743-6700
Jeffrey L Ventura, *President*
John H Pinkerton, *Chairman*
Alan W Farquharson, *Senior VP*
Roger S Manny, *CFO*
Jeffrey Bynum,
EMP: 100
SQ FT: 24,000
SALES (est): 204MM
SALES (corp-wide): 3.2B **Publicly Held**
WEB: www.gl-energy.com
SIC: 1382 Oil & gas exploration services
PA: Range Resources Corporation
100 Throckmorton St # 1200
Fort Worth TX 76102
817 870-2601

(G-2625)
REFRIGERATION CARE INC
Also Called: Refrigeration Care & Ice
111 Orchard Ave (15317-1526)
PHONE................................724 746-1525
Irma Tatano, *President*
Angelo Tatano Jr, *Admin Sec*
EMP: 15
SQ FT: 15,000
SALES (est): 1.7MM **Privately Held**
SIC: 2097 Manufactured ice

(G-2626)
RENAISSANCE GLASSWORKS INC
3311 Washington Rd (15317-3194)
PHONE................................724 969-9009
H B Mertz, *President*
EMP: 8
SQ FT: 16,800
SALES (est): 1.2MM **Privately Held**
SIC: 1793 3231 Glass & glazing work; stained glass: made from purchased glass

(G-2627)
RICE DRILLING B LLC
2200 Rice Dr (15317-1001)
PHONE................................274 281-7200
David Porges, *CEO*
EMP: 20

SALES (est): 14.3MM
SALES (corp-wide): 4.5B **Publicly Held**
SIC: 1382 Oil & gas exploration services
HQ: Eqt Re, Llc
2200 Rice Dr
Canonsburg PA 15317
274 271-7200

(G-2628)
RICE DRILLING D LLC
400 Woodcliff Dr (15317-5851)
PHONE................................274 281-7200
David Porges, *CEO*
EMP: 91
SALES (est): 18.8MM
SALES (corp-wide): 4.5B **Publicly Held**
SIC: 1382 Oil & gas exploration services
HQ: Eqt Re, Llc
2200 Rice Dr
Canonsburg PA 15317
274 271-7200

(G-2629)
RICE OLYMPUS MIDSTREAM LLC
400 Woodcliff Dr (15317-5851)
PHONE................................724 746-6720
David Porges, *President*
EMP: 68
SALES (est): 7.7MM
SALES (corp-wide): 4.5B **Publicly Held**
SIC: 1311 Crude petroleum & natural gas
HQ: Eqt Re, Llc
2200 Rice Dr
Canonsburg PA 15317
274 271-7200

(G-2630)
RICE POSEIDON MIDSTREAM LLC
400 Woodcliff Dr (15317-5851)
PHONE................................724 746-6720
David Porges, *President*
EMP: 125
SALES (est): 11.2MM
SALES (corp-wide): 4.5B **Publicly Held**
SIC: 1311 Crude petroleum & natural gas
HQ: Eqt Re, Llc
2200 Rice Dr
Canonsburg PA 15317
274 271-7200

(G-2631)
ROC SERVICE COMPANY LTD
125 Technology Dr Ste 200 (15317-9557)
PHONE................................724 745-3319
Christy L Hass, *Principal*
Chase Johnson, *Vice Pres*
EMP: 5 EST: 2009
SALES (est): 665.1K **Privately Held**
SIC: 1389 Oil field services

(G-2632)
SARRIS CANDIES INC
511 Adams Ave (15317-2103)
PHONE................................724 745-4042
Frank H Sarris, *President*
William Sarris, *Principal*
Renie Pihiou, *Vice Pres*
Bill Sarris, *Vice Pres*
William F Sarris, *Vice Pres*
EMP: 300
SQ FT: 120,000
SALES (est): 20.3MM **Privately Held**
WEB: www.sarriscandies.com
SIC: 5812 2066 2064 Ice cream stands or dairy bars; chocolate candy, solid; candy & other confectionery products

(G-2633)
SEAHORSE OILFIELD SERVICES LLC
2400 Ansys Dr Ste 102 (15317-0403)
PHONE................................724 597-2039
Mark G Avery, *Mng Member*
EMP: 5 EST: 2016
SQ FT: 300
SALES (est): 72K **Privately Held**
SIC: 1389 Impounding & storing salt water, oil & gas field

▲ = Import ▼=Export
◆ =Import/Export

(G-2634)
SENTRY WELLHEAD SYSTEMS LLC
100 Beta Dr (15317-8700)
PHONE....................724 422-8108
Nathan Simmers, *Branch Mgr*
EMP: 23
SALES (corp-wide): 15MM **Privately Held**
SIC: 1389 Oil & gas wells: building, repairing & dismantling
PA: Sentry Wellhead Systems, Llc
1780 Hughes
Spring TX 77380
281 210-0070

(G-2635)
SHEARERS FODS CANONSBURG PLANT
42 Swihart Rd (15317-6021)
PHONE....................724 746-1162
EMP: 5
SALES (est): 537.6K **Privately Held**
SIC: 2052 Mfg Cookies/Crackers

(G-2636)
SIEMENS INDUSTRY INC
100 Southpointe Blvd (15317-9559)
PHONE....................724 743-5913
EMP: 92
SALES (corp-wide): 83.5B **Privately Held**
SIC: 3613 3621 3625 3612 Mfg Switchgear/Boards Mfg Motors/Generators Mfg Relay/Indstl Control
HQ: Siemens Industry, Inc.
1000 Deerfield Pkwy
Buffalo Grove IL 60089
847 215-1000

(G-2637)
SILVER CREEK SERVICES INC
601 Technology Dr Ste 310 (15317-9523)
PHONE....................724 710-0440
Charles Williams, *President*
Marc Cassel, *Business Mgr*
Dillon Kuehl, *Senior VP*
Gregory Kail, *CFO*
Hollan Puskarich, *Finance*
EMP: 34
SALES: 12MM **Privately Held**
SIC: 1389 Well plugging & abandoning, oil & gas; fishing for tools, oil & gas field; oil consultants; oil field services

(G-2638)
SOUTHERN OHIO COAL COMPANY
1000 Consol Energy Dr (15317-6506)
PHONE....................740 338-3100
B J Hyita, *President*
Stephen W Johnson, *Vice Pres*
David M Khani, *Treasurer*
Michael J Baker, *Admin Sec*
EMP: 3 EST: 1956
SQ FT: 10,000
SALES (est): 327.1K
SALES (corp-wide): 4.8B **Publicly Held**
WEB: www.consolenergy.com
SIC: 1222 Bituminous coal-underground mining
PA: Murray Energy Corporation
46226 National Rd
Saint Clairsville OH 43950
740 338-3100

(G-2639)
STALLION OILFIELD SERVICES LTD
300 Woodcliff Dr Ste 201 (15317-5868)
PHONE....................724 743-4801
Cameron Simion, *Branch Mgr*
EMP: 40 **Privately Held**
SIC: 1389 Oil field services
HQ: Stallion Oilfield Services Ltd.
950 Corbindale Rd Ste 400
Houston TX 77024
713 528-5544

(G-2640)
STEEL CITY GRAPHICS INC
Also Called: Signal Graphics Printing
3529 Washington Rd (15317-2952)
PHONE....................724 942-5699
Roy Crumrine, *President*
Sandra Crumrine, *Vice Pres*

David Ingram, *Manager*
EMP: 5
SQ FT: 2,000
SALES (est): 550K **Privately Held**
SIC: 2752 3993 Commercial printing, offset; signs & advertising specialties

(G-2641)
STRATA PRODUCTS WORLDWIDE LLC
130 Technology Dr (15317-9563)
PHONE....................724 745-5030
Fritz Boesch, *Principal*
EMP: 3
SALES (est): 528.7K **Privately Held**
SIC: 3532 Mining machinery

(G-2642)
SUEZ WTS SYSTEMS USA INC
30 Curry Ave (15317-1786)
PHONE....................724 743-0270
EMP: 125
SALES (corp-wide): 51.4MM **Privately Held**
SIC: 3589 3444 Mfg Service Industry Machinery Mfg Sheet Metalwork
HQ: Suez Wts Systems Usa, Inc.
4636 Somerton Rd
Trevose PA 19053
781 359-7000

(G-2643)
SUPERIOR APPLCHIAN PPELINE LLC
4000 Town Center Blvd # 202 (15317-5837)
PHONE....................724 746-6744
Larry Pinkston, *President*
Tanner Means, *Plant Supt*
Ty Godwin, *Plant Mgr*
EMP: 3
SALES (est): 308K **Privately Held**
SIC: 1382 Oil & gas exploration services

(G-2644)
T N T MANUFACTURING
1 Caley Dr (15317-5900)
PHONE....................724 745-6242
Edgar F Leasure, *Partner*
Richard Leasure, *Partner*
EMP: 3
SALES: 150K **Privately Held**
SIC: 2759 Screen printing

(G-2645)
TATANO WIRE AND STEEL INC (PA)
2 Iron St (15317-1332)
P.O. Box 247, Houston (15342-0247)
PHONE....................724 746-3118
Edgar S Lauther, *President*
Charles Tatano, *Exec VP*
Anthony Spin, *Treasurer*
EMP: 25
SQ FT: 180,000
SALES (est): 3.2MM **Privately Held**
SIC: 3315 3496 Wire & fabricated wire products; miscellaneous fabricated wire products

(G-2646)
TECHNIPFMC US HOLDINGS INC
1001 Corporate Dr Ste 260 (15317-8589)
PHONE....................724 820-5023
Xavier Tison, *Regional Mgr*
EMP: 29
SALES (corp-wide): 15B **Privately Held**
SIC: 3533 Oil & gas field machinery
HQ: Fmc Technologies, Inc.
11740 Katy Fwy Energy Tow
Houston TX 77079
281 591-4000

(G-2647)
TEMTEK SOLUTIONS INC
264 Valley Brook Rd (15317-3256)
P.O. Box 398, Mc Kees Rocks (15136-0398)
PHONE....................724 980-4270
Scott Carter, *President*
Terry Medovitch, *Corp Secy*
EMP: 9

SALES (est): 1.8MM **Privately Held**
SIC: 2655 3441 8711 Fiber cans, drums & similar products; fabricated structural metal; engineering services

(G-2648)
TROYER INC
Also Called: Troyer Farms
42 Swihart Rd (15317-6021)
PHONE....................724 746-1162
Fax: 724 746-1167
EMP: 50
SALES (corp-wide): 753.7MM **Publicly Held**
SIC: 2052 5145 5149 2099 Mfg Cookies/Crackers Whol Confectionery Whol Groceries Mfg Food Preparations
HQ: Troyer, Inc.
1000 W College Ave
York PA 17404
814 796-2611

(G-2649)
U S WEATHERFORD L P
121 Hillpointe Dr (15317-9535)
PHONE....................724 745-7050
EMP: 24 **Privately Held**
SIC: 1389 Construction, repair & dismantling services
HQ: U S Weatherford L P
179 Weatherford Dr
Schriever LA 70395
985 493-6100

(G-2650)
UNI-REF UNITED REFRACTORIES CO (PA)
264 Valley Brook Rd (15317-3256)
PHONE....................724 941-9390
Douglas R Niesen, *President*
Raymond Niesen, *Owner*
Robert J Bahl, *Vice Pres*
▼ EMP: 1
SQ FT: 110,000
SALES (est): 4.7MM **Privately Held**
SIC: 3297 Alumina fused refractories

(G-2651)
UNITED HYDROGEN GROUP INC
1900 Main St Ste 223 (15317-5861)
PHONE....................866 942-7763
Brent Konski, *COO*
Zachary Payne, *Accounting Mgr*
EMP: 15
SQ FT: 25,000
SALES: 3MM **Privately Held**
SIC: 2813 Hydrogen

(G-2652)
UNIVERSAL ELECTRIC CORPORATION
Also Called: Starline Busway Systems
168 Georgetown Rd (15317-5611)
PHONE....................724 597-7800
Joel C Ross, *CEO*
Steven L Ross, *COO*
Brian Maden, *Materials Mgr*
Doug Childers, *Opers Staff*
Francine Petrichevich, *Buyer*
▲ EMP: 350 EST: 1968
SQ FT: 170,000
SALES (est): 105.3MM **Privately Held**
WEB: www.uecorp.com
SIC: 3643 3699 3536 Current-carrying wiring devices; bus bars (electrical conductors); electrical equipment & supplies; hoists, cranes & monorails

(G-2653)
VANTAGE ENERGY LLC
2200 Rice Dr (15317-1001)
PHONE....................724 746-6720
EMP: 57
SALES (est): 179.8K
SALES (corp-wide): 3.3B **Publicly Held**
SIC: 1382 Oil/Gas Exploration Services
HQ: Eqt Re, Llc
2200 Rice Dr
Canonsburg PA 15317
274 271-7200

(G-2654)
WALLACE PHARMACEUTICALS INC
1000 Mylan Blvd (15317-5853)
PHONE....................732 564-2700
Jeffrey Hostler, *CFO*
David Vernieri, *Admin Sec*
EMP: 140
SALES (est): 457.8K
SALES (corp-wide): 204.1K **Privately Held**
WEB: www.wallacepharmaceuticals.com
SIC: 2834 Pharmaceutical preparations
HQ: Mylan Inc
1000 Mylan Blvd
Canonsburg PA 15317
724 514-1800

(G-2655)
WASNYDER AN SON LLC
107 Lexington Dr (15317-3639)
PHONE....................724 260-0695
EMP: 3
SALES (est): 188.9K **Privately Held**
SIC: 3625 Control equipment, electric

(G-2656)
WEATHERFORD INTERNATIONAL LLC
121 Hillpointe Dr Ste 300 (15317-9535)
PHONE....................724 745-7050
David Sommerville, *Opers-Prdtn-Mfg*
EMP: 12 **Privately Held**
WEB: www.allegheny-wireline.com
SIC: 1389 Oil field services
HQ: Weatherford International, Llc
2000 Saint James Pl
Houston TX 77056
713 693-4000

(G-2657)
WELD TOOLING CORPORATION (PA)
Also Called: Bug-O Systems International
280 Technology Dr (15317-9564)
PHONE....................412 331-1776
Herbert E Cable Jr, *CEO*
Matthew Cable, *President*
Matt Cable, *Vice Pres*
Larry Johnson, *VP Mfg*
Bill Gregory, *Warehouse Mgr*
▲ EMP: 70 EST: 1948
SQ FT: 31,000
SALES (est): 14.5MM **Privately Held**
WEB: www.bugo.com
SIC: 3549 Assembly machines, including robotic

(G-2658)
WELD TOOLING CORPORATION
Also Called: Bug-O Systems International
280 Technology Dr (15317-9564)
PHONE....................412 331-1776
Herbert Cable, *Branch Mgr*
EMP: 45
SQ FT: 7,000
SALES (corp-wide): 14.5MM **Privately Held**
WEB: www.bugo.com
SIC: 3679 3548 Electronic circuits; welding apparatus
PA: Weld Tooling Corporation
280 Technology Dr
Canonsburg PA 15317
412 331-1776

(G-2659)
WILD WELL CONTROL INC
380 Southpointe Blvd (15317-8561)
PHONE....................724 873-5083
EMP: 5 **Publicly Held**
SIC: 1389 Fire fighting, oil & gas field
HQ: Wild Well Control, Inc.
2202 Oil Center Ct
Houston TX 77073
281 784-4700

(G-2660)
WILSON CREEK ENERGY LLC (PA)
4600 J Barry Ct Ste 220 (15317)
PHONE....................724 754-0028
George Dethlefsen, *CEO*
EMP: 50
SQ FT: 18,000

SALES (est): 19.2MM **Privately Held**
SIC: **1222** 5052 Bituminous coal-under-ground mining; coal & other minerals & ores

(G-2661)
WOOD GROUP USA INC
4600 Jbarry Ct Ste 210 (15317-5854)
PHONE..................................724 514-1600
EMP: 3
SALES (corp-wide): 5.3B **Privately Held**
SIC: **1389** Oil field services
HQ: Wood Group Usa, Inc.
   17325 Park Row
   Houston TX 77084
   832 809-8000

Canton
Bradford County

(G-2662)
ARCHROCK SERVICES LP
9070 Route 414 (17724-7537)
PHONE..................................570 567-7162
EMP: 3 **Publicly Held**
SIC: **1389** 4225 Gas compressing (natural gas) at the fields; general warehousing
HQ: Archrock Services, L.P.
   9807 Katy Fwy Ste 100
   Houston TX 77024
   281 836-8000

(G-2663)
CARREON PUBLISHING LLC
Also Called: Canton Independent Sentinel
10 W Main St (17724-1503)
P.O. Box 128 (17724-0128)
PHONE..................................570 673-5151
Joseph Carreon, *Mng Member*
Ryan Allen,
Teresa Allen,
Amanda Carreon,
EMP: 4
SALES (est): 220K **Privately Held**
SIC: **2711** 5994 Newspapers, publishing & printing; news dealers & newsstands

(G-2664)
E&J CONSTRUCTION
1261 Masten Rd (17724)
PHONE..................................570 924-4455
Edward Minnier,
Julie Minnier,
EMP: 11
SALES: 475K **Privately Held**
SIC: **1411** Sandstone, dimension-quarrying

(G-2665)
LANDONS CAR WASH AND LAUNDRY
51 S Center St (17724-1510)
PHONE..................................570 673-4188
Brian L Landon, *Owner*
EMP: 5 EST: 1975
SALES: 900K **Privately Held**
WEB: www.landonscarwash.com
SIC: **3589** 7215 5087 Car washing machinery; coin-operated laundries & cleaning; carwash equipment & supplies

(G-2666)
PARKER MACHINE AND FABRICATION
Road 1 Route 14 S (17724)
P.O. Box 67 (17724-0067)
PHONE..................................570 673-4160
Scott Parker, *President*
Homer Parker Jr, *Corp Secy*
Craig Parker, *Vice Pres*
EMP: 9
SQ FT: 8,000
SALES: 1MM **Privately Held**
SIC: **3545** Tools & accessories for machine tools

(G-2667)
RPC INC
Also Called: Cudd Pressure Services
2897 Route 414 (17724-7223)
PHONE..................................570 673-5965
EMP: 28

SALES (corp-wide): 1.6B **Publicly Held**
SIC: **1389** 7359 Oil/Gas Field Services Equipment Rental/Leasing
PA: Rpc, Inc.
   2801 Buford Hwy Ne # 520
   Brookhaven GA 30329
   404 321-2140

(G-2668)
RSJ TECHNOLOGIES LLC
184 S Minnequa Ave (17724-1815)
P.O. Box 86 (17724-0086)
PHONE..................................570 673-4173
Gary Jolly, *CEO*
Michael Reed,
EMP: 20
SQ FT: 10,000
SALES (est): 4MM **Privately Held**
SIC: **3599** Custom machinery; machine shop, jobbing & repair

Carbondale
Lackawanna County

(G-2669)
BECKLEY PERFORATING CORP
166 Dundaff St (18407-1565)
PHONE..................................570 267-2092
Fred Warner, *President*
EMP: 5
SALES (est): 245.2K **Privately Held**
SIC: **1389** Perforating well casings

(G-2670)
CERRA SIGNS INC
Also Called: Embroidery Plus
24 6th Ave (18407-2319)
PHONE..................................570 282-6283
Michael Cerra, *Owner*
EMP: 3
SQ FT: 3,500
SALES (est): 290.8K **Privately Held**
WEB: www.cerrasigns.com
SIC: **3993** 2752 Signs & advertising specialties; poster & decal printing, lithographic

(G-2671)
CFC MANUFACTURING CO INC
56 Dundaff St (18407-1802)
PHONE..................................570 281-9605
Tim Smith, *President*
EMP: 8
SQ FT: 27,000
SALES (est): 1MM **Privately Held**
SIC: **3444** Concrete forms, sheet metal

(G-2672)
CONCRETE FORM CONSULTANTS INC (PA)
56 Dundaff St (18407-1802)
PHONE..................................570 281-9605
Tim Smith, *President*
EMP: 12
SQ FT: 27,000
SALES: 1MM **Privately Held**
WEB: www.concreteform.net
SIC: **3444** Concrete forms, sheet metal

(G-2673)
CREW SYSTEMS CORPORATION
10 Enterprise (18407-1880)
PHONE..................................570 281-9221
William Radzelovage, *President*
Maureen Brennan, *Vice Pres*
Gary Piorkowski, *Vice Pres*
Mike Gillott, *Engineer*
EMP: 9
SQ FT: 6,000
SALES (est): 1.3MM **Privately Held**
WEB: www.crewsystemscorp.com
SIC: **3842** Surgical appliances & supplies

(G-2674)
DYVEX INDUSTRIES INC
26 N Scott St (18407-1834)
PHONE..................................570 281-7141
Eugene Pazzaglia, *President*
David Pettinato, *Vice Pres*
Robert Strony, *Vice Pres*
Joseph De Poti, *Admin Sec*
EMP: 15
SQ FT: 16,000

SALES (est): 3.4MM **Privately Held**
WEB: www.dyvex.com
SIC: **2842** Deodorants, nonpersonal

(G-2675)
FRED FAIRBURN
Also Called: Dunkin' Donuts
40 N Main St (18407-2315)
PHONE..................................570 282-3364
Fred Fairburn, *Owner*
EMP: 20
SALES (est): 399.7K **Privately Held**
SIC: **5461** 2051 Doughnuts; bread, cake & related products

(G-2676)
G & W INSTRUMENTS INC
277 Brooklyn St (18407-2829)
PHONE..................................570 282-7352
Robert Griebel, *President*
Ferdinand M Weiss, *Office Mgr*
▲ EMP: 9
SQ FT: 6,000
SALES (est): 1.1MM **Privately Held**
WEB: www.gandwinstruments.com
SIC: **3823** Hydrometers, industrial process type; thermometers, filled system: industrial process type

(G-2677)
HENDRICK MANUFACTURING COMPANY (PA)
17th Ave (18407)
PHONE..................................570 282-1010
Michael D Drake, *CEO*
Alicia McHale, *Vice Pres*
Tom Mosca, *Vice Pres*
Jonathan Watt, *Plant Mgr*
Darin Drake, *CFO*
▲ EMP: 3
SALES (est): 34.1MM **Privately Held**
WEB: www.hendrickmfg.com
SIC: **3469** 3496 3444 Perforated metal, stamped; screening, woven wire: made from purchased wire; sheet metalwork

(G-2678)
J&B TREE SERVICE
47 Pearl St (18407-2617)
PHONE..................................570 282-1193
Robert D Allen, *Partner*
EMP: 5
SALES (est): 318.3K **Privately Held**
SIC: **2411** Logging

(G-2679)
JC PRINTING
176 N Scott St (18407-1836)
PHONE..................................570 282-1187
James Cuce, *Owner*
EMP: 3 EST: 1979
SALES (est): 246.9K **Privately Held**
SIC: **2752** Commercial printing, offset

(G-2680)
JC VINYL FENCE RAIL & DECK (PA)
Also Called: J. C. Vinyl Siding
128 Pike St (18407-2753)
PHONE..................................570 282-2222
EMP: 3
SQ FT: 12,000
SALES: 1MM **Privately Held**
SIC: **5211** 3089 Ret Building Materials & Mfg Vinyl Windows

(G-2681)
MARGARET MARY MUSIC PUBLISHING
161 Belmont St (18407-1680)
PHONE..................................570 282-3503
Joe Demark, *Owner*
EMP: 3
SALES (est): 113.1K **Privately Held**
SIC: **2711** Newspapers

(G-2682)
METAL INTEGRITY LLC
47 N Scott St (18407-1833)
PHONE..................................570 281-2303
Les Gorton, *Purchasing*
David Rollison, *Mng Member*
EMP: 12
SQ FT: 11,000

SALES (est): 2.4MM **Privately Held**
SIC: **3444** Sheet metalwork

(G-2683)
MILLENNIUM PACKAGING SVC INC
100 Enterprise (18407-1890)
PHONE..................................570 282-2990
Dean Sposto, *CEO*
Greg Brotzman, *Admin Sec*
EMP: 45
SALES (est): 6.8MM **Privately Held**
SIC: **2441** Boxes, wood

(G-2684)
PLEASANT MOUNT WELDING INC
45 Dundaff St (18407-1801)
PHONE..................................570 282-6164
Robert Non, *President*
Paul McGraw, *Vice Pres*
Michael Non, *Treasurer*
Frank O'Neil, *Sales Mgr*
Vicki Bradley, *Admin Sec*
EMP: 70
SQ FT: 45,000
SALES: 10MM **Privately Held**
WEB: www.pmwi.net
SIC: **3441** 3446 Building components, structural steel; architectural metalwork

(G-2685)
QUALITY PERFORATING INC
166 Dundaff St (18407-1565)
PHONE..................................570 267-2092
Robert W Farber, *President*
Jim Bradley, *COO*
William Farber, *Vice Pres*
Mike Gilboy, *Vice Pres*
Rodney Williams, *Vice Pres*
◆ EMP: 60
SQ FT: 95,000
SALES (est): 18.9MM **Privately Held**
WEB: www.qualityperf.com
SIC: **3496** 3469 3089 1761 Screening, woven wire: made from purchased wire; perforated metal, stamped; plastic hardware & building products; sheet metalwork

(G-2686)
TIMOTHY R BRENNAN JR
Also Called: Tim Brennan's Heavy Equipment
Rr 1 Box 1357 (18407)
PHONE..................................570 281-9504
Timmothy R Brennan Jr, *Owner*
EMP: 4
SALES (est): 386.9K **Privately Held**
SIC: **1389** Construction, repair & dismantling services

(G-2687)
TRULITE GL ALUM SOLUTIONS LLC
Clidco Dr (18407)
P.O. Box 313 (18407-0313)
PHONE..................................570 282-6711
EMP: 60 **Privately Held**
SIC: **3211** 5039 Manufacturing Fabricating And Distributing Glass Products
PA: Trulite Glass & Aluminum Solutions, Llc
   800 Fairway Dr Ste 200
   Deerfield Beach FL 30269

Carlisle
Cumberland County

(G-2688)
ALACER CORP
Also Called: Pfizer Global Supply
219 Allen Rd Ste 300 (17013-9447)
PHONE..................................717 258-2000
Ronald Fugate, *CEO*
James Turner, *Ch of Bd*
Ken Vargha, *Vice Pres*
Larry Batina, *CFO*
Debbie Clark, *Controller*
▲ EMP: 165
SQ FT: 131,000

SALES (est): 51.5MM
SALES (corp-wide): 53.6B **Publicly Held**
WEB: www.alacer.com
SIC: **2834** 5169 Vitamin preparations; adhesives, chemical
PA: Pfizer Inc.
235 E 42nd St
New York NY 10017
212 733-2323

(G-2689)
AMES COMPANIES INC
Also Called: Carlisle Distribution Center
1 True Temper Dr (17015-6905)
PHONE..................................717 258-3001
Bruce Ebright, *General Mgr*
Ruth Bucher, *Transptn Dir*
Brian Ripple, *Safety Mgr*
Fred Sauer, *Branch Mgr*
Richard Bevins, *Manager*
EMP: 200
SALES (corp-wide): 1.9B **Publicly Held**
WEB: www.ames.com
SIC: **3423** 3524 Garden & farm tools, including shovels; lawn & garden equipment
HQ: The Ames Companies Inc
465 Railroad Ave
Camp Hill PA 17011
717 737-1500

(G-2690)
ATLANTIC DEV CORP OF PA
Also Called: Pizza Hut
819 E High St (17013-2610)
PHONE..................................717 243-0212
Stephen Cpowell, *Branch Mgr*
EMP: 17
SALES (est): 380.6K
SALES (corp-wide): 18.9MM **Privately Held**
WEB: www.adcpa.net
SIC: **5812** 2038 Pizzeria, chain; frozen specialties
PA: Atlantic Development Corp Of Pennsylvania Inc
1445 N Rock Rd Ste 200
Wichita KS 67206
316 634-2133

(G-2691)
BELTONE CORPORATION
850 Walnut Bottom Rd (17013-3615)
PHONE..................................717 386-5640
EMP: 3
SALES (corp-wide): 1.6B **Privately Held**
SIC: **3842** Hearing aids
HQ: Beltone Corporation
2601 Patriot Blvd
Glenview IL 60026
847 832-3300

(G-2692)
CAREYS DUMPSTER SERVICES
61 Heisers Ln (17015-9205)
PHONE..................................717 258-1400
Ray Carey, *Owner*
EMP: 3
SALES (est): 247K **Privately Held**
SIC: **3443** Dumpsters, garbage

(G-2693)
CARLISLE CONSTRUCTION MTLS INC
1555 Ritner Hwy (17013-9380)
PHONE..................................717 245-7142
EMP: 35
SALES (corp-wide): 4.4B **Publicly Held**
WEB: www.premiumroofs.com
SIC: **2952** 3069 2295 Roof cement: asphalt, fibrous or plastic; roofing, membrane rubber; leather, artificial or imitation
HQ: Carlisle Construction Materials, Llc
1285 Ritner Hwy
Carlisle PA 17013

(G-2694)
CARLISLE CONSTRUCTION MTLS LLC
Also Called: CCM
1603 Industrial Dr (17013)
PHONE..................................717 245-7000
EMP: 3

SALES (corp-wide): 4.4B **Publicly Held**
SIC: **2952** 3069 Roof cement: asphalt, fibrous or plastic; roofing, membrane rubber
HQ: Carlisle Construction Materials, Llc
1285 Ritner Hwy
Carlisle PA 17013

(G-2695)
CARLISLE CONSTRUCTION MTLS LLC (HQ)
Also Called: Carlisle Syntec Systems
1285 Ritner Hwy (17013-9381)
P.O. Box 7000 (17013-0925)
PHONE..................................717 245-7000
Nick Shears, *President*
Mary Brunot, *HR Admin*
Chad Buhrman, *Marketing Mgr*
Robert King, *Manager*
Robert Reale, *Manager*
◆ EMP: 500
SQ FT: 550,000
SALES (est): 1B
SALES (corp-wide): 4.4B **Publicly Held**
WEB: www.premiumroofs.com
SIC: **2952** 3069 5031 2899 Roof cement: asphalt, fibrous or plastic; roofing, membrane rubber; building materials, exterior; chemical preparations; adhesives & sealants
PA: Carlisle Companies Incorporated
16430 N Scottsdale Rd # 400
Scottsdale AZ 85254
480 781-5000

(G-2696)
CARLISLE FOODS INC
1605 Shearer Dr (17013-9605)
PHONE..................................717 218-9880
Kevin Talhelm, *Manager*
▲ EMP: 250
SALES (est): 25.7MM **Privately Held**
SIC: **2051** Bakery: wholesale or wholesale/retail combined

(G-2697)
CARLISLE MACHINE SHOP INC
17 Donegal Dr (17013-1768)
PHONE..................................717 243-0289
Warren E Anderson, *President*
Catherine Anderson, *Admin Sec*
EMP: 3 EST: 1959
SQ FT: 6,000
SALES: 150K **Privately Held**
SIC: **3599** Machine shop, jobbing & repair

(G-2698)
CARLISLE TPO INC
1285 Ritner Hwy (17013-9381)
PHONE..................................717 245-7000
John Calogero, *Controller*
EMP: 1
SALES (est): 3.8MM
SALES (corp-wide): 4.4B **Publicly Held**
SIC: **3089** Thermoformed finished plastic products
HQ: Carlisle Construction Materials, Llc
1285 Ritner Hwy
Carlisle PA 17013

(G-2699)
CARLISLE VAULT LLC
31 S Hanover St Ste 4 (17013-3324)
PHONE..................................717 382-8588
John J Bogonis, *Principal*
EMP: 3
SALES (est): 234.1K **Privately Held**
SIC: **3272** Burial vaults, concrete or precast terrazzo

(G-2700)
CMS ORTHOTIC LAB LLC
405 N East St Ste 110 (17013-2044)
PHONE..................................717 329-9301
EMP: 3 EST: 2011
SALES (est): 184.6K **Privately Held**
SIC: **3842** Mfg Surgical Appliances/Supplies

(G-2701)
COATING CONCEPTS LLC
405 N East St Ste 100 (17013-2044)
PHONE..................................717 240-0010
Shari Kyle, *Principal*
EMP: 3 EST: 2012

SALES (est): 294.3K **Privately Held**
SIC: **3479** Coating of metals & formed products

(G-2702)
COMBAT ARMS LLC
871 Burnt House Rd (17015-9107)
PHONE..................................412 245-0824
Vincent Garrahan, *Principal*
EMP: 6
SALES (est): 320K **Privately Held**
SIC: **3484** 8731 Guns (firearms) or gun parts, 30 mm. & below; electronic research

(G-2703)
COUNTRY BUTCHER SHOP (PA)
Also Called: North Mountain Butcher Shop
286 Mcallister Church Rd (17015-9504)
PHONE..................................717 249-4691
Mary Finkenbinder, *Owner*
EMP: 12
SQ FT: 4,000
SALES (est): 936.7K **Privately Held**
SIC: **2011** 5421 Meat packing plants; meat markets, including freezer provisioners

(G-2704)
CUMBERLAND VALLEY WLDG & REPR
1129 Harrisburg Pike # 4 (17013-1668)
PHONE..................................717 249-1129
Robert Mc Coy, *Owner*
EMP: 4
SALES (est): 363K **Privately Held**
SIC: **7692** 7538 Welding & Automotive Repair

(G-2705)
CUMBERLAND WOODCRAFT CO INC
10 Stover Dr (17015-9782)
P.O. Box 609 (17013-0609)
PHONE..................................717 243-0063
Randolph G Reese, *Ch of Bd*
Donald E Stevens, *Exec VP*
EMP: 30
SQ FT: 30,000
SALES (est): 4MM **Privately Held**
SIC: **2431** Woodwork, interior & ornamental

(G-2706)
D G A INC
Also Called: Infinity Print Graphics
121 N Pitt St (17013-2334)
PHONE..................................717 249-8542
Michael Guion, *President*
Vickie Guion, *Manager*
EMP: 7
SQ FT: 4,500
SALES (est): 941.6K **Privately Held**
WEB: www.infinityprintgraphics.com
SIC: **2752** 5199 Commercial printing, offset; advertising specialties

(G-2707)
DAYNIGHT TRANSPORT LLC
135 C St (17013-1919)
P.O. Box 290528, Wethersfield CT (06129-0528)
PHONE..................................800 288-4996
Mirnes Mustasic,
Hazim Hasamovic,
Mersad Mustasic,
EMP: 8
SALES: 800K **Privately Held**
SIC: **3537** Industrial trucks & tractors

(G-2708)
DUFF AL BAG SCREENPRINTING CO
254 E North St (17013-2538)
PHONE..................................717 249-8686
Rod Yentzer, *President*
Les Russell, *Vice Pres*
EMP: 3
SALES: 400K **Privately Held**
SIC: **2759** Screen printing

(G-2709)
EDMIL FUELS INC
501 Shatto Dr (17013-2108)
PHONE..................................717 249-4901
Michael E Miller, *Principal*

EMP: 6
SALES (est): 738K **Privately Held**
SIC: **2869** Fuels

(G-2710)
EPE INDUSTRIES USA INC
Also Called: Epe Industries USA Harrisburg
1501 Distribution Dr (17013-7400)
PHONE..................................800 315-0336
Mike Hoover, *Branch Mgr*
EMP: 9
SALES (corp-wide): 44.5MM **Privately Held**
SIC: **3086** Packaging & shipping materials, foamed plastic
HQ: Epe Industries Usa, Inc.
17654 Newhope St Ste A
Fountain Valley CA 92708

(G-2711)
FACTOR X GRAFFICS LLC
145 Salem Church Rd Ste 2 (17015)
PHONE..................................717 458-8336
Chad W Mullen,
EMP: 10
SALES (est): 1.2MM **Privately Held**
SIC: **5131** 3993 Labels; signs & advertising specialties

(G-2712)
FILSON WATER TREATMENT INC
11 Roadway Dr Ste A (17015-8836)
PHONE..................................717 240-0763
Rob Filson, *President*
Barry Losh, *Vice Pres*
Jeff Kintz, *VP Sls/Mktg*
EMP: 12
SALES (est): 1.4MM **Privately Held**
WEB: www.filsonwater.com
SIC: **5999** 3589 Water purification equipment; sewage & water treatment equipment

(G-2713)
FLENNIKEN & FLENNIKEN PC
30 State Ave (17013-4431)
PHONE..................................717 249-7777
Eileen Boulden, *Principal*
EMP: 4
SALES (est): 404.2K **Privately Held**
SIC: **3843** Enamels, dentists'

(G-2714)
FORTNEY PACKAGES INC
11 E High St (17013-3058)
P.O. Box 708, Shippensburg (17257-0708)
PHONE..................................717 243-1826
Glen Collier, *CEO*
EMP: 5 EST: 1949
SQ FT: 1,800
SALES (est): 527.8K **Privately Held**
WEB: www.fortneypackages.com
SIC: **2621** Paper mills

(G-2715)
FROG SWITCH AND MFG CO
600 E High St (17013-2654)
PHONE..................................717 243-2454
Lee Hughey, *CEO*
Raphael Hays II, *Ch of Bd*
John Richards, *Vice Pres*
William Walters, *Vice Pres*
Todd Shellenberger, *Engineer*
▼ EMP: 180 EST: 1881
SQ FT: 300,000
SALES (est): 50.8MM **Privately Held**
WEB: www.frogswitch.com
SIC: **3325** 3531 Steel foundries; crushers, grinders & similar equipment

(G-2716)
GALLIKER DAIRY COMPANY
Also Called: Carlisle Depot
1513 Commerce Ave (17015-9166)
PHONE..................................717 258-6199
Sean Melvin, *Manager*
EMP: 6
SALES (corp-wide): 105.3MM **Privately Held**
WEB: www.gallikers.com
SIC: **2026** Buttermilk, cultured
PA: Galliker Dairy Company
143 Donald Ln
Johnstown PA 15904
814 266-8702

(G-2717)
HOFFMAN MATERIALS LLC
321 Cherry St (17013-1838)
PHONE................................717 243-2011
Diana Rauchfuss, *CEO*
Mark Rauchfuss,
EMP: 16
SQ FT: 16,000
SALES (est): 3.1MM **Privately Held**
SIC: 3674 Wafers (semiconductor devices)

(G-2718)
HOFFMAN MATERIALS INC
321 Cherry St (17013-1838)
PHONE................................717 243-2011
Tom Hardy, *CEO*
Diana Rauchfuss, *Ch of Bd*
Marci E Staudte, *Ch of Bd*
Mark S Rauchfuss, *President*
EMP: 25
SQ FT: 40,000
SALES (est): 3.7MM **Privately Held**
SIC: 3679 Quartz crystals, for electronic
application

(G-2719)
LAND OLAKES INC
405 Park Dr (17015-9270)
PHONE................................717 486-7000
William L Schreiber, *General Mgr*
EMP: 110
SQ FT: 48,000
SALES (corp-wide): 10.4B **Privately Held**
WEB: www.landolakes.com
SIC: 2026 2021 2023 Fluid milk; cream-
ery butter; powdered whey
PA: Land O'lakes, Inc.
4001 Lexington Ave N
Arden Hills MN 55126
651 375-2222

(G-2720)
LANE ENTERPRISES INC
Lane Technical Coatings Div
1244 Claremont Rd (17015-9742)
PHONE................................717 249-8342
Greg L Weaver, *Enginr/R&D Mgr*
EMP: 52
SQ FT: 10,000
SALES (corp-wide): 70.5MM **Privately
Held**
WEB: www.lanepipe.com
SIC: 5039 3479 Metal guardrails; painting,
coating & hot dipping
PA: Lane Enterprises, Inc.
3905 Hartzdale Dr Ste 514
Camp Hill PA 17011
717 761-8175

(G-2721)
**LEE ENTERPRISES INC
SENTINEL (DH)**
Also Called: Sentinel, The
327 B St (17013-1825)
P.O. Box 130 (17013-0130)
PHONE................................717 240-7135
Robert Howard, *President*
Jacob Adams, *Editor*
Gary Van Pelt, *Foreman/Supr*
Patrick Doane, *Purch Agent*
Jeff Pratt, *Loan Officer*
EMP: 110
SALES (est): 8MM
SALES (corp-wide): 576.6MM **Publicly
Held**
SIC: 2711 2752 Commercial printing &
newspaper publishing combined; com-
mercial printing, lithographic
HQ: Lee Publications, Inc.
201 N Harrison St Ste 600
Davenport IA 52801
563 383-2100

(G-2722)
LEE PUBLICATION INC
457 E North St (17013-2655)
PHONE................................717 240-7167
Ott Shirley, *Editor*
Beth Holtry, *Business Mgr*
Leanna Faruki, *Personnel Exec*
Karen Robinson, *Sales Staff*
Pat Doane, *Manager*
EMP: 5
SALES (est): 109.9K **Privately Held**
SIC: 2711 Newspapers, publishing & print-
ing

(G-2723)
MACHINING AMERICA INC
1257 Claremont Rd (17015-9726)
PHONE................................717 249-8635
David Coulston, *President*
Jeanette Coluston, *Corp Secy*
EMP: 10
SQ FT: 14,000
SALES: 800K **Privately Held**
SIC: 3599 Machine shop, jobbing & repair

(G-2724)
MASTER SOLUTIONS INC
Also Called: Ats Equipment
20 Wolfs Bridge Rd (17013-8834)
P.O. Box 4444 (17013-0914)
PHONE................................717 243-6849
David W Lutz, *President*
◆ **EMP:** 35
SQ FT: 25,000
SALES (est): 12.9MM **Privately Held**
WEB: www.mastersi.com
SIC: 3715 3535 Truck trailers; conveyors
& conveying equipment

(G-2725)
MASTERBRAND CABINETS INC
219 Allen Rd (17013-9447)
PHONE................................717 359-4131
Ricky Creedmore, *Branch Mgr*
Andy Auchey, *Manager*
EMP: 600
SALES (corp-wide): 5.4B **Publicly Held**
WEB: www.mbcabinets.com
SIC: 2434 Wood kitchen cabinets
HQ: Masterbrand Cabinets, Inc.
1 Masterbrand Cabinets Dr
Jasper IN 47546
812 482-2527

(G-2726)
MOHAWK INC
400 Creek Rd (17013-9645)
PHONE................................717 243-9231
Lawrence Foxx, *President*
Jeffrey E Foxx, *Vice Pres*
EMP: 3
SALES (est): 220K **Privately Held**
SIC: 3085 3083 Plastics bottles; plastic
finished products, laminated

(G-2727)
**MOLLY PITCHER BREWING
COMPANY**
10 E South St (17013-3426)
PHONE................................717 609-0969
Michael Moll,
EMP: 4
SALES (est): 321.8K **Privately Held**
SIC: 2082 Near beer

(G-2728)
**PA PACKING PRODUCTS &
SVCS INC**
433 Zion Rd (17015-7112)
PHONE................................717 486-8100
EMP: 5
SALES (est): 470K **Privately Held**
SIC: 2449 Mfg Wood Containers

(G-2729)
PATRIOT-NEWS CO
101 Noble Blvd Ste 103 (17013-4100)
PHONE................................717 243-1758
Ivey Dejesus, *Manager*
EMP: 8
SALES (corp-wide): 55MM **Privately
Held**
WEB: www.pennlive.com
SIC: 2711 Newspapers
PA: The Patriot-News Co
2020 Tech Pkwy Ste 300
Mechanicsburg PA 17050
717 255-8100

(G-2730)
PPG INDUSTRIES INC
Also Called: PPG Pittsburgh Paints
24 W South St (17013-3431)
PHONE................................717 218-5400
EMP: 4
SALES (corp-wide): 15.3B **Publicly Held**
SIC: 2851 Paints & allied products

PA: Ppg Industries, Inc.
1 Ppg Pl
Pittsburgh PA 15272
412 434-3131

(G-2731)
PPG INDUSTRIES INC
400 Park Dr (17015-9271)
PHONE................................412 820-8116
EMP: 15
SALES (corp-wide): 15.3B **Publicly Held**
SIC: 2851 Paints & allied products
PA: Ppg Industries, Inc.
1 Ppg Pl
Pittsburgh PA 15272
412 434-3131

(G-2732)
**PR HOFFMAN MACHINE PDTS
INC**
1517 Commerce Ave (17015-9166)
PHONE................................717 243-9900
Jong Wang, *CEO*
James Ellis, *Mfg Mgr*
Rod Ansel, *Purchasing*
Andy Leber, *Design Engr*
Ashley Pennabaker, *Sales Staff*
▲ **EMP:** 40
SQ FT: 22,000
SALES: 12MM
SALES (corp-wide): 164.5MM **Publicly
Held**
WEB: www.prhoffman.com
SIC: 3542 3541 Machine tools, metal
forming type; machine tools, metal cutting
type
PA: Amtech Systems, Inc.
131 S Clark Dr
Tempe AZ 85281
480 967-5146

(G-2733)
PYROTEK INCORPORATED
1285 Claremont Rd (17015-9727)
PHONE................................717 249-2075
Steve Kime, *Branch Mgr*
EMP: 52
SQ FT: 16,550
SALES (corp-wide): 592MM **Privately
Held**
WEB: www.pyrotek.info
SIC: 2655 3297 Fiber cans, drums & simi-
lar products; nonclay refractories
PA: Pyrotek Incorporated
705 W 1st Ave
Spokane WA 99201
509 926-6212

(G-2734)
RATCHET RAKE LLC
405 N East St (17013-2045)
PHONE................................717 249-1228
Barbara Kostyak,
▲ **EMP:** 3 **EST:** 2009
SALES (est): 457.3K **Privately Held**
SIC: 3531 Construction machinery

(G-2735)
REACTION ORTHOTICS
405 N East St Ste 110 (17013-2044)
PHONE................................717 609-2361
Steven Miller, *Owner*
EMP: 3
SALES (est): 196.9K **Privately Held**
SIC: 3842 Orthopedic appliances

(G-2736)
RITNER STEEL INC
131 Stover Dr (17015-9782)
PHONE................................717 249-1449
Joseph Dorbian, *President*
Babett Freund, *CFO*
EMP: 32
SQ FT: 15,000
SALES (est): 12.3MM **Privately Held**
SIC: 3441 Building components, structural
steel

(G-2737)
ROWE PRINTING SHOP
350 E High St (17013-2522)
PHONE................................717 249-5485
Michael Rowe, *Owner*
Jon Adams, *Human Res Dir*
EMP: 10
SQ FT: 11,000

SALES (est): 981.5K **Privately Held**
WEB: www.rowesprintshop.com
SIC: 2752 2759 7334 Commercial printing, offset; letterpress printing; photocopying & duplicating services

(G-2738)
S E MOULDING INC
155 Garfield Dr (17015-9199)
PHONE................................717 385-4119
Sidney Ege, *President*
▲ **EMP:** 4 **EST:** 1998
SQ FT: 9,700
SALES (est): 675K **Privately Held**
WEB: www.semoulding.com
SIC: 3089 Injection molding of plastics

(G-2739)
**SPECIALTY PAINTS COATINGS
INC**
608 Alexander Spring Rd (17015)
PHONE................................717 249-5523
Max E Crider, *President*
EMP: 5
SALES (est): 981.6K **Privately Held**
SIC: 2851 Paints & allied products

(G-2740)
SUPERIOR METALWORKS INC
Also Called: S M I
1779 W Trindle Rd Ste B (17015-9766)
PHONE................................717 245-2446
Robert Sgrignoli Jr, *President*
EMP: 12
SQ FT: 25,000
SALES (est): 2.3MM **Privately Held**
WEB: www.superiormetalworks.com
SIC: 3444 1761 3443 Hoods, range:
sheet metal; sheet metalwork; fabricated
plate work (boiler shop)

(G-2741)
TEX VISIONS LLC
10 Pine Hill Dr (17013-8415)
PHONE................................717 240-0213
Kayla Showers, *President*
Nicki Kaufman, *General Mgr*
Nicki Wilson, *General Mgr*
Douglas McGarvey, *Exec VP*
Shawn Reddington, *Purchasing*
◆ **EMP:** 60
SALES (est): 4.5MM **Privately Held**
WEB: www.texvisions.com
SIC: 2759 Screen printing

(G-2742)
**TOTEM POLE RANCH AND
WINERY**
940 Cranes Gap Rd (17013-9634)
PHONE................................717 448-8370
Donald Hopler, *Owner*
Joan Hopler, *Co-Owner*
EMP: 4
SALES (est): 116.1K **Privately Held**
SIC: 2084 Wines

(G-2743)
**TRI-BORO CONSTRUCTION
SUPS INC**
1490 Ritner Hwy (17013-9395)
PHONE................................717 249-6448
Douglas White, *General Mgr*
Tim Kenyon, *Sales Staff*
EMP: 25
SQ FT: 18,000
SALES (est): 1.9MM
SALES (corp-wide): 90.9MM **Privately
Held**
WEB: www.borosupplies.com
SIC: 5082 3273 5251 Masonry equipment
& supplies; ready-mixed concrete; tools,
hand
PA: Tri-Boro Construction Supplies, Inc.
465 E Locust St
Dallastown PA 17313
717 246-3095

(G-2744)
**TUCKEY METAL FABRICATORS
INC**
150 Stover Dr (17015-9782)
PHONE................................717 249-8111
Kenneth Tuckey, *President*
EMP: 35
SQ FT: 30,000

▲ = Import ▼=Export
◆ =Import/Export

SALES (est): 6.8MM **Privately Held**
SIC: 3444 1761 Sheet metal specialties, not stamped; sheet metalwork

(G-2745)
UNION QUARRIES INC
Also Called: Union Quarries At Bonny Brook
102 Bonnybrook Rd (17013-9287)
P.O. Box 686 (17013-0686)
PHONE...............................717 249-5012
Sandra R Diehl, *President*
Vicki Fahnestock, *Admin Sec*
EMP: 31 **EST:** 1961
SQ FT: 10,000
SALES (est): 6.9MM **Privately Held**
SIC: 1422 3273 Crushed & broken limestone; ready-mixed concrete

(G-2746)
USA SPARES INC
1729 W Trindle Rd (17015-9758)
PHONE...............................717 241-9222
Stewart W Byers, *President*
Thomas B Morrison, *Vice Pres*
Ben Breneman, *Manager*
Stewart Wbyers, *Admin Sec*
EMP: 35
SQ FT: 15,000
SALES (est): 7.8MM **Privately Held**
WEB: www.usaspares.com
SIC: 3541 Machine tool replacement & repair parts, metal cutting types; numerically controlled metal cutting machine tools

(G-2747)
VERSICO INCORPORATED
1285 Ritner Hwy (17013-9381)
P.O. Box 1289 (17013-6289)
PHONE...............................717 960-4024
Robert McNeill, *General Mgr*
EMP: 30
SALES (est): 7.8MM
SALES (corp-wide): 4.4B **Publicly Held**
WEB: www.versico.com
SIC: 5169 2952 Synthetic resins, rubber & plastic materials; adhesives & sealants; asphalt felts & coatings
HQ: Carlisle Corporation
11605 N Community House R
Charlotte NC 28277

(G-2748)
VITRO FLAT GLASS LLC
Also Called: Vitro Architectural Glass
400 Park Dr (17015-9271)
PHONE...............................717 486-3366
Tom Abbas, *Manager*
EMP: 343 **Privately Held**
SIC: 3211 Float glass
HQ: Vitro Flat Glass Llc
400 Guys Run Rd
Cheswick PA 15024
412 820-8500

(G-2749)
W S DISPLAY
6 Pine Hill Dr (17013-8415)
PHONE...............................717 460-3485
Scott Wong, *Manager*
EMP: 3
SALES (est): 264.1K **Privately Held**
SIC: 3999 Manufacturing industries

(G-2750)
WAVE CENTRAL LLC
99 Garden Pkwy Ste C (17013-9201)
PHONE...............................717 503-7157
Anthony Sangiovanni, *VP Sales*
Jeffrey Winemiller, *Mng Member*
EMP: 12
SALES (est): 1.2MM **Privately Held**
SIC: 3663 7359 Microwave communication equipment; equipment rental & leasing

(G-2751)
WILSON PAVING INC
480 W Old York Rd (17015-9257)
PHONE...............................717 249-3227
Ward L Wilson, *President*
Dwight A Wilson, *Vice Pres*
Mark L Wilson, *Treasurer*
Edward A Wilson, *Admin Sec*
EMP: 20
SQ FT: 1,000

SALES (est): 4.7MM **Privately Held**
SIC: 2951 1771 Asphalt & asphaltic paving mixtures (not from refineries); blacktop (asphalt) work

(G-2752)
Z-BAND TECHNOLOGIES LLC
848 N Hanover St Ste B (17013-1521)
PHONE...............................717 249-2606
Jacque Brissette, *President*
Daniel Helfrick, *Vice Pres*
Robert Mautino, *CTO*
EMP: 3
SQ FT: 9,200
SALES: 4MM **Privately Held**
SIC: 3679 Video triggers, except remote control TV devices

Carlton
Mercer County

(G-2753)
RANGE RSURCES - APPALACHIA LLC
1369 Cochranton Rd (16311-1605)
PHONE...............................817 870-2601
Doug Tabar, *Production*
Linda Lindsay, *Production*
Jeff Utwiler, *Supervisor*
EMP: 55
SALES (corp-wide): 3.2B **Publicly Held**
WEB: www.gl-energy.com
SIC: 1382 Oil & gas exploration services
HQ: Range Resources - Appalachia, Llc.
3000 Town Center Blvd
Canonsburg PA 15317
724 743-6700

Carmichaels
Greene County

(G-2754)
BRODAK MANUFACTURING & DISTRG
100 Park Ave (15320-1132)
PHONE...............................724 966-2726
John Brodak, *President*
Sandy Bruce, *General Mgr*
▲ **EMP:** 5
SALES (est): 533.1K **Privately Held**
SIC: 3944 Airplane models, toy & hobby

(G-2755)
BRODAK PRINTING COMPANY
100 Park Ave (15320-1132)
PHONE...............................724 966-5178
John Brodak, *Owner*
EMP: 3
SQ FT: 1,200
SALES (est): 234.5K **Privately Held**
SIC: 2752 Commercial printing, offset

(G-2756)
ENERGY CORPORATION OF AMERICA
205 Carmichaels Plz (15320-9642)
PHONE...............................724 966-9000
Roy Ricker, *Principal*
EMP: 3 **EST:** 2009
SALES (est): 261.8K **Privately Held**
SIC: 1382 Oil & gas exploration services

(G-2757)
HOTRONIX LLC
1 Paisley Park (15320)
PHONE...............................800 727-8520
EMP: 3
SALES (est): 109.4K
SALES (corp-wide): 33.4MM **Privately Held**
SIC: 3599 Industrial machinery
PA: Stahls' Inc.
6353 E 14 Mile Rd
Sterling Heights MI 48312
800 478-2457

(G-2758)
IMPRINTABLES WAREHOUSE LLC
1 Posley Pike (15320)
P.O. Box 711, Masontown (15461-0711)
PHONE...............................724 966-8599
Jon A Daniel, *CEO*
▲ **EMP:** 3
SALES (est): 520.9K **Privately Held**
SIC: 3585 4225 Evaporative condensers, heat transfer equipment; general warehousing

(G-2759)
JOHN WALL INC
440 W Greene St (15320-1608)
PHONE...............................724 966-9255
John R Wall, *President*
▲ **EMP:** 13
SALES (est): 2.3MM **Privately Held**
SIC: 3089 Fences, gates & accessories: plastic

(G-2760)
STAHLS HOTRONIX
1 Posley Park (15320)
PHONE...............................724 966-5996
Ted Stahl, *Principal*
◆ **EMP:** 7
SALES (est): 420K **Privately Held**
SIC: 3599 Amusement park equipment

(G-2761)
STALLION LITTLEFIELD SERVICES
12 Industrial Park Rd (15320-9600)
PHONE...............................724 966-2272
EMP: 5
SALES (est): 295.2K **Privately Held**
SIC: 1389 Oil field services

(G-2762)
VELOCITY MUNITIONS INC
480 Jacobs Ferry Rd (15320-1696)
PHONE...............................724 966-2140
Paul Williams, *President*
William Faddis, *Admin Sec*
EMP: 4
SQ FT: 1,750
SALES: 100K **Privately Held**
SIC: 3482 Small arms ammunition

Carnegie
Allegheny County

(G-2763)
AMPCO-PITTSBURGH CORPORATION (PA)
726 Bell Ave Ste 301 (15106-1138)
P.O. Box 457 (15106-0457)
PHONE...............................412 456-4400
J Brett McBrayer, *CEO*
Leonard M Carroll, *Ch of Bd*
Maria Trainor, *Vice Pres*
Michael G McAuley, *CFO*
Roscoe Carrier, *Business Dir*
▲ **EMP:** 71 **EST:** 1929
SQ FT: 165,900
SALES: 419.4MM **Publicly Held**
WEB: www.ampcopgh.com
SIC: 3312 3561 3351 3353 Blast furnaces & steel mills; pumps & pumping equipment; copper & copper alloy pipe & tube; coils, sheet aluminum

(G-2764)
ARDAGH METAL PACKAGING USA INC (HQ)
600 N Bell Ave (15106-4301)
PHONE...............................412 923-1080
James H Willich, *CEO*
John Boyas, *CFO*
◆ **EMP:** 28
SQ FT: 5,000
SALES (est): 320.7MM
SALES (corp-wide): 242.1K **Privately Held**
WEB: www.impresspkg.com
SIC: 3565 Packaging machinery

PA: Ard Holdings Sa
Rue Charles Martel 56
Luxembourg
262 585-55

(G-2765)
CHEM-CLAY CORPORATION
Also Called: Standard Ceramic Supply Co
24 Chestnut St (15106-2072)
P.O. Box 16240, Pittsburgh (15242-0240)
PHONE...............................412 276-6333
James A Turnbull, *President*
James G Turnbull, *Vice Pres*
Sadie Kanownik, *Opers Mgr*
Julie B Hregdovic, *Research*
Lee Grice, *Treasurer*
▲ **EMP:** 22
SQ FT: 22,000
SALES (est): 4.6MM **Privately Held**
WEB: www.standardceramic.com
SIC: 3269 2851 Filtering media, pottery; plastics base paints & varnishes

(G-2766)
DELTA USA INC (DH)
600 N Bell Ave Ste 180 (15106-4325)
PHONE...............................412 429-3574
Jean-Francois Parisot, *President*
Vladimir Fonarev, *Corp Secy*
Jay Kane, *Sales Mgr*
EMP: 4
SQ FT: 1,300
SALES: 3MM
SALES (corp-wide): 776.3K **Privately Held**
WEB: www.delta-usa.com
SIC: 3823 Industrial process measurement equipment
HQ: Delta
1 Rue Foch
Mundolsheim 67450
390 226-122

(G-2767)
FERRI DESIGN
Also Called: Phablab
34 Woodridge Dr (15106-3071)
PHONE...............................412 276-3700
Christopher Ferri, *Owner*
EMP: 4
SQ FT: 6,000
SALES (est): 305.9K **Privately Held**
SIC: 3993 Signs & advertising specialties

(G-2768)
FUTURE-ALL INC
Hammond Gregg St Bldg 21 (15106)
P.O. Box 528 (15106-0528)
PHONE...............................412 279-2670
Charles R King Sr, *President*
C Richard King Jr, *Vice Pres*
Becky King, *Admin Sec*
▲ **EMP:** 40
SQ FT: 60,000
SALES (est): 10.4MM **Privately Held**
WEB: www.future-all.com
SIC: 3531 Construction machinery

(G-2769)
GLEN CARBIDE INC
1054 Campbells Run Rd (15106-1901)
P.O. Box 498 (15106-0498)
PHONE...............................412 279-7500
Edwarddennis Fawcettking, *CEO*
Dennis J King, *President*
Dennis King, *President*
Michael Kennelly, *Vice Pres*
Joseph Makar, *Admin Sec*
EMP: 45 **EST:** 1958
SQ FT: 31,000
SALES (est): 8.2MM **Privately Held**
WEB: www.glencarbide.com
SIC: 3544 Dies & die holders for metal cutting, forming, die casting

(G-2770)
GREENWOOD ENTERPRISES
313 W Main St 315 (15106-2623)
PHONE...............................412 429-6800
L C Greenwood, *President*
James Mc Donald, *Vice Pres*
EMP: 25
SALES (est): 2.1MM **Privately Held**
SIC: 1221 Strip mining, bituminous

(G-2771)
JENNISON CORPORATION
Also Called: Jennison Manufacturing Group
54 Arch St (15106-2040)
P.O. Box 861 (15106-0861)
PHONE..............................412 429-0500
Thomas Jennison, *President*
Shaun Hong, *Managing Dir*
Paul Sirney, *Vice Pres*
J Bradley Holmes, *Purchasing*
Michael T Jennison, *Admin Sec*
◆ **EMP:** 43
SQ FT: 44,000
SALES (est): 10.5MM **Privately Held**
WEB: www.jennisonqc.com
SIC: 3544 3599 Punches, forming &
stamping; machine shop, jobbing & repair

(G-2772)
JENNISON ICE LLC
54 Arch St (15106-2040)
PHONE..............................412 596-5914
Micheal Jennison, *Mng Member*
EMP: 5
SQ FT: 7,000
SALES (est): 869.3K **Privately Held**
SIC: 3581 Automatic vending machines

(G-2773)
JENNISON PRECISION MACHINE INC
54 Arch St (15106-2040)
P.O. Box 861 (15106-0861)
PHONE..............................412 279-3007
Thomas A Jennison, *President*
Thomas H Beattie, *Vice Pres*
Debra Holmes, *Shareholder*
Michael T Jennison, *Shareholder*
EMP: 37
SQ FT: 18,000
SALES (est): 4.9MM **Privately Held**
SIC: 3599 Machine shop, jobbing & repair

(G-2774)
KRAFT HEINZ FOODS COMPANY
86 Pilgrim St (15106-1022)
PHONE..............................412 237-5715
Ronald Trombetta, *Branch Mgr*
EMP: 25
SALES (corp-wide): 26.2B **Publicly Held**
SIC: 2032 Canned specialties
HQ: Kraft Heinz Foods Company
　1 Ppg Pl Ste 3200
　Pittsburgh PA 15222
　412 456-5700

(G-2775)
LANE HOLDINGS LLC
12 Noblestown Rd (15106-1633)
PHONE..............................412 279-1234
Jonnine Kelly, *Mng Member*
EMP: 28 **EST:** 1935
SQ FT: 142,000
SALES (est): 6.2MM **Privately Held**
WEB: www.lane-holdings.com
SIC: 3271 3273 Blocks, concrete or cinder: standard; ready-mixed concrete

(G-2776)
MALLET AND COMPANY INC (DH)
51 Arch St (15106-2022)
P.O. Box 474 (15106-0474)
PHONE..............................412 276-9000
Robert E Campanale, *President*
Robert I Mallet, *Principal*
Arlene Kobos, *Exec VP*
Peter J Chiappa, *CFO*
Donald S Aleski, *Admin Sec*
◆ **EMP:** 2 **EST:** 1939
SQ FT: 8,073
SALES (est): 10.3MM
SALES (corp-wide): 1.4B **Privately Held**
WEB: www.malletoil.com
SIC: 2099 2079 3556 Food preparations;
oil, hydrogenated: edible; food products
machinery
HQ: Vantage Specialty Chemicals, Inc.
　4650 S Racine Ave
　Chicago IL 60609
　800 833-2864

(G-2777)
MCS INC
Bldg 16 (15106)
P.O. Box 536 (15106-0536)
PHONE..............................412 429-8991
Kenneth Sharek, *President*
Leonard Klemencic, *Vice Pres*
EMP: 26
SALES (est): 6.5MM **Privately Held**
SIC: 3498 Piping systems for pulp paper &
chemical industries

(G-2778)
PHASE GUARD CO INC
Also Called: Manufcturer Electronic Contrls
400 Logan St (15106-2229)
P.O. Box 171 (15106-0171)
PHONE..............................412 276-3415
EMP: 3
SALES (est): 200K **Privately Held**
SIC: 3674 Mfg Semiconductors/Related
Devices

(G-2779)
PITTSBURGH DESIGN SERVICES INC
Hammond & Gregg Sts (15106)
P.O. Box 469 (15106-0469)
PHONE..............................412 276-3000
Beth Noonan, *President*
G Timothy Noonan, *Treasurer*
Tim Noonan, *Finance*
Douglas Kelly, *Sales Mgr*
Rich Dunhoff, *Sales Executive*
▲ **EMP:** 11 **EST:** 1970
SALES (est): 3.7MM **Privately Held**
WEB: www.pittsdesign.com
SIC: 5084 3536 3444 Cranes, industrial;
hoists; hoists, cranes & monorails; sheet
metalwork

(G-2780)
PITTSBURGH FENCE CO INC
Also Called: Butler Fence Builders
551 E Main St (15106-2000)
P.O. Box 522 (15106-0522)
PHONE..............................724 775-6550
Robert F Wible, *President*
Virginia C Wible, *Vice Pres*
EMP: 25
SQ FT: 800
SALES (est): 3.7MM **Privately Held**
SIC: 1799 3496 3444 Fence construction;
miscellaneous fabricated wire products;
sheet metalwork

(G-2781)
PPG INDUSTRIES INC
416 Washington Ave (15106-2779)
PHONE..............................412 276-1922
Randy Hamm, *Manager*
EMP: 3
SALES (corp-wide): 15.3B **Publicly Held**
WEB: www.westmorelandsupply.com
SIC: 2851 Paints & allied products
PA: Ppg Industries, Inc.
　1 Ppg Pl
　Pittsburgh PA 15272
　412 434-3131

(G-2782)
PRECISIONS SIGNS AND AWNING (PA)
3 Glass St (15106-2401)
PHONE..............................412 278-0400
Michael Morrow Sr, *President*
Doc Scholler, *General Mgr*
EMP: 9
SQ FT: 5,000
SALES (est): 2MM **Privately Held**
SIC: 3993 7389 Electric signs; lettering &
sign painting services

(G-2783)
PROVA INC
Also Called: Apple Printing Co
1703 E Railroad St (15106-4028)
PHONE..............................412 278-3010
Ray Losego, *President*
EMP: 7
SQ FT: 4,000
SALES (est): 898.2K **Privately Held**
SIC: 2752 Commercial printing, offset

(G-2784)
REACTION NUTRITION LLC
230 E Main St (15106-2700)
PHONE..............................412 276-7800
▲ **EMP:** 10
SQ FT: 10,000
SALES (est): 2.6MM **Privately Held**
SIC: 2833 Mfg Medicinal/Botanical Products

(G-2785)
RED VALVE COMPANY INC (HQ)
Also Called: R K L Controls Div
600 N Bell Ave Ste 300 (15106-4324)
P.O. Box 548 (15106-0548)
PHONE..............................412 279-0044
Chris M Raftis, *President*
Jeff Kelly, *General Mgr*
Kaikun Zou, *Managing Dir*
Derek Szpak, *Plant Mgr*
Benny Lonchar, *Natl Sales Mgr*
▲ **EMP:** 70
SQ FT: 15,000
SALES (est): 34.6MM **Publicly Held**
SIC: 3491 Pressure valves & regulators,
industrial

(G-2786)
RED VALVE COMPANY INC
500 N Bell Ave (15106-4303)
P.O. Box 548 (15106-0548)
PHONE..............................412 279-0044
David Maggi, *Manager*
EMP: 30 **Publicly Held**
SIC: 3491 Pressure valves & regulators,
industrial
HQ: Red Valve Company, Inc
　600 N Bell Ave Ste 300
　Carnegie PA 15106
　412 279-0044

(G-2787)
RETROHAIR INC
427 Jane St (15106-2046)
PHONE..............................412 278-2383
William Gunzburg, *President*
EMP: 3
SALES (est): 348.4K **Privately Held**
SIC: 2844 Toilet preparations

(G-2788)
ROO TEES INC
300 Noblestown Rd Ste 1 (15106-1216)
PHONE..............................412 279-9889
Brian Cross, *President*
Fran Cross, *President*
EMP: 5
SALES (est): 627.4K **Privately Held**
WEB: www.rootees.com
SIC: 2759 Screen printing

(G-2789)
S P KINNEY ENGINEERS INC (PA)
143 1st Ave (15106-2501)
P.O. Box 445 (15106-0445)
PHONE..............................412 276-4600
Craig S Kinney, *President*
Kerry Trachok, *Corp Secy*
Greg Billigen, *Vice Pres*
Robert E Yeager, *Vice Pres*
Jim Comis, *Purch Agent*
▼ **EMP:** 49 **EST:** 1942
SQ FT: 24,000
SALES (est): 9.1MM **Privately Held**
WEB: www.spkinney.com
SIC: 3491 3569 3547 3494 Industrial
valves; liquid automation machinery &
equipment; rolling mill machinery; valves
& pipe fittings; heating equipment, except
electric

(G-2790)
SCOTT METALS INC
730 Superior St Ste 2 (15106-3466)
PHONE..............................412 279-7021
Edward Cipriano Jr, *President*
Leonard A Klemencic, *Vice Pres*
Leonard J Klemencic, *Vice Pres*
Brad Beach, *Project Mgr*
Jim Coddington, *Project Mgr*
EMP: 35
SQ FT: 39,000

SALES (est): 8.1MM **Privately Held**
WEB: www.scottmetals.com
SIC: 3498 3613 3443 Pipe sections fabricated from purchased pipe; panelboards
& distribution boards, electric; liners, industrial: metal plate

(G-2791)
SDC NUTRITION INC
230 E Main St (15106-2700)
PHONE..............................412 276-7800
EMP: 10
SALES (corp-wide): 11.6MM **Privately Held**
SIC: 2833 Medicinals & botanicals
PA: Sdc Nutrition, Inc.
　170 Industry Dr
　Pittsburgh PA 15275
　412 275-3351

(G-2792)
SHAMROCK BUILDING SERVICES INC
535 Forest Ave (15106-2808)
P.O. Box 16223, Pittsburgh (15242-0223)
PHONE..............................412 279-2800
Andrew Breen, *President*
Peter Breen, *Vice Pres*
Paul Vandergraft, *Manager*
EMP: 45
SQ FT: 1,000
SALES (est): 8.1MM **Privately Held**
SIC: 1741 3993 7349 Tuckpointing or
restoration; signs & advertising specialties; window cleaning

(G-2793)
SKY OXYGEN INC
Also Called: Vinces Gas & Welding Supply
Co
2790 Idlewood Ave (15106-1113)
PHONE..............................412 278-3001
Vince Cirrincione III, *President*
Vincent J Cirrincione Jr, *Vice Pres*
Laurie Waller, *Vice Pres*
Garrett Cirrincione, *Sales Staff*
Shawn Lane, *Sales Staff*
EMP: 30
SQ FT: 6,500
SALES (est): 15.6MM **Privately Held**
WEB: www.sky-oxygen.com
SIC: 5085 5984 7692 Welding supplies;
liquefied petroleum gas dealers; welding
repair

(G-2794)
SSKJ ENTERPRISES INC
Also Called: Vital Signs
2812 Idlewood Ave (15106-1238)
PHONE..............................412 494-3308
Sandy F Burkett, *President*
Steven L Burkett, *Vice Pres*
EMP: 4
SQ FT: 2,000
SALES (est): 490.1K **Privately Held**
WEB: www.vitalsignspgh.com
SIC: 3993 Signs & advertising specialties

(G-2795)
SUPERBOLT INC
1000 Gregg St (15106)
P.O. Box 683 (15106-0683)
PHONE..............................412 279-1149
William Myers, *President*
▲ **EMP:** 85
SQ FT: 18,000
SALES (est): 26.5MM
SALES (corp-wide): 1.1B **Privately Held**
WEB: www.superbolt.com
SIC: 3452 Nuts, metal
HQ: Nord Lock Inc
　1000 Gregg St
　Carnegie PA 15106
　412 279-1149

(G-2796)
SUPERCLEANSCOM INC
969 Bell Ave (15106-1162)
PHONE..............................412 429-1640
Rita Harper, *President*
▲ **EMP:** 2
SQ FT: 6,000
SALES: 1.3MM **Privately Held**
SIC: 3635 Household vacuum cleaners

▲ = Import ▼=Export
◆ =Import/Export

(G-2797)
SUPPLY TECHNOLOGIES LLC
Also Called: Sabina Mfg.
1200 Arch St Ste 1 (15106-1824)
PHONE......................724 745-8877
Larry Calvert, *General Mgr*
EMP: 40
SALES (corp-wide): 1.6B **Publicly Held**
WEB: www.deloscrew.com
SIC: 3444 Sheet metalwork
HQ: Supply Technologies Llc
6065 Parkland Blvd Ste 2
Cleveland OH 44124
440 947-2100

(G-2798)
TRINITY FIBRGLS COMPOSITES LLC
1000 Gregg St (15106)
PHONE......................412 855-3398
Donald M Holtkamp,
Jane Moffitt,
EMP: 8
SQ FT: 8,000
SALES (est): 590.6K **Privately Held**
SIC: 3296 Fiberglass insulation

(G-2799)
TROPHY WORKS
1001 Campbells Run Rd (15106-1902)
PHONE......................412 279-0111
Barbara Atkins, *Owner*
EMP: 4
SQ FT: 2,400
SALES (est): 407.7K **Privately Held**
SIC: 3914 5999 2796 Trophies; trophies & plaques; platemaking services

(G-2800)
UNION ELECTRIC STEEL CORP (HQ)
726 Bell Ave Ste 101 (15106-1137)
P.O. Box 465 (15106-0465)
PHONE......................412 429-7655
Rodney L Scagline, *President*
Steve Wiard, *Superintendent*
Amy McCormick, *Vice Pres*
Virginia Oberleitner, *Vice Pres*
George A Ott, *Vice Pres*
◆ EMP: 60 EST: 1923
SQ FT: 50,000
SALES (est): 97.9MM
SALES (corp-wide): 419.4MM **Publicly Held**
WEB: www.uniones.com
SIC: 3325 3398 3312 Rolling mill rolls, cast steel; metal heat treating; blast furnaces & steel mills
PA: Ampco-Pittsburgh Corporation
726 Bell Ave Ste 301
Carnegie PA 15106
412 456-4400

(G-2801)
UNIPAPER RECYCLING COMPANY (DH)
73 Noblestown Rd Ste D (15106-1676)
PHONE......................412 429-8522
Gabe Hudock, *President*
EMP: 10
SALES (est): 8.2MM
SALES (corp-wide): 14.9B **Publicly Held**
SIC: 4953 2611 Recycling, waste materials; pulp mills

(G-2802)
UNIVERSAL CARNEGIE MFG
66a Arch St (15106-2040)
PHONE......................800 867-9554
EMP: 4
SALES (est): 195.1K **Privately Held**
SIC: 3714 Radiators & radiator shells & cores, motor vehicle

(G-2803)
VAUTID NORTH AMERICA INC
554 Washington Ave Ste 3 (15106-2878)
PHONE......................412 429-3288
Ralph Wolf, *Principal*
Dave Davis, *Manager*
▲ EMP: 9
SALES (est): 1.1MM
SALES (corp-wide): 2.1B **Privately Held**
SIC: 3441 Fabricated structural metal

HQ: Vautid Gmbh
Brunnwiesenstr. 5
Ostfildern 73760
711 440-40

(G-2804)
VOLLMER OF AMERICA CORP (DH)
105 Broadway St (15106-2421)
PHONE......................412 278-0655
Peter Allen, *President*
George Brown, *Regional Mgr*
Joerg Vollmer, *Vice Pres*
Stacy Kraus, *Materials Mgr*
Hugh Nevin, *Treasurer*
▲ EMP: 13
SALES (est): 2.7MM, **Privately Held**
WEB: www.vollmer-us.com
SIC: 3541 Machine tools, metal cutting type
HQ: Vollmer Werke Maschinenfabrik Gesellschaft Mit Beschrankter Haftung
Ehinger Str. 34
Biberach An Der RiB 88400
735 157-10

(G-2805)
VON MACHINE CO
338 Logan St (15106-2395)
PHONE......................412 276-4505
Erik V Steding, *President*
David Steding, *Vice Pres*
Eileen Steding, *Treasurer*
EMP: 6
SQ FT: 2,400
SALES (est): 753.6K **Privately Held**
WEB: www.vonmachine.com
SIC: 3599 Machine shop, jobbing & repair

(G-2806)
WEST HILLS SPECIALTY SUPPLY CO
Also Called: West Hills Specialty Dntl Lab
312 2nd Ave (15106-2509)
PHONE......................412 279-6766
Werner Schmidt, *Owner*
EMP: 4
SALES (est): 404.8K **Privately Held**
SIC: 3843 5085 Dental equipment & supplies; industrial supplies

---

Carrolltown
Cambria County

(G-2807)
DIVERSIFIED FABRICATIONS INC
514 Deveaux St (15722-8400)
PHONE......................814 344-8434
John Munjack, *President*
EMP: 8
SALES (est): 1.2MM **Privately Held**
SIC: 3449 Bars, concrete reinforcing: fabricated steel

(G-2808)
E P BENDER COAL COMPANY
198 S Main St (15722)
PHONE......................814 344-8063
Martha A Bender, *President*
Edward C Bender, *Corp Secy*
John E Bender, *Treasurer*
EMP: 30 EST: 1948
SQ FT: 3,500
SALES (est): 5.2MM **Privately Held**
SIC: 1221 1241 Surface mining, bituminous; coal mining services

(G-2809)
R ILLIG MACHINING
314 Deveaux St (15722-8506)
P.O. Box 119 (15722-0119)
PHONE......................814 344-6202
Richard Illig, *Partner*
Robert Illig, *Partner*
EMP: 7
SQ FT: 7,300
SALES (est): 800K **Privately Held**
SIC: 3599 Machine shop, jobbing & repair

(G-2810)
STARFIRE CORPORATION (PA)
682 Cole Rd (15722-7902)
PHONE......................814 948-5164
Audrey Jean Terrizzi, *President*
Linda M Terrizzi, *Corp Secy*
▲ EMP: 2
SALES (est): 1MM **Privately Held**
WEB: www.starfirecorporation.com
SIC: 2899 7999 7389 Fireworks; fireworks display service;

Castanea
Clinton County

(G-2811)
SOLVAY USA INC
Also Called: Wsp Solvay
400 W Brown St (17726)
PHONE......................570 748-4450
William Frost, *CEO*
EMP: 21
SALES (corp-wide): 10MM **Privately Held**
SIC: 2819 Industrial inorganic chemicals
HQ: Solvay Usa Inc.
504 Carnegie Ctr
Princeton NJ 08540
609 860-4000

Catasauqua
Lehigh County

(G-2812)
AD-RAX PRODUCTIONS LLC
1225 7th St (18032-2146)
PHONE......................610 264-8405
Kim Sivonva, *Mng Member*
Kim Sivonda,
Zaheer Rahaman,
▲ EMP: 8
SALES: 1MM **Privately Held**
SIC: 2759 Commercial printing

(G-2813)
ALLENTOWN STEEL FABG CO INC
260 Race St (18032-1961)
PHONE......................610 264-2815
John D Svoboda, *President*
Maryann Felegy, *Admin Sec*
EMP: 10 EST: 1956
SQ FT: 50,000
SALES (est): 1.6MM **Privately Held**
SIC: 3443 Fabricated plate work (boiler shop)

(G-2814)
ARCHER INSTRUMENTS LLC
411 Race St (18032-1148)
PHONE......................215 589-0356
Andrew Morgan, *Mng Member*
EMP: 5
SALES: 1.3MM **Privately Held**
SIC: 3821 5169 5999 Chemical laboratory apparatus; chemicals & allied products; medical apparatus & supplies

(G-2815)
JOHN BACHMAN HVAC
739 2nd St (18032-2345)
PHONE......................610 266-3877
John Bachman, *Owner*
EMP: 5
SALES: 550K **Privately Held**
SIC: 3585 1731 Refrigeration & heating equipment; electrical work

(G-2816)
PHOENIX FORGING COMPANY INC (PA)
Also Called: Phoenix Hotform
800 Front St (18032-2343)
PHONE......................610 264-2861
John E Rodgers, *President*
Nick Thee, *COO*
Robert Harron, *Vice Pres*
Barry Avate, *Plant Mgr*
Nicholas I Thee, *Treasurer*
▲ EMP: 9

SQ FT: 110,000
SALES (est): 11.5MM **Privately Held**
SIC: 3462 3494 Iron & steel forgings; valves & pipe fittings

(G-2817)
ROCK HILL MATERIALS COMPANY (PA)
339 School St Ste 3 (18032-1897)
PHONE......................610 264-5586
Glenn Buskirk, *President*
Jeff Buskirk, *Vice Pres*
Mark Buskirk, *Vice Pres*
Mike Buskirk, *Controller*
EMP: 50 EST: 1947
SQ FT: 8,000
SALES (est): 7.5MM **Privately Held**
SIC: 3273 4212 7359 Ready-mixed concrete; local trucking, without storage; equipment rental & leasing

---

Catawissa
Columbia County

(G-2818)
FUNCTION INC
Also Called: Function of Beauty
236 Parrs Mill Rd (17820-8324)
PHONE......................570 317-0737
Zahir Dossa, *CEO*
EMP: 4 **Privately Held**
SIC: 2844 Cosmetic preparations

(G-2819)
JAMES G BEAVER
Also Called: North Branch Industries
251 Airport Rd (17820-8775)
PHONE......................570 799-0388
James G Beaver, *Owner*
EMP: 3
SQ FT: 2,000
SALES (est): 262.7K **Privately Held**
WEB: www.numidiaairport.com
SIC: 3599 Machine shop, jobbing & repair

(G-2820)
MECHANTECH INC
162 Little Mountain Rd (17820-8105)
PHONE......................570 389-1039
EMP: 12
SALES: 1.5MM **Privately Held**
SIC: 3663 Install Communication

Cecil
Washington County

(G-2821)
AARON J MICHAEL
119 Valleycrest Dr (15321-1181)
PHONE......................724 745-0656
Michael Aaron, *Principal*
EMP: 4
SALES (est): 361.8K **Privately Held**
SIC: 3829 Polygraph devices

(G-2822)
M & M CABINETS LLC
3265 Millers Run Rd (15321-1183)
PHONE......................412 220-9663
Michael Perry,
Steven Stern,
EMP: 9
SALES (est): 858.5K **Privately Held**
SIC: 2431 Millwork

Center Valley
Lehigh County

(G-2823)
AESCULAP IMPLANT SYSTEMS LLC (DH)
3773 Corp Pkwy Ste 200 (18034)
PHONE......................610 984-9000
Charles Dinardo, *Mng Member*
Andrea Vovk, *Manager*
EMP: 9
SALES (est): 10.3MM **Privately Held**
SIC: 3841 Surgical & medical instruments

HQ: Aesculap, Inc.
3773 Corp Pkwy Ste 200
Center Valley PA 18034
610 797-9300

(G-2824)
ALLERGAN INC
4647 Saucon Creek Rd # 101
(18034-9007)
PHONE...................................610 691-2880
Dave Le Cause, *Manager*
EMP: 51 **Privately Held**
SIC: 2834 5122 Drugs acting on the central nervous system & sense organs; pharmaceuticals
HQ: Allergan, Inc.
5 Giralda Farms
Madison NJ 07940
862 261-7000

(G-2825)
COOPERSBURG ASSOCIATES INC
Also Called: Coopersburg Sports
2600 Saucon Valley Rd (18034-9418)
PHONE...................................610 282-1360
Scott Pino, *President*
Anthony P Pino, *Vice Pres*
Dorrit A Pino, *Treasurer*
Edward Emerich, *Admin Sec*
▲ **EMP:** 25 **EST:** 1791
SQ FT: 11,200
SALES (est): 4.8MM **Privately Held**
WEB: www.coopersburgsports.com
SIC: 2511 Novelty furniture: wood

(G-2826)
COOPERSBURG PRODUCTS LLC
2600b Saucon Valley Rd (18034-9418)
PHONE...................................610 282-1360
▲ **EMP:** 3
SALES (est): 274.5K **Privately Held**
SIC: 2329 Men's & boys' sportswear & athletic clothing

(G-2827)
FOUR WINDS CONCRETE INC
Also Called: Four Winds Concrete Company
4401 Camp Meeting Rd (18034-9467)
PHONE...................................610 865-1788
Sherri Casilio, *Branch Mgr*
EMP: 41
SALES (corp-wide): 5.1MM **Privately Held**
SIC: 3273 5211 Ready-mixed concrete; sand & gravel
PA: Four Winds Concrete, Inc.
925 Harvard Ave
Bethlehem PA 18015
610 865-1788

(G-2828)
MICRO MATIC USA INC
4601 Saucon Creek Rd (18034-9005)
PHONE...................................610 625-4464
Jack Thompson, *Opers Mgr*
Scott Beidleman, *Sales Staff*
Jim Barnett, *Manager*
Matt Sabol, *Supervisor*
Leo Murphy, *Info Tech Mgr*
EMP: 10
SALES (corp-wide): 323.5MM **Privately Held**
SIC: 3585 Refrigeration & heating equipment
HQ: Micro Matic Usa, Inc.
2386 Simon Ct
Brooksville FL 34604
352 544-1081

(G-2829)
SBI SURVIVOR CORPORATION (PA)
Also Called: Skee-Ball Amusement Games
3810 Clover Dr (18034-9409)
PHONE...................................215 997-8900
Joseph W Sladek, *President*
John N Irwin, *Vice Pres*
▲ **EMP:** 105
SQ FT: 40,000
SALES (est): 12.6MM **Privately Held**
WEB: www.skeeball.com
SIC: 3599 Amusement park equipment

(G-2830)
SHAMASEEN HAMZAH
Also Called: Royal Service
6137 Main St (18034-8472)
PHONE...................................484 557-5051
Hamzah Shamaseen, *Owner*
EMP: 5 **EST:** 2014
SALES (est): 231.4K **Privately Held**
SIC: 3582 Rug cleaning, drying or napping machines: commercial; building & office cleaning services;

(G-2831)
SPIRAX SARCO INC
4647 Saucon Creek Rd (18034-9006)
PHONE...................................610 807-3500
Ed Beedle, *Branch Mgr*
Flora Cathers, *Manager*
EMP: 7
SALES (corp-wide): 1.3B **Privately Held**
WEB: www.spiraxsarco-usa.com
SIC: 3491 3494 3561 Steam traps; pressure valves & regulators, industrial; line strainers, for use in piping systems; pumps & pumping equipment
HQ: Spirax Sarco, Inc.
1150 Northpoint Blvd
Blythewood SC 29016
803 714-2000

Centerport
Berks County

(G-2832)
BEVERAGE COASTERS INC
589 Centerport Rd (19516)
P.O. Box 99 (19516-0099)
PHONE...................................610 916-4864
Greg Krasnick, *President*
EMP: 6
SQ FT: 12,000
SALES (est): 1.3MM **Privately Held**
SIC: 2679 Paperboard products, converted

Centerville
Crawford County

(G-2833)
CLLN DIRECTIONAL DRILLING INC
37016 State Highway 77 (16404-3646)
PHONE...................................814 460-0248
Catherine I Miller, *President*
Randy E Miller, *Vice Pres*
Shannon M Miller, *Admin Sec*
EMP: 5
SALES (est): 426.7K **Privately Held**
SIC: 3541 Drilling & boring machines

(G-2834)
K & M WOOD PRODUCTS
36529 Tryonville Rd (16404-4537)
PHONE...................................814 967-4613
Wesley Martin, *Partner*
Phillip Kupfer, *Partner*
EMP: 10
SQ FT: 6,000
SALES (est): 744.5K **Privately Held**
SIC: 2431 Panel work, wood

(G-2835)
SANSOM TOOL & DIE INC
37414 Bowmaster Rd (16404-5824)
PHONE...................................814 967-4985
Steven Sansom, *President*
Tracy Sansom, *Vice Pres*
EMP: 3
SALES (est): 200K **Privately Held**
SIC: 3544 Special dies & tools

(G-2836)
TRUE CUT SAWMILLS INC
40021 Dorn Rd (16404-6417)
PHONE...................................814 694-2192
EMP: 3 **EST:** 2016
SALES (est): 214.2K **Privately Held**
SIC: 2421 Sawdust, shavings & wood chips

(G-2837)
VERGONA OUTDOORS LLC
12391 Leboeuf Trail Rd (16404-5305)
PHONE...................................814 967-4844
Fawn Vergona, *CFO*
Michael Vergona, *Mng Member*
EMP: 3 **EST:** 2007
SALES (est): 284.9K **Privately Held**
SIC: 3949 5941 Archery equipment, general; hunting equipment

Central City
Somerset County

(G-2838)
GREENLEY ENGERY HOLDINGS OF PA (PA)
153 Wilson St (15926-1047)
PHONE...................................724 238-8177
Rick Harkcom, *President*
Dominic Ciarimboli, *Corp Secy*
EMP: 3
SALES (est): 804K **Privately Held**
SIC: 1221 Bituminous coal & lignite-surface mining

(G-2839)
INDIAN LAKE MARINA INC
234 S Shore Trl (15926-7611)
PHONE...................................814 754-4774
Marc Alaia, *President*
EMP: 7
SQ FT: 20,000
SALES (est): 850K **Privately Held**
SIC: 5551 3732 4493 Motor boat dealers; boat building & repairing; boat yards, storage & incidental repair

Centre Hall
Centre County

(G-2840)
CENTRE PUBLICATIONS INC
163 Mountainside Ln (16828-8206)
P.O. Box 345 (16828-0345)
PHONE...................................814 364-2000
Gene Kneller, *President*
EMP: 7
SALES (est): 777.2K **Privately Held**
WEB: www.centrepublications.com
SIC: 2741 7311 Atlas, map & guide publishing; advertising agencies

(G-2841)
HANOVER FOODS CORPORATION
3008 Penns Valley Pike (16828-8405)
P.O. Box 193 (16828-0193)
PHONE...................................814 364-1482
Carl Anderson, *Manager*
EMP: 200
SALES (corp-wide): 292MM **Publicly Held**
WEB: www.hanoverfoods.com
SIC: 2033 Canned fruits & specialties
PA: Hanover Foods Corporation
1486 York St
Hanover PA 17331
717 632-6000

(G-2842)
JAYBIRD MANUFACTURING INC
135 Summer Ln (16828-8975)
PHONE...................................814 364-1800
Darren Figart, *President*
Kathy Fye, *Manager*
EMP: 6
SQ FT: 5,000
SALES (est): 1.3MM **Privately Held**
WEB: www.jaybird-mfg.com
SIC: 3564 5191 Blowers & fans; greenhouse equipment & supplies

(G-2843)
MORTON BUILDINGS INC
2789 Earlystown Rd (16828-9144)
P.O. Box 361 (16828-0361)
PHONE...................................814 364-9500
William Shanahan, *Branch Mgr*
EMP: 15

SALES (corp-wide): 463.7MM **Privately Held**
WEB: www.mortonbuildings.com
SIC: 3448 Prefabricated metal buildings
PA: Morton Buildings, Inc.
252 W Adams St
Morton IL 61550
800 447-7436

(G-2844)
STRAUB INDUSTRIES INC
234 Goodhart Rd (16828-9008)
PHONE...................................814 364-9789
Judith Podgorn, *President*
Robert V Straub, *Vice Pres*
Marry Ann Herber, *Treasurer*
Jane Hodkin, *Admin Sec*
EMP: 5
SQ FT: 5,000
SALES (est): 550K **Privately Held**
SIC: 1382 Oil & gas exploration services

(G-2845)
VICTORIAN LIGHTING WORKS INC
251 S Pennsylvania Ave (16828-8701)
P.O. Box 469 (16828-0469)
PHONE...................................814 364-9577
Bryant Musser, *President*
Mark Musser, *Vice Pres*
EMP: 4
SQ FT: 4,500
SALES (est): 330K **Privately Held**
WEB: www.vlworks.com
SIC: 3645 Residential lighting fixtures

(G-2846)
YARGER PRECISION MACHINING
2848 Earlystown Rd (16828-9108)
P.O. Box 282 (16828-0282)
PHONE...................................814 364-1961
Duane E Yarger Sr, *President*
Duane E Yarger, *President*
Ruth Ann Floray, *Corp Secy*
Robert Yarger, *Vice Pres*
Robert A Yarger, *Treasurer*
EMP: 10
SALES (est): 1.5MM **Privately Held**
WEB: www.yargerprecision.com
SIC: 3599 Machine shop, jobbing & repair

Chadds Ford
Delaware County

(G-2847)
AQUACAP PHARMACEUTICAL INC
4 Hillman Dr Ste 190 (19317-9780)
PHONE...................................610 361-2800
Christopher R Lientz, *President*
EMP: 10
SQ FT: 18,000
SALES (est): 2.8MM
SALES (corp-wide): 90.8B **Privately Held**
WEB: www.atrium-bio.com
SIC: 2834 Pharmaceutical preparations
HQ: Atrium Innovations Inc
3500 Boul De Maisonneuve O Bureau 2405
Westmount QC H3Z 3
514 205-6240

(G-2848)
ASSOCIATED PACKAGING ENTPS INC
Also Called: Associated Packaging Tech
1 Dickinson Dr Ste 100 (19317-9665)
PHONE...................................484 785-1120
Arthur Hagg, *General Mgr*
▲ **EMP:** 465
SALES (est): 62MM
SALES (corp-wide): 5.3B **Publicly Held**
WEB: www.aptechnologies.com
SIC: 3089 Plastic containers, except foam
PA: Sonoco Products Company
1 N 2nd St
Hartsville SC 29550
843 383-7000

2019 Harris Pennsylvania
Manufacturers Directory

▲ = Import ▼ =Export
◆ =Import/Export

(G-2849)
CHADDSFORD WINERY LTD (PA)
632 Baltimore Pike (19317-9305)
PHONE..................................610 388-6221
Corey Krejcik, *President*
EMP: 29
SALES (est): 2.9MM **Privately Held**
WEB: www.chaddsford.com
SIC: 2084 5921 Wines; wine

(G-2850)
CORREVIO LLC
3 Dickinson Dr Ste 101 (19317-8800)
PHONE..................................610 833-6050
Jrgen Raths, *CEO*
Bert Van Den Bergh, *Ch of Bd*
Michael Grau, *CFO*
EMP: 12
SQ FT: 2,913
SALES (est): 2MM **Privately Held**
SIC: 2834 Pharmaceutical preparations

(G-2851)
GAADT PERSPECTIVES LLC
251 S Fairville Rd (19317-9438)
PHONE..................................610 388-7641
John Gaadt,
Suzzane Gaadt,
EMP: 5
SALES: 300K **Privately Held**
WEB: www.gaadt.com
SIC: 8748 3669 Environmental consultant;
visual communication systems

(G-2852)
KEBEICO INC
6 Dickinson Dr Ste 114 (19317-9689)
PHONE..................................610 241-8163
Steve Pai, *President*
EMP: 20
SALES (est): 1.5MM **Privately Held**
SIC: 3365 3431 Machinery castings, alu-
minum; plumbing fixtures: enameled iron
cast iron or pressed metal

(G-2853)
KYNECTIV INC
1820 Masters Way (19317-9710)
P.O. Box 461 (19317-0461)
PHONE..................................484 899-0746
Robert J Yayac, *CEO*
Jack Lavender, *Vice Pres*
EMP: 17
SALES (est): 190.8K **Privately Held**
SIC: 7372 Business oriented computer
software

(G-2854)
LANE DISPLAY INC
Also Called: Lane Signs
210 Wilmington W (19317)
PHONE..................................610 361-1110
Edward Protesto, *CEO*
Gary Brick, *Vice Pres*
Bernard Hilman, *Treasurer*
EMP: 3
SALES (est): 226.4K **Privately Held**
SIC: 3993 Signs & advertising specialties

(G-2855)
MCNS TECHNOLOGIES LLC
608 Chadds Ford Dr # 300 (19317-7364)
PHONE..................................610 269-2891
Michael Magann,
Donna Madden,
EMP: 3
SQ FT: 380
SALES (est): 168.9K **Privately Held**
SIC: 7372 7373 5734 4899 Business ori-
ented computer software; office computer
automation systems integration; value-
added resellers, computer systems; per-
sonal computers; communication signal
enhancement network system

(G-2856)
MIVATEK GLOBAL LLC
6 Dickinson Dr Ste 215 (19317-9689)
PHONE..................................610 358-5120
Brendan Hogan, *Mng Member*
EMP: 12
SQ FT: 3,000
SALES: 11MM **Privately Held**
SIC: 3559 Semiconductor manufacturing
machinery

(G-2857)
NUVANNA LLC
225 Wilmington W Chester (19317-9011)
PHONE..................................844 611-2324
Alvaro Vaselli,
EMP: 5
SALES (est): 215.1K **Privately Held**
SIC: 2515 Mattresses, containing felt, foam
rubber, urethane, etc.

(G-2858)
PERDUE FARMS INC
314 Kennett Pike (19317-8211)
P.O. Box 142, Mendenhall (19357-0142)
PHONE..................................610 388-1385
EMP: 191
SALES (corp-wide): 5.7B **Privately Held**
SIC: 2015 Poultry slaughtering & process-
ing
PA: Perdue Farms Inc.
31149 Old Ocean City Rd
Salisbury MD 21804
410 543-3000

(G-2859)
RADIUS SYSTEMS LLC
101 Ponds Edge Dr Ste 201 (19317-8302)
P.O. Box 75 (19317-0075)
PHONE..................................610 388-9940
Ken Kozma, *Opers Staff*
Joshua Holohan, *Engineer*
Nolan Kinslow, *Engineer*
James Tiefenthaler, *Engineer*
Eric Wittendorf, *Engineer*
EMP: 38
SALES (est): 2.2MM **Privately Held**
WEB: www.radiussystemsllc.com
SIC: 1731 5084 3822 1796 Computer-
ized controls installation; energy manage-
ment controls; instruments & control
equipment; controlling instruments & ac-
cessories; temperature controls, auto-
matic; installing building equipment

(G-2860)
SPITZ INC
700 Brandywine Dr (19317-9669)
P.O. Box 198 (19317-0198)
PHONE..................................610 459-5200
Johnathan Shaw, *President*
John Fogleman, *Vice Pres*
Rys Hess, *Engineer*
Brad Thompson, *Engineer*
Paul L Dailey Jr, *CFO*
▲ EMP: 58 EST: 1945
SQ FT: 46,000
SALES (est): 13.2MM
SALES (corp-wide): 37.1MM **Publicly
Held**
WEB: www.spitzinc.com
SIC: 3861 3827 Projectors, still or motion
picture, silent or sound; screens, projec-
tion; optical instruments & lenses
PA: Evans & Sutherland Computer Corpo-
ration
770 S Komas Dr
Salt Lake City UT 84108
801 588-1000

(G-2861)
TOMARK-WORTHEN LLC
64 Watkin Ave (19317-9025)
PHONE..................................610 978-1889
Andreas Rothacker, *Vice Pres*
David Santoleri,
EMP: 3
SALES (est): 237.2K **Privately Held**
SIC: 3083 Thermoplastic laminates: rods,
tubes, plates & sheet

Chalfont
Bucks County

(G-2862)
A & S OLIVE OIL COMPANY INC
1240 Lower State Rd (18914-3418)
PHONE..................................267 483-8379
Helen Seelig, *Principal*
EMP: 3 EST: 2009
SALES (est): 121.3K **Privately Held**
SIC: 2079 Olive oil

(G-2863)
**AMERICAN CULTURE PUBLS
LLC**
Also Called: Africvan American Publications
127 Statesman Rd (18914-3580)
PHONE..................................267 608-9734
Harold Tate, *Mng Member*
EMP: 5 EST: 2014
SALES: 110K **Privately Held**
SIC: 2741 Miscellaneous publishing

(G-2864)
BYERS CHOICE LTD
4355 County Line Rd (18914-1825)
P.O. Box 158 (18914-0158)
PHONE..................................215 822-6700
Robert L Byersjr, *President*
Joyce F Byers, *Corp Secy*
Jeffrey D Byers, *Vice Pres*
Dave Dai, *Vice Pres*
Pat Chiarelli, *Production*
▲ EMP: 125 EST: 1978
SQ FT: 95,000
SALES (est): 16.4MM **Privately Held**
WEB: www.byerschoice.com
SIC: 3999 Miniatures

(G-2865)
C CROUTHAMEL & CO INC
186 New Galena Rd (18914-1316)
PHONE..................................215 822-1911
Carl M Crouthamel III, *President*
Linda Glitzer, *Corp Secy*
Carl M Crouthamel Jr, *Vice Pres*
EMP: 5 EST: 1965
SQ FT: 3,800
SALES (est): 700.9K **Privately Held**
SIC: 3599 Machine shop, jobbing & repair

(G-2866)
CIMA NETWORK INC
121 New Britain Blvd (18914-1833)
PHONE..................................267 308-0575
William Lockett, *President*
Keith Denny, *Vice Pres*
Erika Bitzer, *Project Mgr*
James Bussire, *Controller*
Stephanie Duffy, *Controller*
EMP: 70 EST: 2008
SALES: 16.4MM **Privately Held**
SIC: 3993 Signs & advertising specialties

(G-2867)
COLORCON INC
171 New Britain Blvd (18914-1833)
PHONE..................................267 695-7700
Anica Niedziela, *Project Mgr*
Bob Pavitt, *Business Anlyst*
Dennis Cummings, *Branch Mgr*
EMP: 19
SALES (corp-wide): 2.9B **Privately Held**
SIC: 2834 Pharmaceutical preparations
HQ: Colorcon, Inc.
420 Moyer Blvd
West Point PA 19486
215 699-7733

(G-2868)
COMPUTER SOFTWARE INC
Also Called: C S I
100 Highpoint Dr Ste 104 (18914-3926)
PHONE..................................215 822-9100
Jeffery O Smith, *President*
Kenneth A Strongin, *Vice Pres*
EMP: 21
SQ FT: 4,100
SALES (est): 2.5MM **Privately Held**
WEB: www.computersoftwareinc.com
SIC: 7372 Business oriented computer
software

(G-2869)
**CORE TECHNOLOGY GROUP
INC**
140 Independence Ln (18914-1842)
PHONE..................................215 822-0120
J Philip Altomare Jr, *Principal*
John F Iannuzzi, *Principal*
Nicholas Silva, *Principal*
John Iannuzzi, *Engineer*
Gerald D Corkery, *CFO*
EMP: 5
SALES (est): 470.8K **Privately Held**
SIC: 3825 Instruments to measure electric-
ity

(G-2870)
CRANE MAN INC
237 Schoolhouse Rd (18914-1814)
P.O. Box 370 (18914-0370)
PHONE..................................215 996-1033
Pete Nieves-Sosa, *Principal*
EMP: 7
SALES (est): 902.6K **Privately Held**
SIC: 3536 Hoists, cranes & monorails

(G-2871)
DATACAP SYSTEMS INC
100 New Britain Blvd (18914-1832)
PHONE..................................215 997-8989
Terry Zeigler, *President*
Leon Morsillo, *Vice Pres*
Gale Peters, *Vice Pres*
Roland Sigal, *Director*
EMP: 20
SQ FT: 20,000
SALES (est): 4.1MM **Privately Held**
WEB: www.datacapsystems.com
SIC: 3578 3643 3575 Point-of-sale de-
vices; current-carrying wiring devices;
computer terminals

(G-2872)
DELTRONIC LABS INC
120 Liberty Ln (18914-1820)
PHONE..................................215 997-8616
Stephen Horniak, *President*
Molly A Horniak, *Corp Secy*
Brian Mohan, *Prdtn Mgr*
Gary Todd, *Human Res Dir*
◆ EMP: 30
SQ FT: 17,000
SALES (est): 5.9MM **Privately Held**
WEB: www.deltroniclabs.com
SIC: 3679 3993 3625 3613 Electronic
switches; signs & advertising specialties;
relays & industrial controls; switchgear &
switchboard apparatus; computer periph-
eral equipment

(G-2873)
ENDRESS + HAUSER INC
500 Horizon Dr Ste 502 (18914-3962)
PHONE..................................317 535-7138
Wendy Scamuffo, *Engineer*
EMP: 7
SALES (corp-wide): 2.6B **Privately Held**
SIC: 3823 Industrial instrmnts msrmnt dis-
play/control process variable
HQ: Endress + Hauser Inc
2350 Endress Pl
Greenwood IN 46143
317 535-7138

(G-2874)
**EUREKA STONE QUARRY INC
(PA)**
Also Called: Sterling Quarry
Lower Stte Pickertown Rds (18914)
P.O. Box 249 (18914-0249)
PHONE..................................215 822-0593
James D Morrissey, *President*
Robert V Albert, *Vice Pres*
Mary A Morrissey, *Treasurer*
John Stenken, *Sales Executive*
Scott Barcusky, *Admin Sec*
EMP: 20 EST: 1955
SQ FT: 2,400
SALES (est): 24.4MM **Privately Held**
SIC: 2951 5032 Asphalt & asphaltic
paving mixtures (not from refineries);
sand, construction; gravel; stone, crushed
or broken

(G-2875)
FROG CREEK SOCKS
779 N Limekiln Pike (18914-1528)
PHONE..................................215 997-6104
Kathleen Katsarakes, *Owner*
EMP: 4
SALES (est): 191.6K **Privately Held**
SIC: 2252 Socks

(G-2876)
GENOMIND LLC
100 Highpoint Dr Ste 102 (18914-3926)
PHONE..................................877 895-8658
Michael Koffler, *President*
Nancy Grden, *General Mgr*
Scott A Storrer, *COO*
Zia Choudhry, *Senior VP*
Bryce Kasuba, *Vice Pres*

EMP: 25 EST: 2011
SALES (est): 5.7MM Privately Held
SIC: 2834 2836 Medicines, capsuled or
ampuled; biological products, except diagnostic

(G-2877)
**JOHN BEAN TECHNOLOGIES
CORP**
Jbt
400 Highpoint Dr (18914-3924)
PHONE..................................215 822-4600
David C Burdakin, *Exec VP*
Barry Douglas, *Branch Mgr*
EMP: 150 Publicly Held
SIC: 3556 Food products machinery
PA: John Bean Technologies Corporation
70 W Madison St Ste 4400
Chicago IL 60602

(G-2878)
**JOHN R BROMILEY COMPANY
INC**
105 Bristol Rd (18914-3202)
PHONE..................................215 822-7723
John R Bromiley, *President*
Jason E Bromiley, *Vice Pres*
Bradley Landis, *Purchasing*
▲ EMP: 45 EST: 1977
SQ FT: 23,000
SALES (est): 8.6MM Privately Held
WEB: www.bromileymachine.com
SIC: 3599 3545 3541 3451 Machine
shop, jobbing & repair; machine tool ac-
cessories; machine tools, metal cutting
type; screw machine products

(G-2879)
K & B AQUA EXPRESS CO LLC
3169 County Line Rd (18914-3711)
PHONE..................................215 343-2247
Gary Butterworth,
EMP: 5
SALES (est): 350K Privately Held
SIC: 3531 Batching plants, for aggregate
concrete & bulk cement

(G-2880)
**KEMET INVESTMENT LTD
PARTNR**
200 Highpoint Dr Ste 215 (18914-3925)
PHONE..................................215 822-1550
Joe Pierce III, *President*
EMP: 3
SALES (est): 171K Privately Held
SIC: 3675 Electronic capacitors

(G-2881)
KEMET INVESTMENTS INC
200 Highpoint Dr Ste 215 (18914-3925)
PHONE..................................215 822-1550
Tom Lomax, *CFO*
EMP: 10
SQ FT: 3,000
SALES (est): 828.6K Privately Held
SIC: 3675 Electronic capacitors

(G-2882)
KINDLE CREATIONS INC
4355 County Line Rd (18914-1825)
P.O. Box 158 (18914-0158)
PHONE..................................215 997-6878
Jeff Byers, *President*
EMP: 20
SALES (est): 1.4MM Privately Held
SIC: 3089 Novelties, plastic

(G-2883)
**ME KEN + JEN CRATIVE SVCS
LLC**
Also Called: Mkj Creative
303 Nottingham Pl (18914-2454)
PHONE..................................215 997-2355
Jennifer M Whitesell,
EMP: 4
SALES (est): 535.3K Privately Held
WEB: www.mkjcreative.com
SIC: 7336 7389 2791 7335 Graphic arts
& related design; ; typesetting, computer
controlled; commercial photography; ad-
vertising agencies; marketing consulting
services

(G-2884)
**PRIME IMAGE DELAWARE INC
(PA)**
200 Highpoint Dr Ste 215 (18914-3925)
PHONE..................................215 822-1561
W Thomas Lomax, *CFO*
Gary Gatchell, *CFO*
EMP: 6
SALES: 950K Privately Held
SIC: 3663 Radio & TV communications
equipment

(G-2885)
ROLL FORMER CORPORATION
140 Independence Ln (18914-1842)
PHONE..................................215 997-2511
Phil Altomare, *President*
Gerald D Corkery, *Chairman*
Bob Schultz, *Vice Pres*
Robert Schultz, *Vice Pres*
Jesse Scott, *Prdtn Mgr*
▼ EMP: 28
SQ FT: 17,000
SALES (est): 5.8MM Privately Held
WEB: www.rollformercorp.com
SIC: 3444 Sheet metalwork

(G-2886)
ROMAN PRESS INC
Also Called: Todays Hospitalist
142 Upper Stump Rd (18914-1509)
PHONE..................................215 997-9650
Ed Doyle, *CEO*
Phyllis Maguire, *Editor*
Ashley Doyle, *CFO*
Dianne McNally, *Manager*
EMP: 6
SALES: 486K Privately Held
WEB: www.todayshospitalist.com
SIC: 2721 5192 Magazines: publishing
only, not printed on site; magazines

(G-2887)
SIEMENS INDUSTRY INC
100 Highpoint Dr Ste 101 (18914-3926)
PHONE..................................215 712-0280
Dale Berschner, *Manager*
EMP: 43
SALES (corp-wide): 95B Privately Held
SIC: 3823 Water quality monitoring & con-
trol systems
HQ: Siemens Industry, Inc.
1000 Deerfield Pkwy
Buffalo Grove IL 60089
800 743-6367

(G-2888)
SMITH PRINTS INC
74 Park Ave Ste G2 (18914-2947)
PHONE..................................215 997-8077
Michael J Smith, *President*
Susan Smith, *Bookkeeper*
EMP: 7
SALES: 500K Privately Held
WEB: www.smithprints.com
SIC: 5699 2759 2395 7389 T-shirts, cus-
tom printed; commercial printing; embroi-
dery & art needlework; advertising,
promotional & trade show services

(G-2889)
SOCIETY OF CLINICAL
Also Called: Socra
530 W Butler Ave Ste 2 (18914-3209)
PHONE..................................215 822-8644
Erich Lukas, *Exec Dir*
EMP: 12
SALES (est): 3.7MM Privately Held
WEB: www.socra.org
SIC: 8299 7372 Educational services; ap-
plication computer software

(G-2890)
SUN PRIME ENERGY LLC
1100 Horizon Cir (18914-3971)
PHONE..................................215 962-4196
EMP: 3 EST: 2010
SALES (est): 176.3K Privately Held
SIC: 3674 Solar cells

(G-2891)
**TEVA PHARMACEUTICALS USA
INC**
111 New Britain Blvd (18914-1833)
PHONE..................................215 591-3000

Sharon Jones, *Director*
EMP: 91
SALES (corp-wide): 18.8B Privately Held
SIC: 2834 Pharmaceutical preparations
HQ: Teva Pharmaceuticals Usa, Inc.
1090 Horsham Rd
North Wales PA 19454
215 591-3000

(G-2892)
TIKI KEVS
3462 Limekiln Pike (18914-3608)
PHONE..................................267 718-4527
Kevin Dunn, *Principal*
EMP: 4
SALES (est): 268.7K Privately Held
SIC: 2511 Wood household furniture

(G-2893)
TOWER HILL BERERY
237 W Butler Ave (18914-3020)
PHONE..................................267 308-8992
EMP: 4
SALES (est): 292.4K Privately Held
SIC: 2082 Beer (alcoholic beverage)

(G-2894)
**WEARFORCE NORTH AMERICA
LLC**
69 Bristol Rd (18914-3201)
PHONE..................................215 996-1770
Kevin Chapman, *Mng Member*
▲ EMP: 10
SALES (est): 2.7MM Privately Held
SIC: 5084 3441 Drilling equipment, ex-
cluding bits; fabricated structural metal

Chalk Hill
Fayette County

(G-2895)
**CHRISTIAN W KLAY WINERY
INC**
Also Called: Fayette Springs Farm
412 Fayette Springs Rd (15421)
P.O. Box 309 (15421-0309)
PHONE..................................724 439-3424
Sharon Klay, *President*
EMP: 10
SALES (est): 1MM Privately Held
WEB: www.cwklaywinery.com
SIC: 2084 Wines

Chambersburg
Franklin County

(G-2896)
A KUHNS CABINETS
2979 Newcomer Rd (17202-6714)
PHONE..................................717 263-4306
Adrian Kuhns, *Principal*
EMP: 4
SALES (est): 384.7K Privately Held
SIC: 2434 Wood kitchen cabinets

(G-2897)
**ADVANCED ELECTRONICS
SYSTEMS (PA)**
Also Called: Stediwatt
2005 Lincoln Way E (17202-3391)
PHONE..................................717 263-5681
Richard L Diller, *President*
EMP: 6
SQ FT: 6,500
SALES (est): 1MM Privately Held
WEB: www.stediwatt.com
SIC: 3629 3679 Electronic generation
equipment; electronic loads & power sup-
plies

(G-2898)
AFCO C&S LLC
5121 Coffey Ave (17201-4127)
PHONE..................................717 264-9147
Mike Hinkle, *CEO*
EMP: 9 EST: 2012
SALES (est): 975.5K Privately Held
SIC: 2842 3441 2992 Cleaning or polish-
ing preparations; fabricated structural
metal; lubricating oils & greases

(G-2899)
ALEX C FERGUSSON LLC (PA)
Also Called: Afco
5121 Coffey Ave Ste D (17201-4127)
PHONE..................................717 264-9147
Michael Hinkle, *President*
Thomas Curtis, *CFO*
Misty Runyon, *Marketing Staff*
Tarantino Chris, *Consultant*
Matt Reed, *Info Tech Mgr*
◆ EMP: 65
SALES (est): 21.8MM Privately Held
WEB: www.afco.net
SIC: 2842 3441 2992 2841 Cleaning or
polishing preparations; fabricated struc-
tural metal; lubricating oils & greases;
soap & other detergents

(G-2900)
**ALPHA SPACE CONTROL CO
INC**
1580 Gabler Rd (17201-9501)
PHONE..................................717 263-0182
Richard W Pryor, *President*
Christopher S Meighan, *Vice Pres*
Ashley Sawyer, *Sales Staff*
Bernadette Sevast, *Admin Sec*
EMP: 7
SQ FT: 7,300
SALES: 6.3MM Privately Held
WEB: www.alphaspacecontrol.com
SIC: 1721 7389 3669 Pavement marking
contractor; sign painting & lettering shop;
pedestrian traffic control equipment

(G-2901)
**ALTERNATE HEATING SYSTEMS
LLC**
Also Called: Ahs Acquisition
1086 Wayne Ave (17201-2917)
PHONE..................................717 261-0922
Scott Mentzer,
Brian Wise,
EMP: 35
SALES (est): 3.6MM Privately Held
WEB: www.woodgun.com
SIC: 3443 Fabricated plate work (boiler
shop)

(G-2902)
ALTRA INDUSTRIAL MOTION
440 5th Ave (17201-1763)
PHONE..................................781 917-0600
EMP: 3
SALES (est): 243.7K Privately Held
SIC: 3568 Power transmission equipment

(G-2903)
**ALTRA INDUSTRIAL MOTION
CORP**
86 Monroe Dr (17201-7914)
PHONE..................................717 261-2550
EMP: 3
SALES (corp-wide): 1.1B Publicly Held
SIC: 3568 Power transmission equipment
PA: Altra Industrial Motion Corp.
300 Granite St Ste 201
Braintree MA 02184
781 917-0600

(G-2904)
**AMERICAN STAIR & CABINETRY
INC**
5171 Innovation Way (17201-4187)
PHONE..................................717 709-1061
John Lombardozzi, *CEO*
Jeff Rainess, *President*
Michael Troiano, *CFO*
EMP: 120
SQ FT: 100,000
SALES (est): 10.1MM
SALES (corp-wide): 86.7MM Privately
Held
WEB: www.signaturecos.com
SIC: 2431 Staircases, stairs & railings
PA: The Laminate Company
6612 James Madison Hwy
Haymarket VA 20169
703 753-0699

GEOGRAPHIC

(G-2905)
APPLEGATE INSUL SYSTEMS INC
Also Called: Applegate Manufacturing
1050 Superior Ave Bldg 53 (17201-7859)
PHONE.....................................717 709-0533
John Powlison, *Manager*
EMP: 30 **Privately Held**
SIC: 2493 2499 Insulation & roofing material, reconstituted wood; mulch or sawdust products, wood
PA: Applegate Insulation Systems, Inc.
1000 Highview Dr
Webberville MI 48892

(G-2906)
ART SIGN COMPANY
470 Nelson St (17201-1618)
PHONE.....................................717 264-4211
Edwin L Patterson, *Owner*
Jason Fisher,
EMP: 8
SQ FT: 5,300
SALES (est): 605K **Privately Held**
SIC: 7389 3993 Sign painting & lettering shop; signs & advertising specialties

(G-2907)
ATLAS INSTRUMENT CO INC
144 Oyler Dr (17201-3287)
PHONE.....................................717 267-1250
Terry Olson, *President*
Julie Olson, *Corp Secy*
Gary Olson, *Vice Pres*
Julie M Olson, *Manager*
EMP: 8
SQ FT: 10,000
SALES: 800K **Privately Held**
WEB: www.atlasinstrument.com
SIC: 3827 7699 Optical instruments & apparatus; optical instrument repair; surveying instrument repair; nautical & navigational instrument repair

(G-2908)
B WISE TRAILERS
1086 Wayne Ave (17201-2917)
PHONE.....................................717 261-0922
Brian Wise, *Principal*
EMP: 13 EST: 2012
SALES (est): 4.3MM **Privately Held**
SIC: 3499 Fire- or burglary-resistive products

(G-2909)
BAXTER GROUP INC
941 Progress Rd (17201-3273)
PHONE.....................................717 263-7341
Jocelyne Melton, *President*
Pat Grove, *Senior Mgr*
Tiffany Weathersby, *Director*
Heather Bess, *Administration*
EMP: 17
SQ FT: 3,200
SALES: 2.1MM **Privately Held**
WEB: www.baxtergroupinc.com
SIC: 1799 2851 7532 1742 Asbestos removal & encapsulation; paint removers; interior repair services; insulation, buildings

(G-2910)
BELDEN INC
Hirschmann Electronics
518 Cleveland Ave Ste 2a (17201-3400)
PHONE.....................................717 263-7655
Bernard Baruffalo, *Engineer*
John Mower, *Engineer*
Mark Hendel, *Branch Mgr*
EMP: 26
SALES (corp-wide): 2.5B **Publicly Held**
SIC: 3625 3678 5065 Relays & industrial controls; electronic connectors; communication equipment
PA: Belden Inc.
1 N Brentwood Blvd Fl 15
Saint Louis MO 63105
314 854-8000

(G-2911)
BLACK LOGGING
3880 Crottlestown Rd (17202-8027)
PHONE.....................................717 263-6446
Kevin Black, *Principal*
EMP: 3

SALES (est): 160K **Privately Held**
SIC: 2411 Logging

(G-2912)
BLUE MOUNTAIN SPORTS AP INC
763 S 2nd St (17201-3530)
PHONE.....................................717 263-4124
Jeremy Smith, *President*
Robert Ellis, *Vice Pres*
EMP: 8
SALES: 550K **Privately Held**
WEB: www.bluemountainsportsonline.com
SIC: 2759 2395 5699 Screen printing; embroidery & art needlework; sports apparel

(G-2913)
BRI-MAR MANUFACTURING LLC
1086 Wayne Ave Ste 2 (17201-2917)
PHONE.....................................717 263-6116
Kevin Kelley, *President*
Kevin Killer, *COO*
Brian Wise,
EMP: 50
SQ FT: 10,000
SALES (est): 4.6MM **Privately Held**
WEB: www.bri-mar.com
SIC: 3715 3799 3999 Truck trailers; trailers & trailer equipment; atomizers, toiletry

(G-2914)
BURNSIDE AMERICA INC
5900 Coffey Ave (17201-4102)
PHONE.....................................717 414-1509
Joe Sabol, *General Mgr*
EMP: 3
SALES: 300K
SALES (corp-wide): 48.5MM **Privately Held**
SIC: 3593 Fluid power cylinders, hydraulic or pneumatic
PA: Burnside Autocyl (Tullow) Limited
Tullow Industrial Estate
Carlow
599 151-200

(G-2915)
CASTEK INNOVATIONS INC
4450 Sunset Pike (17202-9601)
PHONE.....................................717 267-2748
Kurt A Grigg, *President*
Richard C Petek, *Treasurer*
Daniel C Petek, *Admin Sec*
EMP: 20
SQ FT: 14,400
SALES (est): 3.8MM **Privately Held**
WEB: www.dcpattern.com
SIC: 3543 3544 Industrial patterns; special dies, tools, jigs & fixtures

(G-2916)
CHAMBERSBURG MACHINE CO INC
250 Sunset Blvd W (17202-9602)
PHONE.....................................717 264-7111
Brian Bakner, *President*
Brian W Bakner, *President*
Brian A Seniw, *President*
EMP: 12
SQ FT: 30,000
SALES (est): 1.9MM **Privately Held**
SIC: 3599 Machine shop, jobbing & repair

(G-2917)
CHAMBERSBURG OPTICAL SERVICE
227 Southgate Mall (17201-2448)
PHONE.....................................717 263-4898
EMP: 4 EST: 1972
SQ FT: 1,400
SALES: 170K **Privately Held**
SIC: 3851 Mfg Ophthalmic Goods

(G-2918)
CHAMBERSBURG SCREEN PRINT EMB
1495 Lincoln Way E # 105 (17202-3395)
PHONE.....................................717 262-2111
Anton Ha, *Principal*
EMP: 5
SALES (est): 391K **Privately Held**
SIC: 2752 Commercial printing, lithographic

(G-2919)
COM PROS INC
584 W Loudon St (17201-2030)
PHONE.....................................717 264-2769
Dave Crouse, *Branch Mgr*
EMP: 5
SALES (corp-wide): 4.6MM **Privately Held**
WEB: www.comprosinc.com
SIC: 3679 Headphones, radio
PA: Com Pros, Inc.
400 Highland Ave
Altoona PA 16602
814 946-8100

(G-2920)
CONSOLIDATED CONTAINER CO LLC
1501 Orchard Dr (17201-4812)
PHONE.....................................717 267-3533
Ken Gabler, *Manager*
EMP: 13
SALES (corp-wide): 14B **Publicly Held**
WEB: www.mesa-industries.com
SIC: 3089 Plastic containers, except foam
HQ: Consolidated Container Company, Llc
2500 Windy Ridge Pkwy Se # 1400
Atlanta GA 30339
678 742-4600

(G-2921)
CRESTON E LOCKBAUM INC
89 Industrial Dr (17201-3233)
PHONE.....................................717 414-6885
Ray E Lockbaum, *President*
EMP: 4
SQ FT: 8,500
SALES (est): 465.5K **Privately Held**
SIC: 3444 Sheet metalwork

(G-2922)
CUSTOM STAIR BUILDERS INC
1271 Candice Ln (17201-8912)
PHONE.....................................717 261-0551
Steven Guyer, *President*
Andrew P Frey, *Treasurer*
EMP: 3
SALES (est): 442.2K **Privately Held**
WEB: www.customstairs.com
SIC: 2431 1521 Millwork; single-family housing construction

(G-2923)
DAWSON PERFORMANCE INC
Also Called: Dp Machining & Fabrication
5274 Sunset Pike (17202-9604)
PHONE.....................................717 261-1414
Margaret L Dawson, *President*
Larry Idawson, *Vice Pres*
James Cdawson, *Treasurer*
Jim Dawnson, *Director*
James C Dawson, *Admin Sec*
▼ EMP: 14
SALES (est): 3.3MM **Privately Held**
WEB: www.dawsonperformance.com
SIC: 3599 3993 Machine shop, jobbing & repair; signs & advertising specialties

(G-2924)
DEETAG USA INC
1683 Opputunity Ave (17201)
PHONE.....................................828 465-2644
EMP: 8
SALES (corp-wide): 14.7MM **Privately Held**
SIC: 3545 Machine tool accessories
HQ: Deetag U.S.A. Inc.
1232 Fedex Dr Sw
Conover NC 28613
828 465-2644

(G-2925)
DIETRICH BROS DREAM CATCHR FLY
416 Cumberland Ave (17201-3743)
PHONE.....................................717 267-0515
Wyatt Dietrich, *Principal*
EMP: 3 EST: 2007
SALES (est): 146.3K **Privately Held**
SIC: 2048 Fish food

(G-2926)
E-LYNXX CORPORATION
Also Called: Elynxx Solutions
1051 Sheffler Dr Ste W (17201-4851)
PHONE.....................................717 709-0990
Michael Jackson, *CEO*
William Gindlesperger, *Chairman*
Maxine L Gindlesperger, *COO*
Nathan Rotz, *COO*
Debbie Snider, *Senior VP*
EMP: 23
SQ FT: 14,000
SALES (est): 3.9MM **Privately Held**
WEB: www.e-lynxx.com
SIC: 7372 Application computer software

(G-2927)
EDGE RUBBER LLC
811 Progress Rd (17201-3257)
PHONE.....................................717 660-2353
Sam Kauffman,
EMP: 22
SALES: 2MM **Privately Held**
SIC: 3999 Manufacturing industries

(G-2928)
EDGE RUBBER RECYCLING LLC
811 Progress Rd (17201-3257)
PHONE.....................................717 660-2353
Derek Martin,
EMP: 22
SALES (est): 762.1K
SALES (corp-wide): 8MM **Privately Held**
SIC: 3069 Fabricated rubber products
PA: Hti Recycling, Llc
490 Ohio St
Lockport NY 14094
716 433-9294

(G-2929)
EFFECTIVE SOFTWARE PRODUCTS
Also Called: ESP
2038 Lincoln Way E Ste A (17202-3362)
PHONE.....................................717 267-2054
John L Hockensmith Jr, *President*
EMP: 7
SQ FT: 6,800
SALES (est): 700K **Privately Held**
SIC: 5734 5112 3571 7378 Computer software & accessories; business forms; personal computers (microcomputers); computer maintenance & repair

(G-2930)
EPIROC USA LLC
5105 Technology Ave (17201-7876)
PHONE.....................................717 552-9694
EMP: 9
SALES (corp-wide): 85.5MM **Privately Held**
SIC: 3532 Drills, bits & similar equipment
PA: Epiroc Usa Llc
3700 E 68th Ave
Commerce City CO 80022
303 287-8822

(G-2931)
F&M SURFACES INC
Also Called: Urns & Ivy
2295 Molly Pitcher Hwy (17202-9202)
PHONE.....................................717 267-3799
Dale Frey, *President*
Chris Coblentz, *Warehouse Mgr*
Rachel Frey, *Admin Sec*
▲ EMP: 9
SQ FT: 19,000
SALES (est): 1.6MM **Privately Held**
WEB: www.fmsurfaces.com
SIC: 5713 3272 Vinyl floor covering; stone, cast concrete

(G-2932)
FRANKLIN CLOTHING COMPANY INC
5121 Innovation Way # 6 (17201-4187)
PHONE.....................................717 264-5768
Mark Falcone, *CEO*
Spencer Hays, *President*
▲ EMP: 150
SQ FT: 60,000

SALES (est): 15.7MM
SALES (corp-wide): 631.4MM **Privately Held**
WEB: www.ashertrousers.com
SIC: 2253 Pants, slacks or trousers, knit
PA: Tom James Company
263 Seaboard Ln
Franklin TN 37067
615 771-1122

(G-2933)
FRANKLIN SHOPPER
Also Called: Franklin Shopper, The
25 Penncraft Ave Ste 405 (17201-1677)
PHONE.................................717 263-0359
Margaret Ehle, *President*
Athena Emond, *Accounts Exec*
Pamela Fridinger, *Accounts Exec*
Bryan Rotz, *Web Dvlpr*
EMP: 15 **EST:** 1946
SQ FT: 2,000
SALES (est): 940.8K **Privately Held**
WEB: www.mix95.com
SIC: 2711 Newspapers: publishing only,
not printed on site

(G-2934)
FREYS FARM DAIRY LLC
1587 Newcomer Rd (17202-9016)
PHONE.................................717 860-8015
Curtis Frey, *Partner*
EMP: 4
SALES (est): 288.2K **Privately Held**
SIC: 1241 Coal mining services

(G-2935)
GATES CORPORATION
1675 Orchard Dr (17201-9206)
PHONE.................................717 267-7000
Dennis Conway, *General Mgr*
EMP: 236
SALES (corp-wide): 3.3B **Publicly Held**
SIC: 3052 Rubber belting
HQ: The Gates Corporation
1144 15th St Ste 1400
Denver CO 80202
303 744-1911

(G-2936)
GOSHORN INDUSTRIES LLC
Also Called: D & D Sawmill Parts and Svc
3911 Jack Rd (17202-9206)
PHONE.................................717 369-3654
Shawn A Goshorn, *Mng Member*
EMP: 3
SALES: 250K **Privately Held**
SIC: 3599 5211 7699 Machine shop, job-
bing & repair; planing mill products & lum-
ber; industrial equipment services

(G-2937)
HAMMAKER EAST
118 Siloam Rd (17201-8901)
PHONE.................................717 263-0434
Jeff Statlor, *Manager*
EMP: 3
SALES (corp-wide): 195.6MM **Privately
Held**
SIC: 2951 Asphalt paving mixtures &
blocks
HQ: Hammaker East
285 Kappa Dr Ste 300
Pittsburgh PA 15238

(G-2938)
**HANGER PRSTHETCS & ORTHO
INC**
Also Called: Teufel & Sons
765 5th Ave Ste D (17201-4228)
PHONE.................................717 264-7117
Brent Shein, *General Mgr*
EMP: 5
SALES (corp-wide): 1B **Publicly Held**
SIC: 3842 Orthopedic appliances
HQ: Hanger Prosthetics & Orthotics, Inc.
10910 Domain Dr Ste 300
Austin TX 78758
512 777-3800

(G-2939)
**HAWK INDUSTRIAL SERVICES
LLC**
4593 Coontown Rd (17202-9225)
PHONE.................................717 658-4332
Kevin Hawk,
EMP: 12

SALES (est): 1MM **Privately Held**
SIC: 8744 7692 7699 Base maintenance
(providing personnel on continuing basis);
welding repair; industrial machinery &
equipment repair

(G-2940)
**HIRSCHMANN ELECTRONICS
INC**
1665 Orchard Dr (17201-9206)
PHONE.................................717 217-2200
Mark Hendle, *President*
Christopher Bala, *Vice Pres*
David Joy, *Vice Pres*
Brian Mell, *Opers Staff*
Ruth Clem,
EMP: 15
SALES: 25MM **Privately Held**
SIC: 5013 5065 3669 3825 Automotive
supplies & parts; connectors, electronic;
communication equipment; transportation
signaling devices; instruments to measure
electricity; electronic connectors; radio &
TV communications equipment

(G-2941)
INGERSOLL-RAND COMPANY
1280 Superior Ave (17201-7839)
PHONE.................................717 532-9181
John Carmack, *Branch Mgr*
EMP: 90 **Privately Held**
WEB: www.ingersoll-rand.com
SIC: 3561 Pumps & pumping equipment
HQ: Ingersoll-Rand Company
800 Beaty St Ste B
Davidson NC 28036
704 655-4000

(G-2942)
**INTERNATIONAL MARKETING
INC (PA)**
Also Called: IMI
3183 Black Gap Rd (17202-9771)
PHONE.................................717 264-5819
Robert D Fogal Sr, *CEO*
Robert D Fogal Jr, *President*
Warren Whitsel, *Vice Pres*
Bernard Kotula, *CFO*
Thomas Eisenhart, *Director*
◆ **EMP:** 17 **EST:** 1973
SQ FT: 4,100
SALES (est): 5.8MM **Privately Held**
WEB: www.imiproducts.com
SIC: 3011 3559 2851 Tire sundries or tire
repair materials, rubber; automotive re-
lated machinery; paints & allied products

(G-2943)
**INTERNATIONAL ROAD
DYNAMICS**
1002 S Main St (17201-3240)
PHONE.................................717 264-2077
Bruce Myers, *Principal*
EMP: 3
SALES (corp-wide): 49.3MM **Privately
Held**
SIC: 7372 Prepackaged software
PA: International Road Dynamics Inc
702 43rd St E
Saskatoon SK S7K 3
306 653-6600

(G-2944)
ITT CORPORATION
1425 Excel Ave (17201-7849)
PHONE.................................717 262-2945
EMP: 4
SALES (corp-wide): 2.7B **Publicly Held**
SIC: 3594 Fluid power pumps & motors
HQ: Itt Llc
1133 Westchester Ave N-100
White Plains NY 10604
914 641-2000

(G-2945)
J S H INDUSTRIES LLC
5110 Technology Ave (17201-7876)
PHONE.................................717 267-3566
John Hopple,
▲ **EMP:** 4
SQ FT: 3,000
SALES (est): 572.2K **Privately Held**
WEB: www.jshindustries.com
SIC: 3714 5085 Bearings, motor vehicle;
bearings

(G-2946)
JOHN H BRICKER WELDING
1354 Sollenberger Rd (17202-8635)
PHONE.................................717 263-5588
John H Bricker, *Owner*
EMP: 10
SQ FT: 12,000
SALES (est): 729.6K **Privately Held**
SIC: 7692 3523 3441 Welding repair;
farm machinery & equipment; fabricated
structural metal

(G-2947)
**KEYSTONE METAL
STRUCTURES LLC**
792 Coble Rd (17202-9429)
PHONE.................................717 816-3631
Keith Sensenig, *Mng Member*
EMP: 4
SALES: 250K **Privately Held**
SIC: 3448 Prefabricated metal buildings

(G-2948)
KNEPPERS KLEEN WATER
2793 Wiles Rd (17202-9387)
PHONE.................................717 264-9715
Loren Knepper, *Owner*
EMP: 3
SALES (est): 423.1K **Privately Held**
SIC: 3589 Water treatment equipment, in-
dustrial

(G-2949)
**KNOUSE FOODS COOPERATIVE
INC**
421 Grant St (17201-1631)
PHONE.................................717 263-9177
William Schnabel, *Manager*
EMP: 264
SALES (corp-wide): 281.7MM **Privately
Held**
SIC: 2033 Fruit juices: fresh
PA: Knouse Foods Cooperative, Inc.
800 Pach Glen Idaville Rd
Peach Glen PA 17375
717 677-8181

(G-2950)
L&S STONE LLC
Also Called: L & S Fireplace Shoppe
462 Gateway Ave (17201-7351)
PHONE.................................717 264-3559
Eugene Strite, *Branch Mgr*
EMP: 15 **Privately Held**
WEB: www.lsfireplace.com
SIC: 3281 Cut stone & stone products
HQ: L&S Stone Llc
1370 Grand Ave Ste B
San Marcos CA 92078
760 736-3232

(G-2951)
LEGACY MARK LLC
284 Overhill Dr (17202-3173)
P.O. Box 333 (17201-0333)
PHONE.................................800 444-9260
Robert Mills,
EMP: 5
SALES (est): 122.1K **Privately Held**
SIC: 0782 7372 Cemetery upkeep serv-
ices; application computer software

(G-2952)
LESHER MACHINE SHOP INC
5522 Wayne Rd (17202-6701)
PHONE.................................717 263-0673
Dana Lesher, *President*
EMP: 5
SQ FT: 4,000
SALES: 700K **Privately Held**
SIC: 3599 Machine shop, jobbing & repair

(G-2953)
LEWRENE INTERIORS
110 Industrial Dr (17201-3217)
PHONE.................................717 263-8300
Jimmy Freeze, *President*
Deborah A Schreiber Ott, *President*
EMP: 8 **EST:** 1965
SQ FT: 12,000
SALES: 570.7K **Privately Held**
WEB: www.lewreneinteriors.com
SIC: 2391 5023 Draperies, plastic & tex-
tile: from purchased materials; draperies;
curtains

(G-2954)
**LOCKHEED MARTIN
CORPORATION**
Also Called: Missiles and Fire Control
Advantage Ave Bldg 13 (17201)
PHONE.................................717 267-5796
Tom Whiteway, *Manager*
EMP: 17 **Publicly Held**
SIC: 3812 Search & navigation equipment
PA: Lockheed Martin Corporation
6801 Rockledge Dr
Bethesda MD 20817

(G-2955)
MACHINE SPECIALTIES
600 Paper Mill Rd (17201-9280)
PHONE.................................717 264-0061
Gene Martin, *Owner*
EMP: 3
SALES: 150K **Privately Held**
SIC: 3599 7692 7699 Machine shop, job-
bing & repair; welding repair; industrial
equipment services; agricultural equip-
ment repair services

(G-2956)
MAJESTIC WINDSOCKS
Also Called: Majestic Flyers
2690 Williamsburg Cir (17202-9752)
P.O. Box 73, Scotland (17254-0073)
PHONE.................................717 264-3113
Mary Ellen Bongiorno, *Owner*
Ray Bongiorno, *Owner*
EMP: 5
SALES: 225K **Privately Held**
SIC: 2399 5131 Banners, pennants &
flags; flags & banners

(G-2957)
**MARTINS FMOUS PSTRY
SHOPPE INC (PA)**
1000 Potato Roll Ln (17202-8897)
PHONE.................................717 263-9580
James A Martin, *President*
Ronald Gipe, *Exec VP*
Ronald G Gipe, *Vice Pres*
James Martin, *Vice Pres*
Tony Martin, *Vice Pres*
◆ **EMP:** 250
SQ FT: 39,000
SALES (est): 152.9MM **Privately Held**
WEB: www.mfps.com
SIC: 2051 Rolls, bread type: fresh or
frozen; buns, bread type: fresh or frozen

(G-2958)
**MARTINS FMOUS PSTRY
SHOPPE INC**
1000 Potato Roll Ln (17202-8897)
PHONE.................................717 263-9580
Sharie Flair, *Manager*
EMP: 200
SALES (corp-wide): 152.9MM **Privately
Held**
WEB: www.mfps.com
SIC: 2051 Rolls, bread type: fresh or
frozen; buns, bread type: fresh or frozen
PA: Martin's Famous Pastry Shoppe, Inc.
1000 Potato Roll Ln
Chambersburg PA 17202
717 263-9580

(G-2959)
**MCCLEARY HEATING &
COOLING LLC**
Also Called: Honeywell Authorized Dealer
198 Sunset Blvd E (17202-7953)
PHONE.................................717 263-3833
Matthew R McCleary,
EMP: 15 **EST:** 2008
SALES (est): 565K **Privately Held**
SIC: 3564 3433 1711 Filters, air: fur-
naces, air conditioning equipment, etc.;
heating equipment, except electric; heat-
ing systems repair & maintenance; heat-
ing & air conditioning contractors; warm
air heating & air conditioning contractor

(G-2960)
MITITECH LLC
Also Called: Mitigation Technologies
40 N 2nd St (17201-1820)
P.O. Box 231, Mercersburg (17236-0231)
PHONE.................................410 309-9447
Craig Schwartz, *Mng Member*

▲ = Import ▼=Export
◆ =Import/Export

Sarah Reed,
EMP: 4
SALES (est): 903.2K **Privately Held**
SIC: 3699 Security devices

(G-2961)
MORLATTON POST CARD CLUB
806 Stanley Ave (17201-2838)
PHONE..................................717 263-1638
Leon Rowe, *President*
EMP: 20 EST: 1975
SALES (est): 1MM **Privately Held**
SIC: 2752 Post cards, picture: lithographed

(G-2962)
NITTERHOUSE CONCRETE PDTS INC
2655 Molly Pitcher Hwy (17202-7220)
P.O. Box 2013 (17201-0813)
PHONE..................................717 207-7837
Mark T Taylor, *President*
Lindsey S Lemaster, *Corp Secy*
John H Gorrell Jr, *Vice Pres*
John M Jones, *Vice Pres*
Clifford Miles, *Vice Pres*
▲ **EMP:** 165 EST: 1923
SQ FT: 127,770
SALES (est): 29.7MM **Privately Held**
WEB: www.nitterhouse.com
SIC: 3272 5999 Prestressed concrete products; concrete products, precast; concrete products, pre-cast

(G-2963)
NITTERHOUSE MASONRY PDTS LLC
859 Cleveland Ave (17201-3728)
P.O. Box 692 (17201-0692)
PHONE..................................717 268-4137
Matt Diller, *General Mgr*
Barry A Diller, *Vice Pres*
Derek Little, *Sales Staff*
Karen Nitterhouse Diller,
William K Nitterhouse,
▲ **EMP:** 64
SQ FT: 60,000
SALES (est): 12.9MM **Privately Held**
SIC: 3271 5032 Blocks, concrete or cinder: standard; brick, stone & related material

(G-2964)
NORTH MOUNTAIN STRUCTURES LLC
9035 Fort Mccord Rd (17202-9570)
PHONE..................................717 369-3400
John L Byers, *Mng Member*
EMP: 5
SALES: 948K **Privately Held**
SIC: 2452 Prefabricated wood buildings

(G-2965)
NUTRIENT CONTROL SYSTEMS INC
130 Industrial Dr (17201-3255)
PHONE..................................717 261-5711
Tim Rensch, *President*
Bradford Whitsel, *Chairman*
Michael Hurt, *Chairman*
▲ **EMP:** 7
SQ FT: 2,000
SALES: 0 **Privately Held**
WEB: www.nutrientcontrol.com
SIC: 2879 5083 Agricultural chemicals; agricultural machinery & equipment

(G-2966)
OLYMPIC STEEL INC
1599 Nitterhouse Dr (17201-4825)
PHONE..................................717 709-1515
Kirk Casey, *General Mgr*
Scott Varner, *Manager*
EMP: 50
SALES (corp-wide): 1.3B **Publicly Held**
WEB: www.olysteel.com
SIC: 5051 3312 Steel; hot-rolled iron & steel products
PA: Olympic Steel, Inc.
22901 Millcreek Blvd # 650
Cleveland OH 44122
216 292-3800

(G-2967)
PAPER AND INK OF PA LLC
Also Called: Applegate Mfg
1050 Superior Ave (17201-7859)
PHONE..................................717 709-0533
Aaron Applegate,
▼ **EMP:** 40
SALES (est): 5.4MM **Privately Held**
SIC: 2899 0723 Insulating compounds; crop preparation services for market

(G-2968)
PARKER-HANNIFIN CORPORATION
Also Called: Parker Service Center
1201a Sheffler Dr (17201-4815)
PHONE..................................717 263-5099
Tom Boyer, *Branch Mgr*
EMP: 126
SALES (corp-wide): 12B **Publicly Held**
WEB: www.parker.com
SIC: 3594 Fluid power pumps; fluid power motors
PA: Parker-Hannifin Corporation
6035 Parkland Blvd
Cleveland OH 44124
216 896-3000

(G-2969)
PRECAST SYSTEMS LLC
859 Cleveland Ave (17201-3728)
PHONE..................................717 267-4500
W K Nitterhouse,
Jason Nitterhouse,
EMP: 40
SQ FT: 22,000
SALES (est): 5.6MM **Privately Held**
SIC: 3272 Concrete products, precast

(G-2970)
PRECISION BUSHING INC
1151 Sheffler Dr (17201-4844)
PHONE..................................717 264-6461
Paul Victor Wolff Jr, *President*
Duane Allen Wolff, *Vice Pres*
EMP: 12
SQ FT: 12,000
SALES (est): 2MM **Privately Held**
SIC: 3366 Bushings & bearings

(G-2971)
PRINTAWAY INC
29 S Main St (17201-2275)
PHONE..................................717 263-1839
Evelyn M Guldin, *President*
Helman Tracy, *Human Res Dir*
Steve Gray, *Office Mgr*
EMP: 6
SQ FT: 3,000
SALES (est): 877K **Privately Held**
WEB: www.printawayinc.com
SIC: 2752 Commercial printing, offset

(G-2972)
RAYTHEON COMPANY
1 Letterkenny Army Depot (17201-4117)
PHONE..................................717 267-4200
Bobby Combs, *Branch Mgr*
EMP: 8
SALES (corp-wide): 27B **Publicly Held**
SIC: 3812 Sonar systems & equipment
PA: Raytheon Company
870 Winter St
Waltham MA 02451
781 522-3000

(G-2973)
ROBERT L BAKER
Also Called: Summit Architectural Metals
975 Wayne Ave (17201-3895)
PHONE..................................443 617-0164
Robert L Baker, *Owner*
EMP: 10 EST: 2012
SALES (est): 250K **Privately Held**
SIC: 1793 3446 3469 Glass & glazing work; architectural metalwork; architectural panels or parts, porcelain enameled

(G-2974)
RYDERS WELDING LLC
Also Called: Ryders Aluminum Welding
3959 Warm Spring Rd (17202-7103)
PHONE..................................717 369-5198
Brad Ryder, *Mng Member*
Marlin Ryder,

EMP: 4
SALES: 275K **Privately Held**
SIC: 7692 Welding repair

(G-2975)
S & S ELECTRIC MOTORS INC
125 Falling Spring Rd (17202-9001)
PHONE..................................717 263-1919
Michael Sollenberger, *President*
Jennifer Sollenberger, *Treasurer*
Gwendolyn Sollenberger, *Admin Sec*
EMP: 9
SQ FT: 9,000
SALES: 940K **Privately Held**
WEB: www.earlsollenberger.com
SIC: 7694 5999 Electric motor repair; motors, electric

(G-2976)
SOLLENBERGER SILOS LLC
2216 Wayne Rd (17202-8867)
PHONE..................................717 264-9588
Randy Lynn Gayman, *Principal*
Fred Bull, *Office Mgr*
EMP: 7
SALES (est): 679.5K **Privately Held**
SIC: 3448 Silos, metal

(G-2977)
SOUTH PENN RESTORATION SHOP
Also Called: Oak Bows
122 Ramsey Ave (17201-1293)
PHONE..................................717 264-2602
Richard Kesselring, *Owner*
EMP: 3
SALES (est): 159K **Privately Held**
SIC: 7532 2499 Antique & classic automobile restoration; decorative wood & woodwork

(G-2978)
STATLER BODY WORKS INC
1266 N Franklin St (17201-8700)
PHONE..................................717 261-5936
John Myers, *President*
Brenda Myers, *Corp Secy*
EMP: 4 EST: 1987
SALES (est): 499.9K **Privately Held**
SIC: 3713 7532 Truck & bus bodies; top & body repair & paint shops

(G-2979)
STATLERS REPAIR SHOP
1053 Paper Mill Rd (17202-9496)
PHONE..................................717 263-5074
EMP: 3
SALES (est): 160K **Privately Held**
SIC: 3599 Mfg Industrial Machinery

(G-2980)
SUNNYWAY FOODS INC
Also Called: Sunnyway Foods 2
49 Warm Spring Rd (17202-7546)
PHONE..................................717 264-6001
Mike Martin, *Manager*
EMP: 100
SALES (est): 4.4MM
SALES (corp-wide): 25MM **Privately Held**
SIC: 5411 2051 Grocery stores, independent; bread, cake & related products
PA: Sunnyway Foods, Inc
212 N Antrim Way
Greencastle PA 17225
717 597-7121

(G-2981)
SUPERIOR FLRCVGS KITCHENS LLC
254 E King St (17201-1809)
PHONE..................................717 264-9096
Gregory Meyers, *Mng Member*
EMP: 9
SALES (est): 1.7MM **Privately Held**
SIC: 5713 5722 2541 1799 Carpets; kitchens, complete (sinks, cabinets, etc.); table or counter tops, plastic laminated; kitchen & bathroom remodeling; customized furniture & cabinets

(G-2982)
SWEETDREAMS BRUSTERS LLC
500 Gateway Ave (17201-8107)
PHONE..................................717 261-1484
Jim Schmutzler, *Principal*
EMP: 3
SALES (est): 173.1K **Privately Held**
SIC: 2024 Ice cream & frozen desserts

(G-2983)
TB WOODS INCORPORATED (HQ)
440 5th Ave (17201-1763)
PHONE..................................717 264-7161
Carl R Christenson, *President*
Christian Storch, *Vice Pres*
Pat Kelly, *Mfg Mgr*
Lew Crist, *Facilities Mgr*
Don Rundle, *Purch Mgr*
◆ **EMP:** 214
SQ FT: 440,000
SALES (est): 77.8MM
SALES (corp-wide): 1.1B **Publicly Held**
WEB: www.tbwoods.com
SIC: 3568 Power transmission equipment
PA: Altra Industrial Motion Corp.
300 Granite St Ste 201
Braintree MA 02184
781 917-0600

(G-2984)
TBJ INCORPORATED
1671 Orchard Dr (17201-9206)
PHONE..................................717 261-9700
Todd E Campbell, *President*
Bryan Campbell, *Vice Pres*
Cynthia D Campbell, *Admin Sec*
◆ **EMP:** 18
SQ FT: 24,000
SALES (est): 4.4MM **Privately Held**
SIC: 3821 3441 Laboratory apparatus, except heating & measuring; fabricated structural metal

(G-2985)
TERRY BAKER
Also Called: Baker Beverage
2045 Country Rd (17202-8568)
PHONE..................................717 263-5942
Terry Baker, *Owner*
EMP: 9 EST: 1958
SQ FT: 8,000
SALES (est): 3.7MM **Privately Held**
SIC: 2082 2086 Beer (alcoholic beverage); carbonated soft drinks, bottled & canned

(G-2986)
TOM JAMES COMPANY
Also Called: Iag Distribution Center
5121 Innovation Way (17201-4187)
PHONE..................................717 264-5768
Ron Garland, *Warehouse Mgr*
Doris Quail, *Accountant*
EMP: 77
SALES (corp-wide): 631.4MM **Privately Held**
SIC: 2311 3161 2325 2323 Suits, men's & boys': made from purchased materials; luggage; men's & boys' trousers & slacks; men's & boys' neckwear; men's & boys' furnishings; men's & boys' clothing stores
PA: Tom James Company
263 Seaboard Ln
Franklin TN 37067
615 771-1122

(G-2987)
TORCOMP USA LLC
1690 Opportunity Ave (17201-7851)
PHONE..................................717 261-1530
Fabrizio Giovannini, *President*
EMP: 2
SQ FT: 6,000
SALES (est): 1.3MM **Privately Held**
SIC: 6153 3751 3714 3599 Financing of dealers by motor vehicle manufacturers organ.; motorcycles, bicycles & parts; motor vehicle parts & accessories; machine shop, jobbing & repair

G
E
O
G
R
A
P
H
I
C

(G-2988)
TRICKLING SPRINGS CREAMERY LLC
2330 Molly Pitcher Hwy (17202-9299)
PHONE...................................717 709-0711
Lee Roy Strite, General Mgr
David Lambert, VP Opers
Kathleen Kennedy, Store Mgr
Heidi Farrar, Sales Mgr
Chris Horn, Sales Staff
EMP: 23
SQ FT: 7,200
SALES (est): 5.9MM Privately Held
WEB: www.tricklingspringscreamery.com
SIC: 2024 2026 Ice cream & frozen
   desserts; fluid milk; cream, sweet; half &
   half

(G-2989)
TRIM P A C LLC
2823 Molly Pitcher Hwy (17202-7232)
PHONE...................................717 375-2366
Patricia A Connor, Owner
EMP: 7
SALES (est): 372.2K Privately Held
SIC: 1799 2511 Home/office interiors fin-
   ishing, furnishing & remodeling; lawn fur-
   niture: wood

(G-2990)
TRUCKCRAFT CORPORATION
5751 Molly Pitcher Hwy (17202-7708)
PHONE...................................717 375-2900
Gary Shoup, President
Gerald Pool, Vice Pres
EMP: 20
SQ FT: 12,000
SALES (est): 4.2MM Privately Held
WEB: www.truckcraft.com
SIC: 3713 Truck bodies (motor vehicles)

(G-2991)
TUSCARORA USA INC
1626 Majestic Dr (17202-8049)
P.O. Box 516 (17201-0516)
PHONE...................................717 491-2861
Benjamin Pietsch, President
Cheryl Pietsch, Vice Pres
EMP: 6
SALES (est): 480K Privately Held
SIC: 3652 4939 Pre-recorded records &
   tapes; combination utilities

(G-2992)
VACON LLC
1500 Nitterhouse Dr (17201-4824)
PHONE...................................717 261-5000
Vesa Laisi, CEO
Tom Doring, President
Claudio Baccarelli, Managing Dir
Daniel Isakkson, Vice Pres
Thomas Fitzkee, Mfg Staff
▲ EMP: 103
SQ FT: 67,000
SALES (est): 28.4MM
SALES (corp-wide): 6.8B Privately Held
WEB: www.vacon.com
SIC: 3625 Motor starters & controllers,
   electric
HQ: Vacon Oy
   Runsorintie 7
   Vaasa 65380
   201 212-1

(G-2993)
VALLEY QUARRIES INC
Chambersburg Transit Mix Div
3593 Stone Quarry Rd (17202-7729)
PHONE...................................717 263-9186
Tedd Everts, Superintendent
EMP: 21
SALES (corp-wide): 651.9MM Privately
Held
WEB: www.valleyquarries.com
SIC: 1422 Crushed & broken limestone
HQ: Valley Quarries, Inc.
   297 Quarry Rd
   Chambersburg PA 17202
   717 267-2244

(G-2994)
VALLEY QUARRIES INC (HQ)
Also Called: Valley Transit Mix
297 Quarry Rd (17202-9099)
P.O. Box 2009 (17201-0809)
PHONE...................................717 267-2244

Paul Detweiler III, President
Joseph Zimmerman, Exec VP
Donald Detweiler, Vice Pres
Paul Detweiler Jr, Vice Pres
Randall Vanscyoc, Vice Pres
EMP: 10
SQ FT: 5,000
SALES (est): 19.3MM
SALES (corp-wide): 651.9MM Privately
Held
WEB: www.valleyquarries.com
SIC: 3273 1422 1442 2951 Ready-mixed
   concrete; crushed & broken limestone;
   construction sand & gravel; asphalt & as-
   phaltic paving mixtures (not from refiner-
   ies); highway & street construction
PA: New Enterprise Stone & Lime Co., Inc.
   3912 Brumbaugh Rd
   New Enterprise PA 16664
   814 224-6883

(G-2995)
VALLEY QUARRIES INC
3587 Stone Quarry Rd (17202-8894)
PHONE...................................717 264-4178
Andrew Barnes, Manager
EMP: 35
SALES (corp-wide): 651.9MM Privately
Held
WEB: www.valleyquarries.com
SIC: 3273 2951 1442 1422 Ready-mixed
   concrete; asphalt paving mixtures &
   blocks; construction sand & gravel;
   crushed & broken limestone
HQ: Valley Quarries, Inc.
   297 Quarry Rd
   Chambersburg PA 17202
   717 267-2244

(G-2996)
VALLEY QUARRIES INC
2921 Stone Quarry Rd (17202-7726)
PHONE...................................717 264-5811
Dale Whitmer, Manager
EMP: 6
SALES (corp-wide): 651.9MM Privately
Held
WEB: www.valleyquarries.com
SIC: 1422 Crushed & broken limestone
HQ: Valley Quarries, Inc.
   297 Quarry Rd
   Chambersburg PA 17202
   717 267-2244

(G-2997)
VENTURA FOODS LLC
1501 Orchard Dr (17201-4817)
PHONE...................................717 263-6900
Tom Waterhouse, Manager
EMP: 250 Privately Held
WEB: www.venturafoods.com
SIC: 2079 5149 2035 Vegetable shorten-
   ings (except corn oil); shortening, veg-
   etable; pickles, sauces & salad dressings
PA: Ventura Foods, Llc
   40 Pointe Dr
   Brea CA 92821

(G-2998)
WARRIOR ROOFING MFG INC
323 Development Ave (17201-4125)
PHONE...................................717 709-0323
Suzanne Cunningham, Treasurer
Dennie Swain, Manager
EMP: 34 Privately Held
WEB: www.warriorroofing.net
SIC: 2952 Roofing materials
PA: Warrior Roofing Manufacturing, Inc.
   3050 Warrior Rd
   Tuscaloosa AL 35404

(G-2999)
WIPRO ENTERPRISES INC
1101 Sheffler Dr (17201-4844)
P.O. Box 371 (17201-0371)
PHONE...................................717 496-8877
Eric Olson, General Mgr
EMP: 7
SQ FT: 33,000
SALES (est): 1.1MM Privately Held
SIC: 3593 Fluid power cylinders, hydraulic
   or pneumatic

(G-3000)
WOODS COMPANY INC
2121 Carbaugh Ave (17201-4126)
PHONE...................................717 263-6524
Barry Stup, President
▼ EMP: 36
SQ FT: 90,000
SALES (est): 5.6MM Privately Held
WEB: www.thewoodscompany.com
SIC: 2491 Flooring, treated wood block

(G-3001)
Y B WELDING INC
Also Called: Yb
990 Progress Rd (17201)
PHONE...................................717 267-0104
Jonas Byers, President
Eric Yoder, Vice Pres
Gene Sarvis, Purchasing
EMP: 5
SALES (est): 1.5MM Privately Held
SIC: 7692 Welding repair

(G-3002)
ZERO ICE CORPORATION
42 Siloam Rd (17201-8951)
PHONE...................................717 264-7912
Peter Neuder, President
Frances Neuder, Corp Secy
EMP: 4
SALES (est): 793.6K Privately Held
WEB: www.zeroicecorp.com
SIC: 2097 4222 Manufactured ice; refrig-
   erated warehousing & storage

Champion
Westmoreland County

(G-3003)
CHAMPION LUMBER COMPANY INC
1195 Nebo Rd (15622)
PHONE...................................724 455-3401
Richard E Naugle, President
Tammy Naugle, Corp Secy
EMP: 18 EST: 1948
SQ FT: 2,000
SALES (est): 1.3MM Privately Held
SIC: 2421 2491 Lumber: rough, sawed or
   planed; wood preserving

Charleroi
Washington County

(G-3004)
AD FORMS LLC
821 Jane Ave (15022-1018)
PHONE...................................724 379-6022
EMP: 4
SQ FT: 8,000
SALES (est): 619.9K Privately Held
SIC: 2752 Lithographic Commercial Print-
   ing

(G-3005)
ALSTOM GRID LLC
T & D High Voltage
1 Power Ln (15022-1082)
PHONE...................................724 483-7308
John Blicen, Manager
EMP: 64
SALES (corp-wide): 121.6B Publicly
Held
SIC: 3613 Switchgear & switchboard appa-
   ratus
HQ: Alstom Grid Llc
   130 3rd St Nw
   Canton OH 44702
   330 452-8428

(G-3006)
AMERICAN AIR DUCT INC
300 Arentzen Blvd (15022-1063)
P.O. Box 10984, Pittsburgh (15236-0984)
PHONE...................................724 483-8057
EMP: 25
SQ FT: 48,000
SALES (est): 3.3MM Privately Held
SIC: 3498 3444 Mfg Fabricated Pipe/Fit-
   tings Mfg Sheet Metalwork

(G-3007)
CANARY LLC
2975 Marginal W (15022)
PHONE...................................724 483-2224
Mark Miller, Branch Mgr
EMP: 18 Privately Held
SIC: 1389 Oil field services
PA: Canary, Llc
   410 17th St Ste 310
   Denver CO 80202

(G-3008)
CONSPEC CONTROLS INC (HQ)
6 Guttman Blvd (15022-1015)
PHONE...................................724 489-8450
Nancy McCullough, CEO
Enzo Ucci, President
Annabelle Garland, Corp Secy
Jennifer L Chiocchio, Manager
Frank Muchnok Jr, Manager
EMP: 18
SQ FT: 11,000
SALES (est): 2.9MM Privately Held
SIC: 3826 3823 3812 Analytical instru-
   ments; industrial instrmnts msrmnt dis-
   play/control process variable; search &
   navigation equipment
PA: Conspec Controls Limited
   25 Klondike Dr
   North York ON M9L 1
   416 661-0500

(G-3009)
DESTEFANOS HARDWOOD LUMBER
19 Holly Dr (15022-3106)
PHONE...................................724 483-6196
Joann Destefano, Owner
Don Destefano, Principal
EMP: 4
SQ FT: 1,200
SALES: 40K Privately Held
SIC: 2511 5211 Wood household furniture;
   lumber products

(G-3010)
DS SERVICES GROUP CORP
Also Called: Mon Valley Signs
10 Chamber Plz (15022-1601)
PHONE...................................724 350-6429
David Zahand, President
EMP: 10
SQ FT: 10,500
SALES (est): 1.4MM Privately Held
WEB: www.ds-services.com
SIC: 3993 Signs & advertising specialties

(G-3011)
DUCTMATE INDUSTRIES INC (PA)
Also Called: Dmi Companies
210 5th St (15022-1514)
PHONE...................................800 990-8459
Raymond W Yeager, President
Timothy N Omstead, Vice Pres
David Jackson, Warehouse Mgr
Doug Gudenburr, Opers Staff
Alvin Jefferson, Engineer
▲ EMP: 50
SQ FT: 150,000
SALES (est): 50.1MM Privately Held
WEB: www.ductmate.com
SIC: 3444 Ducts, sheet metal

(G-3012)
EXIDE TECHNOLOGIES
106 Simko Blvd Ste 106 # 106
(15022-3487)
PHONE...................................724 239-2006
George Herman, Manager
EMP: 6
SALES (corp-wide): 2.4B Privately Held
WEB: www.exideworld.com
SIC: 5013 3629 Automotive batteries; bat-
   tery chargers, rectifying or nonrotating
PA: Exide Technologies
   13000 Deerfield Pkwy # 200
   Milton GA 30004
   678 566-9000

(G-3013)
FOURTH STREET BARBECUE INC
3 Arentzen Blvd (15022-1060)
PHONE...................................724 483-2000

▲ = Import ▼=Export
◆ =Import/Export

David Barbe Sr, *President*
EMP: 200 **EST:** 2012
SQ FT: 60,000
SALES: 56MM **Privately Held**
SIC: 2015 2032 Chicken, processed: cooked; macaroni: packaged in cans, jars, etc.

(G-3014)
GARDNER DENVER NASH LLC
200 Simko Blvd (15022-3493)
PHONE..................724 239-1522
Chuck Kruzan, *Branch Mgr*
EMP: 40
SALES (corp-wide): 2.6B **Publicly Held**
WEB: www.nasheng.com
SIC: 3561 Cylinders, pump
HQ: Gardner Denver Nash Llc
2 Trefoil Dr
Trumbull CT 06611
203 459-3923

(G-3015)
GARDNER DENVER NASH LLC
Also Called: Nash Engineering
200 Simko Blvd (15022-3493)
PHONE..................203 459-3923
John Edman, *Branch Mgr*
EMP: 5
SALES (corp-wide): 2.6B **Publicly Held**
SIC: 5084 3563 8711 3561 Compressors, except air conditioning; air & gas compressors including vacuum pumps; engineering services; pumps & pumping equipment
HQ: Gardner Denver Nash Llc
2 Trefoil Dr
Trumbull CT 06611
203 459-3923

(G-3016)
MON VALLEY INDEPENDENT
111 Fallowfield Ave (15022-1402)
P.O. Box 144 (15022-0144)
PHONE..................724 314-0030
Keith Bassi, *Principal*
EMP: 3
SALES (est): 106.3K **Privately Held**
SIC: 2711 Newspapers, publishing & printing

(G-3017)
NATIONAL POLYMERS INC
9 Guttman Blvd (15022-1016)
PHONE..................724 483-9300
Edward B Dunlap, *President*
Ruth K Simpson, *Corp Secy*
Albert Daugherty, *Vice Pres*
Keith Bailey, *Sales Staff*
Steve Dunlap, *Sales Staff*
◆ **EMP:** 30
SQ FT: 22,000
SALES (est): 9.9MM **Privately Held**
WEB: www.nationalpolymers.com
SIC: 3069 Rubber floor coverings, mats & wallcoverings; roofing, membrane rubber

(G-3018)
NIX OPTICAL CO INC
216 Lincoln Avenue Ext # 1 (15022-3079)
PHONE..................724 483-6527
Jeffrey Nix, *President*
James Nix, *Asst Treas*
EMP: 4
SALES (est): 426.9K **Privately Held**
SIC: 5995 3851 Eyeglasses, prescription; lenses, ophthalmic

(G-3019)
PROGENY SYSTEMS CORPORATION
106 Simko Blvd Ste 100 (15022-3487)
PHONE..................724 239-3939
Terry Harr, *Purch Agent*
Richard Ames, *Engineer*
Katrina Youschak, *Engineer*
Chuck Dreer, *Branch Mgr*
EMP: 16 **Privately Held**
WEB: www.progeny.net
SIC: 3571 Electronic computers
PA: Progeny Systems Corporation
9500 Innovation Dr
Manassas VA 20110

(G-3020)
QUALITY PASTA COMPANY LLC
100 Chamber Plz (15022-1603)
PHONE..................855 878-9630
Paul De Stefano, *President*
Anthony Schelich,
▼ **EMP:** 8 **EST:** 2013
SALES: 6.5MM **Privately Held**
SIC: 2099 Packaged combination products: pasta, rice & potato; pasta, uncooked: packaged with other ingredients

(G-3021)
RTS PACKAGING LLC
98 3rd St (15022-1422)
P.O. Box 116 (15022-0116)
PHONE..................724 489-4495
Jack Lacarte, *Principal*
EMP: 126
SALES (corp-wide): 14.8B **Publicly Held**
WEB: www.rtspackaging.com
SIC: 2653 Hampers, solid fiber: made from purchased materials
HQ: Rts Packaging, Llc
504 Thrasher St
Norcross GA 30071
800 558-6984

(G-3022)
TRI-STATE HYDRAULICS INC
Also Called: Glass Sports Cylinder Works
1250 Mckean Ave (15022-2284)
PHONE..................724 483-1790
Janice M Palmer, *President*
Cheryl P Wall, *Corp Secy*
James D Palmer II, *Vice Pres*
EMP: 50
SQ FT: 63,000
SALES (est): 41.6MM **Privately Held**
WEB: www.tristatehyd.com
SIC: 5084 7699 3593 Pneumatic tools & equipment; hydraulic systems equipment & supplies; aircraft & heavy equipment repair services; hydraulic equipment repair; fluid power cylinders & actuators

(G-3023)
VALLEY RETREADING INC (PA)
Also Called: Valley Retreading of Charleroi
15 Mckean Ave (15022-1436)
PHONE..................724 489-4483
James F Stankiewicz, *President*
EMP: 12
SQ FT: 15,500
SALES (est): 1.4MM **Privately Held**
SIC: 3011 Tires & inner tubes

(G-3024)
WEAHTERFORD MANUFACTURING
100 Vista Dr (15022-3486)
PHONE..................724 239-1404
EMP: 9
SALES (est): 1.5MM **Privately Held**
SIC: 3999 Manufacturing industries

(G-3025)
WENDELL H STONE COMPANY INC
Also Called: Stone & Company
201 2nd St (15022)
PHONE..................724 483-6571
Mike Cozura, *Manager*
EMP: 30
SALES (corp-wide): 35MM **Privately Held**
WEB: www.stoneco.com
SIC: 5032 3273 3271 1442 Concrete building products; ready-mixed concrete; concrete block & brick; construction sand & gravel
PA: Wendell H. Stone Company, Inc.
606 Mccormick Ave
Connellsville PA 15425
724 836-1400

(G-3026)
WESTMORELAND ADVANCED MTLS INC
501 Mckean Ave Ste 3 (15022-1558)
PHONE..................724 684-5902
Kenneth McGowan, *President*
Robert Cullen, *Vice Pres*
Peter Kacheris, *Regl Sales Mgr*
Pete Beaulieu, *Marketing Mgr*

▲ **EMP:** 7
SQ FT: 22,000
SALES (est): 1.3MM **Privately Held**
WEB: www.westadmat.com
SIC: 3273 Ready-mixed concrete

Cheltenham
Montgomery County

(G-3027)
CATHEDRAL STAINED GL STUDIOS
202 Franklin Ave (19012-2224)
PHONE..................215 379-5360
Chandler Coleman, *President*
EMP: 4 **EST:** 1966
SQ FT: 3,000
SALES (est): 454.6K **Privately Held**
WEB: www.cathedralstainedglassinc.com
SIC: 1793 3231 5231 Glass & glazing work; stained glass: made from purchased glass; glass, leaded or stained

(G-3028)
GOLDFAM INC
Also Called: Helen's Pure Foods
301 Ryers Ave (19012-2113)
PHONE..................215 379-6433
Richard Goldberg, *President*
Helen Popeck, *Treasurer*
EMP: 8
SQ FT: 1,500
SALES (est): 883.3K **Privately Held**
SIC: 2099 Food preparations

(G-3029)
H H FLUORESCENT PARTS INC
104 Beecher Ave (19012-2295)
P.O. Box 65 (19012-0065)
PHONE..................215 379-2750
Robert J Hillen Sr, *President*
Robert J Hillen Jr, *Vice Pres*
Kathy Hillen, *Treasurer*
▲ **EMP:** 60 **EST:** 1942
SQ FT: 30,000
SALES (est): 9.6MM **Privately Held**
WEB: www.furniture-info.com
SIC: 3641 3643 3599 Electric lamps & parts for generalized applications; outlets, electric: convenience; fluorescent starters; machine shop, jobbing & repair

(G-3030)
J A EMILIUS SONS INC
Also Called: Emilius, J A Sons
537 Woodland Ave (19012-2119)
PHONE..................215 379-6162
Carl A Emilius III, *President*
Elizabeth Emilius, *Business Mgr*
Bonnie Lehe Emilius, *Admin Sec*
EMP: 15 **EST:** 1935
SQ FT: 7,200
SALES (est): 2.7MM **Privately Held**
WEB: www.emilius.com
SIC: 3599 3535 Machine shop, jobbing & repair; conveyors & conveying equipment

Cherry Tree
Indiana County

(G-3031)
BAKERS LUMBER COMPANY INC
1481 Shawna Rd (15724-9002)
PHONE..................814 743-6671
Robert Larry Baker, *President*
Jack C Myers, *Corp Secy*
EMP: 14 **EST:** 1935
SALES: 1.3MM **Privately Held**
SIC: 2421 Lumber: rough, sawed or planed

(G-3032)
ELICK LOGGING INC
1434 Dogwood Rd (15724-6614)
PHONE..................814 743-5546
Robert J Elick, *President*
John W Elick, *Vice Pres*
Jennifer A Elick, *Treasurer*
Judith A Elick, *Admin Sec*
EMP: 4

SALES (est): 352K **Privately Held**
SIC: 2411 Logging camps & contractors

(G-3033)
NEUROLOGIX TECHNOLOGIES INC
297 Shepherd Rd (15724-8504)
PHONE..................512 914-7941
Frank Carruba, *President*
EMP: 10
SALES (est): 126.2K **Privately Held**
SIC: 3841 8742 7389 Diagnostic apparatus, medical; management information systems consultant;

(G-3034)
PAUL SCALESE
Also Called: Scalese Mill Works
2353 Cherry Tree Rd (15724-8027)
PHONE..................814 743-5121
Paul Scalese, *Owner*
EMP: 3
SQ FT: 2,000
SALES: 250K **Privately Held**
WEB: www.scalesemillworks.com
SIC: 2434 Wood kitchen cabinets

(G-3035)
RANDALL INDS LTD LIABLILITY CO
4565 Hemlock Rd (15724-7223)
PHONE..................814 743-6630
Gregory R Spencer, *CEO*
EMP: 12
SQ FT: 30,000
SALES (est): 2MM **Privately Held**
SIC: 2842 Specialty cleaning preparations

(G-3036)
SPRING HILL WOODWORKS
625 Arcadia Rd (15724-7435)
PHONE..................724 762-0111
Micah Brubaker, *Principal*
EMP: 4
SALES (est): 205.2K **Privately Held**
SIC: 2431 Millwork

Chester
Delaware County

(G-3037)
AERIAL SIGNS & AWNINGS INC
2333 Concord Rd (19013-2447)
PHONE..................610 494-1415
Steve Mc Connell, *President*
Ronald J Corrento Jr, *Vice Pres*
EMP: 10
SQ FT: 3,500
SALES (est): 1.5MM **Privately Held**
SIC: 3993 2394 Signs, not made in custom sign painting shops; awnings, fabric: made from purchased materials

(G-3038)
ALLOY SURFACES COMPANY INC (DH)
121 N Commerce Dr (19014-3205)
PHONE..................610 497-7979
Lawrence M Dandrea, *President*
Lawrence M D'Andrea, *President*
Joseph Verbitski, *General Mgr*
Anne Clements, *Vice Pres*
John A Lafemina, *Vice Pres*
▼ **EMP:** 146 **EST:** 1958
SQ FT: 80,600
SALES (est): 20.2MM
SALES (corp-wide): 734.6MM **Privately Held**
WEB: www.alloysurfaces.com
SIC: 3489 Ordnance & accessories

(G-3039)
AMERICAN WOOD DESIGN INC
201 Fulton St (19013-4127)
PHONE..................302 792-2100
Mike Gilhool, *President*
EMP: 11
SALES (est): 1.1MM **Privately Held**
SIC: 2431 Millwork

GEOGRAPHIC

(G-3040)
BOB ALLEN & SONS INC
Also Called: Sandrose Trophies
1 W 9th St (19013)
PHONE..................610 874-4391
Jason Allen, *President*
EMP: 3
SALES (est): 54K **Privately Held**
SIC: 3914 5091 Trophies; sporting &
recreation goods

(G-3041)
BRANDYWINE FUEL INC
913 Macadam St (19013-5814)
P.O. Box 147, Chester Heights (19017-
0147)
PHONE..................610 455-0123
Michael J Sanders, *Principal*
EMP: 7
SALES (est): 731.5K **Privately Held**
SIC: 2869 Fuels

(G-3042)
BYRNE CHIARLONE LP
Also Called: WM A SCHMIDT & SONS
418 W Front St (19013-4107)
P.O. Box 300 (19016-0300)
PHONE..................610 874-8436
Donald Byrne, *Partner*
Michael Chiarlone, *General Ptnr*
▲ EMP: 35 EST: 1948
SQ FT: 60,000
SALES: 10.6MM **Privately Held**
WEB: www.wasinc.com
SIC: 3443 3441 3444 Industrial vessels,
tanks & containers; fabricated structural
metal; sheet metal specialties, not
stamped

(G-3043)
**COMMUNITY LIGHT & SOUND
INC**
Also Called: Community Prof Loudspeakers
333 E 5th St (19013-4511)
PHONE..................610 876-3400
Bruce Howze, *President*
Chris Howze, *General Mgr*
John Wiggins, *Vice Pres*
Eric Smith, *Facilities Mgr*
Michael Ermilio, *Engineer*
▲ EMP: 100
SQ FT: 78,000
SALES (est): 23.7MM **Privately Held**
WEB: www.loudspeakers.net
SIC: 3651 Loudspeakers, electrodynamic
or magnetic; public address systems

(G-3044)
CONCURE INC
710 Trainer St (19013-1749)
PHONE..................610 497-0198
H Keith Loflin, *President*
Russel Geaneotes, *Vice Pres*
EMP: 7
SQ FT: 15,000
SALES (est): 1.3MM **Privately Held**
SIC: 3281 2891 Marble, building: cut &
shaped; epoxy adhesives

(G-3045)
DAN ORNER SIGNS
1131 Mulberry St (19015-3045)
PHONE..................610 876-6042
Daniel Orner, *Owner*
EMP: 3
SALES (est): 319.7K **Privately Held**
SIC: 3993 Signs & advertising specialties

(G-3046)
DEE PAPER COMPANY INC
100 Broomall St (19013-3413)
PHONE..................610 876-9285
Stephen Harrell, *President*
Andrew Poth, *CFO*
▼ EMP: 90 EST: 1921
SQ FT: 100,000
SALES: 20MM **Privately Held**
WEB: www.deepaper.com
SIC: 2653 Boxes, corrugated: made from
purchased materials

(G-3047)
DELCO MINI MIX LLC
325 Ulrich St (19013-3831)
P.O. Box 26 (19016-0026)
PHONE..................610 809-0316
EMP: 4
SALES (est): 284.4K **Privately Held**
SIC: 3273 Ready-mixed concrete

(G-3048)
DL1 PROCESSING LLC
805b W 2nd St (19013-3600)
PHONE..................215 582-3263
Nicholas Rostock, *CFO*
EMP: 7
SQ FT: 6,500
SALES (est): 489.5K **Privately Held**
SIC: 2869 Industrial organic chemicals

(G-3049)
ERIC SNOW
Also Called: E&M Tile Restoration
320 Townsend St (19013-2539)
PHONE..................267 602-3522
Eric Snow, *Owner*
EMP: 4
SALES (est): 141.8K **Privately Held**
SIC: 3253 Ceramic wall & floor tile

(G-3050)
EVONIK CORPORATION
Also Called: Specialty Resin Systems
1200 W Front St (19013-3438)
P.O. Box 494, West Chester (19381-0494)
PHONE..................610 990-8100
Nick Karaolis, *Opers Mgr*
Teresa Wells, *Buyer*
Houston Nickelson, *Maintence Staff*
EMP: 9
SALES (corp-wide): 2.4B **Privately Held**
SIC: 2819 Industrial inorganic chemicals
HQ: Evonik Corporation
299 Jefferson Rd
Parsippany NJ 07054
973 929-8000

(G-3051)
FISHER TANK COMPANY (PA)
3131 W 4th St (19013-1899)
PHONE..................610 494-7200
P M Szelak, *Principal*
Robert M Borst, *Chairman*
John Fisher, *Vice Pres*
Ken Jensen, *Vice Pres*
Jim Miller, *Vice Pres*
EMP: 50 EST: 1951
SQ FT: 7,200
SALES (est): 33.7MM **Privately Held**
WEB: www.fishertank.com
SIC: 1791 3443 Storage tanks, metal:
erection; tanks, standard or custom fabri-
cated: metal plate; fuel tanks (oil, gas,
etc.): metal plate; water tanks, metal plate

(G-3052)
JM WELDING COMPANY INC
916 Lamokin St (19013-3541)
PHONE..................610 872-2049
James Meehan, *President*
Joe Meehan, *Vice Pres*
EMP: 5
SQ FT: 15,000
SALES: 2MM **Privately Held**
SIC: 3312 Rails, steel or iron

(G-3053)
**KIMBERLY-CLARK
CORPORATION**
1 Avenue Of The States (19013-4471)
PHONE..................610 874-4331
Richard Craig, *Vice Pres*
Gary Tohill, *Engineer*
Thomas Lisinski, *Electrical Engi*
EMP: 100
SALES (corp-wide): 18.4B **Publicly Held**
WEB: www.kimberly-clark.com
SIC: 2621 2676 Sanitary tissue paper; in-
fant & baby paper products
PA: Kimberly-Clark Corporation
351 Phelps Dr
Irving TX 75038
972 281-1200

(G-3054)
KYJS BAKERY (PA)
2702 W 3rd St (19013-2223)
PHONE..................610 494-9400
Lydia Kyj, *President*
Christine Pluta, *Vice Pres*
EMP: 20
SQ FT: 1,500
SALES (est): 2.5MM **Privately Held**
SIC: 5461 2051 Bakeries; bread, cake &
related products

(G-3055)
LARAN BRONZE INC
310 E 6th St (19013-6036)
PHONE..................610 874-4414
Lawrence E Welker, *President*
Diane Welker, *Treasurer*
Randall Welker, *Admin Sec*
EMP: 9
SQ FT: 42,600
SALES (est): 1.4MM **Privately Held**
WEB: www.laranbronze.com
SIC: 3366 Copper foundries

(G-3056)
M & M INDUSTRIES INC (PA)
800 W Front St Ste 2a (19013-3654)
PHONE..................610 447-0663
Ernesto Mayser, *CEO*
▼ EMP: 23 EST: 1998
SQ FT: 53,000
SALES: 6MM **Privately Held**
SIC: 3369 Nonferrous foundries

(G-3057)
**MARINO INDUS SYSTEMS SVCS
INC**
805 W 2nd St Ste A (19013-3667)
PHONE..................610 872-3630
Brendan A Stanton, *President*
Jean Stanton, *Shareholder*
Ann Beddia, *Maintence Staff*
◆ EMP: 20
SQ FT: 14,000
SALES (est): 11.7MM **Privately Held**
SIC: 5063 3625 3621 Electrical fittings &
construction materials; industrial controls:
push button, selector switches, pilot; mo-
tors, electric

(G-3058)
NORQUAY TECHNOLOGY INC
800 W Front St (19013-3654)
P.O. Box 468 (19016-0468)
PHONE..................610 874-4330
Robert W Heldt, *President*
Peter Litak, *Research*
Kathleen Donahue, *Manager*
Don Morrison, *Director*
◆ EMP: 29
SQ FT: 53,000
SALES (est): 9.1MM **Privately Held**
WEB: www.norquaytech.com
SIC: 2869 2834 2899 Industrial organic
chemicals; pharmaceutical preparations;
chemical preparations
HQ: Mpd Chemicals, Llc
340 Mathers Rd
Ambler PA 19002

(G-3059)
PQ CORPORATION
1201 W Front St (19013-3496)
PHONE..................610 447-3900
Alan Rogers, *Opers-Prdtn-Mfg*
EMP: 39
SALES (corp-wide): 1.6B **Publicly Held**
WEB: www.pqcorp.com
SIC: 2819 Industrial inorganic chemicals
HQ: Pq Corporation
300 Lindenwood Dr
Malvern PA 19355
610 651-4200

(G-3060)
**PRECISION PRODUCTION
TURNING**
1128 Chestnut St (19013-6119)
PHONE..................610 872-8557
Robert Renshaw, *Owner*
EMP: 3
SQ FT: 4,000
SALES (est): 191.1K **Privately Held**
SIC: 3599 Machine shop, jobbing & repair

(G-3061)
ROE FABRICATORS INC
3304 W 2nd St (19013-1800)
PHONE..................610 485-4990
Brett Roe, *President*
▲ EMP: 10 EST: 1999
SALES (est): 1.7MM **Privately Held**
SIC: 3993 Signs, not made in custom sign
painting shops

(G-3062)
SIG COMBIBLOC INC
Also Called: Parent Co Is Sig Holdg USA
2501 Seaport Dr Ste Rf100 (19013-1894)
PHONE..................610 546-4200
Eduardo Gatica, *President*
Jerome Blanc, *Project Mgr*
Denis Pokidyshev, *QC Mgr*
Ian Williamson, *QC Mgr*
Michele Needham, *Treasurer*
◆ EMP: 50
SQ FT: 23,000
SALES (est): 15.2MM **Privately Held**
SIC: 2631 3554 Container, packaging &
boxboard; box making machines, paper
PA: Sig Combibloc Inc
2425 Matheson Blvd E Flr 8
Mississauga ON L4W 5
905 361-2829

(G-3063)
SPEC INDUSTRIES INC
101 Engle St 103 (19013-2526)
PHONE..................610 497-4220
Charles Klenotiz, *Owner*
Lori Klenotiz, *Admin Sec*
EMP: 6 EST: 1971
SQ FT: 11,000
SALES: 550K **Privately Held**
SIC: 3479 Coating of metals with plastic or
resins

(G-3064)
SPIRIT MEDIA GROUP INC
Also Called: Chester Spirit
1109 Remington St (19013-6414)
P.O. Box 464, Glenolden (19036-0464)
PHONE..................610 447-8484
Paul A Bennett, *President*
EMP: 3
SALES: 200K **Privately Held**
SIC: 2711 Newspapers

(G-3065)
**SPM GLOBAL SERVICES INC
(PA)**
Also Called: Synygy
2501 Seaport Dr Ste Sh103 (19013-2266)
PHONE..................610 340-2828
Mark A Stiffler, *President*
Daniel L Ganse, *Vice Pres*
EMP: 65
SALES (est): 11.5MM **Privately Held**
WEB: www.synygy.com
SIC: 8742 7372 Management information
systems consultant; prepackaged soft-
ware

(G-3066)
**SYKES-SCHOLTZ-COLLINS LBR
INC**
Also Called: SSC Distributors
3130 W 4th St (19013-1845)
PHONE..................610 494-2700
Barry Scholtz, *President*
Keith Scholtz, *Vice Pres*
Linda Gular, *Director*
EMP: 20 EST: 1960
SQ FT: 30,000
SALES (est): 6.3MM **Privately Held**
WEB: www.sscdistributors.com
SIC: 5031 2434 Kitchen cabinets; vanities,
bathroom: wood

(G-3067)
WEST PHILA BRONZE CO INC
500 Concord Ave (19013-4344)
P.O. Box 448 (19016-0448)
PHONE..................610 874-1454
Ralph V Cacciutti, *CEO*
Charles M Cacciutti, *President*
EMP: 30
SQ FT: 70,000

SALES (est): 7.5MM **Privately Held**
WEB: www.westphilabronze.com
SIC: 3364 3363 Brass & bronze die-castings; aluminum die-castings

(G-3068)
WHITEHILL MFG CORP
2540 Green St Ste 1 (19013-1445)
P.O. Box 356, Media (19063)
PHONE..............................610 494-2378
A Simeon Whitehill, *President*
Elizabeth Huntley, *COO*
Rita Gourley, *Engineer*
Mark Huntley, *Engineer*
Victoria Whitehill, *CFO*
◆ EMP: 40
SQ FT: 60,000
SALES (est): 7.5MM **Privately Held**
SIC: 2298 Rope, except asbestos & wire; cable, fiber

(G-3069)
WIRE WORKS ENTERPRISES INC
Also Called: Ron Francis Wire Works
200 Keystone Rd Ste 1 (19013-1422)
PHONE..............................610 485-1981
Scott M Bowers, *President*
EMP: 18
SQ FT: 15,000
SALES (est): 3.3MM **Privately Held**
WEB: www.ronfranciswiring.com
SIC: 3679 Harness assemblies for electronic use: wire or cable

Chester Springs
Chester County

(G-3070)
AIR VENTURES BALLOON RIDES
2145 Conestoga Rd (19425-3703)
P.O. Box 711, Paoli (19301-0711)
PHONE..............................610 827-2138
Debbie Harding, *President*
EMP: 7
SALES: 150K **Privately Held**
SIC: 3721 7999 Balloons, hot air (aircraft); hot air balloon rides

(G-3071)
AMTEL SYSTEMS CORPORATION
1955 Ticonderoga Blvd # 800 (19425-9553)
PHONE..............................610 458-3320
Franklin C Markle Jr, *President*
Edward E Gardiner, *Treasurer*
John E Tayman Jr, *VP Mktg*
EMP: 8
SQ FT: 2,400
SALES (est): 900K **Privately Held**
WEB: www.amtelsystemscorp.com
SIC: 3661 Telephone & telegraph apparatus

(G-3072)
BLUE AVIONICS INC
542 Black Horse Rd (19425-3521)
PHONE..............................310 433-9431
Ross Cairns,
EMP: 10
SALES (est): 1MM **Privately Held**
SIC: 3812 3728 Aircraft flight instruments; aircraft parts & equipment

(G-3073)
BUSINESS CMMUNICATIONS SYSTEMS
1856 Art School Rd (19425-1300)
PHONE..............................610 827-7061
Donald Taggart, *President*
Marion Taggart, *Vice Pres*
EMP: 5
SALES (est): 834.7K **Privately Held**
SIC: 3669 7389 Intercommunication systems, electric; music & broadcasting services

(G-3074)
COMPLETE IMAGING CORP
1924 Art School Rd (19425-1301)
PHONE..............................610 827-1561
Andrew Taylor, *President*
David Martino, *Vice Pres*
Maria Thompson, *Treasurer*
EMP: 4
SALES (est): 546.4K **Privately Held**
WEB: www.completeimagingproducts.com
SIC: 3299 Images, small: gypsum, clay or papier mache

(G-3075)
DMW MARINE GROUP LLC
1123 Saint Matthews Rd (19425-2701)
PHONE..............................610 827-2032
Mark Gregory, *Vice Pres*
Bo Weidner, *Mng Member*
▲ EMP: 4
SALES (est): 787.7K **Privately Held**
WEB: www.dmwmarinegroup.com
SIC: 3536 Hoists, cranes & monorails

(G-3076)
EAGLE DESIGN GROUP
45 Senn Dr (19425-9539)
PHONE..............................610 321-2488
Melissa Schroth Doyle, *President*
Walter D Schroth, *President*
Alfred T Myles, *CFO*
▲ EMP: 25
SQ FT: 18,000
SALES (est): 6.9MM **Privately Held**
WEB: www.eagledesigngroup.com
SIC: 3678 Communication wire

(G-3077)
EAGLE DESIGN INNOVATION LLC
Also Called: Eagle Design Group
45 Senn Dr (19425-9539)
PHONE..............................610 321-2488
Melissa Doyle, *President*
EMP: 19
SALES (est): 2.9MM **Privately Held**
SIC: 3678 Electronic connectors

(G-3078)
FABRITECH INC
935 Skyline Dr (19425-1900)
PHONE..............................610 430-0027
Michael J O'Neill, *President*
Brian O'Neill, *Vice Pres*
EMP: 7
SQ FT: 10,000
SALES (est): 1.3MM **Privately Held**
WEB: www.fabritechinc.net
SIC: 3053 Gasket materials

(G-3079)
GLOBAL TRADE LINKS LLC
2610 Rockledge Ct (19425-3892)
PHONE..............................888 777-1577
Rajesh Sreedharan, *CEO*
Ommen Mathew, *Purch Mgr*
Divya Eganathan, *Buyer*
▼ EMP: 20
SQ FT: 1,500
SALES (est): 4.5MM **Privately Held**
SIC: 3491 3823 3494 Industrial valves; regulators (steam fittings); industrial flow & liquid measuring instruments; fluid power pumps & motors; valves & pipe fittings; power wire & cable; electric tools

(G-3080)
HOHMANN & BARNARD INC
1985 Ticonderoga Blvd # 15 (19425-9556)
PHONE..............................610 873-0070
Jonathan Giza, *Branch Mgr*
EMP: 9
SALES (corp-wide): 225.3B **Publicly Held**
SIC: 3496 Miscellaneous fabricated wire products
HQ: Hohmann & Barnard, Inc.
30 Rasons Ct
Hauppauge NY 11788
631 234-0600

(G-3081)
J M SCHMIDT PRECISION TOOL CO
931 Newcomen Rd (19425-2018)
PHONE..............................610 436-5010
Robert Harple Jr, *President*
Barbar Kurkjian, *Vice Pres*
Barbara Kurkjian, *Vice Pres*
EMP: 15 EST: 1960
SALES (est): 2.9MM **Privately Held**
WEB: www.precisiontoolco.com
SIC: 3599 Machine shop, jobbing & repair

(G-3082)
LASER-VIEW TECHNOLOGIES INC
Also Called: Dimetix USA
205 Byers Rd (19425-9506)
P.O. Box 195, Lionville (19353-0195)
PHONE..............................610 497-8910
Steven Lubeck, *President*
◆ EMP: 10
SALES: 2MM **Privately Held**
SIC: 3812 Detection apparatus: electronic/magnetic field, light/heat

(G-3083)
O C TANNER COMPANY
74 Pottstown Pike # 1006 (19425-9500)
PHONE..............................610 458-1245
Peter Di Nicola, *Manager*
Joe Obrien, *Director*
EMP: 4
SALES (corp-wide): 341.9MM **Privately Held**
WEB: www.octanner.com
SIC: 3911 Jewelry, precious metal
PA: O. C. Tanner Company
1930 S State St
Salt Lake City UT 84115
801 486-2430

(G-3084)
PUP E LUV LLC
112 Magnolia Dr (19425-3611)
PHONE..............................610 458-5280
Glenn Gardone, *President*
EMP: 53
SQ FT: 5,500
SALES (est): 5.2MM **Privately Held**
SIC: 2047 Dog & cat food

(G-3085)
QUALITY SYSTEMS INTEGRATORS
Also Called: Q S I
148 Magnolia Dr (19425-3611)
P.O. Box 91, Uwchland (19480-0091)
PHONE..............................610 458-0539
Marti Turocy, *President*
Renee Cabrey, *Manager*
John Karcher, *Technology*
EMP: 9
SQ FT: 1,500
SALES (est): 710K **Privately Held**
WEB: www.qsi-inc.com
SIC: 7371 7372 Computer software systems analysis & design, custom; prepackaged software

(G-3086)
SWEETWATER NATURAL PDTS LLC (PA)
Also Called: Sweetwater 100
976 Pottstown Pike (19425-3509)
PHONE..............................610 321-1900
Thomas O Donnell, *Partner*
Scott Risbon, *Partner*
EMP: 5
SQ FT: 3,000
SALES (est): 2.1MM **Privately Held**
SIC: 5039 3271 Prefabricated structures; blocks, concrete: landscape or retaining wall

(G-3087)
WAZA INC
Also Called: Food Medication Interactions
19 Red Rock Ln (19425-2718)
P.O. Box 204, Birchrunville (19421-0204)
PHONE..............................610 827-7800
Walter Pronsky, *CEO*
Zaneta Pronsky, *Corp Secy*
EMP: 5
SQ FT: 1,200

SALES (est): 500K **Privately Held**
WEB: www.foodmedinteractions.com
SIC: 2731 Book publishing

Chester Township
Delaware County

(G-3088)
AJM ELECTRIC INC
2333 Concord Rd (19013-2447)
PHONE..............................610 494-5735
Anne R McConnell, *President*
EMP: 7
SALES (est): 1.2MM **Privately Held**
SIC: 3699 Electrical work

Chesterbrook
Delaware County

(G-3089)
ANIMAS LLC (HQ)
965 Chesterbrook Blvd (19087-5614)
PHONE..............................610 644-8990
Katherine D Crothall, *President*
Juan Toro, *President*
Astrid Matthysse, *Partner*
Audrey Finkelstein, *Exec VP*
Audrey Greenfield, *Vice Pres*
▲ EMP: 287
SQ FT: 50,000
SALES (est): 47.9MM
SALES (corp-wide): 81.5B **Publicly Held**
WEB: www.jnj.com
SIC: 3842 Surgical appliances & supplies
PA: Johnson & Johnson
1 Johnson And Johnson Plz
New Brunswick NJ 08933
732 524-0400

(G-3090)
CUTANEA LIFE SCIENCES INC
1500 Liberty Ridge Dr # 3000 (19087-5581)
PHONE..............................484 568-0100
Robert J Bitterman, *President*
Robert Ferrara, *CFO*
EMP: 30
SALES: 5MM
SALES (corp-wide): 771MM **Privately Held**
SIC: 2834 Pharmaceutical preparations
PA: Maruho Co., Ltd.
1-5-22, Nakatsu, Kita-Ku
Osaka OSK 531-0
663 718-876

(G-3091)
CUTE LOOPS
36 Independence Pl (19087-5825)
PHONE..............................484 318-7175
Elaine Staunton, *Principal*
EMP: 3 EST: 2011
SALES (est): 199.1K **Privately Held**
SIC: 2339 Women's & misses' accessories

(G-3092)
ENVIRONMENTAL SYSTEMS RESEARCH
Also Called: Esri
1325 Morris Dr Ste 201 (19087-5521)
PHONE..............................909 793-2853
James Higgins, *Branch Mgr*
EMP: 38
SALES (corp-wide): 1B **Privately Held**
SIC: 5045 7371 7372 7373 Computer software; custom computer programming services; prepackaged software; computer integrated systems design; computer related maintenance services; computer related consulting services
PA: Environmental Systems Research Institute, Inc.
380 New York St
Redlands CA 92373
909 793-2853

(G-3093)
LIFESCAN INC (HQ)
965 Chesterbrook Blvd (19087-5614)
PHONE..............................800 227-8862
Valerie Asbury, *President*

Amy Van Zandbergen, *Research*
James Buschmeier, *CFO*
▲ **EMP:** 1000
SQ FT: 45,000
SALES (est): 415.3MM **Privately Held**
WEB: www.lifescan.com
SIC: 2835 3841 Blood derivative diagnostic agents; medical instruments & equipment, blood & bone work
PA: Lifescan Global Corporation
965 Chesterbrook Blvd
Chesterbrook PA 19087
800 227-8862

(G-3094)
LIFESCAN GLOBAL CORPORATION (PA)
965 Chesterbrook Blvd (19087-5614)
PHONE...................................800 227-8862
EMP: 10
SALES (est): 415.3MM **Privately Held**
SIC: 3841 Medical instruments & equipment, blood & bone work

(G-3095)
POWSUS INC
14 Woodstream Dr (19087-5874)
PHONE...................................610 296-2237
Donald Mac Elwee, *Managing Dir*
Glyn Miller, *Managing Dir*
Harry Stewart, *Director*
EMP: 15
SALES (est): 1.2MM **Privately Held**
SIC: 2819 Chemicals, high purity: refined from technical grade

(G-3096)
SHIRE HOLDINGS US AG (HQ)
725 Chesterbrook Blvd (19087-5637)
PHONE...................................484 595-8800
John Lee, *Exec VP*
Shawn Fitzpatrick, *Manager*
Sue Hatfield, *Director*
Jonathan Patroni, *Director*
Ivan Tosques, *Director*
EMP: 13
SALES (est): 2MM
SALES (corp-wide): 15.1B **Privately Held**
SIC: 2834 Pharmaceutical preparations
PA: Shire Plc
1 Kingdom Street
London W2 6B
125 689-4003

(G-3097)
SHIRE PHARMACEUTICALS LLC (HQ)
1200 Morris Dr (19087-5507)
PHONE...................................484 595-8800
John Miller, *President*
Michael Cola, *President*
James Cavanaugh, *Chairman*
John Marshall, *Business Mgr*
Jim McNinch, *Business Mgr*
EMP: 170
SALES (est): 785MM
SALES (corp-wide): 212.8K **Privately Held**
SIC: 2834 Pharmaceutical preparations
PA: Shire Biopharmaceuticals Holdings
Hampshire International Business Park
Basingstoke HANTS RG24
125 689-4000

(G-3098)
SHIRE US MANUFACTURING INC (DH)
1200 Morris Dr (19087-5507)
PHONE...................................484 595-8800
John Miller, *President*
Julie Mervine, *General Mgr*
Mike F Cola, *Exec VP*
Mike Yasick, *Senior VP*
Scotty Bowman, *Vice Pres*
▲ **EMP:** 44
SQ FT: 90,000
SALES (est): 55.2MM
SALES (corp-wide): 15.1B **Privately Held**
SIC: 2834 Powders, pharmaceutical
HQ: Shire Us Inc.
300 Shire Way
Lexington MA 02421
781 482-9222

(G-3099)
TREVENA INC
955 Chesterbrook Blvd # 200 (19087-5615)
PHONE...................................610 354-8840
Leon O Moulder Jr, *Ch of Bd*
Carrie L Bourdow, *President*
Michael W Lark, *Senior VP*
John M Limongelli, *Senior VP*
Robert T Yoder, *Senior VP*
EMP: 53
SQ FT: 16,000
SALES: 3.7MM **Privately Held**
SIC: 2834 Pharmaceutical preparations

Cheswick
Allegheny County

(G-3100)
ALLOY AMERICA LLC
820 Route 910 (15024-9716)
P.O. Box 38481, Pittsburgh (15238-8481)
PHONE...................................412 828-8270
Tom Finn,
Bill Versaw,
▲ **EMP:** 12
SALES: 5MM **Privately Held**
SIC: 3354 Aluminum extruded products

(G-3101)
ARMINA STONE INC
780 Route 910 Ste 100 (15024-9703)
PHONE...................................412 406-8442
Emre Basman, *President*
Mark Akscyn, *CFO*
EMP: 7 **EST:** 2016
SALES (est): 340K
SALES (corp-wide): 2.5MM **Privately Held**
SIC: 5032 3281 Brick, stone & related material; cut stone & stone products
PA: Porto Exim Usa, Llc
780 Route 910 Ste 100
Cheswick PA 15024
412 406-8442

(G-3102)
BUBCO ENTERPRISE INC
Also Called: The Graphic Garage
1415 Pittsburgh St (15024-1448)
PHONE...................................724 274-4930
Ken Fricchione, *President*
Lisa Fricchione, *Bookkeeper*
EMP: 4
SQ FT: 1,900
SALES: 200K **Privately Held**
SIC: 7336 2759 Silk screen design; screen printing

(G-3103)
C E HOLDEN INC
938 Route 910 (15024-4014)
PHONE...................................412 767-5050
Clarence Holden, *President*
Geraldine M Holden, *Corp Secy*
Edward J Holden, *Vice Pres*
EMP: 10 **EST:** 1950
SQ FT: 16,800
SALES (est): 1.9MM **Privately Held**
WEB: www.ceholdeninc.com
SIC: 3451 Screw machine products

(G-3104)
CEMLINE CORPORATION
808 Freeport Rd (15024)
PHONE...................................724 274-5430
William Chappell, *CEO*
Charles L Chappell, *President*
Hugh K Chappell, *Treasurer*
Tony Dipardo, *Sales Staff*
Brenda Vozar, *Manager*
EMP: 54
SQ FT: 100,000
SALES (est): 13.5MM **Privately Held**
WEB: www.cemline.com
SIC: 3639 3443 Hot water heaters, household; water tanks, metal plate

(G-3105)
CURTISS-WRIGHT ELECTRO-(HQ)
Also Called: Electro-Mechanical Division
1000 Wright Way (15024-1008)
PHONE...................................724 275-5000
David C Linton, *President*
James Drake, *General Mgr*
Jim Drake, *General Mgr*
Martin R Benante, *Chairman*
John Higgins, *Opers Mgr*
▲ **EMP:** 800
SALES (est): 193.8MM
SALES (corp-wide): 2.4B **Publicly Held**
SIC: 3561 3621 3511 Pumps & pumping equipment; motors & generators; turbines & turbine generator sets
PA: Curtiss-Wright Corporation
130 Harbour Place Dr # 300
Davidson NC 28036
704 869-4600

(G-3106)
DEVELOPED RESOURCES INC
21 Low Grade Rd (15024)
PHONE...................................724 274-6956
David E Icovino, *President*
EMP: 4
SQ FT: 480
SALES (est): 338K **Privately Held**
SIC: 1389 Oil & gas wells: building, repairing & dismantling; well plugging & abandoning, oil & gas

(G-3107)
EXPRESS PRTG & GRAPHICS INC
1801 Pittsburgh St (15024-1527)
PHONE...................................724 274-7700
Michael S Kelly, *President*
Nadine L Kelly, *Vice Pres*
Shawn Sabo, *Prdtn Mgr*
Rob Plocki, *Marketing Mgr*
EMP: 7
SQ FT: 8,000
SALES (est): 1MM **Privately Held**
SIC: 2752 Commercial printing, lithographic

(G-3108)
FILMET COLOR LAB INC
1051 Russellton Rd (15024-1045)
PHONE...................................724 275-1700
Richard L Bachelder, *CEO*
EMP: 65
SQ FT: 65,000
SALES (est): 9.4MM **Privately Held**
WEB: www.filmet.com
SIC: 7384 2759 2752 Photofinishing laboratory; photograph developing & retouching; commercial printing; commercial printing, lithographic

(G-3109)
FILTER SERVICE & INSTALLATION
600 Watercrest Way (15024-1370)
P.O. Box 175 (15024-0175)
PHONE...................................724 274-5220
Edmund J Watson, *President*
Dennis Petronka, *Corp Secy*
EMP: 5
SQ FT: 200,000
SALES (est): 730K **Privately Held**
SIC: 3564 Filters, air: furnaces, air conditioning equipment, etc.

(G-3110)
GRAPHIC GARAGE
1415 Pittsburgh St (15024-1448)
PHONE...................................724 274-4930
Ken Fricchione, *President*
Lisa Fricchione, *Principal*
EMP: 3
SALES (est): 227.1K **Privately Held**
SIC: 2759 Screen printing

(G-3111)
M & M MANUFACTURING CO
Also Called: Vision Products Ic
460 Nixon Rd (15024-1081)
PHONE...................................724 274-0767
Ronald J Marginian, *President*
Fred Coope, *Principal*
Albert J Ortenzio, *Principal*

Warren H Pritchard, *Principal*
Maureen Marginian, *Admin Sec*
EMP: 50
SQ FT: 90,000
SALES (est): 6.5MM **Privately Held**
WEB: www.mandmmfg.com
SIC: 2542 3161 2789 2782 Office & store showcases & display fixtures; luggage; bookbinding & related work; blankbooks & looseleaf binders; wood partitions & fixtures; automotive & apparel trimmings

(G-3112)
NICK MULONE & SON
109 S Highland Ave (15024-1619)
PHONE...................................724 274-3221
Nicklas Mulone, *Owner*
Dennis Tafi, *Manager*
EMP: 9
SALES (est): 1.2MM **Privately Held**
SIC: 3861 Screens, projection

(G-3113)
NORTH AMERICAN FENCING CORP
1005 Pittsburgh St (15024-1307)
P.O. Box 217 (15024-0217)
PHONE...................................412 362-3900
Richard W Holsing, *President*
Robert Sodini, *Corp Secy*
Sue Holsing, *Office Mgr*
EMP: 35
SQ FT: 6,000
SALES (est): 3.9MM **Privately Held**
WEB: www.nafence.com
SIC: 1799 3496 Fence construction; miscellaneous fabricated wire products

(G-3114)
PACKAGING CORPORATION AMERICA
Also Called: Pca/Cheswick 379
499 Nixon Rd (15024-1037)
PHONE...................................724 275-3700
EMP: 87
SALES (corp-wide): 7B **Publicly Held**
SIC: 2653 Boxes, corrugated: made from purchased materials
PA: Packaging Corporation Of America
1 N Field Ct
Lake Forest IL 60045
847 482-3000

(G-3115)
PORTO EXIM USA LLC (PA)
Also Called: Armina Stone
780 Route 910 Ste 100 (15024-9703)
PHONE...................................412 406-8442
Emre Basman, *Principal*
Lisa Curry, *Principal*
EMP: 6
SALES (est): 2.5MM **Privately Held**
SIC: 5032 3281 1799 Granite building stone; cut stone & stone products; kitchen & bathroom remodeling

(G-3116)
PPG INDUSTRIES INC
Also Called: PPG Glass Technology Ctr - GL
400 Guys Run Rd (15024-9464)
PHONE...................................412 820-8500
Dr Mehran Arbab, *Director*
EMP: 250
SALES (corp-wide): 15.3B **Publicly Held**
WEB: www.ppg.com
SIC: 2851 3211 Paints & allied products; flat glass
PA: Ppg Industries, Inc.
1 Ppg Pl
Pittsburgh PA 15272
412 434-3131

(G-3117)
REDLAND BRICK INC
Also Called: Redland Brick Inc Harmar Plant
230 Rich Hill Rd (15024)
PHONE...................................412 828-8046
Wes Fravel, *Manager*
EMP: 50
SALES (corp-wide): 8.1MM **Privately Held**
WEB: www.redlandbrick.com
SIC: 5211 3255 2951 Brick; clay refractories; asphalt paving mixtures & blocks

HQ: Redland Brick Inc.
15718 Clear Spring Rd
Williamsport MD 21795
301 223-7700

(G-3118)
SMOOTH LINE INC
780 Route 910 Ste 400 (15024-9703)
PHONE..............................412 828-3599
John Sussenegger, *President*
EMP: 8 **EST:** 1998
SQ FT: 5,000
SALES: 1MM **Privately Held**
SIC: 3089 Automotive parts, plastic

(G-3119)
TRADEMARK SPECIALTIES
Also Called: Trademark Threads
700 Watercrest Way # 740 (15024-1374)
PHONE..............................412 353-3752
EMP: 5 **EST:** 2004
SQ FT: 4,500
SALES (est): 186.2K **Privately Held**
SIC: 2321 Uniform shirts: made from pur-
chased materials

(G-3120)
**TRULITE GL ALUM SOLUTIONS
LLC**
100 Business Center Dr (15024-1069)
PHONE..............................724 274-9050
Michael Crawford, *Manager*
EMP: 16 **Privately Held**
SIC: 3355 Aluminum rolling & drawing
PA: Trulite Glass & Aluminum Solutions, Llc
403 Westpark Ct Ste 201
Peachtree City GA 30269

(G-3121)
VISION PRODUCTS INC
460 Nixon Rd Ste 100 (15024-1081)
PHONE..............................724 274-0767
James Young, *CEO*
Mike Ryan, *CEO*
EMP: 52
SQ FT: 55,000
SALES (est): 6.2MM **Privately Held**
WEB: www.visionprod.com
SIC: 3993 Displays & cutouts, window &
lobby

(G-3122)
VITRO FLAT GLASS LLC (HQ)
Also Called: Vitro Architectural Glass
400 Guys Run Rd (15024-9464)
PHONE..............................412 820-8500
Richard Beuke,
EMP: 184
SALES (est): 176.7MM **Privately Held**
SIC: 3211 Flat glass

(G-3123)
**ZOLL MANUFACTURING
CORPORATION**
1000 Commerce Dr (15024)
PHONE..............................412 968-3333
Richard Blattenberger, *Manager*
EMP: 90
SALES (corp-wide): 18.3MM **Privately
Held**
SIC: 3845 Electromedical equipment
PA: Zoll Manufacturing Corporation
121 Gamma Dr
Pittsburgh PA 15238
412 968-3333

(G-3124)
ZOLL MEDICAL CORPORATION
Also Called: Zoll Lifevest
1001 Commerce Dr (15024-9768)
PHONE..............................412 968-3333
EMP: 6
SALES (est): 518.2K **Privately Held**
SIC: 3845 Electromedical equipment

Chicora
Butler County

(G-3125)
AHT INC (DH)
Also Called: CMC Defense Products
1024 Kittanning Pike (16025-2030)
PHONE..............................724 445-2155

Gary Hudson, *CEO*
Clyde Selig, *President*
Stanley A Rabin, *Vice Pres*
Bob Unfried, *Vice Pres*
Louis A Federle, *Treasurer*
EMP: 68
SQ FT: 12,000
SALES (est): 11.7MM
SALES (corp-wide): 4.6B **Publicly Held**
SIC: 3398 Annealing of metal
HQ: Cmc Steel Holding Company
802 N West St Ste 302
Wilmington DE 19801
302 691-6200

(G-3126)
DENNIS FILGES CO INC
238 Center Dr (16025-3706)
PHONE..............................724 287-3735
Dennis J Filges, *President*
EMP: 25 **EST:** 1972
SQ FT: 25,000
SALES (est): 4.7MM **Privately Held**
WEB: www.dennisfilges.com
SIC: 3444 Sheet metal specialties, not
stamped

(G-3127)
HUNTER RUSSELL GROUP
758 Christopher Ln (16025-2055)
PHONE..............................724 445-7228
Charles R Morris, *Partner*
Charles Morris, *Partner*
Gilbert Morris, *Partner*
EMP: 4
SALES (est): 390K **Privately Held**
SIC: 3841 Medical instruments & equip-
ment, blood & bone work

(G-3128)
OIL & VINEGAR
350 Bryce Ln (16025-3432)
PHONE..............................724 840-9656
Angela McMasters, *Principal*
EMP: 3 **EST:** 2014
SALES (est): 178.9K **Privately Held**
SIC: 2099 Vinegar

(G-3129)
SPIDERS DEN INC
120 Paradise Ln (16025-2608)
PHONE..............................724 445-7450
Dennis Tefft, *President*
Karen Tefft, *Corp Secy*
EMP: 6 **EST:** 1982
SALES: 200K **Privately Held**
SIC: 3199 Novelties, leather

(G-3130)
ZAVILLAS OIL CO
1479 State Route 4011 (16025-4413)
PHONE..............................724 445-3702
Jack Zavilla, *Owner*
EMP: 4
SALES: 17K **Privately Held**
SIC: 1311 Crude petroleum & natural gas

Childs
Lackawanna County

(G-3131)
MARILAKE WINERY LLC
209 Main St (18407-2938)
PHONE..............................570 536-6575
Alan T Granza, *Manager*
EMP: 4
SALES (est): 83K **Privately Held**
SIC: 2084 Wines

Chinchilla
Lackawanna County

(G-3132)
SPRINT PRINT INC
322 Northern Blvd (18410)
P.O. Box 421 (18410-0421)
PHONE..............................570 586-5947
William D Stevens, *President*
EMP: 9

SALES (est): 1.5MM **Privately Held**
WEB: www.sprintprintscranton.com
SIC: 2752 Commercial printing, offset

Christiana
Lancaster County

(G-3133)
BELL MANUFACTURING
195 Bell Rd (17509-9510)
PHONE..............................717 529-2600
David Smucker, *Principal*
EMP: 3
SALES (est): 248.8K **Privately Held**
SIC: 3599 Industrial machinery

(G-3134)
CHARLES BOND COMPANY
11 Green St (17509-1409)
P.O. Box 105 (17509-0105)
PHONE..............................610 593-5171
Charles C Bond III, *President*
Louis Bond, *Vice Pres*
Mark Bond, *Vice Pres*
Ellen B Erb, *Admin Sec*
EMP: 10 **EST:** 1888
SQ FT: 36,000
SALES (est): 1.5MM **Privately Held**
SIC: 3566 5084 Speed changers (power
transmission equipment), except auto;
gears, power transmission, except auto-
motive; drives, high speed industrial, ex-
cept hydrostatic; materials handling
machinery

(G-3135)
HONEYBROOK WOODWORKS
98 Williams Run Rd (17509-9706)
PHONE..............................610 593-6884
Melvin Kauffman, *Owner*
EMP: 10
SALES: 3MM **Privately Held**
SIC: 2499 5039 5211 Fencing, docks &
other outdoor wood structural products;
prefabricated structures; prefabricated
buildings

(G-3136)
**INNOVATIVE PLASTICS OF PA
LLC**
1084 Noble Rd (17509-9740)
PHONE..............................717 529-2699
Steve Stoltzfus, *Partner*
John Stoltzfus,
EMP: 2
SALES: 1MM **Privately Held**
SIC: 2673 Bags: plastic, laminated &
coated

(G-3137)
**J D KAUFFMAN MACHINE SP
INC (PA)**
Also Called: Teco Mfg Co
414 Newport Ave (17509-9671)
P.O. Box 219 (17509-0219)
PHONE..............................610 593-2033
Robert Bills, *President*
Joan Bills, *Corp Secy*
Mike Dagen, *Vice Pres*
▼ **EMP:** 12 **EST:** 1949
SQ FT: 11,000
SALES (est): 1.4MM **Privately Held**
SIC: 3599 Machine shop, jobbing & repair

(G-3138)
**J D KAUFFMAN MACHINE SP
INC**
Teco Mfg Div
414 Newport Ave (17509-9671)
P.O. Box 219 (17509-0219)
PHONE..............................610 593-2033
Robert Bills, *President*
EMP: 12
SALES (corp-wide): 1.4MM **Privately
Held**
SIC: 3599 Machine shop, jobbing & repair
PA: J. D. Kauffman Machine Shop, Inc.
414 Newport Ave
Christiana PA 17509
610 593-2033

(G-3139)
JACOB B KAUFFMAN
Also Called: Kauffman Woodwork
315 Bell Rd (17509-9777)
PHONE..............................717 529-6522
Jacob Kauffman, *Owner*
EMP: 6
SQ FT: 8,000
SALES (est): 771.6K **Privately Held**
SIC: 2452 Prefabricated wood buildings

(G-3140)
JAKE STOLTZFUS
Also Called: J & M Woodworks
1644 Georgetown Rd (17509-9610)
PHONE..............................717 529-4082
Jake Stoltzfus, *Owner*
EMP: 11
SALES (est): 550K **Privately Held**
SIC: 3944 Dollhouses & furniture

(G-3141)
**LITTLE WASH FABRICATORS
INC**
52 Mill St (17509-1608)
PHONE..............................717 768-7356
Douglas L Howe, *President*
Jones Stoltzfus, *Vice Pres*
EMP: 15 **EST:** 1999
SALES (est): 3.2MM **Privately Held**
SIC: 3449 Bars, concrete reinforcing: fabri-
cated steel

(G-3142)
MILLERS WELDING & REPAIR
54 Christiana Pike (17509-9798)
PHONE..............................610 593-6112
John S Miller, *Owner*
EMP: 5 **EST:** 1998
SALES (est): 200K **Privately Held**
SIC: 7692 Welding repair

(G-3143)
**NOBLE ROAD WOODWORKS
LLC**
732 Noble Rd (17509-9608)
PHONE..............................610 593-5122
Aaron Beiler, *Managing Prtnr*
Ephraim Beiler, *Partner*
Ike Esh, *Partner*
EMP: 3
SALES (est): 378.5K **Privately Held**
SIC: 2452 Prefabricated wood buildings

(G-3144)
WALTER AND JACKSON INC
44 Gay St (17509-1712)
P.O. Box 160 (17509-0160)
PHONE..............................610 593-5195
George Walter, *Ch of Bd*
EMP: 70
SALES (corp-wide): 19.4MM **Privately
Held**
WEB: www.walterandjackson.com
SIC: 5211 5251 2426 Lumber & other
building materials; hardware; hardwood
dimension & flooring mills
PA: Walter And Jackson, Inc.
44 Gay St
Christiana PA 17509
610 593-5195

(G-3145)
ZOOKS SAWMILL LLC
1205 Smyrna Rd (17509-9682)
PHONE..............................610 593-1040
John E Zooks,
EMP: 5
SALES (est): 525.9K **Privately Held**
SIC: 2421 Sawmills & planing mills, gen-
eral

Clairton
Allegheny County

(G-3146)
AKJ INDUSTRIES INC
1500 N State St (15025-3952)
PHONE..............................412 233-7222
John Bielich, *Branch Mgr*
EMP: 7

SALES (corp-wide): 8MM **Privately Held**
WEB: www.akjindustries.com
SIC: **4953** 8748 2992 Recycling, waste materials; environmental consultant; re-refining lubricating oils & greases
PA: Akj Industries, Inc.
10175 Ben C Pratt 6 Mi
Fort Myers FL 33966
239 939-1696

(G-3147)
ALS CONEZONE
1211 State Route 885 (15025-3821)
PHONE................................412 405-9601
Larry Colaianni, *Owner*
EMP: 4
SALES (est): 230.7K **Privately Held**
SIC: **2052** Cones, ice cream

(G-3148)
D & S FABRICATING & WELDING
678 Cochran Mill Rd (15025-3210)
PHONE................................412 653-9185
John Schubert, *Owner*
EMP: 6
SALES (est): 270K **Privately Held**
SIC: **7692** 3441 1799 Welding repair; fabricated structural metal; welding on site

(G-3149)
D/R MACHINE & WELD CO INC
Also Called: D & R Machine Co
668 Cochran Mill Rd (15025-3210)
PHONE................................412 655-4452
Ronald Batykefer, *President*
Pamela Batykefer, *Corp Secy*
EMP: 3
SQ FT: 3,200
SALES (est): 412.5K **Privately Held**
SIC: **3599** Machine shop, jobbing & repair

(G-3150)
EVANS MACHINING SERVICE INC
314 State St (15025-1914)
PHONE................................412 233-3556
Allen R Evans, *CEO*
EMP: 8
SQ FT: 10,000
SALES (est): 1.4MM **Privately Held**
WEB: www.evansmachine.com
SIC: **3469** Machine parts, stamped or pressed metal

(G-3151)
JAMES F KEMP INC
709 Miller Ave (15025-1491)
PHONE................................412 233-8166
Richard Kemp, *President*
EMP: 6 EST: 1931
SQ FT: 20,000
SALES (est): 1.2MM **Privately Held**
SIC: **3443** Pipe, large diameter: metal plate; tanks, standard or custom fabricated: metal plate

(G-3152)
JORDAN DRAFT SERVICE
1002 Oak St (15025-3112)
PHONE................................412 382-4299
Rob Stosic, *Principal*
EMP: 5
SALES (est): 411.7K **Privately Held**
WEB: www.jordandraftservice.com
SIC: **2086** 5078 Bottled & canned soft drinks; refrigerated beverage dispensers

(G-3153)
LOUIS MATTES JR (PA)
1231 Gill Hall Rd (15025-3406)
PHONE................................412 653-1266
Louis Mattes Jr, *Owner*
EMP: 3
SALES (est): 231.6K **Privately Held**
SIC: **3599** Machine shop, jobbing & repair

(G-3154)
MPW INDUSTRIAL SERVICES INC
400 State St (15025-1855)
PHONE................................412 233-4060
Monty Black, *Owner*
EMP: 3

SALES (corp-wide): 208.7MM **Privately Held**
SIC: **3589** Vacuum cleaners & sweepers, electric: industrial
HQ: Mpw Industrial Services, Inc.
9711 Lancaster Rd
Hebron OH 43025
800 827-8790

(G-3155)
PETERSEN MACHINE SHOP INC
1014 Neng Hollow Rd (15025)
PHONE................................412 233-8077
Daniel Petersen, *Principal*
Kathleen Kovtun, *Treasurer*
Eileen Rossi, *Admin Sec*
EMP: 10 EST: 1948
SQ FT: 4,000
SALES (est): 1.5MM **Privately Held**
SIC: **3599** Machine shop, jobbing & repair

(G-3156)
PRINCE PRINTING
Also Called: SpeeDee Shirts.com
517 Saint Clair Ave (15025-1434)
PHONE................................412 233-3555
Christopher Ledonne, *Owner*
EMP: 3 EST: 1963
SQ FT: 5,200
SALES (est): 250K **Privately Held**
WEB: www.speedeeshirts.com
SIC: **2752** 2759 2262 Commercial printing, offset; letterpress printing; screen printing; screen printing: manmade fiber & silk broadwoven fabrics

(G-3157)
PRINT CHARMING DESIGN
1391 Peterson Dr (15025-2717)
PHONE................................412 519-5226
Marlow Robert, *Owner*
EMP: 4
SALES (est): 341.5K **Privately Held**
SIC: **2752** Commercial printing, lithographic

(G-3158)
TYK AMERICA INC (HQ)
301 Brickyard Rd (15025-3650)
PHONE................................412 384-4259
S Ushigone, *Ch of Bd*
Andy Elksnitis, *President*
Kenichi Sasaki, *President*
James Karamanos, *Vice Pres*
Nobuhiro Ichihara, *Manager*
▲ EMP: 50
SQ FT: 5,000
SALES (est): 15.8MM
SALES (corp-wide): 212.9MM **Privately Held**
WEB: www.tykamerica.com
SIC: **3624** 3255 3297 3354 Carbon & graphite products; clay refractories; non-clay refractories; aluminum extruded products
PA: Tyk Corporation
2-11-1, Konan
Minato-Ku TKY 108-0
364 332-888

(G-3159)
VANGURA IRON INC
1020 Neng Hollow Rd (15025)
PHONE................................412 461-7825
Kenneth Senka, *President*
Beth Vangura, *Corp Secy*
Marlene Scheidemantle, *Admin Sec*
EMP: 12
SQ FT: 5,000
SALES (est): 1MM **Privately Held**
SIC: **3446** 3441 Architectural metalwork; fabricated structural metal

(G-3160)
VANGURA TOOL INC
440 Waddell Ave (15025-1556)
PHONE................................412 233-6401
Mark D Ebbitt, *President*
Jerry Hinerman, *Vice Pres*
Erica Beard, *Project Mgr*
EMP: 30
SQ FT: 25,000
SALES (est): 5.5MM **Privately Held**
WEB: www.vanguratool.com
SIC: **3599** 3544 Machine shop, jobbing & repair; special dies, tools, jigs & fixtures

(G-3161)
C & C WELDING AND FABG INC
803 Clarence Rd (16829-8111)
P.O. Box 245 (16829-0245)
PHONE................................814 387-6556
James Hall, *President*
EMP: 6
SQ FT: 6,400
SALES (est): 649.9K **Privately Held**
SIC: **7692** 3449 Welding repair; miscellaneous metalwork

(G-3162)
C/C WELDING/FABRICT INC
803 Main St (16829)
P.O. Box 245 (16829-0245)
PHONE................................814 364-9460
George Chicko, *President*
James Hall, *Vice Pres*
Stephanie Chicko, *Treasurer*
Jymee Chicko, *Admin Sec*
EMP: 5 EST: 1989
SALES (est): 264.7K **Privately Held**
SIC: **7692** Welding repair

(G-3163)
CINGLE BROTHERS MACHINE SHOP
105 Dairy St (16829-8024)
P.O. Box 126 (16829-0126)
PHONE................................814 387-4994
William Cingle, *Owner*
EMP: 7
SQ FT: 25,000
SALES: 500K **Privately Held**
SIC: **3599** Machine shop, jobbing & repair

(G-3164)
MOUNTAINTOP WELDING
1262 Ridge Rd (16829-7801)
PHONE................................814 387-9353
Albert Puhalla, *Owner*
EMP: 5
SALES (est): 210.9K **Privately Held**
SIC: **7692** Welding repair

(G-3165)
SNOW SHOE REFRACTORIES LLC
895 Clarence Rd (16829-8111)
PHONE................................814 387-6811
Robert Wilder, *CFO*
Brett Blair,
Brent Porterfield,
EMP: 46
SQ FT: 200,000
SALES (est): 8MM **Privately Held**
SIC: **3255** 3297 Clay refractories; graphite refractories: carbon bond or ceramic bond

(G-3166)
ALLEGHENY TOOL MOLD & MFG INC
15300 Route 6 (16313-1238)
PHONE................................814 726-0200
Mark Hazeltine, *President*
Tim Hazeltine, *Vice Pres*
Shelly Massa, *Admin Sec*
EMP: 15 EST: 1977
SQ FT: 3,500
SALES (est): 2.4MM **Privately Held**
WEB: www.alleghenytool.com
SIC: **3544** Special dies & tools; dies & die holders for metal cutting, forming, die casting; jigs & fixtures

(G-3167)
BINGAMAN & SON LUMBER INC
22 Brown Ave (16313)
P.O. Box 407 (16313-0407)
PHONE................................814 723-2612
Maurice Bennett, *Manager*
EMP: 40

SALES (corp-wide): 65MM **Privately Held**
WEB: www.bingamanlumber.com
SIC: **5031** 2421 Lumber: rough, dressed & finished; sawmills & planing mills, general
PA: Bingaman & Son Lumber, Inc.
1195 Creek Mountain Rd
Kreamer PA 17833
570 374-1108

(G-3168)
CODY WELL SERVICE
Block 1385 F Rr 1 (16313)
P.O. Box 923, Warren (16365-0923)
PHONE................................814 726-3542
Bill Epling, *Partner*
Jennifer Epling, *Partner*
EMP: 4
SALES (est): 374.1K **Privately Held**
SIC: **1382** Oil & gas exploration services

(G-3169)
I L GEER AND SONS
14232 Route 6 (16313-4104)
PHONE................................814 723-7569
Nancy Monaghan, *Principal*
EMP: 5
SALES (est): 288.4K **Privately Held**
SIC: **1389** Oil & gas field services

(G-3170)
M & D INDUSTRIES INC
251 S Main St (16313-1001)
PHONE................................814 723-2381
Michael Cole, *President*
Susan Cole, *Corp Secy*
EMP: 15 EST: 1974
SQ FT: 35,000
SALES (est): 3MM **Privately Held**
WEB: www.mdindustries.com
SIC: **3443** 3441 Fabricated plate work (boiler shop); fabricated structural metal

(G-3171)
TRU-GAS INC
Rd 1 Rr 6 (16313)
PHONE................................814 723-9260
Bruce Scroxton, *President*
EMP: 8
SQ FT: 15,000
SALES: 2MM **Privately Held**
WEB: www.tru-gasinc.com
SIC: **3533** Gas field machinery & equipment

(G-3172)
C & K COAL COMPANY
1062 E Main St (16214-1208)
P.O. Box 69 (16214-0069)
PHONE................................814 226-6911
Gary C Wilson, *President*
Susan Cherico, *Admin Sec*
EMP: 70 EST: 1952
SQ FT: 12,000
SALES (est): 4.9MM **Privately Held**
SIC: **1241** Coal mining services
HQ: Gre Mining Company
1062 E Main St
Clarion PA 16214
814 226-6911

(G-3173)
CLARION PRINTING - LITHO
645 Main St (16214-1137)
P.O. Box 122 (16214-0122)
PHONE................................814 226-9453
Homer Watson, *Owner*
EMP: 4
SQ FT: 2,500
SALES (est): 365.3K **Privately Held**
WEB: www.clarionprinting.biz
SIC: **2752** Commercial printing, lithographic

(G-3174)
CLARION RIVER BREWING CO
600 Main St (16214-1108)
PHONE................................814 297-8399
EMP: 4

▲ = Import ▼=Export
◆ =Import/Export

SALES (est): 211K **Privately Held**
SIC: 2082 Beer (alcoholic beverage)

(G-3175)
COMMODORE CORPORATION
20898 Paint Blvd (16214)
P.O. Box 349 (16214-0349)
PHONE.............................814 226-9210
Victor Ewy, *Manager*
EMP: 236
SALES (corp-wide): 134.8MM **Privately Held**
WEB: www.commodorehomes.com
SIC: 2451 Mobile homes
PA: The Commodore Corporation
    1423 Lincolnway E
    Goshen IN 46526
    574 533-7100

(G-3176)
DERRICK PUBLISHING COMPANY
Also Called: Enango Newspapers, The
860 S 5th Ave (16214-8601)
PHONE.............................814 226-7000
Mary Louise Logue, *Branch Mgr*
EMP: 25
SALES (corp-wide): 14.5MM **Privately Held**
SIC: 2711 Newspapers, publishing & printing
PA: Derrick Publishing Company
    1510 W 1st St
    Oil City PA 16301
    814 676-7444

(G-3177)
DONALD W DEITZ
489 Lilac Ln (16214-3215)
PHONE.............................814 745-2857
Donald W Deitz, *Owner*
EMP: 5 EST: 1961
SALES (est): 344.7K **Privately Held**
SIC: 1381 8721 Directional drilling oil & gas wells; accounting services, except auditing

(G-3178)
GRE MINING COMPANY (HQ)
1062 E Main St (16214-1208)
P.O. Box 69 (16214-0069)
PHONE.............................814 226-6911
Gary C Wilson, *President*
EMP: 7
SQ FT: 18,000
SALES (est): 5.2MM **Privately Held**
SIC: 1221 Bituminous coal & lignite-surface mining

(G-3179)
GRE VENTURES INC
1062 E Main St (16214-1208)
P.O. Box 69 (16214-0069)
PHONE.............................814 226-6911
Gary Wilson, *President*
EMP: 7
SALES (est): 289.6K **Privately Held**
SIC: 1221 Bituminous coal surface mining
HQ: G R E Mining Company
    1062 E Main St
    Clarion PA 16214
    814 226-6911

(G-3180)
JANUS BIOGENICS LLC
330 N Point Dr (16214-3873)
PHONE.............................814 215-3013
Ronald Bouch, *CEO*
Douglas Smith, *President*
Christopher Kenyon, *Chairman*
EMP: 3
SALES (est): 123.2K **Privately Held**
SIC: 2836 Vaccines & other immunizing products

(G-3181)
KRIEBEL GAS INC (PA)
633 Mayfield Rd (16214-6161)
P.O. Box 765 (16214-0765)
PHONE.............................814 226-4160
James E Kriebel, *CEO*
Milissa Bauer, *Vice Pres*
EMP: 75
SQ FT: 19,000

SALES (est): 8.6MM **Privately Held**
SIC: 1381 1311 Drilling oil & gas wells; natural gas production

(G-3182)
KRIEBEL MINERALS INC
633 Mayfield Rd (16214-6161)
PHONE.............................814 226-4160
James Kriebel, *President*
James E Kriebel, *President*
Milissa Bauer, *Exec VP*
Gregory R Kriebel, *Vice Pres*
Milissa S Bauer, *Treasurer*
EMP: 43 EST: 1993
SALES: 9.7MM **Privately Held**
SIC: 4924 1311 Natural gas distribution; crude petroleum & natural gas production

(G-3183)
KRIEBEL WELLS
633 Mayfield Rd (16214-6161)
PHONE.............................814 226-4160
James E Kriebel, *Principal*
EMP: 3
SALES (est): 174.5K **Privately Held**
SIC: 1321 Natural gas liquids

(G-3184)
MR TS SIXPACK
540 Main St (16214-1136)
PHONE.............................814 226-8890
Edward Flannigan, *General Mgr*
EMP: 3
SALES (est): 135.1K **Privately Held**
SIC: 2086 Mfg Bottled/Canned Soft Drinks

(G-3185)
OWENS-BROCKWAY GLASS CONT INC
151 Grand Ave (16214-1708)
PHONE.............................814 226-0500
Jerry Jamar, *Manager*
EMP: 230
SALES (corp-wide): 6.8B **Publicly Held**
SIC: 3221 Packers' ware (containers), glass; milk bottles, glass
HQ: Owens-Brockway Glass Container Inc.
    1 Michael Owens Way
    Perrysburg OH 43551
    567 336-8449

(G-3186)
REA JOBBER INC (PA)
204 Grand Ave (16214-1710)
PHONE.............................814 226-9552
Dennis Painter, *President*
EMP: 6
SQ FT: 2,700
SALES: 1.5MM **Privately Held**
SIC: 5023 5031 2541 Carpets; kitchen cabinets; counter & sink tops

(G-3187)
WESTERN PA NEWSPPR CO
Also Called: Clairon News
860 S 5th Ave Ste 4 (16214-8601)
PHONE.............................814 226-7000
Ed Boyle, *Ch of Bd*
Patrick C Boyle, *President*
Pat Boyle, *Chairman*
Ann L Pelachi, *Admin Sec*
EMP: 14 EST: 1840
SQ FT: 3,800
SALES: 300K **Privately Held**
SIC: 2711 Newspapers: publishing only, not printed on site

Clark
Mercer County

(G-3188)
CMG PROCESS INC
Also Called: Apex Engineered Products
2659 Lake Rd (16113)
P.O. Box 312 (16113-0312)
PHONE.............................724 962-8717
Mark P Grasso, *President*
Thomas Bunk, *CFO*
▲ EMP: 25
SQ FT: 18,000

SALES (est): 8.8MM **Privately Held**
WEB: www.apexep.com
SIC: 3399 Brads: aluminum, brass or other nonferrous metal or wire

Clarks Green
Lackawanna County

(G-3189)
NEW HOME WINDOW SHADE CO INC
106 Greenbrier Dr (18411-1114)
PHONE.............................570 346-2047
Lawrence Mandel, *President*
EMP: 40 EST: 1926
SQ FT: 35,000
SALES (est): 3.8MM **Privately Held**
WEB: www.newhomewindow.com
SIC: 2591 5023 3429 Window blinds; venetian blinds; window shades; blinds vertical; window furnishings; venetian blinds; window shades; vertical blinds; manufactured hardware (general)

Clarks Summit
Lackawanna County

(G-3190)
CUMMINGS CUSTOM SAW MILLING
109 Cummings Pond Rd (18411-9511)
PHONE.............................570 586-3277
Robert J Cummings, *Principal*
EMP: 4
SALES (est): 374.9K **Privately Held**
SIC: 2653 Corrugated & solid fiber boxes

(G-3191)
D-K TRADING CORPORATION INC (PA)
41 Marshwood Bnd (18411-9174)
P.O. Box E (18411-0240)
PHONE.............................570 586-9662
David Kirtland, *President*
Susann Tully, *Controller*
Robert Spalding, *Sales Associate*
Susan Tully, *Admin Sec*
EMP: 3
SQ FT: 2,000
SALES (est): 2.9MM **Privately Held**
WEB: www.dk-t.com
SIC: 5113 4953 2678 5084 Industrial & personal service paper; recycling, waste materials; newsprint tablets & pads: made from purchased materials; materials handling machinery; materials mgmt. (purchasing, handling, inventory) consultant

(G-3192)
EPIC INDUSTRIES INC
1133 S Abington Rd Unit 3 (18411-2264)
PHONE.............................570 586-0253
Mark D Colombo, *President*
EMP: 5
SQ FT: 2,500
SALES (est): 985.9K **Privately Held**
SIC: 1542 2521 Commercial & office building contractors; desks, office: wood

(G-3193)
G F C INC
Also Called: Creavey Seal Co
91 Quinton Rd (18411)
PHONE.............................570 587-4588
Bernadette J Chrysler, *President*
EMP: 35 EST: 1962
SQ FT: 3,500
SALES (est): 3.5MM **Privately Held**
WEB: www.creavey.com
SIC: 3053 Gaskets, packing & sealing devices

(G-3194)
INTERSTATE SAFETY SERVICE INC
1301 Winola Rd (18411-9445)
PHONE.............................570 563-1161
Susan Colombo, *President*
Christopher Colombo, *Vice Pres*
Jeffrey Colombo, *Asst Sec*

EMP: 25
SQ FT: 6,000
SALES (est): 4.9MM **Privately Held**
SIC: 3272 7359 Building materials, except block or brick: concrete; work zone traffic equipment (flags, cones, barrels, etc.)

(G-3195)
J & B PRINTING
400 S State St Ste 1 (18411-1589)
P.O. Box 584 (18411-0584)
PHONE.............................570 587-4427
Jack Kester, *Partner*
Robert Kester, *Partner*
EMP: 3
SALES: 100K **Privately Held**
SIC: 2752 Commercial printing, offset

(G-3196)
J P R PUBLICATIONS INC
Also Called: Happening's Magazine
115 N State St (18411-1085)
P.O. Box 61 (18411-0061)
PHONE.............................570 587-3532
Paula Mackarey, *President*
Rosemary Nye, *Consultant*
Peter Salerno, *Director*
Linette Manley, *Representative*
EMP: 13 EST: 1969
SQ FT: 1,200
SALES (est): 1.5MM **Privately Held**
WEB: www.happeningsmagazinepa.com
SIC: 2721 Magazines: publishing only, not printed on site; periodicals: publishing only

(G-3197)
LOH ENTERPRISES LLC
Also Called: Loh Medical
318 Davis St Ste 1 (18411-1873)
PHONE.............................570 737-4143
Perry Loh, *President*
▼ EMP: 21
SALES (est): 3.2MM **Privately Held**
SIC: 3841 Anesthesia apparatus

(G-3198)
PIKE CREEK SALT COMPANY
43 Marshwood Bnd (18411-9174)
PHONE.............................570 585-8818
Julianne Bitchko, *President*
Eugene Bitchko, *Vice Pres*
▲ EMP: 11
SALES (est): 1.5MM **Privately Held**
SIC: 2899 Salt

Clarksburg
Indiana County

(G-3199)
ROSEBUD MINING COMPANY
1878 Saltsburg Rd (15725-8057)
PHONE.............................724 459-4970
Jim Anderson, *Branch Mgr*
EMP: 35
SALES (corp-wide): 605.3MM **Privately Held**
SIC: 1241 Coal mining services
PA: Rosebud Mining Company
    301 Market St
    Kittanning PA 16201
    724 545-6222

(G-3200)
TWIN PINES MANUIFACTURING CORP
Also Called: Twin Pines Manufacturing
5779 Newport Rd (15725-9129)
PHONE.............................724 459-3850
Robert J Kovalcik, *President*
EMP: 9
SQ FT: 75,000
SALES (est): 1MM **Privately Held**
SIC: 3599 Machine shop, jobbing & repair; valves & pipe fittings

G E O G R A P H I C

Claysburg
Blair County

(G-3201)
CARPET AND FURNITURE DEPOT INC
Also Called: Carpet Depot Home Center
12756 Dunnings Hwy Ste 3 (16625-8276)
PHONE..................................814 239-5865
Dennis Burket, *President*
Kay Burket, *Treasurer*
EMP: 5
SQ FT: 15,000
SALES (est): 475K **Privately Held**
SIC: 5713 2511 Carpets; wood household furniture

(G-3202)
CENTRAL STATES MFG INC
402 Corporate Blvd (16625-8349)
PHONE..................................814 239-2764
Mike White, *Branch Mgr*
EMP: 30
SALES (corp-wide): 219.5MM **Privately Held**
SIC: 3448 Buildings, portable: prefabricated metal
PA: Central States Manufacturing, Inc.
302 Jane Pl
Lowell AR 72745
800 356-2733

(G-3203)
DIVELY MANUFACTURE CO INC
Also Called: Econo Trailer
1600 Locust Hollow Rd (16625-8529)
PHONE..................................814 239-5441
John A Dively, *President*
Coletta Dively, *Vice Pres*
Amy Slagenweit, *Treasurer*
Mary Dively, *Office Mgr*
EMP: 11
SQ FT: 16,240
SALES (est): 1.8MM **Privately Held**
SIC: 3715 5531 Truck trailers; truck equipment & parts

(G-3204)
HARBISONWALKER INTL INC
2926 Quarry Rd (16625-8330)
PHONE..................................814 239-2111
Doug Hilman, *Branch Mgr*
EMP: 82
SALES (corp-wide): 703.8MM **Privately Held**
SIC: 3255 Clay refractories
HQ: Harbisonwalker International, Inc.
1305 Cherrington Pkwy # 100
Moon Township PA 15108

(G-3205)
NATIONAL IMPRINT CORPORATION (DH)
William Ward Indus Park (16625)
PHONE..................................814 239-8141
Casey T Campbell, *President*
Vanessa Mc Elwaney, *Administration*
EMP: 30
SQ FT: 60,000
SALES (est): 56.3MM
SALES (corp-wide): 370.1MM **Publicly Held**
WEB: www.nationalimprint.com
SIC: 2677 2678 2679 Envelopes; stationery: made from purchased materials; memorandum books, except printed: purchased materials; labels, paper: made from purchased material
HQ: Printegra Corp
5040 Highlands Pkwy Se
Smyrna GA 30082
770 487-5151

(G-3206)
NATIONAL IMPRINT CORPORATION
114 Ward Dr (16625-8217)
P.O. Box 7310, Elgin IL (60123)
PHONE..................................814 239-5116
Dina Nesler, *Manager*
EMP: 26

SALES (corp-wide): 370.1MM **Publicly Held**
WEB: www.nationalimprint.com
SIC: 2677 2759 2752 Envelopes; commercial printing; commercial printing, lithographic
HQ: National Imprint Corporation
William Ward Indus Park
Claysburg PA 16625
814 239-8141

(G-3207)
NPC INC (PA)
13710 Dunnings Hwy (16625-7802)
P.O. Box 373 (16625-0373)
PHONE..................................814 239-8787
Mark N Barnhart, *Ch of Bd*
Mark Kelly, *President*
Fred Tromm, *Business Mgr*
Tim McCarthy, *Exec VP*
Timothy McCarthy, *Exec VP*
EMP: 450 **EST:** 1931
SQ FT: 180,000
SALES (est): 136.4MM **Privately Held**
WEB: www.npcweb.com
SIC: 2752 2789 2759 Commercial printing, offset; bookbinding & related work; commercial printing

(G-3208)
SHIRLEYS COOKIE COMPANY INC
153 William Ward Dr (16625)
P.O. Box 312 (16625-0312)
PHONE..................................814 239-2208
William Z Feathers, *President*
Bryon Shaw, *Vice Pres*
Patricia Shaw, *Vice Pres*
Tyler Shaw, *Human Res Dir*
Bruce Woodring, *Executive*
EMP: 100 **EST:** 1967
SQ FT: 32,000
SALES (est): 15.9MM **Privately Held**
WEB: www.shirleyscookies.com
SIC: 2052 Cookies

Claysville
Washington County

(G-3209)
UNITED FABRICATING INC (PA)
4522 State Route 40 (15323)
P.O. Box 726 (15323-1726)
PHONE..................................724 663-5891
Camille Sushel, *Principal*
Amy Levine, *Shareholder*
John Sushel, *Shareholder*
EMP: 10
SQ FT: 8,400
SALES (est): 3.1MM **Privately Held**
WEB: www.unitedfabricating.com
SIC: 3441 3599 3469 Fabricated structural metal; machine shop, jobbing & repair; stamping metal for the trade

Clearfield
Clearfield County

(G-3210)
ALPHA COAL SALES CO
51 Airport Rd (16830-6124)
PHONE..................................304 256-1015
Ed Ratay, *Manager*
EMP: 3
SALES (est): 119.8K **Privately Held**
SIC: 1221 Bituminous coal & lignite-surface mining

(G-3211)
ALPHA SAFETY USA
9118 Clearfield Curwensvi (16830-3539)
PHONE..................................814 236-3344
Samuel Scribe, *Partner*
EMP: 3
SQ FT: 2,000
SALES (est): 72.6K **Privately Held**
SIC: 1241 1382 8748 7389 Mining services: anthracite; mining services: bituminous; oil & gas exploration services; safety training service; safety inspection service

(G-3212)
APPALACHIAN WOOD PRODUCTS INC
171 Appalachian Dr (16830-6012)
PHONE..................................814 765-2003
Dennis L McCahan, *President*
Bob Witmer, *Vice Pres*
Robert L Witmer, *Vice Pres*
Jim Bedison, *Plant Mgr*
Coty Soult, *Engineer*
◆ **EMP:** 300
SALES (est): 49.8MM **Privately Held**
WEB: www.appwood.com
SIC: 2426 2431 Hardwood dimension & flooring mills; millwork

(G-3213)
BIONOL CLEARFIELD LLC
250 Technology Dr (16830-2663)
PHONE..................................814 913-3100
Stephen J Gatto, *Mng Member*
EMP: 13 **EST:** 2006
SALES (est): 2.2MM **Privately Held**
SIC: 2869 Ethyl alcohol, ethanol

(G-3214)
CLEARFIELD MACHINE COMPANY
520 S 3rd St (16830-2004)
P.O. Box 992a (16830-0993)
PHONE..................................814 765-6544
David G Gallaher Sr, *Ch of Bd*
David G Gallaher Jr, *Vice Pres*
David Semelsberger, *Purch Mgr*
EMP: 18 **EST:** 1868
SQ FT: 64,000
SALES (est): 4.6MM **Privately Held**
WEB: www.clearfieldmachine.com
SIC: 3321 3559 Gray iron castings; foundry machinery & equipment

(G-3215)
CLEARFIELD METAL TECH INC
114 Appalachian Dr (16830-6012)
PHONE..................................814 765-7860
Jim Killian, *President*
Tim Britton, *Vice Pres*
Jason Bloom, *VP Mfg*
Chris Britton, *Design Engr*
Craig Boswell, *CFO*
EMP: 17 **EST:** 2011
SALES: 3.3MM **Privately Held**
SIC: 3542 Mechanical (pneumatic or hydraulic) metal forming machines

(G-3216)
COMMERCIAL JOB PRINTING INC
Also Called: Action Graphics
2079 Turnpike Avenue Ext (16830-7244)
PHONE..................................814 765-1925
Dave Tihansky, *President*
Anita G Graham, *Admin Sec*
EMP: 7
SQ FT: 4,500
SALES (est): 931.8K **Privately Held**
WEB: www.printingandsigns.net
SIC: 2752 Commercial printing, offset

(G-3217)
COMMERCIAL PRTG & OFF SUPPY
Also Called: Commercial Printing & Off Sup
17 S 3rd St (16830-2324)
P.O. Box 23 (16830-0023)
PHONE..................................814 765-4731
Randal K Hurley, *President*
Donna L Hurley, *Vice Pres*
EMP: 3
SQ FT: 2,000
SALES (est): 366.4K **Privately Held**
SIC: 2752 5943 Commercial printing, offset; office forms & supplies

(G-3218)
E M BROWN INCORPORATED
329 Mount Joy Rd (16830-2926)
P.O. Box 767 (16830-0767)
PHONE..................................814 765-7519
Robert E Brown, *President*
Allan M Brown, *Corp Secy*
EMP: 25 **EST:** 1939
SQ FT: 2,000

SALES (est): 2.8MM **Privately Held**
WEB: www.embrown.com
SIC: 1611 3273 General contractor, highway & street construction; ready-mixed concrete

(G-3219)
GANT MEDIA LLC
219 S 2nd St (16830-2205)
P.O. Box 746 (16830-0746)
PHONE..................................814 765-5256
Christene Dahlem, *President*
EMP: 8
SALES (est): 534.6K **Privately Held**
SIC: 2711 Newspapers, publishing & printing

(G-3220)
GRAHAM SIGN COMPANY
290 Wolf Run Rd (16830-6032)
PHONE..................................814 765-7199
Roy Graham, *Owner*
EMP: 3
SALES: 200K **Privately Held**
SIC: 3993 7312 Neon signs; billboard advertising

(G-3221)
J L W VENTURES INCORPORATED
Also Called: Johnson Machine Co
290 Bigler Ave (16830-2662)
P.O. Box 669 (16830-0669)
PHONE..................................814 765-9648
Jack L Woodford, *President*
Michael Boyle, *Opers Staff*
EMP: 16 **EST:** 1930
SALES: 1.1MM **Privately Held**
SIC: 3544 Industrial molds; special dies & tools

(G-3222)
KURTZ BROS (PA)
400 Reed St (16830-2585)
P.O. Box 392 (16830-0392)
PHONE..................................814 765-6561
Monty Kunes, *CEO*
Dana Jagger, *General Mgr*
Paul Bojalad, *Buyer*
Stacy Soltys, *Buyer*
Matthew C Hoover, *CFO*
▲ **EMP:** 92
SQ FT: 130,000
SALES: 20MM **Privately Held**
WEB: www.kurtzbros.com
SIC: 2621 2752 Tablet paper; promotional printing, lithographic

(G-3223)
LITTLE PINE RESOURCES
2 E Market St Ste 1 (16830-2428)
PHONE..................................814 765-6300
Zachary Hunter Hill, *Principal*
EMP: 20
SALES (est): 880.8K **Privately Held**
SIC: 1382 Oil & gas exploration services

(G-3224)
MAYER ELECTRIC SUPPLY CO INC
1145 Fullerton St (16830-1167)
PHONE..................................814 765-7531
Joe Rumsky, *Manager*
EMP: 8
SALES (corp-wide): 911.3MM **Privately Held**
WEB: www.hiteco.com
SIC: 3629 5064 Electronic generation equipment; electric household appliances
PA: Mayer Electric Supply Company, Inc.
3405 4th Ave S
Birmingham AL 35222
205 583-3500

(G-3225)
MINE DRILLING SERVICES LL
615 Tipple Ln (16830-4267)
PHONE..................................814 765-1075
Grant Wise,
Randy May,
EMP: 15
SALES (est): 864.8K **Privately Held**
SIC: 1381 Drilling oil & gas wells

▲ = Import ▼=Export
◆ =Import/Export

GEOGRAPHIC

(G-3226)
NABORS DRILLING TECH USA
143 Cresswood Dr (16830-6127)
PHONE................................814 768-4640
Eric Anton, *Branch Mgr*
EMP: 5 Privately Held
SIC: 1381 Drilling oil & gas wells
HQ: Nabors Drilling Technologies Usa, Inc.
515 W Greens Rd Ste 1200
Houston TX 77067
281 874-0035

(G-3227)
OIL STATES ENERGY SERVICES LLC
Also Called: Well Testing
15106 Clrfeld Shwvlle Hwy (16830)
PHONE................................814 290-6755
EMP: 4
SALES (corp-wide): 1B Publicly Held
SIC: 1389 Oil field services
HQ: Oil States Energy Services, L.L.C.
333 Clay St Ste 2100
Houston TX 77002
713 425-2400

(G-3228)
PENNSYLVANIA GRAINS PROC LLC
250 Technology Dr (16830-2663)
PHONE................................877 871-0774
Brian Terborg, *CFO*
Laura Handel, *Manager*
Daniel Meeuwsen,
Denny Owens, *Maintence Staff*
EMP: 41
SALES (est): 22.5MM Privately Held
SIC: 2869 Ethanolamines

(G-3229)
PROGRESSIVE PUBLISHING COMPANY (PA)
615 Elm Ave (16830-2139)
PHONE................................814 765-5051
Margaret Krebs, *President*
Ann K Law, *Admin Sec*
EMP: 100 EST: 1913
SQ FT: 7,500
SALES (est): 10.6MM Privately Held
SIC: 2711 Newspapers, publishing & printing; newspapers: publishing only, not printed on site

(G-3230)
RES COAL LLC (PA)
51 Airport Rd (16830-6124)
P.O. Box 228, Armagh (15920-0228)
PHONE................................814 765-7525
Dan Benitt, *Mng Member*
EMP: 31
SALES (est): 17.7MM Privately Held
SIC: 1241 Coal mining services

(G-3231)
SWISHER CONCRETE PRODUCTS INC
9428 Clearfield Cwnvl Hwy (16830)
PHONE................................814 765-9502
Jeannine Swisher, *President*
EMP: 9 EST: 1989
SQ FT: 9,300
SALES (est): 1.4MM Privately Held
SIC: 3271 5085 Blocks, concrete or cinder: standard; industrial supplies

(G-3232)
SWISHER CONTRACTING INC
Mt Joy Rd (16830)
P.O. Box 1223 (16830-5223)
PHONE................................814 765-6006
Leonard Swisher Jr, *President*
EMP: 15
SALES (est): 2.4MM Privately Held
SIC: 1222 Bituminous coal-underground mining

(G-3233)
VICTOR LLC
Also Called: Ctor Tipple
3056 Washington Ave (16830-3537)
PHONE................................814 765-5681
Gary V Waroquier, *Principal*
EMP: 3

SALES (est): 111.5K Privately Held
SIC: 1221 Bituminous coal & lignite-surface mining

(G-3234)
VISION QUALITY COMPONENTS INC
1433 Industrial Park Rd (16830-6002)
PHONE................................814 765-1903
Denny Johns, *Principal*
EMP: 12
SALES (est): 2MM Privately Held
WEB: www.visionqci.com
SIC: 3399 Metal powders, pastes & flakes

(G-3235)
WAROQUIER COAL INC (PA)
Rr 879 (16830)
PHONE................................814 765-5681
Joseph Waroquier Jr, *President*
Gary Waroquier, *Corp Secy*
▲ **EMP: 3**
SQ FT: 800
SALES (est): 24.8MM Privately Held
SIC: 5052 1221 Coal; strip mining, bituminous

(G-3236)
WAROQUIER COAL INC
3056 Washington Ave (16830-3537)
P.O. Box 128 (16830-0128)
PHONE................................814 765-5681
Joseph Waroquier, *Manager*
EMP: 40
SALES (corp-wide): 24.8MM Privately Held
SIC: 1222 Bituminous coal-underground mining
PA: Waroquier Coal, Inc.
Rr 879
Clearfield PA 16830
814 765-5681

(G-3237)
WARREN C HARTMAN CONTRACTING
Also Called: Hartman, Warren G
5003 Bigler Rd (16830-1752)
PHONE................................814 765-8842
EMP: 3 EST: 1952
SALES (est): 325K Privately Held
SIC: 1221 Bituminous Coal/Lignite Surface Mining

Clearville
Bedford County

(G-3238)
BEEGLE SAW MILL
Also Called: Beegles Logs and Lumber
1656 Rock Hill Church Rd (15535-5131)
PHONE................................814 784-5697
Geraldine Beegle, *Owner*
EMP: 3
SALES (est): 199.4K Privately Held
SIC: 2421 Sawmills & planing mills, general

(G-3239)
CESSNA BROS LUMBER
150 Cessna Sawmill Rd (15535-7928)
PHONE................................814 767-9518
Dennis Cessna, *Partner*
Carl Cessna, *Partner*
Clifford Cessna, *Partner*
Donald Cessna Sr, *Partner*
EMP: 15
SALES (est): 2.3MM Privately Held
SIC: 2421 5211 Sawmills & planing mills, general; lumber & other building materials

(G-3240)
CLB LOGGING
323 Rock Hill Church Rd (15535-5046)
PHONE................................814 784-3301
Christopher Beegle, *Owner*
EMP: 3
SALES (est): 233.5K Privately Held
SIC: 2411 Logging

(G-3241)
DONALD EBY
2301 Beans Cove Rd (15535-7915)
PHONE................................814 767-9406
Donald EBY, *Partner*
Arnold EBY, *Partner*
Conrad EBY, *Partner*
Daurel EBY, *Partner*
EMP: 5
SALES (est): 390K Privately Held
SIC: 2421 0139 Sawmills & planing mills, general; hay farm

(G-3242)
EBY SAWMILL
Also Called: Durrel
2319 Beans Cove Rd (15535-7915)
PHONE................................814 767-8060
Leo EBY, *Partner*
Arnold EBY, *Partner*
Conrad EBY, *Partner*
Donald R EBY, *Partner*
Llewellyn EBY, *Partner*
EMP: 35 EST: 1990
SQ FT: 14,200
SALES (est): 5.7MM Privately Held
SIC: 2421 Lumber: rough, sawed or planed

(G-3243)
PLEASANT VALLEY SAW MILL
422 Beans Cove Rd (15535-8023)
PHONE................................814 767-9016
William G Robosson, *Principal*
EMP: 9
SALES (est): 906.7K Privately Held
SIC: 2421 Sawmills & planing mills, general

Cleona
Lebanon County

(G-3244)
HAUCK MANUFACTURING COMPANY (DH)
Also Called: Hauck Mfg Kromschroder Contrls
235 W Penn Ave (17042-3230)
P.O. Box 90, Lebanon (17042-0090)
PHONE................................717 272-3051
Michael Shay, *President*
Jim Feese, *Vice Pres*
Craig Wolse, *Director*
▼ **EMP: 63**
SQ FT: 45,000
SALES (est): 25.8MM
SALES (corp-wide): 2.3MM Privately Held
WEB: www.hauckburner.com
SIC: 3564 3433 Blowers & fans; oil burners, domestic or industrial
HQ: Elster Gmbh
SteinernstraBe 19-21
Mainz-Kastel 55252
613 460-50

(G-3245)
MARCAN ADVERTISING INC
537 E Maple St (17042-2536)
P.O. Box 1111, Lebanon (17042-1111)
PHONE................................717 270-6929
Gary L Ludwig, *President*
EMP: 3
SALES (est): 250K Privately Held
SIC: 2752 2741 Commercial printing, lithographic; miscellaneous publishing

Clifford
Susquehanna County

(G-3246)
KOCHMER GRAPHICS
Also Called: Kochmer Graphics & Auto Svc
82 Main St (18413)
P.O. Box 163 (18413-0163)
PHONE................................570 222-5713
Robert Kochmer, *Owner*
EMP: 4
SALES (est): 290K Privately Held
SIC: 3993 Signs & advertising specialties

Clifford Township
Susquehanna County

(G-3247)
BIDWELL MACHINING INC
Also Called: Royal Plastic Lockers
1431 Oswald Johnson Rd (18441-7749)
PHONE................................570 222-5575
Richard P Bidwell, *President*
Diane E Bidwell, *Corp Secy*
EMP: 3
SQ FT: 9,000
SALES (est): 486.3K Privately Held
SIC: 3089 Injection molding of plastics; plastic processing

(G-3248)
IDLEWILD SKI SHOP INC
7471 State Route 374 (18470-7345)
PHONE................................570 222-4200
Jane G Matthews, *President*
Charles W Matthews III, *Vice Pres*
Constance Gerber, *Admin Sec*
EMP: 15
SQ FT: 4,000
SALES (est): 1.4MM Privately Held
WEB: www.idlewildskishop.com
SIC: 5941 2339 Skiing equipment; snow suits: women's, misses' & juniors'

(G-3249)
R E B BLOXHAM INC
4344 State Route 106 (18470-7596)
PHONE................................570 222-4693
Richard Bloxham, *President*
Robert Bloxham, *Vice Pres*
EMP: 5
SALES (est): 504.8K Privately Held
SIC: 2411 Logging

Clifton Heights
Delaware County

(G-3250)
ACE METAL INC
227 E Madison Ave (19018-2616)
P.O. Box 190 (19018-0190)
PHONE................................610 623-2204
Richard Medoff, *President*
◆ **EMP: 25**
SQ FT: 35,000
SALES (est): 5.7MM Privately Held
WEB: www.acemetalinc.com
SIC: 3441 3444 Fabricated structural metal; sheet metalwork

(G-3251)
DE LUCAS DRAPERYS
195 N Springfield Rd (19018-1535)
PHONE................................610 284-2464
Robert De Luca, *Owner*
EMP: 5 EST: 1954
SALES: 500K Privately Held
SIC: 2391 1799 Curtains & draperies; drapery track installation

(G-3252)
DESIGNER CABINETS AND HDWR CO
Also Called: DCI Products
415 S Penn St (19018-2600)
PHONE................................610 622-4455
Jack Henderson, *President*
EMP: 20
SQ FT: 24,000
SALES (est): 1.6MM Privately Held
SIC: 3444 2952 Sheet metalwork; roofing materials

(G-3253)
HATCRAFTERS INC
20 N Springfield Rd Ste 1 (19018-1497)
PHONE................................610 623-2620
Victor H Haentze, *President*
Linda Haentze, *Corp Secy*
John Scott, *Vice Pres*
EMP: 6
SQ FT: 6,000

SALES (est): 616.4K **Privately Held**
WEB: www.hatcrafters.com
SIC: **2353** 2326 Hats & caps; men's &
boys' work clothing

(G-3254)
LPG INDUSTRIES INC
307 N Sycamore Ave (19018-1536)
P.O. Box 600 (19018-0600)
PHONE..................................610 622-2900
Kenneth R Gabriel, *CEO*
EMP: 22 EST: 1968
SQ FT: 2,500
SALES: 1.5MM **Privately Held**
WEB: www.lpgindustriesinc.com
SIC: **3829** Thermocouples; pressure trans-
ducers

(G-3255)
MARIANO WELDING CORP
Baltimore & Marple Ave (19018)
PHONE..................................610 626-0975
Joseph R Mariano, *President*
June Mariano, *Admin Sec*
EMP: 4
SQ FT: 3,300
SALES (est): 437.9K **Privately Held**
SIC: **7692** 5013 Welding repair; truck parts
& accessories

(G-3256)
NEWSHAMS WOODSHOP INC
Merion Ave Bldg 2 (19018)
P.O. Box 249, Rutledge (19070-0249)
PHONE..................................610 622-5800
Tom Newsham, *President*
Lisa M Newsham, *Vice Pres*
EMP: 7
SQ FT: 8,000
SALES (est): 906K **Privately Held**
SIC: **2449** 2499 Rectangular boxes &
crates, wood; decorative wood & wood-
work

(G-3257)
**NICE THREADS
INTERNATIONAL**
Also Called: NTI
4 Rockbourne Rd Ste 501 (19018-1739)
PHONE..................................610 259-0788
EMP: 4
SQ FT: 25,000
SALES: 300K **Privately Held**
SIC: **2395** Embroidery

(G-3258)
SR ROSATI INC
Also Called: Rosati Italian Water Ice
201 E Madison Ave (19018-2616)
PHONE..................................610 626-1818
Richard Trotter, *President*
David Schumacher, *Vice Pres*
Michelle Schomacher, *Treasurer*
Rosmarie Salomone, *Admin Sec*
▲ EMP: 10 EST: 1962
SQ FT: 14,300
SALES (est): 1.9MM **Privately Held**
SIC: **2024** Ices, flavored (frozen dessert)

(G-3259)
TRI-COM INC
359 E Madison Ave (19018-2612)
PHONE..................................610 259-7400
Stephen Flanagan, *President*
Edward Boudjouk, *Admin Sec*
▲ EMP: 20
SQ FT: 16,500
SALES (est): 9.7MM **Privately Held**
WEB: www.tricom-sales.com
SIC: **5065** 3496 Electronic parts; cable,
uninsulated wire: made from purchased
wire

Clifton Twp
Wayne County

(G-3260)
AMIES AIRPARTS LLC
11 Sunnyside Rd (18424-7794)
PHONE..................................570 871-7991
Michelle Adams-Taylor, *President*
EMP: 3

SALES (est): 117.8K **Privately Held**
SIC: **3728** Aircraft parts & equipment

Clinton
Beaver County

(G-3261)
CIECO INC
2401 Hookstown Grade Rd (15026-1813)
PHONE..................................412 262-5581
Ronald Cejer, *President*
Chris Cejer, *Vice Pres*
Kenneth Cejer, *Vice Pres*
EMP: 8
SQ FT: 6,300
SALES (est): 1.2MM **Privately Held**
WEB: www.ciecocontrols.com
SIC: **3625** Control circuit relays, industrial

(G-3262)
**FLABEG SOLAR US
CORPORATION**
2201 Sweeney Dr (15026-1818)
PHONE..................................724 899-4622
▲ EMP: 25
SALES (est): 283.4K **Privately Held**
SIC: **3433** Solar heaters & collectors
HQ: Flabeg Us Holding Inc.
1000 Church St
Naugatuck CT 06770

(G-3263)
**KNEPPER PRESS
CORPORATION**
2251 Sweeney Dr (15026-1818)
PHONE..................................724 899-4200
Ted Ford, *CEO*
Bob Hreha, *President*
David Gilbreath, *Vice Pres*
Emma Logue, *Vice Pres*
Monica Supinsky, *Production*
▲ EMP: 200 EST: 1873
SQ FT: 38,000
SALES: 35MM **Privately Held**
WEB: www.knepperpress.com
SIC: **2752** Commercial printing, offset

(G-3264)
OTX LOGISTICS INC
1730 Route 30 (15026-1794)
PHONE..................................412 567-8821
EMP: 3 **Privately Held**
SIC: **3669** Mfg Communications Equip-
ment
HQ: Otx Logistics, Inc.
16030 Arthur St
Cerritos CA 90703
310 851-8500

(G-3265)
PG PUBLISHING COMPANY
Also Called: Pittsburgh Post Gazette
2201 Sweeney Dr (15026-1818)
PHONE..................................412 263-1100
Joseph Pete, *President*
David M Beihoff, *Principal*
John R Block, *Vice Pres*
David M Shribman, *Vice Pres*
Robert J Stamm, *Finance*
▲ EMP: 825
SALES (est): 79.6MM
SALES (corp-wide): 921.6MM **Privately
Held**
WEB: www.pgaddesk.com
SIC: **2711** Commercial printing & newspa-
per publishing combined; newspapers,
publishing & printing
PA: Block Communications, Inc.
405 Madison Ave Ste 2100
Toledo OH 43604
419 724-6212

(G-3266)
PRECISION KIDD STEEL CO INC
Lncln Hy & Mtchtt Rr 30 (15026)
PHONE..................................724 695-2216
Tom Milhollan, *President*
EMP: 22 **Privately Held**
WEB: www.precisionkidd.com
SIC: **3316** 3315 3312 Cold finishing of
steel shapes; steel wire & related prod-
ucts; blast furnaces & steel mills

PA: Precision Kidd Steel Co., Inc.
1 Quality Way
Aliquippa PA 15001

(G-3267)
TYPE & PRINT INC (PA)
2251 Sweeney Dr (15026-1818)
PHONE..................................412 241-6070
Larry D Saltzman, *President*
EMP: 30 EST: 1971
SQ FT: 6,000
SALES: 3.5MM **Privately Held**
WEB: www.typeandprint.com
SIC: **2791** 2752 Typesetting; commercial
printing, offset

(G-3268)
VODVARKA SPRINGS
1251 Route 30 (15026)
PHONE..................................724 695-3268
Joseph Vodvarka, *Owner*
EMP: 5
SQ FT: 4,800
SALES: 300K **Privately Held**
SIC: **3495** Wire springs

Clymer
Indiana County

(G-3269)
AMFIRE MINING CO
Plant Off Hwy 403 (15728)
PHONE..................................724 254-9554
Kerry Mears, *Principal*
EMP: 4
SALES (est): 179.6K **Privately Held**
SIC: **1241** Coal mining services

(G-3270)
**CHERRYHILL MANUFACTURING
CORP**
3231 Laurel Run Rd (15728-8576)
PHONE..................................724 254-2185
Cyrus Kirsch, *President*
EMP: 18
SQ FT: 26,000
SALES (est): 232.9K **Privately Held**
WEB: www.cherryhillmfg.com
SIC: **3541** Machine tools, metal cutting
type

(G-3271)
CLYMER QUALITY HARDWOOD
15 Rayne Run Rd (15728)
PHONE..................................724 463-1827
Brian Short, *President*
EMP: 4
SALES (est): 359.7K **Privately Held**
SIC: **2426** Hardwood dimension & flooring
mills

(G-3272)
G L R MINING INC
410 Franklin St (15728-1182)
P.O. Box 105 (15728-0105)
PHONE..................................724 254-4043
Raymond Martin, *President*
Larry Martin, *Corp Secy*
Gary Martin, *Vice Pres*
EMP: 6
SQ FT: 225
SALES (est): 469.9K **Privately Held**
SIC: **1221** Surface mining, bituminous

(G-3273)
GILLO BROTHERS
7015 Rte 33 Hwy (15728)
PHONE..................................724 254-4845
George Gillo, *President*
EMP: 5 EST: 1947
SALES: 145K **Privately Held**
SIC: **2013** Sausages & other prepared
meats

(G-3274)
TWIN BROOK COAL CO
410 Franklin St (15728-1182)
P.O. Box 225 (15728-0225)
PHONE..................................724 254-4030
Dennis Bence, *Partner*
Donald Miller, *Partner*
EMP: 3
SQ FT: 225

SALES (est): 357.8K **Privately Held**
SIC: **1221** Surface mining, bituminous

Coal Center
Washington County

(G-3275)
DREBO AMERICA INC
500 Technology Dr (15423-1054)
P.O. Box 577, California (15419-0577)
PHONE..................................724 938-0690
Wayne Chappell, *President*
EMP: 63
SQ FT: 35,000
SALES: 20MM **Privately Held**
SIC: **4213** 3545 Trucking, except local;
drill bits, metalworking

(G-3276)
PERRYMAN COMPANY
625 Technology Dr (15423-1057)
PHONE..................................724 746-9390
Kevin Vonscio, *Branch Mgr*
EMP: 11
SALES (corp-wide): 66.2MM **Privately
Held**
SIC: **3312** 3356 3316 3315 Bar, rod &
wire products; nonferrous rolling & draw-
ing; cold finishing of steel shapes; steel
wire & related products
PA: The Perryman Company
213 Vandale Dr
Houston PA 15342
724 743-4239

(G-3277)
ROSE PLASTIC USA LLLP
525 Technology Dr (15423-1053)
P.O. Box 698, California (15419-0698)
PHONE..................................724 938-8530
Ken Donahue, *President*
Peter Hess, *Exec VP*
David Windmueller, *Vice Pres*
Kevin Dawson, *Prdtn Mgr*
Pete Logan, *Purch Mgr*
▲ EMP: 67
SALES (est): 17.9MM **Privately Held**
WEB: www.rose-plastic.com
SIC: **2655** 3081 Fiber cans, drums & simi-
lar products; packing materials, plastic
sheet

(G-3278)
WESTROCK USC INC
400 Technology Dr (15423-1043)
PHONE..................................724 938-3020
Dannis Mehiel, *President*
Dennis McCullough, *Vice Pres*
Lawrence Grossman, *Treasurer*
Anna-Marie Cotter, *Admin Sec*
EMP: 4 EST: 1985
SALES (est): 274.9K **Privately Held**
SIC: **2653** Boxes, corrugated: made from
purchased materials

Coal Township
Northumberland County

(G-3279)
KEYSTONE EXPRESSIONS LTD
583 N Oak St (17866-1510)
PHONE..................................570 648-5785
EMP: 20
SALES (est): 1.2MM **Privately Held**
SIC: **2759** Commercial Printing

(G-3280)
**KEYSTONE PRTG & GRAPHICS
INC**
583 N Oak St (17866-1510)
PHONE..................................570 648-5785
EMP: 9
SQ FT: 15,000
SALES (est): 640K **Privately Held**
SIC: **2759** 2752 Commercial Letterpress &
Offset Printing

(G-3281)
SHAMOKIN FILLER CO INC
Also Called: Shamokin Carbons
453-455 Venn Access Rd (17866)
P.O. Box 568, Shamokin (17872-0568)
PHONE....................570 644-0437
Don A Rosini, *President*
William J Rosini, *Treasurer*
▲ EMP: 41 EST: 1957
SQ FT: 25,000
SALES (est): 8.6MM **Privately Held**
WEB: www.shamokinfiller.com
SIC: 3295 3624 Graphite, natural: ground, pulverized, refined or blended; carbon & graphite products

(G-3282)
STANSONS KITCHENS & VANITIES
729 S 5th St (17866-3601)
PHONE....................570 648-4660
Victor Ginitz, *President*
Frank Ginitz, *Vice Pres*
EMP: 4
SQ FT: 10,000
SALES (est): 300K **Privately Held**
SIC: 2434 Wood kitchen cabinets

Coalport
Clearfield County

(G-3283)
INTERIOR MOTIVES INC
1168 Maple Rd (16627-9333)
PHONE....................814 672-3100
Samantha J Tarr, *President*
Eric T Tarr, *Vice Pres*
EMP: 7
SALES (est): 664.5K **Privately Held**
SIC: 2511 Wood household furniture

Coatesville
Chester County

(G-3284)
ADVANCED PDT DESIGN & MFG INC
735 Fox Chase Ste 107 (19320-1897)
PHONE....................610 380-9140
Lewis Filo, *President*
Paul Bednar, *Engineer*
Mike Gearhart, *Engineer*
Khanh Tran, *Engineer*
Ann Sonntag, *Sales Staff*
EMP: 20
SQ FT: 10,000
SALES (est): 4.1MM **Privately Held**
WEB: www.apdmfg.com
SIC: 3699 Electrical equipment & supplies

(G-3285)
AERZEN USA CORP (DH)
Also Called: Aerzener Maschinenfabrik
108 Independence Way (19320-1653)
PHONE....................610 380-0244
Pierre Noack, *President*
Michelle Abney, *Project Mgr*
Joseph Shields, *Project Mgr*
Hugh Sinn, *Project Mgr*
Joe Lynch, *Buyer*
◆ EMP: 52
SQ FT: 60,000
SALES (est): 17MM
SALES (corp-wide): 450.2MM **Privately Held**
WEB: www.aerzenusa.com
SIC: 3563 Air & gas compressors
HQ: Aerzener Maschinenfabrik
Gesellschaft Mit Beschrankter Haftung
Reherweg 28
Aerzen 31855
515 481-0

(G-3286)
AIR LIQUIDE AMERICA LP
Modena Rd (19320)
PHONE....................610 383-5500
Tom Manix, *Office Mgr*
EMP: 25

SALES (corp-wide): 125.9MM **Privately Held**
SIC: 2813 3569 Oxygen, compressed or liquefied; generators: steam, liquid oxygen or nitrogen
HQ: Air Liquide America L.P.
9811 Katy Fwy Ste 100
Houston TX 77024
713 624-8000

(G-3287)
AMERICAN LIFTING PRODUCTS INC (HQ)
1227 W Lincoln Hwy (19320-1858)
PHONE....................610 384-1300
Reitzel O Swaim, *President*
Ronald Space, *Treasurer*
▼ EMP: 44
SQ FT: 20,000
SALES (est): 20.5MM
SALES (corp-wide): 66.8MM **Privately Held**
SIC: 3496 5051 Miscellaneous fabricated wire products; rope, wire (not insulated)
PA: Alp Industries, Inc.
512 N Market St Ste 100
Lancaster PA 17603
610 384-1300

(G-3288)
ANNALEE WOOD PRODUCTS INC (PA)
Also Called: Thrifty Pallet
789 Cedar Knoll Rd (19320-1019)
PHONE....................610 436-0142
William Fairbairn, *President*
EMP: 12
SALES (est): 1.5MM **Privately Held**
SIC: 2448 Pallets, wood; cargo containers, wood

(G-3289)
ARCELORMITTAL PLATE LLC
201 Stoyer Rd (19320-6539)
PHONE....................610 383-2000
Michael G Rippey, *CEO*
Laura Bickhart, *Engineer*
◆ EMP: 1132
SALES (est): 228.8MM
SALES (corp-wide): 9.1B **Privately Held**
SIC: 3312 Plate, steel; stainless steel; iron & steel: galvanized, pipes, plates, sheets, etc.
HQ: Arcelormittal Usa Llc
1 S Dearborn St Ste 1800
Chicago IL 60603
312 346-0300

(G-3290)
ARCELORMITTAL USA LLC
Also Called: Arcelormittal Plate
139 Modena Rd (19320-4036)
P.O. Box 3001 (19320-0900)
PHONE....................610 383-2000
Ed Frey, *General Mgr*
Benjamin Guyer, *Engineer*
Timothy Moore, *Engineer*
Jonathan Hayes, *Plant Engr*
Eric Hayes, *Project Engr*
EMP: 79
SALES (corp-wide): 9.1B **Privately Held**
SIC: 3312 Blast furnaces & steel mills
HQ: Arcelormittal Usa Llc
1 S Dearborn St Ste 1800
Chicago IL 60603
312 346-0300

(G-3291)
ARMSTRONG ENGRG ASSOC INC (PA)
1845 W Strasburg Rd (19320-4814)
PHONE....................610 436-6080
Edward Johann, *President*
Eric A Nicholas, *President*
Walter Kuchlak, *CFO*
▲ EMP: 54 EST: 1947
SQ FT: 10,000
SALES: 10MM **Privately Held**
WEB: www.rmarmstrong.com
SIC: 3443 3567 Heat exchangers, plate type; electrical furnaces, ovens & heating devices, exc. induction

(G-3292)
AUGERS UNLIMITED INC
735 Fox Chase Ste 114 (19320-1897)
PHONE....................610 380-1660
Desi T Baker, *President*
EMP: 20
SQ FT: 21,000
SALES (est): 2.9MM **Privately Held**
WEB: www.augersunlimited.com
SIC: 3423 3535 Edge tools for woodworking: augers, bits, gimlets, etc.; conveyors & conveying equipment

(G-3293)
BALLYMORE HOLDINGS INC (PA)
Also Called: Ballymore Company
501 Gunnard Carlson Dr (19320-1691)
PHONE....................610 593-5062
William F Frame, *President*
Phil Damm, *General Mgr*
Diane Catron, *Vice Pres*
Jim Cockerill, *Vice Pres*
Russell Arment, *Prdtn Mgr*
◆ EMP: 50 EST: 1998
SQ FT: 60,000
SALES (est): 11.5MM **Privately Held**
SIC: 3499 3537 3441 Ladders, portable: metal; tables, lift: hydraulic; fabricated structural metal

(G-3294)
BRANDYWINE INDUSTRIAL PAPER
104 Sycamore Ln (19320-4402)
PHONE....................610 212-9949
Donald B Ramaley, *President*
EMP: 5 EST: 2013
SALES (est): 492.3K **Privately Held**
SIC: 2631 Paperboard mills

(G-3295)
BRANDYWINE VALLEY FABRICATORS
1102 Foundry St (19320-2238)
P.O. Box 111 (19320-0111)
PHONE....................610 384-7440
John H Crane, *President*
Lynne Crane, *Vice Pres*
Lynne A Crane, *Vice Pres*
EMP: 12
SQ FT: 66,000
SALES (est): 2.7MM **Privately Held**
WEB: www.brandywinevalleyfab.com
SIC: 3441 3498 3449 3444 Fabricated structural metal; fabricated pipe & fittings; miscellaneous metalwork; sheet metalwork; fabricated plate work (boiler shop); secondary nonferrous metals

(G-3296)
CIGAS MACHINE SHOP INC
1245 Manor Rd (19320-1301)
PHONE....................610 384-5239
Craig Cigas, *President*
Lance Groff, *Maint Spvr*
EMP: 30 EST: 1958
SQ FT: 5,000
SALES (est): 5.5MM **Privately Held**
WEB: www.cigasmachine.com
SIC: 3599 Machine shop, jobbing & repair

(G-3297)
CNC MANUFACTURING INC
Also Called: C N C
131 Birch St (19320-4014)
PHONE....................610 444-4437
Tom Walser, *President*
Jim Rowland, *Vice Pres*
Ray Cruz, *QC Mgr*
Charles Skoch, *QC Mgr*
EMP: 25 EST: 1997
SQ FT: 9,000
SALES (est): 6MM **Privately Held**
SIC: 3599 Machine shop, jobbing & repair

(G-3298)
CNC TECHNOLOGY INC
131 Birch St (19320-4014)
PHONE....................610 444-4437
Regina Prince, *Principal*
Jim Rowland, *Vice Pres*
EMP: 4
SALES (est): 381.7K **Privately Held**
SIC: 3549 Metalworking machinery

(G-3299)
COATESVILLE SCRAP IR MET INC
1000 S 1st Ave (19320-4039)
P.O. Box 751 (19320-0751)
PHONE....................610 384-9230
David Simon, *President*
Ken Simon, *Vice Pres*
Ed Skiles, *Transptn Dir*
Karen Wilson, *Office Mgr*
James Nixdorf, *Manager*
EMP: 25
SQ FT: 3,000
SALES (est): 7.9MM **Privately Held**
WEB: www.coatesvillescrap.com
SIC: 5093 3341 Ferrous metal scrap & waste; nonferrous metals scrap; secondary nonferrous metals

(G-3300)
DAILY
2590 Strasburg Rd (19320-4228)
PHONE....................610 384-0372
Marianne Daily, *Principal*
EMP: 3 EST: 2010
SALES (est): 169.1K **Privately Held**
SIC: 2711 Newspapers, publishing & printing

(G-3301)
DONALD TRAMMELL
Also Called: Donbar Shea Butter Products
935 W Main St (19320-2636)
PHONE....................484 238-5467
Donald Trammell, *Owner*
EMP: 3
SALES (est): 165.1K **Privately Held**
SIC: 2844 Face creams or lotions

(G-3302)
EWALD A STELLRECHT INC
Also Called: E S E Machines
21 S Caln Rd (19320-2401)
PHONE....................610 363-1141
Ewald A Stellrecht, *President*
▲ EMP: 15
SALES (est): 2.3MM **Privately Held**
SIC: 3547 Rolling mill machinery

(G-3303)
FARASON CORPORATION
855 Fox Chase (19320-1895)
PHONE....................610 383-6224
Jay Paul Hershey, *President*
William Collister, *Vice Pres*
Joyce Hurley, *Purch Mgr*
Rick Jacobs, *Engineer*
Ryan Preston, *Engineer*
EMP: 40
SQ FT: 18,000
SALES (est): 15.6MM **Privately Held**
WEB: www.farason.com
SIC: 3565 Packaging machinery

(G-3304)
GENERAL TRANSERVICE INC (HQ)
Also Called: Rampmaster
211 Stewart Huston Dr (19320-1688)
PHONE....................610 857-1900
Leighton Yohannan, *CEO*
Robert G Watkinsi Jr, *Ch of Bd*
Michael J Wilkinson, *President*
Owen Watkins, *Vice Pres*
Dan Watkins, *CFO*
◆ EMP: 34
SQ FT: 30,000
SALES (est): 5.2MM **Privately Held**
SIC: 3537 7699 Trucks, tractors, loaders, carriers & similar equipment; aircraft & heavy equipment repair services

(G-3305)
GLOBAL CAPITAL CORP (PA)
Also Called: Rampmaster
140 Stewart Huston Dr (19320-1646)
PHONE....................610 857-1900
Robert G Watkins Jr, *Ch of Bd*
Mike Matza, *President*
Tim Porter, *Prdtn Mgr*
Kyle Fox, *Engineer*
Robert Watkins, *CIO*
EMP: 1
SQ FT: 30,000

SALES (est): 5.6MM **Privately Held**
SIC: 3537 6159 Trucks, tractors, loaders, carriers & similar equipment; machinery & equipment finance leasing

(G-3306)
GRID ELECTRIC INC
Also Called: Grid Sign Systems
8 Steven Way (19320-1242)
P.O. Box 536, Glenmoore (19343-0536)
PHONE.................................610 466-7030
EMP: 28
SQ FT: 23,000
SALES (est): 1.4MM **Privately Held**
SIC: 1799 3993 3444 2394 Special Trade Contractor Mfg Signs/Ad Specialties Mfg Sheet Metalwork Mfg Canvas/Related Prdts

(G-3307)
HAZEL AND ASH ORGANICS LLC
14 Spaulding Ave (19320-4185)
PHONE.................................717 521-9593
Andrea Keith,
EMP: 3
SALES (est): 75.4K **Privately Held**
SIC: 2032 0181 2033 Ethnic foods: canned, jarred, etc.; seeds, vegetable: growing of; vegetables & vegetable products in cans, jars, etc.

(G-3308)
HONEYBROOK WOODS
22 Martins Corner Rd (19320-1096)
PHONE.................................610 380-7108
Paul Yacoe, *Owner*
EMP: 7
SALES (est): 565.9K **Privately Held**
WEB: www.honeybrookwoods.com
SIC: 2441 Boxes, wood

(G-3309)
JGM FABRICATORS & CONSTRS LLC
1201 Valley Rd (19320-2848)
PHONE.................................484 698-6201
Joseph Messner, *CEO*
EMP: 80 **EST:** 2017
SALES (est): 3MM **Privately Held**
SIC: 3441 1541 Building components, structural steel; industrial buildings, new construction

(G-3310)
JGM WELDING & FABG SVCS INC
1201 Valley Rd (19320-2848)
PHONE.................................610 873-0081
Joseph G Messner Jr, *President*
Dominic Bonura, *Superintendent*
Joe Pardo, *Superintendent*
Joe Messner Sr, *Exec VP*
Neal Horter, *Purch Mgr*
EMP: 85
SQ FT: 5,000
SALES (est): 26.6MM **Privately Held**
WEB: www.jgminc.us
SIC: 3441 1541 1542 8711 Fabricated structural metal; industrial buildings & warehouses; commercial & office building contractors; engineering services

(G-3311)
JOHN ROCK INC
500 Independence Way (19320-1689)
P.O. Box 250, Sadsburyville (19369-0250)
PHONE.................................610 857-8080
William McCauley, *Principal*
▲ **EMP:** 90 **EST:** 1972
SQ FT: 30,000
SALES (est): 17.6MM **Privately Held**
WEB: www.johnrock.com
SIC: 2448 Pallets, wood

(G-3312)
L D KALLMAN INC
Also Called: Dairy Sales
1001 E Chestnut St (19320-3326)
P.O. Box 671 (19320-0671)
PHONE.................................610 384-1200
Gary R Kallman, *President*
Helene Kallman, *Admin Sec*
EMP: 15

SALES (est): 10MM **Privately Held**
WEB: www.dairysales.com
SIC: 2021 2079 Whey butter; margarine, including imitation

(G-3313)
LEADING EDGE COMPOSITES INC
645 Sands Ct Ste 101 (19320-1802)
PHONE.................................610 932-9055
Brian Arni, *President*
Charlene Arni, *Vice Pres*
Matthew Bonner, *Engineer*
Jeff Tatum, *Accounts Mgr*
Sue Corby, *Manager*
EMP: 32
SQ FT: 40,000
SALES (est): 7.2MM **Privately Held**
WEB: www.lec-composites.com
SIC: 3599 Machine shop, jobbing & repair

(G-3314)
LS STEEL INC
1318 W Kings Hwy (19320-1147)
PHONE.................................717 669-4581
Levi Stoltzfus, *Principal*
EMP: 3 **EST:** 2011
SALES (est): 1.4MM **Privately Held**
SIC: 5051 4213 3531 Steel; heavy hauling; construction machinery

(G-3315)
LUKENS INC
Also Called: Lukens Steel
50 S 1st Ave (19320-3418)
PHONE.................................610 383-2000
R William Van Sant, *CEO*
T Grant John, *Senior VP*
Frederick J Smith, *Senior VP*
P Blaine Clemens, *Vice Pres*
Charles B Houghton, *Vice Pres*
▼ **EMP:** 100
SQ FT: 75,000
SALES (est): 15.1MM **Privately Held**
SIC: 3312 Plate, steel; stainless steel

(G-3316)
MANLEY FENCE CO
301 Reeceville Rd (19320-1521)
PHONE.................................610 842-8833
Rene Gilbaugh, *President*
EMP: 4 **EST:** 1958
SQ FT: 5,400
SALES (est): 320K **Privately Held**
WEB: www.manleyfence.com
SIC: 1799 2499 3496 3446 Fence construction; fencing, wood; miscellaneous fabricated wire products; architectural metalwork

(G-3317)
MOTOR ACTUATOR SPECIALTIES INC
20 Vivian Dr (19320-4600)
PHONE.................................215 919-1437
Audrey A Lehman, *President*
EMP: 3
SALES: 80K **Privately Held**
SIC: 3566 Speed changers, drives & gears

(G-3318)
MTI PRECISION PRODUCTS LLC
Also Called: MTI Dental
131 Birch St (19320-4014)
PHONE.................................610 679-5280
Peter Miranda, *Mng Member*
EMP: 15
SALES: 2MM **Privately Held**
SIC: 3843 Hand pieces & parts, dental

(G-3319)
NATIONAL DUMPSTER SERVICE LLC
116 Country Run Dr (19320-3068)
PHONE.................................484 949-1060
Casey Hart, *Principal*
EMP: 3
SALES (est): 232K **Privately Held**
SIC: 3443 Dumpsters, garbage

(G-3320)
PACER INDUSTRIES INC
Also Called: DPR INDUSTRIES
200 Red Rd (19320-2765)
PHONE.................................610 383-4200

Joseph F Moran, *President*
Thomas Linkins, *VP Sales*
Jane Myers, *Manager*
EMP: 14 **EST:** 1979
SQ FT: 46,000
SALES: 3.1MM **Privately Held**
WEB: www.pacerindustries.com
SIC: 3291 Wheels, abrasive

(G-3321)
PATWELL PHRM SOLUTIONS LLC
555 Fox Chase Ste 102 (19320-1885)
PHONE.................................610 380-7101
Dave Popplewell,
EMP: 9
SALES (est): 1MM **Privately Held**
WEB: www.patwell.us
SIC: 2834 Emulsions, pharmaceutical

(G-3322)
PAULSONBILT LTD
1000 W 11th Ave (19320-2811)
PHONE.................................610 384-6112
Jacob R Paulson, *President*
E Grace Paulson, *Admin Sec*
EMP: 15
SQ FT: 13,000
SALES (est): 3.4MM **Privately Held**
WEB: www.paulsonbilt.com
SIC: 3469 Garbage cans, stamped & pressed metal

(G-3323)
PELETS WELDING INC
19 N 12th Ave (19320-3577)
PHONE.................................610 384-5048
John M Pelet, *President*
Michael Pelet Jr, *President*
Douglas Pelet, *Vice Pres*
Tim Pelet, *QC Mgr*
EMP: 30
SQ FT: 67,000
SALES: 3MM **Privately Held**
WEB: www.peletwelding.com
SIC: 7692 3441 Brazing; fabricated structural metal

(G-3324)
PHARMACEUTICAL PROCUREMENT
Also Called: PP&I
324 Martingale Cir (19320-4663)
PHONE.................................610 680-7708
Meghan Capuzzi,
Peter Fassbender,
EMP: 12
SALES (est): 2.2MM **Privately Held**
SIC: 2834 4213 Pharmaceutical preparations; trucking, except local

(G-3325)
SAHA INDUSTRIES INC
Also Called: R-A-S Industries
717 E Chestnut St (19320-3314)
P.O. Box 790 (19320-0790)
PHONE.................................610 383-5070
Richard A Saha, *President*
Richard A Saha Jr, *Treasurer*
EMP: 6 **EST:** 1960
SQ FT: 12,000
SALES (est): 1MM **Privately Held**
WEB: www.sahaindustries.com
SIC: 3442 Store fronts, prefabricated, metal

(G-3326)
SPECIALTY ADHESIVES INC
535 Misty Patch Rd (19320-4605)
PHONE.................................484 524-5324
EMP: 4
SALES (est): 154.1K **Privately Held**
SIC: 2891 Adhesives

(G-3327)
UNEK DESIGNS EMB & SEW SP LLC
1108 W Lincoln Hwy (19320-1837)
PHONE.................................610 563-6676
Tamara Shreve, *Mng Member*
Sandra Hodson,
James C Shreve,
EMP: 5
SALES (est): 608.8K **Privately Held**
SIC: 2326 7389 Work uniforms;

(G-3328)
UTICOM SYSTEMS INC
109 Independence Way (19320-1654)
PHONE.................................610 857-2655
Paul W Keeler, *President*
Alan T Martin, *Admin Sec*
▲ **EMP:** 20
SALES (est): 6MM **Privately Held**
WEB: www.uticom.net
SIC: 2752 2759 Decals, lithographed; commercial printing

(G-3329)
WEAVER MULCH LLC
3186 Strasburg Rd (19320-4155)
PHONE.................................610 383-6818
David Weaver, *Info Tech Mgr*
David L Weaver,
▲ **EMP:** 20
SALES (est): 3.4MM **Privately Held**
SIC: 2499 Mulch, wood & bark

(G-3330)
WIRE AND CABLE SPECIALTIES INC (PA)
Also Called: American Fishing Wire Div
440 Highland Blvd (19320-5808)
PHONE.................................610 466-6200
James F Clark, *President*
Douglas I Clark, *Vice Pres*
▲ **EMP:** 60
SQ FT: 50,000
SALES (est): 12.2MM **Privately Held**
WEB: www.wire-cablespecialties.com
SIC: 3496 3315 Miscellaneous fabricated wire products; steel wire & related products

(G-3331)
WITMER PUBLIC SAFETY GROUP INC (PA)
Also Called: Thefire Store.com
104 Independence Way (19320-1653)
PHONE.................................800 852-6088
James A Witmer, *President*
Pat Phelan, *President*
Kevin Greenlee, *Vice Pres*
Ruth E Witmer, *Vice Pres*
Ruth Witmer, *Vice Pres*
EMP: 75
SQ FT: 35,000
SALES (est): 53.8MM **Privately Held**
WEB: www.thefirestore.com
SIC: 3469 5021 5099 Helmets, steel; shelving; safety equipment & supplies

(G-3332)
Z PUBLICATION LLC
Also Called: Your Town Magazine
143 Milbury Rd (19320-5604)
PHONE.................................484 574-5321
John Zwirzina, *Owner*
EMP: 4
SALES (est): 220.2K **Privately Held**
SIC: 2721 Magazines: publishing & printing; magazines: publishing only, not printed on site

---

Coburn
Centre County

(G-3333)
MARTINS FEED MILL INC
534 Main St (16832)
P.O. Box 17 (16832-0017)
PHONE.................................814 349-8787
Elaiza J Walton, *President*
EMP: 11
SQ FT: 400
SALES: 2.3MM **Privately Held**
SIC: 2048 Livestock feeds

Cochranton
Crawford County

(G-3334)
AETNA MACHINE COMPANY
203 N Franklin St (16314-9715)
P.O. Box 97 (16314-0097)
PHONE.................................814 425-3881

Richard J Mc Clure, *CEO*
Bridget A Sheehan, *President*
Dan Steinbeck, *Purchasing*
Mary Beth Hummel, *Manager*
EMP: 12 **EST:** 1965
SQ FT: 9,600
SALES (est): 1.3MM **Privately Held**
WEB: www.aetnamachine.com
SIC: 3469 Machine parts, stamped or pressed metal

(G-3335)
AREA SHOPPER
Also Called: Millers Publishing and Prtg
4095 Us Highway 19 (16314-3915)
PHONE..............................814 425-7272
Simon Miller, *Owner*
Lon Wilson, *General Mgr*
Bryan Miller, *Principal*
Kevin Miller, *Principal*
Kenny Miller, *Treasurer*
EMP: 7
SALES (est): 529.9K **Privately Held**
WEB: www.areashopper.com
SIC: 2711 Newspapers, publishing & printing

(G-3336)
BECKMAN PRODUCTION SVCS INC
3052 St Rt 173 (16314)
PHONE..............................814 425-1066
Robert Coon, *Principal*
EMP: 3
SALES (corp-wide): 827.1MM **Publicly Held**
SIC: 1382 Oil & gas exploration services
HQ: Beckman Production Services, Inc.
3786 Beebe Rd
Kalkaska MI 49646
231 258-9524

(G-3337)
COINCO INC (PA)
Also Called: Morco
23727 Us Highway 322 (16314-6733)
P.O. Box 248 (16314-0248)
PHONE..............................814 425-7407
James A Cokley, *President*
David E Hart, *Treasurer*
▲ **EMP:** 35 **EST:** 1960
SQ FT: 50,000
SALES (est): 14.3MM **Privately Held**
WEB: www.coinco.org
SIC: 3469 3999 3993 3544 Stamping metal for the trade; calendars, framed; advertising novelties; dies, steel rule; metalworking machinery

(G-3338)
COINCO INC
Also Called: Morco
125 High St (16314-8611)
PHONE..............................814 425-7476
David E Hart, *Manager*
EMP: 35
SALES (corp-wide): 14.3MM **Privately Held**
WEB: www.coinco.org
SIC: 3993 3499 3999 3544 Advertising novelties; novelties & giftware, including trophies; burnt wood articles; dies, steel rule; measuring & controlling devices; automotive & apparel trimmings
PA: Coinco, Inc.
23727 Us Highway 322
Cochranton PA 16314
814 425-7407

(G-3339)
COMOR INC
23697 Us Highway 322 (16314-6731)
P.O. Box 248 (16314-0248)
PHONE..............................814 425-3943
David Hart, *President*
James Cokley, *Vice Pres*
Dave Harts, *Sales Staff*
Dan Bresee, *Maintence Staff*
EMP: 8
SQ FT: 46,000
SALES (est): 1.5MM **Privately Held**
WEB: www.comor.com
SIC: 3089 Injection molding of plastics

(G-3340)
CURTIS BAKER LUMBER INC
Also Called: Baker Curtis Lumber Sawmill
751 Old Route 322 (16314-1843)
PHONE..............................814 425-3020
Curtis P Baker, *President*
Robert Baker, *Vice Pres*
Steven Baker, *Vice Pres*
Janet L Baker, *Admin Sec*
EMP: 17
SALES (est): 1.7MM **Privately Held**
SIC: 2421 Sawmills & planing mills, general

(G-3341)
DE VORE TOOL CO INC
136 S Smith St (16314-8610)
P.O. Box 173 (16314-0173)
PHONE..............................814 425-2566
Doug De Vore, *President*
EMP: 4
SQ FT: 2,500
SALES (est): 400K **Privately Held**
SIC: 3544 Special dies & tools

(G-3342)
DRAFTO CORPORATION
100 Pressler Ave (16314-8668)
P.O. Box 158 (16314-0158)
PHONE..............................814 425-7445
Peter J Wassmer, *President*
EMP: 60 **EST:** 1934
SQ FT: 40,000
SALES (est): 6.1MM **Privately Held**
WEB: www.drafto.com
SIC: 3596 Industrial scales
PA: Zurex Corporation
100 Pressler Ave
Cochranton PA 16314

(G-3343)
J-M MANUFACTURING COMPANY INC
Also Called: Meadville Plant
15661 Delano Rd (16314-4457)
PHONE..............................814 337-7675
Brian Shull, *Plant Mgr*
Dave Slawson, *Branch Mgr*
EMP: 87
SALES (corp-wide): 1B **Privately Held**
SIC: 2821 5051 3084 Polyvinyl chloride resins (PVC); pipe & tubing, steel; plastics pipe
PA: J-M Manufacturing Company, Inc.
5200 W Century Blvd
Los Angeles CA 90045
800 621-4404

(G-3344)
MEARS TOOL & DIE INC
24668 Us Highway 322 (16314-6412)
P.O. Box 434 (16314-0434)
PHONE..............................814 425-8304
William Fanning, *President*
H David Mears, *Vice Pres*
EMP: 13 **EST:** 1975
SQ FT: 14,000
SALES (est): 2.1MM **Privately Held**
SIC: 3544 Special dies & tools

(G-3345)
MILLER PRINTING & PUBLISHING
Also Called: The Area Shopper
Perry Hwy Rr 19 (16314)
PHONE..............................814 425-7272
Simon Miller, *President*
Kenneth Miller, *Treasurer*
Kevin Miller, *Admin Sec*
EMP: 25
SALES (est): 1.4MM **Privately Held**
SIC: 2741 2759 2711 Shopping news; publishing & printing; newspapers: printing; newspapers

(G-3346)
NORTHWEST PA BURIAL SERVICE
22996 Us Highway 322 (16314-6716)
PHONE..............................814 425-2436
Ken Schutz, *President*
EMP: 4
SQ FT: 5,000

SALES (est): 350K **Privately Held**
SIC: 3272 7359 Precast terrazo or concrete products; tent & tarpaulin rental

(G-3347)
PITTSBURGH GLASS WORKS LLC
Also Called: Pgw Division 5
5123 Victory Blvd (16314-3969)
PHONE..............................814 336-4411
Chris Kuppinger, *QC Mgr*
Brian Burnette, *Office Mgr*
Perry Johnson, *Branch Mgr*
Thomas Waterloo, *Maintence Staff*
EMP: 275 **Privately Held**
SIC: 2851 Paints & allied products
HQ: Pittsburgh Glass Works, Llc
30 Isabella St Ste 500
Pittsburgh PA 15212

(G-3348)
POUX PLASTICS INC
5605 State Highway 173 (16314-7751)
PHONE..............................814 425-2100
Michael Poux, *CEO*
Michael Carter, *Vice Pres*
EMP: 9
SQ FT: 7,000
SALES: 1MM **Privately Held**
SIC: 3089 Fittings for pipe, plastic

(G-3349)
REALCO DIVERSIFIED INC
3688 Bailey Rd (16314-5210)
PHONE..............................814 638-0800
Raymond Coon, *President*
Gordon B Coon, *Vice Pres*
Tina M Learn, *Treasurer*
Melanie L McKay, *Admin Sec*
EMP: 21
SQ FT: 17,000
SALES: 2MM **Privately Held**
WEB: www.realcodiversified.com
SIC: 3544 Special dies, tools, jigs & fixtures

(G-3350)
RILEY TOOL INCORPORATED
18908 Adamsville Rd (16314-4606)
PHONE..............................814 425-4140
Lawrence E Riley, *President*
EMP: 17
SALES (est): 2.4MM **Privately Held**
SIC: 2499 Tool handles, wood

(G-3351)
SPECIALTY GROUP PRINTING INC (PA)
126 E Adams St (16314-8604)
P.O. Box 187 (16314-0187)
PHONE..............................814 425-3061
Shirley Sheehan, *President*
Jim Sheehan, *Manager*
EMP: 10
SQ FT: 9,820
SALES (est): 966.8K **Privately Held**
SIC: 2759 5712 5943 2791 Screen printing; office furniture; office forms & supplies; typesetting; bookbinding & related work; commercial printing, lithographic

(G-3352)
SUGAR SHACK
29950 Lake Creek Rd (16314-8010)
PHONE..............................814 425-2220
Sharon Carlson, *President*
EMP: 10
SALES (est): 710K **Privately Held**
SIC: 2062 Cane sugar refining

(G-3353)
ZUREX CORPORATION (PA)
Also Called: Drafto
100 Pressler Ave (16314-8668)
P.O. Box 158 (16314-0158)
PHONE..............................814 425-7445
Peter J Wassmer, *President*
Bruce Wesley, *General Mgr*
EMP: 20
SALES (est): 10.9MM **Privately Held**
SIC: 3596 Industrial scales

Cochranville
Chester County

(G-3354)
BRANDYWINE ENVELOPE CORP
151 Hood Rd (19330-9475)
P.O. Box 70 (19330-0070)
PHONE..............................800 887-9399
Daron Boyd, *President*
Clark Butts, *Treasurer*
EMP: 9
SALES (est): 1.1MM **Privately Held**
WEB: www.brandywineenvelope.com
SIC: 2759 Envelopes: printing

(G-3355)
BUTTS TICKET COMPANY INC
Also Called: Toledo Tickets
151 Hood Rd (19330-9475)
P.O. Box 70 (19330-0070)
PHONE..............................610 869-7450
Thomas Clark Butts Sr, *President*
Johnetta McCown, *Prdtn Mgr*
Bill Gratton, *Sales Staff*
Carmen Butts, *Admin Sec*
EMP: 18 **EST:** 1965
SQ FT: 27,542
SALES: 2MM **Privately Held**
WEB: www.buttsticket.com
SIC: 2752 2759 5199 Commercial printing, offset; tickets, lithographed; flexographic printing; novelties, paper

(G-3356)
T L KING CABINETMAKER
155 Hood Rd (19330-9475)
PHONE..............................610 869-4220
Timothy L King,
EMP: 3
SQ FT: 11,000
SALES (est): 750K **Privately Held**
WEB: www.tlking.com
SIC: 2511 2541 Wood household furniture; cabinets, except refrigerated: show, display, etc.: wood

---

Codorus
York County

(G-3357)
BAUM & HERSH INC
11 Hanover St (17311)
P.O. Box 188 (17311-0188)
PHONE..............................717 229-2255
Thomas Baum, *President*
Sharon Baum, *Treasurer*
Laura Baum, *Admin Sec*
EMP: 4
SQ FT: 12,000
SALES (est): 561.3K **Privately Held**
SIC: 3543 Industrial patterns

Cogan Station
Lycoming County

(G-3358)
ANDREW E TRAUTNER & SONS INC
Also Called: Trautners Well Drilling & Svc
115 Elizabeth St (17728-9507)
PHONE..............................570 494-0191
David Trautner, *President*
Bruce Trautner, *President*
EMP: 3
SALES (est): 270K **Privately Held**
SIC: 1381 Drilling water intake wells

(G-3359)
DONNELLEY JR JOSEPH
3835 State Route 973 W (17728-8660)
PHONE..............................570 998-2541
Joseph Donnelley Jr, *Owner*
EMP: 3
SALES (est): 173.6K **Privately Held**
SIC: 2411 4212 Logging camps & contractors; timber trucking, local

GEOGRAPHIC

(G-3360)
DRESSEL WELDING SUPPLY INC
4450 Lycoming Creek Rd (17728-7757)
PHONE..................................570 505-1994
Bryan Kearney, *Branch Mgr*
EMP: 4
SALES (corp-wide): 125.9MM **Privately Held**
SIC: 7692 5999 5084 Welding repair; welding supplies; petroleum industry machinery
HQ: Dressel Welding Supply, Inc.
1270 Roosevelt Ave
York PA 17404
717 848-6224

(G-3361)
LEMCO TOOL CORPORATION
1850 Metzger Ave (17728-8351)
PHONE..................................570 494-0620
Michael Miller, *President*
Michael Counsil, *Foreman/Supr*
Debra Weisbrod, *Purchasing*
▲ **EMP:** 30
SQ FT: 47,000
SALES (est): 6.1MM **Privately Held**
WEB: www.lemco-tool.com
SIC: 3546 3531 Power-driven handtools; construction machinery

(G-3362)
STALLION OILFIELD SERVICES LTD
297 Beautys Run Rd (17728-8632)
P.O. Box 1103, Williamsport (17703-1103)
PHONE..................................570 494-0760
EMP: 7 **Privately Held**
SIC: 1389 Oil field services
HQ: Stallion Oilfield Services Ltd.
950 Corbindale Rd Ste 400
Houston TX 77024
713 528-5544

(G-3363)
WINTERS LUMBER CO
6765 Pleasant Valley Rd (17728-8551)
PHONE..................................570 435-2231
Gary Winter, *President*
Larry Winter, *Vice Pres*
Barry Winter, *Treasurer*
Tarry Winter, *Admin Sec*
EMP: 4
SQ FT: 4,660
SALES (est): 719.9K **Privately Held**
SIC: 2421 Sawmills & planing mills, general

Cokeburg
Washington County

(G-3364)
ROYAL HYDRAULIC SVC & MFG INC
2 Washington St (15324)
P.O. Box 122 (15324-0122)
PHONE..................................724 945-6800
George Morrell Jr, *President*
Gary Morrell, *Admin Sec*
EMP: 24
SQ FT: 5,000
SALES (est): 4.4MM **Privately Held**
SIC: 7699 7692 7694 Hydraulic equipment repair; welding repair; armature rewinding shops

---

Collegeville
Montgomery County

(G-3365)
7106 DOW CHEMICAL
400 Arcola Rd (19426-2914)
PHONE..................................610 244-6000
EMP: 11 **EST:** 2013
SALES (est): 2.2MM **Privately Held**
SIC: 2821 Plastics materials & resins

(G-3366)
A & T NEWS SERVICE
1005 Brassington Dr (19426-4005)
PHONE..................................610 454-7787
Ran Yu, *Owner*
EMP: 3
SALES (est): 112.9K **Privately Held**
SIC: 2711 Newspapers, publishing & printing

(G-3367)
AMERI PRINT FLAG INC
202 Jordan Ct (19426-2847)
PHONE..................................610 409-9603
Doug Cornish, *President*
EMP: 6
SQ FT: 10,000
SALES (est): 745.5K **Privately Held**
WEB: www.ameriprintflag.com
SIC: 2399 Banners, pennants & flags

(G-3368)
ANALYTICAL TECHNOLOGY INC (PA)
Also Called: ATI
6 Iron Bridge Dr (19426-2045)
PHONE..................................610 917-0991
John J Becker, *President*
Raymond B Cromer, *Exec VP*
Patrick J O'Dowd, *Vice Pres*
Calvin Krusen, *Engineer*
James Worobetz, *Sales Associate*
EMP: 14
SQ FT: 24,000
SALES (est): 7.2MM **Privately Held**
WEB: www.analyticaltechnology.com
SIC: 3829 3823 Gas detectors; water quality monitoring & control systems

(G-3369)
ANTHONY MIECZKOWSKI
Also Called: The Swedish Pastry Shop
928 Dogwood Ln (19426-1160)
PHONE..................................610 489-2523
Anthony Mieczkowski, *Owner*
EMP: 3
SQ FT: 1,000
SALES (est): 96K **Privately Held**
SIC: 2051 Bread, cake & related products

(G-3370)
APPLIED MATERIALS INC
71 Longacre Dr (19426-2898)
PHONE..................................610 409-9187
Daniel Muller, *Branch Mgr*
EMP: 3
SALES (corp-wide): 17.2B **Publicly Held**
SIC: 3674 Semiconductors & related devices
PA: Applied Materials, Inc.
3050 Bowers Ave
Santa Clara CA 95054
408 727-5555

(G-3371)
CDI LAWN EQUIPMENT & GRDN SUP
3474 Germantown Pike (19426-1504)
PHONE..................................610 489-3474
Joe Ianella, *Owner*
Ann Iannella, *Vice Pres*
Dan Iannella, *Vice Pres*
EMP: 20
SQ FT: 5,548
SALES (est): 1.7MM **Privately Held**
SIC: 5084 3546 Engines, gasoline; saws & sawing equipment

(G-3372)
COALISLAND CAST STONE INC
1670 Shefley Ln (19426-1446)
PHONE..................................610 476-1683
Donal Gates, *President*
EMP: 15
SALES (est): 1MM **Privately Held**
SIC: 3272 Cast stone, concrete

(G-3373)
CREATIVE SYSTEMS USA LLC
505 Second Ave (19426-2516)
P.O. Box 26035 (19426-0035)
PHONE..................................610 450-6580
Jason Hendrie, *Partner*
Greg Beese, *Partner*
Harry Blanchard, *Sales Engr*
EMP: 7
SALES (est): 580K **Privately Held**
SIC: 7812 3861 7922 Audio-visual program production; cameras, still & motion picture (all types); lighting, theatrical

(G-3374)
DDP SPECIALTY ELECTRONIC MA (DH)
400 Arcola Rd (19426-2914)
PHONE..................................610 244-6000
Mark A Bachman, *President*
EMP: 4
SALES (est): 456.5K **Privately Held**
SALES (corp-wide): 85.9B **Publicly Held**
SIC: 2821 2869 2891 3569 Plastics materials & resins; industrial organic chemicals; adhesives & sealants; filters; plastics foam products; specialty cleaning, polishes & sanitation goods
HQ: The Dow Chemical Company
2211 H H Dow Way
Midland MI 48642
989 636-1000

(G-3375)
DOW CHEMICAL COMPANY
400 Arcola Rd (19426-2914)
PHONE..................................215 641-7000
Aaron Sarafinas, *Principal*
EMP: 75
SALES (corp-wide): 85.9B **Publicly Held**
SIC: 2819 Industrial inorganic chemicals
HQ: The Dow Chemical Company
2211 H H Dow Way
Midland MI 48642
989 636-1000

(G-3376)
EVANSBURG TOOL CORPORATION
16 Crosskeys Rd (19426-3129)
P.O. Box 26006 (19426-0006)
PHONE..................................610 489-7580
Alan C Stadlin, *President*
Helen Meyer, *Corp Secy*
EMP: 8 **EST:** 1947
SQ FT: 5,000
SALES (est): 1.2MM **Privately Held**
SIC: 3544 Special dies & tools

(G-3377)
FIS DATA SYSTEMS INC (HQ)
200 Campus Dr (19426-4903)
PHONE..................................484 582-2000
Glenn H Hutchins, *Ch of Bd*
Russell P Fradin, *President*
Christopher Breakiron, *Vice Pres*
Charles J Neral, *CFO*
Patricia K Cassidy, *Officer*
EMP: 37
SALES (est): 2.5B
SALES (corp-wide): 8.4B **Publicly Held**
WEB: www.sungard.com
SIC: 7374 7372 Data processing service; business oriented computer software
PA: Fidelity National Information Services, Inc.
601 Riverside Ave
Jacksonville FL 32204
904 438-6000

(G-3378)
FIS SYSTEMS INTERNATIONAL LLC (HQ)
Also Called: Sungard
200 Campus Dr (19426-4903)
PHONE..................................484 582-2000
James Ashton, *President*
Thomas McDugall, *Vice Pres*
Michael Ruane, *Treasurer*
Leslie Brush, *Admin Sec*
EMP: 80
SALES (est): 106.2MM
SALES (corp-wide): 8.4B **Publicly Held**
SIC: 7372 Business oriented computer software
PA: Fidelity National Information Services, Inc.
601 Riverside Ave
Jacksonville FL 32204
904 438-6000

(G-3379)
GLAXOSMITHKLINE LLC
1250 S Collegeville Rd (19426-2990)
PHONE..................................610 917-4941
EMP: 28
SALES (corp-wide): 39.8B **Privately Held**
SIC: 2834 Pharmaceutical preparations
HQ: Glaxosmithkline Llc
5 Crescent Dr
Philadelphia PA 19112
215 751-4000

(G-3380)
GLAXOSMITHKLINE LLC
Also Called: Data Center
1000 Black Rock Rd (19426-2921)
PHONE..................................610 917-3493
Eric Manning, *Branch Mgr*
EMP: 12
SALES (corp-wide): 39.8B **Privately Held**
SIC: 2834 Pharmaceutical preparations
HQ: Glaxosmithkline Llc
5 Crescent Dr
Philadelphia PA 19112
215 751-4000

(G-3381)
H Y K CONSTRUCTION CO INC (PA)
430 Rahns Rd (19426-1895)
P.O. Box 1247, Skippack (19474-1247)
PHONE..................................610 489-2646
Paul Yerk, *President*
Daniel Condiles, *General Mgr*
John B Haines IV, *Vice Pres*
John R Kibblehouse, *Treasurer*
EMP: 100 **EST:** 1956
SQ FT: 4,000
SALES (est): 25.1MM **Privately Held**
SIC: 3273 3272 Ready-mixed concrete; prestressed concrete products

(G-3382)
MOBINOL FUEL COMPANY
119 Hunt Club Dr (19426-3967)
PHONE..................................484 432-9007
John J Savarese, *President*
EMP: 3
SALES (est): 166.3K **Privately Held**
WEB: www.mobinolfuel.com
SIC: 2869 Fuels

(G-3383)
MONTICELLO GRANITE LTD
101 Cherry Tree Blvd (19426-4015)
PHONE..................................215 677-1000
▲ **EMP:** 10
SALES (est): 670K **Privately Held**
SIC: 3281 Mfg Cut Stone/Products

(G-3384)
MORTON INTERNATIONAL LLC (DH)
Also Called: Rohm and Haas Powder Coatings
400 Arcola Rd (19426-2914)
PHONE..................................989 636-1000
Lawrence A Looby, *President*
Elizabeth Nohe, *Vice Pres*
Wallace Shayn, *Vice Pres*
Dan Thompson, *Vice Pres*
Fady Guirguis, *Prdtn Mgr*
◆ **EMP:** 250 **EST:** 1848
SALES (est): 792.6MM
SALES (corp-wide): 85.9B **Publicly Held**
WEB: www.mortonintl.com
SIC: 2891 2851 2822 1479 Adhesives; lacquers, varnishes, enamels & other coatings; polysulfides (thiokol); salt & sulfur mining; salt

(G-3385)
OT MEDICAL LLC
100 Springhouse Dr # 108 (19426-4709)
P.O. Box 1737, Southeastern (19399-1737)
PHONE..................................484 588-2063
Michael Leedle, *Engineer*
William Rhoda,
EMP: 3
SALES (est): 293.1K **Privately Held**
SIC: 3841 Surgical & medical instruments

(G-3386)
PCA CORRUGATED AND DISPLAY LLC
Timbar Packaging & Display
5 Iron Bridge Dr (19426-2042)
PHONE................................610 489-8740
Dennis Wood, *Branch Mgr*
Michael Borneman, *Maintnce Staff*
EMP: 9
SALES (corp-wide): 7B **Publicly Held**
SIC: 2652 2653 Setup paperboard boxes; boxes, corrugated: made from purchased materials
HQ: Pca Corrugated And Display Llc
    1955 W Field Ct
    Lake Forest IL 60045
    847 482-3000

(G-3387)
PFIZER INC
Also Called: Wyeth
500 Arcola Rd (19426-3982)
PHONE................................484 865-5000
EMP: 4
SALES (corp-wide): 53.6B **Publicly Held**
WEB: www.wyeth.com
SIC: 2834 Pharmaceutical preparations
PA: Pfizer Inc.
    235 E 42nd St
    New York NY 10017
    212 733-2323

(G-3388)
PFIZER INC
200 Campus Dr (19426-4903)
PHONE................................484 865-0288
EMP: 8
SALES (corp-wide): 53.6B **Publicly Held**
SIC: 2834 Pharmaceutical preparations
PA: Pfizer Inc.
    235 E 42nd St
    New York NY 10017
    212 733-2323

(G-3389)
PRINTERS PRINTER INC
14 Iron Bridge Dr (19426-2046)
PHONE................................610 454-0102
Michael P Hasler, *President*
Lori Hasler, *Vice Pres*
EMP: 10 EST: 1981
SALES (est): 1.6MM **Privately Held**
WEB: www.theprintersprinter.com
SIC: 2759 7334 Thermography; photocopying & duplicating services

(G-3390)
RAHNS CONSTRUCTION MATERIAL CO
430 Rahns Rd (19426-1895)
P.O. Box 1247, Skippack (19474-1247)
PHONE................................610 584-8500
Paul Yerk, *President*
Dane Condiles, *General Mgr*
John R Kibblehouse, *Corp Secy*
John B Haines IV, *Vice Pres*
Jim Bowman, *Sales Staff*
EMP: 5
SALES (est): 573K **Privately Held**
SIC: 3273 3272 Ready-mixed concrete; prestressed concrete products

(G-3391)
ROHM AND HAAS CHEMICALS LLC (HQ)
Also Called: Dow Bar Roman House
400 Arcola Rd (19426-2914)
PHONE................................989 636-1000
Raj L Gupta, *Mng Member*
◆ EMP: 230
SALES (est): 792.6MM
SALES (corp-wide): 85.9B **Publicly Held**
SIC: 2899 Chemical preparations
PA: Dowdupont Inc.
    2030 Dow Ctr
    Midland MI 48674
    989 636-1000

(G-3392)
ROHM AND HAAS COMPANY (DH)
400 Arcola Rd (19426-2914)
PHONE................................989 636-1000
I M Peribere, *President*
Pierre R Brondeau, *President*

Robert A Lonergan, *Exec VP*
Anne M Wilms, *Exec VP*
I A Barbour, *Vice Pres*
◆ EMP: 1100 EST: 1917
SQ FT: 200,000
SALES: 3.8B
SALES (corp-wide): 85.9B **Publicly Held**
WEB: www.rohmhaas.com
SIC: 2819 2851 2891 2899 Chemicals, high purity: refined from technical grade; paints & paint additives; adhesives & sealants; salt
HQ: The Dow Chemical Company
    2211 H H Dow Way
    Midland MI 48642
    989 636-1000

(G-3393)
SIRTRIS PHARMACEUTICALS INC
Also Called: (A DEVELOPMENT STAGE COMPANY)
1250 S Collegeville Rd (19426-2990)
PHONE................................585 275-5774
Christoph Westphal MD, *President*
Garen Bohlin, *COO*
Peter Elliott PHD, *Senior VP*
Michael Jirousek PHD, *Senior VP*
EMP: 57
SQ FT: 47,786
SALES (est): 5.4MM
SALES (corp-wide): 39.8B **Privately Held**
WEB: www.sirtrispharma.com
SIC: 2834 Pharmaceutical preparations
PA: Glaxosmithkline Plc
    980 Great West Road
    Brentford MIDDX TW8 9
    208 047-5000

(G-3394)
STAUROWSKY WOODWORKING
Also Called: Staurowsky, Gary F Woodworking
3454 Germantown Pike (19426-1504)
PHONE................................610 489-0770
Gary Staurowsky, *Owner*
EMP: 3
SQ FT: 6,000
SALES (est): 379.1K **Privately Held**
SIC: 5712 2541 2431 5211 Cabinet work, custom; wood partitions & fixtures; woodwork, interior & ornamental; millwork & lumber; decorative wood & woodwork; cabinet & finish carpentry

(G-3395)
SUMMERS LABORATORIES INC
103 G P Clement Dr (19426-2044)
PHONE................................610 454-1471
Michael J Precopio, *President*
Rita Precopio, *Treasurer*
Frank M Precopio, *Shareholder*
Ernest G Szoke, *Shareholder*
EMP: 19 EST: 1985
SQ FT: 15,000
SALES (est): 5.5MM **Privately Held**
WEB: www.sumlab.com
SIC: 2834 Dermatologicals; ointments

(G-3396)
SUNGARD ASSET MGT SYSTEMS INC (DH)
200 Campus Dr (19426-4903)
PHONE................................610 251-6500
Andrew P Bronstein, *Vice Pres*
Michael J Ruane, *CFO*
Lawrence A Gross, *Admin Sec*
EMP: 117
SALES (est): 18.5MM
SALES (corp-wide): 8.4B **Publicly Held**
WEB: www.sungardams.com
SIC: 7374 7372 Data processing service; prepackaged software
HQ: Fis Data Systems Inc.
    200 Campus Dr
    Collegeville PA 19426
    484 582-2000

(G-3397)
TRANSICOIL LLC (DH)
Also Called: Ads/Transicoil
9 Iron Bridge Dr (19426-2042)
PHONE................................484 902-1100
Aaron Veres, *VP Opers*
Debbie Lockhoff, *Manager*
Jack Planchak,

EMP: 116
SALES (est): 14.9MM
SALES (corp-wide): 3.8B **Publicly Held**
WEB: www.adstcoil.com
SIC: 3728 3612 Aircraft parts & equipment; transformers, except electric
HQ: Aviation Technologies, Inc.
    1301 E 9th St Ste 3000
    Cleveland OH 44114
    216 706-2960

(G-3398)
UNISOURCE ASSOCIATES INC
Also Called: Salter's Industries
105 G P Clement Dr (19426-2044)
PHONE................................610 489-5799
Barry Salter, *President*
Dorothy Salter, *Admin Sec*
▼ EMP: 30
SALES (est): 8.8MM **Privately Held**
WEB: www.deckspiralstair.com
SIC: 3446 Railings, bannisters, guards, etc.: made from metal pipe

(G-3399)
WILLIAM H HAMMONDS & BROS
21 Crosskeys Rd (19426-3128)
PHONE................................610 489-7924
William H Hammonds, *President*
Brian Drumheller, *Vice Pres*
EMP: 6
SQ FT: 6,900
SALES (est): 762.7K **Privately Held**
SIC: 2431 Window trim, wood

(G-3400)
WILLIAM J JUDGE
Also Called: Judge Excavating and Pav Ink
3938 Ridge Pike Ste 6 (19426-3159)
PHONE................................610 348-8070
EMP: 15
SALES (est): 1.3MM **Privately Held**
SIC: 1794 3281 Excavation Contractor Mfg Cut Stone/Products

(G-3401)
WILLIAMS COMPANY LIMITED
256 Freeland Dr (19426-2677)
PHONE................................610 409-0520
Susan Williams, *President*
EMP: 4
SALES (est): 307.1K **Privately Held**
SIC: 2721 Statistical reports (periodicals): publishing & printing

---

Collingdale
Delaware County

(G-3402)
AIR CONWAY INC
1116 Macdade Blvd Ste 6 (19023-4000)
PHONE................................610 534-0500
Brian Conway, *President*
James Conway, *Vice Pres*
EMP: 11
SQ FT: 10,000
SALES: 1.3MM **Privately Held**
SIC: 7336 2752 2395 Silk screen design; commercial printing, offset; embroidery & art needlework

(G-3403)
ALESSI MANUFACTURING CORP
19 Jackson Ave (19023-3327)
PHONE................................610 586-4200
Richard M Alessi Jr, *President*
▲ EMP: 20
SQ FT: 11,800
SALES (est): 3.9MM **Privately Held**
SIC: 3511 3599 Turbines & turbine generator sets; machine & other job shop work

(G-3404)
FREE ENERGY SYSTEMS INC
Also Called: Ribbons and More
17 S Macdade Blvd 101-1 (19023-1510)
PHONE................................610 583-2640
Douglas Wright, *President*
John McMahon, *Vice Pres*
Marianne Wright, *Treasurer*
EMP: 20
SQ FT: 3,400

SALES (est): 2.6MM **Privately Held**
WEB: www.ribbonsandmore.com
SIC: 5112 3999 Office supplies; lawn ornaments

(G-3405)
J G MUNDY MACHINE LLC
Also Called: J G Mundy Machine Shop
1224 Macdade Blvd (19023-4021)
PHONE................................610 583-1200
Byron Mundy,
Joe Mundy,
EMP: 3 EST: 1945
SQ FT: 5,000 **Privately Held**
SIC: 3599 7629 Machine shop, jobbing & repair; electrical repair shops

(G-3406)
LIBERTY SPRING COMPANY INC
109 Willows Ave (19023-4024)
PHONE................................484 652-1100
Christopher Stewart, *President*
Joseph Marturano, *Principal*
EMP: 10
SALES: 750K **Privately Held**
SIC: 3495 Wire springs

(G-3407)
MERLIN MACHINE & TOOL CO INC
17 S Macdade Blvd (19023-1510)
PHONE................................215 493-6322
Sunnie T Joseph, *President*
EMP: 3 EST: 1994
SQ FT: 2,000
SALES: 150K **Privately Held**
SIC: 3544 Special dies, tools, jigs & fixtures

(G-3408)
MULTIFLEX PLATING COMPANY INC
Also Called: Multi Flex Plating
109 Willows Ave (19023-4024)
PHONE................................610 461-7700
Janet Corr, *President*
David Sugg, *General Mgr*
Joseph Corr, *Vice Pres*
EMP: 20
SQ FT: 26,000
SALES (est): 2.8MM **Privately Held**
SIC: 3471 Electroplating of metals or formed products

(G-3409)
PENN PANEL & BOX COMPANY
Willows Ave (19023)
P.O. Box 1458 (19023-8458)
PHONE................................610 586-2700
Jeffrey C Craven, *President*
Norman M McCausland, *Treasurer*
Douglas Stell, *Sales Engr*
Stefan Darczuk, *Sales Associate*
EMP: 36
SQ FT: 20,000
SALES (est): 12.3MM **Privately Held**
WEB: www.pennpanel.com
SIC: 3613 3644 Switchboards & parts, power; panelboards & distribution boards, electric; switchgear & switchgear accessories; junction boxes, electric

(G-3410)
SIMCO SIGN STUDIOS INC
Also Called: Simco Graphics
50 Jackson Ave (19023)
P.O. Box 255, Glenolden (19036-0255)
PHONE................................610 534-5550
David Lucidi, *President*
David C Lucidi, *Principal*
Tom Fitch Sr, *Vice Pres*
Kathy Lucidi, *Treasurer*
EMP: 13
SQ FT: 20,000
SALES: 4MM **Privately Held**
SIC: 3993 Letters for signs, metal; name plates: except engraved, etched, etc.: metal; advertising artwork; displays & cutouts, window & lobby

---

Colmar
Montgomery County

(G-3411)
CONSTANTIA COLMAR LLC
Also Called: Constantia Colmar, Inc.
92 County Line Rd (18915-9606)
PHONE..................................215 997-6222
Jerry Decker, *CEO*
Ja Homan, *Chairman*
Debbie Gressel, *Sales Executive*
▲ EMP: 90
SQ FT: 95,000
SALES (est): 20.3MM **Privately Held**
WEB: www.hnpack.com
SIC: 2759 2671 Commercial printing; plastic film, coated or laminated for packaging
HQ: Constantia Flexibles Germany Gmbh
   Pirkmuhle 14-16
   Pirk 92712

(G-3412)
CPD LIGHTING LLC
66 Bethlehem Pike (18915-9404)
PHONE..................................215 361-6100
Don Sowers, *Opers Staff*
EMP: 3 EST: 2015
SALES (est): 120.6K **Privately Held**
SIC: 3229 Glass lighting equipment parts

(G-3413)
CRYOGUARD CORPORATION
151 Discovery Dr Ste 107 (18915-9783)
PHONE..................................215 712-9018
EMP: 4
SALES (est): 273K **Privately Held**
SIC: 3823 Industrial instrmnts msrmnt display/control process variable

(G-3414)
CUSTOM PLATECRAFTERS INC (PA)
Also Called: Custom Graphic and Plates
230 Bethlehem Pike (18915-9761)
P.O. Box 545 (18915-0545)
PHONE..................................215 997-1990
Anthony J Spering, *President*
Rob Spering Sr, *Vice Pres*
EMP: 14
SQ FT: 10,000
SALES (est): 2.3MM **Privately Held**
WEB: www.platecrafters.com
SIC: 3555 Printing plates

(G-3415)
CUSTOM SYSTEMS TECHNOLOGY INC
Also Called: Wmi Group
3075 Advance Ln (18915-9420)
PHONE..................................215 822-2525
EMP: 5
SALES: 65K **Privately Held**
SIC: 3643 3679 Mfg Conductive Wiring Devices Mfg Electronic Components

(G-3416)
DORMAN PRODUCTS INC (PA)
3400 E Walnut St (18915-9768)
P.O. Box 1800 (18915-0902)
PHONE..................................215 997-1800
Steven L Berman, *Ch of Bd*
Kevin M Olsen, *President*
Kevin Olsen, *President*
Michael B Kealey, *Exec VP*
Jeffrey L Darby, *Senior VP*
▲ EMP: 166
SQ FT: 342,000
SALES: 973.7MM **Publicly Held**
WEB: www.dormanautoparts.com
SIC: 3714 3231 3965 Motor vehicle parts & accessories; mirrors, truck & automobile: made from purchased glass; fasteners

(G-3417)
INFRAMARK LLC
3000 Advance Ln (18915-9432)
PHONE..................................215 822-2258
Joe Walsh, *Branch Mgr*
EMP: 53

SALES (corp-wide): 72.1MM **Privately Held**
SIC: 3589 Water treatment equipment, industrial
PA: Inframark, Llc
   220 Gibraltar Rd Ste 200
   Horsham PA 19044
   215 646-9201

(G-3418)
PRECISION TRANSMISSION INC (PA)
159 Discovery Dr (18915-9759)
PHONE..................................215 822-8300
David W Macfarland, *President*
Denise Mac Farland, *Admin Sec*
▲ EMP: 4
SALES (est): 3.2MM **Privately Held**
WEB: www.precisiontrans.com
SIC: 3714 Motor vehicle parts & accessories

(G-3419)
RB DISTRIBUTION INC
3400 E Walnut St (18915-9768)
PHONE..................................215 997-1800
Richard Berman, *Ch of Bd*
Ronald R Montgomery, *Senior VP*
Barry D Myers, *Senior VP*
Mathias J Barton, *CFO*
Steven L Berman, *Treasurer*
▲ EMP: 500
SALES (est): 134.2MM
SALES (corp-wide): 973.7MM **Publicly Held**
WEB: www.dormanautoparts.com
SIC: 3714 3231 Motor vehicle parts & accessories; mirrors, truck & automobile: made from purchased glass
PA: Dorman Products, Inc.
   3400 E Walnut St
   Colmar PA 18915
   215 997-1800

(G-3420)
THOMAS MILLER & CO INC
3101 E Walnut St (18915-9415)
PHONE..................................215 822-3118
Thomas Miller, *President*
Cathie Miller, *Corp Secy*
◆ EMP: 11
SQ FT: 12,000
SALES (est): 1.9MM **Privately Held**
SIC: 2095 Roasted coffee

(G-3421)
THOMAS PENNISE JR
Also Called: Concept 1 County Furniture
2522 Lenhart Rd (18915-9425)
PHONE..................................215 822-1832
Thomas V Pennise, *Owner*
EMP: 5
SQ FT: 5,100
SALES (est): 295.9K **Privately Held**
SIC: 2499 Woodenware, kitchen & household

(G-3422)
VALIDUS INC
3075 Advance Ln (18915-9420)
PHONE..................................215 822-2525
Huasheng Wolstenholme, *President*
Andrew Wilkins, *Business Mgr*
James Wolstenholme, *Admin Sec*
EMP: 4
SALES (est): 154.7K **Privately Held**
SIC: 3812 Search & navigation equipment

(G-3423)
WM INDUSTRIES INC
3075 Advance Ln (18915-9420)
PHONE..................................215 822-2525
Bob Wolstenhome, *President*
Andrew Wilkins, *Business Mgr*
EMP: 3
SQ FT: 16,500
SALES (est): 90.5K **Privately Held**
SIC: 8742 3699 Sales (including sales management) consultant; electrical equipment & supplies

(G-3424)
WM ROBOTS, LLC
3075 Advance Ln (18915-9420)
P.O. Box 587 (18915-0587)
PHONE..................................215 822-2525

EMP: 10
SALES (est): 2.1MM **Privately Held**
SIC: 3699 8711 3812 Cleaning equipment, ultrasonic, except medical & dental; engineering services; aviation &/or aeronautical engineering; electronic detection systems (aeronautical)

(G-3425)
WMI GROUP INC
3075 Advance Ln (18915-9420)
PHONE..................................215 822-2525
Robert Wolstenholme, *President*
A Gene Samsi, *Vice Pres*
Clay Fox, *Manager*
▲ EMP: 15
SQ FT: 18,000
SALES (est): 3.8MM **Privately Held**
WEB: www.wmrobots.com
SIC: 3679 Harness assemblies for electronic use: wire or cable

(G-3426)
YUM-YUM COLMAR INC
Also Called: Yum-Yum Bakers
100 Bethlehem Pike (18915)
PHONE..................................215 822-9468
Bruce Conley, *President*
Glen Conley, *Vice Pres*
EMP: 25
SQ FT: 1,600
SALES (est): 936K **Privately Held**
SIC: 5461 2051 2095 Doughnuts; doughnuts, except frozen; roasted coffee

Columbia
Lancaster County

(G-3427)
ANVIL INTERNATIONAL LLC
800 Malleable Rd (17512-9477)
PHONE..................................717 684-4400
EMP: 3
SALES (corp-wide): 4.8B **Privately Held**
SIC: 3498 Fabricated pipe & fittings
HQ: Anvil International, Llc
   2 Holland Way
   Exeter NH 03833
   603 418-2800

(G-3428)
ANVIL INTERNATIONAL LLC
1411 Lancaster Ave (17512-1939)
PHONE..................................717 684-4400
Karen Gaus, *Production*
Mike Millhouse, *Engineer*
Paul Benos, *Branch Mgr*
Ron Porretta, *Manager*
EMP: 116
SALES (corp-wide): 4.8B **Privately Held**
WEB: www.anvilint.com
SIC: 3494 Valves & pipe fittings
HQ: Anvil International, Llc
   2 Holland Way
   Exeter NH 03833
   603 418-2800

(G-3429)
ANVIL INTERNATIONAL LLC
1411 Lancaster Ave (17512-1939)
PHONE..................................256 238-0579
Paul Campbell, *Branch Mgr*
EMP: 160
SALES (corp-wide): 4.8B **Privately Held**
SIC: 3498 Fabricated pipe & fittings
HQ: Anvil International, Llc
   2 Holland Way
   Exeter NH 03833
   603 418-2800

(G-3430)
ART PRINTING CO OF LANCASTER
131 Locust St (17512-1108)
PHONE..................................717 397-6029
Chris Raudabaugh, *President*
EMP: 5
SQ FT: 7,200
SALES (est): 817.6K **Privately Held**
SIC: 2752 2759 Commercial printing, offset; invitation & stationery printing & engraving

(G-3431)
BECKY KENS DUCK & GEESE CREAT
725 Poplar St (17512-2134)
PHONE..................................717 684-0252
Ken Kramer, *Owner*
EMP: 4 **Privately Held**
SIC: 3499 5947 5199 Novelties & giftware, including trophies; novelties; gifts & novelties
PA: Becky & Ken's Duck & Geese Creations
   725 Poplar St
   Columbia PA 17512

(G-3432)
BUCKEYE CORRUGATED INC
Also Called: All-Size Corrugated
3950 Continental Dr (17512-9778)
PHONE..................................717 684-6921
Scott Trayer, *Branch Mgr*
Pam Snader, *CIO*
EMP: 44
SQ FT: 30,000
SALES (corp-wide): 188.4MM **Privately Held**
WEB: www.buckeyecorrugated.com
SIC: 2653 Boxes, corrugated: made from purchased materials
PA: Buckeye Corrugated, Inc
   822 Kumho Dr Ste 400
   Fairlawn OH 44333
   330 576-0590

(G-3433)
COLEBROOK SUPPLY
1040 Prospect Rd (17512-8931)
PHONE..................................717 684-6287
Harry E Bechtold, *Owner*
EMP: 5
SALES (est): 270K **Privately Held**
SIC: 2448 Pallets, wood

(G-3434)
COLONIAL METALS CO (PA)
217 Linden St (17512-1179)
P.O. Box 311 (17512-0311)
PHONE..................................717 684-2311
Craig Friedman, *President*
Allan Sabol, *Vice Pres*
Pat Weber, *Human Res Mgr*
◆ EMP: 105
SQ FT: 100,000
SALES (est): 40.7MM **Privately Held**
WEB: www.colonialmetalsco.com
SIC: 3341 5093 Secondary nonferrous metals; nonferrous metals scrap

(G-3435)
COLUMBIA MOTOR PARTS INC (PA)
138 Lancaster Ave (17512-1596)
PHONE..................................717 684-2501
Carl W Dietrich, *President*
Michael Dietrich, *Admin Sec*
EMP: 7
SQ FT: 8,460
SALES (est): 3.2MM **Privately Held**
SIC: 5531 3599 Automobile & truck equipment & parts; automotive parts; machine shop, jobbing & repair

(G-3436)
COLUMBIA ORGAN WORKS INC
Also Called: Columbia Organ Leathers
915 Lancaster Ave (17512-1851)
PHONE..................................717 684-3573
Larry Pruett, *President*
William Duck, *Vice Pres*
EMP: 8
SQ FT: 23,000
SALES (est): 982.5K **Privately Held**
WEB: www.columbiaorgan.com
SIC: 7699 5948 3931 3111 Organ tuning & repair; leather goods, except luggage & shoes; organs, all types: pipe, reed, hand, electronic, etc.; cutting of leather; leather processing

(G-3437)
DOUBLE D SERVICE CENTER LLC
1338 Johnson Mill Ln (17512-8733)
PHONE..................................717 201-2800
Vincent M Dastra,

▲ = Import ▼=Export
◆ =Import/Export

EMP: 15
SALES (est): 2MM **Privately Held**
SIC: 3589 Service industry machinery

(G-3438)
HANDRAIL DESIGN INC
Also Called: Hdi Railings
3905 Continental Dr (17512-9779)
PHONE...........................717 285-4088
Kevin Downs, *President*
Tracy Downs, *Corp Secy*
▲ **EMP:** 91
SQ FT: 14,514
SALES (est): 18.9MM **Privately Held**
WEB: www.hdirailings.com
SIC: 3446 Railings, bannisters, guards, etc.: made from metal pipe

(G-3439)
INGRAIN CONSTRUCTION LLC
845 Wright St (17512-1542)
PHONE...........................717 205-1475
EMP: 9
SALES (est): 918.5K
SALES (corp-wide): 2.7MM **Privately Held**
SIC: 2511 Wood household furniture
PA: Ingrain Construction Llc
735 Lafayette St
Lancaster PA 17603
717 205-1475

(G-3440)
KEYSTONE CAP CO INC
927 Blunstone St (17512)
P.O. Box 67 (17512-0067)
PHONE...........................717 684-3716
Dorothy Lynch, *President*
EMP: 8 EST: 1930
SQ FT: 7,000
SALES (est): 1.2MM **Privately Held**
SIC: 3466 Closures, stamped metal

(G-3441)
LANCASTER COMPOSITE INC
1000 Houston St (17512-1600)
PHONE...........................717 872-8999
Robert H Greene, *President*
EMP: 10
SALES (est): 743.2K **Privately Held**
SIC: 2491 Poles, posts & pilings: treated wood

(G-3442)
LANCASTER CONTAINER INC
100 Bridge St (17512-1199)
P.O. Box 18, Washington Boro (17582-0018)
PHONE...........................717 285-3312
Barbara Kuhns, *Manager*
EMP: 20
SALES (corp-wide): 12.2MM **Privately Held**
WEB: www.lancastercontainer.com
SIC: 3412 Barrels, shipping: metal
PA: Lancaster Container, Inc.
27 Penn St
Washington Boro PA 17582
717 285-3312

(G-3443)
MIFFLIN PRESS INC
336 Locust St (17512-1121)
P.O. Box 20849, York (17402-0184)
PHONE...........................717 684-2253
Mark Miller, *President*
Pauline Miller, *Admin Sec*
EMP: 7
SQ FT: 6,000
SALES (est): 1MM **Privately Held**
SIC: 2752 2759 Commercial printing, offset; letterpress printing

(G-3444)
MUKIES/MCCARTY SEAL COATING C
913 Chestnut St (17512-1315)
PHONE...........................717 684-2799
Barry McCarty, *Principal*
EMP: 3
SALES (est): 238.5K **Privately Held**
SIC: 1771 2951 1611 Driveway contractor; asphalt paving mixtures & blocks; surfacing & paving

(G-3445)
ON LINE PUBLISHERS INC
3912 Abel Dr (17512-9031)
P.O. Box 8049, Lancaster (17604-8049)
PHONE...........................717 285-1350
Donna Anderson, *Principal*
EMP: 7
SALES (est): 883.8K **Privately Held**
SIC: 8748 2721 Publishing consultant; periodicals

(G-3446)
PAUL W ZIMMERMAN FOUNDRIES CO
Also Called: Erie Landmark
637 Hempfield Hill Rd (17512-9024)
PHONE...........................717 285-5253
Paul Zimmerman Jr, *President*
David Zimmerman, *Vice Pres*
EMP: 15
SQ FT: 8,000
SALES (est): 2.3MM **Privately Held**
SIC: 3366 3365 Bronze foundry; aluminum foundries

(G-3447)
PEERLESS HARDWARE MFG CO
210 Chestnut St (17512-1154)
P.O. Box 351 (17512-0351)
PHONE...........................717 684-2889
James P Speitel, *President*
Peter Speitel, *Vice Pres*
▲ **EMP:** 16
SQ FT: 62,000
SALES (est): 4.6MM **Privately Held**
WEB: www.peerlesshardware.com
SIC: 3452 3429 Screws, metal; metal fasteners

(G-3448)
RENEE AWAD ND
Also Called: Avalon Natural Health Center
259 N 6th St (17512-2107)
PHONE...........................717 875-3056
Renee Awad, *Owner*
EMP: 3
SALES (est): 170K **Privately Held**
SIC: 2834 Medicines, capsuled or ampuled

(G-3449)
RICK DEGEORGE
Also Called: PA Pallet Exchange
2560 Ironville Pike (17512-8913)
PHONE...........................717 684-4555
EMP: 4
SALES (est): 230K **Privately Held**
SIC: 2448 Pallets, wood & wood with metal

(G-3450)
SCANTRON CORPORATION
3975 Continental Dr (17512-9779)
PHONE...........................717 684-4600
Brian Schreiber, *Vice Pres*
EMP: 207 **Privately Held**
SIC: 2752 Commercial printing, lithographic
HQ: Scantron Corporation
1313 Lone Oak Rd
Eagan MN 55121
651 683-6000

(G-3451)
SUSQUEHANNA GLASS CO
731 Avenue H (17512-1379)
PHONE...........................717 684-2155
Walter Rowen, *President*
Catherine Rowen, *Vice Pres*
Chad F Yaw, *Vice Pres*
▲ **EMP:** 50 EST: 1910
SQ FT: 30,000
SALES (est): 6.9MM **Privately Held**
WEB: www.susquehannaglass.com
SIC: 5399 5719 3231 3555 Catalog showrooms; glassware; cut & engraved glassware: made from purchased glass; bronzing or dusting machines for the printing trade

(G-3452)
TYCO FIRE PRODUCTS LP
Also Called: Tyco Fire Protection Products
1411 Lancaster Ave (17512-1939)
PHONE...........................256 238-0579
James Keeton, *Manager*
Clint Decuir,

EMP: 25 **Privately Held**
SIC: 3569 Sprinkler systems, fire: automatic
HQ: Tyco Fire Products Lp
1400 Pennbrook Pkwy
Lansdale PA 19446
215 362-0700

Colver
Cambria County

(G-3453)
DAMIAN HNTZ LOCOMOTIVE SVC INC
Also Called: Wheel & Axel Division
494 Twenty Row Rd (15927-4108)
PHONE...........................814 748-7222
Germaine Krul, *Branch Mgr*
EMP: 6
SALES (corp-wide): 862.8K **Privately Held**
WEB: www.hantzlocomotive.com
SIC: 3462 3743 Railroad wheels, axles, frogs or other equipment: forged; railroad equipment
PA: Damian Hantz Locomotive Service, Inc.
4000 Clements Rd
Pittsburgh PA
412 793-7282

(G-3454)
GREYSTONE MATERIALS BT
272 Interpower Dr (15927-4305)
P.O. Box 529 (15927-0529)
PHONE...........................814 748-7652
Jerry Panczak, *Branch Mgr*
EMP: 4
SALES (corp-wide): 649.5K **Privately Held**
WEB: www.greystone-materials.com
SIC: 1422 Crushed & broken limestone
PA: Greystone Materials Bt
617 Urban Rd
Herndon PA 17830
570 244-2082

Commodore
Indiana County

(G-3455)
ZURENKO WELDING & FABRICATING
2902 Hemlock Rd (15729-8530)
PHONE...........................724 254-1131
Michael Zurenko, *Owner*
EMP: 3
SQ FT: 2,000
SALES (est): 339.4K **Privately Held**
SIC: 3441 3599 Fabricated structural metal; machine shop, jobbing & repair

Concordville
Delaware County

(G-3456)
COTT BEVERAGES WYOMISSING INC
20 Aldan Ave (19331)
P.O. Box 626 (19331-0626)
PHONE...........................484 840-4800
▲ **EMP:** 235 EST: 1951
SQ FT: 84,000
SALES (est): 27.3MM
SALES (corp-wide): 2.1B **Privately Held**
SIC: 2086 Mfg Bottled/Canned Soft Drinks
PA: Cott Corporation
6525 Viscount Rd
Mississauga ON L4V 1
905 672-1900

(G-3457)
LA FRANCE CORP (PA)
Also Called: Jat Creative Pdts Div Lafrance
1 Lafrance Way (19331)
P.O. Box 5002 (19331-5002)
PHONE...........................610 361-4300
George Barrar, *President*
Fran Vespa, *General Mgr*

John J Teti, *Chairman*
Jerrold Helbein, *Vice Chairman*
Brian Spicer, *Regional Mgr*
◆ **EMP:** 144
SQ FT: 50,000
SALES: 148MM **Privately Held**
WEB: www.lafrancecorp.com
SIC: 3089 3364 3993 5013 Injection molded finished plastic products; zinc & zinc-base alloy die-castings; name plates: except engraved, etched, etc.: metal; automotive supplies & parts; design services

(G-3458)
ROCWEL INDUSTRIES INC
277 Conchester Hwy (19331)
P.O. Box 1114 (19331-1114)
PHONE...........................610 459-5490
Anthony Valente, *President*
EMP: 4
SQ FT: 7,500
SALES (est): 862.5K **Privately Held**
SIC: 5072 3452 Bolts; nuts (hardware); screws; rivets; bolts, metal; nuts, metal; screws, metal; rivets, metal

(G-3459)
SOUTHCO INC (HQ)
210 N Brinton Lake Rd (19331)
PHONE...........................610 459-4000
Brian M Mc Neill, *President*
Shane Oconnor, *General Mgr*
Tommy Scattolino, *General Mgr*
Steve Spatig, *General Mgr*
Michael Post, *Business Mgr*
▲ **EMP:** 1000 EST: 1899
SQ FT: 90,000
SALES (est): 681.2MM
SALES (corp-wide): 681.3MM **Privately Held**
WEB: www.southco.com
SIC: 3965 Fasteners
PA: Touchpoint, Inc.
210 N Brinton Lake Rd
Concordville PA 19331
610 459-4000

(G-3460)
TOUCHPOINT INC (PA)
210 N Brinton Lake Rd (19331)
PHONE...........................610 459-4000
Brian M Mc Neill, *President*
Raymond Canzanese, *Vice Pres*
Michael Mc Philmy, *Vice Pres*
Chuck Zimmer, *QC Mgr*
Alan Eisen, *Admin Sec*
EMP: 800 EST: 1899
SQ FT: 150,000
SALES (est): 681.3MM **Privately Held**
SIC: 6512 3452 Commercial & industrial building operation; nuts, metal; bolts, metal; screws, metal

Conestoga
Lancaster County

(G-3461)
TOWN & COUNTRY FUEL LLC
1082 Letort Rd (17516-9312)
PHONE...........................717 252-2152
Wendell Shertzer, *Principal*
EMP: 10
SALES (est): 1.3MM **Privately Held**
SIC: 2869 Fuels

(G-3462)
TURKEY HILL LP
Also Called: Turkey Hill Dairy
2601 River Rd (17516-9327)
PHONE...........................717 872-5461
John Cox, *Branch Mgr*
EMP: 477
SALES (corp-wide): 2.5B **Privately Held**
SIC: 2024 Mfg Ice Cream/Frozen Desert
HQ: Turkey Hill, L.P.
257 Centerville Rd
Lancaster PA 17603
717 299-8908

Confluence
Somerset County

(G-3463)
BEGGS BROTHERS PRINTING CO
472 Latrobe Ave (15424-1058)
PHONE.................................814 395-3241
Connie Conway, *Owner*
EMP: 6
SALES (est): 697.6K **Privately Held**
WEB: www.beggsprinting.com
SIC: 2752 Commercial printing, offset

(G-3464)
DOUBLE DS ROADHOUSE LLC
7966 Kingwood Rd (15424-2328)
PHONE.................................814 395-3535
Darlene Harrington,
Donna Smith,
EMP: 5
SALES (est): 528.1K **Privately Held**
SIC: 2834 2599 Tablets, pharmaceutical; food wagons, restaurant

(G-3465)
HARDWOODS MILLWORKING
300 Whites Creek Rd (15424)
PHONE.................................814 395-5474
William Moravetz, *Owner*
EMP: 5
SQ FT: 12,000
SALES (est): 344.6K **Privately Held**
SIC: 2431 Millwork

(G-3466)
IMMERSION RESEARCH INC (PA)
808 Oden St (15424-1038)
P.O. Box 100 (15424-0100)
PHONE.................................814 395-9191
John Weld, *President*
Kara R Weld, *Vice Pres*
Hayley Collins, *Office Mgr*
Todd Baker, *Manager*
Jess Whittemore, *Director*
▲ EMP: 10
SALES (est): 1MM **Privately Held**
WEB: www.immersionresearch.com
SIC: 2231 Apparel & outerwear broadwoven fabrics

(G-3467)
JERRY G MARTIN
Also Called: Ram Cat Farms
1427 Sugar Loaf Rd (15424-1946)
P.O. Box 115 (15424-0115)
PHONE.................................814 395-5475
EMP: 3
SALES (est): 170K **Privately Held**
SIC: 2431 Mfg Millwork

(G-3468)
QUALITY CANVAS
148 Mae West Rd (15424-2000)
PHONE.................................724 329-1571
Donald B Berton, *Owner*
EMP: 4
SALES (est): 205.5K **Privately Held**
SIC: 2394 Canvas & related products

(G-3469)
ROBIN MORRIS
Also Called: Dunnmorr Studio
255 Paddlers Ln (15424-2637)
PHONE.................................814 395-9555
Robin Morris, *Owner*
EMP: 4
SALES (est): 292.9K **Privately Held**
SIC: 3269 5032 5719 Pottery cooking & kitchen articles; tile & clay products; pottery

Conneaut Lake
Crawford County

(G-3470)
CLASSIC BEDDING MFG CO INC
10212 Old State Rd (16316-3132)
PHONE.................................800 810-0930
Ron Novosel, *President*
EMP: 4
SALES (est): 360K **Privately Held**
SIC: 2515 Mattresses & bedsprings

(G-3471)
DO-CO INC
560 Water St (16316-7226)
P.O. Box 5137 (16316-5137)
PHONE.................................814 382-8339
Margaret A Blair, *President*
EMP: 11
SQ FT: 7,000
SALES (est): 2MM **Privately Held**
SIC: 3544 Special dies & tools

(G-3472)
ESMARK EXCALIBUR LLC (DH)
Also Called: Steel City Plate Company
9723 Us Highway 322 (16316-1941)
P.O. Box 605 (16316-0605)
PHONE.................................814 382-5696
Randy Stanton, *CFO*
Jerry Boyle, *Controller*
David A Luptak, *Mng Member*
EMP: 29
SQ FT: 5,800
SALES (est): 26.1MM
SALES (corp-wide): 249.1MM **Privately Held**
SIC: 3441 Fabricated structural metal

(G-3473)
GEORGE J ANDERTON
Also Called: Pinehurst Tool & Die
9908 Louderman Rd (16316-2656)
PHONE.................................814 382-9201
George J Anderton, *Owner*
EMP: 8
SQ FT: 3,200
SALES: 200K **Privately Held**
SIC: 3544 3823 3369 Special dies & tools; industrial instrmnts msrmnt display/control process variable; nonferrous foundries

(G-3474)
LAKELAND PRECISION INC
Also Called: Lakeland Precision Tool
13236 Phelps Rd (16316-5742)
PHONE.................................814 382-6811
Jeffrey Battles, *President*
Jeffery Battles, *Human Res Mgr*
EMP: 6
SQ FT: 6,000
SALES (est): 575K **Privately Held**
WEB: www.lakelandprecision.com
SIC: 3544 Special dies & tools

(G-3475)
LAKELAND SAND & GRAVEL INC
11203 Ellion Rd (16316-4335)
PHONE.................................724 588-7020
James E Adzima, *President*
EMP: 30
SQ FT: 10,000
SALES (est): 3.9MM **Privately Held**
SIC: 1442 Construction sand mining; gravel mining

(G-3476)
LAKESIDE STOP-N-GO LLC
12211 Lakeside Dr (16316-4305)
PHONE.................................814 213-0202
EMP: 5
SALES (est): 132.8K **Privately Held**
SIC: 2911 Petroleum refining

(G-3477)
MEADVILLE TOOL GRINDING INC
570 State St (16316-7304)
PHONE.................................814 382-1201
Stacey Ewing, *President*
EMP: 12
SQ FT: 3,500
SALES (est): 1.5MM **Privately Held**
SIC: 7699 3999 Industrial tool grinding; atomizers, toiletry

(G-3478)
RAM TOOL CO INC
195 N 3rd St (16316)
P.O. Box 190 (16316-0190)
PHONE.................................814 382-1842
David White, *President*
EMP: 10
SQ FT: 15,000
SALES (est): 1.3MM **Privately Held**
SIC: 3544 Special dies & tools

(G-3479)
STITCH ART CUSTOM EMBROIDERY
14058 Conneaut Lake Rd (16316-6828)
PHONE.................................814 382-2702
Susan Shrock, *Partner*
Nancy Helmreich, *Partner*
Christine Moyers, *Sales Staff*
EMP: 5
SALES (est): 440.4K **Privately Held**
WEB: www.stitch-art.com
SIC: 2395 Embroidery products, except schiffli machine; embroidery & art needlework

(G-3480)
T E FLETCHER SNOWMOBILES
Also Called: Fletcher's Sales and Service
10492 Mohawk Rd (16316-3238)
PHONE.................................724 253-3225
Thomas E Fletcher, *Owner*
EMP: 3
SALES (est): 265.4K **Privately Held**
SIC: 3799 5599 Snowmobiles; snowmobiles

(G-3481)
TAMMY WILLIAMS
Also Called: Creekside Tanning
10509 Mohawk Rd (16316-3243)
PHONE.................................814 654-7127
Tammy Williams, *Owner*
EMP: 4
SALES (est): 75.4K **Privately Held**
SIC: 7299 3543 Tanning salon; industrial patterns

(G-3482)
VIKING TOOL & GAGE INC
11210 State Highway 18 (16316-3699)
PHONE.................................814 382-8691
Brian L Burns, *President*
Joe Simpson, *Prdtn Mgr*
Patty Gessler, *Production*
Tracy Reynolds, *QC Mgr*
James Anderton, *Design Engr*
▼ EMP: 140 EST: 1966
SQ FT: 65,000
SALES (est): 35.3MM **Privately Held**
WEB: www.vikingtg.com
SIC: 3365 3544 Aluminum foundries; special dies & tools

Conneautville
Crawford County

(G-3483)
INLET TOOLS INC
11694 Dicksonburg Rd (16406-1724)
PHONE.................................814 382-3511
Marvin N Hamilton, *President*
EMP: 5
SQ FT: 10,000
SALES: 1MM **Privately Held**
SIC: 3544 Special dies, tools, jigs & fixtures

(G-3484)
PRO TECH MACHINING INC
21382 N Norrisville Rd (16406-6744)
PHONE.................................814 587-3200
Edward Nelson, *Principal*
Susan Schwab, *Manager*
EMP: 21
SALES (est): 2.3MM **Privately Held**
SIC: 3542 Machine tools, metal forming type

(G-3485)
PROTECT MACHINING INC
21382 N Norrisville Rd (16406-6744)
PHONE.................................814 587-3200
Edward Nelson, *President*
Susan Smock, *Treasurer*
Jesse Nelson, *Admin Sec*
EMP: 16
SQ FT: 5,000
SALES (est): 1.5MM **Privately Held**
SIC: 3599 Machine shop, jobbing & repair

(G-3486)
PS FURNITURE INC
Also Called: Palmer Snyder Furniture
801 High St (16406-7129)
PHONE.................................814 587-6313
Jim Groves, *Branch Mgr*
EMP: 50
SALES (corp-wide): 15.7MM **Privately Held**
SIC: 2531 5021 2511 Chairs, portable folding; chairs, table & arm; chairs; wood household furniture
PA: Ps Furniture, Inc.
1339 W Mequon Rd Ste 215
Mequon WI 53092
414 224-3045

(G-3487)
SPRING VLY ALTRNTIVE FUELS LLC
21810 Palmer Rd (16406-4746)
PHONE.................................814 587-3002
Ann Bortnick, *Owner*
EMP: 4
SALES (est): 188.5K **Privately Held**
SIC: 2869 Fuels

(G-3488)
TROYER ROPE CO
Also Called: Birds' Paradise, The
20785 Morris Rd (16406-6117)
PHONE.................................814 587-3879
Andrew M Troyer, *Co-Owner*
Timothy Fisher, *Co-Owner*
Adam Troyer, *Co-Owner*
▲ EMP: 8 EST: 1977
SQ FT: 8,305
SALES: 2.3MM **Privately Held**
SIC: 2298 Cordage & twine

Connellsville
Fayette County

(G-3489)
ARISTO-TEC METAL FORMS INC
401 Ridge Blvd (15425-1951)
P.O. Box 614 (15425-0614)
PHONE.................................724 626-5900
Joseph F Ocasek, *President*
Fred J Elcock, *Admin Sec*
EMP: 20
SQ FT: 30,000
SALES (est): 3.1MM **Privately Held**
WEB: www.aristo-tec.com
SIC: 3496 3315 Woven wire products; wire & fabricated wire products

(G-3490)
BAILEY MACHINE COMPANY
1516 Morrell Ave (15425-3811)
PHONE.................................724 628-4730
Thomas R Bailey, *President*
Janice E Bailey, *Vice Pres*
George E Bailey, *Treasurer*
Eleanor L Bailey, *Admin Sec*
EMP: 33 EST: 1947
SQ FT: 12,000
SALES (est): 4.2MM **Privately Held**
SIC: 7699 3599 7692 Welding equipment repair; machine shop, jobbing & repair; welding repair

(G-3491)
BASINGER LOGGING
3051 Springfield Pike (15425-6463)
PHONE.................................724 455-1067
William Basinger, *Partner*
Eric Basinger, *Partner*
EMP: 3
SALES (est): 258.4K **Privately Held**
SIC: 2411 Logging camps & contractors

(G-3492)
COLEBROOK CHOCOLATE CO LLC
830 Vanderbilt Rd (15425-6241)
PHONE.....................724 628-8383
Mia Miller, *Opers Mgr*
Rose Mary Brooks,
John Coleman,
Susan Coleman,
EMP: 7
SQ FT: 1,900
SALES: 249.7K **Privately Held**
SIC: 2066 5149 Chocolate & cocoa products; chocolate

(G-3493)
CROWN CORK & SEAL USA INC
Also Called: Anchor Hocking Packaging
1840 Baldridge Ave (15425-5236)
PHONE.....................724 626-0121
Owen Gaebel, *Financial Exec*
Mark Craven, *Manager*
EMP: 250
SALES (corp-wide): 11.1B **Publicly Held**
WEB: www.crowncork.com
SIC: 3411 Metal cans
HQ: Crown Cork & Seal Usa, Inc.
770 Township Line Rd # 100
Yardley PA 19067
215 698-5100

(G-3494)
DEW ELECTRIC INC
189 Enterprise Ln (15425-6617)
PHONE.....................724 628-9711
David Wiltrout, *President*
Wendy Wiltrout, *Vice Pres*
EMP: 5
SQ FT: 5,000
SALES (est): 906K **Privately Held**
WEB: www.dewelectric.com
SIC: 1731 3625 Electronic controls installation; relays & industrial controls

(G-3495)
DIVERSATECH INDUSTRIAL LLC
3234 Richey Rd (15425-9737)
PHONE.....................724 887-4199
David Myers,
EMP: 5
SALES: 500K **Privately Held**
SIC: 3569 Filter elements, fluid, hydraulic line

(G-3496)
ED NICHOLSON & SONS LUMBER CO
2451 Springfield Pike (15425-6427)
P.O. Box D, Normalville (15469-0164)
PHONE.....................724 628-4440
Randy Nicholson, *President*
Scott Nicholson, *President*
Randall Nicholson, *Vice Pres*
EMP: 13 EST: 1948
SQ FT: 9,600
SALES (est): 1.9MM **Privately Held**
SIC: 2421 2431 2426 Lumber: rough, sawed or planed; millwork; hardwood dimension & flooring mills

(G-3497)
GALLO DESIGN GROUP
232 N 7th St (15425-2530)
PHONE.....................724 628-0198
EMP: 6
SALES (est): 311.7K **Privately Held**
SIC: 3993 Mfg Signs/Advertising Specialties

(G-3498)
HANSON AGGREGATES BMC INC
Also Called: Commercial Asphalt Products
2200 Springfield Pike (15425-6412)
PHONE.....................724 626-0080
Douglas Ferris, *Sales Staff*
Adam Minnick, *Sales Staff*
Bob Bunting, *Branch Mgr*
Colleen King, *Manager*
Colleen Turner, *Administration*
EMP: 15

SALES (corp-wide): 20.6B **Privately Held**
SIC: 1771 1422 1222 1221 Blacktop (asphalt) work; crushed & broken limestone; bituminous coal-underground mining; bituminous coal & lignite-surface mining
HQ: Hanson Aggregates Bmc, Inc.
852 Swamp Rd
Penns Park PA
215 598-3152

(G-3499)
INDEPENDENT-OBSERVER
Also Called: Mount Pleasant Journal
127 W Apple St (15425-3132)
PHONE.....................724 547-5722
Debbie Brehun, *Principal*
EMP: 5
SALES (corp-wide): 4.3MM **Privately Held**
SIC: 2711 Newspapers
PA: Independent-Observer
228 Pittsburgh St
Scottdale PA 15683
724 887-7400

(G-3500)
KAREN HOLBROOK
Also Called: Ink Spot, The
411 E Youghiogheny Ave (15425-5351)
PHONE.....................724 628-3858
Karen Holbrook, *Owner*
EMP: 3
SALES: 150K **Privately Held**
SIC: 2759 2752 Commercial printing; commercial printing, lithographic

(G-3501)
KCA ENTERPRISES
122 W Apple St (15425-3133)
PHONE.....................724 880-2534
Clarence Conn, *Owner*
Kristen Conn, *Vice Pres*
EMP: 5 EST: 2010
SALES (est): 424.9K **Privately Held**
SIC: 3312 1791 Blast furnaces & steel mills; precast concrete structural framing or panels, placing of

(G-3502)
LYNDAN CABINETS INC
27 Wills Rd (15425-3700)
PHONE.....................724 626-9630
Windy Tuffs, *President*
EMP: 5
SALES (est): 558.5K **Privately Held**
WEB: www.lyndancabinets.com
SIC: 2434 Wood kitchen cabinets

(G-3503)
LYNDAN DESIGNS INC
27 Wills Rd (15425-3700)
PHONE.....................724 626-9630
Daniel Froble, *President*
Zach Froble, *Opers Mgr*
EMP: 8
SALES: 500K **Privately Held**
SIC: 2434 Wood kitchen cabinets

(G-3504)
MUSTANG TRAILER MFG
402 S Arch St (15425-4028)
PHONE.....................724 628-1000
Mark Stone, *Owner*
EMP: 10 EST: 2007
SALES (est): 159.5K **Privately Held**
SIC: 5599 5531 3799 Utility trailers; trailer hitches, automotive; trailers & trailer equipment

(G-3505)
NATIONAL HYDRAULIC SYSTEMS LLC
915 W Crawford Ave (15425-2407)
PHONE.....................724 628-4010
Terry Mascioli, *Managing Prtnr*
EMP: 4
SQ FT: 3,000
SALES (est): 472K **Privately Held**
SIC: 3492 7699 5084 Hose & tube fittings & assemblies, hydraulic/pneumatic; hydraulic equipment repair; hydraulic systems equipment & supplies

(G-3506)
PSI PACKAGING SERVICES INC
Also Called: PSI Industries
2245 Industrial Dr (15425-6181)
PHONE.....................724 626-0100
Vernon E Litzinger, *President*
Roger Russo, *General Mgr*
Wayne B Ruck, *Corp Secy*
Jerry F Morris, *Vice Pres*
Wayne Ruck, *Treasurer*
EMP: 75
SQ FT: 120,000
SALES (est): 17.9MM **Privately Held**
WEB: www.psipa.com
SIC: 2653 Boxes, corrugated: made from purchased materials

(G-3507)
RUFFCUTT TIMBER LLC
132 E End Rd (15425-9360)
PHONE.....................724 626-7306
Matthew Ruff, *Principal*
EMP: 6 EST: 2007
SALES (est): 556.5K **Privately Held**
SIC: 2411 Timber, cut at logging camp

(G-3508)
SHALLENBERGER CONSTRUCTION INC (PA)
195 Enterprise Ln (15425-6617)
PHONE.....................724 628-8408
Terrance C Shallenberger, *President*
Tuffy Shallenberger, *President*
Ray Jacobs, *Principal*
George Milne, *Principal*
Norma Shallenberger, *Corp Secy*
EMP: 76
SALES (est): 31.9MM **Privately Held**
SIC: 1794 1389 Excavation work; building oil & gas well foundations on site

(G-3509)
UH STRUCTURES INC
Also Called: Ebtech Industrial
2241 Industrial Dr Ste A (15425-6181)
PHONE.....................724 628-6100
Mario Kyd, *President*
Don Travis, *Sales Staff*
Donald Travis, *Admin Sec*
Dean Danner, *Administration*
▼ EMP: 10
SALES (est): 2MM **Privately Held**
SIC: 3448 Prefabricated metal buildings

(G-3510)
WENDELL H STONE COMPANY INC (PA)
Also Called: Stone & Co
606 Mccormick Ave (15425-2733)
P.O. Box 776 (15425-0776)
PHONE.....................724 836-1400
Mark Stone, *President*
Gregory Stone, *Treasurer*
Carrie Armstrong, *Manager*
EMP: 16
SQ FT: 3,000
SALES: 35MM **Privately Held**
WEB: www.stoneco.com
SIC: 3273 Ready-mixed concrete

(G-3511)
WENDELL H STONE COMPANY INC
Also Called: Stone & Company
606 Mccormick Ave (15425-2733)
PHONE.....................724 224-7688
Jeff Santone, *Manager*
EMP: 34
SALES (corp-wide): 35MM **Privately Held**
WEB: www.stoneco.com
SIC: 3273 Ready-mixed concrete
PA: Wendell H. Stone Company, Inc.
606 Mccormick Ave
Connellsville PA 15425
724 836-1400

(G-3512)
YOUGHIOGHENY OPALESCENT GL INC
300 S 1st St (15425-3051)
P.O. Box 800 (15425-0800)
PHONE.....................724 628-3000
John W Triggs, *President*
EMP: 41

SQ FT: 5,600
SALES (est): 4.5MM **Privately Held**
WEB: www.youghioghenyglass.com
SIC: 3211 2899 3231 2865 Cathedral glass; opalescent glass, flat; frit; products of purchased glass; cyclic crudes & intermediates

---

Connoquenessing
Butler County

(G-3513)
STARFLITE SYSTEMS INC
116 Dogwood Ln (16027)
P.O. Box 421 (16027-0421)
PHONE.....................724 789-9200
Robert Daquelente, *President*
Andrea Daquelente, *Corp Secy*
Ron Scaife, *Vice Pres*
EMP: 20
SQ FT: 25,000
SALES (est): 3.2MM **Privately Held**
WEB: www.starflitesystems.com
SIC: 1796 3448 Millwright; prefabricated metal buildings

Conshohocken
Montgomery County

(G-3514)
9DOTS MANAGEMENT CORP LLC
1010 Spring Mill Ave # 200 (19428-2391)
PHONE.....................610 825-2027
David Libesman, *President*
Amy Wright, *Vice Pres*
Sam Florio, *Marketing Staff*
Michael Marotta, *Manager*
Tom Hagan, *Consultant*
EMP: 25
SQ FT: 6,000
SALES (est): 3.6MM **Privately Held**
WEB: www.satorigroup.com
SIC: 7372 8748 Business oriented computer software; business consulting

(G-3515)
A JACOBY & COMPANY
300 Conshohocken State Rd # 180
(19428-3816)
PHONE.....................610 828-0500
Arthur Jacoby, *President*
EMP: 7
SALES (est): 470K **Privately Held**
SIC: 3911 Jewelry apparel

(G-3516)
ADAPT TECHNOLOGIES LLC
24 Portland Rd Ste 200 (19428-2717)
PHONE.....................610 896-7274
Joseph Wolf, *President*
EMP: 7
SQ FT: 30,000
SALES (est): 587.8K **Privately Held**
SIC: 3641 Electric lamps

(G-3517)
ALCOBRA INC
101 W Elm St Ste 350 (19428-2014)
PHONE.....................610 940-1630
Yaron Daniely, *CEO*
David Baker, *Officer*
EMP: 5
SQ FT: 1,000
SALES (est): 336.4K **Privately Held**
SIC: 2834 Druggists' preparations (pharmaceuticals)

(G-3518)
AMEKOR INDUSTRIES INC
500 Brook Rd Ste 100 (19428-3209)
PHONE.....................610 825-6747
Mun R Chung, *President*
Harry Moon, *General Mgr*
Kay Cho, *Comptroller*
Sean Park, *Sales Mgr*
Janet Mun, *Office Mgr*
◆ EMP: 58
SQ FT: 10,000

GEOGRAPHIC

SALES (est): 5.2MM
SALES (corp-wide): 330.2MM **Privately Held**
WEB: www.esteticadesigns.com
SIC: 3999 5199 7389 Wigs, including doll wigs, toupees or wiglets; wigs; styling, wigs
HQ: Aderans Hair Goods, Inc.
9135 Independence Ave
Chatsworth CA 91311
818 428-1626

(G-3519)
AMERICAN CNSLD MFG CO INC
Also Called: Amco International
2 Union Hill Rd Bldg 2 # 2 (19428-2701)
PHONE..................................610 825-2630
Fred Slack, *President*
Frederick Slack IV, *President*
Tonya Adams, *General Mgr*
Tonya Owens, *General Mgr*
Bob Maxwell, *Mfg Staff*
▲ **EMP:** 35 **EST:** 1950
SQ FT: 18,500
SALES (est): 11MM **Privately Held**
WEB: www.nsinails.com
SIC: 5087 2891 3843 Beauty parlor equipment & supplies; adhesives & sealants; sealing wax; orthodontic appliances

(G-3520)
AMERICAN REF & BIOCHEM INC
Also Called: Franklin Advanced Materials
100 4 Falls Corporate Ctr (19428-2950)
PHONE..................................610 940-4420
Harry R Halloran Jr, *CEO*
Kathy Coffey, *President*
Gina Wallace, *Controller*
Robert Kelly, *Investment Ofcr*
Carol White, *Admin Sec*
EMP: 6
SALES (est): 37.2K **Privately Held**
SIC: 2911 Petroleum refining

(G-3521)
ARCELORMITTAL USA LLC
900 Conshohocken Rd (19428-1038)
P.O. Box 842 (19428)
PHONE..................................610 825-6020
Kirk Martini, *Engineer*
Gary Sarpen, *Manager*
Robert Damron, *Manager*
EMP: 320
SALES (corp-wide): 9.1B **Privately Held**
SIC: 3312 Blast furnaces & steel mills
HQ: Arcelormittal Usa Llc
1 S Dearborn St Ste 1800
Chicago IL 60603
312 346-0300

(G-3522)
BIMBO BAKERIES USA INC
Stroehmann Bakeries 53
1113 W Ridge Pike (19428-1017)
PHONE..................................610 825-1140
Doug Taschner, *President*
Dan Babin, *Accountant*
EMP: 446 **Privately Held**
SIC: 2051 Bread, all types (white, wheat, rye, etc): fresh or frozen
HQ: Bimbo Bakeries Usa, Inc
255 Business Center Dr # 200
Horsham PA 19044
215 347-5500

(G-3523)
BMC SOFTWARE INC
200 Barr Harbor Dr # 400 (19428-2977)
PHONE..................................610 941-2750
David Pearl, *Branch Mgr*
Jerry Oakes, *Sr Consultant*
EMP: 32
SALES (corp-wide): 1.3B **Privately Held**
WEB: www.bmc.com
SIC: 7372 Prepackaged software
HQ: Bmc Software, Inc.
2103 Citywest Blvd # 2100
Houston TX 77042
713 918-8800

(G-3524)
BOHLINGER INC
600 E Elm St (19428-1999)
PHONE..................................610 825-0440
J Jerry Bohlinger, *President*

Maryanne S Bohlinger, *Corp Secy*
Steve Speak, *Purch Mgr*
▼ **EMP:** 4
SQ FT: 5,000
SALES: 950K **Privately Held**
WEB: www.bohlinger.net
SIC: 5013 3621 5088 Automotive supplies & parts; motors, electric; transportation equipment & supplies

(G-3525)
BRAIN-PAD INCORPORATED
322 Fayette St (19428-1902)
P.O. Box 420, Worcester (19490-0410)
PHONE..................................610 397-0893
▲ **EMP:** 4
SQ FT: 3,000
SALES: 1.7MM **Privately Held**
SIC: 3949 Mfg Sporting/Athletic Goods

(G-3526)
CANTICLE PHARMACEUTICALS INC
200 Barr Harbor Dr # 400 (19428-2977)
PHONE..................................404 380-9263
Rebecca Taub, *CEO*
EMP: 4
SALES (est): 115.9K **Publicly Held**
SIC: 2834 Pharmaceutical preparations
PA: Madrigal Pharmaceuticals, Inc.
200 Barr Harbor Dr # 400
Conshohocken PA 19428

(G-3527)
CHEMALLOY COMPANY LLC (DH)
1301 Conshohocken Rd (19428-1027)
P.O. Box 350 (19428-0350)
PHONE..................................610 527-3700
Geir Kvernmo, *President*
Madge A Malone, *Corp Secy*
▲ **EMP:** 22 **EST:** 1960
SQ FT: 2,000
SALES: 23.7MM
SALES (corp-wide): 945.2MM **Privately Held**
WEB: www.chemalloy.com
SIC: 3399 3295 2819 2899 Powder, metal; minerals, ground or treated; industrial inorganic chemicals; chemical preparations

(G-3528)
CIRIGHT AUTOMATION LLC
7 Union Hill Rd (19428-2718)
PHONE..................................855 247-4448
Gregory Pfeiffer, *COO*
David Schwartz, *Vice Pres*
Scott Knecht, *Sales Staff*
Angela Destefano, *Manager*
Florina Handel, *Officer*
EMP: 4
SALES (est): 68.4K **Privately Held**
SIC: 7372 Application computer software

(G-3529)
CLEARFIELD ENERGY INC
101 E Matsonford Rd (19428-2531)
PHONE..................................610 293-0410
EMP: 3
SALES (corp-wide): 7.7B **Publicly Held**
SIC: 3366 Castings (except die): bronze
HQ: Clearfield Energy Inc
5 Radnor Corp Ctr Ste 400
Radnor PA 19087
610 293-0410

(G-3530)
COMCAST SPOTLIGHT
4 Tower Brigde 200 Bar (19428)
PHONE..................................610 784-2560
Leigh Sauter, *Supervisor*
EMP: 3
SALES (est): 228.6K **Privately Held**
SIC: 3648 Mfg Lighting Equipment

(G-3531)
COMPUTUTOR INC
Also Called: Compu-Tutor
101 E 8th Ave Ste 102 (19428-1779)
P.O. Box 687, Plymouth Meeting (19462-0687)
PHONE..................................610 260-0300
William Conner, *President*
Ryan Hunter, *Software Dev*
Anthony Kanak, *Director*

Tony Kanak, *Business Dir*
EMP: 9
SALES (est): 1MM **Privately Held**
WEB: www.compu-tutor.net
SIC: 7372 8243 7371 Application computer software; software training, computer; computer software development

(G-3532)
CONCRETE SERVICE MATERIALS CO
630 E Elm St (19428-1915)
P.O. Box 447 (19428-0447)
PHONE..................................610 825-1554
Thomas Sovin, *President*
Donna Sovin, *Corp Secy*
EMP: 6 **EST:** 1939
SQ FT: 9,000
SALES (est): 1.4MM **Privately Held**
WEB: www.concreteservicematerials.com
SIC: 2899 2891 5082 Waterproofing compounds; adhesives & sealants; general construction machinery & equipment

(G-3533)
CONSHOHOCKEN ITALIAN BAKERY
79 Jones St (19428-1943)
PHONE..................................610 825-9334
Frank Mansi, *President*
Dominic Gambone, *Vice Pres*
Clara Gambone, *Treasurer*
EMP: 30
SQ FT: 5,000
SALES (est): 5.7MM **Privately Held**
WEB: www.conshybakery.com
SIC: 5149 5461 2051 Bakery products; bakeries; bread, cake & related products

(G-3534)
COOPERS CREEK CHEMICAL CORP
884 River Rd (19428-2699)
PHONE..................................610 828-0375
E Alan Morris, *President*
Elwood Alan Morris, *President*
William A Connelly, *Principal*
Beth A Vogel, *Corp Secy*
Mark A Morris, *Vice Pres*
▲ **EMP:** 30 **EST:** 1915
SQ FT: 10,000
SALES (est): 12MM **Privately Held**
WEB: www.cooperscreekchemical.com
SIC: 2865 2951 2911 2899 Cyclic crudes, coal tar; asphalt paving mixtures & blocks; petroleum refining; chemical preparations; gum & wood chemicals; paints & allied products

(G-3535)
D A R INDUSTRIAL PDTS INC (PA)
2 Union Hill Rd Bldg 1 (19428-2701)
PHONE..................................610 825-4900
Paul Lanoche, *President*
Augustine Lanoche, *Vice Pres*
▲ **EMP:** 6 **EST:** 1935
SQ FT: 3,000
SALES (est): 3.5MM **Privately Held**
WEB: www.darindustrial.com
SIC: 3053 Gaskets, all materials; packing materials

(G-3536)
DAVIDS BRIDAL INC
444 E North Ln (19428-2220)
PHONE..................................610 943-6210
Anthony Coccerino, *Opers Staff*
Roslyn Braddick, *Manager*
Nicole Jones, *Manager*
EMP: 25 **Privately Held**
WEB: www.davidsbridal.com
SIC: 2335 5621 Bridal & formal gowns; bridal shops
PA: David's Bridal, Inc.
1001 Washington St
Conshohocken PA 19428

(G-3537)
DEGADAN CORP
Also Called: AlphaGraphics
950 Colwell Ln Ste 2 (19428-1132)
PHONE..................................610 940-1282
Dan Wisiniewski, *President*
EMP: 8

SALES (est): 1.1MM **Privately Held**
SIC: 2752 7334 2789 7389 Commercial printing, offset; photocopying & duplicating services; binding only: books, pamphlets, magazines, etc.; printers' services: folding, collating

(G-3538)
DIGITAL MEDIA SOLUTIONS LLC
1100 E Hector St Ste 210 (19428-2378)
PHONE..................................610 234-3834
Luis A Ruelas, *Exec VP*
John Dougherty, *Vice Pres*
Andrew Milner, *Vice Pres*
Dan Sheer, *Vice Pres*
EMP: 3
SALES (est): 53.3K **Privately Held**
SIC: 4813 3577 ; data conversion equipment, media-to-media: computer

(G-3539)
DISPERSION TECH SYSTEMS LLC
Also Called: Bfr Hydraulics
1002 W Ridge Pike Ste 100 (19428-1016)
P.O. Box 758, Camp Hill (17001-0758)
PHONE..................................610 832-2040
Joe Knox, *Mng Member*
EMP: 3
SQ FT: 1,500
SALES (est): 184.4K **Privately Held**
SIC: 7699 5084 3492 Hydraulic equipment repair; hydraulic systems equipment & supplies; hose & tube fittings & assemblies, hydraulic/pneumatic

(G-3540)
EAST-WEST LABEL CO INC
1000 E Hector St (19428-2310)
P.O. Box 306 (19428-0306)
PHONE..................................610 825-0410
William Wilson Sr, *Ch of Bd*
Christopher Wilson, *President*
William Wilson Jr, *Vice Pres*
Christina Wilson, *Treasurer*
Roseanne Wilson, *Treasurer*
EMP: 23
SQ FT: 14,000
SALES (est): 4.8MM **Privately Held**
WEB: www.ewlabel.com
SIC: 2679 Labels, paper: made from purchased material

(G-3541)
EDRO ENGINEERING INC
Also Called: Edro Specialty Steel
1027 Conshohocken Rd A (19428-1051)
PHONE..................................610 940-1993
Eric Henn, *President*
Ben Davis, *Sales Staff*
EMP: 12
SALES (corp-wide): 16B **Privately Held**
WEB: www.edro.com
SIC: 3441 Fabricated structural metal
HQ: Edro Engineering, Inc.
20500 Carrey Rd
Walnut CA 91789
909 594-5751

(G-3542)
EMC CORPORATION
300 Conshohocken State Rd # 700 (19428-3804)
PHONE..................................610 834-0471
Chris Lehman, *President*
Chip Smith, *Vice Pres*
Martin Estrada, *Engineer*
John Albanese, *Manager*
EMP: 270
SALES (corp-wide): 90.6B **Publicly Held**
WEB: www.emc.com
SIC: 3572 Computer storage devices
HQ: Emc Corporation
176 South St
Hopkinton MA 01748
508 435-1000

(G-3543)
EPHARMASOLUTIONS
625 W Ridge Pike Ste E402 (19428-3202)
PHONE..................................610 832-2100
Nathan King, *Manager*
Clay Harmony, *Associate Dir*
EMP: 5

▲ = Import ▼=Export
◆ =Import/Export

SALES (est): 239.8K **Privately Held**
SIC: 2834 Pharmaceutical preparations

(G-3544)
EQUISOL LLC
200 Barr Harbor Dr # 400 (19428-2977)
PHONE........................866 629-7646
Curt Given, *CEO*
EMP: 15
SQ FT: 3,000
SALES (est): 990.9K **Privately Held**
WEB: www.equisolgp.com
SIC: 5084 3589 Water pumps (industrial);
water treatment equipment, industrial
PA: Environmental Infrastructure Holdings
Corp.
200 Barr Harbor Dr # 400
Conshohocken PA 19428

(G-3545)
FACTORY LINENS INC (PA)
40 Portland Rd (19428-2717)
PHONE........................610 825-2790
Howard Steidle, *President*
EMP: 22
SQ FT: 8,000
SALES (est): 2.5MM **Privately Held**
WEB: www.johnritz.net
SIC: 2211 2392 Dishcloths; laundry nets;
dust cloths: made from purchased materi-
als

(G-3546)
FAIRMOUNT AUTOMATION INC
10 Clipper Rd (19428-2721)
PHONE........................610 356-9840
Andres Lebaudy, *President*
Bob Forlenza, *COO*
Gary Cane, *Vice Pres*
James Newell, *Engineer*
Robert Forlenza, *Info Tech Mgr*
EMP: 18
SQ FT: 5,200
SALES (est): 5MM **Privately Held**
WEB: www.fairmountautomation.com
SIC: 3823 7371 Industrial instrmnts
msrmnt display/control process variable;
computer software development & appli-
cations

(G-3547)
FINE GRINDING CORPORATION
241 E Elm St (19428-2029)
P.O. Box 71 (19428-0071)
PHONE........................610 828-7250
H Timothy Everett, *President*
▲ EMP: 20 EST: 1960
SQ FT: 50,000
SALES (est): 6.1MM **Privately Held**
WEB: www.finegrindingcorp.com
SIC: 2819 2869 Industrial inorganic chem-
icals; industrial organic chemicals

(G-3548)
**FLORIG R & J INDUSTRIAL CO
INC**
910 Brook Rd (19428-1158)
PHONE........................610 825-6655
Robert J Florig, *President*
John A Florig, *Corp Secy*
▲ EMP: 30
SQ FT: 52,000
SALES (est): 7.5MM **Privately Held**
WEB: www.rjflorig.com
SIC: 3449 3599 1799 Bars, concrete rein-
forcing: fabricated steel; machine shop,
jobbing & repair; hydraulic equipment, in-
stallation & service

(G-3549)
**FRANCIS L FREAS GLASS
WORKS**
148 E 9th Ave (19428-1504)
PHONE........................610 828-0430
Norma Freas Ramey, *President*
Douglas Marzella, *Vice Pres*
Dennis Marzella, *Shareholder*
Francis Marzella, *Shareholder*
EMP: 36 EST: 1905
SQ FT: 25,000

SALES (est): 3.1MM **Privately Held**
WEB: www.freasglass.com
SIC: 3231 3823 3829 3825 Scientific &
technical glassware: from purchased
glass; hydrometers, industrial process
type; thermometers, industrial process
type; filled system: indus-
trial process type; measuring & controlling
devices; instruments to measure electricity

(G-3550)
FRONTLINE GRAPHICS INC (PA)
200 Barr Harbor Dr # 400 (19428-2977)
PHONE........................610 941-2750
David Pearl, *President*
EMP: 4
SQ FT: 500
SALES (est): 606.3K **Privately Held**
WEB: www.frontlinegraphics.com
SIC: 2759 Commercial printing

(G-3551)
GLAXOSMITHKLINE LLC
893 River Rd (19428-2631)
PHONE........................610 270-4800
George Post, *Controller*
EMP: 20
SALES (corp-wide): 39.8B **Privately Held**
WEB: www.delks.com
SIC: 2834 Pharmaceutical preparations
HQ: Glaxosmithkline Llc
5 Crescent Dr
Philadelphia PA 19112
215 751-4000

(G-3552)
H & C GIAMO INC
200 Center St (19428-2411)
PHONE........................610 941-0909
Harry Giamo, *President*
Charles Giamo, *Vice Pres*
EMP: 3
SQ FT: 500
SALES: 340K **Privately Held**
SIC: 3443 4953 Dumpsters, garbage; re-
fuse collection & disposal services

(G-3553)
HARAEUC INC CERMALLOY DIV
24 Union Hill Rd (19428-2719)
PHONE........................610 825-8387
Tom Lorenzo, *Principal*
EMP: 4
SALES (est): 252.5K **Privately Held**
SIC: 2891 Adhesives & sealants

(G-3554)
HAWK GRIPS
1495 Alan Wood Rd Ste 201 (19428-1182)
PHONE........................484 351-8050
Frank Osborne, *President*
Sean Mc Neal, *Vice Pres*
EMP: 9
SALES (est): 859.9K **Privately Held**
SIC: 3829 Aircraft & motor vehicle meas-
urement equipment

(G-3555)
HERAEUS INCORPORATED HIC
24 Union Hill Rd (19428-2719)
P.O. Box 306 (19428-0306)
PHONE........................610 825-6050
Thomas Lorandeau, *General Mgr*
David Holmes, *Vice Pres*
John Jancso, *QC Mgr*
Virginia Garcia, *Research*
Lindsey Karpowich, *Research*
EMP: 127
SALES (corp-wide): 96.1K **Privately Held**
WEB: www.heraeuspm.com
SIC: 3399 2891 Metal powders, pastes &
flakes; adhesives & sealants
HQ: Heraeus Incorporated
770 Township Line Rd # 300
Yardley PA 19067
215 944-9981

(G-3556)
**HERAEUS PRECIOUS METALS
NOR**
24 Union Hill Rd (19428-2719)
P.O. Box 306 (19428-0306)
PHONE........................610 825-6050
Jan Rinnert, *Ch of Bd*
Jan Doets, *President*
Ryydiger Schmitz, *President*

Frank Stietz, *President*
Jyyrgen Heraeus, *Chairman*
◆ EMP: 150
SQ FT: 65,000
SALES: 34.3MM
SALES (corp-wide): 96.1K **Privately Held**
WEB: www.heraeuspm.com
SIC: 3399 2834 3674 Metal powders,
pastes & flakes; pharmaceutical prepara-
tions; semiconductors & related devices
HQ: Heraeus Holding Gesellschaft Mit
Beschrankter Haftung
Heraeusstr. 12-14
Hanau 63450
618 135-0

(G-3557)
HIGHWAY MATERIALS INC
5100 Joshua Rd (19428)
PHONE........................610 828-9525
Eric Friend, *Manager*
EMP: 3
SALES (corp-wide): 10.1MM **Privately
Held**
WEB: www.highwaymaterials.com
SIC: 2951 Asphalt paving mixtures &
blocks
PA: Highway Materials, Inc.
409 Stenton Ave
Flourtown PA 19031
610 832-8000

(G-3558)
HOPE PAIGE DESIGNS LLC
100 Front St Ste 300 (19428-2894)
PHONE........................610 234-0093
Shelly L Fisher, *Mng Member*
▲ EMP: 20
SALES (est): 2.1MM **Privately Held**
WEB: www.hopepaige.com
SIC: 5944 5094 2759 Jewelry, precious
stones & precious metals; jewelry; promo-
tional printing

(G-3559)
**IKEA INDIRECT MTL & SVCS
LLC**
400 Alan Wood Rd (19428-1141)
PHONE........................610 834-0150
▲ EMP: 3
SALES (est): 447.2K **Privately Held**
SIC: 5712 3469 Furniture stores; kitchen
fixtures & equipment: metal, except cast
aluminum

(G-3560)
IMMUNOCORE
181 Washington St (19428-2068)
PHONE........................484 534-5261
EMP: 6
SALES (est): 813.3K **Privately Held**
SIC: 2834 Pharmaceutical preparations

(G-3561)
IMPACT COLORS INC
201 E Elm St (19428-2029)
PHONE........................302 224-8310
Doug Thornley, *President*
H Douglas Thornley, *President*
Anamaria Tanase, *Manager*
▲ EMP: 25
SALES: 10MM **Privately Held**
SIC: 2816 5094 8052 Color pigments;
pearls; personal care facility

(G-3562)
INFINITY PUBLISHING (PA)
1094 New Dehaven St (19428-2705)
PHONE........................610 941-9999
Mark Gregory, *Principal*
Maria Arnt, *Author*
EMP: 14
SALES (est): 1.2MM **Privately Held**
SIC: 2741 Miscellaneous publishing

(G-3563)
**INFRASTRUCTURE H
ENVIRONMENTAL (PA)**
200 Barr Harbor Dr # 400 (19428-2977)
PHONE........................866 629-7646
Michael D Parrish, *Ch of Bd*
Kurt M Given, *Treasurer*
James K Weber, *Admin Sec*
EMP: 12

SALES: 1.7MM **Privately Held**
SIC: 3589 Water treatment equipment, industrial

(G-3564)
**INQUIRER & DAILY NEWS FED
CU (PA)**
800 River Rd (19428-2652)
PHONE........................610 292-6762
Rene Ruzzo, *Principal*
EMP: 5
SALES (est): 393.6K **Privately Held**
SIC: 2711 Newspapers, publishing & print-
ing

(G-3565)
INVIBIO INC
300 Conshohocken State Rd # 120
(19428-3823)
PHONE........................484 342-6004
Michael J Callahan, *President*
Ian Johns, *Engineer*
Jonathan Parr, *Finance Dir*
Michael Wallick, *Technical Staff*
Dr John Devine, *Director*
EMP: 25
SALES (est): 1.8MM
SALES (corp-wide): 415.6MM **Privately
Held**
SIC: 3841 Surgical & medical instruments
HQ: Invibio Limited
Hillhouse International Site
Thornton-Cleveleys LANCS FY5 4
125 389-8000

(G-3566)
J A BROWN COMPANY
Also Called: Process Constractors
1013 Conshohocken Rd # 213
(19428-1034)
PHONE........................610 832-0400
Robert S Wagner, *President*
Courtis Quaintance, *CFO*
EMP: 5
SALES (est): 1.2MM **Privately Held**
SIC: 3625 8711 Noise control equipment;
engineering services

(G-3567)
JACOB SIEGEL LP (DH)
625 W Ridge Pike Ste B105 (19428-1191)
PHONE........................610 828-8400
Bernard Fishman, *Partner*
Stephen R Saft, *Partner*
◆ EMP: 9
SALES (est): 1.5MM
SALES (corp-wide): 164MM **Publicly
Held**
WEB: www.escg.jacobs.com
SIC: 2311 5136 Men's & boys' suits &
coats; men's & boys'
HQ: F&T Apparel Llc
4000 Chemical Rd Ste 500
Plymouth Meeting PA 19462
646 839-7000

(G-3568)
JADE INDUSTRIES INC
Also Called: Jade Yoga
101 Washington St (19428-2052)
PHONE........................610 828-4830
Dean Jerrehian, *President*
Jodi Schatz, *Sales Staff*
▼ EMP: 9
SALES (est): 1MM **Privately Held**
SIC: 2299 Batting, wadding, padding & fill-
ings

(G-3569)
JOHN PASQUARELLO
147 W 3rd Ave (19428-1837)
PHONE........................610 825-3069
John Pasquarello, *Principal*
EMP: 3
SALES (est): 236.7K **Privately Held**
SIC: 3479 Painting, coating & hot dipping

(G-3570)
KLENZOID INC
Also Called: Diox Water Hygiene
912 Spring Mill Ave (19428-2316)
P.O. Box 389 (19428-0389)
PHONE........................610 825-9494
Joseph Hannigan, *President*
Ken Gray, *Plant Mgr*
Paul Zeoli, *Technical Mgr*

Steven Douglas, *Sales Staff*
Dana Hannigan, *Marketing Staff*
EMP: 16
SQ FT: 6,000
SALES (est): 5.1MM **Privately Held**
SIC: 2899 Water treating compounds

(G-3571)
LAMBERTI USA INCORPORATED
161 Wshington St Ste 1000 (19428)
PHONE....................610 862-1400
Diane Hibbs, *Manager*
EMP: 4 **Privately Held**
SIC: 2819 2899 2869 Industrial inorganic chemicals; chemical preparations; industrial organic chemicals
HQ: Lamberti Usa, Incorporated
　　Us 59 & County Rd 212
　　East Bernard TX 77435
　　281 342-5675

(G-3572)
LIBRARY VIDEO COMPANY (PA)
Also Called: Schlessinger Media
300 Barr Harbor Dr # 700 (19428-3901)
P.O. Box 680 (19428-0680)
PHONE....................610 645-4000
Andrew Schlessinger, *CEO*
Timothy Beekman, *President*
Mike Hall, *Vice Pres*
Mike Miller, *CFO*
Dana Digiambattista, *Credit Staff*
EMP: 70
SALES (est): 15.4MM **Privately Held**
WEB: www.libraryvideo.com
SIC: 2741 3571 3661 3577 Miscellaneous publishing; electronic computers; telephone & telegraph apparatus; computer peripheral equipment; radio & TV communications equipment; computers, peripherals & software

(G-3573)
MADRIGAL PHARMACEUTICALS INC (PA)
200 Barr Harbor Dr # 400 (19428-2977)
PHONE....................484 380-9263
Paul A Friedman, *Ch of Bd*
Marc R Schneeaman, *CFO*
Rebecca Taub, *Chief Mktg Ofcr*
EMP: 8
SQ FT: 1,000
SALES (est): 1.1MM **Publicly Held**
WEB: www.syntapharma.com
SIC: 2834 Drugs affecting neoplasms & endrocrine systems

(G-3574)
MATTHEY JOHNSON INC
900 Schuylkill River Rd (19428)
PHONE....................610 292-4300
Matthey Johnson, *Principal*
EMP: 18
SALES (corp-wide): 15B **Privately Held**
SIC: 3341 Platinum group metals, smelting & refining (secondary); gold smelting & refining (secondary)
HQ: Matthey Johnson Inc
　　435 Devon Park Dr Ste 600
　　Wayne PA 19087
　　610 971-3000

(G-3575)
MENISCUS LIMITED
18 Elizabeth St Ste 100 (19428-2933)
PHONE....................610 567-2725
Lois Trench-Hines, *President*
Deborah L Faust, *Vice Pres*
George C Hines, *Vice Pres*
Kathleen Dicicco, *CFO*
EMP: 55
SQ FT: 5,000
SALES (est): 5.1MM **Privately Held**
SIC: 2741 2731 Miscellaneous publishing; book publishing

(G-3576)
MONDO USA INC (DH)
1100 E Hector St Ste 160 (19428-2374)
PHONE....................610 834-3835
Federico Stroppiana, *President*
Greg Stamer, *Sales Staff*
Lisa Wolffe, *Sales Staff*
Michael Tovar, *Director*
Isabelle Giroux, *Executive Asst*

▲ **EMP:** 5
SALES (est): 3MM **Privately Held**
SIC: 3069 Floor coverings, rubber
HQ: Societe Mondo America Inc
　　2655 Av Francis-Hughes
　　Sainte-Rose QC H7L 3
　　450 967-5800

(G-3577)
MONTGOMERY CHEMICALS LLC (PA)
Also Called: Montbrite
901 Conshohocken Rd (19428-1054)
PHONE....................610 567-0877
Thomas Evans,
Charles A Lumsden,
Jim McStratick,
◆ **EMP:** 35
SALES (est): 8.4MM **Privately Held**
WEB: www.montchem.com
SIC: 2899 Chemical preparations

(G-3578)
MONTGOMERY SIGNS INC
539 Ford St Ste C (19428-2905)
PHONE....................610 834-5400
Alan Glickman, *President*
Nina Glickman, *Vice Pres*
EMP: 5
SALES (est): 681.6K **Privately Held**
WEB: www.montgomerysigns.com
SIC: 3993 Signs, not made in custom sign painting shops

(G-3579)
MURLIN CHEMICAL INC
10 Balligomingo Rd Ste Q (19428-2738)
PHONE....................610 825-1165
Edward C Murray, *President*
John F Devlin, *Vice Pres*
◆ **EMP:** 10 **EST:** 1978
SQ FT: 20,000
SALES (est): 990K **Privately Held**
WEB: www.murlinchemical.com
SIC: 2819 Industrial inorganic chemicals

(G-3580)
OPERATING ROOM SAFETY LLC
Also Called: or Safety
960 Brook Rd Ste 2 (19428-1100)
P.O. Box 556, Warminster (18974-0632)
PHONE....................866 498-6882
Howard Brokenshire, *Director*
Sean Nevins,
EMP: 5
SALES (est): 498.4K **Privately Held**
SIC: 3841 Surgical & medical instruments

(G-3581)
ORACLE CORPORATION
300 Barr Harbor Dr # 400 (19428-2998)
PHONE....................610 667-8600
Thomas Lasalle, *Controller*
Min LI, *Branch Mgr*
John Sharkey, *Program Mgr*
Marko Vranich, *Senior Mgr*
Steve Thein, *Software Engr*
EMP: 76
SALES (corp-wide): 39.8B **Publicly Held**
WEB: www.oracle.com
SIC: 7372 Prepackaged software
PA: Oracle Corporation
　　500 Oracle Pkwy
　　Redwood City CA 94065
　　650 506-7000

(G-3582)
ORACLE SYSTEMS CORPORATION
300 Barr Harbor Dr # 400 (19428-2998)
PHONE....................610 729-3600
Nikki De Necochea, *Human Res Dir*
Lloyd Walters, *Manager*
EMP: 240
SALES (corp-wide): 39.8B **Publicly Held**
WEB: www.forcecapital.com
SIC: 7372 Business oriented computer software
HQ: Oracle Systems Corporation
　　500 Oracle Pkwy
　　Redwood City CA 94065
　　650 506-7000

(G-3583)
ORACLE SYSTEMS CORPORATION
100 4 Falls Corp Ctr # 515 (19428-2950)
PHONE....................610 260-9000
Clare Matlock, *Manager*
EMP: 80
SALES (corp-wide): 39.8B **Publicly Held**
WEB: www.forcecapital.com
SIC: 7372 Prepackaged software
HQ: Oracle Systems Corporation
　　500 Oracle Pkwy
　　Redwood City CA 94065
　　650 506-7000

(G-3584)
OTHERA PHARMACEUTICALS INC
200 Barr Harbor Dr # 400 (19428-2977)
PHONE....................484 879-2800
David S Joseph, *CEO*
William L Matier, *President*
Ghanshyam Patil, *Vice Pres*
Phillip Heifetz, *Finance Dir*
Frederick R Rickles, *Security Dir*
EMP: 8
SQ FT: 7,000
SALES (est): 576.9K
SALES (corp-wide): 1.6MM **Privately Held**
WEB: www.othera.com
SIC: 2834 Penicillin preparations
PA: Colby Pharmaceutical Company
　　1095 Colby Ave Ste C
　　Menlo Park CA 94025
　　650 333-3150

(G-3585)
PAK-RAPID INC
1050 Colwell Ln Ste F (19428-1197)
PHONE....................610 828-3511
Ben Karpowicz III, *President*
Nancy Karpowicz, *Admin Sec*
EMP: 7 **EST:** 1945
SQ FT: 10,000
SALES (est): 1.2MM **Privately Held**
WEB: www.pakrapid.com
SIC: 3565 8711 Packaging machinery; designing: ship, boat, machine & product

(G-3586)
PHILADELPHIA MEDIA NETWORK PBC
Also Called: Schuylkill Printing Plant
1150 Schuylkill River Rd (19428)
PHONE....................610 292-6389
Tracy O'Rourke, *Manager*
EMP: 14
SALES (est): 1.2MM **Privately Held**
SIC: 2711 Newspapers, publishing & printing
PA: Philadelphia Media Network, Pbc
　　801 Market St 300
　　Philadelphia PA 19107

(G-3587)
PHILADELPHIA NEWSPAPERS INC
800 River Rd (19428-2632)
PHONE....................610 292-6200
Lynn Steely, *Principal*
Walter Naedele, *Sales Staff*
EMP: 13 **EST:** 1989
SALES (est): 1.9MM **Privately Held**
SIC: 2711 Newspapers, publishing & printing

(G-3588)
PHILDELPHIA-NEWSPAPERS-LLC
800 River Rd (19428-2632)
PHONE....................610 292-6200
Rich Allen, *COO*
EMP: 1001
SALES (corp-wide): 232.9MM **Privately Held**
SIC: 2711 Newspapers, publishing & printing
PA: Phildelphia-Newspapers-Llc
　　801 Market St Ste 300
　　Philadelphia PA 19107
　　215 854-2000

(G-3589)
POTTERS INDUSTRIES LLC
280 Cedar Grove Rd (19428-2247)
PHONE....................610 651-4600
EMP: 4
SALES (corp-wide): 1.6B **Publicly Held**
SIC: 3231 Products of purchased glass
HQ: Potters Industries, Llc
　　300 Lindenwood Dr
　　Malvern PA 19355
　　610 651-4700

(G-3590)
POWER LINE PACKAGING INC
1304 Conshohocken Rd (19428-1061)
PHONE....................610 239-7088
Melissa Johanningsmeier, *President*
Diane Vernon, *Corp Secy*
John T Vernon, *Vice Pres*
John Vernon, *Vice Pres*
Lisa Johanningsmeier, *Purchasing*
▲ **EMP:** 29
SQ FT: 30,000
SALES: 7.5MM **Privately Held**
WEB: www.powerlinepackaging.com
SIC: 2844 Toilet preparations

(G-3591)
PQ CORPORATION
Also Called: P Q
280 Cedar Grove Rd (19428-2253)
PHONE....................610 651-4600
Kofi Assan, *Vice Pres*
Neil Miller, *Opers Mgr*
Bjorn Moden, *Research*
Niel Miller, *Manager*
Joe Leddy, *Manager*
EMP: 100
SALES (corp-wide): 1.6B **Publicly Held**
WEB: www.pqcorp.com
SIC: 2819 8731 Industrial inorganic chemicals; commercial physical research
HQ: Pq Corporation
　　300 Lindenwood Dr
　　Malvern PA 19355
　　610 651-4200

(G-3592)
PRISCILLA OF BOSTON INC (HQ)
1001 Washington St (19428-2356)
PHONE....................610 943-5000
Patricia A Kaneb, *President*
Terry Mc Gonigal, *Purch Agent*
Anthony Spinale, *Controller*
▲ **EMP:** 60 **EST:** 1993
SQ FT: 25,000
SALES (est): 10.4MM
SALES (corp-wide): 3.7B **Privately Held**
WEB: www.priscillaofboston.com
SIC: 2335 2396 Wedding gowns & dresses; veils & veiling: bridal, funeral, etc.
PA: Leonard Green & Partners, L.P.
　　11111 Santa Monica Blvd # 2000
　　Los Angeles CA 90025
　　310 954-0444

(G-3593)
PROTHERICS INC
300 Barr Harbor Dr # 800 (19428-3902)
PHONE....................615 327-1027
Andrew Heath, *CEO*
Saul Komisar, *President*
Cindy Miller, *Manager*
EMP: 187
SALES (est): 7.1MM **Privately Held**
SIC: 8731 2834 8721 Medical research, commercial; pharmaceutical preparations; accounting, auditing & bookkeeping
HQ: Btg Management Services Limited
　　5 Fleet Place
　　London EC4M

(G-3594)
Q-LINX INC
200 Barr Harbor Dr Ste 40 (19428-2977)
PHONE....................610 941-2756
Gilbert F Casellas, *CEO*
Deepa Michsler, *COO*
James Daniel Bosse, *Vice Pres*
David Schwartz, *Vice Pres*
EMP: 5
SQ FT: 2,000

▲ = Import ▼=Export
◆ =Import/Export

SALES: 25K **Privately Held**
WEB: www.qlinx.com
SIC: 7372 Prepackaged software

(G-3595)
QUAKER CHEMICAL CORPORATION (PA)
901 E Hector St (19428-2380)
PHONE..................................610 832-4000
Michael F Barry, *Ch of Bd*
Jeffry Benoliel, *Vice Pres*
Sheldon Weinstein, *Vice Pres*
Dan Nicholson, *Engineer*
John Accurso, *Project Engr*
EMP: 630 **EST:** 1918
SALES: 820MM **Publicly Held**
WEB: www.quakerchem.com
SIC: 2992 2899 2869 2891 Lubricating oils; corrosion preventive lubricant; hydraulic fluids, synthetic base; sealants

(G-3596)
QUANTUM RESTORATION LLC
539 Ford St (19428-2905)
PHONE..................................215 259-3402
Joel Heffelfinger, *Principal*
EMP: 3 **EST:** 2016
SALES (est): 94.5K **Privately Held**
SIC: 3572 Computer storage devices

(G-3597)
RAYMOND SHERMAN CO INC
1304 Conshohocken Rd # 160
(19428-1007)
PHONE..................................610 272-4640
Raymond Sherman, *President*
Rosalie Sherman, *Vice Pres*
EMP: 4
SQ FT: 5,000
SALES (est): 750K **Privately Held**
SIC: 2652 2675 Boxes, newsboard, metal edged: made from purchased materials; die-cut paper & board

(G-3598)
RB CONCEPTS LLC
1100 E Hector St Ste 220 (19428-2388)
PHONE..................................484 351-8211
Richard Banks,
Jerry Thomas,
EMP: 4
SALES (est): 408K **Privately Held**
WEB: www.rbconcepts.net
SIC: 2759 7331 Commercial printing; direct mail advertising services

(G-3599)
RDP TECHNOLOGIES INC
960 Brook Rd Ste 8 (19428-1100)
PHONE..................................610 650-9900
Richard W Christy, *President*
Paul Christy, *Vice Pres*
Robert W Christy, *Vice Pres*
Michael J Quici, *Admin Sec*
▲ **EMP:** 15
SQ FT: 8,000
SALES (est): 3.8MM **Privately Held**
WEB: www.rdptech.com
SIC: 3625 3589 Relays & industrial controls; sewage & water treatment equipment

(G-3600)
REX MEDICAL INC
555 E North Ln Ste 5035 (19428-2208)
PHONE..................................610 940-0665
William W Gardner, *President*
James Mc Guckin, *Principal*
Steve Defonzo, *Vice Pres*
James F McGuckin Jr, *Vice Pres*
John A Henry, *Admin Sec*
EMP: 20
SQ FT: 13,000
SALES (est): 4MM **Privately Held**
WEB: www.rexmedical.com
SIC: 3841 8731 Medical instruments & equipment, blood & bone work; commercial physical research

(G-3601)
RIO BRANDS LLC
100 Front St Ste 1350 (19428-2826)
PHONE..................................610 629-6200
Doug Putnam, *President*
Warren Cohen, *Branch Mgr*
EMP: 60

SALES (corp-wide): 40.5MM **Privately Held**
SIC: 2514 5021 Metal lawn & garden furniture; cots, household: metal; camp furniture: metal; household furniture; office furniture
PA: Rio Brands, Llc
10981 Decatur Rd
Philadelphia PA 19154
215 632-2800

(G-3602)
RMH IMAGE GROUP LLC
950 Colwell Ln Ste 2 (19428-1132)
PHONE..................................610 731-0050
Dan Wisneiwski,
Warren Marchese Jr,
Brian W Rhodenbaugh,
EMP: 7 **EST:** 2000
SQ FT: 7,500
SALES (est): 984.8K **Privately Held**
WEB: www.rmhimagegroup.com
SIC: 2759 Advertising literature: printing

(G-3603)
SCHANK PRINTING INC
520 Wells St (19428-1782)
PHONE..................................610 828-1623
Walter E Schank Jr, *President*
Marylou Donovan, *Corp Secy*
William J Donovan, *Vice Pres*
EMP: 15 **EST:** 1938
SQ FT: 8,000
SALES (est): 2.3MM **Privately Held**
WEB: www.schankprinting.com
SIC: 2752 2759 Commercial printing, offset; letterpress printing

(G-3604)
SCHATZIE LTD
Also Called: Oreland Sheet Metal
601 Washington St (19428-2364)
P.O. Box 510 (19428-0510)
PHONE..................................610 834-1240
EMP: 5 **EST:** 1956
SQ FT: 26,100
SALES (est): 3.9MM **Privately Held**
SIC: 1761 1711 3444 Roofing/Siding Contr Plumbing/Heat/Ac Contr Mfg Sheet Metalwork

(G-3605)
SOURCE HALTHCARE ANALYTICS LLC
1001 E Hector St Ste 400 (19428-2395)
PHONE..................................602 381-9500
Bruce Lenz,
EMP: 99
SALES (est): 15.6MM **Privately Held**
SIC: 2741 7374 8011 Miscellaneous publishing; data processing service; offices & clinics of medical doctors

(G-3606)
SQUID WIRE LLC
1950 Butler Pike Pmb 231 (19428-1202)
PHONE..................................484 235-5155
Eric Wright, *President*
Samantha Herson, *Sales Staff*
Michelle King,
EMP: 6
SALES (est): 506.8K **Privately Held**
SIC: 2298 5051 Cable, fiber; cable; wire

(G-3607)
STITCH CRAZY
360 Arden Rd (19428-2506)
PHONE..................................610 526-0154
John A Krawiec, *Principal*
EMP: 3 **EST:** 2001
SALES (est): 156.2K **Privately Held**
SIC: 2395 Embroidery & art needlework

(G-3608)
STRAINSERT COMPANY
12 Union Hill Rd (19428-2793)
PHONE..................................610 825-3310
Timothy Foley, *President*
Dorothy Foley, *Admin Sec*
EMP: 28 **EST:** 1960
SQ FT: 12,500
SALES (est): 6.3MM **Privately Held**
WEB: www.strainsert.com
SIC: 3825 3829 Instruments to measure electricity; pressure transducers

(G-3609)
SUNSHINE POLISHING SYSTEMS
379 New Dehaven St (19428-2635)
PHONE..................................610 828-6197
Jay Wilfong, *Owner*
EMP: 3
SALES (est): 162.4K **Privately Held**
SIC: 3471 Polishing, metals or formed products

(G-3610)
SUPERIOR GROUP INC (PA)
100 Front St Ste 525 (19428-2887)
PHONE..................................610 397-2040
William G Warden IV, *CEO*
Peter G Gould, *President*
William G Warden III, *Chairman*
John M Morrash, *Vice Pres*
Carol Riley, *Vice Pres*
▲ **EMP:** 20
SQ FT: 16,000
SALES (est): 179MM **Privately Held**
WEB: www.superior-group.com
SIC: 5051 3357 3317 3491 Tubing, metal; nonferrous wiredrawing & insulating; tubing, mechanical or hypodermic sizes: cold drawn stainless; industrial valves; metal stampings; packaging & labeling services

(G-3611)
TELEFACTOR ROBOTICS LLC
1094 New Dehaven St (19428-2705)
PHONE..................................610 940-6040
Martha Jane Chatten,
EMP: 6
SALES (est): 1.1MM **Privately Held**
SIC: 3827 8711 8731 7372 Lenses, optical: all types except ophthalmic; engineering services; commercial physical research; prepackaged software

(G-3612)
TERRAVIZ GEOSPATIAL INC (PA)
1 W Elm St Ste 400 (19428-4135)
PHONE..................................717 938-3591
Greg Condon, *President*
Matt Davis, *COO*
Carl Davis, *CFO*
EMP: 3
SQ FT: 2,000
SALES (est): 328.1K **Privately Held**
SIC: 8713 1382 Surveying services; aerial geophysical exploration oil & gas

(G-3613)
TRANSCELERATE BIOPHARMA
1001 Cnshohocken State Rd (19428-2908)
PHONE..................................484 539-1236
David Nicholson, *Chairman*
EMP: 7
SALES (est): 600.9K **Privately Held**
SIC: 2834 Pharmaceutical preparations

(G-3614)
TWIN SPECIALTIES CORPORATION
15 E Ridge Pike Ste 210 (19428-2121)
PHONE..................................610 834-7900
Samuel B Petrosky, *President*
Michael W Petrosky, *Vice Pres*
Lynn C Gross, *Treasurer*
Maxine W Petrosky, *Admin Sec*
EMP: 4 **EST:** 1955
SQ FT: 750
SALES: 2MM **Privately Held**
SIC: 2992 Cutting oils, blending: made from purchased materials; rust arresting compounds, animal or vegetable oil base; oils & greases, blending & compounding; re-refining lubricating oils & greases

(G-3615)
VALIRA LLC
1300 Fayette St Apt 100 (19428-1347)
PHONE..................................973 216-5803
Lakshmisri M Vangala, *CEO*
EMP: 3

SALES (est): 142K **Privately Held**
SIC: 3845 7379 8711 8748 Surgical support systems: heart-lung machine, exc. iron lung; computer related consulting services; engineering services; systems analysis & engineering consulting services; technical writing

(G-3616)
VISUAL RESOURCES LLC
1950 Butler Pike Ste 225 (19428-1202)
PHONE..................................484 351-8100
Jonathan Goldring, *Officer*
▲ **EMP:** 3
SALES (est): 259.1K **Privately Held**
SIC: 2759 Commercial printing

(G-3617)
WIRECARD NORTH AMERICA INC
Also Called: Citi Prepaid Services
555 E North Ln Ste 5040 (19428-2233)
PHONE..................................610 234-4410
Deirdre Ives, *Managing Dir*
Seth Brennan, *Vice Pres*
EMP: 100
SALES (est): 2.4MM
SALES (corp-wide): 1.7B **Privately Held**
SIC: 8748 3629 Telecommunications consultant; electronic generation equipment
HQ: Wirecard Acquiring & Issuing Gmbh
Einsteinring 35
Aschheim
894 424-0400

(G-3618)
YOUNG WINDOWS INC
680 Colwell Ln (19428-1167)
PHONE..................................610 828-5036
Lewis H Cook, *CEO*
Kathryn H Cook, *Ch of Bd*
Stephanie Cook, *President*
Joseph Lepo III, *Vice Pres*
Kiran C Patel, *Chief Engr*
▲ **EMP:** 60 **EST:** 1950
SQ FT: 45,000
SALES (est): 18.1MM **Privately Held**
WEB: www.youngwindows.com
SIC: 3714 3231 3442 Windshield frames, motor vehicle; products of purchased glass; metal doors, sash & trim

---

Conway
Beaver County

(G-3619)
ANDRITZ HERR-VOSS STAMCO INC
Herr-Voss Stamco Conway Div
1500 1st Ave (15027-1499)
PHONE..................................724 538-3180
Jerry Brenaman, *Branch Mgr*
EMP: 54
SQ FT: 15,000
SALES (corp-wide): 6.9B **Privately Held**
WEB: www.gen-world.com
SIC: 3599 Machine shop, jobbing & repair
HQ: Andritz Herr-Voss Stamco, Inc.
130 Main St
Callery PA 16024
724 538-3180

Cooksburg
Forest County

(G-3620)
COOK FOREST SAW MILL CENTER (PA)
Cooks Forest State Park (16217)
P.O. Box 180 (16217-0180)
PHONE..................................814 927-6655
Cindy Ban, *Director*
EMP: 16
SQ FT: 20,000
SALES: 174.1K **Privately Held**
SIC: 3944 7999 Craft & hobby kits & sets; arts & crafts instruction

GEOGRAPHIC

Coolspring
Jefferson County

(G-3621)
CNG MTOR FUELS CLARION CNTY LP
5349 Route 36 (15730-8524)
PHONE..................................814 590-4498
Abraham Calleros, *President*
EMP: 4
SALES (est): 243.4K **Privately Held**
SIC: 2869 Fuels

(G-3622)
ORIGINAL FUELS INC
Also Called: Grange Lime & Stone
91 Coolspring Rd (15730)
PHONE..................................814 938-5171
David Osikowicz, *President*
EMP: 25
SQ FT: 2,000
SALES (est): 5.9MM **Privately Held**
SIC: 1221 Strip mining, bituminous; bituminous coal surface mining

Coopersburg
Lehigh County

(G-3623)
ACRYL8 LLC
6517 Sugar Maple Cir (18036-3063)
PHONE..................................484 695-6209
Jim Tobin, *President*
EMP: 4
SALES (est): 164.1K **Privately Held**
SIC: 3845 Magnetic resonance imaging device, nuclear

(G-3624)
ADVANTAGE LEARNING TECHNOLOGY
6255 Robin Ln (18036-9590)
PHONE..................................610 217-8022
Bobbe G Baggio, *Owner*
EMP: 6
SALES (est): 326.5K **Privately Held**
WEB: www.a-l-t.com
SIC: 7372 Educational computer software

(G-3625)
CHERNAY PRINTING INC (PA)
7483 S Main St (18036-2459)
P.O. Box 199 (18036-0199)
PHONE..................................610 282-3774
Edmond Ward, *President*
Richard Knapp, *Vice Pres*
▲ **EMP:** 75 **EST:** 1966
SQ FT: 65,000
SALES (est): 11.6MM **Privately Held**
WEB: www.chernay.com
SIC: 2752 2791 2789 Commercial printing, offset; typesetting; bookbinding & related work

(G-3626)
CREATIVE AWNINGS INC
425 Springfield St (18036-2203)
PHONE..................................610 282-3305
Robert Bozzuto, *President*
EMP: 20
SALES (est): 1.3MM **Privately Held**
SIC: 2394 Awnings, fabric: made from purchased materials

(G-3627)
EAST COAST ATV INC
313 S 3rd St (18036-2111)
PHONE..................................267 733-7364
Dave Gibson, *Principal*
▲ **EMP:** 11
SALES (est): 1.6MM **Privately Held**
SIC: 3479 5571 7699 Hot dip coating of metals or formed products; all-terrain vehicles; motorcycle parts & accessories; motorcycle repair service

(G-3628)
H Y K CONSTRUCTION CO INC
Also Called: Rahn's Construction Material
7700 Keewayden St (18036-2141)
PHONE..................................610 282-2300
Danny Cordiolus, *Manager*
EMP: 20
SALES (corp-wide): 25.1MM **Privately Held**
SIC: 3273 Ready-mixed concrete
PA: H. Y. K. Construction Co., Inc.
430 Rahns Rd
Collegeville PA 19426
610 489-2646

(G-3629)
HIGHPOINT WOODWORKS LLC
1387 Parkland Rd (18036-9671)
PHONE..................................610 346-7739
Kelly O Carney, *President*
EMP: 4
SALES (est): 400.7K **Privately Held**
SIC: 2431 Millwork

(G-3630)
LEXMARK INTERNATIONAL INC
7631 Victoria Ln (18036-3445)
PHONE..................................610 966-8283
EMP: 19
SALES (corp-wide): 2.5B **Privately Held**
SIC: 3577 Mfg Computer Peripheral Equipment
PA: Lexmark International, Inc.
740 W New Circle Rd
Lexington KY 40511
859 232-2000

(G-3631)
MAKEFIELD COLLECTION INC
6028 Old Hickory Rd (18036-9433)
PHONE..................................610 496-4649
Patricia Husted, *President*
EMP: 15
SALES (est): 2.1MM **Privately Held**
SIC: 3645 Residential lighting fixtures

(G-3632)
OEM GROUP EAST INC
416 S 4th St (18036-2039)
PHONE..................................610 282-0105
Vincent McGinty, *President*
Larry Viano, *Vice Pres*
▲ **EMP:** 58 **EST:** 1996
SQ FT: 30,000
SALES (est): 14.3MM
SALES (corp-wide): 26.2MM **Privately Held**
WEB: www.rhetechinc.com
SIC: 3674 Semiconductors & related devices
PA: Oem Group, Llc
2120 W Guadalupe Rd
Gilbert AZ 85233
480 609-8565

(G-3633)
PENNY POWER LTD
202 S 3rd St Ste 6 (18036-2150)
P.O. Box 250 (18036-0250)
PHONE..................................610 282-4808
Cecile Brogran, *Manager*
Tim Ambrose, *Executive*
EMP: 13 **EST:** 1981
SALES (est): 1MM **Privately Held**
WEB: www.pennypowerads.com
SIC: 2711 Newspapers

(G-3634)
PRECISION TECHNICAL SALES LLC
1876 Salem Rd (18036-2202)
PHONE..................................610 282-4541
Owen Jones,
EMP: 3
SALES (est): 100K **Privately Held**
SIC: 3699 Laser systems & equipment

(G-3635)
PRINT SOLUTIONS LTD
512 Thomas St (18036-2030)
PHONE..................................484 538-3938
Richard Poole, *President*
EMP: 3

SALES: 1.2MM **Privately Held**
SIC: 2671 Plastic film, coated or laminated for packaging

(G-3636)
STRUCTURAL SERVICES INC
7001 N Route 309 Ste 169 (18036-1100)
PHONE..................................610 282-5810
EMP: 6
SALES (corp-wide): 2.7MM **Privately Held**
SIC: 3449 1611 Steel Reinforcing And Highway Construction
PA: Structural Services Inc
3735 Kim St
Bethlehem PA 18017
610 282-5810

Cooperstown
Venango County

(G-3637)
JOHN WALLACE
693 Bradleytown Rd (16317-1909)
PHONE..................................814 374-4619
John Wallace, *Owner*
EMP: 3
SALES (est): 189.4K **Privately Held**
SIC: 1311 Crude petroleum & natural gas

Coplay
Lehigh County

(G-3638)
ADVANCED MOBILE POWER SYSTEMS
876 Barbara Dr (18037-1723)
PHONE..................................610 440-0195
Scott Hubler, *President*
EMP: 3
SALES (est): 260K **Privately Held**
SIC: 3621 7629 Frequency converters (electric generators); electrical repair shops

(G-3639)
ARROWWOOD CONSTRUCTION
4245 Hill St (18037-2249)
PHONE..................................610 799-6040
Brian Bucks, *Owner*
EMP: 5
SALES: 150K **Privately Held**
SIC: 1389 Construction, repair & dismantling services

(G-3640)
BASEBALL INFO SOLUTIONS INC
41 S 2nd St (18037-1205)
PHONE..................................610 261-4316
Steve Noyer, *President*
EMP: 10
SQ FT: 7,372
SALES (est): 853.8K **Privately Held**
SIC: 3949 Baseball equipment & supplies, general

(G-3641)
C RUFFS MINI MART FUEL
4563 Court St (18037-2300)
PHONE..................................484 619-6832
EMP: 3
SALES (est): 204.2K **Privately Held**
SIC: 2869 Fuels

(G-3642)
CROSS WORKS EMBROIDERY SP INC
129 S 2nd St (18037-1001)
PHONE..................................610 261-1690
Matt Gonnella, *President*
Marie Vinup, *Principal*
Kristine Gonnella, *Vice Pres*
EMP: 8
SALES (est): 629.7K **Privately Held**
SIC: 2395 2759 Embroidery products, except schiffli machine; letterpress & screen printing

(G-3643)
FIREWLKERS SMALL BTCH DIST LLC
2296 Creekside Dr (18037-2075)
PHONE..................................610 737-7900
EMP: 3
SALES (est): 75.4K **Privately Held**
SIC: 2082 Malt beverages

(G-3644)
INWELD CORPORATION (PA)
3962 Portland St (18037-2224)
PHONE..................................610 261-1900
Jerome L Robinson, *President*
Rhianna Miller, *Sales Staff*
Kathy Wanner, *Sales Staff*
◆ **EMP:** 15
SALES (est): 3MM **Privately Held**
SIC: 3355 3312 3356 Aluminum rolling & drawing; blast furnaces & steel mills; non-ferrous rolling & drawing

(G-3645)
L & P MACHINE SHOP INC
177 S Front St (18037-1007)
PHONE..................................610 262-7356
Frank Paukovits, *President*
EMP: 6
SALES: 160K **Privately Held**
SIC: 3599 3714 Machine shop, jobbing & repair; instrument board assemblies, motor vehicle

(G-3646)
MULTICOLOR CORP
52 N 2nd St Ste 2 (18037-1251)
PHONE..................................610 262-8420
Jorge Aguayo, *President*
EMP: 4
SALES: 300K **Privately Held**
SIC: 3089 5091 Plastic containers, except foam; sporting & recreation goods

(G-3647)
ROBINSON TECHNICAL PDTS CORP
Also Called: Inweld
3962 Portland St (18037-2224)
PHONE..................................610 261-1900
Jerry Robinson, *President*
▲ **EMP:** 26 **EST:** 1981
SALES (est): 436K **Privately Held**
WEB: www.inweldcorporation.com
SIC: 5084 3356 Welding machinery & equipment; welding rods

(G-3648)
SIGN FUEL
4618 Mary Ann Cir (18037-2346)
PHONE..................................989 245-6284
EMP: 3
SALES (est): 175.5K **Privately Held**
SIC: 2869 Mfg Industrial Organic Chemicals

(G-3649)
SKRAPITS CONCRETE COMPANY
2550 Quarry St (18037-2054)
PHONE..................................610 442-5355
George Skrapits, *Manager*
EMP: 10
SQ FT: 14,000
SALES (est): 760.1K
SALES (corp-wide): 1.2MM **Privately Held**
SIC: 3273 Ready-mixed concrete
PA: Skrapits Concrete Company
2650 Howertown Rd 3
Northampton PA 18067
610 262-8830

(G-3650)
STABLER COMPANIES INC
2500 Quarry St (18037-2054)
PHONE..................................610 799-2421
EMP: 4
SALES (corp-wide): 651.9MM **Privately Held**
SIC: 1422 Crushed & broken limestone
HQ: Stabler Companies Inc.
635 Lucknow Rd
Harrisburg PA 17110
717 236-9307

G
E
O
G
R
A
P
H
I
C

Coraopolis
Allegheny County

(G-3651)
A F PAUL COMPANY
859 2nd Ave (15108-3913)
PHONE................................412 264-2111
Thomas Paul, *President*
Eleanor J Paul, *Vice Pres*
EMP: 10 EST: 1952
SQ FT: 4,000
SALES (est): 1.4MM **Privately Held**
SIC: 3599 Machine shop, jobbing & repair

(G-3652)
A P GREEN SERVICES INC
1305 Cherrington Pkwy # 100
(15108-4355)
PHONE................................412 375-6600
Guenter Karhut, *President*
EMP: 13
SALES (est): 1.3MM **Privately Held**
SIC: 3297 Nonclay refractories

(G-3653)
A STUCKI COMPANY (PA)
360 Wright Brothers Dr (15108-6807)
PHONE................................412 424-0560
Bill Kiefer, *CEO*
A Stucki, *CEO*
David Lendt, *President*
David W Lendt, *CFO*
Daniel A Bruno, *Asst Treas*
▲ EMP: 20
SQ FT: 25,000
SALES (est): 26.7MM **Privately Held**
WEB: www.stucki.com
SIC: 3743 3569 5088 Freight cars &
    equipment; filters, general line: industrial;
    railroad equipment & supplies

(G-3654)
AEG HOLDINGS INC
Also Called: Atlas America
311 Rouser Rd (15108-6801)
P.O. Box 611 (15108-0611)
PHONE................................412 262-2830
James Omara, *CEO*
Frank Carolis, *Vice Pres*
EMP: 50
SALES (est): 4.8MM **Privately Held**
SIC: 1382 Oil & gas exploration services

(G-3655)
AMERICAN BRIDGE MFG CO
(DH)
Also Called: Grid Division
1000 American Bridge Way (15108-1266)
PHONE................................412 631-3000
Michael Flowers, *CEO*
Rob Conroy, *Project Mgr*
Kelly N Gilliland, *Technology*
EMP: 22
SALES (est): 4.6MM
SALES (corp-wide): 180MM **Privately
Held**
SIC: 3441 Fabricated structural metal for
    bridges; bridge sections, prefabricated
    highway; bridge sections, prefabricated
    railway
HQ: American Bridge Company
    1000 American Bridge Way
    Coraopolis PA 15108
    412 631-1000

(G-3656)
AMERICAN BRIDGE MFG CO
1000 American Bridge Way (15108-1266)
P.O. Box 236, Reedsport OR (97467-0236)
PHONE................................541 271-1100
Oren Sanders, *Manager*
EMP: 8
SQ FT: 60,000
SALES (corp-wide): 180MM **Privately
Held**
SIC: 3441 Fabricated structural metal for
    bridges; bridge sections, prefabricated
    highway; bridge sections, prefabricated
    railway
HQ: American Bridge Manufacturing Co
    1000 American Bridge Way
    Coraopolis PA 15108
    412 631-3000

(G-3657)
AMERICAN LEAK DETECTION
113 Nanton Way (15108-3466)
P.O. Box 15676, Pittsburgh (15244-0676)
PHONE................................412 859-6000
Wayne Nowakowski, *Owner*
EMP: 3
SALES (est): 342.4K **Privately Held**
SIC: 3599 3829 Water leak detectors; liq-
    uid leak detection equipment

(G-3658)
ANGELL INDUSTRIES INC
400 Chess St (15108-3927)
PHONE................................412 269-2956
EMP: 6
SALES (est): 730K **Privately Held**
SIC: 3523 Mfg Farm Machinery/Equipment

(G-3659)
ATLAS AMERICA PUBLIC 10 LTD
311 Rouser Rd (15108-6801)
PHONE................................412 262-2830
EMP: 3
SALES: 347.1K **Privately Held**
SIC: 1381 Drilling oil & gas wells

(G-3660)
ATLAS ENERGY OPERATING CO
LLC
311 Rouser Rd (15108-2849)
P.O. Box 611 (15108-0611)
PHONE................................412 262-2830
Michael L Staines, *Principal*
EMP: 261
SALES (est): 5.9MM **Publicly Held**
SIC: 1381 Drilling oil & gas wells
HQ: Targa Energy, L.P.
    1000 Commerce Dr Ste 400
    Pittsburgh PA 15275

(G-3661)
ATLAS RSRCES PUB 18-2009 B
LP
Also Called: Atlas Energy
Westpointe Corp Ctr One (15108)
PHONE................................330 896-8510
Edward E Cohen, *General Ptnr*
EMP: 1
SALES: 1.5MM **Publicly Held**
SIC: 1311 Crude petroleum & natural gas
HQ: Targa Energy, L.P.
    1000 Commerce Dr Ste 400
    Pittsburgh PA 15275

(G-3662)
BBM TECHNOLOGIES INC
845 4th Ave (15108-1517)
PHONE................................412 269-4546
Fax: 412 269-1415
EMP: 3
SALES: 200K **Privately Held**
SIC: 3479 Aircraft Coatings

(G-3663)
BOOKHAVEN PRESS LLC
302 Scenic Ct (15108-9783)
PHONE................................412 494-6926
Dennis Damp, *Mng Member*
EMP: 3
SALES (est): 284.5K **Privately Held**
WEB: www.bookhavenpress.com
SIC: 2741 Miscellaneous publishing

(G-3664)
BP OIL CO SVC STNS DIESL
FUEL
921 Brodhead Rd (15108-2351)
PHONE................................412 264-6140
Josh Gerhard, *Principal*
EMP: 3
SALES (est): 188.2K **Privately Held**
SIC: 2911 Diesel fuels

(G-3665)
BRIGHTON ELECTRIC
107 Patton Dr (15108-2517)
PHONE................................412 269-7000
EMP: 5
SALES (est): 484K **Privately Held**
SIC: 3325 Steel foundries

(G-3666)
C & E PLASTIC EAST
Also Called: Crighton Plastics
392 Flaugherty Run Rd (15108-9798)
PHONE................................724 457-0594
Christopher Crighton, *Owner*
EMP: 17
SALES (est): 1.7MM **Privately Held**
SIC: 3089 Injection molding of plastics

(G-3667)
CAB TECHNOLOGIES &
PRINTING SO
438 Skylark Dr (15108-8944)
PHONE................................724 457-8880
Charles Basil, *Principal*
EMP: 4
SALES (est): 482.8K **Privately Held**
SIC: 2752 Commercial printing, offset

(G-3668)
CALGON CARBON
CORPORATION
Also Called: Hyde Marine
2000 Mcclaren Woods Dr (15108-7768)
PHONE................................724 218-7001
Tom Mackey, *President*
EMP: 10
SALES (corp-wide): 5.3B **Privately Held**
SIC: 2819 Industrial inorganic chemicals
HQ: Calgon Carbon Corporation
    3000 Gsk Dr
    Moon Township PA 15108
    412 787-6700

(G-3669)
CALGON CARBON
INVESTMENTS INC (DH)
3000 Gsk Dr (15108-1381)
PHONE................................412 787-6700
John S Stanik, *President*
Steve Butterworth, *General Mgr*
Steve Nolder, *Vice Pres*
William Zinsser, *Vice Pres*
Tim Duckwall, *Plant Mgr*
EMP: 44
SALES (est): 8.6MM
SALES (corp-wide): 5.3B **Privately Held**
SIC: 2819 Industrial inorganic chemicals
HQ: Calgon Carbon Corporation
    3000 Gsk Dr
    Moon Township PA 15108
    412 787-6700

(G-3670)
CALGON CARBON UV TECH
LLC
Also Called: Hyde Marine
2000 Mcclaren Woods Dr (15108-7768)
PHONE................................724 218-7001
Randall Sdearth, *President*
Robert Pobrien, *Vice Pres*
Chad Whalen, *Admin Sec*
EMP: 9
SALES (est): 143.1K
SALES (corp-wide): 5.3B **Privately Held**
SIC: 3429 Marine hardware
HQ: Calgon Carbon Corporation
    3000 Gsk Dr
    Moon Township PA 15108
    412 787-6700

(G-3671)
CAMERON TECHNOLOGIES US
INC (DH)
Also Called: Caldon Ultrasonics Div
1000 Mcclaren Woods Dr (15108-7766)
P.O. Box 1212, Houston TX (77251-1212)
PHONE................................724 695-3798
James E Wright, *President*
J E Wright, *President*
Pat Holley, *Vice Pres*
Tom Simms, *Vice Pres*
Charles M Sledge, *Vice Pres*
◆ EMP: 100
SQ FT: 1,000
SALES (est): 64.7MM **Publicly Held**
SIC: 1389 1382 Oil/Gas Field Services
    Oil/Gas Exploration Services

(G-3672)
CAMERON TECHNOLOGIES US
INC
Caldon Ultrasonics Tech Ctr
1000 Mcclaren Woods Dr (15108-7766)
PHONE................................724 273-9300
Kyle Briggs, *General Mgr*
EMP: 55 **Publicly Held**
SIC: 3823 Industrial flow & liquid measur-
    ing instruments
HQ: Cameron Technologies Us, Inc.
    1000 Mcclaren Woods Dr
    Coraopolis PA 15108
    724 695-3798

(G-3673)
CAMERON TECHNOLOGIES US
INC
Also Called: Cameron Measurements Sys-
tems
1000 Mcclaren Woods Dr (15108-7766)
PHONE................................724 273-9300
Cal Hastings, *Manager*
EMP: 14 **Publicly Held**
SIC: 3823 Industrial process control instru-
    ments
HQ: Cameron Technologies Us, Inc.
    1000 Mcclaren Woods Dr
    Coraopolis PA 15108
    724 695-3798

(G-3674)
CENTRIA INC
Also Called: H H Robertson Floor Systems
1005 Beaver Grade Rd # 2 (15108-2964)
PHONE................................724 251-2208
Albert F Smith, *Manager*
EMP: 20
SALES (corp-wide): 2B **Publicly Held**
SIC: 2426 Flooring, hardwood
HQ: Centria, Inc.
    1005 Beaver Grade Rd # 2
    Moon Township PA 15108
    412 299-8000

(G-3675)
CHAMP PRINTING COMPANY
INC
730 4th Ave (15108-3920)
PHONE................................412 269-0197
Robert Champ, *President*
Todd Young, *Sales Staff*
Jeff Wittebort, *Admin Sec*
EMP: 42
SQ FT: 11,000
SALES (est): 8.2MM **Privately Held**
WEB: www.champprinting.com
SIC: 2752 2791 2789 2759 Commercial
    printing, offset; typesetting; bookbinding &
    related work; commercial printing

(G-3676)
CHARTERS FABG PWDR
COATING LLC
200 Main St (15108-1461)
PHONE................................412 203-5421
William Kammerer, *Mng Member*
Peter Wassen,
EMP: 20
SQ FT: 43,000
SALES (est): 3MM **Privately Held**
SIC: 3441 Fabricated structural metal

(G-3677)
CHEVRON USA INC
700 Cherrington Pkwy (15108-4315)
PHONE................................412 262-2830
Dick Redmond, *Branch Mgr*
EMP: 41
SALES (corp-wide): 166.3B **Publicly
Held**
SIC: 5541 5511 2911 5171 Filling sta-
    tions, gasoline; automobiles, new & used;
    gasoline blending plants; petroleum bulk
    stations
HQ: Chevron U.S.A. Inc.
    6001 Bollinger Canyon Rd D1248
    San Ramon CA 94583
    925 842-1000

(G-3678)
CM TECHNOLOGIES CORPORATION
Also Called: Ecad Division
1026 4th Ave (15108-1604)
PHONE................................412 262-0734
Sheldon Lefkowitz, *President*
Kathryn Lefkowitz, *Treasurer*
Linda Lukart, *Admin Sec*
EMP: 18
SALES (est): 2.5MM Privately Held
WEB: www.ecadusa.com
SIC: 3629 7629 Electronic generation equipment; electrical measuring instrument repair & calibration

(G-3679)
COATING INNOVATIONS LLC
900 Commerce Dr Ste 908 (15108-4746)
PHONE................................412 269-0100
Sean Carlin, *Principal*
EMP: 10
SALES (est): 1.1MM
SALES (corp-wide): 118.3MM Privately Held
SIC: 2851 Shellac (protective coating)
PA: Tnemec Company, Inc.
6800 Corporate Dr
Kansas City MO 64120
816 483-3400

(G-3680)
CORAOPOLIS LIGHT METAL INC
1221 3rd Ave (15108-1462)
PHONE................................412 264-2252
Clarence Brenner Jr, *President*
Dorothy Brenner, *Corp Secy*
Doug Brenner, *Vice Pres*
EMP: 3
SALES (est): 250K Privately Held
SIC: 3444 1761 Sheet metalwork; sheet metalwork

(G-3681)
CRIGHTON PLASTICS INC
392 Flaugherty Run Rd (15108-9798)
PHONE................................724 457-0594
Chistopher G Crighton, *President*
Amy Crighton, *Corp Secy*
EMP: 21
SQ FT: 12,000
SALES (est): 4.8MM Privately Held
SIC: 3089 Thermoformed finished plastic products; plastic processing

(G-3682)
CULVERTS INC
330 Pittsburgh Ave (15108-3391)
P.O. Box 271 (15108-0271)
PHONE................................412 262-3111
Josh Montgomery, *President*
William N Chapin, *President*
EMP: 6 EST: 1958
SQ FT: 12,000
SALES (est): 1.1MM Privately Held
WEB: www.culverts.com
SIC: 3444 Culverts, sheet metal

(G-3683)
D & S INDUSTRIAL CONTG INC
3100 Casteel Dr (15108-9787)
PHONE................................412 490-3215
Delbert Celaschi, *President*
Roland Burns, *Partner*
Stephen M Celaschi, *Vice Pres*
EMP: 22
SALES (est): 6.6MM
SALES (corp-wide): 15.3MM Privately Held
SIC: 3536 Cranes, overhead traveling
PA: H & K Equipment, Inc.
4200 Casteel Dr
Coraopolis PA 15108
412 490-5300

(G-3684)
DEBENHAM MEDIA GROUP
416 Mill St (15108-1648)
PHONE................................412 264-2526
Stuart Debenham, *Owner*
Gregory Murdzak, *Manager*
EMP: 10
SQ FT: 5,000

SALES: 1MM Privately Held
WEB: www.3516.com
SIC: 7812 3861 7819 Industrial motion picture production; cameras, still & motion picture (all types); video tape or disk reproduction

(G-3685)
EATON CORPORATION
Also Called: Moon Township Office
1000 Cherrington Pkwy (15108-4312)
PHONE................................412 893-3300
Eugen Borsan, *Business Mgr*
Lenny Bonyak, *Project Mgr*
Fred Chabala, *Project Mgr*
Curtis Garmen, *Project Mgr*
Mike Hines, *Project Mgr*
EMP: 400 Privately Held
WEB: www.eaton.com
SIC: 3625 Relays & industrial controls
HQ: Eaton Corporation
1000 Eaton Blvd
Cleveland OH 44122
440 523-5000

(G-3686)
EKOPAK INC
1120 Stevenson Mill Rd (15108-2446)
P.O. Box 914 (15108-0914)
PHONE................................412 264-9800
EMP: 11
SQ FT: 53,000
SALES (est): 4.5MM Privately Held
SIC: 5113 3086 Whol Industrial/Service Paper Mfg Products

(G-3687)
ELKEM HOLDING INC (HQ)
Also Called: Elkem Metal
Airport Office Park Bldg (15108)
P.O. Box 266, Pittsburgh (15230-0266)
PHONE................................412 299-7200
Geir I Kvernmo, *Principal*
Bjorn Sandberg, *Business Mgr*
Anders Malvik, *Vice Pres*
Knut MO, *Finance Mgr*
Jorgen Rosten, *Finance Mgr*
◆ EMP: 337
SALES: 91MM
SALES (corp-wide): 25MM Privately Held
SIC: 3313 Ferroalloys
PA: Neh Inc
400 Rouser Rd 6airport
Coraopolis PA 15108
412 299-7200

(G-3688)
ELKEM MATERIALS INC
400 Rouser Rd Ste 600 (15108-2767)
P.O. Box 266, Pittsburgh (15230-0266)
PHONE................................412 299-7200
Mark Nilsen, *President*
Simon Wilson, *Vice Pres*
Kimberly Petrisko, *CFO*
◆ EMP: 8
SALES (est): 1MM Privately Held
WEB: www.microblock.net
SIC: 3313 Ferroalloys

(G-3689)
EMC METALS INC
400 Rouser Rd Ste 600 (15108-2767)
PHONE................................412 299-7200
David W Renfrew, *President*
EMP: 5
SALES (est): 246.1K Privately Held
SIC: 3572 Computer storage devices

(G-3690)
FAB-TEC INDUSTRIES INC
3500 University Blvd # 1 (15108-4251)
PHONE................................412 262-1144
Daniel Kohley, *President*
Phillip Kohley, *Treasurer*
John Kohley, *Admin Sec*
▲ EMP: 40
SQ FT: 150,000
SALES (est): 12.5MM Privately Held
WEB: www.fab-tecindustries.com
SIC: 3441 3443 Fabricated structural metal; fabricated plate work (boiler shop)

(G-3691)
FT PITT ACQUISITION CORP
Also Called: Roffler
400 Chess St (15108-3927)
PHONE................................412 269-2950
Sam Leopold, *President*
EMP: 50
SQ FT: 4,000
SALES (est): 3MM Privately Held
SIC: 3999 Barber & beauty shop equipment

(G-3692)
GENERAL FABRICATING SVCS LLC
Also Called: GFS
1 Lewis Ave (15108-3369)
P.O. Box 286 (15108-0286)
PHONE................................412 262-1131
John Hnath,
EMP: 17
SQ FT: 170,000
SALES (est): 3.2MM Privately Held
SIC: 3443 3498 3433 Chutes & troughs; fabricated pipe & fittings; couplings, pipe: fabricated from purchased pipe; burners, furnaces, boilers & stokers

(G-3693)
GENERAL RUBBER CORPORATION
200 Commerce Dr Ste 212 (15108-3189)
PHONE................................412 424-0270
Julie Benzer, *Manager*
EMP: 11
SALES (corp-wide): 5.6MM Privately Held
SIC: 3069 Hard rubber products; molded rubber products; tubing, rubber; valves, hard rubber
PA: General Rubber Corporation
2201 E Ganley Rd
Tucson AZ 85706
201 935-1900

(G-3694)
GFS LLC
1 Lewis Ave (15108-3369)
P.O. Box 286 (15108-0286)
PHONE................................412 262-1131
Michael Morgan, *President*
Carl D Jungers, *Corp Secy*
Todd A Volker, *Vice Pres*
John D Hnath,
▲ EMP: 51 EST: 2005
SALES (est): 10.9MM Privately Held
SIC: 3441 Fabricated structural metal

(G-3695)
GLENN MACHINE CO
422 Flaugherty Run Rd (15108-9799)
PHONE................................724 457-7750
Glenn C Buzza III, *President*
EMP: 13
SQ FT: 6,000
SALES (est): 1.8MM Privately Held
SIC: 3599 Machine shop, jobbing & repair

(G-3696)
H & K EQUIPMENT INC (PA)
4200 Casteel Dr (15108-9725)
PHONE................................412 490-5300
George C Koch, *President*
Peter A Cicero Jr, *Vice Pres*
Terry A Hopkins, *Admin Sec*
EMP: 75
SQ FT: 25,000
SALES (est): 15.3MM Privately Held
WEB: www.hkequipment.com
SIC: 3599 5084 Machine shop, jobbing & repair; materials handling machinery

(G-3697)
HAMILTONIAN SYSTEMS INC
117 Hunters Run Dr (15108-9734)
PHONE................................412 327-7204
Ravishankar Venkatraman, *President*
David Radin, *Vice Pres*
EMP: 12
SALES: 2MM Privately Held
SIC: 7372 7389 Business oriented computer software;

(G-3698)
HORIBA INSTRUMENTS INC
1002 Harvest Ct (15108-9015)
PHONE................................724 457-2424
EMP: 75
SALES (corp-wide): 1.7B Privately Held
SIC: 3823 Mfg Process Control Instruments
HQ: Horiba Instruments Incorporated
9755 Research Dr
Irvine CA 92618
949 250-4811

(G-3699)
IDEAL BUILDING FASTENERS INC
920 2nd Ave Ste 2 (15108-1486)
PHONE................................412 299-6199
Jay Levy, *President*
Joe Jospe, *Vice Pres*
Jack Jospe, *Admin Sec*
▲ EMP: 17
SQ FT: 40,000
SALES (est): 6.8MM Privately Held
SIC: 5085 3965 Fasteners, industrial: nuts, bolts, screws, etc.; fasteners

(G-3700)
JON SWAN INC (PA)
Also Called: Swan Label & Tag Co
929 2nd Ave (15108-1434)
P.O. Box 308 (15108-0308)
PHONE................................412 264-9000
Jon L Swan, *President*
Debbie Nolder, *Technology*
EMP: 30
SQ FT: 10,000
SALES (est): 8.2MM Privately Held
WEB: www.swanlabel.com
SIC: 5131 2754 2672 Labels; labels: gravure printing; coated & laminated paper

(G-3701)
LEE METALS INC
102 Freedom Ct (15108-9020)
P.O. Box 141 (15108-0141)
PHONE................................412 331-8630
▲ EMP: 7
SQ FT: 5,000
SALES (est): 1.3MM Privately Held
SIC: 3341 Secondary Nonferrous Metal Producer

(G-3702)
LOMBARDO INDUSTRIES
1813 Madison Dr (15108-1198)
PHONE................................412 264-4588
D Lombardo, *Principal*
EMP: 3
SALES (est): 142K Privately Held
SIC: 3999 Manufacturing industries

(G-3703)
MAGNETIC LIFTING TECH US LLC (PA)
4200 Casteel Dr (15108-9725)
PHONE................................412 490-5300
George C Koch, *Mng Member*
EMP: 4 EST: 2010
SQ FT: 25,000
SALES (est): 1MM Privately Held
SIC: 3599 Machine shop, jobbing & repair

(G-3704)
MASTER MACHINE AND MFG
1220 2nd Ave (15108-1441)
PHONE................................412 262-1550
Fred Cornell, *President*
EMP: 3
SQ FT: 10,000
SALES (est): 343.9K Privately Held
SIC: 3599 Machine shop, jobbing & repair

(G-3705)
MOLYNEUX INDUSTRIES INC
621 Cliff Mine Rd (15108-9386)
P.O. Box 772 (15108-0772)
PHONE................................724 695-3406
George M Molyneux, *President*
Chip Miller, *VP Sales*
▲ EMP: 10 EST: 1976
SQ FT: 10,000

SALES (est): 1.8MM **Privately Held**
WEB: www.molyneuxindustries.com
SIC: 3312 Blast furnaces & steel mills

(G-3706)
NEH INC (PA)
400 Rouser Rd 6airport (15108-2842)
P.O. Box 266, Pittsburgh (15230-0266)
PHONE...............................412 299-7200
Geir I Kvernmo, *President*
Al Woodrich, *CFO*
Roland Hennigfeld, *Marketing Staff*
David W Renfrew, *Admin Sec*
◆ EMP: 359
SALES (est): 25MM **Privately Held**
SIC: 3313 6719 Electrometallurgical products; investment holding companies, except banks

(G-3707)
NIKE INC
3000 Gsk Dr Ste 300 (15108-1383)
PHONE...............................412 922-3660
Garry Borroughs, *Manager*
EMP: 8
SALES (corp-wide): 36.4B **Publicly Held**
WEB: www.nike.com
SIC: 3021 Rubber & plastics footwear
PA: Nike, Inc.
   1 Sw Bowerman Dr
   Beaverton OR 97005
   503 671-6453

(G-3708)
OHIO VALLEY INDUS SVCS INC
620 Moon Clinton Rd (15108-3806)
PHONE...............................412 335-5237
Doug Robinson, *Manager*
EMP: 14
SALES (est): 1.8MM
SALES (corp-wide): 6.3MM **Privately Held**
WEB: www.ovisinc.com
SIC: 3296 5085 Fiberglass insulation; filters, industrial
PA: Ohio Valley Industrial Services, Inc.
   530 Moon Clinton Rd Ste B
   Moon Township PA 15108
   412 269-0020

(G-3709)
ORACLE AMERICA INC
Also Called: Sun Microsystems
1550 Coraopls Hgts Rd 4 (15108-2973)
PHONE...............................412 859-6051
Bill Haas, *Manager*
EMP: 30
SALES (corp-wide): 39.8B **Publicly Held**
SIC: 7372 Prepackaged software
HQ: Oracle America, Inc.
   500 Oracle Pkwy
   Redwood City CA 94065
   650 506-7000

(G-3710)
ORACLE SYSTEMS CORPORATION
1550 Coraopols Hts Rd 400 (15108-2973)
PHONE...............................412 262-5200
John Lerda, *Sales Staff*
Wendy McHale, *Sales Staff*
Mary Turner, *Manager*
Jeffrey Muth, *Manager*
Antoinette Hall, *Sr Software Eng*
EMP: 5
SALES (corp-wide): 39.8B **Publicly Held**
WEB: www.forcecapital.com
SIC: 7372 Prepackaged software
HQ: Oracle Systems Corporation
   500 Oracle Pkwy
   Redwood City CA 94065
   650 506-7000

(G-3711)
PARK CORPORATION
210 Airside Dr (15108-2793)
PHONE...............................412 472-0500
Dan Park, *Branch Mgr*
EMP: 8

SALES (corp-wide): 568.1MM **Privately Held**
WEB: www.parkcorp.com
SIC: 3547 1711 3443 5084 Rolling mill machinery; boiler maintenance contractor; mechanical contractor; boilers: industrial, power, or marine; industrial machinery & equipment; commercial & industrial building operation; exposition operation
PA: Park Corporation
   6200 Riverside Dr
   Cleveland OH 44135
   216 267-4870

(G-3712)
PERPETUAL ENTERPRISES INC (PA)
2511 Beaver Grade Rd (15108-9703)
PHONE...............................412 299-6356
Ken Hoff, *President*
Tom Hoff, *Principal*
Dennis Hoff, *Vice Pres*
Dick Hoff, *Admin Sec*
EMP: 7
SALES (est): 1.2MM **Privately Held**
SIC: 2522 Office furniture, except wood

(G-3713)
PERPETUAL ENTERPRISES INC
701 4th Ave (15108-3919)
PHONE...............................412 299-6356
Kenneth Hoff, *Branch Mgr*
EMP: 6
SALES (corp-wide): 1.2MM **Privately Held**
SIC: 2522 Office furniture, except wood
PA: Perpetual Enterprises Inc
   2511 Beaver Grade Rd
   Coraopolis PA 15108
   412 299-6356

(G-3714)
PETROLEUM PRODUCTS CORP
520 Narrows Run Rd (15108-1117)
PHONE...............................412 264-8242
Rick Hesfelfinger, *Principal*
EMP: 3
SALES (est): 308.1K **Privately Held**
SIC: 2911 5172 Petroleum refining; petroleum products

(G-3715)
PHOENIX DESIGN & PRINT INC
614 5th Ave (15108-1524)
PHONE...............................412 264-4895
Chistopher J Connolly, *President*
Chistopher Connolly, *President*
Christina C Carlisle, *Vice Pres*
EMP: 13
SALES: 1.5MM **Privately Held**
SIC: 2752 7336 Commercial printing, offset; graphic arts & related design

(G-3716)
PINNACLE SYSTEMS
2504 State Ave (15108-2238)
P.O. Box 100088, Pittsburgh (15233-0088)
PHONE...............................412 262-3950
Kenneth Baron, *President*
Gary Kovac, *Vice Pres*
Darrin Kohn, *Engineer*
Donna Bauer, *Admin Asst*
EMP: 7
SQ FT: 1,664
SALES (est): 844.9K **Privately Held**
WEB: www.pinnaclesystems.com
SIC: 3444 5085 Machine guards, sheet metal; industrial supplies

(G-3717)
PRECISE GRAPHIC PRODUCTS INC
311 Smallwood Dr (15108-2624)
PHONE...............................412 481-0952
Thomas Strusienski, *President*
William Krause, *Chairman*
EMP: 4
SQ FT: 3,100
SALES: 650K **Privately Held**
SIC: 2752 Commercial printing, lithographic

(G-3718)
PRINTING PRESS
246 Moon Clinton Rd # 101 (15108-2490)
PHONE...............................412 264-3355

Derek Danko, *Partner*
Sang GE Lee, *Partner*
EMP: 3
SQ FT: 2,000
SALES: 200K **Privately Held**
SIC: 2752 Commercial printing, offset

(G-3719)
PROCESS DEVELOPMENT & CTRL LLC
1075 Montour West Ind Par (15108-9308)
PHONE...............................724 695-3440
Alina Craig, *Controller*
Gary Lee, *Mng Member*
EMP: 30
SALES (est): 1.2MM **Privately Held**
SIC: 3494 Valves & pipe fittings

(G-3720)
QUALITY MACHINE TOOLS LLC
Also Called: Precision Matthews McHy Co
1060 Montour West Ind Par (15108-9307)
PHONE...............................412 787-2876
Matt Nadeja, *Owner*
EMP: 3
SALES (est): 222.4K **Privately Held**
SIC: 3545 Precision tools, machinists'

(G-3721)
RIVERSIDE BUILDERS SUPPLY
Also Called: Riverside Cement Company
889 Pennsylvania Ave (15108-3999)
PHONE...............................412 264-8835
Joseph Homitsky Sr, *President*
EMP: 35
SQ FT: 1,000
SALES (est): 5.9MM **Privately Held**
WEB: www.riversideconcrete.com
SIC: 5211 3273 Lumber & other building materials; ready-mixed concrete

(G-3722)
ROCKWELL AUTOMATION INC
510 Lindbergh Dr (15108-2750)
PHONE...............................724 741-4000
Carol Voll, *Branch Mgr*
EMP: 53 **Publicly Held**
SIC: 3625 Relays & industrial controls
PA: Rockwell Automation, Inc.
   1201 S 2nd St
   Milwaukee WI 53204

(G-3723)
ROCKWELL AUTOMATION INC
510 Lindbergh Dr (15108-2750)
PHONE...............................412 375-4700
Ralph Lovette, *Principal*
EMP: 9 **Publicly Held**
SIC: 3625 3663 3621 3566 Relays & industrial controls; television closed circuit equipment; motors, electric; speed changers (power transmission equipment), except auto
PA: Rockwell Automation, Inc.
   1201 S 2nd St
   Milwaukee WI 53204

(G-3724)
RONALD E KOLLER WELDING
Also Called: Lewis Emmil Ornamental Iron Co
33 Evelyn Dr (15108-3433)
PHONE...............................412 859-6781
Ronald E Koller, *President*
EMP: 6
SALES (est): 217.1K **Privately Held**
SIC: 7692 Welding repair

(G-3725)
SABRE EQUIPMENT INC
802 Pennsylvania Ave (15108-3958)
PHONE...............................412 262-3080
Frank Bellay, *President*
Bonnie Bellay, *Treasurer*
Jean Dee, *Bookkeeper*
Alexandra Bellay, *Shareholder*
EMP: 23
SQ FT: 27,800
SALES: 6.7MM **Privately Held**
WEB: www.sabreequipment.com
SIC: 5012 5531 3713 Truck bodies; truck equipment & parts; specialty motor vehicle bodies

(G-3726)
STITCH WIZARDS INC
1009 4th Ave (15108-1603)
PHONE...............................412 264-9973
Bettie A Stephenson, *Principal*
EMP: 3
SALES (est): 247.9K **Privately Held**
SIC: 2395 Embroidery products, except schiffli machine; embroidery & art needlework

(G-3727)
TECNOMASIUM INC
Also Called: Control & Data Technologies
105 Bertley Ridge Dr (15108-9762)
PHONE...............................412 264-7364
Roberto Le Donne, *President*
Giovanni Le Donne, *Vice Pres*
EMP: 18
SQ FT: 5,000
SALES (est): 1.2MM **Privately Held**
SIC: 3699 8731 Security control equipment & systems; electronic research

(G-3728)
TPL PLASTIC ENGRAVING
265 Forest Grove Rd (15108-3747)
PHONE...............................412 771-3773
Thomas Lachowicz, *Owner*
EMP: 4
SALES (est): 225K **Privately Held**
SIC: 3089 Engraving of plastic

(G-3729)
TRI-STATE PLASTICS INC
392 Flaugherty Run Rd (15108-9798)
PHONE...............................724 457-2847
Michael A Lopez, *President*
EMP: 15 EST: 1966
SQ FT: 35,000
SALES (est): 3.6MM **Privately Held**
WEB: www.tsplastics.com
SIC: 3089 Thermoformed finished plastic products; injection molding of plastics

(G-3730)
UNIVERSAL REFRACTORIES INC
Universal Specialities
500 Beaver Grade Rd (15108-9732)
PHONE...............................412 787-7220
Alex George, *Manager*
EMP: 30
SALES (corp-wide): 47.8MM **Privately Held**
SIC: 3297 3255 Cement refractories, nonclay; ramming mixes, nonclay; clay refractories
PA: Universal Refractories, Inc.
   915 Clyde St
   Wampum PA 16157
   724 535-4374

(G-3731)
VICTORY MEDIA INC
Also Called: G.I. Jobs
420 Rouser Rd Ste 101 (15108-3090)
P.O. Box 26, Sewickley (15143-0026)
PHONE...............................412 269-1663
Richard McCormack, *President*
Chris Hale, *Chairman*
Mike Stevens, *COO*
Joann Conner, *Vice Pres*
Matthew Stewart, *Accountant*
EMP: 9
SQ FT: 1,500
SALES (est): 1.6MM
SALES (corp-wide): 2.4MM **Privately Held**
WEB: www.gijobs.net
SIC: 2721 8742 Magazines: publishing only, not printed on site; marketing consulting services
PA: Neptune Holdings, Inc.
   420 Rouser Rd Ste 101
   Coraopolis PA 15108
   412 269-1663

(G-3732)
VULCAN INDUSTRIES INC
701 4th Ave (15108-3919)
PHONE...............................412 269-7655
Kenneth M Hoff, *President*
Edward Beals Jr, *Vice Pres*
EMP: 12

SALES (est): 3.8MM **Privately Held**
SIC: 3441 Fabricated structural metal

(G-3733)
WINDURANCE LLC
1300 Commerce Dr (15148-4747)
PHONE.................................412 424-8900
Terry L Havens-Turner, *Corp Secy*
Tod A George, *CFO*
Richard E Turner Jr,
Stephen Jones,
Paul J Rowan,
▲ EMP: 370
SQ FT: 25,000
SALES: 11.6MM **Privately Held**
SIC: 3699 3511 Electrical equipment &
supplies; turbines & turbine generator
sets
HQ: Matric Limited
2099 Hill City Rd
Seneca PA 16346
814 677-0716

(G-3734)
WOJANIS SUPPLY COMPANY
(PA)
1001 Montour West Ind Par (15108-9308)
PHONE.................................724 695-1415
Douglas Goldstrohm, *President*
Keith Goldstrohm, *President*
Christine Simcic, *Corp Secy*
▼ EMP: 22 EST: 1980
SQ FT: 5,000
SALES: 9MM **Privately Held**
WEB: www.wojanis.com
SIC: 5084 3594 Hydraulic systems equip-
ment & supplies; fluid power pumps &
motors

(G-3735)
WTK HOLDINGS INC
1075 Montour West Ind Par (15108-9308)
PHONE.................................724 695-3440
Gary Lee, *President*
Wt Keegan, *President*
Mark Parry, *Prdtn Mgr*
Ron Koch, *Chief Engr*
Alina Craig, *Accounting Mgr*
▲ EMP: 30 EST: 1970
SQ FT: 14,500
SALES (est): 6.5MM **Privately Held**
WEB: www.pdcvalve.com
SIC: 3494 Valves & pipe fittings

(G-3736)
XECOL CORPORATION
200 Marshall Dr Fl 2 (15108-2840)
PHONE.................................412 262-5222
Roy F Johns Jr, *President*
Richard Kattan, *Corp Secy*
Tom Weaver, *Vice Pres*
EMP: 6
SQ FT: 500
SALES (est): 437.6K **Privately Held**
SIC: 1221 Strip mining, bituminous

Cornwall
Lebanon County

(G-3737)
BRENNER MACHINE CO
64 Rexmont Rd (17016)
PHONE.................................717 274-3411
Janis Herschkowitz, *President*
Charles L Lantz, *Vice Pres*
L Saylor Zimmerman III, *Treasurer*
George Heck, *Mktg Dir*
EMP: 125 EST: 1914
SQ FT: 14,000
SALES (est): 12.2MM
SALES (corp-wide): 46.9MM **Privately
Held**
SIC: 3599 Machine shop, jobbing & repair
PA: P R L Inc
64 Rexmont Rd
Cornwall PA 17016
717 273-2470

(G-3738)
CONRAD ENTERPRISES INC
200 Rexmont Rd (17016)
PHONE.................................717 274-5151
EMP: 23

SQ FT: 38,000
SALES (est): 4.4MM **Privately Held**
SIC: 3713 3792 3714 3537 Mfg
Truck/Bus Bodies Mfg Trailers/Campers
Mfg Motor Vehicle Parts Mfg Indstl
Truck/Tractor Mfg Construction Mach

(G-3739)
P R L INC (PA)
64 Rexmont Rd (17016)
P.O. Box 142 (17016-0142)
PHONE.................................717 273-2470
Janis Herschkowitz, *President*
Ronald C Bailor, *Vice Pres*
Barbara Herschkowitz, *Vice Pres*
Joel Valigorsky, *Human Res Dir*
Greg Raudenbush, *Technical Staff*
EMP: 22
SQ FT: 2,500
SALES (est): 46.9MM **Privately Held**
SIC: 3399 3599 8741 Laminating steel;
machine shop, jobbing & repair; manage-
ment services

(G-3740)
PRL INDUSTRIES INC
64 Rexmont Rd (17016)
P.O. Box 142 (17016-0142)
PHONE.................................717 273-6787
Janis Herschkowitz, *President*
L Saylor Zimmerman III, *Corp Secy*
EMP: 45 EST: 1969
SQ FT: 20,000
SALES (est): 11MM
SALES (corp-wide): 46.9MM **Privately
Held**
SIC: 3369 8734 3462 3444 Castings, ex-
cept die-castings, precision; testing labo-
ratories; iron & steel forgings; sheet
metalwork
PA: P R L Inc
64 Rexmont Rd
Cornwall PA 17016
717 273-2470

Corry
Erie County

(G-3741)
A C A SAND & GRAVEL
19144 Route 89 (16407-9554)
PHONE.................................814 665-6087
Anne Zawacki, *Owner*
EMP: 6
SALES (est): 977.6K **Privately Held**
SIC: 1442 Construction sand & gravel

(G-3742)
ADVANTAGE PUCK
TECHNOLOGIES
1 Plastics Rd Ste 6 (16407-8538)
PHONE.................................814 664-4810
Pat Roche, *Principal*
EMP: 9
SALES (est): 1.1MM **Privately Held**
SIC: 3535 Belt conveyor systems, general
industrial use

(G-3743)
AL XANDER CO INC (PA)
Also Called: Axco Valve
36 E South St (16407-1913)
P.O. Box 98 (16407-0098)
PHONE.................................814 665-8268
John A Xander, *President*
Randy Strader, *Vice Pres*
Thomas Xander, *Vice Pres*
Albert Xander, *Treasurer*
Gary Xander, *Shareholder*
EMP: 20
SQ FT: 30,000
SALES (est): 11.1MM **Privately Held**
WEB: www.alxander.com
SIC: 5084 3545 3498 3492 Pneumatic
tools & equipment; hydraulic systems
equipment & supplies; machine tool ac-
cessories; fabricated pipe & fittings; fluid
power valves & hose fittings; industrial
valves; gaskets, packing & sealing de-
vices

(G-3744)
BALLISTIC SCIENTIFIC USA
LLC
1 Plastics Rd Ste 1a (16407-8538)
PHONE.................................267 282-6666
Bernie Montana,
David Fricke,
Richard Peterson,
EMP: 4 EST: 2017
SQ FT: 300
SALES (est): 155.8K **Privately Held**
SIC: 3482 Small arms ammunition

(G-3745)
BARNES GROUP INC
Associated Spring
226 S Center St (16407-1935)
PHONE.................................814 663-6082
Cindy Applebee, *Principal*
Greg Cutshaw, *Plant Engr*
Paulo Leandro, *VP Bus Dvlpt*
EMP: 150
SALES (corp-wide): 1.5B **Publicly Held**
WEB: www.barnesgroupinc.com
SIC: 3495 3469 Wire springs; metal
stampings
PA: Barnes Group Inc.
123 Main St
Bristol CT 06010
860 583-7070

(G-3746)
BROTHERS WOOD COMPANY
Enterprise Rd (16407)
PHONE.................................814 462-2422
Jon Wood, *President*
EMP: 5
SALES (est): 253.3K **Privately Held**
SIC: 2096 Potato chips & similar snacks

(G-3747)
CHASE MANUFACTURING
9 Pennsylvania Ave (16407-1603)
P.O. Box 37 (16407-0037)
PHONE.................................814 664-9069
Bryan Anderson, *Partner*
Richard E Chase, *General Ptnr*
EMP: 40
SQ FT: 47,500
SALES (est): 8.2MM **Privately Held**
SIC: 3469 Machine parts, stamped or
pressed metal

(G-3748)
CORRY CONTRACT INC
21 Maple Ave (16407-1690)
PHONE.................................814 665-8221
William Kafferlin, *CEO*
Douglas H Kafferlin, *President*
Steve Crawford, *Vice Pres*
Linda Melnick, *Production*
Frederick D Davids, *Treasurer*
▲ EMP: 112
SQ FT: 140,000
SALES: 10.8MM **Privately Held**
WEB: www.corrycontract.com
SIC: 3444 Sheet metal specialties, not
stamped

(G-3749)
CORRY FORGE COMPANY (HQ)
441 E Main St (16407-2013)
PHONE.................................814 664-9664
Daniel P Hamilton, *President*
David E Barensfeld, *Vice Pres*
Shaun Powell, *Buyer*
Bentraum D Huffman, *Treasurer*
Susan A Apel, *Admin Sec*
EMP: 34
SALES (est): 8.8MM
SALES (corp-wide): 775.5MM **Privately
Held**
WEB: www.mcinnesrolledrings.com
SIC: 3462 Iron & steel forgings
PA: Ellwood Group, Inc.
600 Commercial Ave
Ellwood City PA 16117
724 752-3680

(G-3750)
CORRY JOURNAL INC
Also Called: Samples News Group
28 W South St (16407-1810)
PHONE.................................814 665-8291
Bob Williams, *President*
Julie Shaver, *Graphic Designe*

EMP: 18
SALES (est): 1.2MM **Privately Held**
WEB: www.thecorryjournal.com
SIC: 2711 Newspapers: publishing only,
not printed on site

(G-3751)
CORRY LASER TECHNOLOGY
INC
Also Called: Corrylaser.com
1530 Enterprise Rd (16407-8574)
PHONE.................................814 664-7212
Scott A Brady, *President*
Madi Rathinavelu, *General Mgr*
Madiajagane K Rathinavelu, *Senior VP*
Madi Rathin, *Vice Pres*
Susan Martin, *Administration*
EMP: 10
SQ FT: 18,000
SALES (est): 1.8MM **Privately Held**
WEB: www.corrylaser.com
SIC: 7699 7692 Miscellaneous automotive
repair services; aircraft & heavy equip-
ment repair services; automotive welding

(G-3752)
CORRY MANUFACTURING
COMPANY
320 W Main St (16407-1843)
PHONE.................................814 664-9611
Mike Bierzienski, *President*
EMP: 200
SQ FT: 13,000
SALES (corp-wide): 26.3MM **Privately
Held**
WEB: www.corrymfg.com
SIC: 3714 3724 Motor vehicle engines &
parts; aircraft engines & engine parts
PA: Corry Manufacturing Company
519 W Main St
Corry PA 16407
814 664-9611

(G-3753)
CORRY METAL PRODUCTS INC
46500 Route 6 (16407-4320)
P.O. Box 297 (16407-0297)
PHONE.................................814 664-7087
Randall Owens, *President*
Richard Owens, *Admin Sec*
EMP: 4
SQ FT: 15,000
SALES (est): 430K **Privately Held**
WEB: www.corrymetalproducts.com
SIC: 3451 Screw machine products

(G-3754)
CORRY MICRONICS INC (PA)
1 Plastics Rd Ste 1a (16407-8538)
PHONE.................................814 664-7728
Don Pavlek, *President*
Tim McCarthy, *Treasurer*
Rick Peterson, *Director*
Terry Peterson, *Director*
▲ EMP: 13
SQ FT: 14,050
SALES: 5.2MM **Privately Held**
WEB: www.cormic.com
SIC: 3679 Microwave components

(G-3755)
CORRY OPOTHECARY
612 W Sweet St (16407)
PHONE.................................814 452-4220
EMP: 4
SALES (est): 200.6K **Privately Held**
SIC: 2834 Mfg Pharmaceutical Prepara-
tions

(G-3756)
CORRY PEAT PRODUCTS CO
INC
515 Turnpike Rd (16407-9065)
PHONE.................................814 665-7101
Roger Roth, *President*
EMP: 5 EST: 1951
SQ FT: 900
SALES (est): 492.5K **Privately Held**
SIC: 1479 Fertilizer mineral mining

(G-3757)
CORRY RUBBER CORPORATION
601 W Main St (16407-1799)
PHONE.................................814 664-2313
Ernest B Ferro, *President*

Jeffery Ferro, *Vice Pres*
Jeffrey A Ferro, *Vice Pres*
Jennifer Gourley, *Treasurer*
EMP: 35 **EST:** 1961
SQ FT: 150,000
SALES (est): 9.3MM **Privately Held**
WEB: www.corryrubber.com
SIC: 3432 3052 3061 Plumbing fixture fittings & trim; rubber & plastics hose & beltings; appliance rubber goods (mechanical)

(G-3758)
D&E MACHINING LTD
150 Industrial Dr (16407-8560)
PHONE.................................814 664-3531
Roland Bauer, *Principal*
Janet Demay, *Vice Pres*
Mand Rehder, *CFO*
Mandi Rehder, *Controller*
Frank Polanski, *Sales Staff*
EMP: 33
SQ FT: 34,000
SALES (est): 10.3MM **Privately Held**
WEB: www.demachining.com
SIC: 3599 Machine shop, jobbing & repair
PA: The Cypress Companies Inc
   670 W Market St
   Akron OH 44303

(G-3759)
ENTECH PLASTICS INC
1 Plastics Rd Ste 5 (16407-8538)
PHONE.................................814 664-7205
Kevin J Gearity, *President*
Sally B Gearity, *Vice Pres*
EMP: 43
SQ FT: 60,000
SALES (est): 11MM **Privately Held**
WEB: www.entechplastics.com
SIC: 3089 Injection molding of plastics

(G-3760)
FCA LLC
844 Route 6 Ste 3 (16407-9062)
PHONE.................................309 792-3444
Shawn Lohnes, *Branch Mgr*
EMP: 43 **Privately Held**
SIC: 5085 2653 Industrial supplies; corrugated & solid fiber boxes
PA: Fca, Llc
   7601 John Deere Pkwy
   Moline IL 61265

(G-3761)
FULL STRUT LOGGING LLC
20065 Hammond Rd (16407-7207)
PHONE.................................814 323-5292
Debra A Kean, *Principal*
EMP: 6
SALES (est): 260.5K **Privately Held**
SIC: 2411 Logging

(G-3762)
FXI INC
Also Called: Foamex
466 S Shady Ave (16407-2043)
PHONE.................................814 664-7771
Mike Smith, *Branch Mgr*
EMP: 125 **Privately Held**
SIC: 3086 Packaging & shipping materials, foamed plastic
HQ: Fxi, Inc.
   1400 N Providence Rd # 2000
   Media PA 19063

(G-3763)
GREAT LAKES CASE & CAB CO INC
18433 Sciota Rd (16407)
PHONE.................................814 663-6015
Matthew Wronna, *Principal*
EMP: 5
SALES (corp-wide): 45.7MM **Privately Held**
SIC: 3499 Fire- or burglary-resistive products
PA: Great Lakes Case & Cabinet Co., Inc.
   4193 Route 6n
   Edinboro PA 16412
   814 734-7303

(G-3764)
GREAT LAKES MANUFACTURING INC
1521 Enterprise Rd (16407-8575)
PHONE.................................814 734-2436
Carrie L Lowther, *President*
Robert I Lowther Jr, *Vice Pres*
EMP: 120
SALES (est): 25.2MM **Privately Held**
SIC: 3444 Sheet metal specialties, not stamped

(G-3765)
IRON HOSE COMPANY LLC
844 E Columbus Ave (16407)
PHONE.................................877 277-9035
EMP: 6
SQ FT: 100,000
SALES (est): 1.1MM **Privately Held**
SIC: 3052 Mfg Rubber/Plastic Hose/Belting

(G-3766)
JCS OILFIELD SERVICES LLC
111 Shady Ave (16407-9066)
PHONE.................................814 665-4008
Mark J Frontera,
EMP: 14
SALES (est): 1.6MM **Privately Held**
SIC: 1389 Oil field services

(G-3767)
MICK BROTHERS LUMBER INC
12242 Lovell Rd (16407-9522)
PHONE.................................814 664-8700
Wayne Mick, *President*
Bruce Mick, *Vice Pres*
EMP: 20
SQ FT: 800
SALES (est): 5MM **Privately Held**
SIC: 2426 Lumber, hardwood dimension

(G-3768)
MITCHELTREE BROS
18700 Conelway Rd (16407-8909)
PHONE.................................814 665-4019
EMP: 3
SALES (est): 198.8K **Privately Held**
SIC: 2411 Logging camps & contractors

(G-3769)
MPE MACHINE TOOL INC
27 W Washington St (16407-1524)
P.O. Box 3 (16407-0003)
PHONE.................................814 664-4822
Thomas Fontecchio, *President*
Thomas J Fontecchio, *Principal*
EMP: 20
SQ FT: 14,000
SALES (est): 2.7MM **Privately Held**
WEB: www.mpemachinetool.com
SIC: 3541 Machine tools, metal cutting type

(G-3770)
NIAGARA PISTON RING WORKS INC
18455 Sciota St (16407-8937)
P.O. Box 333, Clymer NY (14724-0333)
PHONE.................................716 782-2307
Mary Ellen Fusco-Sykes, *President*
Joseph Sykes, *Vice Pres*
EMP: 10
SQ FT: 3,600
SALES (est): 1.6MM **Privately Held**
SIC: 3592 Pistons & piston rings

(G-3771)
PENN WEST TRADING CO INC
Scotts Crossing Rd (16407)
P.O. Box 33 (16407-0033)
PHONE.................................814 664-7649
Mark Lea, *President*
Sherry Bidwell, *Manager*
EMP: 3
SQ FT: 5,500
SALES (est): 290K **Privately Held**
SIC: 2411 Logging

(G-3772)
PILOT-RUN STAMPING COMPANY
715 Spring St (16407-2125)
PHONE.................................440 255-8821
Anthony Mitalski, *President*
Jim Tracy, *President*

Marvin Davison, *Vice Pres*
Lawrence Johnson, *Vice Pres*
EMP: 26 **EST:** 1966
SQ FT: 14,000
SALES (est): 3.7MM **Privately Held**
SIC: 3469 3316 Stamping metal for the trade; cold finishing of steel shapes

(G-3773)
SAMPLE NEWS GROUP LLC (PA)
28 W South St (16407-1810)
PHONE.................................814 665-8291
George Sample, *Mng Member*
Bob Williams,
EMP: 138
SQ FT: 10,316
SALES (est): 8MM **Privately Held**
SIC: 2711 Newspapers, publishing & printing

(G-3774)
THERMA-FAB INC
256 Eagle St (16407-1533)
PHONE.................................814 664-9429
Frank Johnson, *Branch Mgr*
EMP: 4
SQ FT: 3,360 **Privately Held**
WEB: www.thermafab.com
SIC: 3443 Fabricated plate work (boiler shop)
PA: Therma-Fab, Inc
   109 W Central Ave
   Titusville PA 16354

(G-3775)
THOMPSON MAPLE PRODUCTS INC
175 Sample Flats Rd (16407)
PHONE.................................814 664-7717
Charles P Henness, *President*
Susan L Henness, *Corp Secy*
▼ **EMP:** 27
SQ FT: 30,000
SALES (est): 4MM **Privately Held**
WEB: www.tmpusa.com
SIC: 2499 2426 Dowels, wood; hardwood dimension & flooring mills

(G-3776)
TONNARD MANUFACTURING CORP
Also Called: Tonnard Manufacturing Corp 715
715 Spring St (16407-2199)
P.O. Box 168 (16407-0168)
PHONE.................................814 664-7794
Brian Bills, *President*
Anthony Mitalski, *Corp Secy*
Anthony Morelle, *Vice Pres*
Mario Pepicelli, *Vice Pres*
Inspection Tonnard, *Opers Mgr*
EMP: 64 **EST:** 1963
SQ FT: 75,000
SALES (est): 14.3MM **Privately Held**
WEB: www.tonnard.com
SIC: 3469 Stamping metal for the trade

(G-3777)
V I P MACHINING INC (PA)
18381 Sciota St (16407-8969)
PHONE.................................814 665-1840
Ron Thompson, *President*
Debra Thompson, *Corp Secy*
EMP: 17
SALES (est): 2.5MM **Privately Held**
SIC: 3599 Machine shop, jobbing & repair

(G-3778)
V I P MACHINING INC
18381 Sciota St (16407-8969)
PHONE.................................814 665-1840
Mitchelle Erickson, *Manager*
EMP: 5
SALES (corp-wide): 2.5MM **Privately Held**
SIC: 3599 Machine shop, jobbing & repair
PA: V I P Machining Inc
   18381 Sciota St
   Corry PA 16407
   814 665-1840

(G-3779)
VPI ACQUISITION LLC (PA)
Also Called: Viking Plastics
1 Viking St (16407-2079)
PHONE.................................814 664-8671
Kelly Goodsel, *President*
Cathy Pitts, *Admin Sec*
EMP: 110
SQ FT: 64,000
SALES (est): 29.1MM **Privately Held**
WEB: www.vikingplastics.com
SIC: 3089 Injection molding of plastics

Coudersport
Potter County

(G-3780)
COUDERSPORT PRECAST INC (PA)
30 W Hebron Rd (16915-7993)
P.O. Box 189 (16915-0189)
PHONE.................................814 274-9634
Charles Gerner, *President*
Ruth Gerner, *Vice Pres*
Kathy Jackson, *Treasurer*
EMP: 10
SQ FT: 1,125
SALES (est): 950.8K **Privately Held**
SIC: 3272 Concrete products, precast

(G-3781)
GABERSECK BROS
141 Troupe Rd (16915-8370)
PHONE.................................814 274-0763
William Gaberseck, *Partner*
Lawrence Gaberseck, *Partner*
William A Gaberseck, *Partner*
EMP: 4
SALES (est): 415.2K **Privately Held**
SIC: 1794 2411 Excavation work; logging

(G-3782)
HORSEPOWER LOGGING
207 A Frame Rd (16915-8059)
PHONE.................................814 274-2236
Ronald Carr, *Principal*
EMP: 3
SALES (est): 219.1K **Privately Held**
SIC: 2411 Logging

(G-3783)
JOSEPH LAGRUA
Also Called: Lagrew Printing Co
557 State Route 49 (16915-8434)
PHONE.................................814 274-7163
Joseph Lagrua, *Owner*
EMP: 4
SALES (est): 357.4K **Privately Held**
SIC: 2791 2789 2759 2396 Typesetting; bookbinding & related work; commercial printing; automotive & apparel trimmings; lithographing on metal

(G-3784)
LIONETTE ENTERPRISES
Also Called: Gary's Putter Golf
156 Cherry Springs Rd (16915-8315)
PHONE.................................814 274-9401
Gary L Reese, *Owner*
Jeanette Reese, *Partner*
EMP: 5
SALES (est): 2MM **Privately Held**
WEB: www.pasfoods.com
SIC: 7999 2035 5099 5812 Miniature golf course operation; pickles, vinegar; signs, except electric; eating places; signs & advertising specialties

(G-3785)
MORGAN ADVANCED MTLS TECH INC
Also Called: Morgan AM&t
1118 E 2nd St (16915-8307)
PHONE.................................814 274-6132
John Stang, *Principal*
Bill Daly, *Engineer*
EMP: 98
SALES (corp-wide): 1.3B **Privately Held**
SIC: 3624 Carbon & graphite products
HQ: Morgan Advanced Materials And Technology, Inc.
   441 Hall Ave
   Saint Marys PA 15857

(G-3786)
NORTHERN HARDWOODS INC
Also Called: T C Specialties Company
17 S Main St (16915-1301)
P.O. Box 192 (16915-0192)
PHONE..............................814 274-8060
Carl G Clark Jr, *President*
Judi L Tucker, *Corp Secy*
EMP: 6
SQ FT: 11,100
SALES (est): 753.5K **Privately Held**
WEB: www.tcspecialties.com
SIC: 2752 Coupons, lithographed

(G-3787)
PENNSYLVANIN FLAGSTONE INC
Also Called: Ostrom Stone Co
307 E Oak St (16915-1536)
PHONE..............................814 544-7575
EMP: 12
SALES (est): 1.5MM **Privately Held**
SIC: 1423 4213 Cuts Flagstone Trucking Operator-Nonlocal

(G-3788)
ROD QUELLETTE
Also Called: Rod's Welding
707 N Main St (16915-1705)
PHONE..............................814 274-8812
Rod Ouellette, *Owner*
EMP: 5
SALES (est): 477.6K **Privately Held**
SIC: 3599 7692 Custom machinery; welding repair

(G-3789)
TIOGA PUBLISHING COMPANY
Also Called: Leader Publishing Co.
6 W 2nd St (16915-1112)
PHONE..............................814 274-8044
Larry Porado, *President*
EMP: 14
SQ FT: 4,500
SALES (est): 623.2K **Privately Held**
WEB: www.potterleaderenterprise.com
SIC: 2711 Commercial printing & newspaper publishing combined; newspapers: publishing only, not printed on site
HQ: Tioga Publishing Company
25 East Ave Frnt Ste
Wellsboro PA 16901

(G-3790)
TRUCK-LITE CO LLC
100 Market St (16915-9617)
PHONE..............................814 274-5400
John Bard, *Manager*
EMP: 89
SALES (corp-wide): 42.4B **Privately Held**
WEB: www.truck-lite.com
SIC: 3647 5063 Motor vehicle lighting equipment; lighting fixtures
HQ: Truck-Lite Co., Llc
310 E Elmwood Ave
Falconer NY 14733

Covington
Tioga County

(G-3791)
BRODRICK HUGHES ENERGY LLC
2050 N Williamson Rd (16917-9514)
PHONE..............................570 662-2464
Bing Hughes, *Partner*
Kathryn Brodrick, *Partner*
EMP: 4
SQ FT: 4,000
SALES (est): 330K **Privately Held**
SIC: 3621 Motors & generators

(G-3792)
PEQUIGNOT LOGGING
526 E Hill Rd (16917-9658)
PHONE..............................570 659-5251
Richard Pequignot, *Owner*
EMP: 8
SALES (est): 820K **Privately Held**
SIC: 2411 Logging camps & contractors

Covington Township
Lackawanna County

(G-3793)
PUCHALSKI INC
46 Kosinski Rd (18444-7863)
PHONE..............................570 842-0361
Lawrence Puchalski, *President*
EMP: 5 EST: 1980
SALES: 500K **Privately Held**
SIC: 2731 3229 Books: publishing & printing; glassware, art or decorative

---

Covington Township
Wayne County

(G-3794)
WILLIAMS GARDEN CENTER INC
516 Drinker Tpke (18424-7833)
PHONE..............................570 842-7277
Debra Williams, *President*
EMP: 9 EST: 1976
SQ FT: 2,400
SALES (est): 1MM **Privately Held**
SIC: 0782 1794 1442 0781 Mowing services, lawn; landscape contractors; excavation & grading, building construction; construction sand & gravel; landscape planning services

---

Cowansville
Armstrong County

(G-3795)
60X CUSTOM STRINGS
1047 State Route 268 (16218-1409)
PHONE..............................724 525-0507
Brad Patsy, *Owner*
▲ EMP: 4 EST: 2012
SALES (est): 360K **Privately Held**
SIC: 3949 Bows, archery

(G-3796)
GREENHEAT LP
125 Pence Rd (16218-1301)
PHONE..............................724 545-6540
EMP: 12
SALES (est): 139K **Privately Held**
SIC: 3211 Mfg Flat Glass

Cranberry
Venango County

(G-3797)
SENECA HARDWOOD LUMBER CO INC
212 Seneca Hardwood Rd (16319-2526)
PHONE..............................814 498-2241
Orie Hepler, *President*
Wayne Hepler, *Vice Pres*
Mary L Eakin, *Treasurer*
Betty M Hepler, *Admin Sec*
EMP: 30 EST: 1940
SALES (est): 5.2MM **Privately Held**
WEB: www.senecahardwoodlumber.com
SIC: 2426 3442 2431 2421 Hardwood dimension & flooring mills; metal doors, sash & trim; millwork; sawmills & planing mills, general

---

Cranberry Township
Butler County

(G-3798)
ACUITY FINISHING LLC
230 W Kensinger Dr Ste B (16066-3432)
PHONE..............................724 935-9190
Rick Ubinger,
Don Stoebe,
▲ EMP: 55
SQ FT: 45,000

SALES (est): 9.5MM **Privately Held**
SIC: 2789 Binding & repair of books, magazines & pamphlets

(G-3799)
ADVANCED CONTROLS INC
243 Peace St (16066-6828)
P.O. Box 1611 (16066-0611)
PHONE..............................724 776-0224
Vikram Rawal, *President*
EMP: 4
SALES (est): 370K **Privately Held**
SIC: 3625 Electric controls & control accessories, industrial

(G-3800)
ALLEGHENY PLASTICS INC
Printed Plastics Division
1224 Freedom Rd (16066-4914)
PHONE..............................724 776-0100
Kathy Hinsman, *COO*
Don Ranalli, *Branch Mgr*
Dave Coyle, *CIO*
Gary Johnson, *Administration*
EMP: 70
SALES (corp-wide): 39.3MM **Privately Held**
SIC: 2396 2752 Printing & embossing on plastics fabric articles; commercial printing, lithographic
PA: Allegheny Plastics, Inc.
Ave A Bldg 3
Leetsdale PA 15056
412 741-4416

(G-3801)
ALSTOM POWER CONVERSION INC (HQ)
100 E Kensinger Dr # 500 (16066-3557)
PHONE..............................412 967-0765
Shoun Kerbaugh, *President*
Kanishka Kumar, *Engineer*
Justin Morse, *Engineer*
◆ EMP: 200
SQ FT: 100,000
SALES (est): 26.2MM
SALES (corp-wide): 121.6B **Publicly Held**
SIC: 3612 3823 3672 Autotransformers, electric (power transformers); power transformers, electric; industrial instrmnts msrmnt display/control process variable; printed circuit boards
PA: General Electric Company
41 Farnsworth St
Boston MA 02210
617 443-3000

(G-3802)
AMERICAN BOTTLING COMPANY
Cotton Club Bottling Co
125 E Kensinger Dr (16066-3551)
PHONE..............................724 776-6111
Bryan McGee, *Branch Mgr*
Brian McGee, *Manager*
Michael Pippi, *Manager*
EMP: 45 **Publicly Held**
WEB: www.cs-americas.com
SIC: 2086 Soft drinks: packaged in cans, bottles, etc.
HQ: The American Bottling Company
5301 Legacy Dr
Plano TX 75024

(G-3803)
AMERICAN MADE LLC
Also Called: U.S. Liner Company
19 Leonberg Rd Ste 1 (16066-3631)
PHONE..............................724 776-4044
Michael Larocco, *President*
Mick Witenski, *Human Res Mgr*
William Guttman,
Ned Pfeifer,
◆ EMP: 165
SQ FT: 77,000
SALES (est): 89.6MM **Privately Held**
WEB: www.uslco.com
SIC: 3083 Laminated plastics plate & sheet

(G-3804)
ARCADIA CONTROLS
392 Plains Church Rd (16066-2730)
PHONE..............................724 538-8931
Arthur Amsler, *President*
Deborah Amsler, *Manager*

EMP: 2 EST: 1968
SALES: 1.5MM **Privately Held**
WEB: www.arcadiahome.com
SIC: 3823 Industrial process measurement equipment

(G-3805)
ASHBY MFG CO INC
12 Leonberg Rd (16066-3602)
PHONE..............................724 776-5566
Tim O' Donell, *President*
Manus O'Donnell, *President*
Kevin O'Donell, *Vice Pres*
EMP: 15
SQ FT: 17,500
SALES (est): 3.3MM **Privately Held**
WEB: www.ashbymfg.com
SIC: 3312 3599 Tool & die steel; machine shop, jobbing & repair

(G-3806)
ATC TECHNOLOGY CORPORATION (DH)
Also Called: Genco-Atc
700 Cranberry Woods Dr (16066-5213)
PHONE..............................412 820-3700
Todd R Peters, *President*
Andy Smith, *President*
Art Smuck, *COO*
John J Machota, *Exec VP*
Bradley Peacock, *Senior VP*
◆ EMP: 27
SALES: 307.3MM
SALES (corp-wide): 65.4B **Publicly Held**
SIC: 1541 3694 4225 Industrial buildings & warehouses; engine electrical equipment; general warehousing & storage

(G-3807)
ATSCO HOLDINGS CORP
25 Leonberg Rd (16066-3601)
PHONE..............................440 701-1021
Richard Horowitz, *President*
EMP: 84
SALES (est): 4.6MM
SALES (corp-wide): 65MM **Publicly Held**
SIC: 3494 3546 Valves & pipe fittings; power-driven handtools
HQ: Hy-Tech Machine, Inc.
25 Leonb Rd Mashu Indus P K A Industrial P
Cranberry Township PA 16066
724 776-6800

(G-3808)
B & C MATERIAL HANDLING INC
9276 Marshall Rd (16066-2858)
PHONE..............................724 814-7910
Stanley Armen, *President*
EMP: 2 EST: 2016
SALES (est): 1.5MM **Privately Held**
SIC: 3535 Overhead conveyor systems

(G-3809)
BOLTZ PRINTING COMPANY LLC
Also Called: Minuteman Press
20325 Route 19 (16066-6132)
PHONE..............................724 772-4911
James B Boltz,
EMP: 6
SALES (est): 887.7K **Privately Held**
SIC: 2752 Commercial printing, lithographic

(G-3810)
CANNON U S A INC (DH)
1235 Freedom Rd (16066-4949)
PHONE..............................724 772-5600
Paolo Spinelli, *President*
Mark Laughery, *Project Mgr*
Rick Schubert, *Mfg Staff*
Jackie Rose, *Inv Control Mgr*
Greg Hunter, *Purch Agent*
◆ EMP: 45 EST: 1977
SQ FT: 50,000
SALES (est): 13.1MM
SALES (corp-wide): 83.5K **Privately Held**
SIC: 3559 Plastics working machinery
HQ: Sergood Corp
1235 Freedom Rd
Cranberry Township PA 16066
724 772-5600

(G-3811)
CONAIR GROUP INC (DH)
200 W Kensinger Dr # 100 (16066-3428)
PHONE.........................724 584-5500
Christopher Keller, *CEO*
▲ EMP: 50
SALES (est): 19.7MM
SALES (corp-wide): 229.1MM **Privately Held**
SIC: 3559 Plastics working machinery
HQ: Ipeg, Inc.
200 W Kensinger Dr # 100
Cranberry Township PA 16066
724 584-5500

(G-3812)
COOPER BUSSMANN LLC
512 Daisy Ct (16066-6322)
PHONE.........................724 553-5449
EMP: 267 **Privately Held**
WEB: www.bussman.com
SIC: 3613 Fuses, electric
HQ: Cooper Bussmann, Llc
114 Old State Rd
Ellisville MO 63021
636 527-1324

(G-3813)
CURBELL INC
250 W Kensinger Dr # 100 (16066-3438)
PHONE.........................724 772-6800
Bob Galbraith, *Principal*
EMP: 3
SALES (est): 22.7K **Privately Held**
SIC: 2295 Resin or plastic coated fabrics

(G-3814)
DANIELI CORPORATION
600 Cranberry Woods Dr # 200
(16066-5230)
PHONE.........................724 778-5400
Luca Rossetto, *CEO*
Ferdinando Palagiano, *Vice Pres*
Blake Jurena, *Purch Mgr*
Lisa Boehmke, *Accountant*
Bikramjit Ghosh, *Finance*
◆ EMP: 70
SALES (est): 19.3MM **Privately Held**
SIC: 3547 Rolling mill machinery
HQ: Danieli Holdings, Inc.
600 Cranberry Woods Dr # 200
Cranberry Township PA 16066
724 778-5400

(G-3815)
DBWAVE TECHNOLOGIES LLC
2009 Mackenzie Way # 100 (16066-5338)
PHONE.........................412 345-8081
Xupeng Liu,
EMP: 3
SALES (est): 138.3K **Privately Held**
SIC: 3679 Microwave components

(G-3816)
DR PEPPER SNAPPLE GROUP
125 E Kensinger Dr (16066-3551)
PHONE.........................724 776-6111
EMP: 5
SALES (est): 206.6K **Privately Held**
SIC: 2086 Soft drinks: packaged in cans, bottles, etc.

(G-3817)
EAGLE PRINTING COMPANY
Also Called: Cranberry Eagle
20701 Route 19 (16066-6009)
PHONE.........................724 776-4270
Bob Schultz, *Manager*
EMP: 7
SALES (corp-wide): 25.4MM **Privately Held**
SIC: 2711 Newspapers, publishing & printing
PA: Eagle Printing Company
114 W Diamond St
Butler PA 16001
724 282-8000

(G-3818)
FILTRTION OF WSTN PNNYSYLVANIA
Also Called: Filter Queen
1445 Market St (16066)
PHONE.........................412 855-7372
Judy McPodough, *Office Mgr*
EMP: 5 EST: 2009
SALES (est): 20.7K **Privately Held**
SIC: 3569 Filters

(G-3819)
FRESH LINK INDUSTRIAL LTD
511 Thomson Park Dr (16066-6425)
PHONE.........................724 779-6880
Mike Trell, *Manager*
▲ EMP: 3
SALES (est): 240K **Privately Held**
SIC: 3561 Industrial pumps & parts

(G-3820)
GE ENRGY PWR CNVERSION USA INC (HQ)
Also Called: Converteam
100 E Kensinger Dr # 500 (16066-3556)
PHONE.........................412 967-0765
Joe Mastrangelo, *CEO*
Michael Archibald, *President*
Garry Rauscher, *COO*
Donald Grau, *Treasurer*
Elaine Gates, *Admin Sec*
▲ EMP: 132
SQ FT: 92,500
SALES (est): 93.5MM
SALES (corp-wide): 121.6B **Publicly Held**
SIC: 3629 Power conversion units, a.c. to d.c.: static-electric
PA: General Electric Company
41 Farnsworth St
Boston MA 02210
617 443-3000

(G-3821)
GIANT EAGLE
20111 Route 19 Ste 35 (16066-6225)
PHONE.........................724 772-1030
Evelyn Sandonato, *President*
Robert Sandonato, *Vice Pres*
EMP: 200
SQ FT: 90,000
SALES (est): 18.7MM **Privately Held**
SIC: 5411 5912 2051 Supermarkets, chain; drug stores & proprietary stores; bread, cake & related products

(G-3822)
HILLSHIRE BRANDS COMPANY
215 Commerce Park Dr (16066-6403)
PHONE.........................724 772-3440
Mike Lyons, *Manager*
EMP: 19
SALES (corp-wide): 40B **Publicly Held**
SIC: 2013 Sausages & other prepared meats
HQ: The Hillshire Brands Company
400 S Jefferson St Fl 1
Chicago IL 60607
312 614-6000

(G-3823)
HY-TECH MACHINE INC (HQ)
25 Leonb Rd Mashu Indus P K A Industrial P (16066)
PHONE.........................724 776-6800
Richard Horowitz, *President*
Maralynn Lee, *Sales Associate*
▲ EMP: 69
SQ FT: 40,000
SALES (est): 28.9MM
SALES (corp-wide): 65MM **Publicly Held**
WEB: www.hy-techinc.com
SIC: 3494 5085 7692 3599 Valves & pipe fittings; industrial supplies; welding repair; machine shop, jobbing & repair; machine tool attachments & accessories
PA: P & F Industries, Inc.
445 Broadhollow Rd # 100
Melville NY 11747
631 694-9800

(G-3824)
HY-TECH MACHINE INC
Thaxton Division
25 Leonberg Rd (16066-3601)
PHONE.........................724 776-2400
Doug Turner, *Marketing Staff*
Patrick Deyle, *Manager*
EMP: 70
SALES (corp-wide): 65MM **Publicly Held**
WEB: www.hy-techinc.com
SIC: 3494 3829 Pipe fittings; measuring & controlling devices

HQ: Hy-Tech Machine, Inc.
25 Leonb Rd Mashu Indus P K A Industrial P
Cranberry Township PA 16066
724 776-6800

(G-3825)
J S PALUCH CO INC
316 Thomson Park Dr (16066-6434)
PHONE.........................724 772-8850
Brian De Haas, *Branch Mgr*
EMP: 22
SALES (corp-wide): 88.3MM **Privately Held**
WEB: www.jspaluch.com
SIC: 2731 Books: publishing only
PA: J. S. Paluch Co., Inc.
3708 River Rd Ste 400
Franklin Park IL 60131
847 678-9300

(G-3826)
JAMES E ROTH INC
9043 Marshall Rd (16066-3607)
PHONE.........................724 776-1910
Tom Roth, *President*
David F Roth, *Treasurer*
David Roth, *Treasurer*
EMP: 75
SQ FT: 10,000
SALES (est): 6.9MM **Privately Held**
WEB: www.jameserothinc.com
SIC: 1711 3441 Warm air heating & air conditioning contractor; ventilation & duct work contractor; fabricated structural metal

(G-3827)
KAWNEER COMMERCIAL WINDOWS LLC
Also Called: Traco
71 Progress Ave (16066-3511)
PHONE.........................724 776-7000
Jon Maloney, *President*
Ralph Tamburro,
EMP: 99
SALES (est): 34.8MM
SALES (corp-wide): 14B **Publicly Held**
SIC: 3442 Window & door frames
HQ: Kawneer Company, Inc.
555 Guthridge Ct
Norcross GA 30092
770 449-5555

(G-3828)
KEPCO PLANT SERVICE & ENGRG CO
1000 Westinghouse Dr (16066-5228)
PHONE.........................412 374-3410
EMP: 5
SALES (est): 209.5K
SALES (corp-wide): 52.9B **Privately Held**
SIC: 3462 Mfg Iron/Steel Forgings
HQ: Kepco Plant Service & Engineering Co., Ltd.
211 Munhwa-Ro
Naju CHN 58326
317 104-114

(G-3829)
KOZIK BROS INC
213 Executive Dr Ste 300 (16066-6405)
PHONE.........................724 443-2230
Ronald Kozik, *President*
Larry Kozik, *Vice Pres*
Kevin Kozik, *Treasurer*
Todd Kozik, *Admin Sec*
EMP: 50
SQ FT: 1,500
SALES (est): 12MM **Privately Held**
SIC: 1623 1794 1389 Electric power line construction; excavation & grading, building construction; grading oil & gas well foundations

(G-3830)
KRONOS INCORPORATED
8050 Rowan Rd Ste 600 (16066-3632)
PHONE.........................724 742-3142
Lisa Gray, *Branch Mgr*
EMP: 4
SALES (corp-wide): 1.1B **Privately Held**
WEB: www.kronos.com
SIC: 7372 Business oriented computer software

HQ: Kronos Incorporated
900 Chelmsford St # 312
Lowell MA 01851
978 250-9800

(G-3831)
LASTING EXPRESSIONS
Also Called: M & J Sales
9103 Marshall Rd (16066-3621)
P.O. Box 2233 (16066-1233)
PHONE.........................724 776-3953
Judy L Moran, *Partner*
Ray Moran, *Partner*
EMP: 4
SALES (est): 398.7K **Privately Held**
WEB: www.lasting-expressions.com
SIC: 3999 5999 5112 Artificial flower arrangements; artificial flowers; computer paper

(G-3832)
LILY KAY DOLL CLOTHES LLC
402 Hidden Meadow Dr (16066-2300)
PHONE.........................724 814-2210
Judy Stanton, *Principal*
EMP: 3
SALES (est): 198.5K **Privately Held**
SIC: 3942 Clothing, doll

(G-3833)
LUTZ AND ASSOCIATES (PA)
Also Called: North Hills Monthly Magazine
20232 Route 19 Ste 5 (16066-6124)
P.O. Box 386, Zelienople (16063-0386)
PHONE.........................724 776-9800
Carl Craig Lutz, *CEO*
EMP: 5
SALES (est): 461.8K **Privately Held**
SIC: 2721 Magazines: publishing only, not printed on site

(G-3834)
MC NORTON CABINET CO
311 Plains Church Rd (16066-2713)
PHONE.........................724 538-5680
Donald Mc Norton, *Owner*
EMP: 3 EST: 1955
SALES (est): 167.9K **Privately Held**
SIC: 2434 1521 Wood kitchen cabinets; general remodeling, single-family houses

(G-3835)
MECCO PARTNERS LLC
Also Called: Mecco Marking & Traceability
290 Executive Dr Ste 200 (16066-6436)
P.O. Box 5004 (16066-1904)
PHONE.........................724 779-9555
Jared Frye, *Opers Mgr*
Chris Wasel, *Purch Mgr*
Ryan Pillar, *Sales Engr*
Dan Prokop, *Marketing Mgr*
Tim Bugaile, *Corp Comm Staff*
EMP: 15
SALES (est): 3.7MM **Privately Held**
WEB: www.meccomark.com
SIC: 3953 3549 Marking devices; marking machines, metalworking

(G-3836)
MINE SAFETY APPLIANCES CO LLC (HQ)
Also Called: M S A
1000 Cranberry Woods Dr (16066-5296)
PHONE.........................724 776-8600
B V Demaria, *Vice Pres*
Ronald N Herring, *Vice Pres*
Douglas K McClaine, *Vice Pres*
Markus H Weber, *Vice Pres*
Stacy McMahan, *CFO*
▲ EMP: 500 EST: 1914
SQ FT: 212,000
SALES: 1.1B
SALES (corp-wide): 1.3B **Publicly Held**
WEB: www.msanet.com
SIC: 3842 3826 3823 3648 Personal safety equipment; gas masks; radiation shielding aprons, gloves, sheeting, etc.; respiratory protection equipment, personal; environmental testing equipment; industrial process control instruments; lighting equipment; gas detectors
PA: Msa Safety Incorporated
1000 Cranberry Woods Dr
Cranberry Township PA 16066
724 776-8600

(G-3837)
MORGARDSHAMMAR INC
600 Cranberry Woods Dr # 200
(16066-5227)
PHONE..................................724 778-5400
Andrew Betts, *President*
▲ EMP: 5
SQ FT: 4,500
SALES: 500K **Privately Held**
SIC: 3312 Hot-rolled iron & steel products
HQ: Danieli Holdings, Inc.
600 Cranberry Woods Dr # 200
Cranberry Township PA 16066
724 778-5400

(G-3838)
**MSA ADVANCED DETECTION
LLC ((HQ)**
1000 Cranberry Woods Dr (16066-5207)
PHONE..................................724 776-8600
Ken Krause, *CFO*
EMP: 4
SALES (est): 441.6K
SALES (corp-wide): 1.3B **Publicly Held**
SIC: 3822 Flame safety controls for fur-
naces & boilers
PA: Msa Safety Incorporated
1000 Cranberry Woods Dr
Cranberry Township PA 16066
724 776-8600

(G-3839)
**MSA SAFETY INCORPORATED
(PA)**
1000 Cranberry Woods Dr (16066-5207)
PHONE..................................724 776-8600
William M Lambert, *Ch of Bd*
Nishan J Vartanian, *President*
Steven C Blanco, *President*
Bob Leenen, *President*
Gavan C M Duff, *COO*
EMP: 277
SQ FT: 212,000
SALES: 1.3B **Publicly Held**
SIC: 3826 3823 3648 3829 Environmen-
tal testing equipment; industrial process
control instruments; lighting equipment;
gas detectors; personal safety equipment

(G-3840)
MSA SAFETY INCORPORATED
1100 Cranberry Woods Dr (16066-5208)
PHONE..................................724 776-7700
Rick Katz, *Principal*
EMP: 80
SALES (corp-wide): 1.3B **Publicly Held**
WEB: www.msanet.com
SIC: 3842 Personal safety equipment
PA: Msa Safety Incorporated
1000 Cranberry Woods Dr
Cranberry Township PA 16066
724 776-8600

(G-3841)
MSA SAFETY SALES LLC
1000 Cranberry Woods Dr (16066-5207)
PHONE..................................724 776-8600
Nishan J Vartanian, *CEO*
Kenneth D Krause, *CFO*
EMP: 4
SALES (est): 149.9K
SALES (corp-wide): 1.3B **Publicly Held**
SIC: 3648 3842 3826 3829 Lighting
equipment; personal safety equipment;
environmental testing equipment; gas de-
tectors; industrial process control instru-
ments
PA: Msa Safety Incorporated
1000 Cranberry Woods Dr
Cranberry Township PA 16066
724 776-8600

(G-3842)
**NORTH PITTSBURGH UPPER
CERVICA**
8050 Rowan Rd Ste 400 (16066-3624)
PHONE..................................724 553-8526
Ian Bulow, *Principal*
EMP: 4
SALES (est): 470.6K **Privately Held**
SIC: 3131 Uppers

(G-3843)
PPG INDUSTRIES INC
20804 Route 19 Ste 2 (16066-6026)
PHONE..................................724 772-0005
EMP: 3
SALES (corp-wide): 15.3B **Publicly Held**
SIC: 2851 Paints & allied products
PA: Ppg Industries, Inc.
1 Ppg Pl
Pittsburgh PA 15272
412 434-3131

(G-3844)
**PRESERVATION
TECHNOLOGIES LP (PA)**
111 Thomson Park Dr (16066-6424)
PHONE..................................724 779-2111
Richard E Spatz, *Partner*
James E Burd, *Partner*
Robert M Gaydos, *Partner*
Lee H Leiner, *Partner*
Jeffrey Spatz, *Partner*
EMP: 67
SQ FT: 15,600
SALES (est): 24.3MM **Privately Held**
WEB: www.ptlp.com
SIC: 2899 Chemical preparations

(G-3845)
PRINT-O-STAT INC
230 Executive Dr Ste 108 (16066-6435)
PHONE..................................724 742-9811
Corine Kelly, *Branch Mgr*
EMP: 10
SALES (corp-wide): 100.1MM **Privately
Held**
WEB: www.digitalblueprinting.com
SIC: 2752 7334 5049 5044 Commercial
printing, offset; blueprinting service; engi-
neers' equipment & supplies; blueprinting
equipment
HQ: Print-O-Stat, Inc.
1011 W Market St
York PA 17404
717 812-9476

(G-3846)
REX ENERGY CORPORATION
600 Cranberry Woods Dr # 250
(16066-5227)
PHONE..................................724 814-3230
Thomas C Stabley, *Branch Mgr*
EMP: 13 **Privately Held**
SIC: 1382 Oil & gas exploration services
PA: Rex Energy Corporation
366 Walker Dr
State College PA 16801

(G-3847)
**SATCOM DIGITAL NETWORKS
LLC**
20 Leonberg Rd Ste E (16066-3630)
P.O. Box 221, Valencia (16059-0221)
PHONE..................................724 824-1699
David Chishol, *CEO*
EMP: 5
SALES: 700K **Privately Held**
SIC: 3663 Satellites, communications

(G-3848)
**SCHMIDT TECHNOLOGY
CORPORATION**
Also Called: Schmidt Feintechnik
280 Executive Dr Ste 1 (16066-6448)
PHONE..................................724 772-4600
Robert Tichauer, *President*
Rolf Schmidt, *Chairman*
David Hollinger, *Engineer*
George Schultz, *Design Engr*
Edward Butina, *Electrical Engi*
EMP: 18
SQ FT: 15,000
SALES (est): 4.8MM
SALES (corp-wide): 56.5MM **Privately
Held**
WEB: www.schmidtpresses.com
SIC: 3542 Presses: forming, stamping,
punching, sizing (machine tools)
PA: Schmidt Technology Gmbh
Feldbergstr. 1
St. Georgen Im Schwarzwald 78112
772 489-90

(G-3849)
SERGOOD CORP (DH)
1235 Freedom Rd (16066-4949)
PHONE..................................724 772-5600
Alfonso Manzillo, *Ch of Bd*
Robert Fortwangler, *Treasurer*
Leon Jacobsen, *Admin Sec*
◆ EMP: 4
SALES (est): 13.1MM
SALES (corp-wide): 83.5K **Privately Held**
SIC: 3559 Chemical machinery & equip-
ment
HQ: Worldwide Polyurethanes B.V.
Prins Bernhardplein 200
Amsterdam
205 214-777

(G-3850)
SIGMA INSTRUMENTS INC
506 Thomson Park Dr (16066-6425)
PHONE..................................724 776-9500
John Crunick, *CEO*
Tamas Becse, *Vice Pres*
Lou Laskey, *Vice Pres*
EMP: 15
SQ FT: 4,000
SALES: 2MM **Privately Held**
WEB: www.sigma-instruments.com
SIC: 3841 Medical instruments & equip-
ment, blood & bone work; physiotherapy
equipment, electrical

(G-3851)
STIMPLE AND WARD COMPANY
Also Called: S & W Wire
45a Progress Ave (16066-3511)
P.O. Box 2517 (16066-1517)
PHONE..................................724 772-0049
Mark Benzio, *Manager*
EMP: 6
SALES (corp-wide): 10.6MM **Privately
Held**
WEB: www.swcoils.com
SIC: 3621 Coils, for electric motors or gen-
erators
PA: Stimple And Ward Company
3400 Babcock Blvd
Pittsburgh PA 15237
412 364-5200

(G-3852)
**THREE DIMENSIONS SYSTEMS
INC**
Also Called: Lazerfit Smart Soles
210 W Kensinger Dr # 400 (16066-3436)
PHONE..................................724 779-3890
Richard Donley Jr, *President*
Roland Edwards, *COO*
EMP: 5
SQ FT: 2,500
SALES (est): 60K **Privately Held**
WEB: www.lazerfit.com
SIC: 3131 Inner parts for shoes

(G-3853)
**THREE RIVERS ALUMINUM
COMPANY**
71 Progress Ave (16066-3511)
PHONE..................................800 837-7002
Robert Randall, *President*
EMP: 3
SALES (est): 97.8K **Privately Held**
SIC: 3442 Metal doors

(G-3854)
**TOLLGRADE COMMUNICATIONS
INC (HQ)**
260 Executive Dr Ste 150 (16066-6451)
PHONE..................................724 720-1400
Ed Kennedy, *President*
James F Andrus, *Vice Pres*
Roger Faulkner, *Engineer*
R Steven Furr, *CFO*
Rick Kwong, *Director*
▲ EMP: 26
SQ FT: 24,500
SALES: 24MM
SALES (corp-wide): 262.6MM **Privately
Held**
WEB: www.tollgrade.com
SIC: 3661 Telephone central office equip-
ment, dial or manual

PA: Enghouse Systems Limited
80 Tiverton Crt Suite 800
Markham ON L3R 0
905 946-3200

(G-3855)
TOOL O MATIC INC
3016 Unionville Rd (16066-3408)
PHONE..................................724 776-3232
Chester A Leighty Jr, *President*
Janet Leighty, *Corp Secy*
EMP: 7
SQ FT: 18,000
SALES (est): 460K **Privately Held**
SIC: 3569 Assembly machines, non-metal-
working

(G-3856)
TRACO DELAWARE INC (DH)
71 Progress Ave (16066-3596)
PHONE..................................724 776-7000
Robert P Randall, *CEO*
John Kalakos, *Vice Pres*
Brett Randall, *Vice Pres*
Fran Stephen, *CFO*
▼ EMP: 19 EST: 1994
SQ FT: 950,000
SALES (est): 198.2MM
SALES (corp-wide): 14B **Publicly Held**
SIC: 3442 3211 3444 3448 Storm doors
or windows, metal; skylight glass; insulat-
ing glass, sealed units; skylights; sheet
metal; greenhouses: prefabricated metal;
aluminum extruded products; public golf
courses
HQ: Arconic Europe Sarl
Rue De La Cite 1
GenCve GE 1204
229 196-000

(G-3857)
**TRI CITY ALUMINUM COMPANY
(DH)**
71 Progress Ave (16066-3511)
PHONE..................................724 799-8917
Robert Randall, *President*
John Kalakos, *COO*
Fran Stephen, *Treasurer*
Rodney L McDonald, *Admin Sec*
▲ EMP: 900 EST: 1943
SQ FT: 950,000
SALES (est): 189MM
SALES (corp-wide): 14B **Publicly Held**
WEB: www.traco.com
SIC: 3442 3354 7992 Storm doors or win-
dows, metal; aluminum extruded prod-
ucts; public golf courses
HQ: Traco Delaware, Inc.
71 Progress Ave
Cranberry Township PA 16066
724 776-7000

(G-3858)
TRU-TECH INDUSTRIES INC (PA)
9025 Marshall Rd (16066-3605)
PHONE..................................724 776-1020
Grant A Colton Jr, *President*
Roy R Schweitzer, *Treasurer*
▲ EMP: 60
SALES (est): 15.4MM **Privately Held**
SIC: 3491 Industrial valves

(G-3859)
**TSB NCLEAR ENRGY USA
GROUP INC**
1000 Westinghouse Dr (16066-5228)
PHONE..................................412 374-4111
Richard Gabbianelli, *President*
F R Coates, *Vice Pres*
Michael F Wilson, *Treasurer*
Nina A Corey, *Admin Sec*
EMP: 4
SALES (est): 4.9B
SALES (corp-wide): 37B **Privately Held**
SIC: 3823 3559 Nuclear reactor controls;
nuclear reactor control rod & drive mech-
anism
HQ: Toshiba Nuclear Energy Holdings (Us)
Inc.
1251 Ave Of Amrcs 400
New York NY 10020

▲ = Import ▼=Export
◆ =Import/Export

(G-3860)
U E C INC
Also Called: Custom Urethane Elastomers
11 Leonberg Rd (16066-3601)
PHONE..................................724 772-5225
Joseph Scaletta Jr, *President*
Joseph Petrocelli, *CFO*
Lisa Golojuh, *Sales Staff*
Robert Pierce, *Marketing Mgr*
Paolo Spinelli, *Manager*
◆ EMP: 95
SQ FT: 90,000
SALES (est): 33MM **Privately Held**
WEB: www.cue-inc.com
SIC: 3083 Thermoplastic laminates: rods,
tubes, plates & sheet

(G-3861)
US CROSSINGS UNLIMITED LLC
20436 Route 19 620-244 (16066-7541)
PHONE...................................888 359-1115
Mike Lind,
EMP: 5 EST: 2014
SQ FT: 20,000
SALES (est): 254.5K **Privately Held**
SIC: 1081 1381 Preparing shafts or tun-
nels, metal mining; test boring, metal min-
ing; drilling oil & gas wells

(G-3862)
VAG USA LLC
9025 Marshall Rd (16066-3605)
PHONE..................................978 544-2511
Kerry Gahm, *Manager*
Mark W Peterson, *Manager*
Patricia M Whaley, *Manager*
EMP: 4 EST: 2016
SALES (est): 289.4K **Privately Held**
SIC: 3494 Valves & pipe fittings

(G-3863)
VERITIV OPERATING COMPANY
Also Called: International Paper
41 Progress Ave Ste A (16066-3511)
PHONE..................................724 776-3122
Art Kort, *Manager*
EMP: 25
SALES (corp-wide): 8.7B **Publicly Held**
WEB: www.internationalpaper.com
SIC: 5111 3089 5113 Printing & writing
paper; thermoformed finished plastic
products; industrial & personal service
paper
HQ: Veritiv Operating Company
1000 Abernathy Rd
Atlanta GA 30328
770 391-8200

(G-3864)
WELLTEC INC
212 Commerce Park Dr (16066-6404)
PHONE..................................724 553-5922
Shannon Scheffe, *Branch Mgr*
EMP: 3
SALES (corp-wide): 172.4MM **Privately
Held**
SIC: 1389 Cementing oil & gas well cas-
ings
HQ: Welltec, Inc.
22440 Merchants Way
Katy TX 77449
281 371-1200

(G-3865)
**WESTINGHOUSE ELECTRIC CO
LLC (HQ)**
1000 Westinghouse Dr (16066-5228)
P.O. Box 3700, Pittsburgh (15230-3700)
PHONE..................................412 374-2020
Shigenori Shiga, *Ch of Bd*
Jose E Gutierrez, *President*
Jack Allen, *President*
Edouard Saab, *President*
Mark Marano, *COO*
◆ EMP: 4000
SALES (est): 5.5B **Privately Held**
WEB: www.westinghousenuclear.com
SIC: 3829 8711 3823 2819 Measuring &
controlling devices; electrical or electronic
engineering; industrial instrmnts msrmnt
display/control process variable; industrial
inorganic chemicals

(G-3866)
**WESTINGHOUSE INDUSTRY
PRODUCTS**
1000 Westinghouse Dr (16066-5228)
PHONE..................................412 374-2020
Lisa J Donahue,
EMP: 5
SALES (est): 162K **Privately Held**
SIC: 3625 Electric controls & control ac-
cessories, industrial
HQ: Westinghouse Electric Company Llc
1000 Westinghouse Dr
Cranberry Township PA 16066
412 374-2020

Cranesville
Erie County

(G-3867)
JEPSON PRECISION TOOL INC
9437 State Rd (16410-1301)
PHONE..................................814 756-4806
Daniel W Jepson, *President*
Gary Smith, *Vice Pres*
EMP: 12
SQ FT: 5,300
SALES (est): 1.8MM **Privately Held**
WEB: www.jepsontool.com
SIC: 3545 3544 Machine tool accessories;
special dies & tools

(G-3868)
LIQUID METER COMPANY INC
Also Called: Limeco
10512 Crosby Cir (16410-9338)
PHONE..................................814 756-5602
Marcia Konopa, *President*
EMP: 5
SALES (est): 1.8MM **Privately Held**
WEB: www.liquidmeterco.com
SIC: 3823 Industrial instrmnts msrmnt dis-
play/control process variable

(G-3869)
RELIANT MOLDING INC
10525 Crosby Cir (16410-9337)
P.O. Box 300 (16410-0300)
PHONE..................................814 756-5522
David Diehl, *President*
Greg Adamson, *Supervisor*
Jen Hartle, *Technology*
EMP: 30
SQ FT: 10,000
SALES (est): 5.6MM **Privately Held**
WEB: www.reliantmolding.com
SIC: 3089 Injection molding of plastics

(G-3870)
**S & S PACKAGING PRODUCTS
INC**
10549 Crosby Cir (16410-9337)
P.O. Box 234 (16410-0234)
PHONE..................................800 633-0272
Dale Stuart, *Owner*
EMP: 25
SQ FT: 28,000
SALES (est): 4.6MM **Privately Held**
WEB: www.sandspackaging.com
SIC: 3081 Packing materials, plastic sheet

(G-3871)
SERVICE RITE
9045 Miller Rd (16410-9618)
PHONE..................................814 774-8716
Michael Harman, *Partner*
EMP: 3
SQ FT: 2,056
SALES (est): 361.2K **Privately Held**
SIC: 2899 Water treating compounds

(G-3872)
TRIPLE CREEK
Also Called: Gerhard Bilek
9225 Fillinger Rd (16410-9611)
PHONE..................................814 756-4500
Gerhard W Bilek, *Owner*
EMP: 4
SALES (est): 114.8K **Privately Held**
SIC: 0831 2099 Gathering of forest prod-
ucts; sugar, industrial maple

Creamery
Montgomery County

(G-3873)
**BROKER BREWING COMPANY
LLC**
1045 Bridge Rd (19430)
PHONE..................................610 304-0822
Kevin Kershner,
EMP: 3 EST: 2015
SALES (est): 101.8K **Privately Held**
SIC: 2082 Malt beverages

Creekside
Indiana County

(G-3874)
ACCURATE LOGGING LLC
153 Aikens Rd (15732-6918)
PHONE..................................724 354-3094
Terry Rayko, *Mng Member*
Beverly Rayko,
Danielle Rayko,
EMP: 7
SQ FT: 5,000
SALES (est): 530K **Privately Held**
SIC: 2411 1629 Logging camps & contrac-
tors; land preparation construction; land
leveling; land clearing contractor

(G-3875)
FAIRMANS ROOF TRUSSES INC
1020 Craig Rd (15732-7031)
PHONE..................................724 349-6778
David A Fairman, *President*
EMP: 32
SQ FT: 14,556
SALES (est): 4.1MM **Privately Held**
SIC: 2439 3444 2952 Trusses, wooden
roof; trusses, except roof: laminated lum-
ber; sheet metalwork; asphalt felts & coat-
ings

(G-3876)
**FAIRMANS WOOD PROCESSING
INC**
1020 Craig Rd (15732-7031)
PHONE..................................724 349-6778
David Fairman, *President*
EMP: 4
SQ FT: 6,000
SALES (est): 1.5MM **Privately Held**
SIC: 2421 Resawing lumber into smaller
dimensions

(G-3877)
STERNS SOFT SERVE LLC
477 Indiana Rd (15732-7606)
P.O. Box 246 (15732-0246)
PHONE..................................724 349-4118
Randy Stern, *Principal*
EMP: 3
SALES (est): 129K **Privately Held**
SIC: 2024 Ice cream, bulk

(G-3878)
WGM GAS COMPANY INC
37 Copper Valley Rd (15732-8500)
PHONE..................................724 397-9600
Mark M Houser, *President*
Garry Houser, *Corp Secy*
Walter L Houser, *Vice Pres*
Mark Houser, *Executive*
EMP: 25
SQ FT: 2,000
SALES (est): 8.4MM **Privately Held**
SIC: 1381 Drilling oil & gas wells

Creighton
Allegheny County

(G-3879)
**AIR PRODUCTS AND
CHEMICALS INC**
500 Freeport Rd (15030-1056)
PHONE..................................724 226-4434
Randy Sobotka, *Branch Mgr*
EMP: 60
SALES (corp-wide): 8.9B **Publicly Held**
WEB: www.airproducts.com
SIC: 2813 5169 Industrial gases; industrial
gases
PA: Air Products And Chemicals, Inc.
7201 Hamilton Blvd
Allentown PA 18195
610 481-4911

(G-3880)
BUHL BROS PRINTING INC
316 Crawford Run Rd (15030-1013)
PHONE..................................724 335-0970
EMP: 10
SQ FT: 4,800
SALES (est): 1.3MM **Privately Held**
SIC: 2752 2759 Lithographic Commercial
Printing Commercial Printing

(G-3881)
**COMPLETE INTRVNOUS
ACCESS SVCS**
828 Front St Rear (15030-1102)
PHONE..................................724 226-2618
George Kabay, *CEO*
Amy Kabay, *President*
EMP: 10
SALES (est): 1.3MM **Privately Held**
WEB: www.ciasinc.com
SIC: 2834 Solutions, pharmaceutical

(G-3882)
CREIGHTON PRINTING INC
917 Freeport Rd (15030-1049)
PHONE..................................724 224-0444
Arthur R Kuchta, *President*
Paul Kuchta, *Vice Pres*
Rose Kuchta, *Treasurer*
Bernard Kuchta, *Admin Sec*
EMP: 4 EST: 1928
SQ FT: 10,000
SALES (est): 596.5K **Privately Held**
SIC: 2752 2759 Commercial printing, off-
set; letterpress printing

(G-3883)
PITT PENN OIL CO LLC
426 Freeport Rd (15030-1068)
P.O. Box 296 (15030-0296)
PHONE..................................813 968-9635
Randy D Rinicella,
EMP: 90
SQ FT: 120,000
SALES (est): 12.9MM
SALES (corp-wide): 7MM **Publicly Held**
WEB: www.industriallubricants.org
SIC: 2899 Chemical preparations
PA: Industrial Enterprises Of America, Inc.
651 Holiday Dr Ste 300
Pittsburgh PA 15220
412 928-2056

(G-3884)
**PITTSBURGH GLASS WORKS
LLC**
150 Ferry St (15030-1101)
P.O. Box 269, Crestline OH (44827-0269)
PHONE..................................419 683-2400
Jen Ingram, *Maint Spvr*
Mark Patterson, *Electrical Engi*
John Felker, *Human Res Dir*
Joe Stas, *Branch Mgr*
EMP: 300 **Privately Held**
SIC: 2851 Paints & allied products
HQ: Pittsburgh Glass Works, Llc
30 Isabella St Ste 500
Pittsburgh PA 15212

(G-3885)
PPG INDUSTRIES INC
150 Ferry St (15030-1101)
PHONE..................................724 224-6500
Randy Johnson, *Principal*
EMP: 24
SALES (corp-wide): 15.3B **Publicly Held**
SIC: 2851 Paints & allied products
PA: Ppg Industries, Inc.
1 Ppg Pl
Pittsburgh PA 15272
412 434-3131

GEOGRAPHIC

Crescent
Allegheny County

(G-3886)
BHM METAL PRODUCTS & INDS LLC (PA)
33 Mcgovern Blvd (15046-5452)
P.O. Box 76, Mongaup Valley NY (12762-0076)
PHONE..................570 785-2032
Robert D Gordon, *CEO*
James S Gordon,
EMP: 5 **EST:** 2012
SQ FT: 22,000
SALES (est): 701.6K **Privately Held**
SIC: 3469 Stamping metal for the trade

(G-3887)
PREMIER PAN COMPANY INC
Also Called: American Pan Company
33 Mcgovern Blvd (15046-5452)
PHONE..................724 457-4220
Russell T Bundy, *President*
David Bundy, *Vice Pres*
John Bundy Jr, *Vice Pres*
John Logan, *Prdtn Mgr*
Tim Podnar, *Engineer*
◆ **EMP:** 75
SALES (est): 20MM **Privately Held**
SIC: 3469 5046 Metal stampings; bakery equipment & supplies

(G-3888)
PRISM POWDER COATING SERVICES
Also Called: Prism Performance
1232 Mckee St (15046-5337)
PHONE..................724 457-2836
Joyce Kriger, *Owner*
EMP: 4
SQ FT: 1,600
SALES: 80K **Privately Held**
SIC: 3471 Plating & polishing

(G-3889)
SPORTIN MY STUFF
148 Mcgovern Blvd (15046-5300)
PHONE..................724 457-7005
Edward Ludwiczak, *Principal*
EMP: 5
SALES (est): 453.9K **Privately Held**
SIC: 5085 5084 2759 Textile printers' supplies; printing trades machinery; equipment & supplies; screen printing

Cresco
Monroe County

(G-3890)
ANDERSON PRODUCTS INCORPORATED
1 Weiler Dr (18326-9804)
PHONE..................570 595-7495
Casper Noto, *President*
Christopher Weiler, *President*
Karl Weiler, *Chairman*
EMP: 80
SQ FT: 250,000
SALES (est): 6.2MM
SALES (corp-wide): 76.5MM **Privately Held**
WEB: www.andersonproducts.com
SIC: 3991 Brooms & brushes
PA: Weiler Corporation
1 Weiler Dr
Cresco PA 18326
570 595-7495

(G-3891)
BILL BARRY EXCAVATING INC
174 Quarry Ln (18326-7967)
PHONE..................570 595-2269
William Barry, *President*
Charlene Barry, *Vice Pres*
EMP: 3
SQ FT: 8,500
SALES: 350K **Privately Held**
SIC: 1794 1442 Excavation work; common sand mining

(G-3892)
CALLIES CANDY KITCHENS INC
Also Called: Callie's Pretzel Factory
Rr 390 (18326)
P.O. Box 126, Mountainhome (18342-0126)
PHONE..................570 595-3257
Mark Reisenwitz, *Manager*
EMP: 24
SALES (corp-wide): 2.6MM **Privately Held**
WEB: www.calliescandy.com
SIC: 2064 Candy & other confectionery products
PA: Callie's Candy Kitchens Inc
1111 Rte 390
Mountainhome PA 18342
570 595-2280

(G-3893)
E M UNITED WLDG & FABRICATION
7404 W Dogwood Ln (18326-7925)
PHONE..................570 595-0695
Eugene Mahon, *President*
EMP: 4
SALES (est): 200K **Privately Held**
SIC: 7692 Welding repair

(G-3894)
KRECO ANTENNAS
Also Called: Herb Kreckman Antennas
3340 Spruce Cabin Rd (18326-7918)
PHONE..................570 595-2212
Glenn Kreckman, *Owner*
EMP: 3 **EST:** 1953
SALES (est): 300K **Privately Held**
WEB: www.krecoantennas.com
SIC: 3663 Antennas, transmitting & communications

(G-3895)
SWIMTECH DISTRIBUTING INC
191 Rr 390 (18326)
PHONE..................570 595-7680
Mark Vultaggio, *President*
EMP: 3
SQ FT: 250
SALES: 650K **Privately Held**
SIC: 3949 5091 Swimming pools, except plastic; swimming pools, equipment & supplies

(G-3896)
WEILER CORPORATION (PA)
1 Weiler Dr (18326-9804)
P.O. Box 149 (18326-0149)
PHONE..................570 595-7495
Karl M Weiler, *Ch of Bd*
Christopher Weiler, *President*
Bob Vogt, *Production*
Treena Williams, *Production*
Pauline Geiger, *Buyer*
◆ **EMP:** 400
SQ FT: 250,000
SALES (est): 76.5MM **Privately Held**
WEB: www.weilercorp.com
SIC: 3991 3291 Brushes, household or industrial; abrasive products

Cresson
Cambria County

(G-3897)
ANTONIOS MANUFACTURING INC
Also Called: Ajax Comb Company
800 2nd St (16630-1142)
P.O. Box 222 (16630-0222)
PHONE..................814 886-8171
Anthony R Romani II, *President*
Gina Romani, *Corp Secy*
EMP: 13
SQ FT: 45,853
SALES (est): 907.5K **Privately Held**
WEB: www.antoniosmfg.com
SIC: 3999 Combs, except hard rubber

(G-3898)
GRAPHIC CONNECTIONS
813 Front St 2 (16630-1115)
PHONE..................814 948-5810
Kim Mason, *Owner*
EMP: 3
SALES (est): 181.5K **Privately Held**
WEB: www.graphicconnections.net
SIC: 2759 Screen printing

(G-3899)
JENNMAR CORPORATION
Also Called: Keystone Bolt Division
Rr 53 Box S (16630)
P.O. Box 187 (16630-0187)
PHONE..................814 886-4121
Mary Goyldyn, *Branch Mgr*
EMP: 100
SALES (corp-wide): 571.6MM **Privately Held**
SIC: 3532 3452 Mining machinery; bolts, nuts, rivets & washers
HQ: Jennmar Of Pennsylvania, Llc
258 Kappa Dr
Pittsburgh PA 15238
412 963-9071

(G-3900)
VICTORY ATHLETICS
324 Laurel Ave (16630-1121)
PHONE..................814 886-4866
Bryon Mazzocco, *Owner*
EMP: 3
SALES: 100K **Privately Held**
SIC: 2759 Screen printing

(G-3901)
WEST PENN MFG TECH LLC
1027 Front St (16630-1179)
PHONE..................814 886-4100
George Bohrer,
EMP: 18
SALES (est): 1.3MM **Privately Held**
SIC: 3999 Manufacturing industries

(G-3902)
WHOLESALE LINENS SUPPLY INC
720 2nd St (16630-1140)
P.O. Box 316 (16630-0316)
PHONE..................814 886-7000
EMP: 4
SALES: 950K **Privately Held**
SIC: 2299 Textile Products

Cressona
Schuylkill County

(G-3903)
CRESSONA TEXTILE WASTE INC
Front And Rail Rd St (17929)
P.O. Box 56 (17929-0056)
PHONE..................570 385-4556
Lee Winston, *President*
EMP: 4
SALES (corp-wide): 1.7MM **Privately Held**
SIC: 2211 Coutil, cotton
PA: Cressona Textile Waste Inc
Front & Railroad St
Cressona PA 17929
570 385-4556

(G-3904)
HYDRO EXTRUSION USA LLC
Also Called: Sapa Industrial Extrusions
53 Pottsville St (17929-1217)
P.O. Box 518, Hazleton (18201-0518)
PHONE..................318 878-9703
Charles Straface, *Principal*
Dennis Menzies, *Director*
EMP: 207
SALES (corp-wide): 13.8B **Privately Held**
WEB: www.alumag.com
SIC: 3354 Aluminum extruded products
HQ: Hydro Extrusion Usa, Llc
6250 N River Rd Ste 5000
Rosemont IL 60018

(G-3905)
KAYTEE PRODUCTS INCORPORATED
55 N Sillyman St (17929-1120)
PHONE..................570 385-1530
Dave Peleschak, *Purchasing*
Skip Conway, *Branch Mgr*
EMP: 50
SALES (corp-wide): 2B **Publicly Held**
SIC: 2048 Bird food, prepared
HQ: Kaytee Products Incorporated
521 Clay St
Chilton WI 53014
920 849-2321

(G-3906)
NORTHEAST PRESTRESSED PDTS LLC
Also Called: N E Prestressed Products
121 River St (17929-1108)
PHONE..................570 385-2352
Gary Frantz, *Purch Agent*
Scott Schwalm, *Purchasing*
Lisa Gehring, *Human Res Mgr*
Daniel R Hawbaker,
Michael Hawbaker,
▲ **EMP:** 139
SALES (est): 25.4MM **Privately Held**
SIC: 3272 Concrete products, precast

(G-3907)
SAPA NORTH AMERICA INC
53 Pottsville St (17929-1224)
PHONE..................877 922-7272
Charlie Straface, *President*
Geir Kvernmo, *Vice Pres*
Todd Presnick, *CFO*
Pete Vandervelde,
▲ **EMP:** 400
SALES (est): 168.4MM
SALES (corp-wide): 13.8B **Privately Held**
SIC: 3354 Aluminum extruded products
HQ: Hydro Extrusion Usa, Llc
6250 N River Rd Ste 5000
Rosemont IL 60018

(G-3908)
ST MARTIN AMERICA INC
Also Called: St, Martin Cabinetry
87 Schuylkill St (17929-1408)
PHONE..................570 593-8596
Peter Lee, *President*
▲ **EMP:** 32
SQ FT: 60,000
SALES (est): 4.4MM
SALES (corp-wide): 8.1MM **Privately Held**
SIC: 2434 Wood kitchen cabinets
PA: Shanghai Teamefforts Wooden Co., Ltd.
No.8, Yanzhao North Road, Donghai Town, Nanhui District
Shanghai 20132
215 826-0430

Croydon
Bucks County

(G-3909)
A B M MOTORS INC
300 Linton Ave (19021-6845)
PHONE..................215 781-9400
Robert Beatty, *President*
EMP: 6
SQ FT: 8,000
SALES (est): 560K **Privately Held**
WEB: www.abmmotors.com
SIC: 3621 Electric motor & generator parts

(G-3910)
ARMOLOY CO OF PHILADELPHIA
1105 Miller Ave (19021-7531)
PHONE..................215 788-0841
William Marko, *President*
Robert G Grosser Sr, *President*
EMP: 5
SQ FT: 4,800
SALES: 480K **Privately Held**
WEB: www.armoloycompany.com
SIC: 3479 Coating of metals & formed products

(G-3911)
B-TEC SOLUTIONS INC
913 Cedar Ave (19021-7501)
PHONE..................215 785-2400
John Brenner Jr, *President*
Warren Geiger, *Vice Pres*
Matt Fisher, *QC Mgr*
Yefim Chernyakhovsky, *Engineer*

Luke Stone, *Manager*
EMP: 75
SQ FT: 73,000
SALES (est): 23.8MM **Privately Held**
WEB: www.btecsolutions.com
SIC: 3599 3544 3469 3089 Machine shop, jobbing & repair; special dies & tools; stamping metal for the trade; plastic processing

(G-3912)
BELLISIMO LLC
2925 State Rd (19021-6960)
PHONE..................................215 781-1700
Nicholas Lynch, *Mng Member*
Michael C Ross,
EMP: 7 **EST:** 1997
SQ FT: 80,000
SALES (est): 1.1MM **Privately Held**
WEB: www.vinylcompounds.com
SIC: 2821 Molding compounds, plastics

(G-3913)
CIPCO INDUSTRIES LLC
956 Washington Ave (19021-7563)
PHONE..................................215 785-2976
James R Cipolloni,
EMP: 5
SALES (est): 619K **Privately Held**
SIC: 3599 Machine shop, jobbing & repair

(G-3914)
COMFORT SPORTSWEAR INC
705 Linton Ave (19021-6850)
PHONE..................................215 781-0300
Harold F Bernhardt, *President*
Fred S Bernhardt, *Vice Pres*
Linda Walker, *Office Mgr*
EMP: 9 **EST:** 1947
SQ FT: 8,000
SALES (est): 72.6K **Privately Held**
SIC: 2252 Socks

(G-3915)
COMFORT STUMP SOCK MFG CO
Also Called: Comfort Products
931 River Rd (19021-7540)
PHONE..................................215 781-0300
Harold Bernhardt, *President*
Fred S Bernhardt, *Vice Pres*
Lorraine Bernhardt, *Treasurer*
▲ **EMP:** 15 **EST:** 1969
SQ FT: 10,000
SALES (est): 1.5MM **Privately Held**
SIC: 3842 Socks, stump

(G-3916)
DOW CHEMICAL COMPANY
2900 River Rd (19021-6946)
PHONE..................................215 785-8000
EMP: 19
SALES (est): 2.9MM **Privately Held**
SIC: 2869 Industrial organic chemicals

(G-3917)
G N F PRODUTS INC
1025 Washington Ave (19021-7568)
PHONE..................................215 781-6222
Sina Pan, *Principal*
◆ **EMP:** 4
SALES (est): 473.3K **Privately Held**
SIC: 2381 Gloves, work: woven or knit, made from purchased materials

(G-3918)
GENERAL PARTITION COMPANY INC
916 Washington Ave (19021-7589)
P.O. Box 97 (19021-0097)
PHONE..................................215 785-1000
James W Houseman, *President*
Florence E Houseman, *Corp Secy*
Richard Houseman, *Vice Pres*
EMP: 32
SQ FT: 10,000
SALES (est): 6.6MM **Privately Held**
WEB: www.generalpartition.com
SIC: 2653 2631 Partitions, corrugated: made from purchased materials; paperboard mills

(G-3919)
INDUSTRIAL DIESEL POWER INC
933 Washington Ave (19021-7562)
P.O. Box 445, Fairless Hills (19030-0445)
PHONE..................................215 781-2378
Michael Shimkus, *President*
Bernie Bernhauser, *Vice Pres*
Jim Ford, *Manager*
Dale Everett, *Admin Sec*
EMP: 12
SQ FT: 8,000
SALES (est): 4.6MM **Privately Held**
WEB: www.idpinc.com
SIC: 5013 7699 3519 Automotive engines & engine parts; engine repair & replacement, non-automotive; diesel, semi-diesel or duel-fuel engines, including marine; diesel engine rebuilding; engines, diesel & semi-diesel or dual-fuel

(G-3920)
J-MAR METAL FABRICATING CO
1025 Washington Ave (19021-7591)
P.O. Box 160 (19021-0160)
PHONE..................................215 785-6521
John Marricone Jr, *President*
John Marricone Sr, *Chairman*
EMP: 8 **EST:** 1965
SQ FT: 25,000
SALES (est): 799.5K **Privately Held**
WEB: www.j-marmetal.com
SIC: 3559 3444 Automotive maintenance equipment; sheet metalwork

(G-3921)
NEM-PAK LLC
1117 Cedar Ave (19021)
PHONE..................................215 785-6430
Robert Enders, *Mng Member*
Gen Oats,
EMP: 5
SALES (est): 726.1K **Privately Held**
SIC: 2655 Hampers, shipping (vulcanized fiber): purchased material

(G-3922)
NORSHEL INDUSTRIES INC
2933 River Rd (19021-6972)
PHONE..................................215 788-2200
Eric Leibowitz, *President*
Norman Leibowitz, *Principal*
Rochelle Leibowitz, *Principal*
Aaron Leibowitz, *Vice Pres*
Jack Rose, *Warehouse Mgr*
▲ **EMP:** 35
SQ FT: 72,000
SALES (est): 6.6MM **Privately Held**
WEB: www.norshel.com
SIC: 2392 Mops, floor & dust

(G-3923)
OLDCASTLE PRECAST INC
1900 Pennsylvania Ave (19021-6800)
PHONE..................................888 965-3227
EMP: 51
SALES (corp-wide): 29.7B **Privately Held**
SIC: 3272 Concrete products
HQ: Oldcastle Infrastructure, Inc.
1002 15th St Sw Ste 110
Auburn WA 98001
253 833-2777

(G-3924)
PRINCETON SECURITY TECH LLC
2925 State Rd (19021-6960)
PHONE..................................609 915-9700
Paul B Weber,
EMP: 4
SALES (est): 100K **Privately Held**
SIC: 3826 Analytical instruments

(G-3925)
PRINT SHOP
945 Washington Ave (19021-7562)
PHONE..................................215 788-1883
George Haas, *President*
EMP: 3
SALES (est): 380K **Privately Held**
SIC: 2752 Commercial printing, offset

(G-3926)
RAILWAY SPECIALTIES CORP
2979 State Rd (19021-6976)
PHONE..................................215 788-9242
Frederic H Calkins Jr, *President*
Thomas E Calkins, *Treasurer*
EMP: 20 **EST:** 1915
SQ FT: 40,000
SALES (est): 4.6MM **Privately Held**
WEB: www.railwayspecialties.com
SIC: 3441 3442 3354 Ship sections, prefabricated metal; metal doors, sash & trim; aluminum extruded products

(G-3927)
ROWA CORPORATION
110 Phyllis Ave (19021-7500)
PHONE..................................609 567-8600
David Baglia, *President*
▲ **EMP:** 1
SALES (est): 4.1MM **Privately Held**
SIC: 2899 Chemical supplies for foundries

(G-3928)
SHEDAKER METAL ARTS INC
519 Browns Ln (19021-6601)
PHONE..................................215 788-3383
Joseph W Shedaker, *President*
John A Shedaker, *Corp Secy*
David Shedaker, *Vice Pres*
Paul Shedaker, *Vice Pres*
Robert J Shedaker, *Vice Pres*
EMP: 25 **EST:** 1961
SQ FT: 14,225
SALES (est): 1.7MM **Privately Held**
SIC: 3446 Ornamental metalwork

(G-3929)
STANDARD FUSEE CORPORATION
Also Called: Orion Safety Products
2975 State Rd (19021-6976)
PHONE..................................215 788-3001
Earl Brown, *Manager*
EMP: 6
SALES (est): 838.6K
SALES (corp-wide): 20.2MM **Privately Held**
WEB: www.orionsignals.com
SIC: 2899 Fusees: highway, marine or railroad; flares; flares, fireworks & similar preparations
PA: Standard Fusee Corporation
28320 Saint Michaels Rd
Easton MD 21601
410 822-0318

(G-3930)
TEK-TEMP INSTRUMENTS INC
401 Magnolia Ave (19021-6009)
PHONE..................................215 788-5528
Rick Ulerick, *President*
Joel Zober, *Vice Pres*
Reynald St Fleur, *Prdtn Mgr*
EMP: 20
SQ FT: 25,000
SALES (est): 3.4MM **Privately Held**
WEB: www.tek-tempinstruments.com
SIC: 3585 Heating & air conditioning combination units

(G-3931)
TELEX METALS LLC
105 Phyllis Ave (19021-7509)
PHONE..................................215 781-6335
James Maguire, *General Mgr*
Lara Welgs, *Sales Staff*
Matthew Danish, *Mng Member*
John Durule,
▲ **EMP:** 31
SQ FT: 18,255
SALES (est): 12.4MM **Privately Held**
SIC: 3341 Recovery & refining of nonferrous metals

(G-3932)
WESTROCK COMPANY
3001 State Rd (19021-6962)
PHONE..................................215 826-2497
EMP: 3
SALES (corp-wide): 16.2B **Publicly Held**
SIC: 2631 Paperboard mills
HQ: Wrkco Inc.
1000 Abernathy Rd
Atlanta GA 30328
770 448-2193

(G-3933)
WESTROCK PACKAGING INC (DH)
3001 State Rd (19021-6962)
PHONE..................................215 785-3350
Ellen Wook, *President*
Brian Michael, *CFO*
▲ **EMP:** 55 **EST:** 1956
SQ FT: 100,000
SALES (est): 11.7MM
SALES (corp-wide): 16.2B **Publicly Held**
WEB: www.gilbrethusa.com
SIC: 2754 3082 2672 3599 Seals: gravure printing; tubes, unsupported plastic; labels (unprinted), gummed: made from purchased materials; custom machinery; packaging paper & plastics film, coated & laminated
HQ: Westrock Converting, Llc
1000 Abernathy Rd Ste 125
Atlanta GA 30328
770 448-2193

(G-3934)
ZAMPELL REFRACTORIES INC
125 Phyllis Ave (19021-7509)
PHONE..................................215 788-3000
James Zampell, *Branch Mgr*
EMP: 31
SALES (corp-wide): 47.4MM **Privately Held**
SIC: 1711 3255 Heating systems repair & maintenance; clay refractories; firebrick, clay
PA: Zampell Refractories, Inc.
3 Stanley Tucker Dr
Newburyport MA 01950
978 465-0055

Crum Lynne
Delaware County

(G-3935)
BAKER PETROLITE LLC
4 Saville Ave (19022)
PHONE..................................610 876-2200
Syvane Fontaine, *Manager*
EMP: 18
SALES (corp-wide): 121.6B **Publicly Held**
WEB: www.bakerpetrolite.com
SIC: 5169 4225 2899 Chemicals & allied products; general warehousing; chemical preparations
HQ: Baker Petrolite Llc
12645 W Airport Blvd
Sugar Land TX 77478
281 276-5400

(G-3936)
DELRI INDUSTRIAL SUPPLIES INC
1431 Chester Pike (19022-1298)
P.O. Box 125 (19022-0125)
PHONE..................................610 833-2070
William F Schollins, *CEO*
A Thomas Nicholl, *President*
Albert T Nicholl, *Vice Pres*
EMP: 7 **EST:** 1964
SQ FT: 15,000
SALES (est): 1.5MM **Privately Held**
WEB: www.delri.com
SIC: 3492 7699 5084 5085 Hose & tube fittings & assemblies, hydraulic/pneumatic; hydraulic equipment repair; hydraulic systems equipment & supplies; industrial supplies

(G-3937)
FIZZANO BROS INC (PA)
1776 Chester Pike (19022-1223)
PHONE..................................610 833-1100
Thomas Fizzano, *President*
John T Fizzano, *Corp Secy*
Guy T Fizzano, *Vice Pres*
EMP: 90
SQ FT: 10,000
SALES (est): 13.4MM **Privately Held**
WEB: www.fizzano.com
SIC: 3271 5211 Blocks, concrete or cinder: standard; concrete & cinder block

Crystal Spring
Fulton County

(G-3938)
RODERICK DUVALL
Also Called: Duvall Lumber
2190 S Valley Rd (15536-7207)
PHONE...........................814 735-4969
Roderick Duvall, *Owner*
Carolyn Duvall, *Co-Owner*
EMP: 4
SALES: 631.2K **Privately Held**
SIC: 2411 2611 4212 2431 Logging; pulp mills; local trucking, without storage; millwork; sawmills & planing mills, general

(G-3939)
WILLIAMS AND SONS LUMBER CO (PA)
12142 Old 126 (15536-8809)
PHONE...........................814 735-4295
James A Williams Sr, *President*
EMP: 20
SQ FT: 4,000
SALES (est): 3.9MM **Privately Held**
SIC: 2421 Lumber: rough, sawed or planed

Cuddy
Allegheny County

(G-3940)
BLACK VIPER ENERGY SERVICES
3 Nicholson Dr (15031-9749)
PHONE...........................432 561-8801
Clemence Floyd, *Manager*
EMP: 74
SALES (corp-wide): 83.5MM **Privately Held**
SIC: 1381 Drilling oil & gas wells
PA: Black Viper Energy Services, Ltd
11220 W County Road 127
Odessa TX 79765
432 561-8801

(G-3941)
BLASTING PRODUCTS INC
710 Millers Run Rd (15031-9742)
PHONE...........................412 221-5722
Alex Senules, *President*
EMP: 35
SQ FT: 12,000
SALES (est): 3.2MM **Privately Held**
SIC: 2892 Explosive cartridges for concussion forming of metal

(G-3942)
EDWIN BELL COOPERAGE COMPANY
Also Called: Bell, Edwin Containers
697 Millers Run Rd (15031-9700)
P.O. Box 294 (15031-0294)
PHONE...........................412 221-1830
James D Clister, *President*
Kevin Brown, *Corp Secy*
Archie Strimel, *Vice Pres*
▲ EMP: 50
SQ FT: 37,500
SALES (est): 20.7MM **Privately Held**
WEB: www.bellcontainers.com
SIC: 2653 Boxes, corrugated: made from purchased materials

(G-3943)
ELITE MIDSTREAM SERVICES INC
3 Nicholson Dr (15031-9749)
P.O. Box 433, Morgan (15064-0433)
PHONE...........................412 220-3082
Keith Keane, *Principal*
EMP: 46 EST: 2013
SALES: 10MM **Privately Held**
SIC: 1623 3491 Pipeline construction; industrial valves

(G-3944)
ZOTTOLA FAB A PA BUS TR
5 Mcclane St (15031-9739)
PHONE...........................412 221-4488

Eugene H Zottola, *President*
Fred Zottola, *Vice Pres*
Darla Zotolla, *Treasurer*
Toni Zottola, *Admin Sec*
EMP: 9
SQ FT: 10,000
SALES (est): 1.1MM **Privately Held**
SIC: 3446 3441 Architectural metalwork; fabricated structural metal

Curryville
Blair County

(G-3945)
BEDFORD FARM BUREAU COOP ASSN
Rr 866 (16631)
PHONE...........................814 793-2721
James Shades, *Branch Mgr*
EMP: 10
SALES (corp-wide): 3.7MM **Privately Held**
SIC: 2041 2048 2875 8699 Flour & other grain mill products; prepared feeds; fertilizers, mixing only; farm bureau
PA: Bedford Farm Bureau Co-Operative Association
102 Industrial Ave
Bedford PA 15522
814 623-6194

Curwensville
Clearfield County

(G-3946)
B D & D SPCLTY FABRICATION MCH
1181 Bailor Rd (16833-1563)
PHONE...........................814 236-3810
Darrell Smith,
William Smochek,
Dennis Sunderlin,
▲ EMP: 20
SALES (est): 3.1MM **Privately Held**
SIC: 3441 Building components, structural steel

(G-3947)
CASEWORK CABINETRY CNSTR
1382 Schofield Street Ext (16833-6850)
PHONE...........................814 236-7601
Robert D Ingram, *Owner*
EMP: 4
SALES (est): 438.5K **Privately Held**
SIC: 5211 3553 Cabinets, kitchen; cabinet makers' machinery

(G-3948)
CHAMPION CHOICE SPORTS
340 State St (16833-1239)
PHONE...........................814 236-2930
Icie Redden, *Partner*
Fred A Redden, *Partner*
Rick R Redden, *Partner*
Kori Swatsworth, *Partner*
EMP: 5
SALES (est): 321.2K **Privately Held**
SIC: 5941 2759 Bicycle & bicycle parts; screen printing

(G-3949)
COULTER LOGGING
456 Ridge Ave (16833-7254)
PHONE...........................814 236-2855
Robert Coulter, *Principal*
EMP: 3
SALES (est): 206.2K **Privately Held**
SIC: 2411 Logging camps & contractors

(G-3950)
CRG RESOURCES LLC
214 Norris Rd (16833-6523)
PHONE...........................814 571-7190
Charles Guarino, *Principal*
EMP: 4 EST: 2012
SALES (est): 276K **Privately Held**
SIC: 1389 7349 Gas field services; cleaning service, industrial or commercial

(G-3951)
GILLENS LOGGING INC
92 Patty Ln (16833-7153)
PHONE...........................814 236-3999
James Gillen, *Principal*
EMP: 3
SALES (est): 202.6K **Privately Held**
SIC: 2411 Logging

(G-3952)
GLOBAL CUSTOM DECORATING INC
82 Water St (16833-1280)
PHONE...........................814 236-2110
Dean Rosow, *President*
Pamela Cordone, *Vice Pres*
▼ EMP: 50
SQ FT: 5,000
SALES (est): 3.8MM **Privately Held**
SIC: 3211 Flat glass

(G-3953)
HIPPS TOOL & DESIGN
146 Bridgeport Rd (16833-7010)
PHONE...........................814 236-3600
Jeff Hipps, *Partner*
Michael Hipps, *Partner*
Aurther Price, *Partner*
Beth Hipps, *General Ptnr*
EMP: 6
SALES: 102K **Privately Held**
WEB: www.hipps-tool.com
SIC: 3441 7389 Fabricated structural metal;

(G-3954)
MOUNT SVAGE SPCLTY RFRACTORIES
4882 Curwensville (16833)
P.O. Box 60 (16833-0060)
PHONE...........................814 236-8370
Jerry Zawlatski, *Partner*
EMP: 12
SALES (est): 907.3K **Privately Held**
SIC: 3297 Brick refractories

(G-3955)
STARR FINANCIAL GROUP INC (PA)
861 Bailey Rd (16833-7174)
PHONE...........................814 236-0910
Ken Starr Sr, *President*
Judy Starr, *Corp Secy*
Ken Richard Starr, *Vice Pres*
EMP: 4
SQ FT: 1,500
SALES: 340K **Privately Held**
SIC: 2084 Wines

(G-3956)
WICKETT & CRAIG AMERICA INC
120 Cooper Rd (16833-1542)
PHONE...........................814 236-2220
John C H Lee, *President*
Prasad Inaganti, *COO*
Stanley Spaid, *Vice Pres*
Chin M Lim, *VP Opers*
Kylie Ruffner, *Sales Staff*
▲ EMP: 90
SALES (est): 19MM **Privately Held**
SIC: 3111 Tanneries, leather

Daisytown
Washington County

(G-3957)
AMERICAN MACHINING INC
715 Scenic Dr (15427-1139)
PHONE...........................724 938-2120
William E Roach Jr, *President*
Donna M Roach, *Vice Pres*
EMP: 7
SALES (est): 1MM **Privately Held**
SIC: 3599 Machine shop, jobbing & repair

Dallas
Luzerne County

(G-3958)
BAL NUT INC (PA)
191 E Center Hill Rd (18612-1101)
PHONE...........................570 675-2712
Vito Balice, *President*
Domicella Balice, *Treasurer*
EMP: 7
SQ FT: 1,800
SALES (est): 918.1K **Privately Held**
SIC: 2068 5441 5145 Salted & roasted nuts & seeds; nuts; nuts, salted or roasted

(G-3959)
BSC TECHNOLOGIES INC
61 Sterling Ave (18612-1517)
PHONE...........................570 825-9196
EMP: 9 EST: 2008
SALES (est): 877.5K **Privately Held**
SIC: 3589 Mfg Service Industry Machinery

(G-3960)
COATES ELECTROGRAPHICS INC
555 Country Club Rd (18612-9241)
PHONE...........................570 675-1131
Ian Gammage, *President*
Dr Nick Ivory, *Exec VP*
James Collins, *Treasurer*
James P Harris Jr, *Admin Sec*
▲ EMP: 40 EST: 1960
SQ FT: 38,000
SALES: 12.5MM
SALES (corp-wide): 7.1B **Privately Held**
SIC: 2899 3861 Chemical preparations; photographic equipment & supplies
HQ: Sun Chemical Corporation
35 Waterview Blvd Ste 100
Parsippany NJ 07054
973 404-6000

(G-3961)
COLUMBIA PORCH SHADE CO
583 Orange Rd (18612-6129)
P.O. Box 248 (18612-0248)
PHONE...........................570 639-1223
Lee R Isaac, *President*
EMP: 4 EST: 1950
SQ FT: 8,500
SALES (est): 330K **Privately Held**
SIC: 2591 Porch shades, wood slat; window shades

(G-3962)
FABWORKS INC
Rr 3 Box 272-4 (18612)
PHONE...........................570 814-1515
Laurie Kutz, *President*
Laurie Barna, *Principal*
EMP: 11
SQ FT: 1,000
SALES: 625K **Privately Held**
SIC: 3541 Machine tools, metal cutting type

(G-3963)
MOTTO GRAPHICS INC
469 Orange Rd (18612-6123)
PHONE...........................570 639-5555
Tom Motovidlak, *President*
EMP: 4
SQ FT: 4,800
SALES (est): 290K **Privately Held**
SIC: 2752 2759 Commercial printing, offset; envelopes: printing

(G-3964)
OFFSET PAPERBACK MFRS INC (DH)
Also Called: Studio Print Group
2211 Memorial Hwy (18612-9205)
PHONE...........................570 675-5261
David Liess, *President*
Jack O'Donnell, *Vice Pres*
Jack Odonnell, *Vice Pres*
Bob Scheifflee, *Plant Mgr*
Dave Thomas, *Prdtn Mgr*
EMP: 725

GEOGRAPHIC

SALES (est): 131.2MM
SALES (corp-wide): 75.3MM **Privately Held**
SIC: 2731 2752 Book publishing; commercial printing, offset

(G-3965)
PAYNE PRINTERY INC
Also Called: Payne Prcsion Clor Lithography
3235 Memorial Hwy (18612-9229)
PHONE.............................570 675-1147
Bretton R Gauntlet, *President*
Bretton R Gauntlett, *President*
Shaun Daney, *Vice Pres*
Joe Sholtis, *Warehouse Mgr*
Bonnie Levy, *Manager*
EMP: 59
SQ FT: 42,000
SALES: 8.3MM **Privately Held**
WEB: www.payneinc.net
SIC: 2759 2752 7336 2796 Letterpress printing; commercial printing, offset; graphic arts & related design; platemaking services; typesetting; bookbinding & related work

(G-3966)
PENNMARK TECHNOLOGIES CORP
Also Called: Pulverman
1170 Lower Demunds Rd (18612-9033)
PHONE.............................570 255-5000
Randy Mark, *President*
Scott Stephenson, *Vice Pres*
Jennifer Williams, *Vice Pres*
Howard Dinstel, *Purch Mgr*
▲ **EMP:** 140
SQ FT: 80,000
SALES (est): 34.3MM **Privately Held**
WEB: www.kingstonsales.com
SIC: 1761 3443 3444 Sheet metalwork; fabricated plate work (boiler shop); sheet metalwork

(G-3967)
QUALITY METAL PRODUCTS INC
718 Orange Rd (18612-6112)
P.O. Box 273 (18612-0273)
PHONE.............................570 333-4248
Alan E Reese, *President*
Barry Reese, *Principal*
EMP: 36
SQ FT: 77,000
SALES (est): 6.1MM **Privately Held**
WEB: www.qualmet.com
SIC: 3541 3544 Machine tools, metal cutting: exotic (explosive, etc.); special dies & tools

(G-3968)
STEVE SHANNON TIRE COMPANY INC
4090 Memorial Hwy (18612-8101)
PHONE.............................570 675-8473
Steve Shannon, *Owner*
EMP: 7
SALES (corp-wide): 25MM **Privately Held**
SIC: 5531 3011 Automotive tires; tires & inner tubes
PA: Steve Shannon Tire Company, Inc.
920 Millville Rd
Bloomsburg PA 17815
570 387-6387

(G-3969)
TONER HOLDINGS LLC
Also Called: Coates Toners
555 Country Club Rd (18612-9241)
P.O. Box 160 (18612-0160)
PHONE.............................570 675-1131
Paul R Clothier, *CEO*
James F Collins, *Controller*
Lawrence Berti,
Paul Clothier,
Jim Collins,
◆ **EMP:** 30
SQ FT: 50,000
SALES (est): 9.8MM **Privately Held**
SIC: 2865 Color lakes or toners

Dallastown
York County

(G-3970)
ALPINE SIGN AND LIGHTING INC
280 N Park St (17313-1915)
P.O. Box 483 (17313-0483)
PHONE.............................717 246-2376
Alesia Bray, *President*
Douglas Bray, *Vice Pres*
EMP: 13
SQ FT: 24,000
SALES: 724.5K **Privately Held**
SIC: 3993 Electric signs

(G-3971)
ANODIZING PLUS INC
Also Called: M&Z Anodizing
165 E Broad St (17313-1834)
PHONE.............................717 246-0584
Brian S Glatfelter, *President*
Tammy K Glatfelter, *Treasurer*
EMP: 7
SALES (est): 470K **Privately Held**
SIC: 3471 Anodizing (plating) of metals or formed products

(G-3972)
BOOK BINDERY CO INC
401 E Locust St Ste 9 (17313-1935)
PHONE.............................717 244-4343
James Johnson, *President*
Paula E Shaffer, *Vice Pres*
EMP: 3 **EST:** 1976
SQ FT: 10,000
SALES (est): 289.7K **Privately Held**
SIC: 2789 Bookbinding & related work

(G-3973)
CHARLESTON MARINE CNTRS INC (DH)
Also Called: CMCI
490 E Locust St (17313-1902)
PHONE.............................843 745-0022
Eric M Demarco, *President*
Richard Selvaggio, *COO*
Michael W Fink, *Vice Pres*
Thomas Mills, *Vice Pres*
Deanna H Lund, *CFO*
◆ **EMP:** 71
SQ FT: 240,000
SALES (est): 20.6MM **Publicly Held**
WEB: www.cmci-containers.com
SIC: 3443 Containers, shipping (bombs, etc.): metal plate

(G-3974)
E L W MANUFACTURING INC
464 E Market Ave (17313-2333)
P.O. Box 62 (17313-0062)
PHONE.............................717 246-6600
Eric Warner, *President*
EMP: 18
SQ FT: 20,000
SALES (est): 2.2MM **Privately Held**
WEB: www.elwmfg.com
SIC: 3544 Dies & die holders for metal cutting, forming, die casting

(G-3975)
FREEDOM CYBER MARKETING LLC (PA)
660 Blossom Hill Ln (17313-9432)
PHONE.............................717 654-2392
Pauletta McKibben, *Mng Member*
EMP: 3 **EST:** 2017
SALES (est): 173.4K **Privately Held**
SIC: 7372 Business oriented computer software

(G-3976)
GICHNER SYSTEMS GROUP INC (DH)
Also Called: Gichner Shelter Systems
490 E Locust St (17313-1902)
P.O. Box 481 (17313-0481)
PHONE.............................877 520-1773
Eric M Demarco, *President*
Richard Selvaggio, *COO*
Michael W Fink, *Vice Pres*
Thomas Mills, *Vice Pres*
Deanna H Lund, *CFO*

EMP: 251
SALES (est): 134.9MM **Publicly Held**
SIC: 3795 Specialized tank components, military

(G-3977)
GICHNER SYSTEMS GROUP LLC
490 E Locust St (17313-1902)
PHONE.............................717 244-7611
Thomas E Mill IV, *Mng Member*
William P Wilson,
▲ **EMP:** 334
SALES (est): 70.7K **Privately Held**
WEB: www.gichner.us
SIC: 3448 2522 Buildings, portable: prefabricated metal; cabinets, office: except wood

(G-3978)
GICHNER SYSTEMS INTL INC (DH)
490 E Locust St (17313-1902)
PHONE.............................717 244-7611
Eric M Demarco, *President*
Michael W Fink, *Vice Pres*
Thomas Mills, *Vice Pres*
Richard Selvaggio, *Vice Pres*
Deanna H Lund, *CFO*
EMP: 3
SALES (est): 676.8K **Publicly Held**
SIC: 3448 Prefabricated metal buildings

(G-3979)
M & M SALT & PALLET
235 Sheffield Dr (17313-9543)
PHONE.............................717 845-4039
Mithcell Maguigine, *Owner*
EMP: 9
SQ FT: 20,000
SALES: 550K **Privately Held**
SIC: 2448 Pallets, wood & wood with metal

(G-3980)
RJ CUSTOM PRODUCTS LLC
33 W Maple St (17313-1604)
P.O. Box 147 (17313-0147)
PHONE.............................717 246-2693
Richard Juliano, *CEO*
Jack Lacesa, *President*
Harry C Zart, *Admin Sec*
EMP: 19
SQ FT: 20,000
SALES (est): 2MM **Privately Held**
WEB: www.rojahnkitchens.com
SIC: 2434 Vanities, bathroom: wood

(G-3981)
SECHRIST BROS INC
32 E Main St (17313-2206)
PHONE.............................717 244-2975
George S Sechrist Jr, *President*
Mary A Sechrist, *Corp Secy*
EMP: 10
SQ FT: 3,750
SALES (est): 750K **Privately Held**
SIC: 2011 5147 5421 Meat packing plants; meats, cured or smoked; meats, fresh; meat markets, including freezer provisioners

(G-3982)
TRI-BORO CONSTRUCTION SUPS INC (PA)
465 E Locust St (17313-1901)
P.O. Box 8 (17313-0008)
PHONE.............................717 246-3095
Glenn C Rexroth, *President*
Glenn C Rexroth Jr, *Vice Pres*
George Randall, *Project Mgr*
Doug White, *Finance*
Cheryl Howard, *Sales Staff*
EMP: 85
SQ FT: 105,000
SALES (est): 90.9MM **Privately Held**
WEB: www.borosupplies.com
SIC: 5082 3496 5251 Masonry equipment & supplies; concrete reinforcing mesh & wire; tools, hand

(G-3983)
WONDERING CANVAS TATTOOS
40 W Main St (17313-1601)
PHONE.............................717 244-8260
Kyle Blacklidge, *Principal*
EMP: 4

SALES (est): 316.9K **Privately Held**
SIC: 2394 Canvas & related products

Dalmatia
Northumberland County

(G-3984)
COUNTY LINE SCREENPRINTING
126 Melody Ln (17017-7263)
PHONE.............................570 758-5397
Lindsay Schlegel, *Principal*
EMP: 3
SALES (est): 309.4K **Privately Held**
SIC: 2759 Screen printing

(G-3985)
PAXTON PRECAST LLC
725 Paxton Dr (17017-9548)
PHONE.............................717 692-5686
Kimberly Schlegel,
EMP: 4
SQ FT: 10,000
SALES (est): 473.5K **Privately Held**
SIC: 3272 Concrete products, precast

(G-3986)
SUNSET VALLEY STRUCTURES
1936 Mahantongo Creek Rd (17017-7223)
PHONE.............................570 758-2840
Daniel Glick, *Owner*
Katie Click, *Vice Pres*
EMP: 5 **EST:** 1994
SALES: 950K **Privately Held**
SIC: 2452 Prefabricated wood buildings

Dalton
Lackawanna County

(G-3987)
MANNING FARM DAIRY
Manning Rd (18414)
PHONE.............................570 563-2016
Paul Manning, *Owner*
Brian Manning,
EMP: 6
SALES (est): 495.4K **Privately Held**
WEB: www.manningfarm.com
SIC: 0241 2024 5812 Milk production; ice cream & frozen desserts; ice cream stands or dairy bars

(G-3988)
WINOLA ICE CO
Rd Lowr Lower (18414)
PHONE.............................570 378-2726
Paul Cannella, *Owner*
Linda Cannella, *Co-Owner*
EMP: 10
SQ FT: 5,000
SALES (est): 688.1K **Privately Held**
SIC: 2097 Block ice; ice cubes

Damascus
Wayne County

(G-3989)
BOYCE PRODUCTS LTD (PA)
205 Conklin Hill Rd (18415-3007)
PHONE.............................570 224-6570
David L Boyce, *President*
David Boyce, *President*
Anna Buczek, *Marketing Staff*
Nancy Weinperl, *Marketing Staff*
▲ **EMP:** 15
SALES (est): 3MM **Privately Held**
WEB: www.boyceproducts.com
SIC: 2541 Wood partitions & fixtures

(G-3990)
CANFIELD LOGGING LLC
120 Maverick Draw (18415-3073)
PHONE.............................570 224-4507
Joe Canfield, *Principal*
EMP: 3
SALES (est): 262.5K **Privately Held**
SIC: 2411 Logging

Danboro
Bucks County

(G-3991)
PENN ENGINEERING & MFG CORP (DH)
5190 Old Easton Rd (18916)
P.O. Box 1000 (18916-1000)
PHONE.............................215 766-8853
Mark Petty, *President*
Joseph Coluzzi, *CFO*
Elliott Israel, *Treasurer*
Eric Hurt, *Program Mgr*
▲ **EMP:** 429 **EST:** 1942
SQ FT: 230,000
SALES (est): 483.7MM **Privately Held**
WEB: www.penn-eng.com
SIC: 3429 3549 8711 Metal fasteners; metalworking machinery; industrial engineers
HQ: P.E.M. Holding Co., Inc.
800 3rd Ave Fl 40
New York NY 10022
212 446-9300

(G-3992)
PENN ENGINEERING & MFG CORP
Pemserter Div
5190 Old Easton Rd (18916)
PHONE.............................215 766-8853
Randy Hoffman, *Accounts Mgr*
Pat McGloane, *Manager*
EMP: 15
SALES (corp-wide): 483.7MM **Privately Held**
WEB: www.penn-eng.com
SIC: 3429 Manufactured hardware (general)
HQ: Penn Engineering & Manufacturing Corp.
5190 Old Easton Rd
Danboro PA 18916
215 766-8853

(G-3993)
PENN ENGINEERING & MFG CORP
Also Called: Pennengineering
5190 Old Easton Rd (18916)
PHONE.............................215 766-8853
Liam Shanahan, *Manager*
EMP: 40
SALES (corp-wide): 483.7MM **Privately Held**
WEB: www.penn-eng.com
SIC: 3452 Rivets, metal
HQ: Penn Engineering & Manufacturing Corp.
5190 Old Easton Rd
Danboro PA 18916
215 766-8853

Danielsville
Northampton County

(G-3994)
MARTIN SPROCKET & GEAR INC
3376 Delps Rd (18038-9515)
PHONE.............................610 837-1841
Butch Kromer, *Plant Mgr*
Ed Wright, *Branch Mgr*
EMP: 60
SALES (corp-wide): 456MM **Privately Held**
SIC: 3566 3537 3462 3429 Gears, power transmission, except automotive; industrial trucks & tractors; iron & steel forgings; manufactured hardware (general); sprockets (power transmission equipment)
PA: Martin Sprocket & Gear, Inc.
3100 Sprocket Dr
Arlington TX 76015
817 258-3000

(G-3995)
SHOCK SOLUTIONS INC
Also Called: Isolation Technologies
3807 Cinnamon Dr (18038-9709)
P.O. Box 736, Cherryville (18035-0736)
PHONE.............................610 767-7090
Thomas L Vetters, *President*
Karen Vetters, *Treasurer*
EMP: 4
SALES: 500K **Privately Held**
SIC: 3812 Search & navigation equipment

Danville
Montour County

(G-3996)
AGRI WELDING SERVICE INC
Also Called: Stainless Systems Service
2468 Continental Blvd (17821-7922)
PHONE.............................570 437-3330
Patrick Pulsifer, *President*
EMP: 10
SQ FT: 10,000
SALES (est): 4.2MM **Privately Held**
WEB: www.stainlesssystemservice.com
SIC: 5122 5046 7692 Pharmaceuticals; restaurant equipment & supplies; welding repair

(G-3997)
AUTO WELD CHASSIS & COMPONENTS
21 Cherokee Rd (17821-9300)
PHONE.............................570 275-1411
Ronald L Showers, *Owner*
EMP: 5
SQ FT: 2,400
SALES (est): 240K **Privately Held**
SIC: 7692 3441 5961 Welding repair; fabricated structural metal; automotive supplies & equipment, mail order

(G-3998)
BOYD STATION LLC
557 Elysburg Rd (17821-7831)
PHONE.............................866 411-2693
Keith Livziey, *Plant Mgr*
Bryan Cotner,
Donald G Cotner Jr,
EMP: 20
SQ FT: 75,000
SALES (est): 14MM **Privately Held**
WEB: www.boydstation.com
SIC: 5153 2076 Grains; vegetable oil mills

(G-3999)
CSS INDUSTRIES INC
350 Wall St (17821)
PHONE.............................570 275-5241
EMP: 4
SALES (corp-wide): 361.9MM **Publicly Held**
SIC: 2771 2679 Greeting cards; gift wrap & novelties, paper; gift wrap, paper: made from purchased material
PA: Css Industries, Inc.
450 Plymouth Rd Ste 300
Plymouth Meeting PA 19462
610 729-3959

(G-4000)
FABTEX INC (PA)
29 Woodbine Ln (17821-8022)
PHONE.............................570 275-7500
Robert W Snyder, *President*
Ralph C Davis, *Vice Pres*
William P Friese, *Vice Pres*
Glenn E Halterman, *Treasurer*
Mary F Snyder, *Admin Sec*
▲ **EMP:** 110
SQ FT: 30,000
SALES (est): 109.6MM **Privately Held**
WEB: www.fabtex.com
SIC: 5072 2221 5023 2512 Miscellaneous fasteners; draperies & drapery fabrics, manmade fiber & silk; bedspreads, silk & manmade fiber; draperies; upholstered household furniture; household furnishings; curtains & draperies

(G-4001)
FABTEX INC
29 Woodbine Ln (17821-8022)
P.O. Box 2222, Lumberton NC (28359-2222)
PHONE.............................910 739-0019
Craig Davis, *Manager*
EMP: 75
SALES (corp-wide): 109.6MM **Privately Held**
WEB: www.fabtex.com
SIC: 2221 5023 2392 2391 Bedspreads, silk & manmade fiber; draperies & drapery fabrics, manmade fiber & silk; draperies; household furnishings; curtains & draperies
PA: Fabtex, Inc.
29 Woodbine Ln
Danville PA 17821
570 275-7500

(G-4002)
FRANK BELLACE WELDING
Also Called: Iron Art
3965 Snydertown Rd (17821-7451)
PHONE.............................856 488-8099
Frank Bellace, *Owner*
EMP: 6
SALES (est): 240K **Privately Held**
SIC: 1799 3599 7692 3446 Ornamental metal work; welding on site; machine shop, jobbing & repair; welding repair; stairs, staircases, stair treads: prefabricated metal

(G-4003)
GEORGE FARMS
Also Called: George's Meats
33 Pottsgrove Rd (17821-7048)
PHONE.............................570 275-0239
Martin George, *Owner*
Peter George, *Partner*
EMP: 10
SALES (est): 610K **Privately Held**
SIC: 2011 0241 0751 5421 Meat byproducts from meat slaughtered on site; milk production; slaughtering: custom livestock services; meat markets, including freezer provisioners

(G-4004)
GREAT DANE LLC
Also Called: Great Dane Trailers
891 Strick Rd (17821-8084)
PHONE.............................570 437-3141
John Jones, *Plant Mgr*
EMP: 400
SALES (corp-wide): 1.5B **Privately Held**
WEB: www.greatdanetrailers.com
SIC: 3715 Demountable cargo containers
HQ: Great Dane Llc
222 N Lasalle St Ste 920
Chicago IL 60601

(G-4005)
HILL CREST LAMINATING LLC
911 Strawberry Ridge Rd (17821-7998)
PHONE.............................570 437-3357
Keith T Fletcher Jr,
EMP: 6
SALES (est): 737.2K **Privately Held**
SIC: 2295 Coated fabrics, not rubberized

(G-4006)
HOYES OUTDOOR PRODUCTS
134 Oak St (17821-1320)
PHONE.............................570 275-2953
David Hoyes, *Partner*
EMP: 4
SALES (est): 180K **Privately Held**
WEB: www.hoyesoutdoor.com
SIC: 3949 Lures, fishing: artificial

(G-4007)
J A & W A HESS INC
Also Called: Dan Ber Concrete & Supply
57 Old Valley School Rd (17821)
PHONE.............................570 271-0227
Walter Faux, *Branch Mgr*
EMP: 10
SALES (corp-wide): 3.3MM **Privately Held**
SIC: 3273 Ready-mixed concrete

PA: J. A. & W. A. Hess, Inc.
10 Hess Rd
Hazleton PA 18202
570 454-3731

(G-4008)
ON FUEL
Also Called: Citgo
614 E Market St (17821-2137)
PHONE.............................570 275-0170
Sherrie Suckow, *Principal*
EMP: 3
SALES (est): 220.1K **Privately Held**
SIC: 2869 Fuels

(G-4009)
PHARMA TECH PRO LLC
95 Erin Dr (17821-8478)
PHONE.............................570 412-4008
EMP: 3
SALES (est): 152.7K **Privately Held**
SIC: 2834 Pharmaceutical preparations

(G-4010)
RIVERVIEW ORTHTICS PROSTHETICS
957 Bloom Rd (17821-1352)
PHONE.............................570 284-4291
Donald Dixon, *Principal*
Timothy Nutgrass, *Principal*
Keith Senn, *Principal*
David Sickles, *Principal*
EMP: 15
SALES (est): 570.8K **Privately Held**
SIC: 3842 Limbs, artificial; braces, orthopedic

(G-4011)
SILVERLINE SCREEN PRINTING
275 Mill St (17821-2055)
PHONE.............................570 275-8866
Charles Brady, *Principal*
EMP: 4
SALES (est): 101.5K **Privately Held**
SIC: 2752 Commercial printing, lithographic

(G-4012)
STRUCTURE MANUFACTURING WORK
5 Walnut St (17821)
PHONE.............................570 271-2880
Linda Hickoff, *Owner*
EMP: 9 **EST:** 1987
SALES (est): 1.4MM **Privately Held**
SIC: 3441 Fabricated structural metal

(G-4013)
TEE-TO-GREEN
2011 Montour Blvd (17821-8698)
PHONE.............................570 275-8335
Richard L Berkheiser, *Owner*
EMP: 9 **EST:** 1973
SQ FT: 3,200
SALES: 250K **Privately Held**
WEB: www.berkheiser.net
SIC: 7999 5941 3949 Miniature golf course operation; golf driving range; golf goods & equipment; shafts, golf club

(G-4014)
TELE-MEDIA SFP LLC
Also Called: Systematic Filing Products
701 Montour Blvd (17821-9185)
PHONE.............................570 271-0810
Thomas Kenly, *Mng Member*
Robert Stemler,
Tom Wolanski,
▲ **EMP:** 20
SQ FT: 100,000
SALES (est): 5MM **Privately Held**
WEB: www.systematicfiling.com
SIC: 2679 2675 2672 Paper products, converted; folders, filing, die-cut: made from purchased materials; coated & laminated paper

(G-4015)
VISUAL DISPLAY PRODUCTS LLC
701b Montour Blvd (17821-9185)
PHONE.............................570 271-0815
Mike Dewalt, *President*
EMP: 5 **EST:** 2012
SQ FT: 10,000

▲ = Import ▼=Export
◆ =Import/Export

SALES (est): 491.5K **Privately Held**
SIC: 2541 2542 Store & office display
cases & fixtures; display fixtures, wood;
shelving, office & store, wood; fixtures:
display, office or store: except wood;
stands, merchandise display: except
wood

(G-4016)
WING DYNAMICS
59 Clark Rd (17821-7025)
PHONE..............................570 275-5502
Jeff Rine, *Owner*
EMP: 3
SALES: 210K **Privately Held**
SIC: 3441 Fabricated structural metal

Darby
Delaware County

(G-4017)
D & A ASSOCIATES
Also Called: D & A Printing
864 Main St 66 (19023-2109)
PHONE..............................610 534-4840
Donald E Allen, *Owner*
EMP: 6 EST: 1976
SQ FT: 22,600
SALES (est): 463.2K **Privately Held**
WEB: www.daprinting.com
SIC: 2752 7319 Business forms, litho-
graphed; distribution of advertising mate-
rial or sample services; circular & handbill
distribution

(G-4018)
GO MAIN DOMAINS LLC
334 Darby Ter (19023-2609)
PHONE..............................480 624-2500
M Feland, *Administration*
EMP: 6
SQ FT: 2,345
SALES (est): 336.1K **Privately Held**
SIC: 3575 Computer terminals

(G-4019)
HORIZON HOUSE INC
418 Franklin St (19023-2841)
PHONE..............................610 532-7423
Sandra Brat, *Principal*
EMP: 3
SALES (est): 179.5K **Privately Held**
SIC: 2297 8082 Nonwoven fabrics; home
health care services

(G-4020)
JET STREAM MANUFACTURING
INC
125 S Front St (19023-2932)
PHONE..............................610 532-6632
John D Laessig, *President*
John Laessig, *Vice Pres*
EMP: 6
SQ FT: 18,000
SALES: 400K **Privately Held**
WEB: www.jetstreammfg.com
SIC: 3281 Cut stone & stone products

(G-4021)
LERRO CANDY CO
601 Columbia Ave (19023-2510)
P.O. Box 106 (19023-0106)
PHONE..............................610 461-8886
Carmella Lerro, *CEO*
John Lerro, *Vice Pres*
Pasquale Lerro, *Vice Pres*
EMP: 10 EST: 1916
SQ FT: 15,000
SALES: 450K **Privately Held**
WEB: www.lerrocandy.com
SIC: 2064 Candy & other confectionery
products

(G-4022)
LIBERTY SPRING USA LLC
109 Willows Ave (19023-4024)
PHONE..............................484 652-1100
Pamela Stewart, *Mng Member*
EMP: 20
SALES (est): 2.1MM **Privately Held**
SIC: 3495 Wire springs

(G-4023)
PERFECT PRECISION
19 S Macdade Blvd (19023-1510)
PHONE..............................610 461-3625
EMP: 6
SALES: 300K **Privately Held**
SIC: 3999 Mfg Misc Products

(G-4024)
PREFERRED SPORTSWEAR INC
520 Pusey Ave Ste 260 (19023-3333)
PHONE..............................484 494-3067
Richard Kreydt, *President*
Greg Niven, *Vice Pres*
Jason Kreydt, *Admin Sec*
EMP: 3
SALES (est): 253.1K **Privately Held**
WEB: www.preferredsportswear.com
SIC: 2395 2759 Embroidery & art needle-
work; commercial printing

Darlington
Beaver County

(G-4025)
DANZER SERVICES INC
119 Aid Dr (16115-1637)
PHONE..............................724 827-3700
Zane T Brown, *CEO*
Rudi Heinzelmann, *General Mgr*
Kevin Falkingham, *Vice Pres*
Bob Pellegrini, *Vice Pres*
Jennifer Jutte, *Controller*
◆ EMP: 23 EST: 1997
SALES: 5.5MM
SALES (corp-wide): 58MM **Privately**
Held
SIC: 2421 Sawmills & planing mills, gen-
eral
PA: Danzer Services, Inc.
206 S Holland St
Edinburgh IN 46124
812 526-2601

(G-4026)
DANZER VENEER AMERICAS
INC (DH)
119 A I D Dr (16115)
PHONE..............................724 827-8366
Hannes Danzer, *President*
Mervin Deeves, *Engineer*
◆ EMP: 100
SALES (est): 18.4MM **Privately Held**
SIC: 2435 Hardwood veneer & plywood
HQ: Danzer Holding Ag
Hintere AchmuhlerstraBe 1
Dornbirn 6850
557 239-4490

(G-4027)
DONOHUE RAILROAD
EQUIPMENT INC
100 Hollow Rd (16115-2206)
P.O. Box 1569, Beaver Falls (15010-6569)
PHONE..............................724 827-8104
Brian Donohue, *President*
EMP: 24
SQ FT: 15,000
SALES (est): 5.3MM **Privately Held**
WEB: www.donohue-railroad.com
SIC: 3743 Railroad equipment

(G-4028)
EVOQUA WATER
TECHNOLOGIES LLC
118 Park Rd (16115-1636)
PHONE..............................724 827-8181
Dave Adams, *Branch Mgr*
EMP: 40
SALES (corp-wide): 1.3B **Publicly Held**
SIC: 2819 2869 2842 Charcoal (carbon),
activated; industrial organic chemicals;
specialty cleaning, polishes & sanitation
goods
HQ: Evoqua Water Technologies Llc
210 6th Ave Ste 3300
Pittsburgh PA 15222
724 772-0044

(G-4029)
INTERFOREST CORP (DH)
Also Called: Interforest Penn Beaver Div
119 Aid Dr (16115-1637)
PHONE..............................724 827-8366
Juergen De Gruyter, *Vice Ch Bd*
James Prescott, *President*
Hans-Joachim Danzer, *Chairman*
Ronald F Seay, *Admin Sec*
Sam Ricci, *Commercial*
◆ EMP: 70
SQ FT: 45,000
SALES (est): 24.2MM **Privately Held**
SIC: 5031 2435 Veneer; lumber: rough,
dressed & finished; hardwood veneer &
plywood
HQ: Danzer Canada Inc
402725 Hwy 4
Durham ON N0G 1
519 369-3310

(G-4030)
MCKAY & GOULD DRILLING INC
267 Taggert Rd (16115-2399)
PHONE..............................724 436-6823
Lynn Gould, *President*
Jack R Gould, *Principal*
Carla Channel, *Admin Sec*
EMP: 25
SQ FT: 8,000
SALES (est): 2.7MM **Privately Held**
SIC: 1781 1081 Water well drilling; metal
mining services

(G-4031)
SARDELLO INC
407 Cannelton Rd (16115-1619)
PHONE..............................724 827-8835
William Duff, *Principal*
▲ EMP: 3
SALES (est): 352.8K **Privately Held**
SIC: 3519 Diesel, semi-diesel or duel-fuel
engines, including marine

Dauberville
Berks County

(G-4032)
APPEELING FRUIT INC
1149 Railroad Rd (19533-8952)
PHONE..............................610 926-6601
Stephen Cygan, *Principal*
Beth Ann Cygan, *Treasurer*
EMP: 12
SQ FT: 4,000
SALES (est): 2.7MM **Privately Held**
WEB: www.appeelingfruit.com
SIC: 2033 5148 Fruits: packaged in cans,
jars, etc.; fresh fruits & vegetables

Dawson
Fayette County

(G-4033)
UNIVERSAL READY MIX &
SUPPLY
400 Dawson Scottdale Rd (15428-1125)
PHONE..............................724 529-2950
Barry Puskar, *Managing Prtnr*
Jay Puskar, *Partner*
EMP: 10
SQ FT: 8,500
SALES (est): 1.4MM **Privately Held**
SIC: 3273 Ready-mixed concrete

Dayton
Armstrong County

(G-4034)
ANDREW E REKEN
Also Called: A E Reken Welding & Fabg
134 Minich Rd (16222-3420)
P.O. Box 286 (16222-0286)
PHONE..............................724 783-7878
Andrew E Reken, *Owner*
EMP: 9
SQ FT: 16,000

SALES (est): 762.3K **Privately Held**
SIC: 7692 5083 5082 Welding repair;
agricultural machinery & equipment; general construction machinery & equipment

(G-4035)
B & B OIL & GAS PRODUCTION
CO
370 Pipeline Rd (16222-5722)
PHONE..............................814 257-8760
Patricia Barrett Hetrick, *Owner*
EMP: 8
SQ FT: 1,200
SALES (est): 640.7K **Privately Held**
SIC: 1311 Crude petroleum production;
natural gas production

(G-4036)
B & C METER INC
119 E Church Ave (16222-6101)
PHONE..............................814 257-8464
Bradley Steffy, *President*
Bernard Steffy Jr, *Vice Pres*
EMP: 4
SALES (est): 318.9K **Privately Held**
SIC: 1389 Construction, repair & disman-
tling services; testing, measuring, survey-
ing & analysis services

(G-4037)
B&B GAS & OIL SHOP
370 Pipeline Rd (16222-5722)
PHONE..............................814 257-8032
Patricia Hetrick, *Owner*
EMP: 7
SALES (est): 652.8K **Privately Held**
SIC: 2911 Petroleum refining

(G-4038)
DAYTON COMPUTER & SIGN INC
Also Called: DCS
107 N School St 3 (16222-6023)
PHONE..............................814 257-8670
Raymond E Barnette, *President*
EMP: 3
SALES: 20K **Privately Held**
WEB: www.daytoncasi.com
SIC: 3993 Signs & advertising specialties

(G-4039)
R C SILIVIS & SONS
565 State Route 1037 (16222-3925)
P.O. Box 37 (16222-0037)
PHONE..............................814 257-8401
Andrew D Silivis, *Owner*
EMP: 8
SALES (est): 371.3K **Privately Held**
SIC: 2011 Meat packing plants

(G-4040)
STAR ENERGY INC
1009 State Route 839 (16222-4325)
PHONE..............................814 257-8485
Kevin Barrett, *President*
Thomas Huff, *Admin Sec*
EMP: 3
SALES (est): 290K **Privately Held**
SIC: 1382 Oil & gas exploration services

(G-4041)
WHITE OAK FARMS INC
1009 State Route 839 (16222-4325)
PHONE..............................814 257-8485
Kevin Barrett, *President*
EMP: 6
SALES (est): 664.3K **Privately Held**
WEB: www.whiteoakfarms.com
SIC: 0116 1382 7992 Soybeans; oil & gas
exploration services; public golf courses

Delaware Water Gap
Monroe County

(G-4042)
CYGNUS TECHNOLOGY INC
74 Broad St (18327)
P.O. Box 219 (18327-0219)
PHONE..............................570 424-5701
Ronald Crank, *President*
Frances Crank, *Corp Secy*
EMP: 7
SQ FT: 1,500

SALES (est): 951.2K **Privately Held**
WEB: www.cygnustech.com
SIC: **3825** Test equipment for electronic &
electric measurement

(G-4043)
LAIRD TECHNOLOGIES INC
Shielding Way (18327)
PHONE..........................570 424-8510
Bonnie J Van Why, *Principal*
Karin De Witte, *Human Res Mgr*
EMP: 8
SALES (corp-wide): 1.2B **Privately Held**
WEB: www.lairdtechnologies.com
SIC: **3053** Gaskets, packing & sealing de-
vices
HQ: Laird Technologies, Inc.
16401 Swingley
Chesterfield MO 63017
636 898-6000

(G-4044)
VERTELLUS DWG LLC
Rr 611 (18327)
P.O. Box 730 (18327-0730)
PHONE..........................800 344-3426
Richard Preziotti, *President*
Anne Frye, *Vice Pres*
Philip Gillespi, *CFO*
EMP: 315
SQ FT: 560,000
SALES: 480MM
SALES (corp-wide): 7.4MM **Privately
Held**
SIC: **2869** Laboratory chemicals, organic
HQ: Vertellus Llc
1500 S Tibbs Ave
Indianapolis IN 46241
317 247-8141

(G-4045)
WESTROCK RKT LLC
Also Called: Rock-Tenn Paperboard Products
1 Paper Mill Rd (18327)
PHONE..........................570 476-0120
Mark Cline, *General Mgr*
EMP: 97
SALES (corp-wide): 14.8B **Publicly Held**
WEB: www.rocktenn.com
SIC: **2631** 2611 Paperboard mills; pulp
mills
HQ: Westrock Rkt, Llc
1000 Abernathy Rd Ste 125
Atlanta GA 30328
770 448-2193

Delmont
Westmoreland County

(G-4046)
**ALLEGHENY PAPER
SHREDDERS CORP**
Old William Penn Hwy E (15626)
P.O. Box 80 (15626-0080)
PHONE..........................800 245-2497
James Wagner, *President*
Judith Golock, *Vice Pres*
Evelyn Jefferson, *Sales Mgr*
Darwin Strider, *Sales Staff*
Joseph Barush, *Marketing Staff*
EMP: 50
SQ FT: 66,000
SALES (est): 11.4MM **Privately Held**
SIC: **3589** 5087 Shredders, industrial &
commercial; shredders, industrial & com-
mercial

(G-4047)
**ALLEGHENY-WAGNER INDS INC
(PA)**
Old William Penn Hwy E (15626)
PHONE..........................724 468-4300
John W Wagner, *President*
Judith Golock, *Vice Pres*
EMP: 47
SQ FT: 66,000
SALES (est): 5.7MM **Privately Held**
SIC: **3589** 3579 3559 5051 Shredders,
industrial & commercial; coin wrapping
machines; perforators (office machines);
recycling machinery; metals service cen-
ters & offices; farm machinery & equip-
ment

(G-4048)
**BEHRENBERG GLASS
COMPANY INC**
57 Mark Dr (15626-1623)
P.O. Box 100 (15626-0100)
PHONE..........................724 468-4181
John P Behrenberg Jr, *President*
John P Behrenberg Sr, *Vice Pres*
Penny Neumann, *Office Mgr*
▲ EMP: 18 EST: 1923
SQ FT: 25,000
SALES (est): 2.7MM **Privately Held**
WEB: www.behrenbergglass.com
SIC: **3231** Decorated glassware: chipped,
engraved, etched, etc.

(G-4049)
**BURTON SPRINGCREST
INTERIORS**
135 Barrington Rdg (15626-1268)
PHONE..........................724 468-3000
Sara Ann Burton, *President*
Robert P Burton, *Vice Pres*
EMP: 3
SQ FT: 3,400
SALES (est): 270K **Privately Held**
WEB: www.springcrestburtons.com
SIC: **5714** 2591 Draperies; curtain & drap-
ery rods, poles & fixtures

(G-4050)
DOYLE EQUIPMENT COMPANY
Rr 66 Box S (15626)
PHONE..........................724 837-4500
Kevin Nelson, *Branch Mgr*
EMP: 8
SALES (corp-wide): 9MM **Privately Held**
WEB: www.doyleequipment.com
SIC: **5082** 5084 3531 General construc-
tion machinery & equipment; processing
& packaging equipment; backhoes, trac-
tors, cranes, plows & similar equipment
PA: Doyle Equipment Company
179 Perry Hwy
Harmony PA 16037
412 322-4500

(G-4051)
**MCKINNEY DRILLING COMPANY
LLC**
Rr 22 (15626)
P.O. Box 78 (15626-0078)
PHONE..........................724 468-4139
Ronald Goga, *Manager*
Lance Shreffler, *Manager*
EMP: 35
SALES (corp-wide): 2.7B **Privately Held**
WEB: www.mckinneydrilling.com
SIC: **1781** 1081 1741 Water well drilling;
metal mining services; foundation building
HQ: Mckinney Drilling Company, Llc
7550 Teague Rd Ste 300
Hanover MD 21076
410 874-1235

(G-4052)
PENNECO OIL COMPANY (PA)
Penneco 6608 Rr 22 (15626)
PHONE..........................724 468-8232
Seaborn Jacobs, *Ch of Bd*
Terrence S Jacobs, *President*
Lawrence B Nydes, *President*
EMP: 15
SQ FT: 3,000
SALES (est): 23.8MM **Privately Held**
WEB: www.penneco.com
SIC: **1381** 6552 Drilling oil & gas wells;
subdividers & developers

(G-4053)
PENNICO OIL CO INC
Also Called: South Bend Lime Stone Co
6608 State Route 22 (15626-2408)
PHONE..........................724 468-8232
Terrance S Jacobs, *President*
Darryl M Jacobs, *Vice Pres*
Cris Faino, *Treasurer*
EMP: 40
SQ FT: 1,000
SALES (est): 4.6MM **Privately Held**
SIC: **1382** Oil & gas exploration services

(G-4054)
QUADRANT HOLDING INC
201 Industrial Dr (15626-1016)
PHONE..........................724 468-7062
Wendi Weiner, *Transportation*
Sheryl Ammons, *Human Res Mgr*
Harold Epps, *Branch Mgr*
EMP: 120 **Privately Held**
WEB: www.quadrantepp.com
SIC: **2824** 3082 2821 3052 Nylon fibers;
acrylic fibers; unsupported plastics profile
shapes; rods, unsupported plastic; tubes,
unsupported plastic; nylon resins; plastic
hose
HQ: Mitsubishi Chemical Advanced Materi-
als Inc.
2120 Fairmont Ave
Reading PA 19605
610 320-6600

(G-4055)
SALEM ANTIQUITIES
1 W Pittsburgh St (15626-1475)
PHONE..........................724 309-1781
Melissa Herman, *Principal*
EMP: 4 EST: 2008
SALES (est): 383.7K **Privately Held**
SIC: **3645** Garden, patio, walkway & yard
lighting fixtures: electric

(G-4056)
SALEM MILLWORK INC
100 Industrial Dr (15626-1013)
PHONE..........................724 468-5701
Michel J Ferris, *President*
Mike Ferris, *COO*
Ralph Showers, *Manager*
Kimberly Ferris, *Admin Sec*
EMP: 30 EST: 1960
SQ FT: 40,000
SALES (est): 5.3MM **Privately Held**
SIC: **2431** 2439 Millwork; structural wood
members

(G-4057)
SALEM PRINTING INC
506 Athena Dr (15626-1005)
PHONE..........................724 468-8604
David Huczko, *President*
Joe Sesti, *Owner*
EMP: 15
SQ FT: 1,500
SALES (est): 1.1MM **Privately Held**
WEB: www.alphabizforms.com
SIC: **2752** Commercial printing, litho-
graphic

(G-4058)
**SEVEN SISTERS MINING
COMPANY (PA)**
200 Route 22 (15626)
PHONE..........................724 468-8232
Darrel M Jacobs Sr, *President*
Seaborn Jacobs, *Chairman*
Terrence Jacobs, *Vice Pres*
Martha Jacobs, *Admin Sec*
EMP: 4
SQ FT: 1,000
SALES (est): 656K **Privately Held**
SIC: **1221** Strip mining, bituminous

(G-4059)
**SOUTH BEND LIMESTONE
COMPANY (PA)**
6608 State Route 22 # 205 (15626-2408)
PHONE..........................724 468-8232
Darryl M Jacobs, *President*
Terrence Jacobs, *Vice Pres*
Mathew S Jacobs, *Asst Sec*
EMP: 2
SQ FT: 1,000
SALES (est): 1.9MM **Privately Held**
SIC: **1411** Limestone, dimension-quarrying

(G-4060)
**THOMPSON GEAR & MACHINE
CO**
135 Cupp Way (15626)
P.O. Box 178 (15626-0178)
PHONE..........................724 468-5625
Ralph C Thompson Jr, *President*
Gilda Thompson, *Corp Secy*
Carrie Luko, *Vice Pres*
Timothy Thompson, *Vice Pres*
EMP: 7

SQ FT: 4,000
SALES (est): 500K **Privately Held**
SIC: **3599** 3462 Machine shop, jobbing &
repair; gears, forged steel

(G-4061)
VALERO SERVICE INC
2718 Route 66 (15626-1011)
PHONE..........................724 468-1010
Carl J Valero Jr, *President*
Brian Ohara, *General Mgr*
Joseph A Valero, *Corp Secy*
Brian O'Hara, *Controller*
EMP: 30
SALES: 950K **Privately Held**
SIC: **3441** Fabricated structural metal

Delta
York County

(G-4062)
PTI MACHINE INC
23 Mccall Rd (17314-9360)
PHONE..........................410 452-8855
Eve Gordon, *President*
Douglas Gordon, *Vice Pres*
EMP: 3
SALES: 3.5MM **Privately Held**
SIC: **3441** Fabricated structural metal

(G-4063)
STAR PRINTING COMPANY
811 Main St (17314-8945)
P.O. Box 47 (17314-0047)
PHONE..........................717 456-5692
Ronald L Sommer, *Partner*
Michael Sommer, *Partner*
Ronald Sommer, *Partner*
EMP: 3
SQ FT: 2,400
SALES (est): 250K **Privately Held**
SIC: **2752** 2759 Commercial printing, off-
set; letterpress printing

(G-4064)
STRASBURG CREAMERY LLC
4850 Delta Rd (17314-9468)
PHONE..........................717 456-7497
Farrell D Whiteford, *Principal*
EMP: 4
SALES (est): 283.5K **Privately Held**
SIC: **2021** Creamery butter

Denver
Lancaster County

(G-4065)
ACORN MANUFACTURING INC
10 Industrial Way (17517-9305)
PHONE..........................717 964-1111
Shaun Schoenberger, *President*
Patrick J Devlin, *Vice Pres*
Andrew Bowne, *Project Mgr*
Richard Broadbent, *Marketing Staff*
EMP: 34
SALES: 6.2MM **Privately Held**
SIC: **2599** 3993 Cabinets, factory; signs &
advertising specialties

(G-4066)
AGRI MARKETING INC
1368 W Route 897 (17517-9536)
PHONE..........................717 335-0379
Terry L Weaver, *President*
▼ EMP: 7 EST: 1998
SQ FT: 16,000
SALES (est): 870K **Privately Held**
WEB: www.usagypsum.com
SIC: **3275** Gypsum products

(G-4067)
BECO TRUCK CAP OUTLET
Also Called: Beco Truck Caps
143 Denver Rd (17517-9314)
PHONE..........................717 336-3141
Larry Beavens, *Owner*
EMP: 10
SALES (est): 570K **Privately Held**
SIC: **3537** Cabs, for industrial trucks &
tractors

▲ = Import ▼=Export
◆ =Import/Export

(G-4068)
BEILER PRINTING LLC
115 N King St (17517-8737)
PHONE....................................717 336-1148
Richard Beiler,
EMP: 5
SALES (est): 793K Privately Held
WEB: www.beilerprinting.com
SIC: 2752 Commercial printing, offset

(G-4069)
BOLLMAN HAT COMPANY
Also Called: Betmar
50 Denver Rd (17517-9334)
PHONE....................................717 336-0545
Dave Manley, Manager
EMP: 65
SALES (corp-wide): 291.8MM Privately
Held
WEB: www.bollmanhats.com
SIC: 2353 Hats & caps
PA: Bollman Hat Company
110 E Main St
Adamstown PA 19501
717 484-4361

(G-4070)
DIRECT WIRE & CABLE INC
412 Oak St (17517-1451)
PHONE....................................717 336-2842
Richard Witwer, CEO
Eric Laubach, President
David Witwer, Co-President
Wade Smith, Vice Pres
Walter Meck, CFO
▲ EMP: 70
SQ FT: 90,000
SALES: 37MM Privately Held
WEB: www.directwire.biz
SIC: 3548 5063 3357 3699 Welding apparatus; welding wire, bare & coated; power wire & cable; appliance fixture wire, nonferrous; extension cords

(G-4071)
DURAWOOD PRODUCTS INC
18 Industrial Way (17517-9305)
PHONE....................................717 336-0220
Craig McDonald, President
Mary Beth McDonald, Corp Secy
▲ EMP: 110
SQ FT: 60,000
SALES (est): 19.9MM Privately Held
WEB: www.durawoodproducts.com
SIC: 2431 Staircases & stairs, wood

(G-4072)
ES KLUFT & CO EAST LLC
412 Oak St (17517-1451)
P.O. Box 116, Hazleton (18201-0116)
PHONE....................................570 384-2800
Earl S Kluft, CEO
▲ EMP: 40
SALES (est): 3.3MM Privately Held
SIC: 2515 Mattresses & bedsprings

(G-4073)
F & M HAT COMPANY INC
103 Walnut St (17517-1605)
P.O. Box 40 (17517-0040)
PHONE....................................717 336-5505
Ashley E Fichthorn, President
Fred B Fichthorn, Chairman
Eric H Fichthorn, Vice Pres
J Bradford Fichthorn, Vice Pres
Richard Fichthorn, Treasurer
▲ EMP: 48
SQ FT: 120,000
SALES (est): 6.6MM Privately Held
WEB: www.fmhat.com
SIC: 2353 Hats: cloth, straw & felt; millinery

(G-4074)
GOLD RUSH INC
920 Stone Hill Rd (17517-9771)
PHONE....................................717 484-2424
Phil Blankford, President
Glenn Hyneman, Principal
Glenn Grubb, Manager
EMP: 25
SQ FT: 43,000
SALES (est): 7MM Privately Held
SIC: 3537 3799 Industrial trucks & tractors; trailers & trailer equipment

(G-4075)
HIGH CONCRETE GROUP LLC (HQ)
Also Called: High Concrete Structures
125 Denver Rd (17517-9315)
P.O. Box 10008, Lancaster (17605-0008)
PHONE....................................717 336-9300
Michael F Shirk, CEO
John J Seroky, President
Jeffrey L Sterner, COO
Ned Schneider, Exec VP
Dean M Glick, Vice Pres
▲ EMP: 500
SQ FT: 225,000
SALES (est): 134.7MM
SALES (corp-wide): 434.6MM Privately
Held
WEB: www.highconcrete.com
SIC: 1791 3272 Precast concrete structural framing or panels, placing of; prestressed concrete products
PA: High Industries Inc.
1853 William Penn Way
Lancaster PA 17601
717 293-4444

(G-4076)
INGHAMS REGROOVING SERVICE INC
Also Called: Ingham's Powder Coating
22 Industrial Way (17517-9305)
PHONE....................................717 336-8473
Frank Mazzacchi, Branch Mgr
EMP: 25 Privately Held
SIC: 3479 1799 Coating of metals & formed products; sandblasting of building exteriors
PA: Inghams Regrooving Service, Inc.
1860 N Reading Rd
Stevens PA 17578

(G-4077)
J & M CUSTOM POWDR COATING LLC
245 S Muddy Creek Rd (17517-9638)
PHONE....................................717 445-4869
Jerry Evans,
EMP: 6
SALES (est): 454.6K Privately Held
SIC: 3479 Coating, rust preventive

(G-4078)
JIM NEIDERMYER POULTRY
324 Tamarack Dr (17517-1718)
PHONE....................................717 738-1036
Jim Neidermyer, Owner
EMP: 3
SALES (est): 119.4K Privately Held
SIC: 2015 Poultry slaughtering & processing

(G-4079)
KALAS MFG INC
80 Denver Rd (17517-9334)
PHONE....................................717 335-0193
Richard P Witwer, Branch Mgr
Antonio Colon, Manager
EMP: 100
SALES (corp-wide): 85.3MM Privately
Held
WEB: www.kalaswire.com
SIC: 3357 Nonferrous wiredrawing & insulating
PA: Kalas Mfg. Inc.
167 Greenfield Rd
Lancaster PA 17601
717 336-5575

(G-4080)
L & D CABINETRY
700 Stone Hill Rd (17517-9604)
PHONE....................................717 484-1272
Leroy M Martin, Owner
EMP: 4 EST: 2011
SALES (est): 393.5K Privately Held
SIC: 2434 Wood kitchen cabinets

(G-4081)
LANCASTER LOG CABINS LLC
1370 Reading Rd (17517-9723)
PHONE....................................717 445-5522
Daniel Smucker, Mng Member
EMP: 2
SALES: 2MM Privately Held
SIC: 2452 Log cabins, prefabricated, wood

(G-4082)
MARTIN LIMESTONE INC
Also Called: New Holland Concrete
74 Kurtz Rd (17517-9316)
PHONE....................................717 335-4523
Richard Salisbury, Principal
EMP: 50
SALES (corp-wide): 651.9MM Privately
Held
WEB: www.martinlimestone.com
SIC: 3273 Ready-mixed concrete
HQ: Martin Limestone, Inc.
3580 Division Hwy
East Earl PA 17519
717 335-4500

(G-4083)
MGS INC (PA)
Also Called: M G S Trailers
178 Muddy Creek Church Rd (17517-9328)
PHONE....................................717 336-7528
Andy Gehman, CEO
Andrew S Gehman, CEO
Phil Hornberger, Vice Pres
Ted Miller, Vice Pres
Chris Steinman, Vice Pres
▲ EMP: 120
SQ FT: 100,000
SALES (est): 22.5MM Privately Held
WEB: www.mgsincorporated.com
SIC: 3621 3799 5561 7539 Motors & generators; trailers & trailer equipment; travel trailers: automobile, new & used; trailer repair; poultry processing machinery; fuel tanks (oil, gas, etc.): metal plate

(G-4084)
MILLER COUNTRY CRAFT
309 Lausch Rd (17517-9011)
PHONE....................................717 336-1318
Kim Miller, Owner
EMP: 4
SALES (est): 180K Privately Held
WEB: www.millercountrycrafts.com
SIC: 2499 Decorative wood & woodwork

(G-4085)
MUSSER MANUFACTURING
1235 W Route 897 (17517-9536)
PHONE....................................717 271-2321
Elizabeth Musser, Principal
EMP: 8 EST: 2010
SALES (est): 924K Privately Held
SIC: 3999 Manufacturing industries

(G-4086)
PARK PLACE PA LLC
412 Oak St (17517-1451)
PHONE....................................717 336-2846
EMP: 70
SALES (est): 344.1K
SALES (corp-wide): 32.3MM Privately
Held
SIC: 2515 Mfg Mattresses/Bedsprings
PA: Park Place Corporation
6801 Augusta Rd
Greenville SC 29605
864 422-8118

(G-4087)
PEPPERIDGE FARM INCORPORATED
Also Called: Campbell Soup Co
2195 N Reading Rd (17517-9147)
PHONE....................................717 336-8500
Ernesto Martinez, Plant Mgr
Steven Grow, Info Tech Mgr
EMP: 9
SALES (corp-wide): 8.6B Publicly Held
WEB: www.pepperidgefarm.com
SIC: 5145 2052 2099 2053 Snack foods; cookies; bread crumbs, not made in bakeries; frozen bakery products, except bread
HQ: Pepperidge Farm, Incorporated
595 Westport Ave
Norwalk CT 06851
203 846-7000

(G-4088)
PRECISION COATING TECH MFG INC
245 S Muddy Creek Rd (17517-9638)
PHONE....................................717 336-5030
Thomas R Kissling, President
Christopher Kissling, Vice Pres
Patricia Kissling, Office Mgr
EMP: 20
SALES (est): 2.5MM Privately Held
WEB: www.precisioncoatingtech.com
SIC: 3479 Coating of metals & formed products; coating of metals with plastic or resins

(G-4089)
PRO GUARD COATINGS INC
1 Industrial Way (17517-9305)
P.O. Box 289 (17517-0289)
PHONE....................................717 336-7900
Helmar Gueldner, President
Sue Nielsen, Vice Pres
EMP: 17 EST: 1950
SQ FT: 25,000
SALES: 2.4MM Privately Held
WEB: www.proguardcoatings.com
SIC: 2851 Paints & paint additives; lacquers, varnishes, enamels & other coatings

(G-4090)
QUALITY ALUMINUM CASTING CO
603 Lauschtown Rd (17517-9603)
PHONE....................................717 484-4545
Elwood Boose, Owner
EMP: 12
SQ FT: 1,500
SALES (est): 890K Privately Held
WEB: www.laaluminum.com
SIC: 3365 Aluminum & aluminum-based alloy castings

(G-4091)
RLB VENTURES INC
Also Called: Acorn Design and Manufacturing
10 Industrial Way (17517-9305)
PHONE....................................717 964-1111
Richard Broadbent, President
Rich Broadbent, Principal
Robert Bunting Jr, Vice Pres
Todd Shertzer, Vice Pres
Andrew Bowne, Project Mgr
▲ EMP: 38
SQ FT: 67,000
SALES (est): 9.2MM Privately Held
WEB: www.acorndisplay.com
SIC: 2541 Display fixtures, wood

(G-4092)
ROECHLING MED LANCASTER LLC (HQ)
Also Called: P M P
44 Denver Rd (17517-9334)
PHONE....................................717 335-3700
Lewis H Carter, President
Tom Kubacki, President
Robert Rhoads, Vice Pres
Brian Tennies, Mfg Staff
Loretta Delaney, QA Dir
▲ EMP: 112
SQ FT: 103,000
SALES (est): 21.7MM
SALES (corp-wide): 2.1B Privately Held
WEB: www.pmp.net
SIC: 3841 Surgical & medical instruments
PA: Rochling Se & Co. Kg
Richard-Wagner-Str. 9
Mannheim 68165
621 440-20

(G-4093)
SENSENIGS WOOD SHAVINGS
375 Lausch Rd (17517-9011)
PHONE....................................717 336-2047
Eugene Sensenig, Owner
EMP: 3
SALES (est): 241.1K Privately Held
SIC: 2421 2499 Sawdust & shavings; decorative wood & woodwork

(G-4094)
STERIL-SIL CO LLC
1241 Grants Pl (17517-8814)
PHONE....................................617 739-2970
Brian Schilling, President
David Stiller, Chairman
▲ EMP: 3 EST: 1938
SQ FT: 9,000

SALES (est): 270K **Privately Held**
SIC: 3469 Porcelain enameled products & utensils

(G-4095)
STURDY BUILT MANUFACTURING LLC
260 S Muddy Creek Rd (17517-9637)
PHONE...............................717 484-2233
Luke Sensenig, *Mng Member*
▲ EMP: 20
SQ FT: 45,000
SALES (est): 6.6MM **Privately Held**
SIC: 3523 Dairy equipment (farm)

(G-4096)
VISUAL INFORMATION SERVICES (PA)
105 Hawk C Corporate Ctr (17517)
P.O. Box 349, Bowmansville (17507-0349)
PHONE...............................800 777-3565
Ed Applegate, *CEO*
EMP: 9 EST: 1989
SALES: 1.1MM **Privately Held**
WEB: www.visualinfocorp.com
SIC: 3993 Displays & cutouts, window & lobby

(G-4097)
WEAVER INDUSTRIES INC
425 S 4th St (17517-1224)
P.O. Box 326 (17517-0326)
PHONE...............................717 336-7507
John K Weaver, *President*
Jim Weaver, *Exec VP*
David R Mowery, *Vice Pres*
Mildred A Weaver, *Treasurer*
Missy Nolt, *Controller*
◆ EMP: 75
SQ FT: 65,000
SALES: 10MM **Privately Held**
WEB: www.weaverind.com
SIC: 3624 Carbon & graphite products

(G-4098)
ZIMM-O-MATIC LLC
1216 Muddy Creek Rd (17517-9784)
PHONE...............................717 445-6432
Michael Zimmerman, *CEO*
EMP: 6
SQ FT: 15,000
SALES (est): 1.3MM **Privately Held**
SIC: 7692 7538 3599 Welding repair; truck engine repair, except industrial; machine shop, jobbing & repair

Derry
Westmoreland County

(G-4099)
ADVANCED CARBIDE GRINDING INC
5369 Route 982 (15627-2726)
PHONE...............................724 537-3393
Martin T Elloitt, *President*
David E Butz, *Vice Pres*
James C Elliotti III, *Treasurer*
Edward H Beck, *Admin Sec*
▲ EMP: 22
SALES (est): 5.4MM **Privately Held**
SIC: 2819 Carbides

(G-4100)
CAMMAN INDUSTRIES INC
111 Strawcutter Rd (15627-3615)
PHONE...............................724 539-7670
Keith Enos, *President*
Patrick Reeves, *Treasurer*
EMP: 45 EST: 1965
SQ FT: 14,000
SALES (est): 10.8MM **Privately Held**
WEB: www.cammanindustries.com
SIC: 3646 Chandeliers, commercial

(G-4101)
GEORGE J BUSH KITCHEN CENTER
1309 W 4th Ave (15627-1511)
PHONE...............................724 694-9533
George Bush Jr, *President*
Harry Bush, *Corp Secy*
EMP: 9

SQ FT: 2,800
SALES: 900K **Privately Held**
SIC: 2514 Kitchen cabinets: metal

(G-4102)
HALFERTY METALS COMPANY INC
294 Bergman Rd (15627-2632)
PHONE...............................724 694-5280
James A Halferty, *President*
Donna E Halferty, *Admin Sec*
▲ EMP: 13
SQ FT: 40,000
SALES (est): 1.6MM **Privately Held**
SIC: 3312 Stainless steel

(G-4103)
HAYES METAL FABRICATION LLC
294 Bergman Rd (15627-2632)
PHONE...............................724 694-5280
Marcus Lawrence,
EMP: 5 EST: 2013
SALES (est): 450K **Privately Held**
SIC: 3441 Fabricated structural metal for bridges

(G-4104)
KALUMETALS INC
116 Pittsburgh St (15627-1089)
P.O. Box 455, Latrobe (15650-0455)
PHONE...............................724 694-2800
David Beltz, *President*
Robert J Beltz, *President*
Terry Sosko, *Plant Mgr*
D Kent Snyder, *Treasurer*
Lee Storey, *Office Mgr*
◆ EMP: 10 EST: 1973
SQ FT: 13,500
SALES (est): 1.5MM **Privately Held**
WEB: www.kalumetals.com
SIC: 3341 Recovery & refining of nonferrous metals

(G-4105)
MG INDUSTRIES INC (PA)
515 W 3rd Ave (15627-1343)
P.O. Box 336, Laughlintown (15655-0336)
PHONE...............................724 694-8290
Amy Carns, *President*
Paul Lundquist, *Vice Pres*
David Shirley, *Treasurer*
EMP: 5
SQ FT: 34,000
SALES (est): 3.4MM **Privately Held**
WEB: www.mean-green.com
SIC: 5013 3462 Motor vehicle supplies & new parts; truck parts & accessories; automotive & internal combustion engine forgings

(G-4106)
PREMIUM MOLDING INC
294 Bergman Rd (15627-2632)
PHONE...............................724 424-7000
EMP: 7
SALES (est): 648.3K **Privately Held**
SIC: 3089 Mfg Plastic Products

(G-4107)
SIMPSON MANUFACTURING INC
Also Called: Eighteenth Century Hardware Co
131 E 3rd St (15627-1607)
PHONE...............................724 694-2708
William Simpson, *President*
EMP: 5 EST: 1944
SQ FT: 4,000
SALES (est): 302.5K **Privately Held**
SIC: 3429 Furniture hardware

(G-4108)
TECHSPEC INC
Also Called: Tsi Titanium
718 Y St (15627-1007)
P.O. Box 69 (15627-0069)
PHONE...............................724 694-2716
Edward F Sobota, *President*
Diane Sobota, *Corp Secy*
Michael Sobota, *Shareholder*
EMP: 42
SQ FT: 90,000
SALES (est): 32MM **Privately Held**
WEB: www.tsititanium.com
SIC: 5051 3356 Metals service centers & offices; nonferrous rolling & drawing

PA: Prv Metals, Llc
200 Fillmore St Ste 200 # 200
Denver CO 80206
303 292-7300

(G-4109)
XPERT MACHINING INC
501 S Bank St (15627-1520)
PHONE...............................724 694-0123
Doris Hankey, *President*
EMP: 3
SALES (est): 265.6K **Privately Held**
SIC: 3599 Machine shop, jobbing & repair

Devault
Chester County

(G-4110)
ALLAN MYERS MATERIALS INC
4045 State Rd (19432)
PHONE...............................610 442-4191
Mike Menkins, *Branch Mgr*
EMP: 5
SALES (corp-wide): 751MM **Privately Held**
WEB: www.americaninfrastructure.com
SIC: 2951 Asphalt paving mixtures & blocks
HQ: Allan Myers Materials, Inc.
1805 Berks Rd
Worcester PA 19355
610 560-7900

(G-4111)
DEVAULT PACKING COMPANY INC
Also Called: Devault Foods
1 Devault Ln (19432)
P.O. Box 587 (19432-0587)
PHONE...............................610 644-2536
Thomas A Fillippo Jr, *President*
Brett A Black, *COO*
Brett Black, *COO*
Henry Jankowski, *Exec VP*
Joanne S Fillippo, *Vice Pres*
▲ EMP: 150 EST: 1949
SQ FT: 100,000
SALES (est): 39.6MM **Privately Held**
WEB: www.devaultfoods.com
SIC: 2013 2011 Boneless meat, from purchased meat; frozen meats from purchased meat; meat packing plants

(G-4112)
PIPE & PRECAST CNSTR PDTS INC
Old Phoenixville Pike (19432)
PHONE...............................610 644-7338
Bruce W Smith, *President*
Ronald S Heacock, *Vice Pres*
EMP: 15
SQ FT: 12,500
SALES (est): 2.1MM **Privately Held**
SIC: 3272 5051 5032 5074 Precast terrazo or concrete products; pipe & tubing, steel; concrete building products; pipes & fittings, plastic; masonry materials & supplies; septic tanks

Devon
Chester County

(G-4113)
LITTLE SOULS INC
222 Berkley Rd (19333-1514)
PHONE...............................610 278-0500
Gretchen Wilson, *President*
Colleen Charleston, *Vice Pres*
EMP: 25
SQ FT: 12,000
SALES (est): 3.1MM **Privately Held**
WEB: www.littlesouls.com
SIC: 3942 Dolls, except stuffed toy animals

(G-4114)
NURTURE INC (PA)
28 S Waterloo Rd Ste 100 (19333-1574)
PHONE...............................610 989-0945
H Griffith Parker, *President*
H Griffith, *President*

EMP: 5
SQ FT: 6,000
SALES (est): 1.5MM **Privately Held**
SIC: 8731 2869 Biotechnical research, commercial; industrial organic chemicals

(G-4115)
OZ WORLD MEDIA LLC
1100 H St Nw Ste M (19333)
PHONE...............................202 470-6757
Alonzo Ellis, *President*
EMP: 20 EST: 2010
SALES (est): 981.2K **Privately Held**
SIC: 2731 Book publishing

(G-4116)
SUSTRANA LLC
15 N Devon Blvd Ste 200 (19333-1554)
PHONE...............................610 651-2870
John Anderson, *Managing Dir*
Ron M Zettlemoyer, *CTO*
Nancy Cleveland, *Info Tech Mgr*
Jennifer K Anderson,
EMP: 3
SQ FT: 1,200
SALES (est): 248.2K **Privately Held**
SIC: 8742 7372 Business planning & organizing services; prepackaged software

(G-4117)
ZYNERBA PHARMACEUTICALS INC
80 Lancaster Ave Ste 300 (19333-1331)
PHONE...............................484 581-7505
Armando Anido, *Ch of Bd*
Terri B Sebree, *President*
James Fickenscher, *Vice Pres*
Carol Oneill, *Vice Pres*
James E Fickenscher, *CFO*
EMP: 10
SQ FT: 3,800
SALES: 86K **Privately Held**
SIC: 2834 Pharmaceutical preparations

Dewart
Northumberland County

(G-4118)
BIOKINETICS INC
Turbot Ave (17730)
P.O. Box 52 (17730-0052)
PHONE...............................570 538-3089
Kevin Witmer, *President*
Jeffery Long, *Corp Secy*
Julie Witmer, *Vice Pres*
EMP: 4
SQ FT: 7,000
SALES (est): 320K **Privately Held**
SIC: 3559 Refinery, chemical processing & similar machinery

Dickson City
Lackawanna County

(G-4119)
BIOTEST PHARMACEUTICALS CORP
1027 Commerce Blvd (18519-1679)
PHONE...............................570 383-5341
EMP: 5
SALES (corp-wide): 741MM **Privately Held**
SIC: 2834 Pharmaceutical preparations
HQ: Biotest Pharmaceuticals Corporation
901 W Yamato Rd Ste 101
Boca Raton FL 33431

(G-4120)
FANGIO ENTERPRISES INC
Also Called: Fangio Lighting
416 Main St Unit 4 (18519-1696)
PHONE...............................570 383-1030
Radwan Badawi, *Owner*
EMP: 5
SALES (est): 640K
SALES (corp-wide): 4.6MM **Privately Held**
SIC: 3641 5023 Electric lamps & parts for generalized applications; lamps: floor, boudoir, desk

PA: Fangio Enterprises, Inc.
905 Stanton Rd
Olyphant PA 18447
570 383-1030

(G-4121)
KISEL PRINTING SERVICE INC
424 Boulevard Ave (18519-1729)
PHONE..................................570 489-7666
James J Kisel, *Ch of Bd*
Mark J Kisel, *President*
Felicia V Kisel, *Treasurer*
EMP: 20 **EST:** 1933
SQ FT: 25,000
SALES (est): 1.3MM **Privately Held**
SIC: 2752 2675 2791 2789 Commercial printing, offset; die-cut paper & board; typesetting; bookbinding & related work; commercial printing

(G-4122)
MOL COMMUNICATIONS & ELEC
821 Enterprise St (18519-1598)
PHONE..................................570 383-3658
James Mol, *Owner*
EMP: 3
SQ FT: 2,200
SALES (est): 214.4K **Privately Held**
SIC: 7622 4812 3824 Communication equipment repair; paging services; mechanical & electromechanical counters & devices

Dickson Cty
Lackawanna County

(G-4123)
CENTER FOR ORTHTIC AND PRSTHTC
1500 Main St Ste 2 (18447-1343)
PHONE..................................570 382-8208
Donald Dixon, *President*
Keith Senn, *COO*
Keith Meyers,
Mike Nattingly,
Kim Nutgraff,
EMP: 10
SQ FT: 2,500
SALES: 690K **Privately Held**
SIC: 3842 Limbs, artificial; abdominal supporters, braces & trusses

(G-4124)
LEONARDS AUTO TAG SERVICE
1500 Main St Ste 4 (18447-1343)
PHONE..................................570 489-4777
Steven Selinski, *Branch Mgr*
EMP: 3 **Privately Held**
SIC: 2679 Tags & labels, paper
PA: Leonard's Auto Tag Service
295 Susquehanna Ave
Wyoming PA 18644

Dilliner
Greene County

(G-4125)
ROGERSON & ASSOCIATES
500 Walnut Hill Rd (15327-1614)
P.O. Box 236 (15327-0236)
PHONE..................................724 943-3934
Larry Rogerson, *Owner*
EMP: 4
SALES (est): 450K **Privately Held**
SIC: 3646 Commercial indusl & institutional electric lighting fixtures

Dillsburg
York County

(G-4126)
DIGITAL-INK INC (PA)
230 Gettysburg St (17019-1255)
P.O. Box 426 (17019-0426)
PHONE..................................717 731-8890
John J Nissley, *President*
Richard B Gensler, *Vice Pres*
Kathy Stedman, *Financial Exec*

EMP: 90
SQ FT: 38,000
SALES (est): 24.1MM **Privately Held**
WEB: www.digitalink-pa.com
SIC: 7389 2791 2789 2621 Printing broker; typesetting; bookbinding & related work; business form paper; commercial printing, lithographic

(G-4127)
DRS PRINTING SERVICES INC
6 N Grantham Rd (17019-9509)
PHONE..................................717 502-1117
Daniel Snyder, *President*
EMP: 8
SQ FT: 6,000
SALES (est): 1.7MM **Privately Held**
SIC: 2752 Commercial printing, offset

(G-4128)
ENERGY FIELD SERVICES LLC
39 S York Rd Ste A (17019-9535)
PHONE..................................717 791-1018
David Ricker,
EMP: 5
SALES (est): 272.2K **Privately Held**
SIC: 1389 Gas field services

(G-4129)
FIT ENGINEERING
Also Called: Sport and Equipment
200 Mount Zion Rd (17019-9650)
PHONE..................................717 432-2626
David C Weber, *Partner*
EMP: 3
SALES (est): 140.3K **Privately Held**
SIC: 3949 Exercise equipment

(G-4130)
GANNETT STLLITE INFO NTWRK LLC
Also Called: Courier, The
507 Harrisburg Pike (17019-1338)
PHONE..................................703 854-6185
EMP: 5
SALES (corp-wide): 2.9B **Publicly Held**
WEB: www.usatoday.com
SIC: 2711 Newspapers, publishing & printing
HQ: Gannett Satellite Information Network, Llc
7950 Jones Branch Dr
Mc Lean VA 22102
703 854-6000

(G-4131)
HARMONY PLUS WOODWORKS INC
300 Old Cabin Hollow Rd (17019-9772)
PHONE..................................717 432-0372
Terry Frankenfield, *President*
EMP: 7
SQ FT: 7,000
SALES (est): 830.5K **Privately Held**
WEB: www.harmonypluswoodworks.com
SIC: 2434 2511 Wood kitchen cabinets; bookcases, household: wood; stands, household, wood

(G-4132)
JOSEPH MACHINE COMPANY INC
595 Range End Rd (17019-1526)
P.O. Box 121 (17019-0121)
PHONE..................................717 432-3442
Joseph Pigliacampo, *President*
Sanjay Parikh, *General Mgr*
Aleta Pigliacampo, *Vice Pres*
Scott Hamm, *Plant Mgr*
Tim Race, *Prdtn Mgr*
▲ **EMP:** 35
SQ FT: 100,000
SALES (est): 13MM **Privately Held**
WEB: www.josephmachineco.com
SIC: 3549 Metalworking machinery

(G-4133)
LEHMAN CABINETRY
16 S Fileys Rd (17019-9542)
PHONE..................................717 432-5014
Kevin Lehman, *Owner*
EMP: 3 **EST:** 1975
SALES: 300K **Privately Held**
SIC: 2511 Wood household furniture

(G-4134)
LIQUID TECH TANK SYSTEMS INC
125 Old Orchard Rd (17019-9623)
PHONE..................................717 796-7056
Brian Badger, *President*
Marlene Badger, *Corp Secy*
Lyndon Conrad, *Vice Pres*
Stacy Shank, *Office Mgr*
EMP: 14
SQ FT: 590
SALES: 2.9MM **Privately Held**
WEB: www.liquidtechtanks.com
SIC: 3443 Tanks, standard or custom fabricated: metal plate

(G-4135)
MARIANI METAL FABRICATORS USA
325 Beaver Creek Rd (17019-8947)
PHONE..................................717 432-9241
Vince Mariani, *President*
EMP: 3
SALES (est): 313.5K **Privately Held**
WEB: www.marianimetal.com
SIC: 3441 Fabricated structural metal

(G-4136)
MARIE CHOMICKI
Also Called: Bargain Sheet, The
31 S Baltimore St (17019-1228)
PHONE..................................717 432-3456
Marie Chomicki, *Owner*
EMP: 5
SQ FT: 1,000
SALES (est): 275K **Privately Held**
SIC: 2711 Newspapers: publishing only, not printed on site

(G-4137)
MAUELL CORPORATION
31 Old Cabin Hollow Rd (17019-8815)
PHONE..................................717 432-8686
Gary Suchy Sr, *CEO*
Cheryl L Hartzman, *President*
Ulrich Mauell, *President*
Helmut Mauell, *Chairman*
EMP: 50
SQ FT: 30,000
SALES (est): 18MM **Privately Held**
WEB: www.mauell-us.com
SIC: 3613 Control panels, electric

(G-4138)
MYERS STEEL WORKS INC
10 Big Oak Rd (17019-9132)
PHONE..................................717 502-0266
Lisa Myers, *President*
John Fadenrecht, *Project Mgr*
EMP: 29
SALES: 10.6MM **Privately Held**
SIC: 3441 Fabricated structural metal

(G-4139)
MYERS WLDG & FABRICATION INC
10 Big Oak Rd (17019-9132)
PHONE..................................717 502-7473
Darrell L Myers, *President*
Lisa Myers, *Vice Pres*
EMP: 9
SALES (est): 944.7K **Privately Held**
SIC: 7692 Welding repair

(G-4140)
STINES EQUIPMENT & MAINTENANCE
680 Ridge Rd (17019-8964)
PHONE..................................717 432-4374
Gary Stine, *Owner*
EMP: 3
SALES (est): 160K **Privately Held**
SIC: 3524 Lawnmowers, residential: hand or power

(G-4141)
U B R LLC
4 Barlo Cir Ste G (17019-1621)
P.O. Box 263 (17019-0263)
PHONE..................................717 432-3490
Linda Ulrich,
Frank Ulrich,
EMP: 4 **EST:** 1999
SQ FT: 2,160

SALES (est): 495.4K **Privately Held**
SIC: 3613 8711 5045 Control panels, electric; engineering services; computers, peripherals & software

Dingmans Ferry
Pike County

(G-4142)
DINGMANS FERRY STONE INC
432 Park Rd (18328)
P.O. Box 686 (18328-0686)
PHONE..................................570 828-2617
Richard Lavanant, *President*
Elaine Lavanant, *Manager*
Suzanne Lavanant, *Admin Sec*
EMP: 6
SALES: 2MM **Privately Held**
SIC: 1442 3281 5261 Construction sand & gravel; cut stone & stone products; nurseries & garden centers

(G-4143)
PROSTHETIC ARTWORKS LLC
123 Orchid Dr (18328)
PHONE..................................570 828-6177
Susan Bannon, *Principal*
EMP: 3
SALES (est): 222.1K **Privately Held**
SIC: 3842 Prosthetic appliances

Donora
Washington County

(G-4144)
A-1 BABBITT CO INC
Also Called: A-1 Babbitt and Machine
1122 Scott Street Ext (15033-3314)
P.O. Box 791 (15033-0791)
PHONE..................................724 379-6588
Brad Rodeheaver, *President*
EMP: 14
SQ FT: 12,000
SALES: 1.4MM **Privately Held**
SIC: 5085 3599 7699 3569 Bearings; machine shop, jobbing & repair; rebabbitting; filter elements, fluid, hydraulic line

(G-4145)
APEX NORTH AMERICA LLC
65 Washington St (15033-1306)
PHONE..................................866 273-9872
Aaron Lessing, *Sales Dir*
Farrah Nuzzo, *Sales Staff*
Ken Ralton,
◆ **EMP:** 43
SQ FT: 1,100
SALES (est): 11.7MM **Privately Held**
WEB: www.apexnorthamerica.com
SIC: 3555 Printing trades machinery

(G-4146)
BADZIK PRINTING SERVICE INC
799 Meldon Ave (15033-1008)
P.O. Box 242 (15033-0242)
PHONE..................................724 379-4299
Timothy D Urda, *President*
Margaret Anne Urda, *Vice Pres*
EMP: 6 **EST:** 1948
SQ FT: 12,200
SALES (est): 762.5K **Privately Held**
SIC: 2752 Promotional printing, lithographic; commercial printing, offset

(G-4147)
BARCHEMY LLC
65 E 1st St (15033-1374)
PHONE..................................724 379-4405
Lawrence Toscano, *Mng Member*
EMP: 30 **EST:** 2015
SQ FT: 30,000
SALES (est): 1.6MM **Privately Held**
SIC: 2026 2064 Milk, chocolate; chocolate candy, except solid chocolate

(G-4148)
BERGEN PIPE SUPPORTS INC
484 Galiffa Dr (15033-1383)
PHONE..................................724 379-5212
EMP: 100

(PA)=Parent Co (HQ)=Headquarters (DH)=Div Headquarters
✿ = New Business established in last 2 years

2019 Harris Pennsylvania
Manufacturers Directory

169

G E O G R A P H I C

SALES (corp-wide): 773.1MM **Privately Held**
WEB: www.bergenpower.com
SIC: 3498 3429 Fabricated pipe & fittings; manufactured hardware (general)
HQ: Bergen Pipe Supports, Inc.
225 Merrimac St
Woburn MA 01801
781 935-9550

(G-4149)
BRENT D BEISTEL
Also Called: Beistel Machining
23 Mckean Ave (15033-1308)
PHONE...................................724 823-0099
Brent D Beistel, *Owner*
EMP: 5
SQ FT: 8,000
SALES: 50K **Privately Held**
SIC: 3599 Machine & other job shop work

(G-4150)
CARPENTER & PATERSON INC
Also Called: Pipe Supports Group
484 Galiffa Dr (15033-1383)
P.O. Box 461 (15033-0461)
PHONE...................................724 379-8461
David P Lynch, *CEO*
Gary Dmitrzak, *CFO*
EMP: 12
SQ FT: 25,000
SALES: 40MM **Privately Held**
SIC: 3494 Valves & pipe fittings

(G-4151)
DONORA SPORTSWEAR COMPANY INC
Also Called: Donora Embroidery Service
585 Galiffa Dr (15033-1386)
PHONE...................................724 929-2387
Joseph A Palli, *President*
Joseph Palli, *President*
Bruce Silverblatt, *Corp Secy*
EMP: 3 **EST:** 1964
SQ FT: 11,000
SALES: 75K **Privately Held**
SIC: 2311 2337 7389 2395 Topcoats, men's & boys': made from purchased materials; women's & misses' capes & jackets; embroidering of advertising on shirts, etc.; pleating & stitching

(G-4152)
DYNO NOBEL INC
1320 Galiffa Dr (15033)
PHONE...................................724 379-8100
James Kohlburn, *Manager*
Orlando Molinaro, *Supervisor*
EMP: 40 **Privately Held**
SIC: 2875 2873 2819 Fertilizers, mixing only; nitrogenous fertilizers; industrial inorganic chemicals
HQ: Dyno Nobel Inc.
2795 E Cottonwood Pkwy # 500
Salt Lake City UT 84121
801 364-4800

(G-4153)
EASTERN ALLOY INC
1138 Meldon Ave (15033-1131)
P.O. Box 261 (15033-0261)
PHONE...................................724 379-5776
James M Kirk, *President*
Lawrence R Swift, *Vice Pres*
EMP: 9
SQ FT: 7,000
SALES (est): 2.5MM **Privately Held**
WEB: www.easternalloy.com
SIC: 3441 Fabricated structural metal

(G-4154)
EASTERN MACHINE & CONVYRS INC (PA)
Also Called: Eastern Machine & Conveyers
482 Gallifa Dr Donora Industrial (15033)
P.O. Box 742 (15033-0742)
PHONE...................................724 379-4701
Richard D Clark, *President*
William Meade, *Vice Pres*
◆ **EMP:** 15
SQ FT: 17,000

SALES (est): 2.7MM **Privately Held**
WEB: www.conveyorbeltusa.com
SIC: 3532 7699 5082 5084 Mining machinery; hydraulic equipment repair; mining machinery & equipment, except petroleum; conveyor systems

(G-4155)
ELLIOTT COMPANY
Also Called: Elliott Turbomachinery Co
1250 Scott St (15033-3397)
PHONE...................................724 379-5440
Frank Kinchington, *Technical Mgr*
Dave Lundy, *Marketing Staff*
Dan Kelso, *Branch Mgr*
Mike Anderson, *Manager*
John Diethorn, *Director*
EMP: 85
SALES (corp-wide): 4.5B **Privately Held**
WEB: www.elliott-turbo.com
SIC: 7699 3568 3563 Compressor repair; bearings, plain; air & gas compressors
HQ: Elliott Company
901 N 4th St
Jeannette PA 15644
724 527-2811

(G-4156)
MATHESON TRI-GAS INC
1 Nitrous Ln (15033-3319)
PHONE...................................724 379-4104
Tenney Nelson, *Manager*
EMP: 10 **Privately Held**
WEB: www.airliquide.com
SIC: 5084 2813 Welding machinery & equipment; safety equipment; nitrogen
HQ: Matheson Tri-Gas, Inc.
150 Allen Rd Ste 302
Basking Ridge NJ 07920
908 991-9200

(G-4157)
MC GREW WELDING AND FABG INC
30 S Washington St (15033-1394)
P.O. Box 87 (15033-0087)
PHONE...................................724 379-9303
Robert Mc Grew, *President*
Thomas Mc Grew, *Corp Secy*
David Mc Grew, *Vice Pres*
George Mc Grew, *Vice Pres*
EMP: 10 **EST:** 1974
SQ FT: 10,000
SALES (est): 1.8MM **Privately Held**
SIC: 3441 Fabricated structural metal

(G-4158)
POWER & INDUSTRIAL SVCS CORP (PA)
95 Washington St (15033-1305)
P.O. Box 211 (15033-0211)
PHONE...................................800 676-7116
Larry Shekell, *President*
Jeffrey R Yannazzo, *CFO*
▲ **EMP:** 45 **EST:** 1978
SQ FT: 40,000
SALES (est): 9.5MM **Privately Held**
WEB: www.piburners.com
SIC: 3291 Abrasive metal & steel products

(G-4159)
POWER PIPE SUPPORTS INC
Also Called: Bergen Power Pipe Supports
484 Galiffa Dr (15033-1383)
P.O. Box 461 (15033-0461)
PHONE...................................724 379-5212
James Bonetti, *President*
Jeanne Bindi, *Office Mgr*
▲ **EMP:** 107
SALES (est): 39.8MM **Privately Held**
SIC: 3441 Fabricated structural metal

(G-4160)
RETAL PA LLC
55 S Washington St (15033-1393)
PHONE...................................724 705-3975
Admir Dobrata, *CEO*
EMP: 12 **EST:** 2016
SALES (est): 929.5K **Privately Held**
SIC: 2673 Bags: plastic, laminated & coated

(G-4161)
SEALMARK MANUFACTURING CORP (PA)
480 Galiffa Dr (15033-1383)
P.O. Box 91 (15033-0091)
PHONE...................................724 379-4442
Anthony R Cupec, *President*
EMP: 9
SQ FT: 1,500
SALES (est): 1.5MM **Privately Held**
WEB: www.sealmarkcoatings.com
SIC: 2851 Paints, waterproof

(G-4162)
SHALE TANK SOLUTIONS LLC
98 E 1st St (15033)
PHONE...................................724 823-0953
Paul Sasko, *President*
James Sasko, *Vice Pres*
Christy Weight, *Admin Sec*
EMP: 10 **EST:** 2014
SALES (est): 396.5K **Privately Held**
SIC: 3795 Tanks & tank components

(G-4163)
THERM-O-ROCK EAST INC
85 Washington St (15033-1391)
PHONE...................................724 379-8604
Dean Rabe, *Supervisor*
EMP: 35
SALES (corp-wide): 17.6MM **Privately Held**
WEB: www.therm-o-rock.com
SIC: 3295 Perlite, aggregate or expanded
PA: Therm-O-Rock East, Inc.
1 Pine St
New Eagle PA 15067
724 258-3670

(G-4164)
VEND NATURAL OF WESTERN PA
309 W 11th St (15033-2026)
PHONE...................................724 518-6594
Robert Fabean Sr, *Principal*
Fred Fabean, *Principal*
Jeff Fabean, *Principal*
EMP: 3
SALES (est): 177.5K **Privately Held**
SIC: 3581 Automatic vending machines

Dornsife
Northumberland County

(G-4165)
ZOOKS WOODWORKING
713 Smeltz Rd (17823-7235)
PHONE...................................570 758-3579
John Zook, *Owner*
EMP: 3
SALES (est): 190K **Privately Held**
SIC: 1542 2431 Nonresidential construction; woodwork, interior & ornamental

Douglassville
Berks County

(G-4166)
ALL TYPE FENCE CO INC (PA)
1600 W Schuylkill Rd (19518-9713)
P.O. Box 715, Ardmore (19003-0715)
PHONE...................................610 718-1151
Christopher J Murray, *President*
EMP: 4 **EST:** 1949
SQ FT: 5,000
SALES (est): 931K **Privately Held**
SIC: 2499 5211 1799 Fencing, wood; fencing; fence construction

(G-4167)
AMERICAN CRANE & EQP CORP
1440 Ben Franklin Hwy E (19518-1614)
PHONE...................................484 945-0420
David Hope, *Branch Mgr*
EMP: 15
SALES (corp-wide): 40.3MM **Privately Held**
SIC: 3536 7389 Hoists; cranes, overhead traveling; crane & aerial lift service

PA: American Crane & Equipment Corporation
531 Old Swede Rd
Douglassville PA 19518
610 385-6061

(G-4168)
AMERICAN CRANE & EQP CORP (PA)
Also Called: Aceco
531 Old Swede Rd (19518-1299)
PHONE...................................610 385-6061
Oddvar Norheim, *President*
Karen Norheim, *Exec VP*
Jim Marmer, *Vice Pres*
Michael Myers, *Vice Pres*
Mike Myers, *Vice Pres*
▲ **EMP:** 180
SQ FT: 230,000
SALES (est): 40.3MM **Privately Held**
WEB: www.americancrane.com
SIC: 3536 7389 Cranes, overhead traveling; hoists; crane & aerial lift service

(G-4169)
AMITY INDUSTRIES INC (PA)
491 Old Swede Rd (19518-1238)
P.O. Box 355 (19518-0355)
PHONE...................................610 385-6075
Edward O Selwyn, *President*
Brad Luft, *Vice Pres*
EMP: 57
SQ FT: 13,500
SALES (est): 10.8MM **Privately Held**
WEB: www.amityindustries.com
SIC: 3444 3443 Sheet metalwork; tanks, lined: metal plate

(G-4170)
BODON INDUSTRIES INC (PA)
1513 Ben Franklin Hwy E (19518-1939)
PHONE...................................610 323-0700
Donald L Faust Sr, *President*
Donald L Faust Jr, *Vice Pres*
EMP: 10
SALES (est): 25.9MM **Privately Held**
SIC: 3272 Concrete products, precast

(G-4171)
BOYERTOWN SHTMTL FBRCATORS INC
1 Shore Ave (19518)
P.O. Box 102, Birdsboro (19508-0102)
PHONE...................................610 689-0991
Michael L Ortlip, *President*
Micheal D Mitchelle, *Vice Pres*
EMP: 4
SQ FT: 4,500
SALES (est): 340K **Privately Held**
SIC: 3444 Sheet metalwork

(G-4172)
CEI-DOUGLASSVILLE INC
447 Old Swede Rd (19518-1238)
PHONE...................................610 385-9500
William Laudien, *President*
John B Hughes, *General Mgr*
Elinor P Hauer, *Vice Pres*
Cliff Keller, *Buyer*
William Zrebiec, *Treasurer*
▲ **EMP:** 60 **EST:** 1999
SQ FT: 293,000
SALES: 16.2MM
SALES (corp-wide): 243.6MM **Privately Held**
WEB: www.hauermfg.com
SIC: 2842 2841 Shoe polish or cleaner; soap & other detergents
HQ: Cosmetic Essence, Llc
2182 Hwy 35
Holmdel NJ 07733
732 888-7788

(G-4173)
CREATIVE EMBROIDERY DESIGNS
158 Random Rd (19518-1943)
PHONE...................................412 793-1923
Robert D Moran, *President*
Mary Ann Moran, *Vice Pres*
EMP: 4
SALES (est): 280.8K **Privately Held**
SIC: 2395 Embroidery & art needlework

(G-4174)
DAVID J KLEIN INC
1343 Ben Franklin Hwy W (19518-1834)
P.O. Box 350 (19518-0350)
PHONE.............................610 385-4888
David J Klein, *President*
Robin Klein, *Treasurer*
EMP: 10
SALES (est): 1.1MM **Privately Held**
SIC: 3537 Trucks: freight, baggage, etc.; industrial, except mining

(G-4175)
EDWARD M ARNOLD JR
Also Called: Edward M Arnold Drilling Contr
95 Pine Forge Rd (19518-9613)
PHONE.............................610 689-5636
Edward M Arnold Jr, *Owner*
EMP: 14
SALES (est): 712K **Privately Held**
SIC: 1422 Chalk mining, crushed & broken-quarrying

(G-4176)
GIFT LUMBER CO INC
7487 Boyertown Pike (19518-9511)
PHONE.............................610 689-9483
Kenneth Gift, *President*
EMP: 8
SALES (est): 1.1MM **Privately Held**
SIC: 2421 5211 Sawmills & planing mills, general; planing mill products & lumber

(G-4177)
GOODWEST INDUSTRIES LLC (PA)
48 Quarry Rd (19518-1909)
P.O. Box 567 (19518-0567)
PHONE.............................215 340-3100
Bill Goodwin, *CEO*
James P West, *President*
Jimmy West, *Opers Mgr*
Judy Karish, *Purchasing*
William T Goodwin, *Treasurer*
EMP: 40
SQ FT: 15,000
SALES (est): 14.5MM **Privately Held**
WEB: www.goodwest.com
SIC: 2599 3585 Carts, restaurant equipment; heating equipment, complete

(G-4178)
HOPEWELL NON-FERROUS FOUNDRY
2261 E Main St (19518-9131)
PHONE.............................610 385-6747
George W Lewis, *President*
Thea G Lewis, *Corp Secy*
EMP: 4
SALES (est): 670K **Privately Held**
SIC: 3369 3365 Zinc & zinc-base alloy castings, except die-castings; aluminum & aluminum-based alloy castings

(G-4179)
POTTSTOWN TRAP ROCK QUARRIES
1 Quarry Rd (19518-1999)
PHONE.............................610 326-5921
Pep Hunsicker, *General Mgr*
EMP: 15
SQ FT: 1,804
SALES (corp-wide): 10MM **Privately Held**
SIC: 3281 Stone, quarrying & processing of own stone products
PA: Pottstown Trap Rock Quarries Inc
394 S Sanatoga Rd
Pottstown PA 19464
610 326-4843

(G-4180)
PROTO-CAST LLC
1460 Ben Franklin Hwy E (19518-1697)
PHONE.............................610 326-1723
Joseph Gizara,
Bill Vanzino, *Administration*
Jack Budnick,
Edward Snyder,
James Snyder,
EMP: 40
SQ FT: 22,000

SALES: 3.5MM **Privately Held**
WEB: www.proto-cast.com
SIC: 3089 3544 Injection molding of plastics; dies, plastics forming

(G-4181)
TECHO-BLOC CORP
23 Quarry Rd (19518-1906)
PHONE.............................610 326-3677
Paul Ober, *Principal*
Brian Beavin, *Regl Sales Mgr*
Chad Kingrey, *Sales Staff*
EMP: 30
SALES (corp-wide): 38.6MM **Privately Held**
SIC: 3272 Concrete products
PA: Techo-Bloc Corp.
852 W Pennsylvania Ave
Pen Argyl PA 18072
610 863-2300

(G-4182)
WOLF TECHNOLOGIES LLC
Also Called: Precision Technology
551 Old Swede Rd (19518-1205)
P.O. Box 185 (19518-0185)
PHONE.............................610 385-6091
Gregory Wolf, *President*
EMP: 40
SQ FT: 31,000
SALES (est): 11.3MM **Privately Held**
SIC: 3324 Steel investment foundries

Dover
York County

(G-4183)
ADVANCE GRAPHICS EQP OF YORK
Also Called: Advanced Graphic Services
4700 Raycom Rd (17315-1303)
PHONE.............................717 292-9183
Dennis Snyder, *President*
Michael Smith, *Vice Pres*
Greg Kline, *Treasurer*
EMP: 35 **EST:** 1951
SQ FT: 20,000
SALES (est): 4.2MM
SALES (corp-wide): 27.9MM **Privately Held**
WEB: www.ageyork.com
SIC: 3555 3599 Printing trades machinery; machine shop, jobbing & repair
PA: Emt International, Inc.
780 Centerline Dr
Hobart WI 54155
920 468-5475

(G-4184)
BALD HILLS DISTILLERY
5061 Carlisle Rd (17315-3054)
PHONE.............................717 858-2152
Trampas Ferree, *Principal*
EMP: 3
SALES (est): 140.7K **Privately Held**
SIC: 2085 Distilled & blended liquors

(G-4185)
BARKBY GROUP INC
Also Called: Landmark Casting Co
127 Cranbrook Dr (17315-1231)
PHONE.............................717 292-4148
Richard Barkby, *Principal*
Harry W Barkby, *Principal*
Eleanor Barkby, *Vice Pres*
EMP: 4
SQ FT: 3,800
SALES (est): 229.8K **Privately Held**
WEB: www.barkbyandbarkbythorpe.leicestershireparish
SIC: 3999 3562 Miniatures; casters

(G-4186)
BELL-MARK SALES CO INC
Jobath Machine Div
4500 W Canal Rd (17315-4051)
PHONE.............................717 292-5641
Ben Dambly, *General Mgr*
Justin Henson, *Engineer*
EMP: 50

SALES (corp-wide): 17MM **Privately Held**
WEB: www.bell-mark.com
SIC: 3542 7692 3555 2893 Marking machines; welding repair; printing trades machinery; printing ink
PA: Bell-Mark Sales Co., Inc.
331 Changebridge Rd Ste 1
Pine Brook NJ 07058
973 882-0202

(G-4187)
BELL-MARK TECHNOLOGIES CORP
4500 W Canal Rd (17315-4051)
PHONE.............................717 292-5641
John Marozzi, *President*
Daniel Hilleary, *Treasurer*
EMP: 50
SALES (est): 18MM **Privately Held**
SIC: 3552 2893 Printing machinery, textile; printing ink

(G-4188)
BILL MACKS ICE CREAM
Also Called: Mack's Bill Ice Cream
3890 Carlisle Rd (17315-4418)
PHONE.............................717 292-1931
Todd A McDaniel, *Owner*
Sharon Freed, *Manager*
EMP: 20
SQ FT: 2,900
SALES: 550K **Privately Held**
SIC: 5812 5143 2024 American restaurant; ice cream & ices; ice cream & frozen desserts

(G-4189)
BURKEY ACQUISITION INC
Also Called: Stone Hedge Farms
1 Popcorn Ln (17315-2152)
PHONE.............................717 292-5611
Tony Tsonis, *President*
EMP: 60 **EST:** 1983
SQ FT: 35,000
SALES (est): 7.8MM **Privately Held**
SIC: 2096 Popcorn, already popped (except candy covered)

(G-4190)
C KNAUB & SONS
1595 Jug Rd (17315-2037)
PHONE.............................717 292-3908
Curtis Knaub, *Owner*
Tanya J Knaub, *Co-Owner*
EMP: 3
SQ FT: 1,500
SALES: 180K **Privately Held**
SIC: 2448 Pallets, wood

(G-4191)
CONCRETE SIMPLICITY CONS
5635 Crone Rd (17315-2407)
PHONE.............................814 857-7500
Karen Reese, *Owner*
EMP: 3
SALES: 250K **Privately Held**
SIC: 3272 Concrete products

(G-4192)
FERGUSON WELDING INC
1030 Buck Rd (17315-2065)
PHONE.............................717 292-4179
Robert Ferguson, *President*
Norma Ferguson, *Admin Sec*
EMP: 10 **EST:** 1972
SQ FT: 6,000
SALES: 375.2K **Privately Held**
SIC: 7692 Welding repair

(G-4193)
KENA CORPORATION
5420 Old Carlisle Rd (17315-2248)
PHONE.............................717 292-7097
Andy Retzlaff, *President*
Dave Hawpecker, *Vice Pres*
EMP: 10
SALES (est): 1.4MM **Privately Held**
SIC: 3089 8711 3599 Injection molded finished plastic products; engineering services; machine shop, jobbing & repair

(G-4194)
KERN INDUSTRIES INC
16 Rachael Rd (17315-1216)
PHONE.............................814 691-4211

George Kern, *Principal*
EMP: 3 **EST:** 2017
SALES (est): 214.5K **Privately Held**
SIC: 3999 Manufacturing industries

(G-4195)
MARLOWES METAL FABRICATING
2111 Palomino Rd (17315-3670)
PHONE.............................717 292-7360
Donald Marlowe Jr, *Owner*
EMP: 3
SALES (est): 240K **Privately Held**
SIC: 3441 Fabricated structural metal

(G-4196)
MG WELDING & FABRICATION
7070 Bull Rd (17315-1742)
PHONE.............................717 292-5206
Mark Gingrich, *Owner*
EMP: 5
SQ FT: 6,500
SALES (est): 486.2K **Privately Held**
WEB: www.cyberia.com
SIC: 3599 Machine shop, jobbing & repair

(G-4197)
NICOLE LYNN INC
6451 Clearview Rd (17315-3209)
PHONE.............................717 292-6130
Nicole Lynn, *President*
EMP: 4
SALES (est): 185.4K **Privately Held**
WEB: www.nicolelynn.com
SIC: 2393 Duffle bags, canvas: made from purchased materials

(G-4198)
PANAGRAPHICS INC
4690 Raycom Rd (17315-1300)
PHONE.............................717 292-5606
Craig Deist, *President*
Herbert Spicer, *Engineer*
Mike Riordan, *Marketing Staff*
Kris Hightman, *Manager*
EMP: 35
SQ FT: 25,000
SALES (est): 11.6MM **Privately Held**
WEB: www.panagraphicsinc.com
SIC: 3444 Sheet metal specialties, not stamped

(G-4199)
POPCORN ALLEY INC
1 Popcorn Ln (17315-2152)
PHONE.............................877 292-5611
Tony Tsonis, *President*
EMP: 12
SALES (est): 1.9MM **Privately Held**
SIC: 2064 Popcorn balls or other treated popcorn products

(G-4200)
PRAIRIE PRODUCTS INC
Also Called: Larue Optical
4660 Raycom Rd (17315-1334)
P.O. Box 100 (17315-0100)
PHONE.............................717 292-0421
Brian Laprairie, *President*
EMP: 3
SQ FT: 3,600
SALES (est): 483.4K **Privately Held**
WEB: www.larueoptical.com
SIC: 3851 Glasses, sun or glare

(G-4201)
PRO PALLET LLC
1730 Butter Rd (17315-1305)
PHONE.............................717 292-5510
Mark Schaffer,
Larry Cirillo,
Steve Hartman, *Representative*
EMP: 120
SQ FT: 42,000
SALES: 8.2MM **Privately Held**
SIC: 2448 Pallets, wood

(G-4202)
R L SNELBECKER INC
90 S Main St (17315-1527)
PHONE.............................717 292-4971
Robert L Snelbecker, *President*
EMP: 3
SQ FT: 1,200

SALES (est): 500K **Privately Held**
SIC: 1731 3625 General electrical contractor; relays & industrial controls

(G-4203)
RAYCOM ELECTRONICS INC (HQ)
1 Raycom Rd (17315)
PHONE..................717 292-3641
Roger C Mayo, *President*
Steve Flickinger, *Vice Pres*
Darryl K Mayo, *Treasurer*
Geraldine R Mayo, *Admin Sec*
EMP: 70
SQ FT: 20,000
SALES (est): 7.4MM
SALES (corp-wide): 74.2MM **Privately Held**
WEB: www.raycomelectronics.com
SIC: 3677 Electronic coils, transformers & other inductors
PA: Electro Technik Industries, Inc.
5410 115th Ave N
Clearwater FL 33760
727 530-9555

(G-4204)
SHILOH INDUSTRIES
3656 Kortni Dr (17315-4751)
PHONE..................717 779-7654
George J Patsoureas, *Owner*
EMP: 3 EST: 2015
SALES (est): 224.1K **Privately Held**
SIC: 3999 Manufacturing industries

(G-4205)
SPRING VALLEY MULCH BRIAN
2770 Mill Creek Rd (17315-2021)
PHONE..................717 292-7945
Brian Klinger, *Owner*
EMP: 7
SALES (est): 1.5MM **Privately Held**
SIC: 2875 5261 Compost; lawn & garden supplies

(G-4206)
VENOM POWER SPORTS
90 S Main St (17315-1527)
PHONE..................717 467-5190
EMP: 3 EST: 2010
SALES (est): 237.6K **Privately Held**
SIC: 2836 Mfg Biological Products

(G-4207)
WEIR KITCHENS
350 S Winding Rd (17315-2803)
PHONE..................717 292-6829
James Weir, *Owner*
EMP: 16
SQ FT: 8,000
SALES (est): 1.5MM **Privately Held**
SIC: 2434 Wood kitchen cabinets

Downingtown
Chester County

(G-4208)
ACCU BOND CORPORATION
Also Called: Accubond
460 Acorn Ln (19335-3040)
PHONE..................610 269-8433
Steve Freeman, *President*
Tom Clark, *Plant Mgr*
Kristi Pannebecker, *Office Mgr*
EMP: 10
SQ FT: 12,000
SALES (est): 2.1MM **Privately Held**
SIC: 2891 Adhesives

(G-4209)
AGC CHEMICALS AMERICAS INC
255 S Bailey Rd (19335-2003)
PHONE..................610 380-6200
Charles Allen, *Branch Mgr*
EMP: 21
SQ FT: 67,212
SALES (corp-wide): 13.5B **Privately Held**
WEB: www.agcchem.com
SIC: 2821 Plastics materials & resins

HQ: Agc Chemicals Americas, Inc.
55 E Uwchlan Ave Ste 201
Exton PA 19341
610 423-4300

(G-4210)
ANTHONY J MASCHERINO PC
341 E Lancaster Ave Ste 1 (19335-2974)
PHONE..................610 269-6833
Anthony J Mascherino, *President*
EMP: 5
SALES (est): 370K **Privately Held**
WEB: www.ajmascherinocpa.com
SIC: 2782 Ledger, inventory & account books

(G-4211)
ASR ENTERPRISES INC
Also Called: Pfm Enterprises
801 E Lancaster Ave (19335-3327)
PHONE..................610 873-7484
Patrick Foley, *President*
Brian Griswold, *Vice Pres*
Maryann Griswold, *Manager*
Andrew Staples, *Manager*
Caryn Menna, *IT/INT Sup*
EMP: 4
SQ FT: 1,500
SALES (est): 200K **Privately Held**
WEB: www.asrenterprises.com
SIC: 3699 Electric sound equipment

(G-4212)
ASTROMETRICS INC
108 Ashland Dr (19335-1767)
PHONE..................610 280-0869
EMP: 5
SALES (est): 390K **Privately Held**
SIC: 3822 Mfg Environmental Controls

(G-4213)
ATLANTEX MANUFACTURING CORP
600 Brandywine Ave # 500 (19335-3412)
P.O. Box 568 (19335-0568)
PHONE..................610 518-6601
Ken Neuhauser, *President*
Peter Mimmo, *Vice Pres*
▲ **EMP:** 18
SQ FT: 20,000
SALES (est): 3.5MM **Privately Held**
WEB: www.atlantexmfg.com
SIC: 2221 Broadwoven fabric mills, man-made

(G-4214)
BAAR PRODUCTS COMPANY
241 Boot Rd (19335-3402)
P.O. Box 60 (19335-0060)
PHONE..................610 873-4591
Bruce Baar, *Owner*
EMP: 8
SALES (est): 907K **Privately Held**
WEB: www.glycothymoline.com
SIC: 3999 Advertising display products

(G-4215)
BLUE BOY PRODUCTS INC (PA)
104 Woodcrest Dr (19335-1353)
PHONE..................610 284-1055
Paul Rucker, *President*
EMP: 6
SALES: 180K **Privately Held**
SIC: 2899 3589 5074 Water treating compounds; water purification equipment, household type; water purification equipment

(G-4216)
BRANDYWINE MACHINE CO INC
Also Called: Bramco Stainless
State Highway 282 (19335)
P.O. Box 202 (19335-0202)
PHONE..................610 269-1221
William F Mc Queen, *President*
Diane Mc Queen, *Vice Pres*
Brian Hughes, *VP Sales*
Tom Shepherd, *VP Sales*
Corri McNeal, *Marketing Mgr*
EMP: 15
SQ FT: 2,612

SALES (est): 6.4MM **Privately Held**
WEB: www.bramcostainless.com
SIC: 5051 3599 3444 3443 Steel; machine & other job shop work; sheet metalwork; fabricated plate work (boiler shop)

(G-4217)
C & S REPAIR CENTER INC
507 W Uwchlan Ave (19335-1756)
PHONE..................610 524-9724
Carl Ressler, *President*
Shirley Lynn, *Vice Pres*
EMP: 6
SQ FT: 2,000
SALES (est): 573.3K **Privately Held**
WEB: www.csrepaircenter.com
SIC: 7694 5999 Rebuilding motors, except automotive; engine & motor equipment & supplies

(G-4218)
CALGON CARBON CORPORATION
1061 Boot Rd (19335-4065)
PHONE..................610 873-3071
Daniel Meuser, *Opers Mgr*
Andrea Swoger, *Cust Mgr*
Harold Nuse, *Branch Mgr*
Garry Lightner, *CIO*
Jim Stratico, *Technical Staff*
EMP: 8
SALES (corp-wide): 5.3B **Privately Held**
WEB: www.calgoncarbon.com
SIC: 2819 Charcoal (carbon), activated
HQ: Calgon Carbon Corporation
3000 Gsk Dr
Moon Township PA 15108
412 787-6700

(G-4219)
CAWLEY ENVIRONMENTAL SVCS INC
637 Jeffers Cir (19335)
PHONE..................610 594-0101
Steven M Cawley, *President*
EMP: 15
SALES (est): 1.7MM **Privately Held**
SIC: 3589 7389 Water treatment equipment, industrial;

(G-4220)
CHIEF TECHNOLOGIES LLC
Also Called: Chief Fire and Rescue
3947 W Lincoln Hwy (19335-5503)
PHONE..................484 693-0750
Kyle Chandler, *Mng Member*
Jim Henle,
EMP: 12
SQ FT: 75,000
SALES (est): 2.2MM **Privately Held**
SIC: 3569 Firefighting apparatus & related equipment

(G-4221)
COATESVLLE COCA COLA BTLG WRKS
Also Called: Coca-Cola
299 Boot Rd Ste 200 (19335-3456)
PHONE..................610 384-4343
Charles W Bitzer, *President*
George Petrovich, *Manager*
EMP: 45
SALES (est): 5.8MM
SALES (corp-wide): 361.4MM **Privately Held**
WEB: www.pressofatlanticcity.com
SIC: 2086 Soft drinks: packaged in cans, bottles, etc.
HQ: Wilmington Trust Sp Services
1105 N Market St Ste 1300
Wilmington DE 19801
302 427-7650

(G-4222)
DENRON SIGN CO INC
4214 W Lincoln Hwy (19335-2225)
PHONE..................610 269-6622
Dennis Mc Laughlin, *President*
Ronald Coccetti, *Vice Pres*
Joe Dale, *Creative Dir*
EMP: 6
SQ FT: 1,800
SALES (est): 823.1K **Privately Held**
WEB: www.denronsigns.com
SIC: 3993 Electric signs

(G-4223)
DIAMOND GRAPHICS INC
456 Acorn Ln (19335-3040)
PHONE..................610 269-7335
Richard Klump, *President*
EMP: 24
SALES (est): 6.6MM **Privately Held**
SIC: 2759 Commercial printing

(G-4224)
DOWNING ENTERPRISES INC
441 Boot Rd Ste 100 (19335-5910)
PHONE..................610 873-0070
Ronald P Hohmann Sr, *President*
Robert H Hohmann, *Vice Pres*
Jack Nappi, *CFO*
◆ **EMP:** 25
SALES (est): 3.7MM
SALES (corp-wide): 225.3B **Publicly Held**
WEB: www.mii.com
SIC: 3086 Plastics foam products
HQ: Mitek Usa, Inc.
16023 Swingley Ridge Rd
Chesterfield MO 63017

(G-4225)
ELECTRONICS BOUTIQUE AMER INC
40 Quarry Rd Ste H (19335-3410)
PHONE..................610 518-5300
Katrina Leplre, *Manager*
EMP: 5
SALES (corp-wide): 8.2B **Publicly Held**
SIC: 7372 Prepackaged software
HQ: Electronics Boutique Of America Inc.
625 Westport Pkwy
Grapevine TX 76051
817 424-2000

(G-4226)
EXIDE TECHNOLOGIES
Also Called: Exide Batteries
472 Boot Rd (19335-3405)
PHONE..................610 269-0429
Anthony Cioffi, *General Mgr*
EMP: 8
SALES (corp-wide): 2.4B **Privately Held**
WEB: www.exideworld.com
SIC: 3691 3629 Storage batteries; battery chargers, rectifying or nonrotating
PA: Exide Technologies
13000 Deerfield Pkwy # 200
Milton GA 30004
678 566-9000

(G-4227)
EXPERT PR-PRESS CONSULTING LTD
Also Called: Expac Pre-Press Service Group
1030 Boot Rd (19335-4067)
PHONE..................484 401-9821
Ed Bernier, *CEO*
EMP: 5
SQ FT: 1,600
SALES: 4MM **Privately Held**
SIC: 3555 7374 Printing plates; computer graphics service

(G-4228)
G O CARLSON INC
350 Marshallton Thorndale (19335-2083)
PHONE..................610 384-2800
W Wood, *QC Mgr*
Greoge Moser, *Branch Mgr*
Thomas Buckley, *Manager*
EMP: 100
SQ FT: 24,495
SALES (corp-wide): 56.2MM **Privately Held**
WEB: www.gocarlson.com
SIC: 3356 5074 3471 3369 Nickel & nickel alloy: rolling, drawing or extruding; titanium & titanium alloy bars, sheets, strip, etc.; plumbing fittings & supplies; pipes & fittings, plastic; plumbing & heating valves; steam fittings; plating & polishing; nonferrous foundries; blast furnaces & steel mills
PA: G. O. Carlson, Inc.
175 Main St
Oil City PA 16301
814 678-4100

▲ = Import ▼=Export
◆ =Import/Export

(G-4229)
GASKET RESOURCES INC (PA)
280 Boot Rd (19335-3403)
PHONE..................................610 363-5800
Gary Chappell, *President*
◆ EMP: 21
SALES (est): 4.5MM **Privately Held**
SIC: 3053 Gaskets, all materials

(G-4230)
GENDX PRODUCTS INC
1349 Pennsridge Pl (19335-3682)
PHONE..................................443 543-5254
EMP: 3
SALES (est): 185.4K **Privately Held**
SIC: 2834 Pharmaceutical preparations

(G-4231)
GTF WORLDWIDE LLC
Also Called: Canopy Foods
454 Acorn Ln (19335-3040)
PHONE..................................610 873-3663
Kyle Buckley, *CEO*
Alex Doak, *CFO*
Gordon Livingstone, *Exec Dir*
Elly Truesdell, *Security Dir*
EMP: 73
SALES (est): 552.2K **Privately Held**
SIC: 2099 Food preparations

(G-4232)
HANSON AGGREGATES PA LLC
499 Quarry Rd (19335-3447)
PHONE..................................610 269-1710
Randy Miles, *Manager*
EMP: 60
SALES (corp-wide): 20.6B **Privately Held**
SIC: 1442 1411 Common sand mining; dimension stone
HQ: Hanson Aggregates Pennsylvania, Llc
7660 Imperial Way
Allentown PA 18195
610 366-4626

(G-4233)
HAWK CONSTRUCTION PRODUCTS
7 Martins Ln (19335-3255)
PHONE..................................610 873-8658
Brian Hawk, *President*
EMP: 9
SALES: 600K **Privately Held**
SIC: 3271 Plinth blocks, precast terrazzo

(G-4234)
HERITAGE METALWORKS LTD
2089 Bondsville Rd (19335-1123)
PHONE..................................610 518-3999
Jon White,
Matt White,
EMP: 8
SALES: 750K **Privately Held**
WEB: www.heritage-metalworks.com
SIC: 3446 Architectural metalwork

(G-4235)
HSM OF AMERICA LLC
419 Boot Rd (19335-3043)
PHONE..................................610 918-4894
Robert Ouellette, *President*
Rebecca Meick, *Vice Pres*
Mary Lou Kelley, *CFO*
Irene Dengler, *Treasurer*
Audra Hannum, *Mktg Coord*
▲ EMP: 25
SQ FT: 61,163
SALES (est): 7.4MM
SALES (corp-wide): 115.5MM **Privately Held**
WEB: www.hsmofamerica.com
SIC: 3589 Shredders, industrial & commercial
PA: Hsm Gmbh + Co. Kg
Austr. 1-9
Frickingen 88699
755 421-000

(G-4236)
JR MACHINE & TOOL INC
1100 Bondsville Rd (19335-1937)
PHONE..................................610 873-4100
Jason B Reichenbacher, *President*
EMP: 5
SALES (est): 300.6K **Privately Held**
SIC: 3599 Machine shop, jobbing & repair

(G-4237)
KMI SURGICAL LTD
110 Hopewell Rd Ste 2d (19335-1047)
PHONE..................................610 518-7110
Kristen Williams, *President*
EMP: 3
SQ FT: 5,000
SALES: 5MM **Privately Held**
WEB: www.kmisurgical.com
SIC: 3841 Surgical instruments & apparatus

(G-4238)
MAIN LINE CONCRETE & SUP INC
1001 Boot Rd (19335-4001)
PHONE..................................610 269-5556
David Aurillo, *President*
Scott Uhl, *Managing Dir*
Gary Aurillo, *Treasurer*
Andy Mooney, *Sales Staff*
Dan Iannelli, *Manager*
EMP: 15 EST: 1978
SQ FT: 10,000
SALES (est): 3.1MM **Privately Held**
SIC: 3273 5211 Ready-mixed concrete; concrete & cinder block

(G-4239)
MARSH CREEK SIGNS INC
240 Little Conestoga Rd (19335-1519)
P.O. Box 371, Uwchland (19480-0371)
PHONE..................................610 458-5503
Marie Jones, *President*
Fred Jones, *Vice Pres*
EMP: 3
SALES (est): 320.7K **Privately Held**
WEB: www.marshcreeksigns.com
SIC: 3993 Signs, not made in custom sign painting shops

(G-4240)
MATTHEY JOHNSON INC
Also Called: Colour Technologies
498 Acorn Ln (19335-3075)
PHONE..................................610 873-3200
Michael Grassie, *Prdtn Mgr*
Jerry Lopez, *Facilities Mgr*
Dave Becker, *Marketing Staff*
Laurent Cabel, *Branch Mgr*
Sujatha Nireshwalia, *Consultant*
EMP: 50
SALES (corp-wide): 19.7B **Privately Held**
SIC: 3341 Platinum group metals, smelting & refining (secondary)
HQ: Matthey Johnson Inc
435 Devon Park Dr Ste 600
Wayne PA 19087
610 971-3000

(G-4241)
MGI SEAGULL INC (PA)
520 Lincoln Ave Ste 300 (19335-3006)
PHONE..................................610 380-6470
Robert Kantner, *President*
Stephen Dudley, *Vice Pres*
Annette McAteer, *Accounting Dir*
EMP: 25
SQ FT: 22,600
SALES (est): 6.2MM **Privately Held**
WEB: www.monetgraphics.com
SIC: 2672 Adhesive papers, labels or tapes: from purchased material

(G-4242)
MOLECULAR DEVICES LLC
402 Boot Rd (19335-3405)
PHONE..................................610 873-5610
Dan Green, *Branch Mgr*
EMP: 25
SALES (corp-wide): 19.8B **Publicly Held**
WEB: www.moleculardevices.com
SIC: 3826 3841 Analytical instruments; surgical & medical instruments
HQ: Molecular Devices, Llc
3860 N 1st St
San Jose CA 95134
408 747-1700

(G-4243)
MY AUNTIES CANDIES
1419 Price Ln (19335-3622)
PHONE..................................610 269-0919
Rebecca Powell, *Principal*
EMP: 3

SALES (est): 148.6K **Privately Held**
SIC: 2066 2064 Chocolate candy, solid; lollipops & other hard candy

(G-4244)
NELSON STUD WELDING INC
260 Boot Rd (19335-3403)
PHONE..................................610 873-0012
David Preston, *Branch Mgr*
EMP: 6
SALES (corp-wide): 3.4B **Privately Held**
SIC: 7692 Welding repair
HQ: Nelson Stud Welding, Inc.
7900 W Ridge Rd
Elyria OH 44035
440 329-0400

(G-4245)
NORTHWEST BAGEL CORPORATION
Also Called: Manhattan Bagel
546 Lancaster Ct (19335-4209)
PHONE..................................610 237-0586
Simon Hong, *President*
EMP: 8
SQ FT: 2,000
SALES (est): 735K **Privately Held**
SIC: 5461 2051 Bagels; bagels, fresh or frozen

(G-4246)
NYE TECHNICAL SALES
1501 Eagle Ridge Dr (19335-3663)
PHONE..................................610 639-9985
Jeff Nye, *Principal*
EMP: 3
SALES (est): 222.1K **Privately Held**
SIC: 2295 Metallizing of fabrics

(G-4247)
PACTIV LLC
461 Boot Rd (19335-3043)
PHONE..................................610 269-1776
Dave Ochipinti, *VP Sales*
Wayne Anderson, *VP Info Sys*
EMP: 207
SALES (corp-wide): 1MM **Privately Held**
SIC: 3089 Plastic containers, except foam
HQ: Pactiv Llc
1900 W Field Ct
Lake Forest IL 60045
847 482-2000

(G-4248)
PAGE 1 PUBLISHERS INC
341 E Lancaster Ave Ste 3 (19335-2974)
PHONE..................................610 380-8264
Robert H Ludwick Jr, *President*
Dennis C Roussey, *Vice Pres*
EMP: 4
SQ FT: 400
SALES (est): 287.4K **Privately Held**
SIC: 2711 Newspapers

(G-4249)
PALACE PACKAGING MACHINES INC
4102 Edges Mill Rd (19335-1954)
PHONE..................................610 873-7252
Paul Taraschi, *President*
Stephen Taraschi, *Vice Pres*
Crhis Taraschi, *Treasurer*
Tom Getchell, *Regl Sales Mgr*
▲ EMP: 39
SQ FT: 36,000
SALES (est): 9.3MM **Privately Held**
WEB: www.unscramblers.com
SIC: 3565 Packaging machinery

(G-4250)
PPG ARCHITECTURAL FINISHES INC
Also Called: Glidden Professional Paint Ctr
255 S Bailey Rd (19335-2003)
PHONE..................................610 380-6200
John Bonner, *Manager*
EMP: 75
SALES (corp-wide): 15.3B **Publicly Held**
WEB: www.gliddenpaint.com
SIC: 2821 3081 2992 2819 Plastics materials & resins; unsupported plastics film & sheet; lubricating oils & greases; industrial inorganic chemicals

HQ: Ppg Architectural Finishes, Inc.
1 Ppg Pl
Pittsburgh PA 15272
412 434-3131

(G-4251)
PRINT BOX INC
3947 W Lincoln Hwy (19335-5503)
PHONE..................................212 741-1381
Jeffrey Huvar, *CEO*
EMP: 4
SQ FT: 2,000
SALES (est): 526.4K **Privately Held**
WEB: www.promobrands.com
SIC: 2752 Commercial printing, lithographic

(G-4252)
PROPIPE
1025 Boot Rd (19335-4001)
PHONE..................................610 518-6320
Tom Dangelo, *Principal*
EMP: 3
SALES (est): 177.8K **Privately Held**
SIC: 3498 Fabricated pipe & fittings

(G-4253)
QOVALENT
1030 Boot Rd (19335-4067)
PHONE..................................610 269-3075
Ronald G Wick, *President*
EMP: 4
SALES (est): 325.2K **Privately Held**
WEB: www.qovalent.com
SIC: 2851 Paints & allied products

(G-4254)
RICHARD SCOFIELD HSTORC LGHTNG
2089 Bondsville Rd (19335-1123)
PHONE..................................860 767-7032
Jon Joslow, *Owner*
Doreen Joslow,
EMP: 10
SALES (est): 1.4MM **Privately Held**
SIC: 3645 Residential lighting fixtures

(G-4255)
RITE ENVELOPE AND GRAPHICS INC
250 Boot Rd (19335-3403)
PHONE..................................610 518-1601
Walter Pangburn, *President*
Walter M Pangburn Jr, *Corp Secy*
EMP: 18
SALES (est): 3.8MM **Privately Held**
SIC: 2759 Envelopes: printing; stationery: printing

(G-4256)
SERV-I-QUIP INC
127 Wallace Ave (19335-2640)
PHONE..................................610 873-7010
Spencer C Deane, *CEO*
Mike Richey, *President*
Charles McGowan, *Design Engr*
Lori Halpin, *Bookkeeper*
Mike Ford, *Technology*
EMP: 30 EST: 1981
SQ FT: 11,000
SALES (est): 7MM **Privately Held**
WEB: www.siqinc.com
SIC: 3823 Industrial process control instruments

(G-4257)
STRATEGIC MFG TECH LLC
505 Trestle Pl (19335-3459)
PHONE..................................610 269-0054
Dave Misher, *Partner*
Eric Vermillion, *Partner*
EMP: 26
SQ FT: 8,000
SALES (est): 5.3MM **Privately Held**
SIC: 3672 Circuit boards, television & radio printed

(G-4258)
THORNDALE PRESS INC
3947 W Lincoln Hwy (19335-5503)
PHONE..................................610 384-3363
Harry Meraklis, *President*
EMP: 5
SQ FT: 200

SALES (est): 418.8K **Privately Held**
SIC: 2752 5112 5943 Commercial printing, offset; stationery; office supplies; office forms & supplies

(G-4259)
UPPER DARBY SIGN COMPANY
Also Called: Pro Signs
251 Boot Rd (19335-3402)
PHONE...............................610 518-5881
Jack Protesto, *CEO*
Vincent Protesto, *President*
Sean Nuttall, *Project Dir*
Amanda Schultz, *Project Mgr*
Peter Uhlman, *CFO*
▼ **EMP:** 70
SQ FT: 73,000
SALES (est): 14.6MM **Privately Held**
WEB: www.prosign.net
SIC: 7389 3993 Sign painting & lettering shop; electric signs

(G-4260)
VICTORIA ORCHARD LLC
1403 Dodd Dr (19335-3560)
PHONE...............................610 873-2848
Brenda Russell,
EMP: 4
SALES (est): 297K **Privately Held**
SIC: 3556 Mixers, commercial, food

(G-4261)
VICTORY BREWING COMPANY LLC (PA)
420 Acorn Ln (19335-3040)
PHONE...............................610 873-0881
Ron Barchet, *CEO*
William J Covaleski, *President*
Karen Lopez, *Production*
Reinhold T Barchet, *CFO*
Ani Meiklejohn, *Sales Staff*
◆ **EMP:** 42
SQ FT: 40,000
SALES (est): 12MM **Privately Held**
WEB: www.victorybeer.com
SIC: 2082 5812 2086 Malt beverages; eating places; bottled & canned soft drinks

(G-4262)
VPAK TECHNOLOGY
638 Perimeter Dr (19335-4800)
PHONE...............................610 458-8600
Richard Weber, *Owner*
EMP: 8 EST: 2012
SALES (est): 354.6K **Privately Held**
SIC: 3993 Signs & advertising specialties

(G-4263)
WESTBROOK WINDOW WASHERS LLC
1510 Waimea Dr (19335-3746)
PHONE...............................610 873-0245
William Westbrook, *Principal*
EMP: 4 EST: 2007
SALES (est): 192.1K **Privately Held**
SIC: 3452 Washers

(G-4264)
WHITE LIGHT PRODUCTIONS
505 Reeds Rd (19335-1230)
PHONE...............................610 518-0644
Mark Hall, *Partner*
Carol Hall, *Vice Pres*
EMP: 10 EST: 1986
SALES (est): 610K **Privately Held**
WEB: www.seaglass.us
SIC: 3915 Jewelers' materials & lapidary work

Doylesburg
Franklin County

(G-4265)
SCROLL PUBLISHING CO
22012 Indian Spring Trl (17219)
PHONE...............................717 349-7033
David Bercot, *Principal*
EMP: 3
SALES: 140K **Privately Held**
SIC: 2741 Miscellaneous publishing

Doylestown
Bucks County

(G-4266)
A FUNKY LITTLE SIGN SHOP
Also Called: Funky Signs of Doylestown
3605 Old Easton Rd (18902-1107)
PHONE...............................215 489-2880
Stephen Dinardo, *Owner*
EMP: 3
SALES (est): 207.2K **Privately Held**
SIC: 7532 5099 2759 Truck painting & lettering; signs, except electric; commercial printing

(G-4267)
ACCO GBC
1411 Whitehall Dr (18901-5837)
PHONE...............................267 880-6797
EMP: 3
SALES (est): 232.4K **Privately Held**
SIC: 2653 Corrugated boxes, partitions, display items, sheets & pad

(G-4268)
ADVANCED MOBILE GROUP LLC
301 S Main St Ste 1n (18901-4870)
PHONE...............................215 489-2538
Mick Gehman, *Engineer*
Wynn Polin,
Karl Herring,
EMP: 15
SQ FT: 1,900
SALES (est): 1.1MM **Privately Held**
SIC: 3577 Bar code (magnetic ink) printers

(G-4269)
AIRCRAFT INSTRUMENTS COMPANY
4039 Skyron Dr (18902-1121)
PHONE...............................215 348-5274
David C Bielecki, *CEO*
Edward M Roberts, *Vice Pres*
Pam Conway, *CIO*
▼ **EMP:** 8 EST: 1957
SQ FT: 8,500
SALES (est): 1.7MM **Privately Held**
WEB: www.aicinpa.com
SIC: 3812 Aircraft flight instruments

(G-4270)
APEX MANUFACTURING COMPANY
4800 Burnt House Hill Rd (18902-9637)
PHONE...............................215 345-4400
Chris Nagle, *Owner*
EMP: 3 EST: 2017
SALES (est): 230K **Privately Held**
SIC: 3999 Manufacturing industries

(G-4271)
ASPX LLC
1730 Lower State Rd (18901-7033)
PHONE...............................215 345-6782
Mark R Fischer,
EMP: 3
SALES (est): 126.5K **Privately Held**
SIC: 2741 Miscellaneous publishing

(G-4272)
AUMAPHARMA LLC
215 Decatur St (18901-3503)
PHONE...............................215 345-4150
Thomas Hofmann, *Principal*
EMP: 3 EST: 2010
SALES (est): 171.2K **Privately Held**
SIC: 2834 Pharmaceutical preparations

(G-4273)
AVANT-GARDE TECHNOLOGY INC
631 Spring Valley Rd (18901-3258)
PHONE...............................215 345-8228
Richard J Tems, *President*
EMP: 4
SQ FT: 7,500
SALES (est): 550K **Privately Held**
WEB: www.avantgardetech.com
SIC: 3678 3315 3489 Electronic connectors; cable, steel: insulated or armored; ordnance & accessories

(G-4274)
BELVIDERE SAND GRAVEL
350 S Main St Ste 207 (18901-4873)
PHONE...............................267 880-2422
EMP: 3
SALES (est): 177K **Privately Held**
SIC: 1442 Construction sand & gravel

(G-4275)
BINDER INDUSTRIES-CANDLEWIC
3765 Old Easton Rd (18902-1126)
PHONE...............................215 230-3601
William Binder Jr, *CEO*
◆ **EMP:** 16
SQ FT: 46,000
SALES (est): 2.7MM **Privately Held**
WEB: www.candlewic.com
SIC: 3999 Candles

(G-4276)
BIOLEAP INC
3805 Old Easton Rd (18902-8400)
PHONE...............................609 575-8645
John Kulp Jr, *President*
EMP: 8
SALES (est): 630K **Privately Held**
SIC: 2834 Pharmaceutical preparations

(G-4277)
BLOCKCOM
Also Called: Blockcom
3667 Old Easton Rd (18902-1127)
P.O. Box 3, Holicong (18928-0003)
PHONE...............................215 794-9575
Chad M Block, *Owner*
EMP: 3
SQ FT: 2,100
SALES: 600K **Privately Held**
WEB: www.chadblock.com
SIC: 3711 5065 Cars, armored, assembly of; paging & signaling equipment

(G-4278)
BOND WITH ME LLC
30 E Swamp Rd (18901-3915)
PHONE...............................267 334-1233
Maureen Karchner, *Mng Member*
EMP: 4
SALES (est): 307.3K **Privately Held**
SIC: 3845 Electromedical equipment

(G-4279)
BRADS RAW CHIPS LLC (PA)
Also Called: Brad's Raw Foods
4049 Landisville Rd (18902-1128)
P.O. Box 210, Pipersville (18947-0210)
PHONE...............................215 766-3739
Robert Brad Gruno, *Mng Member*
Walter Gruger,
▲ **EMP:** 12
SALES: 12.5MM **Privately Held**
SIC: 2099 Food preparations

(G-4280)
BREEZE DRYER
2567 Mill Rd (18902-1661)
PHONE...............................215 794-2421
Sutterlin Gayle, *Owner*
EMP: 3
SALES (est): 218.4K **Privately Held**
SIC: 3999 Manufacturing industries

(G-4281)
BRIDGE ACPUNCTURE NATURAL HLTH
30 Garden Aly (18901-4325)
PHONE...............................215 348-8058
Grace Rollin, *Owner*
EMP: 3
SALES (est): 173K **Privately Held**
SIC: 3728 Accumulators, aircraft propeller

(G-4282)
BUCKS COUNTY HERALD CORP
3828 Lucy Dr (18902-8900)
PHONE...............................215 794-2601
Donald T Gimpel, *Principal*
EMP: 3 EST: 2010
SALES (est): 120.2K **Privately Held**
SIC: 2711 Commercial printing & newspaper publishing combined

(G-4283)
BUCKS MUSICAL INSTRUMENT PDTS
40 S Sand Rd (18901-5123)
PHONE...............................215 345-9442
Karl F Dieterichs, *Owner*
EMP: 3
SQ FT: 5,000
SALES (est): 220K **Privately Held**
SIC: 5736 7699 3931 8299 Musical instrument stores; musical instrument repair services; guitars & parts, electric & nonelectric; string instruments & parts; music school

(G-4284)
C & L ENTERPRISES LLC
287 Fox Hound Dr (18901-5751)
PHONE...............................215 589-4553
Christine Salvitti, *President*
Lynn Maio, *Vice Pres*
EMP: 3
SALES (est): 116.1K **Privately Held**
SIC: 2253 T-shirts & tops, knit

(G-4285)
CALDWELLS OF BUCKS COUNTY
Also Called: Caldwell's Quality Embroidery
248 W State St (18901-3533)
PHONE...............................215 345-1348
Barbara Caldwell, *Owner*
EMP: 7
SQ FT: 700
SALES: 200K **Privately Held**
SIC: 3552 Embroidery machines

(G-4286)
CANAAN CABINETRY INC
415 E Butler Ave Ste A (18901-5263)
PHONE...............................215 348-0551
Neal Hange, *President*
Susan Hange, *Corp Secy*
EMP: 4
SQ FT: 2,500
SALES (est): 600K **Privately Held**
WEB: www.canaancabinetry.com
SIC: 2434 Wood kitchen cabinets

(G-4287)
CANDLEWIC COMPANY
3765 Old Easton Rd (18902-1126)
PHONE...............................215 230-3601
William Binder, *President*
◆ **EMP:** 4
SALES (est): 186.5K **Privately Held**
SIC: 3999 Candles

(G-4288)
CAPNOSTICS LLC
4639 Old Oak Rd (18902-8813)
PHONE...............................610 442-1363
EMP: 3
SALES (est): 178.9K **Privately Held**
SIC: 2834 Pharmaceutical preparations

(G-4289)
CARLETON INC
Also Called: Carleton Package Engineering
30 S Sand Rd (18901-5123)
PHONE...............................215 230-8900
Nicholas Carleton, *President*
Connie McDermott, *General Mgr*
Mark McDermott, *Prdtn Mgr*
Tanner Cornell, *Engineer*
Jon Fox, *CFO*
EMP: 26
SQ FT: 14,000
SALES (est): 5.3MM **Privately Held**
SIC: 8711 3565 7389 Mechanical engineering; packaging machinery; personal service agents, brokers & bureaus

(G-4290)
CAULFIELD ASSOCIATES INC
243 Harvey Ave (18901-3659)
P.O. Box 1448 (18901-0159)
PHONE...............................215 480-1940
Anthony Caulfield, *Owner*
EMP: 26
SQ FT: 10,000
SALES (est): 4.4MM **Privately Held**
WEB: www.floatingdockcentral.com
SIC: 3531 Marine related equipment

GEOGRAPHIC

(G-4291)
CHERRY STEEL CORP
113 Willowbrook Dr (18901-2887)
PHONE..................................215 340-2239
William Cherry, *President*
Anna Marie Zambriczki, *Office Mgr*
EMP: 17 **EST:** 1953
SQ FT: 35,000
SALES: 4MM **Privately Held**
WEB: www.cherrysteel.com
SIC: 3441 Expansion joints (structural shapes), iron or steel

(G-4292)
CHRIS MACHINE CO INC
110 Doyle St (18901-3702)
PHONE..................................215 348-1229
Chris Czerniakowski, *President*
EMP: 12
SQ FT: 5,600
SALES (est): 2.3MM **Privately Held**
WEB: www.chrismachine.com
SIC: 3599 Machine shop, jobbing & repair

(G-4293)
COLD SPRING CABINETRY INC
4050 Skyron Dr Ste G (18902-1143)
PHONE..................................215 348-8001
Brian Vaughan, *Principal*
EMP: 8
SQ FT: 4,840
SALES (est): 724.1K **Privately Held**
WEB: www.coldspringcabinetry.com
SIC: 2434 Wood kitchen cabinets

(G-4294)
CORTINEO CREATIVE LLC
260 N Broad St (18901-3426)
PHONE..................................215 348-1100
William Norcross, *President*
EMP: 10
SQ FT: 6,000
SALES (est): 1.7MM **Privately Held**
WEB: www.speediprintr.com
SIC: 2752 Commercial printing, offset

(G-4295)
DONAWALD ENTERPRISES LLC
13 Independence Way (18901-2253)
PHONE..................................215 962-3635
Joseph Donawald,
EMP: 10
SQ FT: 1,500
SALES: 250K **Privately Held**
WEB: www.donawald.com
SIC: 1389 Construction, repair & dismantling services

(G-4296)
EASTERN ADHESIVES INC
904 Crosskeys Dr (18902-1025)
P.O. Box 1106 (18901-0037)
PHONE..................................215 348-0119
Dale Craig, *CEO*
Joe Craig, *President*
Joseph Craig, *President*
▲ **EMP:** 12
SQ FT: 10,000
SALES (est): 2.9MM **Privately Held**
WEB: www.easternadhesives.com
SIC: 2891 Adhesives; epoxy adhesives

(G-4297)
EDISON QUARRY INC
25 Quarry Rd (18901-2809)
PHONE..................................215 348-4382
Joseph Bucciarelli, *President*
EMP: 5
SQ FT: 4,200
SALES (est): 971.9K **Privately Held**
SIC: 1429 Grits mining (crushed stone)

(G-4298)
EMC GLOBAL TECHNOLOGIES INC
4059 Skyron Dr (18902-1121)
PHONE..................................215 340-0650
Erick A Cindrich, *Vice Pres*
EMP: 6
SALES (est): 469.5K
SALES (corp-wide): 7MM **Privately Held**
SIC: 3589 Commercial cooking & food-warming equipment

PA: Emc Global Technologies, Inc.
1060 Revenue Dr
Telford PA 18969
267 347-5100

(G-4299)
ENHANCED SYSTEMS & PRODUCTS
Also Called: ESP
4700 Watson Dr (18902-1843)
PHONE..................................215 794-6942
Robert Schopf, *President*
EMP: 5
SALES (est): 989.8K **Privately Held**
WEB: www.esppdq.com
SIC: 3569 Filters

(G-4300)
FRANKLIN POTTER ASSOCIATES
3681 Cold Spg Crmry Rd (18902-1101)
PHONE..................................215 345-0844
Richard Williams, *President*
William Smith, *Corp Secy*
EMP: 5
SQ FT: 1,000
SALES: 600K **Privately Held**
WEB: www.designmanager.com
SIC: 7372 7371 Business oriented computer software; custom computer programming services

(G-4301)
GILMORE & ASSOC INC
65 E Butler Ave Ste 100 (18901-5219)
PHONE..................................215 345-4330
Tom Decker, *Principal*
Phil Donatiello, *Manager*
David N Leh, *Associate*
EMP: 11
SALES (est): 2.2MM **Privately Held**
SIC: 2833 Botanical products, medicinal: ground, graded or milled

(G-4302)
GJV PHARMA LLC
995 Ferry Rd (18901-2104)
PHONE..................................267 880-6375
EMP: 3
SALES (est): 179.6K **Privately Held**
SIC: 2834 Pharmaceutical preparations

(G-4303)
GNOSIS USA INC
4259 W Swamp Rd Ste 305 (18902-1033)
PHONE..................................215 340-7960
Marco Berna, *President*
Lorena Carboni, *Area Mgr*
Michael P Petteruti, *Vice Pres*
Mike Petteruti, *Vice Pres*
Joe Kuncewitch, *Executive*
▲ **EMP:** 4
SQ FT: 1,100
SALES (est): 7.8MM
SALES (corp-wide): 933.7K **Privately Held**
HQ: Gnosis Spa
Via Lavoratori Autobianchi 1
Desio 20832
036 248-841

(G-4304)
GRATE CLIP COMPANY INC
212 Decatur St (18901-3504)
PHONE..................................215 230-8015
Phillip Zaks, *President*
EMP: 4
SALES (est): 378.7K **Privately Held**
SIC: 3429 3089 5072 Clamps, metal; hardware, plastic; hardware

(G-4305)
HARRO HOFLIGER PACKG SYSTEMS
Also Called: Harro Hofliger Packg Systems
350 S Main St Ste 315 (18901-4874)
PHONE..................................215 345-4256
Jeff Shane, *President*
Greg Shane, *Vice Pres*
Janet Santiago, *Admin Asst*
▲ **EMP:** 20
SQ FT: 1,500

SALES (est): 4.8MM
SALES (corp-wide): 255.4MM **Privately Held**
WEB: www.hofliger.com
SIC: 3565 Packaging machinery
PA: Harro Hofliger Verpackungsmaschinen Gmbh
Helmholtzstr. 4
Allmersbach Im Tal 71573
719 150-10

(G-4306)
HOSTVEDT PAVONI INC
30 S Pine St (18901-4633)
PHONE..................................215 489-7300
Erik Hostvedt, *President*
EMP: 13
SQ FT: 2,600
SALES (est): 1.5MM **Privately Held**
SIC: 3565 Packaging machinery

(G-4307)
IMMUNOTOPE INC
3805 Old Easton Rd (18902-8400)
PHONE..................................215 489-4945
Ramila Philip, *President*
Mohan Philip, *Corp Secy*
Lorraine Keller, *Vice Pres*
Paul Von Hoegen, *Marketing Staff*
EMP: 8
SALES (est): 768.9K **Privately Held**
SIC: 8731 2836 Biotechnical research, commercial; vaccines

(G-4308)
J PENNER CORPORATION
17 Weldon Dr (18901-2359)
PHONE..................................215 340-9700
Thomas Frazier, *President*
Carol W Gaede, *Vice Pres*
EMP: 43
SQ FT: 20,000
SALES (est): 4.3MM **Privately Held**
SIC: 7389 3991 3577 Packaging & labeling services; brooms & brushes; computer peripheral equipment

(G-4309)
JDL EQUIPMENT CO
107 E Court St Ste 2 (18901-4387)
PHONE..................................215 489-0134
Jack Doyle, *Owner*
▲ **EMP:** 4
SQ FT: 250
SALES (est): 197.5K **Privately Held**
SIC: 3261 Urinals, vitreous china

(G-4310)
K & H PHARMA LLC
3805 Old Easton Rd Ofc 20 (18902-8400)
PHONE..................................267 893-6578
EMP: 3
SALES (est): 158.8K **Privately Held**
SIC: 2834 Pharmaceutical preparations

(G-4311)
KINSLEY INCORPORATED
Also Called: Roltite Capper
901 Crosskeys Dr (18902-1025)
PHONE..................................215 348-7723
Mary T McCarthy, *President*
Timothy G McCarthy, *Vice Pres*
EMP: 8 **EST:** 1957
SQ FT: 6,000
SALES (est): 2MM **Privately Held**
WEB: www.kinsleyinc.com
SIC: 3565 3599 5084 Bottling machinery: filling, capping, labeling; custom machinery; industrial machinery & equipment

(G-4312)
LEXYLINE MILLWORK
196 W Ashland St (18901-4040)
PHONE..................................267 895-1733
Joe Bendick, *Principal*
EMP: 35
SALES: 950K **Privately Held**
SIC: 2431 Millwork

(G-4313)
LISA LELEU STUDIOS INC
100 Mechanics St Ste 1 (18901-3700)
PHONE..................................215 345-1233
Lisa Leleu, *President*
Frederic Leleu, *Vice Pres*
Frederick Leleu, *Vice Pres*

▲ **EMP:** 3
SQ FT: 5,000
SALES (est): 333.5K **Privately Held**
SIC: 2732 3944 Books: printing & binding; games, toys & children's vehicles

(G-4314)
LYNX SPECIALTY TAPES INC
4264 Southview Ln (18902-1533)
PHONE..................................215 348-1382
Don Heywood, *President*
John Coyne, *Vice Pres*
Jim Reed, *Vice Pres*
EMP: 6
SALES (est): 421.1K **Privately Held**
WEB: www.lynxspecialtytapes.com
SIC: 2891 Adhesives

(G-4315)
MERCHANDISING METHODS INC
800 W State St (18901-2250)
PHONE..................................215 262-4842
Matthew Urban, *President*
Lynn Urban, *Vice Pres*
EMP: 25
SQ FT: 2,400
SALES (est): 957.2K **Privately Held**
SIC: 3993 Displays & cutouts, window & lobby; displays, paint process

(G-4316)
MILLENIUM MEDICAL EDUCATIONAL
1980 S Easton Rd Ste 240 (18901-7103)
PHONE..................................215 230-1960
Peg Forster, *President*
Brian Naulty, *Vice Pres*
Molly Whetstone, *Prdtn Dir*
Kelsey Bray, *Production*
Beth Clark, *CFO*
EMP: 20
SQ FT: 4,600
SALES (est): 3.3MM **Privately Held**
SIC: 7313 2741 Radio, television, publisher representatives; miscellaneous publishing

(G-4317)
N-ZYME SCIENTIFICS LLC
3805 Old Easton Rd (18902-8400)
PHONE..................................267 218-1098
David Hamlin,
Nelson Carvalho,
Anand Mehta,
Romano Patrick,
EMP: 4 **EST:** 2013
SQ FT: 874
SALES (est): 228.8K **Privately Held**
SIC: 2835 Enzyme & isoenzyme diagnostic agents

(G-4318)
NAVAL COMPANY INC
4747 Cold Spg Crmry Rd (18902-1208)
PHONE..................................215 348-8982
Renton W Meininger Jr, *President*
Mary Elizabeth Meininger, *Admin Sec*
EMP: 4 **EST:** 1860
SQ FT: 8,000
SALES (est): 723.3K **Privately Held**
WEB: www.navalcompany.com
SIC: 3357 3489 Shipboard cable, nonferrous; cannons & howitzers, over 30 mm.

(G-4319)
NU TECH INC
5985 Carversville Rd (18902-9201)
P.O. Box 1425, Newtown (18940-0886)
PHONE..................................215 297-8889
Charles Trowbridge, *President*
Linda Trowbridge, *Corp Secy*
▲ **EMP:** 21
SQ FT: 1,400
SALES (est): 3.1MM **Privately Held**
SIC: 3646 Commercial indusl & institutional electric lighting fixtures

(G-4320)
ONCORE BIOPHARMA INC
3805 Old Easton Rd (18902-8400)
PHONE..................................215 589-6378
Mark Murry, *CEO*
Bruce Dorsey, *Vice Pres*
Herb Conrad, *Bd of Directors*
EMP: 16

SALES (est): 2.6MM
SALES (corp-wide): 10.7MM **Privately Held**
SIC: 2834 Pharmaceutical preparations
PA: Arbutus Biopharma Corporation
8900 Glenlyon Pky Suite 100
Burnaby BC V5J 5
604 419-3200

(G-4321)
OSPCOM LLC
350 S Main St Ste 107 (18901-4872)
PHONE.................................267 356-7124
Aykut Balkaya,
EMP: 5
SALES (est): 506.6K **Privately Held**
SIC: 3663 3661 3357 3678 Radio & TV communications equipment; telephone & telegraph apparatus; nonferrous wire-drawing & insulating; electronic connectors; visual communication systems

(G-4322)
PENN COLOR INC (PA)
400 Old Dublin Pike (18901-2399)
PHONE.................................215 345-6550
Kevin Putman, President
Thomas Farrell, Vice Pres
James P Garton, Vice Pres
David Owings, Vice Pres
Steve Wise, Plant Mgr
◆ EMP: 30 EST: 1977
SQ FT: 6,360
SALES (est): 183.9MM **Privately Held**
WEB: www.penncolor.com
SIC: 2865 2816 Color pigments, organic; color pigments

(G-4323)
PEREGRINE SURGICAL LTD
51 Britain Dr (18901-5186)
PHONE.................................215 348-0456
John Richmond, President
Leo Zamparelli, Shareholder
EMP: 40
SQ FT: 7,500
SALES (est): 6.6MM **Privately Held**
WEB: www.peregrinesurgical.com
SIC: 3841 Ophthalmic instruments & apparatus

(G-4324)
PERRY ERCOLINO INC
51 E Oakland Ave (18901-4604)
PHONE.................................215 348-5885
Perry S Ercolino, President
EMP: 6
SQ FT: 1,500
SALES: 340K **Privately Held**
WEB: www.perryercolino.com
SIC: 3143 7251 Men's footwear, except athletic; shoe repair shop

(G-4325)
PIONEER BURIAL VAULT CO INC
Crosskeys Rd Rr 611 (18901)
P.O. Box 347 (18901-0347)
PHONE.................................215 766-2943
Herbert Hevener, President
Joseph F Hevener, Corp Secy
EMP: 10
SALES (est): 1.3MM **Privately Held**
SIC: 3272 Burial vaults, concrete or pre-cast terrazzo

(G-4326)
POINT OF VIEW LLC
24 N Main St (18901-4330)
PHONE.................................215 340-1725
Terry Layman, Owner
EMP: 3
SALES (est): 234.2K **Privately Held**
SIC: 3851 Eyeglasses, lenses & frames

(G-4327)
PRESTI GROUP INC
200 Hyde Park (18902-6623)
PHONE.................................215 340-2870
Duane Presti, President
EMP: 15
SQ FT: 6,000
SALES (est): 2MM **Privately Held**
SIC: 3069 Custom compounding of rubber materials

(G-4328)
PRESTIGE INSTITUTE FOR PLASTIC
79 Bittersweet Dr (18901-2774)
PHONE.................................215 275-1011
Joseph Tamburrino MD, Principal
EMP: 5
SALES (est): 119.8K **Privately Held**
SIC: 2821 Plastics materials & resins

(G-4329)
PROPHASE LABS INC (PA)
621 N Shady Retreat Rd (18901-2514)
PHONE.................................215 345-0919
Ted Karkus, Ch of Bd
Monica Brady, CFO
Richard Dillon, Manager
EMP: 46
SQ FT: 13,000
SALES: 13.1MM **Publicly Held**
WEB: www.quigleyco.com
SIC: 8731 2834 Commercial physical research; cold remedies

(G-4330)
PYXIDIS
1050 Crosskeys Dr (18902-1019)
PHONE.................................267 614-8348
David Hollner, Branch Mgr
EMP: 3
SALES (corp-wide): 55.5K **Privately Held**
SIC: 3845 Ultrasonic scanning devices, medical
PA: Emrah Erkaraman
No.22/B Kanal Mah. A. Vefikpasa Cad.
Antalya

(G-4331)
QUALITY SYSTEMS ASSOCIATES (PA)
100 Mechanics St Ste 2 (18901-3700)
PHONE.................................215 345-5575
Robert E Mahoney Jr, President
EMP: 5
SALES (est): 935.3K **Privately Held**
WEB: www.qsa.com
SIC: 7372 Home entertainment computer software

(G-4332)
QUIRE LLC
23 Taylor Ave (18901-4616)
PHONE.................................267 935-9777
Kelly L Stratton, Principal
EMP: 7
SALES (est): 78.7K **Privately Held**
SIC: 7372 Publishers' computer software

(G-4333)
RAGE BULK SYSTEMS LTD
607 Airport Blvd (18902-1004)
P.O. Box 416, Chalfont (18914-0416)
PHONE.................................215 489-5373
Rolfe A Stapenell, CEO
James Baldwin, President
EMP: 30
SQ FT: 25,000
SALES: 1.3MM **Privately Held**
WEB: www.ragebulksystems.com
SIC: 3535 Conveyors & conveying equipment

(G-4334)
REED DRABICK INC
Also Called: Reed Drabick Publishers
3771 Sablewood Dr (18902-6610)
PHONE.................................215 794-2068
David Drabick, President
▲ EMP: 6
SALES (est): 293.3K **Privately Held**
SIC: 2759 Promotional printing

(G-4335)
ROCHESTER PHARMACEUTICALS
43 S Main St (18901-4640)
PHONE.................................215 345-4880
Carol McMorris, Principal
EMP: 4 EST: 2011
SQ FT: 1,300
SALES (est): 87.5K **Privately Held**
SIC: 2834 Pharmaceutical preparations

(G-4336)
SCHNEIDER ELECTRIC IT CORP
3853 E Brandon Way (18902-6229)
PHONE.................................215 230-7270
Domenic Alcaro, Branch Mgr
EMP: 5
SALES (corp-wide): 355.8K **Privately Held**
WEB: www.apcc.com
SIC: 3568 Power transmission equipment
HQ: Schneider Electric It Corporation
132 Fairgrounds Rd
West Kingston RI 02892
401 789-5735

(G-4337)
SEAPOINT ENTERPRISES INC
Also Called: Home Mag The
199 Washington St (18901-4036)
P.O. Box 1881 (18901-0377)
PHONE.................................215 230-6933
Tom Balutis, President
EMP: 5 EST: 2015
SALES (est): 267.3K **Privately Held**
SIC: 2721 Periodicals-Publishing/Printing

(G-4338)
SRM ENTERTAINMENT GROUP LLC (PA)
4030 Skyron Dr Ste C (18902-1135)
PHONE.................................610 825-1039
Chris Fergusan, CEO
Rachele Cheli, CFO
EMP: 15
SALES (est): 1.8MM **Privately Held**
SIC: 3944 7389 Games, toys & children's vehicles; design services

(G-4339)
STEQ AMERICA LLC
1456 Ferry Rd Ste 501 (18901-2394)
PHONE.................................267 644-5477
EMP: 5
SALES (est): 355.6K **Privately Held**
SIC: 3559 8731 Pharmaceutical machinery; biotechnical research, commercial

(G-4340)
SUPERIOR WOODCRAFT INC
160 N Hamilton St (18901-3654)
PHONE.................................215 348-9942
Michelle G Kennedy, President
Michelle Kennedy, President
Sabina Geiger, Vice Pres
Amanda Bertele, Corp Comm Staff
Sandra Dearden, Admin Asst
EMP: 39 EST: 1967
SQ FT: 30,000
SALES (est): 6.2MM **Privately Held**
WEB: www.superiorwoodcraft.com
SIC: 2434 Vanities, bathroom: wood

(G-4341)
TECHNI-FORMS INC
601 Airport Blvd (18902-1004)
PHONE.................................215 345-0333
Patricia D Gorton, President
Patricia Gorton, President
EMP: 20 EST: 1978
SQ FT: 27,000
SALES (est): 2.8MM **Privately Held**
WEB: www.techniforms.com
SIC: 2761 Manifold business forms

(G-4342)
TIN TINKER
3781 Dogwood Ln (18902-6607)
PHONE.................................215 230-9619
Delores T Clauss, Owner
EMP: 3
SALES (est): 184.6K **Privately Held**
SIC: 3356 Tin

(G-4343)
TOHICKON TOOL & DIE CO
Also Called: A C
4130 Stump Rd (18902-9128)
PHONE.................................215 766-8285
Thomas Barany, President
Steven Barany, Vice Pres
Elmer Barany, Treasurer
EMP: 5
SQ FT: 4,000
SALES (est): 791.6K **Privately Held**
SIC: 3544 Special dies & tools

(G-4344)
VOCAM CORP
Also Called: Minuteman Press
451 N Main St Ste A (18901-3427)
PHONE.................................215 348-7115
Ormond Hearn Sr, President
Dorothy Hearn, Admin Sec
EMP: 7
SQ FT: 2,200
SALES: 1.2MM **Privately Held**
SIC: 2752 2791 2789 2759 Commercial printing, offset; typesetting; bookbinding & related work; commercial printing; automotive & apparel trimmings

(G-4345)
WIRELESS EXPERIENCE OF PA INC
4341 W Swamp Rd (18902-1039)
PHONE.................................215 340-1382
Mike Comunale, Director
EMP: 8
SALES (corp-wide): 34.8MM **Privately Held**
SIC: 2451 Mobile homes
PA: The Wireless Experience Of Pa Inc
509 N Main St
Manahawkin NJ 08050
732 552-0050

(G-4346)
WKW ASSOCIATES LLC
Also Called: Tomtec Sales
206 Oneida Ln (18901-5054)
PHONE.................................215 348-1257
Brett Bauz, VP Sls/Mktg
EMP: 12 EST: 2008
SALES (est): 1.1MM **Privately Held**
SIC: 3999 Manufacturing industries

(G-4347)
YOGO FACTORIES
73 Old Dublin Pike (18901-2491)
PHONE.................................215 230-9646
EMP: 4 EST: 2012
SALES (est): 245.3K **Privately Held**
SIC: 2026 Mfg Fluid Milk

(G-4348)
ZAVETA MILLWORK SPC INC
4030 Skyron Dr Ste H (18902-1135)
PHONE.................................215 489-4065
Richard D Zaveta, President
EMP: 6
SALES (est): 963.9K **Privately Held**
SIC: 2431 Millwork

(G-4349)
ZENCO MACHINE & TOOL CO INC
205 N Broad St (18901-3785)
PHONE.................................215 345-6262
Harry Burak, President
EMP: 8
SQ FT: 9,000
SALES (est): 1.1MM **Privately Held**
SIC: 3599 Machine shop, jobbing & repair

Dravosburg
Allegheny County

(G-4350)
A CRANE RENTAL LLC (PA)
200 Washington Ave (15034-1108)
PHONE.................................412 469-1776
William McCade, Mng Member
EMP: 29
SALES (est): 18.4MM **Privately Held**
SIC: 3531 Construction machinery

(G-4351)
KLEEN LINE SERVICE CO INC
Also Called: Kleen-Line Parts Clr Svc Co
524 Washington Ave (15034-1329)
PHONE.................................412 466-6277
Richard Abdulovic, President
Daryl Abdulovic, Vice Pres
EMP: 4
SALES (est): 534.1K **Privately Held**
SIC: 3559 5169 Automotive maintenance equipment; industrial chemicals

Dresher
Montgomery County

(G-4352)
ALLIED CONCRETE & SUPPLY CORP (PA)
1752 Limekiln Pike Ste 1 (19025-1599)
PHONE..................................215 646-8484
Thad Murwin, President
William J Murwin Jr, President
William J Murwin III, Vice Pres
EMP: 26
SQ FT: 50,000
SALES (est): 15.3MM Privately Held
SIC: 3273 4225 4212 Ready-mixed concrete; general warehousing; local trucking, without storage

(G-4353)
AUCH PRINTING INC
1351 Harris Rd (19025-1103)
PHONE..................................215 886-9133
James Auch, President
EMP: 6 EST: 1947
SQ FT: 4,000
SALES (est): 809.8K Privately Held
SIC: 2752 Commercial printing, offset

(G-4354)
EMMA ONE SOCK INC
566 Cardinal Dr (19025-1923)
PHONE..................................215 542-1082
Linda Podietz, President
Eric Podietz, Treasurer
EMP: 3
SALES (est): 314.1K Privately Held
SIC: 2361 Girls' & children's dresses, blouses & shirts

(G-4355)
GENERAL MILLS INC
200 Dryden Rd E Ste 3000 (19025-1049)
PHONE..................................215 784-5100
Jim Healy, Manager
EMP: 100
SALES (corp-wide): 15.7B Publicly Held
WEB: www.generalmills.com
SIC: 5149 2041 Breakfast cereals; flour mixes
PA: General Mills, Inc.
  1 General Mills Blvd
  Minneapolis MN 55426
  763 764-7600

(G-4356)
LRP MAGAZINE GROUP
Also Called: Axon Magazine Group
747 Dresher Rd Ste 500 (19025)
PHONE..................................215 784-0860
Ken Kahn, President
EMP: 300
SALES (est): 14.3MM
SALES (corp-wide): 111.8MM Privately Held
WEB: www.juryverdictresearch.com
SIC: 2721 Magazines: publishing only, not printed on site
PA: Lrp Publications, Inc.
  360 Hiatt Dr
  Palm Beach Gardens FL 33418
  215 784-0860

(G-4357)
ROBERT WOOLER COMPANY
1755 Susquehanna Rd (19025-1508)
PHONE..................................215 542-7600
Philip C Keidel Jr, President
Robert Coyle, Vice Pres
Robert M Coyle, Vice Pres
Robert Keidel, Shareholder
Robert W Keidel, Shareholder
EMP: 35 EST: 1923
SQ FT: 32,000
SALES (est): 8.2MM Privately Held
WEB: www.robertwooler.com
SIC: 3398 Metal heat treating

(G-4358)
SLOAN EQUIPMENT SALES CO INC (PA)
1677 Tuckerstown Rd (19025-1320)
PHONE..................................215 784-0771
Louis Sloan, President

Cynthia Sloan, Vice Pres
EMP: 2
SQ FT: 1,200
SALES (est): 14.5MM Privately Held
WEB: www.sloanequip.com
SIC: 3826 Environmental testing equipment

(G-4359)
TOSHIBA INTERNATIONAL CORP
200 Dryden Rd E (19025-1044)
PHONE..................................215 830-3340
Erica Toshiba, Branch Mgr
EMP: 9
SALES (corp-wide): 37B Privately Held
SIC: 3621 Motors & generators
HQ: Toshiba International Corporation
  13131 W Little York Rd
  Houston TX 77041
  800 231-1412

Drexel Hill
Delaware County

(G-4360)
AVA ELECTRONICS CORP
4000 Bridge St (19026-2799)
P.O. Box 184 (19026-0184)
PHONE..................................610 284-2500
Mario Rafalin, President
EMP: 25 EST: 1965
SQ FT: 30,000
SALES (est): 2.9MM Privately Held
SIC: 3643 Connectors & terminals for electrical devices

(G-4361)
BOSHA DESIGN INC
707 Burmont Rd (19026-3942)
PHONE..................................610 622-4422
Barbara Bosha, President
Sallie Garfield, Manager
EMP: 3
SQ FT: 1,962
SALES (est): 274.4K Privately Held
WEB: www.boshadesign.com
SIC: 7336 3953 8999 Graphic arts & related design; irons, marking or branding; communication services

(G-4362)
CONICELLA-FESSLER DENTAL LAB
409 Shadeland Ave (19026-1437)
PHONE..................................610 622-3298
Hong Mpham, President
William Fessler, Corp Secy
EMP: 5
SQ FT: 3,600
SALES: 450K Privately Held
SIC: 8072 3843 Artificial teeth production; denture production; dental equipment & supplies

(G-4363)
CRADDOCK & LERRO ASSOCIATES
1005 Pontiac Rd Ste 312 (19026-4816)
PHONE..................................610 543-0200
William J Lerro, Owner
EMP: 3
SQ FT: 2,600
SALES (est): 298.7K Privately Held
SIC: 5044 7389 3577 Micrographic equipment; microfilm equipment; microfilm recording & developing service; magnetic ink & optical scanning devices

(G-4364)
HELP EVERY ADDICT LIVE
3816 Berry Ave (19026-3620)
PHONE..................................484 598-3285
Patrick Brennan, President
EMP: 4
SALES (est): 42.4K Privately Held
SIC: 8322 7372 Rehabilitation services; application computer software

(G-4365)
HOODCO INC
1024 Drexel Ave (19026-4002)
PHONE..................................215 236-0951

Phillip Di Donato, President
EMP: 10
SALES (est): 1.3MM Privately Held
SIC: 3312 Stainless steel

(G-4366)
HURLOCK BROS CO INC
547 Forrest Ave (19026-1314)
PHONE..................................610 659-8153
Allen W Beck Jr, President
Gary H Uhrman, Corp Secy
EMP: 17 EST: 1901
SQ FT: 30,000
SALES (est): 1.3MM Privately Held
SIC: 2599 2631 2273 Boards: planning, display, notice; paperboard mills; carpets & rugs

(G-4367)
KELLYS TROPHIES
3621 Garrett Rd (19026-2321)
PHONE..................................610 626-3300
Edward A Kelly Sr, Owner
Ana Davis, Manager
EMP: 10
SQ FT: 5,000
SALES: 1MM Privately Held
SIC: 3914 5094 5999 Trophies, plated (all metals); trophies; trophies & plaques

(G-4368)
KINGDOM EXPOSURE LTD
4633 State Rd (19026-4423)
P.O. Box 673, Pilgrim Gardens (19026-0673)
PHONE..................................215 621-8291
EMP: 3
SALES (est): 146.8K Privately Held
SIC: 2752 Commercial printing, lithographic

(G-4369)
NATION-WIDE SIGN SERVICE INC
3015 Garrett Rd (19026-2216)
P.O. Box 84 (19026-0084)
PHONE..................................888 234-5300
Francis X Hughes, President
▲ EMP: 3
SALES (est): 258.1K Privately Held
WEB: www.nationwidesignservice.com
SIC: 1799 3993 Sign installation & maintenance; signs & advertising specialties

(G-4370)
OGI INC
Also Called: O G Industries
4219 Garrett Rd (19026-5236)
PHONE..................................610 623-6747
Peter Ganz, President
EMP: 3
SALES (est): 327.1K Privately Held
SIC: 2842 Deodorants, nonpersonal

(G-4371)
SOPHISTICAKES INC
4624 Drexelbrook Dr (19026)
PHONE..................................610 626-9991
Cathy Pawlicki, President
Vincent Pawlicki, Vice Pres
EMP: 4
SQ FT: 1,450
SALES: 25K Privately Held
SIC: 2051 2052 Cakes, bakery: except frozen; cookies

(G-4372)
STUCCO CODE INC
918 Shadeland Ave (19026-1723)
PHONE..................................610 348-3905
John Shields, Principal
EMP: 3
SALES (est): 199.1K Privately Held
SIC: 3299 Stucco

(G-4373)
XENSOR CORPORATION
4000 Bridge St (19026-2711)
P.O. Box 188 (19026-0188)
PHONE..................................610 284-2508
Mario Rafalin, President
Dorothy Ryan, Executive
EMP: 50
SQ FT: 30,000

SALES (est): 5MM Privately Held
WEB: www.xensor.com
SIC: 3829 3812 3674 Measuring & controlling devices; search & navigation equipment; semiconductors & related devices

Drifting
Clearfield County

(G-4374)
CUTTING EDGE MACHINING
75 Basin Run Rd (16834)
P.O. Box 248 (16834-0248)
PHONE..................................814 345-6690
Daniel Smitchko, President
Kimberly Smitchko, Corp Secy
▲ EMP: 23
SQ FT: 1,900
SALES: 2MM Privately Held
SIC: 3599 Machine shop, jobbing & repair

(G-4375)
PTS INDUSTRIES CORP
Also Called: Dura-Kan
506 Firehouse Rd (16834)
PHONE..................................814 345-5200
Patrick Shive, CEO
EMP: 11
SQ FT: 16,000
SALES (est): 2.3MM Privately Held
SIC: 3443 5064 Dumpsters, garbage; garbage disposals

Drifton
Luzerne County

(G-4376)
DRIFTON PRECISION MACHINING
Rr 940 (18221)
P.O. Box 250 (18221-0250)
PHONE..................................570 636-1408
Joseph Maduro, Owner
EMP: 3
SALES: 200K Privately Held
SIC: 3599 Machine shop, jobbing & repair

Driftwood
Cameron County

(G-4377)
MASON HILL LOGGING
5838 Mason Hill Rd (15832-4120)
PHONE..................................814 546-2478
Joshua Patton, Principal
EMP: 3
SALES (est): 175.6K Privately Held
SIC: 2411 Logging

Drumore
Lancaster County

(G-4378)
HENRYS WELDING INC
1537 River Rd (17518-9750)
PHONE..................................717 548-2460
Norman Henry Jr, President
Judith E Henry, Vice Pres
EMP: 7
SALES: 300K Privately Held
SIC: 7692 Welding repair

(G-4379)
SCALPY HOLLOW TIMBER SERVICE
1147 Scalpy Hollow Rd (17518-9753)
PHONE..................................717 284-2862
Elmer G Stoltzsus, Partner
Aaron G Stoltzsus, Partner
EMP: 6 EST: 1995
SALES (est): 605K Privately Held
SIC: 2421 2411 Sawmills & planing mills, general; logging

Drums
Luzerne County

(G-4380)
ABF USA LTD
Also Called: Kite Tables
72 Hillside Dr (18222-2150)
PHONE.................................570 788-0888
Darren Buttle, *Principal*
Mike Prendergast, *Principal*
Joe Prendergast, *Vice Pres*
▲ EMP: 5
SALES (est): 248.9K Privately Held
SIC: 2521 Wood office desks & tables

(G-4381)
CHALLENGER FABRICATION
30 N Old Turnpike Rd B (18222-1900)
PHONE.................................570 788-7911
▲ EMP: 4
SALES (est): 339.4K Privately Held
SIC: 3441 Fabricated structural metal

(G-4382)
DW MACHINE & FABRICATING
109 Birch St (18222-2158)
PHONE.................................570 788-8144
Dennis Wenner, *Owner*
EMP: 6
SALES (est): 696.8K Privately Held
SIC: 3599 Machine shop, jobbing & repair

(G-4383)
SIEGWERK USA INC
Also Called: Siegwerk Ink Packaging
80 Hillside Dr (18222-2150)
PHONE.................................570 708-0267
Beth Denim, *Manager*
EMP: 6
SALES (corp-wide): 940.5K Privately
Held
WEB: www.sipana.com
SIC: 2893 Printing ink
HQ: Siegwerk Usa Inc.
    3535 Sw 56th St
    Des Moines IA 50321
    515 471-2100

Dry Run
Franklin County

(G-4384)
NEW ENTERPRISE STONE LIME INC
18746 Dry Run Rd W (17220)
PHONE.................................717 349-2412
Steven Scott, *Manager*
EMP: 7
SALES (corp-wide): 651.9MM Privately
Held
WEB: www.nesl.com
SIC: 1422 3273 Limestones, ground;
    ready-mixed concrete
PA: New Enterprise Stone & Lime Co., Inc.
    3912 Brumbaugh Rd
    New Enterprise PA 16664
    814 224-6883

Du Bois
Clearfield County

(G-4385)
BURKE PARSONS BOWLBY CORP
392 Larkeytown Rd (15801-3940)
P.O. Box 287 (15801-0287)
PHONE.................................814 371-3042
Richard E Bowlby, *Principal*
EMP: 4 EST: 2009
SALES (est): 430.7K Privately Held
SIC: 5031 2421 Lumber, plywood & mill-
    work; railroad ties, sawed

(G-4386)
CARLSON TECHNOLOGIES INC
213 Hahne Ct (15801-1507)
PHONE.................................814 371-5500
Gary Carlson, *CEO*
Debra Carlson, *Vice Pres*
EMP: 17
SQ FT: 200
SALES (est): 1.8MM Privately Held
SIC: 1311 4924 Natural gas production;
    natural gas distribution

(G-4387)
DOMTAR PAPER COMPANY LLC
377 Satterlee Rd (15801-2969)
PHONE.................................814 371-0630
Raymond Royer, *Principal*
Ann Sunealitis, *Purch Agent*
EMP: 25
SALES (corp-wide): 301.1MM Privately
Held
SIC: 2621 Paper mills
HQ: Domtar Paper Company, Llc
    234 Kingsley Park Dr
    Fort Mill SC 29715

(G-4388)
DU PENN INC
Also Called: Igm Carbon
160 Barnoff Rd (15801-4504)
PHONE.................................814 371-6280
Charles T Moore, *President*
Gordon N Place, *Corp Secy*
EMP: 16 EST: 1966
SQ FT: 30,000
SALES (est): 2.1MM Privately Held
WEB: www.igmcarbon.com
SIC: 3295 Graphite, natural: ground, pul-
    verized, refined or blended

(G-4389)
DUBROOK INC (PA)
40 Hoover Ave (15801-2404)
P.O. Box 376, Falls Creek (15840-0376)
PHONE.................................814 371-3113
Rosemary O Barber, *President*
Jeffrey Gankosky, *Credit Staff*
Diana L Peck, *Admin Sec*
EMP: 6 EST: 1946
SQ FT: 3,000
SALES (est): 9.1MM Privately Held
WEB: www.dubrook.com
SIC: 3273 5032 Ready-mixed concrete;
    aggregate

(G-4390)
DUBROOK INC
40 Parkway Dr (15801-2418)
PHONE.................................814 371-3111
Matt Manning, *Manager*
EMP: 30
SALES (corp-wide): 9.1MM Privately
Held
WEB: www.dubrook.com
SIC: 3273 Ready-mixed concrete
PA: Dubrook, Inc.
    40 Hoover Ave
    Du Bois PA 15801
    814 371-3113

(G-4391)
ERICKSON CORPORATION
11 Clear Run Rd (15801-6121)
PHONE.................................814 371-4350
Don H Erickson Jr, *Ch of Bd*
Don H Erickson III, *President*
Marlene Godak, *Corp Secy*
EMP: 20 EST: 1956
SQ FT: 20,000
SALES (est): 3.4MM Privately Held
SIC: 3599 3613 Machine shop, jobbing &
    repair; control panels, electric

(G-4392)
GASBARRE PRODUCTS INC (PA)
Also Called: Sinterite Furnace Division
590 Division St (15801-2530)
P.O. Box 1022 (15801-1022)
PHONE.................................814 371-3015
Thomas G Gasbarre, *CEO*
Alex T Gasbarre, *President*
Alex Gasbarre, *General Mgr*
Benjamin T Gasbarre, *Vice Pres*
Jeffrey W Gasbarre, *Vice Pres*
◆ EMP: 80
SQ FT: 200,000

SALES: 40MM Privately Held
WEB: www.gasbarre.com
SIC: 3542 3567 3544 Machine tools,
    metal forming type; industrial furnaces &
    ovens; special dies, tools, jigs & fixtures

(G-4393)
GKN SINTER METALS - DUBOIS INC
Also Called: GKN Instruments
1 Tom Mix Dr (15801-2547)
P.O. Box 1047 (15801-1047)
PHONE.................................814 375-0938
Randy Norris, *Plant Mgr*
Terri Steighner, *Purch Agent*
Ron London, *Engineer*
Tim Van Slander, *Manager*
Tim Carlson, *Senior Mgr*
◆ EMP: 60
SQ FT: 60,000
SALES (est): 13.9MM
SALES (corp-wide): 2.7B Privately Held
SIC: 3399 3568 3366 Powder, metal;
    power transmission equipment; copper
    foundries
HQ: Gkn Sinter Metals, Llc
    2200 N Opdyke Rd
    Auburn Hills MI 48326
    248 296-7832

(G-4394)
GLOBAL FABRICATION INC
235 Beaver Dr (15801-2517)
P.O. Box 626 (15801-0626)
PHONE.................................814 372-1500
Dennis V Raybuck, *President*
Kenneth J Mitchell, *Vice Pres*
Rebecca F Raybuck, *Vice Pres*
Molly Kelsey, *CFO*
▼ EMP: 65
SQ FT: 50,000
SALES (est): 19.1MM Privately Held
SIC: 3441 Fabricated structural metal

(G-4395)
HEAD TO TOE SPORTSWEAR
128 W Long Ave Apt A (15801-2104)
PHONE.................................814 371-5119
Brian Caruso, *Owner*
Sue Caruso, *Co-Owner*
EMP: 3
SQ FT: 7,500
SALES (est): 368.9K Privately Held
SIC: 2759 Screen printing

(G-4396)
INVENSYS ENERGY METERING CORP
805 Liberty Blvd (15801-2421)
PHONE.................................814 371-3011
Michael Show, *President*
Dan Harness, *Vice Pres*
Jim Thomson, *VP Opers*
Tim Dolan, *Admin Sec*
▲ EMP: 300
SQ FT: 150,000
SALES (est): 38.9MM Publicly Held
SIC: 3824 3829 3674 3613 Gas meters,
    domestic & large capacity: industrial;
    measuring & controlling devices; semi-
    conductors & related devices; switchgear
    & switchboard apparatus; transformers,
    except electric
HQ: Sensus Usa Inc.
    8601 Six Forks Rd Ste 700
    Raleigh NC 27615
    919 845-4000

(G-4397)
J A KOHLEPP AND SONS STONE (PA)
Also Called: Kohlepp Stone Center
650 Dubois St (15801-1831)
P.O. Box 423 (15801-0423)
PHONE.................................814 371-5200
Benjamin Kohlepp, *President*
Jene Painter, *CFO*
EMP: 15
SALES (est): 7.5MM Privately Held
SIC: 3281 Table tops, marble

(G-4398)
J A KOHLHEPP SONS INC (PA)
Also Called: Kohlhepp Stone Center
650 Dubois St (15801-1831)
P.O. Box 423 (15801-0423)
PHONE.................................814 371-5200
Benjamin R Kohlhepp, *President*
Christine Kohlhepp, *Corp Secy*
Andrew J Kohlhepp, *Vice Pres*
Jean Painter, *CFO*
EMP: 94 EST: 1903
SQ FT: 50,000
SALES (est): 23.7MM Privately Held
SIC: 5251 5211 3271 7359 Hardware;
    lumber & other building materials; blocks,
    concrete or cinder: standard; equipment
    rental & leasing

(G-4399)
JERDEN INDUSTRIES INC
Also Called: C W Graphics Co
24 W Washington Ave (15801-7724)
P.O. Box 927 (15801-5927)
PHONE.................................814 375-7822
Jerry R Croasman, *President*
Dennis R Welsh, *Vice Pres*
Rose Croasman, *Admin Sec*
EMP: 10
SQ FT: 12,000
SALES (est): 1.3MM Privately Held
WEB: www.cwgraphics.biz
SIC: 2752 Commercial printing, litho-
    graphic

(G-4400)
KINETIC
2 E Maloney Rd (15801-1316)
PHONE.................................814 603-1131
Kristy Bell, *Principal*
EMP: 3
SALES (est): 158.2K Privately Held
SIC: 3842 Braces, orthopedic

(G-4401)
L B TONEY CO
153 Beaver Dr (15801-2515)
P.O. Box 336 (15801-1023)
PHONE.................................814 375-9974
Lawrence B Toney, *President*
▲ EMP: 10 EST: 1973
SQ FT: 10,000
SALES (est): 660K Privately Held
SIC: 3398 Metal heat treating

(G-4402)
LABUE PRINTING INC
140 Mccracken Run Rd (15801-3616)
PHONE.................................814 371-5059
Craig A Labue, *President*
Lisa A Labue, *President*
Larry Barber, *Treasurer*
EMP: 7
SQ FT: 3,000
SALES (est): 873.1K Privately Held
WEB: www.labueprintinginc.com
SIC: 2752 Commercial printing, offset

(G-4403)
LYKENS CORPORATION
Also Called: Xtreme Wear
336 Aspen Way (15801-4002)
PHONE.................................814 375-9961
Ronald Lykens, *President*
Joanne Lykens, *Corp Secy*
Beth Yohe, *Sales Staff*
EMP: 10
SQ FT: 5,000
SALES: 620.6K Privately Held
WEB: www.xtremewear.com
SIC: 2759 7389 Screen printing; embroi-
    dering of advertising on shirts, etc.

(G-4404)
M D PHARMA CONNECTION LLC
102 E Long Ave (15801-2125)
PHONE.................................814 371-7726
EMP: 3
SALES (est): 166.1K Privately Held
SIC: 2834 Pharmaceutical preparations

▲ = Import ▼ =Export
◆ =Import/Export

(G-4405)
MDC MACHINE INCORPORATED
335 Aspen Way (15801-4003)
P.O. Box 363 (15801-0363)
PHONE..............................814 372-2345
Donald Bohensky, *President*
EMP: 10
SQ FT: 36,000
SALES (est): 1.4MM **Privately Held**
SIC: 3599 Machine & other job shop work

(G-4406)
METALTECH INC
3547 Watson Hwy (15801-5479)
PHONE..............................814 375-9399
Anthony Zaffuto, *President*
Robert Hanak, *Chairman*
EMP: 24
SQ FT: 15,000
SALES (est): 5.4MM **Privately Held**
SIC: 3399 3568 3462 3366 Powder,
metal; power transmission equipment;
iron & steel forgings; copper foundries

(G-4407)
NORTHERN SON INC
1022 Treasure Lk (15801-9024)
PHONE..............................724 548-1137
Frank Schall, *President*
EMP: 20
SALES (est): 9.4MM **Privately Held**
SIC: 1241 Coal mining services

(G-4408)
OLIVER T KORB & SONS INC
15 E Park Ave (15801-2235)
P.O. Box 623 (15801-0623)
PHONE..............................814 371-4545
Joseph Korb, *President*
James Korb, *Vice Pres*
EMP: 7
SQ FT: 30,000
SALES (est): 806.9K **Privately Held**
SIC: 3281 5999 Monuments, cut stone
(not finishing or lettering only); monu-
ments & tombstones

(G-4409)
OPEN FLOW GAS SUPPLY CORP
90 Beaver Dr Ste 110b (15801-2442)
P.O. Box J (15801-0297)
PHONE..............................814 371-2228
Kevin L Shannon, *President*
EMP: 12
SQ FT: 2,000
SALES (est): 1.8MM **Privately Held**
WEB: www.openflowgas.com
SIC: 1311 Crude petroleum & natural gas
production

(G-4410)
PA & IMPLANT SURGERY LLC
90 Beaver Dr (15801-2440)
PHONE..............................814 375-0500
Firas Ali,
Jeffrey Rice,
EMP: 3
SALES (est): 54.1K **Privately Held**
SIC: 8011 3842 Surgeon; implants, surgi-
cal

(G-4411)
**PACE PRECISIONS PRODUCTS
INC**
21 Ohio Ave (15801-1337)
P.O. Box 1064 (15801-1064)
PHONE..............................814 371-6201
Harold K Hannah, *President*
Patricia Hannah, *CFO*
EMP: 22 EST: 1967
SQ FT: 23,000
SALES (est): 4.2MM **Privately Held**
WEB: www.paceprecision.com
SIC: 3544 Die sets for metal stamping
(presses); jigs & fixtures

(G-4412)
PALUMBOS MEATS DUBOIS INC
Also Called: Palumbo's Meat Market
326 W Long Ave (15801-1848)
PHONE..............................814 371-2150
Joseph L Palumbo, *President*
EMP: 40
SQ FT: 37,000

SALES (est): 10.7MM **Privately Held**
SIC: 5147 2013 5411 Meats, fresh;
bologna from purchased meat; sausages
from purchased meat; frankfurters from
purchased meat; grocery stores, independent

(G-4413)
**PENN-CENTRAL INDUSTRIES
INC**
210 Ohio Ave (15801)
P.O. Box 304 (15801-0304)
PHONE..............................814 371-3211
Wendy Weber, *President*
EMP: 5 EST: 1960
SQ FT: 5,775
SALES: 810K **Privately Held**
SIC: 3569 5075 Filters; electrical heating
equipment; ventilating equipment & sup-
plies

(G-4414)
PROSCO INC
Also Called: Ideal Products
1122 S Main St (15801-1128)
PHONE..............................814 375-0484
Sam Prosper, *President*
Jeffrey Rickard, *Vice Pres*
EMP: 40
SQ FT: 42,000
SALES (est): 1.6MM **Privately Held**
SIC: 2329 5091 3949 Hunting coats &
vests, men's; sporting & recreation goods;
sporting & athletic goods

(G-4415)
PTX - PENTRONIX INC
Also Called: PTX Pentronix
590 Division St (15801-2530)
PHONE..............................734 667-2897
Thomas Gasbarre, *President*
Benjamin Gasbarre, *Vice Pres*
William Gasbarre, *Admin Sec*
▲ EMP: 8
SQ FT: 5,000
SALES (est): 2.7MM
SALES (corp-wide): 40MM **Privately
Held**
WEB: www.ptx.com
SIC: 3542 Pressing machines
PA: Gasbarre Products, Inc.
590 Division St
Du Bois PA 15801
814 371-3015

(G-4416)
RICE AESTHETICS LLC
90 Beaver Dr (15801-2440)
PHONE..............................814 503-8540
Jeffery W Rice,
J Ryan Rice,
EMP: 3
SALES (est): 184K **Privately Held**
SIC: 2844 Cosmetic preparations

(G-4417)
SEKULA SIGN CORPORATION
811 S Brady St (15801-1204)
P.O. Box 395 (15801-0395)
PHONE..............................814 371-4650
Paul J Sekula, *President*
Yolanda Sekula, *Treasurer*
Joe Jewell, *Manager*
EMP: 20
SQ FT: 12,500
SALES: 1.3MM **Privately Held**
WEB: www.sekulasigns.com
SIC: 3993 Electric signs

(G-4418)
SENSUS USA INC
Also Called: Sensus Metering Systems
805 Liberty Blvd (15801-2491)
PHONE..............................814 375-8354
Charles McKay, *Engineer*
Daniel Peace, *Engineer*
Janice Wildnauer, *Cust Mgr*
Lee Gelnett, *Branch Mgr*
Paul Honchar, *Manager*
EMP: 200 **Publicly Held**
SIC: 3824 Water meters
HQ: Sensus Usa Inc.
8601 Six Forks Rd Ste 700
Raleigh NC 27615
919 845-4000

(G-4419)
SENSUS USA INC
805 Liberty Blvd (15801-2491)
PHONE..............................800 375-8875
Barry Seneri, *Branch Mgr*
EMP: 200 **Publicly Held**
WEB: www.sensus.com
SIC: 3824 3491 3363 2891 Gas meters,
domestic & large capacity; industrial;
water meters; industrial valves; aluminum
die-castings; sealants
HQ: Sensus Usa Inc.
8601 Six Forks Rd Ste 700
Raleigh NC 27615
919 845-4000

(G-4420)
STAAR DISTRIBUTING LLC
Also Called: Energy Services & Mfg
130a Satterlee Rd (15801-2966)
PHONE..............................814 371-3500
Todd Gordon, *Principal*
EMP: 20
SALES (corp-wide): 27.3MM **Privately
Held**
SIC: 2899 Corrosion preventive lubricant
PA: Staar Distributing Llc.
560 Myrtle St
Reynoldsville PA 15851
814 612-2115

(G-4421)
STELLA-JONES CORPORATION
Also Called: Du Bois Div
392 Larkeytown Rd (15801-3940)
PHONE..............................814 371-7331
Harry Bressler, *Branch Mgr*
EMP: 43
SALES (corp-wide): 250.7K **Privately
Held**
WEB: www.bpbcorp.com
SIC: 2491 2421 2411 Preserving (cre-
osoting) of wood; sawmills & planing
mills, general; logging
HQ: Stella-Jones Corporation
1000 Cliffmine Rd Ste 500
Pittsburgh PA 15275

(G-4422)
STRISHOCK COAL CO
220 Hillcrest Dr (15801-2340)
P.O. Box 1006 (15801-1006)
PHONE..............................814 375-1245
Stephen A Strishock Jr, *Partner*
Paula Foradora, *Mng Member*
Mark Strishock,
EMP: 25 EST: 1955
SALES (est): 2.9MM **Privately Held**
SIC: 1221 Surface mining, bituminous

(G-4423)
SUPERIOR MACHINING INC
317 Aspen Way (15801-4001)
PHONE..............................814 372-2270
Fran Goldbach, *President*
EMP: 10
SQ FT: 11,000
SALES (est): 1.5MM **Privately Held**
SIC: 3599 Machine shop, jobbing & repair

(G-4424)
TIOGA PUBLISHING COMPANY
Also Called: Courier Express
500 Jeffers St (15801-2430)
PHONE..............................814 371-4200
EMP: 600 **Privately Held**
SIC: 2711 2752 Commercial printing &
newspaper publishing combined; com-
mercial printing, lithographic
HQ: Tioga Publishing Company
25 East Ave Frnt Ste
Wellsboro PA 16901

(G-4425)
**TRIANGLE SSPENSION
SYSTEMS INC (DH)**
Also Called: Triangle Spring
47 E Maloney Rd (15801-1315)
PHONE..............................814 375-7211
Richard Kempski, *President*
James Emigh, *Vice Pres*
▲ EMP: 60
SQ FT: 243,000

SALES (est): 12.5MM
SALES (corp-wide): 225.3B **Publicly
Held**
WEB: www.triangleusa.com
SIC: 3493 5013 Leaf springs: automobile,
locomotive, etc.; springs, shock absorbers
& struts

(G-4426)
WCED NEWS TALK
12 W Long Ave (15801-2100)
PHONE..............................814 372-1420
Jay Philippone, *Principal*
EMP: 3
SALES (est): 124.3K **Privately Held**
SIC: 2711 Newspapers, publishing & print-
ing

(G-4427)
WEYERHAEUSER COMPANY
377 Satterlee Rd (15801-2969)
PHONE..............................814 371-0630
Robert Bailey, *Manager*
EMP: 63
SALES (corp-wide): 7.4B **Publicly Held**
SIC: 2679 2621 Paper products, con-
verted; paper mills
PA: Weyerhaeuser Company
220 Occidental Ave S
Seattle WA 98104
206 539-3000

(G-4428)
WINERY OF WILCOX
5522 Shaffer Rd Unit 122 (15801-3318)
PHONE..............................814 375-4501
Carol Williams, *Owner*
EMP: 9
SALES (est): 388.8K **Privately Held**
SIC: 2084 Wines

(G-4429)
WWF OPERATING COMPANY
Also Called: Whitewave Foods
2592 Oklahoma Salem Rd (15801-8988)
PHONE..............................814 590-8511
EMP: 127
SALES (corp-wide): 762.4MM **Privately
Held**
SIC: 2026 Milk processing (pasteurizing,
homogenizing, bottling)
HQ: Wwf Operating Company
12002 Airport Way
Broomfield CO 80021
214 303-3400

Dublin
Bucks County

(G-4430)
AMANITA TECHNOLOGIES LLC
123 N Main St (18917-2107)
P.O. Box 32, Mechanicsville (18934-0032)
PHONE..............................215 353-1984
Terence Kloss, *President*
EMP: 5
SQ FT: 1,200
SALES: 485.4K **Privately Held**
SIC: 3479 Aluminum coating of metal prod-
ucts

(G-4431)
AMERICAN INNOVATIONS INC
123 N Main St (18917-2107)
PHONE..............................215 249-1840
Karl J Douglass, *President*
EMP: 7
SQ FT: 4,800
SALES (est): 660.7K **Privately Held**
SIC: 3674 5065 3842 Semiconductors &
related devices; electronic parts & equip-
ment; technical aids for the handicapped

(G-4432)
**FALCON MANUFACTURING
COMPANY**
107 High St (18917-2313)
P.O. Box 902 (18917-0902)
PHONE..............................215 249-0212
Dieter Falkenstein, *President*
Bruce F Falkenstein, *Vice Pres*
Dolores Falkenstein, *Admin Sec*
EMP: 9 EST: 1975

SQ FT: 8,800
SALES (est): 1.2MM **Privately Held**
SIC: 3599 Machine shop, jobbing & repair

(G-4433)
HIGHLAND HOSIERY MILLS INC
174 S Main St (18917)
P.O. Box 252 (18917-0252)
PHONE...................................215 249-3934
Leonard Fray, *President*
Ramona Zarka, *Treasurer*
EMP: 10 EST: 1949
SQ FT: 14,000
SALES (est): 865.8K **Privately Held**
SIC: 2251 Dyeing & finishing women's full-
& knee-length hosiery; tights, women's

(G-4434)
HILLTOWN SERVICES
614 Dublin Pike Apt C (18917-9702)
PHONE...................................215 249-3694
Chris Bogt, *President*
Thomas Brophy, *Vice Pres*
EMP: 3
SALES (est): 375.1K **Privately Held**
SIC: 3799 5088 Trailers & trailer equip-
ment; golf carts

(G-4435)
MAR-VAN INDUSTRIES INC
117 Middle Rd (18917-2409)
P.O. Box 144 (18917-0144)
PHONE...................................215 249-3336
Jerry Geroni Jr, *President*
Ralph Geroni, *Treasurer*
EMP: 8
SQ FT: 13,200
SALES (est): 1.2MM **Privately Held**
SIC: 2434 Vanities, bathroom: wood

(G-4436)
MORITZ AEROSPACE INC
123 N Main St Ste 257-258 (18917-2107)
P.O. Box 1000 (18917-1000)
PHONE...................................215 249-1300
Claude Mercier, *President*
Simon Cordner, *Vice Pres*
Richard Nace, *CFO*
EMP: 500
SQ FT: 3,000
SALES (est): 210.6K
SALES (corp-wide): 1.1MM **Privately
Held**
WEB: www.moritzaero.com
SIC: 3728 Aircraft parts & equipment
PA: Carling Technologies, Inc.
60 Johnson Ave
Plainville CT 06062
860 793-9281

(G-4437)
WINTERHOUSE FURNITURE INC
112 Maple Ave (18917-2404)
PHONE...................................215 249-3410
John P Buckman, *President*
Michael J Penta, *Treasurer*
EMP: 8
SQ FT: 11,000
SALES (est): 1MM **Privately Held**
SIC: 2521 2511 5712 Wood office furni-
ture; wood household furniture; office fur-
niture; unfinished furniture

Duke Center
Mckean County

(G-4438)
C DCAP MODEM LINE
691 Main St (16729-9800)
PHONE...................................814 966-3954
EMP: 3 EST: 2010
SALES (est): 135.4K **Privately Held**
SIC: 3661 Modems

Dunbar
Fayette County

(G-4439)
DUNBAR MACHINE CO INC
75 Woodvale St (15431-1599)
PHONE...................................724 277-8711

Robert Holsing, *President*
Robert Holsing Jr, *Vice Pres*
Thomas Holsing, *Treasurer*
Michael Holsing, *Admin Sec*
EMP: 3 EST: 1957
SQ FT: 10,000
SALES (est): 300K **Privately Held**
WEB: www.dunbarquiltart.com
SIC: 3599 7692 3444 3441 Machine
shop, jobbing & repair; welding repair;
sheet metalwork; fabricated structural
metal

(G-4440)
HERALD STANDARD
175 Arch Bridge Rd (15431-2341)
PHONE...................................724 626-8345
EMP: 4
SALES (est): 212.6K **Privately Held**
SIC: 2711 Newspapers-Publishing/Printing

(G-4441)
JLE INDUSTRIES LLC (PA)
119 Icmi Rd Ste 100 (15431-2358)
PHONE...................................724 603-2228
Ray Gamrat, *Vice Pres*
Evan Pohaski, *CFO*
Kimberley Bonacci, *Human Res Mgr*
Jason Adamsky, *Mng Member*
Larry Spade Jr,
EMP: 30 EST: 2012
SALES (est): 715K **Privately Held**
SIC: 4212 4731 3599 Local trucking, with-
out storage; freight transportation
arrangement; machine shop, jobbing &
repair

(G-4442)
**KEYSTONE FREWRKS
SPECIALTY SLS**
High St Ext (15431)
P.O. Box 338 (15431-0338)
PHONE...................................724 277-4294
Donald E Newell, *President*
▲ EMP: 4
SALES: 250K **Privately Held**
SIC: 5999 2899 Fireworks; fireworks

(G-4443)
STEFANOS PRINTING INC
266 Furnace Hill Rd (15431-2452)
PHONE...................................724 277-8374
Patrick Stefano, *President*
Tina Stefano, *Vice Pres*
EMP: 7 EST: 1958
SQ FT: 4,000
SALES (est): 1.3MM **Privately Held**
SIC: 2752 5199 Commercial printing, off-
set; advertising specialties

Duncannon
Perry County

(G-4444)
**BUDDY BOY WINERY &
VINEYARD**
111 Barnett Dr (17020-9022)
PHONE...................................717 834-5606
William Warner, *Principal*
EMP: 11
SALES (est): 1.2MM **Privately Held**
SIC: 2084 Wines

(G-4445)
FURNLEY H FRISCH
Also Called: F & R Materials
291 Sawmill Rd (17020-9531)
PHONE...................................717 957-3261
Furnley H Frisch, *Principal*
EMP: 10
SALES (est): 1.2MM **Privately Held**
SIC: 3272 Concrete products

(G-4446)
HIRT POWERSPORTS LLC
11 Kamp St (17020-9565)
PHONE...................................717 834-9126
Charles White, *General Mgr*
Eric Hirt,
EMP: 4 EST: 2016
SQ FT: 5,000

SALES (est): 110.1K **Privately Held**
SIC: 7538 3524 7699 5571 General automotive repair shops; lawn & garden
tractors & equipment; motorcycle repair
service; motorcycle dealers

(G-4447)
LIGHTNING GROUP INC (PA)
722 N Market St (17020-1716)
P.O. Box 8 (17020-0008)
PHONE...................................717 834-3031
Norman Rosen, *President*
Allen Rosen, *Vice Pres*
Harold Rosen, *Admin Sec*
EMP: 7
SQ FT: 40,000
SALES (est): 1.6MM **Privately Held**
SIC: 2511 6512 Juvenile furniture: wood;
nonresidential building operators

(G-4448)
MARSTELLAR CONCRETE INC
2011 State Rd (17020-9572)
PHONE...................................717 834-6200
Scott D Marstellar, *President*
EMP: 6
SALES (est): 791.3K **Privately Held**
SIC: 5211 5032 3273 Cement; concrete &
cinder building products; ready-mixed
concrete

Duncansville
Blair County

(G-4449)
AMERA GLASS INC
2283 Plank Rd (16635-8235)
PHONE...................................814 696-0944
Douglas Herron, *President*
EMP: 6
SALES (est): 381K **Privately Held**
SIC: 3231 Products of purchased glass

(G-4450)
BRUMBAUGH BODY CO INC
71 Jennifer Rd (16635-8435)
P.O. Box 579 (16635-0579)
PHONE...................................814 696-9552
Warren S Emeigh, *President*
W S Emeigh, *President*
Mary C Emeigh, *Treasurer*
EMP: 4 EST: 1918
SQ FT: 16,000
SALES (est): 577.7K **Privately Held**
SIC: 3443 7699 7538 Air coolers, metal
plate; industrial truck repair; snowmobile
repair; diesel engine repair: automotive

(G-4451)
**FREEDOM METALS MFG INC
(PA)**
185 Commerce Dr (16635-4843)
PHONE...................................814 224-4438
Matthew Will, *President*
Linda Gibbs, *Office Mgr*
EMP: 7
SQ FT: 750
SALES (est): 959.7K **Privately Held**
SIC: 3444 Metal roofing & roof drainage
equipment

(G-4452)
**GARDEN POND PROMOTIONS
INC**
1000 Whitetail Ct (16635-6908)
PHONE...................................814 695-4325
Roseanne Conrad, *President*
EMP: 3
SALES (est): 182.2K **Privately Held**
SIC: 2721 Magazines: publishing & printing

(G-4453)
J W HOIST AND CRANE LLC
Also Called: Altoona Hoist & Crane
3269 Route 764 (16635-7805)
P.O. Box 248 (16635-0248)
PHONE...................................814 696-0350
Douglas C Warner, *President*
Rj McManamy, *Vice Pres*
Rick Penatzer, *Engineer*
Robert M Jubeck,
EMP: 9

SALES (est): 2.3MM **Privately Held**
WEB: www.altoonahoist.com
SIC: 7699 3536 Industrial machinery &
equipment repair; hoists, cranes & monorails

(G-4454)
KEITHS TRUCK SERVICE
124 Repair Rd (16635-4820)
PHONE...................................814 696-6008
Loren Keith, *Owner*
EMP: 6
SQ FT: 10,000
SALES (est): 1.1MM **Privately Held**
SIC: 7538 3441 General truck repair; fab-
ricated structural metal

(G-4455)
LINGENFELTER AWNING
Rr 764 (16635)
P.O. Box 217 (16635-0217)
PHONE...................................814 696-4353
Barry Lingenfelter, *Owner*
▲ EMP: 4
SQ FT: 1,500
SALES: 115K **Privately Held**
SIC: 5999 7699 3444 1799 Awnings;
awning repair shop; awnings, sheet
metal; awning installation

(G-4456)
MARZONIES
164 Patchway Rd (16635-8431)
PHONE...................................814 695-2931
Eve Hunter, *General Mgr*
Rich Hollingshead, *District Mgr*
EMP: 97
SALES (est): 693.6K **Privately Held**
SIC: 5812 2082 American restaurant; beer
(alcoholic beverage)

(G-4457)
NEWMETRO DESIGN LLC
141 Nac Dr (16635-9428)
PHONE...................................814 696-2550
Gary Fallowes, *Mng Member*
Michael Herman,
▲ EMP: 4
SQ FT: 500
SALES (est): 1.5MM **Privately Held**
SIC: 3089 Kitchenware, plastic

(G-4458)
**NORTH AMRCN
COMMUNICATIONS INC**
141 Nac Dr (16635-9428)
P.O. Box 39 (16635-0039)
PHONE...................................814 696-3553
Robert Herman, *Branch Mgr*
EMP: 550
SALES (corp-wide): 73.7MM **Privately
Held**
WEB: www.nacmail.com
SIC: 2677 2752 7331 Envelopes; com-
mercial printing, lithographic; direct mail
advertising services
PA: North American Communications, Inc.
7 Edgemont Rd
Katonah NY 10536
914 273-8620

(G-4459)
**PAPER CONVERTING MACHINE
CO**
F. L. Smithe Machine Co
899 Plank Rd Ste 1 (16635-9437)
PHONE...................................814 695-5521
William Hornung, *Branch Mgr*
EMP: 104
SALES (corp-wide): 2.4B **Privately Held**
SIC: 3579 3554 Envelope stuffing, sealing
& addressing machines; paper industries
machinery
HQ: Paper Converting Machine Company
2300 S Ashland Ave
Green Bay WI 54304
920 494-5601

(G-4460)
PCMC
899 Plank Rd (16635-9437)
PHONE...................................814 934-3262
Scott Wible, *Principal*
EMP: 3
SALES (est): 223.4K **Privately Held**
SIC: 3554 Paper industries machinery

(G-4461)
QUALITY CANVAS
411 2nd Ave (16635-9472)
PHONE..........................814 695-8343
Scott Arnold, *Owner*
EMP: 3
SQ FT: 2,550
SALES: 265K **Privately Held**
SIC: 2394 Canvas & related products

(G-4462)
QUALITY CRRCTONS INSPCTONS INC (PA)
Also Called: Quality Crrections Inspections
611 Gildea Dr (16635-8364)
PHONE..........................814 696-3737
Ron Burk, *President*
Doris Burk, *Vice Pres*
Randy Burk, *Vice Pres*
Ronald E Burk, *Treasurer*
Sherri Leach, *Manager*
▲ EMP: 70
SQ FT: 40,000
SALES (est): 27.1MM **Privately Held**
WEB: www.qualitycorrections.com
SIC: 3144 3131 7251 3143 Women's footwear, except athletic; footwear cut stock; shoe repair shops; men's footwear, except athletic; finishing plants, cotton

(G-4463)
SLATES ENTERPRISES INC
Also Called: Capital Press
1147 3rd Ave (16635-1352)
P.O. Box 338 (16635-0338)
PHONE..........................814 695-2851
Katherine Slates, *President*
EMP: 5 EST: 1836
SQ FT: 4,800
SALES (est): 658.6K **Privately Held**
SIC: 2752 Commercial printing, offset

(G-4464)
SNOWBERGER EMBROIDERY
2239 Maple Hollow Rd (16635-6620)
PHONE..........................814 696-6499
Cynthia Snowberger, *Owner*
EMP: 3
SALES: 210K **Privately Held**
SIC: 2395 Embroidery products, except schiffli machine

(G-4465)
VEEDER-ROOT COMPANY
2709 Route 764 (16635-8047)
PHONE..........................814 695-4476
Dawn Whitcomb, *Human Resources*
James Delgrande, *Manager*
EMP: 41
SALES (corp-wide): 6.4B **Publicly Held**
SIC: 3823 3824 Industrial flow & liquid measuring instruments; fluid meters & counting devices; mechanical measuring meters; gas meters, domestic & large capacity: industrial
HQ: Veeder-Root Company
125 Powder Forest Dr Fl 1
Weatogue CT 06089

(G-4466)
WOLF LUMBER AND MILLWORK INC
1984 Maple Hollow Rd (16635-6605)
P.O. Box 665 (16635-0665)
PHONE..........................814 317-5111
Tom Wolf, *President*
Brenda Wolf, *Admin Sec*
EMP: 3
SQ FT: 13,400
SALES: 550K **Privately Held**
WEB: www.wolflumber.com
SIC: 2431 Millwork

```
Dunmore
Lackawanna County
```

(G-4467)
ARCMAN CORPORATION
1200 Meade St (18512-3171)
PHONE..........................570 489-6402
Glen Gillford, *Manager*
EMP: 5

SALES (corp-wide): 350K **Privately Held**
WEB: www.classicmeters.com
SIC: 3641 7699 1799 1795 Electric lamps; antique repair & restoration, except furniture, automobiles; sandblasting of building exteriors; concrete breaking for streets & highways
PA: Arcman Corporation
807 Center St
Throop PA 18512
570 489-6402

(G-4468)
ATS FLEET TRCKING MGT SLUTIONS
138 Willow St (18512-2929)
PHONE..........................570 445-8805
John Occhipinti, *Partner*
EMP: 10
SALES (est): 344K **Privately Held**
SIC: 7372 Prepackaged software

(G-4469)
AUTOMATED COMPONENTS INTL (PA)
1321 E Drinker St (18512-2612)
PHONE..........................570 344-4000
Joseph H Hollander, *President*
▲ EMP: 20
SQ FT: 15,000
SALES (est): 5.4MM **Privately Held**
WEB: www.acpsr.com
SIC: 3552 Textile machinery

(G-4470)
BARRY CALLEBAUT USA LLC
9 Keystone Industrial Par (18512-1516)
PHONE..........................570 342-7556
EMP: 370
SALES (corp-wide): 45.9MM **Privately Held**
SIC: 2066 Chocolate & cocoa products
HQ: Barry Callebaut U.S.A. Llc
600 W Chicago Ave Ste 860
Chicago IL 60654

(G-4471)
COON INDUSTRIES INC
200 Dunda Dr (18512-2660)
P.O. Box 310, Pittston (18640-0310)
PHONE..........................570 341-8033
Don Galli, *Principal*
Richard Miller, *CFO*
EMP: 33
SALES (est): 2.2MM **Privately Held**
SIC: 3273 Ready-mixed concrete

(G-4472)
CUSTOM CARPET & BEDDING INC
105 Corner St (18512-2311)
PHONE..........................570 344-7533
John Domin, *President*
EMP: 4 EST: 1938
SQ FT: 15,000
SALES: 189K **Privately Held**
SIC: 5713 7217 2515 7699 Carpets; carpet & rug cleaning & repairing plant; mattresses & foundations; mattress renovating & repair shop; mattresses

(G-4473)
GERTRUDE HAWK CHOCOLATES INC (PA)
901 Keystone Indus Park (18512-1544)
PHONE..........................570 342-7556
David W Hawk, *Ch of Bd*
William E Auerey, *President*
William Aubrey, *President*
Steve Arling, *CFO*
◆ EMP: 400 EST: 1958
SALES (est): 243.7MM **Privately Held**
WEB: www.gertrudehawkchocolates.com
SIC: 2066 2064 Chocolate & cocoa products; candy & other confectionery products

(G-4474)
H&K GROUP INC
Dunmore Materials
950 Dunham Dr (18512-2665)
PHONE..........................570 347-1800
John Scarcone, *Branch Mgr*
EMP: 3

SALES (corp-wide): 71.6MM **Privately Held**
WEB: www.hkgroup.com
SIC: 1429 Igneous rock, crushed & broken-quarrying
PA: H&K Group, Inc.
2052 Lucon Rd
Skippack PA 19474
610 584-8500

(G-4475)
JOMARR SAFETY SYSTEMS INC
Also Called: Jomarr Products
1000 Meade St (18512-3195)
P.O. Box 309 (18512-0309)
PHONE..........................570 346-5330
Mark Perrella, *President*
EMP: 60
SQ FT: 100,000
SALES (est): 7.3MM **Privately Held**
SIC: 3569 3829 Firefighting apparatus & related equipment; gas detectors

(G-4476)
LACKAWANNA DISTRIBUTOR CORP
60 Keystone Industrial Pa (18512-1503)
PHONE..........................570 342-8245
Barbara A Lynch, *President*
EMP: 4 EST: 2010
SALES (est): 206.3K **Privately Held**
SIC: 2082 Beer (alcoholic beverage)

(G-4477)
LEGACY POLYMER PRODUCTS INC
500 Mill St (18512-2829)
P.O. Box 154 (18512-0154)
PHONE..........................570 344-5019
Ronald Smith, *President*
Mark Kosek, *Corp Secy*
EMP: 2
SQ FT: 14,000
SALES: 3MM **Privately Held**
WEB: www.legacypoly.com
SIC: 3088 Plastics plumbing fixtures

(G-4478)
MCGREGOR INDUSTRIES INC
46 Line St (18512-1432)
PHONE..........................570 343-2436
Robert McGregor, *President*
▲ EMP: 50 EST: 1919
SQ FT: 30,000
SALES: 12MM **Privately Held**
WEB: www.mcgregorindustries.com
SIC: 3446 Architectural metalwork

(G-4479)
PARODI HOLDINGS LLC
Also Called: Avanti Cigar Company
200 Keystone Industrial P (18512-1556)
PHONE..........................570 344-8566
Luciano Simeone, *Mng Member*
EMP: 31
SALES (est): 2.9MM
SALES (corp-wide): 15.4MM **Privately Held**
SIC: 2121 Cigars
HQ: Manifatture Sigaro Toscano Spa
Via Enrico Mattei 780
Lucca LU 55100
058 343-91

(G-4480)
PENNSYLVANIA SEWING RES CO
1321 E Drinker St (18512-2612)
PHONE..........................570 344-4000
Joseph Hollander, *President*
EMP: 12 EST: 1950
SQ FT: 8,000
SALES (est): 860K **Privately Held**
SIC: 3552 Textile machinery

(G-4481)
POLARIZED MEAT CO INC (PA)
Also Called: MAID-RITESTEAKCO
107 Keystone Indus Park (18512-1518)
PHONE..........................570 347-3396
Donald Bernstein, *President*
Michael Bernstein, *Exec VP*
Ken Keizel, *CFO*
Ken Kozel, *Finance*
EMP: 315 EST: 1964

SQ FT: 12,000
SALES: 25K **Privately Held**
SIC: 2013 2011 Frozen meats from purchased meat; meat packing plants

(G-4482)
ROSS MC DONNELL OPTICAL
217 E Drinker St Unit 1 (18512-2589)
PHONE..........................570 348-0464
Dennis Ross, *Partner*
William Mc Donnell, *Partner*
William Ross, *Partner*
EMP: 3
SALES (est): 405.5K **Privately Held**
SIC: 3851 5048 Lenses, ophthalmic; frames & parts, eyeglass & spectacle; ophthalmic goods

(G-4483)
SCHREIBER & GOLDBERG LTD
1321 E Drinker St (18512-2612)
PHONE..........................570 344-4000
Alan Glassman, *President*
EMP: 20 EST: 1919
SALES (est): 1.4MM
SALES (corp-wide): 5.4MM **Privately Held**
WEB: www.acpsr.com
SIC: 3582 Pressing machines, commercial laundry & drycleaning
PA: Automated Components International Inc
1321 E Drinker St
Dunmore PA 18512
570 344-4000

(G-4484)
SUMMER MUSIC FESTIVAL
224 Prospect St (18512-2150)
PHONE..........................570 343-7271
Doug Smith, *Director*
EMP: 4
SALES: 10K **Privately Held**
SIC: 8641 3931 Civic social & fraternal associations; musical instruments

(G-4485)
TASTY BAKING COMPANY
Also Called: Tastykake
120 Monahan Ave Ste 3 (18512-1720)
PHONE..........................570 961-8211
Richard Garofalo, *General Mgr*
EMP: 4
SALES (corp-wide): 3.9B **Publicly Held**
WEB: www.tastykake.com
SIC: 2051 Bread, cake & related products
HQ: Tasty Baking Company
4300 S 26th St
Philadelphia PA 19112
215 221-8500

(G-4486)
UNION NEWS
1256 Oneill Hwy (18512-1708)
P.O. Box 1321, Scranton (18501-1321)
PHONE..........................570 343-4958
Paul Tucker, *Owner*
EMP: 3
SALES (est): 96.2K **Privately Held**
SIC: 2711 Newspapers, publishing & printing

(G-4487)
UNIVERSAL PRINTING COMPANY LLC
1205 Oneill Hwy (18512-1723)
PHONE..........................570 342-1243
Margaret McGrath, *Owner*
Brian Grady, *Vice Pres*
EMP: 100 EST: 1917
SALES (est): 23.8MM **Privately Held**
WEB: www.universalprintingcompany.com
SIC: 2752 Commercial printing, offset

(G-4488)
ZONDERVAN CORPORATION LLC
1000 Keystone Indus Park (18512-1535)
PHONE..........................570 941-1366
See AR Fiche, *Director*
EMP: 161
SALES (corp-wide): 9B **Publicly Held**
SIC: 2731 Books: publishing only

HQ: The Zondervan Corporation L L C
3900 Sparks Dr Se
Grand Rapids MI 49546
616 698-6900

Dupont
Luzerne County

(G-4489)
CENTER FASHIONS INC
216 Center St Ste 101 (18641-1442)
PHONE......................................570 655-2861
Peter J Burgio, *President*
Louise Burgio, *Corp Secy*
EMP: 60 EST: 1949
SQ FT: 4,000
SALES (est): 3.5MM **Privately Held**
SIC: 2335 Women's, juniors' & misses'
dresses

(G-4490)
DUPONT TOOL & MACHINE CO
Also Called: Valley Grinding & Mfg
311 Elm St (18641-1998)
PHONE......................................570 655-1728
Walter Bryk, *Partner*
Vincent Bryk, *Partner*
EMP: 22
SQ FT: 16,500
SALES (est): 3.4MM **Privately Held**
SIC: 3599 Machine shop, jobbing & repair;
custom machinery

(G-4491)
MINICHI INC
Also Called: Minichi Energy
453 Ziegler St (18641-1947)
PHONE......................................570 654-8332
Marc Minichello, *President*
Marvin Gilpin, *General Mgr*
Joe Nocito, *Corp Secy*
Martin Shamro, *Opers Mgr*
Sharon Glover, *Admin Asst*
EMP: 90
SQ FT: 1,500
SALES: 18MM **Privately Held**
SIC: 1081 1622 Preparing shafts or tun-
nels, metal mining; bridge, tunnel & ele-
vated highway

(G-4492)
MINICHI ENERGY LLC
453 Ziegler St (18641-1947)
PHONE......................................570 654-8332
Marc Minichello, *President*
EMP: 5
SALES (est): 470.7K **Privately Held**
SIC: 1622 1311 Bridge, tunnel & elevated
highway; sand & shale oil mining

(G-4493)
OFCG INC
243 Lidy Rd (18641-2149)
PHONE......................................570 655-0804
Louis Posly, *President*
Joan Posly, *Vice Pres*
EMP: 4 EST: 1975
SQ FT: 12,000
SALES (est): 743.1K **Privately Held**
WEB: www.ofcg.com
SIC: 3545 3544 3599 Machine tool ac-
cessories; special dies & tools; custom
machinery; machine shop, jobbing & re-
pair

Duquesne
Allegheny County

(G-4494)
**AMERICAN TEXTILE COMPANY
INC (PA)**
10 N Linden St (15110-3001)
PHONE......................................412 948-1020
Jack Ouellette, *Ch of Bd*
Reid Ruttenberg, *Ch of Bd*
Lance Ruttenberg, *President*
Blake Ruttenberg, *Exec VP*
Traci Hayes, *Vice Pres*
◆ EMP: 225
SQ FT: 190,000

SALES (est): 184MM **Privately Held**
WEB: www.americantextile.com
SIC: 2392 5719 Pillowcases: made from
purchased materials; mattress protectors,
except rubber; bedding (sheets, blankets,
spreads & pillows)

(G-4495)
ANGSTROM SCIENCES INC
40 S Linden St (15110-1091)
PHONE......................................412 469-8466
Mark Bernick, *President*
Kelly Bernick, *Corp Secy*
▲ EMP: 23
SQ FT: 18,000
SALES (est): 13.4MM **Privately Held**
WEB: www.angstromsciences.com
SIC: 5052 3559 2819 5051 Coal & other
minerals & ores; semiconductor manufac-
turing machinery; industrial inorganic
chemicals; metals service centers & of-
fices

(G-4496)
DURA-BOND COATING INC
5 N Linden St (15110-1097)
PHONE......................................412 436-2411
Mike Reeder, *Executive*
EMP: 45
SALES (corp-wide): 119.9MM **Privately
Held**
WEB: www.durabond.com
SIC: 3479 2865 2851 Coating or wrap-
ping steel pipe; cyclic crudes & intermedi-
ates; paints & allied products
HQ: Dura-Bond Coating, Inc.
2658 Puckety Dr
Export PA 15632
724 327-0782

(G-4497)
LUNA COLLISON LTD
316 Grant Ave (15110-1009)
PHONE......................................412 466-8866
Philip Cupelli, *President*
Collison Luna, *Principal*
EMP: 15
SALES (est): 1.9MM **Privately Held**
SIC: 3479 Painting of metal products

(G-4498)
MARLO ENTERPRISES INC
Also Called: Laurel Printing & Graphics
32 S Linden St (15110)
PHONE......................................412 678-3800
Keith Jones, *President*
Kenneth R McCombs, *Corp Secy*
EMP: 11
SQ FT: 10,000
SALES (est): 1MM **Privately Held**
WEB: www.laurelprint.com
SIC: 2752 Commercial printing, litho-
graphic

(G-4499)
**SARCLAD (NORTH AMERICA)
LP**
30 S Linden St (15110-1091)
PHONE......................................412 466-2000
Michael Sorby, *CEO*
Tony Payling, *Vice Pres*
Martin Shelton, *Sales Engr*
Peter Unwin, *Marketing Staff*
Chris Childs, *Technology*
EMP: 10
SQ FT: 6,700
SALES (est): 2.3MM **Privately Held**
WEB: www.sarcladusa.com
SIC: 3827 5084 Metallographs; instru-
ments & control equipment
HQ: Sarclad Limited
Unit 3
Rotherham S60 5
114 293-9300

(G-4500)
**THERMAL TRANSFER
CORPORATION**
50 N Linden St (15110-1067)
PHONE......................................412 460-4004
Timothy Thompson, *General Mgr*
Robert Lydel, *Vice Pres*
Timothy W Ottie, *Vice Pres*
Jason Fabisch, *Engineer*
Jim Kinter, *Engineer*
◆ EMP: 95 EST: 1952

SQ FT: 161,000
SALES (est): 38MM
SALES (corp-wide): 4.3B **Publicly Held**
WEB: www.hamon-thermaltransfer.com
SIC: 3443 5075 Heat exchangers, con-
densers & components; economizers
(boilers); heat exchangers
HQ: Wabtec Corporation
1001 Airbrake Ave
Wilmerding PA 15148

(G-4501)
VEGELY WELDING INC
600 Duquesne Blvd (15110-1520)
PHONE......................................412 469-9808
Ken Vegely, *President*
EMP: 12
SALES (est): 1.6MM **Privately Held**
SIC: 7692 Welding repair

Durham
Bucks County

(G-4502)
DURHAM PRESS INC
892 Durham Rd (18039)
P.O. Box 159 (18039-0159)
PHONE......................................610 346-6133
Jean-Paul Russell, *President*
EMP: 4
SALES (est): 483.1K **Privately Held**
WEB: www.durhampress.com
SIC: 2752 Commercial printing, offset

Duryea
Luzerne County

(G-4503)
**AMERICAN PRECISION GLASS
CORP**
602 Main St (18642-1326)
PHONE......................................570 457-9664
Jack Rowlands, *President*
Janet Rowlands, *Treasurer*
EMP: 8
SQ FT: 3,000
SALES (est): 990K **Privately Held**
SIC: 3827 Lenses, optical: all types except
ophthalmic; optical elements & assem-
blies, except ophthalmic

(G-4504)
POWERRAIL DISTRIBUTION INC
205 Clark Rd (18642-1112)
PHONE......................................570 883-7005
Paul Foster, *President*
Mark Nolan, *Vice Pres*
Ivis Gaudet, *Chief Engr*
Kevin Wright, *CFO*
James Fazio, *Manager*
EMP: 65
SQ FT: 11,000
SALES (est): 1.3MM
SALES (corp-wide): 56.1MM **Privately
Held**
SIC: 5088 3743 Railroad equipment &
supplies; railroad locomotives & parts,
electric or nonelectric
PA: Powerrail Holdings, Inc.
205 Clark Rd
Duryea PA 18642
570 883-7005

(G-4505)
**POWERRAIL HOLDINGS INC
(PA)**
Also Called: Powerrail Distribution
205 Clark Rd (18642-1112)
PHONE......................................570 883-7005
Paul Foster, *President*
Robert Harvilla, *Vice Pres*
Mark Nolan, *Vice Pres*
James Sweat, *Vice Pres*
Gene Loureiro, *Opers Mgr*
▲ EMP: 32
SQ FT: 11,000
SALES (est): 56.1MM **Privately Held**
WEB: www.epowerrail.com
SIC: 5088 3743 Railroad equipment &
supplies; railroad locomotives & parts,
electric or nonelectric

(G-4506)
**PRODUCTION SYSTEMS
AUTOMTN LLC**
201 Clark Rd (18642-1112)
PHONE......................................570 602-4200
EMP: 29
SALES (corp-wide): 2.3MM **Privately
Held**
SIC: 3559 3535 Automotive related ma-
chinery; robotic conveyors
PA: Production Systems Automation, Llc
1 Crozerville Rd
Aston PA 19014
610 358-0500

(G-4507)
SCHOTT NORTH AMERICA INC
400 York Ave Ste B (18642-2026)
PHONE......................................570 457-7485
Stephen Krenitsky, *General Mgr*
Amy Sincavage, *General Mgr*
Thomas J McDonald, *Vice Pres*
Michael Platt, *Mfg Staff*
Len Metzger, *Engineer*
EMP: 4
SALES (corp-wide): 585K **Privately Held**
SIC: 3211 Flat glass
HQ: Schott North America, Inc.
555 Taxter Rd Ste 470
Elmsford NY 10523
914 831-2200

Dushore
Sullivan County

(G-4508)
COMPASS WELDING LLC (PA)
1524 Hayes Rd (18614-8079)
PHONE......................................570 928-7472
Angie Hampton, *Mng Member*
Russell Hampton,
EMP: 7
SALES (est): 1.6MM **Privately Held**
SIC: 7692 Welding repair

(G-4509)
MID-LIFE STONE WORKS LLC
111 Kocher Rd (18614-7706)
PHONE......................................570 928-8802
Mark Beegle, *President*
EMP: 5 EST: 2007
SQ FT: 1,560
SALES: 119.8K **Privately Held**
SIC: 1411 3281 5032 Bluestone, dimen-
sion-quarrying; stone, quarrying & pro-
cessing of own stone products; building
stone

(G-4510)
SEASONS SPECIALTIES INC
Also Called: L D Wood Designs
178 Carpenter St (18614)
PHONE......................................570 928-9522
Daniel A Dunham, *President*
Eileen L Dunham, *Treasurer*
EMP: 16
SQ FT: 30,000
SALES: 1MM **Privately Held**
SIC: 3999 5992 Artificial trees & flowers;
wreaths, artificial; florists

(G-4511)
SULLIVAN REVIEW
101 N Main St (18614)
PHONE......................................570 928-8403
John A Shoemaker, *Owner*
Rodger Dourte, *CIO*
EMP: 6 EST: 1878
SQ FT: 2,000
SALES (est): 317.1K **Privately Held**
SIC: 2711 2752 Commercial printing &
newspaper publishing combined; com-
mercial printing, offset

▲ = Import ▼=Export
◆ =Import/Export

Eagleville
Montgomery County

(G-4512)
CLEAR ALIGN LLC (PA)
2550 Boulevard Of The Gen (19403-3679)
PHONE..................................484 956-0510
Angelique X Irvin, *President*
Ed Mourar, *President*
Hollie Marinecz, *Vice Pres*
EMP: 78
SQ FT: 40,000
SALES (est): 14.4MM **Privately Held**
WEB: www.clearalign.com
SIC: 3812 Defense systems & equipment

(G-4513)
IVIDIX SOFTWARE INC
1401 Reiner Rd (19403-3852)
PHONE..................................484 580-9601
EMP: 3
SALES (est): 166.9K **Privately Held**
SIC: 7372 Prepackaged software

(G-4514)
JAMES R HANLON INC
Also Called: Equivalent Prfmce Polymers
2550 Boulevard Of The (19403)
PHONE..................................610 631-9999
James R Hanlon, *President*
EMP: 30
SQ FT: 30,000
SALES (est): 4.1MM **Privately Held**
SIC: 5093 2824 Plastics scrap; nylon
fibers

(G-4515)
MAINTAIN-IT
Also Called: Maintain It All
18 W Mount Kirk Ave (19403-1540)
PHONE..................................484 684-6766
Gianni Calabretta, *President*
EMP: 35
SALES (est): 2.5MM **Privately Held**
SIC: 2952 0781 Asphalt felts & coatings;
landscape counseling & planning

(G-4516)
SPECTRUM HEALTHCARE INC
20 Eagleville Rd (19403-1476)
PHONE..................................888 210-5576
Brian Allerton, *CEO*
Christopher Allerton, *President*
Nicholas Chiccino, *COO*
Alex Thibadeau, *Sales Mgr*
John McGinley, *Sales Executive*
EMP: 30
SALES (est): 3.4MM **Privately Held**
SIC: 5999 3845 Medical apparatus & sup-
plies; electrotherapeutic apparatus

(G-4517)
STREAMLIGHT INC
30 Eagleville Rd Ste 100 (19403-1422)
PHONE..................................610 631-0600
Raymond Sharrah, *President*
Michael Dineen, *Vice Pres*
Brian Troxel, *Plant Mgr*
Tom Boris, *Project Mgr*
Waleska Lebron, *Mfg Staff*
◆ EMP: 320
SQ FT: 230,000
SALES: 101.1MM **Privately Held**
WEB: www.streamlight.com
SIC: 3648 Flashlights

(G-4518)
THRIFTY DUMPSTER INC
3037 Griffith Rd (19403-1029)
PHONE..................................215 688-1774
EMP: 6
SALES (est): 802.6K **Privately Held**
SIC: 3443 Dumpsters, garbage

East Berlin
Adams County

(G-4519)
BASICALLY NICKEL
2042 Baltimore Pike (17316-9191)
P.O. Box 608 (17316-0608)
PHONE..................................717 292-7232
Ralph V Dixon, *Principal*
EMP: 6
SALES (est): 510.2K **Privately Held**
SIC: 3356 Nickel

(G-4520)
BOWMAN TOOL
1515 Braggtown Rd (17316-9663)
PHONE..................................717 432-1403
Thomas Bowman, *Owner*
EMP: 3
SALES (est): 360.1K **Privately Held**
WEB: www.bowmantool.com
SIC: 3599 8721 Machine shop, jobbing &
repair; accounting, auditing & bookkeep-
ing

(G-4521)
CRISMOR MACHINE INC
225 Blue Hill School Rd (17316-9145)
PHONE..................................717 292-9646
Alan L Crisamore, *President*
Sonya Crisamore, *Admin Sec*
EMP: 4
SQ FT: 5,000
SALES: 275K **Privately Held**
SIC: 3599 Machine shop, jobbing & repair

(G-4522)
HOFF WOODWORKING
200 College Ave (17316)
PHONE..................................717 259-6040
David Hoff, *Principal*
EMP: 4
SALES (est): 331.1K **Privately Held**
SIC: 2431 Millwork

(G-4523)
MARTIN METAL WORKS INC
6711 Davidsburg Rd (17316-9130)
P.O. Box 770 (17316-0770)
PHONE..................................717 292-5691
Dennis Martin, *President*
Wendy Hayes, *Admin Sec*
EMP: 10 EST: 1976
SQ FT: 10,000
SALES (est): 1.4MM **Privately Held**
WEB: www.martinmetalworks.com
SIC: 1761 3444 Sheet metalwork; sheet
metalwork

(G-4524)
**PENN WOOD PRODUCTS INC
(PA)**
Also Called: Pennwood
102 Locust St (17316-7800)
P.O. Box 766 (17316-0766)
PHONE..................................717 259-9551
Newell E Coxon, *President*
Kraig N Coxon, *Vice Pres*
Ryan Peters, *VP Mfg*
Deb Paino, *Safety Dir*
Beth Reindollar, *VP Sls/Mktg*
▲ EMP: 100 EST: 1929
SQ FT: 1,500
SALES (est): 18.6MM **Privately Held**
WEB: www.pennwoodproducts.com
SIC: 2431 2426 Moldings, wood: unfin-
ished & prefinished; hardwood dimension
& flooring mills; dimension, hardwood

(G-4525)
PRESS START GAMES
70 Sedgwick Dr (17316-9351)
PHONE..................................267 253-0595
Joseph Corallo, *Principal*
EMP: 4
SALES (est): 273.5K **Privately Held**
SIC: 2741 Miscellaneous publishing

(G-4526)
**TUCKER INDUS LQUID CATINGS
INC**
407 N Avenue E Berlin (17316)
P.O. Box 1 (17316-0001)
PHONE..................................717 259-8339
Bernard I Tucker, *President*
Brian Tucker, *Vice Pres*
EMP: 20
SQ FT: 36,000
SALES (est): 3MM **Privately Held**
SIC: 3479 Painting, coating & hot dipping

East Brady
Clarion County

(G-4527)
**BRADYS BEND CORPORATION
(PA)**
209 Cove Run Rd (16028-3113)
PHONE..................................724 526-3353
Robert J Bruce, *President*
Gary Bruce, *President*
Dan L Bruce, *Vice Pres*
Brian Eakin, *Administration*
EMP: 2 EST: 1963
SQ FT: 24,000
SALES (est): 8MM **Privately Held**
SIC: 1422 Limestones, ground

(G-4528)
BRADYS BEND CORPORATION
Cove Run Rd (16028)
PHONE..................................724 526-3353
Pam McGinnis, *Corp Secy*
Paul Early, *Manager*
EMP: 20
SALES (corp-wide): 8MM **Privately Held**
SIC: 1422 Limestones, ground
PA: Bradys Bend Corporation
209 Cove Run Rd
East Brady PA 16028
724 526-3353

(G-4529)
**DR G H MICHEL RESTOR-SKIN
CO**
Also Called: Taurus Holdings
202 6th St (16028-1106)
P.O. Box 337 (16028-0337)
PHONE..................................724 526-5551
Gordon Cogley, *Partner*
Charles Buechele, *Partner*
EMP: 4
SQ FT: 8,500
SALES (est): 516.8K **Privately Held**
WEB: www.taurusholdings.com
SIC: 2869 Industrial organic chemicals

East Butler
Butler County

(G-4530)
BALLISTIC APPLICATIONS
Also Called: Bam International
1317 Grant Ave (16029)
P.O. Box 673 (16029-0673)
PHONE..................................724 282-0416
Stephen Fitzgibbon, *Mng Member*
Michael Cattell,
Thomas Divenedetto,
Patrick Maloney,
Linda B Buckner Ttee,
EMP: 10
SQ FT: 30,000
SALES: 5.5MM **Privately Held**
SIC: 4731 8742 3669 Freight transporta-
tion arrangement; business consultant; in-
tercommunication systems, electric

(G-4531)
**CONSOLIDATED GL HOLDINGS
INC (PA)**
500 Grant Ave Ste 201 (16029-2111)
P.O. Box 739 (16029-0739)
PHONE..................................866 412-6977
Paul Cody, *President*
EMP: 7 EST: 2011

SALES (est): 107.4MM **Privately Held**
SIC: 5039 3211 6719 1793 Glass construction materials; flat glass; investment
holding companies, except banks; glass &
glazing work

(G-4532)
**GOLDSBOROUGH & VANSANT
INC**
Also Called: Butler Forge & Metal Works
1200 Railroad St (16029)
P.O. Box 179 (16029-0179)
PHONE..................................724 287-5590
William Julin Jr, *President*
B Cravener, *Branch Mgr*
EMP: 20
SQ FT: 30,000
SALES (corp-wide): 5.2MM **Privately
Held**
WEB: www.butlerforge.com
SIC: 3312 Forgings, iron & steel
PA: Goldsborough & Vansant Inc
6116 Brownsville Road Ext # 108
Finleyville PA 15332
724 782-0393

(G-4533)
KEN-FAB & WELD INC (PA)
Also Called: Butler Steel Supply
145 Valvoline Rd (16029)
P.O. Box 448 (16029-0448)
PHONE..................................724 283-8815
Richard Kennedy, *President*
Cynthia F Kennedy, *Treasurer*
EMP: 5
SQ FT: 12,000
SALES (est): 2.7MM **Privately Held**
SIC: 3441 Fabricated structural metal

(G-4534)
KEN-FAB & WELD INC
Butler Steel Supply Co Div
145 Valvoline Rd (16029)
PHONE..................................724 283-8815
Richard Kennedy, *Branch Mgr*
EMP: 9 **Privately Held**
SIC: 3441 Fabricated structural metal
PA: Ken-Fab & Weld, Inc.
145 Valvoline Rd
East Butler PA 16029

(G-4535)
**METALZED CERAMICS FOR
ELEC INC**
119 Grant Ave (16029)
P.O. Box 86 (16029-0086)
PHONE..................................724 287-5752
Edward Mable, *President*
Byron S Mable, *President*
EMP: 10 EST: 1969
SQ FT: 10,000
SALES (est): 1.4MM **Privately Held**
WEB: www.metalizedceramics.com
SIC: 3269 Pottery cooking & kitchen arti-
cles

(G-4536)
**STANDARD BENT GLASS LLC
(DH)**
136 Lincoln Ave (16029)
P.O. Box 469, Butler (16003-0469)
PHONE..................................724 287-3747
Vincent Nardy, *President*
John Custer, *Exec VP*
Denny Troyan, *Plant Mgr*
Ronald Marzullo, *Prdtn Mgr*
Phillip Won, *CFO*
◆ EMP: 100
SQ FT: 125,000
SALES: 23MM **Privately Held**
WEB: www.standardbent.com
SIC: 3211 3231 Flat glass; structural
glass; glass sheet, bent: made from pur-
chased glass
HQ: Ibis Tek, Inc.
912 Pittsburgh Rd
Butler PA 16002
724 431-3000

GEOGRAPHIC

East Earl
Lancaster County

(G-4537)
AUNT BARBIES
Also Called: Names 'n Things
234 Pleasant Valley Rd (17519-9302)
PHONE.....................................717 445-6386
Moses S Stoltzfus, *Owner*
Barbie Stoltzfus, *Owner*
EMP: 5 **EST:** 1970
SQ FT: 3,600
SALES: 50K **Privately Held**
WEB: www.auntbarbies.com
SIC: 2499 Decorative wood & woodwork

(G-4538)
BRADLEY WALTER MYERS
Also Called: Carlyd Fishers Products
653 Wentzel Rd (17519-9472)
PHONE.....................................717 413-0197
Bradley Walter Myers, *Owner*
EMP: 3
SQ FT: 4,500
SALES: 70K **Privately Held**
SIC: 3949 Fishing tackle, general

(G-4539)
C E SAUDER & SONS LLC
359 Weaverland Valley Rd (17519-9733)
PHONE.....................................717 445-4822
Jay Sauder, *Partner*
Elvin Sauder,
James Bowman,
Donald Fox,
Gary Sauder,
EMP: 23
SQ FT: 8,000
SALES (est): 4.2MM **Privately Held**
WEB: www.sauderfeeds.com
SIC: 3523 Feed grinders, crushers & mixers; cleaning machines for fruits, grains & vegetables

(G-4540)
CONESTOGA WOOD SPC CORP (PA)
245 Reading Rd (17519-9549)
P.O. Box 158 (17519-0158)
PHONE.....................................717 445-6701
Anthony Hahn, *President*
Norman Hahn, *Chairman*
Anthony Mosca, *Area Mgr*
Richard P Baldauf, *Vice Pres*
Jim Frazier, *Materials Mgr*
◆ **EMP:** 820
SQ FT: 440,000
SALES (est): 213MM **Privately Held**
WEB: www.conestogawood.com
SIC: 2431 2521 2434 Doors, wood; trim, wood; moldings, wood: unfinished & prefinished; wood office furniture; cabinets, office: wood; wood kitchen cabinets

(G-4541)
CREEK VIEW MANUFACTURING LLC
1751 Mill Rd (17519-9552)
PHONE.....................................717 445-4922
Brian J Horst, *Principal*
EMP: 8
SALES (est): 711.1K **Privately Held**
SIC: 3999 Manufacturing industries

(G-4542)
E H WOODWORKING
Also Called: Blueridge Furniture
1763 Weaverland Rd (17519-9425)
PHONE.....................................717 445-6595
Sidney Burkholder, *Owner*
EMP: 8
SQ FT: 14,400
SALES (est): 569.4K **Privately Held**
SIC: 2511 Kitchen & dining room furniture

(G-4543)
FACIO CONCEPTS LLC
1564 Main St Ste 504 (17519-9339)
PHONE.....................................717 945-8609
Myron Bauman,
EMP: 4

SALES (est): 174.7K **Privately Held**
SIC: 2426 Furniture stock & parts, hardwood

(G-4544)
HOOVER PRECISION MACHINE WORKS
1981 N Churchtown Rd (17519-9435)
PHONE.....................................717 445-9190
Marlin Hoover, *Owner*
EMP: 4
SQ FT: 1,808
SALES (est): 409.4K **Privately Held**
SIC: 3599 Machine shop, jobbing & repair

(G-4545)
HORNING MANUFACTURING LLC
1647 Union Grove Rd (17519-9433)
PHONE.....................................717 354-5040
David Horning, *General Mgr*
Leon Horning Jr,
Nathaniel Horning,
EMP: 10
SQ FT: 6,000
SALES: 2MM **Privately Held**
SIC: 3523 Dusters, mechanical: agricultural

(G-4546)
JAY ZIMMERMAN
Also Called: Kitchen Craft
859 Broad St (17519-9650)
PHONE.....................................717 445-7246
Jay Zimmerman, *Owner*
Terry Demkiw, *Cust Mgr*
EMP: 8
SALES (est): 748.4K **Privately Held**
SIC: 2434 2431 Wood kitchen cabinets; millwork

(G-4547)
MARTIN CUSTOM CABINETS LLC
1564 Main St Ste 504 (17519-9339)
PHONE.....................................717 721-1859
Leonard Martin, *Principal*
EMP: 7
SALES (est): 292.7K **Privately Held**
SIC: 2499 1751 Decorative wood & woodwork; carpentry work

(G-4548)
MARTIN LIMESTONE INC (HQ)
Also Called: Limeville Quarry
3580 Division Hwy (17519-9217)
P.O. Box 550, Blue Ball (17506-0550)
PHONE.....................................717 335-4500
Howard Winey, *President*
Donald Detwiler, *Vice Pres*
Paul I Detwiler Jr, *Vice Pres*
▼ **EMP:** 26 **EST:** 1933
SQ FT: 14,000
SALES (est): 250.8MM
SALES (corp-wide): 651.9MM **Privately Held**
WEB: www.martinlimestone.com
SIC: 3273 3271 1611 1422 Ready-mixed concrete; blocks, concrete or cinder: standard; highway & street paving contractor; crushed & broken limestone; business management; lumber & other building materials
PA: New Enterprise Stone & Lime Co., Inc.
3912 Brumbaugh Rd
New Enterprise PA 16664
814 224-6883

(G-4549)
MARTIN LIMESTONE INC
Also Called: Weaverland Quarry
3580 Division Hwy (17519-9217)
PHONE.....................................717 354-1370
Jeffrey Rutt, *Manager*
EMP: 300
SQ FT: 1,660
SALES (corp-wide): 651.9MM **Privately Held**
WEB: www.martinlimestone.com
SIC: 1499 3274 1422 Bituminous limestone quarrying; lime; crushed & broken limestone

HQ: Martin Limestone, Inc.
3580 Division Hwy
East Earl PA 17519
717 335-4500

(G-4550)
MEKE CORP
1282 E Earl Rd (17519-9701)
PHONE.....................................717 354-6353
Kim D Spohn, *President*
Tina Capizzi, *Vice Pres*
▲ **EMP:** 10
SQ FT: 20,000
SALES (est): 1.4MM **Privately Held**
SIC: 2329 2339 2369 Men's & boys' sportswear & athletic clothing; women's & misses' outerwear; girls' & children's outerwear

(G-4551)
NEW ENTERPRISE STONE LIME INC
Also Called: Kutztown Quarry
3580 Division Hwy (17519-9217)
PHONE.....................................610 683-3302
Kevin Huck, *Manager*
EMP: 8
SQ FT: 1,056
SALES (corp-wide): 651.9MM **Privately Held**
WEB: www.berksproducts.com
SIC: 1422 5032 Crushed & broken limestone; stone, crushed or broken
PA: New Enterprise Stone & Lime Co., Inc.
3912 Brumbaugh Rd
New Enterprise PA 16664
814 224-6883

(G-4552)
PAUL H NOLT WOODWORKING
Also Called: Nolt Cabinet Shop
795 Terre Hill Rd (17519-9758)
PHONE.....................................717 445-4972
Paul H Nolt, *Owner*
EMP: 3
SQ FT: 2,000
SALES: 30K **Privately Held**
SIC: 2434 Wood kitchen cabinets

(G-4553)
PHOENIX WOODWORKING INC
211 Reading Rd (17519-9530)
P.O. Box 7, Morgantown (19543-0007)
PHONE.....................................610 209-9030
Ralph D Hill, *President*
Jacob T Hill, *Vice Pres*
Larry S Zentz, *Treasurer*
EMP: 16
SALES (est): 2.2MM **Privately Held**
WEB: www.phoenixwoodworking.com
SIC: 2431 Millwork

(G-4554)
REIFF METAL FABRICATIONS
451 Weaverland Valley Rd (17519-9640)
PHONE.....................................717 445-7050
EMP: 6 **EST:** 2015
SALES (est): 163.3K **Privately Held**
SIC: 3499 Fabricated metal products

(G-4555)
SAUDERS NURSERY
1210 E Earl Rd (17519-9583)
PHONE.....................................717 354-9851
Elam Sauder, *Owner*
▲ **EMP:** 10
SALES (est): 1.1MM **Privately Held**
SIC: 5261 2499 5193 0181 Nurseries; mulch, wood & bark; flowers & nursery stock; nursery stock; ornamental nursery products; nursery stock, growing of

(G-4556)
VALLEY PROTEINS INC
693 Wide Hollow Rd (17519-9645)
P.O. Box 369, Terre Hill (17581-0369)
PHONE.....................................717 445-6890
Randy Derrow, *Transptn Dir*
Keith Landis, *Opers-Prdtn-Mfg*
EMP: 85

SALES (corp-wide): 493.7MM **Privately Held**
WEB: www.valleyproteins.com
SIC: 2077 2048 2047 Tallow rendering, inedible; grease rendering, inedible; meat meal & tankage, except an animal feed; prepared feeds; dog & cat food
PA: Valley Proteins (De), Inc.
151 Valpro Dr
Winchester VA 22603
540 877-2533

(G-4557)
WEAVER CARRIAGE SHOP
361 Iron Bridge Rd (17519-9418)
PHONE.....................................717 445-7191
David Weaver, *Owner*
EMP: 4
SALES (est): 306.4K **Privately Held**
SIC: 3799 Carriages, horse drawn

(G-4558)
WEAVER MACHINE & HARDWARE LLC
385 Reading Rd (17519-9605)
PHONE.....................................717 445-9927
Earl Weaver, *Owner*
Marvin Huber, *Partner*
James Nolt, *Partner*
EMP: 8
SQ FT: 420
SALES: 1MM **Privately Held**
SIC: 3599 Machine shop, jobbing & repair

East Freedom
Blair County

(G-4559)
BEAVERTOWN BLOCK CO INC
16637 Dvecchis Spruce Sts (16637)
PHONE.....................................814 695-4448
Phillip Devecchis, *Branch Mgr*
Phillip De Vecchis, *Manager*
EMP: 17
SALES (corp-wide): 10.5MM **Privately Held**
WEB: www.beavertownblock.com
SIC: 3271 Blocks, concrete or cinder: standard
PA: Beavertown Block Co., Inc.
3612 Paxtonville Rd
Middleburg PA
570 837-1744

(G-4560)
BLAIR TOOL & PLASTIC CO INC
Everette Rd (16637)
P.O. Box 124 (16637-0124)
PHONE.....................................814 695-2726
Joseph E Hetrick, *President*
Betty Hetrick, *Corp Secy*
EMP: 20 **EST:** 1970
SQ FT: 4,320
SALES (est): 3MM **Privately Held**
SIC: 3089 7699 Injection molding of plastics; plastics products repair

(G-4561)
BLAIR TOOL AND PLASTICS CO LLC
2846 Everett Rd (16637)
P.O. Box 124 (16637-0124)
PHONE.....................................814 695-2726
Edward Hetrick,
EMP: 6
SQ FT: 10,000
SALES (est): 473.8K **Privately Held**
SIC: 2821 3544 Plastics materials & resins; special dies, tools, jigs & fixtures

(G-4562)
CENTRAL HYDRAULICS INC
366 Travelers Rd (16637-8118)
PHONE.....................................814 224-0375
Christopher E Ritchey, *Branch Mgr*
EMP: 20 **Privately Held**
SIC: 3599 Machine & other job shop work
PA: Central Hydraulics, Inc.
7324 Woodbury Pike
Roaring Spring PA 16673

▲ = Import ▼=Export
◆ =Import/Export

GEOGRAPHIC

(G-4563)
CS TRUCKING LLC (PA)
366 Travelers Rd (16637-8118)
PHONE..................................814 224-0395
Mike Ritchey, *Mng Member*
EMP: 6 EST: 2009
SALES (est): 14.1MM **Privately Held**
SIC: 1389 4213 Oil field services; heavy
hauling

(G-4564)
KEN IMLER
Also Called: Imler's, Ken Garage
795 Mountain Rd (16637-8301)
PHONE..................................814 695-1310
Kenneth L Imler, *Owner*
EMP: 4
SALES (est): 314.9K **Privately Held**
SIC: 7538 3599 General automotive repair
shops; machine shop, jobbing & repair

East Greenville
Montgomery County

(G-4565)
**BLOMMER CHOCOLATE
COMPANY (HQ)**
1101 Blommer Dr (18041-2140)
PHONE..................................800 825-8181
Henry J Blommer Jr, *CEO*
Peter W Blommer, *Vice Pres*
Peter Drake, *Vice Pres*
Peter Blommer, *VP Opers*
Jill Deters, *Production*
◆ EMP: 100 EST: 1939
SQ FT: 340,000
SALES (est): 33.2MM
SALES (corp-wide): 2.8B **Privately Held**
WEB: www.eg.blommer.com
SIC: 2066 Chocolate coatings & syrup;
powdered cocoa; cocoa butter
PA: Fuji Oil Holdings Inc.
3-6-32, Nakanoshima, Kita-Ku
Osaka OSK 530-0
664 590-700

(G-4566)
**BLOMMER CHOCOLATE
COMPANY**
Also Called: Blommer Chocolate Company,
The
1101 Blommer Dr (18041-2140)
PHONE..................................215 679-4472
Steve Blommer, *Branch Mgr*
EMP: 130
SQ FT: 10,000
SALES (corp-wide): 2.8B **Privately Held**
WEB: www.eg.blommer.com
SIC: 2066 Chocolate & cocoa products
HQ: The Blommer Chocolate Company
1101 Blommer Dr
East Greenville PA 18041
800 825-8181

(G-4567)
ENTERPRISE MACHINE
1341 Tagart Rd (18041-1423)
PHONE..................................215 679-7490
Joe Zappo, *Owner*
EMP: 3 EST: 2000
SALES (est): 365.2K **Privately Held**
SIC: 3599 Machine shop, jobbing & repair

(G-4568)
FIBA TECHNOLOGIES INC
1645 State St (18041-2220)
PHONE..................................215 679-7823
Andrew Cutts, *Manager*
EMP: 10
SALES (corp-wide): 53.5MM **Privately
Held**
WEB: www.fibatech.com
SIC: 3799 Trailers & trailer equipment
PA: Fiba Technologies, Inc.
53 Ayer Rd
Littleton MA 01460
508 887-7100

(G-4569)
INTENTS MFG
200 W 4th St (18041-1610)
PHONE..................................215 527-6441
Kevin Leamer, *Principal*
EMP: 3
SALES (est): 121.1K **Privately Held**
SIC: 3999 Manufacturing industries

(G-4570)
KNOLL INC (PA)
1235 Water St (18041-2202)
PHONE..................................215 679-7991
Burton B Staniar, *Ch of Bd*
Andrew B Cogan, *President*
Christopher M Baldwin, *President*
John Finken, *President*
Steven Kleis, *President*
◆ EMP: 100
SQ FT: 735,000
SALES: 1.3B **Publicly Held**
WEB: www.knoll.com
SIC: 2521 2522 2299 Wood office furni-
ture; panel systems & partitions (free-
standing), office: wood; chairs, office:
padded, upholstered or plain: wood; office
furniture, except wood; panel systems &
partitions, office: except wood; chairs, of-
fice: padded or plain, except wood; uphol-
stery filling, textile

(G-4571)
KNOLL INC
329 Railroad St (18041-1633)
PHONE..................................215 679-1218
Charles Lieb, *Vice Pres*
Joseph Deliso, *Purchasing*
Hana Dorani, *Sales Staff*
Susan Bender, *Director*
EMP: 50 **Publicly Held**
WEB: www.knoll.com
SIC: 2521 Panel systems & partitions
(free-standing), office: wood
PA: Knoll, Inc.
1235 Water St
East Greenville PA 18041

(G-4572)
KOCH FILTER CORPORATION
1653 State St (18041-2220)
PHONE..................................215 679-3135
EMP: 18 **Privately Held**
SIC: 3585 Refrigeration & heating equip-
ment
HQ: Koch Filter Corporation
8401 Air Commerce Dr
Louisville KY 40219
502 634-4796

(G-4573)
**PERKIOMEN VALLEY PRINTING
INC**
114 Main St (18041-1403)
P.O. Box 418, Red Hill (18076-0418)
PHONE..................................215 679-4000
Henry Thomas, *President*
Steve Thomas, *Vice Pres*
EMP: 6 EST: 1976
SQ FT: 5,700
SALES (est): 989.9K **Privately Held**
WEB: www.perkprinting.com
SIC: 2759 Commercial printing

(G-4574)
**SCHULTZ RICHARD DESIGN &
MFG**
1235 Water St (18041-2202)
PHONE..................................215 679-2222
◆ EMP: 18
SQ FT: 22,000
SALES (est): 2.2MM **Privately Held**
SIC: 2514 2511 Mfg Metal Household
Furn Mfg Wood Household Furn

(G-4575)
SEIN ORGANIZING SOLUTIONS
4621 E Mill Hill Rd (18041-2632)
PHONE..................................215 932-8837
Sharon Sein, *Owner*
EMP: 3
SALES (est): 196.3K **Privately Held**
SIC: 3089 Injection molding of plastics

(G-4576)
SOS PRODUCTS COMPANY INC
401 W 4th St (18041-1710)
P.O. Box 47 (18041-0047)
PHONE..................................215 679-6262
William Pryor, *President*
Becky Dudek, *Office Mgr*
▲ EMP: 50

SQ FT: 105,000
SALES (est): 8.1MM **Privately Held**
SIC: 2899 Chemical preparations

(G-4577)
TITANIUM FINISHING CO
248 Main St (18041-1405)
P.O. Box 22 (18041-0022)
PHONE..................................215 679-4181
Melanie Faul Cunningham, *President*
Timothy Cunningham, *Vice Pres*
Melinda Cunningham, *Admin Sec*
EMP: 13
SQ FT: 31,000
SALES (est): 2MM **Privately Held**
WEB: www.titaniumfinishing.com
SIC: 3471 Electroplating of metals or
formed products

(G-4578)
TRIMS
2123 Berry Ln (18041-2001)
PHONE..................................215 541-1946
▲ EMP: 15
SQ FT: 5,000
SALES (est): 1.5MM **Privately Held**
SIC: 2241 Narrow Fabric Mill

East Liberty
Allegheny County

(G-4579)
ROME AT HOME
233 Auburn St (15206-3209)
PHONE..................................412 361-3782
Barbara G Stagno, *Manager*
EMP: 3
SALES (est): 170K **Privately Held**
SIC: 2038 Ethnic foods, frozen

(G-4580)
RTR MANUFACTURING CO
204 Auburn St (15206-3210)
PHONE..................................412 665-1500
Jim Householder, *Owner*
Robert Tortorete, *Principal*
EMP: 19
SQ FT: 16,000
SALES (est): 1.4MM **Privately Held**
SIC: 3714 5531 Motor vehicle engines &
parts; transmissions, motor vehicle; auto-
motive parts

(G-4581)
STAGNOS BAKERY INC (PA)
Also Called: Stagno's Italian Accent
233 Auburn St (15206-3209)
PHONE..................................412 441-3485
Frank Stagno, *President*
Theresa Vento, *Treasurer*
Frances Stagno, *Admin Sec*
EMP: 36 EST: 1941
SQ FT: 20,000
SALES (est): 4.2MM **Privately Held**
SIC: 2051 Bakery: wholesale or whole-
sale/retail combined

East Mc Keesport
Allegheny County

(G-4582)
**WENNING ENTERTAINMENT
LLC**
1354 Wilmerding Ave (15035-1623)
PHONE..................................412 292-8776
Eric Wenning, *CEO*
EMP: 10
SALES: 219.5K **Privately Held**
SIC: 7929 7335 3993 Actors; commercial
photography; signs & advertising special-
ties

East Millsboro
Fayette County

(G-4583)
CONSOL ENERGY INC
379 Alicia Rd (15433-1252)
PHONE..................................724 785-6242
Dean Orr, *Branch Mgr*
EMP: 146 **Publicly Held**
SIC: 1221 Bituminous coal & lignite-sur-
face mining
PA: Cnx Resources Corporation
1000 Consol Energy Dr
Canonsburg PA 15317

East Norriton
Montgomery County

(G-4584)
**GILL QUARRIES
INCORPORATED**
3201 Potshop Rd (19403-4630)
P.O. Box 187, Fairview Village (19409-
0187)
PHONE..................................610 584-6061
Irvin Gill, *President*
EMP: 5
SALES (est): 585.6K **Privately Held**
SIC: 3281 Cut stone & stone products

(G-4585)
TRINITY PARTNERS LLC
301 E Germantown Pike (19401-6517)
PHONE..................................610 233-1210
Stephen Gerard, *CEO*
Gary McWalters, *President*
Peter Bittinger, *Senior VP*
John Carro, *Senior VP*
Joe Falcon, *Senior VP*
EMP: 19 EST: 2007
SALES (est): 2.9MM
SALES (corp-wide): 6.9MM **Privately
Held**
SIC: 8742 2834 Management consulting
services; pharmaceutical preparations
PA: Trinity Partners, Llc
230 3rd Ave
Waltham MA 02451
781 487-7300

East Petersburg
Lancaster County

(G-4586)
AWESOME ICE INC
2235 Olde Meadow Ct (17520-1024)
PHONE..................................717 519-2423
Steven K McKinney, *President*
EMP: 15
SALES (est): 710K **Privately Held**
SIC: 2024 Ice cream & frozen desserts

(G-4587)
**FOX CHAPEL PUBLISHING CO
INC**
1970 Broad St (17520-1102)
PHONE..................................800 457-9112
J Alan Giagnocavo, *President*
Jon Deck, *Opers Staff*
Joseph Schott, *Opers Staff*
Elizabeth Martins, *Pub Rel Mgr*
Fred Pickard, *Controller*
▲ EMP: 22
SQ FT: 15,500
SALES (est): 3.7MM **Privately Held**
WEB: www.foxchapelpublishing.com
SIC: 2731 Books: publishing only

(G-4588)
MAC INC
Also Called: Mac Clay Leather
1986 New St (17520-1312)
P.O. Box 134 (17520-0134)
PHONE..................................717 560-0612
Clay Rosenbarker, *President*
Carol Rosenbarker, *Treasurer*
EMP: 4

SQ FT: 3,000
SALES (est): 519.5K **Privately Held**
WEB: www.macclayleather.com
SIC: 3199 Equestrian related leather articles

(G-4589)
RICHTER PRECISION INC (PA)
1021 Commercial Ave (17520-1601)
P.O. Box 159 (17520-0159)
PHONE...................................717 560-9990
J Hans Richter, *President*
Carolyn M Richter, *Corp Secy*
Yasuo Yamazaki, *Engineer*
Bikram Kamboj, *Manager*
Carolyn Richter, *Admin Sec*
▲ **EMP:** 90
SQ FT: 45,000
SALES (est): 28.2MM **Privately Held**
WEB: www.richterprecision.com
SIC: 3545 3479 3544 3398 Cutting tools for machine tools; coating of metals & formed products; special dies, tools, jigs & fixtures; metal heat treating; paints & allied products

(G-4590)
SPECIALTY PRODUCTS & INSUL CO
1097 Commercial Ave (17520-1648)
PHONE...................................717 569-3900
Nancy Schwarzlose, *Branch Mgr*
EMP: 5
SALES (est): 117.6K **Privately Held**
SIC: 3644 Insulators & insulation materials, electrical

(G-4591)
STAUFFER ACQUISITION CORP
Also Called: Spectrum Printing
1160 Enterprise Ct (17520-1647)
P.O. Box 679 (17520-0679)
PHONE...................................717 569-3200
Nicholas G Schafer, *President*
EMP: 35
SQ FT: 16,000
SALES (est): 5.9MM **Privately Held**
SIC: 2752 2789 2791 Commercial printing, offset; bookbinding & related work; typesetting

(G-4592)
SUZA INC
Also Called: Design Originals
1970 Broad St (17520-1102)
PHONE...................................817 877-0067
Suzanne McNeill, *President*
▲ **EMP:** 10
SQ FT: 16,000
SALES (est): 1MM **Privately Held**
WEB: www.d-originals.com
SIC: 2721 Periodicals: publishing & printing

(G-4593)
TANGLED MANES
5313 Main St (17520-1609)
PHONE...................................717 581-0600
Angie Mauer, *Owner*
EMP: 5
SALES (est): 342.8K **Privately Held**
SIC: 3999 Sterilizers, barber & beauty shop

East Pittsburgh
Allegheny County

(G-4594)
ATOMATIC MANUFACTURING CO INC
300 Shadeland Ave (15112-1432)
PHONE...................................412 824-6400
Alexander T Kindling, *CEO*
John Kindling, *President*
EMP: 16 **EST:** 1954
SQ FT: 11,000
SALES (est): 2.4MM **Privately Held**
SIC: 3599 Machine shop, jobbing & repair

(G-4595)
GEORGE I REITZ & SONS INC
805 Wood St (15112-1246)
PHONE...................................412 824-9976

Brian Reitz, *Vice Pres*
Sandy Crawford, *Branch Mgr*
EMP: 8
SALES (corp-wide): 22.8MM **Privately Held**
WEB: www.gireitz.com
SIC: 5084 3443 7692 3714 Pumps & pumping equipment; tanks, standard or custom fabricated: metal plate; welding repair; motor vehicle parts & accessories; sheet metalwork; fabricated structural metal
PA: George I. Reitz & Sons, Inc.
    17214 Route 36
    Brookville PA 15825
    814 849-2308

(G-4596)
INTERVALA LLC
700 Braddock Ave (15112-1242)
PHONE...................................412 829-4800
Teresa Huber, *CEO*
Scott Gustafson, *COO*
Damian Essel, *Opers Mgr*
Jason Eddy, *Engineer*
Melanie Keenan, *CFO*
EMP: 250
SQ FT: 135,500
SALES (est): 76.7MM **Privately Held**
SIC: 3625 Relays, for electronic use

(G-4597)
SIEMENS INDUSTRY INC
664 Linden Ave (15112-1204)
PHONE...................................412 829-7511
Mark Trocki, *Marketing Mgr*
EMP: 13
SALES (corp-wide): 95B **Privately Held**
SIC: 3661 Telephones & telephone apparatus
HQ: Siemens Industry, Inc.
    1000 Deerfield Pkwy
    Buffalo Grove IL 60089
    800 743-6367

(G-4598)
SIGN SERVICES INC
306 North Ave (15112-1423)
PHONE...................................412 996-0824
Mark A Terdle, *Principal*
EMP: 3
SALES (est): 270.3K **Privately Held**
SIC: 3993 Signs & advertising specialties

East Springfield
Erie County

(G-4599)
JB RACING INC
4097 Scott Rd (16411-9427)
PHONE...................................814 922-3523
Jody Bateman, *President*
▲ **EMP:** 8
SALES (est): 883.6K **Privately Held**
SIC: 3799 All terrain vehicles (ATV)

(G-4600)
MEDCOMP TECHNOLOGIES INC
12220 Main St (16411-9622)
PHONE...................................814 504-3328
Howard Miller, *Principal*
EMP: 3
SALES (est): 189.1K **Privately Held**
SIC: 3571 Electronic computers

East Stroudsburg
Monroe County

(G-4601)
A J SMITH ELECTRIC MOTOR SVC
210 Independence Rd (18301-9435)
PHONE...................................570 424-8743
Andrew J Smith, *Owner*
Debra M Smith, *Office Mgr*
EMP: 3
SQ FT: 6,000
SALES (est): 290K **Privately Held**
SIC: 7694 5063 Electric motor repair; motors, electric

(G-4602)
ABCORE FITNESS INC
158 Progress St (18301-9312)
PHONE...................................570 424-1006
Russell Nohejl, *President*
▲ **EMP:** 7
SALES (est): 852.4K **Privately Held**
SIC: 3949 Exercise equipment

(G-4603)
ADVANCED DOOR TECHNOLOGIES INC
34 N Crystal St (18301-2129)
PHONE...................................570 421-5929
Fred Budetti, *President*
Al Franza, *Vice Pres*
Angela Rodrigues, *Vice Pres*
▲ **EMP:** 43
SQ FT: 175,000
SALES: 4MM **Privately Held**
WEB: www.adtdoor.com
SIC: 3442 Metal doors

(G-4604)
AJAY FUEL INC
2579 Milford Rd (18301)
PHONE...................................570 223-1580
Kusham Lata, *Principal*
EMP: 4 **EST:** 2010
SALES (est): 326.4K **Privately Held**
SIC: 2869 Fuels

(G-4605)
AMANDA REICHE
Also Called: Northern Crafts
127 Chariton Dr (18301-9613)
PHONE...................................570 424-0334
Amanda Reiche, *Owner*
Paul Reiche, *Co-Owner*
EMP: 3
SQ FT: 1,500
SALES: 125K **Privately Held**
WEB: www.northerncrafts.com
SIC: 2511 5712 Wood household furniture; furniture stores

(G-4606)
AUCOURANT LLC
140 Deer Path (18302-7711)
PHONE...................................800 682-1623
Susan Horrell, *Partner*
Cesar Ramirez, *Partner*
EMP: 10
SALES (est): 1.2MM **Privately Held**
WEB: www.aucourant.com
SIC: 2844 Face creams or lotions; cosmetic preparations

(G-4607)
AVIDON WELDING INC
205 W 4th St (18301-1408)
PHONE...................................570 421-2307
Edward Valeich, *CEO*
Robert Stavis, *Treasurer*
Steven Walck, *Admin Sec*
EMP: 3
SALES (est): 630K **Privately Held**
SIC: 3317 Welded pipe & tubes

(G-4608)
BASIC POWER INC
530 Seven Bridge Rd (18301-9121)
PHONE...................................570 872-9666
Guy Lestician, *President*
EMP: 8
SQ FT: 5,000
SALES (est): 1.5MM **Privately Held**
SIC: 3613 3825 Control panels, electric; energy measuring equipment, electrical

(G-4609)
CLOUD CHEMISTRY LLC
4543 Milford Rd Ste 50 (18302-9607)
PHONE...................................570 851-1680
Carl Bevacqua, *CEO*
Sean Murray, *COO*
Caprice Velazquez,
EMP: 16
SALES: 1.3MM **Privately Held**
SIC: 3999 Cigarette & cigar products & accessories

(G-4610)
COMMUTERS EXPRESS INC
Also Called: Community Express
6002 Woodale Rd (18301)
PHONE...................................570 476-0601
Mark Feder, *President*
EMP: 6
SALES (est): 157K
SALES (corp-wide): 75.5K **Privately Held**
SIC: 2711 Newspapers, publishing & printing
PA: Commuters Express, Inc
    569 Executive Dr
    Stroudsburg PA

(G-4611)
COMPLEXX GASES INC
62 Mill Creek Rd (18301-7183)
PHONE...................................610 969-6661
EMP: 3 **EST:** 2014
SALES (est): 363.1K **Privately Held**
SIC: 3369 Nonferrous foundries

(G-4612)
CORPORATE GRAPHICS INC
Rr 5 Box 5268 (18301-9805)
PHONE...................................570 424-0475
Donna Debarbieri, *President*
Donna De Barbieri, *President*
EMP: 3
SALES (est): 329.1K **Privately Held**
SIC: 2752 Commercial printing, lithographic

(G-4613)
DIVERSEY INC
880 Crowe Rd (18301-1118)
PHONE...................................570 421-7850
Richard Hartley, *Branch Mgr*
EMP: 63
SALES (corp-wide): 14.2B **Privately Held**
WEB: www.johnsondiversey.com
SIC: 2842 2841 Cleaning or polishing preparations; soap & other detergents
HQ: Diversey, Inc.
    1300 Altura Rd Ste 125
    Fort Mill SC 29708
    800 842-2341

(G-4614)
EDWARD T REGINA
Also Called: Regina Farms
5181 Milford Rd (18302-9147)
PHONE...................................570 223-8358
Edward Regina, *Owner*
EMP: 5
SALES (est): 363K **Privately Held**
SIC: 3524 5261 Lawn & garden equipment; nurseries & garden centers

(G-4615)
HANGER PRSTHETCS & ORTHO INC
Also Called: Hanger P & O
423 Normal St (18301-2716)
PHONE...................................570 421-8221
J Ksiaskiewicz, *Branch Mgr*
Joseph Ksiaskiewicz,
EMP: 7
SALES (corp-wide): 1B **Publicly Held**
SIC: 3842 Orthopedic appliances
HQ: Hanger Prosthetics & Orthotics, Inc.
    10910 Domain Dr Ste 300
    Austin TX 78758
    512 777-3800

(G-4616)
HARMONY LABELS INC
114 Progress St (18301-9312)
PHONE...................................570 664-6700
EMP: 6 **EST:** 2014
SALES (est): 649.5K **Privately Held**
SIC: 2759 Commercial printing

(G-4617)
HARSCO CORPORATION
Patterson-Kelley Division
155 Burson St (18301-2251)
P.O. Box 458 (18301-0458)
PHONE...................................570 421-7500
Mark Lasewicz, *Branch Mgr*
EMP: 112

▲ = Import ▼=Export
◆ =Import/Export

SALES (corp-wide): 1.6B **Publicly Held**
WEB: www.harsco.com
SIC: 3443 2899 3634 3639 Heat exchangers: coolers (after, inter), condensers, etc.; corrosion preventive lubricant; blenders, electric; dryers, electric: hand & face; hot water heaters, household; cement, hydraulic; paints & allied products
PA: Harsco Corporation
350 Poplar Church Rd
Camp Hill PA 17011
717 763-7064

(G-4618)
HARSCO CORPORATION
Also Called: Harsco Indus Patterson-Kelly
155 Burson St (18301-2251)
PHONE..............................570 421-7500
Fax: 570 421-8735
EMP: 23
SALES (corp-wide): 1.4B **Publicly Held**
SIC: 3585 Mfg Refrigeration/Heating Equipment
PA: Harsco Corporation
350 Poplar Church Rd
Camp Hill PA 17011
717 763-7064

(G-4619)
HAYWARD LABORATORIES INC
1921 Paradise Trl (18301-9197)
P.O. Box 386 (18301-0386)
PHONE..............................570 424-9512
Robert Neis, President
▲ EMP: 180
SQ FT: 132,000
SALES (est): 32MM
SALES (corp-wide): 80.3MM **Privately Held**
WEB: www.etbrowne.com
SIC: 2844 Cosmetic preparations
PA: E.T. Browne Drug Co., Inc.
440 Sylvan Ave
Englewood Cliffs NJ 07632
201 894-9020

(G-4620)
INTEL HOMES LTD LIABILITY CO
6518 Moschella Ct (18302-9515)
PHONE..............................570 872-9559
EMP: 3
SALES (est): 155K **Privately Held**
SIC: 3674 Microprocessors

(G-4621)
IRIDIUM INDUSTRIES INC (PA)
Also Called: Artube
147 Forge Rd (18301-2962)
P.O. Box 220333, Great Neck NY (11022-0333)
PHONE..............................570 476-8800
Parviz Nazarian, Ch of Bd
Jacques Sassouni, President
Owen Tarhovicky, Warehouse Mgr
Charles Lumis, CFO
Carol Stewart, Accounts Exec
▲ EMP: 195
SQ FT: 100,000
SALES (est): 37.5MM **Privately Held**
SIC: 3082 Tubes, unsupported plastic

(G-4622)
KISTLER PRINTING CO INC
109 Prospect St (18301-2509)
PHONE..............................570 421-2050
Robert E Mc Master, President
Robert Imcmaster, Vice Pres
EMP: 10 EST: 1946
SQ FT: 6,000
SALES (est): 1.4MM **Privately Held**
WEB: www.kistlerprinting.com
SIC: 2759 2752 Letterpress printing; screen printing; commercial printing, offset

(G-4623)
MORGAN ADVANCED MTLS TECH INC
100 Mill Creek Rd (18301-1122)
PHONE..............................570 421-9921
Michael Cox, Branch Mgr
EMP: 7
SALES (corp-wide): 1.3B **Privately Held**
SIC: 3624 Carbon & graphite products

HQ: Morgan Advanced Materials And Technology, Inc.
441 Hall Ave
Saint Marys PA 15857

(G-4624)
NATIONAL ELEC CARBN PDTS INC
100 Mills Rd (18301)
PHONE..............................570 476-9004
John Stang, Branch Mgr
EMP: 100
SALES (corp-wide): 1.3B **Privately Held**
WEB: www.nationalspecialties.com
SIC: 3624 Carbon & graphite products
HQ: National Electrical Carbon Products, Inc.
251 Forrester Dr
Greenville SC 29607
864 458-7777

(G-4625)
NORTHWOODS PPR CONVERTING INC
830 Crowe Rd (18301-1118)
PHONE..............................570 424-8786
Jon Caldwell, Branch Mgr
EMP: 80
SALES (corp-wide): 21.3MM **Privately Held**
SIC: 2679 Paper products, converted
PA: Northwoods Paper Converting Inc.
230 Corporate Dr
Beaver Dam WI 53916
920 356-9085

(G-4626)
OLDE SLATE MTN COLOR CO INC
248 Lackawanna Ave (18301-2252)
PHONE..............................570 421-8910
Michael Marocchi, CEO
Mary Agnes Marocchi, President
EMP: 6
SQ FT: 30,000
SALES: 1.3MM **Privately Held**
SIC: 3089 Coloring & finishing of plastic products

(G-4627)
POCONO CANDLE WORKS INC (PA)
2712 Wigwam Park Rd (18301-8758)
PHONE..............................570 421-1832
Phyllis L Cobb, President
Phyllis A Cobb, President
Victoria L Cobb, Vice Pres
Rick Cobb, Treasurer
EMP: 10 EST: 1972
SQ FT: 10,000
SALES (est): 1.5MM **Privately Held**
WEB: www.poconocandle.com
SIC: 5999 5947 3999 Candle shops; gift shop; candles

(G-4628)
POCONO TIMES
96 S Courtland St (18301-2827)
PHONE..............................570 421-4800
Tim Holmes, Manager
EMP: 3 EST: 2011
SALES (est): 127.9K **Privately Held**
SIC: 2711 Newspapers, publishing & printing

(G-4629)
POPCORN BUDDHA INC
266 River Rd Ste 104e (18301-8543)
PHONE..............................570 476-5676
Craig R Campeoto, President
EMP: 10
SQ FT: 18,000
SALES: 400K **Privately Held**
SIC: 2064 Candy & other confectionery products

(G-4630)
PREMIER PRINTING SOLUTIONS LLC
405 Airport Rd (18301)
PHONE..............................570 426-1570
Keith Ramos, Principal
EMP: 7
SALES (est): 582.3K **Privately Held**
SIC: 2752 Commercial printing, offset

(G-4631)
PRICE CHOPPER OPER CO OF PA
4547 Milford Rd (18302-9657)
PHONE..............................570 223-2410
Robert G Hinkley, Manager
EMP: 4
SALES (corp-wide): 3.3B **Privately Held**
SIC: 3751 Motorcycles & related parts
HQ: Price Chopper Operating Co. Of Pennsylvania Inc.
501 Duanesburg Rd
Schenectady NY 12306
518 355-5000

(G-4632)
PURTECH INC
124 Progress St (18301-9312)
PHONE..............................570 424-1669
James C Purington, President
Joanne Vickers, Telecomm Mgr
EMP: 10
SQ FT: 7,800
SALES (est): 1.5MM **Privately Held**
WEB: www.purtech.net
SIC: 3479 5085 Coating of metals & formed products; industrial supplies

(G-4633)
R & R HEAT TREATING INC
28 Mill Creek Rd (18301-7183)
PHONE..............................570 424-8750
Michael Reidinger Jr, President
David Daniels, Vice Pres
EMP: 9
SQ FT: 11,000
SALES (est): 600K **Privately Held**
SIC: 3398 Metal heat treating

(G-4634)
ROYAL CHEMICAL COMPANY LTD
1336 Crowe Rd (18301)
PHONE..............................570 421-7850
Barry Martin, Branch Mgr
EMP: 15
SALES (corp-wide): 8.9MM **Privately Held**
WEB: www.royalchemical.com
SIC: 2841 2869 2819 Soap: granulated, liquid, cake, flaked or chip; industrial organic chemicals; industrial inorganic chemicals
HQ: Royal Chemical Company, Ltd.
8679 Freeway Dr
Macedonia OH 44056
330 467-1300

(G-4635)
STANDARD INK & COLOR CORP
Airport Rd (18301)
PHONE..............................570 424-5214
Robert Pittola, President
EMP: 4
SALES (est): 620.8K **Privately Held**
WEB: www.standardinktattoos.com
SIC: 2893 Printing ink

(G-4636)
SUN LITHO PRINT INC
421 N Courtland St (18301-1906)
P.O. Box 444 (18301-0444)
PHONE..............................570 421-3250
Robert E McMaster, President
Greg Duncan, Prdtn Mgr
Daniel McMaster, Finance Mgr
Janne Kowalski, Sales Staff
EMP: 15 EST: 1968
SQ FT: 10,000
SALES (est): 2.9MM **Privately Held**
WEB: www.sunlithoprint.com
SIC: 2752 2759 2789 Commercial printing, offset; letterpress printing; bookbinding & related work

(G-4637)
VACUUM WORKS LLC
370 N Courtland St (18301-1930)
PHONE..............................570 202-8407
Paul Firnestone, Owner
EMP: 4
SALES (est): 519.4K **Privately Held**
SIC: 3563 3561 Vacuum pumps, except laboratory; pumps & pumping equipment

(G-4638)
VIGON INTERNATIONAL INC
127 Airport Rd (18301-7702)
PHONE..............................877 844-6639
Stephen Somers, President
Laura McKain, General Mgr
Steve Somers Jr, Vice Pres
Randy Cornell, Production
Felicia Perryman, QA Dir
▲ EMP: 75
SQ FT: 100,000
SALES (est): 67.8MM **Privately Held**
WEB: www.vigoninternational.com
SIC: 2869 5149 2077 Flavors or flavoring materials, synthetic; perfumes, flavorings & food additives; flavourings & fragrances; animal & marine fats & oils

East Texas
Lehigh County

(G-4639)
SPIDER VENOM RACING PDTS LLC
1805 Willow Ln (18046)
PHONE..............................484 547-1400
Paul Messick, Principal
EMP: 3
SALES (est): 222.1K **Privately Held**
SIC: 2836 Venoms

East Waterford
Juniata County

(G-4640)
DRV METAL FAB LLC
3089 Berry Ridge Rd (17021-7059)
PHONE..............................717 968-9028
Barry Vawn, Owner
Danie Vawn,
Daniel Vawn,
EMP: 12
SALES (est): 2.3MM **Privately Held**
SIC: 3443 Fabricated plate work (boiler shop)

(G-4641)
HAMPTON MACHINING INC
3 Hampton Ln (17021-7093)
P.O. Box 17 (17021-0017)
PHONE..............................717 734-2497
Deric Hampton, President
Natasha Hampton, Vice Pres
Dale S Hampton, Shareholder
David Hampton, Shareholder
EMP: 3
SQ FT: 800
SALES (est): 390.5K **Privately Held**
SIC: 3599 Machine shop, jobbing & repair

(G-4642)
VALLEY BROOM INC
25591 Horse Valley Rd (17021-7340)
PHONE..............................717 349-2614
Doris Sauerwald, President
Charles Sauerwald, Vice Pres
EMP: 6
SALES (est): 857K **Privately Held**
SIC: 3991 3531 5084 Street sweeping brooms, hand or machine; snow plow attachments; industrial machinery & equipment; conveyor systems

Easton
Northampton County

(G-4643)
A & H SPORTSWEAR CO INC (PA)
610 Uhler Rd (18040-7001)
PHONE..............................484 373-3600
Mark Waldman, President
Bruce Waldman, Corp Secy
Mark Greenberg, CFO
Frederick D'Amato, VP Finance
◆ EMP: 100 EST: 1936
SQ FT: 45,000

GEOGRAPHIC

SALES (est): 21.4MM **Privately Held**
SIC: 2339 Bathing suits: women's, misses'
& juniors'

(G-4644)
ACCU MACHINING CENTER INC
3750 Nicholas St (18045-5116)
P.O. Box 3220 (18043-3220)
PHONE....................................610 252-6855
Atul Kharecha, *President*
Pushker Kharecha, *Shareholder*
Shilpa Kharecha, *Shareholder*
▲ EMP: 32
SQ FT: 33,000
SALES (est): 6.2MM **Privately Held**
WEB: www.accu-laser.com
SIC: 3312 3599 3444 7692 Bar, rod &
wire products; machine shop, jobbing &
repair; sheet metalwork; welding repair

(G-4645)
ANVIL CRAFT CORP
1005 Aspen St (18042-7344)
PHONE....................................610 250-9600
Joseph Sklodowsky, *President*
Paul T Sklodowsky, *Treasurer*
Donna Drake, *Director*
Robert M Sklodowsky, *Admin Sec*
EMP: 25
SQ FT: 125,000
SALES (est): 7.1MM **Privately Held**
SIC: 3441 Fabricated structural metal

(G-4646)
APPLIED EQUIPMENT CO
8 Devon Dr (18045-2502)
PHONE....................................610 258-7941
Charles Roseberry, *President*
Frances Roseberry, *Vice Pres*
EMP: 6
SQ FT: 6,500
SALES: 1.5MM **Privately Held**
SIC: 5084 3563 3821 3443 Compressors, except air conditioning; air & gas
compressors including vacuum pumps;
vacuum pumps, laboratory; heat exchangers, condensers & components

(G-4647)
BAKERLY BARN LLC
4300 Braden Blvd E (18040-6556)
PHONE....................................610 829-1500
Brian Regnier, *CFO*
EMP: 30
SQ FT: 8,000
SALES (est): 222.7K **Privately Held**
SIC: 2051 Bread, cake & related products

(G-4648)
**BALDWIN TECHNOLOGY
COMPANY INC**
2 Danforth Dr (18045-7820)
PHONE....................................610 829-4240
EMP: 4 **Privately Held**
SIC: 3555 Printing trades machinery
HQ: Baldwin Technology Company, Inc.
8040 Forsyth Blvd
Saint Louis MO 63105
314 726-2152

(G-4649)
BANGTEES LLC
217 E Madison St (18042-6228)
PHONE....................................484 767-2382
EMP: 3
SALES (est): 133.9K **Privately Held**
SIC: 2759 Screen printing

(G-4650)
BARDOT PLASTICS INC (PA)
10 Mcfadden Rd (18045-7817)
P.O. Box 3369 (18043-3369)
PHONE....................................610 252-5900
Joseph Lee Boucher, *President*
Dorothy L Boucher, *Corp Secy*
James Boucher, *Vice Pres*
Richard L Boucher, *Vice Pres*
Clyde Burd, *Plant Mgr*
▲ EMP: 104
SQ FT: 80,000
SALES (est): 19.6MM **Privately Held**
WEB: www.bardotplastics.com
SIC: 3089 Injection molding of plastics

(G-4651)
BEE OFFSET PRINTING
1130 Church St (18042-3202)
PHONE....................................610 253-0926
Bud Mays, *President*
Mark Mays, *Vice Pres*
David Danner, *Treasurer*
EMP: 3
SQ FT: 2,000
SALES (est): 291.8K **Privately Held**
SIC: 2752 7336 Commercial printing, offset; silk screen design

(G-4652)
BEER BROTHERS
1125 Northampton St (18042-4115)
PHONE....................................610 438-3900
Peter Koorie, *Owner*
EMP: 5
SALES (est): 350.6K **Privately Held**
SIC: 2082 Beer (alcoholic beverage)

(G-4653)
BEER TO GO INC
250 Line St (18042-7239)
PHONE....................................610 253-2954
Rachel Haddad, *Principal*
EMP: 4 EST: 2008
SALES (est): 216K **Privately Held**
SIC: 2082 Beer (alcoholic beverage)

(G-4654)
**BERENFIELD CNTRS
NORTHEAST INC**
7 Mcfadden Rd (18045-7818)
P.O. Box 11, Mason OH (45040-0011)
PHONE....................................610 258-2700
Leonard H Berenfield, *President*
Anthony Boscarino, *Vice Pres*
Haron Wise, *VP Sales*
Gregory Berenfield, *Admin Sec*
EMP: 175
SQ FT: 50,000
SALES (est): 26.6MM
SALES (corp-wide): 1.1B **Privately Held**
WEB: www.berenfield.com
SIC: 3412 Metal barrels, drums & pails
HQ: Mauser Usa, Llc
35 Cotters Ln Ste C
East Brunswick NJ 08816
732 353-7100

(G-4655)
**BETHLEHEM SAUSAGE WORKS
INC**
110 Mort Dr (18040-9202)
PHONE....................................800 478-2302
Kenneth Mayer, *President*
Eric Mayer, *Vice Pres*
EMP: 4
SALES (est): 164K **Privately Held**
SIC: 2013 Sausages & other prepared
meats

(G-4656)
BIMBO BAKERIES USA INC
Also Called: Maier's Bakery
2400 Northampton St (18045-3823)
PHONE....................................610 258-7131
Fax: 610 258-1135
EMP: 315
SQ FT: 100,000
SALES (corp-wide): 13.3B **Privately Held**
SIC: 2051 5461 Mfg Bread/Related Products Retail Bakery
HQ: Bimbo Bakeries Usa, Inc
255 Business Center Dr # 200
Horsham PA 19044
215 347-5500

(G-4657)
BLESSED DOUGH LLC
Also Called: Atm's
3722 Nazareth Rd (18045-8340)
P.O. Box 6032, Lancaster (17607-6032)
PHONE....................................717 368-4109
Judith Grillo, *Mng Member*
EMP: 10 EST: 2011
SALES (est): 1.2MM **Privately Held**
SIC: 3578 Automatic teller machines (ATM)

(G-4658)
BROWN JR MERRITT (PA)
Also Called: Mi-Llon Sales Associates
2906 William Penn Hwy # 308
(18045-5256)
PHONE....................................610 253-0425
Merritt Brown Jr, *Owner*
EMP: 5
SQ FT: 8,000
SALES (est): 527.4K **Privately Held**
SIC: 2653 2631 Boxes, corrugated: made
from purchased materials; container,
packaging & boxboard

(G-4659)
CAFFREY MICHAEL & SONS
Also Called: Caffrey's
820 Newlins Rd E (18040-7247)
PHONE....................................610 252-1299
Michael Caffrey, *Owner*
EMP: 4
SALES (est): 425K **Privately Held**
SIC: 2759 2395 Screen printing; embroidery & art needlework

(G-4660)
**CALIFORNIA MED INNOVATIONS
LLC**
Also Called: CMC Products
55 Hilton St (18042-7335)
PHONE....................................909 621-5871
Yousuf Nathie, *CEO*
▲ EMP: 24
SQ FT: 23,000
SALES (est): 6.2MM **Privately Held**
WEB: www.cal-med-innovations.com
SIC: 3069 Type, rubber

(G-4661)
CHOCODIEM
325 Northampton St (18042-3541)
PHONE....................................908 200-7044
Eveline Hepp, *Owner*
EMP: 5
SALES (est): 432.5K **Privately Held**
SIC: 2066 Chocolate & cocoa products

(G-4662)
**CONSTAFLOW PUMP COMPANY
LLC**
626 Wirebach St (18042-6447)
PHONE....................................610 515-1753
Daniel Faust Jr, *Mng Member*
EMP: 3
SALES (est): 276.4K **Privately Held**
SIC: 2893 Printing ink

(G-4663)
CRAYOLA LLC (DH)
Also Called: Crayola Experience, The
1100 Church Ln (18040-5999)
P.O. Box 431 (18044-0431)
PHONE....................................610 253-6272
Smith Holland, *President*
Rick Stringer, *General Mgr*
Paul Zadorsky, *General Mgr*
Andrew Hamilton, *Business Mgr*
Chuck Linden, *Exec VP*
◆ EMP: 740
SQ FT: 48,000
SALES (est): 590.4MM
SALES (corp-wide): 3.3B **Privately Held**
WEB: www.crayola.com
SIC: 3952 Crayons: chalk, gypsum, charcoal, fusains, pastel, wax, etc.

(G-4664)
CRAYOLA LLC
Also Called: Creative Services Dept
2035 Edgewood Ave (18045-2213)
P.O. Box 431 (18044-0431)
PHONE....................................610 253-6272
Linda Farina, *Buyer*
EMP: 15
SALES (corp-wide): 3.3B **Privately Held**
SIC: 3952 Lead pencils & art goods
HQ: Crayola Llc
1100 Church Ln
Easton PA 18040
610 253-6272

(G-4665)
CRAYOLA LLC
Also Called: Crayola Factory Discovery Ctr
30 Centre Sq Ste 2 (18042-7743)
PHONE....................................610 515-8000
Nedzad Vatrenjak, *Bd of Directors*
EMP: 363
SALES (corp-wide): 3.3B **Privately Held**
SIC: 3952 Lead pencils & art goods
HQ: Crayola Llc
1100 Church Ln
Easton PA 18040
610 253-6272

(G-4666)
**CURTO TOY MANUFACTURING
CO**
425 S 15th St (18042-4658)
PHONE....................................610 438-5241
Guiseppe Curto, *President*
Francesco Curto, *Vice Pres*
▲ EMP: 12
SQ FT: 150,000
SALES (est): 1.8MM **Privately Held**
WEB: www.curtotoy.com
SIC: 3942 Stuffed toys, including animals

(G-4667)
**CUSTOM SCIENTIFIC
INSTRUMENTS**
1125 Conroy Pl (18040-6656)
PHONE....................................610 923-6500
Paul Sud, *President*
EMP: 8
SQ FT: 7,000
SALES (est): 1.3MM **Privately Held**
WEB: www.csi-instruments.com
SIC: 3829 Physical property testing equipment

(G-4668)
DELAWARE ELECTRIC INC
2149 Bushkill Park Dr # 2 (18040-2200)
PHONE....................................610 252-7803
Timothy Christopher, *President*
EMP: 4
SQ FT: 3,000
SALES: 800K **Privately Held**
SIC: 7694 5063 Electric motor repair; motors, electric

(G-4669)
**DEVCOM MANUFACTURING
LLC (PA)**
1434 Knox Ave Ste 104 (18040-8365)
PHONE....................................484 462-4907
Scott Ford, *Vice Pres*
EMP: 4
SALES (est): 228.3K **Privately Held**
SIC: 3069 Roofing, membrane rubber

(G-4670)
DISCOVERY DIRECT INC
Also Called: Bioflect Medical Group
335 Wedgewood Dr (18045-5750)
PHONE....................................610 252-3809
Janette Chakeres, *President*
Bill Johnson, *General Mgr*
EMP: 3
SALES (est): 232.4K **Privately Held**
SIC: 3161 5136 5137 Clothing & apparel
carrying cases; hosiery, men's & boys';
hosiery: women's, children's & infants'

(G-4671)
EASTON PHOTOWORKS INC
Also Called: Real Estate Marketing Services
429 Centre St (18042-6410)
PHONE....................................610 559-1998
Stephen Grotenhuis, *President*
Mary Jane Dimperio, *Vice Pres*
▲ EMP: 7
SQ FT: 2,200
SALES (est): 1.2MM **Privately Held**
WEB: www.eastonchang.com
SIC: 2759 Promotional printing; advertising
literature; printing

(G-4672)
**EASTON PLTG & MET FINSHG
INC**
925 Conroy Pl (18040-6646)
PHONE....................................610 252-9007
Walter Luczyszyn, *Ch of Bd*
John Luczyszyn, *President*

▲ = Import ▼=Export
◆ =Import/Export

EMP: 25
SQ FT: 24,000
SALES (est): 2.9MM Privately Held
SIC: 3471 Electroplating of metals or formed products

(G-4673)
EASTON PUBLISHING COMPANY
30 N 4th St (18042-3528)
PHONE..................................610 258-7171
Edward S Bennett, Owner
David Yanoshik, Vice Pres
EMP: 3 EST: 2012
SALES (est): 252.1K Privately Held
SIC: 2721 Periodicals: publishing only

(G-4674)
EASTON SALSA COMPANY LLC
50 N 18th St (18042-3112)
PHONE..................................610 923-3692
Arthur Skrzenski, Principal
EMP: 3
SALES (est): 164.5K Privately Held
SIC: 2099 Dips, except cheese & sour cream based

(G-4675)
EASTON UPHOLSTERY FURN MFG CO
Also Called: Easton Furn & Upholstery
512 Northampton St # 514 (18042-3517)
PHONE..................................610 252-3169
Edward C Adams, Owner
EMP: 6
SQ FT: 4,000
SALES (est): 357.4K Privately Held
SIC: 7641 2512 5712 Reupholstery; upholstered household furniture; furniture stores

(G-4676)
ECOPAX LLC
3600 Glover Rd (18040-9203)
PHONE..................................484 546-0700
Tom Hessen, Plant Mgr
Chihming Wong,
▲ EMP: 52
SALES (est): 25.7MM Privately Held
SIC: 2656 Sanitary food containers

(G-4677)
EISENHARDT MILLS INC
1510 Richmond Rd (18040-8430)
PHONE..................................610 253-2791
Amanda Zimmerman, President
Donald Lockard, President
James Zdepski, Prdtn Mgr
EMP: 20 EST: 1937
SQ FT: 25,000
SALES: 3MM Privately Held
WEB: www.eisenhardtmills.com
SIC: 2431 Millwork

(G-4678)
ELECTROCELL SYSTEMS INC
Also Called: Electrochem Water Systems
3320 Nazareth Rd (18045-2018)
PHONE..................................610 438-2969
Paul Q McLaine, President
Bill Hannon, Vice Pres
EMP: 5
SALES: 2MM Privately Held
SIC: 3589 Water treatment equipment, industrial

(G-4679)
ELK GROUP INTERNATIONAL LLC
Also Called: Elk Lighting
100 N 3rd St (18042-1869)
PHONE..................................800 613-3261
John Haste, Senior VP
John Sena, Vice Pres
▲ EMP: 7 EST: 2014
SALES (est): 582.7K Privately Held
SIC: 3645 3646 Residential lighting fixtures; commercial indusl & institutional electric lighting fixtures

(G-4680)
ENVIRONMENTAL CHEM & LUBR CO
121 Blenheim Dr (18045-5719)
P.O. Box 3967 (18043-3967)
PHONE..................................610 923-6492
Richard Baker, President
EMP: 4
SALES: 500K Privately Held
WEB: www.envirocl.com
SIC: 2842 Degreasing solvent

(G-4681)
EUCLID CHEMICAL COMPANY
3 Adamson St (18042-6184)
PHONE..................................610 438-2409
Dennis Haldaman, Manager
EMP: 5
SALES (corp-wide): 5.3B Publicly Held
WEB: www.epoxychemicals.com
SIC: 2899 Chemical supplies for foundries; concrete curing & hardening compounds
HQ: The Euclid Chemical Company
19218 Redwood Rd
Cleveland OH 44110
800 321-7628

(G-4682)
EUCLID TECHNOLOGIES INC
450 Milano Dr (18040-7921)
PHONE..................................610 515-1842
Scott Kraft, President
EMP: 3
SALES (est): 133.5K Privately Held
SIC: 2022 Mfg Cheese

(G-4683)
FLUORTEK INC
12 Mcfadden Rd (18045-7817)
PHONE..................................610 438-1800
John P Botti, Ch of Bd
George Antoci, President
John Hilburn, CFO
Diane Erman, Human Res Mgr
EMP: 70
SQ FT: 50,000
SALES (est): 16.3MM Privately Held
WEB: www.fluortek.com
SIC: 3089 3841 3083 Injection molded finished plastic products; surgical & medical instruments; laminated plastics plate & sheet

(G-4684)
FOLLETT LLC (HQ)
Also Called: Follett Corporation
801 Church Ln (18040-6637)
P.O. Box 8500, Philadelphia (19178-8500)
PHONE..................................610 252-7301
Steven R Follett, Ch of Bd
Margaret Neuner, President
Edward Barr, General Mgr
Robert A Bryson Jr, Exec VP
Robert Bryson, Exec VP
◆ EMP: 277
SQ FT: 127,200
SALES (est): 84.4MM
SALES (corp-wide): 2.7B Publicly Held
WEB: www.follettice.com
SIC: 3585 Ice boxes, industrial; ice making machinery; soda fountain & beverage dispensing equipment & parts
PA: The Middleby Corporation
1400 Toastmaster Dr
Elgin IL 60120
847 741-3300

(G-4685)
FRANK CASILIO AND SONS INC
1395 S 25th St (18042)
PHONE..................................610 253-3558
EMP: 5
SALES (corp-wide): 7.5MM Privately Held
SIC: 3273 5169 Mfg Ready-Mixed Concrete Whol Chemicals/Products
PA: Frank Casilio And Sons, Incorporated
1035 Mauch Chunk Rd
Bethlehem PA 18018
610 867-5886

(G-4686)
FRANKLIN HILL VINEYARDS INC
Also Called: Grape Spot
3625 Nazareth Rd (18045-8335)
PHONE..................................610 559-8966

Elaine Austen, Owner
EMP: 6
SALES (corp-wide): 1.7MM Privately Held
WEB: www.franklinhillvineyards.com
SIC: 2084 Wines
PA: Franklin Hill Vineyards Inc
7833 Franklin Hill Rd
Bangor PA 18013
610 588-8708

(G-4687)
GEMINI MACHINING COMPANY INC
610 Bangor Rd (18040-6509)
PHONE..................................610 746-5000
Peter Eibeck, President
Margaret Eibeck, Admin Sec
EMP: 11
SQ FT: 6,000
SALES (est): 1.7MM Privately Held
SIC: 3599 Machine shop, jobbing & repair

(G-4688)
GEORG FISCHER HARVEL LLC (HQ)
Also Called: GF Harvel
300 Kuebler Rd (18040-9290)
PHONE..................................610 252-7355
Earl E Wismer, President
Patrick M Foose, COO
Evan Wismer, Senior VP
John Mattavi, Vice Pres
Virginia Happel, Treasurer
▲ EMP: 148
SQ FT: 250,000
SALES (est): 75.1MM
SALES (corp-wide): 4.6B Privately Held
WEB: www.harvel.com
SIC: 3084 Plastics pipe
PA: Georg Fischer Ag
Amsler-Laffon-Strasse 9
Schaffhausen SH
526 311-111

(G-4689)
GEORG FISCHER HARVEL LLC
Also Called: George Fischer Harvel
300 Kuebler Rd (18040-9290)
PHONE..................................610 252-7355
Gary Cheatwood, Manager
EMP: 24
SALES (corp-wide): 4.6B Privately Held
WEB: www.harvel.com
SIC: 3084 Plastics pipe
HQ: Georg Fischer Harvel Llc
300 Kuebler Rd
Easton PA 18040
610 252-7355

(G-4690)
GEORGIA-PACIFIC LLC
605 Kuebler Rd (18040-9281)
PHONE..................................610 250-1400
David Carmichael, Engineer
Walter Krajci, Engineer
Andrew Warren, Project Engr
Tom Fowler, Manager
Andrew Borger, Manager
EMP: 400
SALES (corp-wide): 42.4B Privately Held
WEB: www.gp.com
SIC: 2653 2656 2631 3089 Boxes, corrugated: made from purchased materials; sanitary food containers; paper cups, plates, dishes & utensils; paperboard mills; cups, plastic, except foam
HQ: Georgia-Pacific Llc
133 Peachtree St Nw
Atlanta GA 30303
404 652-4000

(G-4691)
GEORGIA-PACIFIC LLC
2410 Northampton St (18042-3822)
PHONE..................................610 250-7402
Michele Egry, Branch Mgr
EMP: 50
SALES (corp-wide): 42.4B Privately Held
SIC: 2621 Paper mills
HQ: Georgia-Pacific Llc
133 Peachtree St Nw
Atlanta GA 30303
404 652-4000

(G-4692)
GOTHIC INC
Also Called: Condoms Galore
370 Larry Holmes Dr (18042-4509)
PHONE..................................610 923-9180
Chuck Meek, Manager
EMP: 5 Privately Held
SIC: 3069 Birth control devices, rubber
PA: Gothic Inc
1980 Catasauqua Rd
Allentown PA

(G-4693)
H&K GROUP INC
Also Called: A.B.E. Materials
5137 Lower Mud Run Rd (18040-6430)
PHONE..................................610 250-7700
John Hanes, President
Jack Mack, Division Mgr
EMP: 19
SALES (corp-wide): 71.6MM Privately Held
WEB: www.hkgroup.com
SIC: 1422 Crushed & broken limestone
PA: H&K Group, Inc.
2052 Lucon Rd
Skippack PA 19474
610 584-8500

(G-4694)
H&K GROUP INC
Also Called: Easton Block & Supply
5135 Lower Mud Run Rd (18040-6448)
PHONE..................................610 250-7703
Larry Lennon, Purchasing
Thomas Krehel, Personnel Exec
EMP: 29
SALES (corp-wide): 71.6MM Privately Held
WEB: www.hkgroup.com
SIC: 3271 3272 Blocks, concrete or cinder: standard; concrete products
PA: H&K Group, Inc.
2052 Lucon Rd
Skippack PA 19474
610 584-8500

(G-4695)
HARMONY PRESS INC (PA)
717 W Berwick St (18042-6301)
PHONE..................................610 559-9800
Stephen Grotenhuis, President
Bob Schneebeli, Purchasing
Fred Grotenhuis, Treasurer
Josephine Thompson, Manager
EMP: 35 EST: 1953
SALES (est): 4.3MM Privately Held
WEB: www.harmonypress.com
SIC: 2752 2791 2789 Commercial printing, offset; typesetting; bookbinding & related work

(G-4696)
HARVEL PLASTICS INC
300 Kuebler Rd (18040-9290)
PHONE..................................610 252-7355
Gregory Purtle, Principal
EMP: 7 EST: 2013
SALES (est): 541.1K Privately Held
SIC: 3084 Plastics pipe

(G-4697)
HAYES ENTERPRISES INC (PA)
Also Called: Gymboree Play & Music
306 S Watson St (18045-3729)
PHONE..................................610 252-2530
Michael Hayes, President
Virginia Hayes, Vice Pres
EMP: 3
SALES: 1.2MM Privately Held
SIC: 3599 Amusement park equipment

(G-4698)
HESS WOOD RECYCLING INC
2357 Newlins Mill Rd (18045-7816)
PHONE..................................610 614-9070
Shannon Hess, President
Jerry Hess, Vice Pres
Jeremy Hess, Opers Mgr
Sonya Hess, Treasurer
Michelle Hess, Admin Sec
EMP: 17
SQ FT: 8,500
SALES (est): 1.1MM Privately Held
SIC: 2448 Pallets, wood

(G-4699)
HINDLE POWER INC
1075 Saint John St (18042-6661)
PHONE....................................610 330-9000
William A Hindle, *President*
John Hindle, *Vice Pres*
Ron Larrimore, *Production*
Jonathan Gaul, *Engineer*
Kyle Huggins, *Marketing Mgr*
EMP: 73
SQ FT: 40,000
SALES (est): 20.9MM **Privately Held**
WEB: www.hindlepowerinc.com
SIC: 3612 Transformers, except electric

(G-4700)
HONEY SANDTS CO
Also Called: Sandt's Honey
714 Wagener Ln (18040-8253)
PHONE....................................610 252-6511
John Torrillo, *President*
EMP: 4
SQ FT: 2,500
SALES (est): 1MM **Privately Held**
SIC: 2099 Honey, strained & bottled

(G-4701)
HORIZON LAMPS INC
Also Called: Primarc Uv Technology
2 Danforth Dr (18045-7820)
PHONE....................................610 829-4220
Jeffery Bade, *Manager*
EMP: 14
SALES (corp-wide): 2.2B **Publicly Held**
SIC: 3645 Lamp & light shades
HQ: Horizon Lamps, Inc
28601 Clemens Rd
Cleveland OH

(G-4702)
HUNTER ENGINEERING
COMPANY
2745 Knollwood Way (18040-8722)
PHONE....................................610 330-9024
EMP: 62
SALES (corp-wide): 400MM **Privately Held**
WEB: www.huntersupport.com
SIC: 3559 Sewing machines & hat & zipper making machinery
PA: Hunter Engineering Company Inc
11250 Hunter Dr
Bridgeton MO 63044
314 731-3020

(G-4703)
HV2 ENTERPRISES INC
842 Line St (18042-7354)
PHONE....................................610 330-9300
Les Gallipeau, *President*
EMP: 10
SALES: 1MM **Privately Held**
WEB: www.hv2enterprises.com
SIC: 3999 Custom pulverizing & grinding of plastic materials

(G-4704)
IMAGEWEAR LTD
2 Maplecroft Ave (18045-2461)
PHONE....................................704 999-9979
James E Allshouse, *President*
Matthew J Allshouse, *Vice Pres*
Rose Allshouse, *Admin Sec*
EMP: 3
SQ FT: 800
SALES: 300K **Privately Held**
SIC: 2395 Embroidery products, except schiffli machine

(G-4705)
INDUSTRIAL SERVICE CO LTD
720 Sheridan Dr (18045-5087)
P.O. Box 3547 (18043-3547)
PHONE....................................484 373-0410
Karen Ruby, *President*
Patrick Ruby, *Vice Pres*
EMP: 15
SQ FT: 30,000
SALES (est): 3.8MM **Privately Held**
SIC: 3561 Industrial pumps & parts

(G-4706)
INNOVATIVE CONTROL
SYSTEMS INC
3370 Fox Hill Rd (18045-8014)
PHONE....................................610 881-8061
Cindy Penchishen, *Branch Mgr*
EMP: 20 **Privately Held**
SIC: 3589 Car washing machinery
PA: Innovative Control Systems, Inc.
1349 Jacobsburg Rd
Wind Gap PA 18091

(G-4707)
INNOVATIVE OFFICE PRODUCTS
LLC (HQ)
100 Kuebler Rd (18040-9288)
PHONE....................................610 559-6369
John Becconsall, *Vice Pres*
Jeffrey Wolber, *Vice Pres*
Mike Erney, *Prdtn Mgr*
Mary Jane Bowen, *Purch Mgr*
Peter Carrasquillo, *Engineer*
▲ EMP: 125
SQ FT: 85,000
SALES (est): 24.3MM **Privately Held**
WEB: www.lcdarms.com
SIC: 2522 Office furniture, except wood

(G-4708)
J CLEM KLINE & SON INC
2824 Freemansburg Ave (18045-7112)
PHONE....................................610 258-6071
Barnabas J Veres Jr, *President*
Barney Veres, *President*
EMP: 3
SQ FT: 4,000
SALES: 225K **Privately Held**
SIC: 3543 3364 3363 Industrial patterns; brass & bronze die-castings; aluminum die-castings

(G-4709)
JONATHAN FALLOS
CABINETMAKER
1158 Stones Crossing Rd (18045-5542)
PHONE....................................610 253-4063
Jonathan Fallos, *President*
EMP: 7
SQ FT: 2,800
SALES (est): 1.1MM **Privately Held**
SIC: 2431 Millwork

(G-4710)
KADCO CERAMICS LLC
1175 Conroy Pl (18040-6656)
PHONE....................................610 252-5424
Kenneth W Sherwood,
Dennis Tretter,
EMP: 13
SQ FT: 8,000
SALES: 2MM **Privately Held**
SIC: 3264 Porcelain electrical supplies

(G-4711)
KEYSTONE FOOD PRODUCTS
INC
3767 Hecktown Rd (18045-2350)
P.O. Box 326 (18044-0326)
PHONE....................................610 258-2706
William Corriere Jr, *CEO*
William Corriere Sr, *Ch of Bd*
William Corriere, *President*
Ford Corriere, *Vice Pres*
Donald A Pysher, *Maint Spvr*
▲ EMP: 150 EST: 1946
SQ FT: 131,000
SALES (est): 41.9MM **Privately Held**
WEB: www.keystonesnacks.com
SIC: 2096 Pork rinds

(G-4712)
KORTE & CO INC
364 E Berwick St (18042-6701)
P.O. Box 1086 (18044-1086)
PHONE....................................610 253-9141
Ernest Bossert, *President*
Catherine Vogel, *Vice Pres*
Thomas W Vogel, *Treasurer*
Debra Bossert, *Admin Sec*
EMP: 15 EST: 1935
SQ FT: 2,400
SALES (est): 7MM **Privately Held**
SIC: 5147 2011 Meats, fresh; meat packing plants

(G-4713)
LEES MISTER NOODLE BAR
325 Northampton St (18042-3541)
PHONE....................................610 829-2799
EMP: 3
SALES (est): 100.5K **Privately Held**
SIC: 2098 Noodles (e.g. egg, plain & water), dry

(G-4714)
LEN SABATINE AUTOMOTIVE
5238 S Delaware Dr (18040-6334)
PHONE....................................610 258-8020
Leonard R Sabatine, *Owner*
Vanessa Sabatine, *Co-Owner*
EMP: 3
SQ FT: 10,000
SALES (est): 170K **Privately Held**
SIC: 3599 5531 5013 Machine shop, jobbing & repair; automotive parts; automotive supplies & parts

(G-4715)
LONGEVITY BRANDS LLC
610 Uhler Rd (18040-7001)
PHONE....................................484 373-3600
Mark Waldman, *CEO*
Frederick Damato, *Controller*
EMP: 30
SQ FT: 200,000
SALES (est): 1.9MM **Privately Held**
SIC: 2339 Bathing suits: women's, misses' & juniors'

(G-4716)
MAGNETIC WINDINGS
COMPANY INC
2711 Freemansburg Ave (18045-6099)
PHONE....................................610 253-2751
Albert J Marron, *CEO*
Coleen Gordon, *President*
EMP: 35
SQ FT: 84,000
SALES (est): 3.2MM **Privately Held**
WEB: www.magwindings.com
SIC: 3612 Power transformers, electric

(G-4717)
MAINSTREAM SWIMSUITS INC
Vera Bradley Swimwear
610 Uhler Rd (18040-7001)
PHONE....................................484 373-3600
EMP: 5
SALES (corp-wide): 33.6MM **Privately Held**
SIC: 2339 Bathing suits: women's, misses' & juniors'
PA: Mainstream Swimsuits, Inc.
610 Uhler Rd
Easton PA 18040
484 373-3600

(G-4718)
MAJESTIC ATHLETIC INTL LTD
Also Called: Vf Imagewer Majestic
2320 Newlins Mill Rd (18045-7815)
PHONE....................................610 746-7494
Faust E Capobianco III, *Ch of Bd*
◆ EMP: 1
SALES (est): 13.6MM
SALES (corp-wide): 11.8B **Publicly Held**
WEB: www.majesticathletic.com
SIC: 2339 2329 Athletic clothing: women's, misses' & juniors'; uniforms, athletic: women's, misses' & juniors'; men's & boys' sportswear & athletic clothing; men's & boys' athletic uniforms
HQ: Maroco Ltd.
2320 Newlins Mill Rd
Easton PA 18045
610 746-6800

(G-4719)
MAROCO LTD (DH)
Also Called: Majestic Athletic
2320 Newlins Mill Rd (18045-7815)
PHONE....................................610 746-6800
Faust E Capobianco III, *CEO*
Jeff Green, *COO*
▲ EMP: 500
SQ FT: 134,000

SALES (est): 93.1MM
SALES (corp-wide): 11.8B **Publicly Held**
SIC: 2329 2339 2261 5611 Men's & boys' sportswear & athletic clothing; athletic (warmup, sweat & jogging) suits: men's & boys'; athletic clothing: women's, misses' & juniors'; finishing plants, cotton; clothing, sportswear, men's & boys'; ready-to-wear apparel, women's; uniforms & work clothing; sports apparel
HQ: Vf Imagewear, Inc.
545 Marriott Dr Ste 200
Nashville TN 37214
615 565-5000

(G-4720)
MAUSER USA LLC
7 Mcfadden Rd (18045-7818)
P.O. Box 350, Mason OH (45040-0350)
PHONE....................................610 258-2700
Rob Tiburzi, *Manager*
EMP: 30
SALES (corp-wide): 1.1B **Privately Held**
WEB: www.berenfield.com
SIC: 2655 Drums, fiber: made from purchased material
HQ: Mauser Usa, Llc
35 Cotters Ln Ste C
East Brunswick NJ 08816
732 353-7100

(G-4721)
MERKIN BODY AND HOIST
COMPANY
1539 Church St (18042-3121)
PHONE....................................610 258-6179
Marion Shirley, *Principal*
EMP: 4 EST: 2016
SALES (est): 84.6K **Privately Held**
SIC: 7373 3639 Computer integrated systems design; household appliances

(G-4722)
MILNER ENTERPRISES INC
Also Called: Surf Chemical
115 Kuebler Rd (18040-9289)
PHONE....................................610 252-0700
George Milner, *President*
Marlene Milner, *Corp Secy*
EMP: 11
SQ FT: 15,000
SALES (est): 1.1MM **Privately Held**
SIC: 3083 3356 Laminated plastics plate & sheet; nonferrous rolling & drawing

(G-4723)
MINTEQ INTERNATIONAL INC
Also Called: Pyrogenics Group
640 N 13th St (18042-1431)
PHONE....................................610 250-3000
William P Hudson Jr, *Branch Mgr*
EMP: 20 **Publicly Held**
WEB: www.minteq.com
SIC: 3297 Nonclay refractories
HQ: Minteq International Inc.
35 Highland Ave
Bethlehem PA 18017

(G-4724)
MINUTEMAN PRESS INC
2473 Hay St (18042-5353)
PHONE....................................610 923-9266
David Pike, *President*
EMP: 4 EST: 1996
SQ FT: 1,200
SALES (est): 422.8K **Privately Held**
SIC: 2752 Commercial printing, lithographic

(G-4725)
MOBILE WELDING & BOILER
REPAIR
500 Industrial Dr (18042-7334)
PHONE....................................610 253-9688
John Taylor, *President*
Nancy Frizzell, *Admin Sec*
EMP: 15
SQ FT: 500
SALES (est): 1.5MM **Privately Held**
SIC: 7699 7692 Boiler repair shop; welding repair

▲ = Import ▼=Export
◆ =Import/Export

(G-4726)
MODERN PRECAST CONCRETE INC
3900 Glover Rd (18040-7046)
PHONE..................................484 548-6200
Phil Weber, *Manager*
EMP: 28
SALES (corp-wide): 29.7B **Privately Held**
WEB: www.modcon.com
SIC: 3272 3448 3443 2452 Septic tanks; concrete; manhole covers or frames, concrete; steps, prefabricated concrete; prefabricated metal buildings; fabricated plate work (boiler shop); prefabricated wood buildings
HQ: Vcw Enterprises, Inc.
210 Durham Rd
Ottsville PA 18942
610 847-5112

(G-4727)
MOLDED ACSTCAL PDTS EASTON INC
500 Industrial Dr (18042-7334)
PHONE..................................610 250-6738
EMP: 10
SALES (corp-wide): 98.6MM **Privately Held**
SIC: 3296 Mfg Mineral Wool
PA: Molded Acoustical Products Of Easton, Inc.
3 Danforth Dr
Easton PA 18045
610 253-7135

(G-4728)
N A PETROLEUM CORP
2911 Old Nazareth Rd (18045-2445)
PHONE..................................610 438-5463
EMP: 3 EST: 2012
SALES (est): 164.3K **Privately Held**
SIC: 1311 Crude petroleum & natural gas

(G-4729)
NABI GENMED LLC
12 Starlite Dr (18045)
PHONE..................................610 258-5627
James Shen,
EMP: 4
SALES (est): 298.5K **Privately Held**
WEB: www.nabigenmed.com
SIC: 2833 Medicinals & botanicals

(G-4730)
NANOMAGNETICS INSTRS USA LLC
15 S Bank St Loft 6 (18042)
PHONE..................................610 417-3857
EMP: 3
SALES (est): 256.9K **Privately Held**
SIC: 3826 Magnetic resonance imaging apparatus

(G-4731)
NATIONAL PLAS ACQUISITION LLC
11 Mcfadden Rd (18045-7819)
PHONE..................................610 250-7800
Gabe Scudese, *President*
EMP: 5
SALES (est): 456.6K **Privately Held**
SIC: 2821 Plastics materials & resins

(G-4732)
NOEL INTERACTIVE GROUP LLC
1789 Rhine Dr (18045-5425)
PHONE..................................732 991-1484
Gwenn Noel, *President*
Roger Noel,
EMP: 5
SALES: 400K **Privately Held**
SIC: 2741 8742 7374 7812 Miscellaneous publishing; management consulting services; computer graphics service; motion picture & video production; commercial art & graphic design; advertising agencies

(G-4733)
NORDSON CORPORATION
2 Danforth Frive (18045)
PHONE..................................610 829-4240
Donna Daros, *Manager*
EMP: 432

SALES (corp-wide): 2.2B **Publicly Held**
SIC: 3563 Spraying outfits: metals, paints & chemicals (compressor)
PA: Nordson Corporation
28601 Clemens Rd
Westlake OH 44145
440 892-1580

(G-4734)
ODHNER AND ODHNER FINE WDWKG
3405 William N Hwy (18042)
PHONE..................................610 258-9300
Dirk Odhner, *President*
EMP: 6
SQ FT: 2,400
SALES: 650K **Privately Held**
SIC: 2541 2521 Cabinets, except refrigerated: show, display, etc.: wood; wood office furniture

(G-4735)
OLDCASTLE PRECAST INC
3900 Glover Rd (18040-7046)
PHONE..................................484 548-6200
Eric Bocich, *Project Mgr*
Mike Grapsy, *Branch Mgr*
EMP: 51
SALES (corp-wide): 29.7B **Privately Held**
SIC: 3272 3446 Concrete products, precast; pipe, concrete or lined with concrete; open flooring & grating for construction
HQ: Oldcastle Infrastructure, Inc.
1002 15th St Sw Ste 110
Auburn WA 98001
253 833-2777

(G-4736)
ORBEL CORPORATION
2 Danforth Dr (18045-7820)
PHONE..................................610 829-5000
Kenneth Marino, *President*
Jon Raseley, *General Mgr*
Michael A Palumbo, *Vice Pres*
Yvette Riebel, *Sales Staff*
Ryan Swanton, *Sales Staff*
▲ EMP: 50 EST: 1960
SQ FT: 57,000
SALES (est): 11.1MM **Privately Held**
WEB: www.orbel.com
SIC: 3469 3471 3398 Perforated metal, stamped; plating & polishing; metal heat treating

(G-4737)
PALERMO METAL PRODUCTS INC
3760 Nicholas St (18045-5116)
P.O. Box 3310, Palmer (18043-3310)
PHONE..................................610 253-6230
Liborio Leo Palermo, *President*
Ellen Palermo, *Vice Pres*
Michael Palermo, *Vice Pres*
EMP: 21
SQ FT: 30,000
SALES (est): 3.8MM **Privately Held**
WEB: www.palermometal.com
SIC: 3444 Sheet metalwork

(G-4738)
PALLET EXPRESS INC
2906 William Penn Hwy # 503
(18045-5282)
PHONE..................................610 258-8846
William Hildenbrand, *President*
Karen Hildenbrand, *Corp Secy*
Robert Hildenbrand, *VP Opers*
EMP: 95
SQ FT: 80,000
SALES: 15MM **Privately Held**
WEB: www.palletexpress.net
SIC: 2448 Pallets, wood

(G-4739)
PALMER PLASTICS INC
2906 William Penn Hwy # 505
(18045-5282)
PHONE..................................610 330-9900
Jim Brehove, *President*
EMP: 12
SALES (est): 2.5MM **Privately Held**
SIC: 3089 Extruded finished plastic products

(G-4740)
PARAGON TECHNOLOGIES INC (PA)
101 Larry Holmes Dr # 500 (18042-7727)
PHONE..................................610 252-7321
Hesham M Gad, *CEO*
John C Molloy, *President*
Victor Egberts, *Vice Pres*
Randy Randolph, *Vice Pres*
Marta Marques, *Purch Mgr*
EMP: 24 EST: 1958
SQ FT: 25,000
SALES: 11.5MM **Publicly Held**
WEB: www.ptgamex.com
SIC: 3535 Unit handling conveying systems

(G-4741)
PEERLESS PRINTERY
1211 Butler St (18042-4711)
PHONE..................................610 258-5226
Layne Gehris,
EMP: 3
SQ FT: 1,000
SALES (est): 180K
SALES (corp-wide): 300K **Privately Held**
WEB: www.peerlessprintery.com
SIC: 5136 5137 2396 Shirts, men's & boys'; women's & children's clothing; automotive & apparel trimmings
PA: S.Y.N. Apparel, Llc
18 W 3rd St
Bethlehem PA 18015
484 821-3664

(G-4742)
PENN JERSEY ADVANCE INC (PA)
Also Called: Express-Times
18 Centre Sq (18042-7746)
PHONE..................................610 258-7171
Martin Till, *President*
David Yanoshik, *Sales Staff*
EMP: 275
SQ FT: 60,000
SALES (est): 67.1MM **Privately Held**
SIC: 2711 2759 Newspapers; commercial printing

(G-4743)
POLYTEK DEVELOPMENT CORP (PA)
55 Hilton St (18042-7335)
PHONE..................................610 559-8620
Jonathan Kane, *CEO*
Bill Scheetz, *Technical Staff*
Jill Spohn, *Technical Staff*
▼ EMP: 26
SALES (est): 7.3MM **Privately Held**
SIC: 2822 2821 3087 2891 Synthetic rubber; plastics materials & resins; custom compound purchased resins; adhesives & sealants

(G-4744)
PRECISION FABG GROUP LLC
1 Adamson St (18042-6184)
PHONE..................................610 438-3156
Timothy Robertson, *Mng Member*
Paul Auger,
EMP: 8
SQ FT: 15,000
SALES (est): 500K **Privately Held**
SIC: 3441 Fabricated structural metal

(G-4745)
PURPLE COW CREAMERY LTD
290 Raubsville Rd (18042-8713)
PHONE..................................610 252-5544
Lynn Flanagan, *President*
Dean Titus, *Treasurer*
Mary Michiner, *Admin Sec*
EMP: 3
SALES (est): 214.1K **Privately Held**
SIC: 2024 Ice cream, bulk

(G-4746)
R & R PROVISION CO (PA)
Also Called: R & R Retail Outlet
1240 Pine St (18042)
P.O. Box 889 (18044-0889)
PHONE..................................610 258-5366
Richard W Rogers, *President*
James Everly, *Vice Pres*
Cathy Fainor, *Treasurer*

David A Tomaszewski, *Treasurer*
Richard W Rogers Jr, *Admin Sec*
EMP: 55 EST: 1966
SQ FT: 25,000
SALES (est): 22.9MM **Privately Held**
WEB: www.rrpdirect.com
SIC: 5147 5141 2011 Meats, fresh; groceries, general line; meat packing plants

(G-4747)
RANDOLPH MANUFACTURING CORP
4 Danforth Dr (18045-7820)
PHONE..................................610 253-9626
Daniel Uslar, *President*
Robin North, *Vice Pres*
EMP: 25
SQ FT: 13,000
SALES (est): 4.6MM **Privately Held**
WEB: www.randolphmfg.com
SIC: 3599 Machine shop, jobbing & repair

(G-4748)
RECYCLED OIL
1600 S 25th St (18042-6065)
PHONE..................................610 250-8747
Nick Cirrollo, *Branch Mgr*
EMP: 10
SALES (corp-wide): 112.1K **Privately Held**
WEB: www.recycleoilco.com
SIC: 2611 Pulp mills, chemical & semi-chemical processing
PA: Recycled Oil
2 Madison Ave
Larchmont NY
914 422-0064

(G-4749)
RSI SILICON PRODUCTS LLC
3700 Glover Rd (18040-9285)
PHONE..................................610 258-3100
EMP: 30
SALES (est): 4.2MM **Privately Held**
SIC: 3339 Manufacturing Of High Purity Silicon Metal

(G-4750)
SABROSA SALT COMPANY LLC
4030 Lantern Pl W (18045-6128)
PHONE..................................610 250-9002
Melissa A Quackenbush, *Principal*
EMP: 4
SALES (est): 480.5K **Privately Held**
SIC: 2899 Salt

(G-4751)
SANDT PRINTING CO INC
2333 Northwood Ave (18045-2240)
P.O. Box 680 (18044-0680)
PHONE..................................610 258-7445
Donald G Sandt Jr, *Ch of Bd*
Frederick Sandt, *Vice Pres*
EMP: 5 EST: 1928
SQ FT: 5,000
SALES: 300K **Privately Held**
SIC: 2752 2759 Commercial printing, offset; letterpress printing

(G-4752)
SKYLINE AUTO SUPPLY LLC
2571 Nazareth Rd (18045-2712)
PHONE..................................484 365-4040
Ebony Vassilatos, *President*
Gregory Vassilatos, *Manager*
EMP: 5
SALES: 1.3MM **Privately Held**
SIC: 3711 5531 Automobile assembly, including specialty automobiles; automotive accessories; automotive parts

(G-4753)
SOLE ARTISAN ALES LLC
45 N 2nd St Apt 203 (18042-7406)
PHONE..................................570 977-0053
EMP: 18
SALES (est): 3.1MM **Privately Held**
SIC: 2082 Malt beverages

(G-4754)
SPECIALTY BUILDING SYSTEMS
484 S Nulton Ave (18045-3758)
PHONE..................................610 954-0595
Donald Peterson, *President*
Shirley Peterson, *Treasurer*
EMP: 3

SQ FT: 1,200
SALES (est): 501.4K **Privately Held**
SIC: 3446 5039 Railings, bannisters, guards, etc.: made from metal pipe; wire fence, gates & accessories

(G-4755)
SPECIALTY MINERALS INC
Also Called: Minerals Technologies
640 N 13th St (18042-1431)
PHONE..................................610 250-3000
Keith Hanchett, *Manager*
EMP: 15 **Publicly Held**
WEB: www.specialtyminerals.com
SIC: 3295 Minerals, ground or treated
HQ: Specialty Minerals Inc.
622 3rd Ave Fl 38
New York NY 10017
212 878-1800

(G-4756)
SQUIBB CUSTOM MACHINE INC
4200 Kesslersville Rd (18040-6634)
PHONE..................................610 258-0923
Frank J Barna Jr, *President*
EMP: 7
SALES (est): 811.3K **Privately Held**
SIC: 3599 Machine shop, jobbing & repair

(G-4757)
SURE-LOK INC
400 S Greenwood Ave 302 (18045-3776)
PHONE..................................610 814-0300
Robert M Joseph, *President*
▲ **EMP:** 30
SALES (est): 3.4MM **Privately Held**
WEB: www.sure-lok.com
SIC: 3999 Wheelchair lifts

(G-4758)
SUSSEX WIRE INC (PA)
4 Danforth Dr (18045-7820)
PHONE..................................610 250-7750
Timothy Kardish, *President*
John Malboeuf, *Principal*
Madan Mathevan, *Principal*
Megan Pierzga, *Principal*
Marian Watkins, *Principal*
▲ **EMP:** 55
SALES (est): 14.4MM **Privately Held**
WEB: www.sussexwire.com
SIC: 2816 Metallic & mineral pigments

(G-4759)
SUTHERLAND BASKETS
410 S 16th St (18042-5459)
PHONE..................................610 438-8233
Andreas Bogi, *Owner*
EMP: 7
SALES (est): 390K **Privately Held**
SIC: 2449 5199 Baskets: fruit & vegetable, round stave, till, etc.; baskets

(G-4760)
SY-CON SYSTEMS INC
Also Called: Sy-Con Technology
1700 Northampton St Ste 6 (18042-3144)
PHONE..................................610 253-0900
Michael Assia, *President*
Edward Kline, *Vice Pres*
EMP: 5
SQ FT: 1,800
SALES (est): 531.4K **Privately Held**
WEB: www.syconsystems.com
SIC: 7372 Business oriented computer software

(G-4761)
T H E M SERVICES INC
Also Called: Tsi Competition Engines
647 Garr Rd (18040-6839)
PHONE..................................610 559-9341
Leonard Jaskewicz, *President*
Pamela Jaskewicz, *Admin Sec*
EMP: 4
SALES: 168K **Privately Held**
SIC: 3599 Machine & other job shop work

(G-4762)
TABACOS USA INC
4500 William Penn Hwy (18045-4845)
PHONE..................................610 438-2005
Kim Carpenter, *COO*
Paula Weiland, *CFO*
EMP: 3

SALES (est): 433.7K **Privately Held**
SIC: 2111 Cigarettes

(G-4763)
TORCUP INC
1025 Conroy Pl (18040-6609)
PHONE..................................610 250-5800
David Boivin, *CEO*
John Kovacs, *President*
Thomas R Porter, *Treasurer*
▲ **EMP:** 15
SQ FT: 25,000
SALES (est): 4MM **Privately Held**
WEB: www.torcup.com
SIC: 3546 5084 Power-driven handtools; industrial machinery & equipment

(G-4764)
TRIMACH LLC
1350 Sullivan Trl Ste C (18040-1185)
PHONE..................................610 252-8983
George Weaver, *Owner*
William Weaver, *Owner*
Trisha Weaver, *Office Mgr*
Mike Jiorle,
EMP: 7
SQ FT: 3,000
SALES: 600K **Privately Held**
SIC: 3599 Custom machinery

(G-4765)
UNICAST INC
17 Mcfadden Rd (18045-7819)
P.O. Box 4627 (18043-4627)
PHONE..................................610 559-9998
Peter Molinaro, *President*
Tom Molinaro, *Vice Pres*
Lester Rush, *Plant Mgr*
Ron Faust, *Purchasing*
James B Rogers, *Treasurer*
EMP: 50
SQ FT: 25,000
SALES (est): 9.4MM **Privately Held**
WEB: www.unicastinc.com
SIC: 3069 Boot or shoe products, rubber

(G-4766)
UPREACH INC
2118 Nrthmpton St Ste 100 (18042)
PHONE..................................215 536-8758
Weston Zelenz, *Principal*
EMP: 4
SALES (est): 243.9K **Privately Held**
SIC: 2834 Pharmaceutical preparations

(G-4767)
VECTOR AEROSPACE USA INC
3314 Sturbridge Ave (18045-8138)
PHONE..................................610 559-2191
EMP: 3
SALES (corp-wide): 78.7B **Privately Held**
SIC: 3724 7699 Turbines, aircraft type; aircraft & heavy equipment repair services
HQ: Vector Aerospace Usa, Inc.
1141 Catalina Dr
Livermore CA

(G-4768)
VF IMAGEWEAR INC
2320 Newlins Mill Rd (18045-7815)
PHONE..................................610 746-6800
Stephanie Hartzell, *Branch Mgr*
EMP: 7
SALES (corp-wide): 11.8B **Publicly Held**
SIC: 2321 2339 Men's & boys' sports & polo shirts; women's & misses' athletic clothing & sportswear
HQ: Vf Imagewear, Inc.
545 Marriott Dr Ste 200
Nashville TN 37214
615 565-5000

(G-4769)
VICTAULIC LLC
4901 Kesslersville Rd (18040-6714)
PHONE..................................610 559-3300
EMP: 3
SALES (est): 190.4K **Privately Held**
SIC: 3494 Valves & pipe fittings

(G-4770)
VICTAULIC COMPANY (PA)
Also Called: Victaulic Company of America
4901 Kesslersville Rd (18040-6714)
P.O. Box 31 (18044-0031)
PHONE..................................610 559-3300

John Malloy, *President*
Clark R Hale, *Exec VP*
Gary M Moore, *Exec VP*
Wayne Barefoot, *Vice Pres*
Brian P Bissey, *Vice Pres*
◆ **EMP:** 900 **EST:** 1925
SQ FT: 100,000
SALES (est): 746.3MM **Privately Held**
WEB: www.victaulic.com
SIC: 3321 3491 3494 5085 Ductile iron castings; industrial valves; couplings, except pressure & soil pipe; tools

(G-4771)
VICTAULIC HOLDING COMPANY LLC
4901 Kesslersville Rd (18040-6714)
PHONE..................................610 559-3300
Joseph Trachtenberg, *CEO*
EMP: 5
SALES (est): 552.6K **Privately Held**
SIC: 3494 Pipe fittings

(G-4772)
VICTOR-BALATA BELTING COMPANY
Also Called: Vbbc
2779 Ohio St (18045-8111)
PHONE..................................610 258-2010
Lawrence W O'Neill, *CEO*
Timothy J O'Neill, *Vice Pres*
David L O'Nell, *Treasurer*
Brian O'Neill, *Admin Sec*
▲ **EMP:** 28 **EST:** 1910
SQ FT: 40,000
SALES: 4MM **Privately Held**
SIC: 3728 3496 Aircraft arresting device system; conveyor belts

(G-4773)
W GRAPHICS DIGITAL SERVICES
18 N 4th St 20 (18042-3502)
PHONE..................................610 252-3565
Keith M Frankenfeild, *President*
Brent Brugler, *Vice Pres*
EMP: 5
SQ FT: 2,520
SALES (est): 975.5K **Privately Held**
WEB: www.waldengraphics.com
SIC: 3577 2796 Computer output to microfilm units; platemaking services

(G-4774)
WAKEEM INC
Also Called: Bell Apothecary
2045 Fairview Ave (18042-3915)
PHONE..................................610 258-2311
Maryann Isaac, *President*
Kathleen Kelley, *Corp Secy*
John Isaac, *Vice Pres*
EMP: 14
SQ FT: 1,000
SALES (est): 2.5MM **Privately Held**
SIC: 2834 5047 Druggists' preparations (pharmaceuticals); medical & hospital equipment

(G-4775)
WEYERBACHER BREWING CO
905 Line St Ste G (18042-7379)
PHONE..................................610 559-5561
Daniel Weirback, *President*
Barbara Lampe, *Vice Pres*
Barbara Lamte, *Vice Pres*
Bob Fauteux, *Natl Sales Mgr*
Andy Coulsey, *Regl Sales Mgr*
▲ **EMP:** 7
SQ FT: 7,500
SALES (est): 1.5MM **Privately Held**
WEB: www.weyerbacher.com
SIC: 2082 5813 Beer (alcoholic beverage); drinking places

(G-4776)
WILLIAM H KIES JR
Also Called: Kies, Harry M Moving
1928 Jefferson St (18042-5442)
PHONE..................................610 252-6261
William H Kies Jr, *Owner*
William Kies Jr, *Manager*
EMP: 4 **EST:** 1910

SALES (est): 419.9K **Privately Held**
SIC: 4213 4212 2392 Contract haulers; local trucking, without storage; household furnishings

(G-4777)
WILSON PDTS COMPRESSED GAS CO
3411 Northwood Ave (18045-8006)
PHONE..................................610 253-9608
Bruce Groner, *President*
Terry Halpin, *Vice Pres*
Randy Everett, *CFO*
George Grom Jr, *Treasurer*
Jeff Grieger, *Accounts Exec*
EMP: 22
SQ FT: 5,000
SALES (est): 14.3MM **Privately Held**
WEB: www.wilsonproducts.com
SIC: 5169 5085 2899 2813 Industrial gases; welding supplies; chemical preparations; industrial gases

Ebensburg
Cambria County

(G-4778)
ALFRED NICKLES BAKERY INC
131 Mini Mall Rd (15931-4101)
PHONE..................................814 471-6913
David Dick, *Manager*
EMP: 15
SALES (corp-wide): 205MM **Privately Held**
WEB: www.nicklesbakery.com
SIC: 5461 2051 Bread; bread, cake & related products
PA: Alfred Nickles Bakery, Inc.
26 Main St N
Navarre OH 44662
330 879-5635

(G-4779)
ARM CAMCO LLC
667 Industrial Park Rd (15931-4111)
PHONE..................................814 472-7980
Sam Morello, *President*
EMP: 46
SALES: 8MM
SALES (corp-wide): 17.6MM **Privately Held**
SIC: 7539 7629 3699 Electrical services; electrical equipment repair, high voltage; electrical equipment & supplies
PA: Arm Group, Inc.
1129 W Governor Rd
Hershey PA 17033
717 533-8600

(G-4780)
BABCOCK WLCOX EBNSBURG PWR INC
Also Called: Babcock & Wilcox Pwr Gen
2840 New Germany Rd (15931-3505)
PHONE..................................814 472-1140
Wilcox Babcock, *CEO*
EMP: 8
SALES (est): 902.5K
SALES (corp-wide): 1B **Publicly Held**
SIC: 3443 Fabricated plate work (boiler shop)
HQ: The Babcock & Wilcox Company
20 S Van Buren Ave
Barberton OH 44203
330 753-4511

(G-4781)
BARTOLOTTA VISION CARE LLC
3133 New Germany Rd (15931-4348)
PHONE..................................814 472-8010
Anthony Sossong, *Principal*
EMP: 3
SALES (est): 264K **Privately Held**
SIC: 3851 Eyes, glass & plastic

(G-4782)
CAMBRIA COUNTY ASSO
175 Industrial Park Rd (15931-4109)
PHONE..................................814 472-5077
Allen Smith, *President*
EMP: 125

SALES (est): 2.3MM
SALES (corp-wide): 15.6MM **Privately Held**
WEB: www.ccabh.com
SIC: 8322 8331 3496 3452 Association for the handicapped; job training & vocational rehabilitation services; miscellaneous fabricated wire products; bolts, nuts, rivets & washers
PA: Cambria County Association For The Blind And Handicapped, Inc.
211 Central Ave
Johnstown PA 15902
814 536-3531

(G-4783)
CAMBRIA PLASTICS LLC
502 E Crawford St (15931-1415)
PHONE...............................814 472-6189
Himanshu S Pandya, *Principal*
EMP: 3
SALES (est): 203.8K **Privately Held**
SIC: 2821 Plastics materials & resins

(G-4784)
DAMIN PRINTING CO LLC
122 S Locust St (15931-1662)
P.O. Box 338 (15931-0338)
PHONE...............................814 472-9530
Rene Damin, *Mng Member*
EMP: 8 EST: 1952
SQ FT: 7,200
SALES (est): 1.3MM **Privately Held**
WEB: www.daminprinting.com
SIC: 2752 Commercial printing, offset

(G-4785)
EZ-PLANT SOFTWARE INC
211 E Sample St (15931-1605)
PHONE...............................814 421-6744
David Petrosky, *President*
EMP: 5
SALES (est): 330K **Privately Held**
SIC: 7372 Prepackaged software

(G-4786)
LONGS HARDWOODS INC
Hc 3 (15931)
PHONE...............................814 472-4740
Douglas Long, *President*
Edwin A Long, *Vice Pres*
Scott Long, *Admin Sec*
EMP: 10
SQ FT: 50,000
SALES (est): 1.3MM **Privately Held**
WEB: www.military-graphics.com
SIC: 2431 Moldings & baseboards, ornamental & trim

(G-4787)
LUKAS CONFECTIONS INC
Also Called: Classic Caramel Co The
310 N Locust St (15931-1432)
P.O. Box 1147, York (17405-1147)
PHONE...............................717 843-0921
Robert R Lukas, *Ch of Bd*
EMP: 50
SQ FT: 50,000
SALES (est): 6.5MM **Privately Held**
WEB: www.classiccaramel.com
SIC: 2064 Candy & other confectionery products

(G-4788)
LYONS INDUSTRIES INC
3912 Admiral Peary Hwy (15931-3911)
PHONE...............................814 472-9770
James H Lyons III, *President*
Laurel L Lyons, *Treasurer*
EMP: 25 EST: 1953
SQ FT: 25,600
SALES (est): 5.7MM **Privately Held**
SIC: 3441 Fabricated structural metal

(G-4789)
MAINLINE NEWSPAPERS
975 Rowena Dr (15931-2077)
P.O. Box 777 (15931-0777)
PHONE...............................814 472-4110
Bill Anderson, *Owner*
EMP: 20
SALES (est): 695.5K **Privately Held**
SIC: 2711 Newspapers, publishing & printing

(G-4790)
NEW ENTERPRISE STONE LIME INC
235 Rubisch Rd (15931-4500)
PHONE...............................814 472-4717
Steven Hoover, *Branch Mgr*
EMP: 36
SALES (corp-wide): 651.9MM **Privately Held**
SIC: 3273 Ready-mixed concrete
PA: New Enterprise Stone & Lime Co., Inc.
3912 Brumbaugh Rd
New Enterprise PA 16664
814 224-6883

(G-4791)
P M SUPPLY CO INC (PA)
136 Lazor Rd (15931-3924)
P.O. Box 566 (15931-0566)
PHONE...............................814 472-4430
William Natcher, *President*
Donna R Natcher, *Corp Secy*
Lawrence Natcher, *Vice Pres*
▲ EMP: 29
SQ FT: 9,000
SALES (est): 6.5MM **Privately Held**
SIC: 3599 5085 Machine shop, jobbing & repair; industrial supplies

(G-4792)
PENN WIND ENERGY LLC
3212 Ben Franklin Hwy (15931-7303)
PHONE...............................814 288-8064
Lois Gongloff, *Mng Member*
EMP: 3
SALES (est): 232.9K **Privately Held**
SIC: 3511 Turbines & turbine generator sets

(G-4793)
R F SPECIALTIES PENNSYLVANIA
619 Industrial Park Rd # 200 (15931-4111)
P.O. Box 24 (15931-0024)
PHONE...............................814 472-2000
David K Edmiston Sr, *President*
EMP: 5
SALES (est): 675K **Privately Held**
SIC: 3663 Radio broadcasting & communications equipment

(G-4794)
RNS SERVICES INC
354 Rubisch Rd (15931-4513)
PHONE...............................814 472-5202
Scott Kroh, *President*
Rusty Taylor, *Vice Pres*
EMP: 50
SQ FT: 500
SALES (est): 2.3MM
SALES (corp-wide): 119.2MM **Privately Held**
WEB: www.resfuel.com
SIC: 1241 Coal mining services
PA: Robindale Energy Services Inc
1 Lloyd Ave Fl 2
Latrobe PA 15650
814 446-6700

(G-4795)
ROCHESTER COCA COLA BOTTLING
Also Called: Coca-Cola
108 Barefoot Rd (15931-7621)
P.O. Box 58 (15931-0058)
PHONE...............................814 472-6113
Richard Snyder, *Branch Mgr*
EMP: 100
SALES (corp-wide): 35.4B **Publicly Held**
SIC: 2086 Soft drinks: packaged in cans, bottles, etc.
HQ: Rochester Coca Cola Bottling Corp
300 Oak St
Pittston PA 18640
570 655-2874

(G-4796)
SEDER GAMING INC
3135 New Germany Rd # 43 (15931-4347)
PHONE...............................814 736-3611
David Seder, *President*
EMP: 3
SALES (est): 302.1K **Privately Held**
SIC: 3944 8742 Games, toys & children's vehicles; retail trade consultant

(G-4797)
SOUTHERN ALLEGHENIES ADVG INC
517 W Lloyd St (15931-1811)
PHONE...............................814 472-8593
James Peacock, *President*
Terry Gearhart, *Corp Secy*
Warren Myers, *Vice Pres*
James Wilson, *Vice Pres*
EMP: 8
SQ FT: 2,400
SALES (est): 1.2MM **Privately Held**
WEB: www.southadver.com
SIC: 5199 2261 Advertising specialties; screen printing of cotton broadwoven fabrics

Eddystone
Delaware County

(G-4798)
BARRY CALLEBAUT USA LLC
903 Industrial Hwy (19022-1531)
PHONE...............................610 872-4528
EMP: 21
SALES (corp-wide): 45.9MM **Privately Held**
SIC: 2066 Chocolate & cocoa products
HQ: Barry Callebaut U.S.A. Llc
600 W Chicago Ave Ste 860
Chicago IL 60654

(G-4799)
CLIPPER PIPE & SERVICE INC
11a Eddystone Indl Park (19022)
P.O. Box 148, Crum Lynne (19022-0148)
PHONE...............................610 872-9067
William C Jimick, *President*
Charlotte E Petrone, *Vice Pres*
Sheree M Petrone, *Admin Sec*
EMP: 7
SQ FT: 13,000
SALES (est): 1.8MM **Privately Held**
WEB: www.clipperpipe.com
SIC: 3441 5085 5051 1623 Fabricated structural metal; valves & fittings; bars, metal; oil & gas pipeline construction; fabricated pipe & fittings; fabricated plate work (boiler shop)

(G-4800)
CURTIS GLENCHEM CORP
2000 Industrial Hwy (19022-1500)
PHONE...............................610 876-9906
F Glenn Schaeffer, *President*
P Curtis Trainer, *Exec VP*
EMP: 6
SQ FT: 8,500
SALES: 600K **Privately Held**
WEB: www.curtisglenchem.com
SIC: 2842 Specialty cleaning, polishes & sanitation goods

(G-4801)
ESSITY NORTH AMERICA INC
Also Called: Sca Personal Care
1510 Chester Pike Ste 500 (19022-1380)
PHONE...............................610 499-3700
Janet Lampe, *Human Res Dir*
EMP: 6
SALES (corp-wide): 7.6B **Privately Held**
SIC: 2621 Paper mills
HQ: Essity North America Inc.
2929 Arch St Ste 2600
Philadelphia PA 19104

(G-4802)
FAD CORPORATION
2000 Industrial Hwy Ste 5 (19022-1500)
PHONE...............................610 872-3844
Robert Fad, *President*
Paula Fad, *Vice Pres*
James Rooney, *Plant Mgr*
Ibrahim Mansaray, *Manager*
EMP: 7
SQ FT: 40,000
SALES: 1.3MM **Privately Held**
SIC: 3479 Coating of metals & formed products; coating or wrapping steel pipe

(G-4803)
GENERAL ELECTRIC COMPANY
301 Saville Ave (19022-1526)
PHONE...............................610 876-2200
Sylvane Fontane, *Branch Mgr*
EMP: 7
SALES (corp-wide): 121.6B **Publicly Held**
SIC: 3533 Oil & gas field machinery
PA: General Electric Company
41 Farnsworth St
Boston MA 02210
617 443-3000

(G-4804)
INSPRO TECHNOLOGIES CORP (PA)
Also Called: ITCC
1510 Chester Pike Ste 400 (19022-1379)
PHONE...............................484 654-2200
Donald R Caldwell, *Ch of Bd*
Anthony Verdi, *President*
Anthony R Verdi, *President*
David J Medlock, *Senior VP*
Jim Zolad, *Sales Executive*
EMP: 14
SQ FT: 17,567
SALES: 21.6MM **Publicly Held**
SIC: 7372 Application computer software

(G-4805)
METROPLITAN COMMUNICATIONS INC
Also Called: Radio Communications
940 Eddystone Ave (19022-1412)
PHONE...............................610 874-7100
Roberta Martin, *Branch Mgr*
EMP: 10
SALES (est): 607K
SALES (corp-wide): 4.2MM **Privately Held**
WEB: www.mcsradio.com
SIC: 5999 3663 Electronic parts & equipment; radio broadcasting & communications equipment
PA: Metropolitan Communications, Inc.
309 Commerce Dr Ste 100
Exton PA 19341
610 363-5858

(G-4806)
P G A MACHINE CO INC
914 Simpson St (19022-1433)
PHONE...............................610 874-1335
Pat Anderson, *President*
EMP: 4
SQ FT: 9,000
SALES (est): 870.5K **Privately Held**
SIC: 3469 3452 3449 Metal stampings; bolts, nuts, rivets & washers; miscellaneous metalwork

Edgemont
Delaware County

(G-4807)
PLASTRAC INC (PA)
3928 Miller Rd (19028)
P.O. Box 1067 (19028-1067)
PHONE...............................610 356-3000
Kenneth Bullivant, *President*
EMP: 12
SQ FT: 5,000
SALES (est): 1.5MM **Privately Held**
WEB: www.plastrac.com
SIC: 3559 Refinery, chemical processing & similar machinery

Edinboro
Erie County

(G-4808)
AMTEK INC (PA)
10961 Route 98 (16412-9757)
PHONE...............................814 734-3327
Kathy Brady, *President*
William Zelina Jr, *Vice Pres*
EMP: 19
SQ FT: 8,000

SALES (est): 3MM Privately Held
WEB: www.amtekballast.com
SIC: 3625 Control equipment, electric

(G-4809)
BECK TOOL INC
25741 Fry Rd (16412-4833)
PHONE..................................814 734-8513
Patrick Beck, *President*
Charles Beck, *Treasurer*
Jan Beck, *Admin Sec*
EMP: 20
SQ FT: 3,400
SALES: 894K Privately Held
WEB: www.becktool.com
SIC: 3544 Special dies & tools

(G-4810)
COUNTERFLOW INC
6933 Route 6n (16412-9657)
PHONE..................................814 734-9440
Anthony W Evans, *President*
▲ EMP: 9
SQ FT: 11,000
SALES (est): 1.4MM Privately Held
WEB: www.counterflow.com
SIC: 3443 Heat exchangers, condensers &
components

(G-4811)
EDINBORO INDUSTRIES
4200 Route 6n (16412-1735)
PHONE..................................814 734-1100
Greg Zomcik, *Owner*
EMP: 8
SQ FT: 7,000
SALES (est): 995.2K Privately Held
SIC: 7692 Welding repair

(G-4812)
**GREAT LAKES CASE & CAB CO
INC (PA)**
4193 Route 6n (16412-1736)
P.O. Box 551 (16412-0551)
PHONE..................................814 734-7303
Carrie L Lowther, *CEO*
Robert I Lowther, *Vice Pres*
Thomas Demitras, *Engineer*
Michelle Hartl, *Regl Sales Mgr*
Jessica Tingley, *Sales Staff*
◆ EMP: 220
SQ FT: 110,000
SALES (est): 45.7MM Privately Held
SIC: 3499 Fire- or burglary-resistive prod-
ucts

(G-4813)
HAGERTY PRECISION TOOL
12250 Eureka Rd (16412-1276)
PHONE..................................814 734-8668
Herman R Hagerty, *President*
EMP: 7
SQ FT: 6,000
SALES: 800K Privately Held
SIC: 3544 3442 Special dies, tools, jigs &
fixtures; moldings & trim, except automo-
bile: metal

(G-4814)
HURRY HILL MAPLE SYRUP
11380 Fry Rd (16412-1004)
PHONE..................................814 734-1358
EMP: 3
SALES (est): 80K Privately Held
SIC: 2099 Mfg Food Preparations

(G-4815)
**HYTECH TOOL & DESIGN CO
(PA)**
Also Called: Tri-Tech
12076 Edinboro Rd (16412-1022)
PHONE..................................814 734-6000
Bernard Pelkowski, *President*
Ray Long, *COO*
Walter Bender, *Manager*
David Reiser, *Manager*
EMP: 18
SQ FT: 34,237
SALES (est): 3.2MM Privately Held
SIC: 3544 Die sets for metal stamping
(presses); dies, plastics forming; dies &
die holders for metal cutting, forming, die
casting

(G-4816)
**MEADVILLE REDI-MIX
CONCRETE**
Also Called: Edinboro Redi Mix Concrete
26269 Blicestone Rd (16412)
P.O. Box 785 (16412-0785)
PHONE..................................814 734-1644
Bob Sharple, *Manager*
EMP: 8
SALES (corp-wide): 5.1MM Privately
Held
SIC: 3273 5032 Ready-mixed concrete;
sand, construction; gravel
HQ: Meadville Redi-Mix Concrete Inc
9725 Liberty Street Ext
Meadville PA
814 724-7777

(G-4817)
MOUNTAIN RESOURCES INC
12321 Culbertson Dr (16412-1227)
P.O. Box 116 (16412-0116)
PHONE..................................814 734-1496
Fax: 814 734-1496
EMP: 7 EST: 1990
SALES (est): 500K Privately Held
SIC: 1389 Oilfield Services

(G-4818)
OVERTIME TOOL INC
6020 Crane Rd (16412-3906)
PHONE..................................814 734-0848
Chuck Graham, *President*
Robin Graham, *Treasurer*
EMP: 10
SALES: 920K Privately Held
SIC: 3069 Rubber hardware

(G-4819)
**PARAMOUNT DIE
CORPORATION**
4180 Route 6n (16412-1736)
PHONE..................................814 734-6999
James Griffing, *President*
Jean Griffing, *Vice Pres*
Norman Devore Jr, *Sales Associate*
Erica Dies, *Office Mgr*
EMP: 18 EST: 1959
SQ FT: 13,000
SALES (est): 3.3MM Privately Held
WEB: www.paramountdie.com
SIC: 3544 3423 Dies, steel rule; cutting
dies, except metal cutting

(G-4820)
PENN-UNION CORP (HQ)
229 Waterford St (16412-2381)
PHONE..................................814 734-1631
Brian Cullen, *President*
Robert Amendola, *VP Finance*
▲ EMP: 97
SQ FT: 132,000
SALES: 25MM
SALES (corp-wide): 699.1MM Privately
Held
SIC: 3643 Connectors & terminals for elec-
trical devices
PA: Nesco, Inc.
6140 Parkland Blvd # 110
Cleveland OH 44124
440 461-6000

(G-4821)
WILLIAMS MACHINING CO
2171 Route 6n (16412-1756)
PHONE..................................814 734-3121
Bernard Williams, *Owner*
EMP: 3
SQ FT: 3,000
SALES (est): 160K Privately Held
SIC: 3599 Machine shop, jobbing & repair

Edinburg
Lawrence County

(G-4822)
HONEY-CREEK STONE CO (HQ)
Rte 551 Rr 422 Rt 551 (16116)
P.O. Box 422 (16116-0422)
PHONE..................................724 654-5538
Carmen Shick, *President*
Rose Ambrosia, *Vice Pres*
EMP: 15

SQ FT: 6,600
SALES (est): 1.2MM
SALES (corp-wide): 2.2MM Privately
Held
SIC: 1422 1222 Crushed & broken lime-
stone; bituminous coal-underground min-
ing
PA: Penn Ohio Road Materials Inc
Rr 422
Edinburg PA 16116
724 654-5538

Edwardsville
Luzerne County

(G-4823)
**DANCHCKS EXTINGUISHERS
SVC INC**
512 Northampton St (18704-4560)
PHONE..................................570 589-1610
EMP: 3 EST: 2015
SALES (est): 189.8K Privately Held
SIC: 3999 Fire extinguishers, portable

(G-4824)
R & H MANUFACTURING INC
105 Woodward Hill Rd (18704-2300)
P.O. Box 1492, Kingston (18704-0492)
PHONE..................................570 288-6648
Alan Pollock, *President*
Diane Kocik, *Corp Secy*
Dale Nicholson, *Vice Pres*
EMP: 33 EST: 1957
SQ FT: 40,000
SALES (est): 7.8MM Privately Held
WEB: www.randhmfg.com
SIC: 3429 Clamps, couplings, nozzles &
other metal hose fittings

Effort
Monroe County

(G-4825)
EFFORT WOODCRAFT INC
1 Evergreen Hollow Rd (18330)
PHONE..................................570 629-1160
C Allen Conklin, *President*
Phyllis J Conklin, *Corp Secy*
Tom Conklin, *Vice Pres*
Karen Conklin, *Sales Staff*
EMP: 24 EST: 1952
SALES (est): 320K Privately Held
SIC: 2491 2434 2517 Millwork, treated
wood; wood kitchen cabinets; wood tele-
vision & radio cabinets

(G-4826)
**MULTIPLE METAL PROCESSING
INC**
1906 Silver Maple Rd (18330-8178)
P.O. Box 987 (18330-0987)
PHONE..................................570 620-7254
EMP: 3
SALES (est): 188.3K Privately Held
SIC: 3471 Plating & polishing

(G-4827)
ONE DAY BATHS INC
2241 Suburban Ln (18330-9755)
PHONE..................................570 402-2337
Charles Etgen, *Vice Pres*
EMP: 3
SALES (est): 200K Privately Held
SIC: 2851 Paints & allied products

(G-4828)
RTCSNACKS LLC
225 Sundance Rd (18330-8011)
PHONE..................................570 234-7266
EMP: 3
SALES (est): 75.4K Privately Held
SIC: 2099 Food preparations

(G-4829)
TNA DOORS
243 Matterhorn Dr (18330-7873)
PHONE..................................570 484-5858
Tanisha Alston-Parker, *Owner*
EMP: 7

SALES (est): 327.3K Privately Held
SIC: 3441 Fabricated structural metal

Eighty Four
Washington County

(G-4830)
84 LUMBER COMPANY (PA)
1019 Route 519 (15330-2813)
PHONE..................................724 228-8820
Joe Hardy, *CEO*
Maggie Hardy Magerko, *President*
David Cochran, *President*
Mark Ingersoll, *President*
Cheri Bomar, *Partner*
▼ EMP: 347
SQ FT: 70,000
SALES (est): 1.4B Privately Held
WEB: www.84lumber.com
SIC: 5211 2439 5031 2431 Lumber &
other building materials; structural wood
members; lumber, plywood & millwork;
millwork

(G-4831)
**ACCESS CREDENTIAL
SYSTEMS LLC**
104 Highcroft Cir (15330-1002)
PHONE..................................724 820-1160
William Livolsi,
EMP: 5 EST: 2010
SALES: 800K Privately Held
SIC: 2621 Card paper

(G-4832)
ALBRIGHTEN INDUSTRIES INC
45 Saint Cloud Rd (15330)
P.O. Box 225 (15330-0225)
PHONE..................................724 222-2959
EMP: 12 EST: 2008
SALES (est): 834.5K Privately Held
SIC: 3999 Manufacturing industries

(G-4833)
AMETEK INC
Ametek Specialty Metal Pdts
1085 Route 519 (15330-2813)
PHONE..................................724 225-8400
George Jucha, *Vice Pres*
Timothy Gilliland, *Manager*
Michael Toscano, *Manager*
Lawanda Yannacci, *Assistant*
EMP: 70
SALES (corp-wide): 4.8B Publicly Held
SIC: 3621 Motors & generators
PA: Ametek, Inc.
1100 Cassatt Rd
Berwyn PA 19312
610 647-2121

(G-4834)
BOLSAN COMPANY INC
163 Linnwood Rd (15330-2918)
PHONE..................................724 225-0446
Kim S Ward, *President*
Chris Fetcho, *General Mgr*
Bill Hamilton, *COO*
Tony Gilroy, *Vice Pres*
Howared F Kimberly, *Treasurer*
EMP: 13
SQ FT: 21,000
SALES (est): 3.4MM
SALES (corp-wide): 97.1MM Privately
Held
WEB: www.bolsan.com
SIC: 3499 Shims, metal
HQ: Shimtech Industries Limited
7a/B Millington Road
Hayes MIDDX UB3 4
208 571-0055

(G-4835)
BRYAN MFG CO
279 Valley Rd (15330-2665)
PHONE..................................724 245-8200
EMP: 45
SALES (est): 2.3MM Privately Held
SIC: 2339 2392 Mfg Women's/Misses'
Outerwear Mfg Household Furnishings

(G-4836)
C R AUGENSTEIN INC
2344 Route 136 (15330-2424)
PHONE..............................724 206-0679
Chaz Augenstein, *President*
EMP: 8
SQ FT: 3,000
SALES: 6.5MM **Privately Held**
SIC: 2911 Diesel fuels

(G-4837)
DEEPWELL ENERGY SERVICES LLC
207 Carlton Dr (15330-1823)
PHONE..............................412 316-5243
EMP: 21
SALES (corp-wide): 231.6MM **Privately Held**
SIC: 1381 Drilling oil & gas wells
PA: Deepwell Energy Services, Llc
4025 Highway 35 N
Columbia MS 39429
800 477-2855

(G-4838)
DIVERSIFIED LOGGING
440 Route 519 Unit 2 (15330-2039)
PHONE..............................724 228-4143
Craig Magee, *Manager*
EMP: 6 **EST:** 2009
SALES (est): 821K **Privately Held**
SIC: 2411 Logging

(G-4839)
ENCOTECH INC (PA)
1037 Route 519 (15330-2813)
P.O. Box 305 (15330-0305)
PHONE..............................724 222-3334
Bernard Lalli, *President*
Rosalyn Lalli, *Corp Secy*
EMP: 24
SALES (est): 7MM **Privately Held**
WEB: www.encotech.net
SIC: 8711 3589 7389 Designing; ship, boat, machine & product; water treatment equipment, industrial; filling pressure containers

(G-4840)
FAIRMOUNT MINERALS
1432 Route 519 (15330-2843)
PHONE..............................724 873-9039
EMP: 3
SALES (est): 174.4K **Privately Held**
SIC: 1442 Construction sand & gravel

(G-4841)
FOUR STARS PIPE & SUPPLY INC
72 Wilson Rd (15330-2846)
PHONE..............................724 746-2029
Rocky Bridges Jr, *Principal*
EMP: 4
SQ FT: 12,000
SALES (est): 596.1K **Privately Held**
SIC: 2679 Pipes & fittings, fiber: made from purchased material

(G-4842)
HANSON AGGREGATES BMC INC
339 Somerset Dr (15330)
PHONE..............................724 229-5840
James Walker, *CEO*
EMP: 15
SALES (corp-wide): 20.6B **Privately Held**
SIC: 3273 Ready-mixed concrete
HQ: Hanson Aggregates Bmc, Inc.
852 Swamp Rd
Penns Park PA
215 598-3152

(G-4843)
INTERNATIONAL PAPER COMPANY
10 Wilson Rd (15330-2846)
PHONE..............................724 745-2288
Eric Kreush, *Branch Mgr*
EMP: 17
SALES (corp-wide): 23.3B **Publicly Held**
SIC: 2621 Paper mills
PA: International Paper Company
6400 Poplar Ave
Memphis TN 38197
901 419-9000

(G-4844)
LORD CORPORATION
267 Arrowhead Ln (15330-2689)
PHONE..............................724 260-5541
EMP: 153
SALES (corp-wide): 1B **Privately Held**
SIC: 2891 Adhesives
PA: Lord Corporation
111 Lord Dr
Cary NC 27511
919 468-5979

(G-4845)
POLYMER SURFACE SYSTEMS LLC
307 Roupe Rd (15330-2483)
PHONE..............................724 222-6544
R Bobick, *Principal*
EMP: 9
SALES (est): 1.2MM **Privately Held**
SIC: 3479 Painting, coating & hot dipping

(G-4846)
RICE ELECTRIC COMPANY
30 Linnwood Rd (15330-2920)
P.O. Box 429 (15330-0429)
PHONE..............................724 225-4180
Claudine A Femiani, *President*
Joseph A Femiani, *Vice Pres*
Jeff Churchill, *Sales Staff*
Jeff Kupec, *Sales Staff*
Lori Dethomas, *Maintence Staff*
EMP: 33
SALES (est): 8.8MM **Privately Held**
SIC: 7694 5063 Electric motor repair; motors, electric

(G-4847)
RITTER INDUSTRIES INC
46 Route 519 (15330-2026)
PHONE..............................724 225-6563
Brian Ritter, *President*
Craig Ritter, *Vice Pres*
EMP: 10
SQ FT: 32,000
SALES (est): 1.5MM **Privately Held**
SIC: 3441 Fabricated structural metal

(G-4848)
SELECT ENERGY SERVICES LLC
Also Called: Impact Energy Services
100 Gallaway Dr (15330-1860)
PHONE..............................724 239-2056
EMP: 59
SALES (corp-wide): 1.5B **Publicly Held**
SIC: 1389 Oil field services
HQ: Select Energy Services, Llc
1820 N I 35
Gainesville TX 76240
940 668-1818

(G-4849)
SKC INC (PA)
863 Valley View Rd (15330-8619)
PHONE..............................724 260-0741
Richard Guild, *President*
Lloyd V Guild, *Chairman*
Dennis Lawler, *Vice Pres*
Daniel Baldauff, *Electrical Engi*
Daniel L Guild, *Treasurer*
EMP: 85 **EST:** 1962
SQ FT: 8,500
SALES (est): 25.9MM **Privately Held**
WEB: www.skcinc.com
SIC: 3821 3829 3564 3561 Laboratory equipment: fume hoods, distillation racks, etc.; measuring & controlling devices; blowers & fans; pumps & pumping equipment

(G-4850)
STAMPEDE INDUSTRIES LLC
1019 Route 519 (15330-2813)
PHONE..............................724 239-2104
Joseph A Hardy III, *Principal*
EMP: 8 **EST:** 2011
SALES (est): 706.9K **Privately Held**
SIC: 3999 Manufacturing industries

(G-4851)
WASHINGTON PENN PLASTIC CO INC
Also Called: Preformance Products Div
136 Mitchell Rd (15330)
PHONE..............................724 228-3709
Herb Rawlangs, *Manager*
Adam Galambos, *Info Tech Mgr*
EMP: 50
SALES (corp-wide): 290.9MM **Privately Held**
SIC: 3087 3083 Custom compound purchased resins; laminated plastics plate & sheet
HQ: Washington Penn Plastic Co., Inc.
450 Racetrack Rd
Washington PA 15301
724 228-1260

Eldred
Mckean County

(G-4852)
ALMA GAS INC
379 Loop Rd (16731-3407)
PHONE..............................814 225-3480
John Greeley, *President*
John Farber, *Manager*
EMP: 4
SALES: 328K **Privately Held**
WEB: www.almagas.com
SIC: 1389 Oil consultants

(G-4853)
JOHNSTON MEAT PROCESSING
74 Larabee Rd B (16731-2806)
PHONE..............................814 225-3495
William Johnston, *Principal*
EMP: 3
SALES (est): 140K **Privately Held**
SIC: 2011 Meat packing plants

(G-4854)
OJACKS INC
Also Called: White Hawk Beef
45 Railroad Ave (16731-4629)
P.O. Box 151 (16731-0151)
PHONE..............................814 225-4755
Steven Slavin, *President*
Cynthia Stanley, *Vice Pres*
Kathleen Slavin, *Treasurer*
EMP: 20
SQ FT: 20,000
SALES (est): 8.5MM **Privately Held**
SIC: 5147 2013 2011 Meats, fresh; sausages & other prepared meats; meat packing plants

---

Elizabeth
Allegheny County

(G-4855)
ART TECH DESIGNS
411 Spring Ln (15037-1933)
PHONE..............................412 754-0391
Elaine Taylor, *Partner*
Alberta Mamrose, *Partner*
EMP: 3
SALES (est): 150K **Privately Held**
SIC: 2395 Embroidery & art needlework

(G-4856)
BASIC CARBIDE CORPORATION
900 Blythedale Rd (15037-2702)
PHONE..............................412 754-0060
John Goodrum, *President*
John Hoak, *Plant Mgr*
Jared Filapose, *Info Tech Mgr*
Mike Weager, *Executive*
EMP: 100
SALES (corp-wide): 19.2MM **Privately Held**
WEB: www.basiccarbide.com
SIC: 3291 3544 Tungsten carbide abrasive; special dies, tools, jigs & fixtures
PA: Basic Carbide Corporation
900 Main St
Irwin PA 15642
724 446-1630

(G-4857)
BLANK RIVER SERVICES INC (PA)
1 Chicago Ave Bldg 12 (15037-1766)
PHONE..............................412 384-2489
Richard Blank, *President*
EMP: 20
SALES (est): 2MM **Privately Held**
SIC: 7699 1629 7692 3444 Welding equipment repair; marine construction; welding repair; sheet metalwork; fabricated plate work (boiler shop)

(G-4858)
COSTA INDUSTRIES LLC
600 Hayden Blvd (15037-1600)
PHONE..............................412 384-8170
Jeff Costa, *Principal*
EMP: 16
SALES (est): 2.6MM **Privately Held**
SIC: 3999 Manufacturing industries

(G-4859)
GARY GIOIA COAL CO
319 Karen Dr (15037-2408)
PHONE..............................412 754-0994
Gary Gioia, *Owner*
EMP: 3 **EST:** 1995
SALES (est): 486.6K **Privately Held**
SIC: 1241 Coal mining services

(G-4860)
HOWELL CRAFT INC
Also Called: Howell Craft Memorials
591 Simpson Howell Rd (15037-2817)
PHONE..............................412 751-6861
Herbert K Howell, *President*
Dorothy Howell, *Vice Pres*
Norma Jean Williams, *Treasurer*
EMP: 7 **EST:** 1948
SQ FT: 2,250
SALES (est): 680K **Privately Held**
WEB: www.howellcraft.com
SIC: 3281 1742 5999 Marble, building: cut & shaped; mantel work; monuments & tombstones

(G-4861)
KEYSTONE CSTM FABRICATORS INC
108 Atlantic Ave (15037-1862)
PHONE..............................412 384-9131
Bret A Holdren, *President*
Michael Limberg, *Vice Pres*
William Limberg, *Admin Sec*
EMP: 30
SQ FT: 10,000
SALES (est): 5.4MM **Privately Held**
SIC: 3444 Sheet metal specialties, not stamped

(G-4862)
PITTSBURGH CARBIDE DIE CO LLC
254 Lovedale Rd (15037-1858)
PHONE..............................412 384-5785
Robert A Ahlin,
Matthew Ahlin,
EMP: 10
SQ FT: 6,000
SALES: 1MM **Privately Held**
SIC: 3544 Dies, steel rule; special dies & tools

(G-4863)
PRISM TECHNOLOGIES INC
1011 Lovedale Rd 1 (15037-1870)
PHONE..............................412 751-3090
Richard Borkowski, *President*
EMP: 9
SALES (est): 1.3MM **Privately Held**
WEB: www.prismtechnologies.net
SIC: 3544 Special dies & tools

(G-4864)
WERNER WELDING LLC
475 W Newton Rd (15037-9512)
P.O. Box 142 (15037-0142)
PHONE..............................724 379-4240
Susan Werner, *General Mgr*
Hans Werner,
EMP: 5
SALES: 250K **Privately Held**
SIC: 7692 Welding repair

Elizabethtown
Lancaster County

(G-4865)
AQUATIC CO
Lasco Bathware
40 Industrial Rd (17022-9425)
PHONE....................................717 367-1100
Polly Turner, *President*
Kim Houseal, *Branch Mgr*
EMP: 139
SALES (corp-wide): 133.8MM **Privately Held**
SIC: 3088 Shower stalls, fiberglass & plastic
HQ: Aquatic Co.
1700 N Delilah St
Corona CA 92879

(G-4866)
BENDERS BUFFING & POLISHING
19 Hess Ave (17022-2131)
PHONE....................................717 226-1850
EMP: 3
SALES (est): 209.1K **Privately Held**
SIC: 3471 Polishing, metals or formed products

(G-4867)
BURKHART & QUINN SIGN CO INC
Also Called: Superior Sign
105 Maytown Rd (17022-9326)
PHONE....................................717 367-1375
Terry Burkhart, *President*
Authur Quinn, *President*
EMP: 11
SQ FT: 16,000
SALES (est): 1.5MM **Privately Held**
SIC: 3993 Electric signs

(G-4868)
CFB LLC
214 Dogwood Dr (17022-9533)
PHONE....................................717 769-0857
Frank Miklos, *Mng Member*
Brian McGeehan, *Mng Member*
EMP: 7
SALES: 1.5MM **Privately Held**
SIC: 3272 Building materials, except block or brick: concrete

(G-4869)
CONTINENTAL PRESS INC (PA)
520 E Bainbridge St (17022-2299)
PHONE....................................717 367-1836
Daniel H Raffensperger, *President*
Eric Beck, *President*
Carl T Raffensperger, *Vice Pres*
Gene McFail, *CFO*
Melvyn R Boeman, *Treasurer*
▼ EMP: 190 EST: 1937
SQ FT: 130,000
SALES (est): 31.3MM **Privately Held**
WEB: www.continentalpress.com
SIC: 2731 7372 2752 Textbooks: publishing & printing; pamphlets: publishing & printing; educational computer software; commercial printing, offset

(G-4870)
CUMMINS-WAGNER COMPANY INC
3 Meating Pl (17022-2883)
PHONE....................................717 367-8294
Douglas Ardinger, *CEO*
Fred Marburger, *Sales Staff*
Tom Getty, *Marketing Staff*
Thomas P Getty, *Branch Mgr*
EMP: 23
SALES (corp-wide): 83.3MM **Privately Held**
SIC: 5046 3519 Commercial equipment; internal combustion engines
PA: Cummins-Wagner Company, Inc.
10901 Pump House Rd
Annapolis Junction MD 20701
410 792-4230

(G-4871)
DC WELDING
643 Hereford Rd (17022-9645)
PHONE....................................717 361-9400
David Becker, *Owner*
EMP: 6
SQ FT: 1,560
SALES (est): 722.3K **Privately Held**
SIC: 7692 7699 Welding repair; farm machinery repair

(G-4872)
DESIGNS UNLIMITED
160 S Poplar St Ste 101 (17022-3300)
PHONE....................................717 367-4405
Coreen Shutter, *Owner*
EMP: 6
SQ FT: 7,000
SALES (est): 310K **Privately Held**
SIC: 2395 7336 Embroidery products, except schiffli machine; silk screen design

(G-4873)
ELIZABETHTOWN ADVOCATE
9 S Market St (17022-2308)
P.O. Box 547 (17022-0547)
PHONE....................................717 361-0340
Daniel Robrish, *Owner*
EMP: 6
SALES (est): 264.8K **Privately Held**
SIC: 2711 Commercial printing & newspaper publishing combined; newspapers, publishing & printing

(G-4874)
GRAYBILL FARMS INC
389 Heisey Quarry Rd (17022-9760)
PHONE....................................717 361-8455
Dave Graybill, *President*
EMP: 7
SALES (est): 1.5MM **Privately Held**
SIC: 2611 Pulp manufactured from waste or recycled paper

(G-4875)
ITP OF USA INC
Also Called: Innovative Tech In Print
200 S Chestnut St (17022-2266)
PHONE....................................717 367-3670
Daniel Raffensperger, *CEO*
Buzz Cox, *President*
R Dean Poff, *Vice Pres*
Gene McFail, *CFO*
EMP: 70 EST: 2000
SALES (est): 9.9MM
SALES (corp-wide): 31.3MM **Privately Held**
WEB: www.itpofusa.com
SIC: 2752 Commercial printing, offset
PA: The Continental Press Inc
520 E Bainbridge St
Elizabethtown PA 17022
717 367-1836

(G-4876)
LEBER MINING COMPANY INC
36 S Market St Fl 2 (17022-2352)
P.O. Box 367 (17022-0367)
PHONE....................................717 367-1453
James E Leber, *President*
Paul Nichols, *Exec VP*
Joseph Oless, *Treasurer*
Ralph Weirich, *Treasurer*
EMP: 4
SALES (est): 279.9K **Privately Held**
SIC: 1081 Exploration, metal mining; mine development, metal

(G-4877)
MARS INCORPORATED
295 S Brown St (17022-2192)
PHONE....................................717 367-1500
Michael Murphy, *Branch Mgr*
EMP: 35
SALES (corp-wide): 34.2B **Privately Held**
SIC: 2064 Candy & other confectionery products
PA: Mars, Incorporated
6885 Elm St Ste 1
Mc Lean VA 22101
703 821-4900

(G-4878)
MARS CHOCOLATE NORTH AMER LLC
295 S Brown St (17022-2192)
PHONE....................................717 367-1500
Michael Tucker, *Branch Mgr*
EMP: 500
SALES (corp-wide): 34.2B **Privately Held**
WEB: www.kilic-kalkan.com
SIC: 2066 2064 Chocolate & cocoa products; candy & other confectionery products
HQ: Mars Chocolate North America, Llc
800 High St
Hackettstown NJ 07840
908 852-1000

(G-4879)
MAX MACHINE LLC
39 Industrial Rd (17022-9426)
PHONE....................................717 361-8744
James Max, *Owner*
EMP: 7
SQ FT: 12,000
SALES (est): 1MM **Privately Held**
SIC: 3599 Machine shop, jobbing & repair

(G-4880)
NOAH F BOYLE CABINETS
3043 Steinruck Rd (17022-9063)
PHONE....................................717 944-1007
Noah Boyle, *Owner*
EMP: 3 EST: 1993
SQ FT: 4,725
SALES: 160K **Privately Held**
SIC: 2434 Wood kitchen cabinets

(G-4881)
NYES MACHINE AND DESIGN
90 S Wilson Ave (17022-2165)
PHONE....................................717 533-9514
Bryan Nye, *President*
EMP: 8
SALES (est): 842.2K **Privately Held**
SIC: 3599 Machine shop, jobbing & repair
PA: Nye's Machine And Design
1153 Roush Rd
Hummelstown PA 17036

(G-4882)
QUALITY METAL WORKS INC
385 Anchor Rd (17022-2808)
PHONE....................................717 367-2120
Jack Garner Jr, *President*
Bob Godshall, *Treasurer*
Joi Garner, *Office Mgr*
EMP: 18
SQ FT: 5,600
SALES (est): 4.5MM **Privately Held**
WEB: www.qmwinc.com
SIC: 3441 7692 Fabricated structural metal; welding repair

(G-4883)
READY TRAINING INC
Also Called: Ready Training Online
222 Old Hershey Rd (17022-1351)
P.O. Box 530 (17022-0530)
PHONE....................................717 366-4253
Jeffery E Kahler, *CEO*
George Rivers III, *Principal*
Lydia Thacker, *Graphic Designe*
EMP: 6
SALES: 250K **Privately Held**
SIC: 3273 Ready-mixed concrete

(G-4884)
RS ASPHALT MAINTENANCE INC
99 Cassell Rd (17022-9554)
PHONE....................................717 367-4914
Robert Stanley, *President*
EMP: 8
SALES (est): 1.1MM **Privately Held**
SIC: 2951 Asphalt paving mixtures & blocks

(G-4885)
RUTTS MACHINE INC
300 Jonlyn Dr (17022-9304)
PHONE....................................717 367-3011
J Leon Rutt, *President*
Myra Rutt, *Treasurer*
Brenda Zeager, *Admin Sec*
EMP: 15

SALES (est): 2.3MM **Privately Held**
SIC: 3519 Internal combustion engines

(G-4886)
S WENGER FEED MILL INC
26 Linden Ave (17022-1507)
PHONE....................................717 361-4223
Barry Shaw, *President*
EMP: 3
SALES (est): 199.4K **Privately Held**
SIC: 2048 Prepared feeds

(G-4887)
SHEARERS WELDING INC
240 Heisey Quarry Rd (17022-9760)
PHONE....................................717 361-9196
Barry Shearer, *President*
Lynn Shearer, *Treasurer*
EMP: 4
SQ FT: 6,000
SALES (est): 521.5K **Privately Held**
SIC: 7692 Welding repair

(G-4888)
STELLAR IMAGES IMGES DCRTV GLS
204 S Market St (17022-2420)
PHONE....................................717 367-6500
John Bishop, *Mng Member*
Virginia Bishop,
EMP: 3
SALES (est): 206.1K **Privately Held**
SIC: 3231 Stained glass: made from purchased glass

(G-4889)
T SHIRT PRINTER
251 Poplar Ln (17022-9475)
PHONE....................................717 367-1167
Karen Wenger, *Owner*
Greg Hoover, *Co-Owner*
EMP: 3
SALES: 150K **Privately Held**
SIC: 3552 2396 2395 Silk screens for textile industry; automotive & apparel trimmings; pleating & stitching

(G-4890)
WELD TEK LTD
69 Industrial Rd (17022-9426)
PHONE....................................717 367-0666
Steven Sisson, *President*
EMP: 3
SALES (est): 180K **Privately Held**
SIC: 7692 Welding repair

(G-4891)
WHITE OAK MILLS INC (PA)
419 W High St (17022-2189)
PHONE....................................717 367-1525
John C Wagner, *Ch of Bd*
Mark Wagner, *President*
Todd Cirelli, *Opers Mgr*
Stuart Heisey, *Purchasing*
Jennifer Hampshire, *Sls & Mktg Exec*
EMP: 50
SQ FT: 30,000
SALES (est): 13.1MM **Privately Held**
WEB: www.whiteoakmills.com
SIC: 2048 2041 Prepared feeds; flour & other grain mill products

Elizabethville
Dauphin County

(G-4892)
BROAD MOUNTAIN VINEYARD LLC
45 W Broad St (17023)
PHONE....................................717 362-8044
EMP: 5
SALES (est): 175K **Privately Held**
SIC: 2084 Wines

(G-4893)
EASTERN INDUSTRIES INC
3633 State Route 225 (17023-8833)
PHONE....................................717 362-3388
Gary Bettick, *Branch Mgr*
EMP: 26

▲ = Import ▼=Export
◆ =Import/Export

SALES (corp-wide): 651.9MM **Privately Held**
WEB: www.eastern-ind.com
SIC: **5032** 3273 2951 Paving mixtures; ready-mixed concrete; asphalt paving mixtures & blocks
HQ: Eastern Industries, Inc.
3724 Crescent Ct W 200
Whitehall PA 18052
610 866-0932

(G-4894)
KLINGER MACHINERY CO INC
333 N Church St (17023-8923)
P.O. Box 306 (17023-0306)
PHONE.................................717 362-8656
El Klinger, *President*
EMP: 5 EST: 1958
SQ FT: 21,000
SALES (est): 904.6K **Privately Held**
WEB: www.klingermachinery.com
SIC: **3532** 5082 Rock crushing machinery, stationary; pulverizers (stationary), stone; crushing, pulverizing & screening machinery

(G-4895)
MI WINDOWS AND DOORS INC
Also Called: Rightscreen
4314 State Route 209 (17023-8438)
PHONE.................................717 362-8196
Eric Rothermel, *Vice Pres*
Kathy Hyde, *Production*
Stanley Spozio, *Senior Buyer*
Ray Garries, *VP Engrg*
Sheila Naylor, *Accounting Mgr*
EMP: 481
SALES (corp-wide): 1.1B **Privately Held**
WEB: www.miwd.com
SIC: **3442** Screens, window, metal; screen doors, metal
HQ: Mi Windows And Doors, Inc.
650 W Market St
Gratz PA 17030
717 365-3300

(G-4896)
PINE CREEK CONSTRUCTION LLC
6140 State Route 225 (17023-9359)
PHONE.................................717 362-6974
EMP: 7
SALES (est): 582.8K
SALES (corp-wide): 3.9MM **Privately Held**
SIC: **2511** Storage chests, household: wood
PA: Pine Creek Construction Llc
102 E Market St
Gratz PA 17030
717 365-3770

(G-4897)
RITESCREEN COMPANY LLC (PA)
4314 State Route 209 (17023-8438)
PHONE.................................717 362-7483
Tom Himmel, *CEO*
John Keller, *President*
Jay K Poppleton, *Treasurer*
Teal Gaylord, *VP Human Res*
Sarah Walker Gutherie, *Admin Sec*
EMP: 180
SQ FT: 200,000
SALES (est): 139MM **Privately Held**
WEB: www.ritescreen.com
SIC: **3442** 2431 Metal doors, sash & trim; door screens, metal covered wood

(G-4898)
SWAB WAGON COMPANY
44 S Callowhill St (17023-6601)
P.O. Box 919 (17023-0919)
PHONE.................................717 362-8151
Tony Margerum, *President*
Anthony J Margerum, *President*
Fred M Margerum, *Vice Pres*
Stuart Margerum, *Treasurer*
Dee Green, *Admin Sec*
EMP: 25 EST: 1868
SQ FT: 30,000
SALES: 3MM **Privately Held**
WEB: www.swabwagon.com
SIC: **3713** Specialty motor vehicle bodies

(G-4899)
W W PALLET CO
1318 Mountain Rd (17023-8228)
PHONE.................................717 362-9388
Woodrow Wiest, *Owner*
EMP: 12
SALES: 500K **Privately Held**
SIC: **2448** Pallets, wood

Elkins Park
Montgomery County

(G-4900)
BLUESTAR MARKETING INC
915 Jenkintown Rd (19027-1633)
PHONE.................................215 886-4002
Hal Sheppard, *President*
Larry Altman, *Principal*
Andrea Berger, *Business Mgr*
Fran Sheppard, *Admin Sec*
EMP: 5
SQ FT: 950
SALES: 1MM **Privately Held**
WEB: www.thinkbluestar.com
SIC: **2395** Embroidery products, except schiffli machine

(G-4901)
CHARLENE CRAWFORD
Also Called: Crawford Education Plus
710 Martin Rd (19027-1710)
P.O. Box 605, Huntingdon Valley (19006-0605)
PHONE.................................215 432-7542
Charlene Crawford, *Principal*
Cynthia Cornish, *Vice Pres*
EMP: 3 **Privately Held**
SIC: **9411** 8299 2731 Administration of educational programs; tutoring school; educational service, nondegree granting; continuing educ.; public speaking school; books: publishing only

(G-4902)
EKO SOLUTIONS PLUS INC
7305 Old York Rd Ste 2 (19027-3068)
PHONE.................................215 856-9517
Christopher Chough, *President*
Justin Sung, *Director*
EMP: 3
SQ FT: 500
SALES (est): 290.6K **Privately Held**
WEB: www.ekous.com
SIC: **3699** 7371 3825 7374 Security devices; computer software development; network analyzers; computer graphics service

(G-4903)
FRY INTERNATIONAL LLC
Also Called: This Week's Ad
715 Martin Rd Ofc (19027-1709)
PHONE.................................215 847-6359
Kevin Fry, *Principal*
Jesse Fry, *Principal*
Lisa Fry, *Principal*
EMP: 3 EST: 2013
SALES (est): 190K **Privately Held**
SIC: **7371** 7372 7379 7389 Custom computer programming services; application computer software; computer related consulting services;

(G-4904)
GULDEN OPHTHALMICS INC
Also Called: Gulden, R. O. & Co
225 Cadwalader Ave (19027-2020)
PHONE.................................215 884-8105
Sean Cockley, *President*
▲ EMP: 10
SQ FT: 4,200
SALES (est): 1.8MM **Privately Held**
WEB: www.guldenindustries.com
SIC: **3841** Ophthalmic instruments & apparatus

(G-4905)
HLI RAIL & RIGGING LLC
511 Spring Ave (19027-2616)
PHONE.................................215 277-5558
Ross McLaren, *Branch Mgr*
EMP: 14

SALES (corp-wide): 22.3MM **Privately Held**
SIC: **4011** 3731 Railroads, line-haul operating; marine rigging
PA: Hli Rail & Rigging, Llc
8900 Eastloch Dr Ste 215
Spring TX 77379
718 309-6693

(G-4906)
IAL ASSOC LLC
890 Serpentine Ln (19027-1214)
PHONE.................................215 887-5114
James Lary,
EMP: 20
SALES (est): 2.3MM **Privately Held**
WEB: www.ialassociates.com
SIC: **3589** Commercial cleaning equipment

(G-4907)
IO SOLUTIONS & CONTROLS
Also Called: Electrical Supply
864 Township Line Rd (19027-2001)
PHONE.................................215 635-4480
Robert Hafter, *Owner*
EMP: 12 EST: 2000
SALES (est): 810K **Privately Held**
WEB: www.ioelectric.com
SIC: **3613** Distribution boards, electric

(G-4908)
KOREA DAILY NEWS INC
1135 W Cheltenham Ave # 100 (19027-3000)
PHONE.................................215 277-1112
EMP: 3
SALES (est): 132.3K **Privately Held**
SIC: **2711** Newspapers, publishing & printing

(G-4909)
NORTHEAST DENTAL LABORATORIES
914 Stratford Ave (19027-2922)
PHONE.................................215 725-0950
Terry Stern, *President*
EMP: 6
SQ FT: 2,400
SALES (est): 654.7K **Privately Held**
WEB: www.nedentallab.com
SIC: **3843** 8072 Orthodontic appliances; dental laboratories

(G-4910)
PRISM GRAPHICS INC
7804 Montgomery Ave Ste 7 (19027-2649)
PHONE.................................215 782-1600
David A Rubin, *Owner*
EMP: 5
SALES (est): 575.4K **Privately Held**
SIC: **2759** Commercial printing

(G-4911)
SONIC TRONICS INC
7865 Mill Rd (19027-2796)
PHONE.................................215 635-6520
Horace F Hankinson, *President*
M E Hankinson, *Corp Secy*
EMP: 9
SQ FT: 6,000
SALES (est): 1.2MM **Privately Held**
SIC: **3944** Games, toys & children's vehicles

(G-4912)
SUNDAY TOPIC KOREAN NEWS
Also Called: Sunday Topic News
7300 Old York Rd Ste 210 (19027-3063)
PHONE.................................215 935-1111
Joseph Shin, *Owner*
▲ EMP: 5
SALES (est): 196.1K **Privately Held**
SIC: **2711** Newspapers, publishing & printing

(G-4913)
TOP-NOTCH TRUCKING INC
7766b Penrose Ave (19027-1011)
PHONE.................................267 456-1744
Franklin Cain III, *CEO*
Denise Cain, *CFO*
EMP: 4
SQ FT: 1,000
SALES (est): 309.8K **Privately Held**
SIC: **3537** Industrial trucks & tractors

(G-4914)
WEISMAN NOVELTY CO INC
Also Called: Timely Impressions
608 Webb Rd (19027-2538)
PHONE.................................215 635-0147
Steven Weisman, *President*
Deirdre Weisman, *Vice Pres*
EMP: 15 EST: 1948
SQ FT: 13,005
SALES (est): 1MM **Privately Held**
SIC: **2353** Hats & caps

(G-4915)
WRAPMASTER USA LLC
7401 Old York Rd (19027-3005)
P.O. Box 8876 (19027-0876)
PHONE.................................215 782-2285
Chris Urban,
Christopher Urban,
▲ EMP: 5
SQ FT: 1,600
SALES (est): 538.9K **Privately Held**
SIC: **5023** 3469 Kitchenware; household cooking & kitchen utensils, metal

---

Elkland
Tioga County

(G-4916)
METAMORA PRODUCTS CORP ELKLAND
112 Industrial Pkwy (16920-1457)
PHONE.................................814 258-7122
Jack Lawless, *President*
Richard Mac Leod, *Vice Pres*
Charles Schiedegger, *Vice Pres*
Leonard M Visosky, *Vice Pres*
Thomas A Ward, *Vice Pres*
EMP: 200 EST: 1974
SQ FT: 120,000
SALES (est): 29.8MM **Privately Held**
SIC: **3089** Injection molded finished plastic products
HQ: Metamora Products Corporation Of Elkland
4057 S Oak St
Metamora MI 48455
810 678-2295

(G-4917)
PAINTER MEAT PROCESSING
408 E River St (16920-1455)
PHONE.................................814 258-7283
Rebecca Painter, *Partner*
Charles Painter, *Partner*
Marie Painter, *Partner*
Norman Painter, *Partner*
EMP: 4
SALES (est): 324.8K **Privately Held**
WEB: www.paintersmeats.com
SIC: **2011** Meat packing plants

Elliottsburg
Perry County

(G-4918)
ADVANCED PSTIONING SYSTEMS INC
Also Called: A P S
184 Butcher Shop Ln (17024-9379)
PHONE.................................717 582-3915
Michael Torok, *President*
Robert Dennis, *Vice Pres*
▼ EMP: 3
SQ FT: 1,000
SALES (est): 319.4K **Privately Held**
SIC: **3579** Mailing, letter handling & addressing machines

(G-4919)
BLUE MOUNTAIN PROCESSORS INC
34 Blue Mountain Ln Fl 35 (17024-9115)
PHONE.................................717 438-3296
Jay Horst, *President*
Marlon Reiff, *Principal*
Merle Reiff, *Principal*
▲ EMP: 10
SALES (est): 1.2MM **Privately Held**
SIC: **2499** Mulch, wood & bark

GEOGRAPHIC

(G-4920)
HISTORY WASHER INC
33 Ridge Ln (17024-9025)
PHONE................................717 275-3101
Charles Santee Rollason Jr, *Principal*
EMP: 3 EST: 2010
SALES (est): 139.2K **Privately Held**
SIC: 3452 Washers

(G-4921)
MONTOUR CREEK MINING CO
2302 Shermans Valley Rd (17024-9002)
PHONE................................717 582-7526
Caom Douglas, *Owner*
EMP: 3
SALES (est): 143.7K **Privately Held**
SIC: 1221 Bituminous coal surface mining

(G-4922)
TUSCARORA HARDWOODS INC
2240 Shermans Valley Rd (17024-9182)
P.O. Box 64 (17024-0064)
PHONE................................717 582-4122
Aquillas Peachey, *President*
Charlotte Swartz, *Corp Secy*
▼ EMP: 60
SALES (est): 11.1MM **Privately Held**
WEB: www.tuscarorahardwoods.com
SIC: 2421 2499 Lumber: rough, sawed or planed; mulch, wood & bark

---

Ellwood City
Lawrence County

(G-4923)
ADAMS MANUFACTURING CORP
1 Early St (16117-2255)
PHONE................................724 758-2125
William E Adams, *Manager*
EMP: 8
SALES (est): 36.2K **Privately Held**
SIC: 3083 Plastic finished products, laminated

(G-4924)
ADAMS MFG CORP
1 Early St (16117-2255)
PHONE................................724 758-2125
William E Adams, *Branch Mgr*
EMP: 4 **Privately Held**
WEB: www.adamsrite.com
SIC: 3999 Barber & beauty shop equipment
HQ: Adams Mfg. Corp.
109 W Park Rd
Portersville PA 16051
800 237-8287

(G-4925)
AMERICAN BALING PRODUCTS INC
103 Park Ave (16117-2251)
P.O. Box 230 (16117-0230)
PHONE................................724 758-5566
Jay Fedorka, *President*
EMP: 3 EST: 2001
SALES (est): 304.1K **Privately Held**
SIC: 3523 Balers, farm: hay, straw, cotton, etc.

(G-4926)
AMSTEEL INC
Also Called: American Steel Co
103 Park Ave (16117-2251)
P.O. Box 230 (16117-0230)
PHONE................................724 758-5566
John G Fedorka, *President*
Dominic R Coccagna, *Corp Secy*
Nick Coccagna, *Vice Pres*
Kenneth L Vegely, *Vice Pres*
Jack Kocerka, *Sales Mgr*
EMP: 13
SQ FT: 20,000
SALES (est): 2.3MM **Privately Held**
SIC: 3452 3496 Cotter pins, metal; miscellaneous fabricated wire products

(G-4927)
APPALACHIAN LTG SYSTEMS INC
Also Called: Alled
101 Randolph St (16117-6215)
PHONE................................724 752-0326
James J Wassel, *President*
William Kreuer, *Treasurer*
▲ EMP: 39
SALES (est): 8.8MM **Privately Held**
SIC: 3645 3646 Residential lighting fixtures; commercial indusl & institutional electric lighting fixtures

(G-4928)
BLANK CONCRETE AND SUPPLY
804 Factory Ave (16117-1940)
P.O. Box 591 (16117-0591)
PHONE................................724 758-7596
G William Blank Jr, *President*
John Smith, *Principal*
David J Blank, *Treasurer*
John E Smith, *Admin Sec*
EMP: 15
SQ FT: 21,500
SALES (est): 3.2MM **Privately Held**
SIC: 5032 3273 5039 5983 Concrete mixtures; sand, construction; aggregate; ready-mixed concrete; septic tanks; fuel oil dealers

(G-4929)
DOUG PFERS DEER CTNG SMOKE HSE
1685 Route 65 (16117-5217)
PHONE................................724 758-7965
Douglas Pefer, *Owner*
EMP: 5
SALES (est): 141.6K **Privately Held**
SIC: 2011 Meat packing plants

(G-4930)
ELLCO PRODUCTS INC
107 Jamison Ave (16117-2532)
PHONE................................724 758-3526
William J Miskolcze, *President*
Barbara J Miskolcze, *Corp Secy*
EMP: 6
SQ FT: 5,000
SALES (est): 556.3K **Privately Held**
WEB: www.ellcofood.com
SIC: 3599 3631 Machine shop, jobbing & repair; barbecues, grills & braziers (outdoor cooking)

(G-4931)
ELLWOOD GROUP INC
Also Called: Ellwood City Forge
800 Commercial Ave (16117-2354)
P.O. Box 31 (16117-0031)
PHONE................................724 752-0055
Kim Weingartner, *General Mgr*
Bjorn Young, *Vice Pres*
Jeremy Blum, *Engineer*
John Andreadis, *VP Mktg*
Bill Nardone, *Branch Mgr*
EMP: 260
SALES (corp-wide): 775.5MM **Privately Held**
WEB: www.ellwoodgroup.com
SIC: 3462 Iron & steel forgings
PA: Ellwood Group, Inc.
600 Commercial Ave
Ellwood City PA 16117
724 752-3680

(G-4932)
ELLWOOD SAFETY APPLIANCE CO
Also Called: Sankey
927 Beaver Ave (16117-1820)
P.O. Box 831 (16117-0831)
PHONE................................724 758-7538
Richard Gray, *President*
Cory Gray, *Corp Secy*
Christian Gray, *Vice Pres*
EMP: 11
SQ FT: 5,000
SALES (est): 1.8MM **Privately Held**
WEB: www.ellwoodsafety.com
SIC: 3842 Braces, orthopedic

(G-4933)
GLASS MACHINERY WORKS LLC
594 Chapel Dr (16117-4602)
PHONE................................724 473-0666
Ed Schmalenberger,
Tammy Schmalenberger,
EMP: 3
SALES (est): 515.2K **Privately Held**
WEB: www.glassmw.com
SIC: 3211 Flat glass

(G-4934)
HALL INDUSTRIES INCORPORATED (PA)
514 Mecklem Rd (16117-3028)
PHONE................................724 752-2000
Jonathan C Hall, *President*
H Mark Hall, *Vice Pres*
John Schlafhauser, *Treasurer*
Frank Schlafhauser, *Admin Sec*
◆ EMP: 45 EST: 1966
SALES (est): 39.7MM **Privately Held**
SIC: 3451 3494 3471 Screw machine products; valves & pipe fittings; plating & polishing

(G-4935)
HALL INDUSTRIES INCORPORATED
1 Uss Industrial Park (16117-2169)
PHONE................................724 758-5522
Dave Mc Laughlin, *Branch Mgr*
EMP: 10
SALES (corp-wide): 39.7MM **Privately Held**
SIC: 3451 Screw machine products
PA: Hall Industries, Incorporated
514 Mecklem Rd
Ellwood City PA 16117
724 752-2000

(G-4936)
HALL TECHNICAL SERVICES LLC
514 Mecklem Ln (16117-3028)
PHONE................................724 752-2000
Jonathan C Hall, *Principal*
EMP: 7 EST: 2010
SALES (est): 690.7K **Privately Held**
SIC: 3451 Screw machine products

(G-4937)
I T C INDUSTRIAL TUBE CLEANING (PA)
416 Pittsburgh Cir (16117-2143)
P.O. Box 146 (16117-0146)
PHONE................................724 752-3100
Michael Antal, *President*
Brian Antal, *Vice Pres*
EMP: 14
SQ FT: 20,000
SALES (est): 2.5MM **Privately Held**
SIC: 3541 Machine tools, metal cutting type

(G-4938)
INDUSTRIAL EQP FABRICATORS INC
2 Early St (16117-2254)
PHONE................................724 752-8819
Robert Boyle, *President*
Karen L Wharrey, *Corp Secy*
James R Wharrey Jr, *Vice Pres*
John Tomon, *QC Mgr*
EMP: 14
SQ FT: 20,000
SALES: 2MM **Privately Held**
WEB: www.ief-fab.com
SIC: 3443 3498 Tanks, standard or custom fabricated: metal plate; chutes & troughs; weldments; fabricated pipe & fittings

(G-4939)
INTERNTNAL MTAL RCLAIMING CORP
Also Called: Inmetco
1 Inmetco Dr (16117-6231)
PHONE................................724 758-5515
James M Hensler, *CEO*
Mark Crooks, *Purch Mgr*
▲ EMP: 108
SQ FT: 400,000

SALES (est): 22.7MM **Privately Held**
WEB: www.inmetco.com
SIC: 4953 3341 Recycling, waste materials; secondary nonferrous metals
PA: American Zinc Recycling Llc
4955 Steubenville Pike
Pittsburgh PA 15205

(G-4940)
J & R EMERICK INC
140 Petrie Rd (16117-4608)
PHONE................................724 752-1251
John H Emerick Jr, *President*
Randall L Emerick, *Treasurer*
Carol L Emerick, *Admin Sec*
Christine Emerick, *Asst Sec*
EMP: 5 EST: 1969
SQ FT: 10,000
SALES (est): 967.4K **Privately Held**
SIC: 3441 Fabricated structural metal

(G-4941)
JAMES C RICHARDS
380 Stamm Hollow Rd (16117-5424)
PHONE................................724 758-9032
James Richards, *Owner*
EMP: 3
SALES (est): 50K **Privately Held**
SIC: 2448 2441 Pallets, wood; shipping cases, wood: nailed or lock corner

(G-4942)
JET INDUSTRIES LLC
700 2nd St (16117-2258)
PHONE................................724 758-5601
Don Williams, *CEO*
EMP: 100
SQ FT: 95,000
SALES (est): 17.4MM **Privately Held**
WEB: www.jetmetal.com
SIC: 3441 Fabricated structural metal

(G-4943)
LITE FIBERS LLC
812 Marion Ave (16117-3121)
PHONE................................724 758-0123
Peggy C Rau, *Mng Member*
Bob Rau,
EMP: 5
SALES (est): 1.3MM **Privately Held**
SIC: 2295 Coated fabrics, not rubberized

(G-4944)
MAMA DS BUNS INC
2555 River Rd (16117-3726)
PHONE................................724 752-1700
Cameron Wickline, *President*
EMP: 7
SALES: 500K **Privately Held**
SIC: 2051 Bakery, for home service delivery

(G-4945)
MARK GRIM
Also Called: Value Recharge Service
705 Lawrence Ave Ste 2 (16117-8519)
P.O. Box 461 (16117-0461)
PHONE................................724 758-2270
Mark Grim, *Owner*
EMP: 3
SQ FT: 8,000
SALES: 200K **Privately Held**
SIC: 3955 7629 5943 Print cartridges for laser & other computer printers; business machine repair, electric; office forms & supplies

(G-4946)
MEDART INC
199 Clyde St (16117-2277)
PHONE................................724 752-3555
Jeffrey D Pierce, *President*
James D Pierce, *CFO*
Craig Falk, *Info Tech Dir*
Dean Lutz, *Director*
▲ EMP: 48
SQ FT: 70,000
SALES (est): 12.6MM **Privately Held**
WEB: www.medartengine.com
SIC: 3089 3547 7629 3568 Synthetic resin finished products; straightening machinery (rolling mill equipment); bar mills; electrical repair shops; power transmission equipment

▲ = Import ▼=Export
◆ =Import/Export

(G-4947)
PRECISION METAL PDTS CO INC
1010 Shady Ln (16117-2568)
PHONE...............................724 758-5555
Alex Sansone, *President*
Jackie Sansone, *Admin Sec*
EMP: 14 **EST:** 1959
SQ FT: 10,000
SALES (est): 1MM **Privately Held**
SIC: 3562 Ball bearings & parts

(G-4948)
SABRE TBLAR STRCTURES - PA LLC
700 2nd St (16117-2258)
PHONE...............................724 201-9968
Ralph Gantz,
EMP: 100
SALES (est): 9.8MM
SALES (corp-wide): 6.3B **Privately Held**
SIC: 3441 Tower sections, radio & television transmission
HQ: Sabre Industries, Inc.
8653 E Highway 67
Alvarado TX 76009
817 852-1700

(G-4949)
SIGNS BY SAM
106 Elizabeth Way (16117-3180)
P.O. Box 576 (16117-0576)
PHONE...............................724 752-3711
Sam Ferrante, *Owner*
Elizabeth Ferrante, *Co-Owner*
EMP: 3
SALES (est): 302.3K **Privately Held**
SIC: 3993 Signs & advertising specialties

(G-4950)
STANDARD TOOL & MACHINE CO (PA)
Also Called: Hall Industries & Eqp Div
514 Mecklem Ln (16117-3028)
PHONE...............................724 758-5522
Jonathan C Hall, *President*
John Schlafhauser, *Vice Pres*
Bill Hanna, *QC Dir*
Irwin Dean, *Admin Sec*
EMP: 75 **EST:** 1944
SQ FT: 30,000
SALES (est): 12.8MM **Privately Held**
WEB: www.standard-hall.com
SIC: 3599 Machine shop, jobbing & repair

(G-4951)
STANDARD TOOL & MACHINE CO
Also Called: S T M Co
1 Uss Industrial Park (16117-2169)
PHONE...............................724 758-5522
Daqve McClaughlin, *Manager*
EMP: 35
SALES (corp-wide): 12.8MM **Privately Held**
WEB: www.standard-hall.com
SIC: 3599 3446 3444 3443 Machine shop, jobbing & repair; architectural metalwork; sheet metalwork; fabricated plate work (boiler shop); fabricated structural metal; miscellaneous metalwork
PA: Standard Tool & Machine Co.
514 Mecklem Ln
Ellwood City PA 16117
724 758-5522

(G-4952)
STEELE PRINT INC
420 Wampum Ave (16117-1203)
PHONE...............................724 758-6178
Arthur Smilek, *President*
EMP: 5
SQ FT: 3,600
SALES (est): 696.5K **Privately Held**
SIC: 2752 3993 3953 2761 Commercial printing, offset; signs & advertising specialties; marking devices; manifold business forms; commercial printing; packaging paper & plastics film, coated & laminated

(G-4953)
TALKIN STICK GAME CALLS INC
1285 Fairlane Dr (16117-3237)
PHONE...............................724 758-3869
Charles M Stang, *President*

Melissa Stang, *Vice Pres*
Linda Venn, *CFO*
EMP: 5
SQ FT: 2,000
SALES: 110K **Privately Held**
SIC: 3949 Game calls

(G-4954)
USA PRECISION
1957 Shaffer Rd (16117-7863)
PHONE...............................724 924-2838
Moulton L Ferguson Jr, *Partner*
George A Ferguson, *Partner*
EMP: 5
SALES: 260K **Privately Held**
SIC: 3599 Machine shop, jobbing & repair

(G-4955)
WOLVERINE PLASTICS INC
Also Called: Wpi Solutions
516 Mecklem Ln (16117-3028)
PHONE...............................724 856-5610
Adam Hall, *President*
Shirley T Dowling, *Corp Secy*
Paul G Persson Jr, *Vice Pres*
EMP: 40
SQ FT: 27,000
SALES (est): 8.4MM **Privately Held**
WEB: www.wpisolutions.com/contact.html
SIC: 3089 Injection molding of plastics; blow molded finished plastic products

Elm
Lancaster County

(G-4956)
EXECUTIVE PRINTING COMPANY INC
656 W Newport Rd (17521-5000)
P.O. Box 100 (17521-0100)
PHONE...............................717 664-3636
Joseph Martin, *President*
EMP: 19
SALES (est): 3MM **Privately Held**
WEB: www.executiveprintingcorp.com
SIC: 2752 Commercial printing, offset

Elmhurst Township
Lackawanna County

(G-4957)
EDWARDS CONCRETE
204 State Route 435 (18444-7692)
PHONE...............................570 842-8438
George Edwards, *Partner*
EMP: 10 **EST:** 2007
SALES (est): 1.3MM **Privately Held**
SIC: 3273 Ready-mixed concrete

(G-4958)
G F EDWARDS INC
204 State Route 435 (18444-7692)
PHONE...............................570 842-8438
Ed Edwards, *Principal*
EMP: 3 **EST:** 2013
SALES (est): 223.7K **Privately Held**
SIC: 3273 Ready-mixed concrete

(G-4959)
GF EDWARDS INC (PA)
Also Called: Edwards Sand & Stone
204 State Route 435 (18444-7692)
PHONE...............................570 842-8438
George F Edwards Jr, *President*
Frank P Edwards, *Treasurer*
Edward A Edwards, *Admin Sec*
EMP: 8 **EST:** 1965
SQ FT: 5,000
SALES (est): 4.6MM **Privately Held**
SIC: 3273 5211 Ready-mixed concrete; sand & gravel

Elton
Cambria County

(G-4960)
MIC INDUSTRIES INC
137 Bronze Dr (15934)
PHONE...............................814 266-8226
Frank Lucotic, *Branch Mgr*
EMP: 100
SQ FT: 22,000
SALES (est): 14.3MM
SALES (corp-wide): 33.8MM **Privately Held**
SIC: 3531 3549 Construction machinery; metalworking machinery
PA: M.I.C. Industries, Inc.
11911 Freedom Dr Ste 1000
Reston VA 20190
703 318-1900

Elverson
Chester County

(G-4961)
BIGSHOT ARCHERY LLC
2836 Creek Rd (19520-9161)
P.O. Box 731, Downingtown (19335-0731)
PHONE...............................610 873-0147
Alfred L Perelli, *Mng Member*
▲ **EMP:** 9
SALES (est): 111.2K **Privately Held**
SIC: 3949 Targets, archery & rifle shooting

(G-4962)
BRANDYWINE BRANCH DISTLRS LLC
350 Warwick Rd (19520-8919)
PHONE...............................610 901-3668
Robert D Avellino, *President*
EMP: 6
SALES (est): 504.1K **Privately Held**
SIC: 2085 Distilled & blended liquors

(G-4963)
FRENCH CREEK WOODWORKING INC
392 Trythall Rd (19520-8956)
PHONE...............................610 286-9295
Kent Laidig, *President*
Charles H Stone IV, *Vice Pres*
EMP: 3
SQ FT: 7,500
SALES: 310K **Privately Held**
SIC: 2521 Cabinets, office: wood; panel systems & partitions (free-standing), office: wood

(G-4964)
LAUREL PRODUCTS LLC
47 Park Ave (19520-9645)
P.O. Box 524 (19520-0524)
PHONE...............................610 286-2534
James Downing, *Director*
Ann Willis,
▲ **EMP:** 200
SALES (est): 2.2MM **Privately Held**
SIC: 2819 Industrial inorganic chemicals

(G-4965)
POLYMERIC SYSTEMS INC
Also Called: PSI
47 Park Ave (19520-9645)
P.O. Box 522 (19520-0522)
PHONE...............................610 286-2500
David P Willis Jr, *President*
Deborah Flint, *Corp Secy*
Ted Flint, *Vice Pres*
◆ **EMP:** 55
SQ FT: 70,000
SALES (est): 12.7MM
SALES (corp-wide): 15.3B **Publicly Held**
WEB: www.polymericsystems.com
SIC: 2891 2869 2851 2821 Sealants; industrial organic chemicals; paints & allied products; plastics materials & resins
HQ: Whitford Worldwide Company, Llc
47 Park Ave
Elverson PA 19520
610 286-3500

(G-4966)
SKOTZ MANUFACTURING INC (PA)
Also Called: Magne Rod
2676 Ridge Rd (19520-8911)
PHONE...............................610 286-0710
Scott Mulder, *President*
Sandy Sabatini, *Vice Pres*
Ellen Mulder, *Treasurer*
▲ **EMP:** 7
SQ FT: 8,500
SALES (est): 1.2MM **Privately Held**
WEB: www.magnerod.com
SIC: 2591 5023 Curtain & drapery rods, poles & fixtures; draperies

(G-4967)
WHITFORD CORPORATION (DH)
47 Park Ave (19520-9645)
P.O. Box 80 (19520-0080)
PHONE...............................610 286-3500
David P Willis Jr, *CEO*
Guglielmo Pernice, *Business Mgr*
Edward Sammond, *Business Mgr*
Marjorie Bonamico, *Purch Agent*
Robert Colmery, *Engineer*
◆ **EMP:** 72
SQ FT: 200,000
SALES (est): 18.8MM
SALES (corp-wide): 15.3B **Publicly Held**
WEB: www.whitfordww.com
SIC: 2891 2899 2816 Adhesives & sealants; chemical preparations; inorganic pigments
HQ: Whitford Worldwide Company, Llc
47 Park Ave
Elverson PA 19520
610 286-3500

(G-4968)
WHITFORD WORLDWIDE COMPANY LLC (HQ)
47 Park Ave (19520-9645)
P.O. Box 80 (19520-0080)
PHONE...............................610 286-3500
Anne Willis, *President*
Ginger Ernst, *Purch Agent*
Kurt Mecray, *Technical Mgr*
Tom Sheehan, *CFO*
Jessica Mannino, *Sales Staff*
◆ **EMP:** 73
SQ FT: 70,000
SALES (est): 88.1MM
SALES (corp-wide): 15.3B **Publicly Held**
SIC: 2891 Adhesives & sealants
PA: Ppg Industries, Inc.
1 Ppg Pl
Pittsburgh PA 15272
412 434-3131

(G-4969)
WHOLE HOUSE CABINETRY
30 Chrisman Dr (19520-9736)
PHONE...............................610 286-2901
Pamela Monaco, *President*
EMP: 3
SALES (est): 583.2K **Privately Held**
WEB: www.wholehousecabinetry.com
SIC: 2434 Wood kitchen cabinets

(G-4970)
WPMW INC
Also Called: West Philadelphia Mch Works
50 Shop Dr (19520-9307)
P.O. Box 49 (19520-0049)
PHONE...............................610 286-5071
Howard Griest, *President*
EMP: 11
SQ FT: 10,000
SALES (est): 1.7MM **Privately Held**
WEB: www.westphiladelphiamachineworks.com
SIC: 3599 Machine shop, jobbing & repair

Elysburg
Northumberland County

(G-4971)
BEAR GAP STONE INC
432 Quarry Rd (17824-7046)
PHONE...............................570 337-9831
Bob Kerris, *President*
Dale Kerris, *Vice Pres*

EMP: 8
SQ FT: 2,500
SALES (est): 660K **Privately Held**
SIC: 1429 Sandstone, crushed & broken-quarrying

(G-4972)
BLACK DIAMOND MINING INC
27 S Hickory St (17824-7199)
P.O. Box 81, Mount Carmel (17851-0081)
PHONE................................570 672-9917
EMP: 8
SALES (est): 676.2K **Privately Held**
SIC: 1499 Nonmetallic Mineral Mining

(G-4973)
DANSWAY INCORPORATED
159 Reed Rd (17824-9488)
P.O. Box 339 (17824-0339)
PHONE................................570 672-1550
Patricia Spano, *President*
Daniel Spano, *Vice Pres*
EMP: 5
SQ FT: 40,000
SALES (est): 1MM **Privately Held**
WEB: www.dansway.com
SIC: 5085 3823 Valves & fittings; pressure gauges, dial & digital

(G-4974)
DRUG PLASTICS AND GLASS CO INC
State Rd 4012 (17824)
P.O. Box 340 (17824-0340)
PHONE................................570 672-3215
Craig Olfon, *Branch Mgr*
EMP: 75
SALES (corp-wide): 166.9MM **Privately Held**
SIC: 3089 Plastic containers, except foam
PA: Drug Plastics And Glass Company, Inc.
1 Bottle Dr
Boyertown PA 19512
610 367-5000

(G-4975)
DRUG PLASTICS AND GLASS CO INC
6 Bottle Dr (17824)
P.O. Box 340 (17824-0340)
PHONE................................570 672-3215
Craig Olson, *Manager*
EMP: 80
SALES (corp-wide): 166.9MM **Privately Held**
WEB: www.drugplastics.com
SIC: 3085 Plastics bottles
PA: Drug Plastics And Glass Company, Inc.
1 Bottle Dr
Boyertown PA 19512
610 367-5000

(G-4976)
GREAT DANE TRAILERS INC
207 Progress Rd (17824-6400)
PHONE................................570 221-6920
Brad Harvey, *President*
EMP: 4
SALES (corp-wide): 1.5B **Privately Held**
SIC: 3715 Truck trailers
HQ: Great Dane Trailers, Inc.
131 Technology Cir
Savannah GA 31407
912 644-2100

(G-4977)
JACOB E LEISENRING LUMBER
1145 Bear Gap Rd (17824-9109)
PHONE................................570 672-9793
Jacob E Leisenring Jr, *President*
EMP: 3
SALES (est): 240K **Privately Held**
SIC: 2448 Pallets, wood

(G-4978)
PAPER MAGIC GROUP INC
Grand Award Division
210 Industrial Park Rd (17824-9770)
PHONE................................570 644-0842
Tom Schoepflin, *Opers-Prdtn-Mfg*
EMP: 450
SALES (corp-wide): 361.9MM **Publicly Held**
WEB: www.papermagic.com
SIC: 2771 2759 2675 Greeting cards; calendars: printing; die-cut paper & board

HQ: Paper Magic Group Inc.
54 Glenmra Ntl Blvd
Moosic PA 18507
570 961-3863

(G-4979)
POLAR TECH INDUSTRIES INC
1017 W Valley Ave (17824-7259)
PHONE................................800 423-2749
Virginia Pawelczyk, *Branch Mgr*
EMP: 30
SALES (est): 4.8MM
SALES (corp-wide): 10.8MM **Privately Held**
SIC: 3089 3086 Plastic containers, except foam; packaging & shipping materials, foamed plastic
PA: Polar Tech Industries, Inc.
415 E Railroad Ave
Genoa IL 60135
815 784-9000

(G-4980)
REKORD PRINTING CO
Also Called: Jansen Greetings
1 Madison Ave (17824-9666)
PHONE................................570 648-3231
Richard Jansen, *Partner*
Concetta Jansen, *Partner*
EMP: 5
SQ FT: 7,000
SALES (est): 650K **Privately Held**
WEB: www.jansengreetings.com
SIC: 2771 2752 2672 Greeting cards; commercial printing, lithographic; adhesive backed films, foams & foils

(G-4981)
SHERMAN COAL COMPANY INC
Rr 81 (17824)
P.O. Box 93 (17824-0093)
PHONE................................570 695-2690
William C Vought, *President*
EMP: 5
SALES (est): 460K **Privately Held**
SIC: 1231 5052 5989 Anthracite mining; coal; coal

(G-4982)
SPICES INC
463 Industrial Park Rd (17824-9700)
PHONE................................570 509-2340
Gregory V Patterson, *President*
EMP: 21
SQ FT: 12,750
SALES: 1.8MM **Privately Held**
SIC: 5411 2099 Grocery stores, independent; spices, including grinding

---

Emigsville
York County

(G-4983)
ABERDEEN ROAD COMPANY
Also Called: Herculite Products
105 Sinking Springs Ln (17318-2030)
P.O. Box 435 (17318-0435)
PHONE................................717 764-1192
Peter R McKernan, *President*
Leslie Haddad, *Business Mgr*
Paul R Moeller, *Corp Secy*
Alan Collier, *Vice Pres*
John Evans, *Vice Pres*
◆ **EMP:** 98 **EST:** 1999
SQ FT: 250,000
SALES (est): 34.4MM **Privately Held**
WEB: www.aberdeenroadcompany.com
SIC: 2295 8748 Laminating of fabrics; business consulting

(G-4984)
BECK & NESS WOODWORKING LLC
3337 N George St (17318-2024)
P.O. Box 461 (17318-0461)
PHONE................................717 764-3984
Mark R Ness, *Mng Member*
Walter E Beck II, *Mng Member*
EMP: 9
SQ FT: 18,000
SALES: 500K **Privately Held**
SIC: 2499 Decorative wood & woodwork

(G-4985)
BODYCOTE THERMAL PROC INC
Alpha Heat Treaters Div
270 Emig Rd (17318-2015)
P.O. Box 23 (17318-0023)
PHONE................................717 767-6757
Bob Bratsch, *Branch Mgr*
EMP: 27
SALES (corp-wide): 911.9MM **Privately Held**
WEB: www.mic-houston.com
SIC: 3398 Metal heat treating
HQ: Bodycote Thermal Processing, Inc.
12700 Park Central Dr # 700
Dallas TX 75251
214 904-2420

(G-4986)
DATUM FILING SYSTEMS INC (PA)
Also Called: Datum Storage Solutions
89 Church Rd (17318-2007)
P.O. Box 355 (17318-0355)
PHONE................................717 764-6350
Thomas Potter, *President*
Chris Potter, *Vice Pres*
Stephen Potter, *Vice Pres*
Jim Murtha, *Purch Mgr*
William Potter, *Treasurer*
◆ **EMP:** 127
SQ FT: 120,000
SALES (est): 20.9MM **Privately Held**
WEB: www.datumfiling.com
SIC: 2522 2521 Office furniture, except wood; wood office furniture

(G-4987)
HARMONY PRODUCTS INC
20 Church Rd (17318-2006)
P.O. Box 482 (17318-0482)
PHONE................................717 767-2779
Daniel T Guthrie, *President*
Daniel Guthrie, *President*
EMP: 25
SQ FT: 24,000
SALES (est): 4.1MM **Privately Held**
WEB: www.harmonyspi.com
SIC: 2431 Window screens, wood frame

(G-4988)
HEALTH-CHEM CORPORATION (PA)
101 Sinking Springs Ln (17318-2030)
PHONE................................717 764-1191
Andy E Yurowitz, *CEO*
Ronald J Burghauser, *CFO*
▲ **EMP:** 55
SQ FT: 61,000
SALES (est): 6.7MM **Privately Held**
SIC: 3841 8731 Surgical & medical instruments; commercial physical research

(G-4989)
HERCON LABORATORIES CORP
101 Sinking Springs Ln (17318-2030)
PHONE................................717 764-1191
Don Kauffman, *President*
EMP: 50
SALES (est): 8.8MM **Privately Held**
SIC: 2869 Industrial organic chemicals

(G-4990)
HERCON LABORATORIES INC
Also Called: Health Chem
101 Sinking Springs Ln (17318-2030)
P.O. Box 467 (17318-0467)
PHONE................................717 764-1191
Ronald Burghauser, *CEO*
Andy Yurowitz, *Chairman*
EMP: 52
SALES (est): 8.3MM
SALES (corp-wide): 6.7MM **Privately Held**
WEB: www.herconlabs.com
SIC: 2834 Drugs acting on the cardiovascular system, except diagnostic
PA: Health-Chem Corporation
101 Sinking Springs Ln
Emigsville PA 17318
717 764-1191

(G-4991)
HERCON PHARMACEUTICALS LLC
101 Sinking Springs Ln (17318-2030)
P.O. Box 467 (17318-0467)
PHONE................................717 764-1191
Ron Burghauser, *Mng Member*
▲ **EMP:** 41 **EST:** 2012
SALES (est): 10.5MM
SALES (corp-wide): 865MM **Privately Held**
SIC: 2834 Pharmaceutical preparations
PA: Cadila Healthcare Limited
Zydus Tower, Satellite Cross Road,
Ahmedabad GJ 38001
792 686-8100

(G-4992)
INDUSTRIAL SVC INSTLLATION INC
290 Emig Rd (17318-2015)
P.O. Box 436 (17318-0436)
PHONE................................717 767-1129
Steven Smith, *President*
Victor Prevost, *Vice Pres*
Dan Heathcote, *Buyer*
Benjamin Taylor, *Engineer*
David Anderson, *Design Engr*
EMP: 60
SQ FT: 60,000
SALES (est): 27.5MM **Privately Held**
WEB: www.isi-pa.com
SIC: 3535 Belt conveyor systems, general industrial use

(G-4993)
INTERNATIONAL VECTORS LTD
Also Called: Pen Fabricators
310 Emig Rd (17318)
PHONE................................717 767-4008
Jeffrey Kurth, *CEO*
Robert Hotaling, *President*
Robert Seitz, *Treasurer*
EMP: 30
SQ FT: 35,500
SALES (est): 5MM
SALES (corp-wide): 124MM **Privately Held**
WEB: www.penfab.com
SIC: 3081 3949 Vinyl film & sheet; sporting & athletic goods
PA: Wexco Incorporated
3490 Board Rd
York PA 17406
717 764-8585

(G-4994)
NEW CONCEPT MANUFACTURING LLC
320 Busser Rd (17318-2005)
P.O. Box 297 (17318-0297)
PHONE................................717 741-0840
Thomas Baughman, *President*
Don Hubbard, *Engineer*
Mel Portner, *CFO*
Don Chaisson, *Marketing Staff*
Krista Vaught, *Marketing Staff*
EMP: 160
SALES (est): 26.1MM **Privately Held**
WEB: www.newconceptmfg.com
SIC: 3089 Bands, plastic

(G-4995)
NEW CONCEPT TECHNOLOGY INC
320 Busser Rd (17318-2005)
P.O. Box 297 (17318-0297)
PHONE................................717 741-0840
Thomas Baughman, *President*
Mel Portner, *Principal*
Brian Trout, *Project Mgr*
Nick Campbell, *Info Tech Mgr*
▲ **EMP:** 38
SALES (est): 11.3MM **Privately Held**
SIC: 3089 Bands, plastic

(G-4996)
NEW STANDARD CORPORATION
3310 Connelly Rd (17318-2009)
PHONE................................717 764-2409
Jerry Rinehart, *Vice Pres*
EMP: 350
SALES (corp-wide): 130.8MM **Privately Held**
SIC: 3469 Metal stampings

▲ = Import ▼=Export
◆ =Import/Export

PA: New Standard Corporation
74 Commerce Way
York PA 17406
717 757-9450

(G-4997)
PRECISION TOOL & MFG CORP
70 Church Rd (17318-2006)
P.O. Box 305 (17318-0305)
PHONE...................................717 767-6454
Mark Painter, *President*
EMP: 7 **EST:** 1973
SQ FT: 10,000
SALES (est): 460K **Privately Held**
SIC: 3599 3549 3443 Mfg Industrial Machinery Mfg Metalworking Mach Mfg Dies/Tools/Jigs/Fixt Mfg Fabricated Plate Wrk

(G-4998)
R/W CONNECTION INC
Also Called: Advanced Fluid Connectors
30 Aberdeen Rd (17318-2001)
P.O. Box 451 (17318-0451)
PHONE...................................717 767-3660
Richard Bare, *Branch Mgr*
EMP: 6
SALES (corp-wide): 3.1B **Privately Held**
SIC: 3492 3052 5085 3053 Fluid power valves & hose fittings; air line or air brake hose, rubber or rubberized fabric; industrial supplies; gasket materials
HQ: R/W Connection, Inc.
936 Links Ave
Landisville PA 17538
717 898-5257

(G-4999)
SHARRETTS PLATING CO INC
3315 Connelly Rd (17318-2010)
P.O. Box 157 (17318-0157)
PHONE...................................717 767-6702
Tamara L Friese, *President*
Stephen T Sharretts, *Vice Pres*
Stephen Sharretts, *VP Bus Dvlpt*
Kelly J Renn, *Treasurer*
Thomas P Sharretts, *Admin Sec*
▲ **EMP:** 55
SQ FT: 168,000
SALES (est): 7.2MM **Privately Held**
WEB: www.sharrettsplating.com
SIC: 3471 Electroplating of metals or formed products

(G-5000)
STRINE CORRUGATED PRODUCTS
150 Emig Rd (17318-2012)
P.O. Box 491 (17318-0491)
PHONE...................................717 764-4800
Donald Reidle, *Owner*
Brad Strine, *Owner*
EMP: 4
SQ FT: 13,400
SALES (est): 705.7K **Privately Held**
SIC: 2653 Boxes, corrugated: made from purchased materials

(G-5001)
THE REYNOLDS AND REYNOLDS CO
Also Called: THE REYNOLDS AND REYNOLDS COMPANY (INC)
York County Industrial Pa (17318)
PHONE...................................717 767-5264
Bruce Arvin, *Principal*
EMP: 20
SALES (corp-wide): 1.5B **Privately Held**
WEB: www.reyrey.com
SIC: 2761 Manifold business forms
HQ: The Reynolds And Reynolds Company
1 Reynolds Way
Kettering OH 45430
937 485-2000

(G-5002)
TRENWYTH INDUSTRIES INC (DH)
1 Connelly Rd (17318-2008)
P.O. Box 438 (17318-0438)
PHONE...................................717 767-6868
Jay Toland, *President*
Jason Schmidt, *Vice Pres*
John Stiles, *CFO*
Patrick Smith, *Manager*

▼ **EMP:** 56 **EST:** 1975
SQ FT: 4,000
SALES (est): 19.2MM
SALES (corp-wide): 29.7B **Privately Held**
WEB: www.trenwyth.com
SIC: 3271 Blocks, concrete: glazed face
HQ: Oldcastle Apg Northeast, Inc.
13555 Wellington Cntr Cir
Gainesville VA 20155
703 365-7070

(G-5003)
YORK SAW & KNIFE COMPANY INC
Also Called: Oleson Saw Technology
295 Emig Rd (17318)
PHONE...................................717 767-6402
Michael Pickard, *President*
James O Pickard Sr, *Chairman*
Todd Gladfelter, *Treasurer*
Mary Pickard, *Admin Sec*
▲ **EMP:** 42
SQ FT: 62,000
SALES (est): 11.6MM **Privately Held**
SIC: 3423 3425 Knives, agricultural or industrial; saw blades for hand or power saws

Emlenton
Venango County

(G-5004)
ALLEGHENY MTN HARDWOOD FLRG
Also Called: Allegheny Mtn Hardwood Flrg
501 Main St (16373-9305)
P.O. Box 659 (16373-0659)
PHONE...................................724 867-9441
Larry Hickman, *President*
Dennis Hickman, *Vice Pres*
EMP: 14
SALES (est): 1.3MM **Privately Held**
SIC: 2426 Furniture stock & parts, hardwood; flooring, hardwood

(G-5005)
ALLEGHENY STRL COMPONENTS INC
3778 Oneida Valley Rd (16373-2514)
PHONE...................................724 867-1100
EMP: 4
SALES (est): 470.6K **Privately Held**
SIC: 3441 1752 Joists, open web steel: long-span series; wood floor installation & refinishing

(G-5006)
BERRYS BEVERAGE INC
613 Main St (16373-9207)
P.O. Box 754 (16373-0754)
PHONE...................................724 867-9480
Michael Berry, *Principal*
EMP: 6
SALES (est): 316.4K **Privately Held**
SIC: 2082 Beer (alcoholic beverage)

(G-5007)
FRB MACHINE INC
119 College Street Ext (16373-7809)
PHONE...................................724 867-0111
Mark R Brosnahan, *President*
Evelyn Brosnahan, *Vice Pres*
EMP: 8 **EST:** 1968
SQ FT: 8,500
SALES (est): 1.2MM **Privately Held**
WEB: www.frbmachine.com
SIC: 3599 Machine shop, jobbing & repair

(G-5008)
FUCHS LUBRICANTS CO
Also Called: Fuchs Grafo Colloids Division
105 8th St (16373)
PHONE...................................724 867-5000
Dr Anand Kakar, *Technical Mgr*
Tim Russell, *Branch Mgr*
EMP: 30
SALES (corp-wide): 2.9B **Privately Held**
WEB: www.fuchs.com
SIC: 5172 2992 2899 2891 Lubricating oils & greases; lubricating oils & greases; chemical preparations; adhesives & sealants; paints & allied products

HQ: Fuchs Lubricants Co.
17050 Lathrop Ave
Harvey IL 60426
708 333-8901

(G-5009)
GES GRAPHITE
2 Penn West Way (16373-2530)
PHONE...................................205 838-0820
EMP: 8
SALES (est): 1.1MM **Privately Held**
SIC: 3624 Carbon & graphite products

(G-5010)
HICKMAN LUMBER COMPANY (PA)
501 Main St (16373-9305)
P.O. Box 130 (16373-0130)
PHONE...................................724 867-9441
Larry W Hickman, *President*
Gayle Hickman, *Corp Secy*
Dennis Hickman, *Vice Pres*
EMP: 5 **EST:** 1948
SQ FT: 21,700
SALES (est): 6.2MM **Privately Held**
WEB: www.hickmanwoods.com
SIC: 2421 Lumber: rough, sawed or planed

(G-5011)
HICKMAN LUMBER COMPANY
Also Called: Allegeny Mountain Hardwood
4478 Route 38 (16373)
PHONE...................................814 797-0555
APT Best, *Branch Mgr*
EMP: 10
SALES (corp-wide): 6.2MM **Privately Held**
WEB: www.hickmanwoods.com
SIC: 2421 Lumber: rough, sawed or planed
PA: Hickman Lumber Company
501 Main St
Emlenton PA 16373
724 867-9441

(G-5012)
JAMES IRWIN
Also Called: Irwin Printing
170 De Ly Bro Rd (16373-7814)
PHONE...................................724 867-6083
James Irwin, *Owner*
EMP: 3
SQ FT: 2,800
SALES (est): 292.5K **Privately Held**
SIC: 2752 Commercial printing, lithographic

(G-5013)
OXBOW ACTIVATED CARBON LLC
3539 Oneida Valley Rd (16373)
PHONE...................................724 791-2411
Kenneth Schaeffer, *President*
EMP: 17
SALES (corp-wide): 602.2MM **Privately Held**
SIC: 2819 Charcoal (carbon), activated
HQ: Oxbow Activated Carbon Llc
1601 Forum Pl Ste 1400
West Palm Beach FL 33401
561 907-5400

(G-5014)
PROGRESS NEWS
Also Called: Staab Typographic
410 Main St (16373)
PHONE...................................724 867-2435
David Staab, *Owner*
EMP: 5 **EST:** 1885
SQ FT: 3,200
SALES (est): 405K **Privately Held**
WEB: www.progressnews.net
SIC: 2711 Newspapers: publishing only, not printed on site

(G-5015)
TCC PENNWEST LLC
Also Called: Penn West Homes
4 Penn West Way (16373-2530)
PHONE...................................724 867-0047
Tracy Kirby, *General Mgr*
Barry S Shein, *Vice Pres*
EMP: 170
SQ FT: 7,000

SALES (est): 23.6MM
SALES (corp-wide): 134.8MM **Privately Held**
WEB: www.pennwesthomes.com
SIC: 2452 Modular homes, prefabricated, wood
PA: The Commodore Corporation
1423 Lincolnway E
Goshen IN 46526
574 533-7100

(G-5016)
WLH ENTERPRISE
5939 Route 38 (16373-1609)
PHONE...................................814 498-2040
Sockey Dill, *Principal*
EMP: 3
SALES (est): 290.7K **Privately Held**
SIC: 2421 Sawmills & planing mills, general

Emmaus
Lehigh County

(G-5017)
A & D FASHIONS INC
55 S 7th St (18049-3716)
P.O. Box 532 (18049-0532)
PHONE...................................610 967-1440
Wayne G Chenevert, *President*
Nancy Chenevert, *Vice Pres*
EMP: 3
SQ FT: 20,000
SALES: 100K **Privately Held**
SIC: 2395 Embroidery products, except schiffli machine

(G-5018)
ADVANCED THERMAL SOLUTIONS LLC
154 E Minor St (18049-4103)
P.O. Box 288 (18049-0288)
PHONE...................................610 966-2500
Antoinette Martin, *Principal*
George Apgar, *Sales Staff*
Alan Silverstein,
EMP: 7
SALES (est): 749.1K **Privately Held**
SIC: 3585 Refrigeration & heating equipment

(G-5019)
AMERICAN MLLWK & CABINETRY INC
840 Broad St (18049-3607)
PHONE...................................610 965-0040
George Reitz, *CEO*
David Reitz, *Vice Pres*
John Hennessy, *CFO*
EMP: 25
SQ FT: 31,000
SALES (est): 6.5MM **Privately Held**
SIC: 2434 2431 5031 Wood kitchen cabinets; millwork; millwork

(G-5020)
BAREBO INC
3840 Main Rd E (18049-9598)
PHONE...................................610 965-6018
Christopher V Barebo, *President*
Theresa Barebo, *Chairman*
Carla V Barebo, *Vice Pres*
Charles A Barebo, *Shareholder*
EMP: 42
SQ FT: 42,000
SALES (est): 7.9MM **Privately Held**
WEB: www.otterbine.com
SIC: 3569 3561 3523 Gas producers, generators & other gas related equipment; pumps & pumping equipment; farm machinery & equipment

(G-5021)
BREAKTHROUGH PUBLICATIONS INC
3 Iroquois St (18049-2817)
P.O. Box 693 (18049-0693)
PHONE...................................610 928-4061
Peter Ognidene, *President*
EMP: 3

GEOGRAPHIC

SALES (est): 44.8K **Privately Held**
WEB: www.booksonhorses.com
SIC: **2731** 2721 5192 Books: publishing only; periodicals: publishing only; books, periodicals & newspapers

(G-5022)
BROC SUPPLY CO INC
30 S Keystone Ave (18049-4110)
PHONE..................................610 433-4646
Christopher C Birosik, *President*
Christopher D Romig, *Treasurer*
EMP: 40
SQ FT: 1,000
SALES (est): 4.1MM **Privately Held**
SIC: **2541** Counters or counter display cases, wood; cabinets, except refrigerated: show, display, etc.: wood

(G-5023)
CLEMENS FOOD GROUP LLC
Also Called: Hatfield Quality Meats
4591 Colebrook Ave (18049-1026)
PHONE..................................215 368-2500
Kris Traub, *Plant Supt*
Galen Cassel, *Manager*
EMP: 65
SQ FT: 47,289
SALES (corp-wide): 705.7MM **Privately Held**
WEB: www.hatfieldqualitymeatsfoodservice.com
SIC: **2011** Meat packing plants
HQ: Clemens Food Group, Llc
2700 Clemens Rd
Hatfield PA 19440
215 368-2500

(G-5024)
CREAMERY ON MAIN
4665 Mill Rd (18049-5243)
PHONE..................................610 928-1500
EMP: 4
SALES (est): 269.7K **Privately Held**
SIC: **2021** Creamery butter

(G-5025)
CVIP INC
801 Broad St (18049-3600)
PHONE..................................610 967-1525
David Nguyen, *President*
Jeffery Dorn, *Principal*
Phil Giagnacova, *Principal*
Dave Smith, *Principal*
▲ EMP: 52
SQ FT: 65,000
SALES: 12.1MM **Privately Held**
WEB: www.cvipinc.com
SIC: **3498** Fabricated pipe & fittings

(G-5026)
G&W SOLUTIONS INC
121 Main St (18049-4008)
PHONE..................................610 704-6959
EMP: 4
SALES (est): 227.2K **Privately Held**
SIC: **3643** Mfg Conductive Wiring Devices

(G-5027)
GLOBAL INSERTING SYSTEMS LLC
Also Called: Gis
88 Chestnut Hill Rd (18049-5508)
PHONE..................................610 217-3019
Randy Seidel, *CEO*
EMP: 20
SQ FT: 30,000
SALES: 3.2MM **Privately Held**
SIC: **3555** Printing trades machinery

(G-5028)
IN A WEEK GUARANTEED INC
2701 Sickle Cir (18049-4630)
PHONE..................................610 965-7700
Gabor Czeczon, *President*
EMP: 5
SALES (est): 348.9K **Privately Held**
SIC: **1389** Construction, repair & dismantling services

(G-5029)
J G PRESS INC
Also Called: Compost Science & Utilization
419 State Ave Ste 1 (18049-3097)
PHONE..................................610 967-4135
Rill Ann Goldstein, *President*

Nora Goldstein, *Vice Pres*
EMP: 7
SQ FT: 1,500
SALES (est): 600K **Privately Held**
WEB: www.biocycle.net
SIC: **2721** 8748 Magazines: publishing only, not printed on site; business consulting

(G-5030)
JABOA ENTERPRISES INC
202 S 6th St (18049-3732)
PHONE..................................610 703-5185
Christopher Kline, *CEO*
Michael Irwin, *President*
▲ EMP: 12
SQ FT: 4,000
SALES: 1.5MM **Privately Held**
WEB: www.jaboa.com
SIC: **2542** Fixtures: display, office or store: except wood

(G-5031)
JAS WHOLESALE & SUPPLY CO INC
Also Called: Ice Cream World
4501 Colebrook Ave (18049-1026)
PHONE..................................610 967-0663
Allen Maciver, *President*
James Schmoyer, *President*
Kinberly Maclver, *Corp Secy*
Ruth Watkins, *Office Mgr*
EMP: 30
SQ FT: 2,800
SALES (est): 3.1MM **Privately Held**
WEB: www.jaswholesale.com
SIC: **5451** 2024 5143 Ice cream (packaged); ice cream & frozen desserts; ice cream & ices

(G-5032)
LEHIGH VALLEY CHRONICLE
49 N 6th St (18049-2431)
PHONE..................................610 965-1636
David Hittinger, *Principal*
EMP: 3 EST: 2016
SALES (est): 95.7K **Privately Held**
SIC: **2711** Newspapers

(G-5033)
M SHANKEN COMMUNICATIONS INC
Also Called: Whisky Advocate
167 Main St (18049-4018)
PHONE..................................610 967-1083
John Hansell, *Editor*
EMP: 5
SALES (corp-wide): 26.6MM **Privately Held**
SIC: **2721** Magazines: publishing & printing
PA: M. Shanken Communications, Inc.
825 8th Ave Fl 33
New York NY 10019
212 684-4224

(G-5034)
MICHAEL R SKRIP EXCAVATING
420 S 6th St (18049-3731)
PHONE..................................610 965-5331
Michael R Skrip, *Owner*
Elizabeth R Skrip, *Admin Sec*
EMP: 4
SALES (est): 391.5K **Privately Held**
SIC: **1389** Excavating slush pits & cellars

(G-5035)
OAK HILL CONTROLS LLC (PA)
3433 Oak Hill Rd (18049-4422)
PHONE..................................610 967-3985
Judy Butterfield, *Principal*
Judith A Butterfield, *Mng Member*
Roger R Butterfield, *Principal*
EMP: 4
SALES (est): 2.2MM **Privately Held**
WEB: www.oakhillcontrols.com
SIC: **3495** Wire springs

(G-5036)
OMNITECH AUTOMATION INC
316 Wood St (18049-3932)
PHONE..................................610 965-3279
Fred Hafer Jr, *President*
Donald Jackson Sr, *Exec VP*
EMP: 20
SQ FT: 10,000

SALES (est): 4.4MM **Privately Held**
WEB: www.oai-automation.com
SIC: **3549** Assembly machines, including robotic; welding & cutting apparatus & accessories

(G-5037)
ONLINE DATA SYSTEMS INC
Also Called: Xperia
22 S 2nd St (18049-3984)
PHONE..................................610 967-5821
Gene Bonett, *President*
Kathy Orloski, *Prgrmr*
EMP: 20
SQ FT: 11,000
SALES (est): 6.2MM **Privately Held**
WEB: www.xperiasolutions.com
SIC: **3577** Computer peripheral equipment

(G-5038)
OTTERBINE BAREBO INC
3840 Main Rd E (18049-9579)
PHONE..................................610 965-6018
Theresa Barebo, *CEO*
EMP: 6
SQ FT: 15,262
SALES (est): 801.5K **Privately Held**
SIC: **3589** Water treatment equipment, industrial

(G-5039)
PARKWAY PRINTING
326 S 2nd St (18049-3981)
PHONE..................................610 928-3433
Ron Billman, *Principal*
Ronald Billman, *Webmaster*
EMP: 3
SALES (est): 221.8K **Privately Held**
SIC: **2752** Commercial printing, lithographic

(G-5040)
PRATT INDUSTRIES USA INC
726 Broad St (18049-3605)
PHONE..................................610 967-6027
Peter Tisi, *General Mgr*
EMP: 64
SALES (corp-wide): 2.5B **Privately Held**
SIC: **2621** 2653 Packaging paper; boxes, corrugated: made from purchased materials
PA: Pratt Industries, Inc.
1800 Sarasota Busin Ste C
Conyers GA 30013
770 918-5678

(G-5041)
REINHARDT AWNING CO
550 Dalton St (18049-3009)
PHONE..................................610 965-2544
Neil B Reinhardt, *Owner*
EMP: 5
SQ FT: 2,000
SALES (est): 639.3K **Privately Held**
SIC: **2394** Awnings, fabric: made from purchased materials; liners & covers, fabric: made from purchased materials

(G-5042)
SCHNECK ART OPTICAL CO
720 Harrison St (18049-2211)
PHONE..................................610 965-4066
Susan Schneck, *Owner*
EMP: 13
SQ FT: 3,600
SALES (est): 1.6MM **Privately Held**
SIC: **3851** Ophthalmic goods

(G-5043)
SUPERIOR DUAL LAMINATES INC
750 Broad St (18049-3605)
PHONE..................................610 965-9061
Robert Bunner, *President*
William Ng, *Principal*
Ivan Tim, *Principal*
Guyle McCuaig, *Vice Pres*
EMP: 3 EST: 2016
SALES (est): 121.7K **Privately Held**
SIC: **3083** Thermoplastic laminates: rods, tubes, plates & sheet

(G-5044)
TCW TECHNOLOGIES LLC
2955 Main Rd E (18049-4742)
PHONE..................................610 928-3420

Robert Yerman, *Mng Member*
EMP: 9
SALES (est): 645.1K **Privately Held**
SIC: **3812** Automatic pilots, aircraft

(G-5045)
TRILLION SOURCE INC
1438 Chestnut St Unit 4 (18049-1913)
P.O. Box 505, Macungie (18062-0505)
PHONE..................................631 949-2304
Afolabi Oyerokun, *CEO*
▲ EMP: 10
SALES (est): 2.3MM **Privately Held**
SIC: **2392** 8748 Household furnishings; business consulting

(G-5046)
VOICESTARS INC
214 N 5th St Apt 2 (18049-2461)
PHONE..................................305 902-9666
Mark Paul Braunstein, *President*
EMP: 3
SALES (est): 139.3K **Privately Held**
WEB: www.voicestars.net
SIC: **7372** 7361 Application computer software; employment agencies

(G-5047)
XTREME HUNTING PRODUCTS
4972 Chestnut St (18049-5105)
PHONE..................................610 967-4588
Ed Felegy, *Partner*
EMP: 4
SALES (est): 170K **Privately Held**
WEB: www.xtremehunting.com
SIC: **3949** Hunting equipment

Emporium
Cameron County

(G-5048)
ALSTOM SIGNALING OPERATION LLC
Also Called: GE Transportation Sys
55 S Pine St (15834-1529)
PHONE..................................814 486-0235
Edward Smith, *Branch Mgr*
EMP: 1123
SALES (corp-wide): 1.5B **Privately Held**
WEB: www.proyard.com
SIC: **3621** Electric motor & generator parts
PA: Alstom Signaling Operation, Llc
2901 E Lake Rd Bldg 122
Erie PA 16531
800 825-3178

(G-5049)
ART & INK
Also Called: Hoffman, Catherine
6 W 6th St (15834-1255)
PHONE..................................814 486-0606
Catherine Hoffman, *Partner*
Shirley Condon, *Partner*
EMP: 3
SALES: 70K **Privately Held**
SIC: **2759** Screen printing

(G-5050)
B & B TOOL AND DIE INC
5878 Beechwood Rd (15834-2258)
PHONE..................................814 486-5355
Tony Gerg, *President*
James Brown, *Corp Secy*
EMP: 18 EST: 1985
SQ FT: 34,900
SALES (est): 2.8MM **Privately Held**
SIC: **3399** 3599 Powder, metal; machine shop, jobbing & repair

(G-5051)
CALDWELL CORPORATION
116 W 2nd St (15834-1265)
P.O. Box 230 (15834-0230)
PHONE..................................814 486-3493
Joseph Caldwell, *President*
Thomas Caldwell, *Vice Pres*
EMP: 30
SQ FT: 290,000
SALES (est): 3.9MM **Privately Held**
WEB: www.caldwell-corp.com
SIC: **7539** 3624 7699 7692 Machine shop, automotive; fibers, carbon & graphite; cleaning services; welding repair

▲ = Import ▼=Export
◆ =Import/Export

(G-5052)
CAMERON COUNTY COMMUNITY CHEST
33 E 4th St (15834-1459)
P.O. Box 134 (15834-0134)
PHONE..................................814 486-0612
EMP: 3
SALES (est): 129.1K Privately Held
SIC: 2711 Newspapers: publishing only,
not printed on site

(G-5053)
CAMERON COUNTY ECHO INC
300 S Broad St Ste 1 (15834-1474)
P.O. Box 308 (15834-0308)
PHONE..................................814 486-3711
David Brown, President
Nancy Fragale, Vice Pres
Julie Brown, Treasurer
Steve Brown, Admin Sec
EMP: 8
SQ FT: 10,000
SALES (est): 574.5K Privately Held
SIC: 2711 2752 Commercial printing &
newspaper publishing combined; com-
mercial printing, lithographic

(G-5054)
CROWELL METAL FABRICATION
221 E 2nd St (15834-1306)
PHONE..................................814 486-2664
EMP: 4
SALES (est): 260K Privately Held
SIC: 3441 Structural Metal Fabrication

(G-5055)
EMBASSY POWDERED METALS INC
70 Airport Rd (15834-2002)
P.O. Box 344 (15834-0344)
PHONE..................................814 486-1011
Steve Aharrah, President
Randy Cooney, Vice Pres
James Belin, Treasurer
Jason Novak, Sales Mgr
Alan Ramsey, Officer
EMP: 38
SQ FT: 21,000
SALES: 6.5MM Privately Held
WEB: www.embassypowderedmetals.com
SIC: 3399 Powder, metal

(G-5056)
EMPORIUM CONTRACTORS INC
Rich Valley Rd Rr 46 (15834)
PHONE..................................814 562-0631
Paul Abriatis Sr, President
EMP: 35
SQ FT: 3,000
SALES (est): 3.9MM Privately Held
SIC: 3273 1771 Ready-mixed concrete;
concrete work

(G-5057)
EMPORIUM HARDWOODS OPER CO LLC
15970 Route 120 (15834-3756)
PHONE..................................814 486-3764
Everett Heitz, Finance Dir
Andrew Becker,
▲ EMP: 130
SQ FT: 219,500
SALES: 28.6MM Privately Held
SIC: 2421 5031 Sawmills & planing mills,
general; lumber, plywood & millwork

(G-5058)
EMPORIUM POWDERED METAL INC
140 W 2nd St Ste 3 (15834-1295)
P.O. Box 342 (15834-0342)
PHONE..................................814 486-0136
Joe Holjencin, President
Thomas J Holjencin, Vice Pres
EMP: 15
SQ FT: 32,000
SALES (est): 1.2MM Privately Held
SIC: 3399 Powder, metal

(G-5059)
EMPORIUM SECONDARIES INC
11769 Route 120 (15834-3239)
PHONE..................................814 486-1881
Michael Singer, Owner
Gregory Secco, Vice Pres

EMP: 16
SQ FT: 10,000
SALES: 700K Privately Held
SIC: 3399 Powder, metal

(G-5060)
GKN SINTER METALS LLC
1 Airport Rd (15834-2001)
P.O. Box 493 (15834-0493)
PHONE..................................814 486-3314
Sean Clark, Engineer
Steve Krise, Branch Mgr
Robert Young, Technology
EMP: 900
SALES (corp-wide): 2.7B Privately Held
SIC: 3312 Blast furnaces & steel mills
HQ: Gkn Sinter Metals, Llc
2200 N Opdyke Rd
Auburn Hills MI 48326
248 296-7832

(G-5061)
GKN SINTER METALS LLC
15420 Route 120 (15834-3742)
P.O. Box 493 (15834-0493)
PHONE..................................814 486-9234
Seifi Ghasemi, CEO
EMP: 800
SALES (corp-wide): 2.7B Privately Held
SIC: 3399 Powder, metal
HQ: Gkn Sinter Metals, Llc
2200 N Opdyke Rd
Auburn Hills MI 48326
248 296-7832

(G-5062)
GUARDIAN TACTICAL INC
205 S Maple St (15834-1232)
PHONE..................................814 558-6761
EMP: 3
SALES (est): 226.8K Privately Held
SIC: 3421 3599 Knife blades & blanks;
custom machinery

(G-5063)
J S H ENTERPRISES INC
547 E Allegany Ave 1 (15834-1544)
PHONE..................................814 486-3939
James Hornung, President
Caran Pdekai, Manager
EMP: 25
SALES (est): 4.6MM Privately Held
SIC: 3399 Metal powders, pastes & flakes

(G-5064)
JAMES A & PAULETTE M BERRY
Also Called: Berry Enterprises Tool and Die
34 N Cherry St (15834-1453)
PHONE..................................814 486-2323
James A Berry, Co-Owner
Paulette M Berry, Co-Owner
EMP: 3
SALES (est): 265.8K Privately Held
SIC: 3312 Tool & die steel

(G-5065)
KAL-CAMERON MANUFACTURING
Also Called: Pro America Premium Tools
221 E 2nd St (15834-1306)
P.O. Box 391 (15834-0391)
PHONE..................................814 486-3394
Tom Hayden, General Mgr
EMP: 14
SQ FT: 54,000
SALES (corp-wide): 23.1MM Privately Held
SIC: 5072 3423 3462 Hand tools; hand &
edge tools; iron & steel forgings
HQ: Kal-Cameron Manufacturing Corp
4265 Puente Ave
Baldwin Park CA 91706
626 338-7308

(G-5066)
KEYSTONE AUTOMATIC TECH INC
Also Called: Kat
1 S Maple St (15834-1228)
PHONE..................................814 486-0513
Barry Alexander, President
Charles Blumle, Treasurer
EMP: 30
SQ FT: 55,000

SALES (est): 6.6MM Privately Held
WEB: www.keystoneautomatic.com
SIC: 3496 3694 3452 Miscellaneous fabricated wire products; engine electrical
equipment; bolts, nuts, rivets & washers

(G-5067)
LEW-HOC WOOD PRODUCTS INC
4725 Rich Valley Rd (15834-5025)
PHONE..................................814 486-0359
David Lewis, President
Dale Lewis, Treasurer
EMP: 40
SQ FT: 3,500
SALES (est): 2.6MM
SALES (corp-wide): 3.8MM Privately
Held
WEB: www.lewhoc.com
SIC: 2426 2431 Lumber, hardwood dimen-
sion; panel work, wood
PA: Lewis & Hockenberry Inc
4725 Rich Valley Rd
Emporium PA 15834
814 486-0359

(G-5068)
LEWIS & HOCKENBERRY INC (PA)
4725 Rich Valley Rd (15834-5025)
PHONE..................................814 486-0359
David Lewis, President
▼ EMP: 24 EST: 1945
SQ FT: 40,000
SALES (est): 3.8MM Privately Held
WEB: www.lewhoc.com
SIC: 2426 Hardwood dimension & flooring
mills

(G-5069)
MICRON RESEARCH CORPORATION
13746 Route 120 (15834-3540)
P.O. Box 269 (15834-0269)
PHONE..................................814 486-2444
Fax: 814 486-0605
EMP: 20
SQ FT: 18,000
SALES (est): 2.8MM Privately Held
SIC: 3624 Mfg Carbon/Graphite Products

(G-5070)
NORTH AMERICAN TOOLING INC
6834 Beechwood Rd Ste 2 (15834-2374)
PHONE..................................814 486-3700
Craig Schloder, President
EMP: 6
SQ FT: 5,000
SALES (est): 804.8K Privately Held
SIC: 3544 3599 Special dies & tools; ma-
chine shop, jobbing & repair

(G-5071)
PENNSYLVANIA SINTERED MTLS INC
Also Called: PSM Brownco
2950 Whittimore Rd (15834-2032)
P.O. Box 308 (15834-0308)
PHONE..................................814 486-1768
Steven Brown, President
Julie Brown, Owner
EMP: 34
SQ FT: 50,000
SALES: 5.6MM Privately Held
WEB: www.psmbrownco.com
SIC: 3399 Powder, metal

(G-5072)
QUALITY COMPACTED METALS INC
513 E 2nd St (15834-1505)
PHONE..................................814 486-1500
Scott A Horning, President
Don Reed, Corp Secy
Jeffery Young, Vice Pres
EMP: 12
SQ FT: 9,500
SALES: 1.2MM Privately Held
WEB: www.compactedmetals.com
SIC: 3399 Powder, metal

(G-5073)
RACOH PRODUCTS INC
1751 Rich Valley Rd (15834-3887)
PHONE..................................814 486-3288
Nancy Housler, President
Susan Anthony, Corp Secy
EMP: 40
SQ FT: 5,000
SALES (est): 4.6MM Privately Held
SIC: 3599 Custom machinery

(G-5074)
ROBERT J BROWN
228 W 4th St (15834-1046)
P.O. Box 308 (15834-0308)
PHONE..................................814 486-1768
Robert J Brown, Owner
EMP: 25
SALES (est): 1.6MM Privately Held
SIC: 3524 Lawn & garden mowers & ac-
cessories

(G-5075)
SMOKER LOGGING INC
Rich Vly Rr 1 (15834)
PHONE..................................814 486-2570
George Smoker, CEO
EMP: 4
SALES (est): 483.8K Privately Held
SIC: 2411 Logging camps & contractors

(G-5076)
SUPERIOR TOOLING TECH INC
12027 Route 120 (15834-3245)
PHONE..................................814 486-9498
Rich Guisto, President
Sheila Guisto, Vice Pres
EMP: 10
SQ FT: 7,200
SALES (est): 1.9MM Privately Held
SIC: 3312 Tool & die steel & alloys

(G-5077)
TEUTECH LLC
227 Barton St (15834-2011)
PHONE..................................814 486-1896
Tony Steer, President
Teutech Holdings, Mng Member
EMP: 40
SALES: 3MM Privately Held
SIC: 3581 Mechanisms & parts for auto-
matic vending machines

Endeavor
Forest County

(G-5078)
A & S PRODUCTION INC
666 Yellow Hammer Rd (16322)
P.O. Box 189 (16322-0189)
PHONE..................................814 463-9310
David R Schrader, President
Carol Schrader, Admin Sec
EMP: 7
SALES (est): 760K Privately Held
SIC: 1381 Service well drilling

(G-5079)
ITL CORP
Also Called: Endeavor Lumber
Russell St Rr 666 (16322)
P.O. Box 67 (16322-0067)
PHONE..................................814 463-7701
Randy Beary, Manager
EMP: 80 Privately Held
WEB: www.itlcorp.com
SIC: 5031 2426 Lumber: rough, dressed &
finished; hardwood dimension & flooring
mills
HQ: Itl Corp.
23925 Commerce Park
Cleveland OH 44122
216 831-3140

GEOGRAPHIC

Enola
Cumberland County

(G-5080)
G T WATTS INC
108 Altoona Ave (17025-2599)
PHONE.................................717 732-1111
Bradley E Watts, *President*
Phyllis Watts, *Corp Secy*
EMP: 7 EST: 1932
SQ FT: 2,500
SALES (est): 675.4K **Privately Held**
SIC: 2394 3444 Awnings, fabric: made from purchased materials; awnings & canopies

(G-5081)
L L BROWN INC
348 Sample Bridge Rd (17025-1099)
PHONE.................................717 766-1885
William B Novosat, *President*
Craig Shearer, *Division Mgr*
Tara Brown Novosat, *Corp Secy*
William Novosat, *Vice Pres*
Tara Novosat, *Treasurer*
▲ EMP: 20
SQ FT: 25,000
SALES (est): 3.6MM **Privately Held**
WEB: www.llbrown.com
SIC: 3599 3544 Machine shop, jobbing & repair; special dies, tools, jigs & fixtures

(G-5082)
LAWCO INC
383 Sample Bridge Rd (17025-1022)
PHONE.................................717 691-6965
Kim Law-Brydon, *President*
EMP: 3
SALES (est): 339K **Privately Held**
SIC: 3823 Magnetic flow meters, industrial process type

(G-5083)
PENN SIGN COMPANY
650 S Enola Rd (17025-3015)
PHONE.................................717 732-8900
Anthony Kertulis, *Owner*
EMP: 8
SQ FT: 7,200
SALES (est): 1MM **Privately Held**
SIC: 3993 Signs, not made in custom sign painting shops

(G-5084)
PREFERRED SHEET METAL INC
4417 Valley St (17025-1444)
PHONE.................................717 732-7100
Anthony Forlizzi, *President*
Marlin Keckler, *Vice Pres*
EMP: 32 EST: 1998
SQ FT: 17,000
SALES: 4MM **Privately Held**
WEB: www.herrebros.com
SIC: 1761 3441 3444 Roofing, siding & sheet metal work; fabricated structural metal; sheet metalwork

(G-5085)
R & R AUTOMOTIVE MACHINE SHOP
59 S Enola Dr (17025-2708)
PHONE.................................717 732-5521
Frederick Ricupero, *Owner*
EMP: 3
SQ FT: 1,500
SALES (est): 253.1K **Privately Held**
SIC: 3599 Machine shop, jobbing & repair

(G-5086)
TEETER ENTERPRISES INC
49 Sherwood Cir (17025-1838)
PHONE.................................717 732-5994
Denise Amig, *President*
Kurt Amig, *Vice Pres*
Glen Lewis, *Treasurer*
Carrie Lewis, *Admin Sec*
EMP: 4
SALES (est): 308.4K **Privately Held**
SIC: 2844 Suntan lotions & oils

Enon Valley
Lawrence County

(G-5087)
QUICK CLAMP 2
Also Called: Houston and Funds
533 Enon Rd (16120-1809)
PHONE.................................724 336-5719
Jean Huston, *Partner*
Samuel Huston, *Partner*
EMP: 3
SQ FT: 3,000
SALES (est): 290K **Privately Held**
SIC: 3714 Motor vehicle brake systems & parts

(G-5088)
RONALD J STIDMON
214 Little Beaver Rd (16120-1724)
PHONE.................................724 336-0501
Ron Stidmon, *Principal*
EMP: 5 EST: 2009
SALES: 500K **Privately Held**
SIC: 2035 Spreads, garlic

Ephrata
Lancaster County

(G-5089)
A & W SCREEN PRINTING INC
503 Alexander Dr (17522-9652)
PHONE.................................717 738-2726
Alton Good, *President*
EMP: 12
SQ FT: 19,000
SALES (est): 1.5MM **Privately Held**
SIC: 2262 2396 Screen printing: man-made fiber & silk broadwoven fabrics; automotive & apparel trimmings

(G-5090)
ASTRO MACHINE WORKS INC
470 Wenger Dr (17522-9269)
P.O. Box 328 (17522-0328)
PHONE.................................717 738-4281
Eric Blow, *President*
Alan Ebersole, *Co-President*
▲ EMP: 80
SQ FT: 34,000
SALES: 18MM **Privately Held**
WEB: www.astromachineworks.com
SIC: 3599 Machine shop, jobbing & repair

(G-5091)
AY MACHINE CO
E King St (17522)
PHONE.................................717 733-0335
Richard W Ay, *President*
Claudia Bradley, *Treasurer*
Claudia R Bradley, *Admin Sec*
EMP: 15 EST: 1955
SQ FT: 35,000
SALES (est): 2.4MM **Privately Held**
WEB: www.aymachine.com
SIC: 3599 3549 Custom machinery; metalworking machinery

(G-5092)
AZS BRUSHER EQUIPMENT LLC
Also Called: A Z S Brusher Equipment
821 Crooked Ln (17522-8642)
PHONE.................................717 733-2584
Harvey Shrik, *Owner*
▲ EMP: 6
SQ FT: 100
SALES: 1.5MM **Privately Held**
SIC: 3523 0723 Grading, cleaning, sorting machines, fruit, grain, vegetable; vegetable packing services

(G-5093)
BEMENN WOOD PRODUCTS INC
37 N Church St (17522-2043)
PHONE.................................717 738-3530
Barry Hibshamm, *President*
EMP: 6
SQ FT: 12,000
SALES (est): 400K **Privately Held**
WEB: www.bemennwood.com
SIC: 2499 Decorative wood & woodwork

(G-5094)
C K SPORTWEAR INC
Also Called: CK Sportswear
178 Ridge Ave (17522-2552)
PHONE.................................717 733-4786
Minan Corby, *President*
Joseph Corby, *Corp Secy*
EMP: 40
SQ FT: 12,500
SALES (est): 2.6MM **Privately Held**
SIC: 2329 2389 2339 2326 Men's & boys' sportswear & athletic clothing; apparel for handicapped; women's & misses' athletic clothing & sportswear; men's & boys' work clothing

(G-5095)
CARUSO INC
820 N Reading Rd (17522-8429)
PHONE.................................717 738-0248
Jeff Busch, *President*
EMP: 5
SALES (est): 387.8K
SALES (corp-wide): 83.2MM **Privately Held**
SIC: 3613 Panel & distribution boards & other related apparatus
PA: Caruso, Inc.
3465 Hauck Rd
Cincinnati OH 45241
513 860-9200

(G-5096)
CHARLES R ECKERT SIGNS INC
291 Wabash Rd (17522-9790)
PHONE.................................717 733-4601
Charles R Eckert, *President*
Joanne Eckert, *Vice Pres*
EMP: 6
SQ FT: 3,000
SALES (est): 935.2K **Privately Held**
WEB: www.eckertsigns.com
SIC: 3993 7532 2759 Signs, not made in custom sign painting shops; truck painting & lettering; screen printing

(G-5097)
COUNTERTEK INC
1215 Ridge Ave (17522-9782)
PHONE.................................717 336-2371
Ray Roux, *President*
Sheri Golembiewski, *Vice Pres*
EMP: 29 EST: 2010
SQ FT: 18,000
SALES: 3.8MM **Privately Held**
SIC: 2541 Counter & sink tops; table or counter tops, plastic laminated

(G-5098)
CUSTOM FAB INC
596 W Trout Run Rd (17522-9604)
PHONE.................................717 721-5008
EMP: 5
SALES (corp-wide): 1.5B **Publicly Held**
SIC: 3317 Steel pipe & tubes
HQ: Custom Fab, Inc.
109 5th St
Orlando FL 32824
407 859-3954

(G-5099)
D COOPER WORKS LLC
100 Industrial Dr (17522-9252)
PHONE.................................717 733-4220
David Cooper,
EMP: 5
SALES (est): 140K **Privately Held**
SIC: 3556 5084 Poultry processing machinery; dairy products manufacturing machinery; food product manufacturing machinery; milk products manufacturing machinery & equipment

(G-5100)
DIAMOND ROAD RESAWING LLC
1635 Diamond Station Rd (17522-9513)
PHONE.................................717 738-3741
Lawrence L Hoover,
EMP: 4
SALES (est): 618.9K **Privately Held**
SIC: 2421 5031 Resawing lumber into smaller dimensions; lumber: rough, dressed & finished

(G-5101)
DN PRINTER SOLUTIONS
175 E King St Bldg 6 (17522-2368)
PHONE.................................717 606-6233
Novikov Dimitri, *Principal*
EMP: 6 EST: 2013
SALES (est): 326.6K **Privately Held**
SIC: 2752 Commercial printing, offset

(G-5102)
EXTRA FACTORS
Also Called: Xf Enterprises
99 Locust Bend Rd (17522-2610)
PHONE.................................717 859-1166
Robert Simmons, *General Mgr*
EMP: 12
SALES (est): 2.1MM **Privately Held**
SIC: 2048 Feed supplements

(G-5103)
FLO ANN GARMENTS
602 Gristmill Rd (17522-8908)
PHONE.................................717 445-5268
Florence Zimmerman, *Partner*
Anna Zimmerman, *Partner*
EMP: 4
SALES (est): 31.9K **Privately Held**
SIC: 2341 Slips: women's, misses', children's & infants'

(G-5104)
FOX MEADOWS CREAMERY INC
2475 W Main St (17522-8426)
PHONE.................................717 721-6455
Chad M Fox, *President*
Robert D Fox, *Vice Pres*
Corey R Fox, *Admin Sec*
EMP: 41
SALES (est): 524.2K **Privately Held**
SIC: 2024 Ice cream & frozen desserts

(G-5105)
FOXCRAFT CABINETS
224 Snyder Rd (17522-8712)
PHONE.................................717 859-3261
Raymond Fox, *Partner*
EMP: 3 EST: 1976
SALES (est): 266.2K **Privately Held**
SIC: 2434 Wood kitchen cabinets

(G-5106)
GILEAD ENTERPRISES INC
Also Called: Tranquilities
15 Pleasure Rd (17522-2616)
PHONE.................................717 733-2003
Robert E Miller, *CEO*
James W Shenk, *Exec VP*
EMP: 3
SQ FT: 1,200
SALES (est): 338.9K **Privately Held**
WEB: www.gileadenterprises.com
SIC: 3652 Compact laser discs, prerecorded

(G-5107)
GRACE PRESS INC
Also Called: Conestoga Bookstore
2175 Division Hwy (17522-8967)
PHONE.................................717 354-0475
Ezra B Martin, *President*
Harold Weaver Jr, *Admin Sec*
EMP: 15
SQ FT: 15,000
SALES (est): 1.5MM **Privately Held**
WEB: www.gracepress.com
SIC: 2752 5942 5947 Commercial printing, offset; books, religious; gift shop; greeting cards

(G-5108)
HESS MACHINE INTERNATIONAL
1040b S State St (17522-2355)
P.O. Box 639 (17522-0639)
PHONE.................................717 733-0005
Richard Hess, *President*
E Austin Hess, *Chairman*
Helen Hess, *Admin Sec*
▼ EMP: 1
SQ FT: 4,000

▲ = Import ▼=Export
◆ =Import/Export

SALES: 1.2MM
SALES (corp-wide): 5.9MM **Privately Held**
WEB: www.hessmachine.com
SIC: 3589 Water treatment equipment, industrial
PA: Ozone Solutions, Inc.
451 Black Forest Rd
Hull IA 51239
712 439-6880

(G-5109)
HOCKING PRINTING CO INC
Also Called: Shopping News of Lncaster Cnty
615 E Main St (17522-2537)
P.O. Box 456 (17522-0456)
PHONE.................................717 738-1151
Julie A Hocking, *President*
John W Hocking, *Vice Pres*
Harold Wenger, *Sales Staff*
Debbie Foose, *Advt Staff*
Eric Ford, *Consultant*
EMP: 80 **EST:** 1953
SQ FT: 24,000
SALES (est): 7.4MM **Privately Held**
SIC: 2741 2752 2711 Shopping news: publishing & printing; commercial printing, offset; newspapers

(G-5110)
HOOVER PUMP WORKS
222 Conestoga Creek Rd (17522-8610)
PHONE.................................717 733-0630
Elvin Hoover, *Owner*
EMP: 3
SQ FT: 5,000
SALES: 500K **Privately Held**
SIC: 3561 3433 Pumps, domestic: water or sump; burners, furnaces, boilers & stokers

(G-5111)
IRA G STEFFY AND SON INC
460 Wenger Dr (17522-9269)
PHONE.................................717 626-6500
Dennis Rineer, *President*
Gary R Erb, *President*
Jeff Gehman, *Foreman/Supr*
Ted Leash, *Manager*
Rick Croft, *Administration*
EMP: 75
SQ FT: 20,000
SALES (est): 28.1MM **Privately Held**
WEB: www.iragsteffyandson.com
SIC: 3441 7692 1791 3444 Fabricated structural metal; structural steel erection; sheet metalwork

(G-5112)
JEMSON CABINETRY INC
1060 S State St Ste A (17522-2378)
PHONE.................................717 733-0540
David M Palm, *President*
EMP: 6
SALES (est): 952.2K **Privately Held**
WEB: www.jemsoncabinetry.com
SIC: 2434 Vanities, bathroom: wood

(G-5113)
KEYSTONE MACHINERY CORPORATION
20 Cocalico Creek Rd (17522-9455)
PHONE.................................717 859-4977
Lloyd Hoover, *President*
EMP: 7
SQ FT: 1,200
SALES (est): 800K **Privately Held**
SIC: 3599 Machine shop, jobbing & repair

(G-5114)
KEYSTONE WOOD TURNING
230 S Fairmount Rd (17522-8543)
PHONE.................................717 354-2435
Ammon Zimmerman, *Partner*
Melvin Martin, *Partner*
Justin Zimmerman, *Partner*
Michael Zimmerman, *Partner*
EMP: 6
SQ FT: 6,000
SALES (est): 1MM **Privately Held**
SIC: 2431 Millwork

(G-5115)
KRIMES INDUSTRIAL AND MECH INC
633 W Liton Ave Bldg N0 7 (17522)
PHONE.................................717 628-1301
Doug Krimes, *President*
EMP: 6
SQ FT: 1,300
SALES: 1.4MM **Privately Held**
SIC: 1711 3441 Mechanical contractor; fabricated structural metal

(G-5116)
KRIMES MACHINE SHOP INC
509 W Main St (17522-1716)
P.O. Box 417 (17522-0417)
PHONE.................................717 733-1271
Larry Krimes, *President*
Beverly Krimes, *Corp Secy*
EMP: 3
SQ FT: 6,500
SALES: 380K **Privately Held**
SIC: 3599 5531 Machine shop, jobbing & repair; automotive parts

(G-5117)
L RICHARD SENSENIG CO
183 S Market St (17522-1298)
P.O. Box 715 (17522-0715)
PHONE.................................717 733-0364
Kirby Sensenig, *President*
Brian Fasnacht, *Superintendent*
Kevin Sensenig, *Vice Pres*
Ryk Smith, *Project Mgr*
Cory Sensenig, *Admin Sec*
EMP: 70
SQ FT: 40,000
SALES: 13.1MM **Privately Held**
WEB: www.rsensenig.com
SIC: 1761 7692 Roofing contractor; sheet metalwork; welding repair

(G-5118)
L S MARTIN LLC
891 Rettew Mill Rd (17522-1836)
PHONE.................................717 859-3073
Lawrence S Martin, *Manager*
Paul Clark,
EMP: 5
SALES (est): 496.1K **Privately Held**
SIC: 3498 Fabricated pipe & fittings

(G-5119)
LANCASTER COUNTY WEEKLIES
Also Called: Ephrata Rview Susquehanna Prtg
1 E Main St (17522-2713)
P.O. Box 527 (17522-0527)
PHONE.................................717 626-2191
Bill Burgess, *President*
Melissa Hunnefield, *Editor*
Bruce Morgan, *Editor*
Allison Miller, *Info Tech Mgr*
EMP: 550
SQ FT: 40,000
SALES (est): 29.9MM
SALES (corp-wide): 123.3MM **Privately Held**
WEB: www.lanccounty.com
SIC: 2711 Newspapers, publishing & printing
PA: Lnp Media Group, Inc.
8 W King St
Lancaster PA 17603
717 291-8811

(G-5120)
LASER LAB INC
Also Called: S Corporation
1438 W Main St Ste A (17522-1364)
PHONE.................................717 738-3333
Michele McHenry, *President*
Vincent McHenry, *Vice Pres*
Ellen Reigel, *Manager*
Cathy David, *Business Dir*
Jerry Page, *Associate*
EMP: 15
SQ FT: 5,600
SALES: 1.1MM **Privately Held**
WEB: www.laser-lab.com
SIC: 3955 7378 Print cartridges for laser & other computer printers; computer maintenance & repair

(G-5121)
LNP MEDIA GROUP INC
Also Called: Lancaster Farming
1 E Main St (17522-2713)
P.O. Box 609 (17522-0609)
PHONE.................................717 733-6397
Todd Ruth, *Editor*
Angela Faust, *Prdtn Mgr*
Bill Burgess, *Executive*
EMP: 100
SALES (corp-wide): 123.3MM **Privately Held**
WEB: www.lanccounty.com
SIC: 2711 Newspapers, publishing & printing
PA: Lnp Media Group, Inc.
8 W King St
Lancaster PA 17603
717 291-8811

(G-5122)
MARTIN ASSOCIATES EPHRATA LLC
Also Called: Martin's Ice
280 Pleasant Valley Rd (17522-8606)
PHONE.................................717 733-7968
James Martin, *Partner*
Chris Martin, *Clerk*
EMP: 12 **EST:** 1958
SQ FT: 5,000
SALES (est): 2.2MM **Privately Held**
WEB: www.martinelectricplants.com
SIC: 2097 3621 Ice cubes; generator sets: gasoline, diesel or dual-fuel

(G-5123)
MARTIN LIMESTONE INC
Burkholder Paving Division
621 Martindale Rd (17522-8930)
PHONE.................................717 354-1340
Joseph Carst, *Branch Mgr*
EMP: 100
SQ FT: 1,500
SALES (corp-wide): 651.9MM **Privately Held**
WEB: www.martinlimestone.com
SIC: 1611 2951 Highway & street paving contractor; asphalt paving mixtures & blocks
HQ: Martin Limestone, Inc.
3580 Division Hwy
East Earl PA 17519
717 335-4500

(G-5124)
MARTINDALE WELDING LLC
977 Martindale Rd (17522-8971)
P.O. Box 2334, Martindale (17549-0334)
PHONE.................................717 445-4666
Richard Martin, *Principal*
EMP: 5
SALES (est): 410K **Privately Held**
SIC: 7692 Welding repair

(G-5125)
MARTINS BUILDINGS
1825 W Main St (17522-1109)
PHONE.................................717 733-6689
John W Martin, *Partner*
Dana Martin, *Partner*
David L Martin, *Partner*
Douglas Martin, *Partner*
Dwight Martin, *Partner*
EMP: 6
SALES: 800K **Privately Held**
SIC: 2452 Prefabricated buildings, wood

(G-5126)
MARTINS FURNITURE LLC
230 S Fairmount Rd (17522-8543)
PHONE.................................717 354-5657
Melvin Martin, *Owner*
EMP: 15
SALES: 5MM **Privately Held**
SIC: 2511 2521 5712 Wood household furniture; wood office furniture; custom made furniture, except cabinets

(G-5127)
MICHENERS ENGRAVING INC
307 N State St (17522-2236)
PHONE.................................717 738-9630
James Michener, *President*
Karl Baker, *Division Mgr*
Margaret Michener, *Corp Secy*
Kim Michener, *Vice Pres*
EMP: 4
SQ FT: 2,200
SALES (est): 494.1K **Privately Held**
SIC: 7389 3914 Engraving service; trophies

(G-5128)
MILLER PRINTING INC
336 N Reading Rd (17522-1679)
PHONE.................................717 626-5800
Tammy L Frederick, *President*
Kenneth S Miller, *Vice Pres*
Tracey L Mearig, *Treasurer*
Kelly M Thomas, *Admin Sec*
EMP: 5 **EST:** 1960
SQ FT: 10,000
SALES: 372K **Privately Held**
SIC: 2752 2759 Lithographic Commercial Printing Commercial Printing

(G-5129)
MILLERS FABRICATING
1156 Steinmetz Rd (17522-2634)
PHONE.................................717 733-9311
Abner Miller, *Owner*
EMP: 3
SQ FT: 3,200
SALES (est): 332.2K **Privately Held**
SIC: 2541 Cabinets, except refrigerated: show, display, etc.: wood; store & office display cases & fixtures

(G-5130)
MORGAN TRUCK BODY LLC
485 Wenger Dr (17522-9270)
P.O. Box 588 (17522-0588)
PHONE.................................717 733-8644
Charles Helms, *Principal*
EMP: 135
SALES (corp-wide): 1.2B **Privately Held**
WEB: www.morgancorp.com
SIC: 3713 Truck bodies (motor vehicles)
HQ: Morgan Truck Body, Llc
111 Morgan Way
Morgantown PA 19543
610 286-5025

(G-5131)
MORTON TOOL COMPANY
Also Called: Francis E, Sheriidan
87 Fieldcrest Ln (17522-2913)
P.O. Box 220, Chester Heights (19017-0220)
PHONE.................................717 824-1723
Emmett Sheridan, *President*
Doris Sheridan, *Admin Sec*
EMP: 4
SALES: 400K **Privately Held**
SIC: 3599 Machine shop, jobbing & repair

(G-5132)
NOAH SHIRK SAWMILL
220 Covered Bridge Rd (17522-8611)
PHONE.................................717 354-0192
Noah Shirk, *Owner*
EMP: 3
SALES (est): 160K **Privately Held**
SIC: 2421 2426 Sawmills & planing mills, general; hardwood dimension & flooring mills

(G-5133)
NOLT BROS INC
121 Valley View Dr (17522-9775)
PHONE.................................717 733-8761
Terry L Nolt, *President*
Levi S Nolt, *Vice Pres*
Gilbert S Nolt, *Admin Sec*
EMP: 5
SQ FT: 10,000
SALES (est): 770.6K **Privately Held**
SIC: 3599 Machine shop, jobbing & repair

(G-5134)
NORMAN HOOVER WELDING LLC
750 Gristmill Rd (17522-9326)
PHONE.................................717 445-5333
Norman Hoover, *Principal*
EMP: 5 **EST:** 2009
SALES (est): 445.8K **Privately Held**
SIC: 7692 Welding repair

(G-5135)
ORDNANCE RESEARCH INC
Also Called: Ordnance Research Co.
121 Valley View Dr (17522-9774)
PHONE..................................717 738-6941
Curtis Wolf, *President*
EMP: 12
SALES (est): 1.8MM **Privately Held**
WEB: www.ordnanceresearch.com
SIC: 3599 Machine shop, jobbing & repair

(G-5136)
PARK PLACE TRANSMISSION INC
65 N Church St (17522-2043)
PHONE..................................717 859-2998
Steve Book, *General Mgr*
EMP: 3
SALES (est): 210K **Privately Held**
SIC: 3714 Transmissions, motor vehicle

(G-5137)
PENNSYLVANIA AGRI-FUEL INC
820 Hilltop Rd (17522-8401)
PHONE..................................717 733-1050
Thomas Zartman, *Principal*
EMP: 3
SALES (est): 158.3K **Privately Held**
SIC: 2869 Fuels

(G-5138)
RAYTEC LLC (PA)
Also Called: Raytec Manufacturing
544 Gristmill Rd (17522-9323)
PHONE..................................717 445-0510
Raymond G Zimmerman,
EMP: 38
SQ FT: 40,000
SALES (est): 12.5MM **Privately Held**
WEB: www.raytec.com
SIC: 5031 3599 3596 3523 Trim, sheet metal; machine shop, jobbing & repair; weighing machines & apparatus; barn, silo, poultry, dairy & livestock machinery; downspouts, sheet metal

(G-5139)
SCRATCH CUPCAKES
378 Jeff Ave (17522-2451)
PHONE..................................717 271-2466
Laura Will, *Principal*
EMP: 4
SALES (est): 295.7K **Privately Held**
SIC: 2051 Bread, cake & related products

(G-5140)
SIGNATURE CUSTOM CABINETRY INC
434 Springville Rd (17522-9610)
PHONE..................................717 738-4884
Kent Martin, *President*
Delayne Martin, *Vice Pres*
Merv Zimmerman, *Purch Mgr*
Devon Martin, *Treasurer*
Tim Reynolds, *Accounting Mgr*
EMP: 125
SQ FT: 35,000
SALES (est): 12.7MM **Privately Held**
WEB: www.signaturecab.com
SIC: 2434 5031 Wood kitchen cabinets; kitchen cabinets

(G-5141)
SLATE ROAD SUPPLY LLC
150 Slate Rd (17522-9339)
PHONE..................................717 445-5222
Leon Martin, *Mng Member*
Nancy Maritn,
Nelson Martin,
EMP: 6
SQ FT: 100,000
SALES (est): 209.4K **Privately Held**
SIC: 5211 3272 5031 5722 Lumber & other building materials; building materials, except block or brick: concrete; building materials, exterior; building materials, interior; household appliance stores

(G-5142)
SMEAL LTC LLC
68 Cocalico Creek Rd (17522-9455)
PHONE..................................717 918-1806
Daryl M Adams, *CEO*
EMP: 20

SALES (est): 4.4MM
SALES (corp-wide): 816.1MM **Publicly Held**
SIC: 3569 3711 3537 Firefighting apparatus; fire department vehicles (motor vehicles), assembly of; trucks, tractors, loaders, carriers & similar equipment
HQ: Spartan Motors Usa, Inc.
　　1541 Reynolds Rd
　　Charlotte MI 48813
　　517 543-6400

(G-5143)
SMOKEY MOUNTAIN WOODWORKING
170 Sensenig Rd (17522-9325)
PHONE..................................717 445-5120
Elvin Hoover, *Owner*
EMP: 3
SALES (est): 105K **Privately Held**
SIC: 2431 7389 Millwork;

(G-5144)
SPARTAN MOTORS USA INC
64 Cocalico Creek Rd (17522-9455)
PHONE..................................605 582-4000
James Salmi, *VP Sales*
EMP: 12
SALES (corp-wide): 816.1MM **Publicly Held**
SIC: 3711 Fire department vehicles (motor vehicles), assembly of
HQ: Spartan Motors Usa, Inc.
　　1541 Reynolds Rd
　　Charlotte MI 48813
　　517 543-6400

(G-5145)
SPRING GLEN FRESH FOODS INC (HQ)
314 Spring Glen Dr (17522-9249)
P.O. Box 518 (17522-0518)
PHONE..................................717 733-2201
John A Warehime, *President*
Steven E Robertson, *Treasurer*
Gary T Knisley, *Admin Sec*
▲ EMP: 80 EST: 1944
SQ FT: 45,000
SALES: 30MM
SALES (corp-wide): 292MM **Publicly Held**
WEB: www.springglen.com
SIC: 2099 2033 2035 Ready-to-eat meals, salads & sandwiches; canned fruits & specialties; pickled fruits & vegetables
PA: Hanover Foods Corporation
　　1486 York St
　　Hanover PA 17331
　　717 632-6000

(G-5146)
STAUFFER COMPRESSOR N MACHINE
49 Pleasant Valley Rd (17522-9473)
PHONE..................................717 733-4128
Darwin Davis, *President*
EMP: 4
SQ FT: 13,550
SALES: 400K **Privately Held**
WEB: www.stauffercompressor.com
SIC: 3563 5084 3599 Air & gas compressors; compressors, except air conditioning; machine shop, jobbing & repair

(G-5147)
STAUFFER MANUFACTURING LLC
1058 Martindale Rd (17522)
PHONE..................................717 445-6122
Kevin Stauffer,
EMP: 3
SQ FT: 7,150
SALES: 300K **Privately Held**
SIC: 3799 Trailers & trailer equipment

(G-5148)
STELLA-JONES CORPORATION
206 Kimberly Ln (17522-9669)
PHONE..................................717 721-3113
Jim Jordie, *Manager*
EMP: 3
SALES (corp-wide): 250.7K **Privately Held**
SIC: 2491 Wood preserving

HQ: Stella-Jones Corporation
　　1000 Cliffmine Rd Ste 500
　　Pittsburgh PA 15275

(G-5149)
STEVES VENTURES
19 Sunflower Dr (17522-9136)
PHONE..................................717 808-2501
Steven P Braun, *Principal*
EMP: 3 EST: 2008
SALES (est): 271.1K **Privately Held**
SIC: 2851 Removers & cleaners

(G-5150)
SUPERIOR TECH INC
266 Tobacco Rd (17522)
PHONE..................................717 569-3359
John M Weinlader, *President*
Barbara Weinlader, *Corp Secy*
Andrey Drobot, *Manager*
▼ EMP: 3
SALES (est): 562.9K **Privately Held**
WEB: www.superior-tech.com
SIC: 3523 Fertilizing machinery, farm

(G-5151)
SUPERIOR TRUSSES LLC
465 N Reading Rd (17522-9606)
PHONE..................................717 721-2411
Jordan Martin, *Mng Member*
EMP: 20
SALES (est): 2.4MM **Privately Held**
SIC: 2439 Trusses, wooden roof

(G-5152)
TERRE HILL CONCRETE
400 W Main St Ste 5 (17522-1760)
PHONE..................................717 738-9164
Bill Kissinger, *Principal*
EMP: 18
SALES (est): 2.9MM **Privately Held**
SIC: 3272 Concrete products

(G-5153)
VAN MAR MANUFACTURING
445 Hahnstown Rd (17522-9389)
PHONE..................................717 733-8948
Aaron Martin, *Owner*
EMP: 3 EST: 1998
SALES (est): 337.5K **Privately Held**
SIC: 2449 Containers, plywood & veneer wood

(G-5154)
VILLAGE FARM MARKET
1520 Division Hwy (17522-8829)
PHONE..................................717 733-5340
Allen Burkholder, *Principal*
▲ EMP: 6
SALES (est): 250K **Privately Held**
SIC: 2051 5261 0782 Bread, cake & related products; nurseries; landscape contractors

(G-5155)
WEAVER METAL FAB LLC
150 Industrial Dr (17522-9252)
PHONE..................................717 466-6601
Dave Martin, *Mng Member*
EMP: 14
SALES (est): 1.8MM **Privately Held**
SIC: 3441 3444 Fabricated structural metal; sheet metalwork

(G-5156)
WEAVER SHEET METAL LLC
200 S Market St (17522-1212)
PHONE..................................717 733-4763
Daniel Weaver, *Owner*
▲ EMP: 19
SQ FT: 6,000
SALES (est): 3.5MM **Privately Held**
SIC: 3444 5084 Sheet metal specialties, not stamped; metalworking machinery

(G-5157)
X F ENTERPRISES INC
Also Called: Xfe Products
99 Locust Bend Rd (17522-2699)
PHONE..................................717 859-1166
Robert Simmons, *Division Mgr*
EMP: 20

SALES (corp-wide): 45.8MM **Privately Held**
WEB: www.anipro.net
SIC: 2047 2048 Dog & cat food; prepared feeds
PA: X F Enterprises, Inc.
　　500 S Taylor St Unit 301
　　Amarillo TX 79101
　　806 367-5810

(G-5158)
ZIMMERMAN INDUSTRIES INC
196 Wabash Rd (17522-9662)
PHONE..................................717 733-6166
Jerry L Stoner, *President*
Joan Stoner, *Vice Pres*
Tim Hultzapple, *Production*
Dave Lund, *Purch Agent*
Phil Strogan, *Manager*
◆ EMP: 38
SQ FT: 48,000
SALES (est): 9.6MM **Privately Held**
WEB: www.zimmermanindustries.com
SIC: 3531 Mixers, concrete

Equinunk
Wayne County

(G-5159)
AURA TIEDYE
3095 Hancock Hwy (18417-3155)
PHONE..................................888 474-2872
Daniel Cox, *Owner*
Jane Holzman, *Manager*
EMP: 6
SALES (est): 483.5K **Privately Held**
SIC: 2211 Yarn-dyed fabrics, cotton

(G-5160)
SEPTIC SURGEONS LLC
57 Lester Rd Bldg B (18417-3207)
PHONE..................................570 224-4822
Richard Clark,
Lori Clark,
EMP: 4
SALES (est): 395.6K **Privately Held**
SIC: 3259 Clay sewer & drainage pipe & tile

Erie
Erie County

(G-5161)
4FRONT SOLUTIONS LLC
Also Called: Accuspec Electronics
8140 Hawthorne Dr (16509-4654)
PHONE..................................814 464-2000
Richard P Ward, *President*
Michael Sementelli, *Vice Pres*
Tom Rettger, *Purchasing*
Patty Schenker, *Human Res Mgr*
▲ EMP: 130
SQ FT: 60,500
SALES (est): 40.5MM **Privately Held**
SIC: 3672 Printed circuit boards
PA: Armstrong Group Of Companies, Inc.
　　1 Armstrong Pl
　　Butler PA 16001

(G-5162)
4SIS LLC (PA)
Also Called: Stefanelli's Candies
2054 W 8th St (16505-4742)
PHONE..................................814 459-2451
Kathleen Stanbrook, *Mng Member*
Joseph Stanbrook,
EMP: 25
SQ FT: 3,000
SALES: 1.9MM **Privately Held**
WEB: www.stefanelliscandies.com
SIC: 2064 5145 2066 Chocolate candy, except solid chocolate; candy; chocolate & cocoa products

(G-5163)
926 PARTNERS INC (PA)
Also Called: Pulakos Chocolates
2530 Parade St (16503-2034)
PHONE..................................814 452-4026
Joseph H Hilbert, *President*
George A Pulakos, *Owner*

▲ = Import ▼=Export
◆ =Import/Export

Alicia Boyd, *Sales Staff*
EMP: 19 **EST:** 1903
SQ FT: 25,000
SALES (est): 2.7MM **Privately Held**
WEB: www.pulakoschocolates.com
SIC: 2066 Chocolate

(G-5164)
A ANTHONY & SONS INC
1450 W 21st St (16502-2294)
PHONE..................................814 454-2883
Margaret Anthony, *President*
Michael Anthony, *Vice Pres*
John Zack, *Treasurer*
EMP: 37
SQ FT: 5,000
SALES (est): 6MM **Privately Held**
SIC: 3273 1771 Ready-mixed concrete;
concrete work

(G-5165)
A DUCHINI INC (PA)
Also Called: Ace Hardware
2550 Mckinley Ave (16503-2322)
P.O. Box 10005 (16514-0005)
PHONE..................................814 456-7027
James A Duchini, *President*
Adelmo Duchini, *Chairman*
Frank Duchini, *Vice Pres*
Maria George, *Vice Pres*
Charles D Schlaufman, *Treasurer*
EMP: 45 **EST:** 1932
SQ FT: 12,000
SALES (est): 4MM **Privately Held**
WEB: www.duchini.com
SIC: 3271 5251 Concrete block & brick;
hardware

(G-5166)
ACCU-CUT INDUSTRIES INC
141 E 26th St (16504-1082)
P.O. Box 11224 (16514-1224)
PHONE..................................814 456-6616
John Vargo, *President*
Linda Vargo, *Vice Pres*
EMP: 3
SALES: 150K **Privately Held**
WEB: www.tek-industries.com
SIC: 3599 Machine shop, jobbing & repair

(G-5167)
ACCUDYN PRODUCTS INC (PA)
2400 Yoder Dr (16506-2364)
PHONE..................................814 833-7615
Peg Bly, *President*
Margaret S Bly, *President*
Jim Cullen, *Business Mgr*
Tom C Bly, *Vice Pres*
Bob Graham, *Prdtn Mgr*
▲ **EMP:** 64 **EST:** 1997
SQ FT: 71,000
SALES (est): 23MM **Privately Held**
WEB: www.accudyn.com
SIC: 3089 Injection molding of plastics

(G-5168)
ACCURIDE AKW LP
1015 E 12th St (16503-1520)
PHONE..................................814 459-7589
Richard F Dauch, *President*
EMP: 3
SALES (est): 280K **Privately Held**
SIC: 3462 Iron & steel forgings

(G-5169)
ACCURIDE CORPORATION
1015 E 12th St (16503-1520)
PHONE..................................814 480-6400
David Kinecki, *Branch Mgr*
EMP: 359
SALES (corp-wide): 685.5MM **Privately
Held**
SIC: 3714 Wheels, motor vehicle; wheel
rims, motor vehicle; bumpers &
bumperettes, motor vehicle; brake drums,
motor vehicle
HQ: Accuride Corporation
7140 Office Cir
Evansville IN 47715
812 962-5000

(G-5170)
ACCURIDE ERIE LP
1015 E 12th St Ste 200 (16503-1520)
PHONE..................................814 480-6400
George Tarcia, *Partner*

Gregory A Risch, *Vice Pres*
James H Woodward, *CFO*
▲ **EMP:** 260
SALES (est): 47.2MM
SALES (corp-wide): 685.5MM **Privately
Held**
WEB: www.akwheels.com
SIC: 3363 3544 3354 Aluminum die-cast-
ings; special dies, tools, jigs & fixtures;
aluminum extruded products
HQ: Accuride Corporation
7140 Office Cir
Evansville IN 47715
812 962-5000

(G-5171)
**ACE VIKING ELECTRIC MTR CO
INC**
2222 E 30th St (16510-2552)
PHONE..................................814 897-9445
Patrick Horwath, *President*
Jeffrey Horwath, *Vice Pres*
James Senkalski, *Treasurer*
Roberta Horwath, *Admin Sec*
EMP: 9
SQ FT: 17,500
SALES (est): 3.1MM **Privately Held**
WEB: www.aceviking.com
SIC: 7694 5063 Electric motor repair; mo-
tors, electric

(G-5172)
ACOUSTICSHEEP LLC
2001 Peninsula Dr (16506-2969)
PHONE..................................814 380-9296
WEI-Shin Lai, *CEO*
Colleen Brady, *Sales Mgr*
Tim Murphy, *Sales Mgr*
Kelly Robb, *Cust Mgr*
Greg Radwan, *Manager*
▲ **EMP:** 18
SQ FT: 3,500
SALES (est): 2.3MM **Privately Held**
SIC: 3679 Headphones, radio

(G-5173)
**ACTION PRINTING AND BUS
FORMS**
824 E 9th St (16503-1410)
PHONE..................................814 453-5977
John Kowalski, *President*
Carol Mancuso, *Vice Pres*
Barb Kwiatkowski, *Treasurer*
Marybeth Porath, *Director*
Kathleen Preatzel, *Director*
EMP: 12
SQ FT: 17,500
SALES (est): 1.2MM **Privately Held**
SIC: 2759 5112 Letterpress printing; busi-
ness forms

(G-5174)
**ADVANCED MOLD
TECHNOLOGIES**
2011 E 30th St (16510-2547)
PHONE..................................814 899-1233
Chris Walderman, *President*
Chris Waldemarson, *President*
EMP: 12
SALES (est): 1.6MM **Privately Held**
SIC: 3089 Molding primary plastic

(G-5175)
**ADVANCED SOLUTIONS
NETWORK LLC**
Also Called: Plastics Services Network
5368 Kuhl Rd (16510-4703)
PHONE..................................814 464-0791
Michael Alabran, *President*
Tera Alabran, *Business Mgr*
EMP: 10
SALES (est): 251.4K **Privately Held**
SIC: 8711 8734 2821 3089 Mechanical
engineering; chemical engineering; prod-
uct testing laboratory, safety or perform-
ance; molding compounds, plastics;
injection molding of plastics

(G-5176)
ADVANCED WELDING TECH INC
3110 Pearl Ave (16510-1646)
PHONE..................................814 899-3584
John Stempka, *President*
Michael Stempka, *Vice Pres*
EMP: 35

SQ FT: 45,000
SALES (est): 8.1MM **Privately Held**
SIC: 3443 3494 3599 8734 Fabricated
plate work (boiler shop); pipe fittings;
crankshafts & camshafts, machining; testing laboratories

(G-5177)
AFTON TRUCKING INC
Also Called: Afton Landscape Supply
8955 Wattsburg Rd (16509-6021)
PHONE..................................814 825-7449
Deborah Will, *President*
John T Afton, *Vice Pres*
Charles Will, *Vice Pres*
Rebecca Thomson, *Treasurer*
Lureda Afton, *Admin Sec*
EMP: 10 **EST:** 1974
SALES (est): 2.1MM **Privately Held**
SIC: 4212 1442 4213 Local trucking, with-
out storage; construction sand & gravel;
trucking, except local

(G-5178)
AIR-CON INC
4835 W 23rd St (16506-1471)
PHONE..................................814 838-6373
Donald L Chapman, *President*
Sue McLaughlin, *Purchasing*
Walter Chapman, *Chief Engr*
Becky Buss, *Marketing Staff*
Robert Chapman, *Admin Sec*
▲ **EMP:** 18
SQ FT: 6,500
SALES (est): 3.5MM **Privately Held**
WEB: www.air-convalves.com
SIC: 3491 Automatic regulating & control
valves; process control regulator valves;
valves, automatic control

(G-5179)
**ALBERTS CUSTOM SHTMTL &
WLDG**
209 E 21st St (16503-1924)
PHONE..................................814 454-4461
Mark E Milford, *Owner*
EMP: 3
SALES (est): 408K **Privately Held**
SIC: 3444 Sheet metalwork

(G-5180)
ALL-AMERICAN HOSE LLC
6424 W Ridge Rd (16506-1023)
PHONE..................................814 438-7616
Edward Weirzchowski, *Manager*
EMP: 40 **Privately Held**
WEB: www.snap-titehose.com
SIC: 3052 Rubber & plastics hose & belt-
ings
HQ: Aah Acquisition, Llc
217 Titusville Rd
Union City PA 16438

(G-5181)
ALL-AMERICAN HOSE LLC
6420 W Ridge Rd (16506-1023)
PHONE..................................814 838-3381
EMP: 25 **Privately Held**
SIC: 3052 Mfg Rubber/Plastic Hose/Belting
HQ: All-American Hose Llc
217 Titusville Rd
Union City PA 16438

(G-5182)
ALPONT II INC
1432 Chestnut St (16502-1705)
PHONE..................................814 456-7561
Albert R Puntureri, *President*
EMP: 27
SALES (est): 1MM
SALES (corp-wide): 338.1MM **Privately
Held**
SIC: 2819 Industrial inorganic chemicals
PA: Interstate Chemical Company, Inc.
2797 Freedland Rd
Hermitage PA 16148
724 981-3771

(G-5183)
ALS AWNING SHOP INC
Also Called: Al's Awning Shop & Canvas Pdts
1721 W 26th St (16508-1294)
PHONE..................................814 456-6262
Cynthia Quadri, *President*
EMP: 5 **EST:** 1945
SQ FT: 10,500

SALES (est): 450K **Privately Held**
SIC: 2394 7699 Awnings, fabric: made
from purchased materials; tents: made
from purchased materials; tarpaulins, fabric: made from purchased materials; tent
repair shop; awning repair shop

(G-5184)
**ALSTOM SIGNALING
OPERATION LLC (PA)**
Also Called: GE Transportation Systems
2901 E Lake Rd Bldg 122 (16531-0001)
PHONE..................................800 825-3178
Brian Helm, *Engineer*
Mike Plaza, *Engineer*
Soban Jalil, *Manager*
Stephen Stoicovy, *Manager*
Chris Spriegel, *CTO*
▲ **EMP:** 300 **EST:** 1946
SQ FT: 12,600
SALES (est): 1.5B **Privately Held**
WEB: www.proyard.com
SIC: 3669 5088 3672 3663 Railroad sig-
naling devices, electric; railroad equip-
ment & supplies; printed circuit boards;
radio broadcasting & communications
equipment

(G-5185)
AMATECH INC (PA)
1460 Grimm Dr (16501-1572)
PHONE..................................814 452-0010
David A Amatangelo, *President*
Rick Bittner, *Vice Pres*
Tony Amatangelo, *Vice Pres*
Eric Lyle, *Prdtn Mgr*
Heidi Johnson, *Engineer*
EMP: 50
SQ FT: 20,000
SALES (est): 11.3MM **Privately Held**
SIC: 7336 2671 3086 Package design;
plastic film, coated or laminated for pack-
aging; packaging & shipping materials,
foamed plastic

(G-5186)
AMERICAN CRUISING SAILS INC
2705 W 17th St (16505-4307)
PHONE..................................814 456-7245
Anthony Miceli, *President*
EMP: 4
SALES (est): 267.2K **Privately Held**
SIC: 2394 Sails: made from purchased
materials

(G-5187)
**AMERICAN HOLLOW BORING
COMPANY**
1901 Raspberry St (16502-2414)
P.O. Box 338 (16512-0338)
PHONE..................................800 673-2458
Geoff Ginader, *President*
John Ginader, *President*
Tim Kaercher, *Vice Pres*
EMP: 23 **EST:** 1918
SQ FT: 60,000
SALES (est): 4.7MM **Privately Held**
WEB: www.amhollow.com
SIC: 3462 3568 3545 3443 Iron & steel
forgings; power transmission equipment;
machine tool accessories; fabricated plate
work (boiler shop)

(G-5188)
**AMERICAN RAILING SYSTEMS
INC**
1813 Mcclelland Ave (16510-1347)
PHONE..................................814 899-7677
Mark A Bliley, *President*
Craig Basington, *Vice Pres*
Craig Brasington, *VP Prdtn*
▼ **EMP:** 20
SQ FT: 26,000
SALES (est): 4.2MM **Privately Held**
WEB: www.americanrailing.com
SIC: 3446 Bannisters, made from metal
pipe; railings, bannisters, guards, etc.:
made from metal pipe

(G-5189)
**AMERICAN TINNING
GALVANIZING (PA)**
552 W 12th St (16501-1507)
P.O. Box 1599 (16512-1599)
PHONE..................................814 456-7053

Kathleen A Scheppner, *President*
Dorothy C Scheppner, *Vice Pres*
A C Scheppner, *Treasurer*
Jacqueline Scheppner, *Admin Sec*
EMP: 53 **EST:** 1931
SQ FT: 65,000
SALES (est): 9.7MM **Privately Held**
WEB: www.galvanizeit.com
SIC: 3471 3479 Electroplating of metals or formed products; anodizing (plating) of metals or formed products; rust proofing (hot dipping) of metals & formed products

(G-5190)
AMERICAN TRIM LLC
3120 W 22nd St (16506-2306)
PHONE.................................814 833-7758
Maurice Hough, *Manager*
EMP: 166
SALES (corp-wide): 445.1MM **Privately Held**
SIC: 3469 Porcelain enameled products & utensils
HQ: American Trim, L.L.C.
1005 W Grand Ave
Lima OH 45801

(G-5191)
AMERICAN TURNED PRODUCTS INC
1944 Wager Rd (16509)
PHONE.................................814 824-7600
Harry Eighmy, *Manager*
EMP: 110
SQ FT: 41,804
SALES (corp-wide): 18MM **Privately Held**
WEB: www.atpteam.com
SIC: 3451 Screw machine products
PA: American Turned Products, Inc.
7626 Klier Dr S
Fairview PA 16415
814 474-4200

(G-5192)
AMERIDRIVES INTERNATIONAL LLC (HQ)
Also Called: Ameridrives Couplings
1802 Pittsburgh Ave (16502-1943)
PHONE.................................814 480-5000
John Folga, *Business Mgr*
Jason Wynne, *Business Mgr*
John Young, *Vice Pres*
James Pratt, *Purch Mgr*
Misty Steinecke, *Purch Mgr*
▲ **EMP:** 89
SALES (est): 21.9MM
SALES (corp-wide): 1.1B **Publicly Held**
WEB: www.ameridrives.com
SIC: 3568 Couplings, shaft: rigid, flexible, universal joint, etc.
PA: Altra Industrial Motion Corp.
300 Granite St Ste 201
Braintree MA 02184
781 917-0600

(G-5193)
AMTHOR STEEL INC (PA)
1717 Gaskell Ave (16503-2429)
PHONE.................................814 452-4700
Terry Carrara, *President*
Richard L Carrara, *President*
Patrick S Carrara, *Vice Pres*
EMP: 3 **EST:** 1920
SQ FT: 60,000
SALES (est): 900MM **Privately Held**
SIC: 3441 Fabricated structural metal

(G-5194)
ARROW CASTINGS CO
2645 W 14th St (16505-4301)
P.O. Box 8349 (16505-0349)
PHONE.................................814 838-3561
Karen Prior, *President*
EMP: 13 **EST:** 1959
SQ FT: 21,120
SALES (est): 2.4MM **Privately Held**
WEB: www.arrowcastings.com
SIC: 3366 Copper foundries

(G-5195)
ARVITE TECHNOLOGIES INC
2731 W 11th St (16505-4125)
PHONE.................................814 838-9444
Grover Martin, *President*
Debra Z Zingelewicz, *Purch Mgr*

Chris Kidder, *CFO*
EMP: 11
SQ FT: 4,000
SALES (est): 1.8MM **Privately Held**
SIC: 3444 Sheet metal specialties, not stamped

(G-5196)
AUTO SEAT COVER COMPANY (PA)
Also Called: Hedlund Glass & Auto
2125 Filmore Ave (16506-2940)
PHONE.................................814 453-5897
Samuel McEwen, *President*
EMP: 8
SQ FT: 26,000
SALES (est): 858.6K **Privately Held**
SIC: 7532 2394 7641 Upholstery & trim shop, automotive; convertible tops, canvas or boat: from purchased materials; re-upholstery

(G-5197)
AUTOCLAVE ENGINEERS
Also Called: Parker Autoclave
8325 Hessinger Dr (16509-4679)
PHONE.................................814 860-5700
John Clark, *Owner*
▼ **EMP:** 7
SALES (est): 1MM **Privately Held**
SIC: 3492 Fluid power valves & hose fittings

(G-5198)
AUTOMATED INDUS SYSTEMS INC
4238 W 12th St (16505-3001)
PHONE.................................814 838-2270
Gerald A Ryan, *Ch of Bd*
Robert C Lindenberger, *President*
Ralph Vorse, *Vice Pres*
EMP: 27
SQ FT: 14,000
SALES: 4MM **Privately Held**
WEB: www.asporing.com
SIC: 3542 5044 3953 Marking machines; office equipment; marking devices

(G-5199)
AUTOMATION PRODUCTS INC (HQ)
Also Called: Swanson-Anaheim
814 E 8th St (16503-1490)
PHONE.................................814 453-5841
Douglas L Swanson, *President*
EMP: 17
SALES (est): 1.5MM
SALES (corp-wide): 14.4MM **Privately Held**
WEB: www.swanson-anaheim.com
SIC: 3549 Assembly machines, including robotic
PA: Swanson Systems, Inc.
814 E 8th St
Erie PA 16503
814 453-5841

(G-5200)
AVURE AUTOCLAVE SYSTEMS INC
2820 W 23rd St Ste 6 (16506-2988)
PHONE.................................814 833-4331
Rick Reber, *Branch Mgr*
EMP: 6
SALES (corp-wide): 147.9MM **Privately Held**
WEB: www.avureae.com
SIC: 3823 5084 Pressure measurement instruments, industrial; industrial machinery & equipment
HQ: Avure Autoclave Systems, Inc.
3721 Corp Dr
Columbus OH 43231
614 891-2732

(G-5201)
B ASF CORP
1729 East Ave (16503-2367)
PHONE.................................814 453-7186
Peter Martin, *Principal*
EMP: 5
SALES (est): 956.1K **Privately Held**
SIC: 2869 Industrial organic chemicals

(G-5202)
BARBATO FOODS INC
1707 State St (16501-2209)
PHONE.................................814 899-3721
Nicholas Barbato Jr, *President*
EMP: 10
SALES (est): 558.7K **Privately Held**
SIC: 2032 Italian foods: packaged in cans, jars, etc.

(G-5203)
BARTLETT SIGNS
5148 Peach St Ste 328 (16509-2475)
PHONE.................................814 392-7082
Kent Bartlett, *Principal*
EMP: 3 **EST:** 2010
SALES (est): 370.6K **Privately Held**
SIC: 3993 Electric signs

(G-5204)
BASF CATALYSTS LLC
1729 East Ave (16503-2367)
PHONE.................................814 870-3900
Pat Consiglio, *Branch Mgr*
EMP: 143
SALES (corp-wide): 71.7B **Privately Held**
SIC: 2869 Industrial organic chemicals
HQ: Basf Catalysts Llc
33 Wood Ave S
Iselin NJ 08830
732 205-5000

(G-5205)
BAYCRETE INC
1816 Greengarden Rd (16502-2148)
PHONE.................................814 454-5001
Thomas M Maya, *President*
EMP: 12
SALES (est): 1.7MM **Privately Held**
SIC: 3273 Mfg Ready-Mixed Concrete

(G-5206)
BEAUMONT ADVANCED PROC LLC
1524 E 10th St (16511-1713)
PHONE.................................814 899-6390
John Beaumont, *Mng Member*
John Ralston, *Mng Member*
EMP: 10
SQ FT: 8,000
SALES (est): 496.5K **Privately Held**
SIC: 3089 Injection molding of plastics

(G-5207)
BEAUMONT DEVELOPMENT LLC
6100 W Ridge Rd (16506-1018)
PHONE.................................814 899-6390
John D Ralston, *Mng Member*
David Hoffman, *Manager*
John Beaumont,
EMP: 15
SQ FT: 8,000
SALES: 5MM **Privately Held**
SIC: 3089 8711 Molding primary plastic; consulting engineer; electrical or electronic engineering

(G-5208)
BENETVISON
355 E 9th St (16503-1107)
PHONE.................................814 459-9224
Joan Chittister, *Exec Dir*
EMP: 6 **EST:** 1990
SALES (est): 576.8K **Privately Held**
SIC: 2731 Book publishing

(G-5209)
BERRY GLOBAL INC
316 W 16th St (16502-1807)
PHONE.................................814 455-9051
Missy Pollack, *Cust Mgr*
EMP: 9 **Publicly Held**
SIC: 3089 Plastic containers, except foam
HQ: Berry Global, Inc.
101 Oakley St
Evansville IN 47710
812 424-2904

(G-5210)
BETTER BAKED FOODS LLC
2200 E 38th St (16510-3699)
PHONE.................................814 899-6128
Jerry Pacinelli, *Manager*
Sallie Hayes, *Technician*

EMP: 41
SALES (corp-wide): 5.3B **Privately Held**
WEB: www.betterbaked.com
SIC: 2051 Bread, cake & related products
HQ: Better Baked Foods, Llc
56 Smedley St
North East PA 16428
814 725-8778

(G-5211)
BIMBO BAKERIES USA INC
Stroehmann Bakeries 32
1220 W 20th St (16502-2366)
PHONE.................................814 456-2596
Bill Pilewski, *Manager*
EMP: 31
SQ FT: 40,000 **Privately Held**
SIC: 2051 Bread, cake & related products
HQ: Bimbo Bakeries Usa, Inc
255 Business Center Dr # 200
Horsham PA 19044
215 347-5500

(G-5212)
BIMBO BAKERIES USA INC
1860 W 26th St (16508-1149)
PHONE.................................814 456-4575
EMP: 18 **Privately Held**
SIC: 2051 Bakery: wholesale or wholesale/retail combined
HQ: Bimbo Bakeries Usa, Inc
255 Business Center Dr # 200
Horsham PA 19044
215 347-5500

(G-5213)
BLANCHARD MFG & ENGRG
1322 E 12th St (16503-1717)
PHONE.................................814 454-8995
Richard H Blanchard, *President*
Pia M Blanchard, *Admin Sec*
EMP: 5
SQ FT: 3,000
SALES: 500K **Privately Held**
SIC: 3089 Hardware, plastic

(G-5214)
BLILEY TECHNOLOGIES INC
2545 W Grandview Blvd (16506-4512)
P.O. Box 3428 (16508-0428)
PHONE.................................814 838-3571
Keith Szewczyk, *CEO*
David Curtis, *Principal*
Roger W Richards, *Chairman*
James H Hynes, *Corp Secy*
Dennis Barrick, *Vice Pres*
EMP: 140
SQ FT: 63,600
SALES (est): 31.9MM **Privately Held**
WEB: www.bliley.com
SIC: 3679 Attenuators; oscillators; harness assemblies for electronic use: wire or cable; quartz crystals, for electronic application

(G-5215)
BROOK MEADOW DAIRY COMPANY (DH)
2365 Buffalo Rd (16510-1459)
PHONE.................................814 899-3191
Jed Davis, *President*
William Riley, *President*
Dale Hecox, *Treasurer*
Eric Blanchard, *Admin Sec*
EMP: 120 **EST:** 1932
SQ FT: 51,766
SALES (est): 27.8MM **Publicly Held**
WEB: www.meadowbrookdairy.com
SIC: 2026 2033 2024 Milk processing (pasteurizing, homogenizing, bottling); fruit juices: packaged in cans, jars, etc.; dairy based frozen desserts
HQ: Dean Holding Company
2711 N Haskell Ave
Dallas TX 75204
214 303-3400

(G-5216)
BROWNING-FERRIS INDUSTRIES INC
1863 E 12th St (16511-1725)
PHONE.................................814 453-6608
Tim Adamczak, *Principal*
EMP: 3

▲ = Import ▼=Export
◆ =Import/Export

SALES (corp-wide): 10B **Publicly Held**
SIC: 3999 Barber & beauty shop equipment
HQ: Browning-Ferris Industries, Llc
18500 N Allied Way # 100
Phoenix AZ 85054
480 627-2700

(G-5217)
BUILDING SPECIALTIES
2011 W 12th St (16505-4802)
PHONE...........................814 454-4345
Charles Fine, *Branch Mgr*
Jackie Davila, *Branch Mgr*
EMP: 5 EST: 2011
SALES (est): 511.7K **Privately Held**
SIC: 3272 Building materials, except block
or brick: concrete

(G-5218)
BURNS MANUFACTURING INC
2001 Lowell Ave (16506-2944)
PHONE...........................814 833-7428
Andrew C Burns, *President*
Michael D Burns, *Vice Pres*
▲ EMP: 17 EST: 1965
SQ FT: 20,000
SALES (est): 4.2MM **Privately Held**
WEB: www.burnsmfg.com
SIC: 3442 Metal doors, sash & trim

(G-5219)
BUSH INDUSTRIES OF PA
2455 Robison Rd W (16509-4675)
PHONE...........................814 868-2874
James L Sherbert Jr, *CEO*
James Garde, *Vice Pres*
Jerry Green, *Vice Pres*
Linda Aldridge, *HR Admin*
Neil Frederick, *Admin Sec*
◆ EMP: 115
SALES (est): 24.2MM
SALES (corp-wide): 89.8MM **Privately Held**
SIC: 2521 2511 Bookcases, office: wood;
cabinets, office: wood; desks, office:
wood; panel systems & partitions (free-standing), office: wood; wood household
furniture
PA: Bush Industries, Inc.
1 Mason Dr
Jamestown NY 14701
716 665-2000

(G-5220)
CARLSON ERIE CORPORATION
1115 Cherry St (16501-1592)
P.O. Box 1599 (16512-1599)
PHONE...........................814 455-2768
Jacqueline Scheppner, *President*
Chris Blakeslee, *General Mgr*
Rodney Chiarellli, *Vice Pres*
EMP: 11
SQ FT: 13,000
SALES: 2MM
SALES (corp-wide): 9.7MM **Privately Held**
SIC: 3559 Metal finishing equipment for
plating, etc.
PA: American Tinning & Galvanizing Co
552 W 12th St
Erie PA 16501
814 456-7053

(G-5221)
CARLSONS INDUSTRIAL GRINDING
8959 Perry Hwy (16509-5549)
PHONE...........................814 864-8640
Terry Carlson, *Owner*
Stefanie Carlson, *Manager*
EMP: 3 EST: 1967
SALES (est): 240K **Privately Held**
SIC: 3599 7389 Grinding castings for the
trade; grinding, precision: commercial or
industrial

(G-5222)
CARRARA STEEL INC
Also Called: Carrara Steel Erectors
1717 Gaskell Ave (16503-2429)
PHONE...........................814 452-4600
Richard Carrara, *President*
EMP: 35
SQ FT: 20,000

SALES (est): 7.1MM **Privately Held**
SIC: 3441 Fabricated structural metal

(G-5223)
CAUSCO
944 W 26th St (16508-3208)
PHONE...........................814 452-2004
Paul Morris, *President*
EMP: 3
SALES (est): 263K **Privately Held**
SIC: 5099 3953 Rubber stamps; cancelling stamps, hand: rubber or metal

(G-5224)
CINTAS CORPORATION NO 2
4734 Pittsburgh Ave (16509-6204)
PHONE...........................440 352-4003
EMP: 100
SALES (corp-wide): 6.4B **Publicly Held**
SIC: 2311 Men's & boys' uniforms
HQ: Cintas Corporation No. 2
6800 Cintas Blvd
Mason OH 45040

(G-5225)
CK TOOL & DIE INC
3214 W 22nd St (16506-2308)
PHONE...........................814 836-9600
Carl Krumpe, *Owner*
Sharon Krumpe, *Co-Owner*
EMP: 7
SQ FT: 5,500
SALES (est): 1MM **Privately Held**
SIC: 3544 Special dies & tools

(G-5226)
CLARKE CONTAINER INC
1513 Grimm Dr (16501-1580)
PHONE...........................814 452-4848
Patricia Chiz, *President*
Frank J Chiz, *Treasurer*
EMP: 10 EST: 2000
SQ FT: 28,000
SALES (est): 1.5MM **Privately Held**
WEB: www.clarkecontainer.com
SIC: 3086 Packaging & shipping materials,
foamed plastic

(G-5227)
CLINTON PRESS INC
500 W 12th St (16501-1507)
PHONE...........................814 455-9089
Wayne Zimmer, *President*
Fay Zimmer, *Treasurer*
EMP: 8 EST: 1950
SQ FT: 15,813
SALES (est): 1.2MM **Privately Held**
SIC: 2752 7331 2791 2789 Commercial
printing, offset; mailing service; typesetting; bookbinding & related work

(G-5228)
CMI AMERICA INC
5300 Knowledge Pkwy # 101 (16510-4674)
PHONE...........................814 897-7000
Tom Poklar, *Info Tech Dir*
EMP: 11
SQ FT: 34,000
SALES (est): 857.5K
SALES (corp-wide): 155.4K **Privately Held**
SIC: 3567 5063 Heating units & devices,
industrial: electric; electrical apparatus &
equipment
PA: Cmi Groupe Tva
Avenue A. Greiner 1
Seraing
433 024-44

(G-5229)
COMPOSIFLEX INC
8100 Hawthorne Dr (16509-4654)
PHONE...........................814 866-8616
Alan J Hannibal, *President*
▲ EMP: 60
SQ FT: 33,000
SALES (est): 11.6MM **Privately Held**
WEB: www.composiflex.com
SIC: 3845 Laser systems & equipment,
medical

(G-5230)
COMPRESSED AIR SPECIALISTS CO
Also Called: Casco USA
2022 Filmore Ave Ste 1 (16506-6911)
PHONE...........................814 835-2420
Toll Free:...........................888 -
Ed Vorpagel, *Manager*
EMP: 5
SALES (corp-wide): 18MM **Privately Held**
WEB: www.cascousa.com
SIC: 3561 3053 Pumps & pumping equipment; packing: steam engines, pipe joints,
air compressors, etc.
PA: Compressed Air Specialists Co Inc
370 Meadowlands Blvd
Washington PA 15301
724 746-6500

(G-5231)
CONTINE CORPORATION
1820 Nagle Rd (16510-2126)
PHONE...........................814 899-0006
Constance C Ellrich, *President*
Bob Platz, *Purchasing*
Cheryl Kulich, *Accounting Mgr*
Sally Skelly, *Human Res Mgr*
Sandra Ebert, *Manager*
EMP: 48
SQ FT: 7,300
SALES: 9MM **Privately Held**
WEB: www.continedbe.com
SIC: 3599 Machine shop, jobbing & repair

(G-5232)
CONTROL DESIGN INC
4807 Atlantic Ave (16506-4589)
PHONE...........................814 833-4663
Bill Harrington, *Manager*
EMP: 15
SALES (corp-wide): 7.1MM **Privately Held**
WEB: www.controldesigninc.com
SIC: 3613 Control panels, electric
PA: Control Design, Inc.
211 Ridc Park West Dr
Pittsburgh PA 15275
412 788-2280

(G-5233)
COPY RIGHT PRINTING & GRAPHICS
Also Called: PIP Printing
2827 W 26th St Ste A (16506-3055)
PHONE...........................814 838-6255
Christopher Spoto, *Owner*
EMP: 3 EST: 1980
SQ FT: 1,500
SALES (est): 325K **Privately Held**
SIC: 7334 2752 2791 Mimeographing;
commercial printing, offset; typesetting

(G-5234)
CORRY FORGE COMPANY
1533 E 12th St (16511-1747)
PHONE...........................814 459-4495
Robert Shephard, *Manager*
EMP: 40
SALES (corp-wide): 775.5MM **Privately Held**
SIC: 3462 Iron & steel forgings
HQ: Corry Forge Company
441 E Main St
Corry PA 16407
814 664-9664

(G-5235)
CTC PRESSURE PRODUCTS LLC
2820 W 21st St Ste 1 (16506-2981)
PHONE...........................814 315-6427
EMP: 4
SALES (est): 125.4K **Privately Held**
SIC: 3589 3494 3429 High pressure
cleaning equipment; valves & pipe fittings;
clamps & couplings, hose

(G-5236)
CURRY SPECTACLE SHOP INC
3202 Buffalo Rd (16510-1810)
PHONE...........................814 899-6833
Howard James Curry, *President*
Mary Ann Curry, *Vice Pres*
EMP: 5

SQ FT: 1,800
SALES (est): 340K **Privately Held**
SIC: 5995 3851 Eyeglasses, prescription;
contact lenses, prescription; ophthalmic
goods

(G-5237)
CUSTOM ENGINEERING CO (PA)
2800 Mcclelland Ave (16510-2598)
P.O. Box 10008 (16514-0008)
PHONE...........................814 898-1390
David M Tullio, *President*
Thomas B Hagen, *Chairman*
Darin Hayes, *Materials Mgr*
Troy Miodus, *Engineer*
James B Ohrn, *CFO*
▲ EMP: 151
SQ FT: 140,000
SALES: 28MM **Privately Held**
WEB: www.customeng.com
SIC: 3541 3443 3542 Machine tools,
metal cutting type; weldments; machine
tools, metal forming type

(G-5238)
CUSTOM KITCHENS INC
3014 W 12th St (16505-3837)
PHONE...........................814 833-5338
Ron J Lester, *President*
EMP: 8
SQ FT: 8,620
SALES (est): 966.6K **Privately Held**
SIC: 2541 2821 5032 Counter & sink
tops; acrylic resins; granite building stone

(G-5239)
CUSTOM PLASTIC SPECIALTIES LLC
5678 W Ridge Rd (16506-1012)
PHONE...........................814 838-6471
Eric Enzbrenner, *Principal*
Kippie Helzel, *Principal*
EMP: 120
SALES (est): 2.8MM
SALES (corp-wide): 159.9MM **Privately Held**
SIC: 3993 Advertising novelties
PA: Gen Cap America, Inc.
40 Burton Hills Blvd # 420
Nashville TN 37215
615 256-0231

(G-5240)
CUSTOM PRODUCTS
2250 W 23rd St (16506-2917)
PHONE...........................814 453-6803
Fax: 814 456-2403
EMP: 7
SQ FT: 7,000
SALES (est): 450K **Privately Held**
SIC: 3444 Mfg Sheet Metalwork

(G-5241)
CUSTOM TOOL & DESIGN INC
4962 Pittsburgh Ave (16509-6207)
PHONE...........................814 838-9777
Jeffrey Mertz, *President*
EMP: 30
SQ FT: 25,000
SALES (est): 6MM **Privately Held**
SIC: 3544 Dies, plastics forming

(G-5242)
CYBERINK LLC
Also Called: Goerie.com
205 W 12th St (16534-0002)
PHONE...........................814 870-1600
EMP: 3
SALES (est): 130.2K
SALES (corp-wide): 1.5B **Publicly Held**
SIC: 2759 Publication printing
PA: New Media Investment Group Inc.
1345 Avenue Of The Americ
New York NY 10105
212 479-3160

(G-5243)
CYBERSONICS INC
5340 Fryling Rd Ste 101 (16510-4672)
PHONE...........................814 898-4734
Thomas Peterson, *President*
Jeffery Vaitekunas, *Vice Pres*
Charlie Baker, *Engineer*
Purva Pangaonkar, *Engineer*
Wenyan Wu, *Engineer*
EMP: 4

SALES (est): 907.5K **Privately Held**
SIC: 3841 Surgical & medical instruments

(G-5244)
D & F TOOL INC
4370 Knoyle Rd (16510-5202)
PHONE..................................814 899-6364
David Farrell, *President*
George H Dieter III, *Vice Pres*
EMP: 7
SQ FT: 2,800
SALES (est): 676.9K **Privately Held**
SIC: 3544 Industrial molds

(G-5245)
DENNIS SANDERS
Also Called: Sanders Tool Co
3030 W 25th St (16506-2328)
PHONE..................................814 833-5497
Dennis Sanders, *Owner*
EMP: 6
SQ FT: 5,000
SALES (est): 250K **Privately Held**
SIC: 3544 Forms (molds), for foundry &
plastics working machinery

(G-5246)
DESI S INTERSTATE BEER
2605 Evanston Ave (16506-3128)
PHONE..................................814 528-5914
Long John Desmond, *Owner*
EMP: 5 **EST:** 2012
SALES (est): 288.8K **Privately Held**
SIC: 2082 Beer (alcoholic beverage)

(G-5247)
DH STEEL PRODUCTS LLC
2420 W 15th St (16505-4576)
PHONE..................................814 459-2715
Gil Jacobs, *Vice Pres*
Lisa Schaefer, *Purchasing*
Dave Konsel, *Engineer*
Don Herbe Jr,
Annmarie Jiuliante, *Admin Sec*
EMP: 20
SALES (est): 5.3MM **Privately Held**
WEB: www.dhsteel.org
SIC: 1791 3441 Structural steel erection;
fabricated structural metal

(G-5248)
DISPATCH PRINTING INC (PA)
917 Bacon St (16511-1727)
PHONE..................................814 870-9600
E Joseph Mehl, *President*
Timothy J Mehl, *Vice Pres*
EMP: 16 **EST:** 1917
SQ FT: 42,000
SALES (est): 6.5MM **Privately Held**
WEB: www. coporder.com
SIC: 7389 2752 2791 2759 Packaging &
labeling services; business form & card
printing, lithographic; typesetting; com-
mercial printing; automotive & apparel
trimmings

(G-5249)
DIVERSIFIED MFG SYSTEMS
421 W 12th St Ste 57 (16501-1559)
P.O. Box 317 (16512-0317)
PHONE..................................814 455-2400
Joseph Fedorko, *President*
Jeff Donovan, *Vice Pres*
EMP: 15
SQ FT: 11,000
SALES (est): 2.5MM **Privately Held**
SIC: 3599 Machine shop, jobbing & repair

(G-5250)
DONJON SHIPBUILDING & REPR LLC
220 E Bayfront Pkwy (16507-2402)
PHONE..................................814 455-6442
Ken Boothe, *General Mgr*
Michael Walsh, *Materials Mgr*
Ed Bowes, *Maint Spvr*
Lou Russo, *Opers Staff*
Vicki Waite, *Human Res Mgr*
EMP: 10
SQ FT: 30,000
SALES (est): 4.1MM
SALES (corp-wide): 71.2MM **Privately Held**
SIC: 3731 Shipbuilding & repairing

PA: Donjon Marine Co., Inc.
100 Central Ave
Hillside NJ 07205
908 964-8812

(G-5251)
DRUMM & OHARAH TL & DESIGN INC
8343 Edinboro Rd (16509-4248)
PHONE..................................814 476-1349
David O'Harah, *President*
James Drumm, *Corp Secy*
EMP: 3 **EST:** 1997
SQ FT: 7,300
SALES: 300K **Privately Held**
WEB: www.drumm.org
SIC: 3544 Special dies & tools

(G-5252)
E P M CORPORATION (PA)
7337 Footemill Rd (16509-6730)
P.O. Box 10125 (16514-0125)
PHONE..................................814 825-6650
Deborah E Miller, *President*
Marc E Miller, *Vice Pres*
Rachel E Miller, *Vice Pres*
▼ **EMP:** 15
SQ FT: 20,000
SALES: 2MM **Privately Held**
WEB: www.epmgroup.com
SIC: 2759 5087 5131 2796 Decals: print-
ing; service establishment equipment; la-
bels; engraving on copper, steel, wood or
rubber: printing plates

(G-5253)
EAGLE PRECISION TOOLING INC
4264 1 An A Hlf W 26th St 26 Th (16506)
PHONE..................................814 838-3515
Timothy Schroeck, *President*
Gary Mikovich, *Vice Pres*
EMP: 12
SQ FT: 4,000
SALES (est): 2.2MM **Privately Held**
SIC: 3544 Forms (molds), for foundry &
plastics working machinery; industrial
molds

(G-5254)
EARL E KNOX COMPANY (PA)
Also Called: Knox Western Gas Comprsr Div
1111 Bacon St (16511-1731)
P.O. Box 1248 (16512-1248)
PHONE..................................814 459-2754
David P Sechrist, *President*
Dave Sechrist, *Treasurer*
Kate Openlander, *Human Res Mgr*
Steven J Rhen, *Admin Sec*
EMP: 10
SQ FT: 45,000
SALES (est): 10MM **Privately Held**
WEB: www.eeknoxair.com
SIC: 3563 Air & gas compressors including
vacuum pumps

(G-5255)
EARL E KNOX COMPANY
Also Called: Knox Western
550 Huron St (16502-1744)
P.O. Box 1248 (16512-1248)
PHONE..................................814 459-2754
David Sechrist, *General Mgr*
EMP: 40
SALES (corp-wide): 10MM **Privately Held**
WEB: www.eeknoxair.com
SIC: 3599 3563 Machine shop, jobbing &
repair; air & gas compressors
PA: Earl E. Knox Company
1111 Bacon St
Erie PA 16511
814 459-2754

(G-5256)
EFCO INC
Also Called: Erie Press Systems
1253 W 12th St (16501-1518)
P.O. Box 4061 (16512-4061)
PHONE..................................814 455-3941
Dougald A Currie II, *President*
George M Currie, *Vice Pres*
◆ **EMP:** 45 **EST:** 1895
SQ FT: 137,000

SALES: 19.5MM **Privately Held**
WEB: www.eriepress.com
SIC: 3542 3559 8741 Machine tools;
metal forming type; foundry, smelting, refining & similar machinery; management
services

(G-5257)
EFI CONNECTION LLC
6586 Station Rd (16510-4737)
PHONE..................................814 566-0946
Michael Noonan, *CEO*
EMP: 3
SALES (est): 409.4K **Privately Held**
SIC: 3714 3519 Automotive wiring har-
ness sets; parts & accessories, internal
combustion engines

(G-5258)
EMERALD PRINTING & IMAGING
3212 Cherry St (16508-2605)
PHONE..................................814 899-6959
Brett Swanson, *President*
EMP: 3
SALES (est): 290K **Privately Held**
SIC: 7334 2759 Photocopying & duplicat-
ing services; commercial printing

(G-5259)
ENGINEERED PLASTICS LLC
1241 Camphausen Ave (16511-1759)
PHONE..................................814 452-6632
Denny Scalise, *Office Mgr*
EMP: 100
SQ FT: 60,000
SALES (corp-wide): 24.8MM **Privately Held**
WEB: www.engineeredplastics.com
SIC: 3089 3944 Plastic processing;
games, toys & children's vehicles
PA: Engineered Plastics Llc
1040 Maple Ave
Lake City PA 16423
814 774-2970

(G-5260)
ENJET AERO ERIE INC
8127 Nathan Cir (16509-4685)
PHONE..................................814 860-3104
Bruce Breckenridge, *CEO*
Nick Dibiase, *General Mgr*
Kayla Walker, *Business Mgr*
Russ McClelland, *Prdtn Mgr*
Christopher Ferraro, *CFO*
EMP: 114 **EST:** 2010
SALES (est): 303.1K
SALES (corp-wide): 38MM **Privately Held**
SIC: 3599 3812 Machine shop, jobbing &
repair; acceleration indicators & systems
components, aerospace
PA: Enjet Aero, Llc
9401 Indian Creek Pkwy
Overland Park KS 66210
913 717-7396

(G-5261)
EQUATE SPACE-TIME TECH LLC
2545 W Grandview Blvd (16506-4512)
PHONE..................................814 838-3571
John Cline,
EMP: 6
SALES (est): 506.6K **Privately Held**
SIC: 3679 Electronic components

(G-5262)
ERIE ASPHALT PAVING CO
1902 Cherry St (16502-2648)
PHONE..................................814 898-4151
John H Laver, *President*
EMP: 75
SALES (est): 5MM **Privately Held**
SIC: 5032 2951 Paving materials; asphalt
paving mixtures & blocks

(G-5263)
ERIE BRONZE & ALUMINUM COMPANY
6300 W Ridge Rd (16506-1021)
PHONE..................................814 838-8602
Imothy M Hunter, *President*
Chip Shamburg, *Vice Pres*
Obert W Shephard, *Vice Pres*
◆ **EMP:** 20 **EST:** 1932
SQ FT: 61,000

SALES (est): 5.9MM **Privately Held**
SIC: 3366 3365 Castings (except die):
bronze; masts, cast aluminum

(G-5264)
ERIE COKE CORP
925 E Bay Dr (16507-2201)
P.O. Box 6180 (16512-6180)
PHONE..................................814 454-0177
Robert Bloom, *President*
Kevin Maleski, *Principal*
Joe Campbell, *Human Res Mgr*
Paul Saffrin, *Manager*
EMP: 19 **EST:** 2010
SALES (est): 4.2MM **Privately Held**
SIC: 3312 Blast furnaces & steel mills

(G-5265)
ERIE COKE CORPORATION
Foot Of East Ave (16512)
PHONE..................................814 454-0177
James D Crane, *President*
Mike Durkin, *CFO*
EMP: 130
SQ FT: 1,200
SALES (est): 43.8MM **Privately Held**
WEB: www.eriecoke.com
SIC: 3312 Blast furnaces & steel mills

(G-5266)
ERIE ENERGY PRODUCTS INC
1400 Irwin Dr (16505-4891)
PHONE..................................814 454-2828
Kathy Klahr, *President*
EMP: 12
SALES (est): 1.6MM **Privately Held**
SIC: 2493 2679 Insulation board, cellular
fiber; pressed fiber products from wood
pulp: from purchased goods

(G-5267)
ERIE FORGE AND STEEL INC
Also Called: E F S
1341 W 16th St (16502-1544)
PHONE..................................814 452-2300
John Fitzgerald, *CEO*
Robin Ingols, *President*
Allan E Concoby, *President*
David Harned, *General Mgr*
Brian Fedei, *Materials Mgr*
▲ **EMP:** 74
SQ FT: 800,000
SALES (est): 18.8MM **Privately Held**
SIC: 3312 3462 3731 5051 Forgings,
iron & steel; ingots, steel; iron & steel
forgings; shipbuilding & repairing; forg-
ings, ferrous; turbines & turbine generator
sets & parts

(G-5268)
ERIE HARD CHROME INC
1570 E 12th St (16511-1796)
PHONE..................................814 459-5114
Lon M Akerly, *President*
EMP: 20 **EST:** 1964
SQ FT: 5,000
SALES (est): 2.7MM **Privately Held**
SIC: 3471 Chromium plating of metals or
formed products; electroplating of metals
or formed products

(G-5269)
ERIE M & P COMPANY INC
Also Called: Erie Mill and Press Company
953 E 12th St (16503-1441)
P.O. Box 6349 (16512-6349)
PHONE..................................814 454-1581
John Nowakowski, *President*
Greg Maus, *Vice Pres*
Daniel Nowak, *Engineer*
Dwayne Bednar, *Treasurer*
▲ **EMP:** 30 **EST:** 1982
SQ FT: 225,000
SALES (est): 7.4MM **Privately Held**
WEB: www.empco-inc.com
SIC: 3542 Presses: hydraulic & pneumatic,
mechanical & manual

(G-5270)
ERIE METAL BASKET INC
2643 W 17th St (16505-4305)
PHONE..................................814 833-1745
Tedd Stewart, *President*
Jeff Pahre, *Corp Secy*
EMP: 10
SQ FT: 8,000

SALES (est): 1.7MM **Privately Held**
SIC: 3569 3444 Filters & strainers, pipeline; sheet metalwork

(G-5271)
ERIE OEM INC
1001 State St Ste 1300 (16501-1832)
PHONE..................................814 459-8024
D E Cunningham, *President*
EMP: 300
SALES (est): 31.7MM **Privately Held**
WEB: www.oemerie.com
SIC: 3089 2262 Injection molding of plastics; finishing plants, manmade fiber & silk fabrics

(G-5272)
ERIE PLATING COMPANY
656 W 12th St (16501-1509)
PHONE..................................814 453-7531
David T Briggs, *President*
Lewis T Briggs, *Chairman*
Mike Ripley, *Maintence Staff*
EMP: 65 **EST:** 1925
SQ FT: 100,000
SALES (est): 8.9MM **Privately Held**
WEB: www.erieplating.com
SIC: 3471 Electroplating of metals or formed products; polishing, metals or formed products; anodizing (plating) of metals or formed products

(G-5273)
ERIE PROTECTIVE COATINGS INC
2646 W 14th St (16505-4302)
PHONE..................................814 833-0095
Raj Ghai, *President*
Sandra Ghai, *Admin Sec*
EMP: 5
SQ FT: 20,000
SALES (est): 669K **Privately Held**
WEB: www.erieprotectivecoatings.com
SIC: 3471 8711 Anodizing (plating) of metals or formed products; engineering services

(G-5274)
ERIE SPECIALTY PRODUCTS INC
645 W 11th St (16501-1503)
PHONE..................................814 453-5611
John R Cipriani, *CEO*
David Cipriani, *President*
Thomas J Bloom, *Vice Pres*
Terrance Skarupski, *Treasurer*
Ron Lapping, *Admin Sec*
EMP: 40
SQ FT: 30,000
SALES (est): 9.1MM **Privately Held**
WEB: www.eriespecialty.com
SIC: 3679 3451 Electronic circuits; screw machine products

(G-5275)
ERIE STRAYER COMPANY
1851 Rudolph Ave (16502-1940)
P.O. Box 1031 (16512-1031)
PHONE..................................814 456-7001
Robert F Strayer, *President*
Hamilton W Strayer, *Corp Secy*
Coleen Triana, *Executive Asst*
Joe Bogda, *Admin Sec*
Brian Smith,
▼ **EMP:** 101
SQ FT: 125,000
SALES (est): 34.4MM **Privately Held**
WEB: www.eriestrayer.com
SIC: 3531 3823 3536 3241 Concrete plants; buckets, excavating: clamshell, concrete, dragline, etc.; industrial instrmnts msrmnt display/control process variable; hoists, cranes & monorails; cement, hydraulic; construction sand & gravel

(G-5276)
ERIE TECHNICAL SYSTEMS INC
1239 Applejack Dr (16509-3953)
PHONE..................................814 899-2103
Richard P Sienerth, *President*
Timothy Porco, *Vice Pres*
EMP: 4
SQ FT: 12,500

SALES (est): 405.4K **Privately Held**
WEB: www.erietechnicalsystems.com
SIC: 8711 3535 3565 Consulting engineer; conveyors & conveying equipment; packaging machinery

(G-5277)
ERIE TECHNICAL SYSTEMS INC
4690 Iroquois Ave (16511-2350)
PHONE..................................814 899-2103
Richard Sienercth, *President*
Tim Porco, *Vice Pres*
Aaron Wilson, *Engineer*
Scott Kennemuth, *Sales Staff*
Tara Estes, *Office Mgr*
EMP: 8
SALES (est): 2.3MM **Privately Held**
SIC: 3823 Differential pressure instruments, industrial process type

(G-5278)
ERIE WELD PRODUCTS INC
1709 Franklin Ave (16510-1325)
PHONE..................................814 899-6320
Richard Jarmolowicz, *President*
▼ **EMP:** 14
SQ FT: 9,000
SALES (est): 4.3MM **Privately Held**
WEB: www.erieweld.com
SIC: 3441 7699 Fabricated structural metal; industrial equipment services

(G-5279)
ERIE WOOD PRODUCTS LLC
1835 E 12th St (16511-1725)
PHONE..................................814 452-4961
Vince White,
▲ **EMP:** 15
SQ FT: 27,000
SALES (est): 2.4MM **Privately Held**
WEB: www.eriewoodproducts.com
SIC: 2448 Pallets, wood

(G-5280)
ERIEZ MANUFACTURING CO (PA)
Also Called: Eriez Magnetics
2200 Asbury Rd (16506-1402)
PHONE..................................814 835-6000
Richard Merwin, *Ch of Bd*
Timothy G Shuttleworth, *President*
Lukas Guenthardt, *Exec VP*
Michael J Mankosa, *Exec VP*
Grainne M Blanchette, *Vice Pres*
◆ **EMP:** 315 **EST:** 1942
SQ FT: 145,000
SALES: 148MM **Privately Held**
WEB: www.eriez.com
SIC: 3559 Separation equipment, magnetic

(G-5281)
ERIEZ MANUFACTURING CO
1901 Wager Rd (16509-4055)
PHONE..................................814 520-8540
EMP: 6
SALES (corp-wide): 148MM **Privately Held**
SIC: 3559 Ammunition & explosives, loading machinery
PA: Eriez Manufacturing Co
2200 Asbury Rd
Erie PA 16506
814 835-6000

(G-5282)
ESSENTRA PLASTICS LLC (DH)
Also Called: Essentra Components
3123 Station Rd (16510-6501)
P.O. Box 10277 (16514-0277)
PHONE..................................814 899-7671
Drew De Crease, *Marketing Staff*
▲ **EMP:** 150
SQ FT: 24,100
SALES (est): 41.5MM
SALES (corp-wide): 1.3B **Privately Held**
SIC: 3089 5162 Injection molding of plastics; plastics products
HQ: Essentra Corp.
2 Westbrook Corp Ctr # 200
Westchester IL 60154
814 899-7671

(G-5283)
ESSENTRA POROUS TECH CORP
Also Called: Alliance Plastics Shipg Dept
2614 Mcclelland Ave (16510-2540)
PHONE..................................814 898-3238
Don Ellison, *Branch Mgr*
EMP: 20
SQ FT: 72,000
SALES (corp-wide): 112.5MM **Privately Held**
SIC: 3082 4226 3089 Unsupported plastics profile shapes; special warehousing & storage; injection molding of plastics
PA: Porex Technologies Corporation
1625 Ashton Park Dr Ste A
South Chesterfield VA 23834
804 524-4983

(G-5284)
EXECUTOOL
941 Guetner Ave (16505-1405)
PHONE..................................814 836-1141
Colin A Coffey, *Principal*
Edward Dobson, *Engineer*
Frank Jones, *Engineer*
EMP: 5
SALES (est): 334.4K **Privately Held**
SIC: 3544 Industrial molds

(G-5285)
EXECUTOOL PRCISION TOOLING INC
2727 W 16th St (16505-4214)
PHONE..................................814 836-1141
Gary Mayes, *President*
Eleanor Bowersox, *QC Mgr*
▲ **EMP:** 34
SQ FT: 33,000
SALES (est): 7.8MM **Privately Held**
WEB: www.executool.net
SIC: 3089 Injection molding of plastics

(G-5286)
F & S TOOL INC
2300 Powell Ave (16506-1844)
PHONE..................................814 838-7991
Michael Faulkner, *President*
James D Faulkner, *Vice Pres*
EMP: 50
SQ FT: 21,100
SALES (est): 13.6MM **Privately Held**
WEB: www.fs-tool.com
SIC: 3544 Forms (molds), for foundry & plastics working machinery; industrial molds; dies, plastics forming

(G-5287)
FABRI-WELD LLC
1133 W 18th St (16502-1514)
PHONE..................................814 490-7324
Michael Grudzien, *Mng Member*
EMP: 7 **EST:** 2007
SALES: 700K **Privately Held**
SIC: 7692 1761 Welding repair; architectural sheet metal work

(G-5288)
FAMILY FIRST SPORTS PARK
8155 Oliver Rd Ste 1 (16509-4683)
PHONE..................................814 866-5425
EMP: 40
SALES (est): 4MM **Privately Held**
SIC: 3949 Sports Facility

(G-5289)
FIESLER SAND & GRAVEL LLC
Also Called: Mining
3853 Knoyle Rd (16510-4924)
PHONE..................................814 899-6161
Patricia Fiesler,
EMP: 5
SALES (est): 595.3K **Privately Held**
SIC: 5211 1442 Sand & gravel; construction sand & gravel

(G-5290)
FINISH THOMPSON INC
Also Called: Fti
921 Greengarden Rd (16501-1525)
PHONE..................................814 455-4478
Kasey Bose, *CEO*
Casey D Bowes, *President*
▲ **EMP:** 46 **EST:** 1951
SQ FT: 50,000

SALES (est): 14.8MM **Privately Held**
WEB: www.finishthompson.com
SIC: 3561 4953 3821 Pumps & pumping equipment; refuse systems; distilling apparatus, laboratory type

(G-5291)
FIRST LINE COATINGS INC
901 W 12th St 204 (16501-1577)
PHONE..................................814 452-0046
Brian Brocious, *President*
Gary G Grzegorzewski, *General Mgr*
Gary Grzegorzewski, *Vice Pres*
Brian B Brocious, *Manager*
EMP: 9
SQ FT: 20,000
SALES (est): 1MM **Privately Held**
WEB: www.firstlinecoatings.com
SIC: 3479 Coating of metals with plastic or resins

(G-5292)
FLAGSHIP CITY HARDWOODS
1606 Harper Dr (16505-3949)
P.O. Box 8407 (16505-0407)
PHONE..................................814 835-1178
Thomas E Meehan, *Principal*
EMP: 3
SQ FT: 8,000
SALES (est): 630K **Privately Held**
SIC: 2431 Moldings & baseboards, ornamental & trim

(G-5293)
FLAGSHIP MULTIMEDIA INC
1001 State St Ste 1315 (16501-1832)
PHONE..................................814 314-9364
Brian Graham, *President*
Adam Welsh, *Vice Pres*
EMP: 3 **EST:** 2010
SALES (est): 263.9K **Privately Held**
SIC: 2721 Periodicals: publishing only

(G-5294)
FLEXCUT TOOL CO INC
8105 Hawthorne Dr (16509-4653)
PHONE..................................814 864-7855
Steven Bain, *President*
Matt Shimek, *Opers Mgr*
Matt Bain, *Sales Mgr*
EMP: 28
SQ FT: 10,000
SALES (est): 4.9MM **Privately Held**
WEB: www.flexcut.com
SIC: 3423 2499 Edge tools for woodworking: augers, bits, gimlets, etc.; carved & turned wood

(G-5295)
FM2 INC
Also Called: Directional Systems
2250 W 23rd St (16506-2917)
PHONE..................................814 874-0090
Annie Moks, *President*
EMP: 4
SALES (est): 209K **Privately Held**
SIC: 3993 Signs, not made in custom sign painting shops

(G-5296)
FMC TECHNOLOGIES INC
1602 Wagner Ave (16510-1444)
PHONE..................................814 898-5000
Dale Bohman, *Business Mgr*
Todd Beckes, *Engineer*
Allison Yori, *HR Admin*
Brian Sinicki, *Sales Mgr*
Lidmery Casasola, *Manager*
EMP: 12
SALES (corp-wide): 15B **Privately Held**
SIC: 3824 Fluid meters & counting devices
HQ: Fmc Technologies, Inc.
11740 Katy Fwy Energy Tow
Houston TX 77079
281 591-4000

(G-5297)
FMC TECHNOLOGIES MEASUREMENT S
Also Called: FMC Measurement Solutions
1648 Mcclelland Ave (16510)
P.O. Box 10428 (16514-0428)
PHONE..................................281 591-4000
John T Gremp, *CEO*
Robert L Potter, *President*
Douglas J Pferdehirt, *Exec VP*

Tom Gonda, *Purch Agent*
Dave Resch, *Engineer*
◆ **EMP:** 200
SQ FT: 340,000
SALES (est): 1.1MM
SALES (corp-wide): 15B **Privately Held**
SIC: 3824 3829 3825 3823 Positive displacement meters; turbine meters; measuring & controlling devices; instruments to measure electricity; industrial instrmnts msrmnt display/control process variable
HQ: Fmc Technologies, Inc.
    11740 Katy Fwy Energy Tow
    Houston TX 77079
    281 591-4000

(G-5298)
FOAM FABRICATORS INC
6550 W Ridge Rd (16506-1025)
PHONE..................................814 838-4538
Dan Lafaro, *VP Sales*
John O'Bryan, *Manager*
Dave Kiser, *Manager*
EMP: 18
SQ FT: 5,000 **Publicly Held**
WEB: www.foamfabricators.com
SIC: 2821 3086 Polyurethane resins; plastics foam products
HQ: Foam Fabricators, Inc.
    8722 E San Alberto Dr # 200
    Scottsdale AZ 85258
    480 607-7330

(G-5299)
FOAMBEAK LLC
4219 Knipper Ave (16510-3317)
PHONE..................................814 452-3626
Timothy Sonney,
EMP: 3
SALES: 45K **Privately Held**
SIC: 3429 7389 Clamps, couplings, nozzles & other metal hose fittings;

(G-5300)
GARNON TRUCK EQUIPMENT INC
Also Called: Garnon Mobility Vehicles
1617 Peninsula Dr (16505-4240)
PHONE..................................814 833-6000
James H Garnon, *President*
Charles L Garnon, *Chairman*
Wanda R Garnon, *Vice Pres*
Rich Magalhaes, *Accountant*
Dan Drakes, *Manager*
EMP: 13
SQ FT: 28,000
SALES (est): 3.3MM **Privately Held**
WEB: www.garnon.com
SIC: 5012 3711 Commercial vehicles; truck bodies; motor vehicles & car bodies

(G-5301)
GENERAL ELECTRIC COMPANY
2901 E Lake Rd (16531-0001)
PHONE..................................814 875-2234
Dave Dewolf, *Project Mgr*
Theodore Brown, *Draft/Design*
James Ghofulpo, *Engineer*
Bill Gross, *Engineer*
Hal Hostettler, *Engineer*
EMP: 5
SALES (corp-wide): 121.6B **Publicly Held**
SIC: 3531 3743 Railroad related equipment; railroad equipment
PA: General Electric Company
    41 Farnsworth St
    Boston MA 02210
    617 443-3000

(G-5302)
GENERAL PARTITIONS MFG CORP (PA)
Also Called: Rockfield Partitions
1702 Peninsula Dr (16505-4243)
P.O. Box 8370 (16505-0370)
PHONE..................................814 833-1154
George Zehner, *President*
Dan Draher, *Vice Pres*
Glenna Bartlett, *Treasurer*
Doug Burlingame, *Technology*
▼ **EMP:** 47 **EST:** 1967
SQ FT: 41,000
SALES: 12.9MM **Privately Held**
SIC: 2542 Partitions for floor attachment, prefabricated: except wood

(G-5303)
GEORGE-KO INDUSTRIES INC
4861 W 23rd St (16506-1471)
PHONE..................................814 838-6992
Matthew Koket, *President*
Alicia Koket, *Vice Pres*
Michael T Koket, *Vice Pres*
Sandra D Koket, *Admin Sec*
▼ **EMP:** 50
SQ FT: 22,000
SALES (est): 5.9MM **Privately Held**
WEB: www.georgeko.com
SIC: 3089 Injection molding of plastics

(G-5304)
GLENSIDE READY MIX CONCRETE CO
147 E 4th St (16507-1507)
PHONE..................................215 659-1500
Ralph Clayton, *Owner*
EMP: 5
SALES (est): 247.6K **Privately Held**
SIC: 3273 Ready-mixed concrete

(G-5305)
GRACO HIGH PRESSURE EQP INC
2955 W 17th St (16505-3928)
PHONE..................................800 289-7447
Christian Edward Rothe, *CEO*
EMP: 6
SALES (est): 234.3K
SALES (corp-wide): 1.6B **Publicly Held**
SIC: 3491 Industrial valves
PA: Graco Inc.
    88 11th Ave Ne
    Minneapolis MN 55413
    612 623-6000

(G-5306)
GREAT LAKES METAL FINISHING
1113 W 18th St (16502-1514)
PHONE..................................814 452-1886
Dennis Hartwig, *President*
Philip H Zacks, *Admin Sec*
EMP: 20
SQ FT: 20,000
SALES (est): 3.2MM **Privately Held**
WEB: www.goglmf.com
SIC: 3471 Electroplating of metals or formed products

(G-5307)
GREEN PROSTHETICS & ORTHOTICS (PA)
2241 Peninsula Dr (16506-2954)
PHONE..................................814 833-2311
David Wanner, *President*
Larry Loehrke, *Business Dir*
EMP: 10
SQ FT: 8,500
SALES (est): 1.9MM **Privately Held**
SIC: 3842 Limbs, artificial

(G-5308)
GREEN PROSTHETICS & ORTHOTICS
2241 Peninsula Dr (16506-2954)
PHONE..................................814 833-2311
Michelle Loehrke, *Branch Mgr*
EMP: 7
SALES (corp-wide): 1.9MM **Privately Held**
SIC: 3842 Limbs, artificial
PA: Green Prosthetics & Orthotics, Inc
    2241 Peninsula Dr
    Erie PA 16506
    814 833-2311

(G-5309)
HAMOT IMAGING FACILITY
Also Called: Hamot Breast Health Center
3406 Peach St (16508-2740)
PHONE..................................814 877-5381
Neal Baker, *Director*
EMP: 10
SALES (est): 1.5MM **Privately Held**
SIC: 3826 8071 Magnetic resonance imaging apparatus; medical laboratories

(G-5310)
HARRIER MFG CORP
904 Wilkins Rd (16505-1270)
PHONE..................................814 838-9957
Michele A Chereson, *President*
Jeffery D Chereson, *Treasurer*
EMP: 4
SALES (est): 431.2K **Privately Held**
SIC: 2675 Die-cut paper & board

(G-5311)
HAVACO TECHNOLOGIES INC
3058 W 22nd St (16506-2304)
P.O. Box 942 (16512-0942)
PHONE..................................814 878-5509
EMP: 9 **EST:** 2014
SALES (est): 1.1MM **Privately Held**
SIC: 3433 3444 3585 Heating equipment, except electric; sheet metalwork; air conditioning equipment, complete

(G-5312)
HAVPACK
1507 Wayne St (16503-3405)
PHONE..................................814 452-4989
EMP: 3
SALES (est): 142K **Privately Held**
SIC: 3089 Plastic containers, except foam

(G-5313)
HAYSITE REINFORCED PLAS LLC
5599 Perry Hwy (16509-3562)
PHONE..................................814 868-3691
Mark Anderson, *President*
Anne Shrm-Scp, *Human Res Mgr*
◆ **EMP:** 75
SQ FT: 100,000
SALES (est): 36MM
SALES (corp-wide): 837MM **Privately Held**
SIC: 2821 Plastics materials & resins
PA: Constantia Industries Ag
    Opernring 19
    Wien 1010
    158 845-0

(G-5314)
HEATRON INC
8135 Nathan Cir (16509-4656)
PHONE..................................814 868-8554
EMP: 42
SALES (corp-wide): 1.4B **Privately Held**
SIC: 3634 Electric Housewares And Fans
HQ: Heatron, Inc.
    3000 Wilson Ave
    Leavenworth KS 66048
    913 651-4420

(G-5315)
HEATRON INC
8135 Nathan Cir (16509-4656)
PHONE..................................814 868-8554
Bill Laneve, *Vice Pres*
Rich Giardina, *Engineer*
Linda Farley, *Human Res Dir*
Matter Robert, *Manager*
Julie Mifsud, *Manager*
EMP: 42
SALES (corp-wide): 2.2B **Privately Held**
SIC: 3634 Electric housewares & fans
HQ: Heatron, Inc.
    3000 Wilson Ave
    Leavenworth KS 66048
    913 651-4420

(G-5316)
HESSINGER GROUP INC
Also Called: Megagrafix
216 E 8th St (16503-1004)
PHONE..................................814 480-8912
Robert G Hessinger, *President*
▲ **EMP:** 7
SQ FT: 10,000
SALES: 1MM **Privately Held**
WEB: www.ptideas.com
SIC: 2752 Commercial printing, lithographic

(G-5317)
HI TECH PLATING CO INC
1015 W 18th St (16502-1512)
PHONE..................................814 455-4231
John Weindorf, *President*
Michelle Amann, *Office Mgr*
EMP: 13
SQ FT: 16,000
SALES: 1.4MM **Privately Held**
SIC: 3471 Chromium plating of metals or formed products; electroplating of metals or formed products

(G-5318)
HIGH PRESSURE EQUIPMENT CO INC
2955 W 17th St (16505-3928)
P.O. Box 8248 (16505-0248)
PHONE..................................800 289-7447
Lawrence Loper, *President*
Beau Griebin, *Vice Pres*
Larry Serafin, *Vice Pres*
Bob Jelinek, *Maint Spvr*
John Metalonis, *Engineer*
EMP: 70 **EST:** 1954
SQ FT: 20,000
SALES (est): 18.2MM
SALES (corp-wide): 1.6B **Publicly Held**
WEB: www.highpressure.com
SIC: 3498 Fabricated pipe & fittings
PA: Graco Inc.
    88 11th Ave Ne
    Minneapolis MN 55413
    612 623-6000

(G-5319)
HOROSCHUCK INC
8127 Nathan Cir (16509-4685)
PHONE..................................814 860-3104
Jerry Horoschuck, *President*
Michael Horoschuck, *Vice Pres*
Jason Keith, *Engineer*
Gordon Long, *CFO*
Valerie Horoschuck, *Admin Sec*
EMP: 13
SALES (est): 3.1MM **Privately Held**
WEB: www.aerohelicopters.com
SIC: 3599 Machine shop, jobbing & repair

(G-5320)
HUMBLE ELEPHANT LLC
333 Beverly Dr (16505-2205)
PHONE..................................814 434-1743
EMP: 3
SALES (est): 176.8K **Privately Held**
SIC: 2711 Newspapers

(G-5321)
ICON SCREENPRINTING INC
1710 French St (16501-2204)
PHONE..................................814 454-0086
Kent Jacoby, *President*
Andrea Jacoby, *Vice Pres*
EMP: 6
SQ FT: 6,095
SALES: 300K **Privately Held**
WEB: www.iconscreenprinting.com
SIC: 2759 Screen printing

(G-5322)
INDECK KEYSTONE ENERGY LLC
5340 Fryling Rd Ste 200 (16510-4672)
PHONE..................................814 452-6421
Gerald Forsythe, *Ch of Bd*
Marsha F Fournier, *President*
Gary Blazek, *Principal*
Janet Oldach Fuller, *Principal*
Phil Meehan, *Principal*
▲ **EMP:** 20
SQ FT: 8,000
SALES (est): 11.3MM **Privately Held**
WEB: www.indeck-keystone.com
SIC: 5084 3443 Industrial machinery & equipment; boilers: industrial, power, or marine

(G-5323)
INDEPENDENT PATTERN SHOP
1919 Reed St Ste 1 (16503-2159)
P.O. Box 1174 (16512-1174)
PHONE..................................814 459-2591
Ronald G Strohmeyer Jr, *Owner*
EMP: 3
SQ FT: 2,500
SALES: 500K **Privately Held**
WEB: www.independentpattern.com
SIC: 3543 Industrial patterns

▲ = Import ▼=Export
◆ =Import/Export

(G-5324)
INDUSTRIAL SALES & MFG INC
Also Called: I S M
2609 W 12th St (16505-4343)
PHONE..................................814 833-9876
James J Rutkowski Sr, *President*
Robert Charlie G Rutkowski, *Vice Pres*
James J Rutkowski Jr, *Treasurer*
▲ EMP: 80
SQ FT: 17,500
SALES (est): 22.7MM **Privately Held**
WEB: www.ismerie.com
SIC: 3599 Machine shop, jobbing & repair

(G-5325)
INNOVATIVE ADVG VEND SVCS LLC
Also Called: Innovative Services USA
7790 Clark Rd (16510-5929)
PHONE..................................814 528-7204
Sean M Maloney, *General Mgr*
EMP: 6
SQ FT: 25,000
SALES (est): 530.5K **Privately Held**
SIC: 2096 Potato chips & similar snacks

(G-5326)
INNOVATIVE PRESSURE TECH LLC
Also Called: Swagelok
4922 Pittsburgh Ave (16509-6207)
PHONE..................................814 833-5200
William D Vassen,
Jeffrey P Shuman,
EMP: 52
SQ FT: 30,000
SALES (est): 8.3MM
SALES (corp-wide): 940.1MM **Privately Held**
SIC: 3492 3432 3491 Fluid power valves & hose fittings; plumbing fixture fittings & trim; industrial valves
PA: Swagelok Company
29500 Solon Rd
Solon OH 44139
440 248-4600

(G-5327)
INSUL-BOARD INC
2120 Colonial Ave (16506-1824)
P.O. Box 8103 (16505-0103)
PHONE..................................814 833-7400
Richard Estock, *President*
Thomas T Estock, *Vice Pres*
Jeannine Estock, *Admin Sec*
▲ EMP: 32
SQ FT: 37,000
SALES (est): 5.2MM **Privately Held**
WEB: www.insulboard.com
SIC: 3086 Insulation or cushioning material, foamed plastic

(G-5328)
INTEGRATED MACHINE COMPANY
3952 W 12th St (16505-3344)
PHONE..................................814 835-4949
Mary Joann Light, *President*
EMP: 8
SQ FT: 7,000
SALES (est): 1MM **Privately Held**
SIC: 3751 Motorcycles & related parts

(G-5329)
INTERNATIONAL BAKERY
610 W 18th St (16502-1609)
PHONE..................................814 452-3435
Lawrence S Corsale, *President*
Joseph Corsale, *Vice Pres*
EMP: 30
SQ FT: 4,200
SALES (est): 4.3MM **Privately Held**
SIC: 2051 2099 5461 Bread, all types (white, wheat, rye, etc): fresh or frozen; food preparations; bread

(G-5330)
INTERNATIONAL PAPER COMPANY
32 E 14th St (16501-1901)
PHONE..................................814 454-9001
Dennis Delprince, *Branch Mgr*
EMP: 133
SALES (corp-wide): 23.3B **Publicly Held**
WEB: www.internationalpaper.com
SIC: 2621 Paper mills
PA: International Paper Company
6400 Poplar Ave
Memphis TN 38197
901 419-9000

(G-5331)
INTERSTATE CHEMICAL CO INC
United Erie
1432 Chestnut St (16502-1705)
PHONE..................................724 813-2576
Jenie Zacherl, *Manager*
EMP: 20
SALES (corp-wide): 346.5MM **Privately Held**
WEB: www.interstatechemical.com
SIC: 5169 2819 Chemicals & allied products; industrial inorganic chemicals
PA: Interstate Chemical Company, Inc.
2797 Freedland Rd
Hermitage PA 16148
724 981-3771

(G-5332)
INTERSTATE FOUNDRY PRODUCTS
1432 Chestnut St (16502-1705)
PHONE..................................814 456-4202
Joseph R Puntureri, *President*
Paul Cirillo, *Controller*
EMP: 13
SQ FT: 30,000
SALES (est): 1.3MM **Privately Held**
SIC: 2899 Core oil or binders

(G-5333)
JAMARCO
3316 W 22nd St (16506-5702)
P.O. Box 9158 (16505-8158)
PHONE..................................814 833-3159
Mark Webster, *President*
Tammy Narducci, *Director*
EMP: 5
SALES (est): 200K **Privately Held**
WEB: www.jamarcoind.com
SIC: 3471 Polishing, metals or formed products

(G-5334)
JAN & DANS JEWELRY (PA)
Also Called: Manufacturing Jewelers
28 W 8th St (16501-1309)
PHONE..................................814 452-3336
Janice Niebauer, *President*
Daniel Niebauer, *Vice Pres*
EMP: 4 EST: 1971
SQ FT: 3,000
SALES (est): 1.4MM **Privately Held**
SIC: 5944 5094 3911 Jewelry, precious stones & precious metals; jewelry; precious stones (gems); jewelry, precious metal

(G-5335)
JCR SALES & MFG LLC
Also Called: Green Lighting Led
1133 W 18th St Ste 200 (16502-1514)
PHONE..................................814 897-8870
Joshua Gehly, *Vice Pres*
Bill Gehly, *Mng Member*
Joel Gehly,
EMP: 4 EST: 2007
SALES (est): 580K **Privately Held**
SIC: 3648 Lighting equipment

(G-5336)
JIFFY PRINTING INC
947 W 26th St (16508)
PHONE..................................814 452-2067
John Blatt, *President*
EMP: 3
SALES (est): 23.4K **Privately Held**
SIC: 2752 Commercial printing, offset

(G-5337)
JMJ FINISHING
2640 W 17th St (16505-4306)
PHONE..................................814 838-4050
EMP: 3
SALES (est): 221.1K **Privately Held**
SIC: 3471 Plating/Polishing Service

(G-5338)
JOHN DIBBLE TREE SERVICE
9470 Wattsburg Rd (16509-6038)
PHONE..................................814 825-4543
Dorsia Dibble, *Owner*
EMP: 3
SALES (est): 314.1K **Privately Held**
SIC: 2448 0783 Pallets, wood; removal services, bush & tree

(G-5339)
JOSEPH MCCORMICK CNSTR CO INC (PA)
3340 Pearl Ave (16510-1659)
P.O. Box 176 (16512-0176)
PHONE..................................814 899-3111
Owen Mc Cormick, *President*
Robert B Gwinn, *Vice Pres*
Joe Hosey, *Vice Pres*
Brenda Burt, *Admin Sec*
EMP: 44 EST: 1904
SQ FT: 2,880
SALES: 18.4MM **Privately Held**
SIC: 1611 2951 1795 Highway & street paving contractor; resurfacing contractor; asphalt & asphaltic paving mixtures (not from refineries); wrecking & demolition work

(G-5340)
JTM FOODS LLC
2126 E 33rd St (16510-2554)
PHONE..................................814 899-0886
Craig Hope, *Principal*
Melissa Kotyuk, *Controller*
Michael Brookhart, *Mktg Dir*
Larry Bilello, *Marketing Staff*
Jeff Jung, *Info Tech Dir*
▲ EMP: 90
SQ FT: 64,000
SALES (est): 25.4MM **Privately Held**
WEB: www.jtmfoods.net
SIC: 2051 Cakes, bakery: except frozen

(G-5341)
K & A TOOL CO
5208 Laurelwood Ct (16506-3901)
PHONE..................................814 835-1405
Gary Scalzitti, *Owner*
EMP: 6
SQ FT: 2,000
SALES (est): 553.6K **Privately Held**
WEB: www.katool.com
SIC: 3544 Forms (molds), for foundry & plastics working machinery

(G-5342)
KANE INNOVATIONS INC (PA)
Also Called: Kane Detention Products
2250 Powell Ave (16506-1842)
PHONE..................................814 838-7731
Dean Campbell, *President*
Todd Frederick, *President*
Doug Radcliffe, *Managing Dir*
Lawrence Finazzo, *Vice Pres*
Michael D Show, *Vice Pres*
▲ EMP: 75 EST: 1959
SALES (est): 31MM **Privately Held**
WEB: www.kanescreens.com
SIC: 3442 3211 3496 3446 Storm doors or windows, metal; screen & storm doors & windows; screens, window, metal; screen doors, metal; strengthened or reinforced glass; miscellaneous fabricated wire products; architectural metalwork

(G-5343)
KIMKOPY PRINTING INC
2040 W 8th St (16505-4742)
PHONE..................................814 454-6635
Donald Seiber, *President*
Paul F Sieber, *Corp Secy*
Larry Muehl, *Vice Pres*
Lisa Watkins, *Manager*
EMP: 6
SQ FT: 1,600
SALES (est): 682.1K
SALES (corp-wide): 13.1MM **Privately Held**
WEB: www.kimkopy.com
SIC: 7334 2759 Photocopying & duplicating services; commercial printing
PA: Mccarty Printing Corp.
246 E 7th St
Erie PA 16503
814 454-4561

(G-5344)
KING PRECISION SOLUTIONS LLC
2200 Colonial Ave Ste 2 (16506-1898)
PHONE..................................877 312-3858
Todd King, *President*
EMP: 11
SALES (est): 1.7MM **Privately Held**
SIC: 3089 Injection molding of plastics

(G-5345)
KITCHENS BY MEADE INC
Also Called: Erie Custom Millwork
2035 W 12th St (16505-4802)
PHONE..................................814 453-4888
Richard Petri, *President*
Mark Bennett, *Vice Pres*
Doreen Petri, *Admin Sec*
EMP: 16
SQ FT: 9,000
SALES: 789.2K **Privately Held**
SIC: 5031 5712 2541 2434 Kitchen cabinets; cabinet work, custom; wood partitions & fixtures; wood kitchen cabinets; carpentry work

(G-5346)
KLAFTERS INC
Also Called: Cigarette Express
2663 W 8th St (16505-4034)
PHONE..................................814 833-7444
Roberta Eckendorf, *Manager*
EMP: 6
SALES (corp-wide): 35.4MM **Privately Held**
SIC: 2111 Cigarettes
PA: Klafter's, Inc.
216 N Beaver St
New Castle PA 16101
724 856-3249

(G-5347)
KLEIN PLATING WORKS INC
2020 Greengarden Rd (16502-2194)
PHONE..................................814 452-3793
Larrie Dudenhoeffer, *CEO*
Joe Dudenhoeffer, *President*
Dennis Hultberg, *Prdtn Mgr*
Len Zielinski, *QC Mgr*
Ken Heberle, *Supervisor*
▲ EMP: 60
SQ FT: 25,000
SALES (est): 6.5MM **Privately Held**
WEB: www.kleinplating.com
SIC: 3471 Anodizing (plating) of metals or formed products; electroplating of metals or formed products

(G-5348)
KNOX-WESTERN INC
Also Called: Knox Western Gas Compressors
1111 Bacon St (16511-1731)
P.O. Box 1248 (16512-1248)
PHONE..................................814 459-2754
David Sechrist, *President*
Jeffrey Potts, *Principal*
▲ EMP: 7 EST: 2015
SALES (est): 209.3K **Privately Held**
SIC: 3563 Air & gas compressors

(G-5349)
KOCH INDUSTRIES INC
1710 Greengarden Rd (16501-1569)
PHONE..................................814 453-5444
Brady Ducharme, *Branch Mgr*
EMP: 10
SQ FT: 4,400
SALES (corp-wide): 42.4B **Privately Held**
WEB: www.kochind.com
SIC: 2879 Agricultural disinfectants
PA: Koch Industries, Inc.
4111 E 37th St N
Wichita KS 67220
316 828-5500

(G-5350)
KOLD DRAFT INTERNATIONAL LLC
Also Called: Kold-Draft
1525 E Lake Rd Ste 700 (16511-1089)
PHONE..................................814 453-6761
Leonard Kosar, *Mng Member*
Martin Gardner,
◆ EMP: 30
SQ FT: 46,285

GEOGRAPHIC

SALES (est): 7.7MM
SALES (corp-wide): 200MM **Privately Held**
WEB: www.eriemg.com
SIC: 3585 Ice making machinery
PA: Greenfield World Trade, Inc.
3355 Entp Ave Ste 160
Fort Lauderdale FL 33331
954 202-7419

(G-5351)
KONE CRANES INC
1351 W 12th St (16501-1520)
PHONE..................(814 878-8070
Justin Allaman, *Office Mgr*
EMP: 10
SALES (est): 1.3MM **Privately Held**
SIC: 3536 7538 5082 Cranes, overhead traveling; general truck repair; cranes, construction

(G-5352)
KONECRANES INC
1351 W 12th St (16501-1520)
PHONE..................814 878-8070
Michelle Ames, *Manager*
EMP: 14
SALES (corp-wide): 3.7B **Privately Held**
SIC: 3536 Hoists, cranes & monorails
HQ: Konecranes, Inc.
4401 Gateway Blvd
Springfield OH 45502

(G-5353)
LAKE ERIE BIOFUELS LLC (HQ)
Also Called: Hero Bx
1670 E Lake Rd (16511-1034)
PHONE..................814 528-9200
Michael L Noble, *President*
Chris Peterson, *Vice Pres*
Kavin Lowery, *Plant Mgr*
Tim Keaveney, *VP Sales*
Shawn Triscuit, *Sales Staff*
EMP: 40
SQ FT: 10,000
SALES: 25.3MM
SALES (corp-wide): 5.5MM **Privately Held**
WEB: www.lakeeriebiofuels.com
SIC: 2869 Fuels
PA: Erie Management Group, Llc
1540 E Lake Rd Ste 302
Erie PA 16511
814 528-9000

(G-5354)
LAKE ERIE RUBBER & MFG LLC
6410 W Ridge Rd (16506-1023)
PHONE..................814 835-0170
Jonathan Meighan, *Mng Member*
EMP: 11
SALES (est): 427.6K **Privately Held**
SIC: 3069 Fabricated rubber products

(G-5355)
LAKE ERIE RUBBER WORKS INC
6410 W Ridge Rd (16506-1023)
PHONE..................814 835-0170
Sean F Sculley, *President*
George Nicewonger, *General Mgr*
George Micewonber, *Vice Pres*
Tracy Lockwood, *Plant Mgr*
EMP: 13
SALES (est): 2.1MM **Privately Held**
SIC: 3069 Molded rubber products

(G-5356)
LAKE SHORE INDUSTRIES INC
1817 Poplar St (16502-1624)
P.O. Box 3427 (16508-0427)
PHONE..................814 456-4277
Leo Bruno, *President*
David H Mays, *Vice Pres*
Shirley Bruno, *Admin Sec*
EMP: 19
SQ FT: 20,000
SALES: 1.4MM **Privately Held**
SIC: 3993 Signs, not made in custom sign painting shops

(G-5357)
LAKESHORE ISOTOPES LLC
2727 W 21st St (16506-2962)
PHONE..................814 836-0207

John Tomayko, *President*
Valerie Wilt, *Exec Dir*
EMP: 13
SALES (est): 1.7MM **Privately Held**
WEB: www.lakeshoreisotopes.com
SIC: 3829 Nuclear radiation & testing apparatus

(G-5358)
LAKEVIEW FORGE CO
Also Called: Erie Tool Works
735 W 12th St (16501-1510)
P.O. Box 1030 (16512-1030)
PHONE..................814 454-4518
Matthew Bacon, *Branch Mgr*
EMP: 13
SQ FT: 53,138
SALES (corp-wide): 6.6MM **Privately Held**
WEB: www.lakeviewforge.com
SIC: 3451 Screw machine products
PA: Lakeview Forge Co
1725 Pittsburgh Ave
Erie PA 16505
814 454-4518

(G-5359)
LAMJEN INC
2254 E 30th St (16510-2552)
PHONE..................814 459-5277
Thomas B Hagen, *President*
David M Tullio, *Vice Pres*
John Graeb, *Prdtn Mgr*
Greg Terlitsky, *QC Mgr*
James B Ohrn, *CFO*
EMP: 25 EST: 1968
SQ FT: 20,000
SALES: 4MM **Privately Held**
WEB: www.lamjen.com
SIC: 3599 Custom machinery; machine shop, jobbing & repair

(G-5360)
LARRY D MAYS (PA)
Also Called: Mays Sporting Gds & Award Ctr
4726 Pittsburgh Ave (16509-6204)
PHONE..................814 833-7988
Larry D Mays, *Owner*
Gregory Mays, *Vice Pres*
EMP: 10
SQ FT: 14,000
SALES (est): 21.8MM **Privately Held**
SIC: 2261 5199 5999 2395 Screen printing of cotton broadwoven fabrics; advertising specialties; trophies & plaques; embroidery & art needlework

(G-5361)
LEMAC PACKAGING INC (PA)
2121 Mckinley Ave (16503-2317)
P.O. Box 10788 (16514-0788)
PHONE..................814 453-7652
Gerald D Lee, *President*
Dennis L McKane, *Vice Pres*
EMP: 8
SQ FT: 110,000
SALES (est): 18.5MM **Privately Held**
WEB: www.fleetimage.com
SIC: 5085 2675 2679 2672 Packing, industrial; die-cut paper & board; labels, paper: made from purchased material; coated & laminated paper; corrugated & solid fiber boxes

(G-5362)
LEMAC PACKAGING INC
Also Called: Graphics Concepts Division
645 W 32nd St (16508-2641)
P.O. Box 10788 (16514-0788)
PHONE..................814 866-7469
Jerry Lee III, *Owner*
EMP: 13
SQ FT: 30,250
SALES (corp-wide): 18.5MM **Privately Held**
WEB: www.fleetimage.com
SIC: 2759 Commercial printing
PA: Lemac Packaging, Inc.
2121 Mckinley Ave
Erie PA 16503
814 453-7652

(G-5363)
LEWIS WELDING SERVICES INC
Also Called: Lewis Bawol Welding
3308 W 22nd St (16506-5702)
PHONE..................814 838-1074
Ken Bawol, *President*
Jeff Lewis, *Treasurer*
EMP: 7
SQ FT: 4,500
SALES (est): 1.2MM **Privately Held**
WEB: www.engravewithlasers.com
SIC: 7692 Welding repair

(G-5364)
LIDS CORPORATION
654 Mllcreek Mall Ste 525 (16565)
PHONE..................814 868-1944
Jill Pauley, *Manager*
EMP: 3
SALES (corp-wide): 2.1B **Publicly Held**
WEB: www.hatworld.com
SIC: 2353 5661 Hats & caps; men's shoes
HQ: Lids Corporation
7555 Woodland Dr
Indianapolis IN 46278

(G-5365)
LIGHTHOUSE ELECTRIC CONTRLS CO
1307 Lowell Ave (16505-4333)
PHONE..................814 835-2348
Albert Clement, *Owner*
EMP: 12
SQ FT: 2,400
SALES (est): 1MM **Privately Held**
WEB: www.lighthouseerie.com
SIC: 3613 3812 3444 7373 Control panels, electric; search & navigation equipment; sheet metalwork; office computer automation systems integration

(G-5366)
LINCOLN FOUNDRY INC
1600 Industrial Dr (16505-4351)
P.O. Box 8156 (16505-0156)
PHONE..................814 833-1514
Nir Riazzi Jr, *President*
Christopher Campbell, *Vice Pres*
Vinnie Carpin, *Project Mgr*
Danielle Bukala, *Bookkeeper*
EMP: 32
SQ FT: 22,000
SALES (est): 8.2MM **Privately Held**
WEB: www.lincolnfoundry.com
SIC: 3366 3365 Brass foundry; bronze foundry; aluminum foundries

(G-5367)
LISA MIKOLAJCZAK
Also Called: Jaymar Tool
119 Lake Cliff Dr (16511-1241)
PHONE..................814 898-4700
Michael Mikolajczak, *Owner*
Lisa Mikolajczak, *Owner*
EMP: 5
SALES (est): 238.5K **Privately Held**
SIC: 3441 Fabricated structural metal

(G-5368)
LITESCAPING LLC
2225 Colonial Ave (16506-1894)
P.O. Box 8893 (16505-0893)
PHONE..................814 833-6200
Darin Linhart,
Rebecca Linhart,
EMP: 3
SALES (est): 340K **Privately Held**
SIC: 3648 5063 Outdoor lighting equipment; lighting fixtures

(G-5369)
LOCALEDGE MEDIA INC
Also Called: Talking Phone Book
3715 Zimmerman Rd (16510-2665)
PHONE..................716 875-9100
Rick Lewis, *Manager*
EMP: 22
SQ FT: 5,580
SALES (corp-wide): 12.5MM **Privately Held**
WEB: www.etpb.com
SIC: 7311 2741 Advertising consultant; miscellaneous publishing

PA: Localedge Media, Inc.
61 John Muir Dr
Buffalo NY 14228
800 388-8255

(G-5370)
LONG DROP GAMES LLC
2110 Knoll Ave (16510-2222)
PHONE..................814 460-7961
Shawn Lynch, *CEO*
James Sokolowski,
Quincy Thomas,
EMP: 3
SALES (est): 90.9K **Privately Held**
SIC: 7372 7389 Application computer software;

(G-5371)
LORD CORPORATION
Also Called: Chemical Products Div
2455 Robison Rd W (16509-4675)
P.O. Box 10038 (16514-0038)
PHONE..................814 868-0924
Peter J Jones, *Engineer*
Brian McGill, *Engineer*
Ron Churley, *Manager*
Paul J Ditmore, *Manager*
Russ Tork, *Info Tech Dir*
EMP: 400
SQ FT: 28,362
SALES (corp-wide): 1B **Privately Held**
WEB: www.lordcorp.com
SIC: 3724 2891 7389 3714 Aircraft engines & engine parts; adhesives & sealants; drafting service, except temporary help; motor vehicle parts & accessories; power transmission equipment; plastics materials & resins
PA: Lord Corporation
111 Lord Dr
Cary NC 27511
919 468-5979

(G-5372)
LORD CORPORATION
Also Called: Aerospace Division
2455 Robison Rd W (16509-4675)
P.O. Box 10039 (16514-0039)
PHONE..................814 868-3180
Charles J Hora Jr, *Vice Chairman*
EMP: 450
SALES (corp-wide): 1B **Privately Held**
WEB: www.lordcorp.com
SIC: 5085 3568 Rubber goods, mechanical; power transmission equipment
PA: Lord Corporation
111 Lord Dr
Cary NC 27511
919 468-5979

(G-5373)
LORD CORPORATION
Also Called: Lord Industrial Products
2455 Robison Rd W (16509-4675)
PHONE..................877 275-5673
Lane Miller, *Vice Pres*
Dale Hull, *Project Mgr*
Kathy Gourley, *Buyer*
Greg Baumgratz, *Engineer*
Zach Fuhrer, *Engineer*
EMP: 800
SALES (corp-wide): 1B **Privately Held**
WEB: www.lordcorp.com
SIC: 3069 3823 3651 2891 Reclaimed rubber & specialty rubber compounds; industrial instrmnts msrmnt display/control process variable; household audio & video equipment; adhesives & sealants; paints & allied products; inorganic pigments
PA: Lord Corporation
111 Lord Dr
Cary NC 27511
919 468-5979

(G-5374)
LUKJAN SUPPLY & MANUFACTURING (PA)
4364 W Ridge Rd (16506-1498)
PHONE..................814 838-1328
Paul Lukjanczuk, *President*
Andrew Lukjanczuk, *Corp Secy*
Greg Lukjanczuk, *Vice Pres*
EMP: 12 EST: 1971
SQ FT: 15,000

SALES (est): 4.3MM **Privately Held**
SIC: 5074 3444 Heating equipment (hydronic); sheet metalwork

(G-5375)
LUXOTTICA OF AMERICA INC
Also Called: Lenscrafters
200 Millcreek Plz (16565-5102)
PHONE..................814 868-7502
Mary Barrett, *Site Mgr*
Tony Juliano, *Branch Mgr*
EMP: 23
SALES (corp-wide): 283.5MM **Privately Held**
WEB: www.lenscrafters.com
SIC: 5995 3851 Eyeglasses, prescription; ophthalmic goods
HQ: Luxottica Of America Inc.
4000 Luxottica Pl
Mason OH 45040

(G-5376)
LYONS ELECTRIC MOTOR SERVICE
1427 E 10th St (16503-1713)
PHONE..................814 456-7127
Daniel Lyons, *President*
▲ **EMP:** 4
SQ FT: 3,500
SALES (est): 260K **Privately Held**
SIC: 7694 Electric motor repair

(G-5377)
M&B ENTERPRISES INC
209 E 21st St (16503-1924)
PHONE..................814 454-4461
Mark Milford, *Owner*
EMP: 5
SALES (est): 249.5K **Privately Held**
SIC: 1761 7692 Roofing contractor; welding repair

(G-5378)
MACHINING CONCEPTS INC
1304 Industrial Dr (16505-4326)
PHONE..................814 838-8896
James F Willats, *President*
Mark Wilkosz, *Vice Pres*
EMP: 11
SQ FT: 5,000
SALES (est): 1.8MM **Privately Held**
SIC: 3599 Machine shop, jobbing & repair

(G-5379)
MAKTEAM SOFTWARE LTD CO
3519 Anne Marie Dr (16506-6023)
PHONE..................814 504-1283
Fong Mak, *Principal*
EMP: 3
SALES (est): 99K **Privately Held**
SIC: 7372 Prepackaged software

(G-5380)
MARINE SHEET METAL WORKS
1447 E 10th St (16503-1798)
PHONE..................814 455-9700
Thomas Mc Ginnis Jr, *Partner*
Margaret E Burton, *Partner*
William Mc Ginnis, *Partner*
EMP: 7
SALES (est): 1MM **Privately Held**
SIC: 3444 Sheet metal specialties, not stamped

(G-5381)
MASON JARS COMPANY
1001 State St Ste 1220 (16501-1833)
PHONE..................877 490-5565
Karen Rzepecki, *President*
EMP: 11
SQ FT: 3,000
SALES: 900K **Privately Held**
SIC: 3221 3089 5961 Food containers, glass; plastic kitchenware, tableware & houseware; catalog & mail-order houses

(G-5382)
MATHESON TRI-GAS INC
1313 Chestnut St (16501-1734)
PHONE..................814 453-5637
Cliff Bendig, *Branch Mgr*
EMP: 7 **Privately Held**
SIC: 3548 Welding apparatus

HQ: Matheson Tri-Gas, Inc.
150 Allen Rd Ste 302
Basking Ridge NJ 07920
908 991-9200

(G-5383)
MAYER BROTHERS CONSTRUCTION CO
1902 Cherry St (16502-2648)
PHONE..................814 452-3748
John H Laver, *President*
Richard T Weschler Jr, *Vice Pres*
Deborah A Snyder, *Asst Sec*
EMP: 10
SQ FT: 5,000
SALES (est): 2.4MM **Privately Held**
WEB: www.mayerbros.net
SIC: 3531 1442 1611 2951 Bituminous batching plants; gravel mining; highway & street paving contractor; asphalt paving mixtures & blocks; concrete work

(G-5384)
MBPJ CORPORATION (PA)
420 E Bayfront Pkwy (16507-2404)
PHONE..................814 461-9120
EMP: 2
SALES (est): 38MM **Privately Held**
SIC: 3679 Electronic circuits

(G-5385)
MCCARTY PRINTING CORP (PA)
Also Called: Walco Label & Packaging
246 E 7th St (16503-1002)
P.O. Box 1136 (16512-1136)
PHONE..................814 454-4561
Donald Sieber, *President*
Mike Arnold, *Principal*
Bill Wolford, *Principal*
Shelley Haefner, *Vice Pres*
Derf Sieber, *Vice Pres*
▲ **EMP:** 59 **EST:** 1916
SQ FT: 41,128
SALES (est): 13.1MM **Privately Held**
WEB: www.mccartyprinting.com
SIC: 2791 2796 2759 2789 Typesetting; platemaking services; commercial printing; bookbinding & related work; commercial printing, lithographic

(G-5386)
MCKESSON PTENT CARE SLTONS INC
14 Millcreek Sq (16565-5203)
PHONE..................814 860-8160
Heather A Edmunds, *Principal*
EMP: 59
SALES (corp-wide): 208.3B **Publicly Held**
SIC: 5999 3842 7363 8322 Orthopedic & prosthesis applications; dressings, surgical; medical help service; rehabilitation services
HQ: Mckesson Patient Care Solutions, Inc.
9235 Activity Rd Ste 105
San Diego CA 92126
412 507-0077

(G-5387)
MCSHANE WELDING COMPANY INC
12 Port Access Rd Ste 1 (16507-2297)
PHONE..................814 459-3797
James McShane, *President*
Robert Eggleston, *Vice Pres*
Jeff Manley, *VP Sales*
Tom Carney, *Sales Staff*
Lisa Schaefer, *Manager*
EMP: 30
SQ FT: 20,000
SALES (est): 7.8MM **Privately Held**
WEB: www.mcshanewelding.com
SIC: 3444 3443 7692 3446 Sheet metalwork; fabricated plate work (boiler shop); welding repair; architectural metalwork; fabricated structural metal

(G-5388)
MG INDUSTRIES ERIE INC
2103 E 33rd St Ste W-5 (16510-2530)
PHONE..................814 806-6826
Michael H Gashgarian, *President*
EMP: 7 **EST:** 2011
SALES (est): 1.6MM **Privately Held**
SIC: 2851 Vinyl coatings, strippable

(G-5389)
MICRO MOLD CO INC (PA)
4820 Pittsburgh Ave (16509-6217)
PHONE..................814 838-3404
David G Mead, *President*
Timothy L Katen, *Vice Pres*
EMP: 30 **EST:** 1978
SQ FT: 6,000
SALES (est): 8.1MM **Privately Held**
WEB: www.micromolderie.com
SIC: 3089 Injection molding of plastics

(G-5390)
MICRO PLATING INC
8110 Hawthorne Dr (16509-4654)
PHONE..................814 866-0073
Paul Szymanowski, *President*
John Vali, *QC Dir*
Barbara Albert, *Office Mgr*
EMP: 8
SQ FT: 5,000
SALES (est): 2MM **Privately Held**
WEB: www.microplating.com
SIC: 3471 Plating of metals or formed products

(G-5391)
MIGHTY FINE INC
Also Called: Mighty Fine Donuts
2612 Parade St (16504-2810)
PHONE..................814 455-6408
Glenn K Brigaman, *President*
Nancy G Brigaman, *Vice Pres*
EMP: 51
SQ FT: 2,500
SALES (est): 2.2MM **Privately Held**
WEB: www.fineblueribbon.com
SIC: 5461 5149 2051 Doughnuts; bakery products; bread, cake & related products

(G-5392)
MIKRON VALVE & MFR INC
1282 W 12th St (16501-1519)
PHONE..................814 453-2337
Mike Miczo, *President*
Mike Ziegler, *Plant Mgr*
Patrick Smith, *Engineer*
Carole Miczo, *Treasurer*
Gloria Malone, *Administration*
EMP: 5 **EST:** 1923
SQ FT: 15,000
SALES (est): 1.3MM **Privately Held**
SIC: 3823 3592 3599 7694 Liquid level instruments, industrial process type; valves; machine shop, jobbing & repair; electric motor repair

(G-5393)
MILLCREEK METAL FINISHING INC
2401 W 15th St (16505-4513)
PHONE..................814 833-9045
Charles S Fiscus, *President*
Kathleen Fiscus, *Corp Secy*
Kathleen A Fiscus, *Treasurer*
Kathleen Fiscus, *Treasurer*
EMP: 6
SQ FT: 4,000
SALES (est): 758.4K **Privately Held**
WEB: www.mcmetal.com
SIC: 3471 Electroplating of metals or formed products

(G-5394)
MODERN INDUSTRIES INC (PA)
613 W 11th St (16501-1503)
P.O. Box 399 (16512-0399)
PHONE..................814 455-8061
Dennis J Sweny, *President*
Timothy Sweny, *President*
Dave Sweny, *Vice Pres*
H David Sweny, *Vice Pres*
Matthew Sweny, *Vice Pres*
▲ **EMP:** 200 **EST:** 1946
SQ FT: 350,000
SALES (est): 20MM **Privately Held**
WEB: www.modernind.com
SIC: 3714 3398 8734 3569 Motor vehicle parts & accessories; metal heat treating; metallurgical testing laboratory; industrial shock absorbers

(G-5395)
MORLIN INC
2044 W 20th St (16502-1901)
PHONE..................814 454-5559

David Morphy, *President*
Jean McMillin, *Vice Pres*
Erik Morphy, *Engineer*
▲ **EMP:** 9
SQ FT: 15,000
SALES (est): 1.4MM **Privately Held**
SIC: 3542 5084 Machine tools, metal forming type; measuring & testing equipment, electrical

(G-5396)
MORRIS COUPLING COMPANY (PA)
Also Called: Tennessee Tubebending Division
2240 W 15th St (16505-4510)
PHONE..................814 459-1741
John Whiteman, *CEO*
George Shabla, *Vice Pres*
◆ **EMP:** 60 **EST:** 1941
SQ FT: 37,000
SALES (est): 23.2MM **Privately Held**
WEB: www.morriscoupling.com
SIC: 3568 3498 Couplings, shaft: rigid, flexible, universal joint, etc.; tube fabricating (contract bending & shaping)

(G-5397)
MSH INDUSTRIES
9640 Lake Pleasant Rd (16509-5762)
PHONE..................814 866-0777
Guy Euliano, *Principal*
EMP: 3 **EST:** 2004
SALES (est): 280.2K **Privately Held**
SIC: 3999 Manufacturing industries

(G-5398)
MUNOT PLASTICS INC (PA)
2935 W 17th St (16505-3995)
PHONE..................814 838-7721
Chandler D Rees, *President*
EMP: 24 **EST:** 1963
SQ FT: 35,000
SALES (est): 4.7MM **Privately Held**
WEB: www.munotplastics.com
SIC: 3089 Thermoformed finished plastic products; plastic containers, except foam

(G-5399)
MUNOT PLASTICS INC
2935 W 17th St (16505-3995)
PHONE..................814 838-7721
Bob Rees, *General Mgr*
EMP: 23
SQ FT: 8,752
SALES (corp-wide): 4.7MM **Privately Held**
WEB: www.munotplastics.com
SIC: 3089 Plastic containers, except foam
PA: Munot Plastics, Inc.
2935 W 17th St
Erie PA 16505
814 838-7721

(G-5400)
MVP PRNTING PRMTIONAL PDTS LLC
Also Called: Gohrs On Demand
4734 Pittsburgh Ave (16509-6204)
PHONE..................814 520-8392
Kenneth Menale, *President*
Stacey Janus, *Vice Pres*
EMP: 7 **EST:** 2010
SQ FT: 10,000
SALES (est): 1MM **Privately Held**
SIC: 3861 Printing equipment, photographic

(G-5401)
N M A
1525 E Lake Rd Ste C (16511-1088)
PHONE..................814 453-6787
EMP: 16 **EST:** 2011
SALES: 2.4MM **Privately Held**
SIC: 3312 Blast Furnace-Steel Works

(G-5402)
NIAGARA MACHINE INC (PA)
325 W Front St (16507-1227)
PHONE..................814 455-8838
Gary R Christensen, *President*
Robert C Christensen, *Chairman*
Richard M Seward, *Vice Pres*
Margaret Christensen, *Admin Sec*
▼ **EMP:** 8 **EST:** 1950
SQ FT: 11,000

SALES (est): 1.6MM **Privately Held**
WEB: www.niagaramachine.com
SIC: **3599** 7699 Machine shop, jobbing &
repair; engine repair & replacement, non-
automotive

(G-5403)
NIAGARA MANUFACTURING CO
2725 W 17th St (16505-4307)
P.O. Box 8206 (16505-0206)
PHONE..................................814 838-4511
Edward Haynor, *President*
EMP: 12
SQ FT: 8,500
SALES (est): 1.5MM **Privately Held**
WEB: www.niagaramfg.com
SIC: **3599** 7692 Machine shop, jobbing &
repair; welding repair

(G-5404)
NIAGARA PLASTICS
7090 Edinboro Rd (16509-4497)
PHONE..................................814 464-8169
Craig Brown, *Plant Mgr*
EMP: 8
SALES (est): 230.1K **Privately Held**
SIC: **3089** Injection molding of plastics

(G-5405)
NON MTALLIC MACHINING
ASSEMBLY
1525 E Lake Rd Ste C (16511-1088)
PHONE..................................814 453-6787
EMP: 15
SQ FT: 6,000
SALES (est): 1.7MM **Privately Held**
SIC: **3599** Machine Shop

(G-5406)
NORTH AMERICAN
COMPOUNDING
Also Called: North American Powder Coat-
ings
4680 Iroquois Ave (16511-2350)
PHONE..................................814 899-0621
Alan Goldberg, *President*
A B Kaufman, *Treasurer*
Sara Finburg, *Admin Sec*
EMP: 45
SQ FT: 56,000
SALES (est): 6.1MM **Privately Held**
WEB: www.erieonline.com
SIC: **3479** Coating of metals & formed
products

(G-5407)
NORTH COAST PLASTICS INC
2114 Loveland Ave (16506-2045)
P.O. Box 8617 (16505-0617)
PHONE..................................814 838-1343
William J Clyde Jr, *President*
Dennis Pascarella, *Vice Pres*
Rick Copley, *Accounts Exec*
Joh Noel, *Admin Sec*
EMP: 12
SQ FT: 15,000
SALES (est): 1.5MM **Privately Held**
WEB: www.northcoastplastics.com
SIC: **2673** Plastic bags: made from pur-
chased materials

(G-5408)
OLYMPUS ADVANCED TECH
LLC
2545 W Grandview Blvd (16506-4512)
PHONE..................................814 838-3571
Tommy Reed, *CEO*
EMP: 8
SALES (est): 330.6K **Privately Held**
SIC: **3679** Oscillators

(G-5409)
OMEGA PLASTICS LLC
1507 Wayne St (16503-3405)
PHONE..................................814 452-4989
Michael Rose,
▲ EMP: 15
SQ FT: 5,600
SALES (est): 3MM **Privately Held**
WEB: www.omegaplastics.net
SIC: **3089** Injection molding of plastics

(G-5410)
ORE ENTERPRISES INC
Also Called: Qual Krom Great Lakes
4725a Iroquois Ave (16511-2344)
PHONE..................................814 898-3933
Robert Ore, *President*
▲ EMP: 5
SQ FT: 12,000
SALES: 500K **Privately Held**
WEB: www.qualkrom.com
SIC: **7532** 3471 Antique & classic automo-
bile restoration; cleaning & descaling
metal products

(G-5411)
OTIS ELEVATOR COMPANY
1001 State St Ste 319 (16501-1823)
PHONE..................................814 452-2703
Robert Radice, *Sales/Mktg Mgr*
EMP: 7
SALES (corp-wide): 66.5B **Publicly Held**
WEB: www.otis.com
SIC: **5084** 3534 Elevators; escalators,
passenger & freight
HQ: Otis Elevator Company
1 Carrier Pl
Farmington CT 06032
860 674-3000

(G-5412)
OWENS-BROCKWAY GLASS
CONT INC
316 W 16th St (16502-1807)
PHONE..................................814 461-5100
Mike Towner, *Branch Mgr*
EMP: 190
SQ FT: 10,000
SALES (corp-wide): 6.8B **Publicly Held**
SIC: **3221** Glass containers
HQ: Owens-Brockway Glass Container Inc.
1 Michael Owens Way
Perrysburg OH 43551
567 336-8449

(G-5413)
PARAGON PRINT SYSTEMS INC
2021 Paragon Dr (16510-1135)
PHONE..................................814 456-8331
Robert C Hess, *President*
Sharon D Hess, *Corp Secy*
Sharon Hess, *Treasurer*
Jason Booth, *Sales Staff*
Marcus Carter, *Sales Staff*
EMP: 16
SQ FT: 2,500
SALES (est): 5MM **Privately Held**
WEB: www.barcodefactory.com
SIC: **5112** 3565 Business forms; packag-
ing machinery

(G-5414)
PARKER-HANNIFIN
CORPORATION
8325 Hessinger Dr (16509-4679)
PHONE..................................814 866-4100
Raj Ghaiy, *General Mgr*
Bob Germanoski, *Engineer*
Shane Dobbins, *Branch Mgr*
Stutzman Brett, *Project Leader*
EMP: 725
SALES (corp-wide): 12B **Publicly Held**
SIC: **3494** 3052 3492 Couplings, except
pressure & soil pipe; hose, pneumatic:
rubber or rubberized fabric; fire hose, rub-
ber; control valves, fluid power: hydraulic
& pneumatic
PA: Parker-Hannifin Corporation
6035 Parkland Blvd
Cleveland OH 44124
216 896-3000

(G-5415)
PARKER-HANNIFIN
CORPORATION
Also Called: S T I Creative Division
6424 W Ridge Rd (16506-1023)
PHONE..................................814 860-5700
Gary Clark, *General Mgr*
EMP: 5
SALES (corp-wide): 14.3B **Publicly Held**
WEB: www.snap-tite.com
SIC: **2732** 7812 Pamphlets: printing only,
not published on site; video tape produc-
tion

PA: Parker-Hannifin Corporation
6035 Parkland Blvd
Cleveland OH 44124
216 896-3000

(G-5416)
PARKER-HANNIFIN
CORPORATION
8325 Hessinger Dr (16509-4679)
PHONE..................................814 866-4100
John Clark, *CEO*
EMP: 50
SALES (corp-wide): 12B **Publicly Held**
WEB: www.snap-tite.com
SIC: **3593** Fluid power cylinders & actua-
tors
PA: Parker-Hannifin Corporation
6035 Parkland Blvd
Cleveland OH 44124
216 896-3000

(G-5417)
PATRICK G STINELY
Also Called: Pat Stinely Ceramic & Stone
952 W 28th St (16508-3242)
PHONE..................................814 528-3832
EMP: 3
SALES (est): 110.9K **Privately Held**
SIC: **3281** Mfg Cut Stone/Products

(G-5418)
PEACOCK PRINTING
205 W 12th St (16534-0002)
PHONE..................................814 336-5009
Matt Mead, *Manager*
EMP: 60
SALES (est): 1.9MM **Privately Held**
SIC: **2752** Commercial printing, offset

(G-5419)
PERRY SCREW MACHINE CO
INC
1043 E 20th St (16503-2396)
PHONE..................................814 452-3095
Michael J Dill, *President*
Thomas J Dill, *Vice Pres*
Mark Truitt, *Purch Mgr*
Thomas Dill, *QC Mgr*
EMP: 26
SQ FT: 25,000
SALES (est): 4.9MM **Privately Held**
WEB: www.perryscrewmachine.com
SIC: **3451** Screw machine products

(G-5420)
PLASTEK INDUSTRIES INC (PA)
Also Called: Plastek Group, The
2425 W 23rd St (16506-2920)
PHONE..................................814 878-4400
Joseph J Prischak, *President*
Daniel J Prischak, *Corp Secy*
Narendra Prischak, *Vice Pres*
Dennis J Prischak, *Shareholder*
◆ EMP: 80 EST: 1971
SQ FT: 200,000
SALES (est): 412.7MM **Privately Held**
WEB: www.plastek.com
SIC: **3089** Injection molding of plastics

(G-5421)
PLASTEK INDUSTRIES INC
2200 Yoder Dr (16506-2368)
PHONE..................................814 878-4741
Joseph J Prischak, *Principal*
EMP: 4
SALES (corp-wide): 412.7MM **Privately
Held**
SIC: **3089** Injection molding of plastics
PA: Plastek Industries, Inc.
2425 W 23rd St
Erie PA 16506
814 878-4400

(G-5422)
PLASTEK INDUSTRIES INC
Also Called: Pioneer Tool & Mold Division
3230 W 22nd St (16506-2308)
PHONE..................................814 878-4719
Pat Sculley, *Manager*
EMP: 35
SQ FT: 22,640
SALES (corp-wide): 412.7MM **Privately
Held**
WEB: www.plastek.com
SIC: **3089** Injection molding of plastics

PA: Plastek Industries, Inc.
2425 W 23rd St
Erie PA 16506
814 878-4400

(G-5423)
PLASTEK INDUSTRIES INC
Also Called: Penn-Erie Division
2315 W 23rd St (16506-2918)
PHONE..................................814 878-4601
Tom Hartline, *General Mgr*
EMP: 40
SALES (corp-wide): 412.7MM **Privately
Held**
SIC: **3089** Injection molding of plastics
PA: Plastek Industries, Inc.
2425 W 23rd St
Erie PA 16506
814 878-4400

(G-5424)
PLASTEK INDUSTRIES INC
Also Called: Spectrum Molding Division
2425 W 23rd St (16506-2920)
PHONE..................................814 878-4466
Rob Elchynski, *General Mgr*
EMP: 300
SALES (corp-wide): 412.7MM **Privately
Held**
SIC: **3089** Injection molding of plastics
PA: Plastek Industries, Inc.
2425 W 23rd St
Erie PA 16506
814 878-4400

(G-5425)
PLASTEK INDUSTRIES INC
Also Called: Consumer Products Division
2310 Pittsburgh Ave (16502-1919)
PHONE..................................814 878-4515
Dave Jones, *General Mgr*
EMP: 600
SALES (corp-wide): 412.7MM **Privately
Held**
WEB: www.plastek.com
SIC: **3089** Injection molding of plastics
PA: Plastek Industries, Inc.
2425 W 23rd St
Erie PA 16506
814 878-4400

(G-5426)
PLASTICS SERVICES NETWORK
5451 Mrwin Ln Knwldge Par Knowledge
Prk (16510)
PHONE..................................814 898-6317
Michael Alabran, *Director*
EMP: 6
SALES (est): 772.8K **Privately Held**
SIC: **3089** Plastic containers, except foam

(G-5427)
PLASTIKOS INC
8165 Hawthorne Dr (16509-4655)
PHONE..................................814 868-1656
Timothy L Katen, *President*
Philip A Katen, *President*
Robert D Cooney, *Vice Pres*
Ryan T Katen, *Admin Sec*
EMP: 28
SALES (est): 8.1MM **Privately Held**
WEB: www.plastikoserie.com
SIC: **3089** Injection molding of plastics
PA: Micro Mold Co Inc
4820 Pittsburgh Ave
Erie PA 16509
814 838-3404

(G-5428)
PMI INC
1655 W 20th St (16502-2115)
PHONE..................................814 455-8085
Jeff Hindman, *Principal*
Tom Dorich, *Info Tech Dir*
William Schaaf, *Admin Sec*
EMP: 3
SALES (est): 97.8K **Privately Held**
SIC: **3089** Plastics products

(G-5429)
POLYMER MOLDING INC
1655 W 20th St (16502-2192)
PHONE..................................800 344-7584
John G Sontag, *CEO*
W Patrick Delaney, *President*
William J Schaaf, *Corp Secy*

Daryl Laufenberg, *QC Mgr*
Denise Martucci, *Cust Mgr*
◆ EMP: 47
SQ FT: 88,000
SALES (est): 12.2MM **Privately Held**
WEB: www.polymermolding.com
SIC: 3089 Caps, plastic

(G-5430)
PRECISE POLISH
1405 W 21st St (16502-2204)
PHONE...........................814 453-4220
Joseph Fosco, *Owner*
EMP: 11 EST: 2007
SALES (est): 937.3K **Privately Held**
SIC: 3544 Special dies, tools, jigs & fixtures

(G-5431)
PRECISION POLYMERS INC
1425 Selinger Ave (16505-4519)
PHONE...........................814 838-9288
Robert T Shepard, *President*
Walter R Brown, *Vice Pres*
EMP: 12
SQ FT: 5,000
SALES (est): 1.7MM **Privately Held**
SIC: 3089 Injection molding of plastics; molding primary plastic

(G-5432)
PRECISION REHAB MANUFACTURING
Also Called: Signature 2000
5325 Kuhl Rd (16510-4702)
PHONE...........................814 899-8731
Todd Dinner, *President*
EMP: 8
SALES (est): 970K **Privately Held**
WEB: www.prmrehab.com
SIC: 2392 Cushions & pillows

(G-5433)
PREMIER CONDUIT INC (PA)
1409 S Shore Dr (16505-2523)
PHONE...........................814 451-0898
Lawrence Baumann, *CEO*
Aimee Daunann, *President*
EMP: 7
SQ FT: 10,000
SALES (est): 1.6MM **Privately Held**
WEB: www.premierconduit.com
SIC: 3084 Plastics pipe

(G-5434)
PREMIER CONDUIT INC
3200 W 22nd St (16506-2308)
PHONE...........................814 451-0898
Relix Rodriguez, *Branch Mgr*
EMP: 7
SALES (corp-wide): 1.6MM **Privately Held**
WEB: www.premierconduit.com
SIC: 3084 Plastics pipe
PA: Premier Conduit, Inc
1409 S Shore Dr
Erie PA 16505
814 451-0898

(G-5435)
PRESQUE ISLE ORTHPD LAB INC
Also Called: Presque Isle Medical Tech
2440 W 8th St (16505-4428)
PHONE...........................814 838-0002
Fax: 814 835-8042
EMP: 12 EST: 1978
SQ FT: 4,500
SALES (est): 2MM **Privately Held**
SIC: 3842 Prosthetic appliances; braces, orthopedic

(G-5436)
PRESTA CONTRACTOR SUPPLY INC
2669 W 16th St (16505-4303)
PHONE...........................814 833-0655
Timothy A Presta, *President*
Louis J Presta, *President*
Barbara J Presta, *Admin Sec*
EMP: 24
SQ FT: 30,000

SALES (est): 5.2MM **Privately Held**
WEB: www.prestasupply.com
SIC: 2431 5072 Millwork; builders' hardware

(G-5437)
PRINTING CONCEPTS INC
4982 Pacific Ave (16506-4978)
PHONE...........................814 833-8080
Michael P Martin, *President*
Doug Dunham, *Prdtn Mgr*
Rick Plonski, *Purchasing*
Katy Desanti, *Bookkeeper*
Jamie Taylor, *Sales Staff*
EMP: 44
SQ FT: 28,000
SALES: 5.4MM **Privately Held**
WEB: www.printingconceptsinc.com
SIC: 2752 Commercial printing, offset

(G-5438)
PRINTS & MORE BY HOLLY
621 Indiana Dr (16505-4407)
PHONE...........................814 453-5548
Holly Schaaf, *Partner*
Debbie Hodinko, *Partner*
Karen Sields, *Partner*
Nanette Spaeder, *Partner*
EMP: 4
SALES (est): 469.7K **Privately Held**
SIC: 2759 Commercial printing

(G-5439)
PRODUCTS FINISHING INC
2002 Greengarden Rd (16502-2195)
PHONE...........................814 452-4887
William Espy, *President*
Dawn Mc Bride, *Corp Secy*
EMP: 17 EST: 1951
SQ FT: 12,000
SALES (est): 1MM **Privately Held**
WEB: www.productsfinishing.net
SIC: 3471 3544 Plating of metals or formed products; special dies, tools, jigs & fixtures

(G-5440)
PROTECH POWDER COATINGS
361 W 11th St (16501-1703)
PHONE...........................814 456-1243
Thoma Dietsch, *Opers Mgr*
◆ EMP: 7
SALES (est): 1.4MM **Privately Held**
SIC: 2851 Paints & allied products

(G-5441)
PROTECTIVE INDUSTRIES INC
Also Called: Caplugs Niagara
7090 Edinboro Rd (16509-4447)
PHONE...........................814 868-3671
Fred Zeyfang, *Vice Pres*
Don Vally, *Engineer*
Amy Buerk, *Accountant*
Charles Cole, *Mktg Dir*
John Fay, *Supervisor*
EMP: 127
SALES (corp-wide): 2.9B **Privately Held**
WEB: www.mokon.com
SIC: 3089 Caps, plastic; plastic containers, except foam; carafes, plastic
HQ: Protective Industries, Inc.
2150 Elmwood Ave
Buffalo NY 14207
716 876-9951

(G-5442)
PSB INDUSTRIES INC (PA)
Also Called: General Air Division
1202 W 12th St (16501-1519)
P.O. Box 1318 (16512-1318)
PHONE...........................814 453-3651
Mark D McCain, *President*
Joe Caccavo, *General Mgr*
Joseph Caccavol, *General Mgr*
Jason Walker, *General Mgr*
Jerry Stephens, *Project Mgr*
▲ EMP: 95
SQ FT: 160,000
SALES (est): 27.1MM **Privately Held**
WEB: www.psbindustries.com
SIC: 3569 3441 7699 Gas producers; generators & other gas related equipment; fabricated structural metal; industrial equipment services

(G-5443)
PSNERGY LLC
5368 Kuhl Rd (16510-4703)
PHONE...........................724 581-3845
Brian Stallard, *Manager*
EMP: 3
SALES (est): 154K **Privately Held**
SIC: 3255 Heater radiants, clay

(G-5444)
QUALITY MOLD INC
1302 Irwin Dr (16505-4814)
PHONE...........................814 459-1084
EMP: 8
SALES (est): 998.3K **Privately Held**
SALES (corp-wide): 2MM **Privately Held**
SIC: 3089 Injection molding of plastics
PA: Quality Mold Inc
8130 Hawthorne Dr
Erie PA 16509
814 866-2255

(G-5445)
QUALITY MOLD INC (PA)
8130 Hawthorne Dr (16509-4654)
PHONE...........................814 866-2255
Thomas J Hakel, *President*
Barbara L Hakel, *Corp Secy*
Joanne Hulick, *Controller*
EMP: 22
SQ FT: 7,800
SALES: 2MM **Privately Held**
SIC: 3544 Industrial molds

(G-5446)
QUANTUM PLATING INC
4300 W Ridge Rd (16506-1457)
PHONE...........................814 835-9213
Sally Busko, *President*
Christopher Busko, *Vice Pres*
EMP: 3
SQ FT: 5,000
SALES (est): 209.9K **Privately Held**
WEB: www.quantumplating.com
SIC: 3471 Plating of metals or formed products; cleaning & descaling metal products

(G-5447)
R CONRADER COMPANY
Also Called: Conrader Valve
749 E 18th St (16503-2146)
P.O. Box 924 (16512-0924)
PHONE...........................814 898-2727
Josh Mosher, *President*
Ryan Mosher, *Opers Mgr*
John Prather, *Engineer*
Richard Lattanzie, *Info Tech Mgr*
▲ EMP: 6 EST: 1945
SQ FT: 26,968
SALES (est): 1.3MM **Privately Held**
SIC: 3491 Industrial valves

(G-5448)
R M G ENTERPRISES INC
Also Called: Mass Storage Newsletter
4003 Wood St (16509-1634)
PHONE...........................814 866-2247
John Rick Morgan, *CEO*
Ralph Gammon, *CEO*
EMP: 3
SALES (est): 300K **Privately Held**
WEB: www.rmgenterprises.com
SIC: 2741 Newsletter publishing

(G-5449)
R M KERNER CO (PA)
2208 E 33rd St (16510-2588)
PHONE...........................814 898-2000
Ronald M Kerner, *President*
Chris Kiefer, *Sls & Mktg Exec*
Joan P Kerner, *Treasurer*
Dan Kerner, *Human Res Mgr*
Jack Smith, *Manager*
EMP: 470 EST: 1949
SQ FT: 130,000
SALES (est): 46.2MM **Privately Held**
WEB: www.rmkco.com
SIC: 3599 Machine shop, jobbing & repair

(G-5450)
R M KERNER CO
2000 E 36th St (16510)
PHONE...........................814 898-2000
Ronald M Kerner, *President*
EMP: 125

SALES (corp-wide): 55.9MM **Privately Held**
WEB: www.rmkco.com
SIC: 3599 Machine shop, jobbing & repair
PA: R. M. Kerner, Co.
2208 E 33rd St
Erie PA 16510
814 898-2000

(G-5451)
RABE ENVIRONMENTAL SYSTEMS INC
2300 W 23rd St (16506-2919)
PHONE...........................814 456-5374
Mark Patrizia, *President*
Richard A Patrizia, *Chairman*
Marjorie Patrizia, *Treasurer*
EMP: 100 EST: 1916
SQ FT: 25,000
SALES (est): 28.6MM **Privately Held**
WEB: www.rabeenv.com
SIC: 3444 Awnings & canopies

(G-5452)
RAIL RYDER LLC (PA)
2155 Norcross Rd (16510-4115)
PHONE...........................814 873-1623
Susan Hofius, *President*
EMP: 3
SQ FT: 300
SALES (est): 113.3K **Privately Held**
SIC: 3799 Trailers & trailer equipment

(G-5453)
RAILPOWER LLC
Also Called: R. J. Corman Railpower
2011 Peninsula Dr (16506-2950)
P.O. Box 788, Nicholasville KY (40340-0788)
PHONE...........................814 835-2212
Kristen Brown, *VP Sales*
Bruce Greinke, *Mng Member*
Michael Wester, *Mng Member*
EMP: 200
SALES (est): 30.5MM
SALES (corp-wide): 270.8MM **Privately Held**
SIC: 3647 Locomotive & railroad car lights
PA: R. J. Corman Railroad Group, Llc
101 Rj Corman Dr
Nicholasville KY 40356
859 881-7521

(G-5454)
RAINEATER LLC
2420 W 23rd St (16506-2921)
P.O. Box 8408 (16505-0408)
PHONE...........................814 806-3100
Christina Teliski-Thornton, *Office Mgr*
Lance Thornton, *Mng Member*
▲ EMP: 8
SALES (est): 1.2MM **Privately Held**
SIC: 3714 Windshield wiper systems, motor vehicle; camshafts, motor vehicle

(G-5455)
RAMAC INDUSTRIES INC
Also Called: Sherman Tool & Gage
1624 Cranberry St (16502-1540)
PHONE...........................814 456-6159
Andrew Machuga, *President*
Robert Machuga, *Vice Pres*
EMP: 11
SQ FT: 5,000
SALES (est): 950K **Privately Held**
SIC: 3599 Machine shop, jobbing & repair

(G-5456)
RAPID MOLD SOLUTIONS INC (PA)
Also Called: Bay Rat Lures
4820 Pacific Ave (16506-4946)
PHONE...........................814 833-2721
Damian M Kuzmin, *President*
Scott C Borstorff, *Vice Pres*
Christine A Kuzmin, *Treasurer*
Lisa Landis, *Manager*
▲ EMP: 8
SQ FT: 15,000
SALES (est): 5.5MM **Privately Held**
WEB: www.rapidmoldsolutions.com
SIC: 3544 3089 Special dies & tools; injection molded finished plastic products

(G-5457)
RAS SPORTS INC
Also Called: Creative Imprint Systems
2670 W 11th St (16505-4168)
PHONE..................................814 833-9111
Richard A Santos, *President*
Bonnie J Santos, *Vice Pres*
Jeffrey Santos, *Prdtn Mgr*
Melissa Larson, *Sales Associate*
Loralee Cragle, *Admin Asst*
EMP: 27 **EST:** 1974
SQ FT: 6,850
SALES: 2.8MM **Privately Held**
WEB: www.creativeimprintsystems.com
SIC: 2759 5199 7389 3993 Screen print-
ing; advertising specialties; embroidering
of advertising on shirts, etc.; signs & ad-
vertising specialties; automotive & ap-
parel trimmings; pleating & stitching

(G-5458)
REDDOG INDUSTRIES INC (PA)
Also Called: Anson Mold & Manufacturing
2012 E 33rd St (16510-2597)
PHONE..................................814 898-4321
William M Hilbert, *Ch of Bd*
Bill Hibert J R, *President*
Janeen Himrod, *Materials Mgr*
John Hilbert, *CFO*
Frank Gocal, *Technology*
▲ **EMP:** 65 **EST:** 1966
SQ FT: 98,000
SALES (est): 13.6MM **Privately Held**
WEB: www.reddog-erie.com
SIC: 3544 Industrial molds

(G-5459)
REED MANUFACTURING COMPANY (PA)
1425 W 8th St (16502-1020)
P.O. Box 1321 (16512-1321)
PHONE..................................814 452-3691
Scott Wright, *President*
Mark A Wright, *President*
Tom Fess, *Regional Mgr*
Debbie Sulecki, *Assistant VP*
Rose Peskorski, *Buyer*
◆ **EMP:** 70
SQ FT: 121,000
SALES (est): 22.6MM **Privately Held**
WEB: www.reedmfgco.com
SIC: 3541 3423 Pipe cutting & threading
machines; hand & edge tools

(G-5460)
REHRIG PACIFIC COMPANY
1738 W 20th St (16502-2196)
PHONE..................................814 455-8023
Patty Reilly, *Manager*
Joan Timko, *Executive*
Tom Cook, *Maintence Staff*
EMP: 100 **Privately Held**
SIC: 3089 Pallets, plastic
HQ: Rehrig Pacific Company
4010 E 26th St
Vernon CA 90058
323 262-5145

(G-5461)
RELIANCE WELL SERVICES LLC (PA)
510 Cranberry St Ste 230 (16507-1078)
PHONE..................................814 454-1644
Daniel C Doyle, *Mng Member*
EMP: 28
SALES: 6MM **Privately Held**
SIC: 1389 Hydraulic fracturing wells

(G-5462)
RICHLYN MANUFACTURING INC
3017 W 15th St (16505-3927)
P.O. Box 8143 (16505-0143)
PHONE..................................814 833-8925
Richard Robinson Jr, *President*
Carolyn Robinson, *Corp Secy*
EMP: 20
SQ FT: 3,000
SALES (est): 3.7MM **Privately Held**
SIC: 3451 Screw machine products

(G-5463)
RIDGE TOOL COMPANY
Also Called: Urick Foundry
1501 Cherry St (16502-1732)
PHONE..................................814 454-2461

Edward Group, *Engineer*
Warner Gerbes, *Branch Mgr*
Mark Sullivan, *Software Engr*
EMP: 80
SQ FT: 99,000
SALES (corp-wide): 17.4B **Publicly Held**
WEB: www.ridgid.com
SIC: 3322 3823 Malleable iron foundries;
combustion control instruments
HQ: Ridge Tool Company
400 Clark St
Elyria OH 44035
440 323-5581

(G-5464)
ROBERTSONS INC
Also Called: Robertsons Flrg & Countertops
4101 W 12th St (16505-3198)
PHONE..................................814 838-2313
Scott M Robertson, *President*
Stephen Murray, *Vice Pres*
John Murray, *Treasurer*
EMP: 3 **EST:** 1946
SQ FT: 6,500
SALES: 500K **Privately Held**
SIC: 2541 5713 1752 5211 Table or
counter tops, plastic laminated; floor cov-
ering stores; floor laying & floor work;
counter tops; counter top installation

(G-5465)
ROCHESTER COCA COLA BOTTLING
Also Called: Coca-Cola
2209 W 50th St (16506-4927)
PHONE..................................814 833-0101
Kelly Conboy, *Manager*
EMP: 60
SQ FT: 64,000
SALES (corp-wide): 35.4B **Publicly Held**
SIC: 2086 Bottled & canned soft drinks
HQ: Rochester Coca Cola Bottling Corp
300 Oak St
Pittston PA 18640
570 655-2874

(G-5466)
ROMOLO CHOCOLATES INC
1525 W 8th St (16505-5005)
PHONE..................................814 452-1933
Anthony Stefanelli, *President*
EMP: 30
SQ FT: 4,000
SALES (est): 5.6MM **Privately Held**
WEB: www.romolochocolates.com
SIC: 2064 2066 Chocolate candy, except
solid chocolate; chocolate candy, solid

(G-5467)
RUSSELL UPHOLSTERY CO INC
1923 W 26th St (16508-1152)
PHONE..................................814 455-9021
Patricia Stevens, *President*
EMP: 9 **EST:** 1950
SQ FT: 7,000
SALES (est): 557.5K **Privately Held**
SIC: 7641 2512 Reupholstery; uphol-
stered household furniture

(G-5468)
RUSSO HEATING & COOLING INC
Also Called: Honeywell Authorized Dealer
1406 E 28th St (16504-2946)
P.O. Box 10064 (16514-0064)
PHONE..................................814 454-6263
Michael Russo, *President*
Deborah Russo, *Vice Pres*
EMP: 10
SQ FT: 12,000
SALES (est): 1.2MM **Privately Held**
SIC: 1711 3444 Warm air heating & air
conditioning contractor; heating & air con-
ditioning contractors; sheet metalwork

(G-5469)
SCHULTZ MKTG & COMMUNICATIONS
Also Called: Phoenix Fine Dining
317 W 6th St (16507-1244)
PHONE..................................814 455-4772
Robert Schultz, *President*
EMP: 4
SALES (est): 372.7K **Privately Held**
SIC: 2741 Miscellaneous publishing

(G-5470)
SCHUTTE WOODWORKING & MFG CO
2831 Zimmerman Rd (16510-2699)
PHONE..................................814 453-5110
Dale Bargielski, *Owner*
EMP: 7 **EST:** 1952
SQ FT: 4,000
SALES: 500K **Privately Held**
SIC: 2531 2434 2511 Pews, church; wood
kitchen cabinets; tables, household; wood

(G-5471)
SCULLY ENTERPRISES INC (PA)
6410 W Ridge Rd (16506-1023)
PHONE..................................814 835-0173
Sean Scully, *President*
Thomas Scully, *Corp Secy*
Patrick Scully, *Vice Pres*
▲ **EMP:** 3
SQ FT: 1,500
SALES (est): 663.8K **Privately Held**
WEB: www.scullyenterprises.com
SIC: 3069 3089 Molded rubber products;
injection molded finished plastic products

(G-5472)
SEAWAY MANUFACTURING CORP (PA)
2250 E 33rd St (16510-2556)
PHONE..................................814 898-2255
Michael W Goodrich, *Principal*
Andrew P Snelling, *COO*
EMP: 97 **EST:** 1959
SQ FT: 85,000
SALES: 9MM **Privately Held**
WEB: www.seawaymfg.com
SIC: 3089 3442 Windows, plastic; storm
doors or windows, metal

(G-5473)
SELECT-TRON INDUSTRIES INC
1946 E 12th St (16511-3006)
PHONE..................................814 459-0847
Barbara Santini-Folga, *President*
Barbara Folga, *Vice Pres*
Lynne San, *Vice Pres*
Ryan Folga, *Sales Staff*
Dave Martin, *Manager*
EMP: 10
SQ FT: 5,300
SALES: 1MM **Privately Held**
WEB: www.goselectron.com
SIC: 3471 Electroplating of metals or
formed products

(G-5474)
SENECA MINERAL CO INC
8431 Edinboro Rd (16509-4250)
PHONE..................................814 476-0076
William Shollenberger, *President*
Gary Dudas, *Admin Sec*
EMP: 7 **EST:** 1961
SQ FT: 4,000
SALES (est): 1.5MM **Privately Held**
SIC: 1481 Nonmetallic mineral services

(G-5475)
SENECA MINERAL COMPANY
8431 Edinboro Rd (16509-4250)
PHONE..................................814 476-0076
Denise Shollenberger, *President*
EMP: 6
SALES (est): 1.5MM **Privately Held**
WEB: www.senecamineral.com
SIC: 2899 Deicing or defrosting fluid

(G-5476)
SEPCO ERIE
1221 Robison Rd W (16509-4911)
PHONE..................................814 864-0311
Dan Ignasiak, *Principal*
EMP: 14
SALES (est): 2.3MM **Privately Held**
SIC: 3599 Machine shop, jobbing & repair

(G-5477)
SIDEHILL COPPER WORKS INC
12 Port Access Rd Ste 2 (16507-2298)
PHONE..................................814 451-0400
Andrew L Fynan, *President*
Barbara Fynan, *Vice Pres*
▲ **EMP:** 9
SQ FT: 20,000

SALES (est): 2.1MM **Privately Held**
WEB: www.sidehillcopper.com
SIC: 3443 Fabricated plate work (boiler
shop)

(G-5478)
SIGN HERE INC
Also Called: Fastsigns
144 W 12th St Ste A (16501-1780)
P.O. Box 1357 (16512-1357)
PHONE..................................814 453-6711
Naomi Stutzman, *CEO*
Daniel Stutzman, *COO*
EMP: 14
SQ FT: 15,000
SALES (est): 1.3MM **Privately Held**
SIC: 3993 Signs & advertising specialties

(G-5479)
SIGNS NOW
2232 W 23rd St (16506-2917)
PHONE..................................814 453-6564
Sue Hawley, *Owner*
EMP: 3
SQ FT: 1,600
SALES (est): 271.4K **Privately Held**
SIC: 3993 Signs & advertising specialties

(G-5480)
SKUNKWIRKZ LLC
2672 Hannon Rd (16510-4438)
PHONE..................................814 602-8936
EMP: 5 **EST:** 2013
SALES (est): 317.3K **Privately Held**
SIC: 3949 Cases, gun & rod (sporting
equipment)

(G-5481)
SLATE AND COPPER SALES CO
436 W 12th St (16501-1506)
PHONE..................................814 455-7430
Michael Peterson, *President*
▲ **EMP:** 11
SQ FT: 12,000
SALES (est): 2.3MM **Privately Held**
SIC: 5033 2952 Roofing & siding materi-
als; roofing materials

(G-5482)
SMITH PROVISION CO INC (PA)
Also Called: SMITH'S
1300 Cranberry St (16501-1566)
PHONE..................................814 459-4974
Michael Weber, *Ch of Bd*
John Weber, *President*
Donald Miller, *Plant Engr*
Brian Lewis, *Manager*
Donna Peters, *Admin Mgr*
EMP: 45 **EST:** 1949
SQ FT: 27,200
SALES: 15.5MM **Privately Held**
WEB: www.smithhotdogs.com
SIC: 2013 Sausages & other prepared
meats

(G-5483)
SMITH PROVISION CO INC
1890 W 20th St (16502-2001)
PHONE..................................814 459-4974
Michael Weber, *President*
Sara Kallner, *Project Dir*
Kathleen Haibach, *QA Dir*
Michelle McGee, *Technology*
Janice Skolnick, *Director*
EMP: 3
SQ FT: 26,505
SALES (est): 333.3K
SALES (corp-wide): 15.5MM **Privately
Held**
SIC: 2013 Sausages & other prepared
meats
PA: Smith Provision Co., Inc.
1300 Cranberry St
Erie PA 16501
814 459-4974

(G-5484)
SOLENOID SOLUTIONS INC
2251 Manchester Rd (16506-1001)
PHONE..................................814 838-3190
Desmond I McDonald, *President*
▲ **EMP:** 50
SALES (est): 11.8MM **Privately Held**
SIC: 3491 Industrial valves

▲ = Import ▼=Export
◆ =Import/Export

(G-5485)
SOUTH ERIE PRODUCTION CO INC
1221 Robison Rd W (16509-4911)
PHONE..................................814 864-0311
Daniel Ignasiak, *President*
Timothy Ignajiak, *Vice Pres*
Jane Drum, *Treasurer*
EMP: 30
SQ FT: 7,000
SALES (est): 5.5MM **Privately Held**
WEB: www.sepco-erie.com
SIC: 3451 3599 Screw machine products; machine shop, jobbing & repair

(G-5486)
SPECIALTY PRODUCTS INC
938 E 12th St (16503-1442)
PHONE..................................814 455-6978
Nick Shaffer, *President*
Sharon Shaffer, *Treasurer*
EMP: 8
SQ FT: 13,300
SALES (est): 1MM **Privately Held**
SIC: 3599 3469 Machine shop, jobbing & repair; stamping metal for the trade

(G-5487)
SPECILIZED SVCS PROMOTIONS INC
Also Called: General Exterminating Co
2204 W 38th St (16506-4502)
PHONE..................................814 864-4984
Donna Reese, *President*
Jim Reese, *Vice Pres*
EMP: 7
SQ FT: 3,011
SALES (est): 385K **Privately Held**
SIC: 5947 2879 Gift, novelty & souvenir shop; pesticides, agricultural or household

(G-5488)
SPEKTRA MANUFACTURING INC
2002 Evanston Ave (16506-2933)
PHONE..................................814 454-6879
Drew Larson, *President*
Mary A Larson, *Vice Pres*
EMP: 7
SQ FT: 2,000
SALES (est): 1MM **Privately Held**
SIC: 3599 Machine shop, jobbing & repair

(G-5489)
SPIRAL STAIRS OF AMERICA LLC
4201 Bell St Ste 2 (16511-2821)
PHONE..................................800 422-3700
Jon Whaley, *General Mgr*
Tim Haskins, *Supervisor*
▼ **EMP:** 25
SALES (est): 5.6MM **Privately Held**
WEB: www.spiralstairsofamerica.com
SIC: 3446 Stairs, staircases, stair treads: prefabricated metal

(G-5490)
STANDARD PATTERN WORKS INC
549 Huron St (16502-1792)
PHONE..................................814 455-5145
Mark Behringer, *President*
Urban Behringer, *Vice Pres*
EMP: 7 **EST:** 1910
SQ FT: 12,000
SALES (est): 550K **Privately Held**
SIC: 3543 Foundry patternmaking

(G-5491)
STERILZER RFURBISHING SVCS INC
1039 W 11th St (16502-1144)
PHONE..................................814 882-4116
Frank Lander, *Manager*
EMP: 3
SALES (corp-wide): 1.8MM **Privately Held**
WEB: www.mrgrungy.com
SIC: 3841 Medical instruments & equipment, blood & bone work
PA: Sterilizer Refurbishing Services, Inc.
1039 W 11th St
Erie PA 16502
814 456-2616

(G-5492)
STERILZER RFURBISHING SVCS INC (PA)
1039 W 11th St (16502-1144)
PHONE..................................814 456-2616
Peter Walczak, *President*
Sandra Walczak, *Vice Pres*
EMP: 10
SQ FT: 30,000
SALES (est): 1.8MM **Privately Held**
WEB: www.mrgrungy.com
SIC: 7699 3842 Professional instrument repair services; sterilizers, hospital & surgical

(G-5493)
STERLING DULA ARCHITECTURAL
2250 Powell Ave (16506-1842)
PHONE..................................814 838-7731
James P Mc Brier, *President*
Thomas Hemdal, *Managing Dir*
Lawrence R Finazzo, *Treasurer*
▲ **EMP:** 115 **EST:** 1964
SQ FT: 31,000
SALES (est): 22.2MM
SALES (corp-wide): 31MM **Privately Held**
WEB: www.sterlingdula.com
SIC: 3446 Railings, bannisters, guards, etc.: made from metal pipe
PA: Kane Innovations, Inc.
2250 Powell Ave
Erie PA 16506
814 838-7731

(G-5494)
SUBCON TL/CCTOOL MCH GROUP INC
5301 Iroquois Ave (16511-2529)
PHONE..................................814 456-7797
John Murosky, *President*
Steve Skiwaryk, *Vice Pres*
Jamie Zeiber, *Purchasing*
EMP: 49
SQ FT: 14,000
SALES (est): 7.4MM **Privately Held**
WEB: www.accutool-fasteners.com
SIC: 3599 7692 3544 3452 Machine shop, jobbing & repair; welding repair; special dies, tools, jigs & fixtures; bolts, nuts, rivets & washers; sheet metalwork; fabricated structural metal

(G-5495)
SUBURBAN TOOL & DIE CO INC
4940 Pacific Ave (16506-4978)
PHONE..................................814 833-4882
Kurt Sprynowicz, *President*
Kurt Supronowiccz, *President*
David Myers, *Vice Pres*
Robert Suprynowicz, *Vice Pres*
Jeff Rzepka, *Mfg Mgr*
EMP: 25
SQ FT: 10,000
SALES (est): 5MM **Privately Held**
SIC: 3544 Special dies & tools

(G-5496)
SUPERIOR BRONZE CORPORATION
1901 Poplar St (16502-2575)
P.O. Box 829 (16512-0829)
PHONE..................................814 452-3474
David F Stadler, *President*
David Holtzel, *CTO*
EMP: 12 **EST:** 1918
SQ FT: 30,000
SALES: 1.2MM **Privately Held**
WEB: www.superiorbronze.com
SIC: 3366 Copper foundries

(G-5497)
SUPERMEDIA LLC
Also Called: Verizon
1600 Peninsula Dr Ste 4 (16505-4261)
PHONE..................................814 833-2121
Robert J Miller, *Manager*
EMP: 52
SALES (corp-wide): 1.8B **Privately Held**
WEB: www.verizon.superpages.com
SIC: 2741 Directories: publishing only, not printed on site
HQ: Supermedia Llc
2200 W Airfield Dr
Dfw Airport TX 75261
972 453-7000

(G-5498)
SUZIE BS PRETZELTOWN INC
527 Millcreek Mall (16565-0502)
PHONE..................................814 868-8443
EMP: 6
SALES (est): 417.5K **Privately Held**
SIC: 2052 Pretzels

(G-5499)
SWANSON SYSTEMS INC (PA)
Also Called: Swanson Erie
814 E 8th St (16503-1490)
P.O. Box 1217 (16512-1217)
PHONE..................................814 453-5841
Douglas Swanson, *President*
Sven Swanson, *Vice Pres*
Chris Brocious, *Safety Mgr*
Leslie Sult, *Purch Agent*
Rich Ivanic, *Engineer*
EMP: 60
SQ FT: 11,000
SALES (est): 14.4MM **Privately Held**
WEB: www.swansonsystems.com
SIC: 3569 Assembly machines, non-metalworking

(G-5500)
SWANSON-ERIE CORPORATION
Also Called: Swanson Assembly Systems
814 E 8th St (16503-1490)
PHONE..................................814 453-5841
Douglas L Swanson, *President*
Charles Trudnowski, *Admin Sec*
EMP: 60 **EST:** 1919
SQ FT: 120,000
SALES (est): 10.3MM
SALES (corp-wide): 14.4MM **Privately Held**
WEB: www.swanson-erie.com
SIC: 3569 Assembly machines, non-metalworking
PA: Swanson Systems, Inc.
814 E 8th St
Erie PA 16503
814 453-5841

(G-5501)
SYNERGY APPLICATIONS INC
1341 W 12th St (16501-1520)
PHONE..................................814 454-8803
Jeffrey Demenik, *President*
Jeffrey Enterline, *Treasurer*
EMP: 13
SALES (est): 3.2MM **Privately Held**
WEB: www.synergyapplications.com
SIC: 3569 Filters

(G-5502)
SYNERGY BUSINESS FORMS INC
3802 W Lake Rd (16505-3266)
PHONE..................................814 833-3344
Randy McCracken, *President*
Randell McCracken, *President*
Debbie Fisher, *Graphic Designe*
EMP: 5
SQ FT: 2,000
SALES: 350K **Privately Held**
WEB: www.synergybf.com
SIC: 5112 2752 Business forms; commercial printing, lithographic

(G-5503)
T S K PARTNERS INC (PA)
Also Called: McInnes Rolled Rings
1533 E 12th St (16511-1747)
PHONE..................................814 459-4495
Tim Hunter, *CEO*
Imothy M Hunter, *Corp Secy*
Kevin O'Connell, *Vice Pres*
Robert W Shephard, *Vice Pres*
EMP: 65
SQ FT: 1,000
SALES (est): 18.7MM **Privately Held**
WEB: www.mcrings.com
SIC: 3462 Iron & steel forgings

(G-5504)
TECHNIPFMC US HOLDINGS INC
1602 Wagner Ave (16510-1444)
PHONE..................................303 217-2030
Mark Karr, *Branch Mgr*
EMP: 5
SALES (corp-wide): 15B **Privately Held**
SIC: 3533 Oil & gas field machinery
HQ: Fmc Technologies, Inc.
11740 Katy Fwy Energy Tow
Houston TX 77079
281 591-4000

(G-5505)
TECHSOURCE ENGINEERING INC
2101 W 12th St (16505-4837)
PHONE..................................814 459-2150
Kevin C Cooney, *President*
Mark Platteter, *Vice Pres*
Mark A Platteter, *Treasurer*
EMP: 5
SQ FT: 3,000
SALES: 500K **Privately Held**
WEB: www.tse-inc.com
SIC: 3625 3824 5065 8734 Industrial controls: push button, selector switches, pilot; controls, revolution & timing instruments; electronic parts; product testing laboratories; calibration & certification

(G-5506)
TETRA TOOL COMPANY
1425 Industrial Dr (16505-4393)
PHONE..................................814 833-6127
Thomas S Newman, *President*
EMP: 12
SQ FT: 34,000
SALES (est): 1.9MM **Privately Held**
WEB: www.tetratool.com
SIC: 3089 3544 Injection molding of plastics; special dies, tools, jigs & fixtures

(G-5507)
THERMOCLAD COMPANY (PA)
361 W 11th St (16501-1797)
PHONE..................................814 456-1243
Roger Cramp, *President*
◆ **EMP:** 13 **EST:** 1963
SQ FT: 12,000
SALES (est): 6.3MM **Privately Held**
WEB: www.thermoclad.com
SIC: 2851 3479 3339 Paints & allied products; painting, coating & hot dipping; primary nonferrous metals

(G-5508)
THERMOCLAD COMPANY
4690 Iroquois Ave (16511-2350)
PHONE..................................814 899-7628
Michael Gashgarian, *President*
Dennis Mc Laughlin, *Lab Dir*
EMP: 40
SQ FT: 14,760
SALES (corp-wide): 6.3MM **Privately Held**
WEB: www.thermoclad.com
SIC: 2851 Paints & allied products
PA: The Thermoclad Company
361 W 11th St
Erie PA 16501
814 456-1243

(G-5509)
TIMES PUBLISHING COMPANY (HQ)
Also Called: Erie Times News
205 W 12th St (16534-0001)
PHONE..................................814 453-4691
John Flanagin, *Chairman*
James Dible, *Vice Pres*
Henry Bujalski, *CFO*
Rosanne Cheeseman, *Treasurer*
Marilyn Mead, *Admin Sec*
EMP: 95
SQ FT: 82,000
SALES (est): 26.3MM
SALES (corp-wide): 1.5B **Publicly Held**
WEB: www.goerie.com
SIC: 2711 2752 Newspapers, publishing & printing; commercial printing, lithographic
PA: New Media Investment Group Inc.
1345 Avenue Of The Americ
New York NY 10105
212 479-3160

(G-5510)
TM INDUSTRIAL SUPPLY INC
Also Called: Fluid Engineering
1432 Walnut St (16502-1746)
PHONE...................................814 453-5014
Carl Steiner, *CEO*
Heather Steiner, *President*
Rick Jackson, *Vice Pres*
Kevin Steiner, *Vice Pres*
Marc Steiner, *VP Sales*
▲ EMP: 30 EST: 1976
SQ FT: 2,400
SALES (est): 9.3MM Privately Held
WEB: www.fluideng.com
SIC: 3443 3559 3564 Industrial vessels,
tanks & containers; refinery, chemical pro-
cessing & similar machinery; blowers &
fans

(G-5511)
TOOL & DIE PRODUCTIONS
5424 W Ridge Rd (16506-1224)
PHONE...................................814 838-3304
Peter Kuvshinikov, *Owner*
EMP: 4
SALES: 140K Privately Held
SIC: 3544 Special dies & tools

(G-5512)
TOOL-ALL INC
2053 E 30th St (16510-2594)
PHONE...................................814 898-3917
John C Farrell, *President*
Gregory N Farrell, *Vice Pres*
EMP: 52 EST: 1962
SQ FT: 12,000
SALES (est): 7.4MM Privately Held
WEB: www.toolall.com
SIC: 3544 Industrial molds

(G-5513)
TOP GUN TOOL INC
421 W 12th St (16501-1559)
PHONE...................................814 454-4849
Richard Daubert, *President*
Douglas Loesch, *Vice Pres*
EMP: 9
SQ FT: 5,000
SALES: 750K Privately Held
SIC: 3089 Injection molding of plastics

(G-5514)
TRANSPORTATION EQP SUP CO
Also Called: TESCO
8106 Hawthorne Dr (16509-4654)
PHONE...................................814 866-1952
Chris F Fette, *President*
Mary Fette, *Corp Secy*
John P Fette, *Vice Pres*
Stephen Chilcott, *Engineer*
Chris F Fette Jr, *CFO*
EMP: 21
SQ FT: 35,000
SALES: 6.3MM Privately Held
WEB: www.tescotools.com
SIC: 3423 5088 3546 Mechanics' hand
tools; wrenches, hand tools; railroad
equipment & supplies; power-driven
handtools

(G-5515)
TRAVAGLINI ENTERPRISES INC
Also Called: Perkins Family Restaurant
4334 Buffalo Rd (16510-2114)
PHONE...................................814 898-1212
Carl Bomb, *Manager*
EMP: 50
SALES (corp-wide): 31.5MM Privately
Held
SIC: 5812 2051 Restaurant, family: chain;
bread, cake & related products
PA: Travaglini Enterprises, Inc.
18228 Conneaut Lake Rd
Meadville PA 16335
814 724-1286

(G-5516)
TRI STATE METAL CLEANING INC
4725 Iroquois Ave (16511-2344)
PHONE...................................814 898-3933
Robert G Ore, *President*
Robert Elmendorf, *Vice Pres*
Theresa Elmendorf, *Treasurer*
Patricia Ore, *Admin Sec*
EMP: 6

SQ FT: 12,000
SALES (est): 435.4K Privately Held
SIC: 7532 3471 Antique & classic automobile restoration; cleaning & descaling
metal products

(G-5517)
TRIANGLE TOOL COMPANY INC (PA)
Also Called: Penn Erie Manufacturing Div
3230 W 22nd St (16506-2396)
PHONE...................................814 878-4400
Joseph J Prischak, *President*
Nar Handa, *President*
Daniel Prischak, *Corp Secy*
Michael Dzurik, *Vice Pres*
EMP: 125 EST: 1956
SQ FT: 44,000
SALES (est): 15.2MM Privately Held
WEB: www.triangletool.com
SIC: 3089 Injection molding of plastics

(G-5518)
TRIANGLE TOOL COMPANY INC
Master Mold Company
2425 W 23rd St (16506-2920)
PHONE...................................814 878-4400
Joseph J Prischak, *President*
EMP: 35
SQ FT: 6,000
SALES (corp-wide): 15.2MM Privately
Held
WEB: www.triangletool.com
SIC: 3544 Forms (molds), for foundry &
plastics working machinery
PA: Triangle Tool Company Inc
3230 W 22nd St
Erie PA 16506
814 878-4400

(G-5519)
TRIANGLE TOOL COMPANY INC
Penn Erie Division
2315 W 23rd St (16506-2918)
PHONE...................................814 878-4603
Tom Hartline, *General Mgr*
EMP: 30
SALES (corp-wide): 15.2MM Privately
Held
WEB: www.triangletool.com
SIC: 3544 Industrial molds
PA: Triangle Tool Company Inc
3230 W 22nd St
Erie PA 16506
814 878-4400

(G-5520)
TSRUBNUS LIQUIDATION INC
Also Called: Sunburst Electronics
420 E Bayfront Pkwy (16507-2404)
PHONE...................................814 461-9120
Keith Szewczyk, *President*
James H Hynes, *Treasurer*
Roger W Richards, *Admin Sec*
▲ EMP: 100
SQ FT: 31,000
SALES (est): 38MM Privately Held
WEB: www.sunb.com
SIC: 3679 Electronic circuits
PA: Mbpj Corporation
420 E Bayfront Pkwy
Erie PA 16507
814 461-9120

(G-5521)
TWO TOGETHERS INC
5539 Peach St (16509-2683)
PHONE...................................814 838-1234
Richard Griffith, *President*
EMP: 5
SQ FT: 30,000
SALES: 100K Privately Held
SIC: 3089 Injection molding of plastics

(G-5522)
ULTIMATE TOOL INC
2001 Peninsula Dr Ste 12 (16506-2974)
PHONE...................................814 835-2291
Fax: 814 835-7466
EMP: 15
SQ FT: 3,600
SALES (est): 1MM Privately Held
SIC: 3544 Mfg Tool And Die Molds

(G-5523)
UNION ELECTRIC COMPANY
1712 Greengarden Rd (16501-1562)
PHONE...................................814 452-0587
Thomas McCue, *General Mgr*
Mearl Kean, *Branch Mgr*
EMP: 8
SALES (corp-wide): 6.2B Publicly Held
SIC: 3312 Blast furnaces & steel mills
HQ: Union Electric Company
1901 Chouteau Ave Mc-1370
Saint Louis MO 63103
314 621-3222

(G-5524)
UNITED BRASS WORKS INC
Keystone Foundry
944 W 12th St (16501-1515)
PHONE...................................814 456-4296
Jim Satler, *Sales Mgr*
Samuel Epolito, *Manager*
EMP: 30
SALES (corp-wide): 77.2MM Privately
Held
WEB: www.ubw.com
SIC: 3366 Castings (except die): brass
HQ: United Brass Works, Inc.
714 S Main St
Randleman NC 27317
336 498-2661

(G-5525)
VERT MARKETS INC
Also Called: Jameson Publishing
5340 Fryling Rd Ste 300 (16510-4672)
PHONE...................................814 897-9000
Tom Roberts, *Opers Staff*
Sergey Safronov, *Opers Staff*
Bhavesh Goel, *Manager*
EMP: 70 EST: 2008
SALES (est): 156.8K Privately Held
SIC: 2741 Miscellaneous publishing

(G-5526)
VICTOR GROUP INC
Also Called: Fralo Industries
1651 E 12th St (16511-1721)
PHONE...................................814 899-1079
John Bauman, *President*
Gary Simmons, *Engineer*
Frank B Victor, *Treasurer*
Michael T Victor, *Admin Sec*
EMP: 53
SQ FT: 36,000
SALES (est): 17.3MM Privately Held
WEB: www.fralo.com
SIC: 3444 Sheet metal specialties, not
stamped

(G-5527)
WATERFORD PRECAST & SALES INC (PA)
8260 E Johnson Rd (16509-5243)
PHONE...................................814 864-4956
Donald R Wurst, *President*
Shirley J Wurst, *Treasurer*
EMP: 6
SQ FT: 6,600
SALES (est): 755.1K Privately Held
SIC: 3272 Concrete products

(G-5528)
WEST PENN OPTICAL INC (PA)
Also Called: Lillie, Julie E Od
2576 W 8th St (16505-4416)
PHONE...................................814 833-1194
Regis S Sobers, *President*
EMP: 40
SQ FT: 1,600
SALES (est): 5.3MM Privately Held
SIC: 3851 5995 3842 3229 Lenses, oph-
thalmic; eyeglasses, prescription; surgical
appliances & supplies; pressed & blown
glass

(G-5529)
WINSTON & DUKE INC
Also Called: M T C
2008 W 16th St (16505-4831)
PHONE...................................814 456-0582
John R Churchill Jr, *President*
Susan Churchill, *Marketing Staff*
EMP: 18
SQ FT: 20,000

SALES (est): 4MM Privately Held
WEB: www.merittoolcompany.com
SIC: 3599 Machine shop, jobbing & repair

(G-5530)
WINSTON & DUKE INC
2008 W 16th St (16505-4831)
PHONE...................................814 456-0582
John Churchill, *President*
EMP: 35
SALES (est): 896.7K Privately Held
SIC: 8711 3599 3469 3462 Machine tool
design; machine & other job shop work;
machine parts, stamped or pressed
metal; machinery forgings, ferrous; ma-
chinery forgings, nonferrous

(G-5531)
WLEK INC
Also Called: C P S
645 W 11th St (16501-1503)
PHONE...................................800 772-8247
Leon Bilewitz, *President*
Debbie Batten, *Finance Dir*
Walter Bender Jr, *Admin Sec*
▲ EMP: 120
SQ FT: 100,000
SALES (est): 14.5MM Privately Held
SIC: 3993 Advertising novelties

(G-5532)
WM T SPAEDER CO INC (PA)
1602 E 18th St (16510-1054)
P.O. Box 10066 (16514-0066)
PHONE...................................814 456-7014
Terry Spaeder, *President*
Mary Kay Reber, *Corp Secy*
Jay Spaeder, *Vice Pres*
Steve Spaeder, *Vice Pres*
Matthew Fildes, *Project Mgr*
EMP: 60
SQ FT: 80,000
SALES: 37.5MM Privately Held
WEB: www.wmtspaeder.com
SIC: 1711 3498 Mechanical contractor;
boiler & furnace contractors; fire sprinkler
system installation; fabricated pipe & fit-
tings

(G-5533)
WOODPECKERS WOODCRAFT INC
4040 Stanton St (16510-3448)
PHONE...................................814 397-2282
EMP: 3 EST: 2015
SALES (est): 77.1K Privately Held
SIC: 2511 Wood household furniture

(G-5534)
X-ACT TECHNOLOGY INCORPORATED
2154 Norcross Rd (16510-4116)
PHONE...................................814 824-6811
Donald R Chrzanowski, *President*
Donald R Chrzanowski Sr, *Corp Secy*
EMP: 7
SQ FT: 12,000
SALES (est): 1.3MM Privately Held
SIC: 3089 Injection molding of plastics

(G-5535)
X-CELL MOLDING INC
2125 Filmore Ave (16506-2940)
PHONE...................................814 836-0202
Richard Putnam, *Principal*
EMP: 4
SALES (est): 223.8K Privately Held
SIC: 3089 Molding primary plastic

(G-5536)
ZEYON INC
3408 Mcclelland Ave (16510-2649)
P.O. Box 10024 (16514-0024)
PHONE...................................814 899-3311
Dianne C Porter, *President*
John Yonko, *Vice Pres*
Steve Zaun, *Vice Pres*
Dave Ganska, *Prdtn Mgr*
Christopher S Yonko, *Admin Sec*
EMP: 35 EST: 1968
SQ FT: 27,500
SALES (est): 7.1MM Privately Held
WEB: www.zeyon.com
SIC: 3443 3491 Weldments; pressure
valves & regulators, industrial

▲ = Import ▼=Export
◆ =Import/Export

(G-5537)
ZURN INDUSTRIES LLC (DH)
1801 Pittsburgh Ave (16502-1998)
P.O. Box 13801 (16514-3801)
PHONE......................................814 455-0921
Alex P Marini, *President*
Michael Davidson, *Area Mgr*
Susan Kruse, *Assistant VP*
Bob Saadi, *Vice Pres*
Frank Schaetzke, *Vice Pres*
◆ EMP: 2
SQ FT: 212,300
SALES (est): 87.1MM **Publicly Held**
WEB: www.zurn.com
SIC: 3431 5074 Bathroom fixtures, including sinks; sinks: enameled iron, cast iron or pressed metal; plumbing fittings & supplies
HQ: Rbs Global, Inc.
    4701 W Greenfield Ave
    Milwaukee WI 53214
    414 643-3000

Erwinna
Bucks County

(G-5538)
EAT THIS
75 Headquarters Rd (18920-9234)
PHONE......................................215 391-5807
Gino De Schrijver, *Owner*
EMP: 4
SALES (est): 268.9K **Privately Held**
SIC: 2033 Marmalade: packaged in cans, jars, etc.

(G-5539)
SAND CASTLE WINERY (PA)
755 River Rd (18920)
PHONE......................................610 294-9181
Paul Maxiam, *President*
Joseph Maxiam, *Vice Pres*
EMP: 12
SQ FT: 18,000
SALES (est): 2.6MM **Privately Held**
WEB: www.sandcastlewinery.com
SIC: 2084 0762 5921 Wine cellars, bonded: engaged in blending wines; vineyard management & maintenance services; wine

(G-5540)
TINICUM RESEARCH COMPANY (PA)
17 Roaring Rocks Rd (18920)
PHONE......................................610 294-9390
Stuart Louden, *President*
Dave Louden, *Vice Pres*
EMP: 2
SQ FT: 3,000
SALES (est): 1.6MM **Privately Held**
SIC: 2672 5113 Coated & laminated paper; industrial & personal service paper

---

Essington
Delaware County

(G-5541)
AMERICAN CRANE & EQP CORP
10 Industrial Hwy Hwys (19029-1003)
PHONE......................................610 521-9000
David Hope, *Branch Mgr*
EMP: 10
SALES (corp-wide): 40.3MM **Privately Held**
SIC: 3536 7389 Hoists; cranes, overhead traveling; crane & aerial lift service
PA: American Crane & Equipment Corporation
    531 Old Swede Rd
    Douglassville PA 19518
    610 385-6061

(G-5542)
DRAGONFLY PICTURES INC
600 W End Of 2nd St # 2 (19029)
PHONE......................................610 521-6115
Gregory Piasecki, *CEO*
Michael Piasecki, *President*
EMP: 15

SQ FT: 2,000
SALES: 2MM **Privately Held**
WEB: www.dragonflypictures.com
SIC: 3721 Research & development on aircraft by the manufacturer

(G-5543)
ESSTECH INC
48 W Powhattan Ave (19029-1229)
PHONE......................................610 521-3800
Bruce Farina, *President*
Lou Palermo, *Vice Pres*
Helen Wheeler, *Vice Pres*
Jim Mastroddi, *Production*
Stephen H Morrison, *Treasurer*
EMP: 14
SALES (est): 3.7MM **Privately Held**
SIC: 2869 Industrial organic chemicals
PA: Justi Group, Inc.
    804 Old Lancaster Rd
    Berwyn PA 19312

(G-5544)
MOBILE MINI INC
10 Industrial Hwy Bldg E (19029)
PHONE......................................484 540-9073
Bryan Kavanagh, *Manager*
EMP: 10
SALES (corp-wide): 593.2MM **Publicly Held**
WEB: www.mobilemini.com
SIC: 3448 Buildings, portable: prefabricated metal
PA: Mobile Mini, Inc.
    4646 E Van Buren St # 400
    Phoenix AZ 85008
    480 894-6311

(G-5545)
PARADIES PLEASANT NEWS LL
100 Putcan Ave (19029-1517)
PHONE......................................610 521-2936
Chris Coyle, *Principal*
EMP: 6
SALES (est): 328K **Privately Held**
SIC: 2711 Newspapers, publishing & printing

(G-5546)
PHILADELPHIA SECURITY PDTS INC
5 Poulson Ave (19029-1514)
PHONE......................................610 521-4400
Joseph M Makous, *President*
▲ EMP: 5
SALES (est): 602.7K **Privately Held**
WEB: www.flexguard.com
SIC: 3429 Locks or lock sets

Etters
York County

(G-5547)
BURNDY LLC
825 Old Trail Rd (17319-9392)
PHONE......................................717 938-7258
Scott Durnin, *Vice Pres*
Bryan Mumma, *Project Mgr*
Chris Pendleton, *Project Mgr*
John Riley, *Manager*
Raja Narayanan, *Manager*
EMP: 5
SALES (corp-wide): 4.4B **Publicly Held**
SIC: 3643 Current-carrying wiring devices
HQ: Burndy Llc
    47 E Industrial Park Dr
    Manchester NH 03109

(G-5548)
FCI USA LLC (DH)
Also Called: Fci Electronics
825 Old Trail Rd (17319-9392)
PHONE......................................717 938-7200
Brent Peterman, *President*
Jill Steps, *Senior VP*
Charlie Gross, *Engineer*
Yifan Huang, *Engineer*
Douglas Johnescu, *Engineer*
◆ EMP: 350 EST: 1924
SQ FT: 9,000

SALES: 72MM
SALES (corp-wide): 8.2B **Publicly Held**
WEB: www.fciconnect.com
SIC: 3643 3678 3694 Connectors & terminals for electrical devices; electronic connectors; automotive electrical equipment
HQ: Amphenol Fci Asia Pte. Ltd.
    159 Kampong Ampat
    Singapore 36832
    629 421-28

(G-5549)
HORTON PRINTING
336 Valley Rd (17319-9777)
P.O. Box 6146, Harrisburg (17112-0146)
PHONE......................................717 938-2777
Jim Horton, *Owner*
EMP: 3
SQ FT: 3,600
SALES (est): 170K **Privately Held**
WEB: www.hortonprinting.com
SIC: 2752 Commercial printing, offset

(G-5550)
KBM INDUSTRIES INC
1065b Pines Rd (17319-9204)
PHONE......................................717 938-2870
Mark Burket, *President*
EMP: 6
SALES: 1MM **Privately Held**
SIC: 3441 Fabricated structural metal

(G-5551)
KEIPER TECH LLC
30 Bridle Ct (17319-9447)
PHONE......................................717 938-1674
EMP: 3
SALES (est): 149.1K **Privately Held**
SIC: 2813 Industrial gases

(G-5552)
PLANET RYO
116 Newberry Pkwy (17319-8968)
PHONE......................................717 938-8860
EMP: 3
SALES (corp-wide): 2.5MM **Privately Held**
SIC: 2131 5194 Chewing & smoking tobacco; tobacco & tobacco products
PA: Planet Ryo
    2559 S Queen St
    York PA 17402
    717 741-4972

(G-5553)
T & N EXCAVATING LLC
1365 Valley Rd (17319-9342)
PHONE......................................717 801-5525
Nicholas Avola, *Principal*
EMP: 5
SALES (est): 769.1K **Privately Held**
SIC: 3531 Buckets, excavating: clamshell, concrete, dragline, etc.

(G-5554)
TERRAVIZ GEOSPATIAL INC
60 Maplewood Dr (17319-9143)
PHONE......................................717 512-9658
Matt Davis, *Branch Mgr*
EMP: 5
SALES (corp-wide): 328.1K **Privately Held**
SIC: 8713 1382 Surveying services; aerial geophysical exploration oil & gas
PA: Terraviz Geospatial, Inc.
    1 W Elm St Ste 400
    Conshohocken PA 19428
    717 938-3591

Evans City
Butler County

(G-5555)
A & A CONCRETE PRODUCTS INC
1559 Mars Evans City Rd (16033-9362)
P.O. Box 346 (16033-0346)
PHONE......................................724 538-1114
Alma Long, *President*
Alma Staskiewicz, *Vice Pres*
William S Long, *Shareholder*
EMP: 18

SQ FT: 5,000
SALES (est): 2.9MM **Privately Held**
SIC: 3272 5211 Concrete products, precast; manhole covers or frames, concrete; covers, catch basin: concrete; pre-stressed concrete products; masonry materials & supplies

(G-5556)
CALLERY LLC
1424 Mars Evans City Rd (16033-9360)
PHONE......................................724 538-1200
Harry Rathore, *CEO*
EMP: 4
SALES (est): 118.4K
SALES (corp-wide): 71.7B **Privately Held**
SIC: 2899 Chemical supplies for foundries
HQ: Basf Corporation
    100 Park Ave
    Florham Park NJ 07932
    973 245-6000

(G-5557)
DAN-BECK WELL SERVICES INC
353 Railroad St (16033-1409)
PHONE......................................724 538-1001
Daniel Lynger, *Principal*
EMP: 40
SALES (est): 969.1K **Privately Held**
SIC: 1389 Oil & gas wells: building, repairing & dismantling

(G-5558)
DUBROOK INC
600 S Washington St (16033)
PHONE......................................724 538-3111
Mike Perdew, *Manager*
EMP: 4
SALES (est): 391.6K
SALES (corp-wide): 9.1MM **Privately Held**
WEB: www.dubrook.com
SIC: 3273 Ready-mixed concrete
PA: Dubrook, Inc.
    40 Hoover Ave
    Du Bois PA 15801
    814 371-3113

(G-5559)
HELENA CHEMICAL COMPANY
Also Called: Pittsburgh Specialty
312 Seneca Ln (16033-9312)
PHONE......................................724 538-3304
Tony Poleti, *Branch Mgr*
EMP: 3
SALES (corp-wide): 70.7B **Privately Held**
SIC: 2819 5191 Chemicals, high purity: refined from technical grade; fertilizers & agricultural chemicals; seeds & bulbs
HQ: Helena Agri-Enterprises, Llc
    255 Schilling Blvd # 300
    Collierville TN 38017
    901 761-0050

(G-5560)
PAULS CHROME PLATING INC
90 Pattison St (16033-1410)
PHONE......................................724 538-3367
Fred W Hespenheide, *President*
EMP: 28 EST: 1978
SQ FT: 35,000
SALES (est): 3MM **Privately Held**
WEB: www.paulschrome.com
SIC: 3471 Chromium plating of metals or formed products; plating of metals or formed products

(G-5561)
PITTSBURGH PLUG AND PDTS CORP (PA)
Also Called: Ppp
101 3rd St (16033)
PHONE......................................724 538-4022
Matthew S Kimerer, *President*
John V Kimerer Jr, *Chairman*
Vito Pilosi, *Vice Pres*
EMP: 30 EST: 1942
SQ FT: 78,000
SALES: 8MM **Privately Held**
WEB: www.pittsburghplug.com
SIC: 3494 Pipe fittings

GEOGRAPHIC

(G-5562)
PITTSBURGH PLUG AND PDTS CORP
700 S Washington St (16033-9258)
PHONE..................................724 538-4022
Thomas D Williams, *President*
EMP: 31
SALES (corp-wide): 8MM Privately Held
WEB: www.pittsburghplug.com
SIC: 3494 Valves & pipe fittings
PA: Pittsburgh Plug And Products Corporation
101 3rd St
Evans City PA 16033
724 538-4022

(G-5563)
SMC DIRECT LLC
143 Wagner Rd (16033-9349)
P.O. Box 81238, Pittsburgh (15217-4238)
PHONE..................................800 521-1635
Rachelee Sacks, *CEO*
EMP: 25
SALES (est): 2.8MM Privately Held
SIC: 5122 5047 2835 Druggists' sundries; medical & hospital equipment; in vitro diagnostics

(G-5564)
SPADRE INVESTMENTS INC (PA)
Also Called: Rbw Technologies
433 Hartmann Rd (16033-3211)
PHONE..................................724 452-8440
James Willich, *CEO*
EMP: 35
SQ FT: 40,000
SALES (est): 6MM Privately Held
WEB: www.rbw.com
SIC: 3999 Custom pulverizing & grinding of plastic materials

(G-5565)
WEISER GROUP LLC
122 Beahm Crest Ln (16033-3204)
P.O. Box 186, Zelienople (16063-0186)
PHONE..................................724 452-6535
Mark Weiser, *Mng Member*
EMP: 12
SQ FT: 20,000
SALES (est): 3MM Privately Held
SIC: 2879 Pesticides, agricultural or household

Everett
Bedford County

(G-5566)
BEDFORD MANUFACTURING LP
227 Industrial Blvd (15537-3330)
PHONE..................................717 419-2680
Earl Sensenig, *Owner*
EMP: 3
SALES (est): 343.2K Privately Held
SIC: 3999 Barber & beauty shop equipment

(G-5567)
BLUE TRIANGLE HARDWOODS LLC
156 Industrial Blvd (15537-3326)
PHONE..................................814 652-9111
Deborah Brady, *Executive*
Andrew E Becker,
▼ EMP: 162
SQ FT: 25,000
SALES (est): 23.3MM
SALES (corp-wide): 57.5MM Privately Held
SIC: 2421 Sawmills & planing mills, general
PA: Hardwood Lumber Manufacturing, Inc
567 N Charlotte Ave
Waynesboro VA 22980
540 946-9150

(G-5568)
C CLARK & SONS
322 W Mattie Rd (15537-4002)
PHONE..................................814 652-5370
Betty Clark, *Partner*
Jerry Clark, *Partner*
Todd Clark, *Partner*
Vinvent Clark, *Partner*

EMP: 4 EST: 1999
SALES (est): 320K Privately Held
SIC: 2411 Timber, cut at logging camp

(G-5569)
CRC MANUFACTURING INC
13358 Lincoln Hwy (15537-5909)
PHONE..................................703 408-0645
Rita Calhoun, *President*
Clifford A Calhoun, *Vice Pres*
EMP: 3
SQ FT: 3,500
SALES: 400K Privately Held
SIC: 3599 Machine & other job shop work

(G-5570)
DEASEY MACHINE TL & DIE WORKS
339 Ott Town Rd (15537-6259)
PHONE..................................814 847-2728
Paul Deasey Jr, *President*
Mary Deasey, *Treasurer*
Sharon Deasey, *Admin Sec*
EMP: 4
SQ FT: 6,000
SALES (est): 576.4K Privately Held
WEB: www.deaseymachine.com
SIC: 3599 3544 Machine shop, jobbing & repair; special dies & tools

(G-5571)
EVERITE DOOR COMPANY
122 Armory St (15537-3324)
PHONE..................................814 652-5143
James B Wistar, *President*
EMP: 12
SALES (est): 1.4MM Privately Held
SIC: 2431 Millwork

(G-5572)
FAIRFAX PRECISION MFG
13358 Lincoln Hwy (15537-5909)
PHONE..................................814 348-1184
Clifford A Calhoun, *Treasurer*
Rita Calhoun, *Admin Sec*
EMP: 3 EST: 1973
SQ FT: 7,000
SALES (est): 317K Privately Held
SIC: 3599 Machine shop, jobbing & repair

(G-5573)
HOWELL MANUFACTURING COMPANY
Also Called: Everite Door Co
122 Armory St (15537-3324)
PHONE..................................814 652-5143
Ron Anderson, *Branch Mgr*
EMP: 16
SALES (corp-wide): 2.8MM Privately Held
WEB: www.howell-dor.com
SIC: 2431 3442 Garage doors, overhead: wood; garage doors, overhead: metal
PA: The Howell Manufacturing Company
895 Fernhill Rd
West Chester PA

(G-5574)
LOCKER PLANT LLC
422 E South St (15537-1224)
PHONE..................................814 652-2714
EMP: 3
SALES (est): 127.7K Privately Held
SIC: 2011 Lamb products from lamb slaughtered on site

(G-5575)
MOUNTAIN CITY CABINETS INC
1595 Raystown Rd (15537-4950)
PHONE..................................814 652-3977
Betty Fluke, *Manager*
EMP: 3
SALES (est): 161.6K Privately Held
SIC: 2434 Wood kitchen cabinets

(G-5576)
NEW ENTERPRISE STONE LIME INC
526 Aschom Rd (15537-6842)
PHONE..................................814 652-5121
Mike Shippy, *Manager*
EMP: 75

SALES (corp-wide): 651.9MM Privately Held
WEB: www.nesl.com
SIC: 1422 3273 2951 Limestones, ground; ready-mixed concrete; asphalt paving mixtures & blocks
PA: New Enterprise Stone & Lime Co., Inc.
3912 Brumbaugh Rd
New Enterprise PA 16664
814 224-6883

(G-5577)
PITTMAN BROS LUMBER
184 Pine Hollow Rd (15537-4247)
PHONE..................................814 652-6396
Ruste Pittman, *Partner*
EMP: 4
SALES (est): 443.8K Privately Held
SIC: 2421 Sawmills & planing mills, general

(G-5578)
R L SIPES LOCKER PLANT
14 S St Ext (15537)
PHONE..................................814 652-2714
Richard L Sipes, *Owner*
EMP: 4
SALES: 220K Privately Held
SIC: 2011 4222 Meat packing plants; storage, frozen or refrigerated goods

(G-5579)
V P L INC (PA)
100 Masters Ave (15537-1216)
PHONE..................................814 652-6767
John Swatkoski, *President*
EMP: 9
SQ FT: 10,000
SALES (est): 2.1MM Privately Held
WEB: www.vacpro.com
SIC: 3567 7699 Vacuum furnaces & ovens; boiler & heating repair services; pumps & pumping equipment repair

Everson
Fayette County

(G-5580)
MLP STEEL LLC
800 Brown St (15631-1146)
PHONE..................................724 887-7720
James Philipkosky, *Mng Member*
EMP: 30 Privately Held
SIC: 3315 Steel wire & related products
PA: Mlp Steel Llc
18 Mount Pleasant Rd
Scottdale PA 15683

Exeter
Luzerne County

(G-5581)
BRIDON-AMERICAN CORPORATION
100 Stevens Ln (18643-1219)
PHONE..................................570 822-3349
Larry J Drummond, *Branch Mgr*
EMP: 150
SALES (corp-wide): 799.4K Privately Held
WEB: www.bridonamerican.com
SIC: 3496 Cable, uninsulated wire: made from purchased wire; woven wire products
HQ: Bridon-American Corporation
280 New Commerce Blvd
Hanover Township PA 18706
570 822-3349

(G-5582)
CALFAB AND MACHINE INC
Also Called: Cal Fab Machine & Tool
201 Schooley Ave (18643-1841)
PHONE..................................570 654-4004
Eugene Lippi, *President*
Richard Chihorek, *Treasurer*
EMP: 10
SALES (est): 730K Privately Held
SIC: 3599 Machine shop, jobbing & repair

(G-5583)
MEGA MOTION LLC
Also Called: Windermere Motion
182 Susquehanna Ave (18643-2653)
PHONE..................................800 800-8586
Scott S Meuser, *President*
Thomas Kretchik, *Vice Pres*
Stanley S Meuser, *Treasurer*
Lauren Miller, *Credit Staff*
EMP: 20
SALES (est): 1.2MM Privately Held
SIC: 2512 Couches, sofas & davenports: upholstered on wood frames

(G-5584)
ROYAL BAKE SHOP
1701 Wyoming Ave Frnt 1 (18643-1491)
PHONE..................................570 654-2011
Ray Dubiac, *Owner*
EMP: 4 EST: 1951
SQ FT: 2,284
SALES (est): 130K Privately Held
SIC: 2051 Bread, all types (white, wheat, rye, etc): fresh or frozen; cakes, bakery: except frozen; pastries, e.g. danish: except frozen

(G-5585)
WARP PROCESSING INC
95 Stevens Ln (18643-1232)
PHONE..................................570 655-1275
Danny Dugan, *General Mgr*
EMP: 155
SALES (est): 16.1MM
SALES (corp-wide): 13.3MM Privately Held
SIC: 2281 2282 Yarn spinning mills; winding yarn
PA: Warp Processing Inc
375 Diamond Bridge Ave
Hawthorne NJ 07506
973 238-1800

(G-5586)
WYOMING VALLEY PALLETS INC
240 Slocum Ave (18643-1191)
PHONE..................................570 655-3640
Ted Harris, *Vice Pres*
EMP: 20
SALES (est): 1.6MM Privately Held
SIC: 2448 Pallets, wood

Export
Westmoreland County

(G-5587)
ABLE PATTERN COMPANY
5597 Fox Chase Dr (15632-9224)
PHONE..................................724 327-1401
Robert J Straka, *Owner*
EMP: 11
SQ FT: 7,000
SALES (est): 610K Privately Held
SIC: 3543 Industrial patterns

(G-5588)
ADVANCED MFG TECH INC
Also Called: A M T
9001 Corporate Cir (15632-8971)
PHONE..................................724 327-3001
Thomas I Scanio, *President*
Jeffrey Scanio, *Vice Pres*
Sheila Guzzi, *Buyer*
Paul Tomlinson, *Engineer*
Karen Tomko, *Finance Mgr*
EMP: 65
SQ FT: 35,000
SALES (est): 18MM Privately Held
WEB: www.amtsupport.com
SIC: 3672 Printed circuit boards

(G-5589)
APPLIED CREATIVITY INC
101 Technology Ln (15632-8903)
P.O. Box 322 (15632-0322)
PHONE..................................724 327-0054
Alan Iszauk, *President*
Alicia Ciafre, *Corp Secy*
Gene P Ciafre, *Corp Secy*
EMP: 7
SQ FT: 3,000

SALES: 960K **Privately Held**
WEB: www.gmpgeneralproducts.com
SIC: **2992** 8731 Lubricating oils &
greases; chemical laboratory, except testing

(G-5590)
ARBCO INDUSTRIES LLC
2040 Borland Farm Rd (15632-2503)
P.O. Box O (15632-0281)
PHONE...................................724 327-6300
Paul Hauck, *CEO*
EMP: 40 EST: 1967
SQ FT: 60,000
SALES (est): 8MM **Privately Held**
WEB: www.arbcowheels.com
SIC: **3999** Barber & beauty shop equip-
ment

(G-5591)
B L TEES INC
Also Called: Perspectives
3005 Venture Ct (15632-8950)
PHONE...................................724 325-1882
Debra Levy Green, *President*
Judith Newfeld, *Treasurer*
Keith Patrick, *Technology*
▲ EMP: 15
SQ FT: 23,000
SALES (est): 2.9MM **Privately Held**
SIC: **2759** 5131 2396 Screen printing;
piece goods & other fabrics; automotive &
apparel trimmings

(G-5592)
BAIP INC
Also Called: Bai Document Services
3 Wesco Dr Ste 3 # 3 (15632-3902)
PHONE...................................412 913-9826
Ronald Holtzer Jr, *President*
EMP: 3
SALES: 300K **Privately Held**
SIC: **2741** Art copy: publishing & printing

(G-5593)
BOILERROOM EQUIPMENT INC
2081 Borland Farm Rd B (15632-2571)
PHONE...................................724 327-0077
Barry Alberts, *President*
Vincent Sands, *Vice Pres*
EMP: 3
SALES (est): 506K
SALES (corp-wide): 9.7MM **Privately
Held**
SIC: **3443** Boiler shop products: boilers,
smokestacks, steel tanks
PA: Thermal Energy International Inc
36 Bentley Ave
Ottawa ON K2E 6
613 723-6776

(G-5594)
CHROMAGLASS INC
1201 Randall Ct (15632-8979)
PHONE...................................724 325-1437
Bruce Stephens, *President*
▲ EMP: 13 EST: 2001
SALES (est): 1.5MM **Privately Held**
SIC: **3229** Industrial-use glassware

(G-5595)
CONTROLSOFT INC
1 Technology Ln Ste 1 # 1 (15632-8994)
PHONE...................................724 733-2000
Martha Jordan, *President*
Integrated Software Systems Lt, *Partner*
Kim O'Neal, *Manager*
EMP: 50
SALES (est): 3.3MM **Privately Held**
WEB: www.controlsoft.com
SIC: **3822** Auto controls regulating residntl
& coml environmt & applncs

(G-5596)
CTP CARRERA INC
6009 Enterprise Dr (15632-8969)
PHONE...................................724 733-2994
James Stewart, *Mfg Mgr*
Todd Pierce, *Branch Mgr*
EMP: 60
SALES (corp-wide): 204.8MM **Privately
Held**
SIC: **3089** Injection molding of plastics

HQ: Ctp Carrera, Inc.
600 Depot St
Latrobe PA 15650
724 539-6995

(G-5597)
**DORMONT MANUFACTURING
COMPANY**
6015 Enterprise Dr (15632-8969)
PHONE...................................724 327-7909
Srinivas K Bagepalli, *President*
Joe Dykta, *General Mgr*
Leo D Maguire, *Vice Pres*
Sandy Sabados, *Buyer*
Chris Scarpino, *Purchasing*
▲ EMP: 113 EST: 1946
SQ FT: 100,000
SALES (est): 58.8MM
SALES (corp-wide): 1.5B **Publicly Held**
WEB: www.dormont.com
SIC: **3498** Tube fabricating (contract bend-
ing & shaping)
PA: Watts Water Technologies, Inc.
815 Chestnut St
North Andover MA 01845
978 688-1811

(G-5598)
DURA-BOND COATING INC (HQ)
2658 Puckety Dr (15632-1234)
P.O. Box 518 (15632-0518)
PHONE...................................724 327-0782
Wayne Norris, *President*
Brad Norris, *Vice Pres*
Jason Norris, *Vice Pres*
Richard Heisey, *QC Mgr*
Jim Norris, *Treasurer*
EMP: 42 EST: 1966
SQ FT: 10,000
SALES (est): 26.9MM
SALES (corp-wide): 119.9MM **Privately
Held**
WEB: www.durabond.com
SIC: **3317** 3441 2851 Steel pipe & tubes;
fabricated structural metal; paints & allied
products
PA: Dura-Bond Industries, Inc.
5790 Kennedy Ave
Export PA 15632
724 327-0280

(G-5599)
DURA-BOND STEEL CORP
2658 Puckety Dr (15632-1234)
P.O. Box 518 (15632-0518)
PHONE...................................724 327-0280
Wayne Norris, *President*
John Hopper, *Vice Pres*
Bradley W Norris, *Vice Pres*
Blake Crews, *Purch Mgr*
James A Norris, *Treasurer*
EMP: 223
SQ FT: 44,150
SALES (est): 76.3MM
SALES (corp-wide): 119.9MM **Privately
Held**
WEB: www.dura-bond.com
SIC: **3441** 3317 3443 Fabricated struc-
tural metal; pipes, seamless steel; tanks,
standard or custom fabricated: metal
plate
PA: Dura-Bond Industries, Inc.
5790 Kennedy Ave
Export PA 15632
724 327-0280

(G-5600)
**EA FISCHIONE INSTRUMENTS
(PA)**
9003 Corporate Cir (15632-8971)
PHONE...................................724 325-5444
Paul E Fischione, *President*
Nancy E Fischione, *Corp Secy*
Eugene Fischione, *Vice Pres*
Cheryl Smajda, *Buyer*
Dan Hill, *Engineer*
EMP: 33 EST: 1990
SQ FT: 10,000
SALES (est): 3.9MM **Privately Held**
WEB: www.fischione.com
SIC: **3826** Analytical instruments

(G-5601)
ENDAGRAPH INC
Also Called: An Emagen Company
9000 Corporate Cir (15632-8970)
PHONE...................................724 327-9384
Terry E Lollar, *President*
David Crooks, *Vice Pres*
Jim Nash, *Vice Pres*
Dave Crooks, *CFO*
Cynthia K Lollar, *Treasurer*
EMP: 38
SQ FT: 20,000
SALES (est): 8.5MM **Privately Held**
WEB: www.endagraph.com
SIC: **3993** Signs, not made in custom sign
painting shops

(G-5602)
FJ PERFORMANCE INC
1022 Lexington Dr (15632-9022)
PHONE...................................724 681-7430
Francis R John III, *Principal*
EMP: 4
SALES (est): 479K **Privately Held**
SIC: **3714** Motor vehicle parts & acces-
sories

(G-5603)
FOX IV TECHNOLOGIES INC
6011 Enterprise Dr (15632-8969)
PHONE...................................724 387-3500
Rick Fox, *President*
EMP: 30
SQ FT: 30,000
SALES (est): 8.1MM **Privately Held**
WEB: www.foxiv.com
SIC: **3565** 3577 5943 5045 Labeling ma-
chines, industrial; magnetic ink & optical
scanning devices; bar code (magnetic
ink) printers; office forms & supplies; com-
puters; labels, paper: made from pur-
chased material

(G-5604)
FS-ELLIOTT CO LLC (PA)
5710 Mellon Rd (15632-8948)
PHONE...................................724 387-3200
Paul C Brown, *CEO*
Richard King, *Project Mgr*
Lisa Mercurio, *Buyer*
Mike Demark, *Purchasing*
Ed Czechowski, *Engineer*
◆ EMP: 275
SQ FT: 143,000
SALES (est): 139.7MM **Privately Held**
WEB: www.fs-elliott.com
SIC: **3563** Air & gas compressors including
vacuum pumps

(G-5605)
FS-NORTH AMERICA INC (PA)
5710 Mellon Rd (15632-8900)
PHONE...................................724 387-3200
EMP: 4
SALES (est): 23.9MM **Privately Held**
SIC: **3563** Air & gas compressors

(G-5606)
FULMER COMPANY INC
3004 Vent Ct Westmrelnd I (15632)
PHONE...................................724 325-7140
Leo A Eger, *President*
Marshall H Cole, *Treasurer*
EMP: 4
SALES (est): 163.2K **Privately Held**
SIC: **3493** Automobile springs

(G-5607)
GATEWAY PACKAGING CORP
2240 Boyd Rd (15632-8974)
P.O. Box 33, Murrysville (15668-0033)
PHONE...................................724 327-7400
Benjamin H Getty, *CEO*
Kenneth P Getty, *President*
Benjamin C Getty, *Corp Secy*
Scott A Getty, *Vice Pres*
EMP: 45
SQ FT: 105,000

SALES (est): 16.9MM **Privately Held**
WEB: www.gatepack.com
SIC: **2653** 3083 3082 3081 Boxes, corrugated: made from purchased materials;
laminated plastics plate & sheet; unsupported plastics profile shapes; unsupported plastics film & sheet; bags: plastic,
laminated & coated; setup paperboard
boxes

(G-5608)
GLAXOSMITHKLINE LLC
1042 Lexington Dr (15632-9022)
PHONE...................................412 860-5475
EMP: 26
SALES (corp-wide): 39.8B **Privately Held**
SIC: **2834** Pharmaceutical preparations
HQ: Glaxosmithkline Llc
5 Crescent Dr
Philadelphia PA 19112
215 751-4000

(G-5609)
IRONMASTER LLC
401 Revere Ln (15632-1519)
PHONE...................................412 554-6705
Michael D Sullivan, *Principal*
EMP: 5
SALES (est): 809.1K **Privately Held**
SIC: **3313** Electrometallurgical products

(G-5610)
J F BURNS MACHINE CO INC
Also Called: J F Burns Machine
4583 School Rd S (15632-1818)
PHONE...................................724 327-2870
Donald C Burns, *President*
David Burns, *Vice Pres*
EMP: 26 EST: 1949
SQ FT: 21,000
SALES (est): 4.6MM **Privately Held**
SIC: **3599** 3452 Machine shop, jobbing &
repair; bolts, nuts, rivets & washers

(G-5611)
**JOHN GALT BNDERY PUBL
SVCS INC**
2251 Woodmont Dr (15632-8955)
PHONE...................................724 733-1439
EMP: 21
SALES (est): 1.6MM **Privately Held**
SIC: **2789** Bookbinding/Related Work

(G-5612)
**JORDAN ACQUISITION GROUP
LLC**
Also Called: American Auto-Matrix
1 Technology Ln (15632-8994)
PHONE...................................724 733-2000
Guerry Matthews, *Vice Pres*
Dennis King, *Sales Mgr*
Martha Jordan, *Mng Member*
Linda Diss,
EMP: 52
SQ FT: 20,000
SALES (est): 14MM **Privately Held**
WEB: www.aamatrix.com
SIC: **3822** 3625 Auto controls regulating
residntl & coml environmt & applncs; re-
lays & industrial controls
HQ: Cylon Energy Inc.
1 Sundial Ave Ste 219
Manchester NH 03103
603 782-8870

(G-5613)
KINTON CARBIDE INC
3000 Venture Ct (15632-8949)
PHONE...................................724 327-3141
Patrick Rankin, *President*
Patrick S Rankin, *President*
EMP: 14 EST: 1966
SQ FT: 15,200
SALES (est): 1.1MM **Privately Held**
WEB: www.kintoncarbide.com
SIC: **3398** Brazing (hardening) of metal

(G-5614)
KT-GRANT INC (PA)
Also Called: Kt-Grants
3073 Route 66 (15632-1908)
PHONE...................................724 468-4700
Marc Glasgow, *President*
Tremayne Hadenfelt, *Area Mgr*
Louis A Grant Jr, *Exec VP*
Scott Rubright, *Plant Mgr*

Robert Heitzman, *Opers Mgr*
▲ **EMP:** 75 **EST:** 1997
SQ FT: 15,000
SALES (est): 28.5MM **Privately Held**
WEB: www.rgrantinc.com
SIC: 7353 3441 3433 Earth moving equipment, rental or leasing; ship sections, prefabricated metal; heating equipment, except electric

(G-5615)
LEMM LIQUIDATING COMPANY LLC (DH)
Also Called: Fulmer
3004 Venture Ct (15632-8949)
PHONE..............................724 325-7140
Matt Gardner, *General Mgr*
▲ **EMP:** 68
SQ FT: 41,000
SALES (est): 14MM
SALES (corp-wide): 4.3B **Publicly Held**
WEB: www.fulmercompany.com
SIC: 3621 3544 Electric motor & generator auxillary parts; industrial molds

(G-5616)
LEYBOLD USA INC (DH)
Also Called: Oerlikon Leybold Vacuum USA
5700 Mellon Rd (15632-8900)
PHONE..............................724 327-5700
Guenter Hauck, *President*
▲ **EMP:** 60
SQ FT: 62,000
SALES (est): 19.4MM
SALES (corp-wide): 13.8B **Privately Held**
SIC: 3821 3563 Vacuum pumps, laboratory; vacuum pumps, except laboratory
HQ: Leybold Gmbh
　　Bonner Str. 498
　　Koln 50968
　　221 347-0

(G-5617)
MAGISEAL SERVICES
3825 Wiestertown Rd (15632-9365)
PHONE..............................724 327-3068
Gene Martin, *Owner*
EMP: 5
SALES (est): 294.3K **Privately Held**
WEB: www.magiseal.com
SIC: 2269 Finishing plants

(G-5618)
METALOR ELECTRONICS USA CORP (DH)
1003 Corporate Ln (15632-8908)
PHONE..............................724 733-8332
Philippe Royer, *CEO*
Scott Morrison, *President*
Joel Lacourte, *Chairman*
Karen Ursiny, *Buyer*
Bill Bronson, *Engineer*
▲ **EMP:** 130 **EST:** 1969
SALES (est): 15.2MM
SALES (corp-wide): 9.1B **Privately Held**
WEB: www.amidoduco.com
SIC: 3643 Contacts, electrical
HQ: Metalor Technologies Usa Corp
　　255 John L Dietsch Blvd
　　North Attleboro MA 02763
　　508 699-8800

(G-5619)
MORROW BROS COUNTERTOP LP
Also Called: Morrow Brother's Countertops
104 Technology Ln (15632-8903)
PHONE..............................724 327-8980
Duane Morrow, *Partner*
Dwight Morrow, *Partner*
EMP: 13
SQ FT: 6,200
SALES (est): 1MM **Privately Held**
SIC: 2541 Table or counter tops, plastic laminated; counter & sink tops

(G-5620)
PERMA CAST LLC
9002 Corporate Cir (15632-8970)
PHONE..............................724 325-1662
Leo Eger, *Mng Member*
▲ **EMP:** 30
SQ FT: 15,000

SALES (est): 5MM
SALES (corp-wide): 4.3B **Publicly Held**
WEB: www.permacast.com
SIC: 3366 5099 Castings (except die): copper & copper-base alloy; castings (except die): brass; brass goods
HQ: Lemm Liquidating Company, Llc
　　3004 Venture Ct
　　Export PA 15632
　　724 325-7140

(G-5621)
PIXCONTROLLER INC
1001 Corporate Ln Ste 100 (15632-8908)
PHONE..............................724 733-0970
William H Powers Jr, *President*
Bill Powers, *Sales Mgr*
EMP: 5
SQ FT: 3,000
SALES: 650K **Privately Held**
WEB: www.pixcontroller.com
SIC: 3861 7382 Aerial cameras; protective devices, security

(G-5622)
R T R BUSINESS PRODUCTS INC
5110 Old William Penn Hwy (15632-9336)
P.O. Box 67, Murrysville (15668-0067)
PHONE..............................724 733-7373
Richard L McCormick, *President*
Allen Latta, *Financial Exec*
Greg Klein, *Info Tech Mgr*
Thomas W Cox, *Admin Sec*
EMP: 45 **EST:** 1968
SQ FT: 8,100
SALES (est): 8.3MM **Privately Held**
WEB: www.rtrbusinessproducts.com
SIC: 3577 7629 5112 5943 Printers, computer; business machine repair, electric; office supplies; office forms & supplies

(G-5623)
RALPH A HILLER COMPANY
6005 Enterprise Dr (15632-8969)
PHONE..............................724 325-1200
Robert Arnold, *President*
Randolph J Hiller, *President*
◆ **EMP:** 48 **EST:** 1946
SQ FT: 28,000
SALES (est): 28.1MM
SALES (corp-wide): 848.5MM **Privately Held**
WEB: www.rahiller.com
SIC: 5085 5084 3593 3594 Fluid power cylinders & actuators; fluid power pumps & motors; relays & industrial controls; industrial supplies; hydraulic systems equipment & supplies
HQ: Rotork Controls Inc.
　　675 Mile Crossing Blvd
　　Rochester NY 14624
　　585 247-2304

(G-5624)
RELIANCE PACKAGING & SUPPLY CO
2963 Route 66 (15632-2039)
PHONE..............................724 468-8849
David Byer, *President*
EMP: 4
SQ FT: 15,000
SALES (est): 805.1K **Privately Held**
WEB: www.reliancepackaging.net
SIC: 2653 Boxes, corrugated: made from purchased materials

(G-5625)
RELIANOLOGY INTERNATIONAL LTD
3421 Chapel Hill Ct (15632-9210)
PHONE..............................412 607-1503
EMP: 3
SALES (est): 178.1K **Privately Held**
SIC: 3089 Injection molding of plastics

(G-5626)
SEPARATION TECHNOLOGIES INC (PA)
20 Claridge Rd (15632)
PHONE..............................724 325-4546
Mary Beth Presutti, *President*
Michael Presutti, *Treasurer*
EMP: 4

SQ FT: 1,200
SALES: 1.5MM **Privately Held**
SIC: 5085 3569 Filters, industrial; filters, general line: industrial

(G-5627)
SPECIALIZED WELDING INC
205 Mamont Dr (15632-1942)
PHONE..............................724 733-7801
Daniel Bazella, *President*
Mike McElroy, *President*
Margie Bazella, *Corp Secy*
EMP: 9
SALES (est): 850K **Privately Held**
SIC: 7692 3599 Welding repair; machine shop, jobbing & repair

(G-5628)
SPERANZA SPECIALTY MACHINING
2226 Boyd Rd (15632-8974)
PHONE..............................724 733-8045
Joann Speranza, *Owner*
Richard Speranza, *Co-Owner*
EMP: 6
SQ FT: 7,200
SALES (est): 500K **Privately Held**
WEB: www.ssmachining.com
SIC: 3599 7692 Machine shop, jobbing & repair; welding repair

(G-5629)
TRESCO CONCRETE PRODUCTS INC
1 Plant Rd (15632)
PHONE..............................724 468-4640
James E Guy IV, *President*
EMP: 15
SALES (est): 3.1MM **Privately Held**
SIC: 3273 Ready-mixed concrete

(G-5630)
VENTANA USA
6001 Enterprise Dr (15632-8969)
PHONE..............................724 325-3400
Stefan Schwanekamp, *President*
Christopher Pauly, *Vice Pres*
Michael Pauly, *Vice Pres*
Ann Pauly, *CFO*
◆ **EMP:** 86
SQ FT: 70,000
SALES: 12MM **Privately Held**
WEB: www.ventanainternational.com
SIC: 3089 Windows, plastic

(G-5631)
VERSATECH INCORPORATED
6012 Enterprise Dr (15632-8968)
P.O. Box 608 (15632-0608)
PHONE..............................724 327-8324
Richard Versaw, *President*
Dale Versaw, *Vice Pres*
Debra Bell, *Office Spvr*
EMP: 80
SQ FT: 85,000
SALES (est): 13.9MM **Privately Held**
WEB: www.e-versatech.com
SIC: 3599 7692 Machine shop, jobbing & repair; welding repair

(G-5632)
ZELL MANUFACTURING CO INC
213 Pfeffer Rd (15632-1936)
PHONE..............................724 327-4771
David Zell, *President*
Timothy C Zell, *Treasurer*
Warren Zell, *Admin Sec*
EMP: 6
SQ FT: 7,000
SALES: 900K **Privately Held**
WEB: www.zellmfg.com
SIC: 2499 Decorative wood & woodwork

```
        Exton
    Chester County
```

(G-5633)
21ST CENTURY MEDIA NEWSPPR LLC
390 Eagleview Blvd (19341-1155)
PHONE..............................610 692-3790
EMP: 55

SALES (est): 1.3MM **Privately Held**
SIC: 2711 Newspapers: publishing only, not printed on site

(G-5634)
ABILITY PRSTHTICS ORTHTICS INC (PA)
Also Called: Ability Prosthetics Orthotics
660 W Lincoln Hwy (19341-2514)
PHONE..............................717 337-2277
Jeffrey Brandt, *CEO*
Thomas Barrow, *Principal*
Jeffrey Quelet, *Vice Pres*
EMP: 3
SALES (est): 742.3K **Privately Held**
SIC: 3842 Orthopedic appliances; prosthetic appliances

(G-5635)
ABPS, INC.
Also Called: Genesis Packaging Technologies
435 Creamery Way Ste 100 (19341-2508)
PHONE..............................800 552-9980
▲ **EMP:** 38
SQ FT: 36,000
SALES (est): 9.6MM **Privately Held**
SIC: 3559 Pharmaceutical machinery

(G-5636)
ADELPHIA GRAPHIC SYSTEMS INC
302 Commerce Dr (19341-2606)
PHONE..............................610 363-8150
Alan D Jacobson, *President*
Joshua Jacobson, *Vice Pres*
Neil Jacobson, *Vice Pres*
EMP: 70
SQ FT: 15,000
SALES (est): 13MM **Privately Held**
WEB: www.agsinfo.com
SIC: 3993 Signs, not made in custom sign painting shops

(G-5637)
AIR PRODUCTS CORPORATION (PA)
Also Called: General Air Products
118 Summit Dr (19341-2825)
PHONE..............................800 345-8207
Robert F Fremont Jr, *President*
Raymond Fremont, *President*
R Geoff Pridham, *Vice Pres*
Brian Blankemeyer, *Purchasing*
Brian Eskridge, *Engineer*
▲ **EMP:** 52
SALES (est): 19MM **Privately Held**
SIC: 3563 3569 5084 Air & gas compressors including vacuum pumps; sprinkler systems, fire: automatic; compressors, except air conditioning

(G-5638)
ALFA LAVAL INC
604 Jeffers Cir (19341-2524)
PHONE..............................610 594-1830
Deann Schrack, *Manager*
EMP: 8
SALES (corp-wide): 4.1B **Privately Held**
SIC: 3589 Commercial cleaning equipment
HQ: Alfa Laval Inc.
　　5400 Intl Trade Dr
　　Richmond VA 23231
　　804 222-5300

(G-5639)
ALL-FILL CORPORATION
418 Creamery Way (19341-2536)
PHONE..............................866 255-3455
Ryan Edginton, *CEO*
Ha Dinh, *Vice Pres*
Kyle Edginton, *Vice Pres*
George Hughes, *Opers Mgr*
Teresa Rivera, *Opers Staff*
◆ **EMP:** 80
SQ FT: 65,000
SALES (est): 24.7MM **Privately Held**
WEB: www.all-fill.com
SIC: 3565 3596 3549 Packaging machinery; scales & balances, except laboratory; metalworking machinery

(G-5640)
ALL-FILL INC
418 Creamery Way (19341-2536)
PHONE..............................610 524-7350

▲ = Import ▼=Export
◆ =Import/Export

Ryan Edginton, *President*
Ray Arra, *Exec VP*
Kyle Edginton, *Exec VP*
Ha Dinh, *Vice Pres*
Joe Brennecke, *Prdtn Mgr*
EMP: 6 **EST:** 2016
SQ FT: 65,000
SALES (est): 157.3K **Privately Held**
SIC: 3565 Packaging machinery

(G-5641)
ALMIRALL LLC
707 Eagleview Blvd # 200 (19341-1159)
PHONE....................................610 644-7000
Christopher Cano, *President*
David Crean, *Development*
Ashley Perry, *Sales Staff*
Dom Dicindio, *Mktg Dir*
Jim Alexander, *Manager*
EMP: 57
SALES (est): 21.5MM
SALES (corp-wide): 494.6MM **Privately Held**
WEB: www.aquapharm.com
SIC: 2834 Dermatologicals
PA: Almirall Sa
Ronda General Mitre, 151 - 6
Barcelona
932 913-000

(G-5642)
AMERCAREROYAL LLC (PA)
420 Clover Mill Rd (19341-2501)
PHONE....................................610 384-3400
David M Milberg, *President*
Fred A Strauss, *Corp Secy*
Halaine A Leibowitz, *Vice Pres*
◆ **EMP:** 37
SQ FT: 225,000
SALES (est): 9.7MM **Privately Held**
WEB: www.royalpaper.com
SIC: 2679 Paper products, converted; food dishes & utensils, from pressed & molded pulp; novelties, paper: made from purchased material

(G-5643)
ANALYTICAL GRAPHICS INC (PA)
Also Called: Agi
220 Valley Creek Blvd (19341-2380)
PHONE....................................610 981-8000
Paul L Graziani, *President*
Joseph Sheehan, *President*
Francesco F Linsalata, *COO*
Scott Reynolds, *Vice Pres*
Ronald E Thompson, *Vice Pres*
EMP: 204
SALES (est): 70.2MM **Privately Held**
WEB: www.stk.com
SIC: 7372 Prepackaged software

(G-5644)
APPLE PRESS LTD
307 Commerce Dr (19341-2608)
PHONE....................................610 363-1776
Gary Gehman, *President*
John Jenkins, *Business Mgr*
Ryan Brown, *Controller*
Erin McGuoirk, *Controller*
Ken Church, *Accounts Exec*
EMP: 36
SQ FT: 16,000
SALES (est): 5.4MM **Privately Held**
WEB: www.applepress.net
SIC: 2752 2759 2789 Commercial printing, offset; commercial printing; bookbinding & related work

(G-5645)
APPLIED TECHNOLOGY INTL LTD
Also Called: Fabrifoam Products
900 Springdale Dr (19341-2805)
PHONE....................................610 363-1077
Harry Sherman, *President*
Sharon Auster, *Marketing Staff*
Charlene Buckley, *Director*
EMP: 15
SQ FT: 10,000
SALES (est): 2.5MM **Privately Held**
WEB: www.fabrifoam.com
SIC: 3842 Supports: abdominal, ankle, arch, kneecap, etc.

(G-5646)
ARKEMA INC
Also Called: Sartomer Americas Division
502 Thomas Jones Way (19341-2530)
PHONE....................................610 363-4100
Douglas Sharp, *President*
Thomas Demoss, *Plant Mgr*
Blair Hamerski, *Engineer*
Lisa Caruso, *Manager*
John Piechule, *Manager*
EMP: 120
SALES (corp-wide): 77.8MM **Privately Held**
SIC: 2819 Industrial inorganic chemicals
HQ: Arkema Inc.
900 First Ave
King Of Prussia PA 19406
610 205-7000

(G-5647)
ASPIRE BARIATRICS INC
319 N Pottstown Pike # 202 (19341-2218)
PHONE....................................610 590-1577
Katherine Crothall, *CEO*
Toni Harp, *Vice Pres*
Jim McGee, *Vice Pres*
Ed Schieferstein, *Opers Staff*
Lea Landsmann, *Engineer*
EMP: 29
SALES (est): 4.6MM **Privately Held**
SIC: 3841 Surgical & medical instruments

(G-5648)
AUGER FABRICATION INC
418 Creamery Way (19341-2500)
PHONE....................................610 524-3350
Richard Edginton, *President*
Glenn Edginton, *President*
George Hughes, *Regional Mgr*
Rita Edginton, *Corp Secy*
Eric Edginton, *VP Sales*
▲ **EMP:** 21
SQ FT: 16,884
SALES (est): 3.8MM **Privately Held**
WEB: www.auger-fab.com
SIC: 3423 3444 Edge tools for woodworking: augers, bits, gimlets, etc.; sheet metalwork

(G-5649)
AUTOMATED FINCL SYSTEMS INC (PA)
Also Called: A F S
123 Summit Dr Ste 2 (19341-2842)
PHONE....................................484 875-1250
John H Shain, *President*
Robert H Kahn, *Managing Dir*
Jorgenson Karen, *Managing Dir*
Paul McCarthy, *Managing Dir*
Agnes Bongor, *Vice Pres*
EMP: 280
SQ FT: 65,000
SALES (est): 75.2MM **Privately Held**
WEB: www.afsvision.com
SIC: 7372 Business oriented computer software

(G-5650)
AUTOMATED FINCL SYSTEMS INC
770 Springdale Dr (19341-2850)
PHONE....................................610 594-1037
Linda Ding, *Engineer*
Diane Kauffman, *Engineer*
Sue A Lewalski-Jozwia, *Business Anlyst*
Biagio Natale, *Business Anlyst*
David Nehr, *Business Anlyst*
EMP: 300
SALES (corp-wide): 75.2MM **Privately Held**
WEB: www.afsvision.com
SIC: 7372 Business oriented computer software
PA: Automated Financial Systems, Inc.
123 Summit Dr Ste 2
Exton PA 19341
484 875-1250

(G-5651)
BALL & BALL LLP
463 W Lincoln Hwy (19341-2594)
PHONE....................................610 363-7330
William W Ball Sr, *Partner*
Robert A Ball, *Partner*
▲ **EMP:** 30 **EST:** 1932

SQ FT: 21,270
SALES (est): 4.2MM **Privately Held**
WEB: www.ballandball.com
SIC: 3429 Manufactured hardware (general)

(G-5652)
BENDER ELECTRONICS INC
Also Called: Isotrol Systems
420 Eagleview Blvd (19341-1116)
PHONE....................................610 383-9200
Christian Bender, *President*
Cindy Schaeffer, *Business Mgr*
Marcel Tremblay, *Treasurer*
Dave Bradley, *Sales Executive*
◆ **EMP:** 55
SQ FT: 22,000
SALES (est): 4.4MM
SALES (corp-wide): 672.8K **Privately Held**
WEB: www.isotrolsystems.com
SIC: 3625 Control equipment, electric
PA: Bender Industries Gmbh & Co. Kg
Londorfer Str. 65
Grunberg 35305
640 180-70

(G-5653)
BENTLEY SYSTEMS INCORPORATED
690 Pennsylvania Dr (19341-1127)
PHONE....................................610 458-5000
Gregory Bentley, *President*
Anthony Falcone, *Software Engr*
Feyerer Patsy, *Technical Staff*
EMP: 250
SQ FT: 35,498
SALES (corp-wide): 510.6MM **Privately Held**
WEB: www.allegria.com
SIC: 7372 Application computer software
PA: Bentley Systems, Incorporated
685 Stockton Dr
Exton PA 19341
610 458-5000

(G-5654)
BENTLEY SYSTEMS INCORPORATED (PA)
685 Stockton Dr (19341-1151)
PHONE....................................610 458-5000
Gregory Bentley, *Ch of Bd*
Alton B Cleveland Jr, *President*
Jeffrey Hollings, *President*
David Nation, *President*
Elly Hoinowski, *Principal*
EMP: 450
SQ FT: 80,000
SALES (est): 510.6MM **Privately Held**
WEB: www.allegria.com
SIC: 7372 7373 Application computer software; computer integrated systems design

(G-5655)
BETA INDUSTRIES INC
Also Called: Omega Design
211 Philips Rd (19341-1309)
PHONE....................................610 363-6555
Glenn R Siegele, *President*
John C Campbell, *Vice Pres*
EMP: 5
SQ FT: 1,600
SALES (est): 792.9K **Privately Held**
SIC: 3565 Packaging machinery

(G-5656)
BOY MACHINES INC (PA)
199 Philips Rd (19341-1337)
PHONE....................................610 363-9121
Marko Koorneef, *President*
Marco Koorneef, *President*
Anthony Lengetti, *Treasurer*
Stephen R Foreht, *Admin Sec*
◆ **EMP:** 23
SQ FT: 48,000
SALES (est): 5.4MM **Privately Held**
WEB: www.boymachines.com
SIC: 3556 Food products machinery

(G-5657)
BRILLIANT STUDIO INC (PA)
Also Called: Brilliant Graphics
400 Eagleview Blvd # 104 (19341-1138)
PHONE....................................610 458-7977
Robert Tursak Jr, *CEO*

Peter Philbin, *General Mgr*
Harold Hepler, *Vice Pres*
Marc Belfiore, *Production*
Zhefan Xu, *Engineer*
▲ **EMP:** 3
SALES (est): 3.5MM **Privately Held**
SIC: 2752 Commercial printing, offset

(G-5658)
C&H7 LLC (PA)
Also Called: Comfort & Harmony
717 Constitution Dr # 112 (19341-1140)
PHONE....................................215 887-7411
David Schwartz, *Managing Dir*
Ken Waldman,
EMP: 5
SQ FT: 8,000
SALES (est): 2.5MM **Privately Held**
SIC: 2369 2399 Girls' & children's outerwear; infant carriers

(G-5659)
CAPE PROSTHETICS-ORTHOTICS (HQ)
Also Called: Standard Artifical Limb
855 Springdale Dr Ste 200 (19341-2852)
PHONE....................................610 644-7824
Daniel J Connors, *President*
Maureen Fitzpatrick, *Manager*
EMP: 1
SALES (est): 3.7MM **Privately Held**
SIC: 3842 Limbs, artificial

(G-5660)
CELL-CON INC (PA)
305 Commerce Dr Ste 300 (19341-2612)
PHONE....................................800 771-7139
Steven Fricker, *President*
Eugene Fkiley Sr, *Corp Secy*
Eugene Fkiley, *Vice Pres*
Steve Fricker, *Engineer*
Eugene F Kiley Sr, *Treasurer*
▲ **EMP:** 54
SQ FT: 8,000
SALES (est): 10.4MM **Privately Held**
WEB: www.cell-con.com
SIC: 3691 5063 Batteries, rechargeable; nickel cadmium storage batteries; electrical apparatus & equipment

(G-5661)
CERSELL COMPANY LLC
100 Woodledge Ln (19341-2089)
PHONE....................................484 753-2655
Neil Cersell, *Principal*
▲ **EMP:** 3
SALES (est): 250K **Privately Held**
SIC: 3563 Air & gas compressors

(G-5662)
CLOVER TECHNOLOGIES GROUP LLC
Also Called: MSE - PA
301 National Rd (19341-2640)
PHONE....................................818 407-7500
EMP: 10
SALES (corp-wide): 702.5MM **Privately Held**
WEB: www.gotink.com
SIC: 3861 Printing equipment, photographic
HQ: Clover Technologies Group, Llc
2700 W Higgins Rd Ste 100
Hoffman Estates IL 60169

(G-5663)
CUSTOM PACK INC
662 Exton Cmns (19341-2446)
PHONE....................................610 363-1900
Frank Menichini, *President*
EMP: 13 **EST:** 1972
SQ FT: 36,000
SALES (est): 3.3MM **Privately Held**
WEB: www.cpispecimen.com
SIC: 3089 3086 Thermoformed finished plastic products; plastics foam products

(G-5664)
DFT INC
140 Sheree Blvd (19341-1231)
P.O. Box 566 (19341-0566)
PHONE....................................610 363-8903
David Moser, *President*
Dianne Lowden, *Vice Pres*
Dennis Petrucci, *Mfg Mgr*
Claire Murphy, *Technical Mgr*

Joe Cristaldi, *Engineer*
▲ **EMP:** 50
SALES (est): 12.1MM **Privately Held**
WEB: www.dft-valves.com
SIC: 3491 Process control regulator valves

(G-5665)
DGH TECHNOLOGY INC (PA)
110 Summit Dr Ste B (19341-2838)
PHONE....................................610 594-9100
Earl Henderson, *President*
Marvin L Detweiler, *Vice Pres*
Rafael Ramirez, *Sales Staff*
Lou Detweiler, *Info Tech Mgr*
▲ **EMP:** 10
SQ FT: 5,000
SALES (est): 1.2MM **Privately Held**
WEB: www.pachometer.com
SIC: 3841 Ophthalmic instruments & apparatus

(G-5666)
DGHKOI INC
110 Summit Dr Ste B (19341-2838)
PHONE....................................610 594-9100
Earl Henderson, *President*
EMP: 4
SALES (est): 312.6K **Privately Held**
WEB: www.dghkoi.com
SIC: 3841 Knives, surgical

(G-5667)
DIAMOND POWER INTL INC
Allen Sherman Hoff
457 Creamery Way (19341-2508)
PHONE....................................484 875-1600
Arthur Boone, *Branch Mgr*
EMP: 70
SALES (corp-wide): 1B **Publicly Held**
WEB: www.diamondpower.com
SIC: 3564 Blowers & fans
HQ: Diamond Power International, Inc.
2600 E Main St
Lancaster OH 43130
740 687-6500

(G-5668)
DSM BIOMEDICAL INC (HQ)
Also Called: Kensey Nash Corporation
735 Pennsylvania Dr (19341-1130)
PHONE....................................484 713-2100
Walter Maupay Jr, *Ch of Bd*
Holly Harrity, *President*
Joseph W Kaufmann, *President*
Robert J Bobb, *Principal*
Lisa Earnhardt, *Principal*
EMP: 9
SQ FT: 202,500
SALES (corp-wide): 10.1B **Privately Held**
WEB: www.kenseynash.com
SIC: 3841 Surgical & medical instruments
PA: Koninklijke Dsm N.V.
Het Overloon 1
Heerlen 6411
455 788-111

(G-5669)
DSM BIOMEDICAL INC
Also Called: Nerites
735 Pennsylvania Dr (19341-1130)
PHONE....................................610 321-2720
Shaun C Lonergan, *Manager*
EMP: 5
SALES (corp-wide): 10.1B **Privately Held**
SIC: 2891 Adhesives
HQ: Dsm Biomedical, Inc.
735 Pennsylvania Dr
Exton PA 19341
484 713-2100

(G-5670)
DYNAMIC TEAM SPORTS INC
Also Called: Cycle Venture
15 E Uwchlan Ave Ste 416 (19341-1258)
PHONE....................................610 518-3300
James D Samter, *President*
Scott A Samter, *Vice Pres*
EMP: 60
SQ FT: 40,000
SALES (est): 10.5MM **Privately Held**
WEB: www.dynamicteamsports.com
SIC: 2311 Men's & boys' uniforms

(G-5671)
EDUCATION MGT SOLUTIONS LLC
436 Creamery Way Ste 300 (19341-2556)
PHONE....................................610 701-7002
Anurag Singh, *President*
Sharada Singh, *Vice Pres*
EMP: 78
SQ FT: 27,500
SALES (est): 14.6MM **Privately Held**
WEB: www.emessages.com
SIC: 7372 7371 7379 7373 Educational computer software; custom computer programming services; computer related maintenance services; computer integrated systems design; data processing & preparation; video equipment, electronic

(G-5672)
ENQUIP CO
365 Devon Dr (19341-1748)
PHONE....................................610 363-8275
Douglass McCord, *President*
EMP: 4
SALES (est): 345.6K **Privately Held**
SIC: 3589 Water treatment equipment, industrial

(G-5673)
ESSENTIAL MEDICAL INC
260 Sierra Dr Ste 120 (19341-2245)
PHONE....................................610 557-1009
Greg Walters, *President*
Gary Roubin MD, *Officer*
EMP: 8 **EST:** 2011
SALES (est): 1.2MM
SALES (corp-wide): 2.1B **Publicly Held**
SIC: 3841 Surgical & medical instruments; surgical instruments & apparatus
PA: Teleflex Incorporated
550 E Swedesford Rd # 400
Wayne PA 19087
610 225-6800

(G-5674)
EXPRESSION TEES
161 Philips Rd (19341-1319)
PHONE....................................631 523-5673
EMP: 3
SALES (est): 243.9K **Privately Held**
SIC: 2759 Screen printing

(G-5675)
FARO TECHNOLOGIES INC
290 National Rd (19341-2665)
PHONE....................................407 333-9911
EMP: 20
SQ FT: 90,000
SALES (corp-wide): 403.6MM **Publicly Held**
SIC: 3829 Measuring & controlling devices
PA: Faro Technologies, Inc.
250 Technology Park
Lake Mary FL 32746
407 333-9911

(G-5676)
FASTSIGNS
307 E Lincoln Hwy (19341-2730)
PHONE....................................610 280-6100
Kevin Mengel, *President*
EMP: 6
SALES (est): 759.1K **Privately Held**
SIC: 3993 Signs & advertising specialties

(G-5677)
FEDERAL-MOGUL POWERTRAIN LLC
241 Welsh Pool Rd (19341-1316)
PHONE....................................610 363-2600
Brian Taylor, *Engineer*
Trevor Seibert, *Design Engr*
Lenny Lewullis, *Finance*
Phil Marks, *CTO*
Michael Gerulski, *Director*
EMP: 57
SALES (corp-wide): 11.7B **Publicly Held**
SIC: 3496 3053 Miscellaneous fabricated wire products; gaskets, packing & sealing devices
HQ: Federal-Mogul Powertrain Llc
27300 W 11 Mile Rd # 101
Southfield MI 48034

(G-5678)
FIBROCELL SCIENCE INC (PA)
405 Eagleview Blvd (19341-1117)
PHONE....................................484 713-6000
John Maslowski, *CEO*
Douglas Swirsky, *Ch of Bd*
Michael F Marino, *Senior VP*
Keith A Goldan, *CFO*
EMP: 52
SQ FT: 86,500
SALES: 355K **Publicly Held**
SIC: 2834 2836 Pharmaceutical preparations; biological products, except diagnostic

(G-5679)
FIBROCELL TECHNOLOGIES INC
405 Eagleview Blvd (19341-1117)
PHONE....................................484 713-6000
Declan Daly, *CFO*
EMP: 10 **EST:** 1995
SQ FT: 5,000
SALES (est): 1.6MM **Publicly Held**
WEB: www.isolagen.com
SIC: 2836 Biological products, except diagnostic
PA: Fibrocell Science, Inc.
405 Eagleview Blvd
Exton PA 19341

(G-5680)
FOCUS NOISE LTD LIABILITY CO
Also Called: Eco Fusions
705 Worthington Dr (19341-1647)
PHONE....................................484 886-7242
Robert Pelc, *Partner*
Kenneth Crockett Jr, *Partner*
EMP: 5
SALES (est): 361.8K **Privately Held**
SIC: 3089 Plastics products

(G-5681)
FREEDMAN SEATING COMPANY
150 Gordon Dr (19341-1304)
PHONE....................................610 265-3610
EMP: 113
SALES (corp-wide): 142.1MM **Privately Held**
WEB: www.freedmanseating.com
SIC: 2531 Seats, miscellaneous public conveyances; vehicle furniture; cabs for off-highway trucks
PA: Freedman Seating Company
4545 W Augusta Blvd
Chicago IL 60651
773 524-2440

(G-5682)
FRONTAGE LABORATORIES INC (PA)
700 Pennsylvania Dr (19341-1129)
PHONE....................................610 232-0100
Song LI, *CEO*
Michael S Willett, *President*
Sue Zhou, *Business Mgr*
Zhongping John Lin, *Exec VP*
Abdul Mutlib, *Exec VP*
EMP: 141
SALES: 43.6MM **Privately Held**
WEB: www.frontagelab.com
SIC: 2834 8731 Pharmaceutical preparations; biological research

(G-5683)
FRONTAGE LABORATORIES INC
75 E Uwchlan Ave Ste 100 (19341-1254)
PHONE....................................610 232-0100
Dongmei Wang, *Branch Mgr*
EMP: 37
SALES (corp-wide): 43.6MM **Privately Held**
SIC: 2834 Pharmaceutical preparations
PA: Frontage Laboratories, Inc.
700 Pennsylvania Dr
Exton PA 19341
610 232-0100

(G-5684)
GAMAJET CLEANING SYSTEMS INC
Also Called: Alpha Label Tank Equipment
604 Jeffers Cir (19341-2524)
PHONE....................................610 408-9940
Robert E Delaney, *President*
▲ **EMP:** 19
SALES (est): 2.9MM **Privately Held**
WEB: www.gamajet.com
SIC: 3589 Commercial cleaning equipment

(G-5685)
GENERAL AIR PRODUCTS INC
Also Called: General Blower Company
118 Summit Dr (19341-2825)
P.O. Box 1387, West Chester (19380-0028)
PHONE....................................610 524-8950
Raymond M Fremont, *President*
Robert F Fremont Jr, *Vice Pres*
Michael Dececco, *Sales Staff*
Dave Fremont, *Manager*
▲ **EMP:** 40 **EST:** 1936
SQ FT: 45,546
SALES (est): 15.8MM **Privately Held**
WEB: www.generalairproducts.com
SIC: 3563 5084 3564 Air & gas compressors including vacuum pumps; industrial machinery & equipment; blowing fans: industrial or commercial

(G-5686)
GENERAL ECOLOGY INC
151 Sheree Blvd (19341-1292)
PHONE....................................610 363-7900
Richard T Williams, *President*
Bonnie C Williams, *Treasurer*
Megan Karnbach, *Manager*
▲ **EMP:** 45
SQ FT: 20,000
SALES (est): 9MM
SALES (corp-wide): 22.8MM **Privately Held**
WEB: www.generalecology.com
SIC: 3589 Water purification equipment, household type; water treatment equipment, industrial
PA: Loar Group Inc.
450 Lexington Ave Fl 31
New York NY 10017
212 210-9348

(G-5687)
GENERAL TECHNICAL PLASTICS
424 Creamery Way (19341-2500)
PHONE....................................610 363-5480
J Benson Campbell, *President*
EMP: 39
SQ FT: 30,000
SALES (est): 3.6MM
SALES (corp-wide): 26.4MM **Privately Held**
SIC: 3089 5162 Plastic processing; plastics products
PA: J. Benson Corp.
2201 Reading Ave
Reading PA 19609
610 678-2692

(G-5688)
GENZYME CORPORATION
Genzyme Diagnostics
115 Summit Dr Ste 3 (19341-2840)
PHONE....................................610 594-8590
Allan Murphy, *Branch Mgr*
EMP: 18 **Privately Held**
WEB: www.genzyme.com
SIC: 2834 Pharmaceutical preparations
HQ: Genzyme Corporation
50 Binney St
Cambridge MA 02142
617 252-7500

(G-5689)
GLUTALOR MEDICAL INC
436 Creamery Way Ste 200 (19341-2556)
PHONE....................................610 492-5710
Brian Heald, *CEO*
EMP: 12 **EST:** 2015
SQ FT: 18,000
SALES (est): 892K **Privately Held**
SIC: 3841 Diagnostic apparatus, medical

▲ = Import ▼=Export
◆ =Import/Export

(G-5690)
GOEBEL CABINETRY
308 Commerce Dr (19341-2635)
PHONE..................................610 363-8970
Jack Goebel, *Principal*
Ashley Kunkle, *Marketing Staff*
EMP: 4
SALES (est): 411.6K **Privately Held**
SIC: 2434 Wood kitchen cabinets

(G-5691)
GRAPHEX INC
301 National Rd Ste 400 (19341-2640)
PHONE..................................610 524-9525
John J Henry, *President*
Lisa H Lacek, *Vice Pres*
EMP: 5
SQ FT: 2,800
SALES (est): 537K **Privately Held**
SIC: 2653 Display items, corrugated: made
from purchased materials; display items,
solid fiber: made from purchased materi-
als

(G-5692)
**HUGHES NETWORK SYSTEMS
LLC**
184 Exton Square Mall (19341-2440)
PHONE..................................610 363-1427
EMP: 32 **Publicly Held**
SIC: 3663 Satellites, communications
HQ: Hughes Network Systems, Llc
11717 Exploration Ln
Germantown MD 20876
301 428-5500

(G-5693)
HUNTER KITCHEN & BATH LLC
212 Philips Rd (19341-1308)
PHONE..................................570 926-0777
Chad Hunter, *Principal*
EMP: 4 EST: 2016
SALES (est): 93.7K **Privately Held**
SIC: 3088 3469 Bathroom fixtures, plastic;
kitchen fixtures & equipment, porcelain
enameled

(G-5694)
IDEMIA AMERICA CORP
523 James Hance Ct (19341-2560)
PHONE..................................610 524-2410
Jean Francois Durand, *VP Mfg*
Yann Limelette, *Opers Staff*
Jerome Ajdenbaum, *VP Bus Dvlpt*
Benjamin Clemens, *Manager*
Richard Martinez, *Manager*
EMP: 250
SQ FT: 80,000
SALES (corp-wide): 5B **Privately Held**
WEB: www.oberthurcs.com
SIC: 2821 Plastics materials & resins
HQ: Idemia America Corp.
296 Concord Rd Ste 300
Billerica MA 01821
978 215-2400

(G-5695)
IDERA PHARMACEUTICALS INC
505 Eagleview Blvd # 212 (19341-1246)
PHONE..................................484 348-1600
James A Geraghty, *Ch of Bd*
Vincent J Milano, *President*
R Clayton Fletcher, *Senior VP*
Bryant D Lim, *Senior VP*
Jonathan Yingling, *Senior VP*
EMP: 62
SQ FT: 27,000
SALES: 662K **Privately Held**
WEB: www.iderapharma.com
SIC: 2836 2834 Biological products, ex-
cept diagnostic; pharmaceutical prepara-
tions

(G-5696)
IMMUNOME INC
665 Stockton Dr Ste 300 (19341-1139)
PHONE..................................610 716-3599
Jane H Hollingsworth, *Ch of Bd*
Scott K Dessain, *President*
Joan Lau, *COO*
Joel F Sussman, *CFO*
Loretta Rossino, *Manager*
EMP: 3
SALES: 200K **Privately Held**
SIC: 2834 Pharmaceutical preparations

(G-5697)
**INDUSTRIAL PLAS
FABRICATION**
Also Called: Ipf
151 Philips Rd (19341-1319)
PHONE..................................610 524-7090
Scott Mackenzie, *President*
John Campbell, *Vice Pres*
Randy Casperson, *Treasurer*
Glen Siegle, *Admin Sec*
EMP: 8
SQ FT: 10,000
SALES: 1MM **Privately Held**
SIC: 3089 Plastic processing

(G-5698)
**INFERNO SPORTS & ATHLETICS
LLC**
492 Orchard Cir (19341-2016)
PHONE..................................610 633-0919
EMP: 4
SALES (est): 527.1K **Privately Held**
SIC: 3949 Sporting & athletic goods

(G-5699)
**INNOVTIVE SLUTIONS SUPPORT
INC (PA)**
Also Called: IS&S
720 Pennsylvania Dr (19341-1129)
PHONE..................................610 646-9800
Geoffrey S M Hedrick, *Ch of Bd*
Glen R Bressner, *Vice Ch Bd*
Shahram Askarpour, *President*
Maureen Martin, *Vice Pres*
Relland M Winand, *CFO*
EMP: 55
SQ FT: 45,000
SALES: 13.8MM **Publicly Held**
WEB: www.innovative-ss.com
SIC: 3812 7371 Aircraft/aerospace flight
instruments & guidance systems; aircraft
control instruments; computer software
development & applications

(G-5700)
INTERNET PIPELINE INC (PA)
Also Called: Ipipeline
222 Valley Creek Blvd # 300 (19341-2385)
PHONE..................................484 348-6555
Timothy Wallace, *CEO*
Andrew Damico, *President*
Paul Melchiorre, *President*
Lawrence Berran, *COO*
Steve Meade, *Exec VP*
▲ EMP: 73
SQ FT: 27,000
SALES: 107.6MM **Privately Held**
WEB: www.ipipeline.com
SIC: 7372 Prepackaged software

(G-5701)
**JANSSEN RESEARCH & DEV
LLC**
665 Stockton Dr Ste 104 (19341-1139)
PHONE..................................610 458-2192
EMP: 140
SALES (corp-wide): 70B **Publicly Held**
SIC: 2834 Drug & Agrochemical Discovery
Company
HQ: Janssen Research & Development, Llc
920 Us Highway 202
Raritan NJ 08869
908 704-4000

(G-5702)
JOURNAL REGISTER COMPANY
Also Called: Mercury, The
390 Eagleview Blvd (19341-1155)
P.O. Box 599, Pottstown (19464-0599)
PHONE..................................610 323-3000
Thomas Abbott, *Principal*
EMP: 96
SALES (corp-wide): 661.2MM **Privately
Held**
WEB: www.journalregister.com
SIC: 2711 7313 Newspapers: publishing
only, not printed on site; newspaper ad-
vertising representative
PA: Journal Register Company
5 Hanover Sq Fl 25
New York NY 10004
212 257-7212

(G-5703)
JOURNAL REGISTER COMPANY
Also Called: Suburban Publications,
390 Eagleview Blvd (19341-1155)
PHONE..................................610 280-2295
Garry Copola, *Manager*
EMP: 100
SQ FT: 82,635
SALES (corp-wide): 661.2MM **Privately
Held**
WEB: www.journalregister.com
SIC: 2711 Newspapers, publishing & print-
ing
PA: Journal Register Company
5 Hanover Sq Fl 25
New York NY 10004
212 257-7212

(G-5704)
JOURNAL REGISTER COMPANY
Also Called: Daily Local News
390 Eagleview Blvd (19341-1155)
PHONE..................................610 696-1775
Ed Condra, *Manager*
EMP: 200
SALES (corp-wide): 661.2MM **Privately
Held**
WEB: www.journalregister.com
SIC: 2711 Newspapers, publishing & print-
ing
PA: Journal Register Company
5 Hanover Sq Fl 25
New York NY 10004
212 257-7212

(G-5705)
KEYSTONE CEMENT CO
557 W Uwchlan Ave (19341-3014)
P.O. Box A, Bath (18014-0058)
PHONE..................................610 837-1881
Terry Kinder, *CEO*
◆ EMP: 3
SALES (est): 330K **Privately Held**
SIC: 3241 Cement, hydraulic

(G-5706)
LEICA MICROSYSTEMS INC
Also Called: Leica Imaging Systems
410 Eagleview Blvd # 107 (19341-1137)
PHONE..................................610 321-0434
William Rogers, *Manager*
EMP: 5
SALES (corp-wide): 19.8B **Publicly Held**
WEB: www.leica-microsystems.com
SIC: 3827 Optical instruments & apparatus
HQ: Leica Microsystems Inc.
1700 Leider Ln
Buffalo Grove IL 60089
847 405-0123

(G-5707)
M & G PACKAGING CORP
602 Jeffers Cir Ste 120 (19341-2539)
PHONE..................................610 363-7455
Mark Ferretti, *President*
Janine Ferretti, *Vice Pres*
EMP: 10
SQ FT: 10,000
SALES (est): 2.2MM **Privately Held**
SIC: 2653 Boxes, corrugated: made from
purchased materials

(G-5708)
MATACHANA USA CORP
300 N Pottstown Pike (19341-2215)
PHONE..................................484 873-2763
Manuel Matachana, *CEO*
Wayne Desantis, *Vice Pres*
EMP: 3 EST: 2015
SQ FT: 1,200
SALES: 1MM
SALES (corp-wide): 71.7MM **Privately
Held**
SIC: 3821 Sterilizers
PA: Antonio Matachana, Sociedad Anonima
Calle Almogavers 174
Barcelona 08018
933 008-012

(G-5709)
**MBA DESIGN & DISPLAY PDTS
CORP (HQ)**
35 E Uwchlan Ave Ste 310 (19341-1259)
PHONE..................................610 524-7590
Markus Militzer, *President*
Gottfried Militzer, *Vice Pres*

Joe Techman, *Warehouse Mgr*
▲ EMP: 9
SALES (est): 1.2MM
SALES (corp-wide): 3.8MM **Privately
Held**
WEB: www.mba-usa.com
SIC: 2221 Wall covering fabrics, manmade
fiber & silk
PA: Mba Design & Display Produkt Gmbh
Siemensstr. 32
Reutlingen 72766
712 116-060

(G-5710)
**METAL FINISHING SYSTEMS
INC**
240 Welsh Pool Rd (19341-1313)
PHONE..................................610 524-9336
Earle Bare, *President*
EMP: 28
SQ FT: 10,000
SALES (est): 1.9MM **Privately Held**
WEB: www.sheetmetalfab.com
SIC: 3444 Sheet metalwork

(G-5711)
METAVIS TECHNOLOGIES INC
256 Eagleview Blvd # 258 (19341-1157)
PHONE..................................484 288-2990
Steven Pogrebivsky, *CEO*
Peter Senescu, *President*
EMP: 35
SALES (est): 3.5MM **Privately Held**
SIC: 7372 Business oriented computer
software

(G-5712)
MISKO INC
171 Philips Rd (19341-1337)
PHONE..................................610 524-1881
Robert Misko, *President*
Joseph Scott, *Project Mgr*
EMP: 15
SQ FT: 13,000
SALES (est): 1.3MM **Privately Held**
WEB: www.miskoinc.com
SIC: 1751 2541 Carpentry work; store &
office display cases & fixtures

(G-5713)
**NATIONAL MAIL GRAPHICS
CORP**
Also Called: Nmg
300 Old Mill Ln (19341-2582)
PHONE..................................610 524-1600
John Sikorski, *President*
Bill Stewart, *President*
Cathy Sikorski, *Principal*
Mary Bradley, *Controller*
Doug Propsner, *Accounts Mgr*
EMP: 65
SQ FT: 30,000
SALES (est): 16.4MM **Privately Held**
WEB: www.nmgcorp.com
SIC: 2752 2677 Commercial printing, off-
set; envelopes

(G-5714)
**NETZSCH PUMPS NORTH AMER
LLC (HQ)**
119 Pickering Way (19341-1393)
PHONE..................................610 363-8010
Thomas Netzsch, *Ch of Bd*
Thomas Streubel, *President*
Dr Otto Max Schaefer, *Managing Dir*
Julio Ferreira, *Vice Pres*
John Maguire, *Vice Pres*
▲ EMP: 38 EST: 2009
SQ FT: 85,000
SALES (est): 15.1MM **Privately Held**
WEB: www.netzschusa.com
SIC: 3561 Pumps & pumping equipment

(G-5715)
NTH SOLUTIONS LLC
15 E Uwchlan Ave Ste 412 (19341-1258)
PHONE..................................610 594-2191
Sue Thompson, *Office Mgr*
Eric Canfield, *Mng Member*
Susan Springsteen, *Mng Member*
Eric L Canfield,
EMP: 6
SALES (est): 989.7K **Privately Held**
SIC: 8742 3679 Marketing consulting
services; electronic circuits

(G-5716)
O & P BENCHMARK HOLDINGS INC (DH)
855 Springdale Dr Ste 200 (19341-2852)
PHONE..................................610 644-7824
Martin McGahan, *CEO*
EMP: 1
SALES (est): 4.5MM **Privately Held**
SIC: 3842 6719 Limbs, artificial; personal holding companies, except banks

(G-5717)
OBERTHUR CARD SYSTEMS INC
523 James Hance Ct (19341-2560)
PHONE..................................610 280-2707
Philippe Tartavull, *President*
Pierre Barrial, *Exec VP*
Robert Boettler, *QC Mgr*
Kyle Wood, *Engineer*
Stephen Arnold, *Controller*
▲ EMP: 300
SALES: 20.6MM
SALES (corp-wide): 5B **Privately Held**
SIC: 2752 Offset & photolithographic printing
HQ: Idemia America Corp.
296 Concord Rd Ste 300
Billerica MA 01821
978 215-2400

(G-5718)
OMEGA DESIGN CORPORATION
211 Philips Rd (19341-1336)
PHONE..................................610 363-6555
Glen Siegele, *President*
Randy Caspersen, *Vice Pres*
Len Dube, *Production*
Stefan Misko, *Production*
Gregory T Eyck, *Engineer*
◆ EMP: 60
SQ FT: 43,000
SALES (est): 17.5MM **Privately Held**
WEB: www.omegadesign.com
SIC: 3565 Packaging machinery

(G-5719)
OMEGA FLEX INC (PA)
451 Creamery Way (19341-2509)
PHONE..................................610 524-7272
Stewart B Reed, *Vice Ch Bd*
Kevin R Hoben, *President*
Mark F Albino, *President*
Steven A Treichel, *Senior VP*
Paul J Kane, *CFO*
EMP: 144
SQ FT: 83,000
SALES: 108.3MM **Publicly Held**
WEB: www.omegaflex.com
SIC: 3599 3429 Hose, flexible metallic; clamps, couplings, nozzles & other metal hose fittings

(G-5720)
ONEXIA INC
750 Springdale Dr (19341-2850)
PHONE..................................610 431-7271
Greg Selke, *CEO*
Andrew Cook, *President*
Jacqueline K Hoffman, *Purch Agent*
Jonathan Lewis, *Engineer*
Robbie Wingert, *Engineer*
EMP: 32 EST: 2001
SQ FT: 23,000
SALES (est): 13MM **Privately Held**
WEB: www.onexiainc.com
SIC: 3625 3599 8711 7373 Electric controls & control accessories, industrial; custom machinery; engineering services; computer integrated systems design; electronic parts & equipment

(G-5721)
PAC STRAPPING PRODUCTS INC
307 National Rd (19341-2647)
PHONE..................................610 363-8805
Edwin A Brownley Jr, *President*
Peter J Silvester, *Vice Pres*
◆ EMP: 40 EST: 1980
SQ FT: 35,000
SALES (est): 12.2MM **Privately Held**
WEB: www.strapsolutions.com
SIC: 3089 5085 Bands, plastic; hose, belting & packing

(G-5722)
PALL CORPORATION
770 Pnnsylvnia Dr Ste 100 (19341)
PHONE..................................610 458-9500
Jill Thompson, *Opers Dir*
Luis Camacho, *Engineer*
Ken Bridges, *Sales Engr*
Alison Ray, *Branch Mgr*
Michael Quinlisk, *Technician*
EMP: 55
SQ FT: 25,000
SALES (corp-wide): 19.8B **Publicly Held**
WEB: www.pall.com
SIC: 3569 Filters
HQ: Pall Corporation
25 Harbor Park Dr
Port Washington NY 11050
516 484-5400

(G-5723)
PELONIS TECHNOLOGIES INC
444 Creamery Way Ste 500 (19341-2583)
PHONE..................................888 546-0524
Sam Pelonis, *President*
▲ EMP: 17
SALES (est): 2.6MM **Privately Held**
SIC: 3634 Electric household fans, heaters & humidifiers

(G-5724)
PENNSYLVANIA PROMOTIONS INC
256 Eagleview Blvd (19341-1157)
P.O. Box 1253, Hockessin DE (19707-5253)
PHONE..................................800 360-2800
Fax: 610 622-1596
EMP: 15
SQ FT: 10,000
SALES: 1.7MM **Privately Held**
SIC: 5199 2262 Whol Advertising Specialties And Silk Screen Printing

(G-5725)
QUIGLEY NUTRACEUTICALS LLC
64 E Uwchlan Ave Ste 443 (19341-1203)
PHONE..................................646 499-5100
Daniel L McCaughan, *CEO*
Guy Quigley, *COO*
EMP: 15
SQ FT: 2,200
SALES: 250K **Privately Held**
SIC: 2834 8742 Vitamin, nutrient & hematinic preparations for human use; marketing consulting services

(G-5726)
R-V INDUSTRIES INC
Also Called: Genesis Packaging Technologies
435 Creamery Way Ste 100 (19341-2544)
PHONE..................................800 552-9980
William Seiler, *Branch Mgr*
EMP: 38
SALES (corp-wide): 44.5MM **Privately Held**
SIC: 3559 Pharmaceutical machinery
PA: R-V Industries, Inc.
584 Poplar Rd
Honey Brook PA 19344
610 273-2457

(G-5727)
SABIC INNOVATIVE PLAS US LLC
475 Creamery Way (19341-2546)
PHONE..................................610 363-4500
Nitin Apte, *Branch Mgr*
EMP: 70
SALES (corp-wide): 388.2MM **Privately Held**
WEB: www.sabic-ip.com
SIC: 3087 Custom compound purchased resins
HQ: Sabic Innovative Plastics Us Llc
2500 City W Blvd Ste 100
Houston TX 77042

(G-5728)
SABIC INNOVATIVE PLAS US LLC
475 Creamery Way (19341-2546)
PHONE..................................610 383-8900
Christopher Poirier, *Engineer*
Marcel Verbist, *Engineer*

Harry Wong, *Engineer*
Madurai Babu, *Controller*
Michael Syroney, *Finance Mgr*
EMP: 150
SALES (corp-wide): 388.2MM **Privately Held**
WEB: www.sabic-ip.com
SIC: 2821 Plastics materials & resins
HQ: Sabic Innovative Plastics Us Llc
2500 City W Blvd Ste 100
Houston TX 77042

(G-5729)
SCREENING ROOM INC
305 Commerce Dr Ste 100 (19341-2612)
PHONE..................................610 363-5405
Thomas Schivane, *President*
EMP: 6
SQ FT: 6,000
SALES (est): 605K **Privately Held**
WEB: www.screeningroominc.com
SIC: 2759 2396 Decals: printing; screen printing; automotive & apparel trimmings

(G-5730)
SEKISUI DIAGNOSTICS LLC
102 Pickering Way Ste 501 (19341-1303)
PHONE..................................610 594-8590
EMP: 5
SALES (corp-wide): 10.3B **Privately Held**
SIC: 3841 Diagnostic apparatus, medical
HQ: Sekisui Diagnostics, Llc
4 Hartwell Pl
Lexington MA 02421

(G-5731)
SHIRE VIROPHARMA INCORPORATED
730 Stockton Dr (19341-1171)
PHONE..................................610 644-9929
David Mariano, *Vice Pres*
Carolyn Vanderweghe, *Branch Mgr*
Steve Jadhav, *Manager*
Jian Xi, *Director*
EMP: 25
SALES (corp-wide): 15.1B **Privately Held**
SIC: 2834 Pharmaceutical preparations
HQ: Shire Viropharma Incorporated
300 Shire Way
Lexington MA 02421

(G-5732)
SHOWMARK LLC
410 Eagleview Blvd # 102 (19341-1137)
PHONE..................................610 458-0304
Scott Markovitz,
EMP: 4
SQ FT: 5,000
SALES (est): 470K **Privately Held**
WEB: www.showmarkcorp.com
SIC: 3542 Spinning, spline rolling & winding machines

(G-5733)
SID GLOBAL SOLUTIONS LLC
407 W Lincoln Hwy Ste 500 (19341-2521)
PHONE..................................484 218-0021
Venkat Madipadaga, *CEO*
Raja Sekhar, *CFO*
Ravi Krishna, *CTO*
EMP: 4 EST: 2014
SALES (est): 41.9K **Privately Held**
SIC: 8742 7372 Management consulting services; business oriented computer software

(G-5734)
SUBURBAN ADVERTISER
575 Exton Cmns (19341-2453)
PHONE..................................610 363-2815
Dennis Daylor, *Principal*
EMP: 3
SALES (est): 119.6K **Privately Held**
SIC: 2711 Newspapers

(G-5735)
TAGLINE INC
253 Welsh Pool Rd (19341-1316)
PHONE..................................610 594-9300
George R Siegl Jr, *President*
Christopher P Siegl, *Vice Pres*
Christopher Siegl, *Vice Pres*
Michael T Siegl, *Vice Pres*
▼ EMP: 8 EST: 1994
SQ FT: 22,000

SALES: 4MM **Privately Held**
WEB: www.tagline.com
SIC: 2679 Labels, paper: made from purchased material

(G-5736)
TECH GROUP NORTH AMERICA INC
530 Herman O West Dr (19341-1147)
P.O. Box 645 (19341-0645)
PHONE..................................480 281-4500
EMP: 3
SALES (est): 225.8K **Privately Held**
SIC: 3089 Injection molding of plastics

(G-5737)
TOTAL PTRCHEMICALS REF USA INC
Also Called: Cray Valley
665 Stockton Dr (19341-1139)
PHONE..................................877 871-2729
Thierry Razat, *Branch Mgr*
Carrie Cunningham, *Manager*
EMP: 281
SALES (corp-wide): 8.4B **Publicly Held**
SIC: 2911 2899 2869 Petroleum refining; chemical preparations; fuels
HQ: Total Petrochemicals & Refining Usa, Inc.
1201 La St Ste 1800
Houston TX 77002
713 483-5000

(G-5738)
TOUCHSTONE HOME PRODUCTS INC
611 Jeffers Cir (19341-2525)
PHONE..................................510 782-1282
Jonathan Bradlee, *President*
Frank Quinlisk, *Vice Pres*
◆ EMP: 4
SQ FT: 7,000
SALES (est): 372.7K **Privately Held**
SIC: 2517 Television cabinets, wood

(G-5739)
TROUTMAN MACHINE SHOP INC
424 Creamery Way (19341-2500)
PHONE..................................610 363-5480
Ben Campbell, *Ch of Bd*
EMP: 7 EST: 1960
SQ FT: 38,000
SALES (est): 1.1MM
SALES (corp-wide): 26.4MM **Privately Held**
WEB: www.troutmanind.com
SIC: 3842 Implants, surgical
PA: J. Benson Corp.
2201 Reading Ave
Reading PA 19609
610 678-2692

(G-5740)
TURNER JOHN
Also Called: J T Ltd Custom Woodworking
305 Commerce Dr Ste 200 (19341-2612)
PHONE..................................610 524-2050
John Turner, *Owner*
EMP: 4
SQ FT: 5,000
SALES: 400K **Privately Held**
WEB: www.jtltd.com
SIC: 5712 2431 Custom made furniture, except cabinets; interior & ornamental woodwork & trim

(G-5741)
TW METALS LLC (HQ)
760 Constitution Dr # 204 (19341-1149)
P.O. Box 644 (19341-0644)
PHONE..................................610 458-1300
Barry Ronsheimer, *Vice Pres*
Bill Schmid, *Vice Pres*
Kirk E Moore, *CFO*
Jack H Elrod, *CFO*
◆ EMP: 65 EST: 1907
SQ FT: 15,913
SALES (est): 339.5MM
SALES (corp-wide): 1.8B **Privately Held**
WEB: www.twmetals.com
SIC: 3498 3444 3443 Tube fabricating (contract bending & shaping); pipe, sheet metal; plate work for the metalworking trade

PA: O'neal Industries, Inc
2311 Highland Ave S # 200
Birmingham AL 35205
205 721-2880

(G-5742)
UNITED PLASTICS MACHINERY INC
131 S Whitford Rd (19341-2699)
PHONE......................................610 363-0990
Ronald Roberts, *CEO*
EMP: 30
SQ FT: 12,000
SALES (est): 5.2MM **Privately Held**
WEB: www.unitedplasticsmachine.com
SIC: 3559 Plastics working machinery

(G-5743)
USSC GROUP INC (PA)
Also Called: JG Seating
101 Gordon Dr Ste 1 (19341-1320)
PHONE......................................610 265-3610
Christian Hammarskjold, *President*
Ken Schnarrs, *Corp Secy*
Bill Rymer, *CFO*
▲ **EMP:** 60
SALES (est): 16.8MM **Privately Held**
SIC: 2531 5049 Seats, miscellaneous public conveyances; engineers' equipment & supplies

(G-5744)
USSC LLC
101 Gordon Dr Ste 1 (19341-1320)
PHONE......................................610 265-3610
Christian Hammarskjold, *Mng Member*
◆ **EMP:** 100
SALES (est): 13.8MM **Privately Held**
SIC: 2531 Seats, automobile

(G-5745)
VALLEY FORGE TAPE LABEL CO INC
119 Summit Dr (19341-2889)
PHONE......................................610 524-8900
Paul Myers, *President*
John Pechy, *Purch Agent*
Dennis C Hulton, *Treasurer*
Joseph Casey, *Regl Sales Mgr*
Michael Brennan, *Sales Staff*
EMP: 55 **EST:** 1962
SQ FT: 30,000
SALES (est): 9.6MM **Privately Held**
WEB: www.vftl.com
SIC: 2759 Labels & seals: printing

(G-5746)
VALLEY INSTRUMENT CO INC
491 Clover Mill Rd (19341-2599)
PHONE......................................610 363-2650
James A Magee, *President*
Jean Langdon, *Controller*
EMP: 15
SQ FT: 5,000
SALES (est): 3.5MM **Privately Held**
WEB: www.valley-instrument.com
SIC: 3823 7629 Industrial instrmnts msrmnt display/control process variable; electronic equipment repair

(G-5747)
WEST PHARMACEUTICAL SERVICES D (PA)
530 Herman O West Dr (19341-1147)
PHONE......................................610 594-2900
Bernard Lahendro, *President*
Dale Herbranson, *Vice Pres*
Kim Koning, *Plant Mgr*
Kelly Collins, *Project Mgr*
Cindy Crawford, *Engineer*
EMP: 23
SALES (est): 7MM **Privately Held**
SIC: 3559 Pharmaceutical machinery

(G-5748)
WEST PHARMACEUTICAL SVCS INC (PA)
530 Herman O West Dr (19341-1147)
PHONE......................................610 594-2900
Patrick J Zenner, *Ch of Bd*
Eric M Green, *President*
Scott Leventhal, *Counsel*
George L Miller, *Senior VP*
David Hoo, *Vice Pres*
▲ **EMP:** 320 **EST:** 1923

SALES: 1.7B **Publicly Held**
WEB: www.westpharma.com
SIC: 3069 3466 2673 3085 Medical & laboratory rubber sundries & related products; stoppers, rubber; atomizer bulbs, rubber; medical sundries, rubber; closures, stamped metal; plastic bags: made from purchased materials; plastics bottles; plastic containers, except foam; closures, plastic

(G-5749)
WEST PHRM SVCS DEL INC (HQ)
530 Herman O West Dr (19341-1147)
PHONE......................................610 594-2900
EMP: 11
SALES (est): 1.3MM
SALES (corp-wide): 1.7B **Publicly Held**
SIC: 3069 Medical & laboratory rubber sundries & related products
PA: West Pharmaceutical Services, Inc.
530 Herman O West Dr
Exton PA 19341
610 594-2900

(G-5750)
WILLIAM J DIXON COMPANY
756 Springdale Dr (19341-2837)
PHONE......................................610 524-1131
John K Dixon, *President*
Gary Rittenhouse, *Sales Mgr*
◆ **EMP:** 25
SQ FT: 25,000
SALES (est): 4.5MM **Privately Held**
WEB: www.wjdixon.com
SIC: 2261 2241 Finishing plants, cotton; narrow fabric mills

(G-5751)
WOLFINGTON BODY COMPANY INC (PA)
N Off Pa Tpk Exit Rr 100 (19341)
P.O. Box 218 (19341-0218)
PHONE......................................610 458-8501
Richard I Wolfington, *President*
David P Fitzgerald, *Exec VP*
◆ **EMP:** 109 **EST:** 1932
SQ FT: 25,000
SALES: 122.6MM **Privately Held**
WEB: www.wolfington.com
SIC: 3711 3713 5012 Automobile bodies, passenger car, not including engine, etc.; automobile assembly, including specialty automobiles; bus bodies (motor vehicles); hearse bodies; ambulance bodies; commercial vehicles

(G-5752)
ZOETIS INC
812 Springdale Dr (19341-2803)
PHONE......................................908 901-1116
Ashley Constantine, *Manager*
Shaun Buck, *Manager*
Cheryl Damirgian, *Manager*
Joe Becker, *Senior Mgr*
EMP: 17
SALES (corp-wide): 5.8B **Publicly Held**
SIC: 2834 Pharmaceutical preparations
PA: Zoetis Inc.
10 Sylvan Way Ste 105
Parsippany NJ 07054
973 822-7000

(G-5753)
ZYNITECH MEDICAL INC
347 N Pottstown Pike (19341-2222)
PHONE......................................610 592-0755
David Zeng, *President*
EMP: 8
SALES (est): 1.8MM **Privately Held**
SIC: 3841 Surgical & medical instruments

Eynon
Lackawanna County

(G-5754)
CASKET SHELLS INCORPORATED
Also Called: C S I
432 1st St (18403-1466)
P.O. Box 172, Archbald (18403-0172)
PHONE......................................570 876-2642
Joseph R Semon, *President*

Dr Elizabeth Semon Bonczar, *Senior VP*
Dr Lawrence J Bonczar, *Senior VP*
William J Semon, *Senior VP*
EMP: 2 **EST:** 1953
SQ FT: 50,000
SALES: 20.5MM **Privately Held**
WEB: www.casketshells.com
SIC: 3995 4213 Burial caskets; trucking, except local

(G-5755)
HOOKE MFG LLC
432 1st St (18403-1466)
PHONE......................................570 876-6787
Mary Miller, *Principal*
EMP: 3
SALES (est): 215.9K **Privately Held**
SIC: 3999 Manufacturing industries

Factoryville
Wyoming County

(G-5756)
ELITE TIMBER HARVESTING LLC
795 Bardwell Rd (18419-2202)
PHONE......................................570 836-2453
Robert Sawicki,
Matthew Carney,
EMP: 4
SALES: 427K **Privately Held**
SIC: 2411 Logging camps & contractors

(G-5757)
KARP EXCAVATING LTD
100 Schlesser Rd (18419-2107)
PHONE......................................570 840-9026
Stanley S Karp Sr, *CEO*
EMP: 3 **EST:** 2016
SALES (est): 89.5K **Privately Held**
SIC: 1389 7389 Excavating slush pits & cellars; grading oil & gas well foundations;

(G-5758)
N C STAUFFER & SONS INC
309 Vail Rd (18419-8041)
P.O. Box 325 (18419-0325)
PHONE......................................570 945-3047
John Kleback, *President*
Richard L Stauffer, *Corp Secy*
EMP: 90
SQ FT: 35,000
SALES (est): 12.7MM **Privately Held**
SIC: 3446 3556 3535 3496 Guards, made from pipe; food products machinery; conveyors & conveying equipment; miscellaneous fabricated wire products; sheet metalwork; fabricated structural metal

(G-5759)
NORTHERN PALLET INC
Also Called: Manufacturing Pallets
151 Creek Rd (18419-2614)
PHONE......................................570 945-3920
Steve Gris, *President*
Lois Gris, *Admin Sec*
EMP: 14
SALES (est): 2MM **Privately Held**
WEB: www.northernpallet.com
SIC: 2448 Pallets, wood

(G-5760)
O & N ARCFT MODIFICATION INC
210 Windsock Ln 9n (18419-9351)
P.O. Box 292 (18419-0292)
PHONE......................................570 945-3769
Myron Olson, *President*
EMP: 35
SQ FT: 12,000
SALES (est): 6.9MM **Privately Held**
WEB: www.onaircraft.com
SIC: 3728 3714 7699 Aircraft assemblies, subassemblies & parts; motor vehicle parts & accessories; aircraft & heavy equipment repair services

(G-5761)
ROBVON BACKING RING CO INC
Ring Rd 1 (18419)
P.O. Box 307 (18419-0307)
PHONE......................................570 945-3800
Cecilia Von Ahrens, *President*
EMP: 10 **EST:** 1943
SQ FT: 16,000
SALES (est): 850K **Privately Held**
WEB: www.robvon.com
SIC: 3399 Metal fasteners

(G-5762)
TEFLEX INC
Also Called: Sealmor Industries
101 College Ave (18419-7719)
P.O. Box 136 (18419-0136)
PHONE......................................570 945-9185
James Zigray, *President*
Linda Zigray, *Vice Pres*
EMP: 12
SQ FT: 1,700
SALES: 780K **Privately Held**
WEB: www.sealmorindustries.com
SIC: 2821 5085 Plastics materials & resins; industrial supplies

(G-5763)
WINOLA INDUSTRIAL INC
Rr 1 Box 1070 (18419)
PHONE......................................570 378-3808
Thomas McGlynn, *President*
James T McGlynn, *Treasurer*
Lynn McGlynn, *Shareholder*
EMP: 11
SQ FT: 4,200
SALES (est): 1.6MM **Privately Held**
WEB: www.winolaindustrial.com
SIC: 1799 3644 Rigging & scaffolding; pole line hardware

Fairbank
Fayette County

(G-5764)
TIBERI GUN SHOP
Also Called: Tiberi Service
47 Pala Ave (15435)
P.O. Box 225 (15435-0225)
PHONE......................................724 245-6151
Joseph A Tiberi, *Owner*
EMP: 3
SQ FT: 400
SALES (est): 231.7K **Privately Held**
SIC: 3599 7699 Machine shop, jobbing & repair; gun parts made to individual order

Fairfield
Adams County

(G-5765)
CASE MODERN WORK
2498 Iron Springs Rd (17320-9792)
PHONE......................................717 785-1232
EMP: 4
SALES (est): 87.8K **Privately Held**
SIC: 3523 Mfg Farm Machinery/Equipment

(G-5766)
CRYSTAL SHOWER DOORS
13 Eagle Trl (17320-8104)
PHONE......................................717 642-9689
Max H Feuerstein, *Principal*
EMP: 7
SALES (est): 806.4K **Privately Held**
SIC: 3431 Shower stalls, metal

(G-5767)
FINE TRIM LINE LLC
240 Valley View Ln (17320-7834)
P.O. Box 428, Blue Ridge Summit (17214-0428)
PHONE......................................717 642-9032
Jerrica Ott,
EMP: 6
SALES (est): 967.1K **Privately Held**
SIC: 2241 Trimmings, textile

(G-5768)
QG PRINTING II CORP
Also Called: Quad Graphics
100 N Miller St (17320-9707)
PHONE....................717 642-5871
Vince Vaughn, *Branch Mgr*
EMP: 452
SALES (corp-wide): 4.1B **Publicly Held**
SIC: 2752 Commercial printing, offset
HQ: Qg Printing Ii Corp.
N61w23044 Harrys Way
Sussex WI 53089

(G-5769)
UPINYA BEVERAGES LLC
22 Centennial St (17320-9533)
PHONE....................717 398-7309
William Houck,
EMP: 3
SALES (est): 213.3K **Privately Held**
SIC: 2087 Beverage bases, concentrates,
syrups, powders & mixes

(G-5770)
VALLEY QUARRIES INC
3805 Bullfrog Rd (17320-9377)
PHONE....................717 642-8535
Bruce Giilan, *Manager*
EMP: 8
SALES (corp-wide): 651.9MM **Privately Held**
WEB: www.valleyquarries.com
SIC: 1422 Crushed & broken limestone
HQ: Valley Quarries, Inc.
297 Quarry Rd
Chambersburg PA 17202
717 267-2244

Fairless Hills
Bucks County

(G-5771)
AE POLYSILICON CORPORATION (PA)
150 Roebling Rd (19030-5011)
PHONE....................215 337-8183
York Tsuo, *President*
Andrew Savadelis, *CFO*
EMP: 30
SQ FT: 10,000
SALES (est): 5.8MM **Privately Held**
SIC: 3339 Silicon, pure

(G-5772)
AURELE M GATTI INC
Also Called: A.M. Gatti, Inc
1 Canal Rd (19030-4301)
PHONE....................215 428-4500
Anthony V Ursic, *President*
Bryan Ursic, *Vice Pres*
EMP: 3 EST: 1920
SQ FT: 15,000
SALES (est): 439.2K **Privately Held**
WEB: www.gattiam.com
SIC: 3915 Jewel bearings, synthetic

(G-5773)
BEARD GROUP INC
572 Fernwood Ln (19030-3804)
P.O. Box 4250, Frederick MD (21705-4250)
PHONE....................240 629-3300
Christopher Beard, *President*
EMP: 25 EST: 1986
SALES (est): 2.1MM **Privately Held**
SIC: 2731 Book publishing

(G-5774)
BONLAND INDUSTRIES INC
Also Called: Bonland Fairless Hills
515 S Olds Blvd Ste 202 (19030-3028)
PHONE....................215 949-3720
Bonaface Andrew, *President*
Michael Rowan, *Project Mgr*
EMP: 70
SALES (corp-wide): 70.5MM **Privately Held**
SIC: 3999 Barber & beauty shop equipment
PA: Bonland Industries, Inc.
50 Newark Pompton Tpke
Wayne NJ 07470
973 694-3211

(G-5775)
CONSTRUCTION DYNAMICS INC
Also Called: Silvi Concrete Products
355 Newbold Rd (19030-4313)
PHONE....................215 295-0777
John Silvi, *President*
Don Carpani, *Vice Pres*
Toby Rich, *Vice Pres*
Michael Matalavage, *CFO*
EMP: 93
SQ FT: 40,000
SALES (est): 19.8MM **Privately Held**
SIC: 3273 Ready-mixed concrete

(G-5776)
COURIER TIMES INC
Also Called: Bucks County Courier Times
2 Geoffrey Dr (19030-4310)
PHONE....................215 949-4219
Todd Warner, *Manager*
EMP: 150
SALES (corp-wide): 1.5B **Publicly Held**
WEB: www.buckscountycouriertimes.com
SIC: 2759 Newspapers: printing
HQ: Courier Times, Inc.
8400 Bristol Pike
Levittown PA 19057
215 949-4011

(G-5777)
CSC SUGAR LLC
80 Roebling Rd (19030-5000)
PHONE....................215 428-3670
Dave Funkhouser, *Administration*
EMP: 13
SALES (corp-wide): 77.1MM **Privately Held**
SIC: 5159 2062 2063 Sugar, raw; refined cane sugar from purchased raw sugar or syrup; liquid sugar from sugar beets
PA: Csc Sugar, Llc
36 Grove St Ste 2
New Canaan CT 06840
203 846-5610

(G-5778)
FALLS MFG CO
129 Canal Rd (19030-4303)
PHONE....................215 736-2557
William Jakubek, *President*
John McCabe, *Corp Secy*
▲ EMP: 80
SALES (est): 24.8MM
SALES (corp-wide): 3.6B **Publicly Held**
SIC: 3469 Stamping metal for the trade
PA: Amerco
5555 Kietzke Ln Ste 100
Reno NV 89511
775 688-6300

(G-5779)
FUTURE FOAM INC
259 Canal Rd (19030-4305)
PHONE....................215 736-8611
Nick Petro, *Controller*
Ryan Samhammer, *Office Mgr*
EMP: 55
SALES (corp-wide): 459.1MM **Privately Held**
SIC: 3086 Packaging & shipping materials, foamed plastic
PA: Future Foam, Inc.
1610 Avenue N
Council Bluffs IA 51501
712 323-9122

(G-5780)
GMA GARNET (USA) CORP
25 Sorrels Rd (19030-5017)
PHONE....................215 736-1868
Ryan Moses, *Branch Mgr*
EMP: 45 **Privately Held**
SIC: 1499 Garnet mining
HQ: Gma Garnet (Usa) Corp.
1780 Hughes Landing Blvd # 725
The Woodlands TX 77380
832 243-9300

(G-5781)
GREGG LANE LLC
Also Called: P V C
386 Lincoln Hwy (19030-1203)
PHONE....................215 269-9900
Gary Brenner,
EMP: 2

SQ FT: 7,200
SALES: 1.9MM **Privately Held**
WEB: www.gregglane.com
SIC: 2519 3429 Lawn & garden furniture, except wood & metal; fireplace equipment, hardware: andirons, grates, screens

(G-5782)
HALEX CORPORATION
352 Newbold Rd (19030-4314)
PHONE....................909 622-3537
EMP: 40
SALES (corp-wide): 1.1B **Publicly Held**
WEB: www.halexcorp.com
SIC: 3423 Carpet layers' hand tools
HQ: Halex Corporation
4200 Santa Ana St Ste A
Ontario CA 91761
909 629-6219

(G-5783)
HARSCO CORPORATION
905 Steel Rd S (19030-5006)
PHONE....................215 295-8675
Brian Tucker, *Manager*
EMP: 5
SALES (corp-wide): 1.6B **Publicly Held**
SIC: 2891 Adhesives & sealants
PA: Harsco Corporation
350 Poplar Church Rd
Camp Hill PA 17011
717 763-7064

(G-5784)
HARSCO MINERALS PA LLC
905 Steel Rd S (19030-5006)
PHONE....................717 506-7157
Anthony Budzinski,
EMP: 7
SQ FT: 600
SALES (est): 384.5K **Privately Held**
SIC: 3295 Minerals, ground or treated

(G-5785)
HEUCOTECH LTD A NJ LTD PARTNR (DH)
99 Newbold Rd (19030-4392)
PHONE....................215 736-0712
Robert W Mihalyi, *CEO*
◆ EMP: 55
SQ FT: 65,000
SALES (est): 46.4MM **Privately Held**
WEB: www.heubach.net
SIC: 2865 5198 Color pigments, organic; colors & pigments
HQ: Heubach Gmbh
Heubachstr. 7
Langelsheim 38685
532 652-0

(G-5786)
KEYSTONE NAP LLC
150 Roebling Rd (19030-5011)
PHONE....................215 280-6614
Peter B Ritz, *CEO*
John E Parker, *President*
Shawn R Carey, *Senior VP*
Philip M Lanctot, *Senior VP*
Susan Williams, *Accounts Mgr*
EMP: 4
SALES (est): 322.5K **Privately Held**
SIC: 7374 3825 7371 Data processing service; network analyzers; custom computer programming services

(G-5787)
MARKING DEVICE MFG CO INC
Also Called: Marco Products
225 Lincoln Hwy Bldg Es (19030-1103)
PHONE....................215 632-9583
Michael Gallagher, *President*
Linda Gallagher, *Treasurer*
EMP: 4 EST: 1946
SQ FT: 7,500
SALES: 300K **Privately Held**
SIC: 3953 Marking devices

(G-5788)
MCHUGH RAILROAD MAINT EQP (PA)
Also Called: McHugh Locomotive and Crane Co
225 Lincoln Hwy (19030-1103)
P.O. Box 8 (19030-0008)
PHONE....................215 949-0430

J C McHugh, *President*
Ann Gillaspy-Mchugh, *Corp Secy*
▼ EMP: 15
SALES (est): 1.8MM **Privately Held**
WEB: www.mchughlocomotiveandcrane.com
SIC: 3743 Locomotives & parts

(G-5789)
MORTON SALT INC
Also Called: International Salt
12 Roebling Rd (19030-5000)
PHONE....................215 428-2012
Tad Kizewski, *Manager*
EMP: 19
SALES (corp-wide): 4.6B **Privately Held**
SIC: 2899 Salt
HQ: Morton Salt, Inc.
444 W Lake St Ste 3000
Chicago IL 60606

(G-5790)
OKUMUS ENTERPRISES LTD
Also Called: Star Label Products
42 Newbold Rd (19030-4308)
PHONE....................215 295-3340
Sevket K Okumus, *President*
M Dogan Okumus, *Treasurer*
Sevket Okumus, *Admin Sec*
▲ EMP: 35 EST: 1972
SQ FT: 35,000
SALES (est): 5.9MM **Privately Held**
WEB: www.starlabel.com
SIC: 2759 7336 2752 2671 Letterpress printing; screen printing; flexographic printing; graphic arts & related design; commercial printing, lithographic; packaging paper & plastics film, coated & laminated

(G-5791)
PLS SIGNS LLC
Also Called: Fastsigns
463 S Oxford Valley Rd (19030-4202)
PHONE....................215 269-1400
Peter Sepe, *Mng Member*
Pete Sepe, *Manager*
EMP: 7
SALES (est): 218.9K **Privately Held**
SIC: 3993 3669 Signs & advertising specialties; visual communication systems

(G-5792)
POLONIER CORPORATION
225 Lincoln Hwy Ste H8 (19030-1103)
PHONE....................267 994-1698
Jacky Wang, *President*
David Fluck, *Vice Pres*
▼ EMP: 5
SALES (est): 279.7K **Privately Held**
SIC: 2869 Industrial organic chemicals

(G-5793)
PRE-BLEND PRODUCTS INC
100 Ben Fairless Dr (19030-5001)
PHONE....................215 295-6004
Paul Henning, *President*
Thomas Herzer, *Vice Pres*
Barry E Fleck, *Shareholder*
▲ EMP: 20
SQ FT: 20,000
SALES (est): 3.2MM **Privately Held**
WEB: www.preblend.com
SIC: 3272 Concrete products

(G-5794)
REED MINERALS
905 Steel Rd S (19030-5006)
PHONE....................215 295-8675
Shawn Mc Cormick, *Principal*
▲ EMP: 4
SALES (est): 304.9K **Privately Held**
SIC: 3295 Minerals, ground or treated

(G-5795)
SAXON OFFICE TECHNOLOGY INC
225 Lincoln Hwy (19030-1103)
PHONE....................215 736-2620
Allen B Aaron, *President*
Jinny Viscardi, *President*
Jannina Viscardi, *Treasurer*
Mike Graff, *Accounts Mgr*
Marc Stein, *Accounts Mgr*
EMP: 15
SQ FT: 10,000

GEOGRAPHIC

SALES (est): 3MM **Privately Held**
SIC: 3577 5112 7379 Printers, computer; laserjet supplies; computer related maintenance services

(G-5796)
SIL KEMP CONCRETE INC (PA)
Also Called: Silvi of Englishtown
355 Newbold Rd (19030-4313)
PHONE....................................215 295-0777
Lawrence J Silvi II, *President*
John L Silvi, *Vice Pres*
EMP: 4 EST: 1962
SQ FT: 40,000
SALES (est): 1.1MM **Privately Held**
SIC: 3273 Ready-mixed concrete

(G-5797)
SILVI CONCRETE PRODUCTS INC
355 Newbold Rd (19030-4313)
PHONE....................................215 295-0777
Laurence Silvi, *President*
John Silvi, *Treasurer*
EMP: 200
SQ FT: 40,000
SALES (est): 26.5MM **Privately Held**
SIC: 3272 Concrete products

(G-5798)
SPECIALTY STEEL SUPPLY CO INC
225 Lincoln Hwy (19030-1103)
PHONE....................................215 949-8800
Patricia A Green Campbell, *President*
Jason Nagel, *Office Mgr*
EMP: 10
SQ FT: 40,000
SALES (est): 1.8MM **Privately Held**
WEB: www.225steel.com
SIC: 3441 5051 Fabricated structural metal; metals service centers & offices

(G-5799)
STRICK CORPORATION (PA)
225 Lincoln Hwy (19030-1103)
PHONE....................................215 949-3600
Frank Katz, *Ch of Bd*
Joseph Puchino, *Vice Pres*
George Schmidt, *Vice Pres*
John Badey, *CFO*
▲ EMP: 18 EST: 1936
SQ FT: 265,000
SALES (est): 74.4MM **Privately Held**
WEB: www.stricktrlr.com
SIC: 2426 3713 3537 3715 Flooring, hardwood; truck & bus bodies; industrial trucks & tractors; trailer bodies

(G-5800)
SUGARIGHT LLC
200 Rock Run Rd (19030-4320)
PHONE....................................215 295-4709
Andrew J Reul, *CEO*
EMP: 11
SALES (est): 1.9MM **Privately Held**
SIC: 2062 Cane sugar refining

(G-5801)
SYNERGY ELECTRICAL SALES INC
95 Canal Rd (19030-4301)
PHONE....................................215 428-1130
Lawrence S Low, *President*
Craig W Low, *Vice Pres*
Gina Moretti-Risdon, *Opers Mgr*
Doug Cunningham, *Sales Staff*
Chris Glogowski, *Sales Staff*
EMP: 19
SQ FT: 70,000
SALES (est): 3.8MM **Privately Held**
WEB: www.synergyelectricalsales.com
SIC: 3699 Electrical equipment & supplies

(G-5802)
TAVO PACKAGING INC
2 Canal Rd (19030-4398)
PHONE....................................215 428-0900
Halfred E Taylor, *President*
David F Taylor, *Vice Pres*
Granderson Hanks, *Plant Mgr*
Jeff Taylor, *Opers Mgr*
Richard Schwarz, *Opers Staff*
▲ EMP: 75 EST: 1978

SALES (est): 24MM **Privately Held**
WEB: www.tavopackaging.com
SIC: 2657 Folding paperboard boxes

(G-5803)
TEMPERATURE CTRL PROFESSIONALS
225 Lincoln Hwy Bldg As-6 (19030-1103)
PHONE....................................215 295-1616
Robert Lambeck, *Opers Staff*
Lisa Lambeck, *Mng Member*
EMP: 6
SALES (est): 382.4K **Privately Held**
SIC: 7623 7699 7692 Refrigeration repair service; air conditioning repair; boiler & heating repair services; welding repair

(G-5804)
THIN LABS INC
225 Lincoln Hwy Ste 178 (19030-1103)
PHONE....................................215 269-3322
Mundkur, *CEO*
Jagdish Mundkur, *Principal*
Sachit Baliga, *Engineer*
Amaey Mundkur, *Manager*
EMP: 3
SALES (est): 315.8K **Privately Held**
SIC: 3679 Liquid crystal displays (LCD)

(G-5805)
UNITED STATES STEEL CORP
Also Called: U. S. Steel
Penne Ave S (19030)
PHONE....................................215 736-4000
Dennis Jones, *Branch Mgr*
EMP: 100
SALES (corp-wide): 14.1B **Publicly Held**
SIC: 3312 5051 Blast furnaces & steel mills; metals service centers & offices
PA: United States Steel Corp
600 Grant St Ste 468
Pittsburgh PA 15219
412 433-1121

(G-5806)
UNITED STATES STEEL CORP
400 Berdis Blvd (19030-5014)
PHONE....................................215 736-4600
Dennis Jones, *Branch Mgr*
EMP: 235
SALES (corp-wide): 14.1B **Publicly Held**
SIC: 3317 3356 3312 Steel pipe & tubes; tin; plate, steel
PA: United States Steel Corp
600 Grant St Ste 468
Pittsburgh PA 15219
412 433-1121

(G-5807)
WASTE GAS FABRICATING CO INC
450 Newbold Rd (19030-4316)
PHONE....................................215 736-9240
Kyle Cloman, *President*
EMP: 49
SQ FT: 62,000
SALES (est): 14.9MM **Privately Held**
WEB: www.wastegas.com
SIC: 3441 7692 3444 3443 Fabricated structural metal; welding repair; sheet metalwork; fabricated plate work (boiler shop)

Fairmount City
Clarion County

(G-5808)
DBI INC
Also Called: Utilities and Industries
660 Longview Rd (16224-1802)
PHONE....................................814 653-7625
Brian E Dougherty, *CEO*
Vincent Dougherty, *Ch of Bd*
Sharon Shreckengost, *Corp Secy*
Monica Weaver, *Supervisor*
EMP: 100
SALES: 1.6MM **Privately Held**
SIC: 5084 2259 6531 5941 Industrial machinery & equipment; gloves & mittens, knit; real estate brokers & agents; firearms

Fairview
Erie County

(G-5809)
ACCUDYN PRODUCTS INC
6543 Sterrettania Rd (16415-2921)
PHONE....................................814 835-5088
Steve Michael, *Manager*
EMP: 4
SALES (corp-wide): 23MM **Privately Held**
SIC: 3544 Industrial molds
PA: Accudyn Products, Inc.
2400 Yoder Dr
Erie PA 16506
814 833-7615

(G-5810)
ADVANCED FINISHING USA INC
Also Called: Archi-Texture
7401 Klier Dr (16415-2462)
PHONE....................................814 474-5200
Gregory M Yahn, *President*
Andrew Foyle, *General Mgr*
Terrence Olaughlin, *Vice Pres*
EMP: 39 EST: 1974
SQ FT: 80,000
SALES: 2.6MM **Privately Held**
WEB: www.afusa.net
SIC: 3479 3471 2851 Coating of metals with plastic or resins; plating & polishing; paints & allied products

(G-5811)
AMERICAN MOLDING AND TECH INC
7700 Birkmire Dr (16415-2928)
PHONE....................................814 836-0202
Richard Putnam, *President*
EMP: 28
SQ FT: 18,000
SALES: 3.9MM **Privately Held**
WEB: www.americanmolding.us
SIC: 3089 Injection molding of plastics

(G-5812)
AMERICAN TURNED PRODUCTS INC (PA)
7626 Klier Dr S (16415-2450)
PHONE....................................814 474-4200
B Scott Eighmy, *CEO*
Jerry Eighmy, *President*
Harry S Eighmy, *COO*
Drew Hoffman, *Vice Pres*
Jim Osmanski, *Vice Pres*
▲ EMP: 80
SQ FT: 48,543
SALES: 18MM **Privately Held**
WEB: www.atpteam.com
SIC: 3451 Screw machine products

(G-5813)
AMES ENTERPRISES INC
Also Called: Naturally Yours Whl Foods
7359 W Ridge Rd (16415-1169)
PHONE....................................814 474-2700
Kathleen Ames, *President*
Alvin Ames, *Vice Pres*
EMP: 8
SQ FT: 4,500
SALES (est): 925.6K **Privately Held**
SIC: 2034 5149 Fruits, dried or dehydrated, except freeze-dried; fruits, dried

(G-5814)
AUTOMATION DEVICES INC
Also Called: Peeco
7050 W Ridge Rd (16415-2099)
PHONE....................................814 474-5561
Larry Smith, *President*
Donald G Buseck, *Corp Secy*
Kevin E Smith, *Vice Pres*
Colleen L May, *Admin Sec*
EMP: 30 EST: 1947
SQ FT: 65,000
SALES: 6.9MM **Privately Held**
WEB: www.autodev.com
SIC: 3569 3625 Assembly machines, non-metalworking; control circuit relays, industrial

(G-5815)
CHOICE TOOL
483 Dorothy Ave (16415-1439)
PHONE....................................814 474-4656
Joseph Hanlin, *Owner*
EMP: 4
SQ FT: 1,500
SALES (est): 294.2K **Privately Held**
SIC: 3544 Special dies & tools

(G-5816)
COLETECH
6950 Tow Rd (16415-1915)
PHONE....................................814 474-3370
William Coleman, *Owner*
EMP: 5
SQ FT: 15,000
SALES (est): 350K **Privately Held**
SIC: 3732 5051 Boat building & repairing; wire

(G-5817)
CONCRETE SERVICES CORPORATION
Also Called: Elk Creek Redi-Mix
3000 Blair Rd (16415-1822)
P.O. Box 930 (16415-0930)
PHONE....................................814 774-8807
James Hornyak, *CEO*
Nancy Hornyak, *President*
EMP: 40 EST: 1960
SALES (est): 6.6MM **Privately Held**
SIC: 3273 1794 Ready-mixed concrete; excavation work

(G-5818)
CONNEX INC
7660 Klier Dr N (16415-2448)
PHONE....................................814 474-4550
Andrew Bucher, *President*
S Bucher, *Corp Secy*
Tom Slat, *Senior VP*
Thomas Slat, *Vice Pres*
Todd Hiegel, *Plant Mgr*
▲ EMP: 17
SQ FT: 6,000
SALES (est): 3.3MM **Privately Held**
WEB: www.connexusa.com
SIC: 3452 Spring pins, metal
HQ: Connex Ag
Industriestrasse 15
Reiden LU
627 493-030

(G-5819)
CSI INDUSTRIES INC
6910 W Ridge Rd Unit 1 (16415-2064)
PHONE....................................814 474-9353
Balwinder Takhar, *President*
Tony Gomo, *General Mgr*
Joseph Jeyanayagam, *Treasurer*
▼ EMP: 50
SQ FT: 40,000
SALES (est): 18MM **Privately Held**
WEB: www.csiind.com
SIC: 3444 Sheet metal specialties, not stamped
PA: Chalmers International Holdings Inc
6400 Northam Dr
Mississauga ON L4V 1
905 362-6400

(G-5820)
EAG ELECTRONICS CORP
7700 Birkmire Dr (16415-2928)
PHONE....................................814 836-8080
Edward Gentle, *President*
▲ EMP: 120
SQ FT: 18,000
SALES (est): 14.6MM **Privately Held**
SIC: 3671 Electron tubes

(G-5821)
FAIRVIEW MANUFACTURING CORP
2505 Avonia Rd (16415-1837)
PHONE....................................814 474-5581
Deanna J Klein, *President*
Gerry Klein, *Vice Pres*
Lisa Starr, *Treasurer*
EMP: 11 EST: 1961
SQ FT: 14,700
SALES (est): 1.6MM **Privately Held**
SIC: 3599 Machine shop, jobbing & repair

(G-5822)
FLEX-Y-PLAN INDUSTRIES INC (PA)
6960 W Ridge Rd (16415-2097)
PHONE..................................814 881-3436
Dorothy Hutzelman, *Ch of Bd*
Thomas Hutzelman, *President*
Donald Worthington, *Exec VP*
Stephen Hutzelman, *Admin Sec*
EMP: 40 **EST:** 1964
SQ FT: 90,000
SALES (est): 4.8MM **Privately Held**
WEB: www.fyp.com
SIC: 2522 Panel systems & partitions, office: except wood

(G-5823)
FORMTECH ENTERPRISES INC
Also Called: Yates Division
7301 Klier Dr (16415-2465)
PHONE..................................814 474-1940
Amy Reynallt, *General Mgr*
EMP: 22
SALES (corp-wide): 14MM **Privately Held**
SIC: 3089 3082 Extruded finished plastic products; unsupported plastics profile shapes
PA: Formtech Enterprises, Inc.
3924 Clock Pointe Trl # 101
Stow OH 44224
330 688-2171

(G-5824)
GREENBRIAR INDUS SYSTEMS INC
Also Called: Greenbriar Plastics
7800 Maple St (16415-1830)
PHONE..................................814 474-1400
James D Byrd, *President*
Theresa Byrd, *Treasurer*
EMP: 95 **EST:** 1978
SQ FT: 58,000
SALES: 7MM **Privately Held**
WEB: www.greenbriar1.com
SIC: 3089 3544 3643 3061 Injection molding of plastics; special dies & tools; current-carrying wiring devices; mechanical rubber goods; broadwoven fabric mills, manmade

(G-5825)
GRIMM INDUSTRIES INC (PA)
7070 W Ridge Rd (16415-2096)
P.O. Box 924 (16415-0924)
PHONE..................................814 474-2648
Butch Grimm, *President*
Beatrice Grimm, *Corp Secy*
Steven Grimm, *Vice Pres*
Karl Kenyon, *Site Mgr*
Sherri Stout, *Accountant*
EMP: 200
SQ FT: 70,000
SALES (est): 41.5MM **Privately Held**
WEB: www.grimmsoda.com
SIC: 3089 Injection molding of plastics

(G-5826)
HANES ERIE INC
7601 Klier Dr N (16415-2447)
PHONE..................................814 474-1999
Thomas A Hanes, *President*
Sam Khodzhayan, *Vice Pres*
Patricia A Hanes, *Treasurer*
Theresa Stachera, *Accounts Mgr*
▲ **EMP:** 127
SQ FT: 75,000
SALES: 15MM **Privately Held**
WEB: www.haneserie.com
SIC: 3089 8711 Plastic processing; designing: ship, boat, machine & product

(G-5827)
HARRY RHOADES
Also Called: Lake Erie Molded Plastics
7395 Market Rd (16415-2826)
PHONE..................................814 474-1099
Harry Rhoades, *Owner*
EMP: 10
SQ FT: 24,000
SALES (est): 1.5MM **Privately Held**
SIC: 3089 Injection molding of plastics

(G-5828)
HOWARD INDUSTRIES INC (PA)
6400 Howard Dr (16415-2912)
PHONE..................................814 833-7000
Gary Schneider, *CEO*
Frank Blanco, *President*
Patrick Sutton, *President*
Joyce Lackey, *Purchasing*
Mike Gajewski, *Sales Staff*
EMP: 45
SQ FT: 48,000
SALES (est): 7.2MM **Privately Held**
WEB: www.howardindustries.com
SIC: 3993 Signs & advertising specialties

(G-5829)
HYDRO-PAC INC
7470 Market Rd (16415-2825)
P.O. Box 921 (16415-0921)
PHONE..................................814 474-1511
Walter Robertson Jr, *President*
Jason Robertson, *Vice Pres*
◆ **EMP:** 35
SQ FT: 29,672
SALES (est): 10.5MM **Privately Held**
WEB: www.hydropac.com
SIC: 3563 3561 Air & gas compressors; pumps & pumping equipment

(G-5830)
KIM KRAFT INC (HQ)
Also Called: Dispatch Printing
6485 Fairoaks Cir (16415-1718)
PHONE..................................814 870-9600
E Joseph Mehl, *Ch of Bd*
Timothy J Mehl, *President*
EMP: 19 **EST:** 1962
SQ FT: 35,000
SALES (est): 2MM
SALES (corp-wide): 6.5MM **Privately Held**
SIC: 2759 2754 Commercial printing; calendar & card printing, except business: gravure
PA: Dispatch Printing, Inc.
917 Bacon St
Erie PA 16511
814 870-9600

(G-5831)
LENNYS MACHINE COMPANY
7900 Middle Rd (16415-1855)
PHONE..................................814 474-5510
Leonard Stahlman, *Principal*
EMP: 7 **EST:** 2012
SALES (est): 923.3K **Privately Held**
SIC: 3599 Machine shop, jobbing & repair

(G-5832)
LIGNITECH INC
Also Called: Lignitech Limited
8000c Middle Rd (16415-1854)
PHONE..................................814 474-9590
John St George, *President*
Vlado Benden, *Vice Pres*
EMP: 10
SQ FT: 11,390
SALES: 932K **Privately Held**
WEB: www.lignitechltd.com
SIC: 2431 Millwork

(G-5833)
MAXPRO TECHNOLOGIES INC (PA)
7728 Klier Dr S (16415-2454)
PHONE..................................814 474-9191
Paul T Bowser, *President*
Ronald D Hyziewicz, *Vice Pres*
Shawn Dailey, *Engineer*
EMP: 14
SQ FT: 6,000
SALES (est): 5.2MM **Privately Held**
WEB: www.maxprotech.com
SIC: 3563 5074 3492 Air & gas compressors; plumbing & hydronic heating supplies; fluid power valves & hose fittings

(G-5834)
NAVITEK GROUP INC
8305 Middle Rd (16415-1851)
P.O. Box 97 (16415-0097)
PHONE..................................814 474-2312
Harvey Downey, *President*
Louise Downey, *Corp Secy*
▲ **EMP:** 8 **EST:** 2000
SQ FT: 4,000

SALES (est): 790K **Privately Held**
WEB: www.navitekgroup.com
SIC: 3699 High-energy particle physics equipment

(G-5835)
PARKER WHITE METAL COMPANY
Also Called: Phb Die Casting
7900 W Ridge Rd (16415-1807)
PHONE..................................814 474-5511
William M Hilbert, *Ch of Bd*
Harland Tolhurst, *Vice Pres*
Pete Tolhurst, *CFO*
▲ **EMP:** 550 **EST:** 1906
SQ FT: 350,000
SALES (est): 88MM
SALES (corp-wide): 3.2MM **Privately Held**
SIC: 3363 3364 Aluminum die-castings; zinc & zinc-base alloy die-castings
PA: Phb, Inc.
7900 W Ridge Rd
Fairview PA 16415
814 474-5511

(G-5836)
PERFOMANCE CASTINGS LLC
6101 Bridlewood Dr (16415-2708)
PHONE..................................814 454-1243
Stephen Konzel,
EMP: 3 **EST:** 2015
SALES (est): 155K **Privately Held**
SIC: 3321 Gray & ductile iron foundries

(G-5837)
PHB INC (PA)
Also Called: Phb Tool and Die Division
7900 W Ridge Rd (16415-1899)
PHONE..................................814 474-5511
William M Hilbert Sr, *President*
James O Benson, *Vice Pres*
Harland R Tolhurst Jr, *Treasurer*
Daniel I Langer, *Admin Sec*
EMP: 700
SQ FT: 342,000
SALES: 3.2MM **Privately Held**
WEB: www.phbcorp.com
SIC: 3363 3364 3545 Aluminum die-castings; zinc & zinc-base alloy die-castings; tools & accessories for machine tools

(G-5838)
PHB INC
Also Called: P H B Molding
8152 W Ridge Rd (16415-1805)
PHONE..................................814 474-2683
David Parrish, *Manager*
EMP: 52
SALES (est): 11.3MM
SALES (corp-wide): 3.2MM **Privately Held**
WEB: www.phbcorp.com
SIC: 3363 3061 Aluminum die-castings; mechanical rubber goods
PA: Phb, Inc.
7900 W Ridge Rd
Fairview PA 16415
814 474-5511

(G-5839)
PHB INC
Also Called: Phb Machining Div
8150 W Ridge Rd (16415-1898)
PHONE..................................814 474-1552
William Hilbert, *President*
Marsha Watkins, *Principal*
Dave Parrish, *Manager*
EMP: 200
SALES (corp-wide): 3.2MM **Privately Held**
WEB: www.phbcorp.com
SIC: 3599 3369 2295 Machine shop, jobbing & repair; nonferrous foundries; coated fabrics, not rubberized
PA: Phb, Inc.
7900 W Ridge Rd
Fairview PA 16415
814 474-5511

(G-5840)
PRECISE PLASTICS INC
Also Called: Ppi-Erie
7700 Middle Rd (16415-1897)
P.O. Box 370 (16415-0370)
PHONE..................................814 474-5504

Gregory N Farrell, *President*
Regory N Farrell, *President*
EMP: 64
SQ FT: 25,000
SALES (est): 11.2MM **Privately Held**
WEB: www.preciseplastics.com
SIC: 3089 3678 3643 3544 Injection molded finished plastic products; electronic connectors; current-carrying wiring devices; special dies, tools, jigs & fixtures; laminated plastics plate & sheet

(G-5841)
SEN DEC CORP
8031 Avonia Rd (16415-2829)
PHONE..................................585 425-3390
EMP: 10
SALES (est): 3.3MM **Privately Held**
SIC: 3672 Printed circuit boards

(G-5842)
SPECTRUM CONTROL INC (DH)
Also Called: API Technologies
8061 Avonia Rd (16415-2899)
PHONE..................................814 474-2207
Robert E Tavares, *CEO*
Bel Lazar, *President*
Lawrence Howanitz, *Vice Pres*
Andrew Laurence, *Vice Pres*
Robert McKenna, *Vice Pres*
▲ **EMP:** 277
SQ FT: 43,000
SALES (est): 137.5MM
SALES (corp-wide): 333.6MM **Privately Held**
SIC: 3677 3663 3612 3676 Filtration devices, electronic; amplifiers, RF power & IF; transformers, except electric; thermistors, except temperature sensors

(G-5843)
SPECTRUM CONTROL INC
Electromagnetic Division
8061 Avonia Rd (16415-2899)
PHONE..................................814 474-1571
EMP: 225
SALES (corp-wide): 333.6MM **Privately Held**
SIC: 3677 3675 Filtration devices, electronic; electronic capacitors
HQ: Spectrum Control, Inc.
8061 Avonia Rd
Fairview PA 16415
814 474-2207

(G-5844)
SPECTRUM CONTROL INC
Control Products Division
8061 Avonia Rd (16415-2899)
PHONE..................................814 835-4000
EMP: 250
SALES (corp-wide): 333.6MM **Privately Held**
SIC: 3677 3675 3643 3564 Filtration devices, electronic; electronic capacitors; current-carrying wiring devices; blowers & fans; porcelain electrical supplies
HQ: Spectrum Control, Inc.
8061 Avonia Rd
Fairview PA 16415
814 474-2207

(G-5845)
SPECTRUM CONTROL INC
8031 Avonia Rd (16415-2829)
PHONE..................................814 474-4315
Jude Hoffman, *Vice Pres*
Jay Salorino, *Engineer*
Jan Scopel, *Branch Mgr*
EMP: 4
SALES (corp-wide): 333.6MM **Privately Held**
SIC: 3677 3663 3612 Filtration devices, electronic; amplifiers, RF power & IF; transformers, except electric
HQ: Spectrum Control, Inc.
8061 Avonia Rd
Fairview PA 16415
814 474-2207

(G-5846)
SPECTRUM CONTROL TECH INC
8031 Avonia Rd (16415-2829)
PHONE..................................814 474-2207
Drew Sullivan, *Principal*
EMP: 10

▲ = Import ▼=Export
◆ =Import/Export

SALES (est): 1.2MM
SALES (corp-wide): 333.6MM **Privately Held**
SIC: 3674 Semiconductors & related devices
HQ: Api Technologies Corp.
400 Nickerson Rd Ste 1
Marlborough MA 01752

(G-5847)
SPECTRUM MICROWAVE INC (DH)
Also Called: Spec Adv Spec Prod Grp
8061 Avonia Rd (16415-2829)
PHONE..................................814 474-4300
Richard Southworth, *President*
John Freeman, *CFO*
Jim Seagul, *Treasurer*
James Toohey, *Admin Sec*
◆ EMP: 99
SQ FT: 53,000
SALES: 63.8MM
SALES (corp-wide): 333.6MM **Privately Held**
WEB: www.spectrummicrowave.com
SIC: 3679 Microwave components
HQ: Spectrum Control, Inc.
8061 Avonia Rd
Fairview PA 16415
814 474-2207

(G-5848)
TITAN TOOL COMPANY
7410 W Ridge Rd (16415-1170)
P.O. Box 220 (16415-0220)
PHONE..................................814 474-1583
Brian A McKean, *President*
Edwin McKean, *Vice Pres*
Frank Hodas, *Controller*
▼ EMP: 16
SQ FT: 10,000
SALES (est): 3MM **Privately Held**
WEB: www.titantoolco.com
SIC: 3545 Machine tool attachments & accessories; chucks: drill, lathe or magnetic (machine tool accessories); collets (machine tool accessories)

(G-5849)
WINDSOR BEACH TECHNOLOGIES INC
7321 Klier Dr (16415-2465)
PHONE..................................814 474-4900
Robert A Macyko, *President*
EMP: 40
SQ FT: 28,000
SALES: 3.5MM **Privately Held**
WEB: www.windsorbeach.com
SIC: 3599 Machine shop, jobbing & repair

(G-5850)
X-CELL TOOL AND MOLD INC
7701 Klier Dr S (16415-2455)
PHONE..................................814 474-9100
Ronald J Novel, *President*
EMP: 21
SQ FT: 10,000
SALES (est): 4.6MM **Privately Held**
WEB: www.xcelltoolandmold.com
SIC: 3312 Tool & die steel

Fallentimber
Cambria County

(G-5851)
CONSOLIDATED STEEL SVCS INC (PA)
632 Glendale Valley Blvd (16639-6508)
PHONE..................................814 944-5890
Cynthia A Zack, *President*
Robert Schmit, *Principal*
Ronald B Mazzocco, *Vice Pres*
John Landry, *Safety Mgr*
Jim Kobak, *Technology*
EMP: 41
SQ FT: 80,000
SALES (est): 6.6MM **Privately Held**
WEB: www.csteel.com
SIC: 3441 Fabricated structural metal

Falls
Wyoming County

(G-5852)
DARBY INDUSTRIES INC
2682 Sullivans Trl (18615-7948)
PHONE..................................570 388-6173
Thomas Darby, *President*
▲ EMP: 9
SQ FT: 7,000
SALES: 1.1MM **Privately Held**
SIC: 5531 3714 Automotive accessories; motor vehicle parts & accessories

Falls Creek
Jefferson County

(G-5853)
FORADORA WELDING & MACHINE
904 Sandstone Dr (15840-3620)
PHONE..................................814 375-2176
Mark S Foradora, *President*
EMP: 20
SQ FT: 9,600
SALES (est): 3.2MM **Privately Held**
WEB: www.foradorawelding.com
SIC: 3599 Machine shop, jobbing & repair

(G-5854)
HAWK PRECISION COMPONENTS
409 3rd St (15840-1549)
PHONE..................................814 371-0184
Don Brown, *Principal*
EMP: 3 EST: 2010
SALES (est): 287.3K **Privately Held**
SIC: 3399 Powder, metal

(G-5855)
NETSHAPE TECHNOLOGIES LLC
409 3rd St (15840-1549)
PHONE..................................814 371-0184
Joel Simbeck, *Plant Mgr*
EMP: 150
SALES (corp-wide): 185.3MM **Privately Held**
SIC: 3399 Powder, metal
HQ: Netshape Technologies Llc
14670 Cumberland Rd
Noblesville IN 46060
812 248-9273

(G-5856)
NORDBERG JOHN
Also Called: Laurel Mountain Vineyard
1754 Old Grade Rd (15840-4016)
PHONE..................................814 371-2217
Barbara A Nordberg, *Owner*
EMP: 6
SALES (est): 593.9K **Privately Held**
WEB: www.laurelwines.com
SIC: 5921 2084 Wine; wines, brandy & brandy spirits

Fannettsburg
Franklin County

(G-5857)
BURPEE WILLOW HILL
12844 Creek Rd (17221-9708)
PHONE..................................717 349-0065
Willow Burpee, *Principal*
Jaime Baker, *Manager*
EMP: 6
SALES (est): 1.3MM **Privately Held**
SIC: 2621 Catalog, magazine & newsprint papers

(G-5858)
ROSENBERRY BROS LUMBER CO
6827 Path Valley Rd (17221-9720)
P.O. Box 405 (17221-0405)
PHONE..................................717 349-7196
Dennis D Rosenberry, *President*
Gary Rosenberry, *Vice Pres*
Joseph L Rosenberry, *Vice Pres*
Gardner Rosenberry, *Treasurer*
Stacey Ann Rosenberry, *Treasurer*
EMP: 12
SQ FT: 7,500
SALES: 2.9MM **Privately Held**
SIC: 2421 2431 Lumber: rough, sawed or planed; millwork

(G-5859)
SEIBERTS COMPUTERS
10850 Back Rd (17221-9722)
PHONE..................................717 349-7859
Travis L Seibert, *Principal*
EMP: 3
SALES (est): 204.8K **Privately Held**
SIC: 3572 Computer tape drives & components

Farmington
Fayette County

(G-5860)
CHURCH COMMUNITIES PA INC
Rr Box 381n (15437)
P.O. Box 260 (15437-0260)
PHONE..................................724 329-8573
Richard Kurtz, *Branch Mgr*
EMP: 4
SALES (corp-wide): 4MM **Privately Held**
SIC: 3944 3842 Games, toys & children's vehicles; surgical appliances & supplies
PA: Church Communities Pa Inc.
101 New Meadow Run Dr
Farmington PA
724 329-8573

(G-5861)
GARY FIKE LOGGING
192 Fike Hollow Rd (15437-1040)
PHONE..................................724 329-7175
Gary Fike, *Principal*
EMP: 3
SALES (est): 236.7K **Privately Held**
SIC: 2411 Logging

(G-5862)
GREAT MEADOWS SAWMILL FRM INC
673 Nelson Rd (15437-1209)
PHONE..................................724 329-7771
James Nicholson, *President*
Matthew Nicholson, *Vice Pres*
Terrie Nicholson, *Treasurer*
Connie Nicholson, *Admin Sec*
EMP: 3
SALES (est): 266.1K **Privately Held**
SIC: 2421 0191 7389 Sawmills & planing mills, general; general farms, primarily crop;

(G-5863)
TOM CESARINO LUMBER
433 Camp Riamo Rd (15437-1033)
PHONE..................................724 329-0467
Thomas Cesarino, *Owner*
Jean Cesarino, *Co-Owner*
EMP: 4 EST: 1996
SALES (est): 210K **Privately Held**
SIC: 2421 Sawmills & planing mills, general

(G-5864)
WICKTEK INC
360 Frmington Ohiopyle Rd (15437-1310)
PHONE..................................513 474-4518
Frank R Yantek, *President*
Paul R Wick, *Exec VP*
Robert Toye, *Vice Pres*
William Casey, *Treasurer*
EMP: 5
SQ FT: 8,000
SALES: 900K **Privately Held**
WEB: www.densicrete.com
SIC: 2899 Concrete curing & hardening compounds

Farrell
Mercer County

(G-5865)
A F NECASTRO INC
Also Called: A F Necastro & Associates
713 Martin Luther King Jr (16121-1915)
P.O. Box 450, Sharon (16146-0450)
PHONE..................................724 981-3239
Anthony Necastro, *President*
EMP: 6
SALES: 1,000K **Privately Held**
SIC: 3317 Steel pipe & tubes

(G-5866)
BERTRAM TOOL AND MCH CO INC
1201 Mtn Ltr Kng Jr Blvd (16121)
P.O. Box 141 (16121-0141)
PHONE..................................724 983-2222
Helmut Bertram, *President*
Carolyn F Bertram, *Corp Secy*
EMP: 18
SQ FT: 18,000
SALES (est): 3.1MM **Privately Held**
WEB: www.bertramtool.com
SIC: 3599 Machine shop, jobbing & repair

(G-5867)
DAFFINS INC
Also Called: Daffin's Candy Factory
7 Spearman Ave (16121-2101)
PHONE..................................724 983-8336
Gary Siggler, *Manager*
EMP: 25
SALES (corp-wide): 15MM **Privately Held**
WEB: www.daffins.com
SIC: 2064 2066 Candy & other confectionery products; chocolate & cocoa products
PA: Daffin's, Inc.
496 E State St
Sharon PA 16146
724 342-2892

(G-5868)
KLARIC FORGE & MACHINE INC (PA)
10 Fruit Ave (16121-2134)
PHONE..................................814 382-6290
Kyle Klaric, *CEO*
Charles Diehl, *Vice Pres*
Dave Shoenfelt, *Admin Sec*
▲ EMP: 16
SALES (est): 1.2MM **Privately Held**
SIC: 3462 Iron & steel forgings

(G-5869)
NLMK PENNSYLVANIA LLC
15 Roemer Blvd (16121-2201)
PHONE..................................724 983-6464
Benedict Sciortino, *CEO*
Robert Miller, *President*
James Banker, *COO*
Jason Adams, *Vice Pres*
Frank Fonner, *Sales Staff*
▲ EMP: 500
SALES (est): 102.4MM
SALES (corp-wide): 510MM **Privately Held**
WEB: www.dufercofarrell.com
SIC: 3316 3356 3312 Cold finishing of steel shapes; nonferrous rolling & drawing; blast furnaces & steel mills
HQ: Nlmk, Pao
2 Pl. Metallurgov
Lipetsk 39804
474 244-4069

(G-5870)
PERFORMANCE PROC VENTURES LLC
660 Martin Luther King (16121-1946)
PHONE..................................724 704-8827
Arron Smith, *Principal*
EMP: 5
SALES (est): 454.4K **Privately Held**
SIC: 3441 Fabricated structural metal

GEOGRAPHIC

(G-5871)
PRECISION STEEL SERVICES INC
650 M L King Jr Blvd # 111 (16121-1946)
P.O. Box 72 (16121-0072)
PHONE..................................724 347-2770
Walter Darby, *President*
Lori Darby, *Director*
EMP: 17
SQ FT: 45,000
SALES (est): 4.6MM **Privately Held**
SIC: 3441 Fabricated structural metal

(G-5872)
PREMIER HYDRAULICS LLC
10 Fruit Ave (16121-2134)
P.O. Box 188 (16121-0188)
PHONE..................................724 342-6506
Kyle Klaric, *President*
David Shoenfelt, *Vice Pres*
Reza Liaghat, *Manager*
Gregory Ham, *Executive*
Charles Todd Deihl, *Admin Sec*
▲ **EMP:** 85
SQ FT: 30,000
SALES (est): 12.6MM **Privately Held**
SIC: 3599 Machine shop, jobbing & repair

(G-5873)
ROLL FORMING CORP - SHARON
Also Called: Rfc Sharon
250 Martin Luther King (16121-2084)
PHONE..................................724 982-0400
Kevin Dierking, *President*
Dan Ahern, *CFO*
EMP: 39
SQ FT: 99,590
SALES (est): 13.7MM
SALES (corp-wide): 16B **Privately Held**
WEB: www.scmf.biz
SIC: 3449 Custom roll formed products
HQ: Global Rollforming Corp.
1070 Brooks Industrial Rd
Shelbyville KY 40065
502 633-4435

(G-5874)
SOMERSET ENTERPRISES INC
Also Called: Future Building of America Co
212 Idaho St (16121-1023)
PHONE..................................724 734-9497
Rick Kennett, *President*
Jim Sydlowski, *Admin Sec*
EMP: 12
SQ FT: 12,000
SALES: 1.5MM **Privately Held**
WEB: www.futurebuilding.com
SIC: 1542 2631 2491 Custom builders, non-residential; paperboard mills; structural lumber & timber, treated wood

Fayette City
Fayette County

(G-5875)
JOD CONTRACTING INC
1250 Connellsville Rd (15438-1014)
PHONE..................................724 323-2124
Santos Maldonado, *President*
Jodi Maldonado, *Vice Pres*
EMP: 4
SALES: 950K **Privately Held**
SIC: 8741 5047 3699 Construction management; medical equipment & supplies; electrical equipment & supplies

Fayetteville
Franklin County

(G-5876)
DYMONDS CONCRETE PRODUCTS
Also Called: Dymond Oil
40 Dymond Ave (17222-1417)
PHONE..................................717 352-2321
David Dymond, *President*
EMP: 6
SALES (est): 727.3K **Privately Held**
SIC: 3272 Septic tanks, concrete

(G-5877)
GLEN L MYERS INC
1211 Knob Hill Rd (17222-9727)
PHONE..................................717 352-0035
Glen Myers, *Principal*
EMP: 7
SALES (est): 1MM **Privately Held**
SIC: 3699 Electrical equipment & supplies

(G-5878)
SPEED PARTZ LLC
Also Called: Aerowings
198 Black Gap Rd Trlr 145 (17222-9560)
PHONE..................................513 874-2034
Cory Myers, *Mng Member*
EMP: 5
SALES (est): 362K **Privately Held**
SIC: 3448 Prefabricated metal components

(G-5879)
VALLEY QUARRIES INC
Also Called: Mt. Cydonia Plant I
1071 Mount Cydonia Rd (17222-9514)
P.O. Box M (17222)
PHONE..................................814 766-2211
Fred Crabbs, *Branch Mgr*
EMP: 4
SALES (corp-wide): 651.9MM **Privately Held**
SIC: 1411 5211 5051 5032 Dimension stone; lime & plaster; metals service centers & offices; stone, crushed or broken
HQ: Valley Quarries, Inc.
297 Quarry Rd
Chambersburg PA 17202
717 267-2244

Feasterville Trevose
Bucks County

(G-5880)
A & F HOLDINGS LLC
1641 Loretta Ave Ste B (19053-7351)
PHONE..................................215 289-8300
Ambrose Fasolak, *Mng Member*
EMP: 40
SALES (est): 6.1MM **Privately Held**
SIC: 3554 Paper mill machinery: plating, slitting, waxing, etc.

(G-5881)
A I FLOOR PRODUCTS
Also Called: Iobbi Shellac
4888 Hazel Ave (19053-4816)
PHONE..................................215 355-2798
Alfred Iobbi Jr, *Owner*
Julie Iobbi, *Partner*
EMP: 4
SQ FT: 2,000
SALES (est): 455.2K **Privately Held**
SIC: 3589 2851 Floor sanding machines, commercial; shellac (protective coating); stains: varnish, oil or wax; lacquers, varnishes, enamels & other coatings

(G-5882)
A TASTE OF PHILLY
1801 Bridgetown Pike # 2 (19053-2398)
PHONE..................................215 639-3997
Daren Ebner, *Principal*
EMP: 5
SALES (est): 368.2K **Privately Held**
SIC: 2052 Pretzels

(G-5883)
ADVERTISING SPECIALTY INST INC (PA)
Also Called: A S I
4800 E Street Rd Ste 100a (19053-6698)
PHONE..................................800 546-1350
Norman Cohn, *Ch of Bd*
Matthew Cohn, *Vice Ch Bd*
Tim Andrews, *President*
Richard Fairfield, *Publisher*
James La Moreaux, *Sr Corp Ofcr*
EMP: 400 **EST:** 1950
SQ FT: 200,000
SALES (est): 78.3MM **Privately Held**
WEB: www.bctechpark.com
SIC: 2721 7372 Periodicals: publishing only; publishers' computer software

(G-5884)
ALCATEL-LUCENT TECH INC
34 Polder Dr (19053-1522)
PHONE..................................215 752-1847
Larry Samson, *Principal*
EMP: 3
SALES (est): 160.8K **Privately Held**
SIC: 3661 Telephone & telegraph apparatus

(G-5885)
AQUACHEMPACS LLC
515 Andrews Rd (19053-3432)
PHONE..................................215 396-7200
Stephen Seneca, *Partner*
Doug Frain, *VP Sales*
Jon Horton, *Sales Dir*
Tracy Annis, *Sales Staff*
Jared Seneca, *Sales Staff*
EMP: 25
SALES (est): 6.5MM **Privately Held**
SIC: 2842 Specialty cleaning preparations

(G-5886)
ARC MANUFACTURING CO INC
1651 Loretta Ave (19053-7310)
PHONE..................................215 355-8500
Stephen Feuchter, *President*
Karin L Hazzard, *Vice Pres*
EMP: 35 **EST:** 1968
SQ FT: 27,000
SALES (est): 5.1MM **Privately Held**
WEB: www.arcmfgco.com
SIC: 3599 Machine shop, jobbing & repair

(G-5887)
ASSOCIATED PRTG GRAPHICS SVCS
Also Called: Abss
4570 E Bristol Rd Ste A (19053-4757)
PHONE..................................215 322-6762
Don Ruben, *Owner*
EMP: 5
SALES (est): 275.3K **Privately Held**
WEB: www.assocprint.com
SIC: 7374 2759 Data processing & preparation; commercial printing

(G-5888)
BEAVER TOOL AND MACHINE CO INC
1641 Loretta Ave Ste A (19053-7390)
PHONE..................................215 322-0660
William Galgon, *President*
Fred Galgon, *Treasurer*
Werner Cziriak, *Admin Sec*
EMP: 10
SQ FT: 12,000
SALES (est): 1.4MM **Privately Held**
SIC: 3599 Machine shop, jobbing & repair

(G-5889)
BERGER BUILDING PRODUCTS INC
805 Pennsylvania Blvd (19053-7813)
PHONE..................................215 355-1200
David Stewart, *President*
Mitchell B Lewis, *Vice Pres*
Edward P Caine, *Treasurer*
R Scott Vansant, *Admin Sec*
▲ **EMP:** 8
SALES (est): 795.8K **Privately Held**
SIC: 3089 3444 Plastic hardware & building products; sheet metalwork

(G-5890)
BERGER BUILDING PRODUCTS CORP (HQ)
805 Pennsylvania Blvd (19053-7813)
PHONE..................................215 355-1200
Scott Anderson, *President*
Greg Boatwright, *Vice Pres*
John Gartzke, *Maintence Staff*
▲ **EMP:** 100 **EST:** 1874
SQ FT: 115,000
SALES: 18.8MM
SALES (corp-wide): 861.3MM **Privately Held**
WEB: www.snowbrakes.com
SIC: 3444 Metal roofing & roof drainage equipment; downspouts, sheet metal
PA: Omnimax Holdings, Inc.
303 Research Dr Ste 400
Norcross GA 30092
770 449-7066

(G-5891)
BODY GEMS
875 Pnnsylvnia Blvd Ste 2 (19053)
PHONE..................................215 357-9552
C S Collins, *Owner*
Josh Collins, *Sales Dir*
EMP: 6
SALES (est): 605K **Privately Held**
WEB: www.bodygems.com
SIC: 3911 Jewelry, precious metal

(G-5892)
BOEKEL INDUSTRIES INC (PA)
Also Called: Boekel Scientific
855 Pennsylvania Blvd (19053-7813)
PHONE..................................215 396-8200
Leo Synnestvedt, *Ch of Bd*
Steve Christie, *President*
Larry Van Atta, *Senior VP*
Charles Carney, *Vice Pres*
Amy Jo Frunzi, *Vice Pres*
▲ **EMP:** 40 **EST:** 1868
SALES (est): 7.8MM **Privately Held**
WEB: www.boekelsci.com
SIC: 3826 3821 Analytical instruments; laboratory apparatus & furniture

(G-5893)
BRB TECHNOLOGY CORPORATION
1641 Loretta Ave Ste B (19053-7351)
PHONE..................................215 364-4115
Leo Konowar, *General Mgr*
EMP: 3
SALES (est): 270K **Privately Held**
SIC: 2282 Throwing & winding mills

(G-5894)
BUCKS COUNTY MIDWEEK
2512 Metropolitan Dr (19053-6791)
PHONE..................................215 355-1234
George Troyano, *Principal*
EMP: 3
SALES (est): 154.6K **Privately Held**
SIC: 2711 Newspapers, publishing & printing

(G-5895)
BUCKS CREAMERY LLC
Also Called: Cold Stone Creamery
140 E Street Rd (19053-7604)
P.O. Box 97, Edison NJ (08818-0097)
PHONE..................................732 387-3535
Purvi Gandhi, *Mng Member*
Nirav Gandhi,
EMP: 22
SQ FT: 1,400
SALES (est): 540K **Privately Held**
SIC: 5812 2052 Ice cream stands or dairy bars; cones, ice cream

(G-5896)
BUSINESSONE TECHNOLOGIES INC
1210 Northbrook Dr # 310 (19053-8407)
PHONE..................................215 953-6660
Sudhakar Raju, *CEO*
Sudhakar Rhau, *President*
EMP: 5
SQ FT: 1,005
SALES: 600K **Privately Held**
WEB: www.businessonetech.com
SIC: 7372 7371 Business oriented computer software; custom computer programming services

(G-5897)
C & M MOLD & TOOL INC
2600 W Maple Ave Rear (19053-7247)
PHONE..................................215 741-2081
Mark Dobron, *Vice Pres*
Neil Ellixson, *Officer*
EMP: 4
SALES (est): 402.1K **Privately Held**
SIC: 3089 Injection molding of plastics

(G-5898)
C C B B INC
Also Called: Audubon Sales & Service
850 Pennsylvania Blvd (19053-7814)
PHONE..................................215 364-5377
Stephen I Weiss, *President*
Denard Schivers, *Vice Pres*
EMP: 18
SQ FT: 14,050

▲ = Import ▼=Export
◆ =Import/Export

SALES (est): 6.4MM **Privately Held**
WEB: www.meshbelt.com
SIC: 5084 3535 3496 Conveyor systems; belt conveyor systems, general industrial use; wire cloth & woven wire products

(G-5899)
CABINET CONNECTIONS
81 Bertha St (19053-2313)
PHONE.....................................215 429-9431
Bernadette Moss, *Owner*
EMP: 3
SALES (est): 255.4K **Privately Held**
SIC: 2434 Wood kitchen cabinets

(G-5900)
CONTEMPORY PUBG GROUP E LLC
1032 Millcreek Dr (19053-7321)
PHONE.....................................215 953-8210
Glen Edwards, *Mng Member*
EMP: 5 **EST:** 2012
SALES: 200K **Privately Held**
SIC: 2741 Miscellaneous publishing

(G-5901)
CROWN CORK & SEAL USA INC
3100 Tremont Ave (19053-6644)
PHONE.....................................215 322-5507
Edwin Macuga, *Branch Mgr*
EMP: 118
SALES (corp-wide): 11.1B **Publicly Held**
WEB: www.crowncork.com
SIC: 3411 Metal cans
HQ: Crown Cork & Seal Usa, Inc.
770 Township Line Rd # 100
Yardley PA 19067
215 698-5100

(G-5902)
CROWN HOLDINGS INC
Also Called: H-V Industries
3100 Tremont Ave (19053-6644)
PHONE.....................................215 322-3533
Harry Arnold, *Principal*
EMP: 25
SALES (corp-wide): 11.1B **Publicly Held**
SIC: 3466 3411 Crowns & closures; jar tops & crowns, stamped metal; bottle caps & tops, stamped metal; tin cans
HQ: Crown Cork & Seal Receivables (De) Corporation
5301 Limestone Rd Ste 221
Wilmington DE 19808

(G-5903)
ELECTRONIC INTEGRATION INC
875 Pnnsylvnia Blvd Ste 4 (19053)
PHONE.....................................215 364-3390
Sona Fitapara, *President*
James Kephart, *Engineer*
Harry Patel, *Treasurer*
▲ **EMP:** 15
SQ FT: 3,600
SALES (est): 2.4MM
SALES (corp-wide): 2.5MM **Privately Held**
WEB: www.electronicii.com
SIC: 3672 Printed circuit boards
PA: Fineline Circuits, Inc.
1660 Loretta Ave
Feasterville Trevose PA 19053
215 364-3311

(G-5904)
ELECTROSPRAY INCORPORATED
Also Called: Corro Therm
175 Philmont Ave (19053-6402)
PHONE.....................................215 322-5255
Donald Kirk, *Branch Mgr*
EMP: 11 **Privately Held**
SIC: 1799 3312 Coating, caulking & weather, water & fireproofing; coated or plated products
PA: Electrospray Incorporated
175 Philmont Ave
Feasterville Trevose PA 19053

(G-5905)
ELECTROSPRAY INCORPORATED (PA)
Also Called: Corro Therm
175 Philmont Ave (19053-6402)
PHONE.....................................215 322-5255

Donald C Kirk, *President*
Loretta Blavier, *Purchasing*
EMP: 7
SQ FT: 7,200
SALES (est): 2.5MM **Privately Held**
SIC: 1799 3312 Coating, caulking & weather, water & fireproofing; coated or plated products

(G-5906)
EVENLITE INC
2575 Metropolitan Dr (19053-6737)
PHONE.....................................215 244-4201
William Lynch, *CEO*
Adrian Pavitt, *President*
Jack Desalliers, *Opers Staff*
Karen Floyd, *Production*
Joanne Benner, *Controller*
▲ **EMP:** 36
SQ FT: 30,700
SALES (est): 8.5MM
SALES (corp-wide): 9.5MM **Privately Held**
WEB: www.evenlite.com
SIC: 3648 Lighting equipment
PA: Isolite Corp.
31 Waterloo Ave
Berwyn PA 19312
610 647-8200

(G-5907)
F AND T LP
Also Called: Sign-A-Rama
434 W Street Rd 436 (19053-5961)
PHONE.....................................215 355-2060
Robert Flemming, *Owner*
EMP: 4
SALES (est): 180K **Privately Held**
SIC: 3993 Signs & advertising specialties

(G-5908)
FIBERBLADE LLC
1150 Northbrook Dr # 150 (19053-8409)
PHONE.....................................814 361-8730
Dirk Matthys, *Mng Member*
▲ **EMP:** 220
SALES (est): 27.3MM
SALES (corp-wide): 95B **Privately Held**
SIC: 3621 Windmills, electric generating
HQ: Siemens Gamesa Renewable Energy Usa, Inc.
1150 Northbrook Dr # 300
Feasterville Trevose PA 19053
215 710-3100

(G-5909)
FINELINE CIRCUITS INC (PA)
1660 Loretta Ave (19053-7311)
PHONE.....................................215 364-3311
Sona Sitapara, *President*
Hemang Patel, *Vice Pres*
Ashwin Patel, *Production*
EMP: 20
SQ FT: 12,000
SALES (est): 2.5MM **Privately Held**
WEB: www.finelinepcb.com
SIC: 3672 8711 Circuit boards, television & radio printed; engineering services

(G-5910)
FIZZANO BROS INC
247 Sterner Mill Rd (19053-6515)
PHONE.....................................215 355-6160
Eric Tiger, *Branch Mgr*
EMP: 20
SALES (corp-wide): 13.4MM **Privately Held**
WEB: www.fizzano.com
SIC: 3271 5032 5211 Blocks, concrete or cinder: standard; concrete & cinder block; concrete & cinder block
PA: Fizzano Bros Inc
1776 Chester Pike
Crum Lynne PA 19022
610 833-1100

(G-5911)
FRASER-VOLPE LLC (PA)
Also Called: Fraser Optics
210 Andrews Rd (19053-3428)
PHONE.....................................215 443-5240
Andrew Levy, *CEO*
Andrew A Levy, *Principal*
William Long, *CFO*
William T Long, *CFO*
EMP: 41

SQ FT: 20,000
SALES (est): 7.6MM **Privately Held**
SIC: 3827 Telescopes: elbow, panoramic, sighting, fire control, etc.

(G-5912)
GE INFRASTRUCTURE SENSING (HQ)
Also Called: GE Water & Process Tech
4636 Somerton Rd (19053-6742)
PHONE.....................................617 926-1749
John G Rice, *President*
Joel A Berdine, *President*
Barbara Cameron, *Vice Pres*
Matthew G Cribbins, *Vice Pres*
Adriana Aguilar, *Buyer*
▼ **EMP:** 10
SALES (est): 280.6MM
SALES (corp-wide): 121.6B **Publicly Held**
SIC: 3589 2086 4941 3559 Water purification equipment, household type; water filters & softeners, household type; water treatment equipment, industrial; water, pasteurized: packaged in cans, bottles, etc.; water supply; desalination equipment; water treating compounds; water quality monitoring & control systems
PA: General Electric Company
41 Farnsworth St
Boston MA 02210
617 443-3000

(G-5913)
GO2POWER LLC
2575 Metropolitan Dr (19053-6737)
PHONE.....................................215 244-4202
Guy Teipel, *Partner*
Adrian Pavitt, *Partner*
EMP: 24
SALES (est): 2.4MM **Privately Held**
SIC: 3621 Inverters, rotating: electrical

(G-5914)
JUSTFROYO INC
70 E Street Rd (19053-7603)
PHONE.....................................215 355-7555
EMP: 4
SALES (est): 209.6K **Privately Held**
SIC: 2024 Yogurt desserts, frozen

(G-5915)
K-B LIGHTING MANUFACTURING CO (PA)
2515 Metropolitan Dr (19053-6737)
PHONE.....................................215 953-6663
Gary Kessel, *President*
Dorothy Kessel, *Corp Secy*
Ben Kessel, *Vice Pres*
EMP: 28 **EST:** 1948
SQ FT: 12,000
SALES (est): 5.6MM **Privately Held**
WEB: www.kblighting.com
SIC: 3645 3641 Fluorescent lighting fixtures, residential; electric lamps

(G-5916)
KEAMCO INDUSTRIES INC
1043 Hilton Ave (19053-3512)
PHONE.....................................215 938-6050
Keith Williams, *President*
EMP: 7
SALES (est): 549K **Privately Held**
SIC: 3449 Bars, concrete reinforcing: fabricated steel

(G-5917)
MASON EAST INC
2 Neshaminy Interplex Dr # 205 (19053-6958)
PHONE.....................................631 254-2240
Rafael Burgos, *President*
EMP: 4
SALES (est): 354K **Privately Held**
WEB: www.mason-east-inc.com
SIC: 5085 3625 3069 3052 Industrial supplies; noise control equipment; hard rubber & molded rubber products; rubber hose
PA: Mason East Inc
64 Brook Ave Ste 3
Deer Park NY 11729

(G-5918)
MASON RUBBER CO INC
1819 2nd St Ste A (19053-3362)
PHONE.....................................215 355-3440
Bruce Mason, *President*
▲ **EMP:** 10
SQ FT: 13,120
SALES (est): 1.3MM **Privately Held**
WEB: www.masonrubber.com
SIC: 3069 Molded rubber products

(G-5919)
MENU FOR LESS
2 Park Ln Ste 107 (19053-6004)
PHONE.....................................215 240-1582
Mikhail Slobodskoi, *Principal*
Nathan Herring, *Director*
EMP: 3
SALES (est): 345.4K **Privately Held**
SIC: 3577 Printers & plotters

(G-5920)
MOYERS SERVICE CO
4409 Somers Ave (19053-3470)
PHONE.....................................267 205-1105
Richard Moyer, *Owner*
EMP: 6
SALES: 200K **Privately Held**
SIC: 3443 Autoclaves, industrial

(G-5921)
NATURES PILLOWS INC
Also Called: N P I
2607 Nshminy Interplex Dr (19053-6946)
PHONE.....................................215 633-9801
Bradley Specter, *President*
Bill McCallister, *Vice Pres*
◆ **EMP:** 6
SALES (est): 891.2K **Privately Held**
SIC: 2392 Cushions & pillows

(G-5922)
NEMCO
Also Called: National Engineering and Mfg
900 Pennsylvania Blvd (19053-7885)
PHONE.....................................215 355-2100
Donald Bandurick, *President*
EMP: 50 **EST:** 1955
SQ FT: 50,000
SALES (est): 9MM **Privately Held**
SIC: 3544 3599 Special dies & tools; machine shop, jobbing & repair

(G-5923)
OLIVER-TLAS HLTHCARE PACKG INC
905 Pennsylvania Blvd (19053-7815)
PHONE.....................................215 322-7900
Scott Dickman, *President*
Ann Zambrano, *Business Mgr*
Kevin Huhn, *Engineer*
Kenneth Seeger, *Controller*
Kim Smith, *Finance Mgr*
▲ **EMP:** 200
SQ FT: 48,000
SALES (est): 125.1MM
SALES (corp-wide): 2.9B **Privately Held**
WEB: www.oliver-tolas.com
SIC: 2671 Packaging paper & plastics film, coated & laminated
HQ: Oliver Products Company
445 6th St Nw
Grand Rapids MI 49504
616 456-7711

(G-5924)
OMNIMAX INTERNATIONAL INC
Berger Holdings
805 Pennsylvania Blvd (19053-7813)
PHONE.....................................215 355-1200
Mitchell B Lewis, *CEO*
EMP: 190
SALES (corp-wide): 861.3MM **Privately Held**
SIC: 3444 Sheet metalwork
HQ: Omnimax International, Inc.
30 Technology Pkwy S # 400
Peachtree Corners GA 30092

(G-5925)
PADC 1
2595 Metropolitan Dr (19053-6737)
PHONE.....................................215 322-3300
EMP: 25

SALES (corp-wide): 10.7B **Publicly Held**
SIC: 2844 Mfg Toilet Preparations
HQ: Padc 1
　411 Sinclair Rd
　Bristol PA 19007
　215 781-1600

(G-5926)
PENN EMBLEM COMPANY (PA)
Also Called: Imprints USA
2577 Neshaminy Interplex # 100
(19053-6957)
PHONE....................................215 632-7800
Robert Blumenthal, *President*
Randi Blumenthal-Joseph, *Principal*
Pat Larosa, *Principal*
Jon Joseph, *Senior VP*
John Thompson, *Vice Pres*
▲ EMP: 99 EST: 1947
SQ FT: 30,000
SALES (est): 22.4MM **Privately Held**
WEB: www.imprintsusa.com
SIC: 2395 2399 2672 Emblems, embroidered; emblems, badges & insignia: from purchased materials; tape, pressure sensitive: made from purchased materials

(G-5927)
PRECISION CARBIDE INC
325 Philmont Ave Ste 1 (19053-6478)
PHONE....................................215 355-4220
John Fornito, *President*
Cathy Fornito, *Admin Sec*
EMP: 9
SQ FT: 3,500
SALES (est): 900K **Privately Held**
SIC: 3544 Special dies & tools

(G-5928)
READY SET LIVE INC
15 E Myrtle Ave (19053-4200)
PHONE....................................215 953-1509
Dolores Bojazi Cressee, *Principal*
EMP: 3 EST: 2007
SALES (est): 238.6K **Privately Held**
SIC: 3273 Ready-mixed concrete

(G-5929)
SHIRT GALLERY INC
200 Elmwood Ave Ste A (19053-2395)
PHONE....................................215 364-1212
Charles Bray, *President*
John Kopack, *Treasurer*
EMP: 3
SQ FT: 3,800
SALES (est): 330.3K **Privately Held**
SIC: 2759 Screen printing

(G-5930)
SIEMENS GAMESA RENEWABLE (DH)
Also Called: Gamesa Wind
1150 Northbrook Dr # 300 (19053-8409)
PHONE....................................215 710-3100
Dirk Matthys, *CEO*
◆ EMP: 0
SQ FT: 2,500
SALES (est): 182.3MM
SALES (corp-wide): 95B **Privately Held**
SIC: 6719 3621 Investment holding companies, except banks; windmills, electric generating
HQ: Siemens Gamesa Renewable Energy Sociedad Anonima
　Poligono Teknologi Elkartegia, Edif. 222
　Zamudio　48170
　944 037-352

(G-5931)
STASIK CUSTOM CABINETRY
410 Clearview Ave Ste H (19053-3356)
PHONE....................................215 357-7277
Ernest Stasik, *Principal*
EMP: 8
SALES (est): 678.5K **Privately Held**
SIC: 2434 Wood kitchen cabinets

(G-5932)
TECHNITROL INC
1210 Northbrook Dr (19053-8407)
PHONE....................................215 355-2900
Melliar Smith, *Principal*
EMP: 3 EST: 2016
SALES (est): 139.9K **Privately Held**
SIC: 3399 Primary metal products

(G-5933)
TIROS MACHINE & TOOL COMPANY
285 Andrews Rd (19053-3427)
PHONE....................................215 322-9965
William Pearson, *President*
EMP: 9
SQ FT: 12,000
SALES (est): 1.2MM **Privately Held**
SIC: 3599 Machine shop, jobbing & repair

(G-5934)
U S TEXTILE CORP
1150 Northbrook Dr # 300 (19053-8443)
PHONE....................................828 733-9244
Mike Secrest, *Manager*
EMP: 329
SALES (corp-wide): 18.1MM **Privately Held**
SIC: 2251 Dyeing & finishing women's full- & knee-length hosiery
HQ: U. S. Textile Corp.
　1150 Northbrook Dr # 300
　Feasterville Trevose PA 19053
　803 283-6800

(G-5935)
U S TEXTILE CORP (HQ)
1150 Northbrook Dr # 300 (19053-8443)
PHONE....................................803 283-6800
John T Duncan, *Corp Secy*
Juergen Dirrigl, *Vice Pres*
◆ EMP: 47
SQ FT: 100,000
SALES (est): 10.4MM
SALES (corp-wide): 18.1MM **Privately Held**
SIC: 2251 2671 Women's hosiery, except socks; packaging paper & plastics film, coated & laminated
PA: Sculptz, Inc.
　1150 Northbrook Dr # 300
　Trevose PA 19053
　215 494-2900

(G-5936)
URBAN ENTERPRISES T & M LLC
Also Called: Core Color Graphics
535 Andrews Rd Ste 100 (19053-3400)
P.O. Box 1032, Southampton (18966-0732)
PHONE....................................215 485-5209
Thomas Urban,
EMP: 6 EST: 2007
SALES (est): 505.2K **Privately Held**
SIC: 2759 Commercial printing

(G-5937)
VETSTREET INCORPORATED (DH)
3800 Horizon Blvd Ste 201 (19053-4968)
PHONE....................................267 685-2400
Derrick Kraemer, *President*
EMP: 30
SALES (est): 6.6MM
SALES (corp-wide): 13.2B **Publicly Held**
SIC: 8732 7372 Market analysis, business & economic research; prepackaged software
HQ: Butler Animal Health Supply Llc
　400 Metro Pl N Ste 100
　Dublin OH 43017
　614 761-9095

(G-5938)
VH SERVICE LLC
102 E Pennsylvania Blvd (19053-7843)
PHONE....................................267 808-9745
Vicaliy Hrytsay,
EMP: 5
SALES: 350K **Privately Held**
SIC: 1799 3993 1731 3444 Sign installation & maintenance; welding on site; signs & advertising specialties; lighting contractor; awnings & canopies

(G-5939)
VICTORIA PRECISION INC
410 Clearview Ave Ste C (19053-3356)
PHONE....................................215 355-7576
George Dilks, *President*
James McGee, *Prdtn Mgr*
EMP: 15
SQ FT: 5,200

SALES (est): 1.9MM **Privately Held**
SIC: 3599 Machine shop, jobbing & repair

Felton
York County

(G-5940)
JACKIE L TROUT SEPTIC
57 Church Ave (17322-9036)
PHONE....................................717 244-6640
Jackie L Trout, *Owner*
EMP: 3
SALES: 350K **Privately Held**
SIC: 1389 Excavating slush pits & cellars

(G-5941)
NOVARES US LLC
12367 Mount Olivet Rd (17322-8449)
PHONE....................................717 244-0151
Don Fortenbaugh, *General Mgr*
Teresa Lewis, *Human Res Mgr*
Yvonne Mifsud,
EMP: 60
SQ FT: 90,000
SALES (corp-wide): 76.6MM **Privately Held**
WEB: www.keyplastics.com
SIC: 3089 Injection molding of plastics
HQ: Novares Us Llc
　19575 Victor Pkwy Ste 400
　Livonia MI 48152
　248 449-6100

(G-5942)
NOVARES US LLC
Also Called: York II
12367 Mount Olivet Rd (17322-8449)
PHONE....................................717 244-4581
Todd Lowe, *Branch Mgr*
EMP: 276
SQ FT: 40,000
SALES (corp-wide): 76.6MM **Privately Held**
WEB: www.keyplastics.com
SIC: 3089 Injection molding of plastics
HQ: Novares Us Llc
　19575 Victor Pkwy Ste 400
　Livonia MI 48152
　248 449-6100

(G-5943)
WYATT WOODWORKING
11931 Mount Olivet Rd (17322-8450)
PHONE....................................717 246-8740
Frank Wyatt, *Principal*
EMP: 4
SALES (est): 380.9K **Privately Held**
SIC: 2431 Millwork

Fenelton
Butler County

(G-5944)
CNC MALTING COMPANY
719 Clearfield Rd (16034-8711)
PHONE....................................570 954-4500
Christopher Callaio, *Partner*
EMP: 6 EST: 2016
SALES (est): 501.5K **Privately Held**
SIC: 2082 Malt beverages

(G-5945)
FUELS & LUBES TECHNOLOGIES LLC
152 Mclafferty Rd (16034-8701)
PHONE....................................724 282-8264
John Chovanes, *Principal*
EMP: 5
SALES (est): 523.2K **Privately Held**
SIC: 2869 Fuels

(G-5946)
KENIC GAS & OIL COMPANY
443 Donaldson Rd (16034-9637)
PHONE....................................724 445-7701
Chalace Schaffner, *Partner*
Kenneth Orloski, *Partner*
Trisha Orloski, *Partner*
Nick Schaffner, *Partner*
Chalace Schfmann, *Partner*

EMP: 4
SALES (est): 209.7K **Privately Held**
SIC: 1389 Oil & gas field services

(G-5947)
OESTERLINGS FEED
Also Called: Oesterlngs Grnding Mxing Feeds
3035 Old Route 422 E (16034-9779)
PHONE....................................724 283-1819
Amie Oesterlings, *Branch Mgr*
EMP: 3
SALES (corp-wide): 655.1K **Privately Held**
SIC: 2048 Cereal-, grain-, & seed-based feeds
PA: Oesterling's Feed
　599 Nichola Rd
　Worthington PA 16262
　724 283-1819

(G-5948)
SHULER WOODWORKING
300 Cornetti Rd (16034-9737)
PHONE....................................724 679-5222
EMP: 4
SALES (est): 386.2K **Privately Held**
SIC: 2431 Millwork

(G-5949)
UNIMACH MANUFACTURING
1652 Route 422 E (16034-9713)
PHONE....................................724 285-5505
Douglas Bartosh, *Owner*
EMP: 7 EST: 1979
SQ FT: 4,000
SALES (est): 530K **Privately Held**
WEB: www.unimachmfg.com
SIC: 3599 Machine shop, jobbing & repair

Ferndale
Bucks County

(G-5950)
FEDERAL METAL PRODUCTS INC
174 Center Hill Rd (18921)
P.O. Box 192 (18921-0192)
PHONE....................................610 847-2077
Marianne E Chabot, *President*
William Chabot, *Vice Pres*
EMP: 6
SQ FT: 1,800
SALES: 474.4K **Privately Held**
SIC: 5051 3469 Metals service centers & offices; machine parts, stamped or pressed metal

---

Finleyville
Washington County

(G-5951)
ABEL MILLWORK LLC
550 Mcclelland Rd (15332-9747)
PHONE....................................412 296-2254
Gene Abel, *Owner*
EMP: 6
SALES: 300K **Privately Held**
SIC: 2431 Millwork

(G-5952)
C L I CORPORATION (PA)
6108 Brownsville Road Ext # 201
(15332-4132)
PHONE....................................724 348-4800
William C Stein Jr, *President*
David Hartley, *Vice Pres*
EMP: 4
SALES (est): 7.2MM **Privately Held**
WEB: www.clicorp.com
SIC: 1241 1629 8741 Coal mining services; industrial plant construction; management services

(G-5953)
CICCI DANCE SUPPLY INC
2528 State Route 88 (15332-3538)
PHONE....................................724 348-7359
George Cicci Jr, *President*
Margo Cicci, *Vice Pres*
▲ EMP: 48 EST: 1956

SALES (est): 5.4MM **Privately Held**
WEB: www.ciccidance.com
SIC: **2389** Costumes

(G-5954)
CUSTOM TURF INC
1900 Gill Hall Rd (15332-4240)
PHONE.............................412 384-4111
Robert J Kerns, *President*
Rob Turley, *General Mgr*
William M Kerns, *Admin Sec*
EMP: 9
SALES (est): 797.9K **Privately Held**
WEB: www.customturfinc.com
SIC: **0782 3524** Turf installation services, except artificial; cultivators (garden tractor equipment)

(G-5955)
DOMAR GROUP INC
108 Aragon Pl (15332-1058)
PHONE.............................714 674-0391
Mary Kokladas, *President*
William Kokladas, *Vice Pres*
EMP: 7
SALES (est): 750.3K **Privately Held**
SIC: **2952** Roofing materials

(G-5956)
EAST BANK MACHINE INC
1 Church St (15332)
PHONE.............................412 384-4721
Edward Toth, *President*
Ruth Toth, *Vice Pres*
EMP: 8
SALES (est): 866.7K **Privately Held**
SIC: **3599** Machine & other job shop work

(G-5957)
EI MACHINE INC
3459 Washington Ave (15332-1325)
PHONE.............................724 348-0296
Michael Cummings, *Manager*
EMP: 3
SALES (est): 388.7K
SALES (corp-wide): 434.6MM **Privately Held**
SIC: **3599** Machine shop, jobbing & repair
HQ: Ensinger Industries, Inc.
365 Meadowlands Blvd
Washington PA 15301
724 746-6050

(G-5958)
ELECTRIC MOTOR SERVICE INC
3755 Ann St (15332-1317)
P.O. Box 61, Gastonville (15336-0061)
PHONE.............................724 348-6858
John Resosky, *President*
Else Resosky, *Admin Sec*
EMP: 5
SQ FT: 9,000
SALES (est): 955.2K **Privately Held**
SIC: **7694 5999** Electric motor repair; motors, electric

(G-5959)
GOLDSBOROUGH & VANSANT INC (PA)
Also Called: Butler Forge & Metal Works Div
6116 Brownsville Road Ext # 108 (15332-4130)
PHONE.............................724 782-0393
William K Julin Jr, *President*
William K Julin III, *Vice Pres*
EMP: 4
SQ FT: 3,800
SALES (est): 5.2MM **Privately Held**
WEB: www.butlerforge.com
SIC: **3441 3599 3462 5051** Fabricated structural metal; machine shop, jobbing & repair; machinery forgings, ferrous; forgings, ferrous; castings, rough: iron or steel; castings (except die); open flooring & grating for construction

(G-5960)
HOMER CITY COAL PROC CORP (HQ)
6108 Brownsville Road Ext # 201 (15332-4132)
PHONE.............................724 348-4800
William Stein Jr, *President*
E H Jones, *Vice Pres*
G M Evans, *Treasurer*
David Hartley, *Director*

EMP: 50 EST: 1977
SQ FT: 20,000
SALES: 0
SALES (corp-wide): 7.2MM **Privately Held**
SIC: **1221** Coal preparation plant, bituminous or lignite
PA: C L I Corporation
6108 Brownsville Road Ext # 201
Finleyville PA 15332
724 348-4800

(G-5961)
LILLIPUT PLAY HOMES INC (PA)
6114 Brownsville Road Ext (15332-4123)
PHONE.............................724 348-7071
Stephen Chernicky, *President*
▼ EMP: 4
SQ FT: 5,000
SALES (est): 2.2MM **Privately Held**
WEB: www.lilliputplayhomes.com
SIC: **3949 5941** Playground equipment; playground equipment

(G-5962)
OVEREND & KRILL LUMBER INC
3800 Baltimore St (15332-1332)
P.O. Box 238 (15332-0238)
PHONE.............................724 348-7511
Robert W Overend, *President*
David Overend, *Vice Pres*
EMP: 3
SQ FT: 7,200
SALES (est): 372.4K **Privately Held**
SIC: **7389 2448 2441** Packaging & labeling services; wood pallets & skids; nailed wood boxes & shook

(G-5963)
PITTSBURGH POWDER COAT
4273 Fnleyville Elrama Rd (15332-3118)
PHONE.............................412 419-8434
Antonio Carosella, *Principal*
EMP: 4
SALES (est): 315.1K **Privately Held**
SIC: **3479** Painting, coating & hot dipping

(G-5964)
QUALITY MILLWORK INC
6299 State Route 88 (15332-9650)
PHONE.............................412 831-3500
Willis R Abel, *President*
Donna Criss, *Corp Secy*
Betty Abel, *Vice Pres*
Scott Criss, *Controller*
EMP: 7 EST: 1960
SQ FT: 5,000
SALES (est): 704.4K **Privately Held**
SIC: **8742 2431 7349** Manufacturing management consultant; millwork; cleaning service, industrial or commercial

(G-5965)
WALTER LONG MFG CO INC
86 Walter Long Rd (15332-9667)
P.O. Box 310, South Park (15129-0310)
PHONE.............................724 348-6631
Robert I Long, *President*
David S Long, *Vice Pres*
EMP: 22
SQ FT: 36,000
SALES (est): 4.9MM **Privately Held**
SIC: **3443 3449 3444 3441** Fabricated plate work (boiler shop); miscellaneous metalwork; sheet metalwork; fabricated structural metal

Fleetville
Lackawanna County

(G-5966)
GECCO INC
Rr 407 (18420)
PHONE.............................570 945-3568
Orna Clum, *President*
Gerald Clum, *Vice Pres*
EMP: 3
SQ FT: 60,000
SALES: 289K **Privately Held**
SIC: **3569** Firefighting apparatus & related equipment

Fleetwood
Berks County

(G-5967)
ADVANCED ENVIROMATION INC
Also Called: Honeywell Authorized Dealer
18 W Poplar St (19522-1505)
P.O. Box 138 (19522-0138)
PHONE.............................610 422-3770
Kevin Breisch, *President*
EMP: 7
SALES (est): 1.3MM **Privately Held**
SIC: **3822** Building services monitoring controls, automatic

(G-5968)
BNB FIRE PROTECTION INC
16 Breezy Park Dr (19522-8891)
PHONE.............................610 944-0594
Mathew Harring, *President*
Barry L Unger, *Vice Pres*
Robert C Kolb Jr, *Treasurer*
EMP: 3
SALES (est): 219.6K
SALES (corp-wide): 3.5MM **Privately Held**
WEB: www.bnbmechanical.com
SIC: **1711 3569 5087** Fire sprinkler system installation; sprinkler systems, fire: automatic; sprinkler systems
PA: Bnb Mechanical Inc
16 Breezy Park Dr
Fleetwood PA
610 944-0594

(G-5969)
CUSTOM MIL & CONSULTING INC (PA)
Also Called: C M C
1246 Maidencreek Rd (19522-8685)
P.O. Box 6224, Reading (19610-0224)
PHONE.............................610 926-0984
Joseph Zidik, *President*
Luary Shaffer, *Bookkeeper*
▲ EMP: 32
SQ FT: 26,000
SALES (est): 12.4MM **Privately Held**
WEB: www.cmcmilling.com
SIC: **3541 2865 2899 2851** Milling machines; dyes: azine, azo, azoic; ink or writing fluids; paints & allied products

(G-5970)
DRDAVESBESTBODIES INC
1050 Maidencreek Rd Ste D (19522-8554)
PHONE.............................610 926-5728
David M Woynarowski, *President*
EMP: 4
SALES (est): 149.9K **Privately Held**
SIC: **2711** Newspapers, publishing & printing

(G-5971)
EAST PENN CONTAINER DCTG INC
19 W Poplar St (19522-1512)
P.O. Box 306 (19522-0306)
PHONE.............................610 944-3227
John Tunitis, *President*
EMP: 25
SQ FT: 22,000
SALES: 1.1MM **Privately Held**
SIC: **2396** Stamping fabric articles

(G-5972)
F M BROWNS SONS INCORPORATED
118 W Main St (19522-1221)
P.O. Box 153 (19522-0153)
PHONE.............................610 944-7654
Franklin Brown, *Branch Mgr*
EMP: 22
SALES (corp-wide): 57.1MM **Privately Held**
WEB: www.fmbrown.com
SIC: **2041** Flour mills; cereal (except rice)
PA: F M Brown's Sons Incorporated
205 Woodrow Ave
Reading PA 19608
800 334-8816

(G-5973)
FLEETWOOD BUILDING BLOCK INC
240 W Main St (19522-1223)
PHONE.............................610 944-8385
Carl Adams, *Ch of Bd*
John Adams, *President*
Dale Adams, *Corp Secy*
EMP: 11
SALES (est): 1.9MM **Privately Held**
WEB: www.fleetwoodblock.com
SIC: **3271** Blocks, concrete or cinder: standard

(G-5974)
HOFFMAN ENTERPRISES INC
Also Called: Heffner Printing
562 Blandon Rd Ste 1 (19522-9376)
PHONE.............................610 944-8481
Murray Hoffman, *President*
EMP: 3
SQ FT: 4,000
SALES (est): 582.2K **Privately Held**
WEB: www.heffnerprinting.com
SIC: **2752** Commercial printing, offset

(G-5975)
KURT LEBO
Also Called: Rockland Signs
230 Schweitz Rd (19522-9727)
PHONE.............................610 682-4071
Kurt Lebo, *Owner*
EMP: 3
SQ FT: 1,536
SALES (est): 100K **Privately Held**
SIC: **7389 3993** Lettering & sign painting services; signs & advertising specialties

(G-5976)
LEHIGH CEMENT COMPANY LLC
537 Evansville Rd (19522-8541)
PHONE.............................610 926-1024
Lloyd Lutz, *Vice Pres*
Bryan Denion, *Purch Mgr*
Robert Preyer, *Manager*
EMP: 131
SALES (corp-wide): 20.6B **Privately Held**
WEB: www.lehighcement.com
SIC: **3241 3273** Portland cement; ready-mixed concrete
HQ: Lehigh Cement Company Llc
300 E John Carpenter Fwy
Irving TX 75062
877 534-4442

(G-5977)
P A OFFICE AND CLOSET SYSTEMS
Also Called: Closet Factory
7 Willow Street Indus Par (19522-1800)
PHONE.............................610 944-1333
Robert B Focht, *President*
Joan Focht, *Vice Pres*
EMP: 18
SALES (est): 3.5MM **Privately Held**
SIC: **5211 2542** Closets, interiors & accessories; partitions & fixtures, except wood

(G-5978)
PRICETOWN EPHRATA GAS &F
3123 Pricetown Rd (19522-8736)
PHONE.............................610 939-1701
Bajinder Singh, *Principal*
EMP: 5
SALES (est): 661.9K **Privately Held**
SIC: **2911** Gases & liquefied petroleum gases

(G-5979)
SEMICNDCTOR OZONE SLUTIONS LLC
36 Lake Rd (19522-9000)
PHONE.............................541 936-0844
EMP: 4
SALES (est): 403.1K **Privately Held**
SIC: **3674** Semiconductors & related devices

(G-5980)
SUNSWEET GROWERS INC
105 S Buttonwood St (19522-1639)
PHONE.............................610 944-1005
Richard Cattermole, *General Mgr*
Chris Heckman, *Director*
Richard Saldivar, *Administration*

GEOGRAPHIC

EMP: 120
SALES (corp-wide): 244.8MM **Privately Held**
WEB: www.sunsweet.com
SIC: 2034 2099 2033 Fruits, dried or dehydrated, except freeze-dried; food preparations; canned fruits & specialties
PA: Sunsweet Growers Inc.
　901 N Walton Ave
　Yuba City CA 95993
　800 417-2253

(G-5981)
SUSQUEHANNA GRDN CONCEPTS LLC
20 Breezy Park Dr (19522-8891)
P.O. Box 355, Lampeter (17537-0355)
PHONE.............................717 826-5144
▲ **EMP:** 5
SALES (est): 439.4K **Privately Held**
SIC: 2511 Garden furniture: wood

(G-5982)
W D ZWICKY & SON INC
Also Called: Zwicky Processing & Recycling
220 Buena Vista Rd (19522-8533)
PHONE.............................484 248-5300
W D Zwicky, *President*
Mary Zwicky, *Corp Secy*
EMP: 45
SQ FT: 2,508
SALES (est): 503.7K **Privately Held**
SIC: 2411 1629 1794 Wood chips, produced in the field; land clearing contractor; excavation & grading, building construction

---

Flinton
Cambria County

(G-5983)
GLENDALE VALLEY WINERY
2599 Glendale Valley Blvd (16640-9109)
PHONE.............................814 687-3438
Sylvia Dixon, *Principal*
EMP: 4
SALES (est): 223.1K **Privately Held**
SIC: 2084 Wines

Flourtown
Montgomery County

(G-5984)
ATLANTIC CMMNCATIONS GROUP INC
18 E Mill Rd (19031-2027)
PHONE.............................215 836-4683
Hayden Wilbur, *CEO*
Bob Sadoski, *Project Mgr*
Karen Belle, *Sales Staff*
Alan Wrobel, *Sales Staff*
Bob Mogavero, *Technology*
EMP: 22
SALES (est): 2.1MM **Privately Held**
SIC: 2731 7336 Books: publishing only; commercial art & graphic design

(G-5985)
ATLANTIC PUBLISHING GROUP INC
18 E Mill Rd (19031-2027)
PHONE.............................800 832-3747
Hayden M Wilbur, *President*
EMP: 10
SALES (est): 519.7K **Privately Held**
WEB: www.atlantic4us.com
SIC: 2711 Newspapers

(G-5986)
DE PAUL CONCRETE (PA)
409 Stenton Ave (19031-1327)
P.O. Box 1667, Blue Bell (19422-0465)
PHONE.............................610 832-8000
Peter De Paul, *Owner*
David Bartynski, *Manager*
EMP: 6
SALES (est): 3.8MM **Privately Held**
WEB: www.depaulconcrete.com
SIC: 3273 5211 Ready-mixed concrete; concrete & cinder block

(G-5987)
HIGHWAY MATERIALS INC (PA)
409 Stenton Ave (19031-1327)
PHONE.............................610 832-8000
Peter De Paul, *President*
Fran Callery, *Area Mgr*
Donna Bartynski, *Vice Pres*
William Nemeth, *Vice Pres*
Chris Rumer, *Plant Mgr*
▲ **EMP:** 13 **EST:** 1936
SQ FT: 50,000
SALES (est): 10.1MM **Privately Held**
WEB: www.highwaymaterials.com
SIC: 2951 5032 Road materials, bituminous (not from refineries); stone, crushed or broken; sand, construction

(G-5988)
MOTSON GRAPHICS INC (PA)
1717 Bethlehem Pike (19031-1110)
P.O. Box 234 (19031-0234)
PHONE.............................215 233-0500
Phillip Henderson, *President*
EMP: 19 **EST:** 1927
SQ FT: 16,000
SALES (est): 2.8MM **Privately Held**
WEB: www.motson.com
SIC: 2759 Screen printing

(G-5989)
PAUL DORAZIO CUSTOM FURNITURE
Also Called: D'Orazio Paul Custom Uphl
1410 Bethlehem Pike (19031-2004)
PHONE.............................215 836-1057
Paul Dorazio, *Owner*
Maria Dorazio, *Finance Other*
EMP: 8
SALES (est): 559.9K **Privately Held**
SIC: 2511 7641 Wood household furniture; upholstery work; furniture repair & maintenance

(G-5990)
PIKE GRAPHICS INC
Also Called: Image 360
1200 E Mermaid Ln (19031)
PHONE.............................215 836-9120
James R Pearce, *President*
EMP: 11
SQ FT: 7,125
SALES (est): 151.4K **Privately Held**
SIC: 3993 1799 Signs & advertising specialties; sign installation & maintenance

---

Fogelsville
Lehigh County

(G-5991)
ATLANTIC CRANE INC
7562 Penn Dr Ste 110 (18051)
P.O. Box 728 (18051-0728)
PHONE.............................610 366-1540
James Winkelspecht, *President*
EMP: 10
SQ FT: 4,500
SALES (est): 3.1MM **Privately Held**
WEB: www.atlantic-crane.com
SIC: 3536 7699 Cranes, overhead traveling; construction equipment repair

(G-5992)
CARLISLE SYSTEMS LLC
210 Sunset Dr (18051)
PHONE.............................610 821-4222
Jason Hoffman,
EMP: 3
SALES (est): 132.5K **Privately Held**
SIC: 3444 Sheet metalwork

(G-5993)
CARPENTER CO
Also Called: Carpenter Insulation Co
57 A Olin Way (18051)
P.O. Box 129 (18051-0129)
PHONE.............................610 366-5110
Joe Summer, *CEO*
EMP: 55

SALES (corp-wide): 2B **Privately Held**
WEB: www.carpenter.com
SIC: 3086 1311 2869 Insulation or cushioning material, foamed plastic; carpet & rug cushions, foamed plastic; padding, foamed plastic; crude petroleum & natural gas; industrial organic chemicals
PA: Carpenter Co.
　5016 Monument Ave
　Richmond VA 23230
　804 359-0800

(G-5994)
FIVE THOUSAND FORMS INC (PA)
Also Called: Givemefive.com
8020 Mine St (18051-1622)
PHONE.............................610 395-0900
Linda Levy, *CEO*
Herbert W Levy, *President*
Jessica Goebel, *Treasurer*
Kim Hartung, *Accounts Exec*
David Eiskowitz, *Marketing Staff*
EMP: 17
SQ FT: 11,000
SALES (est): 6.2MM **Privately Held**
SIC: 5112 5199 2752 7336 Business forms; advertising specialties; commercial printing, lithographic; commercial art & graphic design

(G-5995)
HOFFMAN MANUFACTURING INC
2010 Sunset Dr (18051-2343)
PHONE.............................610 821-4222
Jeffery T Hoffman, *President*
Jason C Hoffman, *Vice Pres*
EMP: 18
SQ FT: 45,000
SALES (est): 4.3MM **Privately Held**
WEB: www.hoffmanmanufacturing.com
SIC: 3444 Sheet metal specialties, not stamped

(G-5996)
PLACEMAT PRINTERS INC
Also Called: Mastercraft Printing & Design
10195 Old Rt 22 (18051)
P.O. Box 699 (18051-0699)
PHONE.............................610 285-2255
Darlene Pinto, *President*
EMP: 15
SQ FT: 8,000
SALES (est): 2.2MM **Privately Held**
WEB: www.mastercraftprinting.com
SIC: 2752 Commercial printing, offset

(G-5997)
VIBRO INDUSTRIES INC
Main St (18051)
PHONE.............................717 527-2094
Leroy Johnson, *President*
EMP: 3
SALES (est): 291.6K **Privately Held**
SIC: 3535 Conveyors & conveying equipment

Folcroft
Delaware County

(G-5998)
AMBASSADOR BAGS & SPATS MFG CO
Also Called: Ambassador Spat Co
900 Ashland Ave (19032-1904)
PHONE.............................610 532-7840
Sunita Madhadan, *President*
EMP: 6 **EST:** 1976
SQ FT: 3,000
SALES: 500K **Privately Held**
SIC: 2399 3199 5131 5699 Aprons, breast (harness); spats; textiles, woven; leather garments; leather goods, except footwear, gloves, luggage, belting

(G-5999)
BELLWETHER CORP
622 Grant Rd (19032-1402)
PHONE.............................610 534-5382
James M Anderson, *President*
Elizabeth W Anderson, *Admin Sec*
EMP: 15

SQ FT: 11,000
SALES (est): 1.3MM **Privately Held**
WEB: www.bellwether1.com
SIC: 3444 Sheet metalwork

(G-6000)
BENFAB INC
801 Carpenters Xing Ste 8 (19032-2020)
PHONE.............................610 626-9100
Paola Versano, *Managing Prtnr*
Bill Bendinelli, *Vice Pres*
EMP: 18 **EST:** 1999
SALES (est): 4.3MM **Privately Held**
SIC: 3446 Railings, bannisters, guards, etc.: made from metal pipe

(G-6001)
CORK INDUSTRIES INC (PA)
500 Kaiser Dr (19032-2108)
PHONE.............................610 522-9550
Frank Jmcdonnell, *President*
Frank J McDonnell, *President*
Bernard J Mc Donnell, *Vice Pres*
Susan M McDonnell, *Vice Pres*
Donald P Gaydos, *Treasurer*
▼ **EMP:** 28
SQ FT: 24,000
SALES (est): 9.6MM **Privately Held**
WEB: www.corkind.com
SIC: 2851 Lacquers, varnishes, enamels & other coatings

(G-6002)
DIAMOND AWNING MFG CO
618 Grant Rd (19032-1402)
PHONE.............................610 656-1924
Gary Diamond, *Principal*
EMP: 3
SALES (est): 400K **Privately Held**
SIC: 3444 5039 5999 Awnings, sheet metal; awnings

(G-6003)
GLOBAL POLISHING SOLUTIONS LLC
Also Called: Diamatic Management Services
622 Grant Rd (19032-1402)
PHONE.............................619 295-0893
Caroline Smith, *Branch Mgr*
EMP: 12
SQ FT: 15,000
SALES (corp-wide): 42.5MM **Privately Held**
SIC: 3531 5082 Surfacers, concrete grinding; concrete processing equipment
HQ: Global Polishing Solutions, Llc
　5220 Gaines St
　San Diego CA 92110
　619 295-5505

(G-6004)
H & H MANUFACTURING CO INC
2 Horne Dr (19032-1806)
PHONE.............................610 532-1250
Thomas Tomei, *President*
Vincent Tomei, *Treasurer*
Marie Tomei, *Admin Sec*
EMP: 58
SQ FT: 31,000
SALES (est): 7.1MM **Privately Held**
SIC: 3599 7692 Mfg Industrial Machinery Welding Repair

(G-6005)
HANNMANN MACHINERY SYSTEMS INC
Also Called: Alyan Pump Company
930 Henderson Blvd (19032-1805)
PHONE.............................610 583-6900
Ralph A Hannmann Jr, *President*
Linda Sheckler, *Corp Secy*
Barbara M Hannmann, *Treasurer*
EMP: 21
SQ FT: 10,000
SALES (est): 5.9MM **Privately Held**
WEB: www.alyanpump.com
SIC: 3561 5074 7699 Industrial pumps & parts; plumbing & hydronic heating supplies; heating equipment (hydronic); plumbing fittings & supplies; pumps & pumping equipment repair

▲ = Import ▼ =Export
◆ =Import/Export

(G-6006)
INNOVATIVE MANUFACTURING SVCS
777 Hnderson Blvd Ste 1/2 (19032)
PHONE..................................610 583-4883
▲ EMP: 3
SALES (est): 335.2K **Privately Held**
SIC: 3999 Mfg Misc Products

(G-6007)
INTELIPC
1572 Chester Pike (19032-1006)
PHONE..................................610 534-8268
Cong Nguren, *Partner*
EMP: 3
SALES (est): 128.8K **Privately Held**
SIC: 7372 Prepackaged software

(G-6008)
LEEFSON TOOL & DIE COMPANY
850 Henderson Blvd (19032-1804)
PHONE..................................610 461-7772
Richard J Leefson, *President*
Daniel Leefson, *Treasurer*
Ed Dougherty, *CTO*
▲ EMP: 35 EST: 1946
SQ FT: 24,000
SALES (est): 5.6MM **Privately Held**
WEB: www.keystonemint.com
SIC: 3469 3544 3549 Stamping metal for the trade; special dies & tools; metalworking machinery

(G-6009)
MADHAVAN INC
Also Called: Barnett Canvas Co
900 Ashland Ave (19032-1904)
PHONE..................................610 534-2600
Shan Madhavan, *President*
David Berenato, *Opers Mgr*
EMP: 5 EST: 1920
SALES: 350K **Privately Held**
SIC: 2394 Tarpaulins, fabric: made from purchased materials; sails: made from purchased materials; tents: made from purchased materials

(G-6010)
NP PRECISION INC
5 Horne Dr (19032-1807)
P.O. Box 61, Wallingford (19086-0061)
PHONE..................................610 586-5100
Nicholas Emper, *President*
Kenneth Narzikul, *President*
EMP: 35
SQ FT: 33,000
SALES (est): 8.5MM **Privately Held**
WEB: www.npprecision.com
SIC: 3599 Machine shop, jobbing & repair

(G-6011)
P R FINISHING INC
Also Called: Plate Rite
5 Horne Dr (19032-1807)
PHONE..................................610 565-0378
Kenneth Narzikul, *President*
EMP: 7
SQ FT: 12,000
SALES (est): 600K **Privately Held**
SIC: 3471 Electroplating of metals or formed products

(G-6012)
PENCOYD IRON WORKS INC
4 School Ln (19032-2400)
PHONE..................................610 522-5000
James Heldring, *President*
EMP: 25
SQ FT: 22,000
SALES (est): 4.6MM **Privately Held**
SIC: 3446 1799 Gates, ornamental metal; ornamental metal work

(G-6013)
Q C M CORPORATION
Also Called: Quaker City Mfg Co
116 Darby Commons Ct (19032-2113)
PHONE..................................610 586-4770
Joseph P Fanelli Jr, *President*
Gerald Boyle, *Exec VP*
EMP: 10
SQ FT: 22,000

SALES (est): 750K **Privately Held**
WEB: www.qcminks.com
SIC: 3442 Window & door frames

(G-6014)
RAINBOW AWNINGS INC
620 Grant Rd (19032-1402)
PHONE..................................610 534-5380
James M Anderson, *President*
EMP: 10
SALES (est): 720K **Privately Held**
WEB: www.rainbowawnings.com
SIC: 3444 5999 Awnings, sheet metal; awnings

(G-6015)
SCRUB DADDY INC
6 Horne Dr (19032-1806)
PHONE..................................610 583-4883
Aaron Krause, *President*
George Belkin, *Vice Pres*
John O'Brian, *Vice Pres*
Stephanie Krause, *Manager*
Robin Marsilii, *Graphic Designe*
▲ EMP: 35
SQ FT: 44,000
SALES (est): 972.3K **Privately Held**
SIC: 3069 Sponge rubber & sponge rubber products

(G-6016)
SPERRY GRAPHIC INC
4 Horne Dr (19032-1806)
P.O. Box 208 (19032-0208)
PHONE..................................610 534-8585
Harry S Caruso, *President*
Peter J Agresti, *Vice Pres*
EMP: 30 EST: 1970
SQ FT: 35,000
SALES (est): 4.7MM **Privately Held**
WEB: www.sperrygraphic.com
SIC: 2782 3993 Looseleaf binders & devices; displays & cutouts, window or lobby; displays, paint process

(G-6017)
TAIF INC (PA)
600 Kaiser Dr Ste A (19032-2122)
PHONE..................................610 522-0122
Joseph A Talluto, *President*
Gus Denicola, *Vice Pres*
EMP: 24 EST: 1982
SQ FT: 30,000
SALES (est): 3.5MM **Privately Held**
WEB: www.taifinc.com
SIC: 2032 2098 Italian foods: packaged in cans, jars, etc.; macaroni: packaged in cans, jars, etc.; ravioli: packaged in cans, jars, etc.; macaroni & spaghetti

(G-6018)
UNIVERSAL SERVICES ASSOC INC (PA)
Also Called: USA Medical
5 Horne Dr (19032-1807)
PHONE..................................610 461-0300
Michael Myers, *President*
Gifford Eldredge, *COO*
Emily Saich, *Opers Staff*
Mark Myers, *Treasurer*
Juanita Bailey, *Office Admin*
EMP: 30
SQ FT: 14,500
SALES (est): 11.3MM **Privately Held**
SIC: 7389 7349 3993 Exhibit construction by industrial contractors; building maintenance services; signs & advertising specialties

(G-6019)
USA MEDIA LLC
Also Called: Usafrica Journal
756 Taylor Dr (19032-1521)
P.O. Box 33143, Philadelphia (19142-0143)
PHONE..................................215 571-9241
Latunde Kolawole,
EMP: 15
SALES (est): 329.2K **Privately Held**
SIC: 2721 Magazines: publishing & printing

(G-6020)
WILLIAM F KEMPF & SON INC
900 Ashland Ave (19032-1904)
PHONE..................................610 532-2000
Shan Madhavan, *President*
Sunita Madhavan, *Vice Pres*

◆ EMP: 5 EST: 1908
SQ FT: 10,500
SALES (est): 1.3MM **Privately Held**
WEB: www.coirmats.com
SIC: 5023 3069 Carpets; mats or matting, rubber

(G-6021)
ZENA ASSOCIATES LLC
Also Called: Smart-Hose Technologies
701a Ashland Ave Ste 1 (19032-2007)
PHONE..................................215 730-9000
Charles Mc Murtrie, *CEO*
▲ EMP: 20
SQ FT: 20,000
SALES (est): 4.9MM **Privately Held**
SIC: 3052 Garden hose, plastic

Folsom
Delaware County

(G-6022)
ALLCAMS MACHINE CO
Also Called: Guzzardo Mach Prodts
116 Sycamore Ave (19033-1906)
PHONE..................................610 534-9004
Philip Guzzardo, *President*
Rita Guzzardo, *Corp Secy*
Mike Steinberg, *Manager*
EMP: 10 EST: 1960
SQ FT: 3,500
SALES (est): 600K **Privately Held**
WEB: www.allcams.net
SIC: 3599 Machine shop, jobbing & repair

(G-6023)
GLOBAL CUSTOM
Also Called: Siberian Coolers
101 Sycamore Ave Ofc 101 # 101 (19033-2321)
PHONE..................................844 782-2653
Ronald J Dimedio, *Principal*
Ronald Dimedio, *Purch Mgr*
Kathleen Sellitto, *Controller*
David Cronk, *Mktg Dir*
EMP: 5
SALES (est): 22.5K **Privately Held**
SIC: 2431 Garage doors, overhead: wood

(G-6024)
GOEBELWOOD INDUSTRIES INC
100 Sycamore Ave (19033-1906)
PHONE..................................610 532-4644
John K Goebel, *Ch of Bd*
Ronald C Goebel, *President*
Bruce C Goebel, *Vice Pres*
Dominck Pino, *Shareholder*
▲ EMP: 15
SQ FT: 11,000
SALES (est): 2.9MM **Privately Held**
WEB: www.goebelwood.com
SIC: 2431 2434 Millwork; wood kitchen cabinets

(G-6025)
INTERNATIONAL GATE DEVICES
101 Sycamore Ave Ofc 101 # 101 (19033-2321)
PHONE..................................610 461-0811
Ronald Di Medio, *President*
▲ EMP: 7
SQ FT: 2,000
SALES (est): 1MM **Privately Held**
WEB: www.intlgate.com
SIC: 3446 Fences or posts, ornamental iron or steel

(G-6026)
JAMES MAY COSTUME CO
Also Called: James May Enterprises
450 Macdade Blvd (19033-2505)
PHONE..................................610 532-3430
James May, *Owner*
EMP: 3
SQ FT: 2,500
SALES (est): 300K **Privately Held**
SIC: 2389 6512 6513 Theatrical costumes; commercial & industrial building operation; apartment building operators

(G-6027)
R G S MACHINE INC
101 Sycamore Ave Ste 109 (19033-2321)
PHONE..................................610 532-1850
Raymond Shihadeh, *President*
EMP: 6
SQ FT: 3,400
SALES (est): 700K **Privately Held**
SIC: 3599 7692 Machine shop, jobbing & repair; welding repair

(G-6028)
SIGN CONCEPTS INC
Also Called: Visual Marketing
106 Swarthmore Ave Ste 1 (19033-1693)
PHONE..................................610 586-7070
Carol Warner, *President*
David Warner, *Vice Pres*
EMP: 3
SALES (est): 368.8K **Privately Held**
WEB: www.sign-concepts-inc.com
SIC: 3993 Signs, not made in custom sign painting shops

Fombell
Beaver County

(G-6029)
ACUTRAN LP
1711 Route 588 (16123-1417)
PHONE..................................724 452-4130
Jeffrey Farbacher, *General Ptnr*
Bob Howells, *Sales Mgr*
EMP: 25
SALES (est): 4.3MM **Privately Held**
SIC: 3612 Transformers, except electric

(G-6030)
BOOS BUG STOPPERS LLC
207 Thomas Hill Rd (16123-1915)
PHONE..................................724 601-3223
Joshua Koach, *Mng Member*
EMP: 4
SALES (est): 247K **Privately Held**
SIC: 7342 2879 Pest control services; insecticides & pesticides

(G-6031)
HONEYWELL INTERNATIONAL INC
195 Hartzell School Rd (16123-1207)
PHONE..................................724 452-1300
Ed De Mailo, *Plant Mgr*
Robert Karika, *Manager*
EMP: 90
SALES (corp-wide): 41.8B **Publicly Held**
WEB: www.honeywell.com
SIC: 3724 Aircraft engines & engine parts
PA: Honeywell International Inc.
115 Tabor Rd
Morris Plains NJ 07950
973 455-2000

(G-6032)
HORSE SYSTEMS INC
151 Greenwood Rd (16123-1601)
PHONE..................................724 544-9686
EMP: 3
SALES (est): 147.1K **Privately Held**
SIC: 2834 Pharmaceutical preparations

(G-6033)
JJ KENNEDY INC (PA)
1790 Route 588 (16123-1422)
P.O. Box 69, Zelienople (16063-0069)
PHONE..................................724 452-6260
Paul R Rader, *President*
John H Rader, *Vice Pres*
John Rader, *Vice Pres*
James D Rader, *Treasurer*
Paul R Rader Jr, *Admin Sec*
EMP: 30
SQ FT: 6,600
SALES (est): 10.8MM **Privately Held**
WEB: www.jjkennedy.com
SIC: 3273 5983 7539 Ready-mixed concrete; fuel oil dealers; automotive repair shops

(G-6034)
RAPID TAG & WIRE CO
133 Eckert Stop Rd (16123-1203)
PHONE..................................724 452-7760

GEOGRAPHIC

J Christopher Spencer, *President*
EMP: 5
SALES (est): 500K **Privately Held**
SIC: 3315 Steel wire & related products

(G-6035)
TSO OF OHIO INC
115 West Rd (16123-1425)
PHONE..................................724 452-6161
Bob Strickler, *Principal*
Bob Massaro, *Manager*
EMP: 6
SALES (est): 481.4K **Privately Held**
SIC: 2491 Wood preserving

(G-6036)
VEKA HOLDINGS INC (DH)
Also Called: Veka Innovations
100 Veka Dr (16123-1424)
PHONE..................................724 452-1000
Joe Peilert, *President*
James H Druschel, *Corp Secy*
Glenn H Taborski, *Treasurer*
Tom Prince, *Sales Mgr*
EMP: 32
SQ FT: 600,000
SALES (est): 216.8MM
SALES (corp-wide): 1.2B **Privately Held**
WEB: www.vekadeck.com
SIC: 3089 Extruded finished plastic products
HQ: Veka Ag
Dieselstr. 8
Sendenhorst 48324
252 629-0

(G-6037)
VEKA INC
100 Veka Dr (16123-1424)
PHONE..................................800 654-5589
Joe Peilert, *President*
Edward Baxa, *Production*
Laura Thoma, *Purch Agent*
James H Druschel, *CFO*
Glenn H Taborski, *Treasurer*
◆ **EMP:** 500
SQ FT: 600,000
SALES (est): 199.9MM
SALES (corp-wide): 1.2B **Privately Held**
WEB: www.vekainc.com
SIC: 3089 Extruded finished plastic products
HQ: Veka Holdings, Inc.
100 Veka Dr
Fombell PA 16123

(G-6038)
VEKA WEST INC (DH)
100 Veka Dr (16123-1424)
PHONE..................................724 452-1000
Joe Peilert, *President*
James H Druschel, *Treasurer*
Dana Benson, *Admin Sec*
EMP: 3
SQ FT: 575,000
SALES (est): 12.8MM
SALES (corp-wide): 1.2B **Privately Held**
WEB: www.vekawest.com
SIC: 3089 Extruded finished plastic products

(G-6039)
WRIGHT MEAT PACKING CO INC
689 N Camp Run Rd (16123-1707)
PHONE..................................724 368-8571
William L Wright, *President*
James G Wright, *Vice Pres*
EMP: 7
SALES (est): 665.1K **Privately Held**
SIC: 2011 5421 Meat packing plants; meat markets, including freezer provisioners

Forbes Road
Westmoreland County

(G-6040)
AIR LIQUID SYSTEMS INC
315 Fire Station Rd (15633)
P.O. Box 218 (15633-0218)
PHONE..................................724 834-8090
Walter A Gaffney Jr, *President*
Ryan Gaffney, *Project Engr*
▲ **EMP:** 4
SQ FT: 9,000

SALES (est): 922K **Privately Held**
WEB: www.airliquidsystems.net
SIC: 3569 Filters, general line: industrial

Ford City
Armstrong County

(G-6041)
A & M MCHINING FABRICATION INC
296 Robbs Fording Rd (16226-5520)
PHONE..................................724 842-0314
Alan Weigand, *President*
EMP: 5
SQ FT: 5,000
SALES (est): 434.7K **Privately Held**
SIC: 3599 Machine shop, jobbing & repair

(G-6042)
ARMSTRONG PATTERNS & MFG
1509 Rearick Rd (16226-5235)
P.O. Box 69, Apollo (15613-0069)
PHONE..................................724 845-1452
EMP: 3
SALES: 230K **Privately Held**
SIC: 3543 Mfg Industrial Patterns

(G-6043)
BOCK WORKHOLDING INC
418 3rd Ave Ste 4 (16226-1018)
P.O. Box 391 (16226-0391)
PHONE..................................724 763-1776
Joseph R Cousins, *President*
▲ **EMP:** 6
SQ FT: 350
SALES: 998K **Privately Held**
WEB: www.bockworkholding.com
SIC: 3545 Machine tool attachments & accessories

(G-6044)
BUFFALO LIMESTONE INC
805 Garretts Run Rd (16226-7107)
PHONE..................................724 545-7478
Ronald Stitt, *President*
Brian Stantler, *Office Mgr*
EMP: 6
SALES (est): 750K **Privately Held**
SIC: 5032 3531 Aggregate; aggregate spreaders

(G-6045)
FORD CITY GUN WORKD
502 Main St (16226-1545)
PHONE..................................724 994-9501
Lisa Kondrick, *Principal*
EMP: 4
SALES (est): 129.5K **Privately Held**
SIC: 3484 3679 3599 3672 Guns (firearms) or gun parts, 30 mm. & below; harness assemblies for electronic use: wire or cable; machine & other job shop work; printed circuit boards; small arms ammunition

(G-6046)
FORD CITY NATIONAL BAKERY
821 5th Ave (16226-1108)
PHONE..................................724 763-7684
Michael Lukowsky, *Owner*
Nadine Lukowsky, *Manager*
EMP: 7
SALES (est): 375.1K **Privately Held**
SIC: 2051 5461 Bakery: wholesale or wholesale/retail combined; bakeries

(G-6047)
HERKULES USA CORPORATION (DH)
Also Called: KPM Herkules
101 River St (16226-1165)
P.O. Box 367 (16226-0367)
PHONE..................................724 763-2066
Samuel C Kube, *President*
Lorene Sukala, *General Mgr*
Howard Adams, *Vice Pres*
Robert Curler, *Vice Pres*
Albert Plekker, *Vice Pres*
▲ **EMP:** 108

SALES (est): 26MM
SALES (corp-wide): 133.9MM **Privately Held**
SIC: 3541 3599 7692 Grinding machines, metalworking; machine shop, jobbing & repair; welding repair
HQ: Maschinenfabrik Herkules Gmbh & Co. Kg
Eisenhuttenstr. 21
Siegen 57074
271 690-60

(G-6048)
HERKULES USA CORPORATION
208-209 Mac Industrial Pa (16226)
P.O. Box 367 (16226-0367)
PHONE..................................724 763-2066
Samuel Kube, *General Mgr*
EMP: 60
SALES (corp-wide): 133.9MM **Privately Held**
SIC: 3541 Grinding machines, metalworking
HQ: Herkules Usa Corporation
101 River St
Ford City PA 16226
724 763-2066

(G-6049)
LU-MAC INC
2021 State Route 66 (16226-4425)
PHONE..................................724 763-3750
William A Key, *President*
Patricia Key, *Corp Secy*
Tim A Key, *Vice Pres*
EMP: 16
SQ FT: 27,000
SALES: 1.5MM **Privately Held**
SIC: 3599 Machine shop, jobbing & repair

(G-6050)
NATURES BLEND WOOD PDTS INC
717 1st Ave (16226-1189)
PHONE..................................724 763-7057
Ted Wohlin, *President*
Chester Jonczak, *Corp Secy*
EMP: 100
SQ FT: 80,000
SALES (est): 11.1MM **Privately Held**
WEB: www.natures-blend.com
SIC: 2434 Wood kitchen cabinets

(G-6051)
PROJECTILE TUBE CLEANING INC
110 Valley View Dr (16226-9758)
PHONE..................................724 763-7633
Daniel Lyle, *President*
Edward Simmers, *Opers Staff*
Evan Lyle, *Marketing Staff*
▲ **EMP:** 25
SQ FT: 10,000
SALES (est): 3MM **Privately Held**
WEB: www.projectiletube.com
SIC: 3599 7349 3569 Boiler tube cleaners; chemical cleaning services; cleaning service, industrial or commercial; assembly machines, non-metalworking

(G-6052)
WALDRICH GMBH INC
101 River St (16226-1165)
P.O. Box 246 (16226-0246)
PHONE..................................724 763-3889
Christoph Thoma, *President*
Sam Kube, *CFO*
EMP: 1
SQ FT: 80,000
SALES (est): 3.1MM
SALES (corp-wide): 133.9MM **Privately Held**
SIC: 3531 3541 Laying equipment, rail; grinding machines, metalworking
HQ: Herkules Usa Corporation
101 River St
Ford City PA 16226
724 763-2066

Forest City
Susquehanna County

(G-6053)
FOREST CITY NEWS INC
636 Main St (18421-1430)
PHONE..................................570 785-3800
John P Kameen, *President*
Jennifer Butler, *Advt Staff*
Jean Matoushek, *Office Mgr*
Patricia Striefsky, *Admin Sec*
EMP: 4 **EST:** 1887
SQ FT: 3,000
SALES (est): 464.5K **Privately Held**
SIC: 2711 7215 Newspapers: publishing only, not printed on site; laundry, coin-operated

(G-6054)
KARTRI SALES COMPANY INC (PA)
Also Called: Mi-Jo Enterprises
100 Delaware St (18421-1432)
P.O. Box 126 (18421-0126)
PHONE..................................570 785-3365
Karen Goskowski, *President*
Michael T Goskowski, *Vice Pres*
Patricia Kubus, *Treasurer*
Trish Goskowski, *Sales Mgr*
Samantha Dolph, *Sales Executive*
▲ **EMP:** 25
SQ FT: 53,000
SALES (est): 8.7MM **Privately Held**
SIC: 2392 2395 2391 5023 Shower curtains: made from purchased materials; embroidery products, except schiffli machine; curtains & draperies; home furnishings; management services

(G-6055)
TERIS DELI & BAKERY LLC
104 Main St (18421-1434)
PHONE..................................570 785-7007
Teri Madrid, *Principal*
EMP: 3
SALES (est): 160.9K **Privately Held**
SIC: 2051 5149 Pies, bakery: except frozen; bakery products

Forksville
Sullivan County

(G-6056)
CURTIS LELJEDAL TRADING LOGGN
Also Called: Leljedal Fencing
Pa Rt 154 N (18616)
PHONE..................................570 924-3938
Curtis H Leljedal, *Owner*
EMP: 3
SALES (est): 225K **Privately Held**
SIC: 2411 1799 Logging camps & contractors; fence construction

Fort Loudon
Franklin County

(G-6057)
ATLAS COPCO SECOROC LLC
13278 Lincoln Way W (17224-9702)
P.O. Box 271 (17224-0271)
PHONE..................................717 369-3177
Keith Mackling, *Branch Mgr*
John Souder, *Manager*
EMP: 23
SQ FT: 24,000
SALES (corp-wide): 13.8B **Privately Held**
SIC: 3532 Drills, bits & similar equipment
HQ: Atlas Copco Secoroc Llc
1600 S Great Sw Pkwy
Grand Prairie TX 75051
972 337-9700

(G-6058)
EFFLANDS SAWMILL REPAIR S
10521 Richmond Rd (17224-9762)
PHONE..................................717 369-2391

Samuel D Effland, *Principal*
EMP: 3
SALES (est): 209.8K **Privately Held**
SIC: 2421 Sawmills & planing mills, general

(G-6059)
GISH LOGGING INC (PA)
Also Called: Hot Sticks
4980 Path Valley Rd (17224-9303)
P.O. Box 282 (17224-0282)
PHONE.................................717 369-2783
Ernie P Gish, *President*
Mike Jones, *Vice Pres*
▼ **EMP:** 34
SQ FT: 50,000
SALES (est): 10.5MM **Privately Held**
WEB: www.hotsticks.net
SIC: 5099 2499 Firewood; mulch, wood & bark

(G-6060)
ROSEWOOD COMPANY A PARTNERSHIP
7446 Path Valley Rd (17224-9738)
PHONE.................................717 349-2289
Carl Rosenberry, *Principal*
EMP: 4
SALES (est): 434.6K **Privately Held**
SIC: 2448 Wood pallets & skids

Fort Washington
Montgomery County

(G-6061)
ALFRED ANGELO - THE BRDES STD
1301 Virginia Dr (19034-3231)
PHONE.................................813 872-1881
EMP: 13
SALES (est): 1.2MM **Privately Held**
SIC: 2335 Mfg Women's/Misses' Dresses

(G-6062)
AMEDRA PHARMACEUTICALS LLC
Also Called: Amedra Specialty Generics
602 W Office Center Dr # 200
(19034-3274)
PHONE.................................215 259-3601
Ernest De Paolantonio, *CEO*
David Risk,
EMP: 13
SALES (est): 2.7MM
SALES (corp-wide): 1.6B **Publicly Held**
SIC: 2834 Pharmaceutical preparations
HQ: Tower Holdings, Inc.
30831 Huntwood Ave
Hayward CA 94544
510 240-6000

(G-6063)
AUXILIARY BUSINESS SERVICES
7157 Camp Hill Rd (19034-2205)
P.O. Box 254, Oreland (19075-0254)
PHONE.................................215 836-4833
Carol Block, *President*
EMP: 9
SALES (est): 1.6MM **Privately Held**
WEB: www.absrepro.com
SIC: 2752 Commercial printing, offset

(G-6064)
CANTWELL WOODWORKING LLC
Also Called: Philadelphia Custom Millwork
175 Commerce Dr Ste 500 (19034-2427)
PHONE.................................215 710-3030
Evan Campwell,
Kevin Cantwell,
EMP: 22
SALES (est): 977.9K **Privately Held**
SIC: 2431 Millwork

(G-6065)
COLONIAL AUTO SUPPLY CO (PA)
135 Commerce Dr (19034-2401)
P.O. Box 128 (19034-0128)
PHONE.................................215 643-3699
Joseph Pluck, *President*

Lawrence Pluck, *Corp Secy*
Kevin Pluck, *Admin Sec*
EMP: 235 **EST:** 1905
SALES (est): 16.6MM **Privately Held**
WEB: www.colonialautoparts.ca
SIC: 5013 3599 Automotive supplies; machine shop, jobbing & repair

(G-6066)
CONSTRUCTION EQUIPMENT GUIDE (PA)
470 Maryland Dr Ste 2 (19034-2513)
PHONE.................................215 885-2900
Edwin M Mc Keon Jr, *President*
Ted Mc Keon, *Vice Pres*
EMP: 30 **EST:** 1958
SQ FT: 6,000
SALES (est): 3.7MM **Privately Held**
WEB:
www.constructionequipmentguide.com
SIC: 2721 8611 2711 Trade journals: publishing only, not printed on site; business associations; newspapers

(G-6067)
CORRUGATED SERVICES CORP (PA)
Also Called: Amtech
515 Pennsylvania Ave # 100 (19034-3314)
PHONE.................................215 639-9540
Cosmo T Denicola, *President*
David Abrams, *Engineer*
Lisa Simmons, *Asst Controller*
Glenn Poynor, *Manager*
Gary Poindexter, *Programmer Anys*
EMP: 80 **EST:** 1981
SQ FT: 22,000
SALES (est): 9.9MM **Privately Held**
WEB: www.amtechsoftware.net
SIC: 7372 8742 Business oriented computer software; management consulting services

(G-6068)
EQ TECHNOLOGIC INC (PA)
500 Office Center Dr # 400 (19034-3219)
PHONE.................................215 891-9010
Dinesh Khaladkar, *President*
Joseph Garay, *Vice Pres*
EMP: 10
SALES (est): 30.9MM **Privately Held**
SIC: 7372 Business oriented computer software

(G-6069)
FORT WASHINGTON PHARMA LLC (PA)
500 Office Center Dr # 400 (19034-3219)
PHONE.................................800 279-7434
Andy Gesek,
EMP: 0
SQ FT: 80
SALES (est): 7.6MM **Privately Held**
SIC: 6719 3842 Investment holding companies, except banks; surgical appliances & supplies

(G-6070)
FOUNDATION SURGERY CENTER
467 Pennsylvania Ave # 202 (19034-3420)
PHONE.................................215 628-4300
Amanda Ricca, *Principal*
EMP: 30
SALES (est): 2.3MM **Privately Held**
SIC: 3841 Surgical & medical instruments

(G-6071)
GALLOP PRINTING
1227 Thomas Dr (19034-1646)
PHONE.................................215 542-0887
Howard Gallop, *Partner*
Joseph Gallop, *Partner*
EMP: 3
SQ FT: 350
SALES (est): 443K **Privately Held**
SIC: 2752 Commercial printing, lithographic

(G-6072)
GLOBAL HOME AUTOMATION LLC
7250 Hollywood Rd Ste 4 (19034-2016)
PHONE.................................484 686-7374
Harlan Lee King Jr,

EMP: 4
SALES (est): 226.1K **Privately Held**
SIC: 5043 3651 8731 Projection apparatus, motion picture & slide; home entertainment equipment, electronic; medical research, commercial

(G-6073)
GRANITE GLLRIA FABRICATION INC
425 Delaware Dr Ste C (19034-2732)
PHONE.................................215 283-0341
Preston Oles, *President*
▲ **EMP:** 6
SQ FT: 22,000
SALES (est): 950K **Privately Held**
SIC: 3281 Granite, cut & shaped

(G-6074)
HYUNDAI ROTEM USA CORPORATION
1300 Virginia Dr Ste 103 (19034-3266)
PHONE.................................215 227-6836
O Hyun Kim, *CEO*
Andrew Hyer, *Marketing Staff*
Seok Lee, *Manager*
▲ **EMP:** 15
SALES (est): 2.7MM
SALES (corp-wide): 1.9B **Privately Held**
SIC: 3743 Railroad equipment
PA: Hyundai Rotem Company
488 Changwon-Daero, Uichang-Gu
Changwon 51407
825 527-3134

(G-6075)
IMPAX LABORATORIES INC
Also Called: Global Pharmaceuticals
602 W Office Center Dr # 200
(19034-3274)
PHONE.................................215 289-2220
Barry Edwards, *Co-CEO*
EMP: 58
SALES (corp-wide): 1.6B **Publicly Held**
WEB: www.impaxlabs.com
SIC: 2834 Pharmaceutical preparations
HQ: Impax Laboratories, Llc
30831 Huntwood Ave
Hayward CA 94544
510 240-6000

(G-6076)
IMPAX LABORATORIES LLC
602 W Office Center Dr # 200
(19034-3274)
PHONE.................................215 558-4300
Carol Maimon, *Branch Mgr*
EMP: 58
SALES (corp-wide): 1.6B **Publicly Held**
SIC: 2834 Pharmaceutical preparations
HQ: Impax Laboratories, Llc
30831 Huntwood Ave
Hayward CA 94544
510 240-6000

(G-6077)
IRONRIDGE INC
7250 Hollywood Rd Ste 6 (19034-2016)
PHONE.................................800 227-9523
EMP: 6
SALES (corp-wide): 30.1MM **Privately Held**
SIC: 3444 Sheet metalwork
PA: Ironridge, Inc.
28357 Industrial Blvd
Hayward CA 94545
800 227-9523

(G-6078)
K&S INTERCONNECT INC (HQ)
1005 Virginia Dr (19034-3101)
PHONE.................................267 256-1725
Ross W Mangano, *Ch of Bd*
Carl Zane Close, *President*
Daniel J Hill, *COO*
Michael K Bonham, *Senior VP*
Henry P Scutoski, *Vice Pres*
EMP: 95
SQ FT: 84,000
SALES (est): 43.9MM
SALES (corp-wide): 809MM **Publicly Held**
WEB: www.antarescontech.com
SIC: 3825 5065 Test equipment for electronic & electrical circuits; electronic parts & equipment

PA: Kulicke And Soffa Industries, Inc.
1005 Virginia Dr
Fort Washington PA 19034
215 784-6000

(G-6079)
KAPPA MEDIA LLC (PA)
40 Skippack Pike (19034-1100)
PHONE.................................215 643-5800
Steve Rossi, *President*
EMP: 102
SALES (est): 7.1MM **Privately Held**
SIC: 2752 Commercial printing, lithographic

(G-6080)
KAPPA MEDIA GROUP INC (PA)
40 Skippack Pike (19034-1100)
PHONE.................................215 643-5800
Nick Karabots, *President*
William J Bonner, *Vice Pres*
William Mainwaring, *Treasurer*
Andrea Duloc, *Admin Sec*
EMP: 165
SALES (est): 149.5MM **Privately Held**
SIC: 2721 2741 5111 Magazines: publishing only, not printed on site; miscellaneous publishing; printing paper

(G-6081)
KULICKE AND SOFFA INDS INC (PA)
Also Called: Kulicke & Soffa
1005 Virginia Dr (19034-3101)
PHONE.................................215 784-6000
Garrett E Pierce, *Ch of Bd*
Fusen E Chen, *President*
Chan Pin Chong, *Senior VP*
Irene Lee, *Senior VP*
Deepak Sood, *Vice Pres*
EMP: 233 **EST:** 1951
SQ FT: 88,000
SALES: 889.1MM **Publicly Held**
WEB: www.kns.com
SIC: 3674 Semiconductors & related devices; integrated circuits, semiconductor networks, etc.

(G-6082)
LARON PHARMA INC
500 Office Center Dr # 400 (19034-3219)
PHONE.................................267 575-1470
Afoluso A Adesanya, *CEO*
Afoluso Adesanya, *CEO*
Adenekan H Adesanya, *President*
EMP: 15
SALES: 300MM **Privately Held**
SIC: 2834 5122 Pharmaceutical preparations; pharmaceuticals

(G-6083)
MCNEIL CONSMR PHARMACEUTICALS (DH)
7050 Camp Hill Rd (19034-2210)
PHONE.................................215 273-7700
James T Lenehan, *President*
EMP: 115
SALES (est): 46.1MM
SALES (corp-wide): 81.5B **Publicly Held**
WEB: www.pepcidenjoy.com
SIC: 2834 Druggists' preparations (pharmaceuticals)
HQ: Johnson & Johnson Consumer Inc.
199 Grandview Rd
Skillman NJ 08558
908 874-1000

(G-6084)
METALS USA INC
1300 Virginia Dr Ste 320 (19034-3223)
PHONE.................................215 540-8004
Lourenco Goncalves, *President*
EMP: 11
SALES (corp-wide): 11.5B **Publicly Held**
SIC: 3441 5051 Fabricated structural metal; metals service centers & offices
HQ: Metals Usa, Inc.
4901 Nw 17th Way Ste 405
Fort Lauderdale FL 33309
954 202-4000

(G-6085)
METALS USA INC
1300 Virginia Dr Ste 320 (19034-3223)
PHONE.................................215 540-8004
EMP: 11

SALES (corp-wide): 9.3B **Publicly Held**
SIC: 3441 Structural Metal Fabrication
HQ: Metals Usa, Inc.
2400 E Coml Blvd Ste 905
Fort Lauderdale FL 33309
954 202-4000

(G-6086)
MG FINANCIAL SERVICES INC
Also Called: Oak Systems
575 Virginia Dr Ste D (19034-2731)
PHONE.................................215 364-7555
Martin Klagholz, *Principal*
Gary Shank, *Vice Pres*
EMP: 30
SQ FT: 2,000
SALES: 1MM **Privately Held**
SIC: 3579 7389 Postage meters; financial
services

(G-6087)
NZINGANET INC
Also Called: Ubedesktop
500 Office Ct Dr Ste 400 (19034)
PHONE.................................877 709-6459
Carl Williams, *CEO*
Garth Reid, *COO*
EMP: 4
SALES (est): 856K **Privately Held**
SIC: 4813 7372 7379 ; prepackaged soft-
ware;

(G-6088)
PILLING COMPANY
420 Delaware Dr (19034-2711)
PHONE.................................215 643-2600
John E Mordock, *President*
EMP: 11 EST: 2010
SALES (est): 1.4MM **Privately Held**
SIC: 3841 Surgical & medical instruments

(G-6089)
RAM TECHNOLOGIES INC
275 Commerce Dr Ste 100 (19034-2413)
PHONE.................................215 654-8810
Robert Tulio, *President*
EMP: 50
SQ FT: 5,000
SALES (est): 6.5MM **Privately Held**
WEB: www.ramtechnologies.net
SIC: 7379 7372 7371 Computer related
consulting services; prepackaged soft-
ware; custom computer programming
services

(G-6090)
**RECIRCULATION
TECHNOLOGIES LLC**
550 Pinetown Rd Ste 210 (19034-2607)
PHONE.................................215 682-7099
Stuart Bryan, *CEO*
John Finley, *COO*
Michael Swindells, *Sales Staff*
EMP: 15
SALES (est): 806.2K **Privately Held**
SIC: 2842 7349 Specialty cleaning prepa-
rations; chemical cleaning services

(G-6091)
RTM VITAL SIGNS LLC
439 Dreshertown Rd (19034-3010)
PHONE.................................215 643-1286
Nance Dicciani, *CEO*
Nance K Dicciani, *President*
Jeffery Joseph, *President*
Kelsey Tarzia, *Principal*
Denise Devine, *CFO*
EMP: 4 EST: 2015
SALES (est): 208.5K **Privately Held**
SIC: 3845 Electromedical equipment

(G-6092)
SPECAC INC (DH)
414 Commerce Dr Ste 175 (19034-2621)
PHONE.................................215 793-4044
Paula Miller, *Finance*
EMP: 3
SQ FT: 16,000
SALES: 843.1K
SALES (corp-wide): 15.1MM **Privately
Held**
WEB: www.specac.com
SIC: 3826 Analytical instruments

(G-6093)
**TIMM MEDICAL TECHNOLOGIES
INC**
500 Office Center Dr # 400 (19034-3234)
PHONE.................................484 321-5900
Edward Fiorentino, *CEO*
Christine McManus Forte, *Director*
EMP: 50
SQ FT: 2,500
SALES (est): 6.1MM
SALES (corp-wide): 7.6MM **Privately
Held**
WEB: www.timmmedical.com
SIC: 3841 Diagnostic apparatus, medical
PA: Fort Washington Pharma Llc
500 Office Center Dr # 400
Fort Washington PA 19034
800 279-7434

(G-6094)
**TRANSPOREON GROUP
AMERICAS INC**
500 Office Center Dr # 400 (19034-3219)
PHONE.................................267 281-1555
Florian Dussler, *CEO*
EMP: 22
SALES (est): 768.9K **Privately Held**
SIC: 7372 4789 4731 Application com-
puter software; cargo loading & unloading
services; freight transportation arrange-
ment
HQ: Ticontract Gmbh
Heisinger Str. 12
Kempten (Allgau) 87437
831 575-8550

(G-6095)
VEEVA SYSTEMS INC
601 Office Center Dr # 100 (19034-3275)
PHONE.................................215 422-3356
Cheryl Jessen, *Accounts Exec*
Ryan Brennan, *Consultant*
Matthew Kopecky, *Consultant*
Jacqueline Ferenz, *Director*
EMP: 5 **Publicly Held**
SIC: 7372 7371 7379 Prepackaged soft-
ware; software programming applications;
computer related consulting services
PA: Veeva Systems Inc.
4280 Hacienda Dr
Pleasanton CA 94588

(G-6096)
VERUS SPORTS INC (PA)
1300 Virginia Dr Ste 401 (19034-3221)
PHONE.................................215 283-0153
Gary D Giegerich, *President*
Paul Giegerich, *Vice Pres*
Matthew Hartwig, *Vice Pres*
▲ EMP: 15
SQ FT: 4,000
SALES (est): 1.7MM **Privately Held**
WEB: www.dmisports.com
SIC: 3944 3949 5091 Darts & dart
games; dartboards & accessories; billiard
& pool equipment & supplies, general;
dartboards & accessories; billiard equip-
ment & supplies

(G-6097)
ZAKES CAKES
Also Called: Zakes Cakes & Cafe
444 S Bethlehem Pike (19034-2312)
PHONE.................................215 654-7600
Marlene Zakes, *Owner*
EMP: 5
SQ FT: 3,012
SALES: 150K **Privately Held**
SIC: 2051 Bakery: wholesale or whole-
sale/retail combined

Forty Fort
Luzerne County

(G-6098)
OUT ON A LIMB CREATIONS
140 Center St (18704-5050)
PHONE.................................570 287-3778
EMP: 3
SALES (est): 205.5K **Privately Held**
SIC: 3842 Limbs, artificial

(G-6099)
VALLEY PLASTICS INC
124 Welles St (18704-4949)
P.O. Box 1126, Kingston (18704-0126)
PHONE.................................570 287-7964
Robert Sabatini, *President*
EMP: 7 EST: 1963
SQ FT: 18,000
SALES: 750K **Privately Held**
SIC: 3089 Thermoformed finished plastic
products

Fountain Hill
Northampton County

(G-6100)
SAUCON SOURCE LLC
612 N Hoffert St (18015-4123)
PHONE.................................610 442-3370
Joshua Popichak, *Principal*
EMP: 4 EST: 2014
SALES (est): 173.1K **Privately Held**
SIC: 2711 Newspapers, publishing & print-
ing

Foxburg
Clarion County

(G-6101)
FOXBURG WINE CELLARS INC
65 Main St (16036)
P.O. Box 349 (16036-0349)
PHONE.................................724 659-0021
Arthur Steffee, *President*
EMP: 7
SALES (est): 622.1K **Privately Held**
SIC: 2084 Wines

Frackville
Schuylkill County

(G-6102)
AUTO DIESEL ELECTRIC INC
9 Starter Dr (17931-2702)
PHONE.................................570 874-2100
Dave Ferraiolo, *President*
Jeff Rush, *Executive*
EMP: 4
SQ FT: 4,800
SALES: 300K **Privately Held**
SIC: 7539 3694 Electrical services; engine
electrical equipment

(G-6103)
**BEAR RIDGE MCH &
FABRICATION**
10 S Eleanor Ave (17931-2348)
PHONE.................................570 874-4083
Michael Rich, *President*
John Wittig, *Engineer*
EMP: 25
SALES (est): 4.7MM **Privately Held**
WEB: www.brmf.net
SIC: 3599 Machine shop, jobbing & repair

(G-6104)
CITY SHIRT CO
242 Industrial Park Rd (17931-2701)
P.O. Box 13099, Reading (19612-3099)
PHONE.................................570 874-4251
Joe Boris, *Principal*
EMP: 5 EST: 1984
SALES (est): 434.4K **Privately Held**
SIC: 2254 Shirts & t-shirts (underwear),
knit

(G-6105)
**HOLLANDER SLEEP PRODUCTS
LLC**
32 Industrial Park Rd (17931)
PHONE.................................570 874-2114
Paul Fallon, *Branch Mgr*
EMP: 185

SALES (corp-wide): 927.1MM **Privately
Held**
WEB: www.hollander.com
SIC: 2392 Pillows, bed: made from purchased materials; comforters & quilts:
made from purchased materials; blanket
bags, plastic: made from purchased materials
PA: Hollander Sleep Products, Llc
901 W Yamato Rd Ste 250
Boca Raton FL 33431
561 997-6900

(G-6106)
KESSLER INDUSTRIES LLC
360 S 3rd St (17931-2039)
PHONE.................................570 590-2333
Russel Kessler, *Principal*
EMP: 3 EST: 2016
SALES (est): 162.6K **Privately Held**
SIC: 3999 Manufacturing industries

(G-6107)
ROSINI COAL INC
236 S Ballard (17931)
PHONE.................................570 874-2879
Karyn Mazur, *President*
EMP: 40 EST: 1973
SALES (est): 1.5MM **Privately Held**
SIC: 1241 Coal mining services

(G-6108)
WAGNER INDUSTRIES INC
6 Starter Dr (17931-2702)
PHONE.................................570 874-4400
Kenneth Wagner, *President*
John Mulhall, *COO*
Dolores Wagner, *Vice Pres*
EMP: 12 EST: 1968
SQ FT: 35,000
SALES (est): 1.7MM **Privately Held**
WEB: www.wagnerind.com
SIC: 3599 Machine & other job shop work

(G-6109)
**WASTE MANAGEMENT &
PROCESSORS**
51 Eleanor Ave (17931-2342)
P.O. Box K (17931-0609)
PHONE.................................570 874-2003
John Rich Jr, *President*
Michael Rich, *Admin Sec*
EMP: 50
SQ FT: 2,000
SALES (est): 5.9MM **Privately Held**
WEB: www.ultracleanfuels.com
SIC: 1231 1241 Recovery of anthracite
from culm banks; coal mining services

Franconia
Montgomery County

(G-6110)
**SHREDSTATION EXPRESS OF
MONTGO**
535 Hagey Rd (18924)
PHONE.................................215 723-1694
Jill Dietterich, *Principal*
EMP: 3
SALES (est): 231.3K **Privately Held**
SIC: 3559 Tire shredding machinery

(G-6111)
UNITED OFFSET
429 Harleysville Pike (18924)
PHONE.................................215 721-2251
Matthew Windfelder, *President*
EMP: 5
SQ FT: 2,000
SALES (est): 751.6K **Privately Held**
WEB: www.united-offset.com
SIC: 2752 Commercial printing, offset

Franklin
Venango County

(G-6112)
ABRILL INDUSTRIES
773 Meadville Pike (16323-6123)
PHONE.................................814 437-5354

G
E
O
G
R
A
P
H
I
C

Darry Brink, *Partner*
Merle Alden, *Partner*
William C Hill II, *Partner*
EMP: 5 **EST:** 1978
SQ FT: 3,800
SALES (est): 586.4K **Privately Held**
WEB: www.galaxyfcu.com
SIC: 3599 Machine shop, jobbing & repair

(G-6113)
AIRGAS USA LLC
984 Mercer Rd (16323-4632)
PHONE..............................814 437-2431
Daniel Pokorney, *General Mgr*
Danielle Pokorney, *Branch Mgr*
EMP: 4
SALES (corp-wide): 125.9MM **Privately Held**
WEB: www.us.linde-gas.com
SIC: 2813 5084 Industrial gases; welding machinery & equipment
HQ: Airgas Usa, Llc
259 N Radnor Chester Rd # 100
Radnor PA 19087
610 687-5253

(G-6114)
ALLEGHENY TOOL & SUPPLY INC
725 Grant St (16323-2219)
PHONE..............................814 437-7062
Joshua G Jolley, *President*
Jason Hanna, *Vice Pres*
George Jolley, *Vice Pres*
EMP: 15
SQ FT: 2,000
SALES (est): 4.2MM **Privately Held**
SIC: 3545 5085 Cutting tools for machine tools; industrial supplies

(G-6115)
ALLEGHENY URN COMPANY
4871 Us 322 (16323-7933)
PHONE..............................814 437-3208
EMP: 3
SALES (est): 138.7K **Privately Held**
SIC: 1411 Limestone & marble dimension stone

(G-6116)
BLUE OX TIMBER RESOURCES INC
6708 Us 322 (16323-8052)
PHONE..............................814 437-2019
Rodney Dodow, *President*
EMP: 12
SALES (est): 108.7K **Privately Held**
SIC: 2411 Peeler logs

(G-6117)
BORCHERS AMERICAS INC
Also Called: Omg
240 Two Mile Run Rd (16323-6250)
P.O. Box 111 (16323-0111)
PHONE..............................814 432-2125
Steve Flinchdaugh, *President*
EMP: 31
SALES (corp-wide): 1.4B **Privately Held**
SIC: 2869 Industrial organic chemicals
HQ: Borchers Americas, Inc.
811 Sharon Dr
Westlake OH 44145
440 899-2950

(G-6118)
C AND M SALES CO
1587 Pittsburgh Rd (16323-2011)
P.O. Box 710 (16323-0710)
PHONE..............................814 437-3095
John S Baron, *President*
Kayla Coryea, *QC Mgr*
Joseph I Opolka, *Admin Sec*
▲ **EMP:** 12
SQ FT: 10,000
SALES (est): 3.5MM **Privately Held**
SIC: 3569 5084 8742 Lubrication equipment, industrial; industrial machinery & equipment; business consultant

(G-6119)
CENTURY PROPELLER CORPORATION
687 Bucktail Rd (16323-7719)
PHONE..............................814 677-7100
Robert Eakin, *President*

EMP: 12
SQ FT: 18,000
SALES (est): 113.9K **Privately Held**
SIC: 3469 3366 Machine parts, stamped or pressed metal; propellers

(G-6120)
CNG ONE SOURCE INC
190 Oak Grove Cir (16323-3646)
PHONE..............................814 673-4980
Karen Teslovich, *President*
Darius Teslovich, *Vice Pres*
EMP: 10 **EST:** 2011
SALES (est): 700K **Privately Held**
SIC: 3599 Custom machinery

(G-6121)
COLBURN ORTHOPEDICS INC
302 Grant St (16323-2212)
PHONE..............................814 432-5252
Brian J Colburn, *President*
Judith Colburn, *Corp Secy*
EMP: 3
SALES (est): 277.4K **Privately Held**
SIC: 5999 3842 Orthopedic & prosthesis applications; limbs, artificial

(G-6122)
CONAIR GROUP INC
455 Allegheny Blvd (16323-6209)
P.O. Box 790 (16323-0790)
PHONE..............................814 437-6861
Larry Doyle, *President*
Matt Zelkovich, *General Mgr*
Doug Brewster, *Engineer*
Mark Hoopes, *Engineer*
Alice Castonguay, *Sales Mgr*
EMP: 24
SALES (corp-wide): 229.1MM **Privately Held**
SIC: 3826 Thermal analysis instruments, laboratory type
HQ: The Conair Group Inc
200 W Kensinger Dr # 100
Cranberry Township PA 16066
724 584-5500

(G-6123)
CRANBERRY BEVERAGE CORP
689 Bucktail Rd (16323-7719)
PHONE..............................814 437-7998
Robert Eakin, *CEO*
Tracy Eakin, *President*
EMP: 3
SALES (est): 182.9K **Privately Held**
SIC: 2082 Beer (alcoholic beverage)

(G-6124)
DB & S CABINETS
1728 Keely Rd (16323-6622)
PHONE..............................814 437-2529
Bruce P Smith, *Principal*
EMP: 8 **EST:** 2001
SALES (est): 766.5K **Privately Held**
SIC: 2434 Wood kitchen cabinets

(G-6125)
FRANKLIN BRINE TREATMENT CORP (PA)
5148 Us 322 (16323-7944)
PHONE..............................814 437-3593
Paul Hart, *President*
EMP: 5
SALES (est): 1.4MM **Privately Held**
SIC: 1389 Impounding & storing salt water, oil & gas field

(G-6126)
FRANKLIN BRONZE & ALLOY CO INC
655 Grant St (16323-2217)
PHONE..............................814 437-6891
Bob Barber, *COO*
John Barber, *Treasurer*
Ron Tarr, *Manager*
Rick Motter, *Manager*
Stacy Reiser, *Manager*
EMP: 18
SALES (corp-wide): 71.7MM **Privately Held**
WEB: www.franklinbronze.com
SIC: 3366 Bronze foundry

HQ: Franklin Bronze Precision Components, Llc
655 Grant St
Franklin PA 16323
814 437-6891

(G-6127)
FRANKLIN BRONZE PRECISION COMP (DH)
655 Grant St (16323-2217)
PHONE..............................814 437-6891
RE Barber, *President*
Jt Barber, *Corp Secy*
Lois Barber, *Vice Pres*
MA Barber, *Vice Pres*
James Bankson, *CFO*
▲ **EMP:** 70
SQ FT: 25,000
SALES (est): 16.3MM
SALES (corp-wide): 71.7MM **Privately Held**
WEB: www.franklinbronze.com
SIC: 3366 3364 Bronze foundry; nonferrous die-castings except aluminum
HQ: Wall Colmonoy Corporation
101 W Girard Ave
Madison Heights MI 48071
248 585-6400

(G-6128)
FRANKLIN INDUSTRIES CO
645 Atlantic Ave (16323-2252)
P.O. Box 671 (16323-0671)
PHONE..............................814 437-3726
Daniel E Hill, *CEO*
Peter D Walsh, *President*
Edward Van Dyke, *Engineer*
Dennis W Savitsky, *Treasurer*
EMP: 258
SQ FT: 200,000
SALES (est): 47.1MM **Privately Held**
SIC: 3312 Blast furnaces & steel mills

(G-6129)
FRANKLIN INDUSTRIES INC
Also Called: Franklin Steel Div
600 Atlantic Ave (16323-2298)
P.O. Box 671 (16323-0671)
PHONE..............................814 437-3726
John F O'Toole, *President*
John R McGarrity, *Corp Secy*
W G Miller, *Vice Pres*
Bernard W Nerlich, *Vice Pres*
W Brady, *Treasurer*
▼ **EMP:** 385
SQ FT: 300,000
SALES (est): 64MM **Privately Held**
SIC: 3312 Fence posts, iron & steel; bars & bar shapes, steel, hot-rolled

(G-6130)
FRANKLIN INVESTMENT CORP
Also Called: Franklin Industries
645 Atlantic Ave (16323-2252)
P.O. Box 671 (16323-0671)
PHONE..............................814 437-3726
Nathan Kovalchick, *President*
Gary Harkleroad, *Exec VP*
Gregory Stokes, *Exec VP*
Judy Kovalchick, *Vice Pres*
▼ **EMP:** 150
SALES (est): 28MM **Privately Held**
WEB: www.franklinindustriesco.com
SIC: 3312 Blast furnaces & steel mills

(G-6131)
FRENCHCREEK PRODUCTION INC
100 N 13th St (16323-2352)
PHONE..............................814 437-1808
Carl Wible, *President*
Frank Davison, *Vice Pres*
Chris Williams, *Mfg Mgr*
Benjamin Gray, *Engineer*
Jeffrey Greksa, *Mktg Dir*
▲ **EMP:** 25
SQ FT: 10,000
SALES (est): 5MM **Privately Held**
WEB: www.frenchcreekproduction.com
SIC: 3199 Safety belts, leather; leather belting & strapping

(G-6132)
GERALD BOUGHNER
Also Called: Eclipse Electric
508 Buffalo St (16323-1002)
PHONE..............................814 432-3519
Fax: 814 432-3519
EMP: 3 **EST:** 1950
SQ FT: 2,700
SALES (est): 317.3K **Privately Held**
SIC: 7694 Repairs Electrical Motors

(G-6133)
GRAHAM MACHINE INC
1581 Pittsburgh Rd (16323-2011)
P.O. Box 1140 (16323-5140)
PHONE..............................814 437-7190
Scott Graham, *President*
James Graham, *Vice Pres*
EMP: 26
SQ FT: 6,450
SALES: 2.7MM **Privately Held**
SIC: 3599 Machine shop, jobbing & repair

(G-6134)
HARRINGTON MACHINE AND TOOL CO
1027 Chestnut St (16323-1251)
PHONE..............................814 432-7339
Tom Harrington, *President*
Sue Grampp, *Admin Sec*
EMP: 32
SQ FT: 40,000
SALES (est): 6.4MM **Privately Held**
WEB: www.harringtonmachine.com
SIC: 3599 Machine shop, jobbing & repair

(G-6135)
HONEYWELL INTERNATIONAL INC
1345 15th St (16323-1941)
PHONE..............................814 432-2118
Sha Dhivyansh, *Branch Mgr*
EMP: 147
SALES (corp-wide): 41.8B **Publicly Held**
SIC: 3724 Aircraft engines & engine parts
PA: Honeywell International Inc.
115 Tabor Rd
Morris Plains NJ 07950
973 455-2000

(G-6136)
IA CONSTRUCTION CORPORATION (DH)
24 Gibb Rd (16323-6225)
P.O. Box 568 (16323-0568)
PHONE..............................814 432-3184
Robert Doucet, *President*
Harry Hopkins, *Assistant VP*
Donald Rosenbarger, *Vice Pres*
Dennis States, *Vice Pres*
Fred Shelton, *Treasurer*
EMP: 40 **EST:** 1924
SQ FT: 10,000
SALES (est): 74.5MM
SALES (corp-wide): 83.5MM **Privately Held**
WEB: www.iaconstruction.com
SIC: 1611 2951 1622 1623 General contractor, highway & street construction; road materials, bituminous (not from refineries); bridge construction; highway construction, elevated; water main construction; sewer line construction
HQ: Barrett Industries Corporation
73 Headquarters Plz
Morristown NJ 07960
973 533-1001

(G-6137)
IA CONSTRUCTION CORPORATION
Also Called: I A Construction Western PA
62 Old City Franklin Rd (16323)
PHONE..............................724 368-2140
Harry Hopkins, *Manager*
EMP: 40
SALES (corp-wide): 83.5MM **Privately Held**
WEB: www.iaconstruction.com
SIC: 2951 1771 Asphalt & asphaltic paving mixtures (not from refineries); concrete work

HQ: Ia Construction Corporation
24 Gibb Rd
Franklin PA 16323
814 432-3184

(G-6138)
IPEG INC
455 Allegheny Blvd (16323-6209)
PHONE..................................814 437-6861
Ed Kline, *Purch Mgr*
Jeff Micichi, *Manager*
Chuck Mc Elhinny, *VP Info Sys*
EMP: 180
SALES (corp-wide): 229.1MM **Privately Held**
SIC: 3535 Belt conveyor systems, general industrial use
HQ: Ipeg, Inc.
200 W Kensinger Dr # 100
Cranberry Township PA 16066
724 584-5500

(G-6139)
IPEG INC
455 Allegheny Blvd (16323-6209)
PHONE..................................814 437-6861
Libby Stover, *Branch Mgr*
EMP: 10
SALES (corp-wide): 229.1MM **Privately Held**
WEB: www.ipec.com
SIC: 3089 Coloring & finishing of plastic products
HQ: Ipeg, Inc.
200 W Kensinger Dr # 100
Cranberry Township PA 16066
724 584-5500

(G-6140)
IPEG INC
455 Allegheny Blvd (16323-6209)
PHONE..................................814 437-6861
Chris Keller, *Principal*
EMP: 31
SALES (corp-wide): 229.1MM **Privately Held**
SIC: 3559 Plastics working machinery; robots, molding & forming plastics
HQ: Ipeg, Inc.
200 W Kensinger Dr # 100
Cranberry Township PA 16066
724 584-5500

(G-6141)
J-M MANUFACTURING COMPANY INC
315 Grant St (16323-2211)
PHONE..................................814 432-2166
David Slawson, *Manager*
EMP: 140
SALES (corp-wide): 1B **Privately Held**
SIC: 2821 3084 Polyvinyl chloride resins (PVC); plastics pipe
PA: J-M Manufacturing Company, Inc.
5200 W Century Blvd
Los Angeles CA 90045
800 621-4404

(G-6142)
JOY GLOBAL INC
Also Called: Joy Mining
120 Liberty St (16323-1066)
P.O. Box 791 (16323-0791)
PHONE..................................814 432-1202
Michael W Sutherlin, *Principal*
Eric A Nielsen, *Exec VP*
James M Sullivan, *Exec VP*
Dennis R Winkleman, *Exec VP*
▲ EMP: 183
SALES: 40K **Privately Held**
SIC: 3532 Mining machinery

(G-6143)
JOY GLOBAL UNDERGROUND MIN LLC
Rr 8 Box North (16323)
PHONE..................................814 676-8531
Terry Nicola, *Branch Mgr*
EMP: 80
SALES (corp-wide): 23.4B **Privately Held**
SIC: 3532 Mining machinery
HQ: Joy Global Underground Mining Llc
40 Pennwood Pl Ste 100
Warrendale PA 15086
724 779-4500

(G-6144)
JOY GLOBAL UNDERGROUND MIN LLC
325 Buffalo St (16323-1040)
PHONE..................................814 432-1647
Ralph Jones, *Manager*
EMP: 60
SALES (corp-wide): 23.4B **Privately Held**
SIC: 3532 Mining machinery
HQ: Joy Global Underground Mining Llc
40 Pennwood Pl Ste 100
Warrendale PA 15086
724 779-4500

(G-6145)
JOY GLOBAL UNDERGROUND MIN LLC
120 Liberty St (16323-1066)
PHONE..................................814 437-5731
Henrey Klinar, *Branch Mgr*
EMP: 150
SALES (corp-wide): 23.4B **Privately Held**
SIC: 3532 Mining machinery
HQ: Joy Global Underground Mining Llc
40 Pennwood Pl Ste 100
Warrendale PA 15086
724 779-4500

(G-6146)
LAKE TOOL INC
190 Howard St Ste 400 (16323-2344)
PHONE..................................814 374-4401
Tina Lake, *President*
Guy Lake, *Vice Pres*
EMP: 5
SQ FT: 5,000
SALES (est): 300K **Privately Held**
SIC: 3544 Special dies & tools

(G-6147)
LATROBE SPECIALTY MTLS CO LLC
1680 Debence Dr (16323-2048)
PHONE..................................814 432-8575
Doug Kurtd, *Manager*
EMP: 60
SALES (corp-wide): 2.1B **Publicly Held**
SIC: 3312 Blast furnaces & steel mills
HQ: Latrobe Specialty Metals Company, Llc
2626 Ligonier St
Latrobe PA 15650
724 537-7711

(G-6148)
LIBERTY ELECTRONICS INC
189 Howard St (16323-2347)
PHONE..................................814 432-7505
John Dumot, *President*
Jacqueline Damico, *Business Mgr*
Scott Anderson, *Vice Pres*
Rhonda Exley, *Production*
Matthew Farren, *Production*
▲ EMP: 295
SQ FT: 46,000
SALES (est): 75.8MM **Privately Held**
WEB: www.libertyelectronics.com
SIC: 3679 5051 Harness assemblies for electronic use: wire or cable; miscellaneous nonferrous products

(G-6149)
MARTINOS DELICATESSEN INC
1218 15th St (16323-1942)
PHONE..................................814 432-2525
Fax: 814 432-8849
EMP: 15
SQ FT: 12,000
SALES (est): 1.1MM **Privately Held**
SIC: 3599 Mfg Industrial Machinery

(G-6150)
NEAC COMPRESSOR SVCS USA INC
191 Howard St Ste 204 (16323-2387)
PHONE..................................814 437-3711
Laura Phillips, *Buyer*
Robert Salzer, *Accounts Mgr*
Betty Hollowell, *Sales Associate*
Laney Tran, *Sales Associate*
Dave Pryer, *Branch Mgr*
EMP: 5

SALES (corp-wide): 263MM **Privately Held**
SIC: 5075 3563 3561 Compressors, air conditioning; air & gas compressors; pumps & pumping equipment
HQ: Neac Compressor Services Usa, Inc.
1502 E Summitry Cir
Katy TX 77449

(G-6151)
PERPETUAL ENTERPRISES INC
Also Called: Perpetual Powder Coting
190 Howard St Ste 406 (16323-2344)
PHONE..................................814 437-3705
Kin Hoff, *Branch Mgr*
EMP: 6
SALES (corp-wide): 1.2MM **Privately Held**
SIC: 2522 Office furniture, except wood
PA: Perpetual Enterprises Inc
2511 Beaver Grade Rd
Coraopolis PA 15108
412 299-6356

(G-6152)
PIONEER ELECTRIC SUPPLY CO INC (PA)
405 Allegheny Blvd (16323-6209)
P.O. Box 348 (16323-0348)
PHONE..................................814 437-1342
Victor H Garmong, *President*
Jeffrey Potter, *Vice Pres*
Todd D Plowman, *Treasurer*
Kevin L Garmong, *Admin Sec*
EMP: 9 EST: 1973
SQ FT: 10,000
SALES (est): 3.4MM **Privately Held**
WEB: www.pioneerelec.com
SIC: 5211 5063 3444 Electrical construction materials; electrical supplies; sheet metalwork

(G-6153)
POWDERCO INC
Also Called: Perpetual Powder Coating
190 Howard St Ste 406 (16323-2344)
PHONE..................................814 437-3705
Paul J Lowers, *President*
Patricia Lowers, *Corp Secy*
Michael Hughes, *Vice Pres*
EMP: 7 EST: 2000
SQ FT: 17,000
SALES (est): 821.9K **Privately Held**
SIC: 3599 Machine shop, jobbing & repair

(G-6154)
RAPID GRANULATOR INC
455 Allegheny Blvd (16323-6209)
PHONE..................................814 437-6861
EMP: 10
SALES (corp-wide): 5.8B **Privately Held**
SIC: 3559 Recycling machinery
HQ: Rapid Granulator Inc.
555 W Park Rd
Leetsdale PA 15056
724 584-5220

(G-6155)
RAPID REACTION INC
1618 Debence Dr (16323-2050)
PHONE..................................814 432-9832
Frank Ditzenberger, *CEO*
Jeffrey Latchaw, *Treasurer*
EMP: 13
SQ FT: 5,000
SALES: 500K **Privately Held**
WEB: www.rapidreactioninc.com
SIC: 3449 Miscellaneous metalwork

(G-6156)
SENECA ENTERPRISES INC (PA)
1642 Debence Dr (16323-2050)
P.O. Box 1211 (16323-5211)
PHONE..................................814 432-7890
Dennis Pascarella, *CEO*
Randy L Hicks, *President*
Robert Puleo, *Vice Pres*
Joseph Schwabenbauer, *Vice Pres*
Edward Mc Mullen, *Admin Sec*
EMP: 9
SALES (est): 6.1MM **Privately Held**
WEB: www.senecaprinting.com
SIC: 2752 Tickets, lithographed

(G-6157)
SENECA PRINTING & LABEL INC
Also Called: Seneca Printing Express & Dist
191 Howard St Ste 302 (16323-2357)
PHONE..................................814 437-5364
Jeffrey Steigerwald, *President*
EMP: 70
SALES (corp-wide): 734.8MM **Privately Held**
WEB: www.salemlabel.com
SIC: 2752 Commercial printing, offset
HQ: Seneca Printing & Label, Inc.
1642 Debence Dr
Franklin PA 16323
814 432-7890

(G-6158)
SENECA PRINTING EXPRESS INC
191 Howard St Ste 302 (16323-2357)
PHONE..................................814 437-5364
Jeffrey Steigerwald, *President*
Earnest McAin, *Vice Pres*
EMP: 6
SALES: 650K **Privately Held**
WEB: www.senecaprintingexpress.com
SIC: 2752 Commercial printing, offset

(G-6159)
SHAW INDUSTRIES INC
561 Allegheny Blvd (16323-6211)
P.O. Box 591 (16323-0591)
PHONE..................................814 432-0954
Peggy A Lang, *President*
Steve Knight, *General Mgr*
EMP: 30 EST: 1941
SQ FT: 50,000
SALES (est): 7.1MM **Privately Held**
WEB: www.shawindustry.com
SIC: 3544 3599 Dies, plastics forming; machine shop, jobbing & repair

(G-6160)
SIGELOCK SYSTEMS LLC
191 Howard St Ste 318 (16323-2389)
PHONE..................................814 673-2791
John Fink, *Branch Mgr*
EMP: 3
SALES (corp-wide): 1.1MM **Privately Held**
SIC: 3491 Fire hydrant valves
PA: Sigelock Systems, Llc
3205 Lawson Blvd
Oceanside NY 11572
888 744-3562

(G-6161)
SPECIALTY FABRICATION AND POWD
Also Called: Sfpc
455 Allegheny Blvd (16323-6209)
P.O. Box 790 (16323-0790)
PHONE..................................814 432-6406
Janet Stewart, *Human Res Mgr*
Rodney C Griffin, *Mng Member*
▲ EMP: 95
SQ FT: 40,000
SALES (est): 16MM **Privately Held**
WEB: www.specfab.com
SIC: 1799 3441 Coating, caulking & weather, water & fireproofing; fabricated structural metal

(G-6162)
SPECIALTY FITNESS SYSTEMS LLC
Also Called: Sfs
455 Allegheny Blvd (16323-6209)
P.O. Box 790 (16323-0790)
PHONE..................................814 432-6406
Rodney Griffin,
Melissa Griffin,
EMP: 3
SQ FT: 40,000
SALES (est): 268.9K **Privately Held**
SIC: 3949 Exercise equipment

(G-6163)
SPERIAN FALL PROTECTION INC
Also Called: Miller By Honeywell
1345 15th St (16323-1998)
PHONE..................................814 432-2118

▲ = Import ▼=Export
◆ =Import/Export

Raymond R Quirk, *President*
Richard L Cox, *Vice Pres*
Daniel K Murphy, *Treasurer*
John M Quttmeyer, *Admin Sec*
▲ **EMP:** 140
SALES (est): 19.7MM
SALES (corp-wide): 41.8B **Publicly Held**
SIC: 3199 Safety belts, leather
HQ: Honeywell Safety Products Usa, Inc.
2711 Centerville Rd
Wilmington DE 19808
302 636-5401

(G-6164)
THERMAL CARE INC
455 Allegheny Blvd (16323-6209)
PHONE..............................724 584-5500
EMP: 6 **EST:** 2017
SALES (est): 651.2K **Privately Held**
SIC: 3585 Refrigeration & heating equipment

(G-6165)
TITUSVILLE FABRICATORS INC
191 Howard St Ste 203 (16323-2387)
PHONE..............................814 432-2551
Roy Blair, *Branch Mgr*
EMP: 20
SQ FT: 100
SALES (corp-wide): 9.1MM **Privately Held**
SIC: 3312 Bar, rod & wire products
PA: Titusville Enterprises, Inc.
700 Blaw Ave Ste 300
Pittsburgh PA 15238
412 826-8140

(G-6166)
UHL TECHNOLOGIES LLC
127 Lamberton St (16323-2935)
P.O. Box 1059 (16323-5059)
PHONE..............................814 437-6346
George Uhl, *President*
▼ **EMP:** 5
SALES (est): 313.6K **Privately Held**
SIC: 3545 Machine tool accessories

(G-6167)
VENANGO STEEL INC
1655 Pittsburgh Rd (16323)
PHONE..............................814 437-9353
Michael Ruhlman, *President*
EMP: 26
SQ FT: 80,000
SALES (est): 5.7MM **Privately Held**
WEB: www.venangosteel.com
SIC: 3441 Fabricated structural metal

(G-6168)
WEAVER GLEN A & SON LLC
823 Congress Hill Rd (16323-3613)
PHONE..............................814 432-3013
Paul Weaver, *Mng Member*
Wilma Weaver, *Admin Sec*
Glenn A Weaver,
EMP: 3
SALES (est): 311.5K **Privately Held**
SIC: 1382 Oil & gas exploration services

(G-6169)
WELDING TECHNOLOGIES INC
561 Allegheny Blvd (16323-6211)
P.O. Box 1184, Oil City (16301-0684)
PHONE..............................814 432-0954
David I Fry, *President*
Panni L Fry, *Vice Pres*
Cary D Hall, *Vice Pres*
Luanne Amfler, *Admin Sec*
EMP: 15
SALES (est): 3.8MM **Privately Held**
SIC: 3449 Miscellaneous metalwork

(G-6170)
WOLBERT WELDING INC
191 Howard St Ste 330 (16323-2389)
PHONE..............................814 437-2870
Greg Wolbert, *President*
EMP: 7
SALES (est): 621.5K **Privately Held**
SIC: 7692 Welding repair

Frederick
Montgomery County

(G-6171)
ATOMIC INDUSTRIES INC
2079 Big Rd (19435)
P.O. Box 279 (19435-0279)
PHONE..............................610 754-6400
Louis P Farrell, *President*
Susan Heid, *Vice Pres*
EMP: 13 **EST:** 1962
SQ FT: 8,200
SALES (est): 1.9MM **Privately Held**
SIC: 3356 Lead & lead alloy bars, pipe, plates, shapes, etc.

Fredericksburg
Lebanon County

(G-6172)
BLATTS PATTERN SHOP
760 Meckville Rd (17026-9615)
PHONE..............................717 933-5633
Keith Blatt, *President*
R W Blatt, *General Mgr*
Richard W Blatt, *General Mgr*
Carol Blatt, *Treasurer*
Richard Blatt, *Sales Staff*
EMP: 18
SQ FT: 6,500
SALES (est): 3MM **Privately Held**
WEB: www.blattspatternshop.com
SIC: 3543 3544 Foundry cores; special dies & tools

(G-6173)
CRAYOLA LLC
Also Called: Distribution Center
2869 Route 22 (17026)
PHONE..............................610 253-6271
EMP: 363
SALES (corp-wide): 3.3B **Privately Held**
SIC: 3952 Lead pencils & art goods
HQ: Crayola Llc
1100 Church Ln
Easton PA 18040
610 253-6272

(G-6174)
FARMERS PRIDE INC (HQ)
Also Called: Bell & Evans
154 W Main St (17026-9510)
P.O. Box 39 (17026-0039)
PHONE..............................717 865-6626
J Michael Good, *CEO*
Scott Sechler, *President*
Daniel Chirico, *CFO*
▲ **EMP:** 1000 **EST:** 1939
SQ FT: 180,000
SALES (est): 180.7MM **Privately Held**
WEB: www.bellandevans.com
SIC: 2015 Chicken, slaughtered & dressed
PA: Sechler Family Foods, Inc.
154 W Main St
Fredericksburg PA 17026
717 865-6626

(G-6175)
HAIN PURE PROTEIN CORPORATION (HQ)
220 N Center St (17026-9723)
P.O. Box 10 (17026-0010)
PHONE..............................717 865-2136
Joe Tepippo, *President*
Jenny Schenk, *Sales Staff*
Paula Crumpley, *Manager*
Steve Milwicz, *Analyst*
EMP: 186 **EST:** 1919
SQ FT: 3,000
SALES (est): 53.9MM **Publicly Held**
WEB: www.freebirdchicken.com
SIC: 2015 Poultry, slaughtered & dressed

(G-6176)
SECHLER FAMILY FOODS INC (PA)
154 W Main St (17026-9510)
P.O. Box 39 (17026-0039)
PHONE..............................717 865-6626
Scott I Sechler, *President*

Mark Blazek, *Principal*
Daniel P Chirico, *Treasurer*
EMP: 16
SALES (est): 180.7MM **Privately Held**
SIC: 2015 Chicken, slaughtered & dressed

(G-6177)
VERLS SALADS INC
Rr 343 (17026)
PHONE..............................717 865-2771
Gary L Gingrich, *President*
Scott Gingrich, *Vice Pres*
Keith Gingrich, *Treasurer*
Alberta Gingrich, *Admin Sec*
EMP: 12
SQ FT: 5,000
SALES (est): 925.4K **Privately Held**
SIC: 2099 Salads, fresh or refrigerated

Fredericktown
Washington County

(G-6178)
RUDYS FABRICATING & MCH INC
40 Fishpot Run Rd (15333)
PHONE..............................724 377-1425
Robert Rudy, *President*
▲ **EMP:** 4
SQ FT: 28,000
SALES: 350K **Privately Held**
SIC: 3599 Machine shop, jobbing & repair

Fredonia
Mercer County

(G-6179)
BONSAL AMERICAN INC
97 Main St (16124)
P.O. Box 66 (16124-0066)
PHONE..............................724 475-2511
David Greggs, *Opers-Prdtn-Mfg*
Viola Harpst, *Clerk*
EMP: 28
SALES (corp-wide): 29.7B **Privately Held**
WEB: www.bonsalamerican.com
SIC: 3272 Concrete products
HQ: Bonsal American, Inc.
625 Griffith Rd Ste 100
Charlotte NC 28217
704 525-1621

(G-6180)
GRACE INDUSTRIES INC (PA)
305 Bend Hill Rd (16124-1903)
PHONE..............................724 962-9231
James Campman, *President*
Paul Emmett, *COO*
Grace Campman, *Vice Pres*
John Campman, *Vice Pres*
Robert Campman, *Vice Pres*
EMP: 42
SQ FT: 16,000
SALES (est): 8.5MM **Privately Held**
WEB: www.graceindustries.com
SIC: 3829 Gas detectors

(G-6181)
J C MOORE INDUSTRIES INC (PA)
152 2nd St (16124-2928)
PHONE..............................724 475-3185
Gary A Rhodes, *President*
Christopher Rhodes, *Vice Pres*
Brian Rhodes, *Shareholder*
Sandy Gbur, *Admin Sec*
EMP: 10
SQ FT: 11,000
SALES (est): 1.2MM **Privately Held**
SIC: 3713 3599 2421 Truck bodies (motor vehicles); machine shop, jobbing & repair; sawmills & planing mills, general

(G-6182)
J C MOORE INDUSTRIES SALES
152 2nd St (16124-2928)
P.O. Box 26 (16124-0026)
PHONE..............................724 475-3185
Gary A Rhodes, *President*
Christopher J Rhodes, *Vice Pres*

Bryan A Rhodes, *Admin Sec*
EMP: 8
SQ FT: 8,200
SALES: 500K **Privately Held**
SIC: 3713 Truck bodies (motor vehicles)

(G-6183)
J C MOORE SALES CORP
152 2nd St (16124-2928)
PHONE..............................724 475-4605
Gary Rhodes, *President*
Chris Rhodes, *Vice Pres*
Bryan Rhodes, *Admin Sec*
EMP: 4
SQ FT: 8,000
SALES (est): 320.7K **Privately Held**
SIC: 3713 7692 Truck bodies & parts; welding repair

(G-6184)
J C& WELL SERVICES INC
1554 N Perry Hwy (16124-2714)
P.O. Box 486 (16124-0486)
PHONE..............................724 475-4881
Fax: 724 475-4882
EMP: 50 **Publicly Held**
SIC: 1389 Oil/Gas Field Services
HQ: C&J Well Services, Inc.
3990 Rogerdale Rd
Houston TX 77042
281 874-0035

(G-6185)
JOHN KOLLER AND SON INC
Also Called: Fairview Swiss Cheese
1734 Perry Hwy (16124-2720)
PHONE..............................724 475-4154
Richard Koller, *President*
Mary A Koller, *Admin Sec*
▲ **EMP:** 10 **EST:** 1957
SQ FT: 20,000
SALES (est): 1.5MM **Privately Held**
SIC: 2022 Natural cheese

(G-6186)
LENGYEL ELECTRIC
1657 Mercer Rd (16124-1611)
PHONE..............................724 475-2045
Jason F Lengyel, *Principal*
EMP: 4
SALES (est): 418.8K **Privately Held**
SIC: 3699 1731 Electrical equipment & supplies; electrical work

(G-6187)
TOP NOTCH PRODUCTS INC
109 2nd St (16124-2905)
P.O. Box 33 (16124-0033)
PHONE..............................724 475-2341
Richard L Buchanan, *President*
Linda Sunderland, *Corp Secy*
George Benninghoff, *Vice Pres*
EMP: 5
SALES (est): 685.5K **Privately Held**
SIC: 3088 5023 1799 Bathroom fixtures, plastic; kitchenware; counter top installation

---

Freeburg
Snyder County

(G-6188)
COLONIAL FURNITURE COMPANY
St Frnt Front (17827)
PHONE..............................570 374-6016
Dennis J Vanbenthuysen, *President*
Judy Vanbenthuysen, *Corp Secy*
EMP: 65 **EST:** 1959
SQ FT: 120,000
SALES (est): 7.1MM **Privately Held**
SIC: 5712 2511 Furniture stores; wood bedroom furniture

Freedom
Beaver County

(G-6189)
ECONOMY METAL INC
340 Dunlap Hill Rd (15042-2508)
PHONE....................724 869-2887
Dennis Melnick, *President*
Charles Melnick, *Treasurer*
EMP: 6
SQ FT: 1,200
SALES (est): 974.8K **Privately Held**
SIC: 3441 Fabricated structural metal

(G-6190)
FRESH FOODS
MANUFACTURING
2500 Lovi Rd (15042-9398)
PHONE....................724 683-3639
EMP: 20
SALES (est): 2.7MM **Privately Held**
SIC: 5411 2051 2035 Ret Groceries Mfg
Bread/Related Products Mfg
Pickles/Sauces/Dressing

(G-6191)
MITSUBISHI ELC PWR PDTS INC
110 Commerce Dr (15042-9200)
PHONE....................724 772-2555
Brian Herry, *Principal*
EMP: 113
SALES (corp-wide): 41.5B **Privately Held**
SIC: 3613 Power circuit breakers
HQ: Mitsubishi Electric Power Products,
Inc.
530 Keystone Dr
Warrendale PA 15086
724 772-2555

(G-6192)
THORN HILL PRINTING INC
155 Commerce Dr (15042-9202)
PHONE....................724 774-4700
Bruce Wilson, *President*
Richard E Bushee III, *Vice Pres*
Lawrence Drechsler, *Vice Pres*
Richard Bushee Jr, *Treasurer*
EMP: 48
SQ FT: 40,000
SALES (est): 4.8MM **Privately Held**
WEB: www.thpprint.com
SIC: 2759 Business forms: printing

(G-6193)
TOYO DENKI USA INC
2507 Lovi Rd Bldg 3 (15042-9395)
PHONE....................724 774-1760
Kenzo Terashima, *President*
Ichiro Sueoka, *Vice Pres*
Brad Dunphy, *Manager*
▲ EMP: 25
SQ FT: 20,000
SALES: 22MM
SALES (corp-wide): 391.3MM **Privately**
Held
SIC: 3743 Railroad equipment
PA: Toyo Electric Mfg. Co.,Ltd.
1-4-16, Yaesu
Chuo-Ku TKY 103-0
352 028-121

Freeland
Luzerne County

(G-6194)
EURO FOODS INC (HQ)
Also Called: Citterio U.S.A. Corporation
2008 State Route 940 (18224-3256)
PHONE....................570 636-3171
Michael S Zieminski, *Vice Pres*
Marius Pasca, *Production*
Ron Matisak, *Engineer*
Joseph Petruce, *VP Sls/Mktg*
Edward M Sharp, *Treasurer*
◆ EMP: 250
SQ FT: 200,000
SALES (est): 89MM **Privately Held**
WEB: www.citteriousa.com
SIC: 2013 Luncheon meat from purchased
meat

(G-6195)
M E KMACHINE
450 Ridge St (18224-1805)
PHONE....................570 636-0710
Michael E Kotch, *Owner*
EMP: 3
SALES (est): 259.5K **Privately Held**
SIC: 3599 5261 Machine shop, jobbing &
repair; lawn & garden equipment

(G-6196)
STEPHEN R LECHMAN
Also Called: Freeland Machine Co
1113 Cunnius St (18224-1118)
PHONE....................570 636-3159
Stephen R Lechman, *Owner*
EMP: 7
SALES: 400K **Privately Held**
SIC: 3599 7692 Machine shop, jobbing &
repair; welding repair

Freemansburg
Northampton County

(G-6197)
KARES KRAFTED KITCHEN INC
535 Washington St (18017-6839)
PHONE....................610 694-0180
Marcel Kares, *President*
EMP: 7 EST: 1979
SQ FT: 5,600
SALES: 1MM **Privately Held**
WEB: www.kareskraftedkitchens.com
SIC: 2434 Wood kitchen cabinets

(G-6198)
PAAR PRECISION INDUSTRIES
93 Market St (18017-7201)
PHONE....................610 807-9230
Jay Johnson, *CEO*
EMP: 4
SALES: 300K **Privately Held**
SIC: 3599 Machine shop, jobbing & repair

Freeport
Armstrong County

(G-6199)
AP SERVICES LLC
203 Armstrong Dr (16229-2619)
PHONE....................724 295-6200
Doug Vantassell, *CEO*
Mike Allen,
David Horn,
EMP: 85
SALES (est): 19.2MM
SALES (corp-wide): 2.4B **Publicly Held**
SIC: 3053 Gaskets, packing & sealing de-
vices
PA: Curtiss-Wright Corporation
130 Harbour Place Dr # 300
Davidson NC 28036
704 869-4600

(G-6200)
BOYLE INCORPORATED
102 Cherokee Ct (16229-2424)
PHONE....................724 295-2420
Dan Boyle, *President*
EMP: 1
SQ FT: 14,500
SALES (est): 2MM **Privately Held**
WEB: www.boyleinc.com
SIC: 3544 Special dies & tools

(G-6201)
CARSON INDUSTRIES INC (PA)
Also Called: Carson Home Accents
189 Foreman Rd (16229-1799)
PHONE....................724 295-5147
Brad Carson, *President*
Pam Keller, *Vice Pres*
Heath Keller, *Plant Mgr*
Jennifer Cogley, *Purch Dir*
Jeff Cowan, *Purch Dir*
◆ EMP: 50
SQ FT: 15,000

SALES (est): 12.8MM **Privately Held**
WEB: www.carsonindustries.com
SIC: 3365 3931 3914 3264 Aluminum &
aluminum-based alloy castings; musical
instruments; silverware & plated ware;
porcelain electrical supplies

(G-6202)
CURTISS-WRIGHT FLOW
CONTROL
Also Called: Curtiss- Wright Nuclear Div
203 Armstrong Dr (16229-2619)
PHONE....................724 295-6200
EMP: 4
SALES (corp-wide): 2.4B **Publicly Held**
SIC: 3491 Industrial valves
HQ: Curtiss-Wright Flow Control Service
Corporation
2950 E Birch St
Brea CA 92821
714 982-1898

(G-6203)
DYNAMIC MANUFACTURING
LLC
156 Armstrong Dr (16229-2616)
PHONE....................724 295-4200
Richard Turner, *President*
Ezra Michalcin, *General Mgr*
Terry L Havens-Turner, *Corp Secy*
Cleo Urbina, *Maint Spvr*
Paul Jensen, *Mfg Staff*
EMP: 52
SQ FT: 25,000
SALES (est): 7.3MM **Privately Held**
SIC: 3679 3672 3511 3663 Electronic
switches; printed circuit boards; turbines
& turbine generator sets; radio & TV com-
munications equipment; electronic com-
puters; assembly machines,
non-metalworking
PA: Matric Group Llc
2099 Hill City Rd
Seneca PA 16346

(G-6204)
FLIR GOVERNMENT SYSTEMS
PITTSB
Also Called: Flir Surveillance
183 Northpointe Blvd # 100 (16229-2611)
PHONE....................724 295-2880
William Sundermeier, *President*
Andrew C Teich, *President*
Thomas A Surran, *COO*
Todd M Duchene, *Senior VP*
Jeffrey D Frank, *Senior VP*
◆ EMP: 70
SQ FT: 16,000
SALES (est): 14.9MM
SALES (corp-wide): 1.7B **Publicly Held**
SIC: 3827 8711 Optical instruments &
lenses; engineering services
PA: Flir Systems, Inc.
27700 Sw Parkway Ave
Wilsonville OR 97070
503 498-3547

(G-6205)
HYDRO LAZER INC
134 Armstrong Dr (16229-2616)
PHONE....................724 295-9100
David Passarelli, *President*
John Passarelli, *Vice Pres*
EMP: 4
SALES: 1MM **Privately Held**
WEB: www.hydro-lazer.com
SIC: 3253 Ceramic wall & floor tile

(G-6206)
J A SMITH INC
Also Called: Marathon Metal
709 Market St (16229-1262)
P.O. Box 477 (16229-0477)
PHONE....................724 295-1133
Fax: 724 295-2982
EMP: 5
SALES (est): 320K **Privately Held**
SIC: 3444 Sheet Metal Fabrication

(G-6207)
MANAC TRAILERS INC
1001 Lyn Rd (16229)
PHONE....................724 294-0007
Charles Dutil, *President*
EMP: 5

SQ FT: 1,200
SALES (est): 910.1K **Privately Held**
WEB: www.manac.ca
SIC: 3715 Semitrailers for truck tractors
HQ: Groupe Canam Inc
11505 1re Av Bureau 500
Saint-Georges QC G5Y 7
418 228-8031

(G-6208)
OBERG CARBIDE PUNCH & DIE
Also Called: Oberg Industries
604 Oberg Dr (16229-1615)
P.O. Box 368 (16229-0315)
PHONE....................724 295-2118
Robert Wagner, *President*
EMP: 3
SALES (est): 338.4K **Privately Held**
SIC: 3544 3545 Punches, forming &
stamping; machine tool accessories

(G-6209)
OBERG INDUSTRIES INC (PA)
Also Called: Oberg Medical
2301 Silverville Rd (16229-1630)
P.O. Box 368 (16229-0315)
PHONE....................724 295-2121
Jeffrey M Mattiuz, *President*
Richard Bartek, *COO*
David Rugaber, *Exec VP*
David Getty, *Director*
David L Bonvenuto, *Admin Sec*
◆ EMP: 635 EST: 1948
SQ FT: 450,000
SALES (est): 265.3MM **Privately Held**
WEB: www.oberg.com
SIC: 3469 3545 Stamping metal for the
trade; precision tools, machinists'

(G-6210)
OBERG INDUSTRIES INC
Also Called: Independent Tool and Die
604 Oberg Dr (16229-1615)
P.O. Box 368 (16229-0315)
PHONE....................724 295-5151
Lynn Kirkland, *Division Mgr*
Bob Elphinstone, *Opers Mgr*
Robert Wagner, *Purch Mgr*
Don Rollinger, *Purchasing*
Dave Rugaber, *Marketing Staff*
EMP: 50
SALES (corp-wide): 265.3MM **Privately**
Held
SIC: 3544 Special dies, tools, jigs & fix-
tures
PA: Oberg Industries, Inc.
2301 Silverville Rd
Freeport PA 16229
724 295-2121

(G-6211)
OMNITECH PARTNERS INC (HQ)
108 Kountz Ln (16229-1724)
PHONE....................724 295-2880
Paul Maxin, *President*
Eugene Pochapsky, *Vice Pres*
EMP: 2
SQ FT: 200
SALES (est): 6.1MM
SALES (corp-wide): 1.7B **Publicly Held**
SIC: 3827 Optical instruments & lenses
PA: Flir Systems, Inc.
27700 Sw Parkway Ave
Wilsonville OR 97070
503 498-3547

(G-6212)
OPTICAL SYSTEMS
TECHNOLOGY
Also Called: Osti Startron
183 Northpointe Blvd # 100 (16229-2611)
PHONE....................724 295-2880
Paul Maxin, *President*
Dr Eugene Pochapsky, *Vice Pres*
Pat Lampe, *CFO*
▲ EMP: 40
SALES (est): 6MM
SALES (corp-wide): 1.7B **Publicly Held**
WEB: www.omnitechpartners.com
SIC: 3827 Optical instruments & lenses
HQ: Omnitech Partners, Inc.
108 Kountz Ln
Freeport PA 16229
724 295-2880

▲ = Import ▼=Export
◆ =Import/Export

(G-6213)
PHOENIX ENERGY PRODUCTIONS
Also Called: Phoenix Energy Marketing
419 Riverside Dr (16229-1126)
PHONE..................................724 295-9220
James Hoover, *President*
Mike Hoover, *Vice Pres*
EMP: 3 **EST:** 1996
SALES (est): 1.5MM **Privately Held**
WEB: www.phoenixenergymarketing.com
SIC: 1382 Oil & gas exploration services

(G-6214)
SLATE LICK PRINTING INC
944 Freeport Rd (16229-1848)
PHONE..................................724 295-2053
Frank Noroski, *President*
Darrin Noroski, *Vice Pres*
EMP: 3
SQ FT: 2,600
SALES (est): 462.5K **Privately Held**
SIC: 2752 Commercial printing, offset

(G-6215)
TRIO MOTION TECHNOLOGY LLC
187 Northpointe Blvd # 105 (16229-2621)
PHONE..................................724 472-4100
Edward Novak, *General Mgr*
Christopher Backhouse, *Managing Dir*
Shannon Zema, *Office Admin*
Roy Bamforth,
EMP: 4
SQ FT: 1,200
SALES (est): 1MM
SALES (corp-wide): 162.4MM **Privately Held**
WEB: www.triomotion.com
SIC: 3625 Electric controls & control accessories, industrial
HQ: Trio Motion Technology Limited
  Shannon Way
  Tewkesbury GLOS
  168 429-2333

(G-6216)
ULTRA PRECISION INCORPORATED
Also Called: Utra Precision
2220 Silverville Rd (16229-1629)
P.O. Box E (16229-0305)
PHONE..................................724 295-5161
Frank Paz, *CEO*
James L Paz, *Director*
John N Paz, *Director*
EMP: 46
SQ FT: 24,000
SALES (est): 6.2MM **Privately Held**
WEB: www.ultraprecisioninc.com
SIC: 3544 Special dies & tools

Frenchville
Clearfield County

(G-6217)
KOVALICK LUMBER CO
24338 Shawville Frenchvil (16836)
PHONE..................................814 263-4928
EMP: 11
SQ FT: 10,000
SALES: 1.2MM **Privately Held**
SIC: 2421 2411 2426 Sawmill/Planing Mill Logging Hardwood Dimension/Floor Mill

(G-6218)
QUEHANNA MILLWORK
22792 Shawville Frenchvil (16836)
PHONE..................................814 263-4145
Ed Plubell, *Owner*
EMP: 3
SQ FT: 16,500
SALES: 300K **Privately Held**
SIC: 2431 5211 Floor baseboards, wood; moldings, wood: unfinished & prefinished; lumber products

Friedens
Somerset County

(G-6219)
COAL INNOVATIONS LLC
1134 Stoystown Rd (15541-7502)
PHONE..................................814 893-5790
Norman Caplan, *Mng Member*
EMP: 9
SALES (est): 891.6K **Privately Held**
SIC: 1241 Coal mining services

(G-6220)
GODIN BROS INC
377 Twin Hills Rd (15541)
PHONE..................................814 629-5117
EMP: 10
SALES (corp-wide): 836.2K **Privately Held**
SIC: 1221 Bituminous Coal Surface Mining
PA: Godin Bros., Inc.
  195 E Philadelphia St
  Armagh PA

(G-6221)
MICHAEL Z GEHMAN
Also Called: Sunquest Metal Rollforming
184 Marts Rd (15541-8623)
PHONE..................................814 483-0488
Michael Z Gehman, *Owner*
EMP: 1
SALES: 1.2MM **Privately Held**
SIC: 2621 7389 Building & roofing paper, felts & insulation siding;

(G-6222)
MINCORP INC (HQ)
Rr 281 (15541)
P.O. Box 260 (15541-0260)
PHONE..................................814 443-4668
David L Shanks, *President*
Joseph Gallo, *President*
Peter J Vuljanic, *Vice Pres*
Denis Kulichenko, *CFO*
Dmitry Goryachev, *Treasurer*
EMP: 10
SQ FT: 17,280
SALES (est): 33.1MM
SALES (corp-wide): 6.5B **Privately Held**
SIC: 1221 Strip mining, bituminous
PA: Severstal, Pao
  30 Ul. Mira
  Cherepovets 16260
  820 253-1915

(G-6223)
MOSTOLLERS MFG & DISTRG
1207 Stoystown Rd (15541-7507)
PHONE..................................814 445-7281
Lloyd E Mostoller, *Managing Prtnr*
Virginia Mostoller, *Managing Prtnr*
EMP: 10 **EST:** 1963
SALES (est): 270.3K **Privately Held**
SIC: 5812 2064 Family restaurants; popcorn balls or other treated popcorn products

(G-6224)
NORTH STAR LEASING INC (PA)
147 Mine Rd (15541-9442)
P.O. Box 66, Boswell (15531-0066)
PHONE..................................814 629-6999
Theodore Beahr, *President*
Ted Beahr, *Vice Pres*
George Pipon, *Admin Sec*
EMP: 1
SALES: 4MM **Privately Held**
SIC: 1411 4212 5052 Dimension stone; local trucking, without storage; coal

(G-6225)
PILES CONCRETE PRODUCTS CO INC
Also Called: Scotty's Porta-Potty's
115 Pickett Ln (15541-7413)
PHONE..................................814 445-6619
Thomas Zimmerman, *President*
Brett Zimmerman, *Vice Pres*
Dorthy Zimmerman, *Admin Sec*
EMP: 13
SQ FT: 2,500

SALES (est): 2.4MM **Privately Held**
SIC: 3272 5074 7699 7359 Burial vaults, concrete or precast terrazzo; septic tanks, concrete; pipes & fittings, plastic; septic tank cleaning service; portable toilet rental

(G-6226)
ROXCOAL INC
Also Called: Pbs Coals
1576 Stoystown Rd (15541-7402)
P.O. Box 260 (15541-0260)
PHONE..................................814 443-4668
Robert Scott, *President*
Joseph Hayes, *CFO*
EMP: 100
SALES (est): 16.7MM
SALES (corp-wide): 6.5B **Privately Held**
SIC: 1222 Bituminous coal-underground mining
HQ: Mincorp, Inc.
  Rr 281
  Friedens PA 15541
  814 443-4668

(G-6227)
SOLAR FUEL CO INC
1134 Stoystown Rd (15541-7502)
P.O. Box 488, Somerset (15501-0488)
PHONE..................................814 443-2646
David C Klementik, *President*
Ron Carl, *Vice Pres*
David Dinning, *CFO*
EMP: 3
SQ FT: 3,500
SALES (est): 231.7K **Publicly Held**
SIC: 1241 Coal mining services
HQ: Ak Steel Corporation
  9227 Centre Pointe Dr
  West Chester OH 45069
  513 425-4200

(G-6228)
WILSON CREEK ENERGY LLC
1576 Stoystown Rd (15541-7402)
P.O. Box 260 (15541-0260)
PHONE..................................814 443-4668
Pete Merritts, *Branch Mgr*
EMP: 50
SALES (corp-wide): 19.2MM **Privately Held**
SIC: 1222 5052 Bituminous coal-underground mining; coal & other minerals & ores
PA: Wilson Creek Energy, Llc
  4600 J Barry Ct Ste 220
  Canonsburg PA 15317
  724 754-0028

Friendsville
Susquehanna County

(G-6229)
CLASSIC SHOTSHELL CO INC
Also Called: R S T
784 Turnpike Rd (18818-8694)
PHONE..................................570 553-1651
Morris Baker, *President*
Christine Benjamin, *Manager*
EMP: 6 **EST:** 2005
SQ FT: 5,000
SALES: 500K **Privately Held**
SIC: 3482 Shotgun ammunition: empty, blank or loaded

(G-6230)
SNAKE CREEK LASERS LLC
Also Called: Advanced Photonic Sciences
26741 State Route 267 # 2 (18818-8792)
PHONE..................................570 553-1120
Dr David C Brown, *President*
Lisa Vitali,
EMP: 16
SQ FT: 9,000
SALES (est): 3MM **Privately Held**
WEB: www.snakecreeklasers.com
SIC: 3841 3845 Surgical lasers; laser systems & equipment, medical

Furlong
Bucks County

(G-6231)
INGERSOLL RAND CO
245 Saddle Dr (18925-1019)
PHONE..................................215 345-4470
Paul Wallace, *Principal*
EMP: 3 **EST:** 2011
SALES (est): 208.9K **Privately Held**
SIC: 3131 Rands

(G-6232)
PRECISE MEDICAL
3140 Cloverly Dr (18925-1229)
PHONE..................................215 345-6729
Richard Dywalt, *Mng Member*
EMP: 32
SALES (est): 2.8MM **Privately Held**
WEB: www.precisemedical.org
SIC: 3841 Surgical & medical instruments

(G-6233)
ROYALTY PROMOTIONS INC
Also Called: Royal T'S
1970 Swamp Rd (18925-1124)
PHONE..................................215 794-2707
Pam Lacey, *President*
Sandra Holly, *Corp Secy*
EMP: 4
SQ FT: 2,100
SALES: 120K **Privately Held**
SIC: 2261 2395 Screen printing of cotton broadwoven fabrics; embroidery & art needlework

(G-6234)
T B W INDUSTRIES INC
2389 Forest Grove Rd (18925-1165)
P.O. Box 336 (18925-0336)
PHONE..................................215 794-8070
Robert L Benner, *President*
Virginia Benner, *Corp Secy*
R Lyle Benner, *Vice Pres*
S J Benner, *Vice Pres*
Jack Cole, *Manager*
EMP: 10
SQ FT: 4,000
SALES (est): 1.8MM **Privately Held**
WEB: www.tbwindustries.com
SIC: 3291 3821 Abrasive products; laboratory apparatus & furniture

(G-6235)
VILLAGE PUBLISHING OPERATIONS
73 Valley Dr (18925-1032)
P.O. Box 623 (18925-0623)
PHONE..................................215 794-0202
Howard Elliot, *President*
Gail Elliott, *Treasurer*
EMP: 4
SALES (est): 400.5K **Privately Held**
WEB: www.custodycenter.com
SIC: 2752 Commercial printing, lithographic

Gaines
Tioga County

(G-6236)
GAINES COMPANY
Long Run Rd (16921)
PHONE..................................814 435-2332
D Thomas Eggler, *Owner*
EMP: 9
SQ FT: 6,000
SALES (est): 547.6K **Privately Held**
SIC: 3949 Lures, fishing: artificial

(G-6237)
RON ANDRUS LOGGING
8317 Leetonia Rd (16921-9571)
PHONE..................................814 435-6484
EMP: 3
SALES (est): 245.5K **Privately Held**
SIC: 2411 Logging

Galeton
Potter County

(G-6238)
CATALUS CORPORATION
1251 Route 6 W (16922-9125)
PHONE..................................814 435-6541
Richard Smith, *Branch Mgr*
EMP: 90 **Privately Held**
SIC: 3399 Powder, metal
PA: Catalus Corporation
    286 Piper Rd
    Saint Marys PA 15857

(G-6239)
EARL F DEAN INC
766 Route 6 W (16922-9114)
P.O. Box 249 (16922-0249)
PHONE..................................814 435-6581
Ronald E Dean Jr, *President*
EMP: 7 **EST:** 1930
SQ FT: 6,000
SALES (est): 1.3MM **Privately Held**
SIC: 1442 Construction sand mining;
    gravel mining

(G-6240)
LARIMER & NORTON INC
91 West St (16922-1113)
PHONE..................................814 435-2202
Stan Prouty, *Manager*
EMP: 7
SALES (corp-wide): 96.3MM **Privately
Held**
WEB: www.larimerlounge.com
SIC: 3949 3312 Baseball equipment &
    supplies, general; billets, steel
HQ: Larimer & Norton, Inc.
    800 W Main St
    Louisville KY 40202
    502 585-5226

(G-6241)
PATTERSON LUMBER CO INC
95 West St (16922-1113)
PHONE..................................814 435-2210
Anthony Adami, *Branch Mgr*
EMP: 45
SALES (corp-wide): 3.5MM **Privately
Held**
SIC: 2421 2426 Lumber: rough, sawed or
    planed; hardwood dimension & flooring
    mills
PA: Patterson Lumber Co., Inc.
    34 Fellows Ave
    Wellsboro PA
    570 724-3210

(G-6242)
PAUL FAMILY FARMS LLC
377 Paul Hollow Rd (16922-9409)
PHONE..................................570 772-2420
Travis Paul,
EMP: 4 **EST:** 2015
SALES (est): 140.5K **Privately Held**
SIC: 2099 Sugar, industrial maple

(G-6243)
PETE RICKARD COMPANY
1 Bridge St (16922-1301)
PHONE..................................518 234-3758
Harold Karschner, *Owner*
EMP: 6
SALES (est): 309.4K **Privately Held**
SIC: 3949 Sporting & athletic goods

(G-6244)
PROTEKTOR MODEL
Also Called: Pete Rickard Co
1 Bridge St 11 (16922-1301)
PHONE..................................814 435-2442
Harold Karschner, *Owner*
Krisanne Karschner, *Manager*
EMP: 6
SALES (est): 551.2K **Privately Held**
WEB: www.protektormodel.com
SIC: 3949 Hunting equipment

Gallitzin
Cambria County

(G-6245)
DONALD BEISWENGER INC
Also Called: Sehrer Mill & Hardware
107 S Main St (16641-1517)
PHONE..................................814 886-8341
Donald Beiswenger, *President*
EMP: 4
SQ FT: 2,000
SALES: 100K **Privately Held**
SIC: 2421 5251 2431 Planing mills; hard-
    ware; millwork

(G-6246)
**INTEGRATED MYERS SYSTEMS
LLC**
500 Church St (16641-1306)
PHONE..................................814 937-3958
David Myers, *Managing Prtnr*
EMP: 3 **EST:** 2013
SALES (est): 127.1K **Privately Held**
SIC: 7699 3824 Cash register repair;
    counter type registers

(G-6247)
R & M APPAREL INC
790 Clark St (16641-1734)
PHONE..................................814 886-9272
Christine Fenkelstine, *President*
Rochelle Gorman, *Vice Pres*
EMP: 150
SQ FT: 68,000
SALES (est): 8.2MM **Privately Held**
SIC: 2339 2369 2337 2335 Women's &
    misses' outerwear; girls' & children's out-
    erwear; women's & misses' suits & coats;
    women's, juniors' & misses' dresses;
    women's & misses' blouses & shirts

Gap
Lancaster County

(G-6248)
ALPHABET SIGNS INC
91 Newport Rd Ste 102 (17527-9579)
PHONE..................................800 582-6366
Daniel Keane, *CEO*
EMP: 7
SALES (est): 462.2K **Privately Held**
WEB: www.alphabetsigns.com
SIC: 3993 Signs, not made in custom sign
    painting shops

(G-6249)
DUTCHLAND INC
160 Route 41 (17527-9410)
P.O. Box 549 (17527-0549)
PHONE..................................717 442-8282
Katie B Kauffman, *CEO*
Benjamin M Kauffman, *President*
Lee Kauffman, *Vice Pres*
Mary Ann Stoltzfus, *Vice Pres*
Josh Allen, *Chief Engr*
EMP: 135 **EST:** 1966
SQ FT: 28,700
SALES (est): 32MM **Privately Held**
WEB: www.dutchlandinc.com
SIC: 3272 Concrete products, precast

(G-6250)
EDWARD THOMPSON
Also Called: Twin County Machine
825 Simmontown Rd (17527-9699)
PHONE..................................717 442-4550
Edward I Thompson, *Owner*
EMP: 4 **EST:** 1998
SQ FT: 2,800
SALES (est): 310K **Privately Held**
SIC: 3599 Machine shop, jobbing & repair

(G-6251)
FARM-BILT MACHINE LLC
Also Called: Farm Bilt
633 Quarry Rd (17527-9031)
PHONE..................................717 442-5020
Jonas Beiler, *Mng Member*
Christian Beiler,
Samuel Beiler,

◆ **EMP:** 14
SQ FT: 480
SALES (est): 2.7MM **Privately Held**
SIC: 3523 5051 5083 Farm machinery &
    equipment; bars, metal; farm & garden
    machinery

(G-6252)
LAPP JOHN
Also Called: Millwood Wood Working
5459 Buena Vista Rd (17527-9711)
PHONE..................................717 442-8583
John Lapp, *Owner*
EMP: 4
SALES: 105K **Privately Held**
SIC: 2511 Lawn furniture: wood

(G-6253)
MCCLURES PIE AND SALAD INC
Also Called: McClure's Pies & Salads
18 Newport Rd (17527-9698)
PHONE..................................717 442-4461
Dauglas Kauffman, *President*
Beverly Kauffman, *Admin Sec*
EMP: 12
SQ FT: 5,000
SALES (est): 1.5MM **Privately Held**
SIC: 2051 5149 5411 Pies, bakery: ex-
    cept frozen; groceries & related products;
    delicatessens

(G-6254)
**NEW ENTERPRISE STONE LIME
INC**
Also Called: Limeville Quarry
520 Lime Quarry Rd (17527-9739)
PHONE..................................717 442-4148
Lynn Weaver, *Manager*
EMP: 10
SALES (corp-wide): 651.9MM **Privately
Held**
WEB: www.martinlimestone.com
SIC: 1499 Bituminous limestone quarrying
PA: New Enterprise Stone & Lime Co., Inc.
    3912 Brumbaugh Rd
    New Enterprise PA 16664
    814 224-6883

(G-6255)
PEQUEA PLANTER LLC
561 White Horse Rd (17527-9217)
PHONE..................................717 442-4406
Daniel F Stoltzfus, *Mng Member*
Daniel Stoltzfus, *Mng Member*
Gideon Stoltzfus,
Omar Stoltzfus,
EMP: 10 **EST:** 1970
SALES (est): 3MM **Privately Held**
SIC: 3523 7699 Planting machines, agri-
    cultural; farm machinery repair

(G-6256)
STEVE EVERSOLL
Also Called: Welsh Mountain Woodworking
604 Gault Rd (17527-9754)
PHONE..................................717 768-3298
Steve Eversoll, *Owner*
EMP: 3
SALES (est): 242K **Privately Held**
SIC: 2491 Bridges, treated wood

(G-6257)
WHITE HORSE MACHINE LLC
5566 Old Phladelphia Pike (17527-9769)
PHONE..................................717 768-8313
Rodney Gossert, *Fire Chief*
Henry King,
David King Jr,
Melvin King,
EMP: 16
SQ FT: 16,500
SALES (est): 3.2MM **Privately Held**
SIC: 3599 3523 5251 Machine shop, job-
    bing & repair; plows, agricultural: disc,
    moldboard, chisel, listers, etc.; hardware

(G-6258)
WILMINGTON METALCRAFT
1406 W Kings Hwy (17527-9011)
PHONE..................................717 442-9834
Amos Glick, *Owner*
EMP: 7
SQ FT: 6,000
SALES (est): 400K **Privately Held**
SIC: 3446 Ornamental metalwork

Gardners
Adams County

(G-6259)
BIG HILL WINERY
1365 Gablers Rd (17324-9528)
PHONE..................................717 226-8702
Kishbaugh Benjamin, *Principal*
EMP: 4
SALES (est): 170K **Privately Held**
SIC: 2084 Wines

(G-6260)
HEMPT BROS INC
4700 Carlisle Rd (17324-8964)
PHONE..................................717 486-5111
Bob Turner, *Manager*
EMP: 8
SALES (corp-wide): 88.9MM **Privately
Held**
SIC: 1442 Construction sand mining
PA: Hempt Bros., Inc.
    205 Creek Rd
    Camp Hill PA 17011
    717 774-2911

(G-6261)
**OMALLEY WOOD PRODUCTS
INC**
465 Upper Bermudian Rd (17324-9768)
PHONE..................................717 677-6550
Michael J O'Malley, *President*
Thomas Biddeson, *Treasurer*
EMP: 50
SQ FT: 30,000
SALES (est): 7.2MM **Privately Held**
WEB: www.omalleylumber.com
SIC: 2441 2448 Shipping cases, wood:
    nailed or lock corner; pallets, wood; skids,
    wood

(G-6262)
ZEIGLER BROS INC (PA)
400 Gardners Station Rd (17324-9686)
PHONE..................................717 677-6181
Dr Thomas Zeigler, *President*
Timothy M Zeigler, *Vice Pres*
Matthew Zeigler, *VP Opers*
Keith Smith, *Plant Mgr*
Sidinei Valle, *Opers Mgr*
◆ **EMP:** 48
SQ FT: 10,000
SALES (est): 17.8MM **Privately Held**
SIC: 2048 Livestock feeds

Garland
Warren County

(G-6263)
**TONY L STEC LUMBER
COMPANY**
Hosmer Run Rd (16416)
PHONE..................................814 563-9002
James A Stec, *President*
Vickie L Stec, *Corp Secy*
▼ **EMP:** 14
SQ FT: 1,000
SALES: 2.5MM **Privately Held**
SIC: 2421 5211 Sawmills & planing mills,
    general; planing mill products & lumber

Garnet Valley
Delaware County

(G-6264)
ACCUSTAR INC
Also Called: Touch Pro
3060 Plaza Dr Ste 101 (19060-2127)
PHONE..................................610 459-0123
Lisa Ann Mariotti, *President*
EMP: 5 **EST:** 1997
SQ FT: 3,200

SALES (est): 710.2K **Privately Held**
SIC: 5999 7371 7372 5734 Business machines & equipment; computer software development & applications; computer software development; business oriented computer software; computer software & accessories; systems software development services; computer terminals; computer terminals, monitors & components; keyboards, computer, office machine

(G-6265)
BERM STUDIOS INCORPORATED
Also Called: BSI Exhibits
3070 Mccann Farm Dr # 104 (19060-2131)
P.O. Box 359, Chester Heights (19017-0359)
PHONE.................................610 622-2100
Albert Berman, *President*
Stephen Berman, *Exec VP*
EMP: 70
SQ FT: 175,000
SALES (est): 7.4MM **Privately Held**
WEB: www.bermstudios.com
SIC: 3993 7311 7389 8742 Displays & cutouts, window & lobby; advertising agencies; advertising, promotional & trade show services; trade show arrangement; marketing consulting services

(G-6266)
KUPER TECHNOLOGIES LLC
6 Rigby Ct (19060-1626)
P.O. Box 893, Concordville (19331-0893)
PHONE.................................610 358-5120
Brendan Hogan,
EMP: 5
SQ FT: 1,500
SALES: 5MM **Privately Held**
SIC: 8742 3559 Management consulting services; semiconductor manufacturing machinery

(G-6267)
PCA GROUP INC
Also Called: De Alfredo Foods
3060 Plaza Dr Ste 108 (19060-2127)
PHONE.................................610 558-2802
Paul Pecorari, *President*
Thomas Sheridan, *Director*
▲ EMP: 3
SALES (est): 259.4K **Privately Held**
SIC: 2079 2099 2098 2033 Olive oil; pasta, uncooked: packaged with other ingredients; vinegar; macaroni & spaghetti; spaghetti, dry; tomato products: packaged in cans, jars, etc.

(G-6268)
SEWSATIONS LLC
3405 Half Mile Post N (19060-1033)
PHONE.................................484 842-1024
Edward G Brugel, *Principal*
EMP: 6 EST: 2010
SALES (est): 267.3K **Privately Held**
SIC: 2491 Piles, foundation & marine construction: treated wood

(G-6269)
SUPLEE ENVELOPE CO INC
1743 Ashbrooke Ave (19060-6821)
PHONE.................................610 352-2900
Robert M Suplee, *President*
Jamie Suplee, *Vice Pres*
EMP: 20
SQ FT: 35,000
SALES (est): 2.5MM **Privately Held**
WEB: www.suplee.com
SIC: 5112 2621 2677 Envelopes; file folders; envelope paper; envelopes

(G-6270)
WGS EQUIPMENT & CONTROLS
3060 Plaza Dr Ste 110 (19060-2127)
PHONE.................................610 459-8800
John E Fetrow, *President*
Howard E Brumeaugh, *Vice Pres*
Diane Beresford, *Sales Associate*
Karen O'Hara, *Admin Asst*
▲ EMP: 13
SQ FT: 5,000

SALES (est): 16.5MM **Privately Held**
WEB: www.wgsequipment.com
SIC: 5084 3823 Instruments & control equipment; industrial process measurement equipment

Genesee
Potter County

(G-6271)
D E HYDE CONTRACTING
2048 Kinney Rd (16923-8701)
PHONE.................................814 228-3685
Douglas Hyde, *Owner*
EMP: 3
SALES: 300K **Privately Held**
SIC: 2411 1794 Logging camps & contractors; excavation work

(G-6272)
HERBERT COOPER COMPANY INC
121 Main St (16923-8901)
P.O. Box 40 (16923-0040)
PHONE.................................814 228-3417
Genevieve Cooper, *President*
Rhonda Elmadollar, *Admin Sec*
EMP: 20 EST: 1957
SQ FT: 8,920
SALES (est): 1.1MM **Privately Held**
SIC: 3069 Medical & laboratory rubber sundries & related products; tubing, rubber

(G-6273)
MATTESON LOGGING INC
843 Bingham Center Rd (16923-9108)
PHONE.................................814 848-9863
Vaughn Buffington, *Principal*
EMP: 3
SALES (est): 229K **Privately Held**
SIC: 2411 Logging

Georgetown
Beaver County

(G-6274)
C & E PLASTICS INC
2500 Route 168 (15043)
PHONE.................................724 947-4949
Clifford D Crighton, *President*
Darlene S Crighton, *Office Mgr*
EMP: 35
SQ FT: 30,000
SALES (est): 5.9MM **Privately Held**
WEB: www.ceplastics.com
SIC: 3089 Injection molding of plastics

(G-6275)
EICKHOFF CORPORATION
165 Temple Rd (15043-9660)
PHONE.................................724 218-1856
Paul Rheinlaender, *President*
David Podobinski, *Vice Pres*
Lisa Podobinski, *Accountant*
▲ EMP: 13 EST: 1973
SALES (est): 5.6MM
SALES (corp-wide): 442MM **Privately Held**
WEB: www.eickhoffcorp.com
SIC: 5082 3532 Mining machinery & equipment, except petroleum; mining machinery
HQ: Gebr. Eickhoff Maschinenfabrik U. EisengieBerei Gmbh
Am Eickhoffpark 1
Bochum 44789
234 975-0

(G-6276)
GEORGETOWN SAND & GRAVEL INC
3rd Rd Ext (15043)
PHONE.................................724 573-9518
David Bryan, *CEO*
EMP: 4
SALES (est): 1MM **Privately Held**
SIC: 1442 Construction sand & gravel

(G-6277)
MARTIN MARIETTA MATERIALS INC
3rd St Ext (15043)
P.O. Box 127 (15043-0127)
PHONE.................................724 573-9518
David Bryan, *Owner*
EMP: 12 **Publicly Held**
WEB: www.martinmarietta.com
SIC: 1442 5032 Construction sand & gravel; sand, construction
PA: Martin Marietta Materials Inc
2710 Wycliff Rd
Raleigh NC 27607

Germansville
Lehigh County

(G-6278)
GROTHOUSE LUMBER COMPANY
6104 Buckery Rd (18053-2549)
PHONE.................................610 767-6515
A Paul Grothouse, *Principal*
EMP: 14
SALES (est): 1.9MM **Privately Held**
SIC: 2431 Millwork

(G-6279)
KINGPIN PRODUCTION VANS INC
6341 Memorial Rd (18053-2508)
PHONE.................................305 772-0687
Christopher Golley, *Principal*
EMP: 7
SALES (est): 630.5K **Privately Held**
SIC: 3452 Pins

(G-6280)
LEHIGH VALLEY SIGN & SERVICE
5812 Walter Rd (18053-2840)
PHONE.................................610 760-8590
Daniel Staub, *President*
Barbara Staub, *Admin Sec*
EMP: 5
SALES: 250K **Privately Held**
SIC: 3993 7629 Neon signs; electrical repair shops

Gettysburg
Adams County

(G-6281)
AAR PLASTIC & GLASS LLC
43 E Middle St (17325-2322)
PHONE.................................410 200-6369
Douglas Miller,
EMP: 6
SALES (est): 822.5K **Privately Held**
SIC: 3089 3083 7389 Stock shapes, plastic; thermoformed finished plastic products; bearings, plastic; corrugated panels, plastic; window sheeting, plastic;

(G-6282)
AGRICULTURAL COMMODITIES INC
Agcom
1585 Granite Station Rd (17325-8345)
PHONE.................................717 624-6858
Dan Winters, *Manager*
EMP: 54
SALES (corp-wide): 118.7MM **Privately Held**
SIC: 5191 5153 2874 Feed; grains; phosphatic fertilizers
PA: Agricultural Commodities, Inc.
2224 Oxford Rd
New Oxford PA 17350
717 624-8249

(G-6283)
AGSALT PROCESSING
530 Storms Store Rd (17325-7907)
PHONE.................................717 632-9144
Merle Herr, *CEO*
Dalen Grove, *Partner*
EMP: 6

SALES (est): 821.4K **Privately Held**
SIC: 2819 Magnesium compounds or salts, inorganic

(G-6284)
BATTLEFIELD BREW WORKS
248 Hunterstown Rd (17325-7840)
PHONE.................................717 398-2907
Dan Kulick, *Principal*
EMP: 6 EST: 2013
SALES (est): 498.6K **Privately Held**
SIC: 2082 Malt beverages

(G-6285)
CENTRAL PENN DISTILLING
Also Called: Mason Dickson Distilleri
25 Tamarack Dr (17325)
PHONE.................................717 808-7695
EMP: 3
SALES (est): 204.7K **Privately Held**
SIC: 8741 2085 Management services; distilled & blended liquors

(G-6286)
COMMUNITY RESOURCE SVCS INC
Also Called: CRS
925 Johnson Dr (17325-8903)
PHONE.................................717 338-9100
EMP: 3
SALES (est): 160.6K **Privately Held**
SIC: 8111 2741 2732 Criminal Justice Consulting

(G-6287)
DAL-TILE CORPORATION
211 N 4th St (17325-1604)
PHONE.................................717 334-1181
Joe Majewski, *Branch Mgr*
EMP: 163
SALES (corp-wide): 9.9B **Publicly Held**
WEB: www.mohawk.com
SIC: 5032 3253 Ceramic wall & floor tile; ceramic wall & floor tile
HQ: Dal-Tile Corporation
7834 C F Hawn Fwy
Dallas TX 75217
214 398-1411

(G-6288)
DAVID BREAM
Also Called: Bream's Print Shop
449 W Middle St (17325-2416)
PHONE.................................717 334-1513
David Bream, *Owner*
EMP: 3 EST: 1970
SALES: 200K **Privately Held**
SIC: 2752 2791 2759 Commercial printing, offset; typesetting; commercial printing

(G-6289)
DELAWARE COUNTY LEGAL JOURNAL
111 Baltimore St Rm 117 (17325-2367)
PHONE.................................717 337-9812
EMP: 4
SALES (est): 150.5K **Privately Held**
SIC: 2711 Newspapers, publishing & printing

(G-6290)
ETCHED IN TIME
31 Buford Ave (17325-1131)
P.O. Box 3222 (17325-0222)
PHONE.................................717 334-3600
Joe Spaeolini, *Principal*
EMP: 3
SALES (est): 220.6K **Privately Held**
SIC: 2759 Engraving

(G-6291)
GETTYSBURG CONCRETE CO INC
Also Called: Hanover Concrete
1625 Baltimore Pike (17325-7090)
P.O. Box 3518 (17325-0518)
PHONE.................................717 334-1494
G Ronald Albright, *President*
David R Albright, *Vice Pres*
Michelle M Albright, *Treasurer*
Bonita L Albright, *Admin Sec*
EMP: 4
SALES (est): 613.4K **Privately Held**
SIC: 3273 Ready-mixed concrete

G
E
O
G
R
A
P
H
I
C

(G-6292)
GETTYSBURG TIMES PUBG LLC
1570 Fairfield Rd (17325-7252)
P.O. Box 3669 (17325-0669)
PHONE..................................717 253-9403
Nancy Pritt, *Sales Mgr*
Harry Hartman,
EMP: 30
SALES (est): 2.1MM **Privately Held**
SIC: 2711 Newspapers: publishing only, not printed on site

(G-6293)
GETTYSBURG TRANSFORMER CORP
1380 Old Harrisburg Rd (17325-8147)
P.O. Box 4356 (17325-4356)
PHONE..................................717 334-2191
Charles Ritter, *President*
Dean Bennett, *Vice Pres*
Charlotte Ritter, *Treasurer*
EMP: 50
SQ FT: 525
SALES (est): 7.7MM **Privately Held**
WEB: www.gettysburgtransformer.com
SIC: 3677 3621 3612 Electronic transformers; motors & generators; transformers, except electric

(G-6294)
GETTYSBURG VILLAGE FACTORY STR
Also Called: Coach
1863 Gettysburg Vlg Dr (17325-8989)
PHONE..................................717 334-2332
Ken Balin, *President*
Nancy Brown, *General Mgr*
EMP: 15
SALES (est): 2.3MM **Privately Held**
SIC: 3643 5999 Outlets, electric: convenience; alarm & safety equipment stores

(G-6295)
GRAPHCOM INC (PA)
Also Called: Graphcom Creative
1219 Chambersburg Rd (17325-7384)
PHONE..................................800 699-1664
S Gregory Allen, *CEO*
Matthew D Livelsberger, *President*
Krista Scarlett, *Editor*
Christine D Allen, *Corp Secy*
David C Sandoe, *Exec VP*
EMP: 105
SQ FT: 17,000
SALES (est): 21.3MM **Privately Held**
WEB: www.graphcom.com
SIC: 2752 2761 7336 2399 Commercial printing, offset; manifold business forms; graphic arts & related design; banners, made from fabric; flags, fabric; direct mail advertising services; custom computer programming services

(G-6296)
GREENWOOD PRODUCTS
975 Marsh Creek Rd (17325-6902)
PHONE..................................717 337-2050
Robert Green, *Partner*
Larry Green, *Partner*
Robert Green Jr, *Partner*
EMP: 6
SALES (est): 572.3K **Privately Held**
SIC: 2421 5031 Sawmills & planing mills, general; lumber, plywood & millwork

(G-6297)
HALF PINT CREAMERY LLC
1101 Biglerville Rd (17325-8837)
PHONE..................................717 420-2110
EMP: 5
SALES (est): 145K **Privately Held**
SIC: 2021 Creamery butter

(G-6298)
HAUSER ESTATE INC (PA)
Also Called: Hauser Estate Winery, The
28 W Middle St (17325-2101)
PHONE..................................717 334-4888
Jonathan Apatrono, *President*
Hanna Hauser, *Vice Pres*
Steve Runkle, *CFO*
Melinda Hhutton, *Treasurer*
EMP: 5

SALES (est): 8.2MM **Privately Held**
SIC: 2084 Wine cellars, bonded: engaged in blending wines; wines

(G-6299)
HILLANDALE FARMS OF PA INC
Also Called: Near By Eggs
3910 Oxford Rd (17325-8367)
PHONE..................................717 229-0601
James Minkin, *Manager*
EMP: 50
SALES (corp-wide): 88.2MM **Privately Held**
SIC: 2015 Egg processing
PA: Hillandale Farms Of Pa., Inc.
4001 Crooked Run Rd Ste 2
North Versailles PA 15137
412 672-9685

(G-6300)
HILLANDALE-GETTYSBURG LP
3910 Oxford Rd (17325-8367)
PHONE..................................717 334-1973
Donald C Hershey, *Mng Member*
Orland Bethal,
EMP: 190
SALES (est): 29.6MM **Privately Held**
SIC: 0252 2015 Chicken eggs; poultry slaughtering & processing

(G-6301)
HIWASSEE ACRES LLC
25 Chambersburg St Ste 1 (17325-1167)
PHONE..................................717 334-1381
Ken Fry, *Branch Mgr*
EMP: 3
SALES (corp-wide): 554.8K **Privately Held**
SIC: 2084 Wines
PA: Hiwassee Acres Llc
251 Peach Tree Rd
Orrtanna PA 17353
717 334-4631

(G-6302)
JACOBY TRANSPORTATION INC
2350 Biglerville Rd (17325-8091)
PHONE..................................717 677-7733
Donald L Jacoby, *President*
Claudia M Redding, *Corp Secy*
Sharon N Jacoby, *Vice Pres*
EMP: 23
SALES: 380K **Privately Held**
SIC: 2511 4151 5947 Wood household furniture; school buses; gift shop; gift baskets; novelties

(G-6303)
K-TOOL INC
1045 Storms Store Rd (17325-8322)
PHONE..................................717 632-3015
Dale Keller, *President*
Scott Keller, *Vice Pres*
Judy Keller, *Treasurer*
Daniel Keller, *Admin Sec*
EMP: 15 **EST:** 1979
SQ FT: 6,000
SALES (est): 1.4MM **Privately Held**
SIC: 3545 Cutting tools for machine tools

(G-6304)
LEONARD DICK
Also Called: Len Dick Signs
3000 York Rd (17325-8240)
PHONE..................................717 334-8992
Leonard Dick, *Owner*
Chad Dick, *Co-Owner*
EMP: 3
SQ FT: 2,160
SALES: 100K **Privately Held**
SIC: 3993 Signs, not made in custom sign painting shops

(G-6305)
LEVIS ONLY STORES INC
1863 Gettysburg Vlg Dr (17325-8989)
PHONE..................................717 337-1294
EMP: 8
SALES (corp-wide): 4.7B **Privately Held**
SIC: 2253 Knit Outerwear Mill
HQ: Levi's Only Stores, Inc.
1155 Battery St
San Francisco CA 94111

(G-6306)
MASON-DIXON DISTILLERY
331 E Water St (17325-1528)
PHONE..................................717 314-2070
EMP: 6
SALES (est): 471.6K **Privately Held**
SIC: 2085 Distilled & blended liquors

(G-6307)
MAYA DEVI INC
1980 Biglerville Rd (17325-8037)
PHONE..................................717 420-7060
Dipendra Sah, *Principal*
EMP: 5
SALES (est): 511.1K **Privately Held**
SIC: 2869 Fuels

(G-6308)
MORTON BUILDINGS INC
3370 York Rd (17325-8258)
PHONE..................................717 624-8000
Rodney Weaver, *Principal*
Dave Gisi, *Regl Sales Mgr*
Rod Weaver, *Office Mgr*
EMP: 50
SALES (corp-wide): 463.7MM **Privately Held**
WEB: www.mortonbuildings.com
SIC: 3448 5039 2452 Farm & utility buildings; prefabricated structures; prefabricated wood buildings
PA: Morton Buildings, Inc.
252 W Adams St
Morton IL 61550
800 447-7436

(G-6309)
MYERS ELECTRICAL REPAIRS
1785 Biglerville Rd (17325-8083)
PHONE..................................717 334-8105
Glenn A Myers, *Owner*
Lois L Myers, *Admin Sec*
EMP: 6 **EST:** 1965
SQ FT: 11,000
SALES: 750K **Privately Held**
SIC: 7538 7694 5013 General automotive repair shops; electric motor repair; filters, air & oil

(G-6310)
PELLA CORPORATION
2000 Proline Pl (17325-8297)
PHONE..................................717 334-0099
Skip Barrick, *Manager*
EMP: 64
SALES (corp-wide): 1.8B **Privately Held**
SIC: 2431 Windows & window parts & trim, wood
PA: Pella Corporation
102 Main St
Pella IA 50219
641 621-1000

(G-6311)
QUALASTAT ELECTRONICS INC (PA)
1270 Fairfield Rd Ste 50 (17325-7246)
PHONE..................................717 253-9301
Vernon Judy Sr, *President*
Patricia Judy, *Admin Sec*
EMP: 20
SQ FT: 17,000
SALES (est): 2.9MM **Privately Held**
WEB: www.qualastat.com
SIC: 3643 3679 3229 Current-carrying wiring devices; electronic circuits; fiber optics strands

(G-6312)
RIGGEALS PERFORMANCE FIBRGLS
1741 Goldenville Rd (17325-7440)
PHONE..................................717 677-4167
Gregory Riggeal, *President*
EMP: 5
SQ FT: 12,000
SALES (est): 430K **Privately Held**
WEB: www.riggeals.com
SIC: 1799 3711 Fiberglass work; motor vehicles & car bodies

(G-6313)
ROARING SPRING BLANK BOOK CO
Also Called: Roaring Spring Bottling Co
1325 Hanover Rd (17325-7709)
P.O. Box 4897 (17325-4897)
PHONE..................................717 334-8080
Brent Smith, *Manager*
EMP: 40
SALES (corp-wide): 96.8MM **Privately Held**
WEB: www.roaringspring.com
SIC: 2086 Bottled & canned soft drinks
PA: Roaring Spring Blank Book Company
740 Spang St
Roaring Spring PA 16673
814 224-2306

(G-6314)
SPECTRA-KOTE CORPORATION
301 E Water St (17325-1528)
P.O. Box 3369 (17325-0369)
PHONE..................................717 334-3177
Colin Bailey, *CEO*
Edward V Kellogg, *President*
Charles W Propst Jr, *President*
Eric W Baker, *Plant Mgr*
Kathy Smith, *Cust Mgr*
EMP: 25 **EST:** 1957
SQ FT: 70,000
SALES (est): 9.8MM **Privately Held**
WEB: www.spectra-kote.com
SIC: 2672 2851 Coated paper, except photographic, carbon or abrasive; paints & allied products

(G-6315)
STAN CLARK MILITARY BOOKS
915 Fairview Ave (17325-2906)
PHONE..................................717 337-1728
Stan Clark, *Owner*
EMP: 3
SALES: 500K **Privately Held**
SIC: 2731 5192 Books: publishing only; books

(G-6316)
STRAT-O-SPAN BUILDINGS INC
2020 Chambersburg Rd (17325-7416)
PHONE..................................717 334-4606
Larry L Johnson, *Opers-Prdtn-Mfg*
EMP: 3
SALES (corp-wide): 1.2MM **Privately Held**
WEB: www.strat-o-span.com
SIC: 2452 5039 Farm buildings, prefabricated or portable: wood; metal buildings
PA: Strat-O-Span Buildings, Inc.
7980 Old Us Highway 50
Breese IL 62230
618 526-4566

(G-6317)
THEN DEFENSE GROUP
1480 Highland Avenue Rd (17325-7010)
PHONE..................................717 465-0584
Robert Then, *Principal*
EMP: 3
SALES (est): 162.8K **Privately Held**
SIC: 3812 Defense systems & equipment

(G-6318)
THOMAS
3245 Fairfield Rd (17325-7363)
P.O. Box 3031 (17325-0031)
PHONE..................................717 642-6600
Dean Thomas, *Owner*
EMP: 3
SQ FT: 10,000
SALES (est): 204.3K **Privately Held**
WEB: www.thomaspublications.com
SIC: 2731 5192 Books: publishing only; books

(G-6319)
TRIPWIRE OPERATIONS GROUP LLC
1685 Baltimore Pike Ste C (17325-7974)
PHONE..................................717 648-2792
Ryan J Morris,
EMP: 9
SQ FT: 11,000

▲ = Import ▼=Export
◆ =Import/Export

G E O G R A P H I C

SALES: 750K **Privately Held**
WEB: www.tripwireops.org
SIC: **8748** 8331 2892 Safety training
service; job training & vocational rehabilitation services; explosives

(G-6320)
VALLEY QUARRIES INC
1575 Baltimore Pike (17325-7089)
P.O. Box 3128 (17325-0128)
PHONE..................................717 334-3281
Thomas Zimmerman, *CEO*
Dale Smith, *Opers-Prdtn-Mfg*
EMP: 20
SALES (corp-wide): 651.9MM **Privately
Held**
WEB: www.valleyquarries.com
SIC: **1422** Crushed & broken limestone
HQ: Valley Quarries, Inc.
297 Quarry Rd
Chambersburg PA 17202
717 267-2244

(G-6321)
**WASHINGTON RADIO REPORTS
INC (PA)**
1588 Fairfield Rd (17325-7252)
PHONE..................................717 334-0668
Dan Roberts, *Principal*
EMP: 12
SQ FT: 1,000
SALES (est): 1MM **Privately Held**
SIC: **2721** 2741 Periodicals: publishing
only; miscellaneous publishing

(G-6322)
**WASHINGTON RADIO REPORTS
INC**
1588 Fairfield Rd (17325-7252)
PHONE..................................717 334-0668
Tammy Cooper, *Branch Mgr*
EMP: 10
SALES (corp-wide): 1MM **Privately Held**
SIC: **2721** Periodicals: publishing only
PA: Washington Radio Reports Inc
1588 Fairfield Rd
Gettysburg PA 17325
717 334-0668

Gibsonia
Allegheny County

(G-6323)
**AMERICAN FASTENER TECH
CORP**
9 Frontier Dr (15044-7992)
PHONE..................................724 444-6940
Jeffrey M Dutkovic, *President*
Jeffrey D Dutkovic, *Vice Pres*
Ron Winter, *Purchasing*
Lisa Stipetich, *Controller*
Jeff Dutkovic, *Manager*
EMP: 10
SQ FT: 15,000
SALES (est): 990K **Privately Held**
WEB: www.americanfastener.com
SIC: **3452** 3965 Nuts, metal; fasteners

(G-6324)
AMERICAN LEGION POST 548
3724 Legion Dr (15044-7509)
P.O. Box 171, Bakerstown (15007-0171)
PHONE..................................724 443-0047
Robert Munhall, *Owner*
EMP: 95
SALES (est): 3.1MM **Privately Held**
SIC: **2389** Regalia

(G-6325)
AWARDS & MORE
5418 William Flynn Hwy (15044-9652)
PHONE..................................724 444-1040
Rennae Capizzi, *Owner*
Peter Capizzi, *Co-Owner*
EMP: 5
SQ FT: 2,400
SALES (est): 468.7K **Privately Held**
WEB: www.awardsmore.com
SIC: **7389** 2395 2759 5999 Engraving
service; embroidery & art needlework;
screen printing; trophies & plaques; ad-
vertising specialties

(G-6326)
BIG OAKS LTD PARTNERSHIP II
5360 William Flynn Hwy (15044-9650)
PHONE..................................724 444-0055
Toll Free:....................................888 -
Anthony Sluka, *Partner*
David Good, *Partner*
EMP: 12
SALES: 2MM **Privately Held**
SIC: **2842** Paint & wallpaper cleaners

(G-6327)
BLOCKI FLUTE METHOD LLC
5368 Hardt Rd (15044-9165)
PHONE..................................866 463-5883
Kathy Blocki, *Mng Member*
Marvin Blocki, *Mng Member*
EMP: 5 EST: 2007
SALES: 120K **Privately Held**
SIC: **3931** Musical instruments

(G-6328)
BON TOOL COMPANY (PA)
4430 Gibsonia Rd (15044-7945)
PHONE..................................724 443-7080
Carl A Bongiovanni, *President*
Michele Bender, *Vice Pres*
Paula Wight, *Admin Sec*
◆ EMP: 78 EST: 1958
SQ FT: 120,000
SALES (est): 18.2MM **Privately Held**
WEB: www.bontool.com
SIC: **3423** 3829 3546 3545 Masons'
hand tools; measuring & controlling de-
vices; power-driven handtools; machine
tool accessories; construction machinery;
architectural metalwork

(G-6329)
**BRADLEY COATINGS GROUP
INC (DH)**
2873 W Hardies Rd Ste 1 (15044-8209)
PHONE..................................724 444-4400
Thomas Gillespie, *President*
EMP: 14 EST: 1946
SQ FT: 2,500
SALES (est): 2.5MM
SALES (corp-wide): 17.8MM **Privately
Held**
SIC: **2851** Paints & paint additives; lac-
quers, varnishes, enamels & other coat-
ings
HQ: Lockhart Holdings Inc
2873 W Hardies Rd Ste 1
Gibsonia PA 15044
724 444-1900

(G-6330)
CDI PRINTING SERVICES INC
Rr 910 (15044)
P.O. Box 689 (15044-0689)
PHONE..................................724 444-6160
Horace Britten, *CEO*
Jake Williams, *Partner*
George Williams, *Vice Pres*
Horace J Britton, *Treasurer*
Joseph Williams, *Admin Sec*
EMP: 15
SALES (est): 3.3MM **Privately Held**
SIC: **2752** Commercial printing, offset

(G-6331)
**DIGITAL DSGNS GRPHICS SGNS
LLC**
12 Kelly Ct (15044-7808)
PHONE..................................724 568-1626
Joe Butera,
EMP: 5
SALES (est): 418.8K **Privately Held**
SIC: **3993** Signs, not made in custom sign
painting shops

(G-6332)
DIVISION SEVEN INC
230 Laurel Ave (15044-6003)
PHONE..................................724 449-8400
David Capezzuti Jr, *President*
Patrick Clements, *Manager*
EMP: 4
SQ FT: 3,500
SALES (est): 1.5MM **Privately Held**
WEB: www.divisionseven.net
SIC: **5085** 3444 Fasteners & fastening
equipment; abrasives & adhesives;
valves, pistons & fittings; sheet metalwork

(G-6333)
ETCHED IN GLASS
5424 William Flynn Hwy (15044-9652)
PHONE..................................724 444-0808
George Masche, *Partner*
Donna Masche, *Partner*
April Pickering, *Partner*
EMP: 7
SALES (est): 783.4K **Privately Held**
SIC: **3231** 5999 5947 3229 Ornamental
glass: cut, engraved or otherwise deco-
rated; trophies & plaques; gift shop;
glassware, art or decorative

(G-6334)
**FORM TECH CONCRETE FORMS
INC**
2850 Kramer Rd (15044-9670)
PHONE..................................412 331-4500
Greg Andrews, *Branch Mgr*
EMP: 10
SALES (corp-wide): 43.3MM **Privately
Held**
WEB: www.formtechinc.com
SIC: **3444** Concrete forms, sheet metal
PA: Form Tech Concrete Forms, Inc.
48575 Downing St
Wixom MI 48393
248 344-8260

(G-6335)
GABLE PRINTING
5499 William Flynn Hwy (15044-9675)
PHONE..................................724 443-3444
Eva Eury, *Owner*
EMP: 5
SQ FT: 2,500
SALES: 275K **Privately Held**
SIC: **2752** Commercial printing, litho-
graphic

(G-6336)
GAYDOS EQUIPMENT LLC
5060 Willow Wood Dr (15044-8298)
PHONE..................................724 272-6951
Mike Gaydos,
EMP: 23
SALES: 25K **Privately Held**
SIC: **3569** Assembly machines, non-metal-
working

(G-6337)
**GEMINI PRECISION PRODUCTS
LTD**
104 Isleworth Way (15044-6083)
PHONE..................................724 452-8700
Linda Thurston, *CEO*
EMP: 3
SQ FT: 2,500
SALES (est): 160K **Privately Held**
WEB: www.geminikaleidoscopes.com
SIC: **3944** Games, toys & children's vehi-
cles

(G-6338)
GET-A-GRIP CHAFING PANS
2361 Banks School Rd (15044-8345)
PHONE..................................724 443-6037
Lois Leonard, *President*
Joseph Leonard, *Vice Pres*
EMP: 3
SQ FT: 1,700
SALES: 20K **Privately Held**
SIC: **3469** Household cooking & kitchen
utensils, metal

(G-6339)
HANDLING PRODUCTS INC (PA)
Also Called: H P I
3151 Seneca Ct (15044-8269)
P.O. Box 322, Allison Park (15101-0322)
PHONE..................................724 443-1100
Frank Bankowski, *President*
Gail Wallace, *Admin Sec*
EMP: 3
SALES (est): 1MM **Privately Held**
WEB: www.handlingproducts.com
SIC: **8742** 3535 Sales (including sales
management) consultant; conveyors &
conveying equipment

(G-6340)
**HOPPER T AND J BUILDING
SUPS**
5975 Station Hill Rd (15044-9766)
PHONE..................................724 443-2222
James L Hopper, *President*
Thomas Hopper, *Vice Pres*
Sarah Marie Hopper, *Treasurer*
EMP: 12
SALES (est): 1.3MM **Privately Held**
SIC: **3273** 5032 1794 Ready-mixed con-
crete; building blocks; excavation & grad-
ing, building construction

(G-6341)
KRAFT HEINZ FOODS COMPANY
704 Bristlecone Dr (15044-6135)
PHONE..................................412 237-5868
Marc Brown, *Branch Mgr*
EMP: 25
SALES (corp-wide): 26.2B **Publicly Held**
SIC: **2032** Canned specialties
HQ: Kraft Heinz Foods Company
1 Ppg Pl Ste 3200
Pittsburgh PA 15222
412 456-5700

(G-6342)
LACASA NARCISI WINERY
4578 Gibsonia Rd (15044-7911)
PHONE..................................724 444-4744
Sara Narcisi, *Owner*
Roberto Smiraglio, *Manager*
EMP: 10
SALES (est): 877.8K **Privately Held**
WEB: www.narcisiwinery.com
SIC: **2084** Wines

(G-6343)
LION ENERGY CO LLC
5636 N Montour Rd (15044-9106)
PHONE..................................724 444-7501
John Holko, *Mng Member*
Karl Kimmel,
EMP: 3
SALES (est): 380K **Privately Held**
SIC: **3731** Drilling & production platforms,
floating (oil & gas)

(G-6344)
**LOCKHART CHEMICAL
COMPANY (PA)**
2873 W Hardies Rd (15044-8209)
PHONE..................................724 444-1900
Thomas Gillespie Jr, *Ch of Bd*
Raj Minhas, *President*
Larry Burkestrom, *Vice Pres*
Rajinder Minhas, *Vice Pres*
Charles J Frasca, *Treasurer*
◆ EMP: 30
SQ FT: 15,000
SALES (est): 17.7MM **Privately Held**
WEB: www.bradleycoatings.com
SIC: **2819** 8731 2899 2865 Chemicals,
high purity: refined from technical grade;
commercial physical research; chemical
preparations; cyclic crudes & intermedi-
ates

(G-6345)
LOCKHART COMPANY (PA)
Also Called: Lockhart Industries
2873 W Hardies Rd Ste 1 (15044-8209)
PHONE..................................724 444-1900
Thomas J Gillespie Jr, *President*
Brian K Benjamin, *Vice Pres*
Barbara Hendler, *Controller*
EMP: 25
SQ FT: 340,000
SALES (est): 17.8MM **Privately Held**
WEB: www.lockhartcompany.com
SIC: **2819** 2851 Chemicals, high purity: re-
fined from technical grade; paints & paint
additives; lacquers, varnishes, enamels &
other coatings

(G-6346)
LOCKHART HOLDINGS INC (HQ)
2873 W Hardies Rd Ste 1 (15044-8209)
P.O. Box 8985, Wilmington DE (19899-
8985)
PHONE..................................724 444-1900
Thomas Gillespie Jr, *CEO*
Thomas J Gillespie Sr, *Chairman*
Thomas Gillespie Sr, *Chairman*

Brian K Benjamin, *Vice Pres*
EMP: 20
SQ FT: 15,000
SALES (est): 7.3MM
SALES (corp-wide): 17.8MM **Privately Held**
SIC: 2819 Chemicals, high purity: refined from technical grade
PA: Lockhart Company
2873 W Hardies Rd Ste 1
Gibsonia PA 15044
724 444-1900

(G-6347)
MASTERFLO PUMP INC
23 Dewey Ln Ste A (15044-4918)
PHONE..................................724 443-1122
Bill Frohlich, *President*
Cynthia Frohlich, *Vice Pres*
EMP: 7
SALES (est): 1.7MM **Privately Held**
SIC: 3561 5084 Industrial pumps & parts; water pumps (industrial)

(G-6348)
PANNIER CORPORATION
345 Oak Rd (15044-7994)
PHONE..................................724 265-4900
Jeffrey Heddaeus, *Vice Pres*
Pam Gilbert, *Purch Agent*
Lisa Dvorchak, *VP Mktg*
Jeff Heddeus, *Branch Mgr*
Tim Bland, *Manager*
EMP: 30
SALES (corp-wide): 17.9MM **Privately Held**
WEB: www.pannier.com
SIC: 3953 3993 Marking devices; signs & advertising specialties
PA: The Pannier Corporation
207 Sandusky St
Pittsburgh PA 15212
412 323-4900

(G-6349)
REJNIAKS ALPACA
1187 Logan Rd (15044-7714)
PHONE..................................724 265-4062
Stanley J Rejniak, *Principal*
EMP: 1
SALES (est): 225.8K **Privately Held**
WEB: www.rejniaksalpacas.com
SIC: 2231 Alpacas, mohair: woven

(G-6350)
ROADSAFE TRAFFIC SYSTEMS INC
1623 Middle Road Ext (15044-7913)
PHONE..................................412 559-1396
David Meirick, *CEO*
EMP: 60 **Privately Held**
SIC: 3499 Barricades, metal
PA: Roadsafe Traffic Systems, Inc.
8750 W Bryn Mawr Ave
Chicago IL 60631

(G-6351)
SEALGUARD INC
1015 Foggy Hollow Rd (15044-9671)
PHONE..................................724 625-4550
Eric W Smith, *President*
EMP: 10
SQ FT: 2,000
SALES (est): 2MM **Privately Held**
WEB: www.sealguardinc.com
SIC: 2821 Polyesters

(G-6352)
STEEL CITY OPTRONICS LLC
5149 Prince Phillip Ct (15044-8492)
PHONE..................................412 501-3849
Sara Partee, *CEO*
Beth Kiser,
EMP: 4
SALES (est): 273.4K **Privately Held**
SIC: 3861 Photographic equipment & supplies

(G-6353)
SURGEONEERING LLC
423 Heights Dr (15044-6032)
PHONE..................................412 292-2816
James Burgess,
EMP: 3

SALES (est): 185.4K **Privately Held**
SIC: 3841 Surgical instruments & apparatus

(G-6354)
SWICK ORNAMENTAL IRON
4785 Josephine Dr (15044)
PHONE..................................412 487-5755
Bernie Swick Jr, *Partner*
EMP: 3
SQ FT: 3,000
SALES (est): 455.4K **Privately Held**
SIC: 3446 Ornamental metalwork

(G-6355)
T K PLASTICS INC
4390 Gibsonia Rd Ste 1 (15044-5325)
PHONE..................................724 443-6760
Todd Kaercher, *President*
EMP: 19
SQ FT: 11,000
SALES (est): 3MM **Privately Held**
WEB: www.tkplastics.com
SIC: 3089 Plastic hardware & building products

(G-6356)
TRU-LITE INTERNATIONAL INC
5311 William Flynn Hwy (15044-9644)
PHONE..................................724 443-6821
Robert Williams, *President*
John Williams, *Admin Sec*
EMP: 5 EST: 1978
SQ FT: 2,500
SALES (est): 728.3K **Privately Held**
SIC: 3699 Welding machines & equipment, ultrasonic

(G-6357)
TRUE POSITION INC
3919 Chessrown Ave (15044-9612)
PHONE..................................724 444-0300
John Spudic, *President*
Ivan A Spudic, *Vice Pres*
Jason Spudic, *Vice Pres*
Diane Spudic, *Admin Sec*
EMP: 15
SQ FT: 10,000
SALES (est): 3.2MM **Privately Held**
SIC: 3599 7692 Machine shop, jobbing & repair; welding repair

(G-6358)
WILBUR ENTERPRISES INC
446 Four Lakes Dr (15044-8045)
PHONE..................................724 625-8010
William Lowry, *President*
Angela Lowry, *Admin Sec*
EMP: 6
SALES (est): 343.9K **Privately Held**
SIC: 2095 Coffee, ground: mixed with grain or chicory

(G-6359)
WILLIAMS BUSINESS FORMS LTD
Also Called: Green Business Forms
Middle Rd Ext Rr 910 (15044)
P.O. Box 625 (15044-0625)
PHONE..................................724 444-6771
Joseph Williams, *President*
George H Williams, *Corp Secy*
EMP: 12 EST: 1976
SQ FT: 10,000
SALES (est): 1.8MM **Privately Held**
SIC: 2759 Letterpress printing

Gifford
Mckean County

(G-6360)
PHILLIPS & DART OIL FIELD SVC
3502 Route 646 (16732-1104)
P.O. Box 222 (16732-0222)
PHONE..................................814 465-2292
Ray Dart, *President*
Paul Phillips, *Corp Secy*
EMP: 6
SQ FT: 115
SALES (est): 620K **Privately Held**
SIC: 1389 Well plugging & abandoning, oil & gas

Gilbert
Monroe County

(G-6361)
HERFURTH BROTHERS INC
Rr 209 (18331)
P.O. Box 128 (18331-0128)
PHONE..................................610 681-4515
Stewart Herfurth, *Principal*
EMP: 8 EST: 2011
SALES (est): 803.1K **Privately Held**
SIC: 2011 Meat packing plants

(G-6362)
JIM MANNELLO
Also Called: West End Printing
1356 Route 209 (18331-7738)
PHONE..................................610 681-6467
EMP: 6
SQ FT: 2,000
SALES (est): 460K **Privately Held**
SIC: 2752 2791 2789 Lithographic Commercial Printing Typesetting Services Bookbinding/Related Work

(G-6363)
POCONO PROTECH
732 Gilbert Rd (18331-7733)
PHONE..................................610 681-3550
EMP: 3 EST: 1992
SQ FT: 3,600
SALES (est): 250K **Privately Held**
SIC: 7692 Welding Repair

(G-6364)
TILSIT CORPORATION
Rr 209 (18331)
PHONE..................................610 681-5951
Bill Schierwagen, *President*
EMP: 12
SQ FT: 12,000
SALES (est): 1.6MM **Privately Held**
SIC: 3643 Electric connectors

Gilberton
Schuylkill County

(G-6365)
B D MINING CO INC
10 Gilberton Rd (17934-1009)
PHONE..................................570 874-1602
John W Rich, *President*
EMP: 25
SQ FT: 15,000
SALES (est): 1.9MM **Privately Held**
SIC: 1231 Anthracite mining

(G-6366)
FILTER MEDIA INC
Main St (17934)
PHONE..................................570 874-2537
John W Rich Sr, *President*
Brian Rich, *Vice Pres*
Robert Ryan, *Treasurer*
John Rich Jr, *Admin Sec*
Jack Dalton, *Administration*
EMP: 5 EST: 1978
SQ FT: 500
SALES (est): 500K **Privately Held**
WEB: www.filtermedia.net
SIC: 1231 Preparation plants, anthracite

(G-6367)
GILBERTON COAL COMPANY
10 Gilberton Rd (17934-1009)
PHONE..................................570 874-1602
John W Rich, *President*
Justine Waiksnoris, *Administration*
Mark Wolfe, *Planning*
EMP: 40
SQ FT: 15,000
SALES (est): 4.2MM **Privately Held**
SIC: 1231 Recovery of anthracite from culm banks; preparation plants, anthracite

(G-6368)
GILBERTON ENERGY CORPORATION (PA)
10 Gilberton Rd (17934-1009)
PHONE..................................570 874-1602
John W Rich, *President*
EMP: 9
SALES (est): 1.1MM **Privately Held**
SIC: 2819 Industrial inorganic chemicals

(G-6369)
R & R ENERGY CORP
Also Called: Gilberton Coal
10 Gilberton Rd (17934-1009)
PHONE..................................570 874-1602
John W Rich Sr, *President*
EMP: 20
SQ FT: 15,000
SALES (est): 1.1MM **Privately Held**
SIC: 1231 Preparation plants, anthracite

Gilbertsville
Montgomery County

(G-6370)
BAGATRIX SOLUTIONS LTD
462 Windy Hill Rd (19525-9807)
P.O. Box 248, Coopersburg (18036-0248)
PHONE..................................610 574-9607
Frank Balcavage,
Jake Kuehner,
EMP: 4
SALES (est): 265.7K **Privately Held**
WEB: www.bagatrix.com
SIC: 7372 Publishers' computer software

(G-6371)
COLORWORKS GRAPHIC SVCS INC
480 County Line Rd (19525-9296)
P.O. Box 80, Boyertown (19512-0080)
PHONE..................................610 367-7599
Donald E Smale, *President*
Robin Fox, *Accounts Mgr*
EMP: 28
SQ FT: 17,000
SALES (est): 1.5MM **Privately Held**
SIC: 2754 2791 2752 Commercial printing, gravure; typesetting; commercial printing, lithographic

(G-6372)
FLAGZONE LLC
105a Industrial Dr (19525-8832)
P.O. Box 526 (19525-0526)
PHONE..................................610 367-9900
Elmer Bauer,
Joseph Price,
▲ **EMP:** 105
SQ FT: 80,000
SALES (est): 19.7MM **Privately Held**
WEB: www.theflagzone.com
SIC: 2399 Flags, fabric

(G-6373)
HUTTS GLASS CO INC
3186 N Charlotte St (19525-9628)
PHONE..................................610 369-1028
John Borchers, *Manager*
EMP: 5
SALES (corp-wide): 6.5MM **Privately Held**
WEB: www.huttsglass.com
SIC: 3211 Flat glass
PA: Hutt's Glass Co., Inc.
105 Limekiln Rd 9
Bechtelsville PA 19505
610 369-1028

(G-6374)
I D TECHNOLOGIES INC
3186 N Charlotte St (19525-9628)
PHONE..................................610 652-2418
Heather Helmers, *CEO*
Duff Helmers, *President*
Kathleen Buckingham, *Office Mgr*
EMP: 6
SALES (est): 150K **Privately Held**
SIC: 3492 Hose & tube couplings, hydraulic/pneumatic

(G-6375)
PENFLEX CORPORATION
105b Industrial Dr (19525-8832)
PHONE..................................610 367-2260
Robert P Barker, *President*
Nathaniel S Barker, *Vice Pres*
Lee Dierolf, *Plant Mgr*
▲ EMP: 52
SQ FT: 100,000
SALES (est): 11.3MM **Privately Held**
WEB: www.penflex.com
SIC: 3599 Flexible metal hose, tubing &
  bellows

(G-6376)
S & W METAL PRODUCTS INC
441 County Line Rd (19525-8822)
PHONE..................................610 473-2400
Gretchen Mohen, *President*
Gary Rolls, *Purch Mgr*
◆ EMP: 48 EST: 1974
SQ FT: 110,000
SALES (est): 9.4MM **Privately Held**
WEB: www.swmetal.net
SIC: 3599 Machine shop, jobbing & repair

(G-6377)
S F U LLC
Also Called: Store Fixtures Unlimited
136 Pinehurst Way (19525-8643)
PHONE..................................610 473-0730
Mike Radich,
EMP: 9
SALES (est): 1.2MM **Privately Held**
WEB: www.storefixturesunlimited.com
SIC: 2541 5046 Display fixtures, wood;
  commercial equipment

(G-6378)
TRS WELDING & FABRICATION INC
500 County Line Rd (19525-9295)
PHONE..................................610 369-0897
Tony Rsheha, *Principal*
EMP: 10
SALES (est): 1.9MM **Privately Held**
SIC: 7692 Welding repair

(G-6379)
UNION SEALANTS LLC
35 Ashley Cir (19525-8877)
PHONE..................................610 473-2892
Matthew J McNally, *Principal*
EMP: 4
SALES (est): 451.9K **Privately Held**
SIC: 2891 Sealants

Gillett
Bradford County

(G-6380)
DURA-BILT PRODUCTS INC
17066 Berwick Tpke (16925-9158)
P.O. Box 188, Wellsburg NY (14894-0188)
PHONE..................................570 596-2000
Martin Chalk, *President*
Jeffrey Chalk, *Vice Pres*
Mary Comstock, *Treasurer*
Richard Keyser, *Admin Sec*
EMP: 60 EST: 1958
SQ FT: 60,000
SALES (est): 15.2MM **Privately Held**
WEB: www.durabilt.com
SIC: 3446 3444 3448 3449 Railings, pre-
  fabricated metal; roof deck, sheet metal;
  prefabricated metal buildings; miscella-
  neous metalwork

(G-6381)
HALLS CANDIES LLC
Also Called: Doc's Candies
3426 Thunder Rd (16925-9347)
PHONE..................................570 596-2267
Jeanne Andrews, *Branch Mgr*
EMP: 5
SALES (est): 316.9K
SALES (corp-wide): 300K **Privately Held**
SIC: 2064 5441 Fudge (candy); chewing
  candy, not chewing gum; nuts, candy cov-
  ered; candy

PA: Hall's Candies, Llc
  32740 Route 14
  Gillett PA 16925
  570 596-7688

(G-6382)
MOUNTAIN TOP WELDING & REPAIR
3894 Centerville Rd (16925-9020)
PHONE..................................570 888-7174
Dave Kolb, *Partner*
Leona Kolb, *Partner*
EMP: 3 EST: 1993
SALES (est): 180K **Privately Held**
SIC: 3599 7692 Machine shop, jobbing &
  repair; welding repair

Girard
Erie County

(G-6383)
ADVANCED CAST STONE INC INC
711 Beaver Rd (16417-8411)
PHONE..................................817 572-0018
Peter Boogren, *President*
EMP: 5
SALES (est): 516.9K **Privately Held**
SIC: 3272 Concrete products, precast

(G-6384)
ANDERSON PLASTICS INC
227 Hathaway St E (16417-1552)
PHONE..................................814 774-0076
Linda Anderson, *President*
Steve Anderson, *Principal*
Ivan Greene, *Vice Pres*
◆ EMP: 12
SQ FT: 6,800
SALES (est): 619K **Privately Held**
WEB: www.andersonplastics.com
SIC: 3089 Injection molding of plastics

(G-6385)
CUMMINGS GROUP LTD
Also Called: Erie Powder Coating
227 Hathaway St E (16417-1552)
PHONE..................................814 774-8238
John B Cummings, *President*
Don Stichick, *Vice Pres*
Chuck Cummings, *Director*
Kira Cummings, *Admin Sec*
EMP: 10
SQ FT: 20,000
SALES (est): 500K **Privately Held**
WEB: www.powdercoater.net
SIC: 3479 5169 5084 Coating of metals &
  formed products; chemicals & allied prod-
  ucts; chemical process equipment

(G-6386)
EMSCO INC (PA)
Also Called: Emsco Group
607 Church St (16417-1515)
P.O. Box 151 (16417-0151)
PHONE..................................814 774-3137
David Oas, *President*
Dennis Oas, *Chairman*
Steve Oas, *Vice Pres*
Nancy Bottom, *Accountant*
Dianne Clark, *Admin Sec*
◆ EMP: 110
SQ FT: 450,000
SALES (est): 18.1MM **Privately Held**
WEB: www.emscogroup.com
SIC: 2842 3423 3089 Specialty cleaning,
  polishes & sanitation goods; hand & edge
  tools; garden & farm tools, including shov-
  els; injection molding of plastics

(G-6387)
EMSCO INC
Emsco-Group
306 Shenango St (16417-1560)
P.O. Box 151 (16417-0151)
PHONE..................................814 774-3137
David B Oas, *President*
EMP: 30
SQ FT: 50,000

SALES (corp-wide): 18.1MM **Privately Held**
WEB: www.emscogroup.com
SIC: 3589 Floor washing & polishing machines, commercial; janitors' carts; mop
  wringers
PA: Emsco, Inc.
  607 Church St
  Girard PA 16417
  814 774-3137

(G-6388)
FABRICATING TECHNOLOGY INC
Also Called: Fabtech
409 Noble Rd (16417-8407)
PHONE..................................814 774-4403
David McDonald, *Principal*
EMP: 10
SALES (est): 700K **Privately Held**
SIC: 3545 Machine tool accessories

(G-6389)
G R GRAPHICS
321 Mechanic St (16417-1410)
P.O. Box 393 (16417-0393)
PHONE..................................814 774-9592
Tom Dagit, *Partner*
Wayne Rose, *Partner*
EMP: 4
SALES: 240K **Privately Held**
SIC: 2752 Commercial printing, offset

(G-6390)
GREAT LAKES CAST STONE INC
711 Beaver Rd (16417-8411)
PHONE..................................814 402-1055
Steven Henderson, *President*
EMP: 10
SALES (est): 1.4MM **Privately Held**
SIC: 3272 Concrete products, precast

(G-6391)
IDENTIFICATION SYSTEMS INC
Also Called: Laser Creations
10043 Peach St (16417-9205)
PHONE..................................814 774-9656
Walter Youngs, *CEO*
Mark Youngs, *President*
Scott Smith, *Vice Pres*
EMP: 20
SQ FT: 30,000
SALES (est): 2.9MM **Privately Held**
WEB: www.lasercreations.com
SIC: 2499 3993 Engraved wood products;
  signs & advertising specialties

(G-6392)
JACKBURN CORPORATION
438 Church St (16417-1512)
P.O. Box 166 (16417-0166)
PHONE..................................814 774-3573
Frederick A Rossetti, *President*
EMP: 30
SQ FT: 48,000
SALES (est): 2.4MM
SALES (corp-wide): 10.6MM **Privately Held**
SIC: 3496 Miscellaneous fabricated wire
  products
PA: Knox Enterprises Inc
  830 Post Rd E Ste 205
  Westport CT 06880
  203 226-6408

(G-6393)
JACKBURN MFG INC
438 Church St (16417-1512)
P.O. Box 166 (16417-0166)
PHONE..................................814 774-3573
Mark L Wilson, *President*
Dale Warofka, *COO*
Michael Vadzemnieks, *CFO*
Reed Grunden, *Sales Mgr*
Donald Macinnes, *Manager*
▲ EMP: 12 EST: 1962
SQ FT: 48,000
SALES (est): 4.9MM **Privately Held**
WEB: www.jackburn.com
SIC: 3496 Miscellaneous fabricated wire
  products

(G-6394)
KAUFER ASSOCIATES INC
Also Called: Maple Craft USA
142 Main St E Ste 1 (16417-1740)
PHONE..................................814 756-4997
EMP: 8
SQ FT: 3,750
SALES: 1.2MM **Privately Held**
SIC: 2599 7389 Mfg Furniture/Fixtures
  Business Services

(G-6395)
KLIMEK MOLDING CORP
321 Mechanic St (16417-1410)
PHONE..................................814 774-4051
Donald Klimek, *President*
Jim Klimek, *President*
Fred Klimek, *Treasurer*
EMP: 3 EST: 2001
SALES (est): 285.6K **Privately Held**
SIC: 3089 Molding primary plastic

(G-6396)
LAWRIE TECHNOLOGY INC
227 Hathaway St E (16417-1552)
PHONE..................................814 402-1208
Duncan Lawrie, *President*
EMP: 8
SQ FT: 15,000
SALES (est): 1.2MM **Privately Held**
WEB: www.lawrietechnology.com
SIC: 3083 3089 8711 8734 Thermoset-
  ting laminates: rods, tubes, plates &
  sheet; plastic processing; consulting engi-
  neer; professional engineer; testing labo-
  ratories

(G-6397)
MCDONALD SAND & GRAVEL INC
11425 Neiger Rd (16417-9130)
PHONE..................................814 774-8149
Dan W McDonald, *President*
Jackie McDonald, *Admin Sec*
EMP: 3
SALES (est): 776.2K **Privately Held**
SIC: 1442 Sand mining; gravel mining

(G-6398)
P D Q PEST CONTROL INC
Also Called: PDQ Pest Control
8799 Ridge Rd (16417-9563)
PHONE..................................814 774-8882
John Retcofsky, *President*
EMP: 4 EST: 1981
SALES (est): 358.1K **Privately Held**
SIC: 7342 3822 Pest control services;
  steam pressure controls, residential or
  commercial type

(G-6399)
PENNSIDE MACHINING LLC
Also Called: P S S Company Fax
18 Elk Creek Ave (16417-1106)
PHONE..................................814 774-2075
Richard Knapp, *Owner*
EMP: 4
SQ FT: 3,000
SALES (est): 290K **Privately Held**
WEB: www.pssco.net
SIC: 3599 Machine shop, jobbing & repair

(G-6400)
R & M TARGETS INC
227 Hathaway St E Ste E (16417-1552)
PHONE..................................814 774-0160
EMP: 6
SQ FT: 6,700
SALES (est): 572.5K **Privately Held**
SIC: 3949 5199 Mfg Sporting/Athletic
  Goods Whol Nondurable Goods

(G-6401)
SAMPLE NEWS GROUP LLC
142 Main St E Ste 3 (16417-1742)
PHONE..................................814 774-7073
Bob Williams, *Principal*
EMP: 13
SALES (corp-wide): 8MM **Privately Held**
SIC: 2711 Newspapers, publishing & print-
  ing
PA: Sample News Group, L.L.C.
  28 W South St
  Corry PA 16407
  814 665-8291

(G-6402)
SOUTH MORGAN TECHNOLOGIES LLC
227 Hathaway St E (16417-1552)
PHONE..........................814 774-2000
Kevin Ames,
EMP: 4 EST: 2011
SQ FT: 5,700
SALES (est): 666.3K Privately Held
SIC: 3541 Vertical turning & boring machines (metalworking)

(G-6403)
WALTON PAINT COMPANY INC
Beaver Paint Company
710 Beaver Rd (16417-8412)
P.O. Box 85 (16417-0085)
PHONE..........................814 774-3042
Richard Shannon, Principal
D Michael Walton, VP Sales
EMP: 11
SQ FT: 17,000
SALES (est): 1.3MM
SALES (corp-wide): 3.2MM Privately Held
SIC: 2851 Paints: oil or alkyd vehicle or water thinned; varnishes; lacquer: bases, dopes, thinner
PA: Walton Paint Company Inc
108 Main St
Jamestown PA 16134
724 932-3101

(G-6404)
ZURN ALUMINUM PRODUCTS CO
10884 Ridge Rd (16417-9114)
PHONE..........................814 774-2681
Robert Zurn Sr, President
Kit Kramer, Corp Secy
Robert Zurn Jr, Exec VP
EMP: 9 EST: 1966
SQ FT: 14,000
SALES (est): 1.4MM Privately Held
SIC: 3442 5999 5211 Storm doors or windows, metal; awnings; door & window products

Girardville
Schuylkill County

(G-6405)
GIRARD ESTATE FEE
Also Called: Girard Coal
Rr 54 (17935)
PHONE..........................570 276-1404
Michael Robert Burns, Branch Mgr
EMP: 20
SALES (corp-wide): 72.5MM Privately Held
SIC: 1241 Coal mining services
PA: Girard Estate Fee
21 S 12th St
Philadelphia PA 19107
215 787-2600

(G-6406)
KEYSTONE ANTHRACITE CO INC
259 N 2nd St (17935-1339)
PHONE..........................570 276-6480
Michael R Burns, President
EMP: 21
SALES (est): 5.1MM Privately Held
SIC: 1231 Anthracite mining

Gladwyne
Montgomery County

(G-6407)
FILTER TECHNOLOGY INC
408 Conshohocken State Rd (19035-1454)
P.O. Box 937, Oaks (19456-0937)
PHONE..........................866 992-9490
Eric Guenther, President
EMP: 5

SALES (est): 454.6K Privately Held
WEB: www.ftinc.net
SIC: 3564 3569 3589 3599 Purification & dust collection equipment; filters; commercial cooking & foodwarming equipment; amusement park equipment

(G-6408)
GAIL DAGOWITZ
Also Called: The Perfect Present
1130 Rock Creek Rd (19035-1440)
P.O. Box 423 (19035-0423)
PHONE..........................610 642-7634
Gail Dagowitz, Owner
EMP: 4
SALES: 250K Privately Held
WEB: www.tfairy.com
SIC: 5199 3999 Gifts & novelties; novelties, bric-a-brac & hobby kits

(G-6409)
WATERMARK USA LLC
408 Conshohocken State Rd (19035-1454)
P.O. Box 239 (19035-0239)
PHONE..........................610 983-0500
Edward Guenther, Principal
EMP: 10
SALES (est): 418.4K Privately Held
SIC: 3589 7389 1799 8734 Water purification equipment, household type; water softener service; food service equipment installation; testing laboratories; water leak detectors; liquid leak detection equipment

Glassport
Allegheny County

(G-6410)
COTT MANUFACTURING COMPANY
43 Allegheny Sq (15045-1649)
PHONE..........................412 675-0101
John Schmidt, General Mgr
EMP: 15
SALES (corp-wide): 5.3MM Privately Held
WEB: www.cottmfg.com
SIC: 3644 3661 Junction boxes, electric; telephone & telegraph apparatus
PA: Cott Manufacturing Company
43 Allegheny Sq
Glassport PA 15045
724 625-3730

(G-6411)
COTT MANUFACTURING COMPANY (PA)
43 Allegheny Sq (15045-1649)
P.O. Box 596, Wexford (15090-0596)
PHONE..........................724 625-3730
Jeffrey G Thomas, President
EMP: 25
SALES (est): 5.3MM Privately Held
WEB: www.cottmfg.com
SIC: 3644 3661 1799 3993 Junction boxes, electric; telephone & telegraph apparatus; corrosion control installation; signs & advertising specialties; plastics materials & resins

(G-6412)
EXPORT BOXING & CRATING INC
18 Allegheny Sq (15045-1649)
PHONE..........................412 675-1000
Karen Ganley, President
James Ganley, Vice Pres
EMP: 15
SQ FT: 30,000
SALES (est): 2.3MM Privately Held
WEB: www.exportboxing.com
SIC: 4225 2441 General warehousing; boxes, wood

(G-6413)
MILL SERVICES CORP (HQ)
12 Monongahela Ave (15045-1315)
PHONE..........................412 678-6141
Michael Coslov, CEO
◆ EMP: 10

SALES (est): 111.3MM Privately Held
SIC: 3295 1422 8742 3341 Slag, crushed or ground; cement rock, crushed & broken-quarrying; public utilities consultant; secondary nonferrous metals

(G-6414)
MPI SUPPLY INCORPORATED
25 Allegheny Sq (15045-1649)
PHONE..........................412 664-9320
Geoffrey Popovich, President
EMP: 6 EST: 2017
SALES (est): 268.5K Privately Held
SIC: 3532 5082 Mining machinery; construction & mining machinery

(G-6415)
PINNACLE PRECISION CO
37 Allegheny Sq (15045-1649)
PHONE..........................412 678-6816
Mike Small, Owner
EMP: 12 EST: 1997
SQ FT: 5,000
SALES (est): 2MM Privately Held
WEB: www.pinnacle-precision.com
SIC: 3599 Machine shop, jobbing & repair

(G-6416)
SUPERIOR CUSTOM DESIGNS INC
Allegheny Ave Bldg 42 (15045)
PHONE..........................412 744-0110
Raymond Podvorec, CEO
EMP: 6
SALES (est): 951.5K Privately Held
SIC: 3799 3537 5599 3711 Trailers & trailer equipment; truck trailers, used in plants, docks, terminals, etc.; utility trailers; motor vehicles & car bodies; bus bodies (motor vehicles)

(G-6417)
SUPERIOR WALLS OF COLORADO
Also Called: Superior Fundations of Rockies
25 Allegheny Sq (15045-1649)
PHONE..........................412 664-7788
David Hussey, President
John Popovich, Vice Pres
George Watson, Admin Sec
EMP: 13 EST: 1996
SALES (est): 950K Privately Held
SIC: 3272 1741 Concrete stuctural support & building material; foundation & retaining wall construction

(G-6418)
TECH MET INC
15 Allegheny Sq (15045-1615)
PHONE..........................412 678-8277
Gary Reed, President
EMP: 31
SQ FT: 30,000
SALES: 6MM Privately Held
WEB: www.techmetinc.com
SIC: 3479 Etching on metals

(G-6419)
TMS INTERNATIONAL LLC (DH)
Also Called: Olympic Mill Services Division
12 Monongahela Ave (15045-1315)
P.O. Box 2000 (15045-0600)
PHONE..........................412 678-6141
Raymond Kalouche, CEO
Detlef Mu Ller, Managing Dir
J David Aronson, COO
Hideto Hata, Purchasing
Daniel E Rosati, CFO
◆ EMP: 60 EST: 1987
SQ FT: 20,000
SALES (est): 194.8MM Privately Held
WEB: www.tubecity.com
SIC: 3312 4731 3399 7359 Blast furnaces & steel mills; railroad freight agency; iron, powdered; equipment rental & leasing; trucking, except local
HQ: Tms International Corporation
12 Monongahela Ave
Glassport PA 15045
412 675-8251

(G-6420)
TMS INTERNATIONAL CORP (PA)
12 Monongahela Ave (15045-1315)
P.O. Box 2000 (15045-0600)
PHONE..........................412 678-6141
Joseph Curtin, Ch of Bd
Raymond S Kalouche, President
William R Miller, Exec VP
Daniel E Rosati, CFO
Thomas E Lippard, Admin Sec
EMP: 103
SALES (est): 472.4MM Privately Held
SIC: 3312 4731 3399 7359 Blast furnaces & steel mills; railroad freight agency; iron, powdered; equipment rental & leasing; trucking, except local

(G-6421)
TMS INTERNATIONAL CORPORATION (HQ)
12 Monongahela Ave (15045-1315)
PHONE..........................412 675-8251
Raymond Kalouche, CEO
J David Aronson, President
Chuck Kiss, General Mgr
Pascal Martin, General Mgr
Kevin Shire, General Mgr
◆ EMP: 50
SALES (est): 472.4MM Privately Held
SIC: 3312 4731 3399 7359 Blast furnaces & steel mills; railroad freight agency; iron, powdered; equipment rental & leasing; trucking, except local

(G-6422)
TYE BAR LLC
1050 Ohio Ave (15045-1675)
PHONE..........................412 896-1376
Katey Wood, President
Daniel Lucas, Vice Pres
EMP: 15
SQ FT: 11,000
SALES (est): 5.3MM Privately Held
SIC: 3449 Bars, concrete reinforcing: fabricated steel

Glen Campbell
Indiana County

(G-6423)
BETH MINING CO
815 Rock Run Rd (15742-7806)
PHONE..........................814 845-7390
Stephen Peles, Owner
EMP: 7
SALES (est): 750K Privately Held
SIC: 1221 Strip mining, bituminous

(G-6424)
FRENO JR A J MINING
4707 Gipsy Rd (15742-8211)
PHONE..........................814 845-2286
Andrew J Freno Jr, Owner
EMP: 4 EST: 1975
SALES (est): 348.6K Privately Held
SIC: 1221 Strip mining, bituminous

(G-6425)
T & T MACHINE & WELDING CO
26529 Route 286 Hwy E (15742-8907)
PHONE..........................814 845-9054
Danny Eemchulla, Partner
Jeff Eemchulla, Partner
EMP: 3
SALES (est): 120.9K Privately Held
SIC: 7692 Welding repair

Glen Hope
Clearfield County

(G-6426)
KITKO WOOD PRODUCTS INC
6098 Glen Hope Blvd (16645-4519)
PHONE..........................814 672-3606
Robert Kitko, President
Kenneth Kitko, Corp Secy
EMP: 125
SQ FT: 4,000

SALES (est): 15.3MM **Privately Held**
WEB: www.kitkowoodproducts.com
SIC: 2511 Wood household furniture

Glen Lyon
Luzerne County

(G-6427)
SINKING SHIP PREMIUM JUICE LLC
Also Called: Sinking Ship Vapors
102 E Main St (18617-1321)
P.O. Box 864, Wilkes Barre (18703-0864)
PHONE..................................570 855-2316
Kenneth Czapracki,
EMP: 4
SALES (est): 125.1K **Privately Held**
SIC: 3999 Cigarette & cigar products & accessories

Glen Mills
Delaware County

(G-6428)
25 FATHOMS INTERNATIONAL INC
Also Called: Blue Horizons Dive Center
364 W Chesterpike Ste B7 (19342)
PHONE..................................610 558-1101
Christopher Donnelly, *President*
Kelly Donnelly, *Vice Pres*
EMP: 3
SALES (est): 304.1K **Privately Held**
SIC: 8748 3949 5941 Business consulting; water sports equipment; skin diving equipment, scuba type; water sport equipment; skin diving, scuba equipment & supplies; specialty sport supplies

(G-6429)
A C F LTD
Also Called: American Contracting Fabg
124 Willits Way (19342-1431)
P.O. Box 544, Chester Heights (19017-0544)
PHONE..................................610 459-5397
Helen Dargay, *President*
Patricia Lord, *Corp Secy*
Katherine Q Dargay, *Vice Pres*
Pete Dargay, *Vice Pres*
EMP: 4
SALES: 450K **Privately Held**
WEB: www.acfchefs.org
SIC: 3086 Plastics foam products

(G-6430)
AXALTA COATING SYSTEMS LLC
50 Applied Bank Blvd # 300 (19342-1091)
P.O. Box 69 (19342-0069)
PHONE..................................610 358-2228
EMP: 20
SALES (corp-wide): 4.7B **Publicly Held**
SIC: 2851 3479 Polyurethane coatings; painting, coating & hot dipping
HQ: Axalta Coating Systems, Llc
2001 Market St Ste 3600
Philadelphia PA 19103
215 255-4347

(G-6431)
BRANDYWINE FUEL INC
83 Smithbridge Rd (19342-1463)
PHONE..................................484 357-7683
Michael Saunders, *President*
Chris Panarelloi, *Vice Pres*
EMP: 5 EST: 2012
SALES (est): 494.2K **Privately Held**
SIC: 2869 Fuels

(G-6432)
BREET INCORPORATED
507 Glen Eagle Sq (19342)
PHONE..................................610 558-4006
Edward Camelli, *President*
Brian Havertine, *Treasurer*
EMP: 9
SQ FT: 2,700

SALES (est): 129.9K **Privately Held**
WEB: www.trailcreekoutfitters.com
SIC: 2389 Men's miscellaneous accessories

(G-6433)
DEER CREEK MALTHOUSE LLC (PA)
1629 E Street Rd (19342-9518)
PHONE..................................717 746-6258
Mark Brault,
EMP: 5
SALES (est): 805.1K **Privately Held**
SIC: 2083 Malt

(G-6434)
DEER CREEK MALTHOUSE LLC
1646 E Street Rd (19342-9517)
PHONE..................................717 746-6258
EMP: 7
SALES (corp-wide): 805.1K **Privately Held**
SIC: 2083 Malt
PA: Deer Creek Malthouse Llc
1629 E Street Rd
Glen Mills PA 19342
717 746-6258

(G-6435)
DIRECT LINE PRODUCTIONS INC
151 Creek Rd (19342-1636)
PHONE..................................610 633-7082
Harriet Kessler, *President*
EMP: 4
SALES (est): 220.7K **Privately Held**
SIC: 7336 2677 Commercial art & graphic design; envelopes

(G-6436)
DONNELLEY FINANCIAL LLC
2 Braxton Way Fl 2 # 2 (19342-2379)
PHONE..................................717 293-3725
Crystal Barrow, *Principal*
EMP: 13
SALES (corp-wide): 963MM **Publicly Held**
SIC: 2752 Commercial printing, offset
HQ: Donnelley Financial, Llc
55 Water St Fl 11
New York NY 10041
212 425-0298

(G-6437)
GRACE WINERY LLC
50 Sweetwater Rd (19342-1709)
PHONE..................................610 459-4711
D Christopher Le Vine, *Mng Member*
EMP: 3
SALES (est): 310.1K **Privately Held**
SIC: 2084 Wines

(G-6438)
GRAPHIC SEARCH ASSOCIATES
1075 Powderhorn Dr (19342-9504)
PHONE..................................610 344-0644
EMP: 3
SALES (est): 248.5K **Privately Held**
SIC: 7361 2759 Executive placement; commercial printing

(G-6439)
LUCKY SIGN SHOP INC
1348 Middletown Rd (19342-9662)
PHONE..................................610 459-5825
EMP: 4
SALES (est): 397.2K **Privately Held**
SIC: 3993 Signs & advertising specialties

(G-6440)
PENTEC HEALTH INC (PA)
50 Applied Card Way (19342-1050)
PHONE..................................610 494-8700
Joseph Cosgrove, *President*
Michael Abens, *Exec VP*
Robert Provonche, *Exec VP*
Barbara Knightly, *Vice Pres*
Karen McHenry, *Vice Pres*
EMP: 160
SQ FT: 24,000
SALES (est): 110.5MM **Privately Held**
WEB: www.pentechealth.com
SIC: 2834 8082 Druggists' preparations (pharmaceuticals); home health care services

(G-6441)
REFRESCO BEVERAGES US INC
20 Aldan Ave (19342-2278)
P.O. Box 626, Concordville (19331-0626)
PHONE..................................484 840-4800
John Sheppard, *CEO*
EMP: 13 **Privately Held**
SIC: 2086 Bottled & canned soft drinks
HQ: Refresco Beverages Us Inc.
8112 Woodland Center Blvd
Tampa FL 33614
813 313-1800

(G-6442)
ROCH GRANDE GST WAFFLES LLC
50 Applied Card Way (19342-1050)
PHONE..................................484 840-9179
Rich Cleaver, *Senior VP*
Joseph Crowley, *Treasurer*
EMP: 240
SALES (est): 6.4MM **Privately Held**
SIC: 2045 5149 2041 Pancake mixes, prepared: from purchased flour; flour; flour & other grain mill products

(G-6443)
SAFETY HOUSE INC
99 Alda Ave (19342)
PHONE..................................610 344-0637
Daniel Scully, *President*
EMP: 10 EST: 2008
SALES (est): 20MM **Privately Held**
SIC: 3589 7382 Asbestos removal equipment; security systems services

(G-6444)
SPEAKMAN COMPANY
51 Lacrue Ave (19342-1042)
PHONE..................................302 764-7100
Robert Knoll, *CEO*
Rodman Ward, *CEO*
Rob Cook, *President*
Rob Ames, *Engineer*
Charlie Novak, *Engineer*
▲ EMP: 120 EST: 1889
SALES (est): 26.3MM **Privately Held**
WEB: www.speakmancompany.com
SIC: 3432 3431 Plumbing fixture fittings & trim; bathroom fixtures, including sinks

(G-6445)
SPORTS MANAGEMENT NEWS INC
Also Called: Sporting Goods Intelligence
442 Featherbed Ln (19342-1512)
PHONE..................................610 459-4040
John Horan, *President*
EMP: 4
SQ FT: 500
SALES (est): 335.3K **Privately Held**
SIC: 2741 8732 Newsletter publishing; research services, except laboratory

(G-6446)
UNEQUAL TECHNOLOGIES COMPANY
10 Lacrue Ave (19342-1042)
PHONE..................................610 444-5900
Rob Vito, *President*
Nicole Kohanski, *COO*
Michael Foerster, *Vice Pres*
Maureen Quinlan, *Corp Comm Staff*
Bart Robertson, *CIO*
EMP: 25 EST: 2008
SALES (est): 5.4MM **Privately Held**
SIC: 3131 5661 Inner soles, leather; custom & orthopedic shoes

(G-6447)
UNEQUAL TECHNOLOGIES COMPANY
10 Lacrue Ave (19342-1042)
PHONE..................................610 444-5900
Vito Rob, *Principal*
EMP: 7
SALES (est): 816.3K **Privately Held**
SIC: 3949 5091 Helmets, athletic; bags, golf; golf & skiing equipment & supplies

(G-6448)
VETMED COMMUNICATIONS INC
37 Paul Ln (19342-8833)
P.O. Box 390 (19342-0390)
PHONE..................................610 361-0555
Nick Paolo, *President*
EMP: 4 EST: 2009
SALES (est): 277.2K **Privately Held**
SIC: 2711 Newspapers: publishing only, not printed on site

Glen Rock
York County

(G-6449)
ADHESIVES RESEARCH INC (PA)
400 Seaks Run Rd (17327-9500)
P.O. Box 100 (17327-0100)
PHONE..................................717 235-7979
John Lind, *President*
George Stolakis, *President*
David Koppenhaver, *Business Mgr*
George Cramer, *Vice Pres*
Lynne Durbin, *Vice Pres*
◆ EMP: 342 EST: 1961
SQ FT: 240,000
SALES: 118MM **Privately Held**
SIC: 2891 Adhesives

(G-6450)
AMERICAN BUILT ARMS COMPANY
322 Industrial Rd (17327-8627)
PHONE..................................443 807-3022
Jason Combs, *President*
EMP: 4
SALES (est): 250K **Privately Held**
SIC: 3949 3484 Hunting equipment; shooting equipment & supplies, general; guns (firearms) or gun parts, 30 mm. & below

(G-6451)
ARX LLC
400 Seaks Run Rd (17327-9500)
P.O. Box 100 (17327-0100)
PHONE..................................717 253-7979
Gralying Messersmith, *President*
Beth Dondrak, *Vice Pres*
Todd Sunstrom, *Director*
EMP: 39
SQ FT: 20,000
SALES (est): 5.6MM
SALES (corp-wide): 118MM **Privately Held**
SIC: 2834 Pills, pharmaceutical
PA: Adhesives Research, Inc.
400 Seaks Run Rd
Glen Rock PA 17327
717 235-7979

(G-6452)
BEL CONNECTOR INC (HQ)
Also Called: Stewart Connector
11118 Susquehanna Trl S (17327-9199)
PHONE..................................717 235-7512
Daniel Bernstein, *President*
Peter Bittner, *General Mgr*
Colin Dunn, *Vice Pres*
Craig Brosious, *Finance*
▲ EMP: 80
SQ FT: 65,000
SALES (est): 31.8MM
SALES (corp-wide): 548.1MM **Publicly Held**
SIC: 3678 Electronic connectors
PA: Bel Fuse Inc.
206 Van Vorst St
Jersey City NJ 07302
201 432-0463

(G-6453)
BIMAX INC (PA)
281 Industrial Rd (17327-8601)
PHONE..................................717 235-3136
Ronald W Kreis, *President*
Carl Shervin, *General Mgr*
Dr Chris Sghibartz, *Vice Pres*
Joe Dettinger, *Opers Mgr*
Howard Dottie, *Buyer*
▲ EMP: 50

SQ FT: 5,000
SALES (est): 20.4MM **Privately Held**
SIC: 2819 Industrial inorganic chemicals

(G-6454)
COAX INCORPORATED
4217 Fissels Church Rd (17327-8759)
P.O. Box 247 (17327-0247)
PHONE....................................717 227-0045
Wilhelm J Mintscheff, *President*
EMP: 15
SQ FT: 3,500
SALES (est): 2.3MM **Privately Held**
SIC: 3679 Electronic circuits

(G-6455)
DIESEL PRO INC
99 Manchester St (17327-1330)
PHONE....................................717 235-4996
Lance Donaldson, *President*
EMP: 4
SQ FT: 8,000
SALES: 600K **Privately Held**
SIC: 3714 Fuel pumps, motor vehicle

(G-6456)
DRILL MANAGEMENT INC
3543 Ridge Rd (17327-8763)
PHONE....................................717 227-8189
Tom Tucker, *President*
Dan Thomas, *Treasurer*
EMP: 7
SALES (est): 1.2MM **Privately Held**
SIC: 1241 Mine preparation services

(G-6457)
HIGGINS SAW MILL
6549 Hokes Rd (17327-8869)
PHONE....................................717 235-4189
Wayne Higgins, *Owner*
Rexter Higgins, *Partner*
David Higgens, *Partner*
EMP: 5
SALES: 350K **Privately Held**
SIC: 2421 Sawmills & planing mills, general

(G-6458)
OAKWOOD CONTROLS CORPORATION
159 Industrial Rd (17327-8602)
PHONE....................................717 801-1515
John Harrell, *Vice Pres*
John Huang,
EMP: 18
SQ FT: 7,500
SALES: 950K **Privately Held**
SIC: 7371 3825 3821 3699 Computer software development & applications; digital test equipment, electronic & electrical circuits; time interval measuring equipment, electric (lab type); teaching machines & aids, electronic; timing devices, electronic

(G-6459)
PASADENA SCIENTIFIC INC
Also Called: Pasadena Scientific Industries
5125 Pine View Dr (17327-7702)
PHONE....................................717 227-1220
Robert J Kessler, *President*
EMP: 6
SQ FT: 2,000
SALES (est): 938.5K **Privately Held**
SIC: 3825 Instruments to measure electricity

(G-6460)
PROCESS SCIENCE & INNOVATION
Also Called: PSI
2807 Godfrey Rd (17327-8465)
PHONE....................................717 428-3511
EMP: 3
SALES (est): 284.4K **Privately Held**
SIC: 3462 Mfg Iron/Steel Forgings

(G-6461)
TOPFLIGHT CORPORATION (PA)
277 Commerce Dr (17327-8625)
PHONE....................................717 227-5400
Craig McClenachan, *President*
Lynne Durbin, *Corp Secy*
Richard C Amspacher, *Vice Pres*
Stacy Ferrell, *Production*

Jeff Shultz, *Production*
▲ **EMP:** 125 **EST:** 1946
SQ FT: 95,000
SALES (est): 21.7MM **Privately Held**
SIC: 2672 Adhesive papers, labels or tapes: from purchased material

(G-6462)
WEICHERT MACHINING INC
97 Manchester St (17327-1330)
PHONE....................................717 235-6761
Dennis E Weichert, *President*
Susan Weichert, *Admin Sec*
EMP: 3
SQ FT: 2,000
SALES: 390K **Privately Held**
SIC: 3312 Tool & die steel & alloys

Glenmoore
Chester County

(G-6463)
AUTOMATED ENTERPRISE INTL
632 Greenridge Rd (19343-9500)
PHONE....................................610 458-5810
Ron Cole, *President*
Geralyn Walish, *Vice Pres*
EMP: 5
SALES (est): 343.2K **Privately Held**
WEB: www.aeiaei.com
SIC: 7372 Prepackaged software

(G-6464)
C & M CUSTOM MACHINING INC
237 Sweet Spring Rd (19343-2600)
P.O. Box 83, Uwchland (19480-0083)
PHONE....................................610 458-0897
Charles Brown, *President*
Michael J Dispenziere, *Vice Pres*
EMP: 7
SQ FT: 3,000
SALES (est): 399.5K **Privately Held**
SIC: 3599 Machine shop, jobbing & repair

(G-6465)
DIA DOCE
100 S High St (19343)
PHONE....................................610 476-5684
Thais Da Silva, *Principal*
EMP: 4 **EST:** 2011
SALES (est): 237.9K **Privately Held**
SIC: 2051 Bakery: wholesale or wholesale/retail combined

(G-6466)
FLUIDTECHNIK USA
1699 Horseshoe Pile (19343)
P.O. Box 715, Uwchland (19480-0715)
PHONE....................................610 321-2407
John Palmer, *President*
▲ **EMP:** 1 **EST:** 2000
SQ FT: 15,200
SALES (est): 2MM **Privately Held**
WEB: www.schrupp.com
SIC: 3535 3593 5085 Pneumatic tube conveyor systems; fluid power actuators, hydraulic or pneumatic; pistons & valves

(G-6467)
FOXCROFT EQUIPMENT & SVCS CO
2101 Creek Rd (19343-1421)
P.O. Box 39 (19343-0039)
PHONE....................................610 942-2888
Roger W Irey Jr, *President*
Jacqueline Irey, *Vice Pres*
Leonardo Herrera, *Representative*
EMP: 12 **EST:** 1963
SQ FT: 7,000
SALES: 1MM **Privately Held**
SIC: 3589 Water treatment equipment, industrial

(G-6468)
JP BETZ INC
Also Called: Custom Inserts
18 Normandy Cir (19343-9581)
PHONE....................................610 458-8787
Jonathan Betz, *President*
EMP: 4
SQ FT: 8,000

SALES (est): 264.6K **Privately Held**
WEB: www.custominserts.com
SIC: 3429 Cabinet hardware

(G-6469)
QUALITY MACHINE INC
8 Andover Rd (19343-1040)
PHONE....................................610 942-2488
Ron Kummerer, *President*
EMP: 3
SALES: 200K **Privately Held**
SIC: 3599 Machine shop, jobbing & repair

(G-6470)
STAR CONTINUOUS CARD SYSTEMS
140 Chalfant Rd (19343-2004)
PHONE....................................800 458-1413
D M Kirkpatrick, *President*
Melanie Kirkpatrick, *Treasurer*
EMP: 5 **EST:** 1952
SQ FT: 15,000
SALES (est): 390K **Privately Held**
SIC: 2761 Continuous forms, office & business

Glenolden
Delaware County

(G-6471)
ADVANCE TRANSIT MIX INC
613 W Oak Ln (19036-1229)
PHONE....................................610 461-2182
Dante Panichi Jr, *President*
Dante Panichi III, *Vice Pres*
Ann O'Neill Panichi, *Admin Sec*
EMP: 11 **EST:** 1981
SQ FT: 300
SALES (est): 1.2MM **Privately Held**
SIC: 3273 Ready-mixed concrete

(G-6472)
CORPORATE PRINT SOLUTIONS INC
9 E Glenolden Ave (19036-2106)
PHONE....................................215 774-1119
Kevin Withers, *President*
EMP: 7
SALES: 500K **Privately Held**
SIC: 2759 5699 2752 2732 Commercial printing; T-shirts, custom printed; commercial printing, offset; book printing

(G-6473)
EATON AEROSPACE LLC (DH)
24 E Glenolden Ave (19036-2107)
PHONE....................................610 522-4000
Gilles Saintonge, *Director*
Mike Vecchiolli,
Bradley Morton,
EMP: 100
SALES (est): 14.4MM **Privately Held**
SIC: 3728 3823 3724 3829 Gears, aircraft power transmission; controllers for process variables, all types; aircraft engines & engine parts; measuring & controlling devices; fluid power pumps & motors; turbines & turbine generator sets
HQ: Eaton Corporation
1000 Eaton Blvd
Cleveland OH 44122
440 523-5000

(G-6474)
EATON CORPORATION
Tedeco Div
24 E Glenolden Ave (19036-2107)
PHONE....................................610 522-4059
Frances Eldridge, *General Mgr*
John Kampanis, *Plant Mgr*
Darrell McGinnis, *Mfg Staff*
John Bero, *QC Mgr*
Xin Pu, *Engineer*
EMP: 180 **Privately Held**
WEB: www.eaton.com
SIC: 3728 3823 Gears, aircraft power transmission; controllers for process variables, all types
HQ: Eaton Corporation
1000 Eaton Blvd
Cleveland OH 44122
440 523-5000

(G-6475)
HARRYS FAMOUS PUDDING
5 1/2 N Bartram Ave (19036-1206)
PHONE....................................484 494-6400
John Doucas, *Owner*
EMP: 12
SALES (est): 869.4K **Privately Held**
SIC: 2051 Bread, cake & related products

(G-6476)
PRECIOUS METAL PLATING CO INC
21 S Chester Pike (19036-1830)
PHONE....................................610 586-1500
Bill Feebe, *Manager*
EMP: 4
SALES (corp-wide): 504.1K **Privately Held**
SIC: 3471 Electroplating of metals or formed products
PA: Precious Metal Plating Co Inc
21202 Shannondell Dr
Norristown PA

Glenshaw
Allegheny County

(G-6477)
A LINDEMANN INC
1005 8th Ave (15116-1733)
PHONE....................................412 487-7282
Roger Baker, *President*
▲ **EMP:** 7
SALES (est): 1MM **Privately Held**
SIC: 3425 7699 Saw blades & handsaws; knife, saw & tool sharpening & repair

(G-6478)
ACCU-TURN TOOL COMPANY INC
Also Called: Generic Slides
1049 William Flynn Hwy # 400
(15116-2659)
PHONE....................................412 492-7270
Richard Antoszewski, *President*
▲ **EMP:** 10
SALES (est): 1.7MM **Privately Held**
WEB: www.genericslides.com
SIC: 3599 Machine shop, jobbing & repair

(G-6479)
ADDEV WALCO INC (PA)
1651 E Sutter Rd (15116-1700)
P.O. Box 9 (15116-0009)
PHONE....................................412 486-4400
Wayne Landy, *President*
Pamela Kelly, *Vice Pres*
Nancy Ihrig, *QC Mgr*
Kevin Holt, *CFO*
Helen Behr, *Director*
EMP: 23
SQ FT: 75,000
SALES (est): 5.6MM **Privately Held**
SIC: 3465 5085 Automotive stampings; adhesives, tape & plasters

(G-6480)
ANYTHING SEWS
2208 Mount Royal Blvd (15116-2025)
PHONE....................................412 486-1055
Robert Neely, *Owner*
EMP: 4
SALES (est): 88.6K **Privately Held**
SIC: 7219 5714 2395 Garment making, alteration & repair; drapery & upholstery stores; embroidery products, except schiffli machine

(G-6481)
APONTES LATIN FLAVOR INC (PA)
Also Called: Apontes Foodtrucks
1606 Butler Plank Rd (15116-1730)
PHONE....................................727 247-2001
Hector Aponte, *President*
Barbara M Dreves, *CPA*
EMP: 5
SQ FT: 5,000
SALES: 500K **Privately Held**
SIC: 2599 5963 Food wagons, restaurant; lunch wagon

(G-6482)
ASSOCIATED PRODUCTS LLC
Also Called: California Scents
1901 William Flynn Hwy (15116-1742)
P.O. Box 8 (15116-0008)
PHONE.................................412 486-2255
August Doppes, *CEO*
Linda Doppes, *President*
Donna Hall, *Vice Pres*
EMP: 30
SQ FT: 180,000
SALES (est): 7.4MM
SALES (corp-wide): 1.8B **Publicly Held**
WEB: www.sani-air.com
SIC: 2842 Deodorants, nonpersonal
PA: Energizer Holdings, Inc.
   533 Maryville Univ Dr
   Saint Louis MO 63141
   314 985-2000

(G-6483)
BENSHAW INC
1659 E Sutter Rd (15116-1700)
PHONE.................................412 487-8235
Sandra Schaltenbrand, *Principal*
Doug Yates, *Regl Sales Mgr*
Lou Mannella, *Director*
EMP: 5
SALES (est): 550K **Privately Held**
SIC: 5063 3625 Motor controls, starters & relays: electric; motor controls, electric

(G-6484)
CNT FIXTURE COMPANY INC
1600 William Flynn Hwy (15116-1737)
PHONE.................................412 443-6260
Max Andrzejewski, *President*
EMP: 35
SQ FT: 30,000
SALES (est): 4.1MM **Privately Held**
WEB: www.cntfixture.com
SIC: 2542 2541 3646 Showcases (not refrigerated): except wood; wood partitions & fixtures; commercial indusl & institutional electric lighting fixtures

(G-6485)
CNT MOTION SYSTEMS INC
1600 William Flynn Hwy (15116-1737)
PHONE.................................412 244-5770
Max Andrzejewski, *President*
EMP: 5 **EST:** 1999
SALES (est): 810K **Privately Held**
WEB: www.cntmotion.com
SIC: 3541 Machine tools, metal cutting type

(G-6486)
CONTROLS SERVICE & REPAIR
1648 Butler Plank Rd (15116-1730)
P.O. Box 424 (15116-0424)
PHONE.................................412 487-7310
James Biel, *President*
Jeffery R Biel, *Vice Pres*
EMP: 7
SQ FT: 2,000
SALES (est): 1.1MM **Privately Held**
WEB: www.ctrlsvc.com
SIC: 7629 3679 Electronic equipment repair; electronic circuits

(G-6487)
EAST LIBERTY ELCPLTG INC
1126 Butler Plank Rd (15116-2660)
PHONE.................................412 487-4080
Vincent Kovalik, *President*
Gary Bugel, *Vice Pres*
Jared Bugel, *Vice Pres*
Robert Carmody, *Admin Sec*
EMP: 50 **EST:** 1920
SQ FT: 50,000
SALES (est): 2.2MM **Privately Held**
WEB: www.elepl.com
SIC: 3471 Electroplating of metals or formed products; finishing, metals or formed products

(G-6488)
GATTO MOTO LLC
Also Called: Three Rivers Harley-Davidson
1463 Glenn Ave (15116-2310)
PHONE.................................412 487-3377
George Gatto, *President*
EMP: 33
SALES (est): 4.8MM **Privately Held**
SIC: 3751 Motorcycles, bicycles & parts

(G-6489)
GOSS INC (PA)
1511 William Flynn Hwy (15116-2301)
P.O. Box 57 (15116-0057)
PHONE.................................412 486-6100
Jacqueline F Goss, *President*
Calvin J Goss, *Vice Pres*
Charles T Goss, *Vice Pres*
John C Beck, *Treasurer*
◆ **EMP:** 55
SQ FT: 50,000
SALES (est): 9.4MM **Privately Held**
WEB: www.gossonline.com
SIC: 3548 5084 Gas welding equipment; soldering equipment, except hand soldering irons; welding machinery & equipment

(G-6490)
INDUSTRIAL PUMP & MTR REPR INC
1648 Butler Plank Rd (15116-1730)
P.O. Box 255 (15116-0255)
PHONE.................................412 369-5060
Michael R Locke, *President*
EMP: 16
SALES (est): 2.2MM **Privately Held**
WEB: www.industrialpumpandmotor.com
SIC: 7699 7694 Pumps & pumping equipment repair; motor repair services

(G-6491)
IPI CO INC
Also Called: Insulation Products
517 Glenhaven Dr (15116-1923)
PHONE.................................412 487-3995
David K Clutter, *President*
EMP: 14 **EST:** 1974
SALES (est): 1.8MM **Privately Held**
WEB: www.ipico.com
SIC: 5033 2493 1742 Insulation materials; insulating board, hard pressed; plastering, drywall & insulation

(G-6492)
KELMAN BOTTLES LLC
1101 William Flynn Hwy (15116-2637)
PHONE.................................412 486-9100
Lou Brudnock,
EMP: 16
SALES (est): 3.1MM **Privately Held**
SIC: 3229 Glassware, art or decorative

(G-6493)
KELMAN HOLDINGS LLC
1101 William Flynn Hwy (15116-2637)
PHONE.................................412 486-9100
James L Moles,
EMP: 4
SALES (est): 327K **Privately Held**
SIC: 3221 Water bottles, glass

(G-6494)
KEMOSABE INC
Also Called: Millvale Vault Co
1010 Glenn Ave (15116-2458)
PHONE.................................412 961-0190
EMP: 6
SQ FT: 7,500
SALES (est): 440K **Privately Held**
SIC: 3272 Mfg Concrete Products

(G-6495)
PANNIER CORPORATION
1130 Butler Plank Rd (15116-2660)
PHONE.................................412 492-1400
Dale Sanborn, *Engineer*
John Visconti, *Manager*
Robert Gosnell, *Executive*
EMP: 50
SALES (corp-wide): 17.9MM **Privately Held**
WEB: www.pannier.com
SIC: 3953 3993 Marking devices; signs & advertising specialties
PA: The Pannier Corporation
   207 Sandusky St
   Pittsburgh PA 15212
   412 323-4900

(G-6496)
PENNSYLVNIA PURE DSTLLRIES LLC
1101 William Flynn Hwy (15116-2637)
PHONE.................................412 486-8666
Charles P Orr Jr, *Mng Member*

EMP: 14 **EST:** 2007
SALES (est): 1.8MM **Privately Held**
SIC: 2085 Distilled & blended liquors

(G-6497)
PIMA LLC
1605 Middle Rd (15116-2539)
PHONE.................................412 770-8130
Antonino Febbraro, *CEO*
EMP: 4
SALES (est): 98.3K **Privately Held**
SIC: 7372 Application computer software

(G-6498)
PORT AUGUSTUS GLASS CO LLC
Also Called: The Old Glenshaw Glass
1101 William Flynn Hwy (15116-2637)
PHONE.................................412 486-9100
Fax: 412 486-9252
EMP: 14
SALES (corp-wide): 5.3MM **Privately Held**
SIC: 3229 Manufacture Glassware
PA: Port Augustus Glass Company, Llc
   1900 Liberty St
   Mount Pleasant PA

(G-6499)
REMARKABLE DESIGNS INC
Also Called: Rebecca J'S Gourmet
1216 Willow St (15116-2647)
PHONE.................................412 512-6564
Greg Hannan, *Vice Pres*
EMP: 6
SQ FT: 1,500
SALES (est): 449.1K **Privately Held**
SIC: 2064 Candy & other confectionery products

(G-6500)
ROBERT AGUGLIA
Also Called: A & K Enterprises
1515 William Flynn Hwy (15116-2301)
PHONE.................................412 487-6511
Robert Aguglia, *Owner*
EMP: 11
SQ FT: 6,000
SALES (est): 967.4K **Privately Held**
SIC: 2448 Pallets, wood

(G-6501)
TARGET INDUSTRIAL PRODUCTS
969 William Flynn Hwy (15116-2633)
PHONE.................................412 486-2627
EMP: 3
SALES (est): 224.3K **Privately Held**
SIC: 3053 Gaskets, packing & sealing devices

(G-6502)
VB FABRICATORS INC
1467 Glenn Ave (15116-2310)
P.O. Box 60 (15116-0060)
PHONE.................................412 486-6385
Russell J Baldt, *President*
Doreen F Baldt, *Admin Sec*
EMP: 12
SQ FT: 26,000
SALES (est): 1.6MM **Privately Held**
SIC: 3312 Bar, rod & wire products

Glenside
Montgomery County

(G-6503)
ADVANCED NETWORK PRODUCTS INC
33 E Glenside Ave (19038-4601)
PHONE.................................215 572-0111
David Scott Mulvey, *CEO*
EMP: 20
SQ FT: 10,000
SALES (est): 10.1MM **Privately Held**
WEB: www.anp.net
SIC: 5065 3577 4813 Communication equipment; computer peripheral equipment;

(G-6504)
ALL WELD STEEL CO INC
3041 Chestnut Ave (19038-1696)
PHONE.................................215 884-6985
Richard J Giuliani, *President*
Richard J Giuliani Jr, *Vice Pres*
EMP: 10
SQ FT: 7,600
SALES (est): 1.9MM **Privately Held**
SIC: 3441 Fabricated structural metal

(G-6505)
ARCO SALES CO
1230 E Mermaid Ln Ste 7 (19038-7667)
PHONE.................................215 743-9425
Stephen Jadczak, *President*
EMP: 10
SQ FT: 5,000
SALES (est): 1.1MM **Privately Held**
WEB: www.arco-ampm.com
SIC: 3599 Machine shop, jobbing & repair

(G-6506)
ARDSLEY AUTO TAGS (PA)
2745 Jenkintown Rd (19038-2531)
PHONE.................................215 572-1409
Nick Angleo, *President*
EMP: 5
SALES (est): 713.6K **Privately Held**
SIC: 3469 Automobile license tags, stamped metal

(G-6507)
ATLANTIC EMBROIDERY COMPANY
6 S Easton Rd Frnt Frnt (19038-3437)
PHONE.................................215 514-2154
James W Thompson Jr, *Partner*
Denise Thompson, *Partner*
James Thompson, *Partner*
EMP: 5
SQ FT: 1,000
SALES (est): 389.3K **Privately Held**
SIC: 2395 Embroidery products, except schiffli machine

(G-6508)
BHAGYAS KITCHEN
1010 E Willow Grove Ave (19038-7938)
PHONE.................................215 233-1587
John Lawrence, *Principal*
EMP: 9
SALES (est): 196.5K **Privately Held**
SIC: 5812 5031 2434 Family restaurants; kitchen cabinets; wood kitchen cabinets

(G-6509)
BUILDING INSPECTORS CONTRS INC
3003 Mount Carmel Ave (19038-1633)
PHONE.................................215 481-0606
Virginia Aikon, *Treasurer*
EMP: 7
SQ FT: 1,200
SALES (est): 1MM **Privately Held**
SIC: 7699 3585 7623 1711 Oil burner repair service; air conditioning condensers & condensing units; air conditioning repair; heating & air conditioning contractors

(G-6510)
BYARD F BROGAN INC
124 S Keswick Ave (19038-4510)
P.O. Box 369 (19038-0369)
PHONE.................................215 885-3550
Byard F Brogan Jr, *President*
Peter Cederberg, *Internal Med*
EMP: 17 **EST:** 1908
SQ FT: 9,000
SALES (est): 4MM **Privately Held**
WEB: www.bfbrogan.com
SIC: 3911 Jewelry, precious metal

(G-6511)
CIRCUIT FOIL TRADING INC
115 E Glenside Ave Ste 8 (19038-4618)
PHONE.................................215 887-7255
Silvio Bertling, *Sales Staff*
Brian Fisher, *Manager*
Eric Lambert, *CIO*
▲ **EMP:** 4
SQ FT: 1,500

SALES (est): 501.1K
SALES (corp-wide): 2.5B **Privately Held**
WEB: www.circuitfoil.com
SIC: 3672 Mfg Printed Circuit Boards
HQ: Circuit Foil Luxembourg Sarl
Salzbaach 6
Wiltz
957 551-

(G-6512)
CLARENCE LARKIN ESTATE
2641 Mount Carmel Ave (19038-2911)
P.O. Box 334 (19038-0334)
PHONE...................................215 576-5590
Phil Heinz, *Director*
EMP: 3
SQ FT: 2,500
SALES (est): 96.5K **Privately Held**
WEB: www.larkinestate.com
SIC: 2731 8661 Books: publishing only;
religious organizations

(G-6513)
**D A TOOL AND MACHINE
COMPANY**
415 W Glenside Ave (19038-3315)
PHONE...................................215 887-1673
Dominic Addesi, *President*
Maria Addesi, *Vice Pres*
EMP: 7
SQ FT: 3,600
SALES (est): 590K **Privately Held**
WEB: www.datoolinc.com
SIC: 3599 Machine shop, jobbing & repair

(G-6514)
EASTON BEER
230 S Easton Rd (19038-3901)
PHONE...................................215 884-1252
Woody Chea, *Principal*
EMP: 8
SALES (est): 518.7K **Privately Held**
SIC: 2082 Beer (alcoholic beverage)

(G-6515)
ELECTRO-TECH SYSTEMS INC
3101 Mount Carmel Ave (19038-1039)
PHONE...................................215 887-2196
Stan Weitz, *President*
Joyce Weitz, *Admin Sec*
EMP: 24
SQ FT: 12,000
SALES (est): 5.5MM **Privately Held**
WEB: www.ets2.com
SIC: 3825 8734 Instruments for measuring
electrical quantities; testing laboratories

(G-6516)
ERIC NEMEYER CORPORATION
107 E Glenside Ave A (19038-4628)
PHONE...................................215 887-8880
Eric Nemeyer, *Principal*
EMP: 3 **EST:** 2010
SALES (est): 128.9K **Privately Held**
SIC: 2711 Newspapers, publishing & print-
ing

(G-6517)
FENSTEMAKER JOHN
Also Called: Goldsmith's
32 E Glenside Ave (19038-4520)
PHONE...................................215 572-1444
John Fenstemaker, *Owner*
EMP: 8
SQ FT: 1,125
SALES (est): 410K **Privately Held**
SIC: 3911 5944 Jewelry, precious metal;
jewelry, precious stones & precious met-
als

(G-6518)
**G H FORBES SCREW MACHINE
PDTS**
115 E Glenside Ave Ste A (19038-4618)
PHONE...................................215 884-4343
George H Forbes III, *President*
EMP: 7
SQ FT: 3,000
SALES: 700K **Privately Held**
SIC: 3451 Screw machine products

(G-6519)
GENTLE REVOLUTION PRESS
8801 Stenton Ave (19038-8319)
PHONE...................................215 233-2050

Janet Doman, *Principal*
EMP: 4
SALES (est): 178.3K **Privately Held**
SIC: 2741 Miscellaneous publishing

(G-6520)
GEORGIA WEB INC (PA)
115 Lismore Ave (19038-4010)
PHONE...................................215 887-6600
Martin Rotter, *President*
EMP: 10
SQ FT: 117,000
SALES (est): 1.7MM **Privately Held**
WEB: www.georgiaweb.biz
SIC: 3444 Ventilators, sheet metal

(G-6521)
GLASGOW INC (PA)
104 Willow Grove Ave (19038-2110)
P.O. Box 1089 (19038-6089)
PHONE...................................215 884-8800
Bruce B Rambo, *President*
Lois Glasgow, *Vice Pres*
John Rath, *Vice Pres*
Al Andrews, *Purch Agent*
Craig Stevenson, *Purch Agent*
EMP: 80 **EST:** 1975
SQ FT: 10,000
SALES (est): 102.1MM **Privately Held**
WEB: www.glasgowinc.com
SIC: 2951 1611 1623 Road materials, bi-
tuminous (not from refineries); general
contractor, highway & street construction;
cable laying construction; sewer line con-
struction; underground utilities contractor

(G-6522)
GLASGOW HAULING INC
104 Willow Grove Ave (19038-2110)
PHONE...................................215 884-8800
EMP: 57
SALES (est): 72.4K
SALES (corp-wide): 102.1MM **Privately
Held**
SIC: 1389 Construction, repair & disman-
tling services
PA: Glasgow, Inc.
104 Willow Grove Ave
Glenside PA 19038
215 884-8800

(G-6523)
GOODSTATE INC
722 Avondale Rd (19038-7352)
PHONE...................................215 366-2030
Nicholai Jablokov, *President*
Eugene Jablokov, *Vice Pres*
▲ **EMP:** 7
SALES (est): 1.8MM **Privately Held**
SIC: 2833 5122 7389 Vitamins, natural or
synthetic: bulk, uncompounded; medici-
nals & botanicals;

(G-6524)
JOHN A MANNING JR
Also Called: Penn Wire Working Equipment
709 Bethlehem Pike Ste 2 (19038-8116)
P.O. Box 226, Flourtown (19031-0226)
PHONE...................................215 233-0976
John A Manning Jr, *Owner*
EMP: 4 **EST:** 1920
SQ FT: 500
SALES (est): 510K **Privately Held**
WEB: www.pennbenders.com
SIC: 5084 3549 Industrial machinery &
equipment; metalworking machinery

(G-6525)
**KUSTOM CARDS
INTERNATIONAL**
1018 E Willow Grove Ave (19038-7938)
PHONE...................................215 233-1678
David Kerper, *President*
EMP: 5 **EST:** 1995
SALES (est): 410K **Privately Held**
WEB: www.kustomcards.com
SIC: 2754 Business form & card printing,
gravure

(G-6526)
LEMA NOVELTY CO INC
309 Glenway Rd (19038-7017)
PHONE...................................610 754-7242
Roy Hoffman, *President*
EMP: 3 **EST:** 1938

SALES: 150K **Privately Held**
WEB: www.lemanovelty.com
SIC: 3961 Jewelry apparel, non-precious
metals

(G-6527)
LEON L BERKOWITZ CO
Also Called: L L B Group
2832 Mount Carmel Ave (19038-2211)
PHONE...................................215 654-0800
John B Long, *CEO*
Howard Moed, *Managing Prtnr*
David Viverette, *Partner*
Gil Cox, *Exec VP*
James Boyle, *Production*
◆ **EMP:** 10
SALES (est): 2.8MM **Privately Held**
WEB: www.llbco.com
SIC: 3993 Displays & cutouts, window &
lobby

(G-6528)
**MINUTEMAN PRESS OF
GLENSIDE**
359 N Easton Rd (19038-4910)
PHONE...................................267 626-2706
EMP: 3
SALES (est): 101.5K **Privately Held**
SIC: 2752 Commercial printing, litho-
graphic

(G-6529)
MONGOOSE PRODUCTS INC
115 Lismore Ave (19038-4010)
PHONE...................................215 887-6600
Martin Rotter, *President*
▼ **EMP:** 3
SQ FT: 1,500
SALES: 1MM **Privately Held**
WEB: www.mongooseproductsinc.com
SIC: 3531 Roofing equipment

(G-6530)
MONITOR DATA CORP
3 Limekiln Pike Ste 3g (19038-2923)
P.O. Box 517 (19038-0517)
PHONE...................................215 887-8343
Thomas Mc Hugh, *President*
Craig Elston, *Vice Pres*
Carl Puschak, *Vice Pres*
William Vinal, *Treasurer*
Jodie Henry, *Accounts Mgr*
EMP: 15
SQ FT: 1,750
SALES (est): 2.3MM **Privately Held**
WEB: www.monitordata.com
SIC: 3824 8721 Electromechanical coun-
ters; billing & bookkeeping service

(G-6531)
MOORE PUSH PIN COMPANY
Also Called: Modern Manufacturing Co
1300 E Mermaid Ln (19038-7664)
PHONE...................................215 233-5700
George W Samson, *President*
Robert Hughes, *Vice Pres*
E Lorincz, *Vice Pres*
Elliott Twersky, *Treasurer*
Alice Cataldi, *Director*
▲ **EMP:** 53 **EST:** 1900
SQ FT: 50,000
SALES (est): 5.5MM **Privately Held**
WEB: www.moorecountingsystems.com
SIC: 3965 3315 3499 2542 Pins & nee-
dles; tacks, steel: wire or cut; boxes for
packing & shipping, metal; partitions & fix-
tures, except wood; metal stampings;
coated & laminated paper

(G-6532)
PAUL F ROTHSTEIN INC
Also Called: Enchanted Beauty
39 S Easton Rd (19038)
PHONE...................................215 884-4720
Paul F Rothstein, *President*
Eileen Rothstein, *Admin Sec*
EMP: 11
SQ FT: 2,500
SALES (est): 968.3K **Privately Held**
SIC: 3911 Pearl jewelry, natural or cultured

(G-6533)
PODCON INC
Also Called: Metlab
1000 E Mermaid Ln (19038-8019)
PHONE...................................215 233-2600

James G Conybear, *President*
Mark Podob, *Corp Secy*
▲ **EMP:** 38
SQ FT: 85,000
SALES (est): 10.7MM **Privately Held**
WEB: www.metlabheattreat.com
SIC: 3398 Metal heat treating

(G-6534)
**ROLANDS SPECIAL MILLWORK
INC**
3119 Pennsylvania Ave (19038-1022)
PHONE...................................215 885-5588
Roland Koschorreck, *President*
EMP: 3
SQ FT: 2,000
SALES (est): 240K **Privately Held**
SIC: 2431 Millwork

(G-6535)
SENTECH INC
2851 Limekiln Pike (19038-2233)
PHONE...................................215 887-8665
Mina Patel, *President*
Dipak Patel, *Vice Pres*
Utpal Patel, *Technology*
EMP: 10
SQ FT: 6,000
SALES (est): 1.8MM **Privately Held**
WEB: www.sentechvdt.com
SIC: 3825 Transducers for volts, amperes,
watts, vars, frequency, etc.; transformers,
portable: instrument

(G-6536)
SNELLBAKER PRINTING INC
128 S Keswick Ave (19038-4510)
PHONE...................................215 885-0674
John Snellbaker, *President*
EMP: 4 **EST:** 1932
SQ FT: 1,200
SALES (est): 290K **Privately Held**
SIC: 2752 Letters, circular or form: litho-
graphed; commercial printing, offset

(G-6537)
SOLAR COOL COATINGS
117 Elm Ave Apt 5 (19038-3022)
PHONE...................................267 664-3667
Patrick Scanlon, *President*
EMP: 3
SALES (est): 187.6K **Privately Held**
SIC: 3443 Air coolers, metal plate

(G-6538)
SOLAR LIGHT COMPANY INC
100 E Glenside Ave (19038-4521)
PHONE...................................215 517-8700
Jay Silverman, *President*
Jeffrey Hall, *Exec VP*
EMP: 58
SQ FT: 7,000
SALES (est): 4.1MM **Privately Held**
WEB: www.solar.com
SIC: 3826 3648 3827 3829 Analytical in-
struments; lighting equipment; optical in-
struments & lenses; measuring &
controlling devices

(G-6539)
SPAHR-EVANS PRINTERS
2816 Limekiln Pike (19038-2205)
PHONE...................................215 886-4057
Barry W Evans, *Owner*
EMP: 4 **EST:** 1963
SQ FT: 3,600
SALES: 500K **Privately Held**
SIC: 2752 Commercial printing, offset; pro-
motional printing, lithographic; business
form & card printing, lithographic

(G-6540)
SPRING MILL WOODWORKS
837 Penn Ave (19038-1820)
PHONE...................................267 408-9469
Tina Silverman, *Principal*
EMP: 4
SALES (est): 328.4K **Privately Held**
SIC: 2431 Millwork

(G-6541)
STERLING FINISHING
1300 E Mermaid Ln (19038-7664)
PHONE...................................267 682-0844
Craig Conover, *President*
EMP: 10

SALES (est): 971.8K **Privately Held**
SIC: 2269 Linen fabrics: dyeing, finishing & printing

(G-6542)
VAULT MY KEYS LLC
2710 Laurel Ln (19038-2313)
PHONE.................................267 575-0506
EMP: 3 EST: 2013
SALES (est): 285.5K **Privately Held**
SIC: 3272 Burial vaults, concrete or pre-cast terrazzo

(G-6543)
WATCH MY NET INC
317 W Glenside Ave (19038-3313)
PHONE.................................267 625-6000
AVI Freedman, *CEO*
EMP: 3
SALES (est): 182.2K **Privately Held**
SIC: 3577 Computer peripheral equipment

(G-6544)
WISSAHICKON STONE QUARRY LLC
1 Waverly Rd (19038-7237)
PHONE.................................215 887-3330
Beth A White,
EMP: 3
SALES (est): 258.7K **Privately Held**
SIC: 3272 Stone, cast concrete

Glenville
York County

(G-6545)
LIZZIE BS BAKERY
4250 Krebs Rd (17329-8935)
PHONE.................................717 817-1791
Beth Baer, *Principal*
EMP: 4
SALES (est): 230.1K **Privately Held**
SIC: 2051 Bakery: wholesale or whole-sale/retail combined

Glenwillard
Allegheny County

(G-6546)
ELBACH & JOHNSON INC
1309 Main St (15046-5408)
PHONE.................................724 457-6180
Steven Cable, *President*
Jean Cable, *Treasurer*
EMP: 7
SQ FT: 11,000
SALES (est): 1.2MM **Privately Held**
SIC: 3545 3544 Precision measuring tools; special dies, tools, jigs & fixtures

Gordon
Schuylkill County

(G-6547)
UFP GORDON LLC
Also Called: Universal Forest Products
1 Royer St (17936)
PHONE.................................570 875-2811
Tom Staskel,
EMP: 35
SALES (est): 5.1MM
SALES (corp-wide): 4.4B **Publicly Held**
SIC: 2448 2436 2449 Wood pallets & skids; pallets, wood; skids, wood; soft-wood veneer & plywood; panels, soft-wood plywood; plywood, softwood; rectangular boxes & crates, wood
PA: Universal Forest Products, Inc.
2801 E Beltline Ave Ne
Grand Rapids MI 49525
616 364-6161

Gordonville
Lancaster County

(G-6548)
A & D MANUFACTURING
345 Centerville Rd (17529-9619)
PHONE.................................717 768-7330
David Fisher, *Principal*
EMP: 3
SALES (est): 267K **Privately Held**
SIC: 3999 Manufacturing industries

(G-6549)
BELL WALL & TRUSS LLC
229 Osceola Mill Rd (17529-9715)
PHONE.................................717 768-8338
Elmer King,
Benjamin King,
Leon King,
Mervin King,
EMP: 12
SALES (est): 705.7K **Privately Held**
SIC: 2439 Trusses, wooden roof

(G-6550)
BLUE FLAME HEATER MFG
321 Osceola Mill Rd (17529-9713)
PHONE.................................717 768-0301
EMP: 3 EST: 2013
SALES (est): 170K **Privately Held**
SIC: 3999 Mfg Misc Products

(G-6551)
CENTERVILLE CABINET SHOP
448 Centerville Rd (17529-9616)
PHONE.................................717 351-0708
Samuel King, *Owner*
EMP: 4
SALES (est): 251.7K **Privately Held**
SIC: 2434 Wood kitchen cabinets

(G-6552)
DS MACHINE LLC
Also Called: D S Machine
238b Old Leacock Rd (17529-9501)
PHONE.................................717 768-3853
David E Stoltzfus Sr, *President*
Amos Stoltzfus,
EMP: 25
SQ FT: 15,000
SALES (est): 5.9MM **Privately Held**
SIC: 3433 3312 Heating equipment, except electric; blast furnaces & steel mills

(G-6553)
ELI K LAPP JR
Also Called: Lapps Woodworking
84 Colonial Rd (17529-9752)
PHONE.................................717 768-0258
Eli K Lapp Jr, *Owner*
EMP: 4
SALES (est): 401.1K **Privately Held**
SIC: 2431 Millwork

(G-6554)
FISHER IRON WORKS
3260 E Gordon Rd (17529-9549)
PHONE.................................717 687-7595
Christin Fisher, *Partner*
Leon Fisher, *Partner*
Sarah Fisher, *Partner*
EMP: 4
SALES (est): 553.3K **Privately Held**
SIC: 3444 Sheet metalwork

(G-6555)
GARDENCRAFT MFG
2909 Lincoln Hwy E (17529-9524)
PHONE.................................717 354-3430
Allen Fisher, *Principal*
EMP: 8
SALES (est): 838K **Privately Held**
SIC: 3999 Manufacturing industries

(G-6556)
GLICKS WOODWORKING
4019 Old Phladelphia Pike (17529-9769)
PHONE.................................717 768-8958
EMP: 4 EST: 2009
SALES (est): 240K **Privately Held**
SIC: 2431 Millwork

(G-6557)
HC QUALITY DOORS LLC
48 Queen Rd Ste 1 (17529-9605)
PHONE.................................717 768-7038
Ray Harnish, *Managing Prtnr*
Levi Lantz Jr,
Amos J Lantz,
EMP: 15 EST: 2010
SALES (est): 5MM **Privately Held**
SIC: 3442 Metal doors, sash & trim

(G-6558)
I & J MANUFACTURING LLC
10 S New Holland Rd Ste 2 (17529-9776)
PHONE.................................717 442-9451
Jacob Blank, *Partner*
Moses Duane Blank,
▲ EMP: 7
SQ FT: 12,000
SALES (est): 684K **Privately Held**
SIC: 3523 7699 Farm machinery & equipment; farm machinery repair

(G-6559)
IDEAL MANUFACTURING LLC
10 S New Holland Rd 1 (17529-9776)
PHONE.................................717 629-3751
Eli Ebersol, *Principal*
EMP: 7
SALES (est): 932.1K **Privately Held**
SIC: 3999 Manufacturing industries

(G-6560)
KINGS KOUNTRY KORNER LLC (PA)
Also Called: King's Country Korner
101 Centerville Rd (17529-9623)
PHONE.................................717 768-3425
Raymond King, *Mng Member*
Mark Fisher,
Mary King,
EMP: 3
SQ FT: 1,619
SALES (est): 438.7K **Privately Held**
WEB: www.kingskountrykorner.com
SIC: 2499 5712 Decorative wood & wood-work; furniture stores

(G-6561)
PINE HILL MANUFACTURING LLC
2969 Lincoln Hwy E (17529-9524)
PHONE.................................717 288-2443
Daniel L Petersheim,
EMP: 12
SALES (est): 4.2MM **Privately Held**
SIC: 3715 Trailer bodies

(G-6562)
S & R WOODWORKING
3841 Yost Rd (17529-9603)
PHONE.................................717 354-8628
Omar Esreal, *Partner*
EMP: 3
SALES (est): 255.2K **Privately Held**
SIC: 2511 Wood household furniture

(G-6563)
SADIES SALADS
4021b Old Phila Pike (17529-9769)
PHONE.................................717 768-3774
Sadie Zook, *Owner*
Jacob Zook, *Co-Owner*
EMP: 7
SALES (est): 250K **Privately Held**
SIC: 2099 Salads, fresh or refrigerated

(G-6564)
SCENIC RIDGE COMPANY
Also Called: Scenic Ridge Contruction
48 Queen Rd (17529-9605)
PHONE.................................717 768-7522
J E King, *Mng Member*
Jay E King, *Mng Member*
EMP: 85
SQ FT: 36,000
SALES (est): 32.9MM **Privately Held**
WEB: www.scenicridge.com
SIC: 1541 3441 3448 Steel building con-struction; fabricated structural metal; pre-fabricated metal buildings

(G-6565)
SCENIC ROAD MANUFACTURING
3539 Scenic Rd (17529-9645)
PHONE.................................717 768-7300
David Esh, *Owner*
EMP: 5
SQ FT: 12,000
SALES (est): 1MM **Privately Held**
SIC: 2429 0272 3523 Barrels & barrel parts; horses & other equines; farm ma-chinery & equipment

(G-6566)
VINYL WINDOW WELLS LLC
229 S Groffdale Rd (17529-9627)
PHONE.................................717 768-0618
Samuel B King, *Mng Member*
EMP: 10
SALES (est): 1.6MM **Privately Held**
SIC: 3081 Vinyl film & sheet

Gouldsboro
Wayne County

(G-6567)
BEAVERS LOGGING INC
Rr 435 (18424)
PHONE.................................570 842-4034
Daniel J Beavers, *President*
EMP: 6
SALES (est): 495.8K **Privately Held**
SIC: 2411 Logging camps & contractors

(G-6568)
GUENTHER & SONS ENTERPRISES
Rr 507 Box N (18424)
P.O. Box 803 (18424-0803)
PHONE.................................570 676-0585
Guenther Fenski, *Owner*
EMP: 5
SQ FT: 4,000
SALES: 600K **Privately Held**
SIC: 3089 Food casings, plastic

(G-6569)
MELT ENTERPRISES LLC
Also Called: Babunyas Gourmets Spice
9 Wichita Ct (18424-9022)
P.O. Box 891 (18424-0891)
PHONE.................................570 244-2970
EMP: 4 EST: 2008
SQ FT: 1,000
SALES: 200K **Privately Held**
SIC: 2099 Mfg Spices

(G-6570)
RIVER STREET PEDORTHICS INC
881 Bear Lake Rd (18424-7962)
PHONE.................................570 299-5472
David W McFadden Jr, *President*
Paul Sonday, *Vice Pres*
Terra Wilkins, *Treasurer*
EMP: 4
SALES: 250K **Privately Held**
SIC: 3842 Surgical appliances & supplies

Grampian
Clearfield County

(G-6571)
HEPBURNIA COAL COMPANY (PA)
Also Called: Div-Forest Manor
Haytown Rd (16838)
PHONE.................................814 236-0473
Robert G Spencer, *President*
Tim Morgan, *Human Res Mgr*
Darrell Spencer, *Director*
Ray Spencer, *Director*
Spencer Collins, *Maintence Staff*
EMP: 5 EST: 1947
SQ FT: 2,400
SALES (est): 1.1MM **Privately Held**
SIC: 1221 Surface mining, bituminous

(G-6572)
RUSSELL STONE PRODUCTS INC
2640 Greenville Pike (16838-9201)
PHONE...............................814 236-2449
Cynthia Russell, *President*
▲ EMP: 9
SALES (est): 1.4MM **Privately Held**
SIC: 3281 Stone, quarrying & processing of own stone products

Grand Valley
Warren County

(G-6573)
T&G LOGGING
Rr 1 (16420)
PHONE...............................814 589-1731
Dedand Wakefield, *Owner*
EMP: 3
SALES (est): 129.9K **Privately Held**
SIC: 2411 Logging camps & contractors

Grantville
Dauphin County

(G-6574)
J & S FABRICATION INC
9330 Allentown Blvd (17028-8686)
PHONE...............................717 469-1409
James E Kline, *President*
▲ EMP: 12
SQ FT: 35,000
SALES (est): 2.2MM **Privately Held**
SIC: 1761 3444 Sheet metalwork; sheet metalwork

(G-6575)
KLINE BROS
10083 Allentown Blvd (17028-8715)
PHONE...............................717 469-0699
Glenn Kline, *Owner*
EMP: 14
SQ FT: 25,000
SALES (est): 2.2MM **Privately Held**
WEB: www.klinebroslandscaping.com
SIC: 3444 Sheet metalwork

(G-6576)
WERT BOOKBINDING INC
9975 Allentown Blvd (17028-8709)
PHONE...............................717 469-0626
Gary Wert, *President*
Sharon Bodtorf, *General Mgr*
Rodney Wert, *Vice Pres*
Scott Wert, *Vice Pres*
Paul B Wert, *Treasurer*
▲ EMP: 37
SQ FT: 26,000
SALES (est): 2.5MM **Privately Held**
WEB: www.wertbookbinding.com
SIC: 2789 Binding only: books, pamphlets, magazines, etc.; binding & repair of books, magazines & pamphlets; rebinding books, magazines or pamphlets

Grassflat
Clearfield County

(G-6577)
3NT-3 NIECES TRUCKING INC
108 Mini St (16839-9602)
PHONE...............................360 815-0938
Tim Cole, *Vice Pres*
EMP: 6
SQ FT: 900
SALES: 700K **Privately Held**
SIC: 4212 3715 Local trucking, without storage; truck trailers

Gratz
Dauphin County

(G-6578)
MI WINDOWS AND DOORS INC (HQ)
650 W Market St (17030)
PHONE...............................717 365-3300
Peter Desoto, *CEO*
Jay K Poppleton, *President*
Matt Desoto, *Vice Pres*
Mike Desoto, *Vice Pres*
Jason Kieffer, *Vice Pres*
▼ EMP: 3
SQ FT: 40,000
SALES (est): 609.3MM
SALES (corp-wide): 1.1B **Privately Held**
WEB: www.miwd.com
SIC: 3089 3442 Window frames & sash, plastic; screens, window, metal
PA: J. T. Walker Industries, Inc.
1310 N Hercules Ave Ste A
Clearwater FL 33765
727 461-0501

(G-6579)
MI WINDOWS AND DOORS INC
760 W Market St Route 25 (17030)
PHONE...............................717 365-3300
Peter Desoto, *President*
EMP: 220
SALES (corp-wide): 1.1B **Privately Held**
WEB: www.miwd.com
SIC: 3442 Screens, window, metal; screen doors, metal
HQ: Mi Windows And Doors, Inc.
650 W Market St
Gratz PA 17030
717 365-3300

(G-6580)
MI WINDOWS AND DOORS LLC
650 W Market St (17030)
PHONE...............................717 365-3300
EMP: 8
SALES (est): 157.6K **Privately Held**
SIC: 3442 Metal doors, sash & trim

Great Bend
Susquehanna County

(G-6581)
CUSTOM MCHINING GREAT BEND INC
26122 State Route 11 (18821-9401)
PHONE...............................570 879-2559
Thomas Koes, *President*
Anna Koes, *Vice Pres*
EMP: 15
SALES (est): 2.2MM **Privately Held**
SIC: 3599 Machine shop, jobbing & repair

(G-6582)
IDEAL-PMT MACHINE INC
1 Tannery St (18821-9426)
P.O. Box 585 (18821-0585)
PHONE...............................570 879-2165
Joseph Woosman, *President*
Wes Smith, *Manager*
EMP: 12
SQ FT: 19,500
SALES (est): 1.9MM **Privately Held**
SIC: 3599 Machine shop, jobbing & repair

Greeley
Pike County

(G-6583)
SAEILO INC (HQ)
Also Called: Kahr Arms
105 Kahr Ave (18425-9001)
PHONE...............................845 735-4500
Kook Moon, *President*
Soji Wada, *Corp Secy*
Katsuya Okamoto, *Vice Pres*
EMP: 10
SQ FT: 5,000
SALES (est): 15MM
SALES (corp-wide): 28.7MM **Privately Held**
WEB: www.kahrshop.com
SIC: 3599 3484 7538 5521 Machine & other job shop work; pistols or pistol parts, 30 mm. & below; general automotive repair shops; used car dealers
PA: Saeilo Enterprises Inc
105 Kahr Ave
Greeley PA 18425
845 735-6500

(G-6584)
SAEILO ENTERPRISES INC (PA)
105 Kahr Ave (18425-9001)
PHONE...............................845 735-6500
Kook Jin Moon, *President*
Katsuya Okamoto, *Vice Pres*
EMP: 28
SQ FT: 2,000
SALES (est): 28.7MM **Privately Held**
SIC: 3599 Machine shop, jobbing & repair

(G-6585)
SMI IL INC
Also Called: Saeilo Manufacturing Inds
105 Kahr Ave (18425-9001)
PHONE...............................847 228-0090
George Dikeman, *President*
EMP: 20
SQ FT: 10,000
SALES: 2MM
SALES (corp-wide): 28.7MM **Privately Held**
WEB: www.saeilo.com
SIC: 3599 Machine & other job shop work
PA: Saeilo Enterprises Inc
105 Kahr Ave
Greeley PA 18425
845 735-6500

Green Lane
Montgomery County

(G-6586)
COUNTY OF MONTGOMERY
Also Called: Greenlane Park
2144 Snyder Rd (18054-9508)
PHONE...............................215 234-4528
Pam Murray, *Principal*
EMP: 41 **Privately Held**
WEB: www.is-partner.com
SIC: 2531 Picnic tables or benches, park
PA: County Of Montgomery
530 Port Indian Rd
Norristown PA 19403
610 278-3072

(G-6587)
DESIGN SPACE INPHARMATICS LLC
Also Called: Ds Inpharmatics
1209 Payne Rd (18054-2341)
P.O. Box 532, Harleysville (19438-0532)
PHONE...............................215 272-4275
Jennifer Seibert,
EMP: 7
SALES (est): 630.1K **Privately Held**
SIC: 2834 8748 Pharmaceutical preparations; business consulting

(G-6588)
ESSENCE OF OLD WOODS
2131 Old Woods Rd (18054-9416)
PHONE...............................215 258-0852
George Howard, *Principal*
EMP: 3
SALES (est): 367.4K **Privately Held**
SIC: 2841 Soap & other detergents

(G-6589)
MATTHEW MCKEON
Also Called: K & H Industrial Filtration
120 Hausman Rd (18054-2315)
PHONE...............................215 234-8505
Matthew McKeon, *Owner*
EMP: 8
SQ FT: 3,000
SALES: 500K **Privately Held**
SIC: 3569 Filters, general line: industrial

(G-6590)
MIDGARD INC (PA)
Also Called: Midgard Plastics
1255 Nursery Rd (18054-9423)
PHONE...............................215 536-3174
Robert S Brown, *President*
Brian Byrd, *President*
Lorena Brown, *Corp Secy*
▲ EMP: 60
SQ FT: 40,000
SALES (est): 20.2MM **Privately Held**
SIC: 3089 Injection molding of plastics

(G-6591)
NEWPORT FABRICATORS INC
432 Walnut St (18054-2246)
PHONE...............................215 234-4400
John Slotter, *President*
EMP: 16
SQ FT: 10,000
SALES (est): 2.9MM **Privately Held**
WEB: www.newportfab.com
SIC: 3444 Sheet metal specialties, not stamped

(G-6592)
RESPONSE ELECTRIC INC
6301 Fifth St (18054-2280)
PHONE...............................215 799-2400
Steven A Kriebel, *President*
Amy N Kribel, *Vice Pres*
EMP: 5
SALES (est): 799.7K **Privately Held**
SIC: 3699 Electrical work

(G-6593)
STREAMLINE PROPANE LLC
35 Schultz Rd (18054-2448)
PHONE...............................215 919-4500
Andrew Fallon, *Principal*
EMP: 3
SALES (est): 200K **Privately Held**
SIC: 1321 Propane (natural) production

(G-6594)
WOXALL WOODCRAFT INC
115 Walnut St (18054)
PHONE...............................215 234-8774
David Kendall, *President*
Brooke Kendall, *Vice Pres*
EMP: 5
SQ FT: 7,500
SALES (est): 587.5K **Privately Held**
WEB: www.woxallwoodcraft.com
SIC: 2511 5712 Desks, household: wood; cabinet work, custom

Greencastle
Franklin County

(G-6595)
AMERICAN FIBERTECH CORPORATION
Also Called: Industrial Pallet
255 N Carlisle St (17225-1424)
PHONE...............................717 597-5708
Rob Meister, *CEO*
Jeff Deike, *Plant Mgr*
EMP: 50
SALES (corp-wide): 58.2MM **Privately Held**
WEB: www.ind-pallet-corp.com
SIC: 2448 Pallets, wood
PA: American Fibertech Corporation
4 N New York St
Remington IN 47977
219 261-3586

(G-6596)
AMY SEMLER
Also Called: AMS Services & Designs
175 Hykes Rd E (17225-8421)
PHONE...............................717 593-9243
Amy Semler, *Owner*
Mark Semler, *Co-Owner*
EMP: 3
SALES: 200K **Privately Held**
SIC: 1731 2741 General electrical contractor; shopping news: publishing & printing

▲ = Import ▼=Export
◆ =Import/Export

(G-6597)
ANTRIM MACHINE COMPANY
Also Called: Castle Machine Company
5865 Bullitt Rd (17225-9296)
P.O. Box 187 (17225-0187)
PHONE.....................................717 369-3184
Sam W Gates, *Principal*
EMP: 30
SQ FT: 7,000
SALES (est): 4.4MM **Privately Held**
SIC: 3599 Machine shop, jobbing & repair

(G-6598)
APPALACHIAN MILL INC
2375 Buchanan Trl W (17225-8306)
PHONE.....................................717 328-2805
EMP: 25 **EST:** 1994
SQ FT: 40,000
SALES: 1.2MM **Privately Held**
SIC: 2434 5712 Mfg Wood Kitchen Cabinets Ret Furniture

(G-6599)
BECK MANUFACTURING COMPANY
9170 Molly Pitcher Hwy (17225-9712)
PHONE.....................................717 593-0197
Chris Stotler, *Branch Mgr*
EMP: 10
SALES (corp-wide): 4.8B **Privately Held**
SIC: 3498 Fabricated pipe & fittings
HQ: Beck Manufacturing Company
330 E 9th St
Waynesboro PA 17268
717 762-9141

(G-6600)
BILTWOOD ARCHITECTURAL MLLWK
Also Called: Biltwood Interiors
544 Buchanan Trl W (17225-9370)
PHONE.....................................717 593-9400
James K Hickey II, *President*
Michael Cranston, *Corp Secy*
EMP: 10
SQ FT: 20,000
SALES: 1MM **Privately Held**
SIC: 2431 2521 5211 Millwork; wood office furniture; door & window products

(G-6601)
BUCHANAN TRAIL INDUSTRIES INC
2375 Buchanan Trl W (17225-8306)
PHONE.....................................717 597-7166
Katherine Gordon, *President*
James Rockwell, *Principal*
Laurie A Myers, *Treasurer*
Marjorie B Michael, *Admin Sec*
EMP: 160
SQ FT: 5,000
SALES (est): 26.6MM **Privately Held**
WEB: www.foremosthomes.com
SIC: 2452 Modular homes, prefabricated, wood

(G-6602)
CELF SERVICES LLC
Also Called: Mason-Dixon Bbq Services
1542 Buchanan Trl E (17225-9511)
PHONE.....................................717 643-0039
Eric Forrester, *Mng Member*
EMP: 6
SALES (est): 12.1K **Privately Held**
SIC: 3499 3479 Metal household articles; coating of metals & formed products

(G-6603)
CONCRETE PIPE & PRECAST LLC
401 S Carlisle St (17225-1565)
PHONE.....................................717 597-5000
Gregory Ouimette, *Branch Mgr*
EMP: 46
SALES (corp-wide): 276.3MM **Privately Held**
SIC: 3272 Sewer pipe, concrete; concrete products used to facilitate drainage
PA: Concrete Pipe & Precast, Llc
11352 Virginia Precast Rd
Ashland VA 23005
804 798-6068

(G-6604)
CONTECH ENGNERED SOLUTIONS LLC
600 N Washington St (17225-1295)
PHONE.....................................717 597-2148
Larry Asbury, *Superintendent*
EMP: 20 **Privately Held**
SIC: 3443 Fabricated plate work (boiler shop)
HQ: Contech Engineered Solutions Llc
9025 Centre Pointe Dr # 400
West Chester OH 45069
513 645-7000

(G-6605)
DARCO INC
Also Called: Danco Products
411 S Cedar Ln (17225-1300)
PHONE.....................................717 597-7139
Daniel Reynolds, *President*
Daniel L Reynolds, *President*
William Reynolds, *Vice Pres*
Darlene Reynolds, *Admin Sec*
EMP: 20
SQ FT: 40,000
SALES (est): 4.9MM **Privately Held**
WEB: www.dancoproducts.com
SIC: 3713 Truck bodies (motor vehicles)

(G-6606)
DEL MARTIN SCREEN PRTG & EMB
21 Sarah Susan Ln (17225-8430)
PHONE.....................................717 597-5751
Brad EBY, *President*
Del Martin, *President*
Karen F Martin, *Corp Secy*
EMP: 15
SQ FT: 12,500
SALES (est): 1.4MM **Privately Held**
WEB: www.delprint.com
SIC: 2759 7389 Screen printing; advertising, promotional & trade show services; embroidering of advertising on shirts, etc.

(G-6607)
DJK PROPERTIES LLC
80 Commerce Ave (17225-9470)
PHONE.....................................717 597-5965
Michael Kulpak, *Principal*
EMP: 3
SALES (est): 168.5K **Privately Held**
SIC: 3399 Laminating steel

(G-6608)
DUVINAGE LLC
Mitchell Machine Shop Div
11550 Molly Pitcher Hwy (17225-9043)
P.O. Box 100 (17225-0100)
PHONE.....................................717 283-6111
William Sanders, *Manager*
EMP: 17
SALES (corp-wide): 6.9MM **Privately Held**
SIC: 3599 Machine shop, jobbing & repair
PA: Duvinage Llc
60 W Oak Ridge Dr
Hagerstown MD 21740
301 733-8255

(G-6609)
ECHO PILOT
29 Center Sq (17225-1458)
P.O. Box 159 (17225-0159)
PHONE.....................................717 597-2164
Joyce Nowell, *Principal*
Kristy Yaukey, *Manager*
EMP: 6
SQ FT: 1,200
SALES (est): 362.4K **Privately Held**
WEB: www.echo-pilot.com
SIC: 2711 Newspapers, publishing & printing

(G-6610)
FAB TECH INDUSTRIES
80 Commerce Ave (17225-9470)
PHONE.....................................717 597-4919
EMP: 3 **EST:** 2015
SALES (est): 143.1K **Privately Held**
SIC: 3441 7692 Structural Metal Fabrication Welding Repair

(G-6611)
FAB TECH V INDUSTRIES INC (PA)
68 Commerce Ave (17225)
PHONE.....................................717 597-4919
Michael Kulpak, *President*
Donna Kulpak, *Corp Secy*
Dawn McClain, *COO*
Bart Graham, *Engineer*
Bill Bachtell, *Human Res Dir*
EMP: 30
SQ FT: 10,000
SALES (est): 4MM **Privately Held**
WEB: www.fabtechind.com
SIC: 3441 7692 Fabricated structural metal; welding repair

(G-6612)
FARMERS UNION COOP ASSN
30 E Walter Ave (17225-1294)
PHONE.....................................717 597-3191
David Forester, *President*
EMP: 10
SQ FT: 5,000
SALES (est): 1.3MM **Privately Held**
SIC: 2048 5251 Livestock feeds; hardware

(G-6613)
GANOE PAVING INC
1455 Buchanan Trl W (17225-8305)
PHONE.....................................717 597-2567
Dirk Mowen, *President*
EMP: 20
SALES (est): 2.1MM **Privately Held**
SIC: 1771 1611 3479 Blacktop (asphalt) work; highway & street construction; coating of metals & formed products

(G-6614)
GATE 7 LLC
Also Called: Safetydecals.net
1098 Armada Dr (17225-1618)
PHONE.....................................717 593-0204
Clare Reay, *Vice Pres*
Joshua Chapman, *Corp Comm Staff*
Keith Wickham, *Mng Member*
John Reay,
Audrey Wickham,
EMP: 14
SQ FT: 6,500
SALES (est): 1.7MM **Privately Held**
WEB: www.gate7llc.com
SIC: 2759 Commercial printing

(G-6615)
GHX INDUSTRIAL LLC
151 N Washington St (17225-1231)
PHONE.....................................410 687-7900
Gary Martin, *Branch Mgr*
EMP: 4
SALES (corp-wide): 504.7MM **Privately Held**
SIC: 3492 Hose & tube fittings & assemblies, hydraulic/pneumatic
HQ: Ghx Industrial, Llc
13311 Lockwood Rd
Houston TX 77044
713 676-0282

(G-6616)
GROVE INVESTORS INC
1542 Buchanan Trl E (17225-9511)
P.O. Box 21, Shady Grove (17256-0021)
PHONE.....................................717 597-8121
Jeff Bust, *President*
EMP: 1300
SALES (est): 92.3MM **Privately Held**
SIC: 3531 Cranes

(G-6617)
HARTRONICS
3354 Conococheague Ln (17225-9495)
PHONE.....................................717 597-3931
Barry Hartle, *Principal*
EMP: 3
SALES (est): 213.5K **Privately Held**
SIC: 3625 Relays & industrial controls

(G-6618)
HESS C & SONS CABINETS INC
2361 Buchanan Trl E (17225-9515)
PHONE.....................................717 597-3295
Calvin Hess, *President*
Mathew Hess, *Vice Pres*
EMP: 7

(G-6619)
JAMES G BOHN
Also Called: Bohn Painting & Decorating
2205 Pikeside Dr (17225-8457)
PHONE.....................................717 597-1901
James G Bohn, *Owner*
EMP: 4
SALES: 200K **Privately Held**
SIC: 2851 1711 Paints & paint additives; plumbing, heating, air-conditioning contractors

(G-6620)
JERRDAN CORPORATION
Molly Pitcher Hwy (17225)
PHONE.....................................717 597-7111
Bradley Kresge, *Engineer*
Barry Kerr, *Manager*
Todd Yoter, *Info Tech Mgr*
EMP: 95
SALES (corp-wide): 6.8B **Publicly Held**
WEB: www.jerrdan.com
SIC: 3713 Truck bodies (motor vehicles); automobile wrecker truck bodies
HQ: Jerrdan Corporation
13224 Fountain Head Plz
Hagerstown MD 21742
301 745-5434

(G-6621)
LAWLESS ASSOC PIPE ORGAN INC
501 S Cedar Ln Ste 2 (17225-1364)
PHONE.....................................717 593-0398
Irving Lawless, *President*
EMP: 5
SQ FT: 5,300
SALES (est): 285.6K **Privately Held**
WEB: www.lawlessorgan.com
SIC: 3931 Pipes, organ

(G-6622)
MILLER FABRICATION INC
13130 Worleytown Rd (17225-9655)
PHONE.....................................717 359-4433
Linda Miller, *President*
EMP: 4
SQ FT: 8,500
SALES (est): 485.9K **Privately Held**
SIC: 3441 Fabricated structural metal

(G-6623)
MITCHELL APX MACHINE SHOP INC
Also Called: Mitchell Machine Shop
11550 Molly Pitcher Hwy (17225-9043)
PHONE.....................................717 597-2157
Andrew V Papoutsis, *President*
Garrett R Gordon, *Treasurer*
Jamie L Papoutsis, *Admin Sec*
EMP: 8
SALES (est): 130.1K **Privately Held**
SIC: 3544 3452 Jigs & fixtures; screws, metal

(G-6624)
NELSON COMPANY INC
113 Commerce Ave (17225-9451)
PHONE.....................................717 593-0600
David Caltrider, *President*
Chris Recker, *Manager*
EMP: 6
SALES (est): 758.8K **Privately Held**
SIC: 2448 2441 Pallets, wood; boxes, wood

(G-6625)
NULL MACHINE SHOP INC
95 Commerce Ave (17225-9470)
P.O. Box 7 (17225-0007)
PHONE.....................................717 597-3330
Mike Keebaugh, *President*
EMP: 6 **EST:** 1921
SQ FT: 12,800
SALES (est): 1MM **Privately Held**
SIC: 3599 Machine shop, jobbing & repair

(G-6626)
PLASTIC PROFILES LLC
48 S Antrim Way (17225-1520)
PHONE.....................................717 593-9200
Leon Miller, *Mng Member*

Elwood Martin, *Mng Member*
EMP: 6
SALES (est): 663.2K **Privately Held**
WEB: www.plastecprofiles.com
SIC: 5162 2821 Plastics products; molding
compounds, plastics

(G-6627)
PRE CAST SYSTEMS LLC
5877 Bullitt Rd (17225-9296)
PHONE................................717 369-3773
Matt Diller, *Mng Member*
EMP: 18
SALES (est): 2MM **Privately Held**
SIC: 3272 Concrete products

(G-6628)
PRESSURE-TECH INC
120 E Grant St (17225-1220)
P.O. Box 430 (17225-0430)
PHONE................................717 597-1868
Craig Walck, *President*
Randall Shearer, *Vice Pres*
EMP: 12
SQ FT: 12,800
SALES (est): 2.2MM **Privately Held**
WEB: www.pressure-tech.com
SIC: 3443 3444 Boiler & boiler shop work;
sheet metalwork

(G-6629)
**REESE DARYL C
WALLPAPERING**
9984 Browns Mill Rd (17225-9705)
PHONE................................717 597-2532
Daryl C Reese, *Owner*
EMP: 4
SALES (est): 250K **Privately Held**
SIC: 2679 1721 Wallpaper; painting &
paper hanging

(G-6630)
RICHARD FREEMAN
Also Called: Greencastle Bronze & Granite
400 N Antrim Way (17225-1531)
PHONE................................717 597-4580
Richard Freeman, *Owner*
Marry Freeman, *Owner*
EMP: 4
SALES (est): 558.8K **Privately Held**
SIC: 3281 5999 Monument or burial stone,
cut & shaped; monuments, finished to
custom order

(G-6631)
ROCKWELL LUMBER CO INC
3865 Buchanan Trl W (17225-9388)
PHONE................................717 597-7428
Myers D Rockwell, *President*
Douglas Rockwell, *Vice Pres*
Dirk Rockwell, *Treasurer*
Dolly Rockwell, *Admin Sec*
EMP: 9
SQ FT: 8,000
SALES (est): 1.6MM **Privately Held**
SIC: 2411 2421 2448 Logging camps &
contractors; sawmills & planing mills, gen-
eral; pallets, wood

(G-6632)
**SHADY GROVE CABINET SHOP
INC**
3030 Buchanan Trl E (17225-9156)
P.O. Box 43, Shady Grove (17256-0043)
PHONE................................717 597-0825
Nelson L Hess, *President*
Larry Gipe, *Corp Secy*
Allan Hess, *Vice Pres*
EMP: 9 **EST:** 1959
SQ FT: 4,800
SALES (est): 1.3MM **Privately Held**
SIC: 2434 5211 Wood kitchen cabinets;
millwork & lumber

(G-6633)
SHAFFER PRODUCTS LLC
13062 Grant Shook Rd (17225-9474)
PHONE................................717 597-2688
Rodney Shaffer,
Timothy Shaffer,
EMP: 18
SALES (est): 2.7MM **Privately Held**
WEB: www.shafferstakes.com
SIC: 2421 Custom sawmill

(G-6634)
**SHANK PALLET RECYCLERS
INC (PA)**
1620 Buchanan Trl E (17225-9803)
PHONE................................717 597-3545
Nelson Shank, *President*
EMP: 4 **EST:** 1992
SQ FT: 18,000
SALES: 2.2MM **Privately Held**
SIC: 2448 Pallets, wood

(G-6635)
**SHANK PALLET RECYCLERS
INC**
13132 Gearhart Rd (17225-9518)
PHONE................................717 597-3545
Linda Hall, *Branch Mgr*
EMP: 4
SALES (corp-wide): 2.2MM **Privately
Held**
SIC: 2448 Pallets, wood
PA: Shank Pallet Recyclers, Inc
1620 Buchanan Trl E
Greencastle PA 17225
717 597-3545

(G-6636)
STRAIT STEEL INC
8400 Molly Pitcher Hwy (17225-9036)
P.O. Box 370 (17225-0370)
PHONE................................717 597-3125
Dallas Strait, *CEO*
Gregory A Strait, *President*
Larry Crouse, *Vice Pres*
Charles Tornetta, *Vice Pres*
Chris Reichelderfer, *Project Mgr*
EMP: 65
SQ FT: 150,000
SALES: 40.4MM **Privately Held**
WEB: www.straitsteel.com
SIC: 3441 Building components, structural
steel

(G-6637)
SUNNYWAY FOODS INC (PA)
Also Called: Sunnyway Food Market
212 N Antrim Way (17225-1406)
PHONE................................717 597-7121
Ladean Martin, *President*
Aldine Martin, *Vice Pres*
Margaret Martin, *Treasurer*
Michael Martin, *Admin Sec*
EMP: 85
SQ FT: 41,000
SALES: 25MM **Privately Held**
SIC: 5411 5812 2051 Supermarkets, in-
dependent; eating places; bread, cake &
related products

(G-6638)
TARCO INC
Also Called: Tarco Roofing Materials
8650 Molly Pitcher Hwy (17225-9716)
PHONE................................717 597-1876
Craig Simpson, *General Mgr*
EMP: 50
SALES (corp-wide): 25.3MM **Privately
Held**
WEB: www.tarco.com
SIC: 2952 Roofing materials
PA: Tarco, Inc.
1 Information Way Ste 225
Little Rock AR 72202
501 945-4506

(G-6639)
THOMAS SALES INC
124 S Washington St (17225-1332)
PHONE................................717 597-9366
Barry Thomas, *President*
Raetta Thomas, *Admin Sec*
EMP: 2
SALES: 8MM **Privately Held**
SIC: 3443 Industrial vessels, tanks & con-
tainers

(G-6640)
TIMBER MILL WOODCRAFT LLC
556 Buchanan Trl W (17225-9370)
PHONE................................717 597-7433
Henry Hostetter, *Partner*
Willis Martin, *Partner*
EMP: 5
SQ FT: 7,200

SALES: 1MM **Privately Held**
SIC: 3448 Buildings, portable: prefabricated metal

(G-6641)
TOMA INC
853 Buchanan Trl E (17225-9509)
PHONE................................717 597-7194
John Thomas, *Manager*
EMP: 8 **Privately Held**
SIC: 3273 Mfg Ready-Mixed Concrete
PA: Toma, Inc.
212 Locust St Ste 500
Harrisburg PA 17101

(G-6642)
WERTNER SIGNS
8002 Stone Bridge Rd (17225-9786)
PHONE................................717 597-4502
James Wertner, *Owner*
EMP: 4
SALES (est): 238.4K **Privately Held**
WEB: www.wertnersigns.com
SIC: 3993 Signs, not made in custom sign
painting shops

Greenfield Township
Lackawanna County

(G-6643)
COMPTON QUARRY
Also Called: Milestone Quarry
565 Route 247 (18407-3707)
PHONE................................570 222-9489
George Hampton, *Owner*
EMP: 3
SALES (est): 252.8K **Privately Held**
SIC: 1411 Bluestone, dimension-quarrying

Greenock
Allegheny County

(G-6644)
**CAPO AND KIFER
PULTRUSIONS**
1 Locust Grv (15047-1129)
P.O. Box 195 (15047-0195)
PHONE................................412 751-3489
Joe Capo, *Principal*
EMP: 4
SALES (est): 410.9K **Privately Held**
SIC: 3312 Tool & die steel

(G-6645)
**OTTO DESIGN CASEFIXTURE
INC (PA)**
Also Called: Ottocase
7341 Sandy Ln (15047)
P.O. Box 64 (15047-0064)
PHONE................................412 824-3580
Christopher Amos, *President*
EMP: 7
SQ FT: 7,000
SALES: 350K **Privately Held**
SIC: 2542 Cabinets: show, display or stor-
age: except wood

Greensboro
Greene County

(G-6646)
FRANKS INTERNATIONAL LLC
153 Dora Village Main St (15338-1015)
PHONE................................724 943-3243
Jeffrey Reynolds, *Branch Mgr*
EMP: 6
SALES (corp-wide): 456.5MM **Privately
Held**
SIC: 1389 Oil field services
HQ: Frank's International, Llc
10260 Westheimer Rd
Houston TX 77042
281 966-7300

Greensburg
Westmoreland County

(G-6647)
ABB INC
125 Theobold Ave Ste 10 (15601-5559)
PHONE................................724 838-8622
Tom Roberts, *Branch Mgr*
EMP: 76
SALES (corp-wide): 34.3B **Privately Held**
WEB: www.elsterelectricity.com
SIC: 3612 Transformers, except electric
HQ: Abb Inc.
305 Gregson Dr
Cary NC 27511

(G-6648)
**AGE-CRAFT MANUFACTURING
INC (PA)**
45 Madison Ave (15601-2715)
PHONE................................724 838-5580
Benjamin J Policastro Jr, *CEO*
Benjamin J Policastro III, *President*
Doug Sabatino, *Manager*
EMP: 10
SQ FT: 15,000
SALES (est): 3.5MM **Privately Held**
SIC: 2591 3444 Blinds vertical; mini
blinds; window shades; awnings, sheet
metal

(G-6649)
ALTRIS INCORPORATED
119 Apple Ln (15601-8796)
P.O. Box 293, Delmont (15626-0293)
PHONE................................724 259-8338
Allen Martello, *President*
Tracey Martello, *Treasurer*
EMP: 7
SQ FT: 400
SALES (est): 827.6K **Privately Held**
SIC: 7311 8742 2759 7336 Advertising
agencies; marketing consulting services;
commercial printing; stationery: printing;
commercial art & graphic design

(G-6650)
**AMERICAN TANK & CONCRETE
SVC**
813 Georges Station Rd (15601-6457)
PHONE................................724 837-4410
George K Kucenic, *President*
Jeffrey Kucenic, *Vice Pres*
EMP: 11 **EST:** 1947
SALES (est): 1.5MM **Privately Held**
SIC: 3272 5039 5211 Septic tanks, con-
crete; septic tanks; lumber & other build-
ing materials

(G-6651)
ANDERSON MACHINE CO
1131 Beaver Run Rd (15601-8983)
PHONE................................724 834-5135
William Anderson Sr, *President*
William Anderson Jr, *Vice Pres*
Joanne Anderson, *Treasurer*
EMP: 7
SQ FT: 7,200
SALES: 1MM **Privately Held**
SIC: 3599 Machine shop, jobbing & repair

(G-6652)
**AVANTI ENGINEERING AND MFG
INC**
1666 Business Route 66 (15601-6324)
PHONE................................724 834-0752
Lisa Sebastiani, *President*
Antonio Sebastiani, *Vice Pres*
EMP: 15
SQ FT: 3,200
SALES (est): 2.6MM **Privately Held**
SIC: 3599 Machine shop, jobbing & repair

(G-6653)
**BECKER/WHOLESALE MINE
SUP LLC**
114 Equity Dr Ste E (15601-3500)
PHONE................................724 515-4993
William Hensler, *President*
Robert Gilmer, *Business Mgr*
Joe Dibridge, *COO*
Jim Hensler, *Engineer*

▲ EMP: 20
SQ FT: 18,000
SALES (est): 9.6MM
SALES (corp-wide): 181.9MM Privately
Held
SIC: 3532 Mining machinery
HQ: Becker Mining Systems Ag
Walter-Becker-Str. 1
Friedrichsthal 66299
689 785-70

(G-6654)
CALDER TRANSPORT
Also Called: Calder Enterprises
314 Persian Ln (15601-6933)
PHONE....................................724 787-8390
EMP: 5 EST: 2010
SALES (est): 360K Privately Held
SIC: 1381 Oil/Gas Well Drilling

(G-6655)
CARBOLINE COMPANY
741 S Main St (15601-4136)
PHONE....................................724 838-5750
EMP: 5
SALES (corp-wide): 5.3B Publicly Held
SIC: 2851 Lacquers, varnishes, enamels &
other coatings
HQ: Carboline Company
2150 Schuetz Rd Fl 1
Saint Louis MO 63146
314 644-1000

(G-6656)
CARDIAC TELECOM
CORPORATION
Also Called: Ctc
212 Outlet Way Ste 1 (15601-7197)
PHONE....................................800 355-2594
Lee Ehrlichman, President
Alois A Langer PHD, Vice Pres
EMP: 17
SQ FT: 5,300
SALES (est): 1.2MM Privately Held
WEB: www.cardiactelecom.com
SIC: 3841 5047 Surgical & medical instru-
ments; electro-medical equipment

(G-6657)
CCS MACHINING INC
7728 Rte 22 W (15601)
PHONE....................................724 668-7706
Thomas Ridella, President
Dean Ridella, Corp Secy
EMP: 4
SALES (est): 399.3K Privately Held
SIC: 3599 7699 Machine shop, jobbing &
repair; motorcycle repair service

(G-6658)
CINCINNATUS GROUP
305 S Maple Ave Fl 1 (15601-3218)
PHONE....................................724 600-0221
Andrew C McCaffrey, Principal
EMP: 4
SQ FT: 2,000
SALES (est): 382.8K Privately Held
WEB: www.thecincinnatusgroup.com
SIC: 3999 Manufacturing industries

(G-6659)
DJ MACHINING LLC (PA)
125 Theobold Ave (15601-5562)
PHONE....................................724 938-0812
Dennis Jenko, Mng Member
EMP: 4
SQ FT: 9,000
SALES: 600K Privately Held
SIC: 3545 Precision tools, machinists'

(G-6660)
DONOHOE CORPORATION
Also Called: Kensington Lighting Company
593 Rugh St Ste 6 (15601-5637)
PHONE....................................724 850-2433
Walter F Shirley, President
Gary Whitenight, President
Samuel Scott, Shareholder
EMP: 19
SQ FT: 40,000
SALES (est): 1.5MM Privately Held
WEB: www.kensingtonus.com
SIC: 3646 Commercial indusl & institu-
tional electric lighting fixtures

(G-6661)
DOPPELHAUER
MANUFACTURING
125 Theobold Ave (15601-5562)
PHONE....................................724 691-0763
EMP: 3
SALES (est): 227.8K Privately Held
SIC: 3999 Atomizers, toiletry

(G-6662)
DOROTHY M NELSON
Also Called: Nelsons Arrows
1181 Swede Hill Rd (15601-4914)
PHONE....................................724 837-6210
Dorothy M Nelson, Owner
EMP: 5
SQ FT: 864
SALES (est): 573.4K Privately Held
WEB: www.nelsonsarrows.com
SIC: 5091 3949 Archery equipment;
archery equipment, general

(G-6663)
EDT
110 Danko Ln (15601-6770)
PHONE....................................724 217-4008
Tom Altman, Principal
EMP: 4
SALES (est): 359K Privately Held
SIC: 2819 Industrial inorganic chemicals

(G-6664)
ENCLOSURES DIRECT
CORPORATION
141 Wilson Ave (15601-2522)
PHONE....................................724 837-7600
Dwayne W Altman, Principal
EMP: 4
SALES (est): 685.3K Privately Held
SIC: 3441 Fabricated structural metal

(G-6665)
EXCELA HEALTH HOLDING CO
INC
Also Called: Westmoreland Regional Hospital
532 W Pittsburgh St (15601-2239)
PHONE....................................724 832-4450
Bob Guyne, Manager
EMP: 4
SALES (corp-wide): 687.1MM Privately
Held
WEB: www.excelahealth.com
SIC: 8062 2835 General medical & surgi-
cal hospitals; in vitro & in vivo diagnostic
substances
PA: Excela Health Holding Company, Inc.
532 W Pittsburgh St
Greensburg PA 15601
724 832-4000

(G-6666)
FARZATI MANUFACTURING
CORP
125 Theobold Ave Ste 2 (15601-5562)
PHONE....................................724 836-3508
Frank Farzati Jr, President
Linda Andrews, Corp Secy
Tony Stader, Director
Dennis Stockberger, Director
EMP: 30
SQ FT: 14,000
SALES (est): 5.5MM Privately Held
WEB: www.farzati.com
SIC: 3599 Machine shop, jobbing & repair

(G-6667)
FOTORECORD PRINT CENTER
INC
45 E Pittsburgh St (15601-3324)
PHONE....................................724 837-0530
Paul Nicholas, President
George Nickloff, President
Joan Nickloff, Corp Secy
Paul Nickloff, Vice Pres
Cindy Strayer, Sales Staff
EMP: 6
SALES (est): 1.1MM Privately Held
WEB: www.fotorecord.com
SIC: 2752 7334 5999 7389 Commercial
printing, offset; blueprinting service; draft-
ing equipment & supplies; mailing & mes-
senger services

(G-6668)
GENERAL CARBIDE
CORPORATION
1151 Garden St (15601-6417)
PHONE....................................724 836-3000
Mona Pappafava Ray, Principal
L B Pappafava, Corp Secy
Cheryl L Miedel, Manager
Michael Midlik, Technical Staff
▲ EMP: 160
SQ FT: 77,000
SALES (est): 35MM Privately Held
WEB: www.pappafava.com
SIC: 3544 3568 3545 3312 Special dies
& tools; power transmission equipment;
machine tool accessories; blast furnaces
& steel mills; industrial inorganic chemi-
cals

(G-6669)
GIBSON STAINLESS SPECIALTY
INC
223 Donohoe Rd (15601-6987)
P.O. Box 847 (15601-0847)
PHONE....................................724 838-8320
Joseph G Gibson, President
EMP: 15
SQ FT: 30,000
SALES (est): 2.4MM Privately Held
WEB: www.gibsonstainless.com
SIC: 3644 3429 Electric conduits & fit-
tings; clamps, couplings, nozzles & other
metal hose fittings

(G-6670)
GREENSBURG MCH &
DRIVELINE LLC
145 Talbot Ave (15601-3222)
PHONE....................................724 837-8233
Mark Petros, Owner
EMP: 3
SALES (est): 550.9K Privately Held
SIC: 3714 Differentials & parts, motor vehi-
cle

(G-6671)
HANGER INC
4000 Hempfield Plaza Blvd # 904
(15601-1484)
PHONE....................................724 836-4949
Joe Avolio, Manager
EMP: 33
SALES (corp-wide): 1B Publicly Held
SIC: 3842 Prosthetic appliances
PA: Hanger, Inc.
10910 Domain Dr Ste 300
Austin TX 78758
512 777-3800

(G-6672)
HANGER PRSTHETCS & ORTHO
INC
Also Called: Hanger Clinic
4000 Hempfield Plaza Blvd (15601-1483)
PHONE....................................724 836-4949
Sam Liang, CEO
EMP: 5
SALES (corp-wide): 1B Publicly Held
SIC: 3842 Limbs, artificial
HQ: Hanger Prosthetics & Orthotics, Inc.
10910 Domain Dr Ste 300
Austin TX 78758
512 777-3800

(G-6673)
HEINNICKEL FARMS INC
2207 State Route 119 (15601-6500)
PHONE....................................724 837-9254
Alquin Heinnickel Jr, President
Philip C Heinnickel, Vice Pres
EMP: 9
SALES (est): 1.5MM Privately Held
SIC: 0211 2011 0119 0115 Beef cattle
feedlots; beef products from beef slaugh-
tered on site; oat farm; cereal crop farms;
corn; soybeans

(G-6674)
HODGE ELECTRIC MOTORS INC
524 Tremont Ave Ste 1 (15601-4295)
PHONE....................................724 834-8420
James Gongaware, President
Kathleen Gongaware, Vice Pres
EMP: 4
SQ FT: 600

SALES (est): 272.2K Privately Held
SIC: 7694 5063 Electric motor repair;
electrical supplies

(G-6675)
HUTCHINSON & GUNTER INC
715 Grove St (15601-2897)
PHONE....................................724 837-3200
John Edward Hutchinson, President
Helen Adiscy, Corp Secy
Keith Hutchinson, Vice Pres
EMP: 15 EST: 1949
SALES: 1MM Privately Held
SIC: 3444 Sheet metalwork

(G-6676)
ICE QUBE INC
Also Called: Ice Qube Cooling Systems
141 Wilson Ave (15601-2522)
PHONE....................................724 837-7600
Dwayne Altman, President
John A De Marchis, Exec VP
▲ EMP: 68
SQ FT: 80,000
SALES (est): 19MM Privately Held
WEB: www.iceqube.com
SIC: 3469 3443 Electronic enclosures,
stamped or pressed metal; cooling tow-
ers, metal plate

(G-6677)
INSTANT PRINT
454 S Main St (15601-3015)
PHONE....................................724 261-5153
Samuel Scott, Owner
Linda Markle, Manager
EMP: 3
SALES: 150K Privately Held
SIC: 2759 Commercial printing

(G-6678)
INTERCON PRINTER &
CONSULTANTS
412 Willow Crossing Rd (15601-9122)
PHONE....................................724 837-5428
Donald Bloom Jr, President
EMP: 3
SALES: 500K Privately Held
SIC: 2752 Commercial printing, offset

(G-6679)
IRWIN AUTOMATION INC
715 Cleveland St (15601-2799)
PHONE....................................724 834-7160
David J Ross, President
S Wayne Whitehead, Vice Pres
Donavon Burns, Foreman/Supr
Heather I Taylor, Treasurer
John Rieseck, Treasurer
EMP: 35
SQ FT: 33,000
SALES (est): 11MM Privately Held
WEB: www.irwinautomation.com
SIC: 3599 3398 Machine shop, jobbing &
repair; metal heat treating

(G-6680)
JIOIOS ITALIAN CORNER INC
132 Mount Odin Dr (15601-9327)
PHONE....................................724 837-4576
Joseph Jioio, President
Anthony Jioio, Vice Pres
Shirley Jioio, Treasurer
Annette Moore, Treasurer
EMP: 3
SALES: 200K Privately Held
SIC: 2099 Sauces: gravy, dressing & dip
mixes

(G-6681)
JONES STONE & MARBLE INC
1580 Woodward Drive Ext (15601-6418)
PHONE....................................724 838-7625
Debra L Stevenson, President
George Stevenson Jr, Admin Sec
EMP: 6
SALES (est): 890.9K Privately Held
WEB: www.jonesstonecompany.com
SIC: 3281 5999 5032 Granite, cut &
shaped; marble, building: cut & shaped;
monuments & tombstones; marble build-
ing stone

(G-6682)
KITCHEN GALLERY INC
626 Alwine Curry Rd (15601-7377)
PHONE....................................724 838-0911
Larry Flock Jr, *President*
Jo Ann Flock, *Treasurer*
EMP: 5
SQ FT: 4,000
SALES (est): 701.5K **Privately Held**
SIC: 2434 Wood kitchen cabinets

(G-6683)
LAUREL PARCEL SERVICES INC
Also Called: UPS Stores, The
645 E Pittsburgh St (15601-2781)
PHONE....................................724 850-6245
Jeffrey J Gaudino, *President*
Michelle A Gaudino, *Corp Secy*
EMP: 5
SQ FT: 1,200
SALES (est): 397.8K **Privately Held**
SIC: 7389 3086 Mailbox rental & related
service; packaging & shipping materials,
foamed plastic

(G-6684)
LEESE & CO INC (PA)
768 Old State Route 66 (15601-8245)
PHONE....................................724 834-5810
Christian Klanica, *President*
Susan Fisher, *Admin Sec*
EMP: 38
SQ FT: 2,500
SALES (est): 9MM **Privately Held**
WEB: www.leeseco.com
SIC: 3599 Machine shop, jobbing & repair

(G-6685)
LIONSHARE MEDIA SERVICES
530 Pellis Rd Ste 8000a (15601-7924)
P.O. Box 222987, Carmel CA (93922-2987)
PHONE....................................724 837-9700
Randy Young, *President*
EMP: 4
SALES (est): 262.8K **Privately Held**
SIC: 7311 2741 Advertising agencies; mis-
cellaneous publishing

(G-6686)
M & T INDUSTRIES LLC
1265 Brinkerton Rd (15601-5852)
PHONE....................................724 216-5256
Jeffrey Yonkey, *Principal*
EMP: 3
SALES (est): 155.7K **Privately Held**
SIC: 3999 Manufacturing industries

(G-6687)
MAT PENN COMPANY INC
612 S Urania Ave (15601-3315)
P.O. Box 506 (15601-0506)
PHONE....................................724 837-7060
John Eidemiller III, *President*
Jack Eidemiller, *Vice Pres*
Theresa Eidemiller, *Treasurer*
Deborah Eidemiller, *Admin Sec*
EMP: 4
SQ FT: 3,500
SALES: 500K **Privately Held**
SIC: 3069 Rubber floor coverings, mats &
wallcoverings

(G-6688)
METAL FINISHING INDUSTRIES
1166 Garden St (15601-6417)
P.O. Box 515 (15601-0515)
PHONE....................................724 836-1003
Sharon Liberto, *President*
Leo Liberto Jr, *Vice Pres*
EMP: 5
SQ FT: 3,000
SALES (est): 586.9K **Privately Held**
SIC: 3471 Finishing, metals or formed
products

(G-6689)
MOORE & MORFORD INC (PA)
1030 Broad St (15601-5302)
P.O. Box 759 (15601-0759)
PHONE....................................724 834-1100
James P Morford, *President*
R W Morford, *Chairman*
Richard P Morford, *Vice Pres*
EMP: 45 **EST:** 1965
SQ FT: 14,000

SALES (est): 6.9MM **Privately Held**
WEB: www.mmsteelfab.com
SIC: 3441 Building components, structural
steel

(G-6690)
MOTOROLA SOLUTIONS INC
515 New Alexandria Rd (15601-1444)
PHONE....................................724 837-3030
Judy Bob, *Manager*
EMP: 142
SALES (corp-wide): 7.3B **Publicly Held**
WEB: www.motorola.com
SIC: 3663 Radio broadcasting & communi-
cations equipment
PA: Motorola Solutions, Inc.
500 W Monroe St Ste 4400
Chicago IL 60661
847 576-5000

(G-6691)
MULTI-METALS CO INC (PA)
Also Called: Jeannette Steel & Supply Div
1941 State Route 66 (15601-9297)
P.O. Box 1185 (15601-5185)
PHONE....................................724 836-2720
Timothy Shepherd, *President*
Richard D Smith, *Treasurer*
Richard K Florek, *Admin Sec*
EMP: 56
SQ FT: 6,500
SALES (est): 10.8MM **Privately Held**
SIC: 3446 Stairs, staircases, stair treads:
prefabricated metal; railings, prefabri-
cated metal

(G-6692)
NICEWONGER AWNING CO
512 Euclid Ave (15601-3039)
PHONE....................................724 837-5920
Norman Waugner, *President*
Kasey Waugman, *Vice Pres*
EMP: 4 **EST:** 1949
SQ FT: 2,520
SALES (est): 500K **Privately Held**
SIC: 7699 7641 2394 General household
repair services; awning repair shop; up-
holstery work; awnings, fabric: made from
purchased materials

(G-6693)
NICHOLS ELECTRONICS INC
Also Called: Rfhero
187 Kennan Dr (15601-8460)
PHONE....................................724 668-2526
Edward Nichols, *President*
Natalie R Nichols, *Corp Secy*
EMP: 6 **EST:** 2000
SQ FT: 1,000
SALES (est): 1.3MM **Privately Held**
WEB: www.rfhero.com
SIC: 3679 Electronic circuits

(G-6694)
O AND P SVETZ INC (PA)
600 S Main St (15601-4049)
PHONE....................................724 834-1448
Michelle Svetz, *President*
EMP: 16
SQ FT: 3,500 **Privately Held**
SIC: 3842 Prosthetic appliances; limbs, ar-
tificial

(G-6695)
ORR SCREW MACHINE PRODUCTS
Also Called: Orrco
190 Orr Dr (15601-8456)
PHONE....................................724 668-2256
Thomas W Orr, *President*
Nancy Orr, *Corp Secy*
Randy Gounder, *COO*
Keith R Orr, *Vice Pres*
EMP: 23 **EST:** 1946
SQ FT: 1,846
SALES (est): 5.4MM **Privately Held**
WEB: www.orrcoind.com
SIC: 3561 3451 3541 3599 Pumps &
pumping equipment; screw machine prod-
ucts; numerically controlled metal cutting
machine tools; machine & other job shop
work

(G-6696)
OVERLY DOOR COMPANY (PA)
574 W Otterman St (15601-2148)
P.O. Box 70 (15601-0070)
PHONE....................................724 834-7300
Timothy T Reese, *Ch of Bd*
Tyler Reese, *VP Opers*
Mike McConville, *Engineer*
Jonathan Reese, *VP Sls/Mktg*
Elmer H Knopf, *CFO*
EMP: 75
SQ FT: 90,000
SALES (est): 25.3MM **Privately Held**
WEB: www.overly.com
SIC: 3442 Metal doors

(G-6697)
OVERLY MANUFACTURING COMPANY
1551 Woodward Drive Ext (15601-6418)
P.O. Box 70 (15601-0070)
PHONE....................................724 834-7300
Timothy Reese, *Ch of Bd*
K Lars Held, *Corp Secy*
Charles R Baugh, *Vice Pres*
Richard Watkins, *Sales Staff*
Rion Ridi, *Maintence Staff*
EMP: 25
SQ FT: 100,000
SALES (est): 5.4MM **Privately Held**
SIC: 3446 Architectural metalwork

(G-6698)
P & R ENGINE REBUILDERS
952 W Pittsburgh St (15601-1229)
PHONE....................................724 837-7590
Neil Bainbridge, *Owner*
EMP: 4
SQ FT: 4,200
SALES (est): 310K **Privately Held**
SIC: 3599 7539 Machine shop, jobbing &
repair; machine shop, automotive

(G-6699)
PELLHEAT INC
928 Country Club Dr (15601-1202)
PHONE....................................724 850-8169
Peter J Skrgic, *President*
Nabine Skrgic, *Admin Sec*
EMP: 5
SQ FT: 15,000
SALES: 500K **Privately Held**
SIC: 2421 Fuelwood, from mill waste

(G-6700)
PIAD PRECISION CASTING CORP
Also Called: Piad Cast Precision
112 Industrial Park Rd (15601-6990)
PHONE....................................724 838-5500
Holger Schweisthal, *CEO*
Ed Kerestes, *Senior Buyer*
Kathy Neill, *Sales Associate*
Beth A Chew, *Admin Sec*
Anthony Poploskie, *Admin Sec*
▲ **EMP:** 110
SQ FT: 47,000
SALES (est): 27.9MM
SALES (corp-wide): 24.7MM **Privately
Held**
WEB: www.piad.net
SIC: 3369 3366 Castings, except die-cast-
ings, precision; copper foundries
PA: Piel & Adey Gmbh & Co. Kg
Lehner Str. 19-23
Solingen 42655
212 206-310

(G-6701)
PIONEER SUPPLY COMPANY INC
660 E Pittsburgh St Ste 1 (15601-2677)
PHONE....................................856 314-8299
Jim Mazza, *Branch Mgr*
EMP: 7
SALES (corp-wide): 25MM **Privately
Held**
SIC: 3993 Signs & advertising specialties
PA: Pioneer Supply Company, Inc.
660 E Pittsburgh St Ste 1
Greensburg PA 15601
412 471-5600

(G-6702)
PLUM CORPORATION
1534 Woodward Drive Ext (15601-6418)
P.O. Box 8373, Pittsburgh (15218-0373)
PHONE....................................724 836-7261
David Landis, *President*
EMP: 13
SALES (est): 1MM **Privately Held**
SIC: 3444 Sheet metal specialties, not
stamped

(G-6703)
POLYMER ENTERPRISES INC (PA)
4731 State Route 30 # 401 (15601-7260)
PHONE....................................724 838-2340
Donald D Mateer III, *CEO*
William E Moreau, *Treasurer*
L Leland Fulton, *Admin Sec*
◆ **EMP:** 5 **EST:** 1915
SQ FT: 3,000
SALES (est): 101.1MM **Privately Held**
WEB: www.polymerenterprises.net
SIC: 3069 3011 Rolls, solid or covered
rubber; tires & inner tubes; airplane tires,
pneumatic; industrial tires, pneumatic;
truck or bus tires, pneumatic

(G-6704)
PRECISION METAL CRAFTERS LTD
220 Huff Ave Ste 700 (15601-5376)
PHONE....................................724 837-2511
Doug Phillips, *President*
Doug Craig, *Human Res Dir*
EMP: 45
SQ FT: 10,000
SALES (est): 7.1MM **Privately Held**
SIC: 7692 3479 3599 1799 Welding re-
pair; painting, coating & hot dipping; ma-
chine shop, jobbing & repair; welding on
site

(G-6705)
PROTOS FOODS INC (PA)
449 Glenmeade Rd (15601-1170)
PHONE....................................724 836-1802
W Logan Dickerson, *President*
Ann W Dickerson, *Treasurer*
EMP: 4
SALES: 1MM **Privately Held**
WEB: www.protos-inc.com
SIC: 2013 Snack sticks, including jerky:
from purchased meat

(G-6706)
PROWELD
1100 Swede Hill Rd (15601-4973)
PHONE....................................724 836-0207
Bruce Marsteller Jr, *President*
EMP: 4
SQ FT: 8,000
SALES (est): 460.6K **Privately Held**
SIC: 3443 Buoys, metal

(G-6707)
PTC INC
41 W Otterman St Ste 310 (15601-2322)
PHONE....................................724 219-2600
EMP: 19
SALES (corp-wide): 1.2B **Publicly Held**
SIC: 7372 Application computer software
PA: Ptc Inc.
121 Seaport Blvd
Boston MA 02210
781 370-5000

(G-6708)
QUESTA PETROLEUM CO
255 Lancewood Pl (15601-5907)
P.O. Box 12863, Pittsburgh (15241-0863)
PHONE....................................724 832-7297
Mike Giglotti, *Owner*
Donald Funnell, *Administration*
EMP: 8
SALES (est): 870K **Privately Held**
SIC: 1311 Natural gas production

(G-6709)
R & K NEON INC
731 Santone Dr (15601-4673)
PHONE....................................724 834-8570
Carol Wolfe, *President*
EMP: 3 **EST:** 1962

▲ = Import ▼=Export
◆ =Import/Export

SALES (est): 455.2K **Privately Held**
SIC: 3993 Manufactures Neon Signs

(G-6710)
RASTER MANUFACTURING LLC
609 Richfield Ct (15601-1028)
PHONE.................................724 837-7354
Douglas Long, *Principal*
EMP: 3
SALES (est): 176.6K **Privately Held**
SIC: 3999 Manufacturing industries

(G-6711)
RELYENCE CORPORATION
145 Weavers Rd (15601-6309)
PHONE.................................724 433-1909
Kevin Van Fleet, *CEO*
EMP: 10 EST: 2014
SQ FT: 6,000
SALES (est): 564.2K **Privately Held**
SIC: 7372 Application computer software;
business oriented computer software

(G-6712)
ROCHESTER COCA COLA BOTTLING
Also Called: Coca-Cola
Rr 12 Box 289 (15601)
PHONE.................................724 834-2700
Scott Lucas, *Manager*
EMP: 50
SALES (corp-wide): 35.4B **Publicly Held**
SIC: 2086 Soft drinks: packaged in cans,
bottles, etc.
HQ: Rochester Coca Cola Bottling Corp
300 Oak St
Pittston PA 18640
570 655-2874

(G-6713)
RUBBER TECHNOLOGY INC (HQ)
Berkshire Ctr Ste 401 (15601)
PHONE.................................724 838-2340
A Elaine Anderson, *President*
William Moreau, *Treasurer*
James O Ireland, *Director*
Donald D Mateer III, *Director*
Thomas Schultz, *Director*
▲ EMP: 2
SQ FT: 26,000
SALES: 1.7MM
SALES (corp-wide): 101.1MM **Privately Held**
SIC: 3069 Roll coverings, rubber
PA: Polymer Enterprises, Inc.
4731 State Route 30 # 401
Greensburg PA 15601
724 838-2340

(G-6714)
SIGNS BY TOMORROW
422 E Pittsburgh St (15601-2644)
PHONE.................................724 838-9060
Keith Davis, *Owner*
EMP: 3
SALES (est): 100K **Privately Held**
SIC: 3993 Signs & advertising specialties

(G-6715)
SOUTH GREENSBURG PRINTING CO
409 Coulter Ave Ste A (15601-5436)
PHONE.................................724 834-0295
Glenn Krause, *President*
Frances Krause, *Corp Secy*
EMP: 16
SQ FT: 14,364
SALES (est): 4MM **Privately Held**
SIC: 2752 Commercial printing, offset

(G-6716)
SRM-AVANT INC
Also Called: Security Resource Management
4727 State Route 30 # 204 (15601-7270)
PHONE.................................724 537-0300
Romi Green, *Principal*
EMP: 7
SALES (est): 540K **Privately Held**
SIC: 3953 8734 Marking devices; testing
laboratories

(G-6717)
STANKO PRODUCTS INC
Also Called: Dens-A-Can International
278 Donohoe Rd (15601-6987)
PHONE.................................724 834-8080
Gregory A Stanko, *Vice Pres*
Tammy Stanko, *Purchasing*
Frances M Stanko, *Treasurer*
Jeffrey T Stanko, *Treasurer*
Kelley Stanko, *Manager*
EMP: 15
SQ FT: 17,000
SALES: 950K **Privately Held**
WEB: www.stankoproducts.com
SIC: 3599 3559 3544 3537 Machine
shop, jobbing & repair; recycling machin-
ery; special dies & tools; industrial trucks
& tractors

(G-6718)
TIN LIZZY INC
909 Rolling Meadows Dr D (15601-9052)
PHONE.................................724 836-0281
EMP: 5
SALES (est): 608.7K **Privately Held**
SIC: 3356 Tin

(G-6719)
TRIB TOTAL MEDIA INC
Vally Independent
622 Cabin Hill Dr (15601-1657)
PHONE.................................724 684-5200
Fax: 724 850-2126
EMP: 100
SALES (corp-wide): 202.6MM **Privately Held**
SIC: 2711 Newspapers-Publishing/Printing
PA: Trib Total Media, Inc.
503 Martin Street D L C
Pittsburgh PA 15601
412 321-6460

(G-6720)
TRIB TOTAL MEDIA LLC (PA)
Also Called: Pennysaver
622 Cabin Hill Dr (15601-1657)
PHONE.................................412 321-6460
Jennifer L Bertetto, *President*
Ralph Martin, *President*
Edward Harrell, *Vice Pres*
Fred Aul, *Opers Staff*
Gary Mazzotta, *Production*
EMP: 300 EST: 2003
SALES (est): 157.2MM **Privately Held**
SIC: 2711 Newspapers: publishing only,
not printed on site

(G-6721)
TRIB TOTAL MEDIA LLC
622 Cabin Hill Dr (15601-1657)
PHONE.................................724 834-1151
EMP: 150
SALES (est): 7.5MM **Privately Held**
SIC: 2711 Newspapers-Publishing/Printing

(G-6722)
TUNA ENTERPRISES
Also Called: Garrow's Draft Service
1811 S Broad Street Ext (15601-5506)
P.O. Box 182 (15601-0182)
PHONE.................................724 205-6535
Tony Garrow, *President*
EMP: 6
SALES (est): 774.6K **Privately Held**
SIC: 3585 Beer dispensing equipment

(G-6723)
ULTRAOPTICS INC
507 New Haven Dr (15601-6103)
PHONE.................................724 838-7155
Glenn A Tarris, *President*
Lynn Ann Tarris, *Vice Pres*
EMP: 4 EST: 1982
SQ FT: 4,500
SALES (est): 320K **Privately Held**
WEB: www.ultraoptics.com
SIC: 3841 5048 Cannulae; frames, oph-
thalmic

(G-6724)
UNION ORTHOTICS PROSTHETICS CO
Also Called: Union Orthotics Prosthetics Co
3 Gibralter Way (15601-5613)
PHONE.................................724 836-6656

Jon P Leimkuehler, *President*
EMP: 7
SALES (corp-wide): 8MM **Privately Held**
WEB: www.unionoandp.com
SIC: 3842 5999 Limbs, artificial; artificial
limbs
PA: Union Orthotics & Prosthetics Co.
3424 Liberty Ave
Pittsburgh PA
412 622-2020

(G-6725)
UNITED STATES HARDMETAL
857 S Main St (15601-4166)
PHONE.................................724 834-8381
Raymond Rosborough, *Owner*
EMP: 2
SALES: 1MM **Privately Held**
SIC: 2297 Nonwoven fabrics

(G-6726)
UNITY FABRICATION TECH INC
1235 Marguerite Lake Rd (15601-8532)
PHONE.................................724 423-7500
Timothy A Lamantia, *President*
Donald Pfeifer, *Vice Pres*
Harry Kenney, *Treasurer*
Robert G Miner, *Admin Sec*
EMP: 15 EST: 2008
SALES (est): 1.1MM **Privately Held**
SIC: 7692 Welding repair

(G-6727)
VINCENT LOHUVEY
123 Laskoski Rd (15601-6220)
PHONE.................................724 527-2994
Vincent Lohuvey, *Owner*
EMP: 4
SALES (est): 345.8K **Privately Held**
SIC: 3273 Ready-mixed concrete

(G-6728)
WAUGAMAN AWNINGS
115 Laird St (15601-3205)
PHONE.................................724 837-1239
Clint Waugaman, *President*
Kirk Waugaman, *Treasurer*
Charles Waugaman Jr, *Admin Sec*
EMP: 6 EST: 1957
SQ FT: 2,400
SALES: 500K **Privately Held**
SIC: 2394 7219 Canvas covers & drop
cloths; reweaving textiles (mending serv-
ice)

(G-6729)
WENDELL H STONE COMPANY INC
Also Called: Stone & Co
1718 Roseytown Rd (15601-7000)
P.O. Box 613 (15601-0613)
PHONE.................................724 836-1400
Joseph Santone, *Branch Mgr*
EMP: 40
SALES (corp-wide): 35MM **Privately Held**
WEB: www.stoneco.com
SIC: 3273 5211 3272 Ready-mixed con-
crete; lumber & other building materials;
concrete products
PA: Wendell H. Stone Company, Inc.
606 Mccormick Ave
Connellsville PA 15425
724 836-1400

(G-6730)
WESTINGHOUSE A BRAKE TECH CORP
Also Called: Wabtec Rubber Products
269 Donohoe Rd (15601-6987)
P.O. Box 212 (15601-0212)
PHONE.................................724 838-1317
Darren Beatty, *Principal*
Sean Harr, *Engineer*
EMP: 50
SQ FT: 100,000
SALES (corp-wide): 4.3B **Publicly Held**
WEB: www.wabtecglobalservices.com
SIC: 3743 Railroad equipment
PA: Westinghouse Air Brake Technologies
Corporation
1001 Airbrake Ave
Wilmerding PA 15148
412 825-1000

(G-6731)
WESTMORELAND CONTRACT FUR
1572 Woodward Drive Ext (15601-6418)
PHONE.................................724 838-7748
Durbin John Jr, *Owner*
EMP: 3
SALES (est): 235K **Privately Held**
SIC: 3999 Furs

Greentown
Pike County

(G-6732)
24-7 INNOVATIONS LLC
176 Old Schoolhouse Rd (18426-5007)
PHONE.................................570 676-8888
Chris Maros,
EMP: 3
SQ FT: 5,500
SALES (est): 361.5K **Privately Held**
WEB: www.247innovations.com
SIC: 3732 Boats, fiberglass: building & re-
pairing

(G-6733)
COREY ASSOCIATES INC
Also Called: Cai
120 Corey Way (18426-4135)
PHONE.................................570 676-4800
Karen Kosydar, *President*
Martha Wood, *Vice Pres*
EMP: 20
SQ FT: 6,000
SALES (est): 3.7MM **Privately Held**
WEB: www.coreyassoc.com
SIC: 3679 3699 3643 Power supplies, all
types: static; electrical equipment & sup-
plies; current-carrying wiring devices

(G-6734)
MR LUCK INC
1609 Route 507 (18426-4501)
P.O. Box 246 (18426-0246)
PHONE.................................570 766-8734
Michael Luck, *Principal*
EMP: 4 EST: 2008
SALES (est): 422.5K **Privately Held**
SIC: 2452 Log cabins, prefabricated, wood

(G-6735)
URSA MJOR DRCTNAL CRSSINGS LLC
102 Bartleson Deer Trl (18426-8916)
P.O. Box 1079 (18426-1079)
PHONE.................................866 410-9719
Robert Pollara,
EMP: 11
SALES: 2.5MM **Privately Held**
SIC: 1389 1623 Cementing oil & gas well
casings; sewer line construction

Greenville
Mercer County

(G-6736)
ADVANCED BULK & CONVEYING INC (PA)
59 W Main St (16125-2449)
P.O. Box 31 (16125-0031)
PHONE.................................724 588-9327
Michael Yurisic, *President*
Kathy Henry, *Bookkeeper*
Bruce Dixon, *CIO*
EMP: 12
SQ FT: 4,720
SALES (est): 5.1MM **Privately Held**
WEB: www.advancedbulk.com
SIC: 3535 Conveyors & conveying equip-
ment

(G-6737)
ADVANCED BULK & CONVEYING INC
15 S Water St (16125-2210)
P.O. Box 31 (16125-0031)
PHONE.................................724 588-9327
Bruce Dixon, *Branch Mgr*
EMP: 6

SALES (corp-wide): 5.1MM **Privately Held**
WEB: www.advancedbulk.com
SIC: 3535 Conveyors & conveying equipment
PA: Advanced Bulk & Conveying Inc
59 W Main St
Greenville PA 16125
724 588-9327

(G-6738)
ARTHUR K MILLER
Also Called: U-Haul
182 Sharon Rd (16125-8105)
PHONE...................................724 588-1118
Arthur K Miller, *Owner*
EMP: 3
SQ FT: 3,000
SALES (est): 140K **Privately Held**
SIC: 3751 7699 5571 7519 Motorcycles, bicycles & parts; motorcycle repair service; motorcycle dealers; trailer rental; stores & yards equipment rental; truck rental & leasing, no drivers

(G-6739)
CLIFTON TUBE CUTTING INC
93 Werner Rd (16125-9434)
P.O. Box 8545, Erie (16505-0545)
PHONE...................................724 588-3241
Joseph Podufal, *President*
Elizabeth Podufal, *Admin Sec*
EMP: 25
SALES (est): 4.9MM **Privately Held**
WEB: www.cliftonautomatic.com
SIC: 3451 3599 Screw machine products; machine shop, jobbing & repair

(G-6740)
CUSTOM CORNER SPORTSWEAR
275 Main St (16125-2022)
PHONE...................................724 588-1667
Joel Mc Dowell, *Owner*
EMP: 5 EST: 1980
SQ FT: 7,000
SALES (est): 701.3K **Privately Held**
WEB: www. 1customcorner.com
SIC: 2396 2395 3499 Screen printing on fabric articles; embroidery & art needlework; novelties & giftware, including trophies

(G-6741)
GRANT BELCHER
Also Called: Seven Sons Roofing
120 Clinton St (16125-2001)
PHONE...................................814 853-9640
Grant Belcher, *Owner*
Karen Kresge, *Admin Sec*
EMP: 11
SALES (est): 626.1K **Privately Held**
SIC: 3069 1799 Roofing, membrane rubber; waterproofing

(G-6742)
GREENVILLE RECORD ARGUS INC
10 Penn Ave (16125-2483)
P.O. Box 711 (16125-0711)
PHONE...................................724 588-5000
Robert Bracey, *President*
Tom Chapin, *Editor*
Holly Patterson, *Editor*
Caleb Stright, *Editor*
Lyn Merz, *Business Mgr*
EMP: 33
SQ FT: 15,109
SALES (est): 1.9MM **Privately Held**
SIC: 2711 Newspapers: publishing only, not printed on site

(G-6743)
GREENVILLE WOOD PRODUCTS INC
425 Crestview Dr (16125)
P.O. Box 735 (16125-0735)
PHONE...................................724 646-1193
Levern Swartz, *President*
Matthew Swartz, *Vice Pres*
EMP: 4
SQ FT: 10,000
SALES: 500K **Privately Held**
SIC: 2431 Millwork

(G-6744)
GUARDIAN FILTRATION PDTS LLC
451 2nd St (16125-8260)
PHONE...................................724 646-0450
Matthew McConnell,
EMP: 3
SALES (est): 50K **Privately Held**
SIC: 3589 Swimming pool filter & water conditioning systems

(G-6745)
HIATT THOMPSON CORPORATION
159 Conneaut Lake Rd (16125-9466)
PHONE...................................708 496-8585
▲ EMP: 6
SQ FT: 6,500
SALES: 5MM **Privately Held**
SIC: 3429 8742 Mfg And Whol Handcuffs Restraint Equip/ Law Enforcement Consultant

(G-6746)
HODGE FOUNDRY INC
42 Leech Rd (16125-9724)
PHONE...................................724 588-4100
Bruce Smith, *CEO*
Joseph Simco, *President*
Michael Forsha, *Vice Pres*
Mike McCliman, *Project Mgr*
Mike Forsha, *Engineer*
▲ EMP: 130
SALES (est): 31.6MM
SALES (corp-wide): 85.3MM **Privately Held**
WEB: www.hodgefoundry.com
SIC: 3321 Gray iron castings
PA: Elyria Foundry Company Llc
120 Filbert St
Elyria OH 44035
440 322-4657

(G-6747)
HONEST INDUSTRIES LLC
Also Called: Honest Amish
14 Louisa Ave (16125-2015)
PHONE...................................724 588-1540
Jason Kushner, *Mng Member*
EMP: 27
SQ FT: 5,600
SALES: 9.5MM **Privately Held**
SIC: 2844 Toilet preparations

(G-6748)
ILSCO EXTRUSIONS INC
93 Werner Rd Bldg A (16125-9434)
PHONE...................................724 589-5888
Andrew Quinn, *President*
John Thigpen, *General Mgr*
Kevin Jenkins, *Vice Pres*
James Valentine, *Treasurer*
EMP: 5
SALES (est): 1.3MM **Privately Held**
SIC: 3643 3354 Connectors & terminals for electrical devices; electric connectors; aluminum extruded products

(G-6749)
INTEGRATED FABRICATION MCH INC
639 Keystone Rd (16125-9747)
P.O. Box 307, Sharpsville (16150-0307)
PHONE...................................724 962-3526
Brent Ward, *President*
Gina Brandan, *Purchasing*
Doug Hilton, *Engineer*
Darla Shannon, *Senior Engr*
Diane Ward, *CFO*
EMP: 45
SQ FT: 74,000
SALES (est): 10.2MM **Privately Held**
WEB: www.integratedfab.com
SIC: 3443 Metal parts

(G-6750)
JAMES DERR
Also Called: Derr Industries
201 Oniontown Rd (16125-8431)
PHONE...................................724 475-2094
James Derr, *Owner*
EMP: 4
SQ FT: 4,800
SALES (est): 483K **Privately Held**
SIC: 3499 Metal household articles

(G-6751)
JL HARTMAN STAINLESS LLC
903 Brentwood Dr (16125-8802)
PHONE...................................724 646-1150
Rita Reeher, *Mng Member*
EMP: 3
SALES (est): 533.1K **Privately Held**
SIC: 3498 Tube fabricating (contract bending & shaping)

(G-6752)
JOHNSONS FROG & RAIL WLDG INC
111 Shearer Rd (16125-8453)
PHONE...................................724 475-2305
Norman Johnson, *President*
Sharon Johnson, *Admin Sec*
EMP: 6
SALES: 500K **Privately Held**
SIC: 7692 7389 Welding repair;

(G-6753)
LANDFRIED PAVING INC
172 Crestview Dr (16125)
P.O. Box 615 (16125-0615)
PHONE...................................724 646-2505
Greg Landfried, *President*
Gary Landfried, *Vice Pres*
Joni Biery-Prugh, *Info Tech Mgr*
EMP: 11 EST: 1958
SQ FT: 3,000
SALES (est): 2.1MM **Privately Held**
SIC: 1611 2951 Highway & street paving contractor; road materials, bituminous (not from refineries)

(G-6754)
MEMRS INC
Also Called: Musgraves Elc Mtr Repr Svc
203 S Summit Rd (16125-9292)
PHONE...................................724 589-5567
Denis R Musgrave, *President*
EMP: 3
SALES (est): 100K **Privately Held**
SIC: 3585 Heat pumps, electric

(G-6755)
METAL EXCHANGE CORPORATION
93 Werner Rd (16125-9434)
PHONE...................................724 373-8471
EMP: 8
SALES (corp-wide): 280.5MM **Privately Held**
SIC: 2819 Aluminum oxide
PA: Metal Exchange Corporation
111 West Port Plz Ste 350
Saint Louis MO 63146
314 434-3500

(G-6756)
METAL LITHO AND LAMINATING LLC
242 Reynolds Indus Pk Dr (16125-8216)
PHONE...................................724 646-1222
John R Frangakis,
EMP: 28
SALES (est): 727K
SALES (corp-wide): 38.8MM **Privately Held**
SIC: 3479 Metal coating & allied service
PA: Reynolds Services, Inc.
860 Brentwood Dr
Greenville PA 16125
724 646-2600

(G-6757)
METSO MINERALS INDUSTRIES INC
42 Leech Rd (16125-9724)
P.O. Box 550 (16125-0550)
PHONE...................................210 491-9521
W Scott Hodge, *Manager*
EMP: 154
SQ FT: 200,000
SALES (corp-wide): 3.1B **Privately Held**
WEB: www.metsominerals.com
SIC: 3321 3322 Gray & ductile iron foundries; malleable iron foundries
HQ: Metso Minerals Industries, Inc.
20965 Crossroads Cir
Waukesha WI 53186
262 717-2500

(G-6758)
NEW WERNER HOLDING CO INC (HQ)
93 Werner Rd (16125-9434)
PHONE...................................724 588-2000
William T Allen, *President*
Dave Plotner, *President*
Edward Gericke, *Vice Pres*
Larry Friend, *CFO*
Geoffrey Hartenstein, *Admin Sec*
EMP: 4
SALES (est): 670.2MM **Privately Held**
SIC: 3499 3355 3089 3446 Ladders, portable: metal; extrusion ingot, aluminum: made in rolling mills; synthetic resin finished products; scaffolds, mobile or stationary: metal; stepladders, wood; nonresidential building operators

(G-6759)
NITTANY COATINGS INC
309 3rd St (16125-8204)
P.O. Box 301 (16125-0301)
PHONE...................................724 588-1898
Jean Bonasera, *President*
Dewey Jose, *Manager*
EMP: 5
SQ FT: 5,000
SALES: 300K **Privately Held**
SIC: 3479 Coating of metals with plastic or resins

(G-6760)
NORTHEAST INDUSTRIAL MFG INC
640 Keystone Rd (16125-9748)
PHONE...................................724 588-7711
Howardthomas Cusick, *President*
Howard Thomas Cusick, *President*
Kimberly Cusick, *Treasurer*
Del Cochran, *Sales Staff*
Angela Bolois, *Manager*
EMP: 27
SALES (est): 7.1MM **Privately Held**
WEB: www.northeastind.com
SIC: 3441 3412 3469 Fabricated structural metal; metal barrels, drums & pails; metal stampings

(G-6761)
OAKES & MCCLELLAND CO
Also Called: Custom Truss
1505 Arlington Dr (16125-8820)
PHONE...................................724 588-6400
Clyde W McClelland, *President*
Shirley Sine, *Admin Sec*
EMP: 17 EST: 1946
SQ FT: 40,000
SALES (est): 4.2MM **Privately Held**
SIC: 5211 2439 2431 2426 Home centers; structural wood members; millwork; hardwood dimension & flooring mills; sawmills & planing mills, general

(G-6762)
OLD LADDER CO (PA)
Also Called: Werner Extruded Products
93 Werner Rd (16125-9434)
PHONE...................................888 523-3371
James J Loughlin Jr, *CEO*
Donald M Werner, *Ch of Bd*
Steven P Richman, *President*
Edward Gericke, *President*
Edward W Gericke, *Senior VP*
▼ EMP: 900
SQ FT: 465,000
SALES (est): 186.8MM **Privately Held**
SIC: 3446 3089 3334 3444 Scaffolds, mobile or stationary: metal; synthetic resin finished products; primary aluminum; sheet metalwork; ladders, portable: metal

(G-6763)
PA ARTIFICIAL LIMB & BRACE CO
111 N Main St Ste 101 (16125-1705)
PHONE...................................724 588-6860
William Cummings, *Owner*
EMP: 4
SALES (est): 301K **Privately Held**
SIC: 3842 Braces, orthopedic

▲ = Import ▼=Export
◆ =Import/Export

GEOGRAPHIC

(G-6764)
PENNEX ALUMINUM COMPANY LLC
93 Werner Rd Bldg B (16125-9434)
PHONE..............................724 373-8471
Jim Barcus, *Branch Mgr*
EMP: 30
SALES (corp-wide): 280.5MM **Privately Held**
SIC: 3365 Aluminum & aluminum-based alloy castings
HQ: Pennex Aluminum Company Llc
50 Community St
Wellsville PA 17365

(G-6765)
PENNTECQ INC
106 Kuder Dr (16125-8324)
PHONE..............................724 646-4250
▲ EMP: 225
SQ FT: 125,000
SALES: 35MM **Privately Held**
WEB: www.penntecq.com
SIC: 3714 Motor Vehicle Parts And Accessories

(G-6766)
PRECISION PATTERN & WDWKG
303 Methodist Rd (16125)
P.O. Box 91 (16125-0091)
PHONE..............................724 588-2224
Robert H Adams Jr, *President*
Raymond Holiga, *Partner*
EMP: 6
SQ FT: 7,500
SALES: 400K **Privately Held**
SIC: 3543 Industrial patterns

(G-6767)
PREMIER PRINTING SERVICES INC
275 Main St (16125-2022)
PHONE..............................724 588-5577
Joel McDowell, *Principal*
EMP: 6
SALES (est): 643.6K **Privately Held**
SIC: 2759 Commercial printing

(G-6768)
QUALITY STEEL FABRICATORS
106 Mortensen Rd (16125-8318)
P.O. Box 226 (16125-0226)
PHONE..............................724 646-0500
Ken Montesano, *President*
EMP: 17
SQ FT: 30,000
SALES (est): 3.3MM **Privately Held**
SIC: 3312 Structural shapes & pilings, steel

(G-6769)
REYNOLDS BUILDING SYSTEMS INC
Also Called: Sentry Buildings
205 Arlington Dr (16125-8212)
PHONE..............................724 646-0771
William Rinella, *President*
Linda L Rinella, *Corp Secy*
EMP: 4
SQ FT: 28,000
SALES (est): 675K **Privately Held**
WEB: www.barnkits.com
SIC: 2452 Farm buildings, prefabricated or portable: wood; modular homes, prefabricated, wood

(G-6770)
REYNOLDS SERVICES INC (PA)
Also Called: RSI
860 Brentwood Dr (16125-8865)
PHONE..............................724 646-2600
F John Frangakis, *President*
John R Frangakis, *Corp Secy*
Keith Christy, *Controller*
◆ EMP: 92
SQ FT: 44,000
SALES (est): 38.8MM **Privately Held**
SIC: 3443 Fabricated plate work (boiler shop)

(G-6771)
ROLLING RIDGE METALS LLC
366 Kinsman Rd (16125-9234)
PHONE..............................724 588-2375
Enos Troyer,

EMP: 9
SALES (est): 1.1MM **Privately Held**
SIC: 3399 Powder, metal

(G-6772)
SALEM TUBE INC
951 4th St (16125-8253)
PHONE..............................724 646-4301
Rufino Orce, *President*
Charles Redzinak, *Vice Pres*
Fred Prossen, *CFO*
Mitchell Buchmann, *Admin Sec*
◆ EMP: 110
SQ FT: 160,000
SALES (est): 34.8MM
SALES (corp-wide): 49.6MM **Privately Held**
WEB: www.salemtube.com
SIC: 3317 3356 Steel pipe & tubes; nonferrous rolling & drawing
PA: Tubacex, Sa
Calle Irukurutzeta (Barrio Gardea) 8
Laudio/Llodio 01400
946 719-300

(G-6773)
SHA CO WELDING & FABRICATION
Also Called: Shaco
53 Canal St (16125-2248)
PHONE..............................724 588-0993
Warren Shaw, *Owner*
EMP: 5
SQ FT: 11,500
SALES: 100K **Privately Held**
SIC: 7692 3537 Welding repair; pallets, metal

(G-6774)
TRINITY INDUSTRIES
100 York St (16125-1528)
PHONE..............................724 588-7000
Timothy Wallace, *CEO*
EMP: 8
SALES (est): 835.1K **Privately Held**
SIC: 3325 Railroad car wheels, cast steel

(G-6775)
WERNER CO (DH)
93 Werner Rd (16125-9434)
PHONE..............................724 588-2000
William T Allen, *CEO*
Larry V Friend, *CFO*
Geoffrey Hartenstein, *Admin Sec*
◆ EMP: 160
SALES (est): 670.2MM **Privately Held**
SIC: 3499 3355 3089 3446 Ladders, portable: metal; extrusion ingot, aluminum: made in rolling mills; synthetic resin finished products; scaffolds, mobile or stationary: metal; stepladders, wood

(G-6776)
WERNER HOLDING CO INC
93 Werner Rd (16125-9434)
PHONE..............................888 523-3371
Dennis G Heiner, *CEO*
Steve Richman, *President*
Edward W Gericke, *Vice Pres*
Robert P Tamburrino, *Vice Pres*
Eric J Werner, *Vice Pres*
EMP: 1250 EST: 1922
SQ FT: 465,000
SALES (est): 85.5MM **Privately Held**
SIC: 3499 3355 3089 3446 Ladders, portable: metal; extrusion ingot, aluminum: made in rolling mills; synthetic resin finished products; scaffolds, mobile or stationary: metal; stepladders, wood

(G-6777)
WOODCRAFT INDUSTRIES INC
62 Grant Rd (16125-8328)
PHONE..............................724 638-4044
John Clarin, *Owner*
EMP: 20 **Publicly Held**
WEB: www.woodcraftind.com
SIC: 2434 Wood kitchen cabinets
HQ: Woodcraft Industries, Inc.
525 Lincoln Ave Se
Saint Cloud MN 56304
320 656-2345

(G-6778)
ZERO ERROR RACING INC
660 Keystone Rd A (16125-9748)
PHONE..............................724 588-5898
James D Fitzgerald, *President*
Ruth Schuff, *Vice Pres*
EMP: 5
SQ FT: 2,800
SALES (est): 530K **Privately Held**
WEB: www.zero-error.com
SIC: 3599 Custom machinery

Grindstone
Fayette County

(G-6779)
SHUMARS WELDING & MCH SVC INC
414 Stone Church Rd (15442-1158)
PHONE..............................724 246-8095
Eli R Shumar Jr, *President*
Eli R Shumar, *President*
Richard Shumar, *Vice Pres*
EMP: 90
SQ FT: 3,500
SALES (est): 25.7MM **Privately Held**
WEB: www.shumars.com
SIC: 3441 3535 Fabricated structural metal; conveyors & conveying equipment

Grove City
Mercer County

(G-6780)
BASHLIN INDUSTRIES INC
119 W Pine St (16127-1516)
P.O. Box 867 (16127-0867)
PHONE..............................724 458-8340
Robert Schell, *President*
Rod Paul, *Vice Pres*
Diane Sanford, *Purchasing*
Michael Kenniston, *CFO*
Brad McGill, *Director*
EMP: 65
SQ FT: 22,000
SALES (est): 24.2MM **Privately Held**
WEB: www.bashlin.com
SIC: 5072 3199 3842 3536 Hardware; safety belts, leather; surgical appliances & supplies; hoists, cranes & monorails; personal leather goods; men's & boys' work clothing

(G-6781)
CALCIUM CHLORIDE SALES INC
713 W Main St (16127-1198)
PHONE..............................724 458-5778
James C Mc Lean, *President*
James C McLean, *President*
Larry Bowie, *Corp Secy*
EMP: 9
SQ FT: 5,000
SALES (est): 2.1MM **Privately Held**
SIC: 5169 3271 4213 Calcium chloride; blocks, concrete or cinder: standard; contract haulers

(G-6782)
CREATIVE LOGISTICS LTD
Also Called: Five Filer Brothers Company
23 Tower Rd (16127-4733)
PHONE..............................724 458-6560
Robert F McBryan, *President*
Victoria L McBryan, *Vice Pres*
EMP: 25 EST: 1992
SQ FT: 15,000
SALES (est): 3.4MM **Privately Held**
WEB: www.creativelogistics.com
SIC: 2394 Canvas & related products

(G-6783)
CUSTOM SIGNS INC
1535 Millbrook Rd (16127-7119)
PHONE..............................814 786-7232
Todd Shillito, *President*
Rita Shillito, *Vice Pres*
EMP: 10
SQ FT: 5,000

SALES (est): 1.3MM **Privately Held**
WEB: www.customsignsinc.com
SIC: 3993 7389 1799 Signs, not made in custom sign painting shops; crane & aerial lift service; sign installation & maintenance

(G-6784)
FAULL FABRICATING INC
530 Courtney Mill Rd (16127-3908)
PHONE..............................724 458-7662
Douglas Faull, *President*
Jennifer Faull, *Vice Pres*
EMP: 8 EST: 1964
SQ FT: 8,000
SALES (est): 1.4MM **Privately Held**
WEB: www.faullfab.com
SIC: 3443 7692 Fabricated plate work (boiler shop); welding repair

(G-6785)
FORTA CORPORATION (PA)
100 Forta Dr (16127-6399)
PHONE..............................724 458-5221
Rodger B Lindh, *President*
Michael Binn, *President*
Pauline Golden, *Corp Secy*
Lauren E Camp, *Vice Pres*
John Lindh, *Vice Pres*
◆ EMP: 30 EST: 1978
SQ FT: 24,000
SALES (est): 5.6MM **Privately Held**
WEB: www.fortacorp.com
SIC: 2821 2823 Polypropylene resins; cellulosic manmade fibers

(G-6786)
GEAR RACEWEAR INC
Also Called: Moto Tees
517 Erie St (16127-2511)
PHONE..............................724 458-6336
John Ayers, *President*
Valarie L Morrison, *Corp Secy*
John E Ayers, *Vice Pres*
Rachel Mullins, *Vice Pres*
Sara Williams, *Admin Sec*
▲ EMP: 12
SQ FT: 7,500
SALES (est): 1.7MM **Privately Held**
WEB: www.mototees.com
SIC: 2339 5941 Women's & misses' athletic clothing & sportswear; sporting goods & bicycle shops

(G-6787)
GENERAL ELECTRIC COMPANY
1503 W Main Street Ext (16127-2598)
PHONE..............................724 450-1887
William J Standera, *Principal*
Stephen Oliver, *Mfg Staff*
Dennis Shea, *Engineer*
Cindy Burdette, *VP Mktg*
EMP: 300
SALES (corp-wide): 121.6B **Publicly Held**
SIC: 3714 3519 Motor vehicle engines & parts; internal combustion engines
PA: General Electric Company
41 Farnsworth St
Boston MA 02210
617 443-3000

(G-6788)
GLENN O HAWBAKER INC
106 Hawbaker Blvd (16127)
PHONE..............................724 458-0991
Glenn Hawbaker, *Principal*
EMP: 238
SALES (corp-wide): 300MM **Privately Held**
SIC: 2951 Asphalt & asphaltic paving mixtures (not from refineries)
PA: Glenn O. Hawbaker, Inc.
1952 Waddle Rd Ste 203
State College PA 16803
814 237-1444

(G-6789)
HAL BEN MINING CO
389 Irishtown Rd (16127-4409)
PHONE..............................724 748-4528
Neil Atwell, *Owner*
EMP: 6
SALES: 1.2MM **Privately Held**
SIC: 1221 5032 Strip mining, lignite; limestone

(G-6790)
HERITAGE WINE CELLARS
1911 Leesburg Grove Cy Rd (16127)
PHONE....................................724 748-5070
Jerry Namey, *Owner*
Jerry Holmes, *Co-Owner*
EMP: 5
SALES (est): 371.6K **Privately Held**
SIC: 2084 Wines

(G-6791)
J & K INDUSTRIAL SALES
Also Called: J & K Hydraulic Hose
Rr 58 Box E (16127)
P.O. Box 225 (16127-0225)
PHONE....................................724 458-7670
Harold Denbow, *Owner*
EMP: 3
SQ FT: 5,000
SALES (est): 400K **Privately Held**
SIC: 3492 5084 Hose & tube fittings & as-
semblies, hydraulic/pneumatic; industrial
machinery & equipment

(G-6792)
JOSEPH JENKINS INC
143 Forest Ln (16127-8711)
PHONE....................................814 786-9085
Joseph Jenkins, *Owner*
EMP: 4
SQ FT: 5,000
SALES: 1.1MM **Privately Held**
WEB: www.josephjenkins.com
SIC: 5211 8712 2721 Roofing material;
architectural services; magazines: pub-
lishing & printing

(G-6793)
**KEFFER DEVELOPMENT SVCS
LLC**
Also Called: Athletic Trainer System
24 Village Park Dr (16127-6358)
PHONE....................................724 458-5289
Rhett Keffer, *Mng Member*
Dana Keffer, *Manager*
EMP: 4
SQ FT: 1,300
SALES (est): 285.8K **Privately Held**
SIC: 7372 Application computer software

(G-6794)
LAWN & GARDEN
Also Called: Oesterling Feed & Farm Sups
410 Erie St (16127-1667)
PHONE....................................724 458-6141
Ron Bowers, *Manager*
EMP: 3
SALES (corp-wide): 425K **Privately Held**
SIC: 5261 2048 Fertilizer; prepared feeds
PA: Lawn & Garden
101 S Monroe St
Butler PA 16001
724 287-3745

(G-6795)
LOCAL MEDIA GROUP INC
Also Called: Allied News
201 Erie St Ste A (16127-1659)
P.O. Box 190 (16127-0190)
PHONE....................................724 458-5010
Sharon Sorg, *Principal*
EMP: 15
SALES (corp-wide): 1.5B **Publicly Held**
WEB: www.ottaway.com
SIC: 2711 Newspapers: publishing only,
not printed on site
HQ: Local Media Group, Inc.
40 Mulberry St
Middletown NY 10940
845 341-1100

(G-6796)
LUSCIOUS LAYERS
140 Garden Ave (16127-1416)
PHONE....................................724 967-2357
Lottie Bibza, *Owner*
EMP: 4 EST: 2010
SALES (est): 237.2K **Privately Held**
SIC: 2053 Cakes, bakery: frozen

(G-6797)
**MC DOWELL IMPLEMENT
COMPANY**
1433 Sandy Lake Rd (16127-6699)
PHONE....................................814 786-7955
Harvey Mc Dowell, *President*
Bill Mc Dowell, *Corp Secy*
Ruth Mc Dowell, *Vice Pres*
◆ EMP: 8 EST: 1953
SQ FT: 3,000
SALES (est): 1.1MM **Privately Held**
SIC: 3523 Farm machinery & equipment

(G-6798)
**MONTGOMERY TRUSS & PANEL
INC (PA)**
803 W Main St (16127-1113)
P.O. Box 866 (16127-0866)
PHONE....................................724 458-7500
Charles B Montgomery Jr, *President*
Tim Wetzel, *Prdtn Mgr*
J R Greer, *Treasurer*
Mary Montgomery, *Admin Sec*
EMP: 100 EST: 1921
SQ FT: 55,000
SALES (est): 15.8MM **Privately Held**
WEB: www.montgomerytruss.com
SIC: 2439 Trusses, wooden roof

(G-6799)
OLDE TOWN GROVE CITY
118 S Center St (16127-1507)
PHONE....................................724 458-0301
Mary Jo Palmer, *Manager*
EMP: 3
SALES (est): 180K **Privately Held**
SIC: 3842 Abdominal supporters, braces &
trusses

(G-6800)
PINE ELECTRONICS INC
101 Industrial Dr (16127-1007)
PHONE....................................724 458-6391
Joseph Hines, *President*
Ben N Cain, *Principal*
EMP: 68
SALES (est): 3.4MM **Privately Held**
SIC: 3672 Printed circuit boards

(G-6801)
**PINE INSTRUMENT COMPANY
(PA)**
101 Industrial Dr (16127-1091)
PHONE....................................724 458-6391
Joseph D Hines, *President*
Gloria L Hines, *Corp Secy*
Gloria Hines, *COO*
Jonathan E Stewart, *Treasurer*
Robin Vaughn, *Human Res Mgr*
◆ EMP: 79
SQ FT: 48,000
SALES: 13.6MM **Privately Held**
WEB: www.pineinst.com
SIC: 3625 3672 Industrial controls: push
button, selector switches, pilot; printed cir-
cuit boards

(G-6802)
PRIEST ENTERPRISES
11 Irishtown Rd (16127-4329)
PHONE....................................724 658-7692
Andrew Priest, *Owner*
EMP: 3
SALES (est): 205.4K **Privately Held**
SIC: 0782 1521 3743 Landscape contrac-
tors; new construction, single-family
houses; train cars & equipment, freight or
passenger

(G-6803)
RIVERWOODS CABINETRY
177 Schmidt Rd (16127-4121)
PHONE....................................724 991-0097
EMP: 4
SALES (est): 316.7K **Privately Held**
SIC: 2434 Wood kitchen cabinets

(G-6804)
**STEIGRWALDS KITCHENS
BATHS INC**
120 S Broad St Ste C (16127-1544)
PHONE....................................724 458-0280
Stephen Steigerwald, *President*
Melinda Steigerwald, *Corp Secy*
EMP: 10 EST: 1977
SQ FT: 15,000

SALES: 1.5MM **Privately Held**
WEB: www.steigerwalds.com
SIC: 2434 5211 2431 Wood kitchen cabinets; cabinets, kitchen; bathroom fixtures,
equipment & supplies; millwork

(G-6805)
SYCAMORE PARTNERS MGT LP
1911 Leesburg Grove Cy Rd (16127)
PHONE....................................724 748-0052
EMP: 5 **Privately Held**
SIC: 2752 Commercial printing, litho-
graphic
PA: Sycamore Partners Management, L.P.
9 W 57th St Ste 3100
New York NY 10019

(G-6806)
TEAM OIL TOOLS LP
109 N Madison Ave (16127-1845)
PHONE....................................724 301-2659
EMP: 4
SALES (corp-wide): 818.6MM **Publicly
Held**
SIC: 1389 Oil/Gas Field Services
HQ: Team Oil Tools, L.P.
4310 N Sam Houston Pkwy E
Houston TX 77032
936 242-8825

(G-6807)
VISTA OPTICAL
15 Pine Grove Sq (16127-4447)
PHONE....................................724 458-0333
EMP: 3 EST: 2014
SALES (est): 271.6K **Privately Held**
SIC: 3827 Optical instruments & lenses

Guys Mills
Crawford County

(G-6808)
BLOOM MACHINE WORKS INC
11860 State Highway 198 (16327-2542)
PHONE....................................814 789-4234
Mark A Bloom, *President*
Howard Bloom, *Vice Pres*
EMP: 8
SQ FT: 3,000
SALES (est): 1.1MM **Privately Held**
SIC: 3544 Special dies & tools

(G-6809)
CISCO SYSTEMS INC
30910 Dobie Ln (16327-4746)
PHONE....................................814 789-2990
EMP: 666
SALES (corp-wide): 49.3B **Publicly Held**
SIC: 3577 Data conversion equipment,
media-to-media: computer
PA: Cisco Systems, Inc.
170 W Tasman Dr
San Jose CA 95134
408 526-4000

(G-6810)
CUSTEADS SAWMILL INC
8950 Frenchtown Rd (16327-2620)
PHONE....................................814 425-3863
Gary L Custead, *President*
Carol Custead, *Corp Secy*
EMP: 5
SQ FT: 400
SALES (est): 260K **Privately Held**
SIC: 2421 Sawmills & planing mills, gen-
eral

(G-6811)
MOUNT HOPE LUMBER
29749 State Highway 27 (16327-2819)
PHONE....................................814 789-4953
David Mullet, *Owner*
John Mullet, *Partner*
EMP: 4
SALES: 240K **Privately Held**
SIC: 2421 5031 Sawmills & planing mills,
general; lumber: rough, dressed & fin-
ished

(G-6812)
SHARP TOOL AND DIE INC
25947 Plank Rd (16327-4319)
P.O. Box 869, Saegertown (16433-0869)
PHONE....................................814 763-1133
Leon Proper, *President*
Ken Myers, *Corp Secy*
EMP: 4
SQ FT: 2,700
SALES: 290K **Privately Held**
SIC: 3312 Tool & die steel & alloys

(G-6813)
SUTLEY TOOL CO
25439 Plank Rd (16327-4223)
PHONE....................................814 789-4332
Terry Sutley, *President*
EMP: 4
SQ FT: 4,400
SALES: 800K **Privately Held**
SIC: 3544 Industrial molds

(G-6814)
**WHITEHEAD TOOL & DESIGN
INC**
27014 State Highway 77 (16327-1810)
PHONE....................................814 967-3064
Lester Bates, *President*
EMP: 15
SQ FT: 10,000
SALES (est): 2MM **Privately Held**
SIC: 3544 Special dies & tools

Gwynedd Valley
Montgomery County

(G-6815)
DEXTER ROSETTES INC
1425 Township Line Rd (19437)
P.O. Box 146 (19437-0146)
PHONE....................................215 542-0118
C Dexter Schierenbeck, *President*
EMP: 4
SALES (est): 265.3K **Privately Held**
WEB: www.dexterrosettes.com
SIC: 3911 Pins (jewelry), precious metal

Hadley
Mercer County

(G-6816)
**COMPONENT
INTRTECHNOLOGIES INC (PA)**
Also Called: CIT
2426 Perry Hwy (16130-2924)
PHONE....................................724 253-3161
John Haggearty, *President*
Gary Anderson, *Engineer*
Mark S Nixon, *Controller*
Mark Nixon, *Controller*
▲ EMP: 37
SQ FT: 45,000
SALES (est): 5.1MM **Privately Held**
WEB: www.cit-hadley.com
SIC: 3679 5065 Electronic circuits; semi-
conductor devices

(G-6817)
CONTROLLED MOLDING INC
Also Called: CMI
3043 Perry Hwy (16130-1923)
PHONE....................................724 253-3550
Raymond P Mozes, *President*
Gordon Sindlinger, *Vice Pres*
Tom Mika, *Prdtn Mgr*
Steve Giddings, *Engineer*
Kevin Learn, *Engineer*
EMP: 49
SQ FT: 38,000
SALES (est): 11.9MM **Privately Held**
WEB: www.controlledmolding.com
SIC: 3089 Injection molding of plastics

(G-6818)
CUSICK TOOL INC
Also Called: Machine Shop
19 Larimer Rd (16130-2301)
PHONE....................................724 253-4455
Martin Cusick, *President*
EMP: 10

SQ FT: 10,000
SALES: 1MM **Privately Held**
SIC: 3599 Machine shop, jobbing & repair

(G-6819)
DEIST INDUSTRIES INC
Also Called: Buck's Fabricating Division
3547 Perry Hwy (16130-2325)
PHONE.............................800 233-0867
Matthew Wilson, *President*
Dale W Deist, *President*
Kristen Wilson, *Vice Pres*
Scott McClellan, *Buyer*
Matthew T Wilson, *Treasurer*
EMP: 40
SQ FT: 35,000
SALES (est): 17MM **Privately Held**
WEB: www.bucksfab.com
SIC: 3443 3411 Dumpsters, garbage; bins,
   prefabricated metal plate; metal cans

(G-6820)
NORTHEAST INDUSTRIAL MFG
191 Pearson Rd (16130-2525)
PHONE.............................724 253-3110
Howard Cusick, *Owner*
EMP: 4
SALES (est): 220.4K **Privately Held**
SIC: 3443 Dumpsters, garbage

(G-6821)
TECHNICAL PRECISION INC
2343 Perry Hwy (16130-2921)
P.O. Box 98 (16130-0098)
PHONE.............................724 253-2800
Gregory Carone, *President*
Scott Wells, *Vice Pres*
Harry Romesburg, *Admin Sec*
EMP: 20
SQ FT: 5,000
SALES (est): 2.6MM **Privately Held**
WEB: www.techprec.com
SIC: 3544 Special dies & tools

(G-6822)
VALLEY CAN INC
1264 Fredonia Rd (16130-2612)
PHONE.............................724 253-2038
Richard E Smith, *President*
Dick Smith, *President*
Sharon Smith, *Corp Secy*
EMP: 18
SQ FT: 20,000
SALES (est): 4.3MM **Privately Held**
WEB: www.valleycan.com
SIC: 3443 Dumpsters, garbage

(G-6823)
WILHELM WINERY INC (PA)
590 Georgetown Rd (16130-1098)
PHONE.............................724 253-3700
Gary A Shelling, *President*
Patricia F Shilling, *Corp Secy*
EMP: 6
SALES (est): 456.5K **Privately Held**
SIC: 2084 Wines

Halifax
Dauphin County

(G-6824)
ACCU-MOLD & TOOL COMPANY INC
Also Called: Accu Mold Plastics
18 Powells Valley Rd (17032-9105)
P.O. Box U (17032-0475)
PHONE.............................717 896-3937
Mary Lou Strohecker, *CEO*
Keith Buffington, *President*
Dana Buffington, *Corp Secy*
Tracy Bower, *Vice Pres*
Jack L Strohecker II, *Vice Pres*
▼ EMP: 35
SQ FT: 12,000
SALES (est): 6.1MM **Privately Held**
SIC: 3089 Injection molding of plastics

(G-6825)
BRUNERS SIGN SERVICE INC
97 Lehman Rd (17032-9082)
PHONE.............................717 896-7699
Brian Bruner, *President*
EMP: 3

SALES (est): 231.9K **Privately Held**
SIC: 3993 Signs & advertising specialties

(G-6826)
HEARTH & HOME TECHNOLOGIES LLC
352 Mountain House Rd (17032-9733)
PHONE.............................717 362-9080
EMP: 4
SALES (corp-wide): 2.2B **Publicly Held**
WEB: www.heatnglo.com
SIC: 3429 4925 Fireplace equipment,
   hardware: andirons, grates, screens; gas
   production and/or distribution
HQ: Hearth & Home Technologies, Llc
   7571 215th St W
   Lakeville MN 55044

(G-6827)
PAUL WITHERS
Also Called: Diesel ERA
528 Dunkel School Rd (17032-8986)
PHONE.............................717 896-3173
Paul Withers, *Owner*
EMP: 4
SQ FT: 4,000
SALES (est): 500K **Privately Held**
SIC: 2731 2721 5192 Books: publishing
   only; magazines: publishing & printing;
   books; magazines

(G-6828)
PAULUS & SON CABINET CO
110 S 2nd St (17032-7928)
P.O. Box 53 (17032-0053)
PHONE.............................717 896-3610
Eugene R Paulus, *Partner*
Scott Paulus, *Partner*
EMP: 8
SQ FT: 11,000
SALES (est): 846.4K **Privately Held**
SIC: 2434 Wood kitchen cabinets

(G-6829)
RIDGE MACHINE SHOP INC
158c Hoffman Rd (17032-9646)
PHONE.............................717 896-8348
Thomas Brown, *President*
Michael Brown, *Vice Pres*
EMP: 3 EST: 1967
SQ FT: 3,200
SALES (est): 130K **Privately Held**
WEB: www.rides.webshots.com
SIC: 3599 Machine shop, jobbing & repair

(G-6830)
SCREENPRINTED GRAFIX INC
Also Called: Screen Printing USA
245 Hershey Rd (17032-8831)
PHONE.............................717 564-7464
Tracy Mancini, *President*
Scott Mancini, *Vice Pres*
EMP: 5
SALES (est): 251K **Privately Held**
SIC: 2759 Screen printing

(G-6831)
SENSE TECHNOLOGY INC
1033 Matamoras Rd (17032-8811)
PHONE.............................724 733-2277
Joseph Evans, *President*
EMP: 4
SQ FT: 900
SALES (est): 784K **Privately Held**
SIC: 3679 8711 3845 Electronic circuits;
   engineering services; electromedical ap-
   paratus

Hallstead
Susquehanna County

(G-6832)
DECK MACHINE CO
Liberty Park Rd (18822)
P.O. Box 898 (18822-0898)
PHONE.............................570 879-2833
James M Decker, *Partner*
Nancy Decker, *Partner*
Rick Decker, *Partner*
EMP: 4
SALES (est): 175K **Privately Held**
SIC: 3599 Machine shop, jobbing & repair

(G-6833)
IMEX PA LLC
14 Merrill St (18822-9498)
PHONE.............................607 343-3160
EMP: 5
SALES (est): 556.1K **Privately Held**
SIC: 3545 Diamond cutting tools for turn-
   ing, boring, burnishing, etc.

(G-6834)
NEW WAY HOMES
425 Gontarski Rd (18822-9346)
PHONE.............................570 967-2187
Jeffery Haberle, *Owner*
Diane Haberle, *Partner*
Douglas Haberle, *Partner*
Rodney Haberle, *Partner*
EMP: 4 EST: 1993
SALES: 400K **Privately Held**
WEB: www.newwayhomes.com
SIC: 3281 Flagstones

(G-6835)
P & P STONE LLC
239 Franklin Hill Rd (18822-9405)
PHONE.............................570 967-2279
Bryan G Parks, *Mng Member*
Catherine W Parks,
Francis Parks,
EMP: 4
SALES: 147K **Privately Held**
WEB: www.beenhereandthere.com
SIC: 1411 Flagstone mining

(G-6836)
THOMAS MAGNETIX INC
350 New York Ave (18822)
P.O. Box 812 (18822-0812)
PHONE.............................570 879-4363
William Thomas, *President*
Lorraine Thomas, *Vice Pres*
EMP: 23
SQ FT: 5,000
SALES: 700K **Privately Held**
WEB: www.thomasmagnetix.com
SIC: 3612 Specialty transformers

Hamburg
Berks County

(G-6837)
DOVE PLASTICS INC
111 Valley Rd (19526-9139)
PHONE.............................610 562-2600
Doug Miller, *President*
Allan F Miller, *Treasurer*
Stacie Miller, *Office Mgr*
EMP: 24
SQ FT: 27,000
SALES: 2MM **Privately Held**
WEB: www.doveplastics.com
SIC: 3089 Blow molded finished plastic
   products; injection molding of plastics

(G-6838)
EMS ENGNRED MTLS SOLUTIONS LLC
600 Valley Rd (19526-8387)
PHONE.............................610 562-3841
Jeff Harlow, *Manager*
EMP: 100
SALES (corp-wide): 352.7MM **Privately Held**
SIC: 3479 Bonderizing of metal or metal
   products
HQ: Ems Engineered Materials Solutions,
   Llc
   39 Perry Ave
   Attleboro MA 02703
   508 342-2100

(G-6839)
EVERLAST PLASTIC LUMBER INC
1000 S 4th St (19526-9208)
PHONE.............................610 562-8336
Robert Cougle, *President*
EMP: 13
SALES: 1.4MM **Privately Held**
WEB: www.everlastlumber.com
SIC: 2421 Lumber: rough, sawed or planed

(G-6840)
HAMBURG MANUFACTURING INC (PA)
Also Called: Hmi
221 S 4th St (19526-1207)
P.O. Box 147 (19526-0147)
PHONE.............................610 562-2203
David E Pendergast, *President*
Edward Geschwindt, *Vice Pres*
Beverly Grim, *Admin Sec*
EMP: 44 EST: 1882
SALES (est): 12.8MM **Privately Held**
WEB: www.hamburgmfg.com
SIC: 3321 Gray iron castings

(G-6841)
HILL JOHN M MACHINE CO INC
Also Called: Jmh Trailers
233 Farview Rd (19526-8627)
PHONE.............................610 562-8690
Bart Hill, *President*
Jesse Hill, *Treasurer*
Marie Hill, *Admin Sec*
EMP: 40 EST: 1966
SQ FT: 43,000
SALES (est): 5.2MM **Privately Held**
WEB: www.jmhtrailers.com
SIC: 7539 3599 3713 7692 Automotive
   turbocharger & blower repair; machine
   shop, jobbing & repair; dump truck bod-
   ies; welding repair

(G-6842)
JOE JURGIELEWICZ & SON LTD (PA)
189 Cheese Ln (19526-8057)
P.O. Box 257, Shartlesville (19554-0257)
PHONE.............................610 562-3825
Joseph Jurgielewicz Jr, *President*
Rhonda Adam, *Buyer*
Janice M Loeb, *Human Res Mgr*
Ian Shollenberger, *Sales Staff*
Joseph Jurgielewicz Sr, *Shareholder*
▲ EMP: 20
SQ FT: 5,000
SALES (est): 22.7MM **Privately Held**
WEB: www.joejurgielewicz.com
SIC: 5144 2015 Poultry products; poultry
   slaughtering & processing

(G-6843)
KORE MART LTD
7 Hill Dr (19526)
P.O. Box 175 (19526-0175)
PHONE.............................610 562-5900
Henry Witmyer III, *President*
Henry Witmyer Jr, *Vice Pres*
Robert M Carney, *Admin Sec*
EMP: 28
SQ FT: 1,575
SALES (est): 5.2MM **Privately Held**
SIC: 3543 Foundry cores

(G-6844)
LEHIGH CEMENT COMPANY LLC
204 Windsor Ave (19526-8341)
PHONE.............................610 562-3000
Patrick J Marion, *Manager*
EMP: 9
SQ FT: 13,072
SALES (corp-wide): 20.6B **Privately Held**
WEB: www.lehighcement.com
SIC: 3241 Portland cement
HQ: Lehigh Cement Company Llc
   300 E John Carpenter Fwy
   Irving TX 75062
   877 534-4442

(G-6845)
MARK RIOUX PALLETS
1100 Pennsylvania 61 (19526)
PHONE.............................610 562-7030
Joshua Rioux, *President*
EMP: 8
SALES (est): 1.1MM **Privately Held**
SIC: 2448 Pallets, wood

(G-6846)
MICHAEL J ZELLERS
611 1st Street Ext (19526-8953)
PHONE.............................610 562-2825
EMP: 3
SQ FT: 1,120
SALES (est): 147.2K **Privately Held**
SIC: 3599 Mfg Industrial Machinery

(G-6847)
NIAGARA BOTTLING LLC
316 Front St (19526-1140)
PHONE..................................610 562-2176
Andy Peykoff, *President*
EMP: 25
SALES (corp-wide): 439MM **Privately Held**
SIC: 2086 Water, pasteurized: packaged in cans, bottles, etc.
PA: Niagara Bottling, Llc
2560 E Philadelphia St
Ontario CA 91761
909 230-5000

(G-6848)
PENN GRAPHICS EQUIPMENT INC
139 Mill Hill Rd (19526-7924)
PHONE..................................610 488-7414
Benjamin Scheffler, *President*
Patricia Scheffler, *Corp Secy*
Brian Scheffler, *Vice Pres*
▲ EMP: 21
SALES (est): 3.1MM **Privately Held**
WEB: www.penngraphics.com
SIC: 2759 Commercial printing

(G-6849)
POWARD PLASTICS INCORPORATED
725 Hex Hwy (19526-8903)
PHONE..................................484 660-3690
Paul Billman, *Principal*
▲ EMP: 4
SALES (est): 381.7K **Privately Held**
SIC: 2295 Resin or plastic coated fabrics

(G-6850)
PROGRESSIVE MACHINE WORKS INC
100 S 2nd St (19526)
PHONE..................................610 562-2281
Arthur E Brudereck, *President*
William C Brudereck, *Vice Pres*
Donald Spangler, *Treasurer*
Mary Ann Brudereck, *Admin Sec*
EMP: 10 EST: 1922
SQ FT: 35,000
SALES (est): 1.5MM **Privately Held**
WEB: www.progressivemachineworks.com
SIC: 3599 Machine shop, jobbing & repair

(G-6851)
RANDY BRENSINGER
Also Called: Edenberg Welding Co
149 Pine St (19526-1812)
PHONE..................................610 562-2184
Randy Brensinger, *Owner*
EMP: 4
SQ FT: 7,000
SALES (est): 392.6K **Privately Held**
SIC: 7692 3446 7629 3444 Welding repair; architectural metalwork; electrical repair shops; sheet metalwork

(G-6852)
TILDEN MANUFACTURING INC
229 Lowland Rd (19526-8702)
PHONE..................................610 562-4682
Mike Rhoads Sr, *President*
EMP: 3
SQ FT: 8,000
SALES: 190K **Privately Held**
SIC: 3363 Aluminum die-castings

(G-6853)
TIMBER PALLET & LUMBER CO INC
Also Called: K & R Skids
1008 Mountain Rd (19526-8200)
PHONE..................................610 562-8442
Rick Zerr, *President*
Kerry Brown, *Vice Pres*
EMP: 5
SALES (est): 635K **Privately Held**
SIC: 2441 Packing cases, wood: nailed or lock corner; shipping cases, wood: nailed or lock corner

(G-6854)
TREGA CORPORATION
625 Valley Rd (19526-8377)
PHONE..................................610 562-5558
Bradley O Gammons, *President*

David Gammons, *Chairman*
Jane Gammons, *Vice Pres*
▲ EMP: 14
SQ FT: 12,500
SALES (est): 2.1MM **Privately Held**
WEB: www.tregacorp.com
SIC: 3365 Aluminum & aluminum-based alloy castings

(G-6855)
VOLLMER PATTERNS INC
389 Creamery Rd (19526-8015)
PHONE..................................610 562-7920
Thomas W Vollmer, *President*
EMP: 6 EST: 1972
SQ FT: 4,400
SALES (est): 726.2K **Privately Held**
SIC: 3599 Machine shop, jobbing & repair

(G-6856)
WEST SIDE WOOD PRODUCTS INC (PA)
157 State St (19526-1820)
PHONE..................................610 562-8166
Darrell Kohler, *President*
Julianne Kohler, *Corp Secy*
EMP: 10
SALES (est): 1.1MM **Privately Held**
WEB: www.westsidewoodproducts.com
SIC: 2448 Pallets, wood; skids, wood

(G-6857)
WINDSOR-PRESS INC
6 N 3rd St (19526-1502)
P.O. Box 465 (19526-0465)
PHONE..................................610 562-3624
George T Mitten, *President*
Matthew Figard, *CFO*
▲ EMP: 43 EST: 1958
SQ FT: 5,000
SALES: 2.5MM **Privately Held**
WEB: www.windsorpress.com
SIC: 2711 Commercial printing & newspaper publishing combined

Hamilton
Jefferson County

(G-6858)
PRODUCTION ABRASIVES INC
46 Sheesley Way (15744)
P.O. Box 60 (15744-0060)
PHONE..................................814 938-5490
Richard A Nesbitt, *President*
Ronald Cook, *Vice Pres*
Cathy London, *Treasurer*
Robb Nesditt, *Sales Executive*
Kali Young, *Admin Sec*
▲ EMP: 28
SQ FT: 30,000
SALES (est): 3.6MM **Privately Held**
WEB: www.productionabrasives.com
SIC: 3291 Abrasive products

Hanover
York County

(G-6859)
ABBOTTSTOWN STAMPING CO INC
13 Barnhart Dr (17331-9589)
PHONE..................................717 632-0588
Tammy Althoff, *President*
Dan Althoff, *Vice Pres*
EMP: 10
SQ FT: 12,000
SALES (est): 2.1MM **Privately Held**
WEB: www.asctornado.com
SIC: 3469 3531 Metal stampings; mixers: ore, plaster, slag, sand, mortar, etc.

(G-6860)
AMERICAN WAFFLE COMPANY LLC
1125 Wilson Ave (17331)
P.O. Box 334 (17331-0334)
PHONE..................................717 632-6000
▲ EMP: 20
SQ FT: 5,000

SALES (est): 3.1MM **Privately Held**
SIC: 3556 Bakery machinery

(G-6861)
AQUAPHOENIX SCIENTIFIC INC
860 Gitts Run Rd (17331-8123)
P.O. Box 1042 (17331-7042)
PHONE..................................717 632-1291
Frank Lecrone III, *CEO*
◆ EMP: 56
SQ FT: 50,000
SALES (est): 20.2MM **Privately Held**
WEB: www.aquaphoenixsci.com
SIC: 2835 In vitro & in vivo diagnostic substances

(G-6862)
BEACH FILTER PRODUCTS INC
555 Centennial Ave # 120 (17331-3956)
P.O. Box 505 (17331-0505)
PHONE..................................717 235-1136
Wesley Jones, *President*
Deborah Edds-Bang, *Chairman*
Kathryn Blackburn, *Treasurer*
Lori Prickitt, *Comptroller*
Anne Buckley, *Admin Sec*
EMP: 5 EST: 1945
SQ FT: 1,976
SALES: 1.2MM **Privately Held**
WEB: www.beachfilters.com
SIC: 3564 Blowers & fans

(G-6863)
BITUMINOUS PAV MTLS YORK INC
100 Green Springs Rd (17331-8979)
PHONE..................................717 632-8919
John Sterling, *Manager*
EMP: 3
SALES (corp-wide): 1.1MM **Privately Held**
SIC: 2951 1611 Asphalt & asphaltic paving mixtures (not from refineries); surfacing & paving
PA: Bituminous Paving Materials Of York, Inc.
1300 Zinns Quarry Rd
York PA 17404
717 843-4573

(G-6864)
C & J CLARK AMERICA INC
Also Called: C & J Clarks
455 Madison St (17331-4727)
PHONE..................................717 632-2444
Gale Bartosh, *Branch Mgr*
Richard Wright, *Branch Mgr*
EMP: 80 **Privately Held**
WEB: www.clarks.com
SIC: 3143 5139 Boots, dress or casual: men's; footwear
HQ: C. & J. Clark America, Inc.
60 Tower Rd
Waltham MA 02451
617 964-1222

(G-6865)
C H REED INC (PA)
301 Poplar St (17331-2370)
P.O. Box 524 (17331-0524)
PHONE..................................717 632-4261
Richard Mondorff, *President*
Brian Ginck, *Regional Mgr*
Steve Reed, *Regional Mgr*
Dennis Reed, *Vice Pres*
Jeff Reed, *Vice Pres*
EMP: 50
SQ FT: 60,000
SALES (est): 26.8MM **Privately Held**
WEB: www.chreed.com
SIC: 3563 5085 Air & gas compressors; industrial supplies

(G-6866)
CAM INDUSTRIES INC
Also Called: Peerless Tool Division
215 Philadelphia St (17331-2039)
PHONE..................................717 637-5988
Charles A Mc Gough III, *President*
Charles A Mc Gough III, *President*
Michelle F McGough, *Admin Sec*
◆ EMP: 25 EST: 1965
SQ FT: 28,000

SALES (est): 3.6MM **Privately Held**
WEB: www.camindustries.com
SIC: 3599 3549 3541 Custom machinery; metalworking machinery; machine tools, metal cutting type

(G-6867)
CAM INNOVATION INC
215 Philadelphia St (17331-2039)
PHONE..................................717 637-5988
Charles McGough III, *President*
Michelle McGough, *Admin Sec*
◆ EMP: 27
SQ FT: 52,000
SALES (est): 5.5MM **Privately Held**
SIC: 3599 Custom machinery

(G-6868)
CONDOR SNACK COMPANY
900 High St (17331-1639)
PHONE..................................303 333-6075
George Phillips, *President*
Don Dixon, *Vice Pres*
Julianna Phillips, *Admin Sec*
EMP: 110
SQ FT: 115,000
SALES (est): 20.9MM
SALES (corp-wide): 723.8MM **Privately Held**
WEB: www.condorsnacks.com
SIC: 2096 Potato chips & similar snacks
PA: Utz Quality Foods, Llc
900 High St
Hanover PA 17331
800 367-7629

(G-6869)
CONEWAGO READY MIX
576 Edgegrove Rd (17331-8928)
PHONE..................................717 633-5022
Dave Denharl, *Principal*
EMP: 7
SALES (est): 615.4K **Privately Held**
SIC: 3273 Ready-mixed concrete

(G-6870)
CONRAD PRINTING CO INC
109 3rd St Rear (17331-2436)
PHONE..................................717 637-5414
Donald J Conrad, *President*
Andrew V Conrad, *Corp Secy*
Patsy Conrad, *Vice Pres*
EMP: 4
SQ FT: 2,700
SALES: 200K **Privately Held**
SIC: 2752 2759 Commercial printing, offset; letterpress printing

(G-6871)
CROWN CORK & SEAL USA INC
1650 Broadway (17331-8118)
PHONE..................................717 633-1163
Ron Vansant, *Manager*
EMP: 58
SALES (corp-wide): 11.1B **Publicly Held**
WEB: www.crowncork.com
SIC: 3411 Metal cans
HQ: Crown Cork & Seal Usa, Inc.
770 Township Line Rd # 100
Yardley PA 19067
215 698-5100

(G-6872)
DAILY INFORMER LLC
209 3rd St Apt A (17331-2326)
PHONE..................................717 634-9087
Matthew Deckelman,
EMP: 3 EST: 2017
SALES (est): 88.7K **Privately Held**
SIC: 2711 Newspapers, publishing & printing

(G-6873)
DANIEL GERARD WORLDWIDE INC (PA)
Also Called: Gerard Daniel Worldwide
34 Barnhart Dr (17331-9586)
PHONE..................................800 232-3332
Gary N Shultis, *CEO*
Tina O'Donnell, *General Mgr*
Scott Miller, *Business Mgr*
Robert Milmoe, *Exec VP*
John Johnson, *Vice Pres*
◆ EMP: 60
SQ FT: 80,000

▲ = Import ▼=Export
◆ =Import/Export

SALES (est): 88.2MM **Privately Held**
WEB: www.gerarddaniels.com
SIC: 3496 Woven wire products

(G-6874)
DANIEL GERARD WORLDWIDE INC
762 Wilson Ave (17331-9517)
PHONE..................................717 630-3787
Scott Miller, *Manager*
EMP: 4
SALES (corp-wide): 88.2MM **Privately Held**
SIC: 3496 Miscellaneous fabricated wire products
PA: Daniel Gerard Worldwide Inc
34 Barnhart Dr
Hanover PA 17331
800 232-3332

(G-6875)
DANIEL GERARD WORLDWIDE INC
Also Called: Gdc/Keystone Wire Cloth
150 Factory St (17331)
PHONE..................................717 637-3250
A Edward Miele, *Manager*
EMP: 200
SALES (corp-wide): 88.2MM **Privately Held**
WEB: www.gerarddaniels.com
SIC: 3496 Miscellaneous fabricated wire products
PA: Daniel Gerard Worldwide Inc
34 Barnhart Dr
Hanover PA 17331
800 232-3332

(G-6876)
DEL-WOOD KITCHENS INC
1856 Dubs Church Rd (17331-8581)
PHONE..................................717 637-9320
Thomas C Hasenstab, *President*
EMP: 44 EST: 1986
SQ FT: 40,000
SALES (est): 6.4MM **Privately Held**
SIC: 2434 Wood kitchen cabinets

(G-6877)
DIVERSE TCHNICAL SOLUTIONS LLC
Also Called: Diverse Defense Solutions
72 Joshua Dr (17331-7448)
PHONE..................................717 630-8522
Diane Arthur, *President*
EMP: 6
SALES (est): 420K **Privately Held**
SIC: 3679 Electronic components

(G-6878)
DOCTOR BART AYURVEDA
108 Fair Ave (17331-3343)
PHONE..................................717 524-4208
Bart Staub, *Owner*
EMP: 3
SALES (est): 165.3K **Privately Held**
SIC: 2819 Mfg Industrial Inorganic Chemicals

(G-6879)
DONALD B SMITH INCORPORATED (PA)
450 W Chestnut St (17331-2927)
P.O. Box 78 (17331-0078)
PHONE..................................717 632-2100
Douglas A Smith, *President*
Gregory Willing, *Corp Secy*
Judith Willing, *Vice Pres*
EMP: 48
SQ FT: 5,000
SALES (est): 9.6MM **Privately Held**
SIC: 1761 3444 Roofing contractor; siding contractor; sheet metalwork

(G-6880)
DRI MACHINE SHOP INC
145 Ram Dr (17331-7783)
PHONE..................................717 633-9306
David R Inners, *President*
Lynn Hagerman, *Technology*
EMP: 12
SQ FT: 8,000
SALES (est): 1.9MM **Privately Held**
SIC: 3599 Machine shop, jobbing & repair

(G-6881)
ELM AVE CAR WASH
703 W Elm Ave (17331-4704)
PHONE..................................717 637-7392
Lee Wildasin, *Owner*
EMP: 5
SALES (est): 200K **Privately Held**
SIC: 7542 3589 Carwash, automatic; car washing machinery

(G-6882)
ELSNER ENGINEERING WORKS INC
475 Fame Ave (17331-1584)
P.O. Box 66 (17331-0066)
PHONE..................................717 637-5991
Frank Elsner III, *President*
Frank Elsner Jr, *Chairman*
Bertram Elsner II, *Vice Pres*
Robert Van Sant, *Vice Pres*
Ed Garvick, *Mfg Staff*
▲ EMP: 65 EST: 1934
SQ FT: 55,000
SALES (est): 17.7MM **Privately Held**
WEB: www.elsnereng.com
SIC: 3554 Die cutting & stamping machinery, paper converting

(G-6883)
EMECO INDUSTRIES INC (PA)
805 W Elm Ave (17331-4706)
P.O. Box 179 (17331-0179)
PHONE..................................717 637-5951
Jay Buckbinder, *CEO*
Ronald D Lynne, *President*
◆ EMP: 28
SQ FT: 240,000
SALES (est): 5.9MM **Privately Held**
WEB: www.emeco.net
SIC: 2522 Chairs, office: padded or plain, except wood

(G-6884)
ESAB GROUP INC
Also Called: ESAB Welding & Cutting Pdts
801 Wilson Ave (17331-7948)
PHONE..................................717 637-8911
Nikola Culich, *Manager*
EMP: 300
SALES (corp-wide): 3.6B **Publicly Held**
WEB: www.esab.com
SIC: 3548 3823 3496 3315 Welding apparatus; industrial instrmnts msrmnt display/control process variable; miscellaneous fabricated wire products; steel wire & related products
HQ: The Esab Group Inc
2800 Airport Rd
Denton TX 76207
800 372-2123

(G-6885)
ESAB GROUP INC
Also Called: ESAB Welding & Cutting Pdts
1500 Karen Ln (17331-8122)
PHONE..................................843 673-7700
David Teston, *Manager*
EMP: 220
SQ FT: 200,000
SALES (corp-wide): 3.6B **Publicly Held**
WEB: www.esab.com
SIC: 3356 3548 3496 3315 Welding rods; welding apparatus; miscellaneous fabricated wire products; steel wire & related products
HQ: The Esab Group Inc
2800 Airport Rd
Denton TX 76207
800 372-2123

(G-6886)
ESAB GROUP INC
Also Called: ESAB Welding & Cutting Pdts
1500 Karen Ln (17331-8122)
PHONE..................................717 637-8911
Jhon Dillanburg, *Vice Pres*
EMP: 300
SALES (corp-wide): 3.6B **Publicly Held**
WEB: www.esab.com
SIC: 3548 Electric welding equipment; gas welding equipment
HQ: The Esab Group Inc
2800 Airport Rd
Denton TX 76207
800 372-2123

(G-6887)
FRAZIER MACHINE COMPANY INC
557 Centennial Ave (17331-3936)
PHONE..................................717 632-1101
Robin Bartlett Frazier, *President*
Donald Frazier, *Treasurer*
EMP: 6 EST: 2007
SALES (est): 29.7K **Privately Held**
SIC: 3541 Machine tools, metal cutting type

(G-6888)
GOOD HEALTH NATURAL PDTS INC (HQ)
900 High St (17331-1639)
PHONE..................................336 285-0735
Dylan Lissette, *CEO*
Jeff Martin, *President*
Thomas Lawrence, *Director*
Todd Staub, *Director*
▲ EMP: 15
SQ FT: 56,250
SALES (est): 22MM
SALES (corp-wide): 723.8MM **Privately Held**
SIC: 2096 Potato chips & other potato-based snacks; corn chips & other corn-based snacks
PA: Utz Quality Foods, Llc
900 High St
Hanover PA 17331
800 367-7629

(G-6889)
GREENLINE FOODS INC
26 Industrial Dr (17331-9531)
PHONE..................................717 630-9200
Jason Frost, *Branch Mgr*
EMP: 9
SALES (corp-wide): 524.2MM **Publicly Held**
SIC: 2033 Vegetables: packaged in cans, jars, etc.
HQ: Greenline Foods, Inc.
12700 S Dixie Hwy
Bowling Green OH 43402
419 354-1149

(G-6890)
HALF PINT CREAMERY LLC
3780 Centennial Rd (17331-8625)
PHONE..................................717 634-5459
EMP: 6 EST: 2013
SALES (est): 174.2K **Privately Held**
SIC: 2021 Creamery butter

(G-6891)
HAND CRAFTED FURNITURE CO INC (PA)
Also Called: Waltersdorff Mfg Co
237 Ridge Ave (17331-2030)
PHONE..................................717 630-0036
Daniel R Waltersdorff, *President*
EMP: 9
SQ FT: 72,000
SALES: 2MM **Privately Held**
SIC: 2431 Millwork

(G-6892)
HANOVER BRICK AND BLOCK CO
240 Bender Rd (17331-9079)
PHONE..................................717 637-0500
John Repasky, *President*
Christine Repasky, *Vice Pres*
EMP: 10
SQ FT: 3,000
SALES (est): 1.5MM **Privately Held**
SIC: 3271 Concrete block & brick

(G-6893)
HANOVER CONCRETE CO
2000 Carlisle Pike (17331-7745)
P.O. Box 156 (17331-0156)
PHONE..................................717 637-2288
G R Albright, *Principal*
EMP: 34
SALES (est): 6.2MM **Privately Held**
SIC: 3273 Ready-mixed concrete

(G-6894)
HANOVER FOODS CORPORATION (PA)
1486 York St (17331-7956)
P.O. Box 334 (17331-0334)
PHONE..................................717 632-6000
John A Warehime, *Ch of Bd*
Luis Camacho, *Prdtn Mgr*
Steve Wolfe, *Senior Buyer*
Jeff Shue, *QC Mgr*
Gary T Knisely, *CFO*
◆ EMP: 655
SQ FT: 5,161
SALES: 292MM **Publicly Held**
WEB: www.hanoverfoods.com
SIC: 2032 2037 2038 2099 Canned specialties; beans & bean sprouts, canned, jarred, etc.; macaroni: packaged in cans, jars, etc.; frozen fruits & vegetables; vegetables, quick frozen & cold pack, excl. potato products; frozen specialties; dinners, frozen & packaged; salads, fresh or refrigerated; vegetables: packaged in cans, jars, etc.

(G-6895)
HANOVER FOODS CORPORATION
1550 York St (17331-7958)
PHONE..................................800 888-4646
Jennifer Dutko, *Buyer*
Kent Spencer, *Sales Staff*
Alan Young, *Branch Mgr*
EMP: 500
SALES (corp-wide): 292MM **Publicly Held**
SIC: 2034 Dehydrated fruits, vegetables, soups
PA: Hanover Foods Corporation
1486 York St
Hanover PA 17331
717 632-6000

(G-6896)
HANOVER IRON WORKS INC
463 Gitts Run Rd (17331-9579)
PHONE..................................717 632-5624
Chris Morgret, *Principal*
EMP: 27
SQ FT: 17,000
SALES (est): 6.9MM **Privately Held**
WEB: www.hanoverironworks.com
SIC: 3446 3443 Railings, prefabricated metal; stairs, staircases, stair treads: prefabricated metal; columns (fractioning, etc.): metal plate

(G-6897)
HANOVER PEN CORP
Also Called: Hpc Global
14 Industrial Dr (17331-9531)
P.O. Box 503 (17331-0503)
PHONE..................................717 637-3729
Robert F Houghland, *President*
Cindy Robertson, *Credit Mgr*
Laura Yingling, *Sales Mgr*
Jane Houghland, *Admin Sec*
Sue Conroy, *Administration*
▲ EMP: 25 EST: 1968
SQ FT: 34,000
SALES (est): 7.7MM **Privately Held**
WEB: www.hpcmedx.com
SIC: 3951 3993 Ball point pens & parts; advertising novelties

(G-6898)
HANOVER POTATO PRODUCTS INC
60 Black Rock Rd (17331-4106)
P.O. Box 35 (17331-0035)
PHONE..................................717 632-0700
Kendra Kauffman, *President*
Jeffrey Kauffman, *Corp Secy*
EMP: 3 EST: 1959
SQ FT: 8,700
SALES (est): 331.3K **Privately Held**
SIC: 2099 Food preparations

(G-6899)
HANOVER PREST PAVING COMPANY
Also Called: Hanover Architectural Products
240 Bender Rd (17331-9080)
PHONE..................................717 637-0500
John Repasky, *President*

Christine Repasky, *Corp Secy*
Chris Slusser, *Sales Staff*
Patricia Rosner, *Manager*
Mike Miller, *Info Tech Mgr*
◆ **EMP:** 50
SQ FT: 3,000
SALES (est): 11.6MM **Privately Held**
SIC: 3272 Paving materials, prefabricated concrete

(G-6900)
HANOVER PREST-PAVING COMPANY
Also Called: HANOVER ARCHITECTURA
5000 Hanover Rd (17331-9077)
PHONE..................................717 637-0500
John Repasky, *President*
Christine Repasky, *Corp Secy*
Michelle Repasky, *Human Res Mgr*
Maresa Fisher, *Sales Staff*
Beth Gallagher, *Sales Staff*
◆ **EMP:** 50
SALES (est): 17.1MM **Privately Held**
WEB: www.hanoverpavers.com
SIC: 3559 3272 3271 2951 Concrete products machinery; concrete products; concrete block & brick; asphalt paving mixtures & blocks

(G-6901)
HANOVER PUBLISHING CO
Also Called: The Evening Sun
135 Baltimore St (17331-3111)
PHONE..................................717 637-3736
Doug Cooper, *CEO*
EMP: 140
SALES (est): 6MM
SALES (corp-wide): 4.2B **Privately Held**
WEB: www.eveningsun.com
SIC: 2711 Newspapers, publishing & printing
HQ: Medianews Group, Inc.
101 W Colfax Ave Ste 1100
Denver CO 80202

(G-6902)
HANOVER WIRE CLOTH
500 E Middle St (17331-2027)
PHONE..................................717 637-3795
Barry Douglas, *Principal*
EMP: 5
SALES (est): 627.5K **Privately Held**
SIC: 3496 Miscellaneous fabricated wire products

(G-6903)
INVENTURE FOODS INC (HQ)
900 High St (17331-1639)
PHONE..................................623 932-6200
Dylan B Lissette, *CEO*
Thomas J Flocco, *President*
Brian Foster, *Vice Pres*
Carrie Berger, *Project Mgr*
Sandip Parikh, *Research*
EMP: 271
SALES: 269MM
SALES (corp-wide): 723.8MM **Privately Held**
SIC: 2096 2037 Potato chips & similar snacks; fruits, quick frozen & cold pack (frozen)
PA: Utz Quality Foods, Llc
900 High St
Hanover PA 17331
800 367-7629

(G-6904)
IVAN C DUTTERER INC
115 Ann St (17331-4198)
PHONE..................................717 637-8977
Whitney J Coombs, *President*
Richard L Sasse, *Corp Secy*
EMP: 51 **EST:** 1954
SQ FT: 65,000
SALES (est): 7.9MM **Privately Held**
SIC: 2431 Doors, wood

(G-6905)
IWM INTERNATIONAL LLC (HQ)
500 E Middle St (17331-2027)
PHONE..................................717 637-3795
Guy Fritz, *President*
Lee Ann Seyler, *Purch Mgr*
▲ **EMP:** 123 **EST:** 1928
SQ FT: 225,000

SALES (est): 67.6MM
SALES (corp-wide): 380MM **Privately Held**
WEB: www.newyorkwireind.com
SIC: 3496 Miscellaneous fabricated wire products
PA: Phifer Incorporated
4400 Kauloosa Ave
Tuscaloosa AL 35401
205 345-2120

(G-6906)
J F ROHRBAUGH & CO
1030 Wilson Ave (17331-7961)
PHONE..................................800 800-4353
Bruce R Yelland, *Ch of Bd*
Steve Yelland, *President*
Timothy E Kiick, *CFO*
Timothy Kiick, *CFO*
Thomas Harbin, *Sales Mgr*
EMP: 55 **EST:** 1880
SQ FT: 55,000
SALES (est): 7.8MM **Privately Held**
WEB: www.jfrohrbaugh.com
SIC: 2448 2421 Pallets, wood; sawmills & planing mills, general

(G-6907)
JACOBS TOOL & MFG INC
210 N Blettner Ave Ste 5 (17331-4432)
PHONE..................................717 630-0083
Robert H Jacobs, *President*
Jason D Jacobs, *Corp Secy*
EMP: 6
SQ FT: 2,000
SALES (est): 600K **Privately Held**
SIC: 3599 Machine shop, jobbing & repair

(G-6908)
JANETTE JEWELERS
25 York St (17331-3106)
PHONE..................................717 632-9478
Janet Krenzer, *President*
Steven Krenzer, *Vice Pres*
Erik Krenzer, *Admin Sec*
EMP: 3
SQ FT: 1,000
SALES (est): 315.5K **Privately Held**
SIC: 5944 7631 3911 Jewelry, precious stones & precious metals; jewelry repair services; jewelry, precious metal

(G-6909)
KAPP ADVERTISING SERVICES INC
Also Called: Merchandiser
300 High St (17331-2301)
PHONE..................................717 632-8303
Joseph O'Brien, *Manager*
EMP: 17
SALES (corp-wide): 10.8MM **Privately Held**
WEB: www.themerchandiser.com
SIC: 2711 2741 Newspapers: publishing only, not printed on site; miscellaneous publishing
PA: Kapp Advertising Services, Inc.
100 E Cumberland St
Lebanon PA 17042
717 270-2742

(G-6910)
KLK WELDING INC
15 Barnhart Dr (17331-9589)
PHONE..................................717 637-0080
Kenneth L Kirkpatrick, *President*
Joshua Higgins, *Plant Mgr*
EMP: 17
SQ FT: 6,200
SALES (est): 2.1MM **Privately Held**
WEB: www.klkwelding.com
SIC: 1799 3312 Welding on site; stainless steel

(G-6911)
KOL INDUSTRIES INC
635 Maple Ave (17331-4626)
PHONE..................................717 630-0600
Robert Schatz, *President*
Mark Shaub, *Vice Pres*
EMP: 17
SQ FT: 51,000

SALES (est): 2.4MM **Privately Held**
WEB: www.kolindustries.com
SIC: 2541 1751 Cabinets, except refrigerated: show, display, etc.: wood; cabinet building & installation

(G-6912)
KUHN AUTO ELECTRIC
215 Linden Ave R (17331-4734)
PHONE..................................717 632-4197
Al Kuhn, *Owner*
EMP: 3
SALES (est): 130K **Privately Held**
WEB: www.kuhnautoelectric.com
SIC: 3694 Automotive electrical equipment

(G-6913)
LEGACY VULCAN LLC
Also Called: Hanover Quarry
875 Oxford Ave (17331-7743)
P.O. Box 468 (17331-0468)
PHONE..................................717 637-7121
Joseph Hurtack, *Manager*
EMP: 75 **Publicly Held**
WEB: www.vulcanmaterials.com
SIC: 1442 1422 Construction sand & gravel; crushed & broken limestone
HQ: Legacy Vulcan, Llc
1200 Urban Center Dr
Vestavia AL 35242
205 298-3000

(G-6914)
LEISTERS FURNITURE INC
433 Ridge Ave (17331-9512)
PHONE..................................717 632-8177
Thomas A Leister, *President*
Jay Persing, *Plant Mgr*
Barbara Kennedy, *Admin Sec*
EMP: 60
SQ FT: 125,000
SALES (est): 8MM **Privately Held**
SIC: 2511 Tables, household: wood

(G-6915)
LEONHARDT MANUFACTURING CO INC
800 High St (17331-1736)
PHONE..................................717 632-4150
Jason D Jacobs, *President*
Michael Benjamin, *Corp Secy*
Karen Kuhn, *Accounting Mgr*
EMP: 95
SQ FT: 95,000
SALES (est): 20MM **Privately Held**
WEB: www.tubebending.com
SIC: 7692 3498 3599 3471 Welding repair; tube fabricating (contract bending & shaping); machine shop, jobbing & repair; plating & polishing

(G-6916)
MAJER BRAND COMPANY INC (PA)
557 Centennial Ave (17331-3936)
PHONE..................................717 632-1320
Gordon Kramon, *President*
▲ **EMP:** 11 **EST:** 1942
SQ FT: 2,000
SALES (est): 4.6MM **Privately Held**
SIC: 2325 2311 Men's & boys' trousers & slacks; suits, men's & boys': made from purchased materials

(G-6917)
MARTIN DESIGN GROUP LLC
850 Vogelsong Rd (17331)
PHONE..................................717 633-9214
Jason Martin, *President*
EMP: 5
SALES (est): 510K **Privately Held**
SIC: 2759 Commercial printing

(G-6918)
MCCLARIN PLASTICS LLC (PA)
15 Industrial Dr (17331-9530)
P.O. Box 486 (17331-0486)
PHONE..................................717 637-2241
Jerry Armstrong, *President*
Robin Rebert, *Principal*
Michael J Clifford, *Vice Pres*
John W Kennedy, *Treasurer*
Wilma D Kennedy, *Admin Sec*
◆ **EMP:** 120 **EST:** 1952
SQ FT: 7,000

SALES (est): 64MM **Privately Held**
WEB: www.mcclarinplastics.com
SIC: 3083 Plastic finished products, laminated; thermoplastic laminates: rods, tubes, plates & sheet

(G-6919)
MEDIANEWS GROUP INC
Also Called: Evening Sun, The
135 Baltimore St (17331-3111)
P.O. Box 514 (17331-0514)
PHONE..................................717 637-3736
Lori Goodlin, *Partner*
EMP: 150
SALES (corp-wide): 4.2B **Privately Held**
SIC: 2711 2791 2759 2752 Commercial printing & newspaper publishing combined; typesetting; commercial printing; commercial printing, lithographic
HQ: Medianews Group, Inc.
101 W Colfax Ave Ste 1100
Denver CO 80202

(G-6920)
MILLER CHEMICAL & FERT CORP
120 Radio Rd (17331-1139)
PHONE..................................717 632-8921
Charles Svec, *President*
Anthony Hartlaub, *Treasurer*
Daniel Damstra, *Admin Sec*
EMP: 3
SALES (est): 6.7K **Privately Held**
SIC: 2879 Mfg Agricultural Chemicals

(G-6921)
MINUTEMAN PRESS OF HANOVER
955 Carlisle St Ofc Ofc (17331-1643)
PHONE..................................717 632-5400
Wendell Mulder, *Owner*
EMP: 6
SALES (est): 650.2K **Privately Held**
SIC: 2752 Commercial printing, lithographic

(G-6922)
MISCREATION BREWING
6 Center Sq (17331-3001)
PHONE..................................717 698-3666
Mark Mathias, *Partner*
Brent Stambaugh, *Partner*
Jason Stambaugh, *Partner*
EMP: 5
SALES (est): 293.3K **Privately Held**
SIC: 2082 Beer (alcoholic beverage)

(G-6923)
MORENO WELDING SERVICE
320 Maple Ave (17331-5120)
P.O. Box 994 (17331-6994)
PHONE..................................717 646-0000
Salvador Moreno, *Owner*
Mike Moreno, *Manager*
EMP: 8
SALES (est): 510K **Privately Held**
SIC: 7692 Welding repair

(G-6924)
MOTORAMA ASSOC
Also Called: Trailway Speedway
100 Speedway Ln (17331-8916)
PHONE..................................717 359-4310
Barry Hostetter, *Owner*
EMP: 5
SALES (est): 421.6K **Privately Held**
WEB: www.trail-wayspeedway.com
SIC: 7389 2721 Convention & show services; periodicals

(G-6925)
NEW WAY PACKAGING MACHINERY
210 N Blettner Ave Ste 1 (17331-4432)
PHONE..................................717 637-2133
Edward J Abendschein, *President*
Merle McMaster, *Engineer*
Edward Abendschein, *Network Mgr*
EMP: 7 **EST:** 1928
SQ FT: 43,500
SALES (est): 840K **Privately Held**
WEB: www.labeler.com
SIC: 3565 Packaging machinery

(G-6926)
NEW YORK WIRE COMPANY
500 E Middle St (17331-2027)
PHONE...................................717 637-3795
EMP: 139
SALES (corp-wide): 112.9MM Privately
Held
SIC: 2221 Mfg Synthetic Fabrics
PA: New York Wire Company
500 E Middle St
Hanover PA 17331
717 266-5626

(G-6927)
OX PAPER TUBE AND CORE INC (PA)
600 W Elm Ave (17331-5140)
PHONE...................................800 414-2476
Christopher F Keffer, President
Kathy R Keffer, Treasurer
Sphr A Hartlaub, Human Res Mgr
Elaine Rife, Sales Staff
Brian Emig, Sales Associate
▼ EMP: 45
SALES (est): 14.3MM Privately Held
WEB: www.oxpapertube.com
SIC: 2655 Tubes, fiber or paper: made
from purchased material

(G-6928)
OX PAPERBOARD LLC (PA)
331 Maple Ave (17331-5123)
P.O. Box 70, Halltown WV (25423-0070)
PHONE...................................304 725-2076
Matt Sullivan, Exec VP
Jennifer Brown, Vice Pres
Steven Carr, Regl Sales Mgr
Kevin J Hayward, Mng Member
Christopher Keffer,
EMP: 31
SALES (est): 22.7MM Privately Held
SIC: 2631 Paperboard mills

(G-6929)
PACKAGING CORPORATION AMERICA
Also Called: Pca/Baltimore, 306
435 Gitts Run Rd (17331-9579)
PHONE...................................301 497-9090
Diana Patterson, Sales Mgr
Curtis Smith, Sales Mgr
Kurtis Smith, Manager
Laurie Godfrey, Manager
EMP: 37
SALES (corp-wide): 7B Publicly Held
WEB: www.packagingcorp.com
SIC: 2653 Mfg Corrugated/Solid Fiber
Boxes
PA: Packaging Corporation Of America
1 N Field Ct
Lake Forest IL 60045
847 482-3000

(G-6930)
PACKAGING CORPORATION AMERICA
Also Called: PCA
401 Moulstown Rd (17331-9438)
PHONE...................................717 632-4800
EMP: 3
SALES (corp-wide): 7B Publicly Held
SIC: 2653 Corrugated & solid fiber boxes
PA: Packaging Corporation Of America
1 N Field Ct
Lake Forest IL 60045
847 482-3000

(G-6931)
PACKAGING CORPORATION AMERICA
Also Called: Pca/Hanover 331
435 Gitts Run Rd (17331-9579)
PHONE...................................717 637-3758
Peter Shovlin, Branch Mgr
Nina Kessler, Analyst
EMP: 50
SQ FT: 50,000
SALES (corp-wide): 7B Publicly Held
WEB: www.packagingcorp.com
SIC: 2653 Boxes, corrugated: made from
purchased materials
PA: Packaging Corporation Of America
1 N Field Ct
Lake Forest IL 60045
847 482-3000

(G-6932)
PCA CORRUGATED AND DISPLAY LLC
148 Penn St (17331-1952)
PHONE...................................800 572-6061
EMP: 9
SALES (corp-wide): 7B Publicly Held
SIC: 2653 Boxes, corrugated: made from
purchased materials
HQ: Pca Corrugated And Display Llc
1955 W Field Ct
Lake Forest IL 60045
847 482-3000

(G-6933)
PCA CORRUGATED AND DISPLAY LLC
148 Penn St (17331-1952)
PHONE...................................800 572-6061
EMP: 3
SALES (corp-wide): 7B Publicly Held
SIC: 2653 Boxes, corrugated: made from
purchased materials
HQ: Pca Corrugated And Display Llc
1955 W Field Ct
Lake Forest IL 60045
847 482-3000

(G-6934)
PCA CORRUGATED AND DISPLAY LLC
Also Called: Timbar Packaging & Display
401 Moulstown Rd (17331-9438)
PHONE...................................800 572-6061
Tom Staub, Plant Mgr
Robert Wagaman, Branch Mgr
EMP: 9
SALES (corp-wide): 7B Publicly Held
WEB: www.timbar.com
SIC: 2653 Boxes, corrugated: made from
purchased materials
HQ: Pca Corrugated And Display Llc
1955 W Field Ct
Lake Forest IL 60045
847 482-3000

(G-6935)
PENN MAR CASTINGS INC
Also Called: P M C
500 Broadway (17331-2001)
P.O. Box 1014 (17331-7014)
PHONE...................................717 632-4165
John F Lemmer, President
Nathaniel Burt, Vice Pres
William E Hester, Vice Pres
Douglas G Walker, Treasurer
Tracy Siegle, Sales Mgr
EMP: 80
SQ FT: 100,000
SALES (est): 20.8MM Privately Held
WEB: www.pennmarcastings.com
SIC: 3321 Gray iron castings

(G-6936)
PRECISION CUT INDUSTRIES INC (PA)
115 Ram Dr (17331-7783)
PHONE...................................717 632-2550
Brian S Greenplate, President
Richard S Lucas, Corp Secy
Dawn Hunt, Mfg Staff
Craig Schriver, Production
Christine Foltz, Controller
EMP: 99
SQ FT: 33,000
SALES (est): 35MM Privately Held
WEB: www.precisioncut.com
SIC: 3441 Fabricated structural metal

(G-6937)
PRETZEL LADY
113 S Blettner Ave (17331-5002)
PHONE...................................717 632-7046
Danial L Storm, Owner
Daniel L Storm, Owner
EMP: 5
SALES (est): 328.3K Privately Held
SIC: 2052 Pretzels

(G-6938)
PRO PAC INC
254 Obrien Ln (17331-7741)
PHONE...................................717 646-9555
Dennis Mills, President
EMP: 9 EST: 2001

SALES: 1.1MM Privately Held
WEB: www.pro-pac-pa.com
SIC: 2653 Boxes, corrugated: made from
purchased materials

(G-6939)
QUICK PRINT CENTER PA
16 Centennial Ave (17331-3513)
PHONE...................................717 637-2838
Peter Velencia, Owner
EMP: 6 EST: 1970
SQ FT: 12,700
SALES (est): 647.4K Privately Held
SIC: 2752 2759 2396 Commercial print-
ing, offset; commercial printing; automo-
tive & apparel trimmings

(G-6940)
R & G PRODUCTS INC
Also Called: Duracart
33 Amy Way (17331-6899)
PHONE...................................717 633-0011
Ron Heilig, President
EMP: 10
SQ FT: 10,000
SALES (est): 1MM Privately Held
WEB: www.duracart.com
SIC: 3089 Organizers for closets, drawers,
etc.: plastic

(G-6941)
R H SHEPPARD CO INC (HQ)
101 Philadelphia St (17331-2038)
P.O. Box 877 (17331-0877)
PHONE...................................717 637-3751
Oliver Hoar, President
John Paul, Counsel
Bud Miller, Vice Pres
Neil Poffenberger, Vice Pres
Bob Crouse, Plant Mgr
◆ EMP: 850 EST: 1945
SQ FT: 850,000
SALES (est): 139.1MM Publicly Held
WEB: www.rhsheppard.com
SIC: 3714 3321 3594 Gears, motor vehi-
cle; gray iron castings; ductile iron cast-
ings; pumps, hydraulic power transfer

(G-6942)
R H SHEPPARD CO INC
Also Called: Remanufacturing Division
447 E Middle St (17331-2543)
P.O. Box 877 (17331-0877)
PHONE...................................717 633-4106
Tom Senseney, Manager
EMP: 13 Publicly Held
WEB: www.rhsheppard.com
SIC: 3714 Gears, motor vehicle
HQ: R. H. Sheppard Co., Inc.
101 Philadelphia St
Hanover PA 17331
717 637-3751

(G-6943)
REVONAH PRETZEL LLC
1250 York St (17331-4503)
PHONE...................................717 632-4477
Kevin Biddelspach, President
EMP: 25
SQ FT: 48,000
SALES (est): 2.7MM Privately Held
WEB: www.revonahpretzel.com
SIC: 5145 2052 2099 Snack foods; pret-
zels; food preparations

(G-6944)
RILEY WELDING AND FABG INC
234 Poplar St (17331-2921)
PHONE...................................717 637-6014
John J Riley Jr, President
Josie Keffer, Corp Secy
J J Riley Sr, Vice Pres
Andrea M Taylor, Vice Pres
EMP: 17
SQ FT: 20,000
SALES (est): 3.7MM Privately Held
WEB: www.rileywelding.com
SIC: 7692 Welding repair

(G-6945)
ROCHER INCORPORATED
1856 Dubs Church Rd (17331-8581)
PHONE...................................717 637-9320
EMP: 3 EST: 2006
SALES (est): 212.4K Privately Held
SIC: 2434 Wood kitchen cabinets

(G-6946)
ROLLER PRINTING COMPANY INC
2 Industrial Dr (17331-9531)
PHONE...................................717 632-1433
James Roller, President
Marie Roller, Vice Pres
Geraldine Carbough, Admin Sec
EMP: 8
SQ FT: 2,080
SALES (est): 610K Privately Held
SIC: 2752 Commercial printing, offset

(G-6947)
S E HAGARMAN DESIGNS LLC
207 Eichelberger St (17331-2232)
PHONE...................................717 633-5336
Stacey Hagarman, Mng Member
▲ EMP: 5
SALES (est): 370K Privately Held
SIC: 2771 2621 Greeting cards; paper
mills

(G-6948)
S-L SNACKS REAL ESTATE INC
Also Called: Soh
1250 York St (17331-4503)
P.O. Box 6917 (17331-0917)
PHONE...................................717 632-4477
Carl E Lee, President
Ed Good, Vice Pres
Charles E Good, Treasurer
Shirley Thomas, Business Anlyst
▼ EMP: 2400
SQ FT: 37,800
SALES (est): 1.5MM
SALES (corp-wide): 8.6B Publicly Held
SIC: 2052 2096 Pretzels; potato chips &
other potato-based snacks; corn chips &
other corn-based snacks; tortilla chips
HQ: Snyder's-Lance, Inc.
13515 Balntyn Corp Pl
Charlotte NC 28277
704 554-1421

(G-6949)
SEALED AIR CORPORATION
260 N Blettner Ave (17331-4501)
P.O. Box 337 (17331-0337)
PHONE...................................717 637-5905
Doug Barbour, Manager
Brian Shea, Info Tech Mgr
EMP: 110
SQ FT: 600,000
SALES (corp-wide): 4.7B Publicly Held
WEB: www.sealedair.com
SIC: 2673 Bags: plastic, laminated &
coated
PA: Sealed Air Corporation
2415 Cascade Pointe Blvd
Charlotte NC 28208
980 221-3235

(G-6950)
SHERIDAN GROUP INC (HQ)
450 Fame Ave (17331-1585)
PHONE...................................717 632-3535
John A Saxton, President
Gary Kittredge, President
Robert M Jakobe, CFO
Rob Daniels, Manager
◆ EMP: 61
SQ FT: 10,628
SALES (est): 390MM
SALES (corp-wide): 514.8MM Privately
Held
WEB: www.sheridan.com
SIC: 2752 2732 Commercial printing, off-
set; books: printing & binding
PA: Cjk Group, Inc.
3323 Oak St
Brainerd MN 56401
218 829-2877

(G-6951)
SHERIDAN PRESS INC
450 Fame Ave (17331-1585)
P.O. Box 465 (17331-0465)
PHONE...................................717 632-3535
John A Saxton, CEO
Patricia A Stricker, President
Dennis Smith, Vice Pres
James D Smith, Vice Pres
J M D Hall, Admin Sec
▲ EMP: 4 EST: 1915
SQ FT: 104,000

SALES (est): 97.6MM
SALES (corp-wide): 514.8MM **Privately Held**
WEB: www.sheridan.com
SIC: 2752 Commercial printing, offset
HQ: The Sheridan Group Inc
450 Fame Ave
Hanover PA 17331
717 632-3535

(G-6952)
SIGNS NOW
643 Frederick St (17331-5007)
PHONE....................717 633-5864
Barry B Horst, *Owner*
EMP: 3
SQ FT: 3,200
SALES: 265K **Privately Held**
SIC: 3993 Signs & advertising specialties

(G-6953)
SKF USA INC
Also Called: SKF Hanover
20 Industrial Dr (17331-9531)
PHONE....................717 637-8981
William Helfrich, *QC Mgr*
Richard Hopkins, *Engineer*
Bonnie Sutton, *Engineer*
Steve Teletnick, *Engineer*
Jeffrey Wirfel, *Project Engr*
EMP: 200
SALES (corp-wide): 9.2B **Privately Held**
WEB: www.skfusa.com
SIC: 3568 7538 Bearings, bushings &
blocks; engine repair
HQ: Skf Usa Inc.
890 Forty Foot Rd
Lansdale PA 19446
267 436-6000

(G-6954)
SNYDERS HANOVER MFG INC
1350 York St (17331-7949)
PHONE....................800 233-7125
Michael A Warehime, *Principal*
EMP: 3
SALES (est): 272.4K **Privately Held**
SIC: 2052 Pretzels

(G-6955)
SNYDERS-LANCE INC
1250 York St (17331-4503)
P.O. Box 6917 (17331-0917)
PHONE....................717 632-4477
Dan Klunk, *Engineer*
Melissa Hess, *Human Res Mgr*
Kristin Blake, *Manager*
Douglas Snyder, *Manager*
Seth Beyer, *Technology*
EMP: 76
SALES (corp-wide): 8.6B **Publicly Held**
SIC: 2052 Pretzels
HQ: Snyder's-Lance, Inc.
13515 Balntyn Corp Pl
Charlotte NC 28277
704 554-1421

(G-6956)
SOMETHING WICKED BREWING LLC
34 Broadway (17331-3104)
PHONE....................717 316-5488
Bridget Seidler, *Manager*
EMP: 3
SALES (est): 68.6K **Privately Held**
SIC: 2082 Brewers' grain

(G-6957)
SONOCO PRODUCTS COMPANY
Also Called: Sonoco Consumer Products
310 Pine St (17331-2353)
PHONE....................717 637-2103
Bob Rohrbaugh, *Sales Mgr*
Brett Loadholt, *Manager*
EMP: 115
SALES (corp-wide): 5.3B **Publicly Held**
WEB: www.sonoco.com
SIC: 2655 Containers, laminated phenolic
& vulcanized fiber; containers, liquid tight
fiber: from purchased material
PA: Sonoco Products Company
1 N 2nd St
Hartsville SC 29550
843 383-7000

(G-6958)
STAMBAUGH METAL INC
802 High St (17331-1714)
PHONE....................717 632-5957
Dane Stambaugh, *President*
EMP: 50
SALES (est): 7.3MM **Privately Held**
WEB: www.metalsfinishing.com
SIC: 3441 3471 3444 Fabricated struc-
tural metal; plating & polishing; sheet met-
alwork

(G-6959)
SUBURBAN DEER DEFENSE LLC
1196 Moulstown Rd N (17331-6853)
PHONE....................717 632-8844
Dana Falls, *Principal*
EMP: 3
SALES (est): 248.2K **Privately Held**
SIC: 3812 Defense systems & equipment

(G-6960)
T BAIRD MCILVAIN COMPANY
Also Called: TBM Hardwoods
370 Poplar St (17331-2369)
PHONE....................717 630-0025
Thomas B McIlvain, *Ch of Bd*
Thomas B McIlvain III, *Vice Pres*
John Gallatig, *Treasurer*
Sheila Hertz, *Controller*
Elaine Dettinourn, *Admin Sec*
◆ **EMP:** 153 EST: 1955
SALES (est): 27.6MM **Privately Held**
SIC: 2421 Sawmills & planing mills, gen-
eral

(G-6961)
TODDS SNAX INC
Also Called: Shultz Food Company
680 W Chestnut St (17331-7802)
P.O. Box 993 (17331-6993)
PHONE....................717 637-5931
David Humbert, *President*
David Humbert Jr, *General Mgr*
▼ **EMP:** 220 EST: 1962
SQ FT: 110,000
SALES (est): 23.9MM **Privately Held**
WEB: www.shultzfoods.com
SIC: 2052 2099 Pretzels; food prepara-
tions

(G-6962)
TRENTON GROUP INC (PA)
2000 Carlisle Pike (17331-7745)
P.O. Box 156 (17331-0156)
PHONE....................717 637-2288
G Ronald Albright, *President*
David R Albright, *Vice Pres*
Michelle M Albright, *Treasurer*
Bonita L Albright, *Admin Sec*
EMP: 40 EST: 1946
SALES (est): 4MM **Privately Held**
WEB: www.hanoverconcrete.com
SIC: 3273 Ready-mixed concrete

(G-6963)
TWO COUSINS HOLDINGS LLC
Also Called: Catridge World, LLC
1000 Carlisle St Ste 1350 (17331-1191)
PHONE....................717 637-1311
Darryll Landis, *President*
Tom Landis, *President*
Thomas E Landis, *Principal*
EMP: 3
SQ FT: 1,000
SALES: 350K **Privately Held**
SIC: 2893 Printing ink

(G-6964)
UNITED ELECTRIC SUPPLY CO INC
550 W Elm Ave (17331-5138)
PHONE....................717 632-7640
Bob Crawford, *Principal*
EMP: 3
SALES (corp-wide): 201.7MM **Privately Held**
WEB: www.unitedelectric.com
SIC: 3645 5063 Residential lighting fix-
tures; lighting fixtures
PA: United Electric Supply Company, Inc.
10 Bellecor Dr
New Castle DE 19720
800 322-3374

(G-6965)
UTZ QUALITY FOODS INC
900 High St (17331-1639)
P.O. Box 338 (17331-0338)
PHONE....................717 637-6644
Michael Rice, *President*
Dwayne Schultheis, *District Mgr*
Michael Summa, *District Mgr*
Dylan Lissette, *Senior VP*
Ed Burda, *Vice Pres*
EMP: 58
SALES (corp-wide): 723.8MM **Privately Held**
WEB: www.utzsnacks.com
SIC: 2096 2099 Potato chips & other po-
tato-based snacks; food preparations
PA: Utz Quality Foods, Llc
900 High St
Hanover PA 17331
800 367-7629

(G-6966)
UTZ QUALITY FOODS INC
1437 Broadway (17331-1514)
P.O. Box 338 (17331-0338)
PHONE....................717 637-5666
Larry Reindollar, *Vice Pres*
Fritz Lidelseerger, *Manager*
EMP: 150
SQ FT: 2,400
SALES (corp-wide): 723.8MM **Privately Held**
WEB: www.utzsnacks.com
SIC: 2052 2096 2099 Pretzels; popcorn,
already popped (except candy covered);
food preparations
PA: Utz Quality Foods, Llc
900 High St
Hanover PA 17331
800 367-7629

(G-6967)
UTZ QUALITY FOODS LLC (PA)
900 High St (17331-1639)
P.O. Box 338 (17331-0338)
PHONE....................800 367-7629
Michael W Rice, *President*
Tom Flocco, *President*
Tim Doran, *Regional Mgr*
Brian Greth, *Vice Pres*
Dylan Lissette, *Vice Pres*
◆ **EMP:** 1100 EST: 1947
SQ FT: 500,000
SALES (est): 723.8MM **Privately Held**
WEB: www.utzsnacks.com
SIC: 2096 2052 2099 Potato chips &
other potato-based snacks; corn chips &
other corn-based snacks; cheese curls &
puffs; popcorn, already popped (except
candy covered); pretzels; cookies; food
preparations

(G-6968)
UTZ QUALITY FOODS LLC
25 Wyndfield Dr (17331-8482)
PHONE....................717 698-4032
M Rice, *Branch Mgr*
EMP: 265
SALES (corp-wide): 723.8MM **Privately Held**
SIC: 2096 Potato chips & other potato-
based snacks
PA: Utz Quality Foods, Llc
900 High St
Hanover PA 17331
800 367-7629

(G-6969)
VISION TECHNOLOGY UHS LLC
513 Highland Ave (17331-1921)
PHONE....................717 465-0694
Jim Williams, *President*
James Williams, *Master*
▼ **EMP:** 4
SQ FT: 5,200
SALES: 400K **Privately Held**
SIC: 2842 2869 2819 Floor waxes; indus-
trial organic chemicals; industrial inor-
ganic chemicals

(G-6970)
W H COOKE & CO INC
6868 York Rd (17331-6814)
P.O. Box 893 (17331-0893)
PHONE....................717 630-2222
Wayne H Cooke Jr, *President*

Dan Feeser, *Purchasing*
Matt Wootton, *Sales Staff*
▲ **EMP:** 8
SQ FT: 8,000
SALES (est): 5.1MM **Privately Held**
WEB: www.whcooke.com
SIC: 5065 3823 Electronic parts; thermo-
couples, industrial process type

(G-6971)
WALTERSDORF MANUFACTURING CO
237 Ridge Ave (17331-2030)
PHONE....................717 630-0036
Daniel Waltersdorff, *President*
EMP: 9
SQ FT: 72,000
SALES: 2MM **Privately Held**
WEB: www.waltersdorff.com
SIC: 2499 Decorative wood & woodwork
PA: Hand Crafted Furniture Company, Inc.
237 Ridge Ave
Hanover PA 17331

(G-6972)
WEAVER SCREEN PRINTING INC
24 Baltimore St (17331-3137)
PHONE....................717 632-9158
Joel Weaver, *President*
Karen Weaver, *Admin Sec*
EMP: 3 EST: 1972
SQ FT: 2,200
SALES: 467K **Privately Held**
SIC: 2759 Screen printing

(G-6973)
WEGE PRETZEL CO INC
116 N Blettner Ave (17331-4433)
PHONE....................717 843-0738
Anthony L Laughman, *President*
Stephen D Laughman, *Vice Pres*
Edith Staub, *Vice Pres*
EMP: 85 EST: 1875
SQ FT: 103,000
SALES (est): 8MM
SALES (corp-wide): 292MM **Publicly Held**
WEB: www.wege.com
SIC: 2052 Pretzels
PA: Hanover Foods Corporation
1486 York St
Hanover PA 17331
717 632-6000

(G-6974)
WEL-MAC INC
Also Called: Feltch's Machine Shop
231 Baltimore St (17331-3203)
P.O. Box 1127 (17331-7127)
PHONE....................717 637-6921
John Laughman, *President*
John Feltch, *President*
EMP: 5
SQ FT: 10,800
SALES (est): 683.3K **Privately Held**
SIC: 3599 7699 7692 Custom machinery;
industrial machinery & equipment repair;
welding repair

(G-6975)
WIERMAN DILLER INC
20 W Park Ave (17331-2428)
PHONE....................717 637-3871
Matthew D Wireman, *President*
Judith A Wierman, *Admin Sec*
Hazel Wierman, *Asst Sec*
EMP: 9 EST: 1779
SQ FT: 20,000
SALES (est): 1.3MM **Privately Held**
SIC: 3444 1711 Ducts, sheet metal;
plumbing contractors; warm air heating &
air conditioning contractor

(G-6976)
WILKE ENGINUITY INC
250 Obrien Ln (17331-7741)
PHONE....................717 632-5937
Julia A Wilke, *President*
Fred Wilke, *Corp Secy*
Fred Wilke III, *Vice Pres*
EMP: 20
SQ FT: 28,000
SALES (est): 3.6MM **Privately Held**
WEB: www.wilkeenginuity.com
SIC: 3599 Machine shop, jobbing & repair;
machine & other job shop work

(G-6977)
WIRE COMPANY HOLDINGS INC
Also Called: New York Wire
500 E Middle St (17331-2027)
PHONE...........................717 637-3795
Guy E Fritz Jr, *CEO*
Frank T Gaiteri Jr, *Vice Pres*
Robert Kervian, *CFO*
John D Caley, *Manager*
EMP: 475
SALES (est): 49.5MM **Privately Held**
SIC: 3496 Woven wire products

Hanover Township
Luzerne County

(G-6978)
A RIFKIN CO
1400 Sans Souci Pkwy (18706-6097)
P.O. Box 878, Wilkes Barre (18703-0878)
PHONE...........................570 825-9551
Paul D Lantz, *President*
Bill Culver, *General Mgr*
Arnold Rifkin, *Chairman*
Larry Lantz, *Purch Agent*
Donald Casterline, *Engineer*
◆ EMP: 100 EST: 1892
SQ FT: 70,000
SALES (est): 15.2MM **Privately Held**
WEB: www.arifkin.com
SIC: 2393 Bags & containers, except
sleeping bags: textile

(G-6979)
BEDWICK AND JONES
PRINTING INC
425 New Commerce Blvd (18706-1436)
P.O. Box 1046, Wilkes Barre (18703-1046)
PHONE...........................570 829-1951
Alex E Rogers, *President*
Margaret Jones, *Vice Pres*
Raymond G Bedwick, *Treasurer*
Jane Keller, *Accounts Mgr*
William Wierbowski, *Graphic Designe*
EMP: 16 EST: 1961
SQ FT: 10,000
SALES (est): 4.2MM **Privately Held**
WEB: www.bedwickandjones.com
SIC: 2752 Commercial printing, offset

(G-6980)
BENNY BREWING COMPANY
LLC
1429 Sans Souci Pkwy (18706-6025)
PHONE...........................570 235-6995
Ben Schonfeld, *Principal*
Matt Scartozzi, *Webmaster*
EMP: 4 EST: 2016
SALES (est): 75.4K **Privately Held**
SIC: 2082 Beer (alcoholic beverage)

(G-6981)
BLASI PRINTING INC
Also Called: Barre Engraving Co
1490 Sans Souci Pkwy (18706-6026)
P.O. Box 1162, Wilkes Barre (18703-1162)
PHONE...........................570 824-3557
Michael Blassi, *President*
EMP: 13
SALES (est): 1.7MM **Privately Held**
WEB: www.blasiprinting.com
SIC: 7389 2752 Engraving service; com-
mercial printing, offset

(G-6982)
BRIDON-AMERICAN
CORPORATION (DH)
280 New Commerce Blvd (18706-1497)
PHONE...........................570 822-3349
Chris Dugan, *CEO*
Sue Mergo, *Purch Agent*
Joseph Simkulak, *CFO*
▲ EMP: 358
SQ FT: 4,000
SALES (est): 371.3MM
SALES (corp-wide): 799.4K **Privately
Held**
WEB: www.bridonamerican.com
SIC: 3533 3532 5084 Oil & gas field ma-
chinery; mining machinery; cranes, indus-
trial

HQ: Bridon International Ltd.
Icon Building First Point
Doncaster DN4 5
130 256-5100

(G-6983)
CANVAS SPECIALTIES INC
785 Hazle St (18706-2319)
PHONE...........................570 825-9282
Joseph Yeslavich, *President*
Andrea Yeslavich, *Corp Secy*
EMP: 5
SQ FT: 6,000
SALES (est): 632.8K **Privately Held**
SIC: 2394 5949 5714 Awnings, fabric:
made from purchased materials; liners &
covers, fabric: made from purchased ma-
terials; fabric stores piece goods; uphol-
stery materials

(G-6984)
CCL TUBE INC
Also Called: CCL Container
1 Lasley Ave (18706-1427)
PHONE...........................570 824-8485
Steve Kinkade, *Manager*
Nicole Miller, *Data Proc Staff*
Debbie Otoole, *Executive*
EMP: 100
SALES (corp-wide): 3.7B **Privately Held**
WEB: www.ccltubes.com
SIC: 3089 3083 Air mattresses, plastic;
laminated plastics plate & sheet
HQ: Ccl Tube, Inc.
2250 E 220th St
Carson CA 90810
310 635-4444

(G-6985)
CERTECH INC
Also Called: Morgan Technical Ceramics
550 Stewart Rd (18706-1455)
PHONE...........................570 823-7400
John Stang, *Branch Mgr*
EMP: 150
SALES (corp-wide): 1.3B **Privately Held**
SIC: 3255 Foundry refractories, clay
HQ: Certech Inc
1 Park Pl W
Wood Ridge NJ 07075
201 842-6800

(G-6986)
CHAUCER PRESS INC
535 Stewart Rd (18706-1454)
PHONE...........................570 825-2005
Patricia A Frances, *President*
Frank A Franzo, *COO*
EMP: 52 EST: 1965
SQ FT: 60,000
SALES (est): 14.4MM **Privately Held**
WEB: www.chaucerpress.com
SIC: 2752 Commercial printing, offset; flex-
ographic printing

(G-6987)
DALTECH INC
1420 Sans Souci Pkwy (18706-6026)
PHONE...........................570 823-9911
Eric Rodeghiero, *President*
EMP: 30
SQ FT: 7,000
SALES: 1.3MM **Privately Held**
SIC: 3599 3549 Machine shop, jobbing &
repair; metalworking machinery

(G-6988)
DMS SHREDDING INC
9 Fellows Ave Rear (18706-5231)
P.O. Box 1022, Wilkes Barre (18703-1022)
PHONE...........................570 819-3339
Louis Denaples, *President*
EMP: 12
SALES (est): 2MM **Privately Held**
WEB: www.dmsshredding.com
SIC: 3449 5093 Miscellaneous metalwork;
scrap & waste materials

(G-6989)
HARTE HANKS INC
Also Called: Harte-Hanks Direct Marketing
165 New Commerce Blvd (18706-1439)
PHONE...........................570 826-0414
Norman Sallitt, *Manager*
EMP: 150

SALES (corp-wide): 284.6MM **Publicly
Held**
SIC: 2741 2759 2671 Miscellaneous publishing; commercial printing; packaging
paper & plastics film, coated & laminated
PA: Harte Hanks, Inc.
9601 Mcallister Fwy # 610
San Antonio TX 78216
210 829-9000

(G-6990)
INTEGRATED POWER DESIGNS
INC
Also Called: I P D
300 Stewart Rd (18706-1459)
PHONE...........................570 824-4666
Steve Thompson, *President*
Arnold Thompson, *Principal*
Mike Floersch, *Engineer*
Diane Thompson, *Treasurer*
Jim Kelley, *Sales Staff*
▲ EMP: 100
SQ FT: 60,000
SALES (est): 18.4MM **Privately Held**
WEB: www.ipdpower.com
SIC: 3679 Electronic circuits

(G-6991)
KOEHLER-BRIGHT STAR LLC
380 Stewart Rd (18706-1459)
PHONE...........................570 825-1900
Mark Dusa, *President*
Curt Rodenhouse, *Treasurer*
Laurie Cywinski, *VP Finance*
Robert Webb, *Admin Sec*
◆ EMP: 40 EST: 1996
SQ FT: 65,000
SALES (est): 9.4MM
SALES (corp-wide): 225.3B **Publicly
Held**
SIC: 3641 3648 Lamps, incandescent fila-
ment, electric; flashlights
HQ: The Marmon Group Llc
181 W Madison St Ste 2600
Chicago IL 60602

(G-6992)
LEGGETT & PLATT
INCORPORATED
Also Called: Leggett & Platt 0071
1655 Sans Souci Pkwy (18706-6089)
PHONE...........................570 824-6622
Eric Rose, *Plant Mgr*
Cliff Hess, *Engr R&D*
Darry Mingus, *Manager*
EMP: 60
SQ FT: 60,000
SALES (corp-wide): 4.2B **Publicly Held**
WEB: www.leggett.com
SIC: 2515 Mattresses & bedsprings
PA: Leggett & Platt, Incorporated
1 Leggett Rd
Carthage MO 64836
417 358-8131

(G-6993)
MANCHESTER INDUSTRIES INC
VA
175 Stewart Rd (18706-1462)
PHONE...........................570 822-9308
Jerry Gazinfki, *Manager*
EMP: 22 **Publicly Held**
SIC: 2679 Pressed fiber & molded pulp
products except food products
HQ: Manchester Industries Inc. Of Virginia
200 Orleans St
Richmond VA 23231
804 226-4250

(G-6994)
ME 5 CENTS LLC
1429 Sans Souci Pkwy (18706-6025)
PHONE...........................570 574-4701
Benjamin Schonfeld,
EMP: 15 EST: 2014
SQ FT: 6,000
SALES (est): 919K **Privately Held**
SIC: 2082 5812 Malt beverages; American
restaurant

(G-6995)
MEDICO INDUSTRIES INC
1060 Hanover St (18706-2000)
PHONE...........................570 208-3140
EMP: 113

SALES (corp-wide): 72.9MM **Privately
Held**
SIC: 3489 Artillery or artillery parts, over 30
mm.
PA: Medico Industries, Inc.
1500 Highway 315 Blvd
Wilkes Barre PA 18702
570 825-7711

(G-6996)
MEDICO INDUSTRIES INC
1060 Hanover St (18706-2000)
PHONE...........................570 825-7711
EMP: 28
SALES (corp-wide): 72.9MM **Privately
Held**
SIC: 3489 5211 3795 3483 Artillery or ar-
tillery parts, over 30 mm.; electrical con-
struction materials; tanks & tank
components; ammunition, except for
small arms; iron & steel forgings
PA: Medico Industries, Inc.
1500 Highway 315 Blvd
Wilkes Barre PA 18702
570 825-7711

(G-6997)
MICHAEL MOOTZ CANDIES INC
1246 Sans Souci Pkwy (18706-5230)
PHONE...........................570 823-8272
Michael Mootz, *President*
EMP: 10
SQ FT: 5,200
SALES (est): 750K **Privately Held**
WEB: www.michaelmootzcandies.com
SIC: 5441 2064 Candy; candy & other
confectionery products

(G-6998)
MT DISPLAYS LLC
1081 Hanover St (18706-2028)
PHONE...........................201 636-4144
EMP: 15 EST: 2013
SALES (est): 1.7MM
SALES (corp-wide): 32.9MM **Privately
Held**
SIC: 3993 Signs & advertising specialties
PA: M.T Reklam Anonim Sirketi
No:1 Cumhuriyet Mahallesi
Kocaeli 41400
262 658-8880

(G-6999)
NARDONE BROTHERS BAKING
CO
Also Called: Nardone Bros
420 New Commerce Blvd (18706-1445)
PHONE...........................570 823-0141
Vincent Nardone, *President*
Frank Nardone, *Vice Pres*
Louis J Nardone, *CFO*
Mario Nardone, *Treasurer*
Ula Kalinowski, *Sales Staff*
▲ EMP: 225 EST: 1915
SQ FT: 10,000
SALES (est): 60.5MM **Privately Held**
SIC: 2038 5812 2099 Pizza, frozen; eat-
ing places; food preparations

(G-7000)
NEWTOWN-SLOCOMB MFG INC
(PA)
767 Sans Souci Pkwy (18706-1330)
PHONE...........................570 825-3675
Colin Slocomb, *President*
EMP: 34 EST: 1997
SQ FT: 67,000
SALES (est): 10MM **Privately Held**
WEB: www.slocombwindows.com
SIC: 3089 5211 5031 Plastic hardware &
building products; lumber & other building
materials; lumber, plywood & millwork

(G-7001)
NEWTOWN-SLOCOMB MFG INC
Also Called: Slocomb Windows & Doors
767 Sans Souci Pkwy (18706-1330)
PHONE...........................570 825-3675
Randy Overcash, *VP Sales*
EMP: 8
SALES (corp-wide): 10MM **Privately
Held**
SIC: 3089 5211 5031 Air mattresses,
plastic; lumber products; building materi-
als, exterior

GEOGRAPHIC

PA: Newtown-Slocomb Manufacturing, Inc.
767 Sans Souci Pkwy
Hanover Township PA 18706
570 825-3675

(G-7002)
P R X
1065 Hanover St (18706-2031)
PHONE..............................570 578-0136
EMP: 4
SALES (est): 272.7K **Privately Held**
SIC: 2741 Miscellaneous publishing

(G-7003)
PENN POWER GROUP LLC
Also Called: Penn Power Systems
1081 Hanover St (18706-2028)
PHONE..............................570 208-1192
Payne, *Branch Mgr*
EMP: 25
SALES (corp-wide): 92MM **Privately Held**
SIC: 3519 Internal combustion engines
PA: Penn Power Group, Llc
8330 State Rd
Philadelphia PA 19136
215 335-0500

(G-7004)
POCONO MOUNTAIN LEATHER CO (PA)
Also Called: P M L C
44 E Saint Marys Rd (18706-4103)
PHONE..............................570 814-6672
Carmen D Cesari, *Principal*
EMP: 7
SALES (est): 640.3K **Privately Held**
SIC: 2386 Garments, leather

(G-7005)
SAVELLO USA INCORPORATED
1265 Sans Souci Pkwy (18706-5229)
PHONE..............................570 822-9743
Cesare Gallo, *President*
Palma Gallo, *Corp Secy*
Nick Gallo, *Vice Pres*
Anna Gallo, *Mktg Coord*
▲ EMP: 14
SQ FT: 52,000
SALES (est): 2.6MM **Privately Held**
WEB: www.savellousa.com
SIC: 2099 5141 Food preparations; gro-
ceries, general line

(G-7006)
STANDARD AWNINGS & ALUMINUM
799 Hazle St (18706-2319)
PHONE..............................570 824-3535
Joesph Yesalavich, *President*
Andrea Yesalavich, *Corp Secy*
EMP: 6 EST: 1946
SQ FT: 8,000
SALES: 250K **Privately Held**
WEB: www.standardawning.com
SIC: 3444 5211 Awnings, sheet metal;
doors, storm: wood or metal; windows,
storm: wood or metal

(G-7007)
WILKES BARRE BURIAL VAULT
Also Called: Von-Crete
628 Nanticoke St (18706-5247)
PHONE..............................570 824-8268
Terry A Vonderheid, *Owner*
Mary Ann Husted, *Office Mgr*
EMP: 15
SQ FT: 200
SALES: 1MM **Privately Held**
SIC: 3272 7261 Burial vaults, concrete or
precast terrazzo; crematory

Harborcreek
Erie County

(G-7008)
PORT ERIE PLASTICS INC (PA)
909 Troupe Rd (16421-1018)
PHONE..............................814 899-7602
William C Witkowski, *President*
John T Johnson, *President*
Cheryl Fahey, *Vice Pres*
▲ EMP: 245 EST: 1953

SQ FT: 300,000
SALES (est): 54.9MM **Privately Held**
WEB: www.porterie.com
SIC: 3089 Molding primary plastic; injec-
tion molding of plastics

(G-7009)
PORT ERIE PLASTICS INC
1350 Troupe Rd (16421-1032)
PHONE..............................814 899-7602
Joe Connell, *Branch Mgr*
EMP: 5
SALES (corp-wide): 54.9MM **Privately Held**
SIC: 3089 Injection molding of plastics
PA: Port Erie Plastics, Inc.
909 Troupe Rd
Harborcreek PA 16421
814 899-7602

Harding
Luzerne County

(G-7010)
COLD CASE BEVERAGE LLC
710 Apple Tree Rd (18643-7033)
PHONE..............................570 388-2297
EMP: 3
SALES (est): 204K **Privately Held**
SIC: 3523 Farm machinery & equipment

Harleysville
Montgomery County

(G-7011)
A AND M TOOL LLC
106 Fairway Dr (19438-2517)
PHONE..............................215 513-0968
Adam Andrews,
EMP: 3
SALES (est): 233K **Privately Held**
SIC: 3545 Cutting tools for machine tools

(G-7012)
ACE COMPANY
19 Kratz Rd (19438-3501)
PHONE..............................215 234-4615
John T Wright, *Owner*
EMP: 3
SALES (est): 540K **Privately Held**
SIC: 2891 Adhesives

(G-7013)
ADVANCED STAIR SYSTEMS - PENNS
1547 Gehman Rd (19438-2930)
PHONE..............................215 256-7981
Steven Guenzel,
Bonnie Guenzel,
▲ EMP: 12 EST: 2007
SALES (est): 1.9MM **Privately Held**
SIC: 2431 Stair railings, wood

(G-7014)
AGAPE WATER SOLUTIONS INC
1567 Gehman Rd (19438-2930)
PHONE..............................215 631-7035
Jeffrey Tate, *President*
▼ EMP: 8
SQ FT: 6,500
SALES (est): 1.7MM **Privately Held**
WEB: www.agapewater.com
SIC: 3589 Water treatment equipment, in-
dustrial

(G-7015)
ALCOM PRINTING GROUP INC
140 Christopher Ln (19438-2034)
P.O. Box 570 (19438-0570)
PHONE..............................215 513-1600
William Kuplen, *President*
Dave Bitting, *President*
Don Eichman, *Vice Pres*
Douglas Yeager, *Vice Pres*
Rocco Misero Treas, *CFO*
▲ EMP: 155
SQ FT: 39,000

SALES (est): 58.6MM **Privately Held**
WEB: www.alcomprinting.com
SIC: 2752 2791 2789 Commercial printing, offset; typesetting; bookbinding & related work

(G-7016)
ALDERFER INC (HQ)
382 Main St (19438-2310)
P.O. Box 2 (19438-0002)
PHONE..............................215 256-8819
James Vanstone, *President*
Thomas Leidy, *Vice Pres*
EMP: 60 EST: 1922
SQ FT: 30,000
SALES (est): 22.7MM
SALES (corp-wide): 77.5MM **Privately Held**
WEB: www.alderfermeats.com
SIC: 5147 2013 Meats, fresh; cured meats
from purchased meat
PA: All Holding Company Inc.
382 Main St
Harleysville PA 19438
215 256-8818

(G-7017)
ALLIANCE CONTRACT PHARMA LLC
1510 Delp Dr (19438-2900)
PHONE..............................215 256-5920
Stephen L Schweibenz, *President*
Stephen Clanton, *Vice Pres*
Shawn J Connaghan, *Vice Pres*
Shawn Connaghan, *Vice Pres*
Benjamin W Reed, *Vice Pres*
EMP: 11
SQ FT: 30,000
SALES (est): 2.2MM **Privately Held**
SIC: 2834 8734 Pills, pharmaceutical;
testing laboratories

(G-7018)
AMETEK INC
343 Godshall Dr (19438-2007)
PHONE..............................267 933-2121
Tim Lynch, *Senior Engr*
Don Furmanski, *Sales Staff*
Keith Reazin, *Branch Mgr*
Thomas Garrigus, *Manager*
Alan McCouch, *Manager*
EMP: 68
SALES (corp-wide): 4.8B **Publicly Held**
SIC: 3812 3825 3724 3728 Search &
navigation equipment; instruments to
measure electricity; aircraft engines & en-
gine parts; aircraft parts & equipment
PA: Ametek, Inc.
1100 Cassatt Rd
Berwyn PA 19312
610 647-2121

(G-7019)
AMETEK INC
Also Called: Ametek- Arspc Div Pwr Data Sys
343 Godshall Dr (19438-2007)
PHONE..............................267 933-2121
Keith Reazin, *Branch Mgr*
EMP: 45
SALES (corp-wide): 4.8B **Publicly Held**
SIC: 3812 3825 3724 3728 Search &
navigation equipment; instruments to
measure electricity; aircraft engines & en-
gine parts; aircraft parts & equipment
PA: Ametek, Inc.
1100 Cassatt Rd
Berwyn PA 19312
610 647-2121

(G-7020)
AMETEK INC
Ametek Pittman
343 Godshall Dr (19438-2007)
PHONE..............................215 256-6601
Todd Schlegel, *Plant Mgr*
Sam Wright, *Purch Mgr*
Dave Croll, *Manager*
Beth Prikockis, *Network Mgr*
Diane Simkins, *Technician*
EMP: 68
SALES (corp-wide): 4.8B **Publicly Held**
SIC: 3621 2892 3625 3566 Motors, elec-
tric; emulsions (explosive); relays & in-
dustrial controls; speed changers, drives
& gears

PA: Ametek, Inc.
1100 Cassatt Rd
Berwyn PA 19312
610 647-2121

(G-7021)
AUTOMATIC CONTROL ELEC CO
Also Called: Ace-Co
220 Stahl Rd (19438-1911)
P.O. Box 200264, San Antonio TX (78220-0264)
PHONE..............................210 661-4111
Dan Faubel, *President*
George M Cox, *Advisor*
EMP: 11 EST: 1961
SQ FT: 14,000
SALES (est): 2.4MM **Privately Held**
WEB: www.ace-co.com
SIC: 3823 3822 3625 Industrial instrmnts
msrmnt display/control process variable;
auto controls regulating residntl & coml
environmt & applncs; relays & industrial
controls

(G-7022)
AUTOMTED CONVEYING SYSTEMS INC
1551 Gehman Rd (19438-2930)
PHONE..............................215 368-0500
Ray Cassel, *President*
Steven Thomas, *Corp Secy*
EMP: 5
SQ FT: 13,000
SALES (est): 746.7K **Privately Held**
SIC: 3535 Conveyors & conveying equip-
ment

(G-7023)
BEC SYSTEMS INC
Also Called: BEC Machine Products
100 Christopher Ln (19438-2034)
PHONE..............................215 256-3100
Earl C Bulgier, *President*
Mike Steever, *General Mgr*
Todd Haldeman, *Foreman/Supr*
▲ EMP: 25
SQ FT: 16,000
SALES (est): 5.3MM **Privately Held**
WEB: www.becsystems.com
SIC: 3599 Machine shop, jobbing & repair

(G-7024)
CAREER COMMUNICATIONS INC
Also Called: CCI
303 Maple Ave Ste 4 (19438-2261)
P.O. Box 169 (19438-0169)
PHONE..............................215 256-3130
Steven A Wood, *President*
Michele A Wood, *Treasurer*
Michele Wood, *Executive*
EMP: 3
SALES (est): 277.6K **Privately Held**
WEB: www.careerbookstore.com
SIC: 8732 2721 Business research serv-
ice; statistical reports (periodicals): pub-
lishing only

(G-7025)
CESSNA INDUSTRIES
2188 Old Skippack Rd (19438-1368)
P.O. Box 136, Salfordville (18958-0136)
PHONE..............................610 636-9282
Ronald J Cessna, *Principal*
EMP: 3
SALES (est): 242.3K **Privately Held**
SIC: 3999 Manufacturing industries

(G-7026)
CHADWICK OPTICAL INC
1557 Gehman Rd (19438-2930)
P.O. Box 485, White River Junction VT (05001-0485)
PHONE..............................267 203-8665
Karen Keeney, *President*
EMP: 9
SQ FT: 4,500
SALES: 750K **Privately Held**
WEB: www.chadwickoptical.com
SIC: 3851 Mountings, eyeglass & specta-
cle; intraocular lenses

(G-7027)
CHOP - RITE TWO INC
531 Old Skippack Rd (19438-2203)
PHONE..............................215 256-4620
Nancy Saeger, *President*

▲ = Import ▼=Export
◆ =Import/Export

Donald Saeger, *Vice Pres*
Michael Saeger, *Vice Pres*
Tammy Snyder, *Admin Sec*
EMP: 15 **EST:** 1958
SQ FT: 2,500
SALES (est): 1.8MM **Privately Held**
WEB: www.chop-rite.com
SIC: 3556 Grinders, commercial, food

(G-7028)
CLOSET CITY LTD
Also Called: Closets & Cabinetry By Closet
352 Godshall Dr Ste A (19438-2017)
P.O. Box 779, Montgomeryville (18936-0779)
PHONE.................................215 855-4400
Marvin Hamburg, *President*
John Witlin, *Vice Pres*
Joanne Landis, *Marketing Staff*
Adele Bywaters, *Manager*
Amber Reynolds, *Technology*
EMP: 19
SQ FT: 10,000
SALES (est): 2.8MM **Privately Held**
WEB: www.closetcity.com
SIC: 2434 Wood kitchen cabinets

(G-7029)
COLORCON INC
275 Ruth Rd (19438-1952)
PHONE.................................215 256-7700
William Motzer, *CEO*
Knut Fenner, *General Mgr*
Joe Casey, *Business Mgr*
Michelle Custred, *Business Mgr*
John Jaworski, *Business Mgr*
EMP: 19
SALES (corp-wide): 2.9B **Privately Held**
SIC: 2834 Pharmaceutical preparations
HQ: Colorcon, Inc.
420 Moyer Blvd
West Point PA 19486
215 699-7733

(G-7030)
DERBYSHIRE MARINE PRODUCTS LLC
100 Christopher Ln (19438-2034)
PHONE.................................267 222-8900
Brian Derbyshire,
EMP: 5
SALES (est): 860.3K **Privately Held**
SIC: 3494 3561 Valves & pipe fittings; pumps & pumping equipment

(G-7031)
EAST COAST METALS INC
171 Ruth Rd Ste C (19438-1808)
P.O. Box 8 (19438-0008)
PHONE.................................215 256-9550
Joseph Saner, *President*
Barbara Saner, *Vice Pres*
Bill Talbot, *Buyer*
EMP: 35
SQ FT: 26,500
SALES (est): 21.7MM **Privately Held**
WEB: www.eastcoastmetals.com
SIC: 5051 3452 3312 Bars, metal; bolts, metal; nuts, metal; blast furnaces & steel mills

(G-7032)
EDWARD J DESETA CO INC
1510 Gehman Rd (19438-2929)
PHONE.................................302 691-2040
Bernadette D Buccini, *President*
Christopher F Buccini, *Vice Pres*
Donato R Buccini, *Vice Pres*
Robert E Buccini, *Vice Pres*
▲ **EMP:** 125 **EST:** 1960
SQ FT: 75,000
SALES (est): 29.5MM **Privately Held**
SIC: 1761 3444 Sheet metalwork; sheet metalwork

(G-7033)
EXPANSION SEAL TECHNOLOGIES
334 Godshall Dr (19438-2008)
PHONE.................................215 513-4300
Carol Haigh, *Principal*
EMP: 3
SALES (est): 240.2K **Privately Held**
SIC: 3494 Pipe fittings

(G-7034)
GLAXOSMITHKLINE LLC
570 Centre Ct (19438-2170)
PHONE.................................610 270-5836
EMP: 26
SALES (corp-wide): 39.8B **Privately Held**
SIC: 2834 Pharmaceutical preparations
HQ: Glaxosmithkline Llc
5 Crescent Dr
Philadelphia PA 19112
215 751-4000

(G-7035)
GUNSMITHS STAINLESS CLG RODS
431 Gruber Rd (19438-1716)
PHONE.................................215 256-9208
Jerry Beard, *Owner*
EMP: 3
SALES (est): 104.9K **Privately Held**
SIC: 3484 Guns (firearms) or gun parts, 30 mm. & below

(G-7036)
H P CADWALLADER INC
175 Ruth Rd (19438-1823)
PHONE.................................215 256-6651
Y P Cadwallader, *President*
Al Hanover, *Vice Pres*
▲ **EMP:** 37
SQ FT: 44,000
SALES (est): 8.3MM **Privately Held**
SIC: 2653 Boxes, corrugated: made from purchased materials; sheets, corrugated: made from purchased materials

(G-7037)
HARLEYSVILLE MATERIALS LLC
460 Indian Creek Rd (19438-2119)
P.O. Box 587, Berlin NJ (08009-0587)
PHONE.................................856 768-8493
Dave Smith, *Mng Member*
EMP: 15
SALES (est): 1.4MM **Privately Held**
SIC: 1499 Asphalt mining & bituminous stone quarrying

(G-7038)
HERITAGE MAINTENANCE PDTS LLC
1537 Gehman Rd (19438-2930)
P.O. Box 2178, Blue Bell (19422-0509)
PHONE.................................610 277-5070
John Munera,
Matthew Munera,
EMP: 5
SQ FT: 1,600
SALES (est): 420K **Privately Held**
WEB: www.heritagemaintenance.com
SIC: 3469 Machine parts, stamped or pressed metal

(G-7039)
HERITAGE TRUCK EQUIPMENT LLC
201 Ruth Rd (19438-1825)
P.O. Box 410, Dublin (18917-0410)
PHONE.................................215 256-0951
Eric L Bontrager,
Brian Bontrager,
EMP: 7
SALES (est): 768.4K **Privately Held**
SIC: 3713 Truck bodies & parts

(G-7040)
ISABELLES KITCHEN INC
Also Called: Salad Specialty
417 Main St (19438-2311)
P.O. Box 20, Mainland (19451-0020)
PHONE.................................215 256-7987
Anthony Pupillo, *President*
Vincent Pupillo, *Vice Pres*
Michelle A Cianchetta, *Treasurer*
Nicholas Pupillo, *Admin Sec*
EMP: 60
SQ FT: 15,000
SALES (est): 15.3MM **Privately Held**
WEB: www.isabelleskitchen.com
SIC: 2099 Tortillas, fresh or refrigerated; dessert mixes & fillings; ready-to-eat meals, salads & sandwiches; salads, fresh or refrigerated

(G-7041)
JACOB SCHMIDT & SON INC
1936 Sumneytown Pike (19438-1147)
PHONE.................................215 234-4641
Jacob Schmidt Jr, *President*
Carol Schmidt, *Corp Secy*
Dean F Wampole, *Vice Pres*
Laura Schmidt, *Admin Sec*
EMP: 15
SQ FT: 30,000
SALES (est): 2.8MM **Privately Held**
WEB: www.jschmidtstainless.com
SIC: 3599 5072 5251 Ties, form: metal; hardware; hardware

(G-7042)
JLI ELECTRONICS INC
2080 Detwiler Rd Ste 2a (19438-2911)
P.O. Box 7 (19438-0007)
PHONE.................................215 256-3200
Mark Strong, *President*
Brad Confer, *Opers Mgr*
▲ **EMP:** 4
SQ FT: 8,000
SALES (est): 765.7K **Privately Held**
WEB: www.jlielectronics.com
SIC: 3571 Electronic computers

(G-7043)
KELLERS CREAMERY LLC (HQ)
855 Maple Ave (19438-1031)
P.O. Box 1365, Kulpsville (19443-1365)
PHONE.................................215 256-8871
Frank J Otis,
EMP: 70
SQ FT: 6,500
SALES (est): 23MM
SALES (corp-wide): 14.6B **Privately Held**
WEB: www.kellerscreamery.com
SIC: 2021 2023 Creamery butter; dry, condensed, evaporated dairy products; condensed, concentrated & evaporated milk products
PA: Dairy Farmers Of America, Inc.
1405 N 98th St
Kansas City KS 66111
816 801-6455

(G-7044)
LANSDALE PACKAGED ICE INC
Also Called: Lansdale Ice
2080 Detwiler Rd Ste 4 (19438-2911)
PHONE.................................215 256-8808
EMP: 19
SALES (est): 2.4MM **Privately Held**
SIC: 2097 Mfg Ice

(G-7045)
MARCHO FARMS INC
176 Orchard Ln (19438-1681)
PHONE.................................215 721-7131
Wayne A Marcho, *President*
Martha G Marcho, *Vice Pres*
Wayne Marcho, *Treasurer*
▼ **EMP:** 140 **EST:** 1968
SQ FT: 10,000
SALES (est): 21.9MM **Privately Held**
SIC: 2011 Veal from meat slaughtered on site

(G-7046)
MARTECH MEDICAL PRODUCTS INC (PA)
1500 Delp Dr (19438-2900)
PHONE.................................215 256-8833
David Markel, *President*
Donna Wolfe, *President*
Derrick Moyer, *QC Mgr*
Jack McMahon, *Engineer*
Nick Noell, *Engineer*
EMP: 23
SQ FT: 13,000
SALES (est): 38.8MM **Privately Held**
WEB: www.martechmedical.com
SIC: 3069 3842 3083 Medical & laboratory rubber sundries & related products; surgical appliances & supplies; laminated plastics plate & sheet

(G-7047)
MAXPOWER INC (PA)
141 Christopher Ln (19438-2035)
PHONE.................................215 256-4575
David L Chua, *President*
Dr Hsiu-Ping Lin, *Vice Pres*
Dr Shiow-Chuan Lin, *Treasurer*

Marilyn Chua, *Admin Sec*
EMP: 16
SQ FT: 8,000
SALES (est): 2.8MM **Privately Held**
SIC: 3691 8731 Batteries, rechargeable; energy research

(G-7048)
MIKE STECK
Also Called: Cottage Woodworks
868 Skippack Rd (19438-1465)
PHONE.................................610 287-3518
Mike Steck, *Owner*
EMP: 8 **EST:** 1998
SQ FT: 100,000
SALES (est): 770K **Privately Held**
WEB: www.cottagewoodworks.com
SIC: 2499 Decorative wood & woodwork

(G-7049)
NATURAL MARKETING INST INC
272 Ruth Rd Fl 1 (19438-1927)
PHONE.................................215 513-7300
Mary Ellen Molyneaux, *President*
Steven French, *Treasurer*
Michael Molyneaux, *Admin Sec*
EMP: 23
SQ FT: 5,700
SALES (est): 2.3MM **Privately Held**
SIC: 2721 Statistical reports (periodicals): publishing & printing

(G-7050)
OUTLOOK PRINTING SOLUTIONS INC
2279 Shelly Rd (19438-1220)
PHONE.................................215 680-4014
Mark T Cox, *President*
EMP: 4 **EST:** 2010
SALES (est): 494.6K **Privately Held**
SIC: 2752 Commercial printing, lithographic

(G-7051)
PECORA CORPORATION
165 Wambold Rd (19438-2014)
PHONE.................................215 723-6051
Joseph F Virdone, *CEO*
Robert L Hartzell, *Corp Secy*
Wayne Waters, *Vice Pres*
Robert Heim, *CFO*
◆ **EMP:** 120 **EST:** 1862
SQ FT: 63,000
SALES (est): 58MM **Privately Held**
WEB: www.pecora.com
SIC: 2891 Sealants
PA: Navigation Capital Partners, Inc.
3060 Peachtree Rd Nw
Atlanta GA 30305

(G-7052)
PERRY PRINTING
776 Moccasin Dr (19438-1623)
PHONE.................................215 256-8074
Harrison Perry, *Owner*
EMP: 3
SALES: 250K **Privately Held**
SIC: 2752 Commercial printing, lithographic

(G-7053)
R F CIRCUITS & CAD SERVICES
1500 Breckenridge Pl (19438-3061)
PHONE.................................215 368-6483
Sunil Patel, *Owner*
EMP: 4 **EST:** 2001
SALES (est): 255.4K **Privately Held**
SIC: 3679 Electronic circuits

(G-7054)
R T CALLAHAN MACHINE PDTS INC
230 Stahl Rd (19438-1911)
PHONE.................................215 256-8765
Marie Beebe, *President*
Timothy P Callahan, *Vice Pres*
EMP: 4 **EST:** 1961
SQ FT: 3,000
SALES: 400K **Privately Held**
SIC: 3599 Machine shop, jobbing & repair

(G-7055)
RESPONSELOGIX INC
220 Stahl Rd (19438-1911)
PHONE.................................215 256-1700

G E O G R A P H I C

EMP: 21
SALES (corp-wide): 27.7MM **Privately Held**
SIC: 7373 3823 Computer-aided manufacturing (CAM) systems service; controllers for process variables, all types
PA: Responselogix, Inc.
6991 E Camelback Rd B300
Scottsdale AZ 85251
408 220-6545

(G-7056)
SAEGER MACHINE INC
Also Called: Saeger Machine and Welding
531 Old Skippack Rd (19438-2203)
PHONE..................................215 256-8754
Nancy Saeger, *President*
Don Saeger, *Vice Pres*
Donald Saeger, *Vice Pres*
Michael Saeger, *Vice Pres*
EMP: 13 **EST:** 1961
SQ FT: 3,000
SALES (est): 2.2MM **Privately Held**
WEB: www.saegermachine.com
SIC: 3599 7692 3444 Machine shop, jobbing & repair; welding repair; sheet metalwork

(G-7057)
SCS INC
Also Called: Sable Calibration Services
1523 Gehman Rd (19438-2930)
PHONE..................................866 727-4436
Kathleen Sable, *President*
EMP: 9
SALES (est): 1.5MM **Privately Held**
SIC: 3826 Analytical instruments

(G-7058)
SILVER SPRINGS FARM INC
640 Meetinghouse Rd (19438-2247)
P.O. Box 268 (19438-0268)
PHONE..................................215 256-4321
Daniel T Fillippo, *President*
EMP: 35
SQ FT: 35,000
SALES (est): 5.9MM **Privately Held**
SIC: 2011 2013 Meat packing plants; prepared beef products from purchased beef

(G-7059)
SOFTKOG INC
Also Called: Victoria Leather Company
691 Sumneytown Pike Ste G (19438-1264)
PHONE..................................717 490-1091
Erik Nadeau, *President*
Deanna Nadeau, *Vice Pres*
EMP: 9
SQ FT: 3,000
SALES (est): 656.3K **Privately Held**
SIC: 3171 Women's handbags & purses

(G-7060)
SUBURBAN NEWSPAPER OF AMERICA
304 Morgan Way (19438-2023)
PHONE..................................215 513-4145
Al Cupo, *Principal*
EMP: 3 **EST:** 2010
SALES (est): 115.5K **Privately Held**
SIC: 2711 Newspapers

(G-7061)
SWIRLING SILKS INC
310 Broad St Ste H (19438-2399)
PHONE..................................610 584-5595
Karen Lowe, *President*
EMP: 9
SQ FT: 1,250
SALES (est): 1MM **Privately Held**
WEB: www.swirlingsilks.com
SIC: 2399 Banners, pennants & flags

(G-7062)
TOPIT TOPPINGS LLC
1535 Gehman Rd (19438-2930)
PHONE..................................267 263-2590
EMP: 3
SALES (est): 72.3K **Privately Held**
SIC: 2024 Ice cream & frozen desserts

(G-7063)
V2R2 LLC
Also Called: CD Hardware
672 Main St Ste D (19438-1678)
PHONE..................................215 277-2181

Joseph Moukalled, *President*
EMP: 3
SALES (est): 160.2K **Privately Held**
SIC: 3599 3429 Bellows, industrial: metal; metal fasteners

Harmonsburg
Crawford County

(G-7064)
SIGNATURE VACUUM SYSTEMS INC
10358 Harmonsburg Rd (16422)
P.O. Box 190 (16422-0190)
PHONE..................................814 333-1110
Timothy Horning, *President*
Greg Kimble, *President*
EMP: 9
SALES (est): 1.8MM **Privately Held**
SIC: 3567 Industrial furnaces & ovens

(G-7065)
TARGET PRECISION
10314 Harmonsburg Rd (16422)
P.O. Box 346 (16422-0346)
PHONE..................................814 382-3000
Eric Kinter, *Partner*
Gary Bell, *Partner*
Ron Sousae, *Partner*
Lorrie Devillars, *Office Mgr*
EMP: 18
SQ FT: 6,500
SALES (est): 3MM **Privately Held**
WEB: www.targetprecision.com
SIC: 3089 Injection molding of plastics

Harmony
Butler County

(G-7066)
APT ADVANCED POLYMER TECH CORP (PA)
109 Conica Ln (16037)
P.O. Box 160 (16037-0160)
PHONE..................................724 452-1330
Andreas Schulze Ising, *CEO*
Michael Beyer, *President*
Wesley Baum, *Research*
Jarod Sterrett, *Research*
Rob Carey, *Controller*
▲ **EMP:** 68
SQ FT: 50,000
SALES (est): 31.3MM **Privately Held**
WEB: www.advpolytech.com
SIC: 2851 2821 3949 2822 Paints & allied products; acrylic resins; sporting & athletic goods; synthetic rubber

(G-7067)
FOSSIL ROCK LLC
102 Kotchey Ln (16037-8322)
PHONE..................................724 355-3747
Leslie Kirby McConnell, *Owner*
EMP: 5
SALES (est): 1.2MM **Privately Held**
SIC: 1382 Oil & gas exploration services

(G-7068)
HARMONY PAPER COMPANY LLC
352 Fanker Rd (16037-9222)
PHONE..................................724 991-1110
Jay A Grinnell, *Mng Member*
▲ **EMP:** 2
SQ FT: 1,200
SALES (est): 1MM **Privately Held**
SIC: 2621 Fine paper

(G-7069)
HENDERSON CONSTRUCTION FABRICS
753 Perry Hwy (16037-8713)
PHONE..................................724 368-1145
Matthew Henderson, *President*
EMP: 5
SALES (est): 447.7K **Privately Held**
SIC: 2295 Coated fabrics, not rubberized

(G-7070)
JADCO MANUFACTURING INC (PA)
167 Evergreen Mill Rd (16037-7619)
P.O. Box 465, Zelienople (16063-0465)
PHONE..................................724 452-5252
James A Davison, *CEO*
Susan Z Davison, *Corp Secy*
Scott Kay, *Maint Spvr*
Jodie Dugan, *Human Res Mgr*
Michael Hillery, *Sales Staff*
▲ **EMP:** 50
SQ FT: 15,000
SALES (est): 34.1MM **Privately Held**
WEB: www.jadco-inc.com
SIC: 5051 3564 3312 3448 Steel; blowers & fans; slabs, steel; buildings, portable: prefabricated metal

(G-7071)
JM INDUSTRIES INC
232 E Lancaster Rd (16037-7302)
PHONE..................................724 452-6060
Jill Marburger, *President*
EMP: 4
SALES (est): 402.9K **Privately Held**
SIC: 3069 Linings, vulcanizable rubber

(G-7072)
LASER HAIR ENHANCEMEN
748 Spring St (16037-7636)
PHONE..................................724 591-5670
Beth Polack, *Owner*
William Zillweger, *Director*
EMP: 4
SALES (est): 241K **Privately Held**
SIC: 3845 Laser systems & equipment, medical

(G-7073)
MAIN STEEL LLC
Also Called: Main Steel - Harmony 6010
6 Whitney Dr (16037-7748)
P.O. Box 277 (16037-0277)
PHONE..................................724 453-3000
Dave Yundt, *Branch Mgr*
EMP: 60
SALES (corp-wide): 1.8B **Privately Held**
SIC: 3471 Finishing, metals or formed products
HQ: Main Steel, Llc
2200 Pratt Blvd
Elk Grove Village IL 60007
847 916-1220

(G-7074)
NEW BERRY INC
Also Called: Berry Metal Co
2408 Evans City Rd (16037-7724)
PHONE..................................724 452-8040
Douglas Behling, *Sr Project Mgr*
EMP: 11
SALES (corp-wide): 21.6MM **Privately Held**
WEB: www.berrymetal.com
SIC: 3548 3433 Welding & cutting apparatus & accessories; heating equipment, except electric
PA: New Berry, Inc.
2408 Evans City Rd
Harmony PA 16037
724 452-8040

(G-7075)
PROGRESSIVE POWER TECH LLC
Also Called: Woodings Industrial
100 Precision Dr (16037-7622)
P.O. Box 430, Mars (16046-0430)
PHONE..................................724 452-6064
Robert T Woodings, *Principal*
▲ **EMP:** 17
SQ FT: 120,000
SALES (est): 2.9MM **Privately Held**
WEB: www.woodingsindustrial.com
SIC: 3612 Transformers, except electric

(G-7076)
SMALL PARTS MACHINE INC
252 Mercer Rd (16037-9112)
PHONE..................................724 452-6116
Donald Cravener, *President*
Nancy Cravener, *Corp Secy*
EMP: 4
SQ FT: 6,500

SALES (est): 536.1K **Privately Held**
WEB: www.smallpartsmachine.com
SIC: 3599 Machine shop, jobbing & repair

Harrisburg
Dauphin County

(G-7077)
310 PUBLISHING LLC
Also Called: America In Wwii
4711 Queen St Ste 202 (17109-3125)
PHONE..................................717 564-0161
Heidi Kushlan,
James Kushlan,
EMP: 6
SALES (est): 450K **Privately Held**
WEB: www.americainwwii.com
SIC: 2721 Magazines: publishing & printing

(G-7078)
A & R NISSLEY INC
Also Called: Nissley Vineyards Wine Shop
22 Colonial Park Mall (17109-6220)
PHONE..................................717 541-1004
EMP: 5
SALES (corp-wide): 3.3MM **Privately Held**
SIC: 2084 Mfg Wines/Brandy/Spirits
PA: A & R Nissley Inc
140 Vintage Dr
Bainbridge PA 17502
717 426-3514

(G-7079)
A CLASS CORP
1303 Market St 1 (17103-2232)
PHONE..................................717 695-0597
Rick Collotia, *Principal*
EMP: 3
SALES (est): 209.6K **Privately Held**
SIC: 3999 Cigarette & cigar products & accessories

(G-7080)
ABBOTT LABORATORIES
Also Called: Ross Products Division
2405 Melbourne Dr (17112-1086)
PHONE..................................717 545-8159
Jerry Ellsesser, *Principal*
EMP: 100
SALES (corp-wide): 30.5B **Publicly Held**
WEB: www.abbott.com
SIC: 2834 Druggists' preparations (pharmaceuticals)
PA: Abbott Laboratories
100 Abbott Park Rd
Abbott Park IL 60064
224 667-6100

(G-7081)
ABES BAKERY
1330 Marion St (17102-1722)
PHONE..................................717 232-1330
A David Kopeland, *Principal*
EMP: 4
SALES (est): 244.4K **Privately Held**
SIC: 2051 Bread, cake & related products

(G-7082)
ACUMIX INC (PA)
805 Harrogate Dr (17111-6892)
P.O. Box 6867 (17112-0867)
PHONE..................................717 540-9738
Beth S Lipkin, *CEO*
Andrew Romano III, *Exec VP*
EMP: 7
SALES (est): 500K **Privately Held**
SIC: 3531 Mixers: ore, plaster, slag, sand, mortar, etc.

(G-7083)
ADVANCED COMPOSITE PDTS INC
1740 Mulberry St (17104-1245)
PHONE..................................717 232-8237
Kerry N Hitt, *President*
EMP: 25
SQ FT: 35,000
SALES (est): 3.8MM **Privately Held**
WEB: www.corvetteracebodies.com
SIC: 3089 Molding primary plastic

▲ = Import ▼ =Export
◆ =Import/Export

(G-7084)
ADVANCED EDUCATION SERVICE
3820 Walnut St (17109-2532)
PHONE..................................717 545-8633
EMP: 7
SALES (est): 550K **Privately Held**
SIC: 7372 Prepackaged Software Services

(G-7085)
ALLEGRA MKTG PRINT MAIL 408
Also Called: Allegra Print
6951 Allentown Blvd Ste D (17112-3374)
PHONE..................................717 839-6390
Andy Orons, *Principal*
Jo Orons, *CFO*
Tracy McCracken, *Accounts Exec*
EMP: 4
SALES (est): 239K **Privately Held**
SIC: 2752 Commercial printing, offset

(G-7086)
AMES TRUE TEMPER INC
1500 S Cameron St (17104-3143)
PHONE..................................717 231-7856
Michael Griffie, *Plant Engr Mgr*
Cindy Bell, *Personnel*
Kevin Kelley, *Branch Mgr*
Rob Evinger, *Manager*
EMP: 61
SALES (corp-wide): 1.5B **Publicly Held**
WEB: www.ames.com
SIC: 3423 Garden & farm tools, including shovels
HQ: The Ames Companies Inc
    465 Railroad Ave
    Camp Hill PA 17011
    717 737-1500

(G-7087)
APPALACHIAN BREWING CO INC
50 N Cameron St (17101-2407)
PHONE..................................717 221-1080
Shawn Gallagher, *CEO*
Jack Sproch, *Corp Secy*
Tim Dunkle, *Sales Mgr*
EMP: 65
SQ FT: 55,000
SALES (est): 9.9MM **Privately Held**
WEB: www.abcbrew.com
SIC: 2082 5812 Beer (alcoholic beverage); eating places

(G-7088)
APPAREL PRINT PROMOTIONALS
5010 Linglestown Rd (17112-9198)
PHONE..................................717 233-4277
David Cobb, *President*
EMP: 4
SQ FT: 10,000
SALES (est): 77.7K **Privately Held**
SIC: 2752 5112 Commercial printing, offset; stationery & office supplies

(G-7089)
APPLIED RES & PHOTONICS INC
Also Called: Arp
470 Friendship Rd Ste 10 (17111-1211)
PHONE..................................717 220-1003
Anis Rahman, *President*
EMP: 3
SALES (est): 50K **Privately Held**
WEB: www.arphotonics.net
SIC: 3826 3845 Spectrometers; ultrasonic scanning devices, medical

(G-7090)
ART COMMUNICATION SYSTEMS INC
Also Called: ACS
1340 N 17th St (17103-1248)
PHONE..................................717 232-0144
Park L Cook, *President*
David Cook, *Vice Pres*
EMP: 38
SQ FT: 6,000
SALES (est): 6.3MM **Privately Held**
WEB: www.artcomsys.com
SIC: 2752 7336 Commercial printing, offset; graphic arts & related design

(G-7091)
ART STITCH INC
1308 N Mountain Rd (17112-1756)
PHONE..................................717 652-8992
Leslie Fleg, *President*
Thomas Fleig, *Vice Pres*
EMP: 4
SALES (est): 320.4K **Privately Held**
SIC: 2395 2269 Embroidery products, except schiffli machine; finishing plants

(G-7092)
ARTWORKS SILK SCREEN PRINTERS
4379 N 6th St (17110-1614)
PHONE..................................717 238-5087
Sephi Itzhaki, *Owner*
Clare Itzhaki, *Partner*
Claire Itzhaki, *Co-Owner*
EMP: 4
SQ FT: 8,000
SALES (est): 300K **Privately Held**
SIC: 2341 7336 Women's & children's underwear; commercial art & illustration

(G-7093)
AUTOMTED LGIC CORP KENNESAW GA
6345 Flank Dr Ste 100 (17112-4602)
PHONE..................................717 909-7000
Rick Abney, *Project Mgr*
Marie Disanti, *Project Mgr*
Brian King, *Project Mgr*
Laura Melnick, *Project Mgr*
Ilya Rabinovich, *Senior Buyer*
EMP: 9
SALES (corp-wide): 66.5B **Publicly Held**
SIC: 3625 Electric controls & control accessories, industrial
HQ: Automated Logic Corporation, Kennesaw, Ga
    1150 Roberts Blvd Nw
    Kennesaw GA
    770 421-3280

(G-7094)
BAHRETS CHURCH INTERIORS
135 N Fairville Ave (17112-3721)
PHONE..................................717 540-1747
Joe Bahret, *Owner*
EMP: 4
SALES (est): 337.8K **Privately Held**
SIC: 2531 3231 Church furniture; stained glass: made from purchased glass

(G-7095)
BAXTER HEALTHCARE CORPORATION
931 N 7th St (17102-1414)
PHONE..................................717 232-1901
Brian Vayhnal, *Principal*
EMP: 401
SALES (corp-wide): 11.1B **Publicly Held**
SIC: 3841 Surgical & medical instruments
HQ: Baxter Healthcare Corporation
    1 Baxter Pkwy
    Deerfield IL 60015
    224 948-2000

(G-7096)
BLUE MOUNTAIN BUILDNG STONE CO
80 S Hershey Rd (17112-3851)
PHONE..................................717 671-8711
Robert Finger, *Vice Pres*
Chad Koons, *Manager*
EMP: 7
SALES (est): 651.2K **Privately Held**
SIC: 1429 Boulder, crushed & broken-quarrying

(G-7097)
BLUE MOUNTAIN FARMS LLC
605 Lesentier Ln (17112-9297)
PHONE..................................717 599-5110
Angela Shaw,
Matthew Shaw,
EMP: 5
SALES (est): 432.2K **Privately Held**
SIC: 2299 0139 0219 2099 Scouring: wool, mohair & similar fibers; preparing textile fibers for spinning (scouring & combing); hay farm; general livestock; maple syrup

(G-7098)
BONESHIRE BREW WORKS
7462 Derry St (17111-5228)
PHONE..................................717 469-5007
EMP: 4 EST: 2016
SALES (est): 256.1K **Privately Held**
SIC: 2082 Malt beverages

(G-7099)
BRIGHTBILL INDUSTRIES INC
1901 N Cameron St (17103-1023)
PHONE..................................717 233-4121
Martin Brightbill, *President*
Todd Vright Bill, *Vice Pres*
Nancy R Spicer, *Office Mgr*
EMP: 30 EST: 1997
SQ FT: 10,000
SALES (est): 7.5MM **Privately Held**
SIC: 2541 2434 Cabinets, lockers & shelving; wood kitchen cabinets

(G-7100)
BRUNNER INDUSTRIAL GROUP INC
Also Called: Smith Paint Products
2200 Paxton St (17111-1038)
PHONE..................................717 233-8781
Charles E Brunner, *President*
Charles E Brunner Jr, *Vice Pres*
Mary Plasic, *Admin Sec*
Justin Swilly, *Admin Asst*
▲ EMP: 13 EST: 1929
SALES (est): 3.5MM **Privately Held**
WEB: www.smithpaints.com
SIC: 2851 Paints & paint additives

(G-7101)
BURRELLS INFORMATION SERVICES
Also Called: Mutual Press Cliping
297 Care St Fl 1 (17109-1521)
PHONE..................................717 671-3872
Robert Wagner, *President*
EMP: 40 EST: 1965
SALES (est): 1MM **Privately Held**
SIC: 2711 Newspapers

(G-7102)
BUSY BEE EMBROIDERY & MORE
7044 Linglestown Rd (17112-9442)
P.O. Box 60841 (17106-0841)
PHONE..................................717 540-1955
Cindy Proctor, *Owner*
EMP: 3
SALES (est): 197.2K **Privately Held**
SIC: 2395 7389 Embroidery & art needlework; embroidering of advertising on shirts, etc.; apparel designers, commercial

(G-7103)
CBC CABINETRY & HOME SERVICES
1009 N Mountain Rd (17112-1751)
PHONE..................................717 564-2521
Cliff Ball, *Owner*
EMP: 12
SALES (est): 1.7MM **Privately Held**
SIC: 2434 Wood kitchen cabinets

(G-7104)
CHURCH PUBLISHING INCORPORATED
4475 Linglestown Rd (17112)
PHONE..................................212 592-4229
Perkins Dr Davis, *Exec VP*
▲ EMP: 40
SALES (est): 2MM **Privately Held**
SIC: 2731 Book publishing

(G-7105)
CIGAR N MORE
3830 Union Deposit Rd (17109-5919)
PHONE..................................717 541-1341
Nick Patel, *Principal*
EMP: 8
SALES (est): 739.2K **Privately Held**
SIC: 3999 Cigarette & cigar products & accessories

(G-7106)
CLEAR VISIONS INC
Also Called: Woodlore Builders Studio
2220 Chestnut St Apt 1 (17104-1337)
PHONE..................................717 236-4526
Michael Spangler, *President*
EMP: 6
SQ FT: 25,000
SALES: 1.3MM **Privately Held**
SIC: 2431 Millwork

(G-7107)
CLEVELAND BROTHERS EQP CO INC
5300 Paxton St (17111-2525)
PHONE..................................717 564-2121
Edward Miller, *Principal*
EMP: 14
SALES (corp-wide): 656.5MM **Privately Held**
SIC: 3462 Construction or mining equipment forgings, ferrous
HQ: Cleveland Brothers Equipment Co., Inc.
    4565 William Penn Hwy
    Murrysville PA 15668
    724 325-9421

(G-7108)
CODI INC (PA)
Also Called: Codi Direct
651 E Park Dr Ste 102 (17111-2752)
PHONE..................................717 540-1337
William Olson, *CEO*
Paul Gimeson, *Vice Pres*
Doug Harrison, *Plant Mgr*
Adam Reynolds, *Manager*
▲ EMP: 18
SALES (est): 5.3MM **Privately Held**
WEB: www.codi-inc.com
SIC: 3161 Cases, carrying

(G-7109)
CORPORATE DISTRIBUTION LTD
Also Called: Cdl Printing and Packaging
3930 Chambers Hill Rd (17111-1508)
PHONE..................................717 697-6900
Sheila O Broderick, *President*
Kathleen A O'Donnell, *Senior VP*
Donald Murphy, *CFO*
Edward Broderick, *Director*
EMP: 25
SQ FT: 51,000
SALES (est): 1.8MM **Privately Held**
WEB: www.cdlinc.com
SIC: 2711 2759 Commercial printing & newspaper publishing combined; advertising literature: printing

(G-7110)
CUMMINS INC
4499 Lewis Rd (17111-2541)
PHONE..................................717 564-1344
Larry Shutt, *Manager*
Matt Hubler, *Manager*
EMP: 65
SQ FT: 28,000
SALES (corp-wide): 23.7B **Publicly Held**
SIC: 5084 3519 Engines & parts, diesel; internal combustion engines
PA: Cummins Inc.
    500 Jackson St
    Columbus IN 47201
    812 377-5000

(G-7111)
CUTHBERT & SON INC
Also Called: Middlesworth Potato Chip
5706 Jonestown Rd (17112-4008)
PHONE..................................717 657-1050
George Cuthbert, *President*
EMP: 20
SQ FT: 20,000
SALES (est): 1.9MM **Privately Held**
SIC: 2096 Potato chips & similar snacks

(G-7112)
D & H INC (PA)
2525 N 7th St (17110-2511)
P.O. Box 5967 (17110-0967)
PHONE..................................800 340-1001
Louis Matter, *President*
Helen Hunt, *Chairman*
Damon Kegerise, *Business Mgr*
Janice Murray, *Treasurer*
Andrew Wilsbach, *Credit Staff*

EMP: 4
SQ FT: 18,360
SALES (est): 8.4MM **Privately Held**
SIC: 2752 Business forms, lithographed

(G-7113)
DATATECH SOFTWARE INC
Also Called: Quickandeasy.com
4800 Linglestown Rd # 201 (17112-9183)
PHONE..................................717 652-4344
Paul Endress, *President*
EMP: 15
SALES (est): 1.5MM **Privately Held**
WEB: www.federaljobs.com
SIC: 7371 7372 5045 5961 Computer
software development; prepackaged soft-
ware; computer software; computer soft-
ware, mail order

(G-7114)
DAVID A SMITH PRINTING INC
742 S 22nd St (17104-2773)
PHONE..................................717 564-3719
David A Smith, *CEO*
Matthew D Smith, *President*
EMP: 35 EST: 1967
SQ FT: 13,000
SALES (est): 6.7MM **Privately Held**
WEB: www.dasprint.com
SIC: 2752 Commercial printing, offset

(G-7115)
DAYTON PARTS LLC
Also Called: Dayto-Batco
3500 Industrial Rd Bldg 1 (17110-2908)
PHONE..................................717 255-8548
Scott Burner, *Manager*
EMP: 16
SALES (corp-wide): 94.4MM **Privately
Held**
SIC: 3713 Truck bodies & parts
PA: Dayton Parts, Llc
3500 Industrial Rd Bldg 1
Harrisburg PA 17110
717 255-8500

(G-7116)
DAYTON PARTS LLC (PA)
3500 Industrial Rd Bldg 1 (17110-2908)
PHONE..................................717 255-8500
Gary A Smalley, *President*
Pamela Kreamer, *Purch Mgr*
Larry Paul, *Buyer*
Greg Shortridge, *Project Engr*
Richard Polan Jr, *CFO*
◆ EMP: 150
SQ FT: 15,000
SALES (est): 94.4MM **Privately Held**
SIC: 7539 3714 Automotive springs, re-
building & repair; motor vehicle parts &
accessories

(G-7117)
DEFOREST SIGNS & LIGHTING
INC
780 Elder St (17104-2729)
PHONE..................................717 564-6102
Greg Shughart, *President*
Melody Wilson, *Corp Secy*
Robert Wert, *Vice Pres*
EMP: 12 EST: 1930
SQ FT: 10,000
SALES (est): 1.3MM **Privately Held**
SIC: 3993 Electric signs

(G-7118)
DEMOCRATIC PRINT SHOP
6 Technology Park (17110-2919)
PHONE..................................717 787-3307
Clayton Dressler, *Director*
EMP: 27
SALES (est): 1.9MM **Privately Held**
SIC: 2752 Commercial printing, litho-
graphic

(G-7119)
DIAMOND HVY VHCL
SOLUTIONS LLC
7389 Paxton St (17111-5423)
PHONE..................................717 695-9378
Joseph J Whitman,
EMP: 6
SALES (est): 663.6K **Privately Held**
SIC: 5013 3711 Truck parts & accessories;
truck & tractor truck assembly

(G-7120)
DISPLAYS AND GRAPHICS INC
5321d Jaycee Ave (17112-2938)
PHONE..................................717 540-1481
Todd Felty, *President*
Ryan Felty, *Production*
EMP: 4
SALES (est): 463.7K **Privately Held**
SIC: 3993 Signs & advertising specialties

(G-7121)
DM COATINGS INC
6950 Chatham Dr (17111-4023)
PHONE..................................717 561-1175
Debra McMonigal, *President*
Brad McMonigal, *Vice Pres*
EMP: 30
SALES (est): 3.3MM **Privately Held**
WEB: www.dmcoatings.com
SIC: 3479 Coating of metals & formed
products

(G-7122)
DS SERVICES OF AMERICA INC
Also Called: Crystal Springs
1890 Old Crooked Hill Rd (17110-9403)
PHONE..................................717 901-4620
William Shipley III, *Branch Mgr*
EMP: 15
SALES (est): 2.2B **Privately Held**
SIC: 5074 3589 Water purification equip-
ment; water purification equipment,
household type
HQ: Ds Services Of America, Inc.
2300 Windy Ridge Pkwy Se 500n
Atlanta GA 30339
770 933-1400

(G-7123)
DYECO INC
2300 Academy Dr (17112-1011)
PHONE..................................717 545-1882
Todd Moyer, *President*
Sherry Moyer, *Vice Pres*
EMP: 5
SALES (est): 696.2K **Privately Held**
SIC: 5999 7692 Welding supplies; welding
repair

(G-7124)
EBROKER SOFTWARE LLC
(HQ)
2600 Commerce Dr (17110-9368)
PHONE..................................717 540-3720
David Watton, *President*
EMP: 4
SALES (est): 199.6K **Privately Held**
SIC: 7372 Prepackaged software

(G-7125)
EDWIN L HEIM CO (PA)
Also Called: Heim Company
1918 Greenwood St (17104-2351)
P.O. Box 2247 (17105-2247)
PHONE..................................717 233-8711
Larry Bashore, *President*
Rick Berkheimer, *Vice Pres*
Donald L Culbertson, *Vice Pres*
Seth Fisher, *Vice Pres*
Frederick R Sontheimer, *Vice Pres*
EMP: 30 EST: 1931
SQ FT: 7,000
SALES (est): 70.8MM **Privately Held**
WEB: www.elheim.com
SIC: 1731 7694 3613 3823 General elec-
trical contractor; electric motor repair;
control panels, electric; programmers,
process type

(G-7126)
EMERSON COMPANY
3539 N 6th St (17110-1425)
PHONE..................................310 940-1755
Daniel Norton, *Owner*
EMP: 3
SALES (corp-wide): 581K **Privately Held**
SIC: 3452 5072 Bolts, nuts, rivets & wash-
ers; bolts, nuts & screws
PA: Emerson Company
1915 W Summerland St
Rancho Palos Verdes CA 90275
310 279-6203

(G-7127)
ESTARI INC
1800 Paxton St (17104-2826)
PHONE..................................717 233-1518
Gary L Cochard, *Ch of Bd*
George H Crist Sr, *President*
EMP: 14
SALES (est): 1.1MM **Privately Held**
WEB: www.estari.com
SIC: 5734 7372 Computer peripheral
equipment; prepackaged software

(G-7128)
F & M DESIGNS INC
7412 Derry St (17111-5228)
PHONE..................................717 564-8120
David Manerie, *President*
Brad McClims, *President*
Brandon Fitzpatrick, *Shareholder*
EMP: 5
SQ FT: 4,000
SALES (est): 691.6K **Privately Held**
WEB: www.fmdesigns.com
SIC: 3444 Awnings, sheet metal

(G-7129)
FINE LINE HOMES (PA)
Also Called: Payco
7300 Derry St (17111-5227)
PHONE..................................717 561-2040
George A Parmer, *President*
Kim Mertz, *Corp Secy*
EMP: 12
SALES (est): 1.8MM **Privately Held**
SIC: 2431 5031 Doors, wood; kitchen cab-
inets

(G-7130)
FORTNEY PRINTING
512 Main St (17113-2711)
PHONE..................................717 939-6422
Fred Fortney, *Owner*
EMP: 10
SQ FT: 4,300
SALES: 275K **Privately Held**
WEB: www.fortneyprinting.com
SIC: 2752 Commercial printing, offset

(G-7131)
FRESH EXPRESS MID-ATLANTIC
LLC
7505 Grayson Rd (17111-5146)
PHONE..................................717 561-2900
Steve Taylor, *Ch of Bd*
Corey Vanskike, *Supervisor*
EMP: 160
SALES (est): 24.2MM
SALES (corp-wide): 3B **Privately Held**
WEB: www.freshexpress.com
SIC: 2099 Salads, fresh or refrigerated
HQ: Fresh Express Incorporated
4757 The Grove Dr Ste 260
Windermere FL 34786
407 612-5000

(G-7132)
G2 DIESEL PRODUCTS INC
3990 Paxton St (17111-1423)
PHONE..................................717 525-8709
Dolph Pinkerman, *President*
EMP: 13
SALES (est): 1.2MM **Privately Held**
SIC: 3519 Engines, diesel & semi-diesel or
dual-fuel

(G-7133)
GES AUTOMATION
TECHNOLOGY
2020 Greenwood St (17104-2343)
PHONE..................................717 236-8733
Gary Slatt, *President*
Don Culbertson, *Vice Pres*
Fred Sontheimer, *Vice Pres*
Collier Cline, *Engineer*
R James Saylor, *Treasurer*
EMP: 25
SQ FT: 4,500
SALES: 8.5MM
SALES (corp-wide): 70.8MM **Privately
Held**
WEB: www.gestech.com
SIC: 3823 3613 3625 Programmers,
process type; panelboards & distribution
boards, electric; relays & industrial con-
trols

PA: Edwin L. Heim Co.
1918 Greenwood St
Harrisburg PA 17104
717 233-8711

(G-7134)
GOLDCRAFTERS CORNER
5301 Jonestown Rd Ste 101 (17112-2905)
PHONE..................................717 412-4616
Stephanie Long, *Owner*
EMP: 5
SALES (est): 100K **Privately Held**
WEB: www.golddreams.com
SIC: 3911 5944 Jewelry, precious metal;
jewelry stores

(G-7135)
GOOD TIME ICE
1621 N 7th St (17102-1114)
PHONE..................................717 234-1479
Ed Neuman, *Owner*
EMP: 5 EST: 1929
SQ FT: 5,146
SALES (est): 220K **Privately Held**
SIC: 2097 Ice cubes

(G-7136)
GRIMS PLASTICS
6691 Allentown Blvd (17112-3308)
PHONE..................................717 526-7980
Thomas Miller, *Owner*
EMP: 6
SALES (est): 572K **Privately Held**
SIC: 3083 Plastic finished products, lami-
nated

(G-7137)
GUTH LABORATORIES INC
590 N 67th St (17111-4500)
PHONE..................................717 564-5470
Richard U Guth, *Ch of Bd*
Ted L Pauley, *President*
Christine Benner, *Purchasing*
Nancy F Guth, *Treasurer*
Nancy Guth, *Treasurer*
EMP: 18 EST: 1976
SQ FT: 12,000
SALES (est): 4MM **Privately Held**
WEB: www.guthlabs.com
SIC: 3829 Breathalyzers

(G-7138)
HANGER PRSTHETCS & ORTHO
INC
989 E Park Dr (17111-2803)
PHONE..................................717 564-4521
Thomas Kirk MD, *CEO*
EMP: 7
SALES (corp-wide): 1B **Publicly Held**
SIC: 3842 Orthopedic appliances
HQ: Hanger Prosthetics & Orthotics, Inc.
10910 Domain Dr Ste 300
Austin TX 78758
512 777-3800

(G-7139)
HAPSCO DESIGN AND PRTG
SVCS
4750 Lindle Rd (17111-2428)
P.O. Box 8600 (17105-8600)
PHONE..................................717 564-2323
D Patrick Mazzolla, *President*
John Kauffman, *Treasurer*
Robert Carper, *Admin Sec*
EMP: 5
SALES (est): 190.2K
SALES (corp-wide): 13MM **Privately
Held**
SIC: 8699 2789 2752 Charitable organi-
zation; bookbinding & related work; com-
mercial printing, lithographic
PA: Hospital And Healthsystem Association
Of Pennsylvania
30 N 3rd St Ste 700
Harrisburg PA 17101
717 564-9200

(G-7140)
HARLAN ELECTRIC
1213 Paxton Church Rd (17110-9561)
PHONE..................................717 243-4600
Jon Arganbright, *General Mgr*
EMP: 9
SALES (est): 2.1MM **Privately Held**
SIC: 3699 1731 Electrical equipment &
supplies; electrical work

(G-7141)
HARMAN BEACH CORPORATION
6700 Allentown Blvd (17112-3309)
PHONE................717 652-0556
Albert E Grissinger Jr, *President*
Paul Reisser, *Sales Mgr*
EMP: 12
SALES (est): 1.6MM **Privately Held**
SIC: 2752 Commercial printing, offset

(G-7142)
HARRISBURG DAIRIES INC
2001 Herr St (17103-1624)
PHONE................717 233-8701
Frederick B Dewey Jr, *President*
Jessica Stought, *General Mgr*
Frederick B Dewey Sr, *Chairman*
Matt Zehring, *Chief Mktg Ofcr*
Janis Brown, *Office Mgr*
EMP: 105 EST: 1946
SQ FT: 100,000
SALES (est): 27.6MM **Privately Held**
WEB: www.harrisburgdairies.com
SIC: 2026 5149 Milk processing (pasteurizing, homogenizing, bottling); juices; mineral or spring water bottling

(G-7143)
HARRISBURG MAGAZINE INC
Also Called: Benchmark Group Media
3400 N 6th St (17110-1423)
PHONE................717 233-0109
Davy Goldsmith, *President*
Carol A Morris, *Vice Pres*
EMP: 17
SALES (est): 1.9MM **Privately Held**
WEB: www.harrisburgmagazine.com
SIC: 2721 Magazines: publishing & printing

(G-7144)
HARRISBURG STAMP & STENCIL CO
3362 Paxton St (17111-1420)
PHONE................717 236-9000
John A Collins III, *President*
John A Collins Jr, *President*
EMP: 5
SQ FT: 3,000
SALES: 500K
SALES (corp-wide): 10.3MM **Privately Held**
WEB: www.ams-stamps.com
SIC: 3953 Marking devices
PA: American Marking Systems Inc
1015 Paulison Ave
Clifton NJ 07011
973 478-5600

(G-7145)
HAVECO DIV OF ACE MOBILITY
7917 Derry St Ste 124 (17111-5330)
PHONE................717 558-4301
Keith Siergiej, *Principal*
EMP: 12
SALES: 950K **Privately Held**
SIC: 3842 Surgical appliances & supplies

(G-7146)
HAVECO INC
7917 Derry St Ste 124 (17111-5330)
PHONE................717 558-4301
Greg Seitz, *President*
Bruce Ahnafield, *Principal*
EMP: 8
SALES (est): 540K **Privately Held**
SIC: 3999 Wheelchair lifts

(G-7147)
HEATHERS CUPCAKES N THINGS LLC
421 Friendship Rd (17111-1206)
PHONE................717 329-2324
EMP: 8
SALES (est): 610.4K **Privately Held**
SIC: 2051 Bread, cake & related products

(G-7148)
HERFF JONES LLC
6470 Huntsmen Dr (17111-4889)
PHONE................717 526-4373
EMP: 15
SALES (corp-wide): 1.1B **Privately Held**
SIC: 3911 Jewelry, precious metal

HQ: Herff Jones, Llc
4501 W 62nd St
Indianapolis IN 46268
800 419-5462

(G-7149)
HERSHEY CREAMERY COMPANY (PA)
Also Called: Hershey's Ice Cream
301 S Cameron St (17101-2815)
PHONE................717 238-8134
George H Holder, *President*
Eric Chamberlain, *Area Mgr*
Jon Gall, *Area Mgr*
Jim McElheny, *Area Mgr*
Walter Holder, *Vice Pres*
▲ EMP: 175 EST: 1894
SQ FT: 65,000
SALES (est): 129.1MM **Privately Held**
WEB: www.hersheyicecream.com
SIC: 2024 Ice cream, bulk; sherbets, dairy based

(G-7150)
HOBART SALES AND SERVICE INC
2917 Wayne St (17111-1397)
PHONE................301 733-6560
Kerry Keegan, *Branch Mgr*
EMP: 3
SALES (corp-wide): 14.7B **Publicly Held**
SIC: 3589 Dishwashing machines, commercial
HQ: Hobart Sales And Service, Inc.
701 S Ridge Ave
Troy OH 45373
937 332-3000

(G-7151)
HOLLYS EMBROIDERY
500 Lesentier Ln (17112-9284)
PHONE................717 599-5975
William Houtz, *Partner*
Holly J Houtz, *Partner*
EMP: 3
SQ FT: 1,200
SALES (est): 305.3K **Privately Held**
WEB: www.hollysembroidery.com
SIC: 2395 Embroidery products, except schiffli machine

(G-7152)
HOUCK PRINTING COMPANY INC
4150 Industrial Rd (17110-2949)
PHONE................717 233-5205
Alice Houck, *President*
William Houck Jr, *Vice Pres*
Jean Wiltrout, *Vice Pres*
EMP: 16 EST: 1953
SQ FT: 5,000
SALES (est): 1.9MM **Privately Held**
WEB: www.houckprinting.com
SIC: 2752 2759 Commercial printing, offset; letterpress printing

(G-7153)
IMAGE 360
Also Called: Oak Management
3950 Tecport Dr (17111-1465)
PHONE................717 317-9147
Rob Kaun, *Owner*
Edward Nail, *Manager*
EMP: 5
SALES (est): 114.8K **Privately Held**
SIC: 7335 7389 3993 7336 Photographic studio, commercial; sign painting & lettering shop; electric signs; commercial art & illustration

(G-7154)
IMPERIAL BEVERAGE SYSTEMS INC
1201 S 20th St (17104-2928)
PHONE................717 238-6870
Douglas Stauffer, *President*
Lou Keller, *Opers Staff*
Gary Frederick, *Manager*
EMP: 16
SQ FT: 24,000
SALES (est): 2.6MM **Privately Held**
WEB: www.imperialbeveragesystems.com
SIC: 2087 Beverage bases, concentrates, syrups, powders & mixes

(G-7155)
INTER MEDIA OUTDOORS
6385 Flank Dr (17112-2784)
PHONE................717 695-8171
Mark Olszewski, *Principal*
EMP: 5
SALES (est): 400.7K **Privately Held**
SIC: 7372 Home entertainment computer software

(G-7156)
J & S SIGNCO INC
Also Called: Fastsigns
4315 Jonestown Rd (17109-6259)
PHONE................717 657-3800
S Schreffler, *Vice Pres*
Steven Schreffler, *Vice Pres*
EMP: 6 EST: 2014
SALES (est): 496.5K **Privately Held**
SIC: 3993 Signs & advertising specialties

(G-7157)
J S ZIMMERMAN CO
2701 Elm St (17103-1993)
PHONE................717 232-6842
Lee Zimmerman, *President*
Donna Zimmerman, *Corp Secy*
EMP: 6
SQ FT: 2,400
SALES (est): 738.5K **Privately Held**
SIC: 2099 5441 5145 Peanut butter; candy; nuts; nuts, salted or roasted

(G-7158)
JOHN STEPHEN GOLOB
Also Called: Golob Concrete
895 Shawnee Dr (17112-9030)
PHONE................717 469-7931
John S Golob, *Principal*
EMP: 7
SALES (est): 466.9K **Privately Held**
SIC: 3273 Ready-mixed concrete

(G-7159)
JOHNNYS DISCOUNT FURNITURE
3440 Derry St (17111-1815)
PHONE................717 564-1898
David Newcomer, *President*
EMP: 6
SALES (est): 656.5K **Privately Held**
SIC: 5712 2211 Mattresses; furniture denim

(G-7160)
KAPOTHANASIS GROUP INC
2720 Walnut St (17103-1954)
PHONE................207 939-5680
Constantine Kapothanasis, *President*
EMP: 7
SQ FT: 20,000
SALES (est): 132.1K **Privately Held**
SIC: 0119 2079 5172 6719 Oil grains; olive oil; engine fuels & oils; personal holding companies, except banks; investment holding companies, except banks

(G-7161)
KELLEY-TRON MACHINE COMPANY
115 Aster Dr (17112-2792)
PHONE................717 545-8814
Steve Kelley, *Owner*
EMP: 3 EST: 1983
SQ FT: 3,000
SALES (est): 351K **Privately Held**
SIC: 3599 Machine shop, jobbing & repair

(G-7162)
KEYSTONE SURGICAL SYSTEMS INC
4949 Queen St Ste 104 (17109-3132)
PHONE................717 412-4383
Nick Cargas, *Owner*
EMP: 4 EST: 2010
SALES (est): 482.9K **Privately Held**
SIC: 3842 Orthopedic appliances

(G-7163)
KEYWORD COMMUNICATIONS INC
Also Called: B2b Magazine
788 Winding Ln (17111-2358)
PHONE................717 481-2960

Stephen Shultz, *President*
Ted Byrne, *Manager*
EMP: 3
SQ FT: 1,200
SALES: 350K **Privately Held**
SIC: 2731 Book publishing

(G-7164)
KINETIC CONCEPTS INC
4400 Lewis Rd (17111-2544)
PHONE................717 558-0985
Kim Denty, *Branch Mgr*
EMP: 4
SALES (corp-wide): 1.8B **Privately Held**
SIC: 3842 Surgical appliances & supplies
HQ: Kinetic Concepts, Inc.
12930 W Interstate 10
San Antonio TX 78249
800 531-5346

(G-7165)
KREHLING INDUSTRIES INC
1399 Hagy Way (17110-9298)
PHONE................717 232-7936
Robert Krehling, *President*
Linda Page, *President*
Mona Krehling, *Corp Secy*
Brian D Krehling, *Vice Pres*
Richard G Krehling, *Vice Pres*
EMP: 80
SQ FT: 26,000
SALES (est): 9.7MM **Privately Held**
WEB: www.krehlingcountertops.com
SIC: 3083 2511 2521 5032 Laminated plastics plate & sheet; wood household furniture; wood office furniture; brick, stone & related material; wood partitions & fixtures

(G-7166)
LA PERLA LLC
806 S 29th St Bldg C (17111-1349)
PHONE................717 561-1257
James Patrick Bowen, *Partner*
Virgen De Calderon, *Partner*
Khiem Nguyen, *Partner*
EMP: 3
SALES (est): 278.4K **Privately Held**
SIC: 7389 2395 7336 Advertising, promotional & trade show services; embroidery & art needlework; silk screen design

(G-7167)
LAFAYETTE VENETIAN BLIND INC
Also Called: Lafayette Interior Fashions
5700 Lingstown Rd Ste D (17112)
PHONE................717 652-3750
EMP: 35
SALES (corp-wide): 173.7MM **Privately Held**
SIC: 2591 2391 Ret Misc Homefurnishings
PA: Lafayette Venetian Blind, Inc.
3000 Klondike Rd
West Lafayette IN 47906
765 464-2500

(G-7168)
LARRY ARNOLD
Also Called: Para Science International
1025 Miller Ln (17110-2827)
PHONE................717 236-0080
Larry Arnold, *Owner*
EMP: 3
SALES: 100K **Privately Held**
WEB: www.parascience.com
SIC: 2731 8732 Books: publishing only; sociological research

(G-7169)
LARRY MYERS
Also Called: L. Myers Associates
3901 Derry St Ste A (17111-2236)
PHONE................717 564-8300
Larry Myers, *Owner*
▲ EMP: 8
SQ FT: 13,000
SALES (est): 2MM **Privately Held**
SIC: 2752 7389 Tag, ticket & schedule printing: lithographic; printers' services: folding, collating

(G-7170)
LCCM SOLAR LLC
3029 N Front St Ste 201 (17110-1224)
PHONE....................717 514-0751
Douglas A Neidich,
Stephen J Fonash,
Wookjun Nam,
EMP: 3
SQ FT: 50,000
SALES (est): 160.7K Privately Held
SIC: 3433 Solar heaters & collectors

(G-7171)
LDP INC
Also Called: Leader Services
4807 Jonestown Rd Ste 251 (17109-1744)
PHONE....................717 657-8500
Charles Mason, President
EMP: 8
SALES (corp-wide): 10.2MM Privately
Held
WEB: www.leaderservices.com
SIC: 7372 7374 Prepackaged software;
data processing service
PA: Ldp, Inc.
75 Kiwanis Blvd
West Hazleton PA 18202
570 455-8511

(G-7172)
MACULOGIX INC
3721 Tecport Dr Ste 301 (17111-1200)
PHONE....................717 982-6751
William McPhee, CEO
EMP: 13
SALES: 100K Privately Held
SIC: 3841 Surgical & medical instruments

(G-7173)
MARY ANN PENSIERO INC
Also Called: Bargain Beer & Soda
3514 Ridgeway Rd (17109-1124)
P.O. Box 22, Lewistown (17044-0022)
PHONE....................717 545-8289
Mary Ann Pensiero, Owner
EMP: 4 EST: 1986
SALES: 750K Privately Held
SIC: 2082 Beer (alcoholic beverage)

(G-7174)
MATANGOS CANDIES INC
1501 Catherine St (17104-2249)
PHONE....................717 234-0882
Peter Matangos, President
EMP: 3 EST: 1949
SQ FT: 4,000
SALES: 300K Privately Held
SIC: 2064 5961 2066 Candy & other con-
fectionery products; catalog & mail-order
houses; chocolate & cocoa products

(G-7175)
**MDI MEMBRANE
TECHNOLOGIES INC**
5340 Jaycee Ave Ste A (17112-4938)
PHONE....................717 412-0943
Nalini Kant Gupta, President
Rohit Singhal, Principal
EMP: 6
SALES (est): 399.9K Privately Held
SIC: 3821 Sample preparation apparatus

(G-7176)
MEDTRONIC USA INC
4230 Crums Mill Rd # 201 (17112-2898)
PHONE....................717 657-6140
Louis Rosetti, Consultant
Janet French, Administration
EMP: 3 Privately Held
WEB: www.medtronic.com
SIC: 3841 Surgical & medical instruments
HQ: Medtronic Usa, Inc.
710 Medtronic Pkwy
Minneapolis MN 55432
763 514-4000

(G-7177)
MESSER GT & S
2551 Paxton St (17111-1034)
PHONE....................717 232-3173
Jason Vortez, Principal
EMP: 3 EST: 2010
SALES (est): 160.3K Privately Held
SIC: 2813 Industrial gases

(G-7178)
MILLENNIUM CIRCUITS LIMITED
7703 Derry St (17111-5205)
PHONE....................717 558-5975
Daniel Thau, President
EMP: 10
SQ FT: 1,500
SALES (est): 2.2MM Privately Held
SIC: 3672 Printed circuit boards

(G-7179)
MITCHELL AVIATION LTD
1310 Crooked Hill Rd # 100 (17110-9714)
PHONE....................717 232-7575
Brad M Polon, President
Sanford Polon, Principal
EMP: 4
SQ FT: 4,000
SALES (est): 910K Privately Held
SIC: 5088 3728 Aircraft equipment & sup-
plies; aircraft parts & equipment

(G-7180)
MOLD-BASE INDUSTRIES INC
Also Called: MBI
7501 Derry St (17111-5230)
PHONE....................717 564-7960
Jay M Ebersole, President
Mary Forbes, Principal
Samuel Shiffler, Vice Pres
Steve Eckles, Safety Mgr
Amy Rieck, Safety Mgr
EMP: 72
SQ FT: 70,000
SALES (est): 16MM Privately Held
WEB: www.moldbase.com
SIC: 3544 Industrial molds

(G-7181)
**MSHAR POWER TRAIN
SPECIALISTS**
3525 N 6th St Side 4 (17110-1485)
PHONE....................717 231-3900
Thomas Mshar, President
Ken Mshar, Vice Pres
EMP: 3
SQ FT: 18,000
SALES (est): 310K Privately Held
SIC: 7539 3479 Automotive repair shops;
coating of metals & formed products

(G-7182)
N F STRING & SON INC
1380 Howard St (17104-1189)
PHONE....................717 234-2441
Floyd K String, President
Lois G String, Corp Secy
Gregory String, Vice Pres
Raul Martinez, Technician
▲ EMP: 55
SQ FT: 52,000
SALES (est): 16.9MM Privately Held
WEB: www.coinwrapper.com
SIC: 2679 Wrappers, paper (unprinted):
made from purchased material

(G-7183)
N H LABORATORIES INC
6940 Allentown Blvd (17112-3313)
P.O. Box 6369 (17112-0369)
PHONE....................717 545-3221
Nick Halkias, President
Irene N Halkias, Vice Pres
Lynn Halkias, Admin Sec
EMP: 10 EST: 1977
SQ FT: 10,000
SALES (est): 1.6MM Privately Held
SIC: 2893 3955 Printing ink; ribbons,
inked: typewriter, adding machine, regis-
ter, etc.; print cartridges for laser & other
computer printers

(G-7184)
NOLATRON INC
1259 2nd St (17113-1105)
PHONE....................717 564-3398
Mike Nolan, President
Joyce Klutz, Treasurer
EMP: 6 EST: 1975
SALES (est): 967K Privately Held
WEB: www.nolatron.com
SIC: 3679 Electronic switches

(G-7185)
NYLACAST LLC (DH)
6951 Allentown Blvd Ste K (17112-3374)
PHONE....................717 270-5600
Mussa Mohamad, Mng Member
Mussa Mohammad, Mng Member
Max Fraiser,
Simon Gilbert,
▲ EMP: 5
SALES (est): 738K Privately Held
WEB: www.nylacast.com
SIC: 3089 Plastic containers, except foam
HQ: Nylacast Limited
460-480 Thurmaston Boulevard
Leicester LEICS LE4 9
116 276-8558

(G-7186)
OAK PARK CABINETRY INC
4220 Paxton St (17111-2510)
PHONE....................717 561-4216
Robert Raffensperger, President
Christopher Ditlow, Vice Pres
EMP: 11
SQ FT: 6,000
SALES (est): 1.4MM Privately Held
SIC: 2434 Wood kitchen cabinets

(G-7187)
OC CANVAS STUDIO LLC
15 S 20th St (17104-1307)
PHONE....................717 510-4847
Anatolie Dodu,
▲ EMP: 4
SALES (est): 110K Privately Held
SIC: 2211 7389 Canvas;

(G-7188)
ORACLE CORPORATION
403 N 2nd St (17101-1377)
PHONE....................717 234-5858
Mark Zimmerman, Principal
EMP: 191
SALES (corp-wide): 39.8B Publicly Held
SIC: 7372 Business oriented computer
software
PA: Oracle Corporation
500 Oracle Pkwy
Redwood City CA 94065
650 506-7000

(G-7189)
PASTA ACQUISITION CORP
85 Shannon Rd (17112-2799)
PHONE....................559 485-8110
EMP: 5
SALES (est): 205.7K Privately Held
SIC: 2098 Macaroni & spaghetti

(G-7190)
PAXTON HERALD
Also Called: Graphic Services
101 Lincoln St (17112-2599)
P.O. Box 6310 (17112-0310)
PHONE....................717 545-9868
Annette A Antoun, Owner
EMP: 16
SQ FT: 4,500
SALES (est): 940.7K Privately Held
WEB: www.thepaxtonherald.com
SIC: 2711 Newspapers: publishing only,
not printed on site

(G-7191)
PECKS GRAPHICS LLC
1310 Crooked Hill Rd # 200 (17110-9714)
PHONE....................717 963-7588
Greg Peck, Programmer Anys
EMP: 6
SALES: 366.8K Privately Held
SIC: 7336 2752 7312 Art design services;
advertising posters, lithographed; poster
advertising, outdoor

(G-7192)
**PEDIATRIX MEDICAL GROUP PA
PC**
111 S Front St (17101-2010)
PHONE....................717 782-3127
Margaret Donahue, Principal
EMP: 10 EST: 2012
SALES (est): 1.2MM Privately Held
SIC: 3231 Medical & laboratory glassware:
made from purchased glass

(G-7193)
PENN-MO FIRE BRICK CO INC
825 Paxton St (17104-1643)
PHONE....................717 234-4504
John S Fulton IV, President
EMP: 6
SQ FT: 18,000
SALES (est): 611.1K Privately Held
SIC: 3297 1711 5719 5085 Nonclay re-
fractories; heating systems repair & main-
tenance; pottery; industrial supplies

(G-7194)
**PENNSYLVANIA LEGISLATIVE
SVCS**
240 N 3rd St Ste 1100 (17101-1504)
PHONE....................717 236-6984
Lynn Deary, Owner
Aaron Rider, Editor
Teresa Irvincopenhaver, Co-Owner
Peter Trufahneseock, Co-Owner
EMP: 9
SQ FT: 4,000
SALES (est): 888.3K Privately Held
WEB: www.mypls.com
SIC: 2759 Periodicals: printing

(G-7195)
PENNSYLVANIA SLING CO (HQ)
421 Amity Rd Ste C (17111-1049)
PHONE....................717 657-7700
Shawn Ober, President
▲ EMP: 7
SALES (est): 1.9MM
SALES (corp-wide): 66.8MM Privately
Held
SIC: 3496 Miscellaneous fabricated wire
products
PA: Alp Industries, Inc.
512 N Market St Ste 100
Lancaster PA 17603
610 384-1300

(G-7196)
PENNSYLVANIA SUPPLY INC
1001 Paxton St (17104-1645)
PHONE....................717 567-3197
David Teter, Principal
EMP: 3 EST: 2016
SALES (est): 204.6K Privately Held
SIC: 3273 Ready-mixed concrete

(G-7197)
**PENNSYLVNIA SOC NEWSPPR
EDITOR**
3899 N Front St Fl 1 (17110-1583)
PHONE....................717 703-3000
Ernest Schreiber, Principal
EMP: 3
SALES (est): 124.1K Privately Held
WEB: www.psne.net
SIC: 2711 Newspapers, publishing & print-
ing

(G-7198)
PENSIONPRO SOFTWARE LLC
940 E Park Dr Ste 100 (17111-2800)
PHONE....................717 545-6060
EMP: 6 EST: 2010
SALES (est): 662.3K Privately Held
SIC: 7372 Prepackaged Software Services

(G-7199)
PITNEY BOWES INC
2405 Park Dr Ste 100 (17110-9313)
PHONE....................717 884-1882
Donald Bioty, Manager
EMP: 50
SALES (corp-wide): 3.5B Publicly Held
SIC: 3579 7359 Postage meters; business
machine & electronic equipment rental
services
PA: Pitney Bowes Inc.
3001 Summer St Ste 3
Stamford CT 06905
203 356-5000

(G-7200)
POPPI ALS INC
7750 Allentown Blvd Frnt (17112-3736)
PHONE....................717 652-6263
Sandra L Grigor, President
EMP: 4

SALES (est): 459.4K **Privately Held**
WEB: www.poppials.com
SIC: 2038 Pizza, frozen

(G-7201)
PRINCE COMPANY INC
85 Shannon Rd (17112-2799)
PHONE..................................717 526-2200
EMP: 3
SALES (est): 189.4K **Privately Held**
SIC: 2098 Macaroni & spaghetti

(G-7202)
PRINT WORKS ON DEMAND INC (PA)
Also Called: David Smith Printing Copy Ctrs
5630 Allentown Blvd (17112-4040)
PHONE..................................717 545-5215
Glenn Young, *President*
Glenn R Young Jr, *Corp Secy*
EMP: 9
SQ FT: 3,900
SALES: 965.1K **Privately Held**
WEB: www.syicopies.com
SIC: 2752 2789 2759 Commercial print-
ing, offset; bookbinding & related work;
commercial printing

(G-7203)
R F FAGER COMPANY
3901 Derry St (17111-2236)
PHONE..................................717 564-1166
Darrell Brosius, *Branch Mgr*
EMP: 15
SALES (corp-wide): 82.5MM **Privately
Held**
SIC: 2952 Roofing materials
PA: R. F. Fager Company
2058 State Rd
Camp Hill PA 17011
717 761-0660

(G-7204)
RAINBOW VISION STAINED GL CTR
3105 Walnut St (17109-3556)
PHONE..................................717 657-9737
Michael Johnston, *President*
EMP: 5
SALES (est): 280K **Privately Held**
WEB: www.rainbowvisionsg.com
SIC: 3231 Stained glass: made from pur-
chased glass

(G-7205)
RICHARD ZERBE LTD
3109 Paul Dr (17109-5721)
PHONE..................................717 564-2024
Richard Zerbe, *President*
EMP: 3
SALES (est): 150K **Privately Held**
SIC: 3131 5948 Boot & shoe accessories;
luggage, except footlockers & trunks

(G-7206)
RICHMAN INDUSTRIES INC
810 S 31st St (17111-1335)
P.O. Box 4349 (17111-0349)
PHONE..................................717 561-1766
Linda Fleisher, *President*
EMP: 9
SQ FT: 10,000
SALES: 450K **Privately Held**
WEB: www.richmanindustries.com
SIC: 2759 3993 3089 Engraving; screen
printing; advertising novelties; plastic pro-
cessing

(G-7207)
RIVIANA FOODS INC
85 Shannon Rd (17112-2799)
PHONE..................................717 526-2200
EMP: 150 **Privately Held**
SIC: 2098 Macaroni & spaghetti
HQ: Riviana Foods Inc.
2777 Allen Pkwy Fl 15
Houston TX 77019
713 529-3251

(G-7208)
RMS KUNKLE INC
Also Called: Signs & More In 24
631 S 17th St (17104-2258)
PHONE..................................717 564-8829
Richard Kunkle Jr, *CEO*

Susanne Kunkle, *Vice Pres*
EMP: 7
SQ FT: 3,000
SALES (est): 676.6K **Privately Held**
SIC: 3993 Signs & advertising specialties

(G-7209)
ROXANNE TOSER NON-SPORT ENTPS
Also Called: Non-Sport Update
4019 Green St (17110-1622)
P.O. Box 5858 (17110-0858)
PHONE..................................717 238-1936
Roxanne Toser, *President*
Harris Toser, *Corp Secy*
Marlin Toser, *Vice Pres*
EMP: 3
SALES: 300K **Privately Held**
WEB: www.nonsportupdate.com
SIC: 5961 2721 Magazines, mail order;
cards, mail order; magazines: publishing
only, not printed on site

(G-7210)
ROZEMA PRINTING LLC
Also Called: To Get It Now Print
4790 Derry St (17111-2619)
PHONE..................................717 564-4143
John Rozema,
EMP: 6 EST: 2012
SQ FT: 2,500
SALES: 900K **Privately Held**
SIC: 2752 Commercial printing, offset

(G-7211)
S F SPECTOR INC
608 Brook St (17110-1582)
P.O. Box 5282 (17110-0282)
PHONE..................................717 236-0805
Stephen F Spector, *President*
Morton Spector, *Treasurer*
EMP: 4
SALES: 250K **Privately Held**
SIC: 2431 1796 2511 Millwork; millwright;
wood household furniture

(G-7212)
SAMUEL GERBER INC
Also Called: Gerber Fabrics
6802 Clubhouse Dr Apt L (17111-7007)
PHONE..................................717 761-0250
Lawrence S Gerber, *President*
Ron Gerber, *Corp Secy*
EMP: 8 EST: 1928
SQ FT: 12,000
SALES (est): 290.8K **Privately Held**
SIC: 5949 2392 2391 Fabric stores piece
goods; sewing supplies; bedspreads &
bed sets: made from purchased materi-
als; draperies, plastic & textile: from pur-
chased materials

(G-7213)
SCOTT GORDON
Also Called: Gordon's Hearing Aid Lab
6091 Linglestown Rd (17112-1208)
PHONE..................................717 652-2828
Scott Gordon, *Owner*
EMP: 5
SALES (est): 621K **Privately Held**
SIC: 3842 5999 5047 Hearing aids; hear-
ing aids; medical & hospital equipment

(G-7214)
SEWELL LOGGING
6014 Jacobs Ave (17112-1205)
PHONE..................................814 837-7136
William Sewell, *Owner*
EMP: 4
SALES (est): 332.4K **Privately Held**
SIC: 2411 Logging

(G-7215)
SHEET METAL SPECIALISTS LLC
1731 S 19th St (17104-3204)
PHONE..................................717 910-7000
Anthoney Forlizzi, *Mng Member*
EMP: 20
SALES (est): 3.3MM **Privately Held**
WEB: www.sheetmetalspecialists.com
SIC: 1711 3443 Ventilation & duct work
contractor; fabricated plate work (boiler
shop)

(G-7216)
SMOKERS STOP
11 Kline Vlg (17104-1528)
PHONE..................................717 232-5206
Sue Kotadia, *Principal*
EMP: 3
SALES (est): 175K **Privately Held**
SIC: 3999 Cigarette & cigar products & ac-
cessories

(G-7217)
SPORTSMANSLIQUIDATIONCOM LLC
2201 N Front St (17110-1027)
PHONE..................................717 263-6000
EMP: 6 EST: 2008
SALES (est): 630K **Privately Held**
SIC: 3949 Mfg Sporting/Athletic Goods

(G-7218)
SPRING GATE VINEYARD
5790 Devonshire Rd (17112-3508)
PHONE..................................717 599-5574
Martin Schoffstall, *Principal*
EMP: 14
SALES (est): 2.5MM **Privately Held**
SIC: 2084 Wines

(G-7219)
STABLER COMPANIES INC (HQ)
635 Lucknow Rd (17110-1635)
PHONE..................................717 236-9307
James Van Buren, *President*
Thomas M Minori, *CFO*
Kathyleen S O'Hare, *Asst Sec*
EMP: 15 EST: 1955
SQ FT: 25,000
SALES (est): 141.8MM
SALES (corp-wide): 651.9MM **Privately
Held**
WEB: www.stablercompaniesinc.com
SIC: 5032 3089 7359 3531 Paving mix-
tures; concrete & cinder block; stone,
crushed or broken; stock shapes, plastic;
work zone traffic equipment (flags, cones,
barrels, etc.); road construction & mainte-
nance machinery; highway & street
paving contractor; resurfacing contractor;
lighting equipment
PA: New Enterprise Stone & Lime Co., Inc.
3912 Brumbaugh Rd
New Enterprise PA 16664
814 224-6883

(G-7220)
STATE STREET COPY AND PRESS
500 N 3rd St Fl 1 (17101-1136)
PHONE..................................717 232-6684
George F Freyvogel, *Owner*
Rick Russell, *Advisor*
EMP: 3 EST: 1974
SQ FT: 3,000
SALES (est): 170K **Privately Held**
SIC: 2752 7334 Commercial printing, off-
set; photocopying & duplicating services

(G-7221)
STEWART-AMOS STEEL INC
4400 Paxton St (17111-2542)
P.O. Box 4259 (17111-0259)
PHONE..................................717 564-3931
William A Starr, *President*
Eckland Schulz, *Vice Pres*
Carlton Hughes, *Treasurer*
John Paraschak, *VP Sales*
Hank Morrow, *Sales Engr*
EMP: 44 EST: 1940
SQ FT: 26,000
SALES (est): 13.3MM **Privately Held**
SIC: 3441 Building components, structural
steel

(G-7222)
SUNOCO INC
80 S 40th St (17111-2266)
PHONE..................................717 564-1440
Kenneth Lunday, *Branch Mgr*
Mike Steinbacher, *Manager*
EMP: 35
SQ FT: 4,000

SALES (corp-wide): 54B **Publicly Held**
WEB: www.sunocoinc.com
SIC: 2911 5171 1711 Oils, fuel; petroleum
bulk stations; warm air heating & air conditioning contractor
HQ: Sunoco, Inc.
3801 West Chester Pike
Newtown Square PA 19073
215 977-3000

(G-7223)
SUPERMEDIA LLC
Also Called: Tadford
4000 Crums Mill Rd # 204 (17112-2896)
PHONE..................................717 540-6500
Steve Hunter, *President*
EMP: 254
SALES (corp-wide): 1.8B **Privately Held**
SIC: 2741 Directories, telephone: publish-
ing only, not printed on site
HQ: Supermedia Llc
2200 W Airfield Dr
Dfw Airport TX 75261
972 453-7000

(G-7224)
SURFACE MINING RECLAMATION OFF
Also Called: Harrisburg Field Office
415 Market St Ste 3c (17101-2309)
PHONE..................................717 782-4036
EMP: 8 **Publicly Held**
SIC: 1081 Metal Mining Services
HQ: Office Of Surface Mining Reclamation
& Enforcement
1951 Constitution Ave N
Washington DC 20240

(G-7225)
T C S INDUSTRIES INC
4326 Crestview Rd (17112-2005)
PHONE..................................717 657-7032
Lois Distenfeld, *President*
Jacquelin Distenfeld, *Corp Secy*
EMP: 3 EST: 1980
SALES (est): 230K **Privately Held**
SIC: 1389 Detection & analysis service,
gas

(G-7226)
TAMMY M TIBBENS
Also Called: Your Private Printer
6103 Blue Grass Ave Apt B (17112-2329)
P.O. Box 6272 (17112-0272)
PHONE..................................717 979-3063
Ted Postosheff, *Owner*
EMP: 4
SALES (est): 210.8K **Privately Held**
SIC: 2752 Commercial printing, litho-
graphic

(G-7227)
TASTY BAKING COMPANY
493 Blue Eagle Ave (17112-2314)
PHONE..................................717 651-0307
EMP: 6
SALES (corp-wide): 3.9B **Publicly Held**
SIC: 2051 Cakes, pies & pastries
HQ: Tasty Baking Company
4300 S 26th St
Philadelphia PA 19112
215 221-8500

(G-7228)
TE CONNECTIVITY CORPORATION
2100 Paxton St (17111-1039)
PHONE..................................717 564-0100
Tom England, *President*
EMP: 100
SALES (corp-wide): 13.1B **Privately Held**
WEB: www.raychem.com
SIC: 3678 Electronic connectors
HQ: Te Connectivity Corporation
1050 Westlakes Dr
Berwyn PA 19312
610 893-9800

(G-7229)
TE CONNECTIVITY CORPORATION
449 Eisenhower Blvd (17111-2301)
PHONE..................................717 564-0100
Alex Smith, *Branch Mgr*
EMP: 400

SALES (corp-wide): 13.1B **Privately Held**
SIC: **3678** Electronic connectors
HQ: Te Connectivity Corporation
　　1050 Westlakes Dr
　　Berwyn PA 19312
　　610 893-9800

(G-7230)
TETRA TECHNOLOGIES INC
Also Called: Tetra Tech Inc-Harrisburg
2400 Park Dr (17110-9304)
PHONE.....................................717 545-3580
EMP: 41
SALES (corp-wide): 998.7MM **Publicly Held**
SIC: **2819** Industrial inorganic chemicals
PA: Tetra Technologies, Inc.
　　24955 Interstate 45
　　The Woodlands TX 77380
　　281 367-1983

(G-7231)
THREE BRIDGES MEDIA LLC
2601 N Front St Ste 101 (17110-1123)
PHONE.....................................717 695-2621
Lauren Mills,
EMP: 3 EST: 2008
SALES (est): 158.1K **Privately Held**
SIC: **2721** Magazines: publishing only, not printed on site

(G-7232)
TOMA INC (PA)
Also Called: Toma Concrete & Materials
212 Locust St Ste 500 (17101-1510)
PHONE.....................................717 597-7194
John Thomas, *President*
EMP: 13
SALES (est): 1.4MM **Privately Held**
SIC: **3272** Mfg Concrete Products

(G-7233)
TRACTION SOFTWARE INC
513 Redwood St (17109-4720)
PHONE.....................................401 528-1145
Gregory R Lloyd, *President*
Christopher Nuzum, *Vice Pres*
EMP: 6
SALES (est): 535.9K **Privately Held**
WEB: www.tractionsoftware.com
SIC: **7372** Business oriented computer software

(G-7234)
TRAINING RESOURCE CORPORATION
5 Miller Rd (17109)
PHONE.....................................717 652-3100
Jay B Bowden, *President*
Connie Bowden, *Admin Sec*
EMP: 15
SQ FT: 4,600
SALES (est): 661.8K **Privately Held**
SIC: **7389 2741** Design services; miscellaneous publishing

(G-7235)
TRANE US INC
3909 Tecport Dr (17111-1214)
PHONE.....................................717 561-5400
Steve Wey, *Manager*
EMP: 50 **Privately Held**
SIC: **3585** Heating & air conditioning combination units
HQ: Trane U.S. Inc.
　　3600 Pammel Creek Rd
　　La Crosse WI 54601
　　608 787-2000

(G-7236)
TRANSPORTATION PA DEPT
Also Called: Bureau of Motor Vehicles
1101 S Front St (17104-2570)
PHONE.....................................717 787-2304
Sandy Woltert, *Director*
EMP: 28 **Privately Held**
WEB: www.dot.gov
SIC: **3469** Automobile license tags, stamped metal
HQ: Pennsylvania Dept Of Transportation
　　400 North St Fl 8
　　Harrisburg PA 17120
　　717 787-6875

(G-7237)
TRIAD ISOTOPES INC
4400 Lewis Rd Ste A (17111-2544)
PHONE.....................................717 558-8640
Matt Coccaro, *Branch Mgr*
EMP: 6
SALES (corp-wide): 518.6MM **Privately Held**
SIC: **2834** Pharmaceutical preparations
HQ: Triad Isotopes, Inc.
　　4205 Vineland Rd Ste L1
　　Orlando FL 32811

(G-7238)
TRIANGLE PRESS INC
6720 Allentown Blvd Frnt (17112-3375)
PHONE.....................................717 541-9315
Adrianne Kihm, *CEO*
Eric Baum, *President*
John W Burkholder, *President*
Mary Ann Burkholder, *Corp Secy*
Tammy Shelley, *Vice Pres*
EMP: 28 EST: 1922
SALES (est): 5.5MM **Privately Held**
WEB: www.trianglepress.net
SIC: **2732 7389** Books: printing only; printers' services: folding, collating

(G-7239)
TURCK ENGINEERED PACKAGING
806 Crosby St (17112-1782)
PHONE.....................................717 421-7371
EMP: 5
SALES (est): 442.2K **Privately Held**
SIC: **2631** Container, packaging & boxboard

(G-7240)
UNDERNET GAMING INCORPORATED
1005 Brittany Blvd (17109-1128)
PHONE.....................................484 544-8943
Christopher Gaither, *Principal*
Sutton Sabinash, *Principal*
EMP: 8
SALES (est): 410.6K **Privately Held**
SIC: **5045 7372 5734 7371** Computers, peripherals & software; home entertainment computer software; software, computer games; computer software development & applications

(G-7241)
UNION SQUARE FROG LLC
3911 Union Deposit Rd (17109-5922)
PHONE.....................................717 561-0623
Kaitlin Lukehart, *Branch Mgr*
EMP: 8
SALES (est): 518.8K **Privately Held**
SIC: **2024** Yogurt desserts, frozen

(G-7242)
VERMICULITE ASSOCIATION INC
2207 Forest Hills Dr (17112-1005)
PHONE.....................................717 238-9902
Kathryn Louis, *President*
EMP: 4
SALES: 138.2K **Privately Held**
SIC: **1499 7389** Vermiculite mining;

(G-7243)
W O HICKOK MANUFACTURING CO
900 Cumberland St (17103-1037)
PHONE.....................................717 234-8041
Peter Hickok, *President*
Charles Hickok, *Admin Sec*
▲ EMP: 27 EST: 1844
SQ FT: 30,000
SALES (est): 6.1MM **Privately Held**
WEB: www.hickokmfg.com
SIC: **3569 3555** Assembly machines, nonmetalworking; printing trades machinery

(G-7244)
WATER GEM INC
818 S 28th St (17111-1125)
PHONE.....................................717 561-4440
John Ramsey, *Principal*
EMP: 19

SALES (est): 3.7MM **Privately Held**
SIC: **3589** Water purification equipment, household type; water treatment equipment, industrial

(G-7245)
WATER MASTER INC
818 S 28th St (17111-1125)
PHONE.....................................717 561-4440
Alan Dennis, *President*
EMP: 6 EST: 1966
SALES (est): 560K **Privately Held**
SIC: **3589** Water purification equipment, household type; water treatment equipment, industrial

(G-7246)
WEST HANOVER WINERY INC
7646 Jonestown Rd (17112-9725)
PHONE.....................................717 652-3711
George Kline, *President*
Dan Kline, *Vice Pres*
EMP: 4 EST: 1997
SALES (est): 339K **Privately Held**
WEB: www.westhanoverwinery.com
SIC: **2084** Wines

(G-7247)
WISE PLASTICS
7253 Huntingdon St (17111-5275)
PHONE.....................................847 697-2840
Frederick M Wise, *Partner*
Larry L Wise, *Partner*
EMP: 5 EST: 1973
SQ FT: 2,000
SALES: 300K **Privately Held**
SIC: **3089** Injection molding of plastics

(G-7248)
WM ENTERPRISES INC
Also Called: Graphtech
1310 Crooked Hill Rd # 800 (17110-9768)
PHONE.....................................717 238-5751
Jane Williams, *President*
Jon Williams, *Vice Pres*
EMP: 36
SALES (est): 5.5MM **Privately Held**
WEB: www.graphtechprinting.com
SIC: **2752 7374 5961 7389** Commercial printing, offset; computer graphics service; catalog & mail-order houses; advertising, promotional & trade show services

---

Harrison City
Westmoreland County

(G-7249)
JACKSON & SONS MACHINE CO
104 Johntown St (15636-1506)
P.O. Box 466 (15636-0466)
PHONE.....................................724 744-2116
Richard Jackson, *Partner*
Lois Jackson, *Partner*
EMP: 3
SALES: 200K **Privately Held**
SIC: **3469** Machine parts, stamped or pressed metal

(G-7250)
PENN CROSSING LIMITED
492 Mnr Harrison City Rd (15636-1102)
P.O. Box 82 (15636-0082)
PHONE.....................................724 744-7725
Megahan Torba, *Principal*
EMP: 7 EST: 2001
SALES (est): 578.6K **Privately Held**
SIC: **1241** Coal mining services

(G-7251)
RANBAR ELECTRICAL MTLS LLC
408 Mnr Harrison City Rd (15636-1102)
PHONE.....................................724 864-8200
Randall L C Russell, *President*
Joann Sipos, *CFO*
Rob McCourt, *Natl Sales Mgr*
Mark Hilty, *Supervisor*
Kevin Shimko, *Info Tech Mgr*
◆ EMP: 33
SQ FT: 70,000

SALES (est): 18.4MM **Privately Held**
SALES (corp-wide): 1.9B **Privately Held**
SIC: **2851 3296 3087 2821** Lacquers, varnishes, enamels & other coatings; varnishes; mineral wool; custom compound purchased resins; polyesters
HQ: Gabriel Performance Products, Llc
　　388 S Main St Ste 340
　　Akron OH 44311
　　866 800-2436

Harrisville
Butler County

(G-7252)
ALLEGHENY MINERAL CORPORATION
133 Camp Ground Rd (16038-1301)
PHONE.....................................724 735-2088
Steve Smith, *Manager*
EMP: 35
SALES (corp-wide): 790.5MM **Privately Held**
WEB: www.snydercos.com
SIC: **1499 3274 1442** Asphalt mining & bituminous stone quarrying; lime; construction sand & gravel
HQ: Allegheny Mineral Corporation
　　1 Glade Dr
　　Kittanning PA 16201
　　724 548-8101

(G-7253)
MONTGOMERY BLOCK WORKS INC
4275 William Flynn Hwy (16038-1411)
PHONE.....................................724 735-2931
Wayne C Donaldson, *President*
Mark W Donaldson, *Vice Pres*
EMP: 15 EST: 1976
SQ FT: 5,000
SALES: 1.8MM **Privately Held**
SIC: **3271 3273** Blocks, concrete or cinder: standard; ready-mixed concrete

(G-7254)
PENN GOLD HUGHES
Also Called: Penn-Gold Ice Cream Company
540 County Line Rd (16038-2801)
P.O. Box 39 (16038-0039)
PHONE.....................................724 735-2121
Gary Hughes, *Owner*
EMP: 6
SQ FT: 900
SALES: 130K **Privately Held**
WEB: www.pennstatewrestlingclub.org
SIC: **2024 5441** Ice cream, bulk; candy

(G-7255)
RIVERWOODS CABINETRY LLC
139 Barkey Hoffman Rd (16038-3901)
PHONE.....................................724 807-1045
Jared Broerman, *Mng Member*
EMP: 7 EST: 2009
SALES: 500K **Privately Held**
SIC: **2599** Cabinets, factory

Harveys Lake
Luzerne County

(G-7256)
EARTH FRIENDLY COMPOST INC
2015 Monkey Hollow Rd (18618-7815)
PHONE.....................................570 760-4510
Thomas Arndt, *Principal*
EMP: 3
SALES (est): 188.6K **Privately Held**
SIC: **2875** Compost

Harwick
Allegheny County

(G-7257)
WATSON INDUSTRIES INC (PA)
616 Hite Rd (15049-8945)
PHONE.....................................724 275-1000

▲ = Import ▼=Export
◆ =Import/Export

H Knox Watson III, *Chairman*
Joseph S Wilkoski, *Corp Secy*
Michael Caruso Jr, *Exec VP*
Daniel Monhemius, *Treasurer*
EMP: 50
SQ FT: 85,000
SALES (est): 45.7MM **Privately Held**
SIC: 2851 2899 Paints, asphalt or bitumi-
nous; varnishes; lacquers, varnishes,
enamels & other coatings; ink or writing
fluids

(G-7258)
WATSON STANDARD ADHESIVES CO
616 Hite Rd (15049-8945)
PHONE...................................724 274-5014
H Knox Watson III, *President*
David Winkler, *Corp Secy*
Henry K Watson IV, *Vice Pres*
◆ **EMP:** 8
SQ FT: 20,000
SALES (est): 1.9MM **Privately Held**
SIC: 2851 Lacquers, varnishes, enamels &
other coatings
PA: Watson Industries, Inc.
616 Hite Rd
Harwick PA 15049

(G-7259)
WATSON STANDARD COMPANY (HQ)
616 Hite Rd (15049-8945)
PHONE...................................724 275-1000
H K Watson, *CEO*
H Knox Watson III, *President*
James E Lore, *President*
J S Wilkoski, *Corp Secy*
Henry K Watson IV, *Exec VP*
◆ **EMP:** 70
SQ FT: 85,000
SALES (est): 36.9MM **Privately Held**
WEB: www.watsonstandard.com
SIC: 2851 Paints, asphalt or bituminous;
varnishes

Hastings
Cambria County

(G-7260)
F & G MONUMENT LETTERING LLC
517 Bridge St (16646-9004)
PHONE...................................814 247-5032
Eric Fritz, *Principal*
EMP: 3 **EST:** 2017
SALES (est): 203.9K **Privately Held**
SIC: 3272 Monuments & grave markers,
except terrazo

(G-7261)
HASTINGS MACHINE COMPANY INC
192 Haida Ave (16646-5612)
PHONE...................................814 247-6562
Kim Kunkle, *President*
EMP: 24
SALES (corp-wide): 101.6MM **Privately Held**
WEB: www.hastingsmachine.com
SIC: 3599 3498 3452 Machine shop, job-
bing & repair; fabricated pipe & fittings;
bolts, nuts, rivets & washers
HQ: Hastings Machine Company, Inc.
111 Roosevelt Blvd
Johnstown PA 15906
814 533-5777

(G-7262)
NEFF SPECIALTIES LLC
1505 Main St (16646-8701)
PHONE...................................814 247-8887
Shari Neff, *Mng Member*
EMP: 10
SALES: 1.6MM **Privately Held**
WEB: www.neffspecialties.com
SIC: 5046 5021 3949 Partitions; chairs;
gymnasium equipment

(G-7263)
SPILLTECH ENVIRONMENTAL INC
233 Haida Ave (16646-5610)
PHONE...................................814 247-8566
Chris Hoover, *Manager*
EMP: 7
SALES (corp-wide): 85.6MM **Privately Held**
WEB: www.newpig.com
SIC: 2842 4226 Sweeping compounds, oil
or water absorbent, clay or sawdust; spe-
cial warehousing & storage
HQ: Spilltech Environmental, Inc.
1627 Odonoghue St
Mobile AL 36615
251 694-0102

Hatboro
Montgomery County

(G-7264)
ACME CORRUGATED BOX CO INC
2700 Turnpike Dr (19040-4219)
PHONE...................................215 444-8000
Burton R Cohen, *President*
David Platt, *Vice Pres*
Saikou Diallo, *Production*
Kathryn Reimer, *Buyer*
Jeff Bittner, *QA Dir*
▲ **EMP:** 200
SALES (est): 39.3MM **Privately Held**
WEB: www.acmebox.com
SIC: 2653 Boxes, corrugated: made from
purchased materials

(G-7265)
ADVANCED MACHINING TECH
Also Called: Amt
220 Jacksonville Rd (19040-2721)
P.O. Box 3351, Warminster (18974-0136)
PHONE...................................215 672-4899
Jim Demetriou, *Partner*
Chris Demetriou, *Partner*
George Demetriou Jr, *Partner*
Mike Demetriou, *Partner*
EMP: 4
SQ FT: 2,000
SALES: 150K **Privately Held**
WEB: www.apcompany.com
SIC: 3599 Machine shop, jobbing & repair

(G-7266)
ALENCON ACQUISITION CO LLC
330 S Warminster Rd # 380 (19040-3404)
PHONE...................................484 436-0035
John Bunce, *CEO*
Oleg Fishman, *Ch of Bd*
Ulrich Kw Schwabe, *Vice Pres*
▲ **EMP:** 7 **EST:** 2011
SQ FT: 7,000
SALES (est): 1.4MM **Privately Held**
SIC: 3629 Electronic generation equipment

(G-7267)
AMERICAN CARBIDE SAW CO
320 Springdale Ave (19040-2230)
PHONE...................................215 672-1466
David B Stokes, *President*
EMP: 10
SALES: 840K **Privately Held**
SIC: 3425 7699 5084 Saw blades &
handsaws; knife, saw & tool sharpening &
repair; sawmill machinery & equipment

(G-7268)
AMERITECH NETWORK CORP
2940 Turnpike Dr Ste 6 (19040-4229)
PHONE...................................215 441-8310
Alfred Ferraro, *President*
EMP: 20
SALES (est): 2.6MM **Privately Held**
WEB: www.ameritechnetwork.com
SIC: 3663 Radio broadcasting & communi-
cations equipment

(G-7269)
AML INDUSTRIES INC
3500 Davisville Rd (19040-4248)
PHONE...................................215 674-2424

Louie Lavin, *President*
Myrna Lavin, *General Mgr*
EMP: 70 **EST:** 1945
SQ FT: 20,000
SALES (est): 6.4MM **Privately Held**
SIC: 3569 Centrifuges, industrial

(G-7270)
ARROW TOOL DIE & MACHINE CO (PA)
56 Home Rd (19040-2026)
PHONE...................................215 676-1300
Richard Comly, *President*
Joseph H Wilson, *Vice Pres*
EMP: 16 **EST:** 1945
SQ FT: 16,000
SALES (est): 1.7MM **Privately Held**
SIC: 3544 3599 Special dies & tools; ma-
chine shop, jobbing & repair

(G-7271)
AZTEC MATERIALS LLC
248 E County Line Rd (19040-2116)
PHONE...................................215 675-8900
Mario Diliberto, *Principal*
EMP: 7
SALES (est): 464.1K **Privately Held**
SIC: 1446 Silica sand mining

(G-7272)
AZTEC MATERIALS LLC
348 E County Line Rd (19040)
PHONE...................................215 675-8900
Mario Diliberto, *President*
EMP: 7
SALES (est): 360K **Privately Held**
SIC: 1446 Industrial sand

(G-7273)
BENT GLASS DESIGN INC
3535 Davisville Rd (19040-4208)
PHONE...................................215 441-9101
Steven D Lerner, *President*
Maribeth P Lerner, *Admin Sec*
▲ **EMP:** 34
SQ FT: 52,000
SALES (est): 5.7MM **Privately Held**
WEB: www.bentglassdesign.com
SIC: 3229 5039 Glassware, industrial;
glass construction materials

(G-7274)
BOGGS PRINTING INC
216 N York Rd (19040-2610)
PHONE...................................215 675-1203
Gerald J Boggs Jr, *President*
EMP: 4
SQ FT: 4,000
SALES (est): 565.9K **Privately Held**
WEB: www.boggsprinting.com
SIC: 2752 Commercial printing, offset

(G-7275)
C & L RIVET CO INC
220 Jacksonville Rd (19040-2721)
P.O. Box 767 (19040-0767)
PHONE...................................215 672-1113
Arthur Newcomb, *President*
John Newcomb, *Vice Pres*
EMP: 22
SALES (est): 4.3MM **Privately Held**
WEB: www.clrivet.com
SIC: 3452 Rivets, metal

(G-7276)
CANALLEY PAINTING
Also Called: Corporate Carpentry
400 Lincoln Ave Ste A (19040-2292)
PHONE...................................215 443-9505
Ed Canalley, *Principal*
EMP: 4 **EST:** 2004
SALES (est): 395.3K **Privately Held**
SIC: 3471 Electroplating of metals or
formed products

(G-7277)
D W MACHINE CO INC
220 Jacksonville Rd (19040-2721)
P.O. Box 3045, Warminster (18974-0105)
PHONE...................................215 672-3340
David Warfield, *President*
EMP: 3
SQ FT: 800
SALES (est): 241.6K **Privately Held**
SIC: 3544 7699 Special dies, tools, jigs &
fixtures; industrial equipment services

(G-7278)
DELAWARE VALLEY CON CO INC (PA)
Also Called: DVC
248 E County Line Rd (19040-2116)
P.O. Box 457 (19040-0457)
PHONE...................................215 675-8900
Mario Diliberto, *President*
Elise Diliberto, *Corp Secy*
EMP: 60 **EST:** 1958
SQ FT: 5,000
SALES (est): 33.9MM **Privately Held**
WEB: www.dvc-concrete.com
SIC: 3273 Ready-mixed concrete

(G-7279)
DESIGNS IN STONE INC
163 E County Line Rd (19040-1218)
P.O. Box 523 (19040-0523)
PHONE...................................800 878-6631
Nancy Guenst, *President*
EMP: 5
SQ FT: 3,000
SALES (est): 494.7K **Privately Held**
SIC: 3281 Cut stone & stone products

(G-7280)
DIGIBUDDHA DESIGN LLC
237 Jacksonville Rd (19040-2630)
PHONE...................................267 387-8165
Monika Levy,
Lisa Albaladejo,
EMP: 18 **EST:** 2012
SQ FT: 3,000
SALES: 2.4MM **Privately Held**
SIC: 2678 Stationery products

(G-7281)
DPI INC
2800 Turnpike Dr (19040-4249)
PHONE...................................215 953-9800
Jeffrey P Wolf, *President*
Lance Zeitz, *VP Opers*
EMP: 13 **EST:** 1963
SQ FT: 5,500
SALES (est): 2.2MM **Privately Held**
WEB: www.dpicnc.com
SIC: 3599 Machine shop, jobbing & repair

(G-7282)
DUDLIK INDUSTRIES INC
326 Jacksonville Rd (19040-2298)
PHONE...................................215 674-4383
Edward Dudlik, *President*
Marilyn Dudlik, *President*
Jay Obarowski, *General Mgr*
Jane Dudlik, *Vice Pres*
Gary Hasler, *Opers Staff*
▲ **EMP:** 25 **EST:** 1959
SQ FT: 80,000
SALES (est): 6MM **Privately Held**
WEB: www.dudlik.com
SIC: 3444 3053 3469 Sheet metalwork;
gaskets, all materials; household cooking
& kitchen utensils, metal

(G-7283)
EBERSOLE ENGINEERING
469b Oakdale Ave (19040-4607)
PHONE...................................215 675-0106
Terry Ebersole, *Owner*
EMP: 5
SQ FT: 4,300
SALES (est): 46.5K **Privately Held**
WEB: www.ebersoleengineering.com
SIC: 3599 Machine shop, jobbing & repair

(G-7284)
ELECTRIC REWIND CO INC
706 Burbridge Rd (19040-4524)
PHONE...................................215 675-6912
Nick Cirone, *President*
Florence Cirone, *Vice Pres*
EMP: 3
SQ FT: 3,500
SALES (est): 126.4K **Privately Held**
SIC: 7694 5999 Electric motor repair; mo-
tors, electric

(G-7285)
FAY STUDIOS
308 S Linden Ave (19040-3320)
PHONE...................................215 672-2599
Walter J Fay, *Owner*
EMP: 6

GEOGRAPHIC

SALES (est): 250K **Privately Held**
WEB: www.faystudios.net
SIC: 7922 2391 Scenery design, theatrical; curtains & draperies

(G-7286)
GRAVEL
52 Horseshoe Ln (19040-4004)
PHONE..................................215 675-3960
Ralph Gravel, *Principal*
EMP: 3
SALES (est): 139.2K **Privately Held**
SIC: 1442 Construction sand & gravel

(G-7287)
HOLMES DENTAL COMPANY
50 S Penn St Ste 6a (19040-3246)
P.O. Box 243 (19040-0243)
PHONE..................................215 675-2877
Shelley M Greene MD, *Owner*
EMP: 3 EST: 1974
SQ FT: 1,000
SALES (est): 16.9K **Privately Held**
WEB: www.holmesdental.com
SIC: 3843 Dental equipment & supplies

(G-7288)
KEYSTONE PRINTING
SERVICES
445 Jacksonville Rd (19040-4605)
PHONE..................................215 675-6464
Kevin Sweeney, *Branch Mgr*
EMP: 3
SALES (corp-wide): 581.7K **Privately Held**
SIC: 2752 Commercial printing, offset
PA: Keystone Printing Services
445 Jacksonville Rd
Hatboro PA 19040
215 675-6464

(G-7289)
KEYSTONE PRINTING
SERVICES (PA)
445 Jacksonville Rd (19040-4605)
PHONE..................................215 675-6464
Kevin P Sweeney, *President*
Clare Sweeney, *Manager*
EMP: 3
SQ FT: 4,000
SALES (est): 581.7K **Privately Held**
SIC: 3555 7389 Printing trades machinery; engraving service

(G-7290)
KINGSBURY INC
3615 Davisville Rd Ste 4 (19040-4245)
PHONE..................................215 824-4000
Stephen Burmeister, *Manager*
Gerry Abrams, *Manager*
EMP: 18
SALES (corp-wide): 29MM **Privately Held**
SIC: 3568 Power transmission equipment
PA: Kingsbury, Inc.
10385 Drummond Rd
Philadelphia PA 19154
215 824-4000

(G-7291)
L & M ENGINES INC
246 E County Line Rd 7b (19040-2159)
PHONE..................................215 675-8485
Michael Rauscher, *President*
EMP: 3
SQ FT: 1,000
SALES (est): 490.5K **Privately Held**
WEB: www.lmengines.com
SIC: 3519 7538 Internal combustion engines; engine rebuilding: automotive

(G-7292)
LINDAS STUFF INC
330 S Warminster Rd # 340 (19040-3433)
PHONE..................................215 956-9190
Linda Lightman, *Principal*
Max Lightman, *VP Bus Dvlpt*
Maria Gordon, *Manager*
EMP: 17
SALES (est): 2MM **Privately Held**
SIC: 2339 Women's & misses' accessories

(G-7293)
LUCCIS
Also Called: Luhv Food
101 N York Rd (19040-3111)
PHONE..................................903 600-5848
Silvia Lucci, *President*
Facundo Lucci, *Vice Pres*
EMP: 3
SALES (est): 121.6K **Privately Held**
SIC: 2038 Soups, frozen

(G-7294)
M & S CENTERLESS GRINDING
INC
258 E County Line Rd (19040-2116)
PHONE..................................215 675-4144
John Shegda, *President*
Mark Shegda, *Principal*
Darrin Brown, *Opers Mgr*
Pearl Shegda, *Admin Sec*
EMP: 10
SQ FT: 6,000
SALES (est): 2.3MM **Privately Held**
WEB: www.msgrinding.com
SIC: 3599 3541 Machine shop, jobbing & repair; custom machinery; grinding machines, metalworking

(G-7295)
PARADIGM CORPORATION
Also Called: Paradigm Tool and Mfg
409 Lincoln Ave (19040-2228)
PHONE..................................215 675-9488
Joe Murphy, *President*
Gerard Murphy, *Treasurer*
EMP: 12
SQ FT: 3,800
SALES (est): 1.7MM **Privately Held**
SIC: 8711 3599 Engineering services; machine shop, jobbing & repair

(G-7296)
PCM CONTRACTING INC
Also Called: Pcm Paving & Sealcoating
537 E County Line Rd (19040-1217)
PHONE..................................215 675-8846
Patrick McAnally, *President*
EMP: 5
SALES (est): 401.1K **Privately Held**
SIC: 1771 2951 Concrete work; asphalt paving mixtures & blocks

(G-7297)
PENN FASTENERS INC
220 Jacksonville Rd (19040-2721)
P.O. Box 767 (19040-0767)
PHONE..................................215 674-2772
Charles Mannella, *President*
EMP: 24
SQ FT: 40,000
SALES (est): 2.2MM **Privately Held**
SIC: 3452 5085 Bolts, nuts, rivets & washers; industrial supplies

(G-7298)
PRECISION CUNTERTOPS
MLLWK INC
301a Lincoln Ave (19040-2227)
PHONE..................................215 598-7161
Mark Eisele, *Principal*
EMP: 4
SALES (est): 468.2K **Privately Held**
SIC: 2434 Wood kitchen cabinets

(G-7299)
REBCO MACHINING INC
403 Lincoln Ave (19040-2228)
PHONE..................................215 957-5133
Robert Bridgers, *President*
Bill Joyce, *Vice Pres*
Jean Bridgers, *Admin Sec*
EMP: 5
SQ FT: 5,000
SALES (est): 510.5K **Privately Held**
SIC: 3599 Machine shop, jobbing & repair

(G-7300)
REVELATIONS PERFUME
COSMT INC
2800 Turnpike Dr Ste B (19040-4249)
PHONE..................................215 396-7286
Larry Couey, *President*
George Kalman Jr, *Corp Secy*
▲ EMP: 7

SALES (est): 1.7MM **Privately Held**
WEB: www.revelationsperfume.com
SIC: 2844 Cosmetic preparations

(G-7301)
RHINO INC
Also Called: Sullivan's Scrap Metals
451 Oakdale Ave (19040-4607)
PHONE..................................215 442-1504
Michael P Whalen Jr, *President*
Elise I Whalen, *Vice Pres*
Michael Whalen, *Treasurer*
EMP: 15
SALES (est): 3.4MM **Privately Held**
SIC: 3569 5093 Baling machines, for scrap metal, paper or similar material; junk & scrap

(G-7302)
ROLL YOUR OWN
207 N York Rd (19040-2003)
PHONE..................................215 420-7441
Don Homes, *Owner*
EMP: 4
SALES (est): 296.5K **Privately Held**
SIC: 3911 Cigar & cigarette accessories

(G-7303)
SB GLOBAL FOODS INC
2940 Turnpike Dr Ste 15 (19040-4229)
PHONE..................................215 361-9500
Karl B Brown, *President*
Jeff Juba, *Finance*
▼ EMP: 6
SQ FT: 3,000
SALES (est): 1MM **Privately Held**
WEB: www.sbglobalfoods.com
SIC: 2038 5145 Snacks, including onion rings, cheese sticks, etc.; snack foods

(G-7304)
SENTINEL PROCESS SYSTEMS
INC (PA)
Also Called: Kilolabs.com
3265 Sunset Ln (19040-4528)
PHONE..................................215 675-5700
Paul Tramo, *President*
Joseph Loughran, *General Mgr*
Robert Etramo, *Treasurer*
Mary Tramo, *Human Res Mgr*
Joe Hartey, *Sales Mgr*
▲ EMP: 16
SQ FT: 12,000
SALES (est): 5.7MM **Privately Held**
WEB: www.sentinelprocess.com
SIC: 3229 5085 Art, decorative & novelty glassware; industrial supplies

(G-7305)
SIX PACK CREAMERY LLC
226 Oak Hill Dr (19040-1918)
PHONE..................................267 261-2727
EMP: 3
SALES (est): 68.6K **Privately Held**
SIC: 2024 Dairy based frozen desserts

(G-7306)
STATUS LABEL CORPORATION
2910 Turnpike Dr (19040-4225)
PHONE..................................215 443-0124
Lee L Tompkins, *President*
William Tompkins, *Vice Pres*
EMP: 9
SQ FT: 7,200
SALES (est): 1.5MM **Privately Held**
WEB: www.blackdart.com
SIC: 2672 Labels (unprinted), gummed: made from purchased materials

(G-7307)
STUTZ CANDY COMPANY (PA)
400 S Warminster Rd (19040-4097)
PHONE..................................215 675-2630
John E Glaser, *President*
EMP: 30 EST: 1931
SQ FT: 21,000
SALES (est): 5.8MM **Privately Held**
SIC: 2064 5441 2068 2066 Candy & other confectionery products; candy; salted & roasted nuts & seeds; chocolate & cocoa products

(G-7308)
TRIDENT EMERGENCY
PRODUCTS LLC
2940 Turnpike Dr Ste 9 (19040-4229)
PHONE..................................215 293-0700
Jim Maher, *President*
Nick Capaldo, *Engineer*
▲ EMP: 4
SALES (est): 753.7K **Privately Held**
WEB: www.tridentdirect.com
SIC: 3569 Firefighting apparatus & related equipment

(G-7309)
VILLAGE PRETZELS
36 S York Rd Ste 1 (19040-3332)
PHONE..................................215 674-5070
Steve Leavtion, *Owner*
EMP: 15
SALES (est): 1.3MM **Privately Held**
SIC: 2052 Pretzels

(G-7310)
WALTER E LEE INC
601 High Ave (19040-2415)
PHONE..................................215 443-0271
Walter E Lee, *President*
EMP: 4
SALES (est): 193K **Privately Held**
WEB: www.waltlee.com
SIC: 2499 Kitchen, bathroom & household ware: wood

(G-7311)
YARRINGTON MILLS
CORPORATION
Also Called: Ymc
412 S Warminster Rd (19040-4095)
P.O. Box 397 (19040-0397)
PHONE..................................215 674-5125
James Yarrington, *President*
Mike Bohn, *Manager*
◆ EMP: 34 EST: 1915
SQ FT: 19,000
SALES: 5.1MM **Privately Held**
WEB: www.yarringtonmills.com
SIC: 2396 2241 2259 Apparel findings & trimmings; lace & decorative trim, narrow fabric; shoe linings, knit

---

Hatfield
Montgomery County

(G-7312)
5P CORPORATION
2800 Crystal Dr (19440-1944)
PHONE..................................215 997-5666
Robert Trockels, *Principal*
▲ EMP: 3
SALES (est): 270K **Privately Held**
SIC: 3843 Dental equipment & supplies

(G-7313)
A L FINISHING CO INC
925 Schwab Rd Ste C (19440-3207)
PHONE..................................215 855-9422
Jamie Hemmerle, *President*
Timothy Hemmerle, *Vice Pres*
John Oberholtzer, *Vice Pres*
Judith Hemmerle, *Treasurer*
Cynthia Hemmerle, *Admin Sec*
EMP: 13
SQ FT: 5,000
SALES (est): 1.6MM **Privately Held**
SIC: 3471 Anodizing (plating) of metals or formed products; finishing, metals or formed products

(G-7314)
ACME SPECIALTIES INC
2880 Bergey Rd Ste 100 (19440-1764)
PHONE..................................215 822-5900
Kevin J Shinners, *President*
J Christopher Shinners, *Treasurer*
J Shinners, *Treasurer*
EMP: 9 EST: 1933
SQ FT: 20,000
SALES (est): 1.4MM **Privately Held**
SIC: 2675 Paperboard die-cutting

(G-7315)
AMERICAN MOLDING INCORPORATED
2800 Sterling Dr (19440-1957)
PHONE.....................................215 822-5544
Joel Glickman, *Principal*
EMP: 4
SALES (est): 232.1K **Privately Held**
SIC: 3089 Molding primary plastic; injection molding of plastics

(G-7316)
AMERICOLD LOGISTICS LLC
2525 Bergey Rd (19440-1703)
PHONE.....................................215 721-0700
Steve Souder, *Facilities Mgr*
James Styer, *Branch Mgr*
EMP: 150
SALES (corp-wide): 1.6B **Privately Held**
SIC: 4222 4731 2097 Warehousing, cold storage or refrigerated; transportation agents & brokers; block ice; ice cubes
HQ: Americold Logistics, Llc
    10 Glenlake Pkwy Ste 324
    Atlanta GA 30328
    678 441-1400

(G-7317)
ANDERSON TUBE COMPANY INC
1400 Fairgrounds Rd (19440-2821)
P.O. Box 129 (19440-0129)
PHONE.....................................215 855-0118
Joann Mancuso, *President*
Rick Witte, *Sales Mgr*
Anthony Lupino, *Sales Staff*
Erica Stidham, *Technology*
George W Hoover, *Admin Sec*
▼ **EMP:** 7
SQ FT: 20,200
SALES (est): 1.4MM **Privately Held**
WEB: www.atube.com
SIC: 3443 Fabricated plate work (boiler shop)

(G-7318)
ARS METAL FABRICATORS LLC
3430 Unionville Pike (19440-1829)
PHONE.....................................215 855-6000
Marlin Gehman, *Mng Member*
EMP: 7 EST: 1956
SQ FT: 4,000
SALES (est): 680K **Privately Held**
WEB: www.arsmetal.com
SIC: 3444 Sheet metal specialties, not stamped

(G-7319)
B&G MANUFACTURING CO INC (PA)
3067 Unionville Pike (19440-1822)
P.O. Box 904 (19440-0904)
PHONE.....................................215 822-1925
William A Edmonds, *President*
Richard Edmunds, *COO*
William Baker, *Vice Pres*
Richard F Edmonds Jr, *Vice Pres*
Tom Kramme, *Vice Pres*
▲ **EMP:** 180
SQ FT: 140,000
SALES (est): 54.1MM **Privately Held**
WEB: www.bgmfg.com
SIC: 3452 5085 Bolts, metal; fasteners, industrial: nuts, bolts, screws, etc.

(G-7320)
BAKERS BEST SNACK FOODS INC
1880 N Penn Rd (19440-1950)
PHONE.....................................215 822-3511
Jerry Driver, *President*
EMP: 35
SALES (est): 4.8MM **Privately Held**
SIC: 2052 Pretzels

(G-7321)
BISHOP EQUIPMENT MANUFACTURING
63 E Broad St Ste 1 (19440-2464)
PHONE.....................................215 368-5307
Melonie Mc Veagh, *President*
EMP: 4

SALES (est): 477.9K **Privately Held**
SIC: 3523 Sprayers & spraying machines, agricultural

(G-7322)
BROOKS INSTRUMENT LLC (HQ)
407 W Vine St (19440-3000)
P.O. Box 903 (19440-0903)
PHONE.....................................215 362-3500
Han Choi, *General Mgr*
Sharon Szafranski, *Vice Pres*
Frank Auriemma, *Vice Pres*
Eric Pipal, *Vice Pres*
Sharon Szfranski, *Vice Pres*
EMP: 189
SALES (est): 48.4MM
SALES (corp-wide): 14.7B **Publicly Held**
SIC: 3823 Industrial process measurement equipment
PA: Illinois Tool Works Inc.
    155 Harlem Ave
    Glenview IL 60025
    847 724-7500

(G-7323)
CENTRIC PLASTICS LLC
925 Schwab Rd Ste 1 (19440-3207)
PHONE.....................................215 309-1999
Morton French, *Mng Member*
Nina French,
◆ **EMP:** 6
SQ FT: 5,000
SALES: 750K **Privately Held**
SIC: 3081 5162 Polyethylene film; plastics materials & basic shapes

(G-7324)
CLEMENS FAMILY CORPORATION (PA)
2700 Clemens Rd (19440-4202)
P.O. Box 902 (19440-0902)
PHONE.....................................800 523-5291
Douglas C Clemens, *CEO*
Philip A Clemens, *CEO*
David W Budnick, *Principal*
Philip E Keeler, *Principal*
James B Wood, *Principal*
▼ **EMP:** 1800
SQ FT: 850,000
SALES (est): 705.7MM **Privately Held**
SIC: 0213 2011 4222 8661 Hogs; meat packing plants; warehousing, cold storage or refrigerated; religious organizations

(G-7325)
CLEMENS FOOD GROUP LLC (HQ)
2700 Clemens Rd (19440-4202)
P.O. Box 902 (19440-0902)
PHONE.....................................215 368-2500
Douglas Clemens, *CEO*
Philip A Clemens, *Ch of Bd*
Steve Brown, *President*
Craig H Edsill, *President*
Robert Ruth, *General Mgr*
◆ **EMP:** 1558 EST: 1895
SQ FT: 850,000
SALES (est): 432.7MM
SALES (corp-wide): 705.7MM **Privately Held**
WEB: www.hatfieldqualitymeatsfoodservice.com
SIC: 2011 2013 Pork products from pork slaughtered on site; sausages & other prepared meats
PA: The Clemens Family Corporation
    2700 Clemens Rd
    Hatfield PA 19440
    800 523-5291

(G-7326)
CLIMATIC TESTING SYSTEMS INC (PA)
Also Called: C T S
2367 N Penn Rd Ste 100 (19440-1962)
PHONE.....................................215 773-9322
Alfonso Rombola, *President*
Douglas E Brace, *Vice Pres*
Paula Kelly, *Purch Mgr*
Brian Merritt, *Engineer*
Richard A Alford, *Admin Sec*
◆ **EMP:** 21
SQ FT: 10,000

SALES (est): 6.4MM **Privately Held**
WEB: www.climatictesting.com
SIC: 3826 Instruments measuring thermal properties

(G-7327)
COUNTRY FRESH PENNSYLVANIA LLC
2600 Richmond Rd (19440-1803)
PHONE.....................................215 855-2408
Joe Moser, *Principal*
▲ **EMP:** 125 EST: 2008
SALES (est): 17.1MM **Privately Held**
SIC: 2099 Food preparations

(G-7328)
CURTISS-WRIGHT CORPORATION
2701 Township Line Rd (19440-1770)
PHONE.....................................215 721-1100
Russ Diehl, *Purch Mgr*
EMP: 10
SALES (corp-wide): 2.4B **Publicly Held**
SIC: 3491 Industrial valves
PA: Curtiss-Wright Corporation
    130 Harbour Place Dr # 300
    Davidson NC 28036
    704 869-4600

(G-7329)
CURVEBEAM LLC
2800 Bronze Dr Ste 110 (19440-1954)
PHONE.....................................267 483-8081
Joe Eck, *Prdtn Mgr*
Guy Long, *Opers Staff*
Mark Dry, *Electrical Engi*
Arun Singh, *Mng Member*
Tami Alexander, *Director*
EMP: 20 EST: 2009
SALES (est): 5.9MM **Privately Held**
SIC: 3842 Orthopedic appliances

(G-7330)
CUSTOM POOL COPING INC
3210 Unionville Pike (19440-1827)
PHONE.....................................215 822-9098
Douglas Dahms, *President*
Jo Ann Dahms, *Admin Sec*
EMP: 6
SQ FT: 6,000
SALES (est): 867.1K **Privately Held**
SIC: 3272 Copings, concrete

(G-7331)
D&W FINE PACK LLC
1100 Schwab Rd (19440-3231)
PHONE.....................................215 362-1501
Dave Randall, *CEO*
EMP: 321
SALES (corp-wide): 614.5MM **Privately Held**
SIC: 3089 Plastic processing
HQ: D&W Fine Pack Llc
    777 Mark St Ste 101
    Wood Dale IL 60191

(G-7332)
DECALCRAFT CORP
2750 Bethlehem Pike (19440-1613)
PHONE.....................................215 822-0517
Scott P Tobin, *President*
EMP: 3
SQ FT: 6,000
SALES (est): 148.2K
SALES (corp-wide): 607.3K **Privately Held**
WEB: www.decalcraft.com
SIC: 2759 Decals: printing
PA: National Decal Craft Corp
    2750 Bethlehem Pike
    Hatfield PA 19440
    215 822-0517

(G-7333)
DENTAL IMAGING TECH CORP (HQ)
Also Called: Imaging Sciences International
2800 Crystal Dr (19440-1944)
PHONE.....................................215 997-5666
Amir Aghbabi, *President*
David Cowan, *President*
Ed Marandola, *Vice Pres*
Mike Frank, *Engineer*
Marc Pensa, *CFO*
▲ **EMP:** 83

SQ FT: 6,000
SALES: 200MM
SALES (corp-wide): 19.8B **Publicly Held**
SIC: 3843 5047 Dental equipment; X-ray machines & tubes
PA: Danaher Corporation
    2200 Penn Ave Nw Ste 800w
    Washington DC 20037
    202 828-0850

(G-7334)
DIATOME U S JOINT VENTURE
Also Called: Diatome-US
1560 Industry Rd (19440-3249)
P.O. Box 550 (19440-0550)
PHONE.....................................215 646-1478
Stacie Kirsch, *President*
Stacie Corporation, *Co-Venturer*
▲ **EMP:** 5
SALES (est): 735.9K **Privately Held**
SIC: 3423 Knives, agricultural or industrial

(G-7335)
DP MILLWORK INC
2262 N Penn Rd Ste 200 (19440-1970)
PHONE.....................................215 996-1179
Frank Perri, *President*
EMP: 6 EST: 1996
SQ FT: 20,000
SALES (est): 1MM **Privately Held**
WEB: www.dpmillwork.com
SIC: 2431 Millwork

(G-7336)
DRT MEDICAL LLC
2342 N Penn Rd (19440-1907)
PHONE.....................................215 997-2900
EMP: 46
SALES (corp-wide): 770.6MM **Publicly Held**
SIC: 3841 Surgical & medical instruments
HQ: Drt Medical, Llc
    4201 Little York Rd
    Dayton OH 45414
    937 387-0880

(G-7337)
ELECTROSTATICS INC
63 E Broad St Ste 6 (19440-2464)
PHONE.....................................215 513-0850
Peter Mariani, *President*
EMP: 13
SQ FT: 6,000
SALES (est): 1.3MM **Privately Held**
WEB: www.electrostatics.com
SIC: 3629 Electronic generation equipment

(G-7338)
ELJOBO INC
2800 Sterling Dr (19440-1957)
PHONE.....................................215 822-5544
Joel Glickman, *President*
Robert Glickman, *Corp Secy*
EMP: 75
SQ FT: 122,600
SALES (est): 16.9MM **Privately Held**
WEB: www.rodongroup.com
SIC: 3089 Injection molding of plastics

(G-7339)
EMS ACQUISITION CORP
Also Called: Electron Microscopy Sciences
1560 Industry Rd (19440-3249)
P.O. Box 550 (19440-0550)
PHONE.....................................215 412-8400
Anton Meyer, *Ch of Bd*
Stacie Kirsch, *President*
Kim Denofa, *Assistant*
▲ **EMP:** 35 EST: 1969
SQ FT: 39,000
SALES (est): 13.7MM **Privately Held**
WEB: ems-contract-packaging.com/
SIC: 3826 Analytical instruments

(G-7340)
ENPRO INDUSTRIES INC
1600 Industry Rd (19440-3251)
PHONE.....................................800 618-4701
Stephen E Macadam, *Branch Mgr*
EMP: 29
SALES (corp-wide): 1.5B **Publicly Held**
SIC: 3053 Gaskets & sealing devices
PA: Enpro Industries, Inc.
    5605 Carnegie Blvd # 500
    Charlotte NC 28209
    704 731-1500

GEOGRAPHIC

(G-7341)
ENTERPRISE MACHINE CO
1370 Industry Rd Ste C (19440-3241)
PHONE...................215 855-0868
Bud Garnett, *Owner*
EMP: 3
SQ FT: 4,000
SALES: 275K **Privately Held**
SIC: 3599 Machine shop, jobbing & repair

(G-7342)
ERASEAL TECHNOLOGIES LLC
2970 Cowpath Rd (19440-2339)
PHONE...................215 350-3633
Wayne Rutter, *Principal*
EMP: 3
SALES (est): 223.5K **Privately Held**
SIC: 3053 Gaskets & sealing devices

(G-7343)
FLUID ENERGY PROC & EQP CO
2629 Penn St (19440-2344)
P.O. Box 200 (19440-0200)
PHONE...................215 368-2510
Jerry Leimkuhler, *President*
Keith Goodwin, *Plant Mgr*
EMP: 64
SALES (corp-wide): 16.4MM **Privately Held**
SIC: 3599 3295 3559 Grinding castings for the trade; minerals, ground or treated; stone working machinery
PA: Fluid Energy Processing & Equipment Co Inc
4300 Bethlehem Pike
Telford PA 18969
215 721-8990

(G-7344)
GENISPHERE LLC
2801 Sterling Dr (19440-1956)
PHONE...................215 996-3002
Tom Bliss, *President*
Dana Witlin, *General Mgr*
James Kadushin, *Mng Member*
EMP: 9
SQ FT: 17,000
SALES (est): 2.4MM **Privately Held**
WEB: www.genisphere.com
SIC: 3829 Physical property testing equipment

(G-7345)
HARDY MACHINE INC
2326 N Penn Rd (19440-1907)
PHONE...................215 822-9359
William N Hardy, *President*
David N Hardy, *Vice Pres*
Carol Snieder, *Office Admin*
EMP: 24 EST: 1957
SQ FT: 30,000
SALES: 5.7MM **Privately Held**
WEB: www.hmiinc.com
SIC: 3599 Custom machinery

(G-7346)
HATFIELD MANUFACTURING INC
1447 Leas Way (19440-2629)
PHONE...................215 368-9574
John Dumkc, *Principal*
EMP: 3
SALES (est): 270.4K **Privately Held**
SIC: 3999 Manufacturing industries

(G-7347)
HEFNER MACHINE & TOOL INC
3003 Unionville Pike (19440-1825)
PHONE...................215 721-5900
Michael Hefner, *President*
Bob Duffy, *QC Mgr*
EMP: 24
SQ FT: 12,000
SALES (est): 2MM **Privately Held**
WEB: www.hefnermachine.com
SIC: 3599 Machine shop, jobbing & repair

(G-7348)
HELM FENCING INC
2021 Bethlehem Pike (19440-1306)
PHONE...................215 822-5595
H Peter Helm, *President*
EMP: 25
SQ FT: 2,400

SALES (est): 2.8MM **Privately Held**
WEB: www.helmfencing.com
SIC: 1799 2499 5211 Fence construction; fencing, wood; fencing

(G-7349)
HF GROUP LLC
63 E Broad St Ste 6 (19440-2464)
PHONE...................215 368-7308
Keith Roberts,
EMP: 40
SALES (est): 4.1MM **Privately Held**
SIC: 2789 Binding & repair of books, magazines & pamphlets

(G-7350)
HF GROUP LLC
Also Called: Library Bindery of PA
63 E Broad St Ste 6 (19440-2464)
PHONE...................215 855-2293
Lee Ogden, *Branch Mgr*
EMP: 37
SALES (corp-wide): 28MM **Privately Held**
SIC: 2732 Books: printing & binding
PA: Hf Group, Llc
8844 Mayfield Rd
Chesterland OH 44026
440 729-2445

(G-7351)
HOLLOW BALL GROUP LLC
2280 Amber Dr (19440-1969)
PHONE...................215 822-3380
Drew Cincotta, *Principal*
EMP: 4 EST: 2008
SALES (est): 381.7K **Privately Held**
SIC: 3562 Ball bearings & parts

(G-7352)
ILLINOIS TOOL WORKS INC
Simco Industrial Static Ctrl
2257 N Penn Rd (19440-1906)
PHONE...................215 822-2171
Gary Swink, *Branch Mgr*
EMP: 100
SALES (corp-wide): 14.7B **Publicly Held**
SIC: 3629 5084 Electronic generation equipment; industrial machinery & equipment
PA: Illinois Tool Works Inc.
155 Harlem Ave
Glenview IL 60025
847 724-7500

(G-7353)
IMAGING SCIENCES INTL LLC
Also Called: I Cat
1910 N Penn Rd (19440-1960)
PHONE...................215 997-5666
Matthew Reintjes, *President*
▲ EMP: 33
SALES (est): 8.6MM
SALES (corp-wide): 19.8B **Publicly Held**
SIC: 3844 X-ray apparatus & tubes
PA: Danaher Corporation
2200 Penn Ave Nw Ste 800w
Washington DC 20037
202 828-0850

(G-7354)
INOFAST MANUFACTURING INC
2880 Bergey Rd Ste R (19440-1764)
PHONE...................215 996-9963
Scott Bardsley, *President*
Rich Oldham, *Sales Mgr*
EMP: 3 EST: 1981
SALES (est): 213K **Privately Held**
SIC: 3965 Fasteners

(G-7355)
J AND B PRECISION MACHINE CO
3020 Bethlehem Pike (19440-1621)
PHONE...................215 822-1400
Benjamin Brower, *President*
Janet Brower, *Corp Secy*
Jeffrey Trauger, *Shareholder*
EMP: 6
SQ FT: 6,000
SALES: 500K **Privately Held**
SIC: 3599 7692 Machine shop, jobbing & repair; welding repair

(G-7356)
JET PLASTICA INDUSTRIES INC
1100 Schwab Rd (19440-3234)
PHONE...................800 220-5381
EMP: 288
SALES (corp-wide): 33.3MM **Privately Held**
SIC: 3089 3421 Mfg Plastic Products Mfg Cutlery
HQ: Jet Plastica Industries Inc.
1100 Schwab Rd
Hatfield PA 19440
215 362-1501

(G-7357)
KDL PHARMACEUTICAL CO LTD
606 Edwin Ln (19440-1259)
PHONE...................215 259-3024
Xiaoping Lo, *Partner*
EMP: 3
SALES (est): 253.8K **Privately Held**
SIC: 2834 Pharmaceutical preparations

(G-7358)
KNEX INDUSTRIES INC
2990 Bergey Rd (19440-1735)
PHONE...................215 997-7722
Michael Araten, *CEO*
Joel Glickman, *President*
Bob Haines, *Senior VP*
Joseph Smith, *Senior VP*
Robert Haines, *CFO*
◆ EMP: 160
SQ FT: 125,000
SALES (est): 25.7MM **Privately Held**
WEB: www.knex.com
SIC: 3944 Games, toys & children's vehicles

(G-7359)
KNEX LTD PARTNERSHIP GROUP
2990 Bergey Rd (19440-1735)
PHONE...................215 997-7722
Michael Araten, *CEO*
EMP: 84
SALES (est): 503.8K **Privately Held**
SIC: 3944 Games, toys & children's vehicles

(G-7360)
KOREN PUBLICATIONS INC
777 Schwab Rd Ste K (19440-3272)
PHONE...................267 498-0071
Tedd Koren, *President*
EMP: 7
SQ FT: 2,000
SALES (est): 979.5K **Privately Held**
SIC: 2721 8041 Trade journals: publishing only, not printed on site; offices & clinics of chiropractors

(G-7361)
LABORATORY TESTING INC
Also Called: Lt
2331 Topaz Dr (19440-1936)
PHONE...................215 997-9080
Mike McVaugh, *President*
Joan Bentley, *Corp Secy*
Thomas Mc Vaugh, *Vice Pres*
Loretta Tubiello Harr, *CFO*
Eileen McVaugh, *Admin Sec*
EMP: 105
SQ FT: 54,000
SALES (est): 23.1MM **Privately Held**
WEB: www.labtesting.com
SIC: 8734 3599 Metallurgical testing laboratory; calibration & certification; product testing laboratories; machine shop, jobbing & repair

(G-7362)
LAMINATORS INCORPORATED (PA)
3255 Penn St (19440-1731)
PHONE...................215 723-5285
David J Thompson, *President*
William Annechini, *Vice Pres*
David I Thompson, *Vice Pres*
John Simon, *Vice Pres*
John T Wright, *Vice Pres*
▲ EMP: 68 EST: 1963
SQ FT: 77,000

SALES (est): 16.4MM **Privately Held**
WEB: www.laminatorsinc.com
SIC: 3291 3446 3993 3365 Steel wool; architectural metalwork; signs & advertising specialties; aluminum & aluminum-based alloy castings

(G-7363)
LANEKO ROLL FORM INC
3003 Unionville Pike (19440-1825)
PHONE...................215 822-1930
Ernest Pfeiffer, *President*
Patrick M Otconnell, *Vice Pres*
EMP: 24
SQ FT: 20,000
SALES (est): 3.3MM **Privately Held**
WEB: www.laneko-rollform.com
SIC: 3547 3544 3449 Rolling mill machinery; special dies, tools, jigs & fixtures; miscellaneous metalwork; cold finishing of steel shapes

(G-7364)
LIBERTY PRODUCTS GROUP INC
1500 Industry Rd Ste S (19440-3271)
PHONE...................215 631-1700
Joe Keilman, *President*
David Kelly, *Business Dir*
EMP: 6
SQ FT: 7,000
SALES (est): 983K **Privately Held**
WEB: www.libprint.com
SIC: 2752 Commercial printing, lithographic

(G-7365)
LIBRARY BINDERY CO OF PA INC
Also Called: Information Conservation
63 E Broad St Ste 6 (19440-2464)
PHONE...................215 855-2293
Fax: 215 367-7308
EMP: 40 EST: 1879
SQ FT: 15,000
SALES (est): 3.5MM
SALES (corp-wide): 43.3MM **Privately Held**
SIC: 2789 Bookbinding
PA: Ici Binding Corp
8834 Mayfield Rd Ste A
Chesterland OH 44026
440 729-2445

(G-7366)
LITTLE ROUND INDUSTRIES LLC
2800 Richmond Rd (19440-1807)
PHONE...................215 361-1456
Richard Burk, *Mng Member*
Brendon Burk, *Manager*
EMP: 8 EST: 1999
SQ FT: 8,000
SALES (est): 1.6MM **Privately Held**
SIC: 3444 Sheet metal specialties, not stamped

(G-7367)
MAGNETIZER INDUSTRIAL TECH
Also Called: Miti
2880 Bergey Rd Ste D (19440-1764)
PHONE...................215 766-9150
Garrett J Shivo, *CEO*
Michael Bowen, *President*
Douglas Greene, *Admin Sec*
▼ EMP: 7
SQ FT: 5,000
SALES: 1MM **Privately Held**
WEB: www.magnetizer.com
SIC: 3695 Drums, magnetic

(G-7368)
MERCK SHARP & DOHME CORP
1227 Independence Way (19440-4122)
PHONE...................215 397-2541
Ed Scolnick, *Manager*
EMP: 4
SALES (corp-wide): 42.2B **Publicly Held**
SIC: 2834 Pharmaceutical preparations
HQ: Merck Sharp & Dohme Corp.
2000 Galloping Hill Rd
Kenilworth NJ 07033
908 740-4000

(G-7369)
MICROSS COMPONENTS INC
2294 N Penn Rd (19440-1905)
PHONE................................215 997-3200
Alan Taylor, *CEO*
EMP: 7
SALES (est): 2.1MM **Privately Held**
SIC: 3674 Semiconductors & related devices

(G-7370)
MONTCO MANUFACTURING CO INC
1610 Bethlehem Pike (19440-1602)
PHONE................................215 822-1291
Saju Thomas Ramapuram, *President*
Molly Ramapuram, *Admin Sec*
EMP: 7
SQ FT: 4,500
SALES (est): 734.1K **Privately Held**
SIC: 3599 Machine shop, jobbing & repair

(G-7371)
NATIONAL DECAL CRAFT CORP (PA)
2750 Bethlehem Pike (19440-1613)
PHONE................................215 822-0517
Scott Tobin, *President*
EMP: 5
SQ FT: 6,000
SALES (est): 607.3K **Privately Held**
SIC: 2759 Decals: printing

(G-7372)
NELSON STEEL PRODUCTS INC
3051 Penn Ave (19440-1763)
PHONE................................215 721-9449
John R Nelson, *CEO*
David R Nelson, *President*
Beverly Nelson, *Corp Secy*
Laurie Nelson, *Exec VP*
Richard J Nelson, *Vice Pres*
▲ **EMP:** 35
SQ FT: 48,000
SALES (est): 12.4MM **Privately Held**
WEB: www.nelsonsteelprod.com
SIC: 3315 Wire, steel: insulated or armored

(G-7373)
NELSON WIRE ROPE CORPORATION
3051 Penn St (19440-1726)
PHONE................................215 721-9449
John R Nelson, *CEO*
Richard J Nelson, *President*
Beverly Nelson, *Corp Secy*
David R Nelson, *Vice Pres*
Laurie Nelson, *Vice Pres*
EMP: 10
SQ FT: 48,000
SALES (est): 6.7MM **Privately Held**
SIC: 5051 5085 3496 Rope, wire (not insulated); rope, except wire rope; slings, lifting: made from purchased wire

(G-7374)
NORTH PENN TECHNOLOGY INC
Also Called: Micross Components
2294 N Penn Rd Ste A (19440-1905)
PHONE................................215 997-3200
Richard Kingeon, *CEO*
EMP: 37
SQ FT: 22,500
SALES (est): 12.2MM
SALES (corp-wide): 84.1MM **Privately Held**
WEB: www.northpenntech.com
SIC: 3674 Semiconductors & related devices
PA: Micross Components, Inc.
    7725 N Orange Blossom Trl
    Orlando FL 32810
    407 298-7100

(G-7375)
NUTECH LLC
Also Called: Nutech Hydronic Specialty Pdts
2705 Clemens Rd Ste 101b (19440-4201)
PHONE................................215 361-0373
Clifford Kratz, *President*
EMP: 10 **EST:** 2003

SALES (est): 740.8K **Privately Held**
SIC: 3491 Automatic regulating & control valves

(G-7376)
ORIGINAL LITTLE PEPIS INC
2866 Sandstone Dr 70 (19440-1911)
PHONE................................215 822-9650
Stan Kourakos, *President*
EMP: 12
SALES (est): 2.3MM **Privately Held**
SIC: 3497 Foil containers for bakery goods & frozen foods

(G-7377)
PARKER-HANNIFIN CORPORATION
Porter Instrument
245 Township Line Rd (19440-1752)
P.O. Box 907 (19440-0907)
PHONE................................215 723-4000
Mike Howard, *Principal*
Rob Schwartz, *Design Engr*
Michael Civitello, *Sales Mgr*
EMP: 245
SALES (corp-wide): 14.3B **Publicly Held**
WEB: www.parker.com
SIC: 3841 3823 3824 3625 Surgical & medical instruments; flow instruments, industrial process type; fluid meters & counting devices; relays & industrial controls; transformers, except electric; valves & pipe fittings
PA: Parker-Hannifin Corporation
    6035 Parkland Blvd
    Cleveland OH 44124
    216 896-3000

(G-7378)
PEAK PRECISION INC
3195 Penn St (19440-1728)
PHONE................................215 799-1929
David Webb, *President*
EMP: 6
SQ FT: 12,000
SALES (est): 1MM **Privately Held**
SIC: 3599 7539 Machine shop, jobbing & repair; machine shop, automotive

(G-7379)
PENN COLOR INC
2801 Richmond Rd (19440-1808)
PHONE................................215 997-9206
Wayne Miller, *Manager*
EMP: 175
SALES (corp-wide): 183.9MM **Privately Held**
WEB: www.penncolor.com
SIC: 2865 Color pigments, organic
PA: Penn Color, Inc.
    400 Old Dublin Pike
    Doylestown PA 18901
    215 345-6550

(G-7380)
PENN COLOR INC
2755 Bergey Rd (19440-1758)
PHONE................................215 997-2221
Michael Rubeo, *Vice Pres*
Thomas Yeager, *Research*
Wayne Miller, *Manager*
EMP: 175
SALES (corp-wide): 183.9MM **Privately Held**
WEB: www.penncolor.com
SIC: 2865 2893 2816 Dyes & pigments; printing ink; inorganic pigments
PA: Penn Color, Inc.
    400 Old Dublin Pike
    Doylestown PA 18901
    215 345-6550

(G-7381)
PETER MAMIENSKI
Also Called: Kings Red Barn
2333 Bethlehem Pike (19440-1331)
PHONE................................215 822-3293
Peter Mamienski, *Owner*
EMP: 3
SQ FT: 6,000
SALES (est): 263.2K **Privately Held**
SIC: 3446 3272 Ornamental metalwork; concrete products

(G-7382)
PHILADELPHIA TOBOGGAN COASTER
3195 Penn St (19440-1728)
PHONE................................215 799-2155
Tom Rebbie, *President*
EMP: 11
SQ FT: 46,000
SALES (est): 1.9MM **Privately Held**
WEB: www.philadelphiatoboggancoastersinc.com
SIC: 3599 Amusement park equipment

(G-7383)
PORTER INSTRUMENT
235 Township Line Rd (19440-1752)
PHONE................................215 723-4000
Bill Zinger, *Manager*
EMP: 15
SALES (est): 1.8MM **Privately Held**
SIC: 3841 Surgical & medical instruments

(G-7384)
PREMIER SEMICONDUCTOR SVCS LLC (DH)
Also Called: Micross Components
2294 N Penn Rd (19440-1905)
PHONE................................267 954-0130
Gary Fox, *Finance*
Richard Kingdon,
Susan Chimento, *Administration*
▲ **EMP:** 75
SQ FT: 16,000
SALES (est): 18.4MM
SALES (corp-wide): 84.1MM **Privately Held**
SIC: 7371 3674 Custom computer programming services; semiconductors & related devices
HQ: Chip Supply, Inc.
    7725 N Orange Blossom Trl
    Orlando FL 32810
    407 298-7100

(G-7385)
PRESTIGE FENCE CO INC
Also Called: Fence City
3434 Unionville Pike (19440-1829)
PHONE................................215 362-8200
John Witlin, *President*
Marvin Hamburg, *Treasurer*
Janice Kozminski, *Manager*
◆ **EMP:** 55
SALES (est): 8.3MM **Privately Held**
WEB: www.fencecity.com
SIC: 2499 5211 5031 Fencing, wood; fencing; fencing, wood

(G-7386)
PRESTO PACKAGING INC (PA)
1795 Keystone Dr (19440-1126)
PHONE................................215 822-9598
Jeff Dlugosz, *President*
Maureen Dlugusz, *Vice Pres*
EMP: 6
SALES (est): 783.1K **Privately Held**
WEB: www.prestopackaging.com
SIC: 3086 3547 Packaging & shipping materials, foamed plastic; steel rolling machinery

(G-7387)
PROFINERS INC
2299 Amber Dr Ste 100 (19440-1910)
PHONE................................215 997-1060
Carl Garrison, *President*
EMP: 7
SQ FT: 5,000
SALES (est): 1.1MM **Privately Held**
SIC: 3341 Secondary precious metals

(G-7388)
QUICK ASSEMBLY INC
Also Called: Q A Technology
1500 Industry Rd Ste E (19440-3271)
PHONE................................215 361-4100
Manhar Shah, *President*
Neil Carroll, *VP Sales*
▲ **EMP:** 15
SQ FT: 11,000
SALES (est): 1.9MM **Privately Held**
SIC: 3674 8711 Semiconductors & related devices; electrical or electronic engineering

(G-7389)
REED ASSOCIATES INC
1500 Industry Rd Ste P (19440-3271)
PHONE................................215 256-9572
Michael R Weir, *CEO*
William F Anderson, *President*
Cynthia Anderson, *CFO*
Linda Popow, *Admin Sec*
EMP: 14
SQ FT: 3,500
SALES (est): 16.5MM **Privately Held**
WEB: www.reedassociatesinc.com
SIC: 5021 3821 Office & public building furniture; laboratory furniture

(G-7390)
REUBES PLASTICS CO INC
1001 W Orvilla Rd (19440-3169)
PHONE................................215 368-3010
Richard Reube, *President*
Mark Ruebe, *President*
Laurie Harfman, *Vice Pres*
Nancy Linberger, *Treasurer*
▲ **EMP:** 21
SQ FT: 40,000
SALES (est): 4.6MM **Privately Held**
WEB: www.reubes-plastics.com
SIC: 3089 Injection molding of plastics

(G-7391)
RODON GROUP
2800 Sterling Dr (19440-1957)
PHONE................................215 822-5544
Joel Glickman, *President*
Robert Glickman, *Corp Secy*
Garrett Talley, *Plant Mgr*
Tony Hofmann, *Facilities Mgr*
Bob Dean, *QC Mgr*
EMP: 55
SALES (est): 22.4MM **Privately Held**
SIC: 3089 Injection molding of plastics

(G-7392)
ROSENBERGERS COLD STORAGE
Also Called: Rosenberger's Ice
2525 Bergey Rd (19440-1703)
PHONE................................215 721-0700
Henry L Rosenberger, *CEO*
James B Styer, *President*
Junaid Syed, *General Mgr*
Thomas J Gorman, *Treasurer*
Charlotte Rosenberger, *Admin Sec*
EMP: 325
SQ FT: 350,000
SALES (est): 23MM **Privately Held**
SIC: 4222 4731 2097 Warehousing, cold storage or refrigerated; transportation agents & brokers; block ice; ice cubes

(G-7393)
S-BOND TECHNOLOGIES LLC
2299 Amber Dr Ste 120 (19440-1910)
PHONE................................215 631-7114
Barbara Lane, *Comptroller*
Ronald Smith,
EMP: 3
SALES (est): 437.5K **Privately Held**
WEB: www.s-bond.com
SIC: 2891 Glue

(G-7394)
SAPIENT AUTOMATION LLC
2398 N Penn Rd (19440-1967)
PHONE................................877 451-4044
John C Molloy, *CEO*
Jack Kuppersmith, *Senior Partner*
Erik Hostvedt, *Chairman*
Colman Roche, *Vice Pres*
Tony Perricone, *CFO*
▲ **EMP:** 20 **EST:** 2010
SALES (est): 8.4MM **Privately Held**
SIC: 3535 Bucket type conveyor systems
PA: Motors Drives & Controls, Inc.
    2398 N Penn Rd
    Hatfield PA

(G-7395)
SCHULMERICH BELLS LLC
11 Church Rd (19440-1206)
P.O. Box 903, Sellersville (18960-0903)
PHONE................................215 257-2771
Ken Horen, *CEO*
Jonathan Goldstein, *Chairman*
EMP: 16
SQ FT: 37,000

SALES (est): 3.2MM **Privately Held**
WEB: www.schulmerich.com
SIC: 3931 Carillon bells; bells (musical instruments)

(G-7396)
SIMCO INDUSTRIAL STATIC CNTRL
Also Called: ITW
2257 N Penn Rd (19440-1906)
PHONE....................215 822-2171
Fax: 215 822-3795
EMP: 80
SALES (est): 10.5MM
SALES (corp-wide): 14.4B **Publicly Held**
SIC: 3679 Mfg Electronic Components
PA: Illinois Tool Works Inc.
155 Harlem Ave
Glenview IL 60025
847 724-7500

(G-7397)
SURCO INC
Also Called: Hatfield Rubber Company
271 W Broad St (19440-2960)
P.O. Box 158 (19440-0158)
PHONE....................215 855-9551
Harry Limbert, *President*
Janet Limbert, *Corp Secy*
EMP: 12
SQ FT: 20,000
SALES (est): 2.2MM **Privately Held**
SIC: 3069 Molded rubber products

(G-7398)
TECH TAG & LABEL INC
Also Called: TT&l
1901 N Penn Rd (19440-1961)
PHONE....................215 822-2400
James Alan Thompson, *President*
▲ EMP: 12
SALES (est): 2MM **Privately Held**
WEB: www.techtagandlabel.com
SIC: 2679 Labels, paper: made from purchased material; tags, paper (unprinted): made from purchased paper

(G-7399)
TECHNETICS
1600 Industry Rd (19440-3251)
PHONE....................215 855-9916
Brian Burns, *President*
EMP: 3
SALES (est): 241.2K **Privately Held**
SIC: 2821 Plastics materials & resins

(G-7400)
TELAN CORPORATION
2880 Bergey Rd Ste G (19440-1764)
PHONE....................215 822-1234
Conrad J Nelson, *CEO*
Shawn Goodwin, *Opers Staff*
EMP: 30
SQ FT: 18,000
SALES (est): 5.2MM **Privately Held**
WEB: www.telancorp.com
SIC: 3679 3672 Electronic circuits; printed circuit boards

(G-7401)
TEMPERATSURE LLC (PA)
Also Called: Nordic Ice
2705 Clemens Rd Ste 103 (19440-4201)
PHONE....................775 358-1999
Christopher P Smith, *President*
Brooke L Smith, *Vice Pres*
EMP: 4
SQ FT: 13,000
SALES (est): 6.3MM **Privately Held**
WEB: www.temperatsure.com
SIC: 3086 Packaging & shipping materials, foamed plastic

(G-7402)
TORTEL PRODUCTS
2880 Bergey Rd Ste C (19440-1764)
PHONE....................267 477-1805
EMP: 3
SALES (est): 219.6K **Privately Held**
SIC: 3812 Aircraft/aerospace flight instruments & guidance systems

(G-7403)
TRAFFIC MAINTENANCE ATTENUATOR
1610 Bethlehem Pike (19440-1602)
PHONE....................215 997-1272
EMP: 3 EST: 2013
SALES (est): 187K **Privately Held**
SIC: 3679 Attenuators

(G-7404)
ULTRONIX INC
2880 Bergey Rd Ste M (19440-1764)
PHONE....................215 822-8206
Carl W Wolf, *President*
EMP: 10
SQ FT: 12,000
SALES (est): 1.8MM
SALES (corp-wide): 1.7B **Privately Held**
WEB: www.ultronix.com
SIC: 2842 Degreasing solvent
HQ: Vishay Sa
199 Boulevard De La Madeleine
Nice 06000
493 372-727

(G-7405)
VENTURE 3 SYSTEMS LLC
Also Called: Telikin
2805 Sterling Dr (19440-1956)
PHONE....................267 954-0100
Fred Allegrezza, *CEO*
Nancy Allegrezza, *Principal*
▲ EMP: 15 EST: 2008
SALES (est): 2.5MM **Privately Held**
SIC: 3571 Electronic computers

(G-7406)
YOUNGTRON INC
2873 Sterling Dr (19440-1956)
PHONE....................215 822-7866
Michael Y Kim, *President*
EMP: 50
SQ FT: 24,000
SALES (est): 15.9MM **Privately Held**
WEB: www.youngtron.com
SIC: 3672 Printed circuit boards

Haverford
Montgomery County

(G-7407)
DANMIR THERAPEUTICS LLC
24 Dartmouth Ln (19041-1020)
PHONE....................610 896-8826
Amir Pelleg, *President*
EMP: 4
SALES (est): 267.6K **Privately Held**
SIC: 2834 Pharmaceutical preparations

(G-7408)
DENT-CHEW BRUSH LLC
10 Williams Rd (19041-1126)
PHONE....................610 520-9941
John Gallagher, *Mng Member*
EMP: 3
SALES (est): 240K **Privately Held**
SIC: 3843 Dental equipment & supplies

(G-7409)
DOUGH NUTS FOR DOUGHNUTS LLC (PA)
341 Lancaster Ave Ste 200 (19041-1579)
PHONE....................610 642-6186
Brian Zaslow, *Mng Member*
EMP: 10
SALES (est): 1.5MM **Privately Held**
SIC: 2051 Doughnuts, except frozen

(G-7410)
EGG TO APPLES LLC
355 Lancaster Ave Ste 111 (19041-1594)
PHONE....................610 822-3670
Julian Barkat, *Mng Member*
EMP: 2
SALES: 1.2MM **Privately Held**
SIC: 3571 Personal computers (microcomputers)

(G-7411)
HOME GROWN INC
393 Lancaster Ave (19041-1548)
PHONE....................610 642-3601
Elizabeth Bloom, *President*
EMP: 5
SQ FT: 1,500
SALES (est): 607.6K **Privately Held**
SIC: 2392 Household furnishings

(G-7412)
INTELLIGENT MICRO SYSTEMS LTD
Also Called: Scandura.com
4401 Parkview Dr (19041-2015)
PHONE....................610 664-1207
Joseph M Scandura, *President*
Alice Scandura, *Vice Pres*
EMP: 7
SQ FT: 1,800
SALES: 250K **Privately Held**
SIC: 7372 7373 7371 Application computer software; computer integrated systems design; custom computer programming services

(G-7413)
MIDVALE PAPER BOX COMPANY
409 Richard Knl (19041-1919)
PHONE....................610 649-6992
David Frank, *President*
EMP: 4
SALES (corp-wide): 2.3MM **Privately Held**
SIC: 2657 Folding paperboard boxes
HQ: Midvale Paper Box Company
19 Bailey St
Plains PA 18705
570 824-3577

(G-7414)
ROBERT H BERENSON
Also Called: Harvey-Robert's
104 Woodside Rd Apt C206 (19041-1848)
PHONE....................610 642-9380
Robert H Berenson, *Owner*
EMP: 4 EST: 1947
SQ FT: 720
SALES (est): 248.7K **Privately Held**
SIC: 3479 5094 5099 5162 Etching & engraving; engraving jewelry silverware, or metal; name plates: engraved, etched, etc.; jewelry; signs, except electric; plastics products; badges; jewelry stores

(G-7415)
SWEET SALVATION TRUFFLE
10 Coopertown Rd (19041-1013)
PHONE....................610 220-4157
Cheryl Ames, *Principal*
EMP: 3 EST: 2010
SALES (est): 169.8K **Privately Held**
SIC: 2066 Chocolate

Havertown
Delaware County

(G-7416)
ALUMTIES INC
638 Country Club Ln (19083-4430)
PHONE....................720 570-6259
Christopher Williams, *President*
EMP: 3
SALES (est): 71.1K **Privately Held**
SIC: 7372 Application computer software

(G-7417)
CASHEL LLC
850 W Chester Pike # 200 (19083-4400)
PHONE....................610 853-8227
Thomas M Fitzgerald Jr, *President*
Timothy Bergen,
▼ EMP: 4 EST: 2012
SQ FT: 1,400
SALES (est): 305.8K **Privately Held**
SIC: 2821 Plastics materials & resins

(G-7418)
CHRONO-LOG CORP
2 W Park Rd (19083-4691)
PHONE....................610 853-1130
Paula Freilich, *President*
Thrity Avari, *Marketing Staff*
Nicholas Veriabo, *Exec Dir*
EMP: 23
SQ FT: 3,000
SALES: 5.6MM **Privately Held**
WEB: www.chronolog.com
SIC: 3841 Blood pressure apparatus

(G-7419)
D R M SERVICES CORPORATION
Also Called: Sir Speedy
443 W Chester Pike (19083-4504)
PHONE....................610 789-2685
David McBride, *President*
David Mc Bride, *President*
Michael Brown, *Vice Pres*
EMP: 8
SQ FT: 3,600
SALES (est): 1.2MM **Privately Held**
SIC: 2752 Commercial printing, offset

(G-7420)
DAVY MANUFACTURING INC
Also Called: Creative Apron
101 W Eagle Rd Ste A (19083-2244)
PHONE....................610 583-8240
Michael Kaufman, *President*
Barbara Kaufman, *Vice Pres*
EMP: 10
SQ FT: 12,000
SALES (est): 1MM **Privately Held**
SIC: 2326 Aprons, work, except rubberized & plastic: men's

(G-7421)
F W LANG CO
121 N Concord Ave (19083-5018)
PHONE....................267 401-8293
Gilbert C Graves, *Partner*
William Haines Lang, *Partner*
EMP: 4 EST: 1928
SALES: 250K **Privately Held**
SIC: 3585 3599 3444 Refrigeration equipment, complete; air conditioning condensers & condensing units; machine shop, jobbing & repair; sheet metal specialties, not stamped

(G-7422)
HELLENIC NEWS OF AMERICA INC
Also Called: Hermexpo
26 W Chester Pike (19083-5320)
PHONE....................484 427-7446
Paul Kotrotsios, *President*
Linda Kotrotsios, *Treasurer*
EMP: 5
SALES: 1MM **Privately Held**
SIC: 2711 Newspapers, publishing & printing

(G-7423)
KNIGHT CORPORATION (PA)
2138 Darby Rd (19083-2306)
P.O. Box 332, Ardmore (19003-0332)
PHONE....................610 853-2161
Paul G Knight, *President*
James C Knight Jr, *President*
Geoffrey G Knight, *Vice Pres*
Rose Marie Knight, *Admin Sec*
▲ EMP: 22
SQ FT: 9,000
SALES (est): 21.2MM **Privately Held**
WEB: www.knightcorp.com
SIC: 5085 3569 2674 Filters, industrial; filters; bags: uncoated paper & multiwall

(G-7424)
NUSS PRINTING INC
1225 W Chester Pike (19083-3432)
PHONE....................610 853-3005
David Nuss, *President*
Mark Nuss, *Vice Pres*
Walter Mayer, *Opers Mgr*
EMP: 12
SQ FT: 7,000
SALES (est): 1.7MM **Privately Held**
WEB: www.nussprinting.com
SIC: 2752 Commercial printing, offset

(G-7425)
OGDEN BROTHERS INCORPORATED
Also Called: Ogden Brothers Office Supply
213 N Ormond Ave (19083-5014)
PHONE....................610 789-1258
Fax: 215 925-3241
EMP: 15 EST: 1921
SQ FT: 18,000

SALES (est): 2.3MM **Privately Held**
SIC: **5943** 2752 5712 Ret Stationery Lithographic Commercial Printing Ret Furniture

(G-7426)
PHL COLLECTIVE LLC
544 Virginia Ave (19083-2125)
PHONE.....................610 496-7758
Nick Madonna,
EMP: 6
SALES (est): 407.3K **Privately Held**
SIC: **7372** Prepackaged software

(G-7427)
SHAFFER DESOUZA BROWN INC
17 Mifflin Ave Ste 1 (19083-4619)
PHONE.....................610 449-6400
Richard C Brown, *President*
EMP: 15
SQ FT: 21,000
SALES (est): 2.4MM **Privately Held**
WEB: www.sdbinc.com
SIC: **2221** 2591 5131 Wall covering fabrics, manmade fiber & silk; textile mills, broadwoven: silk & manmade, also glass; drapery hardware & blinds & shades; piece goods & other fabrics

(G-7428)
STRASSHEIM PRINTING CO INC
754 Lawson Ave (19083-4110)
PHONE.....................610 446-3637
William E Strassheim, *President*
Margaret K Strassheim, *Corp Secy*
EMP: 9
SQ FT: 15,000
SALES (est): 1.2MM **Privately Held**
SIC: **2752** Commercial printing, offset

(G-7429)
T M FITZGERALD & ASSOC INC (PA)
Also Called: Tmf
850 W Chester Pike # 303 (19083-4442)
PHONE.....................610 853-2008
Thomas M Fitzgerald, *President*
Deborah D Bergen, *Admin Sec*
EMP: 4
SQ FT: 1,000
SALES (est): 1.1MM **Privately Held**
SIC: **3089** Injection molded finished plastic products

(G-7430)
TETRA TECHNOLOGIES INC
900 N Eagle Rd (19083-2038)
PHONE.....................610 853-1679
Lance Holman, *Principal*
EMP: 23
SALES (corp-wide): 998.7MM **Publicly Held**
SIC: **2819** Brine
PA: Tetra Technologies, Inc.
24955 Interstate 45
The Woodlands TX 77380
281 367-1983

(G-7431)
TMF CORPORATION
850 W Chester Pike # 303 (19083-4442)
PHONE.....................610 853-3080
Thomas M Fitzgerald, *President*
Deborah Bergen, *Director*
EMP: 4
SALES (est): 403.5K
SALES (corp-wide): 1.1MM **Privately Held**
WEB: www.tmfitzgerald.com
SIC: **3089** Plastic containers, except foam
PA: T. M. Fitzgerald & Associates, Inc.
850 W Chester Pike # 303
Havertown PA 19083
610 853-2008

(G-7432)
TRAC PRODUCTS INC (PA)
1509 Lynnewood Dr (19083-1903)
P.O. Box 1147 (19083-0147)
PHONE.....................610 789-7853
William R Rorer, *President*
EMP: 6
SQ FT: 2,400

SALES (est): 615K **Privately Held**
SIC: **3743** 5172 Railroad equipment; lubricating oils & greases

(G-7433)
WOMENS YELLW PAGES GTR PHIL
117 N Concord Ave (19083-5018)
P.O. Box 1002 (19083-0002)
PHONE.....................610 446-4747
Ellen Fisher, *Owner*
EMP: 4
SALES (est): 189K **Privately Held**
SIC: **2741** Directories: publishing only, not printed on site

Hawley
Pike County

(G-7434)
NORTHEAST CABINET CENTER INC
2591 Route 6 Ste 102 (18428-7062)
PHONE.....................570 226-5005
Michael Burkhardt, *President*
EMP: 4
SALES (est): 332.8K **Privately Held**
SIC: **2434** Wood kitchen cabinets

(G-7435)
PIKE COUNTY CONCRETE INC
N Rte 434 Rr 739 (18428)
PHONE.....................570 775-7880
Roger Mitschele Jr, *President*
Keith Mitschele, *Vice Pres*
Kim Frasen, *Treasurer*
EMP: 10
SQ FT: 960
SALES (est): 1.3MM **Privately Held**
SIC: **3273** Ready-mixed concrete

(G-7436)
PROMO GEAR
693 Route 739 Ste 4 (18428-6083)
PHONE.....................570 775-4078
Michael Casey, *Principal*
EMP: 3 EST: 2007
SALES (est): 197K **Privately Held**
SIC: **2759** Screen printing

(G-7437)
RIZWORKS
605 Church St Ste A (18428-1470)
PHONE.....................570 226-7611
Michael Rizzi, *Principal*
EMP: 9
SALES (est): 286K **Privately Held**
SIC: **7542** 3713 3711 Carwashes; truck & bus bodies; automobile bodies, passenger car, not including engine, etc.

(G-7438)
SDI CUSTOM DECOW
1777 Route 590 (18428-7793)
PHONE.....................570 685-7278
Kennith W Sproson, *Ch of Bd*
Derek Sproson, *President*
EMP: 4
SALES: 1.7MM **Privately Held**
SIC: **3269** 5023 Decalcomania work on china & glass; china; glassware

(G-7439)
THOMAS SPINNING LURES INC
316 Wayne Ave (18428-1430)
P.O. Box 153 (18428-0153)
PHONE.....................570 226-4011
Peter R Ridd, *President*
EMP: 8 EST: 1948
SQ FT: 10,000
SALES (est): 500K **Privately Held**
SIC: **3949** Lures, fishing: artificial

(G-7440)
UNITED METAL PRODUCTS CORP
516 Keystone St (18428-1416)
PHONE.....................570 226-3084
John Arigot, *President*
Diane Arigot, *Treasurer*
EMP: 5
SQ FT: 4,000

SALES (est): 871.2K **Privately Held**
SIC: **3444** Sheet metal specialties, not stamped

(G-7441)
VERTEES
324 Spruce St (18428-4569)
PHONE.....................570 630-0678
Lisa Osborne, *Principal*
EMP: 3
SALES (est): 136.4K **Privately Held**
SIC: **2759** Screen printing

Hawley
Wayne County

(G-7442)
RACKEM MFG LLC
1301 Purdytown Tpke (18438-6794)
P.O. Box C (18428-0159)
PHONE.....................570 226-6093
Harold Block, *Sales Staff*
Glenn Johnson,
John Pallay,
EMP: 3
SQ FT: 7,050
SALES: 1.2MM **Privately Held**
WEB: www.rackemmfg.com
SIC: **3441** Fabricated structural metal

Hawthorn
Clarion County

(G-7443)
D K GAS INC
3809 Cherry Aly (16230)
P.O. Box 228 (16230-0228)
PHONE.....................814 365-5621
Michael S Kennemuth, *President*
Darla Kirkpatrick, *Admin Sec*
EMP: 8
SQ FT: 1,000
SALES (est): 571.5K **Privately Held**
SIC: **1381** Drilling oil & gas wells

(G-7444)
EMPIRE ENERGY E&P LLC
Hc 28 (16230)
P.O. Box 228 (16230-0228)
PHONE.....................814 365-5621
EMP: 10
SALES (corp-wide): 13.2MM **Privately Held**
SIC: **3569** Gas producers, generators & other gas related equipment
PA: Empire Energy E&P, Llc
380 Sthpinte Blvd Ste 130
Canonsburg PA 15317
724 483-2070

Hazel Hurst
Mckean County

(G-7445)
HENDERSON RESOURCE GROUP LLC
121 Dewey Ave (16733)
P.O. Box 29 (16733-0029)
PHONE.....................814 203-3226
Steve Henderson, *Mng Member*
EMP: 4 EST: 2008
SALES (est): 410.8K **Privately Held**
SIC: **1389** Oil consultants

Hazelwood
Allegheny County

(G-7446)
LA GOURMANDINE LLC (PA)
5013 2nd Ave (15207-1624)
PHONE.....................412 291-8146
Fabien Moreau,
Lisanne Lorin Moreau,
EMP: 8

SALES (est): 973K **Privately Held**
SIC: **2051** Biscuits, baked: baking powder & raised; bread, all types (white, wheat, rye, etc): fresh or frozen; bakery: wholesale or wholesale/retail combined

Hazle Township
Luzerne County

(G-7447)
BELLEMARQUE LLC
135 Lions Dr (18202-1167)
P.O. Box 618, Sugarloaf (18249-0618)
PHONE.....................855 262-7783
Alec Marcalus,
▲ EMP: 20
SQ FT: 25,000
SALES (est): 4.7MM **Privately Held**
SIC: **2676** Sanitary paper products

(G-7448)
CARGILL COCOA & CHOCOLATE INC
400 Stoney Creek Rd (18202-9722)
PHONE.....................570 453-6825
Erik Lightner, *Owner*
EMP: 325
SALES (corp-wide): 114.7B **Privately Held**
SIC: **2066** Chocolate
HQ: Cargill Cocoa & Chocolate, Inc.
15407 Mcginty Rd W
Wayzata MN 55391
952 742-7575

(G-7449)
COAL CONTRACTORS (1991) INC
Also Called: Stockton Anthracite
100 Hazle Brook Rd (18201-8257)
P.O. Box 39 (18201-0039)
PHONE.....................570 450-5086
Stephen Best, *President*
Christopher Lloyd, *Treasurer*
EMP: 80
SALES (est): 20.3MM **Privately Held**
SIC: **1231** Strip mining, anthracite
PA: Atlantic Carbon Group Plc
1 Mayford House
Durham CO DURHAM DH1 3

(G-7450)
DADE PAPER CO
1119 N Church St (18202-3330)
PHONE.....................570 579-6780
Tony Franz, *President*
EMP: 3
SALES (est): 99.8K **Privately Held**
SIC: **2674** Bags: uncoated paper & multiwall

(G-7451)
DENIS BELL INC
Also Called: Coal Contractors 1991
100 Hazle Brook Rd (18201-8257)
P.O. Box 39, Hazleton (18201-0039)
PHONE.....................570 450-5086
Steven Best, *President*
EMP: 35
SQ FT: 1,000
SALES (est): 6.4MM **Privately Held**
SIC: **1231** Strip mining, anthracite

(G-7452)
EAM-MOSCA CORP (PA)
675 Jaycee Dr (18202-1155)
PHONE.....................570 459-3426
Daniel C Dreher, *CEO*
Dierk Wessel, *Ch of Bd*
Ralph Morini, *President*
Hartmut Boellmann, *Corp Secy*
Robert Leighton, *Vice Pres*
◆ EMP: 130
SQ FT: 150,000
SALES (est): 75.8MM **Privately Held**
WEB: www.eammosca.com
SIC: **5084** 2241 Packaging machinery & equipment; strapping webs

(G-7453)
ECONOCO
575 Oak Ridge Rd (18202-9362)
PHONE.....................570 384-3000

G
E
O
G
R
A
P
H
I
C

Paul Detwiler, *Director*
◆ **EMP:** 36
SALES (est): 4.8MM **Privately Held**
SIC: 2599 Factory furniture & fixtures

(G-7454)
EFS PLASTICS US INC
504 White Birch Rd (18202-9388)
PHONE.................................570 455-0925
EMP: 3
SALES (est): 338.9K **Privately Held**
SIC: 2821 Plastics materials & resins

(G-7455)
ES KLUFT & COMPANY INC
1104 N Park Dr (18202-9744)
P.O. Box 116, Hazleton (18201-0116)
PHONE.................................570 384-2800
Steven Beuch, *Plant Mgr*
EMP: 51
SALES (corp-wide): 65.8MM **Privately Held**
SIC: 2515 Mattresses & bedsprings
PA: E.S. Kluft & Company, Inc.
11096 Jersey Blvd Ste 101
Rancho Cucamonga CA 91730
909 373-4211

(G-7456)
F & D COAL SALES CO INC
803 S Church St (18201-7621)
P.O. Box 84, Hazleton (18201-0084)
PHONE.................................570 455-4745
Dominick J Forte, *President*
EMP: 3 EST: 1954
SQ FT: 10,000
SALES (est): 280.2K **Privately Held**
SIC: 1241 Coal mining services

(G-7457)
FABRI-KAL CORPORATION
150 Lions Dr (18202-1166)
PHONE.................................570 501-2018
Roland Yarbrough, *Mfg Mgr*
Leonard Ewing, *Human Res Mgr*
Eduardo Lopez, *Sales Staff*
Frank Pangonis, *Manager*
Steven Hribik, *Maintence Staff*
EMP: 275
SQ FT: 185,000
SALES (corp-wide): 1MM **Privately Held**
SIC: 3089 Thermoformed finished plastic products
HQ: Fabri-Kal Corporation
600 Plastics Pl
Kalamazoo MI 49001
269 385-5050

(G-7458)
FREEDOM CORRUGATED LLC
595 Oak Ridge Rd (18202-9362)
PHONE.................................570 384-7500
Dave Galasso, *General Mgr*
Conner Powell, *Plant Mgr*
Thomas E Bennett, *Treasurer*
Sam Perry, *Controller*
Fred Huff, *Sales Dir*
EMP: 65
SQ FT: 144,000
SALES (est): 16.6MM **Privately Held**
SIC: 2653 Boxes, corrugated: made from purchased materials

(G-7459)
GONNELLA FROZEN PRODUCTS LLC
301 Parkview Rd (18202-9723)
PHONE.................................570 455-3194
Joe Medvitz, *Maintence Staff*
EMP: 18
SALES (corp-wide): 126.2MM **Privately Held**
SIC: 2051 Bread, all types (white, wheat, rye, etc): fresh or frozen; rolls, bread type: fresh or frozen
HQ: Gonnella Frozen Products, Llc
1117 Wiley Rd
Schaumburg IL 60173
847 884-8829

(G-7460)
GRAHAM PACKAGING COMPANY LP
360 Maplewood Dr (18202-8200)
PHONE.................................570 454-8261
Amber Wilson, *Accountant*

Bill Campbell, *Branch Mgr*
EMP: 40
SALES (corp-wide): 1MM **Privately Held**
SIC: 3089 Plastic containers, except foam
HQ: Graham Packaging Company, L.P.
700 Indian Springs Dr # 100
Lancaster PA 17601
717 849-8500

(G-7461)
HAZLE PARK PACKING CO
260 Washington Ave (18202-1183)
PHONE.................................570 455-7571
Henry Kreisl, *Ch of Bd*
Gary Kreisl, *President*
Wayne Kreisl, *Corp Secy*
▼ **EMP:** 40 EST: 1966
SQ FT: 30,000
SALES (est): 7.4MM **Privately Held**
WEB: www.hazlepark.com
SIC: 2011 2013 Beef products from beef slaughtered on site; pork products from pork slaughtered on site; sausages & other prepared meats

(G-7462)
HAZLETON CUSTOM METAL PDTS INC
5057 Old Airport Rd (18202-3237)
P.O. Box 203, Hazleton (18201-0203)
PHONE.................................570 455-0450
Richard Andrews, *Principal*
EMP: 5 EST: 2009
SALES (est): 606.4K **Privately Held**
SIC: 3441 Fabricated structural metal

(G-7463)
HERSHEY COMPANY
2 Scotch Pine Dr (18202-9760)
P.O. Box 340, Hazleton (18201-0340)
PHONE.................................570 384-3271
Eugene Tannler, *Manager*
EMP: 267
SALES (corp-wide): 7.7B **Publicly Held**
WEB: www.hersheys.com
SIC: 2064 2066 Candy bars, including chocolate covered bars; chocolate & cocoa products
PA: Hershey Company
100 Crystal A Dr
Hershey PA 17033
717 534-4200

(G-7464)
INTERNATIONAL PAPER COMPANY
533 Forest Rd (18202-9387)
PHONE.................................570 384-3251
Joe Olsbewski, *General Mgr*
EMP: 133
SALES (corp-wide): 23.3B **Publicly Held**
SIC: 2621 Paper mills
PA: International Paper Company
6400 Poplar Ave
Memphis TN 38197
901 419-9000

(G-7465)
IVY STEEL & WIRE INC
503a Forest Rd (18202-9387)
PHONE.................................570 450-2090
John Wittstock, *President*
Tammy Hinkle, *Corp Secy*
James M McCall, *Vice Pres*
EMP: 78
SQ FT: 83,000
SALES (est): 11.7MM
SALES (est): 2.4B **Privately Held**
SIC: 3449 3496 3315 Bars, concrete reinforcing: fabricated steel; miscellaneous fabricated wire products; steel wire & related products
HQ: Merchants Metals Llc
211 Perimeter Center Pkwy
Atlanta GA 30346
770 741-0306

(G-7466)
JML INDUSTRIES INC
400 Jaycee Dr (18202-1150)
P.O. Box 56, Lehighton (18235-0056)
PHONE.................................570 453-1201
Jeffrey Lotz, *President*
Jeff Lotz, *President*
▲ **EMP:** 14
SQ FT: 30,000

SALES (est): 2.9MM **Privately Held**
SIC: 3089 Injection molding of plastics

(G-7467)
JOHNS MANVILLE CORPORATION
600 Jaycee Dr (18202-1154)
PHONE.................................570 455-5340
Dan Stott, *Plant Mgr*
EMP: 100
SALES (corp-wide): 225.3B **Publicly Held**
WEB: www.jm.com
SIC: 5211 3086 Roofing material; plastics foam products
HQ: Johns Manville Corporation
717 17th St Ste 800
Denver CO 80202
303 978-2000

(G-7468)
MACHINING TECHNOLOGY INC
1324 Harwood Rd (18202-3019)
PHONE.................................570 459-3440
Donald Shema, *President*
Leeanne Krapf, *Executive*
EMP: 7
SALES (est): 680K **Privately Held**
SIC: 3599 Machine shop, jobbing & repair

(G-7469)
MERCHANTS METALS LLC
Also Called: Meadow Burke Products
565 Oak Ridge Rd (18202-9362)
PHONE.................................570 384-3063
Scott Highland, *Manager*
EMP: 70
SALES (corp-wide): 2.4B **Privately Held**
SIC: 3272 Concrete products, precast
HQ: Merchants Metals Llc
211 Perimeter Center Pkwy
Atlanta GA 30346
770 741-0306

(G-7470)
NATURES BOUNTY CO
10 Simmons Dr (18202-8001)
PHONE.................................570 384-2270
Adrianne Delaraba, *Branch Mgr*
EMP: 19 **Publicly Held**
SIC: 2833 Vitamins, natural or synthetic: bulk, uncompounded
HQ: The Nature's Bounty Co
2100 Smithtown Ave
Ronkonkoma NY 11779
631 200-2000

(G-7471)
PETS UNITED LLC
1 Maplewood Dr (18202-9790)
PHONE.................................570 384-5555
Judy Patterson, *Principal*
▼ **EMP:** 7 EST: 2009
SALES (est): 640K **Privately Held**
SIC: 5199 5149 3999 Pet supplies; pet foods; pet supplies

(G-7472)
PFNONWOVENS LLC (DH)
101 Green Mountain Rd (18202-9246)
PHONE.................................570 384-1600
Allen Bodford, *President*
Marian Rasik, *Treasurer*
Alena Naatz, *Admin Sec*
◆ **EMP:** 315
SQ FT: 220,000
SALES (est): 10.2MM **Privately Held**
SIC: 2297 Spunbonded fabrics
HQ: Pfnonwovens Us Inc.
101 Green Mountain Rd
Hazle Township PA 18202
570 384-1600

(G-7473)
PLASTINETICS INC
613 Oak Ridge Rd (18202-9391)
PHONE.................................570 384-4832
Edward Batta, *Principal*
EMP: 7
SALES (est): 814.6K **Privately Held**
SIC: 3494 Valves & pipe fittings

(G-7474)
POLYGLASS USA INC
555 Oak Ridge Rd (18202-9362)
PHONE.................................570 384-1230

Berneette Chupela, *Manager*
EMP: 20 **Privately Held**
WEB: www.polyglass.com
SIC: 3259 2952 Roofing tile, clay; asphalt felts & coatings
HQ: Polyglass U.S.A., Inc.
1111 W Newport Center Dr
Deerfield Beach FL 33442
775 575-6007

(G-7475)
PROGRESSIVE CONVERTING INC
Also Called: Pro-Con
109 Maplewood Dr (18202-9267)
PHONE.................................570 384-2979
Martin Rothe, *Vice Pres*
Mike Brandtmeier, *Branch Mgr*
Shannon Allhands, *Technology*
Lea Melusky, *Technology*
EMP: 75
SALES (corp-wide): 83.2MM **Privately Held**
WEB: www.pro-con.net
SIC: 2678 2679 Stationery products; paper products, converted
PA: Progressive Converting, Inc.
2430 E Glendale Ave
Appleton WI 54911
800 637-7310

(G-7476)
PVC CONTAINER CORPORATION
Also Called: Novapak
605 Oak Ridge Rd (18202-9391)
PHONE.................................570 384-3930
Jim Graham, *Manager*
EMP: 40
SALES (corp-wide): 141MM **Privately Held**
WEB: www.airopak.com
SIC: 3085 Plastics bottles
HQ: Pvc Container Corporation
15450 South Outer 40 Rd # 120
Chesterfield MO 63017

(G-7477)
QUIK PIKS & PAKS INC
218 Laurel Mall (18202-1200)
PHONE.................................570 459-3099
Thomas Trella, *President*
Robert Deet, *Vice Pres*
EMP: 9
SALES (est): 1.2MM **Privately Held**
SIC: 2823 5993 Cigarette tow, cellulosic fiber; cigarette store

(G-7478)
R E WILDES SHEET METAL INC
253 W 32nd St (18202-9256)
PHONE.................................570 501-3828
Geraldine Wildes, *President*
EMP: 4
SALES (est): 522.6K **Privately Held**
SIC: 3444 Ducts, sheet metal

(G-7479)
SIGNODE INDUSTRIAL GROUP LLC
Also Called: Down River
450 Jaycee Dr (18202-1150)
PHONE.................................570 450-0123
Ed Siegfried, *Manager*
EMP: 33
SALES (corp-wide): 11.1B **Publicly Held**
WEB: www.greif.com
SIC: 2679 2671 2631 Honeycomb core & board: made from purchased material; packaging paper & plastics film, coated & laminated; paperboard mills
HQ: Signode Industrial Group Llc
3650 W Lake Ave
Glenview IL 60026
847 724-7500

(G-7480)
SILGAN WHITE CAP CORPORATION
350 Jaycee Dr (18202-1148)
PHONE.................................570 455-7781
Mark Hewitt, *Plant Mgr*
EMP: 220

SALES (corp-wide): 4.4B **Publicly Held**
WEB: www.silganclosures.com
SIC: **3411** Metal cans
HQ: Silgan White Cap Corporation
4 Landmark Sq Ste 400
Stamford CT 06901

(G-7481)
SKITCO MANUFACTURING INC
Also Called: Skitco Iron Works
1478 S Church St (18201-7615)
PHONE..................................570 929-2100
William Roman Jr, *President*
Modesta Roman, *Treasurer*
EMP: 9 EST: 1973
SQ FT: 9,600
SALES: 920K **Privately Held**
WEB: www.jwmp.com
SIC: **3446** Railings, prefabricated metal

(G-7482)
SPEARS MANUFACTURING CO
613 Oak Ridge Rd (18202-9391)
PHONE..................................570 384-4832
Daniel Prudich, *Principal*
EMP: 6
SALES (corp-wide): 1.6B **Privately Held**
SIC: **3494** 3089 Valves & pipe fittings; injection molded finished plastic products; injection molding of plastics
PA: Spears Manufacturing Co.
15853 Olden St
Sylmar CA 91342
818 364-1611

(G-7483)
TECH PACKAGING INC
20 Cinnamon Oak Dr (18202-8118)
PHONE..................................570 759-7717
Bob L Janes, *President*
Tonya Abel, *Supervisor*
EMP: 40
SQ FT: 18,000
SALES (est): 8MM **Privately Held**
WEB: www.techpackaging.net
SIC: **3081** Unsupported plastics film & sheet

(G-7484)
TONDA INC
1127 Harwood Rd (18202-3015)
PHONE..................................570 454-3323
David A Schriebmaier, *President*
EMP: 4
SALES (est): 604.9K **Privately Held**
SIC: **3312** Blast furnaces & steel mills

(G-7485)
TOOTSIE ROLL INDUSTRIES INC
490 Forest Rd (18202-3635)
PHONE..................................570 455-2975
EMP: 8
SALES (corp-wide): 518.9MM **Publicly Held**
SIC: **2064** Candy & other confectionery products
PA: Tootsie Roll Industries, Inc.
7401 S Cicero Ave
Chicago IL 60629
773 838-3400

(G-7486)
TRANSCONTINENTAL US LLC
3 Maplewood Dr (18202-9790)
PHONE..................................570 384-4674
Clive E Brown, *Branch Mgr*
EMP: 150
SALES (corp-wide): 1.6B **Privately Held**
WEB: www.exopack.com
SIC: **2673** Bags: plastic, laminated & coated
HQ: Transcontinental Us Llc
50 International Dr # 100
Greenville SC 29615
773 877-3300

(G-7487)
TROY HEALTHCARE LLC
130 Lions Dr (18202-1166)
PHONE..................................570 453-5252
Thomas G Cicini, *President*
EMP: 5
SQ FT: 80,000
SALES (est): 618.2K **Privately Held**
SIC: **2834** Analgesics

(G-7488)
TROY MANUFACTURING CO INC
130 Lions Dr (18202-1166)
PHONE..................................570 453-5252
Thomas Cicini, *President*
Anthony Cicini, *Vice Pres*
▲ EMP: 36
SQ FT: 40,000
SALES (est): 7.2MM **Privately Held**
SIC: **2834** Pharmaceutical preparations

(G-7489)
V MENGHINI & SONS INC
Also Called: Menghini's Truss Systems
1052 S Church St (18201-7662)
PHONE..................................570 455-6315
James J Menghini Jr, *President*
Mark Menghini, *Vice Pres*
Teresa Ostrowski, *Treasurer*
John Menghini, *Admin Sec*
EMP: 10
SQ FT: 20,000
SALES (est): 1.2MM **Privately Held**
SIC: **2439** Trusses, wooden roof

(G-7490)
VITA-LINE PRODUCTS INC
1111 N Park Dr (18202-9720)
PHONE..................................570 450-0192
William Behken, *President*
Raymond G Bialick, *CFO*
▲ EMP: 130
SALES (est): 36.5MM
SALES (corp-wide): 400MM **Privately Held**
SIC: **2048** Dry pet food (except dog & cat)
PA: American Nutrition, Inc.
2813 Wall Ave
Ogden UT 84401
801 394-3477

Hazleton
Luzerne County

(G-7491)
AYWON CHALKBOARD CORKBOARD INC
100 E Diamond Ave (18201-5241)
P.O. Box 11 (18201-0011)
PHONE..................................570 459-3490
Patrick Donahue, *President*
Jenifer Donahue, *Vice Pres*
EMP: 30
SALES (est): 3.8MM **Privately Held**
SIC: **2493** 3281 Bulletin boards, cork; blackboards, slate

(G-7492)
C & C MANUFACTURING & FABG
300 S Church St (18201-7606)
PHONE..................................570 454-0819
Victor F Carbe Jr, *Owner*
EMP: 7 EST: 1961
SQ FT: 8,000
SALES (est): 623.1K **Privately Held**
SIC: **3799** 3446 Trailers & trailer equipment; railings, prefabricated metal

(G-7493)
CARGILL MEAT SOLUTIONS CORP
65 Green Mountain Rd (18202-9224)
PHONE..................................570 384-8350
Kevin Knifel, *Branch Mgr*
EMP: 900
SALES (corp-wide): 114.7B **Privately Held**
WEB: www.excelmeats.com
SIC: **2011** Meat packing plants
HQ: Cargill Meat Solutions Corp
151 N Main St Ste 900
Wichita KS 67202
316 291-2500

(G-7494)
CATHOLIC SCL SVCS OF SCRANTON
Also Called: Holy Rosary Church
240 S Poplar St (18201-7154)
PHONE..................................570 454-6693

EMP: 5
SQ FT: 2,850
SALES (corp-wide): 77.2MM **Privately Held**
WEB: www.catholiccharities-cc.org
SIC: **8661** 2711 8211 8322 Catholic Church; newspapers: publishing only, not printed on site; Catholic elementary & secondary schools; youth center; cemetery association
PA: Catholic Social Services Of The Diocese Of Scranton, Inc.
516 Fig St
Scranton PA 18505
570 207-2283

(G-7495)
CITIZEN PUBLISHING COMPANY
262 N Cedar St (18201-5579)
PHONE..................................570 454-5911
Joseph Cammisa, *Owner*
EMP: 4
SQ FT: 2,000
SALES (est): 1MM **Privately Held**
SIC: **2752** 2759 Commercial printing, offset; letterpress printing

(G-7496)
DALLICE PRECIOUS METALS
216 W 21st St (18201-1829)
PHONE..................................570 501-0850
EMP: 4
SALES (est): 152.9K **Privately Held**
SIC: **3339** Primary Nonferrous Metal Producer

(G-7497)
ENGINEERED DEVICES CORPORATION
Also Called: Equipment Distributing
125 Butler Dr (18201-7364)
PHONE..................................570 455-4897
Lucille Gaffney, *Office Mgr*
Anthony Lutz, *Manager*
EMP: 10
SALES (corp-wide): 8.5MM **Privately Held**
WEB: www.edconline.com
SIC: **3542** Machine tools, metal forming type
PA: Engineered Devices Corporation
25 Bergen Tpke
Ridgefield Park NJ 07660
201 641-2880

(G-7498)
FIRST QUALITY ENTERPRISES INC
First Quality Nonwovens
1 Oakridge Rd (18202-9765)
PHONE..................................570 384-1600
Brian Kostik, *Safety Dir*
Mord Turi, *Manager*
EMP: 120 **Privately Held**
SIC: **2676** 7361 2297 Diapers, paper (disposable): made from purchased paper; employment agencies; nonwoven fabrics
PA: First Quality Enterprises Inc
80 Cuttermill Rd Ste 500
Great Neck NY 11021

(G-7499)
GLOBE PRINT SHOP
Also Called: Globe Color
18 N Locust St (18201-5718)
P.O. Box 399 (18201-0399)
PHONE..................................570 454-8031
Mark Bottley, *Owner*
EMP: 4 EST: 1937
SQ FT: 5,000
SALES (est): 550K **Privately Held**
WEB: www.globeprintshop.com
SIC: **2752** 5943 2759 Commercial printing, offset; office forms & supplies; letterpress printing

(G-7500)
HAZLETON CASTING COMPANY (PA)
Rear 225 N Cedar St (18201)
P.O. Box 21, Weatherly (18255-0021)
PHONE..................................570 453-0199
Michael J Leib, *President*
Frank Lee, *QC Mgr*
EMP: 39

SALES (est): 8.4MM **Privately Held**
WEB: www.hazletoncasting.com
SIC: **3325** Alloy steel castings, except investment

(G-7501)
HAZLETON CUSTOM METAL PRODUCTS
Rr 4 (18202)
PHONE..................................570 455-0450
Richard Andrews, *President*
EMP: 10
SQ FT: 7,000
SALES: 550K **Privately Held**
SIC: **3441** 7692 Fabricated structural metal; welding repair

(G-7502)
HAZLETON IRON WORKS INC
154 N Cedar St (18201-5581)
PHONE..................................570 455-0445
James Uston, *President*
Carol Uston, *Vice Pres*
EMP: 9
SQ FT: 11,000
SALES (est): 1.6MM **Privately Held**
SIC: **3441** Fabricated structural metal

(G-7503)
HAZLETON SHAFT CORPORATION
414 Shaft Rd (18201)
P.O. Box 435 (18201-0435)
PHONE..................................570 450-0900
George M Roskos III, *President*
EMP: 33
SALES: 7.5MM **Privately Held**
SIC: **1481** Shaft sinking, nonmetallic minerals

(G-7504)
J A & W A HESS INC (PA)
Also Called: Hess Sand & Stone
10 Hess Rd (18202-3241)
P.O. Box 645 (18201-0645)
PHONE..................................570 454-3731
George Hess, *President*
Walter Fox, *Vice Pres*
EMP: 20
SQ FT: 2,400
SALES (est): 3.3MM **Privately Held**
SIC: **3273** 5032 1442 Ready-mixed concrete; sand, construction; gravel; construction sand & gravel

(G-7505)
KELLY IRON WORKS INC
Also Called: Fabrication Store, The
270 S Pine St Unit 1 (18201-7284)
PHONE..................................610 872-5436
Boina Kelly, *President*
Padraig Kelly, *Vice Pres*
EMP: 7
SQ FT: 30,000
SALES: 750K **Privately Held**
SIC: **3441** 1791 Fabricated structural metal; structural steel erection

(G-7506)
KREISER FUEL SERVICE INC
128 W Green St (18201-5914)
PHONE..................................570 455-0418
EMP: 3
SALES (est): 152.7K **Privately Held**
SIC: **2869** Fuels

(G-7507)
LANG FILTER MEDIA LP
603 S Church St (18201-7611)
PHONE..................................570 459-7005
Robert Dalvet, *Partner*
Jean Durkin, *Partner*
Jim Durkin, *Partner*
Robert Durkin, *Partner*
EMP: 15
SQ FT: 45,000
SALES (est): 2MM **Privately Held**
WEB: www.ceianthracite.com
SIC: **3589** Water treatment equipment, industrial

(G-7508)
LONGOS BAKERY INC
138 W 21st St (18201-1909)
P.O. Box 396 (18201-0396)
PHONE...................................570 233-0558
James N Capriotti, *President*
EMP: 10 **EST:** 1966
SQ FT: 4,000
SALES (est): 1.4MM **Privately Held**
SIC: 2051 Bakery: wholesale or whole-
sale/retail combined; rolls, bread type:
fresh or frozen; bread, all types (white,
wheat, rye, etc): fresh or frozen; pastries,
e.g. danish: except frozen

(G-7509)
MAMA NARDONE BAKING CO INC
Also Called: Mama Nardone Pizza
138 W 21st St (18201-1909)
PHONE...................................570 825-3421
James Capiotti, *President*
EMP: 26 **EST:** 1937
SQ FT: 3,000
SALES (est): 2.6MM **Privately Held**
SIC: 2051 2099 Bakery: wholesale or
wholesale/retail combined; rolls, bread
type: fresh or frozen; bagels, fresh or
frozen; pizza, refrigerated: except frozen;
sandwiches, assembled & packaged: for
wholesale market

(G-7510)
MILLENNIUM MACHINING SPC
34 N Conahan Dr (18201-7355)
PHONE...................................570 501-2002
John Cibulish, *Owner*
EMP: 8
SALES (est): 705.5K **Privately Held**
SIC: 3599 7699 1799 Machine shop, job-
bing & repair; professional instrument re-
pair services; service station equipment
installation, maintenance & repair

(G-7511)
MONUMENTAL EXPRESS
764 Alter St (18201-2967)
PHONE...................................570 501-1009
Isidro Diaz, *Owner*
EMP: 3 **EST:** 2016
SALES (est): 259.9K **Privately Held**
SIC: 3272 Monuments & grave markers,
except terrazo

(G-7512)
MULTI-PLASTICS EXTRUSIONS INC (HQ)
600 Dietrich Ave (18201-7754)
P.O. Box 596 (18201-0596)
PHONE...................................570 455-2021
John Parsio Jr, *President*
Tom Hughes, *Plant Mgr*
John Bales, *Purchasing*
Dave Rossi, *Research*
Rich Antonio, *Controller*
◆ **EMP:** 150
SALES (est): 68.8MM
SALES (corp-wide): 198MM **Privately Held**
SIC: 2821 Plastics materials & resins
PA: Multi-Plastics, Inc.
7770 N Central Dr
Lewis Center OH 43035
740 548-4894

(G-7513)
NICHOLAS CAPUTO
Also Called: Caputo Ice Plant
190 S Pine St (18201-7239)
PHONE...................................570 454-8280
Nicholas Caputo, *Owner*
EMP: 3
SALES (est): 236.2K **Privately Held**
SIC: 2097 Ice cubes

(G-7514)
P & N HOLDINGS INC (PA)
25 N Wyoming St (18201)
PHONE...................................570 455-3636
Paul N Walser, *President*
Noelle Walser, *Admin Sec*
EMP: 200 **EST:** 1866
SQ FT: 8,000

SALES (est): 6.7MM **Privately Held**
WEB: www.standardspeaker.com
SIC: 2711 Newspapers, publishing & print-
ing

(G-7515)
PANEL SOLUTIONS INC
100 E Diamond Ave (18201-5241)
P.O. Box 11 (18201-0011)
PHONE...................................570 459-3490
Jenifer Donohue, *President*
Scott Donohue, *Technology*
Patrick Donohue, *Admin Sec*
▲ **EMP:** 25
SQ FT: 30,000
SALES (est): 3.2MM **Privately Held**
SIC: 3296 2599 3443 Acoustical board &
tile, mineral wool; boards: planning, dis-
play, notice; baffles

(G-7516)
PENNSYLVANIA MONUMENT CO
Rr 924 Box Humboldt (18201)
PHONE...................................570 454-2621
Stanley Bohenek, *Partner*
Betty Bohenek, *Partner*
EMP: 10 **EST:** 1942
SQ FT: 24,000
SALES (est): 1.2MM **Privately Held**
SIC: 3281 5999 Monuments, cut stone
(not finishing or lettering only); tomb-
stones, cut stone (not finishing or lettering
only); monuments, finished to custom
order; tombstones

(G-7517)
PETRUZZI PIZZA MFG INC
138 W 21st St (18201-1909)
PHONE...................................570 454-5887
James Capriotti, *President*
EMP: 20
SALES (est): 2.5MM **Privately Held**
SIC: 2099 2038 Pizza, refrigerated: except
frozen; pizza, frozen

(G-7518)
PETRUZZIS MANUFACTURING INC
Also Called: Petruzzis Home Dlvry Pizzeria
34 W 9th St (18201-3377)
PHONE...................................570 459-5957
Daniel J Petruzzi, *Owner*
EMP: 7
SQ FT: 3,000
SALES (est): 290K **Privately Held**
SIC: 2051 5149 Mfg Bread/Related Prod-
ucts Whol Groceries

(G-7519)
PIDILITE USA INC
Also Called: Sargent Art
100 E Diamond Ave (18201-5241)
PHONE...................................800 424-3596
Tammy Burton, *Manager*
EMP: 7
SALES (corp-wide): 335.6MM **Privately Held**
SIC: 3952 Lead pencils & art goods
HQ: Pidilite Usa, Inc.
902 S Us Highway 1
Jupiter FL 33477
561 775-9600

(G-7520)
PRINTERS EDGE
17 S Hazle Brook Rd (18201-8202)
PHONE...................................570 454-4803
Joan Dancho, *Owner*
EMP: 4
SALES (est): 330.6K **Privately Held**
SIC: 2752 Commercial printing, litho-
graphic

(G-7521)
PRINTMARK INDUSTRIES INC
600 S Poplar St Ste 2 (18201-7723)
PHONE...................................570 501-0547
Alexander Sloot, *President*
John Fay, *Vice Pres*
Jennifer Sloot, *Treasurer*
EMP: 50
SQ FT: 69,000
SALES (est): 4MM **Privately Held**
SIC: 8743 2759 Sales promotion; screen
printing

(G-7522)
QUAD/GRAPHICS INC
Humboldt Indus Park Rr 92 (18202)
PHONE...................................570 459-5700
Bill Lewis, *Branch Mgr*
EMP: 300
SALES (corp-wide): 4.1B **Publicly Held**
SIC: 2752 Commercial printing, offset
PA: Quad/Graphics Inc.
N61w23044 Harrys Way
Sussex WI 53089
414 566-6000

(G-7523)
ROOVERS INC
125 Butler Dr (18201-7364)
PHONE...................................570 455-7548
Nancy Andrasko, *President*
EMP: 6
SQ FT: 6,500
SALES (est): 513.3K **Privately Held**
WEB: www.roovers.com
SIC: 3579 Embossing machines for store &
office use

(G-7524)
S H SHARPLESS & SON INC
61 N Pine St (18201-6059)
PHONE...................................570 454-6685
Robert H Sharpless, *President*
EMP: 7
SQ FT: 13,000
SALES: 1.4MM **Privately Held**
SIC: 1799 3589 5084 Bowling alley instal-
lation; floor sanding machines, commer-
cial; industrial machinery & equipment

(G-7525)
SARGENT REALTY INC
Also Called: Sargent Art, Inc.
100 E Diamond Ave (18201-5241)
PHONE...................................570 454-3596
Bharat Oza, *CEO*
Tom Hudak, *President*
Gary J Capece, *Corp Secy*
◆ **EMP:** 60
SQ FT: 500,000
SALES (est): 11.1MM
SALES (corp-wide): 335.6MM **Privately Held**
WEB: www.sargentart.com
SIC: 3952 2851 Artists' materials, except
pencils & leads; crayons: chalk, gypsum,
charcoal, fusains, pastel, wax, etc.; water
colors, artists'; modeling clay; paints & al-
lied products
HQ: Pidilite Usa, Inc.
902 S Us Highway 1
Jupiter FL 33477
561 775-9600

(G-7526)
SENAPES BAKERY INC
222 W 17th St (18201-2426)
PHONE...................................570 454-0839
Mary Lou Marchetti, *President*
EMP: 36 **EST:** 1940
SQ FT: 5,000
SALES: 1.5MM **Privately Held**
SIC: 2051 5461 Bakery: wholesale or
wholesale/retail combined; bakeries

(G-7527)
SIGN SPOT
420 W 9th St (18201-3129)
PHONE...................................570 455-7775
Robert M Valente, *Owner*
EMP: 3
SQ FT: 1,500
SALES (est): 210K **Privately Held**
SIC: 7312 3993 Outdoor advertising serv-
ices; signs & advertising specialties

(G-7528)
T & L PIEROGIE INCORPORATED
127 W Chestnut St (18201-6305)
PHONE...................................570 454-3198
Theresa Lonczynski, *President*
Thomas Lonczynski, *Vice Pres*
EMP: 22
SQ FT: 45,000
SALES (est): 1.9MM **Privately Held**
SIC: 2099 Packaged combination prod-
ucts: pasta, rice & potato

(G-7529)
THOREN CAGING SYSTEMS INC (PA)
Also Called: Thoren Industries
815 W 7th St (18201-4019)
P.O. Box 586 (18201-0586)
PHONE...................................570 454-3517
William R Thomas, *CEO*
Sally Thomas, *President*
Cathy Ochs, *General Mgr*
Dave Shema, *Manager*
Willard Hallock, *Director*
▲ **EMP:** 5
SQ FT: 20,000
SALES (est): 7.8MM **Privately Held**
WEB: www.thoren.com
SIC: 3821 Laboratory equipment: fume
hoods, distillation racks, etc.

(G-7530)
THOREN INDUSTRIES INC
325 W 7th St (18201-4221)
P.O. Box 586 (18201-0586)
PHONE...................................570 454-3514
William R Thomas, *President*
Janet Hallock, *Accountant*
EMP: 18
SQ FT: 8,800
SALES (est): 2.4MM **Privately Held**
SIC: 3821 Laboratory apparatus & furniture

(G-7531)
TIMES-SHAMROCK
Also Called: Standard Speaker Newspaper
21 N Wyoming St (18201-6068)
PHONE...................................570 501-0278
Nick Walser, *Publisher*
John Patton, *General Mgr*
Lois Grimm, *Editor*
EMP: 60
SALES (est): 3MM **Privately Held**
SIC: 2711 7313 Commercial printing &
newspaper publishing combined; printed
media advertising representatives; news-
paper advertising representative

(G-7532)
URANIA ENGINEERING CO INC
198 S Poplar St (18201-7198)
PHONE...................................570 455-0776
Joseph A Zoba, *President*
Andrew Postupack, *Vice Pres*
EMP: 49
SQ FT: 20,000
SALES (est): 9.8MM **Privately Held**
WEB: www.uraniaeng.com
SIC: 3599 3625 3565 5199 Mfg Industrial
Machinery Mfg Relay/Indstl Control Mfg
Packaging Machinery Whol Nondurable
Goods Business Services

(G-7533)
USA PORK PACKERS INC
328 S Wyoming St (18201-7237)
PHONE...................................570 501-7675
Wayne Kreisl, *President*
▼ **EMP:** 50 **EST:** 1998
SALES (est): 2.9MM **Privately Held**
SIC: 0751 2011 Slaughtering: custom live-
stock services; meat packing plants

(G-7534)
VICTORIAS CANDIES INC (PA)
51 N Laurel St Frnt (18201-5928)
PHONE...................................570 455-6341
Paul Esposito Sr, *President*
Paul Esposito Jr, *Vice Pres*
EMP: 3 **EST:** 1934
SQ FT: 7,000
SALES (est): 2MM **Privately Held**
WEB: www.victoriascandies.com
SIC: 2064 5441 5145 2066 Candy &
other confectionery products; confec-
tionery produced for direct sale on the
premises; confectionery; chocolate &
cocoa products

(G-7535)
VIKING SIGNS INC
Also Called: Eagle Distrg
175 Carleton Ave (18201-7321)
PHONE...................................570 455-4369
Joesph Mooney, *President*
EMP: 3
SALES (est): 149K **Privately Held**
SIC: 3993 Signs & advertising specialties

▲ = Import ▼=Export
◆ =Import/Export

(G-7536)
VSI SALES LLC (PA)
416 Johns Ave (18201)
PHONE..................................724 625-4060
Angela L Disimone, *President*
EMP: 10
SQ FT: 500
SALES (est): 2MM **Privately Held**
SIC: 3441 8711 Fabricated structural metal; tower sections, radio & television transmission; structural engineering

(G-7537)
WEIR HAZLETON INC
Also Called: Hazleton Pumps
225 N Cedar St (18201-5551)
PHONE..................................570 455-7711
John Moscon, *President*
Ed Klein, *Vice Pres*
John McDonald, *Purch Mgr*
Charlie Burrows, *Engineer*
Greg Maduro, *Engineer*
◆ EMP: 80
SQ FT: 30,000
SALES (est): 23.9MM
SALES (corp-wide): 3.1B **Privately Held**
SIC: 3561 3531 3594 Pumps & pumping equipment; construction machinery; fluid power pumps & motors
HQ: Weir Group (Overseas Holdings) Limited
1 West Regent Street
Glasgow
141 637-7111

(G-7538)
WESTROCK RKT LLC
Also Called: Fold Pak
33 Powell Dr (18201-7360)
PHONE..................................570 454-0433
Charlie Mattson, *Branch Mgr*
EMP: 93
SALES (corp-wide): 16.2B **Publicly Held**
WEB: www.rocktenn.com
SIC: 2631 Paperboard mills
HQ: Westrock Rkt, Llc
1000 Abernathy Rd Ste 125
Atlanta GA 30328
770 448-2193

Hegins
Schuylkill County

(G-7539)
ASH/TEC INC
Also Called: Ashland Technologies
218 Dell Rd (17938-9147)
PHONE..................................570 682-0933
Bill Wydra Jr, *President*
Connie Wydra, *Administration*
◆ EMP: 48
SQ FT: 46,000
SALES (est): 12.6MM **Privately Held**
WEB: www.ash-tec.com
SIC: 3599 3519 Machine shop, jobbing & repair; internal combustion engines; engines, diesel & semi-diesel or dual-fuel

(G-7540)
DENNIS SNYDER
Also Called: Snyder Coal Co
66 Snyder Ln (17938-9378)
PHONE..................................570 682-9698
EMP: 10
SALES (est): 425.1K **Privately Held**
SIC: 1231 Anthracite Mining

(G-7541)
FOUNTAIN FABRICATING CO
1657 E Main St (17938-9142)
PHONE..................................570 682-9018
Fax: 570 682-9019
EMP: 7
SQ FT: 9,000
SALES: 850K **Privately Held**
SIC: 7692 3444 Welding Repair Mfg Sheet Metalwork

(G-7542)
KEYSTONE POTATO PRODUCTS LLC
2317 Shermans Mtn Rd (17938)
P.O. Box 27 (17938-0027)
PHONE..................................570 695-0909
Keith Masser, *CEO*
Glenn Weist, *General Mgr*
Mark Moyer, *Engineer*
Scott Wittman, *Sales Staff*
Gwen Reiner, *Manager*
▼ EMP: 53
SQ FT: 5,000
SALES (est): 10.4MM **Privately Held**
WEB: www.keystonepotato.com
SIC: 2034 Potato products, dried & dehydrated

(G-7543)
MI WINDOWS AND DOORS INC
79 Park Ln (17938-9089)
P.O. Box 528 (17938-0528)
PHONE..................................570 682-1206
Douglas Reed, *Manager*
Leonard Carr, *Maintence Staff*
EMP: 150
SALES (corp-wide): 1.1B **Privately Held**
WEB: www.miwd.com
SIC: 3442 3531 Metal doors; millwork
HQ: Mi Windows And Doors, Inc.
650 W Market St
Gratz PA 17030
717 365-3300

(G-7544)
STOLTZFUS SYLVAN LEE
Also Called: Timber Hollow Woodworking
85 Maple Dr (17938-9609)
PHONE..................................570 682-9755
Sylvan Lee Stoltzfus, *Owner*
EMP: 3
SQ FT: 3,200
SALES: 80K **Privately Held**
SIC: 3949 1751 Playground equipment; carpentry work

(G-7545)
SUPERIOR COAL PREP COOP LLC
184 Schwenks Rd (17938-9791)
PHONE..................................570 682-3246
David Himmelburger,
EMP: 10 EST: 1936
SALES (est): 1.1MM **Privately Held**
SIC: 1241 Mining services: anthracite

(G-7546)
WENGER FEEDS LLC
Also Called: Hegins Valley Farm
824 Church Rd (17938-9615)
PHONE..................................570 682-8812
Debra Martz, *Manager*
EMP: 49
SALES (corp-wide): 111.1MM **Privately Held**
WEB: www.easternag.com
SIC: 0252 2048 Chicken eggs; prepared feeds
PA: Wenger Feeds, Llc
101 W Harrisburg Ave
Rheems PA 17570
717 367-1195

(G-7547)
WEST END ELECTRIC INC
896 E Mountain Rd (17938-9509)
PHONE..................................570 682-9292
Greg Otto, *President*
EMP: 10
SALES (est): 1.5MM **Privately Held**
WEB: www.westendelectric.com
SIC: 1731 7694 Electrical work; electric motor repair

Heilwood
Indiana County

(G-7548)
ROSEBUD MINING CO
6314 Route 403 Hwy S (15745)
PHONE..................................814 948-6390
Cliff Forest, *Principal*
EMP: 80

SALES (est): 1.9MM **Privately Held**
SIC: 1241 Coal mining services

Hellam
York County

(G-7549)
BE THE TREE LLC
1241 Chimney Rock Rd (17406-8844)
PHONE..................................717 887-0780
Gregory Blymire, *Mng Member*
EMP: 4
SALES: 50K **Privately Held**
SIC: 5941 3949 Hunting equipment; hunting equipment

(G-7550)
GIBSON GRAPHICS GROUP INC (PA)
4527 Cherry Ln (17406-9380)
P.O. Box 3039, York (17402-0039)
PHONE..................................717 755-7192
Mark Gibson, *President*
EMP: 1
SQ FT: 5,232
SALES (est): 1.1MM **Privately Held**
WEB: www.gibsongraphicsgroup.com
SIC: 8742 2752 Marketing consulting services; commercial printing, lithographic

(G-7551)
GUARDIAN CSC CORPORATION (PA)
6000 Susquehanna Plaza Dr (17406-8911)
PHONE..................................717 848-2540
Bruce Ketrick, *President*
Patricia Ketrick, *Vice Pres*
Trey Deberry, *Manager*
Roger Landis, *Manager*
Marc Silverman, *Manager*
EMP: 10 EST: 1955
SQ FT: 12,000
SALES: 8.4MM **Privately Held**
WEB: www.guardiancsc.com
SIC: 5074 3589 5085 Boilers, steam; gas burners; water treatment equipment, industrial; tanks, pressurized

(G-7552)
SIMPLEX PAPER BOX CORP
100 S Friendship Ave (17406)
PHONE..................................717 757-3611
Carl E Bender Jr, *President*
Sandra L Bender, *Corp Secy*
EMP: 26
SQ FT: 27,800
SALES (est): 2.3MM **Privately Held**
WEB: www.simplexbox.com
SIC: 2652 Setup paperboard boxes

Hellertown
Northampton County

(G-7553)
AMERICAN MANUFACTURED STRUC
1509 Jakes Pl (18055-2641)
PHONE..................................703 403-4656
Kimberly Bradley, *Principal*
Alan Rand, *Director*
Franklin Cox,
Norman Barbera,
EMP: 3
SALES: 950K **Privately Held**
SIC: 3448 Buildings, portable: prefabricated metal

(G-7554)
BETHLEHEM APPARATUS CO INC (PA)
Also Called: Bethlhem Resource Recovery Div
890 Front St (18055-1507)
P.O. Box Y (18055-0221)
PHONE..................................610 838-7034
Eve Metzger, *President*
Rachel Lawrence, *Vice Pres*
Ward Haute, *Technology*
Bruce James Lawrence, *Executive*
Anne Lawrence, *Admin Sec*

◆ EMP: 15 EST: 1948
SQ FT: 35,000
SALES: 20MM **Privately Held**
WEB: www.bethlehemapparatus.com
SIC: 2819 3229 Mercury, redistilled; glassware, industrial

(G-7555)
FIBER QUEST COMPOSITES LLC
1889 Jeanine Way (18055-3404)
PHONE..................................610 419-0387
Kermit Paul, *President*
Marsha G Paul, *Vice Pres*
EMP: 3
SQ FT: 6,000
SALES: 450K **Privately Held**
SIC: 2299 Carbonizing of wool, mohair & similar fibers

(G-7556)
GAS & AIR SYSTEMS INC
1304 Whitaker St (18055-1376)
PHONE..................................610 838-9625
Stephen St Martin, *President*
Robert E Obrien, *Vice Pres*
William Angus, *Treasurer*
William E Angus, *Admin Sec*
▲ EMP: 15
SQ FT: 20,000
SALES (est): 4.1MM **Privately Held**
WEB: www.gasair.net
SIC: 3563 Air & gas compressors

(G-7557)
INTUIDEX INC
1892 Mill Run Ct (18055-2734)
PHONE..................................484 851-3423
William M Pottenger, *CEO*
EMP: 50
SALES (est): 3.8MM **Privately Held**
SIC: 3669 Visual communication systems

(G-7558)
LOST TAVERN BREWING LLC
782 Main St (18055-1540)
PHONE..................................484 851-3980
Robert Grim, *President*
EMP: 11
SQ FT: 4,000
SALES (est): 910.5K **Privately Held**
SIC: 2082 Ale (alcoholic beverage)

(G-7559)
MOBILE TECHNOLOGY GRAPHICS LLC
Also Called: Mtg Sign
3984 Lower Saucon Rd (18055-3239)
PHONE..................................610 838-8075
Michael J Estojak, *Marketing Staff*
▲ EMP: 4 EST: 2005
SALES: 1.5MM **Privately Held**
SIC: 7359 3993 Sign rental; signs & advertising specialties

(G-7560)
PERMEGEAR INC
1815 Leithsville Rd (18055-1774)
PHONE..................................484 851-3688
Andrew Wilt, *President*
EMP: 4
SQ FT: 3,000
SALES (est): 896.9K **Privately Held**
WEB: www.permegear.com
SIC: 5047 3841 Medical equipment & supplies; medical instruments & equipment, blood & bone work

(G-7561)
REACTION CHEMICALS
3767 Elm Ter (18055-3159)
PHONE..................................610 838-5496
Brad Fleming, *President*
EMP: 4
SALES (est): 286.2K **Privately Held**
SIC: 3764 Engines & engine parts, guided missile

(G-7562)
SHANGRI LA PRODUCTIONS
2425 Apple St (18055-3206)
PHONE..................................610 838-5188
John C Harbove, *Owner*
EMP: 5

SALES: 175K **Privately Held**
SIC: 3651 Sound reproducing equipment

(G-7563)
STEEL CITY CHROMIUM PLATING CO
320 Front St (18055-1706)
P.O. Box 330 (18055-0330)
PHONE...................................610 838-8441
Paul J Makl Jr, *President*
EMP: 7 EST: 1943
SQ FT: 10,000
SALES: 500K **Privately Held**
SIC: 3471 Chromium plating of metals or formed products

(G-7564)
VALLEY VOICE INC
1188 Main St (18055-1319)
P.O. Box 147 (18055-0147)
PHONE...................................610 838-2066
Ann Marie Gonsalves, *President*
EMP: 5
SALES: 125K **Privately Held**
SIC: 2711 Newspapers

Henryville
Monroe County

(G-7565)
CAKEWORKS LLC
2110 Post Hill Ct (18332-7849)
PHONE...................................917 744-1375
Gwenet Claud, *Mng Member*
EMP: 4 EST: 2012
SALES (est): 172.7K **Privately Held**
SIC: 2051 Bakery: wholesale or wholesale/retail combined

(G-7566)
D AND S ARTISTIC WDWKG LLC (PA)
144 Salzer Way (18332-7788)
PHONE...................................973 495-7008
Steven Godding, *Principal*
EMP: 4 EST: 2013
SALES (est): 628K **Privately Held**
SIC: 2431 Millwork

(G-7567)
HOUSE OF CANDLES
Rr 715 (18332)
PHONE...................................570 629-1953
Eddie Coover, *Owner*
Debra Coover, *Manager*
EMP: 10
SQ FT: 6,300
SALES (est): 636.4K **Privately Held**
WEB: www.houseofcandles.com
SIC: 5947 3999 Gift shop; candles

Hereford
Berks County

(G-7568)
METVAC INC
7178 Pine Tree Rd (18056-1507)
P.O. Box 282 (18056-0282)
PHONE...................................215 541-4495
William J Metalsky, *President*
EMP: 8
SALES (est): 639.8K **Privately Held**
SIC: 8711 3567 Consulting engineer; vacuum furnaces & ovens

Herminie
Westmoreland County

(G-7569)
BEGONIA TOOL CO
573 Herminie Rd (15637-1737)
PHONE...................................724 446-1102
Muriel Begonia, *Owner*
EMP: 5
SQ FT: 6,000
SALES (est): 300K **Privately Held**
SIC: 3599 Machine shop, jobbing & repair

(G-7570)
FIRST CLASS SPECIALTIES
Also Called: First Class Specialities
218 Sewickley Ave (15637-1334)
PHONE...................................724 446-1000
Avalene Cantini, *Partner*
Gary A Cantini, *Partner*
EMP: 16
SALES (est): 1.1MM **Privately Held**
SIC: 5199 2759 7216 7389 Advertising specialties; commercial printing; drycleaning plants, except rugs; notary publics; wine

Hermitage
Mercer County

(G-7571)
AMERICAN ARTISAN ORTHOTICS
2532 S Neshannock Rd (16148-6305)
PHONE...................................724 776-6030
EMP: 3
SALES (est): 213.2K **Privately Held**
SIC: 3842 Orthopedic appliances

(G-7572)
BRUCE N PELSH INC
Also Called: Shawnee Optical
2926 E State St (16148-2757)
PHONE...................................724 346-2020
Bruce N Pelsh, *Owner*
Neil Callahan, *Site Mgr*
EMP: 6
SALES (est): 726.1K **Privately Held**
SIC: 3851 Eyeglasses, lenses & frames

(G-7573)
CASTLE BUILDERS SUPPLY INC
1325 Broadway Rd (16148-9037)
PHONE...................................724 981-4212
James Carna, *President*
EMP: 28
SALES (corp-wide): 9MM **Privately Held**
SIC: 3271 3273 Blocks, concrete or cinder: standard; ready-mixed concrete
PA: Castle Builders Supply, Inc.
1409 Moravia St
New Castle PA 16101
724 658-5656

(G-7574)
CCL CONTAINER (HERMITAGE) INC
Also Called: CCL Containers
1 Llodio Dr (16148-9015)
PHONE...................................724 981-4420
John Pedroli, *President*
John Bischoff, *Vice Pres*
Lalitha Vaidyanathan, *Vice Pres*
Linda Condon, *Manager*
Christiana Guccione, *Manager*
EMP: 9
SALES (est): 437.7K
SALES (corp-wide): 3.7B **Privately Held**
SIC: 3411 Aluminum cans
PA: Ccl Industries Inc
111 Gordon Baker Rd Suite 801
Toronto ON M2H 3
416 756-8500

(G-7575)
CCL CONTAINER CORPORATION
Also Called: C C L
1 Llodio Dr (16148-9015)
PHONE...................................724 981-4420
Rami Younes, *President*
Steven W Lancaster, *Treasurer*
◆ EMP: 200
SQ FT: 170,000
SALES (est): 88.4MM
SALES (corp-wide): 3.7B **Privately Held**
SIC: 3411 Aluminum cans
PA: Ccl Industries Inc
111 Gordon Baker Rd Suite 801
Toronto ON M2H 3
416 756-8500

(G-7576)
CHAMPION CARRIER CORPORATION (DH)
2755 Kirila Blvd (16148-9019)
PHONE...................................724 981-3328
Dan Sabastian, *President*
Tom Pratt, *Vice Pres*
Vincent Mish, *Treasurer*
Frank Madonia, *Admin Sec*
▲ EMP: 40
SQ FT: 72,500
SALES (est): 29.3MM
SALES (corp-wide): 615.1MM **Publicly Held**
SIC: 3713 Car carrier bodies
HQ: Century Holdings Inc
8503 Hilltop Dr
Ooltewah TN 37363
423 238-4171

(G-7577)
CHARLIES SPECIALTIES INC
2500 Freedland Rd (16148-9022)
PHONE...................................724 346-2350
Jay Thier, *President*
Edward G Byrnes Jr, *Chairman*
Thomas C Byrnes, *Vice Pres*
EMP: 80
SQ FT: 25,000
SALES (est): 11.7MM
SALES (corp-wide): 23MM **Privately Held**
SIC: 2052 5149 5142 2045 Cookies; groceries & related products; packaged frozen goods; prepared flour mixes & doughs
PA: Byrnes And Kiefer Company
131 Kline Ave
Callery PA 16024
724 538-5200

(G-7578)
CLEAN WORLD INDUSTRIES INC
4835 Anne Ln (16148-6556)
P.O. Box 64, Sharpsville (16150-0064)
PHONE...................................724 962-0720
Vincent E Fustos, *CEO*
EMP: 3
SALES (est): 335.7K **Privately Held**
WEB: www.cleanworldinc.com
SIC: 2899 Chemical preparations

(G-7579)
COLONIAL METAL PRODUCTS INC
2350 Quality Ln (16148)
P.O. Box 415, Wheatland (16161-0415)
PHONE...................................724 346-5550
Williams J Thomas Jr, *President*
Williams J Thomas III, *Principal*
Catherine Settlemire, *Vice Pres*
EMP: 32
SQ FT: 76,000
SALES (est): 29.2MM **Privately Held**
WEB: www.colonialmetalproducts.com
SIC: 5051 3316 Steel; cold finishing of steel shapes

(G-7580)
ECM
2727 Freedland Rd (16148-9027)
PHONE...................................724 347-0250
Mike Kamnikar, *Principal*
EMP: 200
SALES (est): 20.9MM **Privately Held**
SIC: 3462 Iron & steel forgings

(G-7581)
ELLWOOD CRANKSHAFT AND MCH CO
Also Called: Ecg Ellwood Crankshaft Group
2727 Freedland Rd (16148-9027)
PHONE...................................724 347-0250
Brian Taylor, *President*
David McBlain, *Analyst*
◆ EMP: 144
SALES (est): 45MM
SALES (corp-wide): 775.5MM **Privately Held**
SIC: 3599 3541 Crankshafts & camshafts, machining; crankshaft regrinding machines

PA: Ellwood Group, Inc.
600 Commercial Ave
Ellwood City PA 16117
724 752-3680

(G-7582)
ELLWOOD GROUP INC
Also Called: Ellwood Crankshaft and Machine
2727 Freedland Rd (16148-9027)
PHONE...................................724 981-1012
Brian C Taylor, *President*
Bentraum Huffman, *COO*
EMP: 200
SALES (corp-wide): 775.5MM **Privately Held**
WEB: www.ellwoodgroup.com
SIC: 3462 3541 Iron & steel forgings; gear cutting & milling machines
PA: Ellwood Group, Inc.
600 Commercial Ave
Ellwood City PA 16117
724 752-3680

(G-7583)
ELLWOOD NAT CRANKSHAFT SVCS (HQ)
2727 Freedland Rd (16148-9027)
PHONE...................................724 342-4965
Brian C Taylor, *President*
Jim Wilkins, *Manager*
▲ EMP: 5
SQ FT: 1,600
SALES (est): 1.3MM
SALES (corp-wide): 775.5MM **Privately Held**
WEB: www.ellwoodgroup.com
SIC: 3599 Crankshafts & camshafts, machining
PA: Ellwood Group, Inc.
600 Commercial Ave
Ellwood City PA 16117
724 752-3680

(G-7584)
FORNEY HOLDINGS INC (PA)
1565 Broadway Rd (16148-9031)
PHONE...................................724 346-7400
Jeff Gziki, *President*
Scott Grumski, *Chief Engr*
◆ EMP: 27
SQ FT: 23,000
SALES (est): 6.2MM **Privately Held**
WEB: www.forneyonline.com
SIC: 3829 Tensile strength testing equipment

(G-7585)
FORTUNE ELECTRIC CO LTD (HQ)
1965 Shenango Valley Fwy (16148-2502)
PHONE...................................724 346-2722
Chuenwei Hsu, *President*
Alex Hsu, *Director*
▲ EMP: 12
SQ FT: 950
SALES (est): 3MM
SALES (corp-wide): 194MM **Privately Held**
WEB: www.fortuneelectric.com
SIC: 3612 Power & distribution transformers; autotransformers, electric (power transformers); distribution transformers, electric; power transformers, electric
PA: Fortune Electric Co., Ltd.
10, Jilin Rd.,
Taoyuan City TAY 32063
345 261-11

(G-7586)
G W BECKER INC
2600 Kirila Blvd (16148-9034)
PHONE...................................724 983-1000
George W Becker, *President*
David Greene, *COO*
Tom Barron, *Vice Pres*
Christopher M Becker, *Vice Pres*
Chris Wilson, *Opers Mgr*
EMP: 60
SQ FT: 35,000
SALES (est): 23.6MM **Privately Held**
WEB: www.gwbcrane.com
SIC: 3531 Aerial work platforms: hydraulic/elec. truck/carrier mounted

(G-7587)
HANGER PRSTHETCS & ORTHO INC
165 N Hermitage Rd (16148-3345)
PHONE.....................724 981-5775
Charles Moore, *Branch Mgr*
EMP: 6
SALES (corp-wide): 1B **Publicly Held**
SIC: 3842 Orthopedic & prosthesis applications
HQ: Hanger Prosthetics & Orthotics, Inc.
10910 Domain Dr Ste 300
Austin TX 78758
512 777-3800

(G-7588)
INTERSTATE CHEMICAL CO INC (PA)
Also Called: United-Erie Division
2797 Freedland Rd (16148-9099)
P.O. Box 1600 (16148-0600)
PHONE.....................724 981-3771
Michael R Puntureri, *President*
Michael Puntureri, *COO*
Jeff Heverley, *Vice Pres*
Joseph Mikolic, *Plant Mgr*
Shannon Reaver, *Purch Dir*
▲ EMP: 150
SQ FT: 14,000
SALES (est): 338.6MM **Privately Held**
WEB: www.interstatechemical.com
SIC: 5169 2819 Industrial chemicals; industrial inorganic chemicals

(G-7589)
JOY CONE CO (PA)
Also Called: Scoopy's Cone Co
3435 Lamor Rd (16148-3097)
PHONE.....................724 962-5747
Joseph George, *Ch of Bd*
David George, *President*
Scott Kalmanek, *COO*
Joe Marincic, *Vice Pres*
Joseph Pozar, *Plant Mgr*
◆ EMP: 400 EST: 1918
SQ FT: 590,000
SALES (est): 82MM **Privately Held**
SIC: 2052 2099 Cones, ice cream; food preparations

(G-7590)
L M STEVENSON COMPANY INC
Also Called: Stevensons
2600 Kirila Blvd (16148-9034)
PHONE.....................724 458-7510
George Becker, *President*
EMP: 3
SQ FT: 2,400
SALES (est): 290K **Privately Held**
SIC: 3599 5085 Machine shop, jobbing & repair; mill supplies

(G-7591)
MILLER INDS TOWING EQP INC
2755 Kirila Blvd (16148-9019)
PHONE.....................724 981-3328
EMP: 6
SALES (corp-wide): 615.1MM **Publicly Held**
SIC: 3799 Trailers & trailer equipment
HQ: Miller Industries Towing Equipment Inc.
8503 Hilltop Dr
Ooltewah TN 37363
423 238-4171

(G-7592)
MINUTEMAN PRESS
3170 E State St (16148-3305)
PHONE.....................724 346-1105
Ron McDermitt, *Principal*
EMP: 4 EST: 2008
SALES (est): 369.7K **Privately Held**
SIC: 2752 Commercial printing, offset

(G-7593)
NEW CENTURIES LLC
Also Called: Shenango Valley Quik Print
1540 E State St (16148-1823)
PHONE.....................724 347-3030
John Moreira,
La Verne Kline,
EMP: 7 EST: 1976
SQ FT: 3,200

SALES (est): 711.6K **Privately Held**
SIC: 2752 7334 Commercial printing, offset; photocopying & duplicating services

(G-7594)
SAMUEL STAMPING TECH LLC
1760 Broadway Rd (16148-9004)
PHONE.....................724 981-5042
Dan Turner Sr,
Dan Turner Jr,
EMP: 25
SQ FT: 60,000
SALES (est): 4.1MM **Privately Held**
SIC: 3544 3542 Die sets for metal stamping (presses); presses: forming, stamping, punching, sizing (machine tools)

(G-7595)
SOLAR ATMOSPHERES WSTN PA INC
30 Industrial Rd (16148-9028)
PHONE.....................742 982-0660
William R Jones, *CEO*
Robert Hill, *President*
Don Jordan, *President*
Kevin Bekelja, *Vice Pres*
Michael Moyer, *Sales Dir*
EMP: 70
SQ FT: 80,000
SALES: 20MM **Privately Held**
SIC: 3398 Metal heat treating

(G-7596)
TRAVAGLINI ENTERPRISES INC
Also Called: Perkins Family Restaurant
2945 E State St (16148-2748)
PHONE.....................724 342-3334
Homer Filson, *General Mgr*
EMP: 45
SALES (corp-wide): 31.5MM **Privately Held**
SIC: 5812 2051 Restaurant, family: chain; bread, cake & related products
PA: Travaglini Enterprises, Inc.
18228 Conneaut Lake Rd
Meadville PA 16335
814 724-1286

Herndon
Northumberland County

(G-7597)
BAUMERTS WOOD SHAVINGS
745 Mountain Top Rd (17830-7155)
PHONE.....................570 758-1744
Marilyn Baumert, *Principal*
EMP: 9
SALES (est): 868.2K **Privately Held**
SIC: 2421 Sawmills & planing mills, general

(G-7598)
GREYSTONE MATERIALS BT (PA)
617 Urban Rd (17830-7231)
PHONE.....................570 244-2082
Jim Ansell, *General Mgr*
EMP: 7 EST: 2011
SALES (est): 649.5K **Privately Held**
SIC: 1422 Crushed & broken limestone

(G-7599)
HERNDON RELOAD COMPANY
386 Pennsylvania Ave (17830-7284)
PHONE.....................570 758-2597
Samuel K Kauffman, *President*
Melvin J Kauffman, *Vice Pres*
Mahlon Esch, *Manager*
EMP: 25
SQ FT: 392
SALES: 6.1MM **Privately Held**
SIC: 5084 4013 2421 Woodworking machinery; railroad terminals; custom sawmill
PA: S & L Spindles, Llc
347 Weaver Rd
Millersburg PA 17061

(G-7600)
KEIMS MACHINE & TOOL CO INC
454 Jackson Twp Rd (17830-6960)
PHONE.....................570 758-2605

David L Keim, *President*
Darin Keim, *Vice Pres*
Nancy Keim, *Treasurer*
EMP: 9
SQ FT: 5,000
SALES (est): 880K **Privately Held**
SIC: 7389 3491 Design, commercial & industrial; valves, automatic control

(G-7601)
MECKLEYS LIMESTONE PDTS INC (PA)
1543 State Route 225 (17830-7332)
PHONE.....................570 758-3011
Matthew G Markunas, *President*
Anthony B Markunas, *Vice Pres*
EMP: 82 EST: 1936
SQ FT: 4,000
SALES (est): 13.7MM **Privately Held**
WEB: www.meckleys.com
SIC: 1422 1771 Limestones, ground; blacktop (asphalt) work

(G-7602)
NOVINGER WELDING REPAIR INC
126 Tulpehocken Path Rd (17830-7428)
PHONE.....................570 758-6592
James Novinger, *President*
Tina Novinger, *Corp Secy*
EMP: 6
SALES (est): 1.1MM **Privately Held**
SIC: 7692 Welding repair

Hershey
Dauphin County

(G-7603)
AMES INDUSTRIES INC
2999 Elizabethtown Rd (17033-9321)
PHONE.....................877 296-9977
Wesley E Ames, *President*
Lou McCloskey, *Vice Pres*
Donette K Ames, *Treasurer*
Suzanne M Williams, *Treasurer*
Shelley McCloskey, *Admin Sec*
▲ EMP: 50
SQ FT: 28,000
SALES (est): 12.2MM **Privately Held**
WEB: www.amesindustries.com
SIC: 3089 3599 3544 Injection molding of plastics; machine shop, jobbing & repair; special dies, tools, jigs & fixtures

(G-7604)
ARTISAN CONFECTIONS COMPANY (HQ)
100 Crystal A Dr (17033-9524)
P.O. Box 810 (17033-0810)
PHONE.....................717 534-4200
John Scharffenberger, *President*
Robert Steinberg, *Chairman*
▲ EMP: 1
SQ FT: 27,000
SALES (est): 6.1MM
SALES (corp-wide): 7.7B **Publicly Held**
SIC: 2066 Chocolate & cocoa products
PA: Hershey Company
100 Crystal A Dr
Hershey PA 17033
717 534-4200

(G-7605)
CARAUSTAR INDUSTRIES INC
515 W Chocolate Ave Rear (17033-1600)
PHONE.....................717 534-2206
Jorge Sanchez, *Plant Mgr*
Jay Marquet, *Manager*
EMP: 3
SALES (corp-wide): 3.8B **Publicly Held**
WEB: www.caraustar.com
SIC: 2631 Paperboard mills
HQ: Caraustar Industries, Inc.
5000 Austell Powder Sprin
Austell GA 30106
770 948-3101

(G-7606)
CHOCOLATECOVERS LTD INC
506 W Caracas Ave (17033-1619)
PHONE.....................717 534-1992
John T Marcucci, *President*
Sarah Haak, *Marketing Staff*

Gina Marcucci, *Administration*
EMP: 5
SALES (est): 58.9K **Privately Held**
WEB: www.chocolatecovers.com
SIC: 2759 Invitation & stationery printing & engraving

(G-7607)
CULLARI VINEYARDS & WINERY INC
2149 Sand Hill Rd (17033-2660)
PHONE.....................717 571-2376
Cathy Cullari, *President*
Salvatore Cullari, *Vice Pres*
EMP: 10
SALES (est): 811.5K **Privately Held**
SIC: 2084 Wines

(G-7608)
DISPLAY SOURCE ALLIANCE LLC
1 W Chocolate Ave Ste 700 (17033-1451)
PHONE.....................717 534-0884
Ken Brady, *Branch Mgr*
EMP: 4
SALES (corp-wide): 42.9MM **Privately Held**
SIC: 3496 Miscellaneous fabricated wire products
HQ: Display Source Alliance, Llc
1371 S Town East Blvd
Mesquite TX 75149

(G-7609)
EPLANS INC
2 Fox Chase Dr (17033-9700)
P.O. Box 915 (17033-0915)
PHONE.....................717 534-1183
Raymond Hedger, *President*
EMP: 5
SALES (est): 343.6K **Privately Held**
SIC: 7372 Application computer software

(G-7610)
EVENT HORIZON LLC
810 Old W Chocolate Ave (17033-1908)
PHONE.....................717 557-1427
EMP: 5
SALES (est): 304.4K **Privately Held**
SIC: 2066 Chocolate & cocoa products

(G-7611)
H & M DIVERSIFIED ENTPS INC
Also Called: H & M Glass
1712r E Chocolate Ave (17033-1121)
PHONE.....................717 531-3490
Micki Geib, *Branch Mgr*
EMP: 3
SALES (corp-wide): 4MM **Privately Held**
SIC: 3355 Aluminum rail & structural shapes
PA: H & M Diversified Enterprises, Inc.
981 Mount Zion Rd
Lebanon PA 17046
717 277-0680

(G-7612)
HERSEHY VETERINARY HOSPITAL
1016 Cocoa Ave (17033-1709)
PHONE.....................717 534-2244
Kevin Schengrund Dvm, *Owner*
EMP: 10
SALES (est): 450K **Privately Held**
SIC: 0742 2836 Animal hospital services, pets & other animal specialties; veterinary biological products

(G-7613)
HERSHEY COMPANY (PA)
100 Crystal A Dr (17033-9524)
P.O. Box 810 (17033-0810)
PHONE.....................717 534-4200
Charles A Davis, *Ch of Bd*
Michele G Buck, *President*
Todd W Tillemans, *President*
Javier H Idrovo, *Senior VP*
Terence L O'Day, *Senior VP*
◆ EMP: 500 EST: 1894

GEOGRAPHIC

SALES: 7.7B **Publicly Held**
WEB: www.hersheys.com
SIC: 2066 2064 2099 Chocolate & cocoa
products; chocolate bars, solid; chocolate
candy, solid; chocolate coatings & syrup;
candy & other confectionery products;
candy bars, including chocolate covered
bars; chocolate candy, except solid
chocolate; licorice candy; baking powder
& soda, yeast & other leavening agents;
dessert mixes & fillings

(G-7614)
HERSHEY COMPANY
925 Reese Ave (17033-2271)
PHONE..................................717 534-4100
Dan Darcy, *Manager*
EMP: 300
SALES (corp-wide): 7.7B **Publicly Held**
WEB: www.hersheys.com
SIC: 2064 2066 Candy & other confec-
tionery products; chocolate & cocoa prod-
ucts
PA: Hershey Company
100 Crystal A Dr
Hershey PA 17033
717 534-4200

(G-7615)
HERSHEY COMPANY
1033 W Chocolate Ave (17033-2243)
PHONE..................................717 534-4200
Bob Smith, *Manager*
EMP: 500
SALES (corp-wide): 7.7B **Publicly Held**
WEB: www.hersheys.com
SIC: 2064 Candy & other confectionery
products
PA: Hershey Company
100 Crystal A Dr
Hershey PA 17033
717 534-4200

(G-7616)
**HERSHEY FOODS
CORPORATION - MA**
100 Crystal A Dr Unit 8 (17033-9702)
PHONE..................................717 534-6799
Kenneth Wolfe, *Principal*
EMP: 15
SALES (est): 3.2MM **Privately Held**
SIC: 2064 Mfg Candy/Confectionery

(G-7617)
IDEA GROUP INC
Also Called: Igi Global
701 E Chocolate Ave # 100 (17033-1200)
PHONE..................................717 533-3673
Mehdi Khosrow-Pour, *President*
▲ EMP: 50
SQ FT: 27,000
SALES (est): 5.8MM **Privately Held**
WEB: www.idea-group.com
SIC: 2731 2721 Book publishing; periodi-
cals: publishing only

(G-7618)
**INTEGRATED SOFTWARE
SERVICES**
1171 Jill Dr Ste 104 (17033)
PHONE..................................717 534-1480
Vance Cole, *President*
EMP: 5
SALES (est): 264.7K **Privately Held**
WEB: www.issIng.com
SIC: 7372 5734 7378 Prepackaged soft-
ware; personal computers; computer
maintenance & repair

(G-7619)
JOHNSON CONTROLS INC
500 University Dr (17033-2360)
PHONE..................................717 531-5371
Brian Payfere, *Manager*
EMP: 22 **Privately Held**
SIC: 3822 3829 Building services monitor-
ing controls, automatic; measuring & con-
trolling devices
HQ: Johnson Controls, Inc.
5757 N Green Bay Ave
Milwaukee WI 53209
414 524-1200

(G-7620)
MAZZOLIS ICE CREAM
72 W Governor Rd (17033-1722)
PHONE..................................717 533-2252
EMP: 9
SQ FT: 800
SALES: 320K **Privately Held**
SIC: 2024 5143 5451 Mfg Ice
Cream/Frozen Desert Whol Dairy Prod-
ucts Ret Dairy Products

(G-7621)
**MENASHA PACKAGING
COMPANY LLC**
245 W Chocolate Ave (17033-1530)
PHONE..................................717 520-5990
Vince Deller, *Branch Mgr*
EMP: 9
SALES (corp-wide): 1.7B **Privately Held**
SIC: 3578 Point-of-sale devices
HQ: Menasha Packaging Company, Llc
1645 Bergstrom Rd
Neenah WI 54956
920 751-1000

(G-7622)
NATIVE FOODS LLC
Also Called: Native Flatbreads
434 Maple Ave (17033-1740)
P.O. Box 663 (17033-0663)
PHONE..................................717 298-6157
David Eberwein, *Mng Member*
EMP: 25 EST: 2012
SQ FT: 5,000
SALES: 300K **Privately Held**
SIC: 2051 Mfg Bread/Related Products

(G-7623)
NEXT REV DISTRIBUTION INC
337 W Chocolate Ave (17033-1674)
PHONE..................................717 576-9050
Samuel Reed, *CEO*
EMP: 4
SQ FT: 3,000
SALES: 2.2MM **Privately Held**
SIC: 3577 Computer peripheral equipment

(G-7624)
**PARMER METERED CONCRETE
INC**
2981 Elizabethtown Rd (17033-9321)
PHONE..................................717 533-3344
Donald Parmer, *President*
EMP: 6
SALES (est): 1.2MM **Privately Held**
SIC: 3273 Ready-mixed concrete

(G-7625)
PENNSYLVANIA PATTERNS
25 Trinidad Ave (17033-1386)
PHONE..................................717 533-4188
EMP: 4
SALES (est): 359K **Privately Held**
SIC: 3543 Industrial patterns

(G-7626)
WESTROCK RKT COMPANY
Also Called: Alliance Display & Packaging
10 W Chocolate Ave # 101 (17033-1472)
PHONE..................................717 520-7600
Michael Yarzinsky, *Branch Mgr*
EMP: 6
SALES (corp-wide): 16.2B **Publicly Held**
WEB: www.rocktenn.com
SIC: 2653 Hampers, solid fiber: made from
purchased materials
HQ: Westrock Rkt, Llc
1000 Abernathy Rd Ste 125
Atlanta GA 30328
770 448-2193

Hesston
Huntingdon County

(G-7627)
KIMBERLY A SPICKLER
Also Called: Stone Creek Hunds Hunting
Sups
11637 Redstone Ridge Rd (16647-8733)
PHONE..................................814 627-2316
Kimberly A Spickler, *Owner*
EMP: 3

SALES: 200K **Privately Held**
SIC: 3199 7389 Dog furnishings: collars,
leashes, muzzles, etc.: leather;

Hickory
Washington County

(G-7628)
GORDON SEAVER
Also Called: Pittsburgh Foam Products
29 Hidden Acres Ln (15340-1145)
PHONE..................................724 356-2313
R Gordon Seaver, *Owner*
Donna Seaver, *Owner*
EMP: 3
SQ FT: 16,000
SALES: 175K **Privately Held**
SIC: 3069 5087 Foam rubber; upholster-
ers' equipment & supplies

(G-7629)
**MOUNT PLSNT TWNSHP-
WSHNGTN CNT**
31 Mccarrell Rd (15340-1147)
PHONE..................................724 356-7974
Larry H Grimm, *Branch Mgr*
EMP: 15
SALES (est): 2.2MM **Privately Held**
SIC: 3589 Water treatment equipment, in-
dustrial
PA: Mount Pleasant Township- Washington
County
31 Mccarrell Rd
Hickory PA 15340
724 356-7974

(G-7630)
R H CARBIDE & EPOXY INC
107 Main St Ste 3 (15340-1120)
P.O. Box 403 (15340-0403)
PHONE..................................724 356-2277
Russell H Connelley, *President*
EMP: 5
SQ FT: 3,500
SALES (est): 987.1K **Privately Held**
SIC: 2819 2891 3398 Tungsten carbide
powder, except abrasive or metallurgical;
epoxy adhesives; brazing (hardening) of
metal

(G-7631)
SHADY ELMS SAWMILL LLC
50 Caldwell Rd (15340-1406)
PHONE..................................724 356-2594
Alex Cowden, *Principal*
EMP: 3
SALES (est): 306.8K **Privately Held**
SIC: 2421 Sawmills & planing mills, gen-
eral

Highspire
Dauphin County

(G-7632)
ENGINE CYCLE INC
30 Vine St (17034-1120)
PHONE..................................717 214-4177
EMP: 4
SALES (est): 157.9K **Privately Held**
SIC: 2493 Bulletin boards, cork

(G-7633)
HOMESTAT FARM LTD
201 Race St (17034-1127)
PHONE..................................717 939-0407
John Hulsizer, *Principal*
EMP: 13
SALES (corp-wide): 6.6MM **Privately
Held**
WEB: www.homestatfarm.com
SIC: 2043 Cereal breakfast foods
PA: Homestat Farm, Ltd.
6065 Frantz Rd Ste 206
Dublin OH 43017
614 718-3060

(G-7634)
PLOUSE MACHINE SHOP INC
Also Called: Plouse Precision Manufacturing
401 Aviation Way (17034-1559)
PHONE..................................717 558-8530
Kermit Seitz, *CEO*
Dale Seitz, *President*
Jeffrey Bertolette, *Purchasing*
David Smith, *Sales Mgr*
EMP: 75 EST: 1957
SQ FT: 21,000
SALES (est): 17.7MM **Privately Held**
SIC: 3599 Machine shop, jobbing & repair

Hillsgrove
Sullivan County

(G-7635)
**DWIGHT LEWIS LUMBER CO
INC**
1895 Route 87 (18619-9001)
P.O. Box A (18619-0901)
PHONE..................................570 924-3507
Marc Lewis, *President*
Melvin Lewis, *Corp Secy*
EMP: 30
SQ FT: 2,400
SALES (est): 4.3MM **Privately Held**
SIC: 2421 5031 Lumber: rough, sawed or
planed; wood chips, produced at mill;
lumber: rough, dressed & finished

Hillsville
Lawrence County

(G-7636)
**SEALMASTER PENNSYLVANIA
INC**
Also Called: Seal-Master Manufacturing
4551w State 3 (16132)
P.O. Box 282 (16132-0282)
PHONE..................................724 667-0444
Larry Rich, *President*
Doris Rich, *Treasurer*
EMP: 15
SQ FT: 13,000
SALES (est): 5.4MM **Privately Held**
SIC: 2865 5072 2951 2899 Cyclic
crudes, coal tar; hardware; asphalt paving
mixtures & blocks; concrete curing &
hardening compounds

Holbrook
Greene County

(G-7637)
**BERDINES CUSTOM
HARDWOODS**
1276 Golden Oaks Rd (15341-1726)
PHONE..................................724 447-2535
John Berdine, *Owner*
Martha Berdine, *Co-Owner*
EMP: 4
SALES (est): 321.5K **Privately Held**
SIC: 2411 5211 Logging; millwork & lum-
ber

Holicong
Bucks County

(G-7638)
**BARC DEVELOPMENTAL
SERVICES (PA)**
4950 York Rd (18928-5038)
P.O. Box 470 (18928-0470)
PHONE..................................215 794-0800
Teresa Manero, *President*
Joan Esling, *Vice Pres*
Phillip J Kerry, *Vice Pres*
Micheal W Mills, *Treasurer*
Robert Schram, *Exec Dir*
EMP: 45
SQ FT: 8,300

SALES: 20.5MM **Privately Held**
WEB: www.barcprograms.org
SIC: 8331 7349 3841 Skill training center; building maintenance services; surgical & medical instruments

Holland
Bucks County

(G-7639)
AJIKABE INC
Also Called: Chemtech Scientific
207 Buck Rd Ste 1c (18966-1700)
P.O. Box 704, Richboro (18954-0704)
PHONE..................................484 424-9415
Alla Kaziyeva, *President*
EMP: 5 EST: 2013
SALES (est): 756.8K **Privately Held**
SIC: 3821 Laboratory apparatus & furniture

(G-7640)
COLLEGECART INNOVATIONS INC
Also Called: CCI
20 Treeline Dr (18966-2835)
PHONE..................................215 813-3900
Melissa Radlow, *President*
Edward S Radlow, *Vice Pres*
EMP: 3 EST: 2009
SALES (est): 243K **Privately Held**
SIC: 3559 Recycling machinery

(G-7641)
MEGAN SWEET BAKING COMPANY
234 Holland Rd (18966)
PHONE..................................267 288-5080
Patti Lerner, *Principal*
EMP: 6
SALES (est): 100.4K **Privately Held**
SIC: 2051 Bakery: wholesale or wholesale/retail combined

Hollidaysburg
Blair County

(G-7642)
ANDERSON ELECTRONICS LLC (PA)
721 Scotch Valley Rd # 200 (16648-9617)
PHONE..................................814 695-4428
Craig Biesinger, *Engineer*
Mark Massimilla, *Info Tech Mgr*
Shari Shultz, *Info Tech Mgr*
Chris Sokol,
EMP: 32 EST: 1959
SALES (est): 472.8K **Privately Held**
WEB: www.aextal.com
SIC: 3679 Oscillators

(G-7643)
CATHOLIC REGISTER
Also Called: Diocese of Altoona Johnstown
927 S Logan Blvd (16648-3035)
PHONE..................................814 695-7563
Joseph V Adamec, *Principal*
EMP: 3
SALES (est): 130K **Privately Held**
SIC: 2711 8661 Newspapers; religious organizations

(G-7644)
COMPOSITE PNELS INNVATIONS LLC
485 Chimney Rocks Rd (16648-3529)
PHONE..................................814 317-5023
Pat Smith, *Principal*
EMP: 5
SALES (est): 550.9K **Privately Held**
SIC: 3089 Reinforcing mesh, plastic

(G-7645)
CURRY RAIL SERVICES INC
1477 Degol Indl Dr (16648)
PHONE..................................814 793-7245
Mark Vritchey, *President*
Brendan Perretta, *Principal*
Luke Jkelly, *Treasurer*
EMP: 6 EST: 2013

SALES (est): 3.8MM **Privately Held**
SIC: 5088 3743 Railroad equipment & supplies; freight cars & equipment

(G-7646)
EAST LOOP SAND COMPANY INC
210 River Rd (16648-3501)
PHONE..................................814 695-3082
John Gentry, *President*
Yvonne Gentry, *Vice Pres*
Jamie Winters, *Office Mgr*
EMP: 15
SQ FT: 4,800
SALES (est): 4.3MM **Privately Held**
SIC: 5032 3295 2899 Sand, construction; minerals, ground or treated; salt

(G-7647)
FINE LINE CABINETS INC (PA)
737 S Logan Blvd (16648-3031)
P.O. Box 467 (16648-0467)
PHONE..................................814 695-8133
Joseph C Irvin, *President*
Douglas Irvin, *Vice Pres*
Linda Irvin, *Treasurer*
EMP: 13
SQ FT: 13,000
SALES (est): 2.3MM **Privately Held**
SIC: 2434 Wood kitchen cabinets

(G-7648)
GAMPE MACHINE & TOOL CO INC
1224 Route 22 (16648-5166)
PHONE..................................814 696-6206
Michael Gampe, *President*
EMP: 21
SQ FT: 10,000
SALES (est): 4.8MM **Privately Held**
SIC: 2821 7699 Plastics materials & resins; industrial machinery & equipment repair

(G-7649)
GRANNAS BROS STONE ASP CO INC
Also Called: Grannas Bros Contracting Co
157 Grannas Rd (16648-7156)
P.O. Box 488 (16648-0488)
PHONE..................................814 695-5021
Samuel P Grannas, *President*
Scott Grannas, *Vice Pres*
Wade A Grannas, *Admin Sec*
EMP: 70
SALES (est): 19.1MM **Privately Held**
SIC: 2951 1423 Asphalt paving mixtures & blocks; crushed & broken granite

(G-7650)
LARET SIGN CO
121 Justice St (16648-1341)
PHONE..................................814 695-4455
Jack Laret, *Owner*
Tina Mock -Ofc, *Manager*
EMP: 4
SQ FT: 7,420
SALES (est): 331.7K **Privately Held**
SIC: 3993 Neon signs

(G-7651)
MCLANAHAN CORPORATION (PA)
200 Wall St (16648-1637)
P.O. Box 229 (16648-0229)
PHONE..................................814 695-9807
Sean McLanahan, *CEO*
George Sidney, *President*
Michael McLanahan, *Chairman*
Astride S Mc Lanahan, *Treasurer*
◆ EMP: 300
SQ FT: 118,000
SALES (est): 149.6MM **Privately Held**
WEB: www.mclanahan.com
SIC: 3532 3321 3599 3523 Crushers, stationary; washers, aggregate & sand; feeders, ore & aggregate; screeners, stationary; gray iron castings; machine shop, jobbing & repair; farm machinery & equipment

(G-7652)
PATTERNMASTER CHOKES LLC
1102 W Loop Rd (16648-8616)
PHONE..................................877 388-2259

EMP: 4
SALES (est): 319.7K **Privately Held**
SIC: 3949 Sporting & athletic goods

(G-7653)
SECRETS OF BIG DOGS
Also Called: Canis Major International
506 Allegheny St Ste 2 (16648-2015)
P.O. Box 275 (16648-0275)
PHONE..................................814 696-0469
Stan Stuchinski, *Owner*
EMP: 3 EST: 2001
SALES (est): 364.5K **Privately Held**
WEB: www.bigdogsecrets.com
SIC: 2731 Book publishing

(G-7654)
SEVEN D INDUSTRIES LP (HQ)
1001 W Loop Rd (16648-8619)
P.O. Box 447 (16648-0447)
PHONE..................................814 317-4077
Gloria J Burgan, *Partner*
Dennis W De Gol, *Partner*
Donald A De Gol, *Partner*
David A Gol, *Partner*
Bruno De Gol Jr, *General Ptnr*
▲ EMP: 123
SQ FT: 116,000
SALES (est): 11.5MM
SALES (corp-wide): 191.1MM **Privately Held**
SIC: 3089 2431 Windows, plastic; windows & window parts & trim, wood
PA: The Degol Organization L P
3229 Pleasant Valley Blvd
Altoona PA 16602
814 941-7777

(G-7655)
SIGN ME UP LLC
224 Woodlawn Ter (16648-2994)
PHONE..................................814 931-0933
Alison Davies,
Bruce Davies,
EMP: 4
SALES (est): 197.1K **Privately Held**
SIC: 3993 Neon signs

Hollsopple
Somerset County

(G-7656)
AMSI US LLC
111 Hoganas Way (15935-6416)
P.O. Box 140 (15935-0140)
PHONE..................................814 479-3380
John Alexander, *Mng Member*
EMP: 4
SALES (est): 454.6K **Privately Held**
SIC: 3325 Steel foundries

(G-7657)
COUNTY OF SOMERSET
458 Mastillo Rd (15935-6503)
PHONE..................................814 629-9460
EMP: 4 **Privately Held**
SIC: 9511 3589 Air, water & solid waste management; water treatment equipment, industrial
PA: County Of Somerset
300 N Center Ave Ste 500
Somerset PA 15501
814 445-1400

(G-7658)
NORTH AMERICAN HOGANAS COMPANY
Also Called: N.A. Hoganas
111 Hoganas Way (15935-6416)
PHONE..................................814 479-3500
Avinash Gore, *President*
Terry Henrich, *Vice Pres*
Dave Johnson, *Vice Pres*
Ronald Solomon, *Vice Pres*
Matthew Smith, *Opers Mgr*
◆ EMP: 355
SQ FT: 400,000
SALES: 234.4MM
SALES (corp-wide): 974.4MM **Privately Held**
SIC: 3399 8734 Metal powders, pastes & flakes; metallurgical testing laboratory

HQ: Hoganas Ab
Bruksgatan 35
Hoganas 263 3
423 380-00

(G-7659)
NORTH AMRCN HGNAS HOLDINGS INC (DH)
111 Hoganas Way (15935-6416)
PHONE..................................814 479-2551
Avinash Gore, *President*
Dean Howard, *Vice Pres*
Sydney Luke, *Vice Pres*
Ronald Solomon, *Vice Pres*
John Jackson, *Production*
◆ EMP: 190
SQ FT: 400,000
SALES (est): 101.9MM
SALES (corp-wide): 974.4MM **Privately Held**
WEB: www.northamericanhoganas.com
SIC: 3462 Ornamental metal forgings, ferrous
HQ: Hoganas Ab
Bruksgatan 35
Hoganas 263 3
423 380-00

(G-7660)
POLAR BLOX INC
650 Gilbert Hollow Rd (15935-7913)
PHONE..................................814 629-7397
Emma Trevorrow, *President*
EMP: 5
SALES (est): 754.2K **Privately Held**
WEB: www.polarblox.com
SIC: 3799 Snowmobiles

Holmes
Delaware County

(G-7661)
EAST COAST CONSTRUCTORS INC
101 Talbot Ave (19043-1422)
PHONE..................................610 532-3650
Carolyn Golden, *President*
EMP: 10
SALES (est): 2.2MM **Privately Held**
SIC: 3498 Fabricated pipe & fittings

(G-7662)
FIDELITY GRAPHICS
238 Holmes Rd (19043-1590)
PHONE..................................610 586-9300
Melvin J Lindauer, *Owner*
EMP: 14
SQ FT: 5,000
SALES (est): 993.5K **Privately Held**
WEB: www.fidelitygraphics.com
SIC: 2791 Typesetting

(G-7663)
KYKAYKE INC
Also Called: TTI
500 Pine St Ste 3a (19043-1452)
PHONE..................................610 522-0106
Richard Snyder, *CEO*
EMP: 9
SALES (est): 192.9K **Privately Held**
SIC: 3999 3699 7629 3663 Manufacturing industries; security devices; security control equipment & systems; electrical repair shops; radio & TV communications equipment; communications equipment

(G-7664)
RICH INDUSTRIAL SERVICES INC
2230 Forrester Ave (19043-1426)
P.O. Box 71 (19043-0071)
PHONE..................................610 534-0195
Deborah Rich, *President*
Suzanne Rich, *Vice Pres*
Tina Rich, *Admin Sec*
EMP: 14
SALES (est): 831.2K **Privately Held**
SIC: 3585 Drinking fountains, mechanically refrigerated

(G-7665)
TACTICAL TECHNOLOGIES INC
500 Pine St Ste 3a (19043-1452)
P.O. Box 91 (19043-0091)
PHONE..................................610 522-0106
Richard Snyder, *President*
Doug Blakeway, *Treasurer*
EMP: 20
SQ FT: 14,500
SALES (est): 3.4MM
SALES (corp-wide): 5.8MM **Privately Held**
WEB: www.tacticaltechnologies.com
SIC: 3699 Security devices
PA: Nanotech Security Corp
3292 Production Way Suite 505
Burnaby BC V5A 4
604 678-5775

(G-7666)
TOWN TALK NEWSPAPERS INC
1914 Parker Ave (19043-1414)
PHONE..................................610 583-4432
Diane Ryan, *Principal*
EMP: 40 **EST:** 1963
SQ FT: 6,000
SALES (est): 1.7MM **Privately Held**
SIC: 2711 Newspapers, publishing & printing

Holtwood
Lancaster County

(G-7667)
GREEN N GROW COMPOST LLC
300 Douts Hill Rd (17532-9630)
PHONE..................................717 284-5710
Stephen R Lehman, *Principal*
EMP: 3
SALES (est): 331.8K **Privately Held**
SIC: 2875 Compost

Home
Indiana County

(G-7668)
E E S AUGERING COMPANY
687 Ambrose Rd (15747-7514)
PHONE..................................724 397-8821
Robert Elkin, *President*
Judy Elkin, *Corp Secy*
EMP: 6 **EST:** 1978
SALES (est): 562K **Privately Held**
SIC: 1221 Auger mining, bituminous

(G-7669)
MASHAN INC
20 Minich Rd (15747-6111)
PHONE..................................724 397-4008
Matthew Kimmel, *President*
Catherine Kimmel, *President*
EMP: 6
SALES (est): 1.5MM **Privately Held**
SIC: 3669 8748 Emergency alarms; telecommunications consultant

---

Homer City
Indiana County

(G-7670)
BABCOCK & WILCOX COMPANY
81 Grover St (15748-1007)
P.O. Box 360291, Pittsburgh (15251-6291)
PHONE..................................724 479-3585
EMP: 5
SALES (corp-wide): 1.5B **Publicly Held**
SIC: 3511 Mfg Turbines/Generator Sets
HQ: The Babcock & Wilcox Company
20 S Van Buren Ave
Barberton OH 44203
330 753-4511

(G-7671)
CAMERON LUMBER LLP
1386 Ridge Rd (15748-5121)
PHONE..................................814 749-9635
Homer A Cameron, *Partner*

Chris Cameron, *Partner*
Shawn Cameron, *Partner*
EMP: 21
SALES (est): 2.4MM **Privately Held**
SIC: 2411 2421 5031 Logging camps & contractors; lumber: rough, sawed or planed; lumber: rough, dressed & finished

(G-7672)
CHEMSTREAM INC
511 Railroad Ave (15748-1422)
PHONE..................................814 629-7118
Michael Kaufman, *President*
Travis Miller, *General Mgr*
Marilyn Kaufman, *Corp Secy*
Jim Sala, *Sales Associate*
EMP: 10 **EST:** 1997
SALES (est): 2.6MM **Privately Held**
WEB: www.chemstream.com
SIC: 2899 Water treating compounds

(G-7673)
CKL AUGERING INC
129 Mazza St (15748-1013)
PHONE..................................724 479-0213
Robert Caylor, *President*
Charles Kelly, *Principal*
Thomas Lytle, *Principal*
EMP: 3
SALES (est): 127.6K **Privately Held**
WEB: www.stargat.com
SIC: 1221 Auger mining, bituminous

(G-7674)
CLARK TRAFFIC CONTROL INC
10125 Route 56 Hwy E (15748-4305)
PHONE..................................724 388-4023
Fax: 814 446-5597
EMP: 10
SQ FT: 30,000
SALES (est): 533.4K **Privately Held**
SIC: 8748 3669 Business Consulting, Nec, Nsk

(G-7675)
HILLSIDE ENTERPRISE
1274 Brush Creek Rd (15748-5827)
PHONE..................................724 479-3678
Andrew Stauffer, *Partner*
Russell Martin, *Partner*
Amon Zimmerman, *Partner*
EMP: 6
SQ FT: 5,000
SALES (est): 808.5K **Privately Held**
SIC: 2511 Bed frames, except water bed frames: wood

(G-7676)
IA CONSTRUCTION CORPORATION
Old Rte 119 (15748)
PHONE..................................724 479-9690
Tom Broady, *Manager*
EMP: 4
SALES (corp-wide): 83.5MM **Privately Held**
WEB: www.iaconstruction.com
SIC: 2951 Asphalt & asphaltic paving mixtures (not from refineries)
HQ: Ia Construction Corporation
24 Gibb Rd
Franklin PA 16323
814 432-3184

(G-7677)
JOY GLOBAL UNDERGROUND MIN LLC
601 Lucerne Rd (15748-7420)
PHONE..................................724 915-2200
Ed Curnow, *Branch Mgr*
EMP: 63
SALES (corp-wide): 23.4B **Privately Held**
SIC: 3535 Bucket type conveyor systems
HQ: Joy Global Underground Mining Llc
40 Pennwood Pl Ste 100
Warrendale PA 15086
724 779-4500

(G-7678)
MGK TECHNOLOGIES INC
57 Cooper Ave (15748-1306)
P.O. Box H, Brookville (15825-0608)
PHONE..................................814 849-3061
David Miller, *President*
Eric D Miller, *Vice Pres*
Kelly G Belfiore, *Admin Secy*

EMP: 50
SALES (est): 9.7MM
SALES (corp-wide): 33.4MM **Privately Held**
SIC: 3443 Metal parts
PA: Miller Welding And Machine Co.
111 2nd St
Brookville PA 15825
814 849-3061

(G-7679)
NONLETHAL TECHNOLOGIES INC
9419 Route 286 Hwy W (15748-9322)
PHONE..................................724 479-5100
James A Oberdick, *Ch of Bd*
Michael S Oberdick, *President*
Jim Oberdick, *CFO*
◆ **EMP:** 48
SQ FT: 10,000
SALES (est): 7.7MM **Privately Held**
WEB: www.nonlethaltechnologies.com
SIC: 3482 2869 3483 3484 Small arms ammunition; industrial organic chemicals; ammunition, except for small arms; small arms; explosives

(G-7680)
PRIME METALS ACQUISITION LLC
Also Called: Prime Metal and Alloys
101 Innovation Dr (15748-7433)
PHONE..................................724 479-4155
Michael Lynn, *Opers Staff*
Richard Knupp, *Mng Member*
Leon Nusselt, *Director*
EMP: 56 **EST:** 2017
SQ FT: 120,000
SALES (est): 16.4MM
SALES (corp-wide): 43.1MM **Publicly Held**
SIC: 3355 3322 Aluminum ingot; malleable iron foundries
PA: Amerinac Holding Corp.
5936 State Route 159
Chillicothe OH 45601
614 836-1050

(G-7681)
SANFORD MILLER INC
150 Ross Rd (15748-6435)
PHONE..................................724 479-5090
Kurt Catob, *President*
Roger Coudriet, *Vice Pres*
Carol Catob, *Admin Sec*
EMP: 3 **EST:** 1998
SQ FT: 1,000
SALES (est): 309.6K **Privately Held**
SIC: 3679 Rectifiers, electronic

(G-7682)
SMITH CONCRETE PRODUCTS
Old Rte 119 N (15748)
PHONE..................................724 349-5858
Robin Smith, *Owner*
EMP: 6
SQ FT: 1,500
SALES (est): 453.5K **Privately Held**
SIC: 3272 Steps, prefabricated concrete; septic tanks, concrete

---

Homestead
Allegheny County

(G-7683)
BLIND AND VISION REHAB
Also Called: Blind & Vision
1800 West St Side (15120-2564)
PHONE..................................412 325-7504
Tara Zimmerman, *General Mgr*
Jeffery Span, *Branch Mgr*
Jeff Span, *Info Tech Dir*
EMP: 15
SALES (corp-wide): 4.3MM **Privately Held**
WEB: www.pghvis.com
SIC: 3993 2326 3991 2819 Signs & advertising specialties; men's & boys' work clothing; brooms & brushes; charcoal (carbon), activated; helmets, steel

PA: Blind And Vision Rehabilitation Services Of Pittsburgh
1816 Locust St
Pittsburgh PA 15219
412 368-4400

(G-7684)
DOWNING MACHINES INC
467 W 8th Ave (15120-1035)
PHONE..................................412 461-0580
George D Amrhein, *Ch of Bd*
Dean Amrhein, *President*
Lois Durkota, *Vice Pres*
EMP: 5
SALES (est): 762.6K **Privately Held**
SIC: 3599 Machine shop, jobbing & repair

(G-7685)
EDINBORO CREATIONS
Also Called: Bee Hempy
1210 Commonwealth Ave (15120-3604)
PHONE..................................412 462-0370
Ward Troetschel, *Owner*
EMP: 5
SALES (est): 190K **Privately Held**
SIC: 3999 5199 Candles; candles

(G-7686)
HOMESTEAD AUTOMOTIVE SUPPLY
4704 Little St (15120-2926)
PHONE..................................412 462-4467
Richard H Solman Jr, *Owner*
EMP: 8
SQ FT: 3,500
SALES (est): 652K **Privately Held**
SIC: 5531 5013 3599 Automotive accessories; automotive supplies & parts; machine shop, jobbing & repair

(G-7687)
INDUSTRIAL CTRL CONCEPTS INC
278 Mifflin St (15120-2376)
PHONE..................................412 464-1905
Andrea Urban, *President*
EMP: 8 **Privately Held**
SIC: 3613 Control panels, electric
PA: Industrial Control Concepts, Inc.
209 Frank St
Homestead PA 15120

(G-7688)
INDUSTRIAL CTRL CONCEPTS INC (PA)
209 Frank St (15120-2323)
PHONE..................................412 464-1905
Andrea Urban, *President*
David Urban, *Treasurer*
EMP: 2
SALES (est): 1.2MM **Privately Held**
SIC: 3613 Control panels, electric

(G-7689)
JENNIFERS CARDS & GIFTS
3411 Main St Ste 1 (15120-3296)
PHONE..................................412 462-8505
Debby Rende, *Owner*
EMP: 3
SALES (est): 329.6K **Privately Held**
SIC: 2771 Greeting cards

(G-7690)
PISCIS
4501 Main St (15120-3331)
PHONE..................................412 464-5181
John Piscitelli, *Principal*
EMP: 4
SALES (est): 441K **Privately Held**
SIC: 2599 Bar, restaurant & cafeteria furniture

(G-7691)
PMI STAINLESS
Also Called: Pittsburgh Mfrs & Installers
Forest & West 8th Ave (15120)
PHONE..................................412 461-1463
Gary Dale Anthony, *President*
Beverly J Anthony, *Corp Secy*
EMP: 20 **EST:** 1971
SQ FT: 34,000
SALES (est): 1.9MM **Privately Held**
WEB: www.pmistainless.com
SIC: 3469 Kitchen fixtures & equipment: metal, except cast aluminum

G E O G R A P H I C

(G-7692)
REYNOLDS SALES CO INC
462 W 7th Ave (15120-1052)
PHONE....................412 461-7877
Thomas Reynolds, *President*
Larry Reynolds, *Treasurer*
Arthur T Reynolds, *Director*
Virginia Reynolds, *Admin Sec*
EMP: 6
SQ FT: 11,000
SALES (est): 805.6K **Privately Held**
SIC: 3441 3443 3599 1541 Fabricated
structural metal; fabricated plate work
(boiler shop); machine shop, jobbing & re-
pair; prefabricated building erection, in-
dustrial

(G-7693)
**SCIULLO MACHINE SHOP &
TOOL CO**
854 Forest Ave (15120-1115)
PHONE....................412 466-9571
Sam Sciullo, *CEO*
EMP: 8
SALES (corp-wide): 480.1K **Privately
Held**
SIC: 3599 Machine shop, jobbing & repair
PA: Sciullo Machine Shop & Tool Co
1061 Kentucky Blue Dr
West Mifflin PA 15122
412 462-1604

(G-7694)
UNITED STATES STEEL CORP
Also Called: Research & Technology Center
800 E Waterfront Dr (15120-5044)
PHONE....................412 810-0286
Keith Jansen, *Branch Mgr*
EMP: 40
SALES (corp-wide): 14.1B **Publicly Held**
SIC: 3312 Blast furnaces & steel mills
PA: United States Steel Corp
600 Grant St Ste 468
Pittsburgh PA 15219
412 433-1121

(G-7695)
UNITED STATES STEEL CORP
Also Called: Research and Technology Cen-
tre
800 E Waterfront Dr (15120-5044)
PHONE....................412 433-7215
Kevin Veik, *General Mgr*
EMP: 235
SALES (corp-wide): 14.1B **Publicly Held**
SIC: 3317 3356 3312 Steel pipe & tubes;
tin; plate, steel
PA: United States Steel Corp
600 Grant St Ste 468
Pittsburgh PA 15219
412 433-1121

(G-7696)
VALLEY MIRROR
Also Called: Valley Mirror The
3315 Main St Ste A (15120-3200)
PHONE....................412 462-0626
Anthony Munson, *President*
EMP: 5 EST: 1913
SQ FT: 1,700
SALES (est): 340.4K **Privately Held**
WEB: www.valleymirror.com
SIC: 2711 Newspapers: publishing only,
not printed on site

(G-7697)
WATERFRONT EMBROIDERY
233 W 8th Ave (15120-1010)
PHONE....................412 337-9269
Jason Farmicks, *Partner*
EMP: 3
SALES (est): 202.8K **Privately Held**
SIC: 2395 Embroidery products, except
schiffli machine

(G-7698)
**WHEMCO-STEEL CASTINGS
INC**
601 W 7th Ave (15120-1064)
PHONE....................724 643-7001
Christopher J Coholich, *Manager*
EMP: 5
SALES (corp-wide): 568.1MM **Privately
Held**
SIC: 3325 Steel foundries

HQ: Whemco - Steel Castings, Inc.
5 Hot Metal St Ste 300
Pittsburgh PA 15203
412 390-2700

Honesdale
Wayne County

(G-7699)
A & B HOMES INC
Also Called: Altier Archery Mfg Div
Rr 6 (18431)
P.O. Box 286 (18431-0286)
PHONE....................570 253-3888
Anthony Altier, *President*
Roseann Altier, *Admin Sec*
EMP: 6 EST: 1967
SQ FT: 960
SALES (est): 938.8K **Privately Held**
SIC: 5211 3949 5941 5091 Modular
homes; archery equipment, general;
archery supplies; archery equipment

(G-7700)
**ALPINE WURST & MEATHOUSE
INC**
1106 Texas Palmyra Hwy (18431-7682)
PHONE....................570 253-5899
Mark Eifert, *President*
Ingrid Eifert, *Corp Secy*
EMP: 22
SQ FT: 4,800
SALES (est): 1.1MM **Privately Held**
WEB: www.thealpineonline.com
SIC: 5812 2013 5147 5421 German
restaurant; sausages from purchased
meat; cured meats from purchased
meat; meats & meat products; meats, cured or
smoked; meat & fish markets; gift shop;
meat packing plants

(G-7701)
B G M FASTENER CO INC
759 Old Willow Ave (18431-4217)
PHONE....................570 253-5046
Judith A Goyette, *President*
Mike Bancroft, *General Mgr*
Philip L Goyette, *Corp Secy*
Pete Goyette, *Vice Pres*
Peter Goyette, *Vice Pres*
EMP: 28
SQ FT: 50,000
SALES (est): 10.9MM **Privately Held**
WEB: www.bgmfastener.com
SIC: 5085 8734 3429 Fasteners, indus-
trial: nuts, bolts, screws, etc.; product
testing laboratory, safety or performance;
metal fasteners

(G-7702)
BATTERY TECH LLC
203 Dunn Rd (18431-3078)
PHONE....................570 253-6908
Barry Zeglen, *Principal*
EMP: 3
SALES (est): 307.8K **Privately Held**
SIC: 3691 Batteries, rechargeable

(G-7703)
BOYDS MILLS PRESS INC
815 Church St (18431-1889)
PHONE....................570 253-1164
Clayton Winters, *President*
Thomas R Mason, *Treasurer*
▲ EMP: 13
SALES (est): 1.2MM
SALES (corp-wide): 216.2MM **Privately
Held**
WEB: www.boydsmillspress.com
SIC: 2731 Books: publishing only
PA: Highlights For Children, Inc.
1800 Watermark Dr
Columbus OH 43215
614 486-0631

(G-7704)
CALKINS CREAMERY LLC
288 Calkins Rd (18431-7951)
PHONE....................570 729-8103
Emily Montgomery, *Owner*
EMP: 13
SALES (est): 1.4MM **Privately Held**
SIC: 2021 Creamery butter

(G-7705)
CARBONDALE NEWS (PA)
Also Called: Gatehouse
220 8th St (18431-1854)
PHONE....................570 282-3300
Steve Fountain, *President*
EMP: 8
SQ FT: 3,000
SALES (est): 898.5K **Privately Held**
SIC: 2711 Newspapers: publishing only,
not printed on site

(G-7706)
CARBONDALE NEWS
Also Called: Moscow Villager, The
220 8th St (18431-1854)
PHONE....................570 282-3300
Don Doyle, *Manager*
EMP: 4
SALES (corp-wide): 898.5K **Privately
Held**
SIC: 2711 Newspapers: publishing only,
not printed on site
PA: Carbondale News
220 8th St
Honesdale PA 18431
570 282-3300

(G-7707)
COCHECTON MILLS INC
18 Crestmont Dr (18431-1332)
PHONE....................570 224-4144
Dennis Nearing, *President*
EMP: 20
SALES (corp-wide): 2.1MM **Privately
Held**
SIC: 0723 5191 2048 Crop preparation
services for market; farm supplies; pre-
pared feeds
PA: Cochecton Mills, Inc.
30 Depot Rd
Cochecton NY 12726
845 932-8282

(G-7708)
CONNECTIONS MAGAZINE
3305 Lake Ariel Hwy (18431-7694)
PHONE....................570 647-0085
Deborah Bailey, *Principal*
EMP: 3
SALES (est): 240.3K **Privately Held**
SIC: 2721 Magazines: publishing & printing

(G-7709)
DANITA CONTAINER INC
1338 Bethany Tpke (18431-4046)
PHONE....................570 448-3606
Jens P Mueller, *President*
EMP: 6
SALES (est): 595.5K **Privately Held**
SIC: 3999 Barber & beauty shop equip-
ment

(G-7710)
DUNNS SAWMILL LLP
217 Navajo Rd (18431-3127)
PHONE....................570 253-5217
John Dunn, *Partner*
Ryan Dunn, *Partner*
William Dunn, *Partner*
James Watson Jr, *Partner*
EMP: 4
SALES (est): 360K **Privately Held**
WEB: www.wiredsp.com
SIC: 2411 5211 Logging camps & contrac-
tors; lumber products

(G-7711)
**ESTEMERWALT LUMBER PDTS
LLC**
505 Adams Pond Rd (18431-3003)
PHONE....................570 729-8572
Kurt I Probst, *Partner*
EMP: 14
SQ FT: 350
SALES (est): 1.4MM **Privately Held**
WEB: www.estemerwalt.com
SIC: 2421 Sawmills & planing mills, gen-
eral

(G-7712)
GATEHOUSE MEDIA LLC
Also Called: Wayne Independent
220 8th St Ofc (18431-1876)
PHONE....................570 253-3055

Don Doyle, *Publisher*
EMP: 35
SALES (corp-wide): 1.5B **Publicly Held**
WEB: www.gatehousemedia.com
SIC: 2711 Newspapers, publishing & print-
ing
HQ: Gatehouse Media, Llc
175 Sullys Trl Fl 3
Pittsford NY 14534
585 598-0030

(G-7713)
**HERE AND NOW BREWING CO
LLC**
645 Main St (18431-1842)
PHONE....................570 647-6085
Allaina Propst, *President*
EMP: 5
SALES (est): 169.2K **Privately Held**
SIC: 2082 Ale (alcoholic beverage)

(G-7714)
**HIGHLIGHTS FOR CHILDREN
INC**
Also Called: Editorial Office
803 Church St (18431-1895)
PHONE....................570 253-1080
Kent L Brown Jr, *Office Mgr*
EMP: 50
SALES (corp-wide): 216.2MM **Privately
Held**
WEB: www.highlights.com
SIC: 8999 2721 Editorial service; periodi-
cals
PA: Highlights For Children, Inc.
1800 Watermark Dr
Columbus OH 43215
614 486-0631

(G-7715)
**HIMALAYAN INTERNATIONAL
INSTIT (PA)**
952 Bethany Tpke Bldg 1 (18431-4194)
PHONE....................570 253-5551
Rolf Fovik, *President*
Rajmani Tigunait, *Chairman*
Gregory Capitolo, *Treasurer*
Stephen Moulton, *Director*
Suzanne Grady, *Admin Sec*
◆ EMP: 40 EST: 1971
SQ FT: 90,000
SALES (est): 2.6MM **Privately Held**
SIC: 7999 2731 Yoga instruction; books:
publishing & printing

(G-7716)
**HIMALAYAN INTL INS OF YOGA
INS**
Also Called: Yoga International
952 Bethany Tpke Bldg 1 (18431-4194)
PHONE....................570 634-5168
John Clarke, *President*
EMP: 8
SALES (corp-wide): 2.6MM **Privately
Held**
SIC: 2759 Commercial printing
PA: Himalayan International Institute Of
Yoga Science & Philosophy
952 Bethany Tpke Bldg 1
Honesdale PA 18431
570 253-5551

(G-7717)
MARTIN ROLLISON INC (PA)
120 Sunrise Ave (18431-1034)
PHONE....................570 253-4141
Martin Rollison, *President*
EMP: 42
SQ FT: 100,000
SALES (est): 4.5MM **Privately Held**
SIC: 3441 Fabricated structural metal

(G-7718)
**NEW WAVE CUSTOM WDWKG
INC**
214 6th St (18431-1801)
P.O. Box 305, White Mills (18473-0305)
PHONE....................570 251-8218
Rudy Schemitz, *President*
Francine Gilson, *Admin Sec*
EMP: 23
SQ FT: 5,000
SALES (est): 1MM **Privately Held**
SIC: 2426 2511 Frames for upholstered
furniture, wood; wood household furniture

(G-7719)
NEWS EAGLE (PA)
220 8th St (18431-1854)
PHONE..................570 226-4547
Dun Doyle, *Principal*
Peter Becker, *Manager*
EMP: 30 EST: 1965
SQ FT: 5,500
SALES (est): 1.2MM Privately Held
WEB: www.neagle.com
SIC: 2711 2752 Newspapers: publishing only, not printed on site; commercial printing, lithographic

(G-7720)
PROMPTON TOOL INC
120 Sunrise Ave Ste 2 (18431-1034)
PHONE..................570 253-4141
Martin Rollison, *President*
Susan Rollison, *Vice Pres*
Terry Loughrey, *Opers Mgr*
John Stachnik, *QC Mgr*
Jan Smoke, *Accounts Mgr*
EMP: 60 EST: 1963
SQ FT: 16,000
SALES (est): 13.5MM Privately Held
WEB: www.promptontool.com
SIC: 3599 7692 Machine shop, jobbing & repair; welding repair

(G-7721)
PTUBES INC
Also Called: Ryno Linesets
84 4th St Ste 1 (18431-1837)
P.O. Box 1107 (18431-6107)
PHONE..................201 560-7127
Nicola Pilone, *CEO*
Richard Ranieri, *Vice Pres*
Rich Ranieri, *VP Sales*
EMP: 12
SALES (est): 452.8K Privately Held
SIC: 3351 Copper & copper alloy pipe & tube

(G-7722)
ROTHROCKS SILVERSMITHS INC
3361 Lake Ariel Hwy (18431-1174)
PHONE..................570 253-1990
Jan Rothrock, *President*
EMP: 4 EST: 1945
SQ FT: 2,000
SALES (est): 545K Privately Held
WEB: www.rothrocks.com
SIC: 5944 3914 Silverware; hollowware, silver

(G-7723)
SERIGRAPH FACTORY
2 Chapel St (18431-2094)
PHONE..................570 647-0644
Cobb Brian, *Principal*
EMP: 3
SALES (est): 216.8K Privately Held
SIC: 2759 Commercial printing

(G-7724)
SPECIALTY PRODUCTS COMPANY
362 Tryon St (18431-3188)
PHONE..................570 729-7192
Nancy Eisele, *President*
Mark Eisele, *Vice Pres*
EMP: 5
SQ FT: 2,000
SALES: 350K Privately Held
SIC: 3944 Trains & equipment, toy: electric & mechanical

(G-7725)
SPENCER PRINTING INC
Also Called: Spencer Printing and Graphics
216 Willow Ave (18431-1110)
PHONE..................570 253-2001
Nathaniel Zaur, *President*
EMP: 6 EST: 1910
SQ FT: 3,000
SALES (est): 1.1MM Privately Held
SIC: 2752 Commercial printing, offset

(G-7726)
ST CLAIR GRAPHICS INC
Also Called: Plastic Packaging & Print Co
406 Erie St (18431-1012)
PHONE..................570 253-6692

Mary St Clair, *President*
Christopher St Clair, *Corp Secy*
Elizabeth Gleim, *Vice Pres*
Jeff Robbins, *Prdtn Mgr*
EMP: 11
SQ FT: 11,000
SALES (est): 860K Privately Held
WEB: www.stclairgraphics.com
SIC: 2752 7374 2789 Commercial printing, offset; color lithography; computer graphics service; binding only: books, pamphlets, magazines, etc.

(G-7727)
STEER MACHINE TOOL & DIE CORP
3113 Lake Ariel Hwy (18431-7604)
PHONE..................570 253-5152
Steven Seeuwen, *President*
Eric Seeuwen, *Vice Pres*
EMP: 12
SQ FT: 10,000
SALES: 800K Privately Held
WEB: www.steermachine.com
SIC: 3544 Special dies & tools

(G-7728)
TLB INDUSTRIES INC
292 Dunn Rd (18431-3002)
PHONE..................570 729-7192
Melissa Meyers, *President*
EMP: 5
SALES (est): 446.3K Privately Held
SIC: 3999 Pet supplies

(G-7729)
TOP NOTCH DISTRIBUTORS INC
80 4th St (18431-1872)
PHONE..................800 233-4210
Jeff Morris, *Branch Mgr*
EMP: 13
SALES (corp-wide): 62.9MM Privately Held
SIC: 3429 Manufactured hardware (general)
PA: Top Notch Distributors, Inc.
80 4th St
Honesdale PA 18431
570 253-5625

(G-7730)
TRASHCANS UNLIMITED LLC
Also Called: Gotta Have It For Less
1114 Texas Palmyra Hwy (18431-7683)
PHONE..................800 279-3615
Dominick Farina, *Mng Member*
EMP: 3
SALES: 800K Privately Held
SIC: 3443 Trash racks, metal plate

(G-7731)
VIP ADVERTISING & PRINTING
Main And Elizabeth (18431)
PHONE..................570 251-7897
Morgan Hatton, *President*
EMP: 6
SALES (est): 277.7K Privately Held
SIC: 7331 2752 Direct mail advertising services; commercial printing, lithographic

(G-7732)
VISION QUEST INC
2065 Great Bend Tpke (18431-6565)
PHONE..................570 448-2845
Nickolas Giannetti, *President*
Joseph Giannetti, *President*
Catherine Giannetti, *Admin Sec*
EMP: 6
SALES: 400K Privately Held
SIC: 3949 Archery equipment, general

(G-7733)
WAYNE COUNTY READY MIX INC
397 Grimms Rd (18431-4076)
PHONE..................570 253-4341
Richard Frisch, *President*
Richard E Frisch, *President*
Thomas Frisch, *Vice Pres*
EMP: 15 EST: 1970
SQ FT: 1,000
SALES (est): 1.9MM Privately Held
SIC: 3273 Ready-mixed concrete

Honey Brook
Chester County

(G-7734)
A J BLOSENSKI INC (PA)
1600 Chestnut Tree Rd (19344-9642)
P.O. Box 392, Elverson (19520-0392)
PHONE..................610 942-2707
Anthony Blosenski, *President*
Joe Strohl, *Regl Sales Mgr*
James Harmon, *Sales Staff*
Robert Hart, *Sales Staff*
Adam Irey, *Sales Staff*
EMP: 66
SQ FT: 2,000
SALES (est): 17.6MM Privately Held
WEB: www.ajblosenski.com
SIC: 2611 3341 3231 4212 Pulp mills; secondary nonferrous metals; products of purchased glass; local trucking, without storage; scrap & waste materials

(G-7735)
AARON KING
Also Called: Pleasantview Welding
665 Pleasant View Rd (19344-1723)
PHONE..................610 273-1365
EMP: 4
SALES (est): 857K Privately Held
SIC: 3443 Mfg Fabricated Plate Work

(G-7736)
AMS LIQUIDATING CO INC
Also Called: AMS Filling Systems
2500 Chestnut Tree Rd (19344-9646)
PHONE..................610 942-4200
Gary Baker, *President*
Brian C Baker, *Vice Pres*
Jack Treptow, *Vice Pres*
Barry Holzhauser, *Purchasing*
Jim Kerr, *Technical Mgr*
EMP: 99
SQ FT: 45,000
SALES (est): 283.4K Privately Held
SIC: 3565 Packaging machinery

(G-7737)
BEAVER DAM WOODWORKS LLC
2060 Beaver Dam Rd (19344-9256)
PHONE..................610 273-7656
Amos K Kauffman, *Mng Member*
EMP: 7
SALES (est): 855.9K Privately Held
SIC: 2431 Millwork

(G-7738)
BENCO TECHNOLOGY LLC (PA)
625 Todd Rd (19344-1301)
PHONE..................610 273-3364
Matt Ford, *Plant Mgr*
Ben Beiler, *Mng Member*
Rob Aronson, *Manager*
Benji Smoker, *Manager*
Ruth Brown,
EMP: 10
SQ FT: 23,000
SALES (est): 4.4MM Privately Held
WEB: www.bencotechnology.com
SIC: 3471 Finishing, metals or formed products

(G-7739)
BVS INC
Also Called: Brainy Valley Sales
949 Poplar Rd (19344-1357)
P.O. Box 250 (19344-0250)
PHONE..................610 273-2842
Robert M Blechman, *President*
Ursita Blechman, *Vice Pres*
Joseph J Meehan, *Treasurer*
EMP: 3
SQ FT: 7,200
SALES: 250K Privately Held
WEB: www.bvssamplers.com
SIC: 3829 Measuring & controlling devices

(G-7740)
CAMBRIDGE SCALE WORKS INC (PA)
5011 Horseshoe Pike (19344-1344)
P.O. Box 670 (19344-0670)
PHONE..................610 273-7040

Larry Buckwalter, *President*
▲ EMP: 10
SALES (est): 2.1MM Privately Held
WEB: www.cambridgescale.com
SIC: 3596 5046 7699 Industrial scales; scales, except laboratory; scale repair service

(G-7741)
CEDAR CRAFT
1113 Park Rd (19344-9240)
PHONE..................610 273-9224
Benjamin K Kauffman, *Owner*
EMP: 3
SALES: 230K Privately Held
SIC: 0191 2499 General farms, primarily crop; decorative wood & woodwork

(G-7742)
CLEAN ENERGY HTG SYSTEMS LLC
625 Todd Rd (19344-1301)
PHONE..................888 519-2347
Larry J Nissley,
EMP: 10
SQ FT: 1,500
SALES: 1.2MM Privately Held
SIC: 3567 Radiant heating systems, industrial process

(G-7743)
CUSTOM WOODWORKING
3400 Horseshoe Pike (19344-8652)
PHONE..................610 273-2907
Levi S Stoltzfus, *Owner*
EMP: 22
SQ FT: 8,000
SALES (est): 2.4MM Privately Held
WEB: www.cabinetsbycw.com
SIC: 2434 Wood kitchen cabinets

(G-7744)
FISHER WOODCRAFT
1045 Compass Rd (19344-1229)
PHONE..................610 273-2076
Elam L Fisher, *Owner*
EMP: 4 EST: 1969
SQ FT: 8,800
SALES: 200K Privately Held
SIC: 3944 Games, toys & children's vehicles

(G-7745)
GOOD FOOD INC
4960 Horseshoe Pike (19344-1361)
P.O. Box 160 (19344-0160)
PHONE..................610 273-3776
Sally Martin, *President*
Larry E Martin, *Corp Secy*
Dean Johnson, *CFO*
Ron Glessner, *Director*
EMP: 160
SQ FT: 100,000
SALES (est): 17MM Privately Held
SIC: 2061 2079 Blackstrap molasses made from sugar cane; cane syrup made from sugar cane; cooking oils, except corn: vegetable refined

(G-7746)
GRIFFIN INDUSTRIES LLC
Also Called: Bakery Feeds
97 Westbrook Dr (19344-1374)
PHONE..................610 273-7014
Frank Wallace, *General Mgr*
EMP: 25
SALES (corp-wide): 3.3B Publicly Held
WEB: www.griffinind.com
SIC: 2077 Animal & marine fats & oils
HQ: Griffin Industries Llc
4221 Alexandria Pike
Cold Spring KY 41076
859 781-2010

(G-7747)
HESSIAN CO LTD (PA)
Also Called: Faddis Concrete Products
2206 Horseshoe Pike (19344-8657)
PHONE..................610 269-4685
Donald M Cooper, *President*
EMP: 50
SQ FT: 28,000
SALES: 23MM Privately Held
WEB: www.faddis.com
SIC: 3272 Lintels, concrete

(G-7748)
HILLSIDE CUSTOM MAC WEL & FAB
Also Called: AMS Filling Systems
2500 Chestnut Tree Rd (19344-9646)
PHONE.............................610 942-3093
Robert D Dixon, *President*
Steve Stringer, *Vice Pres*
Kevin Showalter, *Project Mgr*
Edward Grasmuck, *Opers Staff*
Dave Mitman, *Engineer*
EMP: 17
SQ FT: 9,620
SALES (est): 4MM **Privately Held**
SIC: 7692 3599 3444 Welding repair; machine & other job shop work; sheet metalwork

(G-7749)
HONEY BROOK CSTM CABINETS INC
5166 Horseshoe Pike (19344-1343)
P.O. Box 520 (19344-0520)
PHONE.............................610 273-2436
Ronald Smoker, *President*
Mona Lu, *Vice Pres*
Timothy Brennan, *Opers Mgr*
Timothy J Brennan, *Engineer*
Craig R Weaver, *Cust Mgr*
EMP: 35
SALES (est): 6.2MM **Privately Held**
WEB: www.honeybrookcabinets.com
SIC: 2434 Wood kitchen cabinets

(G-7750)
HONEY BROOK WOODCRAFTS
630 White School Rd (19344-9785)
PHONE.............................610 273-2928
Samuel Stoltzfus, *Owner*
EMP: 3 EST: 2010
SALES (est): 800K **Privately Held**
SIC: 2511 2515 Wood household furniture; mattresses & bedsprings; sleep furniture

(G-7751)
HPI PLASTICS INCORPORATED
373 Poplar Rd (19344-1348)
PHONE.............................610 273-7113
Robert Hartman, *President*
Concetta Hartman, *Admin Sec*
◆ EMP: 15
SQ FT: 60,000
SALES (est): 3.6MM **Privately Held**
SIC: 2679 Paper products, converted
PA: Inteplast Group Corporation
9 Peach Tree Hill Rd
Livingston NJ 07039

(G-7752)
LIMPET INC
1355 Walnut Rd (19344-1233)
PHONE.............................610 273-7155
Begum Jan, *President*
EMP: 10 EST: 1998
SALES (est): 950K **Privately Held**
SIC: 3625 Industrial controls: push button, selector switches, pilot

(G-7753)
M SIMON ZOOK CO (PA)
Also Called: Zook Molasses Co
4960 Horseshoe Pike (19344-1361)
P.O. Box 160 (19344-0160)
PHONE.............................610 273-3776
Sally L Martin, *President*
Larry E Martin, *COO*
Jim Yeingst, *Purch Mgr*
Kimberly Madara, *QC Mgr*
Dean Johnson, *CFO*
◆ EMP: 170
SQ FT: 100,000
SALES (est): 111.3MM **Privately Held**
SIC: 5149 2048 4013 4213 Molasses, industrial; prepared feeds; railroad terminals; trucking, except local

(G-7754)
MICHAEL BRYAN
Also Called: Brandywine Precision
749 Poplar Rd (19344-1346)
PHONE.............................610 273-2535
Michael Bryan, *Owner*
EMP: 4
SQ FT: 7,500

SALES (est): 900.5K **Privately Held**
SIC: 3599 Machine shop, jobbing & repair

(G-7755)
PEAR TREE MFG
1275 Beaver Dam Rd (19344-1278)
PHONE.............................610 273-9281
Steven R Yoder, *Owner*
EMP: 6
SQ FT: 4,253
SALES (est): 810.7K **Privately Held**
WEB: www.peartreeanalysis.com
SIC: 2452 Prefabricated wood buildings

(G-7756)
POWDER COATING CO (PA)
Also Called: Chester County Coating
5177 Horseshoe Pike (19344)
PHONE.............................610 273-9007
Aaron King, *Owner*
EMP: 4
SQ FT: 4,800
SALES (est): 3.5MM **Privately Held**
WEB: www.powdercoating.com
SIC: 3479 Coating of metals with plastic or resins

(G-7757)
PROVELL PHARMACEUTICALS LLC
1801 Horseshoe Pike Ste 1 (19344-8501)
PHONE.............................610 942-8970
Jim Small, *CEO*
Stephen Hodge, *COO*
Kurt Kalm, *CFO*
Thomas Eldered,
EMP: 4
SALES (est): 10MM **Privately Held**
SIC: 2834 Pharmaceutical preparations

(G-7758)
R-V INDUSTRIES INC (PA)
584 Poplar Rd (19344-1347)
PHONE.............................610 273-2457
Kirk A Putt, *President*
Tracey Webster, *General Mgr*
Kevin Putt, *Vice Pres*
David Dixon, *Plant Mgr*
Ken Brownlow, *Opers Mgr*
▲ EMP: 195 EST: 1974
SQ FT: 92,200
SALES (est): 44.5MM **Privately Held**
WEB: www.rvii.com
SIC: 3443 Fabricated plate work (boiler shop)

(G-7759)
ROSE NETWORK SOLUTIONS
109 Acorn Way (19344-9062)
PHONE.............................610 563-1958
Dan Weiner, *President*
EMP: 3
SALES (est): 174.9K **Privately Held**
SIC: 3674 Integrated circuits, semiconductor networks, etc.

(G-7760)
SAM KING
Also Called: Sk Wood Working
450 Beaver Dam Rd (19344-1275)
PHONE.............................610 273-7979
Sam King, *Principal*
EMP: 3
SALES (est): 275.9K **Privately Held**
SIC: 2517 Wood television & radio cabinets

(G-7761)
SANDERS SAWS & BLADES INC
2470 Conestoga Ave (19344-1052)
P.O. Box 310 (19344-0310)
PHONE.............................610 273-3733
Joe Cammerota, *President*
William Chapple, *Production*
Bill Chapple, *Product Mgr*
Jack Oswald, *Admin Sec*
▲ EMP: 20 EST: 1953
SQ FT: 15,000
SALES (est): 4MM **Privately Held**
WEB: www.sanderssaws.com
SIC: 3546 5085 3425 3423 Saws, portable & handheld: power driven; industrial supplies; saw blades & handsaws; hand & edge tools

(G-7762)
SCHNURE MANUFACTURING CO INC
102 Suplee Rd (19344-9713)
PHONE.............................610 273-3352
Robert E Schnure III, *President*
Robert Schnure III, *President*
Beverly Howe, *Vice Pres*
▲ EMP: 15 EST: 1963
SQ FT: 330,000
SALES (est): 3MM **Privately Held**
WEB: www.schnuremfg.com
SIC: 3715 7692 Trailer bodies; welding repair

(G-7763)
STOLTZFUS ENTERPRISES LTD
34 Lauver Cir (19344-9239)
PHONE.............................610 273-9266
Levi Stolzfus, *General Ptnr*
EMP: 9
SALES: 600K **Privately Held**
SIC: 3441 Fabricated structural metal

(G-7764)
STOLTZFUS MANUFACTURING INC
540 White School Rd (19344-9789)
PHONE.............................610 273-3603
Daniel Stoltzfus, *President*
J Daniel Stoltzfus, *President*
Barbara Stoltzfus, *Vice Pres*
EMP: 8
SQ FT: 6,000
SALES (est): 1.8MM **Privately Held**
SIC: 3523 Farm machinery & equipment

(G-7765)
SWAMPY HOLLOW MFG LLC
16 Westbrook Dr (19344-1354)
PHONE.............................610 273-0157
Levi Stoltfus,
Levi Stoltdfus,
EMP: 12
SQ FT: 8,400
SALES: 950K **Privately Held**
SIC: 3353 Tubes, welded, aluminum

(G-7766)
TEDDY WEARS
1469 Telegraph Rd (19344-9044)
PHONE.............................610 273-3234
Denise M Daniels, *Owner*
EMP: 3
SALES (est): 11.1K **Privately Held**
SIC: 3942 Dolls & stuffed toys

(G-7767)
TURF TEQ LLC
Also Called: Spec Fab
699 Todd Rd (19344-1301)
PHONE.............................484 798-6300
James R Day,
Randy Saylor,
▲ EMP: 45 EST: 2000
SQ FT: 30,000
SALES (est): 7.2MM **Privately Held**
SIC: 3589 Commercial cleaning equipment

Honey Grove
Juniata County

(G-7768)
R J JUNK
1165 Mccoysville Rd (17035)
PHONE.............................717 734-3838
Richard J Junk, *Owner*
EMP: 5
SALES (est): 402.6K **Privately Held**
SIC: 2421 Sawmills & planing mills, general

Hookstown
Beaver County

(G-7769)
J B COOPER AND COOPER CO INC
232 Silver Slipper Rd (15050)
PHONE.............................724 573-9860

Jeff Cooper, *President*
EMP: 13
SALES (est): 1.8MM **Privately Held**
SIC: 3441 Fabricated structural metal

Hooversville
Somerset County

(G-7770)
ANGELIE ORIGINAL
Also Called: Costumes Online
1285 Whistler Rd (15936-6905)
PHONE.............................814 798-3312
Angela Rodger, *Owner*
EMP: 3
SALES (est): 134.2K **Privately Held**
WEB: www.costumes-online.com
SIC: 2389 Costumes

(G-7771)
SHERPA MINING CONTRACTORS INC
337 Benny Rd (15936-8906)
PHONE.............................814 754-5560
Andrew Hewitson, *President*
EMP: 22
SALES (est): 4MM **Privately Held**
SIC: 1241 Coal mining services

Hop Bottom
Susquehanna County

(G-7772)
A-ONE MACHINE LLC
3109 State Route 2096 (18824-7690)
PHONE.............................570 289-4347
Roberta Vallone, *Mng Member*
EMP: 5
SQ FT: 3,600
SALES (est): 470.1K **Privately Held**
SIC: 3599 Machine shop, jobbing & repair

(G-7773)
COMPTON FLAGSTONE QUARRY
909 Glenwood Rd (18824-7813)
PHONE.............................570 942-6359
David Compton, *Principal*
EMP: 5
SALES (est): 338.7K **Privately Held**
SIC: 3281 Flagstones

(G-7774)
KENNETH E DECKER
Also Called: D Flagstone
3724 Forest St (18824-7806)
PHONE.............................570 677-3710
Kenneth Decker, *Principal*
EMP: 3 EST: 2010
SALES (est): 254.4K **Privately Held**
SIC: 3281 Flagstones

(G-7775)
RAPHAEL A INGAGLIO
Also Called: Ingaglio Welding and Ir Works
87 Greenwood St (18824-7835)
PHONE.............................570 289-5000
Raphael A Ingaglio, *Owner*
EMP: 3
SQ FT: 2,800
SALES: 200K **Privately Held**
SIC: 1799 7692 1791 Welding on site; welding repair; iron work, structural

---

Hopwood
Fayette County

(G-7776)
CURRY LUMBER CO (PA)
40 Buttermilk Ln (15445)
PHONE.............................724 438-1911
Charles Curry, *Partner*
Louis J Curry, *Partner*
EMP: 3 EST: 1918
SQ FT: 9,000
SALES (est): 30K **Privately Held**
WEB: www.currylumber.com
SIC: 2421 Lumber: rough, sawed or planed

(G-7777)
WASHITA VALLEY ENTERPRISES INC
1152 National Pike (15445-2250)
PHONE...................................724 437-1593
Shelton Chun, *Branch Mgr*
EMP: 14
SALES (corp-wide): 47.2MM **Privately Held**
SIC: 1389 Gas field services
PA: Washita Valley Enterprises, Inc.
1705 Se 59th St
Oklahoma City OK 73129
405 670-5338

Horsham
Montgomery County

(G-7778)
ACRYLICS UNLIMITED
4 School Rd (19044-1849)
PHONE...................................215 443-2365
Alan Jay Patrowich, *Owner*
Alan Patrowich, *Owner*
EMP: 6
SALES (est): 360K **Privately Held**
SIC: 3083 Laminated plastics plate & sheet

(G-7779)
ADDAREN HOLDINGS LLC
Also Called: Wellvue365
418 Caredean Dr Ste 6 (19044-1310)
PHONE...................................267 387-6029
Harvey Grossman, *Principal*
Fred Shapiro, *Principal*
EMP: 6 EST: 2016
SALES (est): 248.9K **Privately Held**
SIC: 3993 Electric signs

(G-7780)
AEGIS INDUSTRIAL SOFTWARE CORP (PA)
Also Called: Aegis Software
5 Walnut Grove Dr Ste 320 (19044-4000)
PHONE...................................215 773-3571
Jason Spera, *CEO*
John Walls, *COO*
Brian Backenstose, *Vice Pres*
Paul Price, *Vice Pres*
Joe Fine, *Engineer*
EMP: 33
SQ FT: 19,000
SALES (est): 11.4MM **Privately Held**
SIC: 7372 Application computer software

(G-7781)
ALL STEEL SUPPLY INC
412 Caredean Dr (19044-1315)
PHONE...................................215 672-0883
Ed McGowan, *Principal*
EMP: 23
SALES (est): 7MM **Privately Held**
SIC: 3315 Steel wire & related products

(G-7782)
AMERICAN ADDITIVE MFG LLC
201 Witmer Rd (19044-2212)
PHONE...................................215 559-1200
James Visnic, *Mng Member*
Leslie Visnic,
EMP: 10
SQ FT: 5,000
SALES (est): 125.8K **Privately Held**
SIC: 3544 2759 Special dies, tools, jigs & fixtures; commercial printing

(G-7783)
AMERICAN PRINTING GROUP INC
935 Horsham Rd Ste P (19044-1230)
PHONE...................................215 442-0500
Ruth Gehring, *President*
EMP: 6
SQ FT: 1,000
SALES (est): 744.4K **Privately Held**
SIC: 5112 2752 Business forms; commercial printing, lithographic

(G-7784)
AMETEK INC
Pmt Products
205 Keith Valley Rd (19044-1408)
PHONE...................................215 355-6900
James Mellon, *Branch Mgr*
EMP: 80
SQ FT: 53,660
SALES (corp-wide): 4.8B **Publicly Held**
SIC: 3621 3823 3829 Motors & generators; industrial instrmnts msrmnt display/control process variable; measuring & controlling devices
PA: Ametek, Inc.
1100 Cassatt Rd
Berwyn PA 19312
610 647-2121

(G-7785)
AMETEK INC
US Gauge Hunter Springs
205 Keith Valley Rd (19044-1408)
PHONE...................................215 355-6900
James Mellon, *Branch Mgr*
EMP: 3
SALES (corp-wide): 4.8B **Publicly Held**
SIC: 3499 3493 Reels, cable: metal; steel springs, except wire
PA: Ametek, Inc.
1100 Cassatt Rd
Berwyn PA 19312
610 647-2121

(G-7786)
ANTARES INSTRUMENTS INC
418 Caredean Dr Ste 4 (19044-1310)
PHONE...................................215 441-5250
David Donaldson, *President*
Sandy Donaldson, *Vice Pres*
EMP: 11
SQ FT: 7,000
SALES (est): 1.8MM **Privately Held**
WEB: www.antaresinc.net
SIC: 3423 5087 Engravers' tools, hand; engraving equipment & supplies

(G-7787)
APEXCO-PPSI LLC
430 Caredean Dr (19044-1315)
PHONE...................................937 935-0164
Lieven Gruwez, *General Mgr*
Bart Feys, *Mng Member*
Tim Butler,
▲ EMP: 9
SQ FT: 12,500
SALES (est): 2MM **Privately Held**
SIC: 3089 3083 2821 Plates, plastic; thermoplastic laminates: rods, tubes, plates & sheet; plastics materials & resins

(G-7788)
ARNOLD FOODS COMPANY INC
Also Called: George Weston Bakeries
255 Business Center Dr # 200 (19044-3424)
P.O. Box 535, Totowa NJ (07511-0535)
PHONE...................................215 672-8010
Gary Prince, *President*
Bill Petersen, *CFO*
Amanda Colburn, *Accountant*
Joe Fitzpatrick, *Sales Staff*
Matt McGuire, *Sales Staff*
◆ EMP: 12000
SALES (est): 228.8MM **Privately Held**
SIC: 2051 5149 Bread, cake & related products; bread, all types (white, wheat, rye, etc): fresh or frozen; rolls, bread type: fresh or frozen; groceries & related products
HQ: Bimbo Bakeries Usa, Inc
255 Business Center Dr # 200
Horsham PA 19044
215 347-5500

(G-7789)
ARRIS GLOBAL SERVICES INC
101 Tournament Dr (19044-3603)
PHONE...................................215 323-1000
EMP: 3
SALES (est): 187.9K **Privately Held**
SIC: 3661 Telephone & telegraph apparatus

(G-7790)
ARRIS TECHNOLOGY INC
101 Tournament Dr (19044-3603)
PHONE...................................215 323-2590
EMP: 18
SALES (corp-wide): 6.6B **Privately Held**
SIC: 3663 Transmitting apparatus, radio or television; cable television equipment; antennas, transmitting & communications
HQ: Arris Technology, Inc.
3871 Lakefield Dr
Suwanee GA 30024
678 473-2907

(G-7791)
ASTEA INTERNATIONAL INC (PA)
240 Gibraltar Rd Ste 300 (19044-2398)
PHONE...................................215 682-2500
Zack Bergreen, *Ch of Bd*
Fredric Etskovitz, *CFO*
George Wrapp, *CFO*
Leonid Blaivas, *Manager*
EMP: 69
SQ FT: 24,000
SALES: 27.4MM **Publicly Held**
WEB: www.astea.com
SIC: 7372 Prepackaged software

(G-7792)
AUGMENTIR INC
425 Caredean Dr (19044-1318)
PHONE...................................949 432-6450
Russell Fadel, *CEO*
EMP: 7
SQ FT: 100
SALES (est): 152.8K **Privately Held**
SIC: 7372 Prepackaged software

(G-7793)
AVO PHOTONICS INC
120 Welsh Rd (19044-3488)
PHONE...................................215 441-0107
Joseph Dallas, *President*
Jeffrey Perkins, *Vice Pres*
Jonathan Goettler, *Engineer*
Kimberly Wheeler, *Treasurer*
Ryan Ehid, *Manager*
EMP: 14
SQ FT: 10,000
SALES (est): 5.2MM
SALES (corp-wide): 1.5B **Privately Held**
WEB: www.avophotonics.com
SIC: 3827 Optical instruments & apparatus
PA: Halma Public Limited Company
Misbourne Court
Amersham BUCKS HP7 0
149 472-1111

(G-7794)
BALL AROSOL SPECIALTY CONT INC
431 Privet Rd (19044-1220)
PHONE...................................215 442-5462
Bhavesh Shah, *Engineer*
Gregg Pearson, *Branch Mgr*
Aftan Chowansky, *Director*
Cindy Armstrong, *Planning*
EMP: 129
SALES (corp-wide): 11.6B **Publicly Held**
SIC: 3411 Metal cans
HQ: Ball Aerosol And Specialty Container Inc.
9308 W 108th Cir
Westminster CO 80021

(G-7795)
BBU INC (HQ)
255 Business Center Dr # 200 (19044-3424)
P.O. Box 976 (19044-0976)
PHONE...................................215 347-5500
Fred Penny, *President*
Matt Brynes, *Area Mgr*
Stephen J Mollick, *Vice Pres*
Shelly W Seligman, *Vice Pres*
Chris Wiseman, *Plant Mgr*
◆ EMP: 250
SALES (est): 8.3B **Privately Held**
SIC: 2051 Bread, cake & related products

(G-7796)
BIMBO BAKERIES USA INC (DH)
255 Business Center Dr # 200 (19044-3424)
PHONE...................................215 347-5500
Alfred Penny, *President*
Brian Muir, *District Mgr*
Rick Lee, *Vice Pres*
Juan Muldoon, *Vice Pres*
Didier Moleres, *VP Opers*
▲ EMP: 450
SALES (est): 8.3B **Privately Held**
WEB: www.bimbobakeriesusa.com
SIC: 2051 Bakery: wholesale or wholesale/retail combined

(G-7797)
BIMBO HUNGRIA COMPANY (DH)
255 Business Center Dr (19044-3424)
P.O. Box 901029, Fort Worth TX (76101-2029)
PHONE...................................866 506-6807
John Lorenzen, *President*
Shelly Seligman, *Vice Pres*
EMP: 14
SALES (est): 9.8MM **Privately Held**
SIC: 2051 Bakery: wholesale or wholesale/retail combined
HQ: Bimbo Bakeries Usa, Inc
255 Business Center Dr # 200
Horsham PA 19044
215 347-5500

(G-7798)
BIO/DATA CORPORATION
155 Gibraltar Rd (19044-2353)
PHONE...................................215 441-4000
Eugene J Messa, *President*
Mark W Messa, *Vice Pres*
William M Trolio, *Vice Pres*
Barry J Bell, *Treasurer*
Joe Lipski, *Manager*
EMP: 23
SALES (est): 5.9MM **Privately Held**
WEB: www.biodatacorp.com
SIC: 2835 3826 In vitro & in vivo diagnostic substances; analytical instruments

(G-7799)
BIOCOAT INCORPORATED
123 Rock Rd (19044)
PHONE...................................215 734-0888
Jim Moran, *President*
Joseph Sandora, *Vice Pres*
Brett Moyer, *Opers Staff*
Susan Cripps, *Purch Mgr*
Steven Bell, *CFO*
◆ EMP: 40
SQ FT: 20,000
SALES (est): 10.9MM
SALES (corp-wide): 8.6MM **Privately Held**
WEB: www.biocoat.com
SIC: 2851 2821 3829 Paints & allied products; plastics materials & resins; measuring & controlling devices
HQ: Biocoat Holdings, Llc
2929 Walnut St Ste 1240
Philadelphia PA 19104
215 662-1315

(G-7800)
BRYN AND DANES LLC
400 Privet Rd (19044-1221)
PHONE...................................844 328-2823
Bryn Davis, *Principal*
Stephanie Johnson, *Manager*
EMP: 5
SALES (est): 519.2K **Privately Held**
SIC: 2741 Miscellaneous publishing

(G-7801)
CD TECHNOLOGIES INC
Also Called: C & D Powercom
200 Precision Rd 150 (19044-1227)
PHONE...................................215 619-2700
Kim Dang, *Manager*
EMP: 50
SQ FT: 48,000
SALES (corp-wide): 680.2MM **Privately Held**
WEB: www.cdtechno.com
SIC: 3691 3692 Storage batteries; primary batteries, dry & wet

PA: C&D Technologies, Inc.
1400 Union Meeting Rd # 110
Blue Bell PA 19422
215 619-2700

(G-7802)
CENTOCOR INC
800 Ridgeview Dr (19044-3607)
PHONE.........................215 325-2297
Hubert Schoemaker, *Ch of Bd*
Elizabeth Anderson, *Vice Pres*
Robert Class, *Research*
David Lyon, *Sales Staff*
Karen Lade, *Mktg Dir*
EMP: 3
SALES (est): 234.7K **Privately Held**
SIC: 2834 Pharmaceutical preparations

(G-7803)
CENTRAL ADMXTURE PHRM SVCS INC
Also Called: C A P S
253 Gibraltar Rd (19044-2305)
PHONE.........................215 706-4001
Sheldon Malitsky, *President*
Kishor Patel, *Pharmacist*
Peter McGarvey, *Manager*
Arnold Rivero, *Manager*
Karen Rosati, *Pharmacy Dir*
EMP: 30 **Privately Held**
WEB: www.capspharmacy.com
SIC: 2834 5122 Pharmaceutical preparations; pharmaceuticals
HQ: Central Admixture Pharmacy Services, Inc.
2525 Mcgaw Ave
Irvine CA 92614

(G-7804)
CITY SIGN SERVICE INC
424 Caredean Dr Ste A (19044-1389)
PHONE.........................800 523-4452
Jeff Carson, *President*
Liz Radlbeck, *Project Mgr*
Connie Carson, *Executive*
John Carson, *Executive*
Patricia Carson, *Shareholder*
EMP: 26 **EST:** 1930
SQ FT: 25,000
SALES (est): 5.1MM **Privately Held**
WEB: www.citysignservice.com
SIC: 7629 3993 3231 Electrical repair shops; neon signs; electric signs; signs, not made in custom sign painting shops; products of purchased glass

(G-7805)
CPM WOLVERINE PROCTOR LLC (DH)
Also Called: California Pallet Mello
251 Gibraltar Rd (19044-2305)
PHONE.........................215 443-5200
Tedd Waitman, *President*
Paul Smith, *Vice Pres*
Doug Ostrich, *CFO*
▲ **EMP:** 83
SQ FT: 180,000
SALES (est): 79.3MM
SALES (corp-wide): 177.7MM **Privately Held**
WEB: www.cpmwolverineproctor.com
SIC: 3542 Mechanical (pneumatic or hydraulic) metal forming machines
HQ: Cpm Acquisition Corp.
2975 Airline Cir
Waterloo IA 50703
319 232-8444

(G-7806)
CRC INDUSTRIES INC (DH)
800 Enterprise Rd Ste 101 (19044-3508)
PHONE.........................215 674-4300
Perry Cozzone, *CEO*
Scott Gray, *President*
Brian Murtaugh, *CFO*
◆ **EMP:** 140
SQ FT: 120,000
SALES (est): 103.8MM
SALES (corp-wide): 2.9B **Privately Held**
WEB: www.crcindustries.com
SIC: 2992 3471 2899 2842 Lubricating oils & greases; plating & polishing; chemical preparations; specialty cleaning, polishes & sanitation goods

HQ: Berwind Industries, Inc
3000 Ctr Sq W 1500 Mkt St
Philadelphia PA 19102
215 563-2800

(G-7807)
CYBERTECH INC
935 Horsham Rd Ste I (19044-1270)
PHONE.........................215 957-6220
Ronald Schmidt, *President*
Lloyd Barnett, *Corp Secy*
EMP: 15
SQ FT: 8,000
SALES (est): 3.4MM **Privately Held**
WEB: www.cbrtech.com
SIC: 3577 Printers, computer

(G-7808)
DAVINCI GRAPHICS INC
Also Called: Stephan Enterprises
433 Horsham Rd (19044-2066)
PHONE.........................215 441-8180
Thomas Mc Callister, *President*
Bill Stephan, *Partner*
EMP: 8
SQ FT: 4,000
SALES: 700K **Privately Held**
WEB: www.davincigraphicsinc.com
SIC: 2752 Commercial printing, offset

(G-7809)
DELTA INFORMATION SYSTEMS INC
Also Called: Gdp Space Systems
300 Welsh Rd Bldg 3-120 (19044-2294)
PHONE.........................215 657-5270
Paul Randall, *Engineer*
Gary Thom, *Branch Mgr*
EMP: 50
SALES (corp-wide): 20.9MM **Privately Held**
WEB: www.gdpspace.com
SIC: 8732 3829 3823 3699 Research services, except laboratory; measuring & controlling devices; industrial instrmnts msrmnt display/control process variable; electrical equipment & supplies; radio & TV communications equipment
PA: Delta Information Systems, Inc.
747 Dresher Rd Ste 100
Horsham PA 19044
215 657-5270

(G-7810)
DRESSER-RAND COMPANY
203 Precision Rd (19044-1279)
PHONE.........................215 441-0400
Patrice Bardon, *Vice Pres*
EMP: 27
SALES (corp-wide): 95B **Privately Held**
WEB: www.dresser-rand.com
SIC: 3563 Air & gas compressors
HQ: Dresser-Rand Company
500 Paul Clark Dr
Olean NY 14760
716 375-3000

(G-7811)
DYNAMIC GRAPHIC FINISHING INC (DH)
945 Horsham Rd (19044-1273)
PHONE.........................215 441-8880
Dave Liess, *President*
Robert J Sorrentino, *Vice Pres*
John O'Donnell, *Opers Mgr*
James H Shacklett III, *Treasurer*
Jack Odonnell, *Admin Sec*
EMP: 47
SQ FT: 36,000
SALES (est): 73.9MM
SALES (corp-wide): 82.3MM **Privately Held**
WEB: www.dynamicgraphic.com
SIC: 2759 Embossing on paper

(G-7812)
E F E LABORATORIES INC
420 Babylon Rd Ste A (19044-1225)
PHONE.........................215 672-2400
Kip Anthony, *President*
John Hayden, *Principal*
John Thomas, *Principal*
Greg Duffy, *VP Mfg*
Grace A Evans, *Treasurer*
EMP: 36
SQ FT: 16,000

SALES (est): 11.4MM **Privately Held**
WEB: www.efelabs.com
SIC: 3825 3823 3699 3643 Electron tube test equipment; industrial instrmnts msrmnt display/control process variable; electrical equipment & supplies; current-carrying wiring devices; switchgear & switchboard apparatus; metal stampings

(G-7813)
EARTHGRAINS DISTRIBUTION LLC (DH)
255 Business Center Dr (19044-3424)
PHONE.........................215 672-8010
Gary J Price,
EMP: 19
SALES (est): 2.4MM **Privately Held**
SIC: 2051 Bakery: wholesale or wholesale/retail combined
HQ: Bimbo Bakeries Usa, Inc
255 Business Center Dr # 200
Horsham PA 19044
215 347-5500

(G-7814)
EDON CORPORATION
Also Called: Edon Fiberglass
1160 Easton Rd (19044-1491)
PHONE.........................215 672-8050
Matthew Axel, *CEO*
Edwin Axel, *Vice Pres*
Adam Axel, *Treasurer*
James Garvey, *Manager*
Laurel Thompson, *Manager*
EMP: 45
SQ FT: 58,000
SALES (est): 11.9MM **Privately Held**
WEB: www.edon.com
SIC: 3089 Plastic hardware & building products

(G-7815)
ENDO PHARMACEUTICAL INC
420 Babylon Rd (19044-1225)
PHONE.........................484 216-2759
Paul V Campanelli, *President*
EMP: 5
SALES (est): 452.7K **Privately Held**
SIC: 2834 Pharmaceutical preparations

(G-7816)
ENERSYS ADVANCED SYSTEMS INC (DH)
104 Rock Rd (19044-2311)
PHONE.........................215 674-3800
Richard W Zuidema, *Ch of Bd*
Michael J Schmidtlein, *Vice Pres*
Thomas L Oneill, *Treasurer*
Joseph G Lewis, *Admin Sec*
▲ **EMP:** 55
SALES (est): 20.2MM
SALES (corp-wide): 2.5B **Publicly Held**
SIC: 3692 3728 Primary batteries, dry & wet; aircraft parts & equipment
HQ: Enersys Capital Inc.
2366 Bernville Rd
Reading PA 19605
610 208-1991

(G-7817)
EVONIK OIL ADDITIVES USA INC (DH)
723 Electronic Dr (19044-4050)
PHONE.........................215 706-5800
Douglas Placek, *President*
Stan McIntosh, *Research*
Robert Berry, *Regl Sales Mgr*
David Gray, *Cust Mgr*
Rebecca Marshall, *Sales Staff*
◆ **EMP:** 65
SALES (est): 23.7MM
SALES (corp-wide): 2.4B **Privately Held**
WEB: www.rohmax.com
SIC: 2869 Industrial organic chemicals
HQ: Evonik Oil Additives Gmbh
Kirschenallee
Darmstadt 64293
615 118-09

(G-7818)
FINISAR CORPORATION
767 Electronic Dr (19044-2228)
PHONE.........................267 803-3800
Mark Colyar, *Vice Pres*
Philip Rocco, *Engineer*

William Lynch, *Manager*
EMP: 160
SALES (corp-wide): 1.3B **Publicly Held**
SIC: 3661 Fiber optics communications equipment
PA: Finisar Corporation
1389 Moffett Park Dr
Sunnyvale CA 94089
408 548-1000

(G-7819)
FREEDOM MANAGEMENT SVCS LLC
Also Called: Prosthtic Orthtic Sltions Intl
440 Horsham Rd Ste 2 (19044-2141)
PHONE.........................215 328-9111
Ben Harder, *Director*
EMP: 5
SALES (est): 516.9K **Privately Held**
WEB: www.prostheticsolutions.com
SIC: 3842 Prosthetic appliances
HQ: Physiotherapy-Bmi Inc
680 American Ave Ste 200
King Of Prussia PA 19406

(G-7820)
GALAXY WIRE AND CABLE INC
903 Sheehy Dr Ste E (19044-1231)
PHONE.........................215 957-8714
Kathleen M Stussy, *President*
EMP: 15
SQ FT: 9,500
SALES (est): 8.3MM **Privately Held**
SIC: 5063 3679 Wire & cable; harness assemblies for electronic use: wire or cable

(G-7821)
GEO SPECIALTY CHEMICALS INC
903 Sheehy Dr Ste E (19044-1231)
PHONE.........................215 773-9280
George Ahrens, *President*
Joseph Hiznay, *Sales Staff*
EMP: 24 **Privately Held**
WEB: www.geosc.com
SIC: 2819 Aluminum sulfate
PA: Geo Specialty Chemicals, Inc.
401 S Earl Ave Ste 3
Lafayette IN 47904

(G-7822)
HAUSSER SCIENTIFIC COMPANY
935 Horsham Rd Ste C (19044-1286)
PHONE.........................215 675-7769
Ernest Behr, *President*
EMP: 7 **EST:** 1986
SQ FT: 4,000
SALES: 2MM **Privately Held**
SIC: 3231 Laboratory glassware

(G-7823)
INFRAMARK LLC (PA)
220 Gibraltar Rd Ste 200 (19044-2340)
PHONE.........................215 646-9201
Stephane Bouvier, *President*
Terry Pearce, *Vice Pres*
David L Chester, *CFO*
Kenneth J Kelly, *Treasurer*
Adele A Stevens, *Admin Sec*
▲ **EMP:** 45 **EST:** 1991
SQ FT: 15,100
SALES (est): 72.1MM **Privately Held**
SIC: 8748 3589 Business consulting; water treatment equipment, industrial

(G-7824)
INTERNATIONAL MILL SERVICE
Also Called: IMS
1155 Bus Ctr Dr Ste 200 (19044)
PHONE.........................215 956-5500
Raymond S Kalouche, *President*
Daniel E Rosati, *Treasurer*
EMP: 1100
SALES (est): 111.3MM **Privately Held**
WEB: www.enso.net
SIC: 3295 3341 1422 8742 Slag, crushed or ground; secondary nonferrous metals; cement rock, crushed & broken-quarrying; public utilities consultant
HQ: Mill Services Corp.
12 Monongahela Ave
Glassport PA 15045
412 678-6141

(G-7825)
INTRA CORPORATION
433 Caredean Dr Ste D (19044-1321)
PHONE..................................215 672-7003
Dan Morrison, *Manager*
EMP: 5
SALES (corp-wide): 24.7MM **Privately Held**
SIC: 3545 Gauges (machine tool accessories)
PA: Intra Corporation
885 Manufacturers Dr
Westland MI 48186
734 326-7030

(G-7826)
J L COMMUNICATIONS INC
Also Called: Handicapped Product Post Cards
415 Horsham Rd (19044-2068)
P.O. Box 220 (19044-0220)
PHONE..................................215 675-9133
Jeffrey Leonard, *President*
Victoria Leonard, *Vice Pres*
EMP: 9
SQ FT: 1,000
SALES (est): 535.1K **Privately Held**
WEB: www.disabilitypostcards.com
SIC: 2741 Miscellaneous publishing

(G-7827)
JANSSEN BIOTECH INC (HQ)
800 Ridgeview Dr (19044-3607)
PHONE..................................610 651-6000
Robert B Bazemore, *President*
Bruce Peacock, *Vice Pres*
Jay Fischbein, *Treasurer*
James Michalak, *Manager*
▲ EMP: 500
SQ FT: 202,000
SALES (est): 778MM
SALES (corp-wide): 81.5B **Publicly Held**
WEB: www.remicade-crohns.com
SIC: 2834 2835 Pharmaceutical preparations; drugs affecting parasitic & infective diseases; drugs acting on the cardiovascular system, except diagnostic; in vitro diagnostics
PA: Johnson & Johnson
1 Johnson And Johnson Plz
New Brunswick NJ 08933
732 524-0400

(G-7828)
JOHNSON CONTROLS INC
550 Blair Mill Rd Ste 110 (19044-2372)
PHONE..................................610 276-3700
Vince Rydzewski, *Branch Mgr*
EMP: 60 **Privately Held**
SIC: 3822 3823 Air conditioning & refrigeration controls; thermostats & other environmental sensors; electric heat controls; industrial instrmnts msrmnt display/control process variable
HQ: Johnson Controls, Inc.
5757 N Green Bay Ave
Milwaukee WI 53209
414 524-1200

(G-7829)
JONERIC PRODUCTS INC (PA)
Also Called: Jordan David
400 Babylon Rd Ste D (19044-1282)
PHONE..................................215 441-9669
Michael Bell, *CEO*
Jonathan Bell, *President*
▲ EMP: 13 EST: 1974
SQ FT: 20,000
SALES (est): 2.4MM **Privately Held**
WEB: www.jordandavid.com
SIC: 3021 Rubber & plastics footwear

(G-7830)
KEEBLER COMPANY
100 Witmer Rd Ste 300 (19044-2646)
PHONE..................................215 752-4010
Joseph Santoro, *Branch Mgr*
EMP: 40
SALES (corp-wide): 13.5B **Publicly Held**
WEB: www.keebler.com
SIC: 2052 Cookies
HQ: Keebler Company
1 Kellogg Sq
Battle Creek MI 49017
269 961-2000

(G-7831)
LIQUENT INC (DH)
101 Gibraltar Rd Ste 200 (19044-2362)
PHONE..................................215 957-6401
Rick Riegel, *CEO*
Kate Courter, *Vice Pres*
Jeff Huntsman, *Vice Pres*
Marybeth Thompson, *Vice Pres*
Karl Jaegr, *CFO*
EMP: 161
SQ FT: 30,300
SALES (est): 20.9MM
SALES (corp-wide): 2.4B **Privately Held**
WEB: www.liquent.com
SIC: 7372 7373 Business oriented computer software; systems software development services; systems integration services
HQ: Parexel International Corporation
195 West St
Waltham MA 02451
781 487-9900

(G-7832)
LRP PUBLICATIONS INC
Also Called: Human Resource Executive
747 Dresher Rd Ste 500 (19044-2231)
P.O. Box 980 (19044-0980)
PHONE..................................215 784-0941
Bill Corsini, *Manager*
EMP: 10
SALES (corp-wide): 111.8MM **Privately Held**
WEB: www.juryverdictresearch.com
SIC: 2721 8111 Magazines: publishing only, not printed on site; legal services
PA: Lrp Publications, Inc.
360 Hiatt Dr
Palm Beach Gardens FL 33418
215 784-0860

(G-7833)
MORNINGSTAR CREDIT RATINGS LLC
220 Gibraltar Rd Ste 300 (19044-2328)
PHONE..................................800 299-1665
Vickie Tillman, *President*
Caitlin Veno, *Editor*
David Sondesky, *Senior VP*
Chandan Banerjee, *Vice Pres*
Calvin Wong, *Ch Credit Ofcr*
EMP: 40
SALES (est): 3.1MM
SALES (corp-wide): 1B **Publicly Held**
SIC: 2721 7375 6722 Statistical reports (periodicals); publishing only; information retrieval services; management investment, open-end; money market mutual funds
PA: Morningstar, Inc.
22 W Washington St # 600
Chicago IL 60602
312 696-6000

(G-7834)
MOTOROLA MOBILITY LLC
101 Tournament Dr (19044-3603)
P.O. Box 568 (19044-0568)
PHONE..................................215 674-4800
Ralph Pini, *Vice Pres*
Rajib Acharya, *Project Mgr*
Sanjay Dhar, *Engineer*
George Standish, *Engineer*
Kyle Stump, *Engineer*
EMP: 58
SQ FT: 110,000
SALES (corp-wide): 43B **Privately Held**
WEB: www.motorola.com
SIC: 3663 Radio & TV communications equipment
HQ: Motorola Mobility Llc
222 Merchandise Mart Plz # 1800
Chicago IL 60654

(G-7835)
NEWAGE TESTING INSTRUMENTS (HQ)
Also Called: Ametek Company
205 Keith Valley Rd (19044-1408)
PHONE..................................215 355-6900
Harald P Caroe, *President*
Eleanor Lukens, *Vice Pres*
Wayne A Wirtz, *Vice Pres*
Greg Bell, *Natl Sales Mgr*
Richard Miller, *Sales Staff*
▲ EMP: 20

SQ FT: 11,000
SALES (est): 1.9MM
SALES (corp-wide): 4.8B **Publicly Held**
WEB: www.hardnesstester.com
SIC: 3829 Hardness testing equipment
PA: Ametek, Inc.
1100 Cassatt Rd
Berwyn PA 19312
610 647-2121

(G-7836)
NICOMATIC LP
Also Called: Nicomatic North America
450 Progress Dr (19044-1300)
PHONE..................................215 444-9580
Armando Zanchetta, *President*
Caroline Lemieux, *Accountant*
◆ EMP: 44
SALES: 9MM
SALES (corp-wide): 31.4MM **Privately Held**
SIC: 3679 Electronic circuits
PA: Nicomatic
Zone Industrielle
Bons En Chablais 74890
450 361-385

(G-7837)
OPPENHEIMER PRECISION PDTS INC
163-175 Gibraltar Rd (19044)
PHONE..................................215 674-9100
Thomas Kirk, *President*
William Mc Manimen, *Senior VP*
Paul Oppenheimer, *Vice Pres*
Michael R Gleeson, *Treasurer*
Cynthia Bareis, *Human Res Dir*
EMP: 75
SQ FT: 45,000
SALES (est): 14.2MM
SALES (corp-wide): 924.5MM **Privately Held**
WEB: www.oppiprecision.com
SIC: 3812 3545 3537 Search & navigation equipment; precision measuring tools; aircraft engine cradles
HQ: Indel, Inc.
10 Indel Ave
Rancocas NJ 08073
609 267-9000

(G-7838)
OPTIUM CORPORATION (HQ)
200 Precision Rd (19044-1227)
PHONE..................................215 675-3105
Mark Colyar, *Senior VP*
Christopher Brown, *Vice Pres*
David C Renner, *CFO*
Anthony Musto, *VP Sales*
▲ EMP: 55
SALES (est): 15.8MM
SALES (corp-wide): 1.3B **Publicly Held**
WEB: www.optiumcorp.com
SIC: 3695 3357 Optical disks & tape, blank; nonferrous wiredrawing & insulating
PA: Finisar Corporation
1389 Moffett Park Dr
Sunnyvale CA 94089
408 548-1000

(G-7839)
PATRIOT PHARMACEUTICALS LLC
200 Tournament Dr (19044-3606)
PHONE..................................215 325-7676
Louis Esgro, *Mng Member*
EMP: 7
SALES (est): 1.2MM
SALES (corp-wide): 81.5B **Publicly Held**
WEB: www.patriotpharmaceuticals.com
SIC: 2834 Pharmaceutical preparations
HQ: Janssen Pharmaceuticals Inc
1125 Trnton Harbourton Rd
Titusville NJ 08560
609 730-2000

(G-7840)
PATRIOT SENSORS & CONTRLS CORP
Also Called: Ametek Drexelbrook
215 Keith Valley Rd (19044-1408)
PHONE..................................336 449-3400
Diane Malachowski, *Principal*
EMP: 112

SALES (corp-wide): 4.8B **Publicly Held**
SIC: 3621 Motors & generators
HQ: Patriot Sensors & Controls Corporation
1080 N Crooks Rd
Clawson MI 48017

(G-7841)
PHARMCEUTICAL MFG RES SVCS INC
Also Called: Pmrs
202 Precision Rd (19044-1227)
PHONE..................................267 960-3300
Edwin Thompson, *President*
Matthew E Anderson, *Director*
Dennis A Dibiagio, *Director*
Joshua R Fantini, *Director*
Thomas Sweeney, *Associate*
▲ EMP: 40
SQ FT: 68,000
SALES (est): 12.2MM **Privately Held**
WEB: www.pmrsinc.com
SIC: 2834 Pharmaceutical preparations

(G-7842)
PRISM ENGINEERING LLC (HQ)
655 Business Center Dr # 100 (19044-3445)
PHONE..................................215 784-0800
John Ewell, *President*
Daniel Wilkes, *Regional Mgr*
Heather Dawe, *Engineer*
John E Tarka, *Treasurer*
Milt Baer, *Accounts Mgr*
◆ EMP: 36
SALES (est): 7.9MM
SALES (corp-wide): 34.3MM **Privately Held**
SIC: 5045 7372 7373 7371 Computer software; prepackaged software; value-added resellers, computer systems; computer software development & applications
PA: Fisher Unitech, Llc
404 E 10 Mile Rd 150
Pleasant Ridge MI 48069
248 577-5100

(G-7843)
RAM PRECISION INC
405 Caredean Dr Ste A (19044-1385)
PHONE..................................215 674-0663
Rudi Bauknecht, *President*
EMP: 7
SQ FT: 12,000
SALES: 2MM **Privately Held**
WEB: www.ramprecision.net
SIC: 3089 3544 Handles, brush or tool: plastic; forms (molds), for foundry & plastics working machinery; paper cutting dies

(G-7844)
REED TECH & INFO SVCS INC (DH)
7 Walnut Grove Dr (19044-2201)
PHONE..................................215 441-6400
Thomas S Barry, *President*
Ethan Eisner, *President*
Sam Hardman, *President*
Mahmud Mamun, *Project Mgr*
Richard Bieber, *Prdtn Mgr*
EMP: 325
SQ FT: 120,000
SALES (est): 144.3MM
SALES (corp-wide): 9.7B **Privately Held**
WEB: www.reedtech.com
SIC: 2791 Typesetting, computer controlled
HQ: Relx Inc.
230 Park Ave Ste 700
New York NY 10169
212 309-8100

(G-7845)
RELIEFBAND TECHNOLOGIES LLC
220 Gibraltar Rd Fl 2 (19044-2300)
PHONE..................................877 735-2263
Nick Spring, *CEO*
EMP: 11
SQ FT: 3,800
SALES: 2.1MM **Privately Held**
SIC: 3829 Kinematic test & measuring equipment

(G-7846)
REMOTE REMOTES
420 Dresher Rd Ste 400 (19044-2010)
PHONE...................................215 420-7934
Jon Ritger, *CEO*
EMP: 7
SALES (est): 608.1K **Privately Held**
SIC: 3694 Ignition apparatus, internal combustion engines

(G-7847)
RUCKUS WIRELESS INC
Also Called: Arris
101 Tournament Dr (19044-3603)
PHONE...................................215 323-1000
Gene Ambrosio, *Vice Pres*
EMP: 24
SALES (corp-wide): 6.6B **Privately Held**
SIC: 3661 3663 Telephone & telegraph apparatus; satellites, communications
HQ: Ruckus Wireless, Inc.
350 W Java Dr
Sunnyvale CA 94089
650 265-4200

(G-7848)
SCHEERER BEARING CORPORATION
436 Caredean Dr (19044-1315)
PHONE...................................215 443-5252
George Rymar, *CEO*
EMP: 22
SALES (corp-wide): 12.6MM **Privately Held**
SIC: 3562 3568 7699 Ball bearings & parts; power transmission equipment; industrial machinery & equipment repair
PA: Scheerer Bearing Corporation
645 Davisville Rd
Willow Grove PA 19090
215 443-5252

(G-7849)
SCHNEDER ELC BLDNGS AMRCAS INC
125 Rock Rd (19044-2310)
PHONE...................................215 441-4389
Neil Eckles, *Branch Mgr*
EMP: 25
SALES (corp-wide): 355.8K **Privately Held**
SIC: 3699 Electrical equipment & supplies
HQ: Schneider Electric Buildings Americas, Inc.
1650 W Crosby Rd
Carrollton TX 75006
972 323-1111

(G-7850)
SOLID STATE EQP HOLDINGS LLC
185 Gibraltar Rd (19044-2303)
PHONE...................................215 328-0700
Herman Itzkowitz, *CEO*
Tom Werthan, *CFO*
Laura Rothman Mauer, *CTO*
EMP: 5
SALES (est): 495.5K
SALES (corp-wide): 542MM **Publicly Held**
SIC: 3699 Electrostatic particle accelerators
PA: Veeco Instruments Inc.
1 Terminal Dr
Plainview NY 11803
516 677-0200

(G-7851)
SPEED RACEWAY
200 Blair Mill Rd (19044-3053)
PHONE...................................215 672-6128
Robert Andrey, *Executive*
▲ EMP: 10
SALES (est): 1.5MM **Privately Held**
SIC: 3644 Raceways

(G-7852)
STANECO CORPORATION
901 Sheehy Dr (19044-1280)
PHONE...................................215 672-6500
Stanley Dworak Jr, *President*
Stanley T Dworak, *Vice Pres*
Mike Moore, *Project Mgr*
Mike Rahn, *Project Mgr*
EMP: 30 EST: 1963

SQ FT: 26,000
SALES (est): 5.9MM **Privately Held**
WEB: www.staneco.com
SIC: 8711 3823 3613 5063 Electrical or electronic engineering; industrial instrmnts msrmnt display/control process variable; control panels, electric; electrical apparatus & equipment; custom computer programming services; business consulting

(G-7853)
STEAM MAD CARPET CLEANERS INC
Also Called: All-Pro
558 Coach Rd (19044-1602)
PHONE...................................215 283-9833
Tony Alicea, *President*
EMP: 3
SALES (est): 250K **Privately Held**
SIC: 2273 7217 Carpets & rugs; carpet & upholstery cleaning

(G-7854)
STRATA SKIN SCIENCES INC (PA)
5 Walnut Grove Dr Ste 140 (19044-2252)
PHONE...................................215 619-3200
Dolev Rafaeli, *CEO*
Uri Geiger, *Ch of Bd*
Matthew Hill, *CFO*
Christina Allgeier, *Treasurer*
EMP: 98
SQ FT: 10,672
SALES: 31.4MM **Publicly Held**
WEB: www.eo-sciences.com
SIC: 3841 8731 Surgical & medical instruments; commercial physical research

(G-7855)
TALARIS INC
417 Caredean Dr (19044-1311)
PHONE...................................215 674-2882
Louis Vitali, *Branch Mgr*
EMP: 8
SALES (corp-wide): 2.1B **Privately Held**
WEB: www.delarue.com
SIC: 3578 3499 Banking machines; safes & vaults, metal
HQ: Talaris Inc.
3333 Warrenville Rd # 310
Lisle IL 60532
630 577-1000

(G-7856)
TEVA NEUROSCIENCE
1090 Horsham Rd (19044-1307)
P.O. Box 1005 (19044-8005)
PHONE...................................215 591-6309
David Korman, *Regional Mgr*
Robert Parra, *Mfg Staff*
Alain Debatisse, *Sales Staff*
Patti Dunham, *Sales Staff*
Mark Haggard, *Sales Staff*
EMP: 9
SALES (est): 682.4K **Privately Held**
SIC: 2834 Pharmaceutical preparations

(G-7857)
TEVA PHARMACEUTICALS USA INC
425 Privet Rd (19044-1220)
PHONE...................................215 591-3000
Joseph Devito, *Vice Pres*
Katie Robinson, *Sales Staff*
Kathleen Locklear, *Branch Mgr*
Itamar Ben-Anat, *Director*
EMP: 91
SALES (corp-wide): 18.8B **Privately Held**
WEB: www.lemmon.com
SIC: 2834 Pharmaceutical preparations
HQ: Teva Pharmaceuticals Usa, Inc.
1090 Horsham Rd
North Wales PA 19454
215 591-3000

(G-7858)
THEODORE FAZEN
Also Called: F W Echonhofer Company
426 Horsham Rd (19044-2012)
P.O. Box 187, Jamison (18929-0187)
PHONE...................................215 672-1122
Theodore Fazen, *Owner*
EMP: 20
SQ FT: 10,000

SALES (est): 2.1MM **Privately Held**
SIC: 2013 5141 Sausages & other prepared meats; groceries, general line

(G-7859)
TMS INTERNATIONAL LLC
1155 Buss Ctr Dr Ste 200 (19044)
PHONE...................................215 956-5500
Michael McGraw, *Vice Pres*
Raymond Kalouche, *Manager*
Paula Jordan, *Manager*
Ralph Swavely, *Info Tech Dir*
EMP: 80 **Privately Held**
SIC: 3295 3341 1422 8742 Slag, crushed or ground; secondary nonferrous metals; cement rock, crushed & brokenquarrying; public utilities consultant
HQ: Tms International, Llc
12 Monongahela Ave
Glassport PA 15045
412 678-6141

(G-7860)
TMS INTERNATIONAL CORP
1155 Business Pa Ctr Dr (19044)
PHONE...................................215 956-5500
John T Dilacqua, *Branch Mgr*
EMP: 50 **Privately Held**
WEB: www.envirosources.com
SIC: 3295 3399 3341 4212 Blast furnace slag; slag, crushed or ground; iron ore recovery from open hearth slag; recovery & refining of nonferrous metals; aluminum smelting & refining (secondary); steel hauling, local; waste disposal plant construction; hazardous waste collection & disposal
PA: Tms International Corp.
12 Monongahela Ave
Glassport PA 15045

(G-7861)
TWO TECHNOLOGIES INC
419 Sargon Way Ste A (19044-1266)
PHONE...................................215 441-5305
David H Young, *President*
Joan Rickards, *Exec VP*
Russell Maynard, *Assistant VP*
Steve Amberg, *Mfg Staff*
Jim Beiter, *Purch Mgr*
▲ EMP: 45
SQ FT: 18,000
SALES (est): 11.9MM **Privately Held**
WEB: www.twotech.com
SIC: 3571 3575 Electronic computers; computer terminals

(G-7862)
UPPER MORELAND
204 Fair Oaks Ave (19044-2409)
PHONE...................................215 773-9880
EMP: 4 EST: 2010
SALES (est): 180K **Privately Held**
SIC: 3131 Mfg Footwear Cut Stock

(G-7863)
VEECO PRECISION SURFC PROC LLC
Also Called: Veeco Psp
185 Gibraltar Rd (19044-2303)
PHONE...................................215 328-0700
Bill Miller, *President*
John Peeler, *Principal*
Shubham Maheshwari, *Exec VP*
Paul Antolli, *Senior VP*
Robert Bradshaw, *Senior VP*
▼ EMP: 90
SQ FT: 50,000
SALES (est): 24.5MM
SALES (corp-wide): 542MM **Publicly Held**
WEB: www.ssecusa.com
SIC: 3559 3565 3999 8741 Semiconductor manufacturing machinery; bottling & canning machinery; barber & beauty shop equipment; business management
PA: Veeco Instruments Inc.
1 Terminal Dr
Plainview NY 11803
516 677-0200

(G-7864)
VERT MARKETS INC (PA)
101 Gibraltar Rd Ste 100 (19044-2366)
PHONE...................................215 675-1800
Richard I Peterson, *President*

Art Glenn, *Director*
EMP: 6
SALES (est): 5.4MM **Privately Held**
WEB: www.vertmarkets.com
SIC: 2721 Magazines: publishing only, not printed on site

(G-7865)
XGEN LLC
Also Called: Xgen Products
201 Precision Rd (19044-1226)
PHONE...................................877 450-9436
Michael Koretsky, *President*
Andy Green, *Vice Pres*
Christopher Lerner, *Sales Executive*
Alissa Gubitoso, *Marketing Staff*
▲ EMP: 15
SQ FT: 6,000
SALES: 12MM **Privately Held**
SIC: 3845 Electromedical equipment

(G-7866)
ZENESCOPE ENTERTAINMENT INC
433 Caredean Dr Ste C (19044-1321)
PHONE...................................215 442-9094
Joe Brusha, *CEO*
Jason Condeelis, *Sales Staff*
Jennifer Bermel, *Director*
▲ EMP: 15
SALES (est): 2.3MM **Privately Held**
SIC: 2741 Miscellaneous publishing

Houston
Washington County

(G-7867)
BUCYRUS AMERICA INC
2045 W Pike St (15342-2009)
PHONE...................................724 743-1200
Joachim Geisler, *President*
EMP: 31
SALES (est): 11MM **Privately Held**
SIC: 3532 Drills, bits & similar equipment

(G-7868)
C & C MARINE MAINTENANCE CO (DH)
201 S Johnson Rd Ste 303 (15342-1351)
P.O. Box 118, Georgetown (15043-0118)
PHONE...................................724 746-9550
Donald A Grimm, *President*
Mark Schroeder, *Vice Pres*
EMP: 220
SQ FT: 5,625
SALES (est): 28.2MM
SALES (corp-wide): 54.6MM **Privately Held**
WEB: www.barges.us
SIC: 3731 3732 Barges, building & repairing; boat building & repairing
HQ: Campbell Transportation Company, Inc.
201 S Johnson Rd Ste 303
Houston PA 15342
724 746-9550

(G-7869)
CATERPILLAR GLOBL MIN AMER LLC (DH)
Also Called: D B T
2045 W Pike St (15342-1000)
PHONE...................................724 743-1200
William Tate, *President*
◆ EMP: 245 EST: 1949
SALES (est): 269.6MM
SALES (corp-wide): 54.7B **Publicly Held**
SIC: 3532 7629 Mining machinery; electrical repair shops
HQ: Caterpillar Global Mining Llc
1100 Milwaukee Ave
South Milwaukee WI 53172
414 768-4000

(G-7870)
CATERPILLAR INC
2045 W Pike St (15342-1000)
PHONE...................................724 743-0566
Douglas Hancock, *Engineer*
Tina Dettinger, *Hum Res Coord*
Russell Walker, *Administration*
EMP: 355

SALES (corp-wide): 54.7B Publicly Held
SIC: 3531 Construction machinery
PA: Caterpillar Inc.
510 Lake Cook Rd Ste 100
Deerfield IL 60015
224 551-4000

(G-7871)
CLORE ENTERPRISE
19 W Pike St (15342-1537)
PHONE...................................724 745-0673
Gretchen Clore, Owner
EMP: 5
SALES (est): 577.6K Privately Held
SIC: 2752 Commercial printing, offset

(G-7872)
JOY GLOBAL UNDERGROUND MIN LLC
Also Called: Joy Mining Machinery
2101 W Pike St (15342-1154)
PHONE...................................724 873-4200
Wayne Hull, Branch Mgr
Mr Tom Monaghan, MIS Staff
EMP: 214
SALES (corp-wide): 23.4B Privately Held
SIC: 3535 Bucket type conveyor systems
HQ: Joy Global Underground Mining Llc
40 Pennwood Pl Ste 100
Warrendale PA 15086
724 779-4500

(G-7873)
JOY GLOBAL UNDERGROUND MIN LLC
2101 W Pike St (15342-1154)
PHONE...................................724 873-4200
EMP: 0 EST: 2014
SALES (est): 3.2MM Privately Held
SIC: 3535 Mfg Conveyors/Equipment

(G-7874)
MCMILLEN WELDING INC
2415 W Pike St (15342-1199)
PHONE...................................724 745-4507
James Mc Millen, President
Cheryl Mc Millen, Corp Secy
Michael Mc Millen, Vice Pres
EMP: 6
SQ FT: 12,400
SALES (est): 1MM Privately Held
SIC: 3441 3599 Fabricated structural
metal; machine shop, jobbing & repair

(G-7875)
PERRYMAN COMPANY
Perryman Fords & Fabrications
149 S Johnson Rd (15342-1327)
PHONE...................................724 745-7272
Pete Hall, Branch Mgr
EMP: 78
SALES (corp-wide): 66.2MM Privately Held
SIC: 3841 Surgical & medical instruments
PA: The Perryman Company
213 Vandale Dr
Houston PA 15342
724 743-4239

(G-7876)
PERRYMAN COMPANY (PA)
213 Vandale Dr (15342-1272)
PHONE...................................724 743-4239
Frank Perryman, CEO
Ingo Grosse, General Mgr
Dave Tenison, General Mgr
James T Perryman Sr, COO
Jim Perryman Jr, COO
▲ EMP: 200
SQ FT: 9,300
SALES (est): 66.2MM Privately Held
WEB: www.perrymanco.com
SIC: 3356 Titanium & titanium alloy bars,
sheets, strip, etc.

(G-7877)
POCKET CROSS INC
Also Called: See-Line
10 Cherry Ave Ste 100 (15342-1557)
PHONE...................................724 745-1140
Gerald Havelka, President
Darlene Havelka, Corp Secy
EMP: 3
SQ FT: 3,200

SALES: 500K Privately Held
WEB: www.see-line.com
SIC: 2679 Novelties, paper: made from
purchased material

(G-7878)
RANDALL LESSO
Also Called: Special Machine Operations
123 S Main St (15342-1812)
PHONE...................................724 746-2100
Randal A Lesso, Owner
EMP: 3
SQ FT: 6,000
SALES (est): 145.2K Privately Held
SIC: 3599 7538 Machine shop, jobbing &
repair; engine repair

(G-7879)
ROCHESTER COCA COLA BOTTLING
Also Called: Coca-Cola
300 Vandale Dr (15342-1257)
PHONE...................................412 787-3610
James Cameron, President
EMP: 80
SALES (corp-wide): 35.4B Publicly Held
SIC: 2086 Bottled & canned soft drinks
HQ: Rochester Coca Cola Bottling Corp
300 Oak St
Pittston PA 18640
570 655-2874

(G-7880)
TATANO WIRE AND STEEL INC
224 Jackson St (15342)
PHONE...................................724 746-3118
Charles Tatano, Manager
EMP: 4
SALES (corp-wide): 3.2MM Privately
Held
SIC: 3312 3496 Wire products, steel or
iron; miscellaneous fabricated wire prod-
ucts
PA: Tatano Wire And Steel, Inc.
2 Iron St
Canonsburg PA 15317
724 746-3118

(G-7881)
TMS INTERNATIONAL LLC
Also Called: IMS
Western Ave (15342)
P.O. Box 241 (15342-0241)
PHONE...................................724 746-5377
EMP: 4
SALES (corp-wide): 282.4MM Privately
Held
SIC: 3295 Processes Slag & Scrap Metal
HQ: Tms International Group Llc
12 Monongahela Ave
Glassport PA 15045
412 678-6141

(G-7882)
TOM RUSSELL
Also Called: Houston Screen Printing
18 W Pike St (15342-1563)
P.O. Box 266 (15342-0266)
PHONE...................................724 746-5029
Tom Russell, Owner
EMP: 4
SALES (est): 288.6K Privately Held
SIC: 2395 2759 2269 Embroidery prod-
ucts, except schiffli machine; screen print-
ing; finishing plants

Houtzdale
Clearfield County

(G-7883)
KRAUSE C W & SON LUMBER
515 David St (16651-1451)
PHONE...................................814 378-8919
Clarence Krause, Owner
Ben Kraus, Partner
Bill Kraus, Partner
Ed Kraus, Partner
Jeff Kraus, Partner
EMP: 3
SALES (est): 252.2K Privately Held
SIC: 2411 5211 Logging; planing mill prod-
ucts & lumber

(G-7884)
RUSTYS OIL AND PROPANE INC
275 Spring St (16651-1406)
PHONE...................................814 497-4423
Rusty Christoff, Owner
EMP: 3 EST: 2016
SALES (est): 99.1K Privately Held
SIC: 1311 Crude petroleum & natural gas

Howard
Centre County

(G-7885)
B E V O L
118 Country Ln (16841-2625)
PHONE...................................570 962-3644
Robert Anderson, Owner
EMP: 4
SALES (est): 256.2K Privately Held
SIC: 3843 Orthodontic appliances

(G-7886)
CENTROID CORPORATION (PA)
159 Gates Rd (16841-4801)
PHONE...................................814 353-9290
Joseph W McCulloch, President
John D Roe, Corp Secy
Steve Boucher, Engineer
Richard Erhard, Project Engr
Liviu Degeratu, Sales Mgr
▲ EMP: 35
SQ FT: 20,000
SALES (est): 4.3MM Privately Held
WEB: www.centroidcnc.com
SIC: 3625 Motor controls, electric

(G-7887)
COCA COLA REFRESHMENTS US
Also Called: Coca-Cola
217 Aqua Penn Dr (16841-4710)
PHONE...................................814 357-8628
Dominic J Depaola, Manager
EMP: 6
SALES (est): 612.2K Privately Held
SIC: 2086 Bottled & canned soft drinks

(G-7888)
CREATIVE MOUNTAIN SOFTWARE LLC
258 Hoy Rd (16841-4102)
PHONE...................................814 383-2685
Carole J Yerick, Mng Member
EMP: 4
SALES (est): 199.1K Privately Held
SIC: 7372 Prepackaged software

(G-7889)
DANIEL D ESH
Also Called: Scenic View Leather Shop
147 Coder Ln (16841-4020)
PHONE...................................814 383-4579
Daniel D Esh, Owner
EMP: 4
SALES (est): 268.7K Privately Held
SIC: 3111 Collar leather; belting leather

(G-7890)
GATES LOGGING LLC
304 Gates Mountain Rd (16841-2720)
PHONE...................................814 353-1238
Lance Gates, Principal
EMP: 3
SALES (est): 234.1K Privately Held
SIC: 2411 Logging camps & contractors

(G-7891)
HELMERICH & PAYNE INTL DRLG CO
912 N Eagle Valley Rd (16841-4602)
PHONE...................................814 353-3450
Ricky Shoalmire, Branch Mgr
EMP: 143
SALES (corp-wide): 1.8B Publicly Held
SIC: 1381 Drilling oil & gas wells
HQ: Helmerich & Payne International
Drilling Co Inc
1437 S Boulder Ave # 1400
Tulsa OK 74119
918 742-5531

(G-7892)
VIDEO DISPLAY CORPORATION
Also Called: Win Tron Technologies
276 Spearing St (16841-2220)
P.O. Box 285, Milesburg (16853-0285)
PHONE...................................770 938-2080
John Nivison, Manager
EMP: 12
SALES (corp-wide): 11.9MM Publicly
Held
WEB: www.videodisplay.com
SIC: 3678 Electronic connectors
PA: Video Display Corporation
1868 Tucker Industrial Rd
Tucker GA 30084
770 938-2080

Hughestown
Luzerne County

(G-7893)
KAPPA GRAPHICS L P (PA)
50 Rock St (18640-3028)
PHONE...................................570 655-9681
Nick G Karabots, Partner
Tom Brisbon, Partner
Andrea Duloc, Partner
Bill Siebert, Senior VP
Timothy Cotter, VP Mfg
▲ EMP: 198
SQ FT: 128,000
SALES (est): 37.9MM Privately Held
SIC: 2759 2789 2752 2721 Magazines:
printing; bookbinding & related work;
commercial printing, lithographic; periodi-
cals

(G-7894)
PARTY TIME MANUFACTURING CO
421 Parsonage St (18640-2813)
P.O. Box 447, Pittston (18640-0447)
PHONE...................................800 346-3847
James Rosentel Sr, President
Karen Evitts, Corp Secy
James Rosentel Jr, Vice Pres
▲ EMP: 5 EST: 1963
SQ FT: 80,000
SALES (est): 971.8K Privately Held
WEB: www.partytimemfg.com
SIC: 2679 Novelties, paper: made from
purchased material

Hughesville
Lycoming County

(G-7895)
KIO LOGGING LLC
654 Beaver Lake Rd (17737-8427)
PHONE...................................570 584-0283
Ron E Kio, Principal
EMP: 3
SALES (est): 154.9K Privately Held
SIC: 2411 Logging camps & contractors

(G-7896)
MERGTECH INC
48 N Main St (17737-1506)
PHONE...................................570 584-3388
Lucy Gilchrist, President
Robert Mertz, Vice Pres
EMP: 9
SALES (est): 532.1K Privately Held
SIC: 5963 7378 3577 Direct selling estab-
lishments; computer maintenance & re-
pair; computer peripheral equipment

(G-7897)
MUNCY LUMINARY
1025 Route 405 Hwy (17737-9069)
PHONE...................................570 584-0111
Sharon Dapp, Office Mgr
EMP: 4
SALES (est): 186.7K Privately Held
SIC: 2711 Newspapers, publishing & print-
ing

▲ = Import ▼=Export
◆ =Import/Export

(G-7898)
OGDEN NEWSPAPERS INC
Also Called: East Lycoming Shopper & News
1025 Route 405 Hwy (17737-9069)
P.O. Box 266 (17737-0266)
PHONE...................................570 584-2134
Sharon Dapp, *Owner*
EMP: 10 **Privately Held**
SIC: 2711 Newspapers: publishing only, not printed on site
HQ: The Ogden Newspapers Inc
1500 Main St
Wheeling WV 26003
304 233-0100

(G-7899)
SEDCO MANUFACTURING
Also Called: Vanco
10823 Route 864 Hwy (17737-8861)
P.O. Box 5085, Williamsport (17702-0885)
PHONE...................................570 323-1232
Charles Waldman, *President*
EMP: 4 EST: 1966
SQ FT: 7,000
SALES (est): 475.3K **Privately Held**
SIC: 3599 3544 Machine shop, jobbing & repair; special dies, tools, jigs & fixtures

---

Hummels Wharf
Snyder County

(G-7900)
NATIONAL BEEF PACKING CO LLC
1811 N Old Trl (17831)
PHONE...................................570 743-4420
Dave Davidson, *Plant Mgr*
Suzie Hurtado, *QC Mgr*
EMP: 150 **Privately Held**
WEB: www.nationalbeef.com
SIC: 2011 Meat packing plants
HQ: National Beef Packing Company, L.L.C.
12200 N Ambassador Dr # 101
Kansas City MO 64163
800 449-2333

Hummelstown
Dauphin County

(G-7901)
3P LTD
286 E Main St (17036-1722)
PHONE...................................717 566-5643
Renee Nfoster, *Admin Sec*
EMP: 4 EST: 2016
SALES (est): 310.7K **Privately Held**
SIC: 2741 Miscellaneous publishing

(G-7902)
BETTER BOWLS LLC
1152 Mae St Ste 101 (17036-9185)
PHONE...................................717 298-1257
Malathy Nair, *Mng Member*
Alexander Blumenthal,
EMP: 4 EST: 2008
SQ FT: 600
SALES (est): 505.4K **Privately Held**
SIC: 2045 Cake mixes, prepared: from purchased flour

(G-7903)
BONDATA INC
245 W High St (17036-2004)
PHONE...................................717 566-5550
Lisa Bontempo, *President*
Frank Moosic, *Vice Pres*
EMP: 4
SALES (est): 390K **Privately Held**
WEB: www.bondata.com
SIC: 3829 7374 Plotting instruments, drafting & map reading; computer graphics service

(G-7904)
BRADLEY E MILLER
Also Called: B & B Pole Buildings
602 W High St (17036-1907)
PHONE...................................717 566-6243
Bradley E Miller, *Owner*

EMP: 6
SALES (est): 655K **Privately Held**
SIC: 3272 Poles & posts, concrete

(G-7905)
CASSEL VINEYARDS HERSHEY LLC
80 Shetland Dr (17036-9238)
PHONE...................................717 533-2008
Chris Cassel, *Co-Owner*
Craig Cassel, *Co-Owner*
EMP: 7
SALES (est): 537.3K **Privately Held**
SIC: 2084 Wine cellars, bonded: engaged in blending wines

(G-7906)
CHEM-TAINER INDUSTRIES INC
187 S Meadow Ln (17036-7359)
PHONE...................................717 469-7316
David R Roush, *Manager*
EMP: 10
SALES (corp-wide): 46.5MM **Privately Held**
WEB: www.chemtainer.com
SIC: 3089 Plastic containers, except foam
PA: Chem-Tainer Industries Inc.
361 Neptune Ave
West Babylon NY 11704
631 422-8300

(G-7907)
CORE HOUSE
34 Sweet Arrow Dr (17036-2718)
PHONE...................................717 566-3810
Philip Cartier, *Owner*
EMP: 3
SALES (est): 121.8K **Privately Held**
SIC: 3999 Models, except toy

(G-7908)
DAIRICONCEPTS LP
8190 Presidents Dr (17036-8619)
PHONE...................................717 566-4500
Neil Walker, *Principal*
EMP: 50
SALES (corp-wide): 14.6B **Privately Held**
WEB: www.dairiconcepts.com
SIC: 2022 2035 Cheese spreads, dips, pastes & other cheese products; pickles, sauces & salad dressings
HQ: Dairiconcepts, L.P.
3253 E Chestnut Expy
Springfield MO 65802
417 829-3400

(G-7909)
ELECTRONIC SERVICE & DESIGN
2118 Church Rd (17036-8200)
PHONE...................................717 243-7743
Frank T English, *President*
EMP: 5
SQ FT: 6,400
SALES (est): 2MM **Privately Held**
WEB: www.esdpcb.com
SIC: 3672 Circuit boards, television & radio printed

(G-7910)
FIRST SUPPLY CHAIN LLC
Also Called: Erp Software Consulting
1150 Chadwick Cir (17036-6812)
PHONE...................................215 527-2264
Nasir Iqbal, *Principal*
EMP: 3 EST: 2009
SALES (est): 104.7K **Privately Held**
SIC: 7371 7372 Computer software systems analysis & design, custom; software programming applications; prepackaged software; application computer software; business oriented computer software

(G-7911)
FRESH PRESS LLC
112 Savannah Dr (17036-7826)
PHONE...................................717 504-9223
EMP: 3
SALES (est): 110.9K **Privately Held**
SIC: 2711 Newspapers

(G-7912)
GLEN BLOOMING CONTRACTORS INC
Handwerk Contractors
1 Old Farm Rd (17036)
PHONE...................................717 566-3711
Rick Mack, *Manager*
Ricky Mack, *Manager*
EMP: 150
SALES (corp-wide): 66.5MM **Privately Held**
SIC: 1611 1794 2951 Surfacing & paving; excavation work; asphalt paving mixtures & blocks
PA: Glen Blooming Contractors Inc
901 Minsi Trl
Blooming Glen PA 18911
215 257-9400

(G-7913)
HIDDIE KITCHEN INC
Also Called: Gladstone Candies
120 W 2nd St (17036-1507)
PHONE...................................717 566-2211
Doug Gautsch, *President*
EMP: 10
SALES (est): 510K **Privately Held**
SIC: 2064 Lollipops & other hard candy

(G-7914)
HYQ RESEARCH SOLUTIONS LLC
Also Called: Hyq Resonance Systems
1258 Jill Dr (17036-9021)
PHONE...................................717 439-9320
Qing Yang, *Principal*
Michael Lanagan, *Principal*
Sebastian Rupprecht, *Principal*
EMP: 3
SALES (est): 177.2K **Privately Held**
SIC: 3841 8731 Diagnostic apparatus, medical; medical research, commercial

(G-7915)
J MAZE CORP
Also Called: PA Biodiesel Supply
85 Overview Dr (17036-9339)
PHONE...................................717 329-8350
Joe Mazenko, *CEO*
Kay Himes, *President*
▲ EMP: 3
SALES (est): 339.7K **Privately Held**
SIC: 2048 Feed supplements

(G-7916)
M4L INC
Also Called: Millwork For Less
8176 Presidents Dr Ste M (17036-8635)
PHONE...................................717 566-1610
Todd Wilfont, *Owner*
Chris Weinhold, *Accounts Mgr*
Alan Rehm, *Sales Executive*
EMP: 6 EST: 2000
SALES (est): 2.8MM **Privately Held**
WEB: www.millworkforless.com
SIC: 5031 2431 Millwork; doors & door parts & trim, wood; door frames, wood; garage doors, overhead: wood; windows & window parts & trim, wood

(G-7917)
MARKOWSKI INTERNATIONAL PUBG
1 Oakglade Cir (17036-9525)
PHONE...................................717 566-0468
Michael A Markowski, *Owner*
Michael Markowski, *Software Dev*
EMP: 3
SALES: 2.5MM **Privately Held**
WEB: www.possibilitypress.com
SIC: 8742 2731 Management consulting services; books: publishing only

(G-7918)
MOYER MUSIC TEST INC
4 Meadowood Dr (17036-9547)
PHONE...................................717 566-8778
Ray Moyer, *President*
EMP: 5
SALES (est): 290K **Privately Held**
SIC: 2731 Textbooks: publishing & printing

(G-7919)
NEWCO INDUSTRIES
25 S Landis St (17036-2026)
PHONE...................................717 566-9560
Patricia Newell, *Owner*
EMP: 10
SALES (est): 892.8K **Privately Held**
SIC: 3569 Assembly machines, non-metal-working

(G-7920)
NYES MACHINE AND DESIGN (PA)
1153 Roush Rd (17036-9621)
PHONE...................................717 533-9514
Brian Nye, *Owner*
Carol Nye, *Office Mgr*
EMP: 13
SALES (est): 2.1MM **Privately Held**
WEB: www.nyemachine.com
SIC: 3599 Machine shop, jobbing & repair

(G-7921)
PENNSY SUPPLY INC
39 Hersey Park Dr (17036)
PHONE...................................717 566-0222
Larry Stine, *Manager*
EMP: 32
SALES (corp-wide): 29.7B **Privately Held**
SIC: 3273 Ready-mixed concrete
HQ: Pennsy Supply, Inc.
1001 Paxton St
Harrisburg PA 17104
717 233-4511

(G-7922)
PRO BARRIER ENGINEERING LLC
228 Grandview Rd (17036-9264)
PHONE...................................717 944-6056
Tom Potter,
Dennis Owen,
EMP: 3
SALES (est): 360.2K **Privately Held**
WEB: www.probarrier.com
SIC: 3499 Barricades, metal

(G-7923)
RBS FAB INC
230 N Hoernerstown Rd (17036-9503)
PHONE...................................717 566-9513
Joann Smith, *CEO*
Terry Smith, *President*
EMP: 16
SQ FT: 50,000
SALES (est): 2.5MM **Privately Held**
WEB: www.rbsfab.com
SIC: 3599 3544 Machine shop, jobbing & repair; special dies, tools, jigs & fixtures

(G-7924)
RENAISSANCE PRESS INC
1071 Stoney Run Rd (17036-8527)
PHONE...................................717 534-0708
Joesph Lewin, *President*
EMP: 3
SALES (est): 104.5K **Privately Held**
SIC: 2731 Books: publishing only

(G-7925)
STONER GRAPHIX INC
163 S Meadow Ln (17036-7358)
PHONE...................................717 469-7716
Kurt Stoner, *President*
Jill Propps, *Principal*
EMP: 9
SALES: 800K **Privately Held**
WEB: www.stonergraphix.com
SIC: 3993 Signs & advertising specialties

(G-7926)
TEESHIP LLC
409 Pleasant View Rd (17036-8007)
PHONE...................................717 497-2970
EMP: 3 EST: 2014
SALES (est): 151K **Privately Held**
SIC: 2759 Screen printing

(G-7927)
VENTURE PRECISION TOOL INC
241 E 2nd St (17036-1705)
P.O. Box 262 (17036-0262)
PHONE...................................717 566-6496
Keith Foreman, *President*

Pam Foreman, *Corp Secy*
Craig Wallace, *Vice Pres*
EMP: 10
SQ FT: 7,500
SALES (est): 1.7MM **Privately Held**
WEB: www.ventureprecisiontool.com
SIC: 3089 Injection molding of plastics;
molding primary plastic

Hunker
Westmoreland County

(G-7928)
GENERAL NUCLEAR CORP
1651 New Stanton (15639)
P.O. Box 400, New Stanton (15672-0400)
PHONE..............................724 925-3565
Duane Lang, *President*
Rick Lang, *President*
Geno Persio, *Exec VP*
Dino S Persio, *Director*
Frederick Planinsek, *Director*
EMP: 55 **EST:** 1966
SQ FT: 17,000
SALES (est): 18.6MM **Privately Held**
WEB: www.generalnuclearcorp.com
SIC: 3599 3829 3823 Machine shop, job-
bing & repair; measuring & controlling de-
vices; industrial instrmnts msrmnt
display/control process variable

(G-7929)
MARIETTA FENCE EXPERTS
LLC
Also Called: Laurel Fence and Railing
126 Emerald Dr (15639-9716)
P.O. Box 409, New Stanton (15672-0409)
PHONE..............................724 925-6100
Annamarie Marietta,
EMP: 8
SALES (est): 371.7K **Privately Held**
SIC: 1799 2411 3089 3315 Fence con-
struction; rails, fence: round or split;
fences, gates & accessories: plastic;
fence gates posts & fittings: steel

(G-7930)
OIL & GAS MANAGEMENT INC
114 Oil Ln (15639-1056)
P.O. Box 1204, Mount Pleasant (15666-
3304)
PHONE..............................724 925-1568
A Bruce Grindle, *CEO*
Cathy Kirsch, *Treasurer*
EMP: 6
SQ FT: 2,000
SALES (est): 997.8K **Privately Held**
SIC: 1382 Oil & gas exploration services

Hunlock Creek
Luzerne County

(G-7931)
COUNTRY IMPRESSIONS INC
Also Called: Suburban News
5724 Main Rd (18621-2932)
PHONE..............................570 477-5000
Duane Updyke, *President*
Allen Updyke, *Corp Secy*
EMP: 12
SALES (est): 700K **Privately Held**
WEB: www.nepafreeads.com
SIC: 2711 Newspapers: publishing only,
not printed on site

(G-7932)
KASMARK & MARSHALL INC
354 Sorbertown Hl (18621-3712)
PHONE..............................570 287-3663
Fax: 570 287-3663
EMP: 4 **EST:** 1965
SQ FT: 10,600
SALES: 250K **Privately Held**
SIC: 3231 1793 5231 Mfg Stained Glass
Shades & Windows

(G-7933)
PIKES CREEK RACEWAY PARK
INC
111 Croop Rd (18621-4401)
PHONE..............................570 477-2226
Annemarie Zimmerman, *President*
Gregory Zimmerman, *Vice Pres*
EMP: 6
SALES (est): 663.3K **Privately Held**
SIC: 3644 Raceways

(G-7934)
S & K VENDING
5843 Main Rd (18621-5010)
PHONE..............................570 675-5180
Stanley D Joseph, *Owner*
EMP: 4
SALES (est): 73.2K **Privately Held**
SIC: 2099 Emulsifiers, food

(G-7935)
TYPE SET PRINT
310 Hartman Rd (18621-3822)
PHONE..............................570 542-5910
Joann Blaine, *Principal*
EMP: 6 **EST:** 2011
SALES (est): 389.6K **Privately Held**
SIC: 2752 Commercial printing, litho-
graphic

Huntingdon
Huntingdon County

(G-7936)
A T J PRINTING INC (PA)
325 Penn St Ste 1 (16652-1470)
P.O. Box 384 (16652-0384)
PHONE..............................814 641-9614
George R Sample III, *President*
Ken Smith, *Treasurer*
EMP: 11
SQ FT: 5,000
SALES (est): 1MM **Privately Held**
WEB: www.getwireless.net
SIC: 2711 Newspapers, publishing & print-
ing

(G-7937)
ADVANCED COLOR GRAPHICS
14660 Happy Hills Rd (16652-3770)
PHONE..............................814 235-1200
Roger Meinhart, *Partner*
Dennis Devlin, *Partner*
EMP: 25
SQ FT: 3,300
SALES (est): 1.3MM **Privately Held**
WEB: www.advancedcolorgraphics.com
SIC: 2752 Commercial printing, offset

(G-7938)
ALLENSVILLE PLANING MILL
INC
10381 Fairgrounds Rd (16652-7149)
PHONE..............................717 543-4954
Chris Stull, *Manager*
EMP: 15
SALES (corp-wide): 47.3MM **Privately**
Held
WEB: www.apm-inc.net
SIC: 5211 2431 1542 Home centers; or-
namental woodwork: cornices, mantels,
etc.; farm building construction; commer-
cial & office building, new construction
PA: Allensville Planing Mill, Inc.
108 E Main St
Allensville PA 17002
717 483-6386

(G-7939)
BERRENA JSEPH T
MCHANICALS INC
279 Standing Stone Ave (16652-1304)
PHONE..............................814 643-2645
Matthew Berrena, *President*
Mike Tucker, *Corp Secy*
Joseph T Berrena, *Vice Pres*
Tony Berrena, *Manager*
Bob Wendle, *Manager*
EMP: 35
SQ FT: 10,000

SALES: 7.2MM **Privately Held**
WEB: www.jtbmechanicals.com
SIC: 1711 1731 3621 Plumbing, heating,
air-conditioning contractors; electrical
work; generating apparatus & parts, electrical

(G-7940)
BRETT W SHOPE
Also Called: B & S Logging
5272 Cold Springs Rd (16652-3135)
PHONE..............................814 643-2921
Brett W Shope, *Owner*
EMP: 5
SALES (est): 330K **Privately Held**
SIC: 2421 4212 4213 Specialty sawmill
products; local trucking, without storage;
trucking, except local

(G-7941)
COPY RITE
105 Mount Vernon Ave (16652-1211)
PHONE..............................814 644-0360
Scott Fhsaffer, *Owner*
EMP: 5
SALES (est): 431.1K **Privately Held**
SIC: 3555 Copy holders, printers'

(G-7942)
E B ENDRES INC
10630 Fairgrounds Rd (16652-7154)
P.O. Box 396 (16652-0396)
PHONE..............................814 643-1860
Richard J Endres Jr, *President*
EMP: 27
SQ FT: 20,000
SALES (est): 5.4MM **Privately Held**
SIC: 2431 5211 Millwork; lumber & other
building materials

(G-7943)
F R P FABRICATORS INC
10168 Frp Rd (16652)
P.O. Box 388 (16652-0388)
PHONE..............................814 643-2525
James Wilson, *President*
EMP: 6 **EST:** 1973
SQ FT: 8,800
SALES (est): 979.5K **Privately Held**
WEB: www.frpfab.com
SIC: 3089 Plastic processing

(G-7944)
HUNTINGDON ELC MTR SVC INC
Also Called: Hems
Penn & 7th St # 7 (16652)
P.O. Box 542 (16652-0542)
PHONE..............................814 643-3921
Leon Hopkins, *President*
EMP: 20
SALES (est): 2.8MM **Privately Held**
WEB: www.huntingdonelec.com
SIC: 7694 Electric motor repair

(G-7945)
HUNTINGDON FIBERGLASS
PDTS LLC
1200 Susquehanna Ave (16652-1950)
PHONE..............................814 641-8129
Paul Geist, *President*
▲ **EMP:** 43 **EST:** 2013
SALES (est): 11.2MM **Privately Held**
SIC: 2221 Fiberglass fabrics

(G-7946)
HUNTINGDON OFFSET
PRINTING CO
1431 Oneida St (16652-2343)
PHONE..............................814 641-7310
Tony Brenneman, *Owner*
EMP: 4
SALES (est): 500K **Privately Held**
WEB: www.huntingdonoffsetprinting.com
SIC: 2759 2282 Screen printing; embroi-
dery yarn: twisting, winding or spooling

(G-7947)
JOHN R WALD COMPANY INC
10576 Fairgrounds Rd (16652-7152)
PHONE..............................814 643-3908
Michael E Rodli, *President*
Herman E Arnold, *Vice Pres*
Marie Z Rodli, *Shareholder*
Lorry E Hicks, *Admin Sec*
▲ **EMP:** 22

SQ FT: 14,000
SALES: 11.9MM **Privately Held**
WEB: www.jrwald.com
SIC: 1796 3599 Machinery installation;
machine shop, jobbing & repair

(G-7948)
JOHNS WELDING SHOP
10321 Fairgrounds Rd (16652-7149)
PHONE..............................814 643-4564
Rick Johns, *Owner*
Clair Johns, *Owner*
EMP: 4
SALES (est): 303.3K **Privately Held**
SIC: 7692 Welding repair

(G-7949)
KUNZ BUSINESS PRODUCTS
INC
1600 Penn St (16652-2034)
PHONE..............................814 643-4320
Tom Henderson, *Ch of Bd*
Dorothy M Henderson, *Corp Secy*
Reed T Henderson, *Vice Pres*
Jim Swaney, *Sales Mgr*
EMP: 125 **EST:** 1894
SQ FT: 30,000
SALES (est): 9.2MM **Privately Held**
WEB: www.jbkunz.com
SIC: 2782 2759 Passbooks: bank, etc.; di-
rectories (except telephone): printing
PA: Henderson's Printing, Inc.
Green Ave & Ninth St 9th
Altoona PA 16601
814 944-0855

(G-7950)
LANEYS FEED MILL INC
850 Ice Plant Rd (16652-1282)
PHONE..............................814 643-3211
John D Rader, *President*
Cecil Jackson, *Vice Pres*
EMP: 12
SQ FT: 14,000
SALES (est): 2.3MM **Privately Held**
SIC: 2048 5191 Livestock feeds; farm
supplies

(G-7951)
MINERAL MANUFACTURING
CORP
10627 Hartslog Valley Rd (16652-4948)
PHONE..............................814 643-0410
Thomas Reed Jr, *President*
EMP: 25 **EST:** 1999
SALES (est): 2.7MM **Privately Held**
SIC: 3999 Barber & beauty shop equip-
ment

(G-7952)
MODERN SPECIALTIES INC
10627 Hartslog Valley Rd (16652-4948)
PHONE..............................814 643-0410
Thomas Reed Jr, *President*
Judith A Reed, *Treasurer*
Patricia R Moberg, *Admin Sec*
EMP: 6
SALES (est): 1.1MM **Privately Held**
SIC: 3353 Aluminum sheet, plate & foil

(G-7953)
MOGLABS USA LLC
419 14th St (16652-1937)
PHONE..............................814 251-4363
Laura White, *Principal*
EMP: 6
SALES (est): 731.3K **Privately Held**
SIC: 3674 Semiconductors & related de-
vices

(G-7954)
OSWALD & ASSOCIATES INC
10517 Raystown Rd Ste A (16652-7545)
PHONE..............................814 627-0300
Leo A Oswald, *President*
EMP: 3
SQ FT: 10,000
SALES (est): 257.2K **Privately Held**
SIC: 8711 3568 Structural engineering;
power transmission equipment

(G-7955)
PARKS DESIGN & INK
719 Washington St (16652-1723)
PHONE..............................814 643-1120

GEOGRAPHIC

Michele Parks, *Owner*
Brian Parks, *Co-Owner*
EMP: 4
SALES: 150K **Privately Held**
SIC: 2752 Commercial printing, lithographic

(G-7956)
STONE VALLEY WELDING LLC
11582 Guyer Rd (16652-6001)
PHONE....................814 667-2046
Steve Stoltzfus, *Owner*
Stephen P Stoltzfus, *Mng Member*
Ben Yoder,
EMP: 20
SQ FT: 10,000
SALES: 6MM **Privately Held**
SIC: 3443 Trash racks, metal plate

(G-7957)
THOMPSONS CANDLE CO
328 Allegheny St (16652-1430)
PHONE....................814 641-7490
Angela Thompson, *CEO*
John Thompson, *President*
EMP: 24
SQ FT: 15,000
SALES (est): 2.5MM **Privately Held**
SIC: 3999 5199 Candles; candles

(G-7958)
US MUNICIPAL SUPPLY INC (PA)
10583 Raystown Rd (16652-7545)
P.O. Box 574 (16652-0574)
PHONE....................610 292-9450
Paul Statler, *President*
Tim Miller, *General Mgr*
Margaret Statler, *Corp Secy*
Alvah B Adam Jr, *Vice Pres*
Lou Libbi, *Opers Staff*
EMP: 45
SQ FT: 20,000
SALES (est): 38.7MM **Privately Held**
WEB: www.usmuni.com
SIC: 5085 3993 5082 Industrial supplies; signs & advertising specialties; road construction equipment

---

Huntingdon Valley
Montgomery County

(G-7959)
A & A GEAR INC
1840 County Line Rd # 204 (19006-1719)
PHONE....................215 364-3952
Barry Antonelli, *President*
EMP: 3
SQ FT: 4,000
SALES (est): 504.8K **Privately Held**
WEB: www.aagearinc.com
SIC: 3462 Gears, forged steel

(G-7960)
A B PATTERNS MODELS
390 Pike Rd Unit 7 (19006-1619)
PHONE....................215 322-8226
John Bauerle, *Owner*
EMP: 4
SALES: 250K **Privately Held**
SIC: 3543 Industrial patterns

(G-7961)
ACCELBEAM PHOTONICS LLC
111 Buck Rd Unit 5001 (19006-1544)
PHONE....................215 715-4345
EMP: 3
SALES (est): 159.4K **Privately Held**
SIC: 3661 Fiber optics communications equipment

(G-7962)
AJAX ELECTRIC COMPANY (PA)
60 Tomlinson Rd (19006-4294)
PHONE....................215 947-8500
John A Barry, *President*
Donna Stelman, *Treasurer*
Emily Arnold, *Executive Asst*
E Schmidt, *Admin Sec*
EMP: 24 **EST:** 1931
SQ FT: 30,000

SALES (est): 3.3MM **Privately Held**
WEB: www.ajaxelectric.com
SIC: 3567 3613 3823 8742 Metal melting furnaces, industrial: electric; metal melting furnaces, industrial: fuel-fired; control panels, electric; industrial instrmnts msrmnt display/control process variable; management consulting services

(G-7963)
AMERICAN BANK NOTE HOLOGRAPHIC
1448 County Line Rd (19006-1810)
PHONE....................215 357-5300
John Lerlo, *Systems Mgr*
EMP: 40
SALES (corp-wide): 880.4MM **Publicly Held**
WEB: www.abnh.com
SIC: 2752 2796 Commercial printing, lithographic; platemaking services
HQ: American Bank Note Holographics, Inc.
2 Applegate Dr
Robbinsville NJ 08691
609 208-0591

(G-7964)
AMERICAN MILITARY TECHNOLOGIES
Also Called: Amitec
2516 Kirk Dr (19006-5429)
PHONE....................215 550-7970
Boris Gmiryansky, *President*
EMP: 3
SQ FT: 2,500
SALES: 500K **Privately Held**
WEB: www.amitec.net
SIC: 3679 Harness assemblies for electronic use: wire or cable

(G-7965)
BENKALU GROUP LMTD TA JAGUAR
1908 County Line Rd (19006-1738)
PHONE....................215 646-5896
Alan Paston, *President*
Adeeb Khan, *Partner*
EMP: 8
SALES (est): 570K **Privately Held**
SIC: 2752 7334 2791 2789 Commercial printing, lithographic; mimeographing; typesetting; bookbinding & related work

(G-7966)
BSG CORPORATION
Also Called: Bs Group
3401 Sorrel Ln (19006-3808)
PHONE....................267 230-0514
Marina Borukhovich, *President*
Paul Borukhovich, *General Mgr*
EMP: 3
SALES (est): 262.1K **Privately Held**
SIC: 3699 Electrical equipment & supplies

(G-7967)
CANDY COTTAGE CO INC
465 Pike Rd Ste 103 (19006-1621)
P.O. Box 24 (19006-0024)
PHONE....................215 322-6618
Albert Palagruto, *President*
Joan Palagruto, *Vice Pres*
EMP: 3
SALES: 215K **Privately Held**
SIC: 2066 Chocolate

(G-7968)
CENTRAL PANEL INC
60 Tomlinson Rd (19006-4219)
PHONE....................215 947-8500
Bruce Arnold, *President*
Donna Stelman, *Corp Secy*
EMP: 7
SQ FT: 30,000
SALES: 500K
SALES (corp-wide): 3.3MM **Privately Held**
WEB: www.ajaxelectric.com
SIC: 3613 Control panels, electric
PA: Ajax Electric Company
60 Tomlinson Rd
Huntingdon Valley PA 19006
215 947-8500

(G-7969)
CF TEXTILE INC
39 Simons Way (19006-4248)
PHONE....................215 817-5867
Jay Cohen, *President*
John Fontana, *Vice Pres*
EMP: 2
SQ FT: 2,500
SALES: 1.5MM **Privately Held**
SIC: 2299 Broadwoven fabrics: linen, jute, hemp & ramie

(G-7970)
COBRA WIRE & CABLE INC
1800 Byberry Rd Ste 810 (19006-3520)
PHONE....................215 674-8773
Peter Sheehan, *CEO*
Bart Reitter, *President*
Paul J Esko, *CFO*
Bryan Holtzman, *CFO*
Paul Jesko, *CFO*
◆ **EMP:** 43
SQ FT: 62,000
SALES (est): 187K **Privately Held**
WEB: www.copflex.com
SIC: 5063 3496 Electronic wire & cable; miscellaneous fabricated wire products

(G-7971)
CONVERTERS INC
1617 Republic Rd (19006-1807)
P.O. Box 910 (19006-0910)
PHONE....................215 355-5400
Daniel A Cipriano Jr, *CEO*
Daniel J Cipriano, *President*
Deborah Cipriano, *Vice Pres*
Rachel Cipriano, *Treasurer*
Jasna Krstic, *Technology*
▲ **EMP:** 22 **EST:** 1968
SQ FT: 23,000
SALES (est): 5.8MM **Privately Held**
WEB: www.converters.com
SIC: 2672 3441 2675 2295 Tape, pressure sensitive: made from purchased materials; fabricated structural metal; die-cut paper & board; coated fabrics, not rubberized

(G-7972)
COPY MANAGEMENT INC (PA)
Also Called: Chambers Group
447 Veit Rd (19006-1617)
PHONE....................215 269-5000
Christopher Chambers, *CEO*
Joe Chambers, *President*
EMP: 11
SALES (est): 8.3MM **Privately Held**
SIC: 2752 2791 2789 Commercial printing, offset; typesetting; bookbinding & related work

(G-7973)
CZAR IMPORTS INC
Also Called: Czar Floors
390 Pike Rd Unit 4 (19006-1619)
PHONE....................800 577-2927
Valeriy Platonov, *President*
Edward Tsvilik, *Vice Pres*
EMP: 100
SALES (est): 7.5MM **Privately Held**
WEB: www.czarfloors.com
SIC: 5713 2426 3281 Carpets; parquet flooring, hardwood; building stone products; marble, building: cut & shaped

(G-7974)
ECCOTROL LLC
111 Buck Rd Unit 307 (19006-1551)
PHONE....................877 322-6876
EMP: 3
SQ FT: 2,200
SALES: 2.5MM **Privately Held**
SIC: 8731 3822 Commercial Physical Research Mfg Environmental Controls

(G-7975)
ECONOTOOL INC
2971 Franks Rd (19006-4214)
PHONE....................215 947-2404
Andrew Middleton, *President*
EMP: 8 **EST:** 1947
SQ FT: 10,500
SALES (est): 1.5MM **Privately Held**
WEB: www.econotool.com
SIC: 3553 Woodworking machinery

(G-7976)
EIS INC
Cobra Wire & Cable
1800 Byberry Rd Ste 810 (19006-3520)
PHONE....................215 674-8773
Bob Thomas, *Manager*
EMP: 43
SALES (corp-wide): 18.7B **Publicly Held**
SIC: 5063 3496 Electronic wire & cable; miscellaneous fabricated wire products
HQ: Eis, Inc.
2018 Powers Ferry Rd Se # 500
Atlanta GA 30339
678 255-3600

(G-7977)
EL-ANA COLLECTION INC
61 Buck Rd (19006-1501)
PHONE....................215 953-8820
Nina Sitkovetsky, *President*
Elaine Vinikoor, *Corp Secy*
Dimitry Sitkovetsky, *Vice Pres*
EMP: 10
SQ FT: 8,351
SALES (est): 933.9K **Privately Held**
SIC: 2253 5199 Sweaters & sweater coats, knit; pants, slacks or trousers, knit; hats & headwear, knit; knit goods

(G-7978)
EROS HOSIERY CO DEL VLY INC
1430 County Line Rd (19006-1801)
PHONE....................215 342-2121
Brad Seiver, *President*
▲ **EMP:** 9
SQ FT: 6,000
SALES (est): 3.2MM **Privately Held**
WEB: www.pantyhosebymail.com
SIC: 5137 5661 2389 Hosiery: women's, children's & infants'; shoe stores; men's miscellaneous accessories

(G-7979)
EVANS HEAT TREATING COMPANY
360 Red Lion Rd (19006-6437)
PHONE....................215 938-8791
Lee Evans, *President*
William Colon, *General Mgr*
Ryan Burnick, *VP Admin*
William Burnick, *Vice Pres*
Bill Burnick, *VP Opers*
EMP: 10
SQ FT: 35,000
SALES (est): 1.6MM **Privately Held**
SIC: 3398 Metal heat treating

(G-7980)
FCE LLC
2600 Philmont Ave (19006-5306)
P.O. Box 796 (19006-0796)
PHONE....................215 947-7333
Fax: 215 947-7334
EMP: 5
SQ FT: 1,700
SALES (est): 755.6K
SALES (corp-wide): 83.5B **Publicly Held**
SIC: 3567 Manufactures Industrial Furnaces And Ovens
HQ: Siemens Industry, Inc.
1000 Deerfield Pkwy
Buffalo Grove IL 60089
847 215-1000

(G-7981)
FIELCO LLC
1957 Pioneer Rd (19006-2505)
PHONE....................215 674-8700
Daniel Fields, *Principal*
▲ **EMP:** 4
SALES (est): 551.4K **Privately Held**
SIC: 2295 Mfg Coated Fabrics

(G-7982)
FIELCO ADHESIVES
1957 Pioneer Rd (19006-2505)
PHONE....................267 282-5311
James I Fields, *Principal*
EMP: 5
SALES (est): 682.2K **Privately Held**
SIC: 2891 Adhesives

(G-7983)
FIELCO INDUSTRIES INC
1957 Pioneer Rd (19006-2505)
PHONE...................................215 674-8700
James Fields, *President*
EMP: 20
SQ FT: 22,000
SALES (est): 3.7MM **Privately Held**
WEB: www.fielco.com
SIC: 2891 3087 Adhesives; sealing com-
pounds, synthetic rubber or plastic; cus-
tom compound purchased resins

(G-7984)
**FIRST CHOICE RADON TESTING
CO**
460 Newell Dr (19006-4036)
P.O. Box 830 (19006-0830)
PHONE...................................215 947-1995
Lewis Nelson, *Owner*
EMP: 4
SALES (est): 381.3K **Privately Held**
SIC: 3826 Gas testing apparatus

(G-7985)
FREDERICKS COMPANY INC
2400 Philmont Ave (19006-6286)
P.O. Box 67 (19006-0067)
PHONE...................................215 947-2500
Heidi Jmckenna, *President*
Andrew Orr, *COO*
William Johnson, *Vice Pres*
Heidi McKenna, *Opers Mgr*
Brian Vierick, *Opers Staff*
EMP: 50 EST: 1935
SQ FT: 32,000
SALES (est): 9MM **Privately Held**
WEB: www.frederickscom.com
SIC: 3231 3823 Products of purchased
glass; industrial instrmnts msrmnt dis-
play/control process variable

(G-7986)
**FUEL TREATMENT SOLUTIONS
LLC**
48 Lee Lynn Ln (19006-7960)
PHONE...................................215 914-1006
Mitchell Ditnes, *Principal*
EMP: 3
SALES (est): 159.2K **Privately Held**
SIC: 2869 Fuels

(G-7987)
G ADASAVAGE LLC
Also Called: Gma Manufacturing
110 Pike Cir (19006-1615)
PHONE...................................215 355-3105
Gerald Adasavage,
EMP: 21
SQ FT: 27,500
SALES (est): 933.3K **Privately Held**
SIC: 3465 3469 3544 3769 Automotive
stampings; metal stampings; special dies,
tools, jigs & fixtures; airframe assemblies,
guided missiles; motor vehicle body com-
ponents & frame

(G-7988)
GAIA ENTERPRISES INC
Also Called: Safe Paw
103 Roy Ln (19006-3119)
P.O. Box 220, Southampton (18966-0220)
PHONE...................................800 783-7841
Steven Greenwald, *CEO*
Steven Vernik, *Director*
EMP: 10
SQ FT: 3,000
SALES (est): 21MM **Privately Held**
SIC: 2097 Manufactured ice

(G-7989)
**GERMANTOWN TOOL MACHINE
SP INC**
Also Called: Germantown Tool & Mfg
1681 Republic Rd (19006-1899)
PHONE...................................215 322-4970
Jeffrey E Perelman, *President*
John Scott, *Vice Pres*
Vickie I Waitsman, *Admin Sec*
EMP: 40 EST: 2010
SALES (est): 5.8MM **Privately Held**
SIC: 3499 Strapping, metal

(G-7990)
GMA MANUFACTURING INC
110 Pike Cir (19006-1615)
PHONE...................................215 355-3105
Gerald Adasavage, *President*
Martin Adasavage, *Vice Pres*
Thomas Lloyd, *Treasurer*
EMP: 10
SQ FT: 18,500
SALES (est): 1.3MM **Privately Held**
SIC: 3544 Special dies & tools

(G-7991)
GMA TOOLING COMPANY
110 Pike Cir (19006-1688)
PHONE...................................215 355-3107
Gerald Adasavage, *President*
Martin Adasavage, *Treasurer*
EMP: 35
SQ FT: 26,200
SALES (est): 5.9MM **Privately Held**
WEB: www.gmamanufacturing.com
SIC: 3544 3469 Special dies & tools;
metal stampings

(G-7992)
GRIFFITH INC (DH)
Also Called: Alpha Systems
458 Pike Rd (19006-1610)
PHONE...................................215 322-8100
Brett Griffith, *President*
Richard Tetzner, *Production*
Scott Griffith, *Treasurer*
Barbara Baldwin, *Admin Sec*
EMP: 200 EST: 1977
SQ FT: 150,000
SALES (est): 28.7MM
SALES (corp-wide): 14.8B **Publicly Held**
WEB: www.alpha-sys.com
SIC: 7389 7379 3861 3577 Microfilm
recording & developing service; disk &
diskette conversion service; photographic
equipment & supplies; computer periph-
eral equipment; computer storage devices
HQ: Databank Imx Llc
620 Freedom Business Ctr
King Of Prussia PA 19406
610 233-0251

(G-7993)
**H AND K TOOL AND MCH CO
INC**
125 Pike Cir (19006-1614)
PHONE...................................215 322-0380
Stanley F Elias Sr, *President*
Stanley Elias Jr, *Vice Pres*
EMP: 42
SQ FT: 28,000
SALES: 8.5MM **Privately Held**
SIC: 3544 3599 Special dies & tools; ma-
chine shop, jobbing & repair

(G-7994)
HOUND DOG CORP
Also Called: Alessandro Working Dog
1612 Bonnie Brae Dr (19006-1304)
PHONE...................................215 355-6424
George Alessandro, *President*
EMP: 8 EST: 1995
SALES (est): 963.8K **Privately Held**
WEB: www.alessandro-products.com
SIC: 3679 Electronic circuits

(G-7995)
**HYDRA-MATIC PACKING CO INC
(PA)**
Also Called: Fabrics For Industry Division
2992 Franks Rd (19006-4283)
P.O. Box 96 (19006-0096)
PHONE...................................215 676-2992
Mark C McKenna, *President*
Gerald McKenna, *Vice Pres*
Joseph T McKenna, *Treasurer*
Kathleen Tressel, *Info Tech Mgr*
▲ EMP: 40 EST: 1945
SQ FT: 75,000
SALES (est): 71.1MM **Privately Held**
WEB: www.hmpffi.com
SIC: 5033 3564 2821 Fiberglass building
materials; insulation, thermal; blowers &
fans; plastics materials & resins

(G-7996)
IMPERIAL TOOL CO
78 Tomlinson Rd Ste E (19006-4244)
PHONE...................................215 947-7650
Steve Magiera, *Owner*
EMP: 5
SQ FT: 1,000
SALES (est): 473.9K **Privately Held**
SIC: 2821 3544 Molding compounds,
plastics; forms (molds), for foundry &
plastics working machinery

(G-7997)
INSTANT RESPONSE INC
111 Buck Rd Unit 600 (19006-1545)
PHONE...................................215 322-1271
Stan Karmazin, *President*
EMP: 5
SALES (est): 290.9K **Privately Held**
SIC: 2752 Commercial printing, litho-
graphic

(G-7998)
J M T MACHINE COMPANY
2115 Byberry Rd (19006-3503)
PHONE...................................215 934-7600
Julius Kamper, *President*
Edwin G Boom, *President*
Thomas Lengyel, *Vice Pres*
EMP: 20 EST: 1960
SQ FT: 25,000
SALES (est): 4.2MM **Privately Held**
WEB: www.jmtmachine.com
SIC: 3599 7692 Machine shop, jobbing &
repair; welding repair

(G-7999)
**JADE EQUIPMENT
CORPORATION (HQ)**
3063 Philmont Ave (19006-4243)
PHONE...................................215 947-3333
Brian T Manley, *President*
Ric Ross, *President*
Charlie Slayton, *Opers Mgr*
Pat Gill, *Safety Mgr*
Dave Gallagher, *Engineer*
▲ EMP: 160
SQ FT: 61,000
SALES (est): 68.1MM **Privately Held**
WEB: www.jadecorp.com
SIC: 3545 3599 3469 3544 Machine tool
accessories; machine & other job shop
work; metal stampings; special dies,
tools, jigs & fixtures

(G-8000)
JADE HOLDINGS INC
3063a Philmont Ave (19006-4243)
PHONE...................................215 947-3333
Joseph P McPartland, *Ch of Bd*
Tom Jubb, *Vice Pres*
▼ EMP: 245 EST: 1947
SQ FT: 61,000
SALES (est): 19.7MM **Privately Held**
SIC: 3545 3599 3469 Precision tools, ma-
chinists'; custom machinery; stamping
metal for the trade
HQ: Jacuzzi Brands Llc
13925 City Center Dr # 200
Chino Hills CA 91709
909 606-1416

(G-8001)
**JADE PRCSION MED
CMPONENTS LLC**
3063 Philmont Ave (19006-4243)
PHONE...................................215 947-5762
Amy L Blaker, *Purch Mgr*
Mark Bucciarelli, *Engineer*
Robert Jeral, *Engineer*
Joshua Luther, *Engineer*
Dan Rassier, *Engineer*
EMP: 5 EST: 2012
SALES (est): 1.2MM **Privately Held**
SIC: 3841 Surgical & medical instruments;
surgical appliances & supplies

(G-8002)
JAN-STIX LLC
2346 Fairway Rd (19006-5633)
PHONE...................................267 918-9561
Edward Marshall, *Mng Member*
EMP: 4

SALES (est): 259.4K **Privately Held**
SIC: 3089 Plastic kitchenware, tableware &
houseware

(G-8003)
JDM MATERIALS (PA)
Also Called: J D M
851 County Line Rd (19006-1111)
P.O. Box 217, Southampton (18966-0217)
PHONE...................................215 357-5505
James D Morrissey Jr, *President*
Jim Morrissey III, *Vice Pres*
Scott Barcusky, *Asst Treas*
Mary F Morrissey, *Admin Sec*
EMP: 50 EST: 1954
SQ FT: 6,000
SALES (est): 18.1MM **Privately Held**
SIC: 3273 Ready-mixed concrete

(G-8004)
**JERRY LISTER CUSTOM
UPHOLSTERI**
111 Buck Rd Unit 900 (19006-1556)
PHONE...................................215 639-3882
Dennis Lister, *Manager*
EMP: 11
SALES (corp-wide): 1.8MM **Privately
Held**
SIC: 2512 7641 2591 Upholstered house-
hold furniture; reupholstery; window
blinds
PA: Jerry Lister Custom Upholstering, Inc.
2075 Byberry Rd Ste 108
Bensalem PA 19020
215 639-3880

(G-8005)
JOHN E STILES JR
Also Called: Optical Guidance Systems
2450a Huntingdon Pike (19006-6112)
PHONE...................................215 947-5571
John E Stiles Jr, *Owner*
EMP: 4
SQ FT: 4,102
SALES: 350K **Privately Held**
WEB: www.opticalguidancesystems.com
SIC: 3827 Telescopes: elbow, panoramic,
sighting, fire control, etc.

(G-8006)
K V INC
1458 County Line Rd Ste B (19006-1884)
PHONE...................................215 322-4044
Eric Wilhelm, *President*
Raymond Lemond, *Managing Dir*
Karl Wilhelm, *Vice Pres*
EMP: 18
SQ FT: 7,000
SALES (est): 3.8MM **Privately Held**
WEB: www.kv-inc.com
SIC: 3544 Special dies & tools

(G-8007)
KHS CORP
2693 Philmont Ave Rear (19006-5324)
PHONE...................................215 947-4010
Katharina Schwemlein, *President*
Karl Schwemlein, *General Mgr*
William Schwemlein, *Controller*
Hans Schwemlein, *Director*
EMP: 35 EST: 1962
SQ FT: 69,000
SALES: 5.8MM **Privately Held**
WEB: www.khscorp.com
SIC: 3599 Machine shop, jobbing & repair

(G-8008)
LEADING EDGE TOOLING INC
1840 County Line Rd # 103 (19006-1718)
PHONE...................................215 953-9717
Frank Leather, *President*
Cherie Leather, *Vice Pres*
EMP: 3
SQ FT: 1,800
SALES: 300K **Privately Held**
SIC: 3599 Machine shop, jobbing & repair

(G-8009)
LRT SENSORS INC
71 Sunflower Way (19006-5450)
PHONE...................................877 299-8595
Leonard Goldman, *Manager*
EMP: 3 EST: 2010
SALES (est): 209.4K **Privately Held**
SIC: 3677 Electronic coils, transformers &
other inductors

(G-8010)
MAL-BER MANUFACTURING COMPANY
2115 Byberry Rd (19006-3503)
PHONE..................................215 672-6440
Ken Sanford, *Vice Pres*
EMP: 25
SALES (corp-wide): 6.7MM Privately Held
SIC: 3544 Special dies & tools
PA: Mal-Ber Manufacturing Company Inc
830 Pennsylvania Blvd
Feasterville Trevose PA
215 672-6440

(G-8011)
MANNCORP INC (PA)
1610 Republic Rd (19006-1808)
PHONE..................................215 830-1200
Henry Mann, *President*
Jeff Mann, *VP Sales*
Chris Ellis, *Sales Mgr*
Sabino De La O, *Sales Staff*
Tom Becklis, *Mktg Dir*
▲ EMP: 14
SQ FT: 18,000
SALES (est): 3.7MM Privately Held
WEB: www.manncorp.com
SIC: 3672 Printed circuit boards

(G-8012)
MEDIA ADVANTAGE INC
3741 Ridgeview Rd (19006-3317)
PHONE..................................800 985-5596
Adriane Thomson, *President*
EMP: 5
SQ FT: 2,000
SALES: 800K Privately Held
SIC: 3993 Signs & advertising specialties

(G-8013)
METCO MANUFACTURING CO INC (PA)
3035 Franks Rd (19006-4216)
P.O. Box 375, Holicong (18928-0375)
PHONE..................................215 518-7400
Bruce Kanter, *President*
EMP: 50
SQ FT: 50,000
SALES (est): 4.3MM Privately Held
SIC: 3544 8711 Special dies, tools, jigs & fixtures; engineering services

(G-8014)
MULTI-FLOW DISPENSERS LP (PA)
Also Called: Gottlieb & Gottlieb
1434 County Line Rd (19006-1801)
PHONE..................................215 322-1800
Bernard Gottlieb, *Partner*
Bryan Gottlieb, *Partner*
▼ EMP: 90 EST: 1964
SQ FT: 7,000
SALES (est): 20.7MM Privately Held
SIC: 3585 5078 7359 Soda fountains, parts & accessories; soda fountain equipment, refrigerated; equipment rental & leasing

(G-8015)
MULTI-FLOW INDUSTRIES LLC (HQ)
1434 County Line Rd (19006-1801)
PHONE..................................215 322-1800
Ken Schnarrs, *CEO*
Jim Pando, *Controller*
EMP: 200
SALES (est): 2.1MM
SALES (corp-wide): 237.7MM Privately Held
SIC: 2087 Beverage bases, concentrates, syrups, powders & mixes
PA: Falconhead Capital, Llc
680 5th Ave Fl 21
New York NY 10019
212 634-3304

(G-8016)
NATIONAL BASIC SENSOR CORP
455 Veit Rd (19006-1617)
PHONE..................................215 322-4700
Daniel McHugh, *President*
Virginia Smith, *Vice Pres*

Bob Mazzei, *Opers Staff*
Steve Long, *Sales Staff*
Howard Dutton, *Manager*
EMP: 13
SQ FT: 8,500
SALES (est): 3MM Privately Held
WEB: www.nationalbasicsensor.com
SIC: 3829 Thermocouples

(G-8017)
NEWTOWN BUSINESS FORMS CORP
Also Called: Cutpasteandprint
1908 County Line Rd (19006-1738)
PHONE..................................215 364-3898
Laurence N Weiss, *CEO*
Jennifer McQuiggan, *Bookkeeper*
EMP: 11 EST: 1969
SQ FT: 3,000
SALES (est): 1.2MM
SALES (corp-wide): 30.6MM Privately Held
SIC: 2752 2741 Commercial printing, off-set; art copy: publishing & printing
PA: Composing Room, Inc.
2001 Market St Ste 2500
Philadelphia PA 19103
215 310-5559

(G-8018)
NORTHERN IRON WORKS INC
Also Called: N I W
2955 Franks Rd (19006-4214)
P.O. Box 1208 (19006-7208)
PHONE..................................215 947-1867
Karl F Zoller, *President*
Nicholas J Zoller, *Corp Secy*
EMP: 12 EST: 1939
SQ FT: 8,000
SALES (est): 2MM Privately Held
WEB: www.niw.com
SIC: 3446 Gratings, open steel flooring; railings, bannisters, guards, etc.: made from metal pipe

(G-8019)
ORION SYSTEMS INC
1800 Byberry Rd Ste 1300 (19006-3525)
PHONE..................................215 346-8200
Frank J Affeldt, *President*
Richard Moors, *Corp Secy*
EMP: 40 EST: 1977
SQ FT: 16,000
SALES: 4MM Privately Held
SIC: 3669 3643 Intercommunication systems, electric; current-carrying wiring devices

(G-8020)
P & M PRECISION MACHINING INC
65 Buck Rd (19006-1501)
PHONE..................................215 357-3313
Paul J Lips, *President*
Matthew Lips, *Vice Pres*
EMP: 8
SQ FT: 7,000
SALES (est): 950.7K Privately Held
SIC: 3599 3451 Machine shop, jobbing & repair; screw machine products

(G-8021)
PB HOLDINGS INC (PA)
Also Called: Jade
3063 Philmont Ave (19006-4243)
PHONE..................................215 947-3333
Robert D Avritt, *President*
John Carlin, *Production*
Frank Shilkitus, *Engineer*
James Szanajda, *Engineer*
Susan Pappas, *Human Res Mgr*
EMP: 2
SQ FT: 61,000
SALES (est): 68.1MM Privately Held
SIC: 3545 3599 3469 Machine tool accessories; machine & other job shop work; metal stampings

(G-8022)
PENN PROTECTIVE COATINGS CORP
470 Veit Rd B (19006-1616)
PHONE..................................215 355-0708
Joseph W Krzaczek, *President*
Brenda H Krzaczek, *Corp Secy*

EMP: 10
SALES (est): 1.3MM Privately Held
SIC: 3479 Coating of metals & formed products

(G-8023)
PENNSYLVANIA STAIR LIFTS INC
2727 Philmont Ave Ste 310 (19006-5313)
PHONE..................................215 914-0800
Brian D Klein, *President*
EMP: 6
SALES (est): 861.1K Privately Held
SIC: 3446 Stairs, staircases, stair treads: prefabricated metal

(G-8024)
PETERS EQUIPMENT CORP
65 Buck Rd (19006-1501)
PHONE..................................215 364-9147
Peter Melville, *President*
EMP: 3
SQ FT: 5,000
SALES (est): 453K Privately Held
SIC: 5084 3565 Packaging machinery & equipment; packaging machinery

(G-8025)
PHILAPACK LLC
1840 County Line Rd (19006-1717)
PHONE..................................215 322-2122
Steve Nipe,
EMP: 4
SALES (est): 114.4K Privately Held
SIC: 3592 Valves, engine

(G-8026)
PLAN B CONSULTANTS LLC
Also Called: Plan B Engineering
475 Veit Rd (19006-1617)
PHONE..................................215 638-0767
John McErlean, *Principal*
Kathy Jones, *Manager*
EMP: 3
SQ FT: 1,000
SALES (est): 610.6K Privately Held
SIC: 3694 Engine electrical equipment

(G-8027)
PRINTED INK LLC
1840 County Line Rd # 301 (19006-1717)
PHONE..................................215 355-1683
Jonathan Merenlender, *Mng Member*
EMP: 6
SALES (est): 380K Privately Held
SIC: 2893 Printing ink

(G-8028)
R M S GRAPHICS INC
1601 Republic Rd Ste 100 (19006-1809)
PHONE..................................215 322-6000
Ronald Trichon, *CEO*
Stephen Robert Bianco, *Vice Pres*
Michael Mark Kalick, *Treasurer*
EMP: 9
SQ FT: 4,500
SALES (est): 1.5MM Privately Held
WEB: www.rmsgraphics.com
SIC: 2752 Commercial printing, lithographic

(G-8029)
RFCIRCUITS INC
1840 County Line Rd # 207 (19006-1717)
PHONE..................................215 364-2450
Pavel Borukhovich, *CEO*
Michael Belaga, *Vice Pres*
Boris Gmiryansky, *Vice Pres*
EMP: 15
SQ FT: 10,000
SALES (est): 2.8MM Privately Held
WEB: www.rfcircuits.com
SIC: 8711 3825 3429 3496 Engineering services; microwave test equipment; harness hardware; miscellaneous fabricated wire products; wiring boards; electrical equipment & supplies

(G-8030)
ROYCO PACKAGING INC
3979 Mann Rd (19006-1805)
PHONE..................................215 322-8082
Roy Vernik, *President*
EMP: 8
SQ FT: 10,000

SALES (est): 1.7MM Privately Held
SIC: 2673 Plastic bags: made from purchased materials

(G-8031)
RUSSELL RIBBON & TRIM CO
1100 Jefferson Ln (19006-6037)
PHONE..................................215 938-8550
Howard Lederer, *President*
EMP: 5
SALES (est): 458.3K Privately Held
SIC: 2241 Narrow fabric mills

(G-8032)
RUUD KAHLE MASTER GOLDSMITH
Also Called: Kahle Ruud
2535 Huntingdon Pike (19006-6133)
PHONE..................................215 947-5050
Ruud Kahle, *President*
Susan Kahle, *Admin Sec*
EMP: 10 EST: 1959
SQ FT: 3,000
SALES (est): 894.2K Privately Held
WEB: www.dwave.com
SIC: 3911 Jewelry, precious metal

(G-8033)
S & H HARDWARE & SUPPLY CO
Also Called: S H Bath
2146-2150 County Line Rd (19006)
PHONE..................................267 288-5950
Stuart Stern, *President*
EMP: 3
SALES (corp-wide): 5.3MM Privately Held
SIC: 5251 5072 3993 Hardware; hardware; signs & advertising specialties
PA: S & H Hardware & Supply Co
6700 Castor Ave
Philadelphia PA 19149
215 745-9375

(G-8034)
SAFEWARE INC
Also Called: Safeware Willow Grove
1601 Republic Rd Ste 105 (19006-1809)
PHONE..................................215 354-1401
Edward Simmons, *President*
EMP: 6
SALES (corp-wide): 75.9MM Privately Held
WEB: www.safeware.com
SIC: 3842 Personal safety equipment
PA: Safeware, Inc.
4403 Forbes Blvd
Lanham MD 20706
301 683-1234

(G-8035)
SCHILLER GROUNDS CARE INC
Also Called: Germantown Tool and Machine
1681 Republic Rd (19006-1807)
PHONE..................................215 322-4970
Greg Sheets, *Branch Mgr*
EMP: 55
SQ FT: 35,000
SALES (corp-wide): 37.7MM Privately Held
WEB: www.littlewonder.com
SIC: 3524 3544 3469 3444 Lawn & garden equipment; special dies, tools, jigs & fixtures; metal stampings; sheet metalwork
PA: Schiller Grounds Care, Inc.
1028 Street Rd
Southampton PA 18966
215 357-5110

(G-8036)
SEA GROUP GRAPHICS INC
1590 Huntingdon Rd (19006-4415)
PHONE..................................215 805-0290
Mindy Mikulik, *President*
William Mikulik, *Principal*
Ken Dinich, *Vice Pres*
EMP: 3
SALES (est): 335.7K Privately Held
SIC: 2759 2731 Advertising literature: printing; pamphlets: publishing & printing

(G-8037)
SETT
1633 Republic Rd (19006-1807)
PHONE..................................215 322-9301
Ilan Shemesh,

▲ **EMP:** 5
SALES (est): 437.1K **Privately Held**
WEB: www.getreadygetsett.com
SIC: 2514 Medicine cabinets & vanities: metal

(G-8038)
SEYBERT CASTINGS INC
1840 County Line Rd # 108 (19006-1718)
PHONE.................................215 364-7115
Marc Roloff, *General Mgr*
Arlene Seybert, *Principal*
EMP: 10
SQ FT: 2,400
SALES (est): 1.3MM **Privately Held**
WEB: www.seybertcastings.com
SIC: 3369 3089 Castings, except die-castings, precision; casting of plastic

(G-8039)
SPORT MANUFACTURING GROUP INC
Also Called: Steel Will
1840 County Line Rd # 111 (19006-1717)
PHONE.................................718 575-1801
Diana Alperovich, *President*
▲ **EMP:** 5 **EST:** 2010
SQ FT: 2,400
SALES (est): 1.2MM **Privately Held**
SIC: 5091 3949 Sporting & recreation goods; sporting & athletic goods

(G-8040)
STATE OF ART PROSTHETICS
Also Called: Apelsteim, James
2910 Franks Rd Ste 2 (19006-4253)
PHONE.................................215 914-1222
James Apelsteim, *Owner*
EMP: 6
SALES (est): 222.2K **Privately Held**
SIC: 3842 Prosthetic appliances

(G-8041)
STRAUSS ENGINEERING COMPANY
Also Called: Strauss Eng Co
80 Tracey Rd (19006-4222)
PHONE.................................215 947-1083
Richard W Strauss, *President*
Manfred P Schurer, *Admin Sec*
EMP: 55
SQ FT: 72,000
SALES (est): 10.3MM **Privately Held**
WEB: www.straussengineering.com
SIC: 3089 Molding primary plastic

(G-8042)
SYNCOM SPECIALTY INC
110 Pike Cir (19006-1615)
PHONE.................................215 322-9708
John A Baurer Jr, *Manager*
EMP: 25
SALES (corp-wide): 1.9MM **Privately Held**
WEB: www.syncomspecialties.com
SIC: 3599 Machine shop, jobbing & repair
PA: Syncom Specialty Inc
16 Arbor Rd
Southampton PA 18966
215 322-9708

(G-8043)
TCG DOCUMENT SOLUTIONS LLC (PA)
447 Veit Rd (19006-1617)
PHONE.................................215 957-0600
Dorothea Chambers,
EMP: 10 **EST:** 2013
SALES (est): 3.1MM **Privately Held**
SIC: 2752 Commercial printing, lithographic

(G-8044)
TRI-STATE EVENTS MAGAZINE INC
Also Called: Mid-Atlantic Events Magazine
1800 Byberry Rd Ste 901 (19006-3521)
PHONE.................................215 947-8600
James Cohn, *President*
EMP: 6
SQ FT: 4,500
SALES (est): 655.6K **Privately Held**
SIC: 2721 Magazines: publishing & printing

(G-8045)
TRIUNE COLOR CORPORATION
1625 Terwood Rd (19006-5702)
PHONE.................................856 829-5600
William R James, *President*
EMP: 72 **EST:** 1976
SQ FT: 53,274
SALES (est): 7.3MM **Privately Held**
WEB: www.triunecolor.com
SIC: 2752 Offset & photolithographic printing; commercial printing, offset

(G-8046)
UNITED PRECISION MFG CO INC
85 Tomlinson Rd (19006-4256)
PHONE.................................215 938-5890
Shaji Mathai, *President*
Manilal Mathai, *Admin Sec*
EMP: 3
SQ FT: 4,000
SALES: 250K **Privately Held**
SIC: 3599 Machine shop, jobbing & repair

Hyde
Clearfield County

(G-8047)
MARTELL SALES & SERVICE INC
Also Called: Martell Sales and Services
1509 Washington Ave (16843)
P.O. Box 409 (16843-0409)
PHONE.................................814 765-6557
Marc A Martell, *President*
Gregory O Martell, *Vice Pres*
▲ **EMP:** 48 **EST:** 1957
SQ FT: 160,000
SALES (est): 6.3MM **Privately Held**
SIC: 3231 Products of purchased glass

Hyndman
Bedford County

(G-8048)
CL LOGGING INC
4255 Hyndman Rd (15545-8242)
PHONE.................................814 842-3725
Calvin Leydig, *Treasurer*
EMP: 3
SALES (est): 151.1K **Privately Held**
SIC: 2411 Logging

(G-8049)
EMERICKS MAPLE PRODUCTS
156 Ridge Rd (15545-8506)
PHONE.................................814 324-4536
Wilma Emerick, *Owner*
EMP: 3
SALES (est): 130K **Privately Held**
WEB: www.emericksmaple.com
SIC: 2087 Flavoring extracts & syrups

(G-8050)
EMERICKS MEAT & PACKING CO
552 Hyndman Rd (15545-7446)
PHONE.................................814 842-6779
David Emerick, *President*
Ronald Emerick, *Vice Pres*
Kenneth Emerick, *Treasurer*
Jeffrey Emerick, *Admin Sec*
EMP: 20
SALES (est): 1.2MM **Privately Held**
SIC: 2011 5421 5147 Meat packing plants; meat markets, including freezer provisioners; meats, fresh

(G-8051)
SHAFFER BROTHERS LUMBER CO
5927 Kennells Mill Rd (15545-7615)
PHONE.................................814 842-3996
John H Shaffer, *Partner*
James H Shaffer, *Partner*
EMP: 5
SALES (est): 476.5K **Privately Held**
SIC: 2421 5211 Sawmills & planing mills, general; planing mill products & lumber

Ickesburg
Perry County

(G-8052)
JUSTIN L ZEHR
Also Called: J L Logging
68 Reisinger Rd (17037-9530)
PHONE.................................717 582-6436
Justin L Zehr, *Principal*
EMP: 3
SALES (est): 300.5K **Privately Held**
SIC: 2411 Logging

(G-8053)
SUPERIOR PALLET LLC
1616 Valentine Rd (17037-9575)
PHONE.................................717 789-9525
John D Fisher,
EMP: 8
SALES (est): 560K **Privately Held**
SIC: 2448 Pallets, wood & wood with metal

Imler
Bedford County

(G-8054)
CORLE BUILDING SYSTEMS INC
404 Sarah Furnace Rd (16655-8438)
PHONE.................................814 276-9611
John J Corle, *President*
Kevin Ziance, *Corp Secy*
Frank Kmetz, *Vice Pres*
John Kmetz, *Manager*
EMP: 256
SQ FT: 185,000
SALES: 70MM **Privately Held**
WEB: www.corle.com
SIC: 3448 Prefabricated metal buildings

(G-8055)
CORLES PRINTING
210 Sound Ln (16655-8650)
P.O. Box 410 (16655-0410)
PHONE.................................814 276-3775
Theresa Coral, *Owner*
EMP: 3
SALES (est): 176K **Privately Held**
SIC: 2752 Commercial printing, offset

Imperial
Allegheny County

(G-8056)
ACCENT SHOP
161 Main St (15126-1018)
PHONE.................................724 695-7580
EMP: 3
SALES (est): 200K **Privately Held**
SIC: 5199 3944 Mfg And Ret Plaster Crafts

(G-8057)
ALLEGHENY METAL FINISHING
8150 Steubenville Pike (15126-9119)
PHONE.................................724 695-3233
Gary A Cruise, *Owner*
Jason Cruise, *Manager*
EMP: 8
SQ FT: 6,000
SALES (est): 782.2K **Privately Held**
SIC: 3471 Finishing, metals or formed products

(G-8058)
ASK IV SCREEN PRINTING
7900 Steubenville Pike (15126-9139)
PHONE.................................412 200-5610
Michael J Rusnock, *Principal*
EMP: 3 **EST:** 2012
SALES (est): 226.3K **Privately Held**
SIC: 2759 Commercial printing

(G-8059)
BAKER HGHES OLFLD OPRTIONS LLC
400 Bakeman (15126)
PHONE.................................724 695-2266
Bill Debo, *Manager*
EMP: 3
SALES (corp-wide): 121.6B **Publicly Held**
WEB: www.bot.bhi-net.com
SIC: 1389 Oil field services
HQ: Baker Hughes Oilfield Operations Llc
17021 Aldine Westfield Rd
Houston TX 77073
713 879-1000

(G-8060)
CHILL FROZEN DESSERTS
420 Penn Lincoln Dr (15126-9781)
PHONE.................................724 695-8855
EMP: 3
SALES (est): 129.9K **Privately Held**
SIC: 2024 Ice cream & frozen desserts

(G-8061)
CRYOCAL
767 Route 30 (15126-1221)
PHONE.................................714 568-0201
EMP: 3
SALES (est): 278.9K **Privately Held**
SIC: 3559 Special industry machinery

(G-8062)
CRYOGNIC INDS SVC CMPANIES LLC
767 State Route 30 (15126-1221)
PHONE.................................724 695-1910
EMP: 3
SALES (est): 97.8K **Privately Held**
SIC: 3443 Cryogenic tanks, for liquids & gases

(G-8063)
DARLING INGREDIENTS INC
Also Called: Torvac
3173 Potato Garden Run Rd (15126-2167)
PHONE.................................724 695-1212
Sam Leonard, *Manager*
EMP: 17
SALES (corp-wide): 3.3B **Publicly Held**
WEB: www.darlingii.com
SIC: 2077 Grease rendering, inedible; tallow rendering, inedible
PA: Darling Ingredients Inc.
251 Oconnor Ridge Blvd
Irving TX 75038
972 717-0300

(G-8064)
DUERR PACKAGING COMPANY INC
8152 Steubenville Pike (15126-9119)
PHONE.................................724 695-2226
David Lafferty, *Manager*
EMP: 30
SALES (est): 2.6MM
SALES (corp-wide): 9MM **Privately Held**
WEB: www.duerrpack.com
SIC: 3086 2653 2657 2652 Packaging & shipping materials, foamed plastic; boxes, corrugated: made from purchased materials; folding paperboard boxes; setup paperboard boxes
PA: Duerr Packaging Company, Inc.
892 Steubenville Pike
Burgettstown PA 15021
724 947-1234

(G-8065)
GENERAL ELECTRIC COMPANY
101 N Campus Dr (15126-2402)
PHONE.................................646 682-5601
Jennifer Cipolla, *Manager*
EMP: 8
SALES (corp-wide): 121.6B **Publicly Held**
SIC: 3313 Alloys, additive, except copper: not made in blast furnaces
PA: General Electric Company
41 Farnsworth St
Boston MA 02210
617 443-3000

(G-8066)
GLAXOSMITHKLINE LLC
1207 Balsam Dr (15126-1167)
PHONE..............................412 726-6041
EMP: 26
SALES (corp-wide): 39.8B **Privately Held**
SIC: 2834 Pharmaceutical preparations
HQ: Glaxosmithkline Llc
5 Crescent Dr
Philadelphia PA 19112
215 751-4000

(G-8067)
IMPERIAL TRUCK BODY & EQP
934 Santiago Rd (15126-9603)
PHONE..............................724 695-3165
Alfred D Marzzarella Jr, *President*
Bea Kisow, *Vice Pres*
Annette Gross, *Admin Sec*
EMP: 17 EST: 1960
SQ FT: 8,500
SALES (est): 3.6MM **Privately Held**
SIC: 3713 Truck bodies (motor vehicles)

(G-8068)
INTERMEC TECHNOLOGIES CORP
237 Roanoke Way (15126-9314)
PHONE..............................724 218-1444
Debbie Tennant, *Manager*
EMP: 15
SALES (corp-wide): 41.8B **Publicly Held**
WEB: www.intermec.net
SIC: 3577 Printers, computer
HQ: Intermec Technologies Corporation
16201 25th Ave W
Lynnwood WA 98087
425 348-2600

(G-8069)
J&R CAD ENTERPRISE LLC
400 Chelsea Dr (15126-9294)
PHONE..............................724 695-4279
Robert M McArdle, *Principal*
EMP: 4
SALES (est): 366.6K **Privately Held**
SIC: 3567 Industrial furnaces & ovens

(G-8070)
LPW TECHNOLOGY INC
110 S Campus Dr (15126-2401)
PHONE..............................844 480-7663
Phil Carroll, *President*
John Hunter, *General Mgr*
EMP: 10
SQ FT: 3,000
SALES: 1MM
SALES (corp-wide): 222K **Privately Held**
SIC: 3499 Friction material, made from
powdered metal
HQ: L.P.W. Technology Limited
Dennis Road,
Widnes WA8 0

(G-8071)
MANCE PLATING CO
255 Main St (15126-1068)
PHONE..............................724 695-0550
Thomas Mance, *Managing Prtnr*
Matthew Mance, *Partner*
Michael Mance, *Partner*
EMP: 3 EST: 1953
SALES: 150K **Privately Held**
SIC: 3471 Plating of metals or formed
products

(G-8072)
MARONDA SYSTEMS INC FLORIDA (HQ)
11 Timberglen Dr (15126-9267)
PHONE..............................724 695-1200
William J Wolf, *President*
Samuel L Katanich, *Vice Pres*
Ronald Wolf, *Admin Sec*
Kelly Campbell, *Asst Sec*
EMP: 2
SALES (est): 41.1MM
SALES (corp-wide): 171.8MM **Privately Held**
SIC: 2439 Trusses, wooden roof
PA: Maronda, Inc.
11 Timberglen Dr
Imperial PA 15126
724 695-1200

(G-8073)
MOLECULAR FINISHING SYSTEMS
1270 Mccaslin Rd (15126-2217)
PHONE..............................724 695-0554
Diane Maffei, *President*
Michael Maffei, *Vice Pres*
EMP: 8
SQ FT: 17,000
SALES: 378K **Privately Held**
SIC: 3471 5085 Finishing, metals or
formed products; fasteners, industrial:
nuts, bolts, screws, etc.

(G-8074)
PENNSYLVANIA DRILLING COMPANY (PA)
Also Called: Penn Drill Manufacturing
281 Route 30 (15126-1240)
PHONE..............................412 771-2110
T B Sturges III, *CEO*
J R Dravenstott, *Vice Pres*
R R Sands, *Treasurer*
R R Kennedy, *Admin Sec*
▲ EMP: 40 EST: 1900
SQ FT: 50,000
SALES (est): 15.6MM **Privately Held**
WEB: www.pennsylvaniadrillingco.com
SIC: 1623 1799 3532 Pipe laying con-
struction; boring for building construction;
drills, core

(G-8075)
RACEWAY BEVERAGE CENTER
1242 Route 30 (15126)
PHONE..............................724 695-3130
David Kyle, *Principal*
EMP: 9
SALES (est): 923.3K **Privately Held**
SIC: 5181 3644 Beer & ale; raceways

(G-8076)
SPEEDBEAR FASTENERS
103 Enlow Rd (15126-1311)
PHONE..............................724 695-3696
Ed Novak, *Owner*
▲ EMP: 6
SALES (est): 330K **Privately Held**
WEB: www.speedbear.net
SIC: 3452 Rivets, metal

(G-8077)
THERMO-ELECTRIC CO
549 Route 30 (15126-1060)
PHONE..............................724 695-2774
Mark E Madson, *President*
Martha Madson, *Corp Secy*
▲ EMP: 3 EST: 1924
SQ FT: 4,500
SALES (est): 603.2K **Privately Held**
SIC: 3826 3841 Analytical instruments;
surgical & medical instruments

(G-8078)
THRU TUBING SOLUTIONS INC
100 S Campus Dr (15126-2401)
PHONE..............................412 787-8060
Frank Stapp, *Principal*
Jeremiah Rodriguez, *Manager*
EMP: 4
SALES (corp-wide): 1.7B **Publicly Held**
SIC: 1389 Oil field services
HQ: Thru Tubing Solutions, Inc.
11515 S Portland Ave
Oklahoma City OK 73170
405 692-1900

Indiana
Indiana County

(G-8079)
AMERICAN CONSERVATORY CO INC
1380 Wayne Ave (15701-3544)
PHONE..............................724 465-1800
Wayne C Gorell, *President*
Arnold Levitt, *CFO*
EMP: 10
SALES (est): 13.2MM **Privately Held**
SIC: 3448 Prefabricated metal buildings

PA: Gorell Enterprises, Inc.
10250 Philipp Pkwy
Streetsboro OH 44241

(G-8080)
ARCHROCK INC
488 Geesey Rd (15701-8910)
PHONE..............................724 464-2291
Joseph Moffa, *Manager*
EMP: 48 **Publicly Held**
SIC: 1389 4225 Gas compressing (natural
gas) at the fields; general warehousing
PA: Archrock Inc.
9807 Katy Fwy Ste 100
Houston TX 77024

(G-8081)
ARCTIC BLAST COVERS
1434 Florence Ave (15701-3239)
PHONE..............................724 213-8460
Dale Conrath, *President*
EMP: 20
SALES (est): 986K **Privately Held**
SIC: 3086 Insulation or cushioning mate-
rial, foamed plastic

(G-8082)
ARDIEM MEDICAL INC
1380 Route 286 Hwy E (15701-1461)
PHONE..............................724 349-0855
James Cupp, *President*
David McMurry, *President*
Nancy Saxman, *Vice Pres*
Barb Reel, *QC Mgr*
Christi Park, *Electrical Engi*
EMP: 12
SQ FT: 18,000
SALES (est): 2.2MM **Privately Held**
WEB: www.ardiemmedical.com
SIC: 3841 Surgical & medical instruments

(G-8083)
ARKMEDICA LLC
1125 Wayne Ave (15701-3513)
PHONE..............................724 349-0856
David McMurry, *CEO*
EMP: 11
SALES (est): 527.5K **Privately Held**
SIC: 3069 Medical & laboratory rubber
sundries & related products

(G-8084)
AUNTIE ANNES SOFT PRETZELS
2334 Oakland Ave Ste 51 (15701-3348)
PHONE..............................724 349-2825
Tomas Schneider, *President*
Dan Speck, *Vice Pres*
EMP: 9
SALES (est): 174.6K **Privately Held**
SIC: 5461 2052 Pretzels; pretzels

(G-8085)
CAMPBELL OIL & GAS INC
280 Indian Springs Rd 222a (15701-3676)
P.O. Box 276 (15701-0276)
PHONE..............................724 465-9199
Frederick W Zimmerman, *President*
Erik Wood, *Opers Mgr*
Natalia V Garmashova, *Admin Sec*
EMP: 5
SALES (est): 862.4K **Privately Held**
WEB: www.cogicgp.com
SIC: 1382 Oil & gas exploration services

(G-8086)
CIMARRON ENERGY
1700 Sleepy Hollow Rd (15701-6866)
PHONE..............................724 801-8517
Tom Newcomer, *President*
EMP: 5 EST: 2016
SALES (est): 308.5K **Privately Held**
SIC: 1389 Oil field services

(G-8087)
CORECO FIBERGLASS INC
1698 Church St (15701-2549)
PHONE..............................724 463-3726
Robert C Conrad, *President*
David Cook, *Corp Secy*
EMP: 11
SQ FT: 11,000
SALES: 2.5MM **Privately Held**
SIC: 3089 Plastic & fiberglass tanks

(G-8088)
CREPS UNITED PUBLICATIONS INC
40 Christy Park Dr (15701-1585)
P.O. Box 746 (15701-0746)
PHONE..............................724 463-9722
E Garson Creps, *Partner*
Courtney Creps, *Marketing Staff*
Tammy King, *Representative*
EMP: 70
SALES (corp-wide): 38.5MM **Privately Held**
WEB: www.crepsunited.com
SIC: 2752 Commercial printing, offset
PA: Creps United Publications, Inc.
4185 Route 286 Hwy W
Indiana PA 15701
724 463-8522

(G-8089)
DANNIC ENERGY CORPORATION
134 Mill Run Dr (15701-1532)
PHONE..............................724 465-6663
Daniel Sinclair, *President*
EMP: 1
SALES (est): 9MM **Privately Held**
SIC: 1311 Natural gas production

(G-8090)
DEAN TECHNOLOGY INC
Also Called: C K E
2866 W Pike Rd (15701-9769)
PHONE..............................724 349-9440
Roger Coudried, *General Mgr*
Rich Gibbons, *Manager*
EMP: 20
SALES (corp-wide): 35.1MM **Privately Held**
SIC: 3674 Semiconductors & related de-
vices
PA: Dean Technology, Inc.
4117 Billy Mitchell Dr
Addison TX 75001
972 248-7691

(G-8091)
DOMINION EXPLORATION AND PROD
303 Airport Rd (15701)
PHONE..............................724 349-4450
Craig Neal, *Manager*
EMP: 5
SALES (corp-wide): 13.3B **Publicly Held**
SIC: 1382 1311 Oil & gas exploration serv-
ices; natural gas production
HQ: Dominion Exploration And Production
Inc
1 Dominion Dr
Jane Lew WV 26378

(G-8092)
DUQUESNE DISTRIBUTING CO
Also Called: Duquesne Beer Distributing
1215 Maple St (15701-2832)
PHONE..............................724 465-6141
Cathy Strong, *President*
EMP: 6
SQ FT: 3,000
SALES (est): 729K **Privately Held**
SIC: 5921 5181 2086 Beer (packaged);
beer & other fermented malt liquors; bot-
tled & canned soft drinks

(G-8093)
EASTERN AMERICAN ENERGY CORP
101 Heritage Run Ste 1 (15701-4501)
PHONE..............................724 463-8400
Mark Cochran, *Manager*
EMP: 5 **Privately Held**
WEB: www.eca-eaec.com
SIC: 1311 Crude petroleum production;
natural gas production
HQ: Eastern American Energy Corp
500 Corporate Lndg
Charleston WV 25311
304 925-6100

(G-8094)
ELK LAKE SERVICES LLC
Also Called: Environmental Land Surveying &
280 Indian Springs Rd (15701-3676)
PHONE..............................724 463-7303
Elizabeth Gregg, *President*

Michael Moyer, *Vice Pres*
EMP: 17
SALES (est): 1.5MM **Privately Held**
SIC: 8711 1389 Civil engineering; testing, measuring, surveying & analysis services

(G-8095)
EOG RESOURCES INC
2039 S 6th St (15701-6012)
PHONE..................................724 349-7620
Carla Henry, *Branch Mgr*
EMP: 10
SALES (corp-wide): 17.2B **Publicly Held**
WEB: www.eogresources.com
SIC: 1382 Oil & gas exploration services
PA: Eog Resources, Inc.
1111 Bagby Sky Lbby 2
Houston TX 77002
713 651-7000

(G-8096)
EP WORLD INC
285 Ben Franklin Rd N (15701-1506)
PHONE..................................814 361-3860
Joseph M Valenzano Jr, *President*
James P McGinnis, *CFO*
Matthew J Valenzano, *VP Sales*
EMP: 8
SALES (est): 594.3K **Privately Held**
SIC: 2721 Magazines: publishing & printing

(G-8097)
ESPRESSO ANALYSTS
135 Stormer Rd (15701-8977)
PHONE..................................724 541-2151
EMP: 4
SALES (est): 419.4K **Privately Held**
SIC: 3589 Coffee brewing equipment

(G-8098)
F P ENGBERT DISCOUNT GUNS
102b Adams Cir (15701-2334)
PHONE..................................724 465-9756
Frank Engbert, *Owner*
EMP: 3
SALES: 90K **Privately Held**
SIC: 5941 2899 Firearms; flares, fireworks & similar preparations

(G-8099)
FAST TIME SCREEN PRINTING
2030 Shelly Dr (15701-2388)
PHONE..................................724 463-9007
Anthony Medvetz, *Owner*
EMP: 10
SALES (est): 926.4K **Privately Held**
WEB: www.fasttimes.net
SIC: 2759 Screen printing

(G-8100)
FORCE INC (PA)
1380 Route 286 Hwy E # 303
(15701-1474)
PHONE..................................724 465-9399
Bryan Force, *President*
Christopher Force, *Vice Pres*
Adam Botsford, *Project Mgr*
Pam Kauffman, *Office Mgr*
Susan Force, *Admin Sec*
EMP: 35
SQ FT: 2,000
SALES: 40MM **Privately Held**
SIC: 4212 3531 1794 Local trucking, without storage; pavers; excavation work

(G-8101)
G C WYANT LTD
Also Called: G C Wyant Fine Jewelry
716 Philadelphia St (15701-3906)
PHONE..................................724 357-8000
Gary Wyant, *Owner*
EMP: 3
SALES: 500K **Privately Held**
SIC: 3911 5944 Jewelry, precious metal; jewelry stores

(G-8102)
GAS ANALYTICAL SERVICES INC
130 Airport Rd (15701-8904)
PHONE..................................724 349-8133
Erica Maynard, *Project Mgr*
Dawn Ghiardi, *Client Mgr*
Mark Bernard, *Manager*
Kevin Elkin, *Technician*
EMP: 5

SALES (corp-wide): 22.8MM **Privately Held**
SIC: 1389 Gas field services
HQ: Gas Analytical Services, Inc.
8444 Water St
Stonewood WV 26301
304 623-0020

(G-8103)
GORDON INDUSTRIES
771 Indian Springs Rd (15701-3543)
PHONE..................................516 354-8888
EMP: 3
SALES (est): 360.3K **Privately Held**
SIC: 3999 Manufacturing industries

(G-8104)
HI-TECH COLOR INC
1163 Water St (15701-1648)
P.O. Box 746 (15701-0746)
PHONE..................................724 463-8522
Jacob Creps, *President*
Christine Creps Hudson, *Treasurer*
EMP: 11
SQ FT: 15,000
SALES (est): 1.1MM
SALES (corp-wide): 38.5MM **Privately Held**
WEB: www.hitechcolor.com
SIC: 2752 Color lithography
PA: Creps United Publications, Inc.
4185 Route 286 Hwy W
Indiana PA 15701
724 463-8522

(G-8105)
INDIANA PRINTING AND PUBG CO (PA)
Also Called: Indiana Gazette
899 Water St (15701-1705)
P.O. Box 10 (15701-0010)
PHONE..................................724 465-5555
Michael J Donnelly, *CEO*
Jason Levan, *Editor*
Mike Petersen, *Editor*
Joseph Geary, *Vice Pres*
Ron Seckar, *Opers Mgr*
EMP: 250
SQ FT: 25,000
SALES (est): 59.3MM **Privately Held**
WEB: www.indianagazette.com
SIC: 2752 2711 Commercial printing, lithographic; commercial printing & newspaper publishing combined

(G-8106)
INDIANA PRINTING AND PUBG CO
Also Called: Gazette Printers
775 Indian Springs Rd (15701-3543)
PHONE..................................724 349-3434
Kevin Huston, *Manager*
Jeannette Byers, *Manager*
Paul Caruso, *Info Tech Mgr*
Michael Colledge, *Representative*
EMP: 125
SALES (est): 13.5MM
SALES (corp-wide): 59.3MM **Privately Held**
WEB: www.indianagazette.com
SIC: 2759 2791 2789 2752 Newspapers: printing; typesetting; bookbinding & related work; commercial printing, lithographic
PA: The Indiana Printing And Publishing Company
899 Water St
Indiana PA 15701
724 465-5555

(G-8107)
INDIANA TOOL & DIE LLC
207 Nibert Rd (15701-6637)
PHONE..................................724 463-0386
Wayne Simmon, *Mng Member*
▼ **EMP:** 4
SQ FT: 6,000
SALES (est): 708K **Privately Held**
SIC: 3544 Die sets for metal stamping (presses)

(G-8108)
INTEGRATED POWER SERVICES LLC
Also Called: Electro-Mec
4470 Lucerne Rd (15701-9498)
PHONE..................................724 479-9066
EMP: 27
SALES (corp-wide): 924.8MM **Privately Held**
SIC: 7694 Armature rewinding shops
HQ: Integrated Power Services Llc
3 Independence Pt Ste 100
Greenville SC 29615

(G-8109)
K & K MINE PRODUCTS INC
200 Airport Rd (15701-8944)
P.O. Box 160 (15701-0160)
PHONE..................................724 463-5000
Ed Kokolis, *President*
Debbie George, *Corp Secy*
Jeff Kokolis, *Vice Pres*
EMP: 50 **EST:** 1975
SQ FT: 5,000
SALES (est): 10.7MM **Privately Held**
SIC: 3535 3532 3537 Conveyors & conveying equipment; mining machinery; industrial trucks & tractors

(G-8110)
KOVALCHICK CORPORATION (PA)
1060 Wayne Ave (15701-2951)
P.O. Box 279 (15701-0279)
PHONE..................................724 349-3300
Joseph Kovalchick, *President*
Judy Kovalchick, *Vice Pres*
EMP: 35
SALES (est): 9.5MM **Privately Held**
SIC: 1241 5093 5088 3341 Coal mining services; metal scrap & waste materials; railroad equipment & supplies; secondary nonferrous metals

(G-8111)
LEONARD ANDERSON
190 Anderson Rd (15701-3262)
PHONE..................................724 463-3615
Leonard Anderson, *Principal*
EMP: 3 **EST:** 2013
SALES (est): 312K **Privately Held**
SIC: 3827 Optical instruments & lenses

(G-8112)
MCM ARCHITECTURAL PRODUCTS LLC
1410 Wayne Ave Ste A (15701-4742)
PHONE..................................240 416-2809
Patrick Anderson, *Mng Member*
Lynn Anderson, *Admin Sec*
EMP: 6 **EST:** 2014
SALES: 400K **Privately Held**
SIC: 5039 3446 Architectural metalwork; architectural metalwork

(G-8113)
MDC ROMANI INC
Also Called: Pennsylvania Academy of Pet Gr
2860 W Pike Rd (15701-9769)
PHONE..................................724 349-5533
Marlene Romani, *President*
Christen Ruby, *Corp Secy*
Doug Romani, *Vice Pres*
EMP: 13
SQ FT: 11,200
SALES (est): 2.9MM **Privately Held**
WEB: www.mdcromani.com
SIC: 3523 0752 Balers, farm: hay, straw, cotton, etc.; grooming services, pet & animal specialties

(G-8114)
MY INSTANT BENEFITS
1707 Warren Rd (15701-2423)
P.O. Box 1275 (15701-5275)
PHONE..................................724 465-6075
Robert Kane, *President*
EMP: 8
SALES (est): 747.9K **Privately Held**
WEB: www.relianthholdings.com
SIC: 2752 Commercial printing, lithographic

(G-8115)
NORTHEAST ENERGY MGT INC
127 College Lodge Rd (15701-4006)
PHONE..................................724 465-7958
Michael Melnick, *President*
William Gregg, *President*
Paul G Ruddy, *Treasurer*
Jack Pisarcik, *Admin Sec*
John M Pisarcik, *Admin Sec*
EMP: 120
SALES (est): 34MM **Privately Held**
SIC: 1381 Directional drilling oil & gas wells

(G-8116)
PARK PRESS INC
333 Elm St (15701-3198)
PHONE..................................724 465-5812
W Dean Overdorff, *President*
Robert Overdorff, *Vice Pres*
EMP: 6 **EST:** 1928
SQ FT: 5,000
SALES (est): 651.5K **Privately Held**
SIC: 2759 2752 Commercial printing; commercial printing, offset

(G-8117)
PENN PRODUCTION GROUP LLC
418 Gompers Ave (15701-2732)
PHONE..................................724 349-6690
Mark Thompson, *CEO*
Mike Cribes, *Vice Pres*
Brad Brothers, *Treasurer*
Christy Tawson, *Admin Sec*
EMP: 6
SQ FT: 2,400
SALES: 2MM **Privately Held**
SIC: 1381 Drilling oil & gas wells

(G-8118)
PENNSYLVANIA PRODUCTION SVCS
1032 Brown Rd (15701-9175)
P.O. Box 421 (15701-0421)
PHONE..................................724 463-0729
Richard Stewart, *President*
Amy Stormer, *Admin Sec*
EMP: 35
SALES: 900K **Privately Held**
SIC: 1389 Oil & gas wells: building, repairing & dismantling

(G-8119)
PETROLEUM SERVICE PARTNERS
1460 Old Route 119 Hwy N (15701-8556)
PHONE..................................724 349-1536
Charles Brown, *President*
EMP: 9
SALES (est): 1.3MM **Privately Held**
SIC: 1389 Oil field services

(G-8120)
PHILLIPS DRILLING COMPANY
598 Lutz School Rd (15701-8548)
PHONE..................................724 479-1135
Sam Fragale, *Branch Mgr*
EMP: 6
SALES (corp-wide): 290.2B **Publicly Held**
WEB: www.lkdrillingcorp.com
SIC: 1381 1781 Drilling oil & gas wells; water well drilling
HQ: Phillips Drilling Company
190 Thorn Hill Rd
Warrendale PA 15086
724 479-1135

(G-8121)
POLYMER TENNESSEE HOLDINGS (HQ)
1600 Washington St (15701-2893)
PHONE..................................724 838-2340
James O Ireland, *President*
A Elaine Anderson, *Vice Pres*
◆ **EMP:** 1
SQ FT: 50,000
SALES (est): 7.7MM
SALES (corp-wide): 101.1MM **Privately Held**
SIC: 3011 Tire & inner tube materials & related products

PA: Polymer Enterprises, Inc.
4731 State Route 30 # 401
Greensburg PA 15601
724 838-2340

(G-8122)
QUINTECH ELEC CMMNICATIONS INC
250 Airport Rd (15701-8944)
PHONE..................................724 349-1412
Frank Elling, *President*
John M Kriak, *Corp Secy*
Nancy Sargent, *Sr Exec VP*
Nancy Rinehart, *VP Admin*
Brad Baker, *Engineer*
EMP: 60
SQ FT: 38,000
SALES (est): 18.8MM
SALES (corp-wide): 288.6MM **Privately Held**
WEB: www.quintechelectronics.com
SIC: 3661 Switching equipment, telephone
HQ: Evertz Usa Inc.
10621 Gateway Blvd
Manassas VA 20110
703 330-3122

(G-8123)
RAWLEE FUELS LLC
555 Philadelphia St (15701-3901)
PHONE..................................724 349-3320
Ralph L Wingrove, *Principal*
EMP: 4 **EST:** 2008
SALES (est): 408.5K **Privately Held**
SIC: 2869 Fuels

(G-8124)
ROYAL OIL & GAS CORPORATION (PA)
1 Indian Springs Rd (15701-3634)
P.O. Box 809 (15701-0809)
PHONE..................................724 463-0246
Stephen R Patchin, *President*
Carl E Patchin Jr, *Vice Pres*
Phyllis M Patchin, *Vice Pres*
Paul F Brown Jr, *Treasurer*
Thomas M Thompson, *Admin Sec*
EMP: 35 **EST:** 1931
SQ FT: 22,000
SALES (est): 15.3MM **Privately Held**
SIC: 1311 1382 Crude petroleum production; natural gas production; oil & gas exploration services

(G-8125)
ROYAL PRODUCTION COMPANY INC
Also Called: Accounting Department
1 Indian Springs Rd (15701-3634)
PHONE..................................724 463-0246
Paul F Brown, *Branch Mgr*
EMP: 25
SALES (corp-wide): 15.3MM **Privately Held**
SIC: 1311 Crude petroleum production; natural gas production
HQ: Royal Production Company, Inc
500 N Shoreline Blvd # 807
Corpus Christi TX 78401

(G-8126)
SCHROTH INDUSTRIES INC
Also Called: Schroth Lumber
145 Martin Rd (15701-7423)
P.O. Box 699 (15701-0699)
PHONE..................................724 465-5701
Walter A Schroth, *President*
EMP: 7
SQ FT: 217,800
SALES: 500K **Privately Held**
SIC: 2491 Structural lumber & timber, treated wood

(G-8127)
SHEEP THRILLS
244 Lower Twolick Dr (15701-6102)
PHONE..................................724 465-2617
Katheryn Schuman, *Owner*
EMP: 3
SALES (est): 124.2K **Privately Held**
SIC: 2399 Automotive covers, except seat & tire covers

(G-8128)
SHOPPERS GUIDE
899 Water St (15701-1705)
P.O. Box 10 (15701-0010)
PHONE..................................724 349-0336
Michael Donnelly, *President*
Heather Eveges, *Principal*
EMP: 3
SALES (est): 119.5K **Privately Held**
SIC: 2711 Newspapers, publishing & printing

(G-8129)
SKY POINT CRANE LLC
188 Wren St (15701-1440)
PHONE..................................724 471-5710
David R Brocious,
EMP: 5
SALES: 300K **Privately Held**
SIC: 1521 3999 1542 1711 Single-family housing construction; manufacturing industries; agricultural building contractors; heating & air conditioning contractors

(G-8130)
STAUFFERS MINI BARNS
1082 Myers Rd (15701-6336)
PHONE..................................724 479-0760
Luke Stauffer, *Owner*
Ruth Stauffer, *Co-Owner*
EMP: 4
SALES: 1MM **Privately Held**
SIC: 2499 Yard sticks, wood

(G-8131)
STREAM-FLO USA LLC
1410 Wayne Ave Ste C (15701-4742)
PHONE..................................724 349-6090
Brad Nokielski, *Branch Mgr*
EMP: 4 **Privately Held**
SIC: 3533 Oil field machinery & equipment
HQ: Stream-Flo Usa Llc
8726 Fallbrook Dr
Houston TX 77064
903 912-1022

(G-8132)
SYNERGY CONTRACTING SVCS LLC
1380 Route 286 Hwy E # 221 (15701-1461)
PHONE..................................724 349-0855
Nancy J Saxman, *Mng Member*
EMP: 30
SQ FT: 18,000
SALES (est): 3.4MM **Privately Held**
WEB: www.groupsynergy.com
SIC: 3699 1611 Electrical equipment & supplies; general contractor, highway & street construction

(G-8133)
VICTORY ENERGY CORPORATION
220 Airport Rd (15701-8944)
PHONE..................................724 349-6366
Lynn A Doverspike, *President*
Cheryl Miller, *Treasurer*
David McCall, *Director*
Chris Baker,
EMP: 45
SQ FT: 2,750
SALES (est): 5.9MM **Privately Held**
WEB: www.victoryenergycorp.com
SIC: 1381 8711 Drilling oil & gas wells; petroleum, mining & chemical engineers

(G-8134)
VINEGAR HILL PICTURE WORKS
65 Bradley Ct (15701-2310)
PHONE..................................724 596-0023
Michael Hartnett, *Owner*
EMP: 3
SALES (est): 229.1K **Privately Held**
SIC: 2099 Vinegar

Indianola
Allegheny County

(G-8135)
BAYER MEDICAL CARE INC (DH)
Also Called: Bayer Healthcare
1 Bayer Dr (15051-9702)
PHONE..................................724 940-6800
San LI Ang-, *President*
San LI Ang, *President*
Joseph B Havrilla, *Senior VP*
James F Kessing, *Senior VP*
Clifford E Kress, *Senior VP*
▼ **EMP:** 800
SQ FT: 266,476
SALES (est): 390MM
SALES (corp-wide): 45.3B **Privately Held**
WEB: www.medrad.com
SIC: 3841 Surgical & medical instruments
HQ: Berlin Schering Inc
100 Bayer Blvd
Whippany NJ 07981
862 404-3000

Industry
Beaver County

(G-8136)
FILTERFAB MANUFACTURING CORP
3847 Midland Beaver Rd (15052-1760)
PHONE..................................724 643-4000
Edward Peglow, *President*
Robin Marshall, *Admin Sec*
▲ **EMP:** 5
SQ FT: 9,000
SALES (est): 1MM **Privately Held**
WEB: www.filterfabmfg.com
SIC: 3569 5084 5085 Filters & strainers, pipeline; industrial machinery & equipment; filters, industrial

Intercourse
Lancaster County

(G-8137)
INTERCOURSE PRETZEL FACTORY
3614 Old Phila Pike (17534)
PHONE..................................717 768-3432
Donna Clark, *President*
EMP: 23 **EST:** 1955
SALES (est): 1.9MM **Privately Held**
WEB: www.intercoursepretzelfactory.com
SIC: 2052 2099 Pretzels; food preparations

(G-8138)
OLD CANDLE BARN INC
Also Called: Old Candle Barn Gift Shop
3551 Main St (17534)
P.O. Box 7 (17534-0007)
PHONE..................................717 768-3231
Fannie Beiler, *President*
▲ **EMP:** 40
SQ FT: 14,400
SALES (est): 4.5MM **Privately Held**
WEB: www.oldcandlebarn.com
SIC: 3999 5947 Candles; gift shop

Irvine
Warren County

(G-8139)
ELLWOOD NATIONAL CRANKSHAFT CO
1 Front St (16329-1801)
PHONE..................................814 563-7522
Brian C Taylor, *President*
David E Barensfeld, *Vice Pres*
Bentraum D Huffman, *Treasurer*
Nancy Kowal Griffen, *Controller*
Susan A Apel, *Admin Sec*
◆ **EMP:** 230
SALES (est): 34.9MM
SALES (corp-wide): 775.5MM **Privately Held**
WEB: www.ellwoodgroup.com
SIC: 3462 Iron & steel forgings
PA: Ellwood Group, Inc.
600 Commercial Ave
Ellwood City PA 16117
724 752-3680

(G-8140)
ELLWOOD NATIONAL FORGE COMPANY
1 Front St (16329-1801)
PHONE..................................814 563-7522
Glenn C Fegley, *President*
David E Barensfeld, *Vice Pres*
Jerry Johnson, *Purch Agent*
Bentraum D Huffman, *Treasurer*
Mike Keister, *Info Tech Mgr*
◆ **EMP:** 125
SALES (est): 23.7MM
SALES (corp-wide): 775.5MM **Privately Held**
WEB: www.ellwoodgroup.com
SIC: 3599 3312 Machine & other job shop work; forgings, iron & steel
PA: Ellwood Group, Inc.
600 Commercial Ave
Ellwood City PA 16117
724 752-3680

Irwin
Westmoreland County

(G-8141)
AIRTEK INC (PA)
76 Clair St (15642-9311)
P.O. Box 466 (15642-0466)
PHONE..................................412 351-3837
Robert C Whisner, *President*
Tamara L Cramer, *Vice Pres*
Daniel M Curtin, *Vice Pres*
Randy Stoner, *Sales Staff*
EMP: 20
SQ FT: 48,000
SALES (est): 27.2MM **Privately Held**
WEB: www.airtek-inc.com
SIC: 5084 3569 Pneumatic tools & equipment; hydraulic systems equipment & supplies; jacks, hydraulic

(G-8142)
ALLOMET CORPORATION
509 Hahntown Wendel Rd (15642-4343)
PHONE..................................724 864-4787
John M Keane, *President*
◆ **EMP:** 14
SQ FT: 30,000
SALES (est): 2.7MM **Privately Held**
SIC: 3312 Rails, steel or iron

(G-8143)
ALLSORCE SCRNING SOLUTIONS LLC
4 W Hempfield Dr (15642)
PHONE..................................724 515-2637
Peter O'Connor, *Mng Member*
◆ **EMP:** 21
SALES: 1MM **Privately Held**
SIC: 2899

(G-8144)
ASTLEY PRECISION MCH CO INC (PA)
160 S Thompson Ln (15642-4546)
PHONE..................................724 861-5000
Carol Astley, *President*
EMP: 13
SQ FT: 10,501
SALES (est): 2.8MM **Privately Held**
WEB: www.astleyprecision.com
SIC: 3599 Machine shop, jobbing & repair

(G-8145)
ASTRO AUTOMATION INC
100 Productivity Pl (15642-4206)
PHONE..................................724 864-2500
James M Reber, *President*
EMP: 8
SQ FT: 42,000

SALES (est): 1.4MM **Privately Held**
WEB: www.astroautomationinc.com
SIC: **3559** 3549 3599 Robots, molding & forming plastics; assembly machines, including robotic; machine shop, jobbing & repair

(G-8146)
BASIC CARBIDE CORPORATION (PA)
900 Main St (15642-4333)
PHONE...................................724 446-1630
John Goodrum, *President*
Jared P Filapose, *Vice Pres*
Jonathan Goodrum, *Vice Pres*
Michael Stampler, *Sales Engr*
Robert Blazevich, *Sales Staff*
▲ EMP: 25 EST: 1981
SQ FT: 70,000
SALES (est): 19.2MM **Privately Held**
WEB: www.basiccarbide.com
SIC: **3291** Tungsten carbide abrasive

(G-8147)
CARLY RAILCAR COMPONENTS LLC
1090 Sandy Hill Rd (15642-4747)
PHONE...................................724 864-8170
Larry Carly, *Mng Member*
EMP: 5
SALES (est): 1.1MM **Privately Held**
SIC: **3743** Railroad equipment

(G-8148)
CLEAN POWER RESOURCES INC
13031 State Route 30 (15642-1326)
PHONE...................................724 863-3768
Lauren Simkovic, *President*
Robert E Price Jr, *Vice Pres*
Cheryl Peters, *Treasurer*
Mary Louise Price, *Admin Sec*
EMP: 3
SQ FT: 18,500
SALES: 296.7K **Privately Held**
WEB: www.cleanpowerresources.com
SIC: **3822** Hydronic pressure or temperature controls

(G-8149)
COMTROL INTERNATIONAL
500 Pennsylvania Ave (15642-3652)
P.O. Box 306 (15642-0306)
PHONE...................................724 864-3800
Allen Quinn, *President*
Joan Liprando, *Corp Secy*
Thomas I Agnew, *Vice Pres*
▲ EMP: 25
SALES (est): 7MM **Privately Held**
WEB: www.comtrol-corp.com
SIC: **3663** 3669 Radio & TV communications equipment; intercommunication systems, electric

(G-8150)
CORESTAR INTERNATIONAL CORP
Also Called: New Stanton Machining Tooling
1044 Sandy Hill Rd (15642-4700)
PHONE...................................724 744-4094
EMP: 9 **Privately Held**
SIC: **3599** Machine shop, jobbing & repair
PA: Corestar International Corporation
1044 Sandy Hill Rd
Irwin PA 15642

(G-8151)
CORESTAR INTERNATIONAL CORP (PA)
Also Called: New Stanton Machining Tooling
1044 Sandy Hill Rd (15642-4700)
PHONE...................................724 744-4094
Edward P Lopez, *President*
Mike Coradi, *Owner*
Sheldon Miller, *General Mgr*
Michael D Coradi, *Vice Pres*
Greg Turley, *Treasurer*
EMP: 40
SQ FT: 20,000
SALES (est): 6.8MM **Privately Held**
WEB: www.corestar-corp.com
SIC: **7373** 7371 7372 Systems integration services; computer software systems analysis & design, custom; prepackaged software

(G-8152)
CREATIVE STITCHES BY DINA INC
11380 State Route 30 (15642-2022)
PHONE...................................724 863-4104
Dina Denning, *President*
EMP: 7
SQ FT: 6,000
SALES (est): 620.1K **Privately Held**
SIC: **2395** 5946 Embroidery & art needlework; camera & photographic supply stores

(G-8153)
CRISP CONTROL INC
Also Called: Rear Dock
200 Productivity Pl (15642-4212)
PHONE...................................724 864-6777
John Momyer, *President*
Ron Halli, *Prdtn Mgr*
Stephanie Jones, *Financial Exec*
Timothy Bryan, *Technical Staff*
EMP: 60
SQ FT: 14,000
SALES (est): 15.1MM **Privately Held**
WEB: www.crispcontrol.com
SIC: **3625** 3613 Control circuit relays, industrial; switchgear & switchboard apparatus

(G-8154)
D & G MACHINE
367 Wendel Rd (15642-4562)
P.O. Box 59, Wendel (15691-0059)
PHONE...................................724 864-0043
Daniel Szekely, *Owner*
EMP: 5
SQ FT: 1,000
SALES (est): 290K **Privately Held**
SIC: **3599** Machine shop, jobbing & repair

(G-8155)
DATA MACHINE LLC
140 Brush Creek Rd (15642-9503)
PHONE...................................724 864-4370
Jeff Astley,
EMP: 30 EST: 2014
SALES: 3MM **Privately Held**
SIC: **3599** Machine shop, jobbing & repair

(G-8156)
DAVIS NE COMPANY INC
Also Called: Nedco
11000 Parker Dr (15642-1634)
PHONE...................................412 751-5122
Neal Davis, *President*
EMP: 7
SQ FT: 3,800
SALES (est): 1MM **Privately Held**
SIC: **3599** Machine shop, jobbing & repair

(G-8157)
DOUBLE NICKEL DELIVERY LLC
620 1st St (15642-9727)
PHONE...................................412 721-0550
David Scarnati, *Principal*
EMP: 6
SALES (est): 756K **Privately Held**
SIC: **3356** Nickel

(G-8158)
ELECTRONIC INSTRUMENT RES LTD
2231 Trolist Dr (15642-4448)
P.O. Box 678 (15642-0678)
PHONE...................................724 744-7028
Gregory A Bertone, *President*
Herbert C Cooper, *Vice Pres*
EMP: 4
SQ FT: 500
SALES: 500K **Privately Held**
SIC: **3625** Electric controls & control accessories, industrial

(G-8159)
ELIZABETH CARBIDE DIE CO
Also Called: Elizabeth-Hata International
14559 State Route 30 (15642-1045)
PHONE...................................412 829-7700
Richard Sanderson, *CEO*
Nikki Sartori, *Purchasing*
Rosario Cipolla, *Sales Staff*
EMP: 23

SALES (est): 3.1MM **Privately Held**
SIC: **3544** Special dies, tools, jigs & fixtures

(G-8160)
ELIZABETH CARBIDE DIE CO INC
Also Called: Elizabeth Hata International
101 Peterson Dr (15642-1098)
PHONE...................................412 829-7700
Ryan Keefer, *Manager*
EMP: 28
SALES (corp-wide): 57MM **Privately Held**
WEB: www.eliz.com
SIC: **3544** 3599 3542 Special dies, tools, jigs & fixtures; custom machinery; machine tools, metal forming type
PA: Elizabeth Carbide Die Co., Inc.
601 Linden St
Mckeesport PA 15132
412 751-3000

(G-8161)
EMSCO DISTRIBUTOR COMPANY
11025 Parker Dr (15642-1634)
PHONE...................................412 754-1236
Ralph Yelenic, *Principal*
Robin J Gales, *Manager*
EMP: 5 EST: 2007
SALES (est): 508.1K **Privately Held**
SIC: **5091** 3949 Swimming pools, equipment & supplies; swimming pools, plastic

(G-8162)
EXTRUDE HONE LLC (HQ)
235 Industry Blvd (15642-3462)
PHONE...................................724 863-5900
URS Signer, *Manager*
▲ EMP: 80 EST: 1969
SQ FT: 105,000
SALES (est): 91.2MM
SALES (corp-wide): 297MM **Privately Held**
WEB: www.extrudehone.com
SIC: **3541** Milling machines; electrochemical milling machines; ultrasonic metal cutting machine tools
PA: Madison Industries Holdings Llc
500 W Madison St Ste 3890
Chicago IL 60661
312 277-0156

(G-8163)
G D C MANUFACTURING INC
Also Called: Gdc Fine Jewelry
12591 State Route 30 (15642-1336)
PHONE...................................724 864-5000
Joseph Hart, *President*
Joan P Hart, *Treasurer*
EMP: 5
SQ FT: 1,500
SALES (est): 460K **Privately Held**
SIC: **3911** Jewelry, precious metal

(G-8164)
GENERAL WELDMENTS INC
585 Pleasant Valley Rd (15642-9493)
P.O. Box 508 (15642-0508)
PHONE...................................724 744-2105
Robert Potter, *President*
Doris Potter, *Corp Secy*
Carol Lunieski, *Admin Sec*
EMP: 15 EST: 1958
SQ FT: 20,000
SALES (est): 2.6MM **Privately Held**
SIC: **3599** 7692 3444 3443 Machine shop, jobbing & repair; welding repair; sheet metalwork; fabricated plate work (boiler shop); fabricated structural metal

(G-8165)
GWIZ PRODUCTS
870 Main St (15642-4339)
PHONE...................................724 864-0200
Tom Gillespy, *Partner*
EMP: 5
SQ FT: 4,000
SALES: 250K **Privately Held**
WEB: www.gwizpro.com
SIC: **2541** Garment racks, wood

(G-8166)
HARLISS SPECIALTIES CORP
Biddle Rd (15642)
P.O. Box Drawer R
PHONE...................................724 863-0321
John Harkobusic, *President*
Jason T Harkobusic, *Vice Pres*
Bob Pelzer, *Purch Mgr*
John I Harkobusic, *Treasurer*
Jason H Harless, *Manager*
EMP: 50
SQ FT: 20,000
SALES (est): 10.9MM **Privately Held**
WEB: www.harliss.com
SIC: **3443** Weldments

(G-8167)
HIGHLAND CARBIDE TOOL CO
741 Northeast Dr (15642-1976)
PHONE...................................724 863-7151
Kevin Degger, *President*
Thomas E Deger, *President*
Kevin Deger, *Vice Pres*
Mary C Deger, *Admin Sec*
EMP: 10 EST: 1943
SQ FT: 7,000
SALES (est): 1.7MM **Privately Held**
WEB: www.highlandcarbide.com
SIC: **3541** Machine tools, metal cutting type

(G-8168)
HOLAN INC
1048 Sandy Hill Rd (15642-4700)
PHONE...................................724 744-1660
Imre Lancz, *President*
John Holba, *Corp Secy*
EMP: 13
SQ FT: 12,000
SALES (est): 2.1MM **Privately Held**
WEB: www.holan.net
SIC: **3599** Machine shop, jobbing & repair

(G-8169)
HORIZONTAL WIRELINE SVCS LLC (HQ)
Also Called: Allied-Hrizontal Wireline Svcs
381 Colonial Manor Rd (15642-1607)
PHONE...................................724 382-5012
Joseph Sites,
EMP: 20
SQ FT: 3,000
SALES (est): 5.9MM **Privately Held**
SIC: **1389** Oil field services

(G-8170)
IMPACT INNOVATIVE PRODUCTS LLC
Also Called: Zoombang Protective Gear
127 Industry Blvd (15642-3461)
PHONE...................................724 864-8440
Alvaro Carraro, *Mng Member*
Julius Jones, *Manager*
EMP: 14
SQ FT: 30,000
SALES: 800K **Privately Held**
WEB: www.zoombang.com
SIC: **3949** Protective sporting equipment

(G-8171)
INNOVATIVE CARBIDE INC (PA)
11040 Parker Dr (15642-1634)
PHONE...................................412 751-6900
Byron Wardropper, *President*
Ronald Geckle, *Vice Pres*
Joel Wardroppe, *Vice Pres*
Bethany Wardropper, *Vice Pres*
Ken Demko, *Project Mgr*
▲ EMP: 53
SQ FT: 37,285
SALES (est): 7.4MM **Privately Held**
WEB: www.innovativecarbide.com
SIC: **3544** 3291 Special dies & tools; synthetic abrasives

(G-8172)
INSTRUMENT & VALVE SERVICES CO
204 Brandywine Dr (15642-9222)
PHONE...................................724 205-3348
Carla Kish, *Principal*
EMP: 50
SALES (corp-wide): 17.4B **Publicly Held**
SIC: **3823** Industrial instrmnts msrmnt display/control process variable

HQ: Instrument & Valve Services Company
205 S Center St
Marshalltown IA 50158

(G-8173)
IRWIN CAR & EQUIPMENT INC
Also Called: Traction Motor Service
9933 Broadway St (15642-1559)
P.O. Box 409 (15642-0409)
PHONE.....................................724 864-5170
Joe Hantz, *Branch Mgr*
EMP: 17
SALES (est): 3.8MM
SALES (corp-wide): 20.1MM **Privately Held**
SIC: 3535 5085 3532 7389 Conveyors & conveying equipment; industrial supplies; mining machinery; industrial & commercial equipment inspection service; mining machinery & equipment, except petroleum; metal heat treating
PA: Irwin Car & Equipment, Inc.
9953 Broadway St
Irwin PA 15642
724 864-8900

(G-8174)
IRWIN CAR & EQUIPMENT INC (PA)
9953 Broadway St (15642-1559)
P.O. Box 409 (15642-0409)
PHONE.....................................724 864-8900
William Baker, *President*
Lester H Miller Jr, *Vice Pres*
▲ **EMP:** 47
SQ FT: 15,000
SALES (est): 20.1MM **Privately Held**
WEB: www.irwincar.com
SIC: 3535 5085 3532 7389 Conveyors & conveying equipment; industrial supplies; mining machinery; industrial & commercial equipment inspection service; mining machinery & equipment, except petroleum; metal heat treating

(G-8175)
J P TINE TOOL CO
Also Called: Tine, J P Tool Mfg
2751 Hahntown Wendel Rd (15642-3056)
PHONE.....................................724 863-0332
EMP: 8
SQ FT: 6,000
SALES: 650K **Privately Held**
SIC: 3599 Machine shop, jobbing & repair

(G-8176)
JAMES E KRACK
Also Called: Krack Sales Co
214 Cameron Dr (15642-9228)
PHONE.....................................724 864-4150
James E Krack, *Owner*
EMP: 2
SALES: 1.2MM **Privately Held**
SIC: 5013 3519 Motor vehicle supplies & new parts; governors, pump, for diesel engines

(G-8177)
JB ANDERSON & SON INC
115 Railroad St (15642-6506)
P.O. Box 505, Manor (15665-0505)
PHONE.....................................724 523-9610
William T Bilott, *CEO*
Benjamin Bilott, *Vice Pres*
EMP: 5 **EST:** 1941
SQ FT: 10,000
SALES (est): 891.8K **Privately Held**
SIC: 3545 Precision measuring tools

(G-8178)
KENNAMETAL INC
1576 Arona Rd (15642-5008)
PHONE.....................................724 864-5900
Ted Honick, *Branch Mgr*
EMP: 126
SALES (corp-wide): 2.3B **Publicly Held**
SIC: 3545 Cutting tools for machine tools
PA: Kennametal Inc.
600 Grant St Ste 5100
Pittsburgh PA 15219
412 248-8000

(G-8179)
KIN-TECH MANUFACTURING INC
2766 Clay Pike (15642-3016)
PHONE.....................................724 446-0777
John R Kinsey Jr, *President*
EMP: 13
SQ FT: 6,000
SALES (est): 2.1MM **Privately Held**
SIC: 3599 Machine shop, jobbing & repair

(G-8180)
KRESS MANUFACTURING INC
378 Main St (15642-4332)
PHONE.....................................724 864-5056
Thomas Carpenter, *President*
Thomas Carpender, *President*
Linda Carpenter, *Corp Secy*
EMP: 5 **EST:** 1966
SQ FT: 6,000
SALES (est): 605K **Privately Held**
WEB: www.kressmfg.com
SIC: 3599 Machine shop, jobbing & repair

(G-8181)
M C E DEVELOPMENT INC
Also Called: M C Enterprises
27 Renaissance Dr (15642-9545)
PHONE.....................................412 952-0918
Mario Contestabile, *President*
EMP: 5
SALES: 3.5MM **Privately Held**
SIC: 3531 5078 Aggregate spreaders; refrigeration equipment & supplies

(G-8182)
MESTA ELECTRONICS INC
11020 Parker Dr (15642-1634)
PHONE.....................................412 754-3000
John N Mandalakas, *President*
Debbie Levntopoulos, *General Mgr*
Peter Leventopoulos, *General Mgr*
Deborah Leventopoulos, *Corp Secy*
Kay Mandalakas, *Vice Pres*
EMP: 17 **EST:** 1977
SQ FT: 15,000
SALES (est): 3.4MM **Privately Held**
WEB: www.mesta.com
SIC: 3674 8748 Solid state electronic devices; business consulting

(G-8183)
MICHAEL DAHMA ASSOCIATES
558 Carroll Dr (15642-2669)
PHONE.....................................412 607-1151
Michael Dahma, *Owner*
EMP: 3
SALES: 500K **Privately Held**
WEB: www.mdapromo.com
SIC: 2759 7389 Promotional printing; interior designer; interior decorating

(G-8184)
NORWIN MFG INC
1061 Main St Ste 18 (15642-7425)
PHONE.....................................724 515-7092
Jennifer Painter, *Principal*
Terry Painter, *Manager*
EMP: 3
SALES: 250K **Privately Held**
SIC: 3494 Valves & pipe fittings

(G-8185)
NUTRITION INC (PA)
580 Wendel Rd Ste 100 (15642-5001)
PHONE.....................................724 978-2100
Gerald Moore, *President*
Edward W Caswell, *President*
Donald Baker, *Corp Secy*
EMP: 40
SQ FT: 5,000
SALES (est): 75.5MM **Privately Held**
WEB: www.thenutritiongroup.biz
SIC: 5812 2099 8099 Contract food services; food preparations; nutrition services

(G-8186)
NUTRITION INC
Also Called: Nuvu Services
580 Wendel Rd 100 (15642-5001)
PHONE.....................................814 382-3656
Dan Bazlack, *Regional Mgr*
EMP: 50

SALES (corp-wide): 75.5MM **Privately Held**
SIC: 5812 2099 Contract food services; food preparations
PA: Nutrition Inc.
580 Wendel Rd Ste 100
Irwin PA 15642
724 978-2100

(G-8187)
OTTO DESIGN CASEFIXTURE INC
14581 Josephine St (15642-4114)
P.O. Box 64, Greenock (15047-0064)
PHONE.....................................412 378-6460
Christopher Amos, *Office Mgr*
EMP: 6
SALES (corp-wide): 350K **Privately Held**
SIC: 2434 1751 Wood kitchen cabinets; cabinet & finish carpentry
PA: Otto Design Casefixture Inc
7341 Sandy Ln
Greenock PA 15047
412 824-3580

(G-8188)
PARKER-HANNIFIN CORPORATION
Also Called: Electromechanical North Amer
1140 Sandy Hill Rd (15642-4742)
PHONE.....................................724 861-8200
Kenneth Sweet, *Branch Mgr*
EMP: 120
SQ FT: 43,893
SALES (corp-wide): 12B **Publicly Held**
WEB: www.parker.com
SIC: 3827 5084 3823 3625 Optical instruments & lenses; industrial machinery & equipment; industrial instrmnts msrmnt display/control process variable; relays & industrial controls; machine tool accessories
PA: Parker-Hannifin Corporation
6035 Parkland Blvd
Cleveland OH 44124
216 896-3000

(G-8189)
PBM INC
Also Called: PBM Valve
1070 Sandy Hill Rd (15642-4747)
PHONE.....................................724 863-0550
Stuart J Zarembo, *President*
Jim Brennan, *Owner*
Matt Cullen, *Regional Mgr*
Terry Thurn, *Regional Mgr*
Nancy Mayer, *Corp Secy*
▲ **EMP:** 78
SQ FT: 65,000
SALES (est): 22.9MM **Privately Held**
WEB: www.pbm.net
SIC: 3492 5085 3593 3494 Control valves, fluid power: hydraulic & pneumatic; industrial supplies; fluid power cylinders & actuators; valves & pipe fittings

(G-8190)
PERFORMANCE MACHINING INC
79 Pennsylvania Ave (15642-3584)
PHONE.....................................724 864-2499
James K Steffey, *President*
Ryan Steffey, *Owner*
EMP: 14
SQ FT: 10,000
SALES (est): 2.5MM **Privately Held**
SIC: 3599 Machine shop, jobbing & repair; machine & other job shop work

(G-8191)
PHYSIIC LLC
320 Main St (15642-3438)
PHONE.....................................424 653-6410
Justin Tuttle, *CEO*
EMP: 2
SALES (est): 133.4K **Privately Held**
SIC: 7372 Application computer software

(G-8192)
PPG INDUSTRIES INC
10739 State Route 30 (15642-2047)
PHONE.....................................724 863-4473
Frank Fanelli, *Branch Mgr*
EMP: 3

SALES (corp-wide): 15.3B **Publicly Held**
SIC: 2851 Paints & allied products
PA: Ppg Industries, Inc.
1 Ppg Pl
Pittsburgh PA 15272
412 434-3131

(G-8193)
PRECISION DEFENSE SERVICES INC
Also Called: PDS INDUSTRIES
1 Quality Way (15642-4262)
PHONE.....................................724 863-1100
Ann J Fleming, *CEO*
Robert J Perkins, *President*
EMP: 115 **EST:** 1957
SQ FT: 65,000
SALES: 16.7MM **Privately Held**
WEB: www.pdsindustries.com
SIC: 3599 Machine shop, jobbing & repair

(G-8194)
QUALITY BRAND PRINTING INC
12120 State Route 30 # 210 (15642-1840)
PHONE.....................................724 864-1731
Jeffrey Spitz, *CEO*
EMP: 6
SALES (est): 857.7K **Privately Held**
WEB: www.qbrand.net
SIC: 2759 Commercial printing

(G-8195)
QUALITY TOOLING & REPAIR INC
139 Penn Manor Rd (15642-6503)
PHONE.....................................724 522-1555
Steve L Poorman, *President*
EMP: 10
SQ FT: 5,000
SALES: 1MM **Privately Held**
SIC: 3599 Machine shop, jobbing & repair

(G-8196)
RELIANT SYSTEMS LLC
6 3rd St (15642-3359)
PHONE.....................................412 496-2580
Larry Cole,
EMP: 4
SALES (est): 172.2K **Privately Held**
SIC: 3699 Security control equipment & systems

(G-8197)
RJC MANUFACTURING SERVICES LLC
7590 Us 30 (15642)
PHONE.....................................724 836-3636
Regis Cibak,
EMP: 9
SALES (est): 1.6MM **Privately Held**
SIC: 3545 Precision tools, machinists'

(G-8198)
RTB PRODUCTS INC
1061 Main St Ste 2g (15642-7425)
PHONE.....................................724 861-2080
Terry Newell, *President*
Bruce T Newell, *Vice Pres*
▲ **EMP:** 10
SQ FT: 5,000
SALES (est): 953.9K **Privately Held**
WEB: www.rtbproductsinc.com
SIC: 1541 3613 Industrial buildings, new construction; regulators, power

(G-8199)
SAGEKING INC
Also Called: Litter Quick
4395 Sage Ln (15642-3474)
PHONE.....................................717 540-0525
James R Sage Jr, *President*
Richard D Stoneking, *President*
Mischell Stoneking, *Admin Dir*
EMP: 3 **EST:** 1996
SALES (est): 170K **Privately Held**
WEB: www.sageking.com
SIC: 3999 Pet supplies

(G-8200)
SIGNS SERVICE & CRANE INC
165 Leger Rd (15642-1114)
PHONE.....................................724 515-5272
William Stockdill, *President*
Jody Stockdill, *Vice Pres*
EMP: 3 **EST:** 2000

SALES (est): 230K **Privately Held**
SIC: 3993 Electric signs

(G-8201)
**SKUTA SIGNS OF ALL KINDS
(PA)**
10649 State Route 30 (15642-2080)
P.O. Box 703, Manor (15665-0703)
PHONE.....................................724 863-6159
J Martin Skuta, *Partner*
Rich Skuta, *Partner*
EMP: 4 EST: 1974
SQ FT: 900
SALES (est): 384.7K **Privately Held**
SIC: 3993 5099 Signs & advertising spe-
cialties; signs, except electric

(G-8202)
SUGAR CREEK CANDLES LLC
40 Carpenter Ln (15642-1210)
PHONE.....................................724 261-1927
Anthony Barravecchio, *Vice Pres*
EMP: 6 EST: 2011
SALES (est): 550K **Privately Held**
SIC: 3999 5199 Candles; candles

(G-8203)
SYLVAN CORPORATION
Also Called: Sylvan Fiberoptics
612 Cedar St (15642-3611)
P.O. Box 501 (15642-0501)
PHONE.....................................724 864-9350
James Fedorka, *President*
Beverly Fedorka, *Admin Sec*
EMP: 5
SQ FT: 1,000
SALES (est): 200K **Privately Held**
SIC: 3648 5047 5999 Lighting equipment;
electro-medical equipment; medical appa-
ratus & supplies

(G-8204)
VANGURA KITCHEN TOPS INC
Also Called: Vangura Surfacing Products
14431 Vangura Ln (15642-3483)
PHONE.....................................412 824-0772
Edward Vangura, *President*
Donald Hornyak, *Vice Pres*
Robert L Vertes, *Vice Pres*
Jim Lewis, *Controller*
Krystal Vangura, *Sales Staff*
EMP: 100 EST: 1971
SQ FT: 60,000
SALES (est): 18.8MM **Privately Held**
WEB: www.vangura.com
SIC: 2431 2541 5031 Millwork; table or
counter tops, plastic laminated; building
materials, interior

```
Ivyland
Bucks County
```

(G-8205)
ATCH-MONT GEAR CO INC
65 Industrial Dr (18974-1444)
PHONE.....................................215 355-5146
Alexander Shilstut, *President*
Ada Shilstut, *Vice Pres*
EMP: 10 EST: 1972
SQ FT: 10,000
SALES: 3MM **Privately Held**
WEB: www.atchmontgear.com
SIC: 3566 Gears, power transmission, ex-
cept automotive

(G-8206)
ATLANTIC ENTERPRISE INC
Also Called: Atlantic Papers
1800 Mearns Rd Ste P (18974-1191)
P.O. Box 1527 Sinkler Rd, Warminster
(18974)
PHONE.....................................800 367-8547
Pavel Vaclov Repisky, *President*
Bernadette J Repisky, *Vice Pres*
▲ EMP: 4
SALES (est): 458.4K **Privately Held**
SIC: 2621 Art paper

(G-8207)
AXIAL MEDICAL
65 Richard Rd (18974-1512)
PHONE.....................................267 961-2600
Vincent Visco, *President*

EMP: 15 EST: 2014
SALES (est): 2.5MM **Privately Held**
SIC: 3842 Implants, surgical

(G-8208)
CUSTOM ULTRASONICS INC
144 Railroad Dr (18974-1449)
P.O. Box 850, Buckingham (18912-0850)
PHONE.....................................215 364-1477
Frank Weber, *President*
Gail Weber, *Corp Secy*
Craig Weber, *Vice Pres*
Mike Costello, *Manager*
George Hernandez, *Technology*
EMP: 55
SQ FT: 12,000
SALES (est): 13.1MM **Privately Held**
WEB: www.customultrasonics.com
SIC: 3699 8099 Cleaning equipment, ul-
trasonic, except medical & dental; surgi-
cal & medical instruments

(G-8209)
DUCO HOLDINGS LLC
Also Called: Duco Plastics and Supply
116 Railroad Dr (18974-1449)
P.O. Box 757, Richboro (18954-0757)
PHONE.....................................215 942-6274
Jason Dunn, *Sales Mgr*
Derek Cohen,
EMP: 3
SALES (est): 193.1K **Privately Held**
SIC: 3452 2869 3083 5072 Screws,
metal; plasticizers, organic: cyclic &
acyclic; plastic finished products, lami-
nated; screws; plastics materials & basic
shapes

(G-8210)
**ECOMM LIFE SAFETY SYSTEMS
LLC**
27 Steam Whistle Dr (18974-1451)
PHONE.....................................215 953-5858
Mark Lawlor, *General Mgr*
Glenn McMinn, *Manager*
EMP: 7
SALES (est): 321K **Privately Held**
SIC: 3669 Intercommunication systems,
electric

(G-8211)
FOX RUN USA LLC (HQ)
Also Called: Fox Run Craftsmen
1907 Stout Dr (18974-3869)
PHONE.....................................215 675-7700
Sean Leonard, *President*
Owen Leonard, *COO*
Brian Wiggins, *Opers Staff*
Stephen Mutascio, *Controller*
Lynn Nowicki, *Mng Member*
▲ EMP: 55 EST: 1970
SQ FT: 100,000
SALES (est): 35.1MM
SALES (corp-wide): 35.2MM **Privately
Held**
SIC: 5023 2064 Kitchenware; candy &
other confectionery products
PA: Fox Run Holdings, Inc
1907 Stout Dr
Warminster PA 18974
215 675-7700

(G-8212)
H & F MANUFACTURING CORP
116 Railroad Dr (18974-1449)
P.O. Box 757, Richboro (18954-0757)
PHONE.....................................215 355-0250
Robert E Dunn, *President*
Deborah F Dunn, *Treasurer*
◆ EMP: 10
SQ FT: 15,000
SALES (est): 2.1MM **Privately Held**
SIC: 3089 Plastic hardware & building
products

(G-8213)
**JIMS SOFT PRETZEL BAKERY
LLC**
27 Sienna Cir (18974-1788)
PHONE.....................................215 431-1045
EMP: 3
SALES (est): 154.3K **Privately Held**
SIC: 2052 Pretzels

(G-8214)
LABEL CONVERTERS INC
4 Ivybrook Blvd (18974-1700)
PHONE.....................................215 675-6900
Patrick Hayes, *President*
Joseph Hartzell, *Treasurer*
EMP: 7
SQ FT: 5,500
SALES (est): 1.1MM
SALES (corp-wide): 30.2MM **Privately
Held**
SIC: 2672 Labels (unprinted), gummed:
made from purchased materials
PA: The Kennedy Group Incorporated
38601 Kennedy Pkwy
Willoughby OH 44094
440 951-7660

(G-8215)
LIFTEX CORPORATION (PA)
48 Vincent Cir Ste D (18974-1538)
PHONE.....................................800 478-4651
Paul E Keating, *CEO*
Derek W McNab, *President*
Paul Keating, *Treasurer*
John Fleming, *Admin Sec*
▲ EMP: 57
SQ FT: 18,000
SALES (est): 34.7MM **Privately Held**
WEB: www.liftex.com
SIC: 3536 Hoisting slings

(G-8216)
LYNN ELECTRONICS CORP (PA)
154 Railroad Dr (18974-1449)
PHONE.....................................215 355-8200
Doron Phillips, *President*
Michael Rosen, *Principal*
Louis Rosen, *Vice Pres*
Linda Yampolsky, *Treasurer*
Michael Yampolsky, *Treasurer*
▲ EMP: 55 EST: 1956
SQ FT: 38,000
SALES (est): 20MM **Privately Held**
WEB: www.lynnelec.com
SIC: 3679 3643 Harness assemblies for
electronic use: wire or cable; connectors
& terminals for electrical devices

(G-8217)
**MARTELLIS MTAL FABRICATION
INC**
4 Louise Dr (18974-1526)
PHONE.....................................215 957-9700
Ernie Martelli III, *President*
EMP: 23
SQ FT: 12,000
SALES (est): 5.6MM **Privately Held**
WEB: www.martellismetalfab.com
SIC: 3449 Miscellaneous metalwork

(G-8218)
MILTON ROY LLC (HQ)
Also Called: Milton Roy Americas
201 Ivyland Rd (18974-1706)
PHONE.....................................215 441-0800
Chris Krieps, *President*
Elmer Doty, *Exec VP*
Kevin McGlinchey, *Vice Pres*
Dorsey Small, *Vice Pres*
David Weir, *Technical Mgr*
▲ EMP: 150
SQ FT: 100,000
SALES (est): 125.4MM
SALES (corp-wide): 389.5MM **Privately
Held**
SIC: 3561 3586 3826 Pumps & pumping
equipment; measuring & dispensing
pumps; spectroscopic & other optical
properties measuring equipment; mass
spectrometers; photometers
PA: Accudyne Industries, Llc
2728 N Harwood St Ste 200
Dallas TX 75201
469 518-4777

(G-8219)
MILTON ROY LLC
Liquid Metronics
201 Ivyland Rd (18974-1706)
PHONE.....................................215 293-0401
EMP: 4

SALES (corp-wide): 389.5MM **Privately
Held**
SIC: 3561 3586 3826 Pumps & pumping
equipment; measuring & dispensing
pumps; spectroscopic & other optical
properties measuring equipment; mass
spectrometers; photometers
HQ: Milton Roy, Llc
201 Ivyland Rd
Ivyland PA 18974
215 441-0800

(G-8220)
PMDI SIGNS INC
10 Council Rock Dr (18974-1427)
PHONE.....................................215 526-0898
Philip M Dubroff, *President*
EMP: 7
SQ FT: 3,000
SALES: 1.5MM **Privately Held**
WEB: www.pmdubroff.com
SIC: 3993 Signs & advertising specialties

(G-8221)
POWER & ENERGY INC
Also Called: P E
106 Railroad Dr (18974-1449)
PHONE.....................................215 942-4600
Peter R Bossard, *President*
Andrew Kaldor, *President*
Noel Leeson, *President*
Paul Bossard, *Vice Pres*
Al Stubbmann, *Vice Pres*
EMP: 16
SQ FT: 10,000
SALES (est): 3.4MM **Privately Held**
WEB: www.powerandenergy.com
SIC: 3674 Semiconductors & related de-
vices

(G-8222)
**TERRA-GLO LIGHTING
CORPORATION**
Also Called: Terraglo Lighting
59 Steam Whistle Dr (18974-1451)
PHONE.....................................267 430-1259
Laura Giuliano, *President*
EMP: 7
SALES (est): 466.6K **Privately Held**
SIC: 3646 Commercial indusl & institu-
tional electric lighting fixtures

(G-8223)
TITAN ABRASIVE SYSTEMS LLC
35 Steam Whistle Dr (18974-1451)
P.O. Box 750, Montgomeryville (18936-
0750)
PHONE.....................................215 310-5055
Brandon Acker, *President*
▼ EMP: 3 EST: 1953
SQ FT: 6,500
SALES (est): 529.3K **Privately Held**
SIC: 3569 Blast cleaning equipment, dust-
less

(G-8224)
TRIMLINE WINDOWS INC
Gingko Industrial K Industrial Pr (18974)
PHONE.....................................215 672-5233
Dennis J Teeling, *President*
Keith Zimmerman, *Vice Pres*
Glenn Zimmerman, *Admin Sec*
EMP: 55
SQ FT: 30,000
SALES (est): 12.5MM **Privately Held**
WEB: www.trimlinewindows.com
SIC: 3442 2431 Window & door frames;
windows & window parts & trim, wood

```
Jackson Center
Mercer County
```

(G-8225)
ALTRA MARINE
782 S Hazzard Rd (16133-1812)
PHONE.....................................814 786-8346
Paul Chandler, *Partner*
Larry Plumber, *Partner*
EMP: 5
SALES (est): 133.1K **Privately Held**
SIC: 3732 Canoes, building & repairing;
boats, fiberglass: building & repairing

▲ = Import ▼=Export
◆ =Import/Export

(G-8226)
CHEVRON AE RESOURCES LLC
101 Mcquiston Dr (16133-1633)
PHONE..............................724 662-0300
Fax: 724 662-3039
EMP: 49
SALES (corp-wide): 129.9B **Publicly Held**
SIC: **1381** 1311 4924 Oil/Gas Well Drilling Crude Petroleum/Natural Gas Production Natural Gas Distribution
HQ: Chevron Ae Resources Llc
1000 Commerce Dr Fl 4
Pittsburgh PA 15275
800 251-0171

(G-8227)
FAIRWINDS MANUFACTURING INC
68 Limber Rd (16133-2312)
PHONE..............................724 662-5210
Michael W Latchaw, *President*
Max Goldman, *Research*
EMP: 4
SALES (est): 59.4K **Privately Held**
SIC: **3446** Gratings, tread: fabricated metal

(G-8228)
INTERNTIONAL TIMBER VENEER LLC
Also Called: I T V
75 Mcquiston Dr (16133-1635)
PHONE..............................724 662-0880
Bo Edwards, *Exec VP*
Mike Rastatter, *Vice Pres*
H Tyler Howerton, *Treasurer*
Spike Mancuso, *Admin Sec*
▼ EMP: 170
SQ FT: 140,000
SALES (est): 121.4MM **Privately Held**
WEB: www.ivcusa.com
SIC: **2435** 5031 Veneer stock, hardwood; composite board products, woodboard
HQ: International Veneer Company, Inc.
1551 Montgomery St
South Hill VA 23970
434 447-7100

(G-8229)
MUSCLE PRODUCTS CORPORATION
752 Kilgore Rd (16133-2618)
PHONE..............................814 786-0166
Sharon Murphy, *President*
George Fennell, *Exec VP*
Amy L Dent, *Treasurer*
▲ EMP: 10
SALES: 2MM **Privately Held**
WEB: www.mpclubricants.com
SIC: **2992** Re-refining lubricating oils & greases

Jacobus
York County

(G-8230)
LEHR DESIGN & MANUFACTURING
12 Valley Rd (17407-1255)
P.O. Box 293 (17407-0293)
PHONE..............................717 428-1828
Stephen R Lehr, *President*
EMP: 5
SQ FT: 3,000
SALES (est): 544.5K **Privately Held**
WEB: www.lehrsforglass.de
SIC: **3544** Special dies & tools

(G-8231)
T & J BOWLING PRODUCTS CORP
250 N Main St (17407-1011)
PHONE..............................717 428-0100
Jerry Douglas Liem, *President*
EMP: 10
SQ FT: 8,000
SALES (est): 933.9K **Privately Held**
SIC: **3949** 5099 Mfg Sporting/Athletic Goods Whol Durable Goods

(G-8232)
TRY TEK MACHINE WORKS INC
250 N Main St (17407-1011)
PHONE..............................717 428-1477
James Anderson III, *President*
Brooks Cutright, *President*
Dennis Burger, *Vice Pres*
Thomas Wingling, *Vice Pres*
Cameron Tome, *Production*
EMP: 30
SQ FT: 65,000
SALES: 750K **Privately Held**
WEB: www.trytek.com
SIC: **3531** Construction machinery

(G-8233)
Z & Z MACHINE INC
12 Valley Rd (17407-1255)
PHONE..............................717 428-0354
Ernie Phillips, *President*
EMP: 3
SQ FT: 3,200
SALES: 200K **Privately Held**
SIC: **3599** Custom machinery; machine shop, jobbing & repair

James Creek
Huntingdon County

(G-8234)
HILLTOP TANK & SUPPLY
19940 Raystown Rd (16657-7916)
PHONE..............................814 658-3915
Glenn E Houp, *Owner*
EMP: 4
SQ FT: 80,000
SALES: 380K **Privately Held**
SIC: **3272** Septic tanks, concrete

Jamestown
Mercer County

(G-8235)
COMBINED SYSTEMS INC
Also Called: Combined Tactical Systems
388 Kinsman Rd (16134-9540)
P.O. Box 506 (16134-0506)
PHONE..............................724 932-2177
Donald Smith, *Ch of Bd*
Jacob Kravel, *President*
Richard Edge, *COO*
Michael Brunn, *Vice Pres*
Drew Shilling, *Prdtn Mgr*
▼ EMP: 230
SQ FT: 6,000
SALES (est): 55.4MM **Privately Held**
WEB: www.combinedsystems.com
SIC: **3483** Ammunition, except for small arms

(G-8236)
COMBINED TACTICAL SYSTEMS INC
388 Kinsman Rd (16134-9540)
P.O. Box 506 (16134-0506)
PHONE..............................724 932-2177
Donald Smith, *President*
Michael Brunn, *President*
Richad G Edge, *COO*
Jacob Kravel, *Senior VP*
Janet Scott, *CFO*
▲ EMP: 236
SALES (est): 37MM **Privately Held**
WEB: www.less-lethal.com
SIC: **3949** 2326 3482 Sporting & athletic goods; medical & hospital uniforms, men's; small arms ammunition

(G-8237)
HI-TEC CUSTOM PAINTING INC
3543 E State Rd (16134-4637)
PHONE..............................724 932-2631
John Satonica, *President*
Michael Juranovich, *President*
Rhoda Satonica, *Corp Secy*
EMP: 14
SALES (est): 780K **Privately Held**
SIC: **3949** Lures, fishing: artificial

(G-8238)
PENN ARMS INC
388 Kinsman Rd (16134-9540)
PHONE..............................814 938-5279
John Mixerock, *President*
Tracy Mixerock, *Principal*
Jacob Kravel, *Treasurer*
EMP: 49
SALES (est): 5MM **Privately Held**
SIC: **3484** Guns (firearms) or gun parts, 30 mm. & below

(G-8239)
ROB RAND ENTERPRISES INC
7299 Snodgrass Rd (16134-5557)
PHONE..............................724 927-6844
Randy Campbell, *Principal*
EMP: 4 EST: 2008
SALES (est): 356K **Privately Held**
SIC: **3131** Rands

(G-8240)
SHENANGO VALLEY SAND AND GRAV
Also Called: Shenango Vallley Sand & Gravel
172 Shine Rd (16134-9562)
PHONE..............................724 932-5600
Jim Harnett, *Manager*
EMP: 3
SALES (est): 176.6K
SALES (corp-wide): 930.7K **Privately Held**
WEB: www.pymatuning.com
SIC: **1442** Sand mining; gravel mining
PA: Shenango Valley Sand And Gravel Inc
7240 Glenwood Ave
Youngstown OH 44512
330 758-9100

(G-8241)
WALTON PAINT COMPANY INC (PA)
Also Called: Beaver Paint Company
108 Main St (16134-8510)
P.O. Box 157 (16134-0157)
PHONE..............................724 932-3101
Richard A Walton, *President*
Joseph M Walton, *Chairman*
D Michael Walton, *Vice Pres*
Joseph P Walton, *Treasurer*
Richard R Walton, *VP Mktg*
EMP: 5 EST: 1982
SQ FT: 2,000
SALES: 3.2MM **Privately Held**
SIC: **2851** Paints & paint additives

Jamison
Bucks County

(G-8242)
AMEGA HOLDINGS LLC
2604 Heron Pt (18929-1258)
PHONE..............................718 775-7188
Andrey Malkim, *Treasurer*
Eugene Groysman, *Mng Member*
EMP: 4
SQ FT: 7,000
SALES: 7.5MM **Privately Held**
SIC: **2051** Bakery: wholesale or wholesale/retail combined

(G-8243)
FRAMELESS SHOWER DOORS
2141 Chapman Cir (18929-1543)
PHONE..............................215 534-0021
John Wikoff, *Principal*
EMP: 3
SALES (est): 194.9K **Privately Held**
SIC: **3088** Shower stalls, fiberglass & plastic

(G-8244)
HBG-UPPER SAUCON INC
2500 York Rd (18929-1068)
PHONE..............................215 491-7736
Charles C Sturges III, *Principal*
EMP: 3
SALES (est): 155.4K **Privately Held**
SIC: **3131** Mfg Footwear Cut Stock

(G-8245)
QUINNOVA PHARMACEUTICALS INC
2500 York Rd Ste 210 (18929-1098)
PHONE..............................215 860-6263
Mats Silvander, *President*
EMP: 3
SALES (est): 81.8K **Privately Held**
SIC: **2834** Pharmaceutical preparations

(G-8246)
RUSHLAND RDGE VINEYARDS WINERY
2665 Rushland Rd (18929-1136)
P.O. Box 150, Rushland (18956-0150)
PHONE..............................215 598-0251
Ed Ullman, *Owner*
EMP: 4
SALES (est): 238K **Privately Held**
SIC: **2084** Wines

Jeannette
Westmoreland County

(G-8247)
B & E CANDY
1286 Hrrison Cy Export Rd (15644-4601)
PHONE..............................724 327-8898
Elma McKee, *Owner*
EMP: 3 EST: 1968
SQ FT: 1,000
SALES: 85K **Privately Held**
SIC: **2064** 5441 Candy & other confectionery products; candy

(G-8248)
BENJAMIN INDUSTRIES AND MFG
Also Called: Benjamin Company
500 S 4th St (15644-2269)
PHONE..............................724 523-9615
Joseph K Benjamin, *Owner*
EMP: 4
SQ FT: 1,500
SALES (est): 315.3K **Privately Held**
SIC: **3843** Dental equipment & supplies

(G-8249)
CASEWORKS INC
203 Jayhawk Dr (15644-3445)
PHONE..............................724 522-5068
Martin R Zundel, *President*
Bruce J Kaufman, *Vice Pres*
EMP: 15
SQ FT: 32,000
SALES (est): 2.6MM **Privately Held**
SIC: **2541** 5047 2599 Cabinets, except refrigerated: show, display, etc.: wood; store fixtures, wood; medical & hospital equipment; hospital furniture, except beds

(G-8250)
CMS EAST INC (PA)
Also Called: Tristate Precast Products Div
400 Agnew Rd (15644-3201)
P.O. Box 630, Greensburg (15601-0630)
PHONE..............................724 527-6700
George F Stoecklein Jr, *President*
David Strobel, *Corp Secy*
Timothy Kernan, *Vice Pres*
Joseph McNemar, *Vice Pres*
EMP: 80
SQ FT: 20,000
SALES (est): 23.2MM **Privately Held**
WEB: www.cmseast.com
SIC: **6553** 3272 Real property subdividers & developers, cemetery lots only; burial vaults, concrete or precast terrazzo

(G-8251)
CUPCAKE MOMMA
1170 Walton Rd (15644-4736)
PHONE..............................724 516-5098
EMP: 4 EST: 2015
SALES (est): 174.1K **Privately Held**
SIC: **2051** Mfg Bread/Related Products

(G-8252)
DIANAS HEAVENLY CUPCAKES
1007 Gaskill Ave (15644-3307)
PHONE..............................412 628-0642
EMP: 4

SALES (est): 188.1K **Privately Held**
SIC: 2051 Bread, cake & related products

(G-8253)
DUDLEY ENTERPRISES INC
Also Called: Scraders Dairy Queen
56 Millersdale Rd (15644-3163)
PHONE...................724 523-5522
Teresa Miller, *President*
Dean Miller, *Principal*
Jon D Miller, *Admin Sec*
EMP: 25
SALES (est): 2.4MM **Privately Held**
SIC: 2024 Ice cream & frozen desserts

(G-8254)
ELLIOTT COMPANY (HQ)
Also Called: Elliott Support Services
901 N 4th St (15644-1474)
PHONE...................724 527-2811
Michael Lordi, *CEO*
Antonio Casillo, *President*
Matthew Stitt, *Area Mgr*
Patrick Sucher, *Area Mgr*
William K Cox, *Vice Pres*
◆ **EMP:** 695
SQ FT: 271,000
SALES (est): 461MM
SALES (corp-wide): 4.5B **Privately Held**
WEB: www.elliott-turbo.com
SIC: 3563 3511 Air & gas compressors;
steam turbines
PA: Ebara Corporation
11-1, Hanedaasahicho
Ota-Ku TKY 144-0
337 436-111

(G-8255)
EXCEL GLASS AND GRANITE
103 Jayhawk Dr (15644-3442)
PHONE...................724 523-6190
William Pecora, *Owner*
Connie Pecora, *CFO*
▲ **EMP:** 24
SALES (est): 106.5K **Privately Held**
SIC: 1799 3281 Counter top installation;
granite, cut & shaped

(G-8256)
FEJES SIGNS
703 Bullitt Ave (15644-3425)
P.O. Box 214 (15644-0214)
PHONE...................724 527-7446
Robert Fejes, *Owner*
EMP: 4
SQ FT: 16,000
SALES (est): 322.5K **Privately Held**
SIC: 3993 Signs & advertising specialties

(G-8257)
JEANNETTE SHADE AND NOVELTY CO
Also Called: Jeannette Specialty Glass
215 N 4th St (15644-1740)
P.O. Box 99 (15644-0099)
PHONE...................724 523-5567
Yester John T, *CEO*
Kathleen R Sarniak, *President*
Theodore Sarniak III, *Chairman*
Douglas E Johnston, *CFO*
David Smitley, *Maintence Staff*
▲ **EMP:** 70
SQ FT: 65,000
SALES (est): 11.9MM **Privately Held**
WEB: www.jeannettespecglass.com
SIC: 3231 3431 3229 Products of pur-
chased glass; bathroom fixtures, including
sinks; blocks & bricks, glass

(G-8258)
JENSEN MANUFACTURING CO INC
Also Called: Jensen Steam Engine Mfg
700 Arlington Ave (15644-1999)
PHONE...................800 525-5245
Thomas H Jensen Jr, *President*
Betty Jensen Meil, *Admin Sec*
EMP: 7 **EST:** 1933
SQ FT: 6,500
SALES (est): 660K **Privately Held**
SIC: 3944 Railroad models: toy & hobby

(G-8259)
KAF-TECH INDUSTRIES INC
1010 Harrison Ave (15644-1343)
PHONE...................724 523-2343

Thomas Kozar, *President*
David Kozar, *Treasurer*
EMP: 9
SQ FT: 6,000
SALES (est): 936.7K **Privately Held**
SIC: 3599 Air intake filters, internal com-
bustion engine, except auto; machine
shop, jobbing & repair

(G-8260)
L P AERO PLASTICS INC
1086 Boquet Rd (15644-4707)
PHONE...................724 744-4448
Thomas N Frey, *President*
George Mesiarik, *Vice Pres*
John Frey, *Treasurer*
EMP: 45
SQ FT: 24,000
SALES (est): 10.8MM **Privately Held**
WEB: www.lpaero.com
SIC: 3089 3728 Windshields, plastic; air-
craft parts & equipment

(G-8261)
LRG CORPORATION
210 Magee Ave (15644-2136)
P.O. Box 490 (15644-0490)
PHONE...................724 523-3131
Lewis R Gainfort, *CEO*
Vickie Gaudi, *Treasurer*
Deneen C Sarocky, *Exec Dir*
EMP: 22
SQ FT: 24,000
SALES (est): 4.4MM **Privately Held**
WEB: www.lrgcorp.com
SIC: 3599 5084 Machine shop, jobbing &
repair; blanks, tips & inserts

(G-8262)
M & P REFINISHING CO
212 S 5th St (15644-2267)
PHONE...................724 527-6360
John Kerlin, *Partner*
Don Kerlin, *Partner*
Gary Kerlin, *Partner*
EMP: 7
SQ FT: 1,000
SALES (est): 125K **Privately Held**
SIC: 7641 7532 3471 Furniture refinish-
ing; customizing services, non-factory
basis; plating of metals or formed prod-
ucts

(G-8263)
OMNOVA SOLUTIONS INC
1001 Chambers Ave (15644-3207)
PHONE...................724 523-5441
Jeff Phelps, *Controller*
Mike Poznick, *Info Tech Dir*
EMP: 300
SALES (corp-wide): 769.8MM **Publicly
Held**
WEB: www.omnova.com
SIC: 3081 2952 Plastic film & sheet; as-
phalt felts & coatings
PA: Omnova Solutions Inc.
25435 Harvard Rd
Beachwood OH 44122
216 682-7000

(G-8264)
SIGNSTAT
412 Harrison Ave (15644-1938)
PHONE...................724 527-7475
Joel Haluck, *Partner*
Lisa Haluck, *Vice Pres*
Ken Vaughan, *Accounts Mgr*
EMP: 12
SQ FT: 3,000
SALES (est): 990K **Privately Held**
SIC: 3993 1799 5046 5999 Signs & ad-
vertising specialties; sign installation &
maintenance; signs, electrical; electronic
parts & equipment

(G-8265)
STELLAR PRCSION COMPONENTS LTD
1201 Rankin Ave (15644-1682)
PHONE...................724 523-5559
Lori Allbright, *President*
William Rodgers, *COO*
Michaele E Vucish, *Vice Pres*
Dan Linhart, *Supervisor*
EMP: 71
SQ FT: 20,000

SALES (est): 16.5MM **Privately Held**
WEB: www.stellarprecision.com
SIC: 3769 Guided missile & space
vehicle parts & aux eqpt, rsch & dev;
electrical discharge machining (EDM)

(G-8266)
SUNNYS FASHIONS
410 Clay Ave (15644-2123)
PHONE...................724 527-1800
EMP: 3
SALES (est): 189.3K **Privately Held**
SIC: 5139 3149 Footwear; footwear, ex-
cept rubber

(G-8267)
WESTMORELAND IRON AND MET LLC
2571 Radebaugh Rd (15644-4061)
PHONE...................724 523-8151
Nicole R Blazowich, *Principal*
EMP: 4
SALES (est): 200.7K **Privately Held**
SIC: 1099 Metal ores

(G-8268)
WILSON CANDY CO INC (PA)
408 Harrison Ave (15644-1997)
PHONE...................724 523-3151
Douglas Wilson, *President*
Carolyn S Wilson, *Vice Pres*
EMP: 12 **EST:** 1946
SQ FT: 11,000
SALES (est): 520K **Privately Held**
SIC: 2064 5441 Chocolate covered dates;
candy

Jefferson
Greene County

(G-8269)
D L MACHINE LLC
134 Reservoir Hill Rd (15344-4149)
PHONE...................724 627-7870
Douglas Laskody, *Owner*
EMP: 10
SQ FT: 7,000
SALES (est): 1.5MM **Privately Held**
SIC: 3441 3599 Fabricated structural
metal; machine shop, jobbing & repair

(G-8270)
DE SIGNS BY BEN POGUE
230 Pumpkin Run Rd (15344-4204)
PHONE...................724 592-5013
EMP: 3
SALES (est): 130K **Privately Held**
SIC: 3993 Mfg Signs/Advertising Special-
ties

(G-8271)
THISTLETHWAITE VINEYARDS
151 Thistlewaite Ln (15344-4136)
PHONE...................724 883-3372
Richard Thistlethwaite, *Principal*
EMP: 4 **EST:** 2014
SALES (est): 164.7K **Privately Held**
SIC: 0762 2084 Vineyard management &
maintenance services; wines

(G-8272)
WILSON GLOBAL INC
Also Called: Keystone Cooperage
1216 Jefferson Rd (15344-4102)
P.O. Box 269 (15344-0269)
PHONE...................724 883-4952
William A Wilson Jr, *President*
Mike Wilson, *Vice Pres*
Brian Wilson, *Treasurer*
V Joyce Wilson, *Admin Sec*
◆ **EMP:** 55
SQ FT: 25,000
SALES (est): 11.8MM **Privately Held**
WEB: www.wilsonforestproducts.com
SIC: 2429 2436 2426 Heading, barrel
(cooperage stock): sawed or split; staves,
barrel: sawed or split; veneer stock, soft-
wood; dimension, hardwood

Jefferson Hills
Allegheny County

(G-8273)
BAW PLASTICS INC (PA)
2148 Century Dr (15025-3654)
PHONE...................412 384-3100
James D Slovonic, *President*
Jane Laporte, *Vice Pres*
Abigail Slovonic, *Treasurer*
Barb Delaney, *Credit Mgr*
John Dush, *Human Res Dir*
EMP: 128
SQ FT: 160,000
SALES (est): 32.4MM **Privately Held**
WEB: www.bawplastics.com
SIC: 3083 Laminated plastics plate & sheet

(G-8274)
EASTMAN CHEMICAL COMPANY
2200 State Rt 837 (15025)
P.O. Box 545, West Elizabeth (15088-
0545)
PHONE...................412 384-2520
Kiyoshi Ito, *Treasurer*
Coleen Buglar, *Branch Mgr*
Deb Wiley, *Manager*
EMP: 50 **Publicly Held**
SIC: 2821 Plastics materials & resins
PA: Eastman Chemical Company
200 S Wilcox Dr
Kingsport TN 37660

(G-8275)
EASTMAN CHEMICAL COMPANY
200 Willcox Dr (15025)
PHONE...................423 229-2000
EMP: 911 **Publicly Held**
SIC: 2821 Plastics materials & resins
PA: Eastman Chemical Company
200 S Wilcox Dr
Kingsport TN 37660

(G-8276)
EASTMAN CHEMICAL RESINS INC
2200 State Rte 837 (15025)
PHONE...................412 384-2520
Suzanne Spell, *Admin Sec*
EMP: 25 **Publicly Held**
SIC: 2821 Molding compounds, plastics
HQ: Eastman Chemical Resins, Inc.
200 S Wilcox Dr
Kingsport TN 37660
423 229-2000

(G-8277)
KURT J LESKER COMPANY (PA)
Also Called: Kurt J Lesker
1925 Route 51 Ste 1 (15025-3681)
PHONE...................412 387-9200
Kurt J Lesker III, *President*
Duane Bingaman, *Vice Pres*
Chuck Deventura, *Vice Pres*
Richard C Johnson, *Vice Pres*
Cindy Lesker, *Vice Pres*
▲ **EMP:** 180
SQ FT: 2,706
SALES (est): 77.6MM **Privately Held**
WEB: www.lesker.com
SIC: 3559 Semiconductor manufacturing
machinery

Jefferson Township
Wayne County

(G-8278)
J R B PRINTING
302 Wimmers Rd (18436-3262)
PHONE...................570 689-9114
John R Boos, *Owner*
EMP: 3
SALES (est): 231.6K **Privately Held**
SIC: 2752 Commercial printing, offset

(G-8279)
SPACE AGE PLASTICS INC
581 Cortez Rd (18436-3816)
PHONE...................570 630-6060
Joseph P Ceresko, *President*

EMP: 15
SQ FT: 20,000
SALES (est): 2.2MM **Privately Held**
WEB: www.ferdinandart.com
SIC: 3089 3432 3088 Plastic processing; plumbing fixture fittings & trim; bathroom fixtures, plastic; tubs (bath, shower & laundry), plastic

(G-8280)
WILLIAM ELSTON INCORPORATED
481 Cortez Rd (18436-3712)
PHONE....................................570 689-2203
William Elston, *President*
Debbie Coyle, *Vice Pres*
EMP: 12
SALES: 925K **Privately Held**
SIC: 5039 3272 Septic tanks; septic tanks, concrete

Jenkintown
Montgomery County

(G-8281)
AMERICAN SILK MILLS LLC
100 West Ave Ste 910 (19046-2642)
PHONE....................................215 561-4901
James Harowicz, *CFO*
Robin Slough, *Branch Mgr*
EMP: 5
SALES (corp-wide): 375.3MM **Privately Held**
SIC: 2211 2221 Cotton broad woven goods; broadwoven fabric mills, man-made
HQ: American Silk Mills Llc
329 S Wrenn St Ste 101
High Point NC 27260
570 822-7147

(G-8282)
COFFEE CUP PUBLISHING
Also Called: Coffee Cup Studio
99 Runnymede Ave (19046-2016)
PHONE....................................215 887-7365
Randolph Garbin, *Owner*
EMP: 4
SALES: 100K **Privately Held**
WEB: www.dinerforsale.com
SIC: 2741

(G-8283)
DESIGNER MICHAEL TODD LLC
1166 Timbergate Dr (19046-2509)
PHONE....................................215 376-0145
Lewis Hendler,
EMP: 10
SALES (est): 830.4K **Privately Held**
SIC: 2844 Toilet preparations

(G-8284)
E Z NET SOLUTIONS INC
728 Rodman Ave (19046-2218)
PHONE....................................215 887-7200
Eric Hall, *Principal*
EMP: 3
SALES (est): 222K **Privately Held**
SIC: 7372 Prepackaged software

(G-8285)
ELYSE AION
Also Called: Berben Insignia Company
820 Fox Chase Rd (19046-4437)
PHONE....................................215 663-8787
Elyse Aion, *Owner*
Charles Brown, *Financial Exec*
Bobbie Hullstrung, *Manager*
Phil Nelson, *Manager*
EMP: 4
SALES (est): 308.9K **Privately Held**
WEB: www.policebadges.com
SIC: 3999 Badges, metal: policemen, firemen, etc.; buttons: Red Cross, union, identification; military insignia

(G-8286)
ENERGIZER BATTERY CO
689 Pembroke Rd (19046-3325)
PHONE....................................215 572-0200
EMP: 3

SALES (est): 255K **Privately Held**
SIC: 3692 5063 5531 Mfg Primary Batteries Whol Electrical Equipment Ret Auto/Home Supplies

(G-8287)
FEDEX OFFICE & PRINT SVCS INC
636 Old York Rd (19046-2858)
PHONE....................................215 576-1687
EMP: 4
SALES (corp-wide): 65.4B **Publicly Held**
WEB: www.kinkos.com
SIC: 2759 4822 5099 7334 Commercial printing; facsimile transmission services; signs, except electric; photocopying & duplicating services
HQ: Fedex Office And Print Services, Inc.
7900 Legacy Dr
Plano TX 75024
800 463-3339

(G-8288)
GOODWAY GRAPHICS INC
Also Called: Igi Printing
261 York Rd Ste 930 (19046)
PHONE....................................215 887-5700
Donald L Wolk, *Ch of Bd*
Noel Doherty, *President*
Robert Perotti, *President*
Beryl J Wolf, *Director*
EMP: 350 **EST:** 1974
SQ FT: 8,000
SALES (est): 38MM **Privately Held**
WEB: www.goodwaygraphics.com
SIC: 2752 7331 7336 3577 Lithographing on metal; direct mail advertising services; graphic arts & related design; graphic displays, except graphic terminals; promotion service

(G-8289)
HAL-JO CORP
Also Called: Phil Stupp Furs
261 York Rd (19046)
P.O. Box 665, Foxcroft Square (19046-7065)
PHONE....................................215 885-4747
Frank Stupp, *President*
Geraldine Stupp, *Corp Secy*
Hal Stupp, *Vice Pres*
EMP: 10
SALES (est): 793.6K **Privately Held**
SIC: 5632 7219 2386 2371 Furriers; fur garment cleaning, repairing & storage; garments, leather; apparel, fur

(G-8290)
HYDROGEN ELECTRICS LLC
1022 Frederick Rd (19046-1102)
PHONE....................................267 334-3155
Joseph B Kejha, *President*
Lucky Kejha, *Vice Pres*
Gigi Rubin, *Admin Sec*
EMP: 3
SALES: 8.6K **Privately Held**
WEB: www.hydroelectronics.com
SIC: 3569 7389 Centrifuges, industrial;

(G-8291)
INDUSTRIAL FLOOR CORPORATION (PA)
Also Called: Infloor
261 Old York Rd Ste 612 (19046-3778)
PHONE....................................215 886-1800
Fred J Coccagna Jr, *President*
Adrienne Coccagna, *Vice Pres*
Fred F Coccana, *Manager*
EMP: 10
SQ FT: 1,000
SALES: 3MM **Privately Held**
WEB: www.floorepoxyindustrial.com
SIC: 3089 1752 2842 Floor coverings, plastic; floor laying & floor work; access flooring system installation; specialty cleaning, polishes & sanitation goods

(G-8292)
KALNIN GRAPHICS INC
261 York Rd Ste A30 (19046)
PHONE....................................215 887-3203
Dianne Kalnin, *President*
Ivar Kalnin, *Admin Sec*
EMP: 26 **EST:** 1973
SQ FT: 10,405

SALES (est): 4.6MM **Privately Held**
WEB: www.kalnin.com
SIC: 2752 7334 Commercial printing, offset; photocopying & duplicating services

(G-8293)
LD DAVIS INDUSTRIES INC (PA)
1725 The Fairway (19046-1400)
PHONE....................................800 883-6199
Louis D Davis III, *President*
Norbert Kroeger, *COO*
Michael Free, *CFO*
▲ **EMP:** 50 **EST:** 1926
SQ FT: 4,000
SALES (est): 11.9MM **Privately Held**
WEB: www.lddavis.com
SIC: 2891 Adhesives; glue

(G-8294)
LESLIE S GEISSEL
Also Called: Jenkintown Electric Company
220 York Rd (19046-3244)
PHONE....................................215 884-1050
Leslie S Geissel, *Owner*
Mike McKenna, *Manager*
▲ **EMP:** 7
SQ FT: 3,700
SALES: 2MM **Privately Held**
SIC: 3639 5064 Major kitchen appliances, except refrigerators & stoves; electrical appliances, major; television sets

(G-8295)
MANAGING EDITOR INC
Also Called: M E I
610 Old York Rd Ste 250 (19046)
PHONE....................................215 517-5116
Dennis Mc Guire, *President*
Craig Roth, *Senior VP*
Robert Baldwin, *Vice Pres*
Linda Bruce, *Vice Pres*
Steven K Haught, *Vice Pres*
EMP: 50
SQ FT: 26,000
SALES (est): 8.3MM **Privately Held**
WEB: www.maned.com
SIC: 7371 7372 Computer software systems analysis & design, custom; computer software development; prepackaged software

(G-8296)
MARGRAF DENTAL MFG INC
611 Harper Ave (19046-3206)
P.O. Box 2004 (19046-0604)
PHONE....................................215 884-0369
Barry Margraf, *President*
James Margraf, *Vice Pres*
EMP: 4
SQ FT: 4,000
SALES: 390K **Privately Held**
WEB: www.margrafcorp.com
SIC: 3843 Dental laboratory equipment

(G-8297)
MY JEWEL SHOP INC
411 Old York Rd (19046)
PHONE....................................215 887-3881
Robert C Stewart, *President*
Linda Stewart, *Vice Pres*
EMP: 5
SQ FT: 1,200
SALES: 300K **Privately Held**
WEB: www.myjewelshop.com
SIC: 3911 5944 Jewelry, precious metal; jewelry, precious stones & precious metals

(G-8298)
PACKAGING ENTERPRISES INC
12 N Penn Ave (19046-4245)
P.O. Box 5038, Philadelphia (19111-0538)
PHONE....................................215 379-1234
Terrance Geyer, *President*
Timothy Geyer, *Vice Pres*
▲ **EMP:** 9
SQ FT: 8,500
SALES (est): 1.7MM **Privately Held**
SIC: 3565 Bottling machinery: filling, capping, labeling

(G-8299)
RAF INDUSTRIES INC (PA)
165 Township Line Rd # 2100 (19046-3587)
PHONE....................................215 572-0738

Robert A Fox, *CEO*
Richard M Horowitz, *President*
Michael F Daly, *CFO*
EMP: 10
SQ FT: 5,000
SALES (est): 353.3MM **Privately Held**
WEB: www.rafind.com
SIC: 8742 3564 Distribution channels consultant; filters, air: furnaces, air conditioning equipment, etc.

(G-8300)
SFA THERAPEUTICS LLC
610 Old York Rd Ste 400 (19046)
PHONE....................................267 584-1080
Ira Spector, *CEO*
EMP: 4
SQ FT: 150
SALES (est): 156.7K **Privately Held**
SIC: 2834 Pharmaceutical preparations

(G-8301)
SIMKINS CORPORATION (PA)
Also Called: National Paperbox
1636 Valley Rd (19046-1142)
PHONE....................................215 739-4033
Morton Simkins, *President*
James Simkins, *Vice Pres*
EMP: 28
SQ FT: 150,000
SALES (est): 37.4MM **Privately Held**
SIC: 2652 3559 7389 Setup paperboard boxes; pharmaceutical machinery; packaging & labeling services

(G-8302)
SPS TECHNOLOGIES LLC (DH)
Also Called: PCC SPS Fastener Division
301 Highland Ave (19046-2692)
PHONE....................................215 572-3000
Mark Donegan, *Mng Member*
Joe Lynn, *Manager*
Steve Pierce, *Manager*
Meg Comegno, *IT/INT Sup*
Kevin Stein,
◆ **EMP:** 1000 **EST:** 2003
SQ FT: 750,000
SALES (est): 1.3B
SALES (corp-wide): 225.3B **Publicly Held**
WEB: www.spst.com
SIC: 3423 3499 3264 3679 Hand & edge tools; magnets, permanent: metallic; magnets, permanent: ceramic or ferrite; cores, magnetic; secondary nonferrous metals; screws, metal
HQ: Precision Castparts Corp.
4650 Sw Mcdam Ave Ste 300
Portland OR 97239
503 946-4800

(G-8303)
SPS TECHNOLOGIES LLC
Also Called: Aerospace Division
301 Highland Ave (19046-2692)
PHONE....................................215 572-3000
Bryant Cranston, *President*
EMP: 1000
SALES (corp-wide): 225.3B **Publicly Held**
WEB: www.spst.com
SIC: 3452 Screws, metal; bolts, metal
HQ: Sps Technologies, Llc
301 Highland Ave
Jenkintown PA 19046
215 572-3000

(G-8304)
WEB AGE SOLUTIONS INC
744 Yorkway Pl (19046-2712)
P.O. Box 158 (19046-0158)
PHONE....................................215 517-6540
Tapas Banerjee, *President*
Laura Banerjee, *Partner*
Greg Wagner, *Vice Pres*
EMP: 25
SALES (est): 2.1MM **Privately Held**
WEB: www.webagesolutions.com
SIC: 7379 8299 7372 ; educational services; educational computer software
PA: Web Age Solutions Inc
821a Bloor St W
Toronto ON M6G 1
416 406-3994

Jermyn
Lackawanna County

(G-8305)
BARDANE MFG CO
317 Delaware St (18433-1436)
P.O. Box 70 (18433-0070)
PHONE...................................570 876-4844
Neil Horvick, *President*
Dom Augustine, *Project Engr*
Joe Paone, *Project Engr*
George Garrick, *Marketing Staff*
Gary Mahalidge, *Manager*
▲ **EMP:** 100
SQ FT: 85,000
SALES: 12MM **Privately Held**
WEB: www.bardane.com
SIC: 3363 3364 Aluminum die-castings;
zinc & zinc-base alloy die-castings

(G-8306)
GOLIATH DEVELOPMENT LLC
(PA)
Also Called: Ago Design Group
136 Route 247 (18433-3603)
PHONE...................................310 748-6288
Matthew Agostini, *Principal*
EMP: 3 **EST:** 2014
SQ FT: 1,000
SALES: 275K **Privately Held**
SIC: 3944 Games, toys & children's vehicles

(G-8307)
J & E INDUSTRIES INC
201 S Washington Ave (18433-1119)
PHONE...................................570 876-1361
Edward Lastauskas, *President*
Jeff Lastauskas, *Vice Pres*
Carla Curtis, *Admin Sec*
EMP: 25
SQ FT: 1,200
SALES: 2.5MM **Privately Held**
WEB: www.jeindustries.net
SIC: 3599 Machine shop, jobbing & repair

(G-8308)
MILLER CASKET COMPANY INC
(PA)
21 Franklin St (18433-1652)
PHONE...................................570 876-3872
Harry Pontone, *President*
Andrew Pontone, *Treasurer*
Louis Pontone, *Admin Sec*
EMP: 53
SQ FT: 10,000
SALES: 7.8MM **Privately Held**
SIC: 3995 Burial caskets

(G-8309)
REEVES AWNING INC
Also Called: John Reeves & Sons Awning
623 Lincoln Ave (18433-1633)
PHONE...................................570 876-0350
Edward Reeves, *President*
John Reeves, *Vice Pres*
EMP: 11
SALES (est): 941.4K **Privately Held**
SIC: 2394 Awnings, fabric: made from purchased materials

Jersey Shore
Lycoming County

(G-8310)
BOWER WIRE CLOTH TL & DIE
INC
328 Railroad St (17740-1123)
PHONE...................................570 398-4488
Michael Bower, *President*
Robert Irvin, *Admin Sec*
EMP: 3
SQ FT: 9,600
SALES (est): 486K **Privately Held**
WEB: www.bowerwirecloth.com
SIC: 3357 3544 Aluminum wire & cable;
extrusion dies; jigs & fixtures; wire drawing & straightening dies

(G-8311)
CLAIR D THOMPSON & SONS
INC
Also Called: Thompson's Packing Co
400 Allegheny St (17740-1304)
P.O. Box 506 (17740-0506)
PHONE...................................570 398-1880
Richard C Thompson, *President*
Kurt A Thompson, *Vice Pres*
EMP: 30
SQ FT: 34,000
SALES (est): 5MM **Privately Held**
SIC: 2013 5147 5144 5146 Sausages &
related products, from purchased meat;
meats, fresh; poultry products; fish &
seafoods; vegetables, frozen; dairy products, except dried or canned

(G-8312)
CLINTON PALLET COMPANY INC
(PA)
51 Municipal Dr (17740-7039)
PHONE...................................570 753-3010
Scott H Kershner, *President*
EMP: 12
SQ FT: 15,225
SALES (est): 1MM **Privately Held**
WEB: www.clintonpallet.com
SIC: 2448 Pallets, wood

(G-8313)
GAS WELL SERVICES 24-7 LLC
515 Joes Run Rd (17740-8326)
PHONE...................................570 398-7879
Shawn W Fink, *Principal*
EMP: 3
SALES (est): 473.5K **Privately Held**
SIC: 1389 Well logging

(G-8314)
HANSON AGGREGATES PA LLC
Also Called: Pinecreek Quarry
503 Quarry Rd (17740-8458)
PHONE...................................570 368-2481
Larry Weidler, *Principal*
EMP: 14
SALES (corp-wide): 20.6B **Privately Held**
SIC: 1442 1422 Common sand mining;
crushed & broken limestone
HQ: Hanson Aggregates Pennsylvania, Llc
7660 Imperial Way
Allentown PA 18195
610 366-4626

(G-8315)
JERSEY SHORE STEEL
COMPANY (PA)
70 Maryland Ave (17740-7113)
P.O. Box 5055 (17740-5055)
PHONE...................................570 753-3000
John C Schultz, *CEO*
Peter D Schultz, *Exec VP*
Mark Scheffey, *Treasurer*
Lori Rauch, *Accountant*
Lorraine Barone, *Human Res Mgr*
◆ **EMP:** 400 **EST:** 1938
SQ FT: 125,000
SALES (est): 135.6MM **Privately Held**
WEB: www.jssteel.com
SIC: 3312 Rails, steel or iron

(G-8316)
KEYSTONE RAIL RECOVERY
LLC
70 Maryland Ave (17740-7113)
PHONE...................................865 567-2166
Russ Clark, *President*
EMP: 7
SALES (est): 356.3K **Privately Held**
SIC: 3743 Railroad equipment

(G-8317)
LEONARD BLOCK COMPANY
INC
560 Old Us Highway 220 (17740-7819)
PHONE...................................570 398-3376
Richard A Leonard, *CEO*
Linda York, *Corp Secy*
EMP: 7 **EST:** 1956
SQ FT: 5,800
SALES: 1.3MM **Privately Held**
WEB: www.leonardblockcompany.com
SIC: 3271 Blocks, concrete or cinder: standard

(G-8318)
MARTINA GUERRA GOLDSMITH
1102 Allegheny St (17740-1106)
PHONE...................................570 398-1833
Martina Guerra, *Principal*
EMP: 3 **EST:** 2007
SALES (est): 247.4K **Privately Held**
SIC: 3914 Silversmithing

(G-8319)
P STONE INC
Also Called: Fine Thankyou
1430 Route 880 Hwy (17740-7705)
P.O. Box 254 (17740-0254)
PHONE...................................570 745-7166
James P Mc Keag, *President*
EMP: 7
SQ FT: 2,400
SALES (est): 822.1K **Privately Held**
WEB: www.pstone.com
SIC: 1422 Crushed & broken limestone

(G-8320)
PREMIUM TOOL CO INC
1082 Penn Ave (17740-7008)
PHONE...................................570 753-5070
Michael Koch, *President*
Daniel Lazorka, *Vice Pres*
EMP: 13
SQ FT: 6,000
SALES (est): 1.5MM **Privately Held**
SIC: 3599 Machine shop, jobbing & repair

(G-8321)
PROCESS CONTROL SPC INC
1854 Dutch Hollow Rd (17740-6902)
PHONE...................................570 753-5799
Dennis Socling, *President*
Garrett Socling, *Vice Pres*
Kelly Socling, *Treasurer*
Pattie Socling, *Admin Sec*
EMP: 4
SQ FT: 4,200
SALES (est): 683.9K **Privately Held**
WEB: www.pcspecialties.com
SIC: 3823 Computer interface equipment
for industrial process control

(G-8322)
R PS MACHINERY SALES INC
175 Old Rt 220 Hwy (17740)
P.O. Box 507 (17740-0507)
PHONE...................................570 398-7456
Sharon Fisher, *President*
Diane Beiter, *Vice Pres*
EMP: 20
SQ FT: 53,600
SALES (est): 4.9MM **Privately Held**
SIC: 3441 1629 Bridge sections, prefabricated highway; bridge sections, prefabricated railway; expansion joints (structural
shapes), iron or steel; drainage system
construction

(G-8323)
TIADAGHTON EMBROIDERY
110 Charles St (17740-1149)
PHONE...................................570 398-4477
Chris Fravel, *President*
EMP: 3
SALES (est): 178.5K **Privately Held**
SIC: 5699 2395 Customized clothing &
apparel; embroidery products, except
schiffli machine

(G-8324)
WATTS WELDING SHOP LLC
11282 W Route 973 Hwy (17740-8787)
PHONE...................................570 398-1184
Cleon Watts Jr, *Mng Member*
Lynnette R Watts,
EMP: 5
SALES (est): 66.5K **Privately Held**
SIC: 7692 Welding repair

(G-8325)
WEST PHARMACEUTICAL SVCS
INC
347 Oliver St (17740-1923)
PHONE...................................570 398-5411
Warren Crouse, *QC Mgr*
Michael Dincher, *Engineer*
Deb Gibson, *Engineer*
Donald Hill, *Engineer*
Chris Stabley, *Engineer*

EMP: 200
SQ FT: 64,000
SALES (corp-wide): 1.7B **Publicly Held**
WEB: www.westpharma.com
SIC: 2834 Pharmaceutical preparations
PA: West Pharmaceutical Services, Inc.
530 Herman O West Dr
Exton PA 19341
610 594-2900

Jessup
Lackawanna County

(G-8326)
ANGELO NIETO INC
Also Called: N & N Drilling Supply
200 Clarkson Ave (18434-1608)
P.O. Box 95, Peckville (18452-0095)
PHONE...................................570 489-6761
Greg M Nieto, *President*
Gary Geldhof, *Vice Pres*
Bill Henry, *Vice Pres*
John Van Wert, *Design Engr*
Tina Clemo, *Business Anlyst*
▼ **EMP:** 19 **EST:** 1966
SQ FT: 13,000
SALES (est): 9.6MM **Privately Held**
SIC: 3532 Drills, core

(G-8327)
BAKKAVOR FOODS USA INC
46 Alberigi Dr (18434-1827)
PHONE...................................570 383-9800
Michael Falsetti, *Branch Mgr*
EMP: 18
SALES (corp-wide): 2.4B **Privately Held**
SIC: 2051 5149 Bakery: wholesale or
wholesale/retail combined; groceries & related products
HQ: Bakkavor Foods Usa, Inc.
18201 Central Ave
Carson CA 90746
704 522-1977

(G-8328)
C S M BOTTLING INC
Also Called: Mid Valley Bottling Co
214 Flynn St (18434-1307)
PHONE...................................570 489-6071
John Cirba, *President*
Kevin Swift, *Treasurer*
Stacey Menta, *Admin Sec*
EMP: 4
SQ FT: 2,000
SALES: 250K **Privately Held**
SIC: 2086 Soft drinks: packaged in cans,
bottles, etc.

(G-8329)
CARDINAL LG COMPANY
42 Archbald Heights Rd (18434-1156)
PHONE...................................570 489-6421
EMP: 10
SALES (corp-wide): 1B **Privately Held**
SIC: 3231 Products of purchased glass
HQ: Cardinal Lg Company
250 Griffin St E
Amery WI 54001

(G-8330)
LBP MANUFACTURING LLC
7 Alberigi Dr (18434-1831)
PHONE...................................570 291-5463
EMP: 26
SALES (corp-wide): 171.3MM **Privately
Held**
SIC: 2671 Folding paperboard boxes
PA: Lbp Manufacturing Llc
1325 S Cicero Ave
Cicero IL 60804
800 545-6200

(G-8331)
LOCKHEED MARTIN
CORPORATION
1270 Mid Valley Dr (18434-1819)
PHONE...................................570 307-1590
Joe Borys, *Manager*
EMP: 435 **Publicly Held**
SIC: 3812 Search & navigation equipment
PA: Lockheed Martin Corporation
6801 Rockledge Dr
Bethesda MD 20817

▲ = Import ▼=Export
◆ =Import/Export

(G-8332)
MATERIAL TECH & LOGISTICS INC
Also Called: M T L
1325 Veterans Memorial Dr (18434-1825)
PHONE....................................570 487-6162
Michael J Hillebrand, *President*
Tony Poplawski, *Controller*
▲ EMP: 70
SQ FT: 53,000
SALES (est): 14.7MM **Privately Held**
SIC: 2221 Specialty broadwoven fabrics, including twisted weaves

(G-8333)
MINI-GOLF INC
202 Bridge St (18434-1302)
PHONE....................................570 489-8623
Joseph C Rogari, *President*
Joseph J Buckshon Jr, *Vice Pres*
EMP: 20 EST: 1920
SQ FT: 8,000
SALES (est): 2.1MM **Privately Held**
WEB: www.minigolfinc.com
SIC: 3949 Golf equipment

(G-8334)
NORTHEAST LAMINATED GLASS CORP
14 Alberigi Dr (18434-1827)
PHONE....................................570 489-6421
Thomas Zaccone, *President*
Laurence Tumminia, *Vice Pres*
EMP: 5
SQ FT: 64,000
SALES (est): 923.9K **Privately Held**
SIC: 3211 5023 Laminated glass; glassware

(G-8335)
PLUMPYS PIEROGIES INC
Also Called: Plumpy's Homemade
515 Delaware St Ste 1 (18434-1470)
PHONE....................................570 489-5520
Mike Cortazar, *President*
Kathy Cortazar, *Admin Sec*
EMP: 5
SQ FT: 1,000
SALES (est): 199.6K **Privately Held**
SIC: 2045 Doughs, frozen or refrigerated: from purchased flour

(G-8336)
SCRANTON WILBERT VAULT INC
1260 Mid Valley Dr (18434-1819)
PHONE....................................570 489-5065
Randy Sandt, *President*
Vivian Smith, *Corp Secy*
Larry Bruen, *Vice Pres*
Ron Lehman, *Manager*
EMP: 18
SQ FT: 13,500
SALES (est): 1.5MM **Privately Held**
SIC: 3272 Burial vaults, concrete or pre-cast terrazzo

Jim Thorpe
Carbon County

(G-8337)
BIG CREEK VINEYARD
27 Race St (18229-2003)
PHONE....................................570 325-8138
Dominic Stroahien, *Owner*
EMP: 3 EST: 1996
SALES (est): 132.2K **Privately Held**
SIC: 2084 Wines

(G-8338)
CLOSET CASES
44 Bluebell Ln (18229-9315)
PHONE....................................570 262-9092
Michelle Griffin, *Principal*
EMP: 3
SALES (est): 321.5K **Privately Held**
SIC: 3523 Farm machinery & equipment

(G-8339)
CROW VALLEY POTTERY
61 W Broadway (18229-1931)
PHONE....................................360 376-4260

Jeffri Coleman, *Partner*
Micheal Rivkin, *Partner*
EMP: 4
SALES: 450K **Privately Held**
WEB: www.crowvalley.com
SIC: 3269 5719 5947 5999 Figures: pottery, china, earthenware & stoneware; pottery; gift, novelty & souvenir shop; art dealers

(G-8340)
FOSTER-KMETZ WOODWORKING
165 W Broadway 167 (18229-1930)
PHONE....................................570 325-8222
Gerald Kmetz, *Partner*
Farley Foster, *Partner*
Tim Herman, *Partner*
EMP: 8
SQ FT: 12,000
SALES (est): 1MM **Privately Held**
SIC: 2431 5031 5211 1521 Millwork; hardboard; millwork & lumber; single-family home remodeling, additions & repairs

(G-8341)
LUICANA INDUSTRIES INC
99 Packer Hl (18229-1221)
PHONE....................................570 325-9699
Donald G Luicana, *President*
Sandra J Luicana, *Corp Secy*
EMP: 9
SQ FT: 9,000
SALES: 1.4MM **Privately Held**
SIC: 3281 1799 5211 Marble, building: cut & shaped; kitchen & bathroom remodeling; bathroom fixtures, equipment & supplies

(G-8342)
MILAN PRINTING
1012 North St (18229-1715)
PHONE....................................570 325-2649
David Miller, *Owner*
Judith Miller, *Co-Owner*
EMP: 3
SALES: 110K **Privately Held**
SIC: 2759 2752 Letterpress printing; commercial printing, lithographic

Johnsonburg
Elk County

(G-8343)
ACCU-GRIND INC
451 Center St (15845-1304)
P.O. Box 195 (15845-0195)
PHONE....................................814 965-5475
William Shuey, *President*
Donna Shuey, *Treasurer*
EMP: 52
SQ FT: 22,000
SALES (est): 6.3MM **Privately Held**
SIC: 3399 3471 Powder, metal; finishing, metals or formed products

(G-8344)
CHEMTRADE CHEMICALS CORP
1224 E Center St (15845)
PHONE....................................814 965-4118
Randy Welder, *Principal*
EMP: 7
SALES (corp-wide): 1.1B **Privately Held**
SIC: 2819 Aluminum sulfate
HQ: Chemtrade Chemicals Corporation
90 E Halsey Rd Ste 301
Parsippany NJ 07054
973 515-0900

(G-8345)
DIIULIO LOGGING
1797 Bendigo Rd (15845-2917)
PHONE....................................814 965-3183
Robert Diiulio, *Principal*
EMP: 6
SALES (est): 599.6K **Privately Held**
SIC: 2411 Logging

(G-8346)
DOMTAR PAPER COMPANY LLC
100 W Center St (15845-1444)
PHONE....................................814 965-2521
John Murdock, *Buyer*

Bob Grygotis, *Manager*
Samuel Rosenhoover, *Manager*
Daniel Comes, *Technology*
Marsha Muroski, *Admin Asst*
EMP: 600
SALES (corp-wide): 301.1MM **Privately Held**
SIC: 2621 Paper mills
HQ: Domtar Paper Company, Llc
234 Kingsley Park Dr
Fort Mill SC 29715

(G-8347)
JOHNSONBURG PRESS INC
Also Called: Johnsonburg Press Ofc
517 Market St (15845-1294)
PHONE....................................814 965-2503
John Fowler, *President*
EMP: 3 EST: 1892
SQ FT: 2,000
SALES (est): 140K **Privately Held**
SIC: 2711 Job printing & newspaper publishing combined

(G-8348)
OMYA PCC USA INC (DH)
499 Glen Ave (15845-1277)
PHONE....................................814 965-3400
Anthony Colak, *President*
EMP: 20
SALES (est): 1.8MM
SALES (corp-wide): 3.9B **Privately Held**
SIC: 2819 Calcium compounds & salts, inorganic
HQ: Omya Inc.
9987 Carver Rd Ste 300
Blue Ash OH 45242
513 387-4600

Johnstown
Cambria County

(G-8349)
ALEX FROEHLICH PACKING CO
77 D Street Ext (15906-2908)
PHONE....................................814 535-7694
David E Froehlich, *President*
EMP: 12
SQ FT: 10,800
SALES (est): 1.9MM **Privately Held**
SIC: 5147 5421 2013 2011 Meat brokers; meat markets, including freezer provisioners; sausages & other prepared meats; meat packing plants

(G-8350)
ALLEGHENY MFG & ELEC SVC INC
107 Station St (15905-3922)
PHONE....................................814 288-1597
Andrew Stager, *President*
Dean Gindlesperger, *Managing Prtnr*
Russell Stager, *Sales Staff*
EMP: 27
SQ FT: 12,000
SALES (est): 3.9MM **Privately Held**
SIC: 7699 3621 7694 Industrial machinery & equipment repair; electric motor & generator parts; armature rewinding shops

(G-8351)
ALMAC MACHINE CO
205 Morgan Pl (15901-1136)
P.O. Box 786 (15907-0786)
PHONE....................................814 539-5539
Gregory B Lunko, *President*
Virginia A Lunko, *Vice Pres*
EMP: 6
SALES (est): 700K **Privately Held**
SIC: 3599 Machine shop, jobbing & repair

(G-8352)
ALPHA PRINTING
215 Franklin St (15901-1901)
PHONE....................................814 536-8721
Joseph Tavalski, *Partner*
EMP: 6
SALES (est): 750K **Privately Held**
WEB: www.alphaprinting.net
SIC: 2759 Commercial printing

(G-8353)
ALTERNATIVE BURIAL CORPORATION
146 Chandler Ave (15906-2243)
PHONE....................................814 533-5832
Bill Hindman, *President*
EMP: 3
SALES (est): 289.4K **Privately Held**
SIC: 3272 Burial vaults, concrete or pre-cast terrazzo

(G-8354)
AURORA COMPUTER SYSTEMS INC
151 Freidhoff Ln (15902-1402)
PHONE....................................814 535-8371
Kathleen Freidhoff, *President*
Tom Laverick, *Vice Pres*
EMP: 3
SALES: 900K **Privately Held**
WEB: www.aurora-pc-systems.com
SIC: 3571 Computers, digital, analog or hybrid

(G-8355)
BAM FUEL LLC
1023 Willett Dr (15905-1237)
PHONE....................................814 255-1689
Lester Stephenson, *Principal*
EMP: 3
SALES (est): 154.6K **Privately Held**
SIC: 2869 Fuels

(G-8356)
BASIC - PSA INC
269 Jari Dr (15904-6949)
P.O. Box 753, Kennebunk ME (04043-0753)
PHONE....................................814 266-8646
William Louder, *President*
Celinee Bourgoine, *Vice Pres*
Grant Nelson, *Vice Pres*
Rick Schween, *Prdtn Mgr*
Robert Sakmar, *QC Mgr*
EMP: 20
SQ FT: 20,000
SALES (est): 5.2MM
SALES (corp-wide): 4.8B **Privately Held**
WEB: www.basicpsa.com
SIC: 3593 Fluid power cylinders & actuators
HQ: Anvil International, Llc
2 Holland Way
Exeter NH 03833
603 418-2800

(G-8357)
BEST GROUP HOLDINGS INC (PA)
Also Called: Best Window & Door Company
501 Broad St (15906-2522)
PHONE....................................814 536-1422
Barry Ritko Jr, *President*
Tammy Burnheimer, *CFO*
Jaclyn Ritko, *Sales Staff*
EMP: 43
SQ FT: 16,000
SALES (est): 4MM **Privately Held**
SIC: 3442 5031 2431 3089 Sash, door or window: metal; storm doors or windows, metal; building materials, exterior; doors & windows; windows; windows & window parts & trim, wood; fiberglass doors

(G-8358)
BLAINE BORING CHOCOLATES
123 Market St (15901-1608)
PHONE....................................814 539-6244
Steven McAnesy, *Principal*
EMP: 6
SQ FT: 1,500
SALES (est): 368.8K **Privately Held**
WEB: www.mcaneny.biz
SIC: 2064 5441 2066 Candy & other confectionery products; confectionery; chocolate & cocoa products

(G-8359)
BORCO EQUIPMENT INC
Also Called: Borco Equipment Company
50 Johns St (15901-1534)
P.O. Box 255, Tire Hill (15959-0255)
PHONE....................................814 535-1400
John E Bortoli, *President*
Anna Marie Bortoli, *Corp Secy*

GEOGRAPHIC

▼ **EMP**: 45
SQ FT: 17,000
SALES (est): 5.3MM **Privately Held**
SIC: 3715 Truck trailers

(G-8360)
CAMBRIA COUNTY ASSO (PA)
211 Central Ave (15902-2406)
PHONE..............................814 536-3531
Thomas J Bach, *Ch of Bd*
Richard C Bosserman, *President*
Tara Gowarty, *Managing Dir*
Denise Studinary, *Comptroller*
Doug Hughes, *Marketing Staff*
EMP: 365
SQ FT: 50,000
SALES: 15.6MM **Privately Held**
WEB: www.ccabh.com
SIC: 8322 8331 3496 2393 Association
for the handicapped; job training & voca-
tional rehabilitation services; miscella-
neous fabricated wire products; textile
bags; broadwoven fabric mills, manmade

(G-8361)
CAMBRIA PLASTICS LLC
840 Horner St (15902-2226)
PHONE..............................814 535-5467
EMP: 5 **EST**: 2011
SALES (est): 310K **Privately Held**
SIC: 3082 Mfg Plastic Profile Shapes

(G-8362)
CAMBRIA SPRINGS SERVICE INC
151 Horner St (15902-1995)
PHONE..............................814 539-1629
Daniel Fregly, *President*
Rose Fregly, *Corp Secy*
Doug Fregly, *Vice Pres*
EMP: 6 **EST**: 1938
SQ FT: 2,000
SALES (est): 751.6K **Privately Held**
SIC: 3493 7538 7539 Automobile springs;
general automotive repair shops; frame &
front end repair services

(G-8363)
CDR CONTRACTING
1208 Rebecca Dr (15902-3862)
PHONE..............................814 536-7675
Chris Ritko, *Owner*
EMP: 8
SALES: 95K **Privately Held**
SIC: 3292 Asbestos products

(G-8364)
CENTRAL ORTHOTIC PROSTHETIC CO (PA)
725 Franklin St (15901-2823)
PHONE..............................814 535-8221
Thomas C Been, *President*
Amanda Miller, *CFO*
Nancy Been, *Admin Sec*
EMP: 16 **EST**: 1976
SQ FT: 1,000
SALES (est): 1.6MM **Privately Held**
WEB: www.centraloandp.com
SIC: 3842 5999 Orthopedic appliances;
orthopedic & prosthesis applications

(G-8365)
CFM AIR INC
Also Called: J-Air
84 Iron St (15906-2618)
P.O. Box 1286 (15907-1286)
PHONE..............................814 539-6922
William Polacek, *CEO*
Tom Polacek, *COO*
Dudinack Robert, *Buyer*
Matt Hughes, *Business Dir*
▲ **EMP**: 5
SALES: 450K **Privately Held**
SIC: 3563 Air & gas compressors

(G-8366)
CRAIG HOLLERN (PA)
Also Called: American Egle Screen Print EMB
1107 Cushon St (15902-1110)
PHONE..............................814 539-2974
Craig Hollern, *Owner*
Ray Lohr, *Controller*
EMP: 20 **EST**: 1997
SQ FT: 6,500

SALES (est): 20MM **Privately Held**
SIC: 2261 5199 2396 2395 Screen printing of cotton broadwoven fabrics; advertising specialties; automotive & apparel
trimmings; pleating & stitching

(G-8367)
CRICHTON DIVERSFD VENTURES LLC
Also Called: Minahan Sign
636 Tire Hill Rd (15905-7300)
PHONE..............................814 288-1561
David Crichton,
EMP: 7 **EST**: 2008
SALES (est): 652.7K **Privately Held**
SIC: 3993 Neon signs; advertising artwork

(G-8368)
DIAMOND MT INC
213 Chestnut St (15906-2724)
PHONE..............................814 535-3505
Melvin M Popovich, *President*
Sean Horn, *Vice Pres*
Thomas Horn, *Vice Pres*
Lloyd Duso, *Plant Mgr*
Mark Rager, *Marketing Mgr*
▲ **EMP**: 37
SQ FT: 11,000
SALES (est): 6.5MM **Privately Held**
WEB: www.diamond-mt.com
SIC: 3672 Printed circuit boards

(G-8369)
DOLANS WLDG STL FBRICATION INC
118 Venture St (15909-4224)
PHONE..............................814 749-8639
Thomas Dolan Sr, *President*
Ken Dressler, *Purchasing*
Mary Dolan, *Treasurer*
Cindy Wilson, *Admin Sec*
EMP: 41 **EST**: 1967
SQ FT: 55,000
SALES (est): 7.6MM **Privately Held**
WEB: www.dolanswelding.com
SIC: 1799 3443 3441 Welding on site;
fabricated plate work (boiler shop); fabri-
cated structural metal

(G-8370)
DRS LAUREL TECHNOLOGIES (DH)
246 Airport Rd (15904-7224)
PHONE..............................814 534-8900
William J Lynn, *CEO*
Katherine A Krebel, *Counsel*
Joseph Militano, *Senior VP*
Blake M Guy, *Vice Pres*
Patrick R Marion, *Vice Pres*
EMP: 277
SQ FT: 110,000
SALES (est): 103.2MM
SALES (corp-wide): 9.2B **Privately Held**
SIC: 3672 3315 Printed circuit boards;
cable, steel: insulated or armored; wire
products, ferrous/iron: made in wiredraw-
ing plants
HQ: Leonardo Drs, Inc.
2345 Crystal Dr Ste 1000
Arlington VA 22202
703 416-8000

(G-8371)
ELEMENTS SKIN CARE LLC
1753 Lyter Dr (15905-1207)
PHONE..............................814 254-4227
EMP: 3
SALES (est): 85.8K **Privately Held**
SIC: 2819 Mfg Industrial Inorganic Chemi-
cals

(G-8372)
FI-HOFF CONCRETE PRODUCTS INC
240 Bentwood Ave (15904-1399)
PHONE..............................814 266-5834
Von Parkins, *President*
Kai Hoffman, *Vice Pres*
Eileen B Dibartola, *Treasurer*
Chad Tessari, *Sales Staff*
EMP: 16
SQ FT: 75,000

SALES (est): 4.2MM **Privately Held**
WEB: www.fi-hoff.com
SIC: 3273 3272 5989 Ready-mixed concrete; burial vaults, concrete or precast
terrazzo; septic tanks, concrete; manhole
covers or frames, concrete; coal

(G-8373)
FRIENDLY CITY BOX CO INC
520 Oakridge Dr (15904-6915)
PHONE..............................814 266-6287
Larry Blackburn, *President*
Eric Blackburn, *Vice Pres*
EMP: 11
SQ FT: 85,000
SALES (est): 1.9MM **Privately Held**
SIC: 2652 Setup paperboard boxes

(G-8374)
GALLIKER DAIRY COMPANY (PA)
Also Called: Galliker's Quality Chekd
143 Donald Ln (15904-2829)
P.O. Box 159 (15907-0159)
PHONE..............................814 266-8702
Charles Price, *President*
Louis G Galliker, *Chairman*
Bill Livingston, *Vice Pres*
William Livingston, *Vice Pres*
Charles D Price, *Vice Pres*
EMP: 210 **EST**: 1914
SQ FT: 94,000
SALES (est): 105.3MM **Privately Held**
WEB: www.gallikers.com
SIC: 2026 2086 2024 Buttermilk, cultured;
eggnog, fresh: non-alcoholic; milk drinks,
flavored; tea, iced: packaged in cans, bot-
tles, etc.; ice cream & ice milk

(G-8375)
GAP POLLUTION & ENVMTL CTRL
100 Gapvax Ln (15904-2855)
PHONE..............................814 266-9469
Gary Poborsley, *CEO*
Randy Johnson, *President*
James Griffith, *Principal*
Rose Pobosky, *Treasurer*
EMP: 50
SALES (est): 9.1MM **Privately Held**
SIC: 3563 Vacuum (air extraction) sys-
tems, industrial

(G-8376)
GAUTIER STEEL LTD
80 Clinton St (15901-2200)
PHONE..............................814 535-9200
Darryl Diorio, *President*
Jack Mazur, *Vice Pres*
Ken Smith, *Opers Mgr*
Tom McCall, *Electrical Engi*
Jackie Kulback, *CFO*
EMP: 90 **EST**: 1998
SQ FT: 1,200,000
SALES (est): 28.7MM **Privately Held**
WEB: www.gautiersteel.com
SIC: 3312 3325 Blast furnaces & steel
mills; rolling mill rolls, cast steel
PA: Reserve Group Management Company
3560 W Market St Ste 300
Fairlawn OH 44333

(G-8377)
GERBER CHAIR MATES INC
1171 Ringling Ave (15902-3864)
PHONE..............................814 266-6588
Dorothy Gerber, *President*
Dorothy Ann Gerber, *Treasurer*
EMP: 5 **EST**: 1989
SALES: 100K **Privately Held**
WEB: www.gerberchairmates.com
SIC: 3842 Prosthetic appliances

(G-8378)
GLAXOSMITHKLINE LLC
151 Raymond Dr (15909-1115)
PHONE..............................814 243-0366
EMP: 26
SALES (corp-wide): 39.8B **Privately Held**
SIC: 2834 Pharmaceutical preparations
HQ: Glaxosmithkline Llc
5 Crescent Dr
Philadelphia PA 19112
215 751-4000

(G-8379)
HANSON READY MIX INC
248 Solomon Run Rd (15904-7101)
PHONE..............................814 269-9600
Bryan Montorie, *Branch Mgr*
EMP: 16
SALES (corp-wide): 20.6B **Privately Held**
SIC: 3273 Ready-mixed concrete
HQ: Hanson Ready Mix, Inc.
3251 Bath Pike
Nazareth PA 18064

(G-8380)
HASTINGS MACHINE COMPANY INC (HQ)
111 Roosevelt Blvd (15906-2736)
PHONE..............................814 533-5777
Kim Kunkle, *President*
Michael F Brosig Sr, *Corp Secy*
Steve Oyler, *Exec VP*
Wayne E Close, *Vice Pres*
John Glosky, *Treasurer*
EMP: 1 **EST**: 1977
SALES (est): 2.3MM
SALES (corp-wide): 101.6MM **Privately
Held**
WEB: www.hastingsmachine.com
SIC: 3599 Machine shop, jobbing & repair
PA: Laurel Holdings Inc
111 Roosevelt Blvd
Johnstown PA 15906
814 533-5777

(G-8381)
HOFF ENTERPRISES INC
151 Freidhoff Ln (15902-1402)
PHONE..............................814 535-8371
Kurt Freidhoff, *President*
Walter Freidhoff, *Vice Pres*
Brian Pannone, *Project Mgr*
Matt Shaffer, *Prdtn Mgr*
Kathleen Freidhoff, *Treasurer*
EMP: 34
SQ FT: 35,000
SALES (est): 7.9MM **Privately Held**
WEB: www.hoffent.com
SIC: 2541 3083 2434 2431 Wood parti-
tions & fixtures; laminated plastics plate &
sheet; wood kitchen cabinets; millwork

(G-8382)
INTEGRATED TECH SVCS INTL LLC
Also Called: Itsi-Biosciences
633 Napoleon St (15901-2615)
PHONE..............................814 262-7332
Richard Somiari, *Mng Member*
Ya Njie, *Software Dev*
Richard I Somiari,
EMP: 10
SQ FT: 10,000
SALES: 900K **Privately Held**
SIC: 8731 2836 8999 Biotechnical re-
search, commercial; biological products,
except diagnostic; scientific consulting

(G-8383)
J W T HOLDING CORP (PA)
Also Called: Johnstown Wire Technologies
124 Laurel Ave (15906-2246)
PHONE..............................814 532-5600
Walt Robertson, *President*
J Thomas Clark, *Principal*
Jack Leffler, *Vice Pres*
Anthony Garcia, *Treasurer*
Ron Shaffer, *Treasurer*
◆ **EMP**: 265
SQ FT: 650,000
SALES (est): 171.5MM **Privately Held**
WEB: www.johnstownwire.com
SIC: 3312 Bar, rod & wire products

(G-8384)
JBM METALCRAFT CORP
2309 Shannon Way (15905-1511)
PHONE..............................814 241-0448
James Sutt, *President*
EMP: 6
SQ FT: 5,200
SALES (est): 708.5K **Privately Held**
SIC: 3599 Machine & other job shop work

▲ = Import ▼=Export
◆ =Import/Export

(G-8385)
JIGGING TECH LLC DBA ATOLL
950 Riders Rd (15906-2620)
PHONE..................................814 619-5187
EMP: 4
SALES (est): 270.1K **Privately Held**
SIC: 1499 Miscellaneous nonmetallic minerals

(G-8386)
JIGGING TECHNOLOGIES LLC
Also Called: Atoll
1008 Club Dr (15905-1912)
PHONE..................................814 254-4376
Louis Eybers,
EMP: 4
SALES (est): 390.2K **Privately Held**
SIC: 1099 Antimony ore mining

(G-8387)
JOEL FREIDHOFF
Also Called: Hoff Machining
151 Freidhoff Ln (15902-1402)
PHONE..................................814 536-6458
Joel Freidhoff, *Owner*
EMP: 4
SQ FT: 6,000
SALES (est): 242K **Privately Held**
SIC: 3599 7692 Machine shop, jobbing & repair; welding repair

(G-8388)
JOHNSTOWN AMERICA CORPORATION (HQ)
Also Called: Freight Car Division
129 Industrial Park Rd (15904-1940)
PHONE..................................877 739-2006
Joseph E McNeely, *Treasurer*
Tim Mann, *Manager*
Laurence M Trusdell, *Admin Sec*
◆ EMP: 86
SALES (est): 69.8MM
SALES (corp-wide): 316.5MM **Publicly Held**
SIC: 3743 Freight cars & equipment
PA: Freightcar America, Inc.
2 N Rverside Plz Ste 1300
Chicago IL 60606
800 458-2235

(G-8389)
JOHNSTOWN FOUNDRY CASTINGS INC
548 Horner St (15902-2044)
PHONE..................................814 539-8840
Alberto Jablonski, *President*
EMP: 5
SALES (est): 521.1K **Privately Held**
SIC: 3544 7389 Forms (molds), for foundry & plastics working machinery;

(G-8390)
JOHNSTOWN MCHNING FBRCTION INC
210 Iolite Ave (15901-1416)
PHONE..................................814 539-2209
Tom Polazek, *President*
Tom Polacek, *President*
EMP: 40
SALES (est): 5.1MM
SALES (corp-wide): 81.1MM **Privately Held**
WEB: www.jwfi.com
SIC: 3599 Custom machinery
PA: Johnstown Welding And Fabrication, Inc.
84 Iron St
Johnstown PA 15906
800 225-9353

(G-8391)
JOHNSTOWN SPECIALTY CASTINGS
545 Central Ave (15902-2600)
PHONE..................................814 535-9002
Charles R Novelli, *President*
Ken Hall, *General Mgr*
Carl Maskiewicz, *Treasurer*
Robert J Peterson, *Admin Sec*
EMP: 260
SQ FT: 800,000

SALES (est): 37.5MM
SALES (corp-wide): 516.8MM **Privately Held**
WEB: www.whemco.com
SIC: 3312 Stainless steel
HQ: Whemco Inc.
5 Hot Metal St Ste 300
Pittsburgh PA 15203
412 390-2700

(G-8392)
JOHNSTOWN TUBE LASER LLC
Also Called: Tube Laser Industries
195 Jari Dr Ste 300 (15904-6945)
PHONE..................................814 532-4121
Michael Vigne,
EMP: 30
SQ FT: 2,000
SALES (est): 5.4MM **Privately Held**
SIC: 3011 Industrial inner tubes

(G-8393)
JOHNSTOWN WIRE TECH INC
124 Laurel Ave (15906-2246)
PHONE..................................814 532-5600
Gregg Sherrill, *President*
Jack Leffler, *Vice Pres*
Joseph E McNeely, *Treasurer*
Terry D Buxbaum, *Admin Sec*
▲ EMP: 260
SQ FT: 638,000
SALES (est): 61.2MM
SALES (corp-wide): 171.5MM **Privately Held**
WEB: www.johnstownwire.com
SIC: 3312 Bar, rod & wire products
PA: J W T Holding Corp.
124 Laurel Ave
Johnstown PA 15906
814 532-5600

(G-8394)
JOHNSTOWN WLDG FABRICATION INC (PA)
Also Called: Jwf Industries
84 Iron St (15906-2618)
P.O. Box 1286 (15907-1286)
PHONE..................................800 225-9353
William C Polacek, *President*
Kevin Schropp, *General Mgr*
Christina Galasso, *Business Mgr*
Dan Allshouse, *Project Mgr*
Ron Wilson, *Opers Mgr*
▲ EMP: 200
SQ FT: 360,000
SALES (est): 81.1MM **Privately Held**
WEB: www.jwfi.com
SIC: 3441 7692 3479 Fabricated structural metal; welding repair; etching & engraving

(G-8395)
JOINT AMMUNITION AND TECH INC
300 Market St (15901-1702)
PHONE..................................703 926-5509
Paul F Lucas, *President*
Polly Gebhardt, *Admin Sec*
EMP: 12
SALES (est): 896.8K **Privately Held**
SIC: 3482 Small arms ammunition

(G-8396)
JWF DEFENSE SYSTEMS LLC
84 Iron St (15906-2618)
P.O. Box 1286 (15907-1286)
PHONE..................................814 539-6922
Tom Polacek, *COO*
Victoria Long, *Buyer*
John Skelley, *Human Res Mgr*
John Polacek,
William C Polacek,
▲ EMP: 64
SQ FT: 400,000
SALES (est): 10.3MM **Privately Held**
WEB: www.jwfdefensesystems.com
SIC: 3599 Machine shop, jobbing & repair

(G-8397)
KEYSTONE TYPEWRITER COMPANY
1268 Oconnor St (15905-4553)
PHONE..................................814 539-6077
EMP: 3
SQ FT: 2,400

SALES: 160K **Privately Held**
SIC: 3579 7699 Mfg Office Machines Repair Services

(G-8398)
KITRON INC (PA)
160 Jari Dr Ste 160 # 160 (15904-6948)
PHONE..................................814 619-0523
Dag Songedal, *CEO*
Dale Vernon, *President*
Israel Losada Salvador, *COO*
Werner Wernersen, *Production*
Nerijus Kanapienis, *Engineer*
EMP: 32
SALES (est): 21.1MM **Privately Held**
SIC: 3812 Search & navigation equipment

(G-8399)
KONGSBERG INTEGRATED TACTICAL
210 Industrial Park Rd # 105 (15904-1933)
PHONE..................................814 269-5700
Egil Haugsdal, *CEO*
Asmund Groven, *President*
EMP: 30
SQ FT: 23,600
SALES (est): 4.5MM
SALES (corp-wide): 1.7B **Privately Held**
SIC: 8711 3669 3612 Engineering services; visual communication systems; power & distribution transformers
PA: Kongsberg Gruppen Asa
Kirkegardsveien 45
Kongsberg 3616
322 882-00

(G-8400)
KONGSBERG PROTECH SYSTEMS (DH)
210 Industrial Park Rd (15904-1933)
PHONE..................................814 269-5700
Gunnar Pedersen, *President*
Jeffrey Wood, *General Mgr*
Greg Platee, *Vice Pres*
Jeff Wood, *Vice Pres*
Troy Long, *Facilities Mgr*
▲ EMP: 71
SALES (est): 30.6MM
SALES (corp-wide): 1.7B **Privately Held**
SIC: 3489 Ordnance & accessories

(G-8401)
KORNS GALVANIZING COMPANY INC
Also Called: C.C. Korns
75 Bridge St (15902-2902)
PHONE..................................814 535-3293
David J Sheehan, *CEO*
Larry Caprous, *President*
Kathleen Ortel, *President*
John E Sheehan, *President*
Paul Heubeck, *Corp Secy*
EMP: 45 EST: 1916
SQ FT: 39,000
SALES (est): 6.1MM **Privately Held**
WEB: www.kornsgalvanizing.com
SIC: 3479 Hot dip coating of metals or formed products

(G-8402)
LAUREL HOLDINGS INC (PA)
111 Roosevelt Blvd (15906-2736)
PHONE..................................814 533-5777
Kim Kunkle, *President*
Mike Brosig, *Treasurer*
EMP: 6
SQ FT: 20,000
SALES (est): 101.6MM **Privately Held**
SIC: 4941 5063 3599 4724 Water supply; batteries, dry cell; machine shop, jobbing & repair; travel agencies; janitorial service, contract basis

(G-8403)
LEE REGIONAL HEALTH SYSTEM INC
Also Called: Walnut Uniforms and Embroidery
1236 Scalp Ave (15904-3136)
PHONE..................................814 254-4716
John Reed, *Branch Mgr*
EMP: 6
SALES (corp-wide): 18.9MM **Privately Held**
SIC: 2395 Embroidery & art needlework

PA: Lee Regional Health System, Inc.
132 Walnut St Ste 3
Johnstown PA 15901
814 533-0751

(G-8404)
LOCKHEED MARTIN AEROPARTS
211 Industrial Park Rd (15904-1961)
PHONE..................................814 262-3000
Rebeca Z Styles, *President*
Kevin Ott, *General Mgr*
Richard F Horvath, *Vice Pres*
Allan Wynne, *Opers Staff*
Kenneth R Possenriede, *Treasurer*
EMP: 107
SQ FT: 60,000
SALES (est): 24.3MM **Publicly Held**
WEB: www.lockheedmartin.com
SIC: 3724 3728 3444 Aircraft engines & engine parts; aircraft parts & equipment; sheet metalwork
PA: Lockheed Martin Corporation
6801 Rockledge Dr
Bethesda MD 20817

(G-8405)
LOCKHEED MARTIN CORPORATION
211 Industrial Park Rd (15904-1961)
PHONE..................................814 262-3000
John Przybyla, *Manager*
EMP: 458 **Publicly Held**
SIC: 3728 Aircraft parts & equipment
PA: Lockheed Martin Corporation
6801 Rockledge Dr
Bethesda MD 20817

(G-8406)
MARQUISE MINING CORP
3889 Menoher Blvd (15905-5105)
PHONE..................................724 459-5775
John Lee, *President*
Claudia Lee, *Admin Sec*
EMP: 18
SALES: 4MM **Privately Held**
SIC: 1222 Bituminous coal-underground mining

(G-8407)
MARTIN-BAKER AMERICA INC
169 Jari Dr (15904-6945)
PHONE..................................814 262-9325
John Martin, *President*
Mike Santoro, *General Mgr*
Robert Martin, *Vice Pres*
John Rovan, *Mfg Staff*
Ernie Lee, *Manager*
▲ EMP: 115
SQ FT: 58,000
SALES: 30MM
SALES (corp-wide): 346.7MM **Privately Held**
WEB: www.m-bamerica.com
SIC: 3728 Seat ejector devices, aircraft; military aircraft equipment & armament
PA: Killinchy Aerospace Holdings Limited
Lower Road
Uxbridge MIDDX UB9 5
189 583-2214

(G-8408)
MG INDUSTRIAL PRODUCTS INC
1248 Laurelview Dr (15905-1508)
PHONE..................................814 255-2471
Linda C Grados, *Treasurer*
EMP: 3 EST: 2000
SALES (est): 310.1K **Privately Held**
SIC: 2899 Metal treating compounds

(G-8409)
MINAHAN CORPORATION
Also Called: Minahan Signs
636 Tire Hill Rd (15905-7300)
PHONE..................................814 288-1561
Edward Minahan, *President*
Andrea Minahan, *Treasurer*
EMP: 7
SALES (est): 862K **Privately Held**
WEB: www.minahansigns.com
SIC: 3993 Signs & advertising specialties

(G-8410)
MOUNTAIN MOULDINGS
112 Schneider St (15906)
PHONE..................................814 535-8563

GEOGRAPHIC

Joe Rodkey, *Partner*
August Rodkey, *Partner*
▼ EMP: 10
SQ FT: 15,000
SALES (est): 1.1MM Privately Held
SIC: 2431 Millwork

(G-8411)
MOXHAM LUMBER CO
150 Dupont St (15902-2399)
PHONE...................................814 536-5186
Richard E Hayes, *President*
Ernest Lichtenfels, *Vice Pres*
Sam Pantana, *Treasurer*
Bradford Gordon, *Admin Sec*
EMP: 21
SQ FT: 15,000
SALES (est): 2.7MM Privately Held
SIC: 2421 5211 5031 2431 Planing mills; lumber & other building materials; lumber: rough, dressed & finished; building materials, exterior; building materials, interior; millwork

(G-8412)
NEWSPAPER HOLDING INC (DH)
Also Called: Johnstown Tribune Democrat
425 Locust St (15901-1817)
P.O. Box 340 (15907-0340)
PHONE...................................814 532-5102
Donna Barrett, *President*
Keith Blevins, *Vice Pres*
Mike Reed, *Treasurer*
EMP: 70 EST: 1902
SALES (est): 602.7MM Privately Held
WEB: www.tribune-democrat.com
SIC: 2711 Commercial printing & newspaper publishing combined; newspapers: publishing only, not printed on site

(G-8413)
NORTH AMER HOGANAS HIGH ALLOYS
101 Bridge St (15902-2904)
PHONE...................................814 361-6800
Nasser Ahmad, *Vice Pres*
Michele McClelland, *Human Res Mgr*
Avinash Gore,
Robin Muscatello, *Technician*
◆ EMP: 100
SQ FT: 175,000
SALES: 68.8MM
SALES (corp-wide): 974.4MM Privately Held
SIC: 3399 Powder, metal
HQ: North American Hoganas Holdings, Inc.
111 Hoganas Way
Hollsopple PA 15935
814 479-2551

(G-8414)
OSHEAS CANDIES (PA)
1118 Solomon St (15902-3743)
PHONE...................................814 536-4800
Robert O'Shea, *Partner*
Karen Brubaker, *Partner*
EMP: 10 EST: 1934
SQ FT: 10,000
SALES (est): 1.5MM Privately Held
SIC: 2064 5947 5441 2066 Candy & other confectionery products; greeting cards; confectionery produced for direct sale on the premises; chocolate & cocoa products

(G-8415)
OSHEAS CANDIES
2451 Bedford St (15904-1438)
PHONE...................................814 266-7041
Robert Oshea, *Branch Mgr*
EMP: 5
SALES (corp-wide): 1.5MM Privately Held
SIC: 2064 Candy & other confectionery products
PA: O'shea's Candies
1118 Solomon St
Johnstown PA 15902
814 536-4800

(G-8416)
OSRAM SYLVANIA INC
224 W Oakmont Blvd (15904-1316)
PHONE...................................814 269-1418

Sylvania Osram, *Principal*
EMP: 299
SALES (corp-wide): 4.7B Privately Held
SIC: 3641 Electric lamps
HQ: Osram Sylvania Inc
200 Ballardvale St # 305
Wilmington MA 01887
978 570-3000

(G-8417)
OTO MELARA NORTH AMERICA INC
Also Called: Finmeccanica North America
246 Airport Rd (15904-7224)
PHONE...................................314 707-4223
Raymond Scott Rettig, *CEO*
EMP: 5 EST: 2004
SALES (est): 1.7MM
SALES (corp-wide): 9.2B Privately Held
SIC: 3812 4789 Defense systems & equipment; pipeline terminal facilities, independently operated
HQ: Leonardo Drs, Inc.
2345 Crystal Dr Ste 1000
Arlington VA 22202
703 416-8000

(G-8418)
OUR TOWN
500 Galleria Dr Ste 198 (15904-8902)
P.O. Box 638, Somerset (15501-0638)
PHONE...................................814 269-9704
Todd F Schurz, *President*
Craig Springer, *General Mgr*
EMP: 10
SALES: 1MM Privately Held
SIC: 2711 Commercial printing & newspaper publishing combined; newspapers, publishing & printing

(G-8419)
PARRISH R VARNISH
Also Called: P Varnish Contractors
602 Demuth St (15904-1607)
PHONE...................................814 242-1786
Parrish Varnish, *Owner*
EMP: 6
SALES (est): 694.6K Privately Held
SIC: 2851 Varnishes

(G-8420)
PBG JOHNSTOWN
167 Allenbill Dr (15904-1937)
PHONE...................................814 262-1125
Chris Moyer, *Principal*
EMP: 6
SALES (est): 234.5K Privately Held
SIC: 2086 Bottled & canned soft drinks

(G-8421)
PENN MACHINE COMPANY (DH)
Also Called: PMC
106 Station St (15905-3995)
PHONE...................................814 288-1547
Dennis Racine, *President*
H Karl Wiegand, *Vice Pres*
Rosemary Palusko, *Opers Staff*
Jason T Ligas, *Treasurer*
Robert W Webb, *Admin Sec*
▲ EMP: 70
SQ FT: 210,000
SALES: 29.8MM
SALES (corp-wide): 225.3B Publicly Held
WEB: www.pmcgearbox.com
SIC: 3532 3462 3714 Mining machinery; iron & steel forgings; wheels, motor vehicle

(G-8422)
PEPSI-COLA METRO BTLG CO INC
166 Allenbill Dr (15904-1938)
PHONE...................................814 266-9556
Randy Kaiser, *Director*
EMP: 230
SALES (corp-wide): 64.6B Publicly Held
WEB: www.joy-of-cola.com
SIC: 2086 Soft drinks: packaged in cans, bottles, etc.
HQ: Pepsi-Cola Metropolitan Bottling Company, Inc.
1111 Westchester Ave
White Plains NY 10604
914 767-6000

(G-8423)
PEPSICO INC
429 Industrial Park Rd (15904-1943)
PHONE...................................814 266-6005
Randy Kaiser, *Manager*
Caitlin Brophy, *Manager*
Brian Chesla, *Maintence Staff*
EMP: 300
SALES (corp-wide): 64.6B Publicly Held
WEB: www.pepsico.com
SIC: 2086 Carbonated soft drinks, bottled & canned
PA: Pepsico, Inc.
700 Anderson Hill Rd
Purchase NY 10577
914 253-2000

(G-8424)
PRESS BISTRO
110 Franklin St Ste 110 # 110 (15901-1829)
PHONE...................................814 254-4835
Jeremy Shearer, *Principal*
EMP: 4
SALES (est): 350.7K Privately Held
SIC: 2741 Miscellaneous publishing

(G-8425)
PUDLINERS PACKING
Also Called: Pudliner Packing
167 Norton Rd (15906-2906)
PHONE...................................814 539-5422
Andrew Pudliner, *Owner*
EMP: 11 EST: 1920
SALES (est): 366K Privately Held
SIC: 5147 5421 2011 Meats, fresh; meat markets, including freezer provisioners; meat packing plants

(G-8426)
QUAKER SALES CORPORATION (PA)
Rear 83 Cooper Ave (15906)
P.O. Box 880 (15907-0880)
PHONE...................................814 536-7541
Donald C Overdorff, *President*
Calvin C Overdorff, *Corp Secy*
James Costello, *Vice Pres*
Kevin McLaughlin, *Vice Pres*
Tom Beyer, *Manager*
EMP: 10 EST: 1929
SQ FT: 3,200
SALES (est): 3MM Privately Held
WEB: www.quakersales.com
SIC: 1611 2951 Highway & street paving contractor; asphalt & asphaltic paving mixtures (not from refineries)

(G-8427)
QUAKER SALES CORPORATION
2 Asphalt Rd (15907)
P.O. Box 880 (15907-0880)
PHONE...................................814 539-1376
Dennis Grube, *Manager*
EMP: 7
SALES (corp-wide): 3MM Privately Held
WEB: www.quakersales.com
SIC: 2951 Asphalt paving mixtures & blocks
PA: Quaker Sales Corporation
Rear 83 Cooper Ave
Johnstown PA 15906
814 536-7541

(G-8428)
R R DONNELLEY & SONS COMPANY
Also Called: Moore Business Forms
334 Bloomfield St (15904-3268)
PHONE...................................814 266-6031
Paul Seitz, *Manager*
EMP: 7
SALES (corp-wide): 6.8B Publicly Held
WEB: www.moore.com
SIC: 2759 Screen printing
PA: R. R. Donnelley & Sons Company
35 W Wacker Dr Ste 3650
Chicago IL 60601
312 326-8000

(G-8429)
REDSTONE CORPORATION
469 Airport Rd Hngr 9 (15904-7200)
PHONE...................................321 213-2135
Michael Kruse, *President*

Thorwald Eide, *Vice Pres*
Dominic Gilbert, *CFO*
EMP: 9
SQ FT: 10,000
SALES (est): 514.7K Privately Held
WEB: www.redstonecorp.us
SIC: 3728 8711 8742 Aircraft parts & equipment; engineering services; aviation &/or aeronautical engineering; management consulting services

(G-8430)
RICHARD RHODES
Also Called: PA Vault Co
846 Benshoff Hill Rd (15906-3901)
PHONE...................................814 535-3633
Richard Rhodes, *General Mgr*
EMP: 10
SALES (corp-wide): 900K Privately Held
SIC: 3272 Burial vaults, concrete or precast terrazzo
PA: Richard Rhodes
846 Benshoff Hill Rd
Johnstown PA
814 535-3633

(G-8431)
RICHLAND PLASTICS & ENGRAVING
624 Lamberd Ave (15904-1618)
PHONE...................................814 266-3002
Thomas W Haberkorn, *President*
James R Duncan, *Exec VP*
EMP: 4
SALES (est): 475K Privately Held
WEB: www.richlandplastics.com
SIC: 3993 7389 3953 3914 Signs, not made in custom sign painting shops; engraving service; date stamps, hand: rubber or metal; numbering stamps, hand: rubber or metal; trophies, plated (all metals); trophies

(G-8432)
SAYLOR INDUSTRIES INC
757 Tire Hill Rd (15905-7712)
PHONE...................................814 479-4964
Frank D Saylor, *President*
Leona Saylor, *Vice Pres*
Lydia Naugle, *Treasurer*
EMP: 5
SQ FT: 45,000
SALES: 1MM Privately Held
WEB: www.clipperelite.com
SIC: 3524 Lawn & garden mowers & accessories

(G-8433)
SENDER ORNAMENTAL IRON WORKS
742 Cooper Ave (15906-1033)
PHONE...................................814 536-5139
Wilfred E Sender, *Owner*
EMP: 30 EST: 1953
SALES (est): 3.4MM Privately Held
SIC: 3441 Fabricated structural metal

(G-8434)
SHEARER ELBIE
Also Called: Pheasant & Shearer Contractors
204 Atlantic St (15904-1026)
PHONE...................................814 266-7548
Elbie Shearer, *Owner*
EMP: 5
SALES (est): 340.9K Privately Held
SIC: 1389 3296 Excavating slush pits & cellars; cementing oil & gas well casings; insulation: rock wool, slag & silica minerals

(G-8435)
SHETLER MEMORIALS INC
935 Tire Hill Rd (15905-7705)
PHONE...................................814 288-1087
Rich Bailey, *Mng Member*
EMP: 7
SALES (est): 680.8K Privately Held
SIC: 5999 3272 Monuments, finished to custom order; monuments, concrete

▲ = Import ▼=Export
◆ =Import/Export

(G-8436)
SOUTH FORK HARDWARE COMPANY
Also Called: Tirechain.com
115 Haynes St (15901-2548)
PHONE..................................814 248-3375
David Goldblatt, *President*
Michael Goldblatt, *Vice Pres*
Rema Goldblatt, *Admin Sec*
▲ EMP: 4
SALES (est): 493.3K **Privately Held**
SIC: 3496 Tire chains

(G-8437)
SOUTHSIDE BREW-THRU LLC
114 Bridge St (15902-2903)
PHONE..................................814 254-4828
Todd Holbay,
EMP: 3
SALES (est): 177.9K **Privately Held**
SIC: 2082 Malt liquors

(G-8438)
TMS INTERNATIONAL LLC
240 Parkhill Dr (15945-1142)
PHONE..................................814 535-1911
EMP: 5 **Privately Held**
SIC: 3312 Blast furnaces & steel mills
HQ: Tms International, Llc
12 Monongahela Ave
Glassport PA 15045
412 678-6141

(G-8439)
TMS INTERNATIONAL LLC
240 Parkhill Dr (15945-1142)
PHONE..................................814 535-5081
EMP: 10
SALES (corp-wide): 216.9MM **Privately Held**
SIC: 1422 5032 Crushed/Broken Limestone Whol Brick/Stone Material
HQ: Tms International Group Llc
12 Monongahela Ave
Glassport PA 15045
412 678-6141

(G-8440)
UNITED FOUNDRY COMPANY INC
548 Horner St (15902-2044)
PHONE..................................814 539-8840
William Sawrinski, *President*
John M Calandra, *Vice Pres*
William E Kirwan, *Treasurer*
Perry Yahn, *Manager*
J Phillip Saylor, *Admin Sec*
EMP: 24
SQ FT: 30,000
SALES (est): 4.2MM **Privately Held**
SIC: 3366 3599 Machinery castings: brass; castings (except die): brass; machine shop, jobbing & repair

(G-8441)
UNITED INDUSTRIAL ELECTRO
163 Cramer Pike (15906-1157)
PHONE..................................814 539-6115
Matthew R Wilks, *President*
Shawn Oxford, *Principal*
EMP: 52
SALES (est): 8.9MM **Privately Held**
SIC: 3441 Fabricated structural metal

(G-8442)
VALLEY PRINTING AND DESIGN CO
Also Called: Valley Printing Co
667 Main St Ste 667 # 667 (15901-2187)
PHONE..................................814 536-5990
Micheal Migut, *CEO*
EMP: 6 EST: 1940
SQ FT: 2,200
SALES (est): 660K **Privately Held**
SIC: 2759 Letterpress printing; screen printing

(G-8443)
WEST END BEER MART
119 Fairfield Ave (15906-2333)
PHONE..................................814 536-1846
Sylvia McCall, *Partner*
EMP: 3
SALES (est): 212.3K **Privately Held**
SIC: 2082 Beer (alcoholic beverage)

(G-8444)
WESTERN PA WEATHER LLC
557 Russell Ave (15902-2647)
PHONE..................................814 341-5086
Albert Baldish, *Principal*
EMP: 3
SALES (est): 212.4K **Privately Held**
SIC: 2241 Webbing, woven

(G-8445)
WILSON CREEK ENERGY LLC
334 Budfield St Ste 180 (15904-3345)
P.O. Box 260, Friedens (15541-0260)
PHONE..................................814 619-4600
Tina L Phillips, *Owner*
EMP: 7 EST: 2010
SALES (est): 807.5K **Privately Held**
SIC: 1241 Coal mining services

(G-8446)
WPP DOUGH COMPANY INC
1280 Saint Clair Rd (15905-1410)
PHONE..................................814 539-7799
Michael Omahne, *President*
Jackie Omahne, *Treasurer*
EMP: 15
SQ FT: 20,000
SALES: 2.3MM **Privately Held**
SIC: 2041 Pizza dough, prepared

(G-8447)
YORK INTERNATIONAL CORPORATION
395 Industrial Park Rd (15904-1941)
PHONE..................................814 479-4005
Tim Thomas, *Branch Mgr*
EMP: 16 **Privately Held**
SIC: 3585 Air conditioning equipment, complete; refrigeration equipment, complete
HQ: York International Corporation
631 S Richland Ave
York PA 17403
717 771-7890

Jones Mills
Westmoreland County

(G-8448)
SIX PAK SHACK
339 State Route 711 (15646-1108)
P.O. Box 115 (15646-0115)
PHONE..................................724 593-2401
Terry Shaffer, *Owner*
Joan Shaffer, *Co-Owner*
EMP: 6
SALES (est): 300.7K **Privately Held**
SIC: 2086 Bottled & canned soft drinks

Jonestown
Lebanon County

(G-8449)
BENEFICIAL ENRGY SOLUTIONS LLC (HQ)
Also Called: Bes
2632 State Route 72 (17038-8101)
PHONE..................................844 237-7697
Corey C Wolff, *CEO*
EMP: 4 EST: 2015
SQ FT: 7,000
SALES (est): 2MM **Privately Held**
SIC: 1711 3585 Solar energy contractor; refrigeration & heating equipment
PA: Bfhj Holdings, Inc.
26 Chestnut Ridge Rd
Montvale NJ 07645
908 730-6280

(G-8450)
MIKEY GS
3 Old Route 22 Trlr 2 (17038-8932)
PHONE..................................717 820-4053
Michael Geeseman, *Owner*
EMP: 3 EST: 2012
SALES (est): 175K **Privately Held**
SIC: 3465 Body parts, automobile: stamped metal

(G-8451)
SUPREME MID-ATLANTIC CORP (DH)
411 Jonestown Rd (17038-9513)
P.O. Box 779 (17038-0779)
PHONE..................................717 865-0031
Kim Korth, *President*
Robert Wilson, *President*
Omer Kropf, *Chairman*
William I Barrett, *Vice Pres*
Crystal Marko, *Buyer*
▲ EMP: 74 EST: 1900
SQ FT: 92,000
SALES (est): 32MM
SALES (corp-wide): 2.2B **Publicly Held**
SIC: 3713 Truck bodies (motor vehicles)
HQ: Supreme Industries, Inc.
2581 Kercher Rd
Goshen IN 46528
574 642-3070

(G-8452)
TE CONNECTIVITY CORPORATION
3155 State Route 72 (17038-8741)
PHONE..................................717 861-5000
Andrew Domovich, *Branch Mgr*
EMP: 500
SALES (corp-wide): 13.1B **Privately Held**
WEB: www.raychem.com
SIC: 3678 3643 Electronic connectors; current-carrying wiring devices; connectors & terminals for electrical devices
HQ: Te Connectivity Corporation
1050 Westlakes Dr
Berwyn PA 19312
610 893-9800

(G-8453)
V AND S LBANON GALVANIZING LLC
153 Micro Dr (17038-8743)
PHONE..................................717 861-7777
Werner Niehaus,
Brian Miller Sr,
EMP: 48
SQ FT: 100,000
SALES (est): 6.7MM
SALES (corp-wide): 773.1MM **Privately Held**
WEB: www.hotdipgalvanizing.com
SIC: 3479 Galvanizing of iron, steel or end-formed products
HQ: Voigt & Schweitzer Llc
987 Buckeye Park Rd
Columbus OH 43207
614 449-8281

(G-8454)
VOIGT & SCHWEITZER LLC
Also Called: V & S Lebanon Galvanizing
153 Micro Dr (17038-8743)
PHONE..................................717 861-7777
Hans De Meyer, *Manager*
EMP: 33
SALES (corp-wide): 773.1MM **Privately Held**
WEB: www.hotdipgalvanizing.com
SIC: 3479 Etching & engraving; galvanizing of iron, steel or end-formed products
HQ: Voigt & Schweitzer Llc
987 Buckeye Park Rd
Columbus OH 43207
614 449-8281

Julian
Centre County

(G-8455)
GRANDVILLE HOLLOW POTTERY INC
1090 Railroad Ave (16844-9734)
PHONE..................................814 355-7928
Daniel T Harvey, *President*
Mark Essig, *Corp Secy*
EMP: 8
SQ FT: 5,000
SALES (est): 888.5K **Privately Held**
SIC: 3269 5719 Stoneware pottery products; pottery

(G-8456)
SPICER WLDG & FABRICATION INC
1593 S Eagle Valley Rd (16844-9408)
PHONE..................................814 355-7046
Olivia Confer, *President*
EMP: 5
SALES (est): 410K **Privately Held**
SIC: 7692 Welding repair

(G-8457)
VILLAGE CRAFT IRON & STONE INC
Also Called: V C I Quality Masonry Contrs
4725 S Eagle Valley Rd (16844-9708)
P.O. Box 177 (16844-0177)
PHONE..................................814 353-1777
Brian Mannino, *President*
Joseph Mannino, *Vice Pres*
EMP: 38
SALES (est): 2.6MM **Privately Held**
SIC: 2511 2514 7359 Wood household furniture; metal household furniture; furniture rental

---

Kane
Mckean County

(G-8458)
ALLEGHENY MOUNTAIN RACEWAY
505 Gunsmoke Rd (16735-7811)
PHONE..................................814 598-9077
Harry Spaulding, *Principal*
EMP: 3
SALES (est): 228.3K **Privately Held**
SIC: 3644 Raceways

(G-8459)
ARG RESOURCES INC
285 Custom Lumber Ln (16735-6405)
PHONE..................................814 837-7477
Harvey Golubock, *President*
EMP: 38
SALES (corp-wide): 3.3MM **Privately Held**
SIC: 1311 Crude petroleum & natural gas production
PA: Arg Resources, Inc.
100 Four Fls Ste 215
West Conshohocken PA 19428
610 940-4420

(G-8460)
CAROL ZUZEK
Also Called: Zuzek Lumber
Off Rte 66 Rr 2 (16735)
PHONE..................................814 837-7090
Carol Zuzek, *Owner*
EMP: 7
SALES (est): 752.7K **Privately Held**
SIC: 2421 2426 Sawmills & planing mills, general; hardwood dimension & flooring mills

(G-8461)
COLLINS PINE COMPANY
Kane Hardwood Div
W Of Kane Rr 6 (16735)
P.O. Box 807 (16735-0807)
PHONE..................................814 837-6941
Connie Grenz, *Branch Mgr*
EMP: 100
SALES: 6.3MM
SALES (corp-wide): 139MM **Privately Held**
WEB: www.collinswood.com
SIC: 5031 2435 2426 2421 Lumber: rough, dressed & finished; hardwood veneer & plywood; hardwood dimension & flooring mills; sawmills & planing mills, general
PA: Collins Pine Company
29190 Sw Town Center Loop
Wilsonville OR 97070
503 227-1219

(G-8462)
DANGELOS CUSTOM BUILT MFG LLC
Also Called: Dangelo Autobody and Towing
2 Poplar St (16735-5519)
P.O. Box 160 (16735-0160)
PHONE.................................814 837-6053
Derek D'Angelo, *Mng Member*
EMP: 11
SALES (est): 2.1MM **Privately Held**
WEB: www.dangeloautobody.com
SIC: 7532 3711 Body shop, automotive; wreckers (tow truck), assembly of

(G-8463)
GARY T ROSSMAN
Also Called: Rossman, Gary Logging
326 Birch St (16735-1215)
PHONE.................................814 837-7017
Gary T Rossman, *Owner*
EMP: 8
SALES (est): 500K **Privately Held**
SIC: 2411 Logging

(G-8464)
GEORGIA-PACIFIC BLDG PDTS LLC
147 Temple Dr (16735-5343)
PHONE.................................814 778-6000
Lori Smith, *General Mgr*
EMP: 14
SALES (corp-wide): 42.4B **Privately Held**
SIC: 2653 Corrugated & solid fiber boxes
HQ: Georgia-Pacific Building Products Llc
133 Peachtree St Ne
Atlanta GA 30303

(G-8465)
GEORGIA-PACIFIC LLC
149 Temple Dr (16735-5343)
PHONE.................................814 778-6000
Chuck Stevens, *General Mgr*
EMP: 140
SQ FT: 300,000
SALES (corp-wide): 42.4B **Privately Held**
SIC: 2493 Particleboard products
HQ: Georgia-Pacific Llc
133 Peachtree St Nw
Atlanta GA 30303
404 652-4000

(G-8466)
HIGHLAND FOREST RESOURCES INC (HQ)
Rr 6 Box 84 (16735)
PHONE.................................814 837-6760
James A Beck, *President*
Calvin H Fridrich, *Treasurer*
William Pemecky, *Admin Sec*
▼ EMP: 30
SQ FT: 720
SALES (corp-wide): 1.5B **Publicly Held**
SIC: 2421 5031 2426 Sawmills & planing mills, general; lumber: rough, dressed & finished; hardwood dimension & flooring mills
PA: National Fuel Gas Company
6363 Main St
Williamsville NY 14221
716 857-7000

(G-8467)
JIM AIRGOOD PRESSURE WASHER
22 Old Mill Rd (16735-3528)
PHONE.................................814 837-7626
EMP: 8
SALES (est): 992.9K **Privately Held**
SIC: 3452 Mfg Bolts/Screws/Rivets

(G-8468)
JOHN R HOLT
5531 Highland Rd (16735-7737)
PHONE.................................814 837-8687
John R Holt, *Principal*
EMP: 3
SALES (est): 324K **Privately Held**
SIC: 2411 Logging

(G-8469)
KANE INNOVATIONS INC
Sterling Dula Archtchtral Pdts
226 Chestnut St (16735-1659)
PHONE.................................814 838-7731

Michael E Carpenter, *Manager*
EMP: 56
SALES (corp-wide): 31MM **Privately Held**
WEB: www.kanescreens.com
SIC: 3442 3355 Metal doors, sash & trim; aluminum rail & structural shapes
PA: Kane Innovations, Inc.
2250 Powell Ave
Erie PA 16506
814 838-7731

(G-8470)
KANE REPUBLICAN
200 N Fraley St (16735-1197)
PHONE.................................814 837-6000
Cindy Hullings, *General Mgr*
EMP: 4
SQ FT: 3,000
SALES (est): 302.6K **Privately Held**
WEB: www.clintonnc.com
SIC: 2711 8651 Newspapers: publishing only, not printed on site; political action committee

(G-8471)
LITTLE BEAR CREEK ALPACAS
971 Ogrin Rd (16735-6619)
PHONE.................................814 788-0971
EMP: 5 EST: 2015
SALES (est): 358.6K **Privately Held**
SIC: 2231 Alpacas, mohair: woven

(G-8472)
NATIONAL FUEL GAS DIST CORP
5405 Highland Rd (16735-7733)
PHONE.................................814 837-9585
Ronald Morse, *Branch Mgr*
EMP: 6
SALES (corp-wide): 1.5B **Publicly Held**
SIC: 2869 Fuels
HQ: National Fuel Gas Distribution Corporation
6363 Main St
Williamsville NY 14221
716 857-7000

(G-8473)
NEW GROWTH RESOURCES INC
51 Gregory Dr (16735-3009)
P.O. Box 805 (16735-0805)
PHONE.................................814 837-2206
Michael J Kocjancic, *President*
EMP: 1
SALES (est): 1.1MM **Privately Held**
SIC: 2411 1629 2421 Wood chips, produced in the field; land clearing contractor; lumber: rough, sawed or planed

(G-8474)
NORTHWEST LOGGING LLC
326 Birch St (16735-1215)
PHONE.................................814 598-1350
Gary T Rossman, *Principal*
EMP: 3
SALES (est): 233.5K **Privately Held**
SIC: 2411 Logging

(G-8475)
OAKES GAS CO INC
47 E Brick Yard Rd (16735-3905)
P.O. Box 442 (16735-0442)
PHONE.................................814 837-7972
Garold Oakes, *President*
EMP: 6
SALES (est): 550K **Privately Held**
SIC: 1389 Pumping of oil & gas wells

(G-8476)
ON FUEL
159 Fraley St (16735-1386)
PHONE.................................814 837-1017
Kay Hannah, *Manager*
EMP: 3 EST: 2014
SALES (est): 150.5K **Privately Held**
SIC: 2869 Fuels

(G-8477)
PERRY S SWANSON LOGGING
421 Haines St (16735-1434)
PHONE.................................814 837-7020
Perry Swanson, *Principal*
EMP: 3

SALES (est): 288.4K **Privately Held**
SIC: 2411 Logging camps & contractors

(G-8478)
SHIELDS LOGGING LLC
8592 Route 6 (16735-4532)
PHONE.................................814 778-6183
Daniel E Shields, *Principal*
EMP: 3 EST: 2010
SALES (est): 328.5K **Privately Held**
SIC: 2411 Logging

(G-8479)
TWISTED VINE WINERY
13106 Route 948 (16735-6504)
PHONE.................................814 512-4330
EMP: 4
SALES (est): 221K **Privately Held**
SIC: 2084 Wines

Karns City
Butler County

(G-8480)
CALUMET KARNS CITY REF LLC
138 Petrolia St (16041-9222)
PHONE.................................724 756-9212
David Baum, *Manager*
Victor Rozic, *Manager*
Ryan Campbell, *Technology*
William Powers, *Maintence Staff*
EMP: 4
SALES (corp-wide): 3.5B **Publicly Held**
SIC: 2911 Petroleum refining
HQ: Calumet Karns City Refining, Llc
2780 Waterfront
Indianapolis IN 46214

(G-8481)
N-JAY MACHINES
355 Fredericksburg Rd (16041-2209)
PHONE.................................724 232-0110
Imre Nagy, *Principal*
EMP: 4
SALES (est): 300K **Privately Held**
SIC: 3594 Fluid power pumps & motors

(G-8482)
PENNZOIL-QUAKER STATE COMPANY
138 Petrolia St (16041-9222)
PHONE.................................724 756-0110
Charlie Boguf, *Branch Mgr*
EMP: 300
SALES (corp-wide): 305.1B **Privately Held**
WEB: www.pzl.com
SIC: 1311 2911 2992 Crude petroleum production; petroleum refining; lubricating oils & greases
HQ: Pennzoil-Quaker State Company
150 N Dairy Ashford Rd
Houston TX 77079
713 245-4800

Karthaus
Clearfield County

(G-8483)
PHILIP REESE COAL CO INC
3513 Main St (16845)
PHONE.................................814 263-4231
George Philip Reese, *President*
James W Reese, *Treasurer*
EMP: 6 EST: 1946
SALES: 500K **Privately Held**
SIC: 1221 Bituminous coal & lignite-surface mining

(G-8484)
RIVER HILL COAL CO INC
Hwy 879 (16845)
P.O. Box 69 (16845-0069)
PHONE.................................814 263-4506
Elwood King, *Manager*
EMP: 5

SALES (est): 311.7K
SALES (corp-wide): 12.6MM **Privately Held**
SIC: 1221 Bituminous coal & lignite-surface mining
PA: River Hill Coal Co, Inc
S Second St
Kylertown PA 16847
814 345-5642

(G-8485)
RIVER HILL COAL CO INC
Hauseman Dr (16845)
P.O. Box 141, Kylertown (16847-0141)
PHONE.................................814 263-4506
Elwood King, *Manager*
EMP: 10
SALES (corp-wide): 12.6MM **Privately Held**
SIC: 1221 Strip mining, bituminous
PA: River Hill Coal Co, Inc
S Second St
Kylertown PA 16847
814 345-5642

(G-8486)
RIVER HILL COAL CO INC
Potter St (16845)
PHONE.................................814 263-4341
J Hoffman, *Manager*
EMP: 15
SALES (corp-wide): 12.6MM **Privately Held**
SIC: 1221 Bituminous coal & lignite-surface mining
PA: River Hill Coal Co, Inc
S Second St
Kylertown PA 16847
814 345-5642

Kelayres
Schuylkill County

(G-8487)
MCADOO MACHINE COMPANY
51 4th St (18231)
P.O. Box 67 (18231-0067)
PHONE.................................570 929-3717
Mathew Sobolewski, *President*
Douglas Sobolewski, *Admin Sec*
EMP: 16
SQ FT: 6,000
SALES (est): 1.3MM **Privately Held**
SIC: 3599 Machine shop, jobbing & repair

Kelton
Chester County

(G-8488)
GOURMET SPECIALTY IMPORTS
Also Called: G S I
171 Jennersville Rd (19346)
P.O. Box 483, Avondale (19311-0483)
PHONE.................................610 345-1113
Cary Rosenthal, *President*
Richard Rosenthal,
▲ EMP: 12 EST: 2001
SALES: 1MM **Privately Held**
SIC: 2035 Onions, pickled

Kempton
Berks County

(G-8489)
ALBRIGHTS MILL LLC
9927 Kistler Valley Rd (19529-9074)
P.O. Box 195 (19529-0195)
PHONE.................................610 756-6022
Ronald R Wessner,
Gary A Wessner,
Robert G Wessner,
Stephanie Wessner, *Associate*
EMP: 25
SQ FT: 10,000
SALES (est): 8.3MM **Privately Held**
WEB: www.albrightsmill.com
SIC: 5153 2048 5191 Grains; livestock feeds; feed

▲ = Import ▼=Export
◆ =Import/Export

(G-8490)
BAILEY WOOD PRODUCTS INC
441 Mountain Rd (19529-9336)
PHONE..................................610 756-6827
Jeff Schucker, *President*
Tina Schucker, *Office Mgr*
EMP: 5
SQ FT: 2,400
SALES (est): 870.8K **Privately Held**
WEB: www.baileywp.com
SIC: 2421 5211 5031 Lumber: rough,
sawed or planed; lumber & other building
materials; lumber: rough, dressed & fin-
ished

(G-8491)
**EXTRUDED PLASTIC
SOLUTIONS**
8891 Kings Hwy (19529-8916)
PHONE..................................610 756-6602
Bill Felker, *President*
Stewart Ohlinger, *Opers Mgr*
Manny Dijamco, *Marketing Staff*
Sandy Felker, *Office Mgr*
EMP: 7 EST: 2010
SALES (est): 736.6K **Privately Held**
SIC: 2821 Polyvinyl chloride resins (PVC)

(G-8492)
HISTORIC DOORS LLC
Also Called: Hendricks' Woodworking
67 Vole Hollow Rd (19529-8811)
P.O. Box 139 (19529-0139)
PHONE..................................610 756-6187
Wendy Wyncoll, *Finance Mgr*
Steve Hendricks,
Wendi Wenkle,
EMP: 8
SALES (est): 750K **Privately Held**
WEB: www.historicdoors.com
SIC: 2431 Interior & ornamental woodwork
& trim; doors & door parts & trim, wood;
moldings, wood: unfinished & prefinished

(G-8493)
**NATIONAL DERMALOGY IMAGE
CORP**
Also Called: Derma Medical
253 Quaker City Rd (19529-9354)
PHONE..................................610 756-0065
Elizabeth Finch, *President*
Patrick Merrigan, *Vice Pres*
Matthew Merrigan, *Treasurer*
Maura Merrigan, *Admin Sec*
▲ **EMP:** 9
SALES (est): 764.9K **Privately Held**
WEB: www.derma-international.com
SIC: 2844 7231 2752 Cosmetic prepara-
tions; beauty schools; commercial print-
ing, lithographic

(G-8494)
**SPITZENBURG CIDER HOUSE
LLC**
Also Called: Stony Run Winery
67 Kempton Rd (19529-8755)
P.O. Box 167 (19529-0167)
PHONE..................................484 357-2058
Lawrence Shrawder, *Manager*
EMP: 3 EST: 2015
SQ FT: 6,000
SALES (est): 110.1K **Privately Held**
SIC: 2084 Wines

(G-8495)
SPOONWOOD INC (PA)
Also Called: Jonathan Spoon
3716 Route 737 (19529-9187)
PHONE..................................610 756-6464
Jonathan Simons, *President*
EMP: 9
SQ FT: 1,200
SALES (est): 943.4K **Privately Held**
WEB: www.woodspoon.com
SIC: 2499 Woodenware, kitchen & house-
hold

(G-8496)
TIMBERSTRONG LLC
441 Mountain Rd (19529-9336)
PHONE..................................484 357-8730
EMP: 3
SALES (est): 224.3K **Privately Held**
SIC: 2421 Sawmills & planing mills, gen-
eral

Kennerdell
Venango County

(G-8497)
BELL GRAPHICS
338 Donaldson Rd (16374-1403)
P.O. Box 226, Clintonville (16372-0226)
PHONE..................................814 385-6222
Richard R Bell, *Owner*
Marylou Bell, *Co-Owner*
EMP: 5
SALES: 131K **Privately Held**
SIC: 7389 7335 2262 Laminating service;
commercial photography; printing: man-
made fiber & silk broadwoven fabrics

(G-8498)
**LIPINSKI LOGGING AND LBR
INC**
3731 State Route 208 (16374-1515)
PHONE..................................814 385-4101
Walter Lipinski Jr, *President*
Laurie Hanna, *Manager*
EMP: 3
SALES (est): 649K **Privately Held**
SIC: 2411 2421 Logging camps & contrac-
tors; lumber: rough, sawed or planed

(G-8499)
**WITHERUP FBRCTION
ERECTION INC (PA)**
Also Called: We
431 Kennerdell Rd (16374-2007)
P.O. Box 55 (16374-0055)
PHONE..................................814 385-6601
Kevin L Witherup, *President*
Robert A Witherup Jr, *Vice Pres*
Jason Woolcock, *Vice Pres*
Troy Stahlman, *Opers Mgr*
Brian Kratzer, *Project Engr*
EMP: 50
SQ FT: 40,000
SALES (est): 20.5MM **Privately Held**
SIC: 3443 Tanks, standard or custom fabri-
cated: metal plate

Kennett Square
Chester County

(G-8500)
ABBOTT LABORATORIES
Ross Products Division
148 W State St Ste 103 (19348-3055)
PHONE..................................610 444-9818
Tom Sausen, *General Mgr*
EMP: 5
SALES (corp-wide): 30.5B **Publicly Held**
WEB: www.abbott.com
SIC: 3826 3841 2835 2834 Blood testing
apparatus; diagnostic apparatus, medical;
medical instruments & equipment, blood
& bone work; IV transfusion apparatus; in
vitro & in vivo diagnostic substances;
blood derivative diagnostic agents; hemo-
tology diagnostic agents; microbiology &
virology diagnostic products; druggists'
preparations (pharmaceuticals)
PA: Abbott Laboratories
100 Abbott Park Rd
Abbott Park IL 60064
224 667-6100

(G-8501)
ADMIRAL VALVE LLC
Also Called: Cpv Manufacturing
503 School House Rd (19348-1741)
PHONE..................................215 386-6508
Thomas Moran, *Sales Mgr*
Robert Neal, *Sales Staff*
Ira Perlmuter, *Manager*
EMP: 35 EST: 1915
SQ FT: 30,000
SALES: 5.7MM **Privately Held**
WEB: www.cpvmfg.com
SIC: 3498 3492 Fabricated pipe & fittings;
control valves, fluid power: hydraulic &
pneumatic

(G-8502)
ADVANTAGE MILLWORK INC
Also Called: Studio Technology
529 Rosedale Rd Ste 103 (19348-2435)
PHONE..................................610 925-2785
Vince Fiola, *President*
Robin Fiola, *Bookkeeper*
EMP: 8
SALES (est): 1MM **Privately Held**
WEB: www.studiotechnology.com
SIC: 2511 Wood household furniture

(G-8503)
CHADDS FORD CABINET INC
1100 E Baltimore Pike (19348-2304)
PHONE..................................610 388-6005
Beverly L Price, *President*
EMP: 3 EST: 1982
SQ FT: 2,000
SALES (est): 415.8K **Privately Held**
WEB: www.chaddsfordcabinet.com
SIC: 5712 2434 Cabinet work, custom;
wood kitchen cabinets

(G-8504)
CHERYL NASH APPAREL LLC
210a Gale Ln (19348-1734)
PHONE..................................610 692-1919
Marc A Ham, *Mng Member*
Cheryl Nash,
▲ **EMP:** 5 EST: 2012
SALES (est): 677.6K **Privately Held**
SIC: 2339 Women's & misses' outerwear

(G-8505)
CHROMAGEN VISION LLC
326 W Cedar St Ste 1 (19348-3275)
PHONE..................................610 628-2941
Joseph J Sanitate Jr, *Owner*
EMP: 5
SALES (est): 524.1K **Privately Held**
SIC: 3851 Protectors, eye

(G-8506)
CLEARNAV INSTRUMENTS
256 Old Kennett Rd (19348-2710)
PHONE..................................610 925-0198
Brxan Lawrence, *President*
EMP: 3 EST: 2010
SALES (est): 359.7K **Privately Held**
SIC: 3639 Household appliances

(G-8507)
**CONCENTRATED KNOWLEDGE
CORP**
511 School House Rd # 300 (19348-1915)
PHONE..................................610 388-5020
Joseph A Clement, *President*
Robert Carter, *Vice Pres*
EMP: 27
SQ FT: 16,000
SALES (est): 2.1MM **Privately Held**
SIC: 2731 Book publishing

(G-8508)
E VICTOR PESCE
Also Called: At-Mar Glass
611 W State St (19348-3030)
PHONE..................................610 444-5903
E Victor Pesce, *President*
EMP: 8
SQ FT: 2,000
SALES (est): 1.1MM **Privately Held**
SIC: 3229 7699 Scientific glassware; labo-
ratory instrument repair

(G-8509)
EAGLE ENERGY SYSTEMS LTD
500 N Walnut Rd (19348-1714)
PHONE..................................610 444-3388
Joseph Nolan, *Partner*
Brian Nolan, *Partner*
Joe Nolan, *Partner*
Jeff Oswald, *Vice Pres*
Mike Baker, *CFO*
EMP: 30
SQ FT: 10,000
SALES (est): 6.1MM **Privately Held**
SIC: 3699 Security devices

(G-8510)
FARO LASER DIVISION LLC
222 Gale Ln (19348-1734)
PHONE..................................610 444-2300
Jim West, *General Mgr*

Brad Lyold, *Manager*
EMP: 4
SALES (est): 365K
SALES (corp-wide): 403.6MM **Publicly
Held**
SIC: 3699 7389 7371 Laser systems &
equipment; industrial & commercial equip-
ment inspection service; computer soft-
ware development
PA: Faro Technologies, Inc.
250 Technology Park
Lake Mary FL 32746
407 333-9911

(G-8511)
**GALER ESTATES VINYRD &
WINERY**
700 Folly Hill Rd (19348-1506)
PHONE..................................484 899-8013
EMP: 4
SALES (est): 83K **Privately Held**
SIC: 2084 Brandy & brandy spirits; wines

(G-8512)
GLORY FIBERS
293 W Street Rd (19348-1615)
PHONE..................................610 444-5646
Jennifer Cauffman, *Owner*
EMP: 4
SALES: 50K **Privately Held**
WEB: www.gloryfibers.com
SIC: 2741 Art copy: publishing & printing

(G-8513)
GOOD NEIGHBORS INC
224 E Street Rd Ste 2 (19348-1705)
PHONE..................................610 444-1860
Yunsuk Ko, *Managing Dir*
Rob Ellis, *Principal*
EMP: 16
SALES (est): 601.4K **Privately Held**
SIC: 3089 Organizers for closets, drawers,
etc.: plastic

(G-8514)
IKOR INDUSTRIES INC
103 Indian Springs Rd (19348-2553)
P.O. Box 238, Yorklyn DE (19736-0238)
PHONE..................................302 456-0280
Paul Lesniak, *President*
Stephen Coons, *Treasurer*
Daniel Maisano, *Admin Sec*
EMP: 100 EST: 1998
SALES: 3MM **Privately Held**
SIC: 3677 2311 5047 Filtration devices,
electronic; tailored dress & sport coats:
men's & boys'; medical equipment & sup-
plies

(G-8515)
JOB TRAINING SYSTEMS INC
410 Dean Dr (19348-1627)
P.O. Box 868, Unionville (19375-0868)
PHONE..................................610 444-0868
Doak Conn, *President*
EMP: 3
SALES (est): 251.9K **Privately Held**
WEB: www.jobtraining.com
SIC: 2731 Books: publishing only

(G-8516)
JOYCE LANGELIER
Also Called: Langelier Designs
463 N Mill Rd (19348-2401)
P.O. Box 525, Unionville (19375-0525)
PHONE..................................610 659-8859
Joyce Langelier, *Owner*
Matt Langelier, *Vice Pres*
EMP: 15
SQ FT: 8,000
SALES (est): 957.7K **Privately Held**
SIC: 3999 Boutiquing: decorating gift items
with sequins, fruit, etc.; plaques, picture,
laminated

(G-8517)
JT-MESH DIAGNOSTICS LLC
900 Merrybell Ln (19348-2733)
PHONE..................................610 299-7482
Thais Sielecki, *CEO*
EMP: 3
SALES (est): 81.8K **Privately Held**
SIC: 2835 In vivo diagnostics

(G-8518)
KELLY FUEL CO INC
615 S Broad St (19348-3345)
PHONE....................................610 444-5055
Arlene Kelly, *Principal*
EMP: 3
SALES (est): 175.9K **Privately Held**
SIC: 2869 Fuels

(G-8519)
KENNETT ADVANCE PRINTING HOUSE
101 S Walnut St (19348-3131)
PHONE....................................610 444-5840
Justin D'Antonio, *President*
Justin D'Antonio Jr, *Corp Secy*
Sandra D Antonio, *Vice Pres*
EMP: 4 **EST:** 1965
SQ FT: 7,000
SALES (est): 507.4K **Privately Held**
SIC: 3555 Printing presses; presses, envelope, printing

(G-8520)
KENNETT SQUARE SPECIALTIES LLC
Also Called: Kennett Steak and Mushroom
546 Creek Rd (19348-2620)
P.O. Box 652 (19348-0652)
PHONE....................................610 444-8122
Jeffrey D Guest,
Louis J Caputo Jr,
EMP: 90
SALES (est): 18.6MM **Privately Held**
WEB: www.historickennettsquare.com
SIC: 2499 Mulch or sawdust products, wood

(G-8521)
KEYSTONE STRUCTURES INC
705 Terminal Way (19348-3662)
PHONE....................................610 444-9525
Michael Dougherty, *President*
Anthony Hutchinson, *Corp Secy*
EMP: 27
SQ FT: 25,000
SALES (est): 6MM **Privately Held**
WEB: www.keystonestructures.com
SIC: 3448 Buildings, portable: prefabricated metal

(G-8522)
LESTER WATER INC
920 S Union St (19348-2638)
PHONE....................................610 444-4660
David McKeon, *President*
EMP: 10
SQ FT: 5,000
SALES (est): 2.2MM **Privately Held**
WEB: www.lesterwater.com
SIC: 3589 7389 Water filters & softeners, household type; water softener service

(G-8523)
LONGWOOD MANUFACTURING CORP
816 E Baltimore Pike (19348-1890)
PHONE....................................610 444-4200
Thomas J Piacentino Jr, *President*
John Piacentino, *Corp Secy*
Mark Piacentino, *Vice Pres*
EMP: 16
SQ FT: 50,000
SALES (est): 3.1MM **Privately Held**
WEB: www.lmconline.com
SIC: 3599 3443 7692 3441 Mfg Industrial Machinery Mfg Fabricated Plate Wrk Welding Repair Structural Metal Fabrctn

(G-8524)
M AND P CUSTOM DESIGN INC
510 S Walnut St (19348-3343)
P.O. Box 14 (19348-0014)
PHONE....................................610 444-0244
James M De Fazio, *President*
James M Defazio, *President*
Patricia A De Fazio, *Treasurer*
Patti Defazio, *Office Mgr*
EMP: 10
SQ FT: 2,500
SALES (est): 1.6MM **Privately Held**
WEB: www.mpcustom.com
SIC: 3443 3599 7692 Metal parts; machine & other job shop work; welding repair

(G-8525)
MARTRA LLC
Also Called: Optical Interlinks
206 Gale Ln (19348-1734)
P.O. Box 401 (19348-0401)
PHONE....................................610 444-9469
EMP: 5
SALES: 500K **Privately Held**
SIC: 3229 Mfg Fiber Optics

(G-8526)
MCGRORY INC
576 Rosedale Rd (19348-2441)
P.O. Box 999 (19348-0999)
PHONE....................................610 444-1512
Timothy McGrory, *President*
EMP: 60
SQ FT: 20,000
SALES (est): 15.3MM **Privately Held**
WEB: www.mcgroryinc.com
SIC: 2541 Counter & sink tops

(G-8527)
METAL SERVICES LLC (HQ)
Also Called: Phoenix Services
148 W State St Ste 301 (19348-3054)
PHONE....................................610 347-0444
Kip Smith, *President*
Michael Glowa, *Vice Pres*
Allen Barkman, *Site Mgr*
Robert Gorski, *Supervisor*
Clint McGinty, *Director*
▲ **EMP:** 20
SALES (est): 10MM **Privately Held**
SIC: 3295 Perlite, aggregate or expanded

(G-8528)
MICROSPHERE INC
455 Birch St (19348-3609)
PHONE....................................610 444-3450
EMP: 3
SALES (corp-wide): 502K **Privately Held**
SIC: 3679 Microwave components
PA: Microsphere Inc.
640 Snyder Ave Ste B
West Chester PA
610 719-1521

(G-8529)
MIRADOR GLOBAL LP
148 W State St Ste 303 (19348-3054)
PHONE....................................302 983-3430
Chuck Peipher, *Partner*
EMP: 6
SALES: 1.2MM **Privately Held**
SIC: 2834 Pharmaceutical preparations

(G-8530)
MIX EARL
131 Knoxlyn Farm Dr (19348-2738)
PHONE....................................610 444-3245
Earl Mix, *Principal*
EMP: 3
SALES (est): 269.5K **Privately Held**
SIC: 3273 Ready-mixed concrete

(G-8531)
MOLDCRAFT CO
503 School House Rd (19348-1741)
PHONE....................................610 399-1404
George Bonadio, *President*
Robert Angle, *Shareholder*
EMP: 11 **EST:** 1946
SQ FT: 6,400
SALES (est): 1.9MM **Privately Held**
SIC: 3599 Machine shop, jobbing & repair

(G-8532)
MTEKKA LLC
124 Knoxlyn Farm Dr (19348-2700)
PHONE....................................610 619-3555
EMP: 4
SALES (est): 242K **Privately Held**
SIC: 7379 7371 3572 Computer Related Services Custom Computer Programing Mfg Computer Storage Devices

(G-8533)
OLIVE KASTANIA OIL
759 Northbrook Rd (19348-1535)
PHONE....................................610 347-6736
EMP: 3 **EST:** 2015
SALES (est): 139.4K **Privately Held**
SIC: 2079 Olive oil

(G-8534)
OPTICAL CROSSLINKS INC
206 Gale Ln (19348-1734)
P.O. Box 411 (19348-0411)
PHONE....................................610 444-9469
EMP: 4
SQ FT: 13,000
SALES (est): 330K **Privately Held**
SIC: 3827 Mfg Optical Interconnection Components

(G-8535)
PERFECT IMPRESSION
340 N Mill Rd Ste 1 (19348-2800)
PHONE....................................610 444-9493
EMP: 3
SALES (est): 92.3K **Privately Held**
SIC: 2752 Commercial printing, lithographic

(G-8536)
PREMIER CHEMICALS LLC
120 Marshall Bridge Rd (19348-2706)
PHONE....................................610 420-7500
John Ahl, *Principal*
EMP: 4
SALES (est): 190.4K **Privately Held**
SIC: 1499 Miscellaneous nonmetallic minerals

(G-8537)
PURELAND SUPPLY LLC
210 Gale Ln (19348-1734)
P.O. Box 534, Unionville (19375-0534)
PHONE....................................610 444-0590
Lisa Herman, *Engineer*
Robin Huber, *Sales Mgr*
Jon T Felter, *Mng Member*
EMP: 10
SALES (est): 1.9MM **Privately Held**
WEB: www.purelandsupply.com
SIC: 3641 Electric lamps

(G-8538)
RECREATION RESOURCE USA LLC
425 Mcfarlan Rd Ste 100 (19348-2483)
PHONE....................................610 444-4402
Sylvia Umbreit, *Managing Prtnr*
Kevin Umbreit, *Vice Pres*
EMP: 6
SQ FT: 1,550
SALES (est): 4.4MM **Privately Held**
WEB: www.recreation-resource.com
SIC: 3949 5091 Playground equipment; sporting & recreation goods

(G-8539)
RED ORTHODONTIC LAB
Also Called: Red Orthodontic Laboratories
906 Mitchell Farm Ln (19348-1320)
PHONE....................................610 237-1100
Ronald Doerr, *Owner*
Jim Macnulty, *Manager*
EMP: 5
SQ FT: 3,200
SALES (est): 604.3K **Privately Held**
SIC: 3843 8072 Orthodontic appliances; orthodontic appliance production

(G-8540)
ROCKWELL COLLINS INC
503 School House Rd (19348-1741)
PHONE....................................610 925-5844
Doug Minnick, *Manager*
EMP: 16
SALES (corp-wide): 66.5B **Publicly Held**
WEB: www.seosdisplays.com
SIC: 3861 1731 3699 Screens, projection; voice, data & video wiring contractor; electrical equipment & supplies
HQ: Rockwell Collins, Inc.
400 Collins Rd Ne
Cedar Rapids IA 52498

(G-8541)
SARRO SIGNS INC
116 W Street Rd (19348-1614)
P.O. Box 157, Unionville (19375-0157)
PHONE....................................610 444-2020
Penny Sarro, *President*
John Sarro, *Vice Pres*
EMP: 4 **EST:** 2005
SALES (est): 506K **Privately Held**
SIC: 3993 Electric signs

(G-8542)
SENSORTEX INC
948 Wawaset Rd (19348-1342)
PHONE....................................302 444-2383
William Biter, *President*
EMP: 5
SQ FT: 10,000
SALES (est): 585K **Privately Held**
WEB: www.sensortex.com
SIC: 3674 8711 Radiation sensors; engineering services

(G-8543)
SOVANA BISTRO INC
696 Unionville Rd Ste 8 (19348-1763)
PHONE....................................610 444-5600
Nick Farell, *President*
Adam Junkins, *General Mgr*
▲ **EMP:** 60
SALES (est): 5.9MM **Privately Held**
WEB: www.sovanabistro.com
SIC: 2599 Bar, restaurant & cafeteria furniture

(G-8544)
STENGELS WELDING SHOP INC
810 E Baltimore Pike (19348)
PHONE....................................610 444-4110
Frederick C Stengel, *President*
EMP: 4 **EST:** 1956
SALES (est): 587.1K **Privately Held**
SIC: 7692 8711 3523 Welding repair; designing: ship, boat, machine & product; farm machinery & equipment

(G-8545)
STEPHENS EXCAVATING SVC LLC
115 Corman Dr (19348-1655)
P.O. Box 291, Unionville (19375-0291)
PHONE....................................484 888-1010
Timothy E Stephens, *Mng Member*
EMP: 9
SQ FT: 400
SALES (est): 1.3MM **Privately Held**
SIC: 1455 1522 Kaolin & ball clay; residential construction

(G-8546)
STRATEGIC MEDICINE INC
231 Deepdale Dr (19348-1882)
PHONE....................................814 659-5450
Michael N Liebman, *President*
Michael Liebman, *Managing Dir*
EMP: 6
SALES (est): 565K **Privately Held**
SIC: 3641 2834 Health lamps, infrared or ultraviolet; medicines, capsuled or ampuled

(G-8547)
SYNCHRONY MEDICAL LLC
2 W Market St Fl 5 Flr 5 (19348)
PHONE....................................484 947-5003
Rod Hughes,
EMP: 28
SQ FT: 3,750
SALES (est): 3.5MM **Privately Held**
SIC: 2834 Druggists' preparations (pharmaceuticals)

(G-8548)
TASTE OF PUEBLA
201 Birch St (19348-3605)
PHONE....................................484 467-8597
Christopher Castaneda, *Owner*
EMP: 4
SALES (est): 144K **Privately Held**
SIC: 5812 2032 Mexican restaurant; Mexican foods: packaged in cans, jars, etc.

(G-8549)
TEXTURED YARN CO INC
Also Called: Techniservice
738 W Cypress St (19348-2416)
P.O. Box 817 (19348-0817)
PHONE....................................610 444-5400
Nathan Schwartz, *President*
Ethan Schwartz, *Engineer*
EMP: 6 **EST:** 1953
SQ FT: 15,000
SALES (est): 1.1MM **Privately Held**
WEB: www.techniservice.com
SIC: 3552 Textile machinery

(G-8550)
TRAFFIC & SAFETY SIGNS INC
703 Terminal Way (19348-3662)
PHONE....................610 925-1990
Anthony P Hutchinson, *CEO*
Bonnie Dougherty, *President*
Jake McKinley, *Vice Pres*
EMP: 5
SQ FT: 2,000
SALES (est): 749.5K **Privately Held**
WEB: www.trafficsafetysigns.com
SIC: 3993 Signs, not made in custom sign
painting shops

(G-8551)
X-BAR DIAGNOSTICS SYSTEMS INC
77 Deer Path (19348-2345)
PHONE....................610 388-2071
James Lipscomb, *President*
EMP: 3
SALES (est): 192.9K **Privately Held**
SIC: 3829 Medical diagnostic systems, nu-
clear

(G-8552)
YS MANUFACTURING INC
101 Blue Spruce Dr (19348-4114)
PHONE....................610 444-4832
WEI Yang, *President*
Norbert Aubuchon, *Vice Pres*
WEI Ming, *Vice Pres*
▲ **EMP:** 52
SALES (est): 5MM **Privately Held**
SIC: 3599 Machine shop, jobbing & repair

Kersey
Elk County

(G-8553)
ALAN MAZZAFERRO
Also Called: Al's Machining
375 Main St (15846-9127)
PHONE....................814 885-6744
Alan Mazzaferro, *Owner*
EMP: 10 **EST:** 1987
SALES (est): 295K **Privately Held**
SIC: 3599 Machine shop, jobbing & repair

(G-8554)
CHECON POWDER MET CONTACTS LLC
600 Industrial Park Rd (15846-8912)
PHONE....................814 753-4466
D Allen Conaway, *President*
Michael Degrange, *Accounts Mgr*
EMP: 7
SALES (est): 721.7K **Privately Held**
SIC: 3643 Contacts, electrical

(G-8555)
DINSMORE WLDG FABRICATION INC
31 Innovative Dr (15846-8917)
P.O. Box 73, Dagus Mines (15831-0073)
PHONE....................814 885-6407
Mel Dinsmore, *Owner*
EMP: 8
SQ FT: 8,000
SALES (est): 1.2MM **Privately Held**
WEB: www.dinsmorewelding.com
SIC: 3441 Fabricated structural metal

(G-8556)
DOUBLE A LOGGING LLC
5237 Boone Mountain Rd (15846-2119)
PHONE....................814 885-6844
Adam L Vollmer, *Principal*
EMP: 6 **EST:** 2010
SALES (est): 500.5K **Privately Held**
SIC: 2411 Logging camps & contractors

(G-8557)
ELCO SINTERED ALLOYS CO INC
269 Fairview Rd (15846-9213)
P.O. Box 183 (15846-0183)
PHONE....................814 885-8031
Peter Herzing, *President*
Joan Herzing, *Vice Pres*
EMP: 50 **EST:** 1952
SQ FT: 40,000

SALES (est): 9.1MM **Privately Held**
SIC: 3399 Powder, metal

(G-8558)
EUGENE FLYNN LOGGING
856 Kemmer Rd (15846-9520)
PHONE....................814 772-1219
Eugene Flynn, *Principal*
EMP: 3 **EST:** 2009
SALES (est): 406.4K **Privately Held**
SIC: 2411 Logging

(G-8559)
GKN SINTER METALS LLC
319 Uhl Rd (15846-2621)
PHONE....................814 885-8053
John Gurosik, *Engineer*
Jackie Lenox, *Human Res Mgr*
Jody Meyer, *Branch Mgr*
EMP: 52
SALES (corp-wide): 2.7B **Privately Held**
SIC: 3399 Powder, metal
HQ: Gkn Sinter Metals, Llc
2200 N Opdyke Rd
Auburn Hills MI 48326
248 296-7832

(G-8560)
GKN SINTER METALS LLC
Also Called: Gnk Sinter Metals - St Marys 1
104 Fairview Rd (15846-2710)
PHONE....................814 781-6500
Brian Slusarick, *Branch Mgr*
Jody Meyer, *Manager*
EMP: 200
SALES (corp-wide): 2.7B **Privately Held**
SIC: 3399 Powder, metal
HQ: Gkn Sinter Metals, Llc
2200 N Opdyke Rd
Auburn Hills MI 48326
248 296-7832

(G-8561)
GKN SINTER METALS LLC
Also Called: GKN Saint Marys
104 Fairview Rd (15846-2710)
PHONE....................814 781-6500
Brian Slusarick, *Branch Mgr*
EMP: 200
SALES (corp-wide): 2.7B **Privately Held**
SIC: 2819 Tungsten carbide powder, ex-
cept abrasive or metallurgical
HQ: Gkn Sinter Metals, Llc
2200 N Opdyke Rd
Auburn Hills MI 48326
248 296-7832

(G-8562)
KERSEY TOOL AND DIE CO INC
272 Fairview Rd (15846-8916)
PHONE....................814 885-8045
Richard Bush Jr, *President*
Paul Holtzhauser, *Vice Pres*
EMP: 6 **EST:** 1964
SQ FT: 6,000
SALES (est): 500K **Privately Held**
SIC: 3544 Special dies & tools; jigs & fix-
tures

(G-8563)
LIBERTY PRESSED METALS LLC
151 Irishtown Rd (15846-2609)
P.O. Box 193 (15846-0193)
PHONE....................814 885-6277
Richard Uhl Jr, *Mng Member*
Rajeev Ranadive,
Doug Gaffey,
Rajeev D Ranadive,
EMP: 11
SQ FT: 12,000
SALES (est): 1.6MM **Privately Held**
WEB: www.libertypressedmetals.com
SIC: 3399 Powder, metal

(G-8564)
MODERN INDUSTRIES INC
Also Called: U.S. Heat Treaters
129 Green Rd (15846-8905)
PHONE....................814 885-8514
Pamela Gerarge, *Branch Mgr*
EMP: 12

SALES (corp-wide): 20MM **Privately Held**
SIC: 3398 3714 8734 3569 Metal heat
treating; motor vehicle parts & accessories; metallurgical testing laboratory; industrial shock absorbers
PA: Modern Industries, Inc.
613 W 11th St
Erie PA 16501
814 455-8061

(G-8565)
PENN METAL STAMPING INC
130 Sunset Rd (15846-2934)
P.O. Box 221, Saint Marys (15857-0221)
PHONE....................814 834-7171
Jude Weis, *President*
Edward F Crowe, *Vice Pres*
EMP: 47
SQ FT: 22,900
SALES (est): 11.1MM **Privately Held**
WEB: www.pennmetal.com
SIC: 3469 Stamping metal for the trade

(G-8566)
PRECISION SECONDARY MACHINING
157 Dagus Mines Rd (15846-2501)
PHONE....................814 885-6572
Michael Swanson, *Partner*
Michael Curley, *Partner*
EMP: 5
SQ FT: 2,500
SALES (est): 486.3K **Privately Held**
SIC: 3599 Machine shop, jobbing & repair

(G-8567)
QUALITY DISPERSIONS INC
1413 Million Dollar Hwy (15846-9327)
P.O. Box 575, Saint Marys (15857-0575)
PHONE....................814 781-7927
Patrick J Catalone, *President*
Robert G Catalone, *Treasurer*
Betty L Catalone, *Admin Sec*
▲ **EMP:** 12 **EST:** 1971
SQ FT: 20,280
SALES (est): 2.1MM **Privately Held**
SIC: 3471 2893 Coloring & finishing of
aluminum or formed products; printing
ink; screen process ink

(G-8568)
REBCO INC
650 Brandy Camp Rd (15846-1904)
PHONE....................814 885-8035
Kenneth L Huey, *President*
Corey Mesbitt, *General Mgr*
Grace Doran, *Treasurer*
Rhonda Bonfardin, *Admin Sec*
EMP: 114
SQ FT: 49,000
SALES (est): 5.9MM **Privately Held**
SIC: 3399 Powder, metal

(G-8569)
SIDELINGER BROS TOOL & DIE
Also Called: Sidelinger Brothers Tool & Die
500 Main St (15846-1912)
P.O. Box 185 (15846-0185)
PHONE....................814 885-8001
John M Sidelinger, *President*
Timothy Sidelinger, *Corp Secy*
EMP: 8
SQ FT: 3,200
SALES (est): 460K **Privately Held**
SIC: 3599 3544 Machine shop, jobbing &
repair; special dies, tools, jigs & fixtures

(G-8570)
SINTERFIRE INC
200 Indl Pk Rd (15846)
PHONE....................814 885-6672
Brandon Graves, *President*
Joseph C Benini, *President*
Catherine G Benini, *Treasurer*
EMP: 13
SQ FT: 12,000
SALES (est): 2.9MM **Privately Held**
WEB: www.sinterfire.com
SIC: 3399 Metal powders, pastes & flakes

(G-8571)
STRUBLES FIRE AND SAFETY
185 Struble Rd (15846-2727)
P.O. Box 190 (15846-0190)
PHONE....................814 594-0840

Thomas P Struble, *Principal*
EMP: 4 **EST:** 2010
SALES (est): 489.5K **Privately Held**
SIC: 3822 Auto controls regulating residntl
& coml environmt & applncs

(G-8572)
WORLDWIDE EDM GRAPHITE INC
1215 Million Dollar Hwy (15846-9429)
PHONE....................814 781-6939
Anthony Gerg, *CEO*
Mike Kronenwetter, *President*
Todd W Hanes, *Vice Pres*
Laura Resch, *Vice Pres*
EMP: 3
SALES (est): 201.8K **Privately Held**
SIC: 3295 Graphite, natural: ground, pul-
verized, refined or blended

Kimberton
Chester County

(G-8573)
HENRY COMPANY LLC
336 Cold Stream Rd (19442)
P.O. Box 368 (19442-0368)
PHONE....................610 933-8888
Daniel Rob, *Business Mgr*
Matt Stosko, *Branch Mgr*
Robert Beck, *Manager*
Randy Russell, *Manager*
Darrin Williams, *Supervisor*
EMP: 300 **Publicly Held**
WEB: www.henry.com
SIC: 2951 2952 2851 Asphalt paving mix-
tures & blocks; asphalt felts & coatings;
coating compounds, tar; paints & allied
products
HQ: Henry Company Llc
999 N Pacific Coast Hwy
El Segundo CA 90245
310 955-9200

(G-8574)
SHELLY ENTERPRISES -US LBM LLC
Also Called: Shelly Building Supply
629 Pike Spgs Rd (19442)
P.O. Box 418 (19442-0418)
PHONE....................610 933-1116
Thaddeus Brzezicki, *General Mgr*
EMP: 11
SALES (corp-wide): 2B **Privately Held**
WEB: www.shellys.cc
SIC: 5211 2431 Lumber & other building
materials; millwork
HQ: Shelly Enterprises -Us Lbm, Llc
3110 Old State Rd
Telford PA 18969
215 723-5108

King of Prussia
Montgomery County

(G-8575)
A J PRINTING
Also Called: Sir Speedy
150 Allendale Rd Ste 11 (19406-2926)
PHONE....................610 337-7468
James Moser, *President*
EMP: 12
SQ FT: 4,200
SALES (est): 1.1MM **Privately Held**
WEB: www.sirspeedykop.com
SIC: 2752 7334 2789 2759 Commercial
printing, lithographic; photocopying & du-
plicating services; bookbinding & related
work; commercial printing

(G-8576)
ABBOTT LABORATORIES
920 E 8th Ave (19406-1302)
PHONE....................610 265-9100
Tony McElhinny, *Manager*
EMP: 50
SALES (corp-wide): 30.5B **Publicly Held**
WEB: www.abbott.com
SIC: 2834 Pharmaceutical preparations

PA: Abbott Laboratories
　　100 Abbott Park Rd
　　Abbott Park IL 60064
　　224 667-6100

(G-8577)
ACUTEDGE INC
660 American Ave Ste 204 (19406-4032)
PHONE.................................484 846-6275
Sandeep Banga, *CEO*
Thilo Marg-Bracken, *Director*
EMP: 7
SALES: 1MM **Privately Held**
SIC: 7372 8742 7371 Business oriented computer software; management information systems consultant; computer software systems analysis & design, custom

(G-8578)
ALTUGLAS INTERNATIONAL
900 1st Ave (19406-1308)
PHONE.................................610 878-6423
EMP: 4
SALES (est): 272.7K **Privately Held**
SIC: 2819 Industrial inorganic chemicals

(G-8579)
AMD PENNSYLVANIA LLC
3400 Horizon Dr Ste 400 (19406-2675)
PHONE.................................610 485-4400
Rivkind Gregg, *Owner*
EMP: 11
SALES (est): 1.3MM **Privately Held**
SIC: 2741 Miscellaneous publishing

(G-8580)
AMERICAN AUTO WASH INC
Also Called: Motor Fuels Management
508 S Henderson Rd (19406-3515)
PHONE.................................610 265-3222
Fax: 610 265-3222
EMP: 12
SALES (corp-wide): 72MM **Privately Held**
SIC: 3589 7542 5541 Mfg Service Industry Machinery Carwash Gasoline Service Station
PA: American Auto Wash, Inc.
　　512 E King Rd
　　Malvern PA 19355

(G-8581)
AMERICAN BAPTST HM MISSION SOC
Also Called: National Ministries
588 N Gulph Rd Ste C (19406-2831)
P.O. Box 851, Valley Forge (19482-0851)
PHONE.................................610 768-2465
Michaele Bardsall, *Treasurer*
Margaret A Cowden, *Treasurer*
Jeff Haggray, *Exec Dir*
Jeffrey Haggray, *Exec Dir*
EMP: 90
SQ FT: 50,000
SALES: 2.7MM **Privately Held**
SIC: 2731 2721 8661 Books: publishing only; pamphlets: publishing only, not printed on site; periodicals: publishing only; Baptist Church

(G-8582)
ARKEMA DELAWARE INC (DH)
900 First Ave (19406-1308)
PHONE.................................610 205-7000
Bernard Roche, *President*
Steve Zuk, *Business Mgr*
Patricia McCarthy, *Vice Pres*
Abdel Ramadane, *Mfg Mgr*
Robert Greco, *Treasurer*
◆ **EMP:** 600
SALES (est): 3B
SALES (corp-wide): 77.8MM **Privately Held**
SIC: 2812 2819 2869 2891 Chlorine, compressed or liquefied; caustic soda, sodium hydroxide; industrial inorganic chemicals; sodium compounds or salts, inorg., ex. refined sod. chloride; sodium sulfate, glauber's salt, salt cake; peroxides, hydrogen peroxide; industrial organic chemicals; solvents, organic; adhesives; metal treating compounds; lubricating oils & greases

HQ: Arkema Ameriques Sas
　　420 Rue D Estienne D Orves
　　Colombes
　　149 008-080

(G-8583)
ARKEMA INC
Research & Development Center
900 1st Ave (19406-1308)
P.O. Box 61536 (19406-0936)
PHONE.................................610 878-6500
Danny Tan, *Business Mgr*
Virginia Richmond, *Purch Agent*
Ryan Dirkx, *Manager*
EMP: 290
SALES (corp-wide): 77.8MM **Privately Held**
SIC: 2812 8731 Alkalies & chlorine; commercial physical research
HQ: Arkema Inc.
　　900 First Ave
　　King Of Prussia PA 19406
　　610 205-7000

(G-8584)
ARON LIGHTING LLC
307 E Church Rd Ste 3 (19406-2668)
PHONE.................................484 681-5687
Craig Aronchick,
Terence E Yeo,
EMP: 5
SALES (est): 759.1K **Privately Held**
SIC: 3674 Light emitting diodes

(G-8585)
ART OF SHAVING - FL LLC
160 N Gulph Rd Ste 2184 (19406-2953)
PHONE.................................610 962-1000
EMP: 6
SALES (corp-wide): 66.8B **Publicly Held**
SIC: 5999 2844 3421 5122 Hair care products; toilet preparations; razor blades & razors; razor blades
HQ: The Art Of Shaving - Fl Llc
　　6100 Blue Lagoon Dr # 150
　　Miami FL 33126

(G-8586)
ASPIRE TECHNOLOGIES
970 Pulaski Dr (19406-2802)
P.O. Box 415, Skippack (19474-0415)
PHONE.................................610 491-8162
EMP: 3 **EST:** 2011
SALES (est): 232.7K **Privately Held**
SIC: 3089 Bottle caps, molded plastic

(G-8587)
BEAUTIFULBODY SKINCARE LLC
444 Dorothy Dr (19406-2005)
PHONE.................................610 255-2255
Marty McCommons, *Mng Member*
EMP: 10
SALES: 100K **Privately Held**
SIC: 2844 Shampoos, rinses, conditioners: hair; lotions, shaving; face creams or lotions; suntan lotions & oils

(G-8588)
BIOCHEM TECHNOLOGY INC
601 S Henderson Rd # 153 (19406-4241)
PHONE.................................484 674-7003
George Lee, *President*
Tilo Stahl, *Vice Pres*
Gregory Duffy, *Engineer*
Steve Kestel, *Engineer*
Jim Zhang, *Engineer*
▲ **EMP:** 9
SQ FT: 8,000
SALES (est): 750K **Privately Held**
WEB: www.biochemtech.com
SIC: 3841 Surgical & medical instruments

(G-8589)
C-E MINERALS INC
901 E 8th Ave Ste 200 (19406-1354)
PHONE.................................610 768-8800
Fax: 610 337-7163
EMP: 6
SALES (corp-wide): 2.6MM **Privately Held**
SIC: 3295 Mfg Minerals-Ground/Treated
HQ: C-E Minerals, Inc.
　　100 Mansell Ct E Ste 615
　　Roswell GA 30076
　　770 225-7900

(G-8590)
CAMERON COMPRESSION SYSTEMS
156 Anderson Rd (19406-1902)
PHONE.................................610 265-2410
EMP: 3 **EST:** 2009
SALES (est): 212.6K **Privately Held**
SIC: 3563 Air & gas compressors

(G-8591)
CATALOGS BY DESIGN
590 N Gulph Rd (19406-2800)
PHONE.................................610 337-9133
Sebastian Pistritto, *President*
Lorna Rudick, *President*
EMP: 26
SALES (est): 2.5MM **Privately Held**
SIC: 2752 Catalogs, lithographed

(G-8592)
CHILTERN INTERNATIONAL INC
Also Called: Theorem Clinical Research
1016 W 9th Ave Ste 300 (19406-1221)
PHONE.................................484 679-2400
John Potthoff PHD, *CEO*
S Hogue, *Partner*
Douglas Lytle, *Business Mgr*
Scott Treiber, *Exec VP*
Brian Mooney, *Vice Pres*
EMP: 44 **Publicly Held**
SIC: 8731 8071 2834 Medical research, commercial; biotechnical research, commercial; medical laboratories; pharmaceutical preparations
HQ: Chiltern International Inc.
　　3147 S 17th St Ste 300
　　Wilmington NC 28412
　　910 338-4760

(G-8593)
COLONIAL CONCRETE INDUSTRIES
364 E Church Rd (19406-2624)
PHONE.................................610 279-2102
Anthony Di Lella III, *President*
Angela Di Lella, *Corp Secy*
EMP: 10
SALES (est): 1.5MM **Privately Held**
SIC: 3272 Burial vaults, concrete or precast terrazzo

(G-8594)
COLONIAL CONCRETE INDUSTRIES
364 E Church Rd (19406-2624)
PHONE.................................610 279-2102
Fax: 610 279-7402
EMP: 9
SALES (corp-wide): 733K **Privately Held**
SIC: 3272 5211 5087 Mfg Concrete Products Ret Lumber/Building Materials Whol Service Establishment Equipment
PA: Colonial Concrete Industries Inc
　　231 Barren Rd
　　Newtown Square PA 19406
　　610 279-2102

(G-8595)
COLONIAL EP LLC
Also Called: Colonnial Generators
473 S Henderson Rd (19406-3512)
PHONE.................................844 376-9374
Nikos Papadotoulos, *CEO*
Michael Mazzola, *Vice Pres*
EMP: 50
SQ FT: 190,000
SALES: 35MM **Privately Held**
SIC: 3621 Power generators
PA: Ntp Marble, Inc.
　　475 S Henderson Rd
　　King Of Prussia PA 19406

(G-8596)
COMPLEAT STRATEGIST INC
580 Shoemaker Rd (19406-4205)
PHONE.................................610 265-8562
Ross White, *Manager*
EMP: 4
SALES (corp-wide): 2.1MM **Privately Held**
WEB: www.thecompleatstrategist.com
SIC: 3944 5945 Games, toys & children's vehicles; toys & games

PA: The Compleat Strategist Inc
　　11 E 33rd St Fl 1
　　New York NY 10016
　　212 685-3880

(G-8597)
COOPER INTERCONNECT INC
620 Allendale Rd Ste 175 (19406-7400)
P.O. Box 13700, Philadelphia (19175)
PHONE.................................630 248-4007
Michael Carter, *Branch Mgr*
EMP: 30 **Privately Held**
WEB: www.vikcon.com
SIC: 3678 3643 Electronic connectors; current-carrying wiring devices
HQ: Cooper Interconnect, Inc.
　　750 W Ventura Blvd
　　Camarillo CA 93010
　　805 484-0543

(G-8598)
CORDRAY CORPORATION
420 Feheley Dr Ste D (19406-2664)
P.O. Box 1001, Paoli (19301-0907)
PHONE.................................610 644-6200
Peter H Cordray, *President*
▲ **EMP:** 19
SQ FT: 20,000
SALES (est): 3.7MM **Privately Held**
WEB: www.cordraycorp.com
SIC: 3399 Metal fasteners

(G-8599)
CORE ESSENCE ORTHOPEDICS INC
1000 Continental Dr # 240 (19406-2848)
PHONE.................................215 660-5014
EMP: 11
SALES (est): 1.4MM **Privately Held**
SIC: 3842 Mfg Surgical Appliances/Supplies

(G-8600)
COUNTRY FRESH BATTER INC (PA)
Also Called: Hope's Cookies
221 King Manor Dr Ste B (19406-2502)
PHONE.................................610 272-5751
Hope Spivak, *President*
EMP: 54
SQ FT: 34,000
SALES (est): 20.8MM **Privately Held**
WEB: www.hopescookies.com
SIC: 2052 5461 2045 Cookies; prepared flour mixes & doughs

(G-8601)
CSL BEHRING LLC (HQ)
1020 1st Ave (19406-1310)
P.O. Box 61501 (19406-0901)
PHONE.................................610 878-4000
Paul Perreault, *President*
Ingolf Sieper, *President*
John B Neff, *Counsel*
Karen Etchberger, *Exec VP*
Paul R Perreault, *Exec VP*
▲ **EMP:** 400
SALES (est): 2.6B
SALES (corp-wide): 6.9B **Privately Held**
SIC: 2836 Blood derivatives; plasmas
PA: Csl Limited
　　45 Poplar Rd
　　Parkville VIC 3052
　　393 891-911

(G-8602)
CSLB HOLDINGS INC (HQ)
1020 1st Ave (19406-1310)
PHONE.................................610 878-4000
Paul R Perreault, *President*
Karen Neave, *Treasurer*
Gregory Boss, *Admin Sec*
John Neff Jr, *Asst Sec*
EMP: 128
SALES (est): 10.9MM **Privately Held**
SIC: 2834 Pharmaceutical preparations

(G-8603)
CTI KING OF PRUSSIA LLC
400 Drew Ct (19406-2608)
PHONE.................................610 879-2868
Bobby Horowitz,
▼ **EMP:** 1 **EST:** 2012

▲ = Import ▼=Export
◆ =Import/Export

SALES (est): 1.1MM
SALES (corp-wide): 2.5MM Privately Held
SIC: 2011 Meat packing plants
HQ: Cti Foods, Llc
22303 Highway 95
Wilder ID 83676
208 482-7844

(G-8604)
DAMBROSIO BAKERY LLC (PA)
1040 1st Ave Ste 435 (19406-1345)
P.O. Box 626, Devault (19432-0626)
PHONE.................................610 560-4700
Edward Merry,
EMP: 33
SQ FT: 30,000
SALES (est): 2.5MM Privately Held
WEB: www.dambrosiobakery.com
SIC: 2051 5149 Bread, cake & related
products; groceries & related products

(G-8605)
DE TECHNOLOGIES INC (PA)
100 Queens Dr (19406-3562)
PHONE.................................610 337-2800
George Ch Chou, President
Hoa Lam, Research
Bob Colbert, Project Engr
Mary Ann C T C Chou, Treasurer
John Grossi, Manager
EMP: 26
SALES (est): 4.5MM Privately Held
WEB: www.detk.com
SIC: 8711 3369 Consulting engineer; cast-
ings, except die-castings, precision

(G-8606)
DECON LABORATORIES INC
Also Called: Decon Labs
460 Glennie Cir (19406-2682)
PHONE.................................610 755-0800
Peter Taylor, President
Bill Fox, President
William F Fox, Corp Secy
Elizabeth W Heffner, Corp Secy
Tim Gordon, Exec VP
EMP: 24 EST: 1979
SQ FT: 2,600
SALES (est): 5.3MM Privately Held
WEB: www.deconlabs.com
SIC: 2842 2844 3842 Specialty cleaning
preparations; industrial plant disinfectants
or deodorants; face creams or lotions;
personal safety equipment; radiation
shielding aprons, gloves, sheeting, etc.

(G-8607)
**DEVON INTERNATIONAL GROUP
INC (PA)**
Also Called: Devon Health Services
700 American Ave Ste 100 (19406-4031)
P.O. Box 61927 (19406-0140)
PHONE.................................866 312-3373
John A Bennett, President
Francis A Lutz, CFO
Felicia Swesey, Relations
▲ EMP: 56
SALES (est): 25.4MM Privately Held
SIC: 3571 Electronic computers

(G-8608)
DEVON IT INC
700 American Ave Ste 100 (19406-4031)
PHONE.................................610 757-4220
Joe Makoid, President
Frank Diaz, COO
Ian Geiser, Vice Pres
Francis A Lutz, CFO
John A Bennett, Treasurer
▲ EMP: 35
SALES (est): 6MM Privately Held
WEB: www.devonit.com
SIC: 3571 Electronic computers
PA: Devon International Group Inc
700 American Ave Ste 100
King Of Prussia PA 19406

(G-8609)
**DICKSON INVESTMENT HDWR
INC**
386 E Church Rd (19406-2640)
PHONE.................................610 272-0764
Robert C Dickson, President
Theresa Dickson, Corp Secy
EMP: 30

SQ FT: 20,000
SALES (est): 7.2MM Privately Held
SIC: 3325 Alloy steel castings, except in-
vestment

(G-8610)
DIGITAL GRAPES LLC
Also Called: Remindermedia
1100 1st Ave Ste 200 (19406-1327)
PHONE.................................866 458-4226
Steve Acree, CEO
Michael Caiola, Accounts Exec
Ross Frank, Accounts Exec
Regina Hammeke, Sales Staff
Shannon Mosser, Corp Comm Staff
EMP: 50
SALES (est): 7.6MM Privately Held
SIC: 2741 Miscellaneous publishing

(G-8611)
**DIVERSIFIED DESIGN & MFG
INC**
Also Called: Diversified Designing & Mfg
161 Boro Line Rd (19406-2112)
PHONE.................................610 337-1969
Edward Cicutti, President
▲ EMP: 6
SQ FT: 7,000
SALES: 1MM Privately Held
SIC: 3599 Custom machinery; machine
shop, jobbing & repair

(G-8612)
DREAM PUBLISHING
1150 1st Ave Ste 501 (19406-1316)
PHONE.................................610 945-2017
Lorna L Samuels, Owner
EMP: 6 EST: 2007
SALES: 100K Privately Held
SIC: 2741 Miscellaneous publishing

(G-8613)
DUNKIN DONUTS
251 W Dekalb Pike Apt 132 (19406-2421)
PHONE.................................610 992-0111
Denney Katrelle, Co-Owner
EMP: 8
SQ FT: 1,580
SALES (est): 240K Privately Held
SIC: 5461 2051 Doughnuts; doughnuts,
except frozen

(G-8614)
DYNA EAST CORPORATION
3620 Horizon Dr (19406-4706)
PHONE.................................610 270-9900
Pei CHI Chou, President
Rosalind Chou, Treasurer
Clara Schultheiss, Manager
EMP: 25
SALES (est): 2.3MM Privately Held
SIC: 8711 3469 8734 Consulting engi-
neer; metal stampings; product testing
laboratory, safety or performance

(G-8615)
DYNAMIC BALANCING CO INC
831 Crooked Ln (19406-3552)
PHONE.................................610 337-2757
Rick Broendale, President
EMP: 7
SALES (est): 845K Privately Held
SIC: 3545 Balancing machines (machine
tool accessories)

(G-8616)
**DYNAMIC CONTROL SYSTEMS
INC**
600 Clark Ave Ste 1 (19406-1433)
PHONE.................................484 674-1408
Ed Devine, Manager
Judy Pietryka, Admin Sec
EMP: 3 EST: 1999
SALES (est): 339.4K Privately Held
SIC: 3829 Measuring & controlling devices

(G-8617)
**EVERGREEN SYNERGIES LLC
(PA)**
Also Called: East Coast Liquid Filling
221 King Manor Dr (19406-2502)
PHONE.................................610 239-9425
Howard Levine, President
▲ EMP: 28

SALES (est): 3.2MM Privately Held
SIC: 3471 2841 Cleaning & descaling
metal products; soap & other detergents

(G-8618)
FIRST QUALITY PRODUCTS INC
Also Called: Kendall Healthcare Products
601 Allendale Rd (19406-1417)
PHONE.................................610 265-5000
Doug Strohemeier, Principal
Gary Beagle, Sales Dir
Larry Raymer, Sales Staff
Jim Schuler, Sales Staff
Benjamin Termine, Manager
EMP: 400 Privately Held
SIC: 2676 8748 Diapers, paper (dispos-
able): made from purchased paper; busi-
ness consulting
HQ: First Quality Products, Inc
80 Cuttermill Rd Ste 500
Great Neck NY 11021
516 829-4949

(G-8619)
**FIRST QUALITY RETAIL SVCS
LLC (HQ)**
601 Allendale Rd (19406-1417)
PHONE.................................610 265-5000
Doug Strohmier, CEO
Fred Ackerman, Manager
Kristy Hickernell, Manager
Nader Damaghi,
▲ EMP: 110
SQ FT: 650,000
SALES (est): 314.2MM Privately Held
SIC: 3822 Building services monitoring
controls, automatic

(G-8620)
GLASGOW INC
Glasgow Quarry Div
550 E Church Rd (19406-2649)
P.O. Box 1089, Glenside (19038-6089)
PHONE.................................610 279-6840
Dennis Fitzwater, Manager
EMP: 30
SALES (corp-wide): 102.1MM Privately
Held
WEB: www.glasgowinc.com
SIC: 1411 5032 Dimension stone; stone,
crushed or broken
PA: Glasgow, Inc.
104 Willow Grove Ave
Glenside PA 19038
215 884-8800

(G-8621)
GLAXOSMITHKLINE LLC
801 River Rd (19406)
PHONE.................................610 270-7125
Chris Pastore,
EMP: 60
SALES (corp-wide): 39.8B Privately Held
WEB: www.delks.com
SIC: 2834 Pharmaceutical preparations
HQ: Glaxosmithkline Llc
5 Crescent Dr
Philadelphia PA 19112
215 751-4000

(G-8622)
GLAXOSMITHKLINE LLC
Also Called: Gck US Processing
709 Swedeland Rd (19406-2711)
PHONE.................................610 270-4692
Ilse I Blumentals, Director
EMP: 28
SALES (corp-wide): 39.8B Privately Held
SIC: 2834 Pharmaceutical preparations
HQ: Glaxosmithkline Llc
5 Crescent Dr
Philadelphia PA 19112
215 751-4000

(G-8623)
GLAXOSMITHKLINE LLC
820 3rd Ave (19406-1412)
PHONE.................................610 768-3150
Brian Herman, Manager
EMP: 11
SALES (corp-wide): 39.8B Privately Held
WEB: www.delks.com
SIC: 2834 Pharmaceutical preparations

HQ: Glaxosmithkline Llc
5 Crescent Dr
Philadelphia PA 19112
215 751-4000

(G-8624)
GLAXOSMITHKLINE LLC
Also Called: Gsk Technical Sourcing
709 Swedeland Rd (19406-2711)
PHONE.................................610 270-4800
Wendy Oakes, Branch Mgr
EMP: 27
SALES (corp-wide): 39.8B Privately Held
SIC: 2834 Cough medicines
HQ: Glaxosmithkline Llc
5 Crescent Dr
Philadelphia PA 19112
215 751-4000

(G-8625)
GMP NUTRACEUTICALS INC
711 1st Ave Ste B (19406-4058)
PHONE.................................484 924-9042
Paul Lariviere, President
Eugene Long, Corp Secy
Keith Drinkwater, Opers Mgr
Kevin Stranen, Research
Julie Drenkhahn, Admin Asst
EMP: 15
SQ FT: 6,000
SALES (est): 3.4MM Privately Held
WEB: www.GMP-Nutraceuticals.com
SIC: 2099 Food preparations

(G-8626)
**GREENWOOD BUSINESS
PRINTING**
Also Called: PIP Printing
950 W Valley Forge Rd # 1 (19406-4534)
PHONE.................................610 337-8887
Rich Greenwood, President
Joellen Greenwood, Vice Pres
EMP: 4
SQ FT: 3,500
SALES (est): 453K Privately Held
SIC: 2752 Commercial printing, offset

(G-8627)
**HAMBURGER COLOR COMPANY
INC**
555 E Church Rd (19406-2600)
PHONE.................................610 279-6450
Jack Dunnous, President
Claudia Dunnous, CFO
▲ EMP: 17
SQ FT: 40,000
SALES (est): 2.7MM Privately Held
WEB: www.hamburgercolor.com
SIC: 2865 Dyes & pigments
PA: Nudam Investments N.V.
C/O: Caribbean Management Com-
pany N.V.
Willemstad

(G-8628)
HAVEN HOMES INC (HQ)
555 Croton Rd Ste 200 (19406-3171)
PHONE.................................410 694-0091
David Ballard, President
Donald Dick Jr, Corp Secy
EMP: 110 EST: 1970
SQ FT: 4,000
SALES (est): 15.5MM
SALES (corp-wide): 153MM Privately
Held
WEB: www.havenhomes.com
SIC: 2452 Prefabricated buildings, wood
PA: American Manufacturing Corporation
555 Croton Rd Ste 200
King of Prussia PA 19406
610 962-3770

(G-8629)
HEALTH MARKET SCIENCE INC
2700 Horizon Dr (19406-2677)
PHONE.................................610 940-4002
Matt Reichert, CEO
Jeff Klein, President
Nancy Bostock, Business Mgr
Rick Hlavacek, Business Mgr
Ramaswamy Kuppuswamy, Technical Mgr
EMP: 200
SQ FT: 65,000

SALES (est): 31.4MM
SALES (corp-wide): 9.7B **Privately Held**
WEB: www.hmsonline.com
SIC: 7371 7372 Computer software development; prepackaged software
HQ: Lexisnexis Risk Solutions Inc.
　1000 Alderman Dr
　Alpharetta GA 30005
　678 694-6000

(G-8630)
HELICOPTER TECH INC
452 Swedeland Rd (19406-2715)
PHONE..................................610 272-8090
Rachel Carson, *President*
EMP: 12
SALES (est): 2.2MM **Privately Held**
SIC: 3728 Aircraft parts & equipment

(G-8631)
HI-TEC MAGNETICS INC
109 Walker Ln (19406-2322)
PHONE..................................484 681-4265
Dave Carlberg, *President*
EMP: 4
SALES (est): 340K **Privately Held**
SIC: 3499 Magnets, permanent: metallic

(G-8632)
ICEUTICA INC
3602 Horizon Dr Ste 160 (19406-2669)
PHONE..................................267 546-1400
Matthew Callahan, *CEO*
Humphrey J Harte, *Senior VP*
Paul Hemsley, *Senior VP*
Rohit C Mehta, *Senior VP*
Olalekan Andrew Bayode, *Vice Pres*
EMP: 5
SALES (est): 862.1K **Privately Held**
WEB: www.iceutica.com
SIC: 2834 Pharmaceutical preparations
PA: Iroko Pharmaceuticals Llc
　1 Kew Pl 150 Rouse Blvd St 1 Kew
　Pla
　Philadelphia PA 19112

(G-8633)
ICU MEDICAL SALES INC
920 E 8th Ave (19406-1302)
PHONE..................................610 265-9100
EMP: 3
SALES (corp-wide): 1.4B **Publicly Held**
SIC: 3841 IV transfusion apparatus; catheters
HQ: Icu Medical Sales, Inc.
　951 Calle Amanecer
　San Clemente CA 92673
　949 366-2183

(G-8634)
INNOVATION PLUS LLC
Also Called: Load Control Technologies
3630 Horizon Dr (19406-4701)
PHONE..................................610 272-2600
Ian E Kibblewhite,
Robert Molsbergen,
▲ EMP: 9
SALES (est): 1.6MM **Privately Held**
WEB: www.innovationplus.com
SIC: 3965 Fasteners

(G-8635)
IP LASSO LLC
1045 First Ave Ste 120 (19406-1358)
PHONE..................................484 352-2029
David Jannetta, *President*
Peter Gordon, *Accounts Mgr*
EMP: 6
SALES (est): 430K **Privately Held**
SIC: 7372 Business oriented computer software

(G-8636)
JOHN MIDDLETON CO
418 W Church Rd (19406-3134)
P.O. Box 85108, Richmond VA (23285-5108)
PHONE..................................804 274-2000
Craig G Schwartz, *Senior VP*
EMP: 16
SALES (corp-wide): 25.3B **Publicly Held**
SIC: 2121 Cigars
HQ: John Middleton Co.
　2325 Bells Rd
　Richmond VA 23234
　610 792-8000

(G-8637)
LANE ENTERPRISES INC
377 Crooked Ln (19406-2601)
PHONE..................................610 272-4531
Marlin Cathers, *Opers-Prdtn-Mfg*
EMP: 25
SQ FT: 10,000
SALES (corp-wide): 70.5MM **Privately Held**
WEB: www.lanepipe.com
SIC: 3479 5033 5051 Coating or wrapping steel pipe; asphalt felts & coating; pipe & tubing, steel
PA: Lane Enterprises, Inc.
　3905 Hartzdale Dr Ste 514
　Camp Hill PA 17011
　717 761-8175

(G-8638)
LAVENDER BADGE LLC
Also Called: Neely By Vnb
840 First Ave Ste 200 (19406-4062)
PHONE..................................610 994-9476
Victoria Burch,
Charlotte Burch,
Robert Burch,
Daniel Gorge,
EMP: 4 EST: 2014
SALES (est): 417.5K **Privately Held**
SIC: 2339 5661 Women's & misses' accessories; women's boots; women's shoes

(G-8639)
LE BUS BAKERY INC (PA)
480 Shoemaker Rd (19406-4237)
PHONE..................................610 337-1444
David Braverman, *CEO*
Ruth Drye, *Treasurer*
Winnie Clowry, *Exec Dir*
EMP: 41
SALES (est): 63.9MM **Privately Held**
WEB: www.lebusbakery.com
SIC: 5149 5461 2051 Bakery products; bakeries; bread, cake & related products

(G-8640)
LEVI STRAUSS & CO
640 W Dekalb Pike # 1216 (19406-5035)
PHONE..................................610 337-0388
EMP: 19
SALES (corp-wide): 4.6B **Privately Held**
SIC: 2325 Mfg Men's/Boy's Trousers
PA: Levi Strauss & Co.
　1155 Battery St
　San Francisco CA 94111
　415 501-6000

(G-8641)
LOCKHEED MARTIN CORPORATION
Also Called: Rotary and Mission Systems
230 Mall Blvd (19406-2902)
PHONE..................................610 382-3200
Dean George, *Purchasing*
John P Zimmerman, *Purchasing*
Brian Anderson, *Engineer*
Richard August, *Engineer*
Kristen Cavanaugh, *Engineer*
EMP: 1000 **Publicly Held**
SIC: 3812 3761 Search & navigation equipment; guided missiles & space vehicles
PA: Lockheed Martin Corporation
　6801 Rockledge Dr
　Bethesda MD 20817

(G-8642)
LOCKHEED MARTIN CORPORATION
230 Mall Blvd (19406-2902)
P.O. Box 61511 (19406-0911)
PHONE..................................610 354-3083
James Burget, *Engineer*
Mindy Goodman, *Manager*
James Richvalsky, *Network Mgr*
John Campbell, *Technology*
EMP: 3000 **Publicly Held**
WEB: www.lockheedmartin.com
SIC: 3812 Search & navigation equipment
PA: Lockheed Martin Corporation
　6801 Rockledge Dr
　Bethesda MD 20817

(G-8643)
LOCKHEED MARTIN CORPORATION
230 Mall Blvd (19406-2902)
PHONE..................................610 531-7400
Mike Berdeguez, *Manager*
EMP: 3000 **Publicly Held**
WEB: www.lockheedmartin.com
SIC: 3812 3761 Search & navigation equipment; guided missiles & space vehicles
PA: Lockheed Martin Corporation
　6801 Rockledge Dr
　Bethesda MD 20817

(G-8644)
LOCKHEED MARTIN CORPORATION
230 Mall Blvd (19406-2902)
PHONE..................................610 962-4954
Mark Robinson, *General Mgr*
Terry Ford, *Director*
EMP: 500 **Publicly Held**
WEB: www.lockheedmartin.com
SIC: 3812 Search & navigation equipment
PA: Lockheed Martin Corporation
　6801 Rockledge Dr
　Bethesda MD 20817

(G-8645)
LOCKHEED MARTIN CORPORATION
7000 Geerdes Blvd (19406-1525)
P.O. Box 61511 (19406-0911)
PHONE..................................610 531-7400
Stanton D Sloane, *President*
Edward Nichlas, *Senior Engr*
EMP: 150 **Publicly Held**
WEB: www.lockheedmartin.com
SIC: 3812 Search & navigation equipment
PA: Lockheed Martin Corporation
　6801 Rockledge Dr
　Bethesda MD 20817

(G-8646)
LOCKHEED MARTIN CORPORATION
700 American Ave Ste 101 (19406-4031)
PHONE..................................610 962-2264
Mike McGinn, *Branch Mgr*
EMP: 4 **Publicly Held**
WEB: www.lockheedmartin.com
SIC: 3812 Search & navigation equipment
PA: Lockheed Martin Corporation
　6801 Rockledge Dr
　Bethesda MD 20817

(G-8647)
LUXOTTICA OF AMERICA INC
Also Called: Lenscrafters
160 N Gulph Rd Ste 1065 (19406-2937)
PHONE..................................610 962-5945
Mary Lyons, *Branch Mgr*
EMP: 25
SALES (corp-wide): 283.5MM **Privately Held**
WEB: www.lenscrafters.com
SIC: 5995 3851 Optical goods stores; ophthalmic goods
HQ: Luxottica Of America Inc.
　4000 Luxottica Pl
　Mason OH 45040

(G-8648)
MARIOS TREE SERVICE INC
453 Crooked Ln (19406-2606)
PHONE..................................610 637-1405
Michael Dippolito, *President*
EMP: 7
SALES (est): 301.8K **Privately Held**
WEB: www.mariostreeservice.com
SIC: 0783 3999 Removal services, bush & tree; custom pulverizing & grinding of plastic materials

(G-8649)
MCDAL CORPORATION (PA)
475 E Church Rd (19406-2623)
PHONE..................................800 626-2325
Frank McMullan III, *President*
EMP: 16
SALES (est): 5.2MM **Privately Held**
WEB: www.mcdal.com
SIC: 1796 3536 Installing building equipment; hoists, cranes & monorails

(G-8650)
MEDICAL ALARM CONCEPTS LLC
Also Called: Medipendant
200 W Church Rd Ste 2 (19406-3221)
PHONE..................................877 639-2929
Allen Polsky, *Vice Pres*
Haword Teicher, *Mng Member*
Ronnie Adams,
Jennifer Loria,
▲ EMP: 7
SQ FT: 5,000
SALES (est): 650K **Privately Held**
SIC: 3669 Emergency alarms

(G-8651)
MICROSOFT CORPORATION
160 N Gulph Rd Ste 1644 (19406-2904)
PHONE..................................484 754-7600
P Jobs, *Branch Mgr*
EMP: 5
SALES (corp-wide): 110.3B **Publicly Held**
SIC: 7372 Prepackaged software
PA: Microsoft Corporation
　1 Microsoft Way
　Redmond WA 98052
　425 882-8080

(G-8652)
MONTCO INDUSTRIES
100 Ross Rd Ste 203 (19406-2110)
PHONE..................................610 233-1081
EMP: 3
SALES (est): 172.7K **Privately Held**
SIC: 3999 Manufacturing industries

(G-8653)
NABRIVA THERAPEUTICS US INC
1000 Continental Dr # 600 (19406-2848)
PHONE..................................610 816-6640
Colin Broom, *CEO*
William T Prince, *Senior VP*
Werner Heilmayer, *Vice Pres*
Stefan Reisinger, *Vice Pres*
Ralf Schmid, *CFO*
EMP: 12
SALES (est): 2.9MM **Privately Held**
SIC: 5122 2833 8731 Pharmaceuticals; antibiotics; biological research
HQ: Nabriva Therapeutics Gmbh
　LeberstraBe 20
　Wien 1110
　174 093-0

(G-8654)
NEOPOST USA INC
3100 Horizon Dr Ste 100 (19406-2660)
P.O. Box 4240, Harrisburg (17111-0240)
PHONE..................................717 939-2700
EMP: 4
SALES (corp-wide): 53.4MM **Privately Held**
SIC: 3579 7359 7629 Postage meters; business machine & electronic equipment rental services; business machine repair, electric
HQ: Neopost Usa Inc.
　478 Wheelers Farms Rd
　Milford CT 06461
　203 301-3400

(G-8655)
NESTLE USA INC
3000 Horizon Dr (19406-2626)
PHONE..................................818 549-6000
EMP: 132
SALES (corp-wide): 90.8B **Privately Held**
SIC: 2023 2033 2064 2047 Evaporated milk; canned milk, whole; cream substitutes; fruits: packaged in cans, jars, etc.; tomato paste: packaged in cans, jars, etc.; tomato sauce: packaged in cans, jars, etc.; candy & other confectionary products; breakfast bars; dog food; cat food; pasta, uncooked: packaged with other ingredients; canned specialties
HQ: Nestle Usa, Inc.
　1812 N Moore St
　Rosslyn VA 22209
　818 549-6000

▲ = Import ▼=Export
◆ =Import/Export

(G-8656)
NEWSLINE PUBLISHING INC
661 Moore Rd Ste 100 (19406-1317)
PHONE................................610 337-1050
G Patrick Polli, *President*
Aaron Snader, *Partner*
Christopher Polli, *Vice Pres*
Eric Smoger, *Info Tech Mgr*
EMP: 30
SALES (est): 2.4MM **Privately Held**
WEB: www.newslinepublishing.com
SIC: 2741 2721 Miscellaneous publishing; periodicals

(G-8657)
NOCOPI TECHNOLOGIES INC (PA)
480 Shoemaker Rd Ste 104 (19406-4237)
PHONE................................610 834-9600
Michael A Feinstein, *Ch of Bd*
Terry W Stovold, *COO*
Rudolph A Lutterschmidt, *CFO*
EMP: 5
SQ FT: 6,100
SALES: 3.3MM **Publicly Held**
WEB: www.nocopi.com
SIC: 2754 3952 3944 6794 Security certificates: gravure printing; facsimile letters: gravure printing; ink, drawing: black & colored; games, toys & children's vehicles; patent owners & lessors

(G-8658)
PACKAGING SCIENCE INC
105 Town Center Rd Ste 7 (19406-2394)
PHONE................................610 992-9991
Thomas C Hough, *President*
EMP: 16
SQ FT: 800
SALES (est): 1.2MM **Privately Held**
SIC: 3081 5162 Packing materials, plastic sheet; plastics film

(G-8659)
PAPYRUS INC
Also Called: Gold Leaf The
160 N Gulph Rd Ste 2650 (19406-5003)
PHONE................................610 354-9480
Veronica Balassone, *President*
Virginia Balassone, *Vice Pres*
EMP: 10
SALES (est): 675K **Privately Held**
SIC: 5947 2759 Greeting cards; invitation & stationery printing & engraving

(G-8660)
PARATEK PHARMACEUTICALS INC
1000 1st Ave Ste 200 (19406-1333)
PHONE................................484 751-4920
Evan Loh M D, *President*
EMP: 9
SALES (est): 1MM **Privately Held**
SIC: 2834 Pharmaceutical preparations

(G-8661)
PERGAMON CORP
380 Crooked Ln Ste 3 (19406-2567)
PHONE................................610 239-0721
John R Artman, *President*
Len Youngberg, *Sales Staff*
Jerry Dengler, *Info Tech Mgr*
▲ **EMP:** 15
SQ FT: 4,000
SALES (est): 3.1MM **Privately Held**
WEB: www.pergamon-corp.com
SIC: 3672 Printed circuit boards

(G-8662)
PINDAR SET INC
2201 Renaissance Blvd (19406-2707)
PHONE................................610 731-2921
Sally Weaver, *CEO*
John Tooher, *President*
Carol Dalton - Slover, *Director*
EMP: 170
SQ FT: 200,000
SALES (est): 10.5MM **Privately Held**
SIC: 7311 2791 Advertising agencies; typesetting

(G-8663)
PINNACLE TEXTILE INDS LLC
440 Drew Ct (19406-2608)
PHONE................................800 901-4784

Patrick Methven, *President*
Bill Terrell, *Manager*
David Gurss,
Robert Lazarus,
◆ **EMP:** 49
SQ FT: 47,000
SALES (est): 13.3MM **Privately Held**
WEB: www.pinnacletextile.com
SIC: 2326 2299 5136 5137 Medical & hospital uniforms, men's; linen fabrics; uniforms, men's & boys'; uniforms, women's & children's; linens & towels

(G-8664)
PRINT-O-STAT INC
489 Shoemaker Rd Ste 109 (19406-4235)
PHONE................................610 265-5470
Richard Laskoski, *Branch Mgr*
EMP: 7
SQ FT: 1,000
SALES (corp-wide): 100.1MM **Privately Held**
WEB: www.digitalblueprinting.com
SIC: 2752 5999 7334 5065 Commercial printing, offset; drafting equipment & supplies; blueprinting service; facsimile equipment; drafting supplies; blueprinting equipment
HQ: Print-O-Stat, Inc.
1011 W Market St
York PA 17404
717 812-9476

(G-8665)
PRO-MIC CORP
20135 Valley Forge Cir (19406-1112)
PHONE................................610 783-7901
John Walsh Jr, *President*
James Walsh, *Vice Pres*
EMP: 4
SQ FT: 5,000
SALES (est): 505.7K **Privately Held**
WEB: www.pro-mic.com
SIC: 3823 5084 Coulometric analyzers, industrial process type; instruments & control equipment

(G-8666)
PROTARGA INC
2200 Renaissance Blvd # 200 (19406-2755)
PHONE................................610 260-4000
Nigel Webb, *Ch of Bd*
Lee P Schachter, *Senior VP*
Charles L Swindell, *Senior VP*
Forrest Anthony, *Vice Pres*
Robert Dickey, *CFO*
EMP: 9
SQ FT: 3,000
SALES (est): 840K **Privately Held**
SIC: 2834 8011 Pharmaceutical preparations; offices & clinics of medical doctors

(G-8667)
PSI PHARMA SUPPORT AMERICA INC
875 1st Ave (19406-1403)
PHONE................................267 464-2500
Nickolai Sinakevich, *President*
Lynn Schneider, *Human Res Mgr*
Carmella Guzik, *Office Mgr*
Olga Golubeva, *Manager*
Elena Pekarskaya, *Manager*
EMP: 105
SALES: 15.3MM **Privately Held**
SIC: 2834 Pharmaceutical preparations
HQ: Psi Cro Ag
Baarerstrasse 113a
Zug ZG 6300
412 281-000

(G-8668)
REILLY FOAM CORP (PA)
751 5th Ave (19406-1413)
P.O. Box 137, Eagleville (19408-0137)
PHONE................................610 834-1900
Charles J Reilly, *President*
Kathleen Reilly, *Vice Pres*
Megan Wagenmann, *Human Res Mgr*
◆ **EMP:** 75 **EST:** 1972
SALES (est): 33.5MM **Privately Held**
SIC: 3069 5199 Foam rubber; foam rubber

(G-8669)
RENMATIX INC (PA)
660 Allendale Rd (19406-1418)
PHONE................................484 681-9246
Mike Hamilton, *CEO*
Timothy Brown, *General Mgr*
Mark Schweiker, *Governor*
Mark S Schweiker, *Senior VP*
Debra Kurucz, *Vice Pres*
EMP: 80
SQ FT: 28,000
SALES (est): 16MM **Privately Held**
SIC: 2836 Biological products, except diagnostic

(G-8670)
ROCKWOOD PIGMENTS NA INC
555 Church St (19406)
PHONE................................610 279-6450
Jack Dunnous, *Principal*
EMP: 16
SALES (est): 2.8MM **Privately Held**
SIC: 2816 2895 2299 5169 Zinc pigments: zinc oxide, zinc sulfide; carbon black; yarn, metallic, ceramic or paper fibers; chemicals & allied products

(G-8671)
S & S MACHINE & TOOL COMPANY
150 W Church Rd (19406-3230)
PHONE................................610 265-1582
James Nadwodny, *President*
EMP: 3
SQ FT: 4,500
SALES (est): 336.5K **Privately Held**
SIC: 3599 Machine shop, jobbing & repair

(G-8672)
SFK VENTURES INC
Also Called: Kempf Building Materials
381 Brooks Rd (19406-3107)
PHONE................................610 825-5151
Steven F Kempf, *President*
Bob Kehs, *Opers Mgr*
Jan Dalina, *VP Finance*
Matt Brophy, *Sales Staff*
Sean Henderson, *Sales Staff*
EMP: 60
SQ FT: 172,500
SALES (est): 19.2MM
SALES (corp-wide): 2.5B **Publicly Held**
SIC: 1542 2421 Commercial & office building contractors; building & structural materials, wood
PA: Gms Inc.
100 Crescent Center Pkwy
Tucker GA 30084
800 392-4619

(G-8673)
SHEEN KLEEN INC
Also Called: S K I
3000 Valley Forge Cir G9 (19406-1176)
PHONE................................610 337-3969
Al Cowling, *President*
Mary Conway, *Vice Pres*
EMP: 3
SALES (est): 210K **Privately Held**
SIC: 2655 Containers, liquid tight fiber: from purchased material

(G-8674)
SHINGLE BELTING INC
420 Drew Ct Ste A (19406-2681)
PHONE................................610 825-5500
Renwick Keating, *President*
Bob Frasetto, *Vice Pres*
Frank Manley, *CFO*
Paul Dunay, *Manager*
Jim Raudenbush, *Manager*
◆ **EMP:** 25
SQ FT: 30,000
SALES (est): 8.2MM **Privately Held**
WEB: www.shinglebelting.com
SIC: 3535 3052 Conveyors & conveying equipment; transmission belting, rubber

(G-8675)
SIKKENS INC
310 Hansen Access Rd (19406-2442)
PHONE................................610 337-8710
Dave Matthews, *Principal*
EMP: 3 **EST:** 2011

SALES (est): 213K **Privately Held**
SIC: 3465 Body parts, automobile: stamped metal

(G-8676)
SILGAN CONTAINERS MFG CORP
620 Freedom Business Ctr (19406-1330)
PHONE................................610 337-2203
Ronald Lee, *Branch Mgr*
EMP: 80
SALES (corp-wide): 4.4B **Publicly Held**
WEB: www.silgancontainers.com
SIC: 3411 Metal cans
HQ: Silgan Containers Manufacturing Corporation
21600 Oxnard St Ste 1600
Woodland Hills CA 91367

(G-8677)
SINACOM NORTH AMERICA INC
Also Called: Sinocom North America
1020 W 8th Ave (19406-1322)
PHONE................................610 337-2250
Alan Zheng, *President*
Peipei Chow, *Vice Pres*
▲ **EMP:** 22
SQ FT: 2,000
SALES (est): 3.3MM **Privately Held**
WEB: www.sinacom.com
SIC: 3699 3399 3599 5044 Electrical equipment & supplies; metal powders, pastes & flakes; machine & other job shop work; mailing machines; management services; malleable iron foundries
PA: Sinacom China Limited
No. 855,No.1 Building Middle Part (Layer), Xiangyang Road, Minha Shanghai
213 430-4200

(G-8678)
SOUTHERN GLAZER S WINE AND SP (DH)
Also Called: Sgws of PA
460 American Ave (19406-1405)
P.O. Box 60384 (19406-0384)
PHONE................................610 265-6800
Sheldon Margolis, *CEO*
Wayne E Chaplin, *President*
Pat Pokorny, *Exec VP*
Mark Santangelo, *Business Anlyst*
Debbie Carabini, *Manager*
▲ **EMP:** 145
SALES (est): 60.6MM
SALES (corp-wide): 7.2B **Privately Held**
SIC: 5182 3993 Wine; liquor; displays & cutouts, window & lobby

(G-8679)
SPECIALTY SURFACES INTL INC
Also Called: Sprinturf
660 American Ave Ste 101 (19406-4032)
PHONE................................877 686-8873
Stanley H Greene, *President*
Joel Cardis, *Admin Sec*
▼ **EMP:** 170 **EST:** 1999
SALES (est): 21.3MM **Privately Held**
WEB: www.sprinturf.com
SIC: 2426 1799 Hardwood dimension & flooring mills; artificial turf installation
HQ: Its-Sprinturf
900 Circle 75 Pkwy Se
Atlanta GA 30339

(G-8680)
STEELWAY CELLAR DOORS LLC
Also Called: Steelway Custom Cellar Doors
290 E Church Rd (19406-2604)
PHONE................................610 277-9988
Norman McAvoy,
Carter Williams,
▲ **EMP:** 10
SQ FT: 7,500
SALES (est): 1.9MM **Privately Held**
WEB: www.cellardoors.com
SIC: 3442 3711 Metal doors; motor homes, self-contained, assembly of

(G-8681)
SUGARTOWN WORLDWIDE LLC
160 N Gulph Rd Ste 2333 (19406-2953)
PHONE................................610 265-7607
EMP: 11

SALES (corp-wide): 1.1B **Publicly Held**
SIC: 2389 5137 Apparel for handicapped; women's & children's clothing
HQ: Sugartown Worldwide Llc
800 3rd Ave
King Of Prussia PA 19406

(G-8682)
SUGARTOWN WORLDWIDE LLC (HQ)
Also Called: Lilly Pulitzer
800 3rd Ave (19406-1412)
PHONE..................................610 878-5550
Scott A Beaumont, *CEO*
James B Bradbeer Jr, *President*
Blair Morrison, *Production*
Libby Saylor, *Opers-Prdtn-Mfg*
Julie Colbert, *Human Res Dir*
▲ EMP: 150
SQ FT: 100,000
SALES (est): 172.4MM
SALES (corp-wide): 1.1B **Publicly Held**
WEB: www.lillypulitzer.com/
SIC: 2339 2361 5136 5611 Sportswear, women's; girls' & children's dresses, blouses & shirts; sportswear, men's & boys'; clothing, sportswear, men's & boys'
PA: Oxford Industries, Inc.
999 Peachtree St Ne # 688
Atlanta GA 30309
404 659-2424

(G-8683)
SWAROVSKI US HOLDING LIMITED
Also Called: Swarovski Botique
160 N Gulph Rd (19406-2941)
PHONE..................................610 992-9661
Figen Caner, *Branch Mgr*
EMP: 5
SALES (corp-wide): 3.7B **Privately Held**
SIC: 3961 Costume jewelry
HQ: Swarovski U.S. Holding Limited
1 Kenney Dr
Cranston RI 02920
401 463-6400

(G-8684)
TECH TUBE INC
750 Vandenburg Rd (19406-1423)
PHONE..................................610 491-8000
Gary J Johnson, *President*
Matt Mankus, *Controller*
EMP: 90
SALES (est): 17.7MM **Privately Held**
SIC: 3317 Tubing, mechanical or hypodermic sizes: cold drawn stainless

(G-8685)
TENEX SYSTEMS INC (PA)
2011 Renaissance Blvd # 100 (19406-2782)
PHONE..................................610 239-9988
Donald Roskos, *President*
Joseph W Roskos, *Corp Secy*
EMP: 10
SALES (est): 3.8MM **Privately Held**
WEB: www.tenexsys.com
SIC: 7371 7372 Computer software development; prepackaged software

(G-8686)
TESLA INC
160 N Gulph Rd Ste 1926 (19406-2937)
PHONE..................................484 235-5858
Chris Vance, *Branch Mgr*
EMP: 10
SALES (corp-wide): 21.4B **Publicly Held**
SIC: 3711 Motor vehicles & car bodies
PA: Tesla, Inc.
3500 Deer Creek Rd
Palo Alto CA 94304
650 681-5000

(G-8687)
THEODORE PRESSER COMPANY (HQ)
Also Called: Merien Music
588 N Gulph Rd Ste B (19406-2831)
PHONE..................................610 592-1222
Hayden Connor, *President*
Daniel Dorff, *Vice Pres*
Sonya Kim, *Vice Pres*
Jennifer Colon, *Accounting Mgr*
Jackie Bach, *Sales Associate*

▲ EMP: 40
SQ FT: 30,000
SALES (est): 7.7MM **Privately Held**
WEB: www.presser.com
SIC: 2741 5736 Music, sheet: publishing only, not printed on site; sheet music

(G-8688)
THUNDER BASIN CORPORATION (HQ)
555 Croton Rd Ste 200 (19406-3171)
PHONE..................................610 962-3770
Russell C Ball III, *Ch of Bd*
Tim Dwyer, *CFO*
Paul Brennan, *Admin Sec*
EMP: 17
SALES (est): 99.2MM
SALES (corp-wide): 153MM **Privately Held**
SIC: 3566 2298 Gears, power transmission, except automotive; speed changers (power transmission equipment), except auto; drives, high speed industrial, except hydrostatic; rope, except asbestos & wire; twine
PA: American Manufacturing Corporation
555 Croton Rd Ste 200
King of Prussia PA 19406
610 962-3770

(G-8689)
TIMKEN GEARS & SERVICES INC (HQ)
Also Called: Philadelphia Gear
901 E 8th Ave Ste 100 (19406-1354)
PHONE..................................610 265-3000
Christopher Coughlin, *President*
Glen Olivi, *General Mgr*
Tracy Achuff, *Chairman*
Malcolm Steven, *Business Mgr*
Philip Fracassa, *Vice Pres*
▲ EMP: 220
SQ FT: 15,000
SALES (est): 59.6MM
SALES (corp-wide): 3.5B **Publicly Held**
SIC: 3462 Gear & chain forgings; gears, forged steel; anchors, forged
PA: The Timken Company
4500 Mount Pleasant St Nw
North Canton OH 44720
234 262-3000

(G-8690)
TRILION QUALITY SYSTEMS LLC (PA)
651 Park Ave (19406-1408)
PHONE..................................215 710-3000
Holly Hoch, *CFO*
John Tyson, *Mng Member*
Tim Schmidt,
EMP: 40 EST: 1998
SQ FT: 8,000
SALES (est): 12.1MM **Privately Held**
WEB: www.trilion.com
SIC: 3545 8711 Precision measuring tools; engineering services

(G-8691)
TUMBLING WITH JOJO
970 Pulaski Dr (19406-2802)
PHONE..................................267 574-5074
Joelle Decarlo, *Principal*
EMP: 3 EST: 2017
SALES (est): 139.7K **Privately Held**
SIC: 3471 Plating & polishing

(G-8692)
UGI EUROPE INC (PA)
460 N Gulph Rd (19406-2815)
PHONE..................................610 337-1000
John Walsh, *President*
Amy Hunt, *VP Opers*
Ivanovic Diana, *Manager*
Brian Yost, *Manager*
EMP: 7 EST: 2001
SALES: 8.2B **Privately Held**
SIC: 1321 Cycle condensate production (natural gas)

(G-8693)
UGI NEWCO LLC
460 N Gulph Rd (19406-2815)
PHONE..................................610 337-7000
Bradley C Hall, *Mng Member*
Brad Hall, *Mng Member*

EMP: 202
SQ FT: 88,741
SALES (est): 2.8MM
SALES (corp-wide): 7.6B **Publicly Held**
SIC: 1389 Gas field services
HQ: Ugi Enterprises, Inc.
460 N Gulph Rd
Valley Forge PA 19482

(G-8694)
UPL NA INC (DH)
Also Called: United Phosphorus Inc.
630 Freedom Business Ctr (19406-1331)
PHONE..................................610 491-2800
Vicente Gongora, *President*
Madeline Palac, *CFO*
William Herbert, *Admin Sec*
▲ EMP: 30 EST: 1996
SQ FT: 2,100
SALES (est): 201.2MM
SALES (corp-wide): 655.5K **Privately Held**
WEB: www.upi-usa.com
SIC: 5191 2879 Chemicals, agricultural; agricultural chemicals
HQ: Upl Europe Ltd
First Floor The Centre
Warrington WA3 6
192 581-9999

(G-8695)
VENATOR AMERICAS LLC
555 E Church Rd (19406-2600)
PHONE..................................610 279-6450
EMP: 114
SALES (corp-wide): 9.3B **Publicly Held**
WEB: www.rockwoodpigments.com
SIC: 2816 Zinc pigments: zinc oxide, zinc sulfide
HQ: Venator Americas Llc
7011 Muirkirk Rd
Beltsville MD 20705
301 210-3400

(G-8696)
VF OUTDOOR LLC
690 W Dekalb Pike # 2049 (19406-2943)
PHONE..................................610 265-2193
EMP: 4
SALES (corp-wide): 11.8B **Publicly Held**
WEB: www.timberland.com
SIC: 3144 2386 2329 2321 Women's footwear, except athletic; boots, canvas or leather: women's; coats & jackets, leather & sheep-lined; coats (oiled fabric, leatherette, etc.): men's & boys'; jackets (suede, leatherette, etc.), sport: men's & boys'; sweaters & sweater jackets: men's & boys'; men's & boys' furnishings; men's & boys' trousers & slacks; boots, dress or casual: men's
HQ: Vf Outdoor, Llc
2701 Harbor Bay Pkwy
Alameda CA 94502
510 618-3500

(G-8697)
VIKING ELECTRONIC SERVICES
620 Allendale Rd Ste 175 (19406-7400)
PHONE..................................610 992-0400
William Lirraob, *President*
Ray King, *Managing Dir*
John Hewitt, *Opers Mgr*
Andy Johannsen, *Sales Staff*
Jay Cohen, *Director*
▲ EMP: 40
SQ FT: 20,000
SALES (est): 5.1MM
SALES (corp-wide): 448.5MM **Privately Held**
SIC: 3953 Figures (marking devices), metal
HQ: Tyden Group Holdings Corp.
409 Hoosier Dr
Angola IN 46703
740 420-6777

(G-8698)
WEARABLE HEALTH SOLUTIONS INC (HQ)
200 W Church Rd Ste B (19406-3221)
PHONE..................................877 639-2929
Ronnie Adams, *Ch of Bd*
Allen Polsky, *Exec VP*
EMP: 10

SALES: 1.3MM **Publicly Held**
SIC: 3669 Emergency alarms
PA: D2cf, Llc
108 Coccio Dr
West Orange NJ 07052
973 699-4111

(G-8699)
WIKOFF COLOR CORPORATION
445 Hillview Rd (19406-2310)
PHONE..................................484 681-4065
Kathy Gratz, *Principal*
EMP: 3
SALES (corp-wide): 150MM **Privately Held**
SIC: 2893 Printing ink
PA: Wikoff Color Corporation
1886 Merritt Rd
Fort Mill SC 29715
803 548-2210

(G-8700)
XIII TOUCHES PRINTING
1150 First Ave Ste 530 (19406-1334)
PHONE..................................484 754-6504
EMP: 10
SALES (est): 291K **Privately Held**
SIC: 2396 7336 7389 Mfg Auto/Apparel Trim Coml Art/Graphic Design Bus Servs Non-Comcl Site

(G-8701)
ZAVANTE THERAPEUTICS INC
1000 Continental Dr # 600 (19406-2848)
PHONE..................................610 816-6640
Ted Schroeder, *CEO*
Kevin Finney, *COO*
Evelyn Ellis-Grosse, *Security Dir*
EMP: 8
SQ FT: 10,000
SALES (est): 1.3MM **Privately Held**
SIC: 2834 Drugs affecting parasitic & infective diseases
PA: Nabriva Therapeutics Public Limited Company
25-28 North Wall Quay
Dublin 1

Kingsley
Susquehanna County

(G-8702)
CARL J KAETZEL
Also Called: Carl J Kaetzel Flagstone
203 Reynolds Rd (18826-6913)
PHONE..................................570 434-2391
Carl J Kaetzel, *Principal*
EMP: 3
SALES (est): 119.5K **Privately Held**
SIC: 3281 Flagstones

(G-8703)
DIAZ STONE AND PALLET INC
7822 N Weston Rd (18826-7211)
PHONE..................................570 289-8760
Tim Washeurn, *Branch Mgr*
EMP: 15
SALES (corp-wide): 4.8MM **Privately Held**
SIC: 3281 Cut stone & stone products
PA: Diaz Stone And Pallet, Inc.
7686 State Route 167
Kingsley PA 18826
570 289-8760

(G-8704)
DIAZ STONE AND PALLET INC (PA)
7686 State Route 167 (18826-6966)
PHONE..................................570 289-8760
Adam M Diaz, *President*
EMP: 35
SQ FT: 14,000
SALES (est): 4.8MM **Privately Held**
WEB: www.diazstoneandpallet.com
SIC: 3281 2448 Cut stone & stone products; pallets, wood & wood with metal

(G-8705)
HARFORD STONE COMPANY
1060 Bartholomew Rd (18826-7773)
P.O. Box 1 (18826-0001)
PHONE..................................570 434-9141

▲ = Import ▼=Export
◆ =Import/Export

David Morales, *Owner*
EMP: 10 **EST:** 1993
SALES (est): 630K **Privately Held**
SIC: 3281 2653 Flagstones; solid fiber boxes, partitions, display items & sheets

(G-8706)
HERB KILMER & SONS FLAGSTONE
11308 State Route 106 (18826-6940)
P.O. Box 129 (18826-0129)
PHONE...................................570 434-2060
Herb Kilmer, *President*
Trail Stewards, *Business Mgr*
Jeff Kilmer, *Vice Pres*
Tom Kilmer, *Vice Pres*
EMP: 50
SALES (est): 4.7MM **Privately Held**
WEB: www.herbkilmerflagstone.com
SIC: 3281 Flagstones

(G-8707)
ROSS FEEDS INC (PA)
6 Mill St (18826-7771)
P.O. Box 14 (18826-0014)
PHONE...................................570 289-4388
Ernest Blachek, *President*
Faye Blachek, *Corp Secy*
EMP: 14
SALES (est): 2.1MM **Privately Held**
SIC: 2048 5251 2041 Prepared feeds; hardware; flour & other grain mill products

(G-8708)
STONE SUPPLY INC
2432 Orphan School Rd (18826-6772)
PHONE...................................570 434-2076
Marlene Rhodes, *President*
Nelson Rhodes, *General Mgr*
▲ **EMP:** 5
SQ FT: 2,200
SALES (est): 771.9K **Privately Held**
SIC: 3545 Diamond cutting tools for turning, boring, burnishing, etc.

(G-8709)
STONEY LONESOME QUARRY INC
1475 Orphan School Rd (18826-6765)
PHONE...................................570 434-2509
Julie Lepre, *President*
EMP: 4
SALES (est): 360K **Privately Held**
SIC: 1411 Bluestone, dimension-quarrying

(G-8710)
WILDER DIAMOND BLADES INC
5638 State Route 92 (18826-7072)
PHONE...................................570 222-9590
Mary Wilder, *President*
Glenn G Wilder, *Vice Pres*
Glenn Wilder, *Vice Pres*
▲ **EMP:** 6 **EST:** 2007
SQ FT: 8,000
SALES (est): 1.4MM **Privately Held**
SIC: 3291 5084 3425 3281 Abrasive wheels & grindstones, not artificial; abrasive metal & steel products; metallic abrasive; metalworking tools (such as drills, taps, dies, files); saw blades & handsaws; saw blades, chain type; saw blades for hand or power saws; saws, hand: metalworking or woodworking; cut stone & stone products; curbing, granite or stone; granite, cut & shaped; wire springs; custom pulverizing & grinding of plastic materials

Kingston
Luzerne County

(G-8711)
4 DAUGHTERS LLC
1 Korn St (18704-2637)
PHONE...................................570 283-5934
Moshe Granit, *Marketing Mgr*
Moshe Granite,
▲ **EMP:** 52
SQ FT: 74,000
SALES (est): 7.6MM **Privately Held**
WEB: www.4daughters.net
SIC: 2431 Exterior & ornamental woodwork & trim

(G-8712)
AZAR INTERNATIONAL INC
232 Division St (18704-2761)
PHONE...................................570 288-0786
Ben Cohen, *Branch Mgr*
EMP: 5
SALES (est): 481.9K
SALES (corp-wide): 8.5MM **Privately Held**
SIC: 3999 8742 Advertising display products; distribution channels consultant
PA: Azar International Inc.
80 W Century Rd Ste 400
Paramus NJ 07652
845 624-8808

(G-8713)
CARBON CLEAN INDUSTRIES INC
216 Courtdale Ave (18704-1123)
P.O. Box E (18704-0920)
PHONE...................................570 288-1155
Ernest J Clamar, *Owner*
EMP: 23
SALES (est): 15MM **Privately Held**
SIC: 2842 Cleaning or polishing preparations

(G-8714)
COR-RITE CORRUGATED INC
195 Slocum St (18704-2935)
PHONE...................................570 287-1718
Marlene T Wright, *President*
EMP: 12
SALES (est): 1.1MM **Privately Held**
SIC: 2653 Boxes, corrugated: made from purchased materials

(G-8715)
CRYO TEMPERING TECH OF NE PA
189 River St (18704-5038)
PHONE...................................570 287-7443
Duane E Kersteen, *President*
EMP: 8
SALES (est): 943.1K **Privately Held**
SIC: 3399 Cryogenic treatment of metal

(G-8716)
ECCO INDUSTRIES INC
215 Courtdale Ave (18704-1148)
PHONE...................................570 288-1226
Bill Cochren, *Principal*
EMP: 3
SALES (est): 203.8K **Privately Held**
SIC: 3999 Manufacturing industries

(G-8717)
FORTUNE FABRICS INC
Also Called: Wyoming Weavers
315 Simpson St (18704-3098)
P.O. Box 1589 (18704-0589)
PHONE...................................570 288-3666
Robert Fortinsky, *President*
Shirley Fortinsky, *Corp Secy*
Jill S Schwartz, *Vice Pres*
EMP: 30 **EST:** 1949
SQ FT: 32,000
SALES (est): 4.5MM **Privately Held**
SIC: 2221 2295 Upholstery fabrics, manmade fiber & silk; coated fabrics, not rubberized

(G-8718)
GOLDEN BROTHERS INC
Also Called: Golden Technologies
263 Schuyler Ave (18704-3321)
PHONE...................................570 714-5002
EMP: 48
SALES (corp-wide): 60.7MM **Privately Held**
SIC: 2512 Chairs: upholstered on wood frames; living room furniture: upholstered on wood frames
PA: Golden Brothers, Inc.
401 Bridge St
Old Forge PA 18518
570 457-0867

(G-8719)
HELFRAN GLASS
416 Northampton St (18704-4542)
PHONE...................................570 287-8105
Frances McGough, *Owner*
EMP: 3

SALES (est): 231.3K **Privately Held**
SIC: 5719 3479 Glassware; etching & engraving

(G-8720)
L&D MILLWORK INC
161 Eley St (18704-3931)
PHONE...................................570 285-3200
Linda Grosso, *CEO*
EMP: 8
SQ FT: 2,000
SALES (est): 2MM **Privately Held**
SIC: 2542 Office & store showcases & display fixtures

(G-8721)
LIBERTY THROWING COMPANY
214 Pringle St (18704-2719)
P.O. Box 1387 (18704-0387)
PHONE...................................570 287-1114
Dennis Wagner, *President*
Charles M Epstein Jr, *Chairman*
EMP: 60 **EST:** 1919
SQ FT: 35,000
SALES (est): 7MM **Privately Held**
SIC: 2241 2284 Thread, elastic: fabric covered; thread mills

(G-8722)
LOCO YOCO
26 Pierce St (18704-4634)
PHONE...................................570 331-4529
Nanda Palissery, *Owner*
EMP: 4
SALES (est): 232.6K **Privately Held**
SIC: 2026 Yogurt

(G-8723)
M ROBZEN INC
Also Called: Customers Choice Brand
734 Milford Dr (18704-5308)
PHONE...................................570 283-1226
Mark Robzen, *President*
EMP: 25 **EST:** 1997
SQ FT: 18,000
SALES (est): 3.8MM **Privately Held**
SIC: 2011 2013 Meat packing plants; frozen meats from purchased meat

(G-8724)
PDQ PRINT CENTER
Also Called: P D Q Instant Print Center
502 Market St (18704-4530)
PHONE...................................570 283-0995
David Price, *President*
EMP: 3
SALES (est): 184.7K **Privately Held**
WEB: www.pdqprint.com
SIC: 2759 Commercial printing

(G-8725)
PENN LOCK CORP
21 Noyes Ave (18704-2298)
PHONE...................................570 288-5547
Brian Thimot, *President*
Mike Rifkin, *Vice Pres*
Paul Lantz, *Treasurer*
▲ **EMP:** 24
SQ FT: 20,000
SALES (est): 4.6MM **Privately Held**
WEB: www.pennlockcorp.com
SIC: 3429 Keys, locks & related hardware

(G-8726)
WYOMING VALLEY TIMES JURNL INC
16 Bidlack St (18704-4121)
PHONE...................................570 288-8362
George Maguschak, *Principal*
EMP: 3
SALES (est): 124.5K **Privately Held**
SIC: 2711 Newspapers, publishing & printing

Kintnersville
Bucks County

(G-8727)
GLENN A HISSIM WOODWORKING LLC
4770 Route 212 (18930-9787)
PHONE...................................610 847-8961
Glenn Hissim, *Principal*

EMP: 5
SALES (est): 278.2K **Privately Held**
SIC: 2431 Millwork

(G-8728)
J A K MACHINE CO
4740 Lehnenberg Rd (18930-9753)
PHONE...................................610 346-6906
Jeff Kapralick, *Owner*
EMP: 3
SALES: 300K **Privately Held**
SIC: 3599 Machine shop, jobbing & repair

(G-8729)
JONES CRAFTS INC
1860 Stony Garden Rd (18930-9436)
PHONE...................................610 346-6247
Robert M Jones, *President*
Patricia Jones, *Admin Sec*
EMP: 3
SALES (est): 262.8K **Privately Held**
SIC: 2499 Engraved wood products

(G-8730)
WOODS WINGS
85 Traugers Crossing Rd (18930-9615)
PHONE...................................610 417-5684
Darren Kyle, *Owner*
EMP: 3
SALES (est): 100K **Privately Held**
SIC: 2035 5149 5812 Seasonings, meat sauces (except tomato & dry); sauces; caterers

Kinzers
Lancaster County

(G-8731)
ADVANCED TRIM SPECIALTIES
Also Called: Advanced Trim and Kitchens
4966 Lincoln Hwy (17535-9789)
P.O. Box 120 (17535-0120)
PHONE...................................717 442-8098
Jennifer Engel, *CEO*
Merv Engel, *President*
Mervin Angle, *Principal*
Nikki Deritis, *Sales Staff*
Tom Weeple, *Sales Staff*
EMP: 49
SQ FT: 31,000
SALES (est): 8.6MM **Privately Held**
WEB: www.atsbuild.com
SIC: 2431 Ornamental woodwork: cornices, mantels, etc.

(G-8732)
B & L WOODWORKING
250 Snake Ln (17535-9726)
PHONE...................................717 354-5430
Leon S Lapp, *Principal*
EMP: 4
SALES (est): 339.1K **Privately Held**
SIC: 2431 Millwork

(G-8733)
BREEO LLC
5002 Lincoln Hwy (17535-9789)
PHONE...................................800 413-9848
Brandon Schlabach, *Mng Member*
EMP: 19
SALES (est): 3MM **Privately Held**
SIC: 3631 Household cooking equipment

(G-8734)
BYERSTOWN WOODWORK SHOP
5031 Newport Rd (17535-9713)
PHONE...................................717 442-8586
Samuel Fisher, *Owner*
EMP: 5
SQ FT: 7,600
SALES: 600K **Privately Held**
SIC: 2499 Decorative wood & woodwork

(G-8735)
CAPITAL COATING INC
7 S Kinzer Rd (17535-9766)
P.O. Box 365, Intercourse (17534-0365)
PHONE...................................717 442-0979
Mervin Fisher, *President*
Daryl Pilon, *Engineer*
EMP: 10

G E O G R A P H I C

SALES (est): 1.4MM **Privately Held**
SIC: 2851 1721 Paints & allied products; painting & paper hanging

(G-8736)
DAVCO ADVERTISING INC
89 N Kinzer Rd (17535-9705)
P.O. Box 288 (17535-0288)
PHONE..................................717 442-4155
Jerry L Esh, *CEO*
Rick D Esh, *President*
Elsie R Esh, *Corp Secy*
Donald L Esh, *Vice Pres*
Daryl Stoltzfus, *Sales Staff*
EMP: 40
SQ FT: 35,000
SALES: 5.8MM **Privately Held**
WEB: www.davcoadvertising.com
SIC: 5199 2752 2791 2789 Advertising specialties; commercial printing, offset; typesetting; bookbinding & related work

(G-8737)
ELS MANUFACTURING LLC
5270 Amish Rd (17535-9744)
PHONE..................................717 442-8569
Elam Stoltzfus,
EMP: 16
SQ FT: 5,450
SALES: 1.1MM **Privately Held**
SIC: 3523 Loaders, farm type: manure, general utility

(G-8738)
GAP RIDGE CONTRACTORS LLC
5206 Old Strasburg Rd (17535-9750)
PHONE..................................717 442-4386
David Lapp, *Managing Prtnr*
EMP: 17
SALES (est): 1.4MM **Privately Held**
SIC: 1751 3585 Carpentry work; refrigeration & heating equipment

(G-8739)
KINGS WOODWORK SHOP
181 Snake Ln (17535-9725)
PHONE..................................717 768-7721
David L King, *Owner*
EMP: 4
SALES: 450K **Privately Held**
SIC: 2499 Decorative wood & woodwork

(G-8740)
PEQUEA STORAGE SHEDS LLC
211 S New Holland Rd (17535-9729)
PHONE..................................717 768-8980
Abner F King, *President*
Rebecca King, *Vice Pres*
EMP: 12
SALES (est): 1.7MM **Privately Held**
SIC: 2452 7389 Prefabricated buildings, wood; business services

(G-8741)
RIEHL QUALITY STOR BARNS LLC
4940 Lincoln Hwy (17535-9788)
P.O. Box 123 (17535-0123)
PHONE..................................717 442-8655
Elam S Riehl, *Mng Member*
EMP: 16
SQ FT: 7,000
SALES (est): 2.2MM **Privately Held**
SIC: 2452 Prefabricated buildings, wood

(G-8742)
SAM BEILER
Also Called: Wolf Rock Furniture
3533 Lincoln Hwy E (17535-9701)
PHONE..................................717 442-8990
Sam Beiler, *Owner*
EMP: 5
SALES: 1.2MM **Privately Held**
SIC: 2511 Wood household furniture

(G-8743)
STOLTZFOOS LAYERS (PA)
1003 Gap Rd (17535-9752)
PHONE..................................717 826-0371
Clifford Stoltzfoos, *Partner*
Joshua Stoltzfoos, *Partner*
EMP: 4
SQ FT: 718,740
SALES: 350K **Privately Held**
SIC: 0252 2451 Chicken eggs; mobile homes

Kirkwood
Lancaster County

(G-8744)
BLACK ROCK REPAIR LLC
858 Pumping Station Rd (17536-9727)
PHONE..................................717 529-6553
Leroy King, *Mng Member*
Levi Stoltzfus, *Mng Member*
EMP: 4
SALES: 900K **Privately Held**
SIC: 3441 Fabricated structural metal

(G-8745)
CONESTOGA MFG LLC
1867 Kirkwood Pike (17536-9711)
PHONE..................................717 529-0199
Aaron Glick, *Principal*
EMP: 8
SALES (est): 820.5K **Privately Held**
SIC: 3523 Farm machinery & equipment

(G-8746)
COOPER MACHINE LLC
Also Called: Cooper Saws
245 Cooper Dr (17536-9728)
PHONE..................................717 529-6155
Andrew L Stoltzfus,
EMP: 7
SALES (est): 649.5K **Privately Held**
SIC: 3599 Machine shop, jobbing & repair

(G-8747)
DANIEL B PROFFITT JR
195 Schoolhouse Rd (17536-9606)
PHONE..................................717 529-2194
Daniel B Proffitt, *Owner*
EMP: 15
SALES (est): 2.2MM **Privately Held**
SIC: 3535 Unit handling conveying systems

(G-8748)
DS FABRICATION
Also Called: D & J Metal Tech
834 Pumping Station Rd (17536-9727)
PHONE..................................717 529-2282
Daniel E Stoltzfus, *Owner*
EMP: 8
SALES (est): 752.1K **Privately Held**
SIC: 3561 Pumps & pumping equipment

(G-8749)
JEFFREY R KNUDSEN
Also Called: Knudsen's Woodworking
6150 Street Rd (17536-9647)
PHONE..................................717 529-4011
Jeffrey R Knudsen, *Owner*
EMP: 6
SQ FT: 6,000
SALES (est): 531.6K **Privately Held**
SIC: 2431 2434 Millwork; wood kitchen cabinets

(G-8750)
LOCUST RIDGE WOODWORKS LLC
56 Schoolhouse Rd (17536-9635)
PHONE..................................610 350-6029
EMP: 4 EST: 2010
SALES (est): 445.7K **Privately Held**
SIC: 2431 Millwork

(G-8751)
MAGNUM MODEL CONCEPTS INC
886 King Pen Rd (17536-9765)
PHONE..................................717 529-0912
Stephen C Holup, *President*
EMP: 3
SALES (est): 123.3K **Privately Held**
SIC: 3999 Models, general, except toy

(G-8752)
OAK SHADE CHEESE LLC
286 Reath Rd (17536-9655)
PHONE..................................717 529-6049
Israel Kinsinger,
EMP: 3
SQ FT: 3,676

SALES (est): 252.3K **Privately Held**
SIC: 2022 Cheese, natural & processed

Kittanning
Armstrong County

(G-8753)
ALLEGHENY MINERAL CORPORATION (HQ)
1 Glade Dr (16201-7139)
P.O. Box 1022 (16201-5022)
PHONE..................................724 548-8101
Dennis C Snyder, *President*
Richard Snyder, *Division Mgr*
Charles Snyder Jr, *Chairman*
Jonathan Kolbe, *Vice Pres*
Richard G Snyder, *Vice Pres*
EMP: 5 EST: 1952
SALES (est): 33.8MM
SALES (corp-wide): 790.5MM **Privately Held**
WEB: www.snydercos.com
SIC: 3281 3295 3274 Limestone, cut & shaped; minerals, ground or treated; agricultural lime
PA: Snyder Associated Companies, Inc.
1 Glade Park Dr
Kittanning PA 16201
724 548-8101

(G-8754)
APPALACHIAN DRILLERS LLC
409 Butler Rd Ste A (16201-4403)
PHONE..................................724 548-2501
Michael D Snyder, *President*
Randall L Morris Jr, *Vice Pres*
Jason C Knapp, *Admin Sec*
EMP: 3
SALES (est): 12.2MM **Privately Held**
SIC: 1381 Drilling oil & gas wells

(G-8755)
ASBURY GRAPHITE MILLS INC
Also Called: Anthracite
280 Linde Rd (16201-4718)
P.O. Box 1 (16201-0001)
PHONE..................................724 543-1343
Roger Master, *Branch Mgr*
EMP: 52
SALES (corp-wide): 126.7MM **Privately Held**
WEB: www.asbury.com
SIC: 3295 3624 Graphite, natural: ground, pulverized, refined or blended; carbon & graphite products
HQ: The Asbury Graphite Mills Inc
405 Old Main St
Asbury NJ 08802
908 537-2155

(G-8756)
BAUER COMPANY INC
1 Glade Dr (16201-7139)
PHONE..................................724 548-8101
David E Snyder, *President*
Charles H Snyder Jr, *Chairman*
Dennis C Snyder, *Vice Pres*
Mark A Snyder, *Admin Sec*
EMP: 5 EST: 1901
SALES (est): 565.8K
SALES (corp-wide): 790.5MM **Privately Held**
WEB: www.farmersnatl.com
SIC: 3271 3272 Blocks, concrete or cinder: standard; septic tanks, concrete
PA: Snyder Associated Companies, Inc.
1 Glade Park Dr
Kittanning PA 16201
724 548-8101

(G-8757)
BERGAD INC
Also Called: Bergad Spclty Foams Composites
11858 State Route 85 (16201-3720)
PHONE..................................724 763-2883
Paul Bergad, *President*
Saul Bergad, *Treasurer*
▼ EMP: 20
SQ FT: 60,000

SALES (est): 4.7MM **Privately Held**
WEB: www.bergad.com
SIC: 3086 2515 Padding, foamed plastic; mattresses & foundations

(G-8758)
BLX INC
233 North Park Dr (16201-7123)
PHONE..................................724 543-5743
Stanley J Berdell, *President*
EMP: 4
SALES (est): 1.3MM **Privately Held**
SIC: 1311 Natural gas production

(G-8759)
BUTTER MILK FALLS INC
Also Called: Walker Printer
341 N Grant Ave Ste C (16201-1343)
PHONE..................................724 548-7388
Donald Cole, *President*
EMP: 5
SQ FT: 3,040
SALES: 250K **Privately Held**
SIC: 2752 Commercial printing, offset

(G-8760)
CARSON INDUSTRIES INC
15 Glade Dr (16201-7139)
PHONE..................................724 295-5147
EMP: 7
SALES (corp-wide): 12.8MM **Privately Held**
SIC: 3365 Aluminum & aluminum-based alloy castings
PA: Carson Industries, Inc.
189 Foreman Rd
Freeport PA 16229
724 295-5147

(G-8761)
CHEMSTREAM HOLDINGS INC
301 Market St (16201-1504)
PHONE..................................724 545-6222
J Clifford Forrest III, *President*
EMP: 4 EST: 2012
SALES (est): 241.1K **Privately Held**
SIC: 1221 1222 Strip mining, bituminous; bituminous coal-underground mining

(G-8762)
COOKPORT COAL CO INC
425 E Market St Ste 1 (16201-1433)
PHONE..................................814 938-4253
Charles Sheesley Jr, *President*
Eva Sheesley, *Corp Secy*
EMP: 3
SALES: 355K **Privately Held**
SIC: 1221 Strip mining, bituminous

(G-8763)
CURTIS SURE-GRIP INC
Also Called: Curtis Industries
105 West Park Dr (16201-7125)
PHONE..................................724 545-8333
John Curtis, *President*
EMP: 11
SQ FT: 4,000
SALES (est): 1.8MM **Privately Held**
SIC: 3599 Machine shop, jobbing & repair

(G-8764)
CUSTOM FAB TRAILERS INC
12478 Us Route 422 (16201-5148)
PHONE..................................724 548-5529
Waqar Siddiqi, *President*
EMP: 3
SQ FT: 10,000
SALES (est): 192K **Privately Held**
SIC: 3715 Demountable cargo containers

(G-8765)
D & S BUSINESS SERVICES INC
529 Butler Rd (16201-1989)
PHONE..................................724 545-3143
Wendell Davis, *Principal*
EMP: 6 EST: 2001
SALES (est): 581.7K **Privately Held**
SIC: 2752 Commercial printing, offset

(G-8766)
DIELECTRIC SALES LLC (PA)
Also Called: Allegheny Glass Technologies
1655 Orr Ave (16201-1015)
PHONE..................................724 543-2333
Howard A Kadar,
EMP: 5

2019 Harris Pennsylvania
Manufacturers Directory

▲ = Import ▼=Export
◆ =Import/Export

SALES: 5MM **Privately Held**
SIC: 3229 Glass fiber products

(G-8767)
DRUG PLASTICS AND GLASS CO INC
104 West Park Dr (16201-7124)
PHONE..................................724 548-5654
Dayton Dudas, *Manager*
EMP: 65
SALES (corp-wide): 166.9MM **Privately Held**
WEB: www.drugplastics.com
SIC: 3085 Plastics bottles
PA: Drug Plastics And Glass Company, Inc.
1 Bottle Dr
Boyertown PA 19512
610 367-5000

(G-8768)
EXCO RESOURCES LLC (HQ)
13448 State Route 422 # 1 (16201-3620)
PHONE..................................724 720-2500
Douglas H Miller, *Ch of Bd*
Stephen F Smith, *President*
Harold L Hickey, *COO*
William L Boeing, *Vice Pres*
Ronald G Edelen, *Vice Pres*
EMP: 81
SALES (est): 287MM
SALES (corp-wide): 394MM **Privately Held**
WEB: www.northcoastenergy.com
SIC: 1382 1381 1311 8741 Oil & gas exploration services; drilling oil & gas wells; crude petroleum & natural gas; management services; brokers, security
PA: Exco Resources, Inc.
12377 Merit Dr Ste 1700
Dallas TX 75251
214 368-2084

(G-8769)
FAMILY-LIFE MEDIA-COM INC
Also Called: Kittaning Paper
114 S Jefferson St (16201-2408)
PHONE..................................724 543-6397
David Croyle, *President*
Reuben A Bogley, *Treasurer*
Paul A Price, *Admin Sec*
EMP: 10
SALES (est): 740.5K **Privately Held**
WEB: www.familylifetv.com
SIC: 4833 2711 4832 Television broadcasting stations; newspapers, publishing & printing; radio broadcasting stations

(G-8770)
FIRST CLASS ENERGY LLC
409 Butler Rd A (16201-4403)
PHONE..................................724 548-2501
EMP: 39
SALES (corp-wide): 32.5MM **Privately Held**
SIC: 4939 1381 Combination utilities; drilling oil & gas wells
PA: First Class Energy, Llc
409 Butler Rd Ste A
Kittanning PA 16201
724 548-2501

(G-8771)
FIRST CLASS ENERGY LLC (PA)
409 Butler Rd Ste A (16201-4403)
PHONE..................................724 548-2501
Michael D Snyder, *President*
Michael Knapp, *Vice Pres*
Wayne Branan, *Manager*
EMP: 29
SALES (est): 32.5MM **Privately Held**
SIC: 1381 Drilling oil & gas wells

(G-8772)
FUZION TECHNOLOGIES INC
114 West Park Dr (16201-7124)
PHONE..................................724 545-2223
William Sabo, *Branch Mgr*
EMP: 10 **Privately Held**
SIC: 3297 Brick refractories; cement refractories
PA: Fuzion Technologies, Inc.
570 Morrison Rd
Rossville TN 38066

(G-8773)
GLACIAL SAND & GRAVEL CO (HQ)
1 Glade Dr (16201-7139)
PHONE..................................724 548-8101
Mark A Snyder, *CEO*
Charles Snyder Jr, *Vice Pres*
Thomas C Snyder, *Vice Pres*
David E Snyder, *Treasurer*
Dennis Synder, *Admin Sec*
EMP: 5
SQ FT: 500
SALES (est): 7.3MM
SALES (corp-wide): 790.5MM **Privately Held**
SIC: 1442 Sand mining; gravel mining
PA: Snyder Associated Companies, Inc.
1 Glade Park Dr
Kittanning PA 16201
724 548-8101

(G-8774)
GLOBAL CERAMIC SERVICES INC
238 North Park Dr (16201-7122)
PHONE..................................724 545-7224
Frank Dlubak, *President*
▲ EMP: 10
SALES (est): 1.3MM **Privately Held**
WEB: www.globalceramicservices.com
SIC: 3999 Custom pulverizing & grinding of plastic materials

(G-8775)
J BROWN MACHINE LLC
991 Butler Rd (16201-7011)
PHONE..................................724 543-4044
Jeffrey Brown, *Principal*
EMP: 3
SALES (est): 277.8K **Privately Held**
SIC: 3599 Machine shop, jobbing & repair

(G-8776)
JJ KENNEDY INC
10373 State Route 85 (16201-6131)
PHONE..................................724 783-6081
EMP: 12
SALES (corp-wide): 10.8MM **Privately Held**
SIC: 3273 Ready-mixed concrete
PA: J.J Kennedy Inc
1790 Route 588
Fombell PA 16123
724 452-6260

(G-8777)
LENS CONTACT CENTER
Also Called: Dr Opalka's Office
131 N Mckean St (16201-1565)
P.O. Box 946 (16201-0946)
PHONE..................................724 543-2702
Paul Opalka Od, *Partner*
Dr John Opalka, *Partner*
EMP: 6
SALES (est): 748K **Privately Held**
SIC: 3851 8042 Ophthalmic goods; offices & clinics of optometrists

(G-8778)
M/D GAS INC
409 Butler Rd Ste A (16201-4403)
PHONE..................................724 548-2501
Michael D Snyder, *President*
Jason C Knapp, *Vice Pres*
EMP: 5 EST: 2006
SQ FT: 4,000
SALES (est): 274.4K
SALES (corp-wide): 14.2MM **Privately Held**
SIC: 1321 Natural gasoline production
PA: Mds Associated Companies, Inc.
409 Butler Rd Ste A
Kittanning PA 16201
724 548-2501

(G-8779)
MARK TK WELDING INC
11771 State Route 85 (16201-3715)
PHONE..................................724 545-2001
Scott A Walter, *President*
EMP: 15
SQ FT: 7,880
SALES (est): 1.7MM **Privately Held**
SIC: 7692 Welding repair

(G-8780)
MDS ASSOCIATED COMPANIES INC (PA)
409 Butler Rd Ste A (16201-4403)
PHONE..................................724 548-2501
Michael D Snyder, *President*
Jason C Knapp, *Vice Pres*
EMP: 100 EST: 2007
SALES (est): 14.2MM **Privately Held**
SIC: 6719 1321 Investment holding companies, except banks; natural gasoline production

(G-8781)
MDS ENERGY DEVELOPMENT LLC
409 Butler Rd Ste A (16201-4403)
PHONE..................................724 548-2501
Michael Snyder, *President*
EMP: 20
SQ FT: 3,000
SALES (est): 722.3K **Privately Held**
SIC: 1311 Crude petroleum & natural gas production

(G-8782)
MDS ENERGY PARTNERS GP LLC
409 Butler Rd Ste A (16201-4403)
PHONE..................................724 548-2501
Jason Knapp, *Vice Pres*
EMP: 3 EST: 2014
SQ FT: 2,500
SALES (est): 104.3K **Privately Held**
SIC: 1311 Crude petroleum & natural gas production

(G-8783)
MDS SECURITIES LLC
409 Butler Rd Ste A (16201-4403)
PHONE..................................724 548-2501
Jason Knapp, *Mng Member*
EMP: 6
SALES: 1.6MM **Privately Held**
SIC: 6211 1389 Security brokers & dealers; cementing oil & gas well casings

(G-8784)
MDS WELL HOLDINGS LLC
409 Butler Rd Ste A (16201-4403)
PHONE..................................724 548-2501
Michael Snyder, *President*
Jason Knapp, *Vice Pres*
EMP: 3 EST: 2017
SQ FT: 2,500
SALES (est): 104.3K **Privately Held**
SIC: 1311 Crude petroleum & natural gas

(G-8785)
MYERS VACUUM REPAIR SVCS INC (PA)
1155 Myers Ln (16201-4129)
PHONE..................................724 545-8331
Dean M Myers, *President*
Brandy Myers, *Corp Secy*
EMP: 13
SQ FT: 2,500
SALES (est): 801.8K **Privately Held**
WEB: www.myers-vacuum.com
SIC: 3563 7699 Air & gas compressors including vacuum pumps; industrial machinery & equipment repair

(G-8786)
NORTHERN HOT SHOT SERVICES LLC
126 N Jefferson St (16201-1536)
PHONE..................................724 664-5477
Kent Walker, *Principal*
EMP: 5
SALES (est): 413.2K **Privately Held**
SIC: 1389 Hot shot service

(G-8787)
PARKWOOD RESOURCES INC
301 Market St (16201-1504)
PHONE..................................724 479-4090
John Garcia, *President*
EMP: 25
SALES (est): 2.1MM **Privately Held**
SIC: 1241 Coal mining services

(G-8788)
PROFESSIONAL HEARING AID SVC (PA)
Also Called: Beltone Hearing Center
141 S Jefferson St (16201-2409)
PHONE..................................724 548-4801
Judith Bonatch, *Owner*
EMP: 4
SALES (est): 511.7K **Privately Held**
SIC: 3842 5999 7629 Hearing aids; hearing aid sales; hearing aid repair

(G-8789)
ROSEBUD COAL SALES INC
301 Market St (16201-1504)
PHONE..................................724 545-6222
Cliff Forrest, *President*
EMP: 4
SALES (est): 103.9K **Privately Held**
SIC: 1241 Coal mining services

(G-8790)
ROSEBUD MINING COMPANY (PA)
301 Market St (16201-1504)
PHONE..................................724 545-6222
J Clifford Forrest III, *President*
James R Barker, *Vice Pres*
Clifford Forest, *Vice Pres*
EMP: 43
SQ FT: 15,000
SALES (est): 605.3MM **Privately Held**
WEB: www.rosebudmining.com
SIC: 1222 1221 Bituminous coal-underground mining; strip mining, bituminous

(G-8791)
S & S SLIDES INC
11771 State Route 85 (16201-3715)
PHONE..................................724 545-2001
Scott A Walter, *President*
Alan Polka, *Vice Pres*
James Szalkiewicz, *Treasurer*
EMP: 3
SALES: 1.1MM **Privately Held**
SIC: 3462 Construction or mining equipment forgings, ferrous

(G-8792)
SINTERMET LLC
222 North Park Dr Ste 1 (16201-7142)
PHONE..................................724 548-7631
Paul C Fleiner,
▲ EMP: 65
SQ FT: 50,000
SALES (est): 18.8MM
SALES (corp-wide): 2.3MM **Privately Held**
WEB: www.sintermet.com
SIC: 3356 Tungsten, basic shapes
PA: Sintermet Acquisition Co., Llc
209 4th Ave
Pittsburgh PA

(G-8793)
SNYDER ASSOD COMPANIES INC (PA)
Also Called: Sylvan
1 Glade Park Dr (16201-7001)
P.O. Box 1022 (16201-5022)
PHONE..................................724 548-8101
Charles H Snyder Jr, *Ch of Bd*
Monir K Elzalaki, *President*
David E Snyder, *President*
Darrel Lewis, *Chief Engr*
Thomas C Snyder, *Treasurer*
◆ EMP: 45
SQ FT: 1,000
SALES (est): 790.5MM **Privately Held**
WEB: www.farmersnatl.com
SIC: 1442 3281 1222 Sand mining; gravel mining; limestone, cut & shaped; bituminous coal-underground mining

(G-8794)
SNYDER BROTHERS INC (HQ)
1 Glade Dr (16201-7139)
P.O. Box 1022 (16201-5022)
PHONE..................................724 548-8101
David E Snyder, *President*
Bryan Snyder, *Division Mgr*
Daniel Boylstein, *Vice Pres*
Dave Ohara, *Vice Pres*
Chuck Snyder, *Vice Pres*
EMP: 30

SALES (est): 13.1MM
SALES (corp-wide): 790.5MM **Privately Held**
SIC: 1382 Oil & gas exploration services
PA: Snyder Associated Companies, Inc.
1 Glade Park Dr
Kittanning PA 16201
724 548-8101

(G-8795)
SNYDER ENTERPRISES INC
Also Called: Aleghaney Mineral
1 Glade Dr (16201-7139)
P.O. Box 1022 (16201-5022)
PHONE..................724 548-8101
Chuck Snyder Jr, *President*
David Snyder, *President*
Dennis C Snyder, *President*
Elmer Snyder, *President*
Mark Snyder, *Admin Sec*
EMP: 6
SALES (est): 387.8K
SALES (corp-wide): 790.5MM **Privately Held**
SIC: 1222 Bituminous coal-underground mining
HQ: Snyder Brothers, Inc.
1 Glade Dr
Kittanning PA 16201

(G-8796)
SNYDER EXPLORATION CO
Also Called: Snyder's Associated Co
1 Glade Dr (16201-7139)
P.O. Box 1022 (16201-5022)
PHONE..................724 548-8101
Chuck Snyder Jr, *President*
EMP: 3
SALES (est): 253.8K **Privately Held**
SIC: 1241 Exploration, bituminous or lignite mining

(G-8797)
STATE INDUSTRIES INC (HQ)
1 Glade Dr (16201-7139)
P.O. Box 1022 (16201-5022)
PHONE..................724 548-8101
Thomas C Snyder, *President*
C H Snyder, *Vice Pres*
Elmer A Snyder, *Vice Pres*
Mark A Snyder, *Treasurer*
Richard G Snyder, *Admin Sec*
EMP: 3
SQ FT: 2,000
SALES (est): 512.7K
SALES (corp-wide): 790.5MM **Privately Held**
SIC: 1221 Strip mining, bituminous
PA: Snyder Associated Companies, Inc.
1 Glade Park Dr
Kittanning PA 16201
724 548-8101

(G-8798)
SYLVAN BIO INC
Also Called: Sylvan Bioproducts, Inc.
90 Glade Dr (16201-7116)
PHONE..................724 543-3900
Mark Wach, *General Mgr*
▲ EMP: 7
SALES (est): 639.7K
SALES (corp-wide): 790.5MM **Privately Held**
WEB: www.sylvaninc.com
SIC: 2836 Biological products, except diagnostic
HQ: Sylvan Inc.
90 Glade Dr
Kittanning PA 16201
724 543-3900

(G-8799)
T & L WELDING
162 Farster Rd (16201-4310)
P.O. Box 219, Elderton (15736-0219)
PHONE..................724 354-3538
Timothy Altman, *Principal*
EMP: 13
SALES (est): 1.4MM **Privately Held**
SIC: 7692 Welding repair

(G-8800)
TRIB TOTAL MEDIA LLC
Also Called: Leader-Times Daily Newspaper
1270 N Water St (16201-1055)
PHONE..................724 543-1303

Nick Monaco, *Manager*
EMP: 42
SALES (corp-wide): 157.2MM **Privately Held**
SIC: 2711 Newspapers: publishing only, not printed on site
PA: Trib Total Media, Llc
622 Cabin Hill Dr
Greensburg PA 15601
412 321-6460

(G-8801)
VALLEY WHOLESALE & SUPPLY
10307 Ste Rte 85 (16201)
P.O. Box 325, Yatesboro (16263-0325)
PHONE..................724 783-6531
John P Wasilko, *Owner*
John Wasilko, *Owner*
EMP: 20
SQ FT: 15,000
SALES: 5MM **Privately Held**
SIC: 2842 5198 5169 5084 Degreasing solvent; paints; paint brushes, rollers, sprayers; noncorrosive products & materials; cleaning equipment, high pressure, sand or steam

(G-8802)
VILLAGE IDIOT DESIGNS
12157 Us Route 422 (16201-9559)
PHONE..................724 545-7477
James R Hileman II, *Owner*
EMP: 3 EST: 1981
SALES: 150K **Privately Held**
SIC: 2261 7299 Screen printing of cotton broadwoven fabrics; stitching, custom

(G-8803)
VISTA METALS INC
189 Nolpe Dr (16201)
PHONE..................724 545-7750
Greg Riley, *Manager*
EMP: 8
SALES (corp-wide): 35.9MM **Privately Held**
WEB: www.vistametalsinc.com
SIC: 3545 Machine tool accessories
PA: Vista Metals, Inc.
1024 E Smithfield St
Mckeesport PA 15135
412 751-4600

(G-8804)
ZAMBOTTI COLLISION & WLDG CTR
138 Zambotti St (16201-3760)
PHONE..................724 545-2305
Joe Zambotti Jr, *President*
Karen Zambotti, *Vice Pres*
EMP: 6 EST: 1969
SALES: 50K **Privately Held**
SIC: 7538 7692 3444 General automotive repair shops; welding repair; sheet metalwork

Klingerstown
Schuylkill County

(G-8805)
BENIGNAS CREEK VNYRD WNERY INC
1585 Ridge Rd (17941-9649)
PHONE..................570 523-4997
Mirt Masser, *President*
Michael Masser, *Vice Pres*
Jopsephine Masser, *Admin Sec*
EMP: 4
SALES (est): 356.1K **Privately Held**
SIC: 2084 Wines

(G-8806)
BIG B MANUFACTURING INC (PA)
17 Municipal Rd (17941-9631)
PHONE..................570 648-2084
Russell Blyler Jr, *President*
Josh Blyler, *Vice Pres*
EMP: 50
SALES (est): 12.7MM **Privately Held**
WEB: www.bigbmfg.com
SIC: 3599 3441 Machine shop, jobbing & repair; fabricated structural metal

(G-8807)
CRYSTAL FRMS REFRIGERATED DIST
Also Called: Quaker State Farms
68 Spain Rd (17941-9656)
PHONE..................570 425-2910
Greg Ostrander, *President*
Mark B Anderson, *President*
Carolyn V Wolski, *Admin Sec*
EMP: 310 **Publicly Held**
SIC: 5142 2015 Packaged frozen goods; eggs, processed: frozen
HQ: Crystal Farms Dairy Company
301 Carlson Pkwy Ste 400
Minnetonka MN 55305

(G-8808)
SPEEDWELL GARAGE
Also Called: Baker's Maple
689 Salem Rd (17941-7714)
PHONE..................607 434-2376
Reed Baker, *Owner*
EMP: 7
SQ FT: 2,500
SALES (est): 866.1K **Privately Held**
SIC: 5051 2099 Metals service centers & offices; maple syrup

Knox
Clarion County

(G-8809)
EDEN INC
210 Miller St (16232-1920)
PHONE..................814 797-1160
G Barrett Garbarino, *President*
Dan Hurrelbrink, *Vice Pres*
▲ EMP: 40
SQ FT: 30,000
SALES (est): 9.6MM **Privately Held**
SIC: 5031 2431 Doors & windows; millwork

(G-8810)
FOUR THREE ENERGY SERVICES LLC
7313 Route 338 (16232-4927)
PHONE..................814 797-0021
John Bachman, *Mng Member*
EMP: 2
SALES: 3MM **Privately Held**
SIC: 1321 Natural gas liquids

(G-8811)
SWARTFAGER WELDING INC
199 Boyle Memorial Dr (16232-5561)
P.O. Box 484 (16232-0484)
PHONE..................814 797-0394
Kenneth L Swartfager, *President*
Kimberly D Swartfager, *Vice Pres*
EMP: 73
SQ FT: 149,000
SALES (est): 7.6MM **Privately Held**
SIC: 7692 7699 Automotive welding; industrial machinery & equipment repair

Knoxville
Tioga County

(G-8812)
MSPI ENTERPRISES LLC
Also Called: Bear Paw Hand Cleaner
10726 Route 249 (16928-9692)
PHONE..................814 258-7500
Jeremy Freeman,
EMP: 4
SALES (est): 381.8K **Privately Held**
SIC: 2842 5169 Sanitation preparations, disinfectants & deodorants; specialty cleaning & sanitation preparations

Koppel
Beaver County

(G-8813)
ARA CORPORATION
Also Called: A Ra
5227 Fifth Ave (16136)
PHONE..................724 843-5378
Brian Wisbith, *CEO*
Ronald S Wisbith, *President*
Sue Ellen Wisbith, *Treasurer*
Amy Tyger, *Director*
EMP: 8 EST: 1963
SQ FT: 3,500
SALES: 500K **Privately Held**
SIC: 2752 7311 Commercial printing, offset; advertising consultant

(G-8814)
IPSCO KOPPEL TUBULARS LLC (DH)
Also Called: Tmk-Ipsco
6403 6th Ave (16136)
P.O. Box 750, Beaver Falls (15010-0750)
PHONE..................724 847-6389
David Mitch, *President*
Piotr Galitzine, *Chairman*
Scott Barnes, *Senior VP*
Prasenjit Adhikari, *Vice Pres*
Greg Doll, *Info Tech Mgr*
▲ EMP: 370
SQ FT: 680,000
SALES (est): 230.6MM
SALES (corp-wide): 355.8K **Privately Held**
SIC: 3312 Pipes & tubes

(G-8815)
PENN STATE SPECIAL METALS LLC
7544 State Rte 18 Big Bea (16136)
P.O. Box Q (16136-0617)
PHONE..................724 847-4623
Duane Maietta, *President*
Joseph Hanrahan,
▲ EMP: 28
SQ FT: 156,000
SALES (est): 3.6MM **Privately Held**
WEB: www.pennstatespecialmetals.com
SIC: 3317 Tubes, seamless steel

(G-8816)
SUMMERILL TUBE CORPORATION
220 Franklin St (16136)
PHONE..................724 887-9700
Joseph Handrahan, *President*
EMP: 4
SALES (est): 510K **Privately Held**
SIC: 3312 Tubes, steel & iron

Kreamer
Snyder County

(G-8817)
DEAN W BROUSE & SONS
E Main St (17833)
P.O. Box 65 (17833-0065)
PHONE..................570 374-7695
Dean Brouse, *Owner*
Scott Brouse, *Partner*
William Brouse, *Partner*
EMP: 3
SALES: 200K **Privately Held**
SIC: 2411 Logging

(G-8818)
KREAMER FEED INC
215 Kreamer Ave (17833)
PHONE..................570 374-8148
George W Robinson, *Ch of Bd*
William D Robinson, *President*
Julie Eriksson, *Corp Secy*
Edward G Robinson, *Vice Pres*
Tom Hennessey, *VP Sales*
EMP: 50
SQ FT: 3,000
SALES: 70.6MM **Privately Held**
WEB: www.kreamerfeed.com
SIC: 2048 Prepared feeds

(G-8819)
WOOD-MODE INCORPORATED (PA)
1 Second St (17833-5000)
P.O. Box 250 (17833-0250)
PHONE..................................570 374-2711
Robert L Gronlund, CEO
R Brooks Gronlund, President
Fred Richetta, President
Robert Gessner, General Mgr
Jim Campbell, Editor
▲ EMP: 910
SQ FT: 1,200,000
SALES (est): 1B Privately Held
WEB: www.wood-mode.com
SIC: 2434 Vanities, bathroom: wood

Kresgeville
Monroe County

(G-8820)
CLARK F BURGER INC
Off Rte 534 (18333)
PHONE..................................610 681-4762
Clark F Burger, President
EMP: 6 EST: 1930
SALES (est): 477.3K Privately Held
SIC: 2421 Sawmills & planing mills, general

Kulpmont
Northumberland County

(G-8821)
ALERT ENTERPRISES LTD LBLTY CO
Also Called: Alert Security Service
1109 Maple St (17834-1113)
PHONE..................................570 373-2821
Keith Tamborelli, Principal
EMP: 6
SQ FT: 5,000
SALES (est): 111.6K Privately Held
SIC: 7381 7389 3699 1731 Guard services; ; security control equipment & systems; safety & security specialization; security control equipment & systems

(G-8822)
CHERI-LEE INC
1349 Scott St (17834-1625)
PHONE..................................570 339-4195
Ronald Smith, President
Theresa Smith, Corp Secy
EMP: 8
SALES (est): 1.1MM Privately Held
SIC: 2892 1795 Explosives; demolition, buildings & other structures

Kulpsville
Montgomery County

(G-8823)
ALINE COMPONENTS INC
1830 Tomlinson Rd (19443)
P.O. Box 263 (19443-0263)
PHONE..................................215 368-0300
Harry Davis, President
Mark Davis, Vice Pres
Charles Knaefler, Manager
EMP: 25
SQ FT: 16,500
SALES (est): 4.6MM Privately Held
WEB: www.alinecomponents.com
SIC: 3089 Injection molding of plastics

(G-8824)
BISSINGER AND STEIN INC
1500 Industrial Blvd (19443)
PHONE..................................215 256-1122
Philip C Stein Jr, President
Gary Schuler, Plant Mgr
Manik Vasagar, Chief Engr
Donald Findley, Project Engr
Anthony Maggio, Sales Executive
EMP: 44 EST: 1960
SQ FT: 60,000

SALES (est): 5.8MM Privately Held
SIC: 3599 7692 Machine shop, jobbing & repair; welding repair

(G-8825)
DAVIS TOOL COMPANY
1830 Tomlinson Rd (19443)
P.O. Box 263 (19443-0263)
PHONE..................................215 368-0300
Harry Davis, President
Mark Davis, Vice Pres
EMP: 5
SQ FT: 4,000
SALES: 1MM Privately Held
SIC: 3544 Special dies, tools, jigs & fixtures

(G-8826)
ELEMENTS FOR MOTION LLC
Also Called: E F M
1515 Gehman Rd (19443)
P.O. Box 493, Chalfont (18914-0493)
PHONE..................................215 768-1641
Sam Kromstain, President
▲ EMP: 5 EST: 2012
SALES (est): 408.9K Privately Held
SIC: 2819 Industrial inorganic chemicals

(G-8827)
GREENE TWEED & CO INC (PA)
2075 Detwiler Rd (19443)
PHONE..................................215 256-9521
Felix Paino, CEO
Michael Delfiner, President
Michelle Appleby, Vice Pres
Brent Regan, Vice Pres
Brian Green, Warehouse Mgr
◆ EMP: 629 EST: 1903
SQ FT: 200,000
SALES (est): 280.7MM Privately Held
SIC: 3053 Gaskets & sealing devices

(G-8828)
GRIFFIN SEALING LLC
900 Forty Foot Rd (19443)
PHONE..................................267 328-6600
Carl F Hulfish, Mng Member
Eric Duffy,
Sebastian Marano,
EMP: 8
SQ FT: 30,000
SALES (est): 1.9MM Privately Held
SIC: 3399 Metal fasteners

(G-8829)
GT SERVICES LLC
Also Called: Greene Tweed
1510 Gehman Rd (19443)
PHONE..................................215 256-9521
Felix Paino, Mng Member
Wanda Bonasera, Manager
EMP: 25
SALES (est): 3.5MM Privately Held
SIC: 3083 3533 Thermoplastic laminates: rods, tubes, plates & sheet; gas field machinery & equipment

(G-8830)
HODGSONS QUICK PRINTING
1510 Franklin St (19443)
PHONE..................................215 362-1356
Patricia Allen, Owner
EMP: 3
SQ FT: 720
SALES (est): 200K Privately Held
SIC: 7334 2752 2741 Photocopying & duplicating services; commercial printing, offset; business service newsletters: publishing & printing

(G-8831)
STEIN SEAL COMPANY (PA)
1500 Industrial Blvd (19443)
P.O. Box 316 (19443-0316)
PHONE..................................215 256-0201
Phillip C Stein Jr, President
Robert J Schmal, Vice Pres
Sciutto Steve, Opers Mgr
Gary Schuler, Mfg Mgr
Craig Duvall, Production
◆ EMP: 170 EST: 1970
SQ FT: 40,000

SALES (est): 42.2MM Privately Held
WEB: www.steinseal.com
SIC: 3724 3053 3624 Aircraft engines & engine parts; gaskets & sealing devices; carbon & graphite products

Kunkletown
Monroe County

(G-8832)
D & B SERVICES INC
Fiddletown Rd (18058)
PHONE..................................610 381-2848
Edmund P Dicker, President
Daniel G Bodnar, Treasurer
▲ EMP: 10
SQ FT: 7,600
SALES (est): 940K Privately Held
SIC: 3599 8711 Machine shop, jobbing & repair; consulting engineer

(G-8833)
GETZ PAVING
1038 Scenic Dr (18058-7935)
PHONE..................................570 629-3007
EMP: 7
SALES: 390K Privately Held
SIC: 2951 Mfg Asphalt Mixtures/Blocks

(G-8834)
PATRICK AIELLO CABINETRY LLC
225 Berger St (18058-2665)
PHONE..................................610 681-7167
Patrick Aiello, Principal
EMP: 4
SALES (est): 357.2K Privately Held
SIC: 2434 Wood kitchen cabinets

(G-8835)
STAUFFER CON PDTS & EXCVTG INC
Rr 534 (18058)
PHONE..................................570 629-1977
Leonard J Stauffer, President
Dave Stauffer, Corp Secy
EMP: 4
SQ FT: 4,800
SALES (est): 795.4K Privately Held
SIC: 3272 1794 Septic tanks, concrete; excavation work

Kutztown
Berks County

(G-8836)
BANC TECHNIC INC
Also Called: Firelock Fireproof Vaults
7 Tedway Ave (19530-9080)
PHONE..................................610 756-4440
Hugh Smith, President
Joyce Smith, Corp Secy
Trudy Smith, Corp Secy
EMP: 10
SQ FT: 3,200
SALES: 3MM Privately Held
SIC: 3499 7389 Locks, safe & vault: metal; design services

(G-8837)
COLORFIN LLC
65 Willow St (19530-1535)
P.O. Box 825 (19530-0825)
PHONE..................................484 646-9900
Bernadatte Ward,
Lad Forsline,
▲ EMP: 4
SALES (est): 451.8K Privately Held
SIC: 3952 Lead pencils & art goods

(G-8838)
CRAIG A SCHOLEDICE INC
Also Called: Kutztown Woodworking Company
58 Willow St (19530-1538)
PHONE..................................610 683-8910
Craig Scholedice, President
EMP: 12
SQ FT: 12,000

SALES (est): 1.7MM Privately Held
SIC: 2431 5031 Millwork; millwork

(G-8839)
CRYSTAL CUSTOM KITCHENS INC
755 Crystal Cave Rd (19530-8885)
PHONE..................................610 683-8187
EMP: 3
SQ FT: 4,000
SALES: 300K Privately Held
SIC: 2434 Mfg Custom Wood Cabinets

(G-8840)
EAST PENN MANUFACTURING CO
Kutztown Wire and Cable
191 Willow St (19530)
P.O. Box 147, Lyon Station (19536-0147)
PHONE..................................610 682-6361
George Sproesser, Vice Pres
EMP: 27
SALES (corp-wide): 2.5B Privately Held
WEB: www.eastpenn-deka.com
SIC: 3691 3694 Lead acid batteries (storage batteries); battery cable wiring sets for internal combustion engines
PA: East Penn Manufacturing Co.
102 Deka Rd
Lyon Station PA 19536
610 682-6361

(G-8841)
EAST PENN WELDING INC
110 S Maple St (19530-1523)
PHONE..................................610 682-2290
Barry Moyer, President
Lewis Nolt, General Mgr
Nina Bailey, Manager
EMP: 8
SQ FT: 10,000
SALES (est): 1.4MM Privately Held
SIC: 7692 Welding repair

(G-8842)
EASTERN INDUSTRIES INC
210 Hinterleiter Rd (19530-9262)
PHONE..................................610 683-7400
Jim Holderman, Manager
EMP: 30
SALES (corp-wide): 651.9MM Privately Held
WEB: www.eastern-ind.com
SIC: 1442 5032 Sand mining; paving materials
HQ: Eastern Industries, Inc.
3724 Crescent Ct W 200
Whitehall PA 18052
610 866-0932

(G-8843)
FOLINO ESTATE LLC
Also Called: Folino Estate Winery
340 Old Route 22 (19530-9023)
PHONE..................................484 256-5300
Marco Folino, Principal
Stefano Folino, Principal
EMP: 3
SALES (est): 153.1K Privately Held
SIC: 5812 2084 Italian restaurant; wine cellars, bonded: engaged in blending wines

(G-8844)
HESSIAN CO LTD
Also Called: Faddis Concrete Products
210 Hinterleiter Rd (19530-9262)
PHONE..................................610 683-5464
EMP: 3
SALES (corp-wide): 23MM Privately Held
SIC: 3272 Concrete products
PA: Hessian Co., Ltd.
2206 Horseshoe Pike
Honey Brook PA 19344
610 269-4685

(G-8845)
HESSIAN CO LTD
Also Called: Faddis Concrete Products
210 Hinterleiter Rd (19530-9262)
PHONE..................................610 683-0067
Clarence Mauser, President
EMP: 3

G E O G R A P H I C

SALES (corp-wide): 23MM **Privately Held**
SIC: 3272 Lintels, concrete
PA: Hessian Co., Ltd.
2206 Horseshoe Pike
Honey Brook PA 19344
610 269-4685

(G-8846)
HESSIAN CO LTD
210 Hinterleiter Rd (19530-9262)
PHONE...................................610 683-0067
Clarence Mauser, *Principal*
EMP: 6
SALES (corp-wide): 23MM **Privately Held**
SIC: 3272 Lintels, concrete
PA: Hessian Co., Ltd.
2206 Horseshoe Pike
Honey Brook PA 19344
610 269-4685

(G-8847)
KUTZTOWN BOTTLING WORKS INC
78 S Whiteoak St 80 (19530-1622)
PHONE...................................610 683-7377
Donald Miller, *President*
Audrey Miller, *Corp Secy*
Thomas Miller, *Vice Pres*
EMP: 8
SQ FT: 4,500
SALES (est): 1.6MM **Privately Held**
WEB: www.kutztownbottlingworks.com
SIC: 5181 5921 2086 Beer & other fermented malt liquors; beer (packaged); carbonated beverages, nonalcoholic: bottled & canned

(G-8848)
KUTZTOWN OPTICAL CORP
Also Called: Weinman Eye Center
126 W Main St (19530-1712)
PHONE...................................610 683-5544
Joel B Weinman, *President*
EMP: 3
SQ FT: 970
SALES (est): 346.6K **Privately Held**
SIC: 3851 5995 Lens grinding, except prescription: ophthalmic; optical goods stores

(G-8849)
MCCONWAY & TORLEY LLC
230 Railroad St (19530-1199)
PHONE...................................610 683-7351
Donald Reinard, *Branch Mgr*
EMP: 10
SALES (corp-wide): 1.4B **Publicly Held**
WEB: www.mcconway.com
SIC: 3325 Steel foundries
HQ: Mcconway & Torley, Llc
109 48th St
Pittsburgh PA 15201
412 622-0494

(G-8850)
MULTICELL NORTH INC
240 Broad St (19530-1502)
PHONE...................................610 683-9000
Paul Miller, *President*
Paul F Miller, *President*
Craig Sudderth, *Engineer*
Thomas D Collins, *Treasurer*
Bob Weller, *Maintence Staff*
EMP: 10
SALES (est): 2MM **Privately Held**
WEB: www.multicellpkg.com
SIC: 2653 Boxes, corrugated: made from purchased materials

(G-8851)
NEW ENTERPRISE STONE LIME INC
80 Willow St (19530-1538)
PHONE...................................610 374-5131
Fax: 610 683-6535
EMP: 80
SALES (corp-wide): 651.9MM **Privately Held**
SIC: 2452 2439 5211 Mfg Prefabricated Wood Buildings Mfg Structural Wood Members Ret Lumber/Building Materials
PA: New Enterprise Stone & Lime Co., Inc.
3912 Brumbaugh Rd
New Enterprise PA 16664
814 224-6883

(G-8852)
PALRAM 2000 INC
9735 Commerce Cir (19530-8579)
PHONE...................................610 285-9918
Ron Dvir, *President*
Rico Rojas, *Export Mgr*
Mitchell Stull, *Treasurer*
Lea Kotler, *VP Human Res*
Lahr Phillip, *Natl Sales Mgr*
▲ EMP: 26
SQ FT: 92,000
SALES (est): 17.1MM **Privately Held**
SIC: 2821 Polycarbonate resins
HQ: Paltough Industries (1998) Ltd.
Kibbutz
Ramat Yochanan
484 599-00

(G-8853)
PALRAM AMERICAS INC
Also Called: Palram 2000
9735 Commerce Cir (19530-8579)
PHONE...................................610 285-9918
Yuval Hen, *President*
Roy Rimon, *Managing Dir*
Amon Wirthiem, *Exec VP*
Manuel Liebembuk, *Vice Pres*
John Seiffert, *Vice Pres*
◆ EMP: 71
SQ FT: 92,000
SALES (est): 45.7MM **Privately Held**
WEB: www.palramhort.com
SIC: 2821 Plastics materials & resins
HQ: Palram Israel Ltd.
Kibbutz
Ramat Yochanan
484 599-00

(G-8854)
PALRAM PANELS INC
Also Called: Palram Industries 1990
9735 Commerce Cir (19530-8579)
PHONE...................................610 285-9918
Amon Wirthiem, *President*
Mitchell Stull, *Treasurer*
◆ EMP: 2
SALES (est): 2.5MM **Privately Held**
SIC: 3081 Plastic film & sheet
HQ: Palram U.S.A., Inc.
9741 Commerce Cir
Kutztown PA 19530
610 285-9918

(G-8855)
PINNACLE RIDGE WINERY
407 Old Route 22 (19530-9027)
PHONE...................................610 756-4481
Bradley J Knapp, *Partner*
EMP: 4
SALES (est): 340K **Privately Held**
WEB: www.pinridge.com
SIC: 2084 Wines

(G-8856)
PRINCETON TRADE CONSULTING GRO
Also Called: Cleftstone Works, The
760 Seem Dr (19530-9649)
PHONE...................................610 683-9348
Peter F Galgano, *President*
◆ EMP: 20
SQ FT: 20,000
SALES: 2MM **Privately Held**
SIC: 5032 1411 3281 3253 Granite building stone; dimension stone; cut stone & stone products; ceramic wall & floor tile

(G-8857)
PROCESS MASTERS CORPORATION
940 Krumsville Rd (19530-9175)
PHONE...................................610 683-5674
David Owen, *President*
Naomi Owen, *Admin Sec*
EMP: 6
SALES (est): 1MM **Privately Held**
WEB: www.processmasters.net
SIC: 3589 Swimming pool filter & water conditioning systems

(G-8858)
RADIUS CORPORATION
40 Willow St (19530-1538)
PHONE...................................484 646-9122
Kevin Foley, *President*

◆ EMP: 21
SQ FT: 12,000
SALES (est): 4.1MM **Privately Held**
WEB: www.radiustoothbrush.com
SIC: 3991 3843 Toothbrushes, except electric; dental equipment & supplies

(G-8859)
RODALE INSTITUTE (PA)
611 Siegfriedale Rd (19530-9749)
PHONE...................................610 683-6009
Rosalba Messina, *CEO*
Judy Kuhns, *Production*
Hannah Pechter, *Sales Staff*
EMP: 42
SQ FT: 2,000
SALES: 4.3MM **Privately Held**
WEB: www.kidsregen.com
SIC: 8733 2731 2721 Educational research agency; research institute; books: publishing & printing; magazines: publishing & printing

(G-8860)
SAW ROCKING HORSE
Also Called: Saw Horse Woodworking
83 Sieger Rd (19530-8858)
PHONE...................................610 683-8075
Michael Campanelli, *Owner*
EMP: 3 EST: 1979
SALES: 150K **Privately Held**
SIC: 2511 Chairs, household, except upholstered: wood; tables, household: wood; desks, household: wood

(G-8861)
SORRELLI INC
Also Called: Sorrelli Jewelry Co
125 W Main St (19530-1711)
PHONE...................................610 894-9857
Lisa Oswald, *President*
Kermit Oswald, *Vice Pres*
▲ EMP: 15
SQ FT: 3,800
SALES: 1.5MM **Privately Held**
WEB: www.sorrelli.com
SIC: 3961 Costume jewelry

(G-8862)
SUNTUF 2000 INC
9735 Commerce Cir (19530-8579)
PHONE...................................610 285-6968
Arnon Eshed, *CEO*
EMP: 4
SALES (est): 213.7K **Privately Held**
SIC: 3089 Plastics products

(G-8863)
WILLIAM LAMMERS
Also Called: Lammers Micro Drill
973 Saucony Rd (19530-8907)
PHONE...................................610 894-9502
William Lammers, *Owner*
EMP: 3
SQ FT: 4,000
SALES (est): 190K **Privately Held**
SIC: 3545 Precision tools, machinists'

(G-8864)
XODE INC
15519 Kutztown Rd (19530-9743)
PHONE...................................610 683-8777
J M Seitzinger, *CEO*
J J Tkach, *President*
Mary Ann Seitzinger, *Corp Secy*
Pete Sietzinger, *Vice Pres*
EMP: 25
SQ FT: 25,000
SALES (est): 14.2MM **Privately Held**
WEB: www.xode.com
SIC: 5085 2672 Adhesives, tape & plasters; labels (unprinted), gummed: made from purchased materials

Kylertown
Clearfield County

(G-8865)
H & B ENTERPRISES INC
Also Called: HB Hardware
Int 80 Exit 21 St I (16847)
P.O. Box 66 (16847-0066)
PHONE...................................814 345-6416

Dennis Diviney, *Principal*
Janet Larson, *Principal*
Allen Larson, *Vice Pres*
EMP: 8
SALES (est): 1MM **Privately Held**
WEB: www.hbenterprises.com
SIC: 3429 Manufactured hardware (general)

(G-8866)
LARSON ENTERPRISES INC
Larson Rd (16847)
P.O. Box 96 (16847-0096)
PHONE...................................814 345-5101
Roger Larson, *President*
Alan Larson, *Corp Secy*
EMP: 12
SALES (est): 675.6K **Privately Held**
WEB: www.larsonenterprises.com
SIC: 1221 Strip mining, bituminous

(G-8867)
RIVER HILL COAL CO INC (PA)
S Second St (16847)
PHONE...................................814 345-5642
Harry Hanchar, *President*
EMP: 70
SQ FT: 2,500
SALES (est): 12.6MM **Privately Held**
SIC: 1221 Strip mining, bituminous

(G-8868)
W W ENGINE AND SUPPLY INC (PA)
Also Called: Shaw Mack Sales & Service-Div
Old Route 53 (16847)
P.O. Box 68 (16847-0068)
PHONE...................................814 345-5693
John P Niebauer Jr, *President*
Diane Niebauer, *Corp Secy*
EMP: 30
SQ FT: 28,000
SALES (est): 59.5MM **Privately Held**
SIC: 5084 3519 3714 5012 Engines & parts, air-cooled; internal combustion engines; motor vehicle parts & accessories; trucks, noncommercial; trucks, commercial; engine repair & replacement, non-automotive; automobiles, new & used

La Plume
Lackawanna County

(G-8869)
DARLINGS LOCKER PLANT
Also Called: La Plume Country Market
And 11 Rr 6 (18440)
P.O. Box 1 (18440-0001)
PHONE...................................570 945-5716
Howard Darling, *Owner*
EMP: 6
SQ FT: 10,000
SALES (est): 367K **Privately Held**
SIC: 2011 5411 Meat packing plants; grocery stores, independent

Laceyville
Wyoming County

(G-8870)
BRICKHOUSE SERVICES
2 Main St (18623)
PHONE...................................570 869-1871
Richard N Sherman, *Owner*
EMP: 3
SQ FT: 6,000
SALES (est): 508.1K **Privately Held**
SIC: 3524 5251 7539 5945 Lawn & garden equipment; hardware; alternators & generators, rebuilding & repair; toys & games; toiletries, cosmetics & perfumes

(G-8871)
J & E FLAGSTONE
2512 Whitney Rd (18623-7814)
PHONE...................................570 869-2718
Elaine Helvig, *Partner*
John Helvig, *Partner*
EMP: 14

SALES (est): 1.1MM **Privately Held**
SIC: **1411** Bluestone, dimension-quarrying; flagstone mining

(G-8872)
LACEYVILLE LUMBER INC
227 Main St (18623-6709)
PHONE................................570 869-1212
Elwood Sickler, *President*
EMP: 5
SALES (est): 1.5MM **Privately Held**
SIC: **2421** Building & structural materials, wood

(G-8873)
PICKETT QUARRIES INC
167 River Ln (18623-6731)
PHONE................................570 869-1817
William C Pickett, *Principal*
EMP: 3
SALES (est): 150.1K **Privately Held**
SIC: **1422** Crushed & broken limestone

(G-8874)
ROMAX HOSE INC
Rr 367 (18623)
PHONE................................570 869-0860
Emil J Wirth, *President*
EMP: 17
SALES (est): 661.9K **Privately Held**
SIC: **3083** Thermoplastic laminates: rods, tubes, plates & sheet

(G-8875)
WEMCO INC
3087 State Route 367 (18623-7791)
PHONE................................570 869-9660
Emil J Wirth, *President*
Redelle Wirth, *Corp Secy*
EMP: 15
SQ FT: 3,000
SALES (est): 1.3MM **Privately Held**
SIC: **3542** Sheet metalworking machines

Lackawaxen
Pike County

(G-8876)
QUARRY MANAGEMENT LLC
237 Masthope Plank Rd (18435-9791)
PHONE................................646 599-5893
Steven Carusso, *Mng Member*
Joshua Abramson,
EMP: 10
SQ FT: 5,000
SALES: 8MM **Privately Held**
SIC: **1422** Cement rock, crushed & broken-quarrying

Lafayette Hill
Montgomery County

(G-8877)
BOEING COMPANY
853 Hamilton Dr (19444-1746)
PHONE................................610 828-7764
Kevin Allen, *General Mgr*
EMP: 80
SALES (corp-wide): 101.1B **Publicly Held**
SIC: **3721** Aircraft
PA: The Boeing Company
100 N Riverside Plz
Chicago IL 60606
312 544-2000

(G-8878)
DIXON-SAUNDERS ENTERPRISES
Also Called: Dixon-Saunders Printing
4504 Briar Hl W (19444-1024)
PHONE................................215 335-2150
Morton T Saunders, *President*
Deirdre Saunders, *Corp Secy*
Barbara Feeney, *Vice Pres*
EMP: 7
SALES: 500K **Privately Held**
SIC: **2752** Lithographing on metal; commercial printing, offset

(G-8879)
EDWARD C RINCK ASSOCIATES INC
462 Germantown Pike Ste 5 (19444-1818)
PHONE................................610 397-1727
Edward Rinck, *President*
Eileen Rinck, *Admin Sec*
▲ EMP: 2
SQ FT: 700
SALES (est): 4.5MM **Privately Held**
SIC: **3331** Refined primary copper products

(G-8880)
FLEXIBLE INFORMATICS LLC
600 Germantown Pike B (19444-1800)
PHONE................................215 253-8765
Craig Scott, *President*
Jeremy Ke, *Software Engr*
Evan Bellinger,
Jonathan Bishop,
Kevin Duffy,
EMP: 5
SALES (est): 261.7K **Privately Held**
SIC: **7371 7372** Custom computer programming services; business oriented computer software

(G-8881)
JAY WEISS CORPORATION
Also Called: Marc Publishing Company
600 Germantown Pike Ste 1 (19444-1800)
PHONE................................610 834-8585
Jay Weiss, *President*
Sandra Weiss, *Corp Secy*
EMP: 4 EST: 1960
SQ FT: 1,500
SALES (est): 438.3K **Privately Held**
WEB: www.marcpub.com
SIC: **7331 2741** Mailing list brokers; directories, telephone: publishing & printing

(G-8882)
JERRY JAMES TRDNG AS MNLS BSC
Also Called: Manuals-Basic Business Forms
4104 Fountain Green Rd (19444-1203)
PHONE................................425 255-0199
Jerome Gaines, *Owner*
EMP: 5 EST: 1962
SALES: 350K **Privately Held**
SIC: **2621 5112 5045 2759** Business form paper; business forms; computers, peripherals & software; computer software; commercial printing; management consulting services; real estate consultant; brokers' services

(G-8883)
JOSEPH LEE & SON INC
38 Scarlet Oak Dr (19444-2423)
PHONE................................610 825-1944
Irving Lee, *President*
Sharon Lee, *Corp Secy*
EMP: 6 EST: 1902
SQ FT: 10,000
SALES (est): 440K **Privately Held**
SIC: **3446** Ornamental metalwork

(G-8884)
RJJ WAYNE LLC
9223 Eagleview Dr (19444-1740)
PHONE................................215 796-1935
John Thain,
Bob Bauer,
Jason Klotkowski,
EMP: 5
SALES (est): 190K **Privately Held**
SIC: **2052** Cones, ice cream

Lahaska
Bucks County

(G-8885)
OAKLAWN METAL CRAFT SHOP INC
Also Called: David John Metal Artisan
5752 York Rd (18931)
P.O. Box 13 (18931-0013)
PHONE................................215 794-7387
David B John, *President*
EMP: 5

SQ FT: 3,750
SALES: 350K **Privately Held**
SIC: **3645** Residential lighting fixtures

Lairdsville
Lycoming County

(G-8886)
BIG BEAR CONCRETE WORKS
213 Mill Ln (17742)
P.O. Box 7 (17742-0007)
PHONE................................570 584-0107
EMP: 5
SQ FT: 9,000
SALES: 400K **Privately Held**
SIC: **3272** Mfg Architectural Precast Concrete Products

Lake Ariel
Wayne County

(G-8887)
ADVANCED AUTOMATED CONTROLS CO
Also Called: Advanced Automated Contrls Inc
473 Easton Tpke (18436-4716)
PHONE................................570 842-5842
John M Kernoschak, *President*
EMP: 17
SALES (est): 4.8MM
SALES (corp-wide): 549.3MM **Privately Held**
SIC: **3823** Programmers, process type
HQ: Bearing Distributors, Inc.
8000 Hub Pkwy
Cleveland OH 44125
216 642-9100

(G-8888)
FOTO-WEAR INC (PA)
473 Easton Tpke Ste D (18436-4716)
PHONE................................570 307-3600
Bob Rozema, *President*
Devin Blizzard, *Principal*
Donald Hare, *Chairman*
Paul Jetter, *Senior VP*
Mark Sawchak, *Vice Pres*
EMP: 6
SQ FT: 5,000
SALES (est): 456.5K **Privately Held**
WEB: www.fotowear.com
SIC: **2678** Stationery products

(G-8889)
K J SHAFFER MILLED PRODUCTS
Also Called: Lake Ariel Wood Products
136 Wallace Rd (18436-4901)
PHONE................................570 698-8650
Greg Cutler, *President*
Jerry Strackbein, *Vice Pres*
EMP: 15
SALES (est): 1.2MM **Privately Held**
SIC: **2411** Logging camps & contractors

(G-8890)
R J S WOOD PRODUCTS INC
308 Sawmill Rd (18436-3352)
PHONE................................570 689-7630
Roger Shaffer, *President*
EMP: 6
SQ FT: 25,000
SALES: 150K **Privately Held**
SIC: **2421** Lumber: rough, sawed or planed

(G-8891)
RUBY CUSTOM WOODCRAFT INC
138 Deacon Hill Rd (18436-4211)
PHONE................................570 698-7741
John J Ruby III, *President*
EMP: 3
SQ FT: 25,000
SALES: 100K **Privately Held**
SIC: **2541 2511** Bar fixtures, wood; cabinets, lockers & shelving; wood household furniture

(G-8892)
SPRING HILL LASER SERVICES
6 Industrial Park Rd A (18436-5618)
P.O. Box 79, Sterling (18463-0079)
PHONE................................570 689-0970
Jeff Kulick, *President*
Charlie Childress, *President*
Jeffrey Kulick, *Vice Pres*
Charlie Shinert, *Vice Pres*
EMP: 30
SQ FT: 22,000
SALES (est): 4.1MM **Privately Held**
WEB: www.springhilllaser.com
SIC: **2759** Laser printing

(G-8893)
STEVE A VITELLI
Also Called: American Molding
347 Tisdel Rd (18436-4113)
PHONE................................570 937-4546
Steve A Vitelli, *Owner*
EMP: 3
SALES: 150K **Privately Held**
SIC: **2499** Picture frame molding, finished

(G-8894)
TEAM BIONDI LLC
248 Easton Tpke (18436-4792)
PHONE................................570 503-7087
Michael Biondi, *Mng Member*
EMP: 28
SQ FT: 3,200
SALES (est): 400MM **Privately Held**
SIC: **3537** Trucks, tractors, loaders, carriers & similar equipment

(G-8895)
UNIVERSAL GLASS CNSTR INC
95 Purdytown Tpke (18436-9391)
P.O. Box 44 (18436-0044)
PHONE................................570 390-4900
Dennis Eisloeffer, *Principal*
EMP: 9
SALES (est): 865.1K **Privately Held**
SIC: **3211** Construction glass

(G-8896)
WATT ENTERPRISES INC
1117 Easton Tpke (18436-4843)
P.O. Box 185 (18436-0185)
PHONE................................570 698-8081
Stephen Watt, *President*
EMP: 6
SALES (est): 951.6K **Privately Held**
SIC: **3444** Sheet metalwork

Lake City
Erie County

(G-8897)
ALLEGHENY WOOD WORKS INC
10003 Railroad St (16423-1414)
PHONE................................814 774-7338
David Haag, *President*
Stefan Kraus, *Vice Pres*
James Steigerwald, *Vice Pres*
EMP: 30 EST: 1997
SQ FT: 90,000
SALES (est): 4.4MM **Privately Held**
SIC: **2431** Doors, wood

(G-8898)
CARON ENTERPRISES INC
2700 Mechanic St (16423-2023)
PHONE................................814 774-5658
Ronald D Greer, *President*
Carol Greer, *Admin Sec*
EMP: 475
SQ FT: 30,000
SALES (est): 42MM
SALES (corp-wide): 208.8MM **Privately Held**
WEB: www.caronenterprises.com
SIC: **3679** Electronic circuits
PA: Airborn Interconnect, Inc.
3500 Airborn Cir
Georgetown TX 78626
512 863-5585

GEOGRAPHIC

(G-8899)
ENGINEERED PLASTICS LLC (PA)
1040 Maple Ave (16423-2528)
PHONE...................................814 774-2970
Kurt Duska, *President*
Terry Maloney,
▲ **EMP:** 60
SQ FT: 62,000
SALES (est): 24.8MM **Privately Held**
WEB: www.engineeredplastics.com
SIC: 3089 Injection molding of plastics

(G-8900)
GOOD IDEAS INC
10047 Keystone Dr (16423-1061)
P.O. Box 299, Girard (16417-0299)
PHONE...................................814 774-8231
Gregory A Cronkhite, *President*
Cary Quigley, *Vice Pres*
Ross Smith, *Info Tech Mgr*
▲ **EMP:** 38 **EST:** 2001
SQ FT: 100,000
SALES (est): 7.4MM **Privately Held**
SIC: 3524 Lawn & garden equipment

(G-8901)
GREAT LAKES AUTOMTN SVCS INC
Also Called: Clifton Machining Division
9937 Sampson Ave (16423-1543)
PHONE...................................814 774-3144
EMP: 15
SALES (corp-wide): 12MM **Privately Held**
SIC: 3599 Crankshafts & camshafts, machining
PA: Great Lakes Automation Services, Inc.
8835 Walmer Dr
Mc Kean PA 16426
814 476-7710

(G-8902)
LAKE CITY POWER SYSTEMS LLC
2170 Rice Ave (16423-1533)
PHONE...................................814 774-2034
John Baldwin, *Mng Member*
EMP: 7
SALES (est): 990.2K **Privately Held**
SIC: 3621 5063 Motors & generators; electrical apparatus & equipment

(G-8903)
LAKE CY MANUFACTURED HSING INC (PA)
10068 Keystone Dr (16423-1060)
PHONE...................................814 774-2033
Gerald R Garity, *President*
Geoffery G Garity, *Vice Pres*
Linda Garity, *Treasurer*
EMP: 25
SQ FT: 13,000
SALES (est): 10.1MM **Privately Held**
WEB: www.lakecityhomes.com
SIC: 2452 Modular homes, prefabricated, wood

(G-8904)
LENNYS MACHINE COMPANY
10047 Keystone Dr 200 (16423-1061)
P.O. Box 107, Fairview (16415-0107)
PHONE...................................814 490-4407
Leonard Stahlman, *Owner*
EMP: 3
SALES (est): 200K **Privately Held**
SIC: 3599 Machine shop, jobbing & repair

(G-8905)
MAPLE DONUTS INC
Also Called: Maple Donuts Erie
10307 Hall Ave (16423-1226)
P.O. Box 327, Girard (16417-0327)
PHONE...................................814 774-3131
Nathanial Burnside, *Branch Mgr*
EMP: 100
SALES (corp-wide): 83.9MM **Privately Held**
WEB: www.mapledonuts.com
SIC: 2051 5461 Doughnuts, except frozen; bakeries
PA: Maple Donuts, Inc.
3455 E Market St
York PA 17402
717 757-7826

(G-8906)
NORTH COAST TOOL INC
9843 Martin Ave (16423-1526)
PHONE...................................814 836-7685
Dale Rapela, *President*
Terrance Amon, *Vice Pres*
Eric Rapela, *Vice Pres*
Diane Rapela, *Treasurer*
▲ **EMP:** 17
SQ FT: 32,000
SALES (est): 3MM **Privately Held**
WEB: www.nctm.com
SIC: 3544 Special dies, tools, jigs & fixtures

(G-8907)
NORTHWESTERN WELDING & MCH CO
Also Called: Northwestern Manufacturing
9704 Martin Ave (16423-1523)
PHONE...................................814 774-2866
Kevin C Cashdollar, *President*
Justin Cashdollar, *Vice Pres*
Mollie Bennett, *Corp Comm Staff*
EMP: 8
SQ FT: 5,000
SALES (est): 1.9MM **Privately Held**
WEB: www.nwwelding.com
SIC: 3599 7699 3441 Machine shop, jobbing & repair; metal reshaping & replating services; fabricated structural metal

(G-8908)
STERLING TECHNOLOGIES INC
10047 Keystone Dr (16423-1061)
PHONE...................................814 774-2500
Gregory Cronkhite, *CEO*
Cary P Quigley, *President*
Tony Montefiori, *Plant Mgr*
Doug Walker, *Prdtn Mgr*
Michael Moats, *Warehouse Mgr*
▲ **EMP:** 103 **EST:** 1997
SQ FT: 24,000
SALES (est): 9.3MM **Privately Held**
WEB: www.sterlingtechinc.com
SIC: 3089 Injection molding of plastics

(G-8909)
VAN AIR INC (PA)
2950 Mechanic St (16423-2023)
PHONE...................................814 774-2631
James A Currie Jr, *President*
Steve Fenner, *Electrical Engi*
Mark J Sunseri, *CFO*
Tom Vignolini, *Cust Mgr*
Mike Caldwell, *Sales Staff*
◆ **EMP:** 49 **EST:** 1944
SQ FT: 8,000
SALES (est): 16MM **Privately Held**
WEB: www.vanairsystems.com
SIC: 3563 3669 3433 2819 Air & gas compressors; smoke detectors; heating equipment, except electric; industrial inorganic chemicals

(G-8910)
VANICEK PRECISION MACHINING CO
9192 Middle Rd (16423-2120)
PHONE...................................814 774-9012
Robert Vanicek, *Owner*
EMP: 7
SQ FT: 4,200
SALES (est): 430K **Privately Held**
WEB: www.bvprecisionmach.com
SIC: 3544 Forms (molds), for foundry & plastics working machinery

(G-8911)
YORK-SEAWAY INDUS PDTS INC
9843 Martin Ave (16423-1526)
PHONE...................................814 774-7080
Rick R York, *President*
Rick York, *President*
Janet York, *Corp Secy*
EMP: 76
SALES (est): 13.8MM **Privately Held**
WEB: www.seawayindustrial.com
SIC: 3599 Machine shop, jobbing & repair

Lake Winola
Wyoming County

(G-8912)
TURNER TOOL & DIE INC
Orchard Dr (18625)
PHONE...................................570 378-3233
John Turner, *President*
Sanford Vanderveken, *Partner*
EMP: 10
SQ FT: 3,500
SALES (est): 1.3MM **Privately Held**
SIC: 3544 Special dies & tools

Lakeville
Wayne County

(G-8913)
SCULPTED ICE WORKS INC
311 Purdytown Tpke (18438-4005)
PHONE...................................570 226-6246
Mark S Crouthamel, *President*
EMP: 14
SALES (est): 1.7MM **Privately Held**
WEB: www.icework.net
SIC: 3299 5999 2097 Architectural sculptures: gypsum, clay, papier mache, etc.; ice; block ice

(G-8914)
SUPREME ZIPPER INDUSTRIES
1076 Purdytown Tpke (18438-4021)
PHONE...................................570 226-9501
Jim Zumpone, *Principal*
▲ **EMP:** 3
SALES (est): 260.2K **Privately Held**
SIC: 3999 5131 Manufacturing industries; zippers

Lakewood
Wayne County

(G-8915)
MASTERS CONCRETE
Main St (18439)
P.O. Box 25, Kingsley (18826-0025)
PHONE...................................570 798-2680
Richard Masters, *President*
EMP: 40
SALES (est): 5MM **Privately Held**
WEB: www.mastersconcrete.com
SIC: 3273 Ready-mixed concrete

(G-8916)
WC WELDING SERVICES
162 Beaver Hollow Rd (18439-4062)
PHONE...................................570 798-2300
Wes Carnes, *Principal*
EMP: 4
SALES (est): 626.8K **Privately Held**
SIC: 3533 Oil & gas field machinery

Lampeter
Lancaster County

(G-8917)
EXIDE TECHNOLOGIES
829 Paramount Ave (17537)
P.O. Box 427 (17537-0427)
PHONE...................................717 464-2721
William Hozza, *General Mgr*
Mark Bosworth, *Manager*
EMP: 220
SALES (corp-wide): 2.4B **Privately Held**
WEB: www.exideworld.com
SIC: 3691 3629 Lead acid batteries (storage batteries); battery chargers, rectifying or nonrotating
PA: Exide Technologies
13000 Deerfield Pkwy # 200
Milton GA 30004
678 566-9000

Lancaster
Lancaster County

(G-8918)
A H EMERY COMPANY
Also Called: Pennsylvania Scale Co
665 N Reservoir St (17602-2140)
PHONE...................................717 295-6935
William Fischer, *Branch Mgr*
EMP: 11
SALES (corp-wide): 14MM **Privately Held**
SIC: 3596 Industrial scales
PA: The A H Emery Company
73 Cogwheel Ln
Seymour CT 06483
203 881-9333

(G-8919)
AAVID THERMACORE INC (DH)
780 Eden Rd Ofc (17601-4276)
PHONE...................................717 569-6551
Jerome Toth, *President*
Gernert Nelson, *President*
James Rothenberger, *CFO*
Kevin Lynn, *Manager*
▲ **EMP:** 168
SQ FT: 50,000
SALES (est): 37.3MM
SALES (corp-wide): 1B **Privately Held**
WEB: www.thermacore.com
SIC: 3999 8731 Heating pads, nonelectric; commercial physical research
HQ: Aavid Thermalloy, Llc
1 Aavid Cir
Laconia NH 03246
603 528-3400

(G-8920)
ABACUS SURFACES INC
2330 Dairy Rd (17601-2308)
PHONE...................................717 560-8050
Susan Proud, *CEO*
EMP: 16
SALES (est): 1.6MM **Privately Held**
WEB: www.abacussurfaces.com
SIC: 3069 Flooring, rubber: tile or sheet

(G-8921)
ADVANCED COOLING TECH INC
Also Called: Act
1046 New Holland Ave (17601-5606)
PHONE...................................717 208-2612
Zhijun Zuo, *President*
Jon Zuo, *President*
Diane Baldassarre, *Business Mgr*
Scott D Garner, *Vice Pres*
Mohammed Ababneh, *Research*
EMP: 100
SALES (est): 18.8MM **Privately Held**
WEB: www.1-act.com
SIC: 3433 8731 Heating equipment, except electric; commercial physical research

(G-8922)
AHF HOLDING INC (PA)
2500 Columbia Ave (17603-4117)
PHONE...................................800 233-3823
EMP: 0
SALES (est): 34.1MM **Privately Held**
SIC: 6719 3996 Investment holding companies, except banks; hard surface floor coverings

(G-8923)
AHF PRODUCTS LLC
Also Called: Armstrong Flooring
2500 Columbia Ave (17603-4117)
P.O. Box 3001 (17604-3001)
PHONE...................................800 233-3823
Frank J Ready, *CEO*
Howard J Maymon, *Vice Pres*
Jeff Steed, *CFO*
Thomas Waters, *Treasurer*
Robert J Sandkuhler, *Admin Sec*
◆ **EMP:** 1700
SQ FT: 60,000
SALES (est): 206.7MM
SALES (corp-wide): 34.1MM **Privately Held**
WEB: www.trianglepacific.com
SIC: 2426 Flooring, hardwood

PA: Ahf Holding, Inc.
2500 Columbia Ave
Lancaster PA 17603
800 233-3823

(G-8924)
AIN PLASTICS
499 Running Pump Rd # 116 (17601-2225)
PHONE...................................717 291-9300
Terry Tewel, *General Mgr*
EMP: 9
SALES (est): 1.1MM **Privately Held**
SIC: 3089 Injection molding of plastics

(G-8925)
AIR PRODUCTS AND CHEMICALS INC
3250 Hempland Rd (17601-1314)
PHONE...................................717 291-1617
Barry Van Leer, *Manager*
EMP: 60
SALES (corp-wide): 8.9B **Publicly Held**
WEB: www.airproducts.com
SIC: 2813 Nitrogen; oxygen, compressed or liquefied
PA: Air Products And Chemicals, Inc.
7201 Hamilton Blvd
Allentown PA 18195
610 481-4911

(G-8926)
ALCOA N AMERCN ROLLED PROUDCTS
1480 Manheim Pike (17601-3152)
PHONE...................................717 393-9641
Brenda Martin, *CEO*
EMP: 5
SALES (est): 358.2K **Privately Held**
SIC: 3353 Aluminum sheet, plate & foil

(G-8927)
ALFRED AND SAM ITALIAN BAKERY
17 Fairview Ave (17603-5512)
PHONE...................................717 392-6311
Salvatore Borsellino, *President*
EMP: 11
SQ FT: 8,000
SALES (est): 810K **Privately Held**
SIC: 2051 Breads, rolls & buns

(G-8928)
ALL AMERICA THREADED PDTS INC
731 Martha Ave (17601-4560)
PHONE...................................317 921-3000
L G Broderick, *President*
EMP: 74 **Privately Held**
SIC: 3452 5085 Bolts, nuts, rivets & washers; industrial supplies
HQ: All America Threaded Products, Inc.
4661 N Monaco St
Denver CO 80216

(G-8929)
ALLEGRA PRINT & IMAGING
Also Called: Allegra Print & Imaging no.233
1770 Hempstead Rd (17601-6706)
P.O. Box 11027 (17605-1027)
PHONE...................................717 397-3440
Joyce Meyers, *Owner*
EMP: 20
SQ FT: 8,000
SALES (est): 2.1MM **Privately Held**
WEB: www.allegrapa.com
SIC: 2752 Commercial printing, offset

(G-8930)
ALUMAX MILL PRODUCTS INC
1480 Manheim Pike (17601-3152)
PHONE...................................717 393-9641
Brenda Martin, *President*
◆ **EMP:** 22
SQ FT: 6,686
SALES (est): 5.5MM
SALES (corp-wide): 14B **Publicly Held**
SIC: 3353 Aluminum sheet & strip
HQ: Alumax Llc
201 Isabella St
Pittsburgh PA 15212
412 553-4545

(G-8931)
AMERICAN PERIOD LIGHTING INC
Also Called: Salt Box, The
118 Weaver Rd (17603-9709)
PHONE...................................717 392-5649
Jack Cunningham, *President*
EMP: 3
SALES (est): 455.1K **Privately Held**
SIC: 3645 3646 5719 5063 Lamp shades, metal; light shades, metal; ornamental lighting fixtures, commercial; lighting fixtures; lighting fixtures, residential; lighting fixtures, commercial & industrial

(G-8932)
AMES CONSTRUCTION INC
351 Sprecher Rd (17603-9462)
PHONE...................................717 299-1395
Gerry Breneman, *Branch Mgr*
EMP: 30
SALES (corp-wide): 23MM **Privately Held**
SIC: 1542 2541 2517 2511 Commercial & office building, new construction; commercial & office buildings, renovation & repair; wood partitions & fixtures; wood television & radio cabinets; wood household furniture; wood kitchen cabinets
PA: Ames Construction, Inc.
826 E Main St
Ephrata PA 17522
717 733-4141

(G-8933)
AMETEK INC
Hamilton Precision Metals
1780 Rohrerstown Rd (17601-2320)
PHONE...................................717 569-7061
Barry A Brandt, *Division Pres*
EMP: 85
SALES (corp-wide): 4.8B **Publicly Held**
SIC: 3621 Motors & generators
PA: Ametek, Inc.
1100 Cassatt Rd
Berwyn PA 19312
610 647-2121

(G-8934)
ANDREW W NISSLY INC
544 W Mill Ave (17603-3426)
P.O. Box 633 (17608-0633)
PHONE...................................717 393-3841
Andrew W Nissly, *President*
EMP: 5 **EST:** 1935
SQ FT: 18,000
SALES (est): 340K **Privately Held**
SIC: 3479 3993 3552 Enameling, including porcelain, of metal products; signs & advertising specialties; silk screens for textile industry

(G-8935)
APP-TECHS CORPORATION
505 Willow Ln (17601-5624)
PHONE...................................717 735-0848
Daniel Fritsch, *President*
Nancy Beauregard, *Sales Staff*
Jenny Romanosky, *Sales Staff*
EMP: 10
SQ FT: 16,000
SALES: 1.8MM **Privately Held**
WEB: www.app-techs.com
SIC: 7382 7373 3663 Security systems services; systems software development services; radio & TV communications equipment

(G-8936)
APPLE BELTING COMPANY
3501 Hempland Rd (17601-1319)
PHONE...................................717 293-8903
Barry Hershey, *Administration*
EMP: 8
SQ FT: 7,000
SALES (est): 577.4K
SALES (corp-wide): 39.5MM **Privately Held**
WEB: www.transply.com
SIC: 3496 Conveyor belts; fabrics, woven wire
PA: Transply, Inc.
1005 Vogelsong Rd
York PA 17404
717 767-1005

(G-8937)
ARCOBALENO LLC
160 Greenfield Rd (17601-5815)
PHONE...................................717 394-1402
Maja Adiletta, *Vice Pres*
Antonio Adeletta,
▲ **EMP:** 15
SQ FT: 30,000
SALES: 3.8MM **Privately Held**
SIC: 3556 Pasta machinery; bakery machinery

(G-8938)
ARCONIC INC
Also Called: Alcoa
1480 Manheim Pike (17601-3152)
P.O. Box 3167 (17604-3167)
PHONE...................................717 393-9641
John Nied, *Opers Mgr*
Russel Gwynne, *Branch Mgr*
EMP: 135
SALES (corp-wide): 14B **Publicly Held**
SIC: 3353 3444 Aluminum sheet & strip; sheet metalwork
PA: Arconic Inc.
390 Park Ave Fl 12
New York NY 10022
212 836-2758

(G-8939)
ARMA CO LLC
1048 New Holland Ave (17601-5606)
PHONE...................................717 295-6805
Richard Armellino,
EMP: 20
SALES (est): 2.5MM **Privately Held**
SIC: 3842 Bulletproof vests

(G-8940)
ARMSTRONG FLOORING INC (PA)
Also Called: AFI
2500 Columbia Ave (17603-4117)
P.O. Box 3025 (17604-3025)
PHONE...................................717 672-9611
Larry S McWilliams, *Ch of Bd*
Donald R Maier, *President*
John C Bassett, *Senior VP*
Douglas B Bingham, *CFO*
Christopher S Parisi, *Ch Credit Ofcr*
EMP: 1596 **EST:** 1891
SALES: 728.2MM **Publicly Held**
SIC: 3996 2426 Hard surface floor coverings; hardwood dimension & flooring mills; flooring, hardwood

(G-8941)
ARMSTRONG HARDWOOD FLOORING CO
Also Called: Armstrong Flooring
2500 Columbia Ave (17603-4117)
P.O. Box 3001 (17604-3001)
PHONE...................................717 672-9611
Donald Maier, *President*
Charles J Wilson, *Vice Pres*
Douglas Bingham, *Treasurer*
Christopher S Parisi, *Admin Sec*
▲ **EMP:** 955 **EST:** 1946
SALES (est): 202.8MM
SALES (corp-wide): 728.2MM **Publicly Held**
SIC: 2426 Flooring, hardwood; parquet flooring, hardwood
PA: Armstrong Flooring, Inc.
2500 Columbia Ave
Lancaster PA 17603
717 672-9611

(G-8942)
ARMSTRONG WORLD INDUSTRIES INC (PA)
2500 Columbia Ave (17603-4117)
P.O. Box 3001 (17604-3001)
PHONE...................................717 397-0611
Victor D Grizzle, *President*
Greg Estabrook, *General Mgr*
Ellen R Romano, *Senior VP*
Beverley Doody, *Vice Pres*
Donald F Martin, *Vice Pres*
EMP: 1000 **EST:** 1891
SALES: 975.3MM **Publicly Held**
WEB: www.armstrong.com
SIC: 3646 3296 Ceiling systems, luminous; acoustical board & tile, mineral wool

(G-8943)
ART CRAFT CABINETS INC
720 Lafayette St (17603-5515)
PHONE...................................717 397-7817
Richard E Artz, *President*
Judith W Artz, *Admin Sec*
EMP: 4
SQ FT: 2,300
SALES: 500K **Privately Held**
SIC: 2434 Vanities, bathroom: wood

(G-8944)
ART RESEARCH ENTERPRISES
3050 Industry Dr (17603-4024)
PHONE...................................717 290-1303
Becky Ault, *President*
Mike Cunningham, *Vice Pres*
EMP: 30
SQ FT: 30,000
SALES (est): 7MM **Privately Held**
WEB: www.thinksculpture.com
SIC: 3366 8999 Castings (except die): bronze; art restoration

(G-8945)
ASM INDUSTRIES INC (HQ)
Also Called: Pacer Pumps
41 Industrial Cir (17601-5927)
PHONE...................................717 656-2161
Jack H Berg, *President*
Carole L Berg, *Corp Secy*
◆ **EMP:** 2
SQ FT: 50,000
SALES (est): 18.1MM
SALES (corp-wide): 62.5MM **Privately Held**
SIC: 3561 Industrial pumps & parts
PA: Service Filtration Corp.
2900 Macarthur Blvd
Northbrook IL 60062
847 509-2900

(G-8946)
ASM INDUSTRIES INC
Pacer Pumps
41 Industrial Cir (17601-5927)
PHONE...................................717 656-2161
Jack H Berg, *Branch Mgr*
EMP: 50
SALES (corp-wide): 62.5MM **Privately Held**
SIC: 3561 Industrial pumps & parts
HQ: Asm Industries, Inc
41 Industrial Cir
Lancaster PA 17601
717 656-2161

(G-8947)
AUNTIE ANNES INC (DH)
48-50 W Chestnut St # 200 (17603-3791)
PHONE...................................717 435-1435
William P Dunn Jr, *President*
Michael Mercado, *President*
Russel Umphenour, *President*
Lenore Krentz, *Vice Pres*
Dom Portanova, *Vice Pres*
EMP: 73
SQ FT: 30,000
SALES (est): 199MM
SALES (corp-wide): 4.7B **Privately Held**
SIC: 6794 2051 5461 Franchises, selling or licensing; bread, cake & related products; pretzels
HQ: Focus Brands, Inc.
5620 Glenridge Dr
Atlanta GA 30342
404 255-3250

(G-8948)
BARRICK DESIGN INC
541 N Mulberry St (17603-2958)
PHONE...................................717 295-4800
Richard D Faulkner Jr, *President*
Marion L Faulkner, *Admin Sec*
EMP: 5
SQ FT: 5,000
SALES (est): 350K **Privately Held**
WEB: www.barrickdesign.com
SIC: 3999 Candles

(G-8949)
BARTS PNEUMATICS CORP
Also Called: All Aboard Railroad
1952 Landis Valley Rd (17601-5406)
PHONE...................................717 392-1568
Catherine Board, *President*

G E O G R A P H I C

Robert Board, *Corp Secy*
EMP: 5 **EST:** 1945
SQ FT: 12,000
SALES (est): 620K **Privately Held**
WEB: www.allaboardrailroad.com
SIC: 5084 3563 Compressors, except air
conditioning; air & gas compressors in-
cluding vacuum pumps

(G-8950)
BED BATH & BEYOND INC
2350 Lincoln Hwy E # 100 (17602-1199)
PHONE....................................717 397-0206
Erin Warner, *Branch Mgr*
EMP: 5
SALES (corp-wide): 12.3B **Publicly Held**
SIC: 5719 2844 2299 Beddings & linens;
cosmetic preparations; linen fabrics
PA: Bed Bath & Beyond Inc.
650 Liberty Ave
Union NJ 07083
908 688-0888

(G-8951)
BERRY GLOBAL INC
1846 Charter Ln (17601-6773)
PHONE....................................717 393-3498
EMP: 7 **Publicly Held**
SIC: 3089 Plastic containers, except foam
HQ: Berry Global, Inc.
101 Oakley St
Evansville IN 47710
812 424-2904

(G-8952)
BERRY GLOBAL INC
1706 Hempstead Rd (17601-6706)
P.O. Box 8527 (17604-8527)
PHONE....................................717 299-6511
Michael Makhlouf, *Project Mgr*
Jimmy Sawmiller, *Maint Spvr*
Joe Bruchman, *Branch Mgr*
EMP: 50 **Publicly Held**
SIC: 3089 Bottle caps, molded plastic
HQ: Berry Global, Inc.
101 Oakley St
Evansville IN 47710
812 424-2904

(G-8953)
BINDERY ASSOCIATES INC
2025 Horseshoe Rd (17602-1007)
PHONE....................................717 295-7443
Robert L Drummond, *President*
Keith Siemon, *General Mgr*
Russell Richelderfer, *Vice Pres*
Eugene Sowers, *Admin Sec*
EMP: 40 **EST:** 1963
SQ FT: 30,000
SALES (est): 5.4MM **Privately Held**
SIC: 2789 Binding only: books, pamphlets,
magazines, etc.; paper cutting

(G-8954)
**BIRD-IN-HAND WOODWORKS
INC**
3031 Industry Dr (17603-4073)
PHONE....................................717 397-5686
William Brugmann, *Opers Staff*
Jackie Rampulla, *Human Res Dir*
Gary Polak, *Admin Asst*
◆ **EMP:** 70 **EST:** 1970
SQ FT: 70,000
SALES: 21.6MM
SALES (corp-wide): 658.3MM **Publicly
Held**
SIC: 2511 2531 Children's wood furniture;
public building & related furniture
PA: School Specialty, Inc.
W6316 Design Dr
Greenville WI 54942
920 734-5712

(G-8955)
**BISMOLINE MANUFACTURING
CO**
411 S Queen St (17603-5617)
PHONE....................................717 394-8795
Robert Schroeder, *President*
Martin Keen, *Corp Secy*
Arthur Keen, *Vice Pres*
EMP: 3
SQ FT: 2,000

SALES: 150K **Privately Held**
WEB: www.bismoline.com
SIC: 2844 5999 Powder: baby, face, tal-
cum or toilet; cosmetics

(G-8956)
BLACK BEAR ASSOCIATES LLC
Also Called: Hot Shot Tactical
923 E Orange St Unit 1 (17602-3213)
PHONE....................................610 470-6477
Richard Masho,
EMP: 5 **EST:** 2011
SALES (est): 337.8K **Privately Held**
SIC: 3648 Lighting equipment

(G-8957)
**BOSCH SECURITY SYSTEMS
INC**
1706 Hempstead Rd (17601-6706)
PHONE....................................717 735-6300
Karla Pratt, *Plant Mgr*
Robert Richards, *Branch Mgr*
John Homan, *Manager*
Bruce Magid, *Technical Staff*
EMP: 475
SALES (corp-wide): 301.8MM **Privately
Held**
WEB: www.telex.com
SIC: 3699 Security control equipment &
systems
HQ: Bosch Security Systems, Inc.
130 Perinton Pkwy
Fairport NY 14450
585 223-4060

(G-8958)
BREEZECRAFT LLC
946 Gypsy Hill Rd (17602-1214)
PHONE....................................717 397-8584
Paul Tyson, *Principal*
EMP: 3
SALES (est): 322.9K **Privately Held**
SIC: 2431 Millwork

(G-8959)
BRENNEMAN PRINTING INC
1909 Olde Homestead Ln (17601-5824)
P.O. Box 11147 (17605-1147)
PHONE....................................717 299-2847
Jennifer Hostetter, *CEO*
Jennifer Brenneman-Hostetter, *CEO*
Jill Pyle, *Vice Pres*
Ed Nevling, *CFO*
Jennifer Brenneman, *VP Human Res*
EMP: 35 **EST:** 1969
SQ FT: 25,000
SALES (est): 6.5MM **Privately Held**
WEB: www.brenprint.com
SIC: 2752 3993 Commercial printing, off-
set; signs & advertising specialties

(G-8960)
BRONTECH INDUSTRIES INC
1115 Marietta Ave Apt 16 (17603-2552)
P.O. Box 4667 (17604-4667)
PHONE....................................717 672-0240
Kenneth Gabron, *President*
EMP: 6
SALES (est): 701.2K **Privately Held**
SIC: 3645 5063 Residential lighting fix-
tures; lighting fixtures

(G-8961)
**BROOKSHIRE PRINTING INC
(PA)**
200 Hazel St (17603-5630)
PHONE....................................717 392-1321
L James Weaver, *President*
Steven L Weaver, *Vice Pres*
Elva J Weaver, *Treasurer*
Cynthia Yoder, *Admin Sec*
▲ **EMP:** 20
SQ FT: 15,000
SALES (est): 1.6MM **Privately Held**
WEB: www.brookshireprinting.com
SIC: 2752 2791 2789 2731 Commercial
printing, offset; typesetting; bookbinding &
related work; book publishing; periodicals;
newspapers

(G-8962)
BROWNS GRAPHIC SOLUTIONS
1397 Arcadia Rd Ste 100 (17601-3190)
PHONE....................................717 721-6160
EMP: 3 **EST:** 2017

SALES (est): 266.3K **Privately Held**
SIC: 3993 Signs & advertising specialties

(G-8963)
BRUBAKER KITCHENS INC
1121 Manheim Pike (17601-3195)
PHONE....................................717 394-5622
Jerry Berkowitz, *President*
Michael D Snyder, *Treasurer*
Rita Berkowitz, *Sales Executive*
EMP: 35
SQ FT: 17,000
SALES (est): 4.4MM **Privately Held**
SIC: 2434 Wood kitchen cabinets

(G-8964)
BURNHAM HOLDINGS INC (PA)
1241 Harrisburg Ave (17603-2515)
P.O. Box 3245 (17604-3245)
PHONE....................................717 390-7800
Albert Morrison III, *Ch of Bd*
Douglas S Brossman, *President*
Greg White, *General Mgr*
Chris Drew, *Exec VP*
Christopher Drew, *Vice Pres*
▲ **EMP:** 29 **EST:** 2002
SQ FT: 10,800
SALES: 172.4MM **Publicly Held**
SIC: 3433 Boilers, low-pressure heating:
steam or hot water

(G-8965)
BURNHAM LLC
Also Called: Burnham Commercial
1237 Harrisburg Ave (17603-2515)
P.O. Box 3939 (17604-3939)
PHONE....................................717 293-5839
Dave Lackmann, *President*
Kenneth Sturtz, *Vice Pres*
Roger Pepper, *QC Mgr*
Jim Knauss, *Engineer*
Doug Springer, *Controller*
EMP: 69
SALES (est): 14.9MM
SALES (corp-wide): 172.4MM **Publicly
Held**
WEB: www.burnhamcommercial.com
SIC: 3443 Boilers: industrial, power, or ma-
rine
PA: Burnham Holdings, Inc.
1241 Harrisburg Ave
Lancaster PA 17603
717 390-7800

(G-8966)
BUTZ SIGN CO
915 N Ann St (17602-1928)
PHONE....................................717 397-8565
Michael Butz, *Partner*
Jean Butz, *Partner*
Kathleen Butz, *Partner*
EMP: 4
SALES (est): 200K **Privately Held**
SIC: 3993 Signs, not made in custom sign
painting shops

(G-8967)
C-B TOOL CO (PA)
Also Called: Lancaster Pump & Water Trtmnt
640 Bean Hill Rd (17603-9525)
PHONE....................................717 397-3521
John D Wenzel, *Ch of Bd*
John D Wenzel Jr, *Park Mgr*
▲ **EMP:** 26 **EST:** 1939
SQ FT: 44,000
SALES (est): 8.3MM **Privately Held**
WEB: www.lancasterpump.com
SIC: 3561 3599 3589 Pumps, domestic:
water or sump; machine shop, jobbing &
repair; water filters & softeners, house-
hold type

(G-8968)
C-B TOOL CO
640 Bean Hill Rd (17603-9525)
PHONE....................................717 393-3953
John D Wentzel Jr, *Manager*
EMP: 36
SALES (corp-wide): 8.3MM **Privately
Held**
WEB: www.lancasterpump.com
SIC: 3561 Industrial pumps & parts
PA: C-B Tool Co
640 Bean Hill Rd
Lancaster PA 17603
717 397-3521

(G-8969)
**CAMBRIDGE FARMS HANOVER
LLC**
201 Granite Run Dr # 250 (17601-6807)
PHONE....................................717 945-5178
Gary Gregory, *President*
▲ **EMP:** 7
SALES (est): 1.2MM **Privately Held**
SIC: 2037 5142 Frozen fruits & vegeta-
bles; frozen vegetables & fruit products

(G-8970)
**CARAUSTAR INDUSTRIAL AND
CON**
Also Called: Lancaster Tube Plant
1820 Olde Homestead Ln (17601-5836)
P.O. Box 10516 (17605-0516)
PHONE....................................717 295-0047
EMP: 30
SALES (corp-wide): 1.1B **Privately Held**
SIC: 2655 Mfg Spiral Wound Tubes
HQ: Caraustar Industrial And Consumer
Products Group Inc
2031 Carolina Place Dr
Fort Mill SC 30106
803 548-5100

(G-8971)
CAROL FANELLI
Also Called: Minuteman Press
118 Parklawn Ct (17601-2653)
PHONE....................................717 945-7418
Carol A Fanelli, *Owner*
Thomas Fanelli, *Co-Owner*
EMP: 5
SQ FT: 1,500
SALES (est): 333.4K **Privately Held**
SIC: 2752 Commercial printing, litho-
graphic

(G-8972)
**CEDARS WDWKG &
RENOVATIONS LLC**
Also Called: Cedars Woodworking & Intr Pntg
630 W Fulton St (17603-3415)
PHONE....................................717 392-1736
Steven Schmucker, *Mng Member*
EMP: 7
SALES (est): 337K **Privately Held**
SIC: 2541 2431 Cabinets, except refriger-
ated: show, display, etc.: wood; millwork

(G-8973)
**CENTRAL DISTRIBUTION CO
INC (PA)**
11b Meadow Ln (17601-3701)
PHONE....................................717 393-4851
Chris Sullivan, *President*
EMP: 3
SALES (est): 343.2K **Privately Held**
SIC: 2671 5162 Plastic film, coated or
laminated for packaging; plastics sheets
& rods

(G-8974)
**CENTRAL PENN WIRE AND
CABLE**
360 Steel Way A (17601-3183)
PHONE....................................717 945-5540
David Breinieh, *Principal*
Brett Stromberg, *Sales Staff*
EMP: 4
SALES (est): 158.4K **Privately Held**
SIC: 4841 3612 Cable television services;
transmission & distribution voltage regula-
tors

(G-8975)
CENVEO WORLDWIDE LIMITED
3575 Hempland Rd (17601-6912)
PHONE....................................717 285-9095
Craig Fausnacht, *Safety Mgr*
Kathy Delmotte, *Warehouse Mgr*
EMP: 11
SALES (corp-wide): 1.6B **Privately Held**
SIC: 2677 Envelopes
HQ: Cenveo Worldwide Limited
200 First Stamford Pl # 2
Stamford CT 06902
203 595-3000

▲ = Import ▼=Export
◆ =Import/Export

(G-8976)
CERTIFIED CARPET SERVICE INC
Also Called: Carpet Steam Rentals
932 High St (17603-5406)
P.O. Box 1746 (17608-1746)
PHONE....................717 393-3012
Darren Fritz, *Manager*
EMP: 53
SALES (corp-wide): 13.4MM **Privately Held**
SIC: 7217 5713 3069 7299 Carpet & rug cleaning & repairing plant; carpets; vinyl floor covering; mats or matting, rubber; rental of personal items, except for recreation & medical
PA: Certified Carpet Service, Inc.
1855 Columbia Ave 65
Lancaster PA 17603
717 394-3731

(G-8977)
CHARLES & ALICE INC
2870 Yellow Goose Rd (17601-1814)
PHONE....................717 537-4700
Thierry Goubault, *President*
Dominique Sagne, *Vice Pres*
James Schneider, *Vice Pres*
Philipple Moullee, *CFO*
Tim Kennedy, *Admin Sec*
EMP: 20
SQ FT: 65,000
SALES (est): 4.4MM
SALES (corp-wide): 547.8MM **Privately Held**
SIC: 2033 Apple sauce: packaged in cans, jars, etc.
HQ: Charles & Alice
Charles Et Alice Zone Industrielle
Allex 26400

(G-8978)
CK MANUFACTURING LLC
Also Called: CK Replacement Stalls
330 Millwood Rd (17603-9601)
PHONE....................717 442-8912
Christ King, *President*
▲ **EMP:** 43
SQ FT: 300
SALES: 2.7MM **Privately Held**
SIC: 3523 Dairy equipment (farm); cabs, tractors & agricultural machinery

(G-8979)
CLARK FILTER INC (DH)
3649 Hempland Rd (17601-1323)
PHONE....................717 285-5941
Norm Johnson, *Ch of Bd*
Richard Kurcina, *VP Opers*
Mark Kern, *Maint Spvr*
Bruce Klein, *Treasurer*
Jamie Breisch, *Manager*
▼ **EMP:** 2
SQ FT: 168,000
SALES (est): 339.8MM
SALES (corp-wide): 14.3B **Publicly Held**
WEB: www.clarkfilter.com
SIC: 3564 3714 Filters, air: furnaces, air conditioning equipment, etc.; motor vehicle parts & accessories
HQ: Clarcor Inc.
840 Crescent Centre Dr # 600
Franklin TN 37067
615 771-3100

(G-8980)
CM INDUSTRIES INC
Also Called: Hope Hosiery Mills
158 Hamilton Rd (17603-4734)
PHONE....................717 336-4545
Charles Milner Jr, *President*
Mark Fuhrer, *Vice Pres*
▲ **EMP:** 150 **EST:** 1903
SQ FT: 60,000
SALES (est): 17.5MM **Privately Held**
SIC: 2252 Socks

(G-8981)
CNH INDUSTRIAL AMERICA LLC
7100 Durand Ave Ste 300 (17604)
P.O. Box 71277, Philadelphia (19176-6277)
PHONE....................262 636-6011
Sergio Marchionne, *Chairman*
EMP: 374
SALES (corp-wide): 27.9B **Privately Held**
SIC: 3523 Farm machinery & equipment

HQ: Cnh Industrial America Llc
700 State St
Racine WI 53404
262 636-6011

(G-8982)
COMPASS GROUP USA INC
Also Called: Canteen
1640 Crooked Oak Dr (17601-4208)
PHONE....................717 569-2671
Doug Pickett, *Manager*
EMP: 60
SALES (corp-wide): 29.6B **Privately Held**
WEB: www.compass-usa.com
SIC: 5962 2099 Sandwich & hot food vending machines; food preparations
HQ: Compass Group Usa, Inc.
2400 Yorkmont Rd
Charlotte NC 28217
704 328-4000

(G-8983)
COMPUTER PRINT INC
2132 Oreville Rd (17601-2625)
PHONE....................717 397-9174
Ernest A Rojahn, *President*
Sandra Rojahn, *Manager*
EMP: 6
SALES (est): 753.1K **Privately Held**
SIC: 2752 Commercial printing, offset

(G-8984)
CONESTOGA DATA SERVICES INC
Also Called: Cds Solutions Group
46 E King St (17602-2850)
PHONE....................717 569-7728
Nadim R Baker, *President*
Ren Baker, *Vice Pres*
Ronay Wolaver, *Vice Pres*
Donald Welsh, *Treasurer*
Nadim Baker, *Info Tech Mgr*
EMP: 17
SQ FT: 7,100
SALES (est): 2.6MM **Privately Held**
WEB: www.cdsgroup.com
SIC: 7372 Business oriented computer software

(G-8985)
CONNECTEDSIGN LLC
480 New Holland Ave # 6202 (17602-2291)
PHONE....................717 490-6431
Loren Bucklin,
Brigitte Bucklin,
EMP: 3
SALES: 1MM **Privately Held**
WEB: www.connectedsign.com
SIC: 7372 Application computer software

(G-8986)
COOPER PRINTING INC
Also Called: Cooper Printing,
2094 New Danville Pike (17603-9512)
PHONE....................717 871-8856
David W Cooper, *Owner*
Mark Miller, *Sales Staff*
EMP: 9
SQ FT: 2,500
SALES (est): 899.5K **Privately Held**
SIC: 2752 Commercial printing, offset

(G-8987)
CREATIVE EMBEDMENTS
1851 Wickersham Ln (17603-2327)
PHONE....................717 299-0385
Charles P Reynolds, *Owner*
EMP: 8
SALES (est): 539.1K **Privately Held**
SIC: 3914 Trophies, plated (all metals)

(G-8988)
CREATIVE FLAVOR CONCEPTS INC
350 Richardson Dr (17603-4034)
PHONE....................949 705-6584
Jeferay Lehman, *Branch Mgr*
EMP: 4
SALES (corp-wide): 9.2MM **Privately Held**
SIC: 2087 Powders, flavoring (except drink)
HQ: Creative Concepts Holdings, Llc
580 Garcia Ave
Pittsburg CA 94565

(G-8989)
D & SR INC (PA)
500 E Oregon Rd (17601)
P.O. Box 5319 (17606-5319)
PHONE....................717 569-3264
Donald K Roseman, *President*
Scott Reighard, *President*
Sheila W Roseman, *Treasurer*
▲ **EMP:** 99 **EST:** 1956
SQ FT: 40,000
SALES (est): 7.1MM **Privately Held**
WEB: www.acornpress.com
SIC: 2752 2789 2759 Commercial printing, offset; bookbinding & related work; commercial printing

(G-8990)
DAIRY CONVEYOR CORP
2173 Embassy Dr (17603-2387)
PHONE....................717 431-3121
Dirk Harkopf, *Principal*
EMP: 4
SALES (corp-wide): 29.4MM **Privately Held**
SIC: 3535 Conveyors & conveying equipment
PA: Dairy Conveyor Corp.
38 Mount Ebo Rd S
Brewster NY 10509
845 278-7878

(G-8991)
DANIEL BAUM COMPANY
1383 Arcadia Rd Ste 102 (17601-3149)
PHONE....................717 509-5724
Daniel Baum, *President*
Ilsa Bender, *Office Mgr*
EMP: 12
SALES (est): 1.9MM **Privately Held**
SIC: 2834 Vitamin, nutrient & hematinic preparations for human use

(G-8992)
DART CONTAINER CORP PA
110 Pitney Rd (17602-2616)
PHONE....................717 397-1032
EMP: 1447
SALES (corp-wide): 265.3MM **Privately Held**
SIC: 3086 Cups & plates, foamed plastic
PA: Dart Container Corporation Of Pennsylvania
60 E Main St
Leola PA 17540
717 656-2236

(G-8993)
DENTALEZ INC
Star Dental
1816 Colonial Village Ln (17601-5807)
PHONE....................717 291-1161
Greg Myer, *Safety Mgr*
Amanda Wirls, *Safety Mgr*
John Brunozzi, *Opers-Prdtn-Mfg*
Luther Gates, *Engineer*
R Patrick St Clair, *Persnl Mgr*
EMP: 135
SALES (corp-wide): 59.5MM **Privately Held**
WEB: www.dentalez.com
SIC: 3843 5047 Dental equipment; medical & hospital equipment
PA: Dentalez, Inc.
2 W Liberty Blvd Ste 160
Malvern PA 19355
610 725-8004

(G-8994)
DENTSPLY SIRONA INC
Also Called: Llc, Dentsply
1800 Cloister Dr (17601-2359)
PHONE....................717 849-7747
Maeve Bowers, *Engineer*
EMP: 111
SALES (corp-wide): 3.9B **Publicly Held**
SIC: 3843 Dental equipment & supplies
PA: Dentsply Sirona Inc.
221 W Philadelphia St
York PA 17401
717 845-7511

(G-8995)
DEP TECHNOLOGIES LLC
1000 New Holland Ave (17601-5606)
PHONE....................800 578-7929
Gregory Bell, *Principal*

EMP: 3
SALES (est): 173.3K **Privately Held**
SIC: 3812 Search & detection systems & instruments

(G-8996)
DESTECH PUBLICATIONS INC (PA)
439 N Duke St Ste 3 (17602-4967)
PHONE....................717 290-1660
Anthony Deraco, *President*
Joseph Eckenrode, *Senior VP*
Steven Spangler, *Senior VP*
▼ **EMP:** 4
SQ FT: 1,000
SALES (est): 368.8K **Privately Held**
WEB: www.destechpub.com
SIC: 2731 Books: publishing only

(G-8997)
DIG FAMILY BUSINESS LLC
Also Called: Calloway House
451 Richardson Dr (17603-4035)
P.O. Box 4844 (17604-4844)
PHONE....................717 299-5703
Dustin Knarr, *CEO*
Monica Knarr, *President*
Kim McCall, *Vice Pres*
Steven Reed, *Vice Pres*
EMP: 11
SQ FT: 40,000
SALES (est): 1.6MM **Privately Held**
SIC: 3999 Education aids, devices & supplies

(G-8998)
DIVERSIFIED MACHINE INC
430 N Franklin St (17602-2409)
PHONE....................717 397-5347
James Haines, *President*
Tammy Haines, *Corp Secy*
Jennifer Ely, *Personnel*
EMP: 20
SQ FT: 66,000
SALES (est): 3.7MM **Privately Held**
WEB: www.diversifiedracing.com
SIC: 3599 Machine shop, jobbing & repair

(G-8999)
DMM WOODWORKING
518 Fremont St (17603-5231)
PHONE....................717 390-2828
Mike Sahd, *Partner*
EMP: 4
SALES (est): 464.3K **Privately Held**
SIC: 2431 Millwork

(G-9000)
DOGS IN CAST STONE
175 N Concord St (17603-3503)
PHONE....................717 291-9696
Nancy Vandermolen, *Principal*
EMP: 3
SALES (est): 209.1K **Privately Held**
SIC: 3272 Concrete products

(G-9001)
DONNA KARAN COMPANY LLC
801 Stanley K Tanger Blvd (17602-1492)
PHONE....................717 299-1706
EMP: 157
SALES (corp-wide): 279MM **Privately Held**
SIC: 2335 Mfg Women/Misses Dresses
HQ: The Donna Karan Company Llc
550 Fashion Ave Fl 14
New York NY 10018
212 789-1500

(G-9002)
DOODAD PRINTING LLC
1842 Clnl Vlg Ln 101 (17601)
PHONE....................800 383-6973
Keith Bartlett, *COO*
Elizabeth Bagley, *Marketing Staff*
Scott Levy,
Thomas McCloskey,
EMP: 52
SQ FT: 60,000
SALES (est): 10.6MM **Privately Held**
SIC: 2752 Commercial printing, offset

GEOGRAPHIC

(G-9003)
DUNCAN ASSOCIATES INC
517 High St (17603-5207)
P.O. Box 1232 (17608-1232)
PHONE..................................717 299-6940
Gene Duncan, *President*
Linda Duncan, *Corp Secy*
Mel Glick, *Vice Pres*
EMP: 3
SQ FT: 1,000
SALES: 210K **Privately Held**
SIC: 3569 Firefighting apparatus & related equipment

(G-9004)
DUTCH GOLD HONEY INC (PA)
2220 Dutch Gold Dr (17601-1997)
PHONE..................................717 393-1716
Nancy J Gamber, *President*
William R Gamber II, *Chairman*
William Gamber, *Chairman*
Marianne M Gamber, *Corp Secy*
◆ **EMP:** 60 **EST:** 1946
SQ FT: 100,000
SALES: 159.8MM **Privately Held**
WEB: www.dutchgoldhoney.com
SIC: 2099 5149 Honey, strained & bottled; honey

(G-9005)
E S H POULTRY
2316 Norman Rd Ste 1 (17601-5960)
PHONE..................................717 517-9535
Samuel Lantz, *Owner*
EMP: 15
SQ FT: 5,250
SALES: 480K **Privately Held**
SIC: 2099 2034 2015 Salads, fresh or refrigerated; soup mixes; sausage, poultry

(G-9006)
EASTERN SYSTEMS MANAGEMENT
1860 Charter Ln Ste 207 (17601-6755)
PHONE..................................717 391-9700
EMP: 5
SQ FT: 1,626
SALES: 1.5MM **Privately Held**
SIC: 7371 5045 7372 Computer Programming Services & Whol Computer Systems

(G-9007)
ECORE INTERNATIONAL INC (PA)
715 Fountain Ave (17601-4547)
P.O. Box 989 (17608-0989)
PHONE..................................717 295-3400
Arthur B Dodge III, *President*
Bo Barber, *Vice Pres*
Rich Campbell, *Vice Pres*
John McFalls, *Vice Pres*
Mike Sage, *Vice Pres*
◆ **EMP:** 130
SQ FT: 380,000
SALES: 51.5MM **Privately Held**
WEB: www.regupol.com
SIC: 3069 2499 Hard rubber & molded rubber products; sheets, hard rubber; cork & cork products

(G-9008)
ELECTRONIC TEST EQP MFG CO
Also Called: Etemco
1370 Arcadia Rd (17601-3165)
P.O. Box 4651 (17604-4651)
PHONE..................................717 393-9653
Edward I Hockenberry, *President*
Stephen Jliebl, *Vice Pres*
Steve Liebl, *Vice Pres*
▲ **EMP:** 40 **EST:** 1952
SQ FT: 30,000
SALES (est): 11.9MM **Privately Held**
WEB: www.etemco.net
SIC: 3672 Printed circuit boards

(G-9009)
ENGLE PRINTING & PUBG CO INC (PA)
Also Called: Engle Online
1100 Corporate Blvd (17601-1278)
P.O. Box 500, Mount Joy (17552-0500)
PHONE..................................717 653-1833
Charles A Engle, *President*
Denise Sater, *Editor*

Dennis Engle, *Vice Pres*
Audrey Rutt, *Treasurer*
Gregory March, *Sales Staff*
EMP: 200 **EST:** 1975
SQ FT: 28,000
SALES: 76.7MM **Privately Held**
SIC: 2791 2752 2721 2741 Typesetting; commercial printing, offset; magazines: publishing & printing; miscellaneous publishing

(G-9010)
ENGLE PRINTING & PUBG CO INC
1100 Corporate Blvd (17601-1278)
PHONE..................................717 892-6800
Eric Tapman, *Branch Mgr*
EMP: 11
SALES (corp-wide): 76.7MM **Privately Held**
SIC: 2752 2721 Commercial printing, offset; magazines: publishing & printing
PA: Engle Printing & Publishing Co., Inc.
1100 Corporate Blvd
Lancaster PA 17601
717 653-1833

(G-9011)
ERIC HERR
2125 S View Rd (17602-1842)
PHONE..................................717 464-1829
EMP: 3 **EST:** 2008
SALES (est): 295.1K **Privately Held**
SIC: 3331 Primary Copper Producer

(G-9012)
EVANS CANDY LLC
2100 Willow Street Pike (17602-4838)
PHONE..................................717 295-7510
Duane Evans, *Partner*
Harriet Evans, *Partner*
Karen Evans, *Partner*
Steve Evans,
Jay Evans,
EMP: 5
SQ FT: 7,000
SALES (est): 290K **Privately Held**
WEB: www.evanscandy.com
SIC: 5441 2064 Candy; chocolate candy, except solid chocolate

(G-9013)
FAB-RICK INDUSTRIES INC
28 Penn Sq Fl 1 (17603-4297)
PHONE..................................717 859-5633
EMP: 22
SQ FT: 23,760
SALES (est): 4.5MM **Privately Held**
SIC: 3441 1799 Structural Metal Fabrication Trade Contractor

(G-9014)
FAMILY READY LABOR INC
53 N Plum St (17602-2969)
PHONE..................................717 615-4900
Yoeun Kim, *President*
EMP: 4
SALES (est): 207.2K **Privately Held**
SIC: 3273 Ready-mixed concrete

(G-9015)
FENNER INC
Also Called: Fenner Drives
1421 Arcadia Rd (17601-3107)
PHONE..................................717 665-2421
EMP: 8
SALES (corp-wide): 855.1MM **Privately Held**
SIC: 3568 Power transmission equipment
HQ: Fenner, Inc.
311 W Stiegel St
Manheim PA 17545
717 665-2421

(G-9016)
FIG INDUSTRIES LLC
1411 Fieldstead Ln (17603-4665)
PHONE..................................803 414-3950
Matt Brandt, *CFO*
EMP: 3 **EST:** 2010
SALES (est): 169.9K **Privately Held**
SIC: 3999 Manufacturing industries

(G-9017)
FLEX-CELL PRECISION
833 2nd St (17603-3235)
PHONE..................................717 393-3335
Anthony Fanning, *Principal*
EMP: 5
SALES (est): 502.4K **Privately Held**
SIC: 3599 Machine shop, jobbing & repair

(G-9018)
FLEX-CELL PRECISION INC
1151 S Duke St (17602-4660)
PHONE..................................717 824-4086
Tony Fanning, *President*
EMP: 6
SQ FT: 6,100
SALES (est): 1.3MM **Privately Held**
WEB: www.flex-cellinc.com
SIC: 3599 Machine shop, jobbing & repair

(G-9019)
FLEXSTEEL INDUSTRIES INC
107 Pitney Rd (17602-2615)
PHONE..................................717 392-4161
Craig Adams, *General Mgr*
Lois Killian, *Principal*
EMP: 140
SALES (corp-wide): 489.1MM **Publicly Held**
WEB: www.flexsteel.com
SIC: 2512 Living room furniture: upholstered on wood frames
PA: Flexsteel Industries, Inc.
385 Bell St
Dubuque IA 52001
563 556-7730

(G-9020)
FLINT GROUP US LLC
3575 Hempland Rd (17601-6912)
PHONE..................................717 285-5454
Paul Sato,
EMP: 4
SALES (corp-wide): 3.2B **Privately Held**
WEB: www.flintink.com
SIC: 2899 Ink or writing fluids
PA: Flint Group Us Llc
14909 N Beck Rd
Plymouth MI 48170
734 781-4600

(G-9021)
FLINT GROUP US LLC
Also Called: Flint Ink North America Div
216 Greenfield Rd (17601-5817)
PHONE..................................717 392-1953
Jad Batchelder, *Manager*
EMP: 8
SALES (corp-wide): 3.2B **Privately Held**
WEB: www.flintink.com
SIC: 2893 Printing ink
PA: Flint Group Us Llc
14909 N Beck Rd
Plymouth MI 48170
734 781-4600

(G-9022)
FLORIDA KEY WEST
1308 Kelley Dr (17601-7148)
PHONE..................................717 208-3084
Cappie Hose, *Principal*
EMP: 5
SALES (est): 458.2K **Privately Held**
SIC: 2033 Canned fruits & specialties

(G-9023)
FLURY FOUNDRY COMPANY
1160 Elizabeth Ave (17601-4384)
PHONE..................................717 397-9080
Calvin K Flury Jr, *President*
Jason H Flury, *Vice Pres*
Tom Needham, *Treasurer*
EMP: 15 **EST:** 1939
SQ FT: 10,500
SALES (est): 2.7MM **Privately Held**
WEB: www.fluryfoundry.com
SIC: 3366 Castings (except die): brass; castings (except die): bronze

(G-9024)
FLY MAGAZINE
Also Called: Barfly Monthly
2144 Kentwood Dr (17601-3016)
PHONE..................................717 293-9772
John Villella, *Owner*
EMP: 6

SALES (est): 345.9K **Privately Held**
WEB: www.flymagazine.net
SIC: 2711 7922 Newspapers, publishing & printing; theatrical producers & services

(G-9025)
FREY LUTZ CORP
Also Called: Honeywell Authorized Dealer
1195 Ivy Dr (17601-1123)
PHONE..................................717 394-4635
Richard Donnelly Jr, *CEO*
Scott P Rhoads, *President*
Robert W Wagner, *Vice Pres*
Nancy Daub, *Treasurer*
EMP: 150
SQ FT: 20,000
SALES: 39MM **Privately Held**
WEB: www.freylutz.com
SIC: 1711 1761 3446 3444 Plumbing contractors; warm air heating & air conditioning contractor; sheet metalwork; architectural metalwork; sheet metalwork; fabricated structural metal

(G-9026)
G G SCHMITT & SONS INC (PA)
2821 Old Tree Dr (17603-7301)
PHONE..................................717 394-3701
Ronald Schmitt, *President*
Gervase A Schmitt, *Vice Pres*
Steve Schmitt, *Vice Pres*
Nanette Smith, *Administration*
▲ **EMP:** 15 **EST:** 1951
SQ FT: 50,000
SALES (est): 20.6MM **Privately Held**
SIC: 3429 3743 Marine hardware; railroad equipment

(G-9027)
GENERGY POWER LLC
1812 Olde Homestead Ln (17601-6710)
P.O. Box 10731 (17605-0731)
PHONE..................................717 584-0375
Craig Consylman, *Accounts Mgr*
Angel Benfer, *Marketing Staff*
Edgar Molina,
Jack Witwer,
EMP: 6
SALES (est): 519.9K **Privately Held**
SIC: 3357 Building wire & cable, nonferrous

(G-9028)
GERHART COFFEE CO
224 Wohlsen Way (17603-4043)
PHONE..................................717 397-8788
Charles W Braungard Jr, *Owner*
Troy Hartman, *Manager*
EMP: 3 **EST:** 1880
SQ FT: 4,200
SALES (est): 160K **Privately Held**
WEB: www.gerhartcoffee.com
SIC: 2095 5149 Coffee roasting (except by wholesale grocers); tea; spices & seasonings; specialty food items

(G-9029)
GLAXOSMITHKLINE LLC
2937 Hearthside Ln (17601-1475)
PHONE..................................717 898-6853
Robert Scheid, *Principal*
EMP: 26
SALES (corp-wide): 39.8B **Privately Held**
WEB: www.delks.com
SIC: 2834 Antibiotics, packaged
HQ: Glaxosmithkline Llc
5 Crescent Dr
Philadelphia PA 19112
215 751-4000

(G-9030)
GOODHART SONS INC
2515 Horseshoe Rd (17601-5998)
P.O. Box 10308 (17605-0308)
PHONE..................................717 656-2404
Gary W Goodhart, *CEO*
Chad E Goodhart, *Division Pres*
Marc W Goodhart, *Division Pres*
Michael B Goodhart, *Vice Pres*
Jack Graham, *Controller*
EMP: 160
SQ FT: 200,000

▲ = Import ▼=Export
◆ =Import/Export

SALES (est): 27.7MM **Privately Held**
WEB: www.goodhartsons.com
SIC: 3443 3441 1796 1731 Fabricated
plate work (boiler shop); fabricated structural metal; pollution control equipment installation; electrical work; machine shop,
jobbing & repair

(G-9031)
**GRAHAM PACKAGING
COMPANY INC (DH)**
700 Indian Springs Dr # 100 (17601-7801)
P.O. Box 20009, York (17402-0139)
PHONE..............................717 849-8500
Herm Koch, *Mfg Dir*
Don Waud, *Plant Mgr*
Dave Brown, *Purchasing*
Steve Ream, *Purchasing*
Greg Taylor, *Engineer*
▲ EMP: 147 EST: 1997
SALES (est): 3.8B
SALES (corp-wide): 1MM **Privately Held**
SIC: 5199 3089 5162 Packaging materi-
als; plastic containers, except foam; plas-
tics materials
HQ: Reynolds Group Holdings Limited
Floor 9, 148 Quay Street
Auckland 1010
935 912-68

(G-9032)
GRETCHEN MASER
142 Cliff Ave (17602-4700)
PHONE..............................717 295-9426
Gretchen Maser, *Owner*
EMP: 3
SALES (est): 259.7K **Privately Held**
SIC: 2841 Soap: granulated, liquid, cake,
flaked or chip

(G-9033)
GROFFS CANDIES
3587 Blue Rock Rd (17603-9776)
PHONE..............................717 872-2845
Marvin R Groff, *Owner*
EMP: 3 EST: 1969
SALES (est): 238K **Privately Held**
SIC: 2064 Fudge (candy)

(G-9034)
GSM INDUSTRIAL INC
3249 Hempland Rd (17601-6913)
PHONE..............................717 207-8985
John S Gooding, *Ch of Bd*
Brian Dombach, *President*
William H Gooding, *Corp Secy*
John Kleinfelter, *Vice Pres*
Jeffrey Ream, *Vice Pres*
▲ EMP: 112
SQ FT: 60,000
SALES (est): 29.4MM **Privately Held**
WEB: www.gsmindustrial.com
SIC: 3444 1711 Sheet metalwork; me-
chanical contractor

(G-9035)
H & H GRAPHICS INC (PA)
Also Called: Sir Speedy
854 N Prince St (17603-2752)
PHONE..............................717 393-3941
Mary Kohler, *President*
Deb Williams, *CFO*
Joshua Rittenhouse, *Marketing Mgr*
Dan Schwebel, *Manager*
EMP: 20
SQ FT: 5,000
SALES: 5MM **Privately Held**
SIC: 2752 Commercial printing, litho-
graphic

(G-9036)
H & H GRAPHICS INC
Also Called: Sir Speedy
1893 Commerce Park E (17601-5808)
PHONE..............................717 393-3941
Mary Elliot, *Manager*
EMP: 35
SALES (corp-wide): 5MM **Privately Held**
SIC: 2752 7334 Commercial printing, off-
set; photocopying & duplicating services
PA: H & H Graphics, Inc.
854 N Prince St
Lancaster PA 17603
717 393-3941

(G-9037)
HALEY PAINT COMPANY (PA)
Also Called: Finnaren & Haley Company
194 Greenfield Rd (17601-5832)
PHONE..............................717 299-6771
Robert A Haley Jr, *CEO*
Joseph Giandonato, *President*
Regina Haley Pakradooni, *President*
Haley Lancaster, *Store Mgr*
Francis X Connell, *Treasurer*
▼ EMP: 80
SQ FT: 100,000
SALES (est): 36.7MM **Privately Held**
WEB: www.fhpaint.com
SIC: 5231 2851 Paints: oil or alkyd vehicle
or water thinned; paint

(G-9038)
**HAMMOND PRETZEL BAKERY
INC**
Also Called: Hammond's Old Fashnd Hnd
Made
716 S West End Ave Rear (17603-5050)
PHONE..............................717 392-7532
Brian Nicklaus, *President*
Karen Achtermann, *Vice Pres*
EMP: 20 EST: 1931
SQ FT: 4,000
SALES (est): 1.2MM **Privately Held**
WEB: www.hammondpretzels.com
SIC: 2052 Pretzels

(G-9039)
HARROWGATE FINE FOODS INC
2322 Hancock Dr (17601-2818)
PHONE..............................717 823-6855
Ron Steele, *President*
EMP: 3
SALES (est): 239.5K **Privately Held**
SIC: 2099 Tea blending

(G-9040)
HAVERSTICK BROS INC
2111 Stone Mill Rd (17601-6099)
PHONE..............................717 392-5722
H C Haverstick, *President*
James Haverstick, *Vice Pres*
EMP: 14 EST: 1947
SQ FT: 10,000
SALES: 2.9MM **Privately Held**
SIC: 5084 5085 3599 7692 Hydraulic
systems equipment & supplies; power
transmission equipment & apparatus; ma-
chine shop, jobbing & repair; welding re-
pair

(G-9041)
HEILIG DEFENSE LLC
171 Eshelman Rd (17601-5643)
PHONE..............................717 490-6833
EMP: 3
SALES (est): 165.9K **Privately Held**
SIC: 3812 Defense systems & equipment

(G-9042)
HEISEY MACHINE CO INC
78 Pitney Rd (17602-2614)
PHONE..............................717 293-1373
Winston L Heisey, *President*
EMP: 9
SALES: 800K **Privately Held**
WEB: www.heiseymachine.com
SIC: 3541 3533 Drilling machine tools
(metal cutting); oil & gas field machinery

(G-9043)
HERLEY INDUSTRIES INC
Ultra Electronics Herley
3061 Industry Dr (17603-4092)
PHONE..............................717 397-2777
Deanna Lund, *CEO*
Richard Poirier, *President*
EMP: 292
SALES (corp-wide): 1B **Privately Held**
WEB: www.herley.com
SIC: 3812 3679 Search & navigation
equipment; microwave components
HQ: Herley Industries, Inc.
3061 Industry Dr
Lancaster PA 17603
717 397-2777

(G-9044)
HERLEY INDUSTRIES INC
Also Called: Stewart Warner Electronics
3061 Industry Dr (17603-4092)
PHONE..............................717 397-2779
George Rounsaville, *Branch Mgr*
EMP: 5
SALES (corp-wide): 1B **Privately Held**
WEB: www.herley.com
SIC: 3679 Microwave components
HQ: Herley Industries, Inc.
3061 Industry Dr
Lancaster PA 17603
717 397-2777

(G-9045)
HERSHEY COMPANY
400 Running Pump Rd (17603-2269)
PHONE..............................717 509-9795
Gary Young, *Purchasing*
Louis Mendoza, *QC Dir*
Ken Ewing, *Personnel*
Pete Sydorko, *Branch Mgr*
Douglas Hartman, *Admin Sec*
EMP: 767
SALES (corp-wide): 7.7B **Publicly Held**
WEB: www.hersheys.com
SIC: 2064 Licorice candy
PA: Hershey Company
100 Crystal A Dr
Hershey PA 17033
717 534-4200

(G-9046)
HIGH INDUSTRIES INC (PA)
1853 William Penn Way (17601-6713)
P.O. Box 10008 (17605-0008)
PHONE..............................717 293-4444
Michael F Shirk, *CEO*
S Dale High, *Ch of Bd*
Jeffrey L Sterner, *President*
Jason Schultz, *General Mgr*
Sandy Knoll, *Principal*
EMP: 280
SQ FT: 80,000
SALES (est): 434.6MM **Privately Held**
SIC: 1791 3272 5051 3441 Structural
steel erection; prestressed concrete prod-
ucts; steel; fabricated structural metal

(G-9047)
HIGH STEEL STRUCTURES LLC
144 Greenfield Rd (17601-5815)
PHONE..............................717 390-4227
Chuck Gillenwater, *Principal*
EMP: 13
SALES (corp-wide): 434.6MM **Privately
Held**
SIC: 3441 Fabricated structural metal
HQ: High Steel Structures Llc
1915 Old Phladelphia Pike
Lancaster PA 17602

(G-9048)
**HIGH STEEL STRUCTURES LLC
(HQ)**
1915 Old Phladelphia Pike (17602-3410)
P.O. Box 10008 (17605-0008)
PHONE..............................717 299-5211
Michael F Shirk, *CEO*
Brian Laborde, *President*
Steven M Bussanmas, *Senior VP*
Dean M Glick, *Vice Pres*
Paul A Lipinsky, *Vice Pres*
▲ EMP: 430
SQ FT: 330,000
SALES: 166.2MM
SALES (corp-wide): 434.6MM **Privately
Held**
WEB: www.highsteel.com
SIC: 3441 Fabricated structural metal
PA: High Industries Inc.
1853 William Penn Way
Lancaster PA 17601
717 293-4444

(G-9049)
HIGH STEEL STRUCTURES LLC
Also Called: High Steel Structures Div
1915 Old Phladelphia Pike (17602-3410)
PHONE..............................717 299-5211
Pat Lofpus, *President*
EMP: 9

(G-9050)
HOBART CORPORATION
165 Independence Ct (17601-5838)
PHONE..............................717 397-5100
Linford Sensenig, *Branch Mgr*
EMP: 21
SALES (corp-wide): 14.7B **Publicly Held**
WEB: www.hobartcorp.com
SIC: 3589 3554 3531 Sewage & water
treatment equipment; paper industries
machinery; construction machinery
HQ: Hobart Llc
701 S Ridge Ave
Troy OH 45374
937 332-3000

(G-9051)
HODGE TOOL CO INC
2831 Old Tree Dr (17603-7301)
PHONE..............................717 393-5543
Edward R Hodgen, *President*
Mary Ann Nagle, *Admin Sec*
▲ EMP: 45 EST: 1979
SQ FT: 30,000
SALES (est): 7.8MM **Privately Held**
WEB: www.hodgetool.com
SIC: 3544 Special dies & tools

(G-9052)
**HUEPENBECKER ENTERPRISES
INC**
Also Called: Sir Speedy
854 N Prince St (17603-2752)
PHONE..............................717 393-3941
Camilla Huepenbecker, *President*
Mary Kohler, *Corp Secy*
EMP: 15
SQ FT: 11,000
SALES (est): 1.5MM **Privately Held**
WEB: www.3speedys.com
SIC: 2752 7334 2241 Commercial print-
ing, offset; photocopying & duplicating
services; bindings, textile

(G-9053)
IC&S DISTRIBUTING CO
Also Called: Ilva USA
1833 William Penn Way (17601-6712)
P.O. Box 10845 (17605-0845)
PHONE..............................717 391-6250
Nelson W Baker, *President*
▲ EMP: 20
SQ FT: 50,000
SALES (est): 3.2MM **Privately Held**
WEB: www.ics-company.com
SIC: 2851 Paints & allied products

(G-9054)
**IDEAL PRTG CO LANCASTER
INC**
Also Called: PIP Printing
1136 Elizabeth Ave (17601-4364)
PHONE..............................717 299-2643
Emil Vanlierde, *President*
EMP: 4
SQ FT: 3,000
SALES (est): 382.9K **Privately Held**
SIC: 2752 Commercial printing, offset

(G-9055)
IEHLE ENTERPRISES INC
Also Called: Lehle Enterprises
1305 Manheim Pike Ste 2 (17601-3194)
PHONE..............................717 859-1113
Doug Iehle, *President*
EMP: 35
SALES (est): 2.4MM **Privately Held**
WEB: www.ieembroidery.com
SIC: 5199 2395 Advertising specialties;
pleating & stitching

SALES (corp-wide): 434.6MM **Privately
Held**
SIC: 3441 1791 5051 3272 Fabricated
structural metal; structural steel erection;
metals service centers & offices; concrete
products; industrial buildings & warehouses; nonresidential construction
HQ: High Steel Structures Llc
1915 Old Phladelphia Pike
Lancaster PA 17602

(G-9056)
INDOOR CITY GRANITE & MBL INC
1284 Loop Rd (17601-3114)
PHONE...................................717 393-3931
Frank Barrett, *President*
EMP: 10
SQ FT: 8,000
SALES (est): 1.2MM **Privately Held**
SIC: 3281 Cut stone & stone products

(G-9057)
INGRAIN CONSTRUCTION LLC (PA)
735 Lafayette St (17603-5514)
PHONE...................................717 205-1475
Tom Grab, *CEO*
EMP: 16
SALES (est): 2.7MM **Privately Held**
SIC: 3423 2511 Carpenters' hand tools, except saws: levels, chisels, etc.; wood household furniture

(G-9058)
INTEGRATED METAL PRODUCTS INC
Also Called: Advancing Alternative
2016 Single Tree Ln (17602-1021)
PHONE...................................717 824-4052
David S Stoltzfus, *President*
EMP: 6
SALES (est): 1MM **Privately Held**
SIC: 3448 2441 Greenhouses: prefabricated metal; flats, wood: greenhouse

(G-9059)
INTERFACE SOLUTIONS INC
216 Wohlsen Way (17603-4043)
PHONE...................................717 824-8009
EMP: 3
SALES (est): 160.1K **Privately Held**
SIC: 3053 Gaskets, packing & sealing devices

(G-9060)
INTERNATIONAL PAPER COMPANY
801 Fountain Ave (17601-4532)
PHONE...................................717 391-3400
James P Bonifas, *Branch Mgr*
EMP: 110
SALES (corp-wide): 23.3B **Publicly Held**
WEB: www.internationalpaper.com
SIC: 2621 Paper mills
PA: International Paper Company
6400 Poplar Ave
Memphis TN 38197
901 419-9000

(G-9061)
INTERVIDEO INC
35 E Orange St (17602-2801)
PHONE...................................717 435-9433
Matt Drake,
EMP: 3 EST: 2014
SALES (est): 308K **Privately Held**
SIC: 3674 Microprocessors

(G-9062)
INTRICATE EDM LLC
Also Called: Intricate Precision Mfg
2970 Old Tree Dr (17603-4058)
PHONE...................................717 392-8244
Thomas H Frick Jr, *President*
EMP: 8
SALES (est): 850K **Privately Held**
SIC: 3599 Machine shop, jobbing & repair

(G-9063)
INTRICATE PRECISION MFG LLC
2970 Old Tree Dr (17603-4058)
PHONE...................................717 392-8244
Thomas Frick, *President*
EMP: 8
SALES (est): 1.1MM **Privately Held**
SIC: 3599 Machine shop, jobbing & repair

(G-9064)
IRON COMPASS MAP COMPANY
313 W Liberty St Ste 239 (17603-2748)
P.O. Box 8966 (17604-8966)
PHONE...................................717 295-1194
John Fix, *President*
EMP: 5

SALES (est): 594.5K **Privately Held**
WEB: www.ironcompassmap.com
SIC: 7372 Application computer software

(G-9065)
ITT CORPORATION
33 Centerville Rd (17603-4004)
PHONE...................................717 509-2200
Michael J Garrison, *General Mgr*
Paul Kisner, *Purch Mgr*
Hui Lee, *Engineer*
James Daniels, *Senior Engr*
Heather Sandoe, *Sls & Mktg Exec*
EMP: 260
SALES (corp-wide): 2.7B **Publicly Held**
WEB: www.ittind.com
SIC: 3625 Control equipment, electric
HQ: Itt Llc
1133 Westchester Ave N-100
White Plains NY 10604
914 641-2000

(G-9066)
ITT ENGINEERED VALVES LLC
33 Centerville Rd (17603-4068)
PHONE...................................717 509-2200
Robert J Pagano, *Principal*
Kurt Haegele, *Buyer*
Erik Albright, *Financial Analy*
Darrin Erickson, *Manager*
EMP: 19
SALES (corp-wide): 2.7B **Publicly Held**
SIC: 3491 Industrial valves
HQ: Itt Engineered Valves, Llc
240 Fall St
Seneca Falls NY 13148
662 257-6982

(G-9067)
J & L LOGGING
46b Hartman Bridge Rd (17602-1412)
PHONE...................................717 687-8096
John Stoltzfus, *Partner*
Levi Stoltzfus, *Partner*
EMP: 9
SALES (est): 950K **Privately Held**
SIC: 2411 Logging camps & contractors

(G-9068)
J C SNAVELY & SONS INC
Snavely's
3149 Hempland Rd (17601-1311)
PHONE...................................717 291-8989
Alan Simpson, *Manager*
EMP: 45
SALES (corp-wide): 30.4MM **Privately Held**
SIC: 2431 Millwork
PA: J C Snavely & Sons Inc
150 Main St
Landisville PA 17538
717 898-2241

(G-9069)
J THOMAS LTD
300 Richardson Dr (17603-4034)
PHONE...................................717 397-3483
Margaret F Thomas, *CEO*
Daniel J Thomas, *President*
EMP: 42
SQ FT: 32,000
SALES: 2.1MM **Privately Held**
SIC: 3443 3713 3441 Mfg Fabricated Plate Work Mfg Truck/Bus Bodies Structural Metal Fabrication

(G-9070)
JAMES K WALLICK
25 Dickinson Ave (17603-4429)
PHONE...................................717 471-8152
James K Wallick, *Owner*
EMP: 3
SALES (est): 173.6K **Privately Held**
SIC: 3471 Finishing, metals or formed products

(G-9071)
JAMES RICHARD WOODWORKING
Also Called: Richard James Woodworking
727 W Vine St (17603-5539)
PHONE...................................717 397-4790
James Barndollar, *Owner*
EMP: 10
SALES (est): 780K **Privately Held**
SIC: 2431 Millwork

(G-9072)
JAREN ENTERPRISES INC
Also Called: Curry Copy Center
155 E King St (17602-2803)
PHONE...................................717 394-2671
James V Abbarno, *President*
Carole Gerz, *Vice Pres*
Irene Abbarno, *Treasurer*
EMP: 4
SQ FT: 1,000
SALES (est): 390K **Privately Held**
SIC: 2752 2759 Commercial printing, offset; menus: printing

(G-9073)
JL CLARK LLC
Also Called: Lancaster Metals
303 N Plum St (17602-2401)
PHONE...................................717 392-4125
Rick Jones, *General Mgr*
Fred Wilds II, *Project Mgr*
Emily Karel, *Mfg Staff*
B Andrews Smith, *Engrg Mgr*
James Fidler, *Manager*
EMP: 150
SQ FT: 244,000
SALES (corp-wide): 1.5B **Privately Held**
SIC: 3411 3444 Metal cans; sheet metalwork
HQ: J.L. Clark Llc
923 23rd Ave
Rockford IL 61104
815 961-5609

(G-9074)
JOHNSON & JOHNSON CONSUMER INC
1838 Colonial Village Ln (17601-6700)
PHONE...................................717 207-3500
Donna Humski, *General Mgr*
EMP: 227
SALES (corp-wide): 81.5B **Publicly Held**
SIC: 2834 Pharmaceutical preparations
HQ: Johnson & Johnson Consumer Inc.
199 Grandview Rd
Skillman NJ 08558
908 874-1000

(G-9075)
JS&D GRAPHICS INC
1770 Hempstead Rd (17601-6706)
P.O. Box 11027 (17605-1027)
PHONE...................................717 397-3440
Joyce Morris, *President*
Stephen Morris, *Vice Pres*
EMP: 8
SALES: 380K **Privately Held**
SIC: 2711 Commercial printing & newspaper publishing combined

(G-9076)
K&L PLATING COMPANY INC
524 E Mifflin St (17602-3720)
PHONE...................................717 397-9819
James Struck, *President*
Sandra Riger, *Senior VP*
David Riger, *Vice Pres*
EMP: 19
SQ FT: 15,000
SALES (est): 2.8MM **Privately Held**
SIC: 3471 Plating of metals or formed products

(G-9077)
K2 CONCEPTS INC
114 Prince St (17603)
PHONE...................................717 207-0820
Bryan Kepner, *President*
EMP: 12
SALES (est): 1.2MM **Privately Held**
WEB: www.k2concepts.net
SIC: 2899 Chemical supplies for foundries

(G-9078)
KALAS MFG INC (PA)
167 Greenfield Rd (17601-5814)
PHONE...................................717 336-5575
Jack Witwer, *President*
Jon J Wiig, *Vice Pres*
Dennis M Melnyk, *CFO*
Janelle Meyer, *Accountant*
Frederick Wagaman, *Info Tech Mgr*
▲ EMP: 100
SQ FT: 100,000

SALES (est): 85.3MM **Privately Held**
WEB: www.kalaswire.com
SIC: 3357 3694 Nonferrous wiredrawing & insulating; engine electrical equipment

(G-9079)
KELLOGG COMPANY
2050 State Rd (17601-1821)
P.O. Box 3006 (17604-3006)
PHONE...................................717 898-0161
Steve Harvey, *Branch Mgr*
EMP: 508
SALES (corp-wide): 13.5B **Publicly Held**
WEB: www.kelloggs.com
SIC: 2043 Cereal breakfast foods
PA: Kellogg Company
1 Kellogg Sq
Battle Creek MI 49017
269 961-2000

(G-9080)
KELLY PRECISION MACHINING CO
1895 Commerce Park E (17601-5808)
PHONE...................................717 396-8622
Wayne Coleman, *Partner*
Rachel Coleman, *Partner*
EMP: 3
SQ FT: 5,000
SALES: 300K **Privately Held**
SIC: 3599 Machine & other job shop work

(G-9081)
KEN LEAMAN SIGNS
2060 Lincoln Hwy E (17602-5910)
PHONE...................................717 295-4531
Ken Leaman, *Owner*
EMP: 3
SALES (est): 196.4K **Privately Held**
SIC: 3993 Signs, not made in custom sign painting shops

(G-9082)
KERR GROUP LLC (DH)
1846 Charter Ln Ste 209 (17601-6773)
PHONE...................................812 424-2904
Richard D Hofmann, *President*
Steven Rafter, *President*
Peter A Siebert, *COO*
Lawrence C Caldwell, *Exec VP*
Bruce T Cleevely, *Vice Pres*
◆ EMP: 20 EST: 1903
SQ FT: 33,000
SALES (est): 102.8MM **Publicly Held**
WEB: www.kerrgroup.com
SIC: 3089 Closures, plastic; jars, plastic; tubs, plastic (containers); plastic containers, except foam
HQ: Berry Global, Inc.
101 Oakley St
Evansville IN 47710
812 424-2904

(G-9083)
KERR GROUP LLC
1846 Charter Ln Ste 209 (17601-6773)
PHONE...................................812 424-2904
R Beeler, *Branch Mgr*
EMP: 136 **Publicly Held**
SIC: 3089 Plastic containers, except foam
HQ: Kerr Group, Llc
1846 Charter Ln Ste 209
Lancaster PA 17601
812 424-2904

(G-9084)
KEYSTONE GRANITE TILE INC
1905 Olde Homestead Ln (17601-5824)
PHONE...................................717 394-4972
Mustafa Ayaz, *Principal*
▲ EMP: 18 EST: 2012
SALES (est): 3.4MM **Privately Held**
SIC: 1423 5032 Diorite, crushed & broken-quarrying; marble building stone

(G-9085)
KEYSTONE WOOD SPECIALTIES INC
2225 Old Phladelphia Pike (17602-3416)
P.O. Box 10127 (17605-0127)
PHONE...................................717 299-6288
Samuel D Stoltzfus, *President*
David Landis, *Safety Mgr*
Rolph Kullander, *Mktg Dir*
Jane Shenk, *Admin Asst*
Jean Troy, *Assistant*

▼ **EMP:** 56
SQ FT: 63,267
SALES (est): 9MM **Privately Held**
SIC: 2431 Doors, wood

(G-9086)
KING ASSOCIATES LTD
Also Called: Kord King Company
62 Industrial Cir (17601-5928)
PHONE..................................717 556-5673
Tom King, *President*
Timothy King, *President*
Carol E King, *Corp Secy*
Thomas King, *Vice Pres*
▲ **EMP:** 100
SQ FT: 30,000
SALES (est): 28.2MM **Privately Held**
WEB: www.kordking.com
SIC: 3643 Connectors, electric cord

(G-9087)
KIRBY AGRI INC (PA)
Also Called: Margro
500 Running Pump Rd (17601-2241)
P.O. Box 6277 (17607-6277)
PHONE..................................717 299-2541
Carroll Kirby Jr, *President*
Carroll Kirby III, *Senior VP*
Rick Kirby, *Vice Pres*
Thomas Calcaterra, *Treasurer*
EMP: 25
SQ FT: 60,000
SALES (est): 23.3MM **Privately Held**
WEB: www.kirbyagri.com
SIC: 2875 5191 Fertilizers, mixing only;
chemicals, agricultural; fertilizer & fertil-
izer materials

(G-9088)
KREIDER FOODS INC
1555 Sylvan Rd (17601-7138)
PHONE..................................717 898-3372
Frank Kreider, *President*
Dale Kreider, *Vice Pres*
Barbara Sheaffer, *Admin Sec*
EMP: 15
SALES: 3.5MM **Privately Held**
SIC: 2037 Frozen fruits & vegetables

(G-9089)
KUNZLER & COMPANY INC (PA)
652 Manor St (17603-5108)
P.O. Box 4747 (17604-4747)
PHONE..................................717 299-6301
Christian C Kunzler III, *President*
John S Kunzler, *Vice Pres*
Bill Lambert, *Prdtn Mgr*
Bob Reese, *Production*
Cory Sharpe, *Production*
EMP: 330 **EST:** 1901
SQ FT: 132,816
SALES (est): 117.4MM **Privately Held**
SIC: 2011 2013 Meat packing plants;
smoked meats from purchased meat

(G-9090)
LANCASTER BREWING COMPANY
302 N Plum St (17602-2402)
PHONE..................................717 391-6258
Peter Keares, *CEO*
Irene Keares, *President*
Irene S Keares, *Corp Secy*
Prentice Macdougall, *Manager*
Brenda Yeager, *Manager*
EMP: 35
SQ FT: 16,000
SALES (est): 7.3MM **Privately Held**
WEB: www.lancasterbrewing.com
SIC: 2082 5169 Beer (alcoholic bever-
age); alcohols

(G-9091)
LANCASTER COMPOSITE
131 Stable Dr (17603-9788)
PHONE..................................717 872-8999
Harrison Greene, *Principal*
EMP: 7 **EST:** 2010
SALES (est): 870.5K **Privately Held**
SIC: 3443 Pile shells, metal plate

(G-9092)
LANCASTER CONTACT LENS INC
Also Called: Lancaster Artificial Eye
700 Eden Rd Ste 2 (17601-4700)
PHONE..................................717 569-7386
Dominic C Siviglia, *President*
EMP: 7
SQ FT: 9,000
SALES (est): 750K **Privately Held**
WEB: www.lancastercontactlens.com
SIC: 5995 3851 Eyeglasses, prescription;
contact lenses, prescription; contact
lenses; eyes, glass & plastic

(G-9093)
LANCASTER EXTRUSION INC
212 Hazel St (17603-5630)
PHONE..................................717 392-9622
Mya Lau, *President*
EMP: 3
SQ FT: 18,000
SALES: 250K **Privately Held**
WEB: www.lancasterextrusion.com
SIC: 2673 Plastic bags: made from pur-
chased materials

(G-9094)
LANCASTER FINE FOODS INC
501 Richardson Dr Ste 100 (17603-4276)
PHONE..................................717 397-9578
Michael S Thompson, *CEO*
Michael Thompson, *CEO*
D Cahill, *President*
Mark Thompson, *Treasurer*
Scott Goldsmith, *Admin Sec*
EMP: 50
SQ FT: 33,000
SALES (est): 12.2MM **Privately Held**
WEB: www.beaniesoflancaster.com
SIC: 2035 5963 Seasonings & sauces, ex-
cept tomato & dry; mustard, prepared
(wet); food services, direct sales
PA: Earth Pride Organics, Llc
501 Richardson Dr Ste 200
Lancaster PA 17603

(G-9095)
LANCASTER GENERAL SVCS BUS TR (DH)
Also Called: Print Shop , The
607 N Duke St (17602-2269)
PHONE..................................717 544-5474
Andre W Renna, *President*
EMP: 12
SQ FT: 1,500
SALES (est): 7.7MM
SALES (corp-wide): 9.1MM **Privately Held**
SIC: 4226 6512 2752 2789 Document &
office records storage; nonresidential
building operators; commercial printing,
lithographic; bookbinding & related work;
miscellaneous publishing
HQ: Lancaster General Health
555 N Duke St
Lancaster PA 17602
717 290-5511

(G-9096)
LANCASTER GENERAL SVCS BUS TR
Print Shop, The
555 N Duke St (17602-2250)
PHONE..................................800 341-2121
Susan Frey, *Manager*
Keith Cromwell, *Manager*
Manny Perez, *Manager*
Donna Ricketts, *Manager*
Joye Mahler, *Supervisor*
EMP: 11
SALES (corp-wide): 9.1MM **Privately Held**
SIC: 2752 Commercial printing, offset
HQ: Lancaster General Services Business
Trust
607 N Duke St
Lancaster PA 17602
717 544-5474

(G-9097)
LANCASTER LEAF TOB CO PA INC (DH)
198 W Liberty St (17601-2712)
P.O. Box 897 (17608-0897)
PHONE..................................717 394-2676
Freidrich G Bossert, *President*
T K Walsh Jr, *President*
Claude Martin, *Chairman*
D C Moore, *Corp Secy*
T E Stephenson, *Vice Pres*
◆ **EMP:** 40 **EST:** 1941
SQ FT: 100,000
SALES (est): 44.5MM
SALES (corp-wide): 2B **Publicly Held**
SIC: 5159 2141 Tobacco distributors &
products; tobacco stemming & redrying

(G-9098)
LANCASTER LEAF TOB CO PA INC
207 Pitney Rd (17601-5626)
PHONE..................................717 291-1528
Ernest Blachek, *Manager*
John Chism, *Manager*
EMP: 21
SALES (corp-wide): 2B **Publicly Held**
SIC: 2141 Tobacco stemming & redrying
HQ: Lancaster Leaf Tobacco Company Of
Pennsylvania, Inc.
198 W Liberty St
Lancaster PA 17603
717 394-2676

(G-9099)
LANCASTER LEAF TOB CO PA INC
850 N Water St (17603-2711)
PHONE..................................717 393-1526
Joe Everett, *Principal*
EMP: 5
SALES (corp-wide): 2B **Publicly Held**
SIC: 5159 2141 Tobacco distributors &
products; tobacco stemming & redrying
HQ: Lancaster Leaf Tobacco Company Of
Pennsylvania, Inc.
198 W Liberty St
Lancaster PA 17603
717 394-2676

(G-9100)
LANCASTER LIME WORKS
1630 Millersville Pike (17603-6217)
PHONE..................................717 207-7014
John Ellins, *Mng Member*
EMP: 11
SALES (est): 908.7K **Privately Held**
SIC: 3274 Building lime

(G-9101)
LANCASTER METAL MFG INC
1548 Fruitville Pike (17601-4056)
P.O. Box 3245 (17604-3245)
PHONE..................................717 293-4480
Paul Spradling, *President*
Thomas L Wickenheiser, *Vice Pres*
EMP: 66
SALES (est): 14.3MM
SALES (corp-wide): 172.4MM **Publicly
Held**
WEB: www.govrad.com
SIC: 3443 Fabricated plate work (boiler
shop)
PA: Burnham Holdings, Inc.
1241 Harrisburg Ave
Lancaster PA 17603
717 390-7800

(G-9102)
LANCASTER METALS SCIENCE CORP
Also Called: LMS
826 N Queen St (17603-2740)
PHONE..................................717 299-9709
Ralph Ludewig, *President*
Robert Ludewig, *Corp Secy*
Carmen Ailes, *Vice Pres*
EMP: 21
SQ FT: 18,000
SALES (est): 5.2MM **Privately Held**
WEB: www.lancastermetals.com
SIC: 3599 Chemical milling job shop

(G-9103)
LANCASTER PARTS & EQP INC
Also Called: Lsc Equipment
2008 Horseshoe Rd (17602-1008)
PHONE..................................717 299-3721
Omar S Smucker, *President*
Rachel H Smucker, *Admin Sec*
◆ **EMP:** 11 **EST:** 1967
SQ FT: 8,000
SALES: 6.7MM **Privately Held**
WEB: www.lancastersilo.com
SIC: 5083 3523 7699 Agricultural machin-
ery & equipment; farm equipment parts &
supplies; farm machinery & equipment;
agricultural equipment repair services;
farm machinery repair

(G-9104)
LANCASTER PROPANE GAS INC (PA)
2860 Yellow Goose Rd (17601-1814)
PHONE..................................717 898-0800
Paul S Wheaton, *President*
Heidi F Wheaton, *Treasurer*
EMP: 10
SQ FT: 20,000
SALES (est): 6MM **Privately Held**
WEB: www.lancasterpropanegas.com
SIC: 1321 5085 5722 5984 Propane
(natural) production; tanks, pressurized;
household appliance stores; propane gas,
bottled

(G-9105)
LANCASTER PUMP
Also Called: Lancaster Pump & Water Trtmnt
1340 Manheim Pike (17601-3196)
PHONE..................................717 397-3521
John Wenzel, *CEO*
EMP: 26
SALES (est): 3.4MM **Privately Held**
SIC: 3589 Service industry machinery

(G-9106)
LANCASTER SIGN SOURCE INC
Also Called: Fastsigns
121 Centerville Rd (17603-4006)
PHONE..................................717 569-7606
Ark Wynne, *President*
Albert Hall, *Senior VP*
EMP: 18 **EST:** 1998
SQ FT: 3,550
SALES (est): 2.3MM **Privately Held**
SIC: 3993 Signs & advertising specialties

(G-9107)
LANDIS NEON SIGN CO INC
425 Rohrerstown Rd (17603-2234)
PHONE..................................717 397-0588
Kevin Landis, *Owner*
EMP: 6
SALES (est): 290K **Privately Held**
SIC: 3993 Neon signs

(G-9108)
LASER IMAGING SYSTEMS INC
Also Called: Lis
2100 State Rd (17601-1812)
PHONE..................................717 266-1700
Ned Ensmiger, *President*
Larry Begelfer, *Vice Pres*
Lori Baum, *Admin Sec*
EMP: 35
SALES (est): 5MM
SALES (corp-wide): 20MM **Privately
Held**
WEB: www.laserlis.com
SIC: 2759 Laser printing
HQ: Pemcor Printing Company, Llc
330 Eden Rd
Lancaster PA 17601
717 898-1555

(G-9109)
LEGGS HANES BALI FACTORY OTLT
104 Stanley K Tanger Blvd (17602-1468)
PHONE..................................717 392-2511
Jodie Moore, *Principal*
EMP: 3 **EST:** 2010
SALES (est): 197K **Privately Held**
SIC: 3643 Outlets, electric: convenience

(G-9110)
LENOX MACHINE INC
833 2nd St Ste I (17603-3235)
PHONE................................717 394-8760
William P Lenox, *President*
Diane Lenox, *Corp Secy*
Mathew Lenox, *Vice Pres*
William Lenox Jr, *Vice Pres*
EMP: 4
SQ FT: 5,000
SALES: 250K **Privately Held**
SIC: 3599 Machine shop, jobbing & repair

(G-9111)
LIGHTHOUSE STUDIOS INC
439 E Ross St (17602-1943)
PHONE................................717 394-1300
Daniel Martin, *Principal*
EMP: 3
SALES (est): 269.9K **Privately Held**
SIC: 2759 Screen printing

(G-9112)
LINEAR ACOUSTIC INC
108 Foxshire Dr (17601-3982)
PHONE................................717 735-6142
Fax: 717 735-3612
EMP: 9
SALES (est): 1.6MM **Privately Held**
SIC: 3663 Mfg Radio/Tv Communication
Equipment

(G-9113)
LINK SOFTWARE CORP
815 E Madison St (17602-2423)
PHONE................................717 399-3023
Hai Banh, *President*
Loi Banh, *Vice Pres*
EMP: 6 EST: 1997
SQ FT: 700
SALES: 1.5MM **Privately Held**
SIC: 7372 Prepackaged software

(G-9114)
LONGS HORSERADISH
2192 W Ridge Dr (17603-6150)
PHONE................................717 872-9343
Michael J Long, *President*
EMP: 3
SALES (est): 190K **Privately Held**
SIC: 2035 Pickles, sauces & salad dress-
ings

(G-9115)
LPW RACING PRODUCTS INC
632 E Marion St (17602-3136)
PHONE................................717 394-7432
Douglas K Fellenbaum, *President*
EMP: 3
SALES (est): 371.8K **Privately Held**
SIC: 3714 Motor vehicle parts & acces-
sories

(G-9116)
LSC COMMUNICATIONS US LLC
1375 Harrisburg Pike (17601-2612)
PHONE................................717 392-4074
EMP: 980
SQ FT: 2,584
SALES (corp-wide): 3.8B **Publicly Held**
WEB: www.rrdonnelley.com
SIC: 2752 2789 2759 Commercial print-
ing, offset; bookbinding & related work;
commercial printing
HQ: Lsc Communications Us, Llc
191 N Wacker Dr Ste 1400
Chicago IL 60606
844 572-5720

(G-9117)
LUMSDEN CORPORATION (PA)
Also Called: Hoyt Wire Cloth Div
10 Abraso St (17601-3104)
P.O. Box 4647 (17604-4647)
PHONE................................717 394-6871
Glenn P Farrell, *CEO*
Arthur Lumsden, *President*
Tom Boaman, *Vice Pres*
Gina Mitchell, *Vice Pres*
Alexander D Lumsden, *Treasurer*
▲ EMP: 125
SQ FT: 63,000

SALES (est): 24.2MM **Privately Held**
WEB: www.lumsdencorp.com
SIC: 3496 3535 Screening, woven wire;
made from purchased wire; belt conveyor
systems, general industrial use

(G-9118)
LUXOTTICA OF AMERICA INC
Also Called: Lenscrafters
1158 Park City Ctr (17601-2726)
PHONE................................717 295-3001
Mary Lyons, *Branch Mgr*
EMP: 25
SALES (corp-wide): 283.5MM **Privately
Held**
WEB: www.lenscrafters.com
SIC: 5995 3851 Eyeglasses, prescription;
ophthalmic goods
HQ: Luxottica Of America Inc.
4000 Luxottica Pl
Mason OH 45040

(G-9119)
**LYDALL PERFORMANCE MTLS
US INC**
310 Running Pump Rd (17603-2249)
PHONE................................717 207-6000
EMP: 135
SALES (corp-wide): 785.9MM **Publicly
Held**
SIC: 3053 Gasket materials
HQ: Lydall Performance Materials (Us), Inc.
216 Wohlsen Way
Lancaster PA 17603

(G-9120)
**LYDALL PERFORMANCE MTLS
US INC**
320 Running Pump Rd (17603-2249)
PHONE................................717 207-6025
EMP: 135
SALES (corp-wide): 785.9MM **Publicly
Held**
SIC: 3053 Gasket materials
HQ: Lydall Performance Materials (Us), Inc.
216 Wohlsen Way
Lancaster PA 17603

(G-9121)
**LYDALL PERFORMANCE MTLS
US INC (DH)**
216 Wohlsen Way (17603-4043)
PHONE................................717 390-1886
Victor Swint, *President*
Krishna Venkataswamy, *Senior VP*
Alex Konya, *Vice Pres*
Bob Rathsam, *CFO*
◆ EMP: 50
SALES (est): 117.3MM
SALES (corp-wide): 785.9MM **Publicly
Held**
WEB: www.sealinfo.com
SIC: 3053 Gasket materials
HQ: Susquehanna Capital Acquisition Co
216 Wohlsen Way
Lancaster PA 17603
800 942-7538

(G-9122)
MAC-IT CORPORATION
275 E Liberty St (17602-1999)
PHONE................................717 397-3535
Michael Stillman, *President*
Jean Zymnis, *Manager*
Rob Stillman, *Executive*
EMP: 25
SQ FT: 43,000
SALES (est): 4.1MM **Privately Held**
WEB: www.macit.com
SIC: 3451 3452 Screw machine products;
bolts, nuts, rivets & washers

(G-9123)
**MACHINED PRODUCTS
COMPANY**
82 Pitney Rd (17602-2614)
P.O. Box 10456 (17605-0456)
PHONE................................717 299-3757
Gerard Gammache, *President*
Kathleen Saul, *Corp Secy*
Barry Enos, *Vice Pres*
Michael Gammache, *Vice Pres*
Kathy Saul, *CPA*
EMP: 35
SQ FT: 25,000

SALES (est): 7.4MM **Privately Held**
WEB: www.mpco.net
SIC: 3599 Machine shop, jobbing & repair

(G-9124)
MAKES SCENTS LLC
336 N Charlotte St # 100 (17603-3073)
PHONE................................717 824-3094
Heather Kreider, *Owner*
EMP: 5
SALES (est): 221.7K **Privately Held**
SIC: 2844 Cosmetic preparations

(G-9125)
**MARTINS DRAPERIES &
INTERIORS**
1520 Commerce Dr (17601-2749)
PHONE................................717 239-0501
Dorothy Martin, *President*
Larry Martin, *Vice Pres*
EMP: 9
SALES: 870K **Privately Held**
SIC: 2391 7389 Curtains & draperies; inte-
rior designer

(G-9126)
**MAUGUS MANUFACTURING INC
(PA)**
Also Called: Nnbc
505 E Fulton St (17602-3022)
PHONE................................717 299-5681
Ruth N Lamb, *Ch of Bd*
Richard Seavey, *President*
Michael Simms, *President*
Ronald Vellucci, *Vice Pres*
Tom Young, *Vice Pres*
◆ EMP: 12 EST: 1947
SQ FT: 4,200
SALES (est): 16.7MM **Privately Held**
WEB: www.nnbc-pa.com
SIC: 3991 3466 Brooms & brushes;
crowns & closures

(G-9127)
MAUGUS MANUFACTURING INC
708 E Walnut St (17602-2435)
PHONE................................717 481-4823
Richard Seavey, *Branch Mgr*
EMP: 98
SALES (corp-wide): 16.7MM **Privately
Held**
WEB: www.nnbc-pa.com
SIC: 3991 Brooms & brushes
PA: Maugus Manufacturing, Inc.
505 E Fulton St
Lancaster PA 17602
717 299-5681

(G-9128)
**MAX INTRNTIONAL
CONVERTERS INC**
2360 Dairy Rd (17601-2308)
PHONE................................717 898-0147
Laura C Douglas, *CEO*
Michael Vigunas, *President*
Dianne Hulbert, *Vice Pres*
◆ EMP: 35
SQ FT: 40,000
SALES: 16.5MM **Privately Held**
WEB: www.maxintl.com
SIC: 2679 5112 Paper products, con-
verted; inked ribbons

(G-9129)
MAXIMA TECH & SYSTEMS INC
Also Called: Stewart Warner
1090 N Charlotte St (17603-2764)
PHONE................................717 569-5713
Oddie V Leopando, *President*
Avee Poston, *CFO*
EMP: 300
SALES (est): 35.1MM
SALES (corp-wide): 1.1B **Publicly Held**
WEB: www.stewartwarner.com
SIC: 3089 Automotive parts, plastic
HQ: Maxima Technologies & Systems Llc
1090 N Charlotte St # 101
Lancaster PA 17603
717 581-1000

(G-9130)
**MAXIMA TECH & SYSTEMS LLC
(HQ)**
1090 N Charlotte St # 101 (17603-2764)
PHONE................................717 581-1000

Brian West, *District Mgr*
Matthew Sturdy, *Vice Pres*
Brady Umberger, *Plant Mgr*
Mario Marmolejo, *Purchasing*
Cecilia Mireles, *Purchasing*
▲ EMP: 170 EST: 2003
SALES (est): 69.1MM
SALES (corp-wide): 1.1B **Publicly Held**
WEB: www.maximatech.com
SIC: 3823 3824 3825 3812 Industrial in-
strmnts msrmnt display/control process
variable; tachometer, centrifugal;
speedometers; elapsed time meters, elec-
tronic; search & navigation equipment;
switchgear & switchboard apparatus
PA: Actuant Corporation
N86w12500 Westbrook Xing
Menomonee Falls WI 53051
262 293-1500

(G-9131)
MEDICINE SHOPPE
625 S Duke St (17602-4509)
PHONE................................717 208-3415
EMP: 4
SALES (est): 371.7K **Privately Held**
SIC: 2834 Syrups, pharmaceutical

(G-9132)
**MERCHANDISING SOLUTIONS
INC**
2882 Yellow Goose Rd (17601-1814)
PHONE................................717 898-1800
Thomas Burns, *President*
Jessica Burns, *Manager*
EMP: 4
SALES (est): 429.9K **Privately Held**
SIC: 2541 Store & office display cases &
fixtures

(G-9133)
**MICRO PRECISION
CORPORATION**
Also Called: Esquire Holdings
200 Centerville Rd (17603-4074)
PHONE................................717 393-4100
Michael Peck, *President*
Kevin Curtis, *CFO*
Baron Abel, *Treasurer*
EMP: 55 EST: 1967
SQ FT: 20,000
SALES (est): 8.7MM **Privately Held**
WEB: www.mpcind.com
SIC: 3599 Machine & other job shop work

(G-9134)
MID ATLANTIC MUNICIPAL LLC
Also Called: Lancaster Truck Bodies
310 Richardson Dr (17603-4034)
PHONE................................717 394-2647
Paul Statler, *President*
Luis Olmeda, *Vice Pres*
John F Benton, *CFO*
EMP: 20
SALES: 4MM **Privately Held**
SIC: 3713 Truck bodies (motor vehicles)

(G-9135)
MIESSE CANDIES CORP
118 N Water St Ste 102 (17603-3873)
PHONE................................717 299-5427
Therese Walton, *Branch Mgr*
EMP: 5
SALES (corp-wide): 1MM **Privately Held**
SIC: 2064 5145 5441 Chocolate candy,
except solid chocolate; candy; confec-
tionery produced for direct sale on the
premises
PA: Miesse Candies Corp
877 N Hwy A1a
Indialantic FL

(G-9136)
**MILLER J WALTER COMPANY
INC**
411 E Chestnut St (17602-3016)
PHONE................................717 392-7428
Milton Morgan III, *President*
Thomas Oheher, *General Mgr*
Geoffrey Wolpert, *QC Mgr*
Helaina Sipe, *Controller*
Theresa Castrenze, *Manager*
EMP: 40 EST: 1887
SQ FT: 80,000

GEOGRAPHIC (vertical tab)

SALES (est): 8.6MM **Privately Held**
WEB: www.jwaltermiller.com
SIC: 3369 3366 Nonferrous foundries;
brass foundry

(G-9137)
MJJM ENTERPRISES INC
Also Called: Lancaster Reprographics
19 Prestige Ln (17603-4076)
PHONE....................................717 392-1711
James M Miklos, *President*
Michael Jones, *Vice Pres*
Greg Stauffer, *Production*
Susan Vidzicki, *Sales Mgr*
Diane Dungan, *Supervisor*
EMP: 30
SQ FT: 24,000
SALES (est): 5.5MM **Privately Held**
SIC: 2752 Commercial printing, offset

(G-9138)
MPC INDUSTRIES LLC
200 Centerville Rd (17603-4074)
PHONE....................................717 393-4100
Michael Rote, *Sales Mgr*
Michael Peck,
▲ EMP: 36
SALES (est): 7.2MM **Privately Held**
SIC: 3449 Miscellaneous metalwork

(G-9139)
MSI ACQUISITION CORP (DH)
3061 Industry Dr Ste 200 (17603-4025)
PHONE....................................717 397-2777
Deanna Lund, *CEO*
Eric Demarco, *President*
Michael Fink, *Vice Pres*
Laura Siegal, *Treasurer*
Deborah Butera, *Admin Sec*
EMP: 9
SALES (est): 7.3MM
SALES (corp-wide): 1B **Privately Held**
SIC: 3812 Search & navigation equipment
HQ: Herley Industries, Inc.
3061 Industry Dr
Lancaster PA 17603
717 397-2777

(G-9140)
MVP SPORTS & GAMES CO
50 Redwood Dr (17603-4404)
PHONE....................................302 250-4836
EMP: 4
SALES (est): 427.4K **Privately Held**
SIC: 3949 Darts & table sports equipment
& supplies

(G-9141)
MXL INDUSTRIES INC
1764 Rohrerstown Rd (17601-2320)
PHONE....................................717 569-8711
James Eberle, *President*
Russell E Priest, *COO*
John C Belknap, *Vice Pres*
Manny Rodriguez, *Vice Pres*
Manuel Rodriguez Jr, *Vice Pres*
▲ EMP: 65
SQ FT: 33,000
SALES (est): 16MM **Privately Held**
WEB: www.mxl-industries.com
SIC: 3544 3089 3479 3851 Special dies
& tools; injection molding of plastics; coat-
ing of metals with plastic or resins; oph-
thalmic goods; motorcycles, bicycles &
parts; paints & allied products

(G-9142)
**NATIONAL HOT ROD
ASSOCIATION**
Also Called: Nhra Northeast Division
2420 Gehman Ln Ste 200 (17602-1139)
PHONE....................................717 584-1200
EMP: 65
SALES (corp-wide): 99.2MM **Privately
Held**
SIC: 7948 2711 2741 Automotive race
track operation; newspapers: publishing
only, not printed on site; miscellaneous
publishing
PA: National Hot Rod Association
2035 E Financial Way
Glendora CA 91741
626 914-4761

(G-9143)
NAUTICA OF LANCASTER
35 S Willowdale Dr # 105 (17602-1472)
PHONE....................................717 396-9414
Alicia Cook, *Manager*
EMP: 15
SALES (est): 667K **Privately Held**
SIC: 2329 Men's & boys' sportswear & ath-
letic clothing
HQ: Nautica Retail Usa Llc
40 W 57th St Fl 3
New York NY 10019

(G-9144)
**NEFRA COMMUNICATION
CENTER**
Also Called: Nefra Communications Center
3011 Columbia Ave (17603-4010)
PHONE....................................717 509-1430
Frances Courtright, *CEO*
EMP: 30
SALES (est): 1.4MM **Privately Held**
SIC: 2759 Commercial printing

(G-9145)
NEWSLETTERS INK CORP
700 Eden Rd Ste 2 (17601-4700)
P.O. Box 4008 (17604-4008)
PHONE....................................717 393-1000
John Richey, *President*
Greg Gilson, *Vice Pres*
Kim Reiff, *Prdtn Mgr*
Kim Taylor, *HR Admin*
Sandi Beach, *Technology*
EMP: 25
SQ FT: 18,000
SALES (est): 2.4MM **Privately Held**
SIC: 2741 Miscellaneous publishing

(G-9146)
**NISSIN FOODS USA COMPANY
INC**
Also Called: Eastern Production Division
2901 Hempland Rd (17601-1386)
PHONE....................................717 291-5901
Clay Baker, *Purch Agent*
Billie Dangro, *Purch Agent*
Melinda Levinsky, *QC Dir*
Kazuyoshi Taniguchi, *Branch Mgr*
Dave Cedeno, *Manager*
EMP: 150
SALES (corp-wide): 4.8B **Privately Held**
WEB: www.nissinfoods.com
SIC: 2098 2099 Noodles (e.g. egg, plain &
water), dry; food preparations
HQ: Nissin Foods (U.S.A.) Company, Inc.
2001 W Rosecrans Ave
Gardena CA 90249
310 327-8478

(G-9147)
NOODLE KING
216 N Duke St (17602-2710)
PHONE....................................717 299-2799
Trang Vu, *Owner*
EMP: 5
SALES (est): 333.4K **Privately Held**
SIC: 2098 5812 Noodles (e.g. egg, plain &
water), dry; Vietnamese restaurant

(G-9148)
NUCOR CORPORATION
201 Granite Run Dr # 280 (17601-6807)
PHONE....................................717 735-7766
Ken Nichols, *Manager*
Bruce Wirth, *Manager*
EMP: 4
SALES (corp-wide): 25B **Publicly Held**
SIC: 3448 Prefabricated metal components
PA: Nucor Corporation
1915 Rexford Rd Ste 400
Charlotte NC 28211
704 366-7000

(G-9149)
OAKWOOD BINDERY
1133 Manheim Pike (17601-3185)
PHONE....................................717 396-9559
Thomas Peterson, *President*
EMP: 35
SQ FT: 22,000

SALES (est): 2.4MM **Privately Held**
SIC: 2789 5961 3542 Binding only:
books, pamphlets, magazines, etc.; mail
order house; machine tools, metal forming type

(G-9150)
**OCEAN THERMAL ENERGY
CORP (PA)**
800 S Queen St (17603-5818)
PHONE....................................717 299-1344
Jeremy P Feakins, *Ch of Bd*
EMP: 10 EST: 1987
SQ FT: 28,000
SALES (est): 5.8MM **Publicly Held**
WEB: www.tetridyn.com
SIC: 4911 3585 Electric services; refriger-
ation & heating equipment

(G-9151)
OLDE MILL LIGHTING LIMITED
Also Called: Olde Mill Lighting Ltd Shop
833 2nd St Ste E (17603-3235)
PHONE....................................717 299-7240
Jerry Landis, *President*
EMP: 4
SALES (est): 350K **Privately Held**
SIC: 3646 Ornamental lighting fixtures,
commercial

(G-9152)
OMNIMAX INTERNATIONAL INC
Amerimax Home Products
450 Richardson Dr (17603-4036)
PHONE....................................717 299-3711
Mitchell B Lewis, *CEO*
EMP: 49
SALES (corp-wide): 861.3MM **Privately
Held**
SIC: 3444 Sheet metalwork
HQ: Omnimax International, Inc.
30 Technology Pkwy S # 400
Peachtree Corners GA 30092

(G-9153)
OMNIMAX INTERNATIONAL INC
Fabral
3449 Hempland Rd (17601-1317)
PHONE....................................717 397-2741
Mitchell B Lewis, *CEO*
EMP: 330
SALES (corp-wide): 861.3MM **Privately
Held**
SIC: 3444 Sheet metalwork
HQ: Omnimax International, Inc.
30 Technology Pkwy S # 400
Peachtree Corners GA 30092

(G-9154)
ON LINE PUBLISHERS INC
808 Paddington Dr (17601-1462)
P.O. Box 8049 (17604-8049)
PHONE....................................717 285-1350
Donna Anderson, *President*
EMP: 5
SALES (est): 44.4K **Privately Held**
SIC: 2741 Miscellaneous publishing

(G-9155)
OPSEC SECURITY INC (DH)
1857 Colonial Village Ln (17601-6702)
P.O. Box 10155 (17605-0155)
PHONE....................................717 293-4110
Richard Cremona, *CEO*
Diane Albano, *Exec VP*
Michael T Banahan, *Vice Pres*
Michael Currie, *Finance Dir*
Kees Riphagen, *Manager*
◆ EMP: 100
SQ FT: 24,500
SALES (est): 42.2MM
SALES (corp-wide): 84.6MM **Privately
Held**
WEB: www.opsecsecurity.com
SIC: 2671 3953 Packaging paper & plas-
tics film, coated & laminated; embossing
seals & hand stamps
HQ: Opsec Security Group, Inc.
7333 W Jefferson Ave # 165
Lakewood CO 80235
720 639-2832

(G-9156)
**OPTIMA PLUS INTERNATIONAL
LLC**
436 Mahogany Dr (17602-7010)
PHONE....................................717 207-9037
Richard Ferrucci, *Principal*
EMP: 4 EST: 2007
SALES (est): 330K **Privately Held**
SIC: 3651 Audio electronic systems

(G-9157)
PACCAR INC
3001 Industry Dr (17603-4025)
PHONE....................................717 397-4111
Allen Austin, *Manager*
EMP: 25
SALES (corp-wide): 23.5B **Publicly Held**
WEB: www.paccar.com
SIC: 3711 Truck & tractor truck assembly
PA: Paccar Inc
777 106th Ave Ne
Bellevue WA 98004
425 468-7400

(G-9158)
PACKAGING CORP O
1530 Fruitville Pike (17601-4093)
PHONE....................................717 293-2877
Bill Noon, *Principal*
Robert Spicer, *Sales Staff*
Mike Wills, *Manager*
EMP: 3
SALES (est): 109.8K **Privately Held**
SIC: 2653 Boxes, corrugated: made from
purchased materials

(G-9159)
**PACKAGING CORPORATION
AMERICA**
Also Called: Pca/Lancaster 344
1530 Fruitville Pike (17601-4093)
PHONE....................................717 397-3591
Michael Snyder, *General Mgr*
William Harp, *Mfg Staff*
Timothy Grady, *Sales Mgr*
Bill Noon, *Marketing Mgr*
Henderson Julie, *Executive*
EMP: 150
SALES (corp-wide): 7B **Publicly Held**
WEB: www.packagingcorp.com
SIC: 2653 Boxes, corrugated: made from
purchased materials
PA: Packaging Corporation Of America
1 N Field Ct
Lake Forest IL 60045
847 482-3000

(G-9160)
PAP TECHNOLOGIES INC
1813 Colonial Village Ln (17601-6702)
PHONE....................................717 399-3333
Mike R Owner, *President*
Peggy Seibert, *Vice Pres*
EMP: 47
SQ FT: 25,000
SALES (est): 14MM **Privately Held**
WEB: www.papsecurity.com
SIC: 2752 Tickets, lithographed; business
form & card printing, lithographic

(G-9161)
PDS PAINT INC
334 Mill St (17603-5308)
P.O. Box 8495 (17604-8495)
PHONE....................................717 393-5838
EMP: 13
SQ FT: 32,000
SALES (est): 2MM **Privately Held**
SIC: 3559 Mfg Misc Industry Machinery

(G-9162)
**PEMCOR PRINTING COMPANY
LLC (HQ)**
330 Eden Rd (17601-4218)
PHONE....................................717 898-1555
Scott Eshelman, *Human Resources*
Jeffery J Bozzi, *Mng Member*
Joseph Simon, *Executive*
EMP: 77
SQ FT: 20,000

SALES (est): 10MM
SALES (corp-wide): 20MM **Privately Held**
WEB: www.pemcor.com
SIC: 2759 7374 2752 7331 Commercial printing; data processing service; commercial printing, lithographic; mailing service
PA: Intellicor Llc
  330 Eden Rd
  Lancaster PA 17601
  717 291-3100

(G-9163)
PENN VETERINARY SUPPLY INC
53 Industrial Cir (17601-5927)
PHONE................................717 656-4121
Richard K Sexton, *President*
John Beck, *Vice Pres*
Thomas Jones, *Vice Pres*
Lita Shillenn, *Vice Pres*
Mark Weiss, *Opers Mgr*
EMP: 55 **EST:** 1981
SALES (est): 31.5MM **Privately Held**
WEB: www.pennvet.com
SIC: 5047 3999 Veterinarians' equipment & supplies; education aids, devices & supplies

(G-9164)
PENN WIRE PRODUCTS CORPORATION (PA)
481 Richardson Dr (17603-4035)
P.O. Box 4804 (17604-4804)
PHONE................................717 393-2352
David T Sneath, *President*
Margaret A Sneath, *Vice Pres*
▲ **EMP:** 2
SQ FT: 6,000
SALES (est): 1.6MM **Privately Held**
WEB: www.pennwire.com
SIC: 3496 Mesh, made from purchased wire; conveyor belts

(G-9165)
PENNSY SUPPLY INC
1060 Manheim Pike (17601-3118)
PHONE................................717 397-0391
EMP: 3
SALES (corp-wide): 29.7B **Privately Held**
SIC: 3273 Ready-mixed concrete
HQ: Pennsy Supply, Inc.
  1001 Paxton St
  Harrisburg PA 17104
  717 233-4511

(G-9166)
PENNSYLVANIA DRY MIX
499 Running Pump Rd # 102 (17601-2225)
PHONE................................717 509-3520
Chris Payonk, *General Mgr*
Bob Kelser, *Principal*
EMP: 3
SALES (est): 274.2K **Privately Held**
SIC: 3269 Vases, pottery

(G-9167)
PENNSYLVANIA EQUESTRIAN
336 E Orange St (17602-2963)
PHONE................................717 509-9800
Stephanie Lawson, *Owner*
EMP: 4
SALES (est): 354.6K **Privately Held**
SIC: 2741 Miscellaneous publishing

(G-9168)
PEPPER ITALIAN BISTRO
486 Royer Dr (17601-5151)
PHONE................................717 392-3000
EMP: 3
SALES (est): 108.9K **Privately Held**
SIC: 2899 Salt

(G-9169)
PERFUSION MANAGEMENT GROUP
555 N Duke St (17602-2250)
PHONE................................717 392-4112
Ricky G Smith, *President*
Craig J Gassmann, *Treasurer*
Mark S Campbell, *Admin Sec*
EMP: 10
SALES (est): 1.3MM **Privately Held**
SIC: 3845 Heart-lung machine

(G-9170)
PHOTONIS DEFENSE INC (DH)
Also Called: Photonis USA Pennsylvania Inc
1000 New Holland Ave (17601-5606)
PHONE................................717 295-6000
Larry J Stack, *President*
Lori Suter, *General Mgr*
Jeffrey Baker, *Vice Pres*
JM Baker, *Vice Pres*
Joseph Scholly, *Vice Pres*
▲ **EMP:** 61
SQ FT: 106,000
SALES: 30MM
SALES (corp-wide): 3.4MM **Privately Held**
WEB: www.burle.com
SIC: 3671 2796 3812 Vacuum tubes; electrotype plates; electronic detection systems (aeronautical)

(G-9171)
PHOTONIS DIGITAL IMAGING LLC
1000 New Holland Ave (17601-5606)
PHONE................................972 987-1460
EMP: 1
SALES (est): 1.4MM
SALES (corp-wide): 3.4MM **Privately Held**
SIC: 3829 Measuring & controlling devices
HQ: Photonis Defense, Inc.
  1000 New Holland Ave
  Lancaster PA 17601
  717 295-6000

(G-9172)
POLAR PEACH LLC
2481 Lincoln Hwy E Ste 3 (17602-1482)
PHONE................................717 517-9497
EMP: 3
SALES (est): 194.5K **Privately Held**
SIC: 2026 Yogurt

(G-9173)
POPULTION HLTH INNOVATIONS LLC
313 W Liberty St (17603-2798)
PHONE................................717 735-8105
Robert Gillio, *CEO*
EMP: 5 **EST:** 2014
SALES (est): 434.9K **Privately Held**
SIC: 7336 7372 Graphic arts & related design; creative services to advertisers, except writers; educational computer software

(G-9174)
PRAXAIR DISTRIBUTION INC
1311-15 Harrisburg Pike (17603)
PHONE................................717 393-3681
Matt Hall, *Manager*
EMP: 9
SQ FT: 2,500 **Privately Held**
SIC: 2813 Industrial gases
HQ: Praxair Distribution, Inc.
  10 Riverview Dr
  Danbury CT 06810
  203 837-2000

(G-9175)
PRIMITIVES BY KATHY INC
1817 William Penn Way (17601-5830)
PHONE................................717 394-4220
Kathy Phillips, *President*
Stacy McAdams, *Partner*
Tori Shank, *Partner*
Lisa Dicostanzo, *Vice Pres*
Ken Seaman, *VP Opers*
▲ **EMP:** 95
SQ FT: 77,000
SALES: 54.7MM **Privately Held**
WEB: www.primitivesbykathy.com
SIC: 5023 3499 Decorative home furnishings & supplies; novelties & specialties, metal

(G-9176)
PROSOURCE OF LANCASTER
2969 Old Tree Dr (17603-4060)
PHONE................................717 299-5680
Kristie Cobb, *President*
EMP: 3
SALES (est): 318.2K **Privately Held**
SIC: 5023 7359 2273 Carpets; floor maintenance equipment rental; carpets & rugs

(G-9177)
PTB RICE NOODLE
401 Parkwynne Rd (17601-2819)
PHONE................................717 569-0330
Vy Banh, *Principal*
EMP: 3
SALES (est): 111.3K **Privately Held**
SIC: 2098 Noodles (e.g. egg, plain & water), dry

(G-9178)
PURINA ANIMAL NUTRITION LLC
3029 Hempland Rd (17601-1309)
PHONE................................717 393-1361
Rick Race, *Manager*
EMP: 9
SALES (corp-wide): 10.4B **Privately Held**
SIC: 2048 Prepared feeds
HQ: Purina Animal Nutrition Llc
  100 Danforth Dr
  Gray Summit MO 63039

(G-9179)
PURINA MILLS LLC
3029 Hempland Rd (17601-1309)
PHONE................................717 393-1299
Carl Espenshade, *Branch Mgr*
EMP: 7
SALES (corp-wide): 10.4B **Privately Held**
WEB: www.purina-mills.com
SIC: 2048 Prepared feeds
HQ: Purina Mills, Llc
  555 Maryvle Univ Dr 200
  Saint Louis MO 63141

(G-9180)
QUANTA TECHNOLOGIES INC
1036 New Holland Ave (17601-5606)
PHONE................................610 644-7101
Jay Reyher, *CEO*
Thomas Culp, *Principal*
Michael Neff, *Principal*
John Siegel, *Principal*
EMP: 3
SALES: 950K **Privately Held**
SIC: 2869 Industrial organic chemicals

(G-9181)
QUANTA TECHNOLOGIES INC
1004 New Holland Ave (17601-5606)
PHONE................................610 644-7101
▼ **EMP:** 7
SALES (est): 725K **Privately Held**
SIC: 3296 Fiberglass insulation

(G-9182)
R M METALS INC
32 Industrial Cir (17601-5928)
PHONE................................717 656-8737
Robert J Mellinger, *President*
Jennifer Mellinger, *Corp Secy*
EMP: 4
SQ FT: 39,100
SALES: 1.8MM **Privately Held**
WEB: www.rmmetals.com
SIC: 5039 3444 Architectural metalwork; metal buildings; roof deck, sheet metal

(G-9183)
R R DONNELLEY & SONS COMPANY
Also Called: R R Donnelley
391 Steel Way (17601-3153)
P.O. Box 3780 (17604-3780)
PHONE................................717 295-4002
Mark Ramey, *Director*
EMP: 600
SALES (corp-wide): 6.8B **Publicly Held**
WEB: www.rrdonnelley.com
SIC: 2759 Commercial printing
PA: R. R. Donnelley & Sons Company
  35 W Wacker Dr Ste 3650
  Chicago IL 60601
  312 326-8000

(G-9184)
R R DONNELLEY & SONS COMPANY
Also Called: R R Donnelley
1905 Horseshoe Rd (17602-1005)
PHONE................................717 209-7700
Stephanie Windsor, *Manager*
EMP: 200

SALES (corp-wide): 6.8B **Publicly Held**
WEB: www.rrdonnelley.com
SIC: 2752 Commercial printing, lithographic
PA: R. R. Donnelley & Sons Company
  35 W Wacker Dr Ste 3650
  Chicago IL 60601
  312 326-8000

(G-9185)
RADIANCE
9 W Grant St (17603-3801)
PHONE................................717 290-1517
Sarah Campbell, *Principal*
EMP: 5 **EST:** 2007
SALES (est): 323.8K **Privately Held**
SIC: 2099 Seasonings & spices

(G-9186)
RAGNASOFT INC
117 S West End Ave Ste 12 (17603-3396)
P.O. Box 4903 (17604-4903)
PHONE................................866 471-2001
Christian Yecker, *President*
EMP: 11 **EST:** 1999
SALES (est): 453K **Privately Held**
WEB: www.ragnasoft.com
SIC: 7372 7373 Prepackaged software; systems software development services

(G-9187)
RETTEW FIELD SERVICES INC (PA)
Also Called: Energy Construction Services
3020 Columbia Ave (17603-4011)
PHONE................................717 697-3551
Dawn Gamble, *President*
Mark Kayruekllo, *Principal*
George Rettew, *Principal*
Gregorty Young, *Principal*
Joel Young, *Principal*
EMP: 24
SALES (est): 6.2MM **Privately Held**
SIC: 1623 1389 Oil & gas pipeline construction; pipe laying construction; hydraulic fracturing wells

(G-9188)
RIDLEY USA INC
Also Called: Hubbard Feeds
3349 Hempland Rd (17601-1315)
PHONE................................717 509-1078
Grant Lebo, *Branch Mgr*
EMP: 13
SALES (corp-wide): 1.7B **Privately Held**
WEB: www.hubbardfeeds.net
SIC: 2048 Livestock feeds
HQ: Ridley Usa Inc.
  111 W Cherry St Ste 500
  Mankato MN 56001
  507 388-9400

(G-9189)
ROB KEI INC
Also Called: Crystal Palace
142 Park City Ctr (17601-2706)
PHONE................................717 293-8991
EMP: 4 **EST:** 1980
SALES (est): 200K **Privately Held**
SIC: 3229 5719 5699 5611 Mfg/Ret Sculpted Objects/Complete Line Of Renaissance Clothing/

(G-9190)
ROCHESTER COCA COLA BOTTLING
Also Called: Coca-Cola
1428 Manheim Pike (17601-3126)
PHONE................................717 209-4411
Robert Klan, *Branch Mgr*
EMP: 70
SALES (corp-wide): 35.4B **Publicly Held**
SIC: 2086 Bottled & canned soft drinks
HQ: Rochester Coca Cola Bottling Corp
  300 Oak St
  Pittston PA 18640
  570 655-2874

(G-9191)
SCHMITT MAR STERING WHEELS INC
1001 Ranck Mill Rd (17602-2503)
PHONE................................717 431-2316
Timothy J Schmitt, *President*
Tim Schmitt, *Manager*

GEOGRAPHIC

▲ **EMP**: 6
SQ FT: 13,000
SALES (est): 1MM **Privately Held**
WEB: www.schmittsteering.com
SIC: 3429 5091 5088 Marine hardware; sporting & recreation goods; transportation equipment & supplies

(G-9192)
SENSING DEVICES LLC
625 2nd St (17603-5113)
PHONE.................................717 295-4735
Catherine Nickel, *Principal*
Christopher Edie, *Principal*
EMP: 16
SALES (est): 926.2K **Privately Held**
SIC: 3823 Industrial instrmnts msrmnt display/control process variable

(G-9193)
SENSING DEVICES INC
625 2nd St (17603-5113)
PHONE.................................717 295-4735
Steve Cornibert, *President*
EMP: 20
SALES (est): 1.2MM **Privately Held**
WEB: www.sensingdevices.com
SIC: 3823 3829 3812 Temperature instruments: industrial process type; measuring & controlling devices; search & navigation equipment

(G-9194)
SERVICE FILTRATION CORP
Also Called: Pacer Pumps
41 Industrial Cir (17601-5927)
PHONE.................................717 656-2161
Denzel Stoops, *Manager*
EMP: 35
SALES (corp-wide): 62.5MM **Privately Held**
WEB: www.pacerpumps.com
SIC: 3569 3561 Filters, general line: industrial; pumps & pumping equipment
PA: Service Filtration Corp.
2900 Macarthur Blvd
Northbrook IL 60062
847 509-2900

(G-9195)
SHENKS FOODS INC
1980 New Danville Pike (17603-9615)
PHONE.................................717 393-4240
Karl Achtermann, *President*
EMP: 3
SQ FT: 6,000
SALES (est): 150K **Privately Held**
WEB: www.shenks.com
SIC: 2033 2022 Jams, jellies & preserves: packaged in cans, jars, etc.; cheese spreads, dips, pastes & other cheese products

(G-9196)
SIEMENS PRODUCT LIFE MGMT SFTW
301 Post Oak Rd (17603-9448)
PHONE.................................717 299-1846
Chuck Grindstaff, *CEO*
EMP: 3
SALES (corp-wide): 95B **Privately Held**
SIC: 7372 Business oriented computer software
HQ: Siemens Product Lifecycle Management Software Inc.
5800 Granite Pkwy Ste 600
Plano TX 75024
972 987-3000

(G-9197)
SIGMA TECHNOLOGY SYSTEMS LLC
1148 Elizabeth Ave Ste 6 (17601-4359)
PHONE.................................717 569-2926
Diane Hohenwarter, *Sls & Mktg Exec*
Barry Gardner, *Sales Mgr*
Bill Swilley, *Mng Member*
EMP: 11
SQ FT: 13,000
SALES (est): 850K **Privately Held**
SIC: 3651 Audio electronic systems

(G-9198)
SIGN MEDIX INC
2153 Columbia Ave (17603-4332)
PHONE.................................717 396-9749
Phillip Saunders, *President*
Phil Saunders, *Owner*
EMP: 11
SALES (est): 1.1MM **Privately Held**
WEB: www.signmedix.com
SIC: 1799 3993 7629 Sign installation & maintenance; electric signs; electrical equipment repair services

(G-9199)
SIGNARAMA
Also Called: Sign-A-Rama
1748 Columbia Ave Ste 1 (17603-4366)
PHONE.................................717 397-3173
Mark Boss, *President*
EMP: 10 **EST**: 1996
SALES (est): 395.6K **Privately Held**
SIC: 3993 Signs & advertising specialties

(G-9200)
SIGNATURE STONE INC
1005 Willow Street Pike (17602-4655)
PHONE.................................717 397-2364
Jeffrey Hess, *President*
EMP: 3
SALES (est): 464.7K **Privately Held**
WEB: www.signaturestoneinc.com
SIC: 2435 Veneer stock, hardwood

(G-9201)
SIGNS BY DESIGN
2273 Lititz Pike (17601-3603)
PHONE.................................717 626-6212
Brett Groff, *Principal*
EMP: 5
SALES (est): 422.1K **Privately Held**
SIC: 3993 Signs & advertising specialties

(G-9202)
SOMAT COMPANY
165 Independence Ct (17601-5838)
PHONE.................................717 397-5100
Nancy Kauffman, *Principal*
Will Saylor, *Buyer*
EMP: 30
SALES (est): 5.8MM **Privately Held**
SIC: 3589 Dishwashing machines, commercial

(G-9203)
SOUTHERN CONTAINER CORP
Also Called: Rocktemn
500 Richardson Dr (17603-4096)
PHONE.................................717 393-0436
Wayne Marchant, *Branch Mgr*
EMP: 200
SALES (corp-wide): 16.2B **Publicly Held**
WEB: www.southerncontainer.com
SIC: 2653 2657 Boxes, corrugated: made from purchased materials; display items, corrugated: made from purchased materials; folding paperboard boxes
HQ: Westrock - Southern Container, Llc
133 River Rd
Cos Cob CT 06807
631 232-5704

(G-9204)
STAR-H CORPORATION
48-50 W Chestnut St (17603-3791)
PHONE.................................717 826-7587
Milton Machalek, *President*
EMP: 4 **EST**: 1999
SALES (est): 300K **Privately Held**
WEB: www.star-h.com
SIC: 3663 Radio & TV communications equipment

(G-9205)
STECKEL PRINTING INC
2100 State Rd (17601-1829)
PHONE.................................717 898-1555
Faye L Givler, *President*
Faye Givler, *Owner*
EMP: 95 **EST**: 1931
SQ FT: 55,000
SALES (est): 6.6MM **Privately Held**
SIC: 2752 Commercial printing, offset

(G-9206)
STEEL FAB ENTERPRISES LLC
623 Baumgardner Rd (17603-9649)
PHONE.................................717 464-0330
Steve Fisher Jr, *CEO*
Chip Martin, *Exec VP*
Kurt Fisher, *Vice Pres*
Paul Reiter, *Project Mgr*
Mary Ober, *Sales Staff*
EMP: 30
SQ FT: 16,000
SALES (est): 11.1MM **Privately Held**
WEB: www.enterprisesteelfab.com
SIC: 3441 Fabricated structural metal

(G-9207)
STOLTZFUS WOODWORKING
324 Willow Rd (17601-6020)
PHONE.................................717 656-4823
EMP: 4
SALES (est): 217.1K **Privately Held**
SIC: 2431 Millwork

(G-9208)
STONER INCORPORATED
1813 William Penn Way (17601-5830)
PHONE.................................800 227-5538
Mike Fasano, *Branch Mgr*
EMP: 10
SALES (corp-wide): 15.6MM **Privately Held**
SIC: 2992 Lubricating oils & greases
PA: Stoner Incorporated
1070 Robert Fulton Hwy
Quarryville PA 17566
717 786-7355

(G-9209)
SUPERIOR RESPIRATORY HOME CARE
Also Called: T & W Traffic Control
1505 Rohrerstown Rd (17601-2317)
PHONE.................................717 560-7806
Judith A Warfel, *President*
Denise Warfel, *Vice Pres*
Mike Warfel, *Treasurer*
Don Warfel, *Admin Sec*
EMP: 8 **EST**: 1958
SQ FT: 4,000
SALES: 11MM **Privately Held**
SIC: 7359 3993 Work zone traffic equipment (flags, cones, barrels, etc.); signs, not made in custom sign painting shops

(G-9210)
SUSQUEHANNA CAPITL ACQUISITION (HQ)
216 Wohlsen Way (17603-4043)
PHONE.................................800 942-7538
Robert C Rathsam, *CFO*
EMP: 536
SALES (est): 133.1MM
SALES (corp-wide): 785.9MM **Publicly Held**
SIC: 3053 6719 Gasket materials; investment holding companies, except banks
PA: Lydall, Inc.
1 Colonial Rd
Manchester CT 06042
860 646-1233

(G-9211)
TAKE AWAY REFUSE
810 Pinetree Way (17601-6606)
PHONE.................................717 490-9258
Jeffrey Scott Weit, *Owner*
EMP: 3
SALES (est): 339.1K **Privately Held**
SIC: 2611 Pulp manufactured from waste or recycled paper

(G-9212)
TASTY BAKING COMPANY
Also Called: Tastykake Lancaster Dist Ctr
1127 Elizabeth Ave (17601-4365)
PHONE.................................717 295-2530
EMP: 3
SALES (corp-wide): 3.7B **Publicly Held**
SIC: 2051 Mfg Bread/Related Products
HQ: Tasty Baking Company
4300 S 26th St
Philadelphia PA 19112
215 468-4024

(G-9213)
TEAM APPROACH INC
Also Called: Center For Internal Change
2174 Old Philadelphia Pik (17602-3433)
PHONE.................................847 259-0005
Susan Stamm, *President*
Richard Stamm, *Vice Pres*
Bob Jackson, *Director*
EMP: 4
SQ FT: 500
SALES (est): 3MM **Privately Held**
WEB: www.teamapproach.com
SIC: 8742 7372 Training & development consultant; application computer software; business oriented computer software

(G-9214)
TECHNICOLOR USA INC
Also Called: Thomson Consumer Electronics
1002 New Holland Ave (17601-5606)
PHONE.................................717 295-6100
Robert K Lorch, *Vice Pres*
EMP: 250
SALES (corp-wide): 62.9MM **Privately Held**
SIC: 3651 8731 Household audio & video equipment; commercial physical research
HQ: Technicolor Usa, Inc.
101 W 103rd St
Indianapolis IN 46290
317 587-4287

(G-9215)
TEE PRINTING INC
124 College Ave (17603-3394)
PHONE.................................717 394-2978
Donald Linton, *President*
EMP: 5
SQ FT: 1,600
SALES (est): 509.6K **Privately Held**
SIC: 2262 Printing: manmade fiber & silk broadwoven fabrics

(G-9216)
THERMACORE INTERNATIONAL INC
780 Eden Rd Ofc (17601-4794)
PHONE.................................717 569-6551
L Ronald Hoover, *Ch of Bd*
Donald M Ernst, *Vice Pres*
James E Rothenberger, *Vice Pres*
EMP: 267
SQ FT: 30,000
SALES (est): 17.1MM
SALES (corp-wide): 2.1B **Publicly Held**
SIC: 8731 3443 Commercial physical research; fabricated plate work (boiler shop)
PA: Modine Manufacturing Company Inc
1500 Dekoven Ave
Racine WI 53403
262 636-1200

(G-9217)
THERMAL SOLUTIONS PRODUCTS LLC
1175 Manheim Pike Ste 7 (17601-3175)
P.O. Box 3244 (17604-3244)
PHONE.................................717 239-7642
Jim Schnorr, *President*
Brian Pedersen, *Engineer*
Randy Witmer, *Engineer*
Ed Deal, *Controller*
Joyce Vino, *Technical Staff*
▲ **EMP**: 34
SQ FT: 40,000
SALES (est): 7.3MM
SALES (corp-wide): 172.4MM **Publicly Held**
WEB: www.thermalsolutions.com
SIC: 3443 Boilers: industrial, power, or marine
PA: Burnham Holdings, Inc.
1241 Harrisburg Ave
Lancaster PA 17603
717 390-7800

(G-9218)
THORN HILL VINEYARDS
2076 Fruitville Pike (17601-7200)
PHONE.................................717 517-7839
Amy Thorn, *Principal*
EMP: 7 **EST**: 2011
SALES (est): 512.9K **Privately Held**
SIC: 2084 Wines

(G-9219)
TITAN SECURITY GROUP LLC
79 Millrace Dr (17603-9320)
PHONE....................................914 474-2221
Liann Francisco,
EMP: 10
SALES: 100K **Privately Held**
SIC: 3699 Security control equipment &
systems

(G-9220)
TMU INC
Also Called: Dombach, C B & Son
252 N Prince St Side (17603-3535)
PHONE....................................717 392-0578
Scott Underwood, *President*
John Thomas, *Treasurer*
Larry Metz, *Admin Sec*
EMP: 12
SQ FT: 17,500
SALES (est): 907.5K **Privately Held**
SIC: 2394 7359 2211 Awnings, fabric:
made from purchased materials;
canopies, fabric: made from purchased
materials; tent & tarpaulin rental; decora-
tive trim & specialty fabrics, including twist
weave

(G-9221)
**TOTAL DOCUMENT RESOURCE
INC**
19 Prestige Ln (17603-4076)
PHONE....................................717 648-6234
Michael Jones, *Vice Pres*
EMP: 3
SALES: 950K **Privately Held**
SIC: 2752 Commercial printing, litho-
graphic

(G-9222)
TRI COUNTY SPORTS INC
Also Called: Volleyball Corner
2007 Lincoln Hwy E (17602-3397)
PHONE....................................717 394-9169
Bill Helm, *Owner*
EMP: 3
SALES (corp-wide): 490K **Privately Held**
WEB: www.volleyballcorner.com
SIC: 3949 5941 Sporting & athletic goods;
team sports equipment
PA: Tri County Sports Inc
233 Cliff Ln
Elizabethtown PA 17022
717 367-0861

(G-9223)
**TRUE PRECISION PLASTICS
LLC**
310 Running Pump Rd (17603-2249)
PHONE....................................717 358-9251
Dennis Rote, *Vice Pres*
Eric Leaman, *Marketing Staff*
Dennis E Rote,
▲ **EMP:** 25
SALES (est): 2.2MM **Privately Held**
SIC: 3089 Injection molding of plastics
HQ: Restech Plastic Molding, Llc
34 Tower St
Hudson MA 01749
978 567-1000

(G-9224)
TURNMATIC
2878 Yellow Goose Rd (17601-1814)
P.O. Box 336, Landisville (17538-0336)
PHONE....................................717 898-3200
Donald Vogtman, *Owner*
EMP: 4
SQ FT: 2,800
SALES (est): 210K **Privately Held**
SIC: 3451 Screw machine products

(G-9225)
TWO LETTERS INK
Also Called: News Letters Ink
700 Eden Rd Ste 2 (17601-4700)
PHONE....................................717 393-8989
EMP: 29
SALES (est): 1.3MM **Privately Held**
SIC: 2759 Commercial Printing

(G-9226)
U S DURUM PRODUCTS LIMITED
1812 William Penn Way (17601-5831)
P.O. Box 10126 (17605-0126)
PHONE....................................717 293-8698
Carlo Stephano Franchetti, *Ch of Bd*
Jeffrey Dewey, *Vice Pres*
▲ **EMP:** 10
SQ FT: 16,500
SALES (est): 1.5MM **Privately Held**
WEB: www.usdurum.com
SIC: 2099 Packaged combination prod-
ucts: pasta, rice & potato

(G-9227)
**UDS HOME MEDICAL
EQUIPMENT LLC**
2270 Erin Ct (17601-1965)
PHONE....................................717 665-1490
William Kepner, *President*
EMP: 7
SALES (est): 899.7K
SALES (corp-wide): 7.6MM **Privately
Held**
SIC: 3842 Wheelchairs
PA: United Disabilities Services
2270 Erin Ct
Lancaster PA 17601
717 397-1841

(G-9228)
UNDER ARMOUR INC
35 S Willowdale Dr # 207 (17602-1472)
PHONE....................................717 393-7671
EMP: 50
SALES (corp-wide): 5.1B **Publicly Held**
SIC: 2353 Hats, caps & millinery
PA: Under Armour, Inc.
1020 Hull St Ste 300
Baltimore MD 21230
410 454-6428

(G-9229)
US BOILER COMPANY INC
Residential Steel Boiler
1548 Fruitville Pike (17601-4056)
P.O. Box 3079 (17604-3079)
PHONE....................................717 397-4701
Jim Dietz, *Buyer*
Donald Sweigart, *Manager*
Matt Kozak, *Director*
EMP: 130
SALES (corp-wide): 172.4MM **Publicly
Held**
WEB: www.govrad.com
SIC: 3443 Boilers: industrial, power, or ma-
rine
HQ: U.S. Boiler Company, Inc.
2920 Old Tree Dr
Lancaster PA 17603

(G-9230)
VANRODEN INC
Also Called: Wellspring Gift Lancaster
747 Flory Mill Rd (17601-2733)
PHONE....................................717 509-2600
Albert C Van Roden III, *President*
Cindy Henry, *Vice Pres*
▲ **EMP:** 25
SQ FT: 25,000
SALES (est): 5.7MM **Privately Held**
WEB: www.wellspringgift.com
SIC: 2678 2731 Tablets & pads; books:
publishing & printing

(G-9231)
VANS INC
569 Park City Ctr (17601-2713)
PHONE....................................717 291-8936
EMP: 4
SALES (corp-wide): 11.8B **Publicly Held**
SIC: 3021 Rubber & plastics footwear
HQ: Vans, Inc.
1588 S Coast Dr
Costa Mesa CA 92626
855 909-8267

(G-9232)
VELOCITY COLOR INC
841 N Prince St (17603-2751)
PHONE....................................717 431-2591
Mark S Gibson, *Principal*
EMP: 6
SALES (est): 520K **Privately Held**
SIC: 2752 Commercial printing, offset

(G-9233)
VERITAS PRESS INC
1805 Olde Homestead Ln (17601-5837)
PHONE....................................717 519-1974
Marlin Detweiler, *President*
David Heinaman, *Business Mgr*
Laurie K Detweiler, *Exec VP*
Carl Petticoffer, *Exec VP*
Vpsa Griffin, *Vice Pres*
EMP: 10 EST: 1996
SALES (est): 1.1MM **Privately Held**
WEB: www.veritaspress.com
SIC: 2741 5192 5961 Miscellaneous pub-
lishing; books, periodicals & newspapers;
catalog & mail-order houses

(G-9234)
**VERTICAL ACCESS SOLUTIONS
LLC**
120 N Lime St (17602-2923)
PHONE....................................412 787-9102
EMP: 12 **Privately Held**
SIC: 2591 Blinds vertical
HQ: Vertical Access Solutions Llc
4465 Campbells Run Rd
Pittsburgh PA 15205
412 787-9102

(G-9235)
WARREN INSTALLATIONS INC
1842 William Penn Way (17601-6714)
PHONE....................................717 517-9321
Bob Warren, *President*
EMP: 10 EST: 2011
SALES (est): 1.7MM **Privately Held**
SIC: 3663 5013 7532 7538 Radio & TV
communications equipment; automotive
supplies & parts; interior repair services;
body shop, automotive; general automotive repair shops; communication equipment repair

(G-9236)
**WATSON METAL PRODUCTS
CORP (PA)**
731 Martha Ave (17601-4560)
PHONE....................................908 276-2202
Gary Ostermueller, *President*
Karen Sidlowski, *Exec VP*
Vance Gorayeb, *CFO*
EMP: 65
SQ FT: 50,000
SALES (est): 7MM **Privately Held**
WEB: www.watsonmetal.com
SIC: 3444 3452 3356 Studs & joists,
sheet metal; bolts, metal; nonferrous
rolling & drawing

(G-9237)
**WEIDENHAMMER SYSTEMS
CORP**
25 N Queen St Ste 501 (17603-4094)
PHONE....................................610 378-1149
Doug Barge, *Branch Mgr*
EMP: 25
SALES (corp-wide): 40MM **Privately
Held**
WEB: www.hammer.net
SIC: 7372 Prepackaged software
PA: Weidenhammer Systems Corp
935 Berkshire Blvd
Reading PA 19610
610 378-1149

(G-9238)
WENGER FEEDS LLC
3579 Hempland Rd (17601-1319)
PHONE....................................717 367-1195
J Michael Lutz, *Admin Sec*
EMP: 300
SALES (corp-wide): 111.1MM **Privately
Held**
SIC: 2048 5144 0252 Poultry feeds; eggs;
chicken eggs
PA: Wenger Feeds, Llc
101 W Harrisburg Ave
Rheems PA 17570
717 367-1195

(G-9239)
WESTROCK RKT LLC
500 Richardson Dr (17603-4038)
PHONE....................................717 393-0436
Joseph Milhollen, *Branch Mgr*
EMP: 161

SALES (corp-wide): 14.8B **Publicly Held**
WEB: www.rocktenn.com
SIC: 2653 2652 2631 Boxes, corrugated:
made from purchased materials; setup
paperboard boxes; paperboard mills
HQ: Westrock Rkt, Llc
1000 Abernathy Rd Ste 125
Atlanta GA 30328
770 448-2193

(G-9240)
WHITE OAK GROUP INC
1180 Dillerville Rd (17601-3110)
P.O. Box 4945 (17604-4945)
PHONE....................................717 291-2222
David B Wisehaupt, *President*
Jack Greenawalt, *Exec VP*
David Miller, *Vice Pres*
Jeffery Shoop, *Treasurer*
Denise Royer, *Human Res Mgr*
EMP: 39
SQ FT: 20,000
SALES (est): 7.5MM **Privately Held**
WEB: www.whiteoaknet.com
SIC: 2752 Commercial printing, offset

(G-9241)
WILLIAMS COMPANIES INC
1848 Charter Ln (17601-5896)
PHONE....................................717 490-6857
EMP: 98
SALES (corp-wide): 8.6B **Publicly Held**
SIC: 4924 1311 1321 4922 Natural gas
distribution; natural gas production; natu-
ral gas liquids; pipelines, natural gas
PA: The Williams Companies Inc
1 Williams Ctr
Tulsa OK 74172
918 573-2000

(G-9242)
**WILLIAMS RICHARD H
PHARMACIST**
1405 Center Rd (17603-4729)
PHONE....................................717 393-6708
Richard Williams, *Principal*
EMP: 4 EST: 2007
SALES (est): 298.4K **Privately Held**
SIC: 5912 5122 2834 Drug stores & pro-
prietary stores; pharmaceuticals; pharma-
ceutical preparations

(G-9243)
WINDY HILL CONCRETE INC
1760 Windy Hill Rd (17602-1352)
P.O. Box 10727 (17605-0727)
PHONE....................................717 464-3889
Paul S Smucker, *President*
EMP: 3
SALES (est): 506.9K **Privately Held**
SIC: 3272 Concrete products, precast

(G-9244)
YURCHAK PRINTING INC
1781 Hidden Ln (17603-2382)
PHONE....................................717 399-9551
John Yurchak Jr, *President*
EMP: 4
SALES (est): 413.4K **Privately Held**
SIC: 2752 Commercial printing, offset

(G-9245)
ZIEL TECHNOLOGIES LLC
590 Sylvan Rd Ste 341 (17601)
PHONE....................................717 951-7485
Iris He, *Mng Member*
EMP: 3 EST: 2010
SALES: 200K **Privately Held**
SIC: 3672 7389 Printed circuit boards;

Landenberg
Chester County

(G-9246)
24K GOLD PLATING
124 Woodhaven Dr (19350-1133)
PHONE....................................610 255-4676
Kathryn Glenn, *Principal*
EMP: 3
SALES (est): 150.6K **Privately Held**
SIC: 3471 Plating of metals or formed
products

(G-9247)
BRIAN M PALLET
860 Penn Green Rd (19350-9209)
PHONE...............................484 720-8052
Brian M Pallet, *Principal*
EMP: 4
SALES (est): 286.7K **Privately Held**
SIC: 2448 Pallets, wood & wood with metal

(G-9248)
D&D SECURITY SOLUTIONS LLC
192 Sawmill Rd (19350-9302)
PHONE...............................484 614-7024
David Sampson, *Owner*
EMP: 5 EST: 2009
SALES (est): 530.4K **Privately Held**
SIC: 3699 Security control equipment &
systems

(G-9249)
HAMPDEN PAPERS INC
3 Meadow Wood Ln (19350-1246)
PHONE...............................610 255-4166
Sean Connors, *Manager*
EMP: 3
SALES (est): 181.4K
SALES (corp-wide): 27.1MM **Privately
Held**
SIC: 2621 Paper mills
PA: Hampden Papers, Inc.
100 Water St
Holyoke MA 01040
413 536-1000

(G-9250)
HOPE GOOD HARDWOODS INC
1627 New London Rd (19350-1109)
PHONE...............................610 350-1556
Norman Hughes, *President*
Dolores Hughes, *Corp Secy*
EMP: 3
SALES: 500K **Privately Held**
SIC: 2426 Dimension, hardwood; flooring,
hardwood; lumber, hardwood dimension

(G-9251)
LAUREL VALLEY FARMS INC
Also Called: Laurel Valley Soils
705 Penn Green Rd (19350-9204)
P.O. Box 70 (19350-0070)
PHONE...............................610 268-2074
Clint Blackwell, *President*
Joseph Dinorscia, *President*
Mario Basciani, *Vice Pres*
Edmond Sannini, *Treasurer*
Don Phillips, *Shareholder*
▲ EMP: 44
SQ FT: 10,000
SALES (est): 11.5MM **Privately Held**
WEB: www.laurelvalleysoils.com
SIC: 0139 2875 2873 Food crops; fertiliz-
ers, mixing only; nitrogenous fertilizers

(G-9252)
PARADOCX VINEYARD LLC
1833 Flint Hill Rd (19350-1513)
PHONE...............................610 255-5684
Mark Harris, *Partner*
Kelly Daly, *General Mgr*
John Caldwell, *Manager*
EMP: 4 EST: 2010
SALES (est): 376.7K **Privately Held**
SIC: 2084 Wines

(G-9253)
**STERLING COMPUTER SALES
LLC**
11 Laetitia Ln (19350-1051)
PHONE...............................610 255-0198
Wolfgang Brunke, *Partner*
Nancy Brunke, *Manager*
Jeffrey Brunke,
EMP: 7
SQ FT: 1,800
SALES (est): 746.3K **Privately Held**
WEB: www.sterlingcomputersales.com
SIC: 5734 3571 Computer & software
stores; personal computers (microcom-
puters)

(G-9254)
THOMAS W SPRINGER INC
227 Buttonwood Rd (19350-9397)
PHONE...............................610 274-8400
Thomas W Springer, *President*

Patricia A Springer, *Corp Secy*
EMP: 32
SQ FT: 20,000
SALES (est): 6.3MM **Privately Held**
WEB: www.twspringer.com
SIC: 3451 Screw machine products

(G-9255)
W L GORE & ASSOCIATES INC
380 Starr Rd (19350-9221)
PHONE...............................610 268-1864
Les Barnard, *Engineer*
Wayne Bruhn, *Engineer*
Chris Ericksen, *Engineer*
Drew Marlett, *Engineer*
Rafael Pinto, *Engineer*
EMP: 550
SALES (corp-wide): 3.4B **Privately Held**
WEB: www.gore.com
SIC: 3357 2821 Nonferrous wiredrawing &
insulating; polytetrafluoroethylene resins
(teflon)
PA: W. L. Gore & Associates, Inc.
555 Paper Mill Rd
Newark DE 19711
302 738-4880

Landisburg
Perry County

(G-9256)
COLLINS DECK SEALING
121 Indiana Rd (17040-9331)
PHONE...............................717 789-3322
Tammy Fittry, *Principal*
EMP: 4
SALES (est): 428.2K **Privately Held**
SIC: 3589 High pressure cleaning equip-
ment

(G-9257)
D&J PALLET SERVICES INC
548 Landisburg Rd (17040-9328)
P.O. Box 212, Shermans Dale (17090-
0212)
PHONE...............................717 275-1064
Brenda Hartman, *President*
John Hartman, *Vice Pres*
EMP: 4
SALES (est): 481.8K **Privately Held**
SIC: 2448 Pallets, wood & wood with metal

Landisville
Lancaster County

(G-9258)
AUD-A-BUD CERAMICS
3090 Harrisburg Pike (17538-1823)
PHONE...............................717 898-7537
Charles Hauser Jr, *Owner*
EMP: 3
SQ FT: 6,000
SALES: 75K **Privately Held**
SIC: 3269 5945 8299 Art & ornamental
ware, pottery; ceramics supplies; ceramic
school

(G-9259)
**ELECTRON ENERGY
CORPORATION (PA)**
Also Called: E E C
924 Links Ave (17538-1621)
PHONE...............................717 898-2294
Michael H Walmer, *President*
Kathryn Hambleton, *Treasurer*
Scott Murr, *Business Dir*
Tina Manley, *Personnel Assit*
▲ EMP: 50
SQ FT: 40,000
SALES (est): 17.7MM **Privately Held**
WEB: www.electronenergy.com
SIC: 3499 Magnets, permanent: metallic

(G-9260)
**GENESYS CONTROLS
CORPORATION**
1908 Mcfarland Dr (17538-1829)
PHONE...............................717 291-1116
Matthew W Anater, *President*
Thomas J Anater, *Admin Sec*

EMP: 3 EST: 2003
SALES (est): 97.2K **Privately Held**
SIC: 3613 Control panels, electric

(G-9261)
**GENESYS CONTROLS
CORPORATION**
1917 Olde Homestead Ln (17538)
P.O. Box 5117, Lancaster (17606-5117)
PHONE...............................717 291-1116
Matthew W Anater, *President*
Thomas J Anater, *Corp Secy*
Stephen Anater, *Opers Mgr*
Daron Boyd, *Marketing Staff*
Harry Flawd III, *Manager*
EMP: 16
SQ FT: 20,000
SALES (est): 4.1MM **Privately Held**
WEB: www.genesyscontrols.com
SIC: 3613 3679 Control panels, electric;
electronic circuits

(G-9262)
J C SNAVELY & SONS INC (PA)
150 Main St (17538-1295)
PHONE...............................717 898-2241
Charles B Fessler, *President*
Stephan Snavely, *Vice Pres*
James R Snavely, *Treasurer*
EMP: 122 EST: 1878
SQ FT: 50,000
SALES (est): 30.4MM **Privately Held**
SIC: 2439 5211 2452 2435 Trusses, ex-
cept roof: laminated lumber; lumber &
other building materials; panels & sec-
tions, prefabricated, wood; hardwood ve-
neer & plywood

(G-9263)
LIFT-TECH INC (PA)
1909 Mcfarland Dr (17538-1810)
PHONE...............................717 898-6615
Jeffrey M Klibert, *President*
Charles T Anton, *Corp Secy*
John D Roberts, *Vice Pres*
Jeffrey R Kauffman, *Asst Treas*
▲ EMP: 4
SQ FT: 59,000
SALES (est): 26.2MM **Privately Held**
SIC: 3315 2298 Wire & fabricated wire
products; ropes & fiber cables

(G-9264)
PINTER INDUSTRIES INC
3152 Woodridge Dr (17538-1347)
PHONE...............................717 898-9517
John T Goserude, *President*
▲ EMP: 3
SALES (est): 250K **Privately Held**
SIC: 3999 Coin-operated amusement ma-
chines

(G-9265)
PROSPECT CONCRETE INC
Also Called: Prospect Aggregates
1591 Quarry Rd (17538)
PHONE...............................717 898-2277
Donald C Emich, *President*
H Lee Ober, *Corp Secy*
J Barry Emich, *Vice Pres*
Edward Rick, *Vice Pres*
EMP: 15
SALES (est): 1.4MM **Privately Held**
SIC: 3273 Ready-mixed concrete

(G-9266)
R/W CONNECTION INC (DH)
936 Links Ave (17538-1615)
P.O. Box 287, Silver Spring (17575-0287)
PHONE...............................717 898-5257
Donald S Fritzinger, *President*
Scott Priestner, *Vice Pres*
▲ EMP: 46
SQ FT: 33,000
SALES (est): 53.5MM
SALES (corp-wide): 3.1B **Privately Held**
SIC: 5085 3052 3492 3053 Hose, belting
& packing; air line or air brake hose, rub-
ber or rubberized fabric; fluid power
valves & hose fittings; gasket materials
HQ: Hampton Rubber Company
1669 W Pembroke Ave
Hampton VA 23661
757 722-9818

(G-9267)
**TE CONNECTIVITY
CORPORATION**
1590 Kauffman Rd (17538-1400)
PHONE...............................717 898-4302
Ped Young, *Manager*
EMP: 125
SALES (corp-wide): 13.1B **Privately Held**
WEB: www.raychem.com
SIC: 3679 Electronic circuits
HQ: Te Connectivity Corporation
1050 Westlakes Dr
Berwyn PA 19312
610 893-9800

(G-9268)
**WARWICK MACHINE & TOOL
COMPANY**
1917 Mcfarland Dr (17538-1810)
PHONE...............................717 892-6814
Brian Shank, *President*
Becky Shank, *Vice Pres*
▲ EMP: 25
SQ FT: 12,000
SALES (est): 5MM **Privately Held**
WEB: www.warwickmachine.com
SIC: 3599 Machine shop, jobbing & repair

(G-9269)
YURCHAK PRINTING INC
920 Links Ave (17538-1615)
PHONE...............................717 399-0209
John Yurchak Jr, *CEO*
John W Yurchak, *President*
Bruce Jackson, *COO*
Jason Yurchak, *Vice Pres*
Paul Gimeson, *CFO*
EMP: 40
SQ FT: 18,000
SALES (est): 8MM **Privately Held**
SIC: 2759 2752 Commercial printing;
commercial printing, lithographic

Langeloth
Washington County

(G-9270)
**LANGELOTH METALLURGICAL
CO LLC**
10 Langeloth Plant Dr (15054)
P.O. Box 608 (15054-0608)
PHONE...............................724 947-2201
Robert Dorfler, *General Mgr*
Tom Ondrejko, *Manager*
Mark Wilson,
◆ EMP: 135
SQ FT: 350,000
SALES (est): 35.1MM
SALES (corp-wide): 760.7MM **Privately
Held**
WEB: www.langeloth.com
SIC: 2899 1061 Acid resist for etching; fer-
roalloy ores, except vanadium
HQ: Thompson Creek Mining Co.
26 W Dry Creek Cir # 225
Littleton CO 80120

Langhorne
Bucks County

(G-9271)
A & R JADCZAK COMPANY
135 Green St (19047-5543)
PHONE...............................215 752-3438
Richard Jadczak, *Owner*
EMP: 3
SQ FT: 1,250
SALES: 160K **Privately Held**
SIC: 3599 Machine shop, jobbing & repair

(G-9272)
**ACTIVE CHEMICAL
CORPORATION (PA)**
4511 Old Lincoln Hwy (19053-8421)
PHONE...............................215 322-0377
Janet White, *President*
Daniel Weidman, *Principal*
EMP: 12
SQ FT: 3,000

SALES (est): 2.3MM **Privately Held**
SIC: 5074 7349 2819 Water purification equipment; water softeners; chemical cleaning services; industrial inorganic chemicals

(G-9273)
ADVANCED INDUSTRIAL TECH CORP
30 Goldfields Ave (19047-3412)
PHONE..................201 483-7235
Jerry C Wang, *President*
EMP: 12 EST: 1967
SQ FT: 500
SALES: 8MM **Privately Held**
WEB: www.advantechnology.com
SIC: 3564 8711 Air purification equipment; pollution control engineering

(G-9274)
AEROPRINT GRAPHICS INC
134 W Lincoln Hwy Rear (19047-5200)
PHONE..................215 752-1089
Mark J Sorrentino, *President*
Anita Sorrentino, *Vice Pres*
EMP: 4
SQ FT: 1,728
SALES (est): 266.2K **Privately Held**
WEB: www.edumedia.com
SIC: 2752 7334 Commercial printing, offset; photolithographic printing; photocopying & duplicating services

(G-9275)
ALLIQUA BIOMEDICAL INC (PA)
2150 Cabot Blvd W Ste B (19047-1852)
PHONE..................215 702-8550
Jerome Zeldis, *Ch of Bd*
David Johnson, *President*
Brad Barton, *COO*
Bradford Barton, *COO*
Rick Rhode, *Engineer*
EMP: 72
SQ FT: 9,000
SALES: 2.2MM **Publicly Held**
WEB: www.hepalife.com
SIC: 2834 3841 Pharmaceutical preparations; surgical & medical instruments

(G-9276)
APPLE ALLEY ASSOCIATES-II LP
413 Executive Dr (19047-8003)
PHONE..................215 817-2828
EMP: 4
SALES (est): 206.9K **Privately Held**
SIC: 3571 Mfg Electronic Computers

(G-9277)
AQUAMED TECHNOLOGIES INC
2150 Cabot Blvd W Ste B (19047-1852)
PHONE..................215 702-8550
Richard Rosenblum, *President*
Steven Berger, *CFO*
EMP: 12
SQ FT: 16,500
SALES (est): 305.6K **Publicly Held**
SIC: 3842 8733 Bandages & dressings; dressings, surgical; medical research
PA: Alliqua Biomedical, Inc.
2150 Cabot Blvd W Ste B
Langhorne PA 19047

(G-9278)
ARCHER-DANIELS-MIDLAND COMPANY
Also Called: ADM
100 Cabot Blvd E (19047-1841)
PHONE..................215 547-8424
Mike Bojakowski, *Manager*
EMP: 40
SALES (corp-wide): 64.3B **Publicly Held**
WEB: www.admworld.com
SIC: 2041 Flour & other grain mill products
PA: Archer-Daniels-Midland Company
77 W Wacker Dr Ste 4600
Chicago IL 60601
312 634-8100

(G-9279)
ARKAY TOOL & DIE INC
41 Terry Dr (19053-6517)
PHONE..................215 322-2039
Mike Falcone, *President*
Judith Keil, *Treasurer*

EMP: 11
SQ FT: 4,400
SALES: 600K **Privately Held**
SIC: 3544 3599 Special dies & tools; machine shop, jobbing & repair

(G-9280)
BBK INDUSTRIES LLC
Also Called: Ace Overhead Door Co.
585 Heatons Mill Dr (19047-1521)
P.O. Box 7305, Penndel (19047-7305)
PHONE..................215 676-1500
Sherry Calvert,
Jacklyn Capille,
EMP: 8
SALES (est): 798.9K **Privately Held**
SIC: 3442 1751 Metal doors; fire doors, metal; hangar doors, metal; rolling doors for industrial buildings or warehouses, metal; garage door, installation or erection

(G-9281)
BRISTOL INDUSTRIES PENNSYLV
131 Old Oxford Valley Rd (19047-1838)
PHONE..................215 493-7230
Richard Coleman, *President*
EMP: 8
SALES (est): 765.1K **Privately Held**
SIC: 3999 Manufacturing industries

(G-9282)
BRISTOL TANK & WELDING CO INC
Also Called: Tank Heads
2400 Big Oak Rd (19047-1910)
PHONE..................215 752-8727
Vito Marseglia, *President*
Dan Marseglia, *Vice Pres*
Joseph Marseglia, *Treasurer*
Joanne Masterson, *Office Mgr*
EMP: 11 EST: 1949
SQ FT: 25,000
SALES (est): 1MM **Privately Held**
WEB: www.tankheads.com
SIC: 3443 Fuel tanks (oil, gas, etc.): metal plate

(G-9283)
BUCK COUNTY PRINT
17 Lady Slipper Ln (19047-3420)
PHONE..................215 741-3250
EMP: 4
SALES (est): 239.6K **Privately Held**
SIC: 2752 Commercial printing, lithographic

(G-9284)
CHOICE THERAPEUTICS INC
2150 Cabot Blvd W Ste B (19047-1852)
PHONE..................508 384-0425
EMP: 4
SALES (est): 470.9K **Publicly Held**
SIC: 5047 2834 Develops And Manufactures Its Therabond 3d Antimicrobial Barrier Systems Wound Dressings
PA: Alliqua Biomedical, Inc.
2150 Cabot Blvd W Ste B
Langhorne PA 19047

(G-9285)
CONNOR SIGN GROUP LTD
101 Spring St (19047-5353)
PHONE..................215 741-1299
Michael F Connor, *President*
Jane Connor, *Vice Pres*
EMP: 8 EST: 1944
SQ FT: 8,000
SALES: 1MM **Privately Held**
SIC: 3993 Signs, not made in custom sign painting shops; neon signs

(G-9286)
CONSOLIDATED PACKAGING LLC
304 Corporate Dr E (19047-8009)
PHONE..................215 968-6260
Joe Pfender,
Jim Ferrero,
▲ EMP: 4
SALES (est): 662.4K **Privately Held**
WEB: www.consolidatedpackaging.com
SIC: 2673 Plastic & pliofilm bags

(G-9287)
CREATIVE IMPRESSIONS ADVG LLC
1209 Ridge Rd Ste B (19053-3566)
PHONE..................215 357-1228
Adele L Tidman,
▲ EMP: 7
SQ FT: 5,000
SALES: 950K **Privately Held**
WEB: www.creativeimpressionspa.com
SIC: 2759 5947 Promotional printing; gifts & novelties

(G-9288)
DARLING BLENDS LLC
433 White Swan Way (19047-2371)
PHONE..................215 630-2802
Matthew Coleman, *Mng Member*
EMP: 4
SALES (est): 114.8K **Privately Held**
SIC: 2393 2099 5149 5499 Tea bags, fabric: made from purchased materials; tea blending; tea; tea

(G-9289)
DAVID CRAIG JEWELERS LTD
10 Summit Sq Shopg Ctr Shopping Ctr (19047)
PHONE..................215 968-8900
David C Rotenberg, *President*
Deborah Rotenberg, *Corp Secy*
EMP: 4
SQ FT: 1,600
SALES (est): 355.1K **Privately Held**
SIC: 5944 3911 Jewelry, precious stones & precious metals; jewelry, precious metal

(G-9290)
DIGITAL CARD INC
Also Called: Digital Card Media
303 Corporate Dr E (19047-8009)
PHONE..................215 275-7100
Darren Smith, *President*
EMP: 11 EST: 1997
SQ FT: 2,000
SALES: 1MM **Privately Held**
SIC: 3663 Digital encoders

(G-9291)
E INSTRUMENTS GROUP LLC
402 Middletown Blvd # 216 (19047-1818)
PHONE..................215 750-1212
Ray Biarnes,
EMP: 9
SQ FT: 3,500
SALES: 900K **Privately Held**
WEB: www.einstrumentsgroup.com
SIC: 3695 Instrumentation type tape, blank

(G-9292)
EASTERN MANUFACTURING LLC
2151 Cabot Blvd W (19047-1808)
PHONE..................215 702-3600
George Schafer, *President*
EMP: 4
SALES (corp-wide): 104.6MM **Privately Held**
SIC: 3564 3312 Blowers & fans; tubes, steel & iron
HQ: Eastern Manufacturing, Llc
2151 Cabot Blvd W
Langhorne PA 19047
215 702-3600

(G-9293)
EASTERN MANUFACTURING LLC (HQ)
Also Called: Eastern Catalytic
2151 Cabot Blvd W (19047-1808)
PHONE..................215 702-3600
George Schafer, *President*
James Derrah, *General Mgr*
Ken Schafer, *Vice Pres*
William Schafer, *Treasurer*
Joe Senek, *Controller*
◆ EMP: 66
SALES: 17.2MM
SALES (corp-wide): 104.6MM **Privately Held**
WEB: www.easterncatalytic.com
SIC: 3567 3498 ; fabricated pipe & fittings

PA: Ap Emissions Technologies, Llc
300 Dixie Trl
Goldsboro NC 27530
919 580-2000

(G-9294)
ERNIE SAXTON
Also Called: Motorsports Sponship Mktg News
1448 Hollywood Ave (19047-7417)
PHONE..................215 752-7797
Ernie Saxton, *President*
Marilyn Saxton, *Treasurer*
EMP: 3
SALES (est): 320K **Privately Held**
WEB: www.saxtonsponsormarket.com
SIC: 8742 8743 2741 Marketing consulting services; promotion service; newsletter publishing

(G-9295)
EUSA PHARMA (USA) INC (DH)
1717 Langhorne Newtown Rd (19047-1085)
PHONE..................215 867-4900
James Mitchum, *President*
Jeffrey S Hackman, *President*
Thu Dang, *VP Finance*
▲ EMP: 49
SQ FT: 16,100
SALES (est): 6.1MM **Privately Held**
WEB: www.cytogen.com
SIC: 2834 2836 Pharmaceutical preparations; biological products, except diagnostic
HQ: Jazz Pharmaceuticals, Inc.
3170 Porter Dr
Palo Alto CA 94304
650 496-3777

(G-9296)
EXPRESS SCREENPRINTING
Also Called: Express Screen Printing
219 Shady Brook Dr (19047-8030)
PHONE..................215 579-8819
Stan Cowen, *Owner*
EMP: 3
SALES: 250K **Privately Held**
SIC: 2752 Commercial printing, lithographic

(G-9297)
FIT FUEL FOODS LLC
Also Called: Prepped Delivery
18 Oxford Ct (19047-1645)
PHONE..................267 342-1559
Ted Elonis,
Andy Bronstein,
EMP: 6
SALES (est): 621K **Privately Held**
SIC: 2099 Ready-to-eat meals, salads & sandwiches

(G-9298)
FIZZANO BROS CONCRETE PDTS INC
247 Sterner Mill Rd (19053-6515)
PHONE..................215 355-6160
Eric Tiger, *Manager*
EMP: 9
SALES (corp-wide): 10MM **Privately Held**
SIC: 3271 3272 Concrete block & brick; concrete products, precast
PA: Fizzano Bros. Concrete Products, Inc.
1776 Chester Pike
Crum Lynne PA 19022
610 833-1100

(G-9299)
FUEL7 INC
13 Summit Square Ctr (19047-1078)
PHONE..................267 980-7888
Tomas Gonzalez, *Principal*
EMP: 3
SALES (est): 240.6K **Privately Held**
SIC: 2869 Fuels

(G-9300)
GE BETZ INTERNATIONAL INC (DH)
4636 Somerton Rd (19053-6742)
PHONE..................215 957-2200
Heinrich Markhoff, *President*
William W Booth, *Vice Pres*
William C Brafford, *Asst Sec*

EMP: 20 EST: 1969
SALES (est): 28.4MM
SALES (corp-wide): 94.7MM **Privately Held**
WEB: www.betzdearborn.com
SIC: 2899 Water treating compounds
HQ: Suez Wts Usa, Inc.
4636 Somerton Rd
Trevose PA 19053
215 355-3300

(G-9301)
HENDRICKS WELDING SERVICE INC
293 Hulmeville Rd (19047-2713)
PHONE......................................215 757-5369
Richard James Jones, *President*
Helen Jones, *Corp Secy*
EMP: 3 EST: 1960
SALES (est): 210K **Privately Held**
SIC: 7692 3446 Welding repair; architectural metalwork

(G-9302)
HERAEUS KULZER LLC
1 Summit Square Ctr # 403 (19047-1091)
PHONE......................................215 944-9968
Yuri Rozenfeld, *Principal*
EMP: 6 EST: 2012
SALES (est): 643.2K **Privately Held**
SIC: 3339 Precious metals

(G-9303)
ICON/INFORMATION CONCEPTS INC
1 Oxford Vly Ste 312 (19047-3312)
PHONE......................................215 545-6700
Alan Krigman, *President*
EMP: 4
SQ FT: 1,100
SALES (est): 352.6K **Privately Held**
WEB: www.icon-info.com
SIC: 2741 8999 Business service newsletters: publishing & printing; newspaper column writing

(G-9304)
JAZZ PHARMACEUTICALS (DH)
1717 Langhorne Newtown Rd (19047-1085)
PHONE......................................215 867-4900
Bryan Morton, *President*
Todd Rufner, *Regl Sales Mgr*
Erin Fitzpatrick, *Sales Staff*
EMP: 23
SALES (est): 12.7MM **Privately Held**
SIC: 2834 Pharmaceutical preparations
HQ: Jazz Pharmaceuticals, Inc.
3170 Porter Dr
Palo Alto CA 94304
650 496-3777

(G-9305)
JUST NORMLICHT INC
2000 Cabot Blvd W Ste 120 (19047-2408)
PHONE......................................267 852-2200
Michael Gall, *CEO*
James Summers, *Vice Pres*
Evan Zimmerman, *Opers Mgr*
▲ EMP: 3
SQ FT: 6,000
SALES (est): 514.6K **Privately Held**
WEB: www.justnormlicht.com
SIC: 3648 5063 Lighting equipment; lighting fixtures, commercial & industrial
PA: Just Vermogensverwaltungsges. Mbh
Otto-Hahn-Str. 2
Weilheim An Der Teck
702 395-040

(G-9306)
KEITH BUSH ASSOCIATES INC
1709 Langhorne Newtown Rd # 4 (19047-1010)
PHONE......................................215 968-5255
Keith Busch, *Principal*
EMP: 7
SALES (est): 523.5K **Privately Held**
SIC: 3296 Acoustical board & tile, mineral wool

(G-9307)
LANGHORNE METAL SPINNING INC
1095 Wood Ln (19047-1754)
PHONE......................................215 497-8876
Michael J Kearney, *President*
Kathy Kearney, *Manager*
EMP: 3
SALES (est): 262.5K **Privately Held**
SIC: 3469 Spinning metal for the trade

(G-9308)
LIFE SUPPORT INTERNATIONAL
2250 Cabot Blvd W Ste 255 (19047-1807)
PHONE......................................215 785-2870
Gregory Yerkes, *President*
Chris Belmonte, *Vice Pres*
▼ EMP: 20
SQ FT: 20,000
SALES: 6MM **Privately Held**
WEB: www.lifesupportintl.com
SIC: 5047 2399 3842 3069 Medical equipment & supplies; industrial safety devices: first aid kits & masks; parachutes; personal safety equipment; clothing, fire resistant & protective; life jackets, inflatable: rubberized fabric; life rafts, rubber

(G-9309)
LOEFFLER CORPORATION
201 E Lincoln Hwy (19047-4029)
PHONE......................................215 757-2404
Margaret Loeffler, *CEO*
Joe Loeffler, *President*
Frank Loeffler, *Vice Pres*
EMP: 11
SQ FT: 12,000
SALES (est): 600K **Privately Held**
WEB: www.loefflercorp.com
SIC: 5088 3731 Ships; submarines, building & repairing

(G-9310)
LORENZO FST FLW CYLINDER HEADS
112 Reetz Ave (19047-5891)
PHONE......................................215 750-8324
Lorenzo Damore, *President*
EMP: 3
SALES (est): 385.1K **Privately Held**
SIC: 3599 Machine shop, jobbing & repair

(G-9311)
MIKE BARTA AND SONS INC
1036 Woodbourne Rd (19047-1371)
PHONE......................................215 757-1162
Mike Barta, *President*
Joann Barta, *Corp Secy*
▼ EMP: 7
SQ FT: 5,360
SALES (est): 1.1MM **Privately Held**
SIC: 7699 3728 Aircraft & heavy equipment repair services; fuel tanks, aircraft

(G-9312)
NAILED IT II LLC
314 W Lincoln Hwy Ste 2 (19047-5168)
PHONE......................................215 803-2060
EMP: 4
SALES (est): 451.5K **Privately Held**
SIC: 2434 Wood kitchen cabinets

(G-9313)
NATIONAL RFRGN & AC PDTS INC
Also Called: National Refrigeration Pdts
985 Wheeler Way (19047-1705)
PHONE......................................215 638-8909
William Morrison, *Vice Pres*
Julia Realey, *Branch Mgr*
EMP: 15
SALES (corp-wide): 77MM **Privately Held**
WEB: www.nationalcomfortproducts.com
SIC: 3585 5078 Refrigeration & heating equipment; refrigeration equipment & supplies
PA: National Refrigeration & Air Conditioning Products, Inc.
539 Dunksferry Rd
Bensalem PA 19020
215 244-1400

(G-9314)
NEWTOWN GAZETTE
341 Rumpf Ave (19047-5523)
P.O. Box 7195 (19047-7195)
PHONE......................................215 702-3405
Donna Allen, *Principal*
EMP: 3 EST: 2008
SALES (est): 193.6K **Privately Held**
SIC: 2711 Commercial printing & newspaper publishing combined

(G-9315)
NOBLESOFT SOLUTIONS INC
405 Executive Dr (19047-8003)
P.O. Box 924, Plainsboro NJ (08536-0924)
PHONE......................................713 480-7510
Heather Lynn Rawla, *President*
Rakesh Rawla, *Vice Pres*
Nidhi Khanna, *Human Res Mgr*
Jeff Mutschler, *Director*
EMP: 3
SALES (est): 310.4K **Privately Held**
SIC: 7371 7372 Computer software systems analysis & design, custom; computer software development & applications; prepackaged software

(G-9316)
NORTHAMPTON HERALD
341 Rumpf Ave (19047-5523)
PHONE......................................215 702-3405
Donna Allen, *Principal*
EMP: 3
SALES (est): 101.3K **Privately Held**
SIC: 2711 Commercial printing & newspaper publishing combined

(G-9317)
PENNDEL HYDRAULIC SLS & SVC CO
77 W Lincoln Hwy (19047-5293)
PHONE......................................215 757-2000
Shari Farley, *President*
EMP: 3 EST: 1962
SQ FT: 4,000
SALES (est): 394.1K **Privately Held**
SIC: 3492 3594 7699 Hose & tube fittings & assemblies, hydraulic/pneumatic; pumps, hydraulic power transfer; hydraulic equipment repair

(G-9318)
PHILADELPHIA PHOTO REVIEW
Also Called: Photo Review, The
140 E Richardson Ave # 3 (19047-2857)
PHONE......................................215 364-9185
Stephen Perloff, *Owner*
EMP: 3 EST: 1976
SALES (est): 151.7K **Privately Held**
WEB: www.photoreview.org
SIC: 2741 Miscellaneous publishing

(G-9319)
PIPE DREAMS PLUMBING SUP INC
579 Heatons Mill Dr (19047-1521)
PHONE......................................215 741-0889
Wayne Asciolla, *Principal*
EMP: 3
SALES (est): 510.5K **Privately Held**
SIC: 5074 3432 Plumbing fittings & supplies; plumbing fixture fittings & trim

(G-9320)
POPIT INC
250 Woodbourne Rd (19047-7000)
PHONE......................................215 752-8410
Mary Geragi, *President*
EMP: 3
SQ FT: 2,000
SALES (est): 191.2K **Privately Held**
SIC: 3089 Fittings for pipe, plastic

(G-9321)
PREMIUM PET DIVISION
Also Called: Provident Marketing
325 Andrews Rd (19053-3429)
PHONE......................................215 364-0211
Jay Belding, *President*
EMP: 3
SALES (est): 225.4K **Privately Held**
WEB: www.providentmarketing.com
SIC: 3999 5999 Pet supplies; pet supplies

(G-9322)
ROBERT J FLEIG INC
750 Parker St (19047-5058)
PHONE......................................215 702-7676
Robert J Fleig, *President*
EMP: 3
SALES (est): 280K **Privately Held**
SIC: 3088 Shower stalls, fiberglass & plastic

(G-9323)
S D L CUSTOM CABINETRY INC
4570 E Bristol Rd (19053-4757)
PHONE......................................215 355-8188
David Kotovnikov, *President*
EMP: 6
SQ FT: 7,000
SALES (est): 400K **Privately Held**
WEB: www.sdlcustomcabinetry.com
SIC: 2511 1751 Wood household furniture; carpentry work

(G-9324)
SEAN S ZUNIGA
Also Called: Silgan Plastics
227 E Maple Ave (19047-1657)
PHONE......................................215 757-2676
Sean S Zuniga, *Owner*
EMP: 4
SALES (est): 348.4K **Privately Held**
SIC: 3085 Plastics bottles

(G-9325)
SILGAN PLASTICS LLC
121 Wheeler Ct (19047-1701)
PHONE......................................215 727-2676
Kevin Grevera, *Manager*
EMP: 100
SALES (corp-wide): 4.4B **Publicly Held**
WEB: www.silganplastics.com
SIC: 3089 3085 Plastic containers, except foam; plastics bottles
HQ: Silgan Plastics Llc
14515 North Outer 40 Rd # 210
Chesterfield MO 63017
800 274-5426

(G-9326)
STANLEY BLACK & DECKER INC
Also Called: Stanley Security Solution
2000 Cabot Blvd W (19047-2407)
PHONE......................................215 710-9300
John F Lundgren, *CEO*
EMP: 125
SALES (corp-wide): 13.9B **Publicly Held**
SIC: 3429 Builders' hardware
PA: Stanley Black & Decker, Inc.
1000 Stanley Dr
New Britain CT 06053
860 225-5111

(G-9327)
SWAROVSKI NORTH AMERICA LTD
2300 E Lincoln Hwy (19047-1824)
PHONE......................................215 752-3198
Emory Wallace, *Branch Mgr*
EMP: 4
SALES (corp-wide): 3.7B **Privately Held**
SIC: 3961 Costume jewelry
HQ: Swarovski North America Limited
1 Kenney Dr
Cranston RI 02920
401 463-6400

(G-9328)
TECH CYCLE PERFORMANCE PDTS
169 W Lincoln Hwy Ste 1 (19047-5271)
PHONE......................................215 702-8324
Jason Bowman, *President*
EMP: 6
SQ FT: 7,500
SALES (est): 1MM **Privately Held**
SIC: 3751 7699 Motorcycles & related parts; motorcycle repair service

(G-9329)
TIMES PUBG NEWSPAPERS INC
341 Rumpf Ave (19047-5523)
P.O. Box 7195 (19047-7195)
PHONE......................................215 702-3405
Donna Allen, *President*
EMP: 10

SALES (est): 560.1K **Privately Held**
WEB: www.timespub.com
SIC: 2711 Newspapers, publishing & printing

(G-9330)
VANTAGE LEARNING USA LLC
444 Oxford Valley Rd (19047-8300)
PHONE.............................800 230-2213
Tam Kirby, *President*
EMP: 50
SALES (corp-wide): 100MM **Privately Held**
SIC: 7372 Educational computer software
PA: Vantage Learning Usa, Llc
6805 Route 202
New Hope PA 18938
800 230-2213

(G-9331)
VIRTUS PHARMACEUTICALS LLC (HQ)
Also Called: New Virtus Pharmaceuticals
2050 Cabot Blvd W Ste 200 (19047-1811)
PHONE.............................267 938-4850
Tina Guilder, *CEO*
Birdget Higginbotham, *VP Opers*
Damian Finio, *CFO*
Gerard Funck, *Accountant*
Warren Pefley, *VP Sales*
▲ **EMP:** 50
SQ FT: 1,500
SALES (est): 2.1MM
SALES (corp-wide): 9.7MM **Privately Held**
SIC: 2834 Pharmaceutical preparations
PA: Virtus Pharmaceuticals Holdings, Llc
2050 Cabot Blvd W Ste 200
Langhorne PA 19047
267 938-4850

(G-9332)
VIRTUS PHRMCTCALS HOLDINGS LLC (PA)
2050 Cabot Blvd W Ste 200 (19047-1811)
PHONE.............................267 938-4850
Louis Sanchez, *Mng Member*
EMP: 5
SQ FT: 5,000
SALES (est): 9.7MM **Privately Held**
SIC: 2834 6719 Pharmaceutical preparations; investment holding companies, except banks

(G-9333)
VIRTUS PHRMCTICALS OPCO II LLC (HQ)
2050 Cabot Blvd W Ste 200 (19047-1811)
PHONE.............................267 938-4850
Tina Guilder, *CEO*
Damian Fieno, *CFO*
EMP: 9
SQ FT: 1,500
SALES (est): 7.3MM
SALES (corp-wide): 9.7MM **Privately Held**
WEB: www.virtusrx.com
SIC: 2834 Pharmaceutical preparations
PA: Virtus Pharmaceuticals Holdings, Llc
2050 Cabot Blvd W Ste 200
Langhorne PA 19047
267 938-4850

(G-9334)
VORNHOLD WALLPAPERS INC
501 Main St (19047)
PHONE.............................215 757-6641
Frederick W Vornhold, *President*
James Vornhold, *Vice Pres*
EMP: 6 EST: 1905
SQ FT: 6,000
SALES (est): 1.6MM **Privately Held**
SIC: 2621 Wallpaper (hanging paper)

(G-9335)
WESCOTT STEEL INC
425 Andrews Rd (19053-3498)
PHONE.............................215 364-3636
Jeffrey B Burke, *President*
James B Burke, *Admin Sec*
EMP: 26
SQ FT: 13,200

SALES (est): 3.5MM **Privately Held**
WEB: www.wescottsteel.com
SIC: 3325 3312 Bushings, cast steel: except investment; blast furnaces & steel mills

(G-9336)
WORLD WIDE PLASTICS INC (PA)
Also Called: Key Instruments
250 Andrews Rd (19053-3428)
PHONE.............................215 357-0893
Donald C Frick, *President*
Robert B Jackson, *Vice Pres*
Myra Frick, *Admin Sec*
EMP: 32
SQ FT: 25,000
SALES (est): 5.4MM **Privately Held**
WEB: www.keyinstruments.com
SIC: 3823 3825 3824 3494 Flow instruments, industrial process type; instruments to measure electricity; fluid meters & counting devices; valves & pipe fittings; industrial valves; products of purchased glass

(G-9337)
ZIRCON CORP
348 Main St (19047-5802)
PHONE.............................215 757-7156
John A Zitkus, *President*
Alvera R Zitkus, *Corp Secy*
EMP: 4
SQ FT: 2,500
SALES: 300K **Privately Held**
SIC: 3089 Injection molding of plastics

Lansdale
Montgomery County

(G-9338)
21ST CNTURY MDIA NEWPAPERS LLC
307 Derstine Ave (19446-3532)
PHONE.............................215 368-6973
EMP: 3
SALES (est): 76.2K **Privately Held**
SIC: 2711 Newspapers, publishing & printing

(G-9339)
A M INDUSTRIES INC
151 Green St (19446-3667)
PHONE.............................215 362-2525
Anthony M Morrelli, *President*
P A Morrelli, *Corp Secy*
EMP: 7
SQ FT: 4,000
SALES (est): 1.3MM **Privately Held**
WEB: www.amindustriesinc.com
SIC: 3369 Castings, except die-castings, precision

(G-9340)
AMERICAN PAPER PRODUCTS OF PHI
Also Called: American Tube & Paper Co Div
1802 Beth Ln (19446-5004)
PHONE.............................215 855-3327
Howard Goldberg, *Manager*
EMP: 30
SALES (corp-wide): 7.1MM **Privately Held**
WEB: www.americanpaperproducts.com
SIC: 2655 Tubes, fiber or paper: made from purchased material
PA: American Paper Products Of Philadelphia, Inc.
2113 E Rush St 25
Philadelphia PA 19134
215 739-5718

(G-9341)
AMERICAN PAPER PRODUCTS OF PHI
1802 Beth Ln (19446-5004)
PHONE.............................508 879-1141
Rick Segal, *Manager*
EMP: 35

SALES (corp-wide): 7.1MM **Privately Held**
WEB: www.americanpaperproducts.com
SIC: 2655 2631 Fiber cans, drums & similar products; paperboard mills
PA: American Paper Products Of Philadelphia, Inc.
2113 E Rush St 25
Philadelphia PA 19134
215 739-5718

(G-9342)
APANTEC LLC (PA)
805 W 5th St Ste 13 (19446-2279)
PHONE.............................267 436-3991
Sudhakar Pandey, *President*
Patri D Prasad, *Vice Pres*
Charles M Williams, *Vice Pres*
Charlie Williams, *Vice Pres*
Mark E Hiegl, *Engineer*
▲ **EMP:** 10
SQ FT: 5,000
SALES: 2.4MM **Privately Held**
WEB: www.apantec.com
SIC: 3823 3829 Nuclear reactor controls; nuclear radiation & testing apparatus

(G-9343)
ARCHITECTURAL STL & ASSOD PDTS
864 W 5th St (19446-2248)
P.O. Box 1233 (19446-0721)
PHONE.............................215 368-8113
Edward J Hinks, *President*
EMP: 18
SQ FT: 40,000
SALES (est): 4.1MM **Privately Held**
SIC: 3441 Fabricated structural metal

(G-9344)
BELA PRINTING & PACKAGING CORP
650 N Cannon Ave (19446-1874)
PHONE.............................215 664-7090
Ahmed Aijazi, *President*
EMP: 3
SALES (est): 252K **Privately Held**
SIC: 2752 2732 Commercial printing, lithographic; books: printing & binding

(G-9345)
BEST BAKERY INC
Also Called: Patel, Satyn & Pragness
804 W 2nd St (19446-2132)
PHONE.............................215 855-3831
Pragness Patel, *President*
Satyn Patel, *Admin Sec*
▲ **EMP:** 3
SQ FT: 1,425
SALES (est): 131.7K **Privately Held**
WEB: www.unknown.com
SIC: 5461 2051 Bakeries; bread, cake & related products

(G-9346)
BESTWAY PRINTING
Also Called: Bestway Printing Service
300 S Broad St (19446-3896)
PHONE.............................215 368-4140
John L Swartz, *Owner*
EMP: 5
SQ FT: 2,849
SALES (est): 403.7K **Privately Held**
WEB: www.bestway.com
SIC: 2752 2789 2672 2671 Commercial printing, offset; bookbinding & related work; coated & laminated paper; packaging paper & plastics film, coated & laminated

(G-9347)
BETTER AIR MANAGEMENT LLC
810 E Hancock St (19446-3929)
P.O. Box 341 (19446-0341)
PHONE.............................215 362-5677
Kumasi Morris,
EMP: 4
SQ FT: 1,000
SALES (est): 343.8K **Privately Held**
WEB: www.betterair.net
SIC: 8744 2842 ; specialty cleaning preparations

(G-9348)
BOARDROOM SPIRITS LLC
Also Called: Boardroom Spirits Distillery
575 W 3rd St (19446-2127)
PHONE.............................215 815-5351
▲ **EMP:** 8
SALES (est): 187.8K **Privately Held**
SIC: 3556 5182 5813 Distillery machinery; wine & distilled beverages; drinking places

(G-9349)
BUX MONT AWARDS
122 S Broad St (19446-3815)
PHONE.............................215 855-5052
Gregory Bencsik, *President*
EMP: 4 **Privately Held**
SIC: 7389 3993 Engraving service; signs & advertising specialties
PA: Bux Mont Awards
225 N Main St
Sellersville PA 18960

(G-9350)
CAPITOL SIGN COMPANY INC
Also Called: Capital Manufacturing
Broad St & Rte 309 (19446)
PHONE.............................215 822-0166
Piero Cappelli, *President*
EMP: 85
SQ FT: 50,000
SALES (est): 9.7MM **Privately Held**
WEB: www.capitalpa.com
SIC: 3993 Electric signs

(G-9351)
COBHAM ADV ELEC SOL INC (HQ)
305 Richardson Rd (19446-1495)
PHONE.............................215 996-2000
Jill Kale, *President*
Paul Carroll, *Safety Mgr*
Tom Bleam, *Buyer*
Brian Drzewiecki, *Treasurer*
Hardik Lagad, *Accounts Exec*
EMP: 277
SALES (est): 820.6MM
SALES (corp-wide): 2.7B **Privately Held**
WEB: www.cobham.com
SIC: 3812 Acceleration indicators & systems components, aerospace
PA: Cobham Plc
Brook Road
Wimborne BH21
120 288-2020

(G-9352)
CONNECTWO LLC
121 Misty Meadow Ln (19446-4452)
PHONE.............................215 421-4225
Eric Burlingame, *Partner*
EMP: 3
SALES (est): 93.5K **Privately Held**
SIC: 7372 Prepackaged software

(G-9353)
CONSIDINE STUDIOS INC
751 Maple Ave Unit B (19446-1846)
PHONE.............................215 362-8922
Tom Considine, *President*
EMP: 3
SALES: 200K **Privately Held**
WEB: www.considinestudios.com
SIC: 3366 Castings (except die): bronze

(G-9354)
CRETE NYCE CO INC
Iron & 6th St # 6 (19446)
P.O. Box 64418, Souderton (18964-0418)
PHONE.............................215 855-4628
James D NYCE, *President*
EMP: 20 EST: 1942
SQ FT: 20,000
SALES (est): 2.2MM **Privately Held**
SIC: 3271 3273 Blocks, concrete or cinder: standard; ready-mixed concrete

(G-9355)
CRYSTAL INC - PMC (HQ)
601 W 8th St (19446-1809)
PHONE.............................215 368-1661
P M Chakrabarti, *President*
Henry Witte, *Human Res Mgr*
▲ **EMP:** 60

SALES (est): 85.6MM **Privately Held**
WEB: www.crystalinc-pmc.com
SIC: 2899 2842 Chemical preparations; specialty cleaning, polishes & sanitation goods

(G-9356)
D G WOODWORKS LLC
675 W 3rd St (19446-2109)
PHONE.................................215 368-8001
Dan Gordman, *Principal*
EMP: 4
SALES (est): 412.2K **Privately Held**
SIC: 2431 Millwork

(G-9357)
DAVRO OPTICAL SYSTEMS INC
500 N Cannon Ave (19446-1816)
PHONE.................................215 362-3870
EMP: 9
SALES (est): 730K **Privately Held**
SIC: 3827 5049 Mfg Optical Instruments/Lenses Whol Professional Equipment

(G-9358)
DEAN FOODS COMPANY
880 Allentown Rd (19446-5206)
PHONE.................................215 855-8205
Ed Sweeney, *Principal*
Robert Dugan, *Engineer*
Maria Nevin, *Manager*
EMP: 8 EST: 2013
SALES (est): 798.7K **Privately Held**
SIC: 2026 Fluid milk

(G-9359)
DELUXE CORPORATION
1180 Church Rd Ste A (19446-3976)
PHONE.................................215 631-7500
Edward Coll, *Branch Mgr*
EMP: 248
SALES (corp-wide): 2B **Publicly Held**
WEB: www.dlx.com
SIC: 2782 Checkbooks
PA: Deluxe Corporation
3680 Victoria St N
Shoreview MN 55126
651 483-7111

(G-9360)
DEMESTIA BAKING COMPANY LLC
402 Bonnie Ln (19446-1521)
PHONE.................................215 896-2289
Julia Dischell, *Manager*
EMP: 5
SALES (est): 285K **Privately Held**
SIC: 2051 Bread, cake & related products

(G-9361)
DIMPTER WOODWORKING
35 E Blaine St (19446)
PHONE.................................215 855-2335
James Dimpter, *Owner*
EMP: 3
SALES (est): 249.4K **Privately Held**
WEB: www.dimpterwoodworking.com
SIC: 2431 Millwork

(G-9362)
DIVERSIFIED MECH SVCS INC
618 Knapp Rd (19446-2968)
PHONE.................................215 368-3084
Charles W Hahl Jr, *CEO*
EMP: 6 EST: 1999
SALES (est): 785K **Privately Held**
SIC: 4789 7692 Railroad maintenance & repair services; welding repair

(G-9363)
DOW CHEMICAL CO ✪
4602 Merchant Square Pl (19446-4087)
PHONE.................................610 244-7101
EMP: 3 EST: 2018
SALES (est): 168.1K **Privately Held**
SIC: 2819 Industrial inorganic chemicals

(G-9364)
EAST HILL VIDEO PROD CO LLC
Also Called: East Hill Media
157 S Broad St Ste 103 (19446-3831)
P.O. Box 461 (19446-0461)
PHONE.................................215 855-4457
Mary Stallings-Whiting, *COO*

Evelyn Watson-Bey, *CFO*
Daniel P Watson-Bey, *Mng Member*
EMP: 13
SQ FT: 2,500
SALES (est): 138K **Privately Held**
WEB: www.easthillvideo.com
SIC: 7812 3651 7221 1731 Video tape production; household audio & video equipment; photographic studios, portrait; electrical work; television broadcasting stations; data communication services

(G-9365)
EVANS JOHN SONS INCORPORATED
1 Spring Ave (19446-1883)
P.O. Box 885 (19446-0651)
PHONE.................................215 368-7700
Samuel A Davey, *President*
Paetrus F Banmiller, *Vice Pres*
Pate Banmiller, *Vice Pres*
Bob L Catlett, *Vice Pres*
Keith Kannengieszer, *Plant Mgr*
▲ EMP: 70 EST: 1850
SQ FT: 52,000
SALES: 20MM **Privately Held**
WEB: www.springcompany.com
SIC: 3495 3829 Wire springs; measuring & controlling devices

(G-9366)
EZNERGY LLC
411 Shipwrighter Way (19446-4022)
PHONE.................................215 361-7332
Coranne C Brown, *Mng Member*
James Brown,
EMP: 6
SALES (est): 355.7K **Privately Held**
SIC: 1711 3089 1781 3511 Solar energy contractor; automotive parts, plastic; geothermal drilling; steam turbines;

(G-9367)
FENG SHUI LIGHTING INC
1925 S Broad St (19446-5547)
PHONE.................................215 393-5500
Lawrence Berman, *President*
EMP: 4
SALES (est): 447.9K **Privately Held**
SIC: 3648 Lighting equipment

(G-9368)
FMC TECHNOLOGIES INC
2750 Morris Rd Ste A100 (19446-6680)
PHONE.................................215 822-4485
Hesham Mahmoud, *Managing Dir*
Arlo EBY, *Engineer*
Lori Donis, *Branch Mgr*
EMP: 15
SALES (corp-wide): 15B **Privately Held**
SIC: 3533 Oil field machinery & equipment
HQ: Fmc Technologies, Inc.
11740 Katy Fwy Energy Tow
Houston TX 77079
281 591-4000

(G-9369)
FOX BINDERY INC
Also Called: Fox Specialties
2750 Morris Rd (19446-6008)
PHONE.................................215 538-5380
Henry J Fox, *President*
Georgina Kolotello, *Human Res Dir*
Bill Smith, *Manager*
EMP: 150
SQ FT: 40,000
SALES (est): 25.8MM **Privately Held**
WEB: www.foxbind.com
SIC: 2789 Gold stamping on books

(G-9370)
FOX GROUP INC
2750 Morris Rd Ste E1 (19446-6682)
PHONE.................................215 538-5380
Mark Rotenberger, *President*
Tim Higgins, *Store Mgr*
Joe Minguez, *Production*
Luis Rodriguez, *Manager*
Jesse Serricca, *Info Tech Dir*
EMP: 36
SALES (est): 7MM **Privately Held**
SIC: 2789 Bookbinding & related work

(G-9371)
FOX SPECIALTIES INC
Mac Direct
2750 Morris Rd Ste C (19446-6046)
PHONE.................................215 822-5775
Phillip Murray, *Branch Mgr*
EMP: 9
SALES (est): 782.4K
SALES (corp-wide): 20.1MM **Privately Held**
SIC: 2789 Binding only: books, pamphlets, magazines, etc.
PA: Fox Specialties, Inc.
2750 Morris Rd Ste C
Lansdale PA 19446
215 822-5775

(G-9372)
GENTHERM INCORPORATED
215 Musket Cir (19446-4052)
PHONE.................................215 362-9191
Art Morse, *Principal*
EMP: 3
SALES (corp-wide): 1B **Publicly Held**
SIC: 3612 Transformers, except electric
PA: Gentherm Incorporated
21680 Haggerty Rd Ste 101
Northville MI 48167
248 504-0500

(G-9373)
GREAT ATLANTIC GRAPHICS INC
2750 Morris Rd Ste A120 (19446-6045)
PHONE.................................610 296-8711
Fred Duffy Jr, *President*
Kurt Wise, *Vice Pres*
Fred Aduffy Jr, *Admin Sec*
EMP: 77
SQ FT: 32,500
SALES (est): 32.4MM **Privately Held**
WEB: www.gagraph.com
SIC: 2752 7389 7336 7331 Lithographic Coml Print Business Services Coml Art/Graphic Design Direct Mail Ad Svcs

(G-9374)
GUYS ROUND BREWING COMPANY
324 W Main St (19446-2006)
PHONE.................................215 368-2640
Diliberto Rich, *Principal*
EMP: 12 EST: 2011
SALES (est): 1.4MM **Privately Held**
SIC: 2082 Malt beverages

(G-9375)
HANDELOK BAG COMPANY INC
Also Called: Hbc Packaging
701 W 5th St Ste A (19446-2269)
PHONE.................................215 362-3400
Craig Banet, *President*
▲ EMP: 20
SALES (est): 4.7MM **Privately Held**
WEB: www.handelokbag.com
SIC: 2674 Shopping bags: made from purchased materials

(G-9376)
HERITAGE STONE & MARBLE INC
1045 Archer Ln (19446-4820)
PHONE.................................610 222-0856
Charles Szuchan, *President*
EMP: 6 EST: 2000
SALES (est): 557.4K **Privately Held**
SIC: 3281 Stone, quarrying & processing of own stone products

(G-9377)
J D ENTERPRISE-MP LLC
Also Called: Minuteman Press
427 W Main St Ste 1 (19446-2007)
PHONE.................................215 855-4003
Joshua L Clemens,
EMP: 3
SALES (est): 528.1K **Privately Held**
SIC: 2752 Commercial printing, lithographic

(G-9378)
JAREX ENTERPRISES
1141 W 8th St (19446-1953)
PHONE.................................215 855-2149
Nick Novak, *Engineer*

John Rex,
EMP: 3
SALES (est): 413.9K **Privately Held**
SIC: 8711 3398 Heating & ventilation engineering; metal heat treating

(G-9379)
JASINSKI DENTAL LAB INC
Also Called: New Tech Dental Training Ctr
1141 Smile Ln (19446-5396)
PHONE.................................215 699-8861
Hubert Jasinski, *President*
Karen Jasinski, *Vice Pres*
Seung Lee, *Vice Pres*
Steve Hardy, *Controller*
Todd Hydock, *Lab Dir*
EMP: 20
SQ FT: 2,500
SALES (est): 3.3MM **Privately Held**
WEB: www.ndlsmile.com
SIC: 3843 8072 Dental equipment & supplies; denture production

(G-9380)
JBR ASSOCIATES INC
200 W Mount Vernon St (19446-3657)
P.O. Box 928 (19446-0660)
PHONE.................................215 362-1318
Ken Koons, *President*
EMP: 7
SQ FT: 4,800
SALES (est): 1.2MM **Privately Held**
SIC: 3089 2796 2759 Engraving of plastic; engraving on copper, steel, wood or rubber: printing plates; screen printing

(G-9381)
JDP THERAPEUTICS INC
823 Jays Dr (19446-7501)
PHONE.................................215 661-8557
Josh Tarnoff, *CEO*
Jie Du, *President*
EMP: 6
SQ FT: 500
SALES (est): 807.1K **Privately Held**
SIC: 2834 Pharmaceutical preparations

(G-9382)
JOURNAL REGISTER COMPANY
Also Called: Reporter, The
307 Derstine Ave (19446-3532)
PHONE.................................215 368-6976
Fax: 215 855-3432
EMP: 90
SALES (corp-wide): 894.1MM **Privately Held**
SIC: 2711 Newspapers, publishing & printing
PA: Journal Register Company
5 Hanover Sq Fl 25
New York NY 10004
212 257-7212

(G-9383)
KEENEY PRINTING GROUP INC
816 W 2nd St (19446-2132)
PHONE.................................215 855-6116
Margaret Keeney, *President*
Michael S Keeney, *Admin Sec*
EMP: 7 EST: 1975
SQ FT: 3,200
SALES (est): 1MM **Privately Held**
WEB: www.keeneyprinting.com
SIC: 2752 7334 2791 7389 Commercial printing, offset; photocopying & duplicating services; typesetting; design services

(G-9384)
LASER VGINAL REJUVENATION INST
2017 Cedars Hill Rd (19446-5897)
PHONE.................................610 584-0584
Donald J Debrakeleer, *Principal*
EMP: 5
SALES (est): 398.3K **Privately Held**
SIC: 3845 Laser systems & equipment, medical

(G-9385)
MANCINO MANUFACTURING CO INC
1180 Church Rd Ste 400 (19446-3976)
PHONE.................................800 338-6287
Robert Mancino, *Principal*
Sherry Everett, *Principal*
Rebecca Mancino, *Vice Pres*

GEOGRAPHIC

Thomas Bair, *Representative*
▲ **EMP:** 17
SQ FT: 33,000
SALES (est): 2.5MM **Privately Held**
WEB: www.mancinomats.com
SIC: 3949 Gymnasium equipment

(G-9386)
MERCK SHARP DHME ARGENTINA INC
333 S Broad St (19446-3804)
PHONE..................................215 996-3806
Samantha Hagerman, *Engineer*
Louise Pearcy, *Branch Mgr*
Vanessa Gaynor, *Sr Project Mgr*
EMP: 11
SQ FT: 2,600
SALES (corp-wide): 42.2B **Publicly Held**
SIC: 2834 Pharmaceutical preparations
HQ: Merck Sharp & Dohme (Argentina) Inc.
1 Merck Dr
Whitehouse Station NJ 08889

(G-9387)
METSO AUTOMATION USA INC
2750 Morris Rd Ste A100 (19446-6680)
PHONE..................................215 393-3900
EMP: 4
SALES (corp-wide): 3.1B **Privately Held**
SIC: 3625 Control equipment, electric
HQ: Metso Automation Usa Inc.
2750 Morris Rd Ste A100
Lansdale PA 19446

(G-9388)
METSO AUTOMATION USA INC (DH)
2750 Morris Rd Ste A100 (19446-6680)
PHONE..................................215 393-3947
John Quinlivan, *President*
Edward M Coll, *Principal*
Jeffrey Hass, *Vice Pres*
Michael McGoulbrick, *Director*
▲ **EMP:** 48
SQ FT: 85,000
SALES (est): 7.8MM
SALES (corp-wide): 3.1B **Privately Held**
SIC: 3625 Control equipment, electric

(G-9389)
MONTCO SCIENTIFIC INC
565 W 3rd St (19446-2127)
PHONE..................................215 699-8057
Gary Schillo, *President*
EMP: 4
SQ FT: 5,000
SALES (est): 493.6K **Privately Held**
SIC: 2759 Screen printing

(G-9390)
NANOSCAN IMAGING LLC
2250 Berks Rd (19446-6026)
PHONE..................................215 699-1703
Clinton H Brown, *Vice Pres*
Don Skerrett,
Joseph Patterson,
Donlon Skerrett,
EMP: 3
SQ FT: 1,000
SALES (est): 230K **Privately Held**
WEB: www.nanoscanimaging.com
SIC: 2834 Pharmaceutical preparations

(G-9391)
NASH PRINTING LLC
1617 N Line St Apt A (19446-1692)
PHONE..................................215 855-4267
Martin Wolfe, *President*
EMP: 17 **EST:** 1929
SQ FT: 5,000
SALES (est): 2.8MM
SALES (corp-wide): 4.2MM **Privately Held**
WEB: www.nashprinting.com
SIC: 2752 2759 Commercial printing, offset; screen printing
PA: Printworks & Company, Inc.
1617 N Line St Apt A
Lansdale PA 19446
215 721-8500

(G-9392)
NEXT GENERATION SOFTWARE
30 E Main St Ste 2 (19446-2517)
PHONE..................................215 361-2754
Roger Hammond, *President*

EMP: 4
SALES (est): 210.7K **Privately Held**
WEB: www.nextgenwt.com
SIC: 7372 Prepackaged software

(G-9393)
NORTH PENN ART INC
720 S Broad St (19446-5295)
PHONE..................................215 362-2494
Paul Kraynak, *President*
EMP: 11
SQ FT: 3,600
SALES (est): 1.3MM **Privately Held**
WEB: www.northpennart.com
SIC: 2499 7699 7336 Picture & mirror frames, wood; lasts, boot & shoe; picture framing, custom; commercial art & illustration

(G-9394)
NORTHERN MILLWORK INC
505 N Mitchell Ave (19446-2236)
PHONE..................................215 393-7242
William Guerrieri, *President*
Kevin F Dempter, *Vice Pres*
Francis Belfield, *Admin Sec*
EMP: 10
SQ FT: 13,000
SALES (est): 1.6MM **Privately Held**
WEB: www.northernmillwork.com
SIC: 2431 Millwork

(G-9395)
OPHTHALMIC ASSOCIATES PC
Also Called: Schwartz, Louis W MD
1000 N Broad St Ste 2 (19446-1138)
PHONE..................................215 368-1646
Ronald E Robinson, *Partner*
Robert W Connor MD, *Principal*
EMP: 22
SQ FT: 3,000
SALES (est): 3.7MM **Privately Held**
SIC: 3827 8011 5048 Optical instruments & lenses; medical centers; lenses, ophthalmic

(G-9396)
OVERHEAD DOOR CORPORATION
Also Called: Advanced Door Service
1441 Industry Rd (19446)
PHONE..................................215 368-8700
Kathy Meledy, *Manager*
EMP: 65
SALES (corp-wide): 3.6B **Privately Held**
SIC: 3442 2431 3699 3537 Garage doors, overhead: metal; doors, wood; door opening & closing devices, electrical; industrial trucks & tractors; vacuum cleaners & sweepers, electric: industrial
HQ: Overhead Door Corporation
2501 S State Hwy 121 Ste
Lewisville TX 75067
469 549-7100

(G-9397)
PENNS VALLEY PUBLISHERS
154 E Main St Ste 1 (19446-8501)
PHONE..................................215 855-4948
Thomas Cleary, *Owner*
Kathleen Cleary, *Co-Owner*
EMP: 5
SQ FT: 24,000
SALES (est): 265.9K **Privately Held**
WEB: www.pennsvalleypublishers.com
SIC: 2741 Miscellaneous publishing

(G-9398)
PERRY C RITTER
685 Jones Ave (19446-5621)
PHONE..................................215 699-7079
Perry C Ritter, *Owner*
EMP: 3
SALES (est): 190K **Privately Held**
SIC: 3469 Machine parts, stamped or pressed metal

(G-9399)
PRICE MACHINE TOOL REPAIR
422 W 6th St (19446-2262)
PHONE..................................215 631-9440
David Price, *Principal*
EMP: 4
SALES (est): 449.3K **Privately Held**
SIC: 3541 Machine tool replacement & repair parts, metal cutting types

(G-9400)
PRINTWORKS & COMPANY INC (PA)
1617 N Line St Apt A (19446-1692)
PHONE..................................215 721-8500
Martin Wolfe, *President*
Jim Fagan, *Sales Staff*
EMP: 24
SQ FT: 3,100
SALES (est): 4.2MM **Privately Held**
WEB: www.bonekemper.com
SIC: 2752 2791 Commercial printing, offset; typesetting

(G-9401)
PROBES UNLIMITED INC
836 W 8th St (19446-1932)
PHONE..................................267 263-0400
Ernest W Delany, *President*
Lisa Lyons, *Corp Secy*
Elizaabeth L Delany, *Vice Pres*
Michelle Brienza, *Treasurer*
◆ **EMP:** 33
SQ FT: 7,800
SALES (est): 6.7MM **Privately Held**
WEB: www.temp-probes.com
SIC: 3829 3822 Thermometers & temperature sensors; auto controls regulating residntl & coml environmt & applncs

(G-9402)
PRODUCTION COMPONENTS CORP
701 W 5th St Ste D (19446-2269)
PHONE..................................215 368-7416
Marsha Stanek, *President*
Joseph Walsh, *President*
EMP: 38 **EST:** 1981
SQ FT: 35,000
SALES (est): 6.7MM **Privately Held**
SIC: 3444 Sheet metal specialties, not stamped

(G-9403)
RE PACK INC
500 N Cannon Ave (19446-1816)
P.O. Box 1271, North Wales (19454-0271)
PHONE..................................215 699-9252
Richard W Surprise, *President*
Gary Rutherford, *Prdtn Mgr*
Penny Nezaj, *Sales Staff*
Dawn Kilgariff, *Office Mgr*
▲ **EMP:** 6
SQ FT: 3,200
SALES (est): 1.2MM **Privately Held**
WEB: www.re-pack.com
SIC: 3565 Packaging machinery

(G-9404)
REUBES MACHINE & TOOL CO INC
1239 Welsh Rd (19446-1359)
PHONE..................................215 368-0200
William E Reube, *President*
William R Reube Jr, *Vice Pres*
EMP: 8
SQ FT: 6,300
SALES (est): 931.5K **Privately Held**
SIC: 3544 7389 Special dies & tools; grinding, precision: commercial or industrial

(G-9405)
REX HEAT TREAT -LANSDALE INC (PA)
951 W 8th St (19446-1933)
PHONE..................................215 855-1131
John W Rex, *President*
John Sherman, *Vice Pres*
EMP: 64
SQ FT: 100,000
SALES (est): 20.9MM **Privately Held**
WEB: www.rexheattreat.com
SIC: 3398 Metal heat treating

(G-9406)
ROBERT BOONE COMPANY
806 W 5th St (19446-2248)
PHONE..................................215 362-2577
Robert Boone, *President*
EMP: 4
SQ FT: 7,000
SALES (est): 609.9K **Privately Held**
SIC: 3545 Tools & accessories for machine tools; thread cutting dies

(G-9407)
ROTONDO WEIRICH ENTPS INC
1240 S Broad St Ste 120 (19446-5395)
PHONE..................................215 256-7940
Steven J Weirich, *CEO*
Carrie Davis, *Vice Pres*
Mario Rotondo, *Vice Pres*
EMP: 90
SALES (est): 27.2MM **Privately Held**
SIC: 3272 Concrete products, precast

(G-9408)
SAFEGUARD BUSINESS SYSTEMS INC
1180 Church Rd Ste A (19446-7723)
PHONE..................................215 631-7500
Herb Berkelback, *Manager*
EMP: 110
SALES (corp-wide): 2B **Publicly Held**
WEB: www.gosafeguard.com
SIC: 5112 2761 2752 Business forms; manifold business forms; commercial printing, lithographic
HQ: Safeguard Business Systems, Inc.
8585 N Stemmons Fwy 600n
Dallas TX 75247
800 523-2422

(G-9409)
SCATTON BROS MFG CO
Also Called: Msgo Manufacturing Company
1680 Bridle Path Dr (19446-4746)
PHONE..................................215 362-6830
Christina M Masucci, *President*
EMP: 20 **EST:** 1949
SQ FT: 40,000
SALES (est): 4.1MM **Privately Held**
SIC: 3442 3444 3448 Storm doors or windows, metal; awnings, sheet metal; screen enclosures

(G-9410)
SICOM SYSTEMS INC (HQ)
1684 S Broad St Ste 300 (19446-5422)
PHONE..................................215 489-2500
William Terry Doan, *President*
Gene Holland, *Vice Chairman*
Barbara McGinnity, *Exec VP*
Scott Meyer, *Senior VP*
William Robert, *Senior VP*
◆ **EMP:** 74
SQ FT: 40,000
SALES (est): 159.8MM
SALES (corp-wide): 3.3B **Publicly Held**
WEB: www.sicomasp.com
SIC: 5045 3578 7379 Terminals, computer; point-of-sale devices; computer related consulting services
PA: Global Payments Inc.
3550 Lenox Rd Ne Ste 3000
Atlanta GA 30326
770 829-8000

(G-9411)
SKF MOTION TECHNOLOGIES LLC (DH)
890 Forty Foot Rd Ste 105 (19446-4303)
PHONE..................................267 436-6000
Tarek Bugaighis, *President*
Steve Hammen, *Project Engr*
EMP: 25 **EST:** 2017
SALES (est): 551.6K
SALES (corp-wide): 9.2B **Privately Held**
SIC: 3562 Ball & roller bearings

(G-9412)
SPIN-A-LATTE TM
Also Called: Spin-A-Latte Tm Laundry
642 Cowpath Rd 292 (19446-1586)
PHONE..................................215 285-1567
Carolyn Robinson, *Principal*
EMP: 3
SALES: 50K **Privately Held**
SIC: 2051 Bread, cake & related products

(G-9413)
TAKRAF USA INC
2750 Morris Rd Ste A120 (19446-6045)
PHONE..................................215 822-4485
Thomas Gramling, *President*
EMP: 17
SALES (corp-wide): 355.8K **Privately Held**
SIC: 1081 Metal mining services

2019 Harris Pennsylvania
Manufacturers Directory

▲ = Import ▼=Export
◆ =Import/Export

HQ: Takraf Usa, Inc.
4643 S Ulster St Ste 900
Denver CO 80237

(G-9414)
THEBATHOUTLET LLC
1953 W Point Pike (19446-5627)
PHONE..............................877 256-1645
WEB: www.tyco-fire.com
William Shuhaibar, *CEO*
Yazan Shuhaibar, *COO*
EMP: 15
SALES: 6.5MM **Privately Held**
SIC: 5211 7372 Bathroom fixtures, equipment & supplies; application computer software

(G-9415)
TRI-KRIS CO INC
1001 Walnut St (19446-1124)
PHONE..............................215 855-5183
William E Carling, *Principal*
William Carling, *Treasurer*
EMP: 6 EST: 2012
SALES (est): 171.7K **Privately Held**
SIC: 3599 Machine shop, jobbing & repair

(G-9416)
TRI-KRIS COMPANY
1001 Walnut St (19446-1124)
P.O. Box 785 (19446-0631)
PHONE..............................215 855-5183
William E Carling, *President*
William I Carling, *Vice Pres*
Kerry Detwiler, *Supervisor*
EMP: 18 EST: 1946
SQ FT: 15,500
SALES (est): 3.1MM **Privately Held**
SIC: 3599 Machine shop, jobbing & repair

(G-9417)
TRITECH APPLIED SCIENCES INC
650 N Cannon Ave 20 (19446-1874)
PHONE..............................215 362-6890
George Stone, *President*
Karen M Stone, *Corp Secy*
EMP: 6
SALES (est): 835.6K **Privately Held**
SIC: 8711 3499 1799 Consulting engineer; magnetic shields, metal; airwave shielding installation

(G-9418)
TROEMEL LANDSCAPING
2027 Wentz Church Rd (19446-5715)
PHONE..............................215 783-3150
Mike Troemel, *Owner*
EMP: 4 EST: 1996
SALES (est): 360.5K **Privately Held**
WEB: www.troemellandscaping.com
SIC: 3271 Architectural concrete: block, split, fluted, screen, etc.

(G-9419)
TULIP BIOLABS INC
2031 N Broad St Ste 139 (19446-1063)
P.O. Box 334, West Point (19486-0334)
PHONE..............................610 584-2706
John R Simon, *President*
EMP: 5
SALES (est): 750.4K **Privately Held**
WEB: www.tulipbiolabs.com
SIC: 2836 Biological products, except diagnostic

(G-9420)
TUSCAN/LEHIGH DAIRIES INC
Also Called: Lehigh Valley Dairies
880 Allentown Rd (19446-5206)
PHONE..............................215 855-8205
Paulette Brunetti, *General Mgr*
Pat Egbert, *Manager*
Jim Macri, *Exec Dir*
EMP: 19 **Publicly Held**
SIC: 2026 Milk processing (pasteurizing, homogenizing, bottling)
HQ: Tuscan/Lehigh Dairies, Inc.
117 Cumberland Blvd
Burlington NJ 08016
570 385-1884

(G-9421)
TYCO FIRE PRODUCTS LP (DH)
Also Called: Tyco Fire Sppression Bldg Pdts
1400 Pennbrook Pkwy (19446-3840)
PHONE..............................215 362-0700

Colleen Repplier, *Partner*
Robert Roche, *Partner*
Ryan K Stafford, *Partner*
Melissa McClain, *Manager*
Carolyn Wilks, *Manager*
▼ EMP: 150 EST: 1984
SQ FT: 166,000
SALES (est): 535.7MM **Privately Held**
WEB: www.tyco-fire.com
SIC: 3569 3494 3321 5085 Sprinkler systems, fire: automatic; valves & pipe fittings; sprinkler systems, field; water pipe, cast iron; valves & fittings
HQ: Tyco International Management Company, Llc
9 Roszel Rd Ste 2
Princeton NJ 08540
609 720-4200

(G-9422)
VERAIL TECHNOLOGIES INC
650 N Cannon Ave (19446-1874)
PHONE..............................513 454-8192
Tom Mack, *President*
Thomas Mack, *President*
Nigel Horsley, *Treasurer*
Peter Roosen, *Admin Sec*
EMP: 4 EST: 2014
SALES (est): 82.8K **Privately Held**
SIC: 3743 Railroad locomotives & parts, electric or nonelectric

(G-9423)
VICTOR ASSOCIATES INC
453 Country Club Dr (19446-1464)
PHONE..............................215 393-5437
Art Huster, *President*
EMP: 8
SQ FT: 7,000
SALES: 1.7MM **Privately Held**
SIC: 3674 Semiconductors & related devices

(G-9424)
VILLAGE HNDCRFTED CBINETRY INC
Also Called: Village Wood Shop
200 W 8th St (19446-1802)
PHONE..............................215 393-3040
Gary Marks, *President*
Gina Trave, *Partner*
Joseph Trave, *Vice Pres*
Katy Pellegrino, *Project Mgr*
David Stremme, *Project Mgr*
EMP: 3
SALES: 500K **Privately Held**
WEB: www.villagehandcrafted.com
SIC: 2434 Wood kitchen cabinets

(G-9425)
VINYL DIZZIGN
1106 Elm St (19446-1912)
PHONE..............................267 246-7725
Randall L Rosenberg, *Owner*
EMP: 3
SALES (est): 151.1K **Privately Held**
SIC: 3993 Signs & advertising specialties

(G-9426)
VR ENTERPRISES LLC
1170 Troxel Rd (19446-4768)
PHONE..............................215 932-1113
Michael Dardzinski,
EMP: 7
SALES (est): 351.7K **Privately Held**
SIC: 7532 7538 7692 7699 Mobile home & trailer repair; general truck repair; automotive welding; aircraft & heavy equipment repair services

(G-9427)
WEBTRANS LIMITED LLC
701 W 5th St Ste D (19446-2269)
P.O. Box 1435, Kulpsville (19443-1435)
PHONE..............................215 260-3313
Eric El Duffy,
Scott Duffy,
EMP: 20
SALES (est): 2.1MM **Privately Held**
SIC: 3743 Railroad equipment

(G-9428)
ZEIGLERS BEVERAGES LLC
1513 N Broad St (19446-1111)
PHONE..............................215 855-5161
Art Balzereit, *CFO*

Tim Kulig, *Manager*
▲ EMP: 50
SALES (est): 15MM
SALES (corp-wide): 247.9MM **Privately Held**
SIC: 2086 Bottled & canned soft drinks
PA: Lidestri Foods, Inc.
815 Whitney Rd W
Fairport NY 14450
585 377-7700

Lansdowne
Delaware County

(G-9429)
APPLIGENT INC
22 E Baltimore Ave (19050-2202)
PHONE..............................610 284-4006
Virginia Gavin, *President*
Heather Woodward, *Info Tech Mgr*
Mark Gavin, *Officer*
EMP: 21
SQ FT: 6,000
SALES (est): 2.7MM **Privately Held**
WEB: www.appligent.com
SIC: 7372 7371 Prepackaged software; computer software development & applications

(G-9430)
ARTISTWORKS WHOLESALE INC
Also Called: Image Connections
456 Penn St (19050-3017)
PHONE..............................610 622-9940
Michael Markowicz, *President*
Mark Shoham, *Treasurer*
▲ EMP: 5
SALES (est): 410K **Privately Held**
SIC: 2741 5199 Art copy & poster publishing; art goods

(G-9431)
BONINFANTE FRICTION INC
Also Called: Boninfante Enterprises
555 Industrial Park Dr (19050-3012)
PHONE..............................610 626-2194
Rob Boninfante, *CEO*
Elliott Pickett, *Opers Staff*
Bob Malloy, *Production*
Drew Farnese, *QC Mgr*
EMP: 33
SQ FT: 20,000
SALES (est): 8.1MM **Privately Held**
SIC: 3714 Clutches, motor vehicle

(G-9432)
F CREATIVE IMPRESSIONS INC
240 Lexington Ave (19050-2516)
PHONE..............................215 743-7577
Richard Freas, *President*
EMP: 9 EST: 1996
SALES: 900K **Privately Held**
SIC: 3444 3993 Awnings & canopies; signs, not made in custom sign painting shops

(G-9433)
GRIFFITHS PRINTING CO
Also Called: Griffiths Printing
404 E Baltimore Ave (19050-2596)
PHONE..............................610 623-3822
Roy Bell Jr, *President*
James Bell, *Vice Pres*
Edward Bell, *Shareholder*
EMP: 19 EST: 1946
SQ FT: 4,000
SALES (est): 2.5MM **Privately Held**
WEB: www.griffithsprint.com
SIC: 2752 2759 2791 2789 Commercial printing, offset; letterpress printing; typesetting; bookbinding & related work

(G-9434)
HENRY MARGU INC
540 Commerce Dr (19050-3088)
PHONE..............................610 622-0515
Andrew Marguiles, *President*
Steven Margulies, *Vice Pres*
Joan Whalen, *Accountant*
Linda Bridgins, *Bookkeeper*
▲ EMP: 12
SQ FT: 10,000

SALES (est): 1.4MM **Privately Held**
WEB: www.henrymarguwigs.com
SIC: 3999 Wigs, including doll wigs, toupees or wiglets

(G-9435)
J R FINIO & SONS INC
555 Baily Rd (19050-3103)
PHONE..............................610 623-5800
Nicholas Finio, *President*
EMP: 10
SQ FT: 6,000
SALES (est): 770K **Privately Held**
SIC: 2752 Commercial printing, offset

(G-9436)
JENARD CORPORATION
451 Penn St (19050-3016)
PHONE..............................610 622-3600
Peter Keay, *President*
EMP: 4
SALES (est): 285.5K **Privately Held**
SIC: 3089 Plastics products

(G-9437)
LAURA J DESIGNS
109 Walsh Rd (19050-2116)
PHONE..............................610 213-1082
Laura Jackson, *Owner*
EMP: 3 EST: 2010
SALES: 150K **Privately Held**
SIC: 7389 3961 Design services; costume jewelry, ex. precious metal & semi-precious stones

(G-9438)
MGK PRODUCE CO
610 Industrial Park Dr (19050-3035)
PHONE..............................610 853-3678
Ilias Pagiotas, *Principal*
EMP: 4 EST: 1983
SALES (est): 187.2K **Privately Held**
SIC: 2037 Fruits, quick frozen & cold pack (frozen)

(G-9439)
NAVARRO SPRING COMPANY
550 Commerce Dr (19050-3077)
PHONE..............................610 259-3177
John Navarro, *President*
Joan Mary Navarro, *Corp Secy*
Jill Navarro, *Opers Mgr*
EMP: 7
SQ FT: 6,000
SALES (est): 991.4K **Privately Held**
WEB: www.navarrospring.com
SIC: 3495 Wire springs

(G-9440)
OMNI PUBLLISHING EASTERN PA
615 Penn St (19050-3131)
PHONE..............................610 626-8819
Thomas Abrams, *Owner*
EMP: 3
SALES (est): 150K **Privately Held**
SIC: 2741 Telephone & other directory publishing

(G-9441)
PHILLYS BEST STEAK COMPANY INC
619 Indl Park Dr (19050)
PHONE..............................610 259-6000
Odyssefs Akranis, *President*
Zafeiris Akranis, *VP Opers*
Edd Culbertson, *Sales Staff*
EMP: 18
SQ FT: 6,000
SALES (est): 3.6MM **Privately Held**
WEB: www.phillysbeststeak.com
SIC: 2011 Meat packing plants

(G-9442)
RIDGWAY INDUSTRIES INC
6250 Baltimore Ave Ste 22 (19050-2700)
P.O. Box 660, Darby (19023-0660)
PHONE..............................610 259-5534
Bradford Daggy, *President*
Robert Firedel, *Vice Pres*
EMP: 18
SALES: 2.5MM **Privately Held**
WEB: www.ridgwayindustries.com
SIC: 2819 Industrial inorganic chemicals

(G-9443)
SCHERMERHORN BROS CO
610 Industrial Park Dr (19050-3035)
PHONE....................................610 284-7402
Dennis Carson, *Manager*
EMP: 5
SALES (corp-wide): 14.3MM **Privately Held**
SIC: 2298 5085 Twine; mill supplies
PA: Schermerhorn Bros. Co.
340 Eisenhower Ln N
Lombard IL 60148
630 627-9860

(G-9444)
SOUTHWEST VINYL WINDOWS INC
6250 Baltimore Ave Ste 7 (19050-2700)
PHONE....................................610 626-8826
Albert Dixon, *CEO*
James Dixon, *Vice Pres*
Christine Dixon, *Admin Sec*
EMP: 18
SQ FT: 12,000
SALES (est): 3.2MM **Privately Held**
SIC: 3089 3444 3442 Windows, plastic; awnings & canopies; metal doors

(G-9445)
THERMIGATE LLC
617 Glenwood Ave (19050-2643)
PHONE....................................610 931-1023
EMP: 4 EST: 2014
SALES (est): 250K **Privately Held**
SIC: 1629 3674 Heavy Construction, Nec, Nsk

Lanse
Clearfield County

(G-9446)
LARRY D BAUMGARDNER COAL CO
421 Knox Run Rd (16849)
P.O. Box 186 (16849-0186)
PHONE....................................814 345-6404
Larry D Baumgardner, *President*
Marjorie L Baumgardner, *Corp Secy*
EMP: 10
SALES (est): 1.2MM **Privately Held**
SIC: 1221 Strip mining, bituminous

Lansford
Carbon County

(G-9447)
HILLS MACHINE SHOP
1 Dock St (18232-1200)
PHONE....................................570 645-8787
Kenneth Hill, *Owner*
EMP: 6 EST: 1964
SALES: 1MM **Privately Held**
SIC: 3599 7692 Machine shop, jobbing & repair; welding repair

(G-9448)
JOAN VADYAK PRINTING INC
321 W Ridge St (18232-1115)
PHONE....................................570 645-5507
Harry Vadyak Sr, *President*
Harry Vadyak Jr, *Vice Pres*
Joan Vadyak, *Treasurer*
EMP: 3
SQ FT: 1,500
SALES (est): 271.8K **Privately Held**
SIC: 2752 Commercial printing, lithographic

(G-9449)
SILBERLINE MFG CO INC
201 Dock St (18232-1213)
PHONE....................................570 668-6050
Tori Ng, *Finance Mgr*
Steven Tate, *Manager*
Graham Berry, *Manager*
EMP: 100

SALES (corp-wide): 113.8MM **Privately Held**
WEB: www.silberline.com
SIC: 2816 2819 Inorganic pigments; industrial inorganic chemicals
PA: Silberline Manufacturing Co., Inc.
130 Lincoln Dr
Tamaqua PA 18252
570 668-6050

(G-9450)
THIS LIFE FOREVER INC
106 W Ridge St (18232-1310)
PHONE....................................707 733-0383
Russell Fletcher, *CEO*
EMP: 3
SQ FT: 7,000
SALES (est): 121.6K **Privately Held**
SIC: 2085 Distilled & blended liquors

Larimer
Westmoreland County

(G-9451)
FEDCO MANUFACTURING INC
11585 Rte 993 (15647)
P.O. Box 357 (15647-0357)
PHONE....................................724 863-2252
Fred Pferdehirt, *President*
Edward Pferdehirt, *Vice Pres*
EMP: 18
SQ FT: 20,000
SALES (est): 3.4MM **Privately Held**
WEB: www.fedcomfg.com
SIC: 3444 1721 Sheet metalwork; interior commercial painting contractor

Latrobe
Westmoreland County

(G-9452)
A E PAKOS INC
1106 Burns St (15650-2149)
PHONE....................................724 539-1790
Allen Pakos, *President*
Karen Ohara, *Corp Secy*
EMP: 6
SQ FT: 3,200
SALES (est): 765.5K **Privately Held**
SIC: 3643 Current-carrying wiring devices

(G-9453)
ALLEGHENY LUDLUM LLC
Also Called: ATI Allegheny Ludlum
Rr 981 Box N (15650)
PHONE....................................724 537-5551
Joe Dowfer, *Superintendent*
Stephen Nelson, *Plant Engr*
EMP: 10 **Publicly Held**
SIC: 3312 Blast furnaces & steel mills
HQ: Allegheny Ludlum, Llc
1000 Six Ppg Pl
Pittsburgh PA 15222
412 394-2800

(G-9454)
ALUMINA CERAMIC COMPONENTS INC
4532 State Route 982 (15650-5298)
PHONE....................................724 532-1900
Jack Lininger, *CEO*
Tim Lininger, *Sales Mgr*
EMP: 10
SQ FT: 15,000
SALES (est): 1.4MM **Privately Held**
WEB: www.alumina-ceramic.com
SIC: 3253 3264 Mosaic tile, glazed & unglazed: ceramic; porcelain electrical supplies

(G-9455)
AMFIRE MINING COMPANY LLC (HQ)
1 Energy Pl Ste 3000 (15650-9646)
P.O. Box 1020, Waynesburg (15370-3020)
PHONE....................................724 532-4307
EMP: 15
SALES (est): 64.6MM
SALES (corp-wide): 4.2B **Publicly Held**
SIC: 1241 Coal Mining Services

PA: Alpha Natural Resources Inc
1 Alpha Pl
Bristol VA 37620
276 619-4410

(G-9456)
APPALACHIAN MILLWORK
166 Menasha Ln (15650)
PHONE....................................724 539-1944
Paul Church, *Owner*
EMP: 3
SALES (est): 191.9K **Privately Held**
SIC: 2431 Millwork

(G-9457)
ARTCRAFT PRINTERS INC
400 Weldon St (15650-1517)
P.O. Box 284 (15650-0284)
PHONE....................................724 537-5231
Marybeth Elder, *President*
EMP: 4
SQ FT: 1,500
SALES: 400K **Privately Held**
SIC: 2752 Commercial printing, offset

(G-9458)
ARTHUR R WARNER COMPANY (PA)
701 Depot St (15650-1620)
P.O. Box 1 (15650-0001)
PHONE....................................724 539-9229
Michael Warner, *President*
Kevin Greene, *Vice Pres*
Jennifer Warner, *Vice Pres*
Mathias Packe, *VP Opers*
Roxanne Warner, *Info Tech Dir*
▼ EMP: 18 EST: 1961
SQ FT: 9,000
SALES: 1.9MM **Privately Held**
WEB: www.arwarnerco.com
SIC: 3541 3544 Machine tools, metal cutting type; special dies & tools

(G-9459)
BARMAH CO
Center Dr Bldg 1 (15650)
P.O. Box 526 (15650-0526)
PHONE....................................724 539-8477
Fax: 724 539-8476
EMP: 4
SQ FT: 20,000
SALES (est): 310K **Privately Held**
SIC: 2431 Mfg Millwork

(G-9460)
BOQUET TOOL & DIE
143 Shawley Ln (15650-5249)
PHONE....................................724 539-8250
Bonny Shawley, *Owner*
Wiles Shawley, *Owner*
EMP: 3 EST: 1974
SQ FT: 1,200
SALES (est): 338.2K **Privately Held**
SIC: 3599 Machine shop, jobbing & repair

(G-9461)
BRIDGE DECK SOLUTIONS LLC
298 Cherry Hills Dr (15650-4677)
PHONE....................................724 424-1001
Nathan Kurek, *Mng Member*
EMP: 20
SQ FT: 100,000
SALES (est): 2.5MM **Privately Held**
SIC: 3479 Galvanizing of iron, steel or endformed products

(G-9462)
CBC LATROBE ACQUISITION LLC
100 33rd St (15650-1477)
PHONE....................................724 532-5444
George Parke, *President*
EMP: 200
SALES (est): 31.8MM
SALES (corp-wide): 210.7MM **Privately Held**
SIC: 2086 Bottled & canned soft drinks
PA: City Brewing Company, Llc
925 3rd St S
La Crosse WI 54601
608 785-4200

(G-9463)
CERATIZIT USA INC
5369 Rte 982 (15650)
PHONE....................................724 694-8100
Andreas Olthoff, *President*
EMP: 13
SALES (est): 1.4MM **Privately Held**
SIC: 3291 Tungsten carbide abrasive

(G-9464)
CHESTNUT RIDGE FOAM INC
443 Warehouse Dr (15650-3573)
P.O. Box 781 (15650-0781)
PHONE....................................724 537-9000
Carl Ogburn, *President*
Carl M Ogburn, *Exec VP*
Dale Horner, *Opers Mgr*
Brandon Hohman, *Prdtn Mgr*
Henry Kubistek, *Maint Spvr*
▲ EMP: 120
SQ FT: 155,000
SALES (est): 37.9MM **Privately Held**
WEB: www.chestnutridgefoam.com
SIC: 3069 2821 2515 2392 Foam rubber; plastics materials & resins; mattresses & bedsprings; household furnishings

(G-9465)
CI MEDICAL TECHNOLOGIES INC (DH)
149 Devereux Dr (15650-2662)
PHONE....................................724 537-9600
Robert P Subasic Jr, *CEO*
John D Pearson, *COO*
Richard Cobb, *Engineer*
Eduardo Saenz, *Engineer*
Frank Tomaselli, *Engineer*
EMP: 29
SALES (est): 14MM **Privately Held**
SIC: 3089 Injection molding of plastics
HQ: Technimark Llc
180 Commerce Pl
Asheboro NC 27203
336 498-4171

(G-9466)
CITY BREWING
100 33rd St (15650-1477)
PHONE....................................724 532-5454
Simon Thorpe, *Principal*
Kirk Riffer, *Warehouse Mgr*
Stephen Mead, *Production*
Randy Hull, *Engineer*
Craig May, *Electrical Engi*
EMP: 12
SALES (est): 1.3MM **Privately Held**
SIC: 2082 Beer (alcoholic beverage)

(G-9467)
CRAFT MANUFACTURING INC
315 Linden St (15650-1709)
P.O. Box 779 (15650-0779)
PHONE....................................724 532-2702
Dave Quicquaro, *President*
Darlene Potts, *Purch Mgr*
Tina Dillon, *Admin Sec*
EMP: 19
SQ FT: 13,000
SALES (est): 4.6MM **Privately Held**
SIC: 3556 Food products machinery

(G-9468)
CTP CARRERA INC (HQ)
Also Called: Carclo Technical Plastics
600 Depot St (15650-1617)
PHONE....................................724 539-6995
Mark Charbonneu, *CEO*
Todd Pierce, *COO*
Diane McNealy, *CFO*
Mary Smetak, *Human Res Dir*
Rob Stutzman, *Mktg Dir*
▲ EMP: 117
SQ FT: 16,000
SALES: 48.3MM
SALES (corp-wide): 204.8MM **Privately Held**
SIC: 3229 3827 3089 Optical glass; reflectors, optical; injection molding of plastics
PA: Carclo Plc
Po Box 88
Ossett WF5 9
207 067-0000

(G-9469)
CUSTOM CARBIOE GRINDING
303 State Route 217 (15650-3457)
PHONE.................................724 539-8826
Dennis Liberoni, *President*
Craig Liberoni, *Vice Pres*
Cannelle Bianco, *Admin Sec*
EMP: 13
SALES (est): 1.6MM **Privately Held**
SIC: 3599 Machine shop, jobbing & repair

(G-9470)
D & Z PRINTERS
1101 Ligonier St (15650-1919)
PHONE.................................724 539-8922
Elton Weeks, *Principal*
EMP: 4
SQ FT: 1,000
SALES: 220.5K **Privately Held**
SIC: 2752 Commercial printing, offset

(G-9471)
DERRY CONSTRUCTION CO INC (PA)
527 State Route 217 (15650-3451)
PHONE.................................724 539-7600
Richard S Hudocki Jr, *President*
Mark Visconti, *Corp Secy*
Daniel G Slavek Jr, *Vice Pres*
EMP: 10
SQ FT: 4,200
SALES (est): 10.2MM **Privately Held**
WEB: www.derryconstruction.com
SIC: 1771 2951 Blacktop (asphalt) work;
asphalt paving mixtures & blocks

(G-9472)
DERRY STONE & LIME CO INC
523 State Route 217 (15650-3451)
PHONE.................................724 459-3971
Daniel Slevak III, *President*
Sandy Kramer, *Manager*
EMP: 11 **EST:** 2000
SALES (est): 1.3MM **Privately Held**
SIC: 3281 Stone, quarrying & processing
of own stone products

(G-9473)
DYNAMIC SEALING SYSTEMS LLC
5927 State Route 981 # 7 (15650-2687)
P.O. Box 235 (15650-0235)
PHONE.................................724 537-6315
Lee V Freeman, *President*
EMP: 5
SALES: 200K **Privately Held**
SIC: 3053 Gaskets, packing & sealing de-
vices

(G-9474)
ELIZABETH CARBIDE COMPONENTS
200 Monastery Dr (15650-2656)
PHONE.................................724 539-3574
Richard A Pagliari, *CEO*
David Keefer, *President*
EMP: 32
SALES (est): 8.5MM
SALES (corp-wide): 57MM **Privately Held**
SIC: 3545 Machine tool accessories
PA: Elizabeth Carbide Die Co., Inc.
601 Linden St
Mckeesport PA 15132
412 751-3000

(G-9475)
EXTRAMET PRODUCTS LLC (PA)
2890 Ligonier St (15650-4218)
PHONE.................................724 532-3041
Wayne Douglas, *Mng Member*
Denise Douglas,
EMP: 17
SQ FT: 3,500
SALES (est): 2.1MM **Privately Held**
SIC: 3291 Synthetic abrasives

(G-9476)
FLEURI LLC
105 Redwood Cir (15650-2517)
PHONE.................................724 539-7566
Ted Morris,
Lorraine Morris,
EMP: 5

SQ FT: 600
SALES: 250K **Privately Held**
SIC: 3171 5137 Handbags, women's;
handbags

(G-9477)
G V D INC
Also Called: Jay-Mari Company
1305 Spring St (15650-2233)
P.O. Box 350 (15650-0350)
PHONE.................................724 537-5586
Henry Di Pietro, *Principal*
Gene Christner, *Opers Mgr*
EMP: 7
SQ FT: 18,000
SALES: 700K **Privately Held**
WEB: www.gvd.com
SIC: 3479 Coating of metals & formed
products; painting of metal products

(G-9478)
GBY CORPORATION
1001 Lloyd Ave (15650-2652)
PHONE.................................724 539-1626
Nancy S Robbins, *Ch of Bd*
James Stupakoff Robbins, *Vice Pres*
EMP: 80 **EST:** 1957
SQ FT: 46,000
SALES (est): 9.9MM **Privately Held**
WEB: www.latronicscorp.com
SIC: 3679 Hermetic seals for electronic
equipment

(G-9479)
GUTCHESS LUMBER CO INC
185 Devereux Dr (15650-2662)
PHONE.................................724 537-6447
Richard Porteus, *Manager*
EMP: 87
SALES (corp-wide): 150MM **Privately Held**
SIC: 2491 2426 2421 Millwork, treated
wood; lumber, hardwood dimension; plan-
ing mills
PA: Gutchess Lumber Co., Inc.
890 Mclean Rd
Cortland NY 13045
607 753-3393

(G-9480)
HYDRO CARBIDE INC (HQ)
4439 State Route 982 (15650-3700)
PHONE.................................724 539-9701
Randy L Greely, *CEO*
Thomas Pozda, *CEO*
Mark R Dyll, *CFO*
Robert Sirac, *Treasurer*
Michael T Clancey, *Admin Sec*
▲ **EMP:** 111
SALES (est): 22.7MM
SALES (corp-wide): 261.6MM **Privately Held**
WEB: www.ramet.com
SIC: 2819 Carbides
PA: Hbd Industries Inc
5200 Upper Metro
Dublin OH 43017
614 526-7000

(G-9481)
INDUSTRIAL SHIPPING PDTS ISP
2404 State Route 130 (15650-4207)
PHONE.................................724 423-6533
Frank Rozik, *President*
EMP: 4
SQ FT: 7,000
SALES (est): 530K **Privately Held**
SIC: 2441 2431 Packing cases, wood:
nailed or lock corner; planing mill, mill-
work

(G-9482)
J M S FABRICATED SYSTEMS INC
647 Donohoe Rd (15650-3524)
PHONE.................................724 832-3640
Joe Torrero, *President*
John Torrero, *Vice Pres*
EMP: 32
SQ FT: 3,500
SALES: 9.3MM **Privately Held**
SIC: 3441 3297 3444 Fabricated struc-
tural metal; nonclay refractories; sheet
metalwork

(G-9483)
JE LYONS CONSTRUCTION INC
174 Smiths Hill Rd (15650-5448)
PHONE.................................724 686-3967
Jon E Lyons, *President*
EMP: 8 **EST:** 2015
SALES: 1.5MM **Privately Held**
SIC: 1521 3448 Single-family housing
construction; farm & utility buildings

(G-9484)
JEFFREY SHEPLER
Also Called: Walters Electric Co
10 W 2nd Ave (15650-1166)
PHONE.................................724 537-7411
Jeffrey Shepler, *Owner*
Renee Shepler, *Office Mgr*
EMP: 5
SQ FT: 2,600
SALES (est): 219.6K **Privately Held**
SIC: 7694 1731 Electric motor repair;
electrical work

(G-9485)
K CASTINGS INC
523 Lloyd Ave (15650-1721)
PHONE.................................724 539-9753
Chris A Adams, *President*
Larry Wallisch, *Corp Secy*
EMP: 8 **EST:** 1969
SQ FT: 8,000
SALES: 1MM **Privately Held**
SIC: 3363 3364 Aluminum die-castings;
brass & bronze die-castings

(G-9486)
KENNAMETAL INC
Rr 981 Box S (15650)
P.O. Box 231 (15650-0231)
PHONE.................................412 539-5000
Lawrence W Stranghoener, *Ch of Bd*
Sean Garrett, *Engineer*
Elie Khoury, *Engineer*
Mia Ramaekers, *Finance Mgr*
Donna Hixson, *Human Res Mgr*
EMP: 700
SALES (corp-wide): 2.3B **Publicly Held**
SIC: 3545 Cutting tools for machine tools;
bits for use on lathes, planers, shapers,
etc.; tool holders
PA: Kennametal Inc.
600 Grant St Ste 5100
Pittsburgh PA 15219
412 248-8000

(G-9487)
LANG SPECIALITY TRAILERS LLC
321 Cherry Hills Dr (15650-4628)
PHONE.................................724 972-6590
Adam Ghrist, *Mng Member*
EMP: 9
SALES (est): 343.2K **Privately Held**
SIC: 3715 7389 Truck trailers; financial
services

(G-9488)
LATROBE ASSOCIATES INC
Also Called: Westmoreland Plastics Company
135 Gertrude St (15650-2901)
P.O. Box 29 (15650-0029)
PHONE.................................724 539-1612
Fred Crocker, *President*
Alfred A Crocker Jr, *Principal*
John Adams, *Director*
Michael Sullivan, *Director*
EMP: 45
SQ FT: 36,500
SALES (est): 14.3MM **Privately Held**
WEB: www.westmorelandplastics.com
SIC: 3089 Injection molding of plastics

(G-9489)
LATROBE FOUNDRY MCH & SUP CO (PA)
5655 State Route 981 (15650-5303)
P.O. Box 431 (15650-0431)
PHONE.................................724 537-3341
Ted Steiner, *President*
Michael Steiner, *Vice Pres*
EMP: 17 **EST:** 1933
SQ FT: 10,000

SALES (est): 3.5MM **Privately Held**
WEB: www.latrobefoundry.com
SIC: 3365 Aluminum & aluminum-based
alloy castings

(G-9490)
LATROBE GLASS & MIRROR INC
4915 State Route 982 (15650-2387)
PHONE.................................724 539-2431
Bob Kramer, *President*
Bob Craymon, *Owner*
EMP: 5
SALES (est): 567.3K **Privately Held**
SIC: 3231 1793 Cut & engraved glass-
ware: made from purchased glass; glass
& glazing work

(G-9491)
LATROBE PALLET INC
1284 State Route 981 (15650-4146)
PHONE.................................724 537-9636
Scott Himler, *President*
Scott Harr, *Vice Pres*
EMP: 7
SQ FT: 5,000
SALES: 1MM **Privately Held**
SIC: 2448 Pallets, wood

(G-9492)
LATROBE PATTERN CO
523 Lloyd Ave (15650-1799)
PHONE.................................724 539-9753
Chris Adams, *President*
Allan Wallisch, *Treasurer*
Larry Wallisch, *Admin Sec*
EMP: 20 **EST:** 1946
SQ FT: 8,000
SALES (est): 3.2MM **Privately Held**
WEB: www.kccastings.com
SIC: 3543 Foundry patternmaking

(G-9493)
LATROBE PRINTING AND PUBG CO
Also Called: Latrobe Bulletin
1211 Ligonier St (15650-1921)
PHONE.................................724 537-3351
Chris P Miles, *President*
Marlene Sample, *Vice Pres*
George Sample, *Treasurer*
Allen Martello, *Marketing Staff*
EMP: 26 **EST:** 1902
SQ FT: 10,000
SALES (est): 1.6MM **Privately Held**
SIC: 2711 Commercial printing & newspa-
per publishing combined; newspapers:
publishing only, not printed on site

(G-9494)
LATROBE SPECIALTY MTLS CO LLC (HQ)
Also Called: Carpenter Technology
2626 Ligonier St (15650-3246)
P.O. Box 31 (15650-0031)
PHONE.................................724 537-7711
Toni Thene, *CEO*
Dale Mikus, *Vice Pres*
David Havemann, *Controller*
Eric Thomson, *Technology*
James R Bucci, *Admin Sec*
◆ **EMP:** 650 **EST:** 1913
SQ FT: 250,000
SALES (est): 230.3MM
SALES (corp-wide): 2.1B **Publicly Held**
WEB: www.latrobesteel.com
SIC: 3312 3369 Tool & die steel; castings,
except die-castings, precision
PA: Carpenter Technology Corporation
1735 Market St Fl 15
Philadelphia PA 19103
610 208-2000

(G-9495)
LAUREL CARBIDE INC
920 Lloyd Ave (15650-2650)
PHONE.................................724 537-4810
David A Snyder, *President*
EMP: 3
SQ FT: 2,000
SALES (est): 239.6K **Privately Held**
WEB: www.laurelcarbide.com
SIC: 3291 Synthetic abrasives

(G-9496)
LAUREL ENERGY LP
1 Energy Pl Ste 7500 (15650-9627)
PHONE..............................724 537-5731
EMP: 3
SALES (est): 140K **Privately Held**
SIC: 1241 Coal Mining

(G-9497)
LAUREL HIGHLANDS FINISHING
319 Unity St (15650-1743)
PHONE..............................724 537-9850
EMP: 3
SQ FT: 3,000
SALES: 150K **Privately Held**
SIC: 3479 Metal Coatings/ Metal Finishing

(G-9498)
LAUREL VALLEY GRAPHICS INC
1511 Monastery Dr (15650-5207)
PHONE..............................724 539-4545
John R Watson, *President*
Diane L Watson, *Vice Pres*
Dave Kornides, *Sales Staff*
EMP: 19
SQ FT: 100,000
SALES (est): 4.9MM **Privately Held**
WEB: www.lvgraphics.net
SIC: 2752 Commercial printing, offset

(G-9499)
LEHIGH SPECIALTY MELTING INC
107 Gertrude St (15650-2963)
PHONE..............................724 537-7731
Charles F Ireland, *President*
Jerald Krueger, *Principal*
Chad Ireland, *Vice Pres*
EMP: 65
SALES (est): 19.5MM
SALES (corp-wide): 568.1MM **Privately Held**
SIC: 3312 Blast furnaces & steel mills
HQ: Whemco Inc.
5 Hot Metal St Ste 300
Pittsburgh PA 15203
412 390-2700

(G-9500)
LIGONIER STONE & LIME COMPANY
Also Called: Derry Stone & Lime Co
117 Marcia St (15650-4300)
PHONE..............................724 537-6023
David Herrholtz, *President*
David S Herrholtz, *President*
Cathy A Herrholtz, *Corp Secy*
EMP: 28
SALES (est): 6.3MM **Privately Held**
SIC: 3273 Ready-mixed concrete

(G-9501)
LUXCELIS TECHNOLOGIES LLC
45 Bay Hill Dr (15650-4665)
PHONE..............................724 424-1800
EMP: 3
SALES (est): 264.6K **Privately Held**
SIC: 3599 Machine shop, jobbing & repair

(G-9502)
MASTER-LEE ENGINEERED PRODUCTS
5631 State Route 981 (15650-5303)
PHONE..............................724 537-6002
Richard Douds, *President*
Mike Cortese, *Vice Pres*
EMP: 3
SQ FT: 1,200
SALES (est): 509.6K **Privately Held**
SIC: 3823 Industrial instrmnts msrmnt display/control process variable

(G-9503)
MASTROROCCO MACHINE
Rr 2 (15650)
PHONE..............................724 539-4511
Anthony Mastrocco, *Owner*
EMP: 4
SALES (est): 260.6K **Privately Held**
SIC: 3599 Machine shop, jobbing & repair

(G-9504)
MENASHA PACKAGING COMPANY LLC
131 Menasha Ln (15650-1674)
P.O. Box 678 (15650-0678)
PHONE..............................800 783-4563
EMP: 80
SALES (corp-wide): 1.7B **Privately Held**
WEB: www.menashapackaging.com
SIC: 2653 Corrugated & solid fiber boxes
HQ: Menasha Packaging Company, Llc
1645 Bergstrom Rd
Neenah WI 54956
920 751-1000

(G-9505)
MORGAN ADVANCED CERAMICS INC
580 Monastery Dr (15650-2659)
PHONE..............................724 537-7791
John Stang, *Branch Mgr*
EMP: 80
SALES (corp-wide): 1.3B **Privately Held**
WEB: www.morganelectroceramics.com
SIC: 2899 Fluxes: brazing, soldering, galvanizing & welding
HQ: Morgan Advanced Ceramics, Inc
2425 Whipple Rd
Hayward CA 94544

(G-9506)
O & S MACHINE CO INC
718 Ashland Dr (15650-2639)
PHONE..............................724 539-9431
John G Orzehowski, *President*
Richard J Stemmler, *Corp Secy*
Eileen Orzehowski, *Trustee*
Carol Stemmler, *Trustee*
EMP: 6 EST: 1963
SQ FT: 6,000
SALES (est): 579.2K **Privately Held**
SIC: 3599 Machine shop, jobbing & repair

(G-9507)
OPCO INC
205 W Harrison Ave (15650-3115)
P.O. Box 101 (15650-0101)
PHONE..............................724 537-9300
Michael K Payne, *President*
Deborah A Payne, *Admin Sec*
▲ EMP: 20
SQ FT: 60,000
SALES (est): 3.5MM **Privately Held**
WEB: www.opcodirect.com
SIC: 2821 5162 Polystyrene resins; plastics materials & basic shapes; resins

(G-9508)
OTW TOOL CO
939 Donohoe Rd (15650-3530)
PHONE..............................724 539-8952
Donald E Smith, *President*
Windy Hill, *Admin Sec*
EMP: 10
SQ FT: 9,000
SALES (est): 1.1MM **Privately Held**
WEB: www.otwtool.com
SIC: 3599 Machine shop, jobbing & repair

(G-9509)
PANTHERA PRODUCTS INC
5055 Center Dr (15650-5202)
P.O. Box 900, Luxor (15662-0900)
PHONE..............................724 532-3362
Albert M Kairys Jr, *President*
EMP: 8
SQ FT: 10,000
SALES (est): 1.3MM **Privately Held**
SIC: 3089 Plastic containers, except foam

(G-9510)
PRECISIONEERING INC
5420 Pleasant Unity Rd (15650-5502)
PHONE..............................724 423-2472
Fax: 724 423-2472
EMP: 3
SALES (est): 280K **Privately Held**
SIC: 3599 Mfg Industrial Machinery

(G-9511)
PREMIUM PLASTICS SOLUTIONS LLC
Also Called: P P S
59 Bay Hill Dr (15650-4665)
PHONE..............................724 424-7000

John Hatch, *CFO*
Christopher Scarazzo,
EMP: 68
SQ FT: 5,000
SALES (est): 16.8MM **Privately Held**
SIC: 3089 Plastic containers, except foam

(G-9512)
QUALITY MOULD INC
110 Dill Ln Bldg 2 (15650-5205)
PHONE..............................724 532-3678
David A Danko, *CEO*
Dj Danko, *President*
EMP: 29
SQ FT: 15,000
SALES (est): 5.9MM **Privately Held**
WEB: www.qualitymould.com
SIC: 3599 3544 Machine shop, jobbing & repair; special dies, tools, jigs & fixtures

(G-9513)
QUIKRETE COMPANIES LLC
Also Called: Quikrete/Pittsburgh
519 Red Barn Ln (15650-6402)
PHONE..............................724 539-6600
Lloyd C Miller, *Manager*
Robert Turberville, *Manager*
EMP: 50 **Privately Held**
WEB: www.quikrete.com
SIC: 3272 3241 Concrete products; cement, hydraulic
HQ: The Quikrete Companies Llc
5 Concourse Pkwy Ste 1900
Atlanta GA 30328
404 634-9100

(G-9514)
R AND M MACHINING COMPANY INC
2412 Raymond Ave (15650-3348)
PHONE..............................724 532-0890
Mario Venzin, *President*
Ray Venzin, *Vice Pres*
EMP: 10
SQ FT: 24,000
SALES (est): 800K **Privately Held**
SIC: 3599 Machine shop, jobbing & repair

(G-9515)
R K NEON COMPANY
410 Unity St (15650-1342)
PHONE..............................724 539-9605
Carol Wolfe, *Owner*
EMP: 3 EST: 2010
SALES (est): 294.4K **Privately Held**
SIC: 2813 Neon

(G-9516)
RAVEN INDUSTRIES INC
5049 Center Dr (15650-5202)
PHONE..............................724 539-8230
Ken White, *President*
John Comunale, *Plant Mgr*
Aj Waitkus, *Project Mgr*
Mike Bache, *Purch Dir*
Kevin Williams, *Controller*
◆ EMP: 72
SQ FT: 56,000
SALES (est): 15.2MM **Privately Held**
WEB: www.ravenindustries.com
SIC: 3861 2899 2893 Toners; prepared photographic (not made in chemical plants); ink or writing fluids; printing ink

(G-9517)
ROBINDALE EXPORT LLC
Also Called: Robindale Energy
11 Lloyd Ave Ste 200 (15650-1711)
PHONE..............................724 879-4264
Judson Kroh, *Mng Member*
EMP: 500
SALES (est): 15.6MM **Privately Held**
SIC: 8731 6282 1081 Energy research; investment research; metal mining services; metal mining exploration & development services

(G-9518)
SAINT-GOBAIN CERAMICS PLAS INC
4702 Route 982 (15650-3280)
PHONE..............................724 539-6000
John Hickey, *Manager*
EMP: 100

SALES (corp-wide): 215.9MM **Privately Held**
WEB: www.sgceramics.com
SIC: 3297 Nonclay refractories
HQ: Saint-Gobain Ceramics & Plastics, Inc.
750 E Swedesford Rd
Valley Forge PA 19482

(G-9519)
SENATE COAL MINES (PA)
1 Energy Pl Ste 5100 (15650-9627)
PHONE..............................724 537-2062
Hans J Mende, *President*
Mary Walker, *Corp Secy*
EMP: 6
SALES (est): 832.8K **Privately Held**
SIC: 1221 Coal preparation plant, bituminous or lignite

(G-9520)
SIEM TOOL COMPANY INC
131 Turnberry Cir (15650-4621)
PHONE..............................724 520-1904
John Siemering Jr, *President*
Leslie Siemering, *Treasurer*
EMP: 30
SALES: 1.5MM **Privately Held**
SIC: 2819 Carbides

(G-9521)
SOSKO MANUFACTURING INC
410 Unity St Ste 500 (15650-1342)
PHONE..............................724 879-4117
Jason Sosko, *President*
EMP: 6
SALES (est): 279K **Privately Held**
SIC: 3499 Wheels: wheelbarrow, stroller, etc.; stamped metal

(G-9522)
SPECIALTY SEAL GROUP INC
1001 Lloyd Ave (15650-2644)
PHONE..............................724 539-1626
Jay Renton, *President*
Allyson Dinsmore, *Purchasing*
EMP: 20
SALES (est): 3.5MM **Privately Held**
SIC: 3229 Tableware, glass or glass ceramic

(G-9523)
SUN STAR INC
4427 State Route 982 (15650-3700)
PHONE..............................724 537-5990
David Carrera, *CEO*
Michael Berry, *President*
Mike Berry, *President*
Denny Wasko, *Plant Mgr*
Mike Kozar, *QC Mgr*
EMP: 30
SQ FT: 21,000
SALES (est): 8.7MM **Privately Held**
WEB: www.sunstar-inc.com
SIC: 3089 Injection molding of plastics

(G-9524)
TOOLING SPECIALISTS INC (PA)
433 Fayette St (15650-5341)
P.O. Box 828 (15650-0828)
PHONE..............................724 539-2534
Theodore Prettiman, *President*
Paul M Prettiman, *Senior VP*
Troy Prettiman, *Assistant VP*
Antonio Sebastian, *VP Mfg*
Kathleen Osinkoski, *Admin Sec*
EMP: 100 EST: 1960
SQ FT: 80,000
SALES: 7.5MM **Privately Held**
SIC: 3599 7692 Machine shop, jobbing & repair; welding repair

(G-9525)
TOOLING SPECIALISTS INC
Alexandria Rd (15650)
P.O. Box 383 (15650-0383)
PHONE..............................724 837-0433
Troy Prettiman, *Manager*
EMP: 5
SALES (corp-wide): 7.5MM **Privately Held**
SIC: 3599 Machine & other job shop work
PA: Tooling Specialists, Inc.
433 Fayette St
Latrobe PA 15650
724 539-2534

(G-9526)
UNITED STATES THERMOAMP INC
Also Called: Heat Siphon
1223 Heat Siphon Ln (15650-6205)
P.O. Box 694 (15650-0694)
PHONE................................724 537-3500
William Bernardi, *President*
Sue Giannini, *Corp Secy*
▼ EMP: 25
SQ FT: 13,000
SALES (est): 6.1MM **Privately Held**
WEB: www.heatsiphon.com
SIC: 3585 Heat pumps, electric

(G-9527)
UNITY PRINTING COMPANY INC
5848 State Route 981 (15650-9525)
PHONE................................724 537-5800
James L Ernette, *President*
Joe Frederick, *COO*
George I Frederick, *Vice Pres*
Brenda S Ernette, *Admin Sec*
▲ EMP: 20
SQ FT: 12,500
SALES (est): 4.1MM **Privately Held**
WEB: www.unityprinting.com
SIC: 2752 3953 2791 2789 Commercial printing, offset; marking devices; typesetting; bookbinding & related work

(G-9528)
WEST MORELAND PRECISION TOOL
151 Kingston St (15650-3801)
P.O. Box 365, Youngstown (15696-0365)
PHONE................................724 537-6558
Dean Sheffler, *Mng Member*
EMP: 8
SALES (est): 854.8K **Privately Held**
WEB: www.wptcllc.com
SIC: 3599 Machine shop, jobbing & repair

(G-9529)
ZAPPONE BROS FOODS
Also Called: Lucy's Foods
408 Longs Rd (15650-3506)
PHONE................................724 539-1430
Nicholas D Zappone, *Owner*
EMP: 3
SQ FT: 5,000
SALES: 1.2MM **Privately Held**
SIC: 2099 Packaged combination products: pasta, rice & potato

Lattimer Mines
Luzerne County

(G-9530)
HUNTER HIGHWAY INC
30 Lauren Ln (18234)
P.O. Box 295, Drums (18222-0295)
PHONE................................570 454-8161
Robert Tarapchak, *President*
EMP: 14 EST: 2014
SQ FT: 18,000
SALES (est): 790.2K **Privately Held**
SIC: 3449 Miscellaneous metalwork

Laughlintown
Westmoreland County

(G-9531)
BULLSKIN STONE & LIME LLC
1350 Route 30 (15655-1018)
P.O. Box 528, Latrobe (15650-0528)
PHONE................................724 537-7505
David S Herrholtz, *Principal*
EMP: 10
SALES (est): 146.2K **Privately Held**
SIC: 3274 Lime

Laurys Station
Lehigh County

(G-9532)
BRADERS WOODCRAFT INC
5440 Route 145 (18059-1307)
P.O. Box C (18059-0963)
PHONE................................610 262-3452
Edwin Brader, *President*
EMP: 15 EST: 1956
SQ FT: 10,000
SALES (est): 1.5MM **Privately Held**
SIC: 2434 2511 Wood kitchen cabinets; wood household furniture

Lawrence
Washington County

(G-9533)
ACS INVESTORS LLC (DH)
1000 Park Dr (15055-1018)
PHONE................................724 746-5500
Timothy C Huffmyer, *President*
Guy Lammers, *Accounts Mgr*
EMP: 6
SALES (est): 6.3MM
SALES (corp-wide): 1.8MM **Privately Held**
SIC: 3577 Computer peripheral equipment
HQ: Black Box Corporation
1000 Park Dr
Lawrence PA 15055
724 746-5500

(G-9534)
ALLEGHENY MILLWORK PBT (PA)
104 Commerce Blvd (15055)
P.O. Box 493 (15055-0493)
PHONE................................724 873-8700
Richard A Serdy, *CEO*
David Priselac, *Vice Pres*
Virgil Beeman, *Project Mgr*
Vladimir Kshiminskiy, *Project Mgr*
Tyler Tronzo, *Project Mgr*
EMP: 110
SQ FT: 80,000
SALES (est): 25.6MM **Privately Held**
WEB: www.alleghenymillwork.com
SIC: 2431 5211 Millwork; lumber products; door & window products; insulation & energy conservation products

(G-9535)
BLACK BOX CORPORATION (DH)
1000 Park Dr (15055-1018)
PHONE................................724 746-5500
Deepak Bansal, *President*
Lori Martin, *District Mgr*
Michael Carney, *Corp Secy*
Ronald Basso, *Exec VP*
Amie Burr, *Project Mgr*
◆ EMP: 3
SQ FT: 352,000
SALES: 774.6MM
SALES (corp-wide): 1.8MM **Privately Held**
WEB: www.blackbox.com
SIC: 3577 3679 3661 5045 Computer peripheral equipment; electronic switches; harness assemblies for electronic use: wire or cable; modems; computer peripheral equipment; modems, computer; electronic parts; electrical apparatus & equipment; electronic wire & cable
HQ: Bbx Inc.
1000 Park Dr
Lawrence PA 15055
724 746-5500

(G-9536)
BLACK BOX SERVICES COMPANY
1000 Park Dr (15055-1018)
PHONE................................724 746-5500
Timothy C Huffmyer, *President*
Dusten Schiefert, *Manager*
EMP: 6

SALES (est): 1.5MM
SALES (corp-wide): 1.8MM **Privately Held**
SIC: 3577 Computer peripheral equipment
HQ: Black Box Corporation
1000 Park Dr
Lawrence PA 15055
724 746-5500

(G-9537)
INDUSTRIAL CONTROLS & EQP INC
Also Called: Ice
2 Park Dr (15055)
PHONE................................724 746-3705
Thomas Santacroce, *President*
William Eurich, *General Mgr*
James Neville, *Vice Pres*
Greg Winslow, *Project Mgr*
Pam Barrett, *Engineer*
EMP: 50
SQ FT: 15,000
SALES (est): 8.3MM **Privately Held**
WEB: www.ice-vip.com
SIC: 7699 3491 Industrial equipment services; industrial valves
PA: Synergistic Partners, Inc.
2 Pk Dr
Lawrence PA 15055

(G-9538)
NCRX OPTICAL SOLUTIONS INC
106 Commerce Blvd (15055)
P.O. Box 38004, Pittsburgh (15238-8004)
PHONE................................724 745-1011
John Traina, *CEO*
EMP: 5
SQ FT: 2,000
SALES (corp-wide): 1.5MM **Privately Held**
SIC: 3827 Optical test & inspection equipment
PA: Ncrx Optical Solutions Inc.
105 Executive Pkwy # 401
Hudson OH 44236
330 239-5353

(G-9539)
POWER IGN CNTRLS APPLACHIA LLC
2 Park Dr (15055)
P.O. Box 614 (15055-0614)
PHONE................................724 746-3700
Larry Guess, *General Mgr*
Dale Robertson, *CFO*
Mary Jo Simon, *Manager*
EMP: 7
SQ FT: 26,000
SALES: 2MM **Privately Held**
SIC: 1389 Cementing oil & gas well casings
HQ: Equipment & Controls, Inc.
2 Park Dr
Lawrence PA 15055
724 746-3700

(G-9540)
ROSEMOUNT INC
2 Park Dr (15055)
PHONE................................724 746-3400
Bob Tracy, *Manager*
EMP: 10
SALES (corp-wide): 17.4B **Publicly Held**
WEB: www.rosemount.com
SIC: 3823 Manometers, industrial process type
HQ: Rosemount Inc.
8200 Market Blvd
Chanhassen MN 55317
952 906-8888

Lawrenceville
Tioga County

(G-9541)
EFFECTIVE CD LLC
51b Main St (16929-9472)
P.O. Box 116 (16929-0116)
PHONE................................607 351-5949
Eric L Edwards, *President*
EMP: 5
SALES (est): 479.8K **Privately Held**
SIC: 3577 Computer peripheral equipment

(G-9542)
FARRS MEAT PROCESSING
367 Erickson Rd (16929-8426)
PHONE................................570 827-2241
Jim Farr, *Principal*
EMP: 3
SALES (est): 173.7K **Privately Held**
SIC: 2011 Meat packing plants

Le Raysville
Bradford County

(G-9543)
THOMAN LOGGING
662 Main St (18829-7767)
PHONE................................570 265-4993
EMP: 3 EST: 2012
SALES (est): 220.5K **Privately Held**
SIC: 2411 Logging

Lebanon
Lebanon County

(G-9544)
A ARCHERY AND PRINTING PLACE
Also Called: Colemans
1705 E Cumberland St # 2 (17042-8306)
PHONE................................717 274-1811
Jamie I Brungart, *President*
Jody Chernich, *President*
EMP: 4
SALES (est): 388.6K **Privately Held**
SIC: 2752 5941 Commercial printing, offset; archery supplies

(G-9545)
ACORN TRAIL WOODCRAFT
1010 E Maple St (17046-2237)
PHONE................................717 279-0261
Eugene Fox, *Owner*
EMP: 4
SALES (est): 250.5K **Privately Held**
SIC: 2511 Wood household furniture

(G-9546)
AUMAN MACHINE COMPANY INC (PA)
1525 Joel Dr (17046-8376)
PHONE................................717 273-4604
Timothy I Auman, *President*
▲ EMP: 41 EST: 1949
SQ FT: 30,000
SALES (est): 10.7MM **Privately Held**
WEB: www.aumanmachine.com
SIC: 3599 7692 Mfg Industrial Machinery Welding Repair

(G-9547)
BEMIS PACKAGING INC
Bemis North America
5 Keystone Dr (17042-9791)
PHONE................................717 279-5000
Bray Brunkhurst, *Branch Mgr*
EMP: 50
SALES (corp-wide): 4B **Publicly Held**
WEB: www.milprint.com
SIC: 2671 2891 Plastic film, coated or laminated for packaging; adhesives & sealants
HQ: Bemis Packaging, Inc.
3550 Moser St
Oshkosh WI 54901
920 527-7300

(G-9548)
BRENTWOOD INDUSTRIES INC
2101 Lehman St (17046-2757)
PHONE................................717 274-1827
James Riegel, *Manager*
EMP: 77
SALES (corp-wide): 194.6MM **Privately Held**
WEB: www.brentw.com
SIC: 3089 3564 3443 Molding primary plastic; blowers & fans; fabricated plate work (boiler shop)

PA: Brentwood Industries, Inc.
500 Spring Ridge Dr
Reading PA 19610
610 374-5109

(G-9549)
BUDGET PORTABLE WELDING MCH
2197 State Route 72 N (17046-8064)
PHONE..................................717 865-0473
James A Young, *Owner*
EMP: 3
SALES (est): 110K **Privately Held**
SIC: 7692 Welding repair

(G-9550)
BVI C/O GENCO
1629 Willow St (17042-4580)
PHONE..................................712 228-3338
Nicole Bicksler, *Principal*
EMP: 3
SALES (est): 193.5K **Privately Held**
SIC: 2834 Pharmaceutical preparations

(G-9551)
C L STURKEY INC (PA)
824 Cumberland St Ste 3 (17042-5256)
PHONE..................................717 274-9441
Christopher Tarsa, *President*
Michelle A Tarsa, *Corp Secy*
Leon F Tarsa, *Vice Pres*
EMP: 8
SQ FT: 1,000
SALES (est): 2.8MM **Privately Held**
WEB: www.sturkey.com
SIC: 3841 7699 Knives, surgical; surgical
instrument repair

(G-9552)
CARGILL INCORPORATED
320 N 16th St (17046-4511)
PHONE..................................717 273-1133
Dennis De Long, *Manager*
Rod Isham, *Manager*
EMP: 12
SALES (corp-wide): 114.7B **Privately Held**
WEB: www.cargill.com
SIC: 5153 2075 2046 2048 Grain & field
beans; wheat; corn; soybeans; soybean
oil, cake or meal; corn oil, refined; corn
oil, meal; gluten feed; high fructose corn
syrup (HFCS); prepared feeds; meat
packing plants; beef products from beef
slaughtered on site; pork products from
pork slaughtered on site; poultry slaughtering & processing
PA: Cargill, Incorporated
15407 Mcginty Rd W
Wayzata MN 55391
952 742-7575

(G-9553)
CARPENTER ENGINEERING INC
808 Patmar Dr (17046-2132)
PHONE..................................717 274-8808
Richard A Carpenter, *President*
EMP: 8
SQ FT: 2,000
SALES (est): 1.5MM **Privately Held**
WEB: www.carpenter-eng-inc.com
SIC: 3613 8711 Control panels, electric;
consulting engineer

(G-9554)
CHOO R CHOO SNACKS INC
Also Called: Buffalo Bills
1547 Joel Dr (17046-8376)
P.O. Box 866 (17042-0866)
PHONE..................................717 273-7499
Pat Sherburne, *President*
Paul Squires, *Treasurer*
Evelyn Sherburne, *Admin Sec*
EMP: 5
SQ FT: 6,000
SALES (est): 2.4MM **Privately Held**
WEB: www.ccrsnacks.com
SIC: 2099 Food preparations

(G-9555)
COLORATURA INC
544 Louser Rd (17042-4829)
P.O. Box 157, Annville (17003-0157)
PHONE..................................717 867-1144
Alan J Resnick, *President*
EMP: 4

SALES (est): 414.6K **Privately Held**
WEB: www.coloratura.com
SIC: 2369 5632 Coats; girls', children's &
infants'; women's accessory & specialty
stores

(G-9556)
COLORTECH INC
232 S 9th St (17042-5902)
PHONE..................................717 450-5416
Patrick A Sullivan, *President*
Austin Sullivan, *Sales Executive*
George Gassert, *Supervisor*
▲ EMP: 30
SQ FT: 10,200
SALES (est): 5.3MM **Privately Held**
WEB: www.colortechinc.com
SIC: 2796 2752 Color separations for
printing; commercial printing, offset

(G-9557)
D A R A INC
1650 N 7th St (17046-2159)
PHONE..................................717 274-1800
Danny J Alexander, *President*
L Jeanne Alexander, *Treasurer*
EMP: 17 EST: 1982
SQ FT: 30,300
SALES: 1.9MM **Privately Held**
WEB: www.daraplastics.com
SIC: 3084 3089 Plastics pipe; stock
shapes, plastic

(G-9558)
DANIEL WEAVER COMPANY INC
Also Called: Weavers Famous Lebanon
Bologna
1415 Weavertown Rd (17046-2276)
P.O. Box 525 (17042-0525)
PHONE..................................717 274-6100
Robert Trider, *President*
John C Tuten Jr, *Admin Sec*
Dan Baum, *Asst Sec*
EMP: 36 EST: 1885
SQ FT: 10,000
SALES (est): 5.6MM
SALES (corp-wide): 91MM **Privately
Held**
WEB: www.godshalls.com
SIC: 2013 Sausages from purchased
meat; bologna from purchased meat;
smoked meats from purchased meat;
ham, smoked: from purchased meat
PA: Godshall's Quality Meats, Inc.
675 Mill Rd
Telford PA 18969
215 256-8867

(G-9559)
DAVIES PRECISION MACHINING INC
2400 Colebrook Rd (17042-9562)
PHONE..................................717 273-5495
Pearl Davies, *President*
Gene Martin, *General Mgr*
Jean Martin, *Principal*
David Davies, *Treasurer*
EMP: 12 EST: 1978
SQ FT: 24,000
SALES (est): 2.5MM **Privately Held**
SIC: 3599 Machine shop, jobbing & repair

(G-9560)
DEAN FOODS COMPANY
Also Called: Swiss Premium Dairy
2401 Walnut St (17042-9444)
PHONE..................................717 228-0445
John Wengert, *Principal*
Keith Kreiser, *Plant Engr*
EMP: 200 **Publicly Held**
SIC: 2026 Milk processing (pasteurizing,
homogenizing, bottling)
PA: Dean Foods Company
2711 N Haskell Ave
Dallas TX 75204

(G-9561)
DONALD BLYLER OFFSET INC
2101 Fonderwhite Rd (17042-9139)
PHONE..................................717 949-6831
Donald Blyler, *President*
EMP: 76
SQ FT: 40,000

SALES (est): 8.3MM **Privately Held**
WEB: www.dboprinting.com
SIC: 2752 2791 2789 Commercial printing, offset; typesetting; bookbinding & related work

(G-9562)
DWELL AMERICA LLC
1349 Cumberland St Ste 1 (17042-4504)
P.O. Box 233, East Petersburg (17520-
0233)
PHONE..................................717 272-4666
Sloan Caplan, *President*
EMP: 3
SQ FT: 25,000
SALES (est): 127.7K **Privately Held**
SIC: 2211 2221 Draperies & drapery fab-
rics, cotton; jacquard woven fabrics, cot-
ton; jacquard woven fabrics, manmade
fiber & silk

(G-9563)
DWELL AMERICA HOLDINGS INC (HQ)
Also Called: Keystone Weaving
1349 Cumberland St Ste 1 (17042-4504)
P.O. Box 233, East Petersburg (17520-
0233)
PHONE..................................717 272-4665
Sloan D Caplan, *President*
Perry C Caplan, *Vice Pres*
Eli Caplan, *Treasurer*
▲ EMP: 32 EST: 1946
SQ FT: 200,000
SALES (est): 6.2MM **Privately Held**
WEB: www.keystoneweaving.com
SIC: 2221 Marquisettes, manmade fiber;
flat crepes; comforters & quilts, manmade
fiber & silk

(G-9564)
DYNA-TECH INDUSTRIES LTD
Also Called: Tiger Power
120 N 25th St (17042-2501)
PHONE..................................717 274-3099
Lyndon B Risser, *General Ptnr*
EMP: 15
SQ FT: 30,000
SALES (est): 4.4MM **Privately Held**
WEB: www.dynagen.com
SIC: 7629 5063 3621 7623 Generator re-
pair; generators; electric motor & genera-
tor parts; refrigeration service & repair

(G-9565)
E & E METAL FABRICATIONS INC
110 N 16th St (17042-4507)
PHONE..................................717 228-3727
Wilfred E Erb, *President*
Steven R Erb, *Vice Pres*
Liane Erb, *Treasurer*
EMP: 23
SQ FT: 12,750
SALES (est): 6.6MM **Privately Held**
WEB: www.e-emetalfab.com
SIC: 3441 Fabricated structural metal

(G-9566)
EAST INDIES COFFEE & TEA
Also Called: Walter Progner
7 Keystone Dr (17042-9791)
PHONE..................................717 228-2000
Walter Progner, *Owner*
▲ EMP: 10
SALES (est): 601.9K **Privately Held**
SIC: 5499 2099 2095 Coffee; tea; food
preparations; roasted coffee

(G-9567)
FINETEX ROTARY ENGRAVING INC
Also Called: Finetex Textile Group
1431 Willow St (17046-4542)
PHONE..................................717 273-6841
Dave Hammond, *President*
▲ EMP: 8 EST: 1957
SQ FT: 40,000
SALES: 2MM **Privately Held**
SIC: 3552 7389 Silk screens for textile in-
dustry; textile & apparel services

(G-9568)
FISHER-KLOSTERMAN INC
Buell
200 N 7th St Ste 2 (17046-5040)
PHONE..................................717 274-7280
Tom Luger, *Branch Mgr*
EMP: 12
SQ FT: 7,000
SALES (corp-wide): 337.3MM **Publicly
Held**
WEB: www.fkinc.com
SIC: 2911 Acid oil
HQ: Fisher-Klosterman, Inc.
10000 Shelbyville Rd # 101
Louisville KY 40223
502 572-4000

(G-9569)
FITZ SECURITY CO INC
2 Pershing Ave (17042-5460)
PHONE..................................717 272-5020
John Fitzgibbons, *President*
Richard M Fitzgibbons, *Vice Pres*
EMP: 3 EST: 1979
SALES: 100K **Privately Held**
SIC: 3699 Security devices; electric sound
equipment

(G-9570)
FIVES N AMERCN COMBUSTN INC
819 Wheatfield Ln (17042-6405)
PHONE..................................717 228-0714
Robert Kopp, *Manager*
EMP: 43
SALES (corp-wide): 4.5MM **Privately
Held**
SIC: 3433 Heating equipment, except elec-
tric
HQ: Fives North American Combustion, Inc.
4455 E 71st St
Cleveland OH 44105
216 271-6000

(G-9571)
FLINTWOOD METALS INC
205 N 5th Ave (17046-4011)
PHONE..................................717 274-9481
Michael Glant, *President*
Michael O Glant, *Vice Pres*
Robynn M Glant, *Admin Sec*
EMP: 24
SQ FT: 145,000
SALES (est): 5.4MM **Privately Held**
WEB: www.flintwoodmetals.com
SIC: 3441 Fabricated structural metal

(G-9572)
FRESH DONUTS
1202 Cumberland St (17042-4526)
PHONE..................................717 273-8886
Elaine Minn, *Owner*
EMP: 6
SALES (est): 442.1K **Privately Held**
SIC: 2051 5812 Doughnuts, except
frozen; eating places

(G-9573)
GILL ROCK DRILL COMPANY INC
903 Cornwall Rd 905 (17042-7040)
PHONE..................................717 272-3861
James E Gill, *President*
Ronald J Birch, *Vice Pres*
Eric Crosson, *Vice Pres*
Edward Killian, *CFO*
Deborah L Gill, *Admin Sec*
▲ EMP: 35 EST: 1915
SQ FT: 130,000
SALES (est): 9.3MM **Privately Held**
WEB: www.gillrockdrill.com
SIC: 3532 7353 7699 1381 Drills &
drilling equipment, mining (except oil &
gas); heavy construction equipment
rental; industrial machinery & equipment
repair; drilling oil & gas wells; oil & gas
field machinery; blast furnaces & steel
mills

(G-9574)
GINGRICH MEMORIALS INC
424 Maple St 434 (17046-2959)
PHONE..................................717 272-0901
James R Gingrich, *President*
Jack Brown, *President*

▲ = Import ▼=Export
◆ =Import/Export

Richard D Ebling, *Corp Secy*
Mark Gingrich, *Vice Pres*
EMP: 16
SQ FT: 1,100
SALES (est): 1.4MM **Privately Held**
WEB: www.gingrichmemorials.com
SIC: 3281 5999 Marble, building: cut &
shaped; granite, cut & shaped; slate prod-
ucts; monuments & tombstones

(G-9575)
GOLDEN SPECIALTIES LTD
Also Called: O'Donnell, B T Goldsmith
604 Cornwall Rd (17042-7008)
P.O. Box 32 (17042-0032)
PHONE.................................717 273-9731
Brian O'Donnell, *Partner*
EMP: 7
SALES (est): 610K **Privately Held**
SIC: 3911 Jewelry, precious metal

(G-9576)
GRAPHIC DISPLAY SYSTEMS
308 S 1st St (17042-5427)
PHONE.................................717 274-3954
Robert Tobias, *Owner*
Karen Ramos, *Admin Sec*
EMP: 10
SALES (est): 912.1K **Privately Held**
WEB: www.graphicdisplaysystems.com
SIC: 3952 2542 Lead pencils & art goods;
partitions & fixtures, except wood

(G-9577)
**H & M DIVERSIFIED ENTPS INC
(PA)**
Also Called: H & M Glass
981 Mount Zion Rd (17046-2243)
PHONE.................................717 277-0680
Ammon Meyer, *President*
Corey Hoffert, *Vice Pres*
Debra Hoffert, *Treasurer*
Tina Hoffert, *Admin Sec*
EMP: 30
SQ FT: 17,500
SALES (est): 4MM **Privately Held**
SIC: 3355 Aluminum rolling & drawing

(G-9578)
HAINS PATTERN SHOP INC
521 S 14th Ave (17042-8807)
PHONE.................................717 273-6351
Gordon Hains, *President*
Shirley Hains, *Corp Secy*
Timothy Hains, *Vice Pres*
EMP: 12
SQ FT: 15,000
SALES (est): 1.7MM **Privately Held**
WEB: www.hainspattern.com
SIC: 3543 Industrial patterns

(G-9579)
HERB SHEET METAL INC
630 N 5th St (17046-3759)
PHONE.................................717 273-8001
Jack S Herb Jr, *President*
EMP: 13
SQ FT: 21,000
SALES (est): 900.6K **Privately Held**
SIC: 1761 3444 Sheet metalwork; sheet
metalwork

(G-9580)
HEWEY WELDING
1045 Wampler Ln (17042-4831)
PHONE.................................717 867-5222
Henry E Wampler, *Owner*
EMP: 5
SQ FT: 9,000
SALES (est): 1.2MM **Privately Held**
SIC: 3713 Truck bodies (motor vehicles)

(G-9581)
HIDDEN STILL INC
435 Willow St (17046-4866)
PHONE.................................717 270-1753
David E Stein, *President*
EMP: 7
SALES (est): 100.4K **Privately Held**
SIC: 2085 Cordials & premixed alcoholic
cocktails

(G-9582)
INGRETEC LTD
1500 Lehman St (17046-3337)
PHONE.................................717 273-0711

Philippe Jallon, *President*
▲ **EMP:** 10
SALES (est): 1.4MM **Privately Held**
WEB: www.ingretec.com
SIC: 2022 Natural cheese

(G-9583)
INNOVATIVE DESIGN INC (PA)
210 Weidman St (17046-3765)
P.O. Box 900, Jonestown (17038-0900)
PHONE.................................717 202-1306
William R Bixler, *President*
Kristy L Bixler, *Treasurer*
Gary J Fox, *Admin Sec*
EMP: 32
SQ FT: 100,000
SALES (est): 6.7MM **Privately Held**
WEB: www.innovativedesigninc.com
SIC: 3541 Machine tool replacement & re-
pair parts, metal cutting types

(G-9584)
J R RAMOS DENTAL LAB INC
Also Called: Jr Ramos Recording
21 S 7th St (17042-5202)
PHONE.................................717 272-5821
Wilfredo Ramos, *Owner*
EMP: 5
SQ FT: 1,000
SALES (est): 249.4K **Privately Held**
SIC: 8072 3843 Denture production; den-
tal equipment & supplies

(G-9585)
K & S CASTINGS INC
402 Schaeffer Rd (17042-9741)
PHONE.................................717 272-9775
Kenneth R Fair, *President*
Shiela Fair, *Admin Sec*
EMP: 45 **EST:** 1974
SQ FT: 25,000
SALES (est): 5.3MM **Privately Held**
WEB: www.cornwallaluminum.com
SIC: 3365 3369 Aluminum & aluminum-
based alloy castings; nonferrous
foundries

(G-9586)
K MACHINE & TOOL INC
554 E Walnut St (17042-5651)
PHONE.................................717 272-2241
Kenneth Miller, *President*
Terrence Remlinger, *Vice Pres*
Belva Miller, *Treasurer*
EMP: 8
SQ FT: 5,000
SALES (est): 1MM **Privately Held**
SIC: 3599 Machine shop, jobbing & repair

(G-9587)
**KAPP ADVERTISING SERVICES
INC (PA)**
Also Called: Merchandiser, The
100 E Cumberland St (17042-5485)
P.O. Box 840 (17042-0840)
PHONE.................................717 270-2742
Robert S Kapp, *President*
Herbert M Kapp, *Vice Pres*
Forrest Okelly, *Opers Mgr*
Erma Kapp, *Treasurer*
Randy Miller, *Sales Mgr*
EMP: 53 **EST:** 1950
SQ FT: 12,000
SALES (est): 10.8MM **Privately Held**
WEB: www.themerchandiser.com
SIC: 2711 Newspapers, publishing & print-
ing

(G-9588)
**KAUFFMANS ANIMAL HEALTH
INC**
21 Keystone Dr (17042-9791)
PHONE.................................717 274-3676
David Kauffman, *President*
Thomas Kauffman, *Vice Pres*
▲ **EMP:** 9
SQ FT: 17,000
SALES (est): 2MM **Privately Held**
WEB: www.ka-hi.com
SIC: 2833 Animal based products

(G-9589)
**KEENER ELECTRIC MOTORS
INC**
705 State Dr (17042-6345)
PHONE.................................717 272-7686
Jeffrey Keener, *President*
David Keener, *Vice Pres*
EMP: 8 **EST:** 1962
SQ FT: 7,000
SALES (est): 1.2MM **Privately Held**
SIC: 7694 5063 5999 Electric motor re-
pair; motors, electric; motors, electric

(G-9590)
KELLY MACHINE WORKS
604 N 22nd St (17046-2717)
PHONE.................................717 273-0303
Ryan E Kelly, *Owner*
EMP: 4
SALES (est): 371.6K **Privately Held**
SIC: 3599 Machine shop, jobbing & repair

(G-9591)
KERCHER ENTERPRISES INC
Also Called: Kercher Machine Works
920 Mechanic St (17046-1936)
PHONE.................................717 273-2111
Curtis Snyder, *President*
Anthony Kury, *Controller*
EMP: 28 **EST:** 2016
SQ FT: 7,000
SALES (est): 1MM **Privately Held**
SIC: 3599 Machine & other job shop work

(G-9592)
KERCHER INDUSTRIES INC
920 Mechanic St (17046-1936)
PHONE.................................717 273-2111
Edwin C Kercher, *President*
Helen Kercher, *Corp Secy*
James Kercher Jr, *Vice Pres*
Tony Kury, *Controller*
▲ **EMP:** 30
SQ FT: 75,000
SALES (est): 4.8MM **Privately Held**
SIC: 3559 7699 Brick making machinery;
industrial machinery & equipment repair

(G-9593)
**KERCHER MACHINE WORKS
INC**
Also Called: Kercher Industries
920 Mechanic St (17046-1936)
PHONE.................................717 273-2111
Edwin C Kercher, *President*
Helen Kercher, *Corp Secy*
EMP: 32 **EST:** 1946
SQ FT: 75,000
SALES (est): 3.3MM **Privately Held**
SIC: 3599 Machine shop, jobbing & repair

(G-9594)
KEYSTONE SPIKE
255 N Lincoln Ave (17046-3949)
PHONE.................................717 270-2700
Walter Pohl, *President*
Joseph Kijak, *Vice Pres*
EMP: 6
SQ FT: 280,000
SALES (est): 690K **Privately Held**
SIC: 3743 3315 3312 Railroad equip-
ment; steel wire & related products; blast
furnaces & steel mills

(G-9595)
KREICO LLC
609 S 4th St (17042-6808)
PHONE.................................717 228-7312
Kenneth Kreitz,
EMP: 3
SALES (est): 150K **Privately Held**
SIC: 3449 Miscellaneous metalwork

(G-9596)
KWIK QUALITY PRESS INC
732 Locust St (17042-6029)
PHONE.................................717 273-0005
Douglas Suereth, *President*
Cheron Suereth, *Corp Secy*
Scott Gass, *Vice Pres*
EMP: 8
SQ FT: 1,500
SALES (est): 720K **Privately Held**
WEB: www.kwikquality.com
SIC: 2752 Commercial printing, offset

(G-9597)
LANCO INDUSTRIES
2605 Prescott Rd (17042-9210)
PHONE.................................717 949-3435
David Lantz, *Owner*
EMP: 3 **EST:** 1995
SALES (est): 353.1K **Privately Held**
SIC: 3411 Metal cans

(G-9598)
LASERFAB INC
26 Lebanon Valley Pkwy (17042-9745)
PHONE.................................717 272-0060
Leon Zimmerman, *President*
Dain Zimmerman, *Business Mgr*
Joel Gockley, *Production*
Joel S Gockley, *Treasurer*
Anthony Martin, *Manager*
EMP: 10
SQ FT: 20,000
SALES (est): 3.5MM **Privately Held**
WEB: www.laserfab.net
SIC: 3699 Laser welding, drilling & cutting
equipment

(G-9599)
LEBANON DAILY NEWS
718 Poplar St (17042-6755)
P.O. Box 600 (17042-0600)
PHONE.................................717 272-5615
Jerry Grilly, *President*
EMP: 15
SALES (est): 1MM **Privately Held**
SIC: 2711 Commercial printing & newspa-
per publishing combined; newspapers,
publishing & printing

(G-9600)
**LEBANON GASKET AND SEAL
INC**
Also Called: Lebanon Gasket & Seal
2380 Colebrook Rd (17042-9530)
P.O. Box 1066 (17042-1066)
PHONE.................................717 274-3684
William A Sprecher, *President*
▲ **EMP:** 5
SALES (est): 766.9K **Privately Held**
SIC: 3069 2822 Rubberized fabrics; syn-
thetic rubber

(G-9601)
**LEBANON MACHINE & MFG CO
LLC**
Also Called: Tiburon Waterjet Services
2380 Colebrook Rd (17042-9530)
PHONE.................................717 274-3636
Josh Sprecher,
EMP: 7
SALES: 850K **Privately Held**
SIC: 3441 Fabricated structural metal

(G-9602)
LEBANON PARTS SERVICE INC
335 S 9th St (17042-5907)
PHONE.................................717 272-0181
Randall Kehler, *President*
EMP: 5
SALES (est): 636.6K **Privately Held**
SIC: 5531 5074 3599 Automotive parts;
plumbing & hydronic heating supplies;
machine shop, jobbing & repair

(G-9603)
LEBANON PATTERN SHOP INC
504 E Canal St (17046-4050)
PHONE.................................717 273-8159
Joseph G Woelfling, *President*
EMP: 6 **EST:** 1966
SQ FT: 25,000
SALES: 600K **Privately Held**
SIC: 3544 3543 Special dies, tools, jigs &
fixtures; industrial patterns

(G-9604)
LEBANON TOOL CO INC
Also Called: Ltc
330 N 7th Ave (17046-4000)
P.O. Box 29 (17042-0029)
PHONE.................................717 273-3711
Janis Herschkowitz, *President*
L Saylor Zimmerman III, *Corp Secy*
Ronald C Bailor, *Vice Pres*
EMP: 125
SQ FT: 19,700

SALES (est): 21.1MM
SALES (corp-wide): 46.9MM **Privately Held**
SIC: 3599 Machine shop, jobbing & repair
PA: P R L Inc
　　64 Rexmont Rd
　　Cornwall PA 17016
　　717 273-2470

(G-9605)
LEBANON VALLEY ENGRAVING INC (PA)
Also Called: Lebanon Valley Engraving Co
1245 Chestnut St (17042-4519)
PHONE....................................717 273-7913
Neil Rhine, *President*
Gary Rhine, *Vice Pres*
Jon Wagner, *Vice Pres*
▲ EMP: 14 EST: 1949
SQ FT: 30,000
SALES (est): 2.2MM **Privately Held**
WEB: www.lebanonvalleyengraving.com
SIC: 2759 Textile printing rolls: engraving

(G-9606)
LEBANON WATER TREATMENT PLANT
12 E Behney St (17046-9318)
PHONE....................................717 865-2191
Ron Luciotti, *Principal*
Jonathan Beers, *Exec Dir*
EMP: 18
SALES (est): 1.6MM **Privately Held**
SIC: 3589 Water treatment equipment, industrial

(G-9607)
MAJOR LEAGUE SCREEN PRTG & EMB
19 S 5th Ave (17042-5613)
PHONE....................................717 270-9511
Douglas Bartal, *President*
Sharon Bartal, *Vice Pres*
Kevin Bartal, *Manager*
EMP: 10
SQ FT: 6,000
SALES (est): 940K **Privately Held**
SIC: 2759 Screen printing

(G-9608)
MARK HERSHEY FARMS INC
479 Horseshoe Pike (17042-9260)
PHONE....................................717 867-4624
Michael T Morris, *CEO*
Daryl L Alger, *President*
EMP: 45
SQ FT: 5,744
SALES (est): 14.5MM **Privately Held**
WEB: www.markhersheyfarms.com
SIC: 2048 Prepared feeds

(G-9609)
MHP INDUSTRIES INC
2402 E Cumberland St (17042-9214)
PHONE....................................717 450-4753
Mathew Heisey, *President*
EMP: 25
SALES (est): 4.8MM **Privately Held**
SIC: 2448 Wood pallets & skids

(G-9610)
MICRO MACHINE DESIGN INC
1555 Joel Dr (17046-8376)
P.O. Box 201 (17042-0201)
PHONE....................................717 274-3500
Tom Zentz, *President*
Nate Schickling, *Vice Pres*
EMP: 11
SALES (est): 1.8MM **Privately Held**
SIC: 3599 Machine shop, jobbing & repair

(G-9611)
MILLET PLASTICS INC
21 Lebanon Valley Pkwy (17042-9744)
PHONE....................................717 277-7404
Alain Mermet, *President*
Warren Wohlfahrt, *Vice Pres*
Millet Mari, *Shareholder*
▲ EMP: 25
SQ FT: 43,000
SALES (est): 9.3MM **Privately Held**
SIC: 3089 Injection molding of plastics

(G-9612)
MURRYS OF MARYLAND INC
Also Called: Murry's Plant
1501 Willow St (17046-4578)
PHONE..............................301 420-6400
Tony Lucci, *Vice Pres*
Matt Wickenheiser, *Vice Pres*
Jon Stager, *Supervisor*
Louis Ford, *Data Proc Staff*
EMP: 230
SALES (corp-wide): 103.9MM **Privately Held**
SIC: 2038 2015 2013 2011 Frozen specialties; poultry slaughtering & processing; sausages & other prepared meats; meat packing plants
HQ: Murry's Of Maryland, Inc.
　　7852 Walker Dr Ste 420
　　Greenbelt MD 20770
　　888 668-7797

(G-9613)
MYERSTOWN SHEDS
513 King St Apt E (17042-9164)
PHONE....................................717 866-7644
Clair Martin, *Managing Prtnr*
Larry Stauffer, *Partner*
EMP: 5
SQ FT: 4,800
SALES (est): 430K **Privately Held**
SIC: 2452 5211 3496 Prefabricated wood buildings; prefabricated buildings; fencing, made from purchased wire

(G-9614)
PALMYRA BOLOGNA COMPANY
Also Called: Seltzers Bologna
1035 Willow St (17046-4937)
PHONE....................................717 273-9581
Frank Kettering, *Manager*
EMP: 6
SALES (corp-wide): 14MM **Privately Held**
WEB: www.seltzerslebanonbologna.com
SIC: 2011 Meat packing plants
PA: Palmyra Bologna Company
　　230 N College St
　　Palmyra PA 17078
　　717 838-6336

(G-9615)
PATRICIA MORRIS
Also Called: Elco Machine & Tool
21 Lehman St (17046-3871)
PHONE....................................717 272-5594
Patricia Morris, *President*
Jerry Morris, *Vice Pres*
EMP: 5
SQ FT: 10,000
SALES (est): 500K **Privately Held**
SIC: 3599 Machine shop, jobbing & repair

(G-9616)
PAULHUS AND ASSOCIATES INC
8 Keystone Dr (17042-9791)
PHONE....................................717 274-5621
Cheryl E Paulhus, *President*
George Cannon, *Vice Pres*
Dorie Lessig, *Treasurer*
Nancy Cameron, *Admin Sec*
EMP: 15
SQ FT: 7,000
SALES (est): 3MM **Privately Held**
WEB: www.paulhus.net
SIC: 5045 5734 7372 Computer software; software, business & non-game; business oriented computer software

(G-9617)
PEAK INDUSTRIES INC
Also Called: Conestoga Log Cabins
246 N Lincoln Ave (17046-3948)
PHONE....................................717 306-4490
Ronald Myer, *President*
EMP: 30
SQ FT: 86,000
SALES (est): 5.7MM **Privately Held**
SIC: 2452 Log cabins, prefabricated, wood

(G-9618)
PEAK VENTURES INC
Also Called: Conestoga Log Cabins and Homes
246 N Lincoln Ave (17046-3948)
PHONE....................................717 306-4490

Robert Cook, *Ch of Bd*
Ronald Myers, *President*
EMP: 35
SALES (est): 3MM **Privately Held**
SIC: 2452 Log cabins, prefabricated, wood

(G-9619)
PENNSY SUPPLY INC
201 Prescott Rd Ste A (17042-9222)
PHONE....................................717 274-3661
Kevin Smith, *Manager*
EMP: 75
SALES (corp-wide): 29.7B **Privately Held**
SIC: 1422 3273 2951 1442 Limestones, ground; ready-mixed concrete; asphalt paving mixtures & blocks; construction sand & gravel
HQ: Pennsy Supply, Inc.
　　1001 Paxton St
　　Harrisburg PA 17104
　　717 233-4511

(G-9620)
PENNSYLVANNIA PRECISION CAST P
Also Called: Ppcp
521 N 3rd Ave (17046-3965)
P.O. Box 1429 (17042-1429)
PHONE....................................717 273-3338
Andrew Miller, *President*
Richard Miller, *Chairman*
Dan Hummel, *Vice Pres*
Paul Pfautz, *Vice Pres*
Rick Schmidt, *Vice Pres*
EMP: 150
SQ FT: 52,000
SALES (est): 37.7MM **Privately Held**
WEB: www.ppcpinc.com
SIC: 3324 Steel investment foundries

(G-9621)
PHARMALOZ MANUFACTURING INC
Also Called: Simon Candy Co
500 N 15th Ave (17046-8303)
PHONE....................................717 274-9800
Ted Karkus, *CEO*
Robert V Cuddihy Jr, *COO*
Jennifer Herman, *Director*
▲ EMP: 30 EST: 2004
SQ FT: 57,000
SALES (est): 440.3K
SALES (corp-wide): 13.1MM **Publicly Held**
WEB: www.prophaselabs.com
SIC: 2064 Lollipops & other hard candy; cough drops, except pharmaceutical preparations
PA: Prophase Labs, Inc.
　　621 N Shady Retreat Rd
　　Doylestown PA 18901
　　215 345-0919

(G-9622)
PLAINS LPG SERVICES
2397 Quentin Rd Ste A (17042-9236)
PHONE....................................717 376-0830
Jason Balash, *President*
EMP: 5
SALES (est): 278.7K **Privately Held**
SIC: 1321 Propane (natural) production

(G-9623)
PLASTIC SYSTEM PACKAGING MILLE
17 Lebanon Valley Pkwy (17042-9744)
PHONE....................................717 277-7404
Warren Wohlfahrt, *President*
EMP: 19
SALES (est): 4.2MM **Privately Held**
SIC: 3089 Blow molded finished plastic products
HQ: Millet Marius
　　3 Rue Gerard Millet
　　Lavans-Les-Saint-Claude 39170
　　384 421-717

(G-9624)
PRECISION CUSTOM AMMUNITION
373 Acorn Cir (17042-8886)
PHONE....................................717 274-8762
Fred Wright, *President*
▲ EMP: 3

SALES: 100K **Privately Held**
WEB: www.pcammoinc.com
SIC: 3482 Pellets & BB's, pistol & air rifle ammunition

(G-9625)
REGAL CAST INC
307 N 9th Ave (17046-8105)
P.O. Box 1170 (17042-1170)
PHONE....................................717 270-1888
Janis Herschkowitz, *President*
L Saylor Zimmerman III, *Corp Secy*
EMP: 12
SQ FT: 20,000
SALES (est): 2.5MM
SALES (corp-wide): 46.9MM **Privately Held**
SIC: 3325 3369 Steel foundries; nonferrous foundries
PA: P R L Inc
　　64 Rexmont Rd
　　Cornwall PA 17016
　　717 273-2470

(G-9626)
REGUPOL AMERICA LLC (HQ)
11 Ritter Way (17042-9761)
PHONE....................................717 675-2198
George Soukas, *President*
Dirk Hainbach, *COO*
John Aten, *VP Sales*
◆ EMP: 25 EST: 2008
SQ FT: 84,000
SALES (est): 7.5MM
SALES (corp-wide): 88.3MM **Privately Held**
SIC: 3069 Floor coverings, rubber
PA: Bsw Berleburger Schaumstoffwerk Gmbh
　　Am Hilgenacker 24
　　Bad Berleburg 57319
　　275 180-30

(G-9627)
SCHNUPPS GRAIN ROASTING LLC
Also Called: Roast-A-Matic
416 Union Rd (17046-7826)
PHONE....................................717 865-6611
Nelson Zimmerman, *Sales Staff*
Joel Stauffer, *Mng Member*
EMP: 15 EST: 1971
SQ FT: 15,400
SALES: 2MM **Privately Held**
SIC: 3556 0723 Roasting machinery: coffee, peanut, etc.; grain drying services

(G-9628)
SCHOTT NORTH AMERICA INC
Also Called: Schott Pharmaceutical Packg
30 Lebanon Valley Pkwy (17042-9745)
PHONE....................................717 228-4200
Stanley Nazarchuk, *President*
Simon Williams, *President*
Blair Campbell, *Info Tech Mgr*
EMP: 140
SALES (corp-wide): 585K **Privately Held**
SIC: 3221 Vials, glass
HQ: Schott North America, Inc.
　　555 Taxter Rd Ste 470
　　Elmsford NY 10523
　　914 831-2200

(G-9629)
SENECA FOODS CORPORATION
30 Keystone Dr (17042-9791)
P.O. Box 202 (17042-0202)
PHONE....................................717 675-2074
Mike Moore, *Branch Mgr*
EMP: 31
SALES (corp-wide): 1.3B **Publicly Held**
SIC: 2099 Food preparations
PA: Seneca Foods Corporation
　　3736 S Main St
　　Marion NY 14505
　　315 926-8100

(G-9630)
SHYDAS SERVICES INC
Lincoln Traps Division
2360 Colebrook Rd Frnt (17042-9588)
PHONE....................................717 274-8676
Rod Shyda, *Branch Mgr*
EMP: 6 **Privately Held**
SIC: 3949 Trap racks (clay targets)

PA: Shyda's Services, Inc.
2360 Colebrook Rd
Lebanon PA

(G-9631)
SIMONE ASSOCIATES INC
845 Cumberland St (17042-5238)
PHONE......................717 274-3621
William C Simone, *President*
Mary Hossler, *Manager*
Art Clagett, *Director*
EMP: 6
SQ FT: 6,000
SALES (est): 380K **Privately Held**
WEB: www.simoneassociates.com
SIC: 3993 7335 Advertising artwork; commercial photography

(G-9632)
SNITZ CREEK CABINET SHOP LLC
2020 Cornwall Rd (17042-7413)
PHONE......................717 273-9861
Dean Zook,
Glendon Zook,
Loren Zook,
▲ **EMP:** 15
SQ FT: 16,500
SALES: 1.8MM **Privately Held**
WEB: www.snitzcreek.com
SIC: 2434 Wood kitchen cabinets

(G-9633)
SOLIDAYS MILLWORK
36 Weidman St (17046-3755)
PHONE......................717 274-2841
Raymon R Soliday, *Owner*
EMP: 3
SALES (est): 237.3K **Privately Held**
SIC: 2431 Planing mill, millwork

(G-9634)
STEEL PLUS INC
Also Called: Flintwood Metals
205 N 5th Ave (17046-4011)
PHONE......................717 274-9481
Michael Glant, *President*
Robynn Glant, *Vice Pres*
EMP: 26
SQ FT: 100,000
SALES: 5MM **Privately Held**
SIC: 3441 Fabricated structural metal

(G-9635)
SWEET SANCTIONS
323 Bricker Ln (17042-4109)
PHONE......................717 222-1859
Elizabeth Reddinger, *Principal*
EMP: 4 **EST:** 2012
SALES (est): 362.5K **Privately Held**
SIC: 3421 Table & food cutlery, including butchers'

(G-9636)
TREYCO MANUFACTURING INC
1500 Chestnut St (17042-4524)
PHONE......................717 273-6504
John B Stehman Jr, *President*
EMP: 26
SALES (est): 6.6MM **Privately Held**
SIC: 2951 Concrete, asphaltic (not from refineries)

(G-9637)
VAN TONGEREN AMERICA LLC
518 S 8th St (17042-6717)
PHONE......................717 450-3835
James Miller, *Mng Member*
EMP: 6 **EST:** 2016
SQ FT: 3,000
SALES: 3MM **Privately Held**
SIC: 2911 5084 Petroleum refining; industrial machinery & equipment
PA: Van Tongeren International Limited
Van Tongeren House
Godalming

(G-9638)
WEABER INC (HQ)
Also Called: Weaber Hardwoods
1231 Mount Wilson Rd (17042-4785)
PHONE......................717 867-2212
Matthew Weaber, *President*
Michelle Knamm, *Vice Pres*
Michael Potts, *Maint Spvr*
Maney Rivera, *Production*

Sean Downs, *Buyer*
▼ **EMP:** 216
SQ FT: 840,500
SALES (est): 180.8MM **Privately Held**
WEB: www.weaberlumber.com
SIC: 2426 Dimension, hardwood
PA: Wt Hardwoods Group, Inc.
1231 Mount Wilson Rd
Lebanon PA 17042
717 867-2212

(G-9639)
WT HARDWOODS GROUP INC (PA)
Also Called: Weaber Lumber
1231 Mount Wilson Rd (17042-4785)
PHONE......................717 867-2212
Matthew Weaber, *CEO*
H William Campoll, *CFO*
EMP: 12
SALES (est): 180.8MM **Privately Held**
SIC: 2426 Hardwood dimension & flooring mills

(G-9640)
ZIMMERMAN CHAIR SHOP
1486 Colebrook Rd (17042-9507)
PHONE......................717 273-2706
Glen Zimmerman, *Partner*
Wesley Zimmerman, *Partner*
EMP: 20 **EST:** 1974
SQ FT: 20,000
SALES (est): 3MM **Privately Held**
SIC: 2511 Chairs, household, except upholstered: wood

Leechburg
Armstrong County

(G-9641)
ALPHA CARB ENTERPRISES INC
691 Hyde Park Rd (15656-8241)
PHONE......................724 845-2500
Louis Leibert, *President*
Rob Rollinger, *General Mgr*
Russ Mundy, *Vice Pres*
John Rozic, *Vice Pres*
Bob Myers, *Production*
▲ **EMP:** 50
SQ FT: 28,500
SALES (est): 6.8MM **Privately Held**
WEB: www.alphacarb.com
SIC: 3544 Special dies & tools

(G-9642)
C & C TOOLING INC
120 Siberian Ave (15656-1251)
PHONE......................724 845-0939
Clyde M Ross, *President*
EMP: 10
SQ FT: 22,500
SALES (est): 1.2MM **Privately Held**
SIC: 3544 Special dies & tools

(G-9643)
COMPOSIDIE INC
Toolex Div
River Rd (15656)
P.O. Box 607 (15656-0607)
PHONE......................724 845-8602
Dean Hoch, *General Mgr*
EMP: 30
SALES (corp-wide): 60.5MM **Privately Held**
WEB: www.composidie.com
SIC: 3312 3544 3469 Tool & die steel; special dies, tools, jigs & fixtures; metal stampings
PA: Composidie, Inc.
1295 Route 380
Apollo PA 15613
724 845-8602

(G-9644)
DG SERVICES LLC
1057 State Route 356 A (15656-2029)
PHONE......................724 845-7300
Chad Dupill, *CEO*
EMP: 6
SALES: 1MM **Privately Held**
SIC: 1389 Gas field services; oil field services

(G-9645)
FRENCH QUATERS
1140 State Route 356 (15656-2030)
PHONE......................724 845-7387
Linda Gavasto, *Principal*
EMP: 3 **EST:** 2007
SALES (est): 245.1K **Privately Held**
SIC: 3131 Quarters

(G-9646)
KISKI PRECISION INDUSTRIES LLC
Also Called: ALLE-KISKI INDUSTRIES
531 Hyde Park Rd (15656-8969)
PHONE......................724 845-2799
Kevin Hartford, *President*
Ed Newell, *Vice Pres*
Liane Newell, *CFO*
EMP: 32
SQ FT: 27,000
SALES: 4.8MM **Privately Held**
SIC: 3599 7692 Machine shop, jobbing & repair; welding repair

(G-9647)
LEADING TECHNOLOGIES INC
1153 Industrial Pk Rd (15656)
P.O. Box 628 (15656-0628)
PHONE......................724 842-3400
Chester A Jonczak, *President*
L T Wohlin, *Chairman*
Chester Jonczak Jr, *Treasurer*
▲ **EMP:** 43
SQ FT: 70,000
SALES (est): 6.7MM
SALES (corp-wide): 60.5MM **Privately Held**
WEB: www.composidie.com
SIC: 3471 Plating & polishing
PA: Composidie, Inc.
1295 Route 380
Apollo PA 15613
724 845-8602

(G-9648)
LEECHBURG CONTACT LENS LAB
Also Called: Duppstadt, Arthur G, Od
84 2nd St (15656-1345)
PHONE......................724 845-7777
Arthur G Duppstadt, *President*
Sandy Catchpole, *Admin Sec*
EMP: 3
SQ FT: 700
SALES (est): 231.5K **Privately Held**
SIC: 8042 3851 Offices & clinics of optometrists; contact lenses

(G-9649)
MINUTEMAN PRESS
541 Hyde Park Rd (15656-8969)
PHONE......................724 236-0261
Tony Colecchi, *Principal*
EMP: 4
SALES (est): 361.1K **Privately Held**
SIC: 2752 Commercial printing, lithographic

(G-9650)
PRECISE TOOL & DIE INC
1711 Piper Rd (15656-9425)
PHONE......................724 845-1285
Jeff Swartzlander, *President*
Holly Swartzlander, *Corp Secy*
EMP: 30
SQ FT: 12,000
SALES (est): 4.3MM **Privately Held**
WEB: www.precisetd.com
SIC: 3544 Special dies & tools

(G-9651)
R E DUPILL & ASSOCIATES LTD
Also Called: Dupill Group
1057 State Route 356 (15656-2029)
PHONE......................724 845-7300
Raymond Dupill, *Principal*
Linda Dupill, *General Ptnr*
Alana Carr, *COO*
EMP: 7
SQ FT: 1,650
SALES (est): 1.4MM **Privately Held**
WEB: www.larslapusa.com
SIC: 3546 Power-driven handtools

(G-9652)
RENT-A-CENTER INC
397 Hyde Park Rd Ste B (15656-9687)
PHONE......................724 845-1070
Jeremiah Williams, *Branch Mgr*
EMP: 5
SALES (corp-wide): 2.6B **Publicly Held**
WEB: www.rentacenter.com
SIC: 3639 Major kitchen appliances, except refrigerators & stoves
PA: Rent-A-Center, Inc.
5501 Headquarters Dr
Plano TX 75024
972 801-1100

(G-9653)
SCHULTZ PRECISION TOOLING
111 Kathleen Rd (15656-2065)
PHONE......................724 334-4491
Keith A Schultz, *Owner*
EMP: 7
SALES (est): 924.2K **Privately Held**
SIC: 3544 Special dies, tools, jigs & fixtures

(G-9654)
W E KELLER MACHINING WELDING
327 Phillips Ln (15656-8311)
PHONE......................724 337-8327
Fax: 724 337-9408
EMP: 8
SALES (est): 584.8K **Privately Held**
SIC: 3599 Mfg Industrial Machinery

Leeper
Clarion County

(G-9655)
HEARTLAND KITCHENS & BATH
1758 Anderson Dr (16233)
PHONE......................814 744-8266
Brad Sthamaber, *Partner*
Craig Malm, *Partner*
Brad Schmaber, *Partner*
EMP: 5
SALES (est): 409K **Privately Held**
SIC: 2499 Kitchen, bathroom & household ware: wood

(G-9656)
KAHLES KITCHENS INC
7422 Route 36 (16233-3628)
PHONE......................814 744-9388
David A Kahle, *President*
Barbara A Kahle, *Admin Sec*
EMP: 100
SQ FT: 79,551
SALES (est): 8.3MM **Privately Held**
WEB: www.kahles.com
SIC: 2434 Wood kitchen cabinets

Leesport
Berks County

(G-9657)
ASHLEY FURNITURE INDS INC
45 Ashley Way (19533-8663)
PHONE......................610 926-0897
Michael Pitman, *Vice Pres*
Jerry Katz, *Manager*
EMP: 907
SALES (corp-wide): 4.7B **Privately Held**
SIC: 2511 2512 Wood household furniture; upholstered household furniture
PA: Ashley Furniture Industries, Inc.
1 Ashley Way
Arcadia WI 54612
608 323-3377

(G-9658)
ATLANTIC TRACK & TURNOUT CO
5 S Cntre Ave Ste 200 (19533)
PHONE......................610 916-2840
EMP: 5
SALES (corp-wide): 89.8MM **Privately Held**
SIC: 3531 Cranes, ship

PA: Atlantic Track & Turnout Co.
400 Broadacres Dr Ste 415
Bloomfield NJ 07003
973 748-5885

(G-9659)
BALDWIN HARDWARE CORPORATION
225 Peach St (19533-8644)
PHONE...................................610 777-7811
Dave Konopka, *Manager*
EMP: 418
SALES (corp-wide): 3.1B **Publicly Held**
SIC: 3429 Builders' hardware
HQ: Baldwin Hardware Corporation
19701 Da Vinci
Foothill Ranch CA 92610
949 672-4000

(G-9660)
BRIGHT SIGN AND MAINT CO INC
1025 James Dr (19533-8841)
P.O. Box 461 (19533-0461)
PHONE...................................610 916-5100
James H Mandolos, *President*
Randy Seaman, *Vice Pres*
EMP: 25 **EST:** 1958
SQ FT: 12,000
SALES (est): 2.3MM **Privately Held**
SIC: 3993 7353 Signs & advertising specialties; cranes & aerial lift equipment, rental or leasing

(G-9661)
EAGLE METALS INC (PA)
1243 Old Bernville Rd (19533-9115)
PHONE...................................610 926-4111
Charles J Bernard, *President*
Jon Anderton, *Purchasing*
Brian Murphy, *Sales Staff*
George Eisenhower, *Supervisor*
▲ **EMP:** 50 **EST:** 1963
SQ FT: 50,000
SALES (est): 8.6MM **Privately Held**
WEB: www.eaglebrass.com
SIC: 3351 3356 Strip, copper & copper alloy; brass rolling & drawing; bronze rolling & drawing; nickel & nickel alloy: rolling, drawing or extruding

(G-9662)
EMPIRE BUILDING PRODUCTS INC (HQ)
Also Called: Empire Surplus Home Center
2741 Bernville Rd (19533-8807)
PHONE...................................610 926-0500
Harry J O Neill III, *President*
Harry J O Neill, *Vice Pres*
Todd O Neill, *Vice Pres*
Thomas Chambers, *CFO*
Douglas E Wood, *Treasurer*
▲ **EMP:** 15
SQ FT: 8,000
SALES (est): 2.4MM
SALES (corp-wide): 39.2MM **Privately Held**
WEB: www.empiresurplus.com
SIC: 2434 Wood kitchen cabinets
PA: Empire Group Of Reading, Pa, Inc.
1420 Clarion St Ofc
Reading PA 19601
610 372-6511

(G-9663)
ENTRANCE INC
2651 Leiscz's Bridge Rd (19533-9333)
PHONE...................................610 926-0126
Ed M Collins III, *President*
EMP: 14
SALES: 1MM **Privately Held**
WEB: www.entranceinc.com
SIC: 3089 Floor coverings, plastic

(G-9664)
GROWMARK FS LLC
Also Called: Milford Fertilizer
119 E Wall St (19533)
P.O. Box 703 (19533-0703)
PHONE...................................610 926-6339
Adrian Robinson, *Area Mgr*
Mike Layton, *Safety Mgr*
Tim Kleinsmith, *Manager*
EMP: 25
SQ FT: 12,132

SALES (corp-wide): 7.2B **Privately Held**
WEB: www.growmarkfs.com
SIC: 2874 5191 Phosphatic fertilizers; pesticides
HQ: Growmark Fs, Llc
308 Ne Front St
Milford DE 19963
302 422-3002

(G-9665)
HAILIANG AMERICA CORPORATION
1001 James Dr Ste B38 (19533-8869)
PHONE...................................877 515-4522
Feng Jiang, *President*
Zhihong Xu, *Admin Sec*
▲ **EMP:** 13 **EST:** 2009
SALES (est): 2MM **Privately Held**
SIC: 3494 Pipe fittings

(G-9666)
HAWK MOUNTAIN EDITIONS LTD
Also Called: Hawk Mountain Art Papers
314 Ziegler Rd (19533-9402)
P.O. Box 145 (19533-0145)
PHONE...................................484 220-0524
EMP: 7
SQ FT: 20,000
SALES: 630K **Privately Held**
SIC: 5999 2621 Misc Ret Stores Mfg Speciality Paper

(G-9667)
KUSTOM KOMPONENTS
2670 Leiscz's Bridge Rd # 300 (19533-9433)
PHONE...................................484 671-3076
Chad Rochotte, *President*
Jay Lehrbach, *Technician*
EMP: 6
SQ FT: 3,500
SALES: 700K **Privately Held**
WEB: www.kustomkomponents.com
SIC: 3822 Air conditioning & refrigeration controls

(G-9668)
NEW ENTERPRISE STONE LIME INC
167 New Enterprise Dr (19533-8948)
PHONE...................................610 374-5131
Paul J Detwiler Jr, *Ch of Bd*
EMP: 325
SALES (corp-wide): 651.9MM **Privately Held**
SIC: 5031 3273 5983 5172 Lumber: rough, dressed & finished; millwork; ready-mixed concrete; fuel oil dealers; fuel oil; trusses, wooden roof; warm air heating & air conditioning contractor
PA: New Enterprise Stone & Lime Co., Inc.
3912 Brumbaugh Rd
New Enterprise PA 16664
814 224-6883

(G-9669)
NEW ENTERPRISE STONE LIME INC
Rte 73 Rr 61 (19533)
PHONE...................................610 678-1913
James Marks, *Plant Mgr*
EMP: 5
SALES (corp-wide): 651.9MM **Privately Held**
SIC: 1611 1771 2951 Highway & street construction; parking lot construction; asphalt & asphaltic paving mixtures (not from refineries)
PA: New Enterprise Stone & Lime Co., Inc.
3912 Brumbaugh Rd
New Enterprise PA 16664
814 224-6883

(G-9670)
NOLL PALLET & LUMBER CO (PA)
61 Cider Mill Run (19533-8615)
P.O. Box 706 (19533-0706)
PHONE...................................610 926-3502
Kim Noll, *President*
Jo Ellen Youse, *Manager*
Elizabeth Noll, *Admin Sec*
EMP: 30 **EST:** 1973
SQ FT: 5,100

SALES (est): 4.3MM **Privately Held**
SIC: 2448 Pallets, wood; skids, wood

(G-9671)
NOLL PALLET INC
Also Called: No Pallett
61 Cider Mill Run (19533-8615)
P.O. Box 706 (19533-0706)
PHONE...................................610 926-2500
Kim Noll, *President*
EMP: 30
SALES: 3MM **Privately Held**
SIC: 5031 2421 2448 Lumber: rough, dressed & finished; sawmills & planing mills, general; wood pallets & skids

(G-9672)
NORTHEIMER MANUFACTURING
Also Called: Northeimer Engineering & Mfg
2670 Leiscz's Bridge Rd (19533-9432)
PHONE...................................610 926-1136
Gary L Northeimer, *CEO*
William Butler, *President*
Sergio Ulloa, *Vice Pres*
Niny RAO, *CFO*
Gary Northeimer, *Treasurer*
EMP: 35
SQ FT: 20,000
SALES (est): 8.6MM **Privately Held**
WEB: www.northeimer.com
SIC: 3679 8711 3699 3694 Harness assemblies for electronic use: wire or cable; consulting engineer; electrical equipment & supplies; engine electrical equipment; miscellaneous fabricated wire products

(G-9673)
READING PRECAST INC
5494 Pottsville Pike (19533-8645)
PHONE...................................610 926-5000
R Timothy Achenbach, *Ch of Bd*
Michael A Achenbach, *President*
Karen L Achenbach, *Corp Secy*
EMP: 22
SQ FT: 20,000
SALES (est): 4.5MM **Privately Held**
WEB: www.readingprecast.com
SIC: 3272 Concrete products, precast

(G-9674)
SOLAR TECHNOLOGY SOLUTIONS
2670 Leiscz's Bridge Rd # 100 (19533-9432)
PHONE...................................610 916-0864
Andrew M Lacey, *Principal*
EMP: 3 **EST:** 2010
SALES (est): 152.3K **Privately Held**
SIC: 3433 Solar heaters & collectors

(G-9675)
ZEB MACHINE CO INC
331 Kindt Corner Rd (19533-8624)
PHONE...................................610 926-4766
David Zebertavage, *President*
Brian Zebertavage, *Treasurer*
Joan Anderton, *Admin Sec*
EMP: 5
SQ FT: 3,000
SALES (est): 436.6K **Privately Held**
WEB: www.zebpalmer.com
SIC: 3599 Machine shop, jobbing & repair

Leetsdale
Allegheny County

(G-9676)
ABTREX INDUSTRIES INC
112 Ross Way (15056-1302)
PHONE...................................724 266-5425
David Graham, *Branch Mgr*
EMP: 23
SALES (corp-wide): 18.4MM **Privately Held**
WEB: www.abtrex.com
SIC: 3443 3498 3317 3088 Tanks, standard or custom fabricated: metal plate; fabricated pipe & fittings; steel pipe & tubes; plastics plumbing fixtures; unsupported plastics film & sheet; organic fibers, noncellulosic

PA: Abtrex Industries, Inc.
28530 Reynolds St
Inkster MI 48141
734 728-0550

(G-9677)
AIR PRODUCTS AND CHEMICALS INC
360 Leetsdale Indus Dr (15056-1013)
PHONE...................................724 266-1563
Mike Colangelo, *Manager*
EMP: 23
SALES (corp-wide): 8.9B **Publicly Held**
SIC: 2869 2842 2821 2891 Amines, acids, salts, esters; acetates: amyl, butyl & ethyl; methyl alcohol, synthetic methanol; ammonia, household; thermoplastic materials; thermosetting materials; adhesives; gas producers, generators & other gas related equipment; gas separators (machinery); separators for steam, gas, vapor or air (machinery); oxygen, compressed or liquefied
PA: Air Products And Chemicals, Inc.
7201 Hamilton Blvd
Allentown PA 18195
610 481-4911

(G-9678)
ALLEGHENY PERFORMANCE PLAS LLC
3 Avenue A (15056-1304)
PHONE...................................412 741-4416
Gregory Shoup, *President*
EMP: 40
SQ FT: 3,500
SALES (est): 1.5MM **Privately Held**
SIC: 3089 Injection molding of plastics

(G-9679)
ALLEGHENY PLASTICS INC (PA)
Also Called: Allegheny Performance Plastics
Ave A Bldg 3 (15056)
PHONE...................................412 741-4416
Walter M Yost II, *President*
Gregory J Shoup, *President*
Shevey Westbrook, *Business Mgr*
Richard Berdik, *Vice Pres*
William Pugh, *Vice Pres*
▲ **EMP:** 150 **EST:** 1936
SQ FT: 56,000
SALES (est): 39.3MM **Privately Held**
SIC: 3559 3089 3443 Plastics working machinery; plastic processing; injection molding of plastics; fabricated plate work (boiler shop)

(G-9680)
ALLEGHENY PLASTICS INC
Performance Plastics Division
3 Avenue A (15056-1304)
PHONE...................................412 741-4416
Walter M Yost, *President*
EMP: 50
SALES (corp-wide): 39.3MM **Privately Held**
SIC: 3089 Bearings, plastic; molding primary plastic; laminating of plastic
PA: Allegheny Plastics, Inc.
Ave A Bldg 3
Leetsdale PA 15056
412 741-4416

(G-9681)
ALMATIS INC (DH)
501 W Park Rd (15056-1018)
PHONE...................................412 630-2800
Emre Timurkan, *CEO*
Bob Crouse, *General Mgr*
Peter Post, *Vice Pres*
Leslie Power, *Vice Pres*
George Lucey, *Plant Mgr*
◆ **EMP:** 100
SQ FT: 40,000
SALES: 179.5MM
SALES (corp-wide): 8B **Privately Held**
WEB: www.almatis.com
SIC: 2819 Industrial inorganic chemicals
HQ: Almatis B.V.
Theemsweg 30
Botlek Rotterdam 3197
181 270-100

(G-9682)
APPALACHIAN TANK CAR SVCS INC
Multiservice Supply Division
Ferry St & Ave C (15056)
PHONE....................................412 741-1500
Jim Crone, *Principal*
Timothy Crone, *Manager*
EMP: 55
SALES (corp-wide): 110MM **Privately Held**
SIC: 3492 3743 Fluid power valves & hose fittings; brakes, air & vacuum: railway
HQ: Appalachian Tank Car Services, Inc.
3915 Hydro St
Lynchburg VA 24503
434 384-6200

(G-9683)
AUGUST TRANSPORT INC
17 Ferry St (15056-1141)
P.O. Box 4, Freedom (15042-0004)
PHONE....................................724 462-1445
James R August Jr, *President*
EMP: 22
SALES (est): 2.1MM **Privately Held**
SIC: 4953 3531 Dumps, operation of; trucks, off-highway

(G-9684)
BIMBO BAKERIES USA INC
Also Called: Stroehmann Bakeries 34
140 Ferry St (15056-1154)
PHONE....................................724 251-0971
Gary Stom, *Sales/Mktg Mgr*
EMP: 32 **Privately Held**
SIC: 2051 Bakery: wholesale or whole-sale/retail combined
HQ: Bimbo Bakeries Usa, Inc
255 Business Center Dr # 200
Horsham PA 19044
215 347-5500

(G-9685)
BIMBO BAKERIES USA INC
140 Ferry St Bldg 24c (15056-1154)
PHONE....................................412 443-3499
Gary Stom, *Manager*
EMP: 18 **Privately Held**
SIC: 2051 Bakery: wholesale or whole-sale/retail combined
HQ: Bimbo Bakeries Usa, Inc
255 Business Center Dr # 200
Horsham PA 19044
215 347-5500

(G-9686)
C E N INC
Buncher Commerce Pk Ave A (15056)
PHONE....................................412 749-0442
Christopher Pappas, *President*
▲ EMP: 9
SALES (est): 1.8MM **Privately Held**
SIC: 2821 Plastics materials & resins
HQ: Nova Chemicals Inc.
1555 Coraopolis Hts Rd
Moon Township PA 15108
412 490-4000

(G-9687)
C M R USA LLC
940 Riverside Pl (15056-1036)
PHONE....................................724 452-2200
John Gatto, *Principal*
EMP: 17
SQ FT: 3,800
SALES (est): 3.9MM **Privately Held**
WEB: www.cmr-us.com
SIC: 3679 Electronic circuits
PA: C.M.R. U.S.A., Inc.
940 Riverside Pl
Leetsdale PA 15056

(G-9688)
CARROLL MANUFACTURING CO LLC
Also Called: B C I Engineering
80 Leetsdale Indstrl 30 (15056-1034)
PHONE....................................724 266-0400
Matthew P Carroll,
Beth A Carroll,
▲ EMP: 4

SALES (est): 706.8K **Privately Held**
SIC: 3441 3644 3365 8711 Fabricated structural metal; insulators & insulation materials, electrical; aluminum & aluminum-based alloy castings; machinery castings, aluminum; engineering services

(G-9689)
CMR USA INC (PA)
940 Riverside Pl (15056-1036)
PHONE....................................724 452-2200
John Gatto, *President*
▲ EMP: 17
SQ FT: 3,800
SALES: 5.3MM **Privately Held**
SIC: 3679 Electronic circuits

(G-9690)
COUGAR METALS INC (PA)
100 Washington St (15056-1000)
PHONE....................................724 251-9030
Roy D Allen, *President*
EMP: 2
SALES (est): 1MM **Privately Held**
SIC: 3679 Commutators, electronic

(G-9691)
GREAT LAKES POWER PRODUCTS INC
Also Called: John Deere Authorized Dealer
450 Riverport Dr (15056-1020)
PHONE....................................724 266-4000
Brian Frank, *Manager*
EMP: 6
SALES (corp-wide): 31.9MM **Privately Held**
WEB: www.glpowerlift.com
SIC: 3714 5082 Transmissions, motor vehicle; construction & mining machinery
PA: Great Lakes Power Products, Inc.
7455 Tyler Blvd
Mentor OH 44060
440 951-5111

(G-9692)
HAEMONETICS CORPORATION
Avenue C Bldg 18 (15056)
PHONE....................................412 741-7399
Tim Kerrigan, *Engineer*
Jim Foley, *Manager*
Mark Shafranich, *Director*
Brian Eldridge, *Technician*
EMP: 110
SALES (corp-wide): 903.9MM **Publicly Held**
WEB: www.haemonetics.com
SIC: 3841 5047 Medical instruments & equipment, blood & bone work; surgical equipment & supplies
PA: Haemonetics Corporation
400 Wood Rd
Braintree MA 02184
781 848-7100

(G-9693)
HCL LIQUIDATION LTD (PA)
Also Called: Hussey Fabricated Products
100 Washington St (15056-1000)
PHONE....................................724 251-4200
David Ziolkowski, *Business Mgr*
Rebecca J Kozar, *Senior Buyer*
Bill Bianco, *Buyer*
Josh Boocks, *Buyer*
Arnold Goode, *Buyer*
▲ EMP: 697
SQ FT: 300,000
SALES (est): 205.2MM **Privately Held**
WEB: www.husseycopper.com
SIC: 3351 Rails, copper & copper alloy

(G-9694)
HUSSEY MARINE ALLOYS LTD
100 Washington St (15056-1000)
PHONE....................................724 251-4200
Marine Alloys Corporation, *General Ptnr*
Roy Allen, *Ltd Ptnr*
EMP: 40
SALES (est): 5.4MM **Privately Held**
SIC: 3463 3369 Nonferrous forgings; nonferrous foundries

(G-9695)
IMPACT GUARD LLC
31 Leetsdale Indus Dr (15056-1011)
PHONE....................................724 318-8800
Sam Osten,

▲ EMP: 30
SALES (est): 13.2MM **Privately Held**
SIC: 2821 Thermoplastic materials

(G-9696)
INDUSTRIAL WELDING AND FABG (PA)
Also Called: Industrial Welding & Fabg
80 Leetsdale Indus Dr (15056-1033)
P.O. Box 35 (15056-0035)
PHONE....................................724 266-2887
Richard Gratton, *President*
EMP: 7
SALES (est): 1.2MM **Privately Held**
SIC: 5084 3441 Welding machinery & equipment; fabricated structural metal

(G-9697)
LIBERTAS COPPER LLC (PA)
Also Called: Hussey Copper
100 Washington St (15056-1000)
PHONE....................................724 251-4200
John Harrington, *CEO*
Brian Benjamin, *CFO*
Jim Carroll, *Credit Mgr*
Bruce Dennison, *Supervisor*
Mark Webb, *Supervisor*
▲ EMP: 575 EST: 1848
SQ FT: 16,600
SALES (est): 228.8MM **Privately Held**
SIC: 3366 3351 Copper foundries; copper rolling & drawing

(G-9698)
LUCKY VITAMIN LLC
Also Called: Luckyvitamin.com
Ave B And Ferry St Bldg 8 (15056)
PHONE....................................412 741-2598
Bill Monk, *Branch Mgr*
EMP: 218 **Privately Held**
SIC: 2834 Vitamin, nutrient & hematinic preparations for human use
PA: Lucky Vitamin, Llc
555 E North Ln Ste 6050
Conshohocken PA 19428

(G-9699)
MILLWOOD INC
200 Leetsdale Indus Blvd (15056-1016)
PHONE....................................724 266-7030
Shawn Scott, *Branch Mgr*
EMP: 17 **Privately Held**
SIC: 3565 5084 Packaging machinery; packaging machinery & equipment
PA: Millwood, Inc.
3708 International Blvd
Vienna OH 44473

(G-9700)
NATIONAL OILWELL VARCO LP
Also Called: Nov Fluid Control
201 Center Ave (15056-1313)
PHONE....................................570 862-2548
EMP: 30
SALES (corp-wide): 7.3B **Publicly Held**
SIC: 3533 Mfg Oil/Gas Field Machinery
HQ: National Oilwell Varco, L.P.
7909 Parkwood Circle Dr
Houston TX 77036
713 960-5100

(G-9701)
PITTSBURGH POST GAZETTE
144 Ferry St (15056-1154)
PHONE....................................724 266-2701
J Smith, *Principal*
EMP: 3
SALES (est): 169.9K **Privately Held**
SIC: 2711 Newspapers, publishing & printing

(G-9702)
RAPID GRANULATOR INC (DH)
555 W Park Rd (15056-1018)
PHONE....................................724 584-5220
Bengt Rimark, *President*
Daniel Boll, *Principal*
▲ EMP: 14
SQ FT: 2,000
SALES: 3MM
SALES (corp-wide): 5.8B **Privately Held**
WEB: www.rapidgranulator.com
SIC: 3559 Recycling machinery

HQ: Rapid Granulator Ab
Industrivagen 4
Bredaryd 333 7
370 865-00

(G-9703)
ROPPA INDUSTRIES LLC
698 Avenue C (15056-1329)
PHONE....................................412 749-9250
Brian Roppa, *Principal*
EMP: 7
SALES (est): 814.7K **Privately Held**
SIC: 3999 Manufacturing industries

(G-9704)
SCHROEDER INDUSTRIES LLC
580 W Park Rd (15056-1025)
PHONE....................................724 318-1100
Ernest Reeves, *President*
Gus Schroeder, *President*
Michael Lamers, *Exec VP*
Robert Adams, *Production*
Mindy Thoerig, *Production*
▲ EMP: 90
SALES (est): 30.6MM
SALES (corp-wide): 216.7MM **Privately Held**
WEB: www.schroeder-ind.com
SIC: 3569 Filters
HQ: Hydac Technology Corp.
2260 Cy Line Rd Ste 2280
Bethlehem PA 18017
205 520-1220

(G-9705)
SHAW INDUSTRIES GROUP INC
780 Brickworks Dr (15056)
PHONE....................................724 266-0315
Bob Shaw, *President*
Jerrod Fry, *Manager*
EMP: 28
SALES (corp-wide): 225.3B **Publicly Held**
SIC: 2273 Carpets & rugs
HQ: Shaw Industries Group, Inc.
616 E Walnut Ave
Dalton GA 30721
800 446-9332

(G-9706)
VSMPO-TIRUS US INC
401 Riverport Dr (15056-1019)
PHONE....................................724 251-9400
Chris Chmura, *Materials Mgr*
Andy McElwee, *Branch Mgr*
Tammie M McDonald, *Manager*
Liz Burkert, *Executive*
EMP: 6
SALES (corp-wide): 50.2K **Privately Held**
WEB: www.vsmpo-tirus.com
SIC: 3356 Nonferrous rolling & drawing
HQ: Vsmpo-Tirus, U.S., Inc.
1745 Shea Center Dr # 330
Highlands Ranch CO 80129
720 746-1023

Lehigh Valley
Northampton County

(G-9707)
STEEL STONE MANUFACTURING CO
6693 Ruch Rd (18002)
P.O. Box 20203 (18002-0203)
PHONE....................................610 837-9966
Clementina Pollack, *President*
Bernard Pollack, *Vice Pres*
EMP: 15
SQ FT: 12,000
SALES: 300K **Privately Held**
SIC: 3272 Siding, precast stone

Lehighton
Carbon County

(G-9708)
A W EVERETT FURNITURE FRAMES
95 Reber St (18235-9382)
PHONE....................................610 377-0170

GEOGRAPHIC

Steve Everett, *President*
EMP: 12 **EST:** 1958
SQ FT: 12,000
SALES: 650K **Privately Held**
SIC: 2426 Frames for upholstered furniture, wood

(G-9709)
ACTION MATERIALS INC
155157 Interchange Rd (18235)
PHONE..................................610 377-3037
James Walsh, *President*
EMP: 3
SALES (est): 300.4K **Privately Held**
WEB: www.actionmaterials.com
SIC: 3442 3312 3469 Rolling doors for industrial buildings or warehouses, metal; moldings & trim, except automobile: metal; forgings, iron & steel; stamping metal for the trade

(G-9710)
BLUE MOUNTAIN MACHINE INC
725 State Rd (18235-2851)
PHONE..................................610 377-4690
Philip L Myers Sr, *President*
Philip L Myers Jr, *Treasurer*
Elizabeth Yoder, *Office Mgr*
EMP: 75
SQ FT: 25,000
SALES (est): 15.6MM **Privately Held**
WEB: www.bluemtmachine.com
SIC: 3599 Machine shop, jobbing & repair

(G-9711)
DONALD B REMMEY INC (PA)
Also Called: Remmey The Pallet Company
523 Mill Rd (18235-9560)
PHONE..................................570 386-5379
Donald Remmey Jr, *President*
Arthur Mertz, *Prdtn Mgr*
Ben Remmey, *Manager*
EMP: 9 **EST:** 1956
SQ FT: 3,000
SALES (est): 16.6MM **Privately Held**
SIC: 2448 2671 Pallets, wood; packaging paper & plastics film, coated & laminated

(G-9712)
DONALD B REMMEY INC
Also Called: Remmey The Pallet Company
523 Mill Rd (18235-9560)
PHONE..................................570 386-5379
Donald Remmey, *President*
Bill Usignea, *Vice Pres*
EMP: 39
SALES (corp-wide): 16.6MM **Privately Held**
SIC: 2448 Pallets, wood; skids, wood
PA: Donald B. Remmey Inc.
　　523 Mill Rd
　　Lehighton PA 18235
　　570 386-5379

(G-9713)
ECOLUTION ENERGY LLC
565 Lake Dr (18235-5966)
PHONE..................................908 707-1400
Jason Billingsby, *Mng Member*
EMP: 4
SALES (est): 297.8K **Privately Held**
SIC: 5211 3621 Solar heating equipment; power generators

(G-9714)
FLOW MEASUREMENT TECHNOLOGIES
Also Called: F M T
1464 Lower Nis Hollow Dr (18235-8732)
PHONE..................................610 377-6050
Hal Hoover, *President*
Joseph Concilio, *Vice Pres*
EMP: 7
SQ FT: 2,000
SALES (est): 1MM **Privately Held**
WEB: www.flowmeasurement.com
SIC: 3823 Industrial instrmnts msrmnt display/control process variable

(G-9715)
HEALTH SOLUTIONS INC
1001 Mahoning St Unit 3a (18235-1123)
PHONE..................................610 379-0300
Charles Thomas, *CEO*
EMP: 3

SALES (est): 255K **Privately Held**
SIC: 3842 Respiratory protection equipment, personal

(G-9716)
ICA INC (PA)
Also Called: Hamfab Products
500 S 9th St (18235-2509)
P.O. Box 436, South Plainfield NJ (07080-0436)
PHONE..................................610 377-6100
Robert March, *President*
Jocelyn Holland, *Cust Mgr*
EMP: 17
SQ FT: 65,000
SALES: 7.2MM **Privately Held**
SIC: 3296 3086 Fiberglass insulation; plastics foam products

(G-9717)
J & R SLAW INC
Also Called: Slaw Precast
438 Riverview Rd (18235-3435)
P.O. Box D, Bowmanstown (18030-0516)
PHONE..................................610 852-2020
Robert A Slaw Jr, *President*
Nick Keeler, *Project Mgr*
Timothy Slaw, *Treasurer*
Chris Slaw, *Admin Sec*
EMP: 90
SQ FT: 35,000
SALES (est): 20.5MM **Privately Held**
WEB: www.slawprecast.com
SIC: 3272 Concrete products, precast

(G-9718)
LEHIGHTON ELECTRONICS INC (PA)
208 Memorial Dr (18235-2300)
P.O. Box 328 (18235-0328)
PHONE..................................610 377-5990
Austin Blew, *President*
Joanne Blew, *Corp Secy*
Michael Barrasso, *Opers Staff*
Danh Nguyen, *Products*
EMP: 12 **EST:** 1963
SQ FT: 10,000
SALES (est): 1.8MM **Privately Held**
WEB: www.lehighton.com
SIC: 3825 Integrated circuit testers

(G-9719)
MAJESTIC FIRE APPAREL INC
255 Wagner St (18235-9281)
P.O. Box 248 (18235-0248)
PHONE..................................610 377-6273
Michael A Leggett, *President*
Janeane Matula, *Sales Staff*
▲ **EMP:** 20
SQ FT: 7,000
SALES (est): 3.9MM **Privately Held**
WEB: www.majesticfireapparel.com
SIC: 2326 Work apparel, except uniforms

(G-9720)
MORNING CALL LLC
179 Interchange Rd (18235-2824)
PHONE..................................610 379-3200
Ralanbo Pujol, *Manager*
EMP: 18
SALES (corp-wide): 1B **Publicly Held**
WEB: www.mcall.com
SIC: 2711 Newspapers, publishing & printing
HQ: The Morning Call Llc
　　101 N 6th St
　　Allentown PA 18101
　　610 820-6500

(G-9721)
PENCOR SERVICES INC
Times News, The
594 Blakeslee Blvd Dr W (18235-9818)
P.O. Box 239 (18235-0239)
PHONE..................................570 386-2660
Scott Masenheimer, *General Mgr*
EMP: 125
SALES (corp-wide): 108.7MM **Privately Held**
WEB: www.pennspeak.com
SIC: 2711 2752 Newspapers: publishing only, not printed on site; commercial printing, lithographic

PA: Pencor Services, Inc.
　　613 3rd Street Palmerton
　　Palmerton PA 18071
　　610 826-2115

(G-9722)
PRINTING 4U
1895 Indian Hill Rd (18235-9261)
PHONE..................................610 377-0111
David R Koch, *Owner*
EMP: 4
SALES (est): 305.5K **Privately Held**
SIC: 2752 Commercial printing, offset

(G-9723)
RADICAL WINE COMPANY
511 Mahoning Dr E Ste 1 (18235-8889)
PHONE..................................610 365-7969
Brandon Borger, *CEO*
EMP: 3
SALES (est): 134.3K **Privately Held**
SIC: 2084 Wines

(G-9724)
RC & DESIGN COMPANY
180 James Ln (18235-5703)
PHONE..................................484 626-1216
Thomas Zimmerman, *Director*
EMP: 4 **EST:** 2011
SALES (est): 77.5K **Privately Held**
SIC: 7948 8711 3645 3648 Motorcycle racing; mechanical engineering; residential lighting fixtures; decorative area lighting fixtures; commercial indusl & institutional electric lighting fixtures; computer-aided design (CAD) systems service

(G-9725)
RITTER PRECISION MACHINING
839 Blakeslee Blvd Dr E (18235-8712)
PHONE..................................610 377-2011
Scott Ritter, *President*
Cindy Ritter, *Vice Pres*
EMP: 3
SALES: 200K **Privately Held**
SIC: 7539 7538 3519 Machine shop, automotive; engine rebuilding: automotive; gas engine rebuilding

(G-9726)
SEMILAB USA LLC
208 Memorial Dr (18235-2300)
PHONE..................................610 377-5990
Mark Benjamin, *Co-Mgr*
EMP: 12
SALES (corp-wide): 10.8MM **Privately Held**
SIC: 3699 3825 3674 Electrical equipment & supplies; instruments to measure electricity; semiconductors & related devices
PA: Semilab Usa Llc
　　10770 N 46th St Ste E700
　　Tampa FL 33617
　　813 977-2244

(G-9727)
SERVICE CONSTRUCTION CO INC
701 Bridge St Ste 102 (18235-1800)
PHONE..................................610 377-2111
W Frey, *President*
Woody Frey, *President*
EMP: 11
SALES (est): 1.5MM **Privately Held**
SIC: 1521 1542 2452 New construction, single-family houses; nonresidential construction; log cabins, prefabricated, wood

(G-9728)
STANDARD METAL INDUSTRIES LLC
500 S 9th St (18235-2509)
PHONE..................................610 377-5400
Robert March, *Mng Member*
▲ **EMP:** 8
SALES (est): 1.4MM **Privately Held**
SIC: 3449 Miscellaneous metalwork

(G-9729)
TECHNA-PLASTIC SERVICES INC (PA)
164 Seneca Rd (18235-9724)
P.O. Box 298 (18235-0298)
PHONE..................................570 386-2732
Keith Foreman, *Owner*
Robert Ziola, *General Mgr*
EMP: 20
SQ FT: 55,000
SALES (est): 2MM **Privately Held**
SIC: 3089 Injection molding of plastics; thermoformed finished plastic products

(G-9730)
TECHNICAL PROCESS & ENGRG INC
892 Blakeslee Blvd Dr W (18235-9793)
PHONE..................................570 386-4777
Harold Schafer, *CEO*
Kelly Ziegenfus, *President*
Jim Hower, *Project Engr*
Roy Bradbury, *Technical Staff*
EMP: 22
SQ FT: 20,000
SALES (est): 2.1MM **Privately Held**
WEB: www.tpei.com
SIC: 8711 7699 3559 Consulting engineer; industrial machinery & equipment repair; plastics working machinery

---

Lemasters
Franklin County

(G-9731)
BILL STRALEY PRINTING
4879 Steele Ave (17231)
P.O. Box 58 (17231-0058)
PHONE..................................717 328-5404
Bill Straley, *Owner*
EMP: 3
SALES: 50K **Privately Held**
SIC: 2741 2752 Miscellaneous publishing; commercial printing, lithographic

---

Lemont Furnace
Fayette County

(G-9732)
ADVANCED ACOUSTIC CONCEPTS LLC
Also Called: AAC
1080 Eberly Way (15456-1010)
PHONE..................................724 434-5100
Brian Boyle, *President*
Michael Carnovale, *Vice Pres*
Lindsey Kovach, *Director*
EMP: 60
SALES (est): 8.6MM **Privately Held**
SIC: 3812 7371 Acceleration indicators & systems components, aerospace; computer software development

(G-9733)
BUDDYS BREWS
60 Nickman Plz (15456-9732)
PHONE..................................724 970-2739
James Nickman, *Owner*
EMP: 4 **EST:** 2007
SALES (est): 271.6K **Privately Held**
SIC: 2082 Malt beverages

(G-9734)
CENTER INDEPENDENT OIL COMPANY
1346 Connerville St (15456)
PHONE..................................724 437-6607
Lisa Smith, *Manager*
EMP: 6
SALES (corp-wide): 16.4MM **Privately Held**
SIC: 1311 Crude petroleum & natural gas production
PA: Center Independent Oil Company
　　407 Rowes Run Rd
　　Smock PA

(G-9735)
CUDD PRESSURE CONTROL INC
Also Called: Cudd Energy Services
90 Brittany Ln (15456-1310)
PHONE.................................570 250-9043
EMP: 49
SALES (corp-wide): 1.7B **Publicly Held**
SIC: 1389 Oil field services
HQ: Cudd Pressure Control, Inc.
2828 Tech Forest Blvd
The Woodlands TX 77381
832 295-5555

(G-9736)
PROVANCE TRUSS LLC
119 Republic St (15456)
PHONE.................................724 437-0585
Regis B Provance, *Principal*
EMP: 3
SQ FT: 6,000
SALES (est): 440K **Privately Held**
SIC: 2439 Trusses, wooden roof

(G-9737)
SLAVIC GROUP INC
1189 Connellsville Rd (15456-1071)
PHONE.................................724 437-6756
Ronald Slavic Jr, *President*
EMP: 6
SQ FT: 8,000
SALES: 1MM **Privately Held**
SIC: 2759 3993 Screen printing; neon signs

(G-9738)
STK LLC (PA)
2282 University Dr Ste 1 (15456-1024)
PHONE.................................724 430-2477
Kent Buckingham,
▼ EMP: 13
SQ FT: 7,500
SALES (est): 1.3MM **Privately Held**
SIC: 3714 Pickup truck bed liners

(G-9739)
UNIVERSAL WELL SERVICES INC
2198 University Dr (15456-1026)
PHONE.................................724 430-6201
Kurt Williams, *Branch Mgr*
EMP: 110
SALES (corp-wide): 3.3B **Publicly Held**
WEB: www.univwell.com
SIC: 1389 Oil field services
HQ: Universal Well Services, Inc.
13549 S Mosiertown Rd
Meadville PA 16335
814 337-1983

Lemoyne
Cumberland County

(G-9740)
ADS LLC
Also Called: ADS Environmental Services
319 S 3rd St Lowr 3 (17043-1976)
PHONE.................................717 554-7552
Joseph Scarcia, *Principal*
EMP: 3
SALES (corp-wide): 2.4B **Publicly Held**
SIC: 3823 7699 8748 Water quality monitoring & control systems; professional instrument repair services; mechanical instrument repair; industrial equipment services; scientific equipment repair service; systems analysis or design
HQ: Ads Llc
340 The Bridge St Ste 204
Huntsville AL 35806
256 430-3366

(G-9741)
ADVANCED FABRICATION SVCS INC
Also Called: Afs Energy Systems
420 Oak St (17043-1674)
P.O. Box 170 (17043-0170)
PHONE.................................717 763-0286
Mark T Leach, *President*
Jay Clark, *Vice Pres*
John A Frailey, *Vice Pres*

Mike Wildasin, *Manager*
▲ EMP: 20
SALES (est): 6.6MM **Privately Held**
WEB: www.afsenergy.com
SIC: 3441 Fabricated structural metal

(G-9742)
AMAX SOLUTIONS INC
717 Market St Ste 221 (17043-1581)
PHONE.................................717 798-8070
Iffat Ershad, *Director*
EMP: 3
SALES (est): 226.8K **Privately Held**
SIC: 3841 Diagnostic apparatus, medical

(G-9743)
DEAD LIGHTNING DISTILLERY LLC
233 Plum St (17043-1961)
PHONE.................................717 798-2021
Eric Montgomery, *Principal*
EMP: 3
SALES (est): 158.8K **Privately Held**
SIC: 2085 Distilled & blended liquors

(G-9744)
FORMEX BUSINESS PRINTING
328 Market St (17043-1627)
PHONE.................................717 737-3430
Paul Yeager, *Principal*
EMP: 3
SALES (est): 233.6K **Privately Held**
SIC: 2752 Commercial printing, lithographic

(G-9745)
HAAS PRINTING CO INC
1000 Hummel Ave (17043-1740)
PHONE.................................717 761-0277
Royce Haas, *President*
Lois G Haas, *Vice Pres*
EMP: 21
SQ FT: 13,620
SALES (est): 3.8MM **Privately Held**
WEB: www.haas-printing.com
SIC: 2752 Commercial printing, offset

(G-9746)
KEYSTONE DISPLAYS CORPORATION
230 S 2nd St (17043-1315)
PHONE.................................717 612-0340
Sean Farrell, *President*
EMP: 6
SQ FT: 5,000
SALES (est): 1.2MM **Privately Held**
WEB: www.keystonedisplays.com
SIC: 2653 7336 Display items, solid fiber: made from purchased materials; graphic arts & related design

(G-9747)
ORACLE AMERICA INC
Also Called: Sun Microsystems
645 N 12th St Ste 101 (17043-1219)
PHONE.................................717 730-5501
Scott Nealy, *Branch Mgr*
EMP: 5
SALES (corp-wide): 39.8B **Publicly Held**
SIC: 7372 Prepackaged software
HQ: Oracle America, Inc.
500 Oracle Pkwy
Redwood City CA 94065
650 506-7000

(G-9748)
PPG INDUSTRIES INC
1039 Columbus Ave (17043-1715)
PHONE.................................717 763-1030
EMP: 7
SALES (corp-wide): 15.3B **Publicly Held**
SIC: 2851 Paints & allied products
PA: Ppg Industries, Inc.
1 Ppg Pl
Pittsburgh PA 15272
412 434-3131

(G-9749)
PURPOSE 1 LLC
309 S 10th St (17043-1706)
PHONE.................................717 232-9077
Daniel Liberatore,
Dorothy McDermott,
EMP: 4

SALES: 800K **Privately Held**
SIC: 7319 3993 7336 7389 Display advertising service; distribution of advertising material or sample services; signs & advertising specialties; graphic arts & related design; trade show arrangement

(G-9750)
REARDEN STEEL FABRICATION INC
100 Market St (17043-1390)
P.O. Box 198 (17043-0198)
PHONE.................................717 503-1989
Steven J Capuano, *President*
EMP: 15
SALES: 5MM **Privately Held**
SIC: 5051 7699 3999 Steel; cash register repair; atomizers, toiletry

(G-9751)
ROADSAFE TRAFFIC SYSTEMS INC
1011 Mumma Rd Ste 101 (17043-1143)
PHONE.................................904 350-0080
Terry Lester, *Manager*
EMP: 10 **Privately Held**
SIC: 3531 7359 Construction machinery; equipment rental & leasing
PA: Roadsafe Traffic Systems, Inc.
8750 W Bryn Mawr Ave
Chicago IL 60631

(G-9752)
ROCHESTER COCA COLA BOTTLING
Also Called: Coca-Cola
230 S 10th St Ste A (17043-1784)
PHONE.................................717 730-2100
Frank Anderson, *Manager*
EMP: 55
SALES (corp-wide): 35.4B **Publicly Held**
SIC: 2086 Bottled & canned soft drinks
HQ: Rochester Coca Cola Bottling Corp
300 Oak St
Pittston PA 18640
570 655-2874

(G-9753)
SIGNS BY TOMORROW INC
333 S Front St (17043-1306)
PHONE.................................717 975-2456
Gary Zimmerman, *President*
Richard Wojnar, *Corp Secy*
EMP: 4
SALES (est): 392.1K **Privately Held**
SIC: 3993 Signs & advertising specialties

(G-9754)
STUART KRANZEL
415 Bosler Ave (17043-1966)
PHONE.................................717 737-7223
Stuart Kranzel, *Principal*
EMP: 4
SALES (est): 270K **Privately Held**
SIC: 3644 Raceways

(G-9755)
WHITE BOX SYSTEMS LLC
418 Plum St (17043-1964)
PHONE.................................717 612-9911
William Hersh, *Mng Member*
Alycia Knoll,
EMP: 4
SALES: 150K **Privately Held**
WEB: www.whiteboxsystems.com
SIC: 3571 Electronic computers

Lenhartsville
Berks County

(G-9756)
BOYESEN INC (PA)
8 Rhoades Rd (19534-9595)
PHONE.................................610 756-6818
Allen M Leech, *President*
Bengt Boyesen, *Vice Pres*
EMP: 27 EST: 1971
SQ FT: 22,000

SALES (est): 4.6MM **Privately Held**
WEB: www.boyesen.com
SIC: 3714 5531 5013 3751 Motor vehicle engines & parts; automotive parts; motor vehicle supplies & new parts; motorcycles, bicycles & parts; internal combustion engines

(G-9757)
CLAYPOOLE HEX SIGNS
227 Schock Rd (19534-9331)
PHONE.................................610 562-8911
Eric Claypoole, *Principal*
EMP: 3
SALES (est): 150.2K **Privately Held**
SIC: 3577 Computer peripheral equipment

(G-9758)
DODIE SABLE
Also Called: New Promise Farms
593 Old 22 (19534-9232)
PHONE.................................610 756-3836
Marc Sable, *President*
Dodie Sable, *General Mgr*
EMP: 5
SALES: 120K **Privately Held**
WEB: www.newpromisefarms.com
SIC: 3944 Craft & hobby kits & sets

(G-9759)
MECK MANUFACTURING
30 Donat Rd (19534-9695)
PHONE.................................610 756-6284
Steven Meck, *Owner*
EMP: 3
SALES (est): 236.1K **Privately Held**
SIC: 3599 Machine & other job shop work

(G-9760)
PERMA-COLUMN EAST
65 Penn St (19534-9302)
P.O. Box 87 (19534-0087)
PHONE.................................610 562-7161
Allen Homan, *General Mgr*
Beverly E Kistler, *Principal*
EMP: 6
SALES (est): 855K **Privately Held**
SIC: 3272 Concrete products

Lenni
Delaware County

(G-9761)
DERMAMED USA INC
394 Parkmount Rd (19052)
P.O. Box 198 (19052-0198)
PHONE.................................610 358-4447
Mark Kinsley, *President*
Kevin Hilden, *Purchasing*
EMP: 15
SQ FT: 15,000
SALES (est): 2.4MM **Privately Held**
WEB: www.dermamedusa.com
SIC: 3841 Surgical instruments & apparatus

(G-9762)
SCHUBERT PLASTICS INC
245 Lundgreen Rd (19052)
P.O. Box 126 (19052-0126)
PHONE.................................610 358-4920
Charles Schubert, *President*
EMP: 15
SQ FT: 21,000
SALES (est): 1.4MM **Privately Held**
SIC: 3089 Injection molding of plastics

(G-9763)
WESTLAKE PLASTICS COMPANY (PA)
490 Lenni Rd (19052-1002)
P.O. Box 127 (19052-0127)
PHONE.................................610 459-1000
Amy Gaylord, *President*
Joe Derrickson, *Business Mgr*
Foucauld Thery, *COO*
Neil Brown, *Vice Pres*
Edward F Westlake Jr, *Vice Pres*
▲ EMP: 160 EST: 1951
SQ FT: 50,000

SALES (est): 45.5MM Privately Held
WEB: www.westlakeplastics.com
SIC: 3082 3081 Tubes, unsupported plastic; unsupported plastics film & sheet

Leola
Lancaster County

(G-9764)
A R GROFF TRANSPORT INC
Also Called: Artwear
20 Trinity Dr (17540-1955)
PHONE...................................717 859-4661
Anthony Groff, President
EMP: 4
SALES (est): 155.6K Privately Held
SIC: 2395 Embroidery & art needlework

(G-9765)
ACHENBACHS PASTRY INC
375 E Main St (17540-1928)
PHONE...................................717 656-6671
John Burkeholder, President
Earl H Hess, President
Sharon Martin, Exec VP
Anita Hess, Admin Sec
EMP: 35 EST: 1954
SALES: 1.3MM Privately Held
SIC: 5461 5149 2051 Pastries; pies; cakes; bread; crackers, cookies & bakery products; bread, cake & related products

(G-9766)
ADVANCED BUILDING PRODUCTS (PA)
Also Called: Renaissance Conservatories
132 Ashmore Dr (17540-2007)
PHONE...................................717 661-7520
Mark Barrocco, President
Angie Renzi, General Mgr
Bob Sawyer, Vice Pres
Jason Sawyer, Vice Pres
▲ EMP: 1
SQ FT: 900
SALES (est): 2.9MM Privately Held
SIC: 3448 1542 Sunrooms, prefabricated metal; prefabricated metal buildings; commercial & office buildings, renovation & repair

(G-9767)
AGGREGATES EQUIPMENT INC
Also Called: A E I
9 Horseshoe Rd (17540-1812)
P.O. Box 39 (17540-0039)
PHONE...................................717 656-2131
Len Stairs, President
David Stairs, Vice Pres
Steven Buchanan, Engineer
Mary Jane Stairs, Admin Sec
▲ EMP: 40
SQ FT: 60,000
SALES (est): 18MM Privately Held
WEB: www.aggregatesequipment.com
SIC: 5084 3535 Crushing machinery & equipment; bulk handling conveyor systems

(G-9768)
ALLAN MYERS MANAGEMENT INC (PA)
330 Quarry Rd (17540-9733)
PHONE...................................717 656-2411
Ruth E Stoltzfus, Ch of Bd
Donald Brubaker, President
Eric Nordstrom, Admin Sec
EMP: 54 EST: 1914
SQ FT: 1,900
SALES (est): 14.6MM Privately Held
WEB: www.dmstoltzfus.com
SIC: 1422 Limestones, ground

(G-9769)
ASM INDUSTRIES INC
Polymar Div
1 Lark Ave (17540-9566)
PHONE...................................717 656-2166
John Wolf, General Mgr
Evelyn Neff, Regional Mgr
Ed Ladoski, Manager
EMP: 50

SALES (corp-wide): 62.5MM Privately Held
SIC: 3561 2821 Industrial pumps & parts; molding compounds, plastics
HQ: Asm Industries, Inc
41 Industrial Cir
Lancaster PA 17601
717 656-2161

(G-9770)
ATLAS MOLDING LLC
36 Glenbrook Rd (17540-1301)
PHONE...................................717 556-8193
Amos Glick, Principal
Brian Horst, COO
Bryan Horst, COO
▲ EMP: 11
SALES (est): 1.8MM Privately Held
SIC: 3089 Molding primary plastic

(G-9771)
BAREVILLE WOODCRAFT CO
70 Farmland Rd (17540-1999)
PHONE...................................717 656-6261
J Louis Oberholtzer, Partner
Edward Oberholtzer, Partner
▲ EMP: 13 EST: 1968
SQ FT: 13,100
SALES (est): 1.7MM Privately Held
WEB: www.barevillewoodcraft.com
SIC: 2511 2426 Wood household furniture; furniture stock & parts, hardwood

(G-9772)
BEILERS MANUFACTURING & SUPPLY
290 S Groffdale Rd (17540-9523)
PHONE...................................717 656-2179
Chris Beiler, Branch Mgr
EMP: 12
SALES (est): 1MM
SALES (corp-wide): 1.5MM Privately Held
SIC: 2399 5191 Horse harnesses & riding crops, etc.: non-leather; harness equipment
PA: Beiler's Manufacturing & Supply
3025 Harvest Dr
Ronks PA 17572
717 768-0174

(G-9773)
BELMONT MACHINE CO
40 Hess Rd (17540-9512)
PHONE...................................717 556-0040
Jacob P King, President
Evelyn H King, Vice Pres
EMP: 3
SALES (est): 624.1K Privately Held
SIC: 3715 Truck trailers

(G-9774)
C EVERWINE MACHINE LLC
Also Called: Everwine Machine Services
2 Site Rd (17540-1849)
PHONE...................................717 656-5451
Charles M Everwine Sr,
Charles Everwine Jr,
EMP: 6
SQ FT: 8,000
SALES (est): 560K Privately Held
SIC: 3599 Machine shop, jobbing & repair

(G-9775)
CREEKSIDE STRUCTURES LLC
745 E Millport Rd (17540-9759)
PHONE...................................717 627-5267
John L King, Mng Member
EMP: 3
SALES (est): 291.6K Privately Held
SIC: 2511 Storage chests, household: wood

(G-9776)
CUSTOM CABINETRY UNLIMITED LLC
20 S Groffdale Rd (17540-9555)
PHONE...................................717 656-9170
Mervin L Beiler, Principal
EMP: 4
SALES (est): 306.9K Privately Held
SIC: 2434 Wood kitchen cabinets

(G-9777)
DART CONTAINER CORP PA (PA)
60 E Main St (17540-1940)
P.O. Box 546 (17540-0546)
PHONE...................................717 656-2236
Robert Dart, President
Beston S Chitala, Vice Pres
Gary Collins, Vice Pres
Clarence Wenger, Plant Mgr
Jim Woodring, Engineer
◆ EMP: 3
SQ FT: 50,000
SALES (est): 265.3MM Privately Held
SIC: 3086 Cups & plates, foamed plastic

(G-9778)
DUTCHIE MANUFACTURING LLC
Also Called: DMC
21 School Rd (17540-9545)
PHONE...................................717 656-2186
Lina Mae, Mng Member
C Hester Hoover,
EMP: 4
SQ FT: 1,800
SALES (est): 484.6K Privately Held
SIC: 3799 3599 Trailers & trailer equipment; machine shop, jobbing & repair

(G-9779)
EARL WEST INDUSTRIES
164 Butter Rd (17540-9562)
PHONE...................................717 656-6600
Martin Herr, Owner
EMP: 6
SQ FT: 3,000
SALES (est): 448.5K Privately Held
SIC: 2514 Kitchen cabinets: metal

(G-9780)
ELVIN B ZIMMERMAN
Also Called: E Z Storage Barns
275 W Farmersville Rd (17540-9752)
PHONE...................................717 656-9327
Elvin B Zimmerman, Owner
EMP: 3
SALES: 500K Privately Held
WEB: www.ezstoragebarns.com
SIC: 1542 2452 Commercial & office building, new construction; prefabricated wood buildings

(G-9781)
EVANS EAGLE BURIAL VAULTS INC (PA)
15 Graybill Rd (17540-1998)
PHONE...................................717 656-2213
William Evans, President
Deborah Wyble, Treasurer
Allison Evans, Admin Sec
EMP: 16 EST: 1916
SQ FT: 18,800
SALES: 1.6MM Privately Held
WEB: www.evanseagle.com
SIC: 3272 Burial vaults, concrete or precast terrazzo

(G-9782)
FOREST HILL MANUFACTURING LLC
240 Forest Hill Rd (17540-9728)
PHONE...................................717 556-0363
Isaiah Miller,
Joseph Glick,
EMP: 6 EST: 1995
SQ FT: 10,000
SALES (est): 1.2MM Privately Held
SIC: 3315 Fence gates posts & fittings: steel

(G-9783)
FUTURE GENERATION AG LLC
20 Keystone Ct Ste 20 # 20 (17540-2207)
PHONE...................................844 993-3311
Wayne Ebersole,
Samuel Lapp,
Konrad Martin,
Joshua Riker,
EMP: 4
SQ FT: 900
SALES (est): 183.1K Privately Held
SIC: 3999 Seeds, coated or treated, from purchased seeds

(G-9784)
GIBSON JOURNAL
41 N Hershey Ave (17540-1617)
PHONE...................................717 656-2582
Randolph S Gibson, Principal
EMP: 3
SALES (est): 135.6K Privately Held
SIC: 2711 Newspapers, publishing & printing

(G-9785)
GROFFDALE MACHINE CO INC
194 S Groffdale Rd (17540-9556)
PHONE...................................717 656-3249
Leon F Stoltzfus, President
▲ EMP: 8
SQ FT: 12,000
SALES (est): 1MM Privately Held
SIC: 3599 3523 5191 3441 Machine shop, jobbing & repair; farm machinery & equipment; farm supplies; fabricated structural metal

(G-9786)
HAYLOFT CANDLES
99 S Groffdale Rd (17540-9533)
PHONE...................................717 656-9463
David Yoder, Owner
Benjamin K Smoker, Owner
EMP: 7 EST: 1971
SQ FT: 1,540
SALES (est): 310K Privately Held
SIC: 5947 3999 2024 Gift shop; candles; ice cream, bulk

(G-9787)
IRONSTONE MILLS INC
334 Quarry Rd (17540-9733)
PHONE...................................717 656-4539
Frank L Diem, President
Franklin Diem, Corp Secy
EMP: 5
SQ FT: 10,000
SALES (est): 480K Privately Held
SIC: 2499 Logs of sawdust & wood particles, pressed

(G-9788)
J & R METAL PRODUCTS LLC
Also Called: Jr Metal
52 Hess Rd (17540-9512)
PHONE...................................717 656-6241
John Peterson, CEO
Ervin Miller, Vice Pres
EMP: 4
SQ FT: 6,000
SALES (est): 772.2K Privately Held
SIC: 3469 Stamping metal for the trade

(G-9789)
K & L MACHINING INC
Also Called: K&L Machining
50 Trinity Dr (17540-1955)
PHONE...................................717 656-0948
Michael Linetty, President
Francis Linetty, Vice Pres
Ted Stitzel, Purchasing
Michael Kastanidis, Treasurer
Mike Linetty, Sales Executive
EMP: 28
SQ FT: 24,000
SALES (est): 4.4MM Privately Held
WEB: www.klmachining.com
SIC: 3599 Machine shop, jobbing & repair

(G-9790)
KEYSTONE QUALITY PRODUCTS LLC
83 S Groffdale Rd (17540-9533)
P.O. Box 185, New Holland (17557-0185)
PHONE...................................717 354-2762
Ben Kauffman,
EMP: 32
SALES: 2.4MM Privately Held
SIC: 2512 5021 5199 Upholstered household furniture; furniture; gifts & novelties

(G-9791)
KREIDERS CANVAS SERVICE INC
73 W Main St (17540-1803)
PHONE...................................717 656-7387
Leslie Kreider, President
Lester Kreider, President
EMP: 7 EST: 1975

SQ FT: 3,500
SALES: 1MM Privately Held
SIC: 2394 Awnings, fabric: made from purchased materials

(G-9792)
LANTZ STRUCTURES LLC
162 Newport Rd (17540-1824)
PHONE....................................717 656-9418
Melvin Fisher, Mng Member
EMP: 9
SALES (est): 1.2MM Privately Held
SIC: 2452 Prefabricated buildings, wood

(G-9793)
LIBERTY HOMES INC
21 S Groffdale Rd (17540-9533)
PHONE....................................717 656-2381
Warren Keyes, General Mgr
Kathy Fausnacht, Controller
EMP: 120
SALES (corp-wide): 19.3MM Privately Held
WEB: www.libertyhomesinc.com
SIC: 2451 Mobile homes, except recreational
PA: Liberty Homes Inc
    1101 Eisenhower Dr N
    Goshen IN 46526
    574 533-0438

(G-9794)
MILLCREEK STRUCTURES
429 Hess Rd (17540-9518)
PHONE....................................717 656-2797
Emanuel J Lantz, Partner
Emanuel S Esh, Partner
Ruben S Esh, Partner
Lloyd M King, Partner
Amos B Lantz, Partner
EMP: 15
SQ FT: 7,200
SALES (est): 2.2MM Privately Held
SIC: 2452 Prefabricated buildings, wood

(G-9795)
NEW HEIGHTS LLC
49 Eagle Dr (17540-1987)
PHONE....................................717 768-0070
Jeremiah Weaver, Prdtn Mgr
David Beiler, Marketing Staff
Aaron Beiler, Mng Member
EMP: 7
SALES (est): 1.6MM Privately Held
SIC: 2493 5211 Insulation & roofing material, reconstituted wood; roofing material

(G-9796)
NYP CORP (FRMR NY-PTERS CORP)
Pennsylvania Division
10 Site Rd (17540-1849)
PHONE....................................717 656-0299
Jerry Tombach, Manager
EMP: 4
SALES (corp-wide): 16.8MM Privately Held
WEB: www.nyp-corp.com
SIC: 2393 Textile bags
PA: Nyp Corp. (Formerly New Yorker-Peters Corporation)
    805 E Grand St
    Elizabeth NJ 07201
    908 351-6550

(G-9797)
PIONEER WOODCRAFTS LLC
35 Graybill Rd (17540-1910)
PHONE....................................717 656-0776
Samuel Stoltzfus, Mng Member
EMP: 10
SALES (est): 1.4MM Privately Held
SIC: 2431 Millwork

(G-9798)
QUALITY CUSTOM CABINETRY INC
Also Called: Bareville Furniture
295 E Main St (17540-1923)
P.O. Box 321 (17540-0321)
PHONE....................................717 661-6565
Doug Sensenig, Branch Mgr
EMP: 11

SALES (est): 769.2K
SALES (corp-wide): 37.9MM Privately Held
WEB: www.qualitycabinetry.com
SIC: 2434 Wood kitchen cabinets
PA: Quality Custom Cabinetry, Inc.
    125 Peters Rd
    New Holland PA 17557
    717 656-2721

(G-9799)
QUALITY WIRE FORMING
120 Brick Church Rd (17540-9705)
PHONE....................................717 656-4478
Leon Stolzfus, Owner
▲ EMP: 5
SALES (est): 1MM Privately Held
SIC: 3315 5051 Wire & fabricated wire products; metal wires, ties, cables & screening

(G-9800)
RISSLER CUSTOM KITCHENS
90 Brethren Church Rd (17540-9715)
PHONE....................................717 656-6101
John M Rissler, Owner
Alice Rissler, Co-Owner
EMP: 5 EST: 1958
SALES (est): 384.2K Privately Held
SIC: 2434 5722 Wood kitchen cabinets; kitchens, complete (sinks, cabinets, etc.)

(G-9801)
ROSS SECURITY SYSTEMS LLC
104 N Maple Ave (17540-9799)
P.O. Box 646 (17540-0646)
PHONE....................................717 656-2200
Daniel Hobson,
Andrew Jones,
Donald Speicher,
▼ EMP: 50
SALES (est): 2.9MM Privately Held
SIC: 3699 Security devices

(G-9802)
ROTATION DYNAMICS CORPORATION
Also Called: Rotadyne Company
21 Zimmerman Rd (17540-1949)
PHONE....................................717 656-4252
Len Kruizenga, Mfg Dir
Ron Ellison, Manager
Theresa Hilken, Manager
Darrell Baker, Consultant
EMP: 20
SALES (corp-wide): 164.4MM Privately Held
SIC: 3547 Primary rolling mill equipment
PA: Rotation Dynamics Corporation
    1101 Windham Pkwy
    Romeoville IL 60446
    630 769-9255

(G-9803)
SKYLINE CHAMPION CORPORATION
Also Called: Skyline Homes
99 Horseshoe Rd (17540-1763)
P.O. Box 220 (17540-0220)
PHONE....................................717 656-2071
Mike Scheid, Branch Mgr
Jim Holbritter, Manager
EMP: 22
SALES (corp-wide): 1.5B Publicly Held
SIC: 2451 Mobile homes
PA: Skyline Champion Corporation
    2520 Bypass Rd
    Elkhart IN 46514
    574 294-6521

(G-9804)
SMG FAB INC
129 Ashmore Dr (17540-2007)
PHONE....................................717 556-8263
Gary Snyder, President
Jeff Jones, Exec VP
Douglas Weaver, VP Opers
EMP: 15
SALES (est): 3MM Privately Held
SIC: 3441 Fabricated structural metal

(G-9805)
STEFFYS PATTERN SHOP
297 E Main St (17540-1923)
PHONE....................................717 656-6032
Randall Steffy, Owner

EMP: 3 EST: 1926
SQ FT: 3,000
SALES: 303K Privately Held
WEB: www.northernthunder.com
SIC: 3543 Industrial patterns

(G-9806)
SUPERIOR PLASTIC PRODUCTS LLC
33 Hess Rd (17540-9511)
PHONE....................................717 556-3240
EMP: 3
SALES (est): 185.9K Privately Held
SIC: 3089 Fences, gates & accessories: plastic

(G-9807)
SWING KINGDOM LLC
Also Called: Sk
36 Glenbrook Rd (17540-1301)
PHONE....................................717 656-4449
Amos Glick, Owner
EMP: 19
SALES (est): 2MM Privately Held
SIC: 3949 7999 Playground equipment; recreation center

(G-9808)
WHITLEY EAST LLC (DH)
64 Hess Rd (17540-9512)
PHONE....................................717 656-2081
Simon Dragan,
EMP: 51
SALES (est): 17.5MM Privately Held
SIC: 3281 Building stone products
HQ: Whitley Evergreen Inc
    201 W First St
    South Whitley IN 46787
    260 723-5131

(G-9809)
YODER INDUSTRIES LLC
83 S Groffdale Rd (17540-9533)
PHONE....................................717 656-6770
David Yoder, Council Mbr
EMP: 7
SQ FT: 18,000
SALES (est): 1.2MM Privately Held
SIC: 3599 Machine shop, jobbing & repair

Levittown
Bucks County

(G-9810)
A & E MANUFACTURING CO INC
Also Called: A&E
2110 Hartel Ave (19057-4597)
PHONE....................................215 943-9460
Armin AST, President
Erick AST, President
Eric AST, Controller
Ralph Murray, Chief Mktg Ofcr
Dan McLane, Manager
EMP: 110
SQ FT: 50,000
SALES (est): 20.9MM Privately Held
WEB: www.ae-mfg.com
SIC: 3444 Sheet metal specialties, not stamped

(G-9811)
A C GRINDING & SUPPLY CO INC
1917 Hartel Ave (19057)
PHONE....................................215 946-3760
Robert Albert Jr, President
Albert Rob, CFO
David Albert, Sales Staff
EMP: 7
SQ FT: 10,000
SALES (est): 1MM Privately Held
SIC: 3599 5085 5051 Grinding castings for the trade; industrial supplies; steel

(G-9812)
ADVANCED POLYMER COATINGS INC (PA)
6000 Hibbs Ln (19057-4304)
PHONE....................................215 943-1466
Bruce G Pelham, President
Debbie Arbuckle, Treasurer
EMP: 4

SALES (est): 703.9K Privately Held
SIC: 3479 Coating of metals & formed products

(G-9813)
ADVENTEK CORPORATION
Also Called: Nylomatic
10 Headley Pl (19054-1401)
PHONE....................................215 736-0961
Kenneth Brandt, President
Howard Park, Vice Pres
Anita Tracey, Sales Dir
Franz Beismann, Administration
EMP: 24
SQ FT: 45,000
SALES (est): 4.8MM Privately Held
WEB: www.nylomatic.com
SIC: 3089 3083 Injection molding of plastics; laminated plastics plate & sheet

(G-9814)
AIRGAS SAFETY INC (DH)
2501 Green Ln (19057-4146)
PHONE....................................215 826-9000
Donald S Carlino, President
John W Smith, Vice Pres
Thomas M Smyth, Vice Pres
David Levin, Treasurer
Robert H Young, Admin Sec
▲ EMP: 200
SQ FT: 1,000
SALES (est): 422.7MM
SALES (corp-wide): 125.9MM Privately Held
WEB: www.airgassafety.com
SIC: 5084 5085 3561 3841 Safety equipment; welding supplies; cylinders, pump; surgical & medical instruments
HQ: Airgas, Inc.
    259 N Radnor Chester Rd # 100
    Radnor PA 19087
    610 687-5253

(G-9815)
ALE HYDRAULIC MCHY CO LLC
6215 Airport Rd (19057-4701)
PHONE....................................215 547-3351
Al Zwiebel,
Edward Deck,
Curtis Seida,
EMP: 12
SQ FT: 17,000
SALES (est): 1.9MM Privately Held
SIC: 3599 5084 7699 Custom machinery; hydraulic systems equipment & supplies; hydraulic equipment repair

(G-9816)
ANTONIO CENTENO LAWNKEEPING
73 Kingwood Ln (19055-2422)
PHONE....................................267 580-0443
Antonio Centeno, Owner
EMP: 5
SALES (est): 400K Privately Held
SIC: 3524 Lawn & garden equipment

(G-9817)
API AMERICAS INC
47 Runway Dr Ste G (19057-4738)
PHONE....................................785 842-7674
EMP: 13 EST: 2013
SALES (est): 1.4MM Privately Held
SIC: 1411 2541 Dimension Stone Quarry Mfg Wood Partitions/Fixtures

(G-9818)
BASF CONSTRUCTION CHEM LLC
6450 Bristol Pike (19057-4916)
PHONE....................................215 945-3900
George Tessier, Branch Mgr
EMP: 8
SALES (corp-wide): 71.7B Privately Held
WEB: www.chemrex.com
SIC: 2899 Concrete curing & hardening compounds
HQ: Basf Construction Chemicals, Llc
    889 Valley Park Dr
    Shakopee MN 55379
    952 496-6000

(G-9819)
BRIDGE AUTO TAGS
34 Indian Park Rd (19057-2214)
PHONE....................................215 946-8026

Lucille La Penna, *Owner*
EMP: 7
SALES (est): 323.8K **Privately Held**
SIC: 3469 Automobile license tags, stamped metal

(G-9820)
BRISTOL ALUMINUM CO
5514 Bristol Emilie Rd (19057-2511)
PHONE..................215 946-1566
Paul Mathias, *President*
Clark Mathias, *Treasurer*
Calvin Mathias, *Warden*
Paul H Mathias, *Admin Sec*
EMP: 45
SQ FT: 25,000
SALES (est): 11.2MM **Privately Held**
WEB: www.bristolaluminum.com
SIC: 3354 Aluminum extruded products

(G-9821)
BRISTOL ROLLING DOOR INC
1990 Hartel Ave (19057-4519)
PHONE..................215 949-9090
Jerry Gauvreau III, *President*
Reid Balard, *Vice Pres*
Lou Maisonet, *Prdtn Mgr*
EMP: 6
SQ FT: 14,000
SALES (est): 978.1K **Privately Held**
SIC: 3442 Rolling doors for industrial buildings or warehouses, metal

(G-9822)
CALKINS MEDIA INCORPORATED (PA)
Also Called: Montgomery County Record
8400 Bristol Pike (19057-5117)
PHONE..................215 949-4000
Mark G Contreras, *CEO*
Mike Jameson, *President*
Art Lanham, *General Mgr*
Jeff Benninghoff, *Vice Pres*
Shirley Ellis, *Vice Pres*
EMP: 200 **EST:** 1804
SQ FT: 20,000
SALES (est): 207.2MM **Privately Held**
WEB: www.phillyburbs.com
SIC: 2711 Commercial printing & newspaper publishing combined

(G-9823)
CASNER FABRICS
922 Woodbourne Rd Ste 244 (19057-1001)
PHONE..................215 946-3334
Cathleen Spicer Kubat, *Owner*
EMP: 8
SALES (est): 622.4K **Privately Held**
SIC: 2211 5945 Broadwoven fabric mills, cotton; arts & crafts supplies

(G-9824)
CASTROL INDUSTRIAL N AMER INC
2201 Green Ln (19057-4112)
PHONE..................877 641-1600
EMP: 57
SALES (corp-wide): 240.2B **Privately Held**
SIC: 2992 2899 Lubricating oils & greases; corrosion preventive lubricant; rust resisting compounds
HQ: Castrol Industrial North America Inc.
150 W Warrenville Rd
Naperville IL 60563
877 641-1600

(G-9825)
CLARANCE J VENNE INC
6300 Mcpherson St (19057-4728)
PHONE..................215 547-7110
Richard A Venne, *President*
John Venne, *Corp Secy*
Clarence J Venne, *Vice Pres*
EMP: 3
SALES (est): 223.4K **Privately Held**
SIC: 2891 Glue

(G-9826)
CONSOLIDATED COATINGS INC
Also Called: Master Terrazzo Technologies
8000 Bristol Pike (19057-5104)
PHONE..................215 949-1474
James Guy, *President*
Joyce Wenzke, *Vice Pres*
EMP: 7 **EST:** 1950

SALES (est): 1.3MM **Privately Held**
SIC: 2851 Paints & paint additives

(G-9827)
COREN-INDIK INC
6300 Bristol Pike (19057-4914)
PHONE..................267 288-1200
David Indik, *President*
Larry Indik, *Treasurer*
EMP: 15 **EST:** 1957
SQ FT: 50,000
SALES (est): 1.3MM **Privately Held**
SIC: 2281 Yarn spinning mills

(G-9828)
COURIER TIMES INC (HQ)
Also Called: Bucks County Courier Times
8400 Bristol Pike (19057-5117)
P.O. Box 368, Langhorne (19047-0368)
PHONE..................215 949-4011
Mike Jameson, *President*
Michael White, *Treasurer*
Charles Smith, *Admin Sec*
EMP: 655
SQ FT: 60,000
SALES (est): 191.9MM
SALES (corp-wide): 1.5B **Publicly Held**
WEB: www.buckscountycouriertimes.com
SIC: 2711 Commercial printing & newspaper publishing combined
PA: New Media Investment Group Inc.
1345 Avenue Of The Americ
New York NY 10105
212 479-3160

(G-9829)
CUSTOM FINISHING INC
7205 Hibbs Ln (19057-4303)
PHONE..................215 269-7500
James Gross, *President*
William Blaney, *Vice Pres*
Sylvia Hicks, *Office Mgr*
Jim Hampton, *Manager*
EMP: 12
SQ FT: 10,000
SALES (est): 2.1MM **Privately Held**
WEB: www.cfsigns.com
SIC: 3993 Signs & advertising specialties

(G-9830)
DAJR ENTERPRISES INC
Also Called: Penn Valley Paint
8000 Bristol Pike (19057-5104)
PHONE..................215 949-0800
EMP: 16 **EST:** 1944
SQ FT: 21,000
SALES (est): 3.1MM **Privately Held**
SIC: 2851 Mfg Paints/Allied Products

(G-9831)
DIGITAL CARE SYSYTEMS INC
2000 Hartel Ave (19057-4523)
PHONE..................215 946-7700
Richard Bowman, *President*
EMP: 15
SALES (est): 2.4MM **Privately Held**
SIC: 3669 Emergency alarms

(G-9832)
DIGITAL DESIGNS INC
37 Scarlet Oak Rd (19056-1701)
PHONE..................215 781-2525
EMP: 14
SQ FT: 2,500
SALES (est): 1.3MM **Privately Held**
SIC: 8711 3699 Engineering Services Mfg Electrical Equipment/Supplies

(G-9833)
DJF PRINT XPRESS
47 Locust Ln (19054-3917)
PHONE..................215 964-1258
EMP: 4
SALES (est): 373.5K **Privately Held**
SIC: 2752 Commercial printing, lithographic

(G-9834)
ECLAT INDUSTRIES INC
1604 Hanford St (19057-4712)
PHONE..................215 547-2684
Wenjue Liu, *CEO*
Tao Cheng, *COO*
Rong Nie, *CFO*
▲ **EMP:** 4

SALES: 600K **Privately Held**
WEB: www.eclatcoating.com
SIC: 3479 Etching & engraving; painting, coating & hot dipping

(G-9835)
EXPORT USA LLC
103 Verdant Rd (19057-4226)
PHONE..................215 949-3380
Monica Dionne, *President*
EMP: 4
SALES: 7MM **Privately Held**
SIC: 3325 Alloy steel castings, except investment

(G-9836)
FIBERGLASS TECHNOLOGIES INC
1610 Hanford St Ste P (19057-4712)
PHONE..................215 943-4567
Scott Kennedy, *President*
Eugene G Kennedy Jr, *Treasurer*
EMP: 25
SQ FT: 22,000
SALES (est): 5.4MM **Privately Held**
WEB: www.fiberglasstechnologies.com
SIC: 3089 Plastic hardware & building products

(G-9837)
FSI INDUSTRIES INC
8 Nancia Dr (19054-1412)
PHONE..................215 295-0552
Michael Mormando, *President*
EMP: 3
SALES (est): 208.5K **Privately Held**
SIC: 3999 Manufacturing industries

(G-9838)
GARRETT LINERS INC
295 Lower Morrisville Rd (19054-1406)
PHONE..................215 295-0200
Kenneth H Garrett, *CEO*
Roger Morley, *Vice Pres*
Matt Rodgers, *Department Mgr*
▲ **EMP:** 35
SQ FT: 36,000
SALES (est): 4.4MM **Privately Held**
WEB: www.garrettliners.com
SIC: 2394 3949 Liners & covers, fabric: made from purchased materials; sporting & athletic goods

(G-9839)
GEMINI PLASTICS INC
7 Headley Pl (19054-1401)
PHONE..................215 736-1313
Alan S Breece, *President*
Ken Pugh, *Principal*
Drew Wildonger, *Vice Pres*
James M Breece, *Treasurer*
▲ **EMP:** 45
SQ FT: 80,000
SALES (est): 12.3MM **Privately Held**
WEB: www.geminiplastics.net
SIC: 3089 Injection molding of plastics

(G-9840)
GIBBYS ICE CREAM INC
20 Candle Rd (19057-1402)
PHONE..................215 547-7253
Richard Purcell, *President*
Jean Purcell, *Corp Secy*
EMP: 12
SQ FT: 1,200
SALES (est): 1.6MM **Privately Held**
SIC: 2024 5451 Ice cream, bulk; ice cream (packaged)

(G-9841)
GITTENS CORP
Also Called: Valley Enterprises
1415 Hardy St (19057-4729)
P.O. Box 743 (19058-0743)
PHONE..................215 945-0944
Douglas Gittens Jr, *President*
Lee Gittens, *Corp Secy*
EMP: 4 **EST:** 1959
SQ FT: 2,400
SALES: 600K **Privately Held**
SIC: 3599 Machine shop, jobbing & repair

(G-9842)
GRIFF AND ASSOCIATES LP (PA)
Also Called: Griff & Associates
275 Lower Morrisville Rd (19054-1406)
P.O. Box 658 (19058-0658)
PHONE..................215 428-1075
Alex J Phinn, *Partner*
John Phinn, *Sales Staff*
Todd Phinn, *Manager*
John Dearing, *IT/INT Sup*
Robert Phinn, *Products*
▲ **EMP:** 60
SQ FT: 90,000
SALES (est): 12MM **Privately Held**
WEB: www.paperandfilm.com
SIC: 5113 3674 Industrial & personal service paper; photovoltaic devices, solid state

(G-9843)
HIGLEY ENTERPRISES
Also Called: Kool Stuff 4 Kids
1339 Oakland Ave (19056-2105)
P.O. Box 142, Wernersville (19565-0142)
PHONE..................610 693-4039
Ron Higley, *Owner*
EMP: 5
SALES (est): 472.2K **Privately Held**
WEB: www.koolstuff4kids.com
SIC: 3944 Craft & hobby kits & sets

(G-9844)
LABELWORX INC
51 Runway Dr (19057-4700)
PHONE..................215 945-5645
Jack Lang, *President*
Gerard E Toepfer, *President*
Paula Parrish, *General Mgr*
Kathryn Bartusis, *Facilities Mgr*
John R Long, *Admin Sec*
EMP: 8
SALES (est): 1.9MM **Privately Held**
WEB: www.labelworx.biz
SIC: 2672 Labels (unprinted), gummed: made from purchased materials

(G-9845)
LEVITTOWN PRINTING INC
1433 Haines Rd (19057-5033)
PHONE..................215 945-8156
E Steven Martino, *President*
Judy Hadalski, *Corp Secy*
EMP: 5
SQ FT: 3,300
SALES (est): 600K **Privately Held**
WEB: www.lpiprint.com
SIC: 2759 2752 Letterpress printing; commercial printing, offset

(G-9846)
LIBERTY PRESS LLC
4510 New Falls Rd (19056-3011)
P.O. Box 1017 (19058-1017)
PHONE..................215 943-3788
Ralph W Liberty Jr,
EMP: 3
SQ FT: 1,200
SALES (est): 396.1K **Privately Held**
SIC: 2752 Photo-offset printing; commercial printing, offset

(G-9847)
LOOMIS PRODUCTS COMPANY
5500 Bristol Emilie Rd (19057-2599)
PHONE..................215 547-2121
Karl Kahlefeld, *President*
Joan Kahlefeld, *Admin Sec*
▲ **EMP:** 15
SQ FT: 17,000
SALES (est): 4.8MM **Privately Held**
WEB: www.loomisproducts.com
SIC: 3542 Presses: forming, stamping, punching, sizing (machine tools)

(G-9848)
M SQUARED ELECTRONICS INC
1610 Manning Blvd Ste C (19057-4733)
PHONE..................215 945-6658
Frederick Robinson, *President*
Mark Robinson, *Vice Pres*
◆ **EMP:** 10
SQ FT: 5,000

SALES (est): 1.9MM **Privately Held**
WEB: www.msquaredelectronics.com
SIC: 3829 3625 7373 8711 Testing
equipment: abrasion, shearing strength,
etc.; control circuit devices, magnet &
solid state; computer systems analysis &
design; engineering services

(G-9849)
**MOA INSTRUMENTATION INC
(PA)**
1606 Manning Blvd Ste 1 (19057-4732)
PHONE.....................................609 352-9329
Amy S Borlaug, *President*
Marshall Borlaug, *Vice Pres*
EMP: 12
SQ FT: 3,000
SALES (est): 2.6MM **Privately Held**
SIC: 3826 Spectrometers

(G-9850)
MODERN BLENDING TECH INC
2061 Hartel Ave (19057-4506)
PHONE.....................................267 580-1000
Robert Stempel, *President*
Irina Burd, *President*
EMP: 10
SQ FT: 23,000
SALES (est): 2.1MM **Privately Held**
WEB: www.modernblending.com
SIC: 2891 Adhesives & sealants

(G-9851)
MOLDAMATIC LLC
3911 Nebraska Ave (19056-3333)
PHONE.....................................215 785-2356
Peter Paden, *General Mgr*
EMP: 8
SQ FT: 19,516
SALES (corp-wide): 26.6MM **Privately
Held**
WEB: www.moldamatic.com
SIC: 3089 Injection molding of plastics
PA: Moldamatic, Llc
29 Noeland Ave
Penndel PA 19047
215 757-4819

(G-9852)
**NATIONAL GENERIC
DISTRIBUTORS**
Also Called: High Chemical Company
3901 Nebraska Ave Ste A (19056-3374)
PHONE.....................................215 788-3113
Nalin Barikh, *President*
EMP: 6 **EST:** 1945
SQ FT: 35,000
SALES (est): 1.3MM **Privately Held**
WEB: www.sarapin.com
SIC: 2834 Pharmaceutical preparations

(G-9853)
PATTERSON PLASTICS & MFG
253 Lower Morrisville Rd (19054-1406)
PHONE.....................................215 736-3020
Roger Patterson, *President*
Amy Flannery, *Office Mgr*
EMP: 7
SALES (est): 754K **Privately Held**
SIC: 3543 Industrial patterns

(G-9854)
**PERFORMANCE COATINGS
CORP**
1610 Manning Blvd Ste A (19057-4733)
PHONE.....................................610 525-1190
Ernest Korchak, *President*
◆ **EMP:** 10
SQ FT: 15,000
SALES (est): 1.7MM **Privately Held**
WEB: www.performancecoatings.biz
SIC: 2851 2891 2899 2952 Paints & al-
lied products; adhesives & sealants;
chemical preparations; asphalt felts &
coatings; etching & engraving; metal foil &
leaf

(G-9855)
PHOENIX LABORATORIES INC
1a Headley Pl (19054-1401)
PHONE.....................................215 295-5222
George Wooley, *President*
Marilyn Wooley, *Corp Secy*
EMP: 10 **EST:** 1975
SQ FT: 5,000

SALES (est): 1.2MM **Privately Held**
SIC: 2899 Water treating compounds

(G-9856)
PITNEY BOWES INC
42 Runway Dr (19057-4731)
PHONE.....................................215 946-2863
John F Thompson, *President*
EMP: 35
SALES (corp-wide): 3.5B **Publicly Held**
SIC: 3579 7359 Postage meters; business
machine & electronic equipment rental
services
PA: Pitney Bowes Inc.
3001 Summer St Ste 3
Stamford CT 06905
203 356-5000

(G-9857)
POLYCUBE COMPANY LLC
30a Runway Dr (19057-4731)
PHONE.....................................215 946-2823
Carola Berina, *Principal*
EMP: 12
SALES (est): 2.2MM **Privately Held**
SIC: 3089 Plastics products

(G-9858)
**POLYMERIC EXTRUDED
PRODUCTS**
6000 Hibbs Ln (19057-4304)
PHONE.....................................215 943-1288
Bruce Pelham, *President*
Scott Pelham, *Vice Pres*
James D Klatt, *Administration*
EMP: 5
SQ FT: 3,200
SALES (est): 786.1K **Privately Held**
SIC: 3052 3069 Air line or air brake hose,
rubber or rubberized fabric; tubing, rubber

(G-9859)
POPIT INC
922 Woodbourne Rd 333 (19057-1001)
PHONE.....................................215 945-5201
Mary Geragi, *President*
EMP: 4
SALES (est): 320K **Privately Held**
WEB: www.popit.com
SIC: 3494 Pipe fittings

(G-9860)
PRECISION CONTROLS LLC
47 Crystal Pl (19057-1413)
PHONE.....................................267 337-9812
Bruce Kerr, *President*
EMP: 1
SALES (est): 2.5MM **Privately Held**
SIC: 5084 3592 Controlling instruments &
accessories; valves, engine

(G-9861)
RIBARCHIK JOHN
Also Called: Bucks County Equipment
1606 Unit C2 Levittown 2 C (19055)
P.O. Box 2037, Bristol (19007-0837)
PHONE.....................................215 547-8901
John Ribarchik, *Owner*
EMP: 4
SQ FT: 3,500
SALES (est): 250K **Privately Held**
SIC: 7699 3549 Construction equipment
repair; metalworking machinery

(G-9862)
**RTJ INC A CLOSE
CORPORATION**
Also Called: American Conveyor Systems
1601 Harmer St Ste C (19057-4724)
PHONE.....................................215 943-9220
Thomas Gramlich, *President*
John Gramlich, *Vice Pres*
Bud Marshall, *Engineer*
◆ **EMP:** 13
SQ FT: 125,000
SALES (est): 3.8MM **Privately Held**
WEB: www.american-conveyor.com
SIC: 3535 5084 Belt conveyor systems,
general industrial use; industrial machin-
ery & equipment

(G-9863)
SIMTECH INDUSTRIAL PDTS INC
47 Runway Dr Ste A (19057-4738)
PHONE.....................................215 547-0444

Peter Vagell, *President*
Kundla Peter, *Corp Secy*
◆ **EMP:** 16
SALES (est): 4.3MM **Privately Held**
WEB: www.simtechusa.com
SIC: 2821 Thermoplastic materials

(G-9864)
**SOLID WOOD CABINET
COMPANY LLC (PA)**
Also Called: Interstock Premium Cabinetry
6300 Bristol Pike (19057-4914)
PHONE.....................................267 288-1200
Nick Renzulli, *Project Mgr*
Steve Newton, *Mng Member*
Matt Sharp, *Consultant*
Jack Catzman,
David Indick,
▲ **EMP:** 120
SQ FT: 200,000
SALES (est): 26.2MM **Privately Held**
WEB: www.interstockcabinets.com
SIC: 2434 Wood kitchen cabinets

(G-9865)
**SPECIALTY SUPPORT SYSTEMS
INC**
2100 Hartel Ave (19057-4508)
P.O. Box 226, Morrisville (19067-0226)
PHONE.....................................215 945-1033
Joseph M Silva, *President*
Palmira R Silva, *Treasurer*
Phyllis Silva, *Admin Sec*
EMP: 12
SQ FT: 10,000
SALES (est): 2.2MM **Privately Held**
WEB: www.specialtysupportsystems.com
SIC: 3441 5085 8711 5072 Fabricated
structural metal; industrial supplies; engi-
neering services; bolts; nuts (hardware);
screws

(G-9866)
**SUPER CAN INDUSTRIES INC
(PA)**
Also Called: F.I.R.E.S. Group
6913 Bristol Pike (19057-4925)
PHONE.....................................215 945-1075
Joseph Nelson, *President*
EMP: 5
SQ FT: 4,500
SALES: 460K **Privately Held**
SIC: 3842 Respiratory protection equip-
ment, personal

(G-9867)
TELAMON CORPORATION
45 Runway Dr Ste A (19057-4737)
PHONE.....................................800 945-8800
Barbara Hiller, *Branch Mgr*
Jo A Jaquays, *Administration*
EMP: 30
SALES (corp-wide): 497.5MM **Privately
Held**
WEB: www.ibuybroadband.com
SIC: 5065 3661 Communication equip-
ment; telephone equipment; telephones &
telephone apparatus
PA: Telamon Corporation
1000 E 116th St
Carmel IN 46032
317 818-6888

(G-9868)
**TOBACCO PLUS CASH
CHECKING**
8612 New Falls Rd (19054-1712)
PHONE.....................................267 585-3802
EMP: 3
SALES (est): 291.3K **Privately Held**
SIC: 6099 5194 2111 Check cashing
agencies; smoking tobacco; cigarettes

(G-9869)
TORRENT PHARMA INC
2091 Hartel Ave (19057-4506)
PHONE.....................................215 949-3711
Sanjay Gupta, *Manager*
EMP: 100 **Privately Held**
SIC: 2834 Pharmaceutical preparations
HQ: Torrent Pharma Inc.
150 Allen Rd Ste 102
Basking Ridge NJ 07920

(G-9870)
ZURN INDUSTRIES LLC
37 Runway Dr (19057-4700)
PHONE.....................................215 946-0216
Mike Gonzalez, *Branch Mgr*
EMP: 6 **Publicly Held**
SIC: 3431 Bathroom fixtures, including
sinks; sinks: enameled iron, cast iron or
pressed metal
HQ: Zurn Industries, Llc
1801 Pittsburgh Ave
Erie PA 16502
814 455-0921

Lewis Run
Mckean County

(G-9871)
**BRADFORD ALLEGHENY
CORPORATION (PA)**
Also Called: Top Line Process Equipment
1522 South Ave (16738-9704)
P.O. Box 264, Bradford (16701-0264)
PHONE.....................................814 362-2590
Daniel P McCune, *President*
Chuck Ridenour, *Regional Mgr*
John H Satterwhite, *Vice Pres*
John Satterwhite, *Vice Pres*
Staci Frantz, *VP Opers*
◆ **EMP:** 161
SQ FT: 28,000
SALES (est): 50.3MM **Privately Held**
WEB: www.alleghenybradford.com
SIC: 3556 3494 3317 3559 Food prod-
ucts machinery; valves & pipe fittings;
steel pipe & tubes; pharmaceutical ma-
chinery

(G-9872)
**BRADFORD ALLEGHENY
CORPORATION**
1522 South Ave (16738-9704)
P.O. Box 200, Bradford (16701-0200)
PHONE.....................................814 362-2591
EMP: 11
SALES (est): 1.6MM **Privately Held**
SIC: 3443 Mfg Fabricated Plate Work

(G-9873)
**BRADFORD ALLEGHENY
CORPORATION**
Also Called: Allegheny Surface Technology
14 Egbert Ln (16738-3802)
P.O. Box 200, Bradford (16701-0200)
PHONE.....................................814 368-4465
Thomas Hoffmann, *General Mgr*
Sue Langianese, *Sales Mgr*
Matthew Irwin, *Sales Staff*
Thomas Hoffman, *Manager*
EMP: 16
SALES (corp-wide): 50.3MM **Privately
Held**
WEB: www.alleghenybradford.com
SIC: 3471 Finishing, metals or formed
products; polishing, metals or formed
products
PA: Bradford Allegheny Corporation
1522 South Ave
Lewis Run PA 16738
814 362-2590

(G-9874)
**BRADFORD ALLEGHENY
CORPORATION**
16 Valley Hunt Dr (16738-9716)
P.O. Box 200, Bradford (16701-0200)
PHONE.....................................814 362-2593
Amy Tompkins, *Principal*
Steven Moyer, *Manager*
Shandra Wilson, *Personnel Assit*
EMP: 80
SALES (corp-wide): 50.3MM **Privately
Held**
SIC: 3556 3564 3494 3444 Food prod-
ucts machinery; blowers & fans; valves &
pipe fittings; sheet metalwork; fabricated
plate work (boiler shop); steel pipe &
tubes
PA: Bradford Allegheny Corporation
1522 South Ave
Lewis Run PA 16738
814 362-2590

(G-9875)
ESCHRICH AND SON LOGGING
20 Twin Buck Rd (16738-3534)
PHONE..............................814 362-1371
EMP: 3
SALES (est): 254.7K Privately Held
SIC: 2411 Logging

(G-9876)
KEYSTONE POWDERED METAL CO
8 Hanley Dr (16738-3804)
PHONE..............................814 368-5320
Terri Niver, QC Mgr
William Hirsh, Manager
EMP: 100
SALES (corp-wide): 28.9B Privately Held
SIC: 3399 3568 Metal powders, pastes & flakes; power transmission equipment
HQ: Keystone Powdered Metal Co
251 State St
Saint Marys PA 15857
814 781-1591

(G-9877)
MCCOURT LABEL CABINET COMPANY
Also Called: McCourt Label Company
20 Egbert Ln (16738-3802)
PHONE..............................800 458-2390
David G Ferguson, President
Mary E Reiley, Treasurer
Jane Luzzi, Admin Sec
EMP: 70
SQ FT: 41,000
SALES (est): 15.1MM Privately Held
WEB: www.mccourtlabel.com
SIC: 2752 2679 2759 2671 Commercial printing, lithographic; labels, paper: made from purchased material; commercial printing; packaging paper & plastics film, coated & laminated

(G-9878)
MSL OIL & GAS CORP
Marshburg Rd Rr 59 (16738)
P.O. Box 151, Bradford (16701-0151)
PHONE..............................814 362-6891
Shelly Floyd, General Mgr
Robert Merry, Branch Mgr
EMP: 24
SALES (corp-wide): 8.5MM Privately Held
SIC: 1389 Oil field services
PA: Msl Oil & Gas Corp
6161 Fuller Ct
Alexandria VA 22310
703 971-8805

Lewisberry
York County

(G-9879)
A G MAURO COMPANY
580 Industrial Dr (17339-9538)
PHONE..............................717 938-4671
Jerry Richmond, Opers-Prdtn-Mfg
EMP: 35
SALES (corp-wide): 36.9MM Privately Held
SIC: 5072 3429 Builders' hardware; manufactured hardware (general)
PA: The A G Mauro Company
310 Alpha Dr
Pittsburgh PA 15238
412 782-6600

(G-9880)
ARTHUR L BAKER ENTERPRISES
Also Called: Baker WD & Coal Burning Stoves
711 E Mount Airy Rd (17339-9732)
PHONE..............................717 432-9788
Nancy Baker, President
EMP: 4
SQ FT: 20,000
SALES (est): 584.5K Privately Held
SIC: 3433 3799 Stoves, wood & coal burning; furnaces, domestic steam or hot water; trailers & trailer equipment

(G-9881)
BEST DRESSED ASSOCIATES INC
Also Called: Gazebo Room Salad Dressing
641 Lowther Rd (17339-9527)
PHONE..............................717 938-2222
Nick G Gekas, President
Steven G Gekas, Vice Pres
EMP: 10 EST: 1990
SQ FT: 70,000
SALES (est): 1.3MM Privately Held
WEB: www.gazeboroom.com
SIC: 2035 Dressings, salad: raw & cooked (except dry mixes)

(G-9882)
CULVER TOOL & DIE INC
688 Yorktown Rd Ste E (17339-9216)
PHONE..............................717 932-2000
Mark Culver, President
EMP: 7
SQ FT: 3,500
SALES (est): 1MM Privately Held
SIC: 3544 Industrial molds

(G-9883)
DI CHEM CONCENTRATE INC
509 Fishing Creek Rd (17339-9517)
PHONE..............................717 938-8391
Dewayn Buchholz, President
EMP: 33
SALES (corp-wide): 6.7MM Privately Held
WEB: www.dichem-us.com
SIC: 5169 2833 Chemicals & allied products; medicinals & botanicals
PA: Di Chem Concentrate Inc
12297 Ensign Ave N
Champlin MN 55316
763 422-8311

(G-9884)
DIMESOL USA LLC
509 Fishing Creek Rd (17339-9517)
PHONE..............................717 938-0796
Daniel Rangel, President
Stephen Callaghan, CFO
▼ EMP: 13
SALES (est): 5.6MM Privately Held
SIC: 2899 Acids

(G-9885)
ELK SYSTEMS INC
303 Heck Hill Rd (17339-9145)
PHONE..............................717 884-9355
Jeffrey A Schmidt, President
EMP: 5
SALES (est): 648.4K Privately Held
SIC: 3571 7373 7389 Electronic computers; computer integrated systems design;

(G-9886)
FLIGHT SYSTEMS AUTO GROUP LLC (HQ)
Also Called: Flight Systems Elec Group
505 Fishing Creek Rd (17339-9517)
PHONE..............................717 932-7000
Mark Digiampietro, President
Tom Davidson Jr, General Mgr
Tim Stechschulte, Business Mgr
Ralph Rulli, Vice Pres
Justin Mayberry, Buyer
▲ EMP: 105
SQ FT: 140,000
SALES (est): 19.2MM
SALES (corp-wide): 40.4MM Privately Held
WEB: www.fseg.net
SIC: 3694 Automotive electrical equipment
PA: Cignet, L.L.C.
24601 Capital Blvd
Clinton Township MI 48036
586 307-3790

(G-9887)
HYDROFLEX SYSTEMS INC
1009 Silver Lake Rd (17339-9119)
PHONE..............................717 480-4200
Thomas A Stayer, Principal
Thomas Marasciullo, Mfg Dir
Cathleen Carver, CFO
EMP: 16
SALES (est): 2.5MM Privately Held
SIC: 3443 Breechings, metal plate

(G-9888)
LEIPHART ENTERPRISES LLC
Also Called: Sheaffer Signs
688 Yorktown Rd Ste A (17339-9216)
P.O. Box 131 (17339-0131)
PHONE..............................717 938-4100
Todd Leiphart, President
EMP: 4
SQ FT: 3,000
SALES (est): 266.2K Privately Held
SIC: 3993 7389 Neon signs; sign painting & lettering shop; lettering service

(G-9889)
OPTIMA TECHNOLOGY ASSOC INC
515 Fishing Creek Rd (17339-9517)
PHONE..............................717 932-5877
Paul A Anastasio, President
Rick Defrank, Purch Mgr
Joe Vandzura, Design Engr
Paul J Anastasio, Treasurer
▲ EMP: 90
SQ FT: 5,000
SALES: 6.6MM Privately Held
WEB: www.optimatech.net
SIC: 3678 8711 Electronic connectors; consulting engineer; electrical or electronic engineering

(G-9890)
PFIZER INC
543 Industrial Dr B (17339-9532)
PHONE..............................717 932-3701
D Perritt, Branch Mgr
EMP: 300
SALES (corp-wide): 53.6B Publicly Held
WEB: www.pfizer.com
SIC: 5122 2834 Pharmaceuticals; pharmaceutical preparations
PA: Pfizer Inc.
235 E 42nd St
New York NY 10017
212 733-2323

(G-9891)
PFIZER INC
543 Industrial Dr Ste B (17339-9532)
PHONE..............................717 932-3701
Charles Thorwarth, Branch Mgr
EMP: 11
SALES (corp-wide): 53.6B Publicly Held
SIC: 2834 Pharmaceutical preparations
PA: Pfizer Inc.
235 E 42nd St
New York NY 10017
212 733-2323

(G-9892)
PIONEER ENTERPRISES INC
Also Called: Ron Eppley Pioneer Enterprises
1008 Pinetown Rd (17339-9148)
PHONE..............................717 938-9388
Ron Eppley, President
EMP: 3
SQ FT: 4,000
SALES (est): 500K Privately Held
SIC: 3949 Sporting & athletic goods

(G-9893)
SPEARS MANUFACTURING CO
590 Industrial Dr Ste 100 (17339-9665)
PHONE..............................717 938-8844
Vivian Yinger, Manager
John Adkins, Manager
EMP: 27
SALES (corp-wide): 1.6B Privately Held
WEB: www.spearsmfg.com
SIC: 3084 5162 Plastics pipe; plastics materials & basic shapes
PA: Spears Manufacturing Co.
15853 Olden St
Sylmar CA 91342
818 364-1611

(G-9894)
WATER TREATMENT BY DESIGN LLC
730 Seitz Dr (17339-9714)
PHONE..............................717 938-0670
Mark J Coldren,
EMP: 5
SALES: 950K Privately Held
SIC: 3589 Water treatment equipment, industrial

(G-9895)
ZOETIS LLC
543 Industrial Dr (17339-9532)
PHONE..............................717 932-3702
EMP: 9
SALES (est): 1.3MM Privately Held
SIC: 2834 Pharmaceutical preparations

Lewisburg
Union County

(G-9896)
ALLEN ZIMMMERMAN
Also Called: Zimmerman Deisel
360 Young Rd (17837-7833)
PHONE..............................570 966-6924
Allen Zimmerman, Owner
EMP: 4
SALES (est): 405K Privately Held
SIC: 0212 3599 Beef cattle except feedlots; machine shop, jobbing & repair

(G-9897)
AMERICAN SLAR ENVMTL TECHNOLOG
Also Called: Aset
220 S 3rd St (17837-1912)
PHONE..............................570 279-0338
Judith Karr, Principal
Roan Confer, COO
EMP: 4
SALES: 250K Privately Held
SIC: 8999 3433 Earth science services; solar heaters & collectors

(G-9898)
BESSIE GROVE
Also Called: H & C Ggrove Mills
268 Wolfland Rd (17837-7537)
PHONE..............................570 524-2436
Bessie Grove, Owner
EMP: 3
SQ FT: 10,000
SALES (est): 110K Privately Held
SIC: 2041 2048 Flour: blended, prepared or self-rising; prepared feeds

(G-9899)
CENTRAL BUILDERS SUPPLY CO
520 Saint Mary St (17837-1440)
PHONE..............................570 524-9147
EMP: 6
SALES (corp-wide): 14.9MM Privately Held
SIC: 3273 Mfg Ready-Mixed Concrete
PA: Central Builders Supply Company
125 Bridge Ave
Sunbury PA 17801
570 286-6461

(G-9900)
COLONIAL CANDLECRAFTERS
165 Brookpark Cir (17837-6804)
PHONE..............................570 524-4556
Patricia L Bird Hess, Partner
Gregory A Hess, Partner
EMP: 3
SQ FT: 2,500
SALES (est): 190K Privately Held
WEB: www.colonialcandlecrafters.com
SIC: 3999 5199 5999 Candles; candles; candle shops

(G-9901)
COUNTRY TEES & GRAFX LLC
2794 Crossroads Dr (17837-7428)
PHONE..............................570 568-0973
Loree Brown,
EMP: 5 EST: 2008
SALES (est): 438.1K Privately Held
SIC: 2759 Screen printing

(G-9902)
CUSTOM CONTAINER SOLUTIONS LLC
391 Wolfland Rd (17837-7538)
P.O. Box 133 (17837-0133)
PHONE..............................570 524-7835
Todd Vonderheid, Mng Member
EMP: 15

SALES (est): 4.2MM **Privately Held**
SIC: 3448 Prefabricated metal buildings

(G-9903)
CUSTOM CONTAINER VLY CAN LLC
Also Called: Valley Can Custom Container
391 Wolfland Rd (17837-7538)
PHONE..................................724 253-2038
Todd Vonderheid, *Manager*
EMP: 18
SALES (est): 962.8K **Privately Held**
SIC: 3443 Dumpsters, garbage

(G-9904)
D&E COMMUNICATIONS LLC
20 S 2nd St (17837-1902)
P.O. Box 350 (17837-0350)
PHONE..................................570 524-2200
Marcia Wolfe, *Branch Mgr*
EMP: 4
SALES (corp-wide): 5.7B **Publicly Held**
SIC: 3661 Telephones & telephone apparatus
HQ: D&E Communications, Llc
124 E Main St Fl 6
Ephrata PA 17522

(G-9905)
ELMWOOD
25 Cedar Dr (17837-7575)
PHONE..................................570 524-9663
Jacob A Riehl Jr, *President*
▲ EMP: 10
SQ FT: 15,000
SALES (est): 1.3MM **Privately Held**
SIC: 2499 2511 Shoe trees; wood lawn & garden furniture

(G-9906)
FEDERAL PRISON INDUSTRIES
Also Called: Unicor
2400 Robert F Miller Dr (17837-6850)
P.O. Box 1000 (17837-1000)
PHONE..................................570 524-0096
Ray Laws, *Superintendent*
EMP: 370 **Publicly Held**
WEB: www.unicor.gov
SIC: 2511 2542 2514 9223 Wood household furniture; partitions & fixtures, except wood; metal household furniture;
HQ: Federal Prison Industries, Inc
320 1st St Nw
Washington DC 20534
202 305-3500

(G-9907)
FERO VINEYARDS AND WINERY LLC
758 Moores School Rd (17837-7323)
PHONE..................................570 568-0846
Daneen K Zaleski, *Principal*
EMP: 10
SALES (est): 867.1K **Privately Held**
SIC: 2084 Wines

(G-9908)
FOGLE FOREST PRODUCTS
521 Hoffa Mill Rd (17837-6906)
PHONE..................................570 524-2580
Donald C Fogle, *Owner*
EMP: 4
SALES (est): 180K **Privately Held**
SIC: 2499 5989 Mulch or sawdust products, wood; mulch, wood & bark; coal

(G-9909)
FRANK GRIFFITH
Also Called: Frank Griffith Remdlng/Cstm CB
2297 Pheasant Ridge Rd (17837-7073)
PHONE..................................570 524-7175
Frank Griffith, *Owner*
EMP: 4
SQ FT: 2,500
SALES (est): 380K **Privately Held**
SIC: 1521 2434 General remodeling, single-family houses; wood kitchen cabinets

(G-9910)
FRIESENS WELDING
Also Called: Friesens Welding & Mfg
3266 Col John Kelly Rd (17837-7473)
PHONE..................................570 523-3580
Bernhard R Friesen, *Partner*
Marvin Peachey, *Partner*

EMP: 5
SALES: 120K **Privately Held**
SIC: 7692 Automotive welding

(G-9911)
HUNA DESIGNS LTD
1000 Buffalo Rd (17837-9702)
PHONE..................................570 522-9800
Matthew Miller, *President*
Kelly L Barrick, *Corp Secy*
Steve Malriat, *CFO*
EMP: 3
SQ FT: 1,000
SALES (est): 160K **Privately Held**
SIC: 3949 Playground equipment

(G-9912)
I FUEL
71 Walter Dr (17837-7400)
PHONE..................................570 524-6851
Usman Bajwa, *Manager*
EMP: 5
SALES (est): 399.7K **Privately Held**
SIC: 2869 Fuels

(G-9913)
JAMES A MARQUETTE
Also Called: Catherman's Home Made Candy
209 N Front St (17837-1509)
PHONE..................................570 523-3873
James A Marquette, *Owner*
EMP: 4
SQ FT: 6,000
SALES (est): 194.2K **Privately Held**
SIC: 5441 5145 2064 Candy, nut & confectionery stores; candy; chocolate candy, except solid chocolate; fudge (candy); nuts, candy covered

(G-9914)
KUHNS BROS LUMBER CO INC
434 Swartz Rd (17837-7659)
PHONE..................................570 568-1412
Leonard Kuhns, *President*
Timothy Kuhns, *Corp Secy*
Thomas Kuhns, *Vice Pres*
Vicki Hoffman, *Accounting Mgr*
David Kuhns, *Asst Treas*
▼ EMP: 50
SQ FT: 2,200
SALES (est): 8.3MM **Privately Held**
WEB: www.kuhnsbroslumber.com
SIC: 2421 2448 2499 Lumber: rough, sawed or planed; planing mills; pallets; wood; mulch, wood & bark

(G-9915)
LOCAL MEDIA GROUP INC
Also Called: Daily Item
328 Market St Ste 4 (17837-2404)
PHONE..................................570 524-2261
EMP: 5
SALES (corp-wide): 1.2B **Publicly Held**
SIC: 2711 Newspaper
HQ: Local Media Group, Inc.
40 Mulberry St
Middletown NY 10940
845 341-1100

(G-9916)
PLAYPOWER INC
Also Called: Playworld
1000 Buffalo Rd (17837-9702)
PHONE..................................570 522-9800
Matthew Miller, *Manager*
EMP: 300 **Publicly Held**
SIC: 3949 Playground equipment
HQ: Playpower, Inc.
11515 Vanstory Dr Ste 100
Huntersville NC 28078
704 875-6550

(G-9917)
PLAYWORLD SYSTEMS INCORPORATED (DH)
Also Called: Playword
1000 Buffalo Rd (17837-9795)
PHONE..................................570 522-5435
Dale Miller, *President*
Karla Cooper, *Treasurer*
◆ EMP: 29 EST: 1952
SQ FT: 260,000
SALES: 65MM **Publicly Held**
WEB: www.playworldsystems.com
SIC: 3949 Playground equipment

HQ: Playpower, Inc.
11515 Vanstory Dr Ste 100
Huntersville NC 28078
704 875-6550

(G-9918)
R R DONNELLEY & SONS COMPANY
Also Called: Moore Document Solutions
1601 Industrial Blvd (17837-1274)
PHONE..................................570 524-2224
Ed Rigby, *Branch Mgr*
EMP: 182
SALES (corp-wide): 6.8B **Publicly Held**
WEB: www.rrdonnelley.com
SIC: 2752 Commercial printing, lithographic
PA: R. R. Donnelley & Sons Company
35 W Wacker Dr Ste 3650
Chicago IL 60601
312 326-8000

(G-9919)
STOLTZFUS STEEL MANUFACTURING
Also Called: Stolzfus Transport
391 Wolfland Rd (17837-7538)
PHONE..................................570 524-7835
Daniel K Stolzfus, *Owner*
EMP: 6
SQ FT: 6,000
SALES (est): 823K **Privately Held**
SIC: 3443 Dumpsters, garbage

(G-9920)
SUSQUEHANNA LIFE MAGAZINE
217 Market St (17837-1543)
P.O. Box 421 (17837-0421)
PHONE..................................570 522-0149
Erica Shanes, *Owner*
EMP: 3
SALES (est): 251K **Privately Held**
WEB: www.susquehannalife.com
SIC: 2721 Magazines: publishing only, not printed on site

(G-9921)
TILO INDUSTRIES
2738 Buffalo Rd (17837-7726)
PHONE..................................570 524-9990
Timothy Yoder, *Partner*
Linus Yoder, *Opers Staff*
Keith Bingaman, *Office Mgr*
David Swartzentruber, *Office Mgr*
EMP: 23
SQ FT: 16,207
SALES (est): 3.4MM **Privately Held**
WEB: www.tiloindustries.com
SIC: 2431 Millwork

(G-9922)
TIMBERHAVEN LOG HOMES LLC
434a Swartz Rd (17837-7659)
PHONE..................................570 568-1422
Joseph Folker, *Principal*
Glenn Salsman, *Controller*
▼ EMP: 15 EST: 2013
SALES (est): 2.5MM **Privately Held**
SIC: 2452 5099 Farm buildings, prefabricated or portable: wood; timber products, rough

(G-9923)
VARGO OUTDOORS INCORPORATED
214 Market St Rear (17837-1544)
PHONE..................................570 437-0990
Brian Vargo, *President*
Chad North, *Marketing Staff*
▲ EMP: 3
SQ FT: 8,000
SALES: 1.1MM **Privately Held**
SIC: 3356 Battery metal

Lewistown
Mifflin County

(G-9924)
ALLENSVILLE PLANING MILL INC
Also Called: APM Home Center
101 Kish Pike (17044-1368)
PHONE..................................717 248-9688
Dave Strouse, *Manager*
EMP: 17
SALES (corp-wide): 47.3MM **Privately Held**
WEB: www.apm-inc.net
SIC: 5211 1521 2431 Millwork & lumber; single-family housing construction; millwork
PA: Allensville Planing Mill, Inc.
108 E Main St
Allensville PA 17002
717 483-6386

(G-9925)
CHESTER A ASHER INC
19 Susquehanna Ave (17044-2332)
PHONE..................................717 248-8613
John L Asher Jr, *Branch Mgr*
EMP: 5
SALES (corp-wide): 23MM **Privately Held**
SIC: 2064 Candy & other confectionery products
PA: Chester A. Asher, Inc.
80 Wambold Rd
Souderton PA 18964
215 721-3000

(G-9926)
CLELAN INDUSTRIES INC
600 Middle Rd (17044-8051)
PHONE..................................717 248-5061
Gerald B Clelan, *President*
Beverly Clelan, *Vice Pres*
EMP: 7
SALES: 700K **Privately Held**
SIC: 3949 Lures, fishing: artificial

(G-9927)
COLLINS TOOL CORPORATION
3254 Old Stage Rd (17044-7632)
PHONE..................................717 543-6070
Patty Rhodes, *Manager*
EMP: 22
SALES (est): 3.4MM **Privately Held**
SIC: 2421 Sawmills & planing mills, general

(G-9928)
FIRST QUALITY BABY PDTS LLC
97 Locust Rd (17044-9340)
PHONE..................................717 247-3516
Julie Rogers, *Human Resources*
Nader Damaghi,
Babak Damaghi,
Kambiz Damaghi,
Karen Molek,
◆ EMP: 800
SALES (est): 228.8MM **Privately Held**
SIC: 2676 Diapers, paper (disposable): made from purchased paper
PA: First Quality Enterprises Inc
80 Cuttermill Rd Ste 500
Great Neck NY 11021

(G-9929)
FOXPRO INC
14 Fox Hollow Dr (17044-2763)
PHONE..................................717 248-2507
John C Dillon, *President*
Mike Dillon, *General Mgr*
Tom Steel, *Prdtn Mgr*
Corrinne Pierce, *Controller*
Sue Burge, *Manager*
▲ EMP: 35
SQ FT: 40,000
SALES (est): 7.7MM **Privately Held**
WEB: www.gofoxpro.com
SIC: 3949 Game calls

(G-9930)
FREEDOM COMPONENTS INC
262 Roundhouse Rd (17044-7846)
PHONE..................................717 242-0101

Norita J Rowe, *President*
David L Rowe, *President*
EMP: 6
SQ FT: 15,000
SALES (est): 679.4K **Privately Held**
SIC: 3599 3541 3441 3451 Machine shop, jobbing & repair; machine tools, metal cutting type; fabricated structural metal; screw machine products; metal stampings; sheet metalwork

(G-9931)
FREEDOM TECHNOLOGIES INC
855 Roundhouse Rd (17044-2406)
PHONE...................................717 242-0101
Jean A Daer, *President*
EMP: 9
SALES (est): 1.5MM **Privately Held**
SIC: 3599 Machine shop, jobbing & repair

(G-9932)
GARY FOSTER
Also Called: Foster's Monuments
702 W 4th St (17044-1901)
PHONE...................................717 248-5322
Gary Foster, *Owner*
EMP: 4
SALES (est): 320K **Privately Held**
SIC: 3281 Monuments, cut stone (not finishing or lettering only)

(G-9933)
GUARDIAN INDUSTRIES LLC
Also Called: Guardian Auto Glass
6395 State Route 103 N # 35
(17044-7899)
PHONE...................................717 242-2571
Tim Wilkins, *Manager*
EMP: 90
SALES (corp-wide): 42.4B **Privately Held**
WEB: www.guardian.com
SIC: 3211 Flat glass
HQ: Guardian Industries, Llc
2300 Harmon Rd
Auburn Hills MI 48326
248 340-1800

(G-9934)
HARTLEYS POTATO CHIP MFG
2157 Back Maitland Rd (17044-7311)
PHONE...................................717 248-0526
Carl Hartley, *President*
Kellie Johnson, *Corp Secy*
Daniel Hartley, *Vice Pres*
EMP: 12 **EST:** 1934
SALES (est): 1.8MM **Privately Held**
WEB: www.hartleyschips.com
SIC: 2096 Potato chips & other potato-based snacks

(G-9935)
HAWSTONE HOLLOW WINERY LLC
11 Hawstone Rd (17044-7812)
PHONE...................................717 953-9613
Mary Naylor, *Manager*
EMP: 4 **EST:** 2013
SALES (est): 107.8K **Privately Held**
SIC: 2084 5921 Wines; wine

(G-9936)
IRA MIDDLESWARTH AND SON INC
520 Princeton St (17044-1661)
PHONE...................................717 248-3093
EMP: 3
SALES (est): 137.2K **Privately Held**
SIC: 2096 Potato chips & similar snacks

(G-9937)
JUNIATA CONCRETE CO
2 Silversand Ave (17044-1962)
PHONE...................................717 248-9677
Jo Patkalitsky, *Manager*
EMP: 6
SALES (corp-wide): 6.3MM **Privately Held**
SIC: 3273 5999 Ready-mixed concrete; concrete products, pre-cast
PA: Juniata Concrete Co.
721 Smith Rd
Mifflintown PA 17059
717 436-2176

(G-9938)
LEWISTOWN MANUFACTURING INC
1 Belle Ave Bldg 1 # 1 (17044-2432)
P.O. Box 146 (17044-0146)
PHONE...................................717 242-1468
David O'Hayon, *President*
Vince Snyder, *General Mgr*
EMP: 12
SQ FT: 5,500
SALES: 1MM **Privately Held**
SIC: 3469 Stamping metal for the trade

(G-9939)
LEWISTOWN SENTINEL INC
Also Called: Infoline
375 6th St (17044-1233)
PHONE...................................717 248-6741
Jay McCaulley, *Principal*
Michele Jordan, *Admin Asst*
EMP: 11
SALES (est): 777.7K **Privately Held**
SIC: 2711 Newspapers, publishing & printing

(G-9940)
NITTANY PAPER MILLS INC
Also Called: NP
6395 State Route 103 N (17044-7899)
PHONE...................................888 288-7907
Dave Fowler, *Plant Mgr*
Kevin Dressler, *Engineer*
Patrick Stewart, *CFO*
Emily Royer, *Sales Dir*
Chris Tressler, *Accounts Mgr*
◆ **EMP:** 63
SQ FT: 120,000
SALES (est): 21.3MM **Privately Held**
WEB: www.nittanypapermills.com
SIC: 2621 Paper mills

(G-9941)
OGDEN NEWSPAPERS OF PA
Also Called: The Sentinel
352 6th St (17044-1213)
P.O. Box 588 (17044-0588)
PHONE...................................717 248-6741
EMP: 70
SALES (est): 4.3MM
SALES (corp-wide): 683.9MM **Privately Held**
SIC: 2711 Newspapers-Publishing & Printing
PA: The Ogden Newspapers Inc
1500 Main St
Wheeling WV 26003
304 233-0100

(G-9942)
OVERHEAD DOOR CORPORATION
23 Industrial Park Rd (17044-9337)
P.O. Box 110 (17044-0110)
PHONE...................................717 248-0131
Brad Kanble, *Manager*
EMP: 500
SQ FT: 8,000
SALES (corp-wide): 3.6B **Privately Held**
WEB: www.overheaddoor.com
SIC: 1751 2431 Garage door, installation or erection; doors, wood
HQ: Overhead Door Corporation
2501 S State Hwy 121 Ste
Lewisville TX 75067
469 549-7100

(G-9943)
PENN STATE CNSTR J&D LLC
27 State St (17044-1974)
PHONE...................................717 953-9200
David Miller,
Jason Miller,
John Miller,
EMP: 5
SALES (est): 2.4MM **Privately Held**
SIC: 3448 1542 1521 Buildings, portable: prefabricated metal; commercial & office building contractors; commercial & office buildings, renovation & repair; single-family housing construction

(G-9944)
PENNSYLVANIA INSULATING GLASS
6395 State Route 103 N (17044-7899)
PHONE...................................717 247-0560
Dave Newlen, *Opers Mgr*
EMP: 13
SALES (est): 2.1MM **Privately Held**
WEB: www.pennsylvaniaig.com
SIC: 3211 Flat glass

(G-9945)
RAM-WOOD CUSTOM CABINETRY LLC
6395 Belle Ave Ste 1 (17044)
PHONE...................................717 242-6357
Ryan Benny,
EMP: 9
SQ FT: 6,500
SALES: 380K **Privately Held**
SIC: 2434 Wood kitchen cabinets

(G-9946)
RECOGNITION ENGRAVING (PA)
100 S Main St (17044-2154)
PHONE...................................717 242-1166
Ruth H Raup, *Owner*
EMP: 4
SALES (est): 284.6K **Privately Held**
WEB: www.recognition-engraving.com
SIC: 5999 3555 Trophies & plaques; printing trades machinery

(G-9947)
RYAN KANASKIE
306 Country Club Rd (17044-8022)
PHONE...................................717 248-9822
Ryan Kanaskie, *Principal*
EMP: 3 **EST:** 2011
SALES (est): 324.3K **Privately Held**
SIC: 3949 Shafts, golf club

(G-9948)
SPIGELMYER WOOD PRODUCTS INC
2316 Hawstone Rd (17044-7828)
PHONE...................................717 248-6555
Toby Spigelmyer, *President*
Beth Spigelmyer, *Admin Sec*
EMP: 13
SQ FT: 3,000
SALES (est): 1.6MM **Privately Held**
SIC: 2421 2411 Sawmills & planing mills, general; logging

(G-9949)
TN TS
9210 Us Highway 522 S (17044-8910)
PHONE...................................717 248-2278
Tom Shirey, *Principal*
EMP: 3
SALES (est): 254.7K **Privately Held**
SIC: 2759 Screen printing

(G-9950)
TRINITY PLASTICS INC
13 Industrial Park Rd (17044-9342)
PHONE...................................717 242-2355
Dale Ridenour, *Manager*
EMP: 323 **Privately Held**
SIC: 2673 Plastic bags: made from purchased materials
HQ: Trinity Plastics Inc.
9 Peach Tree Hill Rd
Livingston NJ 07039
973 994-8018

Liberty
Tioga County

(G-9951)
BUTTONWOOD LUMBER COMPANY INC
1418 Beuterstown Rd (16930-9287)
PHONE...................................570 324-3421
Arthur W Ulmer, *President*
Kathy R Ulmer, *Treasurer*
EMP: 5
SALES (est): 350K **Privately Held**
SIC: 2421 Sawmills & planing mills, general

(G-9952)
WHEELAND LUMBER CO INC
3558 Williamson Trl (16930-9065)
PHONE...................................570 324-6042
Ray E Wheeland, *President*
Regina Wheeland, *Vice Pres*
Mark Dibble, *Project Mgr*
Kathy Price, *CFO*
Chris Kemp, *Sales Staff*
◆ **EMP:** 70
SQ FT: 5,000
SALES (est): 13MM **Privately Held**
WEB: www.wheelandlumber.com
SIC: 2421 2426 Lumber: rough, sawed or planed; kiln drying of lumber; hardwood dimension & flooring mills

---

Library
Allegheny County

(G-9953)
AD POST GRAPHICS INC
6321 Library Rd Bldg 2 (15129-8502)
P.O. Box 300 (15129-0300)
PHONE...................................412 405-9163
Mary C Staley, *CEO*
EMP: 13
SALES (est): 2.1MM **Privately Held**
WEB: www.adpostgraphics.com
SIC: 2752 Commercial printing, offset

(G-9954)
DYNAMIC SYSTEMS
6420 Pleasant St (15129-9717)
PHONE...................................412 835-6100
Roger Oldaker, *President*
EMP: 10 **EST:** 2001
SALES (est): 1.2MM **Privately Held**
SIC: 2759 2752 Commercial printing; color lithography

(G-9955)
JOSEPH RIEPOLE CONSTRUCTION
2728 Gould Dr (15129-8560)
PHONE...................................412 833-6611
Joseph Riepole, *Owner*
EMP: 4
SALES (est): 262.7K **Privately Held**
SIC: 1771 3272 Concrete work; cast stone, concrete

Ligonier
Westmoreland County

(G-9956)
A BETTER POWER LLC
116 Timberlane Dr (15658-9720)
PHONE...................................412 498-6537
Julius Vrana,
William Gimmos,
Deg Walters,
EMP: 3
SALES (est): 160.1K **Privately Held**
SIC: 2842 7389 Specialty cleaning preparations;

(G-9957)
ARC DIAMOND TOOLING
494 Bethel Church Rd (15658-2075)
PHONE...................................724 593-5814
Roger Lenhart, *Owner*
Lenita Lenhart, *Co-Owner*
EMP: 4
SALES (est): 210K **Privately Held**
SIC: 3545 Diamond cutting tools for turning, boring, burnishing, etc.

(G-9958)
COAL LOADERS INC
210 E Main St (15658-1318)
P.O. Box 346 (15658-0346)
PHONE...................................724 238-6601
G Gray Garland, *Ch of Bd*
James W Cooper, *President*
Donald Lupyan, *Vice Pres*
Mark Klonicke, *Buyer*
Debra Oyler, *Admin Sec*
EMP: 13

SALES (est): 2.2MM **Privately Held**
SIC: **1221** 4789 Coal preparation plant, bituminous or lignite; car loading

(G-9959)
INDEPENDENT-OBSERVER
Also Called: Laurel Group Newspapers
112 W Main St (15658-1243)
PHONE..................................724 238-2111
Richard Schwarb, *Manager*
EMP: 4
SALES (corp-wide): 4.3MM **Privately Held**
SIC: **2711** Newspapers
PA: Independent-Observer
228 Pittsburgh St
Scottdale PA 15683
724 887-7400

(G-9960)
KENCO CONSTRUCTION PDTS INC
170 State Route 271 (15658-2677)
P.O. Box 576 (15658-0576)
PHONE..................................724 238-3387
William Douglas, *President*
Helen Marie Douglas, *Treasurer*
Daun Palmer, *Office Mgr*
Michael Scott Douglas, *Admin Sec*
EMP: 15
SQ FT: 3,000
SALES (est): 2.9MM **Privately Held**
WEB: www.kenco.com
SIC: **3531** Construction machinery

(G-9961)
LIGONIER OUTFITTERS NEWSSTANDS
Also Called: Ligonier Newsstand
127 W Main St (15658-1252)
PHONE..................................724 238-4900
Danny McMaster, *Owner*
EMP: 3
SQ FT: 9,000
SALES (est): 300K **Privately Held**
SIC: **2678** 5251 5994 Newsprint tablets & pads; made from purchased materials; hardware; news dealers & newsstands

(G-9962)
OSCAR & BANKS LLC
110 Maple Dr (15658-8745)
PHONE..................................701 922-1005
Einar Sigurdsson,
EMP: 4 EST: 2017
SALES (est): 116.1K **Privately Held**
SIC: **2047** 5149 Dog food; dog food

(G-9963)
PATRICK DONOVAN
105 Deerfield Rd (15658-9714)
PHONE..................................724 238-9038
Patrick Donovan, *Principal*
EMP: 3 EST: 2010
SALES (est): 236K **Privately Held**
SIC: **2491** 4212 2411 Structural lumber & timber, treated wood; lumber (log) trucking, local; logging

(G-9964)
ROYAL WELSH WINERY
125 W Main St (15658-1394)
PHONE..................................724 396-7560
Renee Downing, *Principal*
EMP: 4
SALES (est): 174.4K **Privately Held**
SIC: **2084** Wines

(G-9965)
SLC SALES AND SERVICE INC
132 Presidents Dr (15658-8525)
PHONE..................................724 238-7692
Jeffrey Cmar, *President*
Julie Leblanc, *Vice Pres*
EMP: 3
SQ FT: 4,000
SALES (est): 210K **Privately Held**
SIC: **3089** Blow molded finished plastic products

(G-9966)
STONEBRAKER JOHN
Also Called: Stonebraker's Jewelers
946 Bridlewood Ln (15658-2671)
PHONE..................................724 238-6466

John Stonebraker, *Owner*
EMP: 3
SQ FT: 2,000
SALES: 177K **Privately Held**
WEB: www.stoney-designs.com
SIC: **5944** 7631 3911 Jewelry stores; jewelry repair services; jewelry, precious metal

(G-9967)
THOMAS GROSS WOODWORKING
135 Greenbriar Dr (15658-2138)
PHONE..................................724 593-7044
Thomas Gross, *Owner*
EMP: 3
SALES: 150K **Privately Held**
SIC: **2426** 2431 5211 Flooring, hardwood; millwork; millwork & lumber

Limekiln
Berks County

(G-9968)
SHAPE TEC LTD
860 Limekiln Rd (19535)
PHONE..................................610 689-8940
William D Beards, *President*
▲ EMP: 8
SQ FT: 5,000
SALES: 2.5MM **Privately Held**
WEB: www.shapetec.com
SIC: **3089** Injection molding of plastics

Limerick
Montgomery County

(G-9969)
M & Q PLASTIC PRODUCTS CO (PA)
Also Called: Pan Saver
542 N Lewis Rd Ste 206 (19468-3521)
PHONE..................................484 369-8906
Iiichael Schmal, *President*
Curt Rubenstein, *Principal*
Ernie Bachert, *Vice Pres*
Tim Blucher, *Vice Pres*
John Menges, *Vice Pres*
▲ EMP: 12 EST: 1956
SQ FT: 80,000
SALES (est): 51MM **Privately Held**
WEB: www.pansaver.com
SIC: **3089** Blow molded finished plastic products

(G-9970)
MARINE ACQUISITION US INC
Also Called: Seastar Solutions
640 N Lewis Rd (19468-1228)
PHONE..................................610 495-7011
Juan Vargues, *CEO*
Dave Wolfe, *General Mgr*
Kimberly Koennecker, *Vice Pres*
Jeffrey Hoffman, *Design Engr*
Peter Kjellberg, *CFO*
▲ EMP: 43 EST: 2011
SALES (est): 117.9MM
SALES (corp-wide): 1.6B **Privately Held**
SIC: **3531** 5551 Marine related equipment; marine supplies & equipment
HQ: Dometic Sweden Ab
Hemvarnsgatan 156tr
Solna
850 102-500

(G-9971)
SEASTAR SOLUTIONS
640 N Lewis Rd (19468-1228)
PHONE..................................610 495-7011
EMP: 3
SALES (est): 97.2K **Privately Held**
SIC: **3625** Motor controls & accessories

(G-9972)
YARDE METALS INC
1200 Enterprise Dr (19468-4202)
PHONE..................................610 495-7545
EMP: 6

SALES (corp-wide): 11.5B **Publicly Held**
SIC: **5051** 3499 Metal wires, ties, cables & screening; safe deposit boxes or chests, metal
HQ: Yarde Metals, Inc.
45 Newell St
Southington CT 06489
860 406-6061

Lincoln University
Chester County

(G-9973)
COURTNEY METAL DESIGN
Also Called: Courtney Design
458 Elkdale Rd Fl 3 (19352-9730)
PHONE..................................610 932-6065
Courtney Peterson, *Owner*
Lee Peterson, *Vice Pres*
EMP: 8
SQ FT: 4,826
SALES (est): 799.8K **Privately Held**
WEB: www.courtneydesign.com
SIC: **3911** Jewelry, precious metal

(G-9974)
PROTOSTAR TECHNOLOGIES
202 S Deer Run Dr (19352-9108)
PHONE..................................484 988-0964
Jim Sullivan, *Mng Member*
EMP: 3
SALES: 100K **Privately Held**
SIC: **3081** Unsupported plastics film & sheet

(G-9975)
SNYDER & SONS TREE SURGEONS
480 Mount Hope Rd (19352-8910)
PHONE..................................610 932-2966
Steve Snyder, *Owner*
EMP: 3
SALES (est): 188.4K **Privately Held**
SIC: **2411** Logging

Line Lexington
Bucks County

(G-9976)
HOOD & SON INC
31 Maple Ave (18932-9508)
PHONE..................................215 822-5750
Barbara K Hood, *President*
Robert Hood, *General Mgr*
EMP: 6
SQ FT: 3,200
SALES: 180K **Privately Held**
SIC: **3599** Custom machinery; machine shop, jobbing & repair

(G-9977)
TRIJAY SYSTEMS INC
10 Maple Ave (18932-9508)
P.O. Box 109 (18932-0109)
PHONE..................................215 997-5833
Manuel Arevalo, *President*
Ken Radley, *Project Mgr*
Greg Kucza, *Manager*
Julie Tobias, *Admin Sec*
▲ EMP: 15 EST: 1980
SQ FT: 10,000
SALES (est): 4.1MM **Privately Held**
WEB: www.trijay.com
SIC: **3589** 8711 Sewage & water treatment equipment; engineering services

Linesville
Crawford County

(G-9978)
BUCKEYE ALUMINUM FOUNDRY INC
5906 W Center Rd (16424-7752)
PHONE..................................814 683-4011
Peter S Otterman, *President*
EMP: 25

SALES (corp-wide): 2MM **Privately Held**
WEB: www.buckeyealuminum.com
SIC: **3365** Aluminum & aluminum-based alloy castings
PA: Buckeye Aluminum Foundry, Inc.
457 N Lake St
Madison OH 44057
440 428-7180

(G-9979)
COMMUNITY NEWSPAPER
109 N Mercer St (16424-9229)
P.O. Box 451 (16424-0451)
PHONE..................................814 683-4841
David Schaef, *Owner*
EMP: 6
SALES: 100K **Privately Held**
SIC: **2711** Newspapers, publishing & printing

(G-9980)
DICK WARNER SALES & CONTG
17385 Tighe Rd (16424-7030)
PHONE..................................814 683-4606
Dick Warner, *Principal*
EMP: 3
SALES (est): 167.9K **Privately Held**
SIC: **2448** Wood pallets & skids

(G-9981)
HEWLETT MANUFACTURING CO
Also Called: Jewelstik
7343 Harmonsburg Rd (16424-8235)
P.O. Box 100 (16424-0100)
PHONE..................................814 683-4762
Lloyd Hewlett, *President*
Brian Hewlett, *Vice Pres*
EMP: 6 EST: 1975
SQ FT: 7,200
SALES (est): 951.2K **Privately Held**
WEB: www.jewelstik.com
SIC: **3545** 3423 3291 Shaping tools (machine tool accessories); hand & edge tools; abrasive products

(G-9982)
HIMES MACHINE INC
9842 Espy Rd (16424-3530)
PHONE..................................724 927-6850
Michael Himes, *President*
Melanie Himes, *Corp Secy*
Timothy Himes, *Vice Pres*
EMP: 12
SQ FT: 10,000
SALES: 1MM **Privately Held**
SIC: **3312** Tool & die steel

(G-9983)
HINES FLASK DIV BCKEYE ALNIMUM
5906 W Center Rd (16424-7752)
PHONE..................................814 683-4420
Chip Otterman, *Vice Pres*
EMP: 25
SALES (est): 2.6MM **Privately Held**
SIC: **3366** Copper foundries

(G-9984)
MOLDED FIBER GLASS COMPANIES
Molded Fiberglass Tray Co
6175 Us Highway 6 (16424-5921)
PHONE..................................814 683-4500
Tom Lezenhagen, *President*
Johnathan Thompson, *Mfg Spvr*
Robin Tighe, *Purch Mgr*
Mike Carr, *Manager*
Rob Prenatt, *Manager*
EMP: 150
SALES (corp-wide): 589.3MM **Privately Held**
WEB: www.moldedfiberglass.com
SIC: **3089** 3559 3537 2441 Plastic kitchenware, tableware & houseware; plastics working machinery; industrial trucks & tractors; nailed wood boxes & shook
PA: Molded Fiber Glass Companies
2925 Mfg Pl
Ashtabula OH 44004
440 997-5851

(G-9985)
MURPHY PRINTING FREE PRESS
1887 State Highway 285 (16424-4035)
PHONE.................................724 927-2222
Thomas M Murphy, *President*
EMP: 20
SQ FT: 3,600
SALES (est): 1.2MM **Privately Held**
SIC: 2752 Commercial printing, offset

(G-9986)
R-G-T PLASTICS COMPANY
600 Penn St (16424-9756)
P.O. Box 8 (16424-0008)
PHONE.................................814 683-2161
Robert Drnek, *President*
Thelma Drnek, *Vice Pres*
EMP: 6
SQ FT: 12,000
SALES (est): 909.3K **Privately Held**
SIC: 3089 Injection molding of plastics

Linfield
Montgomery County

(G-9987)
BENGAL CONVERTING SERVICES INC
1155 Main St (19468-1113)
PHONE.................................610 787-0900
Scott H Korn, *President*
Dylan O'Donnell, *VP Opers*
▲ EMP: 30
SQ FT: 250,000
SALES (est): 17.9MM **Privately Held**
WEB: www.bengalconverting.com
SIC: 2679 Paper products, converted

(G-9988)
BENGAL DIRECT LLC
1155 Main St (19468-1113)
PHONE.................................610 245-5901
Scott Korn, *President*
Arlene Korn,
EMP: 11
SQ FT: 125,000
SALES: 10MM **Privately Held**
SIC: 2679 Paperboard products, converted; paper products, converted

---

Linwood
Delaware County

(G-9989)
ESSCHEM INC (HQ)
Also Called: Estech Division
4000 Columbia Ave (19061-3925)
PHONE.................................610 497-9000
Michael D Norquist, *President*
Michael Getz, *Production*
Stephen H Morrison, *Treasurer*
John Burrell, *Sales Staff*
Stephen Height, *Manager*
▲ EMP: 80
SQ FT: 61,000
SALES (est): 13.4MM **Privately Held**
WEB: www.esschem.com
SIC: 2821 Plastics materials & resins

(G-9990)
MIMCO EQUIPMENT INC
1509 Chichester Ave (19061-4207)
PHONE.................................610 494-7400
Joseph D Melloni, *President*
Kenneth I Melloni, *Vice Pres*
Robert Melloni, *Treasurer*
Gloria Felicione, *Admin Sec*
EMP: 18
SQ FT: 5,000
SALES (est): 4.3MM **Privately Held**
WEB: www.mimcoequip.com
SIC: 5084 3612 Pumps & pumping equipment; power & distribution transformers

(G-9991)
SAI HYDRAULICS INC
168 E Ridge Rd Ste 106 (19061-4360)
PHONE.................................610 497-0190
Mariano Pecorari, *President*

Giuseppe Pecorari, *Vice Pres*
Shawn Warner, *Engineer*
▲ EMP: 20
SALES (est): 2.1MM **Privately Held**
WEB: www.saihyd.com
SIC: 3241 Cement, hydraulic

Lititz
Lancaster County

(G-9992)
ACORN PRESS INC
500 E Oregon Rd (17543-8398)
PHONE.................................717 569-3264
Donald Roseman, *Principal*
EMP: 4
SALES (est): 306.1K **Privately Held**
SIC: 2741 Miscellaneous publishing

(G-9993)
ALUMINUM 2000 INC
595 E Oregon Rd (17543-9201)
P.O. Box 1200, Charlestown NH (03603-1200)
PHONE.................................717 569-2300
Andrew H Secker, *President*
Marjorie Secker, *Corp Secy*
▲ EMP: 25
SQ FT: 30,000
SALES: 2.2MM **Privately Held**
SIC: 3442 Metal doors; screen & storm doors & windows

(G-9994)
BAKER BALLISTICS LLC
112 Koser Rd (17543-7605)
PHONE.................................717 625-2016
Gregory Stern, *General Mgr*
Richard Armellino, *General Mgr*
Richard A Armellino,
Stephen E Armellino,
Alfred J Baker,
▼ EMP: 15
SQ FT: 13,600
SALES: 900K **Privately Held**
WEB: www.bakerbatshield.com
SIC: 2399 Flags, fabric

(G-9995)
CAPRI CORK LLC
Also Called: Lititz Flooring Company
215 Bucky Dr (17543-7600)
PHONE.................................717 627-5701
Dave Cipalla, *Mng Member*
Margaret Buchholz,
▲ EMP: 13
SQ FT: 25,000
SALES: 11.5MM **Privately Held**
WEB: www.capricork.com
SIC: 3069 Flooring, rubber: tile or sheet

(G-9996)
CARPENTER CO
Also Called: Er Carpentry
400 Arrowhead Dr (17543-8703)
PHONE.................................717 627-1878
Gregg Austin, *General Mgr*
EMP: 18
SALES (corp-wide): 2B **Privately Held**
WEB: www.carpenter.com
SIC: 3086 Plastics foam products
PA: Carpenter Co.
5016 Monument Ave
Richmond VA 23230
804 359-0800

(G-9997)
CHELATE INCORPORATED
218 Ironstone Dr (17543-9468)
PHONE.................................717 203-0415
Lawrence Letch, *President*
EMP: 5
SALES (est): 290K **Privately Held**
SIC: 3499 Fabricated metal products

(G-9998)
CHROMA ACRYLICS INC
205 Bucky Dr (17543-7600)
PHONE.................................717 626-8866
James Cobb, *President*
Don Rossi, *Business Mgr*
Mark Kline, *Vice Pres*
Kathryn Betz, *Mktg Coord*

▲ EMP: 30
SQ FT: 34,000
SALES (est): 6.5MM **Privately Held**
WEB: www.chromaonline.com
SIC: 2851 Paints: oil or alkyd vehicle or water thinned
PA: Chroma Australia Pty Limited
17 Mundowi Rd
Mount Kuring-Gai NSW 2080

(G-9999)
CLASSIC FURNITURE (PA)
546c E 28th Division Hwy (17543-9766)
PHONE.................................717 738-0088
John Earl Hollinger, *Partner*
Jeremy Horst, *Partner*
EMP: 3
SALES (est): 419.7K **Privately Held**
SIC: 2511 Wood household furniture

(G-10000)
CLEMENTINES
695 Sue Dr (17543-8891)
PHONE.................................717 626-1378
Donna Grivin, *Owner*
EMP: 4
SALES (est): 243.3K **Privately Held**
SIC: 3111 Accessory products, leather

(G-10001)
CONDOR CORPORATION
Also Called: Keystone Pretzels
124 W Airport Rd (17543-7624)
PHONE.................................717 560-1882
George M Phillips, *President*
Shawn Cunningham, *Prdtn Mgr*
Mark Hasson, *Prdtn Mgr*
Bob Wenger, *Maint Spvr*
Lori Trostle, *Human Res Mgr*
▲ EMP: 110
SQ FT: 50,000
SALES (est): 19.2MM **Privately Held**
WEB: www.oatzels.com
SIC: 2052 Pretzels

(G-10002)
COOK & FREY INC
38 Wade Dr (17543-3110)
PHONE.................................717 336-1200
Ralph A Cook, *President*
Michael W Frey, *Vice Pres*
▲ EMP: 40
SQ FT: 70,000
SALES (est): 10.1MM **Privately Held**
WEB: www.integrityplastics.com
SIC: 3089 Injection molding of plastics

(G-10003)
CORNERSTONE PRINTING SERVICES
Also Called: Integra Graphics
160 Koser Rd (17543-9353)
PHONE.................................717 626-7895
Larry Hess, *President*
David Kunkle, *Accounts Mgr*
Linda Johnson, *Manager*
EMP: 4
SALES (est): 2MM **Privately Held**
WEB: www.printintegra.com
SIC: 2759 Commercial printing

(G-10004)
COUNTRYSIDE WOODCRAFTS INC
802 Scott Ln (17543-8866)
PHONE.................................717 627-5641
Brian Bomgardner, *President*
▲ EMP: 12
SALES (est): 1.1MM **Privately Held**
WEB: www.countrysidewoodcrafts.com
SIC: 2499 5712 Decorative wood & woodwork; furniture stores

(G-10005)
EDM CO
Also Called: Lititz Planing Mill Co
302 Front St (17543-1604)
PHONE.................................717 626-2186
Edward D Maley, *President*
Francis Musso, *Treasurer*
EMP: 22 EST: 1912
SQ FT: 20,000

SALES: 1.6MM **Privately Held**
SIC: 2431 3442 2541 2434 Planing mill, millwork; metal doors, sash & trim; wood partitions & fixtures; wood kitchen cabinets; sawmills & planing mills, general

(G-10006)
EMW INC
10 W 2nd Ave (17543-2304)
PHONE.................................717 626-0248
Charles Harach, *President*
Dennis Hollingsworth, *Vice Pres*
EMP: 10
SQ FT: 15,000
SALES (est): 920K **Privately Held**
SIC: 3646 3824 Fluorescent lighting fixtures, commercial; mechanical & electromechanical counters & devices

(G-10007)
FEEDMOBILE INC
727 Furnace Hills Pike (17543-9503)
PHONE.................................717 626-8318
Samuel E High Jr, *President*
John Withmyer, *Treasurer*
Betty M High, *Admin Sec*
EMP: 10
SQ FT: 12,600
SALES (est): 1.5MM **Privately Held**
WEB: www.feedmobile.com
SIC: 5999 5012 3523 Swimming pools, above ground; spas & hot tubs; truck bodies; feed grinders, crushers & mixers

(G-10008)
FLUID CONDITIONING PDTS INC
101 Warwick St (17543-1018)
P.O. Box 407 (17543-0407)
PHONE.................................717 627-1550
Karl K Reinhart, *CEO*
Susan E Niggel, *President*
Mary Asghar, *Buyer*
Galen Shaud, *Treasurer*
Tammy Johnson, *Manager*
EMP: 34
SQ FT: 48,000
SALES (est): 5.3MM **Privately Held**
WEB: www.fcp-filters.com
SIC: 7389 3569 Metal cutting services; filters

(G-10009)
FOUNDATION PRINT SOLUTIONS
304 Dorchester Dr (17543-8011)
PHONE.................................717 330-0544
Paul Mosser, *Owner*
EMP: 3
SALES (est): 197.3K **Privately Held**
SIC: 2752 Commercial printing, offset

(G-10010)
FOXS COUNTRY SHEDS
537 E 28th Division Hwy (17543-9766)
PHONE.................................717 626-9560
Adam Kontis, *Co-Owner*
Gennie Kontis, *Co-Owner*
EMP: 14
SQ FT: 15,000
SALES (est): 1.8MM **Privately Held**
WEB: www.foxsheds.com
SIC: 2452 5941 3949 Prefabricated buildings, wood; playground equipment; playground equipment

(G-10011)
GAMUT ENTERPRISES INC
Also Called: Whiff Roasters
219 E Main St (17543-2011)
PHONE.................................717 627-5282
Peggy Woods, *President*
Dennis Tessen, *Vice Pres*
EMP: 3
SQ FT: 1,900
SALES (est): 293.6K **Privately Held**
SIC: 2095 Roasted coffee

(G-10012)
GENENTECH
5 Meadowbrook Ln (17543-7928)
PHONE.................................717 572-8001
EMP: 3
SALES (est): 179.5K **Privately Held**
SIC: 2834 Pharmaceutical preparations

(G-10013)
GRAYBILL MACHINES INC
221 W Lexington Rd (17543-9412)
PHONE...................................717 626-5221
David D Fyock, *President*
Karl Popma, *Engineer*
Don Winger, *Engineer*
Tyler Newswanger, *Design Engr*
Rob Wolfgang, *Sales Engr*
EMP: 20
SALES (est): 4.9MM **Privately Held**
WEB: www.graybillmachines.com
SIC: 3556 Food products machinery

(G-10014)
HENRY H ROSS & SON INC
121 Koser Rd (17543-7602)
PHONE...................................717 626-6268
James H Ross, *President*
Michael Ross, *Vice Pres*
EMP: 30 EST: 1982
SQ FT: 8,000
SALES (est): 4.1MM **Privately Held**
WEB: www.hhross.com
SIC: 1799 2541 Kitchen cabinet installation; counter & sink tops

(G-10015)
HENRY S ESH
95 W Newport Rd (17543-9427)
PHONE...................................717 627-2585
Henry Esh, *Principal*
EMP: 6
SQ FT: 3,168
SALES (est): 320K **Privately Held**
SIC: 3272 Concrete products

(G-10016)
HERR INDUSTRIAL INC (PA)
610 E Oregon Rd (17543-8435)
P.O. Box 5249, Lancaster (17606-5249)
PHONE...................................717 569-6619
Timothy Herr, *Ch of Bd*
Thomas Herr, *President*
Chris Herr, *COO*
Kent Kise, *COO*
Mike Lightner, *Safety Mgr*
▼ EMP: 45
SQ FT: 27,000
SALES: 6MM **Privately Held**
WEB: www.herrindustrial.com
SIC: 3559 1796 Paint making machinery; machine moving & rigging

(G-10017)
HIGHWAY MATERIALS INC
859 Woodcrest Ave (17543-8765)
PHONE...................................717 626-8571
Ron Fleagle, *Superintendent*
EMP: 5
SALES (corp-wide): 10.1MM **Privately Held**
WEB: www.highwaymaterials.com
SIC: 2951 Asphalt & asphaltic paving mixtures (not from refineries)
PA: Highway Materials, Inc.
    409 Stenton Ave
    Flourtown PA 19031
    610 832-8000

(G-10018)
HOT SAUCE SPOT LLC
9 Owl Hill Rd (17543-8685)
PHONE...................................717 341-7573
Wesley Blount,
EMP: 5
SALES (est): 15.8K **Privately Held**
SIC: 2033 Canned fruits & specialties

(G-10019)
INTEGRA GRAPHIX INC
Also Called: Integra Graphics Synergy
160 Koser Rd (17543-9353)
PHONE...................................717 626-7895
Larry Hess, *President*
Kerry Lodish, *Vice Pres*
Eric Gearhart, *Manager*
EMP: 5
SALES (est): 605.4K **Privately Held**
SIC: 2759 7389 Commercial printing; printing broker

(G-10020)
J & J PRECISION TECH LLC
10 W 2nd Ave (17543-2304)
PHONE...................................717 625-0130

Jody Brown, *Principal*
EMP: 12
SALES (est): 1.9MM **Privately Held**
SIC: 3451 Screw machine products

(G-10021)
KEYSTONE KOATING LLC (HQ)
295 Wood Corner Rd (17543-9165)
PHONE...................................717 738-2148
Sylvan Martin, *Purchasing*
Richard Gehman,
EMP: 22
SALES (est): 5.5MM
SALES (corp-wide): 49.8MM **Privately Held**
SIC: 3479 Coating of metals & formed products
PA: Paul B Zimmerman Inc
    50 Wood Corner Rd
    Lititz PA 17543
    717 738-0380

(G-10022)
LIME ROCK GAZEBOS LLC
33 Limerock Rd (17543-8751)
PHONE...................................717 625-4066
Ben Stoltzfus,
Eli Stoltzfus,
EMP: 5
SQ FT: 6,000
SALES (est): 500K **Privately Held**
SIC: 2511 Wood lawn & garden furniture

(G-10023)
LITITZ RECORD EXPRESS INC
22 E Main St (17543-1947)
P.O. Box 366 (17543-0366)
PHONE...................................717 626-2191
Robert G Campbell, *President*
Mike Steis, *President*
Bill Burgess, *Manager*
Lucinda T Campbell, *Admin Sec*
EMP: 6 EST: 1870
SQ FT: 18,000
SALES (est): 312.6K **Privately Held**
SIC: 2711 Newspapers: publishing only, not printed on site

(G-10024)
LITITZ SIGN COMPANY
400 N Cedar St Rear (17543-1154)
PHONE...................................717 626-7715
Thomas Benjamin, *Owner*
EMP: 5
SQ FT: 3,000
SALES: 85K **Privately Held**
WEB: www.lititzsignco.com
SIC: 3993 Electric signs

(G-10025)
NEVCO SERVICE CO LLC
102 Chestnut St (17543-8926)
PHONE...................................717 626-1479
Nevin Martin, *Mng Member*
EMP: 5
SALES: 1.2MM **Privately Held**
SIC: 3585 Heating & air conditioning combination units

(G-10026)
NOLT SERVICES LLC
Also Called: Nolt's Services
728 Rettew Mill Rd (17543-9163)
PHONE...................................717 738-1066
Nelson Nolt, *Partner*
EMP: 7 EST: 1998
SQ FT: 2,544
SALES (est): 440K **Privately Held**
SIC: 1481 Pumping or draining, nonmetallic mineral mines

(G-10027)
OLIVE OLIO OILS AND BALSAMICS
41 S Broad St B (17543-1415)
PHONE...................................717 627-0088
Peter Desimone, *Vice Pres*
EMP: 3
SALES (est): 243.1K **Privately Held**
SIC: 2079 Olive oil

(G-10028)
PACK PRO TECHNOLOGIES LLC
204 Bucky Dr Ste A (17543-7695)
P.O. Box 5209, Lancaster (17606-5209)
PHONE...................................717 517-9065
Jarrett Chaffee,
EMP: 5
SALES (est): 967.4K **Privately Held**
SIC: 3565 Wrapping machines

(G-10029)
PBZ LLC
Also Called: Cropcare
295 Wood Corner Rd (17543-9165)
PHONE...................................800 578-1121
Richard Gehman, *President*
Mark Zimmerman, *President*
EMP: 37
SALES (est): 7.2MM
SALES (corp-wide): 40.6MM **Privately Held**
SIC: 3523 3479 3444 Dairy equipment (farm); lacquering of metal products; sheet metalwork
PA: Paul B Zimmerman Inc
    50 Wood Corner Rd
    Lititz PA 17543
    717 738-0380

(G-10030)
PENN MANUFACTURING
393 W Lexington Rd (17543-9439)
PHONE...................................717 626-8879
Mahlon S Martin, *Partner*
Claire Garman, *Partner*
Kenneth Kreider, *Partner*
Leonard Nolt, *Partner*
Lee Wagner, *Partner*
EMP: 5 EST: 1972
SQ FT: 14,000
SALES (est): 490K **Privately Held**
SIC: 3433 3537 Stoves, wood & coal burning; dollies (hand or power truck), industrial except mining

(G-10031)
PENNSYLVANIA FIREMAN INC
632 E Roegon Rd (17543)
PHONE...................................717 397-9174
Bill Hall, *President*
Ernest Rojohn, *Treasurer*
EMP: 10
SALES (est): 750K **Privately Held**
SIC: 2731 Book publishing

(G-10032)
PFIZER INC
400 W Lincoln Ave (17543-8701)
PHONE...................................717 627-2211
Paul Di Paolo, *Engineer*
David Burton, *Manager*
Jill Steinig, *Manager*
EMP: 875
SQ FT: 482,000
SALES (corp-wide): 53.6B **Publicly Held**
WEB: www.pfizer.com
SIC: 2834 Pharmaceutical preparations
PA: Pfizer Inc.
    235 E 42nd St
    New York NY 10017
    212 733-2323

(G-10033)
POMPANETTE LLC
Aluminum 2000
595 E Oregon Rd (17543-9201)
PHONE...................................717 569-2300
Andrew H Secker, *Manager*
EMP: 25
SALES (corp-wide): 24.8MM **Privately Held**
WEB: www.pompanette.com
SIC: 3442 Metal doors; screen & storm doors & windows
PA: Pompanette, Llc
    73 Southwest St
    Charlestown NH 03603
    717 569-2300

(G-10034)
POTS BY DEPERROT
201 S Locust St (17543-2108)
PHONE...................................717 627-6789
Steve Deperrot, *Owner*
EMP: 3

SALES: 50K **Privately Held**
SIC: 3269 Cookware: stoneware, coarse earthenware & pottery

(G-10035)
PRECISIONFORM INCORPORATED
148 W Airport Rd (17543-7624)
PHONE...................................717 560-7610
Rick Frey, *COO*
James G Corckran, *Vice Pres*
Steve Kleckner, *Purchasing*
Bill Guscott, *Engineer*
John C Corckran Jr, *Treasurer*
EMP: 100
SQ FT: 105,000
SALES (est): 25.2MM **Privately Held**
WEB: www.precisionform.com
SIC: 3451 Screw machine products

(G-10036)
PREMIER SCREEN PRINTING INC
519b Airport Rd (17543-9339)
PHONE...................................717 560-9088
Keith Parke, *President*
Marsha Parke, *Manager*
EMP: 8
SQ FT: 12,000
SALES (est): 662.7K **Privately Held**
SIC: 2759 Screen printing

(G-10037)
RECOVERY ENVIRONMENT INC
324 North Ln (17543-1611)
PHONE...................................717 625-0040
EMP: 4
SALES (est): 130.8K **Privately Held**
SIC: 2899

(G-10038)
RED ROSE CABINETRY
740 Rothsville Rd (17543-8504)
PHONE...................................717 625-4456
Carl Gehman, *Principal*
EMP: 8
SALES (est): 1MM **Privately Held**
SIC: 2434 Wood kitchen cabinets

(G-10039)
RED ROSE SCREEN PRTG AWRDS INC
30 Wright Ave (17543-9343)
PHONE...................................717 625-1581
Melissa A Walton, *Principal*
▲ EMP: 3
SALES (est): 375.6K **Privately Held**
SIC: 2759 Screen printing

(G-10040)
RENEWAL KOMBUCHA LLC
200 Leaman St (17543-1214)
PHONE...................................484 525-3575
EMP: 4
SALES (est): 253.4K **Privately Held**
SIC: 2086 Tea, iced: packaged in cans, bottles, etc.

(G-10041)
REPLICANT METALS
330 Snavely Mill Rd (17543-9623)
PHONE...................................717 626-1618
EMP: 4
SALES (est): 540.2K **Privately Held**
SIC: 3441 Fabricated structural metal

(G-10042)
ROCKY RIDGE STEEL LLC
Also Called: Leon O'Berholtzer
1501 E Newport Rd (17543-9118)
PHONE...................................717 626-0153
Leon O'Berholtzer,
EMP: 1
SALES: 1.4MM **Privately Held**
SIC: 3315 Steel wire & related products

(G-10043)
ROHRERS QUARRY INC (PA)
Also Called: Rohrer's Concrete
70 Lititz Rd (17543-9383)
P.O. Box 365 (17543-0365)
PHONE...................................717 626-9760
Wilbur G Rohrer, *President*
Travis Rohrer, *President*
Vernon O Martin, *Vice Pres*

Tom Kifolo, *CFO*
Timothy Rohrer, *Treasurer*
EMP: 95
SQ FT: 2,000
SALES (est): 22.4MM **Privately Held**
WEB: www.rohrersquarry.com
SIC: 1422 3273 3274 7549 Crushed & broken limestone; ready-mixed concrete; agricultural lime; automotive maintenance services

(G-10044)
ROHRERS QUARRY INC
16 Lititz Rd (17543-9383)
PHONE..............................717 626-9756
Wilbur Rohrer, *President*
EMP: 5
SALES (corp-wide): 22.4MM **Privately Held**
WEB: www.rohrersquarry.com
SIC: 1422 3273 Crushed & broken limestone; ready-mixed concrete
PA: Rohrer's Quarry, Inc.
　　70 Lititz Rd
　　Lititz PA 17543
　　717 626-9760

(G-10045)
SANITARY PROCESS SYSTEMS INC
945 Fruitville Pike (17543-9357)
PHONE..............................717 627-6630
Thomas M Fischer, *President*
Don Heinly, *General Mgr*
David Fink, *Vice Pres*
Dave Kazmerski, *Vice Pres*
EMP: 35
SQ FT: 20,000
SALES (est): 7MM **Privately Held**
WEB: www.sanitaryprocesssystems.com
SIC: 1799 3444 Welding on site; sheet metalwork

(G-10046)
SCHUYLKILL VALLEY SPORTS INC
701 S Broad St Ste B (17543-2804)
PHONE..............................717 627-0417
Scott Goebel, *Branch Mgr*
EMP: 82
SALES (corp-wide): 118.6MM **Privately Held**
SIC: 2759 5941 Screen printing; sporting goods & bicycle shops
PA: Schuylkill Valley Sports, Inc.
　　118 Industrial Dr Ste 1
　　Pottstown PA 19464
　　610 495-8813

(G-10047)
SENORET CHEMICAL COMPANY
69 N Locust St (17543-1714)
PHONE..............................717 626-2125
Miquel Nistal, *CEO*
▲ **EMP:** 40
SQ FT: 35,000
SALES (est): 4.7MM
SALES (corp-wide): 167.7MM **Privately Held**
WEB: www.terro.com
SIC: 2842 2879 Specialty cleaning, polishes & sanitation goods; insecticides & pesticides
HQ: Woodstream Corporation
　　69 N Locust St
　　Lititz PA 17543
　　717 626-2125

(G-10048)
SENSENICH PROPELLER COMPANY
519 Airport Rd (17543-9339)
PHONE..............................717 560-3711
Joe Maus, *President*
EMP: 20 **EST:** 1993
SALES (est): 3.1MM **Privately Held**
SIC: 3366 Propellers

(G-10049)
SENSENIGS SPOUTING
265 E Meadow Valley Rd (17543-9143)
PHONE..............................717 627-6886
Nelson Sensenig, *Owner*
EMP: 18
SQ FT: 18,000

SALES: 1.9MM **Privately Held**
SIC: 1761 3444 Gutter & downspout contractor; siding contractor; spouts, sheet metal

(G-10050)
SNAVELYS MILL INC (PA)
333 Snavely Mill Rd (17543-9624)
PHONE..............................717 626-6256
Douglas E Snavely, *President*
Daniel L Snavely, *Vice Pres*
David M Snavely, *Treasurer*
EMP: 3 **EST:** 1875
SQ FT: 10,000
SALES (est): 3.5MM **Privately Held**
SIC: 2041 Wheat flour

(G-10051)
TAIT TOWERS INC
9 Wynfield Dr (17543-8001)
PHONE..............................717 626-9571
Michael Tait, *CEO*
James Sairorth, *President*
Adam Davis, *Vice Pres*
Jennifer Spear, *Vice Pres*
Todd Vernon, *Project Mgr*
▲ **EMP:** 65
SQ FT: 40,000
SALES (est): 13.4MM **Privately Held**
SIC: 3999 3648 Theatrical scenery; lighting equipment

(G-10052)
TAIT TOWERS MANUFACTURING LLC
401 W Lincoln Ave (17543-8701)
PHONE..............................717 626-9571
Jim Love, *President*
Rowly Walker, *Sr Project Mgr*
Matthew Gola, *Manager*
EMP: 6
SALES (corp-wide): 5.5MM **Privately Held**
SIC: 3999 Barber & beauty shop equipment
PA: Tait Towers Manufacturing Llc
　　9 Wynfield Dr
　　Lititz PA 17543
　　717 626-9571

(G-10053)
TELL DOORS & WINDOWS LLC
18 Richard Dr (17543-7796)
PHONE..............................717 625-2990
Patrick Tell, *President*
EMP: 4
SALES (est): 421.5K **Privately Held**
SIC: 3442 Metal doors, sash & trim

(G-10054)
TELL MANUFACTURING INC (PA)
18 Richard Dr (17543-7796)
PHONE..............................717 625-2990
Patrick J Tell, *President*
Katie Smarilli, *Principal*
Jane Getz, *COO*
Kathleen Tell, *Vice Pres*
Thomas Gamon, *Finance*
◆ **EMP:** 35
SQ FT: 4,500
SALES (est): 9.5MM **Privately Held**
WEB: www.tellmfg.com
SIC: 3429 5031 Manufactured hardware (general); doors & windows; paneling, wood

(G-10055)
TSHUDY SNACKS INC
Also Called: Sturgis Pretzel Company
219 E Main St (17543-2011)
PHONE..............................717 626-4354
Tim Snyder, *President*
EMP: 16
SQ FT: 10,900
SALES (est): 2MM **Privately Held**
SIC: 2052 2099 Pretzels; food preparations

(G-10056)
UTC FIRE SEC AMERICAS CORP INC
40 Citation Ln (17543-7604)
PHONE..............................717 569-5797
Robert Hager, *General Mgr*

EMP: 150
SALES (corp-wide): 66.5B **Publicly Held**
SIC: 3861 Photographic equipment & supplies
HQ: Utc Fire & Security Americas Corporation, Inc.
　　8985 Town Center Pkwy
　　Lakewood Ranch FL 34202

(G-10057)
VERSATEK ENTERPRISES LLC
508 Front St (17543-1708)
PHONE..............................717 626-6390
Earl Furman, *President*
Ron Eshleman, *Materials Mgr*
Jacquelin Gumpper, *CFO*
EMP: 60 **EST:** 1998
SQ FT: 200,000
SALES (est): 11.8MM **Privately Held**
WEB: www.versatekllc.com
SIC: 2541 Display fixtures, wood

(G-10058)
WEEKLY PIPER LTD
112 S Spruce St (17543-1818)
PHONE..............................717 341-3726
David R Hughes, *Principal*
EMP: 3
SALES (est): 105.7K **Privately Held**
SIC: 2711 Newspapers

(G-10059)
WEST PHARMACEUTICAL SVCS INC
179 W Airport Rd (17543-9260)
PHONE..............................717 560-8460
Joel Worman, *Plant Mgr*
Pam Ruhl, *Controller*
EMP: 22
SALES (corp-wide): 1.7B **Publicly Held**
WEB: www.westpharma.com
SIC: 2834 Pharmaceutical preparations
PA: West Pharmaceutical Services, Inc.
　　530 Herman O West Dr
　　Exton PA 19341
　　610 594-2900

(G-10060)
WOODSTREAM CORPORATION (HQ)
69 N Locust St (17543-1714)
P.O. Box 327 (17543-0327)
PHONE..............................717 626-2125
Miguel A Nistal, *President*
Simon Ragdale, *Managing Dir*
Harry E Whaley, *Principal*
Andrew Church, *Exec VP*
Elizabeth Ricca, *Vice Pres*
◆ **EMP:** 49 **EST:** 1924
SQ FT: 150,000
SALES (est): 90.8MM
SALES (corp-wide): 167.7MM **Privately Held**
WEB: www.woodstream.com
SIC: 3496 Cages, wire; traps, animal & fish
PA: Brockway Moran & Partners, Inc.
　　225 Ne Mizner Blvd # 700
　　Boca Raton FL 33432
　　561 750-2000

(G-10061)
ZAREBA SYSTEMS INC (DH)
69 N Locust St (17543-1714)
PHONE..............................763 551-1125
Dale A Nordquist, *President*
Donald G Dalland, *Vice Pres*
John Kelnberger, *Vice Pres*
Jeffrey S Mathiesen, *CFO*
▼ **EMP:** 84 **EST:** 1960
SQ FT: 6,895
SALES (est): 11.6MM
SALES (corp-wide): 167.7MM **Privately Held**
WEB: www.wtrs.com
SIC: 3699 5065 Electric fence chargers; security control equipment & systems
HQ: Woodstream Corporation
　　69 N Locust St
　　Lititz PA 17543
　　717 626-2125

Littlestown
Adams County

(G-10062)
ADAMS COUNTY LASER LLC
1789 Frederick Pike (17340-9046)
PHONE..............................717 359-4030
David Updike, *Mng Member*
EMP: 4
SALES (est): 489.4K **Privately Held**
SIC: 3499 3541 Machine bases, metal; machine tools, metal cutting type

(G-10063)
BAR-RAY PRODUCTS INC
90 E Lakeview Dr (17340-1704)
PHONE..............................717 359-9100
Jeff Stein, *Principal*
Mary Stein, *Admin Sec*
▲ **EMP:** 70
SQ FT: 15,000
SALES (est): 13.8MM **Privately Held**
WEB: www.bar-ray.com
SIC: 3842 Radiation shielding aprons, gloves, sheeting, etc.

(G-10064)
BRANDT TOOL & DIE CO INC
1908 Frederick Pike (17340-9056)
P.O. Box 22 (17340-0022)
PHONE..............................717 359-5995
Brian Bixler, *President*
Zickie Brown, *Admin Sec*
EMP: 9 **EST:** 1945
SQ FT: 4,000
SALES (est): 1.3MM **Privately Held**
SIC: 3544 Special dies & tools

(G-10065)
CRAFT LITE INC
100 Craftway Dr (17340-1651)
PHONE..............................717 359-7131
Chris Hammelef, *Principal*
EMP: 3
SALES (est): 291.2K **Privately Held**
SIC: 3645 Residential lighting fixtures

(G-10066)
HAWK INDUSTRIES INC
1880 White Hall Rd (17340-9588)
P.O. Box 342 (17340-0342)
PHONE..............................717 359-4138
Fred E Clark, *President*
Scott Hawk, *General Mgr*
Larry Hawk, *Vice Pres*
EMP: 10
SQ FT: 6,000
SALES (est): 1.7MM **Privately Held**
WEB: www.therestaurantstore.com
SIC: 2599 Restaurant furniture, wood or metal

(G-10067)
HERITAGE GALLERY OF LACE & INT
Also Called: Quiltpatch Fabric Furn & Gifts
1897 Hanover Pike (17340-9608)
PHONE..............................717 359-4121
Lewis Hillard,
EMP: 5
SQ FT: 4,000
SALES (est): 468.3K **Privately Held**
SIC: 2395 5719 Quilting & quilting supplies; bedding (sheets, blankets, spreads & pillows); lighting, lamps & accessories; pictures & mirrors; wicker, rattan or reed home furnishings

(G-10068)
KEYSTONE MACHINE INC
115 Newark St (17340-1232)
PHONE..............................717 359-9256
Patrick J Sweeney Sr, *President*
Patrick J Sweeney, *Vice Pres*
▲ **EMP:** 25
SQ FT: 37,624
SALES (est): 5.2MM **Privately Held**
WEB: www.keystonemachine.com
SIC: 3451 3546 Screw machine products; power-driven handtools

▲ = Import ▼=Export
◆ =Import/Export

(G-10069)
LEE SANDUSKY CORPORATION (PA)
80 Keystone St (17340-1664)
PHONE.................................717 359-4111
Mitchell Liss, *President*
Mark Kelbaugh, *Manager*
▲ EMP: 45
SALES (est): 22.8MM **Privately Held**
SIC: 5021 2514 Furniture; metal household furniture

(G-10070)
LIBERTY VIEW CREAMERY LLC
467 Orphanage Rd (17340-9728)
PHONE.................................717 359-8206
Matt Carman, *Principal*
EMP: 4
SALES (est): 195.6K **Privately Held**
SIC: 2021 Creamery butter

(G-10071)
M & M TOOL & DIE INC (PA)
10 E King St (17340-1612)
PHONE.................................717 359-7178
Karl J Mullinix, *President*
Patricia Mullinix, *President*
EMP: 5 EST: 1972
SQ FT: 25,000
SALES: 1MM **Privately Held**
SIC: 3544 Special dies & tools

(G-10072)
M & M TOOL & DIE INC
10 E King St (17340-1612)
PHONE.................................717 359-7178
EMP: 4
SALES (corp-wide): 1MM **Privately Held**
SIC: 3544 Mfg Tool & Die
PA: M & M Tool & Die, Inc.
    10 E King St
    Littlestown PA 17340
    717 359-7178

(G-10073)
OFFICE MATS INC
51 N Queen St (17340-1336)
PHONE.................................717 359-9571
Lloyd R Harner Jr, *President*
EMP: 4
SALES: 150K **Privately Held**
SIC: 2273 Mats & matting

(G-10074)
P & L SPORTSWEAR INC
950 Bulk Plant Rd (17340-9653)
PHONE.................................717 359-9000
Luan Le, *President*
Phuong Le, *Vice Pres*
EMP: 3
SQ FT: 3,000
SALES: 600K **Privately Held**
WEB: www.plsportswear.com
SIC: 2353 2339 Hats & caps; women's & misses' outerwear

(G-10075)
PHILIPS-HADCO
100 Craftway Dr (17340-1651)
PHONE.................................717 359-7131
Felix Llibre, *Managing Dir*
Nashiba Mohammed, *Executive Asst*
EMP: 19 EST: 2017
SALES (est): 4.4MM **Privately Held**
SIC: 3645 Residential lighting fixtures

(G-10076)
ROCKAFELLOW JOHN
Also Called: Essential Images
382 Schottie Rd (17340-9748)
PHONE.................................717 359-4276
John Rockafellow, *Owner*
EMP: 4
SALES (est): 275K **Privately Held**
SIC: 5946 2231 Camera & photographic supply stores; weaving mill, broadwoven fabrics: wool or similar fabric

---

Liverpool
Perry County

(G-10077)
BAKER OUTLAW FUEL SYSTEMS
130 Peach Rd Apt A (17045-9246)
PHONE.................................717 795-9383
Steve Baker, *Manager*
EMP: 6
SALES (est): 465.2K **Privately Held**
SIC: 2869 Fuels

(G-10078)
HUNTER VALLEY WINERY
3 Orchard Rd (17045-9241)
PHONE.................................717 444-7211
William Kvaternik, *Owner*
EMP: 3
SQ FT: 2,000
SALES (est): 140K **Privately Held**
WEB: www.huntersvalleywines.com
SIC: 2084 5921 Wine cellars, bonded: engaged in blending wines; wine

(G-10079)
S S SALVAGE RECYCLING INC
600 Susquehanna Trl (17045-9177)
PHONE.................................717 444-0008
EMP: 13 EST: 2013
SALES (est): 2.7MM **Privately Held**
SIC: 4953 5093 3547 Refuse System Whol Scrap/Waste Material Mfg Rolling Mill Machinery

(G-10080)
WEAVER SAWMILL
305 Sawmill Rd (17045-8526)
PHONE.................................570 539-8420
Steve Weaver, *Owner*
Stephen Weaver, *Partner*
EMP: 12
SQ FT: 5,000
SALES: 104K **Privately Held**
WEB: www.mywebpage.net
SIC: 5031 2448 Lumber, plywood & millwork; wood pallets & skids

---

Lock Haven
Clinton County

(G-10081)
ADDIES INC
Also Called: Addie's Jewels
202 E Main St (17745-1312)
PHONE.................................570 748-2966
Peter Rinella Sr, *President*
Anthony Rinella III, *Corp Secy*
Adeline M Rinella, *Vice Pres*
EMP: 6
SQ FT: 10,000
SALES (est): 700K **Privately Held**
SIC: 5944 3479 Jewelry stores; engraving jewelry silverware, or metal

(G-10082)
ADDIES AWARDS & PRINTING LLC
125 E Main St (17745-1322)
PHONE.................................570 484-9060
Steve Brion, *Mng Member*
Deanna Heggen Staller,
EMP: 3
SQ FT: 3,000
SALES: 50K **Privately Held**
SIC: 3993 Signs & advertising specialties

(G-10083)
AIR PARTS OF LOCK HAVEN
1084 E Water St (17745-7800)
P.O. Box 418 (17745-0418)
PHONE.................................570 748-0823
Bob Larsen, *President*
Robert Larsen, *President*
George McKinney, *Vice Pres*
EMP: 10
SALES (est): 1.5MM **Privately Held**
WEB: www.airpartsoflockhaven.com
SIC: 3728 Aircraft parts & equipment

(G-10084)
ALBERT MILLER LOGGING INC
143 Davis Ln (17745-8769)
PHONE.................................570 295-4040
Butch Miller, *Owner*
EMP: 3
SALES (est): 277.1K **Privately Held**
SIC: 2411 Logging camps & contractors

(G-10085)
CENTRE CONCRETE COMPANY
357 E Walnut St (17745-3508)
PHONE.................................570 748-7747
David Harstly, *Branch Mgr*
EMP: 10
SALES (corp-wide): 16.5MM **Privately Held**
SIC: 3273 Ready-mixed concrete
PA: Centre Concrete Company
    629 E Rolling Ridge Dr
    Bellefonte PA 16823
    814 238-2471

(G-10086)
CLINTON CONTROLS INC
860 Woodward Ave (17745-1727)
PHONE.................................570 748-4042
Mark Miller, *President*
EMP: 7
SQ FT: 1,800
SALES (est): 1.3MM **Privately Held**
SIC: 3613 Control panels, electric

(G-10087)
COASTAL DEFENSE
360 Proctor St (17745-9527)
PHONE.................................570 858-1139
Mike Holmes, *President*
EMP: 3 EST: 2015
SALES (est): 156.9K **Privately Held**
SIC: 3812 Defense systems & equipment

(G-10088)
FABER BURNER COMPANY
Also Called: Faber Fab
1000 E Bald Eagle St (17745-2269)
PHONE.................................570 748-4009
Samuel G Probst, *President*
Troy A Probst, *Corp Secy*
Robert Kelly, *Sales Mgr*
Tom Bechtol, *Info Tech Mgr*
EMP: 35
SQ FT: 17,000
SALES (est): 22.7MM **Privately Held**
WEB: www.faberburner.com
SIC: 5074 3433 Boilers, steam; burners, furnaces, boilers & stokers

(G-10089)
FIRST QUALITY TISSUE LLC
904 Woods Ave (17745-3348)
PHONE.................................570 748-1200
Dan Corbett, *Prdtn Mgr*
Jennifer Cohen, *Buyer*
Debra R Phr, *Human Res Mgr*
Jeff Willard, *Train & Dev Mgr*
Matt Hiller, *Marketing Staff*
▲ EMP: 380
SALES (est): 218.9MM **Privately Held**
WEB: www.firstqualitytissue.com
SIC: 2621 Tissue paper
PA: First Quality Enterprises Inc
    80 Cuttermill Rd Ste 500
    Great Neck NY 11021

(G-10090)
LOCK HAVEN EXPRESS
Also Called: Express, The
9 W Main St (17745-1217)
P.O. Box 208 (17745-0208)
PHONE.................................570 748-6791
Fax: 570 748-1544
EMP: 44 EST: 1917
SQ FT: 2,100
SALES: 30.9K
SALES (corp-wide): 683.9MM **Privately Held**
SIC: 2711 2752 Newspapers-Publishing/Printing Lithographic Commercial Printing
PA: The Ogden Newspapers Inc
    1500 Main St
    Wheeling WV 26003
    304 233-0100

(G-10091)
RANDALL A REESE
Also Called: Reese's Print Shop
7 E Main St (17745-1303)
PHONE.................................570 748-6528
Randall A Reese, *Owner*
Judy Reese, *Office Mgr*
EMP: 5
SALES: 422K **Privately Held**
WEB: www.reesesprintshop.com
SIC: 2759 Letterpress printing

(G-10092)
SERVANT PC RESOURCES INC
220 Woodward Ave Ste 1 (17745-1757)
PHONE.................................570 748-2800
Ed Newman, *President*
Janet Newman, *Vice Pres*
EMP: 16
SALES (est): 500K **Privately Held**
WEB: www.servantpc.com
SIC: 7372 7371 Prepackaged software; custom computer programming services

(G-10093)
WAGNER MASTERS CUSTOM WDWKG
Also Called: New Look Kitchens
700 Maple St (17745-3214)
PHONE.................................570 748-9424
Gurney Wagner, *President*
Anne Wagner, *Admin Sec*
EMP: 5
SQ FT: 5,000
SALES: 200K **Privately Held**
SIC: 2434 2431 1799 Wood kitchen cabinets; doors & door parts & trim, wood; moldings, wood: unfinished & prefinished; counter top installation

---

Loganton
Clinton County

(G-10094)
EKS VINYL STRUCTURES
816 E Valley Rd (17747-9211)
PHONE.................................570 725-3439
Emanuel K Peachey, *Owner*
EMP: 3 EST: 1998
SALES (est): 463.6K **Privately Held**
SIC: 3089 Panels, building: plastic

(G-10095)
FISHERS WOODWORKING
158 Country Ln (17747-9314)
PHONE.................................570 725-2310
Jacob Fisher, *Owner*
EMP: 4
SALES (est): 422.6K **Privately Held**
SIC: 2431 Millwork

(G-10096)
NICHOLAS MEAT LLC
508 E Valley Rd (17747-9207)
P.O. Box 95 (17747-0095)
PHONE.................................570 725-3511
Eugene Nicholas, *General Mgr*
Jeanette Lamey, *Purch Agent*
EMP: 87 EST: 2005
SALES: 3MM **Privately Held**
SIC: 2011 Boxed beef from meat slaughtered on site

(G-10097)
NICHOLAS MEAT PACKING CO
508 E Valley Rd (17747-9207)
PHONE.................................570 725-3511
Eugene A Nicholas, *President*
Deborah A Nicholas, *Corp Secy*
EMP: 108
SALES (est): 16.3MM **Privately Held**
SIC: 2011 5154 2013 Beef products from beef slaughtered on site; cattle; sausages & other prepared meats

(G-10098)
SCAFFS ENTERPRISES INC
2550 E Valley Rd (17747-9165)
P.O. Box 66 (17747-0066)
PHONE.................................570 725-3497
Marilyn Y Scaff, *Owner*
EMP: 7
SQ FT: 8,400

SALES (est): 722.2K **Privately Held**
WEB: www.scaffsenterprises.com
SIC: 0971 3089 Hunting services; clo-
sures, plastic

(G-10099)
SUGAR VALLEY COLLAR SHOP INC
18 Wagon Wheel Ln (17747-9564)
PHONE....................................570 725-3499
Amos K Fisher, *President*
EMP: 3
SALES: 430K **Privately Held**
SIC: 3111 7389 Collar leather;

(G-10100)
WOOD YA LIKE CABINETS
2455 E Valley Rd (17747-9361)
PHONE....................................570 725-2523
Daniel Stoltzfus, *Principal*
EMP: 3
SALES (est): 199.2K **Privately Held**
SIC: 2434 Wood kitchen cabinets

Loganville
York County

(G-10101)
ALLEN MCKINNEY INC
Also Called: Carman Ice Cream
24 N Main St (17342)
P.O. Box 155 (17342-0155)
PHONE....................................717 428-2321
Allen McKinney, *President*
EMP: 4
SQ FT: 1,364
SALES (est): 350K **Privately Held**
WEB: www.allenmckinney.com
SIC: 5451 2024 Ice cream (packaged); ice
cream, packaged: molded, on sticks, etc.

Loretto
Cambria County

(G-10102)
E & E LOGGING & SONS
6721 Admiral Peary Hwy (15940-6403)
PHONE....................................814 886-4440
Eugene Krug, *Partner*
Alan Krug, *Partner*
Edward Krug, *Partner*
Jeff Krug, *Partner*
EMP: 6 EST: 1920
SALES (est): 520K **Privately Held**
SIC: 2411 Logging camps & contractors

(G-10103)
HIGH COUNTRY MOTORS LLC
6512 Admiral Peary Hwy (15940-6400)
PHONE....................................814 886-9375
James Panaro, *President*
Jud Kroh, *Vice Pres*
Steven McMullen, *Vice Pres*
Denise Schildt, *CFO*
Samuel Shirley, *Treasurer*
EMP: 30
SALES (est): 1.7MM **Privately Held**
SIC: 3537 Trucks, tractors, loaders, carri-
ers & similar equipment

(G-10104)
HIGH VIEW INC
Also Called: Vale Wood Farms
517 Vale Wood Rd (15940-6605)
PHONE....................................814 886-7171
William C Itle, *President*
T Mathew Itle, *Vice Pres*
Jennifer Itle, *VP Prdtn*
Timothy A Itle, *Treasurer*
EMP: 45 EST: 1933
SQ FT: 10,000
SALES (est): 10.7MM **Privately Held**
WEB: www.valewoodfarms.com
SIC: 0241 2033 2026 2024 Milk produc-
tion; canned fruits & specialties; fluid milk;
ice cream & frozen desserts; creamery
butter

Lower Burrell
Westmoreland County

(G-10105)
CCX INC
Also Called: Braeburn Alloy Steel
101 Braeburn Rd (15068-2259)
PHONE....................................724 224-6900
Richard Rinaldi, *President*
Dennis J McGillicuddy, *Chairman*
Francis X Feeney, *VP Finance*
W Edward Wood, *Director*
EMP: 49 EST: 1944
SALES: 4.9MM **Privately Held**
SIC: 3325 Steel foundries

(G-10106)
HETRICK MFG INC
210 Reimer St (15068-2850)
PHONE....................................724 335-0455
Donald Burk, *President*
George H Grattan, *Vice Pres*
Debbie Burk, *Treasurer*
Dave Danik, *Marketing Staff*
Elizabeth Grattan, *Admin Sec*
EMP: 12 EST: 1974
SQ FT: 14,000
SALES (est): 3.2MM **Privately Held**
WEB: www.hetrickmfg.com
SIC: 3599 7692 7629 3541 Machine
shop, jobbing & repair; welding repair;
electrical repair shops; machine tools,
metal cutting type

(G-10107)
OVERHEAD CRANE SALES SVC LLC
2644 Leechburg Rd (15068-3087)
PHONE....................................724 335-1415
Brian Sagath, *Mng Member*
Susan Sagath, *Mng Member*
EMP: 4 EST: 2016
SALES: 800K **Privately Held**
SIC: 3536 Hoists, cranes & monorails

(G-10108)
WOLFE METAL FAB INC (PA)
Also Called: Saxon Turf Equipment
299 Greensburg Rd (15068-3915)
PHONE....................................724 339-7790
Kevin D Wolfe, *President*
Janet F Wolfe, *Treasurer*
EMP: 2
SQ FT: 11,500
SALES (est): 2MM **Privately Held**
WEB: www.wolfemetalfab.com
SIC: 3523 3443 Turf equipment, commer-
cial; fabricated plate work (boiler shop)

Lower Merion
Delaware County

(G-10109)
SOUTHWIND STUDIOS LTD
901 Beechwood Rd (19083-2623)
PHONE....................................610 664-4110
Gloria Rioux, *Partner*
Francis M Rioux, *Partner*
EMP: 5 EST: 1963
SQ FT: 7,000
SALES (est): 520K **Privately Held**
SIC: 2679 5719 5947 Wallboard, deco-
rated: made from purchased material; pic-
tures, wall; gift shop

Loyalhanna
Westmoreland County

(G-10110)
DAVID KOVALCIK
Also Called: Kodyn Products Company
922 Industrial Blvd (15661-1002)
P.O. Box 286, Latrobe (15650-0286)
PHONE....................................724 539-3181
David Kovalcik, *Owner*
EMP: 7
SQ FT: 4,000

SALES (est): 500K **Privately Held**
WEB: www.dyna-frame.com
SIC: 3599 5084 Custom machinery; in-
struments & control equipment

(G-10111)
GOG PAINTBALL USA
100 Station St (15661-9702)
PHONE....................................724 520-8690
Adam Gardner, *Principal*
▲ EMP: 3
SALES (est): 715.3K **Privately Held**
SIC: 3484 Pellet & BB guns

(G-10112)
PACE INDUSTRIES LLC
Airo Division
1004 Industrial Blvd (15661-1028)
PHONE....................................724 539-4527
Marshall Haines, *Division Pres*
EMP: 275
SALES (corp-wide): 101.3MM **Privately Held**
SIC: 3363 Aluminum die-castings
HQ: Pace Industries, Llc
481 S Shiloh Dr
Fayetteville AR 72704
479 443-1455

(G-10113)
SPECIAL-LITE PRODUCTS LLC
1634 Latrobe Derry Rd (15661-1022)
PHONE....................................724 537-4711
Edward Lamolinara, *President*
Joanna Lamolinara, *Admin Sec*
▲ EMP: 19 EST: 1967
SQ FT: 10,000
SALES (est): 3.9MM **Privately Held**
WEB: www.specialliteproducts.com
SIC: 3648 Lighting equipment

Loysville
Perry County

(G-10114)
FISHER STRUCTURES
183 Memory Ln (17047-9298)
PHONE....................................717 789-4569
Dave Fisher, *Partner*
EMP: 4
SALES (est): 854.7K **Privately Held**
SIC: 2452 Prefabricated buildings, wood

(G-10115)
GLICKS WOODCRAFT LLC
321 Meadowlark Ln (17047-9664)
PHONE....................................717 536-3670
EMP: 4
SALES (est): 375.9K **Privately Held**
SIC: 2434 Wood kitchen cabinets

(G-10116)
JAMES K REISINGER
2877 Dobbs Rd (17047-9537)
PHONE....................................717 275-2124
James K Reisinger, *Principal*
EMP: 3
SALES (est): 298K **Privately Held**
SIC: 2411 Logging

Lucernemines
Indiana County

(G-10117)
DEAN TECHNOLOGY INC
Also Called: C.K.E.
1000 Lucerne Rd (15754)
PHONE....................................724 479-3533
Raj Maharaj, *Engineer*
Pamela Brank, *Mktg Dir*
Rich Gibbons, *Branch Mgr*
Jeff Learn, *Maintence Staff*
EMP: 30
SALES (corp-wide): 35.1MM **Privately Held**
SIC: 3674 3676 3675 3643 Diodes, solid
state (germanium, silicon, etc.); rectifiers,
solid state; electronic resistors; electronic
capacitors; current-carrying wiring de-
vices

PA: Dean Technology, Inc.
4117 Billy Mitchell Dr
Addison TX 75001
972 248-7691

Ludlow
Mckean County

(G-10118)
JAMES CONFER
Also Called: Confer Logging
37 Church St (16333)
PHONE....................................814 945-7013
James Confer, *Owner*
EMP: 3
SALES (est): 211.7K **Privately Held**
SIC: 2411 7389 Timber, cut at logging
camp;

(G-10119)
JOHN F BIEL
6 Willow Ln (16333)
P.O. Box 253 (16333-0253)
PHONE....................................814 945-6306
John F Biel, *Owner*
EMP: 3
SALES: 200K **Privately Held**
SIC: 2411 Logging

Luthersburg
Clearfield County

(G-10120)
ACE PANELS COMPANY
436 Evergreen Rd (15848-3508)
PHONE....................................814 583-5015
Aaron Hershberger, *Owner*
EMP: 8
SALES (est): 995.8K **Privately Held**
SIC: 3069 Stair treads, rubber

(G-10121)
COLONIAL HARDWOODS & LOGGING
Also Called: Herbalife Distributor
384 Evergreen Rd (15848-3506)
PHONE....................................814 583-5901
Enos Kurtz, *Owner*
EMP: 18 EST: 1993
SQ FT: 10,000
SALES (est): 1.5MM **Privately Held**
SIC: 2426 Lumber, hardwood dimension

(G-10122)
COLONIAL LOGGING
384 Evergreen Rd (15848-3506)
PHONE....................................814 583-5901
Enice Kurtz, *Owner*
EMP: 13
SQ FT: 5,500
SALES: 2MM **Privately Held**
SIC: 2411 Logging

(G-10123)
ED RE INVENT
366 Carson Hill Rd (15848-4304)
PHONE....................................814 590-0771
EMP: 5
SALES (est): 354.1K **Privately Held**
SIC: 2512 Upholstered household furniture

Luzerne
Luzerne County

(G-10124)
GREAT ADDITIONS INC
265 Charles St (18709-1511)
PHONE....................................570 675-0852
Deborah K Deubler, *President*
EMP: 17
SQ FT: 10,000
SALES (est): 2.8MM **Privately Held**
WEB: www.greatadditions.com
SIC: 3448 1521 Sunrooms, prefabricated
metal; general remodeling, single-family
houses

(G-10125)
KMS FAB LLC
Also Called: Kms of Pennsylvania
100 Parry St (18709-1040)
PHONE..............................570 338-0200
Jeffrey S Dickson,
▲ EMP: 45
SQ FT: 78,000
SALES (est): 12MM
SALES (corp-wide): 11.5B **Publicly Held**
SIC: 3444 5051 5999 Sheet metal spe-
cialties, not stamped; metals service cen-
ters & offices; electronic parts &
equipment
PA: Reliance Steel & Aluminum Co.
350 S Grand Ave Ste 5100
Los Angeles CA 90071
213 687-7700

(G-10126)
LIGUS ELECTRIC MTR & PUMP
SVC
340 Union St (18709-1430)
PHONE..............................570 287-1272
Jake Hassaj, *Owner*
EMP: 4
SQ FT: 6,500
SALES (est): 425.5K **Privately Held**
SIC: 5063 5084 7694 Motors, electric;
pumps & pumping equipment; electric
motor repair

(G-10127)
LUZERNE IRONWORKS INC
Also Called: Luzerne Iron Works
300 Sly St (18709-1546)
PHONE..............................570 288-1950
Anthony Fasciano, *President*
EMP: 8
SQ FT: 78,000
SALES (est): 1.2MM **Privately Held**
SIC: 3312 Blast furnaces & steel mills

(G-10128)
ON FUEL
Also Called: Citgo
360 Main St (18709-1014)
PHONE..............................570 288-5805
Shannon Doan, *Manager*
EMP: 5
SALES (est): 419.4K **Privately Held**
SIC: 2869 Fuels

Lykens
Dauphin County

(G-10129)
ALFA LAVAL INC
300 Chestnut St (17048-1446)
PHONE..............................717 453-7143
Chris Naurer, *Manager*
EMP: 55
SQ FT: 60,000
SALES (corp-wide): 4.1B **Privately Held**
SIC: 3433 3443 Heating equipment, ex-
cept electric; fabricated plate work (boiler
shop)
HQ: Alfa Laval Inc.
5400 Intl Trade Dr
Richmond VA 23231
804 222-5300

(G-10130)
BRADY INSTRUMENTS
1315 Pottsville St (17048-9625)
PHONE..............................717 453-7171
Jeremy Krebs, *Principal*
Bill Kaster, *Marketing Staff*
▲ EMP: 6
SALES (est): 878.4K **Privately Held**
SIC: 3821 Laboratory apparatus & furniture

(G-10131)
CEDAR LANE PALLETS
2253 Luxemburg Rd (17048-8631)
PHONE..............................717 365-4014
EMP: 4
SALES (est): 356.7K **Privately Held**
SIC: 2448 Pallets, wood & wood with metal

(G-10132)
DONS LYKENS FOOD MARKET
INC
Also Called: Don's Food Rite
672 Main St (17048-1309)
P.O. Box 76 (17048-0076)
PHONE..............................717 453-7042
Carla Sauve, *President*
Bill Jones, *Manager*
EMP: 97
SQ FT: 26,000
SALES (est): 6.4MM **Privately Held**
WEB: www.donsfoodrite.com
SIC: 5411 2051 Grocery stores, independ-
ent; bread, cake & related products

(G-10133)
GESSNER LOGGING & SAWMILL
INC
496 Luxemburg Rd (17048-8500)
PHONE..............................717 365-3883
Vernon Gessner, *President*
EMP: 19
SALES (est): 1.9MM **Privately Held**
SIC: 2411 2421 Logging camps & contrac-
tors; sawmills & planing mills, general

(G-10134)
REIFF & NESTOR COMPANY
(PA)
50 Reiff St W (17048)
P.O. Box 147 (17048-0147)
PHONE..............................717 453-7113
Patrick J Savage, *President*
Mary M Nestor, *Vice Pres*
Mary Nestor, *Vice Pres*
Donald E Nestor, *Treasurer*
▲ EMP: 67
SQ FT: 40,600
SALES (est): 6MM **Privately Held**
WEB: www.rntap.com
SIC: 3545 Taps, machine tool

(G-10135)
S DON FOOD MARKET INC
Also Called: Don Fooderte Food Market
672 Main St (17048-1309)
P.O. Box 32 (17048-0032)
PHONE..............................717 453-7470
Carla Sauve, *President*
EMP: 30
SALES (est): 1MM **Privately Held**
SIC: 5411 5812 2051 Grocery stores; eat-
ing places; bread, cake & related prod-
ucts

Lyndora
Butler County

(G-10136)
SR JAN FISHER
Also Called: Omni One Group of Pennsylva-
nia
716 Hansen Ave (16045-1408)
PHONE..............................724 841-0508
Jan Fisher Sr, *Owner*
Laura Narry, *Assistant*
EMP: 9 EST: 2017
SQ FT: 3,048
SALES: 183.4K **Privately Held**
SIC: 3842 Wheelchairs

Mackeyville
Clinton County

(G-10137)
APC INTERNATIONAL LTD
Also Called: American Piezo Ceramics
213 Duck Run Rd (17750)
P.O. Box 180 (17750-0180)
PHONE..............................570 726-6961
Ian Henderson, *President*
Ronald Staut, *President*
Brian Julius, *Plant Mgr*
Eddie Kahler, *Technical Staff*
Todd Cable, *Business Dir*
▲ EMP: 35
SQ FT: 29,000

SALES: 7MM **Privately Held**
WEB: www.americanpiezo.com
SIC: 3679 Power supplies, all types: static

Macungie
Lehigh County

(G-10138)
ADVANCED RESEARCH
SYSTEMS INC
7476 Industrial Park Way (18062-9687)
PHONE..............................610 967-2120
Ravi Bains, *President*
EMP: 20
SQ FT: 5,500
SALES (est): 5.1MM **Privately Held**
WEB: www.arscryo.com
SIC: 3399 Cryogenic treatment of metal

(G-10139)
ALLEN INTEGRATED
ASSEMBLIES
150 Locust St (18062-1165)
PHONE..............................610 966-2200
Teresa O'Malley, *President*
Curtis Rosevelt, *Purch Mgr*
Teresa Omalley, *Human Res Dir*
EMP: 6
SALES (est): 845.3K **Privately Held**
SIC: 3672 Printed circuit boards

(G-10140)
ANDROMEDA LED LIGHTING
LLC
2188 Greenmeadow Dr (18062-8444)
PHONE..............................610 336-7474
Tai-Yin Huang, *President*
EMP: 4 EST: 2012
SALES (est): 244.5K **Privately Held**
SIC: 3646 3645 Commercial indusl & insti-
tutional electric lighting fixtures; residen-
tial lighting fixtures

(G-10141)
AOC ACQUISITION INC (PA)
150 Locust St (18062-1165)
P.O. Box 36 (18062-0036)
PHONE..............................610 966-2200
Steven Markowitz, *President*
EMP: 271
SALES (est): 24.9MM **Privately Held**
SIC: 3672 Printed circuit boards

(G-10142)
BENEBONE LLC
7089 Queenscourt Ln (18062-8988)
PHONE..............................610 366-3718
Peter Toolan, *Mng Member*
EMP: 3
SALES (est): 188.5K **Privately Held**
SIC: 2048 Dry pet food (except dog & cat)

(G-10143)
BETHLEHEM PRE-CAST INC
(PA)
Also Called: Bethlehem Precast
4702 Indian Creek Rd (18062-9171)
P.O. Box 247, Bethlehem (18016-0247)
PHONE..............................610 967-5531
Thomas Engelman, *President*
Joseph G Engelman, *Vice Pres*
Mary Eastland, *Treasurer*
Sharon Saylor, *Info Tech Mgr*
Kathleen Scapellati, *Admin Sec*
EMP: 4 EST: 1974
SQ FT: 15,000
SALES (est): 8.9MM **Privately Held**
WEB: www.bethlehemprecast.com
SIC: 3272 Concrete products, precast

(G-10144)
CMMUNICATIONS U KRIENR-
PTTHOFF
6970 Beech Cir (18062-9422)
PHONE..............................484 547-5261
Philip Kriener, *President*
EMP: 4 EST: 2014
SALES (est): 153.8K **Privately Held**
SIC: 2731 Books: publishing only

(G-10145)
F & H WAX WORKS LTD
6070 Eli Cir (18062-8215)
PHONE..............................610 336-0308
EMP: 25
SQ FT: 42,000
SALES (est): 1.9MM **Privately Held**
SIC: 5199 3999 Whol Nondurable Goods
Mfg Misc Products

(G-10146)
GARDNER S CONSTRUCTION
6613 Saint Peters Rd (18062-9161)
P.O. Box 187, Breinigsville (18031-0187)
PHONE..............................610 395-6614
Peter Gardner, *Owner*
EMP: 5
SALES: 350K **Privately Held**
SIC: 2452 1522 Modular homes, prefabri-
cated, wood; residential construction

(G-10147)
HOFFMAN POWDER COATING
221 Benfield Rd (18062-2073)
PHONE..............................610 845-1422
Jeff Hoffman, *Principal*
EMP: 4
SALES (est): 220K **Privately Held**
SIC: 3479 Coating of metals & formed
products

(G-10148)
I2R ELECTRONICS INC
7448 Industrial Park Way (18062-9687)
PHONE..............................610 928-1045
Justin Miller, *President*
Michael Bearish, *Controller*
Milton Padgett, *Director*
EMP: 20 EST: 2011
SQ FT: 17,000
SALES (est): 3.3MM **Privately Held**
SIC: 3812 Search & navigation equipment

(G-10149)
LEHIGH CEMENT COMPANY LLC
1718 Spring Creek Rd (18062-9784)
PHONE..............................610 366-0500
Cindy Troxell, *Manager*
EMP: 3
SALES (corp-wide): 20.6B **Privately Held**
SIC: 3273 Ready-mixed concrete
HQ: Lehigh Cement Company Llc
300 E John Carpenter Fwy
Irving TX 75062
877 534-4442

(G-10150)
LEHIGH CONSUMER PRODUCTS
LLC
Also Called: Lehigh Group The
2834 Schoeneck Rd (18062-9679)
PHONE..............................484 232-7100
EMP: 5
SALES (corp-wide): 14.7B **Publicly Held**
SIC: 3965 Mfg Fasteners/Buttons/Pins
HQ: Lehigh Consumer Products Llc
3901 Liberty St
Aurora IL 60504
630 851-7330

(G-10151)
LEHIGH PRINT & DATA LLC
16 Lehigh St (18062-1318)
PHONE..............................610 421-8891
Tahera Sumar, *Principal*
Ed Sumar, *Prdtn Mgr*
EMP: 5
SALES (est): 795.4K **Privately Held**
SIC: 2752 Commercial printing, offset

(G-10152)
LEHIGH SERVICES INC
142 W Main St Ste 3 (18062-1176)
P.O. Box 3535, Allentown (18106-0535)
PHONE..............................610 966-2525
Justin Huddleston, *Principal*
EMP: 6
SALES (est): 525.6K **Privately Held**
SIC: 5531 3446 3444 1799 Automotive
parts; railings, bannisters, guards, etc.:
made from metal pipe; sheet metalwork;
welding on site

(G-10153)
LEO TAUR TECHNOLOGY GROUP INC
Also Called: Lehigh Surfaces
111 Lehigh St (18062-1302)
PHONE....................................610 966-3484
Narsu Tatikole, *President*
▲ EMP: 10
SALES (est): 1.2MM **Privately Held**
SIC: 3088 2434 Tubs (bath, shower & laundry), plastic; wood kitchen cabinets

(G-10154)
MACK TRUCKS INC
Macungie Operations
7000 Alburtis Rd (18062-9631)
PHONE....................................610 966-8800
Jim Doodell, *General Mgr*
Mike Maddox, *Vice Pres*
Stefan Seghers, *Mfg Staff*
Thomas H Campbell, *Senior Buyer*
John Bolich, *Engineer*
EMP: 840
SALES (corp-wide): 39.6B **Privately Held**
WEB: www.macktrucks.com
SIC: 3711 3537 Truck tractors for highway use, assembly of; industrial trucks & tractors
HQ: Mack Trucks, Inc.
 7900 National Service Rd
 Greensboro NC 27409
 336 291-9001

(G-10155)
NATURAL TEXTILES SOLUTIONS LLC
3648 Gehman Rd (18062-9629)
PHONE....................................484 660-4085
Tarit Chatterjee,
EMP: 5
SALES (est): 692K **Privately Held**
SIC: 5131 2284 2299 5199 Textiles, woven; thread from natural fibers; flax yarns & roving; hemp yarn, thread, roving & textiles; woolen & worsted yarns

(G-10156)
POINT 2 POINT WIRELESS INC
6690 Hauser Rd Apt K203 (18062-8115)
PHONE....................................347 543-5227
Ralph Winn,
Dawayadah Winn,
EMP: 5 EST: 2017
SALES (est): 213.6K **Privately Held**
SIC: 3357 Nonferrous wiredrawing & insulating

(G-10157)
PUREOPTIX LED LLC
6986 Periwinkle Ct (18062-8966)
PHONE....................................610 301-9767
EMP: 3 EST: 2014
SALES (est): 159.4K **Privately Held**
SIC: 3646 Commercial indusl & institutional electric lighting fixtures

(G-10158)
SITKA ENTERPRISES INC
2490 Lantern Ct S (18062-9792)
P.O. Box 150, East Texas (18046-0150)
PHONE....................................610 393-6708
Brian P Roy, *President*
Kevin Baker, *Vice Pres*
EMP: 3
SALES (est): 220K **Privately Held**
SIC: 3645 Residential lighting fixtures

(G-10159)
SMOOTH-ON INC (PA)
5600 Lower Macungie Rd (18062-9030)
PHONE....................................610 252-5800
Sal A Bianco, *President*
Dominick Finocchio, *Vice Pres*
Clay Western, *Vice Pres*
Craig Greenwood, *Plant Mgr*
Matt Earles, *Prdtn Mgr*
◆ EMP: 125 EST: 1895
SQ FT: 50,000
SALES (est): 43.5MM **Privately Held**
WEB: www.smooth-on.com
SIC: 2821 2822 2891 Epoxy resins; polyurethane resins; polysulfides (thiokol); sealants; sealing compounds, synthetic rubber or plastic

(G-10160)
UNISTRESS CORP
5071 Bridlepath Dr (18062-9023)
PHONE....................................610 395-5930
Mark Dipietro, *Principal*
EMP: 4
SALES (est): 263.5K **Privately Held**
SIC: 3272 Concrete products

(G-10161)
WELLTECH PRODUCTS INC
7823 Sweetwood Dr (18062-9104)
PHONE....................................610 417-8928
Kris Bickford, *President*
EMP: 5
SQ FT: 14,500
SALES: 400K **Privately Held**
SIC: 3826 1382 Environmental testing equipment; seismograph surveys

Madera
Clearfield County

(G-10162)
D D J MANUFACTURING INC
46 Shoff Ln (16661-9124)
PHONE....................................814 378-7625
David Campolong, *President*
Dennis Campolong, *Corp Secy*
EMP: 70
SQ FT: 23,000
SALES (est): 4.3MM **Privately Held**
SIC: 2337 2339 2325 Skirts, separate: women's, misses' & juniors'; slacks: women's, misses' & juniors'; men's & boys' trousers & slacks

(G-10163)
EUGENE ZAPSKY
Also Called: Central Manufacturing Company
266 Alexander Rd (16661-9246)
PHONE....................................814 378-6157
Eugene Zapsky, *Owner*
EMP: 4
SALES (est): 280K **Privately Held**
SIC: 3465 Body parts, automobile: stamped metal

(G-10164)
WALTER MCCLELLAND JR LLC
102 Mcclelland Dr (16661-9232)
PHONE....................................814 378-7434
Walter McClelland, *Principal*
EMP: 3
SALES (est): 304.7K **Privately Held**
SIC: 7692 Welding repair

Madison
Westmoreland County

(G-10165)
ESSAY PRECISION MACHINING
233 W Newton Rd (15663)
P.O. Box 284 (15663-0284)
PHONE....................................724 446-2422
Jeffrey J Essay, *Owner*
EMP: 6
SQ FT: 5,000
SALES (est): 484K **Privately Held**
SIC: 3599 Machine shop, jobbing & repair; machine & other job shop work

(G-10166)
REUSS INDUSTRIES INC
195 Waltz Mill Flat Rd (15663)
P.O. Box 22 (15663-0022)
PHONE....................................724 722-3300
Melanie T Reuss, *President*
James Reuss, *Corp Secy*
EMP: 25
SQ FT: 10,000
SALES: 2MM **Privately Held**
WEB: www.reussindustries.com
SIC: 3441 3599 Fabricated structural metal; machine & other job shop work

(G-10167)
WESTMRLAND STL FABRICATION INC
371 Middletown Rd (15663-1101)
P.O. Box 281 (15663-0281)
PHONE....................................724 446-0555
Robert Whisner, *President*
Michelle Kosker, *Treasurer*
EMP: 20
SQ FT: 10,500
SALES: 2.3MM **Privately Held**
WEB: www.westmorelandsteel.com
SIC: 3441 7692 1799 Fabricated structural metal; welding repair; welding on site

Madison Township
Lackawanna County

(G-10168)
DOWN HOME RICE PUDDING
Also Called: Downhome Homemade Rice Pudding
1580 Aberdeen Rd (18444-7129)
PHONE....................................570 945-5744
Stacy Selig, *Principal*
EMP: 6
SQ FT: 3,200
SALES (est): 540K **Privately Held**
WEB: www.ricepudding.com
SIC: 2032 Puddings, except meat: packaged in cans, jars, etc.

(G-10169)
KEYSTONE TRUCK & TRAILER LLC
4171 Quicktown Rd (18444-6941)
PHONE....................................570 903-1902
Kevin May, *Mng Member*
EMP: 4
SALES (est): 215.9K **Privately Held**
SIC: 3444 Sheet metalwork

Mahaffey
Clearfield County

(G-10170)
BOWSER LUMBER CO INC
8530 Colonel Drake Hwy (15757-7505)
PHONE....................................814 277-9956
Marlin D Bowser, *President*
Edwin R Bowser, *Principal*
Ronald E Bowser, *Principal*
Shirley Bowser, *Corp Secy*
EMP: 14 EST: 1961
SQ FT: 12,000
SALES: 1.5MM **Privately Held**
SIC: 2421 5211 Lumber: rough, sawed or planed; millwork & lumber

(G-10171)
MAHONING OUTDOOR FURNACE INC
208 Whiskey Run Rd (15757-7415)
PHONE....................................814 277-6675
Robin Weaver, *President*
Jodie Irwin, *Administration*
EMP: 30
SQ FT: 31,000
SALES (est): 4.9MM **Privately Held**
WEB: www.mahoningoutdoorfurnaces.com
SIC: 3433 Burners, furnaces, boilers & stokers

(G-10172)
NORTHWESTERN ENERGY CORP
1214 Mcgees Mills Rd (15757-7149)
PHONE....................................814 277-9935
EMP: 3
SALES (corp-wide): 1.3B **Publicly Held**
SIC: 1311 Crude Petroleum/Natural Gas Production
HQ: Northwestern Energy Corporation
 3010 W 69th St
 Sioux Falls SD 57108
 605 978-2900

Mahanoy City
Schuylkill County

(G-10173)
FABCON EAST LLC
1200 Morear (17948)
PHONE....................................610 530-4470
Ernie Wargo, *Plant Mgr*
Michael L Lejeune,
▲ EMP: 100
SALES (est): 38.3MM **Privately Held**
SIC: 3272 Panels & sections, prefabricated concrete
PA: Fabcon Companies, Llc
 6111 Highway 13 W
 Savage MN 55378

(G-10174)
SKY TOP COAL COMPANY INC
State Hwy New Boston (17948)
P.O. Box 330 (17948-0330)
PHONE....................................570 773-2000
Ettore Di Casimirro, *President*
Jen Conna, *Admin Sec*
Eileen Di Casimirro, *Admin Sec*
EMP: 5 EST: 1967
SALES (est): 529.6K **Privately Held**
SIC: 1231 Preparation plants, anthracite

Mainland
Montgomery County

(G-10175)
R & R WOOD PRODUCTS INC
645 Fretz Rd (19451)
P.O. Box 51065 (19451-0065)
PHONE....................................215 723-3470
Reginald Bishop, *President*
R David Bishop, *Vice Pres*
Brooke Ziegler, *Admin Sec*
EMP: 23
SQ FT: 19,000
SALES (est): 4.3MM **Privately Held**
WEB: www.rrwood.com
SIC: 2448 5031 Pallets, wood; skids, wood; lumber: rough, dressed & finished

Malvern
Chester County

(G-10176)
3SI SECURITY SYSTEMS INC (HQ)
101 Lindenwood Dr Ste 200 (19355-1764)
PHONE....................................800 523-1430
David Stanks, *President*
EMP: 63
SALES (est): 33.8MM
SALES (corp-wide): 55.4MM **Privately Held**
SIC: 3699 Security control equipment & systems
PA: Llr Partners, Inc.
 2929 Arch St Ste 1650
 Philadelphia PA 19104
 215 717-2900

(G-10177)
3SI SECURITY SYSTEMS HOLDG INC
101 Lindenwood Dr Ste 200 (19355-1764)
PHONE....................................610 280-2000
Thomas Oxenfeld, *President*
EMP: 1
SALES (est): 26.9MM **Privately Held**
SIC: 3483 3699 3873 3643 Ammunition, except for small arms; electrical equipment & supplies; watches, clocks, watchcases & parts; current-carrying wiring devices; relays & industrial controls
PA: Stirling Square Capital Partners, Llp
 10 Duke Of York Square
 London SW3 4

(G-10178)
A G F MANUFACTURING CO INC
100 Quaker Ln (19355-2479)
PHONE..................................610 240-4900
George McHugh III, *President*
Ben Gleeson, *Engineer*
Don Medon, *Controller*
▲ **EMP:** 30
SALES (est): 7.1MM **Privately Held**
WEB: www.testandrain.com
SIC: 3569 Sprinkler systems, fire: auto-
matic

(G-10179)
ACCUTOME INC (HQ)
3222 Phoenixville Pike # 100 (19355-9610)
PHONE..................................800 979-2020
Brian Chandler, *President*
Matt Virgilio, *Vice Pres*
Frederic B Kremer, *Treasurer*
Mike Ahern, *VP Finance*
Jennifer Krantz, *Accountant*
▲ **EMP:** 28
SQ FT: 24,000
SALES (est): 12MM
SALES (corp-wide): 1.5B **Privately Held**
WEB: www.accutome.com
SIC: 3827 3841 Optical instruments &
lenses; surgical & medical instruments
PA: Halma Public Limited Company
Misbourne Court
Amersham BUCKS HP7 0
149 472-1111

(G-10180)
**ADVANCED METALS GROUP
LLC (PA)**
18 Mystic Ln (19355-1942)
PHONE..................................610 408-8006
Keith Sterling, *President*
John Thach,
EMP: 18
SALES (est): 62.8MM **Privately Held**
SIC: 3365 3321 Aluminum foundries; cast
iron pipe & fittings

(G-10181)
AIRSOURCES INC
17 Country Ln (19355-9671)
PHONE..................................610 983-0102
Betty Scott, *President*
EMP: 6
SALES: 500K **Privately Held**
SIC: 3444 Sheet metalwork

(G-10182)
**ALPHA SCIENTIFIC
INSTRUMENT**
Also Called: A S I
287 Great Valley Pkwy (19355-1308)
PHONE..................................610 647-7000
David Levine, *President*
Dan Levine, *Vice Pres*
EMP: 7
SQ FT: 5,400
SALES (est): 539.3K **Privately Held**
WEB: www.alpha-scientific.com
SIC: 3842 Surgical appliances & supplies
PA: Alpha Scientific Corporation
820 Springdale Dr
Exton PA 19341

(G-10183)
**AMERICAN ACCESS CARE
HOLDINGS (HQ)**
40 Valley Stream Pkwy (19355-1407)
PHONE..................................717 235-0181
Raymond Figueroa, *CEO*
EMP: 1
SALES (est): 35MM
SALES (corp-wide): 18.9B **Privately Held**
SIC: 3844 Gamma ray irradiation equip-
ment
PA: Fresenius Medical Care Ag & Co. Kgaa
Else-Kroner-Str. 1
Bad Homburg 61352
617 260-90

(G-10184)
**AMERICAN ACCESS CARE
INTERMEDI (DH)**
40 Valley Stream Pkwy (19355-1407)
PHONE..................................717 235-0181
Raymond Figueroa, *CEO*
EMP: 1

SALES (est): 23.1MM
SALES (corp-wide): 18.9B **Privately Held**
SIC: 3844 Gamma ray irradiation equip-
ment

(G-10185)
**AMERICAN DIRECTORY
SYSTEMS CO**
255 Great Valley Pkwy # 120 (19355-1300)
PHONE..................................610 640-1774
Scott Sawin, *President*
Dean Hodges, *Exec VP*
EMP: 16 **EST:** 1967
SQ FT: 7,000
SALES (est): 1.9MM **Privately Held**
SIC: 2791 Photocomposition, for the print-
ing trade

(G-10186)
**AMERICAN FUTURE SYSTEMS
INC (PA)**
Also Called: Progressive Gifts & Incentives
370 Technology Dr (19355-1315)
P.O. Box 3019 (19355-0719)
PHONE..................................610 695-8600
Edward M Satell, *President*
Susan Wade, *Editor*
Tom Schubert, *COO*
James Brown, *Vice Pres*
Christine Dougherty, *Sales Staff*
EMP: 100 **EST:** 1973
SQ FT: 80,000
SALES (est): 134.8MM **Privately Held**
WEB: www.pbp.com
SIC: 2741 5199 7311 Newsletter publish-
ing; advertising specialties; advertising
consultant

(G-10187)
**AMERICAN MEDICAL SYSTEMS
INC**
1400 Atwater Dr (19355-8701)
PHONE..................................512 808-4974
Marrit Gill, *President*
EMP: 15 **EST:** 2006
SALES (est): 2.4MM **Privately Held**
SIC: 2834 Pharmaceutical preparations

(G-10188)
AUGER MFG SPECIALISTS CO
22a N Bacton Hill Rd (19355-1006)
PHONE..................................610 647-4677
William Day, *President*
Karen Kerr, *Technology*
EMP: 28 **EST:** 1973
SQ FT: 8,800
SALES (est): 1.8MM **Privately Held**
WEB: www.augermfg.com
SIC: 3423 Hand & edge tools

(G-10189)
**AUXILIUM PHARMACEUTICALS
LLC (HQ)**
1400 Atwater Dr (19355-8701)
PHONE..................................484 321-5900
Adrian Adams, *President*
Mark A Glickman, *Senior VP*
Rigo Canal, *Opers Staff*
Andrew Saik, *CFO*
James P Tursi, *Chief Mktg Ofcr*
EMP: 145 **EST:** 1999
SQ FT: 75,000
SALES (est): 133.4MM **Privately Held**
WEB: www.auxilium.com
SIC: 2834 Hormone preparations

(G-10190)
**B E WALLACE PRODUCTS
CORP**
Also Called: Wallace Cranes
71 N Bacton Hill Rd (19355-1005)
PHONE..................................610 647-1400
Sherry J De Carville, *President*
James Finkel, *Engineer*
Diane Grim, *Treasurer*
Diane Grimm, *Treasurer*
Bart Sunderland, *Sales Mgr*
▼ **EMP:** 15
SQ FT: 30,000
SALES (est): 4.8MM **Privately Held**
WEB: www.wallacecranes.com
SIC: 3536 Cranes, industrial plant

(G-10191)
B V LANDSCAPE SUPPLIES INC
Also Called: Sunrise Mulch
154 Lancaster Ave (19355-2123)
PHONE..................................610 316-1099
Barbara D Kamp, *President*
EMP: 3
SALES (est): 161.3K **Privately Held**
SIC: 2499 3271 Mulch, wood & bark;
blocks, concrete: landscape or retaining
wall

(G-10192)
BACON PRESS
215 Lancaster Ave (19355-1874)
PHONE..................................484 328-3118
EMP: 4
SALES (est): 263.5K **Privately Held**
SIC: 2741 Miscellaneous publishing

(G-10193)
BIOTELEMETRY INC (PA)
1000 Cedar Hollow Rd (19355-2300)
PHONE..................................610 729-7000
Kirk E Gorman, *Ch of Bd*
Joseph H Capper, *President*
Fred Broadway III, *Senior VP*
Peter Ferola, *Senior VP*
George Hrenko, *Senior VP*
EMP: 87
SQ FT: 61,000
SALES (est): 399.4MM **Publicly Held**
SIC: 3845 8093 Electromedical equip-
ment; specialty outpatient clinics

(G-10194)
BODINE BUSINESS PRODUCTS
2099 Bodine Rd Ste 100 (19355-8615)
PHONE..................................610 827-0138
Christopher Zubyk, *President*
▲ **EMP:** 8 **EST:** 1996
SALES (est): 850K **Privately Held**
WEB: www.bbp-kerfeal.com
SIC: 2311 Men's & boys' suits & coats

(G-10195)
**BROCADE CMMNCTIONS
SYSTEMS INC**
5 Great Valley Pkwy # 325 (19355-1426)
PHONE..................................610 648-3915
Tm Fradeneck, *Accounts Mgr*
EMP: 3
SALES (corp-wide): 20.8B **Publicly Held**
SIC: 3577 Computer peripheral equipment
HQ: Brocade Communications Systems Llc
130 Holger Way
San Jose CA 95134

(G-10196)
BROOKE PRODUCTION INC
730 Monument Rd (19355-2861)
PHONE..................................610 296-9394
Brooke Drinkwater, *Architect*
Skipp Drinkwater, *Director*
EMP: 3
SALES (est): 264K **Privately Held**
SIC: 3652 Master records or tapes, prepa-
ration of

(G-10197)
**BURCH SUPPLIES COMPANY
INC**
Also Called: Burch Materials & Supplies
380 Lapp Rd (19355-1210)
PHONE..................................610 640-4877
Charles Burch, *President*
Jeffrey Nelson, *Vice Pres*
EMP: 5
SALES (est): 572.3K **Privately Held**
SIC: 3532 Mining machinery

(G-10198)
**BUSINESS & DECISION NORTH
AMER (HQ)**
5 Great Valley Pkwy # 210 (19355-1426)
PHONE..................................610 230-2500
Robin Kearon, *CEO*
Christian Oram, *General Mgr*
Jenessa Boniface, *Business Mgr*
William Carbajal, *Vice Pres*
Michele Dozier, *Accountant*
EMP: 150

SALES (est): 96.8MM
SALES (corp-wide): 18.1MM **Privately
Held**
WEB: www.mi-services.net
SIC: 7372 Business oriented computer
software
PA: Business & Decision
153 Rue De Courcelles
Paris
156 212-121

(G-10199)
CARDIONET INC
1000 Cedar Hollow Rd (19355-2300)
PHONE..................................888 312-2328
Ronate Wright, *Partner*
Peter R Kowey MD, *Chairman*
Peter Ferola, *Vice Pres*
Heather Getz, *CFO*
Maria Mastrocola, *Marketing Staff*
EMP: 6 **EST:** 2016
SALES (est): 196.5K **Privately Held**
SIC: 3845 Pacemaker, cardiac

(G-10200)
CATALENT MICRON TECH INC
Also Called: Catalent Micron Tehcnologies
333 Phoenixville Pike (19355-9603)
PHONE..................................610 251-7400
Joseph Drost, *President*
EMP: 100
SQ FT: 84,000
SALES (est): 23MM **Publicly Held**
SIC: 2834 Antibiotics, packaged
PA: Catalent, Inc.
14 Schoolhouse Rd
Somerset NJ 08873

(G-10201)
CEDAR HOLLOW SALES INC
1101 Church Rd (19355-9729)
PHONE..................................610 644-2660
Ted Heffernen, *President*
EMP: 3
SALES (est): 750K **Privately Held**
SIC: 3479 Name plates: engraved, etched,
etc.

(G-10202)
**CENTER EDCTN & EMPYMNT
LAW**
370 Technology Dr (19355-1315)
PHONE..................................800 365-4900
Edward Satell, *Owner*
EMP: 50
SALES (est): 3.4MM **Privately Held**
SIC: 2731 Book publishing

(G-10203)
CEPHALON INC (HQ)
41 Moores Rd (19355-1113)
P.O. Box 4011 (19355-0992)
PHONE..................................610 344-0200
J Kevin Buchi, *CEO*
William Marth, *President*
Tracey Johnson, *Principal*
Thomas Lyons, *Principal*
Jennifer Pokorny, *Principal*
▲ **EMP:** 706
SQ FT: 190,000
SALES (est): 633.2MM
SALES (corp-wide): 18.8B **Privately Held**
WEB: www.cephalon.com/
SIC: 2834 Mfg Pharmaceutical Prepara-
tions
PA: Teva Pharmaceutical Industries Limited
5 Bazel
Petah Tikva 49510
392 672-67

(G-10204)
**CERTAINTEED CORPORATION
(DH)**
Also Called: Saint-Gobain
20 Moores Rd (19355-1114)
P.O. Box 860, Valley Forge (19482-0860)
PHONE..................................610 893-5000
Frank Cahouet, *Chairman*
Robert J Panaro, *CFO*
John J Sweeney III, *Treasurer*
Timothy L Feagans, *General Counsel*
Carol Gray, *Admin Sec*
◆ **EMP:** 450 **EST:** 1904
SQ FT: 177,000

SALES (est): 2.3B
SALES (corp-wide): 215.9MM **Privately Held**
WEB: www.certainteed.net
SIC: 3221 3292 3259 3084 Glass containers; roofing, asbestos felt roll; roofing tile, clay; plastics pipe; plastic hardware & building products; plastic plumbing fixture fittings, assembly

(G-10205)
CERTAINTEED CORPORATION
Also Called: Certainteed/Saint-Gobain
18 Moores Rd (19355-1114)
PHONE..............................610 651-8706
Debra Vanderhorst, *Principal*
EMP: 6
SALES (corp-wide): 215.9MM **Privately Held**
SIC: 3221 3292 3259 3084 Glass containers; roofing, asbestos felt roll; roofing tile, clay; plastics pipe; plastic hardware & building products; plastic plumbing fixture fittings, assembly
HQ: Certainteed Corporation
20 Moores Rd
Malvern PA 19355
610 893-5000

(G-10206)
CERTAINTEED GYPSUM INC (DH)
20 Moores Rd (19355-1114)
PHONE..............................610 893-6000
David Engelhardt, *President*
Keith C Campbell, *CFO*
◆ **EMP:** 60
SQ FT: 40,000
SALES (est): 358.9MM
SALES (corp-wide): 215.9MM **Privately Held**
WEB: www.bpb-na.com
SIC: 3275 Gypsum products
HQ: Lapeyre
Lapeyrepro Lapeyre La Maison Tour Les Miroirs La Defense 3
Courbevoie 92400
148 117-400

(G-10207)
CHEMGENEX PHARMACEUTICALS INC
41 Moores Rd (19355-1113)
PHONE..............................650 804-7660
Greg R Collier, *CEO*
Dennis M Brown, *President*
EMP: 14
SQ FT: 10,500
SALES (est): 1.6MM
SALES (corp-wide): 18.8B **Privately Held**
SIC: 2834 Pharmaceutical preparations
HQ: Teva Pharmaceuticals Australia Pty Ltd
L 2 37-39 Epping Rd
Macquarie Park NSW 2113

(G-10208)
CIMBERIO VALVE CO INC
100 Quaker Ln (19355-2479)
PHONE..............................610 560-0802
James McHugh, *President*
Tom Pratt, *Sales Executive*
▲ **EMP:** 4
SQ FT: 25,000
SALES (est): 550K **Privately Held**
WEB: www.cimberiovalve.com
SIC: 5074 3432 Plumbing & heating valves; plumbing fixture fittings & trim

(G-10209)
CIRCA HEALTHCARE LLC
10 Valley Stream Pkwy # 201
(19355-1447)
PHONE..............................610 954-2340
Steve Kirton, *President*
Ike Carpenter, *COO*
EMP: 4
SALES (est): 733K **Privately Held**
SIC: 3829 Medical diagnostic systems, nuclear

(G-10210)
CISCO SYSTEMS INC
301 Lindenwood Dr Ste 210 (19355-1774)
PHONE..............................610 695-6000
Jeff Gottsegen, *Engineer*
Ron Hinderer, *Engineer*

Jeff Hoch, *Engineer*
Anthony Maiale, *Engineer*
Victor Nunes, *Engineer*
EMP: 70
SALES (corp-wide): 49.3B **Publicly Held**
WEB: www.cisco.com
SIC: 3577 5045 Data conversion equipment, media-to-media: computer; computers, peripherals & software
PA: Cisco Systems, Inc.
170 W Tasman Dr
San Jose CA 95134
408 526-4000

(G-10211)
CLEAR MICROWAVE INC
5 Great Valley Pkwy # 210 (19355-1426)
PHONE..............................610 844-6421
Lin He, *President*
EMP: 10
SQ FT: 2,000
SALES: 1MM **Privately Held**
SIC: 3679 Microwave components

(G-10212)
CLINICAL SUPPLIES MGT LLC
300 Technology Dr (19355-1315)
PHONE..............................215 596-4356
Gerald Finken, *CEO*
EMP: 11
SALES (est): 753.2K **Privately Held**
SIC: 2834 Tablets, pharmaceutical

(G-10213)
COATING TECHNOLOGY INC
26 N Bacton Hill Rd B (19355-1006)
PHONE..............................610 296-7722
EMP: 9
SQ FT: 8,150
SALES: 1.2MM **Privately Held**
SIC: 3479 Coating/Engraving Service

(G-10214)
COIL COMPANY LLC
3223 Phoenixville Pike B (19355-9628)
P.O. Box 956, Paoli (19301-0956)
PHONE..............................610 408-8361
Thomas Jacobs, *President*
Robert Jacobs, *Corp Secy*
David McCool, *Vice Pres*
John Lyons, *Manager*
▼ **EMP:** 40
SQ FT: 10,000
SALES (est): 8.5MM
SALES (corp-wide): 10.2MM **Privately Held**
WEB: www.coilcompany.com
SIC: 3585 3498 Heating & air conditioning combination units; fabricated pipe & fittings
PA: Usa Coil & Air, Inc.
11 General Warren Blvd # 2
Malvern PA 19355
610 296-9668

(G-10215)
COMMUNIMETRICS GROUP LLC
127 Watch Hill Ln (19355-2177)
PHONE..............................215 260-5382
Ivan Masanga,
EMP: 5
SALES: 150K **Privately Held**
SIC: 7372 Prepackaged software

(G-10216)
CONNIE FOGARTY
1151 Shadow Oak Dr (19355-2311)
PHONE..............................610 647-3172
Consuela M Fogarty, *Principal*
Cathryn Smith, *Accountant*
Mona Thorsen, *Administration*
Laurie Harding, *Advisor*
EMP: 3 **EST:** 2011
SALES (est): 171.2K **Privately Held**
SIC: 2834 Pharmaceutical preparations

(G-10217)
COPY MANAGEMENT INC
Also Called: CMI
147 Pnnsylvania Ave Ste 3 (19355)
PHONE..............................610 993-8686
Paul Chambers, *Vice Pres*
EMP: 6

SALES (est): 601.9K
SALES (corp-wide): 8.3MM **Privately Held**
SIC: 2752 2791 2789 Commercial printing, offset; typesetting; bookbinding & related work
PA: Copy Management, Inc.
447 Veit Rd
Huntingdon Valley PA 19006
215 269-5000

(G-10218)
CRANE PAYMENT INNOVATIONS INC (HQ)
Also Called: CPI
3222 Phoenixville Pike # 200 (19355-9615)
PHONE..............................610 430-2700
Kurt Gallo, *President*
Mary Rampe, *Vice Pres*
Brian Wedderspoon, *Vice Pres*
Stephen Marsh, *Technical Mgr*
Pat Erbe, *Engineer*
◆ **EMP:** 268
SALES (est): 183.8MM
SALES (corp-wide): 3.3B **Publicly Held**
WEB: www.meiglobal.com
SIC: 3578 Change making machines
PA: Crane Co.
100 1st Stamford Pl # 300
Stamford CT 06902
203 363-7300

(G-10219)
CRNCTE LLC
1013 W King Rd (19355-2004)
PHONE..............................610 648-0419
Charles Haines,
James Shaugnessy,
EMP: 12
SQ FT: 5,000
SALES (est): 748.4K **Privately Held**
SIC: 3089 Plastic containers, except foam

(G-10220)
DARKAR RAILWAY EQUIPMENT INC
Also Called: Darkar Railway Supplies
641 Lancaster Ave # 1008 (19355-1831)
P.O. Box 2150 (19355-0812)
PHONE..............................610 296-5712
Karla E Kalman, *President*
Darla J Kalman, *Corp Secy*
James H Kalman, *Vice Pres*
EMP: 3
SQ FT: 5,000
SALES (est): 240K **Privately Held**
SIC: 3531 Railway track equipment

(G-10221)
DATA PRINT
147 Pennsylvania Ave (19355-2496)
PHONE..............................484 329-7553
EMP: 3
SALES (est): 258.6K **Privately Held**
SIC: 2752 Commercial printing, offset

(G-10222)
DELTA/DUCON CONVEYING TECHLGY
33 Sproul Rd (19355-1951)
PHONE..............................610 695-9700
Ron Grabowski, *VP Sales*
Cathy Heinser, *Marketing Staff*
Ronald Tempesta, *Officer*
Matthew Delpizzo, *Admin Sec*
EMP: 24
SQ FT: 8,200
SALES (est): 7.6MM **Privately Held**
SIC: 3535 Conveyors & conveying equipment

(G-10223)
DENTALEZ INC (PA)
Also Called: Dentalez Integrated Solutions
2 W Liberty Blvd Ste 160 (19355-1472)
PHONE..............................610 725-8004
Gordon Hagder, *President*
Don Smuck, *Safety Mgr*
David Reagan, *Engineer*
Clay Dean, *Design Engr*
George Mick, *CFO*
▲ **EMP:** 22
SQ FT: 3,000

SALES (est): 59.5MM **Privately Held**
WEB: www.dentalez.com
SIC: 3843 Dental equipment; dental materials

(G-10224)
DIMENSION DATA NORTH AMER INC
301 Lindenwood Dr Ste 330 (19355-1775)
PHONE..............................484 362-2563
Elva Harrison, *Manager*
EMP: 26
SALES (corp-wide): 110.7B **Privately Held**
SIC: 7372 7373 Application computer software; systems integration services
HQ: Dimension Data North America, Inc.
1 Penn Plz
New York NY 10119
212 613-1220

(G-10225)
DUPLI GRAPHICS CORPORATION
Dupli Envelope & Graphics
2533 Yellow Springs Rd # 1 (19355-1452)
PHONE..............................610 644-4188
Jeff Timinski, *Accounts Exec*
Peg Lauber, *Mktg Dir*
John Hudak, *Branch Mgr*
Cecelia McCabe,
EMP: 20
SALES (corp-wide): 49.5MM **Privately Held**
WEB: www.duplionline.com
SIC: 2759 2754 Envelopes: printing; envelopes: gravure printing
HQ: Dupli Graphics Corporation
6761 Thompson Rd
Syracuse NY 13211
315 234-7286

(G-10226)
EAGLE TOOL & DIE CO INC
183 Pennsylvania Ave (19355-2418)
P.O. Box 592, Downingtown (19335-0592)
PHONE..............................610 264-6011
Eric Reitelbach, *President*
EMP: 7 **EST:** 1952
SQ FT: 6,000
SALES: 670K **Privately Held**
SIC: 3544 Special dies & tools

(G-10227)
ECO SERVICES OPERATIONS CORP (DH)
300 Lindenwood Dr (19355-1740)
PHONE..............................610 251-9118
Belgacem Chariag, *CEO*
Dave Taylor, *President*
EMP: 74
SALES (est): 254.5MM
SALES (corp-wide): 1.6B **Publicly Held**
SIC: 2819 Sulfuric acid, oleum
HQ: Pq Corporation
300 Lindenwood Dr
Malvern PA 19355
610 651-4200

(G-10228)
EGGLANDS BEST INC
70 E Swedesford Rd # 150 (19355-1454)
PHONE..............................610 265-6500
Charles Lanktree, *President*
Steve Michella, *Vice Pres*
Kurt Misialek, *Vice Pres*
Bart Slaugh, *QA Dir*
Javier Bou, *Sales Dir*
EMP: 22
SQ FT: 3,000
SALES (est): 4.3MM **Privately Held**
WEB: www.eggland.com
SIC: 2015 Egg processing

(G-10229)
ELLUCIAN SUPPORT INC
4 Country View Rd (19355-1408)
PHONE..............................610 647-5930
John Speer III, *President*
Michael Chamberlain, *President*
Paul Cunningham, *Senior VP*
Jorge Green, *Senior VP*
Mark D Jones, *Senior VP*
EMP: 119

▲ = Import ▼=Export
◆ =Import/Export

SALES (est): 19.9MM **Privately Held**
SIC: 7372 Business oriented computer software

(G-10230)
EMERGENSEE INC
1620 Minden Ln (19355-8769)
PHONE..................................610 804-9007
Philip A Reitnour, *CEO*
EMP: 20 **EST:** 2012
SQ FT: 1,500
SALES: 4MM **Privately Held**
SIC: 3699 Security control equipment & systems

(G-10231)
ENDO FINANCE CO
1400 Atwater Dr (19355-8701)
PHONE..................................484 216-0000
Paul V Campanelli, *President*
EMP: 3
SALES (est): 191.6K **Privately Held**
SIC: 2834 Pharmaceutical preparations

(G-10232)
ENDO HEALTH SOLUTIONS INC (HQ)
1400 Atwater Dr (19355-8701)
PHONE..................................484 216-0000
Rajiv De Silva, *President*
Joseph J Ciaffoni, *President*
Don Degolyer, *COO*
Susan Hall PHD, *Exec VP*
Dan A Rudio, *Vice Pres*
EMP: 385 **EST:** 1997
SQ FT: 80,000
SALES (est): 4.9B **Privately Held**
WEB: www.endo.com
SIC: 2834 Analgesics

(G-10233)
ENDO PHARMACEUTICALS INC (DH)
1400 Atwater Dr (19355-8701)
PHONE..................................484 216-0000
Paul Campanelli, *CEO*
Armando Cortaas, *Vice Pres*
Blaine Davis, *Vice Pres*
Al Ayes, *Purch Mgr*
Karen C Adler, *Treasurer*
▲ **EMP:** 15
SQ FT: 14,000
SALES: 4.5B **Privately Held**
WEB: www.lidoderm.com
SIC: 2834 Pharmaceutical preparations
HQ: Endo Health Solutions Inc.
1400 Atwater Dr
Malvern PA 19355
484 216-0000

(G-10234)
ENDO PHRMCTICALS SOLUTIONS INC (DH)
1400 Atwater Dr (19355-8701)
PHONE..................................484 216-0000
David P Holveck, *CEO*
Rajiv De Silva, *CEO*
Glenn L Cooper MD, *Ch of Bd*
Eric Gordon, *Partner*
Don Degolyer, *COO*
EMP: 46
SQ FT: 53,200
SALES (est): 36.2MM **Privately Held**
WEB: www.interneuron.com
SIC: 2834 Pharmaceutical preparations
HQ: Endo Pharmaceuticals, Inc.
1400 Atwater Dr
Malvern PA 19355
484 216-0000

(G-10235)
FIZZANO BROS CONCRETE PDTS INC
201 Phoenixville Pike (19355-1136)
PHONE..................................610 363-6290
Steven Fizzano, *Branch Mgr*
EMP: 27
SALES (corp-wide): 10MM **Privately Held**
WEB: www.fizzano.com
SIC: 3271 5211 Concrete block & brick; lumber & other building materials

PA: Fizzano Bros. Concrete Products, Inc.
1776 Chester Pike
Crum Lynne PA 19022
610 833-1100

(G-10236)
FLOTRAN EXTON INC
249 Planebrook Rd Ste 2 (19355-1580)
PHONE..................................610 640-4141
Ray Pepe, *President*
EMP: 5
SALES (est): 644.8K **Privately Held**
SIC: 5084 3492 Hydraulic systems equipment & supplies; hose & tube fittings & assemblies, hydraulic/pneumatic

(G-10237)
FLW OF PA INC
Also Called: F L W of PA
527 Lancaster Ave (19355-1870)
PHONE..................................610 251-9700
Morrell Jacobs, *President*
Kathy Jacobs, *Office Mgr*
EMP: 3
SQ FT: 2,500
SALES: 1.5MM **Privately Held**
SIC: 3823 Industrial instrmnts msrmnt display/control process variable

(G-10238)
GAS BREAKER INC
17 Lee Blvd Ste D (19355-1234)
PHONE..................................610 407-7200
John B McGowan Jr, *CEO*
C Dean McGowan, *President*
EMP: 28
SQ FT: 9,570
SALES: 100MM **Privately Held**
SIC: 3491 Gas valves & parts, industrial

(G-10239)
GENERICS INTERNATIONAL US INC (DH)
Also Called: Qualitest Pharmaceuticals
1400 Atwater Dr (19355-8701)
PHONE..................................256 859-2575
Rajiv De Silva, *President*
▲ **EMP:** 9
SALES (est): 183.8MM **Privately Held**
SIC: 2834 Pharmaceutical preparations
HQ: Endo Pharmaceuticals, Inc.
1400 Atwater Dr
Malvern PA 19355
484 216-0000

(G-10240)
GLASGOW INC
660 N Morehall Rd (19355-1415)
PHONE..................................610 251-0760
Bill McGrath, *General Mgr*
Perry Phillips, *Manager*
EMP: 30
SALES (corp-wide): 102.1MM **Privately Held**
WEB: www.glasgowinc.com
SIC: 3272 5032 3274 1422 Stone, cast concrete; paving materials; lime; crushed & broken limestone
PA: Glasgow, Inc.
104 Willow Grove Ave
Glenside PA 19038
215 884-8800

(G-10241)
GOOD CROP INC
8 Lee Blvd Ste 3 (19355-1231)
PHONE..................................585 944-7982
Douglas Gilman, *President*
Rita Gilman, *Vice Pres*
Samuel Schulick, *Manager*
EMP: 10
SQ FT: 12,500
SALES: 1MM
SALES (corp-wide): 28.2MM **Privately Held**
SIC: 2033 Fruit juices: fresh; vegetable juices: fresh
PA: G.L. - ImportaCAo E ExportaCAo, S.A.
Estrada Nacional 3 Km 5,7, Parque Industrial Da Azambuja
Vila Nova Da Rainha 2050-
263 857-000

(G-10242)
GRAPHIC ARTS CAMERA SERVICE
Also Called: Graphic Art Imaging
1 Golfview Ln (19355-1522)
P.O. Box 733 (19355-0904)
PHONE..................................610 647-6395
Carl Lotz, *President*
EMP: 3
SQ FT: 1,000
SALES (est): 368.4K **Privately Held**
SIC: 2791 Typesetting

(G-10243)
GRAPHIC IMPRESSIONS OF AMERICA
179 Lancaster Ave (19355-2122)
PHONE..................................610 296-3939
George Kazanjian Jr, *President*
Edward Kazanjian, *Vice Pres*
EMP: 4
SQ FT: 15,000
SALES (est): 614.8K **Privately Held**
WEB: www.giacopy.com
SIC: 2752 Commercial printing, offset

(G-10244)
GRUED CORPORATION
63 Lancaster Ave (19355-2120)
PHONE..................................610 644-1300
Dr Gerald Paul, *President*
Felix Zandman PHD, *Chairman*
EMP: 150
SQ FT: 10,000
SALES: 7.4MM
SALES (corp-wide): 1.7B **Privately Held**
SIC: 3676 Electronic resistors
HQ: Vishay Ltd.
Suite 7a, Tower House
Sunderland
191 516-8584

(G-10245)
HIGHWAY MATERIALS INC
29 Morehall Rd (19355)
PHONE..................................610 647-5902
Steve Fox, *Manager*
EMP: 5
SQ FT: 15,468
SALES (corp-wide): 10.1MM **Privately Held**
WEB: www.highwaymaterials.com
SIC: 2951 5032 Road materials, bituminous (not from refineries); paving materials
PA: Highway Materials, Inc.
409 Stenton Ave
Flourtown PA 19031
610 832-8000

(G-10246)
HILL LABORATORIES CO
3 N Bacton Hill Rd (19355-1005)
P.O. Box 2028 (19355-0810)
PHONE..................................610 644-2867
Howard A Hill, *President*
Tim Anderson, *QC Mgr*
▲ **EMP:** 40 **EST:** 1932
SQ FT: 15,000
SALES (est): 8.6MM **Privately Held**
WEB: www.hilllabs.com
SIC: 3841 Muscle exercise apparatus, ophthalmic; operating tables

(G-10247)
HMP CMMUNICATIONS HOLDINGS LLC (PA)
83 General Warren Blvd (19355-1209)
PHONE..................................610 560-0500
Jeff Hennessy, *CEO*
Joshua D Hartman, *Vice Pres*
Daniel Rice, *CFO*
Tim Shaw, *Manager*
EMP: 5
SALES (est): 136.3MM **Privately Held**
SIC: 2721 7389 Trade journals: publishing only, not printed on site; advertising, promotional & trade show services

(G-10248)
HMP COMMUNICATIONS LLC
Also Called: Hmp Publications
70 E Swedesford Rd # 100 (19355-1476)
PHONE..................................610 560-0500
Julie Gould, *Editor*

Peter Norris, *Exec VP*
Joshua D Hartman, *Senior VP*
Kristi Shelly, *Project Mgr*
Rich Lancia, *Human Resources*
EMP: 49
SQ FT: 13,400
SALES (est): 11.7MM **Privately Held**
WEB: www.hmpcommunications.com
SIC: 2721 7389 Trade journals: publishing only, not printed on site; advertising, promotional & trade show services
PA: Hmp Communications Holdings, Llc
83 General Warren Blvd
Malvern PA 19355

(G-10249)
ICE BUTLER
44 Malin Rd (19355-1734)
PHONE..................................610 644-3243
Mark Tillman, *Owner*
EMP: 4 **EST:** 2007
SALES (est): 231.1K **Privately Held**
SIC: 2097 Manufactured ice

(G-10250)
IDEAL PRODUCTS AMERICA LP
3239 Phoenixville Pike (19355-9006)
PHONE..................................484 320-6194
Larry Rice, *Principal*
Maryann Merlino, *Principal*
▲ **EMP:** 15 **EST:** 2010
SALES (est): 2.5MM **Privately Held**
SIC: 2311 3499 Tailored suits & formal jackets; aerosol valves, metal

(G-10251)
IFCO ENTERPRISES INC (PA)
14 Lee Blvd 46 (19355-1235)
PHONE..................................610 651-0999
Richard D Mellinger, *President*
John McDevitt, *Opers Mgr*
Jeffrey E Hanhausen, *CFO*
William H Annesley III, *Admin Sec*
EMP: 120
SQ FT: 34,000
SALES (est): 5.6MM **Privately Held**
WEB: www.invisiblefence.com
SIC: 3699 0752 3612 Electrical equipment & supplies; animal specialty services; transformers, except electric

(G-10252)
IFM EFECTOR INC (DH)
1100 Atwater Dr (19355-8731)
PHONE..................................800 441-8246
Roger Zarma, *President*
Vincent R Zagar, *Corp Secy*
Joseph T Kelly, *Vice Pres*
Michael McGowan, *Prdtn Mgr*
Ernie Maddox, *Natl Sales Mgr*
▲ **EMP:** 145
SQ FT: 59,000
SALES (est): 59.1MM
SALES (corp-wide): 1B **Privately Held**
WEB: www.ifmefector.com
SIC: 3679 Electronic switches
HQ: Ifm Electronic Gmbh
Friedrichstr. 1
Essen 45128
201 242-20

(G-10253)
INFINITY MARKETING INC
1065 S Wisteria Dr (19355-2330)
PHONE..................................610 296-0653
Lida Bonner, *President*
EMP: 3
SALES (est): 180.5K **Privately Held**
SIC: 3089 Plastics products

(G-10254)
INFOR (US) INC
40 General Warren Blvd # 110 (19355-1251)
PHONE..................................678 319-8000
Riaz Raihan, *Vice Pres*
Soma Sundaeram, *Manager*
Peter Cullen, *Software Engr*
Dennis Dixon, *Executive*
EMP: 50
SALES (corp-wide): 3.1B **Privately Held**
SIC: 7372 Prepackaged software
HQ: Infor (Us), Inc.
13560 Morris Rd Ste 4100
Alpharetta GA 30004
678 319-8000

G E O G R A P H I C

(G-10255)
INK SPOT PRINTING & COPY CTR
Also Called: The Ink Spot
14 Church Rd (19355-1509)
P.O. Box 812 (19355-0912)
PHONE..................................610 647-0776
Steve Blatman, *President*
Maria Hurley, *Corp Secy*
EMP: 4
SQ FT: 2,500
SALES: 250K **Privately Held**
WEB: www.inkspot.net
SIC: 2752 7334 Commercial printing, off-set; photocopying & duplicating services

(G-10256)
ITT WATER & WASTEWATER USA INC
Also Called: Slygt
2330 Yellow Springs Rd (19355-9758)
PHONE..................................610 647-6620
Mark Umile, *Manager*
EMP: 20 **Publicly Held**
WEB: www.flygtus.com
SIC: 5084 3561 3511 Pumps & pumping equipment; pumps & pumping equipment; turbines & turbine generator sets
HQ: Itt Water & Wastewater U.S.A., Inc.
　　1 Greenwich Pl Ste 2
　　Shelton CT 06484
　　262 548-8181

(G-10257)
J & L BUILDING MATERIALS INC (PA)
600 Lancaster Ave (19355-1846)
PHONE..................................610 644-6311
David Moretzsohn, *President*
David Barnes, *Vice Pres*
Paul Craskey, *Vice Pres*
Rob Tyre, *Warehouse Mgr*
Mike Drozda, *Purch Agent*
▲ **EMP:** 200 **EST:** 1958
SQ FT: 50,000
SALES (est): 106.2MM **Privately Held**
SIC: 3089 5072 5031 5033 Window frames & sash, plastic; hardware; windows; roofing, asphalt & sheet metal; siding, except wood

(G-10258)
JAECO FLUID SOLUTIONS INC
Also Called: Jaeco Fluid Systems
100 Quaker Ln (19355-2479)
PHONE..................................610 407-7207
James McHugh, *President*
▼ **EMP:** 4
SQ FT: 22,000
SALES (est): 1MM **Privately Held**
WEB: www.jaecofs.com
SIC: 3561 3586 5084 Pumps & pumping equipment; measuring & dispensing pumps; industrial machinery & equipment

(G-10259)
JANSSEN BIOTECH INC
260 Great Valley Pkwy (19355-1318)
PHONE..................................610 407-0194
EMP: 3
SALES (corp-wide): 71.8B **Publicly Held**
SIC: 2834 2835 Mfg Pharmaceutical Preparations Mfg Diagnostic Substances
HQ: Janssen Biotech, Inc.
　　800 Ridgeview Dr
　　Horsham PA 19044
　　610 651-6000

(G-10260)
JANSSEN BIOTECH INC
200 Great Valley Pkwy (19355-1307)
PHONE..................................610 651-6000
Robert Betz, *Principal*
Philip Silkoff, *Research*
Julie Killeen, *Human Res Mgr*
Frederick Barbara, *Manager*
John Levitt, *Technology*
EMP: 74
SALES (corp-wide): 81.5B **Publicly Held**
SIC: 2834 Pharmaceutical preparations
HQ: Janssen Biotech, Inc.
　　800 Ridgeview Dr
　　Horsham PA 19044
　　610 651-6000

(G-10261)
JANSSEN BIOTECH INC
155 Great Valley Pkwy (19355-1321)
PHONE..................................215 325-4250
Brett Chronister, *Branch Mgr*
Peter Glind, *Manager*
EMP: 3
SALES (corp-wide): 81.5B **Publicly Held**
WEB: www.remicade-crohns.com
SIC: 2834 Pharmaceutical preparations
HQ: Janssen Biotech, Inc.
　　800 Ridgeview Dr
　　Horsham PA 19044
　　610 651-6000

(G-10262)
JANSSEN BIOTECH INC
52 Great Valley Pkwy (19355-1303)
PHONE..................................610 651-6000
Joe Hofmann, *Branch Mgr*
EMP: 3
SALES (corp-wide): 81.5B **Publicly Held**
SIC: 2834 2835 Pharmaceutical preparations; in vitro diagnostics
HQ: Janssen Biotech, Inc.
　　800 Ridgeview Dr
　　Horsham PA 19044
　　610 651-6000

(G-10263)
JD DELTA COMPANY INC
136 Pennsylvania Ave (19355-2418)
PHONE..................................484 320-7600
Robert Dettore, *Director*
EMP: 3
SALES (est): 151.8K **Privately Held**
SIC: 3546 Power-driven handtools

(G-10264)
KEELER INSTRUMENTS INC
3222 Phoenixville Pike # 100 (19355-9610)
PHONE..................................610 353-4359
EMP: 21
SALES (est): 3.6MM **Privately Held**
SIC: 3841 Surgical & medical instruments

(G-10265)
LAWSON LABS INC
3217 Phoenixville Pike (19355-9600)
PHONE..................................610 725-8800
Thomas E Lawson, *President*
Anita H Lawson, *Corp Secy*
EMP: 7
SQ FT: 3,700
SALES: 655.9K **Privately Held**
WEB: www.lawsonlabs.com
SIC: 3823 Industrial instrmnts msrmnt display/control process variable

(G-10266)
LEGNINI RC ARCHITECTURAL MLLWK
Also Called: Studio Technology
46 Pennsylvania Ave (19355-2417)
PHONE..................................610 640-1227
Mitch Handman, *President*
Fran Handman, *Principal*
EMP: 11
SALES (est): 1MM **Privately Held**
SIC: 2531 Public building & related furniture

(G-10267)
LIBERTY UPLINK INC
2547 Yellow Springs Rd (19355-1443)
PHONE..................................215 964-5222
Adam Sirkin, *Principal*
EMP: 3
SALES (est): 425.7K **Privately Held**
SIC: 3663 Satellites, communications

(G-10268)
LIFESENSORS INC
Also Called: Gene Transcription Tech
271 Great Valley Pkwy (19355-1308)
PHONE..................................610 644-8845
Tauseef Butt PHD, *President*
EMP: 15 **EST:** 1996
SQ FT: 10,000
SALES (est): 3MM **Privately Held**
WEB: www.lifesensors.com
SIC: 3841 Diagnostic apparatus, medical

(G-10269)
LIFEWATCH SERVICES INC (HQ)
1000 Cedar Hollow Rd # 102 (19355-2300)
PHONE..................................847 720-2100
Stephan Rietiker, *CEO*
Roger K Richardson, *President*
Yacov Geva, *Principal*
Kobi Ben Efraim, *CFO*
Michael Turchi, *CFO*
EMP: 370
SQ FT: 56,000
SALES (est): 247.3MM
SALES (corp-wide): 399.4MM **Publicly Held**
WEB: www.lifewatchinc.com
SIC: 5047 8099 3845 8071 Patient monitoring equipment; electro-medical equipment; physical examination service; insurance; health screening service; physical examination & testing services; electrocardiographs; testing laboratories
PA: Biotelemetry, Inc.
　　1000 Cedar Hollow Rd
　　Malvern PA 19355
　　610 729-7000

(G-10270)
LOCKHEED MARTIN CORPORATION
2111 Yellow Springs Rd (19355-9602)
P.O. Box 61511, King of Prussia (19406-0911)
PHONE..................................610 337-9560
Mark Hansen, *President*
Beth Moretti, *Research*
Kory Boyden, *Engineer*
Keith Lynn, *Engineer*
Robert Marx, *Engineer*
EMP: 3 **Publicly Held**
WEB: www.lockheedmartin.com
SIC: 3721 Surgical & medical instruments
PA: Lockheed Martin Corporation
　　6801 Rockledge Dr
　　Bethesda MD 20817

(G-10271)
LOCKHEED MARTIN CORPORATION
590 Lancaster Ave (19355-3606)
P.O. Box 4001 (19355-0985)
PHONE..................................610 531-5640
EMP: 435 **Publicly Held**
WEB: www.lockheedmartin.com
SIC: 3761 3721 Space vehicles, complete; guided missiles, complete; ballistic missiles, complete; guided missiles & space vehicles, research & development; research & development on aircraft by the manufacturer
PA: Lockheed Martin Corporation
　　6801 Rockledge Dr
　　Bethesda MD 20817

(G-10272)
MAGRITEK INC
103 Great Valley Pkwy (19355-1309)
PHONE..................................855 667-6835
Andrew Coy, *President*
Hector Robert, *General Mgr*
EMP: 4
SQ FT: 1,500
SALES (est): 571.9K **Privately Held**
SIC: 3826 Analytical instruments
HQ: Magritek Limited
　　Unit 3,6 Hurring Place
　　Wellington
　　492 076-71

(G-10273)
MAINLINE BIOSCIENCES LLC
40 Lloyd Ave Ste 309 (19355-3092)
PHONE..................................610 643-4881
Junge Zhang, *CEO*
Yunqi Lu, *Vice Pres*
EMP: 7
SALES (est): 453.1K **Privately Held**
SIC: 2834 Pharmaceutical preparations

(G-10274)
MALVERN SCALE DATA SYSTEMS (PA)
Also Called: Malvern Systems
81 Lancaster Ave Ste 216 (19355-2145)
PHONE..................................610 296-9642
James M Stuart, *President*

Thomas Andrew Stuart, *President*
EMP: 8
SQ FT: 2,000
SALES (est): 919.8K **Privately Held**
WEB: www.malvernsys.com
SIC: 3679 3625 3596 Electronic loads & power supplies; relays & industrial controls; scales & balances, except laboratory

(G-10275)
MARKET SERVICE CORP
641 S Warren Ave (19355-2950)
P.O. Box 522 (19355-0522)
PHONE..................................610 644-6211
John Marshall Salyers, *President*
Mari Lynn Salyers, *Corp Secy*
EMP: 3
SALES (est): 286.9K **Privately Held**
SIC: 3821 Clinical laboratory instruments, except medical & dental

(G-10276)
MASLO COMPANY INC (PA)
11 Lee Blvd (19355-1234)
PHONE..................................610 540-9000
Robert S Loose Jr, *President*
Stephen M Loose, *President*
▼ **EMP:** 17
SQ FT: 100,000
SALES: 25MM **Privately Held**
WEB: www.maslocompany.com
SIC: 2611 Pulp manufactured from waste or recycled paper

(G-10277)
MERIT MEDICAL
65 Great Valley Pkwy (19355-1302)
PHONE..................................610 651-5000
Fred Lampropoulos, *CEO*
EMP: 5 **EST:** 2013
SALES (est): 1.1MM **Privately Held**
SIC: 3841 Surgical & medical instruments

(G-10278)
MICROSOFT CORPORATION
45 Liberty Blvd Ste 210 (19355-1419)
PHONE..................................610 240-7000
Michael Ferreri, *Manager*
Emily Keefe, *Manager*
EMP: 130
SALES (corp-wide): 110.3B **Publicly Held**
WEB: www.microsoft.com
SIC: 7372 Application computer software
PA: Microsoft Corporation
　　1 Microsoft Way
　　Redmond WA 98052
　　425 882-8080

(G-10279)
MID ATLANTIC RETRACTABLE
641 Lancaster Ave # 1011 (19355-1831)
P.O. Box 2143, West Chester (19380-0090)
PHONE..................................610 496-8062
Robert Madding,
EMP: 4
SALES (est): 316.7K **Privately Held**
SIC: 3442 Screen doors, metal

(G-10280)
MODEVITY LLC
Also Called: Araloc
20 Valley Stream Pkwy # 265 (19355-1428)
PHONE..................................610 251-0700
Jim Coyne, *President*
Tom Canova, *Chief Mktg Ofcr*
EMP: 22
SQ FT: 6,000
SALES (est): 1.6MM **Privately Held**
WEB: www.modevity.com
SIC: 7372 Application computer software

(G-10281)
MULTITHERM HEAT TRANSFER
11 General Warren Blvd (19355-1216)
P.O. Box 579, Devault (19432-0579)
PHONE..................................610 408-8361
Mark E Smith, *President*
Matt Edie, *General Mgr*
Jeff Paolizzi, *General Mgr*
Thomas Jacobs, *Principal*
David McCool, *Vice Pres*
EMP: 8 **EST:** 1977

SQ FT: 6,500
SALES (est): 2.3MM **Privately Held**
WEB: www.multitherm.com
SIC: 3443 Fabricated plate work (boiler shop)

(G-10282)
MYTAMED INC
274 Lancaster Ave Ste 208 (19355-3255)
PHONE..................................877 444-6982
David Burke, *President*
EMP: 3
SALES (est): 443.7K **Privately Held**
SIC: 3841 Surgical & medical instruments

(G-10283)
NATURE FLOORING INDUSTRIES INC
40 Lloyd Ave Ste 306 (19355-3057)
P.O. Box 596, Downingtown (19335-0596)
PHONE..................................610 280-9800
Ren Fang, *Director*
Luxia Hong, *Admin Sec*
▲ EMP: 28
SALES (est): 5.6MM **Privately Held**
SIC: 2431 Floor baseboards, wood

(G-10284)
NECO EQUIPMENT COMPANY
Also Called: Neco Pumping Systems
458 E King Rd Ste 1 (19355-3266)
PHONE..................................215 721-2200
David Cox, *President*
EMP: 8
SALES (est): 1.8MM **Privately Held**
WEB: www.necoequipment.com
SIC: 3561 Pumps & pumping equipment

(G-10285)
NEURONETICS INC
3222 Phoenixville Pike # 300 (19355-9610)
PHONE..................................610 640-4202
Brian Farley, *Ch of Bd*
Gregory Harper, *Vice Pres*
Yelena Tropsha, *Vice Pres*
Peter Donato, *CFO*
Daniel Guthrie, *Ch Credit Ofcr*
EMP: 126
SQ FT: 32,000
SALES: 52.7MM **Privately Held**
WEB: www.neuronetics.com
SIC: 3841 Surgical & medical instruments

(G-10286)
NIAGARA HOLDINGS INC
300 Lindenwood Dr (19355-1740)
PHONE..................................610 651-4200
Michael R Boyce, *President*
Michael R Imbriani, *President*
Scott Randolph, *President*
James P Cox, *CFO*
EMP: 1300
SALES (est): 52.1MM
SALES (corp-wide): 2.4B **Publicly Held**
SIC: 2819 3231 Sodium & potassium compounds, exc. bleaches, alkalies, alum.; sodium hyposulfite, sodium hydrosulfite; potassium compounds or salts, except hydroxide or carbonate; products of purchased glass
PA: The Carlyle Group L P
1001 Pennsylvania Ave Nw 220s
Washington DC 20004
202 729-5626

(G-10287)
NO FEAR INC
Also Called: Reino's Design Print Mail
99 Great Valley Pkwy (19355-1309)
PHONE..................................484 527-8000
Michael A Reino, *President*
Linda Reino, *President*
Dennis Fluck, *Treasurer*
EMP: 10
SQ FT: 6,000
SALES (est): 1.6MM **Privately Held**
WEB: www.reinos.net
SIC: 3552 Printing machinery, textile

(G-10288)
NOVAVAX EXECOFFICE
508 Lapp Rd (19355-1214)
PHONE..................................484 913-1200
Rahul Singhvi, *Principal*
EMP: 4

SALES (est): 531.2K **Privately Held**
SIC: 2836 Biological products, except diagnostic

(G-10289)
NUPATHE INC
41 Moores Rd (19355-1113)
PHONE..................................610 232-0800
Armando Anido, *CEO*
Terri B Sebree, *President*
Michael F Marino, *Vice Pres*
Keith A Goldan, *CFO*
EMP: 14
SQ FT: 11,075
SALES (est): 4MM
SALES (corp-wide): 18.8B **Privately Held**
WEB: www.nupathe.com
SIC: 2834 Drugs acting on the central nervous system & sense organs
HQ: Teva Pharmaceuticals Usa, Inc.
1090 Horsham Rd
North Wales PA 19454
215 591-3000

(G-10290)
ORACLE AMERICA INC
Also Called: Sun Microsystems
400 Chesterfield Pkwy (19355-7700)
P.O. Box 8500s-4020, Philadelphia (19178-0001)
PHONE..................................610 647-8530
EMP: 3
SALES (corp-wide): 39.8B **Publicly Held**
SIC: 7372 Prepackaged software
HQ: Oracle America, Inc.
500 Oracle Pkwy
Redwood City CA 94065
650 506-7000

(G-10291)
ORTHOVITA INC
Also Called: Stryker Orthobiologics
45 Great Valley Pkwy (19355-1302)
PHONE..................................610 640-1775
Kevin Lobo, *President*
Teutsch Eric, *Vice Pres*
▲ EMP: 256
SQ FT: 13,700
SALES (est): 44.7MM
SALES (corp-wide): 13.6B **Publicly Held**
SIC: 3841 Medical instruments & equipment, blood & bone work
PA: Stryker Corporation
2825 Airview Blvd
Portage MI 49002
269 385-2600

(G-10292)
OXICOOL INC (PA)
508 Lapp Rd (19355-1214)
PHONE..................................215 462-2665
Ravikant Barot, *CEO*
Dave Martin, *President*
John Engels, *Principal*
EMP: 6
SQ FT: 8,500
SALES (est): 1.1MM **Privately Held**
WEB: www.oxicool.com
SIC: 3585 8731 Air conditioning units, complete: domestic or industrial; commercial physical research

(G-10293)
PAR PHARMACEUTICAL 2 INC
1400 Atwater Dr (19355-8701)
PHONE..................................484 216-7741
Paul Campanelli, *CEO*
Cheryl Matz, *Manager*
EMP: 90
SALES (est): 5MM **Privately Held**
SIC: 2834 Pharmaceutical preparations

(G-10294)
PEACE PRODUCTS CO INC
143 Pnnsylvania Ave Ste 2 (19355)
PHONE..................................610 296-4222
Kenneth R Trimble, *President*
Stephen R Trimble, *Vice Pres*
Kenneth D Trimble, *Admin Sec*
▼ EMP: 22 EST: 1970
SQ FT: 40,000
SALES (est): 8MM **Privately Held**
WEB: www.peaceproducts.com
SIC: 2673 Plastic bags: made from purchased materials; food storage & frozen food bags, plastic

(G-10295)
PHASEBIO PHARMACEUTICALS INC
1 Great Valley Pkwy # 30 (19355-1423)
PHONE..................................610 981-6500
Jonathan P Mow, *CEO*
Clay B Thorp, *Ch of Bd*
Susan Arnold, *Vice Pres*
James Ballance, *Vice Pres*
Michael York, *Vice Pres*
EMP: 18
SQ FT: 16,000
SALES (est): 668K **Privately Held**
WEB: www.phasebio.com
SIC: 2834 Pharmaceutical preparations

(G-10296)
PHLEXGLOBAL INC
400 Chesterfield Pkwy (19355-7700)
PHONE..................................484 324-7921
John McNeill, *CEO*
Stella Donoghue, *President*
Kathleen Vangeri, *HR Admin*
Mariangelis Smith, *Marketing Staff*
James Horstmann, *Manager*
EMP: 60
SALES (est): 8.6MM
SALES (corp-wide): 20.8MM **Privately Held**
SIC: 3679 Electronic loads & power supplies
PA: Phlexglobal Limited
Mandeville House
Amersham BUCKS HP7 0
149 472-0420

(G-10297)
POTTERS HOLDINGS II LP
300 Lindenwood Dr (19355-1740)
PHONE..................................610 651-4200
Joe Kwapinski, *Mng Member*
EMP: 4 EST: 2011
SALES (est): 250K
SALES (corp-wide): 1.6B **Publicly Held**
SIC: 3231 Reflector glass beads, for highway signs or reflectors
HQ: Pq Corporation
300 Lindenwood Dr
Malvern PA 19355
610 651-4200

(G-10298)
POTTERS INDUSTRIES LLC (DH)
300 Lindenwood Dr (19355-1740)
P.O. Box 841, Valley Forge (19482-0841)
PHONE..................................610 651-4700
Scott Randolph, *President*
Hector Martinez-Rossier, *Vice Pres*
Maxwell James Singleton, *Vice Pres*
Allan Kressig, *Plant Mgr*
Bob Schult, *Plant Mgr*
◆ EMP: 45 EST: 1914
SALES (est): 186.9MM
SALES (corp-wide): 1.6B **Publicly Held**
WEB: www.flexolite.com
SIC: 3231 Reflector glass beads, for highway signs or reflectors
HQ: Pq Corporation
300 Lindenwood Dr
Malvern PA 19355
610 651-4200

(G-10299)
PQ CORPORATION (DH)
300 Lindenwood Dr (19355-1740)
P.O. Box 840, Valley Forge (19482-0840)
PHONE..................................610 651-4200
Belgacem Chariag, *CEO*
Steve Dervin, *CEO*
Joe Cistone, *Vice Pres*
Paul Ferrall, *Vice Pres*
Scott Randolph, *Vice Pres*
◆ EMP: 150 EST: 1904
SALES (est): 885MM
SALES (corp-wide): 1.6B **Publicly Held**
WEB: www.pqcorp.com
SIC: 3231 2819 Products of purchased glass; sodium silicate, water glass
HQ: Pq Holding, Inc.
300 Lindenwood Dr
Malvern PA 19355
610 651-4400

(G-10300)
PQ EXPORT COMPANY
Also Called: PQ International, Inc.
300 Lindenwood Dr (19355-1740)
P.O. Box 840, Valley Forge (19482-0840)
PHONE..................................610 651-4200
Michael R Imbriani, *President*
EMP: 7
SALES (est): 712.6K
SALES (corp-wide): 1.6B **Publicly Held**
WEB: www.pqcorp.com
SIC: 2819 Industrial inorganic chemicals
HQ: Pq Corporation
300 Lindenwood Dr
Malvern PA 19355
610 651-4200

(G-10301)
PQ GROUP HOLDINGS INC (PA)
300 Lindenwood Dr (19355-1740)
PHONE..................................610 651-4400
James F Gentilcore, *Ch of Bd*
Belgacem Chariag, *President*
Scott Randolph, *President*
David J Taylor, *Exec VP*
Paul Ferrall, *Senior VP*
EMP: 15 EST: 2007
SQ FT: 33,000
SALES: 1.6B **Publicly Held**
SIC: 2819 Catalysts, chemical

(G-10302)
PQ HOLDING INC (HQ)
300 Lindenwood Dr (19355-1740)
PHONE..................................610 651-4400
Michael Boyce, *Ch of Bd*
John M Steitz, *President*
Alan McIlroy, *CFO*
William Sichko Jr, *Officer*
EMP: 13 EST: 1977
SQ FT: 33,000
SALES (est): 885MM
SALES (corp-wide): 1.6B **Publicly Held**
SIC: 2819 Sodium silicate, water glass
PA: Pq Group Holdings Inc.
300 Lindenwood Dr
Malvern PA 19355
610 651-4400

(G-10303)
PRINT A TOOTH INC
155 Planebrook Rd (19355-1526)
PHONE..................................610 647-6990
James Cadmus, *President*
EMP: 3
SALES (est): 172.4K **Privately Held**
SIC: 3843 Dental equipment & supplies

(G-10304)
QILU PHARMA INC
101 Lindenwood Dr Ste 225 (19355-1762)
PHONE..................................484 443-2935
Chen Lianbing, *President*
EMP: 60
SALES (est): 3.6MM **Privately Held**
SIC: 2834 Pharmaceutical preparations
HQ: Qilu Pharmaceutical Co., Ltd.
No.317, Xinluo St., High-Tech Zone
Jinan 25010
531 831-2666

(G-10305)
QUEEN OF HEARTS INC
Also Called: Queen of Hearts Catering
189 Pennsylvania Ave (19355-2418)
PHONE..................................610 889-0477
Stephanie Nichols, *President*
EMP: 20
SALES (est): 2MM **Privately Held**
WEB: www.queenofheartscatering.com
SIC: 2051 5812 Bakery: wholesale or wholesale/retail combined; caterers

(G-10306)
R H BENEDIX CONTRACTING
77 N Bacton Hill Rd (19355-1005)
PHONE..................................610 889-7472
Robert H Benedix Jr, *Owner*
EMP: 3
SQ FT: 4,708
SALES (est): 431.8K **Privately Held**
SIC: 7692 3441 Welding repair; fabricated structural metal

(G-10307)
RAJANT CORPORATION (PA)
200 Chesterfield Pkwy (19355-8704)
PHONE................................484 595-0233
Robert J Schena, *President*
Scott Beer, *COO*
Geoff Smith, *Exec VP*
Michael J Van Rassen, *Exec VP*
Gary Anderson, *Senior VP*
EMP: 90
SQ FT: 5,000
SALES: 26MM **Privately Held**
WEB: www.rajant.com
SIC: 3661 Communication headgear, telephone

(G-10308)
REALM THERAPEUTICS INC (PA)
Also Called: Puricore
267 Great Valley Pkwy (19355-1308)
PHONE................................484 321-2700
Greg Bosch, *President*
Paul J Donnelly, *President*
Michael Rd Ashton, *Chairman*
Tom H Daniel, *Senior VP*
Mark Sampson, *Vice Pres*
EMP: 92
SALES (est): 18.5MM **Privately Held**
WEB: www.sterilox.com
SIC: 3589 Water treatment equipment, industrial

(G-10309)
RECRO PHARMA INC (PA)
490 Lapp Rd (19355-1212)
PHONE................................484 395-2470
Wayne B Weisman, *Ch of Bd*
Gerri A Henwood, *President*
Michael Celano, *COO*
Mike Choi, *Vice Pres*
John Harlow, *Vice Pres*
EMP: 55
SQ FT: 22,313
SALES: 77.3MM **Publicly Held**
SIC: 2834 Pharmaceutical preparations

(G-10310)
RIVERBED TECHNOLOGY INC
5 Great Valley Pkwy (19355-1426)
PHONE................................610 648-3819
Jack Knezo, *Principal*
EMP: 3
SALES (corp-wide): 1.2B **Privately Held**
SIC: 3577 Computer peripheral equipment
HQ: Riverbed Technology, Inc.
680 Folsom St Ste 500
San Francisco CA 94107
415 247-8800

(G-10311)
RUSTICRAFT FENCE CO
439 E King Rd (19355-2552)
P.O. Box 1429 (19355-0629)
PHONE................................610 644-6770
John Diguseppe, *President*
Steve Lauriello, *Vice Pres*
EMP: 7 EST: 1918
SQ FT: 25,000
SALES (est): 706K **Privately Held**
WEB: www.rusticraftfence.com
SIC: 2499 5211 Fencing, wood; fencing

(G-10312)
RWG COMPANY
333 Lancaster Ave Apt 804 (19355-1829)
P.O. Box 6191, Philadelphia (19115-6191)
PHONE................................215 552-9541
EMP: 3 EST: 1996
SALES (est): 120K **Privately Held**
SIC: 2741 Publisher Of Newsletter

(G-10313)
SAINT-GOBAIN CORPORATION (DH)
20 Moores Rd (19355-1114)
PHONE................................610 893-6000
Thomas Kinisky, *President*
Carmen Ferrigno, *President*
Timothy Feagans, *Senior VP*
Philippe Mouailhac, *Senior VP*
Timothy Guyer, *Vice Pres*
▲ EMP: 750
SQ FT: 200,000

SALES (est): 9.1B
SALES (corp-wide): 215.9MM **Privately Held**
SIC: 2891 3269 2493 3275 Adhesives; laboratory & industrial pottery; insulation & roofing material, reconstituted wood; gypsum products
HQ: Spafi-Soc Particip Financiere Industriel
Tour Les Miroirs Tour Saint Gobain
Courbevoie
147 623-000

(G-10314)
SAMUELSON LEATHER LLC
2309 Woodview Way (19355-3229)
PHONE................................484 328-3273
EMP: 6
SALES (est): 491.4K
SALES (corp-wide): 1.2MM **Privately Held**
SIC: 2386 3199 5651 Garments, leather; leather garments; unisex clothing stores
PA: Samuelson Leather Llc
638 Metro Ct
West Chester PA 19380
610 719-7391

(G-10315)
SIEMENS MED SOLUTIONS USA INC (DH)
Also Called: Nuclear Systems Group
40 Liberty Blvd (19355-1418)
PHONE................................888 826-9702
Jeffrey Bundy, *CEO*
Britta Fuenfstueck, *CEO*
John Glaser, *CEO*
Michael Reitermann, *President*
Viola Fernandes, *Principal*
◆ EMP: 453
SQ FT: 150,000
SALES (est): 1.5B
SALES (corp-wide): 95B **Privately Held**
WEB: www.siemensmedical.com
SIC: 3845 3842 3843 5047 Electromedical apparatus; pacemaker, cardiac; orthopedic appliances; hearing aids; dental equipment & supplies; medical equipment & supplies
HQ: Siemens Corporation
300 New Jersey Ave Nw # 10
Washington DC 20001
202 434-4800

(G-10316)
SIGNAGE UNLIMITED INC
197 Pennsylvania Ave (19355-2418)
PHONE................................610 647-6962
Henry Mc Curdy, *President*
John Povey, *Treasurer*
Daniel Mc Curdy, *Admin Sec*
EMP: 18
SQ FT: 8,000
SALES (est): 2.4MM **Privately Held**
WEB: www.signageunlimited.com
SIC: 3993 1799 Electric signs; sign installation & maintenance

(G-10317)
SILICON POWER CORPORATION (PA)
280 Great Valley Pkwy (19355-1313)
PHONE................................610 407-4700
Harshad Mehta, *President*
Jack Ladden, *Vice Pres*
Vic Temple, *Vice Pres*
EMP: 100
SQ FT: 11,000
SALES (est): 19.7MM **Privately Held**
SIC: 3674 3679 3643 3612 Switches, silicon control; electronic switches; current-carrying wiring devices; transformers, except electric

(G-10318)
SIXTH WHEEL INC
23 Deer Run Ln (19355-1613)
PHONE................................610 647-0880
David McGrew, *President*
James Himler, *Treasurer*
EMP: 3
SALES (est): 260K **Privately Held**
WEB: www.sixthwheel.net
SIC: 3713 Truck bodies & parts

(G-10319)
SKYLINE TECHNOLOGY INC
44 Pennsylvania Ave (19355-2417)
PHONE................................610 296-7501
John B Rugh, *President*
Patricia Rugh, *Corp Secy*
EMP: 3
SQ FT: 1,000
SALES (est): 130K **Privately Held**
SIC: 2399 Money belts

(G-10320)
SLATE PHARMACEUTICALS INC
1400 Atwater Dr (19355-8701)
PHONE................................484 321-5900
Bob Whitehead, *Principal*
Matt Tetzold, *CFO*
EMP: 65
SQ FT: 2,500
SALES: 400MM **Privately Held**
SIC: 2834 Pharmaceutical preparations

(G-10321)
SMC INDUSTRIES INC (PA)
Also Called: Sproule Mfg.
3239 Phnxvlle Pike Bldg 1 (19355)
PHONE................................610 647-5687
Charles Sproule III, *President*
George Bauer, *Vice Pres*
Chris Diegel, *Controller*
Shanon Yarbrough, *Manager*
EMP: 8
SQ FT: 25,000
SALES (est): 5.6MM **Privately Held**
WEB: www.sproule-mfg.com
SIC: 3296 5033 Insulation: rock wool, slag & silica minerals; insulation materials

(G-10322)
SMITHS GROUP NORTH AMERICA INC (HQ)
101 Lindenwood Dr Ste 125 (19355-1755)
P.O. Box 2349, Castro Valley CA (94546-0349)
PHONE................................772 286-9300
R C Albrecht, *Vice Pres*
Ronald C Albrecht, *Vice Pres*
Walter Orme, *Asst Sec*
◆ EMP: 16
SALES (est): 951.1MM
SALES (corp-wide): 4.1B **Privately Held**
SIC: 3812 3841 3679 Aircraft control systems, electronic; navigational systems & instruments; surgical instruments & apparatus; harness assemblies for electronic use: wire or cable
PA: Smiths Group Plc
4th Floor
London SW1Y
207 004-1600

(G-10323)
SOUTHEASTERN PA TRNSP AUTH
Also Called: Septa
32 Sproul Rd (19355-1952)
PHONE................................215 580-7800
EMP: 319
SALES (corp-wide): 528.1MM **Privately Held**
SIC: 2542 4111 Postal lock boxes, mail racks & related products; local & suburban transit
PA: Southeastern Pennsylvania Transportation Authority
1234 Market St Fl 4
Philadelphia PA 19107
215 580-7800

(G-10324)
STRYKER ORTHOBIOLOGICS
67 Great Valley Pkwy (19355-1302)
PHONE................................610 407-5259
EMP: 3
SALES (est): 358.3K **Privately Held**
SIC: 3841 Surgical & medical instruments

(G-10325)
SYNCHRGNIX INFO STRATEGIES INC
5 Great Valley Pkwy # 359 (19355-1426)
PHONE................................302 892-4800
Trish Moroz, *Branch Mgr*
EMP: 6 **Privately Held**

SIC: 2721 8999 8742 8731 Magazines: publishing only, not printed on site; writing for publication; management consulting services; commercial physical research
HQ: Synchrogenix Information Strategies, Llc
2 Righter Pkwy Ste 205
Wilmington DE 19803
302 892-4800

(G-10326)
T M P REFINING CORPORATION
23 Long Ln (19355-2946)
PHONE................................484 318-8285
Thomas Parvesse, *President*
EMP: 3
SALES (est): 4.5MM **Privately Held**
SIC: 3339 Platinum group metal refining (primary)

(G-10327)
TALEXMEDICAL LLC
5 Great Valley Pkwy # 210 (19355-1426)
PHONE................................888 327-2221
Kimberly Coffey, *President*
Scott Bartlett,
EMP: 6
SALES (est): 657.3K **Privately Held**
SIC: 3841 Surgical & medical instruments

(G-10328)
TETRALGIC PHARMACEUTICALS CORP (PA)
343 Phoenixville Pike (19355-9603)
P.O. Box 1305, Paoli (19301-5305)
PHONE................................610 889-9900
Andrew Pecora, *Ch of Bd*
J Kevin Buchi, *President*
C Glenn Begley, *Senior VP*
Richard L Sherman, *Senior VP*
Pete A Meyers, *CFO*
EMP: 11
SQ FT: 16,190
SALES (est): 2.8MM **Publicly Held**
WEB: www.tetralogicpharma.com
SIC: 2834 Pharmaceutical preparations

(G-10329)
TEVA BRANDED PHRM PDTS R&D INC (DH)
41 Moores Rd (19355-1113)
PHONE................................215 591-3000
Richard Egosi, *Principal*
Erez Vigodman, *COO*
Lori Queisser, *Vice Pres*
Renee Thompson, *Production*
Lewis Murray, *Buyer*
EMP: 1
SALES (est): 8.3MM
SALES (corp-wide): 18.8B **Privately Held**
WEB: www.barrlabs.com
SIC: 2834 Penicillin preparations; drugs acting on the respiratory system; drugs acting on the cardiovascular system, except diagnostic
HQ: Teva Pharmaceuticals Usa, Inc.
1090 Horsham Rd
North Wales PA 19454
215 591-3000

(G-10330)
TEVA RESPIRATORY LLC
41 Moores Rd (19355-1113)
PHONE................................610 344-0200
Phillip Frost, *Chairman*
Ken Hochberg, *Production*
Dianne Pfueller, *Accountant*
Kevin McKernan, *HR Admin*
Matthew Kramin, *Regl Sales Mgr*
EMP: 60
SALES (est): 28.6MM **Privately Held**
SIC: 2834 Mfg Pharmaceutical Preparations

(G-10331)
TIMKEN COMPANY
7 Great Valley Pkwy # 140 (19355-1425)
PHONE................................215 654-7606
Fax: 215 654-7171
EMP: 6
SALES (corp-wide): 2.6B **Publicly Held**
SIC: 3562 Mfg Ball/Roller Bearings
PA: The Timken Company
4500 Mount Pleasant St Nw
North Canton OH 44720
234 262-3000

▲ = Import ▼=Export
◆ =Import/Export

(G-10332)
TITAN MANUFACTURING INC (PA)
1 Rapps Run Dr (19355-9663)
PHONE..............................610 935-8203
Don Seadey, *President*
EMP: 9
SALES (est): 882.9K **Privately Held**
SIC: 3841 Surgical instruments & apparatus

(G-10333)
TITAN MANUFACTURING INC
1 Rapps Run Dr (19355-9663)
PHONE..............................781 767-1963
Donald A Seavey, *President*
Gastao Dacamara, *Vice Pres*
EMP: 8
SALES: 600K **Privately Held**
WEB: www.titanmfg.com
SIC: 3841 5047 Surgical instruments & apparatus; instruments, surgical & medical

(G-10334)
TOWERSTAR PETS LLC
Also Called: Neater Pet Brands
2350 Yellow Springs Rd # 2 (19355-9758)
PHONE..............................610 296-4970
Tony Hill, *Mfg Staff*
Jackie Becattini, *Marketing Staff*
Fernando Becattini Jr,
▲ EMP: 8
SALES (est): 1.4MM **Privately Held**
SIC: 3999 Pet supplies

(G-10335)
TRI-STATE TUBULAR RIVET CO
382 Lancaster Ave (19355-1804)
P.O. Box 4006 (19355-0990)
PHONE..............................610 644-6060
Thomas J Ryan, *President*
Dennis Diginto, *Sales Staff*
EMP: 10
SQ FT: 25,000
SALES: 2.5MM **Privately Held**
WEB: www.tristaterivet.com
SIC: 3452 Rivets, metal

(G-10336)
USA COIL & AIR INC (PA)
Also Called: USA Coil and Air
11 General Warren Blvd # 2 (19355-1216)
P.O. Box 578, Devault (19432-0578)
PHONE..............................610 296-9668
Melissa Selfridge, *President*
Brian Schnepp, *Corp Secy*
Brian Cosgrove, *Vice Pres*
Michael Walrath, *Vice Pres*
Jean Kirk Hindley, *Controller*
EMP: 45
SQ FT: 10,056
SALES (est): 15.6MM **Privately Held**
WEB: www.usacoil.com
SIC: 3585 3564 3433 Air conditioning units, complete: domestic or industrial; heating equipment, complete; blowers & fans; heating equipment, except electric

(G-10337)
VALIDITY LLC
101 Lindenwood Dr Ste 225 (19355-1762)
PHONE..............................610 768-8042
Tracey White,
EMP: 7
SQ FT: 1,000
SALES (est): 564.5K **Privately Held**
SIC: 5734 5045 3663 7372 Computer & software stores; computers, peripherals & software; computer software; encryption devices; business oriented computer software; software training, computer

(G-10338)
VELTEK ASSOCIATES INC
Also Called: Vai
15 Lee Blvd (19355-1234)
PHONE..............................610 644-8335
Arthur L Vellutato Jr, *President*
Josephine P Vellutato, *Vice Pres*
Walt Baker, *VP Opers*
Patricia Choquette, *Export Mgr*
Gary O'Dell, *Controller*
◆ EMP: 50

SALES (est): 17.2MM **Privately Held**
WEB: www.sterile.com
SIC: 2842 Sanitation preparations, disinfectants & deodorants

(G-10339)
VENATORX PHARMACEUTICALS INC
30 Spring Mill Dr (19355-1200)
PHONE..............................610 644-8935
Christopher J Burns, *President*
Daniel Pevear, *Vice Pres*
James G Murphy, *CFO*
EMP: 8
SALES (est): 1.7MM **Privately Held**
SIC: 8731 2833 Biological research; antibiotics

(G-10340)
VINTAGE PHARMACEUTICALS LLC (DH)
1400 Atwater Dr (19355-8701)
PHONE..............................256 859-2222
William S Propst, *President*
EMP: 59
SALES (est): 36.1MM **Privately Held**
SIC: 2834 Vitamin, nutrient & hematinic preparations for human use

(G-10341)
VISHAY INTERTECHNOLOGY INC (PA)
63 Lancaster Ave (19355-2120)
PHONE..............................610 644-1300
Marc Zandman, *Ch of Bd*
Gerald Paul, *President*
Werner Gebhardt, *Exec VP*
Joel Smejkal, *Exec VP*
Clarence TSE, *Exec VP*
EMP: 277 EST: 1962
SALES: 3B **Publicly Held**
WEB: www.vishay.com
SIC: 3677 3675 3674 3613 Electronic coils, transformers & other inductors; electronic capacitors; semiconductors & related devices; switchgear & switchboard apparatus; transformers, except electric; resistor networks

(G-10342)
VISHAY PRECISION FOIL INC (HQ)
3 Great Valley Pkwy # 150 (19355-1478)
PHONE..............................484 321-5300
Ziv Shoshani, *CEO*
Willian Clancy, *CFO*
Steven Klausner, *Treasurer*
EMP: 1122
SALES (est): 87.9MM
SALES (corp-wide): 299.7MM **Publicly Held**
SIC: 3676 Electronic resistors
PA: Vishay Precision Group, Inc.
3 Great Valley Pkwy # 150
Malvern PA 19355
484 321-5300

(G-10343)
VISHAY PRECISION GROUP INC (PA)
Also Called: Vpg
3 Great Valley Pkwy # 150 (19355-1478)
PHONE..............................484 321-5300
Marc Zandman, *Ch of Bd*
Ziv Shoshani, *President*
Roland B Desilets, *Vice Pres*
Benny Shaya, *Vice Pres*
Dubi Zandman, *Vice Pres*
EMP: 85
SQ FT: 8,000
SALES: 299.7MM **Publicly Held**
SIC: 3676 3823 Electronic resistors; pressure measurement instruments, industrial

(G-10344)
VISHAY SILICONIX LLC
63 Lancaster Ave (19355-2120)
PHONE..............................408 567-8177
EMP: 636 EST: 1999
SALES (est): 4.6MM
SALES (corp-wide): 3B **Publicly Held**
SIC: 3674 Semiconductors & related devices

HQ: Siliconix Incorporated
2585 Junction Ave
San Jose CA 95134
408 988-8000

(G-10345)
VITABRU EMBROIDERY
115 Great Valley Pkwy (19355-1309)
PHONE..............................610 296-0181
Bruce Korn, *Owner*
EMP: 3
SALES: 120K **Privately Held**
SIC: 2395 Embroidery products, except schiffli machine

(G-10346)
WILLIAM T JENKINS
Also Called: Jenkins Competition
460 E King Rd (19355-3049)
PHONE..............................610 644-7052
William T Jenkins, *Owner*
Jake Barbato, *Manager*
EMP: 5
SQ FT: 8,500
SALES (est): 155.1K **Privately Held**
WEB: www.williamtjenkins.com
SIC: 7948 3711 Racing, including track operation; motor vehicles & car bodies

(G-10347)
WIRE CRAFTERS
3119 Phnxvlle Pike Unit 2 (19355)
PHONE..............................610 296-2538
Frank Fullam, *Principal*
EMP: 75
SALES (est): 7.1MM **Privately Held**
SIC: 3496 Miscellaneous fabricated wire products

(G-10348)
WOODSHOP LLC
Also Called: Thal, David
214 N Warren Ave (19355-2425)
PHONE..............................610 647-4190
David Thal,
EMP: 3
SQ FT: 6,000
SALES: 500K **Privately Held**
SIC: 2431 2434 Millwork; wood kitchen cabinets

(G-10349)
WORKMASTER INC
284 Three Tun Rd (19355-3981)
PHONE..............................866 476-9217
Jo Anna Dougherty, *President*
EMP: 3
SALES (est): 176.3K **Privately Held**
SIC: 3321 Railroad car wheels & brake shoes, cast iron

(G-10350)
WORTHINGTON ARMSTRONG INTL LLC (HQ)
9 Old Lincoln Hwy Ste 200 (19355-2551)
PHONE..............................610 722-1200
Debbie Burch, *Admin Asst*
EMP: 4
SALES (est): 2.1MM **Privately Held**
SIC: 3446 5051 Acoustical suspension systems, metal; iron & steel (ferrous) products

(G-10351)
WORTHINGTON ARMSTRONG VENTURE (PA)
Also Called: Wave
101 Lindenwood Dr Ste 350 (19355-1744)
PHONE..............................610 722-1200
Rose Mary Clyburn, *President*
Doug Wisel, *CFO*
▲ EMP: 230
SQ FT: 130,000
SALES (est): 141MM **Privately Held**
SIC: 3446 5051 Acoustical suspension systems, metal; iron & steel (ferrous) products

(G-10352)
ZEOLYST INTERNATIONAL
300 Lindenwood Dr (19355-1740)
PHONE..............................610 651-4200
Belgacem Chariag, *President*
Bill Cormier, *Vice Pres*
Harry Spink, *Analyst*

EMP: 45
SALES: 287.5MM **Privately Held**
WEB: www.zeolyst.com
SIC: 2819 Industrial inorganic chemicals

(G-10353)
ZEOMEDIX INC
26 Ashlawn Cir (19355-1133)
PHONE..............................610 517-7818
John Aybar, *CEO*
EMP: 4
SALES (est): 316.6K **Privately Held**
SIC: 2834 Pharmaceutical preparations

Manchester
York County

(G-10354)
ALLEGHENY-YORK CO
Also Called: Konsep Co
3995 N George Street Ext (17345-9202)
P.O. Box 3327, York (17402-0327)
PHONE..............................717 266-6617
Herbert I Konrad III, *President*
Judy Watkins, *Corp Secy*
Chip Konrad, *Manager*
▲ EMP: 45
SQ FT: 20,000
SALES (est): 17.7MM **Privately Held**
WEB: www.alleghenyyork.com
SIC: 5085 3053 Pipeline wrappings, anticorrosive; seals, industrial; gaskets, packing & sealing devices

(G-10355)
B&B METAL FINISHING INC
401 N Main St (17345-1511)
PHONE..............................717 764-8941
Aaron Schwartz, *President*
EMP: 3
SQ FT: 6,500
SALES (est): 133.6K **Privately Held**
SIC: 3471 Electroplating of metals or formed products

(G-10356)
FLINCHBAUGH COMPANY INC (PA)
245 Beshore School Rd (17345-9536)
PHONE..............................717 266-2202
Greogory Jenkins, *President*
Kurt R Weber, *Treasurer*
EMP: 29
SQ FT: 34,600
SALES (est): 9.2MM **Privately Held**
WEB: www.flinchbaugh.com
SIC: 3599 7692 1721 7389 Custom machinery; welding repair; commercial painting; grinding, precision: commercial or industrial

(G-10357)
MANCHESTER HYDRAULICS INC
3775 N George Street Ext (17345-9675)
PHONE..............................717 764-5226
Owen Rumburg, *President*
Delilah Rumburg, *Admin Sec*
EMP: 7
SQ FT: 3,500
SALES (est): 1.4MM **Privately Held**
SIC: 3593 3594 Fluid power cylinders, hydraulic or pneumatic; fluid power pumps & motors

(G-10358)
NAVISTAR INC
105 Steam Boat Blvd (17345-9339)
PHONE..............................717 767-3800
Margy Designic, *Branch Mgr*
EMP: 66
SALES (corp-wide): 10.2B **Publicly Held**
WEB: www.internationaldelivers.com
SIC: 3711 Truck & tractor truck assembly
HQ: Navistar, Inc.
2701 Navistar Dr
Lisle IL 60532
331 332-5000

(G-10359)
NOVAPAK CORPORATION
1 Devco Dr (17345-1337)
PHONE..............................717 266-6687

William Bergen, *President*
William J Bergen, *President*
Joel F Roberts, *Vice Pres*
Jeffrey Shapiro, *Treasurer*
Herbert S Meeker, *Admin Sec*
EMP: 11 **EST:** 2008
SALES (est): 2MM **Privately Held**
SIC: 3085 Plastics bottles

(G-10360)
PENNTEX INDUSTRIES INC (PA)
202 Plaza Dr (17345-1340)
PHONE..................................717 266-8762
Thomas J Lucas, *President*
EMP: 3
SQ FT: 12,000
SALES (est): 2.4MM **Privately Held**
WEB: www.penntexusa.com
SIC: 3694 Alternators, automotive; automotive electrical equipment

(G-10361)
POLYVISIONS HOLDINGS INC (PA)
25 Devco Dr (17345-1337)
PHONE..................................717 266-3031
Scott Howard, *CEO*
Dave Altland, *Opers Staff*
Larry Bourland, *Technology*
EMP: 13
SALES (est): 1.4MM **Privately Held**
SIC: 2821 Plastics materials & resins

(G-10362)
PRETIUM PACKAGING LLC
1 Devco Dr (17345-1337)
PHONE..................................717 266-6687
Mike Euler, *Plant Mgr*
Alex Myers, *Production*
Michael Euler, *Branch Mgr*
Scott Koprowski, *Maintence Staff*
Matt Towzey, *Maintence Staff*
EMP: 103
SALES (corp-wide): 141MM **Privately Held**
SIC: 3089 Plastic containers, except foam; plastic processing; closures, plastic
HQ: Pretium Packaging, L.L.C.
15450 S Outer Forty Dr St
Chesterfield MO 63017
314 727-8200

(G-10363)
PVC CONTAINER CORPORATION
Also Called: Airopek
50 Devco Dr (17345)
PHONE..................................717 266-9100
Mike Euler, *Manager*
EMP: 100
SALES (corp-wide): 141MM **Privately Held**
WEB: www.airopak.com
SIC: 3085 Plastics bottles
HQ: Pvc Container Corporation
15450 South Outer 40 Rd # 120
Chesterfield MO 63017

(G-10364)
QUIGLEY MOTOR COMPANY INC
100 Sunset Dr (17345-1330)
PHONE..................................717 266-5631
William H Quigley Jr, *CEO*
Michael Quigley, *President*
Mario Iocco, *Exec VP*
Angie Quigley, *VP Opers*
Steve Hooper, *Purchasing*
▼ **EMP:** 55 **EST:** 1966
SQ FT: 59,700
SALES (est): 10.5MM **Privately Held**
WEB: www.quigley4x4.com
SIC: 3714 3566 5521 Motor vehicle transmissions, drive assemblies & parts; speed changers, drives & gears; used car dealers

(G-10365)
WAGMAN MANUFACTURING INC
215 Beshore School Rd (17345-9536)
P.O. Box 428 (17345-0428)
PHONE..................................717 266-5616
Harold Wagman, *CEO*
Chris Wagman, *President*
Craig Wagman, *President*
Shauna Rofier, *Admin Sec*
EMP: 12 **EST:** 1959

SQ FT: 11,100
SALES: 1,000K **Privately Held**
WEB: www.wagmanmfg.com
SIC: 3451 3599 Screw machine products; machine shop, jobbing & repair

---

Manheim
Lancaster County

(G-10366)
3 T SECUIRTY LLC
3045 Back Run Rd (17545-8131)
PHONE..................................717 653-0019
Kevin Stauffer,
EMP: 6
SALES (est): 535.1K **Privately Held**
SIC: 3699 Security devices

(G-10367)
AMISH COUNTRY GAZEBOS INC
340 Hostetter Rd (17545-8597)
PHONE..................................717 665-0365
Chester Beiler, *President*
Elizabeth Greiner, *General Mgr*
Sharon Beiler, *Treasurer*
Julie Strubel, *Office Admin*
◆ **EMP:** 5
SALES (est): 540K **Privately Held**
WEB: www.amishgazebos.com
SIC: 2394 Tents: made from purchased materials

(G-10368)
B & B MACHINE INC
8820 S Chiques Rd (17545)
PHONE..................................717 898-3081
Charles Beard, *President*
EMP: 7
SQ FT: 6,400
SALES (est): 420K **Privately Held**
SIC: 3599 Machine shop, jobbing & repair

(G-10369)
BALLEWS ALUMINUM PRODUCTS INC
166 Arrowhead Dr (17545-8682)
PHONE..................................717 492-8956
EMP: 17
SALES (corp-wide): 15.8MM **Privately Held**
SIC: 3354 Aluminum extruded products
PA: Ballew's Aluminum Products, Inc.
2 Shelter Dr
Greer SC 29650
864 272-4453

(G-10370)
BIGBEE STEEL AND TANK COMPANY (PA)
Also Called: Highland Tank
4535 Elizabethtown Rd (17545-8367)
PHONE..................................814 893-5701
Charles A Frey Jr, *President*
Tom Schoendorf, *Division Mgr*
John W Jacob, *Vice Pres*
John Schmucker, *Plant Mgr*
Michael Vanlenten, *Treasurer*
EMP: 150
SQ FT: 110,000
SALES (est): 42.1MM **Privately Held**
WEB: www.highlandtank.com
SIC: 3443 3714 Tanks, standard or custom fabricated: metal plate; motor vehicle parts & accessories

(G-10371)
BIGBEE STEEL AND TANK COMPANY
4535 Elizabethtown Rd (17545-8367)
PHONE..................................717 664-0600
EMP: 64
SALES (corp-wide): 42.1MM **Privately Held**
SIC: 3443 Tanks, standard or custom fabricated: metal plate
PA: Bigbee Steel And Tank Company Inc
4535 Elizabethtown Rd
Manheim PA 17545
814 893-5701

(G-10372)
BOND CASTER AND WHEEL CORP (PA)
Also Called: Bond Machine and Fabrication
230 S Penn St (17545-2018)
PHONE..................................717 665-2275
Louis J Bond, *President*
Kimberly L Bond, *Vice Pres*
Alex Bond, *VP Opers*
Dale Bezzard, *Purchasing*
EMP: 10
SQ FT: 60,000
SALES (est): 4.4MM **Privately Held**
SIC: 3499 Wheels: wheelbarrow, stroller, etc.: disc, stamped metal

(G-10373)
BOND MACHINE & FABRICATION LLC
230 S Penn St (17545-2018)
P.O. Box 339 (17545-0339)
PHONE..................................717 665-9030
Karen Von Clef, *Marketing Staff*
Louis J Bond, *Mng Member*
Kimberly L Bond,
EMP: 20
SQ FT: 60,000
SALES (est): 2.8MM
SALES (corp-wide): 4.4MM **Privately Held**
SIC: 3599 Machine shop, jobbing & repair
PA: Bond Caster And Wheel Corporation
230 S Penn St
Manheim PA 17545
717 665-2275

(G-10374)
CAREL USA INC
385 S Oak St (17545-1600)
PHONE..................................410 497-5128
Bill Sitler, *COO*
Nick Patton, *Production*
Bryan Bomberger, *Engineer*
Wanda Gonzalez, *Sales Staff*
EMP: 5
SALES (corp-wide): 195.9MM **Privately Held**
SIC: 3585 Humidifiers & dehumidifiers
HQ: Carel Usa, Inc
385 S Oak St
Manheim PA 17545
717 664-0500

(G-10375)
CBH OF LANCASTER COMPANY
Also Called: National Bearings Company
311 W Stiegel St (17545-1747)
PHONE..................................717 569-0485
Jessica H May, *President*
▲ **EMP:** 55 **EST:** 1917
SQ FT: 45,000
SALES (est): 14.1MM
SALES (corp-wide): 855.1MM **Privately Held**
WEB: www.nationalbearings.com
SIC: 3562 3451 3568 Ball bearings & parts; screw machine products; power transmission equipment
HQ: Fenner, Inc.
311 W Stiegel St
Manheim PA 17545
717 665-2421

(G-10376)
CHESTNUT VLY CTRL SYSTEMS LLC
1470 S Colebrook Rd (17545-8663)
PHONE..................................717 330-2356
Scott A Durdock,
EMP: 5
SALES (est): 858.1K **Privately Held**
SIC: 3625 7389 Control equipment, electric;

(G-10377)
CLAIR BROS AUDIO ENTPS INC (PA)
1 Clair Blvd (17545-1699)
P.O. Box 396, Lititz (17543-0396)
PHONE..................................717 626-4000
Barry Clair, *President*
Roy Clair, *President*
Harry Witz, *General Mgr*
Eugene Clair, *Principal*
Rochelle Clair, *Principal*

▲ **EMP:** 100 **EST:** 1966
SQ FT: 50,000
SALES (est): 29MM **Privately Held**
SIC: 7359 3651 Sound & lighting equipment rental; household audio & video equipment

(G-10378)
CONESTOGA DPI LLC
181 E Stiegel St Ste 100 (17545-1738)
PHONE..................................717 665-0298
Sharon K O'Neal,
Sharon A O'Neal,
Shawn O'Neal,
EMP: 3
SQ FT: 1,100
SALES (est): 468.8K **Privately Held**
SIC: 2752 Commercial printing, lithographic

(G-10379)
DUAL CORE LLC (HQ)
Also Called: Identicard Systems Worldwide
148 E Stiegel St (17545-1627)
PHONE..................................800 233-0298
Robert L Hager, *CEO*
Tim Bupp, *General Mgr*
Marcus Vaughn, *Regional Mgr*
Sameer Dattu, *Purchasing*
Tom Faith, *Regl Sales Mgr*
◆ **EMP:** 55
SQ FT: 52,000
SALES (est): 17.6MM
SALES (corp-wide): 1.1B **Publicly Held**
WEB: www.identicard.com
SIC: 3089 3861 3699 Identification cards, plastic; photographic equipment & supplies; security control equipment & systems
PA: Brady Corporation
6555 W Good Hope Rd
Milwaukee WI 53223
414 358-6600

(G-10380)
FENNER INC
Fenner Drives
311 W Stiegel St (17545-1747)
PHONE..................................717 665-2421
Don Burzen, *Manager*
EMP: 225
SALES (corp-wide): 855.1MM **Privately Held**
WEB: www.fennerdrives.com
SIC: 3052 3714 3613 3568 Rubber & plastics hose & beltings; motor vehicle parts & accessories; switchgear & switchboard apparatus; power transmission equipment; conveyors & conveying equipment; copper foundries
HQ: Fenner, Inc.
311 W Stiegel St
Manheim PA 17545
717 665-2421

(G-10381)
FENNER INC
250 S Penn St (17545-2018)
PHONE..................................717 665-2421
John Krecek, *President*
EMP: 100
SALES (corp-wide): 855.1MM **Privately Held**
SIC: 2399 3052 3568 Belting & belt products; rubber belting; power transmission equipment
HQ: Fenner, Inc.
311 W Stiegel St
Manheim PA 17545
717 665-2421

(G-10382)
FENNER INC (DH)
Also Called: Fenner Drives
311 W Stiegel St (17545-1747)
PHONE..................................717 665-2421
John Krecek, *President*
Stacey Penn, *Partner*
Eric Mosser, *Project Mgr*
Jesse Mutchler, *Opers Mgr*
Jason Kinney, *Mfg Mgr*
▲ **EMP:** 4

SALES (est): 74.8MM
SALES (corp-wide): 855.1MM **Privately Held**
WEB: www.fennerdrives.com
SIC: 2399 3052 3568 Belting & belt products; rubber belting; power transmission equipment

(G-10383)
FENNER PRECISION INC
250 S Penn St (17545-2018)
PHONE.................................800 327-2288
Jeffrey Oak, *President*
Mike Thompson, *President*
John Mullineaux Jr, *Vice Pres*
Glyn Geary, *Technical Mgr*
Ben Ficklen, *Treasurer*
▲ **EMP:** 110
SQ FT: 90,000
SALES (est): 16.6MM
SALES (corp-wide): 855.1MM **Privately Held**
WEB: www.winfield-inds.com
SIC: 3089 3061 2869 2821 Synthetic resin finished products; mechanical rubber goods; industrial organic chemicals; plastics materials & resins
HQ: Fenner, Inc.
311 W Stiegel St
Manheim PA 17545
717 665-2421

(G-10384)
FEROTEC FRICTION INC
150 Shellyland Rd (17545-8679)
P.O. Box 387, Mount Joy (17552-0387)
PHONE.................................717 492-9600
Brad Smith, *Principal*
Blaine Lowry, *Finance Mgr*
▲ **EMP:** 10
SQ FT: 25,000
SALES (est): 4MM **Privately Held**
WEB: www.investorsinternational.com
SIC: 3069 Brake linings, rubber

(G-10385)
FLSMIDTH INC
236 S Cherry St (17545-2006)
PHONE.................................717 665-2224
Frank Olejack, *Branch Mgr*
EMP: 130
SALES (corp-wide): 2.8B **Privately Held**
SIC: 3563 3535 Air & gas compressors including vacuum pumps; conveyors & conveying equipment
HQ: Flsmidth Inc.
2040 Avenue C
Bethlehem PA 18017
610 264-6011

(G-10386)
GETAWAYS ON DISPLAY INC
Also Called: Great Display Company
147 Arrowhead Dr (17545-8680)
P.O. Box 116, Landisville (17538-0116)
PHONE.................................717 653-8070
James C Morrison, *President*
Carrie Irwin, *Manager*
EMP: 11
SQ FT: 15,000
SALES: 1.1MM **Privately Held**
WEB: www.getawaysondisplay.com
SIC: 7319 2542 Distribution of advertising material or sample services; racks, merchandise display or storage: except wood

(G-10387)
HAMPTON CABINET SHOP
Also Called: Hampton's
2730 Shenck Rd (17545-9113)
PHONE.................................717 898-7806
Gary L Hampton, *Partner*
Gary Hampton, *Partner*
Garry Longenecker, *Partner*
▲ **EMP:** 9 **EST:** 1968
SQ FT: 4,000
SALES: 900K **Privately Held**
SIC: 2431 2511 2434 Millwork; wood household furniture; vanities, bathroom: wood

(G-10388)
HARRINGTON HOISTS INC (HQ)
401 W End Ave (17545-1703)
PHONE.................................717 665-2000
Edward W Hunter, *President*

Edward Hunter, *Exec VP*
Yoshio Morita, *Vice Pres*
Guy Haney, *Plant Mgr*
Mark Snavely Corp, *Controller*
◆ **EMP:** 110
SQ FT: 72,000
SALES (est): 28.6MM
SALES (corp-wide): 449.9MM **Privately Held**
WEB: www.harringtonhoists.com
SIC: 3536 Hoists, cranes & monorails
PA: Kito Corporation
2000, Tsuijiarai, Showa-Cho
Nakakoma-Gun YMA 409-3
552 757-521

(G-10389)
HONEY BUTTER PRODUCTS CO INC
Also Called: Downey's Honey Butter
103 S Heintzelman St (17545-1723)
P.O. Box 430 (17545-0430)
PHONE.................................717 665-9323
Kevin Sadd, *President*
EMP: 7 **EST:** 1942
SQ FT: 10,000
SALES (est): 830K **Privately Held**
SIC: 2021 Creamery butter

(G-10390)
IK STOTZFUS SERVICE CORP
1896 Auction Rd (17545-9164)
PHONE.................................717 397-3503
John Stoltzfus, *CEO*
John Stotzfus, *President*
EMP: 25
SALES (est): 2.1MM **Privately Held**
WEB: www.ikstoltzfus.com
SIC: 3443 Fabricated plate work (boiler shop)

(G-10391)
J & S MACHINING CORP
3491 Back Run Rd (17545-8136)
PHONE.................................717 653-6358
Harold Turner, *President*
Ella Mae Turner, *Vice Pres*
EMP: 10
SQ FT: 3,800
SALES (est): 650K **Privately Held**
WEB: www.jsmachining.com
SIC: 3599 7692 3549 Machine shop, jobbing & repair; welding repair; metalworking machinery

(G-10392)
KAUFFMANS WELDING IRON WO
3111 Sunnyside Rd (17545-8329)
PHONE.................................717 361-9844
Todd Kauffman, *Principal*
EMP: 3
SALES (est): 407.3K **Privately Held**
SIC: 3446 Architectural metalwork

(G-10393)
MANHEIM SPECIALTY MACHINE
76 W End Dr (17545-9380)
P.O. Box 143 (17545-0143)
PHONE.................................717 665-5400
Robert B Miller, *President*
Bob Miller, *Vice Pres*
Philip Miller, *Vice Pres*
EMP: 17
SQ FT: 16,000
SALES (est): 1.6MM **Privately Held**
SIC: 3599 Machine shop, jobbing & repair

(G-10394)
MAZZA VINEYARDS INC (PA)
Also Called: Mount Hope Estate & Winery
2775 Lebanon Rd (17545-8711)
PHONE.................................717 665-7021
Heather Bowser, *President*
Barbara Lacek, *Vice Pres*
EMP: 35
SALES (est): 4.5MM **Privately Held**
SIC: 7999 2084 5947 Tourist attraction, commercial; wines; gift, novelty & souvenir shop

(G-10395)
MC CRACKENS FEED MILL INC (PA)
Also Called: Pet Feed and Supply
63 New Charlotte St (17545-2098)
PHONE.................................717 665-2186
Peter B Mc Cracken, *President*
EMP: 13 **EST:** 1946
SQ FT: 13,500
SALES (est): 2.4MM **Privately Held**
SIC: 2048 5999 Poultry feeds; livestock feeds; feed & farm supply; pet food; pet supplies

(G-10396)
NAIL CENTRAL
605 Goldfinch Ln (17545-8589)
PHONE.................................717 664-5051
Jenna Jahnigen, *Principal*
EMP: 4
SALES (est): 344K **Privately Held**
SIC: 2844 Manicure preparations

(G-10397)
NOT FOR RADIO LLC
2750 Shenck Rd (17545-9113)
PHONE.................................484 437-9962
Patrick Kelsey, *Managing Prtnr*
EMP: 5
SALES (est): 502.3K **Privately Held**
SIC: 3571 Electronic computers

(G-10398)
PACKAGING CORPORATION AMERICA
Also Called: PCA Supply Services 302
109 Arrowhead Dr Bldg 2 (17545-8680)
PHONE.................................717 653-0420
Dan Hofer, *General Mgr*
EMP: 15
SALES (corp-wide): 7B **Publicly Held**
WEB: www.packagingcorp.com
SIC: 2653 Boxes, corrugated: made from purchased materials
PA: Packaging Corporation Of America
1 N Field Ct
Lake Forest IL 60045
847 482-3000

(G-10399)
PENN WIRE PRODUCTS CORPORATION
280 S Penn St (17545-2018)
P.O. Box 4804, Lancaster (17604-4804)
PHONE.................................717 664-4411
Robert G Sneath, *Manager*
EMP: 6
SQ FT: 1,080
SALES (corp-wide): 1.6MM **Privately Held**
WEB: www.pennwire.com
SIC: 3496 Mesh, made from purchased wire; conveyor belts
PA: Penn Wire Products Corporation
481 Richardson Dr
Lancaster PA 17603
717 393-2352

(G-10400)
PENNSY SUPPLY INC
2743 Lancaster Rd (17545-8887)
PHONE.................................717 569-2623
Jeffrey Sweigart, *Principal*
EMP: 7
SALES (corp-wide): 29.7B **Privately Held**
SIC: 3273 Ready-mixed concrete
HQ: Pennsy Supply, Inc.
1001 Paxton St
Harrisburg PA 17104
717 233-4511

(G-10401)
PFA INC
Also Called: Pro-Fab Associates
280 Hostetter Rd (17545-8549)
P.O. Box 492 (17545-0492)
PHONE.................................717 664-4216
Randy S Kaylor, *President*
Jesse H Edwards, *Corp Secy*
EMP: 6
SALES: 675K **Privately Held**
SIC: 3444 5012 Sheet metalwork; truck tractors

(G-10402)
PHILLIPS GRAPHIC FINISHING LLC
150 Arrowhead Dr (17545-8682)
PHONE.................................717 653-4565
Andrew Hoffman, *President*
Kris Harchuska, *Prdtn Mgr*
Dave Gochnauer, *Cust Mgr*
Cindy Eckerd, *Office Admin*
EMP: 80 **EST:** 1957
SQ FT: 40,000
SALES (est): 19MM **Privately Held**
WEB: www.pgfinish.com
SIC: 2675 Die-cut paper & board

(G-10403)
PINCH ROAD SAWMILL
2770 Pinch Rd (17545-8790)
PHONE.................................717 665-1096
Barry McFarland, *Principal*
EMP: 4
SALES (est): 239.2K **Privately Held**
SIC: 2421 Sawmills & planing mills, general

(G-10404)
SPORTING VALLEY FEEDS LLC
934 Junction Rd (17545-9103)
PHONE.................................717 665-6122
Elden Rider, *Mng Member*
John Neuenschwander,
EMP: 20
SQ FT: 500
SALES: 30MM **Privately Held**
SIC: 2048 Prepared feeds

(G-10405)
TE CONNECTIVITY CORPORATION
209 Shellyland Rd (17545-8681)
PHONE.................................717 492-2000
Steve Mc Intire, *Branch Mgr*
EMP: 117
SALES (corp-wide): 13.1B **Privately Held**
WEB: www.raychem.com
SIC: 3679 Electronic circuits
HQ: Te Connectivity Corporation
1050 Westlakes Dr
Berwyn PA 19312
610 893-9800

(G-10406)
WHITE OAK WOODCRAFT
2407 Newport Rd (17545-9204)
PHONE.................................717 665-4738
David J Sensenig, *Managing Prtnr*
Irvin B Heisey, *Partner*
Darren Sensenig, *Partner*
Dustin Sensenig, *Partner*
EMP: 4
SQ FT: 4,800
SALES (est): 300K **Privately Held**
SIC: 2511 Chairs, household, except upholstered: wood

(G-10407)
WILLIAM F AND KATHY A YEAGER
Also Called: Auto Graphics Company
62 Doe Run Rd (17545-9314)
PHONE.................................717 665-6964
William F Yeager, *Owner*
EMP: 6
SQ FT: 25,000
SALES (est): 400K **Privately Held**
SIC: 7532 7389 3993 Lettering, automotive; customizing services, non-factory basis; sign painting & lettering shop; signs & advertising specialties

---

Manns Choice
Bedford County

(G-10408)
BEDFORD MATERIALS CO INC
7676 Allegheny Rd (15550-8967)
PHONE.................................800 773-4276
William Gates, *President*
Ronald Dandrea, *Vice Pres*
Leo Manganello, *Vice Pres*
▲ **EMP:** 91
SQ FT: 65,000

GEOGRAPHIC

SALES (est): 25MM **Privately Held**
SIC: 3644 Insulators & insulation materials, electrical

Manor
Westmoreland County

(G-10409)
B6 SYSTEMS INC
B 7 Manor Vly Plz Rte 993 (15665)
P.O. Box 553 (15665-0553)
PHONE......................724 861-8080
Deborah Berardi, *President*
Mark Berardi, *Vice Pres*
EMP: 5
SQ FT: 1,000
SALES (est): 435.8K **Privately Held**
SIC: 7372 Business oriented computer software

(G-10410)
FIRST RATE MET FABRICATION LLC
1 Penn St (15665-9739)
PHONE......................724 515-7005
Linda L Pence,
Howard J Pence,
▼ **EMP:** 14
SQ FT: 16,000
SALES (est): 1.8MM **Privately Held**
SIC: 3444 Metal housings, enclosures, casings & other containers

(G-10411)
H AND H FOUNDRY MACHINE CO
Also Called: Jeannette Machine & Die
1570 Rte 993 (15665)
PHONE......................724 863-3251
C R Lessig Jr, *Ch of Bd*
A R Lessig, *President*
Eleanor E Lessig, *Admin Sec*
Marsha J Lessig, *Admin Sec*
EMP: 8 **EST:** 1926
SQ FT: 18,396
SALES (est): 1.1MM **Privately Held**
SIC: 3321 Gray iron castings

Mansfield
Tioga County

(G-10412)
CHAD CROSS
Also Called: Cross Excavating
19316 Route 6 (16933-9524)
PHONE......................570 549-3234
Chad Cross, *Owner*
EMP: 28
SALES: 950K **Privately Held**
SIC: 1442 Construction sand & gravel

(G-10413)
COSTYS ENERGY SERVICES
2329 S Main St (16933-9311)
PHONE......................570 662-2752
Matthew Kurzejewski, *President*
Ray McIlroy, *Opers Mgr*
EMP: 7 **EST:** 2015
SALES (est): 105.4K **Privately Held**
SIC: 1389 Oil field services

(G-10414)
ENERGY WORX INC
11 Vosburg St (16933-1038)
PHONE......................321 610-4676
Coley Wood, *President*
EMP: 3
SALES (est): 126.4K
SALES (corp-wide): 39.2MM **Privately Held**
SIC: 1389 Oil field services
PA: Energy Worx Inc
2801 E Interstate 20
Midland TX
432 685-9958

(G-10415)
GEC ENTERPRISES INC
Also Called: Sign Shop, The
15491 Route 6 (16933-9192)
PHONE......................570 662-8898
James Cooper, *President*
Sandra Cooper, *Corp Secy*
EMP: 3 **EST:** 1964
SALES: 250K **Privately Held**
SIC: 3993 Signs & advertising specialties

(G-10416)
HOUSE WOOD PRODUCTS CO
1 Lutes Ave (16933-1237)
P.O. Box 277 (16933-0277)
PHONE......................570 662-3868
Eugene F House, *Owner*
EMP: 8 **EST:** 1948
SQ FT: 15,000
SALES: 1MM **Privately Held**
SIC: 2448 Pallets, wood

(G-10417)
KEANE FRAC LP (HQ)
Also Called: Ultra Tech Frac Services
14235 Route 6 (16933-8828)
PHONE......................570 302-4050
James Stewart, *CEO*
Louis Wilpitz, *President*
M Paul Debonis Jr, *COO*
Ian J Henkes, *Vice Pres*
James J Venditto, *Engineer*
EMP: 20
SALES (est): 47.7MM
SALES (corp-wide): 2.1B **Publicly Held**
SIC: 1381 Drilling oil & gas wells
PA: Keane Group, Inc.
1800 Post Oak Blvd # 450
Houston TX 77056
713 357-9490

(G-10418)
KEANE FRAC TX LLC
14235 Route 6 (16933-8828)
PHONE......................570 302-4050
EMP: 8
SALES (corp-wide): 21.9MM **Privately Held**
SIC: 1381 8711 Drilling oil & gas wells; engineering services
PA: Keane Frac Tx, Llc
2121 Sage Rd
Houston TX 77056
713 960-0381

(G-10419)
KEANE GROUP HOLDINGS LLC
14235 Route 6 (16933-8828)
PHONE......................570 302-4050
Stewart James, *Branch Mgr*
EMP: 21
SALES (corp-wide): 2.1B **Publicly Held**
SIC: 3541 Drill presses
HQ: Keane Group Holdings, Llc
5825 N Sam Houston Pkwy W # 600
Houston TX 77086
713 960-0381

(G-10420)
KEYSTONE NORTH INC
Also Called: Keystone Welding & Fabricaton
310 S Main St (16933-1511)
PHONE......................570 662-3882
Karen Russel, *President*
Robert Dalton, *Treasurer*
Adrienne Russell, *Controller*
Adrian Sanford, *Admin Sec*
EMP: 38
SQ FT: 12,000
SALES (est): 7.2MM **Privately Held**
SIC: 3562 3469 Ball & roller bearings; metal stampings

(G-10421)
MAPLE MOUNTAIN INDUSTRIES INC
Also Called: Maple Mountain Equipment
845 Route 660 (16933-8851)
PHONE......................570 662-3200
Leroy Wilson, *Manager*
EMP: 21 **Privately Held**
WEB: www.maplemountain.com
SIC: 2512 Upholstered household furniture
PA: Maple Mountain Industries Inc
1820 Mulligan Hill Rd
New Florence PA 15944

(G-10422)
NORTH COUNTRY WOODWORKING INC
9646 N Elk Run Rd (16933-8217)
PHONE......................570 549-8105
Peter McLelland, *President*
Gerard Cormier, *Treasurer*
EMP: 9
SQ FT: 9,050
SALES: 322.2K **Privately Held**
SIC: 2431 5211 2434 Woodwork, interior & ornamental; cabinets, kitchen; bathroom fixtures, equipment & supplies; vanities, bathroom: wood

(G-10423)
NORTHERN TIER BEVERAGE INC
133 N Main St (16933-1305)
PHONE......................570 662-2523
Anthony Fiamingo, *President*
Brian Alexander, *General Mgr*
George Koury, *Admin Sec*
▲ **EMP:** 5
SALES: 380K **Privately Held**
SIC: 2086 5181 Bottled & canned soft drinks; beer & ale

(G-10424)
PENNY MANSFIELD SAVER INC (PA)
Also Called: Wellsboro Advertiser
98 N Main St (16933-1304)
P.O. Box 37 (16933-0037)
PHONE......................570 662-3277
Richard Colegrove, *President*
EMP: 6 **EST:** 1947
SQ FT: 5,000
SALES (est): 456.5K **Privately Held**
WEB: www.mansfieldpennysaver.com
SIC: 2711 2752 2741 Newspapers: publishing only, not printed on site; commercial printing, offset; shopping news: publishing only, not printed on site

(G-10425)
PETTA ENTERPRISES
299 S Main St (16933-1512)
PHONE......................607 857-5915
William Petta, *Owner*
EMP: 3
SALES (est): 180K **Privately Held**
SIC: 1389 Oil field services

(G-10426)
TETRA TECHNOLOGIES INC
2467 S Main St (16933-9389)
PHONE......................570 659-5357
Jared Hale, *Manager*
EMP: 41
SALES (corp-wide): 998.7MM **Publicly Held**
SIC: 2819 1389 Brine; oil & gas wells: building, repairing & dismantling
PA: Tetra Technologies, Inc.
24955 Interstate 45
The Woodlands TX 77380
281 367-1983

(G-10427)
WOLVERINE ENTERPRISE LLC
2740 S Main St (16933-9479)
PHONE......................570 463-4103
Bradley Robinson, *CEO*
EMP: 48
SQ FT: 4,000
SALES (est): 1.3MM **Privately Held**
SIC: 1389 Gas field services

(G-10428)
WOODHOUSE POST & BEAM
Rr 549 (16933)
P.O. Box 219 (16933-0219)
PHONE......................570 549-6232
C Stephen Keller, *CEO*
Patrick Seaman, *Owner*
Joe Crance, *Manager*
EMP: 40
SQ FT: 2,700
SALES (est): 6MM **Privately Held**
WEB: www.woodhouse-pb.com
SIC: 2452 Prefabricated buildings, wood

Maple Glen
Montgomery County

(G-10429)
EASY WALKING INC
1478 Dillon Rd (19002-4039)
PHONE......................215 654-1626
Eli Razon, *CEO*
Giora Klainer, *Sales Staff*
EMP: 4
SALES (est): 591.7K **Privately Held**
WEB: www.easy-walking.com
SIC: 3841 Surgical & medical instruments

(G-10430)
HOLTEC INTERNATIONAL
1838 Howe Ln (19002-2916)
PHONE......................215 646-5842
Joseph Odrain, *Principal*
▲ **EMP:** 3 **EST:** 2013
SALES (est): 241.1K **Privately Held**
SIC: 3724 Aircraft engines & engine parts

Mapleton Depot
Huntingdon County

(G-10431)
PAUL DANFELT
Also Called: Danfelt Paul Logging Contr
Rr 1 (17052)
PHONE......................814 448-2592
Paul Danfelt, *Owner*
EMP: 3
SALES (est): 234K **Privately Held**
SIC: 2411 Logging

(G-10432)
U S SILICA COMPANY
Also Called: Mapleton
1885 Rte 1 (17052)
PHONE......................814 542-2561
Les Vanalstyne, *Principal*
EMP: 70
SALES (corp-wide): 1.5B **Publicly Held**
WEB: www.u-s-silica.com
SIC: 1446 Industrial sand
HQ: U. S. Silica Company
8490 Progress Dr Ste 300
Frederick MD 21701
301 682-0600

Marble
Clarion County

(G-10433)
ALLEGHENY WOOD PDTS INTL INC
Awpi Mill 7
17761 Route 208 (16334-1817)
P.O. Box 30 (16334-0030)
PHONE......................814 354-7304
John Crites II, *Ch of Bd*
Patricia Crites, *Admin Sec*
EMP: 32 **Privately Held**
SIC: 2421 Sawmills & planing mills, general
PA: Allegheny Wood Products International, Inc.
240 Airport Rd
Petersburg WV 26847

(G-10434)
ALLEGHENY WOOD PRODUCTS INC
Also Called: Awp Mill 7
17761 Route 208 (16334-1817)
P.O. Box 30 (16334-0030)
PHONE......................814 354-7304
John Crites, *Ch of Bd*
Kevin Stout, *Manager*
EMP: 70
SALES (corp-wide): 119MM **Privately Held**
WEB: www.alleghenywood.com
SIC: 2421 2426 Lumber: rough, sawed or planed; kiln drying of lumber; hardwood dimension & flooring mills

▲ = Import ▼=Export
◆ =Import/Export

PA: Allegheny Wood Products, Inc.
240 Airport Rd
Petersburg WV 26847
304 257-1082

(G-10435)
CLARION BATHWARE INC
16273 Route 208 (16334-1515)
P.O. Box 20 (16334-0020)
PHONE.................................814 782-3016
David Groner, Branch Mgr
EMP: 120
SALES (corp-wide): 20.8MM Privately Held
SIC: 3088 Tubs (bath, shower & laundry), plastic
PA: Clarion Bathware, Inc.
44 Amsler Ave
Shippenville PA 16254
814 226-5374

(G-10436)
CLARION BATHWARE INC
16273 Route 208 (16334-1515)
PHONE.................................814 782-3016
David Groner, President
EMP: 85
SALES (corp-wide): 20.8MM Privately Held
WEB: www.clarionbathware.com
SIC: 3088 3444 Tubs (bath, shower & laundry), plastic; shower stalls, fiberglass & plastic; bathroom fixtures, plastic; sheet metalwork
PA: Clarion Bathware, Inc.
44 Amsler Ave
Shippenville PA 16254
814 226-5374

Marcus Hook
Delaware County

(G-10437)
AUTOMATING MOLDING TECH LLC
203 E 10th St Ste 16 (19061-4605)
PHONE.................................610 497-7162
EMP: 3
SALES (est): 149.7K Privately Held
SIC: 3089 Molding primary plastic

(G-10438)
BRASKEM AMERICA INC
750 W 10th St (19061-4500)
PHONE.................................610 497-8378
Conway Yee, Prdtn Mgr
Jim McKenna, Sales Staff
EMP: 106 Privately Held
SIC: 2821 2865 2869 Polypropylene resins; polyesters; acrylic resins; plasticizer/additive based plastic materials; cyclic crudes & intermediates; phenol, alkylated & cumene; aniline, nitrobenzene; diphenylamines; acetone, synthetic; alcohols, non-beverage
HQ: Braskem America, Inc.
1735 Market St Fl 28
Philadelphia PA 19103
215 841-3100

(G-10439)
CONGOLEUM CORPORATION
4401 Ridge Rd (19061-5094)
PHONE.................................609 584-3000
Rob Sheater, Manager
EMP: 340
SALES (corp-wide): 116.7MM Privately Held
WEB: www.congoleum.com
SIC: 3996 Hard surface floor coverings
PA: Congoleum Corporation
3500 Quakerbridge Rd
Trenton NJ 08619
609 584-3000

(G-10440)
CRUSADER PRECISION SHTMTL CO
1581 Chichester Ave (19061-4208)
PHONE.................................610 485-4321
Phillip B Kline, President
EMP: 8 EST: 1959
SQ FT: 9,200

SALES (est): 993K Privately Held
SIC: 3444 Sheet metal specialties, not stamped

(G-10441)
FLUID GEAR PRODUCTS LLC
115 Market St (19061-4823)
PHONE.................................484 480-3923
Steven Kolesar, Mng Member
Stephanie Leone,
▲ EMP: 2
SALES: 1MM Privately Held
SIC: 3462 Iron & steel forgings

(G-10442)
GEORGE KRANICH
Also Called: Marine Performance Products
201 E 10th St (19061-4605)
PHONE.................................610 295-2039
George D Kranich, Owner
EMP: 4
SQ FT: 4,500
SALES (est): 299.7K Privately Held
SIC: 3732 Boats, fiberglass: building & repairing

(G-10443)
GEORGEOS WATER ICE INC (PA)
409 Green St (19061-4807)
P.O. Box 242 (19061-0242)
PHONE.................................610 494-4975
George Swayngim, President
Debbie Swayngim, General Mgr
Sean Swayngim, General Mgr
Kyle Fwayngim, Vice Pres
Kyle Swayngim, Vice Pres
▲ EMP: 16
SQ FT: 6,125
SALES: 2.3MM Privately Held
WEB: www.georgeoswaterice.com
SIC: 2038 2024 Frozen specialties; yogurt desserts, frozen

(G-10444)
GUIDA INC (PA)
Also Called: Ornamental Iron Works
7 Chelsea Pkwy Ste 705 (19061-1300)
PHONE.................................215 727-2222
Francis Lomonaco, President
Ron Lomonaco, Treasurer
Danielle Sheehan, Manager
John Lomonaco, Asst Sec
EMP: 35
SALES (est): 6.7MM Privately Held
WEB: www.guidadoors.com
SIC: 3449 3466 3442 3446 Miscellaneous metalwork; crowns & closures; metal doors; architectural metalwork

(G-10445)
H & G DINERS CORP
Also Called: Wicks Kitchen
3305 W 2nd St (19061-5101)
PHONE.................................610 494-5107
George Bostwick Jr, President
Em Bostwrck, Office Mgr
EMP: 20 EST: 1955
SQ FT: 1,300
SALES (est): 3.7MM Privately Held
SIC: 2092 Fish, frozen: prepared

(G-10446)
K WAGNER MACHINE INC
701 Chestnut St (19061-5006)
PHONE.................................610 485-3831
Kurt Wagner, Owner
EMP: 5
SQ FT: 14,000
SALES (est): 810K Privately Held
SIC: 3599 Machine shop, jobbing & repair

(G-10447)
LOUSTON INTERNATIONAL INC
168 E Ridge Rd Ste 202 (19061-4365)
PHONE.................................610 859-9860
John Peng, President
Yuejunzheng Zheng, Admin Sec
EMP: 5
SQ FT: 200
SALES (est): 450K Privately Held
WEB: www.louston.com
SIC: 2834 Pharmaceutical preparations

(G-10448)
MARBLE CRAFTERS INC
Also Called: Marble Crafters USA
11 Nealy Blvd (19061-5312)
PHONE.................................610 497-6000
Robert Capoferri, President
Annemarie Alexander, Principal
Ray Peslar, Project Mgr
David Eppley, Design Engr
Jeanne Amoroso, Controller
◆ EMP: 100
SQ FT: 40,000
SALES (est): 22.2MM Privately Held
WEB: www.marblecrafters.com
SIC: 1411 5211 Granite, dimension-quarrying; paving stones

(G-10449)
MIPC LLC
4101 Post Rd (19061-5052)
PHONE.................................610 364-8660
EMP: 400
SALES (est): 27.8MM Privately Held
SIC: 2911 Petroleum refining

(G-10450)
MRLRX LLC
Also Called: Marcus Hook Pharmacy
46 E 10th St (19061-4515)
P.O. Box 428 (19061-0428)
PHONE.................................610 485-7750
Mark Lawson,
EMP: 19
SALES: 12MM Privately Held
SIC: 5047 5122 2834 5912 Medical equipment & supplies; pharmaceuticals; druggists' sundries; druggists' preparations (pharmaceuticals); drug stores

(G-10451)
MUNRO PRTG GRAPHIC DESIGN LLC
815 Market St (19061-4725)
PHONE.................................610 485-1966
Brian Munro, Sales Associate
John Munro,
Gail Munro,
EMP: 4
SQ FT: 4,200
SALES (est): 588.4K Privately Held
SIC: 2752 2759 7336 Commercial printing, offset; letterpress printing; commercial art & graphic design

(G-10452)
OH RYANS IRISH POTATOES
168 E Ridge Rd Ste 201 (19061-4365)
PHONE.................................610 494-7123
David Lamparelli, Owner
EMP: 15
SALES: 800K Privately Held
SIC: 2064 Candy & other confectionery products

(G-10453)
QUINLAN SCENIC STUDIO INC
203 E 10th St (19061-4648)
PHONE.................................610 859-9130
Frank Quinlan, President
Jan Supco, Treasurer
EMP: 12
SALES (est): 924.2K Privately Held
WEB: www.qscenic.com
SIC: 3999 Theatrical scenery; advertising display products

(G-10454)
SCREEN SERVICE TECH INC
Also Called: Extec Eastern
22 Nealy Blvd (19061-5312)
PHONE.................................610 497-3555
Hugh Quinn, Owner
EMP: 7 EST: 1997
SALES (est): 460K Privately Held
WEB: www.exteceastern.com
SIC: 3531 Construction machinery

(G-10455)
SUNOCO INC (R&M)
Cavern 5 Hewes Post Rd (19061)
P.O. Box 426 (19061-0426)
PHONE.................................610 859-1000
John Rossi, Manager
EMP: 1000

SALES (corp-wide): 54B Publicly Held
SIC: 2911 Petroleum refining
HQ: Sunoco (R&M), Llc
3801 West Chester Pike
Newtown Square PA 19073
215 977-3000

Marianna
Washington County

(G-10456)
CREOTECH INDUSTRIES LLC
Also Called: Bico Machine and Tool
72 Little Creek Rd (15345-1200)
PHONE.................................724 267-3100
Adam Johnston,
Walter Moore,
EMP: 4 EST: 2014
SALES (est): 240.1K Privately Held
SIC: 3599 Machine shop, jobbing & repair

Marienville
Forest County

(G-10457)
HIGHLAND FOREST RESOURCES INC
237 Highland Dr (16239-4009)
PHONE.................................814 927-2226
Fred Carrier, Principal
EMP: 40
SALES (corp-wide): 1.5B Publicly Held
SIC: 2421 Sawmills & planing mills, general
HQ: Highland Forest Resources Inc
Rr 6 Box 84
Kane PA 16735
814 837-6760

(G-10458)
NATIONAL FOREST PRODUCTS LTD
S Forest St (16239)
P.O. Box 612 (16239-0612)
PHONE.................................814 927-5622
Ronald Songer, President
EMP: 1
SQ FT: 8,000
SALES: 1.2MM Privately Held
WEB: www.nationalforestproducts.com
SIC: 2434 Wood kitchen cabinets

(G-10459)
STEVEN E TACHOIR
977 Watson Farm Rd (16239-6127)
PHONE.................................814 726-1572
Steven E Tachoir, Owner
EMP: 3
SALES (est): 146.6K Privately Held
SIC: 1389 Oil field services

Marietta
Lancaster County

(G-10460)
ARMSTRONG WORLD INDUSTRIES INC
1507 River Rd (17547-9403)
PHONE.................................717 426-4171
Mark Chesko, Vice Pres
Michael Miller, Facilities Mgr
James Winkey, Technology
EMP: 12
SALES (corp-wide): 975.3MM Publicly Held
WEB: www.armstrong.com
SIC: 3996 Hard surface floor coverings
PA: Armstrong World Industries, Inc.
2500 Columbia Ave
Lancaster PA 17603
717 397-0611

(G-10461)
BF HIESTAND HOUSE
722 E Market St (17547-1810)
PHONE.................................717 426-8415
Pam Fritz, Principal

EMP: 4
SALES (est): 521.1K **Privately Held**
WEB: www.bfhiestandhouse.com
SIC: 3011 7011 Tires & inner tubes; hotels
& motels

(G-10462)
GLAXOSMITHKLINE
Also Called: Glaxosmithkline Upsu
325 N Bridge St (17547-1134)
PHONE....................717 426-6644
Mike Simansky, *Principal*
EMP: 23
SALES (est): 6.1MM **Privately Held**
SIC: 2834 Pharmaceutical preparations

(G-10463)
GOHN MFG
18 N Pine St (17547-1629)
PHONE....................717 426-3875
Lois Gohn, *Owner*
EMP: 4
SALES (est): 197.9K **Privately Held**
SIC: 3999 Military insignia

(G-10464)
HILTZ PROPANE SYSTEMS INC
693 W Market St (17547-1020)
PHONE....................717 799-4322
Matt Hiltz, *Principal*
EMP: 26 **EST:** 2013
SALES (est): 10.4MM **Privately Held**
SIC: 5171 8711 3795 Petroleum bulk sta-
tions; mechanical engineering; tanks &
tank components

(G-10465)
NEW JERSEY SHELL CASTING CORP
21 S Decatur St (17547-1007)
P.O. Box 86 (17547-0086)
PHONE....................717 426-1835
William Nagy Jr, *President*
Mary Lou Nagy, *Corp Secy*
EMP: 26
SQ FT: 17,738
SALES (est): 3.3MM **Privately Held**
SIC: 3366 3365 Castings (except die):
brass; castings (except die): bronze; alu-
minum & aluminum-based alloy castings

(G-10466)
PERDUE FARMS INC
1609 River Rd (17547-9504)
PHONE....................717 426-1961
Greg Douts, *Manager*
EMP: 447
SALES (corp-wide): 5.7B **Privately Held**
SIC: 2015 Poultry slaughtering & process-
ing
PA: Perdue Farms Inc.
31149 Old Ocean City Rd
Salisbury MD 21804
410 543-3000

(G-10467)
SMART AVIONICS INC
186 Airport Rd (17547-9105)
PHONE....................717 928-4360
Benjamin Travis, *President*
EMP: 6
SQ FT: 10,000
SALES (est): 1.2MM **Privately Held**
WEB: www.smartavionics.com
SIC: 3812 Search & navigation equipment

(G-10468)
STRUBE INC
629 W Market St (17547-1011)
PHONE....................717 426-1906
J Patrick Rieder, *President*
Tammie Dallmeyer, *Treasurer*
Jpatrick Rieder, *Officer*
Robert B Burns, *Admin Sec*
EMP: 12
SQ FT: 13,000
SALES (est): 2.4MM **Privately Held**
WEB: www.strubeinc.net
SIC: 3812 3728 3824 3566 Aircraft flight
instruments; aircraft parts & equipment;
fluid meters & counting devices; gears,
power transmission, except automotive

(G-10469)
TRANSPORT FOR CHRIST INC (PA)
Also Called: Transport For Christ Intl
1525 River Rd (17547-9403)
P.O. Box 117 (17547-0117)
PHONE....................717 426-9977
Scott Weidner, *President*
Robert Thompson, *Chairman*
Dwayne Johnson, *Vice Pres*
Leon Faddis, *Treasurer*
Bunny O'Hare, *Director*
EMP: 7
SQ FT: 2,000
SALES (est): 5.4MM **Privately Held**
WEB: www.transportforchrist.org
SIC: 2721 8661 Magazines: publishing &
printing; religious instruction

Marion
Franklin County

(G-10470)
WADE HOLDINGS LLC
Also Called: Statler Body Works
5573 Main St (17235)
P.O. Box 19, Chambersburg (17201-0019)
PHONE....................717 375-2251
EMP: 3 **EST:** 2013
SALES (est): 180K **Privately Held**
SIC: 3713 Truck And Bus Bodies, Nsk

(G-10471)
WILLARD AGRI-SERVICE INC
Also Called: Willard Agri Service of Marion
5325 3rd St (17235)
PHONE....................717 375-2229
Pete Surgeon, *Branch Mgr*
EMP: 11
SALES (corp-wide): 2MM **Privately Held**
SIC: 2874 Phosphatic fertilizers
PA: Willard Agri-Service, Inc.
50 S Wisner St
Frederick MD 21701
301 662-8100

Marion Center
Indiana County

(G-10472)
CUTTING EDGE COUNTERTOPS
10064 Route 119 Hwy N (15759-7013)
PHONE....................724 397-8605
Kerry Gardner, *Owner*
EMP: 3
SALES (est): 200K **Privately Held**
WEB: www.cutting-edge-countertops.com
SIC: 3441 Fabricated structural metal

(G-10473)
MARION CENTER SUPPLY INC (PA)
517 Church St (15759-9003)
P.O. Box 173 (15759-0173)
PHONE....................724 397-5505
Edith Elliott, *President*
Bill Elliott, *Vice Pres*
Penny Wallace, *Executive*
EMP: 10
SQ FT: 1,500
SALES (est): 2MM **Privately Held**
SIC: 3273 3272 Ready-mixed concrete;
concrete products, precast

(G-10474)
MUNICIPAL PUBLICATIONS
1369 Wrigden Run Rd (15759-6703)
P.O. Box 308, Home (15747-0308)
PHONE....................724 397-9812
Malcolm Hermann, *President*
Elizabeth Hermann, *Vice Pres*
EMP: 3
SALES (est): 216.9K **Privately Held**
WEB: www.municipalpublications.org
SIC: 2273 Door mats: paper, grass, reed,
coir, sisal, jute, rags, etc.

(G-10475)
NICKLES INDUSTRIES
1425 Olson Rd (15759-4912)
PHONE....................724 422-7211
Brent Elkin, *Owner*
EMP: 4
SALES (est): 210K **Privately Held**
SIC: 3511 Gas turbines, mechanical drive

(G-10476)
R P NEESE & SONS LLC
2425 Tanoma Rd (15759-8109)
PHONE....................724 465-5718
John Gascoine,
EMP: 3
SALES (est): 1MM **Privately Held**
SIC: 1389 Construction, repair & disman-
tling services

(G-10477)
ROBERT A CROOKS
1485 Pollock Rd (15759-6907)
PHONE....................724 541-2746
Robert A Crooks, *Principal*
EMP: 3 **EST:** 2014
SALES (est): 240.6K **Privately Held**
SIC: 2411 Logging

(G-10478)
WILMOTH INTERESTS INC
550 Hastings Rd (15759-4515)
P.O. Box 203 (15759-0203)
PHONE....................724 397-5558
Harry C Wilmoth Sr, *President*
Ann Wilmoth, *Treasurer*
Lori Lomman, *Accountant*
EMP: 7
SALES (est): 986.9K **Privately Held**
WEB: www.wilmothinterests.com
SIC: 1311 Crude petroleum production

Markleysburg
Fayette County

(G-10479)
APPALACHIAN TIMBER PRODUCTS
5441 National Pike (15459-1023)
PHONE....................724 329-1990
John Merschat, *President*
▼ **EMP:** 10 **EST:** 1998
SQ FT: 30,000
SALES (est): 1.2MM **Privately Held**
SIC: 2411 Logging camps & contractors

(G-10480)
DENNIS LUMBER AND CONCRETE
Also Called: Floral Mountain True Value
4888 National Pike (15459-1028)
P.O. Box 37 (15459-0037)
PHONE....................724 329-5542
Jubal Margroff, *President*
Jennifer Margroff, *Vice Pres*
EMP: 27
SQ FT: 3,500
SALES: 5MM **Privately Held**
SIC: 5251 3272 Hardware; septic tanks,
concrete

(G-10481)
LEONARD FOREST PRODUCTS
114 Mudd Pike Rd (15459-1108)
PHONE....................724 329-4703
Gale Leonard, *Owner*
EMP: 10
SALES (est): 1.4MM **Privately Held**
SIC: 5031 2421 Lumber: rough, dressed &
finished; lumber: rough, sawed or planed

(G-10482)
MOUNTAIN METAL STUDIO INC
190 Thomas Rd (15459-1182)
PHONE....................724 329-0238
Mark Susko, *President*
EMP: 3
SALES (est): 300K **Privately Held**
SIC: 3446 Fences or posts, ornamental
iron or steel

(G-10483)
P S COMPOSITES INC
311 Friendsville Rd (15459-1207)
PHONE....................724 329-4413
Paul Schreiner Sr, *President*
EMP: 3
SALES (est): 236.9K **Privately Held**
WEB: www.customkayak.com
SIC: 3732 Kayaks, building & repairing

(G-10484)
SUMMIT FOREST RESOURCES INC
5441 National Pike (15459-1023)
PHONE....................724 329-3314
John R Merschat, *President*
Linda Merschat, *Corp Secy*
EMP: 29
SALES (est): 3.7MM **Privately Held**
SIC: 2421 Sawmills & planing mills, gen-
eral

Mars
Butler County

(G-10485)
A CUBED CORPORATION (PA)
Also Called: Concast Metal Products Com-
pany
131 Myoma Rd (16046-2227)
P.O. Box 816 (16046-0816)
PHONE....................724 538-4000
Alfred D Barbour, *President*
John Dorsey, *COO*
Martin Little, *Exec VP*
Harry Libengood, *Vice Pres*
Dean Mora, *Vice Pres*
▲ **EMP:** 129
SQ FT: 74,000
SALES (est): 38.5MM **Privately Held**
SIC: 3366 Castings (except die): brass;
castings (except die): bronze; castings
(except die): copper & copper-base alloy

(G-10486)
AMERICAN METALS COMPANY
311 Clark St (16046)
PHONE....................724 625-8666
Ying Jia, *President*
Frank LI, *Vice Pres*
EMP: 5
SALES (est): 454.4K **Privately Held**
WEB: www.metalshims.com
SIC: 3444 Sheet metalwork

(G-10487)
ATLAS SIGN GROUP LLC
508 Pittsburgh St Ste 104 (16046)
P.O. Box 703 (16046-0703)
PHONE....................724 935-2160
EMP: 5 **EST:** 2014
SALES (est): 16.4K **Privately Held**
SIC: 3993 Signs & advertising specialties

(G-10488)
BISHOPS INC
1022 Sophia Ln (16046-2142)
PHONE....................412 821-3333
Rhea Nicotra, *President*
Sam Nicotra, *Vice Pres*
EMP: 8
SQ FT: 5,000
SALES (est): 931.9K **Privately Held**
SIC: 2591 2391 5023 Drapery hardware
& blinds & shades; curtains & draperies;
window furnishings

(G-10489)
CARL STRUTZ & COMPANY INC (PA)
440 Mars Valencia Rd (16046)
P.O. Box 509 (16046-0509)
PHONE....................724 625-1501
Carl Strutz Jr, *President*
C James Strutz, *Treasurer*
Edward Dimarzio, *Manager*
Frank C Strutz Jr, *Admin Sec*
EMP: 33
SQ FT: 25,000
SALES (est): 8.4MM **Privately Held**
WEB: www.strutz.com
SIC: 3559 Glass making machinery: blow-
ing, molding, forming, etc.

(G-10490)
CARL STRUTZ & COMPANY INC
Strutz Intl Div Strutz Carl Co
440 Mars Valencia Rd (16046)
P.O. Box 509 (16046-0509)
PHONE..............................724 625-1501
John C Strutz, *Branch Mgr*
EMP: 51
SALES (corp-wide): 8.4MM **Privately Held**
WEB: www.strutz.com
SIC: 3559 Glass making machinery: blowing, molding, forming, etc.
PA: Carl Strutz & Company Inc
440 Mars Valencia Rd
Mars PA 16046
724 625-1501

(G-10491)
COMPUTER PWR SOLUTIONS PA INC
624 Route 228 (16046-3028)
PHONE..............................724 898-2223
Ralph G Jockel Jr, *President*
Chris Jockel, *Vice Pres*
EMP: 10
SQ FT: 2,000
SALES (est): 964.7K **Privately Held**
SIC: 7699 3621 Battery service & repair; generators for storage battery chargers

(G-10492)
CONCAST METAL PRODUCTS COMPANY
131 Myoma Rd (16046-2227)
P.O. Box 816 (16046-0816)
PHONE..............................724 538-4000
Alfred D Barbour, *President*
John Dorsey, *COO*
Martin Little, *Exec VP*
Dean Mora, *Vice Pres*
Thomas Zadan, *CFO*
▲ EMP: 129
SQ FT: 74,000
SALES (est): 24.9MM
SALES (corp-wide): 38.5MM **Privately Held**
WEB: www.concast.com
SIC: 3366 Castings (except die): brass; castings (except die): bronze; castings (except die): copper & copper-base alloy
PA: A Cubed Corporation
131 Myoma Rd
Mars PA 16046
724 538-4000

(G-10493)
CUPOLADUA OVEN LLC
137 Grand Ave Ste 1 (16046)
PHONE..............................412 592-5378
Stephanie M Santoso,
EMP: 5
SQ FT: 1,000
SALES (est): 50K **Privately Held**
SIC: 2052 Cookies & crackers

(G-10494)
DOERSCHNER MACHINE
114 Grand Ave (16046)
PHONE..............................724 625-1350
John Sheridan, *Principal*
EMP: 3
SALES (est): 248K **Privately Held**
SIC: 3449 Miscellaneous metalwork

(G-10495)
DREXLER ASSOCIATES INC
112 Olivia Ave (16046-3545)
PHONE..............................724 888-2042
Nora Drexler, *President*
Raymond G Drexler, *Vice Pres*
EMP: 3
SQ FT: 900
SALES: 115K **Privately Held**
SIC: 2741 Miscellaneous publishing

(G-10496)
ESM GROUP INC
130 Myoma Rd (16046-2228)
PHONE..............................724 538-8974
Eugene Flemming, *Director*
EMP: 26 **Privately Held**
WEB: www.esmgroup.com
SIC: 2819 Industrial inorganic chemicals

HQ: Esm Group Inc.
300 Corporate Pkwy 118n
Amherst NY 14226
716 446-8914

(G-10497)
FBC CHEMICAL CORPORATION (PA)
634 Route 228 (16046-3028)
P.O. Box 599 (16046-0599)
PHONE..............................724 625-3116
Dave J Hudac, *President*
Chris Hudac, *CFO*
Christopher Hudac, *CFO*
Laura Augustine, *Sales Staff*
Mark Hudac, *Marketing Staff*
▼ EMP: 2
SQ FT: 14,000
SALES (est): 60MM **Privately Held**
WEB: www.fbcchem.com
SIC: 5169 2952 Chemicals, industrial & heavy; roofing felts, cements or coatings

(G-10498)
GREG NORTON
209 Oakland Ave (16046)
P.O. Box 412 (16046-0412)
PHONE..............................724 625-3426
Greg Norton, *Mng Member*
EMP: 50
SALES (est): 3.2MM **Privately Held**
WEB: www.gregnorton.net
SIC: 3661 Telephone & telegraph apparatus

(G-10499)
HOUSE OF PRICE INC
177 Brickyard Rd (16046-3001)
PHONE..............................724 625-3415
Robert Price, *Vice Pres*
EMP: 5
SALES (est): 343K **Privately Held**
SIC: 2273 Rugs, braided & hooked

(G-10500)
INDUSTRIAL BRAKE COMPANY INC
300 Clay Ave (16046)
P.O. Box 670 (16046-0670)
PHONE..............................724 625-0010
Eric E Timko, *President*
Claudia Timko, *Corp Secy*
EMP: 9
SQ FT: 7,500
SALES (est): 1.6MM **Privately Held**
WEB: www.industrialbrakemars.com
SIC: 3714 Motor vehicle brake systems & parts

(G-10501)
INTERSOURCE INC
Also Called: S & S Refractories
946 Route 228 (16046-2326)
PHONE..............................724 940-2220
Joseph L Stein, *President*
Brian J Stein, *Vice Pres*
Philip J Scarsella, *Treasurer*
Maureen Kelley, *Controller*
Laynn V Tyssel, *Manager*
▲ EMP: 10
SQ FT: 3,000
SALES (est): 1.3MM **Privately Held**
SIC: 3297 5085 Nonclay refractories; industrial supplies

(G-10502)
J BAUR MACHINING INC
241 Clay Avenue Ext (16046-3301)
P.O. Box 924 (16046-0924)
PHONE..............................724 625-2680
Jeffrey Baur, *President*
Tim Hart, *Foreman/Supr*
Kelly Baur, *Manager*
John Pro, *Maintence Staff*
EMP: 15
SALES (est): 2.4MM **Privately Held**
SIC: 3599 Machine shop, jobbing & repair

(G-10503)
J W STEEL FABRICATING CO (PA)
Also Called: Fey Steel Fabricating
100 Fey Ln (16046)
P.O. Box 814 (16046-0814)
PHONE..............................724 625-1355

Robert J Fey, *President*
Ginette Novak, *Treasurer*
Ginny Novak, *Executive*
▲ EMP: 50
SQ FT: 30,000
SALES: 2.3MM **Privately Held**
SIC: 3441 3535 3444 3443 Fabricated structural metal; conveyors & conveying equipment; sheet metalwork; tanks, standard or custom fabricated; metal plate

(G-10504)
JAMES AUSTIN COMPANY (PA)
115 Downieville Rd (16046)
PHONE..............................724 625-1535
Harry G Austin III, *CEO*
John T Austin Sr, *Ch of Bd*
Robert Downie, *Ch of Bd*
J Douglas Austin, *Vice Pres*
John T Austin Jr, *Vice Pres*
EMP: 112 EST: 1889
SQ FT: 180,000
SALES (est): 71.6MM **Privately Held**
WEB: www.jamesaustin.com
SIC: 2841 2842 Soap: granulated, liquid, cake, flaked or chip; specialty cleaning, polishes & sanitation goods

(G-10505)
LECTROMAT INC
Mars Valencia Rd (16046)
P.O. Box 608 (16046-0608)
PHONE..............................724 625-3502
Ken Fleeson, *President*
Chris Fleeson, *Treasurer*
Gerald Fleeson, *Admin Sec*
▲ EMP: 15
SQ FT: 10,000
SALES (est): 3.7MM **Privately Held**
WEB: www.lectromat.com
SIC: 2621 5063 Saturated felts; insulators, electrical

(G-10506)
MARS LUMBER INC
1084 Mars Evans City Rd (16046-3332)
PHONE..............................724 625-2224
Robert Sarver, *President*
Holly Sarver, *Vice Pres*
Susan Sarver, *Vice Pres*
EMP: 7
SQ FT: 13,000
SALES (est): 693K **Privately Held**
WEB: www.marslumber.com
SIC: 2435 5211 2431 Hardwood veneer & plywood; lumber products; moldings, wood: unfinished & prefinished

(G-10507)
MIKE WOODSHOP
205 Hespenheide Rd (16046-2311)
PHONE..............................724 272-0259
Mike Santa, *Owner*
EMP: 3
SALES (est): 800K **Privately Held**
SIC: 2435 Plywood, hardwood or hardwood faced

(G-10508)
MILLER SCREEN & DESIGN INC
449 Mars Valencia Rd (16046)
P.O. Box 506 (16046-0506)
PHONE..............................724 625-1870
Henry L Miller, *President*
Michael J Miller, *Treasurer*
Anita Jordan, *Sales Staff*
Tammy Stauffer, *Office Mgr*
Rita M Miller, *Director*
EMP: 14 EST: 1966
SQ FT: 4,500
SALES (est): 1.4MM **Privately Held**
WEB: www.millerscreen.com
SIC: 3552 Silk screens for textile industry

(G-10509)
NORTHERN WINDING INC
270 Myoma Rd (16046-2116)
PHONE..............................724 776-4983
Roberta Huffman, *President*
EMP: 3
SQ FT: 2,304
SALES: 350K **Privately Held**
SIC: 3677 3575 Coil windings, electronic; inductors, electronic; keyboards, computer, office machine

(G-10510)
PRIMROSE CONSULTING INC
Also Called: Heart of The Home
125 Majestic Dr (16046-5001)
PHONE..............................724 816-5769
Jeff Martin, *President*
Chris Claypoole, *Project Mgr*
EMP: 4
SALES (est): 380.7K **Privately Held**
SIC: 2521 2522 Cabinets, office: wood; office cabinets & filing drawers: except wood

(G-10511)
TUTORGEN INC
505 Linden Ct (16046-7167)
PHONE..............................704 710-8445
John Stamper, *CEO*
EMP: 4
SALES (est): 289.7K **Privately Held**
SIC: 7372 Educational computer software

(G-10512)
WALTCO INC
1100 Mars Evans City Rd (16046-2216)
P.O. Box 422 (16046-0422)
PHONE..............................724 625-3110
Walter G Frank Jr, *President*
Shari Frank, *Treasurer*
EMP: 22
SALES (est): 4.8MM **Privately Held**
SIC: 3441 7389 Fabricated structural metal;

(G-10513)
WEL INSTRUMENT CO
106 Camp Trees Rd (16046-2804)
PHONE..............................724 625-9041
Kendra Leonard, *President*
EMP: 3
SALES (est): 260K **Privately Held**
SIC: 3826 Microscopes, electron & proton

(G-10514)
WOODINGS DOWELING TECH INC
Also Called: Wdt
218 Clay Avenue Ext (16046)
PHONE..............................724 625-3131
Robert T Woodings III, *President*
David Draskovic, *Controller*
EMP: 8 EST: 1948
SQ FT: 51,000
SALES (est): 1.1MM **Privately Held**
SIC: 3531 Construction machinery attachments

(G-10515)
WOODINGS INDUSTRIAL CORP (PA)
218 Clay Ave (16046)
P.O. Box 851 (16046-0851)
PHONE..............................724 625-3131
Robert T Woodings III, *President*
Donald E Howell, *Vice Pres*
Rick Bralich, *CFO*
David Draskovic, *Admin Sec*
W Eric Hench, *Asst Sec*
◆ EMP: 109
SQ FT: 95,000
SALES (est): 59.1MM **Privately Held**
SIC: 3541 3443 3441 3546 Drilling machine tools (metal cutting); cylinders, pressure: metal plate; fabricated structural metal; power-driven handtools; hand & edge tools

(G-10516)
WOODWARD INC
Also Called: Mars Mineral
128 Myoma Rd (16046-2228)
P.O. Box 719 (16046-0719)
PHONE..............................724 538-3110
Earl R Woodward Jr, *CEO*
Clayton Woodward, *President*
Earl Jr R Woodward, *Vice Pres*
William C Hamm Jr, *Treasurer*
EMP: 35 EST: 1962
SQ FT: 45,000
SALES (est): 9.4MM **Privately Held**
WEB: www.marsmineral.com
SIC: 3312 Plate, steel

Martins Creek
Northampton County

(G-10517)
AGRI-DYNAMICS INC
6574 S Delaware Dr (18063-9706)
P.O. Box 267 (18063-0267)
PHONE.................................610 250-9280
Regina Marinelli, *President*
EMP: 5
SALES (est): 194.3K **Privately Held**
WEB: www.agri-dynamics.com
SIC: 3999 5149 Pet supplies; pet foods

Martinsburg
Blair County

(G-10518)
21ST N COLLEGE
1863 Piney Creek Rd (16662-7111)
PHONE.................................814 502-1542
Nevins Ty, *Principal*
EMP: 3
SALES (est): 267.8K **Privately Held**
SIC: 2752 Commercial printing, lithographic

(G-10519)
AAA COLOR CARD COMPANY
115 S Wall St (16662-1114)
PHONE.................................814 793-2342
Sally Wright, *President*
EMP: 3
SQ FT: 2,000
SALES (est): 259K **Privately Held**
WEB: www.aaacolorcard.com
SIC: 2752 Commercial printing, offset

(G-10520)
CARGILL INCORPORATED
965 Frederick Rd (16662-8866)
PHONE.................................814 793-3701
Jody Harker, *Manager*
EMP: 20
SALES (corp-wide): 114.7B **Privately Held**
WEB: www.cargill.com
SIC: 2048 Mineral feed supplements
PA: Cargill, Incorporated
15407 Mcginty Rd W
Wayzata MN 55391
952 742-7575

(G-10521)
CARGILL INCORPORATED
106 S Railroad St (16662-1334)
PHONE.................................814 793-2137
David Rockwell, *Plant Mgr*
EMP: 24
SALES (corp-wide): 114.7B **Privately Held**
WEB: www.pennfield.com
SIC: 5191 2048 Feed; prepared feeds
PA: Cargill, Incorporated
15407 Mcginty Rd W
Wayzata MN 55391
952 742-7575

(G-10522)
COVE STAKE & WOOD PRODUCTS GP
1434 Curryville Rd (16662-8729)
PHONE.................................814 793-3257
Irvin Zimmerman, *Partner*
EMP: 7
SALES (est): 1MM **Privately Held**
SIC: 2499 2452 2448 Handles, poles, dowels & stakes: wood; surveyors' stakes, wood; prefabricated wood buildings; pallets, wood

(G-10523)
HH BROWN SHOE COMPANY INC
107 Highland St (16662-1424)
PHONE.................................814 793-3786
John Swenney, *General Mgr*
EMP: 50

SALES (corp-wide): 225.3B **Publicly Held**
WEB: www.coveshoe.com
SIC: 3143 Work shoes, men's
HQ: H.H. Brown Shoe Company, Inc.
124 W Putnam Ave 1a
Greenwich CT 06830
203 661-2424

(G-10524)
HH BROWN SHOE COMPANY INC
Cove Shoe Company
107 Highland St (16662-1424)
PHONE.................................814 793-3786
Chuck Covatch, *President*
EMP: 100
SALES (corp-wide): 225.3B **Publicly Held**
WEB: www.coveshoe.com
SIC: 3143 3144 3021 Men's footwear, except athletic; women's footwear, except athletic; rubber & plastics footwear
HQ: H.H. Brown Shoe Company, Inc.
124 W Putnam Ave Ste 1a
Greenwich CT 06830
203 661-2424

(G-10525)
KEITHS CABINET COMPANY
2181 Curryville Rd (16662-7607)
PHONE.................................814 793-2614
Roger L Keith, *Owner*
EMP: 20
SALES (est): 1.7MM **Privately Held**
SIC: 2426 5712 Frames for upholstered furniture, wood; cabinet work, custom

(G-10526)
MARTIN TRUCK BODIES INC
279 Cross Roads Ln (16662-8203)
PHONE.................................814 793-3353
Shawn Martin, *President*
Nelson Martin, *Treasurer*
Travis Martin, *Admin Sec*
EMP: 24
SQ FT: 22,000
SALES: 4.1MM **Privately Held**
SIC: 3599 7699 Custom machinery; industrial machinery & equipment repair

(G-10527)
MORRISONS COVE HERALD INC
113 N Market St (16662-1207)
PHONE.................................814 793-2144
Allen Bassler, *President*
Karen Bassler, *President*
David Snyder, *President*
David Synder, *President*
EMP: 7 **EST:** 1865
SQ FT: 3,000
SALES: 325K **Privately Held**
SIC: 2711 5943 Job printing & newspaper publishing combined; office forms & supplies

(G-10528)
PRECISION WOOD WORKS
356 Spring Farm Rd (16662-8949)
PHONE.................................814 793-9900
Kevin Z Zimmerman, *Owner*
EMP: 3
SALES (est): 236.1K **Privately Held**
SIC: 2434 Wood kitchen cabinets

(G-10529)
RITCHEYS DAIRY INC
2130 Cross Cove Rd (16662-7619)
PHONE.................................814 793-2157
Reid E Ritchey, *President*
Andrew Ritchey, *Info Tech Mgr*
EMP: 50 **EST:** 1940
SQ FT: 10,000
SALES: 8.9MM **Privately Held**
WEB: www.ritcheysdairy.com
SIC: 2026 2024 Fluid milk; ice cream & frozen desserts

(G-10530)
ROARING SPRING BLANK BOOK CO
270 Martin Ln (16662-7613)
PHONE.................................814 793-3744
Randy Oeffner, *Branch Mgr*
EMP: 250

SALES (corp-wide): 96.8MM **Privately Held**
WEB: www.roaringspring.com
SIC: 2678 Stationery: made from purchased materials
PA: Roaring Spring Blank Book Company
740 Spang St
Roaring Spring PA 16673
814 224-2306

Marysville
Perry County

(G-10531)
ALLEN P SUTTON
Also Called: Sutton Brothers
222 Verbeke St (17053-1325)
PHONE.................................717 957-2047
Fax: 717 957-3214
EMP: 6 **EST:** 1971
SQ FT: 10,000
SALES (est): 319.8K **Privately Held**
SIC: 1771 1721 3599 Pavement Sealer Specialists Repairs Pavements Power Sweeping

(G-10532)
ROCK PROOF BOATS
407 Mountain Rd (17053-9701)
PHONE.................................717 957-3282
Brent Kauffman, *Principal*
EMP: 3
SALES (est): 341.3K **Privately Held**
SIC: 3732 Boat building & repairing

(G-10533)
SPECIALTY BAKERS LLC
450 S State Rd (17053-1009)
PHONE.................................717 626-8002
Paul Durlacher, *President*
EMP: 100 **EST:** 1963
SQ FT: 75,000
SALES (est): 22MM
SALES (corp-wide): 57.5MM **Privately Held**
WEB: www.sbiladyfingers.com
SIC: 2051 Mfg Bread/Related Products
PA: Specialty Bakers Holding Company Llc
450 S State Rd
Marysville PA 17053
717 957-2131

(G-10534)
VALLEY CUSTOM CABINETRY
109 Tower Rd (17053-9422)
PHONE.................................717 957-2819
Neal A Barrik, *Owner*
EMP: 3
SALES (est): 193.1K **Privately Held**
SIC: 2434 Wood kitchen cabinets

Masontown
Fayette County

(G-10535)
DURANT EXCAVATING
18 N Ross St (15461-1764)
PHONE.................................724 583-9800
Mark J Durant, *Owner*
EMP: 3
SALES: 60K **Privately Held**
SIC: 1794 1221 Excavation work; strip mining, bituminous

(G-10536)
SHAFFERS FABRICATING INC (PA)
Also Called: Shaffers Fabg & Diesl Svc
417 N Water St (15461)
PHONE.................................724 583-2833
William Shaffer Sr, *President*
Jackie Shay, *Admin Sec*
EMP: 7
SALES (est): 350K **Privately Held**
SIC: 3549 Wiredrawing & fabricating machinery & equipment, ex. die

(G-10537)
STAHLS SPECIAL PROJECTS INC
Also Called: Stahl's Hotronix
1 Stahls Dr (15461-2585)
PHONE.................................724 583-1176
Richard Ellsworth, *President*
Ted Stahl, *Chairman*
Ted A Stahl, *Treasurer*
Brian Stahl, *Shareholder*
Darla Early, *Administration*
▲ **EMP:** 50
SQ FT: 65,000
SALES (est): 14.1MM
SALES (corp-wide): 33.4MM **Privately Held**
SIC: 3552 Textile machinery
PA: Stahls' Inc.
6353 E 14 Mile Rd
Sterling Heights MI 48312
800 478-2457

(G-10538)
WILLIAM AUPPERLE
Also Called: Gigantes Bakery
1892 Mcclellandtown Rd (15461-2508)
PHONE.................................724 583-8310
William Aupperle, *Owner*
EMP: 5
SQ FT: 3,000
SALES (est): 440K **Privately Held**
SIC: 5411 2051 5141 5461 Grocery stores, independent; bakery: wholesale or wholesale/retail combined; groceries, general line; bakeries

Matamoras
Pike County

(G-10539)
JALITE INC
202 7th St (18336-1500)
PHONE.................................570 491-2205
John Creek, *President*
Alex Yost, *Opers Dir*
▲ **EMP:** 4
SQ FT: 22,000
SALES (est): 513.3K **Privately Held**
WEB: www.jaliteusa.com
SIC: 5099 3993 Luminous products (non-electrical); signs & advertising specialties

(G-10540)
SIGN HERE SIGN CO INC
808 Pennsylvania Ave (18336-1540)
PHONE.................................845 858-6366
Howard Vovis, *President*
Gail Bowdoin, *Manager*
EMP: 5
SQ FT: 10,000
SALES (est): 609.7K **Privately Held**
WEB: www.signheresignco.com
SIC: 3993 1799 Signs & advertising specialties; sign installation & maintenance

Mayfield
Lackawanna County

(G-10541)
JAM WORKS LLC
889 Route 6 (18433-1515)
PHONE.................................570 972-1562
John Mele, *President*
Harry Morgan, *Project Mgr*
Kristina Galati, *Office Mgr*
EMP: 6 **EST:** 2007
SQ FT: 3,000
SALES (est): 1.4MM **Privately Held**
SIC: 3535 Robotic conveyors

(G-10542)
P A HUTCHISON COMPANY
400 Penn Ave (18433-1813)
PHONE.................................570 876-4560
Philip O Hutchison, *CEO*
Christian Hutchison, *President*
Christian P Hutchison, *President*
EMP: 140
SQ FT: 150,000

SALES (est): 37.9MM **Privately Held**
WEB: www.pahutch.com
SIC: 2732 2752 2791 Book printing; commercial printing, offset; typesetting

(G-10543)
TE STONE PRODUCTS LLC
301 Whitmore Ave (18433-1740)
PHONE...................................570 335-4921
Todd Erb,
EMP: 4 EST: 2011
SALES (est): 162.9K **Privately Held**
SIC: 1481 Mine & quarry services, nonmetallic minerals

(G-10544)
UNITED LAMINATIONS INC
1311 Lackawanna Ave (18433-1998)
PHONE...................................570 876-1360
Herbert Perry, *President*
Thomas Perry, *Vice Pres*
EMP: 18
SQ FT: 45,000
SALES (est): 3.3MM **Privately Held**
SIC: 3081 3083 Unsupported plastics film & sheet; laminated plastic sheets

(G-10545)
WESTLAKE UNITED CORPORATION (PA)
91 Hickory St (18433-1919)
PHONE...................................570 876-0222
E F Westlake Sr, *President*
Herbert Perry, *Corp Secy*
Gary Allen, *Manager*
Andrew Anderlonis, *Supervisor*
EMP: 18
SQ FT: 3,000
SALES (est): 3.6MM **Privately Held**
SIC: 3089 3081 Plastic hardware & building products; unsupported plastics film & sheet

Mayport
Clarion County

(G-10546)
MAYPORT COTTONS & QUILT SHOP
68 Paradise Rd (16240-2804)
PHONE...................................814 365-2212
Patty Toy, *Owner*
EMP: 3
SALES (est): 126.7K **Privately Held**
SIC: 2395 Quilted fabrics or cloth

(G-10547)
TATY BUG INC
Also Called: Woodland Pavarn
8631 Route 28 (16240-2119)
PHONE...................................814 856-3323
Kevin Hoffman, *President*
EMP: 5 EST: 2010
SALES (est): 304.5K **Privately Held**
SIC: 3523 7389 Barn, silo, poultry, dairy & livestock machinery;

Mc Alisterville
Juniata County

(G-10548)
CROWNWOOD LLC
Also Called: Crownwood Custom Cabinetry
1739 Main St (17049-8465)
PHONE...................................717 463-2942
Andrew Fisher,
Melvin Beiler,
Daniel Esh,
EMP: 4
SQ FT: 7,500
SALES (est): 430K **Privately Held**
SIC: 2434 7389 Wood kitchen cabinets; engraving service

(G-10549)
EVERGREEN PALLET COMPANY
2647 Free Spring Ch Rd (17049-8597)
PHONE...................................717 463-3217
John A Peachy, *Owner*
EMP: 8

SALES (est): 490K **Privately Held**
SIC: 2448 Pallets, wood

(G-10550)
L & R LUMBER INC
5374 Mountain Rd (17049-8338)
P.O. Box 246 (17049-0246)
PHONE...................................717 463-3411
Larry E Bowersox, *Partner*
L Russell Bowersox, *Partner*
Russell Bowersox, *Vice Pres*
EMP: 9
SALES (est): 1.4MM **Privately Held**
SIC: 2421 5031 5211 Lumber: rough, sawed or planed; lumber: rough, dressed & finished; lumber & other building materials

(G-10551)
OLIVEROS VINEYARD LLC
1271 Troyer Rd (17049-8080)
PHONE...................................717 856-4566
William E Dressler,
EMP: 4
SALES (est): 278.1K **Privately Held**
SIC: 2084 Wines

(G-10552)
SHADE MOUNTAIN COUNTERTOPS
75 Steves Woods Dr (17049-8161)
PHONE...................................717 463-2729
Aaron Petersheim, *Owner*
EMP: 10
SALES: 1.6MM **Privately Held**
SIC: 2541 7389 Counter & sink tops;

(G-10553)
WEAVER PALLET COMPANY LLC
2107 Free Spring Ch Rd (17049-8591)
PHONE...................................717 463-2770
Paul Weaver,
Saloma Weaver,
EMP: 9
SQ FT: 15,000
SALES: 3MM **Privately Held**
SIC: 2448 Pallets, wood

(G-10554)
YODER LUMBER CO INC
114 Yoder Ln (17049-8075)
PHONE...................................717 463-9253
Steven Yoder, *Partner*
EMP: 8
SQ FT: 3,200
SALES (est): 993.3K
SALES (corp-wide): 30.3MM **Privately Held**
SIC: 2421 Sawmills & planing mills, general
PA: Yoder Lumber Co., Inc.
 4515 Township Road 367
 Millersburg OH 44654
 330 893-3121

Mc Clellandtown
Fayette County

(G-10555)
C & J WELDING & CNSTR LLC
116 Moonlite Dr (15458)
PHONE...................................724 564-7120
Charles Jason Foster, *President*
▲ EMP: 112
SALES (est): 7.5MM
SALES (corp-wide): 3B **Privately Held**
SIC: 7699 1241 Welding equipment repair; mine preparation services
HQ: Rema Tip Top Ag
 Gruber Str. 65
 Poing 85586
 812 170-7100

(G-10556)
SOUTH PENN RESOURCES LLC (PA)
334 Livinggood Hollow Rd (15458-1512)
PHONE...................................724 880-5882
James Collins,
Vincent Frazier,
Michael Sandzimier,
EMP: 16

SALES (est): 2.7MM **Privately Held**
SIC: 1241 Coal mining services

Mc Clure
Mifflin County

(G-10557)
ARMSTRONGS
130 Armstrong Ln (17841-9246)
PHONE...................................717 543-5488
Robin Armstrong, *Partner*
Wanda Armstrong, *Partner*
EMP: 3
SALES (est): 275.5K **Privately Held**
SIC: 2899 Water treating compounds

(G-10558)
GERALD LAUB
Also Called: G L Laub Surplus
Specht St (17841)
P.O. Box 279 (17841-0279)
PHONE...................................570 658-2609
Gerald Laub, *Owner*
EMP: 4
SALES (est): 222.8K **Privately Held**
SIC: 3949 Balls: baseball, football, basketball, etc.

(G-10559)
JAMES P WOLFLEY
7718 Old Stage Rd (17841)
PHONE...................................570 541-0414
James P Wolfley, *Principal*
EMP: 4
SALES (est): 384.4K **Privately Held**
SIC: 3531 Backhoes

(G-10560)
LOZIER CORPORATION
48 E Ohio St (17841-8884)
PHONE...................................570 658-8111
Scoot Spotts, *Branch Mgr*
Sharon Hess, *Assistant*
EMP: 120
SALES (corp-wide): 545.7MM **Privately Held**
WEB: www.lozier.com
SIC: 2541 5046 Store fixtures, wood; store fixtures
PA: Lozier Corporation
 6336 John J Pershing Dr
 Omaha NE 68110
 402 457-8000

(G-10561)
SNOOKS RHINE & ARNOLD
113 Log Ln (17841-8122)
PHONE...................................570 658-3410
Lynn Snook, *Partner*
Sheldon Arnold, *Partner*
Ronald Rhine, *Partner*
Alton Snook, *Partner*
Donald Snook, *Partner*
EMP: 6
SALES (est): 410K **Privately Held**
SIC: 2421 Sawmills & planing mills, general

Mc Connellsburg
Fulton County

(G-10562)
ANTIETAM IRON WORKS LLC
201 Lincoln Way W Ste 100 (17233-1320)
PHONE...................................717 485-5557
Austin Fred Gunnell,
EMP: 7
SALES (est): 579.8K **Privately Held**
WEB: www.antietamironworks.com
SIC: 1799 3479 Ornamental metal work; welding on site; coating of metals & formed products

(G-10563)
CONAIR CORPORATION
Also Called: Wearing Products
1 Crystal Dr (17233-1208)
PHONE...................................717 485-4871
Thomas H Kilby, *Branch Mgr*
EMP: 85

SALES (corp-wide): 2B **Privately Held**
WEB: www.conair.com
SIC: 3634 5064 3556 Electric housewares & fans; electrical appliances, television & radio; food products machinery
PA: Conair Corporation
 1 Cummings Point Rd
 Stamford CT 06902
 203 351-9000

(G-10564)
ENERGY PRODUCTS & TECHNOLOGIES
433 Peach Orchard Rd (17233-8554)
P.O. Box 436 (17233-0436)
PHONE...................................717 485-3137
Randy Keefer, *President*
Jeff Mellott, *General Mgr*
Bonnie Keefer, *Vice Pres*
EMP: 5
SALES: 250K **Privately Held**
SIC: 3679 3585 Harness assemblies for electronic use: wire or cable; parts for heating, cooling & refrigerating equipment

(G-10565)
FULTON COUNTY NEWS
417 E Market St (17233-1131)
P.O. Box 635 (17233-0635)
PHONE...................................717 485-4513
Jamie S Greathead, *Owner*
EMP: 10
SQ FT: 8,400
SALES (est): 620.7K **Privately Held**
SIC: 2711 Commercial printing & newspaper publishing combined; newspapers, publishing & printing

(G-10566)
FULTON COUNTY REPORTER
50 Hillside Ests (17233-8178)
PHONE...................................717 325-0079
EMP: 4
SALES (est): 122.4K **Privately Held**
SIC: 2711 Newspapers, publishing & printing

(G-10567)
FULTON PRECISION INDS INC
300 Success Dr (17233-8656)
P.O. Box 526 (17233-0526)
PHONE...................................717 485-5158
Walter R Barmont III, *President*
Greg G Fuller Sr, *Vice Pres*
Brandon Waters, *Plant Mgr*
Larry Zimmerman, *QC Mgr*
George Fuller, *Sales Mgr*
▲ EMP: 45
SQ FT: 78,000
SALES (est): 9.7MM **Privately Held**
WEB: www.fultonprecision.com
SIC: 3599 Machine shop, jobbing & repair

(G-10568)
JLG INDUSTRIES INC (HQ)
Also Called: J L G
1 J L G Dr (17233-9533)
PHONE...................................717 485-5161
Frank Nerenhausen's, *President*
Chaz Carr, *District Mgr*
Dennis Hess, *District Mgr*
Aaron Moss, *District Mgr*
Charles Foreman, *Business Mgr*
▼ EMP: 1501
SALES (est): 2.1B
SALES (corp-wide): 7.7B **Publicly Held**
WEB: www.jlg.com
SIC: 3531 Aerial work platforms: hydraulic/elec. truck/carrier mounted
PA: Oshkosh Corporation
 2307 Oregon St
 Oshkosh WI 54902
 920 235-9151

(G-10569)
JLG INDUSTRIES INC
221 Success Dr (17233-8899)
PHONE...................................717 485-5161
Eugene Swope, *Director*
EMP: 200
SALES (corp-wide): 6.8B **Publicly Held**
WEB: www.jlg.com
SIC: 3531 7353 3535 Construction machinery; heavy construction equipment rental; conveyors & conveying equipment

HQ: Jlg Industries, Inc.
1 J L G Dr
Mc Connellsburg PA 17233
717 485-5161

(G-10570)
JLG INDUSTRIES INC
220 Success Dr (17233-8899)
PHONE...................................717 485-6464
Denny Buterbaugh, *Director*
EMP: 50
SALES (corp-wide): 6.8B **Publicly Held**
WEB: www.jlg.com
SIC: 3531 Aerial work platforms: hydraulic/elec. truck/carrier mounted
HQ: Jlg Industries, Inc.
1 J L G Dr
Mc Connellsburg PA 17233
717 485-5161

(G-10571)
MERCERSBURG JOURNAL
115 Lincoln Way E Ste A (17233-1423)
PHONE...................................717 485-3162
Vernon Leese, *Partner*
Barbara Leese, *General Ptnr*
EMP: 3 EST: 1843
SALES (est): 210.3K **Privately Held**
WEB: www.mercersburginternet.com
SIC: 2711 Newspapers, publishing & printing

Mc Donald
Washington County

(G-10572)
DONART ELECTRONICS INC
1005 Robinson Hwy (15057-2021)
P.O. Box 27 (15057-0027)
PHONE...................................724 796-3011
John Salvadori, *President*
Halene Salvadori, *Treasurer*
EMP: 5 EST: 1959
SQ FT: 6,000
SALES (est): 1MM **Privately Held**
WEB: www.donartelectronics.com
SIC: 3825 Test equipment for electronic & electrical circuits; digital test equipment, electronic & electrical circuits

(G-10573)
FEDINETZ SAWMILL
Also Called: Fedinetz Co
40 Belgium Hollow Rd (15057-2922)
PHONE...................................724 796-9461
Troy Fedinetz, *Owner*
EMP: 5
SALES: 200K **Privately Held**
SIC: 2421 Specialty sawmill products

(G-10574)
FULL THROTTLE INDUSTRIES LLC
328 E Lincoln Ave (15057-1430)
PHONE...................................724 926-2140
EMP: 8
SALES (est): 705.8K **Privately Held**
SIC: 3999 Manufacturing industries

(G-10575)
MATT NABEJA
Also Called: Quality Machine Tools
3193 Old Oakdale Rd (15057-3536)
PHONE...................................412 787-2876
Matt Nabeja, *Owner*
▲ EMP: 4
SALES (est): 621K **Privately Held**
WEB: www.machinetoolonline.com
SIC: 3599 Machine shop, jobbing & repair

(G-10576)
MCC HOLDINGS COMPANY LLC
Also Called: Miller Centrifugal Casting
110 Centrifugal Ct (15057-2448)
PHONE...................................724 745-0300
Ian Sadler, *President*
Roger Chambers, *Vice Pres*
Rod Francis, *Vice Pres*
Giri Rajendran, *Vice Pres*
Lance Shomo, *Vice Pres*
◆ EMP: 56
SQ FT: 53,000

SALES (est): 9.6MM **Privately Held**
WEB: www.millercentrifugal.com
SIC: 3369 Nonferrous foundries
HQ: Eisenwerk Sulzau-Werfen, R. & E. Weinberger Aktiengesellschaft
BundesstraBe 4
Tenneck 5451
646 852-850

(G-10577)
MCC INTERNATIONAL INC
Also Called: Miller Centrifugal Casting Co
110 Centrifugal Ct (15057-2448)
PHONE...................................724 745-0300
Ian Sadler, *President*
Roger Chambers, *Vice Pres*
Rod Francis, *Vice Pres*
Giri Rajendran, *Vice Pres*
▲ EMP: 53
SQ FT: 53,900
SALES (est): 9MM **Privately Held**
SIC: 3549 3559 Metalworking machinery; foundry, smelting, refining & similar machinery
HQ: Eisenwerk Sulzau-Werfen, R. & E. Weinberger Aktiengesellschaft
BundesstraBe 4
Tenneck 5451
646 852-850

(G-10578)
POST GAZETTE
26 Ridgewood Dr (15057-4444)
PHONE...................................412 965-6738
Scott Campbell, *Principal*
EMP: 4 EST: 2010
SALES (est): 216.1K **Privately Held**
SIC: 2711 Newspapers

(G-10579)
PROMARK INDUSTRIES INC
45 Casey Rd (15057-2938)
P.O. Box 1149, West End NC (27376-1149)
PHONE...................................724 356-4060
Thomas B Gaffney, *President*
Joy Gaffney, *Vice Pres*
Tj Balaban, *Marketing Staff*
EMP: 4
SALES (est): 462.6K **Privately Held**
WEB: www.promark-ind.com
SIC: 2752 3993 Decals, lithographed; name plates: except engraved, etched, etc.: metal

(G-10580)
REAXIS INC
941 Robinson Hwy (15057-2213)
PHONE...................................412 517-6070
Marco R Van Der Poel, *President*
Coleen Pangan, *Chairman*
Clint Wilson, *Business Mgr*
Charles J Zimmerman, *Exec VP*
Charles Zmmerman, *Exec VP*
◆ EMP: 43 EST: 1935
SQ FT: 25,000
SALES (est): 32.5MM
SALES (corp-wide): 14.5MM **Privately Held**
WEB: www.reaxis.com
SIC: 2819 Tin (stannic/stannous) compounds or salts, inorganic; catalysts, chemical
PA: Gicc Holdings, Inc.
941 Robinson Hwy
Mc Donald PA 15057
724 796-1511

(G-10581)
SCHAEFER MACHINE INC
727 Robinson Hwy (15057-2209)
P.O. Box 239 (15057-0239)
PHONE...................................724 796-7755
Len Schaefer, *President*
Ginny Schaefer, *Office Mgr*
EMP: 9
SQ FT: 11,000
SALES (est): 650K **Privately Held**
SIC: 3599 Machine shop, jobbing & repair

(G-10582)
SUMMIT MATERIALS LLC
1274 Oakridge Rd (15057-2632)
PHONE...................................412 260-8048
Eric Bono,
EMP: 4

SALES (est): 300K **Privately Held**
SIC: 3399 Metal powders, pastes & flakes

(G-10583)
SUPERIOR POWDER COATING INC
785 Millers Run Rd (15057-2539)
PHONE...................................412 221-8250
Robert A Olson Jr, *President*
EMP: 9 EST: 2001
SALES (est): 903.3K **Privately Held**
SIC: 3399 Powder, metal

(G-10584)
WORLD CHRONICLE INC
105 William St (15057-4446)
PHONE...................................724 745-3808
Tarache L Armstead, *President*
EMP: 5
SALES: 150K **Privately Held**
SIC: 2759 Commercial printing

Mc Elhattan
Clinton County

(G-10585)
BRODART CO
Contract Furniture Division
280 North Rd (17748)
P.O. Box 360 (17748-0360)
PHONE...................................570 769-7412
Randall McKenzie, *Vice Pres*
EMP: 190
SALES (corp-wide): 431.1MM **Privately Held**
SIC: 2531 2599 Public building & related furniture; factory furniture & fixtures
PA: Brodart Co.
500 Arch St
Williamsport PA 17701
570 326-2461

(G-10586)
BRODART CO
Supplies and Furnishings Div
100 North Rd (17748)
P.O. Box 360 (17748-0360)
PHONE...................................570 769-3265
Randall Mackenzie, *Principal*
Douglas Boob, *Engineer*
EMP: 138
SALES (corp-wide): 431.1MM **Privately Held**
SIC: 2679 5961 Book covers, paper; catalog & mail-order houses
PA: Brodart Co.
500 Arch St
Williamsport PA 17701
570 326-2461

(G-10587)
FIRST QUALITY HYGIENIC INC (HQ)
121 North Rd (17748-9601)
PHONE...................................570 769-6900
Nader Damaghi, *President*
Kambiz Damaghi, *Treasurer*
▲ EMP: 3
SALES (est): 1.2MM **Privately Held**
SIC: 2676 Feminine hygiene paper products

(G-10588)
FIRST QUALITY PRODUCTS INC
121 North Rd (17748-9601)
P.O. Box 270 (17748-0270)
PHONE...................................570 769-6900
Bob Damaghi, *Owner*
Sherry Zell, *General Mgr*
Jim Fritz, *Plant Mgr*
Ken Flerlage, *Info Tech Mgr*
Jesse Rearick, *Info Tech Mgr*
EMP: 400 **Privately Held**
SIC: 2676 2621 Towels, napkins & tissue paper products; toweling tissue, paper; tissue paper
HQ: First Quality Products, Inc
80 Cuttermill Rd Ste 500
Great Neck NY 11021
516 829-4949

(G-10589)
NUTEK DISPOSABLES INC (HQ)
121 North Rd (17748-9601)
PHONE...................................570 769-6900
Kambiz Damaghi, *President*
Ken Adams, *Vice Pres*
▲ EMP: 60 EST: 1997
SALES (est): 22.2MM **Privately Held**
SIC: 2676 Sanitary paper products

(G-10590)
TRUCK-LITE CO LLC
786 Mcelhattan Rd (17748)
P.O. Box 329 (17748-0329)
PHONE...................................570 769-7231
Jack Dingess, *Plant Mgr*
EMP: 55
SALES (corp-wide): 42.4B **Privately Held**
WEB: www.truck-lite.com
SIC: 3647 Vehicular lighting equipment
HQ: Truck-Lite Co., Llc
310 E Elmwood Ave
Falconer NY 14733

Mc Kean
Erie County

(G-10591)
GREAT LAKES AUTOMTN SVCS INC (PA)
Also Called: Great Lakes Automtn Machining
8835 Walmer Dr (16426-1142)
PHONE...................................814 476-7710
Kenneth Fisher, *CEO*
Mark Fatica, *President*
Bryan Brooks, *Vice Pres*
Vicki Fisher, *Sales Mgr*
Vanessa Fremer, *Manager*
EMP: 30
SQ FT: 35,000
SALES: 12MM **Privately Held**
WEB: www.glasi.us
SIC: 3599 Machine shop, jobbing & repair

(G-10592)
SPX CORPORATION
5620 West Rd (16426-1504)
PHONE...................................814 476-5800
Roderic Karpen, *Ch of Bd*
EMP: 16
SALES (corp-wide): 1.5B **Publicly Held**
WEB: www.spx.com
SIC: 3491 Industrial valves
PA: Spx Corporation
13320a Balntyn Corp Pl
Charlotte NC 28277
980 474-3700

(G-10593)
SPX FLOW US LLC
5620 West Rd (16426-1504)
PHONE...................................814 476-5842
Chris Kearney, *Mng Member*
Robert B Foreman,
Jeremy Smeltser,
EMP: 3
SALES (est): 1.1MM **Privately Held**
SIC: 3494 Valves & pipe fittings

(G-10594)
SPX FLOW US LLC
Also Called: SPX Valves & Controls
5620 West Rd (16426-1504)
PHONE...................................814 476-5800
Corey Erven, *Mfg Mgr*
John P Campolo, *VP Finance*
▲ EMP: 1
SQ FT: 47,500
SALES (est): 13.2MM
SALES (corp-wide): 2B **Publicly Held**
SIC: 3494 3443 3567 7359 Valves & pipe fittings; boilers: industrial, power, or marine; heat exchangers, condensers & components; industrial furnaces & ovens; equipment rental & leasing; industrial equipment services; heating equipment (hydronic); plumbing fittings & supplies
HQ: M & J Valve Company
19191 Hempstead Hwy
Houston TX 77065
281 469-0550

▲ = Import ▼=Export
◆ =Import/Export

(G-10595)
TRI-TECH INJECTION MOLDING INC
8556 Edinboro Rd (16426-1338)
PHONE................................814 476-7748
Walter Rbender, *President*
Dan Mandus, *Principal*
Walter Bender, *Manager*
EMP: 22
SALES (est): 4.6MM **Privately Held**
SIC: 3089 Injection molding of plastics

Mc Kees Rocks
Allegheny County

(G-10596)
1998 EQUIPMENT LEASING CORP
400 Island Ave (15136-3250)
PHONE................................412 771-2944
Arnold Davis, *CEO*
Shawn Davis, *Admin Sec*
EMP: 4
SALES: 380K **Privately Held**
SIC: 3448 Prefabricated metal buildings

(G-10597)
5 GENERATION BAKERS LLC
Also Called: Jenny Lee Swirl Breads
1100 Chartiers Ave (15136-3642)
P.O. Box 71, Zelienople (16063-0071)
PHONE................................412 444-8200
Scott A Baker,
▼ EMP: 43
SQ FT: 21,500
SALES (est): 1.1MM **Privately Held**
SIC: 2051 Bakery: wholesale or whole-sale/retail combined

(G-10598)
A J DRGON ASSOCIATES INC
201 Chamber St (15136-3264)
PHONE................................412 771-5160
Anthony Drgon Sr, *President*
Anthony Drgon Jr, *Vice Pres*
EMP: 6 EST: 1979
SQ FT: 2,000
SALES: 500K **Privately Held**
SIC: 3599 8711 Machine shop, jobbing & repair; engineering services

(G-10599)
A MAMAUX & SON INC
102 Ella St (15136-2756)
PHONE................................412 771-8432
Edward J Coleman, *President*
Theresa R Coleman, *Admin Sec*
EMP: 12 EST: 1865
SQ FT: 44,000
SALES (est): 930K **Privately Held**
SIC: 2394 5712 Awnings, fabric: made from purchased materials; tarpaulins, fabric: made from purchased materials; tents: made from purchased materials; outdoor & garden furniture

(G-10600)
ACACIA CORP
Also Called: Plymouth Interiors
7 Crawford St (15136-3633)
PHONE................................412 771-6144
Bernadette Gardy, *President*
Ralph Trainer, *Corp Secy*
Peter Gardy, *Vice Pres*
EMP: 18
SALES: 2MM **Privately Held**
SIC: 3444 2591 Sheet metalwork; drapery hardware & blinds & shades

(G-10601)
ACE WIRE SPRING & FORM CO INC
1105 Thompson Ave (15136-3824)
PHONE................................412 331-3353
Richard D Froehlich, *President*
Linda Froehlich, *Corp Secy*
Joseph Vodvarka, *Vice Pres*
Al Carmichael, *Prdtn Mgr*
Ritchy Froehlich, *Engineer*
◆ EMP: 50 EST: 1939
SQ FT: 50,000

SALES (est): 14.2MM **Privately Held**
WEB: www.acewire.com
SIC: 3315 3493 3495 3496 Steel wire & related products; steel springs, except wire; wire springs; miscellaneous fabricated wire products

(G-10602)
ADVANCED INTEGRATION GROUP INC
1 Mccormick Rd Ste A (15136-1429)
PHONE................................412 722-0065
Donna D Chappel, *President*
EMP: 25 EST: 1997
SQ FT: 4,500
SALES (est): 8.5MM **Privately Held**
WEB: www.advancedintegrationgroup.net
SIC: 8711 3699 Electronic generation equipment

(G-10603)
ARMSTRONG/KOVER KWICK INC
401 Sproul St (15136-2883)
P.O. Box 337 (15136-0337)
PHONE................................412 771-2200
Robert H Wolf, *President*
Kenneth L Simon, *Vice Pres*
Linda S Simon, *Vice Pres*
Susan L Wolf, *Vice Pres*
▲ EMP: 30 EST: 1925
SQ FT: 57,000
SALES (est): 5.9MM **Privately Held**
WEB: www.akkinc.com
SIC: 2299 2211 2231 2392 Carbonized rags; cheesecloth; felts, woven: wool, mohair or similar fibers; household furnishings; nonwoven fabrics

(G-10604)
BECKERS CAFE
315 Olivia St (15136-2725)
PHONE................................412 331-1373
Conrad Becker, *Partner*
EMP: 4
SQ FT: 2,160
SALES: 150K **Privately Held**
SIC: 5813 2066 Bar (drinking places); chocolate & cocoa products

(G-10605)
BPI INC
Also Called: By-Products Industries
149 Nichol Ave Ste 2 (15136-2627)
PHONE................................412 771-8176
Jerry Graham, *Branch Mgr*
EMP: 10
SALES (corp-wide): 20.5MM **Privately Held**
WEB: www.bpiminerals.com
SIC: 2899 3312 3295 Oxidizers, inorganic; blast furnaces & steel mills; minerals, ground or treated
PA: Bpi, Inc.
   612 S Trenton Ave
   Pittsburgh PA 15221
   412 371-8554

(G-10606)
CONCRETE CONCEPTS INC
Also Called: Bryan Material Group
1095 Thompson Ave (15136-3850)
P.O. Box 272 (15136-0272)
PHONE................................412 331-1500
David Bryan, *President*
EMP: 10
SQ FT: 6,000
SALES (est): 1.7MM **Privately Held**
SIC: 3272 Panels & sections, prefabricated concrete

(G-10607)
ERNEST RICCI
Also Called: Ricci Italian Sausage
5888 Steubenville Pike # 1 (15136-1347)
PHONE................................412 490-9531
Ernest Ricci, *Owner*
Sherry Ricci, *Corp Secy*
EMP: 5
SQ FT: 3,500
SALES (est): 392.9K **Privately Held**
WEB: www.riccisausage.net
SIC: 2013 Sausages from purchased meat

(G-10608)
EVERFRESH JUICE CO PGH
1 Sexton Rd (15136-2758)
PHONE................................412 777-9660
John Federici, *Principal*
EMP: 5
SALES (est): 440.6K **Privately Held**
SIC: 2086 Fruit drinks (less than 100% juice): packaged in cans, etc.

(G-10609)
FRANK BRYAN INC (PA)
1263 Chartiers Ave (15136-3643)
PHONE................................412 331-1630
Thomas J Bryan III, *President*
James P Bryan Jr, *Vice Pres*
Tom Bryan, *Engineer*
Samuel P Bryan, *Treasurer*
J Robert Bryan, *Admin Sec*
EMP: 6
SQ FT: 2,400
SALES (est): 17.5MM **Privately Held**
SIC: 3273 Ready-mixed concrete

(G-10610)
G I S INC
23 Furnace Street Ext (15136-3831)
PHONE................................412 771-8860
David Guiliani, *President*
John H Hartzell III, *Vice Pres*
EMP: 11
SQ FT: 22,000
SALES (est): 6.3MM **Privately Held**
WEB: www.gisinsulation.com
SIC: 5033 3086 Insulation materials; insulation or cushioning material, foamed plastic

(G-10611)
GAZETTE TWO DOT O
706 Broadway Ave (15136-2271)
PHONE................................412 458-1526
EMP: 3
SALES (est): 108K **Privately Held**
SIC: 2711 Newspapers

(G-10612)
GENERAL WIRE SPRING COMPANY
1101 Thompson Ave (15136-3899)
PHONE................................412 771-6300
Lee Silverman, *President*
David Silverman, *Exec VP*
Arthur A Silverman, *Vice Pres*
Robert Silverman, *Vice Pres*
Kurt Perschy, *Foreman/Supr*
▲ EMP: 162 EST: 1930
SALES (est): 66.7MM **Privately Held**
WEB: www.generalwirespring.com
SIC: 3589 3495 3493 3423 Sewer cleaning equipment, power; wire springs; steel springs, except wire; hand & edge tools

(G-10613)
GRACO INC
10 Thomas St (15136-2556)
PHONE................................412 771-5774
Thomas Andrews, *Branch Mgr*
EMP: 1000
SALES (corp-wide): 1.6B **Publicly Held**
WEB: www.graco.com
SIC: 3714 Lubrication systems & parts, motor vehicle
PA: Graco Inc.
   88 11th Ave Ne
   Minneapolis MN 55413
   612 623-6000

(G-10614)
HORIX MANUFACTURING COMPANY (PA)
1384 Island Ave (15136-2593)
PHONE................................412 771-1111
Linda M Szramowski, *CEO*
Christopher Sweeney, *Vice Pres*
◆ EMP: 25 EST: 1929
SQ FT: 80,000
SALES (est): 8.8MM **Privately Held**
WEB: www.horix.net
SIC: 5084 3565 Processing & packaging equipment; bottling machinery: filling, capping, labeling

(G-10615)
J & B BLENDING & TECHNOLOGIES
163 Nichol Ave (15136-2623)
PHONE................................412 331-2850
Richard J Pelot, *President*
Walter Gremba Jr, *Treasurer*
EMP: 4
SQ FT: 50,000
SALES (est): 626.1K **Privately Held**
SIC: 2869 2819 Industrial organic chemicals; industrial inorganic chemicals

(G-10616)
J & L PROFESSIONAL SALES INC
200 Meteor Cir (15136)
PHONE................................412 788-4927
Paul Wischmann, *Principal*
EMP: 3 EST: 2010
SALES (est): 217K **Privately Held**
SIC: 3535 3532 Conveyors & conveying equipment; cleaning machinery, mineral

(G-10617)
JEAN ALEXANDER COSMETICS INC
815 7th St (15136-2121)
PHONE................................412 331-6069
Joseph Scioscia, *CEO*
Oreste V Scioscia, *President*
Christine McLean, *Marketing Staff*
▲ EMP: 5
SQ FT: 7,000
SALES (est): 971.7K **Privately Held**
WEB: www.jeanalexander.com
SIC: 2844 5122 Hair coloring preparations; hair preparations, including shampoos; cosmetics, perfumes & hair products

(G-10618)
KEYSTONE FIRE APPARATUS INC
1751 Mckees Rocks Rd (15136-1607)
PHONE................................412 771-7722
Thomas Ball, *President*
Paula B Ball, *President*
EMP: 9
SQ FT: 7,800
SALES (est): 1.8MM **Privately Held**
WEB: www.keystonefireapp.com
SIC: 7538 3569 General truck repair; firefighting apparatus & related equipment

(G-10619)
MARTIN COMMUNICATIONS INC
1639 Pine Hollow Rd Ste C (15136-1707)
PHONE................................412 498-0157
Donald L Martin, *President*
EMP: 10 EST: 1999
SALES: 1MM **Privately Held**
SIC: 5999 3699 1731 5065 Alarm & safety equipment stores; security devices; safety & security specialization; security control equipment & systems; security systems services; protective devices, security

(G-10620)
MCKEES ROCKS FORGINGS INC
75 Nichol Ave (15136-2625)
PHONE................................412 778-2020
Tim R Wallace, *President*
Jeff Coombs, *Vice Pres*
K W Lewis Sr, *Vice Pres*
Dean Phelps, *Vice Pres*
Johnny Harmon, *Purchasing*
EMP: 56
SQ FT: 50,000
SALES: 10.5MM
SALES (corp-wide): 1.4B **Publicly Held**
WEB: www.mckeesrocksforgings.com
SIC: 3462 Railroad wheels, axles, frogs or other equipment: forged
HQ: Standard Forged Products, Llc
   500 N Akard St
   Dallas TX 75201
   214 631-4420

GEOGRAPHIC

(G-10621)
MSSI REFRACTORY LLC
2 John St (15136-3266)
PHONE...............................412 771-5533
Douglas S Carter, *President*
Joel Hammer, *Vice Pres*
Steven Wake, *Treasurer*
Marinko Milos, *Admin Sec*
EMP: 20
SQ FT: 70,000
SALES (est): 1.9MM **Privately Held**
SIC: 3297 3255 5085 Cement: high tem-
perature, refractory (nonclay); alumina
fused refractories; clay refractories; indus-
trial supplies

(G-10622)
PATTERSON FURNITURE CO
701 Yunker St (15136-3625)
PHONE...............................412 771-0600
Nary Patterson, *President*
Claude D Patterson Jr, *President*
EMP: 5
SALES (est): 363.8K **Privately Held**
SIC: 2512 5712 2522 2511 Upholstered
household furniture; furniture stores; of-
fice furniture, except wood; wood house-
hold furniture

(G-10623)
**PENNSYLVANIA DRILLING
COMPANY**
Also Called: Penn Drill Manufacturing
500 Thompson Ave (15136-3828)
PHONE...............................412 771-2110
Robert Kennedy, *Branch Mgr*
EMP: 22
SALES (corp-wide): 15.6MM **Privately
Held**
SIC: 3532 Drills & drilling equipment, min-
ing (except oil & gas)
PA: Pennsylvania Drilling Company
281 Route 30
Imperial PA 15126
412 771-2110

(G-10624)
PEPSI BEVERAGES COMPANY
400 Graham St (15136-2755)
PHONE...............................412 778-4552
Pat Liberaski, *Mfg Mgr*
Melanie Hill, *Accounts Mgr*
EMP: 22
SALES (est): 4.4MM **Privately Held**
SIC: 2086 Soft drinks: packaged in cans,
bottles, etc.

(G-10625)
**PEPSI-COLA METRO BTLG CO
INC**
Also Called: Pepsico
400 Graham St (15136-2755)
PHONE...............................412 331-6775
Dina Liberta, *Project Mgr*
Mark Gresh, *Sales Staff*
Lisa Sarneso, *Manager*
Richard Gordon, *Manager*
Thomas Vukic, *Manager*
EMP: 20
SALES (corp-wide): 64.6B **Publicly Held**
WEB: www.joy-of-cola.com
SIC: 2086 Carbonated soft drinks, bottled
& canned
HQ: Pepsi-Cola Metropolitan Bottling Com-
pany, Inc.
1111 Westchester Ave
White Plains NY 10604
914 767-6000

(G-10626)
PLYMOUTH BLIND CO INC
Also Called: Plymouth Interiors
7 Crawford St (15136-3633)
PHONE...............................412 771-8569
Barry Ross, *President*
Lou Stempler, *Sales Mgr*
Ralph Trainer, *Admin Sec*
EMP: 20 EST: 1961
SQ FT: 32,000
SALES (est): 1.5MM **Privately Held**
WEB: www.plymouthinteriors.com
SIC: 2591 2391 Venetian blinds; curtains
& draperies

(G-10627)
PLYMOUTH INTERIORS LP
7 Crawford St (15136-3633)
PHONE...............................412 771-8569
Barry Roth, *Principal*
EMP: 10
SALES (est): 1.6MM **Privately Held**
SIC: 2591 2391 Drapery hardware &
blinds & shades; curtains & draperies

(G-10628)
PROCESS TECHNOLOGIES INC
1641 Pine Hollow Rd (15136-1782)
PHONE...............................412 771-8555
Jenni Haushalter, *Principal*
Mark Cohen, *Sales Staff*
EMP: 5
SALES (corp-wide): 10.1MM **Privately
Held**
SIC: 3053 Packing materials
PA: Process Technologies, Inc.
619 Franklin St Rear 1
Reading PA 19611
610 603-7525

(G-10629)
QUALITOX LABORATORIES LLC
109 William Cir (15136-2076)
PHONE...............................412 458-5431
EMP: 3 EST: 2016
SALES (est): 162K **Privately Held**
SIC: 2834 Pharmaceutical preparations

(G-10630)
R & D COATINGS INC
1320 Island Ave (15136-2518)
P.O. Box 418 (15136-0418)
PHONE...............................412 771-8110
Donald Eshenbaugh, *President*
Leo Belknap, *Vice Pres*
Bob Graham, *Plant Engr*
Joseph B Weinzierl, *Treasurer*
Tony Kingera, *Manager*
▲ EMP: 12
SALES (est): 3MM **Privately Held**
WEB: www.rdcoatings.com
SIC: 2851 Paints & paint additives

(G-10631)
RIDELTIN POWDER METAL INC
221 Waterford Dr (15136-1375)
PHONE...............................412 788-0956
Richard A Wendel, *President*
EMP: 8 EST: 2001
SALES (est): 580K **Privately Held**
SIC: 3399 Metal powders, pastes & flakes

(G-10632)
RUGANI & RUGANI LLC
64a Locust St (15136-1712)
PHONE...............................412 223-6472
Vincent Rugani Jr, *Partner*
Raquel Rugani, *Partner*
Diane Darnley,
Belinda Shlapak,
Dave Shlapak,
EMP: 4
SALES (est): 461.7K **Privately Held**
SIC: 2842 Specialty cleaning, polishes &
sanitation goods

(G-10633)
**SANTUCCI PROCESS
DEVELOPMENT (PA)**
121 Beaver Grade Rd (15136-1103)
PHONE...............................412 787-0747
Randall Santucci, *President*
Maria Santucci, *Admin Sec*
EMP: 5
SALES (est): 663.7K **Privately Held**
WEB: www.santuccipd.com
SIC: 3556 3599 Food products machinery;
machine shop, jobbing & repair

(G-10634)
**SHAKE AND TWIST CHARTIERS
AVE**
1238 Chartiers Ave (15136-3644)
PHONE...............................412 331-9606
Robert Chiff, *Partner*
EMP: 4 EST: 2009
SALES (est): 231.9K **Privately Held**
SIC: 2024 Ice cream, bulk

(G-10635)
SILVER STAR MEATS INC (PA)
Also Called: Alfery Sausage
1720 Middletown Rd (15136-1602)
P.O. Box 393 (15136-0393)
PHONE...............................412 771-5539
Robert Germony, *President*
Dominick Bovalina, *Vice Pres*
Randall K Hite, *Treasurer*
Ginger Nemscik, *Accountant*
Karen Bovalina, *Office Mgr*
EMP: 62
SQ FT: 55,000
SALES (est): 13.8MM **Privately Held**
WEB: www.silverstarmeats.com
SIC: 2013 2011 Sausages & other pre-
pared meats; hams & picnics from meat
slaughtered on site

(G-10636)
**SMART PRINT TECHNOLOGIES
INC**
312 Thompson Ave (15136-3821)
PHONE...............................412 771-8307
Joseph O'Brien, *President*
Michael O'Brien, *Admin Sec*
Ryan Walton,
EMP: 4
SALES (est): 361.4K **Privately Held**
SIC: 2752 Commercial printing, litho-
graphic

(G-10637)
**STANDARD FORGED
PRODUCTS LLC**
Also Called: McKees Rock Forging
75 Nichol Ave (15136-2625)
PHONE...............................412 778-2020
Helmut Hvizdalek, *Vice Pres*
Jerry McRill, *Manager*
EMP: 80
SQ FT: 20,000
SALES (corp-wide): 1.4B **Publicly Held**
WEB: www.standardforgedproductsinc.com
SIC: 3312 Axles, rolled or forged: made in
steel mills
HQ: Standard Forged Products, Llc
500 N Akard St
Dallas TX 75201
214 631-4420

(G-10638)
STEEL FACTORY CORP
Also Called: American Steel Span
200 Bradley St (15136-3256)
PHONE...............................412 771-2944
Arnold Davis, *President*
Gary J Bonacci, *Principal*
Bill Suhoski, *CFO*
William A Suhoski, *Treasurer*
William Suhoski, *Treasurer*
▲ EMP: 15
SQ FT: 45,000
SALES (est): 3.3MM **Privately Held**
SIC: 3448 Prefabricated metal buildings

(G-10639)
TIME TECH INDUSTRIES INC
226 Field Club Cir (15136-1033)
PHONE...............................412 670-5498
Brian Paulin, *President*
Aime Paulin, *Corp Secy*
EMP: 4
SQ FT: 10,000
SALES (est): 350K **Privately Held**
WEB:
www.pittsburgh.homeconnections.com
SIC: 3585 Air conditioning equipment,
complete

(G-10640)
UNIQUE MACHINE & TOOL
365 Munson Ave (15136-2721)
PHONE...............................412 331-2717
Martin Rubeo Jr, *Owner*
EMP: 10
SQ FT: 12,000
SALES (est): 1.2MM **Privately Held**
SIC: 3599 3544 Machine shop, jobbing &
repair; special dies, tools, jigs & fixtures

(G-10641)
**WENDELL H STONE AND
COMPANY**
149 Nichol Ave (15136-2627)
PHONE...............................412 331-1944
EMP: 5
SALES (est): 470.3K **Privately Held**
SIC: 3273 Ready-mixed concrete

Mc Keesport
Allegheny County

(G-10642)
M GLOSSER & SONS INC
Also Called: Tygart Steel Division
1 Douglas St (15134)
P.O. Box 276, McKeesport (15134-0276)
PHONE...............................412 751-4700
Greg Glosser, *Principal*
EMP: 25
SALES (corp-wide): 21MM **Privately
Held**
WEB: www.glossernet.com
SIC: 5051 3443 Steel; plate work for the
metalworking trade
PA: M. Glosser & Sons, Inc.
72 Messenger St
Johnstown PA 15902
814 533-2800

Mc Murray
Washington County

(G-10643)
**ADVANCED CNSTR ESTIMATING
LLC**
240 Center Church Rd (15317-3062)
PHONE...............................724 747-7032
EMP: 18
SALES (est): 381.7K **Privately Held**
SIC: 1742 1751 3446 Drywall/Insulation
Contr Carpentry Contractor Mfg Architec-
tural Mtlwrk

(G-10644)
**EVOLUTION ENERGY SERVICES
LLC**
3935 Washington Rd # 1191 (15317-2532)
PHONE...............................412 946-1371
Michael Slavik, *Mng Member*
EMP: 75
SQ FT: 37,000
SALES (est): 4.9MM **Privately Held**
SIC: 1382 Oil & gas exploration services

(G-10645)
MAN PAN LLC
309 Buffalo Ridge Rd (15317-6611)
PHONE...............................724 942-9500
EMP: 6
SALES (est): 569.1K **Privately Held**
SIC: 3321 Manhole covers, metal

(G-10646)
STELKAST INC
200 Hidden Valley Rd (15317-2659)
PHONE...............................888 273-1583
Peter Stephans, *CEO*
James M Byer, *Treasurer*
Joan R Stephans, *Asst Treas*
Connie J Allen, *Admin Sec*
EMP: 25
SQ FT: 16,000
SALES (est): 3.7MM **Privately Held**
SIC: 3842 Orthopedic appliances
PA: Trigon Holding, Inc.
124 Hidden Valley Rd
Mc Murray PA 15317

(G-10647)
TRIGON HOLDING INC (PA)
124 Hidden Valley Rd (15317-2604)
PHONE...............................724 941-5540
Peter N Stephans, *President*
James Byer, *Treasurer*
Joan R Stephans, *Asst Treas*
Connie Allen, *Admin Sec*
EMP: 23
SQ FT: 40,000

▲ = Import ▼ =Export
◆ =Import/Export

SALES (est): 26.7MM **Privately Held**
SIC: 3728 3842 Aircraft parts & equipment; surgical appliances & supplies

(G-10648)
TRIGON INCORPORATED
Also Called: Fpd Company
124 Hidden Valley Rd (15317-2604)
PHONE...................................724 941-5540
Peter N Stephans, *President*
David Tenison, *Vice Pres*
▲ **EMP:** 99
SQ FT: 40,000
SALES (est): 22.9MM **Privately Held**
SIC: 3728 3842 Aircraft parts & equipment; surgical appliances & supplies
PA: Trigon Holding, Inc.
124 Hidden Valley Rd
Mc Murray PA 15317

Mc Sherrystown
Adams County

(G-10649)
ALLEGHENY SOLID SURFC TECH LLC
Also Called: A.S.S.T.
350 South St (17344-1720)
PHONE...................................717 630-1251
Russell Berry, *President*
Mike Keefer, *Project Mgr*
Bob Hannigan, *Sr Project Mgr*
EMP: 28
SQ FT: 30,000
SALES (est): 9.4MM **Privately Held**
WEB: www.asst.com
SIC: 2541 Counter & sink tops

(G-10650)
F X SMITHS SONS CO
372 North St (17344-1402)
PHONE...................................717 637-5232
Craig Smith, *President*
EMP: 13 **EST:** 1863
SQ FT: 7,500
SALES (est): 1.3MM **Privately Held**
SIC: 2121 Cigars

(G-10651)
HARVEST MOON WOODWORKING
360 Fairview Ave (17344-1411)
PHONE...................................717 521-4204
Jeffrey Warner, *Principal*
EMP: 3 **EST:** 2014
SALES (est): 167.5K **Privately Held**
SIC: 2431 Millwork

(G-10652)
SAY PLASTICS INC
165 Oak Ln (17344-1320)
P.O. Box 76 (17344-0076)
PHONE...................................717 633-6333
Louie Smith, *President*
Denise Conrad, *General Mgr*
Ron Staub, *Vice Pres*
Ronald J Staub, *Vice Pres*
Tj Hefner, *Plant Mgr*
▲ **EMP:** 30
SQ FT: 17,000
SALES (est): 6.2MM **Privately Held**
WEB: www.sayplastics.com
SIC: 3089 Thermoformed finished plastic products; blow molded finished plastic products

Mc Veytown
Mifflin County

(G-10653)
KURTZS MACHINING LLC
56 Flower Dr (17051-8319)
PHONE...................................717 899-6125
Janelle Kurtz, *Principal*
Thomas Kurtz,
EMP: 6
SALES: 56K **Privately Held**
SIC: 3545 Machine tool accessories

(G-10654)
ZOOKS PALLETS LLC
260 Riverside Dr (17051-8625)
PHONE...................................717 899-5212
EMP: 3 **EST:** 2011
SALES (est): 149.2K **Privately Held**
SIC: 2448 Mfg Wood Pallets/Skids

McAdoo
Schuylkill County

(G-10655)
ALTADIS USA INC
Also Called: Consolidated Cigar
1000 Tresckow Rd (18237-2504)
PHONE...................................570 929-2220
Joseph Shimanski, *Personnel*
John McGoff, *Manager*
Diana Andrewcavage, *Manager*
Joseph Lewis, *Data Proc Staff*
Atul Govil, *Director*
EMP: 52
SALES (corp-wide): 38.9B **Privately Held**
WEB: www.altadisusa.com
SIC: 2121 Cigars
HQ: Altadis U.S.A. Inc.
5900 N Andrews Ave # 600
Fort Lauderdale FL 33309
954 772-9000

(G-10656)
POSTIES BEVERAGES INC
55 S Manning St (18237-1417)
PHONE...................................570 929-2464
James Dvorshock, *President*
EMP: 6 **EST:** 1919
SALES (est): 840K **Privately Held**
SIC: 5181 2086 Beer & other fermented malt liquors; soft drinks: packaged in cans, bottles, etc.

(G-10657)
POSTUPACK RUSSELL CULM CORP
Also Called: Postupack Oil
109 Silverbrook Rd (18237-3106)
PHONE...................................570 929-1699
Russel Postupack, *President*
EMP: 2
SALES (est): 1.9MM **Privately Held**
SIC: 1231 5983 1794 Anthracite mining; fuel oil dealers; excavation work

(G-10658)
PSI CONTAINER INC
1057 Tresckow Rd (18237-2509)
PHONE...................................570 929-1600
Vernon F Litzinger, *President*
Jerry F Morris, *Vice Pres*
Jimmy Olson, *Sales Mgr*
Nathan Mulcahy, *Accounts Mgr*
Dereck Hewitt, *Cust Mgr*
EMP: 62
SQ FT: 82,000
SALES (est): 14.1MM **Privately Held**
WEB: www.psicontainer.com
SIC: 2653 Boxes, corrugated: made from purchased materials

(G-10659)
UNIVERSAL TRLR CRGO GROUP INC
Also Called: Haulmark of Pennsylavania
6 Banks Ave (18237-2507)
PHONE...................................570 929-3761
Jack Zimmerman, *Branch Mgr*
EMP: 11
SALES (corp-wide): 894.8MM **Privately Held**
SIC: 3715 Demountable cargo containers
HQ: Universal Trailer Cargo Group, Inc.
14054 C R 4
Bristol IN 46507
574 264-9661

Mckees Rocks
Allegheny County

(G-10660)
GATEWAY PUBLICATIONS
Also Called: Signal Item
5500 Stbnvlle Pike Ste 1a (15136)
PHONE...................................412 856-7400
Angelo Donofrio, *Manager*
EMP: 5
SALES (corp-wide): 37.2MM **Privately Held**
SIC: 2711 Commercial printing & newspaper publishing combined
PA: Gateway Publications
610 Beatty Rd Ste 2
Monroeville PA 15146
412 856-7400

(G-10661)
GORDON TERMINAL SERVICE CO PA (PA)
1000 Ella St (15136)
PHONE...................................412 331-9410
Robert N Gorden, *President*
Robert M Gordon Jr, *President*
Tim Gordon, *COO*
Thomas P Gordon, *Vice Pres*
Ernie Solomon, *Purch Mgr*
EMP: 160 **EST:** 1935
SQ FT: 250,000
SALES (est): 29.8MM **Privately Held**
SIC: 4789 4226 2992 4613 Pipeline terminal facilities, independently operated; petroleum & chemical bulk stations & terminals for hire; lubricating oils; refined petroleum pipelines

McKeesport
Allegheny County

(G-10662)
CHARLES CASTURO
Also Called: Casturo Iron & Metal
750 W 5th Ave (15132-3505)
PHONE...................................412 672-1407
Charles Casturo, *Owner*
EMP: 4
SALES: 150K **Privately Held**
SIC: 5093 3341 Ferrous metal scrap & waste; secondary nonferrous metals

(G-10663)
CLEARVIEW MIRROR AND GLASS
2801 5th Ave (15132-1190)
PHONE...................................412 672-4122
Susan Frencik, *President*
Emma Frencik, *Corp Secy*
Henry Frencik, *Vice Pres*
EMP: 9
SQ FT: 11,000
SALES: 292.2K **Privately Held**
SIC: 3231 3442 Mirrored glass; metal doors

(G-10664)
COMPACTING TOOLING INC
403 Wide Dr (15135-1021)
P.O. Box 89 (15135-0089)
PHONE...................................412 751-3535
Kenneth Lasica, *President*
Robert Fellabaum, *Vice Pres*
Donald Trust, *Vice Pres*
Marshall Black, *Treasurer*
James Houck, *Admin Sec*
EMP: 28
SQ FT: 18,000
SALES (est): 4.4MM **Privately Held**
WEB: www.compactingtooling.com
SIC: 3544 Dies, steel rule

(G-10665)
CP INDUSTRIES HOLDINGS INC
2214 Walnut St (15132-7098)
PHONE...................................412 664-6604
Michael Larsen, *President*
Nicole Rebyanski, *Engrg Mgr*
Roger L Seese, *Treasurer*
Bill Yurek, *Controller*

John Crupi, *Human Res Mgr*
◆ **EMP:** 100
SQ FT: 600,000
SALES (est): 30.6MM
SALES (corp-wide): 49.4MM **Privately Held**
SIC: 3443 Industrial vessels, tanks & containers
HQ: Ekc Hungary Korlatolt Felelossegu Tarsasag
Koer Utca 2/A. C. ep.
Budapest 1103

(G-10666)
DURA-BOND PIPE LLC
301 4th Ave (15132-2603)
PHONE...................................412 672-0764
EMP: 3
SALES (corp-wide): 119.9MM **Privately Held**
SIC: 5051 3479 Metals service centers & offices; painting, coating & hot dipping
HQ: Dura-Bond Pipe, L.L.C.
2716 S Front St
Steelton PA 17113
717 986-1100

(G-10667)
ELIZABETH CARBIDE DIE CO INC (PA)
601 Linden St (15132-6525)
P.O. Box 95 (15135-0095)
PHONE...................................412 751-3000
R A Pagliari, *CEO*
D A Keefer, *President*
Kenneth Spiegel, *Vice Pres*
Tara Becker, *Traffic Mgr*
Brian Jordan, *Opers Staff*
◆ **EMP:** 127 **EST:** 1954
SQ FT: 47,000
SALES (est): 57MM **Privately Held**
WEB: www.eliz.com
SIC: 3544 3542 Die sets for metal stamping (presses); machine tools, metal forming type

(G-10668)
GLW GLOBAL INC
3009 Boyd St (15132-1943)
PHONE...................................412 664-7946
Gilbert West, *CEO*
Michael West, *COO*
Erica Gordon, *Treasurer*
EMP: 3
SALES (est): 192.5K **Privately Held**
SIC: 3069 7389 Reclaimed rubber (reworked by manufacturing processes);

(G-10669)
H B SOUTH PRINTING
428 Eden Park Blvd (15132-7798)
PHONE...................................412 751-1300
Mark South, *President*
W James South, *Partner*
Marlin South, *Vice Pres*
EMP: 10 **EST:** 1892
SQ FT: 13,000
SALES (est): 1.2MM **Privately Held**
SIC: 2752 Commercial printing, offset

(G-10670)
HKP METALS INC
301 Wide Dr (15135-1019)
PHONE...................................412 751-0500
EMP: 3
SALES (est): 101.9K **Privately Held**
SIC: 3471 Plating of metals or formed products

(G-10671)
HOME TOWN SPORTS INC
3213 Orchard St (15132-5944)
PHONE...................................412 672-2242
Jim Miller, *CEO*
EMP: 3
SALES (est): 178.6K **Privately Held**
SIC: 2395 Embroidery products, except schiffli machine

(G-10672)
HYRDOGEN CORP
2 Juniper St (15132-6026)
PHONE...................................412 405-1000
Leo Blomen, *Principal*
EMP: 3

GEOGRAPHIC

SALES (est): 244.5K **Privately Held**
SIC: 2813 Hydrogen

(G-10673)
INDUTEX INC (PA)
528 Eden Park Blvd (15132-7797)
PHONE..................................724 935-1482
EMP: 11
SQ FT: 8,500
SALES (est): 860.5K **Privately Held**
SIC: 2394 Mfg Canvas/Related Products

(G-10674)
KENBERN STORM DOORS
2801 5th Ave (15132-1134)
PHONE..................................412 678-7210
Henry Frencik, *Principal*
EMP: 3 **EST:** 2010
SALES (est): 163.2K **Privately Held**
SIC: 3442 Screen & storm doors & windows

(G-10675)
LEXMARUSA INC
627 Market St (15132-2729)
PHONE..................................412 896-9266
Jonathan Stark, *Principal*
EMP: 3
SALES (est): 252.1K **Privately Held**
SIC: 3281 1799 Cut stone & stone products; kitchen & bathroom remodeling; kitchen cabinet installation

(G-10676)
MRG FOOD LLC
800 Manning Ave (15132-3624)
P.O. Box 98039, Pittsburgh (15227-0439)
PHONE..................................412 482-7430
Mehmet Gurakar, *Mng Member*
EMP: 11 **EST:** 2008
SQ FT: 20,000
SALES (est): 1.4MM **Privately Held**
SIC: 2011 Meat packing plants

Mckeesport
Allegheny County

(G-10677)
P D Q TOOLING INC
Also Called: Pdqtooling.com
940 Grnock Buena Vista Rd (15135)
PHONE..................................412 751-2214
Brian Bailey, *President*
EMP: 8
SQ FT: 30,000
SALES: 450K **Privately Held**
WEB: www.pdqtooling.com
SIC: 3544 3399 Dies, steel rule; metal powders, pastes & flakes

---

McKeesport
Allegheny County

(G-10678)
PRADA COMPANY INC
Also Called: Generation Stoneworks
2000 Donner St (15135-1204)
PHONE..................................412 751-4900
Joseph L Castagnola, *President*
Donna Glagola, *Regional Mgr*
Anthony Castagnola, *Corp Secy*
Joseph C Castagnola, *Vice Pres*
EMP: 12
SALES (est): 1.6MM **Privately Held**
WEB: www.stonecompany.net
SIC: 3281 Building stone products

(G-10679)
RENDULIC PACKING COMPANY
Also Called: Nema Food Co
800 Manning Ave (15132-3624)
PHONE..................................412 678-9541
Beyhan Nakiboglu, *President*
Abdullah Nakiboglu, *Vice Pres*
▲ **EMP:** 23 **EST:** 1928
SQ FT: 45,000
SALES: 4.4MM
SALES (corp-wide): 1.2MM **Privately Held**
WEB: www.nemahalal.com
SIC: 2011 Meat packing plants

PA: Nema Usa, Inc.
2535 Washington Rd # 1121
Pittsburgh PA 15241
412 678-9541

(G-10680)
SCHWEBEL BAKING CO OF PA INC
Also Called: Schwebel Baking Co PA
4315 Walnut St (15132-6114)
PHONE..................................412 751-4080
Joseph Schwebel, *President*
Paul Schwebel, *Exec VP*
Barry Solomon, *Senior VP*
Alyson Winick, *Senior VP*
Joseph Winick, *Senior VP*
EMP: 110
SQ FT: 38,000
SALES (est): 8.2MM
SALES (corp-wide): 170MM **Privately Held**
WEB: www.schwebels.com
SIC: 5149 2051 5461 Bakery products; bread, cake & related products; bread
PA: Schwebel Baking Company
965 E Midlothian Blvd
Youngstown OH 44502
330 783-2860

(G-10681)
SIL-BASE COMPANY INC
4 Juniper St (15132-6026)
PHONE..................................412 751-2314
Carole Nguyen, *CEO*
Carole L Suey Nguyen, *President*
Ngoc Nguyen, *Vice Pres*
EMP: 35
SQ FT: 85,000
SALES (est): 4.4MM **Privately Held**
SIC: 3297 3433 3251 Castable refractories, nonclay; heating equipment, except electric; brick & structural clay tile

(G-10682)
SQUIBB ALVAH M COMPANY INC
637 Long Run Rd (15132-7426)
P.O. Box 428 (15134-0428)
PHONE..................................412 751-2301
Donald E Squibb, *President*
Jeffrey Squibb, *Vice Pres*
Julie Squibb-Howell, *Treasurer*
EMP: 17
SQ FT: 18,000
SALES (est): 2.2MM **Privately Held**
WEB: www.amsquibb.com
SIC: 2732 5112 Books: printing & binding; stationery

(G-10683)
STEFFAN INDUSTRIES INC
950 E Smithfield St (15135-1004)
PHONE..................................412 751-4484
Frank C Steffan, *President*
EMP: 6
SALES (est): 1MM **Privately Held**
SIC: 1799 7353 3441 Rigging & scaffolding; cranes & aerial lift equipment, rental or leasing; fabricated structural metal

(G-10684)
STRAINSENSE ENTERPRISES INC
1080 Long Run Rd (15132-7448)
PHONE..................................412 751-3055
Layne D Vranka, *President*
Sandra L Vranka, *Corp Secy*
EMP: 4
SQ FT: 5,000
SALES (est): 696.3K **Privately Held**
WEB: www.strainsense.com
SIC: 3629 7629 Electronic generation equipment; electronic equipment repair

(G-10685)
VISTA METALS INC (PA)
1024 E Smithfield St (15135-1031)
PHONE..................................412 751-4600
William F Riley, *President*
Gregg Riley, *Exec VP*
Brian Riley, *Vice Pres*
Mark Shelleby, *Treasurer*
▲ **EMP:** 112
SQ FT: 72,000

SALES (est): 35.9MM **Privately Held**
WEB: www.vistametalsinc.com
SIC: 3545 Machine tool attachments & accessories

(G-10686)
WESTCOM WIRELESS INC
1025 Lysle Blvd (15132)
PHONE..................................412 228-5507
Dave Fakars, *Branch Mgr*
EMP: 4
SALES (corp-wide): 4.7MM **Privately Held**
WEB: www.westcomwireless.com
SIC: 4813 3663 ; radio broadcasting & communications equipment
PA: Westcom Wireless, Inc.
2773 Leechburg Rd
New Kensington PA 15068
724 337-1400

(G-10687)
WHEATON & SONS INC
Also Called: Wheaton & Son's Iron Works
2121 5th Ave (15132-1112)
PHONE..................................412 351-0405
Ronald Wheaton, *President*
Claude Wheaton, *Treasurer*
EMP: 10
SQ FT: 26,000
SALES (est): 176.3K **Privately Held**
SIC: 3441 3443 Fabricated structural metal; fabricated plate work (boiler shop)

McKnight
Allegheny County

(G-10688)
SAFETY GUARD STEEL FABG CO
220 Lincoln Ave (15237)
PHONE..................................412 821-1177
William Campbell, *Manager*
EMP: 13
SALES (corp-wide): 2.4MM **Privately Held**
SIC: 7699 3441 Welding equipment repair; fabricated structural metal
PA: Safety Guard Steel Fabricating Company
113 Lincoln Ave
Millvale PA
412 821-3533

Meadow Lands
Washington County

(G-10689)
ACCUDIE INC
175 S Country Club Rd (15347)
P.O. Box 786 (15347-0786)
PHONE..................................724 222-8447
Grant Boland, *President*
Denise Boland, *Admin Sec*
EMP: 6
SQ FT: 6,000
SALES (est): 1MM **Privately Held**
WEB: www.accudie.com
SIC: 3544 Special dies & tools

(G-10690)
IGS INDUSTRIES INC
200 Country Club Rd (15347)
P.O. Box 368 (15347-0368)
PHONE..................................724 222-5800
Richard Disalle, *Ch of Bd*
David C Sphar, *President*
Dan Bird, *Vice Pres*
Dave Sphar, *CFO*
Bill Sutton, *Controller*
▲ **EMP:** 110 **EST:** 1961
SQ FT: 45,000
SALES (est): 32MM **Privately Held**
WEB: www.igscorp.com
SIC: 3499 3469 3053 Shims, metal; stamping metal for the trade; gaskets, all materials

(G-10691)
LONGWALL SERVICES INC
63 S Country Club Rd (15347)
P.O. Box 737 (15347-0737)
PHONE..................................724 228-9898
Ceriog Hughes, *President*
John Whitfield, *Vice Pres*
▲ **EMP:** 6 **EST:** 1996
SQ FT: 47,000
SALES (est): 1.2MM **Privately Held**
WEB: www.longwallservices.com
SIC: 3532 Auger mining equipment

(G-10692)
RUBBER ROLLS INC
Also Called: Industrial Rubber Products Co
50 Rockwood Dr (15347)
P.O. Box 398 (15347-0398)
PHONE..................................724 225-9240
Michael C Kerestes, *Principal*
EMP: 40
SALES (corp-wide): 10.3MM **Privately Held**
SIC: 3069 3061 Rolls, solid or covered rubber; mechanical rubber goods
PA: Rubber Rolls Inc
726 Trumbull Dr
Pittsburgh PA 15205
412 276-6400

Meadville
Crawford County

(G-10693)
2W TECHNOLOGIES LLC (PA)
1009 Water St Ste 2 (16335-3465)
P.O. Box 762 (16335-6762)
PHONE..................................814 333-3117
Diana Whitinger, *Mng Member*
Bill Whitinger,
EMP: 2
SQ FT: 3,000
SALES (est): 1.4MM **Privately Held**
WEB: www.2wtech.com
SIC: 7372 Business oriented computer software

(G-10694)
ACTCO TOOL & MFG CO
14421 Baldwin Street Ext (16335-9462)
P.O. Box 675 (16335-0675)
PHONE..................................814 336-4235
Rob Gruber II, *President*
Dennis Heffern, *Vice Pres*
Scott Gruber, *Treasurer*
EMP: 40 **EST:** 1964
SQ FT: 20,000
SALES (est): 6.8MM **Privately Held**
SIC: 3544 Special dies & tools

(G-10695)
ACUTEC PRECISION AEROSPACE INC
13555 Broadway (16335-8307)
PHONE..................................814 336-2214
Elisabeth Smith, *President*
Aaron Patterson, *Plant Mgr*
Dan Leicht, *Opers Mgr*
Sam Fischer, *Buyer*
Ron Renner, *Buyer*
▲ **EMP:** 300
SQ FT: 300,000
SALES (est): 67.5MM **Privately Held**
SIC: 3724 3728 Aircraft engines & engine parts; aircraft landing assemblies & brakes

(G-10696)
ADVANTAGE PRECISION PLASTICS
10246 Mercer Pike (16335-6289)
P.O. Box 456 (16335-0456)
PHONE..................................814 337-8535
Theodore Styborski, *President*
Karen Styborski, *Treasurer*
EMP: 23
SALES: 2MM **Privately Held**
WEB: www.advantagemold.com
SIC: 3089 Injection molding of plastics

(G-10697)
AINSWORTH PET NTRTN PARENT LLC (DH)
18746 Mill St (16335-3644)
PHONE..................................814 724-7710
Barry C Dunaway, *President*
EMP: 4
SALES (est): 48.9MM
SALES (corp-wide): 7.3B **Publicly Held**
SIC: 2047 Dog food
HQ: Nu Pet Company
1 Strawberry Ln
Orrville OH 44667
330 682-3000

(G-10698)
AINSWORTH PET NUTRITION LLC (DH)
18746 Mill St (16335-3644)
PHONE..................................814 724-7710
Jeff Watters, *President*
EMP: 14
SALES (est): 48.9MM
SALES (corp-wide): 7.3B **Publicly Held**
SIC: 2047 Dog food
HQ: Ainsworth Pet Nutrition Parent, Llc
18746 Mill St
Meadville PA 16335
814 724-7710

(G-10699)
AINSWORTH PET NUTRITION LLC
18746 Mill St (16335-3644)
PHONE..................................814 724-7710
EMP: 200
SALES (corp-wide): 7.3B **Publicly Held**
SIC: 2047 Dog food
HQ: Ainsworth Pet Nutrition, Llc
18746 Mill St
Meadville PA 16335
814 724-7710

(G-10700)
ALLEGHENY TOOL & MFG CO
19320 Cochranton Rd (16335-9033)
P.O. Box 422 (16335-0422)
PHONE..................................814 337-2795
William Lynn, *President*
Sheila Ledford, *Manager*
EMP: 15
SQ FT: 6,000
SALES (est): 1.1MM **Privately Held**
SIC: 3544 Special dies & tools

(G-10701)
ALPHA LASER-US
7799 Mchenry St (16335-9004)
PHONE..................................814 724-3666
Blair Learn, *Principal*
EMP: 4 EST: 2017
SALES (est): 600.2K **Privately Held**
SIC: 3599 Machine shop, jobbing & repair

(G-10702)
AMERICAN FUTURE SYSTEMS INC
660 Terrace St (16335-1727)
PHONE..................................814 724-2035
Jennifer Maziarz, *Branch Mgr*
EMP: 27
SALES (corp-wide): 134.8MM **Privately Held**
SIC: 2759 Publication printing
PA: American Future Systems, Inc.
370 Technology Dr
Malvern PA 19355
610 695-8600

(G-10703)
AREA TOOL & MANUFACTURING INC
181 Baldwin Street Ext (16335-7919)
P.O. Box 1409 (16335-0909)
PHONE..................................814 724-3166
John Wehrle, *President*
Roberta McBride, *Corp Secy*
Ashleigh Smith, *Office Mgr*
EMP: 15
SQ FT: 20,000
SALES (est): 2.3MM **Privately Held**
WEB: www.areatool.com
SIC: 3544 Special dies & tools

(G-10704)
ARRO FORGE INC
Kebert Industrial Park (16335)
P.O. Box 1293 (16335-0793)
PHONE..................................814 724-4223
Fax: 814 333-6365
EMP: 15
SQ FT: 12,000
SALES (est): 2.1MM **Privately Held**
SIC: 3462 Mfg Iron & Steel Forgings

(G-10705)
BAYFRONT BREWING CO
13388 Leslie Rd (16335-8038)
PHONE..................................814 333-8641
William Eaton, *President*
EMP: 5
SALES (est): 326.7K **Privately Held**
SIC: 2082 Beer (alcoholic beverage)

(G-10706)
BELCO TOOL & MFG INC
225 Terrace Street Ext (16335-7917)
PHONE..................................814 337-3403
John Brunot, *President*
David Easly, *Vice Pres*
EMP: 16
SQ FT: 6,100
SALES (est): 3.4MM **Privately Held**
SIC: 3544 3089 Special dies, tools, jigs & fixtures; molding primary plastic

(G-10707)
BKTS INC
1347 S Main St (16335-3036)
PHONE..................................814 724-1547
Garth Faivre, *President*
Karen Faivre, *Treasurer*
Terry Denton, *Admin Sec*
EMP: 4
SALES (est): 472.9K **Privately Held**
WEB: www.bktsinc.com
SIC: 2449 Baskets: fruit & vegetable, round square, till, etc.

(G-10708)
BRA-VOR TOOL & DIE CO INC
11189 Murray Rd (16335-3863)
PHONE..................................814 724-1557
Scott Devore, *President*
Todd Devore, *Corp Secy*
John Merritt, *Technology*
EMP: 20
SQ FT: 15,000
SALES (est): 2.8MM **Privately Held**
WEB: www.bra-vor.com
SIC: 3544 3469 Die sets for metal stamping (presses); metal stampings

(G-10709)
C & J INDUSTRIES INC
760 Water St (16335-3338)
P.O. Box 499 (16335-0499)
PHONE..................................814 724-4950
Robert Marut, *President*
Candace Harvey, *Corp Secy*
Jerry Sargeant, *Vice Pres*
▲ EMP: 300
SQ FT: 214,000
SALES: 35MM **Privately Held**
SIC: 3089 Injection molding of plastics

(G-10710)
CANTO TOOL CORPORATION
11494 Airport Rd (16335-3888)
P.O. Box 533 (16335-0533)
PHONE..................................814 724-2865
Dale Cummings, *President*
Dale Johnston, *Vice Pres*
EMP: 15
SALES (est): 1.7MM **Privately Held**
WEB: www.cantotool.com
SIC: 3544 Special dies & tools

(G-10711)
CHANNELLOCK INC (PA)
1306 S Main St (16335-3035)
PHONE..................................814 337-9200
William S De Arment, *Ch of Bd*
Jonathan S Dearment, *President*
Stephen Sada, *Corp Secy*
Jon Dearment, *COO*
Donald Hornstein, *Vice Pres*
▲ EMP: 400
SQ FT: 143,000

SALES (est): 84MM **Privately Held**
WEB: www.channellock.com
SIC: 3423 Hand & edge tools

(G-10712)
CHIPBLASTER INC
13605 S Mosiertown Rd (16335-8346)
PHONE..................................814 724-6278
Greg S Antoun, *President*
Boyd A Armstrong Jr, *Corp Secy*
▲ EMP: 65
SQ FT: 23,425
SALES: 27.3MM **Privately Held**
WEB: www.chipblaster.com
SIC: 3585 Refrigeration & heating equipment
HQ: L.N.S. America, Inc.
4621 E Tech Dr
Cincinnati OH 45245
513 528-5674

(G-10713)
COLEMAN WATER SERVICES
14022 Coleman Rd (16335-7820)
PHONE..................................814 382-8004
Ronald H Coleman, *Owner*
EMP: 3
SALES: 130K **Privately Held**
SIC: 3561 Pumps, domestic: water or sump

(G-10714)
CORRUGATED SPECIALTIES
10677 Mchenry St (16335-9068)
PHONE..................................814 337-5705
Marty Krendar, *Manager*
EMP: 10
SALES (corp-wide): 1.5MM **Privately Held**
SIC: 4225 2657 3086 General warehousing; folding paperboard boxes; plastics foam products; insulation or cushioning material, foamed plastic; packaging & shipping materials, foamed plastic
PA: Corrugated Specialties
10677 Mchenry St
Meadville PA 16335
814 337-5705

(G-10715)
CORRUGATED SPECIALTIES (PA)
10677 Mchenry St (16335-9068)
P.O. Box 426 (16335-0426)
PHONE..................................814 337-5705
Martin C Kundar, *Owner*
EMP: 10
SQ FT: 7,500
SALES (est): 1.5MM **Privately Held**
SIC: 2657 3086 7336 2653 Folding paperboard boxes; plastics foam products; insulation or cushioning material, foamed plastic; packaging & shipping materials, foamed plastic; package design; corrugated & solid fiber boxes

(G-10716)
D&M TOOL INC
10976 Mchenry St (16335-9094)
PHONE..................................814 724-6743
Wayne Karastury, *President*
Michael Karastury, *Admin Sec*
EMP: 18
SQ FT: 7,200
SALES (est): 2.1MM **Privately Held**
WEB: www.dmtool.com
SIC: 3544 Die sets for metal stamping (presses); dies, plastics forming; forms (molds), for foundry & plastics working machinery

(G-10717)
DACH DIME MANUFACTURE
15926 S Mosiertown Rd (16335-7876)
P.O. Box 1296 (16335-0796)
PHONE..................................814 336-2376
Charles Beatty, *Owner*
EMP: 5
SALES: 500K **Privately Held**
SIC: 2448 Pallets, wood

(G-10718)
DAN DONAHUE
Also Called: Donahue's Classic Auto
21717 Ryan Rd (16335-5453)
PHONE..................................814 336-3262

Dan Donahaue, *Owner*
EMP: 3
SALES (est): 235.2K **Privately Held**
SIC: 3711 Reconnaissance cars, assembly of

(G-10719)
DPC PET SPECIALTIES LLC
Also Called: Ainsworth Pet Nutrition
18746 Mill St (16335-3644)
P.O. Box 451 (16335-0451)
PHONE..................................814 724-7710
Sean P Lang, *President*
Douglas A Lang, *Vice Pres*
Richard D Moyer, *Treasurer*
James D Lang, *Admin Sec*
EMP: 37 EST: 2007
SALES (est): 6.9MM
SALES (corp-wide): 7.3B **Publicly Held**
SIC: 2047 Cat food; dog food
PA: The J M Smucker Company
1 Strawberry Ln
Orrville OH 44667
330 682-3000

(G-10720)
E-SLINGER LLC
14527 State Highway 98 (16335-7885)
PHONE..................................412 848-1742
John Lubimir,
EMP: 3 EST: 2014
SALES (est): 147.3K **Privately Held**
SIC: 3089 Injection molded finished plastic products

(G-10721)
ESMARK EXCALIBUR LLC
Also Called: Steel City Plate Company
10730 Mchenry St (16335-9096)
P.O. Box 605, Conneaut Lake (16316-0605)
PHONE..................................814 382-5696
Cindi Cortney, *Branch Mgr*
Jeff Keas, *Prgrmr*
EMP: 29
SALES (corp-wide): 249.1MM **Privately Held**
SIC: 3315 Steel wire & related products
HQ: Esmark Excalibur, Llc
9723 Us Highway 322
Conneaut Lake PA 16316

(G-10722)
EVOLUTION MLDING SOLUTIONS INC
1099 Morgan Village Rd (16335-2735)
PHONE..................................814 807-1982
Jamie Holler, *President*
Joshua Sindlinger, *Vice Pres*
EMP: 7 EST: 2010
SALES (est): 76.3K **Privately Held**
SIC: 2821 3089 Thermoplastic materials; injection molding of plastics

(G-10723)
EVOLUTION PRINTING SYSTEMS
217 North St (16335-3322)
PHONE..................................814 724-5831
EMP: 4
SALES (est): 326.6K **Privately Held**
SIC: 2752 Commercial printing, lithographic

(G-10724)
EXCELLENT TOOL INC
18879 E Cole Rd (16335-9663)
PHONE..................................814 337-7705
Ellen Durfee, *Owner*
David Durfee, *Principal*
Dawn Jones, *Manager*
EMP: 5
SQ FT: 2,500
SALES (est): 442.8K **Privately Held**
WEB: www.excellenttool.com
SIC: 3599 7699 3544 Machine & other job shop work; cash register repair; special dies & tools

(G-10725)
FAIVRE MCH & FABRICATION INC
1369 S Main St (16335-3072)
PHONE..................................814 724-7160
Garth Faivre, *President*

Karen Faivre, *Treasurer*
EMP: 6
SQ FT: 11,000
SALES (est): 935.8K **Privately Held**
SIC: 3541 3089 Machine tools, metal cutting type; plastic processing

(G-10726)
FINE PRINT COMMERCIAL PRINTERS
287 Chestnut St (16335-3266)
PHONE..................814 337-7468
Joseph W Fonner, *President*
Daniel V Crandall, *Vice Pres*
EMP: 9
SQ FT: 6,000
SALES (est): 1.3MM **Privately Held**
SIC: 2752 Commercial printing, offset

(G-10727)
FOSTERMATION INC
Also Called: Foster-Tobin
200 Valleyview Dr (16335-7916)
PHONE..................814 336-6211
Susan Ritchey, *Branch Mgr*
EMP: 4
SALES (est): 295.5K
SALES (corp-wide): 2MM **Privately Held**
WEB: www.fostermation.com
SIC: 3451 Screw machine products
PA: Fostermation, Inc
200 Valleyview Dr
Meadville PA 16335
814 336-6211

(G-10728)
FOSTERMATION INC (PA)
200 Valleyview Dr (16335-7916)
PHONE..................814 336-6211
Susan F Ritchey, *President*
Tom Pavlik, *CFO*
Tammy Sterling, *Admin Sec*
EMP: 15
SQ FT: 1,300
SALES (est): 2MM **Privately Held**
WEB: www.fostermation.com
SIC: 3451 Screw machine products

(G-10729)
GRAHAM TECH INC
9245 Williamson Rd (16335-5188)
PHONE..................814 807-1778
Mark Graham, *President*
Valerie Graham, *Admin Sec*
EMP: 3
SQ FT: 3,100
SALES (est): 720K **Privately Held**
WEB: www.graham-tech.com
SIC: 3544 Special dies & tools

(G-10730)
GREEN PROSTHETICS & ORTHOTICS
279 North St (16335-2521)
PHONE..................814 337-1159
Dave Wanner, *President*
EMP: 7
SALES (corp-wide): 1.9MM **Privately Held**
SIC: 3842 5999 Limbs, artificial; orthopedic & prosthesis applications
PA: Green Prosthetics & Orthotics, Inc
2241 Peninsula Dr
Erie PA 16506
814 833-2311

(G-10731)
GSG MANUFACTURING INC
18544 Cussewago Rd (16335-3510)
PHONE..................814 336-4287
George Gisewhite, *President*
Patricia Gisewhite, *Vice Pres*
Christina Gisewhite, *Admin Sec*
EMP: 3
SQ FT: 3,300
SALES (est): 220K **Privately Held**
SIC: 3599 Machine shop, jobbing & repair

(G-10732)
H AND H TOOL
384 Clark Rd (16335-4136)
PHONE..................814 333-4677
Herman A Hargenrater, *Managing Prtnr*
Stephen R Hargenrater, *Partner*
EMP: 6
SQ FT: 3,500

SALES (est): 1.3MM **Privately Held**
SIC: 3544 7692 Special dies & tools; welding repair

(G-10733)
HALSIT HOLDINGS LLC
Also Called: Abbatron
13680 S Mosiertown Rd (16335-8312)
PHONE..................814 724-6440
Kris Gamble, *COO*
Joseph Halloran,
EMP: 23
SALES (est): 4.3MM **Privately Held**
SIC: 3643 3678 3677 3679 Connectors & terminals for electrical devices; connectors, electric cord; electronic connectors; electronic coils, transformers & other inductors; harness assemblies for electronic use: wire or cable

(G-10734)
HAMILTON TOOL CO INC
13887 Middle Rd (16335-7574)
PHONE..................814 382-3419
Martin Hamilton, *President*
Marvin Hamilton, *President*
Darwin Hamilton, *Manager*
EMP: 4
SQ FT: 8,000
SALES: 350K **Privately Held**
SIC: 3545 Cutting tools for machine tools

(G-10735)
HILLS MICRO WELD INC
1134 Water St (16335-4317)
PHONE..................814 336-4511
Kevin Hill, *President*
EMP: 3
SALES (est): 360.5K **Privately Held**
SIC: 7373 7692 Computer-aided manufacturing (CAM) systems service; welding repair

(G-10736)
HOLBROOK TOOL & MOLDING INC
10696 Perry Hwy (16335-6570)
P.O. Box 60 (16335-0060)
PHONE..................814 336-4113
Richard Lockwood, *President*
Michael Lockwood, *Vice Pres*
Christopher Knierman, *Treasurer*
Mark Arbucle, *Asst Treas*
Karen Newman, *Admin Sec*
EMP: 37 **EST:** 1978
SQ FT: 22,800
SALES (est): 6.6MM **Privately Held**
WEB: www.holbrooktool.com
SIC: 3089 3544 Injection molding of plastics; special dies, tools, jigs & fixtures

(G-10737)
IMPERIAL NEWBOULD INC
15256 Harmonsburg Rd (16335-8776)
PHONE..................814 337-8155
Kenneth T Gunn, *President*
EMP: 10
SQ FT: 10,000
SALES (est): 1.6MM **Privately Held**
WEB: www.imperialnewbould.com
SIC: 3541 5085 3544 Grinding machines, metalworking; tools; special dies, tools, jigs & fixtures

(G-10738)
INDEPENDENT TOOL & MFG
422 Park Ave (16335-1561)
P.O. Box 1304 (16335-0804)
PHONE..................814 336-5168
Robert F Beier Sr, *President*
Robert F Beier Jr, *Vice Pres*
EMP: 6 **EST:** 1981
SQ FT: 2,500
SALES (est): 900.9K **Privately Held**
SIC: 3469 3089 Machine parts, stamped or pressed metal; injection molded finished plastic products

(G-10739)
JEGLINSKI GROUP INC
18075 Woodland Dr (16335-8325)
PHONE..................814 807-0681
Matthew R Jeglinski, *President*
EMP: 25

SALES (est): 803.5K **Privately Held**
SIC: 3599 Machine tools, metal cutting type

(G-10740)
JONNY T FLETCHER
Also Called: Jt Industries
10921 Murray Rd Ste 540 (16335-3871)
PHONE..................814 724-6687
Jonny T Fletcher, *Owner*
EMP: 4 **EST:** 2001
SQ FT: 5,000
SALES (est): 273.8K **Privately Held**
WEB: www.jdhillinc.com
SIC: 3599 Machine shop, jobbing & repair

(G-10741)
K & S TOOL & DIE INC
15256 Harmonsburg Rd (16335-8776)
PHONE..................814 336-6932
Andrew Speck, *President*
Michael Keefer, *Corp Secy*
EMP: 8
SQ FT: 6,000
SALES: 500K **Privately Held**
SIC: 3599 3544 Machine shop, jobbing & repair; special dies, tools, jigs & fixtures

(G-10742)
KAPANICK CONSTRUCTION INC
17547 State Highway 98 (16335-7735)
PHONE..................814 763-3681
John Lee Kapanick, *President*
EMP: 10 **EST:** 1956
SALES (est): 941.7K **Privately Held**
SIC: 1521 1542 1389 New construction; single-family houses; commercial & office building, new construction; oil field services

(G-10743)
KEYSTONE PRECISION INC
1379 S Main St (16335-3072)
P.O. Box 42, Guys Mills (16327-0042)
PHONE..................814 336-2187
Lawrence Sniezek, *President*
EMP: 5
SQ FT: 4,000
SALES (est): 859.4K **Privately Held**
WEB: www.keystoneprecisioninc.com
SIC: 3544 5085 Special dies, tools, jigs & fixtures; tools

(G-10744)
KONO CO
13517a Broadway (16335-8307)
PHONE..................724 462-3333
John G Rushlander, *President*
Clinton Rushlander, *Corp Secy*
EMP: 6
SALES (est): 716.1K **Privately Held**
WEB: www.konoco.com
SIC: 3599 Machine shop, jobbing & repair

(G-10745)
KREM CARS/RACING INC
10204 Perry Hwy (16335-6450)
PHONE..................814 336-6619
Allen Krem, *President*
EMP: 5
SALES (est): 80K **Privately Held**
SIC: 7948 5511 3999 Motor vehicle racing & drivers; automobiles, new & used; barber & beauty shop equipment

(G-10746)
KREM SPEED EQUIPMENT INC
10204 Perry Hwy (16335-6450)
PHONE..................814 724-4806
Alan Krem, *President*
EMP: 5
SQ FT: 3,600
SALES: 200K **Privately Held**
WEB: www.krem-enterprises.com
SIC: 3714 Motor vehicle engines & parts

(G-10747)
KUHN TOOL & DIE CO
21371 Blooming Valley Rd (16335-5067)
P.O. Box 574 (16335-0574)
PHONE..................814 336-2123
Kenneth Kuhn, *President*
Bonnie Kuhn, *Vice Pres*
EMP: 20 **EST:** 1963
SQ FT: 41,615

SALES (est): 2MM **Privately Held**
WEB: www.kuhntool.com
SIC: 3544 Special dies & tools

(G-10748)
LAYKE TOOL & MANUFACTURING CO
23877 State Highway 77 (16335-5473)
P.O. Box 438 (16335-0438)
PHONE..................814 333-1169
Douglas Sheets, *President*
Lisa Sheets, *Admin Sec*
EMP: 20
SQ FT: 8,200
SALES: 2.9MM **Privately Held**
WEB: www.layke.com
SIC: 3545 3544 Gauges (machine tool accessories); special dies, tools, jigs & fixtures

(G-10749)
LEECH INC
Also Called: Leech Carbide
1085 Lamont Dr (16335-8197)
P.O. Box 539 (16335-0539)
PHONE..................814 724-5454
Daniel J Leech, *President*
Daniel T Leech, *Vice Pres*
Faye Gorman, *Purchasing*
Heather McKinney, *Bookkeeper*
Kathy Stainbrook, *Payroll Mgr*
▲ **EMP:** 60 **EST:** 1965
SQ FT: 40,000
SALES (est): 15.5MM **Privately Held**
WEB: www.leechcarbide.com
SIC: 3356 Tungsten, basic shapes

(G-10750)
LUBRITE LLC (HQ)
Also Called: Lubrite Technologies
18649 Brake Shoe Rd (16335-9603)
P.O. Box 458 (16335-0458)
PHONE..................814 337-4234
Tom Seringer, *CEO*
Dan Higham, *President*
David Del Propost,
EMP: 26
SQ FT: 375,000
SALES (est): 3.8MM
SALES (corp-wide): 15MM **Privately Held**
SIC: 3568 Bearings, bushings & blocks
PA: U.S. Bronze Foundry And Machine, Inc.
18649 Brake Shoe Rd
Meadville PA 16335
814 337-4234

(G-10751)
LWE INC
Also Called: Lubiniecki Welding & Equipment
17071 Cussewago Rd (16335-9591)
PHONE..................814 336-3553
Mark A Lubiniecki, *President*
Patty Lubiniecki, *Corp Secy*
Walter D Lubiniecki, *Vice Pres*
EMP: 8 **EST:** 1957
SQ FT: 12,000
SALES (est): 1.3MM **Privately Held**
WEB: www.lwe-inc.com
SIC: 3599 5084 5083 7699 Machine & other job shop work; welding machinery & equipment; lawn machinery & equipment; tractors, agricultural; agricultural equipment repair services; tractor repair

(G-10752)
MAC TOOL & DIE INC
18836 Cussewago Rd (16335-3606)
PHONE..................814 337-9105
Charles Mc Cullough, *President*
EMP: 7
SQ FT: 3,500
SALES: 700K **Privately Held**
SIC: 3544 Die sets for metal stamping (presses); special dies & tools

(G-10753)
MALONEY PLASTICS INC
10890 Mercer Pike (16335-6231)
P.O. Box 379 (16335-0379)
PHONE..................814 337-8417
Edward A Maloney, *President*
Gary Smith, *QC Mgr*
Tonya Nemeth, *Office Mgr*
Luke Wellmon, *Maintence Staff*
EMP: 20 **EST:** 1997

SALES (est): 4.9MM **Privately Held**
WEB: www.maloneycos.com
SIC: 3089 Injection molding of plastics

(G-10754)
MALONEY TOOL & MOLD INC
10890 Mercer Pike (16335-6231)
P.O. Box 379 (16335-0379)
PHONE..................814 337-8407
Edward Maloney, *President*
EMP: 50
SQ FT: 16,000
SALES: 5.1MM **Privately Held**
SIC: 3544 Special dies & tools

(G-10755)
MANDELBROKS
16226 Conneaut Lake Rd (16335-3804)
PHONE..................814 813-5555
Dawn Biggs, *Principal*
EMP: 4
SALES (est): 284.4K **Privately Held**
SIC: 2752 Commercial printing, lithographic

(G-10756)
MARCIES HOMEMADE ICE CREAM (PA)
18 Forest Ave (16335-1319)
PHONE..................814 336-1749
Randy Fyock, *Principal*
EMP: 4
SALES (est): 499K **Privately Held**
SIC: 2024 Ice cream & frozen desserts

(G-10757)
MARLAN TOOL INC
13385 Denny Rd (16335-7615)
PHONE..................814 382-2744
Marlan Jones, *President*
Dale Berlin, *Engineer*
Sherry Jones, *Treasurer*
Karen Whitesmith, *Office Mgr*
EMP: 20 EST: 1979
SQ FT: 6,800
SALES (est): 2.8MM **Privately Held**
WEB: www.marlantool.com
SIC: 3544 Special dies & tools

(G-10758)
MEADVILLE FORGING COMPANY LP (HQ)
Also Called: MFC
15309 Baldwin Street Ext (16335-9401)
P.O. Box 459 (16335-0459)
PHONE..................814 332-8200
John Keller, *Partner*
William P Glavin, *Partner*
James Martin, *Partner*
▲ EMP: 280
SQ FT: 187,000
SALES (est): 75.4MM
SALES (corp-wide): 98.2MM **Privately Held**
WEB: www.meadvillepa.com
SIC: 3462 Iron & steel forgings
PA: Keller Group, Inc.
1 Northfield Plz Ste 510
Northfield IL 60093
847 446-7550

(G-10759)
MEADVILLE NEW PRODUCTS INC
Also Called: Baco Plastics
15850 Conneaut Lake Rd (16335-4728)
P.O. Box 405 (16335-0405)
PHONE..................814 336-2174
John Bainbridge, *President*
EMP: 14 EST: 1962
SQ FT: 12,000
SALES (est): 1.2MM **Privately Held**
WEB: www.mnplasticbaskets.com
SIC: 3089 3083 3082 3081 Plastic containers, except foam; laminated plastics plate & sheet; unsupported plastics profile shapes; unsupported plastics film & sheet

(G-10760)
MEADVILLE PLATING COMPANY INC
10775 Franklin Pike (16335-9060)
PHONE..................814 724-1084
Donald C McBride, *President*
Wilma McBride, *Corp Secy*

Ron Weikal, *Sales Mgr*
EMP: 14 EST: 1969
SQ FT: 9,475
SALES (est): 1.8MM **Privately Held**
WEB: www.meadvilleplating.com
SIC: 3471 Chromium plating of metals or formed products; electroplating of metals or formed products

(G-10761)
MEADVILLE TOOL & MANUFACTURING
696 Hickory St (16335-2114)
PHONE..................814 337-7555
Terril John Gutowski, *Owner*
EMP: 5
SALES (est): 398.7K **Privately Held**
SIC: 3599 Machine shop, jobbing & repair

(G-10762)
MICHAEL CAIN
Also Called: Tower 23
576 Washington St (16335-2445)
PHONE..................814 333-1852
Michael Cain, *Owner*
EMP: 10
SALES (est): 410K **Privately Held**
WEB: www.tower23.com
SIC: 3999 Education aids, devices & supplies

(G-10763)
MICRO PLASTICS INC
13561 Broadway Ste A (16335-8307)
PHONE..................814 337-0781
Mark Sisco, *President*
EMP: 6
SALES (est): 584.1K
SALES (corp-wide): 2.4MM **Privately Held**
WEB: www.microtool-plastic.com
SIC: 3089 Injection molding of plastics
PA: Micro Tool & Mfg., Inc.
1425 Liberty St
Meadville PA
814 724-4704

(G-10764)
MINCO TOOL & MOLD INC
370 Linden St (16335-3026)
PHONE..................814 724-1376
Rick L Minman, *President*
EMP: 4
SQ FT: 1,800
SALES (est): 350K **Privately Held**
SIC: 3544 Special dies & tools

(G-10765)
MODERN INDUSTRIES INC
Also Called: Free-Col Laboratories
16285 Conneaut Lake Rd # 99
(16335-3885)
PHONE..................814 724-6242
Patrick Vargo, *Branch Mgr*
EMP: 30
SALES (est): 1.6MM
SALES (corp-wide): 20MM **Privately Held**
SIC: 3599 Machine shop, jobbing & repair
PA: Modern Industries, Inc.
613 W 11th St
Erie PA 16501
814 455-8061

(G-10766)
MOLDEX TOOL & DESIGN CORP
823 Bessemer St (16335-1859)
PHONE..................814 337-3190
Brian Shorey, *President*
J Michael Griffin, *Info Tech Mgr*
▲ EMP: 70
SQ FT: 40,000
SALES (est): 11MM **Privately Held**
WEB: www.moldexcorp.com
SIC: 3544 Industrial molds

(G-10767)
NEON MOON
891 Market St (16335-3317)
PHONE..................814 332-0302
Linda Narpes, *Principal*
EMP: 3 EST: 2014
SALES (est): 181.1K **Privately Held**
SIC: 2813 Neon

(G-10768)
NEW FRONTIER INDUSTRIES INC (HQ)
18649 Brake Shoe Rd (16335-9603)
P.O. Box 458 (16335-0458)
PHONE..................814 337-4234
Dan Higham, *President*
Dan Higam, *President*
David McRight, *Engineer*
David Del Propost, *Treasurer*
Barb Lucas, *Director*
EMP: 9
SALES (est): 1.4MM
SALES (corp-wide): 15MM **Privately Held**
SIC: 3341 Copper smelting & refining (secondary)
PA: U.S. Bronze Foundry And Machine, Inc.
18649 Brake Shoe Rd
Meadville PA 16335
814 337-4234

(G-10769)
NEWSPAPER HOLDING INC
Also Called: Meadville Tribune
947 Federal Ct Ste 49 (16335-3234)
PHONE..................814 724-6370
Melody Ferry, *Manager*
EMP: 80 **Privately Held**
WEB: www.clintonnc.com
SIC: 2711 2752 Newspapers: publishing only, not printed on site; commercial printing, lithographic
HQ: Newspaper Holding, Inc.
425 Locust St
Johnstown PA 15901
814 532-5102

(G-10770)
ONEIDA INSTANT LOG
300 Allegheny St (16335-1643)
PHONE..................814 336-2125
Sharon E Diley, *President*
Kathleen Smith, *Vice Pres*
EMP: 25 EST: 1958
SALES (est): 2MM **Privately Held**
SIC: 3679 2891 Electronic circuits; adhesives & sealants

(G-10771)
OPTICAL FILTERS USA LLC
13447 S Mosiertown Rd A (16335-8321)
PHONE..................814 333-2222
Michael Dent, *President*
Thomas Lord, *Manager*
▲ EMP: 39
SQ FT: 28,000
SALES (est): 5.2MM **Privately Held**
WEB: www.opticalfiltersusa.com
SIC: 3229 Glass furnishings & accessories

(G-10772)
ORVILLE BRONZE AND ALUM LLC
18649 Brake Shoe Rd (16335-9603)
PHONE..................330 948-1231
EMP: 5
SALES (est): 633.9K **Privately Held**
SIC: 3568 Power transmission equipment

(G-10773)
P & C TOOL INC
8111 Pettis Rd (16335-9165)
PHONE..................814 425-7050
Paul Drazina, *President*
EMP: 10
SALES (est): 927.3K **Privately Held**
SIC: 3089 Injection molded finished plastic products

(G-10774)
PARDEES JEWELRY & ACCESSORIES
664 Tremont St (16335-4142)
PHONE..................814 282-1172
Susan Pardee, *President*
EMP: 6
SALES (est): 374K **Privately Held**
SIC: 3961 Costume jewelry

(G-10775)
PENN WELD INC
1057 French St (16335-3572)
PHONE..................814 332-3682
Bill Starn, *President*

Timothy J Mullen, *Vice Pres*
Pam Mullen, *Bookkeeper*
EMP: 7
SQ FT: 1,800
SALES (est): 1.1MM **Privately Held**
WEB: www.pennweld.com
SIC: 7692 3441 Welding repair; fabricated structural metal

(G-10776)
PENNCO TOOL & DIE INC
99 Mead Ave (16335-3528)
PHONE..................814 336-5035
Philip W Passilla, *President*
EMP: 30 EST: 1980
SQ FT: 12,500
SALES: 2.2MM **Privately Held**
WEB: www.penncotool.com
SIC: 3544 Special dies & tools

(G-10777)
PENNHEAT LLC
360 Chestnut St (16335-3211)
PHONE..................814 282-6774
Therman L Kantzm, *Owner*
James McWilliams, *Vice Pres*
Therman Kantzm, *Mng Member*
EMP: 20 EST: 2012
SQ FT: 1,200
SALES: 3MM **Privately Held**
SIC: 3441 3315 Fabricated structural metal; wire & fabricated wire products

(G-10778)
PENNSYLVANIA TOOL & GAGES INC
16906 Pa Tool & Gauge Dr (16335-3768)
P.O. Box 534 (16335-0534)
PHONE..................814 336-3136
Kathleen Glover, *President*
Mark Burns, *Corp Secy*
James Burns, *Vice Pres*
Jim Burns, *VP Opers*
Scott McKinney, *CTO*
EMP: 34 EST: 1954
SQ FT: 52,000
SALES: 3.3MM **Privately Held**
WEB: www.patool.com
SIC: 3599 Machine shop, jobbing & repair

(G-10779)
PETERS HEAT TREATING INC (PA)
215 Race St (16335-1829)
P.O. Box 624 (16335-0624)
PHONE..................814 333-1782
Douglas Peters, *President*
J Douglas Peters, *President*
Jacqueline Peters, *Treasurer*
EMP: 26
SQ FT: 6,000
SALES: 3.2MM **Privately Held**
WEB: www.petersheattreat.com
SIC: 3398 Brazing (hardening) of metal

(G-10780)
PLASMA AUTOMATION INCORPORATED
10346 Mercer Pike (16335-6264)
PHONE..................814 333-2181
Christopher Hamilton, *Plant Mgr*
Mark Weigel, *Regl Sales Mgr*
Brian Owens, *Manager*
EMP: 15
SALES (est): 2.2MM **Privately Held**
WEB: www.plasma-automation.com
SIC: 3541 Machine tools, metal cutting: exotic (explosive, etc.)
PA: Plasma Automation Incorporated
1801 Artic Ave
Bohemia NY 11716

(G-10781)
PRISM PLASTICS INC
Also Called: Tech Molded Plastics
1045 French St (16335-3572)
PHONE..................814 724-8222
EMP: 150
SALES (corp-wide): 225.3B **Publicly Held**
SIC: 3089 Molding primary plastic
HQ: Prism Plastics, Inc.
52111 Sierra Dr
Chesterfield MI 48047
810 292-6300

G E O G R A P H I C

(G-10782)
PROGRESSIVE TOOL & DIE INC
13693 Broadway Ste A (16335-8322)
PHONE..............................814 333-2992
Michael A Setta, *President*
William Latta, *Vice Pres*
Nancy Setta, *Manager*
EMP: 15
SQ FT: 7,500
SALES: 1.1MM **Privately Held**
SIC: 3544 Special dies, tools, jigs & fixtures

(G-10783)
PTR TOOL & PLASTICS LLC
150 Baldwin Street Ext (16335-7920)
P.O. Box 338, Wheatland (16161-0338)
PHONE..............................814 724-6979
Philip Moroco II, *Mng Member*
Richard Moroco,
Charles Todd,
▲ **EMP:** 40
SQ FT: 5,000
SALES (est): 10.3MM **Privately Held**
SIC: 3089 Plastic containers, except foam
PA: Ptr Group, Lp
54 Buhl Blvd
Sharon PA 16146

(G-10784)
QTD PLASTICS INC
21398 Blooming Valley Rd (16335-5044)
PHONE..............................814 724-1641
Chad Kearns, *CEO*
Robert Gregg, *President*
EMP: 35
SQ FT: 20,000
SALES (est): 3.3MM **Privately Held**
SIC: 3089 Jars, plastic

(G-10785)
QUALITY TOOL & DIE INC
21398 Blooming Valley Rd (16335-5044)
PHONE..............................814 336-6364
Jeff Barnard, *President*
Robert Gregg, *Partner*
Rebert Greg, *Vice Pres*
Tom Mason, *Vice Pres*
Chad Kearns, *Treasurer*
EMP: 18
SQ FT: 7,500
SALES (est): 3.8MM **Privately Held**
WEB: www.qualitytoolanddie.com
SIC: 3545 Machine tool attachments & accessories

(G-10786)
QUANTUM CONNECTION
10553 Shaffer Rd (16335-9337)
PHONE..............................814 333-9398
Guy Burchill, *Owner*
EMP: 3
SALES (est): 213.8K **Privately Held**
SIC: 3572 Computer storage devices

(G-10787)
RHKG HOLDINGS INC
10890 Mercer Pike (16335-6231)
P.O. Box 379 (16335-0379)
PHONE..............................814 337-8407
Paul Huber, *CEO*
Robert Douglas, *President*
Paul Kelyman Sr, *Vice Pres*
Gary Rodgers, *Vice Pres*
EMP: 47
SQ FT: 26,243
SALES (est): 4.9MM **Privately Held**
SIC: 3544 3089 Special dies & tools; injection molding of plastics

(G-10788)
SB SPECIALTY METALS LLC
99 W Poplar St (16335-3536)
PHONE..............................814 337-8804
Steve McKeever, *Manager*
EMP: 9 **Privately Held**
WEB: www.crucible.com
SIC: 3312 5051 Blast furnaces & steel mills; steel
HQ: Sb Specialty Metals Llc
1020 7th North St Ste 140
Liverpool NY 13088

(G-10789)
SCHWEBEL BAKING COMPANY
813 Water St (16335-3420)
PHONE..............................814 333-2498
Sandy Thress, *Manager*
EMP: 3
SALES (corp-wide): 170MM **Privately Held**
WEB: www.schwebels.com
SIC: 2051 Bakery: wholesale or wholesale/retail combined
PA: Schwebel Baking Company
965 E Midlothian Blvd
Youngstown OH 44502
330 783-2860

(G-10790)
SECO/VACUUM TECHNOLOGIES LLC
180 Mercer St (16335-3618)
PHONE..............................814 332-8520
Piotr Zawistowski,
EMP: 9
SALES (est): 408.7K **Privately Held**
SIC: 3567 Vacuum furnaces & ovens

(G-10791)
SECO/WARWICK CORPORATION
180 Mercer St (16335-3618)
P.O. Box 908 (16335-6908)
PHONE..............................814 332-8400
Jonathan Markley, *President*
Jeffrey W Boswell, *Vice Pres*
Arthur V Russo, *CFO*
Jason Mackerman, *Treasurer*
Bill St Thomas, *Regl Sales Mgr*
◆ **EMP:** 100 **EST:** 1900
SQ FT: 130,000
SALES: 20MM
SALES (corp-wide): 73.5MM **Privately Held**
WEB: www.secowarwick.com
SIC: 3567 Induction heating equipment; kilns; metal melting furnaces, industrial: electric; metal melting furnaces, industrial: fuel-fired
PA: Seco Warwick S A
Ul. Sobieskiego 8
Swiebodzin 66-20
486 838-2050

(G-10792)
STANDARD PRECISION MFG INC
13617 Broadway (16335-8375)
PHONE..............................814 724-1202
Frank Repko, *President*
Christopher Repko, *Vice Pres*
EMP: 26
SQ FT: 8,000
SALES (est): 4.4MM **Privately Held**
WEB: www.standardprecisionmfg.com
SIC: 3544 Special dies & tools

(G-10793)
STARLITE GROUP INC
246 Race St (16335-1830)
PHONE..............................814 333-1377
Chris Coldren, *President*
Doug Samuels, *Engineer*
EMP: 7
SQ FT: 130,000
SALES (est): 2MM **Privately Held**
WEB: www.starlitegroup.com
SIC: 3599 5084 6512 Machine shop, jobbing & repair; industrial machinery & equipment; commercial & industrial building operation

(G-10794)
STARN TOOL & MANUFACTURING CO (PA)
20524 Blooming Valley Rd (16335-8099)
P.O. Box 209 (16335-0209)
PHONE..............................814 724-1057
William E Starn, *President*
Tim Mullen, *Vice Pres*
Linda Maloney, *Admin Sec*
▲ **EMP:** 55 **EST:** 1945
SQ FT: 18,000
SALES (est): 8.4MM **Privately Held**
WEB: www.starn.com
SIC: 3544 3545 Special dies & tools; machine tool accessories

(G-10795)
SUBURBAN PRECISON MOLD COMPANY
19370 Cochranton Rd (16335-9034)
PHONE..............................814 337-3413
David J Mc Guire, *President*
Stephen Reitz, *Accounts Exec*
EMP: 15
SALES: 1.5MM **Privately Held**
WEB: www.suburbanprecision.com
SIC: 3544 Special dies & tools

(G-10796)
SUIT-KOTE CORPORATION
10965 Mchenry St (16335-9067)
PHONE..............................814 337-1171
Earl Koon, *General Mgr*
Steeve San Filipo, *Branch Mgr*
EMP: 100
SALES (corp-wide): 234.8MM **Privately Held**
SIC: 1611 2951 Highway & street paving contractor; asphalt & asphaltic paving mixtures (not from refineries)
PA: Suit-Kote Corporation
1911 Lorings Crossing Rd
Cortland NY 13045
607 753-1100

(G-10797)
TALBAR INC
10991 Liberty St (16335-8179)
P.O. Box 401 (16335-0401)
PHONE..............................814 337-8400
Thomas Parks, *President*
Tamara Parks, *Vice Pres*
Carol Parks, *Admin Sec*
EMP: 25 **EST:** 1967
SQ FT: 30,000
SALES (est): 4.8MM **Privately Held**
WEB: www.talbar.com
SIC: 3544 Special dies & tools

(G-10798)
TAMARACK PACKAGING LTD
11124 Mercer Pike (16335-6200)
P.O. Box 693 (16335-0693)
PHONE..............................814 724-2860
William S Dearment, *CEO*
Stephen Sada, *Corp Secy*
Ronald Proper, *Vice Pres*
Martha Babcock, *Sales Mgr*
EMP: 25 **EST:** 1962
SQ FT: 12,000
SALES (est): 4.3MM **Privately Held**
WEB: www.tamarackpackaging.com
SIC: 2782 3089 7336 Looseleaf binders & devices; plastic processing; commercial art & graphic design

(G-10799)
TAPCO TUBE COMPANY
10748 S Water Street Ext (16335-9098)
PHONE..............................814 336-2201
Chester Marshall Jr, *President*
Jeff Bresler, *Chief Mktg Ofcr*
EMP: 40
SALES (est): 14.2MM **Privately Held**
WEB: www.tapcotube.com
SIC: 3317 Steel pipe & tubes

(G-10800)
THEODORE W STYBORSKI
Also Called: Advantage Mold & Design
10246 Mercer Pike (16335-6289)
P.O. Box 455 (16335-0455)
PHONE..............................814 337-8535
Theodore W Styborski, *Owner*
Karen Styborski, *Office Mgr*
EMP: 9
SQ FT: 8,000
SALES: 325K **Privately Held**
SIC: 3544 3089 Industrial molds; plastic processing; molding primary plastic

(G-10801)
TIGER BRAND JACK POST CO
10721 S Water Street Ext (16335-9097)
PHONE..............................814 333-4302
Chester R Marshall Jr, *President*
EMP: 20
SALES (est): 2.3MM **Privately Held**
WEB: www.tigerbrandjackpost.com
SIC: 3325 Steel foundries

(G-10802)
TOOL CITY WELDING LLC
280 Baldwin Street Ext (16335-9425)
PHONE..............................814 333-9353
Karl J Brown,
Nicole Fies,
EMP: 6
SQ FT: 7,000
SALES: 700K **Privately Held**
WEB: www.toolcitywelding.com
SIC: 3441 1799 Fabricated structural metal; welding on site

(G-10803)
TRIO PLASTICS INC
21398 Blooming Valley Rd (16335-5044)
PHONE..............................814 724-1640
Bob Riordan, *CEO*
James R Burek, *President*
Thomas Phelps, *Vice Pres*
Robert C Riordan, *Treasurer*
Walter L Johnston, *Admin Sec*
EMP: 14 **EST:** 1999
SALES (est): 1.7MM **Privately Held**
SIC: 3089 Plastic processing

(G-10804)
TROJAN INC
Also Called: Hytron Electric Products Div
114 W Poplar St (16335-3537)
P.O. Box 404 (16335-0404)
PHONE..............................814 336-4468
Susan Pompano, *Branch Mgr*
EMP: 50
SALES (corp-wide): 15.7MM **Privately Held**
WEB: www.trojan.com
SIC: 3089 3641 3357 Molding primary plastic; electric light bulbs, complete; nonferrous wiredrawing & insulating
PA: Trojan, Inc.
198 Trojan St
Mount Sterling KY 40353
859 498-0526

(G-10805)
UNITED TOOL & DIE INC
275 Terrace Street Ext (16335-7917)
P.O. Box 213, Saegertown (16433-0213)
PHONE..............................814 763-1133
Ronald Wilcox, *President*
Stuart Wilcox, *Vice Pres*
Jane Wilcox, *Treasurer*
Douglas Wilcox, *Admin Sec*
EMP: 14
SQ FT: 6,000
SALES: 1MM **Privately Held**
SIC: 3544 Industrial molds

(G-10806)
UNIVERSAL PRESSURE PUMPING INC
18360 Technology Dr (16335-8333)
PHONE..............................814 373-3226
Roy Irwin, *Sr Project Mgr*
EMP: 5
SALES (corp-wide): 3.3B **Publicly Held**
SIC: 1381 Drilling oil & gas wells
HQ: Universal Pressure Pumping, Inc.
6 Desta Dr Ste 4400
Midland TX 79705

(G-10807)
UNIVERSAL WELL SERVICES INC (HQ)
13549 S Mosiertown Rd (16335-8317)
PHONE..............................814 337-1983
Roger Willis, *President*
Daniel Mesley, *Principal*
John Stansfield, *VP Admin*
Kyle Brocious, *Engineer*
Joseph Pinkhouse, *Engineer*
EMP: 40
SQ FT: 15,000
SALES (est): 415.8MM
SALES (corp-wide): 3.3B **Publicly Held**
WEB: www.univwell.com
SIC: 1389 1382 Hydraulic fracturing wells; oil & gas exploration services
PA: Patterson-Uti Energy, Inc.
10713 W Sam Houston Pkwy
Houston TX 77064
281 765-7100

(G-10808)
UNIVERSAL WELL SERVICES INC
18360 Technology Dr 4 (16335-8333)
PHONE..................................814 333-2656
Charles Curry, *Opers Mgr*
Jamie Gordon, *Treasurer*
Evert Sanders, *Manager*
Brandon Hill, *IT/INT Sup*
EMP: 45
SALES (corp-wide): 3.3B **Publicly Held**
WEB: www.univwell.com
SIC: 1389 Hydraulic fracturing wells; cementing oil & gas well casings
HQ: Universal Well Services, Inc.
13549 S Mosiertown Rd
Meadville PA 16335
814 337-1983

(G-10809)
UNIVERSAL WELL SERVICES INC
18360 Technology Dr (16335-8333)
PHONE..................................814 368-6175
Frank Covine, *General Mgr*
EMP: 50
SALES (corp-wide): 3.3B **Publicly Held**
WEB: www.univwell.com
SIC: 7353 1389 Oil well drilling equipment, rental or leasing; oil field services
HQ: Universal Well Services, Inc.
13549 S Mosiertown Rd
Meadville PA 16335
814 337-1983

(G-10810)
US BRONZE FOUNDRY & MCH INC (PA)
18649 Brake Shoe Rd (16335-9603)
P.O. Box 458 (16335-0458)
PHONE..................................814 337-4234
Daniel E Higham, *President*
Aaron Reibel, *General Mgr*
Tom Herrick, *Maint Spvr*
David Delpropost, *Treasurer*
Thomas Seringer, *Admin Sec*
EMP: 55
SQ FT: 375,000
SALES (est): 14.9MM **Privately Held**
SIC: 3341 3369 Copper smelting & refining (secondary); nonferrous foundries

(G-10811)
VISION TOOL & MANUFACTURING
10670 Mercer Pike (16335-6230)
PHONE..................................814 724-6363
Jim Wilson, *President*
Joseph T Berces, *Vice Pres*
EMP: 20
SQ FT: 7,000
SALES (est): 3.3MM **Privately Held**
WEB: www.visiontool.com
SIC: 3544 Special dies, tools, jigs & fixtures

(G-10812)
WELLSVILLE FOUNDRY INC
24939 State St (16335-8843)
PHONE..................................330 532-2995
Chuck H Gilmore, *President*
Patsy Frontone, *Principal*
Gerald M Kelly, *Principal*
James K Kelly, *Principal*
EMP: 30
SQ FT: 17,000
SALES (est): 7.6MM **Privately Held**
WEB: www.wellsvillefoundry.com
SIC: 3321 Gray/Ductile Iron Foundry

(G-10813)
WIRE TECH & TOOL INC
350 Linden St (16335-3026)
PHONE..................................814 333-3175
Terry L Faivre, *Owner*
Karen Faivre, *Office Mgr*
EMP: 5
SQ FT: 5,500
SALES: 300K **Privately Held**
SIC: 3599 Machine shop, jobbing & repair

(G-10814)
WOODSTOCK MFG SERVICES INC
831 Mulberry St (16335-3413)
P.O. Box 1357 (16335-0857)
PHONE..................................814 336-4426
David Call, *President*
Karen Struckel, *Principal*
EMP: 6
SALES (est): 731.8K **Privately Held**
SIC: 3599 Machine shop, jobbing & repair

Mechanicsburg
Cumberland County

(G-10815)
486 ASSOCIATES INC
486 Covinton St (17055)
PHONE..................................717 691-7077
Joseph M Hummer Sr, *Ch of Bd*
Joseph M Hummer II, *President*
Frances Hummer, *Vice Pres*
EMP: 23 **EST:** 1975
SQ FT: 26,500
SALES (est): 2.5MM **Privately Held**
SIC: 5074 5075 3444 Heating equipment (hydronic); air conditioning & ventilation equipment & supplies; ventilating equipment & supplies; sheet metalwork

(G-10816)
ADVANCE CENTRAL SERVICES PA
1900 Patriot Dr (17050-9499)
PHONE..................................717 255-8400
Paul Thomas, *President*
EMP: 3
SALES (est): 197.1K **Privately Held**
SIC: 2759 Commercial printing

(G-10817)
ALCOLOCK PA INC
273 Mulberry Dr Ste 2 (17050-7914)
PHONE..................................800 452-1759
Felix Comeau, *President*
EMP: 5
SALES (est): 441.3K **Privately Held**
SIC: 3694 Ignition apparatus & distributors

(G-10818)
ALL AMERICAN HOMES COLO LLC
4900 Ritter Rd Ste 130 (17055-6929)
PHONE..................................970 587-0544
Del Herr, *President*
EMP: 50
SQ FT: 124,058
SALES (est): 5.8MM **Privately Held**
WEB: www.coachmen.com
SIC: 2452 Modular homes, prefabricated, wood
HQ: All American Group, Inc.
2831 Dexter Dr
Elkhart IN 46514
574 262-0123

(G-10819)
ALPHAGRAPHICS
4609 Gettysburg Rd (17055-4324)
PHONE..................................717 731-8444
David Boone, *Owner*
EMP: 9
SQ FT: 4,500
SALES (est): 1MM **Privately Held**
SIC: 2752 2791 7334 Commercial printing, offset; typesetting; photocopying & duplicating services

(G-10820)
AQUA TREATMENT SERVICES INC
Also Called: A T S
194 Hempt Rd (17050-2666)
PHONE..................................717 697-4998
John R Filson II, *President*
David Rishell, *President*
Jim Heinbaugh, *Vice Pres*
Barry Duncan, *Opers Mgr*
Ed Wood, *Opers Mgr*
▲ **EMP:** 45
SQ FT: 22,000

SALES (est): 14MM **Privately Held**
WEB: www.aquat.com
SIC: 3589 3821 Water filters & softeners, household type; water purification equipment, household type; water treatment equipment, industrial; sterilizers

(G-10821)
B AND B SIGNS AND GRAPHICS
Also Called: Fastsigns
4713 Carlisle Pike (17050-7714)
PHONE..................................717 737-4467
Ryan Bowman, *President*
EMP: 5 **EST:** 1997
SALES (est): 330K **Privately Held**
SIC: 3993 Signs & advertising specialties

(G-10822)
BARKLEIGH PRODUCTIONS INC
Also Called: Barkleigh Publications
970 W Trindle Rd (17055-4071)
PHONE..................................717 691-3388
Sally J Liddick, *President*
Rebecca Shipman, *Editor*
Gwen Shelly, *Vice Pres*
Martha Lucas, *Prdtn Mgr*
Lance Williams, *Production*
EMP: 12
SQ FT: 3,500
SALES (est): 1.5MM **Privately Held**
WEB: www.barkleigh.com
SIC: 2741 Catalogs: publishing only, not printed on site

(G-10823)
BAYER HLTHCARE PHRMCTICALS INC
260 Salem Church Rd (17050-2895)
P.O. Box 416, Pittsburg (15230)
PHONE..................................717 713-7173
EMP: 212
SALES (corp-wide): 45.3B **Privately Held**
SIC: 2834 Pharmaceutical preparations
HQ: Bayer Healthcare Pharmaceuticals Inc.
100 Bayer Blvd
Whippany NJ 07981
862 404-3000

(G-10824)
BFHJ ENRGY SOLUTIONS LTD LBLTY
6427 Carlisle Pike (17050-2385)
PHONE..................................717 458-0927
EMP: 3
SALES (corp-wide): 2MM **Privately Held**
SIC: 3674 Photovoltaic devices, solid state
HQ: Beneficial Energy Solutions Llc
2632 State Route 72
Jonestown PA 17038
844 237-7697

(G-10825)
BIOWERK USA INC
1115 S York St (17055-4742)
PHONE..................................717 697-3310
EMP: 4
SQ FT: 3,840
SALES (est): 242K **Privately Held**
SIC: 3842 Mfg Orthopedic Supports

(G-10826)
CAPPELLI ENTERPRISES INC
Also Called: Future Home Technology
4900 Ritter Rd Ste 130 (17055-6929)
PHONE..................................845 856-9033
Louis Cappelli, *Chairman*
EMP: 120 **Privately Held**
SIC: 2452 Modular homes, prefabricated, wood
PA: Cappelli Enterprises, Inc.
7 Renaissance Sq Fl 4
White Plains NY 10601

(G-10827)
CMI PRINTGRAPHIX INC
937 Nixon Dr Ste 2 (17055-7507)
P.O. Box 141135, Staten Island NY (10314-1135)
PHONE..................................717 697-4567
EMP: 3 **EST:** 2009
SALES (est): 330K **Privately Held**
SIC: 2759 7331 Commercial Printing Direct Mail Advertising Services

(G-10828)
COLLECTIVE INTELLIGENCE INC
6 Kacey Ct Ste 203 (17055-9237)
PHONE..................................717 545-9234
Daren Stonesifer, *President*
Chuck Russell, *Treasurer*
EMP: 9
SALES (est): 1.7MM **Privately Held**
WEB: www.collectiveintelligence.com
SIC: 7372 Prepackaged software

(G-10829)
COMMERCIAL FLRG PROFESSIONALS
6029 Carlisle Pike (17050-2426)
P.O. Box 99, Grantham (17027-0099)
PHONE..................................717 576-7847
Joy Macdonald, *President*
James Macdonald II, *Admin Sec*
EMP: 4 **EST:** 2011
SALES (est): 466.9K **Privately Held**
SIC: 1752 3996 Carpet laying; vinyl floor tile & sheet installation; wood floor installation & refinishing; hard surface floor coverings; asphalted-felt-base floor coverings: linoleum, carpet

(G-10830)
COMPUTER DEV SYSTEMS LLC
220 Cumberland Pkwy Ste 8 (17055-5683)
PHONE..................................717 591-0995
Jonathan Ebersole, *Mng Member*
Lee Longland, *Consultant*
Jennifer Ebersole, *Software Dev*
EMP: 5 **EST:** 1997
SALES (est): 442K **Privately Held**
WEB: www.parss.net
SIC: 7372 7371 7374 Prepackaged software; custom computer programming services; computer graphics service

(G-10831)
COUNTRY FOOD LLC
Also Called: Country Food USA
937 Nixon Dr Ste D (17055-7522)
PHONE..................................717 506-0393
Mesut Baysal,
Erdogan Ceylan,
Birol Guler,
EMP: 3 **EST:** 2013
SALES (est): 75.4K **Privately Held**
SIC: 2026 Yogurt

(G-10832)
CREES WLDG & FABRICATION INC
320 E Allen St (17055-3307)
PHONE..................................717 795-8711
Ray F Cree Jr, *President*
EMP: 3
SQ FT: 1,300
SALES (est): 541.9K **Privately Held**
SIC: 7699 3498 Boiler repair shop; fabricated pipe & fittings

(G-10833)
CRESLINE PLASTIC PIPE CO INC
264 Silver Spring Rd (17050-2840)
PHONE..................................717 766-9262
Richard Schroeder, *President*
EMP: 75
SALES (est): 10.2MM
SALES (corp-wide): 142.3MM **Privately Held**
WEB: www.creslinepipe.com
SIC: 3084 Plastics pipe
PA: Cresline Plastic Pipe Co Inc
600 N Cross Pointe Blvd
Evansville IN 47715
812 428-9300

(G-10834)
CROCKETT LOG HOMES OF PA INC
58 Sunset Dr (17050-1624)
PHONE..................................717 697-6198
Douglas Dodson, *President*
EMP: 3
SALES (est): 380K **Privately Held**
SIC: 2452 Log cabins, prefabricated, wood

G E O G R A P H I C

(G-10835)
CUMBERLAND TOOL & DIE INC
6 Brenneman Cir (17050-2658)
PHONE..................................717 691-1125
Kenneth Brown, *President*
Lester Lightner, *Corp Secy*
Dave Nesmith, *Manager*
EMP: 30
SALES (est): 3.8MM **Privately Held**
SIC: 3469 3544 Machine parts, stamped
　or pressed metal; special dies & tools

(G-10836)
DAIRY FARMERS AMERICA INC
4825 Old Gettysburg Rd (17055)
PHONE..................................717 691-4141
Kevin Bankos, *Principal*
Joe Yentzer, *Warehouse Mgr*
James Kurtz, *Manager*
EMP: 46
SALES (corp-wide): 14.6B **Privately Held**
WEB: www.dfamilk.com
SIC: 2026 Fluid milk
PA: Dairy Farmers Of America, Inc.
　1405 N 98th St
　Kansas City KS 66111
　816 801-6455

(G-10837)
DLA DOCUMENT SERVICES
5450 Crlsle Pike Bldg 410 (17055)
P.O. Box 2020 (17055-0788)
PHONE..................................717 605-3777
George Gianos, *Manager*
EMP: 18 **Publicly Held**
SIC: 2752 9711 Commercial printing, litho-
　graphic; national security
HQ: Dla Document Services
　5450 Carlisle Pike Bldg 9
　Mechanicsburg PA 17050
　717 605-2362

(G-10838)
DOTTED QUARTER MUSIC
1563 English Dr (17055-5687)
PHONE..................................724 541-4211
David Stockton, *Principal*
EMP: 3 EST: 2013
SALES (est): 120K **Privately Held**
SIC: 3131 Quarters

(G-10839)
DULL KNIFE TERMINATOR INC
5005 Inverness Dr (17050-8314)
PHONE..................................717 512-8596
John S Moesta, *President*
EMP: 3
SALES (est): 381.3K **Privately Held**
SIC: 3199 5085 Novelties, leather; knives,
　industrial

(G-10840)
E-HARVEST SYSTEMS
5124 Erbs Bridge Rd (17050-2432)
PHONE..................................908 832-0400
Robert C Klein Jr, *Owner*
EMP: 3
SALES (est): 177.5K **Privately Held**
SIC: 3511 Turbines & turbine generator
　sets

(G-10841)
ECHO DELTA CHARLIE INC
458 N Locust Point Rd (17050-1518)
PHONE..................................267 278-7598
EMP: 3
SALES (est): 291.2K **Privately Held**
SIC: 3999 Manufacturing industries

(G-10842)
FACTOR X GRAFFICS
Also Called: Fxg Fine and Label
145 Salem Church Rd (17050-2813)
PHONE..................................717 590-7402
Ted Muelen, *Mng Member*
EMP: 4 EST: 2014
SALES (est): 637.9K **Privately Held**
SIC: 2621 Fine paper

(G-10843)
FAIRYLOGUE PRESS
4173 Grouse Ct Apt 115 (17050-7636)
PHONE..................................717 713-5788
Megan Heaton, *Principal*
EMP: 4 EST: 2014

SALES (est): 154.6K **Privately Held**
SIC: 2711 Newspapers

(G-10844)
FLIGHT SYSTEMS INC (PA)
207 Hempt Rd (17050-2607)
PHONE..................................717 590-7330
Robert York, *CEO*
Robert D Shaffner, *President*
Jean-Luc Calvo, *Production*
Anthony Misiti, *Info Tech Mgr*
Karl Thompson, *Software Engr*
▲ EMP: 20 EST: 1968
SQ FT: 250,000
SALES (est): 2.6MM **Privately Held**
WEB: www.flightsystems.com
SIC: 3571 Electronic computers

(G-10845)
FOUST MACHINE & TOOL
6380 Basehore Rd (17050-2801)
PHONE..................................717 766-7841
Ronald L Foust, *Owner*
EMP: 5 EST: 1968
SQ FT: 6,000
SALES (est): 360K **Privately Held**
SIC: 3545 Precision tools, machinists';
　thread cutting dies

(G-10846)
FRY COMMUNICATIONS INC (PA)
800 W Church Rd (17055-3198)
PHONE..................................717 766-0211
Mike Lukas, *CEO*
Henry Fry, *Ch of Bd*
Calvin Groff, *President*
Tom Dyson, *General Mgr*
Dawn Felts, *General Mgr*
▲ EMP: 1050 EST: 1934
SQ FT: 1,000,000
SALES (est): 292MM **Privately Held**
WEB: www.frycomm.com
SIC: 2752 Lithographic Commercial Print-
　ing

(G-10847)
G CASE INC
11 Devonshire Sq (17050-6876)
PHONE..................................717 737-5000
George Case, *President*
Carol Case, *Vice Pres*
EMP: 5
SALES (est): 781.9K **Privately Held**
WEB: www.gcase.com
SIC: 2599 7389 Factory furniture & fix-
　tures; interior designer

(G-10848)
G&R DESIGNS LLC
Also Called: Little Bits
102a W Main St Unit A (17055-6229)
PHONE..................................717 697-4538
Mr John Gram,
EMP: 3
SALES (est): 256.1K **Privately Held**
SIC: 2759 3577 Screen printing; printers &
　plotters

(G-10849)
GLOBAL DATA CONSULTANTS LLC
4700 Westport Dr (17055-6788)
PHONE..................................717 697-7500
Rob Meier, *President*
EMP: 20
SALES (corp-wide): 71MM **Privately Held**
SIC: 3575 7373 7379 Computer termi-
　nals, monitors & components; systems in-
　tegration services; computer related
　maintenance services
PA: Global Data Consultants, Llc
　1144 Kennebec Dr
　Chambersburg PA 17201
　717 262-2080

(G-10850)
GREENRAY INDUSTRIES INC
840 W Church Rd (17055-3199)
PHONE..................................717 766-0223
Miklos Vendel, *Chairman*
Brian T McCarthy, *CFO*
Margaritha E Werren, *Admin Sec*
EMP: 25 EST: 1958
SALES (est): 18,300

SALES (est): 5.4MM
SALES (corp-wide): 75.1MM **Privately Held**
WEB: www.greenrayindustries.com
SIC: 3679 Oscillators
PA: Technicorp International li, Inc.
　512 N Main St
　Orange CA 92868
　714 639-7810

(G-10851)
HARSCO CORPORATION
Also Called: Reed Minerals
5020 Ritter Rd Ste 205 (17055-4837)
P.O. Box 515, Camp Hill (17001-0515)
PHONE..................................717 506-2071
Jene Iannazzo, *President*
EMP: 10
SALES (corp-wide): 1.6B **Publicly Held**
SIC: 3443 Fuel tanks (oil, gas, etc.): metal
　plate; cryogenic tanks, for liquids &
　gases; cylinders, pressure: metal plate;
　heat exchangers: coolers (after, inter),
　condensers, etc.
PA: Harsco Corporation
　350 Poplar Church Rd
　Camp Hill PA 17011
　717 763-7064

(G-10852)
HERFF JONES LLC
5502 Gloucester St Unit B (17055-4413)
PHONE..................................717 697-0649
EMP: 4
SALES (corp-wide): 1.1B **Privately Held**
WEB: www.herffjones.com
SIC: 3911 Rings, finger: precious metal
HQ: Herff Jones, Llc
　4501 W 62nd St
　Indianapolis IN 46268
　800 419-5462

(G-10853)
HOMESTEAD INSPECTION SERVICE
2471 Cope Dr (17055-5355)
PHONE..................................717 691-1586
James Benson, *Owner*
▲ EMP: 3
SALES (est): 163.9K **Privately Held**
SIC: 1389 Construction, repair & disman-
　tling services

(G-10854)
HOPE GOOD ANIMAL CLINIC
6108 Carlisle Pike # 120 (17050-5243)
PHONE..................................717 766-5535
Curt Barnett, *Owner*
EMP: 4
SALES (est): 290K **Privately Held**
SIC: 0742 3999 5999 5231 Animal hospi-
　tal services, pets & other animal special-
　ties; pet supplies; trophies & plaques;
　paint, glass & wallpaper; fire sprinkler
　system installation

(G-10855)
HOT FROG PRINT MEDIA LLC
118 W Allen St (17055-6203)
PHONE..................................717 697-2204
James Geedy, *CEO*
EMP: 26
SALES (est): 4.6MM **Privately Held**
SIC: 2752 Commercial printing, litho-
　graphic

(G-10856)
ICEBLOX INC
Also Called: Snoblox-Snojax
1405 Brandton Rd (17055-6739)
PHONE..................................717 697-1900
Brion McMullen, *President*
Dondra McMullen, *Admin Sec*
EMP: 7
SALES (est): 1MM **Privately Held**
SIC: 3524 Snowblowers & throwers, resi-
　dential

(G-10857)
IGNEOUS ROCK GALLERY
4702 Carlisle Pike Ste 25 (17050-3099)
PHONE..................................717 774-4074
Robert Wertz, *Principal*
EMP: 7 EST: 2010
SALES (est): 602.4K **Privately Held**
SIC: 3272 Cast stone, concrete

(G-10858)
INDUSTRIAL CONTROLS INC
Also Called: Johnson Contrls Authorized Dlr
837 W Trindle Rd (17055-4077)
P.O. Box 693 (17055-0693)
PHONE..................................717 697-7555
David Kratzer, *President*
Edwin Kratzer, *Vice Pres*
EMP: 8 EST: 1958
SQ FT: 9,500
SALES (est): 1.5MM **Privately Held**
SIC: 8748 3625 5075 5084 Business
　consulting; control equipment, electric;
　warm air heating & air conditioning; indus-
　trial machinery & equipment; boilers,
　power (industrial); oil burners

(G-10859)
INNOVATIVE BUILDING SYSTEMS, L (PA)
4900 Ritter Rd Ste 130 (17055-6929)
PHONE..................................717 458-1400
EMP: 12
SALES (est): 73.3MM **Privately Held**
SIC: 2452 Prefabricated wood buildings

(G-10860)
JUMPERS SHOE SERVICE
106 E Main St Frnt (17055-3822)
PHONE..................................717 766-3422
Rodger M Jumper, *Partner*
EMP: 4
SQ FT: 840
SALES: 80K **Privately Held**
SIC: 3842 5661 Extension shoes, orthope-
　dic; shoe stores

(G-10861)
K-SYSTEMS INC
2104 Aspen Dr (17055-5507)
P.O. Box 1459 (17055-1459)
PHONE..................................717 795-7711
Joseph Kuhn, *President*
EMP: 19
SQ FT: 5,400
SALES: 4.5MM **Privately Held**
SIC: 7372 7373 Prepackaged software;
　value-added resellers, computer systems

(G-10862)
KEEBLER COMPANY
5045 Ritter Rd (17055-4884)
PHONE..................................717 790-9886
Robert E Dunham, *Manager*
EMP: 18
SALES (corp-wide): 13.5B **Publicly Held**
WEB: www.keebler.com
SIC: 2052 Cookies
HQ: Keebler Company
　1 Kellogg Sq
　Battle Creek MI 49017
　269 961-2000

(G-10863)
KEYSCRIPTS LLC
1970 Technology Pkwy (17050-8507)
PHONE..................................866 446-2848
Raymond W Hoover Jr, *President*
EMP: 3 EST: 2006
SALES (est): 330K **Privately Held**
SIC: 3841 8082 5047 Diagnostic appara-
　tus, medical; home health care services;
　medical equipment & supplies

(G-10864)
KEYSTONE SIGN SYSTEMS INC
Also Called: Central Sign Systems
703 W Simpson St Ste 1 (17055-3708)
PHONE..................................717 319-2265
Darby Miller, *President*
EMP: 7
SALES (est): 791.3K **Privately Held**
WEB: www.centralsignsystems.com
SIC: 3993 Signs, not made in custom sign
　painting shops

(G-10865)
KNOCK ON WOODWORK
320 Contemdra Dr (17055-7513)
PHONE..................................717 579-8179
Gregory S Dorie, *Principal*
EMP: 8 EST: 2010
SALES (est): 937.2K **Privately Held**
SIC: 2431 Millwork

▲ = Import ▼=Export
◆ =Import/Export

(G-10866)
LOT MADE GALLERY LLC
43 W Main St (17055-6262)
PHONE....................................717 458-8716
EMP: 3
SALES (est): 72.2K Privately Held
SIC: 8412 3211 Museum/Art Gallery Mfg
Flat Glass

(G-10867)
M & B MACHINE INC
10 Long Ln Ste 102 (17050-2676)
PHONE....................................717 766-7879
Jeffry Matesevac, President
Jeff Matesevac, Founder
EMP: 5
SQ FT: 2,000
SALES: 500K Privately Held
WEB: www.mbmachine.com
SIC: 3599 Machine shop, jobbing & repair

(G-10868)
MEREDITH BANZHOFF LLC (PA)
2308 Stumpstown Rd (17055-5784)
PHONE....................................717 919-5074
Meredith Banzhoff,
EMP: 3
SQ FT: 750
SALES (est): 198K Privately Held
SIC: 2331 2389 Blouses, women's & jun-
iors': made from purchased material; ap-
parel for handicapped

(G-10869)
MILLWOOD INC
435 Independence Ave (17055-5495)
PHONE....................................717 790-9118
Jeff Speese, Branch Mgr
EMP: 17 Privately Held
SIC: 3565 5084 Packaging machinery;
packaging machinery & equipment
PA: Millwood, Inc.
3708 International Blvd
Vienna OH 44473

(G-10870)
MINLEON INTL USA LTD LLC
4902 Carlisle Pike (17050-3079)
PHONE....................................717 991-1432
Dean Stiteler, Owner
▲ EMP: 3
SALES (est): 275.9K Privately Held
SIC: 3641 Electric light bulbs, complete

(G-10871)
MINNICH LIMITED
Also Called: Cumberland Printing Co
4 W Allen St (17055-6211)
PHONE....................................717 697-2204
Scott Minnich, President
EMP: 7
SQ FT: 4,000
SALES (est): 750K Privately Held
WEB: www.cprint.net
SIC: 2752 Commercial printing, offset

(G-10872)
NESTLE PURINA PETCARE COMPANY
Also Called: Nestle Purina Factory
6509 Brandy Ln (17050-2817)
P.O. Box 1190 (17055-1190)
PHONE....................................717 795-5454
John Bear, Branch Mgr
Craig Van Gundy, Maintence Staff
EMP: 240
SALES (corp-wide): 90.8B Privately Held
WEB: www.purina.com
SIC: 2047 2048 Dog & cat food; prepared
feeds
HQ: Nestle Purina Petcare Company
1 Checkerboard Sq
Saint Louis MO 63164
314 982-1000

(G-10873)
NEW HARRISBURG TRUCK BODY CO
408 Sheely Ln (17050-3605)
P.O. Box 568 (17055-0568)
PHONE....................................717 766-7651
W Stephen Forrest, President
Carol Forrest, Corp Secy
EMP: 45
SQ FT: 22,000

SALES (est): 7.4MM Privately Held
WEB: www.nhtbco.com
SIC: 7538 5012 3713 General automotive
repair shops; truck bodies; truck & bus
bodies

(G-10874)
NOVARTIS PHARMACEUTICALS CORP
300 Salem Church Rd (17050-2959)
PHONE....................................717 901-1916
Joe Hile, Manager
EMP: 7
SALES (corp-wide): 49.1B Privately Held
WEB: www.pharma.us.novartis.com
SIC: 2834 Pharmaceutical preparations
HQ: Novartis Pharmaceuticals Corporation
1 Health Plz
East Hanover NJ 07936
862 778-8300

(G-10875)
PATRIOT-NEWS CO (PA)
2020 Tech Pkwy Ste 300 (17050)
P.O. Box 2265, Harrisburg (17105-2265)
PHONE....................................717 255-8100
John Kirkpatrick, President
Kelly Gambini, Mfg Staff
EMP: 350 EST: 1965
SQ FT: 70,000
SALES (est): 55MM Privately Held
WEB: www.pennlive.com
SIC: 2711 Newspapers, publishing & print-
ing

(G-10876)
PATRIOT-NEWS CO
1900 Patriot Dr (17050-9405)
PHONE....................................717 255-8100
John Kirkpatrick, Branch Mgr
EMP: 7
SALES (corp-wide): 55MM Privately
Held
SIC: 2711 Newspapers: publishing only,
not printed on site
PA: The Patriot-News Co
2020 Tech Pkwy Ste 300
Mechanicsburg PA 17050
717 255-8100

(G-10877)
PATTON PICTURE COMPANY
Also Called: Patton Wall Decor
207 Lynndale Ct (17050-2805)
PHONE....................................717 796-1508
William A Patton, President
Scott Sanders, Vice Pres
Beth Bucher, Opers Mgr
Michael Clark, Engineer
Kelly Gorman, Design Engr
▲ EMP: 200
SALES (est): 34.5MM Privately Held
WEB: www.pattonpicture.com
SIC: 2499 5023 Picture & mirror frames,
wood; frames & framing, picture & mirror
HQ: Home Decor Holding Company
4325 Executive Dr Ste 150
Southaven MS 38672
662 996-2440

(G-10878)
PDQ PRINTING SERVICES
325 Hemlock Rd (17055-5822)
PHONE....................................717 691-4777
Jeffery Zinn, Owner
EMP: 5
SQ FT: 10,000
SALES: 425K Privately Held
SIC: 2759 Commercial printing

(G-10879)
PENNSY SUPPLY INC
5450 Carlisle Pike (17050-2411)
PHONE....................................717 766-7676
Mike Culver, Manager
EMP: 20
SALES (corp-wide): 29.7B Privately Held
SIC: 3273 Ready-mixed concrete
HQ: Pennsy Supply, Inc.
1001 Paxton St
Harrisburg PA 17104
717 233-4511

(G-10880)
PIN HSUN KUO
1041 Brookwood Dr (17055-6765)
PHONE....................................717 795-7297
Pin Hsun Kuo, Principal
EMP: 5 EST: 2009
SALES (est): 456.4K Privately Held
SIC: 3452 Pins

(G-10881)
PRECISION MEDICAL DEVICES INC
5020 Ritter Rd Ste 211 (17055-4837)
PHONE....................................717 795-9480
William M Murray, President
Wilson C Everhart Jr, Corp Secy
EMP: 7
SQ FT: 4,000
SALES (est): 520K Privately Held
WEB: www.precisionmedicaldevices.com
SIC: 3841 8731 Surgical & medical instru-
ments; commercial physical research

(G-10882)
PRINT-O-STAT INC
5040 Louise Dr (17055-4897)
PHONE....................................717 795-9255
Richard Laskowski, Owner
EMP: 12
SQ FT: 1,200
SALES (corp-wide): 100.1MM Privately
Held
WEB: www.digitalblueprinting.com
SIC: 7334 2752 5999 Blueprinting serv-
ice; commercial printing, offset; drafting
equipment & supplies
HQ: Print-O-Stat, Inc.
1011 W Market St
York PA 17404
717 812-9476

(G-10883)
RECKITT BENCKISER LLC
360 Independence Ave (17055-8306)
PHONE....................................717 506-0165
Rakesh Kapoor, CEO
Chris McGettigan, Principal
EMP: 140
SALES (corp-wide): 15.2B Privately Held
WEB: www.reckittprofessional.com
SIC: 2842 2035 Specialty cleaning, pol-
ishes & sanitation goods; pickles, sauces
& salad dressings
HQ: Reckitt Benckiser Llc
399 Interpace Pkwy # 101
Parsippany NJ 07054
973 404-2600

(G-10884)
REHOBOTH SIGNS
5221 Simpson Ferry Rd (17050-3532)
PHONE....................................717 458-8520
Maria Pasquel, Owner
EMP: 3 EST: 2011
SALES (est): 211.4K Privately Held
SIC: 3993 Signs, not made in custom sign
painting shops

(G-10885)
ROCK IT PRINTWEAR
416 Ricky Rd (17055-4976)
PHONE....................................717 697-3983
Mike Heimbuch, Co-Owner
EMP: 4
SALES (est): 238.3K Privately Held
SIC: 2759 Screen printing

(G-10886)
RYDER GRAPHICS
701 W Simpson St (17055-3716)
PHONE....................................717 697-0187
Scott Ryder, Owner
EMP: 3
SALES: 225K Privately Held
WEB: www.rydergraphics.com
SIC: 3993 Signs & advertising specialties

(G-10887)
SGRIGNOLI BROTHERS
97 Texaco Rd (17050-2623)
PHONE....................................717 766-2812
Vince Sgrignoli, Partner
EMP: 5
SQ FT: 3,200

SALES (est): 410K Privately Held
SIC: 3728 Military aircraft equipment & armament

(G-10888)
SHENK ATHLETIC EQUIPMENT CO (PA)
Also Called: Shenk Company
5010 E Trindle Rd Ste 203 (17050-3631)
PHONE....................................717 766-6600
Owen P Shenk, President
Michael Girard Shenk, Treasurer
Judith C Shenk, Admin Sec
EMP: 10
SQ FT: 13,000
SALES (est): 38.8MM Privately Held
SIC: 2261 2396 2395 Screen printing of
cotton broadwoven fabrics; automotive &
apparel trimmings; pleating & stitching

(G-10889)
SLOAN VALVE COMPANY
5031 Richard Ln Ste 101 (17055-6904)
PHONE....................................717 387-3959
EMP: 5
SALES (corp-wide): 222.9MM Privately
Held
SIC: 3592 Mfg Carburetors/Pistons/Rings
PA: Sloan Valve Company
10500 Seymour Ave
Franklin Park IL 60131
847 671-4300

(G-10890)
SMART FUELS LLC
2145 Canterbury Dr (17055-5769)
PHONE....................................717 645-8983
Cynthia Poiesz, Principal
EMP: 3 EST: 2017
SALES (est): 183.4K Privately Held
SIC: 2869 Fuels

(G-10891)
STANHOPE MICROWORKS
614 Apple Dr (17055-3471)
PHONE....................................717 796-9000
Michael Shiebley, Owner
EMP: 3
SALES (est): 110K Privately Held
SIC: 5947 3861 Novelties; photographic
equipment & supplies

(G-10892)
SUNBURY PRESS
50 W Main St (17055-6249)
P.O. Box 548, Boiling Springs (17007-
0548)
PHONE....................................717 254-7274
Lawrence Knorr, Principal
Jennifer Cappello, Editor
EMP: 4 EST: 2013
SALES (est): 273.8K Privately Held
SIC: 2741 Miscellaneous publishing

(G-10893)
SWEET JUBILEE GOURMET
275 Mulberry Dr (17050-3174)
PHONE....................................717 691-9782
EMP: 6
SALES (est): 571.6K Privately Held
SIC: 2066 Chocolate & cocoa products

(G-10894)
TAYLOR-WHARTON INTL LLC
4718 Old Gettysburg Rd # 300
(17055-8414)
PHONE....................................717 763-5060
Eric Rottier, CEO
EMP: 3
SALES (est): 158.1K Privately Held
SIC: 3491 Gas valves & parts, industrial

(G-10895)
TE CONNECTIVITY CORPORATION
1311 S Market St (17055-5632)
PHONE....................................717 691-5842
Garry Calhoun, Manager
EMP: 79
SALES (corp-wide): 13.1B Privately Held
WEB: www.raychem.com
SIC: 3679 5065 4226 Electronic circuits;
electronic parts & equipment; special
warehousing & storage

HQ: Te Connectivity Corporation
1050 Westlakes Dr
Berwyn PA 19312
610 893-9800

(G-10896)
TERRANETTIS ITALIAN BAKERY
844 W Trindle Rd (17055-4079)
PHONE..................................717 697-5434
Terrence Mc Mahon, *President*
Thomas Mc Mahon, *Opers Mgr*
Timothy McMahon, *Plant Engr*
Timothy Mc Mahon, *Admin Sec*
EMP: 50
SQ FT: 25,000
SALES (est): 8.3MM **Privately Held**
WEB: www.terranettis.com
SIC: 5149 2051 Bakery products; bread, cake & related products

(G-10897)
TICKET COUNTER
4902 Carlisle Pike (17050-3079)
PHONE..................................717 536-3092
Robin Urbach, *Principal*
EMP: 3
SALES (est): 254K **Privately Held**
SIC: 3131 Counters

(G-10898)
TORCHBEARER SAUCES LLC
1110 E Powderhorn Rd (17050-2002)
PHONE..................................717 697-3568
David Lynch, *Mng Member*
Tom Lynch,
Tricia Lynch,
Ben Smith,
Tim Wortman,
EMP: 5
SALES (est): 683.8K **Privately Held**
WEB: www.torchbearersauces.com
SIC: 2099 Sauces: dry mixes

(G-10899)
TRAFCON INDUSTRIES INC
81 Texaco Rd (17050-2665)
PHONE..................................717 691-8007
Shawn Gallagher, *President*
Scott Ward, *General Mgr*
Matthew Johnson, *Vice Pres*
Don Eisenhower, *Purch Mgr*
Joseph Devers, *Controller*
▲ **EMP:** 25
SQ FT: 35,000
SALES (est): 4.1MM **Privately Held**
SIC: 3993 Signs, not made in custom sign painting shops

(G-10900)
TURRI ASSOCIATES INCORPORATED
Also Called: Advanced Coating Technology
327 W Allen St (17055-6248)
PHONE..................................717 795-9936
Joseph Turri Jr, *President*
Jon Taylor, *Prdtn Mgr*
Kathleen Groome, *Office Mgr*
EMP: 17
SQ FT: 29,739
SALES (est): 2.1MM **Privately Held**
WEB:
www.advancedcoatingtechnology.com
SIC: 3479 Coating of metals & formed products

(G-10901)
UAV AVIATION SERVICES
827 W Trindle Rd (17055-4058)
PHONE..................................717 691-8882
Gary Kopperman, *CEO*
Benjamin Smith, *President*
EMP: 4
SALES (est): 95.7K **Privately Held**
SIC: 7389 1389 8713 Pipeline & power line inspection service; servicing oil & gas wells;

(G-10902)
UNIGRAPHICS COMMUNICATIONS
1 Jeffrey Rd (17050-6805)
PHONE..................................717 697-8132
Brigitte Benedict, *Owner*
EMP: 3 **EST:** 1972
SQ FT: 4,000

SALES: 150K **Privately Held**
SIC: 2752 Commercial printing, offset

(G-10903)
UNIVERSAL PROTECTIVE PACKG INC (PA)
61 Texaco Rd (17050-2623)
PHONE..................................717 766-1578
Rodney Rumberger, *President*
Timothy Ritter, *Vice Pres*
Robert Wineland, *CFO*
◆ **EMP:** 75
SQ FT: 70,000
SALES (est): 16.1MM **Privately Held**
WEB: www.uppi.com
SIC: 3089 3411 2671 Plastic containers, except foam; metal cans; packaging paper & plastics film, coated & laminated

(G-10904)
VERSATILE CREDIT INC
4900 Ritter Rd Ste 100 (17055-6930)
PHONE..................................800 851-1281
Michael May, *CEO*
Sam Mittelstaedt, *Marketing Staff*
EMP: 25
SALES (est): 15.8MM
SALES (corp-wide): 15.9MM **Privately Held**
WEB: www.poss.com
SIC: 7372 Prepackaged software
PA: Mass Ventures Holdings 1 Corporation
308 Congress St Fl 5
Boston MA 02210
617 723-4920

(G-10905)
WAVELINE DIRECT LLC
192 Hempt Rd (17050-2668)
PHONE..................................717 795-8830
Stewart Taylor,
Brenda Kern, *Graphic Designe*
Vinnie Taylor,
EMP: 50
SQ FT: 16,300
SALES (est): 8.7MM **Privately Held**
WEB: www.printingbuyersguide.com
SIC: 2752 Commercial printing, offset

(G-10906)
WENDELLS PRFMCE TRCK SP LLC
Also Called: Line-X of Cumberland County
5253 Simpson Ferry Rd (17050-3541)
PHONE..................................717 458-8404
Wendell B Chilcote, *Mng Member*
EMP: 3
SQ FT: 2,480
SALES (est): 721.3K **Privately Held**
SIC: 5013 2851 5169 Body repair or paint shop supplies, automotive; undercoatings, paint; lacquers, varnishes, enamels & other coatings; polyurethane coatings; anti-corrosion products

(G-10907)
WESKEM TECHNOLOGIES INC
Also Called: Stevenson Machine Shop
49 Texaco Rd (17050-2623)
PHONE..................................717 697-8228
Wayne Stevenson, *President*
EMP: 5
SQ FT: 6,000
SALES (est): 708.9K **Privately Held**
SIC: 3599 Machine shop, jobbing & repair

(G-10908)
WEST SHORE PRTG & DIST CORP
304 Mulberry Dr (17050-3108)
PHONE..................................717 691-8282
Robert Bruckner, *President*
EMP: 20
SQ FT: 15,000
SALES (est): 3.4MM **Privately Held**
SIC: 2752 Commercial printing, offset

(G-10909)
WESTROCK RKT COMPANY
Also Called: Alliance Display
300 Salem Church Rd (17050-2959)
PHONE..................................717 790-1596
EMP: 8
SALES (corp-wide): 14.1B **Publicly Held**
SIC: 2653 Mfg Paper Products

HQ: Westrock Rkt Company
504 Thrasher St
Norcross GA 30328
770 448-2193

(G-10910)
WILLIAM A FRASER INC
5521 Carlisle Pike (17050-2419)
PHONE..................................717 766-1126
John Martin, *Sales Executive*
EMP: 17
SALES (corp-wide): 47.6MM **Privately Held**
SIC: 3579 Mailing, letter handling & addressing machines
PA: William A. Fraser Inc.
320 Penn Ave
Reading PA 19611
610 378-0101

Mechanicsville
Bucks County

(G-10911)
DEK MACHINE CO INC
4794 Mechanicsville Rd (18934-9506)
PHONE..................................215 794-5791
Walter Breithaupt, *President*
EMP: 3 **EST:** 2000
SALES (est): 322K **Privately Held**
SIC: 3449 Miscellaneous metalwork

(G-10912)
MC MAHON WELDING INC
Also Called: McMahon's Welding
5248 Mechanicsville Rd (18934-9511)
P.O. Box 386 (18934-0386)
PHONE..................................215 794-0260
Scott Mc Mahon, *CEO*
EMP: 6
SQ FT: 9,000
SALES (est): 697.3K **Privately Held**
SIC: 1761 3444 Sheet metalwork; sheet metalwork

Media
Delaware County

(G-10913)
ACRYMAX TECHNOLOGIES INC
221 Brooke St (19063-3699)
PHONE..................................610 566-7470
Scott Bennung, *President*
EMP: 10 **EST:** 1951
SQ FT: 20,000
SALES (est): 2.3MM **Privately Held**
WEB: www.acrymax.com
SIC: 2899 2891 Chemical preparations; adhesives

(G-10914)
ADM PUBLICATIONS INC
326 W State St (19063-2616)
P.O. Box 132, Thornton (19373-0132)
PHONE..................................610 565-8895
Fax: 610 566-5854
EMP: 4 **EST:** 1994
SQ FT: 1,000
SALES: 350K **Privately Held**
SIC: 2759 7336 Graphic Design & Commercial Printing

(G-10915)
BEVANS CANDIES INC
Also Called: Bevan's Own Make Candies
141 E Baltimore Ave # 143 (19063-3427)
PHONE..................................610 566-0581
Randy Bevan, *President*
EMP: 12 **EST:** 1959
SQ FT: 1,000
SALES (est): 1.5MM **Privately Held**
SIC: 2064 5441 2066 Candy & other confectionery products; candy; chocolate & cocoa products

(G-10916)
BROWN INDUSTRIES INC
344 W Front St Ste 100 (19063-2640)
PHONE..................................610 544-8888
Amber L Flynn, *President*
Edward J Ardis Jr, *Vice Pres*

Tim Holt, *Human Res Mgr*
Robert Grasberger, *Director*
Alice L Ardis, *Admin Sec*
EMP: 20 **EST:** 1946
SQ FT: 15,000
SALES (est): 3.3MM **Privately Held**
WEB: www.browninc.com
SIC: 3911 Jewelry, precious metal

(G-10917)
CEDAR FOREST PRODUCTS COMPANY (PA)
Also Called: Farmer's Lumber & Supply Co.
27 E Forge Rd (19063-4346)
PHONE..................................815 946-3994
Donald W Much, *President*
EMP: 12 **EST:** 1988
SQ FT: 60,000
SALES (est): 1.6MM **Privately Held**
WEB: www.cedarforestproducts.com
SIC: 2452 5211 1521 1542 Prefabricated wood buildings; lumber & other building materials; new construction, single-family houses; commercial & office building contractors; farm building construction

(G-10918)
CHESAPEAKE DEL BREWING CO LLC
Also Called: Iron Hill Brewery & Restaurant
30 E State St (19063-2904)
PHONE..................................610 627-9000
Eric Maney, *Manager*
EMP: 120
SALES (corp-wide): 20.1MM **Privately Held**
WEB: www.ironhillbrewery.com
SIC: 5812 5813 2082 American restaurant; drinking places; malt beverages
PA: Chesapeake & Delaware Brewing Company Llc
2502 W 6th St
Wilmington DE 19805
302 888-2739

(G-10919)
COUNTRY PRESS INC
Also Called: Lima Quick Print
10 S Pennell Rd (19063-5715)
P.O. Box 10 (19063-0010)
PHONE..................................610 565-8808
Keith M Cox, *President*
EMP: 10 **EST:** 1956
SQ FT: 3,800
SALES (est): 1.7MM **Privately Held**
WEB: www.countrypressonline.com
SIC: 2752 Commercial printing, offset

(G-10920)
DELAWARE COUNTY PENNSYLVANIA
Also Called: County Delaware, The
201 W Front St Frnt (19063-2700)
PHONE..................................610 891-4865
Barbara Hatton, *Regional Mgr*
Beverlee Barnes, *Manager*
Grace Speck, *Supervisor*
Evelyn Yancoskie, *Director*
Patrick Oconnell, *Director*
EMP: 7 **Privately Held**
SIC: 3823 Industrial process measurement equipment
PA: Delaware County, Pennsylvania
201 W Front St
Media PA 19063
610 891-4000

(G-10921)
DIGITAL DESIGNED SOLUTIONS LLC
96 E Lincoln St (19063-3765)
P.O. Box 1857 (19063-8857)
PHONE..................................484 440-9665
Adam Creed,
Margarette Creed,
EMP: 4 **EST:** 2017
SQ FT: 6,000
SALES: 80K **Privately Held**
SIC: 2599 Boards: planning, display, notice

(G-10922)
DIVERSIFIED MODULAR CASEWORK
60 State Rd Ste A (19063-1452)
PHONE..................................484 442-8007

▲ = Import ▼=Export
◆ =Import/Export

GEOGRAPHIC

William Henderson, *President*
EMP: 3
SQ FT: 2,400
SALES (est): 430.9K **Privately Held**
WEB: www.dmclabs.com
SIC: 3821 Laboratory apparatus & furniture

(G-10923)
ELIZABETH C BAKER
Also Called: Baker Print Design
10 W State St (19063-3311)
PHONE...............................610 566-0691
Elizabeth C Baker, *Owner*
EMP: 10 EST: 1922
SQ FT: 6,000
SALES (est): 1.4MM **Privately Held**
WEB: www.baker-printing.com
SIC: 2752 7334 Commercial printing, offset; photocopying & duplicating services

(G-10924)
FOAMEX INTERNATIONAL INC
1400 N Providence Rd (19063-2043)
PHONE...............................610 744-2300
John G Johnson Jr, *President*
James B Gamache, *Chairman*
Paul A Haslanger, *Exec VP*
Darrell Nance, *Exec VP*
Robert S Graham, *Senior VP*
◆ EMP: 160
SQ FT: 47,000
SALES (est): 140.2MM **Privately Held**
WEB: www.foamex.com
SIC: 3086 Carpet & rug cushions, foamed plastic
PA: Fxi Holdings, Inc.
     1400 N Providence Rd # 2000
     Media PA 19063

(G-10925)
FOAMEX LP (PA)
1400 N Providence Rd # 2000
(19063-2081)
PHONE...............................610 565-2374
Raymond Maybus, *Partner*
Gregory Ciston, *Partner*
▲ EMP: 85
SQ FT: 45,000
SALES (est): 385.3MM **Privately Held**
SIC: 3086 Carpet & rug cushions, foamed plastic

(G-10926)
FXI INC (HQ)
Also Called: Rose Tree Corporate Center II
1400 N Providence Rd # 2000
(19063-2081)
PHONE...............................610 744-2300
John Cowles, *President*
David J Prilutski, *COO*
Donald W Phillips, *Exec VP*
Kurt W Werth, *Exec VP*
Robert Dimartino, *Senior VP*
◆ EMP: 101
SALES (est): 1B **Privately Held**
SIC: 3086 Carpet & rug cushions, foamed plastic

(G-10927)
FXI BUILDING PRODUCTS CORP
1400 N Providence Rd # 2000
(19063-2043)
PHONE...............................610 744-2230
John G Johnson, *President*
Andrew Prusky, *President*
David J Prilutski, *COO*
Donald W Phillips, *Exec VP*
EMP: 204
SALES (est): 48MM **Privately Held**
SIC: 3069 Foam rubber
HQ: Fxi, Inc.
     1400 N Providence Rd # 2000
     Media PA 19063

(G-10928)
FXI HOLDINGS INC (PA)
Also Called: Fxi Foamex Innovations
1400 N Providence Rd # 2000
(19063-2081)
PHONE...............................610 744-2300
John Cowles, *President*
David M Minning, *General Mgr*
John M Smail Jr, *General Mgr*
Philippe Knaub, *Senior VP*
Andrew R Prusky, *Senior VP*
▼ EMP: 101

SALES (est): 1.2B **Privately Held**
SIC: 3086 Carpet & rug cushions, foamed plastic

(G-10929)
GLEN MILLS SAND & GRAVEL INC
Also Called: Big Trucking Co
5400 Pennell Rd (19063-6511)
PHONE...............................610 459-4988
Bruce Snyder, *President*
EMP: 25
SQ FT: 8,000
SALES (est): 5.4MM **Privately Held**
SIC: 5032 5031 1442 Sand, construction; gravel; building materials, exterior; building materials, interior; lumber: rough, dressed & finished; construction sand & gravel

(G-10930)
GREEN SCENES LANDSCAPE INC
520 S Old Middletown Rd (19063-4910)
PHONE...............................610 566-3154
David Zawisza, *President*
Renee Zawisza, *Admin Sec*
EMP: 3
SALES (est): 324.6K **Privately Held**
SIC: 3271 Blocks, concrete: landscape or retaining wall

(G-10931)
GROKAS INC
722 Hemlock Rd (19063-1710)
PHONE...............................610 565-1498
Chris Grossi, *Corp Secy*
Joe Grossi, *Manager*
EMP: 10
SALES (est): 849.8K **Privately Held**
SIC: 3585 Air conditioning units, complete: domestic or industrial

(G-10932)
H & P MANUFACTURING
41 S New Middletown Rd (19063-4601)
PHONE...............................610 565-7344
Ronald Geoffrey Pridham, *President*
Alan Hooper, *Vice Pres*
EMP: 3
SALES (est): 100K **Privately Held**
SIC: 3441 Fabricated structural metal

(G-10933)
H&K GROUP INC
Pyramid Hardscape & Ldscp Sups
414 W Knowlton Rd (19063-5964)
PHONE...............................610 494-5364
Haines Kibbles, *Branch Mgr*
EMP: 29
SALES (corp-wide): 71.6MM **Privately Held**
SIC: 3271 Architectural concrete: block, split, fluted, screen, etc.
PA: H&K Group, Inc.
     2052 Lucon Rd
     Skippack PA 19474
     610 584-8500

(G-10934)
INTERFORM CORPORATION
Also Called: Consolidated Graphic Comm
7046 Snow Drift Rd (19063)
PHONE...............................610 566-1515
Craig Lafreniere, *Principal*
EMP: 10 **Publicly Held**
WEB: www.interformsolutions.com
SIC: 5943 2759 Office forms & supplies; promotional printing
HQ: Interform Corporation
     1901 Mayview Rd
     Bridgeville PA 15017
     412 221-7321

(G-10935)
KRAS CORPORATION
Also Called: Kras Worldwide
2 Old Mill Ln (19063-4238)
PHONE...............................610 566-0271
Lawrence L Plummer Sr, *Ch of Bd*
EMP: 20 EST: 1960
SQ FT: 15,000

SALES (est): 7MM **Privately Held**
SIC: 3559 5084 Electronic component making machinery; plastics working machinery; industrial machinery & equipment; hydraulic systems equipment & supplies

(G-10936)
LASERSENSE INC
230 N Monroe St (19063-2908)
PHONE...............................856 207-5701
John Zarroli, *President*
EMP: 5
SALES (est): 463.1K **Privately Held**
WEB: www.lasersense.net
SIC: 3829 Measuring & controlling devices

(G-10937)
MAGUIRE PRODUCTS INC
400 W Knowlton Rd (19063-5964)
PHONE...............................610 494-6566
F B Maguire, *Branch Mgr*
EMP: 3
SALES (corp-wide): 11.9MM **Privately Held**
WEB: www.maguire.com
SIC: 3824 Fluid meters & counting devices
PA: Maguire Products, Inc.
     11 Crozerville Rd
     Aston PA 19014
     610 459-4300

(G-10938)
MEDIA QUARRY CO INC
500 Beatty Rd (19063-1614)
P.O. Box 667 (19063-0667)
PHONE...............................610 566-6667
John W Scala, *President*
EMP: 25 EST: 1954
SALES (est): 2.6MM **Privately Held**
SIC: 1411 3281 Dimension stone; cut stone & stone products

(G-10939)
METRO MANUFACTURING & SUPPLY (PA)
524 N Providence Rd (19063-3056)
PHONE...............................610 891-1899
Harry C Noerenberg, *President*
EMP: 7
SQ FT: 3,500
SALES (est): 3.1MM **Privately Held**
WEB: www.metromfginc.com
SIC: 3465 5013 Body parts, automobile: stamped metal; motor vehicle supplies & new parts

(G-10940)
NEW VIEW GIFTS & ACC LTD (PA)
311 E Baltimore Ave # 300 (19063-3500)
PHONE...............................610 627-0190
Sied Narzikul, *CEO*
John J Brennan, *President*
Ann Marie Mendlow, *Exec VP*
◆ EMP: 35
SQ FT: 8,000
SALES (est): 8MM **Privately Held**
SIC: 3499 Giftware, brass goods; giftware, copper goods

(G-10941)
ODHNER CORPORATION
400 W Knowlton Rd (19063-5964)
PHONE...............................610 364-3200
Roy Hollabaugh, *President*
Lou Fow, *Vice Pres*
Jerry Horner, *Vice Pres*
EMP: 3
SQ FT: 2,460
SALES (est): 190K **Privately Held**
WEB: www.skybrush.com
SIC: 3952 Eraser guides & shields

(G-10942)
PAYSERV INC
104 W Front St (19063-3208)
PHONE...............................610 524-3251
Jay Schneider, *Owner*
EMP: 4
SALES (est): 360.9K **Privately Held**
WEB: www.payservinc.com
SIC: 7372 8721 Prepackaged software; accounting, auditing & bookkeeping

(G-10943)
PORTICO GROUP LLC
Also Called: Media Copy
11 E State St Ste 1 (19063-2935)
PHONE...............................610 566-8499
Richard Lee,
Jeffrey Plourde,
EMP: 6
SQ FT: 1,500
SALES (est): 800.9K **Privately Held**
WEB: www.mediacopyonline.com
SIC: 2752 7334 5999 Commercial printing, offset; photocopying & duplicating services; business machines & equipment

(G-10944)
PROFESSIONAL DUPLICATING INC (PA)
33 E State St (19063-2917)
P.O. Box 1910 (19063-8910)
PHONE...............................610 891-7979
Thomas Hgregory, *President*
Thomas Gregory Sr, *President*
Lori Gasorowski, *Bookkeeper*
Joe Spaventa, *Manager*
Larry Clark, *Executive*
EMP: 20
SQ FT: 3,000
SALES (est): 3.3MM **Privately Held**
WEB: www.produpe.com
SIC: 2752 Commercial printing, offset

(G-10945)
PROTEUS OPTICS LLC
4 Locust Ln (19063-1733)
PHONE...............................215 204-5241
Robert J Levis, *President*
EMP: 6
SALES: 1,000K **Privately Held**
WEB: www.proteusoptics.com
SIC: 3827 Optical instruments & lenses

(G-10946)
ROBERTS FILTER HOLDING COMPANY (PA)
Also Called: Robert Water Technologies
214 N Jackson St (19063-2807)
PHONE...............................610 583-3131
R Lee Roberts, *President*
Matthew Roberts, *Vice Pres*
Michelle Guerrero, *Plant Mgr*
Roderick Mellott, *Production*
Andre Razeek, *Engineer*
EMP: 4
SQ FT: 40,000
SALES (est): 5.5MM **Privately Held**
WEB: www.robertsfiltergroup.com
SIC: 3589 Water treatment equipment, industrial; sewage treatment equipment

(G-10947)
SANDA CORPORATION
19 W Third St (19063-2803)
PHONE...............................502 510-8782
Trude Sadtler, *President*
EMP: 3
SQ FT: 2,000
SALES (est): 348.3K **Privately Held**
WEB: www.sanda.com
SIC: 3826 2869 Titrimeters; industrial organic chemicals

(G-10948)
SERENDIB IMPORTS INC
116 Moore Dr (19063-4955)
PHONE...............................610 203-3070
Meghan Edge, *President*
EMP: 2
SALES (est): 1.5MM **Privately Held**
SIC: 3949 Winter sports equipment

(G-10949)
SERVICES UNLIMITED MSTR PRTG
451 W Baltimore Ave (19063-2610)
P.O. Box 1801 (19063-8801)
PHONE...............................610 891-7877
William T Mulloney, *President*
Joan Mulloney, *President*
EMP: 6
SALES: 420K **Privately Held**
SIC: 2752 2759 Color lithography; commercial printing

(G-10950)
SINCLAIR TECHNOLOGIES LLC
200 E State St Ste 301 (19063-3434)
PHONE....................................610 296-8259
Lawrence Husick, *Professor*
EMP: 3
SALES (est): 321.2K **Privately Held**
SIC: 7372 Application computer software

(G-10951)
STERLING-FLEISCHMAN INC
198 Martins Run (19063-1042)
PHONE....................................610 647-1717
Stephen Fleischman, *President*
Ruth Fleischman, *Admin Sec*
EMP: 10 EST: 1955
SQ FT: 13,000
SALES (est): 1MM **Privately Held**
SIC: 3537 3312 Cradles, drum; stainless steel

(G-10952)
TED J TEDESCO
Also Called: Tedesco & Son Products
473 Linville Rd (19063-5429)
PHONE....................................215 316-8303
Ted J Tedesco, *Owner*
Barbara Cross-Tedesco, *Treasurer*
EMP: 6
SQ FT: 3,000
SALES: 950K **Privately Held**
SIC: 3672 Printed circuit boards

(G-10953)
TERRASOURCE GLOBAL CORPORATION
1400 N Providence Rd # 3000 (19063-2060)
PHONE....................................610 544-7200
Ernest Oliver, *Branch Mgr*
Andrew Mikula, *Director*
EMP: 45 **Publicly Held**
SIC: 3532 Mining machinery
HQ: Terrasource Global Corporation
100 N Broadway Ste 1600
Saint Louis MO 63102
618 641-6966

(G-10954)
TIN ROOF ENTERPRISES LLC
342 W Second St (19063-2302)
PHONE....................................610 659-3989
Bradley D Good, *Principal*
EMP: 3 EST: 2007
SALES (est): 160K **Privately Held**
SIC: 3356 Tin

(G-10955)
ULTIMATE SCREW MACHINE PDTS
641 Painter St (19063-3624)
PHONE....................................610 565-1565
Andre Horne, *Owner*
EMP: 4
SQ FT: 3,000
SALES (est): 516.5K **Privately Held**
WEB: www.ultimatescrew.com
SIC: 3451 5941 Screw machine products; sporting goods & bicycle shops

(G-10956)
VEGA APPLICATIONS DEVELOPMENT
176 S New Middletown Rd # 204 (19063-5255)
P.O. Box 502, Glen Riddle Lima (19037-0502)
PHONE....................................610 892-1812
Michael L Brachman, *President*
EMP: 6
SQ FT: 3,000
SALES (est): 469.4K **Privately Held**
WEB: www.vegadevelopment.com
SIC: 7371 7372 Computer software development; prepackaged software

---

Mehoopany
Wyoming County

(G-10957)
PROCTER & GAMBLE PAPER PDTS CO
Rr 87 (18629)
PHONE....................................570 833-5141
Alex Fried, *Vice Pres*
Raul Moliva, *Manager*
Jody Wells, *Manager*
Don Sutton, *Senior Mgr*
EMP: 302
SALES (corp-wide): 66.8B **Publicly Held**
SIC: 2676 Towels, paper: made from purchased paper
HQ: The Procter & Gamble Paper Products Company
1 Procter And Gamble Plz
Cincinnati OH 45202
513 983-1100

Mercer
Mercer County

(G-10958)
ABB INSTALLATION PRODUCTS INC
Also Called: Thomas & Betts
150 Mckinley Ave (16137-1326)
PHONE....................................724 662-4400
Mike Sherd, *Branch Mgr*
EMP: 457
SALES (corp-wide): 34.3B **Privately Held**
WEB: www.tnb.com
SIC: 3433 Space heaters, except electric
HQ: Abb Installation Products Inc.
860 Ridge Lake Blvd
Memphis TN 38120
901 252-5000

(G-10959)
AMERICANA ART CHINA CO INC (PA)
316 Manito Trl (16137-9326)
PHONE....................................330 938-6133
Joan Mercer, *President*
Deborah Estell, *Principal*
James P Puckett, *Corp Secy*
EMP: 14 EST: 1948
SQ FT: 30,000
SALES: 1.5MM **Privately Held**
SIC: 5199 3269 3993 3231 Glassware, novelty; decalcomania work on china & glass; firing & decorating china; signs & advertising specialties; products of purchased glass

(G-10960)
CARRIERS WRECKERS BY KIMES
7294 W Market St (16137-6602)
PHONE....................................724 342-2930
Ron Kimes, *President*
Mary K Ondick, *Treasurer*
EMP: 5
SQ FT: 6,100
SALES: 184.6K **Privately Held**
SIC: 1541 3711 Truck & automobile assembly plant construction; chassis, motor vehicle

(G-10961)
EAST PENN TRUCK EQP W INC
7298 W Market St (16137-6602)
PHONE....................................724 342-1800
John H Oberly III, *President*
Casey Smith, *Vice Pres*
Amy Persing, *Office Mgr*
EMP: 9 EST: 2007
SQ FT: 26,000
SALES (est): 5MM **Privately Held**
SIC: 5531 5511 3713 Automotive parts; automobiles, new & used; truck & bus bodies

---

(G-10962)
HAPEMAN ELECTRONICS INC (PA)
761 N Cottage Rd (16137-5309)
PHONE....................................724 475-2033
Bryan Hapeman, *President*
Sheri Hapeman, *Admin Sec*
EMP: 6
SQ FT: 10,000
SALES (est): 1.1MM **Privately Held**
WEB: www.hapeman.com
SIC: 7373 3825 8711 Office computer automation systems integration; digital test equipment, electronic & electrical circuits; engineering services

(G-10963)
HOWARD & SON MEATPACKING
8392 Sharon Mercer Rd (16137-3162)
PHONE....................................724 662-3700
Darrel Howard, *Owner*
EMP: 3
SALES (est): 200.3K **Privately Held**
SIC: 2011 Meat packing plants

(G-10964)
IMPERIAL SYSTEMS INC
7320 W Market St (16137-6604)
PHONE....................................724 662-2801
Richard J Wann, *President*
EMP: 31
SQ FT: 6,250
SALES (est): 10.7MM **Privately Held**
SIC: 3564 Dust or fume collecting equipment, industrial

(G-10965)
INTERSTATE SELF STORAGE
Also Called: U-Haul
410 N Cottage Rd (16137-5304)
PHONE....................................724 662-1186
Judy McQuiston, *Owner*
EMP: 3
SALES (est): 210.8K **Privately Held**
SIC: 2511 3993 4225 7513 Storage chests, household: wood; signs & advertising specialties; warehousing, self-storage; truck rental & leasing, no drivers

(G-10966)
LEGGETT & PLATT INCORPORATED
966 Perry Hwy (16137-3622)
PHONE....................................724 748-3057
Jimmy Prinos, *Branch Mgr*
EMP: 92
SALES (corp-wide): 4.2B **Publicly Held**
SIC: 2515 Box springs, assembled
PA: Leggett & Platt, Incorporated
1 Leggett Rd
Carthage MO 64836
417 358-8131

(G-10967)
LISA THOMAS
Also Called: North Pittsburgh Steel
1046 Perry Hwy (16137-3628)
PHONE....................................724 748-3600
Lisa Thomas, *Owner*
EMP: 3
SALES (est): 176K **Privately Held**
SIC: 3325 Steel foundries

(G-10968)
MERCER FORGE CORPORATION (DH)
Also Called: Fia
315 S Erie St Ste E (16137-1555)
PHONE....................................724 662-2750
James Ackerman, *President*
▲ EMP: 150
SQ FT: 130,000
SALES (est): 47.6MM
SALES (corp-wide): 433.9MM **Privately Held**
WEB: www.mercerforge.com
SIC: 3462 Iron & steel forgings
HQ: Neenah Foundry Company
2121 Brooks Ave
Neenah WI 54956
920 725-7000

(G-10969)
MOBILE MEDICAL INNOVATIONS
700 Coolspring Church Rd (16137-4822)
PHONE....................................724 646-2200
Brian Nount, *President*
Eric Nount, *Admin Sec*
EMP: 3
SQ FT: 6,000
SALES (est): 366.5K **Privately Held**
WEB: www.mobilemedicalinnovations.com
SIC: 3845 Electromedical equipment

(G-10970)
RAIL CAR SERVICE CO (PA)
Also Called: Pennsylvania Rail Car Co
584 Fairground Rd (16137-5113)
P.O. Box 129 (16137-0129)
PHONE....................................724 662-3660
Sam Ryan, *President*
Robert L Gilkey, *Vice Pres*
Dave Stanley, *Vice Pres*
Rick Winder, *Plant Mgr*
Dave Smith, *Sales Staff*
EMP: 9
SQ FT: 40,000
SALES (est): 8.1MM **Privately Held**
WEB: www.parailcar.com
SIC: 3743 Railroad equipment

(G-10971)
REZNOR LLC
150 Mckinley Ave (16137-1326)
PHONE....................................724 662-4400
Marcel Ferrere, *President*
Steve Mattocks, *Opers Mgr*
▲ EMP: 1321 EST: 2013
SALES (est): 292.7MM
SALES (corp-wide): 2.7B **Privately Held**
SIC: 3585 Heating equipment, complete
HQ: Nortek, Inc.
8000 Phoenix Pkwy
O Fallon MO 63368
636 561-7300

(G-10972)
RMS SYSTEMS INC
1850 Mercer Grove City Rd (16137-6336)
P.O. Box 507 (16137-0507)
PHONE....................................724 458-7580
Richard Slagle, *President*
W Kinsey, *Sales Executive*
EMP: 3
SQ FT: 1,000
SALES: 500K **Privately Held**
SIC: 8742 3571 Industry specialist consultants; electronic computers

(G-10973)
RUSSELL STANDARD CORPORATION
12 Penn Perry Hwy (16137)
P.O. Box 509 (16137-0509)
PHONE....................................724 748-3700
Bert Rodgers, *Manager*
EMP: 6
SALES (corp-wide): 195.6MM **Privately Held**
WEB: www.russellstandard.com
SIC: 2951 2819 Asphalt & asphaltic paving mixtures (not from refineries); industrial inorganic chemicals
PA: Russell Standard Corporation
285 Kappa Dr Ste 300
Pittsburgh PA 15238
412 449-0700

(G-10974)
SAFARI TOOLS INC
383 N Perry Hwy (16137-5043)
PHONE....................................717 350-9869
Nirmal Patel, *Partner*
EMP: 58 EST: 2016
SALES (est): 2.3MM **Privately Held**
SIC: 3462 Iron & steel forgings

(G-10975)
SHANNONS KANDY KITCHEN (PA)
225 N Erie St (16137-1101)
PHONE....................................724 662-5211
Lawrence Shannon, *Owner*
EMP: 3
SQ FT: 1,800

▲ = Import ▼=Export
◆ =Import/Export

SALES: 200K **Privately Held**
SIC: **2064** 5947 Chocolate candy, except solid chocolate; gift shop

(G-10976)
STEVENS CLOGGING SUPPLIES INC
49 Franklin Rd (16137-5117)
P.O. Box 112 (16137-0112)
PHONE....................................724 662-0808
Carolyn Stevens, *Principal*
EMP: 4
SALES (est): 437.8K **Privately Held**
SIC: **3131** Footwear cut stock

(G-10977)
VICIOUS CYCLE WORKS LLC
1684 Pulaski Mercer Rd (16137-3216)
PHONE....................................724 662-0581
Thomas A Davanzo Sr,
Tammy Davanzo,
EMP: 3
SALES: 280K **Privately Held**
WEB: www.viciouscycleworks.us
SIC: **3751** 7389 Motorcycles & related parts; design services

(G-10978)
WALTERS MLDING FABRICATION LLC
339 Stonepile Rd (16137-3345)
PHONE....................................724 662-4836
Mark Walters, *Principal*
EMP: 3 EST: 2009
SALES (est): 189.4K **Privately Held**
SIC: **3089** Molding primary plastic

(G-10979)
WENDELL AUGUST FORGE INC (PA)
111 Amercian Way (16137-4025)
P.O. Box 109, Grove City (16127-0109)
PHONE....................................724 748-9500
Ken Durrett, *CEO*
Frank W Knecht IV, *President*
V Constance Knecht, *Vice Pres*
Robert L Thompson Jr, *Treasurer*
Deborah I Fetter, *Admin Sec*
▲ EMP: 79 EST: 1932
SQ FT: 33,000
SALES (est): 19.8MM **Privately Held**
SIC: **5947** 3463 3914 3499 Gift shop; aluminum forgings; pewter ware; silverware; stainless steel ware; novelties & giftware, including trophies; catalog & mail-order houses

(G-10980)
YOUNGSTOWN ALLOY & CHAIN CORP
364 Yankee Ridge Rd (16137-2522)
PHONE....................................724 347-1920
Peter C George, *President*
Charles T George, *Treasurer*
EMP: 3
SQ FT: 10,000
SALES: 100K **Privately Held**
SIC: **3441** Fabricated structural metal

Mercersburg
Franklin County

(G-10981)
APX ENCLOSURES INC (PA)
200 Oregon St (17236-1630)
PHONE....................................717 328-9399
Andrew V Papoutsis, *President*
Rebel Edleblute, *Purchasing*
Ron Beckley, *Engineer*
Terry Reagan, *Sales Mgr*
Colby Winters, *Sales Staff*
▲ EMP: 34
SQ FT: 28,000
SALES (est): 7.9MM **Privately Held**
WEB: www.apx-enclosures.com
SIC: **3444** Sheet metal specialties, not stamped; metal housings, enclosures, casings & other containers

(G-10982)
C & T MACHINING INC
Also Called: C & T Industrial Supply Co
12991 Buchanan Trl W (17236-9403)
PHONE....................................717 328-9572
John E Carmack Jr, *President*
Ricky R Twine, *Vice Pres*
Rick R Twine, *Site Mgr*
Shawn Hill, *Sales Executive*
Gregg Foreman, *Manager*
EMP: 28
SQ FT: 13,000
SALES: 7MM **Privately Held**
SIC: **7692** 3599 Welding repair; machine shop, jobbing & repair

(G-10983)
CLAYLICK ENTERPRISES LLC
Also Called: Claylick Fabrication
10278 Clay Lick Rd (17236-8713)
PHONE....................................717 328-9876
Jason Petre, *Owner*
Michael Petre, *Mng Member*
EMP: 10
SALES (est): 294.7K **Privately Held**
SIC: **1799** 7692 Welding on site; welding repair

(G-10984)
D L MARTIN CO (PA)
25 D L Martin Dr (17236)
PHONE....................................717 328-2141
Preston Spohr, *Ch of Bd*
Donnie L Martin, *Ch of Bd*
Daniel J Fisher, *President*
Thomas Sims, *General Mgr*
William C Oneill, *Vice Pres*
▲ EMP: 175 EST: 1946
SQ FT: 120,000
SALES (est): 34.9MM **Privately Held**
WEB: www.dlmartin.com
SIC: **3569** 3537 Jacks, hydraulic; trucks, tractors, loaders, carriers & similar equipment

(G-10985)
DANOWSKI
Also Called: Fast Ink Screen Prtg & EMB Co
111 N Main St (17236-1723)
PHONE....................................717 328-5057
Barbara Danowski, *General Mgr*
EMP: 3
SALES (est): 315.7K **Privately Held**
SIC: **2759** 5199 2395 Screen printing; advertising specialties; embroidery & art needlework

(G-10986)
FAST INK APPAREL
111 N Main St (17236-1723)
P.O. Box 232 (17236-0232)
PHONE....................................717 328-5057
Timothy Howley, *Owner*
EMP: 3 EST: 2001
SALES (est): 409.1K **Privately Held**
WEB: www.fastink.com
SIC: **2759** Screen printing

(G-10987)
HICKS SIGNS
8941 Oellig Rd (17236-9497)
PHONE....................................717 328-3300
John Hicks, *Owner*
EMP: 8
SQ FT: 8,000
SALES (est): 400K **Privately Held**
SIC: **3993** Signs & advertising specialties

(G-10988)
JWI ARCHITECTURAL MILLWORK INC
209 Oregon St (17236-1629)
PHONE....................................717 328-5880
Gary Marshall, *President*
Alice Ahalt, *Vice Pres*
Randy Barnhart, *Vice Pres*
EMP: 30
SQ FT: 60,000
SALES (est): 2.7MM **Privately Held**
SIC: **2431** Windows, wood; moldings, wood: unfinished & prefinished

(G-10989)
KNOUSE FOODS COOPERATIVE INC
9332 Heisey Rd (17236-8557)
PHONE....................................717 328-3065
Robert Souders, *Principal*
EMP: 3
SQ FT: 62,500
SALES (corp-wide): 281.7MM **Privately Held**
SIC: **2033** Canned fruits & specialties
PA: Knouse Foods Cooperative, Inc.
800 Pach Glen Idaville Rd
Peach Glen PA 17375
717 677-8181

(G-10990)
LEIDYS CUSTOM WOODWORKING
11427 Church Hill Rd (17236-9664)
PHONE....................................717 328-9323
David Leidy, *Owner*
Connie Duvall, *Sales Staff*
EMP: 9
SALES (est): 1.1MM **Privately Held**
SIC: **2431** Millwork

(G-10991)
LOUDON INDUSTRIES INC (PA)
Also Called: L I
140 Landis Dr (17236-1754)
PHONE....................................717 328-9808
Tracy L Hill, *President*
Loren Myers, *President*
Marc Cree, *General Mgr*
Lynn Ross, *General Mgr*
Tim Hill, *Corp Secy*
EMP: 48
SQ FT: 15,000
SALES (est): 12.1MM **Privately Held**
WEB: www.loudonindustries.com
SIC: **3545** 3599 Machine tool accessories; machine shop, jobbing & repair

(G-10992)
MERCERSBURG JOURNAL
11 S Main St (17236-1501)
P.O. Box 239 (17236-0239)
PHONE....................................717 328-3223
Barbara Leese, *Owner*
Vernon Leese, *Co-Owner*
Melanie Gordon, *Admin Sec*
EMP: 8
SQ FT: 150
SALES (est): 351.9K **Privately Held**
SIC: **2711** Newspapers, publishing & printing

(G-10993)
MERCERSBURG PRINTING INC (PA)
9964 Buchanan Trl W (17236-9586)
PHONE....................................717 328-3902
Don Shenberger, *President*
Julie Swain, *Partner*
Doug Shenberger, *Manager*
EMP: 40
SQ FT: 16,000
SALES (est): 7.3MM **Privately Held**
WEB: www.mercersburg.net
SIC: **2752** 2759 Commercial printing, offset; laser printing

(G-10994)
R VBRIDENDOLPH & SONS INC
14144 Buchanan Trl W (17236-9459)
PHONE....................................717 328-3650
Betty Bridendolph, *President*
Barbara Bridendolph, *Corp Secy*
EMP: 3 EST: 1929
SQ FT: 5,000
SALES (est): 210K **Privately Held**
SIC: **2421** Sawmills & planing mills, general

(G-10995)
RELIABLE PRODUCTS INTL LLC
Also Called: Rocky Mountain Air Purifiers
218 N Main St (17236-1746)
P.O. Box 300 (17236-0300)
PHONE....................................717 261-1291
Dennis Cook, *Mng Member*
Charla Cook,
▲ EMP: 5
SQ FT: 3,200

SALES (est): 634K **Privately Held**
SIC: **3585** Heating equipment, complete

Merion Station
Montgomery County

(G-10996)
ACK DISPLAYS INC
232 Standish Rd (19066-1135)
PHONE....................................215 236-3000
Allen Actman, *President*
EMP: 6 EST: 1946
SALES (est): 653.1K **Privately Held**
WEB: www.ackdisplays.com
SIC: **3944** Games, toys & children's vehicles

(G-10997)
FORTMEX CORPORATION
249 Stoneway Ln (19066-1819)
PHONE....................................215 990-9688
EMP: 4
SALES (est): 318.6K **Privately Held**
SIC: **3357** 5065 Communication wire; communication equipment

(G-10998)
R & E INTERNATIONAL INC (HQ)
136 Broome Ln (19066-1702)
PHONE....................................610 664-5637
Clement Nahmias, *President*
Elizabeth Nahmias, *Admin Sec*
EMP: 10
SALES (est): 1.6MM
SALES (corp-wide): 3.9B **Publicly Held**
WEB: www.randeint.com
SIC: **8711** 3674 Engineering services; integrated circuits, semiconductor networks, etc.
PA: Microchip Technology Inc
2355 W Chandler Blvd
Chandler AZ 85224
480 792-7200

(G-10999)
VETPACK ENTERPRISES LLC
113 Winchester Rd (19066-1319)
PHONE....................................215 680-8637
Stuart W Boyer Jr, *Owner*
EMP: 6
SALES: 100K **Privately Held**
SIC: **2679** Converted paper products

Mertztown
Berks County

(G-11000)
ATLAS MINERALS & CHEMICALS INC
1227 Valley Rd (19539-8827)
P.O. Box 38 (19539-0038)
PHONE....................................800 523-8269
George P Gabriel, *CEO*
Francis X Hanson, *President*
Edward Ehret, *CFO*
◆ EMP: 45 EST: 1892
SQ FT: 102,000
SALES (est): 13.9MM **Privately Held**
WEB: www.atlasmin.com
SIC: **2891** 2952 3089 2951 Cement, except linoleum & tile; asphalt felts & coatings; plastic processing; asphalt paving mixtures & blocks

(G-11001)
BLAIR VINEYARDS
62 Five Points Rd (19539-9214)
PHONE....................................610 682-0075
Carol Blair, *Principal*
EMP: 4
SALES (est): 247.3K **Privately Held**
SIC: **2084** Wines

(G-11002)
CONCEPT PRODUCTS CORPORATION
62 Five Points Rd (19539-9214)
PHONE....................................610 722-0830
Leonard Blair, *President*
EMP: 5

SQ FT: 2,500
SALES (est): 729.4K **Privately Held**
WEB: www.conceptproducts.com
SIC: 3567 2652 3589 Incinerators, metal: domestic or commercial; filing boxes, paperboard: made from purchased materials; shredders, industrial & commercial

(G-11003)
ROCKLAND COACH WORKS LLC
24 High View Ln (19539-9727)
PHONE.................................610 682-2830
Brian L Gabel,
Susan Gabel,
EMP: 6
SQ FT: 22,000
SALES (est): 2.2MM **Privately Held**
SIC: 3711 Buses, all types, assembly of

(G-11004)
SOLTS SAWMILL INC
33 S Park Ave (19539-9000)
PHONE.................................610 682-6179
Paul L Solt, President
Kerry Solt, Vice Pres
EMP: 20
SQ FT: 3,600
SALES (est): 1MM **Privately Held**
SIC: 2421 Sawmills & planing mills, general

Meshoppen
Wyoming County

(G-11005)
ALDERDICE INC
524 Sr 4015 (18630-8136)
PHONE.................................570 996-1609
William Ruark, President
EMP: 70 EST: 2001
SALES (est): 4.6MM **Privately Held**
SIC: 1389 Oil field services

(G-11006)
DAVID R KIPAR
451 Mcgavin Rd (18630-7862)
PHONE.................................570 833-4068
Patrick Kipar, President
David R Kipar, Vice Pres
EMP: 27
SALES (est): 2MM **Privately Held**
SIC: 3281 Flagstones

(G-11007)
MESHOPPEN STONE INCORPORATED
131 Frantz Rd (18630)
P.O. Box 127 (18630-0127)
PHONE.................................570 833-2767
William Ruark, President
Steven Ciprich, Vice Pres
EMP: 115 EST: 1976
SQ FT: 1,200
SALES (est): 21.8MM **Privately Held**
WEB: www.meshoppenstone.com
SIC: 3281 Flagstones

Meyersdale
Somerset County

(G-11008)
APEX SCREEN PRINTING & EMB
102 Meyers Ave (15552-1126)
P.O. Box 120 (15552-0120)
PHONE.................................814 634-5992
Jeff Daniels, CEO
EMP: 8
SALES (est): 1.1MM **Privately Held**
WEB: www.apexplasticinc.com
SIC: 2759 Screen printing

(G-11009)
B & T FABRICATION
187 Maple Valley Rd (15552-6838)
P.O. Box 304 (15552-0304)
PHONE.................................814 634-0638
Bill Rugg, Owner
Tammy Rugg, Owner
EMP: 4

SQ FT: 4,000
SALES (est): 469K **Privately Held**
SIC: 3441 Fabricated structural metal

(G-11010)
FOUR GUYS STNLESS TANK EQP INC
Also Called: 4 GUY'S FIRETRUCKS
230 Industrial Park Rd (15552-7258)
P.O. Box 90 (15552-0090)
PHONE.................................814 634-8373
Alma Lauver, President
Melvin Shaulis, CIO
Eric Shaulis, Director
Jeanne K Cross, Shareholder
Ruth Ann Imhoff, Shareholder
EMP: 53
SQ FT: 30,000
SALES (est): 21.2MM **Privately Held**
WEB: www.4guysfire.com
SIC: 7699 3443 3561 3432 Tank repair; tanks, standard or custom fabricated: metal plate; pumps & pumping equipment; plumbing fixture fittings & trim

(G-11011)
HOOVER CNVYOR FABRICATION CORP (PA)
262 Industrial Park Rd (15552-7258)
PHONE.................................814 634-5431
Jerry Hoover, President
Jerell D Hoover, President
Melanie Hoover, Corp Secy
Dave Thomas, Sales Staff
EMP: 35
SQ FT: 26,000
SALES (est): 6.9MM **Privately Held**
SIC: 3535 3537 3444 Conveyors & conveying equipment; platforms, cargo; sheet metalwork

(G-11012)
INTERNATIONAL TRAILERS INC
Also Called: ITI
8535 Mason Dixon Hwy (15552-7100)
PHONE.................................814 634-1922
Robert Lohr, President
Lenny Lottig, Vice Pres
Larry Whitt, Vice Pres
Tim Buterbaugh, Purch Agent
Tim Yoder, Purchasing
EMP: 84
SQ FT: 6,500
SALES (est): 12.1MM **Privately Held**
SIC: 3715 Trailer bodies

(G-11013)
ITI TRAILERS & TRCK BODIES INC
8535 Mason Dixon Hwy (15552-7100)
P.O. Box 59 (15552-0059)
PHONE.................................814 634-0080
Leonard Lottig, President
Karen Lauver, Finance Mgr
Barb Oester, Financial Exec
Karl Testa, Manager
Larry Sanner, Admin Sec
EMP: 48
SALES (est): 14MM **Privately Held**
SIC: 3715 Trailer bodies

(G-11014)
JOHNSON MEMORIAL CO (PA)
20 Salisbury St (15552-1359)
P.O. Box 177 (15552-0177)
PHONE.................................814 634-0622
Gerald B Johnson, Owner
Carl Deal, Nurse
EMP: 7
SQ FT: 6,000
SALES (est): 500K **Privately Held**
SIC: 5999 3536 Monuments, finished to custom order; hoists, cranes & monorails

(G-11015)
MAPLE MOUNTAIN INDUSTRIES INC
Also Called: Furniture Factory
150 6th Ave (15552-1453)
PHONE.................................814 634-0674
Fax: 814 634-9397
EMP: 5 **Privately Held**
SIC: 2514 2512 Mfg Metal Household Furniture Mfg Upholstered Household Furniture

PA: Maple Mountain Industries Inc
1820 Mulligan Hill Rd
New Florence PA 15944

(G-11016)
MARK R STAIRS
4914 Brush Creek Rd (15552-7631)
PHONE.................................814 634-0871
Mark Stairs, Principal
EMP: 6
SALES (est): 466.1K **Privately Held**
SIC: 2411 Logging camps & contractors

(G-11017)
NEW REPUBLIC
688 Creek Rd (15552-5910)
PHONE.................................814 634-8321
Linda A Gindlesperger, President
EMP: 5 EST: 2001
SALES (est): 189.8K **Privately Held**
SIC: 2711 Newspapers, publishing & printing

(G-11018)
PONFEIGH DISTILLERY INC
3954 Brush Creek Rd (15552-7724)
PHONE.................................919 606-0526
Maximilian Merrill, President
EMP: 4 EST: 2012
SALES (est): 167.4K **Privately Held**
SIC: 2085 Distilled & blended liquors

(G-11019)
SAND PATCH MILL LLC
134 Deal Rd (15552-7547)
PHONE.................................814 634-9772
Arlen L Miller, Principal
EMP: 9
SALES (est): 590K **Privately Held**
SIC: 2421 Lumber: rough, sawed or planed

(G-11020)
VICTORIAN PUBLISHING CO INC
Also Called: New Republic Newspaper
145 Center St (15552-1320)
P.O. Box 239 (15552-0239)
PHONE.................................814 634-8321
Linda Gindlesperger, President
EMP: 6
SALES (est): 389.3K **Privately Held**
SIC: 2711 2791 Newspapers, publishing & printing; typesetting

Middleburg
Snyder County

(G-11021)
APEX HOMES INC
7172 Route 522 (17842-9488)
P.O. Box 77b (17842)
PHONE.................................570 837-2333
Chriss R Nipple, President
Harry L Kuhns, Vice Pres
Sue E Nerhood, Treasurer
Kent L Jenkins, VP Finance
Timothy Krouse, Manager
EMP: 200
SQ FT: 85,000
SALES (est): 27.4MM **Privately Held**
WEB: www.apexhomesinc.com
SIC: 2452 Modular homes, prefabricated, wood

(G-11022)
APEX HOMES OF PA LLC
7172 Route 522 (17842-9488)
PHONE.................................570 837-2333
Lynn Kuhns, President
EMP: 107
SQ FT: 150,000
SALES (est): 18MM **Privately Held**
SIC: 2452 Modular homes, prefabricated, wood

(G-11023)
ARCHITCTRAL PRCAST INNOVATIONS
3369 Paxtonville Rd (17842-8819)
PHONE.................................570 837-1774
Steve Kenepp, CEO
EMP: 80
SALES: 18MM **Privately Held**
SIC: 3272 Concrete products, precast

(G-11024)
DAVCO PALLET
837 Hartman Rd (17842-8514)
PHONE.................................570 837-5910
Michael Hornberger,
EMP: 5
SALES (est): 1.3MM **Privately Held**
SIC: 2448 Pallets, wood

(G-11025)
HASSINGER DIESEL SERVICE LLC
75 Diesel Rd (17842-9346)
PHONE.................................570 837-3412
Byron H Hassinger,
EMP: 3
SALES (est): 335.7K **Privately Held**
WEB: www.hassingerdiesel.com
SIC: 3519 Diesel engine rebuilding

(G-11026)
KEYSTONE PRECAST INC
3671 Paxtonville Rd (17842-8816)
PHONE.................................570 837-1864
Dale Kein, President
EMP: 4
SQ FT: 2,000
SALES (est): 599.4K **Privately Held**
SIC: 3272 Concrete products, precast

(G-11027)
LARRY PAIGE
Also Called: Top Flight Wings
45 Top Flight Ln (17842-8865)
PHONE.................................570 374-5650
Larry Paige, Owner
EMP: 4
SQ FT: 1,872
SALES (est): 300K **Privately Held**
SIC: 3429 Luggage racks, car top

(G-11028)
LEON SPANGLER
Also Called: Country Print Shop, The
44 N Shuman St (17842-1227)
PHONE.................................570 837-7903
Leon Spangler, Owner
EMP: 13
SQ FT: 2,000
SALES (est): 750K **Privately Held**
WEB: www.countryprint.com
SIC: 2752 2741 2789 2711 Lithographing on metal; shopping news: publishing & printing; bookbinding & related work; newspapers

(G-11029)
MIDDLEBURG PRE CAST LLC
Rr 522 Box N (17842)
P.O. Box 88 (17842-0088)
PHONE.................................570 837-1463
Emmitt Kreamer, Mng Member
Dean L Kartzer,
Donald L Kartzer,
EMP: 10
SALES (est): 1.5MM **Privately Held**
SIC: 3272 3273 1781 Septic tanks, concrete; ready-mixed concrete; water well drilling

(G-11030)
MIDDLESWARTH AND SON INC (PA)
250 Furnace Rd (17842-9159)
PHONE.................................570 837-1431
David Middlesworth, President
EMP: 80
SQ FT: 60,000
SALES (est): 69.5K **Privately Held**
SIC: 2096 Potato chips & similar snacks

(G-11031)
MIKE DUPUY HAWK FOOD
4552 Troxelville Rd (17842-8476)
PHONE.................................570 837-1551
Mike Dupuy, Owner
Christine Astin, Manager
EMP: 7
SALES (est): 130K **Privately Held**
SIC: 2048 Prepared feeds

(G-11032)
MITCHEL LOADING CREW
45 Black Bear Dr (17842-8444)
PHONE.................................570 837-5907

Gale Smith, *Owner*
EMP: 15
SALES (est): 1.4MM **Privately Held**
SIC: 2015 Chicken, processed

(G-11033)
NATIONAL LIMESTONE QUARRY
3499 Quarry Rd (17842)
P.O. Box 397 (17842-0397)
PHONE..................................570 837-1635
Eric Stahl, *President*
Eric E Stahl II, *Vice Pres*
John C Stahl III, *Vice Pres*
Robert Smith, *Admin Sec*
EMP: 34 **EST:** 1921
SQ FT: 2,000
SALES (est): 6.2MM **Privately Held**
SIC: 1422 Limestones, ground

(G-11034)
NORTHWAY INDUSTRIES INC
434 Paxtonville Rd (17842-9535)
P.O. Box 277 (17842-0277)
PHONE..................................570 837-1564
Donald O'Hora, *President*
Don O'Hora, *General Mgr*
C K Battram, *Principal*
Joseph E Callender, *Corp Secy*
Don Ohoro, *COO*
EMP: 133
SQ FT: 93,000
SALES (est): 16MM **Privately Held**
WEB: www.northwayind.com
SIC: 2542 3083 2541 Partitions & fix-
tures, except wood; laminated plastics
plate & sheet; wood partitions & fixtures

(G-11035)
POWDER COATING
148 Pitzer Rd (17842-8605)
PHONE..................................570 837-3325
Thomas Tice, *Principal*
EMP: 4
SALES (est): 308.2K **Privately Held**
SIC: 3479 Coating of metals & formed
products

(G-11036)
**PROFESSIONAL BLDG
SYSTEMS INC (PA)**
Also Called: P B S
72 E Market St (17842-1064)
PHONE..................................570 837-1424
William French, *President*
Dave Kojura, *CFO*
David Konjura, *CFO*
Cory Messimer, *Marketing Staff*
Nick Lust, *Executive*
EMP: 113
SQ FT: 300,000
SALES (est): 62.9MM **Privately Held**
WEB: www.pbsmodular.com
SIC: 2452 1521 Prefabricated wood build-
ings; single-family housing construction

(G-11037)
REFINED PALLET
1406 Breon Rd (17842-8615)
PHONE..................................570 238-9455
Nathan Sanders, *Principal*
EMP: 3 **EST:** 2016
SALES (est): 149.3K **Privately Held**
SIC: 2448 Pallets, wood

(G-11038)
**RIDGEVIEW MDLAR HSING
GROUP LP**
7172 Route 522 (17842-9488)
PHONE..................................570 837-2333
Jeffrey Reber, *Co-Owner*
Thomas Gates, *Co-Owner*
H Lynn Kuhns, *Co-Owner*
Susan Nerhood, *Co-Owner*
EMP: 99
SALES (est): 3.8MM **Privately Held**
SIC: 2452 Modular homes, prefabricated,
wood

(G-11039)
**ROWE SPRINKLER SYSTEMS
INC**
7993 Route 522 (17842-9483)
P.O. Box 407 (17842-0407)
PHONE..................................570 837-7647
Cathy R Church, *President*

George Church, *Principal*
Kevin Hunt, *COO*
Doug Eddy, *Project Mgr*
Carolyn J Waple, *CFO*
EMP: 26
SQ FT: 7,000
SALES (est): 11.5MM **Privately Held**
WEB: www.rowesprinkler.com
SIC: 3569 1711 3432 Sprinkler systems,
fire: automatic; fire sprinkler system in-
stallation; lawn hose nozzles & sprinklers

(G-11040)
**SHADE MOUNTAIN WINERY INC
(PA)**
16140 Route 104 (17842-8792)
PHONE..................................570 837-3644
Karl Zimmerman, *President*
EMP: 8
SQ FT: 15,000
SALES (est): 864.2K **Privately Held**
SIC: 2084 Wines

(G-11041)
SNYDER COUNTY TIMES
405 E Main St (17842-1215)
P.O. Box 356 (17842-0356)
PHONE..................................570 837-6065
Sue Weaver, *Owner*
EMP: 5
SALES (est): 278.2K **Privately Held**
WEB: www.snydercountytimes.com
SIC: 2711 6411 Newspapers, publishing &
printing; insurance agents, brokers &
service

(G-11042)
ZEIGLERS MACHINE SHOP
650 E Hollow Rd (17842-8212)
PHONE..................................570 374-5535
Roger Zeigler Sr, *Partner*
EMP: 3
SALES (est): 474K **Privately Held**
SIC: 3599 Machine shop, jobbing & repair

Middlebury Center
Tioga County

(G-11043)
CORNELL BROS INC (PA)
1 Mill St (16935)
PHONE..................................570 376-2471
D Edward Cornell, *President*
Edward D Cornell, *President*
Jess Cornell, *Principal*
EMP: 16 **EST:** 1949
SQ FT: 18,500
SALES (est): 3.7MM **Privately Held**
SIC: 2041 2875 5251 2048 Grain mills
(except rice); fertilizers, mixing only; hard-
ware; prepared feeds

(G-11044)
**DIETRICHS MILK PRODUCTS
LLC**
Also Called: Dairy Farmers of America
72 Milk Plant Rd (16935)
PHONE..................................570 376-2001
Alan Sauter, *Manager*
EMP: 70
SALES (corp-wide): 20.4MM **Privately
Held**
SIC: 2021 2023 Creamery butter; pow-
dered milk
HQ: Dietrich's Milk Products Llc
100 Mckinley Ave
Reading PA 19605
610 929-5736

Middleport
Schuylkill County

(G-11045)
**KUPERAVAGE ENTERPRISES
INC**
Also Called: Tuscarora Coal Company
Old Rte 209 (17953)
P.O. Box 99 (17953-0099)
PHONE..................................570 668-1633
Dave Kuperavage, *President*

Bernard Kuperavage, *President*
EMP: 20 **EST:** 1976
SALES (est): 2.2MM **Privately Held**
SIC: 1231 Preparation plants, anthracite

(G-11046)
MIDDLEPORT MATERIALS INC
730 Mountain Rd (17953)
PHONE..................................570 277-0335
Brian L Carpenter, *President*
Gary M Carpenter, *Vice Pres*
Regina S Carpenter, *Treasurer*
William G Carpenter, *Admin Sec*
EMP: 10
SALES (est): 579.9K **Privately Held**
WEB: www.mmstone.net
SIC: 1442 Common sand mining

Middletown
Dauphin County

(G-11047)
**ALTO GARAGE DOOR
MANUFACTURING**
1451 Stoneridge Dr (17057-5967)
PHONE..................................717 546-0056
Thomas Pagliaro, *CEO*
James M Pagliaro Sr, *Vice Pres*
EMP: 7 **EST:** 1978
SQ FT: 25,000
SALES (est): 72K **Privately Held**
SIC: 3442 Garage doors, overhead: metal

(G-11048)
APPLY POWDER & COATING
394 Parkmount Rd (17057)
PHONE..................................610 361-1889
Jim Snyder, *President*
EMP: 7
SALES (est): 439.7K **Privately Held**
SIC: 3479 Coating of metals & formed
products

(G-11049)
BRICK WALL MINISTRIES
1371 Spring House Rd (17057-5947)
PHONE..................................717 592-1798
Charles Gray Jr, *Owner*
Renee Gray, *Senior VP*
EMP: 4
SALES: 1K **Privately Held**
SIC: 2731 Books: publishing only

(G-11050)
**CFC LEOLA PROPERTIES INC
(HQ)**
1301 Fulling Mill Rd # 3000 (17057-5975)
P.O. Box 902, Hatfield (19440-0902)
PHONE..................................717 390-1978
Philip A Clemens, *CEO*
Jim Woods, *President*
Philip E Keeler, *Admin Sec*
EMP: 14
SQ FT: 30,000
SALES (est): 5.8MM
SALES (corp-wide): 705.7MM **Privately
Held**
SIC: 2013 Prepared beef products from
purchased beef
PA: The Clemens Family Corporation
2700 Clemens Rd
Hatfield PA 19440
800 523-5291

(G-11051)
**COMPASS GROUP USA
INVESTMENTS**
3201 Fulling Mill Rd (17057-3174)
PHONE..................................717 939-1200
Dave Hurley, *General Mgr*
EMP: 13
SALES (corp-wide): 29.6B **Privately Held**
SIC: 3581 Automatic vending machines
HQ: Compass Group Usa Investments Llp
2400 Yorkmont Rd
Charlotte NC 28217
704 328-4000

(G-11052)
**ELEGANT MARBLE PRODUCTS
INC**
416 Richardson Rd (17057-5513)
PHONE..................................717 939-0373
Richard Scherba, *President*
Rick Scherba, *Purchasing*
EMP: 12
SQ FT: 6,000
SALES (est): 1.2MM **Privately Held**
SIC: 3088 2434 3281 Plastics plumbing
fixtures; wood kitchen cabinets; house-
hold articles, except furniture: cut stone

(G-11053)
EMKA-INCORPORATED
1961 Fulling Mill Rd (17057-3125)
PHONE..................................717 986-1111
Peter Macnussen, *President*
▲ **EMP:** 28
SQ FT: 10,000
SALES (est): 13.2MM
SALES (corp-wide): 91.8MM **Privately
Held**
WEB: www.emkausa.com
SIC: 5085 3429 Fasteners, industrial:
nuts, bolts, screws, etc.; gaskets; manu-
factured hardware (general)
PA: Emka Beschlagteile Gmbh & Co. Kg
Langenberger Str. 32
Velbert 42551
205 127-30

(G-11054)
GLEN-GERY CORPORATION
2750 Commerce Dr (17057-3200)
PHONE..................................717 939-6061
Sarah Coburn, *Human Res Dir*
Duane Luckenbill, *Branch Mgr*
EMP: 7
SALES (corp-wide): 1.2MM **Privately
Held**
SIC: 3251 Brick & structural clay tile
HQ: Glen-Gery Corporation
1166 Spring St
Reading PA 19610
610 374-4011

(G-11055)
**HALDEX BRAKE PRODUCTS
CORP**
Also Called: Haldex Midland
2700 Commerce Dr (17057-3200)
PHONE..................................717 939-5928
Fred Moeslein, *Manager*
EMP: 15
SALES (corp-wide): 528.7MM **Privately
Held**
WEB: www.hbsna.com
SIC: 3714 Motor vehicle brake systems &
parts
HQ: Haldex Brake Products Corporation
10930 N Pomona Ave
Kansas City MO 64153
816 891-2470

(G-11056)
**HENDERSONS TARPAULIN
COVERS**
8 Ann St Side (17057-1382)
P.O. Box 188 (17057-0188)
PHONE..................................717 944-5865
Gregory Henderson, *President*
John Henderson, *Corp Secy*
EMP: 7 **EST:** 1955
SQ FT: 6,560
SALES (est): 480.7K **Privately Held**
WEB: www.hendersontarp.com
SIC: 2394 Awnings, fabric: made from pur-
chased materials

(G-11057)
**HYDROWORX INTERNATIONAL
INC**
Also Called: Hydrotrack
1420 Stoneridge Dr Ste C (17057-5989)
PHONE..................................717 902-1923
Timothy McArthy, *CEO*
Katon Tressler, *Controller*
Mike McHugh, *Sales Staff*
Rob Miller, *Sales Staff*
▼ **EMP:** 46
SQ FT: 2,982

SALES: 20MM **Privately Held**
WEB: www.hydroworx.com
SIC: 3842 Whirlpool baths, hydrotherapy equipment

(G-11058)
IWI US INC
1441 Stoneridge Dr (17057-5977)
PHONE........................717 695-2081
Shlomo Sabag, *President*
Michael Kassnar, *Vice Pres*
Casey Flack, *Sales Staff*
EMP: 27
SQ FT: 26,000
SALES: 24MM **Privately Held**
SIC: 3484 Guns (firearms) or gun parts, 30 mm. & below

(G-11059)
JST CORPORATION
1501 Fulling Mill Rd (17057-3117)
PHONE........................717 920-7700
Atsuhiro Nishimoto, *CEO*
EMP: 6
SALES (est): 974.3K **Privately Held**
SIC: 2655 Tubes, for chemical or electrical uses: paper or fiber

(G-11060)
LEGRAND HOME SYSTEMS INC (DH)
Also Called: On Q Home
301 Fulling Mill Rd Ste G (17057-5966)
P.O. Box 60907, Harrisburg (17106-0907)
PHONE........................717 702-2532
Douglas Fikse, *President*
Stu Rutherford, *President*
Bob Fallert, *Vice Pres*
Robert Julian, *Vice Pres*
Fritz Werder, *Vice Pres*
▲ **EMP:** 96
SQ FT: 25,000
SALES (est): 17.6MM
SALES (corp-wide): 20.7MM **Privately Held**
WEB: www.onqhome.com
SIC: 3661 3315 3651 3577 Telephone & telegraph apparatus; wire & fabricated wire products; household audio & video equipment; computer peripheral equipment
HQ: Legrand Holding, Inc.
60 Woodlawn St
West Hartford CT 06110
860 233-6251

(G-11061)
LEGRAND HOME SYSTEMS INC
Also Called: On Q Home
1001 Aip Dr (17057-5970)
PHONE........................717 702-2532
Jeff Eberle, *Branch Mgr*
EMP: 20
SALES (corp-wide): 20.7MM **Privately Held**
WEB: www.onqhome.com
SIC: 3577 3651 Computer peripheral equipment; household audio & video equipment
HQ: Legrand Home Systems, Inc.
301 Fulling Mill Rd Ste G
Middletown PA 17057
717 702-2532

(G-11062)
LESHER INC
Also Called: Lesher Metal Stone and Tiles
2400 Swatara Creek Rd (17057-3576)
PHONE........................717 944-4431
Frank Lesher, *President*
EMP: 17 **EST:** 1997
SQ FT: 15,000
SALES: 3MM **Privately Held**
WEB: www.lesher.net
SIC: 7349 1743 3281 Cleaning service, industrial or commercial; marble installation, interior; granite, cut & shaped

(G-11063)
LIBRANDI MACHINE SHOP INC
Also Called: Librandi's Plating
93 Airport Dr (17057-5022)
PHONE........................717 944-9442
Thomas C Librandi, *CEO*
Todd A Librandi, *President*
Marle J Librandi, *Corp Secy*

EMP: 85 **EST:** 1972
SQ FT: 50,000
SALES (est): 12.9MM **Privately Held**
WEB: www.carchrome.com
SIC: 3471 3599 3544 Plating & polishing; machine shop, jobbing & repair; special dies, tools, jigs & fixtures

(G-11064)
MACK TRUCKS INC
Also Called: Remanufacturing Center
2800 Commerce Dr (17057-3294)
PHONE........................717 939-1338
Kristine Cowfer, *Accountant*
Steven Edelund, *Manager*
Kevin Miller, *Manager*
EMP: 178
SQ FT: 17,000
SALES (corp-wide): 39.6B **Privately Held**
WEB: www.macktrucks.com
SIC: 3711 3714 3519 Truck tractors for highway use, assembly of; motor vehicle parts & accessories; internal combustion engines
HQ: Mack Trucks, Inc.
7900 National Service Rd
Greensboro NC 27409
336 291-9001

(G-11065)
MSJC INC
643 Southward St (17057)
PHONE........................717 930-0718
Janet Ai, *Manager*
▲ **EMP:** 4
SALES (est): 180K **Privately Held**
SIC: 2399 Fabricated textile products

(G-11066)
NEOPOST USA INC
1201 Fulling Mill Rd (17057-3111)
P.O. Box 4240, Harrisburg (17111-0240)
PHONE........................717 939-2700
Andrew J Orons, *General Mgr*
EMP: 24
SALES (corp-wide): 53.4MM **Privately Held**
SIC: 3579 7359 7629 Postage meters; business machine & electronic equipment rental services; business machine repair, electric
HQ: Neopost Usa Inc.
478 Wheelers Farms Rd
Milford CT 06461
203 301-3400

(G-11067)
PENN CENTRAL SPRING CORP
1451 Stoneridge Dr (17057-5967)
PHONE........................717 564-6792
Barry Pagliaro, *President*
EMP: 8
SQ FT: 17,000
SALES (est): 1.2MM **Privately Held**
SIC: 3495 Wire springs

(G-11068)
PHOENIX CONTACT DEV & MFG INC (PA)
586 Fulling Mill Rd (17057-2966)
PHONE........................717 944-1300
John L Nehlig, *President*
Kent H Patterson, *Vice Pres*
Kevin Zak, *Vice Pres*
Joel A Ness, *Treasurer*
EMP: 310
SQ FT: 136,000
SALES (est): 86MM **Privately Held**
SIC: 5063 3678 3643 Electrical apparatus & equipment; electronic connectors; current-carrying wiring devices

(G-11069)
PHXCO LLC
Also Called: Parts Now
1451 Stoneridge Dr Ste B (17057-5992)
PHONE........................608 203-1500
Matt Wilbur, *Branch Mgr*
EMP: 80 **Privately Held**
SIC: 3577 Printers, computer
HQ: Phxco, Llc
48 N 49th Ave
Glendale AZ 85306
608 266-4671

(G-11070)
PRATT & WHITNEY AMERICON INC
181 Fulling Mill Rd Ste 1 (17057-5702)
PHONE........................717 546-0220
Scott Deitrich, *Engineer*
Kelly Livingston, *Personnel Assit*
◆ **EMP:** 120 **EST:** 1998
SQ FT: 88,000
SALES (est): 20.8MM
SALES (corp-wide): 66.5B **Publicly Held**
WEB: www.amerconinc.com
SIC: 3728 3724 Aircraft parts & equipment; airfoils, aircraft engine
PA: United Technologies Corporation
10 Farm Springs Rd
Farmington CT 06032
860 728-7000

(G-11071)
PRESS AND JOURNAL
Also Called: Press & Journal Publications
20 S Union St (17057-1466)
PHONE........................717 944-4628
Joseph Sukale, *President*
Joe Sukle, *Editor*
Jason Maddux, *Editor*
Gloria Brown, *Accounts Exec*
Nancy Brown, *Manager*
EMP: 40 **EST:** 1854
SALES (est): 2.7MM **Privately Held**
WEB: www.harrisburg.com
SIC: 2711 2752 2741 Newspapers, publishing & printing; commercial printing, offset; miscellaneous publishing

(G-11072)
ROYALTON TOOL AND DIE INC
412 Wyoming St (17057-1649)
PHONE........................717 944-5838
John I Burkett III, *President*
Kelly E Kreiser, *Vice Pres*
Lisa Taylor, *Treasurer*
Dale Burkett, *Admin Sec*
EMP: 9
SQ FT: 6,880
SALES (est): 680K **Privately Held**
SIC: 3599 Machine shop, jobbing & repair

(G-11073)
RUTTER BROS DAIRY INC
2800 Vine St (17057-3032)
PHONE........................717 388-1665
EMP: 16
SALES (corp-wide): 23.2MM **Privately Held**
SIC: 2026 Milk processing (pasteurizing, homogenizing, bottling)
PA: Rutter Bros. Dairy, Inc.
2100 N George St
York PA 17404
717 848-9827

(G-11074)
SCHNEIDER ELECTRIC IT CORP
Also Called: American Power Company
201 Fulling Mill Rd (17057-2921)
PHONE........................717 948-1200
Robert Jones, *Manager*
Timothy Harbaugh, *Info Tech Mgr*
EMP: 300
SALES (corp-wide): 355.8K **Privately Held**
SIC: 3629 3612 3677 7372 Power conversion units, a.c. to d.c.: static-electric; transformers, except electric; line voltage regulators; voltage regulators, transmission & distribution; filtration devices, electronic; prepackaged software
HQ: Schneider Electric It Corporation
132 Fairgrounds Rd
West Kingston RI 02892
401 789-5735

(G-11075)
SEBASTIAN BROTHERS
Also Called: Sebastiani Concrete
4189 E Harrisburg Pike (17057-4654)
PHONE........................717 930-8797
EMP: 12 **EST:** 1958
SQ FT: 4,000
SALES: 2MM **Privately Held**
SIC: 1771 3273 Asphalt Paving Contractor & Mfg Metered Concrete

(G-11076)
SHERIDAN CONSTRUCTION GROUP
950 Swatara Creek Rd (17057-3854)
PHONE........................717 948-0507
Lane Schultz, *President*
Robert Rahsman, *Treasurer*
EMP: 2 **EST:** 1995
SALES: 1MM **Privately Held**
SIC: 1481 Mine & quarry services, non-metallic minerals; mine development, nonmetallic minerals

(G-11077)
SMITHFIELD FOODS INC
Also Called: Smithfield Global Product
370 Maple Rd (17057)
PHONE........................215 752-1090
EMP: 619 **Privately Held**
WEB: www.smithfield.com
SIC: 2011 Meat packing plants
HQ: Smithfield Foods, Inc.
200 Commerce St
Smithfield VA 23430
757 365-3000

(G-11078)
TE CONNECTIVITY CORPORATION
3101 Fulling Mill Rd # 128 (17057-3172)
P.O. Box 3608, Harrisburg (17105-3608)
PHONE........................717 564-0100
EMP: 200
SALES (corp-wide): 13.1B **Privately Held**
WEB: www.raychem.com
SIC: 3678 3643 Electronic connectors; current-carrying wiring devices; connectors & terminals for electrical devices
HQ: Te Connectivity Corporation
1050 Westlakes Dr
Berwyn PA 19312
610 893-9800

(G-11079)
TE CONNECTIVITY CORPORATION
Also Called: AMP
2801 Fulling Mill Rd (17057-3143)
PHONE........................717 986-3028
James Schroeder, *Branch Mgr*
EMP: 198
SALES (corp-wide): 13.1B **Privately Held**
WEB: www.raychem.com
SIC: 3643 Connectors & terminals for electrical devices
HQ: Te Connectivity Corporation
1050 Westlakes Dr
Berwyn PA 19312
610 893-9800

(G-11080)
TE CONNECTIVITY CORPORATION
2800 Fulling Mill Rd (17057-3142)
P.O. Box 3608, Harrisburg (17105-3608)
PHONE........................866 743-6440
Thomas Lynch, *Branch Mgr*
EMP: 756
SALES (corp-wide): 13.1B **Privately Held**
WEB: www.raychem.com
SIC: 3678 Electronic connectors
HQ: Te Connectivity Corporation
1050 Westlakes Dr
Berwyn PA 19312
610 893-9800

(G-11081)
TE CONNECTIVITY CORPORATION
2900 Fulling Mill Rd (17057-3144)
P.O. Box 3608, Harrisburg (17105-3608)
PHONE........................717 986-3743
Bob Leggett, *Branch Mgr*
EMP: 281
SALES (corp-wide): 13.1B **Privately Held**
WEB: www.raychem.com
SIC: 3678 3827 3613 Electronic connectors; optical instruments & lenses; switchgear & switchboard apparatus
HQ: Te Connectivity Corporation
1050 Westlakes Dr
Berwyn PA 19312
610 893-9800

▲ = Import ▼=Export
◆ =Import/Export

(G-11082)
TE CONNECTIVITY CORPORATION
2901 Fulling Mill Rd (17057-3170)
PHONE.................................717 564-0100
Juergen W Gromer, *Manager*
EMP: 281
SALES (corp-wide): 13.1B Privately Held
WEB: www.raychem.com
SIC: 3678 Electronic connectors
HQ: Te Connectivity Corporation
1050 Westlakes Dr
Berwyn PA 19312
610 893-9800

(G-11083)
TREMCO INCORPORATED
46 Hillcrest Dr (17057-3600)
PHONE.................................717 944-9702
EMP: 100
SALES (corp-wide): 5.3B Publicly Held
SIC: 2891 7389 Sealants;
HQ: Tremco Incorporated
3735 Green Rd
Beachwood OH 44122
216 292-5000

(G-11084)
UNIVAR USA INC
532 E Emaus St Ste 1 (17057-2200)
PHONE.................................717 944-7471
Jim Reardon, *General Mgr*
Jeffrey Silcox, *Managing Dir*
Roger Crane, *Maint Spvr*
Jack Umholtz, *Manager*
EMP: 97
SALES (corp-wide): 8.6B Publicly Held
SIC: 5169 2842 2819 2812 Industrial
chemicals; specialty cleaning, polishes &
sanitation goods; industrial inorganic
chemicals; alkalies & chlorine
HQ: Univar Usa Inc.
3075 Highland Pkwy # 200
Downers Grove IL 60515
331 777-6000

(G-11085)
WOOLF STEEL INC
170 Fulling Mill Rd (17057-5921)
PHONE.................................717 944-1423
Mervin G Woolf, *Ch of Bd*
Jerry L Woolf, *President*
Bill Woolf, *Vice Pres*
William A Woolf, *Vice Pres*
EMP: 20
SQ FT: 13,500
SALES (est): 5.3MM Privately Held
WEB: www.woolfsteel.com
SIC: 3441 Building components, structural
steel

(G-11086)
YORK BUILDING PRODUCTS CO INC
Also Called: Harrisburg Building Units
325 Fulling Mill Rd (17057-2999)
PHONE.................................717 944-1488
Dick Boombec, *Manager*
EMP: 15
SALES (corp-wide): 56.4MM Privately
Held
SIC: 3271 Blocks, concrete or cinder: stan-
dard
PA: York Building Products Co., Inc.
950 Smile Way
York PA 17404
717 848-2831

Midland
Beaver County

(G-11087)
M I P INC
1066 Midland Ave (15059-1640)
PHONE.................................724 643-5114
James Furgiuele, *President*
EMP: 7
SQ FT: 14,000
SALES (est): 828K Privately Held
SIC: 3599 Machine & other job shop work;
custom machinery; machine shop, job-
bing & repair

(G-11088)
VISTA MANUFACTURING INC
728 Railroad Ave (15059-1423)
PHONE.................................724 495-6860
Barbara A Mc Gaffic, *President*
EMP: 4 Privately Held
SIC: 3599 Machine shop, jobbing & repair
PA: Vista Manufacturing Inc
1201 State Route 18
Aliquippa PA 15001

(G-11089)
WHEMCO - STEEL CASTINGS INC
1 12th St (15059-1645)
PHONE.................................724 643-7001
Chris Slingluff, *Vice Pres*
Charles Scherrer, *Branch Mgr*
EMP: 14
SALES (corp-wide): 568.1MM Privately
Held
SIC: 3325 Alloy steel castings, except in-
vestment
HQ: Whemco - Steel Castings, Inc.
5 Hot Metal St Ste 300
Pittsburgh PA 15203
412 390-2700

Midway
Washington County

(G-11090)
COXS MACHINE SHOP
312 Eaton St (15060-1114)
PHONE.................................724 796-7815
Richard Cox, *Owner*
EMP: 3
SALES (est): 158.3K Privately Held
SIC: 3599 Machine shop, jobbing & repair

Mifflin
Juniata County

(G-11091)
TUSCARORA STRUCTURES INC
152 Tuscarora Ln (17058-7070)
PHONE.................................717 436-5591
David S Glick, *President*
EMP: 8
SQ FT: 3,500
SALES (est): 1.2MM Privately Held
SIC: 2452 Farm buildings, prefabricated or
portable: wood

Mifflinburg
Union County

(G-11092)
ALVIN REIFF WOODWORKING
1190 Green Ridge Rd (17844-7435)
PHONE.................................570 966-1149
Alvin M Reiff, *Partner*
Landis Reiff, *Partner*
Marvis Reiff, *Partner*
EMP: 4
SQ FT: 7,000
SALES (est): 500.7K Privately Held
SIC: 2434 2431 2511 Wood kitchen cabi-
nets; ornamental woodwork: cornices,
mantels, etc.; wood household furniture

(G-11093)
EAST WEST DRILLING INC
157 Buffalo Creek Rd (17844-7769)
PHONE.................................570 966-7312
Stelios Xagorarakis, *President*
Michael Dover, *Vice Pres*
◆ EMP: 20
SALES (est): 4.4MM Privately Held
WEB: www.eastwestdrilling.com
SIC: 3599 7699 Machine shop, jobbing &
repair; compressor repair; industrial ma-
chinery & equipment repair; construction
equipment repair; hydraulic equipment re-
pair

(G-11094)
ELKAY WOOD PRODUCTS COMPANY
Also Called: Yorktowne Cabinets
5 N 8th St (17844-1003)
PHONE.................................570 966-1076
Rod Holtzhepple, *Opers-Prdtn-Mfg*
EMP: 500
SALES (corp-wide): 1.3B Privately Held
SIC: 2434 Wood kitchen cabinets
HQ: Elkay Wood Products Company
1 Medallion Way
Waconia MN 55387
952 442-5171

(G-11095)
HORNINGS PALLET FORKS
370 Stahl Rd (17844-7356)
PHONE.................................570 966-1025
Mervin Horning, *Principal*
EMP: 6
SALES (est): 783.8K Privately Held
SIC: 2448 Pallets, wood & wood with metal

(G-11096)
IDDINGS QUARRY INC (PA)
900 Chestnut St (17844-1235)
PHONE.................................570 966-1551
David Iddings, *President*
Jeremy Boney, *Principal*
EMP: 2 EST: 1950
SALES (est): 1.1MM Privately Held
SIC: 1422 Crushed & broken limestone

(G-11097)
MARTINS STEEL LLC
2050 Swengle Rd (17844-8153)
PHONE.................................570 966-3775
Irvin Martin, *Mng Member*
Anna Mae Martin,
David Martin,
Eugene Martin,
John Martin,
EMP: 8
SQ FT: 23,000
SALES (est): 1.8MM Privately Held
SIC: 7692 5051 3599 Welding repair;
steel; machine shop, jobbing & repair

(G-11098)
MIFFLINBURG FARMERS EXCHANGE
Also Called: Country Farm & Home Center
Rr 45 Box E (17844)
P.O. Box 26 (17844-0026)
PHONE.................................570 966-4030
Kris Schuck, *Manager*
EMP: 8
SALES (est): 528.7K
SALES (corp-wide): 3.1MM Privately
Held
SIC: 5261 5947 2339 5621 Garden sup-
plies & tools; gift shop; women's &
misses' accessories; women's clothing
stores
PA: Mifflinburg Farmers Exchange Inc
660 Mulberry St
Mifflinburg PA 17844
570 966-1001

(G-11099)
MIFFLINBURG TELEGRAPH INC
358 Walnut St (17844-1153)
P.O. Box 189 (17844-0189)
PHONE.................................570 966-2255
John Stamm, *President*
EMP: 6
SQ FT: 5,500
SALES (est): 868.8K Privately Held
WEB: www.mifflinburgtelegraph.com
SIC: 2752 2711 2791 2789 Commercial
printing, offset; newspapers: publishing
only, not printed on site; typesetting;
bookbinding & related work; commercial
printing

(G-11100)
PREMIER AUTOMOTIVE
925 Grand Valley Rd (17844-7959)
PHONE.................................570 966-0363
Roger Stahl, *Owner*
EMP: 3 EST: 1995
SALES: 250K Privately Held
SIC: 3613 Switches, electric power except
snap, push button, etc.

(G-11101)
RED BANK WELDING
53 Red Bank Rd (17844-6800)
PHONE.................................570 966-0695
Barry Delcamp, *Owner*
EMP: 3
SALES: 250K Privately Held
SIC: 7692 Welding repair

(G-11102)
S & H LOGGING LLC
745 White Springs Rd (17844-8113)
PHONE.................................570 966-8958
Hanselman Steve, *Owner*
EMP: 3
SALES (est): 253.6K Privately Held
SIC: 2411 Logging camps & contractors

(G-11103)
THREE BELLE CHEESE
137 Dice Rd (17844-7463)
PHONE.................................570 713-8722
Tammy Rhyne, *Owner*
Derrick Rhyne, *Owner*
EMP: 4
SALES: 1K Privately Held
SIC: 2022 Natural cheese

(G-11104)
VICKSBURG BUGGY SHOP
1400 Beaver Run Rd (17844-6706)
PHONE.................................570 966-3658
Isaac M Reiff, *Owner*
EMP: 5
SQ FT: 5,600
SALES: 150K Privately Held
WEB: www.sbsequine.com
SIC: 3799 7699 Carriages, horse drawn;
horse drawn vehicle repair

(G-11105)
WHISPERING PINE WOODWORKING
235 Diehl Rd (17844-7948)
PHONE.................................570 922-4530
Noah Zimmerman, *Principal*
EMP: 3
SALES (est): 241K Privately Held
SIC: 2431 Millwork

(G-11106)
WILD CAT PUBLISHING LLC
229 E Chestnut St (17844-9322)
PHONE.................................570 966-1120
EMP: 4
SALES (est): 226.5K Privately Held
SIC: 2741 Miscellaneous publishing

Mifflintown
Juniata County

(G-11107)
A W SAWMILL
2144 Locust Run Rd (17059-8950)
PHONE.................................717 535-5081
Samuel Peight, *Owner*
EMP: 3
SALES (est): 216.9K Privately Held
SIC: 2421 Sawmills & planing mills, gen-
eral

(G-11108)
ADVANCE PUBLICATIONS
Juniata Sentinel
Old Rte 22 W (17059)
PHONE.................................717 436-8206
Carol Smith, *Manager*
EMP: 12
SALES (corp-wide): 1.4B Privately Held
SIC: 2711 Job printing & newspaper pub-
lishing combined
HQ: Advance Publications Of Perry & Juni-
ata Counties, Inc.
51 Church St
New Bloomfield PA 17068
717 582-4305

(G-11109)
ALBERT GRAY
Also Called: Gray's Pallets
Off Rte 32222 (17059)
PHONE.................................717 436-8585
Albert Gray, *Owner*

GEOGRAPHIC

EMP: 15
SQ FT: 16,000
SALES (est): 1.9MM **Privately Held**
SIC: 2448 Pallets, wood

(G-11110)
BIOFUEL BOILER TECH LLC
600 Airport Dr (17059-8408)
PHONE....................717 436-9300
Bruce Lisle, *Principal*
EMP: 4
SALES (est): 331.1K **Privately Held**
SIC: 2869 Fuels

(G-11111)
CAMEO KITCHENS INC
Old Rt 22 (17059)
P.O. Box 191 (17059-0191)
PHONE....................717 436-9598
John T Shellenberger, *President*
Roy Knepp, *Vice Pres*
Gary Felmlee, *Admin Sec*
EMP: 28
SQ FT: 13,700
SALES: 1.5MM **Privately Held**
WEB: www.cameokitchens.net
SIC: 2434 Wood kitchen cabinets

(G-11112)
CROWN HARDWOOD WEST INC
26960 Route 75 N (17059-7886)
PHONE....................717 436-9677
Peter Schlobauch, *President*
EMP: 3
SALES (est): 180.2K **Privately Held**
SIC: 2411 Logging

(G-11113)
E K HOLDINGS INC (HQ)
Rr 5 (17059)
PHONE....................717 436-5921
Jeff Brown, *CEO*
EMP: 7
SALES (est): 83.7MM **Publicly Held**
SIC: 2015 Chicken, processed

(G-11114)
EMPIRE KOSHER POULTRY INC (DH)
Also Called: Matterns Hatchery
Chicken Plant Rd (17059)
PHONE....................717 436-5921
Greg Rosenbaum, *CEO*
Paul Simkus, *Exec VP*
Lisa Nelson, *Senior VP*
William Walters, *Mfg Mgr*
James Tatum, *Purchasing*
◆ **EMP:** 900 **EST:** 1992
SQ FT: 240,000
SALES (est): 55.6MM **Publicly Held**
WEB: www.empirekosher.com
SIC: 5812 2015 Eating places; chicken, processed
HQ: E. K. Holdings Inc.
   Rr 5
   Mifflintown PA 17059
   717 436-5921

(G-11115)
ENERGEX INC
95 Energex Dr (17059-7748)
PHONE....................717 436-2400
John Burrows, *President*
Sherry Montis, *General Mgr*
Michael Shertzer, *Plant Mgr*
Kathy Gilson, *Human Resources*
EMP: 4
SALES (est): 333.4K **Privately Held**
SIC: 2411 Logging
PA: Energex Corporation
   95 Energex Dr
   Mifflintown PA 17059

(G-11116)
ENERGEX AMERICAN INC
95 Energex Dr (17059-7748)
PHONE....................717 436-2400
Bruce Lisle, *Principal*
Darryl Rose, *Vice Pres*
Max Beraud, *Plant Mgr*
Michael Derosa, *Treasurer*
Adam Becker, *Accounts Exec*
EMP: 38

SALES (est): 9.5MM
SALES (corp-wide): 15.3MM **Privately Held**
SIC: 2493 Reconstituted wood products
PA: Granules Combustibles Energex Inc
   3891 Rue Du President-Kennedy
   Lac-Megantic QC G6B 3
   819 583-5131

(G-11117)
ENERGEX CORPORATION (PA)
95 Energex Dr (17059-7748)
PHONE....................717 436-2400
John Burrows, *President*
▼ **EMP:** 82
SALES (est): 9.7MM **Privately Held**
SIC: 2493 Reconstituted wood products

(G-11118)
FLINT ROAD WELDING
540 Center Rd (17059-8162)
PHONE....................717 535-5282
Christie Kanagy, *Owner*
EMP: 6 **EST:** 2013
SQ FT: 7,200
SALES: 650K **Privately Held**
SIC: 7692 3441 5211 Welding repair; fabricated structural metal; lumber & other building materials

(G-11119)
GRAYS AUTOMOTIVE SPEED EQP
713 Washington Ave (17059-1417)
PHONE....................717 436-8777
Timothy E Gray, *Owner*
EMP: 3
SALES: 230K **Privately Held**
SIC: 5531 3621 Automotive & home supply stores; motors & generators

(G-11120)
H & M LUMBER
35 Petersheim Dr (17059-7568)
PHONE....................717 535-5080
Harvey Petersheim, *Owner*
EMP: 4
SALES (est): 238.8K **Privately Held**
SIC: 2448 7389 Pallets, wood;

(G-11121)
HAZARDS DISTILLERY INC
241 Nicholson Dr (17059-9010)
PHONE....................717 994-4860
Robert Hazard, *Principal*
EMP: 4
SALES (est): 300.5K **Privately Held**
SIC: 2085 Distilled & blended liquors

(G-11122)
HEIRLOOM CABINETRY PA INC
977 Nelson Rd (17059-8035)
PHONE....................717 436-8091
Theodore E Wagner, *President*
Robin A Wagner, *Admin Sec*
EMP: 12
SQ FT: 3,000
SALES (est): 1.3MM **Privately Held**
SIC: 2434 Wood kitchen cabinets

(G-11123)
IMPRESSIONS PRINTING & PUBG
5196 W River Rd (17059-7891)
PHONE....................717 436-2034
Sally Leaper, *Owner*
EMP: 4
SALES: 140K **Privately Held**
SIC: 2759 Commercial printing

(G-11124)
J & M PALLET LLC
506 Oak Dr (17059-8653)
PHONE....................717 463-9205
Barbara Peachey, *Mng Member*
Nelson Peachey, *Manager*
Andrew Peachey,
EMP: 8
SALES (est): 660K **Privately Held**
SIC: 2448 Pallets, wood; pallets, wood & wood with metal

(G-11125)
JUNIATA CONCRETE CO (PA)
721 Smith Rd (17059-7456)
PHONE....................717 436-2176
John E Groninger Jr, *President*
Kim Bomberger, *Corp Secy*
Dave Bomberger, *Vice Pres*
EMP: 20
SQ FT: 20,000
SALES: 6.3MM **Privately Held**
SIC: 3273 3272 5051 Ready-mixed concrete; concrete products, precast; steel decking

(G-11126)
K S M ENTERPRISES INC
224 White Pine Ln (17059-9818)
PHONE....................717 463-2383
EMP: 6
SQ FT: 16,000
SALES (est): 603.5K **Privately Held**
SIC: 2452 Mfg Prefabricated Wood Buildings

(G-11127)
KEYSTONE KOATING LLC
583 E Industrial Dr (17059-8296)
PHONE....................717 436-2056
Paul Zimmerman, *President*
EMP: 66
SALES (corp-wide): 40.6MM **Privately Held**
WEB: www.pbzinc.com
SIC: 3479 Etching & engraving
HQ: Keystone Koating Llc
   295 Wood Corner Rd
   Lititz PA 17543

(G-11128)
LAUREL RUN PALLET COMPANY LLC
975 Billyville Rd (17059-8610)
PHONE....................717 436-5428
Allen Wengerd, *Mng Member*
Donna Saner, *Manager*
EMP: 14
SALES (est): 2.2MM **Privately Held**
SIC: 2448 Pallets, wood

(G-11129)
LOST CREEK SHOE SHOP INC
643 Oakland Rd (17059-8659)
PHONE....................717 463-3117
David Troyer, *President*
Mary Troyer, *Treasurer*
EMP: 4
SQ FT: 4,368
SALES (est): 609.5K **Privately Held**
WEB: www.lostcreekgolfpa.com
SIC: 5661 3827 5941 Shoe stores; sighting & fire control equipment, optical; saddlery & equestrian equipment

(G-11130)
MEXICO HEAT TREATING
Rr 2 (17059-9802)
PHONE....................717 535-5034
Brenda Shaffer, *Owner*
EMP: 5
SALES (est): 541.4K **Privately Held**
SIC: 3398 Metal heat treating

(G-11131)
NORTH EAST LOUVERS INC
481 E Industrial Park Dr (17059)
PHONE....................717 436-5300
Robert J Allen, *President*
Michael Allen, *Vice Pres*
Robert W Allen, *Vice Pres*
EMP: 10
SALES (est): 740K **Privately Held**
SIC: 3446 Louvers, ventilating

(G-11132)
POWERSAFE INC
4311 William Penn Hwy (17059-7895)
PHONE....................717 436-5380
John Groninger Jr, *President*
EMP: 3
SQ FT: 1,000
SALES: 1.6MM **Privately Held**
WEB: www.powersafeusa.com
SIC: 3643 Current-carrying wiring devices

(G-11133)
R&F PALLET CO
Rr 1 (17059-9801)
PHONE....................717 463-3560
R Keith Nipple, *Principal*
EMP: 6
SALES (est): 830.3K **Privately Held**
SIC: 2448 Pallets, wood & wood with metal

(G-11134)
ROSEWOOD KITCHENS INC
12 Industrial Cir (17059-9572)
P.O. Box 141 (17059-0141)
PHONE....................717 436-9878
Robert J Rowles, *President*
Elizabeth Rowles, *Vice Pres*
EMP: 20
SALES (est): 2MM **Privately Held**
SIC: 2434 Wood kitchen cabinets

(G-11135)
SHADY HILL HARDWOOD INC
Rr 2 Box 1225 (17059)
PHONE....................717 463-9475
Henry Kanagy, *President*
Samuel Kanagy, *President*
EMP: 4
SQ FT: 3,500
SALES (est): 564.3K **Privately Held**
SIC: 2421 Sawmills & planing mills, general

(G-11136)
TREEN BOX & PALLET CORP (PA)
400 Center Rd (17059-8160)
P.O. Box 368, Bensalem (19020-0368)
PHONE....................717 535-5800
George P Geiges, *President*
Delores Fisher, *Corp Secy*
Albert Geiges, *Vice Pres*
EMP: 50 **EST:** 1948
SQ FT: 2,000
SALES (est): 8.1MM **Privately Held**
SIC: 2448 2449 2441 Pallets, wood; rectangular boxes & crates, wood; nailed wood boxes & shook

(G-11137)
TROYER PALLET COMPANY
81 Center Rd (17059-8156)
PHONE....................717 535-4499
Raymond Troyer, *Park Mgr*
EMP: 7
SALES: 520K **Privately Held**
SIC: 2448 Pallets, wood

(G-11138)
TRUSS-TECH INC
98 E Industrial Dr (17059-8253)
PHONE....................717 436-9778
Jeffery Whitesel, *President*
Kathy Whitesel, *Admin Sec*
EMP: 30
SQ FT: 15,000
SALES (est): 3.6MM **Privately Held**
SIC: 2439 Trusses, wooden roof

(G-11139)
ULTRA PURE PRODUCTS INC
Also Called: Mountain Pure Water Systems
46 N Main St (17059-1003)
P.O. Box 589, Millerstown (17062-0589)
PHONE....................717 589-7001
Fax: 717 436-8291
EMP: 20
SQ FT: 30,000
SALES: 1.2MM **Privately Held**
SIC: 3589 5084 5074 Water Treatment Retail Sales & Service

(G-11140)
VALLEY PROTEINS INC
687 Cleck Rd (17059-9117)
P.O. Box 1 (17059-0001)
PHONE....................717 436-0004
John Hamzik, *General Mgr*
Shane Taylor, *Transptn Dir*
Wade Cleck, *Manager*
Jamie Faison, *Manager*
R Hutson, *Manager*
EMP: 60

SALES (corp-wide): 493.7MM **Privately Held**
WEB: www.valleyproteins.com
SIC: 2077 Rendering
PA: Valley Proteins (De), Inc.
151 Valpro Dr
Winchester VA 22603
540 877-2533

(G-11141)
WALKER WOOD PRODUCTS INC
1060 Smith Rd (17059-7460)
PHONE...............................717 436-2105
Bill Mac Cauley, *CEO*
Douglas R Hostler, *President*
Vernon Troier, *Vice Pres*
EMP: 15 EST: 1996
SQ FT: 47,000
SALES (est): 2.4MM **Privately Held**
SIC: 2449 Wood containers

(G-11142)
WEAVER PALLET COMPANY
2107 Free Springs Ch Rd (17059)
PHONE...............................717 463-3037
EMP: 10 EST: 2007
SALES (est): 570K **Privately Held**
SIC: 2448 Mfg Wood Pallets/Skids

(G-11143)
WEBER ELECTMOTOR SERVICE
310 Henry St (17059-7610)
PHONE...............................717 436-8120
Joe Weber, *Owner*
EMP: 4
SALES (est): 383.1K **Privately Held**
SIC: 7694 Electric motor repair

(G-11144)
WENGERD PALLET COMPANY
1824 Rockland Rd (17059-8826)
PHONE...............................717 463-3274
Raymond Troyer, *Partner*
Eli Troyer, *Partner*
Wayne Troyer, *Partner*
EMP: 20
SALES: 8MM **Privately Held**
SIC: 2448 Pallets, wood

Mifflinville
Columbia County

(G-11145)
WILKES POOL CORP
Interstate 80 Exit 242 (18631)
P.O. Box F (18631-0486)
PHONE...............................570 759-0317
Gerald Stancavage, *President*
EMP: 40
SQ FT: 30,000
SALES (est): 4.4MM **Privately Held**
WEB: www.wilkespools.com
SIC: 3949 Swimming pools, plastic

Milan
Bradford County

(G-11146)
COLE CONSTRUCTION INC
27315 Route 220 (18831-9624)
PHONE...............................570 888-5501
Alan Cole, *President*
Murray Cole, *Officer*
Leo Drabinski, *Officer*
EMP: 3
SALES: 1MM **Privately Held**
SIC: 2951 Asphalt & asphaltic paving mixtures (not from refineries)

(G-11147)
D & R STEEL CONSTRUCTION INC
28463 Route 220 (18831-7753)
P.O. Box 108, Towanda (18848-0108)
PHONE...............................570 265-6216
Robert Reeves, *President*
EMP: 12
SQ FT: 700

SALES (est): 1.6MM **Privately Held**
SIC: 1799 3498 7349 1791 Welding on site; pipe fittings, fabricated from purchased pipe; air duct cleaning; structural steel erection

(G-11148)
R L KINGSLEY LUMBER COMPANY
3404 Milan Rd (18831-7724)
PHONE...............................570 596-3575
Rex L Kingsley, *Owner*
Sarah Kingsley, *Admin Sec*
EMP: 15
SALES (est): 1.2MM **Privately Held**
SIC: 2421 5031 5211 Sawmills & planing mills, general; lumber, plywood & millwork; lumber & other building materials

(G-11149)
R S W ENTERPRISES INC
1 Railroad St (18831)
P.O. Box 58 (18831-0058)
PHONE...............................570 888-2184
Fax: 570 888-9255
EMP: 6
SQ FT: 8,600
SALES (est): 781.9K **Privately Held**
SIC: 2451 5271 Mfg Mobile Homes Ret Mobile Homes

(G-11150)
SOUTO MOULD
1283 Laurel Hill Rd (18831-7840)
PHONE...............................570 596-3128
Len Suoto, *Managing Prtnr*
Len Suoto, *Managing Prtnr*
Liz Ross, *Partner*
EMP: 3
SALES: 170K **Privately Held**
SIC: 2431 Moldings, wood: unfinished & prefinished

Milesburg
Centre County

(G-11151)
HILEX POLY CO LLC
606 Old Curtin Rd (16853)
P.O. Box 258 (16853-0258)
PHONE...............................814 355-7410
Jim Lassiger, *Branch Mgr*
EMP: 122
SALES (corp-wide): 3B **Privately Held**
SIC: 2673 Plastic bags: made from purchased materials
HQ: Hilex Poly Co. Llc
101 E Carolina Ave
Hartsville SC 29550
843 857-4800

(G-11152)
JERRY D WATSON JR
Also Called: Cabinet Fashions
329 Old 220 Rd 220th (16853)
P.O. Box 598 (16853-0598)
PHONE...............................814 355-7104
Jerry D Watson Jr, *Owner*
EMP: 6 EST: 1972
SQ FT: 8,000
SALES: 850K **Privately Held**
WEB: www.cabinetfashions.com
SIC: 2434 Wood kitchen cabinets

Milford
Pike County

(G-11153)
ALL CLIMATE SERVICING
103 Dove Ct (18337-5024)
PHONE...............................570 686-4629
William E Welch, *Principal*
EMP: 5
SALES (est): 232.7K **Privately Held**
SIC: 1389 Roustabout service

(G-11154)
ALTEC LANSING INC
535 Route 6 And 209 (18337-7847)
PHONE...............................570 296-4434

Nick Jonas, *Principal*
EMP: 13 EST: 2014
SALES (est): 1.1MM **Privately Held**
SIC: 3651 Household audio & video equipment

(G-11155)
ALTERNATIVE PETROLEUM SVCS LLC
301 W Ann St (18337-1413)
P.O. Box 820 (18337-0820)
PHONE...............................570 807-1797
Shelly Sciascia, *Principal*
EMP: 4
SALES (est): 142.4K **Privately Held**
SIC: 1381 Drilling oil & gas wells

(G-11156)
ARCHITECTURAL IRON COMPANY
Also Called: Capital Crestings
104 Ironwood Ct (18337-9066)
P.O. Box 126 (18337-0126)
PHONE...............................570 296-7722
Donald G Quick, *President*
EMP: 22
SQ FT: 16,400
SALES (est): 3.4MM **Privately Held**
WEB: www.architecturaliron.com
SIC: 3462 Iron & steel forgings

(G-11157)
CLARION SAFETY SYSTEMS LLC
190 Old Milford Rd (18337-7601)
P.O. Box 1174 (18337-2174)
PHONE...............................570 296-5686
Geoffrey Peckham, *CEO*
Annette Martin, *Vice Pres*
Mark Stevens, *CFO*
Tammie Samartina, *Sales Staff*
Sonya Scott, *Sales Staff*
EMP: 45
SALES (est): 6.2MM **Privately Held**
WEB: www.safetylabel.com
SIC: 2759 Decals: printing

(G-11158)
DANIEL PARENT
Also Called: Astrocomix
102 Link Rd (18337-4227)
PHONE...............................914 850-5473
Dan Parent, *Owner*
EMP: 3
SALES (est): 178.5K **Privately Held**
SIC: 2721 Comic books: publishing & printing

(G-11159)
EDGELL COMMUNICATIONS
Also Called: Consumer Goods Manufacturing
134 Vandermark Dr (18337-9480)
PHONE...............................570 296-8330
Douglas Edgell, *President*
EMP: 25
SALES (est): 1MM **Privately Held**
SIC: 2721 Periodicals

(G-11160)
EUREKA STONE QUARRY INC
460 Route 6 (18337-7279)
PHONE...............................570 296-6632
George McCracken, *Manager*
EMP: 6
SALES (corp-wide): 24.4MM **Privately Held**
SIC: 3281 Cut stone & stone products
PA: Eureka Stone Quarry, Inc.
Lower Stte Pickertown Rds
Chalfont PA 18914
215 822-0593

(G-11161)
ICBRIDAL LLC
322 Broad St (18337-1345)
PHONE...............................570 409-6333
EMP: 5
SALES (est): 211.4K **Privately Held**
SIC: 2335 Mfg Women's/Misses' Dresses

(G-11162)
LUPOSELLO ENTERPRISES
107 Bull Run N (18337-7690)
PHONE...............................570 994-2500
John Luposello, *Owner*

EMP: 10
SQ FT: 4,000
SALES (est): 563.6K **Privately Held**
SIC: 2759 Commercial printing; sports apparel; glassware; banners, flags, decals & posters

(G-11163)
NEW GEAR BRANDS LLC
214 W Harford St Unit 2 (18337-1140)
PHONE...............................407 674-6850
Gail Backal, *Owner*
▲ EMP: 9
SALES (est): 1.2MM **Privately Held**
SIC: 3111 Bag leather

(G-11164)
NEWS EAGLE
301 E Harford St (18337-1000)
PHONE...............................570 296-4547
J W Johnson, *Principal*
EMP: 8
SALES (est): 295.7K
SALES (corp-wide): 1.2MM **Privately Held**
WEB: www.neagle.com
SIC: 2711 Newspapers, publishing & printing
PA: The News Eagle
220 8th St
Honesdale PA 18431
570 226-4547

(G-11165)
NORTH AMERICAN PACKAGING LLC
Also Called: Econo Pak
535 Route 6 And 209 Ste A (18337-7847)
PHONE...............................570 296-4200
Bob Szyani, *Principal*
▲ EMP: 100
SALES (est): 36.3MM **Privately Held**
SIC: 2043 Cereal breakfast foods

(G-11166)
PIKE COUNTY DISPATCH INC
105 W Catherine St (18337-1417)
P.O. Box 186 (18337-0186)
PHONE...............................570 296-2611
Sue Doty Lloyd, *President*
EMP: 15
SQ FT: 3,200
SALES (est): 1MM **Privately Held**
SIC: 2711 7313 Newspapers, publishing & printing; newspaper advertising representative

(G-11167)
POWER SYSTEMS SPECIALISTS INC
103 Route 6 (18337-1240)
PHONE...............................570 296-4573
Dave Naples, *Branch Mgr*
Ray Kissane, *Technical Staff*
EMP: 10
SALES (corp-wide): 1.9MM **Privately Held**
WEB: www.p-s-s.com
SIC: 3612 Transformers, except electric
PA: Power Systems Specialists, Inc.
103 Route 6
Milford PA 18337
888 305-1555

(G-11168)
WILLIAM DELEEUW CO
102 Schocopee Ct (18337-9337)
PHONE...............................570 296-2694
EMP: 4
SALES (est): 359K **Privately Held**
SIC: 3083 Mfg Laminated Plastic Plate/Sheet

Mill Creek
Huntingdon County

(G-11169)
WORLD MARKETING OF AMERICA (PA)
12256 William Penn Hwy (17060)
P.O. Box 192 (17060-0192)
PHONE...............................814 643-6500
Delmont R Sunderland, *President*

GEOGRAPHIC

Suzanne Beezer, *Purchasing*
Steve Koval, *Controller*
Janelle Sunderland, *Accounting Mgr*
Dodie Price, *Sales Staff*
◆ **EMP:** 25
SQ FT: 32,000
SALES (est): 7.8MM **Privately Held**
SIC: 7389 5074 3567 Labeling bottles, cans, cartons, etc.; heating equipment (hydronic); heating units & devices, industrial: electric

Mill Hall
Clinton County

(G-11170)
APPALACHIAN WOODCRAFTS LLC
88 Airstrip Dr (17751-9398)
PHONE..................................570 726-7149
Lloyd Stoltzfus,
EMP: 8
SQ FT: 10,000
SALES (est): 1.3MM **Privately Held**
SIC: 2452 Modular homes, prefabricated, wood

(G-11171)
AUTOMATED UNMANNED VEHICLE SYS
155 Orchard Hill Ln (17751-8890)
PHONE..................................570 748-3844
Jeffrey Parker,
Alison Parker, *Admin Sec*
EMP: 6
SALES: 950K **Privately Held**
SIC: 3714 Motor vehicle parts & accessories

(G-11172)
AVERY DENNISON CORPORATION
Also Called: Ad Performance Polymers USA
171 Draketown Rd (17751-8608)
PHONE..................................570 748-7701
Don Eyer, *Buyer*
Bill Bottorf, *Research*
Lance Karstetter, *Research*
Nathaniel Weiner, *Branch Mgr*
Sue Caris, *Technician*
EMP: 75
SALES (corp-wide): 7.1B **Publicly Held**
WEB: www.avery.com
SIC: 2672 Coated paper, except photographic, carbon or abrasive
PA: Avery Dennison Corporation
207 N Goode Ave Ste 500
Glendale CA 91203
626 304-2000

(G-11173)
BINGAMAN & SON LUMBER INC
Also Called: Pine Creek Lumber, Co
60 Lizardville Rd (17751-8845)
PHONE..................................570 726-7795
Bob Shields, *Manager*
EMP: 20
SALES (corp-wide): 65MM **Privately Held**
WEB: www.bingamanlumber.com
SIC: 5211 2426 2421 Millwork & lumber; hardwood dimension & flooring mills; sawmills & planing mills, general
PA: Bingaman & Son Lumber, Inc.
1195 Creek Mountain Rd
Kreamer PA 17833
570 374-1108

(G-11174)
CONDOS INCORPORATED
Also Called: Condo's Welding
131 Draketown Rd (17751-8608)
PHONE..................................570 748-9265
Glenn M Condo Jr, *President*
Terry Condo, *Corp Secy*
Thomas Condo, *Vice Pres*
EMP: 22 **EST:** 1973
SQ FT: 1,200
SALES (est): 3.8MM **Privately Held**
SIC: 1711 7539 7692 Mechanical contractor; radiator repair shop, automotive; welding repair

(G-11175)
CRODA INC
8 Croda Way (17751-8727)
PHONE..................................570 893-7650
Dave Johnson, *Manager*
EMP: 47
SALES (corp-wide): 1.8B **Privately Held**
WEB: www.crodausa.com
SIC: 2833 2899 Medicinals & botanicals; chemical preparations
HQ: Croda, Inc.
300 Columbus Cir Ste A
Edison NJ 08837
732 417-0800

(G-11176)
EAST END WELDING
31 Welders Ln (17751-9305)
PHONE..................................570 726-7925
Gillian Spoltzs, *Owner*
EMP: 5
SALES: 400K **Privately Held**
SIC: 7692 7699 Welding repair; hydraulic equipment repair

(G-11177)
H M SPENCER WIRE
Also Called: Johnston Dandy Company, The
1004 Ridge Rd (17751-8712)
PHONE..................................570 726-7495
Daniel Johnston, *President*
Robert Johnston, *Vice Pres*
EMP: 5
SALES (est): 589.8K **Privately Held**
SIC: 3554 Paper industries machinery

(G-11178)
KITCO TOOL INC
21 Water St (17751)
P.O. Box 184 (17751-0184)
PHONE..................................570 726-6190
Charles L Stevenson, *President*
Hazel A Stevenson, *Corp Secy*
EMP: 6 **EST:** 1966
SQ FT: 7,500
SALES (est): 719.3K **Privately Held**
SIC: 3561 Pumps & pumping equipment

(G-11179)
MILL HALL CLAY PRODUCTS INC
2 Homestead Dr (17751-9623)
PHONE..................................570 726-6752
A R Thorson, *President*
Richard Campbell, *Vice Pres*
David McGinniss, *Vice Pres*
Robert Campbell, *Treasurer*
Lynn Thorson, *Treasurer*
EMP: 39 **EST:** 1947
SQ FT: 10,000
SALES (est): 2.5MM **Privately Held**
SIC: 3259 5719 Flue lining, clay; drain tile, clay; sewer pipe or fittings, clay; chimney pipe & tops, clay; pottery

(G-11180)
PHILLIPS WOOD PRODUCTS INC
479 Sugar Run Rd (17751-8580)
PHONE..................................570 726-3515
Carl Phillips, *President*
Neil Phillips, *Vice Pres*
EMP: 16
SQ FT: 2,100
SALES (est): 1.8MM **Privately Held**
SIC: 2421 Wood chips, produced at mill; lumber: rough, sawed or planed

(G-11181)
RENNINGERS CABINETREE INC
Also Called: Clinton County Cabinetry
225 Long Run Rd (17751-8867)
PHONE..................................570 726-6494
Ernest E Renninger, *President*
Nancy Renninger, *Corp Secy*
EMP: 24
SQ FT: 12,000
SALES (est): 2.2MM **Privately Held**
SIC: 2434 1751 2511 Wood kitchen cabinets; cabinet building & installation; wood household furniture

(G-11182)
SNAVELYS MILL INC
22 Fishing Creek Rd (17751-9127)
PHONE..................................570 726-4747
Al Brandt, *General Mgr*
Dan Snavely, *Manager*
EMP: 13
SALES (corp-wide): 3.5MM **Privately Held**
SIC: 2041 Wheat flour
PA: Snavely's Mill, Inc.
333 Snavely Mill Rd
Lititz PA 17543
717 626-6256

(G-11183)
TRIPLE D TRUSS LLC
168 Sunrise Ln (17751-8924)
PHONE..................................570 726-7092
John Stoltzfus, *Mng Member*
Daniel Fisher,
EMP: 32
SALES (est): 9.1MM **Privately Held**
SIC: 2439 Trusses, wooden roof

(G-11184)
WEBBS SUPER-GRO PRODUCTS INC
30 Pennsylvania Ave (17751-1806)
P.O. Box C (17751-0166)
PHONE..................................570 726-4525
James P Webb Jr, *President*
Jennifer Babcock, *Admin Sec*
EMP: 24 **EST:** 1963
SQ FT: 2,800
SALES (est): 9.1MM **Privately Held**
WEB: www.webbsupergro.com
SIC: 5191 2875 0711 Chemicals, agricultural; pesticides; fertilizers, mixing only; fertilizer application services

Mill Run
Fayette County

(G-11185)
AMERIHOHL MINING
940 Jim Mountain Rd (15464-1355)
PHONE..................................724 455-4450
Rich Hall, *Principal*
EMP: 3
SALES (est): 161K **Privately Held**
SIC: 1241 Mining services: lignite

Millersburg
Dauphin County

(G-11186)
ADVANCED SCIENTIFICS INC
Also Called: A S I
163 Research Ln (17061-9402)
PHONE..................................717 692-2104
Carl Martin, *CEO*
Kent Smeltz, *President*
Jay Martin, *Vice Pres*
▲ **EMP:** 320
SQ FT: 70,000
SALES (est): 93.8MM
SALES (corp-wide): 24.3B **Publicly Held**
WEB: www.advancedscientifics.com
SIC: 3069 Medical & laboratory rubber sundries & related products; tubes, hard rubber
PA: Thermo Fisher Scientific Inc.
168 3rd Ave
Waltham MA 02451
781 622-1000

(G-11187)
ALVORD-POLK INC
Also Called: Ampm
125 Gehrhart St (17061-1295)
PHONE..................................800 925-2126
Pat Panza, *President*
John Panza, *Vice Pres*
Mike Demale, *Bd of Directors*
Maryann Kost, *Admin Sec*
EMP: 4 **EST:** 1976
SQ FT: 4,000

SALES: 431K **Privately Held**
WEB: www.ampmfasteners.com
SIC: 3728 3452 Aircraft parts & equipment; bolts, nuts, rivets & washers

(G-11188)
ALVORD-POLK INC (PA)
Also Called: Alvord-Polk Tool Company
125 Gehrhart St (17061-1295)
P.O. Box 97 (17061-0097)
PHONE..................................605 847-4823
Ronald E Boyer, *President*
Robert Rissinger, *Corp Secy*
Bill Lahr, *Vice Pres*
Gene Paul, *Plant Mgr*
Dennis Youells, *Maint Spvr*
▲ **EMP:** 85
SQ FT: 40,000
SALES: 14MM **Privately Held**
WEB: www.alvordpolk.com
SIC: 3545 3991 Reamers, machine tool; brushes, household or industrial

(G-11189)
ALVORD-POLK INC
Morton Machine Works
135 Gehrhart St (17061-1295)
PHONE..................................717 692-2128
David Boyer, *General Mgr*
EMP: 15
SALES (corp-wide): 14MM **Privately Held**
WEB: www.alvordpolk.com
SIC: 3544 5085 Jigs & fixtures; industrial supplies
PA: Alvord-Polk, Inc.
125 Gehrhart St
Millersburg PA 17061
605 847-4823

(G-11190)
ANGEL PINS AND MORE
2141 State Route 209 (17061-8237)
PHONE..................................717 692-5086
Donna Beitman, *Principal*
EMP: 3
SALES (est): 190.3K **Privately Held**
SIC: 3452 Pins

(G-11191)
BRUBAKER TOOL CORPORATION (PA)
200 Front St (17061-1399)
PHONE..................................717 692-2113
William F Coyle Jr, *President*
EMP: 296 **EST:** 1881
SQ FT: 125,000
SALES (est): 29.2MM **Privately Held**
WEB: www.brubakertool.com
SIC: 3541 5084 3545 Machine tools, metal cutting type; tapping attachments; machine tool accessories

(G-11192)
DAUPHIN PRECISION TOOL LLC
Also Called: Talbot
200 Front St (17061-1324)
PHONE..................................800 522-8665
William Coyle Jr, *President*
Gary Lahr, *Manager*
Hellan Rodichok, *Admin Sec*
▲ **EMP:** 140
SALES: 15MM
SALES (corp-wide): 21.8MM **Privately Held**
SIC: 3545 Cutting tools for machine tools
PA: Harpoint Holdings, Inc
200 Front St
Millersburg PA 17061
717 692-2113

(G-11193)
DIE BOTSCHAFT
420 Weaver Rd (17061-9509)
PHONE..................................717 433-4417
EMP: 5
SALES (est): 354.8K **Privately Held**
SIC: 3544 Special dies & tools

(G-11194)
HARPOINT HOLDINGS INC (PA)
200 Front St (17061-1324)
PHONE..................................717 692-2113
William F Coyle Jr, *President*
David R Pelizzon, *Vice Pres*
EMP: 2

SALES (est): 21.8MM **Privately Held**
SIC: 3545 Cutting tools for machine tools

(G-11195)
MANUGRAPH AMERICAS INC
Also Called: Manugraph Dgm
158 Damhill Rd (17061)
P.O. Box 573, Elizabethville (17023-0573)
PHONE....................................717 362-3243
Andrew Welker, *President*
William Hummer, *Corp Secy*
Ron Ehrhardt, *Vice Pres*
Kyle Monroe, *Vice Pres*
Matt Chubb, *Opers Staff*
▲ EMP: 29 EST: 1973
SQ FT: 80,000
SALES: 8.5MM
SALES (corp-wide): 27.5MM **Privately Held**
WEB: www.dauphingraphic.com
SIC: 3555 7699 Printing trades machinery; printing trades machinery & equipment repair
PA: Manugraph India Limited
1st Floor, Sidhwa House
Mumbai MH 40000
222 287-0620

(G-11196)
MI METALS INC
1517 Rte 209 (17061)
PHONE....................................717 692-4851
Richard Schylaske, *Branch Mgr*
EMP: 19
SALES (corp-wide): 27.7MM **Privately Held**
SIC: 3354 Aluminum extruded products
HQ: Mi Metals, Inc.
301 Commerce Blvd
Oldsmar FL 34677
813 855-5695

(G-11197)
MOUNTAIN RIDGE METALS LLC
1517 Rte 209 (17061)
PHONE....................................717 692-4851
Kevin Sponsler,
EMP: 130
SQ FT: 115,000
SALES (est): 12.3MM **Privately Held**
SIC: 3354 Aluminum extruded products

(G-11198)
PROPLASTIX INTERNATIONAL INC
1519 State Route 209 (17061-8217)
PHONE....................................717 692-4733
Peter Desoto, *CEO*
Sara W Guthrie, *Ch of Bd*
Jay K Poppleton, *President*
Jeffrey P Paradise, *Vice Pres*
Janet L Fasenmyer, *VP Finance*
EMP: 120
SQ FT: 103,000
SALES (est): 16.4MM
SALES (corp-wide): 1.1B **Privately Held**
SIC: 3081 3089 Vinyl film & sheet; fences, gates & accessories: plastic
PA: J. T. Walker Industries, Inc.
1310 N Hercules Ave Ste A
Clearwater FL 33765
727 461-0501

(G-11199)
REAL SCENT
667 Wert Rd (17061-8788)
PHONE....................................717 692-0527
Elam Lapp, *Owner*
EMP: 4
SALES (est): 210K **Privately Held**
SIC: 5941 3949 Hunting equipment; hunting equipment

(G-11200)
SEAL GLOVE MFG INC
Also Called: Ark Safety
525 North St (17061-2421)
PHONE....................................717 692-4837
William A Specht III, *President*
Sheri Hess, *Treasurer*
Robin Stoner, *Treasurer*
William Specht, *Mktg Dir*
Janet E Specht, *Admin Sec*
EMP: 15 EST: 1906
SQ FT: 32,500

SALES (est): 2.9MM **Privately Held**
WEB: www.sealglove.com
SIC: 7382 3842 Protective devices, security; respiratory protection equipment, personal

(G-11201)
SUNRISE NATURALS LLC
420 Weaver Rd (17061-9509)
PHONE....................................717 350-6169
EMP: 6
SALES (est): 587.1K **Privately Held**
SIC: 2082 Malt beverages

(G-11202)
TALBOT HOLDINGS LLC
200 Front St (17061-1324)
PHONE....................................717 692-2113
Robert C McKee, *President*
EMP: 120
SQ FT: 70,000
SALES (est): 7.6MM **Privately Held**
WEB: www.talbotholdings.com
SIC: 3545 3542 3541 Cutting tools for machine tools; machine tools, metal forming type; machine tools, metal cutting type

(G-11203)
THERMO FISHER SCIENTIFIC INC
163 Research Ln (17061-9402)
PHONE....................................717 692-2104
Josh Easter, *Info Tech Mgr*
EMP: 320
SALES (corp-wide): 24.3B **Publicly Held**
SIC: 3069 Medical & laboratory rubber sundries & related products; tubes, hard rubber
PA: Thermo Fisher Scientific Inc.
168 3rd Ave
Waltham MA 02451
781 622-1000

Millerstown
Perry County

(G-11204)
HALLS ICE CREAM INC
861 Raccoon Valley Rd (17062-8902)
PHONE....................................717 589-3290
Allen R Hall, *President*
Margrett Hall Raub, *Corp Secy*
EMP: 15
SQ FT: 3,584
SALES: 500K **Privately Held**
WEB: www.hallsicecream.com
SIC: 2024 5451 Ice cream, packaged: molded, on sticks, etc.; ice cream (packaged)

(G-11205)
LLC SNYDER GATES
2339 Highland Rd (17062-8331)
PHONE....................................877 621-0195
Nolan Snyder, *Owner*
▲ EMP: 4 EST: 2008
SALES (est): 364.3K **Privately Held**
SIC: 3089 Fences, gates & accessories: plastic

(G-11206)
MILL RUN CARRIAGE
355 Lyons Rd (17062-9239)
PHONE....................................717 438-3149
Jason G Stoltzfus, *President*
EMP: 7
SALES (est): 1.1MM **Privately Held**
WEB: www.millruncarriage.com
SIC: 3523 Trailers & wagons, farm

(G-11207)
PERRY PALLET INC
5124 Sugar Run Rd (17062-8763)
PHONE....................................717 589-3345
Keith Scheaffer, *President*
EMP: 24
SALES: 5MM **Privately Held**
SIC: 2448 5211 Pallets, wood; lumber & other building materials

(G-11208)
RONALD KAUFFMAN
Also Called: Shallenberger Lumber Co
100 Owl Hollow Rd (17062-9215)
PHONE....................................717 589-3789
EMP: 7
SALES (est): 350K **Privately Held**
SIC: 2421 Sawmill/Planing Mill

Millersville
Lancaster County

(G-11209)
ADVANCED MACHINE TECHNOLOGIES
19 Russet Ln (17551-1348)
PHONE....................................717 871-9724
Jonathan Price, *President*
Michael J Stranko, *Treasurer*
William J Beck, *Admin Sec*
EMP: 3
SALES: 75K **Privately Held**
SIC: 3569 Filters

(G-11210)
COLOR IMPRESSIONS INC
433 Brook View Dr (17551-2001)
PHONE....................................717 872-2666
Michael Kilheffer, *President*
Patrick Reinhart, *Corp Secy*
EMP: 4
SQ FT: 7,000
SALES (est): 485.6K **Privately Held**
SIC: 2752 Commercial printing, offset

(G-11211)
LIBERTY CRAFTSMEN INC
202 Springdale Ln (17551-9529)
PHONE....................................717 871-0125
J Frank Young Jr, *President*
Bruce Hampton, *Vice Pres*
EMP: 4 EST: 1930
SQ FT: 4,000
SALES: 300K **Privately Held**
SIC: 2752 3953 2759 Commercial printing, offset; marking devices; letterpress printing

(G-11212)
MILLER METALCRAFT INC
113 E Charlotte St (17551-1505)
PHONE....................................717 399-8100
Lee Zipf, *Vice Pres*
Rob Lieblein, *Treasurer*
Zen Tgarf, *Admin Sec*
EMP: 35
SQ FT: 18,000
SALES (est): 6.3MM **Privately Held**
WEB: www.millermetalcraft.com
SIC: 3441 Fabricated structural metal

(G-11213)
MILLERSVILLE UNIVERSITY PA
Also Called: Snapper, The
Student Memrl Ctr Mu 18 (17551)
PHONE....................................717 871-4636
Gene Ellis, *Branch Mgr*
EMP: 20 **Privately Held**
WEB: www.millersv.edu
SIC: 2711 8221 9411 Newspapers, publishing & printing; university; administration of educational programs;
HQ: Millersville University Of Pennsylvania
1 S George St
Millersville PA 17551

Millerton
Tioga County

(G-11214)
BIO SUN SYSTEMS INC
7088 Route 549 Ste 2 (16936-9350)
PHONE....................................570 537-2200
Donna J White, *President*
Allen White, *Technical Staff*
EMP: 6
SQ FT: 3,000
SALES: 1MM **Privately Held**
WEB: www.biosunsystems.com
SIC: 2842 Sanitation preparations

(G-11215)
JAMES F SARGENT
6350 Route 549 (16936-9447)
PHONE....................................570 549-2168
James Sargent, *Principal*
EMP: 3
SALES: 160K **Privately Held**
SIC: 2041 Flour & other grain mill products

(G-11216)
T-M-T GRAVEL AND CONTG INC
8792 Route 549 (16936-7789)
PHONE....................................570 537-2647
Charlton Dygert, *President*
John Shannon, *CFO*
Brian Latshaw, *Manager*
Erin Dygert, *Admin Sec*
EMP: 10
SALES (est): 1.3MM **Privately Held**
SIC: 1442 Construction sand & gravel

Millheim
Centre County

(G-11217)
CENTRE COUNTY WOMENS JOURNAL
165 Main St (16854)
PHONE....................................814 349-8202
Terre Rill, *Principal*
EMP: 6 EST: 2007
SALES (est): 192.8K **Privately Held**
SIC: 2711 Newspapers, publishing & printing

(G-11218)
GOOD SCENTS CANDLE CO INC
115 E Main St (16854)
P.O. Box 30 (16854-0030)
PHONE....................................814 349-5848
Judy Shawver, *President*
Wayne Shawver, *Treasurer*
▲ EMP: 6
SQ FT: 3,000
SALES (est): 702.4K **Privately Held**
SIC: 3999 5947 5199 Candles; gift shop; candles

Millmont
Union County

(G-11219)
CATANIA FOLK INSTRUMENTS INC
521 Paddy Mountain Rd (17845-9429)
PHONE....................................570 922-4487
Steven J Catania, *President*
Tami Catania, *Vice Pres*
EMP: 3
SALES: 200K **Privately Held**
SIC: 3931 Musical instruments

(G-11220)
THOMAS HENRY POTOESKI
Also Called: Potoeski Decal Aplicat Svcs
17355 Old Turnpike Rd (17845-9334)
PHONE....................................570 922-3361
Thomas Potoeski, *Owner*
EMP: 4
SALES: 113K **Privately Held**
SIC: 3993 Signs & advertising specialties

(G-11221)
WILLIAM BENDER TRIMMING
1290 Shirk Rd (17845-8912)
PHONE....................................570 922-4274
William Bender, *Owner*
EMP: 3
SALES (est): 190K **Privately Held**
SIC: 2431 Interior & ornamental woodwork & trim

Mills
Potter County

(G-11222)
KIBBES CONCRETE
4617 State Route 49 W (16937-9632)
P.O. Box 59 (16937-0059)
PHONE..................................814 334-5537
Doug Kibbe, *Owner*
EMP: 2
SALES: 1.1MM **Privately Held**
SIC: 3273 Ready-mixed concrete

Millvale
Allegheny County

(G-11223)
GREATER PTTSBRGH SPCIALTY ADVG
112 Lincoln Ave (15209-2620)
PHONE..................................412 821-5976
Klaas Brian T A, *Principal*
EMP: 50
SALES (est): 3.4MM **Privately Held**
SIC: 7389 2395 Design services; embroidery & art needlework

Millville
Columbia County

(G-11224)
COLUMBIA WOOD INDUSTRIES INC
1000 State St (17846)
P.O. Box 94 (17846-0094)
PHONE..................................570 458-4311
Wayne Dennis, *President*
David W Dennis, *Vice Pres*
EMP: 12
SQ FT: 10,000
SALES (est): 980K **Privately Held**
SIC: 2448 Pallets, wood

(G-11225)
GREENWOOD TOWNSHIP
90 Shed Rd (17846-9148)
PHONE..................................570 458-0212
Keith Bangs, *Ch of Bd*
Joe Farr, *Corp Secy*
Jon Beck, *Supervisor*
EMP: 5 **Privately Held**
SIC: 9111 3531 City & town managers' offices; road construction & maintenance machinery

(G-11226)
P K CHOPPERS MOBILE
1205 State Route 254 (17846-9122)
PHONE..................................570 458-6983
Keith Gordner, *Owner*
EMP: 3
SALES (est): 264.2K **Privately Held**
SIC: 3751 Motorcycles & related parts

(G-11227)
RM BATTERY DOCTORS LLC
67 Reese Ln (17846-8810)
PHONE..................................570 441-9184
Jeff Machamer, *Partner*
EMP: 3
SALES (est): 200.9K **Privately Held**
SIC: 3691 Storage batteries

Milroy
Mifflin County

(G-11228)
BEAR SPRINGS MANUFACTURING
107 S Main St (17063-8610)
P.O. Box 863 (17063-0863)
PHONE..................................717 667-3200
Devin B Decker, *President*
EMP: 5 **EST:** 2000

SQ FT: 2,000
SALES (est): 705.6K **Privately Held**
WEB: www.bearspringsmfg.com
SIC: 3599 Machine shop, jobbing & repair

(G-11229)
D K HOSTETLER INC
Also Called: Hostetler Truck Bodies & Trlrs
5015 Old Us Hwy 322 (17063)
PHONE..................................717 667-3921
Ruth Knarr, *President*
EMP: 12
SQ FT: 14,500
SALES: 5MM **Privately Held**
WEB: www.dkhostetler.com
SIC: 5012 3713 Truck bodies; trailers for trucks, new & used; dump truck bodies; truck beds

(G-11230)
EASTERN INDUSTRIES INC
475 Naginey Rd (17063-9000)
PHONE..................................717 667-2015
Gary Cutler, *Branch Mgr*
EMP: 20
SALES (corp-wide): 651.9MM **Privately Held**
WEB: www.eastern-ind.com
SIC: 5032 1422 Paving materials; crushed & broken limestone
HQ: Eastern Industries, Inc.
3724 Crescent Ct W 200
Whitehall PA 18052
610 866-0932

(G-11231)
LEWISTOWN CABINET CENTER INC
20 Water St (17063-9475)
P.O. Box 507, Reedsville (17084-0507)
PHONE..................................717 667-2121
Douglas Kerstetter, *President*
William Ruble, *Vice Pres*
Duane Kerstetter, *Treasurer*
Denise Kerstetter, *Admin Sec*
EMP: 65
SQ FT: 7,500
SALES (est): 7.7MM **Privately Held**
SIC: 2434 Wood kitchen cabinets

Milton
Northumberland County

(G-11232)
ACF INDUSTRIES LLC
417 N Arch St (17847-1320)
PHONE..................................570 742-7601
Mark Pawling, *Opers-Prdtn-Mfg*
EMP: 57
SALES (corp-wide): 955MM **Privately Held**
WEB: www.acfindustries.com
SIC: 3743 Railroad equipment, except locomotives
HQ: Acf Industries Llc
101 Clark St
Saint Charles MO 63301
636 949-2399

(G-11233)
B & B BEVERAGE
1220 N Front St Frnt (17847-9609)
PHONE..................................570 742-7782
Louis Engle, *Owner*
EMP: 4
SALES (est): 200K **Privately Held**
SIC: 2082 Beer (alcoholic beverage)

(G-11234)
BLUE HERON SPORTSWEAR INC
Also Called: Blue Heron Sporstwear
Rr 405 Box S (17847)
PHONE..................................570 742-3228
David M Lilley, *President*
EMP: 3
SQ FT: 3,500
SALES (est): 453.2K **Privately Held**
SIC: 2262 5941 Screen printing: manmade fiber & silk broadwoven fabrics; sporting goods & bicycle shops

(G-11235)
CATHYS CREAMERY
25 Sylvan Ct (17847-8928)
PHONE..................................570 916-3386
Bradley W Alvey, *Principal*
EMP: 3
SALES (est): 124.5K **Privately Held**
SIC: 2021 Creamery butter

(G-11236)
CONAGRA BRANDS INC
30 Marr St (17847-1598)
PHONE..................................570 742-7621
Steven Smith, *Branch Mgr*
EMP: 801
SALES (corp-wide): 7.9B **Publicly Held**
WEB: www.conagra.com
SIC: 2099 Food preparations
PA: Conagra Brands, Inc.
222 Merchandise Mart Plz
Chicago IL 60654
312 549-5000

(G-11237)
CONAGRA BRANDS INC
50 Cameron Ave (17847)
PHONE..................................570 742-6607
Brian Williams, *Manager*
EMP: 108
SALES (corp-wide): 7.9B **Publicly Held**
WEB: www.conagra.com
SIC: 2099 Food preparations
PA: Conagra Brands, Inc.
222 Merchandise Mart Plz
Chicago IL 60654
312 549-5000

(G-11238)
CONAGRA BRANDS INC
60 N Industrial Park Rd (17847)
PHONE..................................570 742-8910
Del Hames, *Branch Mgr*
EMP: 42
SALES (corp-wide): 7.9B **Publicly Held**
WEB: www.conagra.com
SIC: 2099 Food preparations
PA: Conagra Brands, Inc.
222 Merchandise Mart Plz
Chicago IL 60654
312 549-5000

(G-11239)
GATEHOUSE MEDIA LLC
Also Called: Standard Journal Newspapers
21 N Arch St (17847-1211)
PHONE..................................570 742-9671
Amy Moyer, *Manager*
EMP: 35
SALES (corp-wide): 1.5B **Publicly Held**
WEB: www.gatehousemedia.com
SIC: 2711 Newspapers: publishing only, not printed on site
HQ: Gatehouse Media, Llc
175 Sullys Trl Fl 3
Pittsford NY 14534
585 598-0030

(G-11240)
HANSON AGGREGATES PA LLC
3 Quarry Rd (17847-8981)
PHONE..................................570 437-4068
Jim Wolfe, *Manager*
EMP: 10
SALES (corp-wide): 20.6B **Privately Held**
SIC: 1442 Common sand mining
HQ: Hanson Aggregates Pennsylvania, Llc
7660 Imperial Way
Allentown PA 18195
610 366-4626

(G-11241)
HOFFMANS MACHINE SHOP INC
Also Called: Hoffman Machine
330 Limestone Rd (17847-8968)
PHONE..................................570 437-2788
Fred Hoffman, *President*
Sandra Hoffman, *Corp Secy*
EMP: 5
SALES (est): 350K **Privately Held**
SIC: 3599 Machine shop, jobbing & repair

(G-11242)
HRI INC
653 Narehood Rd (17847)
PHONE..................................570 437-4315
Glenn Shoals, *Manager*

EMP: 4
SALES (corp-wide): 83.5MM **Privately Held**
SIC: 2951 1771 Asphalt paving mixtures & blocks; blacktop (asphalt) work
HQ: Hri, Inc.
73 Headquarters Plz
Morristown NJ 07960
973 290-9082

(G-11243)
ISTIL (USA) MILTON INC
230 Lower Market St (17847-1508)
PHONE..................................570 742-7420
Sohail Masood, *President*
Nancy Martin, *Vice Pres*
EMP: 50
SALES (est): 3.9MM **Privately Held**
SIC: 3312 Structural shapes & pilings, steel

(G-11244)
JERACO ENTERPRISES INC
135 Sodom Rd (17847-9232)
PHONE..................................570 742-9688
Gary Fawcett, *President*
Larry Fawcett, *President*
Gary L Fawcett, *Vice Pres*
EMP: 60
SQ FT: 100,000
SALES (est): 7.1MM **Privately Held**
WEB: www.jeraco.com
SIC: 3792 Travel trailers & campers

(G-11245)
KEYSTONE PALLET AND RECYCL LLC
13 Industrial Park Rd # 4 (17847-9204)
PHONE..................................570 279-7236
Matthew Roberts,
EMP: 12
SQ FT: 50,000
SALES (est): 1.4MM **Privately Held**
WEB: www.keystonepallet.com
SIC: 2448 Pallets, wood

(G-11246)
KEYSTONE SPORTING ARMS LLC
155 Sodom Rd (17847-9232)
PHONE..................................570 742-2066
Aaron Clevell, *Engineer*
Anthony Snyder, *Engineer*
Steve McNeal, *VP Sales*
Caleb Baney, *Sales Staff*
Nathan Hallman, *Sales Staff*
▲ **EMP:** 62
SQ FT: 4,000
SALES (est): 14.8MM **Privately Held**
SIC: 3484 Rifles or rifle parts, 30 mm. & below

(G-11247)
LIMESTONE MOBILE CONCRETE
122 Strick Rd (17847-8930)
PHONE..................................570 437-2640
Dennis Swardz, *Owner*
EMP: 3
SALES (est): 210K **Privately Held**
SIC: 3273 5211 Ready-mixed concrete; masonry materials & supplies

(G-11248)
MARQUIP WARD UNITED
318 Yocum Rd (17847-7501)
PHONE..................................570 742-7859
Dave Stotler, *Vice Pres*
EMP: 4
SALES (est): 336.7K **Privately Held**
SIC: 3554 Paper industries machinery

(G-11249)
MILTON HOME SYSTEMS INC
55 Patton Dr (17847-7438)
P.O. Box 85, Selinsgrove (17870-0085)
PHONE..................................800 533-4402
Richard Rowe, *President*
Mark Bowman, *Vice Pres*
Tim McWilliams, *Vice Pres*
Martin Sickle, *Vice Pres*
Mike Steimling, *Vice Pres*
EMP: 80
SQ FT: 70,000

GEOGRAPHIC

SALES (est): 8.6MM **Privately Held**
WEB: www.integritybuild.com
SIC: **1521 2452** Mfg Prefabricated Wood Buildings Single-Family House Construction

(G-11250)
VORTX UNITED INC
318 Yocum Rd (17847-7501)
PHONE....................................570 742-7859
Keith Sickafoose, *President*
Dave Stotler, *Vice Pres*
EMP: 9
SQ FT: 12,000
SALES (est): 1.1MM **Privately Held**
WEB: www.vortx-united.com
SIC: **3599 8711 5084** Custom machinery; engineering services; industrial machinery & equipment

(G-11251)
WILLIAM J KOSHINSKIE
Also Called: B & K Sheet Metal Products
100 Hepburn St (17847-1710)
PHONE....................................570 742-4969
William J Koshinskie, *Owner*
EMP: 3 EST: 1965
SQ FT: 5,000
SALES: 150K **Privately Held**
SIC: **3444 1711 1761** Ducts, sheet metal; gutters, sheet metal; sheet metal specialties, not stamped; ventilators, sheet metal; ventilation & duct work contractor; gutter & downspout contractor; sheet metalwork

Mineral Point
Cambria County

(G-11252)
MOGNET INDUSTRIES LLC
265 Wess Rd (15942-5200)
PHONE....................................814 418-0864
EMP: 3
SALES (est): 102.2K **Privately Held**
SIC: **3999** Manufacturing industries

Minersville
Schuylkill County

(G-11253)
ALIG LLC
Also Called: Sterling Compress Gas
125 S Delaware Ave (17954-2005)
PHONE....................................570 544-2540
Toll Free:.............................877 -
Steve Swartz, *Branch Mgr*
EMP: 5
SALES (corp-wide): 125.9MM **Privately Held**
WEB: www.mgindustries.com
SIC: **2813** Oxygen, compressed or liquefied
HQ: Alig Llc
    2700 Post Oak Blvd
    Houston TX 77056
    212 626-4936

(G-11254)
FEDERAL PRISON INDUSTRIES
Also Called: Unicor
Interstate 81 & Route 901 Rt 901 (17954)
PHONE....................................570 544-7343
Dave Kranzel, *Branch Mgr*
EMP: 35 **Publicly Held**
WEB: www.unicor.gov
SIC: **2521 9223** Wood office furniture; correctional institutions;
HQ: Federal Prison Industries, Inc
    320 1st St Nw
    Washington DC 20534
    202 305-3500

(G-11255)
JAMES W QUANDEL & SONS INC
9 Schaeffers Hill Rd (17954)
P.O. Box 220 (17954-0220)
PHONE....................................570 544-2261
Jean K Quandel, *CEO*
James W Quandel Jr, *President*

Bonnie Rowlands, *Treasurer*
Katie Carr, *Mktg Dir*
EMP: 35
SALES (est): 6.1MM **Privately Held**
WEB: www.quandelconcrete.com
SIC: **3273** Ready-mixed concrete

Mingoville
Centre County

(G-11256)
KENUM DISTRIBUTION LLC
229 Hecla Rd (16856)
P.O. Box 67 (16856-0067)
PHONE....................................814 383-2626
EMP: 3 EST: 2013
SALES (est): 120.7K **Privately Held**
SIC: **2992 2329** Lubricating oils & greases; athletic (warmup, sweat & jogging) suits: men's & boys'

(G-11257)
RIGHTNOUR MANUFACTURING CO INC
229 Hecla Rd (16856)
PHONE....................................800 326-9113
Don Foreman, *President*
▲ EMP: 23
SQ FT: 15,000
SALES (est): 2.8MM **Privately Held**
WEB: www.rmcsports.com
SIC: **3599 3949** Custom machinery; archery equipment, general; hunting equipment

Modena
Chester County

(G-11258)
ORGANIC MECHANICS SOIL CO LLC
12 Union St Rear Warehouse (19358)
P.O. Box 272 (19358-0272)
PHONE....................................484 557-2961
Mark Highland, *Mng Member*
Jim Flanigan,
EMP: 7
SQ FT: 16,000
SALES: 60K **Privately Held**
SIC: **2875** Potting soil, mixed

(G-11259)
SEALED AIR CORPORATION
Paper Mill Div
22 Meredith Rd (19358)
P.O. Box 158 (19358-0158)
PHONE....................................610 384-2650
Michael Feeney, *Manager*
EMP: 36
SALES (corp-wide): 4.7B **Publicly Held**
WEB: www.sealedair.com
SIC: **3086 2621** Packaging & shipping materials, foamed plastic; paper mills
PA: Sealed Air Corporation
    2415 Cascade Pointe Blvd
    Charlotte NC 28208
    980 221-3235

Mohnton
Berks County

(G-11260)
BLAZING TECHNOLOGIES INC
4631 Morgantown Rd (19540-8249)
PHONE....................................484 722-4800
Donald Blasdell, *President*
Robert Backer, *Vice Pres*
Brenda Blasdell, *Treasurer*
EMP: 8
SQ FT: 4,400
SALES (est): 104.1K **Privately Held**
WEB: www.blazingtech.net
SIC: **3531** Airport construction machinery

(G-11261)
DANIEL G BERG
Also Called: Bergs Custom Furniture
477 Alleghenyville Rd (19540-8111)
PHONE....................................610 856-7095
Daniel Berg, *Owner*
EMP: 3
SALES: 200K **Privately Held**
WEB: www.bergscustomfurniture.com
SIC: **2511** Chairs, household, except upholstered: wood

(G-11262)
DILULLO GRAPHICS INC
448 Imperial Dr (19540-8342)
PHONE....................................610 775-4360
Thomas J Dilullo, *President*
Betty C Dilullo, *Corp Secy*
EMP: 21
SQ FT: 15,000
SALES (est): 2.2MM **Privately Held**
WEB: www.pgprinting.com
SIC: **2791 2752 2789 2759** Typesetting; commercial printing, offset; bookbinding & related work; commercial printing

(G-11263)
FALVEY STEEL CASTINGS
862 Maple Grove Rd (19540-7789)
PHONE....................................484 678-2174
Dale Martin, *Principal*
EMP: 3
SALES (est): 177.2K **Privately Held**
SIC: **3325** Steel foundries

(G-11264)
HUBBELL INCORPORATED DELAWARE
100 E Wyomissing Ave (19540)
PHONE....................................574 234-7151
Jonathan Dumas, *Branch Mgr*
EMP: 300
SALES (corp-wide): 4.4B **Publicly Held**
SIC: **3669** Emergency alarms
HQ: Hubbell Incorporated (Delaware)
    40 Waterview Dr
    Shelton CT 06484
    475 882-4000

(G-11265)
I H RISSLER MFG LLC
448 Orchard Rd (19540-9440)
PHONE....................................717 484-0551
Ivan H Rissler, *Mng Member*
Jason Rissler,
EMP: 8
SALES: 2MM **Privately Held**
SIC: **3523 7389** Feed grinders, crushers & mixers;

(G-11266)
INDUSTRIAL CONSORTIUM INC
40 S Church St (19540-1702)
PHONE....................................610 775-5760
Richard Raffauf, *Manager*
EMP: 4
SALES (corp-wide): 1.7MM **Privately Held**
SIC: **3599** Amusement park equipment
PA: Industrial Consortium Inc
    40 S Church St
    Mohnton PA 19540
    610 777-1653

(G-11267)
INDUSTRIAL CONSORTIUM INC (PA)
40 S Church St (19540-1702)
PHONE....................................610 777-1653
Richard S Raffauf Sr, *President*
Richard S Raffauf Jr, *President*
Theda Raffauf, *Admin Sec*
EMP: 10 EST: 1971
SQ FT: 1,200
SALES (est): 1.7MM **Privately Held**
SIC: **3599 5084 8742** Machine & other job shop work; metalworking machinery; industrial consultant

(G-11268)
KINGS POTATO CHIP COMPANY
Also Called: Kings Quality Foods
1451 Reading Rd (19540-9421)
PHONE....................................717 445-4521
Glenn Weber, *President*

EMP: 20
SQ FT: 22,000
SALES (est): 3.1MM **Privately Held**
WEB: www.kingsqualityfoods.com
SIC: **2096 2052** Potato chips & other potato-based snacks; pretzels; corn chips; nuts, salted or roasted; popcorn & supplies; candy

(G-11269)
ROAD RUNNER RACE FUELS LLC
2645 Welsh Rd (19540-8855)
PHONE....................................717 587-1693
EMP: 4
SALES (est): 298.8K **Privately Held**
SIC: **2869** Fuels

(G-11270)
STAR BRANDS NORTH AMERICA INC
Also Called: Demet's Candy Company
11 Main St (19540-2012)
PHONE....................................610 775-4100
Michael Anderson, *Regl Sales Mgr*
James Reazor, *Branch Mgr*
Guy Pauley, *Maintence Staff*
EMP: 8 **Privately Held**
SIC: **2052** Pretzels
HQ: Star Brands North America, Inc.
    10 Bank St Ste 1011
    White Plains NY 10606
    914 355-9750

(G-11271)
UNIQUE TECHNOLOGIES INC
111 Chestnut St (19540-1601)
PHONE....................................610 775-9191
Luther Hoffman, *President*
EMP: 17
SQ FT: 13,500
SALES (est): 2MM **Privately Held**
WEB: www.unique-tech-inc.com
SIC: **3841** Surgical knife blades & handles

(G-11272)
VAN BENNETT FOOD CO INC
Also Called: Betty's Salads
62 Shea Dr (19540-9273)
PHONE....................................610 374-8348
John Marcinko, *President*
Beatrice Bennett, *Admin Sec*
EMP: 42 EST: 1940
SQ FT: 22,000
SALES (est): 15.1MM **Privately Held**
WEB: www.vanbennett.com
SIC: **5141 2038 2099** Food brokers; frozen specialties; salads, fresh or refrigerated

Mohrsville
Berks County

(G-11273)
ALPHA PACKAGING CORPORATION
589 Centerport Rd (19541)
PHONE....................................610 926-5100
Harold R Leh Jr, *President*
EMP: 17
SQ FT: 180,000
SALES (est): 4.4MM **Privately Held**
SIC: **2653** Boxes, corrugated: made from purchased materials

(G-11274)
BLATTS PRINTING CO
637 Main St (19541-8847)
PHONE....................................610 926-2289
Larry Blatts, *Owner*
EMP: 5
SALES (est): 211.8K **Privately Held**
SIC: **2752** Commercial printing, lithographic

(G-11275)
BULK CHEMICALS INC
809 Old Mohrsville Rd (19541)
PHONE....................................610 926-4128
Bertram Schaeffer, *Vice Pres*
EMP: 12
SQ FT: 480

SALES (est): 1.8MM
SALES (corp-wide): 10.2MM **Privately Held**
SIC: 2819 2899 2851 2841 Phosphates, except fertilizers: defluorinated & ammoniated; chemical preparations; paints & allied products; soap & other detergents
PA: Bulk Chemicals, Inc.
1074 Stinson Dr
Reading PA 19605
610 926-4128

(G-11276)
J/M FENCE & DECK COMPANY
2209 Shartlesville Rd (19541-9081)
PHONE..................................610 488-7382
Carl J Spatz Jr, *Partner*
James W Brown, *Partner*
EMP: 5
SQ FT: 1,584
SALES (est): 623.6K **Privately Held**
SIC: 1799 5211 2499 Fence construction; lumber & other building materials; fencing; fencing, wood

(G-11277)
LEONARD LEIBENSPERGER
Also Called: Lenny's Automotive
26 Railroad Rd (19541-8884)
PHONE..................................610 926-7491
Leonard Leivensperger, *Owner*
EMP: 3
SQ FT: 6,360
SALES (est): 150K **Privately Held**
SIC: 7538 3496 General automotive repair shops; miscellaneous fabricated wire products

(G-11278)
PATHFNDER EQINE PBLCATIONS LLC
243 N Garfield Rd (19541-9248)
PHONE..................................610 488-1282
Camille Matthews, *Principal*
EMP: 3
SALES (est): 140K **Privately Held**
SIC: 2759 Publication printing

Monaca
Beaver County

(G-11279)
ALLEGHENY TECHNOLOGIES INC
2070 Pennsylvania Ave (15061-1854)
PHONE..................................724 775-1554
Charlene Edwards, *Principal*
EMP: 10 **Publicly Held**
SIC: 3471 Finishing, metals or formed products
PA: Allegheny Technologies Incorporated
1000 Six Ppg Pl
Pittsburgh PA 15222

(G-11280)
ATI PRECISION FINISHING LLC
Also Called: ATI Flat Rolled Products
2070 Pennsylvania Ave (15061-1854)
PHONE..................................724 775-2618
EMP: 10 **Publicly Held**
SIC: 3312 Stainless steel
HQ: Ati Precision Finishing, Llc
499 Delaware Ave
Rochester PA 15074
724 775-1664

(G-11281)
BASF CORPORATION
370 Frankfort Rd (15061-2210)
PHONE..................................724 728-6900
Mark Todd, *Opers-Prdtn-Mfg*
EMP: 106
SALES (corp-wide): 71.7B **Privately Held**
WEB: www.basf.com
SIC: 2869 Industrial organic chemicals
HQ: Basf Corporation
100 Park Ave
Florham Park NJ 07932
973 245-6000

(G-11282)
BEAVER CONCRETE & SUPPLY INC
10 Industrial Park Rd (15061-1878)
PHONE..................................724 774-5100
Justin Bryan, *President*
EMP: 11
SQ FT: 10,000
SALES (est): 868.9K
SALES (corp-wide): 17.5MM **Privately Held**
SIC: 3273 3531 3271 Ready-mixed concrete; log splitters; architectural concrete: block, split, fluted, screen, etc.
PA: Frank Bryan, Inc.
1263 Chartiers Ave
Mc Kees Rocks PA 15136
412 331-1630

(G-11283)
BEAVER VALLEY ALLOY FOUNDRY CO
4165 Brodhead Rd (15061-2496)
PHONE..................................724 775-1987
John B Forster, *President*
Charles T Forster, *Treasurer*
Margaret I Castellan, *Admin Sec*
EMP: 48 EST: 1919
SQ FT: 36,000
SALES (est): 12.6MM **Privately Held**
WEB: www.bvalley.com
SIC: 3325 3322 3369 Alloy steel castings, except investment; malleable iron foundries; nonferrous foundries

(G-11284)
BEAVER VALLEY SLAG INC
300 Constitution Blvd (15061-2941)
PHONE..................................724 773-0444
Steve Orgovotte, *Branch Mgr*
EMP: 18 **Privately Held**
SIC: 3295 Slag, crushed or ground
PA: Beaver Valley Slag, Inc
3468 Brodhead Rd Ste 3
Monaca PA 15061

(G-11285)
BEAVER VALLEY SLAG INC (PA)
3468 Brodhead Rd Ste 3 (15061-3149)
PHONE..................................724 375-8173
Roxsan R Betters-Albanese, *CEO*
Charles J Betters II, *Corp Secy*
EMP: 2
SALES (est): 1.7MM **Privately Held**
SIC: 2951 Asphalt paving mixtures & blocks

(G-11286)
BVHT INC
1585 Beaver Ave (15061-1441)
P.O. Box 233 (15061-0233)
PHONE..................................724 728-4328
Michael Pitterich, *Principal*
▼ EMP: 6
SALES (est): 621.7K **Privately Held**
SIC: 3398 Metal heat treating

(G-11287)
C & S SPORTS & PROMOTIONS
3433 Brodhead Rd Ste 2 (15061-3189)
PHONE..................................724 775-1655
Deborah L Bianco, *Partner*
Aurelio Bianco, *Partner*
EMP: 4
SQ FT: 1,600
SALES (est): 391.5K **Privately Held**
SIC: 2395 2396 5611 Embroidery products, except schiffli machine; screen printing on fabric articles; clothing, sportswear, men's & boys'

(G-11288)
CHOCOLATE CREATIONS
3465 Brodhead Rd Ste 4 (15061-3144)
PHONE..................................724 774-7675
Donna Unterberger, *President*
EMP: 5
SALES (est): 380.4K **Privately Held**
SIC: 5441 5947 2066 Candy, nut & confectionery stores; gift baskets; chocolate & cocoa products

(G-11289)
CREST ADVERTISING CO
1529 Old Brodhead Rd (15061-2408)
P.O. Box 209 (15061-0209)
PHONE..................................724 774-4413
John Medved, *Owner*
EMP: 10
SQ FT: 2,400
SALES (est): 734.2K **Privately Held**
SIC: 3993 1799 Signs, not made in custom sign painting shops; sign installation & maintenance

(G-11290)
GHP II LLC
Also Called: Phoenix Glass Co The
400 9th St (15061-1862)
PHONE..................................724 775-0010
Kinorea Dickman, *Principal*
EMP: 550
SALES (corp-wide): 682.6MM **Privately Held**
WEB: www.anchorhocking.com
SIC: 3229 5023 Tableware, glass or glass ceramic; glassware, industrial; glassware
HQ: Ghp Ii, Llc
1115 W 5th Ave
Lancaster OH 43130
740 687-2500

(G-11291)
LOWLANDER CORPORATION
105 4th St Apt 306 (15061-1711)
P.O. Box 510 (15061)
PHONE..................................412 221-1240
Karen Hollenden, *President*
Christopher Hollenden, *Admin Sec*
EMP: 3 EST: 1987
SALES (est): 429.1K **Privately Held**
SIC: 2759 5946 Commercial printing; photographic supplies

(G-11292)
NAK INTERNATIONAL CORP
Also Called: NF&m
1729 Penn Ave Ste 7 (15061-1852)
PHONE..................................724 774-9200
Dean Musi, *Branch Mgr*
Bruce Dixon, *Manager*
EMP: 43
SALES (est): 16.7MM
SALES (corp-wide): 14MM **Privately Held**
SIC: 3356 3471 3341 Titanium; plating & polishing; secondary nonferrous metals
PA: Nak International Corp.
108 Forest Ave
Locust Valley NY 11560
516 334-6245

(G-11293)
NOVA CHEMICALS INC
400 Frankfort Rd (15061-2212)
PHONE..................................724 770-5542
Ian Macdonald, *Manager*
Ernest V Dean, *Admin Sec*
EMP: 400 **Privately Held**
SIC: 3081 2821 Polyethylene film; polypropylene film & sheet; plastics materials & resins
HQ: Nova Chemicals Inc.
1555 Coraopolis Hts Rd
Moon Township PA 15108
412 490-4000

(G-11294)
POTTER DISTRIBUTING CO
112 Mowry Rd (15061-2222)
PHONE..................................724 495-3189
Maria Torrence, *President*
EMP: 4
SALES (est): 266.7K **Privately Held**
SIC: 5921 2086 5984 Beer (packaged); bottled & canned soft drinks; propane gas, bottled

(G-11295)
ROBERT URDA JR
Also Called: Ambridge Mobile Welding & Fabg
1990 Beaver Ave (15061-1303)
PHONE..................................724 775-9333
Robert N Urda Jr, *Owner*
EMP: 5
SQ FT: 2,000

SALES: 400K **Privately Held**
SIC: 7692 Welding repair

Monessen
Westmoreland County

(G-11296)
ALUMISOURCE CORPORATION (PA)
1145 Donner Ave (15062-1058)
P.O. Box 398 (15062-0398)
PHONE..................................412 250-0360
Gabriel Hudock, *President*
Keith Miller, *Vice Pres*
Brian Ritchie, *Plant Mgr*
Jimmy Turner, *Plant Mgr*
Kenny White, *Senior Buyer*
EMP: 18
SQ FT: 315,000
SALES (est): 6.5MM **Privately Held**
WEB: www.alumisource.net
SIC: 3334 Primary aluminum

(G-11297)
ARCELORMITTAL HOLDINGS LLC
345 Donner Ave (15062-1156)
PHONE..................................724 684-1000
Scott Wolfe, *Principal*
Jason Hopkins, *Plant Engr*
Frank Indof, *Accounting Mgr*
Jim Burkhart, *Manager*
Vernon Williams, *Maintence Staff*
EMP: 195
SALES (corp-wide): 9.1B **Privately Held**
WEB: www.mittalsteel.com
SIC: 3312 Chemicals & other products derived from coking
HQ: Arcelormittal Holdings Llc
3210 Watling St
East Chicago IN 46312
219 399-1200

(G-11298)
DARRA GROUP INC
63 Overhill Dr (15062-2541)
P.O. Box 48 (15062-0048)
PHONE..................................724 684-6040
Donna M Dalfonso, *Principal*
Joseph A Dalfonso, *Principal*
Bernard A Sarra, *Principal*
Martin St John, *Principal*
EMP: 3
SALES: 150K **Privately Held**
SIC: 2759 Screen printing

(G-11299)
KOPPERS INDUSTRIES INC
345 Donner Ave (15062-1156)
PHONE..................................724 684-1000
Jim Burkhart, *Principal*
EMP: 3
SALES (est): 196.7K **Privately Held**
SIC: 2491 Wood preserving

(G-11300)
MID MON VALLEY PUB
996 Donner Ave (15062)
PHONE..................................724 314-0030
Naz Victoria, *Mng Member*
EMP: 50
SALES (est): 1.1MM **Privately Held**
SIC: 2731 Book publishing

(G-11301)
SANTELLI TEMPERED GLASS INC
Also Called: S T G
240 Riverview Dr (15062-1094)
PHONE..................................724 684-4144
Joe Santelli, *President*
Debra Wise, *Vice Pres*
EMP: 48
SQ FT: 2,000
SALES (est): 5MM **Privately Held**
SIC: 3231 Tempered glass: made from purchased glass

(G-11302)
WYATT INCORPORATED
112 Riverview Dr (15062-1067)
PHONE..................................724 684-7060
Jim Barca, *Manager*

▲ = Import ▼=Export
◆ =Import/Export

EMP: 45
SALES (corp-wide): 96.2MM **Privately Held**
WEB: www.wyatt.com
SIC: 2499 2431 Decorative wood & woodwork; millwork
PA: Wyatt Incorporated
4545 Campbells Run Rd
Pittsburgh PA 15205
412 787-5800

Monongahela
Washington County

(G-11303)
AKZO NOBEL CHEMICALS INC
829 Route 481 (15063-3437)
PHONE................................724 258-6200
Jeff Kszastowski, *Manager*
EMP: 65
SALES (corp-wide): 11.3B **Privately Held**
WEB: www.akzo-nobel.com
SIC: 2819 Sulfur, recovered or refined, incl. from sour natural gas
HQ: Akzo Nobel Chemicals Llc
525 W Van Buren St # 1600
Chicago IL 60607
312 544-7000

(G-11304)
ANTHONY BURNEY
Also Called: 142-Tactical
455 4th St (15063-2548)
PHONE................................412 606-7336
Anthony Burney, *Owner*
EMP: 3
SALES (est): 190.5K **Privately Held**
SIC: 3484 Guns (firearms) or gun parts, 30 mm. & below

(G-11305)
C JTHOMAS SCREENING INC
1213 Prospect St (15063-9735)
PHONE................................412 384-4279
Concetta J Thomas, *President*
Concetta Thomas, *President*
David H Thomas, *Vice Pres*
Sheryf Lyons, *Admin Sec*
EMP: 11
SALES: 350K **Privately Held**
SIC: 2261 Custom Screen Printing

(G-11306)
CASTEC INC (PA)
1462 Delberts Dr (15063-9752)
PHONE................................724 258-8700
Wayne W Hillier, *President*
Pamela Hillier, *Corp Secy*
EMP: 4
SQ FT: 13,500
SALES: 1MM **Privately Held**
WEB: www.castecinc.com
SIC: 3559 Foundry machinery & equipment

(G-11307)
DUCTMATE INDUSTRIES INC
1502 Industrial Dr (15063-9753)
PHONE................................724 258-0500
Fredrick J Arnoldt, *Principal*
EMP: 3
SALES (corp-wide): 50.1MM **Privately Held**
SIC: 3444 Ducts, sheet metal
PA: Ductmate Industries, Inc.
210 5th St
Charleroi PA 15022
800 990-8459

(G-11308)
FLEXSYS AMERICA LP
829 Route 481 (15063-3437)
P.O. Box 481 (15063-0481)
PHONE................................724 258-6200
Jeffery Kszastowski, *Branch Mgr*
EMP: 65 **Publicly Held**
SIC: 3069 Reclaimed rubber & specialty rubber compounds
HQ: Flexsys America L.P.
260 Springside Dr
Akron OH 44333

(G-11309)
KANAWHA SCALES & SYSTEMS INC
579a Park Way (15063-1834)
PHONE................................724 258-6650
Ruth Lipinski, *Branch Mgr*
EMP: 13
SALES (corp-wide): 51.1MM **Privately Held**
SIC: 5046 7699 3822 3596 Scales, except laboratory; scale repair service; auto controls regulating residntl & coml environmt & applncs; scales & balances, except laboratory
PA: Kanawha Scales & Systems, Inc.
111 Jacobson Dr
Poca WV 25159
304 755-8321

(G-11310)
LOCK 3 COMPANY
1469 Delberts Dr (15063-9714)
PHONE................................724 258-7773
Charles H Muse III, *President*
James G Muse, *Corp Secy*
Albert C Muse, *Vice Pres*
▲ **EMP:** 10
SALES (est): 3.1MM **Privately Held**
WEB: www.l3company.com
SIC: 5032 1311 Brick, except refractory; crude petroleum & natural gas

(G-11311)
MIMCO PRODUCTS LLC (PA)
731 E Main St (15063-1403)
PHONE................................724 258-8208
R Wayne Bickerton,
Thomas P Cepaitis,
EMP: 6 **EST:** 1957
SQ FT: 15,000
SALES (est): 685.8K **Privately Held**
SIC: 2899 5411 5085 Chemical preparations; convenience stores, independent; refractory material

(G-11312)
PARNELL ENTERPRISES INC
Also Called: Ernest W Parnell Burial Vaults
787 Dry Run Rd (15063-1226)
PHONE................................724 258-3320
Ernest W Parnell, *President*
Carol Parnell, *Corp Secy*
EMP: 6
SALES (est): 786.1K **Privately Held**
SIC: 3272 Burial vaults, concrete or precast terrazzo

(G-11313)
PENNCRAFT CABINET CO
151 Donora Rd (15063-3712)
PHONE................................724 379-7040
Richard D Wyne, *Owner*
EMP: 3
SQ FT: 9,000
SALES (est): 274.9K **Privately Held**
SIC: 2434 Wood kitchen cabinets

(G-11314)
PITTSBURGH TANK CORPORATION
1500 Industrial Dr (15063-9753)
PHONE................................724 258-0200
James M Bollman, *President*
Philip Duvall, *Vice Pres*
Jeff Farrar, *Engineer*
Philip O Bollman, *Treasurer*
Mary Tedeschi, *Info Tech Dir*
EMP: 36
SQ FT: 70,000
SALES (est): 9MM **Privately Held**
WEB: www.pghtank.com
SIC: 3443 Tanks, standard or custom fabricated: metal plate

(G-11315)
SIGN GUY
770 E Main St (15063-1404)
PHONE................................724 483-2200
Ed Dlutowski, *Principal*
EMP: 5
SALES (est): 465.5K **Privately Held**
SIC: 3993 Signs, not made in custom sign painting shops

(G-11316)
SOLUTIA INC
Also Called: Easttmont Chemical
829 Route 481 (15063-3437)
PHONE................................724 258-6200
Steve Knight, *Branch Mgr*
EMP: 191 **Publicly Held**
SIC: 2824 Organic fibers, noncellulosic
HQ: Solutia Inc.
575 Maryville Centre Dr
Saint Louis MO 63141
423 229-2000

(G-11317)
TAMCO INC
1466 Delberts Dr (15063-9752)
P.O. Box 371 (15063-0371)
PHONE................................724 258-6622
Alan D Citron, *President*
Franklyn Gorell, *Senior VP*
Darryl Pingor, *CFO*
Howard M Alex, *Treasurer*
Rick Varela, *Sales Staff*
▲ **EMP:** 50 **EST:** 1951
SQ FT: 55,000
SALES (est): 10MM **Privately Held**
WEB: www.tamcotools.com
SIC: 3423 3546 3531 Screw drivers, pliers, chisels, etc. (hand tools); hammers (hand tools); drills & drilling tools; construction machinery

(G-11318)
TOP BOX INC
1428 Delberts Dr (15063-9752)
PHONE................................724 258-8966
Clement P Gigliotti, *President*
Frank De Rosa, *Principal*
Barbara Gigliotti, *Principal*
▲ **EMP:** 10
SQ FT: 30,000
SALES (est): 2.2MM **Privately Held**
WEB: www.topboxincus.com
SIC: 2448 Pallets, wood

(G-11319)
WALL FIRMA INC
733 E Main St (15063-1499)
PHONE................................724 258-6873
Kenneth F Codeluppi, *President*
Arlene Everly, *Administration*
▼ **EMP:** 12 **EST:** 1949
SQ FT: 25,000
SALES (est): 1.5MM **Privately Held**
WEB: www.wallfirma.com
SIC: 2899 2891 2999 Waterproofing compounds; adhesives & sealants; waxes, petroleum: not produced in petroleum refineries

Monroeton
Bradford County

(G-11320)
SERVE INC (PA)
Also Called: Secure Rhblttion Vctonal Entps
22 Chiola Ln (18832)
P.O. Box 93 (18832-0093)
PHONE................................570 265-3119
Donald Black, *Exec Dir*
EMP: 6
SQ FT: 12,500
SALES: 1.7MM **Privately Held**
WEB: www.serveinc.com
SIC: 8331 2791 2759 2752 Vocational rehabilitation agency; sheltered workshop; typesetting; commercial printing; commercial printing, lithographic

(G-11321)
SHAFFERS FEED SERVICE INC
8 Dalpiaz Dr (18832-8821)
PHONE................................570 265-3300
Linda Cook, *President*
EMP: 12 **EST:** 1957
SALES (est): 1.7MM **Privately Held**
SIC: 2048 5191 5499 Feed supplements; animal feeds; dried fruit

Monroeville
Allegheny County

(G-11322)
A PLUS STAIR LIFT PITTSBURGH
2828 Broadway Blvd (15146-4675)
PHONE................................412 260-7469
Carl E Alitandero, *Owner*
Carl E Alitandro, *Owner*
EMP: 5 **EST:** 2014
SALES (est): 354.2K **Privately Held**
SIC: 3534 Elevators & moving stairways

(G-11323)
ALL FLOOR SUPPLIES INC
168 Dexter Dr (15146-1033)
PHONE................................412 793-6421
Glenn Whitfield, *Branch Mgr*
EMP: 15
SALES (corp-wide): 10.7MM **Privately Held**
SIC: 2273 5087 Carpets & rugs; carpet installation equipment
PA: All Floor Supplies Inc.
6070 Carey Dr
Cleveland OH 44125
216 642-7330

(G-11324)
AMERICAN INDUSTRIAL PARTS
1610 Mcclure Rd (15146-2061)
PHONE................................800 421-1180
Carol Wagner, *Branch Mgr*
EMP: 4
SALES (corp-wide): 20.1MM **Privately Held**
SIC: 3011 Industrial tires, pneumatic
PA: American Industrial Parts
433 Lane Dr
Florence AL 35630
256 764-2900

(G-11325)
BEN SWANEY
Also Called: Swaney Truck & Equip Co
3704 Northern Pike (15146-2112)
PHONE................................412 372-8109
Ben Swaney, *Owner*
EMP: 3
SALES (est): 180.7K **Privately Held**
SIC: 7538 3441 General truck repair; fabricated structural metal

(G-11326)
C H REED INC
Also Called: C H Reed
205 Seco Rd (15146-1419)
PHONE................................412 380-1334
Dave Diianni, *Branch Mgr*
EMP: 3
SALES (est): 107.4K
SALES (corp-wide): 26.8MM **Privately Held**
SIC: 3563 Air & gas compressors
PA: C. H. Reed Inc.
301 Poplar St
Hanover PA 17331
717 632-4261

(G-11327)
CLAYTON KENDALL INC (PA)
Also Called: Rushimprint
167 Dexter Dr (15146-1034)
PHONE................................412 798-7120
Regina Broudy, *CEO*
Bonnie Faas, *President*
Dave Basista, *Vice Pres*
Michael Broudy, *VP Opers*
Diane Jones, *Purch Agent*
▲ **EMP:** 120 **EST:** 1984
SQ FT: 30,000
SALES: 18.6MM **Privately Held**
WEB: www.claytonkendall.com
SIC: 2759 Promotional printing

(G-11328)
COMPUNETICS INC (PA)
700 Seco Rd Ste 5 (15146-1467)
PHONE................................412 373-8110
Giorgio Coraluppi, *President*
Pier Benci, *General Mgr*
Anthony Silvio, *Engineer*

Jerry Pompa, *Marketing Mgr*
Leslie Stegman, *Marketing Staff*
EMP: 55
SQ FT: 39,993
SALES (est): 19.6MM **Privately Held**
WEB: www.compunetics.com
SIC: 8711 3672 Engineering services; circuit boards, television & radio printed

(G-11329)
COMPUNETIX INC
700 Seco Rd Ste 2 (15146-1464)
PHONE..............................412 373-8110
Deborah Gray, *Accountant*
John Gralewski, *Manager*
EMP: 90
SALES (corp-wide): 56.2MM **Privately Held**
WEB: www.compunetix.com
SIC: 3672 Printed circuit boards
PA: Compunetix Inc.
  2420 Mosside Blvd Ste 1
  Monroeville PA 15146
  412 373-8110

(G-11330)
COMPUNETIX INC (PA)
2420 Mosside Blvd Ste 1 (15146-4253)
PHONE..............................412 373-8110
Giorgio Coraluppi, *President*
Joseph Kasunich, *Vice Pres*
Gerard Pompa, *Vice Pres*
Robert Hannush, *Plant Mgr*
John Sherrow, *Mfg Mgr*
EMP: 270
SQ FT: 103,000
SALES: 56.2MM **Privately Held**
WEB: www.compunetix.com
SIC: 3661 Telephones & telephone apparatus

(G-11331)
CYPHER COMPANY INC (PA)
4790 Old Frankstown Rd (15146-2096)
PHONE..............................412 661-4913
Robert G Cypher, *President*
Brian Brush, *Vice Pres*
Derry Dorman, *Manager*
Jim Sever, *Manager*
▲ **EMP:** 14 **EST:** 1946
SQ FT: 18,500
SALES (est): 3.7MM **Privately Held**
WEB: www.cyphercompany.com
SIC: 3492 5085 Hose & tube fittings & assemblies, hydraulic/pneumatic; hose, belting & packing

(G-11332)
DAVIS SIGN SERVICE LLC (PA)
Also Called: Signs By Tomorrow
4112 Monroeville Blvd (15146-2618)
PHONE..............................412 856-5535
Jeff Davis,
EMP: 3
SQ FT: 1,500
SALES (est): 493.2K **Privately Held**
SIC: 3993 7389 Signs, not made in custom sign painting shops; lettering service

(G-11333)
DUANE GRANT
Also Called: Grant's Tool Company
1367 Foxwood Dr (15146-4461)
PHONE..............................412 856-1357
Duane Grant, *Owner*
Darla Grant, *Principal*
EMP: 5
SALES: 600K **Privately Held**
SIC: 5085 3841 Tools; surgical knife blades & handles

(G-11334)
EJ USA INC
141 Dexter Dr (15146-1034)
PHONE..............................412 795-6000
Mike McGuane, *District Mgr*
Ted Hyman, *Manager*
EMP: 12 **Privately Held**
SIC: 3321 Manhole covers, metal
HQ: Ej Usa, Inc.
  301 Spring St
  East Jordan MI 49727
  800 874-4100

(G-11335)
ELES BROS INC
1000 Thompson Run Rd (15146-2130)
P.O. Box 307 (15146-0307)
PHONE..............................412 824-6161
Carl Eles, *President*
EMP: 5
SALES (corp-wide): 783.8K **Privately Held**
SIC: 3273 Ready-mixed concrete
PA: Eles Bros., Inc.
  1235 Rodi Rd
  Turtle Creek PA
  412 824-6161

(G-11336)
ENLIGHTENING LRNG MINDS LLC
726 Garden City Dr (15146-1116)
PHONE..............................412 880-9601
Mahmoud Arafat, *CEO*
EMP: 12
SALES (est): 256K **Privately Held**
SIC: 7372 Educational computer software

(G-11337)
FEDEX OFFICE & PRINT SVCS INC
4010 William Penn Hwy (15146-2503)
PHONE..............................412 856-8016
Martin Kosut, *Manager*
EMP: 26
SALES (corp-wide): 65.4B **Publicly Held**
WEB: www.kinkos.com
SIC: 7334 2791 2789 Photocopying & duplicating services; typesetting; bookbinding & related work
HQ: Fedex Office And Print Services, Inc.
  7900 Legacy Dr
  Plano TX 75024
  800 463-3339

(G-11338)
FROGURT LLC
507 Pinoak Dr (15146-3165)
PHONE..............................724 263-4299
Adnan Chawdhry,
EMP: 10
SALES: 200K **Privately Held**
SIC: 2024 Ice cream & frozen desserts

(G-11339)
GATEWAY PUBLICATIONS (PA)
Also Called: Gateway Press
610 Beatty Rd Ste 2 (15146-1558)
PHONE..............................412 856-7400
Scott Patterson, *President*
Thomas Bova, *Vice Pres*
EMP: 200 **EST:** 1956
SQ FT: 35,000
SALES (est): 37.2MM **Privately Held**
SIC: 2711 Newspapers, publishing & printing

(G-11340)
HOMEOPATHIC NATURAL HEALING
3824 Northern Pike (15146-2141)
PHONE..............................412 646-4151
EMP: 3
SALES (est): 133.6K **Privately Held**
SIC: 3221 Medicine bottles, glass

(G-11341)
HUNTLEY & HUNTLEY INC
2660 Monroeville Blvd (15146-2302)
PHONE..............................412 380-2355
Keith N Mangini, *President*
Stephen Kenney, *Vice Pres*
Gregory Kline, *Controller*
Frank Garufi, *Shareholder*
Jolene Dillman, *Executive Asst*
EMP: 12
SQ FT: 4,500
SALES (est): 4.8MM **Privately Held**
WEB: www.huntleyandhuntleyinc.com
SIC: 1382 Oil & gas exploration services

(G-11342)
LEE RJ GROUP INC (PA)
350 Hochberg Rd (15146-1516)
PHONE..............................800 860-1775
Richard J Lee, *President*
Alex Sculli, *President*
Gary Casuccio, *Vice Pres*

Duane Conley, *Vice Pres*
David Crawford, *Vice Pres*
EMP: 223
SQ FT: 89,103
SALES (est): 85.1MM **Privately Held**
WEB: www.rjlg.com
SIC: 8731 7372 3826 3825 Industrial laboratory, except testing; prepackaged software; analytical instruments; instruments to measure electricity; industrial instrmnts msrmnt display/control process variable; computer peripheral equipment

(G-11343)
LETS GET PERSONAL
2526 Mnrvlle Blvd Ste 102 (15146)
PHONE..............................412 829-0975
Karen Crandall, *Owner*
John Crandall, *Co-Owner*
EMP: 3
SALES (est): 268.3K **Privately Held**
WEB: www.letsgetpersonalgifts.com
SIC: 2284 Embroidery thread

(G-11344)
LUXOTTICA OF AMERICA INC
Also Called: Lenscrafters
370 Monroeville Mall (15146-2256)
PHONE..............................412 373-2200
Tony Juliano, *Branch Mgr*
EMP: 8
SALES (corp-wide): 283.5MM **Privately Held**
WEB: www.lenscrafters.com
SIC: 5995 3851 Eyeglasses, prescription; ophthalmic goods
HQ: Luxottica Of America Inc.
  4000 Luxottica Pl
  Mason OH 45040

(G-11345)
MIRAGE ADVERTISING INC
Also Called: Mirage Marcom
206 Monroe St (15146-1704)
PHONE..............................412 372-4181
Curtis J Brooks, *President*
Christine Godzin, *Controller*
EMP: 8
SALES: 1MM **Privately Held**
WEB: www.mirageadv.com
SIC: 2759 7311 7819 7812 Advertising literature: printing; advertising agencies; video tape or disk reproduction; motion picture & video production

(G-11346)
MONROEVILLE INK REFILLS INC
2671 Monroeville Blvd (15146-2301)
PHONE..............................412 374-1700
Thomas Laird, *Principal*
EMP: 5
SALES (est): 521.5K **Privately Held**
SIC: 3577 Printers, computer

(G-11347)
OSRAM SYLVANIA INC
9001 Rico Rd (15146-1494)
PHONE..............................412 856-2111
Bryan Pivar, *Manager*
EMP: 62
SALES (corp-wide): 4.7B **Privately Held**
WEB: www.sylvania.com
SIC: 3641 3647 3646 3643 Electric lamps; vehicular lighting equipment; commercial indusl & institutional electric lighting fixtures; current-carrying wiring devices; nonclay refractories
HQ: Osram Sylvania Inc
  200 Ballardvale St # 305
  Wilmington MA 01887
  978 570-3000

(G-11348)
PITTSBURGH POSTGAZETTE
2350 Eldo Rd (15146-1457)
PHONE..............................412 858-1850
EMP: 3
SALES (est): 109.8K **Privately Held**
SIC: 2711 Newspapers

(G-11349)
POMPA TRSSLER CHIROPRACTIC LLC
4905 William Penn Hwy (15146-3757)
P.O. Box 2054, Buckeye Lake OH (43008-2054)
PHONE..............................724 327-5665
Aaron Tressler, *President*
EMP: 3
SALES (est): 242.1K **Privately Held**
SIC: 2834 Pharmaceutical preparations

(G-11350)
PPG INDUSTRIES INC
440 College Park Dr (15146-1553)
PHONE..............................724 327-3000
David McKeough, *Manager*
EMP: 24
SALES (corp-wide): 15.3B **Publicly Held**
WEB: www.ppg.com
SIC: 2851 Paints & allied products
PA: Ppg Industries, Inc.
  1 Ppg Pl
  Pittsburgh PA 15272
  412 434-3131

(G-11351)
R A PALMER PRODUCTS COMPANY
Also Called: Ppi Imaging
2808 Broadway Blvd (15146-4679)
PHONE..............................412 823-5971
Richard A Palmer, *President*
Wayne Palmer, *President*
Jeff Miller, *General Mgr*
Debbie Daniels, *Office Mgr*
Jeff Valco, *Manager*
EMP: 16
SQ FT: 13,000
SALES (est): 2.3MM **Privately Held**
SIC: 2759 Promotional printing

(G-11352)
RAUCMIN SEVEN LLC
Also Called: Fastsigns
4051 William Penn Hwy (15146-2504)
PHONE..............................412 374-1420
Dante Mincin, *Principal*
Traci Mincin, *Principal*
EMP: 5
SALES (est): 255.3K **Privately Held**
SIC: 3993 Signs & advertising specialties

(G-11353)
REL-TEK CORPORATION
4185 Old William Penn Hwy (15146-1619)
PHONE..............................412 373-4417
Albert E Ketler, *President*
Deanna Della Vedova, *Vice Pres*
EMP: 12
SQ FT: 8,000
SALES (est): 930K **Privately Held**
WEB: www.rel-tek.com
SIC: 3829 Gas detectors

(G-11354)
RESPIRONICS INC
Also Called: Philips Respironics
1740 Golden Mile Hwy (15146-2012)
PHONE..............................724 387-4270
EMP: 483
SALES (corp-wide): 20.9B **Publicly Held**
SIC: 3845 3841 3564 8351 Patient monitoring apparatus; surgical & medical instruments; blowers & fans; child day care services; respiratory protection equipment, personal
HQ: Respironics, Inc.
  1001 Murry Ridge Ln
  Murrysville PA 15668
  724 387-5200

(G-11355)
SOLCON USA LLC
1050 Rico Rd (15146-1414)
PHONE..............................724 728-2100
▲ **EMP:** 12
SALES: 3.2MM
SALES (corp-wide): 3.7B **Privately Held**
SIC: 3625 Mfg Relays/Industrial Controls
HQ: Solcon Industries Ltd.
  6 Hacarmel
  Upper Yokneam
  777 711-111

▲ = Import ▼=Export
◆ =Import/Export

(G-11356)
SOUTH HILLS BREWING SUPPLY
2526 Mosside Blvd (15146-3556)
PHONE.............................412 937-0773
Jon Benedict, *Branch Mgr*
EMP: 4
SALES (est): 227.9K **Privately Held**
SIC: 2082 5993 Malt beverages; tobacco stores & stands
PA: South Hills Brewing Supply Inc
2212 Noblestown Rd Ste 6
Pittsburgh PA 15205

(G-11357)
STANLEY SECURITY SOLUTIONS INC
Also Called: Best Access Systems
2350 Eldo Rd Ste B (15146-1457)
PHONE.............................877 476-4968
Louis Visker, *Manager*
EMP: 13
SALES (corp-wide): 13.9B **Publicly Held**
WEB: www.bestlock.com
SIC: 3429 5099 Locks or lock sets; locks & lock sets
HQ: Stanley Security Solutions, Inc.
9998 Crosspoint Blvd # 3
Indianapolis IN 46256
317 849-2255

(G-11358)
STANLEY SECURITY SOLUTIONS INC
Also Called: Best Access Systems
2350 Eldo Rd Ste B (15146-1457)
PHONE.............................888 265-0412
John Quinn, *Manager*
EMP: 15
SALES (corp-wide): 13.9B **Publicly Held**
WEB: www.bestlock.com
SIC: 3429 5072 5099 5063 Locks or lock sets; security devices, locks; locks & lock sets; burglar alarm systems
HQ: Stanley Security Solutions, Inc.
9998 Crosspoint Blvd # 3
Indianapolis IN 46256
317 849-2255

(G-11359)
STAR ORGANIZATION INC
Also Called: Fastsigns
4051 William Penn Hwy (15146-2504)
PHONE.............................412 374-1420
Stephanie Carleton, *President*
James Carleton, *Vice Pres*
EMP: 3
SQ FT: 2,000
SALES (est): 310.3K **Privately Held**
SIC: 3993 Signs & advertising specialties

(G-11360)
TOMDEL INC
Also Called: Sign-A-Rama
4901 Old William Penn Hwy (15146-3770)
PHONE.............................724 519-2697
Tommy Green, *President*
Dolores Green, *Vice Pres*
EMP: 4 EST: 2012
SALES: 420K **Privately Held**
SIC: 3993 Signs & advertising specialties

(G-11361)
UNION SPRING & MFG CORP (PA)
Also Called: Mercer Spring and Wire Div
4268 N Pike Ste 1 (15146)
PHONE.............................412 843-5900
James Whims, *Ch of Bd*
Ray Beacha, *President*
Charles W McWilliams, *President*
Richard Black, *Exec VP*
EMP: 140
SQ FT: 3,500
SALES (est): 22.7MM **Privately Held**
WEB: www.pontotocspring.com
SIC: 3493 Hot formed springs; cold formed springs

(G-11362)
UNIVERSAL NETWORK TECHNOLOGIES
100 Urick Ct (15146-4920)
PHONE.............................412 490-0990

Sofiya Goldsthtein, *President*
Sofiya Goldshtein, *President*
EMP: 3
SQ FT: 1,000
SALES: 70K **Privately Held**
SIC: 2752 Commercial printing, lithographic

(G-11363)
WATER TREATMENT SERVICES INC
Also Called: First Defense Operations MGT
203 Townsend Dr (15146-1065)
PHONE.............................800 817-5116
Bill Campbell, *Principal*
EMP: 12
SALES (est): 285.7K **Privately Held**
WEB: www.wtservicesllc.com
SIC: 2899 Chemical preparations

(G-11364)
WENDELL H STONE COMPANY INC
Also Called: Stone & Co
4135 Old William Penn Hwy (15146)
PHONE.............................412 373-6235
Greg Stone, *Owner*
EMP: 12
SALES (corp-wide): 35MM **Privately Held**
WEB: www.stoneco.com
SIC: 3273 5211 Ready-mixed concrete; brick
PA: Wendell H. Stone Company, Inc.
606 Mccormick Ave
Connellsville PA 15425
724 836-1400

Mont Alto
Franklin County

(G-11365)
SOUDERS INDUSTRIES INC (PA)
Also Called: Sesco
19 Ash St (17237-9645)
PHONE.............................717 749-3900
David S Souders, *President*
Brian Forsythe, *Engineer*
David Cook, *Sales Executive*
Stacie Reeder, *Executive Asst*
Donna Holtry, *Admin Sec*
▲ EMP: 70
SQ FT: 30,000
SALES (est): 14.5MM **Privately Held**
WEB: www.sesco1.com
SIC: 3679 Harness assemblies for electronic use: wire or cable

---

Montandon
Northumberland County

(G-11366)
PARDOES PERKY PEANUTS INC
143 Center St (17850-8016)
P.O. Box 90 (17850-0090)
PHONE.............................570 524-9595
Carl L Pardoe, *President*
Rose Stitzel, *General Mgr*
Chris Schmouder, *Manager*
EMP: 40
SQ FT: 21,000
SALES: 8MM **Privately Held**
WEB: www.pardoesperkypeanuts.com
SIC: 2068 2087 2066 Salted & roasted nuts & seeds; powders, flavoring (except drink); chocolate bars, solid

---

Montgomery
Lycoming County

(G-11367)
B & C AUTO WRECKERS INC
4867 Us Highway 15 (17752-9035)
PHONE.............................570 547-1040
Robert Twigg, *Owner*
EMP: 5

SALES (est): 757.1K **Privately Held**
WEB: www.bandcautowreckers.com
SIC: 3711 5015 Wreckers (tow truck), assembly of; motor vehicle parts, used

(G-11368)
BRODART CO
E S Thomas St (17752)
PHONE.............................570 326-2461
Ammon Henninger, *Principal*
EMP: 42
SALES (corp-wide): 431.1MM **Privately Held**
SIC: 2511 2426 Kitchen & dining room furniture; hardwood dimension & flooring mills
PA: Brodart Co.
500 Arch St
Williamsport PA 17701
570 326-2461

(G-11369)
G&M BANDSAW INC
6124 Us Highway 15 (17752-9634)
PHONE.............................570 547-2386
Chester E James II, *President*
Tracey Jeffreys, *Sales Staff*
Brendon Burton, *Sales Associate*
EMP: 14
SQ FT: 7,000
SALES (est): 3.3MM **Privately Held**
WEB: www.gmbandsaw.com
SIC: 3553 Sawmill machines

(G-11370)
HALLIBURTON COMPANY
Also Called: Halliburton Energy Services
343 Riddell Rd (17752-9244)
PHONE.............................570 547-5800
Douglas Magill, *Branch Mgr*
EMP: 190 **Publicly Held**
SIC: 1389 Oil field services
PA: Halliburton Company
3000 N Sam Houston Pkwy E
Houston TX 77032

(G-11371)
J & M INDUSTRIAL COATINGS INC
163 Bower St (17752)
P.O. Box 186 (17752-0186)
PHONE.............................570 547-1825
Brian Woods, *President*
Felicia Woods, *Vice Pres*
EMP: 5
SQ FT: 3,000
SALES (est): 782.9K **Privately Held**
SIC: 2851 Paints & paint additives

(G-11372)
KEURIG DR PEPPER INC
121 State Route 54 (17752-9027)
PHONE.............................570 547-0777
Wes Davis, *Manager*
EMP: 93 **Publicly Held**
SIC: 2086 Soft drinks: packaged in cans, bottles, etc.
PA: Keurig Dr Pepper Inc.
53 South Ave
Burlington MA 01803

(G-11373)
KOPPERS INDUSTRIES INC
Koppers RR & Utility Pdts Div
50 Koppers Ln (17752-9606)
PHONE.............................570 547-1651
Paul Beswick, *Manager*
EMP: 40
SALES (corp-wide): 1.7B **Publicly Held**
WEB: www.koppers.com
SIC: 2491 Poles, posts & pilings: treated wood; railroad cross bridges & switch ties, treated wood; railroad cross-ties, treated wood
HQ: Koppers Industries Of Delaware Inc.
436 7th Ave Ste 2026
Pittsburgh PA 15219

(G-11374)
LAFARGE RD MARKING INC
79 Montgomery St (17752-1138)
PHONE.............................570 547-1621
John Loehrke, *Director*
EMP: 3
SALES (est): 96.6K **Privately Held**
SIC: 2851 Paints & allied products

(G-11375)
LECLERC FOODS USA INC
44 Park Dr (17752-8534)
PHONE.............................570 547-6295
Denis Leclerc, *President*
Jean Leclerc, *Vice Pres*
Sebastien Leclerc, *Vice Pres*
Line Leclerc, *Admin Sec*
Robert Leclerc, *Admin Sec*
▲ EMP: 100
SQ FT: 10,000
SALES (est): 18.8MM
SALES (corp-wide): 419.3K **Privately Held**
SIC: 2052 5411 Pretzels; supermarkets
HQ: Biscuits Leclerc Ltee
91 Rue De Rotterdam
Saint-Augustin-De-Desmaures QC
G3A 1
418 878-2601

(G-11376)
MILTON DAILY STANDARD
Also Called: Standard Journal
21 Arch St (17752-1101)
PHONE.............................570 742-9077
EMP: 30
SALES (est): 1MM **Privately Held**
SIC: 2711 Newspapers, publishing & printing

(G-11377)
PHOENIX DATA INC
8813 State Route 405 (17752-9587)
P.O. Box 200 (17752-0200)
PHONE.............................570 547-1665
Larry Lovell, *President*
Ronald Way, *Division Mgr*
Sanford J Bernan, *Admin Sec*
EMP: 81
SQ FT: 45,000
SALES (est): 23.6MM **Privately Held**
WEB: www.phoenixdatainc.com
SIC: 2761 2752 Computer forms, manifold or continuous; commercial printing, lithographic

(G-11378)
SPRINGS WINDOW FASHIONS LLC
8467 Route 405 Hwy S (17752)
P.O. Box 500 (17752-0500)
PHONE.............................570 547-6671
Doreen Decker, *Branch Mgr*
EMP: 32
SALES (corp-wide): 3.1B **Privately Held**
WEB: www.springs.com
SIC: 2591 Blinds vertical
HQ: Springs Window Fashions, Llc
7549 Graber Rd
Middleton WI 53562
608 836-1011

(G-11379)
STAGGERT DISPOSAL
147 James Rd (17752-8930)
PHONE.............................570 547-6150
Harris Staggert, *Principal*
EMP: 6
SALES (est): 495.1K **Privately Held**
SIC: 3089 Garbage containers, plastic

(G-11380)
STANLEY ACCESS TECH LLC
270 Dogwood Ridge Rd (17752-9071)
PHONE.............................570 368-1435
EMP: 4
SALES (corp-wide): 13.9B **Publicly Held**
SIC: 3699 Door opening & closing devices, electrical
HQ: Stanley Access Technologies Llc
65 Scott Swamp Rd
Farmington CT 06032

(G-11381)
VT HACKNEY INC
Also Called: Kidron Division
914 Saegers Station Rd (17752-8501)
PHONE.............................570 547-1681
Scott Hope, *Manager*
EMP: 100
SALES (corp-wide): 4.8B **Privately Held**
WEB: www.rescueleader.com
SIC: 5561 3713 Travel trailers: automobile, new & used; beverage truck bodies

HQ: Vt Hackney, Inc.
911 W 5th St
Washington NC 27889
252 946-6521

Montgomeryville
Montgomery County

(G-11382)
ALCAST METALS INC
440 Stump Rd (18936-9630)
P.O. Box 188 (18936-0188)
PHONE..................................215 368-5865
Wolfgang Schmidt, *President*
EMP: 20 **EST:** 1966
SQ FT: 25,000
SALES (est): 437.5K **Privately Held**
SIC: 3363 3566 Aluminum die-castings; gears, power transmission, except automotive; drives, high speed industrial, except hydrostatic

(G-11383)
ALEXANDERWERK INC
102 Commerce Dr (18936-9624)
PHONE..................................215 442-0270
Manfred Felder, *President*
Sean Koontz, *Vice Pres*
▲ **EMP:** 5
SQ FT: 16,400
SALES (est): 1.1MM
SALES (corp-wide): 35.7MM **Privately Held**
WEB: www.alexanderwerk.com
SIC: 3559 Automotive related machinery
PA: Alexanderwerk Ag
Kippdorfstr. 6-24
Remscheid 42857
219 179-50

(G-11384)
ALLIED FOAM TECH CORP
146 Keystone Dr (18936-9637)
PHONE..................................215 540-2666
Harrison Chao, *President*
Lin-Lin Pao-Chao, *Vice Pres*
EMP: 7
SALES (est): 1.2MM **Privately Held**
WEB: www.alliedfoamtech.com
SIC: 3559 2899 Chemical machinery & equipment; foam charge mixtures

(G-11385)
AMERICAN MANUFACTURING & ENGRG
506 Stump Rd (18936-9619)
PHONE..................................215 362-9694
Nand Todi, *President*
Shashi Todi, *Corp Secy*
EMP: 14
SQ FT: 10,000
SALES (est): 2.2MM **Privately Held**
WEB: www.amemfg.com
SIC: 3599 2298 Machine shop, jobbing & repair; cordage & twine

(G-11386)
AMERICAN SAFETY TECHNOLOGIES (PA)
130 Commerce Dr (18936-9624)
PHONE..................................215 855-8450
Steve Danion, *Business Mgr*
▲ **EMP:** 2
SQ FT: 58,000
SALES (est): 3.1MM **Privately Held**
WEB: www.americansafetytech.com
SIC: 3479 3446 Coating of metals & formed products; coating, rust preventive; stairs, staircases, stair treads: prefabricated metal

(G-11387)
AZTEC PRODUCTS INC
201 Commerce Dr (18936-9641)
PHONE..................................215 393-4700
Whitney I Beverly, *President*
Allan H Beverly, *Vice Pres*
◆ **EMP:** 18
SQ FT: 20,000
SALES (est): 5.1MM **Privately Held**
WEB: www.aztecproducts.com
SIC: 3589 3519 5084 Floor washing & polishing machines, commercial; gas engine rebuilding; propane conversion equipment

(G-11388)
CLOSET WORKS INC
160 Commerce Dr (18936-9651)
P.O. Box 839 (18936-0839)
PHONE..................................215 675-6430
David R Cutler, *President*
Annmarie Cutler, *Vice Pres*
Paul Rumer, *Manager*
Jennifer Molinelli, *Consultant*
Brendan Coyne, *Info Tech Mgr*
▲ **EMP:** 50
SQ FT: 30,000
SALES (est): 3.1MM **Privately Held**
WEB: www.closetworksinc.com
SIC: 1751 1799 2511 Cabinet building & installation; closet organizers, installation & design; office furniture installation; unassembled or unfinished furniture, household: wood

(G-11389)
COMMERCE DRIVE ENTERPRISES LLC
Also Called: Numonics
101 Commerce Dr (18936-9623)
PHONE..................................215 362-2766
Alfred N Basilicato, *President*
Jeff Golden, *Business Mgr*
Dan Keelan, *Controller*
Richard Dumler, *Admin Sec*
▲ **EMP:** 60
SQ FT: 20,000
SALES (est): 10.8MM **Privately Held**
WEB: www.interactivewhiteboards.com
SIC: 3577 Plotters, computer

(G-11390)
COMPU-CRAFT FABRICATORS INC
102d Park Dr (18936-9612)
PHONE..................................215 646-2381
Alfred Erpel, *President*
EMP: 35
SQ FT: 25,000
SALES (est): 7.5MM **Privately Held**
WEB: www.metalwork.com
SIC: 3444 3451 3441 Sheet metal specialties, not stamped; screw machine products; fabricated structural metal

(G-11391)
CRAFTWELD FABRICATION CO INC
105 Park Dr (18936-9613)
PHONE..................................267 492-1100
Glenn Spalding, *President*
EMP: 33
SQ FT: 24,000
SALES (est): 6.3MM **Privately Held**
WEB: www.craftweldfab.com
SIC: 3599 3444 3441 Machine shop, jobbing & repair; sheet metalwork; fabricated structural metal

(G-11392)
D B PRODUCTS INC
120 Keystone Dr Unit B (18936-9637)
PHONE..................................215 628-0416
Kyle N Southerling, *President*
Jennifer Southerling, *Director*
▲ **EMP:** 30 **EST:** 2006
SALES (est): 3.7MM **Privately Held**
SIC: 3955 Print cartridges for laser & other computer printers

(G-11393)
EDWARD T CHRISTIANSEN & SONS
Also Called: Christiansen Memorials
697 Bethlehem Pike (18936-9702)
P.O. Box 424 (18936-0424)
PHONE..................................215 368-1001
Edward T Christiansen Jr, *President*
EMP: 7 **EST:** 1946
SALES (est): 618.2K **Privately Held**
SIC: 5999 3272 Monuments, finished to custom order; monuments, concrete

(G-11394)
ELECTRO SOFT INC
113 Keystone Dr (18936-9638)
PHONE..................................215 654-0701
James T Wallace, *President*
Zach Rowand, *Purch Dir*
Mike Tandy, *Purch Mgr*
Sheila B Wallace, *Treasurer*
Sheila Wallace, *Treasurer*
EMP: 30
SQ FT: 20,000
SALES (est): 6.4MM **Privately Held**
WEB: www.electrosoftinc.com
SIC: 3679 3672 3643 3613 Harness assemblies for electronic use: wire or cable; printed circuit boards; current-carrying wiring devices; switchgear & switchboard apparatus

(G-11395)
EMBALL ISO INC
130 Keystone Dr (18936-9637)
P.O. Box 3527, Philadelphia (19122-0527)
PHONE..................................267 687-8570
Ron Stern, *Principal*
▲ **EMP:** 6
SALES: 850K **Privately Held**
SIC: 2671 Thermoplastic coated paper for packaging
PA: Emball iso Sa
Zone Industrielle Des Vernailles
Saint Georges De Reneins 69830

(G-11396)
ENVIRONMENTAL SOLUT WORLD INC (PA)
Also Called: Technology Fabricators
200 Progress Dr (18936-9616)
PHONE..................................215 699-0730
Mark Yung, *Ch of Bd*
Brian Webster, *VP Opers*
Cindy Moffitt, *Purch Agent*
Praveen Nair, *CFO*
Virendra Kumar, *Ch Credit Ofcr*
EMP: 30 **EST:** 1989
SQ FT: 40,000
SALES (est): 25MM **Privately Held**
SIC: 3812 Light or heat emission operating apparatus

(G-11397)
FILTER & WATER TECHNOLOGIES
162 Keystone Dr (18936-9637)
PHONE..................................267 450-4900
Gary Pifer, *President*
Joseph Kidd, *Treasurer*
EMP: 8
SQ FT: 15,000
SALES: 1MM **Privately Held**
SIC: 3589 Water treatment equipment, industrial

(G-11398)
GAMERS VAULT
411 Doylestown Rd G (18936-9636)
PHONE..................................609 781-0938
Robert Healey Jr, *Principal*
EMP: 3
SALES (est): 218.9K **Privately Held**
SIC: 3272 Burial vaults, concrete or precast terrazzo

(G-11399)
ILLINOIS TOOL WORKS INC
ITW Polymers Coatings N Amer
130 Commerce Dr (18936-9624)
PHONE..................................215 855-8450
R Siock, *Branch Mgr*
EMP: 68
SQ FT: 26,000
SALES (corp-wide): 14.7B **Publicly Held**
SIC: 2821 5169 Plastics materials & resins; chemicals & allied products
PA: Illinois Tool Works Inc.
155 Harlem Ave
Glenview IL 60025
847 724-7500

(G-11400)
KEYSTONE CONVERTING INC
108 Park Dr (18936-9612)
PHONE..................................215 661-9004
Frank Schoendorfer, *President*
▲ **EMP:** 10

SQ FT: 13,000
SALES (est): 1.7MM **Privately Held**
WEB: www.keyslit.com
SIC: 2754 5131 2679 Labels: gravure printing; labels; pressed fiber & molded pulp products except food products

(G-11401)
LAURELIND CORP (PA)
Also Called: Fastsigns
724 Bethlehem Pike (18936-9601)
P.O. Box 528 (18936-0528)
PHONE..................................215 368-5800
Stephen Nave, *President*
EMP: 4
SALES (est): 536.1K **Privately Held**
SIC: 3993 Signs & advertising specialties

(G-11402)
LAURELIND CORP
Also Called: Fastsigns
411 Doylestown Rd (18936-9636)
PHONE..................................215 230-4737
Stephen Nave, *President*
EMP: 3
SALES (corp-wide): 536.1K **Privately Held**
SIC: 3993 Signs & advertising specialties
PA: Laurelind Corp.
724 Bethlehem Pike
Montgomeryville PA 18936
215 368-5800

(G-11403)
LEM PRODUCTS INC
147 Keystone Dr (18936-9638)
PHONE..................................800 220-2400
Maureen O'Connor, *President*
Timothy P O'Connor, *Vice Pres*
Jeff Kulp, *Engineer*
Nicole Adamczyk, *Sales Staff*
David Rosen, *Manager*
◆ **EMP:** 37 **EST:** 1967
SQ FT: 42,000
SALES (est): 8.7MM **Privately Held**
WEB: www.lemproductsinc.com
SIC: 2759 2752 Screen printing; labels & seals: printing; tags: printing; commercial printing, lithographic

(G-11404)
LLOYD INDUSTRIES INC (PA)
231 Commerce Dr (18936-9641)
PHONE..................................215 367-5863
William P Lloyd, *Principal*
Eileen Lindsay, *Comptroller*
▲ **EMP:** 35
SQ FT: 40,000
SALES (est): 13.7MM **Privately Held**
WEB: www.firedamper.com
SIC: 3822 3312 Damper operators: pneumatic, thermostatic, electric; tool & die steel

(G-11405)
LUMENOPTIX LLC
203 Progress Dr (18936-9618)
PHONE..................................215 671-2029
Larry Schmidt, *President*
Jay Goodman, *Principal*
Chris Pico, *Director*
David Newman,
EMP: 46
SALES (est): 15.6MM **Privately Held**
SIC: 3646 8748 Commercial indusl & institutional electric lighting fixtures; lighting consultant

(G-11406)
MATHESON TRI-GAS INC
166 Keystone Dr (18936-9637)
PHONE..................................215 641-2700
Rick Kowey, *Vice Pres*
Paul Taylor, *QC Mgr*
EMP: 100
SQ FT: 22,500 **Privately Held**
WEB: www.matheson-trigas.com
SIC: 3533 3569 3824 Oil & gas field machinery; gas producers, generators & other gas related equipment; gas producers (machinery); gas separators (machinery); fluid meters & counting devices
HQ: Matheson Tri-Gas, Inc.
150 Allen Rd Ste 302
Basking Ridge NJ 07920
908 991-9200

▲ = Import ▼=Export
◆ =Import/Export

(G-11407)
MICROSEMI CORP -
MNTGMERYVILLE
140 Commerce Dr (18936-9624)
PHONE......................215 631-9840
Patrick Sireta, *President*
EMP: 45
SQ FT: 20,600
SALES (est): 2.8MM
SALES (corp-wide): 3.9B **Publicly Held**
WEB: www.advancedpower.com
SIC: 3674 Semiconductors & related devices
HQ: Microsemi Corp. - Power Products
Group
405 Sw Columbia St
Bend OR 97702
541 382-8028

(G-11408)
MICROTRAC INC (DH)
215 Keystone Dr (18936-9647)
PHONE......................215 619-9920
Robert Sheng, *President*
EMP: 32
SQ FT: 23,500
SALES (est): 7.2MM
SALES (corp-wide): 1.4B **Privately Held**
WEB: www.microtrac.com
SIC: 3826 5049 Analytical instruments;
analytical instruments

(G-11409)
NATION RUSKIN HOLDINGS INC
(PA)
206 Progress Dr (18936-9616)
PHONE......................267 654-4000
Raymond C Adolf, *President*
Marianne Cardis, *Vice Pres*
▲ EMP: 10
SQ FT: 50,400
SALES (est): 1.9MM **Privately Held**
WEB: www.nationruskin.com
SIC: 3069 3089 3991 Sponge rubber &
sponge rubber products; buckets, plastic;
brushes, household or industrial

(G-11410)
PALETTI USA LLC
145 Keystone Dr (18936-9638)
PHONE......................267 289-0020
Justin Westcott, *Prdtn Mgr*
Helmut Kahl,
John Schmidt,
▲ EMP: 28
SALES (est): 7.9MM **Privately Held**
WEB: www.palettiusa.com
SIC: 3569 3354 Robots, assembly line: industrial & commercial; rods, extruded,
aluminum

(G-11411)
PENN MANUFACTURING INDS
INC
Also Called: P M I
506 Stump Rd (18936-9619)
PHONE......................215 362-1217
Nand K Todi, *President*
Shashi Todi, *Vice Pres*
◆ EMP: 60 EST: 1977
SQ FT: 85,000
SALES (est): 15MM **Privately Held**
WEB: www.pennmfg.com
SIC: 3599 Machine shop, jobbing & repair

(G-11412)
PERFORMANCE CONTROLS
INC (DH)
151 Domorah Dr (18936-9642)
PHONE......................215 619-4920
Perry Walraven, *CEO*
Joseph McKibbin, *President*
Kevin West, *Production*
Michael Lacianca, *Purch Mgr*
Brian Fenstermacher, *Engineer*
▲ EMP: 60
SQ FT: 100,000
SALES (est): 11.1MM
SALES (corp-wide): 87.9B **Privately Held**
WEB: www.pcipa.com
SIC: 3679 Parametric amplifiers
HQ: Hitachi Healthcare Manufacturing, Ltd.
2-1, Shintoyofuta
Kashiwa CHI 277-0
471 314-336

(G-11413)
PERKINELMER INC
221 Commerce Dr (18936-9641)
PHONE......................215 368-6900
Michael Sullivan, *Principal*
EMP: 55
SALES (corp-wide): 2.7B **Publicly Held**
SIC: 3826 Analytical instruments
PA: Perkinelmer, Inc.
940 Winter St
Waltham MA 02451
781 663-6900

(G-11414)
PHILADELPHIA SCIENTIFIC LLC
207 Progress Dr (18936-9618)
PHONE......................215 616-0390
Charles R Snyder, *VP Sales*
William M Jones,
Dan Jones,
▲ EMP: 50
SALES (est): 10.8MM **Privately Held**
WEB: www.phlsci.com
SIC: 3691 Storage batteries

(G-11415)
PHILLYSTRAN INC
Also Called: WireCo World Group
151 Commerce Dr (18936-9628)
PHONE......................215 368-6611
Stephan Kessel, *CEO*
Robert Lombardo, *Managing Dir*
Bob Lombardo, *Opers Mgr*
Steve Hogan, *Facilities Mgr*
Danny Welsh, *Plant Engr*
◆ EMP: 30
SQ FT: 50,000
SALES (est): 5.3MM **Privately Held**
WEB: www.phillystran.com
SIC: 2298 Rope, except asbestos & wire
HQ: Wireco Worldgroup Inc.
2400 W 75th St
Prairie Village KS 66208
816 270-4700

(G-11416)
SAINT-GOBAIN ABRASIVES INC
Also Called: Moyco Precision
200 Commerce Dr (18936-9640)
PHONE......................215 855-4300
Joesph Sternberg, *Manager*
EMP: 45
SALES (corp-wide): 215.9MM **Privately Held**
WEB: www.sgabrasives.com
SIC: 3291 Abrasive products
HQ: Saint-Gobain Abrasives, Inc.
1 New Bond St
Worcester MA 01606
508 795-5000

(G-11417)
SAINT-GOBAIN ABRASIVES INC
Moyco Precision Abrasives
200 Commerce Dr (18936-9640)
PHONE......................267 218-7100
Mark Sternberg, *Manager*
EMP: 35
SALES (corp-wide): 215.9MM **Privately Held**
WEB: www.sgabrasives.com
SIC: 3291 Abrasive products
HQ: Saint-Gobain Abrasives, Inc.
1 New Bond St
Worcester MA 01606
508 795-5000

(G-11418)
SNAPTEX INTERNATIONAL LLC
111a Park Dr (18936-9613)
PHONE......................215 283-0152
Norman Yerusalem,
EMP: 3
SALES: 1MM **Privately Held**
SIC: 3446 Partitions & supports/studs, including accoustical systems

(G-11419)
SONOCO PRTECTIVE
SOLUTIONS INC
Also Called: Thermosafe
161 Corporate Dr (18936-9643)
PHONE......................215 643-5555
Tom Hanslits, *President*
EMP: 35

SALES (corp-wide): 5.3B **Publicly Held**
SIC: 2631 Container, packaging &
boxboard
HQ: Sonoco Protective Solutions, Inc.
1 N 2nd St
Hartsville SC 29550
843 383-7000

(G-11420)
SURGICAL LASER TECH INC
147 Keystone Dr (18936-9638)
PHONE......................215 619-3600
Michael Stewart, *Principal*
Dennis M McGrath, *CFO*
EMP: 9
SALES (est): 1.2MM **Privately Held**
WEB: www.slti.com
SIC: 3845 Electromedical equipment

(G-11421)
TECHNOLOGY FABRICATORS
INC
Also Called: Tfi
200 Progress Dr (18936-9616)
PHONE......................215 699-0731
Mark Young, *CEO*
EMP: 35
SALES (est): 7.9MM **Privately Held**
SIC: 3714 Mufflers (exhaust), motor vehicle

(G-11422)
TEGRANT CORPORATION
Also Called: Tegrant Thermosare Brands
161 Corporate Dr (18936-9643)
PHONE......................215 643-3555
Tom Hanslits, *Manager*
▲ EMP: 11
SALES (est): 1.7MM **Privately Held**
SIC: 3053 Gaskets, packing & sealing devices

(G-11423)
TELEDYNE SCENTIFIC IMAGING
LLC
Also Called: Teledyne Judson Technologies
221 Commerce Dr (18936-9641)
PHONE......................215 368-6900
Henry Yuan, *Engineer*
Kadri Vural, *Manager*
Joe Chang, *Manager*
Janet Miner, *Manager*
Kevin Gaines, *Info Tech Dir*
EMP: 12
SALES (corp-wide): 2.9B **Publicly Held**
WEB: www.teledyne.com
SIC: 3724 Aircraft engines & engine parts
HQ: Teledyne Scientific & Imaging, Llc
1049 Camino Dos Rios
Thousand Oaks CA 91360

(G-11424)
TIMBERLANE INC
150 Domorah Dr (18936-9633)
PHONE......................215 616-0600
Rick Skidmore, *CEO*
▼ EMP: 40
SQ FT: 20,000
SALES (est): 8.2MM **Privately Held**
WEB: www.timberlane.com
SIC: 2431 Window shutters, wood; door
trim, wood

(G-11425)
UNIQUE MACHINE CO
131 Commerce Dr (18936-9628)
PHONE......................215 368-8550
Robert G Barndt, *President*
Richard W Barndt, *Vice Pres*
Mark G Schmid, *Vice Pres*
EMP: 20 EST: 1962
SQ FT: 22,000
SALES (est): 3.2MM **Privately Held**
WEB: www.unique-machine.com
SIC: 3599 3544 Machine shop, jobbing &
repair; special dies & tools

(G-11426)
VINK & BERI LLC
140 Domorah Dr (18936-9633)
PHONE......................215 654-5252
Vipul Chander Beri, *Principal*
▲ EMP: 11
SALES: 2.5MM **Privately Held**
SIC: 2082 Malt beverages

(G-11427)
WSG & SOLUTIONS INC
160 Commerce Dr Ste 100 (18936-9651)
PHONE......................267 638-3000
Stephen B Wilcher, *President*
Angelo R Didonato, *Admin Sec*
▲ EMP: 25
SQ FT: 12,836
SALES (est): 5MM **Privately Held**
WEB: www.wsgandsolutions.com
SIC: 3589 Water treatment equipment, industrial

Montoursville
Lycoming County

(G-11428)
ABBY SIGNS OF PA
1128 Broad St (17754-2550)
PHONE......................570 494-0600
Bill Abernatha, *President*
EMP: 3
SALES (est): 296K **Privately Held**
SIC: 3993 Signs, not made in custom sign
painting shops

(G-11429)
ALBERTS SPRAY SOLUTIONS
LLC
60 Choate Cir (17754-9791)
PHONE......................570 368-6653
Seth Alberts, *Owner*
Edward Alberts, *Owner*
Laurie Alberts-Salita, *Owner*
Brad Vasko, *Division Mgr*
Randy Barton, *Foreman/Supr*
EMP: 7 EST: 2013
SALES: 3.7MM **Privately Held**
SIC: 3086 Plastics foam products

(G-11430)
AMERICAN CREPE
CORPORATION
496 Fairfield Rd (17754-8331)
P.O. Box 31 (17754-0031)
PHONE......................570 433-3319
Scott Slocum, *President*
Judith Odell, *Admin Sec*
EMP: 3
SQ FT: 13,000
SALES (est): 503.3K **Privately Held**
SIC: 2679 2621 Crepe paper or crepe
paper products: purchased material;
paper mills

(G-11431)
APPELLATION CNSTR SVCS
LLC (PA)
999 N Loyalsock Ave Ste C (17754-1005)
PHONE......................570 601-4765
William Emick, *Mng Member*
David Holtzman,
EMP: 72
SQ FT: 4,200
SALES (est): 21.9MM **Privately Held**
SIC: 3498 1731 1623 Fabricated pipe &
fittings; general electrical contractor; natural gas compressor station construction

(G-11432)
BASSLER WLLMSPORT PTTERN
WORKS
430 S Alley (17754-2324)
PHONE......................570 368-2471
Louis M Bassler, *Owner*
Aaron Bassler, *Project Mgr*
EMP: 5
SQ FT: 7,200
SALES: 450K **Privately Held**
WEB: www.basslerwpw.com
SIC: 3543 Industrial patterns

(G-11433)
BEACON CONTAINER
CORPORATION
Also Called: Beacon Container Corp Pennsylv
326 S Maple St (17754-2531)
P.O. Box 117 (17754-0117)
PHONE......................570 433-3800
Chris Winters, *President*
Robert Bower, *QC Dir*

EMP: 20
SALES (corp-wide): 23.6MM **Privately Held**
WEB: www.beaconcontainer.com
SIC: 2653 5113 Boxes, corrugated: made from purchased materials; corrugated & solid fiber boxes
PA: Beacon Container Corporation
700 W 1st St
Birdsboro PA 19508
610 582-2222

(G-11434)
BOWSER MANUFACTURING CO
Also Called: Englishs Model Railroad Supply
201 Streibeigh Ln (17754-2525)
P.O. Box 322 (17754-0322)
PHONE 570 368-5045
Geraldine English, *Vice Pres*
Lewis K English Jr, *Treasurer*
▲ **EMP:** 10 **EST:** 1961
SQ FT: 7,500
SALES (est): 1.6MM **Privately Held**
WEB: www.toytrainheaven.com
SIC: 3944 5945 5092 3366 Railroad models: toy & hobby; models, toy & hobby; hobby goods; copper foundries; steel investment foundries

(G-11435)
CENTRE CONCRETE COMPANY
307 Fairfield Rd (17754-8340)
PHONE 570 433-3186
Sean McCoy, *Manager*
EMP: 22
SALES (corp-wide): 16.5MM **Privately Held**
SIC: 3273 Ready-mixed concrete
PA: Centre Concrete Company
629 E Rolling Ridge Dr
Bellefonte PA 16823
814 238-2471

(G-11436)
CHEMCOAT INC
2790 Canfields Ln (17754-9463)
P.O. Box 188 (17754-0188)
PHONE 570 368-8631
Kathleen D Obrien, *President*
Myral A Bonnell, *Vice Pres*
Todd E Moyer, *Purch Agent*
Stephen J Mondell, *CFO*
Steve Mondell, *CFO*
EMP: 30 **EST:** 1930
SQ FT: 37,500
SALES (est): 9.7MM **Privately Held**
WEB: www.chemcoat.net
SIC: 2851 Paints & paint additives

(G-11437)
CROMAFLOW INC
143 Lumber Ln (17754-8973)
PHONE 570 546-3557
Henry Holcomb, *CEO*
Jose Gerardo Villarreal, *Ch of Bd*
Carvin Malone, *Treasurer*
Ian Baynes, *Admin Sec*
◆ **EMP:** 11 **EST:** 2014
SQ FT: 1,500
SALES (est): 2.1MM **Privately Held**
SIC: 3589 Sewage & water treatment equipment

(G-11438)
FAIRFIELD MANUFACTURING CO INC
213 Streibeigh Ln (17754-2525)
PHONE 570 368-8624
Raymond Marshalek, *President*
Dorothy Marshalek, *Corp Secy*
▼ **EMP:** 18
SQ FT: 8,200
SALES: 1.4MM **Privately Held**
WEB: www.fairfieldmanufacturing.com
SIC: 3599 Machine & other job shop work; machine shop, jobbing & repair

(G-11439)
FLEXSTEEL PIPELINE TECH INC
300 Streibeigh Ln Bldg D (17754-2540)
PHONE 570 505-3491
EMP: 5 **Privately Held**
SIC: 1623 3498 Pipeline construction; coils, pipe: fabricated from purchased pipe

HQ: Flexsteel Pipeline Technologies, Inc.
1201 La St Ste 2700
Houston TX 77002

(G-11440)
GRIT COMMERCIAL PRINTING INC
80 Choate Cir (17754-9700)
PHONE 570 368-8021
Lance Spitler, *President*
Phil Spitler, *Vice Pres*
Michael Bischof, *Sales Staff*
Sean Henderson, *Sales Staff*
EMP: 33
SALES (est): 5.5MM **Privately Held**
WEB: www.gritprinting.com
SIC: 2752 Commercial printing, offset

(G-11441)
IN STITCHES EMBROIDERY
317 Broad St Ste 2 (17754-2205)
PHONE 570 368-5525
Timothy Bower, *Owner*
EMP: 8
SQ FT: 1,000
SALES: 450K **Privately Held**
SIC: 2759 2395 Screen printing; emblems, embroidered

(G-11442)
INFINITY OILFIELD SERVICES LLC
1500 Sycamore Rd (17754-9303)
PHONE 570 327-8114
Daniel A Klingerman, *Principal*
EMP: 3
SALES (est): 298.7K **Privately Held**
SIC: 1389 Oil field services

(G-11443)
JERSEY SHORE STEEL COMPANY
Also Called: Met Fab Division
2800 Canfields Ln (17754-9427)
PHONE 570 368-2601
Peter Schultz, *Exec VP*
Frank Bardo, *Branch Mgr*
EMP: 104
SQ FT: 75,000
SALES (corp-wide): 135.6MM **Privately Held**
WEB: www.jssteel.com
SIC: 3312 2411 Rails, steel or iron; logging
PA: Jersey Shore Steel Company
70 Maryland Ave
Jersey Shore PA 17740
570 753-3000

(G-11444)
JOHN M FINK LUMBER
77 Lumber Ln (17754-8970)
PHONE 570 435-0362
John M Fink, *Owner*
EMP: 3
SALES: 150K **Privately Held**
WEB: www.johnmfink.com
SIC: 2421 5211 Lumber: rough, sawed or planed; resawing lumber into smaller dimensions; planing mill products & lumber

(G-11445)
LOGUE INDUSTRIES INC
120 S Arch St (17754-2304)
PHONE 570 368-2639
Joe Logue, *President*
George E Logue, *Vice Pres*
EMP: 25
SQ FT: 47,000
SALES (est): 3.6MM **Privately Held**
WEB: www.logueind.com
SIC: 7692 3599 3444 Welding repair; machine shop, jobbing & repair; sheet metalwork

(G-11446)
LYCOMING BURIAL VAULT CO INC
Also Called: Lycoming Concrete Septic Tanks
350 Spruce St (17754-1706)
P.O. Box 157 (17754-0157)
PHONE 570 368-8642
Kirk Naugle, *President*
Lucinda Naugle, *Corp Secy*
EMP: 11

SQ FT: 3,000
SALES (est): 1MM **Privately Held**
SIC: 3272 5044 5039 Burial vaults, concrete or precast terrazzo; septic tanks, concrete; vaults & safes; septic tanks

(G-11447)
M & S CONVERSION COMPANY INC
248 Streibeigh Ln (17754-2526)
PHONE 570 368-1991
Ray Mattie, *President*
EMP: 10
SQ FT: 25,000
SALES (est): 3.1MM **Privately Held**
SIC: 3449 Custom roll formed products

(G-11448)
PPK ANIMAL HEALTHCARE LLC
416 Vandine Rd (17754-7984)
PHONE 718 288-4318
Robert Vandine, *President*
EMP: 2 **EST:** 2014
SQ FT: 2,500
SALES: 1.5MM **Privately Held**
SIC: 3841 Surgical & medical instruments

(G-11449)
RAPID PATHOGEN SCREENING INC
416 Vandine Rd (17754-7984)
PHONE 718 288-4318
Robert Vandine,
EMP: 40
SALES (est): 139.2K **Privately Held**
SIC: 2836 2835 5047 Biological products, except diagnostic; in vitro & in vivo diagnostic substances; medical & hospital equipment

(G-11450)
SOONER PIPE LLC
150 S Loyalsock Ave (17754-2212)
PHONE 570 368-4590
EMP: 6
SALES (corp-wide): 20.2B **Privately Held**
SIC: 5084 1389 3491 Oil well machinery, equipment & supplies; instruments & control equipment; oil field services; industrial valves
HQ: Sooner Pipe, L.L.C.
909 Fannin St Ste 3100
Houston TX 77010
713 759-1200

(G-11451)
TASSERON SENSORS INC
140 Choate Cir (17754-9792)
PHONE 570 601-1971
Thomas Vandijk, *President*
Scott Reed, *Opers Mgr*
Len Otto, *Facilities Mgr*
Richard Baaij, *Treasurer*
Todd Stoner, *Sales Staff*
◆ **EMP:** 60
SALES (est): 7.4MM **Privately Held**
SIC: 3829 Temperature sensors, except industrial process & aircraft

(G-11452)
TEAMWORK GRAPHIC INC
227 Streibeigh Ln (17754-2525)
P.O. Box 53 (17754-0053)
PHONE 570 368-2360
Rodney Watson, *President*
Rodney J Watson, *President*
Barbara Watson, *Vice Pres*
Lauren Kelly, *Marketing Staff*
EMP: 4
SQ FT: 4,300
SALES (est): 631K **Privately Held**
WEB: www.teamworkgraphics.com
SIC: 2759 7389 Screen printing; embroidering of advertising on shirts, etc.

(G-11453)
THRU TUBING SOLUTIONS INC
243 Grey Fox Dr Ste 3 (17754-9568)
PHONE 570 546-0323
Tank Johnson, *Branch Mgr*
EMP: 9
SALES (corp-wide): 1.7B **Publicly Held**
SIC: 1389 Oil field services

HQ: Thru Tubing Solutions, Inc.
11515 S Portland Ave
Oklahoma City OK 73170
405 692-1900

(G-11454)
TRANSPORT CUSTOM DESIGNS LLC
240 Streibeigh Ln (17754-2526)
PHONE 570 368-1403
Joseph Reynolds, *Principal*
Jamie Pepperman, *Office Mgr*
EMP: 4
SALES (est): 227.9K **Privately Held**
SIC: 3792 3799 3715 Travel trailers & campers; trailers & trailer equipment; trailer bodies

(G-11455)
UTZ QUALITY FOODS INC
90 Choate Cir (17754-9791)
PHONE 570 368-8050
Dennis Fausey, *Sales Mgr*
Dennis Fozie, *Manager*
EMP: 15
SALES (corp-wide): 723.8MM **Privately Held**
WEB: www.utzsnacks.com
SIC: 2096 Potato chips & other potato-based snacks
PA: Utz Quality Foods, Llc
900 High St
Hanover PA 17331
800 367-7629

(G-11456)
WESTLAB DISTRIBUTION INC
1050 Broad St Ste 5 (17754-2533)
PHONE 800 699-0301
EMP: 9
SALES (est): 1.1MM **Privately Held**
SIC: 2844 Bath salts
PA: Westlab Ltd
57 Dunsfold Park Stovolds Hill
Cranleigh

(G-11457)
WILLIAM SPORT CRANE & RIGGING
214 Brushy Ridge Rd (17754-8313)
PHONE 570 433-3300
Bob Witmer, *President*
EMP: 3
SQ FT: 7,000
SALES: 300K **Privately Held**
SIC: 3531 7389 Cranes; crane & aerial lift service

(G-11458)
XTO ENERGY INC
1050 Broad St (17754-2533)
PHONE 570 368-8920
EMP: 6
SALES (corp-wide): 290.2B **Publicly Held**
SIC: 5211 1311 Energy conservation products; crude petroleum & natural gas production
HQ: Xto Energy Inc.
22777 Sprngwoods Vlg Pkwy
Spring TX 77389

Montrose
Susquehanna County

(G-11459)
BS QUARRIES INC
859 John C Mcnamara Dr (18801-8564)
PHONE 570 278-4901
Timothy M Smith, *President*
Lynn F Bolles, *Treasurer*
EMP: 200
SQ FT: 47,000
SALES (est): 15.9MM **Privately Held**
SIC: 3281 Cut stone & stone products

(G-11460)
CARRIZO (MARCELLUS) LLC
12231 State Route 706 (18801-6995)
PHONE 570 278-7450
Bruce Bonnice, *Superintendent*
EMP: 8 **Publicly Held**
SIC: 1311 Crude petroleum & natural gas

▲ = Import ▼ =Export
◆ =Import/Export

HQ: Carrizo (Marcellus) Llc
500 Dallas St Ste 2300
Houston TX 77002
713 328-1000

(G-11461)
CARRIZO OIL & GAS INC
12231 State Route 706 (18801-6995)
PHONE...................................570 278-7009
Bruce Bonnice, *Manager*
EMP: 5 **Publicly Held**
SIC: 1311 Crude petroleum & natural gas
PA: Carrizo Oil & Gas, Inc.
500 Dallas St Ste 2300
Houston TX 77002

(G-11462)
CHITRA PUBLICATIONS
2 Public Ave (18801-1217)
PHONE...................................570 278-1984
Christiane Meunier, *Owner*
Gildas Conan, *Ltd Ptnr*
George Meunier, *Ltd Ptnr*
Helen Meunier, *Ltd Ptnr*
▲ **EMP:** 22
SQ FT: 6,000
SALES: 2.2MM **Privately Held**
WEB: www.quilttownusa.com
SIC: 2721 5949 Magazines: publishing &
printing; sewing, needlework & piece
goods

(G-11463)
ENDLESS MOUNTAINS SPECIALTIES
873 Old County Rd (18801-7926)
PHONE...................................570 432-4018
Andrew Vaccaro, *President*
EMP: 4
SALES: 280K **Privately Held**
WEB: www.endmo.com
SIC: 3812 Search & navigation equipment

(G-11464)
FROM HEART
2 Public Ave (18801)
PHONE...................................570 278-6343
Christiane Meunier, *Principal*
EMP: 7
SALES (est): 383.3K **Privately Held**
SIC: 2731 Book publishing

(G-11465)
GOLIS MACHINE INC
92 Industrial Dr (18801-8519)
PHONE...................................570 278-1963
Rosemary Franssen, *President*
William Franssen Jr, *Vice Pres*
John Mills, *Sales Mgr*
EMP: 17
SQ FT: 12,600
SALES: 3.2MM **Privately Held**
WEB: www.golis.com
SIC: 3599 3541 Machine shop, jobbing &
repair; machine tools, metal cutting type

(G-11466)
HALSEY INC
State Route 706 W (18801)
PHONE...................................570 278-3610
Harold Turner, *President*
EMP: 15 **EST:** 1950
SQ FT: 40,000
SALES (est): 550K **Privately Held**
SIC: 3089 Plastic kitchenware, tableware &
houseware; dishes, plastic, except foam;
bowl covers, plastic; cups, plastic, except
foam

(G-11467)
JOHNSON & SON STONE WORKS
Rr 4 (18801)
PHONE...................................570 278-9385
Janice Johnson, *Owner*
EMP: 6
SALES (est): 507.7K **Privately Held**
WEB: www.pennsylvaniabluestone.com
SIC: 1411 Dimension stone

(G-11468)
JOS PALLETS
5495 Davis Rd (18801-8094)
PHONE...................................570 278-8935
Joanne Himko, *Owner*

EMP: 3
SALES (est): 130K **Privately Held**
SIC: 2448 Wood pallets & skids

(G-11469)
L & D STONEWORKS INC
Rr 5 Box 112m (18801)
PHONE...................................570 553-1670
David Owens, *President*
Lance Birchard, *President*
EMP: 24
SALES (est): 1.3MM **Privately Held**
SIC: 3281 Cut stone & stone products

(G-11470)
MASTERS RMC INC
Also Called: Masters Ready Mix Concrete Co
Off Route 106 (18801)
P.O. Box 25, Kingsley (18826-0025)
PHONE...................................570 278-3258
Richard S Masters, *Owner*
Rich Masters, *Manager*
EMP: 20
SALES (corp-wide): 4MM **Privately Held**
WEB: www.mastersrmc.com
SIC: 3531 Concrete plants
PA: Masters Rmc Inc
Us Rte 11
Kingsley PA
570 289-4191

(G-11471)
MONTROSE MACHINE WORKS INC (PA)
Rr 29 Box S (18801)
PHONE...................................570 278-7655
Nicholas C Salamone, *President*
▲ **EMP:** 18
SQ FT: 15,000
SALES (est): 1.8MM **Privately Held**
SIC: 3325 3069 Rolling mill rolls, cast
steel; rubber rolls & roll coverings

(G-11472)
NATSTONE LLC
631 State Route 1039 (18801-9790)
PHONE...................................570 278-1611
August Deluca, *Mng Member*
Jon Beizer,
Dan Mytels,
EMP: 38
SQ FT: 42,000
SALES (est): 2.1MM **Privately Held**
SIC: 3281 Cut stone & stone products

(G-11473)
NUFEEDS INC (PA)
200 Jackson St (18801-1286)
PHONE...................................570 278-3767
Glenn P Ely, *President*
David Williams, *Corp Secy*
EMP: 3 **EST:** 1954
SALES (est): 846.7K **Privately Held**
SIC: 2048 Poultry feeds; livestock feeds

(G-11474)
PENNSY SUPPLY INC
15644 State Route 267 (18801-7289)
PHONE...................................570 833-4497
Ronald Powers, *Branch Mgr*
EMP: 6
SALES (corp-wide): 29.7B **Privately Held**
SIC: 3273 Ready-mixed concrete
HQ: Pennsy Supply, Inc.
1001 Paxton St
Harrisburg PA 17104
717 233-4511

(G-11475)
POWERS STONE INC
Stuart Rd (18801)
PHONE...................................570 553-4276
Ronald J Powers, *President*
Mark Powers, *Treasurer*
▲ **EMP:** 30
SALES (est): 5.5MM **Privately Held**
SIC: 1411 3281 Flagstone mining; flag-
stones

(G-11476)
SHEN MANUFACTURING COMPANY INC
Also Called: Ritztex
S Main St (18801)
PHONE...................................570 278-3707

Howard Steidle, *Owner*
EMP: 8
SALES (corp-wide): 2.5MM **Privately
Held**
SIC: 2392 2211 Dust cloths: made from
purchased materials; dishcloths, nonwo-
ven textile: made from purchased materi-
als; laundry nets
PA: Factory Linens, Inc.
40 Portland Rd
Conshohocken PA 19428
610 825-2790

(G-11477)
SMITH LAWTON MILLWORK
Rr 706 (18801)
PHONE...................................570 934-2544
Wayne E Smith, *Owner*
EMP: 9
SALES: 800K **Privately Held**
SIC: 2434 2511 2431 Wood kitchen cabi-
nets; wood household furniture; moldings,
wood: unfinished & prefinished; window
frames, wood; doors, wood

(G-11478)
SPONGE-JET INC
1230 Bare Valley Rd (18801-7775)
PHONE...................................570 278-4563
Michael Merrit, *Branch Mgr*
EMP: 8 **Privately Held**
SIC: 3589 3291 5085 High pressure
cleaning equipment; abrasive buffs,
bricks, cloth, paper, stones, etc.; abra-
sives
PA: Sponge-Jet, Inc.
14 Patterson Ln
Newington NH 03801

(G-11479)
SUSQUEHANNA INDEPENDENT WKNDR
231 Church St (18801-1272)
PHONE...................................570 278-6397
David Barry, *Principal*
Staci Wilson, *Editor*
EMP: 4
SALES (est): 120.9K **Privately Held**
SIC: 2711 Newspapers: publishing only,
not printed on site

Moon Township
Allegheny County

(G-11480)
ATLAS AMERICA PUB 11-2002 LTD
311 Rouser Rd (15108-6801)
PHONE...................................412 262-2830
EMP: 3
SALES: 353.4K **Privately Held**
SIC: 1311 Crude petroleum & natural gas

(G-11481)
BLUESTEM INDUSTRIES PA LLC
944 Beaver Grade Rd (15108-6805)
PHONE...................................412 585-6220
Robert Stone,
EMP: 4
SQ FT: 1,000
SALES (est): 169.6K **Privately Held**
SIC: 3646 3648 Commercial indusl & insti-
tutional electric lighting fixtures; outdoor
lighting equipment; street lighting fixtures

(G-11482)
CALGON CARBON CORPORATION (DH)
3000 Gsk Dr (15108-1381)
P.O. Box 717, Pittsburgh (15230-0717)
PHONE...................................412 787-6700
Stevan R Schott, *President*
James A Coccagno, *Exec VP*
Jim Coccagno, *Vice Pres*
Ken McGuire, *Project Mgr*
Mark Meyers, *Project Mgr*
◆ **EMP:** 226

SALES (est): 619.8MM
SALES (corp-wide): 5.3B **Privately Held**
WEB: www.calgoncarbon.com
SIC: 2819 7699 3589 3564 Charcoal
(carbon), activated; industrial equipment
services; water treatment equipment, industrial; sewage treatment equipment; air
purification equipment
HQ: Kuraray Holdings U.S.A., Inc.
2625 Bay Area Blvd
Houston TX 77058
713 495-7311

(G-11483)
CENTRIA INC (HQ)
1005 Beaver Grade Rd # 2 (15108-2964)
PHONE...................................412 299-8000
Raymond Caudill, *President*
Brian Finnegan, *Regional Mgr*
Curtis Nyssen, *Vice Pres*
Donna Hurd, *Opers Staff*
Greg Tisdale, *Production*
◆ **EMP:** 150 **EST:** 1993
SQ FT: 30,000
SALES (est): 293.2MM
SALES (corp-wide): 2B **Publicly Held**
SIC: 3444 1761 3563 3449 Metal flooring
& siding; metal roofing & roof drainage
equipment; roofing, siding & sheet metal
work; blowers & fans; miscellaneous met-
alwork
PA: Nci Building Systems, Inc.
10943 N Sam Huston Pkwy W
Houston TX 77064
281 897-7788

(G-11484)
EATON CORPORATION
Also Called: Cutler Hammer
1000 Cherrington Pkwy (15108-4312)
PHONE...................................412 893-3300
Andrew Smulski, *Project Mgr*
Thomas Colcombe, *Engrg Mgr*
Victor Epee, *Engineer*
Jess Yenter, *Project Engr*
Rachel Antinone, *Controller*
EMP: 43 **Privately Held**
SIC: 5063 3812 3643 3625 Electrical ap-
paratus & equipment; search & navigation
equipment; current-carrying wiring de-
vices; relays & industrial controls;
switchgear & switchboard apparatus; fluid
power pumps & motors
HQ: Eaton Corporation
1000 Eaton Blvd
Cleveland OH 44122
440 523-5000

(G-11485)
EATON ELECTRICAL INC (DH)
Also Called: Cutler Hammer
1000 Cherrington Pkwy (15108-4312)
PHONE...................................412 893-3300
Alexander M Cutler, *CEO*
David Riggenbach, *Area Mgr*
Barbara F Odell, *Senior VP*
David Bailey, *Vice Pres*
Paul Cody, *Vice Pres*
◆ **EMP:** 35
SALES (est): 74.8MM **Privately Held**
WEB: www.ch.cutler-hammer.com
SIC: 5063 3812 3643 3625 Electrical ap-
paratus & equipment; search & navigation
equipment; current-carrying wiring de-
vices; relays & industrial controls;
switchgear & switchboard apparatus; fluid
power pumps & motors
HQ: Eaton Corporation
1000 Eaton Blvd
Cleveland OH 44122
440 523-5000

(G-11486)
ELKEM MATERIALS INC (DH)
Airpo Offic Parl Bldg 24 (15108)
P.O. Box 266, Pittsburgh (15230-0266)
PHONE...................................412 299-7200
Tony Kojundic, *Business Mgr*
Simon Wilson, *Director*
◆ **EMP:** 5
SALES (est): 3.6MM
SALES (corp-wide): 91MM **Privately
Held**
WEB: www.elkemmaterials.com
SIC: 2899 2819 Chemical preparations;
silica compounds

GEOGRAPHIC

HQ: Elkem Holding, Inc.
Airport Office Park Bldg
Coraopolis PA 15108
412 299-7200

(G-11487)
EZ-FLO INJECTION SYSTEMS INC (PA)
Also Called: Ez-Flo Fertilizing Systems
400 Lee Dr Apt 75 (15108-1231)
PHONE.................................412 996-2161
Dan Gilmore, Ch of Bd
Thomas Patton, President
Darin Brasch, Natl Sales Mgr
EMP: 4
SALES (est): 636.8K Privately Held
SIC: 3523 Fertilizing, spraying, dusting & irrigation machinery

(G-11488)
HARBISNWLKER INTL HOLDINGS INC (PA)
1305 Cherrington Pkwy (15108-4355)
PHONE.................................412 375-6600
Carol Jackson, CEO
Douglas Hall, Senior VP
EMP: 2 EST: 2000
SALES (est): 703.8MM Privately Held
SIC: 3297 1459 3272 Nonclay refractories; magnesite mining; solid containing units, concrete

(G-11489)
HARBISONWALKER INTL FOUNDATION
Also Called: Anh Refractories
1305 Cherrington Pkwy # 100 (15108-4355)
PHONE.................................412 375-6600
Gabriel Faimann, CEO
Guenter Karhut, CEO
Regis Perich, President
Viktor Fischer, Exec VP
Ernest Liedtke, Exec VP
EMP: 198
SALES (est): 18.7MM
SALES (corp-wide): 418.8MM Privately Held
SIC: 3255 Clay refractories
HQ: Rhi Refractories Holding Company
1105 N Market St Ste 1300
Wilmington DE 19801
302 655-6497

(G-11490)
HARBISONWALKER INTL INC (HQ)
1305 Cherrington Pkwy # 100 (15108-4355)
PHONE.................................412 375-6600
Carol Jackson, CEO
Douglas Hall, Senior VP
Brad Cramer, Vice Pres
Colin Rojak, Project Mgr
John Sutton, Director
◆ EMP: 200
SALES (est): 703.8MM Privately Held
SIC: 3297 3272 1459 Nonclay refractories; solid containing units, concrete; magnesite mining
PA: Harbisonwalker International Holdings, Inc.
1305 Cherrington Pkwy
Moon Township PA 15108
412 375-6600

(G-11491)
HWI INTERMEDIATE 1 INC
1305 Cherrington Pkwy # 100 (15108-4355)
PHONE.................................412 375-6800
EMP: 3
SALES (est): 206.9K Privately Held
SIC: 3255 Clay refractories

(G-11492)
HYDRO EXTRUDER LLC (DH)
Also Called: Sapa Extruder LLC
Airport Offc Park (15108)
PHONE.................................412 299-7600
Charlie Straface, President
Geir Kvernmo, Vice Pres
Robert Rubicky, Vice Pres
Todd Presnick, CFO
Robert Kavanaugh, Treasurer

▲ EMP: 156
SALES (est): 276.7MM
SALES (corp-wide): 13.8B Privately Held
SIC: 3354 Aluminum extruded products

(G-11493)
HYDRO EXTRUSION USA LLC
Also Called: Shared Services
400 Rouser Rd Ste 300 (15108-2749)
PHONE.................................877 966-7272
Jerry Jones, Branch Mgr
EMP: 50
SALES (corp-wide): 13.8B Privately Held
WEB: www.alumag.com
SIC: 3354 Aluminum extruded products
HQ: Hydro Extrusion Usa, Llc
6250 N River Rd Ste 5000
Rosemont IL 60018

(G-11494)
INSPIRE CLOSING SERVICES LLC
420 Rouser Rd (15108-3090)
PHONE.................................412 348-8367
Michael Crispeno, Principal
Tom Garner, Principal
Norma Ortega, Principal
Kari Yoder, Principal
EMP: 3 EST: 2017
SALES (est): 282.9K Privately Held
SIC: 6163 7372 Mortgage brokers arranging for loans, using money of others; business oriented computer software

(G-11495)
JAG FABRICATION LLC
392 Flaugherty Run Rd (15108-9798)
PHONE.................................724 457-2347
EMP: 3
SALES (est): 372.3K Privately Held
SIC: 3599 Machine shop, jobbing & repair

(G-11496)
KRAFT HEINZ FOODS COMPANY
121 Wright Brothers Dr (15108-6802)
PHONE.................................412 456-2482
Hj Comp, Branch Mgr
EMP: 261
SALES (corp-wide): 26.2B Publicly Held
SIC: 2033 Tomato sauce: packaged in cans, jars, etc.
HQ: Kraft Heinz Foods Company
1 Ppg Pl Ste 3200
Pittsburgh PA 15222
412 456-5700

(G-11497)
NOVA CHEMICALS INC (DH)
1555 Coraopolis Hts Rd (15108-2927)
PHONE.................................412 490-4000
Todd D Karran, CEO
Randy G Woelfel, Principal
Bruce Davies, Counsel
Chris Bezaire, Senior VP
Bill Greene, Senior VP
▼ EMP: 150
SQ FT: 200,000
SALES (est): 885.2MM Privately Held
WEB: www.novachem.com
SIC: 2821 Polyethylene resins; polystyrene resins
HQ: Nc Holdings Usa Inc.
1555 Coraopolis Hts Rd
Moon Township PA 15108
412 490-4000

(G-11498)
OHIO VALLEY INDUS SVCS INC (PA)
530 Moon Clinton Rd Ste B (15108-3874)
PHONE.................................412 269-0020
Tom Kaminski, President
Bob Steger, Vice Pres
Debbie Rhodes, Admin Sec
EMP: 7
SQ FT: 6,200
SALES (est): 6.3MM Privately Held
WEB: www.ovisinc.com
SIC: 3296 4911 5085 Fiberglass insulation; generation, electric power; industrial supplies

(G-11499)
SAPA PRECISION TUBING LLC (DH)
400 Rouser Rd Ste 300 (15108-2749)
P.O. Box 544, Hazleton (18201-0544)
PHONE.................................412 893-1300
Sergio Luiz Vendrasco, President
EMP: 11
SALES (est): 12.6MM
SALES (corp-wide): 13.8B Privately Held
SIC: 3354 Aluminum extruded products
HQ: Hydro Extruded Solutions Ab
Kanalgatan 1
Finspang 612 3
122 170-00

(G-11500)
SIGNIFICANT DEVELOPMENTS LLC
Also Called: Tailgate Master Truck Steps
1710 Wheatland Ct (15108-9208)
PHONE.................................724 348-5277
Kenneth Puglisi Sr, President
EMP: 4
SALES (est): 336.3K Privately Held
SIC: 3499 Ladders, portable: metal

Moosic
Lackawanna County

(G-11501)
AC FASHION LLC
330 Montage Mountain Rd (18507-1779)
PHONE.................................570 291-5982
Robert Birkland,
◆ EMP: 4
SQ FT: 2,500
SALES: 10MM Privately Held
SIC: 2326 5961 Men's & boys' work clothing; clothing, mail order (except women's)

(G-11502)
ALBRIGHT PRECISION INC
4 Rocky Glen Rd (18507)
P.O. Box 3479, Scranton (18505-0479)
PHONE.................................570 457-5744
Paul J Labelle, President
Michael Schimelfenig, Manager
EMP: 30
SQ FT: 50,000
SALES: 11.1MM Privately Held
WEB: www.albrightprecisioninc.com
SIC: 3444 Sheet metal specialties, not stamped

(G-11503)
ANDREW TORBA
Also Called: Kuhcoon
905 Marion Ln (18507-1431)
P.O. Box 41, Falls (18615-0041)
PHONE.................................570 209-1622
Andrew Torba,
EMP: 4
SALES (est): 272.6K Privately Held
SIC: 7313 7372 Electronic media advertising representatives; application computer software

(G-11504)
COLLINS HARPER PUBLISHERS
Also Called: Harper Collins
53 Glnmura Nat Blvd 300 (18507-2132)
PHONE.................................570 941-1557
Fax: 570 941-1597
▲ EMP: 7 EST: 2009
SALES (est): 2.3MM
SALES (corp-wide): 8.6B Publicly Held
SIC: 2741 Misc Publishing
PA: News Corporation
1211 Ave Of The Americas
New York NY 10036
212 416-3400

(G-11505)
FLOWSERVE CORPORATION
567 Rocky Glen Rd (18507)
P.O. Box 3055, Scranton (18505-3055)
PHONE.................................570 451-2325
Frances Hanley, General Mgr
Sandra Kovach, Buyer
Dave Engles, Purchasing
Ginger Pokorney, Sales Staff
EMP: 100

SALES (corp-wide): 3.8B Publicly Held
SIC: 3561 Industrial pumps & parts
PA: Flowserve Corporation
5215 N Oconnor Blvd Connor
Irving TX 75039
972 443-6500

(G-11506)
GLEEN
523 Orchard St (18507-1053)
PHONE.................................570 457-3858
Robert Smith, Principal
EMP: 6 EST: 2007
SALES (est): 611.9K Privately Held
SIC: 3144 Women's footwear, except athletic

(G-11507)
HARPERCOLLINS PUBLISHERS LLC
53 Glnmura Nat Blvd 300 (18507-2132)
PHONE.................................570 941-1500
Joe Franceschelli, Senior VP
EMP: 200
SALES (corp-wide): 9B Publicly Held
WEB: www.harpercollins.com
SIC: 2731 Books: publishing only
HQ: Harpercollins Publishers L.L.C.
195 Broadway Fl 2
New York NY 10007
212 207-7000

(G-11508)
HARPERCOLLINS PUBLISHERS LLC
53 Glnmura Nat Blvd St300 (18507-2132)
PHONE.................................800 242-7737
EMP: 6
SALES (corp-wide): 9B Publicly Held
SIC: 2741 Miscellaneous publishing
HQ: Harpercollins Publishers L.L.C.
195 Broadway Fl 2
New York NY 10007
212 207-7000

(G-11509)
J&J SNACK FOODS CORP/MIA
Rocky Glenn Industrial Pa (18507)
P.O. Box 3777, Scranton (18505-0777)
PHONE.................................570 457-7431
Arnold J Goldstein, President
Gerald B Shreiber, President
T J Couzens, Vice Pres
Dennis Moore, Vice Pres
Ernest Fogle, QC Dir
▲ EMP: 40
SQ FT: 35,000
SALES (est): 5.6MM
SALES (corp-wide): 1.1B Publicly Held
WEB: www.jjsnack.com
SIC: 2024 Ice milk, bulk; ices, flavored (frozen dessert); juice pops, frozen
PA: J & J Snack Foods Corp.
6000 Central Hwy
Pennsauken NJ 08109
856 665-9533

(G-11510)
NORTHEASTERN PA CARTON CO INC
Also Called: Nepa Carton & Carrier Co.
4820 Birney Ave (18507-1232)
PHONE.................................570 457-7711
Michael Collins, President
Rich Howells, Sales Mgr
▼ EMP: 27
SQ FT: 50,000
SALES (est): 7.5MM Privately Held
WEB: www.nepacartons.com
SIC: 2631 2657 2652 Folding boxboard; folding paperboard boxes; setup paperboard boxes

(G-11511)
PAPER MAGIC GROUP INC (HQ)
54 Glenmra Ntl Blvd (18507-2101)
P.O. Box 428, Berwick (18603-0428)
PHONE.................................570 961-3863
Chris Munyan, President
Lois Karpinski, Vice Pres
Vince Paccapaniccia, CFO
Stefanie Smoke, Treasurer
Mike Santisafci, Admin Sec
▲ EMP: 180 EST: 1974
SQ FT: 30,000

SALES (est): 101.9MM
SALES (corp-wide): 361.9MM **Publicly Held**
WEB: www.papermagic.com
SIC: 2771 2678 2679 3944 Greeting cards; stationery: made from purchased materials; novelties, paper: made from purchased material; games, toys & children's vehicles; cyclic crudes & intermediates; toilet preparations
PA: Css Industries, Inc.
450 Plymouth Rd Ste 300
Plymouth Meeting PA 19462
610 729-3959

(G-11512)
PREFERRED MEAL SYSTEMS INC
4135 Birney Ave (18507-1397)
PHONE....................................570 457-8311
Robert Keen, *Director*
EMP: 200
SQ FT: 45,000
SALES (corp-wide): 18.3MM **Privately Held**
SIC: 5812 2038 Contract food services; frozen specialties
HQ: Preferred Meal Systems, Inc.
5240 Saint Charles Rd
Berkeley IL 60163
800 886-6325

(G-11513)
RED MILL FARMS LLC
Also Called: Jennies Gluten Free Bakery
591 Rocky Glen Rd (18507)
PHONE....................................570 457-2400
Arnold Badner, *President*
Gilbert Shwom,
▼ **EMP:** 17
SQ FT: 10,000
SALES (est): 4.5MM **Privately Held**
SIC: 2051 Bakery: wholesale or wholesale/retail combined

(G-11514)
S W U AUTOMOTIVE MACHINERY LLC
4961 Birney Ave R (18507-1205)
PHONE....................................570 457-4299
Philip Lamberti,
EMP: 3
SQ FT: 2,000
SALES: 150K **Privately Held**
SIC: 3599 Machine shop, jobbing & repair

(G-11515)
SIGNATURE BUILDING SYSTEMS INC
1004 Springbrook Ave (18507-1814)
PHONE....................................570 774-1000
S Bartholomew, *General Mgr*
EMP: 50 **Privately Held**
WEB: www.signaturebuildingsystems.com
SIC: 2452 5211 Modular homes, prefabricated, wood; modular homes
PA: Signature Building Systems, Inc.
1004 Springbrook Ave
Moosic PA 18507

(G-11516)
SIGNATURE BUILDING SYSTEMS INC (PA)
Also Called: Signature Building Systems PA
1004 Springbrook Ave (18507-1814)
P.O. Box 3927, Scranton (18505-0927)
PHONE....................................570 774-1000
Victor A Dephillips, *President*
Charles L Kasko, *President*
Antonio Lesavage, *Accounts Exec*
EMP: 91
SQ FT: 61,000
SALES (est): 19.3MM **Privately Held**
WEB: www.signaturebuildingsystems.com
SIC: 2452 Modular homes, prefabricated, wood

Morgan
Allegheny County

(G-11517)
GEORGE TAYLOR FORKLIFT REPAIR
108 Blythe Rd (15064-9711)
P.O. Box 177 (15064-0177)
PHONE....................................412 221-7206
George Taylor, *President*
Sandra Taylor, *Admin Sec*
EMP: 3
SALES (est): 331.3K **Privately Held**
SIC: 7699 3537 Hydraulic equipment repair; forklift trucks

Morgantown
Berks County

(G-11518)
BEAM S CUSTOM WOODWORKING
95 Oak Tree Ln (19543-9603)
PHONE....................................610 286-9040
Bill Beam, *CEO*
EMP: 14
SALES (est): 2.7MM **Privately Held**
SIC: 2431 Millwork

(G-11519)
CEDAR RIDGE FURNITURE
112 Maxwell Hill Rd (19543-9418)
PHONE....................................610 286-6225
David Esh, *Principal*
EMP: 5 EST: 2007
SALES (est): 716.7K **Privately Held**
SIC: 2531 2521 2511 Public building & related furniture; wood office furniture; wood household furniture

(G-11520)
CHIYODA AMERICA INC
378 Thousand Oaks Blvd (19543-9769)
P.O. Box 470 (19543-0470)
PHONE....................................610 286-3100
Hiroshi Mizumoto, *President*
Steven N Wentzel, *Vice Pres*
R Kenneth Whitlatch, *Admin Sec*
◆ **EMP:** 58
SQ FT: 97,000
SALES (est): 12.9MM
SALES (corp-wide): 97.1MM **Privately Held**
WEB: www.chiamer.com
SIC: 2621 2672 Art paper; coated & laminated paper
PA: Chiyoda Gravure Corporation
1-18-16, Osaki
Shinagawa-Ku TKY 141-0
334 925-311

(G-11521)
DAVID ESH
Also Called: Chests Unlimited
112 Maxwell Hill Rd (19543-9418)
PHONE....................................610 286-6225
David Esh, *Owner*
EMP: 4 EST: 1995
SALES (est): 297.1K **Privately Held**
SIC: 2511 Cedar chests

(G-11522)
EASTERN TECHNOLOGIES INC
60 Thousand Oaks Blvd (19543-8878)
PHONE....................................610 286-2010
Robert Keeler, *President*
Douglas K Flick, *COO*
Jamie Stoudt, *Opers Staff*
Liz Vaughan, *Manager*
EMP: 14
SQ FT: 18,000
SALES (est): 4.3MM **Privately Held**
WEB: www.go2eti.com
SIC: 2899 Water treating compounds

(G-11523)
HAWKE AEROSPACE HOLDINGS LLC (PA)
189a Twin County Rd (19543-9475)
PHONE....................................610 372-5191

Joseph A Hawke,
EMP: 7
SALES (est): 15MM **Privately Held**
WEB: www.hawkaerospace.com
SIC: 3999 Barber & beauty shop equipment

(G-11524)
LEMAR MAST
Also Called: Masthof Press
219 Mill Rd (19543-9516)
PHONE....................................610 286-0258
Lemar Mast, *Owner*
EMP: 8
SQ FT: 3,000
SALES (est): 977.7K **Privately Held**
WEB: www.masthof.com
SIC: 2759 5942 Commercial printing; book stores

(G-11525)
LIGHTHOUSE ENRGY SOLUTIONS LLC
601 Ridgeview Dr (19543-8868)
PHONE....................................610 269-0113
Mary Plank, *Principal*
Ilkka Pyllkkanen, *Principal*
Scott Carter, *Project Mgr*
William Carter,
Jean Carter,
EMP: 5
SALES (est): 323.9K **Privately Held**
SIC: 3699 High-energy particle physics equipment

(G-11526)
LUG-ALL CO INC
604 Hemlock Rd (19543-9710)
P.O. Box 888 (19543-0888)
PHONE....................................610 286-9884
Richard Uhlig, *CEO*
Janet Uhlig, *Treasurer*
▲ **EMP:** 50 EST: 1949
SQ FT: 8,000
SALES (est): 10.4MM **Privately Held**
WEB: www.lug-all.com
SIC: 3536 Hoists

(G-11527)
MCNEILUS TRUCK AND MFG INC
Also Called: McNeilus Company
941 Hemlock Rd (19543-9767)
P.O. Box 219 (19543-0219)
PHONE....................................610 286-0400
Scott Ravert, *Branch Mgr*
EMP: 36
SQ FT: 22,200
SALES (corp-wide): 7.7B **Publicly Held**
WEB: www.mcneiluscompanies.com
SIC: 3713 3565 3531 Cement mixer bodies; packaging machinery; construction machinery
HQ: Mcneilus Truck And Manufacturing, Inc.
524 E Highway St
Dodge Center MN 55927
507 374-6321

(G-11528)
MORGANTOWN EYE CARE CENTER
105 Moreview Blvd (19543-9483)
P.O. Box 617 (19543-0617)
PHONE....................................610 286-0206
Miriam Pearson Od, *Owner*
EMP: 3 EST: 1966
SQ FT: 2,000
SALES (est): 270.2K **Privately Held**
SIC: 8042 3851 5995 Offices & clinics of optometrists; lens coating, ophthalmic; optical goods stores

(G-11529)
NILFISK INC
Also Called: Nilfisk Industrial Vacuums
740 Hemlock Rd Ste 100 (19543-9744)
PHONE....................................800 645-3475
Jamie O'Neill, *General Mgr*
Gerard Geiger, *Business Mgr*
Vincent Dimento, *Info Tech Mgr*
▲ **EMP:** 53
SQ FT: 25,000

SALES (est): 13MM
SALES (corp-wide): 1.2B **Privately Held**
SIC: 3635 Household vacuum cleaners
HQ: Nilfisk, Inc.
9435 Winnetka Ave N
Brooklyn Park MN 55445
800 334-1083

(G-11530)
PHYTOGENX INC
35 Thousand Oaks Blvd (19543-8838)
PHONE....................................610 286-0111
Christof Lelan, *CEO*
Julie Knox, *President*
Scott Knox, *Vice Pres*
EMP: 50
SALES (est): 15.6MM **Privately Held**
WEB: www.phytogenx.com
SIC: 2844 Cosmetic preparations

(G-11531)
PRECAST SERVICES INC
51 Thsand Oaks Blvd Ste A (19543)
PHONE....................................330 425-2880
EMP: 62
SALES (corp-wide): 30MM **Privately Held**
SIC: 3272 Precast terrazo or concrete products
PA: Precast Services, Inc.
8200 Boyle Pkwy Ste 2
Twinsburg OH 44087
330 425-2880

(G-11532)
READING READING BOOKS LLC
508 Quaker Hill Rd (19543-9586)
P.O. Box 6654, Reading (19610-0654)
PHONE....................................757 329-4224
Kris Bonnell,
▲ **EMP:** 4
SALES (est): 323.4K **Privately Held**
SIC: 2731 Books: publishing only

(G-11533)
RPC BRAMLAGE-WIKO-USA INC
1075 Hemlock Rd (19543-9803)
PHONE....................................610 286-0805
Harald Hoika, *President*
Glenn Gehr, *Vice Pres*
Sandra Shannon, *Purchasing*
Maryann Kimes, *Human Res Dir*
Mary Ann Kimes, *Human Res Mgr*
▲ **EMP:** 75
SQ FT: 57,614
SALES (est): 37.1MM **Privately Held**
WEB: www.wiko-usa.com
SIC: 3089 Tubs, plastic (containers)
PA: Rpc Group Plc
Sapphire House
Rushden NORTHANTS NN10

(G-11534)
SHEDS UNLIMITED INC
2025 Valley Rd (19543-9649)
PHONE....................................717 442-3281
Steve Stoltzfus Sr, *President*
Steve Stoltzfus Jr, *Vice Pres*
Chris Stoltzfus, *Admin Sec*
EMP: 15
SQ FT: 25,000
SALES (est): 3.5MM **Privately Held**
SIC: 2452 Prefabricated wood buildings

(G-11535)
SLAWKO RACING HEADS INC
171 Twin County Rd (19543-9475)
PHONE....................................610 286-1822
Tom Slawko, *President*
EMP: 3
SQ FT: 2,000
SALES: 300K **Privately Held**
WEB: www.slawkoracingheads.com
SIC: 3714 Cylinder heads, motor vehicle

(G-11536)
SPRING MILL WOODWORKING
217 S Red School Rd (19543-9588)
PHONE....................................610 286-7051
Brian Martin, *Partner*
Harold Martin, *Partner*
EMP: 4 EST: 2000
SALES: 375K **Privately Held**
SIC: 2499 Decorative wood & woodwork

G E O G R A P H I C

(G-11537)
STOLTZ MFG LLC
Also Called: Stoltzfus Spreaders
121 Morgan Way (19543-7714)
P.O. Box 527 (19543-0527)
PHONE..............................610 286-5146
Bernard Hershberger, *Principal*
Tyler Martikainen, *Engineer*
▼ EMP: 20
SALES (est): 5.1MM **Privately Held**
SIC: 3523 Farm machinery & equipment

(G-11538)
TD & COMPANY
780 Ranck Rd (19543-9551)
PHONE..............................610 637-6100
Tim Detwiler, *Owner*
EMP: 5
SQ FT: 2,000
SALES: 295K **Privately Held**
SIC: 3541 Machine tools, metal cutting type

(G-11539)
TITANIUM METALS CORPORATION
Also Called: Timet
900 Hemlock Rd (19543-9762)
PHONE..............................702 564-2544
William D Cummings, *Plant Mgr*
Jeffrey Lieb, *Engineer*
Patrick Resh, *Treasurer*
Charles Entrekin, *Branch Mgr*
Michelle Schonour, *Director*
EMP: 35
SALES (corp-wide): 225.3B **Publicly Held**
SIC: 3339 3699 3341 Titanium metal, sponge & granules; electrical equipment & supplies; secondary nonferrous metals
HQ: Titanium Metals Corporation
4832 Richmond Rd Ste 100
Warrensville Heights OH 44128
610 968-1300

(G-11540)
TITUS COMPANY
36 Mountain View Rd (19543-8885)
PHONE..............................610 913-9100
Sean Dempsey, *CEO*
Stephen Titus, *President*
Michael Titus, *Vice Pres*
Donna Titus, *Treasurer*
◆ EMP: 24
SQ FT: 8,000
SALES (est): 14.6MM **Privately Held**
SIC: 5084 3569 Compressors, except air conditioning; separators for steam, gas, vapor or air (machinery)

(G-11541)
TOPPAN INTERAMERICA INC
378 Thsnd Oks Bld Crp Ctr (19543)
PHONE..............................610 286-3100
John Sato, *President*
▲ EMP: 27
SALES (est): 5.6MM **Privately Held**
SIC: 2752 Commercial printing, lithographic

(G-11542)
TRANSOL CORPORATION (PA)
604 Hemlock Rd Ste 1 (19543-9711)
PHONE..............................610 527-0234
George Uhlig, *President*
Richard Uhlig, *Vice Pres*
EMP: 2
SQ FT: 8,000
SALES (est): 5.3MM **Privately Held**
SIC: 3536 Cranes, overhead traveling

(G-11543)
VIWINCO INC
851 Hemlock Rd (19543)
P.O. Box 499 (19543-0499)
PHONE..............................610 286-8884
David Barnes, *President*
Michael Duncan, *Admin Sec*
EMP: 175
SQ FT: 140,000
SALES (est): 50MM **Privately Held**
WEB: www.viwinco.com
SIC: 3089 Windows, plastic

Morris
Tioga County

(G-11544)
CHAIR SHOPPE
132 Windsor Ln (16938-9428)
PHONE..............................570 353-2735
Daniel Stoltzfus, *Partner*
EMP: 5
SALES: 400K **Privately Held**
SIC: 2512 Upholstered household furniture

(G-11545)
LEWIS WELDING & XCAVATING
331 Plank Rd (16938-9592)
PHONE..............................570 353-7301
Ron Lewis, *Partner*
James Lewis, *Partner*
Jim Lewis, *Partner*
EMP: 3
SALES (est): 200K **Privately Held**
SIC: 3599 Machine & other job shop work

Morris Run
Tioga County

(G-11546)
M & M WOOD PRODUCTS INC
159 Lake St (16939)
P.O. Box 207 (16939-0207)
PHONE..............................570 638-2234
Tom Mahosky, *President*
Theresa Mahosky, *Treasurer*
EMP: 11
SQ FT: 3,840
SALES: 1MM **Privately Held**
SIC: 2448 Pallets, wood

Morrisdale
Clearfield County

(G-11547)
CENTRAL PENN RIG SERVICE
540 Summit Hill Rd (16858-7536)
PHONE..............................814 342-4800
Rob Fye, *Principal*
EMP: 6
SALES (est): 898.3K **Privately Held**
SIC: 3533 Oil & gas field machinery

(G-11548)
ENERCORP INC
1310 Allport Cutoff (16858-7604)
PHONE..............................814 345-6225
Harvey Bumbarger, *President*
EMP: 3
SALES: 500K **Privately Held**
SIC: 1221 5052 Bituminous coal surface mining; coal

(G-11549)
WARD FABRICATING INC
1930 Palestine Rd (16858-8029)
PHONE..............................814 345-6707
Shawn Ward, *President*
Laurie Ward, *Treasurer*
EMP: 5
SALES (est): 297.9K **Privately Held**
SIC: 3449 Bars, concrete reinforcing; fabricated steel

Morrisville
Bucks County

(G-11550)
ACCU-FIRE FABRICATION INC
Also Called: Mechanical Piping Solutions
8 Progress Dr (19067-3702)
PHONE..............................800 641-0005
Deardra Murphy, *President*
Vince Murphy, *Vice Pres*
Mike Stango, *Vice Pres*
Dan Boice, *Sales Mgr*
Michael Murphy, *Regl Sales Mgr*
▲ EMP: 35

SQ FT: 70,000
SALES (est): 14.4MM **Privately Held**
WEB: www.accu-fire.com
SIC: 3498 5085 Tube fabricating (contract bending & shaping); valves & fittings

(G-11551)
ACES INC
1300 Steel Rd E Ste 3 (19067-3620)
P.O. Box 28, Croydon (19021-0028)
PHONE..............................215 458-7143
EMP: 4
SALES (est): 590.4K **Privately Held**
SIC: 3531 Bituminous, cement & concrete related products & equipment

(G-11552)
AD DISTINCTION
211 Winding Way (19067-4824)
PHONE..............................215 736-0672
Anthony F Disalvo, *Owner*
EMP: 4
SALES (est): 151.7K **Privately Held**
SIC: 2399 Emblems, badges & insignia

(G-11553)
AIR LIQUIDE ELECTRONICS US LP
19 Steel Rd W (19067-3615)
PHONE..............................215 428-4600
EMP: 13
SALES (corp-wide): 125.9MM **Privately Held**
SIC: 2813 Industrial gases
HQ: Air Liquide Electronics U.S. Lp
9101 Lyndon B Johnson Fwy # 800
Dallas TX 75243
972 301-5200

(G-11554)
AIR LIQUIDE ELECTRONICS US LP
19 Steel Rd W (19067-3615)
PHONE..............................215 736-2796
Johnathan Borzio, *Plant Mgr*
John Borzio, *Branch Mgr*
EMP: 37
SALES (corp-wide): 125.9MM **Privately Held**
WEB: www.airliquide.com
SIC: 2813 Industrial gases
HQ: Air Liquide Electronics U.S. Lp
9101 Lyndon B Johnson Fwy # 800
Dallas TX 75243
972 301-5200

(G-11555)
AVANTA ORTHOPAEDICS INC
Also Called: Viscogliosi Brothers Venture
1711 S Pennsylvania Ave (19067-2507)
PHONE..............................215 428-1792
Arthur Mouyard, *President*
Thomas C Bender, *Vice Pres*
Donald A Schumacher, *Treasurer*
EMP: 9
SQ FT: 7,500
SALES (est): 549.5K
SALES (corp-wide): 3.3MM **Privately Held**
WEB: www.vbllc.com
SIC: 3842 Mfg Surgical Appliances/Supplies
PA: Viscogliosi Brothers, Inc.
505 Park Ave Ste 1400
New York NY 10022
212 583-9700

(G-11556)
COVESTRO LLC
1 Progress Dr (19067-3702)
PHONE..............................215 428-4400
Vern Bennett, *President*
EMP: 12
SALES (corp-wide): 16.7B **Privately Held**
SIC: 2822 Mfg Synthetic Rubber
HQ: Covestro Llc
1 Covestro Cir
Pittsburgh PA 15205
412 413-2000

(G-11557)
DAMSEL IN DEFENSE
1588 S Pennsylvania Ave (19067-2504)
PHONE..............................215 262-3643
EMP: 3 EST: 2014

SALES (est): 162.1K **Privately Held**
SIC: 3812 Defense systems & equipment

(G-11558)
ENVISION PRODUCTS INC
1711 S Pennsylvania Ave (19067-2507)
PHONE..............................215 428-1791
EMP: 40
SQ FT: 9,250
SALES (est): 3.3MM **Privately Held**
SIC: 3842 Mfg Surgical Appliances/Supplies

(G-11559)
GARLITS INDUSTRIES INC
Also Called: Garlits Printing
30 N Pennsylvania Ave (19067-1110)
PHONE..............................215 736-2121
Edward E Garlits III, *President*
Brian Garlits, *Manager*
Susan Garlits, *Admin Sec*
EMP: 15
SQ FT: 8,000
SALES (est): 2.6MM **Privately Held**
SIC: 2752 5072 Commercial printing, offset; business form & card printing, lithographic; padlocks

(G-11560)
GELEST INC
1 Progress Dr (19067-3702)
PHONE..............................215 547-1015
Barry Arkles, *President*
EMP: 4
SALES (est): 183.2K **Privately Held**
SIC: 2869 Silicones

(G-11561)
GELEST INC (PA)
11 Steel Rd E (19067-3605)
PHONE..............................215 547-1015
Barry Arkles, *President*
John Sobchak, *CFO*
Jonathan Goff, *Manager*
Youlin Pan, *Manager*
◆ EMP: 50
SALES (est): 24.2MM **Privately Held**
WEB: www.gelest.com
SIC: 2819 Industrial inorganic chemicals

(G-11562)
GELEST REALTY INC
11 Steel Rd E (19067-3605)
PHONE..............................215 547-1015
Barry Arkles, *Principal*
EMP: 3
SALES (est): 205.5K **Privately Held**
SIC: 2819 Industrial inorganic chemicals

(G-11563)
GELEST TECHNOLOGIES INC
11 Steel Rd E (19067-3605)
PHONE..............................215 547-1015
Barry Arkles, *President*
EMP: 4
SALES (est): 178.2K **Privately Held**
SIC: 2819 Industrial inorganic chemicals

(G-11564)
JFI REDI-MIX LLC
18 Steel Rd W (19067-3612)
PHONE..............................215 428-3560
Feher John, *Principal*
EMP: 11
SALES (est): 2.1MM **Privately Held**
SIC: 3273 Ready-mixed concrete

(G-11565)
JOSEPH T RYERSON & SON INC
Also Called: Ryerson Thypin Steel
20 Steel Rd S (19067-3614)
PHONE..............................215 736-8970
Amro Elsabbagh, *Opers-Prdtn-Mfg*
EMP: 10 **Publicly Held**
SIC: 5051 3316 Steel; cold finishing of steel shapes
HQ: Joseph T. Ryerson & Son, Inc.
227 W Monroe St Fl 27
Chicago IL 60606
312 292-5000

▲ = Import ▼=Export
◆ =Import/Export

(G-11566)
K MATKEM OF MORRISVILLE LP
120 Enterprise Ave (19067-3703)
PHONE..................................215 295-4158
Theodorus A Bus, *Branch Mgr*
EMP: 3
SALES (corp-wide): 48MM **Privately Held**
SIC: 3479 Etching & engraving
HQ: K. Matkem Of Morrisville, Lp
    6612 Snowdrift Rd
    Allentown PA 18106
    215 428-3664

(G-11567)
KISTLER & DINAPOLI INC
Also Called: Minuteman Press
364 W Trenton Ave Ste 4 (19067-2004)
PHONE..................................215 428-4740
John Kistler, *President*
Michelle Dinapoli, *Corp Secy*
Joanna Bni, *Mktg Dir*
EMP: 6
SQ FT: 3,500
SALES (est): 913.5K **Privately Held**
SIC: 2752 Commercial printing, offset

(G-11568)
L D H PRINTING LTD INC
Also Called: Ldh Printing Unlimited
30 N Pennsylvania Ave (19067-1110)
PHONE..................................609 924-4664
La Verne D Hebert, *President*
EMP: 12
SALES (est): 850K **Privately Held**
SIC: 2752 2791 Commercial printing, off-
set; typesetting

(G-11569)
LEHIGH MACHINE TOOLS INC
201 Dean Sievers Pl (19067-3700)
PHONE..................................215 493-6446
Steven He, *CEO*
▲ EMP: 5
SQ FT: 1,000
SALES (est): 370.4K **Privately Held**
WEB: www.lehigh-lathe.com
SIC: 3541 Machine tools, metal cutting
type

(G-11570)
LTL COLOR COMPOUNDERS LLC
Also Called: Infinity Ltl
20 Progress Dr (19067-3702)
PHONE..................................215 736-1126
Carlos Carreno, *President*
James Figaniak, *Vice Pres*
Robert Bissinger, *CFO*
▲ EMP: 53
SQ FT: 70,000
SALES: 21.7MM
SALES (corp-wide): 228.8MM **Privately Held**
SIC: 3087 2295 Custom compound pur-
chased resins; resin or plastic coated fab-
rics
PA: Americhem, Inc.
    2000 Americhem Way
    Cuyahoga Falls OH 44221
    330 929-4213

(G-11571)
MICRO-TRAP CORPORATION
1300 Steel Rd E Ste 2 (19067-3620)
P.O. Box 1011 (19067-9011)
PHONE..................................215 295-8208
David J Steil, *President*
EMP: 5
SQ FT: 3,600
SALES: 260K **Privately Held**
WEB: www.microtrapcorp.com
SIC: 3669 7629 Emergency alarms;
smoke detectors; burglar alarm appara-
tus, electric; fire alarm apparatus, electric;
electrical repair shops

(G-11572)
MRS AND SON LLC
765 Old Bristol Pike (19067)
PHONE..................................215 750-7828
Michael Smith Sr, *Owner*
EMP: 3
SQ FT: 5,000

SALES: 600K **Privately Held**
SIC: 3441 Building components, structural
steel

(G-11573)
MTR FUEL LLC
117 Osborne Ave (19067-1129)
PHONE..................................609 610-0783
Michael T Ryan, *Principal*
Michael Ryan, *Principal*
EMP: 3 EST: 2011
SALES (est): 179.8K **Privately Held**
SIC: 2869 Fuels

(G-11574)
OLDCASTLE PRECAST INC
1381 S Pennsylvania Ave (19067-1275)
PHONE..................................215 736-9576
John Bereneo, *President*
EMP: 90
SALES (corp-wide): 29.7B **Privately Held**
WEB: www.oldcastle-precast.com
SIC: 3272 Concrete products
HQ: Oldcastle Infrastructure, Inc.
    1002 15th St Sw Ste 110
    Auburn WA 98001
    253 833-2777

(G-11575)
ONE BREW AT A TIME
229 Plaza Blvd (19067-7601)
PHONE..................................267 797-5437
EMP: 4
SALES (est): 277.6K **Privately Held**
SIC: 2082 Malt beverages

(G-11576)
PENN VALLEY PRINTING COMPANY
1320 Bristol Pike (19067-6199)
PHONE..................................215 295-5755
Edward Glerum, *Owner*
EMP: 4 EST: 1958
SQ FT: 2,400
SALES (est): 422.5K **Privately Held**
SIC: 2752 2759 Commercial printing, off-
set; letterpress printing

(G-11577)
PEXCO LLC
16 Progress Dr (19067-3702)
PHONE..................................215 736-2553
Bruce Cagnetti, *General Mgr*
Bob Scott, *Sales Staff*
EMP: 50
SALES (corp-wide): 6.3B **Privately Held**
SIC: 3089 Plastic hardware & building
products
HQ: Pexco Llc
    2500 Northwinds Pkwy # 472
    Alpharetta GA 30009
    404 564-8560

(G-11578)
PHOENIX CORPORATION
Also Called: Phoenix Metals
600 Dean Sievers Pl (19067-3706)
PHONE..................................215 295-9510
Dave Hutcheson, *Branch Mgr*
EMP: 30
SALES (corp-wide): 11.5B **Publicly Held**
SIC: 3499 Aerosol valves, metal
HQ: Phoenix Corporation
    4685 Buford Hwy
    Peachtree Corners GA 30071
    770 447-4211

(G-11579)
PRAXAIR DISTRIBUTION INC
1 Steel Rd E (19067-3613)
PHONE..................................215 736-8005
Joel Todaro, *Principal*
EMP: 13 **Privately Held**
SIC: 2813 5984 5169 Oxygen, com-
pressed or liquefied; nitrogen; argon;
acetylene; liquefied petroleum gas deal-
ers; chemicals & allied products
HQ: Praxair Distribution, Inc.
    10 Riverview Dr
    Danbury CT 06810
    203 837-2000

(G-11580)
ROGERS FOAM CORPORATION
150 E Post Rd (19067-1295)
PHONE..................................215 295-8720

Dave Hayes, *Manager*
EMP: 100
SALES (corp-wide): 194.7MM **Privately Held**
WEB: www.rogersfoam.com
SIC: 3086 Packaging & shipping materials,
foamed plastic
PA: Rogers Foam Corporation
    20 Vernon St Ste 1
    Somerville MA 02145
    617 623-3010

(G-11581)
SHAWCOR PIPE PROTECTION LLC
Also Called: Encoat
21 Steel Rd S (19067-3614)
PHONE..................................215 736-1111
Sheryl Wright, *Purchasing*
Joanne Conrad, *Finance Other*
Ted Jones, *Systems Mgr*
EMP: 25
SALES (corp-wide): 1.6B **Privately Held**
SIC: 3479 Coating or wrapping steel pipe
HQ: Shawcor Pipe Protection Llc
    3838 N Sam Houston Pkwy E # 300
    Houston TX 77032

(G-11582)
SOLARIS SELECT
18 Sandy Dr (19067-4841)
PHONE..................................267 987-2082
William Johns, *Mng Member*
EMP: 3 EST: 2015
SALES: 200K **Privately Held**
SIC: 3621 Inverters, rotating: electrical

(G-11583)
SUNBEAM MORRISVILLE INC
395 W Trenton Ave (19067-3516)
PHONE..................................215 736-9991
Vijay Padodara, *President*
Padodara R Nilesh, *Vice Pres*
EMP: 7
SALES (est): 630.2K **Privately Held**
SIC: 2053 Mfg Frozen Bakery Products

(G-11584)
TATE LYLE INGRDNTS AMRICAS LLC
E Post Rd (19067)
PHONE..................................215 295-5011
Frank Luciani, *Manager*
EMP: 86
SQ FT: 20,000
SALES (corp-wide): 3.8B **Privately Held**
WEB: www.aestaley.com
SIC: 2046 Corn syrup, dried or unmixed
HQ: Tate & Lyle Ingredients Americas Llc
    2200 E Eldorado St
    Decatur IL 62521
    217 423-4411

(G-11585)
THIN FILM INDUSTRIES INC
1300 Steel Rd E Ste 9 (19067-3620)
PHONE..................................267 316-9999
Scott Bennett, *President*
EMP: 6
SALES (est): 931.2K **Privately Held**
SIC: 3679 Electronic circuits

(G-11586)
VANQUISH FENCING INCORPORATED
1900 S Pennsylvania Ave (19067-2500)
PHONE..................................215 295-2863
Donald E Moore, *President*
Jim Wilson, *Technical Staff*
EMP: 18
SALES (est): 5.7MM **Privately Held**
SIC: 3446 Architectural metalwork

(G-11587)
VISTAPPLIANCES
437 W Bridge St (19067-2303)
P.O. Box 3701, Boynton Beach FL (33424-
3701)
PHONE..................................215 600-1232
EMP: 5 EST: 2016
SALES (est): 99.3K **Privately Held**
SIC: 3639 5719 Floor waxers & polishers,
electric: household; kitchenware

(G-11588)
WALTER R ERLE - MRRISVILLE LLC
14 Steel Rd E (19067-3613)
P.O. Box 728, Farmingdale NJ (07727-
0728)
PHONE..................................215 736-1708
Walter R Erle, *Principal*
EMP: 3
SALES (est): 310.9K **Privately Held**
SIC: 2951 Asphalt paving mixtures &
blocks

Morton
Delaware County

(G-11589)
AMRIT WORKS LLC
Also Called: Geared Apparel
108 Harding Ave (19070-1422)
PHONE..................................267 475-7129
Abhi Agarwal, *Mng Member*
EMP: 4 EST: 2013
SALES: 3MM **Privately Held**
SIC: 2326 2337 Men's & boys' work cloth-
ing; uniforms, except athletic: women's,
misses' & juniors'

(G-11590)
CAPE MAY OLIVE OIL COMPANY
618 N Morton Ave (19070-1126)
PHONE..................................610 256-3667
EMP: 3
SALES (est): 165.4K **Privately Held**
SIC: 2079 Olive oil

(G-11591)
DELCO PALLETS LLC
1916 Pershing Ave (19070-1625)
PHONE..................................267 438-1227
Brian McElvarr, *Principal*
EMP: 4
SALES (est): 109.4K **Privately Held**
SIC: 2448 Pallets, wood & wood with metal

(G-11592)
N VISION GROUP INC
1 N Morton Ave (19070-1514)
PHONE..................................610 278-1900
Rick A Norwood, *President*
▲ EMP: 9
SALES (est): 1.2MM **Privately Held**
SIC: 3827 Optical instruments & lenses

(G-11593)
SURF & TURF ENTERPRISES
Also Called: Signs By Tomorrow
1 Kedron Ave Ste K3 (19070-1540)
PHONE..................................610 338-0274
Joyce Csanady, *Owner*
EMP: 4 EST: 1998
SALES (est): 340K **Privately Held**
SIC: 3993 Signs & advertising specialties

(G-11594)
UTCRAS INC
501 Highland Ave (19070-1204)
P.O. Box 319 (19070-0319)
PHONE..................................610 328-1100
Frank Ursone, *President*
John Martin, *Dept Chairman*
Edward McManamy, *Vice Pres*
Charles Mullen, *Sales Dir*
Steve Persson, *Manager*
▲ EMP: 70
SQ FT: 1,500
SALES: 15.7MM **Privately Held**
SIC: 3743 Railroad equipment

(G-11595)
UTCRAS LLC
501 Highland Ave (19070-1204)
PHONE..................................610 328-1100
Frank Ursone II, *Opers Staff*
Linda Kinworthy, *Controller*
Anthony Ursone, *Director*
EMP: 70
SQ FT: 740,520
SALES: 19MM **Privately Held**
SIC: 3743 Railroad equipment

GEOGRAPHIC

Moscow
Lackawanna County

(G-11596)
EUREKA STONE QUARRY INC
35 Eureka Stone Quarry Rd (18444-9038)
PHONE...................................570 842-7694
Robert Benjamin, *Manager*
EMP: 17
SALES (corp-wide): 24.4MM **Privately Held**
SIC: 3273 Ready-mixed concrete
PA: Eureka Stone Quarry, Inc.
    Lower Stte Pickertown Rds
    Chalfont PA 18914
    215 822-0593

(G-11597)
GLUTEN FREE FOOD GROUP LLC
Also Called: Three Bakers
360 J J Rd (18444-7171)
PHONE...................................570 689-9694
Lyle Hubbard, *CEO*
Eric Shellenback, *President*
EMP: 42
SALES (est): 7MM **Privately Held**
SIC: 2043 5149 Cereal breakfast foods; diet foods

(G-11598)
MALSOM LOGGING
443 Spring Hill Rd (18444-4129)
PHONE...................................570 840-1044
David Malson, *Principal*
EMP: 3
SALES (est): 235.9K **Privately Held**
SIC: 2411 Logging

(G-11599)
NAMMO POCAL INC
Rr 435 (18444)
PHONE...................................570 842-2288
Vince Debelli, *Manager*
EMP: 16
SALES (est): 1.4MM
SALES (corp-wide): 14.2MM **Privately Held**
WEB: www.pocal.com
SIC: 3483 Mortar shells, over 30 mm.
PA: Nammo Pocal Inc.
    100 Electric St
    Scranton PA 18509
    570 961-1999

(G-11600)
POCONO WATER CENTERS INC
307 Rr 502 (18444)
P.O. Box 92 (18444-0092)
PHONE...................................570 839-8012
Anthony Seidita Jr, *President*
Mark Seidita, *Vice Pres*
Peter Seidita, *Admin Sec*
EMP: 3
SALES (est): 244.4K **Privately Held**
SIC: 3589 Swimming pool filter & water conditioning systems

(G-11601)
PROSTHETIC ARTS INC
440 N Main St (18444-9004)
P.O. Box 809 (18444-0809)
PHONE...................................570 842-2929
Ronald F Patane, *Principal*
EMP: 9 EST: 1942
SALES (est): 630K **Privately Held**
SIC: 3843 Dental metal; denture materials; teeth, artificial (not made in dental laboratories)

(G-11602)
RB FARMS INC
Sandy Beach Rd (18444)
PHONE...................................570 842-7246
Jennifer Richards, *President*
EMP: 4
SALES (est): 320.3K **Privately Held**
SIC: 1389 Excavating slush pits & cellars

(G-11603)
RGM HARDWOODS INC
Rr 7 Box 7190 (18444)
PHONE...................................570 842-4533

Robert A Mallery, *Ch of Bd*
Patrick A Mallery, *President*
EMP: 30
SALES (est): 3.6MM **Privately Held**
SIC: 2421 2426 Lumber: rough, sawed or planed; hardwood dimension & flooring mills

Moshannon
Centre County

(G-11604)
YE LOGGING VENEER
Rr 53 Box P (16859)
PHONE...................................814 387-6503
EMP: 3
SALES (est): 170K **Privately Held**
SIC: 2411 Logging

Mount Aetna
Berks County

(G-11605)
RESSLER ENTERPRISES INC
Also Called: Peiffer Machine Division
7650 Lancaster Ave (19544)
P.O. Box 218 (19544-0218)
PHONE...................................717 933-5611
Kelly Terlikosky, *President*
James Ressler, *Corp Secy*
Kristina Houck, *Treasurer*
▲ EMP: 30 EST: 1956
SQ FT: 23,000
SALES (est): 7.4MM **Privately Held**
WEB: www.peiffer-machine.com
SIC: 3541 3599 Machine tool replacement & repair parts, metal cutting types; numerically controlled metal cutting machine tools; machine shop, jobbing & repair

Mount Bethel
Northampton County

(G-11606)
AIR LIQUIDE ELECTRONICS US LP
103 Demi Rd (18343-7702)
PHONE...................................570 897-2000
EMP: 3
SALES (corp-wide): 125.9MM **Privately Held**
SIC: 2813 5084 Industrial gases; blanks, tips & inserts
HQ: Air Liquide Electronics U.S. Lp
    9101 Lyndon B Johnson Fwy # 800
    Dallas TX 75243
    972 301-5200

(G-11607)
BUDD LAKE MACHINE AND TOOL INC
800 Jacoby Creek Rd (18343)
P.O. Box 61 (18343-0061)
PHONE...................................570 897-5899
EMP: 15 EST: 1993
SQ FT: 6,000
SALES (est): 2MM **Privately Held**
SIC: 3599 Job Machine Shop

(G-11608)
CUSTOM HELIARC WELDING & MCH
4136 Church St (18343-5452)
PHONE...................................570 897-0400
EMP: 21 EST: 1990
SQ FT: 3,900
SALES (est): 1.3MM **Privately Held**
SIC: 3599 Mfg Industrial Machinery

(G-11609)
CUSTOM LAMINATING CORPORATION
5000 River Rd (18343-5610)
PHONE...................................570 897-8300
Paul Leonardelli, *President*
John Post, *Corp Secy*
Jacqueline Stafirny, *Purch Mgr*

Jeff Metzger, *Train & Dev Mgr*
David Berner, *Technical Staff*
▲ EMP: 17
SALES (est): 5.3MM **Privately Held**
SIC: 3399 Laminating steel

(G-11610)
FORMICA CORPORATION
Also Called: Formica Surell
1379 S Delaware Dr (18343-5821)
PHONE...................................570 897-6319
Virginia Shelp, *Human Res Mgr*
Jaremy Getz, *Director*
EMP: 60
SALES (corp-wide): 6.5B **Privately Held**
WEB: www.formica.com
SIC: 2679 Cardboard: pasted, laminated, lined, or surface coated
HQ: Formica Corporation
    10155 Reading Rd
    Cincinnati OH 45241
    513 786-3400

(G-11611)
LAMTEC CORPORATION
5010 River Rd (18343-5610)
PHONE...................................570 897-8200
John Post, *President*
Paul Leonardelli, *Vice Pres*
Norman Parker, *Vice Pres*
Charlie Petty, *Technical Mgr*
Robert Hodgetts, *Plant Engr*
◆ EMP: 160 EST: 1975
SQ FT: 260,000
SALES (est): 71.3MM **Privately Held**
WEB: www.lamtec.com
SIC: 2679 5033 Insulating paper: batts, fills & blankets; foil board: made from purchased material; insulation materials

(G-11612)
M C M MACHINE & TOOL INC
2561 N Delaware Dr (18343-5301)
PHONE...................................570 897-5472
Tom Conroy, *President*
EMP: 5
SQ FT: 1,500
SALES (est): 708.5K **Privately Held**
SIC: 3599 Machine shop, jobbing & repair

(G-11613)
MARINE INGREDIENTS LLC (DH)
794 Sunrise Blvd (18343-6004)
PHONE...................................570 260-6900
Olav Sandness, *President*
Nicolas Bonne, *Vice Pres*
Patty Glasgow, *Inv Control Mgr*
Doug Wathne, *Accountant*
Olav Sandnes, *VP Mktg*
▲ EMP: 24 EST: 2011
SALES (est): 41.7MM
SALES (corp-wide): 355.8K **Privately Held**
SIC: 2077 Fish oil
HQ: K.D. Pharma Bexbach Gesellschaft Mit Beschrankter Haftung
    Am Kraftwerk 6
    Bexbach 66450
    682 697-9700

(G-11614)
QUIET VALLEY PRINTING LLC
421 Quiet Valley Rd (18343-5954)
PHONE...................................908 400-3689
Dan Deroche, *Principal*
EMP: 3
SALES (est): 92.3K **Privately Held**
SIC: 2752 Commercial printing, lithographic

(G-11615)
UNITED PANEL INC
8 Wildon Dr (18343)
PHONE...................................610 588-6871
Steve Atkins, *President*
EMP: 30
SQ FT: 35,000
SALES (est): 3.9MM **Privately Held**
WEB: www.unitedpanel.com
SIC: 3469 2439 2435 Architectural panels or parts, porcelain enameled; structural wood members; hardwood veneer & plywood

Mount Braddock
Fayette County

(G-11616)
DMC GLOBAL INC
1138 Industrial Park Dr (15465-1008)
P.O. Box 317 (15465-0317)
PHONE...................................724 277-9710
Curtis Prothe, *Engineer*
Gary Burke, *Manager*
EMP: 45
SALES (corp-wide): 326.4MM **Publicly Held**
WEB: www.dynamicmaterials.com
SIC: 3599 3444 3443 3398 Machine & other job shop work; sheet metalwork; fabricated plate work (boiler shop); metal heat treating; secondary nonferrous metals
PA: Dmc Global Inc.
    5405 Spine Rd
    Boulder CO 80301
    303 665-5700

(G-11617)
GREEN FILTER USA INC
714 Braddock View Dr (15465)
P.O. Box 150 (15465-0150)
PHONE...................................724 430-2050
Mark K German, *President*
Jason Early, *Sales Mgr*
▲ EMP: 20
SALES (est): 5.2MM **Privately Held**
WEB: www.greenfilterusa.com
SIC: 3569 Filters

(G-11618)
GROUND FORCE MARKETING CO
Also Called: Green Filter
714 Braddock View Dr (15465)
P.O. Box 149 (15465-0149)
PHONE...................................724 430-2068
Mark German, *President*
▲ EMP: 30
SQ FT: 47,000
SALES (est): 5.8MM **Privately Held**
WEB: www.groundforce.com
SIC: 3714 Motor vehicle parts & accessories

(G-11619)
HOLT AND BUGBEE COMPANY
Also Called: Holt & Bugbee Hardwoods
1162 Industrial Park Dr (15465-1008)
P.O. Box 123 (15465-0123)
PHONE...................................724 277-8510
Eric Dannolfo, *Principal*
Eric D'Annolfo, *Plant Mgr*
EMP: 38
SALES (corp-wide): 58.7MM **Privately Held**
SIC: 2421 5031 Lumber: rough, sawed or planed; lumber: rough, dressed & finished
PA: Holt And Bugbee Company
    1600 Shawsheen St
    Tewksbury MA 01876
    978 851-7201

(G-11620)
LAUREL MACHINE INC
119 Commerce Dr (15465)
P.O. Box 133 (15465-0133)
PHONE...................................724 438-8661
John S Novak, *President*
David Novak, *Admin Sec*
EMP: 67
SQ FT: 10,000
SALES (est): 14.8MM **Privately Held**
WEB: www.laurelmachine.com
SIC: 3599 Machine shop, jobbing & repair

(G-11621)
SPECIALTY CONDUIT & MFG LLC
760 Bradockview Dr (15465)
P.O. Box 259 (15465-0259)
PHONE...................................724 439-9371
David Kerr,
Daniel Gearing,
EMP: 15
SALES (est): 2.6MM **Privately Held**
SIC: 3644 Electric conduits & fittings

Mount Carmel
Northumberland County

(G-11622)
ACADEMY SPORTS CENTER INC
18 S Oak St 20 (17851-2156)
PHONE..................................570 339-3399
Louanne Walsh, *President*
Robert W Welker, *President*
Caterine Desser, *Corp Secy*
EMP: 5
SQ FT: 3,500
SALES (est): 390K **Privately Held**
SIC: 2261 2262 5812 5941 Screen printing of cotton broadwoven fabrics; screen printing: manmade fiber & silk broadwoven fabrics; restaurant, lunch counter; sporting goods & bicycle shops

(G-11623)
ARCOS INDUSTRIES LLC
394 Arcos Dr (17851-2612)
PHONE..................................570 339-5200
Stacy Tangeman, *Credit Staff*
Ray Cristan, *Manager*
Ken Freed, *Manager*
Harold Wehr, *Manager*
Ottmar Marko,
▲ **EMP:** 95 **EST:** 1919
SQ FT: 180,000
SALES: 21.8MM **Privately Held**
SIC: 3548 Welding apparatus

(G-11624)
FRANCIS LATOVICH
Also Called: Francis Latovich Machine Shop
650 E 3rd St (17851-2401)
PHONE..................................570 339-1059
Francis Latovich, *Owner*
Ian Kanezo, *Engineer*
EMP: 8
SQ FT: 5,000
SALES (est): 610K **Privately Held**
WEB: www.latovichmachine.com
SIC: 3599 Machine shop, jobbing & repair

(G-11625)
INTERNATIONAL PAPER COMPANY
2164 Locust Gap Hwy (17851-2564)
PHONE..................................570 339-1611
Michael Merlo, *Purch Mgr*
Robert Meredith, *Purchasing*
Sandra Hause, *Human Res Mgr*
Richmond Harris, *Branch Mgr*
Joseph Olszewski, *Manager*
EMP: 180
SALES (corp-wide): 23.3B **Publicly Held**
WEB: www.internationalpaper.com
SIC: 2653 Boxes, corrugated: made from purchased materials
PA: International Paper Company
6400 Poplar Ave
Memphis TN 38197
901 419-9000

(G-11626)
MALLARD CONTRACTING CO INC
122 Wilburton Rd (17851-1282)
PHONE..................................570 339-2930
Edward Helfrick Jr, *President*
EMP: 28
SQ FT: 200
SALES (est): 2.1MM **Privately Held**
SIC: 1231 Strip mining, anthracite

(G-11627)
MIDWAY AUTOMOTIVE & INDUS MCH
Also Called: Midway Performance Warehouse
23 State St (17851-1815)
PHONE..................................570 339-2411
Daniel Yastifhak, *Owner*
EMP: 6
SALES (est): 575.1K **Privately Held**
SIC: 3599 Machine shop, jobbing & repair

(G-11628)
OWENS CORNING SALES LLC
1024 Locust Gap Hwy (17851)
PHONE..................................570 339-3374
Gary Fanelli, *Manager*
EMP: 25 **Publicly Held**
WEB: www.owenscorning.com
SIC: 3296 Fiberglass insulation
HQ: Owens Corning Sales, Llc
1 Owens Corning Pkwy
Toledo OH 43659
419 248-8000

(G-11629)
REGENCY PLUS INC
2000 Locust Gap Hwy (17851-2563)
PHONE..................................570 339-1390
Gary Fanelli, *President*
EMP: 50 **EST:** 1998
SQ FT: 120,000
SALES (est): 7.8MM **Privately Held**
WEB: www.window-pros.info
SIC: 3089 Window frames & sash, plastic

(G-11630)
UAE COALCORP ASSOCIATES
1 Harmony Rd (17851-1880)
PHONE..................................570 339-4090
Terence P Okeefe, *Principal*
EMP: 4
SALES (est): 233.7K **Privately Held**
SIC: 1241 Coal mining services

Mount Holly Springs
Cumberland County

(G-11631)
AHLSTROM MOUNT HOLLY SPRNG LLC (DH)
122 W Butler St (17065-1218)
PHONE..................................717 486-3438
Christopher Coates,
▲ **EMP:** 50
SQ FT: 40,000
SALES (est): 13.3MM
SALES (corp-wide): 2.3B **Privately Held**
SIC: 2621 Specialty or chemically treated papers
HQ: Ahlstrom North America Llc
3820 Mansell Rd Ste 200
Alpharetta GA 30022
770 650-2100

(G-11632)
AHLSTROM MOUNT HOLLY SPRNG LLC
Junction 34 94 Yates St 34 Junction (17065)
PHONE..................................717 486-3438
Gary Brown, *Manager*
EMP: 120
SALES (corp-wide): 2.3B **Privately Held**
SIC: 2621 Specialty or chemically treated papers
HQ: Ahlstrom Mount Holly Springs Llc
122 W Butler St
Mount Holly Springs PA 17065
717 486-3438

(G-11633)
CRUMBS
101 Watts St (17065-1825)
PHONE..................................717 609-1120
Mary Ann Skovira, *Owner*
Chuck Skovira, *Co-Owner*
EMP: 12
SALES (est): 116.1K **Privately Held**
SIC: 5812 3499 Cafe; machine bases, metal

(G-11634)
HOLLY WOODCRAFTERS INC
Mill St (17065)
P.O. Box 26 (17065-0026)
PHONE..................................717 486-5862
EMP: 36 **EST:** 1965
SQ FT: 15,000
SALES (est): 233.6K **Privately Held**
SIC: 2541 3944 Mfg Wooden Toys Cabinets & Display Fixtures

(G-11635)
KEYSTONE SIGNS
Also Called: Keystone Sign Service
88 Cedar St (17065-1429)
PHONE..................................717 486-5381
Douglas Bradley, *Owner*
EMP: 4
SALES (est): 389.5K **Privately Held**
WEB: www.keystonesignservice.com
SIC: 3993 Signs & advertising specialties

(G-11636)
MICROSEMI CORP - HIGH
100 Watts St (17065-1821)
PHONE..................................717 486-3411
Scott Benfield, *Branch Mgr*
EMP: 100
SALES (corp-wide): 3.9B **Publicly Held**
WEB: www.emxo.com
SIC: 3674 Semiconductors & related devices
HQ: Microsemi Corp. - High Performance Timing
1 Enterprise
Aliso Viejo CA 92656
949 380-6100

(G-11637)
MT HOLLY SPRNG SPECIALTY PPR
1 Mountain St (17065-1406)
PHONE..................................717 486-8500
Terry Rickert, *President*
Joann Ferringer, *Office Mgr*
▼ **EMP:** 12
SQ FT: 157,000
SALES (est): 3MM **Privately Held**
SIC: 2621 Specialty papers

(G-11638)
PENNSY SUPPLY INC
Mountain View Rd (17065)
PHONE..................................717 486-5414
Harold Kauffman, *Manager*
EMP: 13
SALES (corp-wide): 29.7B **Privately Held**
SIC: 1442 1422 Construction sand mining; crushed & broken limestone
HQ: Pennsy Supply, Inc.
1001 Paxton St
Harrisburg PA 17104
717 233-4511

(G-11639)
SKOVIRA FABRICATION MCH SP INC
101 Watts St (17065-1825)
PHONE..................................717 323-0056
Mary A Skovira, *President*
Charles R Skovira Jr, *Vice Pres*
EMP: 5
SALES (est): 770K **Privately Held**
WEB: www.skovirafab.com
SIC: 3599 Machine shop, jobbing & repair

(G-11640)
VECTRON INTERNATIONAL INC (HQ)
Also Called: Sengenuity
100 Watts St (17065-1821)
PHONE..................................603 598-0070
David W Wightman, *President*
Edward Grant, *Vice Pres*
Aline A Tomaszewski, *Treasurer*
Ram Arvikar, *Director*
EMP: 34 **EST:** 1992
SQ FT: 60,000
SALES (est): 91.8MM
SALES (corp-wide): 826.9MM **Publicly Held**
WEB: www.emxo.com
SIC: 3671 Electron tubes
PA: Knowles Corporation
1151 Maplewood Dr
Itasca IL 60143
630 250-5100

(G-11641)
WAGGONER FBRCTION MLLWRGHT LLC
30 Woodcraft Dr (17065)
PHONE..................................717 486-7533
Byron Waggoner, *President*
EMP: 50

SALES (est): 8.2MM **Privately Held**
WEB: www.landisinc.com
SIC: 3441 Fabricated structural metal

Mount Jewett
Mckean County

(G-11642)
HOWARD DRILLING INC
Also Called: Howard Productions
11 Bridge St Ste 4 (16740)
P.O. Box N (16740-0556)
PHONE..................................814 778-5820
Ted E Howard, *President*
Dale W Howard, *Vice Pres*
EMP: 7
SQ FT: 1,500
SALES (est): 800K **Privately Held**
SIC: 1381 1389 Drilling oil & gas wells; construction, repair & dismantling services

(G-11643)
JAMES SLUGA
Also Called: Sluga Logging
8 Boyd St (16740)
PHONE..................................814 778-5100
James Sluga, *Owner*
EMP: 5
SALES (est): 381.8K **Privately Held**
SIC: 2411 Logging

Mount Joy
Lancaster County

(G-11644)
8 12 INNOVATIONS INC
11 Mount Joy St (17552-1417)
PHONE..................................717 413-7656
Lacey Urban, *Principal*
EMP: 5
SALES (est): 150.7K **Privately Held**
SIC: 3999 Manufacturing industries

(G-11645)
ALVIN ENGLE ASSOCIATES INC
Also Called: Engle Publishing Co
1425 W Main St (17552-9589)
P.O. Box 500 (17552-0500)
PHONE..................................717 653-1833
Denise Sater, *Principal*
EMP: 44
SALES (corp-wide): 2.8MM **Privately Held**
SIC: 2711 Newspapers: publishing only, not printed on site
PA: Alvin Engle Associates Inc
1425 W Main St
Mount Joy PA 17552
717 653-1833

(G-11646)
ALVIN ENGLE ASSOCIATES INC (PA)
Also Called: Merchandiser, The
1425 W Main St (17552-9589)
PHONE..................................717 653-1833
Charlie Engle, *President*
Dennis Engle, *Vice Pres*
Audrey Rutt, *Treasurer*
Joe Larkin, *Sales Staff*
Stephanie Novotny, *Sales Staff*
▲ **EMP:** 6
SQ FT: 28,000
SALES (est): 2.8MM **Privately Held**
SIC: 2711 Newspapers: publishing only, not printed on site

(G-11647)
CARGILL COCOA & CHOCOLATE INC
200 Chocolate Ave (17552-2000)
PHONE..................................717 653-1471
Jeremiah Sheedy, *Superintendent*
EMP: 325
SALES (corp-wide): 114.7B **Privately Held**
SIC: 2066 Chocolate

HQ: Cargill Cocoa & Chocolate, Inc.
15407 Mcginty Rd W
Wayzata MN 55391
952 742-7575

(G-11648)
CHARLOTTE INDUSTRIES INC
630 Clay Aly (17552-2027)
PHONE..................................717 653-6721
Robert Devenburgh, *President*
Todd Devenburgh, *Foreman/Supr*
EMP: 6
SQ FT: 2,000
SALES (est): 1MM **Privately Held**
SIC: 3599 Machine shop, jobbing & repair

(G-11649)
CHILDCRAFT EDUCATION CORP
Also Called: ABC School Supply
1156 Four Star Dr (17552-8884)
PHONE..................................717 653-7500
Ronald Suchodolski, *President*
Ginger Murphy, *Vice Pres*
EMP: 250
SQ FT: 400,000
SALES (est): 19.2MM
SALES (corp-wide): 658.3MM **Publicly Held**
WEB: www.childcrafteducation.com
SIC: 2511 3999 2531 Children's wood furniture; education aids, devices & supplies; public building & related furniture
PA: School Specialty, Inc.
W6316 Design Dr
Greenville WI 54942
920 734-5712

(G-11650)
CLOVERLEAF ALPACAS (PA)
1650 Cloverleaf Rd (17552-8710)
PHONE..................................717 492-0504
Deb Potts-Ragan, *Principal*
EMP: 5 **EST:** 2010
SALES (est): 464.5K **Privately Held**
SIC: 2211 Alpacas, cotton

(G-11651)
COWZ LEAP CREAMERY LLC
369 Kelly Ave (17552-9018)
PHONE..................................717 653-1532
Crystal Ldohner, *Principal*
EMP: 3 **EST:** 2012
SALES (est): 158K **Privately Held**
SIC: 2022 Cheese spreads, dips, pastes & other cheese products

(G-11652)
DEMUTH STEEL PRODUCTS INC
25 Eby Chiques Rd (17552-9317)
PHONE..................................717 653-2239
Eric Vallieres, *President*
EMP: 10
SALES: 2.4MM **Privately Held**
SIC: 3523 Farm machinery & equipment

(G-11653)
DONSCO INC
Also Called: Foundry Div
100 S Jacob St (17552)
PHONE..................................717 653-1851
Jessie Fluck, *Branch Mgr*
EMP: 150
SALES (est): 20.7MM
SALES (corp-wide): 191.5MM **Privately Held**
WEB: www.donsco.com
SIC: 3321 3369 Gray iron castings; nonferrous foundries
PA: Donsco, Inc.
124 N Front St
Wrightsville PA 17368
717 252-1561

(G-11654)
ENGLE PRINTING & PUBG CO INC
Also Called: Auto Locator
1425 W Main St (17552-9589)
P.O. Box 500 (17552-0500)
PHONE..................................717 653-1833
Marty Wilcox, *Manager*
EMP: 11
SALES (corp-wide): 76.7MM **Privately Held**
SIC: 2752 2721 Commercial printing, offset; magazines: publishing & printing

PA: Engle Printing & Publishing Co., Inc.
1100 Corporate Blvd
Lancaster PA 17601
717 653-1833

(G-11655)
ESBENSHADE INC (PA)
Also Called: Esbensade Farms
220 Eby Chiques Rd (17552-8800)
PHONE..................................717 653-8061
Chris Esbenshade, *President*
Glenn Esbenshade, *Principal*
Greg Gillespie, *COO*
Brett Groff, *CFO*
EMP: 160 **EST:** 2008
SQ FT: 100,000
SALES (est): 23.2MM **Privately Held**
SIC: 0252 2048 Chicken eggs; poultry feeds

(G-11656)
EYELAND OPTICAL
769 E Main St (17552-9510)
PHONE..................................888 603-3937
Wes McCully, *Manager*
EMP: 3
SALES (est): 136.4K **Privately Held**
SIC: 5995 5048 3827 Opticians; optometric equipment & supplies; optical instruments & lenses

(G-11657)
FAIRWAY BUILDING PRODUCTS LLC (PA)
53 Eby Chiques Rd (17552-9317)
P.O. Box 37 (17552-0037)
PHONE..................................717 653-6777
Gregory Burkholder, *President*
Charles George, *COO*
EMP: 62
SQ FT: 89,000
SALES (est): 15.1MM **Privately Held**
SIC: 3446 Architectural metalwork

(G-11658)
GLOBAL PACKAGING SOLUTIONS INC
1160 E Main St (17552-9337)
PHONE..................................717 653-2345
Deam Fink, *Vice Pres*
EMP: 5
SALES (est): 319.4K **Privately Held**
SIC: 2653 Corrugated & solid fiber boxes

(G-11659)
GREAT DANE LLC
1155 Four Star Dr (17552-8884)
PHONE..................................717 492-0057
Paul Williams, *Branch Mgr*
EMP: 309
SALES (corp-wide): 1.5B **Privately Held**
SIC: 3715 7539 5013 5012 Truck trailers; trailer repair; trailer parts & accessories; trailers for trucks, new & used
HQ: Great Dane Llc
222 N Lasalle St Ste 920
Chicago IL 60601

(G-11660)
GREINER INDUSTRIES INC
1650 Steel Way (17552-9515)
PHONE..................................717 653-8111
Franklin Greiner Jr, *President*
▼ **EMP:** 275
SQ FT: 400,000
SALES (est): 44MM **Privately Held**
SIC: 3441 1799 7353 3731 Fabricated structural metal; food service equipment installation; cranes & aerial lift equipment, rental or leasing; general electrical contractor

(G-11661)
HIGHLANDS OF DONEGAL LLC
650 Pinkerton Rd (17552-9239)
PHONE..................................717 653-2048
Chlres N Groff, *President*
EMP: 4
SALES (est): 251.1K **Privately Held**
SIC: 3949 Shafts, golf club

(G-11662)
INDUSTRIAL DATA EXCHANGE INC
Also Called: Auto Locater
1425 W Main St (17552-9589)
P.O. Box 500 (17552-0500)
PHONE..................................717 653-1833
EMP: 300
SALES (est): 13MM
SALES (corp-wide): 70.8MM **Privately Held**
SIC: 2721 Periodicals-Publishing/Printing
PA: Engle Printing & Publishing Co., Inc.
1100 Corporate Blvd
Lancaster PA 17601
717 653-1833

(G-11663)
JACK GARNER & SONS INC
1901 Landis Rd (17552-8805)
PHONE..................................717 367-8866
Shirley Y Garner, *President*
Timothy Crider, *Manager*
EMP: 5
SQ FT: 8,400
SALES (est): 879K **Privately Held**
WEB: www.garnerwelding.com
SIC: 7692 3599 Welding repair; machine shop, jobbing & repair

(G-11664)
KINSEYS ARCHERY PRODUCTS INC (PA)
1660 Steel Way (17552-9515)
PHONE..................................717 653-9074
Sherri Gorman, *President*
Rick Kinsey, *Vice Pres*
Keith Arnold, *Buyer*
Drew Arnesen, *Sales Mgr*
Gary Kulp, *Manager*
▲ **EMP:** 57 **EST:** 1967
SQ FT: 48,200
SALES: 48.5MM **Privately Held**
WEB: www.kinseyarchery.com
SIC: 5091 3949 Archery equipment; arrows, archery

(G-11665)
KROESEN TOOL CO INC
Also Called: Ktc
43 Eby Chiques Rd (17552-9317)
P.O. Box 98 (17552-0098)
PHONE..................................717 653-1392
John P Kroesen, *Principal*
Darla A Kroesen, *Corp Secy*
Justin Kroesen, *Plant Mgr*
EMP: 16
SQ FT: 33,000
SALES (est): 3.5MM **Privately Held**
SIC: 3544 Special dies & tools

(G-11666)
MOUNT JOY WIRE CORPORATION
1000 E Main St (17552-9332)
PHONE..................................717 653-1461
Tom R Duff, *CEO*
Ty Krieger, *President*
Jim Lancaster, *Purch Agent*
Scott Badger, *CFO*
Dawn Brunner, *Bookkeeper*
▲ **EMP:** 150
SQ FT: 200,000
SALES (est): 75.1MM **Privately Held**
WEB: www.mjwire.com
SIC: 3315 Wire & fabricated wire products

(G-11667)
NEW STANDARD CORPORATION
170 New Haven St (17552-2226)
PHONE..................................717 757-9450
Morton Zifferer Jr, *President*
EMP: 4
SALES (est): 384.8K **Privately Held**
SIC: 3469 Metal stampings

(G-11668)
PATRICK INDUSTRIES INC
Also Called: Patrick Custom Vynals
20 Eby Chiques Rd (17552-9335)
PHONE..................................717 653-2086
Leo Conova, *Branch Mgr*
EMP: 50

SALES (corp-wide): 2.2B **Publicly Held**
WEB: www.patrickind.com
SIC: 3083 3275 Laminated plastics plate & sheet; gypsum products
PA: Patrick Industries, Inc.
107 W Franklin St
Elkhart IN 46516
574 294-7511

(G-11669)
REIST POPCORN COMPANY (PA)
113 Manheim St (17552-1317)
P.O. Box 155 (17552-0155)
PHONE..................................717 653-8078
David Reist, *President*
Pam Reist, *Corp Secy*
Henry Reist, *Vice Pres*
EMP: 5
SQ FT: 10,000
SALES (est): 825K **Privately Held**
SIC: 2099 Popcorn, packaged: except already popped

(G-11670)
RGM WATCH COMPANY
801 W Main St (17552-1809)
PHONE..................................717 653-9799
Roland Murphy, *President*
Mitchell E Kertzman, *Vice Pres*
EMP: 13
SALES (est): 2.1MM **Privately Held**
WEB: www.rgmwatches.com
SIC: 3873 7631 Chronographs, spring wound; watch repair

(G-11671)
TE CONNECTIVITY CORPORATION
30 S Jacob St (17552-2401)
PHONE..................................717 492-1000
Leo Graham, *Exec VP*
EMP: 13
SALES (corp-wide): 13.1B **Privately Held**
SIC: 3678 Electronic connectors
HQ: Te Connectivity Corporation
1050 Westlakes Dr
Berwyn PA 19312
610 893-9800

(G-11672)
TE CONNECTIVITY CORPORATION
Also Called: Tyco Electronics
1250 E Main St (17552-9338)
PHONE..................................717 653-8151
Janet Wazeter, *Principal*
Chris Chehovin, *Manager*
EMP: 367
SALES (corp-wide): 13.1B **Privately Held**
WEB: www.raychem.com
SIC: 3678 3643 Electronic connectors; electric connectors
HQ: Te Connectivity Corporation
1050 Westlakes Dr
Berwyn PA 19312
610 893-9800

(G-11673)
TYSON FOODS INC
455 Ridge Run Rd (17552-9634)
PHONE..................................717 653-8326
Patrick Eberlin, *Manager*
EMP: 25
SALES (corp-wide): 40B **Publicly Held**
SIC: 2011 Meat packing plants
PA: Tyson Foods, Inc.
2200 W Don Tyson Pkwy
Springdale AR 72762
479 290-4000

(G-11674)
UP-FRONT FOOTWEAR INC
33 N Market St (17552-1303)
PHONE..................................717 492-1875
Harry Dinkle, *Principal*
▲ **EMP:** 7
SALES (est): 741.3K **Privately Held**
SIC: 5139 3149 Shoes; footwear, except rubber

(G-11675)
VINEYARD AT GRANDVIEW LLC
1489 Grandview Rd (17552-8769)
PHONE..................................717 653-4825
Larry Kennel,
Sarah Haines,

▲ = Import ▼ =Export
◆ =Import/Export

Scott Haines,
Marilyn Kennel,
Fran Kratz,
EMP: 6 **EST:** 2011
SALES (est): 458.7K **Privately Held**
SIC: 2084 0762 Wine cellars, bonded: engaged in blending wines; vineyard management & maintenance services

(G-11676)
WENGER FEEDS LLC
230 S Market Ave (17552-1932)
P.O. Box 26, Rheems (17570-0026)
PHONE................................717 367-1195
Charley Doughtrey, *Manager*
J Michael Lutz, *Admin Sec*
EMP: 10
SQ FT: 4,000
SALES (corp-wide): 111.1MM **Privately Held**
WEB: www.easternag.com
SIC: 2048 Prepared feeds
PA: Wenger Feeds, Llc
101 W Harrisburg Ave
Rheems PA 17570
717 367-1195

Mount Morris
Greene County

(G-11677)
AMERICAN OIL & GAS LLC
130 Madow Ridge Rd Ste 26 (15349)
PHONE................................724 852-2222
EMP: 7
SALES (est): 550K **Privately Held**
SIC: 1382 Oil/Gas Exploration Services

(G-11678)
ARRISON H B WEST VIRGINIA INC
Also Called: Inter-State Treated Material
Rr 19 (15349)
PHONE................................724 324-2106
Edward Gene Frazee, *President*
Gary McCarty, *Corp Secy*
EMP: 8
SQ FT: 3,200
SALES (est): 1.2MM **Privately Held**
SIC: 2491 Mine props, treated wood

(G-11679)
BLAIRSVILLE WILBERT BURIAL VLT
Also Called: Tennant Wilbert
Mechanic St (15349)
P.O. Box 524 (15349-0524)
PHONE................................724 324-2010
Donnie Cumberledge, *Manager*
EMP: 5
SALES (corp-wide): 5MM **Privately Held**
SIC: 3272 7261 Burial vaults, concrete or precast terrazzo; funeral service & crematories
PA: Blairsville Wilbert Burial Vault Company Inc
6 Decker St
Blairsville PA 15717
724 459-9677

(G-11680)
EPIROC USA LLC
201 Meadow Ridge Rd (15349-9344)
PHONE................................724 324-2391
EMP: 5
SALES (corp-wide): 13.8B **Privately Held**
SIC: 3532 Mining Machinery
HQ: Epiroc Usa Llc
3700 E 68th Ave
Commerce City CO 80022
303 287-8822

(G-11681)
MINING CLAMPS FASTENERS & MORE
117 Little Shannon Run Rd (15349-3328)
PHONE................................724 324-2430
John Bernosky, *President*
Marilyn Bernosky, *Corp Secy*
Daniel Bernosky, *Vice Pres*
EMP: 4
SALES (est): 630.1K **Privately Held**
SIC: 3532 Mining machinery

(G-11682)
MORGANTOWN TECHNICAL SERVICES
303 Meadow Ridge Rd (15349-9345)
PHONE................................724 324-5433
Thomas I Dewitt, *President*
Gary Cain, *Corp Secy*
Howard Nelson, *Corp Secy*
Douglas M Carter, *Vice Pres*
Mark Carter, *Vice Pres*
EMP: 70
SQ FT: 49,494
SALES (est): 12.7MM
SALES (corp-wide): 3.1B **Privately Held**
WEB: www.swansonindustries.com
SIC: 3593 Fluid power cylinders, hydraulic or pneumatic
HQ: Swanson Industries, Inc.
2608 Smithtown Rd
Morgantown WV 26508
304 292-0021

(G-11683)
NORTH AMERICAN DRILLERS LLC (HQ)
130 Madow Ridge Rd Ste 22 (15349)
PHONE................................304 291-0175
Scott Kiger, *President*
▲ **EMP:** 125
SQ FT: 5,000
SALES (est): 148.7MM
SALES (corp-wide): 213.4MM **Privately Held**
WEB: www.shaftdrillers.com
SIC: 1481 Shaft sinking, nonmetallic minerals
PA: Shaft Drillers International, Llc
130 Madow Ridge Rd Ste 23
Mount Morris PA 15349
800 331-0175

(G-11684)
YOST DRILLING LLC
313 Steel Hill Rd (15349-1203)
P.O. Box 598 (15349-0598)
PHONE................................724 324-2253
Duane Yost, *Mng Member*
Thomas Flynn,
Greg Lemley,
EMP: 85
SALES (est): 11.2MM **Privately Held**
SIC: 1381 Drilling oil & gas wells

Mount Pleasant
Westmoreland County

(G-11685)
ABB INC
Also Called: ABB High Voltage Technology
100 Distribution Cir (15666-1044)
PHONE................................724 696-1300
Scot Naparstek, *Branch Mgr*
EMP: 76
SALES (corp-wide): 34.3B **Privately Held**
WEB: www.elsterelectricity.com
SIC: 3612 Power & distribution transformers
HQ: Abb Inc.
305 Gregson Dr
Cary NC 27511

(G-11686)
APPLIED INDUS TECH — PA LLC
Also Called: Applied Industrial Tech 0118
301 Westec Dr (15666-2763)
PHONE................................724 696-3099
Jeff Girod, *Manager*
EMP: 7
SALES (corp-wide): 3B **Publicly Held**
SIC: 5084 5063 3492 5085 Industrial machine parts; power transmission equipment, electric; hose & tube fittings & assemblies, hydraulic/pneumatic; bearings
HQ: Applied Industrial Technologies — Pa Llc
1 Applied Plz
Cleveland OH 44115

(G-11687)
BAKER HUGHES A GE COMPANY LLC
370 Westec Dr (15666-2762)
PHONE................................724 696-3059
EMP: 87
SALES (corp-wide): 121.6B **Publicly Held**
SIC: 1389 Oil field services
HQ: Baker Hughes, A Ge Company, Llc
17021 Aldine Westfield Rd
Houston TX 77073
713 439-8600

(G-11688)
BETTER BUILT PRODUCTS
320 Moccasin Hollow Rd (15666-3676)
PHONE................................724 423-5268
John Kitz, *Owner*
EMP: 3
SALES (est): 309K **Privately Held**
SIC: 2448 Pallets, wood; skids, wood

(G-11689)
BLAIRSVILLE WILBERT BURIAL VLT
Klocek Burial Vault
153 S Quarry St (15666-1747)
PHONE................................724 547-2865
Jerry Lucia, *Manager*
EMP: 20
SALES (corp-wide): 5MM **Privately Held**
SIC: 3272 5087 Burial vaults, concrete or precast terrazzo; concrete burial vaults & boxes
PA: Blairsville Wilbert Burial Vault Company Inc
6 Decker St
Blairsville PA 15717
724 459-9677

(G-11690)
C-K COMPOSITES CO LLC
361 Bridgeport St (15666)
PHONE................................724 547-4581
F Patrick Kozbelt, *CEO*
Allan Bartek, *President*
▲ **EMP:** 64
SQ FT: 80,800
SALES (est): 14.1MM **Privately Held**
WEB: www.ckcomposites.com
SIC: 3089 Injection molding of plastics

(G-11691)
CENVEO WORLDWIDE LIMITED
1001 Tech Dr Ste 1121 (15666)
PHONE................................724 887-5400
EMP: 141
SALES (corp-wide): 1.6B **Privately Held**
SIC: 2759 Announcements: engraved
HQ: Cenveo Worldwide Limited
200 First Stamford Pl # 2
Stamford CT 06902
203 595-3000

(G-11692)
CINTAS CORPORATION NO 2
320 Westec Dr (15666-2762)
PHONE................................724 696-5640
Tim Ford, *Manager*
EMP: 100
SALES (corp-wide): 6.4B **Publicly Held**
WEB: www.cintas-corp.com
SIC: 7218 2326 2337 7213 Industrial uniform supply; wiping towel supply; treated equipment supply: mats, rugs, mops, cloths, etc.; work uniforms; uniforms, except athletic: women's, misses' & juniors'; uniform supply
HQ: Cintas Corporation No. 2
6800 Cintas Blvd
Mason OH 45040

(G-11693)
COLUMBIA NORTHWEST INC
Also Called: C N W
1297 Kecksburg Rd (15666-3650)
PHONE................................724 423-7440
Clyde E Collins, *President*
Net Counts, *President*
Mark A Tait, *Corp Secy*
Ken Topka, *Buyer*
Linda Wires, *Controller*
◆ **EMP:** 15
SQ FT: 125,000

SALES (est): 3.4MM **Privately Held**
WEB: www.aliner.com
SIC: 3792 Camping trailers & chassis

(G-11694)
COPY CENTER PLUS
311 N Diamond St (15666-1308)
PHONE................................724 547-5850
Paul T Michael, *Owner*
EMP: 3
SQ FT: 5,000
SALES (est): 431K **Privately Held**
SIC: 2752 Commercial printing, offset

(G-11695)
CROWN EQUIPMENT CORPORATION
Also Called: Crown Lift Trucks
300 Westec Dr (15666-2762)
PHONE................................724 696-3533
Toll Free:................................888
Dudley Hawley, *Manager*
EMP: 40
SALES (corp-wide): 3.1B **Privately Held**
SIC: 3537 Lift trucks, industrial: fork, platform, straddle, etc.
PA: Crown Equipment Corporation
44 S Washington St
New Bremen OH 45869
419 629-2311

(G-11696)
DEMARCHI JOHN
Also Called: Mt Pleasant Mine Service
150 Three Mile HI (15666-8875)
PHONE................................724 547-6440
John Demarchi, *Owner*
EMP: 6
SQ FT: 4,500
SALES (est): 605K **Privately Held**
SIC: 3599 3441 5999 5984 Machine shop, jobbing & repair; fabricated structural metal; welding supplies; propane gas, bottled

(G-11697)
DNP IMAGINGCOMM AMERICA CORP
Also Called: Dnp IMS America Corporation
1001 Technology Dr (15666-1782)
PHONE................................724 696-7500
Satoshi Kondo, *Principal*
Dorcas Richmond-David, *Accounts Exec*
Aileen Bell, *Comp Spec*
EMP: 100
SALES (corp-wide): 13.2B **Privately Held**
WEB: www.dnpribbons.com
SIC: 3955 Carbon paper & inked ribbons
HQ: Dnp Imagingcomm America Corporation
4524 Enterprise Dr Nw
Concord NC 28027

(G-11698)
EARLY AMERICAN PITTSBURGH INC
Also Called: Early American Candle Supplies
402 E Main St Ste 100 (15666-1798)
P.O. Box 2227, Cranberry Township (16066-1227)
PHONE................................412 486-6757
John G Byrnes, *President*
Susan B Byrnes, *Vice Pres*
Susan Byrnes, *Treasurer*
EMP: 70
SQ FT: 24,000
SALES (est): 6.6MM **Privately Held**
WEB: www.eacandle.com
SIC: 3999 5999 Candles; candle shops

(G-11699)
EHC INDUSTRIES INC
Also Called: E.H.C. Industries
319 Westec Dr (15666-2763)
PHONE................................724 696-1212
Charles Miller, *President*
Randy Miller, *Vice Pres*
E Earl Miller, *Treasurer*
Justin Crisi, *Supervisor*
Todd Martin, *Admin Sec*
▲ **EMP:** 35
SQ FT: 35,000
SALES (est): 9MM **Privately Held**
WEB: www.ehcind.com
SIC: 3444 Sheet metalwork

GEOGRAPHIC

(G-11700)
GLASSAUTOMATIC INC
Also Called: Rolf Glass
402 E Main St Ste 200 (15666-1794)
PHONE..................................724 547-7500
Rolf Poeting, *President*
Dr Gina Quintana, *Corp Secy*
Joe Rosenberry, *Inv Control Mgr*
Gretchen Sandzimier, *Marketing Staff*
◆ **EMP:** 30
SQ FT: 10,000
SALES: 2.2MM **Privately Held**
SIC: 5085 3231 Industrial supplies; aquariums & reflectors, glass

(G-11701)
INTEGRATION TECH SYSTEMS INC
Also Called: Ice/Stations
271 Westec Dr (15666-2761)
PHONE..................................724 696-3000
John Spangler, *President*
John Nfulham III, *Chairman*
Peter B Orthwein, *Corp Secy*
EMP: 50
SQ FT: 40,000
SALES (est): 12.1MM **Privately Held**
WEB: www.itsenclosures.com
SIC: 3572 Computer storage devices

(G-11702)
ISOLA SERVICES INC
207 Cedar St (15666-1913)
PHONE..................................724 547-5142
Domonic S Isola, *President*
EMP: 3
SALES (est): 242.9K **Privately Held**
SIC: 3083 Plastic finished products, laminated

(G-11703)
JKR PROLIFT
256 Brook Hollow Rd (15666-9178)
PHONE..................................724 547-5955
James Komarinski, *Owner*
EMP: 3
SALES (est): 375.5K **Privately Held**
SIC: 3537 Forklift trucks

(G-11704)
KLOCEK BURIAL VAULT CO
153 S Quarry St (15666-1747)
P.O. Box 7, Blairsville (15717-0007)
PHONE..................................724 547-2865
Fax: 724 547-4786
EMP: 3
SALES (est): 459.7K **Privately Held**
SIC: 3272 Mfg Concrete Products

(G-11705)
MATAMATIC INC
181 Westec Dr (15666-2759)
PHONE..................................724 696-5678
Gary Kovac, *President*
EMP: 7
SQ FT: 15,000
SALES (est): 590K **Privately Held**
WEB: www.matamatic.com
SIC: 3069 3089 Rubber floor coverings, mats & wallcoverings; plastic processing

(G-11706)
MOBILE CONCEPTS BY SCOTTY INC
480 Bessemer Rd (15666-9136)
PHONE..................................724 542-7640
Anne Degre, *President*
Melissa Marks, *Purch Agent*
EMP: 35 **EST:** 2001
SQ FT: 50,000
SALES (est): 8.3MM **Privately Held**
WEB: www.scottyrv.com
SIC: 2451 3792 Mobile homes; travel trailers & campers

(G-11707)
MORTON BUILDINGS INC
615 Valley Ln (15666-9129)
P.O. Box 507, Pleasant Unity (15676-0507)
PHONE..................................724 542-7930
Kirk Melenyzer, *Manager*
EMP: 13

SALES (corp-wide): 463.7MM **Privately Held**
WEB: www.mortonbuildings.com
SIC: 3448 Prefabricated metal buildings
PA: Morton Buildings, Inc.
252 W Adams St
Morton IL 61550
800 447-7436

(G-11708)
NATIONAL HYDRAULICS INC (PA)
1558 Mt Plsant Connell Rd (15666-3672)
P.O. Box 20, Scottdale (15683-0020)
PHONE..................................724 547-9222
Frank C Brush, *President*
David O Hower, *Corp Secy*
EMP: 87 **EST:** 1980
SQ FT: 52,800
SALES: 12.1MM **Privately Held**
WEB: www.nationalhydraulicinc.com
SIC: 7699 3593 3594 3492 Hydraulic equipment repair; fluid power cylinders, hydraulic or pneumatic; fluid power pumps & motors; fluid power valves & hose fittings

(G-11709)
OLD GLORY CORP
4150 State Route 981 (15666-3709)
PHONE..................................724 423-3580
Russell Dunaway, *President*
EMP: 12
SALES (est): 1MM **Privately Held**
SIC: 3914 2821 Pewter ware; plastics materials & resins

(G-11710)
PEERLESS CHAIN COMPANY
Acco Chain & Lifting
1558 Mount Pleasant Conne (15666-3672)
PHONE..................................800 395-2445
Dan Watson, *Manager*
EMP: 15
SALES (corp-wide): 81.2MM **Privately Held**
WEB: www.fkiinc.com
SIC: 5084 3496 3462 Materials handling machinery; miscellaneous fabricated wire products; iron & steel forgings
HQ: Peerless Chain Company
1416 E Sanborn St
Winona MN 55987
507 457-9100

(G-11711)
PITTSBURGH ELECTRIC ENGS INC
Also Called: Peei
402 E Main St Ste 800 (15666-1796)
PHONE..................................724 547-9170
Owen Taylor, *President*
Lawrence T Ratkus, *CFO*
Sarah Dewald, *Director*
Nick Zaharoff, *Admin Sec*
EMP: 15
SQ FT: 15,000
SALES (est): 2.1MM
SALES (corp-wide): 3MM **Privately Held**
WEB: www.pghengine.com
SIC: 3694 Engine electrical equipment
PA: Watt Fuel Cell Corp.
402 E Main St Ste 800
Mount Pleasant PA 15666
724 547-9170

(G-11712)
RED DEVIL BRAKES INC
1378 Old State Route 119 (15666-3510)
PHONE..................................724 696-3744
Gerald Martino, *President*
Robert J Hodge, *Vice Pres*
▲ **EMP:** 10
SALES (est): 1.7MM **Privately Held**
WEB: www.reddevilbrakes.com
SIC: 3714 Motor vehicle brake systems & parts

(G-11713)
REED TOOL & DIE INC
1643 Pleasant Valley Rd (15666-2308)
PHONE..................................724 547-3500
David Reed, *President*
John Reed, *Principal*
William Reed, *Vice Pres*
Minnie Reed, *Treasurer*

EMP: 20
SQ FT: 10,000
SALES: 2.4MM **Privately Held**
SIC: 3545 3544 Cutting tools for machine tools; special dies, tools, jigs & fixtures

(G-11714)
RESPIRONICS INC
Also Called: Philips Respironics
174 Tech Center Dr # 100 (15666-1076)
PHONE..................................724 387-5200
James W Liken, *President*
EMP: 164
SALES (corp-wide): 20.9B **Privately Held**
WEB: www.respironics.com
SIC: 3842 3845 Surgical appliances & supplies; electromedical equipment
HQ: Respironics, Inc.
1001 Murry Ridge Ln
Murrysville PA 15668
724 387-5200

(G-11715)
RESPIRONICS INC
174 Tech Center Dr # 100 (15666-1076)
PHONE..................................724 771-7837
EMP: 5
SALES (corp-wide): 20.9B **Privately Held**
SIC: 3641 Electric light bulbs, complete
HQ: Respironics, Inc.
1001 Murry Ridge Ln
Murrysville PA 15668
724 387-5200

(G-11716)
RFSJ INC
654 W Main St (15666-1815)
PHONE..................................724 547-4457
Robert Smithnosky Jr, *President*
▲ **EMP:** 7
SQ FT: 1,944
SALES (est): 620K **Privately Held**
SIC: 3229 Glassware, art or decorative

(G-11717)
ROCHLING MACHINED PLASTICS
161 Westec Dr (15666-2759)
PHONE..................................724 696-5200
Lewis Carter, *President*
Roechling G Haren, *Ltd Ptnr*
Craig Critchfield, *Sales Mgr*
Steve Hepker, *Sales Engr*
Lisa Bushovsky, *Sales Staff*
▲ **EMP:** 23
SQ FT: 34,000
SALES (est): 5.6MM
SALES (corp-wide): 1.7B **Privately Held**
WEB: www.roechling.biz
SIC: 3644 3083 Insulators & insulation materials, electrical; laminated plastics plate & sheet
HQ: Rochling Engineering Plastics Se & Co. Kg
Rochlingstr. 1
Haren (Ems) 49733
593 470-10

(G-11718)
SMOUSE TRUCKS & VANS INC
Also Called: Stv Rental
207 Smouse Rd (15666-2800)
PHONE..................................724 887-7777
George A Smouse, *President*
EMP: 7
SQ FT: 980
SALES (est): 1.9MM **Privately Held**
WEB: www.smouse.com
SIC: 5599 3799 3523 5084 Snowmobiles; utility trailers; trailers & trailer equipment; trailers & wagons, farm; trailers, industrial; trailers for passenger vehicles

(G-11719)
STOUFFERS ASPHALT CONSTRUCTION
Also Called: Stouffer's Paving
1320 W Laurel Cir (15666-2186)
PHONE..................................724 527-0917
Jim Stouffer, *Owner*
EMP: 5
SALES (est): 664.1K **Privately Held**
SIC: 2951 Asphalt paving mixtures & blocks

(G-11720)
TRI-STATE REBAR COMPANY
1558 Mt Pleasnt Cnl Rd # 72 (15666-3672)
PHONE..................................412 824-4000
Mark Simpson, *Principal*
Edward Durick, *Principal*
Matthew Durick, *Principal*
EMP: 11
SQ FT: 20,000
SALES (est): 1.9MM **Privately Held**
SIC: 3441 Fabricated structural metal

(G-11721)
ULTRA LITE BRAKES AN C
1378 Old State Route 119 (15666-3510)
PHONE..................................724 696-3743
Gerald R Martino, *President*
Robert I Hodge, *Vice Pres*
EMP: 8 **EST:** 2004
SALES (est): 1.1MM **Privately Held**
SIC: 3621 3714 7539 Rotors, for motors; motor vehicle brake systems & parts; brake services

(G-11722)
WATT FUEL CELL CORP (PA)
Also Called: Wfc
402 E Main St Ste 800 (15666-1796)
PHONE..................................724 547-9170
Travis Bradford, *Ch of Bd*
Caine Finnerty, *President*
Sarah Dewald, *Director*
Mike Joyce, *Director*
EMP: 22
SQ FT: 6,000
SALES (est): 3.6MM **Privately Held**
SIC: 2869 Fuels

(G-11723)
WESTINGHOUSE PLASMA CORP
Also Called: Westinghouse Plasma Center
221 Westec Dr (15666-2761)
PHONE..................................724 722-7053
Walter Howard, *CEO*
Richard Fish, *President*
Kent Hicks, *Senior VP*
Thomas J Gdaniec, *Vice Pres*
Kevin Willerton, *Vice Pres*
▼ **EMP:** 17
SQ FT: 20,000
SALES (est): 5.4MM
SALES (corp-wide): 21.2MM **Privately Held**
WEB: www.westinghouse-plasma.com
SIC: 3823 Thermal conductivity instruments, industrial process type
PA: Alter Nrg Corp
227 11 Ave Sw Suite 460
Calgary AB T2R 1
403 806-3875

Mount Pleasant Mills
Snyder County

(G-11724)
A & L WOOD INC
Also Called: A&L Wood Products
2220 Paradise Church Rd (17853-8277)
PHONE..................................570 539-8922
Gary Leitzel, *President*
EMP: 45 **EST:** 1979
SQ FT: 28,000
SALES: 9MM **Privately Held**
WEB: www.alwood.net
SIC: 2448 2421 Pallets, wood; lumber: rough, sawed or planed

(G-11725)
HEISTER HOUSE MILLWORKS INC
1937 Troup Valley Rd (17853-8115)
PHONE..................................570 539-2611
Lorne Nipple, *President*
Jeffrey Hunt, *General Mgr*
Susan Womer, *Corp Secy*
Craig Doak, *Site Mgr*
Sherry Tapper, *Sales Staff*
EMP: 67

▲ = Import ▼=Export
◆ =Import/Export

SALES: 16.4MM **Privately Held**
WEB: www.hhmillworks.com
SIC: 5031 2431 Moldings, wood: unfinished & prefinished; mantels, wood; millwork; doors; windows; customized furniture & cabinets; wood kitchen cabinets

(G-11726)
IRVINS CORP
101 Cedar Ln (17853-8016)
PHONE..................................570 539-8200
Irvin G Hoover, *President*
Steven Hoover, *Manager*
▲ EMP: 72
SQ FT: 9,600
SALES (est): 11.6MM **Privately Held**
WEB: www.countrytinware.com
SIC: 3499 5712 5947 Giftware, copper goods; furniture stores; gift shop

(G-11727)
MEISERVILLE MILLING CO
127 Mill Rd Ofc Rte 104 (17853-8134)
PHONE..................................570 539-8855
Harold S Meiser, *Owner*
Annamary Meiser, *Co-Owner*
EMP: 3 EST: 1956
SQ FT: 3,000
SALES (est): 371.9K **Privately Held**
SIC: 5191 2048 Feed; fertilizer & fertilizer materials; seeds: field, garden & flower; poultry feeds

(G-11728)
MOUNTAIN SIDE SCRN PRNT/DESGN
309 Leister Ln (17853-8015)
PHONE..................................570 539-2400
Barry L Leister, *Owner*
Crystal Leister, *Principal*
EMP: 4
SALES (est): 184.7K **Privately Held**
SIC: 2759 Screen printing

(G-11729)
PORTZLINES PALLETS
Laurel Hill Rd (17853)
PHONE..................................717 694-3951
Anthony Portzline, *Owner*
EMP: 5
SALES: 500K **Privately Held**
SIC: 2421 Sawmills & planing mills, general

(G-11730)
R J & SONS HOFFMAN
1144 Buckwheat Valley Rd (17853-8641)
PHONE..................................570 539-2428
Barry Hoffman, *President*
Mark Hoffman, *Partner*
Daniel Hoffman, *Vice Pres*
Joel Hoffman, *Treasurer*
Jonathan Hoffman, *Admin Sec*
EMP: 21
SALES (est): 1.2MM **Privately Held**
WEB: www.rjhoffmanlumber.com
SIC: 2411 2421 Logging; lumber: rough, sawed or planed

(G-11731)
RALPH STUCK LUMBER COMPANY
684 Maneval Rd (17853-8661)
PHONE..................................570 539-8666
Joe Stuck, *President*
Harold Stuck, *President*
EMP: 4 EST: 1946
SQ FT: 5,000
SALES (est): 399.3K **Privately Held**
SIC: 2421 5211 Kiln drying of lumber; planing mill products & lumber

(G-11732)
SHINE MOON L P
Also Called: Moon Shine Camo
10594 Route 35 (17853-8470)
PHONE..................................570 539-8602
Travis Mattern, *Partner*
▲ EMP: 15 EST: 2008
SALES (est): 1.1MM **Privately Held**
SIC: 3161 5651 Clothing & apparel carrying cases; unisex clothing stores

---

(G-11733)
BYRNE ENERGY CORP
187 Sterling Rd (18344-1005)
PHONE..................................570 895-4333
EMP: 3 EST: 2010
SALES (est): 140K **Privately Held**
SIC: 2992 Mfg Lubricating Oils/Greases

(G-11734)
COCA-COLA REFRESHMENTS USA INC
Industrial Park Dr (18344)
PHONE..................................570 839-6706
Elizabeth Van Houten, *Manager*
EMP: 40
SALES (corp-wide): 35.4B **Publicly Held**
WEB: www.cokecce.com
SIC: 2086 Bottled & canned soft drinks
HQ: Coca-Cola Refreshments Usa, Inc.
   2500 Windy Ridge Pkwy Se
   Atlanta GA 30339
   770 989-3000

(G-11735)
MONADNOCK NON-WOVENS LLC
Also Called: Mnw
5110 Park Ct (18344-1374)
PHONE..................................570 839-9210
Ed Books, *Principal*
Keith Hayward, *Mng Member*
EMP: 44 EST: 1998
SQ FT: 40,000
SALES (est): 14.7MM
SALES (corp-wide): 78.1MM **Privately Held**
WEB: www.mpm.com
SIC: 2297 Nonwoven fabrics
PA: Monadnock Paper Mills, Inc.
   117 Antrim Rd
   Bennington NH 03442
   603 588-3311

(G-11736)
MORITZ EMBROIDERY WORKS INC
405 Industrial Park Dr (18344-1372)
P.O. Box 187 (18344-0187)
PHONE..................................570 839-9600
Carl J Moritz Jr, *President*
Stephen Moritz, *Corp Secy*
Carl J Moritz III, *Vice Pres*
Giselle Beltran, *Sales Staff*
Jane Niering, *Sales Staff*
▲ EMP: 30 EST: 1885
SQ FT: 22,500
SALES: 3.8MM **Privately Held**
SIC: 2395 2397 Emblems, embroidered; schiffli machine embroideries

(G-11737)
SUMMIT AEROSPACE USA INC
Also Called: Summit Aerospace Machining
137 Market Way (18344)
P.O. Box 289 (18344-0289)
PHONE..................................570 839-8615
David Watson, *CEO*
EMP: 15 EST: 2009
SQ FT: 16,200
SALES: 2MM
SALES (corp-wide): 9.7MM **Privately Held**
SIC: 3724 Aircraft engines & engine parts
PA: Plaintree Systems Inc
   10 Didak Dr Suite 100
   Arnprior ON K7S 0
   613 623-3434

(G-11738)
UNITED ENVELOPE LLC
1200 Industrial Park (18344-1352)
P.O. Box 37 (18344-0037)
PHONE..................................570 839-1600
EMP: 280
SALES (corp-wide): 30.2MM **Privately Held**
SIC: 2759 Commercial printing
HQ: United Envelope, Llc
   65 Railroad Ave
   Ridgefield NJ 07657

(G-11739)
BONNEY FORGE CORPORATION (PA)
14496 Croghan Pike (17066-8869)
PHONE..................................814 542-2545
John A Leone, *President*
Melanie Petron, *Editor*
Jason Schirf, *COO*
Glen Gribbell, *Vice Pres*
J Rick Leone, *Vice Pres*
◆ EMP: 295
SQ FT: 150,000
SALES (est): 68.3MM **Privately Held**
WEB: www.bonneyforge.com
SIC: 3462 3498 3494 3451 Flange, valve & pipe fitting forgings, ferrous; fabricated pipe & fittings; valves & pipe fittings; screw machine products

(G-11740)
COLOURS INC
10 N Division St (17066-1308)
PHONE..................................814 542-4215
Deb Ergler, *Owner*
EMP: 4
SALES (est): 192.7K **Privately Held**
SIC: 3465 Body parts, automobile: stamped metal

(G-11741)
CONTAINMENT SOLUTIONS INC
14489 Croghan Pike (17066-8869)
PHONE..................................814 542-8621
John Cormas, *Vice Pres*
Art Decamp, *Branch Mgr*
EMP: 128 **Privately Held**
WEB: www.containmentsolutions.com
SIC: 3443 3088 Fabricated plate work (boiler shop); plastics plumbing fixtures
HQ: Containment Solutions, Inc.
   333 N Rivershire Dr # 190
   Conroe TX 77304

(G-11742)
CURBS PLUS INC
208 N Division St (17066-1314)
PHONE..................................888 639-2872
EMP: 35 **Privately Held**
SIC: 3444 Mfg Sheet Metalwork
PA: Curbs Plus, Inc.
   8767 Alabama Hwy
   Ringgold GA 30736

(G-11743)
CURBS PLUS INC
208 N Division St (17066-1314)
PHONE..................................888 639-2872
John Dannel, *Branch Mgr*
EMP: 35 **Privately Held**
SIC: 3444 Sheet metalwork
PA: Curbs Plus, Inc.
   8767 Alabama Hwy
   Ringgold GA 30736

(G-11744)
EASTER UNLIMITED INC
436 N Industrial Dr (17066-1728)
P.O. Box 187 (17066-0187)
PHONE..................................814 542-8661
Lisa Mifsud, *Accounting Mgr*
Frank Lukins, *Manager*
Michael Pollack, *Technology*
EMP: 50
SALES (corp-wide): 25.6MM **Privately Held**
WEB: www.fun-world.net
SIC: 2671 3081 Packaging paper & plastics film, coated & laminated; unsupported plastics film & sheet
PA: Easter Unlimited, Inc.
   80 Voice Rd
   Carle Place NY 11514
   516 873-9000

(G-11745)
MCVEYS LOGGING & LUMBE
320 Mcvey Rd (17066-9009)
PHONE..................................814 542-2776
Lyle McVey, *Principal*

EMP: 3
SALES (est): 276.7K **Privately Held**
SIC: 2411 Logging camps & contractors

(G-11746)
OIS LLC ✪
10 S Jefferson St (17066-1228)
PHONE..................................717 447-0265
Esther Phares,
Christopher Phares,
EMP: 6 EST: 2018
SALES: 352K **Privately Held**
SIC: 7372 5044 8231 Prepackaged software; office equipment; documentation center

(G-11747)
GEORGIA-PACIFIC LLC
25 Walnut St (17347-6405)
PHONE..................................717 266-3621
Tim Coffey, *General Mgr*
EMP: 115
SQ FT: 150,000
SALES (corp-wide): 42.4B **Privately Held**
WEB: www.gp.com
SIC: 2653 Boxes, corrugated: made from purchased materials
HQ: Georgia-Pacific Llc
   133 Peachtree St Nw
   Atlanta GA 30303
   404 652-4000

(G-11748)
NAYLOR CANDIES INC
289 Chestnut St (17347-7502)
P.O. Box 1018 (17347-0918)
PHONE..................................717 266-2706
Charles E Naylor, *Ch of Bd*
Dennis Naylor, *President*
Anna Mae Naylor, *Vice Pres*
EMP: 15
SQ FT: 8,000
SALES (est): 1.2MM **Privately Held**
WEB: www.naylorcandies.com
SIC: 2064 Nuts, candy covered

(G-11749)
NEW YORK WIRE COMPANY
152 N M St (17347)
PHONE..................................717 266-5626
EMP: 5 EST: 2015
SALES (est): 495.4K **Privately Held**
SIC: 3312 Blast Furnaces And Steel Mills, Nsk

(G-11750)
AMCOR GROUP GMBH
750 Oak Hill Rd (18707-2112)
PHONE..................................570 474-9739
EMP: 3 EST: 2014
SALES (est): 99.3K **Privately Held**
SIC: 4783 3089 Packing & crating; plastics products

(G-11751)
AMERICAN BIT & DRILL STEEL
29 Independence Rd (18707-2318)
PHONE..................................570 474-6788
Frank Janowitz Sr, *President*
Barbara Stacey, *Office Mgr*
EMP: 4
SQ FT: 15,000
SALES: 400K **Privately Held**
SIC: 3532 Drills, bits & similar equipment

(G-11752)
BERRY GLOBAL FILMS LLC
20 Elmwood Ave (18707-2100)
PHONE..................................570 474-9700
David Cron, *Exec VP*
Paul Feeney, *Exec VP*
Steven Garrett, *Plant Mgr*
Lou Pellegrino, *QC Mgr*
EMP: 250 **Publicly Held**
WEB: www.aepinc.com

SIC: 3081 2821 Polyethylene film; plastics materials & resins
HQ: Berry Global Films, Llc
95 Chestnut Ridge Rd
Montvale NJ 07645
201 641-6600

(G-11753)
CARDINAL IG COMPANY
50 Elmwood Ave (18707-2100)
PHONE.................................570 474-9204
Steve Marti, CEO
Steve Dean, Director
EMP: 7
SALES (est): 708.3K Privately Held
SIC: 3231 Products of purchased glass

(G-11754)
CERTAINTEED CORPORATION
1220 Oak Hill Rd (18707-2199)
PHONE.................................570 474-6731
Tomas Weigert, Branch Mgr
EMP: 420
SALES (corp-wide): 215.9MM Privately Held
WEB: www.certainteed.net
SIC: 3296 Fiberglass insulation
HQ: Certainteed Corporation
20 Moores Rd
Malvern PA 19355
610 893-5000

(G-11755)
CIW ENTERPRISES INC (PA)
24 Elmwood Ave (18707-2100)
PHONE.................................800 233-8366
Andrew Cornell, President
G Bruce Burwell, Vice Pres
Steven Gallagher, Vice Pres
Joseph Heller, Vice Pres
Lauretta O'Hara, Vice Pres
EMP: 36
SQ FT: 84,000
SALES (est): 58.2MM Privately Held
SIC: 3442 3446 2431 Rolling doors for industrial buildings or warehouses, metal; open flooring & grating for construction; millwork; doors, wood

(G-11756)
CORNELLCOOKSON LLC
24 Elmwood Ave (18707-2100)
PHONE.................................800 294-4358
Andrew Cornell, President
G Bruce Burwell, Vice Pres
Joseph Heller, Vice Pres
Sean Smith, Vice Pres
Paul Sugarman, CFO
◆ EMP: 350 EST: 1828
SALES (est): 125.4MM
SALES (corp-wide): 1.9B Publicly Held
WEB: www.cornelliron.com
SIC: 3442 Rolling doors for industrial buildings or warehouses, metal
HQ: Clopay Building Products Company, Inc.
8585 Duke Blvd
Mason OH 45040

(G-11757)
CORNELLCOOKSON INC
24 Elmwood Ave (18707-2100)
PHONE.................................570 474-6773
Kevin Yakubowski, Controller
EMP: 120
SALES (corp-wide): 58.2MM Privately Held
SIC: 3442 3446 2431 Rolling doors for industrial buildings or warehouses, metal; open flooring & grating for construction; millwork; doors, wood
HQ: Cornellcookson Inc
1901 S Litchfield Rd
Goodyear AZ 85338
602 272-4244

(G-11758)
CRESTWOOD MEMBRANES INC
Also Called: I 2 M
755 Oak Hill Rd (18707-2150)
PHONE.................................570 474-6741
Christopher L Hackett, President
Bob Riley, CFO
Terri Mc Carthy, Admin Sec
EMP: 75

SALES (est): 21.8MM Privately Held
SIC: 3081 2621 Polyvinyl film & sheet; floor or wall covering, unsupported plastic; building & roofing paper, felts & insulation siding

(G-11759)
FABRI-KAL CORPORATION
955 Oak Hill Rd (18707-2142)
PHONE.................................570 454-6672
Chris Allen, Principal
Dan Braley, Manager
Gary Coghill, Manager
EMP: 125
SALES (corp-wide): 1MM Privately Held
SIC: 3089 Thermoformed finished plastic products
HQ: Fabri-Kal Corporation
600 Plastics Pl
Kalamazoo MI 49001
269 385-5050

(G-11760)
FAIRCHILD SEMICONDUCTOR CORP
125 Crestwood Dr (18707-2107)
PHONE.................................570 474-6761
Susan Jason, General Mgr
Dave Katen, General Mgr
June Martelli, Mfg Staff
Sampat Shekhawat, Engineer
Joe Yedinak, Engineer
EMP: 145
SALES (corp-wide): 5.8B Publicly Held
SIC: 3674 Semiconductors & related devices
HQ: Fairchild Semiconductor Corporation
82 Running Hill Rd
South Portland ME 04106
207 775-8100

(G-11761)
FUEL ONE GAS CNVNIENCE STR LLC
17 Red Coat Ln (18707-2247)
PHONE.................................551 208-3490
Keith A Yanuzzi, Owner
EMP: 3 EST: 2012
SALES (est): 220.4K Privately Held
SIC: 2869 Fuels

(G-11762)
GEO FUELS LLC
36 S Mountain Blvd (18707-1123)
P.O. Box 297, Nanticoke (18634-0297)
PHONE.................................570 331-0800
EMP: 3
SALES (est): 175K Privately Held
SIC: 2869 Fuels

(G-11763)
GRUMA CORPORATION
Also Called: Mission Foods
15 Elmwood Ave (18707-2136)
PHONE.................................570 474-6890
Bud Lung, Manager
EMP: 400 Privately Held
WEB: www.missionfoods.com
SIC: 0723 2096 2099 Flour milling custom services; tortilla chips; food preparations
HQ: Gruma Corporation
5601 Executive Dr Ste 800
Irving TX 75038
972 232-5000

(G-11764)
HYDRO EXTRUDER LLC
330 Elmwood Ave (18707-2116)
PHONE.................................570 474-5935
Walt Brown, Sales Dir
EMP: 200
SALES (corp-wide): 13.8B Privately Held
WEB: www.indalex.com
SIC: 3354 Aluminum extruded products
HQ: Hydro Extruder, Llc
Airport Offc Park
Moon Township PA 15108

(G-11765)
HYDRO EXTRUDER LLC
330 Elmwood Ave (18707-2116)
P.O. Box 638, Hazleton (18201-0638)
PHONE.................................570 474-5935
Walt Brown, Sales Dir
EMP: 196

SALES (corp-wide): 13.8B Privately Held
SIC: 3354 Aluminum extruded products
HQ: Hydro Extruder, Llc
Airport Offc Park
Moon Township PA 15108

(G-11766)
MOUNTAINTOP ANTHRACITE INC
1550 Crestwood Dr (18707-2132)
P.O. Box 568, Shamokin (17872-0568)
PHONE.................................570 474-1222
Robert M Durkin, President
EMP: 12
SALES (est): 1.1MM Privately Held
SIC: 1231 Anthracite mining

(G-11767)
MT CHEMICAL COMPANY LLC
1050 Crestwood Dr (18707-2151)
P.O. Box 508 (18707-0508)
PHONE.................................570 474-2200
Mark Dugan, Vice Pres
EMP: 3 EST: 2009
SQ FT: 5,000
SALES (est): 977.3K Privately Held
SIC: 5169 3999 Alkalines & chlorine; barber & beauty shop equipment

(G-11768)
OHIO MAT LCNSING CMPNNTS GROUP
Also Called: Sealy Component Group
25 Elmwood Ave (18707-2136)
PHONE.................................570 715-7200
Joseph Pale, Branch Mgr
EMP: 70
SQ FT: 200,000
SALES (corp-wide): 2.7B Publicly Held
SIC: 2515 Box springs, assembled
HQ: The Ohio Mattress Company Licensing And Components Group
1 Office Parkway Rd
Trinity NC 27370
336 861-3500

(G-11769)
ON SEMICONDUCTOR
125 Crestwood Dr (18707-2107)
PHONE.................................570 475-6030
Joseph Nichols, Principal
EMP: 3
SALES (est): 281.1K Privately Held
SIC: 3674 Semiconductors & related devices

(G-11770)
POLYONE CORPORATION
855 Oak Hill Rd (18707-2113)
PHONE.................................570 474-7770
Mark Layland, Plant Mgr
EMP: 14 Publicly Held
SIC: 2821 Vinyl resins
PA: Polyone Corporation
33587 Walker Rd
Avon Lake OH 44012

(G-11771)
PRECISION CASTPARTS CORP
701 Crestwood Dr (18707-2143)
PHONE.................................570 474-6371
EMP: 439
SALES (corp-wide): 225.3B Publicly Held
SIC: 3324 3369 3724 3511 Aerospace investment castings, ferrous; nonferrous foundries; airfoils, aircraft engine; turbines & turbine generator sets & parts; parts & accessories, internal combustion engines; prosthetic appliances
HQ: Precision Castparts Corp.
4650 Sw Mcdam Ave Ste 300
Portland OR 97239
503 946-4800

(G-11772)
PRECISION TOOL AND MACHINE CO
1698 Stairville Rd (18707-9047)
PHONE.................................570 868-3920
John Haydt, President
Harry Haydt, Vice Pres
EMP: 15
SQ FT: 23,600

SALES (est): 2.8MM Privately Held
SIC: 3599 3549 Machine shop, jobbing & repair; metalworking machinery

(G-11773)
QTG QU TROP GAT9084
750 Oak Hill Rd Rear (18707-2112)
PHONE.................................570 474-9995
EMP: 6
SALES (est): 281.2K Privately Held
SIC: 2099 Food preparations

(G-11774)
QUAKER OATS COMPANY
750 Oak Hill Rd (18707-2112)
PHONE.................................570 474-3800
Brian Mc Laughlin, Plant Mgr
Vince Gonder, Safety Mgr
Tom Grace, Engineer
Diane Hochreiter, Finance
Alan Brzozowski, Manager
EMP: 250
SALES (corp-wide): 64.6B Publicly Held
WEB: www.quakeroats.com
SIC: 2087 2086 Beverage bases, concentrates, syrups, powders & mixes; bottled & canned soft drinks
HQ: The Quaker Oats Company
555 W Monroe St Fl 1
Chicago IL 60661
312 821-1000

(G-11775)
SK SALES COMPANY INC
980 Crestwood Dr (18707-2154)
P.O. Box 156 (18707-0156)
PHONE.................................570 474-5600
Stanley W Keefe, President
Joanne Hudock, Admin Sec
EMP: 15
SQ FT: 23,000
SALES: 4MM Privately Held
SIC: 3444 Sheet metalwork

(G-11776)
SMITHS AEROSPACE COMPONENTS I
701 Crestwood Dr (18707-2143)
PHONE.................................570 474-3011
Fred Decusatis, CFO
Joseph Phillips, Maintenc Staff
EMP: 5 EST: 2010
SALES (est): 451.1K Privately Held
SIC: 3728 Aircraft parts & equipment

(G-11777)
SVC MANUFACTURING INC
750 Oak Hill Rd (18707-2112)
PHONE.................................623 907-1822
Brian McLaughlin, Manager
EMP: 4
SALES (corp-wide): 64.6B Publicly Held
SIC: 2096 Corn chips & other corn-based snacks
HQ: Svc Manufacturing, Inc.
409 S 104th Ave
Tolleson AZ 85353
623 936-8898

(G-11778)
TEMPUR PRODUCTION USA LLC
Also Called: Mountain Top Foam Co.
25 Elmwood Ave (18707-2136)
PHONE.................................570 715-7200
Paula Hoeft, Financial Exec
Robert Trussell,
EMP: 11 EST: 2015
SQ FT: 225,000
SALES (est): 1.4MM
SALES (corp-wide): 2.7B Publicly Held
SIC: 2515 Mattresses & bedsprings
PA: Tempur Sealy International, Inc.
1000 Tempur Way
Lexington KY 40511
800 878-8889

(G-11779)
TRIVAGORY ENTERPRISES
89 S Main St (18707-1920)
PHONE.................................570 474-6520
John Yuscavage, Partner
Donna Yuscavage,
EMP: 14
SQ FT: 2,000

SALES (est): 890K **Privately Held**
SIC: **3944** Board games, puzzles & models, except electronic

(G-11780)
WHIPPLE BROS INC (PA)
Also Called: Whipples Building Mtls Ctr
34 Pine Tree Rd (18707-1717)
PHONE..................................570 836-6262
Debra Whipple, *CEO*
Clarence B Whipple, *Chairman*
Bruce K Anders, *Corp Secy*
David Sherry, *Vice Pres*
Bruce Phillips, *Admin Sec*
EMP: 4 EST: 1894
SQ FT: 2,000
SALES (est): 3MM **Privately Held**
SIC: **5211** 2452 2439 Home centers; panels & sections, prefabricated, wood; trusses, wooden roof; trusses, except roof: laminated lumber

(G-11781)
WIRELESS ACQUISITION LLC
Also Called: Emcee Communication
395 Oak Hill Rd (18707-2148)
PHONE..................................602 315-9979
Jim Yard,
EMP: 6
SALES (corp-wide): 1.5MM **Privately Held**
WEB: www.emceecom.com
SIC: **3663** Television broadcasting & communications equipment
PA: Wireless Acquisition Llc
1215 S Park Ln Ste 4
Tempe AZ

(G-11782)
WYCHOCKS MOUNTAINTOP BEVERAGE
75 S Mountain Blvd (18707-1122)
PHONE..................................570 474-5577
Mary Wychock, *Owner*
EMP: 3
SALES (est): 310K **Privately Held**
SIC: **5921** 2086 Beer (packaged); bottled & canned soft drinks

(G-11783)
WYMAN-GORDON PENNSYLVANIA LLC (DH)
Also Called: Wyman Gordon - Mountain Top
701 Crestwood Dr (18707-2143)
P.O. Box 68 (18707-0068)
PHONE..................................570 474-6371
Ben Huber, *Mng Member*
▲ EMP: 49
SALES (est): 15.9MM
SALES (corp-wide): 225.3B **Publicly Held**
SIC: **3462** Aircraft forgings, ferrous; flange, valve & pipe fitting forgings, ferrous
HQ: Wyman-Gordon Forgings, Inc.
10825 Telge Rd
Houston TX 77095
281 856-9900

(G-11784)
ZODIAC PRINTING CORPORATION
395 Oak Hill Rd (18707-2148)
PHONE..................................570 474-9220
Thomas Zabroski, *President*
Ann Zabroski, *Corp Secy*
Brian Zabroski, *Vice Pres*
Chuck Allabaugh, *Sales Mgr*
John Puterbaugh, *Manager*
EMP: 20 EST: 1980
SQ FT: 28,000
SALES (est): 3.4MM **Privately Held**
WEB: www.zodiacprinting.com
SIC: **2752** Commercial printing, offset

Mountainhome
Monroe County

(G-11785)
B/E AEROSPACE INC
Also Called: J.A. Reinhardt
Spruce Cabin Rd (18342)
PHONE..................................570 595-7491
Amin J Khoury, *Ch of Bd*

EMP: 5
SALES (corp-wide): 66.5B **Publicly Held**
SIC: **2531** 3728 3647 Seats, aircraft; aircraft parts & equipment; aircraft lighting fixtures
HQ: B/E Aerospace, Inc.
1400 Corporate Center Way
Wellington FL 33414
561 791-5000

(G-11786)
CALLIES CANDY KITCHENS INC (PA)
Also Called: Callie's Pretzel Factory
1111 Rte 390 (18342)
P.O. Box 126 (18342-0126)
PHONE..................................570 595-2280
Gretchen Reisenwitz, *President*
Harry D Callie, *Principal*
Carol Callie, *Corp Secy*
Mark Reisenwitz, *Vice Pres*
Lynn Callie, *Treasurer*
EMP: 15
SQ FT: 10,000
SALES (est): 2.6MM **Privately Held**
WEB: www.calliescandy.com
SIC: **5441** 2064 Confectionery produced for direct sale on the premises; candy & other confectionery products

(G-11787)
J A REINHARDT & CO INC
Also Called: Rockwell Interior Services
3319 Spruce Cabin Rd (18342)
P.O. Box 202 (18342-0202)
PHONE..................................570 595-7491
▲ EMP: 111
SQ FT: 75,000
SALES (est): 23MM
SALES (corp-wide): 66.5B **Publicly Held**
WEB: www.jareinhardt.com
SIC: **3728** Aircraft parts & equipment
HQ: B/E Aerospace, Inc.
1400 Corporate Center Way
Wellington FL 33414
561 791-5000

(G-11788)
YE OLDE VILLAGE WORKSHOP
And Golf Dr Rr 390 (18342)
PHONE..................................570 595-2593
William M Fisher III, *Owner*
EMP: 4
SQ FT: 5,000
SALES (est): 600K **Privately Held**
SIC: **1799** 2434 Kitchen & bathroom remodeling; vanities, bathroom: wood

---

Mountville
Lancaster County

(G-11789)
8 12 ILLUMINATION LLC
200 N Donnerville Rd (17554-1511)
PHONE..................................717 285-9700
Logan Abel, *Opers Mgr*
Ken Urban, *Director*
EMP: 3 EST: 2014
SALES (est): 243K **Privately Held**
SIC: **3646** Commercial indusl & institutional electric lighting fixtures

(G-11790)
BORRIS INFORMATION GROUP INC
306 Primrose Ln (17554-1262)
PHONE..................................717 285-9141
EMP: 8 EST: 1971
SQ FT: 7,000
SALES: 1.1MM **Privately Held**
SIC: **2791** 7311 Typesetting Services Advertising Agency

(G-11791)
CLIPPER MAGAZINE LLC (DH)
3708 Hempland Rd (17554-1542)
PHONE..................................717 569-5100
Steve Hauber, *CEO*
Marina Dick, *Area Mgr*
Kathy Gough, *Area Mgr*
David Marks, *Vice Pres*
Gene Galeschewski, *Opers Staff*
EMP: 325

SQ FT: 120,000
SALES (est): 112.7MM **Privately Held**
WEB: www.clippermagazine.com
SIC: **2754** 2721 Coupons: gravure printing; periodicals
HQ: Valassis Communications, Inc.
19975 Victor Pkwy
Livonia MI 48152
734 591-3000

(G-11792)
CUSTOM TOOL AND DIE INC
103 S Manor St (17554-1615)
PHONE..................................717 522-1440
William Woratyla, *President*
Bernice Woratyla, *Treasurer*
EMP: 19
SQ FT: 10,000
SALES: 1.5MM **Privately Held**
WEB: www.customtoolanddie.com
SIC: **3544** Special dies & tools

(G-11793)
DEAN FOODS COMPANY
3800 Hempland Rd (17554-1500)
PHONE..................................717 522-5653
EMP: 3
SALES (est): 666.1K **Privately Held**
SIC: **2026** Fluid milk

(G-11794)
DUTKA INC
1812 Stony Battery Rd (17554-1300)
PHONE..................................717 285-5880
Gordon P Dutka, *Principal*
EMP: 4 EST: 1998
SALES (est): 520.3K **Privately Held**
SIC: **2541** Counter & sink tops

(G-11795)
GENE FORREY MILLWORK
312 Druid Hill Dr (17554-1206)
PHONE..................................717 285-4046
Eugene K Forrey, *Owner*
Nancy Forrey, *Co-Owner*
EMP: 12
SQ FT: 3,000
SALES: 1.2MM **Privately Held**
SIC: **2431** Millwork

(G-11796)
INFOTECHNOLOGIES INC
Also Called: AG Information Systems
306 Primrose Ln (17554-1262)
PHONE..................................717 285-7105
Corey Mahoney, *President*
Donna Mast, *Business Mgr*
Todd Borris, *Vice Pres*
EMP: 4
SQ FT: 2,500
SALES (est): 477.2K **Privately Held**
SIC: **2791** Typographic composition, for the printing trade

(G-11797)
KAHN-LUCAS-LANCASTER INC (PA)
Also Called: Kahn Lucas
306 Primrose Ln (17554-1262)
PHONE..................................717 537-4140
Andrew L Kahn, *Ch of Bd*
Howard Kahn, *President*
Paul R Beshler, *Vice Pres*
Yuliya Akopova, *Production*
John Zander, *CFO*
◆ EMP: 45 EST: 1889
SQ FT: 12,000
SALES (est): 44.5MM **Privately Held**
WEB: www.kahnlucas.com
SIC: **2369** 2361 Girls' & children's outerwear; dresses: girls', children's & infants'

(G-11798)
MADAME ALEXANDER DOLL CO LLC (HQ)
306 Primrose Ln (17554-1262)
PHONE..................................717 537-4140
Howard Kahn, *CEO*
John Zander, *CFO*
▲ EMP: 24
SALES (est): 15.8MM
SALES (corp-wide): 44.5MM **Privately Held**
SIC: **3942** Dolls, except stuffed toy animals

PA: Kahn-Lucas-Lancaster, Inc.
306 Primrose Ln
Mountville PA 17554
717 537-4140

(G-11799)
MICRO FACTURE LLC
200 N Donnerville Rd (17554-1511)
PHONE..................................717 285-9700
Baron Abel, *CEO*
Sandy Abel, *Chairman*
David Taylor, *QC Mgr*
Norm Huhn, *Manager*
Rich Bushong, *Prgrmr*
EMP: 29
SQ FT: 20,000
SALES (est): 7.8MM **Privately Held**
WEB: www.microfacture.com
SIC: **3599** 3484 3841 3643 Machine shop, jobbing & repair; guns (firearms) or gun parts, 30 mm. & below; surgical & medical instruments; bus bars (electrical conductors); connectors & terminals for electrical devices

(G-11800)
NEXGEN ATS
115 Timber Dr (17554-1868)
PHONE..................................717 779-9580
Robert Doane, *Owner*
EMP: 6
SALES (est): 295K **Privately Held**
SIC: **3812** Air traffic control systems & equipment, electronic

(G-11801)
REIST PRECISION MACHINE INC
156 N Donnerville Rd (17554-1509)
PHONE..................................717 606-3166
Timothy Reist, *President*
Joanne Reist, *Vice Pres*
EMP: 4
SALES (est): 463.3K **Privately Held**
SIC: **3599** Machine shop, jobbing & repair

(G-11802)
SENSIBLE PORTIONS
3775 Hempland Rd (17554-1541)
PHONE..................................717 898-7131
Tom Keenin, *Principal*
EMP: 9
SALES (est): 953.5K **Privately Held**
SIC: **2096** Potato chips & similar snacks

(G-11803)
TEREX CORPORATION
Also Called: D U E C O
180a N Donnerville Rd (17554-1509)
PHONE..................................717 840-0226
Greg Adler, *Manager*
EMP: 25
SALES (corp-wide): 5.1B **Publicly Held**
WEB: www.dueco.com
SIC: **3537** 5531 Industrial trucks & tractors; truck equipment & parts
PA: Terex Corporation
200 Nyala Farms Rd Ste 2
Westport CT 06880
203 222-7170

(G-11804)
WORLD GOURMET ACQUISITION LLC
Also Called: Sensible Portions
3775 Hempland Rd (17554-1541)
PHONE..................................717 285-1884
Jason Cohen,
Jerry Bello,
▲ EMP: 100
SALES (est): 11.1MM **Publicly Held**
SIC: **2096** Potato chips & similar snacks
PA: The Hain Celestial Group Inc
1111 Marcus Ave Ste 100
New Hyde Park NY 11042

Muncy
Lycoming County

(G-11805)
ADVANCED DRAINAGE SYSTEMS INC
173 Industrial Pkwy (17756-6652)
PHONE..................................570 546-7686

GEOGRAPHIC

Dan Kowalchuk, *Manager*
EMP: 28
SALES (corp-wide): 1.3B **Publicly Held**
WEB: www.ads-pipe.com
SIC: 3084 5051 3444 3272 Plastics pipe;
pipe & tubing, steel; sheet metalwork;
concrete products
PA: Advanced Drainage Systems, Inc.
4640 Trueman Blvd
Hilliard OH 43026
614 658-0050

(G-11806)
ANDRITZ INC
336 W Penn St (17756-1210)
PHONE.................................570 546-1253
Dennis Shulick, *Human Resources*
John Dobson, *Technical Staff*
EMP: 400
SALES (corp-wide): 6.9B **Privately Held**
SIC: 3554 3523 Pulp mill machinery; grad-
ing, cleaning, sorting machines, fruit,
grain, vegetable
HQ: Andritz Inc.
500 Technology Dr
Canonsburg PA 15317
724 597-7801

(G-11807)
ANDRITZ INC
35 Sherman St (17756-1227)
PHONE.................................570 546-8211
Edson Aleixo, *Division Mgr*
Scott Shuman, *General Mgr*
Keith Vogel, *General Mgr*
Kristi Cirelli, *Vice Pres*
Klaus Fischbach, *Vice Pres*
EMP: 400
SALES (corp-wide): 6.9B **Privately Held**
SIC: 3554 8711 Pulp mill machinery; in-
dustrial engineers
HQ: Andritz Inc.
500 Technology Dr
Canonsburg PA 15317
724 597-7801

(G-11808)
BEENAH ENTERPRISES LLC
995 Gardner Rd (17756-7388)
PHONE.................................570 546-9388
John W Merrifield,
EMP: 5
SALES (est): 309.4K **Privately Held**
SIC: 2448 Wood pallets & skids

(G-11809)
**BENIGNAS CREEK VINEYARD &
WINE**
300 Lycoming Mall Cir (17756-8072)
PHONE.................................570 546-0744
EMP: 4
SALES (est): 181.6K **Privately Held**
SIC: 2084 5921 Mfg Wines/Brandy/Spirits
Ret Alcoholic Beverages

(G-11810)
BENTLEY & COLLINS COMPANY
195 Parkway Dr (17756-8282)
P.O. Box 142, Montoursville (17754-0142)
PHONE.................................570 546-3250
Kurt C Fritz, *President*
Jeffrey Allen, *Admin Sec*
EMP: 14
SQ FT: 10,000
SALES (est): 1.2MM **Privately Held**
SIC: 2434 2431 Wood kitchen cabinets;
millwork

(G-11811)
**BLACKHAWK SPECIALTY
TOOLS LLC**
285 Marcellus Dr (17756-6647)
PHONE.................................570 323-7100
Billy Brown, *Principal*
EMP: 5
SALES (corp-wide): 456.5MM **Privately
Held**
SIC: 1382 Oil & gas exploration services
HQ: Blackhawk Specialty Tools, Llc
10260 Westheimer Rd # 600
Houston TX 77042
713 466-4200

(G-11812)
**CHARLOTTE PIPE AND
FOUNDRY CO**
100 Industrial Park Rd (17756-8038)
P.O. Box 363 (17756-0363)
PHONE.................................570 546-7666
Wes Webster, *Plant Mgr*
Dave Feggestad, *Manager*
EMP: 40
SALES (corp-wide): 650.2MM **Privately
Held**
WEB: www.charlottepipe.com
SIC: 3084 Plastics pipe
PA: Charlotte Pipe And Foundry Company
2109 Randolph Rd
Charlotte NC 28207
704 372-5030

(G-11813)
**CONSTRUCTION SPECIALTIES
INC**
Decogard Products
6696 Route 405 Hwy (17756-6381)
P.O. Box 380 (17756-0380)
PHONE.................................570 546-2255
Howard Williams, *Vice Pres*
Gary Bartlett, *Vice Pres*
Paul Moulton, *Vice Pres*
EMP: 310
SALES (corp-wide): 379MM **Privately
Held**
WEB: www.c-sgroup.com
SIC: 3354 Aluminum extruded products
PA: Construction Specialties Inc.
3 Werner Way Ste 100
Lebanon NJ 08833
908 236-0800

(G-11814)
**CONSTRUCTION SPECIALTIES
INC**
Also Called: The Cs Group
6696 Route 405 Hwy (17756-6381)
P.O. Box 380 (17756-0380)
PHONE.................................570 546-5941
Ronald Dodd, *CEO*
EMP: 59
SALES (corp-wide): 379MM **Privately
Held**
WEB: www.c-sgroup.com
SIC: 3999 Barber & beauty shop equip-
ment
PA: Construction Specialties Inc.
3 Werner Way Ste 100
Lebanon NJ 08833
908 236-0800

(G-11815)
**ENERFLEX ENERGY SYSTEMS
INC**
160 Logan Dr B (17756-7061)
PHONE.................................570 726-0500
EMP: 89
SALES (corp-wide): 1.2B **Privately Held**
SIC: 3585 Refrigeration equipment, com-
plete; compressors for refrigeration & air
conditioning equipment
HQ: Enerflex Energy Systems Inc.
10815 Telge Rd
Houston TX 77095
281 345-9300

(G-11816)
FMC TECHNOLOGIES INC
320 Marcellus Dr (17756-6650)
PHONE.................................570 546-2441
Jack Hancock, *Branch Mgr*
EMP: 29
SALES (corp-wide): 15B **Privately Held**
SIC: 3533 Oil field machinery & equipment
HQ: Fmc Technologies, Inc.
11740 Katy Fwy Energy Tow
Houston TX 77079
281 591-4000

(G-11817)
FRY & 146 CAST DIVISION
3700 Clarkstown Rd (17756-7774)
PHONE.................................570 546-2109
Bret Gray, *Manager*
EMP: 3
SALES (est): 235.7K **Privately Held**
SIC: 3321 Cast iron pipe & fittings

(G-11818)
HANSON AGGREGATES PA LLC
1918 Lime Bluff Rd (17756)
PHONE.................................570 584-2153
EMP: 14
SALES (corp-wide): 16B **Privately Held**
SIC: 1442 1422 Construction Sand/Gravel
Crushed/Broken Limestone
HQ: Hanson Aggregates Pennsylvania, Llc
7660 Imperial Way
Allentown PA 18195
610 366-4626

(G-11819)
HIGH TECH AQUATICS INC
104 Chas Rd (17756)
PHONE.................................570 546-3557
Henry Holcomb, *President*
EMP: 1
SALES: 1.5MM **Privately Held**
SIC: 3589 7389 Sewage & water treat-
ment equipment;

(G-11820)
**HOUSEKNECHTS MCH & TL CO
INC (PA)**
Also Called: Houseknecht Precision Mch Sp
1064 Old Cement Rd (17756-8055)
PHONE.................................570 584-3010
Galen Houseknecht, *President*
Judy Houseknecht, *Corp Secy*
EMP: 6
SQ FT: 5,000
SALES: 386K **Privately Held**
SIC: 3599 Machine shop, jobbing & repair

(G-11821)
HRI INC
Also Called: Benchmark Mtrials/ Cornerstone
81 Fitness Dr 1 (17756-8393)
PHONE.................................570 322-6737
Glenn Shawl, *Manager*
Dave Baier, *Manager*
EMP: 80
SALES (corp-wide): 83.5MM **Privately
Held**
SIC: 1611 1771 2951 General contractor,
highway & street construction; parking lot
construction; asphalt paving mixtures &
blocks
HQ: Hri, Inc.
73 Headquarters Plz
Morristown NJ 07960
973 290-9082

(G-11822)
JOES WELDING REPAIRS
645 Allen Dr (17756-5714)
PHONE.................................570 546-5223
Joseph Reynolds, *Owner*
EMP: 7
SALES: 750K **Privately Held**
SIC: 7692 3441 Welding repair; fabricated
structural metal

(G-11823)
KELLOGG COMPANY
572 Industrial Park Rd (17756-8059)
PHONE.................................570 546-0200
Dennis Sweeney, *Branch Mgr*
Sam Altemose, *Info Tech Mgr*
EMP: 278
SALES (corp-wide): 13.5B **Publicly Held**
SIC: 2043 2051 Cereal breakfast foods;
bread, cake & related products
HQ: Kellogg Usa Inc.
1 Kellogg Sq
Battle Creek MI 49017

(G-11824)
KEYSTONE FILLER & MFG CO
214 Railroad St (17756-1422)
PHONE.................................570 546-3148
Charles Pfleegor, *CEO*
David W Pfleegor, *President*
David W Pfleegor II, *Vice Pres*
David Pfleegor Jr, *Vice Pres*
◆ **EMP:** 50
SQ FT: 100,000
SALES (est): 10.3MM **Privately Held**
SIC: 3295 Mfg Minerals-Ground/Treated

(G-11825)
M-B COMPANIES INC
95 Blessing Dr (17756-6373)
PHONE.................................570 547-1621
Terrance Cosgrove, *Principal*
James Lakatos, *Electrical Engi*
Jo Anna Johnson, *Persnl Mgr*
EMP: 30
SALES (corp-wide): 355.8K **Privately
Held**
WEB: www.m-bco.com
SIC: 2851 3842 3531 3083 Paints & al-
lied products; surgical appliances & sup-
plies; construction machinery; laminated
plastics plate & sheet
HQ: M-B Companies, Inc.
1200 Park St
Chilton WI 53014
920 849-2313

(G-11826)
MCCARLS INC
56 Blessing Dr (17756-6386)
PHONE.................................724 581-5409
Mike Geyer, *Controller*
Jim Butler, *Branch Mgr*
EMP: 10
SALES (corp-wide): 4.4B **Privately Held**
SIC: 3498 Fabricated pipe & fittings
HQ: Mccarl's Llc
1413 9th Ave
Beaver Falls PA 15010
724 581-5409

(G-11827)
MUNCY HOMES
1567 Route 442 Hwy (17756-6853)
PHONE.................................570 546-2261
Thomas M Saltsgiver, *President*
Jo Ann Saltsgiver, *Corp Secy*
Mike Clementoni, *Exec VP*
Bill Huber, *Vice Pres*
William F Huber, *Vice Pres*
EMP: 450
SALES (est): 60.2MM **Privately Held**
WEB: www.muncyhomes.com
SIC: 2452 Modular homes, prefabricated,
wood

(G-11828)
PALCON LLC (PA)
1759 Lime Bluff Rd (17756-7927)
P.O. Box 235 (17756-0235)
PHONE.................................570 546-9032
Matt Carey,
EMP: 16
SQ FT: 26,000
SALES: 2.5MM **Privately Held**
WEB: www.palconllc.com
SIC: 2448 Pallets, wood

(G-11829)
PALCON LLC
1759 Lime Bluff Rd (17756-7927)
P.O. Box 235 (17756-0235)
PHONE.................................570 546-9032
Matt Carey, *President*
EMP: 11
SALES (corp-wide): 2.5MM **Privately
Held**
WEB: www.palconllc.com
SIC: 2448 Pallets, wood
PA: Palcon, Llc
1759 Lime Bluff Rd
Muncy PA 17756
570 546-9032

(G-11830)
PENN-AMERICAN INC
6840 Susquehanna Trl (17756-5510)
P.O. Box 240 (17756-0239)
PHONE.................................570 649-5173
Randall Stiger, *Owner*
Barbara Stiger, *Vice Pres*
Bill Crowell, *Project Mgr*
Craig Kimble, *Sales Executive*
Carrie Stiger, *Manager*
EMP: 27
SQ FT: 25,000
SALES (est): 9MM **Privately Held**
WEB: www.pennamerican.com
SIC: 3441 Fabricated structural metal

▲ = Import ▼=Export
◆ =Import/Export

(G-11831)
POLY-GROWERS INC
Also Called: Poly Grower Greenhouse Co
161 Fairground St (17756-8205)
P.O. Box 359 (17756-0359)
PHONE..................................570 546-3216
Jack Bartlett, *President*
EMP: 10
SQ FT: 2,000
SALES (est): 1.1MM **Privately Held**
SIC: 3448 1541 Greenhouses: prefabricated metal; prefabricated building erection, industrial

(G-11832)
S & D WELDING INC
1754 John Brady Dr (17756-8105)
PHONE..................................570 546-8772
Wayne L Derrick, *President*
EMP: 7
SQ FT: 14,000
SALES (est): 679.4K **Privately Held**
SIC: 7692 Welding repair

(G-11833)
SPM FLOW CONTROL INC
76 Odell Rd (17756-8403)
PHONE..................................570 546-1005
EMP: 138
SALES (corp-wide): 3.1B **Privately Held**
SIC: 1389 Oil field services
HQ: S.P.M. Flow Control, Inc.
7601 Wyatt Dr
Fort Worth TX 76108
817 246-2461

(G-11834)
TECHNIPFMC US HOLDINGS INC
320 Marcellus Dr (17756-6650)
PHONE..................................570 546-2380
Jack Hancock, *Branch Mgr*
EMP: 29
SALES (corp-wide): 15B **Privately Held**
SIC: 3533 Oil & gas field machinery
HQ: Fmc Technologies, Inc.
11740 Katy Fwy Energy Tow
Houston TX 77079
281 591-4000

(G-11835)
TELEPOLE MANUFACTURING INC
1975 John Brady Dr (17756-7831)
PHONE..................................570 546-3699
Kimon Digenakis, *President*
▲ EMP: 3
SALES (est): 221.2K **Privately Held**
SIC: 5947 2752 Novelties; commercial printing, lithographic

(G-11836)
TROJAN TUBE SLS & FABRICATIONS
Also Called: Trojan Boiler Service
161 W Water St (17756-1011)
PHONE..................................570 546-8860
Jack Decker Jr, *President*
Justin Michael Decker, *Vice Pres*
EMP: 12
SQ FT: 13,000
SALES: 2MM **Privately Held**
SIC: 3498 5051 Pipe sections fabricated from purchased pipe; tube fabricating (contract bending & shaping); pipe & tubing, steel

(G-11837)
VETCO GRAY INC
Also Called: GE Oil & Gas
321 Marcellus Dr (17756-6649)
PHONE..................................570 435-8027
Derreck Falgaut, *Regional Mgr*
EMP: 9
SALES (corp-wide): 121.6B **Publicly Held**
SIC: 3533 Oil & gas field machinery
HQ: Vetco Gray, Llc
4424 W Sam Houston Pkwy N
Houston TX 77041
281 448-4410

(G-11838)
WEATHERFORD ARTIFICIA
25 Energy Dr (17756-7565)
PHONE..................................570 308-3400

EMP: 32 **Privately Held**
SIC: 3561 Pumps, oil well & field
HQ: Weatherford Artificial Lift Systems, Llc
2000 Saint James Pl
Houston TX 77056
713 836-4000

(G-11839)
WEATHERFORD INTERNATIONAL LLC
25 Energy Dr (17756-7565)
PHONE..................................570 326-2754
EMP: 23 **Privately Held**
SIC: 3533 Oil & gas field machinery
HQ: Weatherford International, Llc
2000 Saint James Pl
Houston TX 77056
713 693-4000

(G-11840)
WEATHERFORD INTERNATIONAL LLC
306 Industrial Park Rd (17756-8158)
PHONE..................................570 546-0745
EMP: 100 **Privately Held**
SIC: 3533 Mfg Oil/Gas Field Machinery
HQ: Weatherford International, Llc
2000 Saint James Pl
Houston TX 77056
713 693-4000

(G-11841)
WENGER FEEDS LLC
6829 Route 405 Hwy (17756-6372)
PHONE..................................717 367-1195
Matt Spring, *Manager*
J Michael Lutz, *Admin Sec*
EMP: 7
SALES (corp-wide): 111.1MM **Privately Held**
WEB: www.easternag.com
SIC: 2048 5144 0252 Poultry feeds; livestock feeds; eggs; chicken eggs
PA: Wenger Feeds, Llc
101 W Harrisburg Ave
Rheems PA 17570
717 367-1195

(G-11842)
WODRIG LOGGING CORPORATION
9763 Route 864 Hwy (17756-7992)
PHONE..................................570 435-0783
Harold R Wodrig, *President*
David L Wodrig, *Treasurer*
Norma L Wodrig, *Treasurer*
Rocky G Wodrig, *Admin Sec*
EMP: 3
SALES (est): 293.8K **Privately Held**
SIC: 2411 Logging camps & contractors

Muncy Valley
Sullivan County

(G-11843)
THERMALBLADE LLC (PA)
775 Christian Camp Rd (17758-5297)
PHONE..................................570 995-1425
Harry Kleinsasser, *Mng Member*
Sheryl Laubscher, *Manager*
EMP: 3
SALES (est): 407.6K **Privately Held**
SIC: 3714 Windshield wiper systems, motor vehicle

Munhall
Allegheny County

(G-11844)
MARCEGAGLIA USA INC
1001 E Waterfront Dr (15120-1098)
PHONE..................................412 462-2185
Antonio Marcegaglia, *CEO*
Francesco Tabarrini, *President*
David Cornelius, *President*
Ferdinando Saglio, *COO*
Tammy Bodzenski, *Purch Agent*
◆ EMP: 135
SQ FT: 350,000

SALES (est): 89.7MM
SALES (corp-wide): 27.4MM **Privately Held**
WEB: www.marcegaglia-usa.com
SIC: 3317 3312 Welded pipe & tubes; iron & steel: galvanized, pipes, plates, sheets, etc.; stainless steel
HQ: Marcegaglia Specialties Spa
Via Bresciani 16
Gazoldo Degli Ippoliti MN 46040
037 668-51

Murrysville
Westmoreland County

(G-11845)
AEGIS SOFTWARE CORPORATION
3840 Beatty Ct (15668-1829)
PHONE..................................724 325-5595
Dominic Barnabei, *President*
John Gribik, *Vice Pres*
EMP: 6
SQ FT: 1,200
SALES: 2MM **Privately Held**
SIC: 7372 8711 Publishers' computer software; engineering services

(G-11846)
AMERAQUICK INC
3821 Harwick Ct (15668-1025)
PHONE..................................724 733-5906
Alan Sloan, *President*
EMP: 4
SALES (est): 200K **Privately Held**
SIC: 3993 Signs & advertising specialties

(G-11847)
AMERAQUICK SIGN SYSTEMS
3821 Harwick Ct (15668-1025)
PHONE..................................724 733-5906
Alan Sloan, *President*
Stanley Stavitz, *Principal*
EMP: 4
SALES (est): 200K **Privately Held**
WEB: www.ameraquick.com
SIC: 3993 Signs, not made in custom sign painting shops

(G-11848)
BONDI PRINTING CO INC
3975 William Penn Hwy (15668-1857)
PHONE..................................724 327-6022
August Bondi, *President*
Edana Bondi, *Treasurer*
EMP: 14
SQ FT: 5,500
SALES (est): 2.4MM **Privately Held**
WEB: www.bondiprinting.com
SIC: 2752 Commercial printing, offset

(G-11849)
CELLAR TECH LLC
4530 William Penn Hwy (15668-2002)
PHONE..................................724 519-2139
James Rose, *Principal*
Lynn Rose,
EMP: 25 EST: 2015
SALES (est): 1.3MM **Privately Held**
SIC: 1389 Well logging

(G-11850)
COMPUNETICS INC
Flex Circuits
4060 Norbatrol Ct (15668-1821)
PHONE..................................724 519-4773
EMP: 23
SALES (corp-wide): 19.6MM **Privately Held**
SIC: 3672 Printed circuit boards
PA: Compunetics Inc.
700 Seco Rd Ste 5
Monroeville PA 15146
412 373-8110

(G-11851)
FRANKLIN PENN PUBLISHING CO
Also Called: Penn Trafford News
4021 Old William Penn Hwy (15668-1846)
PHONE..................................724 327-3471
Georgia Boring, *President*
Linda Lyman, *President*

Charlene Word, *Corp Secy*
EMP: 10
SALES (est): 583.3K **Privately Held**
SIC: 2711 Job printing & newspaper publishing combined; newspapers: publishing only, not printed on site

(G-11852)
GRAND OPENINGS INC
3075 Carson Ave (15668-1814)
PHONE..................................724 325-2029
Keith McCauley, *President*
EMP: 7
SQ FT: 6,000
SALES: 720K **Privately Held**
SIC: 3089 Window frames & sash, plastic

(G-11853)
IMAGEWEAR INTERNATIONAL INC
4491 Hilty Rd (15668-9315)
PHONE..................................724 335-2425
Eric Nonnenberg, *President*
EMP: 4
SQ FT: 5,000
SALES (est): 1MM **Privately Held**
SIC: 5136 2389 Uniforms, men's & boys'; uniforms & vestments

(G-11854)
KABINET KONCEPTS INC
4482 William Penn Hwy (15668-1900)
PHONE..................................724 327-7737
James Metar, *President*
EMP: 5
SQ FT: 9,000
SALES: 750K **Privately Held**
SIC: 5211 2434 Cabinets, kitchen; wood kitchen cabinets

(G-11855)
LOG CABIN EMBROIDERY INC
3941 William Penn Hwy # 3 (15668-1866)
PHONE..................................724 327-5929
Deborah Osicowicz, *Corp Secy*
EMP: 5
SQ FT: 1,100
SALES: 400K **Privately Held**
WEB: www.logcabinembroidery.com
SIC: 2395 2396 5699 Embroidery & art needlework; screen printing on fabric articles; uniforms

(G-11856)
MACHINING SOLUTIONS
4000 Saltsburg Rd (15668-9774)
PHONE..................................412 798-6590
Mike Mc Cleary, *Managing Prtnr*
Patty Kriss, *Sales Staff*
EMP: 5
SALES (est): 656.1K **Privately Held**
WEB: www.machiningsolutionsllc.com
SIC: 3599 Machine shop, jobbing & repair

(G-11857)
MARKRAFT COMPANY
104 Artman Ln (15668-9726)
PHONE..................................724 733-3654
Mark Hinebaugh, *Owner*
EMP: 4
SALES (est): 399.8K **Privately Held**
SIC: 2599 2541 2431 Factory furniture & fixtures; bar, restaurant & cafeteria furniture; store & office display cases & fixtures; moldings & baseboards, ornamental & trim

(G-11858)
MSA SAFETY INCORPORATED
Also Called: MSA Worldwide
3880 Meadowbrook Rd (15668-1753)
PHONE..................................724 733-9100
Robert Bilger, *Manager*
EMP: 350
SALES (corp-wide): 1.3B **Publicly Held**
WEB: www.msanet.com
SIC: 3842 3648 3823 Personal safety equipment; miners' lamps; industrial instrmnts msrmnt display/control process variable
PA: Msa Safety Incorporated
1000 Cranberry Woods Dr
Cranberry Township PA 16066
724 776-8600

(G-11859)
MSA SAFETY INCORPORATED
Also Called: Mine Safety Appliance Company
3880 Meadowbrook Rd (15668-1753)
P.O. Box 428, Pittsburgh (15230-0428)
PHONE..................................724 733-9100
Hal Kerstein, *Branch Mgr*
EMP: 650
SALES (corp-wide): 1.3B **Publicly Held**
WEB: www.msanet.com
SIC: 5084 3842 3443 Safety equipment; surgical appliances & supplies; fabricated plate work (boiler shop)
PA: Msa Safety Incorporated
1000 Cranberry Woods Dr
Cranberry Township PA 16066
724 776-8600

(G-11860)
MURRYSVILLE AUTO LLC
Also Called: Choice Auto Sales
4765 Old William Penn Hwy (15668-2012)
PHONE..................................724 387-1607
Kirk Rettger, *Managing Prtnr*
Billy Harris, *Sales Staff*
Ray Murphy, *Sales Staff*
Corey E Bigley, *Manager*
EMP: 10
SALES: 10MM **Privately Held**
SIC: 3711 7542 Motor vehicles & car bodies; washing & polishing, automotive

(G-11861)
PITTSBURGH MEDICAL DEVICE
1008 Summer Ridge Ct (15668-8510)
PHONE..................................724 325-1869
Antonino Servelo, *CEO*
EMP: 10
SALES (est): 1.1MM **Privately Held**
SIC: 3845 Ultrasonic scanning devices, medical

(G-11862)
PROGRESSIVE DOOR CORPORATION
3075 Carson Ave (15668-1814)
PHONE..................................724 733-4636
William Polinski, *President*
EMP: 6
SQ FT: 2,500
SALES: 450K **Privately Held**
SIC: 2431 Doors & door parts & trim, wood

(G-11863)
R L SGATH MCHINING FABRICATION
1111 Spring Hill Rd (15668-2304)
PHONE..................................724 327-3895
Ronald Sagath, *President*
Ilene Sagath, *Treasurer*
EMP: 7
SQ FT: 5,000
SALES (est): 1.1MM **Privately Held**
SIC: 3599 Machine shop, jobbing & repair

(G-11864)
RESPIRONICS INC
1001 Murry Ridge Ln (15668-8550)
PHONE..................................724 733-0200
Jim Laikem, *President*
EMP: 500
SALES (corp-wide): 20.9B **Privately Held**
WEB: www.respironics.com
SIC: 3842 Surgical appliances & supplies
HQ: Respironics, Inc.
1001 Murry Ridge Ln
Murrysville PA 15668
724 387-5200

(G-11865)
RESPIRONICS INC (DH)
Also Called: Philips
1001 Murry Ridge Ln (15668-8550)
P.O. Box 405740, Atlanta GA (30384-5700)
PHONE..................................724 387-5200
Brent Shafer, *CEO*
Gerald E McGinnis, *Ch of Bd*
Pamela Dunlap, *President*
Dennis S Meteny, *Principal*
Craig B Reynolds, *Exec VP*
◆ **EMP:** 90

SALES (est): 1B
SALES (corp-wide): 20.9B **Privately Held**
WEB: www.respironics.com
SIC: 3641 3845 3841 3564 Electric light bulbs, complete; patient monitoring apparatus; surgical & medical instruments; blowers & fans; child day care services

(G-11866)
SIEMENS INDUSTRY INC
100 Sagamore Hill Rd (15668)
PHONE..................................724 733-2569
Dave Paleo, *Branch Mgr*
EMP: 106
SALES (corp-wide): 95B **Privately Held**
WEB: www.sea.siemens.com
SIC: 3625 Control equipment, electric
HQ: Siemens Industry, Inc.
1000 Deerfield Pkwy
Buffalo Grove IL 60089
800 743-6367

(G-11867)
SIGNS OF EXCELLENCE INC
4225 Old William Penn Hwy (15668-1948)
PHONE..................................724 325-7446
Joyce Kelsey, *President*
Scott Kelsey, *Managing Dir*
Ella McGhee, *Graphic Designe*
EMP: 5
SALES: 150K **Privately Held**
SIC: 3993 Signs, not made in custom sign painting shops

(G-11868)
SINGERMAN LABORATORIES
4091 Saltsburg Rd Ste F (15668-8524)
PHONE..................................412 798-0447
Patrick Mahoney, *Owner*
EMP: 5
SALES (est): 480.5K **Privately Held**
WEB: www.ecomade.com
SIC: 2842 Rust removers; specialty cleaning preparations

(G-11869)
TARP AMERICA INC
588 State Route 380 (15668-2200)
PHONE..................................724 339-4771
Trevor Young, *President*
Frank Gazzo, *Vice Pres*
Melinda Young, *Treasurer*
EMP: 5
SQ FT: 4,400
SALES (est): 923.6K **Privately Held**
SIC: 3081 2394 5199 Plastic film & sheet; tarpaulins, fabric: made from purchased materials; tarpaulins

(G-11870)
THERMAL INDUSTRIES INC (DH)
Also Called: Aba Thermal Windows & Doors
3700 Haney Ct (15668-1711)
PHONE..................................724 325-6100
David Rascoe, *President*
Evan Kaffenes, *Vice Pres*
Arthur Poland, *Vice Pres*
Todd Rascoe, *Vice Pres*
EMP: 35 **EST:** 1960
SQ FT: 20,000
SALES (est): 48.3MM
SALES (corp-wide): 2B **Publicly Held**
WEB: www.thermalindustries.com
SIC: 2431 Windows & window parts & trim, wood
HQ: Atrium Windows And Doors, Inc.
959 Profit Dr
Dallas TX 75247
214 583-1840

(G-11871)
THERMAL WINDOWS & DOORS LLC
3700 Haney Ct (15668-1711)
PHONE..................................724 325-6100
Gary Acinapura, *CEO*
EMP: 7 **EST:** 2015
SALES (est): 95.8K **Privately Held**
SIC: 2431 Windows & window parts & trim, wood

Myerstown
Lebanon County

(G-11872)
A & B STEELWORKS LLC
464 E Main Ave (17067-2225)
PHONE..................................717 823-8599
David P Levach,
EMP: 11 **EST:** 2008
SQ FT: 2,000
SALES: 1MM **Privately Held**
SIC: 1799 3315 Insulation of pipes & boilers; welding on site; welded steel wire fabric

(G-11873)
A & H INDUSTRIES INC
837 S Railroad St (17067-1526)
P.O. Box 223 (17067-0223)
PHONE..................................717 866-7591
Frederick Hoffman, *President*
Beryl Hoffman, *Vice Pres*
EMP: 35 **EST:** 1976
SQ FT: 14,000
SALES (est): 5.9MM **Privately Held**
WEB: www.ahtools.com
SIC: 3545 3544 Cutting tools for machine tools; special dies, tools, jigs & fixtures

(G-11874)
BACK 2 EARTH RECYCLING LLC
213 N Locust St (17067-1228)
PHONE..................................717 389-6591
EMP: 5 **EST:** 2012
SALES (est): 197.1K **Privately Held**
SIC: 3089 Plastic processing

(G-11875)
BAYER CORPORATION
400 W Stoever Ave (17067-1421)
PHONE..................................717 866-2141
John Oneill, *Principal*
Dan Mueller, *Mfg Staff*
Joseph Cruz, *Engineer*
Gisselle Talley, *Engineer*
Micahel Mazur, *Project Engr*
EMP: 750
SALES (corp-wide): 45.3B **Privately Held**
SIC: 2834 Pharmaceutical preparations
HQ: Bayer Corporation
100 Bayer Rd Bldg 14
Pittsburgh PA 15205
412 777-2000

(G-11876)
BAYER HEALTHCARE LLC
400 W Stoever Ave (17067-1421)
PHONE..................................717 866-2141
Kevin Showalter, *Branch Mgr*
EMP: 350
SALES (corp-wide): 45.3B **Privately Held**
SIC: 2834 Pharmaceutical preparations
HQ: Bayer Healthcare Llc
100 Bayer Blvd
Whippany NJ 07981
862 404-3000

(G-11877)
BMC EAST LLC
Also Called: Charles Loose & Son
50 W Stoever Ave (17067-1533)
PHONE..................................717 866-2167
Stephen Alley, *Manager*
EMP: 50 **Publicly Held**
WEB: www.stockbuildingsupply.com
SIC: 5211 5031 2431 Lumber & other building materials; lumber, plywood & millwork; millwork
HQ: Bmc East, Llc
8020 Arco Corp Dr Ste 400
Raleigh NC 27617
919 431-1000

(G-11878)
BURKHOLDER S MOTOR REPAIR
115 Martin Rd (17067-2238)
PHONE..................................717 866-9724
Lowell Burkholder,
EMP: 5

SALES: 1MM **Privately Held**
SIC: 7629 7539 7694 Electrical repair shops; frame & front end repair services; electric motor repair

(G-11879)
CHESTNUT ACRES SPECIALTY
156 W Reistville Rd (17067-3047)
PHONE..................................717 949-2875
EMP: 3
SALES (est): 81K **Privately Held**
SIC: 2099 Cole slaw, in bulk

(G-11880)
CORNERSTONE WOODWORKS LLC
101 N Ramona Rd (17067-2152)
PHONE..................................717 866-0230
EMP: 4
SALES (est): 206.1K **Privately Held**
SIC: 2431 Millwork

(G-11881)
COUNTRY CUPOLA LTD (PA)
53 N Ramona Rd (17067-2150)
P.O. Box 349 (17067-0349)
PHONE..................................717 866-8801
Kevin Martin, *Owner*
EMP: 3
SQ FT: 8,000
SALES (est): 1MM **Privately Held**
WEB: www.cupola.ca
SIC: 2499 Decorative wood & woodwork

(G-11882)
DUTCH WOOD LLC
1317 Hilltop Rd (17067-1760)
PHONE..................................717 933-5133
Irvin High,
Jason High,
Lamar High,
EMP: 9
SALES (est): 850.3K **Privately Held**
SIC: 2434 Wood kitchen cabinets

(G-11883)
EASTCOAST CUTTER INC
1940 Camp Swatara Rd (17067-1820)
PHONE..................................717 933-5566
Bill Achenbach, *President*
EMP: 5
SQ FT: 5,000
SALES (est): 1MM **Privately Held**
SIC: 3545 Cutting tools for machine tools

(G-11884)
ELK PREMIUM BUILDING PRODUCTS
401 Weavertown Rd (17067-2401)
P.O. Box 228 (17067-0228)
PHONE..................................717 866-8300
Hank Hummel, *Manager*
EMP: 3
SALES (corp-wide): 2.7B **Privately Held**
SIC: 2952 Roofing materials
HQ: Elk Premium Building Products, Inc
14911 Quorum Dr Ste 600
Dallas TX 75254
972 851-0400

(G-11885)
FARMER BOY AG INC (PA)
50 W Stoever Ave (17067-1533)
PHONE..................................717 866-7565
Dale W Martin, *President*
Leonard R Martin, *Corp Secy*
Dean R Weaver, *Vice Pres*
Jared Moyer, *Sales Staff*
Chad Nolen, *Sales Staff*
▲ **EMP:** 59
SALES (est): 35.9MM **Privately Held**
WEB: www.farmerboyag.com
SIC: 5083 1711 3523 3448 Farm & garden machinery; plumbing, heating, air-conditioning contractors; farm machinery & equipment; prefabricated metal buildings; prefabricated wood buildings; non-residential construction

(G-11886)
HARNISH PRODUCTION MACHINE
360 King St (17067-2525)
P.O. Box 261 (17067-0261)
PHONE..................................717 866-4562

Bryan Harnish, *President*
Susan Harnish, *Corp Secy*
EMP: 7
SQ FT: 6,500
SALES (est): 550K **Privately Held**
SIC: 3599 Machine shop, jobbing & repair

(G-11887)
HORST SIGNS
400 W Lincoln Ave (17067-2327)
PHONE..................................717 866-8899
Howard Horst, *Owner*
EMP: 15
SALES (est): 1.4MM **Privately Held**
SIC: 3993 Signs, not made in custom sign painting shops

(G-11888)
JRM PALLETS INC
212 E Mill Ave (17067-2402)
PHONE..................................717 926-6812
Jacob I Mays, *Principal*
EMP: 4 **EST:** 2010
SALES (est): 491K **Privately Held**
SIC: 2448 Pallets, wood; pallets, wood & wood with metal

(G-11889)
KENNEDYS POWDER COATING
410 E Lincoln Ave (17067-2213)
PHONE..................................717 866-6747
Terry Kennedy, *Owner*
EMP: 12
SQ FT: 20,000
SALES: 1MM **Privately Held**
WEB: www.kennedypowdercoating.com
SIC: 3523 Tractors, farm

(G-11890)
KEYSTONE INDUSTRIES
52 King St (17067-2519)
PHONE..................................717 866-7571
Michael Prozzillo, *Vice Pres*
Derek J Keene, *Vice Pres*
Monica Rocco, *Vice Pres*
▲ **EMP:** 18
SALES (est): 2.4MM **Privately Held**
SIC: 3999 Beekeepers' supplies

(G-11891)
LEATHERSMITH INC
417 Frystown Rd (17067-1923)
PHONE..................................717 933-8084
Shaun Luther, *President*
EMP: 7
SQ FT: 20,000
SALES: 1MM **Privately Held**
WEB: www.leathersmithinc.com
SIC: 3172 2394 Personal leather goods; canvas & related products

(G-11892)
LITTLE MOUNTAIN PRINTING
Also Called: Fish Wrapper, The
234 E Rosebud Rd (17067-1625)
PHONE..................................717 933-8091
Merle Gingrich, *Owner*
Ted Ansel, *Sales Staff*
Anthony Martin, *Consultant*
Karen Gingrich, *Admin Secy*
Ian Brownlie, *Graphic Designe*
EMP: 18
SQ FT: 2,500
SALES: 2MM **Privately Held**
WEB: www.littlemountainprinting.com
SIC: 2752 Commercial printing, offset

(G-11893)
MARTINS WOOD PRODUCTS LLC
Also Called: Keystone Collections
650 Houtztown Rd (17067-2196)
PHONE..................................717 933-5115
James Martin,
Marvin Martin,
EMP: 42
SQ FT: 8,000
SALES (est): 5.9MM **Privately Held**
WEB: www.martinswood.com
SIC: 2434 2511 Wood kitchen cabinets; wood household furniture

(G-11894)
MYERSTOWN SHEDS AND FENCING
694 E Lincoln Ave (17067-2217)
PHONE..................................717 866-7015
Claire Morton, *Partner*
Shelden Beicher, *Partner*
EMP: 5
SALES (est): 677.8K **Privately Held**
SIC: 2452 5722 Prefabricated wood buildings; vacuum cleaners

(G-11895)
OLDE MILL CABINET CO
103 E Main Ave (17067-1118)
PHONE..................................717 866-6504
Pammy Landis, *Partner*
EMP: 9
SQ FT: 5,000
SALES (est): 944K **Privately Held**
WEB: www.oldemillkitchens.com
SIC: 2434 5251 Wood kitchen cabinets; hardware

(G-11896)
RELIGIOUS THEOLOGICAL ABSTRACT
100 W Park Ave (17067-1250)
P.O. Box 215 (17067-0215)
PHONE..................................717 866-6734
William Sailer, *President*
Harold Scanlin, *Vice Pres*
EMP: 4
SALES: 119.6K **Privately Held**
WEB: www.rtabst.org
SIC: 2721 Trade journals: publishing only, not printed on site

(G-11897)
RICHARD HURST
Also Called: Hurst Engineering
516 S Cherry St (17067-1509)
PHONE..................................717 866-2343
Richard Hurst, *Owner*
EMP: 3
SALES: 225K **Privately Held**
WEB: www.hurstengineering.com
SIC: 2434 Wood kitchen cabinets

(G-11898)
SPOHN PERFORMANCE INC
494 E Lincoln Ave (17067-2213)
PHONE..................................717 866-6033
Steven Spohn, *President*
Gordon Spohn, *Vice Pres*
▲ **EMP:** 7
SQ FT: 9,000
SALES (est): 630K **Privately Held**
WEB: www.spohn.net
SIC: 3714 Motor vehicle parts & accessories

Nanticoke
Luzerne County

(G-11899)
COON INDUSTRIES INC
30 Simon St (18634-1321)
PHONE..................................570 735-6852
Don Galli, *Manager*
EMP: 8
SALES (corp-wide): 10MM **Privately Held**
WEB: www.coonindustries.com
SIC: 3273 Ready-mixed concrete
PA: Coon Industries, Inc.
117 Armstrong Rd
Pittston PA
570 654-0211

(G-11900)
NEWPORT AGGREGATE INC
31 N Market St (18634-1410)
PHONE..................................570 736-6612
John Oliver, *Manager*
EMP: 3
SALES (est): 335.1K **Privately Held**
SIC: 1411 Onyx marble, dimension-quarrying

(G-11901)
PENN CIGAR MACHINES INC (PA)
1 Line St (18634-3132)
P.O. Box 149 (18634-0149)
PHONE..................................570 740-1112
Niranjan Gupta, *President*
Namita D Gupta, *Vice Pres*
Pravesh Gupta, *Admin Sec*
▼ **EMP:** 25
SQ FT: 70,000
SALES (est): 4.5MM **Privately Held**
WEB: www.penncigar.com
SIC: 3599 Machine shop, jobbing & repair

(G-11902)
REILLY PLATING COMPANY INC
Also Called: Reilly Finishing Technologies
130 Alden Rd (18634-2198)
PHONE..................................570 735-7777
Joseph J Reilly, *President*
Charles M Reilly, *Chairman*
Florence Reilly, *Corp Secy*
Ralph Emmett, *Vice Pres*
James Reilly, *Vice Pres*
EMP: 95
SALES (est): 14.9MM **Privately Held**
WEB: www.reillyfinishing.com
SIC: 3471 3599 7389 Plating of metals or formed products; machine & other job shop work;

(G-11903)
STELLAR MACHINE INCORPORATED
250 Railroad St (18634-1734)
PHONE..................................570 718-1733
Cory Wasiakowski, *President*
David Morgan, *President*
John Tomasura, *Admin Sec*
EMP: 18
SQ FT: 20,000
SALES: 2.2MM **Privately Held**
SIC: 3469 3499 3599 Machine parts, stamped or pressed metal; furniture parts, metal; custom machinery

(G-11904)
TUNEFLY LLC
371 State St (18634-2511)
PHONE..................................570 392-9239
Elizabeth Klein, *Partner*
Samuel O'Connell, *Partner*
EMP: 3 **EST:** 2016
SALES (est): 86K **Privately Held**
SIC: 7372 Application computer software

Nanty Glo
Cambria County

(G-11905)
CAMPBELL OIL LLC
1021 Wagner St (15943-1449)
PHONE..................................814 749-0002
Jim Campbell, *Principal*
EMP: 4
SALES (est): 325K **Privately Held**
SIC: 1311 Crude petroleum & natural gas

(G-11906)
MOONSHINE MINE DISTILLERY INC
2046 Cardiff Rd (15943-3909)
PHONE..................................814 749-3038
Michael Cocho, *Principal*
EMP: 3
SALES (est): 121.5K **Privately Held**
SIC: 2085 Distilled & blended liquors

Narberth
Montgomery County

(G-11907)
ANSA ELECTRIC VEHICLES LLC
209 Avon Rd (19072-2307)
PHONE..................................610 955-5686
Wayne S Morrison,
EMP: 5

SALES (est): 292K **Privately Held**
SIC: 3714 Motor vehicle parts & accessories

(G-11908)
AU FOURNIL INC
234 Woodbine Ave (19072-1930)
PHONE..................................610 664-0235
Stephane Wojtowiz, *Owner*
EMP: 8
SALES (est): 454.8K **Privately Held**
SIC: 5149 2051 Bakery products; croissants, except frozen

(G-11909)
BRAVE SPIRITS LLC
229 Forrest Ave (19072-1804)
PHONE..................................610 453-3917
David Fox,
EMP: 1
SALES: 15MM **Privately Held**
SIC: 2085 Neutral spirits, except fruit

(G-11910)
EVERIGHT POSITION TECH CORP
114 Forrest Ave Ste 209 (19072-2218)
PHONE..................................856 727-9500
George David Jr, *President*
Leonard Goldman, *CFO*
EMP: 4
SQ FT: 1,000
SALES (est): 1.1MM **Privately Held**
WEB: www.evrtp.com
SIC: 3829 Measuring & controlling devices

(G-11911)
INFOMAT ASSOCIATES INC
Also Called: All So Sites & Bites
215 Forrest Ave (19072-1804)
PHONE..................................610 668-8306
EMP: 3
SALES (est): 170K **Privately Held**
SIC: 2741 7389 Misc Publishing Business Services

(G-11912)
SOLUTION SYSTEMS INC
Also Called: Ssi
201 Sabine Ave Ste 500 (19072-1635)
PHONE..................................610 668-4620
Neil L Kleeman, *President*
Rochelle Kleeman, *Corp Secy*
Scott Kleeman, *Vice Pres*
EMP: 11 **EST:** 1981
SQ FT: 3,700
SALES: 1MM **Privately Held**
WEB: www.solsys.com
SIC: 7374 7372 Data processing & preparation; prepackaged software

(G-11913)
TODD CURYTO
120 Merion Ave (19072-2415)
PHONE..................................215 906-8097
Todd Curyto, *Principal*
EMP: 3
SALES (est): 195.2K **Privately Held**
SIC: 2024 Ices, flavored (frozen dessert)

(G-11914)
VENUS NAIL & SPA
219 Haverford Ave (19072-2210)
PHONE..................................610 660-6180
Jung MI Yun, *Principal*
EMP: 4
SALES (est): 219.6K **Privately Held**
SIC: 2844 Manicure preparations

Narvon
Lancaster County

(G-11915)
A & L IRON WORKS LLC
624 Buchland Rd (17555-9633)
PHONE..................................717 768-0705
Lloyd Beiler, *Mng Member*
Aaron K Beiler,
EMP: 3
SALES (est): 280K **Privately Held**
SIC: 3449 7389 Miscellaneous metalwork;

G E O G R A P H I C

(G-11916)
A+ PACKAGING
2262 Laurel Ridge Rd (17555-9761)
PHONE..................................610 864-1758
Dean Grigsby, *President*
EMP: 3
SALES (est): 148.6K Privately Held
SIC: 2449 Wood containers

(G-11917)
BROOKSIDE WOODWORKS
615 Red Hill Rd (17555-9685)
PHONE..................................717 768-0241
EMP: 3 EST: 2008
SALES (est): 216.2K Privately Held
SIC: 2431 Millwork

(G-11918)
CHURCHTOWNE CABINETRY
281 Gehman Rd (17555-9701)
PHONE..................................717 354-6682
Ben Stoltzfus, *Principal*
EMP: 4
SALES (est): 234.1K Privately Held
SIC: 2434 Wood kitchen cabinets

(G-11919)
CONESTOGA VALLEY CSTM KITCHENS
2042 Turkey Hill Rd (17555-9780)
PHONE..................................717 445-5415
Fax: 717 445-6849
EMP: 20
SQ FT: 12,000
SALES (est): 2MM Privately Held
SIC: 2434 2521 2517 Manufacturers Of Wooden Kitchen Cabinet Wooden Office Furniture And Wooden Television Or Radio Cabinets

(G-11920)
DILWORTH MANUFACTURING CO
6051 Division Hwy (17555-9223)
P.O. Box 158, Honey Brook (19344-0158)
PHONE..................................717 354-8956
William P Dilworth, *President*
Steven Dilworth, *Vice Pres*
EMP: 5
SQ FT: 4,800
SALES (est): 500K Privately Held
WEB: www.windowbubble.com
SIC: 3083 Window sheeting, plastic

(G-11921)
ENVIROSAFE SERVICES OF OHIO
Narvon Products Div
1046 Narvon Rd (17555-9604)
PHONE..................................717 354-1025
EMP: 12 Privately Held
SIC: 3297 Clay Mining Refractory
HQ: Envirosafe Services Of Ohio Inc
876 Otter Creek Rd
Oregon OH 43616
419 698-3500

(G-11922)
H&K GROUP INC
Silver Hill Quarries Div
470 Yellow Hill Rd (17555-9338)
PHONE..................................717 445-0961
Keith Marting, *Facilities Mgr*
Keith Martin, *Branch Mgr*
EMP: 20
SQ FT: 1,000
SALES (corp-wide): 71.6MM Privately Held
WEB: www.hkgroup.com
SIC: 1411 Trap rock, dimension-quarrying
PA: H&K Group, Inc.
2052 Lucon Rd
Skippack PA 19474
610 584-8500

(G-11923)
LANCHESTER WOODWORKING
935 Churchtown Rd (17555-9617)
PHONE..................................717 355-2184
Jacob Stoltzsus, *Partner*
EMP: 6
SALES (est): 550K Privately Held
SIC: 2499 Decorative wood & woodwork

(G-11924)
NARVON CONSTRUCTION LLC
247 S Pool Forge Rd (17555-9580)
PHONE..................................717 989-2026
Ivan K Fisher, *Principal*
EMP: 18
SALES (est): 5.2MM Privately Held
SIC: 3444 7532 Metal roofing & roof drainage equipment; exterior repair services

(G-11925)
SHADY GROVE WOODWORKING
622 Buchland Rd (17555)
PHONE..................................610 273-7038
Benuel Lapp, *Principal*
EMP: 4 EST: 2010
SALES (est): 360.5K Privately Held
SIC: 2431 Millwork

(G-11926)
SHIRK MANUFACTURING
Also Called: Shirk AG Supply
2100 Turkey Hill Rd (17555-9373)
PHONE..................................717 445-9353
Kenneth Shirk, *Owner*
Janet Shirk, *Owner*
EMP: 3
SQ FT: 2,832
SALES: 800K Privately Held
SIC: 3315 Steel wire & related products

(G-11927)
SMUCKERS HARNESS SHOP INC
2016 Main St (17555-9565)
PHONE..................................717 445-5956
Moses Smucker, *President*
Susie Smucker, *Corp Secy*
▲ EMP: 16 EST: 1962
SQ FT: 12,000
SALES (est): 1.3MM Privately Held
WEB: www.smuckersharness.com
SIC: 3199 7699 5941 5191 Equestrian related leather articles; harness repair shop; saddlery & equestrian equipment; equestrian equipment; musical instruments

(G-11928)
SUNSET CREATIONS
203 Churchtown Rd (17555-9658)
PHONE..................................717 768-7663
Sam Blank, *Owner*
EMP: 3
SALES (est): 252.7K Privately Held
SIC: 3441 Fabricated structural metal

(G-11929)
SWEET WATER WOODWORKS LLC
6430 Emery Rd (17555-9556)
PHONE..................................610 273-1270
Jonas Stoltzfus,
Susie Stoltzfus,
EMP: 8 EST: 2010
SALES (est): 35.1K Privately Held
SIC: 2431 Millwork

(G-11930)
TJ MANUFACTURING LLC
10313 Plank Rd (17555)
PHONE..................................717 575-0675
EMP: 4
SALES (est): 498.7K Privately Held
SIC: 3523 Farm machinery & equipment

(G-11931)
WANNER ROAD WOODCRAFT
6011 Wanner Rd (17555-9648)
PHONE..................................717 768-0207
Ervin Stoltzfus, *Partner*
EMP: 4 EST: 1992
SQ FT: 2,061
SALES (est): 205.2K Privately Held
SIC: 2511 Lawn furniture: wood

(G-11932)
WEAVERLINE LLC
180 Boot Jack Rd (17555-9705)
PHONE..................................717 445-6724
Delton Leid, *Accounts Mgr*
Frank Weaver,
▲ EMP: 10 EST: 1965
SQ FT: 16,000

SALES (est): 2.3MM Privately Held
SIC: 3523 Farm machinery & equipment

Natrona Heights
Allegheny County

(G-11933)
ATI FLAT RLLED PDTS HLDNGS LLC
1300 Pacific Ave (15065-1100)
PHONE..................................800 323-1240
EMP: 9
SALES (corp-wide): 1.2MM Privately Held
WEB: www.alleghenyludlum.com
SIC: 5051 3312 Metals service centers & offices; blast furnace & related products
PA: Ati Flat Rolled Products Holdings, Llc
1000 Six Ppg Pl
Pittsburgh PA 15222
412 394-3047

(G-11934)
BAR MACHINING
9 Kuhnert St (15065-2219)
PHONE..................................724 226-1050
Bruce Rusiewicz, *Owner*
EMP: 5
SQ FT: 7,000
SALES (est): 485.3K Privately Held
SIC: 3599 Machine shop, jobbing & repair

(G-11935)
BIAGIO SCHIANO DI COLA DEBORA
Also Called: J & S Pizza
1828 Union Ave (15065-2201)
PHONE..................................724 224-9906
Debora Malvone, *Owner*
EMP: 25
SALES (est): 146.5K Privately Held
SIC: 2086 Soft drinks: packaged in cans, bottles, etc.

(G-11936)
BRUCE BANNING
Also Called: Banning Specialty Co
1546 Saxonburg Rd (15065-1842)
PHONE..................................724 226-0818
Bruce Banning, *Owner*
EMP: 3
SALES (est): 283.6K Privately Held
WEB: www.hightempcoatings.com
SIC: 2295 Metallizing of fabrics

(G-11937)
C&G ARMS LLC
Also Called: C&G Holsters
160 York Dr (15065-1946)
PHONE..................................724 858-2856
Christopher J Burns,
EMP: 4
SALES: 72K Privately Held
SIC: 3199 7997 5941 7389 Holsters, leather; gun club, membership; firearms;

(G-11938)
DLUBAK FABRICATION INC
1487 Saxonburg Rd (15065-1840)
PHONE..................................724 224-5887
James Dlubak, *President*
James E Dlubak, *Admin Sec*
EMP: 17 EST: 1998
SALES (est): 2MM Privately Held
SIC: 3498 Tube fabricating (contract bending & shaping)

(G-11939)
DLUBAK GLASS COMPANY (PA)
1600 Saxonburg Rd (15065-1801)
PHONE..................................724 226-1991
Dave Dlubak, *President*
Mike Muta, *Opers Mgr*
Deb Carnathan, *Manager*
▼ EMP: 11
SQ FT: 20,000
SALES (est): 4MM Privately Held
SIC: 3229 Pressed & blown glass

(G-11940)
DLUBAK GLASS COMPANY
1487 Saxonburg Rd (15065-1840)
PHONE..................................724 224-5887

Jim Dlubak, *Branch Mgr*
EMP: 11
SALES (corp-wide): 4MM Privately Held
SIC: 3229 Pressed & blown glass
PA: Dlubak Glass Company
1600 Saxonburg Rd
Natrona Heights PA 15065
724 226-1991

(G-11941)
ELECTRONIC PROTOTYPE DEV INC
Also Called: Epd Electronics
5 Acee Dr (15065-9700)
PHONE..................................412 767-4111
James Sullivan, *President*
Ellen Sullivan, *Corp Secy*
Nancy Meinert, *Purchasing*
EMP: 22
SQ FT: 10,000
SALES (est): 5.3MM Privately Held
SIC: 8711 3679 8731 3672 Electrical or electronic engineering; electronic circuits; electronic research; printed circuit boards

(G-11942)
ELECTRONIC TECH SYSTEMS INC
Also Called: Etsi
2 Acee Dr (15065-9700)
PHONE..................................724 295-6000
Ron Walko, *President*
Gerald Koch, *Vice Pres*
William Fluhrer, *Treasurer*
EMP: 93
SQ FT: 45,000
SALES: 18MM
SALES (corp-wide): 34.3B Privately Held
SIC: 3823 5085 7699 8742 Industrial instrmnts msrmnt display/control process variable; industrial supplies; industrial equipment services; management consulting services
HQ: Abb Asea Brown Boveri Ltd
Affolternstrasse 44
ZUrich ZH 8050
433 177-111

(G-11943)
GENERAL PRESS CORPORATION (PA)
110 Allegheny Dr (15065-1902)
P.O. Box 316 (15065-0316)
PHONE..................................724 224-3500
Terry L Conroy, *Principal*
Scott Poorbaugh, *Vice Pres*
David Wolffe, *VP Sales*
Dave Wolff, *Chief Mktg Ofcr*
Connie Vickroy, *Marketing Staff*
▲ EMP: 50 EST: 1937
SQ FT: 60,000
SALES: 6.3MM Privately Held
WEB: www.generalpress.com
SIC: 2752 2759 Commercial printing, offset; commercial printing

(G-11944)
JASON A KREINBROOK
1117 Carlisle St (15065-1017)
PHONE..................................724 493-6202
Jason A Kreinbrook, *Principal*
EMP: 4
SALES (est): 302.3K Privately Held
SIC: 2951 Paving blocks

(G-11945)
JV MANUFACTURING CO INC
1603 Burtner Rd (15065-1541)
PHONE..................................724 224-1704
Alan M Vecchi, *President*
Richard C Celecki, *Corp Secy*
Sam Gruber, *Vice Pres*
▲ EMP: 90
SQ FT: 43,000
SALES (est): 25.7MM Privately Held
WEB: www.jvmfgco.com
SIC: 3545 3544 Precision measuring tools; special dies & tools

(G-11946)
METPLAS INC
3 Acee Dr (15065-9736)
PHONE..................................724 295-5200
Russell E Finsness, *President*
Russ Garrett, *Vice Pres*

David Snider, *QC Dir*
Karen Conroy, *Sales Mgr*
Audrey Messer, *Accounts Mgr*
EMP: 60
SQ FT: 24,600
SALES: 8.5MM **Privately Held**
WEB: www.metplas.com
SIC: 3083 3443 Laminated plastics plate
& sheet; fabricated plate work (boiler
shop)

(G-11947)
NATRONA BOTTLING WORKS
INC
Also Called: Natrona Bottling Company
91 River Ave (15065-2672)
PHONE.................................724 224-9224
Vito Gerasole, *CEO*
John Nese, *President*
Noel Nese, *Vice Pres*
Gail Coffin, *Treasurer*
Mary Jane Zdila, *Admin Mgr*
EMP: 3
SQ FT: 5,000
SALES: 600K **Privately Held**
SIC: 2086 Soft drinks: packaged in cans,
bottles, etc.

(G-11948)
ONE SIGN INC
219 Chinkapin Dr (15065-1974)
PHONE.................................412 478-6809
Paul Kehren Jr, *President*
EMP: 5
SALES (est): 328.1K **Privately Held**
SIC: 3993 Signs & advertising specialties

(G-11949)
SUSINI SPECIALTY STEELS INC
Highlands Industr Park 11 Park Nds Indus-
trial (15065)
P.O. Box 232 (15065-0232)
PHONE.................................724 295-6511
Lloyd J Susini, *CEO*
Thomas Susini, *President*
Mary Faix, *Principal*
Karen Less, *Corp Secy*
▲ **EMP:** 10
SQ FT: 8,200
SALES (est): 1.6MM **Privately Held**
SIC: 3312 3356 Stainless steel; nickel &
nickel alloy pipe, plates, sheets, etc.

(G-11950)
TALK EXPRESS
1503 Donnellville Rd (15065-3001)
PHONE.................................412 977-1786
John Kammerdeiner, *Principal*
EMP: 5
SALES (est): 426.1K **Privately Held**
SIC: 3412 Metal barrels, drums & pails

Nazareth
Northampton County

(G-11951)
A & H SPORTSWEAR CO INC
50 Sycamore St (18064-1037)
PHONE.................................610 746-0922
Herman Waldman, *President*
John Duvall, *Branch Mgr*
EMP: 62
SQ FT: 15,000
SALES (corp-wide): 21.4MM **Privately**
Held
SIC: 2339 Bathing suits: women's, misses'
& juniors'
PA: A & H Sportswear Co., Inc.
610 Uhler Rd
Easton PA 18040
484 373-3600

(G-11952)
AIRLITE PLASTICS CO
2860 Bath Pike (18064-8898)
PHONE.................................610 759-0280
Robert Friedman, *Controller*
EMP: 56
SALES (corp-wide): 228.8MM **Privately**
Held
SIC: 3089 Injection molding of plastics

PA: Airlite Plastics Co.
6110 Abbott Dr
Omaha NE 68110
402 341-7300

(G-11953)
AMERICAN TUBE COMPANY INC
603 Gremar Rd (18064-8881)
PHONE.................................610 759-8700
William French, *President*
EMP: 70
SQ FT: 10,000
SALES (est): 7.8MM **Privately Held**
SIC: 3317 Steel pipe & tubes

(G-11954)
AMORE VINEYARDS AND
WINERY
6821 Steuben Rd (18064-9755)
PHONE.................................610 837-1683
Gregg Amore, *Principal*
EMP: 3
SALES (est): 178.5K **Privately Held**
SIC: 2084 Wines

(G-11955)
ANACONDA ENTERPRISES LLC
2104 Fieldview Dr (18064-8408)
PHONE.................................908 910-7150
Lanelle Mikolaitis, *Principal*
Paul Torres, *Mng Member*
EMP: 4
SALES (est): 500K **Privately Held**
SIC: 3648 Lighting equipment

(G-11956)
BATTERYTEST EQUIPMENT CO
539 S Main St (18064-2728)
PHONE.................................610 746-9449
Charles H Trillich, *President*
Mike Lewis, *Sales Staff*
Mary Anne Thear, *Office Mgr*
Jeffrey Quinto, *Admin Sec*
EMP: 4
SALES (est): 495K **Privately Held**
SIC: 3829 Measuring & controlling devices

(G-11957)
C F MARTIN & CO INC
Green St (18064)
PHONE.................................610 759-2837
Christian F Martin IV, *Ch of Bd*
EMP: 600
SALES (corp-wide): 130.5MM **Privately**
Held
WEB: www.mguitar.com
SIC: 3931 String instruments & parts
PA: C. F. Martin & Co., Inc.
510 Sycamore St
Nazareth PA 18064
610 759-2837

(G-11958)
CALANDRA CHEESE (PA)
Also Called: Calandra Salvatore
350 E Lawn Rd (18064-1116)
PHONE.................................610 759-2299
Salvatore Calandra, *Partner*
Charles Calandra, *Partner*
EMP: 7
SQ FT: 1,500
SALES (est): 707.3K **Privately Held**
WEB: www.calandracheese.com
SIC: 2022 5451 Natural cheese; cheese

(G-11959)
CARL AMORE GREENHOUSES
6761 Steuben Rd (18064-9752)
PHONE.................................610 837-7038
Charles Amore, *Owner*
EMP: 4
SQ FT: 4,320
SALES (est): 280.8K **Privately Held**
WEB: www.greenhousegroupy.com
SIC: 2441 Flats, wood: greenhouse

(G-11960)
D & A BUSINESS SERVICES INC
460 Spruce Ln (18064-9607)
PHONE.................................610 837-7748
Diana Fritchman, *President*
Al Fritchman, *Vice Pres*
EMP: 5
SALES (est): 320K **Privately Held**
SIC: 2741 Miscellaneous publishing

(G-11961)
DEFENSE TRAINING
SOLUTIONS LLC
3499 Gun Club Rd (18064-9721)
PHONE.................................484 240-1188
EMP: 3
SALES (est): 227.4K **Privately Held**
SIC: 3812 Defense systems & equipment

(G-11962)
EAGLE INDUSTRIAL
SOLUTIONS
2162 Michael Rd (18064-8715)
PHONE.................................610 509-8275
Joseph Boyle, *President*
EMP: 8
SALES (est): 464.4K **Privately Held**
SIC: 3448 Silos, metal

(G-11963)
ESSROC CORP
401 W Prospect St (18064-2727)
PHONE.................................610 759-4211
Larry Fritchman, *Branch Mgr*
EMP: 19
SALES (corp-wide): 20.6B **Privately Held**
SIC: 3272 3241 Concrete products; ma-
sonry cement
HQ: Essroc Corp.
3251 Bath Pike
Nazareth PA 18064
610 837-6725

(G-11964)
ESSROC CORP (DH)
3251 Bath Pike (18064-8999)
P.O. Box 21750, Lehigh Valley (18002-
1750)
PHONE.................................610 837-6725
Alex Car, *President*
Craig C Becker, *Senior VP*
Roberto Fedi, *Senior VP*
Francois M Perrin, *Senior VP*
Carol Lowry, *Vice Pres*
◆ **EMP:** 5
SQ FT: 25,000
SALES (est): 407.2MM
SALES (corp-wide): 20.6B **Privately Held**
SIC: 5032 3273 3241 Cement; ready-
mixed concrete; masonry cement
HQ: Italcementi Fabbriche Riunite Cemento
Spa Bergamo
Via Stezzano 87
Bergamo BG 24126
035 396-111

(G-11965)
EVERSON TESLA INC
614 Gremar Rd (18064-8788)
PHONE.................................610 746-1520
Gregory Naumovich, *President*
Douglas Hartman, *General Mgr*
Michael Begg, *Managing Dir*
James Ramage, *Chairman*
Richard Harper, *Maint Spvr*
◆ **EMP:** 80
SQ FT: 60,000
SALES (est): 24.2MM **Privately Held**
WEB: www.eversontesla.com
SIC: 3621 3679 3699 3674 Motors &
generators; electronic loads & power sup-
plies; electrical equipment & supplies;
semiconductors & related devices
HQ: Tesla Engineering Limited
Water Lane
Pulborough W SUSSEX RH20

(G-11966)
EXIGO MANUFACTURING INC
3486 Gun Club Rd (18064-9722)
PHONE.................................484 285-0200
Craig Traugher, *President*
Erik Zetterstrand, *Vice Pres*
Robert J Elbich, *Admin Sec*
EMP: 15
SQ FT: 3,600
SALES (est): 3.3MM **Privately Held**
SIC: 3494 Valves & pipe fittings

(G-11967)
FUEL CELL INC
5879 Sullivan Trl (18064-9254)
PHONE.................................610 759-0143
Dennis Einsalt, *President*
EMP: 25

SALES (est): 2.8MM **Privately Held**
SIC: 2869 5541 Fuels; gasoline service
stations

(G-11968)
G SCUDESE CONSULTANTS INC
373 Little Creek Dr (18064-8576)
PHONE.................................610 250-7800
Rosemarie Scudese, *President*
Munish Suri, *President*
▲ **EMP:** 15
SQ FT: 51,000
SALES (est): 4.4MM **Privately Held**
WEB: www.natplasticsinc.com
SIC: 2821 Plastics materials & resins

(G-11969)
GENESIS HEARING SYSTEMS
169 Spring St (18064-2631)
PHONE.................................610 759-0459
Dennis M Barket, *Principal*
EMP: 3
SALES (est): 205.9K **Privately Held**
SIC: 3842 Hearing aids

(G-11970)
GREGORY RACING
FABRICATIONS
Also Called: Racetronics
314 Industrial Park Rd (18064-2419)
PHONE.................................610 759-8217
John W Gregory, *President*
Jo Ann Gregory, *Treasurer*
EMP: 3
SQ FT: 1,000
SALES: 280K **Privately Held**
SIC: 7692 3711 3714 3715 Welding re-
pair; chassis, motor vehicle; transmis-
sions, motor vehicle; trailer bodies

(G-11971)
HANSON READY MIX INC (DH)
3251 Bath Pike (18064-8928)
PHONE.................................610 837-6725
Francesco Carantani, *CEO*
Kevin A Jones, *Treasurer*
EMP: 9
SALES (est): 29MM
SALES (corp-wide): 20.6B **Privately Held**
SIC: 3273 Ready-mixed concrete
HQ: Lehigh Hanson Ecc, Inc.
3251 Bath Pike
Nazareth PA 18064
610 837-6725

(G-11972)
J & P INCORPORATED
Also Called: J & P Men's & Boy's
68 S Main St Frnt (18064-2091)
PHONE.................................610 759-2378
Paul A Koklus, *President*
Jim Sakasits, *Principal*
James Sakasits, *Vice Pres*
Elizabeth Koklus, *Treasurer*
Constance Sakasits, *Admin Sec*
EMP: 6
SQ FT: 6,000
SALES (est): 868.5K **Privately Held**
WEB: www.jpincorporated.com
SIC: 3993 5611 Signs & advertising spe-
cialties; clothing accessories: men's &
boys'

(G-11973)
JEFFERY FAUST
Also Called: Schultz Water Systems
583 Nazareth Pike (18064-8401)
PHONE.................................610 759-1951
Jeffery Faust, *Owner*
EMP: 4
SQ FT: 5,400
SALES (est): 405.4K **Privately Held**
SIC: 3823 7692 Water quality monitoring
& control systems; welding repair

(G-11974)
JMC ENGRAVING INC
802 Colonna Ln (18064-9180)
PHONE.................................610 759-0140
Janice M Carlson, *President*
EMP: 5
SALES (est): 397.4K **Privately Held**
SIC: 7389 3089 Engraving service; en-
graving of plastic

(G-11975)
KRAEMER TEXTILES INC
Also Called: Kraemer Yarn Shop
240 S Main St (18064-2796)
P.O. Box 72 (18064-0072)
PHONE...................................610 759-4030
David T Schmidt, *CEO*
Victor R Schmidt, *Treasurer*
Janice Pintarich, *Office Mgr*
Arthur T Schmidt, *Admin Sec*
▲ EMP: 114 EST: 1907
SQ FT: 150,000
SALES (est): 15.9MM Privately Held
SIC: 2281 Manmade & synthetic fiber
yarns, spun; natural & animal fiber yarns,
spun

(G-11976)
LEHIGH CEMENT COMPANY LLC
3251 Bath Pike (18064-8928)
PHONE...................................610 837-6725
EMP: 3
SALES (corp-wide): 20.6B Privately Held
SIC: 3273 Ready-mixed concrete
HQ: Lehigh Cement Company Llc
300 E John Carpenter Fwy
Irving TX 75062
877 534-4442

(G-11977)
LEHIGH CEMENT COMPANY LLC
3938 Easton Nazareth Hwy (18064-3017)
PHONE...................................610 759-2222
Donald Levonian, *QC Mgr*
EMP: 5
SALES (corp-wide): 20.6B Privately Held
SIC: 3273 Ready-mixed concrete
HQ: Lehigh Cement Company Llc
300 E John Carpenter Fwy
Irving TX 75062
877 534-4442

(G-11978)
LEHIGH HANSON ECC INC (DH)
Also Called: Italcementi Group
3251 Bath Pike (18064-8928)
PHONE...................................610 837-6725
Silvio Panseri, *President*
Craig Becker, *Senior VP*
Alexander Car, *Senior VP*
Glenn Dalrymple, *Senior VP*
Kevin A Jones, *Treasurer*
▲ EMP: 72 EST: 1866
SQ FT: 25,000
SALES (est): 293.8MM
SALES (corp-wide): 20.6B Privately Held
WEB: www.essroc.com
SIC: 3273 Ready-mixed concrete
HQ: Essroc Corp.
3251 Bath Pike
Nazareth PA 18064
610 837-6725

(G-11979)
LEHIGH HANSON ECC INC
3162 Bath Pike 1 (18064-8929)
PHONE...................................610 837-3312
David Williamson, *Branch Mgr*
EMP: 56
SALES (corp-wide): 20.6B Privately Held
WEB: www.essroc.com
SIC: 3273 Ready-mixed concrete
HQ: Lehigh Hanson Ecc, Inc.
3251 Bath Pike
Nazareth PA 18064
610 837-6725

(G-11980)
LEHIGH HANSON ECC INC
Also Called: Essroc Italcementi Group
3938 Easton Nazareth Hwy (18064-3017)
PHONE...................................610 759-2222
Dan Wren, *Branch Mgr*
EMP: 100
SALES (corp-wide): 20.6B Privately Held
WEB: www.essroc.com
SIC: 3273 Ready-mixed concrete
HQ: Lehigh Hanson Ecc, Inc.
3251 Bath Pike
Nazareth PA 18064
610 837-6725

(G-11981)
MCLEAN PACKAGING CORPORATION
Also Called: Quality Box Company
Easton Rd Mp Mp Broad St Amp Amp
(18064)
P.O. Box 180 (18064-0180)
PHONE...................................610 759-3550
Elise Jack, *Controller*
Linda Walker, *Accountant*
David Seidenberg, *Data Proc Exec*
EMP: 150
SALES (corp-wide): 60MM Privately
Held
SIC: 2652 2631 Setup paperboard boxes;
setup boxboard
PA: Mclean Packaging Corporation
1504 Glen Ave
Moorestown NJ 08057
856 359-2600

(G-11982)
MISSING PIECE
462 Bushkill Center Rd (18064-9532)
PHONE...................................610 759-4033
Karen Sampson,
EMP: 4 EST: 2007
SALES (est): 509.7K Privately Held
SIC: 2599 2531 2521 2511 Factory furni-
ture & fixtures; public building & related
furniture; wood office furniture; wood
household furniture

(G-11983)
NAZARETH INDUSTRIAL CORP
595 E Lawn Rd (18064-1211)
P.O. Box 376 (18064-0376)
PHONE...................................610 759-9776
Junichi Mutsuki, *President*
Jeff Queitzsch, *Vice Pres*
EMP: 15
SQ FT: 25,000
SALES (est): 2.3MM
SALES (corp-wide): 345K Privately Held
WEB: www.nazcorp.com
SIC: 3089 Injection molding of plastics
PA: Mutsuki Industry Co. Ltd.
1-8-11, Oyodokita, Kita-Ku
Osaka OSK
664 511-420

(G-11984)
NAZARETH KEY YOUNGS PRESS
127 E High St Frnt (18064-1565)
P.O. Box 419 (18064-0419)
PHONE...................................610 759-5000
Kyle Young, *Owner*
EMP: 4
SALES (est): 215.7K Privately Held
SIC: 2711 2752 Newspapers: publishing
only, not printed on site; commercial print-
ing, lithographic

(G-11985)
PENN QUAKER SITE CONTRS INC
267 Daniels Rd B (18064-8760)
P.O. Box 343 (18064-0343)
PHONE...................................610 614-0401
Arlene Anthony, *CEO*
Larry Anthony, *Admin Sec*
EMP: 9
SALES (est): 2.2MM Privately Held
SIC: 1389 Excavating slush pits & cellars

(G-11986)
PROFORMA GRAPHIC IMPRESSIONS
161 Heyer Rd (18064-8775)
PHONE...................................610 759-2430
Martin Henry, *Owner*
EMP: 6
SALES (est): 502.7K Privately Held
SIC: 2752 Commercial printing, litho-
graphic

(G-11987)
SES INC
4483 Sarah Marie Ct (18064-8595)
PHONE...................................484 767-3280
Robert Oakley, *Principal*
EMP: 4 EST: 2010

SALES (est): 342.8K Privately Held
SIC: 3674 Semiconductors & related devices

(G-11988)
SOFTWARE CONSULTING SVCS LLC
Also Called: S. C. S.
630 Municipal Dr Ste 420 (18064-8990)
PHONE...................................610 746-7700
Martha J Cichelli,
Richard J Cichelli,
EMP: 40
SQ FT: 19,000
SALES (est): 4.4MM Privately Held
WEB: www.newspapersystems.com
SIC: 7372 Publishers' computer software

(G-11989)
STAN BENDER
Also Called: Stans Dental Service
890 Lahr Rd (18064-9545)
PHONE...................................610 759-4021
Stan Bender, *Owner*
EMP: 3
SALES (est): 214.8K Privately Held
SIC: 3843 Dental equipment & supplies

(G-11990)
STARKE MILLWORK INC
671 Bangor Rd (18064-8625)
PHONE...................................610 759-1753
John Starke, *President*
Marianne Starke, *Vice Pres*
▲ EMP: 15
SQ FT: 7,800
SALES (est): 2.4MM Privately Held
WEB: www.starkemillwork.com
SIC: 2431 Millwork

(G-11991)
THERMO FISHER SCIENTIFIC INC
6771 Silver Crest Rd (18064-9746)
PHONE...................................610 837-5091
Bill Hughes, *Branch Mgr*
EMP: 16
SALES (corp-wide): 24.3B Publicly Held
SIC: 3826 Analytical instruments
PA: Thermo Fisher Scientific Inc.
168 3rd Ave
Waltham MA 02451
781 622-1000

(G-11992)
TOSS MACHINE COMPONENTS INC
539 S Main St Ste 1 (18064-2795)
PHONE...................................610 759-8883
Charles H Trillich, *President*
Helma Young, *Vice Pres*
Alice Driber, *Accountant*
EMP: 10
SQ FT: 1,000
SALES (est): 588.5K Privately Held
WEB: www.tossheatseal.com
SIC: 3053 Gaskets & sealing devices

(G-11993)
VICTAULIC COMPANY OF AMERICA
2860 Bath Pike (18064-8898)
PHONE...................................610 614-1261
Sheri Nordstrom, *Manager*
EMP: 8
SALES (est): 1MM Privately Held
SIC: 3325 Steel foundries

(G-11994)
WILEY ELECTRIC SIGN SERVICE
2232 Whitehead Rd (18064-8906)
PHONE...................................610 759-8167
Michael Wiley, *Owner*
EMP: 3
SALES (est): 149.6K Privately Held
SIC: 3993 7629 1799 Electric signs; elec-
trical repair shops; sign installation &
maintenance

(G-11995)
WILLIAMS FRESH SCENTS LLC
501 W Highland Ter (18064-1024)
PHONE...................................484 838-0147
William Gorkos,
Daniel Gorkos,

Susan Gorkos,
Annamarie Jonas,
EMP: 4
SALES (est): 198.2K Privately Held
SIC: 2844 Toilet preparations

Needmore
Fulton County

(G-11996)
MELLOTT WOOD PRESERVING INC (PA)
1398 Sawmill Rd (17238)
P.O. Box 209 (17238-0209)
PHONE...................................717 573-2519
Cecil B Mellott, *President*
Douglas Mellott, *Vice Pres*
Thelma Mellott, *Treasurer*
EMP: 25
SQ FT: 5,000
SALES (est): 4.1MM Privately Held
SIC: 2491 2421 Wood preserving; railroad
ties, sawed

Neelyton
Huntingdon County

(G-11997)
NICOLE M REASNER
22389 Decorum Rd (17239-9400)
PHONE...................................814 259-3827
Nicole M Reasner, *Principal*
EMP: 3
SALES (est): 382.4K Privately Held
SIC: 2411 Logging

Neffs
Lehigh County

(G-11998)
DAVID J HOHENSHILT WELDING LLC
5628 Route 873 (18065-7700)
P.O. Box 13 (18065-0013)
PHONE...................................610 349-2937
David J Hohenshilt,
EMP: 6 EST: 1999
SALES (est): 2.3MM Privately Held
SIC: 3441 Building components, structural
steel

(G-11999)
HOWMEDICA OSTEONICS CORP
5702 Route 873 (18065-7701)
PHONE...................................610 760-7007
Ned Lipes, *Branch Mgr*
EMP: 15
SALES (corp-wide): 13.6B Publicly Held
SIC: 5047 3842 Orthopedic equipment &
supplies; surgical appliances & supplies
HQ: Howmedica Osteonics Corp.
325 Corporate Dr
Mahwah NJ 07430
201 831-5000

Nescopeck
Luzerne County

(G-12000)
DANT ENTERPRISES
226 Overlook Rd (18635-1882)
PHONE...................................570 379-3121
Tom Crawford, *Owner*
EMP: 6
SALES (est): 743.5K Privately Held
WEB: www.plowdolly.com
SIC: 3531 Snow plow attachments

(G-12001)
RAD MFG LLC (PA)
531 Maple St (18635)
PHONE...................................570 752-4514
Gail Portman, *President*
Josh Cantor, *COO*
Michael Sofer, *COO*

▲ = Import ▼=Export
◆ =Import/Export

GEOGRAPHIC

▲ EMP: 65
SQ FT: 80,000
SALES (est): 21MM **Privately Held**
SIC: 2426 2511 Hardwood dimension &
flooring mills; tables, household: wood

(G-12002)
RAD MFG LLC
Maple St (18635)
PHONE..................................570 752-4514
Marvin Michael, *Manager*
EMP: 50
SALES (corp-wide): 21MM **Privately
Held**
SIC: 2431 2426 Millwork; hardwood di-
mension & flooring mills
PA: Rad Mfg. Llc
531 Maple St
Nescopeck PA 18635
570 752-4514

Nesquehoning
Carbon County

(G-12003)
AMETEK INC
Chemical Products Division
42 Mountain Ave (18240-2201)
PHONE..................................570 645-2191
James Visnic, *General Mgr*
Anthony Scioli, *Regl Sales Mgr*
John Kowalchick, *Executive*
EMP: 68
SQ FT: 120,000
SALES (corp-wide): 4.8B **Publicly Held**
SIC: 3621 Motors & generators
PA: Ametek, Inc.
1100 Cassatt Rd
Berwyn PA 19312
610 647-2121

(G-12004)
CRYSTALINE BUS & RAIL INC
442 Industrial Rd (18240-2249)
P.O. Box 1295, Tuckerton NJ (08087-5295)
PHONE..................................570 645-3145
Louis T Albertini, *President*
Christopher Davis, *Corp Secy*
EMP: 15
SQ FT: 18,000
SALES (est): 2.2MM **Privately Held**
SIC: 5075 3585 Air conditioning equip-
ment, except room units; parts for heat-
ing, cooling & refrigerating equipment

(G-12005)
HYDRA-TECH PUMPS INC
167 Stock St (18240-2241)
PHONE..................................570 645-3779
Robert Losse, *President*
Kenneth Reim, *Vice Pres*
◆ EMP: 11
SQ FT: 10,000
SALES (est): 3.5MM **Privately Held**
WEB: www.hydra-tech.com
SIC: 3561 Pump jacks & other pumping
equipment

(G-12006)
KOVATCH CORP
Also Called: K M E
1 Industrial Complex (18240-1499)
PHONE..................................570 669-5130
John I Kovatch, *Ch of Bd*
Brian Mertz, *Plant Mgr*
Frank Smell, *Mfg Mgr*
Nikolas Wasko, *Purch Agent*
John Borovies, *Engineer*
▲ EMP: 75
SQ FT: 500,000
SALES (est): 1.5MM **Privately Held**
WEB: www.kovatch.com
SIC: 3711 7532 Fire department vehicles
(motor vehicles), assembly of; truck &
tractor truck assembly; automobile as-
sembly, including specialty automobiles;
body shop, automotive

(G-12007)
**KOVATCH MOBILE EQUIPMENT
CORP (HQ)**
Also Called: Kme Fire Apparatus
1 Industrial Complex (18240-1499)
PHONE..................................570 669-9461
John I Kovatch, *President*
Philip Gerace, *President*
Tim Besser, *Regional Mgr*
Brittany Bowman, *Purch Agent*
Mark Smith, *Engineer*
◆ EMP: 665
SQ FT: 170,000
SALES (est): 165.5MM **Publicly Held**
SIC: 3711 Chassis, motor vehicle; fire de-
partment vehicles (motor vehicles), as-
sembly of; automobile assembly,
including specialty automobiles

(G-12008)
**PHILADELPHIA VALVE
COMPANY INC**
1 Industrial Complex (18240-1420)
PHONE..................................570 669-9461
John J Kovatch Jr, *President*
EMP: 20
SALES (est): 222.8K **Privately Held**
WEB: www.kovatch.com
SIC: 3592 Valves

(G-12009)
TARACO SPORTSWEAR INC
Also Called: Emcee Knitwear
258 W Columbus Ave (18240-1007)
PHONE..................................570 669-9004
Tony Cusanelli, *President*
Margaret Cusanelli, *Vice Pres*
Alicia Cusanelli, *Admin Sec*
EMP: 4
SQ FT: 15,000
SALES (est): 67K **Privately Held**
SIC: 2321 2331 Men's & boys' dress
shirts; shirts, women's & juniors': made
from purchased materials

(G-12010)
VIKING LLC
Also Called: A Dema Company
512 Industrial Rd (18240-2243)
PHONE..................................570 645-3633
Keith Yurchak, *General Mgr*
Pete Yurchak, *General Mgr*
Kelly McMullen, *Opers Staff*
EMP: 13
SALES (est): 3MM **Privately Held**
SIC: 2842 Dusting cloths, chemically
treated; drain pipe solvents or cleaners

(G-12011)
WHITTCO INC
Also Called: Hydra-Tech Pumps
167 Stock St (18240-2241)
PHONE..................................570 645-3779
Kyle Whittaker, *President*
◆ EMP: 12
SALES: 6MM **Privately Held**
SIC: 3561 Pump jacks & other pumping
equipment

New Albany
Bradford County

(G-12012)
J R KLINE BUTCHERY LLC
3302 Route 220 (18833)
PHONE..................................570 220-4229
Robin Fiester, *Principal*
Jason Kline, *Principal*
EMP: 6
SALES (est): 185.1K **Privately Held**
SIC: 2011 Boxed beef from meat slaugh-
tered on site

(G-12013)
J R KLINE BUTCHERY LLC
3302 Route 220 (18833)
Rr # Rte 220
PHONE..................................570 220-4229
EMP: 6
SQ FT: 5,076
SALES (est): 185.1K **Privately Held**
SIC: 2011 Meat Packing Plant

(G-12014)
PARROT GRAPHICS
807 Iron Bridge Rd (18833-7740)
PHONE..................................570 746-1745
Eleanor Ferguson, *Partner*
Kathy Bradbury, *Partner*
EMP: 3
SALES: 25K **Privately Held**
SIC: 2759 Screen printing

(G-12015)
**R & K WETTLAUFER LOGGING
INC**
3326 Dushore Overton Rd A 1
(18833-8844)
PHONE..................................570 924-4752
Robert Murriel Wettlaufer, *President*
EMP: 3
SALES: 500K **Privately Held**
SIC: 2411 Logging camps & contractors

(G-12016)
**WYOMING CASING SERVICE
INC**
4713 Route 220 N (18833)
P.O. Box 225 (18833-0225)
PHONE..................................570 363-2883
Tim Gross, *Branch Mgr*
EMP: 20
SALES (corp-wide): 182.2MM **Privately
Held**
SIC: 1389 Oil field services; gas field serv-
ices
PA: Wyoming Casing Service, Inc.
198 40th St E
Dickinson ND 58601
701 225-8521

New Alexandria
Westmoreland County

(G-12017)
B B OILFIELD EQUIPMENT
8791 State Route 22 (15670-3018)
P.O. Box 301 (15670-0301)
PHONE..................................724 668-2509
Hal Banks, *President*
EMP: 12
SALES (est): 600K **Privately Held**
SIC: 1389 Oil field services

(G-12018)
EIDEMILLER DOOR CO
176 Skyview Dr (15670-2768)
PHONE..................................724 668-8294
Erik S Eidemiller, *Principal*
EMP: 4
SALES (est): 362.2K **Privately Held**
SIC: 2431 Garage doors, overhead: wood

(G-12019)
HOMER CITY AUTOMATION INC
699 State Park Rd (15670-3522)
PHONE..................................724 479-4503
Stephanie Dileo, *President*
▲ EMP: 5
SALES (est): 1.2MM **Privately Held**
SIC: 3535 Belt conveyor systems, general
industrial use

(G-12020)
RT 66 TRACTOR SUPPLY
Also Called: New Alexandria Tractor Supply
1855 Lions Club Rd (15670-3086)
PHONE..................................724 668-2000
Dennis G Downes, *Owner*
▲ EMP: 9 EST: 1968
SQ FT: 28,800
SALES (est): 1.7MM **Privately Held**
SIC: 5083 3715 Agricultural machinery &
equipment; tractors, agricultural; truck
trailers

New Berlin
Union County

(G-12021)
Q ALUMINUM LLC
Also Called: Qcast Aluminum
10 Willow Pond Rd (17855-8000)
PHONE..................................570 966-2800
Matthew Haggerty, *Mng Member*
David Powers, *Mng Member*
EMP: 12
SALES (est): 621.8K **Privately Held**
SIC: 3365 Aluminum foundries

(G-12022)
Q COMPANY LLC
809 Market St (17855-8054)
PHONE..................................570 966-1017
Matthew Haggerty, *Mng Member*
David Powers, *Mng Member*
EMP: 40
SALES (est): 1.3MM **Privately Held**
SIC: 3545 Machine tool accessories

(G-12023)
**Q-E MANUFACTURING
COMPANY**
809 Market St (17855-8054)
P.O. Box 525 (17855-0525)
PHONE..................................570 966-1017
Dale L Miller, *President*
Kelly Barrick, *Corp Secy*
Matthew Miller, *Vice Pres*
Darryl Chappell, *Technical Staff*
EMP: 45
SQ FT: 10,000
SALES (est): 7.6MM **Privately Held**
WEB: www.qe-man.com
SIC: 3599 3451 3452 3492 Machine
shop, jobbing & repair; screw machine
products; bolts, nuts, rivets & washers;
fluid power valves & hose fittings; valves
& pipe fittings

New Berlinville
Berks County

(G-12024)
B C FABRICATIONS INC
821 N Reading Ave (19545)
P.O. Box 442 (19545-0442)
PHONE..................................610 369-2882
Sharon Bauman, *President*
Barbara Nester, *Vice Pres*
EMP: 5
SALES (est): 771.1K **Privately Held**
WEB: www.bcfabrications.com
SIC: 3462 Railroad wheels, axles, frogs or
other equipment: forged

New Bethlehem
Clarion County

(G-12025)
CHAR-VAL CANDIES
1391 Route 66 (16242-2039)
P.O. Box 285 (16242-0285)
PHONE..................................814 275-1602
Howard H Schreckengost, *Owner*
Janet Schreckengost, *Manager*
EMP: 5
SQ FT: 2,500
SALES (est): 486.2K **Privately Held**
SIC: 2064 Candy & other confectionery
products

(G-12026)
J M SMUCKER PA INC
300 Keck Ave (16242-1151)
PHONE..................................814 275-1323
Timothy P Smucker, *CEO*
Richard K Smucker, *President*
Paul H Smucker, *Chairman*
Allan Mc Falls, *Vice Pres*
Dick Troyak, *Vice Pres*
EMP: 50 EST: 1946
SQ FT: 30,000

SALES (est): 9.1MM
SALES (corp-wide): 7.3B **Publicly Held**
WEB: www.smuckers.com
SIC: 2099 Peanut butter
PA: The J M Smucker Company
　　1 Strawberry Ln
　　Orrville OH 44667
　　330 682-3000

(G-12027)
MCLEAN PUBLISHING CO
Also Called: Leader Vindicator
435 Broad St (16242-1102)
P.O. Box 158 (16242-0158)
PHONE................................814 275-3131
William McLean, *Ch of Bd*
EMP: 10 **EST:** 2004
SALES (est): 580.8K **Privately Held**
SIC: 2711 2752 Job printing & newspaper
　　publishing combined; commercial printing,
　　lithographic

(G-12028)
**NEW BETHLEHEM BURIAL
SERVICE (PA)**
171 Theas Farms Rd (16242)
P.O. Box 100 (16242-0100)
PHONE................................814 275-3333
Dean L Hetrick, *President*
Ann Hetrick, *Corp Secy*
EMP: 14
SQ FT: 1,000
SALES (est): 1.2MM **Privately Held**
SIC: 3272 Burial vaults, concrete or pre-
　　cast terrazzo; septic tanks, concrete

New Bloomfield
Perry County

(G-12029)
ADVANCE PUBLICATIONS (HQ)
Also Called: Duncannon Record
51 Church St (17068-9683)
PHONE................................717 582-4305
Curt Dreibblbis, *Publisher*
Wade Fowler, *Manager*
EMP: 15 **EST:** 1946
SQ FT: 3,000
SALES (est): 2.3MM
SALES (corp-wide): 1.4B **Privately Held**
SIC: 2711 Job printing & newspaper pub-
　　lishing combined
PA: Advance Digital Inc.
　　3100 Harborside Fincl 3
　　Jersey City NJ 07311
　　201 459-2808

(G-12030)
PERRY PRINTING COMPANY
51 Church St (17068-9683)
P.O. Box 85 (17068-0085)
PHONE................................717 582-2838
Lori Little, *President*
EMP: 7
SALES (est): 899.9K **Privately Held**
WEB: www.perryprinting.com
SIC: 2759 2752 Business forms: printing;
　　commercial printing, lithographic

New Brighton
Beaver County

(G-12031)
**BEAVER VALLEY CASH
REGISTER CO**
1408 Lexington Dr (15066-3712)
PHONE................................724 728-0800
Ronald Cooper, *Owner*
EMP: 3
SALES (est): 258.7K **Privately Held**
SIC: 5999 7629 3578 Business machines
　　& equipment; business machine repair,
　　electric; accounting machines & cash reg-
　　isters

(G-12032)
**CERAMIC COLOR AND CHEM
MFG CO**
Also Called: Ceramic Color and Chem Mfg
Co
13th St & 11th Ave (15066)
PHONE................................724 846-4000
Burgess M Hurd, *Ch of Bd*
William F Wenning Jr, *President*
▼ **EMP:** 25
SQ FT: 95,000
SALES (est): 5.7MM **Privately Held**
SIC: 2816 2819 Industrial inorganic chem-
　　icals; inorganic pigments

(G-12033)
**DAN DULLS SPECIALTY
WDWKG**
1027 4th Ave (15066-2015)
PHONE................................724 843-6223
Dan Dulls, *Owner*
EMP: 3
SALES (est): 239.2K **Privately Held**
SIC: 3553 Woodworking machinery

(G-12034)
**DIAMOND MILLING COMPANY
INC (PA)**
313 5th Ave (15066-1733)
P.O. Box 410 (15066-0410)
PHONE................................724 846-0920
Harlan T Richards, *President*
Dan Murphy, *Director*
EMP: 7
SQ FT: 14,500
SALES (est): 1.7MM **Privately Held**
SIC: 2048 5999 5261 Cereal-, grain-, &
　　seed-based feeds; pets & pet supplies;
　　lawn & garden supplies

(G-12035)
ELEMENTS DIRECT LLC
913 6th St (15066-1417)
PHONE................................903 343-5441
Shannon Wilson, *Vice Pres*
Ganelle Jones, *Vice Pres*
EMP: 4
SALES (est): 110K **Privately Held**
SIC: 1389 7389 Oil field services;

(G-12036)
ETA INDUSTRIES INC
1785 Route 68 (15066-4224)
PHONE................................724 453-1722
James Jones, *President*
Paul Jones, *Vice Pres*
EMP: 4
SQ FT: 8,000
SALES (est): 570K **Privately Held**
WEB: www.rolflor.com
SIC: 3535 Belt conveyor systems, general
　　industrial use

(G-12037)
G & K WATTERSON COMPANY
507 2nd Ave (15066-1702)
P.O. Box 314, Darlington (16115-0314)
PHONE................................724 827-2800
Glenn Watterson II, *Owner*
EMP: 5
SQ FT: 3,200
SALES: 750K **Privately Held**
SIC: 1771 1459 Driveway contractor;
　　parking lot construction; shale (common)
　　quarrying

(G-12038)
JEFFERS & LEEK ELECTRIC INC
438 Constitution Blvd (15066-3107)
PHONE................................724 384-0315
EMP: 9
SALES (est): 86.3K **Privately Held**
SIC: 4911 3699 1731 Electric services;
　　electrical equipment & supplies; general
　　electrical contractor

(G-12039)
PAUL GROTH & SONS INC
101 Blockhouse Run Rd (15066)
P.O. Box 383 (15066-0383)
PHONE................................724 843-8086
Paul W Groth, *President*
Dorothy Groth, *Treasurer*
EMP: 12 **EST:** 1960
SQ FT: 6,000

SALES (est): 679.4K **Privately Held**
SIC: 3444 Sheet metal specialties, not
　　stamped

(G-12040)
**ROCHESTER MACHINE
CORPORATION**
1300 Allegheny St (15066-1652)
P.O. Box 94 (15066-0094)
PHONE................................724 843-7820
Jeffrey L Bruce, *President*
Todd Bruce, *Vice Pres*
Charles W Bruce, *Treasurer*
Adam Reed, *Prgrmr*
Angela Jones, *Admin Sec*
EMP: 30
SQ FT: 157,000
SALES (est): 5.7MM **Privately Held**
WEB: www.rochestermachine.com
SIC: 3599 7692 3441 Machine shop, job-
　　bing & repair; welding repair; fabricated
　　structural metal

(G-12041)
ROSALIND CANDY CASTLE INC
1301 5th Ave (15066-2117)
P.O. Box 93 (15066-0093)
PHONE................................724 843-1144
James R Crudden, *President*
Elizabeth S Crudden, *Vice Pres*
EMP: 15 **EST:** 1914
SQ FT: 3,000
SALES (est): 1.9MM **Privately Held**
WEB: www.rosalindcandy.com
SIC: 2064 5441 Chocolate candy, except
　　solid chocolate; candy

(G-12042)
**SPORTS FACTORY
PROMOTIONS INC**
917 3rd Ave (15066-1916)
PHONE................................724 847-2684
Karen A Burns, *President*
Kevin L Burns, *Vice Pres*
EMP: 7
SQ FT: 6,000
SALES (est): 212.5K **Privately Held**
SIC: 5941 2759 Sporting goods & bicycle
　　shops; commercial printing

(G-12043)
STANDARD HORSE NAIL CORP
Also Called: Stanho
1415 5th Ave Ste 2 (15066-2210)
P.O. Box 316 (15066-0316)
PHONE................................724 846-4660
Robert S Merrick Jr, *President*
Ryan Merrick, *President*
Peter Merrick, *Vice Pres*
Roger L Javens, *Admin Sec*
▲ **EMP:** 13 **EST:** 1872
SQ FT: 87,000
SALES (est): 3.3MM **Privately Held**
WEB: www.stanho.com
SIC: 3452 Machine keys

(G-12044)
STEEL VALLEY CASTING LLC
1784a Route 68 (15066-4224)
PHONE................................724 777-4025
EMP: 4
SALES (est): 150.3K **Privately Held**
SIC: 3482 3483 Cores, bullet: 30 mm. &
　　below; ammunition loading & assembling
　　plant

New Britain
Bucks County

(G-12045)
**CHANT ENGINEERING CO INC
(PA)**
59 Industrial Dr (18901-6007)
PHONE................................215 230-4260
James Chant, *CEO*
Philip Chant, *President*
Jules Dirienzo, *Vice Pres*
Tony Oliver, *Opers Mgr*
Jerry Schafer, *Purchasing*
▼ **EMP:** 35
SQ FT: 38,000

SALES (est): 11.5MM **Privately Held**
WEB: www.chantengineering.com
SIC: 3829 8748 Torsion testing equipment;
　　testing equipment: abrasion, shearing
　　strength, etc.; systems engineering con-
　　sultant, ex. computer or professional

(G-12046)
CHANT ENGINEERING CO INC
Hull Industries
59 Industrial Dr (18901-6007)
PHONE................................215 230-4260
Philip E Chant, *Branch Mgr*
Werner Lamberger, *Technical Staff*
EMP: 35
SALES (corp-wide): 11.5MM **Privately
Held**
SIC: 3569 3559 3555 3563 Blast clean-
　　ing equipment, dustless; plastics working
　　machinery; printing trades machinery;
　　vacuum pumps, except laboratory; pumps
　　& pumping equipment; machine tools,
　　metal forming type
PA: Chant Engineering Co., Inc.
　　59 Industrial Dr
　　New Britain PA 18901
　　215 230-4260

(G-12047)
MANGAR INDUSTRIES INC
Also Called: Mangar Medical Packaging
97 Britain Dr (18901-5193)
PHONE................................215 230-0300
Jerry Bennish, *President*
Ann Buckley, *CFO*
▲ **EMP:** 225 **EST:** 1986
SALES (est): 131.9MM
SALES (corp-wide): 2.9B **Privately Held**
SIC: 2671 Packaging paper & plastics film,
　　coated & laminated
HQ: Oliver Products Company
　　445 6th St Nw
　　Grand Rapids MI 49504
　　616 456-7711

(G-12048)
MANGAR MEDICAL INC
97 Britain Dr (18901-5186)
PHONE................................215 230-0300
Don Coleman, *CEO*
John Coleman, *Ch of Bd*
Douglas Coleman, *Principal*
Donald K Hanson, *Corp Secy*
▲ **EMP:** 200
SQ FT: 23,000
SALES (est): 32.6MM **Privately Held**
WEB: www.mangar.com
SIC: 3841 2671 Surgical & medical instru-
　　ments; packaging paper & plastics film,
　　coated & laminated

(G-12049)
MCMILLAN MUSIC CO LLC
15 Britain Dr (18901-5186)
PHONE................................215 441-0212
David Duane,
EMP: 6 **EST:** 1956
SQ FT: 3,000
SALES: 2MM **Privately Held**
WEB: www.mcmillanmusic.com
SIC: 2992 Lubricating oils & greases

(G-12050)
OLIVER PRODUCTS COMPANY
Also Called: Oliver Healthcare Packaging
97 Britain Dr (18901-5186)
PHONE................................215 230-0300
EMP: 4
SALES (corp-wide): 2.9B **Privately Held**
SIC: 3053 Gaskets, packing & sealing de-
　　vices
HQ: Oliver Products Company
　　445 6th St Nw
　　Grand Rapids MI 49504
　　616 456-7711

New Castle
Lawrence County

(G-12051)
A & L TUBULAR SPECIALTIES
5124 Erie St (16102-4006)
PHONE................................724 667-6101
Larry L Loth, *Owner*

▲ = Import ▼=Export
◆ =Import/Export

EMP: 4
SALES (est): 450.4K **Privately Held**
SIC: 3317 Tubes, seamless steel

(G-12052)
A LA HENRI INC
3213 Lexington Dr (16105-1113)
PHONE......................724 856-1374
Edward J De Carbo, *President*
Gerald De Carbo, *Vice Pres*
Donald De Carbo, *Admin Sec*
EMP: 3
SALES (est): 133.2K **Privately Held**
SIC: 2015 5147 Chicken, processed; lard

(G-12053)
ADG FABRICATION LLC
540 Sampson St (16101-2056)
PHONE......................724 658-3000
Daniel Depaolo II, *President*
EMP: 4 EST: 2015
SQ FT: 7,000
SALES (est): 456K **Privately Held**
SIC: 3444 Sheet metalwork

(G-12054)
ADVANCED FEEDSCREWS INC
3307 Us 422 (16101-7963)
P.O. Box 7856 (16107-7856)
PHONE......................724 924-9877
John Fraschetti III, *President*
Wallace Cunningham, *Vice Pres*
Branden Huff, *Sales Mgr*
Philip Cunningham, *Admin Sec*
EMP: 20
SQ FT: 2,000
SALES (est): 3.6MM **Privately Held**
SIC: 3469 Machine parts, stamped or
    pressed metal

(G-12055)
ALLFAB MANUFACTURING INC
1602 Old Princeton Rd (16105-6255)
PHONE......................724 924-2725
Ralph Pisano Sr, *CEO*
Roseann Pisano, *President*
EMP: 7
SQ FT: 4,300
SALES: 200K **Privately Held**
SIC: 3441 Fabricated structural metal

(G-12056)
ALMEGA PLASTICS INC
503 Commerce Ave (16101-7631)
P.O. Box 7524 (16107-7524)
PHONE......................724 652-6411
Mark Claus, *President*
Clemente Bruno, *Vice Pres*
Carl W Heinrich, *Treasurer*
Steve M Llewellyn, *Admin Sec*
EMP: 27
SALES (est): 8.2MM **Privately Held**
SIC: 3089 Injection molding of plastics

(G-12057)
AMERICAN HARD CHROME LLC
925 Industrial St (16102-1329)
PHONE......................412 951-9051
EMP: 3
SALES (est): 251.7K **Privately Held**
SIC: 3471 1446 7699 Sand blasting of
    metal parts; grinding sand mining; indus-
    trial tool grinding

(G-12058)
AMERICAN TOOL & MACHINE CO
1119 Butler Ave (16101-4294)
PHONE......................724 654-0971
Fax: 724 654-6207
EMP: 8
SQ FT: 14,000
SALES (est): 1MM **Privately Held**
SIC: 3599 Mfg Industrial Machinery

(G-12059)
ARMOR MANUFACTURING INC
5220 State Route 18 (16102-3342)
PHONE......................724 658-1848
Thomas M Schrantz, *President*
EMP: 10
SQ FT: 8,000
SALES (est): 1.5MM **Privately Held**
SIC: 3599 Machine shop, jobbing & repair

(G-12060)
AX HEAT TRANSFER INC
420 S Cascade St (16103-3339)
P.O. Box 7158 (16107-7158)
PHONE......................724 654-7747
Jim Andanasaris, *Vice Pres*
EMP: 13
SQ FT: 29,000
SALES (est): 150.2K **Privately Held**
WEB: www.axheattransfer.com
SIC: 3443 Heat exchangers: coolers (after,
    inter), condensers, etc.
PA: Select Industries, Inc.
    420 S Cascade St
    New Castle PA 16101

(G-12061)
AXION POWER BATTERY MFG INC
Also Called: Axion Power International
3601 Clover Ln (16105-5507)
P.O. Box 9366, Youngstown OH (44513-0366)
PHONE......................724 654-9300
Thomas G Granville, *President*
Edward Buiel, *Vice Pres*
Charles Trego, *Treasurer*
▲ EMP: 50
SALES (est): 8.2MM **Privately Held**
SIC: 3692 Primary batteries, dry & wet

(G-12062)
BERNER INDUSTRIES INC
Rr 422 Box E (16101)
PHONE......................724 924-9240
EMP: 19 EST: 1977
SALES (est): 1.5MM **Privately Held**
SIC: 3559 Mfg Misc Industry Machinery

(G-12063)
BERNER INTERNATIONAL LLC (PA)
111 Progress Ave (16101-7601)
PHONE......................724 658-3551
Georgia Berner, *President*
Theresa Foust, *General Mgr*
George M Berner, *Vice Pres*
Joe Miller, *Plant Mgr*
Miranda Berner, *Project Mgr*
EMP: 50 EST: 1956
SQ FT: 62,500
SALES (est): 16.7MM **Privately Held**
WEB: www.berner.com
SIC: 3564 Aircurtains (blower)

(G-12064)
BLAIR STRIP STEEL COMPANY
1209 Butler Ave (16101-4369)
P.O. Box 7159 (16107-7159)
PHONE......................724 658-2611
Bruce A Kinney, *Ch of Bd*
John L Avau, *Vice Pres*
James J Ferraro, *Vice Pres*
Scott A McDowell, *CFO*
Beth Lysinger, *Manager*
▲ EMP: 80 EST: 1923
SQ FT: 150,000
SALES (est): 21MM **Privately Held**
WEB: www.blairstripsteel.com
SIC: 3316 5051 3312 Strip steel, cold-
    rolled: from purchased hot-rolled; metals
    service centers & offices; blast furnaces &
    steel mills

(G-12065)
BOSCHUNG AMERICA LLC
930 Cass St Ste 2 (16101-5241)
PHONE......................724 658-3300
Jay H Bruce,
Justin L Bruce,
Wilbur Henstel,
▲ EMP: 12
SALES (est): 2.3MM **Privately Held**
WEB: www.boschungamerica.com
SIC: 3829 Weather tracking equipment

(G-12066)
BRIDGES & TOWERS INC
923 Industrial St (16102-1329)
P.O. Box 577, Ontario NY (14519-0577)
PHONE......................724 654-6672
Frederick A Nudd Sr, *CEO*
Thomas Nudd, *President*
EMP: 12
SQ FT: 80,000

SALES (corp-wide): 8.5MM **Privately Held**
WEB: www.nuddtowers.com
SIC: 3441 Fabricated structural metal for
    bridges; building components, structural
    steel; tower sections, radio & television
    transmission
PA: Fred A. Nudd Corporation
    1743 State Route 104
    Ontario NY 14519
    315 524-2531

(G-12067)
BRINDLE PRINTING CO INC
401 Sampson St (16101-2094)
P.O. Box 994 (16103-0994)
PHONE......................724 658-8549
Merle Burkes, *President*
Edyce Burkes, *Admin Sec*
EMP: 6 EST: 1957
SQ FT: 4,000
SALES (est): 570K **Privately Held**
SIC: 2752 2759 2791 Commercial print-
    ing, offset; letterpress printing; typesetting

(G-12068)
BRYAN CHINA COMPANY
657 Northgate Cir (16105-5549)
PHONE......................724 658-3098
Bruce A Keagy, *President*
Bruce Keagy, *President*
Matt Keagy, *COO*
▲ EMP: 75 EST: 1980
SQ FT: 33,000
SALES (est): 7.2MM **Privately Held**
WEB: www.bryanchina.com
SIC: 3269 3263 Firing & decorating china;
    semivitreous table & kitchenware

(G-12069)
CARLSON MINING
166 Mount Herman Ch Rd (16101-8042)
PHONE......................724 924-2188
Jack E Carlson, *Partner*
Steven Carlson, *Partner*
EMP: 11
SQ FT: 600
SALES (est): 800K **Privately Held**
SIC: 1221 Strip mining, bituminous

(G-12070)
CASTLE BUILDERS SUPPLY INC (PA)
1409 Moravia St (16101-3968)
P.O. Box 6774, Pittsburgh (15212-0774)
PHONE......................724 658-5656
James R Carna, *Corp Secy*
Jim Carna, *Executive*
EMP: 50
SQ FT: 25,000
SALES (est): 9MM **Privately Held**
SIC: 3273 3271 Ready-mixed concrete;
    blocks, concrete or cinder: standard

(G-12071)
CASTLE MOLD & TOOL CO INC
3932 Wilmington Rd (16105-3822)
PHONE......................724 652-4737
Joseph Smarrelli, *CEO*
Joe Smarrelli, *Engineer*
EMP: 7
SQ FT: 7,000
SALES: 700K **Privately Held**
WEB: www.castlemold.com
SIC: 3544 Industrial molds

(G-12072)
CCT MANUFACTURING & FULFILLMEN
203 Commerce Ave (16101-7625)
PHONE......................724 652-0818
George Comianos, *Mng Member*
John Comianos,
EMP: 10
SALES (est): 1.3MM **Privately Held**
SIC: 2675 7389 4783 Paper die-cutting;
    packaging & labeling services; container-
    ization of goods for shipping

(G-12073)
CITY OF NEW CASTLE
Also Called: Sanitation Billing Office
110 E Washington St (16101-3815)
P.O. Box 1404 (16103-1404)
PHONE......................724 654-1627

Richard A Christopher, *Manager*
EMP: 5 **Privately Held**
SIC: 3589 9111 Sewage & water treatment
    equipment; mayors' offices
PA: City Of New Castle
    City Bldg 230 N Jefferson
    New Castle PA 16101
    724 656-3510

(G-12074)
CONSOLIDATED CONTAINER CO LLC
221 Grove St (16101-4022)
PHONE......................724 658-4570
Nick Shuler, *Branch Mgr*
EMP: 8
SALES (corp-wide): 14B **Publicly Held**
SIC: 3089 Plastic containers, except foam
HQ: Consolidated Container Company, Llc
    2500 Windy Ridge Pkwy Se # 1400
    Atlanta GA 30339
    678 742-4600

(G-12075)
CONSOLIDATED CONTAINER CO LLC
221 Grove St (16101-4022)
PHONE......................724 658-4578
Nick Shuler, *Manager*
Toni Chieze, *Executive*
EMP: 57
SALES (corp-wide): 14B **Publicly Held**
WEB: www.cccllc.com
SIC: 3089 3085 Plastic containers, except
    foam; plastics bottles
HQ: Consolidated Container Company, Llc
    2500 Windy Ridge Pkwy Se # 1400
    Atlanta GA 30339
    678 742-4600

(G-12076)
CONSOLIDATED CONTAINER CO LLC
221 Grove St (16101-4022)
PHONE......................724 658-0549
Paul Sherba, *Principal*
EMP: 5
SALES (corp-wide): 14B **Publicly Held**
SIC: 3089 Plastic containers, except foam
HQ: Consolidated Container Company, Llc
    2500 Windy Ridge Pkwy Se # 1400
    Atlanta GA 30339
    678 742-4600

(G-12077)
CONSOLIDATED GLASS CORPORATION
Also Called: Cgc
1150 N Cedar St (16102-1920)
P.O. Box 430 (16103-0430)
PHONE......................724 658-4541
Louis G Merryman, *President*
Audrey E Merryman, *Corp Secy*
Howard Holesapple, *Vice Pres*
Andrea Schry, *CFO*
▲ EMP: 50 EST: 1967
SQ FT: 45,000
SALES (est): 9MM **Privately Held**
WEB: www.cgcglass.com
SIC: 3231 Products of purchased glass

(G-12078)
COPY SHOP
3447 Wilmington Rd (16105-3211)
PHONE......................724 654-6515
Jim Orrico, *Owner*
EMP: 4
SALES (est): 361K **Privately Held**
SIC: 2759 7334 Invitation & stationery
    printing & engraving; photocopying & du-
    plicating services

(G-12079)
CUSTOM ETCH INC
1813 W State St Ste 1 (16101-1261)
PHONE......................724 652-7117
C H Melonio, *President*
Don Melonio, *Vice Pres*
Pat Woytek, *Plant Mgr*
Donald E Melonio, *Treasurer*
Debbie Heath, *Office Mgr*
EMP: 32
SQ FT: 15,000

SALES: 3MM **Privately Held**
WEB: www.custometch.com
SIC: 3479 Etching on metals

(G-12080)
CUSTOM PALLET RECYCLER
Also Called: Custom Power Recycler
1799 County Line Rd (16101-2948)
PHONE.................................724 658-6086
Rudy Kwiatkowski, *Owner*
EMP: 6
SALES (est): 690.7K **Privately Held**
SIC: 2448 Pallets, wood

(G-12081)
DENNIS DOWNING
Also Called: Downing's Cab
2386 Eastbrook Rd (16105-6510)
PHONE.................................724 598-0043
Dennis Downing, *Owner*
EMP: 3
SALES: 260K **Privately Held**
SIC: 2431 1799 2541 2434 Millwork;
kitchen cabinet installation; wood partitions & fixtures; vanities, bathroom: wood

(G-12082)
DEVIDO RANIER STONE CO
2619 New Butler Rd (16101-3226)
PHONE.................................724 658-8518
Ranier A Devido,
William Devido,
EMP: 20 EST: 1956
SQ FT: 10,700
SALES (est): 2.4MM **Privately Held**
WEB: www.devidostone.com
SIC: 3281 Limestone, cut & shaped

(G-12083)
ELLWOOD CITY FORGE COMPANY
700 Moravia St (16101-3950)
PHONE.................................724 202-5008
William Edwards, *Principal*
EMP: 4
SALES (est): 304.2K **Privately Held**
SIC: 3462 Iron & steel forgings

(G-12084)
ELLWOOD GROUP INC
Also Called: Ellwood City Forge
712 Moravia St 10 (16101-3948)
PHONE.................................724 658-3685
Carrie Rust, *Human Res Dir*
Kim Senchak, *Branch Mgr*
Ryan Catcott, *IT/INT Sup*
EMP: 40
SALES (corp-wide): 775.5MM **Privately Held**
WEB: www.ellwoodgroup.com
SIC: 3462 3312 Iron & steel forgings; ferroalloys, produced in blast furnaces; ingots, steel
PA: Ellwood Group, Inc.
600 Commercial Ave
Ellwood City PA 16117
724 752-3680

(G-12085)
ELLWOOD MILL PRODUCTS COMPANY
710 Moravia St (16101-3948)
PHONE.................................724 752-0055
Kim Senchak, *Principal*
EMP: 49
SALES (corp-wide): 10.4MM **Privately Held**
SIC: 3312 Blast furnaces & steel mills
PA: Ellwood Mill Products Company
712 Moravia St
New Castle PA 16101
724 658-9632

(G-12086)
ELLWOOD MILL PRODUCTS COMPANY (PA)
712 Moravia St (16101-3948)
PHONE.................................724 658-9632
Daniel P Hamilton, *President*
Avid E Barensfeld, *Vice Pres*
Bentraum D Huffman, *Treasurer*
Susan A Apel, *Admin Sec*
▲ EMP: 20 EST: 2003
SALES (est): 10.4MM **Privately Held**
SIC: 3312 Tool & die steel

(G-12087)
ELLWOOD QUALITY STEELS COMPANY
700 Moravia St Ste 7 (16101-3950)
P.O. Box 790, Ellwood City (16117-0790)
PHONE.................................724 658-6502
Robert E Rumcik, *President*
David E Barensfeld, *Vice Pres*
Arthur Mangie, *Engineer*
Thomas McKinney, *Engineer*
Bentraum D Huffman, *Treasurer*
▲ EMP: 178
SALES (est): 99.5MM
SALES (corp-wide): 775.5MM **Privately Held**
WEB: www.ellwoodqualitysteels.com
SIC: 3312 Stainless steel
PA: Ellwood Group, Inc.
600 Commercial Ave
Ellwood City PA 16117
724 752-3680

(G-12088)
ELLWOOD SPECIALTY STEEL CO (HQ)
499 Honey Bee Ln (16105-3807)
PHONE.................................724 657-1160
Scott Boyd, *President*
▲ EMP: 68
SQ FT: 100,000
SALES (est): 45MM
SALES (corp-wide): 775.5MM **Privately Held**
WEB: www.ellwoodgroup.com
SIC: 3312 5051 Tool & die steel; steel
PA: Ellwood Group, Inc.
600 Commercial Ave
Ellwood City PA 16117
724 752-3680

(G-12089)
ENTECH INDUSTRIES
1038 N Cedar St (16102-1326)
PHONE.................................724 244-9805
EMP: 4
SALES (est): 359.7K **Privately Held**
SIC: 3999 Atomizers, toiletry

(G-12090)
EZEFLOW USA INC
Also Called: Flowline Division
1400 New Butler Rd (16101-3026)
P.O. Box 7027 (16107-7027)
PHONE.................................724 658-3711
Marty Caposerri, *President*
Pierre Latendresse, *Vice Pres*
Jacques Latendresse, *Treasurer*
Hannah Jurina, *Controller*
Cory Burick, *Sales Staff*
▲ EMP: 120
SALES (est): 21.7MM **Privately Held**
SIC: 3494 Pipe fittings

(G-12091)
FAIRFIELD CONFECTIONERY
2570 Blossom Ln (16105-1668)
PHONE.................................724 654-3888
Tom Joseph Jr, *Owner*
EMP: 5
SQ FT: 12,000
SALES: 800K **Privately Held**
WEB: www.fairfieldcandies.com
SIC: 3556 Confectionery machinery

(G-12092)
FERGUSON PERFORATING COMPANY
901 Commerce Ave (16101-7634)
P.O. Box 8827 (16107-8827)
PHONE.................................724 657-8703
Howard Turner, *Manager*
EMP: 25
SALES (corp-wide): 11.5B **Publicly Held**
WEB: www.fergusonperf.com
SIC: 3469 3496 Perforated metal, stamped; hardware cloth, woven wire
HQ: Ferguson Perforating Company
130 Ernest St
Providence RI 02905
401 941-8876

(G-12093)
FLEMING STEEL CO
2739 Pulaski Rd (16105-4645)
P.O. Box 5207 (16105-0207)
PHONE.................................724 658-1511
Gary Derrone, *CEO*
Seth Kohn, *President*
Patti F Frabotta, *General Mgr*
John Gavroy, *Vice Pres*
John List, *Prdtn Mgr*
EMP: 19 EST: 1921
SQ FT: 69,500
SALES (est): 5.7MM **Privately Held**
WEB: www.flemingdoors.com
SIC: 3442 Metal doors; hangar doors, metal

(G-12094)
FLOWLINE
1400 Butter Rd (16101)
PHONE.................................724 658-3711
Bill Chappell, *Principal*
Terry Gibbson, *Plant Mgr*
EMP: 14
SALES (est): 2.5MM **Privately Held**
SIC: 3312 Pipes & tubes

(G-12095)
FREW MILL DIE CRAFTS INC
311 W Grant St (16101-2214)
PHONE.................................724 658-9026
Charles Lee Mc Combs, *President*
David McKissick, *Corp Secy*
David Deeulio, *Vice Pres*
EMP: 17
SQ FT: 14,000
SALES (est): 1.6MM **Privately Held**
WEB: www.frewmilldiecrafts.com
SIC: 3544 3545 Special dies & tools; tools & accessories for machine tools

(G-12096)
GAINTENNA
3804 Wilmington Rd (16105-6134)
PHONE.................................724 654-9900
Glen Clark, *President*
EMP: 3 EST: 2010
SALES: 200K **Privately Held**
SIC: 3663 Radio & TV communications equipment

(G-12097)
GLOBAL METAL POWDERS LLC
315 Green Ridge Rd Ste H3 (16105-6145)
PHONE.................................724 654-9171
Henry Brougham, *President*
◆ EMP: 9
SALES (est): 1.8MM **Privately Held**
SIC: 3399 Metal powders, pastes & flakes

(G-12098)
GRAHAM THERMAL PRODUCTS LLC
105 Mahoning Ave (16102-1333)
PHONE.................................724 658-0500
Michael Derosa Jr, *President*
Harry L Derosa, *Admin Sec*
▲ EMP: 45
SQ FT: 45,000
SALES (est): 6MM
SALES (corp-wide): 103.1MM **Privately Held**
WEB: www.keystone-industries.com
SIC: 3442 3444 Storm doors or windows, metal; screens, window, metal; sheet metalwork
PA: Graham Architectural Products Corporation
1551 Mount Rose Ave
York PA 17403
717 849-8100

(G-12099)
HARBOR ORTHODONTIC SERVICES
699 Kings Chapel Rd Ste A (16105-4763)
PHONE.................................724 654-3599
Charles R Shearer, *President*
David C Hamilton, *President*
EMP: 1
SALES (est): 100K **Privately Held**
SIC: 3843 8072 Orthodontic appliances; orthodontic appliance production

(G-12100)
HARBOR STEEL INC
1980 Bnjmin Franklin Pkwy (16101-8706)
PHONE.................................724 658-7748
Jeffrey A Stitt, *President*
Susan Hoover, *Manager*
Judith M Stitt, *Admin Sec*
EMP: 13
SQ FT: 63,000
SALES (est): 2.3MM **Privately Held**
SIC: 3443 3444 Fabricated plate work (boiler shop); sheet metal specialties, not stamped

(G-12101)
HD LASER ENGRV & ETCHING LLC
3374 Princeton Rd (16101-7852)
PHONE.................................724 924-9241
Kodey Young,
EMP: 6
SALES (est): 455.5K **Privately Held**
SIC: 3479 Etching & engraving

(G-12102)
HERMAN GEER COMMUNICATIONS INC
Also Called: Hermes Press
2100 Wilmington Rd (16105-1931)
PHONE.................................724 652-0511
Daniel Herman, *President*
▲ EMP: 5
SALES (est): 142.7K **Privately Held**
SIC: 2741 Miscellaneous publishing

(G-12103)
HESS COMMERCIAL PRINTING INC
703 Wilmington Ave (16101-2144)
PHONE.................................724 652-6802
Richard Hess, *President*
Jason Hess, *Vice Pres*
Leslie Hess, *Sales Staff*
Joe Libbey, *Director*
EMP: 38
SQ FT: 12,000
SALES (est): 5.8MM **Privately Held**
WEB: www.quickprintnc.com
SIC: 2752 Commercial printing, offset

(G-12104)
HESSIAN CO LTD
Also Called: Faddis Concrete Products
205 W Washington St (16101-3944)
PHONE.................................724 658-6638
Donald Cooper, *Branch Mgr*
EMP: 30
SALES (corp-wide): 23MM **Privately Held**
SIC: 3272 Lintels, concrete
PA: Hessian Co., Ltd.
2206 Horseshoe Pike
Honey Brook PA 19344
610 269-4685

(G-12105)
INTERNTIONAL TRACK SYSTEMS INC
221 E Cherry St (16102-1306)
P.O. Box 5189 (16105-0189)
PHONE.................................724 658-5970
Ben Baker, *President*
Bryan Shaffer, *Vice Pres*
EMP: 5
SALES (est): 933.5K **Privately Held**
SIC: 3069 Hard rubber products

(G-12106)
INTERSTATE CONT NEW CASTLE LLC
Also Called: Creative Color Display
792 Commerce Ave (16101-7626)
PHONE.................................724 657-3650
Robert I Galligos, *President*
Russell Taylor, *Controller*
EMP: 29
SQ FT: 120,000
SALES (est): 6MM
SALES (corp-wide): 8B **Privately Held**
SIC: 2759 Flexographic printing
HQ: Interstate Resources, Inc.
1300 Wilson Blvd Ste 1075
Arlington VA 22209
703 243-3355

▲ = Import ▼=Export
◆ =Import/Export

(G-12107)
JAMESONS CANDY INC
3451 Wilmington Rd (16105-3211)
PHONE.................................724 658-7441
Joseph W Jameson, *President*
Dennis Jameson, *Vice Pres*
Betty Poland, *Vice Pres*
Randy Poland, *Treasurer*
Kacelyn Jameson, *Admin Sec*
EMP: 14 EST: 1945
SQ FT: 2,520
SALES (est): 375K **Privately Held**
SIC: 2064 Candy & other confectionery
products

(G-12108)
JB MILL & FABRICATING INC
2851 Eastbrook Volant Rd (16105-6805)
PHONE.................................724 202-6814
Jeff Bloise, *President*
▼ EMP: 50
SQ FT: 200,000
SALES (est): 8.4MM **Privately Held**
SIC: 2441 2448 2449 Nailed wood boxes
& shook; wood pallets & skids; rectangu-
lar boxes & crates, wood

(G-12109)
JF MILL AND LUMBER CO
1032 N Cedar St (16102-1326)
PHONE.................................724 654-9542
John P Fishovitz Jr, *President*
Jane Fishovitz, *Corp Secy*
EMP: 4
SQ FT: 15,000
SALES (est): 523.9K **Privately Held**
SIC: 2431 5211 Window frames, wood;
lumber products

(G-12110)
K D MACHINE INC
600 Gilmore Rd (16102-3774)
PHONE.................................724 652-8833
Pauline Davis, *CEO*
Kenneth J Davis Jr, *President*
EMP: 18
SQ FT: 12,500
SALES (est): 3.9MM **Privately Held**
SIC: 3599 Machine shop, jobbing & repair

(G-12111)
KASGRO RAIL CORP (PA)
121 Rundle Rd (16102-1913)
PHONE.................................724 658-9061
Joseph S Crawford, *President*
Jeffrey A Plut, *Vice Pres*
John M Silseth, *Treasurer*
Predrag Stojanovic, *Admin Sec*
◆ EMP: 53
SQ FT: 58,000
SALES (est): 1.6MM **Privately Held**
SIC: 3743 7699 Railway maintenance
cars; railway motor cars; sleeping cars,
railroad; railroad car customizing

(G-12112)
KENNAMETAL INC
599 Northgate Cir (16105-5547)
PHONE.................................724 657-1967
Josepht Patrick, *Principal*
Kelly Stachnik, *Materials Mgr*
Daniel Bentley, *Production*
Charles Morrison, *Production*
Robert Pepper, *Engineer*
EMP: 10
SALES (corp-wide): 2.3B **Publicly Held**
SIC: 3545 Cutting tools for machine tools
PA: Kennametal Inc.
600 Grant St Ste 5100
Pittsburgh PA 15219
412 248-8000

(G-12113)
**KENNEDY TUBULAR
PRODUCTS INC**
430 S Cascade St (16101-3339)
P.O. Box 7258 (16107-7258)
PHONE.................................724 658-5508
William G Barker, *President*
Naomi Barker, *Treasurer*
EMP: 19
SQ FT: 60,000
SALES (est): 2.1MM **Privately Held**
WEB: www.kennedytubular.com
SIC: 3498 Couplings, pipe: fabricated from
purchased pipe

(G-12114)
LARK ENTERPRISES INC (PA)
315 Green Ridge Rd Ste A1 (16105-6145)
PHONE.................................724 657-2001
Susan Lautenbacher, *CEO*
Dave Freshcorn, *Production*
Alice Sankey, *Exec Dir*
EMP: 27
SALES: 3.7MM **Privately Held**
WEB: www.larkent.org
SIC: 8331 3993 Sheltered workshop;
signs & advertising specialties

(G-12115)
LEE MICHAEL INDUSTRIES INC
Also Called: L M I
124 E Long Ave (16101-4804)
PHONE.................................724 656-0890
Brian L Herr, *President*
EMP: 20
SQ FT: 23,000
SALES (est): 4.6MM **Privately Held**
SIC: 1611 3449 General contractor, high-
way & street construction; bars, concrete
reinforcing: fabricated steel

(G-12116)
LITTLE JOHNS WOODSHOP
2671 Copper Rd (16101-7909)
PHONE.................................724 924-9029
Barb Proch, *Owner*
EMP: 3
SQ FT: 1,380
SALES: 125K **Privately Held**
SIC: 2448 2449 Pallets, wood; wood con-
tainers

(G-12117)
MACRIS SPORTS INC
3132 Wilmington Rd Ste 2 (16105-1180)
PHONE.................................724 654-6065
Beth Krivosh, *President*
Tyler Krivosh, *Vice Pres*
EMP: 4
SQ FT: 1,700
SALES: 750K **Privately Held**
SIC: 3949 Sporting & athletic goods

(G-12118)
**MAGNETIC LIFTING TECH US
LLC**
Also Called: M L T U S
3877 Wilmington Rd (16105-6135)
PHONE.................................724 202-7987
Peter Cicero,
George Koch,
EMP: 15
SQ FT: 10,000
SALES: 3MM **Privately Held**
SIC: 3312 Rods, iron & steel: made in steel
mills

(G-12119)
MARKOVITZ ENTERPRISES INC
Quality Rolls Division
597 Commerce Ave (16101-7633)
PHONE.................................724 658-6575
Walt Russell, *Manager*
EMP: 50
SQ FT: 24,000
SALES (corp-wide): 12.8MM **Privately
Held**
WEB: www.badgerind.com
SIC: 3462 3316 3312 Iron & steel forg-
ings; cold finishing of steel shapes; blast
furnaces & steel mills
PA: Markovitz Enterprises, Inc.
100 Badger Dr
Zelienople PA 16063
724 452-4500

(G-12120)
MAS ENGINEERING LLC
2008 County Line Rd (16101-3012)
PHONE.................................724 652-1367
Gary Miller, *Owner*
Mike Hando, *Principal*
EMP: 17
SALES (est): 2.9MM **Privately Held**
WEB: www.masengineering.com
SIC: 3564 Blowing fans: industrial or com-
mercial

(G-12121)
MOLINARO TOOL & DIE INC
Also Called: M T D
Shenango Commrce Prk Comr (16101)
PHONE.................................724 654-5141
Luca Molinaro, *President*
EMP: 15
SQ FT: 3,750
SALES (est): 2.1MM **Privately Held**
SIC: 3545 Precision tools, machinists'

(G-12122)
**MOMS WHOLESALE FOODS
INC (PA)**
930 Cass St Ste 3 (16101-5241)
PHONE.................................724 856-3049
Phillip Pratt, *President*
EMP: 5
SALES (est): 656.2K **Privately Held**
SIC: 2013 2051 2045 2038 Sausages &
other prepared meats; bread, cake & re-
lated products; prepared flour mixes &
doughs; frozen specialties

(G-12123)
N C B TECHNOLOGIES INC
1220 Frew Mill Rd (16101-7602)
PHONE.................................724 658-5544
Joseph Marinelli, *President*
Anthony Marinelli Jr, *Vice Pres*
EMP: 6
SQ FT: 15,000
SALES (est): 639K **Privately Held**
SIC: 3714 3568 3469 Bearings, motor ve-
hicle; power transmission equipment;
metal stampings

(G-12124)
NCC WHOLESOME FOODS INC
Also Called: Troyer's Wholesome Foods
809 Sampson St (16101-8909)
PHONE.................................724 652-3440
William Nagel, *President*
Albert G Canton, *Vice Pres*
EMP: 10
SQ FT: 30,000
SALES: 2.5MM **Privately Held**
SIC: 2034 5149 5142 2022 Dried & de-
hydrated soup mixes; dried & dehydrated
vegetables; dried or canned foods; fruits,
dried; frozen fish, meat & poultry; cheese,
natural & processed

(G-12125)
NCRI INC (HQ)
3909 Station Rd (16101-6567)
PHONE.................................724 654-7711
Thomas Shaffer, *President*
Thomas A Huffman, *Exec VP*
L Edward Allison, *Vice Pres*
EMP: 36
SQ FT: 325,000
SALES (est): 14.9MM
SALES (corp-wide): 216.3MM **Privately
Held**
SIC: 3255 5084 3297 Clay refractories;
industrial machinery & equipment; non-
clay refractories
PA: Resco Products, Inc.
6600 Steubenville Pike # 1
Pittsburgh PA 15205
888 283-5505

(G-12126)
NELSON COMPANY
Also Called: Associated Box
301 Mahoning Ave (16102-1336)
PHONE.................................724 652-6681
Paul Pascarella, *Branch Mgr*
EMP: 8
SALES (corp-wide): 23.1MM **Privately
Held**
WEB: www.smartrax.net
SIC: 2448 Pallets, wood
PA: The Nelson Company
4517 North Point Blvd
Baltimore MD 21219
410 477-3000

(G-12127)
NEW CASTLE BATTERY MFG CO
Also Called: Turbo Start Battery
3601 Wilmington Rd (16105-5513)
PHONE.................................724 658-5501
Steven F Hoye, *President*
Tim Holler, *Vice Pres*

Dennis Miller, *VP Finance*
Mike Coad, *VP Sales*
Susan Phillips, *Admin Sec*
EMP: 110 EST: 1933
SQ FT: 33,000
SALES: 18.3MM **Privately Held**
SIC: 3691 Lead acid batteries (storage bat-
teries)

(G-12128)
NEW CASTLE COMPANY INC
3812 Wilmington Rd (16105-6134)
P.O. Box 322 (16103-0322)
PHONE.................................724 658-4516
Dennis Alduk, *President*
EMP: 9 EST: 1961
SQ FT: 10,000
SALES (est): 2.2MM **Privately Held**
WEB: www.newcastleco.com
SIC: 3535 3544 Unit handling conveying
systems; dies, steel rule

(G-12129)
NEW CASTLE INDUSTRIES INC
Xaloy
925 Industrial St (16102-1329)
PHONE.................................724 656-5600
Ron Auletta, *President*
Keith E Young, *Treasurer*
EMP: 6
SQ FT: 52,000
SALES (corp-wide): 2.2B **Publicly Held**
WEB: www.newcas.com
SIC: 3471 3443 Plating & polishing; fabri-
cated plate work (boiler shop)
HQ: New Castle Industries, Inc.
375 Victoria Rd Ste 1
Youngstown OH 44515
724 654-2603

(G-12130)
**NEW CASTLE REFACTORIES CO
IN**
606 Mccleary Ave (16101-7502)
PHONE.................................724 654-7711
Thomas E Shaffer, *President*
L Edward Allison Jr, *Vice Pres*
Thomas A Huffman, *VP Mktg*
EMP: 85
SALES (est): 5.3MM **Privately Held**
SIC: 3255 Clay refractories

(G-12131)
NEWSPAPER HOLDING INC
Also Called: New Castle News
27 N Mercer St (16101-3806)
P.O. Box 60 (16103-0060)
PHONE.................................724 654-6651
Max Thomson, *Branch Mgr*
EMP: 52 **Privately Held**
WEB: www.clintonnc.com
SIC: 2711 2752 Newspapers, publishing &
printing; commercial printing, lithographic
HQ: Newspaper Holding, Inc.
425 Locust St
Johnstown PA 15901
814 532-5102

(G-12132)
**NORTH AMERICAN
FORGEMASTERS CO**
710 Moravia St (16101-3948)
PHONE.................................724 656-6440
Mike Kamnikar, *President*
Ben Huffman,
EMP: 31 EST: 1998
SQ FT: 200,000
SALES (est): 10MM **Privately Held**
SIC: 3462 Iron & steel forgings

(G-12133)
**NORTHERN ENGRG PLAS CORP
PR**
1902 New Butler Rd (16101-3123)
PHONE.................................724 658-9019
EMP: 3
SALES (est): 199.7K **Privately Held**
SIC: 3089 Plastics products

(G-12134)
**NORWOOD MANUFACTURE CO
LLC**
224 E Cherry St (16102-1307)
PHONE.................................724 652-0698
William Enscoe, *Mng Member*

EMP: 8
SALES (est): 439.2K **Privately Held**
SIC: 3469 Stamping metal for the trade

(G-12135)
O S A GLOBAL LLC (PA)
2700 Highland Ave Ste 6 (16105-2382)
PHONE...................724 698-7042
Bridget Gerrity, *Principal*
EMP: 8
SALES (est): 5.7MM **Privately Held**
SIC: 2211 Bags & bagging, cotton

(G-12136)
PABCOR INC
925 N Cedar St (16102-1323)
P.O. Box 7528 (16107-7528)
PHONE...................724 652-1930
Gary Grant, *President*
Greg Grant, *Vice Pres*
EMP: 6 EST: 1978
SQ FT: 10,000
SALES (est): 887.6K **Privately Held**
SIC: 3599 3441 Machine shop, jobbing &
repair; fabricated structural metal

(G-12137)
PLASTIC OPTIONS LLC (PA)
2704 Mercer Rd (16105-1422)
PHONE...................724 730-5225
John Williams, *President*
EMP: 7 EST: 2008
SALES (est): 2.8MM **Privately Held**
SIC: 4953 2655 Recycling, waste materi-
als; wastebaskets, fiber: made from pur-
chased material

(G-12138)
POINT SPRING COMPANY
Also Called: Valley Spring
1001 Harbor St (16101-8507)
PHONE...................724 658-9076
Gary Brenneman, *Manager*
EMP: 17
SALES (corp-wide): 51.3MM **Privately
Held**
WEB: www.pointspring.com
SIC: 5013 3714 Truck parts & acces-
sories; drive shafts, motor vehicle
PA: Point Spring Company
7307 Grand Ave
Pittsburgh PA 15225
412 264-3152

(G-12139)
PRECISION FEEDSCREWS INC
373 Commerce Ave (16101)
P.O. Box 7357 (16107-7357)
PHONE...................724 654-9676
James J Fagan, *President*
Eileen J Fagan, *Corp Secy*
Richard Davis, *Vice Pres*
Mary McAnallen, *Plant Mgr*
▲ EMP: 24
SQ FT: 13,000
SALES (est): 4.1MM **Privately Held**
WEB: www.precisionfeedscrews.com
SIC: 3451 3535 Screw machine products;
conveyors & conveying equipment

(G-12140)
PRECISION PLATING CO INC
407 Summit View Dr (16105-1431)
PHONE...................724 652-2393
Richard Davis, *President*
Carol Davis, *Corp Secy*
EMP: 9 EST: 1954
SQ FT: 13,000
SALES (est): 1MM **Privately Held**
SIC: 3471 Plating of metals or formed
products

(G-12141)
RECYCLED PALLETS INC
1603 Hanna St (16102-1513)
PHONE...................724 657-6978
Ted Payne, *Principal*
EMP: 8
SALES (est): 756.9K **Privately Held**
SIC: 2448 Pallets, wood

(G-12142)
**RICHARDSON COOLG
PACKAGES LLC**
Also Called: RCP
1900 New Butler Rd (16101-3123)
P.O. Box 7327 (16107-7327)
PHONE...................724 698-2302
David Richardson,
Carla Richardson,
◆ EMP: 45
SALES (est): 10.5MM **Privately Held**
WEB: www.srfamerica.com
SIC: 3443 Boiler & boiler shop work

(G-12143)
RIGGANS ADVG SPECIALTY CO
2934 Mercer Rd (16105-1320)
PHONE...................724 654-5741
Laraine Riggans-Stock, *Owner*
EMP: 10
SALES: 200K **Privately Held**
WEB: www.riggansadvertising.com
SIC: 5199 5112 2759 Advertising special-
ties; business forms; commercial printing

(G-12144)
ROCCAS ITALIAN FOODS INC
520 S Mill St (16101-4007)
P.O. Box 150 (16103-0150)
PHONE...................724 654-3344
Anthony Rocca, *President*
Victor Rocca, *Corp Secy*
▲ EMP: 10
SALES (est): 871.5K **Privately Held**
SIC: 2038 Ethnic foods, frozen

(G-12145)
ROSSI PRECISION INC
250 Reed Rd (16102-3628)
PHONE...................724 667-9334
Richard Rossi, *President*
EMP: 6
SALES: 317K **Privately Held**
SIC: 3312 Tool & die steel

(G-12146)
RWE HOLDING COMPANY
535 Rundle Rd (16107)
PHONE...................724 752-9082
Bryan Lechner, *Manager*
EMP: 10
SALES (corp-wide): 1.2MM **Privately
Held**
SIC: 3295 5169 Graphite, natural: ground,
pulverized, refined or blended; carbon
black
PA: Rwe Holding Company
372 Rundle Rd
New Castle PA 16102
724 652-2999

(G-12147)
SELECT INDUSTRIES INC (PA)
420 S Cascade St (16101-3339)
P.O. Box 7158 (16107-7158)
PHONE...................724 654-7747
Jeffrey A Gotthardt, *President*
Glenn E Gotthardt, *Corp Secy*
James Andamasaris, *Vice Pres*
▼ EMP: 2
SQ FT: 29,000
SALES (est): 1.8MM **Privately Held**
SIC: 2796 3443 Lithographic plates, posi-
tives or negatives; heat exchangers: cool-
ers (after, inter), condensers, etc.

(G-12148)
SERVEDIO A ELC MTR SVC INC
634 E Washington St (16101-4169)
PHONE...................724 658-8041
Samuel Servedio, *President*
Anthony Servedio, *Vice Pres*
Thomas Servedio, *Sales Staff*
EMP: 16 EST: 1931
SQ FT: 1,800
SALES (est): 6.7MM **Privately Held**
WEB: www.servedio.com
SIC: 5063 7694 3679 7692 Motors, elec-
tric; motor repair services; electric motor
repair; electronic circuits; welding repair;
industrial electrical relays & switches

(G-12149)
**SHENANGO ADVANCED
CERAMICS LLC (HQ)**
Also Called: Resco Products
606 Mccleary Ave (16101-7502)
PHONE...................724 652-6668
William Augur, *Mng Member*
Mike Atkins,
Alina Chand,
Brad Olson,
▲ EMP: 20
SQ FT: 80,000
SALES (est): 17.6MM
SALES (corp-wide): 210.1MM **Privately
Held**
WEB: www.shenac.com
SIC: 3255 Clay refractories
PA: Resco Products, Inc.
6600 Steubenville Pike # 1
Pittsburgh PA 15205
888 283-5505

(G-12150)
SHENANGO AUTO MALL LLC
2515 Ellwood Rd (16101-6201)
PHONE...................724 698-7304
Paul Lapskl, *CEO*
EMP: 150
SALES (est): 4.8MM **Privately Held**
SIC: 3559 Automotive maintenance equip-
ment

(G-12151)
SHENANGO OPERATING INC
792 Commerce Ave (16101-7626)
PHONE...................724 657-3650
Joe Clavelli, *President*
EMP: 40
SQ FT: 225,000
SALES (est): 5.6MM **Privately Held**
WEB: www.ccd-pop.com
SIC: 2653 7389 Display items, solid fiber:
made from purchased materials; balloons,
novelty & toy

(G-12152)
SILGAN IPEC CORPORATION
185 Northgate Cir (16105-5537)
PHONE...................724 658-3004
Joseph Giordano Jr, *President*
EMP: 55
SALES (corp-wide): 4.4B **Publicly Held**
SIC: 3089 Closures, plastic
HQ: Silgan Ipec Corporation
185 Northgate Cir
New Castle PA 16105
724 658-3004

(G-12153)
**SILGAN IPEC CORPORATION
(HQ)**
185 Northgate Cir (16105-5537)
PHONE...................724 658-3004
Joseph Giordano Jr, *President*
Charles J Long Jr, *Corp Secy*
EMP: 75
SALES (est): 21.7MM
SALES (corp-wide): 4.4B **Publicly Held**
SIC: 3089 Closures, plastic
PA: Silgan Holdings Inc.
4 Landmark Sq Ste 400
Stamford CT 06901
203 975-7110

(G-12154)
SOAP PLANT INC
765 Commerce Ave (16101-7635)
PHONE...................724 656-3601
Deborah Spik, *President*
EMP: 5
SALES (est): 1.5MM **Privately Held**
SIC: 2841 Soap & other detergents

(G-12155)
SPOMIN METALS INC
2975 New Butler Rd (16101-3232)
PHONE...................724 924-9718
Robert Esposito, *President*
Joyce Esposito, *Corp Secy*
EMP: 11
SQ FT: 9,500
SALES (est): 1MM **Privately Held**
SIC: 3443 3312 Plate work for the nuclear
industry; blast furnaces & steel mills

(G-12156)
SUMMERS ACQUISITION CORP
Also Called: Quality Hose Div
1101 N Liberty St (16102-1359)
PHONE...................724 652-4673
Joseph Stiles Jr, *Branch Mgr*
EMP: 5
SALES (corp-wide): 3.1B **Privately Held**
WEB: www.summersrubber.com
SIC: 5085 3429 Rubber goods, mechani-
cal; manufactured hardware (general)
HQ: Summers Acquisition Corporation
12555 Berea Rd
Cleveland OH 44111
216 941-7700

(G-12157)
SUMMERS CONSTRUCTION
2196 Copper Rd (16101-7974)
PHONE...................724 924-1700
Mark Summers, *Principal*
EMP: 6
SALES (est): 430K **Privately Held**
SIC: 1442 Construction sand & gravel

(G-12158)
**T C REDI MIX YOUNGSTOWN
INC**
Also Called: T C Redi-Mix
203 W Washington St (16101-3999)
PHONE...................724 652-7878
Rick Carna, *Manager*
EMP: 6
SALES (corp-wide): 4.4MM **Privately
Held**
SIC: 3273 Ready-mixed concrete
PA: T C Redi Mix Of Youngstown, Inc.
2400 Poland Ave
Youngstown OH 44502
330 755-2143

(G-12159)
TMS INTERNATIONAL LLC
208 Rundle Rd (16102-1916)
PHONE...................724 658-2004
EMP: 5 **Privately Held**
SIC: 3312 Blast furnaces & steel mills
HQ: Tms International, Llc
12 Monongahela Ave
Glassport PA 15045
412 678-6141

(G-12160)
TRU TECH VALVE LLC (PA)
3287 Perry Hwy (16101-8447)
PHONE...................724 916-4805
Jeffrey R Ruffing, *Mng Member*
▲ EMP: 4 EST: 2009
SALES (est): 705.1K **Privately Held**
SIC: 3592 Valves

(G-12161)
UNISTEEL LLC
499 Honey Bee Ln (16105-3807)
PHONE...................724 657-1160
Karie Magno, *Principal*
EMP: 3
SALES (est): 242K **Privately Held**
SIC: 3462 Iron & steel forgings

(G-12162)
**VELOCITY EQP SOLUTIONS LLC
(PA)**
2618 W State St (16101-8642)
PHONE...................800 521-1368
Tom Blaszkow, *President*
Mark Trott, *Vice Pres*
Adam Brunke, *Sales Mgr*
Michael Lepore, *Manager*
◆ EMP: 16
SALES (est): 5MM **Privately Held**
SIC: 3089 3565 3545 Blow molded fin-
ished plastic products; bottling machinery:
filling, capping, labeling; tools & acces-
sories for machine tools

(G-12163)
VELOCITY MAGNETICS INC
200 Green Ridge Rd (16105-6140)
PHONE...................724 657-8290
Domenic P Marzano, *President*
Butch Hudak, *Project Engr*
▲ EMP: 8
SQ FT: 1,500

▲ = Import ▼=Export
◆ =Import/Export

SALES (est): 1.8MM **Privately Held**
WEB: www.velocitymagnetics.com
SIC: 3812 Magnetic field detection apparatus

(G-12164)
VELOCITY POWDER COATING LLC
2618 W State St (16101-8642)
PHONE..........................704 287-1024
Thomas Blaszkow, *Mng Member*
Danielle De Paolo,
Mark Trott,
EMP: 5 EST: 1998
SQ FT: 5,000
SALES (est): 313.8K **Privately Held**
SIC: 3479 3599 Etching & engraving; machine shop, jobbing & repair

(G-12165)
VULCAN OILFIELD SERVICES LLC
418 S Cascade St Ste 1 (16101-3384)
P.O. Box 7726 (16107-7726)
PHONE..........................724 698-1008
Matthew Anderson, *Principal*
EMP: 7 EST: 2013
SALES (est): 1.2MM **Privately Held**
SIC: 1389 Oil field services

(G-12166)
WEEKLY BARGAIN BULLETIN INC
1576 Sunrise Dr (16105-5340)
PHONE..........................724 654-5529
Frank Hutchison, *President*
Karen Hutchinson, *Corp Secy*
EMP: 9
SALES (est): 536.5K **Privately Held**
SIC: 2711 Newspapers: publishing only, not printed on site

(G-12167)
WELDING ALLOYS USA
759 Northgate Cir (16105-5551)
PHONE..........................724 202-7497
Adam Smith, *Office Mgr*
EMP: 5
SALES (est): 185K **Privately Held**
SIC: 7692 3548 Welding repair; welding & cutting apparatus & accessories

(G-12168)
WEST PENN PRINTING
103 Riverpark Dr (16101-8919)
PHONE..........................724 546-2020
Brad Susen, *Manager*
Keith Vargo, *Manager*
EMP: 4
SALES (est): 615.4K **Privately Held**
SIC: 2752 Commercial printing, offset

(G-12169)
WESTERN PA STL FABG INC
550 Honey Bee Ln (16105-3810)
PHONE..........................724 658-8575
Fredric J Defiore, *President*
Douglas McFarland, *Purchasing*
Denise De Fiore, *Financial Exec*
Frederic De Fiore, *Sales Executive*
Denise Defiore, *Manager*
EMP: 35
SQ FT: 54,000
SALES (est): 9.7MM **Privately Held**
WEB: www.wpsfinc.com
SIC: 3443 Fabricated plate work (boiler shop)

(G-12170)
XALOY SUPERIOR HOLDINGS INC
1399 County Line Rd (16101-2955)
PHONE..........................724 656-5600
Brad Casale, *Regl Sales Mgr*
James R Jaye, *Director*
EMP: 4
SALES (est): 274.4K
SALES (corp-wide): 2.2B **Publicly Held**
SIC: 3544 Forms (molds), for foundry & plastics working machinery
PA: Nordson Corporation
28601 Clemens Rd
Westlake OH 44145
440 892-1580

(G-12171)
YESCO NEW CASTLE ELEC SUP
218 Old Youngstown Rd (16101-8630)
PHONE..........................724 656-0911
Lee Derose, *President*
Steve Wiseman, *Branch Mgr*
EMP: 6
SALES (est): 1.7MM **Privately Held**
SIC: 5063 3993 Electrical supplies; signs & advertising specialties

(G-12172)
ZAMBELLI FIREWORKS MFG CO
782 Garner Rd (16101)
PHONE..........................724 652-1156
Fax: 724 652-1456
EMP: 5
SALES (corp-wide): 19.5MM **Privately Held**
SIC: 2899 Mfg Chemical Preparations
PA: Zambelli Fireworks Manufacturing Co.

New Castle PA
800 245-0397

New Columbia
Union County

(G-12173)
C M C STEEL FABRICATORS INC
Also Called: CMC Joist & Deck
2093 Old Hwy Ste 15 (17856)
PHONE..........................570 568-6761
Doug Lannert, *Branch Mgr*
EMP: 210
SALES (corp-wide): 4.6B **Publicly Held**
WEB: www.cmcsg.com
SIC: 3441 Joists, open web steel: long-span series
HQ: C M C Steel Fabricators, Inc.
1 Steel Mill Dr
Seguin TX 78155
830 372-8200

(G-12174)
NEW NGC INC
Also Called: Paper Plant
2586 Old Route 15 (17856-9367)
P.O. Box 210, West Milton (17886-0210)
PHONE..........................570 538-2531
Lou Erhardt, *Manager*
EMP: 86
SALES (corp-wide): 685.8MM **Privately Held**
WEB: www.natgyp.com
SIC: 2621 3275 2631 Wallpaper (hanging paper); gypsum products; paperboard mills
HQ: New Ngc, Inc.
2001 Rexford Rd
Charlotte NC 28211

(G-12175)
PILLINGS FRP (PA)
Old Rte 15 (17856)
P.O. Box 119, West Milton (17886-0119)
PHONE..........................570 538-9202
Earl W Pilling, *President*
Richard Pilling, *Principal*
EMP: 15
SQ FT: 15,000
SALES (est): 1.6MM **Privately Held**
SIC: 3714 Tops, motor vehicle

(G-12176)
STANDARD INDUSTRIES INC
Also Called: GAF Materials Corporation
2093 Old Route 15 (17856-9375)
PHONE..........................570 568-7230
EMP: 11
SALES (corp-wide): 2.7B **Privately Held**
SIC: 3089 Injection molded finished plastic products
HQ: Standard Industries Inc.
1 Campus Dr
Parsippany NJ 07054

(G-12177)
TPS LLC (HQ)
Also Called: Thermal Product Solutions
2821 Old Route 15 (17856-9396)
PHONE..........................570 538-7200

Ron Cozean, *Ch of Bd*
David Strand, *President*
Ben Lehman, *Safety Mgr*
Scott Walters, *Purchasing*
Dennis Mendler, *Engineer*
▲ EMP: 150
SQ FT: 70,000
SALES (est): 27.5MM
SALES (corp-wide): 95.3MM **Privately Held**
WEB: www.lunaire.com
SIC: 3567 3821 3842 3564 Industrial furnaces & ovens; ovens, laboratory; incubators, laboratory; sterilizers; calorimeters; surgical appliances & supplies; blowers & fans
PA: The Resilience Fund Iii L P
25101 Chagrin Blvd
Cleveland OH 44122
216 292-0200

(G-12178)
VILLAGE AT OVERLOOK LLC
99 Park Dr (17856-9277)
PHONE..........................570 538-9167
EMP: 3 EST: 2008
SALES (est): 160K **Privately Held**
SIC: 2451 Mfg Mobile Homes

(G-12179)
WA DEHART INC
1130 Old Route 15 (17856-9310)
PHONE..........................570 568-1551
Christian C Trate, *President*
Amy D Woodcock, *Corp Secy*
EMP: 58
SQ FT: 68,000
SALES (est): 25.9MM **Privately Held**
SIC: 5194 5113 2064 Tobacco & tobacco products; cigarettes; cigars; snuff; disposable plates, cups, napkins & eating utensils; dishes, disposable plastic & paper; cups, disposable plastic & paper; napkins, paper; breakfast bars

New Cumberland
Cumberland County

(G-12180)
CAPITOL TOOL & MFG CO INC
429 Old York Rd (17070-3124)
PHONE..........................717 938-6165
Jeffrey R Mathias, *President*
Jeff Mathias, *Vice Pres*
EMP: 15
SQ FT: 5,000
SALES (est): 2.6MM **Privately Held**
WEB: www.captool.com
SIC: 3599 Machine shop, jobbing & repair

(G-12181)
CENTRAL PENNA TOOL & MFG INC
450 Locust Rd (17070-3137)
PHONE..........................717 932-1294
Thomas Long, *President*
Mary Beth Long, *Corp Secy*
EMP: 6
SQ FT: 1,200
SALES: 510K **Privately Held**
SIC: 3544 Industrial molds

(G-12182)
CHARLES L SIMPSON SR
Also Called: Charles Furriers
333 Sharon Dr (17070-3038)
PHONE..........................717 763-7023
Charles L Simpson Sr, *Owner*
EMP: 12
SQ FT: 14,000
SALES: 700K **Privately Held**
SIC: 7219 2371 5632 Fur garment cleaning, repairing & storage; coats, fur; fur apparel, made to custom order

(G-12183)
CHEROKEE SOFTWARE SYSTEMS
334 Hillcrest Dr (17070-3077)
PHONE..........................717 932-5008
Frank Sechrist, *Owner*
EMP: 4

SALES (est): 191.9K **Privately Held**
SIC: 7372 Prepackaged software

(G-12184)
CHOCCOBUTTER INC
1492 Maplewood Dr (17070-2217)
P.O. Box 10628, Harrisburg (17105-0628)
PHONE..........................717 756-5590
Celestin Bedzigui, *President*
Deborah Vereem, *CFO*
▲ EMP: 5
SALES: 1MM **Privately Held**
SIC: 2066 5149 Chocolate liquor; chocolate coatings & syrup; coffee, green or roasted

(G-12185)
DEAD LIGHTNING DISTILLERY
311 Bridge St (17070-2188)
PHONE..........................717 695-0927
EMP: 3
SALES (est): 125.9K **Privately Held**
SIC: 2085 Distilled & blended liquors

(G-12186)
HOT ROD FABRICATIONS LLP
2 Pine Tree Dr (17070-2330)
PHONE..........................717 774-6302
William Lang, *Partner*
Jeff Shores, *Partner*
EMP: 7
SALES (est): 490K **Privately Held**
WEB: www.hotrodfabrications.com
SIC: 3711 Automobile assembly, including specialty automobiles

(G-12187)
JOHNSON CONTROLS
195 Limekiln Rd (17070-2423)
PHONE..........................717 610-8100
John Gehrlein, *Principal*
Steve McCoy, *Technology*
EMP: 97 **Privately Held**
WEB: www.simplexgrinnell.com
SIC: 3669 Emergency alarms
HQ: Johnson Controls Fire Protection Lp
6600 Congress Ave
Boca Raton FL 33487
561 988-7200

(G-12188)
KARL DODSON
Also Called: K D Graphics
464 Big Spring Rd (17070-3103)
PHONE..........................717 938-6132
Karl Dodson, *Owner*
EMP: 3
SALES (est): 208.8K **Privately Held**
SIC: 2396 Screen printing on fabric articles

(G-12189)
MITIGATOR INC
198 Rose Hill Dr (17070-2357)
PHONE..........................717 576-9589
Tiffany Levine, *Principal*
EMP: 4
SALES (est): 416.3K **Privately Held**
SIC: 3826 Moisture analyzers

(G-12190)
ROWE SCREEN PRINT INC
1605 Elm St (17070-1220)
PHONE..........................717 774-8920
Thomas Rowe, *President*
James Rowe, *Vice Pres*
▲ EMP: 10
SQ FT: 11,000
SALES (est): 919.9K **Privately Held**
SIC: 2396 2395 Screen printing on fabric articles; embroidery & art needlework

New Derry
Westmoreland County

(G-12191)
MACHINE REBUILDERS
5722 Route 982 (15671-1004)
PHONE..........................724 694-3190
Thomas Kitchen, *Owner*
EMP: 5

GEOGRAPHIC

SALES: 450K **Privately Held**
SIC: 3542 7699 Machine tools, metal forming type; industrial machinery & equipment repair

(G-12192)
MC CULLOUGH MACHINE INC
116 Atlantic Rd (15671-1023)
PHONE....................................724 694-8485
Scott Mc Cullough, *President*
Barbara Mc Cullough, *Treasurer*
EMP: 17
SQ FT: 9,000
SALES (est): 2.3MM **Privately Held**
SIC: 3599 Machine shop, jobbing & repair

New Eagle
Washington County

(G-12193)
THERM-O-ROCK EAST INC (PA)
Also Called: T R
1 Pine St (15067)
P.O. Box 429 (15067-0429)
PHONE....................................724 258-3670
Edward Jdobkin, *Principal*
▲ EMP: 100
SQ FT: 150,000
SALES (est): 17.6MM **Privately Held**
WEB: www.therm-o-rock.com
SIC: 3295 3296 Perlite, aggregate or expanded; vermiculite, exfoliated; mineral wool

New Enterprise
Bedford County

(G-12194)
NEW ENTERPRISE STONE LIME INC (PA)
Also Called: Buffalo Crushed Stone
3912 Brumbaugh Rd (16664-9137)
P.O. Box 77 (16664-0077)
PHONE....................................814 224-6883
Paul I Detwiler Jr, *Ch of Bd*
Donald L Detwiler, *Vice Ch Bd*
Paul Detwiler III, *President*
James Van Buren, *COO*
Steven B Detwiler, *Senior VP*
EMP: 100 EST: 1924
SQ FT: 4,000
SALES: 651.9MM **Privately Held**
WEB: www.nesl.com
SIC: 1422 1611 Crushed & broken limestone; highway & street paving contractor

(G-12195)
RISSLER E MANUFACTURING LLC
2794 Brumbaugh Rd (16664-8643)
PHONE....................................814 766-2246
John Rissler,
EMP: 7
SALES (est): 1.3MM **Privately Held**
SIC: 3535 3441 Conveyors & conveying equipment; fabricated structural metal

New Florence
Westmoreland County

(G-12196)
EVERCLEAR VALLEY INC (PA)
Also Called: Maple Mountain
1820 Mulligan Rd (15944)
PHONE....................................724 676-4703
Ralph Woods, *President*
EMP: 1
SQ FT: 10,000
SALES (est): 17.5MM **Privately Held**
SIC: 2512 3999 Upholstered household furniture; candles

(G-12197)
GROMAN RESTORATION INC
519 Sugar Run Rd (15944-2325)
PHONE....................................724 235-5000
John Groman, *President*
EMP: 3

SALES: 100K **Privately Held**
SIC: 7641 2499 3842 Antique furniture repair & restoration; laundry products, wood; cosmetic restorations

(G-12198)
MAPLE MOUNTAIN INDUSTRIES INC (PA)
Also Called: Maple Mountain Homes
1820 Mulligan Hill Rd (15944-9549)
PHONE....................................724 676-4703
Cheryl Woods, *President*
William R Woods, *Vice Pres*
Amy McDowell, *CFO*
Amy M McDowell, *Treasurer*
Dave Daucher, *Info Tech Mgr*
▲ EMP: 30
SQ FT: 10,000
SALES (est): 48.6MM **Privately Held**
WEB: www.maplemountain.com
SIC: 2512 2511 5999 7699 Upholstered household furniture; wood household furniture; farm machinery; farm machinery repair; new construction, single-family houses; nonresidential construction

(G-12199)
NAPOTNIK WELDING INC
4225 Power Plant Rd (15944-8815)
PHONE....................................814 446-4500
Norman Napotnik, *President*
Robin Napotnik, *Treasurer*
Bree Napotnik, *Admin Sec*
EMP: 5
SQ FT: 30,000
SALES (est): 1.7MM **Privately Held**
SIC: 7692 Welding repair

New Freedom
York County

(G-12200)
AMAT INC
10 E Franklin St (17349-9506)
PHONE....................................717 235-8003
Roy Kroner, *President*
EMP: 9
SALES: 1.2MM **Privately Held**
SIC: 3545 5085 7389 Cutting tools for machine tools; industrial supplies; abrasives; grinding, precision: commercial or industrial

(G-12201)
BALDUCCI STONEYARD LLC
18159 Susquehanna Trl S (17349-8900)
P.O. Box 305, Maryland Line MD (21105-0305)
PHONE....................................410 627-0594
Gregory Buchman, *Director*
EMP: 5
SALES (est): 729.1K **Privately Held**
SIC: 5211 1411 Masonry materials & supplies; paving stones; bluestone, dimension-quarrying

(G-12202)
BB VINTAGE MAGAZINE ADS
118 Windy Hill Rd (17349-8403)
PHONE....................................717 235-1109
Robert Brulinski, *Principal*
EMP: 3
SALES (est): 174.5K **Privately Held**
SIC: 2721 Periodicals

(G-12203)
CRESCENT INDUSTRIES INC (PA)
70 E High St (17349-9664)
PHONE....................................717 235-3844
Daryl W Paules, *President*
Catherine Allen, *Vice Pres*
Eric Paules, *Vice Pres*
Shawn Hedrick, *Engineer*
Bill Morningstar, *Engineer*
▲ EMP: 153 EST: 1945
SQ FT: 154,000
SALES: 19.6MM **Privately Held**
SIC: 3089 Injection molding of plastics

(G-12204)
CRESCENT INDUSTRIES INC
70 E High St (17349-9664)
PHONE....................................717 235-3844
Darrell Paules, *President*
EMP: 100
SALES (corp-wide): 19.6MM **Privately Held**
SIC: 3089 3544 Injection molding of plastics; special dies, tools, jigs & fixtures
PA: Crescent Industries Inc.
70 E High St
New Freedom PA 17349
717 235-3844

(G-12205)
EBER & WEIN INC
15727 Whitcraft Rd (17349-8119)
PHONE....................................717 759-8065
Rachel Mueck, *Principal*
EMP: 13
SALES (est): 963.9K **Privately Held**
SIC: 2741 Miscellaneous publishing

(G-12206)
EDEN TOOL COMPANY
157 E Main St (17349-9704)
P.O. Box 491 (17349-0491)
PHONE....................................717 235-7009
Michael Eden, *President*
EMP: 5 EST: 2000
SQ FT: 2,600
SALES (est): 685K **Privately Held**
SIC: 3312 Tool & die steel

(G-12207)
ELECTRONIC CONCEPTS INC
223 W Main St (17349-7955)
P.O. Box 601 (17349-0601)
PHONE....................................717 235-9450
Jean Jeffers, *President*
Gary Jeffers, *Vice Pres*
EMP: 5 EST: 1996
SALES (est): 223.8K **Privately Held**
SIC: 8748 3651 Telecommunications consultant; home entertainment equipment, electronic

(G-12208)
EXPRESS MONEY SERVICES INC
Also Called: Express Check Cashing
16 Mccurley Dr (17349-9489)
PHONE....................................717 235-5993
Tom Bond, *President*
Beth Bond, *Vice Pres*
EMP: 3
SALES: 50K **Privately Held**
SIC: 6099 2741 Check cashing agencies; miscellaneous publishing

(G-12209)
ID TECHNOLOGY LLC
Also Called: Epi Labelers
1145 E Wellspring Rd (17349-8426)
PHONE....................................717 235-8345
EMP: 25
SALES (corp-wide): 599.3MM **Privately Held**
SIC: 3565 Labeling machines, industrial
HQ: Id Technology Llc
5051 N Sylvania Ave
Fort Worth TX 76137
817 626-7779

(G-12210)
IDSI LLC
888 Far Hills Dr Ste 200 (17349-8428)
PHONE....................................717 227-9055
Thomas Steidel, *Principal*
James A Hougo,
EMP: 4
SALES (corp-wide): 10MM **Privately Held**
SIC: 3663 Radio & TV communications equipment
HQ: Idsi, Llc
888 Far Hills Dr Ste 200
New Freedom PA 17349

(G-12211)
IDSI LLC (HQ)
888 Far Hills Dr Ste 200 (17349-8428)
PHONE....................................717 235-5474
Christopher Brady,

Thomas Steidel,
EMP: 25
SALES (est): 10MM **Privately Held**
WEB: www.tripointglobal.com
SIC: 3663 Radio & TV communications equipment
PA: Crescend Technologies, L.L.C.
140 E State Pkwy
Schaumburg IL 60173
847 908-5400

(G-12212)
LUMI TRAK INC
230 Orwig Rd (17349-9652)
PHONE....................................717 235-2863
George Townsend, *President*
EMP: 10
SQ FT: 3,000
SALES (est): 1.9MM **Privately Held**
WEB: www.lumitrak.com
SIC: 3648 Lighting equipment

(G-12213)
OAKWORKS INC
923 E Wellspring Rd (17349-8408)
P.O. Box 238, Shrewsbury (17361-0238)
PHONE....................................717 227-0516
Jeffrey Riach, *CEO*
Richard Schuman, *President*
Linda Riach, *Exec VP*
Charles Alcorn, *CFO*
Lisa Severn, *Accounts Exec*
◆ EMP: 100
SQ FT: 90,518
SALES (est): 21.6MM **Privately Held**
WEB: www.oakworks.com
SIC: 2531 3842 3841 Public building & related furniture; stretchers; surgical & medical instruments; operating tables

(G-12214)
POWERHOUSE GENERATOR INC (PA)
454 N Constitution Ave (17349-8813)
PHONE....................................717 759-8535
Tim Paciolla, *CEO*
Jim Wilson, *General Mgr*
EMP: 5 EST: 2010
SALES (est): 964.9K **Privately Held**
SIC: 3621 Power generators

(G-12215)
SIELING AND JONES INC
127 Pleasant Ave (17349)
P.O. Box 159 (17349-0159)
PHONE....................................717 235-7931
Edward G Jones III, *President*
Loren Garner, *Project Mgr*
William Schwenke, *Controller*
▲ EMP: 52 EST: 1949
SQ FT: 45,000
SALES: 7MM **Privately Held**
WEB: www.sielingandjones.com
SIC: 2435 Veneer stock, hardwood

(G-12216)
TECHNICAL FABRICATION INC
Also Called: TEC Fab
15842 Elm Dr Ste 1 (17349-9400)
PHONE....................................717 227-0909
Bruce G Beigel, *President*
EMP: 20
SQ FT: 12,000
SALES (est): 3.8MM **Privately Held**
WEB: www.tecfab-inc.com
SIC: 3672 Printed circuit boards

(G-12217)
TITANIUM FOUNDATION
1550 Elm Dr (17349)
PHONE....................................717 668-8423
Laura Bowman Frazier, *Principal*
EMP: 4 EST: 2010
SALES (est): 356.1K **Privately Held**
SIC: 3356 Titanium

New Freeport
Greene County

(G-12218)
SPRINGHILL WELL SERVICE INC
669 Deep Valley Rd (15352-1761)
PHONE....................................724 447-2449

▲ = Import ▼=Export
◆ =Import/Export

EMP: 20
SALES (est): 1.7MM **Privately Held**
SIC: 1389 Oil & Gas Field Services

(G-12219)
STALNAKER LUMBER
138 Renner Creek Rd (15352-1665)
PHONE..................................724 447-2248
EMP: 3 EST: 1969
SALES (est): 130K **Privately Held**
SIC: 2411 Logging

New Galilee
Beaver County

(G-12220)
BOGNAR AND COMPANY INC
Hc 168 (16141)
P.O. Box 464 (16141-0464)
PHONE..................................724 336-5000
Michael Livingston, *Manager*
EMP: 20
SALES (corp-wide): 7.1MM **Privately Held**
SIC: 2911 Coke, petroleum
PA: Bognar And Company, Inc.
  733 Washington Rd Ste 500
  Pittsburgh PA 15228
  412 344-9900

(G-12221)
MSA PITTSBURGH DIST CTR
1750 Shenango Rd (16141-2224)
PHONE..................................724 742-8090
▲ EMP: 3
SALES (est): 145K **Privately Held**
SIC: 3842 Personal safety equipment

(G-12222)
SOAP ALCHEMY LLC
317 Walker Rd (16141-3607)
PHONE..................................412 671-4278
Jordan Henderson, *Principal*
EMP: 3
SALES (est): 215K **Privately Held**
SIC: 3261 Soap dishes, vitreous china

(G-12223)
WAMPUM HARDWARE CO (PA)
636 Paden Rd (16141-2018)
PHONE..................................724 336-4501
Gerald Davis, *President*
Jay Elkin, *Regional Mgr*
Paul J Davis, *Vice Pres*
Edward C Beck, *Treasurer*
Christine Yoder, *Web Dvlpr*
EMP: 4
SALES (est): 36.1MM **Privately Held**
WEB: www.wampumhardware.com
SIC: 2892 Explosives

New Holland
Lancaster County

(G-12224)
AARON E BEILER
905 W Main St (17557-9224)
PHONE..................................717 656-9596
Aaron Beiler, *Owner*
Aaron E Beiler, *Owner*
EMP: 8 EST: 2010
SALES (est): 793.2K **Privately Held**
SIC: 2499 Wood products

(G-12225)
AARON WENGER
Also Called: Wenger Systems
264 Voganville Rd (17557-9229)
PHONE..................................717 656-9876
Aaron Wenger, *Owner*
EMP: 4
SQ FT: 4,500
SALES (est): 900K **Privately Held**
SIC: 3523 7692 5531 Trailers & wagons, farm; welding repair; automotive tires

(G-12226)
ADVENTURE SYSTEMS INC
172 Orlan Rd (17557-9108)
PHONE..................................717 351-7177
Carl Leaman, *President*

EMP: 7
SQ FT: 33,000
SALES (est): 490K **Privately Held**
WEB: www.adventuresystems.com
SIC: 3949 Playground equipment

(G-12227)
AFP ADVANCED FOOD PRODUCTS LLC (DH)
402 S Custer Ave (17557-9234)
PHONE..................................717 355-8667
Miro Hosek, *CEO*
Lou Gitlin,
▼ EMP: 200 EST: 2001
SQ FT: 10,000
SALES (est): 181.1MM
SALES (corp-wide): 6.3B **Privately Held**
WEB: www.afpllc.com
SIC: 2026 2035 2032 2099 Fluid milk; pickles, sauces & salad dressings; puddings, except meat: packaged in cans, jars, etc.; food preparations; cheese spreads, dips, pastes & other cheese products
HQ: Zausner Foods Corp.
  400 S Custer Ave
  New Holland PA 17557
  717 355-8505

(G-12228)
AFP ADVANCED FOOD PRODUCTS LLC
158 W Jackson St (17557-1607)
PHONE..................................717 354-6560
Howard Covenko, *Manager*
EMP: 30
SALES (corp-wide): 6.3B **Privately Held**
WEB: www.afpllc.com
SIC: 2032 Canned specialties
HQ: Afp Advanced Food Products Llc
  402 S Custer Ave
  New Holland PA 17557
  717 355-8667

(G-12229)
ATI CORPORATION
Also Called: Preseeder
250 Earland Dr (17557-1505)
PHONE..................................717 354-8721
John L Herr, *President*
Jevon Herr, *Vice Pres*
Joann M Herr, *Treasurer*
Jansen Herr, *Admin Sec*
EMP: 20
SQ FT: 39,600
SALES (est): 4.7MM **Privately Held**
WEB: www.preseeder.com
SIC: 3444 3523 Sheet metalwork; soil preparation machinery, except turf & grounds

(G-12230)
BERK-TEK LLC
132 White Oak Rd (17557-8303)
PHONE..................................717 354-6200
Paul Trunk, *President*
Knut Stenseth, *Project Dir*
Knut Lauglo, *Project Mgr*
Glenn Richardson, *Production*
Sharon Strausser, *Buyer*
▼ EMP: 1
SALES (est): 135.1MM **Privately Held**
WEB: www.nexans.com
SIC: 3357 Coaxial cable, nonferrous
HQ: Nexans Usa Inc.
  39 2nd St Nw
  Hickory NC 28601
  828 323-2660

(G-12231)
CASUAL LIVING UNLIMITED LLC
172 Orlan Rd (17557-9108)
PHONE..................................717 351-7177
Joesph Guarino, *CEO*
EMP: 9
SALES (est): 1.5MM **Privately Held**
WEB: www.clunlimited.com
SIC: 3949 2514 Playground equipment; metal lawn & garden furniture
PA: Argosy Real Estate Partners, L.L.C.
  950 W Valley Rd Ste 2900
  Wayne PA 19087

(G-12232)
CHESTNUT RIDGE LLC
475 Voganville Rd (17557-9727)
PHONE..................................717 354-5741
John R Zook,
Linda M Zook,
EMP: 8
SALES (est): 930K **Privately Held**
SIC: 2048 0213 0161 Feed premixes; hogs; cantaloupe farm; asparagus farm; pumpkin farm

(G-12233)
CNH INC
500 Diller Ave (17557-9301)
PHONE..................................717 355-1121
Richard Buckman, *President*
Jim Witmer, *Engineer*
Luke Zerby, *Marketing Staff*
Ken Williford, *Manager*
▼ EMP: 1 EST: 2001
SALES (est): 109.4MM
SALES (corp-wide): 935.8MM **Privately Held**
WEB: www.cnh.net
SIC: 3523 Farm machinery & equipment
PA: New Holland North America, Inc
  300 Diller Ave
  New Holland PA 17557
  717 355-1121

(G-12234)
CNH INDUSTRIAL AMERICA LLC
Also Called: Cnh Industrial Capital's
535 500 Diller Ave (17557)
PHONE..................................800 501-5711
EMP: 21
SALES (est): 12MM **Privately Held**
SIC: 3523 Farm machinery & equipment

(G-12235)
CNH INDUSTRIAL AMERICA LLC
500 Diller Ave (17557-9301)
P.O. Box 1895 (17557-0903)
PHONE..................................717 355-1121
Jean Rosso, *Manager*
Michelle Ruth, *Manager*
EMP: 208
SALES (corp-wide): 27.9B **Privately Held**
SIC: 3523 Farm machinery & equipment
HQ: Cnh Industrial America Llc
  700 State St
  Racine WI 53404
  262 636-6011

(G-12236)
CNH INDUSTRIAL AMERICA LLC
200 George Delp Rd (17557)
PHONE..................................717 355-1902
Robert Craine, *Branch Mgr*
EMP: 208
SALES (corp-wide): 27.9B **Privately Held**
SIC: 3523 3531 Farm machinery & equipment; construction machinery
HQ: Cnh Industrial America Llc
  700 State St
  Racine WI 53404
  262 636-6011

(G-12237)
COLONIAL ROAD WOODWORKS LLC
285 Voganville Rd (17557-9228)
PHONE..................................717 354-8998
Elmer Ebersol, *Mng Member*
EMP: 21
SALES (est): 529.9K **Privately Held**
SIC: 2511 Wood household furniture

(G-12238)
COUNTRY LANE WOODWORKING LLC
Also Called: Country Lane Gazebos
191 Jalyn Dr (17557-9232)
PHONE..................................717 351-9250
Samuel S Stoltzfus, *Owner*
EMP: 30 EST: 1994
SALES (est): 6.1MM **Privately Held**
SIC: 2499 Decorative wood & woodwork

(G-12239)
COZY CABINS LLC
455 Farmersville Rd (17557-9740)
PHONE..................................717 354-3278
David Seibel,

EMP: 9 EST: 1997
SALES (est): 50K **Privately Held**
WEB: www.cozycabins.com
SIC: 2452 Modular homes, prefabricated, wood

(G-12240)
CREATIVE ENERGY DISTRIBUTORS
150 Jalyn Dr (17557-9233)
PHONE..................................717 354-6090
Fred S Umble, *Owner*
EMP: 4 EST: 1995
SALES: 4.5MM **Privately Held**
SIC: 3567 Heating units & devices, industrial: electric

(G-12241)
CREEKSIDE WELDING LLC
137 Meadowcreek Rd (17557-9317)
PHONE..................................717 355-2008
Christ Stoltzsus,
EMP: 4
SQ FT: 3,000
SALES: 450K **Privately Held**
SIC: 3443 Dumpsters, garbage

(G-12242)
CUSTER AVE WOODWORKING LLC
868 S Custer Ave (17557-9326)
PHONE..................................717 354-3999
David Beiler, *Mng Member*
EMP: 2 EST: 1980
SALES (est): 7.5MM **Privately Held**
SIC: 2431 Moldings, wood: unfinished & prefinished

(G-12243)
DL TRUSS LLC
199 Quality Cir (17557-9007)
PHONE..................................717 355-9813
Daniel Lapp, *Mng Member*
EMP: 7
SQ FT: 12,000
SALES (est): 1.3MM **Privately Held**
SIC: 2439 Trusses, wooden roof

(G-12244)
DUTCH CNTRY SOFT PRETZELS LLC
2758 Division Hwy Fl 1 (17557-9650)
PHONE..................................717 354-4493
David Burkholder, *Mng Member*
Jeremy Benshoff, *Mng Member*
EMP: 9 EST: 1994
SALES: 900K **Privately Held**
WEB: www.dutchcountrysoftpretzels.com
SIC: 2052 5145 5461 Pretzels; pretzels; pretzels

(G-12245)
E BEILER CABINETRY
617 New Holland Rd (17557-9531)
PHONE..................................717 354-5515
Elam S Beiler, *Principal*
EMP: 4
SALES (est): 383.9K **Privately Held**
SIC: 2434 Wood kitchen cabinets

(G-12246)
E Z SENSENIG & SON
Also Called: Sensenig, E Z Harness & Son
895 Centerville Rd (17557-9631)
PHONE..................................717 445-5580
Ezra Z Sensenig, *Partner*
Martha Sensenig, *Partner*
Susanna Sensenig, *Partner*
EMP: 7
SALES (est): 979.6K **Privately Held**
SIC: 5191 3199 Harness equipment; harness or harness parts

(G-12247)
EARTH & TURF PRODUCTS LLC
112 S Railroad Ave (17557-1731)
PHONE..................................717 355-2276
John Bentley, *General Mgr*
◆ EMP: 3 EST: 1998
SALES: 500K **Privately Held**
WEB: www.earthandturf.com
SIC: 3523 Farm machinery & equipment

GEOGRAPHIC

(G-12248)
ELITE VINYL RAILINGS LLC (PA)
3431 Division Hwy (17557-9662)
PHONE.............................717 354-0524
Ken Nolt, *Mng Member*
EMP: 9 EST: 1995
SALES (est): 1.2MM **Privately Held**
WEB: www.elitevinylrailings.com
SIC: 2431 Stair railings, wood

(G-12249)
FLEUR DE LAIT EAST LLC
400 S Custer Ave (17557-9220)
PHONE.............................717 355-8580
Greg Gable,
▲ EMP: 8
SALES (est): 1.4MM **Privately Held**
SIC: 2022 Cheese spreads, dips, pastes &
other cheese products

(G-12250)
H & S ELECTRONICS
Also Called: Radioshack
331 E Main St (17557-1336)
PHONE.............................717 354-2200
Stephen Loewen, *Owner*
EMP: 4
SQ FT: 1,500
SALES (est): 357.3K **Privately Held**
SIC: 5731 3663 Consumer electronic
equipment; radios, two-way, citizens'
band, weather, short-wave, etc.; sound
equipment, automotive; radio broadcast-
ing & communications equipment

(G-12251)
HAROLD M HORST INC
Also Called: Horst, H M
340 W Main St (17557-1208)
P.O. Box 486 (17557-0486)
PHONE.............................717 354-5815
Rickey D Horst, *President*
Jeffrey S Horst, *Vice Pres*
Rick Horst, *Manager*
Harold M Horst, *Shareholder*
EMP: 3
SQ FT: 4,000
SALES: 500K **Privately Held**
SIC: 1761 2514 Sheet metalwork; roofing
contractor; kitchen cabinets: metal

(G-12252)
HB SPORTSWEAR INC (PA)
494 W Broad St (17557-1102)
PHONE.............................717 354-2306
James Miller, *President*
Warren Hackman, *Vice Pres*
David Hackman, *Treasurer*
Annette Radcliffe, *Admin Sec*
▲ EMP: 3
SQ FT: 1,000
SALES (est): 539.5K **Privately Held**
WEB: www.hbsports.com
SIC: 2329 2339 2361 2369 Men's &
boys' sportswear & athletic clothing;
women's & misses' athletic clothing &
sportswear; shirts: girls', children's & in-
fants'; warm-up, jogging & sweat suits:
girls' & children's; play suits: girls', chil-
dren's & infants'

(G-12253)
**HORNING MANUFACTURING
LLC**
301 Twin Springs Ct (17557-8789)
PHONE.............................717 354-5040
Leon Horning Jr, *Mng Member*
EMP: 10
SALES (est): 190.8K **Privately Held**
SIC: 3999 Barber & beauty shop equip-
ment

(G-12254)
JOHN CARVELL LOGGING
417 E Main St (17557-1403)
PHONE.............................717 354-8136
Edward Carvell, *Principal*
EMP: 3
SALES (est): 229.8K **Privately Held**
SIC: 2411 Logging

(G-12255)
JOHN M SENSENIG
Also Called: Conestoga Wood Machinery
887 Centerville Rd (17557-9631)
PHONE.............................717 445-4669
John M Sensenig, *Owner*
▲ EMP: 3
SQ FT: 1,800
SALES (est): 697.6K **Privately Held**
SIC: 5084 3553 5999 Woodworking ma-
chinery; woodworking machinery; busi-
ness machines & equipment

(G-12256)
LANCO SHEDS INC
150 Commerce Dr (17557-9115)
PHONE.............................717 351-7100
Sam E King, *President*
EMP: 10 EST: 1998
SQ FT: 10,000
SALES (est): 1.4MM **Privately Held**
SIC: 2452 Prefabricated buildings, wood

(G-12257)
LEROY M SENSENIG INC
Also Called: Sensenig's Feed Mill
115 S Railroad Ave (17557-1730)
PHONE.............................717 354-4756
Kenneth E Sensenig, *President*
Sandra Sensenig, *Admin Sec*
EMP: 30
SQ FT: 11,000
SALES: 9MM **Privately Held**
WEB: www.sensenigsfeedmill.com
SIC: 5191 2048 Feed; prepared feeds

(G-12258)
MARTIN LIMESTONE INC
New Holland Creat
828 E Earl Rd (17557-8510)
PHONE.............................717 354-1200
Brian Demaris, *Branch Mgr*
EMP: 100
SQ FT: 2,360
SALES (corp-wide): 651.9MM **Privately
Held**
WEB: www.martinlimestone.com
SIC: 3273 3272 3271 Ready-mixed con-
crete; concrete products, precast; con-
crete block & brick
HQ: Martin Limestone, Inc.
3580 Division Hwy
East Earl PA 17519
717 335-4500

(G-12259)
MARTIN LIMESTONE INC
Also Called: New Holland Concrete
875 E Earl Rd (17557)
PHONE.............................717 354-1298
Andy Hood, *Branch Mgr*
EMP: 100
SALES (corp-wide): 651.9MM **Privately
Held**
WEB: www.martinlimestone.com
SIC: 3273 Ready-mixed concrete
HQ: Martin Limestone, Inc.
3580 Division Hwy
East Earl PA 17519
717 335-4500

(G-12260)
MARTIN WEAVER R
Also Called: Shady Lane Wagons
192 Amishtown Rd (17557-9717)
PHONE.............................717 354-8970
Weaver R Martin, *Owner*
EMP: 3
SALES (est): 156.1K **Privately Held**
SIC: 3944 Games, toys & children's vehi-
cles

(G-12261)
MEADOWCREEK WELDING LLC
221 Jalyn Dr (17557-9210)
PHONE.............................717 354-7533
Melvin Stoltzsus, *Mng Member*
EMP: 7
SQ FT: 10,000
SALES (est): 917.3K **Privately Held**
SIC: 7692 Welding repair

(G-12262)
**MECHANCAL FBRICATION
GROUP INC**
100 E Franklin St (17557)
P.O. Box 5 (17557-0005)
PHONE.............................717 351-0437
Ray Clugston, *President*
Chris Buck, *Shareholder*
EMP: 5
SALES (est): 931.2K **Privately Held**
SIC: 3441 Fabricated structural metal

(G-12263)
MERIDIAN PRODUCTS INC
124 Earland Dr (17557-1503)
PHONE.............................717 355-7700
Marty Ness, *President*
Elmer R Martin, *President*
Lewis Martin, *Vice Pres*
Dean Youndt, *Engineer*
Mike Hurst, *CFO*
▼ EMP: 75
SQ FT: 66,700
SALES (est): 10.1MM **Privately Held**
WEB: www.meridianproduct.com
SIC: 2434 Wood kitchen cabinets

(G-12264)
**MUSSELMAN LUMBER - US LBM
LLC**
200 Brimmer Ave (17557-1706)
P.O. Box 105 (17557-0105)
PHONE.............................717 354-4321
Galen EBY, *President*
EMP: 63 EST: 2013
SALES (est): 7.5MM
SALES (corp-wide): 2B **Privately Held**
SIC: 2426 2439 Lumber, hardwood dimen-
sion; timbers, structural: laminated lumber
HQ: Us Lbm Holdings, Llc
1000 Corporate Grove Dr
Buffalo Grove IL 60089

(G-12265)
NEW HOLLAND FENCE LLC
917 Walnut St (17557-8500)
PHONE.............................717 355-2204
Aaron E Beiler,
Mervin Beiler,
EMP: 13
SALES (est): 1.4MM **Privately Held**
SIC: 2499 0241 Fencing, wood; milk pro-
duction

(G-12266)
**NEW HOLLAND NORTH
AMERICA**
300 Diller Ave (17557-1631)
PHONE.............................717 354-4514
Allen Rider, *President*
Seth Doman, *Marketing Staff*
EMP: 376
SALES (corp-wide): 935.8MM **Privately
Held**
WEB: www.newholland.com
SIC: 3523 Farm machinery & equipment
PA: New Holland North America, Inc
300 Diller Ave
New Holland PA 17557
717 355-1121

(G-12267)
**NEW HOLLAND NORTH
AMERICA (PA)**
300 Diller Ave (17557-1631)
PHONE.............................717 355-1121
A R Rider, *President*
Barbara Prossen, *President*
Andrew Wood, *Regional Mgr*
Robert Hermsen, *Area Mgr*
Trent Hardy, *Business Mgr*
◆ EMP: 1729
SALES (est): 935.8MM **Privately Held**
WEB: www.newholland.com
SIC: 3523 Farm machinery & equipment

(G-12268)
**NEW HOLLAND NORTH
AMERICA**
300 Diller Ave (17557-1631)
PHONE.............................717 355-1121
EMP: 376

SALES (corp-wide): 935.8MM **Privately
Held**
SIC: 3523 Farm machinery & equipment
PA: New Holland North America, Inc
300 Diller Ave
New Holland PA 17557
717 355-1121

(G-12269)
**NEWSWANGER WOODS
SPECIALTIES**
313 Gristmill Rd (17557-9776)
PHONE.............................717 355-9274
Martha Newswanger, *Partner*
Reuben Newswanger, *General Ptnr*
EMP: 4
SQ FT: 3,000
SALES (est): 750K **Privately Held**
SIC: 2511 Wood household furniture

(G-12270)
NEXANS AEROSPACE USA LLC
132 White Oak Rd (17557-8303)
PHONE.............................252 236-4311
Stephen Hall, *President*
▲ EMP: 125
SALES (est): 20.9MM **Privately Held**
WEB: www.berktek.com
SIC: 3357 Nonferrous wiredrawing & insu-
lating
HQ: Nexans Usa Inc.
39 2nd St Nw
Hickory NC 28601
828 323-2660

(G-12271)
NEXANS USA INC
Berk-Tek
132 White Oak Rd (17557-8303)
PHONE.............................717 354-6200
Kevin St Cyr, *President*
Benjamin Aymard, *Business Mgr*
Giuseppe Borrelli, *Exec VP*
Paul Freese, *Purchasing*
Michael Leed, *Engineer*
EMP: 450 **Privately Held**
WEB: www.berktek.com
SIC: 3357 3827 3643 3315 Coaxial
cable, nonferrous; fiber optic cable (insu-
lated); optical instruments & lenses; cur-
rent-carrying wiring devices; steel wire &
related products
HQ: Nexans Usa Inc.
39 2nd St Nw
Hickory NC 28601
828 323-2660

(G-12272)
PENDU MANUFACTURING INC
718 N Shirk Rd (17557-9721)
PHONE.............................717 354-4348
Marlin J Hurst, *President*
Paul Barnhart, *Prdtn Mgr*
April Morgan, *Asst Controller*
Matt Davis, *Marketing Mgr*
Paul Nolt, *Manager*
▲ EMP: 48
SQ FT: 89,000
SALES (est): 11.4MM **Privately Held**
WEB: www.pendu.com
SIC: 3553 2411 2426 3496 Sawmill ma-
chines; logging; hardwood dimension &
flooring mills; miscellaneous fabricated
wire products

(G-12273)
PROTECHS LLC
Also Called: W. G. Malden
2724 Division Hwy (17557-9650)
P.O. Box 196, East Earl (17519-0196)
PHONE.............................717 768-0800
Phoebe Slingerland, *General Mgr*
David Slingerland,
EMP: 7
SQ FT: 1,800
SALES (est): 809.4K **Privately Held**
SIC: 1623 3589 Water, sewer & utility
lines; service industry machinery

(G-12274)
QLF INC
947 E Earl Rd (17557-9597)
PHONE.............................717 445-6225
Edward Z EBY, *President*
Erma EBY, *Treasurer*
◆ EMP: 25

SALES (est): 3.4MM **Privately Held**
SIC: 2048 Mineral feed supplements

(G-12275)
QUALITY CUSTOM CABINETRY INC (PA)
125 Peters Rd (17557-9205)
P.O. Box 189 (17557-0189)
PHONE.....................................717 656-2721
Glen L Good, *President*
Martin H Weaver, *Chairman*
Jerle Weaver, *Corp Secy*
Sally Brownlee, *Sales Staff*
Gerald Sauder, *Manager*
EMP: 240 EST: 1968
SQ FT: 9,500
SALES (est): 37.9MM **Privately Held**
WEB: www.qualitycabinetry.com
SIC: 2434 2541 Wood kitchen cabinets; wood partitions & fixtures

(G-12276)
QUALITY FENCING & SUPPLY
Also Called: Universal Polly Products
622 N Shirk Rd (17557-9737)
P.O. Box 185 (17557-0185)
PHONE.....................................717 355-7112
John K Lapp Jr, *Partner*
Amos B Lapp, *Partner*
Rubin B Lapp, *Partner*
Reuben Lapp,
EMP: 40
SQ FT: 18,176
SALES (est): 5.7MM **Privately Held**
SIC: 3089 3523 3496 Fences, gates & accessories: plastic; farm machinery & equipment; miscellaneous fabricated wire products

(G-12277)
QUALITY TRAILER PRODUCTS LP
Also Called: Rockwell American
170 Commerce Dr (17557-9115)
PHONE.....................................717 354-7070
Rich McIntyre, *Branch Mgr*
EMP: 10
SALES (corp-wide): 240MM **Privately Held**
SIC: 3714 Motor vehicle parts & accessories
HQ: Quality Trailer Products, Lp
604 W Main St
Azle TX 76020
817 444-4518

(G-12278)
RAYTEC FABRICATING LLC
3340 Division Hwy (17557-9665)
PHONE.....................................717 355-5333
Raymond Zimmerman, *Ltd Ptnr*
EMP: 25
SALES (est): 2.3MM **Privately Held**
SIC: 3444 Gutters, sheet metal

(G-12279)
RIDGE CRAFT
Also Called: Garden Craft
280 Commerce Dr (17557-9671)
PHONE.....................................717 355-2254
Allan Fisher, *Owner*
EMP: 12
SALES (est): 1.9MM **Privately Held**
SIC: 2431 Interior & ornamental woodwork & trim

(G-12280)
SAFEGUARD PRODUCTS INC
Also Called: Val-Co Companies
2710 Division Hwy (17557-9650)
P.O. Box 8 (17557-0008)
PHONE.....................................717 354-4586
Frederick Steudler Jr, *President*
Richard Steudler, *Vice Pres*
Jacob Byer, *Site Mgr*
Rick Benedick, *Engineer*
John S Kurtz, *Treasurer*
▲ EMP: 50 EST: 1982
SQ FT: 70,000
SALES (est): 9.7MM **Privately Held**
WEB: www.safeguardproducts.com
SIC: 3496 Cages, wire

(G-12281)
SAVENCIA CHEESE USA LLC (DH)
Also Called: Fleur De Lait East
400 S Custer Ave (17557-9220)
PHONE.....................................717 355-8500
Dominique Huth, *CEO*
◆ EMP: 75
SALES (est): 221.6MM
SALES (corp-wide): 6.3B **Privately Held**
WEB: www.alouettecheese.com
SIC: 5143 2022 Cheese; cheese, natural & processed
HQ: Zausner Foods Corp.
400 S Custer Ave
New Holland PA 17557
717 355-8505

(G-12282)
SEVEN TREES WOODWORKING LLC
939 E Earl Rd (17557-9597)
PHONE.....................................717 351-6300
Jarin Smoker, *Mng Member*
EMP: 11
SALES (est): 1.3MM **Privately Held**
SIC: 2431 Millwork

(G-12283)
SHIRKS CUSTOM WOOD TURNING
1155 Short Rd (17557-9395)
PHONE.....................................717 656-6295
Norman N Shirk, *Partner*
Earl Ray Shirk, *Partner*
Roy Shirk, *Partner*
EMP: 3
SALES (est): 200K **Privately Held**
SIC: 2431 Woodwork, interior & ornamental

(G-12284)
SIGNAL MACHINE CO
150 King Ct (17557-9216)
PHONE.....................................717 354-9994
David W Defernelmont, *President*
David M Defernelmont, *Vice Pres*
EMP: 9
SQ FT: 4,800
SALES (est): 1.4MM **Privately Held**
SIC: 3544 3441 Special dies & tools; fabricated structural metal

(G-12285)
SMUCKERS SALES & SERVICES LLC
643 Peters Rd (17557-9410)
PHONE.....................................717 354-4158
Dale Smucker, *President*
Amos S Smucker, *Treasurer*
Michael Smucker, *Admin Sec*
EMP: 6
SQ FT: 3,100
SALES (est): 2.1MM **Privately Held**
SIC: 5078 5084 3563 Refrigeration equipment & supplies; engines & parts, diesel; air & gas compressors

(G-12286)
STRUCTURAL GLULAM LLC
199 Quality Cir (17557-9007)
PHONE.....................................717 355-9813
Daniel Lapp, *Mng Member*
Melvin Lapp,
EMP: 20
SALES (est): 1.1MM **Privately Held**
SIC: 2426 Lumber, hardwood dimension

(G-12287)
SUMMITVILLE WOODWORKING
855 S Custer Ave (17557-9326)
PHONE.....................................717 355-5337
Amos Lapp, *Owner*
EMP: 3
SQ FT: 3,131
SALES: 230K **Privately Held**
SIC: 2499 Decorative wood & woodwork

(G-12288)
SUPERIOR PLASTIC PRODUCTS INC (PA)
260 Jalyn Dr (17557-9231)
P.O. Box 185 (17557-0185)
PHONE.....................................717 355-7100

Reuben B Lapp, *President*
Benuel Lapp, *Principal*
John Omar Lapp, *Principal*
EMP: 37
SQ FT: 100,000
SALES (est): 12.4MM **Privately Held**
WEB: www.qualityfence.com
SIC: 3089 Fences, gates & accessories: plastic

(G-12289)
TYSON FOODS INC
403 S Custer Ave (17557-9221)
P.O. Box 1156 (17557-0901)
PHONE.....................................717 354-4211
Rich Johnston, *Plant Mgr*
Leonard Paine, *Plant Mgr*
Leonard Payne, *Plant Mgr*
Albert Gonzalez, *Safety Mgr*
Darren Schiefer, *Production*
EMP: 1200
SALES (corp-wide): 40B **Publicly Held**
SIC: 2015 Chicken slaughtering & processing
PA: Tyson Foods, Inc.
2200 W Don Tyson Pkwy
Springdale AR 72762
479 290-4000

(G-12290)
UHURU MFG LLC
622 Farmersville Rd (17557-9749)
P.O. Box 365, Denver (17517-0365)
PHONE.....................................717 345-3366
Casey Charbonneaux, *Principal*
EMP: 5
SALES (est): 369.2K **Privately Held**
SIC: 3999 Manufacturing industries

(G-12291)
VAL PRODUCTS INC
2710 Division Hwy (17557-9650)
PHONE.....................................717 354-4586
Joseph Wetzel, *President*
Eric Cooper, *Sr Project Mgr*
EMP: 13
SALES (corp-wide): 72.5MM **Privately Held**
SIC: 3523 Farm machinery & equipment
HQ: Val Products, Inc.
2599 Old Phladelphia Pike
Bird In Hand PA 17505
717 392-3978

(G-12292)
VOGAN MFG INC
316 Voganville Rd (17557-9720)
PHONE.....................................717 354-9954
Harvey Burkholder, *President*
Daryl Horning, *Vice Pres*
EMP: 8
SQ FT: 15,000
SALES (est): 1MM **Privately Held**
WEB: www.voganmfg.com
SIC: 3496 Miscellaneous fabricated wire products

(G-12293)
WELLBORN HOLDINGS INC
215 Diller Ave (17557-1611)
PHONE.....................................717 351-1700
Paul Wellborn, *CEO*
William Scott Parnell, *Controller*
EMP: 225
SALES (est): 27.2MM
SALES (corp-wide): 296.3MM **Privately Held**
WEB: www.wellborn.com
SIC: 2434 Wood kitchen cabinets
PA: Wellborn Cabinet, Inc.
38669 Highway 77
Ashland AL 36251
800 762-4475

(G-12294)
WHITE OAK ICE COMPANY LLC (PA)
106 Conestoga Ave (17557-9624)
PHONE.....................................717 354-5322
Nelson Sensenig, *Mng Member*
Jason Senenig,
Jordan Senenig,
Joshua Sensenig,
EMP: 9
SQ FT: 20,000

SALES (est): 1.2MM **Privately Held**
WEB: www.whiteoakice.com
SIC: 2097 Manufactured ice

(G-12295)
YARDCRAFT PRODUCTS LLC
191 Jalyn Dr (17557-9232)
PHONE.....................................866 210-9273
Sam Stoltzfus,
Mike Lapp,
EMP: 9
SALES (est): 1.6MM **Privately Held**
SIC: 2421 Outdoor wood structural products

(G-12296)
ZAUSNER FOODS CORP (DH)
Also Called: Bc USA
400 S Custer Ave (17557-9220)
PHONE.....................................717 355-8505
Jessie Hogan, *President*
Desigalony Olivea, *CFO*
EMP: 300 EST: 1946
SQ FT: 27,000
SALES (est): 429.8MM
SALES (corp-wide): 6.3B **Privately Held**
SIC: 2022 2032 6794 Natural cheese; puddings, except meat: packaged in cans, jars, etc.; soups & broths: canned, jarred, etc.; franchises, selling or licensing
HQ: Savencia Sa
42 Rue Rieussec
Viroflay 78220
134 586-300

New Hope
Bucks County

(G-12297)
APPLIED SOFTWARE INC (PA)
6720 Paxson Rd (18938-9658)
P.O. Box 30698, West Palm Beach FL (33420-0698)
PHONE.....................................215 297-9441
Janis Josephson, *President*
EMP: 9
SQ FT: 4,000
SALES (est): 975.2K **Privately Held**
WEB: www.appliedsoftware.com
SIC: 7372 Application computer software

(G-12298)
BETTS EQUIPMENT INC
3139 Windy Bush Rd (18938-9305)
PHONE.....................................215 598-7501
Calvin J Betts, *President*
Michael Betts, *Principal*
Joan Betts, *Corp Secy*
EMP: 5 EST: 1948
SQ FT: 2,000
SALES: 1MM **Privately Held**
WEB: www.bettseq.com
SIC: 3524 5261 Lawn & garden equipment; lawnmowers & tractors

(G-12299)
BRAZILIAN PAPER CORPORATION (PA)
6 Middle Rd (18938-1101)
PHONE.....................................215 369-7000
Neil Wolf, *President*
Marian Lesavoy, *Vice Pres*
Bradley Wolf, *Vice Pres*
Louise Wollrath, *Admin Sec*
▼ EMP: 3
SQ FT: 1,500
SALES (est): 414.2K **Privately Held**
SIC: 2631 Container board

(G-12300)
CALIBER THERAPEUTICS INC
150 Union Square Dr (18938-1365)
PHONE.....................................215 862-5797
Steve Camp, *Vice Pres*
Eileen B Bailey, *Engineer*
EMP: 14
SALES (est): 2.7MM **Privately Held**
SIC: 2834 Pharmaceutical preparations

(G-12301)
FACTOR MEDICAL LLC
6542 Lower York Rd Ste A (18938-1817)
PHONE.....................................215 862-5345

Sanjay Batra, *Principal*
Joe Fiore,
Richard Goldfarb,
EMP: 6 **EST:** 2016
SALES (est): 338.1K **Privately Held**
SIC: 3842 Cosmetic restorations

(G-12302)
GEORGE NKASHIMA WOODWORKER S A
1847 Aquetong Rd (18938-1140)
PHONE....................215 862-2272
Mira Nakashima, *President*
John Lutz, *General Mgr*
Kevin Nakashima, *Vice Pres*
Soomi Amagasu, *Sales Staff*
EMP: 12 **EST:** 1939
SALES (est): 2.1MM **Privately Held**
WEB: www.nakashimawoodworker.com
SIC: 5712 5211 2511 Furniture stores; lumber & other building materials; dining room furniture: wood

(G-12303)
GIVING TREE INC
Also Called: Cottage Roads
130 Heather Dr (18938-5750)
PHONE....................215 968-2487
Pat Finch, *Owner*
Reed C Finch, *Fmly & Gen Dent*
EMP: 5
SQ FT: 4,000
SALES (est): 314.3K **Privately Held**
SIC: 5947 8999 2759 Gift shop; calligrapher; invitation & stationery printing & engraving

(G-12304)
GREEN HILLS SOFTWARE LLC
325 Brownsburg Rd (18938-9202)
PHONE....................215 862-9474
Erik Vallow, *Branch Mgr*
Jesse Small, *Software Dev*
EMP: 3
SALES (corp-wide): 76.7MM **Privately Held**
SIC: 7372 Prepackaged software
PA: Green Hills Software Llc
30 W Sola St
Santa Barbara CA 93101
805 965-6044

(G-12305)
HERACLITEAN CORPORATION
Also Called: Primrose Press
Phillips Mill Rd (18938)
P.O. Box 302 (18938-0302)
PHONE....................215 862-5518
George Knight, *President*
Patricia Knight, *Corp Secy*
EMP: 10
SALES (est): 676.6K **Privately Held**
WEB: www.heracliteanfire.net
SIC: 2759 Posters, including billboards: printing

(G-12306)
IOTA COMMUNICATIONS INC (PA)
540 Union Square Dr (18938-1368)
PHONE....................855 743-6478
Barclay Knapp, *CEO*
Terrence Defranco, *President*
EMP: 9
SALES: 12MM **Publicly Held**
WEB: www.arkados.com
SIC: 4813 7372 ; prepackaged software

(G-12307)
JB SERVICES OF INDIANA LLC
6931 Ely Rd (18938-9641)
PHONE....................215 862-2515
William H Powderly IV, *Mng Member*
EMP: 6
SALES (est): 35.9K **Privately Held**
SIC: 3229 Glass fiber products

(G-12308)
LOCK AND MANE
30 W Bridge St Ste 2 (18938-1363)
PHONE....................215 221-2131
John Cascarano, *Manager*
EMP: 8
SALES (est): 587.5K **Privately Held**
SIC: 3999 Manufacturing industries

(G-12309)
NELSON BRIDGE INC
6103 Upper York Rd (18938-9606)
P.O. Box 419, Solebury (18963-0419)
PHONE....................908 996-6646
Denise Mpilato-Nelson, *President*
Jonathan M Nelson, *Vice Pres*
EMP: 5
SALES: 1MM **Privately Held**
SIC: 2426 7389 8712 Furniture stock & parts, hardwood; apparel designers, commercial; architectural services

(G-12310)
NEW HOPE CRUSHED STONE LIME CO
6970 Phillips Mill Rd (18938-9684)
PHONE....................215 862-5295
John Mehok, *President*
Daniel Adamczyk, *Vice Pres*
George Riordan, *Vice Pres*
EMP: 25
SQ FT: 3,000
SALES (est): 7.9MM **Privately Held**
SIC: 1422 Lime rock, ground

(G-12311)
OTTE GEAR LLC
6542a Lower York Rd 41 (18938-1824)
P.O. Box 141 (18938-0141)
PHONE....................917 923-6230
Todd Fairbairn,
EMP: 3
SALES (est): 199.7K **Privately Held**
WEB: www.ottegear.com
SIC: 2399 Military insignia, textile

(G-12312)
QUESTAR CORPORATION (PA)
6204 Ingham Rd (18938-9663)
PHONE....................215 862-5277
Don Bandurick, *CEO*
Dr Douglas M Knight, *Ch of Bd*
Donald Bandurick, *General Mgr*
James A Perkins, *VP Opers*
EMP: 27 **EST:** 1950
SQ FT: 10,000
SALES (est): 6MM **Privately Held**
WEB: www.questar-corp.com
SIC: 3827 7371 8732 Optical instruments & apparatus; microscopes, except electron, proton & corneal; telescopes: elbow, panoramic, sighting, fire control, etc.; computer software development; educational research

(G-12313)
QUICKEL INTERNATIONAL CORP
Also Called: Usironline
65 Chapel Rd (18938-1026)
PHONE....................215 862-1313
Stephen Quickel, *President*
EMP: 3
SALES (est): 142.3K **Privately Held**
SIC: 2711 Newspapers

(G-12314)
ROBERT GERENSER
Also Called: Gerenser's Exotic Ice Cream
22 S Main St (18938-1378)
PHONE....................215 646-1853
Robert V Gerenser, *Owner*
Robert Gerenser, *Owner*
EMP: 12
SQ FT: 3,000
SALES: 125K **Privately Held**
SIC: 2024 5812 Ice cream, bulk; ice cream stands or dairy bars

(G-12315)
STOREFLEX LLC
603 Creeks Edge Cir (18938-1111)
PHONE....................856 498-0079
Linda Sarnecki, *Principal*
EMP: 4 **EST:** 2010
SALES (est): 267.7K **Privately Held**
SIC: 2834 Pharmaceutical preparations

(G-12316)
SYNERGY CORE ELEMENTS
560 Union Square Dr (18938-1368)
P.O. Box 552, Holicong (18928-0552)
PHONE....................267 885-5832
Felipe Sanchez, *Principal*

EMP: 3
SALES (est): 233.3K **Privately Held**
SIC: 2819 Mfg Industrial Inorganic Chemicals

(G-12317)
TESTLINK CORP (PA)
73 W Mechanic St (18938-1234)
P.O. Box 4833, Trenton NJ (08650-4833)
PHONE....................267 743-2956
Tony Barbaro, *President*
Joseph O'Neill, *Vice Pres*
EMP: 6
SQ FT: 13,000
SALES: 4MM **Privately Held**
SIC: 3825 Test equipment for electronic & electrical circuits

(G-12318)
VANTAGE LEARNING USA LLC (PA)
6805 Route 202 (18938-1079)
PHONE....................800 230-2213
Tam Kirby, *President*
Gina Vogt, *Info Tech Mgr*
Ken Lafiandra, *General Counsel*
Daniel Filson, *Recruiter*
EMP: 100
SALES (est): 100MM **Privately Held**
SIC: 7372 Educational computer software

(G-12319)
VANTAGE ONLINE STORE LLC
6805 Route 202 (18938-1079)
PHONE....................267 756-1155
Donna Wallace, *Accountant*
Peter Murphy,
EMP: 150
SALES (est): 8.7MM **Privately Held**
SIC: 7372 Prepackaged software

New Kensington
Westmoreland County

(G-12320)
ACCROTOOL INC
401 Hunt Valley Rd (15068-7062)
PHONE....................724 339-3560
William Phillips, *Chairman*
Greg Rundy, *QC Mgr*
Joseph Rady, *Manager*
EMP: 150
SQ FT: 70,000
SALES (est): 34.8MM **Privately Held**
WEB: www.accrotool.com
SIC: 3469 3444 Metal stampings; sheet metalwork

(G-12321)
ACCURATE MARKING PRODUCTS INC
Also Called: Accurate Marking & Mfg
225 Prominence Dr (15068-7077)
PHONE....................724 337-8390
Hank Mulraney, *President*
Michael Weir, *Admin Sec*
EMP: 13
SQ FT: 10,000
SALES (est): 2MM **Privately Held**
SIC: 3953 3089 3544 Printing dies, rubber or plastic, for marking machines; thermoformed finished plastic products; special dies, tools, jigs & fixtures

(G-12322)
ALCOA TECHNICAL CENTER LLC
Also Called: Building G
859 White Cloud Rd (15068-7047)
PHONE....................724 337-5300
EMP: 4
SALES (corp-wide): 13.4B **Publicly Held**
SIC: 3355 Aluminum rolling & drawing
HQ: Alcoa Technical Center Llc
201 Isabella St Ste 500
Pittsburgh PA 15212
412 553-4545

(G-12323)
ALKAB CONTRACT MFG INC
843 Industrial Blvd (15068-6498)
PHONE....................724 335-7050
William Kabazie, *President*

Allison Kabazie, *Corp Secy*
▼ **EMP:** 28
SQ FT: 21,180
SALES (est): 5.3MM **Privately Held**
WEB: www.alkab.com
SIC: 3599 Machine shop, jobbing & repair

(G-12324)
ARCONIC INC
Arconic Technical Center
100 Technical Dr (15068-9001)
PHONE....................724 337-5300
Jim McRickard, *President*
Amit Kundu, *General Mgr*
Markus Heinimann, *Vice Pres*
Eileen M Kenzevich, *Project Mgr*
Jay Ketty, *Facilities Mgr*
EMP: 15
SALES (corp-wide): 14B **Publicly Held**
SIC: 3353 Aluminum sheet, plate & foil
PA: Arconic Inc.
390 Park Ave Fl 12
New York NY 10022
212 836-2758

(G-12325)
ASPOL LLC
1504 Constitution Blvd (15068-4310)
PHONE....................412 628-0078
Shree Chandrasekaran,
Kenneth Ogilvie,
Chandrasekaran Pillai,
EMP: 4
SQ FT: 100,000
SALES (est): 154.7K **Privately Held**
SIC: 3069 Reclaimed rubber (reworked by manufacturing processes)

(G-12326)
BACHARACH INC (PA)
621 Hunt Valley Cir (15068-7074)
PHONE....................724 334-5000
Timothy N Macphee, *President*
Doug Keeports, *President*
Don Oliver, *Senior Buyer*
Michael Conde, *Engineer*
Aaron Kennison, *Engineer*
▲ **EMP:** 115
SQ FT: 60,000
SALES (est): 31.3MM **Privately Held**
WEB: www.mybacharach.com
SIC: 3823 Industrial instrmnts msrmnt display/control process variable

(G-12327)
BAYER MEDICAL CARE INC
2555 7th St (15068-5153)
PHONE....................724 337-8176
Sandra Grates, *Manager*
EMP: 57
SALES (corp-wide): 45.3B **Privately Held**
SIC: 3841 Diagnostic apparatus, medical
HQ: Bayer Medical Care Inc.
1 Bayer Dr
Indianola PA 15051
724 940-6800

(G-12328)
BURRELL GROUP INC (PA)
Also Called: Westmoreland Insurance Svcs
2400 Leechburg Rd Ste 216 (15068-4673)
PHONE....................724 337-3557
C H Booth Jr, *President*
Harvey F Booth, *President*
William Harbaugh, *Vice Pres*
Reid E Rotzler, *Vice Pres*
T J Phillis, *Treasurer*
EMP: 18 **EST:** 1935
SQ FT: 26,200
SALES (est): 18.4MM **Privately Held**
WEB: www.webinsurequote.com
SIC: 6411 3271 6512 Insurance agents; concrete block & brick; nonresidential building operators

(G-12329)
BURRELL MINING PRODUCTS INC (HQ)
2400 Leechburg Rd Ste 216 (15068-4673)
PHONE....................724 339-2511
Charles H Booth Jr, *President*
Harvey F Booth, *Vice Pres*
William Harbaugh, *Vice Pres*
Reid E Rotzler, *Vice Pres*
Rose M Monteleone, *Admin Sec*
EMP: 15

▲ = Import ▼ = Export
◆ = Import/Export

SQ FT: 26,200
SALES (est): 10.5MM
SALES (corp-wide): 18.4MM **Privately Held**
SIC: 3271 Blocks, concrete or cinder: standard
PA: Burrell Group, Inc.
2400 Leechburg Rd Ste 216
New Kensington PA 15068
724 337-3557

(G-12330)
BURRELL MINING SERVICES INC
2400 Leechburg Rd Ste 216 (15068-4673)
PHONE...................................724 339-2220
EMP: 3
SALES (est): 105.7K **Privately Held**
SIC: 1241 Mining services: anthracite

(G-12331)
CANDLEROCK
925 4th Ave (15068-6409)
PHONE...................................724 503-2231
Heather Mackelvey, *Owner*
EMP: 8
SALES (est): 515.6K **Privately Held**
WEB: www.candlerock.com
SIC: 3999 Candles

(G-12332)
CANNON BOILER WORKS INC
Also Called: C B W
510 Constitution Blvd (15068-6599)
PHONE...................................724 335-8541
Arthur P Skelley, *President*
Robert Dull, *General Mgr*
Jim Riggin, *QC Mgr*
Mark Dinsmore, *Engineer*
Madonna J Flinn, *CFO*
▲ EMP: 52
SQ FT: 65,000
SALES (est): 14.1MM **Privately Held**
WEB: www.cannonboilerworks.com
SIC: 3443 7699 Boilers: industrial, power, or marine; finned tubes, for heat transfer; boiler repair shop

(G-12333)
CATORIS CANDIES INC
981 5th Ave (15068-6307)
PHONE...................................724 335-4371
Georgienne Bufalino, *President*
EMP: 17 EST: 1946
SQ FT: 3,000
SALES (est): 2MM **Privately Held**
SIC: 2064 5441 Chocolate candy, except solid chocolate; candy

(G-12334)
CITY BTLG CO OF NEW KENSINGTON
Also Called: Sam's Pop and Beer Shop
1820 5th Ave (15068-4420)
PHONE...................................724 335-3350
Louis Lombardo, *President*
Sandra Lombardo, *Corp Secy*
Sam Lombardo, *Assistant VP*
EMP: 10
SQ FT: 10,000
SALES (est): 1MM **Privately Held**
SIC: 2086 5181 Soft drinks: packaged in cans, bottles, etc.; beer & other fermented malt liquors

(G-12335)
COMFAB INC
2095 Melwood Rd (15068-6855)
PHONE...................................724 339-1750
Harry Beck, *President*
EMP: 5
SALES (est): 875.6K **Privately Held**
WEB: www.comfab.net
SIC: 7692 Welding repair

(G-12336)
CORA LEE CUPCAKES
442 Violet Dr (15068-3340)
PHONE...................................724 681-5498
EMP: 4 EST: 2013
SALES (est): 102.9K **Privately Held**
SIC: 2051 Bread, cake & related products

(G-12337)
CURTISS-WRIGHT CORPORATION
205 Nebraska Dr (15068-3214)
PHONE...................................724 275-5277
EMP: 700
SALES (corp-wide): 2.4B **Publicly Held**
WEB: www.curtisswright.com
SIC: 3491 Industrial valves
PA: Curtiss-Wright Corporation
130 Harbour Place Dr # 300
Davidson NC 28036
704 869-4600

(G-12338)
CUSTOM PRINTING UNLIMITED
1515 5th Ave (15068-4413)
PHONE...................................724 339-3000
Ray Peiranuzi, *Owner*
EMP: 10
SQ FT: 4,500
SALES (est): 664.7K **Privately Held**
SIC: 2759 Letterpress & screen printing; screen printing

(G-12339)
EXTORR INC
307 Columbia Rd (15068-3911)
PHONE...................................724 337-3000
John Hackwelder, *President*
Steve Hackwelder, *Vice Pres*
Lutz Kurzweg, *Vice Pres*
EMP: 10
SALES (est): 1.6MM **Privately Held**
WEB: www.extorr.com
SIC: 3699 Electric sound equipment

(G-12340)
EYE-BOT AERIAL SOLUTIONS LLC
701 5th Ave Ste 108 (15068-6301)
PHONE...................................724 904-7706
Jacob A Lydick,
EMP: 4 EST: 2009
SQ FT: 500
SALES (est): 126.1K **Privately Held**
SIC: 8713 1382 7335 ; aerial geophysical exploration oil & gas; aerial photography, except mapmaking

(G-12341)
GARRETT & CO INC
804 Montclair Dr (15068-6866)
P.O. Box 839, Adamstown (19501-0839)
PHONE...................................800 748-4608
Mark Bansner, *President*
EMP: 3
SQ FT: 1,850
SALES (est): 293.4K **Privately Held**
SIC: 3484 Rifles or rifle parts, 30 mm. & below

(G-12342)
GENERAL GRAPHICS
1608 Leishman Ave (15068-4204)
P.O. Box 3192 (15068-0992)
PHONE...................................724 337-1470
Carlene Gregowich, *Partner*
Craig T Thickey, *Partner*
EMP: 3
SALES (est): 243.2K **Privately Held**
WEB: www.ggbarcode.com
SIC: 2759 Labels & seals: printing

(G-12343)
GRELIN PRESS
1040 5th Ave (15068-6234)
P.O. Box 367 (15068-0367)
PHONE...................................724 334-8240
EMP: 3
SALES (est): 150K **Privately Held**
SIC: 2741 Misc Publishing

(G-12344)
H R EDGAR MACHINING & FABG INC
Also Called: Edgar Industries
931 Merwin Rd (15068-1621)
PHONE...................................724 339-6694
Harry Edgar Jr, *President*
R Edgar, *President*
Harry Edgar Sr, *Corp Secy*
Francis Kwiatek, *Vice Pres*
Harry R Edgar III, *Treasurer*
EMP: 55

SQ FT: 35,000
SALES (est): 12.8MM **Privately Held**
WEB: www.edgarindustries.com
SIC: 3599 3441 3082 Machine shop, jobbing & repair; fabricated structural metal; unsupported plastics profile shapes

(G-12345)
HABSCO INC
Schreiber Industrial Dst (15068)
P.O. Box 65 (15068-0065)
PHONE...................................724 337-9498
George Hubbard, *CEO*
Barbara Hubbard, *President*
EMP: 9
SQ FT: 10,000
SALES (est): 1.8MM **Privately Held**
SIC: 5084 8748 7694 Industrial machinery & equipment; systems engineering consultant, ex. computer or professional; rebuilding motors, except automotive

(G-12346)
INDUSTRIAL TERMINAL SYSTEMS
100 Logans Ferry Rd (15068-2004)
P.O. Box 4127 (15068-1227)
PHONE...................................724 335-9837
Michael Steimer, *President*
Elizabeth Steimer, *Corp Secy*
Todd Glenn, *Shareholder*
Wayne Glenn, *Shareholder*
Nancy Steimer, *Shareholder*
EMP: 50 EST: 1958
SQ FT: 70,000
SALES (est): 6.4MM **Privately Held**
SIC: 7389 2899 Packaging & labeling services; chemical preparations

(G-12347)
J K TOOL DIE CO
148 Prominence Dr (15068-7078)
PHONE...................................724 339-1858
EMP: 5 EST: 2017
SALES (est): 759.8K **Privately Held**
SIC: 3544 Special dies & tools

(G-12348)
JABTEK LLC
450 Industrial Blvd (15068-6634)
PHONE...................................724 796-5656
Thomas Donaldson,
Jeffrey Klinker,
EMP: 3
SALES (est): 380K **Privately Held**
SIC: 3316 Cold-rolled strip or wire

(G-12349)
JADDEN INC
1542 Constitution Blvd (15068-4310)
PHONE...................................724 212-3715
Nachhatar Singh, *Owner*
EMP: 3
SALES (est): 352.1K **Privately Held**
SIC: 2911 Petroleum refining

(G-12350)
K & N ENTERPRISES INC
Also Called: Pennsylvania Art Glass Company
112 Sunny Ridge Ln (15068-1929)
PHONE...................................724 334-0698
Edward Kachurik, *President*
Carol Kachurik, *Admin Sec*
EMP: 3
SQ FT: 1,500
SALES: 300K **Privately Held**
SIC: 3229 Pressed & blown glass

(G-12351)
KEY ENERGY SERVICES INC
2154 Greensburg Rd Ste 1 (15068-1851)
PHONE...................................878 302-3333
David Clark, *Manager*
EMP: 24
SALES (corp-wide): 521.7MM **Publicly Held**
WEB: www.keyenergy.com
SIC: 1389 1381 Servicing oil & gas wells; drilling oil & gas wells
PA: Key Energy Services, Inc.
1301 Mckinney St Ste 1800
Houston TX 77010
713 651-4300

(G-12352)
KEYSTONE RUSTPROOFING INC (PA)
1901 Dr Thomas Blvd Ste 1 (15068-4398)
PHONE...................................724 339-7588
Daniel Paul Wright, *President*
Paul Gunsallus, *Principal*
Patrick W Wright, *Corp Secy*
William Joseph Wright Jr, *Vice Pres*
Patricia Wright Gunsallus, *Treasurer*
EMP: 40
SQ FT: 14,000
SALES (est): 5.4MM **Privately Held**
WEB: www.keystonerustproofing.com
SIC: 3471 Electroplating of metals or formed products

(G-12353)
LOST CREEK MINING
212 Gabrielle Dr (15068-6875)
PHONE...................................724 335-8780
EMP: 3
SALES (est): 125.6K **Privately Held**
SIC: 1221 Bituminous coal surface mining

(G-12354)
MANNIS WASH SYSTEMS
Also Called: Manni's Frank Sales & Service
1131 Greensburg Rd (15068-3800)
PHONE...................................724 337-8255
Franklin Manni, *Owner*
EMP: 7
SQ FT: 7,000
SALES (est): 746.6K **Privately Held**
WEB: www.manniwashsystems.com
SIC: 3589 7542 Car washing machinery; carwash, self-service

(G-12355)
METALWORKING MACHINERY CO INC (PA)
700 Constitution Blvd (15068-6230)
PHONE...................................724 625-3181
Rufus Duff Jr, *President*
C H Duff, *Treasurer*
EMP: 15
SQ FT: 4,000
SALES (est): 1.9MM **Privately Held**
WEB: www.blastcleaningequipment.com
SIC: 3569 Blast cleaning equipment, dustless

(G-12356)
METHOD AUTOMATION SERVICES INC
1801 5th Ave (15068-4419)
PHONE...................................724 337-9064
Paul Konieczny, *President*
EMP: 3
SALES (est): 155.1K **Privately Held**
SIC: 7371 7372 Computer software development & applications; business oriented computer software

(G-12357)
MILL PROFESSIONAL SERVICES
1562 Fairmont Dr (15068-5856)
PHONE...................................724 335-4625
Ruth W Novickoff, *President*
EMP: 15
SALES (est): 940K **Privately Held**
SIC: 7692 1799 Welding repair; rigging & scaffolding

(G-12358)
MINERAL PROCESSING SPC INC
1 Industrial Park Blvd (15068)
PHONE...................................724 339-8630
Don Edwards, *President*
EMP: 8
SALES (est): 913.5K **Privately Held**
SIC: 3532 Separating machinery, mineral

(G-12359)
MITO INSULATION COMPANY
Also Called: Mito Industries
1290 3rd Ave (15068)
P.O. Box 711 (15068-0711)
PHONE...................................724 335-8551
Michael Malcanas, *President*
EMP: 30
SQ FT: 50,000

G E O G R A P H I C

SALES (est): 7.5MM **Privately Held**
WEB: www.mitoinsulation.com
SIC: **3296** 1742 2672 Fiberglass insulation; insulation, buildings; coated & laminated paper

(G-12360)
NAMSCO PLASTICS INDS INC
100 Hunt Valley Rd (15068-7072)
PHONE.....................................724 339-3591
David Namey, *President*
David Johns, *Corp Secy*
▲ EMP: 80 EST: 1978
SQ FT: 67,000
SALES (est): 19.2MM **Privately Held**
WEB: www.namscoplastics.com
SIC: **3089** Injection molding of plastics

(G-12361)
NAMSCO PLASTICS INDUSTRIES
1035 Hunt Valley Cir (15068-7053)
PHONE.....................................724 339-3100
David Namey, *President*
Jamie Gorman, *Principal*
EMP: 30
SALES (est): 8.4MM **Privately Held**
SIC: **3089** Injection molding of plastics

(G-12362)
NATIONAL MATERIAL LP
National Material Company
2001 Dr Thomas Blvd (15068-2102)
PHONE.....................................724 337-6551
Tab Steinhauf, *Branch Mgr*
EMP: 50
SALES (corp-wide): 1B **Privately Held**
WEB: www.nmlp.com
SIC: **5051** 3444 Steel; sheet metalwork
PA: National Material L.P.
1965 Pratt Blvd
Elk Grove Village IL 60007
847 806-7200

(G-12363)
NOGA LOGGING
4825 Garvers Ferry Rd (15068-9531)
PHONE.....................................724 224-6369
Frank Noga, *Owner*
EMP: 3 EST: 1998
SALES (est): 200K **Privately Held**
SIC: **2411** Logging camps & contractors

(G-12364)
OMNI FAB INC
822 Anderson St (15068-6030)
PHONE.....................................724 334-8851
Jim Frank, *President*
Tracey Frank, *Treasurer*
Bruce Wickline, *Sales Mgr*
Terri Bryan, *Manager*
EMP: 19
SQ FT: 30,000
SALES (est): 4.8MM **Privately Held**
WEB: www.omnifab.com
SIC: **3444** 3446 3449 Sheet metal specialties, not stamped; ladders, for permanent installation: metal; railings, bannisters, guards, etc.: made from metal pipe; miscellaneous metalwork

(G-12365)
PENN MANUFACTURING LLC
634 Pleasant Valley Rd (15068-7248)
PHONE.....................................724 845-4682
John Chabal, *President*
John Townsend, *Vice Pres*
EMP: 12
SQ FT: 15,000
SALES (est): 3.4MM **Privately Held**
SIC: **3443** Heat exchangers, condensers & components

(G-12366)
PIONEER TOOL & FORGE INC
101 6th St (15068-6544)
PHONE.....................................724 337-4700
Michael Clougherty, *President*
Thomas Clougherty, *Corp Secy*
▲ EMP: 15
SQ FT: 43,000
SALES (est): 3MM **Privately Held**
WEB: www.breakersteel.com
SIC: **3545** Machine tool attachments & accessories

(G-12367)
PITTSBURGH TECHNOLOGIES INC
1035 Hunt Valley Cir (15068-7053)
PHONE.....................................724 339-0900
David Namey, *President*
EMP: 30
SQ FT: 60,000
SALES (est): 2.8MM **Privately Held**
SIC: **3089** Injection molding of plastics

(G-12368)
PRECISION AUTOMATIC MACHINE CO
134 Prominence Dr (15068-7078)
PHONE.....................................724 339-2360
Walter Stammer, *President*
EMP: 13 EST: 1946
SQ FT: 10,000
SALES (est): 1.4MM **Privately Held**
SIC: **3599** Machine shop, jobbing & repair

(G-12369)
QUALITY MACHINED PDTS MFG INC
134 Prominence Dr (15068-7078)
PHONE.....................................724 339-2360
Walter G Stammer, *President*
Dorothy Stammer, *Corp Secy*
EMP: 34
SALES (est): 6.5MM **Privately Held**
SIC: **3599** Machine shop, jobbing & repair

(G-12370)
RESPIRONICS INC
312 Alvin Dr (15068-7022)
PHONE.....................................724 334-3100
EMP: 164
SALES (corp-wide): 20.9B **Privately Held**
SIC: **3845** 3841 3564 8351 Patient monitoring apparatus; surgical & medical instruments; blowers & fans; child day care services; respiratory protection equipment, personal
HQ: Respironics, Inc.
1001 Murry Ridge Ln
Murrysville PA 15668
724 387-5200

(G-12371)
RICK RADVANSKY & SONS
1578 Fairmont Dr (15068-5856)
PHONE.....................................724 335-7411
Rick Radvansky, *Principal*
EMP: 5
SALES (est): 476.5K **Privately Held**
SIC: **3471** Plating of metals or formed products

(G-12372)
ROCK-BUILT INC
Also Called: Kay Core
1170 2nd Ave (15068-6114)
PHONE.....................................878 302-3978
Rock Ferrone, *President*
EMP: 20
SALES (est): 4.1MM **Privately Held**
WEB: www.rockbuilt.com
SIC: **3537** Industrial trucks & tractors

(G-12373)
S & M MACHINE COMPANY
1500 Queensburg Rd (15068)
P.O. Box 2505 (15068-0747)
PHONE.....................................724 339-2035
Paul Shadle, *President*
Sharon Y Shadle, *Vice Pres*
EMP: 6
SALES (est): 307K **Privately Held**
SIC: **3599** Machine shop, jobbing & repair

(G-12374)
SAKALA STONE PRODUCTS
7230 Guyer Rd (15068-9799)
PHONE.....................................724 339-2224
Cynthia Sakala, *Owner*
EMP: 7
SALES (est): 650.6K **Privately Held**
WEB: www.sakalastoneproducts.com
SIC: **5211** 3272 Masonry materials & supplies; stone, cast concrete

(G-12375)
SIEMENS INDUSTRY INC
Siemens - Large Drives
500 Hunt Valley Rd (15068-7060)
PHONE.....................................724 339-9500
Jennifer Mihalic, *Project Mgr*
Loretta Laughlin, *Purch Agent*
Larry Schaeffer, *Purchasing*
Mark Bolha, *Engineer*
Mark Harshman, *Engineer*
EMP: 166
SALES (corp-wide): 95B **Privately Held**
WEB: www.sea.siemens.com
SIC: **3625** 3651 3594 Control equipment, electric; household audio & video equipment; fluid power pumps & motors
HQ: Siemens Industry, Inc.
1000 Deerfield Pkwy
Buffalo Grove IL 60089
800 743-6367

(G-12376)
SIMPSON REINFORCING INC (PA)
Also Called: Simpson Staff Reinforcement
2001 Dr Thomas Blvd (15068-2102)
PHONE.....................................412 362-6200
Robert M Simpson, *President*
Frances Donatelli, *Vice Pres*
Gary Hartle, *Vice Pres*
Jill Simpson, *Admin Sec*
EMP: 16
SALES (est): 4.1MM **Privately Held**
SIC: **3449** Bars, concrete reinforcing: fabricated steel

(G-12377)
SIR JAMES PRTG & BUS FORMS INC
864 4th Ave (15068-6479)
PHONE.....................................724 339-2122
James M Litterio, *President*
Dorothy Litterio, *Treasurer*
Michele Litterio, *Admin Sec*
EMP: 7
SQ FT: 2,000
SALES (est): 989.5K **Privately Held**
SIC: **2752** 2789 Commercial printing, offset; bookbinding & related work

(G-12378)
SMITHFIELD PACKAGED MEATS CORP
Also Called: North Side Foods
2200 Rivers Edge Dr (15068-4540)
PHONE.....................................724 335-5800
Danny Connery, *Controller*
Dave Holko, *Director*
Rebecca Coward,
EMP: 357 **Privately Held**
SIC: **2011** Meat packing plants
HQ: Smithfield Packaged Meats Corp.
805 E Kemper Rd
Cincinnati OH 45246
513 782-3800

(G-12379)
SPECIALTY ALLOY PROC CO INC
14th St (15068)
P.O. Box 104, Murrysville (15668-0104)
PHONE.....................................724 339-0464
Edward J Moses, *President*
Marlene L Moses, *Vice Pres*
EMP: 8
SALES (est): 460K **Privately Held**
SIC: **3398** Metal heat treating

(G-12380)
STELLAR INDUSTRIES INC
Schreiber Industrial Park (15068)
P.O. Box 677 (15068-0677)
PHONE.....................................724 335-5525
Albert Nicastro, *President*
EMP: 7
SALES: 500K **Privately Held**
SIC: **3645** 3646 5063 Residential lighting fixtures; commercial indusl & institutional electric lighting fixtures; lighting fixtures

(G-12381)
TAYLOR MADE SMILES
2300 Freeport Rd Ste 1b (15068-4686)
PHONE.....................................724 212-3167
Brian Taylor, *Principal*

EMP: 8
SALES (est): 1MM **Privately Held**
SIC: **3843** Enamels, dentists'

(G-12382)
TOOLCO INC
4020 Leechburg Rd (15068-2326)
PHONE.....................................724 337-9119
Michael Malecki, *President*
Carol L Malecki, *Treasurer*
Jim Chicker, *Info Tech Mgr*
Daniel Malecki, *Admin Sec*
EMP: 22 EST: 1975
SQ FT: 14,000
SALES: 2.1MM **Privately Held**
WEB: www.toolcoinc.com
SIC: **3599** Machine shop, jobbing & repair

(G-12383)
TOP HATS DRUM AND BATON CO
451 Longvue Dr (15068-5819)
PHONE.....................................724 339-7861
Arlene Meisner, *Principal*
EMP: 4
SALES (est): 260.5K **Privately Held**
SIC: **3949** Batons

(G-12384)
TRI-FORM INC
2104 Constitution Blvd (15068-2101)
PHONE.....................................724 334-0237
Robert Serafini, *President*
James Chirdon, *Treasurer*
EMP: 12
SQ FT: 10,000
SALES (est): 2MM **Privately Held**
WEB: www.triforminc.com
SIC: **3441** Fabricated structural metal

(G-12385)
VALOS HOUSE OF CANDY
Also Called: Valos Candy
1726 5th Ave (15068-4418)
PHONE.....................................724 339-2669
John Mandak, *Partner*
Vicky Mandak, *Principal*
EMP: 5
SQ FT: 1,500
SALES (est): 424.1K **Privately Held**
SIC: **5441** 2064 Confectionery; candy & other confectionery products

(G-12386)
VERE INC
3 Schreiber Industrial Pa (15068-4549)
PHONE.....................................724 335-5530
Mary Vaerewyck, *President*
Gerard Vaerewyck, *Vice Pres*
Paul Pachura, *Admin Sec*
EMP: 10
SQ FT: 14,000
SALES: 3MM **Privately Held**
WEB: www.vere.com
SIC: **3821** 3826 5049 Worktables, laboratory; analytical optical instruments; optical goods

(G-12387)
VERSA-FAB INC
270 Hunt Valley Rd (15068-7068)
PHONE.....................................724 889-0137
Jim Cullen Jr, *President*
James Cullen, *Principal*
Kathy Miller, *Manager*
Robert Geer, *Shareholder*
EMP: 20
SQ FT: 23,000
SALES (est): 5.4MM **Privately Held**
SIC: **3444** 3599 Sheet metalwork; machine shop, jobbing & repair

(G-12388)
VOLIAN ENTERPRISES INC
122 Kerr Rd Ste 4 (15068-9318)
P.O. Box 410, Murrysville (15668-0410)
PHONE.....................................724 335-3744
Harold Julian, *President*
Kathy Ruffing, *Sr Software Eng*
EMP: 10
SQ FT: 3,600
SALES (est): 1.1MM **Privately Held**
WEB: www.volian.com
SIC: **8711** 7372 Consulting engineer; utility computer software

GEOGRAPHIC

(G-12389)
WHITAKER CORPORATION
Also Called: Anchor Distributors
1030 Hunt Valley Cir (15068-7075)
PHONE..................................724 334-7000
Robert Whitaker Jr, *President*
John Whitaker, *Treasurer*
Mary Whitaker, *Admin Sec*
▼ EMP: 125 EST: 1970
SQ FT: 186,000
SALES (est): 33.9MM Privately Held
WEB: www.anchordistributors.com
SIC: 2731 5192 3652 Books: publishing &
printing; books; pre-recorded records &
tapes

(G-12390)
WOODEN DOOR WINERY LLC
4087 Greenwood Rd (15068)
PHONE..................................724 889-7244
Steven Pollick, *Owner*
EMP: 4
SALES (est): 236.4K Privately Held
SIC: 2084 Wines

(G-12391)
XODUS MEDICAL INC
204 Myles Dr (15068-7046)
PHONE..................................724 337-5500
EMP: 3
SALES (est): 232.8K Privately Held
SIC: 3841 Surgical & medical instruments

(G-12392)
XODUS MEDICAL INC
702 Prominence Dr (15068-7052)
PHONE..................................724 337-5500
Craig E Kaforey, *President*
Mark Kaforey, *Corp Secy*
Carrie Riga, *Buyer*
Kelly Ferace, *Finance*
Alec Head, *VP Sales*
▲ EMP: 42
SQ FT: 40,000
SALES (est): 8.4MM Privately Held
WEB: www.xodusmedical.com
SIC: 3841 Surgical & medical instruments

(G-12393)
YERECIC LABEL CO INC
701 Hunt Valley Rd (15068-7076)
PHONE..................................724 334-3300
Arthur M Yerecic Jr, *President*
Josh Yerecic, *President*
Linda Ciuca, *Vice Pres*
Chris Hurst, *Opers Mgr*
John Boyer, *Purch Mgr*
▼ EMP: 100
SQ FT: 21,000
SALES (est): 29.6MM Privately Held
WEB: www.yereciclabel.com
SIC: 2672 Labels (unprinted), gummed:
made from purchased materials

New Kingstown
Cumberland County

(G-12394)
VALK MANUFACTURING
COMPANY
66 E Main St (17072)
P.O. Box 428 (17072-0428)
PHONE..................................717 766-0711
Ted P Valk, *President*
Robert P Lang, *Senior VP*
Linda Bassler, *Treasurer*
EMP: 100 EST: 1952
SQ FT: 80,000
SALES (est): 38MM Privately Held
WEB: www.valkmfg.com
SIC: 3531 Snow plow attachments; blades
for graders, scrapers, dozers & snow
plows

New Milford
Susquehanna County

(G-12395)
CARPENTER PALLETS
301 Hall Rd (18834-6735)
PHONE..................................570 465-2573
George Carpenter, *Principal*
EMP: 4 EST: 2009
SALES (est): 313.2K Privately Held
SIC: 2448 Pallets, wood & wood with metal

(G-12396)
HEPCO QUARRIES
INCORPORATED
418 Montrose St (18834-7514)
PHONE..................................570 955-8545
Brian Hepler, *Principal*
EMP: 4
SALES (est): 209K Privately Held
SIC: 1422 Crushed & broken limestone

(G-12397)
KOWALEWSKI QUARRIES
3886 E Lake Rd (18834-6938)
PHONE..................................570 465-7025
Donna K Kowalewski, *Principal*
EMP: 3
SALES (est): 147.4K Privately Held
SIC: 1422 Crushed & broken limestone

(G-12398)
MARSHALL FLP LP
70 Mitchell St (18834-2117)
PHONE..................................570 465-3817
William Marshall, *General Ptnr*
EMP: 3
SALES (est): 50K Privately Held
SIC: 1389 7389 Gas field services;

(G-12399)
ROCK LAKE INC
4412 State Route 848 (18834-7877)
P.O. Box 277, Lake Como (18437-0277)
PHONE..................................570 465-2986
Nicholas Shursky, *President*
EMP: 12
SALES (est): 1MM Privately Held
SIC: 1411 Bluestone, dimension-quarrying

(G-12400)
SPECTACULAR FIRE WORKS
USA
1541 Oliver Rd (18834-7515)
PHONE..................................570 465-2100
Kyle Cannon, *Office Mgr*
EMP: 3
SALES (est): 387.5K Privately Held
SIC: 2899 Fireworks

New Oxford
Adams County

(G-12401)
AARON S MYERS
Also Called: Bowlder Metal
630 Cashman Rd (17350-9620)
PHONE..................................717 339-9304
Aaron Myers, *Owner*
EMP: 3
SALES (est): 407K Privately Held
SIC: 3441 3444 Fabricated structural
metal; roof deck, sheet metal

(G-12402)
ADVANCED ASPHALT LLC
59 Kelly Rd (17350-9459)
PHONE..................................717 965-2406
Christopher Adler, *Mng Member*
EMP: 3
SALES: 100K Privately Held
SIC: 2951 Asphalt paving mixtures &
blocks

(G-12403)
AIELLOS INTERNATIONAL INC
60 Shamrock Ln (17350-9264)
PHONE..................................717 451-3910
Justin Aiello, *Principal*
▲ EMP: 14

SALES (est): 1.9MM Privately Held
SIC: 2434 Wood kitchen cabinets

(G-12404)
ALLPURE TECHNOLOGIES INC
80 Progress Ave (17350-8442)
PHONE..................................717 624-3241
Micheal A Zumbrum, *President*
Trish Wilks, *Opers Mgr*
EMP: 4
SALES (est): 1MM
SALES (corp-wide): 1.7B Privately Held
SIC: 2834 Pharmaceutical preparations
HQ: Sartorius Stedim Biotech Gmbh
August-Spindler-Str. 11
Gottingen 37079
551 308-0

(G-12405)
CARMA INDUSTRIAL COATINGS
INC
45 Enterprise Dr (17350-9253)
PHONE..................................717 624-6239
Ronald Howe, *President*
Michele Howe, *Vice Pres*
◆ EMP: 5
SALES (est): 820.9K Privately Held
SIC: 3479 Coating of metals & formed
products

(G-12406)
CLIFFORD CNC TLING
SURGEON LLC
1232 E Berlin Rd (17350-9636)
PHONE..................................717 528-4264
Neil Clifford, *Prgrmr*
Neil F Clifford,
EMP: 7
SALES (est): 430.5K Privately Held
SIC: 3545 Tool holders

(G-12407)
CNC METALWORKS INC
45 Pine Run Rd (17350-8724)
PHONE..................................717 624-8436
Ellery Stonemetz, *President*
EMP: 4
SALES (est): 250K Privately Held
SIC: 3724 Air scoops, aircraft; airfoils, air-
craft engine; cooling systems, aircraft en-
gine; engine mount parts, aircraft

(G-12408)
COVINGTON PLASTIC MOLDING
10 S Bolton St (17350-1602)
PHONE..................................717 624-1111
James Covington, *President*
Scott Covington, *Vice Pres*
EMP: 9 EST: 1998
SQ FT: 6,000
SALES (est): 1.6MM Privately Held
WEB: www.covingtonplasticmolding.com
SIC: 3089 Molding primary plastic

(G-12409)
FRITO-LAY NORTH AMERICA
INC
140 Enterprise Dr Ste A (17350-9261)
PHONE..................................717 624-4206
Wayne Altland, *Branch Mgr*
EMP: 160
SALES (corp-wide): 64.6B Publicly Held
SIC: 2096 Potato chips & similar snacks
HQ: Frito-Lay North America, Inc.
7701 Legacy Dr
Plano TX 75024

(G-12410)
GARDNER ASSOCIATE
ENTERPRISES
2776 Oxford Rd (17350-9640)
PHONE..................................717 624-2003
Patricia Gardner, *President*
EMP: 4
SALES (est): 320K Privately Held
SIC: 3541 Machine tools, metal cutting
type

(G-12411)
HAIN PURE PROTEIN
CORPORATION
Plainville Farms
304 S Water St (17350-9688)
P.O. Box 38 (17350-0038)
PHONE..................................717 624-2191

Barb Quijano, *VP Mktg*
Beatta Carreon, *Branch Mgr*
Linda Adkins, *Manager*
Stanley Firebaugh, *Manager*
EMP: 69 Publicly Held
SIC: 2015 Poultry slaughtering & process-
ing
HQ: Hain Pure Protein Corporation
220 N Center St
Fredericksburg PA 17026
717 865-2136

(G-12412)
K & N MACHINE SHOP LLC
925 Kohler Mill Rd (17350-9239)
PHONE..................................717 624-3403
Allan Naylor, *Mng Member*
David Naylor,
EMP: 3
SQ FT: 3,200
SALES (est): 460K Privately Held
SIC: 3549 Metalworking machinery

(G-12413)
K TOOL INC
99 Enterprise Dr (17350-9253)
PHONE..................................717 624-3866
Dale Keller, *President*
EMP: 3
SALES (est): 693.2K Privately Held
WEB: www.ktoolinc.com
SIC: 3541 Machine tools, metal cutting
type

(G-12414)
KABAR TACK AND FEED
Also Called: Original Horse Tack Company
35 Cashman Rd (17350-9601)
PHONE..................................717 416-0069
Kareen Nichllson, *Owner*
EMP: 3
SALES (est): 283.4K Privately Held
SIC: 2399 Horse & pet accessories, textile;
horse blankets; horse harnesses & riding
crops, etc.: non-leather

(G-12415)
KEN F SMITH CUSTOM SHTMTL
LLC
25 Walker Dr (17350-9313)
P.O. Box 275 (17350-0275)
PHONE..................................717 624-4214
Duane Wright, *Sales Staff*
Denise Weimer, *Manager*
Ken F Smith,
EMP: 9
SQ FT: 14,000
SALES (est): 969.8K Privately Held
SIC: 1761 3441 Sheet metalwork; fabri-
cated structural metal

(G-12416)
MOSSE BLOCKS INC
140 Enterprise Dr Ste C (17350-9261)
PHONE..................................717 624-2597
Steven Brokenshire, *Principal*
EMP: 7
SALES (est): 943.1K Privately Held
SIC: 3599 Machine shop, jobbing & repair

(G-12417)
NEW OXFORD TOOL & DIE INC
186 Poplar Rd (17350-9523)
PHONE..................................717 624-8441
Nancy A Baltzley, *President*
Richard Baltzley, *Vice Pres*
EMP: 5
SQ FT: 2,000
SALES (est): 400K Privately Held
SIC: 3599 8711 Machine shop, jobbing &
repair; machine tool design

(G-12418)
PACKAGING CORPORATION
AMERICA
104 Commerce St (17350-1702)
PHONE..................................717 624-2122
EMP: 3
SALES (corp-wide): 7B Publicly Held
SIC: 2653 Corrugated & solid fiber boxes
PA: Packaging Corporation Of America
1 N Field Ct
Lake Forest IL 60045
847 482-3000

(G-12419)
PACKAGING CORPORATION AMERICA
Also Called: PCA
201 S College St (17350-1725)
P.O. Box 189 (17350-0189)
PHONE..................................717 632-4727
Michael Salloom, *Vice Pres*
June Dutka, *Chief Mktg Ofcr*
James Simpson, *Manager*
EMP: 80
SALES (corp-wide): 7B **Publicly Held**
WEB: www.timbar.com
SIC: 2653 Display items, corrugated: made from purchased materials
PA: Packaging Corporation Of America
1 N Field Ct
Lake Forest IL 60045
847 482-3000

(G-12420)
PCA CORRUGATED AND DISPLAY LLC
201 S College St (17350-1725)
PHONE..................................717 624-3500
EMP: 5 **EST:** 2017
SALES (est): 719.8K **Privately Held**
SIC: 2653 Mfg Corrugated/Solid Fiber Boxes

(G-12421)
PCA CORRUGATED AND DISPLAY LLC
Timbar Packaging & Display
104 Commerce St (17350-1702)
P.O. Box 98 (17350-0098)
PHONE..................................717 624-2122
John Rice, *General Mgr*
Goodwin Michael, *Manager*
Dan Miller, *Manager*
EMP: 80
SALES (corp-wide): 7B **Publicly Held**
WEB: www.timbar.com
SIC: 2653 Boxes, corrugated: made from purchased materials
HQ: Pca Corrugated And Display Llc
1955 W Field Ct
Lake Forest IL 60045
847 482-3000

(G-12422)
POSTAL HISTORY SOCIETY INC
869 Bridgewater Dr (17350-8206)
PHONE..................................717 624-5941
Joseph Geraci, *President*
III Yefalvi, *Corp Secy*
EMP: 11 **EST:** 1952
SALES (est): 790K **Privately Held**
SIC: 2721 8699 Trade journals: publishing & printing; charitable organization

(G-12423)
ROTH WOODWORKING LLC
107 S Water St (17350-9555)
PHONE..................................717 476-8609
Andrew Roth, *Principal*
EMP: 3
SALES (est): 227.4K **Privately Held**
SIC: 2431 Millwork

(G-12424)
SAY PLASTICS INC
2259 Oxford Rd (17350-9614)
PHONE..................................717 624-3222
William Smith, *Principal*
EMP: 3
SALES (est): 178.4K **Privately Held**
SIC: 3089 Injection molding of plastics

(G-12425)
W J STRICKLER SIGNS INC (PA)
Also Called: Hipple Signs
3999 Carlisle Pike (17350-8626)
P.O. Box 175 (17350-0175)
PHONE..................................717 624-8450
Warren J Strickler, *President*
Bryan Strickler, *President*
Peggy Strickler, *Corp Secy*
EMP: 25 **EST:** 1972
SQ FT: 12,000
SALES (est): 4.4MM **Privately Held**
SIC: 3993 Neon signs

(G-12426)
WHERLEYS TRAILER INC
6480 York Rd (17350-8418)
PHONE..................................717 624-2268
Ray Wherley, *President*
Rodney J Wherley, *Vice Pres*
EMP: 5
SALES (est): 460K **Privately Held**
SIC: 3715 7549 Semitrailers for truck tractors; trailer maintenance

(G-12427)
WINTER GARDENS QULTY FOODS INC
304 Commerce St (17350-1723)
P.O. Box 339 (17350-0339)
PHONE..................................717 624-4911
Thomas M Bross III, *President*
Stephen Raines, *Principal*
Thomas Becker, *Vice Pres*
Anh Tran, *Supervisor*
Jason M Bross, *Admin Sec*
EMP: 250 **EST:** 1974
SQ FT: 58,000
SALES (est): 59.3MM **Privately Held**
WEB: www.wintergardens.com
SIC: 2032 2099 Canned specialties; salads, fresh or refrigerated

(G-12428)
YAZOO MILLS INCORPORATED
305 Commerce St (17350-1724)
P.O. Box 369 (17350-0369)
PHONE..................................717 624-8993
Troy E Eckert, *President*
Stephanie Leonard, *General Mgr*
Cedric Noel, *Treasurer*
Charmian E Noel, *Treasurer*
Ryan Stevens, *Manager*
◆ **EMP:** 85 **EST:** 1902
SQ FT: 142,000
SALES (est): 39.9MM **Privately Held**
WEB: www.yazoomills.com
SIC: 2655 Tubes, fiber or paper: made from purchased material; cores, fiber: made from purchased material

New Park
York County

(G-12429)
ELITE CABINETRY INC
501 Marsteller Rd Ste 4 (17352-9568)
PHONE..................................717 993-5269
Michael Wiley, *Principal*
EMP: 4
SALES (est): 350K **Privately Held**
SIC: 2434 3429 Wood kitchen cabinets; cabinet hardware

(G-12430)
FAWN EMBROIDERY PUNCHING SVCS
1537 Main St (17352-9302)
P.O. Box 230 (17352-0230)
PHONE..................................717 382-4855
H William Clarius, *President*
Al Betmarik, *Vice Pres*
Alois Ettmarik, *Vice Pres*
EMP: 6
SALES (est): 374.9K **Privately Held**
WEB: www.fawn.com
SIC: 2395 Embroidery products, except schiffli machine

(G-12431)
FAWN INDUSTRIES INC
1537 Main St (17352-9302)
P.O. Box 230 (17352-0230)
PHONE..................................717 382-4855
H William Clarius, *President*
EMP: 65
SQ FT: 12,000
SALES (est): 5MM **Privately Held**
SIC: 2395 Embroidery products, except schiffli machine; emblems, embroidered

New Philadelphia
Schuylkill County

(G-12432)
J H C FABRICATIONS INC
2 Pine St (17959-1048)
PHONE..................................570 277-6150
Alan Nelson, *Branch Mgr*
EMP: 8
SALES (corp-wide): 3.9MM **Privately Held**
WEB: www.jhclabresin.com
SIC: 3821 Laboratory furniture
PA: J H C Fabrications Inc
595 Berriman St
Brooklyn NY 11208
718 649-0065

New Providence
Lancaster County

(G-12433)
DONER DESIGN INC
2175 Beaver Valley Pike (17560-9605)
PHONE..................................717 786-4172
EMP: 4
SALES (est): 350K **Privately Held**
SIC: 3648 Mfg Lighting Equipment

(G-12434)
LANCASTER SIGN CO INC
1334 Rawlinsville Rd (17560-9737)
PHONE..................................717 284-3500
Silvano J Giannini, *President*
Michael P Labiak, *Supervisor*
EMP: 10
SQ FT: 6,000
SALES (est): 1.1MM **Privately Held**
SIC: 3993 Electric signs; neon signs; signs, not made in custom sign painting shops

(G-12435)
STRONG BODY CARE PRODUCTS INC
1 Lakeside Dr (17560-9698)
P.O. Box 148 (17560-0148)
PHONE..................................717 786-8947
Victoria B Strong, *President*
EMP: 5
SALES (est): 408.3K **Privately Held**
SIC: 2844 Face creams or lotions; cosmetic preparations

(G-12436)
WYOMISSING STRUCTURES LLC
223 Refton Rd (17560-9724)
PHONE..................................610 374-2370
Samuel E Kineg, *Principal*
EMP: 3
SALES (est): 322.9K **Privately Held**
SIC: 2511 Lawn furniture: wood

New Ringgold
Schuylkill County

(G-12437)
COUNTRY TRADITIONS
2174 Sunny Rd (17960-8930)
PHONE..................................570 386-3621
Susan Hoover, *Owner*
EMP: 4
SALES (est): 235.2K **Privately Held**
SIC: 3942 Miniature dolls, collectors'

(G-12438)
E O J INCORPORATED
2401 Summer Valley Rd (17960-9668)
PHONE..................................570 943-2860
Joseph W Zaprazny, *President*
Elizabeth Zaprazny, *Corp Secy*
EMP: 4
SQ FT: 2,000
SALES (est): 276.4K **Privately Held**
SIC: 1231 Strip mining, anthracite

(G-12439)
INNOVATIVE DISPLAYS
1768 W Penn Pike (17960-8938)
PHONE..................................570 386-8121
Jamie Schellhammer, *Owner*
EMP: 4
SALES (est): 422.2K **Privately Held**
SIC: 2431 Millwork

(G-12440)
J W ZAPRAZNY INC
Also Called: Joe's Used Auto Parts Div
2401 Summer Valley Rd (17960-9668)
PHONE..................................570 943-2860
Joseph W Zaprazny, *President*
Elizabeth Zaprazny, *Corp Secy*
EMP: 51
SQ FT: 2,500
SALES (est): 8.6MM **Privately Held**
WEB: www.joesusedautoparts.com
SIC: 5093 5531 3341 Ferrous metal scrap & waste; automotive parts; secondary nonferrous metals

(G-12441)
MILLER BURIAL VAULT CO
17 Dorset Rd (17960-9385)
PHONE..................................570 386-5479
Paul H Bachman, *Partner*
Earl Oliver Zellner, *Partner*
EMP: 8 **EST:** 1967
SALES (est): 520K **Privately Held**
SIC: 3272 Burial vaults, concrete or precast terrazzo

(G-12442)
MOTORSPORT GREEN ENGINEER
2040 W Penn Pike (17960-9398)
PHONE..................................570 386-8600
Peter M Green, *Principal*
EMP: 4
SALES (est): 356.9K **Privately Held**
SIC: 3714 Motor vehicle parts & accessories

(G-12443)
SUMMER VALLEY EMB
2704 Summer Valley Rd (17960-9678)
PHONE..................................570 386-3711
Susan Mantz, *Owner*
EMP: 19
SALES (est): 667.7K **Privately Held**
WEB: www.summervalleyembroidery.com
SIC: 2395 Embroidery & art needlework

(G-12444)
TREE EQUIPMENT DESIGN INC
1392 W Penn Pike (17960-8503)
PHONE..................................570 386-3515
Lee W Squyres, *President*
EMP: 8
SQ FT: 1,000
SALES (est): 1.9MM **Privately Held**
WEB: www.treeequip.com
SIC: 3523 Transplanters

New Salem
Fayette County

(G-12445)
JACKSON FARMS DAIRY
6718 National Pike (15468-1202)
PHONE..................................724 246-7010
William S Jackson, *Owner*
EMP: 22
SALES (est): 2.3MM **Privately Held**
SIC: 0241 2099 2026 2024 Dairy farms; food preparations; fluid milk; ice cream & frozen desserts

(G-12446)
WIRE MESH SALES LLC
1015 New Salem Rd (15468-1175)
PHONE..................................724 245-9577
Marissa Kling, *Manager*
EMP: 20
SALES (corp-wide): 30.8MM **Privately Held**
SIC: 3496 Miscellaneous fabricated wire products

▲ = Import ▼=Export
◆ =Import/Export

HQ: Wire Mesh Sales Llc
25219 Kuykendahl Rd # 290
The Woodlands TX 77375
706 922-5179

New Stanton
Westmoreland County

(G-12447)
CAMPBELL 3
Also Called: Campbell House Publishing
418 Crossbow Dr (15672-9485)
PHONE..................................724 322-1043
Denise Campbell, *Owner*
EMP: 3
SALES (est): 12.8K **Privately Held**
SIC: 2721 8742 Periodicals; hospital &
health services consultant

(G-12448)
**HENRY JACK WATER ON
WHEELS**
124 Ash Brook Ln (15672-1113)
PHONE..................................724 925-1727
John Henry, *Owner*
EMP: 3
SALES (est): 18.7K **Privately Held**
WEB: www.wateronwheels.com
SIC: 3949 Swimming pools, except plastic

(G-12449)
**MASONS MARK STONE VENEER
CORP**
106 Sewickley St (15672-9757)
PHONE..................................724 635-0082
Shawn Miller, *President*
Christopher Miller, *Vice Pres*
EMP: 6 EST: 2013
SQ FT: 9,000
SALES (est): 200K **Privately Held**
SIC: 3272 Building stone, artificial: con-
crete; cast stone, concrete; siding, pre-
cast stone

(G-12450)
SCIENTIFIC TOOL INC
596 Middletown Rd (15672-1176)
PHONE..................................724 446-9311
William Faltz Jr, *President*
EMP: 35 EST: 1941
SQ FT: 8,000
SALES (est): 4.9MM **Privately Held**
WEB: www.scientifictool.com
SIC: 3599 3544 3541 Machine shop, job-
bing & repair; special dies & tools; ma-
chine tools, metal cutting type

(G-12451)
SENTINEL POWER INC
922 Middletown Rd (15672-1168)
PHONE..................................724 925-8181
Kenneth Thomas, *President*
Heather Thomas, *Marketing Staff*
▼ EMP: 4
SALES (est): 408.9K **Privately Held**
WEB: www.sentinelpower.com
SIC: 3674 Microprocessors

(G-12452)
TROTWOOD MANOR
612 Woodmere Dr (15672-9732)
PHONE..................................724 635-3057
EMP: 3
SALES (est): 66.8K **Privately Held**
SIC: 2499 Wood products

New Tripoli
Lehigh County

(G-12453)
**BLUE MTN VINEYARDS &
CELLARS (PA)**
7627 Grape Vine Dr (18066-3726)
P.O. Box 492 (18066-0492)
PHONE..................................610 298-3068
Joseph Greff, *President*
Vickie Greff, *Vice Pres*
EMP: 10

SALES (est): 1MM **Privately Held**
WEB: www.bluemountainwine.com
SIC: 2084 Wines

(G-12454)
CORPORATE ARTS INC
7397 Gun Club Rd (18066-4308)
PHONE..................................610 298-8374
Barry J Cleveland, *President*
EMP: 4
SALES (est): 417.2K **Privately Held**
WEB: www.corparts.com
SIC: 2752 7336 3861 7812 Commercial
printing, offset; graphic arts & related de-
sign; sound recording & reproducing
equipment, motion picture; audio-visual
program production

(G-12455)
**EIGHT OAKS CRAFT
DISTILLERY CO**
Also Called: Eight Oaks Craft Distillers
7189 Route 309 (18066-3808)
PHONE..................................484 387-5287
Chad Butters, *President*
Jesse Tyahla, *Treasurer*
EMP: 5 EST: 2016
SQ FT: 4,500
SALES (est): 204.8K **Privately Held**
SIC: 2085 Distilled & blended liquors

(G-12456)
GRUBER CON SPECIALISTS INC
6638 Jefferson Ct (18066-3652)
PHONE..................................610 760-0925
Allen Gruber Jr, *President*
EMP: 10
SQ FT: 4,836
SALES (est): 590.6K **Privately Held**
SIC: 1771 3251 Concrete work; brick &
structural clay tile

(G-12457)
HAYES-IVY MFG INC
Also Called: United Service Co
6273 Route 309 (18066-2031)
P.O. Box 455 (18066-0455)
PHONE..................................610 767-3865
Peter H Knight, *President*
Ivy Knight, *Corp Secy*
EMP: 25
SQ FT: 6,000
SALES (est): 5.1MM **Privately Held**
WEB: www.unitedserviceco.com
SIC: 3087 Custom compound purchased
resins

(G-12458)
HOFFMAN BROS SPEED
5661 Route 100 (18066-2108)
PHONE..................................610 760-6274
Jim Barr, *Principal*
EMP: 8
SALES (est): 1.1MM **Privately Held**
SIC: 3714 Propane conversion equipment,
motor vehicle

(G-12459)
OSWALDSMILL INC
7002 Gun Club Rd (18066-4301)
PHONE..................................610 298-3271
Jonathan Weiss, *Principal*
EMP: 6
SALES (est): 627.4K **Privately Held**
SIC: 3651 7389 Household audio equip-
ment;

(G-12460)
**PROCESS SLTIONS
CONSULTING INC**
8009 George Rd (18066-2847)
PHONE..................................610 248-2002
Mary Jane Levin, *President*
Lee Levine, *Shareholder*
EMP: 3
SALES: 80K **Privately Held**
SIC: 3674 8748 Semiconductors & related
devices; business consulting

(G-12461)
VERSALOT ENTERPRISES LLC
Also Called: Versalot Sales & Specialty Sup
3540 Alyssa Ct (18066-3052)
PHONE..................................610 213-1017
Joel Berardi, *President*

EMP: 6 EST: 2014
SALES (est): 713.2K **Privately Held**
SIC: 3639 Major kitchen appliances, ex-
cept refrigerators & stoves

(G-12462)
WEATHERED VINEYARDS LLC
7670 Carpet Rd (18066-4548)
PHONE..................................484 560-1528
EMP: 5 EST: 2014
SALES (est): 238.1K **Privately Held**
SIC: 2084 Wines

(G-12463)
WHITE CASTLE SERVICES LLC
9174 Briar Edge Rd (18066-3119)
PHONE..................................484 560-5961
Michael Levitsky,
EMP: 3
SALES (est): 140.2K **Privately Held**
SIC: 2752 Poster & decal printing, litho-
graphic

New Wilmington
Lawrence County

(G-12464)
BYLERS SAW MILL
23 Angel Rd (16142-1701)
PHONE..................................724 964-8528
Benjamin Byler, *Principal*
EMP: 3
SALES (est): 167.3K **Privately Held**
SIC: 2421 Sawmills & planing mills, gen-
eral

(G-12465)
DAIRY FARMERS AMERICA INC
925 State Route 18 (16142-5023)
PHONE..................................724 946-8729
Tim Sallmen, *Vice Pres*
Gary Shivley, *Plant Mgr*
Robin Barbour, *Manager*
Frank Hughes, *Data Proc Exec*
EMP: 100
SALES (corp-wide): 14.6B **Privately Held**
WEB: www.dfamilk.com
SIC: 2026 Milk processing (pasteurizing,
homogenizing, bottling)
PA: Dairy Farmers Of America, Inc.
1405 N 98th St
Kansas City KS 66111
816 801-6455

(G-12466)
**GARDAN MANUFACTURING
COMPANY**
171 State Route 18 # 16142 (16142-3713)
P.O. Box 34, New Castle (16103-0034)
PHONE..................................724 652-8171
Victor H Ross, *President*
Thomas J Bevan, *Corp Secy*
EMP: 8 EST: 1964
SQ FT: 4,000
SALES (est): 907.2K **Privately Held**
WEB: www.gardanmfg.com
SIC: 3599 Bellows, industrial: metal

(G-12467)
**GILLILAND PALLET COMPANY
INC**
Also Called: Gilliland Lumber
71 Auction Rd (16142-2001)
PHONE..................................724 946-2222
Robert Gilliland, *President*
Cindy Guilliland, *Treasurer*
EMP: 9 EST: 1956
SQ FT: 10,000
SALES: 1.3MM **Privately Held**
SIC: 2448 Pallets, wood

(G-12468)
NOVOSEL LLC
Also Called: Novocellars
5253 Old Pulaski Rd (16142-5703)
PHONE..................................724 230-6686
EMP: 7
SALES (est): 933.1K **Privately Held**
SIC: 2084 Wines

(G-12469)
**RIETHMILLER LUMBER MFG
CORP**
171 Riethmiller Rd (16142-2333)
PHONE..................................724 946-8608
Judith Riethmiller, *President*
Harry Riethmiller, *Admin Sec*
EMP: 5
SQ FT: 10,000
SALES (est): 1MM **Privately Held**
SIC: 3559 Kilns, lumber

(G-12470)
ROOFTOP EQUIPMENT INC
4617 New Castle Rd (16142-1729)
PHONE..................................724 946-9999
Robert Burns, *President*
EMP: 4
SALES (est): 852.1K **Privately Held**
WEB: www.rooftopequipment.com
SIC: 3531 Roofing equipment

(G-12471)
TERVO MASONRY LLC
Also Called: Ryder Rock
117 James St (16142-3305)
PHONE..................................724 944-6179
Aaron Tervo, *Mng Member*
EMP: 20
SALES (est): 1.1MM **Privately Held**
SIC: 1741 3272 Stone masonry; building
stone, artificial: concrete

(G-12472)
W W MCFARLAND INC
1103 Pulaski Mercer Rd (16142-2427)
PHONE..................................724 946-9663
William W McFarland, *Owner*
EMP: 4
SALES: 240K **Privately Held**
SIC: 2448 Wood pallets & skids

(G-12473)
WILMINGTON DIE INC
Maple St Ext (16142)
P.O. Box 254 (16142-0254)
PHONE..................................724 946-8020
Ronald G Collins, *President*
Patricia Collins, *Corp Secy*
EMP: 3
SQ FT: 4,600
SALES: 700K **Privately Held**
SIC: 3544 Special dies & tools

Newburg
Cumberland County

(G-12474)
**CHESTNUT RD LUMBER & DRY
KILN**
90 Chestnut Rd (17240-9150)
PHONE..................................717 423-5941
Steven Hostetler, *Owner*
EMP: 3
SALES (est): 298.6K **Privately Held**
SIC: 3559 Kilns

(G-12475)
FRIENDLY FUEL
156 Newville Rd (17240-9379)
PHONE..................................717 254-1932
William Brehm, *Principal*
EMP: 4
SALES (est): 234.6K **Privately Held**
SIC: 2869 Fuels

Newfoundland
Wayne County

(G-12476)
**CADOSIA VALLEY LUMBER
COMPANY**
Rr 191 (18445)
PHONE..................................570 676-3400
EMP: 7
SALES (est): 445.5K
SALES (corp-wide): 2MM **Privately Held**
SIC: 2421 Sawmill/Planing Mill

PA: Cadosia Valley Lumber Company Inc
Cadosia Apex Rd Rr 268
Hancock NY

Newmanstown
Lebanon County

(G-12477)
HORNINGS WOODCRAFT
4574 Stiegel Pike (17073-7011)
PHONE....................................717 949-3524
Lynford Horning, *Principal*
EMP: 4
SALES (est): 390.6K **Privately Held**
SIC: 2599 Furniture & fixtures

(G-12478)
K & H CABINET COMPANY INC
320 Stricklerstown Rd (17073-9173)
PHONE....................................717 949-6551
Lee Hertzog, *President*
Carrie Hertzog, *Treasurer*
EMP: 12
SQ FT: 1,250
SALES (est): 1.2MM **Privately Held**
SIC: 2434 Wood kitchen cabinets

(G-12479)
KOUNTRY KRAFT KITCHENS INC
291 S Sheridan Rd (17073-9192)
P.O. Box 570 (17073-0570)
PHONE....................................610 589-4575
Elvin W Hurst Jr, *President*
Dolores Hurst, *Corp Secy*
Mike R Bobers, *Vice Pres*
Linda Beamesderfer, *Sales Mgr*
Scott Peters, *Manager*
EMP: 120 EST: 1959
SQ FT: 60,000
SALES (est): 15.3MM **Privately Held**
WEB: www.kountrykraft.com
SIC: 2434 2541 2511 Wood kitchen cabinets; wood partitions & fixtures; wood household furniture

(G-12480)
LEBANON VALLEY ENTERPRISES
14 Martin Rd (17073-9129)
PHONE....................................717 866-2030
Earl Zimmerman, *President*
EMP: 3
SALES (est): 172.1K **Privately Held**
SIC: 3272 Concrete products

(G-12481)
MIDDLECREEK WELDING & MFG
201 Hopeland Rd (17073-8903)
PHONE....................................315 853-3936
Daniel Stoltzfus, *Owner*
EMP: 6
SALES (est): 685K **Privately Held**
SIC: 3523 Dairy equipment (farm)

(G-12482)
OCCUPED ORTHOTICS
439 Sunnyside Rd (17073-8849)
PHONE....................................717 949-2377
Daniel Roush, *Principal*
EMP: 3
SALES (est): 197.7K **Privately Held**
SIC: 3842 Prosthetic appliances

(G-12483)
SHANE HOSTETTER
Also Called: Quentin Wood
307 Old Mill Rd (17073-8961)
PHONE....................................717 949-6563
Shane Hostetter, *Owner*
EMP: 4
SALES (est): 304.5K **Privately Held**
SIC: 2431 Doors & door parts & trim, wood; moldings, wood: unfinished & pre-finished

(G-12484)
SHERIDAN SUPPLY COMPANY INC
7 Furnace Rd (17073-9106)
PHONE....................................610 589-4361
Glenn E Wolgemuth, *President*
John H Wolgemuth, *Treasurer*
Loren Wolgemuth, *Admin Sec*
EMP: 3
SALES (est): 313.7K **Privately Held**
SIC: 1081 4225 Metal mining services; general warehousing

(G-12485)
WOODMASTERS CABINETRY INC
204 Rod And Gun Rd (17073-9161)
PHONE....................................717 949-3937
Ronald Schies, *President*
EMP: 30 EST: 1974
SQ FT: 20,000
SALES: 3.2MM **Privately Held**
WEB: www.woodmasterscabinetry.com
SIC: 2434 Wood kitchen cabinets

Newport
Perry County

(G-12486)
ARTISTIC IMAGE
211 N 4th St (17074-1202)
PHONE....................................717 567-7070
Patricia Sharar, *Owner*
EMP: 3
SALES (est): 392.7K **Privately Held**
SIC: 2759 Screen printing

(G-12487)
BRAHMA BUILDING PRODUCTS LLC
224 Red Hill Rd (17074-8602)
P.O. Box 953906, Lake Mary FL (32795-3906)
PHONE....................................717 567-2571
Douglas Flaute, *President*
EMP: 15
SALES (est): 1.9MM **Privately Held**
SIC: 2431 Moldings & baseboards, ornamental & trim

(G-12488)
BUCKS VALLEY SAWMILL LLC
913 Bucks Valley Rd (17074-8210)
PHONE....................................717 567-9663
Derek Smith, *Principal*
EMP: 9
SALES (est): 380K **Privately Held**
SIC: 2421 Sawmills & planing mills, general

(G-12489)
EDGE BUILDING PRODUCTS INC
224 Market St (17074-1516)
P.O. Box 341 (17074-0999)
PHONE....................................717 567-2311
Terry J Heller, *President*
Ronald A Weller, *Treasurer*
Dave Colby, *Shareholder*
Robert King, *Shareholder*
Jeffrey F Nesbitt, *Shareholder*
EMP: 45
SQ FT: 2,000
SALES: 6MM **Privately Held**
WEB: www.permatrimboard.com
SIC: 3272 Building materials, except block or brick: concrete

(G-12490)
H & H PRECISION WIRE LLC
50 Red Hill Ct (17074-8743)
PHONE....................................717 567-9600
Terry J Heller,
Todd J Heller,
EMP: 15
SQ FT: 7,500
SALES (est): 2.1MM **Privately Held**
WEB: www.hmfourslide.com
SIC: 3599 Machine shop, jobbing & repair

(G-12491)
JUNIATA CONCRETE CO
2320 Keystone Way (17074-9449)
PHONE....................................717 567-3183
Joe Walker, *Manager*
EMP: 8
SALES (corp-wide): 6.3MM **Privately Held**
SIC: 3273 3271 Ready-mixed concrete; concrete block & brick

PA: Juniata Concrete Co.
721 Smith Rd
Mifflintown PA 17059
717 436-2176

(G-12492)
N T M INC
222 Red Hill Rd (17074-8602)
PHONE....................................717 567-9374
Ronald Weller, *President*
Mary High, *Prdtn Mgr*
Shayne Knouse, *Manager*
EMP: 35
SQ FT: 13,000
SALES (est): 7.9MM **Privately Held**
WEB: www.ntminc.net
SIC: 3599 3643 3841 Machine shop, jobbing & repair; connectors & terminals for electrical devices; contacts, electrical; surgical & medical instruments

Newtown
Bucks County

(G-12493)
A & C PHARMTECH INC
375 Pheasant Run (18940-3423)
PHONE....................................215 968-5605
Youmao Shi, *President*
▲ EMP: 5
SQ FT: 2,500
SALES: 300K **Privately Held**
SIC: 2834 Pharmaceutical preparations

(G-12494)
ACRA CONTROL INC
15 Terry Dr (18940-1830)
PHONE....................................714 382-1863
Christopher Wiltfey, *General Mgr*
▲ EMP: 4
SQ FT: 3,000
SALES: 6.6MM
SALES (corp-wide): 2.4B **Publicly Held**
WEB: www.acracontrol.com
SIC: 5065 3669 Communication equipment; intercommunication systems, electric
HQ: Curtiss-Wright Controls, Inc.
15801 Brixham Hill Ave # 200
Charlotte NC 28277
704 869-4600

(G-12495)
AJJP CORPORATION
Also Called: Bompadre Division
305 Pheasant Run (18940-3423)
PHONE....................................215 968-6677
Joe Parisi, *President*
Jack Childs, *Vice Pres*
Joseph Parisi, *Vice Pres*
▲ EMP: 110 EST: 1962
SQ FT: 92,000
SALES (est): 18MM **Privately Held**
WEB: www.parisi-royal.com
SIC: 2599 2541 2521 2531 Restaurant furniture, wood or metal; wood partitions & fixtures; wood office furniture; public building & related furniture; office furniture, except wood; millwork

(G-12496)
APPLIED MICRO CIRCUITS CORP
41 University Dr Ste 400 (18940-1873)
PHONE....................................267 757-8722
Jerome L Goodwin, *Principal*
EMP: 27 **Publicly Held**
WEB: www.amcc.com
SIC: 3674 Microcircuits, integrated (semiconductor)
HQ: Applied Micro Circuits Corp
4555 Great America Pkwy # 601
Santa Clara CA 95054
408 542-8600

(G-12497)
ASSOCIATES IN MEDICAL MKTG CO
Also Called: Handbooks & Healthcare
6 Penns Trl (18940-1889)
PHONE....................................215 860-9600
Marvin Anzel, *President*
Stephanie Anzel, *Admin Sec*
EMP: 20
SQ FT: 50,000
SALES: 4.2MM **Privately Held**
WEB: www.hhcbooks.com
SIC: 2741 Technical manuals: publishing only, not printed on site

(G-12498)
BOYD GEYER SIGN CORPORATION
444 S State St Ste C3 (18940-1945)
PHONE....................................215 860-3008
Howard H Geyer, *President*
EMP: 3 EST: 2011
SALES (est): 320.5K **Privately Held**
SIC: 3993 Signs & advertising specialties

(G-12499)
BUCKS COUNTY TYPE & DESIGN INC
Also Called: Bucks County Digital Imaging
90 Walker Ln (18940-1888)
PHONE....................................215 579-4200
Neal Carson, *President*
Howard Carson, *Vice Pres*
EMP: 14
SQ FT: 1,500
SALES (est): 2.3MM **Privately Held**
WEB: www.bucksdigital.com
SIC: 2791 7374 8748 Typographic composition, for the printing trade; service bureau, computer; publishing consultant

(G-12500)
CBD INCORPORATED
10 W Center Ave (18940-3504)
PHONE....................................215 579-6337
Dennis Jenkins, *President*
EMP: 3
SALES (est): 124.5K **Privately Held**
SIC: 3999

(G-12501)
DCM SLOT CAR RACEWAY
26 Thornbury Ln (18940-4218)
PHONE....................................215 805-6887
David Simms, *Principal*
EMP: 4
SALES (est): 247.9K **Privately Held**
SIC: 3644 Raceways

(G-12502)
FOLDED STRUCTURES COMPANY LLC
1044 Durham Rd (18940-4102)
P.O. Box 726, Ringoes NJ (08551-0726)
PHONE....................................908 237-1955
Daniel Kling, *Mng Member*
EMP: 3
SALES (est): 246.7K **Privately Held**
SIC: 2675 Panels, cardboard, die-cut: made from purchased materials

(G-12503)
FRIENDS BOARDING HO BUC QUA ME
50 S Congress St (18940-1906)
PHONE....................................215 968-3346
Mary Ann Brook, *Principal*
EMP: 2
SALES: 2.6MM **Privately Held**
SIC: 2721 Periodicals

(G-12504)
GENUINE PARTS COMPANY
Also Called: NAPA Auto Parts
42 Richboro Newtown Rd (18940-1595)
PHONE....................................215 968-4266
Kevin McHenry, *Branch Mgr*
EMP: 8
SALES (corp-wide): 18.7B **Publicly Held**
SIC: 5013 5531 3492 Automotive supplies & parts; automotive parts; automotive accessories; hose & tube couplings, hydraulic/pneumatic
PA: Genuine Parts Company
2999 Wildwood Pkwy
Atlanta GA 30339
770 953-1700

(G-12505)
GHARDA CHEMICALS LIMITED
760 Newtown Yardley Rd # 110 (18940-4500)
PHONE....................................215 968-9474

Ramanathan Seethapathi, *President*
Frank Sobtka, *President*
Florian Rodrigues, *General Mgr*
Ram Seethapathi, *General Mgr*
Dr K H Charda, *Chairman*
▲ **EMP:** 4
SALES (est): 872.1K **Privately Held**
WEB: www.ghardausa.com
SIC: 2819 Industrial inorganic chemicals

(G-12506)
HAROLD BECK & SONS INC (PA)
Also Called: Beck Electric Actuator
11 Terry Dr (18940-1895)
PHONE....................215 968-4600
Douglas C Beck, *President*
Pamela Thompson, *Buyer*
Adam Miller, *Purchasing*
John Medved, *Engineer*
Brian Scott, *Engineer*
EMP: 115
SQ FT: 90,000
SALES (est): 16.8MM **Privately Held**
WEB: www.haroldbeck.com
SIC: 3625 3566 5084 Actuators, industrial; controls for adjustable speed drives; speed changers, drives & gears; industrial machinery & equipment

(G-12507)
HAZARDOUS MATERIALS MGT TEAM
Also Called: Hmmt Environmental
418 Washington Ave (18940-2130)
P.O. Box 1066 (18940-0857)
PHONE....................215 968-4044
Fax: 215 968-5708
EMP: 4
SALES (est): 332.6K **Privately Held**
SIC: 8748 3826 Environmental Consultants & Mfg Specialty Equipment

(G-12508)
HEARTSINE TECHNOLOGIES LLC (DH)
Also Called: Heartsine Technologies, Inc.
121 Friends Ln Ste 400 (18940-1897)
PHONE....................215 860-8100
Declan O'Mahoney, *CEO*
William Samuel, *President*
Volker Brand, *Vice Pres*
Stephen Garrett, *Vice Pres*
Paul Phillips, *Vice Pres*
◆ **EMP:** 32
SALES (est): 14.9MM **Privately Held**
SIC: 3845 Surgical support systems: heart-lung machine, exc. iron lung

(G-12509)
HEATHA HENRYS LLC
Also Called: Sir Speedy
103 Penns Trl Unit B (18940-1814)
PHONE....................215 968-2080
Debra Ciligan, *General Mgr*
Heather Bradley, *Mng Member*
Brian Bradley,
EMP: 9
SQ FT: 5,000
SALES: 750K **Privately Held**
SIC: 2752 2759 Commercial printing, lithographic; commercial printing

(G-12510)
HELIUS MEDICAL TECH INC (PA)
642 Newtown Yardley Rd # 100
(18940-1775)
PHONE....................215 944-6100
Philippe Deschamps, *Ch of Bd*
Jennifer Laux, *Ch Credit Ofcr*
Jonathan Sackier, *Chief Mktg Ofcr*
Joyce Laviscount, *Officer*
EMP: 10
SQ FT: 10,444
SALES: 478K **Publicly Held**
SIC: 3845 Electromedical apparatus

(G-12511)
HIPPS SONS COINS PRECIOUS MTLS
408 S State St Ste 5 (18940-1947)
PHONE....................215 550-6854
Edward S Hipps, *Principal*
EMP: 4

SALES (est): 462.1K **Privately Held**
SIC: 3339 Precious metals

(G-12512)
IHEADBONES INC
1636 Wrightstown Rd (18940-2814)
PHONE....................888 866-0807
Thomas Buroojy, *Principal*
EMP: 3
SALES (est): 259.3K **Privately Held**
SIC: 3559 Electronic component making machinery

(G-12513)
JUST PLAY
6 Terry Dr Ste 300 (18940-3432)
PHONE....................215 953-1208
Jeffrey Greenberg, *Owner*
EMP: 30
SALES (est): 4.6MM **Privately Held**
SIC: 3944 Games, toys & children's vehicles

(G-12514)
KEYSTONE FOUNDATION SERVICE
910 Creamery Rd (18940-2908)
PHONE....................215 968-2955
Brad Welch, *President*
EMP: 5
SALES (est): 447.5K **Privately Held**
WEB: www.wallfix.com
SIC: 7692 Welding repair

(G-12515)
KVK-TECH INC
100 Campus Dr (18940-1784)
PHONE....................215 579-1842
Anthony Tabasso, *President*
EMP: 40
SALES (corp-wide): 85MM **Privately Held**
SIC: 2834 Pharmaceutical preparations
PA: Kvk-Tech, Inc.
110 Terry Dr
Newtown PA 18940
215 579-1842

(G-12516)
KVK-TECH INC (PA)
110 Terry Dr (18940-3427)
PHONE....................215 579-1842
Anthony Tabasso, *President*
Kishorekumar Kotini, *QA Dir*
Nimish Patel, *QC Mgr*
Orla Nicholl, *Human Resources*
Joe Lefebvre, *Sales Mgr*
▲ **EMP:** 267
SALES (est): 85MM **Privately Held**
SIC: 2834 Pharmaceutical preparations

(G-12517)
LANTICA SOFTWARE LLC
100 Jericho Valley Dr (18940-3632)
PHONE....................215 598-8419
William Halpern,
EMP: 3
SALES (est): 160.4K **Privately Held**
WEB: www.lantica.com
SIC: 7371 7372 Computer software development; prepackaged software

(G-12518)
LEEDOM WELDING & FABRICATING (PA)
434 Penn St (18940-2124)
PHONE....................215 757-8787
Robert H Leedom, *President*
Janet Leedom, *Corp Secy*
EMP: 4
SQ FT: 4,500
SALES (est): 441.8K **Privately Held**
SIC: 3444 Sheet metalwork

(G-12519)
LIONHEART HOLDINGS LLC (PA)
Also Called: Lionheart Ventures
54 Friends Ln Ste 125 (18940-3403)
PHONE....................215 283-8400
David Bovenizer, *CEO*
EMP: 60

SALES (est): 56.8MM **Privately Held**
WEB: www.lionheartventures.com
SIC: 3724 3561 3594 3433 Aircraft engines & engine parts; pumps & pumping equipment; fluid power pumps & motors; heating equipment, except electric; clay refractories; industrial instrmnts msrmnt display/control process variable

(G-12520)
LIONHEART INDUSTRIAL GROUP LLC
54 Friends Ln Ste 125 (18940-3403)
PHONE....................215 283-8400
David S Bovenizer, *CEO*
Patrick R Laphen, *Exec VP*
William S Rymer, *CFO*
Vanessa H MAI, *Marketing Staff*
EMP: 4
SALES (est): 149.7K **Privately Held**
SIC: 3544 Special dies & tools

(G-12521)
MEDIA MANAGEMENT SERVICES INC (PA)
Also Called: MMS Education
105 Terry Dr Ste 120 (18940-1872)
PHONE....................800 523-5948
Susan Keipper, *CEO*
Karen Ellis, *President*
Edward J Meell, *Chairman*
Stacey Moyers, *Vice Pres*
Connie Schofer, *Vice Pres*
EMP: 29
SALES (est): 3.4MM **Privately Held**
WEB: www.mmseducation.com
SIC: 2741 8748 8742 Miscellaneous publishing; business consulting; management consulting services

(G-12522)
MODZORI LLC
Also Called: Sylish
157 Justice Dr (18940-1108)
PHONE....................215 833-3618
Leon Shmureak, *Mng Member*
EMP: 4 **EST:** 2012
SALES: 50K **Privately Held**
SIC: 3144 5661 5139 7389 Dress shoes, women's; women's shoes; shoes;

(G-12523)
MORNINGSTAR CORPORATION (PA)
8 Pheasant Run (18940-1819)
PHONE....................267 685-0500
Lee Gordon, *President*
Yalunallen Wu, *Design Engr*
Russell Borum, *Sales Engr*
Mark McHenry, *Marketing Mgr*
Qing Kou, *Admin Sec*
◆ **EMP:** 16
SQ FT: 4,000
SALES (est): 2.1MM **Privately Held**
WEB: www.morningstarcorp.com
SIC: 3625 Control equipment, electric

(G-12524)
MPOWER SOFTWARE SERVICES LLC (PA)
115 Pheasant Run Ste 110 (18940-1886)
PHONE....................215 497-9730
Edward J Smith, *Partner*
Vaidyanathan Narayanan, *Principal*
Timothy J McNamara, *Principal*
Donald Wilcox, *Principal*
Edward Smith, *Vice Pres*
EMP: 75
SQ FT: 3,500
SALES: 10MM **Privately Held**
SIC: 7372 Prepackaged software

(G-12525)
MRI FLEXIBLE PACKAGING COMPANY
660 Newtown Yardley Rd (18940-1759)
PHONE....................215 860-7676
Greg Lane, *Branch Mgr*
EMP: 15

SALES (corp-wide): 757.8MM **Privately Held**
WEB: www.mriflex.com
SIC: 2679 2672 2673 2621 Labels, paper: made from purchased material; labels (unprinted), gummed: made from purchased materials; food storage & frozen food bags, plastic; printing paper
HQ: Mri Flexible Packaging Company
181 Rittenhouse Cir
Bristol PA 19007

(G-12526)
MSI TECHNOLOGIES LLC
1267 Fountain Rd (18940-3722)
PHONE....................215 968-5068
Dale Baver, *Branch Mgr*
EMP: 5
SALES (est): 283.7K **Privately Held**
WEB: www.msitechnologies.com
SIC: 7372 Prepackaged software
PA: Msi Technologies, Llc
1055 Parsippany Blvd 205a
Parsippany NJ 07054

(G-12527)
NEUROHABILITATION CORPORATION
642 Newtown Yardley Rd # 100
(18940-1775)
PHONE....................215 809-2018
Philippe Deschamps, *CEO*
EMP: 3
SQ FT: 300
SALES (est): 313.9K
SALES (corp-wide): 478K **Publicly Held**
SIC: 3845 Colonoscopes, electromedical
PA: Helius Medical Technologies, Inc.
642 Newtown Yardley Rd # 100
Newtown PA 18940
215 944-6100

(G-12528)
NEWTOWN PRINTING CORP
358 S Lincoln Ave (18940-2122)
PHONE....................215 968-6876
Paul Kajmo, *President*
Kurt Wecker, *Treasurer*
EMP: 5 **EST:** 1976
SQ FT: 3,000
SALES: 1.2MM **Privately Held**
WEB: www.newtownprinting.com
SIC: 2759 2262 Commercial printing; screen printing: manmade fiber & silk broadwoven fabrics

(G-12529)
NTEC INC
12 Penns Trl Ste 102 (18940-1892)
PHONE....................215 768-0261
Bruce Stevens, *President*
EMP: 3
SQ FT: 12,000
SALES (est): 391K **Privately Held**
WEB: www.anodizing-ntec.com
SIC: 3559 Anodizing equipment; metal finishing equipment for plating, etc.

(G-12530)
NUSHIELD INC
2110 S Eagle Rd Ste 400 (18940-1574)
PHONE....................215 500-6426
Mark Ross, *President*
Andrew Serenyi, *Vice Pres*
▼ **EMP:** 4 **EST:** 2001
SALES: 1MM **Privately Held**
WEB: www.nusheild.com
SIC: 3089 Window screening, plastic

(G-12531)
OMPI OF AMERICA INC
41 University Dr Ste 400 (18940-1873)
PHONE....................267 757-8747
Howard Drake, *Principal*
▲ **EMP:** 13
SALES (est): 1.2MM **Privately Held**
SIC: 3221 Medicine bottles, glass

(G-12532)
ONCONOVA THERAPEUTICS INC (PA)
375 Pheasant Run (18940-3423)
PHONE....................267 759-3680
Steven Fruchtman, *CEO*
Michael B Hoffman, *Ch of Bd*
Manoj Maniar, *Senior VP*

GEOGRAPHIC

Abraham Oler, *Vice Pres*
Mark P Guerin, *CFO*
EMP: 16
SQ FT: 9,500
SALES: 1.2MM **Publicly Held**
WEB: www.onconova.com
SIC: 2834 8731 Pharmaceutical preparations; commercial physical research

(G-12533)
PELMOR LABORATORIES INC
401 Lafayette St　(18940-2151)
PHONE..........................215 968-3334
E William Ross Sr, *Chairman*
William Ross Jr, *Vice Pres*
Ross Wilson, *Vice Pres*
Rosemary Nugent, *QC Mgr*
Michael Wuensche, *Controller*
▲ **EMP:** 45 **EST:** 1956
SQ FT: 18,000
SALES (est): 9.7MM
SALES (corp-wide): 6.5MM **Privately Held**
WEB: www.pelmor.com
SIC: 3061 2891 2851 2822 Mechanical rubber goods; adhesives & sealants; paints & allied products; synthetic rubber
PA: Ross Enterprises Inc
401 Lafayette St
Newtown PA 18940
215 968-3334

(G-12534)
PENN MEDICAL EDUCATION LLC
2865 S Eagle Rd B354　(18940-1546)
PHONE..........................215 524-2785
Valerie Crenshaw,
EMP: 5
SALES: 600K **Privately Held**
SIC: 2721 Periodicals

(G-12535)
PHARMA INNVTION SRCING CTR LLC
105 Perry Ln　(18940-1154)
PHONE..........................203 314-8095
Neel Balasubramanian, *President*
EMP: 3
SALES (est): 168.6K **Privately Held**
SIC: 2834 Pharmaceutical preparations

(G-12536)
PLASTIC SOLUTIONS INC
424 Mahogany Walk　(18940-4211)
PHONE..........................215 968-3242
Russell Consentino, *President*
EMP: 4 **EST:** 1998
SALES (est): 301.8K **Privately Held**
SIC: 8742 3089 Manufacturing management consultant; plastic containers, except foam

(G-12537)
PLEASANT LUCK CORP
Also Called: Sir Speedy
46 Blacksmith Rd　(18940-1847)
PHONE..........................215 968-2080
Gadi Naaman, *President*
Carolyn Naaman, *Treasurer*
EMP: 7
SQ FT: 4,000
SALES: 600K **Privately Held**
WEB: www.sirspeedynewtown.com
SIC: 2752 2791 2789 Commercial printing, lithographic; typesetting; bookbinding & related work

(G-12538)
POONAM INTERNATIONAL INC
104 Justice Dr　(18940-1109)
PHONE..........................215 968-1555
Poonam Sood, *CEO*
EMP: 3
SALES (est): 302.5K **Privately Held**
SIC: 3695 Computer software tape & disks: blank, rigid & floppy

(G-12539)
PUBLICATION CONNEXION LLC
6 Terry Dr　(18940-3432)
PHONE..........................215 944-9400
Susan Stein,
EMP: 10
SALES: 950K **Privately Held**
SIC: 2741 Miscellaneous publishing

(G-12540)
QUALTEK MOLECULAR LABORATORIES
300 Pheasant Run　(18940-3422)
PHONE..........................215 504-7402
Steven Bernstein, *Principal*
Frank Lynch, *Vice Pres*
Joell Gramacy, *Manager*
EMP: 6
SALES (est): 395.6K **Privately Held**
SIC: 3841 Diagnostic apparatus, medical

(G-12541)
QUOTIENT BIODIAGNOSTICS INC (PA)
301 S State St Ste S204　(18940-1997)
PHONE..........................215 497-8820
Jeremy Stackawitz, *President*
Stephen Unger, *CFO*
Bill Brady, *VP Sales*
Greg Magda, *Accounts Exec*
Robert Thyret, *Accounts Exec*
EMP: 11
SALES (est): 1.4MM **Privately Held**
SIC: 2836 Biological products, except diagnostic

(G-12542)
RCD TECHNOLOGY INC
Also Called: Vizinex Rfid
670 Pineville Rd　(18940-3008)
PHONE..........................215 529-9440
Kenneth Horton, *CEO*
Sandra Garby, *Vice Pres*
Phil Koppenhofer, *VP Sales*
Robert Oberle, *CTO*
EMP: 15
SQ FT: 7,500
SALES (est): 1.1MM **Privately Held**
WEB: www.rcdtechnology.com
SIC: 3679 Electronic circuits

(G-12543)
RELIABLE PRODUCTS INC
110 Terry Dr Ste 200　(18940-3427)
PHONE..........................215 860-2011
Kalpesh Vepuri, *President*
◆ **EMP:** 5
SALES (est): 590.7K **Privately Held**
SIC: 2834 Pharmaceutical preparations

(G-12544)
RENAISSANCE SSA LLC
411 S State St Ste E100　(18940-1955)
PHONE..........................267 685-0340
John Denman, *President*
Pierre Frechette, *Chairman*
Christine Woolgar, *Treasurer*
David Koo, *Asst Sec*
EMP: 13 **EST:** 2012
SQ FT: 1,000
SALES (est): 945.4K **Privately Held**
SIC: 2834 Proprietary drug products

(G-12545)
ROCKFISH VENTURE LLP (PA)
Also Called: Mom's Bake At Home Pizza
156 N State St　(18940-2043)
PHONE..........................215 968-5054
Maureen Distesano, *Managing Prtnr*
EMP: 15 **EST:** 1961
SQ FT: 7,500
SALES: 550K **Privately Held**
SIC: 2041 Pizza dough, prepared

(G-12546)
ROSS ENTERPRISES INC (PA)
401 Lafayette St　(18940-2151)
PHONE..........................215 968-3334
E William Ross, *President*
EMP: 66
SQ FT: 18,000
SALES (est): 6.5MM **Privately Held**
SIC: 3061 Mechanical rubber goods

(G-12547)
SEACO FOODS INTERNATIONAL
Also Called: Good Catch
2110 S Eagle Rd　(18940-1574)
PHONE..........................844 579-1133
Chris Kerr, *CEO*
Eric Schnell, *Principal*
Marci Zaroff, *Principal*
EMP: 10

SALES (est): 530.8K **Privately Held**
SIC: 2092 Seafoods, frozen: prepared

(G-12548)
SECOND PLAY LLC
6 Terry Dr　(18940-3432)
PHONE..........................267 229-8033
Marvin Greenberg, *Mng Member*
▲ **EMP:** 5
SQ FT: 1,500
SALES (est): 304K **Privately Held**
SIC: 3944 Games, toys & children's vehicles

(G-12549)
SELAS HEAT TECHNOLOGY CO LLC
54 Friends Ln Ste 125　(18940-3403)
PHONE..........................215 646-6600
David Bovenizer, *Principal*
EMP: 4
SALES (est): 64K **Privately Held**
SIC: 3255 Clay refractories

(G-12550)
SMUCKERS SALAD
2150 S Eagle Rd　(18940-1559)
PHONE..........................267 757-0944
David Smucker, *Owner*
EMP: 5
SALES (est): 129.9K **Privately Held**
SIC: 5812 2099 5149 Sandwiches & submarines shop; dessert mixes & fillings; sandwiches

(G-12551)
SOLUTION PEOPLE INC
675 Eagle Rd　(18940-2911)
PHONE..........................215 750-2694
Waldo Alfaro, *Principal*
EMP: 3
SALES (est): 121.6K **Privately Held**
SIC: 3272 Concrete products

(G-12552)
STAUDT MACHINE COMPANY
16 Martindell Dr　(18940-3645)
PHONE..........................215 598-7225
Joseph Staudt, *President*
Dolores Staudt, *Admin Sec*
EMP: 10 **EST:** 1970
SQ FT: 6,000
SALES (est): 970K **Privately Held**
SIC: 3599 Machine shop, jobbing & repair

(G-12553)
STI PHARMA LLC
32 Blacksmith Rd　(18940-1847)
PHONE..........................215 710-3270
Anup Dam, *Chairman*
Michael Stalhamer, *Vice Pres*
Bryan Hallmark, *Technology*
Shrikant Dhoke, *Associate Dir*
Nicholas Heller, *Admin Asst*
EMP: 2
SALES: 10MM **Privately Held**
SIC: 2834 Pharmaceutical preparations

(G-12554)
T T M CONTACTS CORPORATION
7 Garrison Pl　(18940-1711)
PHONE..........................215 497-1078
Henry J Tedds, *President*
John E Antilozi, *President*
EMP: 6
SQ FT: 2,000
SALES (est): 540K **Privately Held**
SIC: 3699 Electrical equipment & supplies

(G-12555)
TELETRONICS TECHNOLOGY CORP
15 Terry Dr　(18940-1830)
P.O. Box 728　(18940-0728)
PHONE..........................267 352-2020
David C Adams, *CEO*
Joyce Haney, *General Mgr*
Allan Symonds, *Vice Pres*
Barbara Bucci, *Prdtn Mgr*
Kevin Redick, *Purch Mgr*
EMP: 209
SQ FT: 93,000

SALES (est): 59.5MM
SALES (corp-wide): 2.4B **Publicly Held**
WEB: www.ttcdas.com
SIC: 3812 Aircraft/aerospace flight instruments & guidance systems; electronic detection systems (aeronautical)
PA: Curtiss-Wright Corporation
130 Harbour Place Dr # 300
Davidson NC 28036
704 869-4600

(G-12556)
TRIM TECH INC
1055 Little Rd　(18940-2735)
PHONE..........................215 321-0841
Donald Jay Glatz, *President*
Britt Glatz, *Treasurer*
EMP: 10
SALES (est): 1MM **Privately Held**
SIC: 2434 Wood kitchen cabinets

(G-12557)
UNITED COLOR MANUFACTURING INC (PA)
660 Newtown Yardley Rd # 205
(18940-1799)
P.O. Box 480　(18940-0480)
PHONE..........................215 860-2165
Thomas E Nowakowski Sr, *President*
Carmella Nowakowski, *Corp Secy*
Thomas E Nowakowski Jr, *Vice Pres*
▲ **EMP:** 19
SQ FT: 5,000
SALES (est): 7.9MM **Privately Held**
SIC: 2865 Dyes & pigments

(G-12558)
UNIVERSAL DISPLAY CORPORATION
2005 Trowbridge Dr　(18940-9438)
PHONE..........................609 671-0980
EMP: 3 **Publicly Held**
SIC: 3674 Semiconductors & related devices
PA: Universal Display Corporation
375 Phillips Blvd Ste 1
Ewing NJ 08618

(G-12559)
VERDER SCIENTIFIC INC
11 Penns Trl Ste 300　(18940-4800)
PHONE..........................267 757-0351
Georg Schick, *President*
Ferdinand Walter, *CFO*
Jurgen Pankratz, *Director*
Patricia Jung, *Admin Sec*
▲ **EMP:** 12
SQ FT: 2,000
SALES (est): 3.7MM
SALES (corp-wide): 183.7K **Privately Held**
WEB: www.retsch-us.com
SIC: 3821 Laboratory apparatus, except heating & measuring; laboratory equipment: fume hoods, distillation racks, etc.
HQ: Retsch Gmbh
Retsch-Allee 1-5
Haan　42781
210 423-3310

(G-12560)
VIA DESIGN & TECHNOLOGIES
12 Penns Trl Ste 125　(18940-1892)
PHONE..........................215 579-5730
Douglas Dixon, *President*
EMP: 4
SALES (est): 338.4K **Privately Held**
SIC: 7372 Prepackaged software

(G-12561)
VIRTUS PHARMACEUTICALS LLC ✪
12 Penns Trl Ste A　(18940-1892)
PHONE..........................813 283-1344
EMP: 3 **EST:** 2018
SALES (est): 187.8K **Privately Held**
SIC: 2834 Pharmaceutical preparations

(G-12562)
WEAVE HUB LLC
41 University Dr Ste 400　(18940-1873)
PHONE..........................215 809-2082
Farheen Naviwala,
Sameed Naviwala,
EMP: 3 **EST:** 2015

SQ FT: 150
SALES (est): 282.7K **Privately Held**
SIC: 2211 Towels, dishcloths & washcloths:
cotton

(G-12563)
WHITE ENGRG SURFACES
CORP
1 Pheas Run Newto Busin (18940)
PHONE..................................215 968-5021
Christopher M Nyland, *President*
Diane W Nyland, *Admin Sec*
▲ **EMP:** 170
SQ FT: 65,000
SALES (est): 61MM **Privately Held**
SIC: 3479 3451 2899 Painting, coating &
hot dipping; screw machine products;
chemical preparations

(G-12564)
WORTHINGTON STOWE FINE
WOODWOR (PA)
1108 Wrightstown Rd (18940-9602)
PHONE..................................215 504-5500
Chance Worthington, *Principal*
Steve Shagen, *Vice Pres*
EMP: 14 **EST:** 2008
SALES (est): 1.5MM **Privately Held**
SIC: 2499 Decorative wood & woodwork

Newtown Square
Delaware County

(G-12565)
APPITUR CO
3553 West Chester Pike (19073-3701)
PHONE..................................215 720-1420
Thomas Rossi,
Michele Coghlan,
Thomas Coghlan,
Kristin Jones,
EMP: 6 **EST:** 2012
SALES (est): 287.3K **Privately Held**
SIC: 7372 Educational computer software

(G-12566)
ARIBA INC
3999 West Chester Pike (19073-2305)
PHONE..................................610 661-8413
Art Bruni, *Vice Pres*
Margaret Smith, *Manager*
Nagesh Naik, *Director*
Gary Schaaf, *Director*
EMP: 12
SALES (est): 881.1K
SALES (corp-wide): 28.2B **Privately Held**
SIC: 7372 Prepackaged software
HQ: Sap America, Inc.
3999 West Chester Pike
Newtown Square PA 19073
610 661-1000

(G-12567)
BOIRON INC (HQ)
6 Campus Blvd (19073-3267)
PHONE..................................610 325-7464
Christian Boiron, *Ch of Bd*
Janick Boudazin, *President*
Ludovic Rassat, *President*
▲ **EMP:** 42 **EST:** 1910
SQ FT: 16,000
SALES (est): 17.2MM
SALES (corp-wide): 576.4MM **Privately**
Held
WEB: www.boiron.com
SIC: 2833 2834 Drugs & herbs: grading,
grinding & milling; pharmaceutical prepa-
rations
PA: Boiron
2 Avenue De L Ouest Lyonnais
Messimy 69510
478 456-100

(G-12568)
CAMPBELL BUSINESS FORMS
INC
3558 Winding Way (19073-3608)
P.O. Box 396 (19073-0396)
PHONE..................................610 356-0626
Thomas Kaufman Jr, *President*
Thomas Kauffman, *Treasurer*
Carol Kauffman, *Admin Sec*
EMP: 7 **EST:** 1943

SQ FT: 5,000
SALES: 800K **Privately Held**
SIC: 2752 2761 Business forms, litho-
graphed; manifold business forms

(G-12569)
CAPTAIN CHUCKYS CRAB
CAKE CO I
5149 West Chester Pike (19073-1101)
PHONE..................................610 355-7525
Nancy Wojciehowski, *President*
Charles Wojciehowski, *Vice Pres*
EMP: 4
SALES (est): 961.1K **Privately Held**
SIC: 5149 3556 Groceries & related prod-
ucts; food products machinery

(G-12570)
CHEMICAL EQUIPMENT LABS
VA INC
Also Called: Chemical Equipment Labs of De
3920 Providence Rd A (19073-2205)
PHONE..................................610 497-9390
Edward Morgan Sr, *President*
Joe Kelly, *Sales Mgr*
Melissa Justice, *Sales Staff*
▲ **EMP:** 30
SALES (est): 10.2MM **Privately Held**
WEB: www.chemicalequipmentlabs.com
SIC: 3589 8742 2899 5169 Water treat-
ment equipment, industrial; management
consulting services; water treating com-
pounds; chemicals & allied products

(G-12571)
D&B TAILORS INC
Also Called: Dannunzio and Battistoni
3620 Chapel Rd (19073-3603)
PHONE..................................610 356-9279
Gabrielle Dannunzio, *President*
EMP: 20 **EST:** 1966
SQ FT: 2,500
SALES (est): 1.1MM **Privately Held**
SIC: 2842 5611 Laundry cleaning prepara-
tions; suits, men's

(G-12572)
DAYS BEVERAGE INC
Also Called: Manischewitz Shelzer Company
529 Guinevere Dr (19073-4433)
PHONE..................................215 990-0983
David P Digirolamo, *President*
Dennis A Digirilamo, *Corp Secy*
David A Digirolamo, *Vice Pres*
EMP: 56 **EST:** 1997
SQ FT: 60,000
SALES: 52MM **Privately Held**
WEB: www.daysbeverage.com
SIC: 2086 5149 Soft drinks: packaged in
cans, bottles, etc.; soft drinks

(G-12573)
G R G TECHNOLOGIES LLC
3954 Miller Rd (19073-2244)
PHONE..................................610 325-6701
Mike Schultheis, *Purch Dir*
M Parker Blatchford, *Mng Member*
Doug Blatchford, *Admin Asst*
EMP: 10
SQ FT: 11,000
SALES (est): 1.5MM **Privately Held**
SIC: 3299 Ornamental & architectural plas-
ter work; columns, papier mache or plas-
ter of paris; moldings, architectural:
plaster of paris

(G-12574)
GIANNA SKIN & LASER LTD
4667 West Chester Pike (19073-2227)
PHONE..................................610 356-7870
Susan Cathcart, *Principal*
EMP: 4
SALES (est): 331.4K **Privately Held**
SIC: 3845 Laser systems & equipment,
medical

(G-12575)
HEY GIRL INC
5105 Cornerstone Dr (19073-4545)
PHONE..................................610 945-6138
EMP: 3
SALES (est): 292.3K **Privately Held**
SIC: 2339 Women's & misses' outerwear

(G-12576)
HILLS QULTY SEAFOOD MKTS
INC
3605 West Chester Pike (19073-3703)
PHONE..................................610 359-1888
Brian Murray, *Branch Mgr*
EMP: 12
SALES (corp-wide): 4.4MM **Privately**
Held
SIC: 2092 Fresh or frozen packaged fish
PA: Hill's Quality Seafood Markets, Inc.
402 W Baltimore Ave
Media PA
610 566-3788

(G-12577)
INNOCOLL INC
3803 West Chester Pike (19073-2333)
PHONE..................................484 406-5200
EMP: 11
SALES (est): 1.8MM **Privately Held**
SIC: 2834 Pharmaceutical preparations

(G-12578)
JCPDS INTERNATIONAL
CENTRE (PA)
12 Campus Blvd (19073-3200)
PHONE..................................610 325-9814
Nicole Ernst, *Editor*
Stacy Gates, *Editor*
James Kaduk, *Chairman*
Helen McDonell, *Marketing Mgr*
Benjamin Hish, *Marketing Staff*
EMP: 38
SQ FT: 25,000
SALES: 6.3MM **Privately Held**
WEB: www.icdd.com
SIC: 2741 Technical papers: publishing
only, not printed on site

(G-12579)
JOBSON MEDICAL
INFORMATION LLC
Also Called: Review of Ophthalmology
11 Campus Blvd Ste 100 (19073-3242)
PHONE..................................610 492-1000
Richard Bay, *President*
Manuel Valle Sanchez, *Web Dvlpr*
Victor Raroque, *Software Dev*
EMP: 30
SALES (corp-wide): 78.7MM **Privately**
Held
WEB: www.revoptom.com
SIC: 2721 Trade journals: publishing &
printing
PA: Jobson Medical Information Llc
395 Hudson St Fl 3
New York NY 10014
212 274-7000

(G-12580)
KOZMER TECHNOLOGIES LTD
950 Beverly Ln (19073-2730)
PHONE..................................610 358-4099
Joseph Kozachick, *President*
Joseph Kozacheck, *President*
Rose Kozacheck, *Corp Secy*
EMP: 4
SALES (est): 371K **Privately Held**
SIC: 2821 Plastics materials & resins

(G-12581)
LAESSIG ASSOCIATES
833 Malin Rd (19073-3515)
PHONE..................................610 353-3543
John D Laessig, *Owner*
EMP: 3
SALES (est): 202.5K **Privately Held**
SIC: 3569 8711 Testing chambers for alti-
tude, temperature, ordnance, power; con-
sulting engineer

(G-12582)
LOUIS NARDELLO COMPANY
124 Cornerstone Dr (19073-4048)
PHONE..................................215 467-1420
Wright B Robert, *Branch Mgr*
EMP: 5
SALES (corp-wide): 4.1MM **Privately**
Held
SIC: 2869 Fuels
PA: Louis Nardello Company
230 Concord St
Eddystone PA 19022
215 467-1420

(G-12583)
LYONDELL CHEMICAL
COMPANY
3801 West Chester Pike (19073-2320)
PHONE..................................610 359-2360
Paul Andrel, *Branch Mgr*
EMP: 79
SALES (corp-wide): 34.5B **Privately Held**
WEB: www.lyondell.com
SIC: 2911 8731 2899 2865 Petroleum
Refining Coml Physical Research
HQ: Lyondell Chemical Company
1221 Mckinney St Ste 300
Houston TX 77010
713 309-7200

(G-12584)
MARTINO SIGNS INC
101 Mulberry Ln (19073-4605)
PHONE..................................610 355-9269
David Martino, *President*
EMP: 3
SALES (corp-wide): 1.3MM **Privately**
Held
SIC: 3993 Signs & advertising specialties
PA: Martino Signs Inc.
453 Penn St
Yeadon PA 19050
610 622-7446

(G-12585)
METCURE INC
18 Campus Blvd Ste 100 (19073-3240)
PHONE..................................813 601-3533
Surendra Ajjarapu, *President*
EMP: 5 **EST:** 2016
SALES (est): 267.6K **Privately Held**
SIC: 2834 Pharmaceutical preparations

(G-12586)
NDS HOLDINGS LP
3811 West Chester Pike (19073-2323)
PHONE..................................610 408-0500
Mike Bradey, *CFO*
EMP: 501
SALES (est): 23MM **Privately Held**
SIC: 3089 Plastic hardware & building
products; fittings for pipe, plastic

(G-12587)
PAYLOADZ INC
3 Richards Rdg (19073-1918)
PHONE..................................609 510-3074
Shannon Sofield, *President*
EMP: 3
SALES (est): 220K **Privately Held**
WEB: www.payloadz.com
SIC: 3663 Digital encoders

(G-12588)
PEAK BEAM SYSTEMS INC
3938 Miller Rd (19073-2229)
P.O. Box 1127, Edgemont (19028-1127)
PHONE..................................610 353-8505
Jean McManus, *President*
Anne Thorne, *Principal*
Robert Kleinhans, *Engineer*
Annie McManus, *Mktg Dir*
EMP: 20
SQ FT: 6,000
SALES (est): 3.5MM **Privately Held**
WEB: www.peakbeam.com
SIC: 3648 Searchlights

(G-12589)
PERSEON CORPORATION
102 Weatherburn Way (19073-1118)
PHONE..................................201 486-5924
EMP: 3
SALES (est): 170K **Privately Held**
SIC: 3845 Electromedical equipment

(G-12590)
PHYSICIAN TRANSFORMATIONS
LLC
17 Bishop Hollow Rd Ste C (19073-3228)
PHONE..................................484 420-4407
Earl M Bryant, *Director*
EMP: 6
SALES (est): 782.8K **Privately Held**
SIC: 2834 7299 Hormone preparations;
scalp treatment service

(G-12591)
SUNOCO INC (DH)
3801 West Chester Pike (19073-2320)
PHONE..215 977-3000
Brian P Macdonald, *President*
Anne-Marie Ainsworth, *Principal*
Theresa Zabawa, *Counsel*
Thomas Luka, *Exec VP*
Stacy L Fox, *Senior VP*
▲ EMP: 90
SALES (est): 2.3B
SALES (corp-wide): 54B **Publicly Held**
WEB: www.sunocoinc.com
SIC: 5541 2911 2869 2865 Filling stations, gasoline; petroleum refining; industrial organic chemicals; acetone, synthetic; phenol, alkylated & cumene; petroleum terminals; coal & coke
HQ: Etp Legacy Lp
8111 Westchester Dr # 600
Dallas TX 75225
214 981-0700

(G-12592)
SUNOCO (R&M) LLC (DH)
Also Called: Sunoco, Inc. R&M
3801 West Chester Pike (19073-2320)
P.O. Box 60541, Philadelphia (19145-0541)
PHONE..215 977-3000
John G Drosdick, *Ch of Bd*
John D Pickering, *President*
Deborah M Fretz, *Senior VP*
Brian P Macdonald, *Vice Pres*
James F Wagner, *Vice Pres*
▲ EMP: 100 EST: 1971
SQ FT: 200,000
SALES (est): 948.4MM
SALES (corp-wide): 54B **Publicly Held**
WEB: www.mvoil.com
SIC: 5541 2869 2911 5411 Filling stations, gasoline; ethylene glycols; petroleum refining; convenience stores, chain
HQ: Sunoco, Inc.
3801 West Chester Pike
Newtown Square PA 19073
215 977-3000

(G-12593)
SUPPLYONE HOLDINGS COMPANY INC (PA)
11 Campus Blvd Ste 150 (19073-3246)
PHONE..484 582-5005
William T Leith, *President*
Jack Keeney, *CFO*
EMP: 54
SALES (est): 439.8MM **Privately Held**
SIC: 2653 5113 Corrugated & solid fiber boxes; industrial & personal service paper

(G-12594)
SUPREME CORQ LLC
3811 West Chester Pike # 200
(19073-2323)
PHONE..610 408-0500
Robert Anderson,
EMP: 1
SALES (est): 1.8MM
SALES (corp-wide): 251.3MM **Privately Held**
SIC: 3089 Caps, plastic
PA: Graham Partners, Inc.
3811 West Chester Pike # 200
Newtown Square PA 19073
610 408-0500

(G-12595)
ULTRAVOICE LTD
Also Called: Deanrosecrans
90 S Newtown Street Rd # 14
(19073-4041)
PHONE..610 356-6443
David Baraff, *Partner*
Rebecca Poultney, *Admin Sec*
EMP: 8
SALES (est): 1.3MM **Privately Held**
SIC: 3679 5999 Voice controls; telephone & communication equipment

(G-12596)
UNIQUELY DIAMONDS
3513 West Chester Pike # 1 (19073-3701)
PHONE..610 356-5025
Robert S Howard, *Owner*
EMP: 3
SQ FT: 1,000

SALES (est): 140K **Privately Held**
SIC: 3911 5944 Jewelry, precious metal; jewelry, precious stones & precious metals

(G-12597)
VISUAL MERCHANDISING LLC
832 Hunt Rd (19073-3522)
PHONE..610 353-7550
Alex Hill,
▲ EMP: 5
SALES (est): 577.9K **Privately Held**
WEB: www.vmideas.com
SIC: 2541 Display fixtures, wood

(G-12598)
W C WOLFF COMPANY
Also Called: Wc Wolff Company
40 Bishop Hollow Rd (19073-4001)
P.O. Box 458 (19073-0458)
PHONE..610 359-9600
Walter C Wolff Jr, *President*
John Andrews, *Vice Pres*
Lynn Wolff, *Treasurer*
Dorothy H Wolff, *Admin Sec*
EMP: 12 EST: 1951
SQ FT: 8,500
SALES (est): 500K **Privately Held**
WEB: www.gunsprings.com
SIC: 3495 5091 5961 Gun springs, precision; hunting equipment & supplies; mail order house

(G-12599)
ZEKELMAN INDUSTRIES INC
2304 Westfield Ct (19073-1085)
PHONE..610 889-3337
Mark Viola, *Branch Mgr*
EMP: 77 **Privately Held**
SIC: 3317 Pipes, seamless steel
PA: Zekelman Industries, Inc.
227 W Monroe St Ste 2600
Chicago IL 60606

Newville
Cumberland County

(G-12600)
DON SAYLORS MARKETS INC
37 Carlisle Rd (17241-9703)
P.O. Box 147 (17241-0147)
PHONE..717 776-7551
Curt Saylor, *President*
Craig Saylor, *Treasurer*
Joanne Smith, *Manager*
Janet Saylor, *Admin Sec*
EMP: 102
SQ FT: 38,000
SALES (est): 12.1MM **Privately Held**
SIC: 5411 5541 2051 Grocery stores, independent; gasoline service stations; bread, cake & related products

(G-12601)
FUNKS DRILLING INCORPORATED
30 Myers Rd (17241-8501)
PHONE..717 423-6688
Lester Funk, *President*
EMP: 17
SQ FT: 5,000
SALES (est): 1MM **Privately Held**
SIC: 3536 1781 3533 Hoists; water well drilling; oil & gas field machinery

(G-12602)
GARNES PARK E JR
Also Called: Medisox
78 Big Spring Ter (17241-9109)
PHONE..757 502-3381
Park E Garnes Jr, *Owner*
EMP: 3
SALES (est): 110.2K **Privately Held**
SIC: 3842 Hosiery, support

(G-12603)
GLAXOSMITHKLINE LLC
48 Sir William Dr (17241-9205)
PHONE..814 935-5693
EMP: 27
SALES (corp-wide): 39.8B **Privately Held**
SIC: 2834 Pharmaceutical preparations

HQ: Glaxosmithkline Llc
5 Crescent Dr
Philadelphia PA 19112
215 751-4000

(G-12604)
KOCHS PORTABLE SAWMILL & LBR
4354 Enola Rd (17241-9789)
PHONE..717 776-7961
Nathan D Koch, *Principal*
EMP: 3
SALES (est): 218.1K **Privately Held**
SIC: 2421 Sawmills & planing mills, general

(G-12605)
LAWRENCE SCHIFF SILK MILLS INC
Newville Ribbon Co
15 Railroad Ave (17241-1513)
PHONE..717 776-4073
Fax: 717 776-6609
EMP: 75
SQ FT: 2,020
SALES (corp-wide): 43.4MM **Privately Held**
SIC: 5131 2396 Piece Goods And Notions, Nsk
PA: Lawrence Schiff Silk Mills Inc.
590 California Rd
Quakertown PA 18951
215 538-2880

(G-12606)
MELVIN LEID
Also Called: LDS Machine Shop
237 Green Hill Rd (17241-9574)
PHONE..717 776-4940
Melvin Leid, *Owner*
EMP: 4
SQ FT: 2,002
SALES (est): 389.1K **Privately Held**
SIC: 3599 Machine shop, jobbing & repair

(G-12607)
MENASHA PACKAGING COMPANY LLC
954 Centerville Rd # 100 (17241-9586)
PHONE..717 776-2900
EMP: 50
SALES (corp-wide): 1.7B **Privately Held**
SIC: 2653 Boxes, corrugated: made from purchased materials
HQ: Menasha Packaging Company, Llc
1645 Bergstrom Rd
Neenah WI 54956
920 751-1000

(G-12608)
NEWVILLE PRINT SHOP
35 S High St (17241-1413)
PHONE..717 776-7673
Daniel Sheaffer, *Owner*
EMP: 5
SQ FT: 2,200
SALES (est): 250K **Privately Held**
SIC: 2752 Commercial printing, offset

(G-12609)
RHOADS SIGN SYSTEMS
225 Farm Rd (17241-9588)
PHONE..717 776-7309
Clark A Rhoads, *Owner*
EMP: 6
SALES (est): 320K **Privately Held**
SIC: 3993 1799 Electric signs; neon signs; signs, not made in custom sign painting shops; sign installation & maintenance

(G-12610)
ROUND RIVER WOODWORKING
457 Meadows Rd (17241-8734)
PHONE..717 776-5876
Mike Bletz, *Principal*
EMP: 4
SALES (est): 176.6K **Privately Held**
SIC: 1751 2499 Cabinet building & installation; decorative wood & woodwork

(G-12611)
UNILEVER
954 Centerville Rd (17241-9586)
PHONE..717 776-2180
EMP: 10

SALES (est): 2.8MM **Privately Held**
SIC: 2844 Toilet preparations

Nicholson
Wyoming County

(G-12612)
BAKERS QUARRY
18712 Dmock To Nchlson Rd (18446-7774)
PHONE..570 942-6005
Dolores Bakers, *Owner*
EMP: 3
SALES (est): 176.6K **Privately Held**
SIC: 3281 Stone, quarrying & processing of own stone products

(G-12613)
GK FLAGSTONE INC
405 State Route 374 (18446-7624)
PHONE..570 942-4393
Gary Kilmer, *Principal*
EMP: 3
SALES (est): 146.3K **Privately Held**
SIC: 3281 Flagstones

(G-12614)
GLENWOOD STONE CO INC
Also Called: Cecil Kilmer Flagstone
Rr 1 Box 1130 (18446)
PHONE..570 942-6420
Cecil Kilmer, *President*
Marilyn Kilmer, *Corp Secy*
EMP: 40
SQ FT: 450
SALES (est): 6.9MM **Privately Held**
SIC: 1411 Flagstone mining

(G-12615)
HOLLY LABEL COMPANY INC
1656 Maloney Hill Rd (18446-7823)
PHONE..570 222-9000
John M Carr Jr, *President*
Jim Phillips, *Purch Mgr*
Candi Barnard, *Sales Staff*
Ruth Oakley, *Sales Staff*
EMP: 25
SQ FT: 15,000
SALES (est): 5.5MM **Privately Held**
WEB: www.hollylabel.com
SIC: 2672 2269 2796 2759 Labels (unprinted), gummed: made from purchased materials; tape, pressure sensitive: made from purchased materials; labels, cotton: printed; platemaking services; commercial printing; packaging paper & plastics film, coated & laminated

(G-12616)
J RYBNICK MECH CONTR INC
1087 State Route 2035 (18446-7613)
PHONE..570 222-2544
Jean Rybnick, *President*
EMP: 5
SALES (est): 462K **Privately Held**
SIC: 1796 5441 3498 1799 Millwright; candy, nut & confectionery stores; fabricated pipe & fittings; welding on site; ; mechanical contractor

(G-12617)
KEYSTONE DIAMOND BLADES INC
363 State Route 374 (18446-7623)
PHONE..570 942-4526
EMP: 6
SQ FT: 690
SALES (est): 500K **Privately Held**
SIC: 3549 Mfg Cutting Blades

Nicktown
Cambria County

(G-12618)
AEROPARTS FABG & MACHINING INC
Also Called: Aerofab
722 Ridge Rd (15762-8603)
PHONE..814 948-6015
Joseph Phillips, *President*
Ray Caretti, *Sales Executive*

EMP: 24
SQ FT: 19,000
SALES (est): 4.7MM Privately Held
WEB: www.aerofabpa.com
SIC: 3496 3444 3469 Miscellaneous fabricated wire products; sheet metalwork; machine parts, stamped or pressed metal

(G-12619)
CAMBRIA MACHINING CO LLC
108 Kinter Rd (15762-8111)
P.O. Box 9 (15762-0009)
PHONE...........................814 948-8128
Michael Dargay, *Partner*
Barbara J Dargay, *Partner*
Michael S Dargay, *Partner*
Timothy Dargay, *Partner*
John Mazenko, *Partner*
EMP: 4
SQ FT: 10,000
SALES (est): 498.8K Privately Held
SIC: 3599 Machine shop, jobbing & repair

(G-12620)
D & D WOOD SALES INC
268 Amadei Rd (15762)
PHONE...........................814 948-8672
Bernard Dumm, *President*
Jamie L Dumm, *Corp Secy*
EMP: 35
SALES (est): 5MM Privately Held
WEB: www.smokingwood.com
SIC: 2421 Sawmills & planing mills, general

(G-12621)
RJC KOHL INC
1927 Killen School Rd (15762-8708)
PHONE...........................814 948-5903
James Cramer Jr, *President*
EMP: 10
SALES (est): 851.3K Privately Held
SIC: 1221 Bituminous coal & lignite-surface mining

(G-12622)
WENTURINE BROS LUMBER INC
Rr 553 Box 66 (15762)
PHONE...........................814 948-6050
John Wenturine Jr, *President*
Kim Wenturine, *Admin Sec*
◆ EMP: 60
SQ FT: 15,000
SALES (est): 7.1MM Privately Held
WEB: www.wblumber.com
SIC: 2421 2426 2411 Sawmills & planing mills, general; hardwood dimension & flooring mills; logging

Normalville
Fayette County

(G-12623)
JE LOGGING
788 Clinton By Pass Rd (15469-1224)
PHONE...........................724 455-5723
Janet Wingard, *Principal*
EMP: 3
SALES (est): 376.5K Privately Held
SIC: 2411 Logging camps & contractors

(G-12624)
MASTOWSKI LUMBER COMPANY INC
Foxburg Rd (15469)
PHONE...........................724 455-7502
Geraldine Mastowski, *President*
Patricia Johnson, *Corp Secy*
Robert D Mastowski, *Vice Pres*
Walter E Mastowski, *Vice Pres*
EMP: 36
SQ FT: 8,000
SALES (est): 1MM Privately Held
SIC: 2421 Lumber: rough, sawed or planed

(G-12625)
QUALITY PROCESS SERVICES
216 Indian Creek Vly Rd (15469-1102)
PHONE...........................724 455-1687
Karen Sagona, *Office Mgr*
EMP: 3

SALES (est): 88.6K Privately Held
SIC: 1389 Oil field services

Norristown
Montgomery County

(G-12626)
2 SPORTS INC
1055 W Germantown Pike # 1
(19403-3912)
PHONE...........................484 679-1225
Mike Pupillo, *Principal*
EMP: 6
SALES (est): 429.3K Privately Held
SIC: 3949 Sporting & athletic goods

(G-12627)
69TH ST COMMERCIAL PRINTERS
Also Called: Sixty Ninth St Coml Prtrs
4030 Redwing Ln (19403-1848)
PHONE...........................610 539-8412
EMP: 8
SQ FT: 2,000
SALES (est): 250K Privately Held
SIC: 2752 2789 2759 Lithographic commercial Printing Bookbinding/Related Work Commercial Printing

(G-12628)
911 SAFETY EQUIPMENT LLC
9 S Forrest Ave Ste 200 (19403-6016)
PHONE...........................610 279-6808
Daniel Silvestri, *Mng Member*
EMP: 17
SQ FT: 8,000
SALES (est): 2.7MM Privately Held
WEB: www.911se.com
SIC: 5087 5999 3842 Firefighting equipment; fire extinguishers; clothing, fire resistant & protective; suits, firefighting (asbestos)

(G-12629)
A & M COMPOST
2650 Audubon Rd (19403-2400)
PHONE...........................215 256-1900
Richard E Valiga, *President*
Harry Keck, *Vice Pres*
Robert C Murtha Jr, *Vice Pres*
Joseph D Grove, *Treasurer*
EMP: 10
SALES (est): 633.2K Privately Held
SIC: 4953 2875 Refuse collection & disposal services; compost

(G-12630)
ACTION CENTERED TRAINING INC
Also Called: Act Government Support Svcs
935 E Main St (19401-4105)
PHONE...........................610 630-3325
Ronald Roberts, *President*
Diane Roberts, *Director*
EMP: 8
SALES: 120K Privately Held
WEB: www.corporateteambuilding.com
SIC: 3944 8249 8742 Board games, children's & adults'; business training services; training & development consultant

(G-12631)
ALL ASPECTS
800 Stanbridge St (19401-3662)
PHONE...........................610 292-1955
Thomas Blakeslee, *Owner*
Dorothy Blakeslee, *Owner*
EMP: 4
SALES (est): 296.1K Privately Held
SIC: 3272 Floor slabs & tiles, precast concrete

(G-12632)
AMATEX CORPORATION (PA)
Also Called: Norfab
1032 Stanbridge St (19401-3666)
P.O. Box 228 (19404-0228)
PHONE...........................610 277-6100
Richard C Howard, *President*
Andrew Weber, *Controller*
Angela Vaillancourt, *Manager*
Stephen Zawislak, *Director*
Dawnn Guay, *Admin Asst*

▲ EMP: 75 EST: 1921
SQ FT: 80,000
SALES (est): 14.2MM Privately Held
WEB: www.amatex.com
SIC: 2221 Fiberglass fabrics

(G-12633)
AMERICAN ALLOY FABRICATORS
2559 Industry Ln (19403-3907)
PHONE...........................610 635-0205
Gerard T Colvin, *President*
Barbara Colvin, *Treasurer*
EMP: 9
SQ FT: 12,000
SALES (est): 1.9MM Privately Held
SIC: 3351 3444 Sheets, copper & copper alloy; sheet metalwork

(G-12634)
AMERICAN REGENT INC
800 Adams Ave Ste 200 (19403-2323)
PHONE...........................610 650-4200
Joseph Kenneth Keller, *CEO*
Robert Vultaggio, *Controller*
Linda Romaine, *Manager*
EMP: 30 Privately Held
SIC: 2834 Pharmaceutical preparations
HQ: American Regent, Inc.
5 Ramsey Rd
Shirley NY 11967
631 924-4000

(G-12635)
APEX MANUFACTURING CO
2706 Hillcrest Ave (19401-1766)
PHONE...........................610 272-0659
Robert Glass Jr, *Owner*
EMP: 5 EST: 1910
SALES: 200K Privately Held
SIC: 3944 Darts & dart games

(G-12636)
ATM BANCORP INC
2938 Dekalb Pike (19401-1597)
PHONE...........................610 279-9550
Marc Rondeau, *President*
Vic Rondeau, *Vice Pres*
EMP: 8
SALES (est): 790K Privately Held
WEB: www.atmbancorp.com
SIC: 6099 7699 3578 Automated teller machine (ATM) network; automated teller machine (ATM) repair; automatic teller machines (ATM)

(G-12637)
AVO INTERNATIONAL INC
2621 Van Buren Ave Ste 40 (19403-2329)
PHONE...........................610 676-8500
EMP: 4 Privately Held
SIC: 3825 Instruments to measure electricity
HQ: Avo International, Inc.
4271 Bronze Way
Dallas TX 75237

(G-12638)
AVO MULTI-AMP CORPORATION
Also Called: Megger
2621 Van Buren Ave # 400 (19403-2329)
P.O. Box 9007, Valley Forge (19485)
PHONE...........................610 676-8501
Jose Aguilar, *Marketing Staff*
James E Udstuen, *Branch Mgr*
Robert Runta, *Manager*
Deborah M Slobodzian, *Manager*
Michael Shookla, *IT/INT Sup*
EMP: 140 Privately Held
WEB: www.megger.com
SIC: 3825 7629 3829 3826 Instruments to measure electricity; electrical repair shops; measuring & controlling devices; analytical instruments
HQ: Avo Multi-Amp Corporation
4271 Bronze Way
Dallas TX 75237
214 330-3201

(G-12639)
AWESOME FOODS INC
329 E Penn St (19401-5022)
PHONE...........................610 757-1048
Bruce Weinstein, *President*
Marsha Weinstein, *Principal*
EMP: 10

SQ FT: 10,000
SALES: 450K Privately Held
SIC: 2099 Ready-to-eat meals, salads & sandwiches

(G-12640)
BACON JAMS
125 Noble St (19401-4470)
PHONE...........................484 681-5674
EMP: 3
SALES (est): 118.9K Privately Held
SIC: 2033 Jams, jellies & preserves: packaged in cans, jars, etc.

(G-12641)
BOSTOCK INC
16 W Indian Ln (19403-3510)
PHONE...........................610 650-9650
Peter Bostock, *President*
EMP: 3 EST: 1995
SALES (est): 446.9K Privately Held
SIC: 3423 Hand & edge tools

(G-12642)
BRANCH MEDICAL GROUP LLC
Also Called: Branch Medical Group, Inc.
1111 Adams Ave (19403-2403)
PHONE...........................877 992-7262
Peter Iswariah, *Opers Mgr*
Glenn Edla, *Opers Staff*
Robert Eplett, *Engineer*
David Divaker, *Finance Dir*
Dennis Jones, *Sales Staff*
EMP: 90 EST: 2004
SALES (est): 16.3MM
SALES (corp-wide): 712.9MM Publicly Held
SIC: 3841 Surgical & medical instruments
PA: Globus Medical, Inc.
2560 Gen Armistead Ave
Audubon PA 19403
610 930-1800

(G-12643)
CAMBER SPORTSWEAR INC
2 Dekalb St (19401-4902)
PHONE...........................610 239-9910
Barry Schwartz, *President*
Irv Moses, *CFO*
EMP: 45
SQ FT: 82,000
SALES: 4MM Privately Held
WEB: www.cambersportswear.com
SIC: 2329 Men's & boys' sportswear & athletic clothing

(G-12644)
CHARACTER TRANSLATION INC
Also Called: Provost Display
501 W Washington St Ste 2 (19401-4572)
PHONE...........................610 279-3970
Ardia Dayton, *President*
EMP: 5
SQ FT: 8,000
SALES (est): 804.4K Privately Held
WEB: www.charactertranslations.com
SIC: 2389 3993 Theatrical costumes; signs & advertising specialties

(G-12645)
COLEMAN & SCHMIDT INC
843 Cherry St (19401-3925)
PHONE...........................610 275-0796
Charles Brown, *President*
Brian Brown, *Vice Pres*
Andrea Brown, *Admin Sec*
EMP: 3
SQ FT: 10,000
SALES (est): 650.6K Privately Held
SIC: 7694 Electric motor repair

(G-12646)
COMPONENT ENTERPRISES CO INC
235 E Penn St (19401-5020)
P.O. Box 189 (19404-0189)
PHONE...........................610 272-7900
Michael Hoffman, *President*
Theodore Hoffman, *Vice Pres*
Bob Getz, *Technical Mgr*
Betty Wilmer, *Controller*
John Hoffman, *Manager*
EMP: 43
SQ FT: 45,000

SALES (est): 19.2MM **Privately Held**
WEB: www.compenco.com
SIC: 5065 3678 Connectors, electronic; electronic connectors

(G-12647)
CRANE CO
2650 Eisenhower Ave 100a (19403-2314)
PHONE..............................610 631-7700
Jeff Porter, *President*
EMP: 100
SALES (corp-wide): 3.3B **Publicly Held**
WEB: www.craneco.com
SIC: 3492 Control valves, fluid power: hydraulic & pneumatic
PA: Crane Co.
100 1st Stamford Pl # 300
Stamford CT 06902
203 363-7300

(G-12648)
CRAZE FOR RAYZ TANNING CENTER
3333 Ridge Pike Apt 1 (19403-5703)
PHONE..............................484 231-1164
Carla Klousetos, *Owner*
EMP: 4
SALES (est): 72.8K **Privately Held**
SIC: 7299 3648 Tanning salon; sun tanning equipment, incl. tanning beds

(G-12649)
CRAZY AARON ENTERPRISES INC
Also Called: Crazy Aaron's Puttyworld
700 E Main St Fl 1rear (19401-4122)
PHONE..............................866 578-2845
Aaron Muderick, *President*
Elizabeth Perry, *Vice Pres*
Judy Carrino, *Plant Mgr*
Jill Walters, *Sales Staff*
Elizabeth Muderick, *Officer*
◆ EMP: 13
SALES (est): 3.7MM **Privately Held**
SIC: 3069 Toys, rubber

(G-12650)
DATAPATH NORTH AMERICA INC
2550 Blvd Of The Generals (19403-3680)
PHONE..............................484 679-1553
Simon Hunt, *Chairman*
Daniel Nye, *Manager*
Russell Healey, *Director*
▲ EMP: 5
SQ FT: 3,300
SALES (est): 741.5K **Privately Held**
SIC: 3577 Decoders, computer peripheral equipment

(G-12651)
DAVID R HOUSER
Also Called: Houser's Mouthpiece Works
10 Clyston Cir (19403-4725)
PHONE..............................610 505-5924
David R Houser, *Owner*
EMP: 6
SQ FT: 2,000
SALES (est): 492.4K **Privately Held**
SIC: 3931 Mouthpieces for musical instruments

(G-12652)
E R SCHANTZ INC
Also Called: E R Shantz
613 W Marshall St (19401-4513)
PHONE..............................610 272-3603
Steven Berry, *President*
EMP: 3
SQ FT: 1,500
SALES (est): 198K **Privately Held**
SIC: 3444 1799 2394 Awnings, sheet metal; awning installation; canvas & related products

(G-12653)
ELBY BEDDING INC
Also Called: Sichel Sleep Products
1210 Stnbridge St Ste 800 (19401)
PHONE..............................610 292-8700
Robert Burwinkle, *President*
Ellen Burwinkle, *Vice Pres*
EMP: 5 EST: 1884

SALES (est): 1.1MM **Privately Held**
WEB: www.sichelbed.com
SIC: 2515 Mattresses & foundations; box springs, assembled; spring cushions

(G-12654)
EMC CORPORATION
80 E Germantown Pike (19401)
PHONE..............................484 322-1000
Jim Dowson, *Principal*
John Albanbse, *Manager*
EMP: 170
SALES (corp-wide): 90.6B **Publicly Held**
WEB: www.emc.com
SIC: 3572 Computer storage devices
HQ: Emc Corporation
176 South St
Hopkinton MA 01748
508 435-1000

(G-12655)
FALLIEN COSMECEUTICALS LTD
Also Called: Fallene
2495 Blvd Of The Generals (19403-5236)
PHONE..............................610 630-6800
Harry Fallick, *President*
▲ EMP: 10
SQ FT: 7,000
SALES (est): 2.2MM **Privately Held**
SIC: 2834 Pharmaceutical preparations

(G-12656)
FARGO ASSEMBLIES
800 W Washington St (19401-4535)
P.O. Box 550 (19404-0550)
PHONE..............................610 272-5726
EMP: 3 EST: 2012
SALES (est): 220.7K **Privately Held**
SIC: 3679 Harness assemblies for electronic use: wire or cable

(G-12657)
FARGO ASSEMBLY OF PA INC (PA)
Also Called: David City Manufacturing
800 W Washington St (19401-4535)
P.O. Box 550 (19404-0550)
PHONE..............................610 272-6850
Dennis Rees, *CEO*
Ron Bergan, *Chairman*
Marilyn Fiorito, *Admin Sec*
▲ EMP: 145
SQ FT: 40,000
SALES (est): 177.8MM **Privately Held**
WEB: www.dillblox.com
SIC: 3679 Harness assemblies for electronic use: wire or cable

(G-12658)
FINE SIGN DESIGNS INC
Also Called: Sign-A-Rama
1848 Markley St (19401-2904)
PHONE..............................610 277-9860
Gene Schneider, *President*
EMP: 3 EST: 1998
SALES (est): 255.6K **Privately Held**
SIC: 3993 Signs & advertising specialties

(G-12659)
FIVE STS DSTLG INTL SPRITS LLC
129 E Main St (19401-4916)
PHONE..............................610 279-5364
John George, *Mng Member*
EMP: 2
SALES (est): 1MM **Privately Held**
SIC: 2085 Distilled & blended liquors

(G-12660)
GAMBONE STEEL COMPANY INC
545 Foundry Rd (19403-3990)
PHONE..............................610 539-6505
Ralph Gambone, *President*
Tracy Gambone, *Accountant*
EMP: 20 EST: 1962
SQ FT: 20,000
SALES: 6.1MM **Privately Held**
SIC: 3441 1799 Fabricated structural metal; welding on site

(G-12661)
GLOBUS MEDICAL INC
2550 General Armistead Av (19403-5214)
PHONE..............................610 930-1800
Julio Gallego, *Managing Dir*
John Davidar, *Vice Pres*
Al Fitch, *Production*
Richard Scargill, *Production*
Christy Buck, *Purch Agent*
EMP: 8
SALES (corp-wide): 712.9MM **Publicly Held**
SIC: 3841 Surgical & medical instruments
PA: Globus Medical, Inc.
2560 Gen Armistead Ave
Audubon PA 19403
610 930-1800

(G-12662)
GOJI SYSTEMS INC
107 W Township Line Rd (19403-4352)
P.O. Box 432, Blue Bell (19422-0432)
PHONE..............................267 309-2000
John E Stout Jr, *President*
EMP: 5
SALES (est): 436.5K **Privately Held**
SIC: 7372 Prepackaged software

(G-12663)
H TROXEL CEMETERY SERVICE INC
1806 W James St (19403-2825)
PHONE..............................610 489-4426
Horace F Troxel, *President*
EMP: 7
SALES (est): 617.5K **Privately Held**
SIC: 1799 0782 3272 Grave excavation; mowing services, lawn; seeding services, lawn; burial vaults, concrete or precast terrazzo

(G-12664)
HANDY & HARMAN TUBE CO INC
Also Called: Handy Tube Company
701 W Township Line Rd (19403)
PHONE..............................610 539-3900
Ronald La Bow, *Ch of Bd*
Paul E Dixon, *Senior VP*
◆ EMP: 303
SQ FT: 109,000
SALES (est): 44.3MM
SALES (corp-wide): 1.5B **Publicly Held**
SIC: 3317 5051 Tubes, seamless steel; metals service centers & offices
HQ: Handy & Harman
C/O Steel Partners
New York NY 10022
212 520-2300

(G-12665)
HANFORD & HOCKENBROCK
Also Called: Frank Jones Sporting Goods
1735 Markley St (19401-2901)
PHONE..............................610 275-5373
Bruce Hockenbrock, *Partner*
Steven Hanford, *Partner*
EMP: 7 EST: 1933
SQ FT: 1,700
SALES (est): 900K **Privately Held**
SIC: 3949 Sporting & athletic goods

(G-12666)
HII HOLDING CORPORATION
945 Madison Ave (19403-2306)
PHONE..............................610 666-0219
David Hayes, *CFO*
EMP: 6
SALES (est): 508.3K **Privately Held**
SIC: 2869 Hydraulic fluids, synthetic base
HQ: Houghton International Inc.
945 Madison Ave
Norristown PA 19403
888 459-9844

(G-12667)
HOMER REPRODUCTIONS INC
Also Called: Homer Group , The
2605 Egypt Rd Ste 100 (19403-2317)
PHONE..............................610 539-8400
Bernard Homer, *President*
Lore Homer, *Corp Secy*
Guy Homer, *Vice Pres*
Kevin Homer, *Vice Pres*
Michael Smith, *Director*

EMP: 14 EST: 1963
SQ FT: 10,000
SALES (est): 2.5MM **Privately Held**
WEB: www.homergroup.com
SIC: 2752 7336 2759 Calendars, lithographed; graphic arts & related design; commercial printing

(G-12668)
HOUGHTON INTERNATIONAL INC (DH)
945 Madison Ave (19403-2306)
P.O. Box 930, Valley Forge (19482-0930)
PHONE..............................888 459-9844
Michael Shannon, *CEO*
Kim Johnson, *Senior VP*
Dave Slinkman, *Senior VP*
Richard R Lovely, *Vice Pres*
Keller Arnold, *CFO*
◆ EMP: 145 EST: 1910
SQ FT: 30,000
SALES (est): 652.9MM **Privately Held**
WEB: www.houghtonintl.com
SIC: 2869 2992 Hydraulic fluids, synthetic base; lubricating oils & greases
HQ: Gh Holdings, Inc.
Madison & Van Buren Ave
Valley Forge PA 19482
610 666-4000

(G-12669)
IN SPECK CORPORATION
208 E Penn St (19401-5021)
PHONE..............................610 272-9500
Kenneth Kaplan, *President*
EMP: 30
SALES (est): 3.5MM **Privately Held**
SIC: 7389 3672 3676 3451 Packaging & labeling services; printed circuit boards; electronic resistors; screw machine products

(G-12670)
INTEPROD LLC
2583 Industry Ln (19403-3923)
PHONE..............................610 650-9002
Paul Hamel, *Program Mgr*
Rick Smethers,
Mary Tammaro, *Administration*
Suzanne Smethers,
EMP: 17
SQ FT: 23,000
SALES (est): 5.1MM **Privately Held**
SIC: 3826 Analytical instruments

(G-12671)
J G MCGINNESS PROSTHETICS
1445 Dekalb St (19401-3405)
PHONE..............................610 278-1866
Jim G Mc Ginness, *President*
Joanne Mc Ginnis, *Admin Sec*
EMP: 10
SALES: 480K **Privately Held**
SIC: 3842 5999 Prosthetic appliances; orthopedic & prosthesis applications

(G-12672)
J MASTROCOLA HAULING INC
2828 Breckenridge Blvd (19403-1200)
PHONE..............................610 631-1773
Joseph Mastrocola, *President*
Joanne Mastrocola, *Treasurer*
EMP: 7
SALES (est): 1.1MM **Privately Held**
SIC: 2421 Building & structural materials, wood

(G-12673)
JAZ FORMS
Also Called: PDQ Printing
318 W Main St (19401-4612)
PHONE..............................610 272-0770
George Parnes, *President*
Ron Burd, *Vice Pres*
▼ EMP: 5
SQ FT: 5,000
SALES (est): 704.2K **Privately Held**
SIC: 2752 Commercial printing, offset

(G-12674)
JOHN W KEPLINGER & SON
2789 Egypt Rd (19403-2254)
PHONE..............................610 666-6191
John W Keplinger, *Owner*
EMP: 3

▲ = Import ▼=Export
◆ =Import/Export

SALES (est): 194.5K **Privately Held**
SIC: 2399 5999 Flags, fabric; pennants; banners, made from fabric; flags; banners; banners, flags, decals & posters

(G-12675)
LINDE GAS NORTH AMERICA LLC
2570 Blvd Of The Generals (19403-3675)
PHONE...............................610 539-6510
Greg Francis, *Sales Mgr*
EMP: 19 **Privately Held**
SIC: 2813 Nitrogen
PA: Linde Gas North America Llc
    200 Somerset Corp Blvd # 7000
    Bridgewater NJ 08807

(G-12676)
LITE TECH INC
975 Madison Ave (19403-2411)
PHONE...............................610 650-8690
Thomas E Krug, *President*
David Krug, *Vice Pres*
▲ EMP: 18
SALES (est): 3.7MM **Privately Held**
SIC: 3842 Clothing, fire resistant & protective

(G-12677)
LOCAL PAGES PUBLISHING LLC
2811 W Crossing Cir (19403-3972)
PHONE...............................610 579-3809
John Rasanello,
EMP: 15
SALES (est): 1.2MM **Privately Held**
SIC: 2741 Telephone & other directory publishing

(G-12678)
LONTEX CORPORATION
8 Dekalb St Fl 4 (19401-4902)
PHONE...............................610 272-5040
Efraim Nathan, *President*
Samantha Nathan, *Personnel*
▲ EMP: 21 EST: 1951
SQ FT: 18,000
SALES (est): 1.7MM **Privately Held**
WEB: www.sweatitout.com
SIC: 2342 Foundation garments, women's

(G-12679)
MAWA INC
Also Called: Erjo Services
15 Woodlyn Ave (19403-1605)
PHONE...............................610 539-5007
Michael A Wagner, *President*
EMP: 7
SQ FT: 10,000
SALES (est): 1.4MM **Privately Held**
SIC: 3491 Compressed gas cylinder valves

(G-12680)
MBR2 GRAPHIC SERVICES LLC
2550 Industry Ln Ste 103 (19403-3915)
PHONE...............................610 490-8996
Chad Miller, *CFO*
Mike Rogers, *Mng Member*
EMP: 5
SQ FT: 6,000
SALES: 1.2MM **Privately Held**
SIC: 2759 7311 Commercial printing; advertising agencies

(G-12681)
MCGINNESS GROUP LLC
1445 Dekalb St (19401-3405)
PHONE...............................610 278-1866
Jim McGinness, *Principal*
EMP: 3
SQ FT: 3,001
SALES (est): 170K **Privately Held**
SIC: 3842 Prosthetic appliances

(G-12682)
MEDISURG LTD
100 W Fornance St (19401-3316)
PHONE...............................610 277-3937
William R Knepsheild, *President*
Dawn Delcampo, *Vice Pres*
EMP: 3
SALES: 500K **Privately Held**
WEB: www.medisurg.com
SIC: 3841 Medical instruments & equipment, blood & bone work

(G-12683)
MICRO DIMENSIONAL PRODUCTS
199 W Spruce St (19401-3863)
PHONE...............................610 239-7940
Sudhir Arya, *CEO*
Jesse S Wright, *Vice Pres*
Jesse Wright, *Vice Pres*
▲ EMP: 85
SQ FT: 800
SALES (est): 13.3MM **Privately Held**
WEB: www.microdimensional.com
SIC: 3089 Injection molding of plastics; plastic processing

(G-12684)
MICROCHIP TECHNOLOGY INC
2490 Genl Armistd Ave 2 (19403-3600)
PHONE...............................610 630-0556
John Yerger, *Manager*
EMP: 11
SALES (corp-wide): 3.9B **Publicly Held**
SIC: 3674 Semiconductor circuit networks
PA: Microchip Technology Inc
    2355 W Chandler Blvd
    Chandler AZ 85224
    480 792-7200

(G-12685)
MINUTEMAN PRESS
545 Swede St Ste 102 (19401-4850)
PHONE...............................610 272-6220
Andrea Grant, *Principal*
EMP: 3
SALES (est): 153K **Privately Held**
SIC: 2752 Commercial printing, lithographic

(G-12686)
MINUTEMAN PRESS INTERNATIONAL
2938 W Main St Ste 100 (19403-1500)
PHONE...............................610 539-6707
Cheryl Messum, *Principal*
EMP: 4
SALES (est): 181.6K **Privately Held**
SIC: 2752 Commercial printing, lithographic

(G-12687)
MONTCO ADVERTISING SPC INC
Also Called: Pedline
9 S Forrest Ave Unit B (19403-6016)
PHONE...............................610 270-9800
Michael Lorah, *President*
EMP: 25
SQ FT: 6,500
SALES (est): 4.1MM **Privately Held**
WEB: www.pedlineusa.com
SIC: 5199 2759 Advertising specialties; screen printing

(G-12688)
MORABITO BAKING CO INC (PA)
Also Called: Morabito Baking Company
757 Kohn St (19401-3739)
PHONE...............................610 275-5419
Michael A Morabito Jr, *President*
Jim Scandlin, *President*
Michael Morabito III, *Vice Pres*
Carla Horosky, *Accountant*
R A Morabito, *Admin Sec*
EMP: 66 EST: 1932
SQ FT: 70,000
SALES (est): 20.1MM **Privately Held**
WEB: www.morabito.com
SIC: 2051 Bakery: wholesale or wholesale/retail combined; bagels, fresh or frozen; bread, all types (white, wheat, rye, etc): fresh or frozen; rolls, bread type: fresh or frozen

(G-12689)
MOUSLEY CONSULTING INC
447 Alexandra Dr (19403-1301)
PHONE...............................610 539-0150
Kirk Mousley, *President*
EMP: 4
SQ FT: 2,000
SALES: 400K **Privately Held**
WEB: www.mousleyconsulting.com
SIC: 7371 7372 Computer software systems analysis & design, custom; prepackaged software

(G-12690)
MVC INDUSTRIES INC
Also Called: Avm Services
2675 Eisenhower Ave (19401-2316)
PHONE...............................610 650-0500
Joseph Valerio Jr, *President*
John Romano, *CFO*
EMP: 53
SQ FT: 42,800
SALES (est): 7.1MM **Privately Held**
WEB: www.avmservices.com
SIC: 7389 5962 2086 Coffee service; candy & snack food vending machines; cold drinks vending machines; hot drinks & soup vending machines; mineral water, carbonated: packaged in cans, bottles, etc.

(G-12691)
MYERS DRUGSTORE INC
Also Called: Myoderm Medical Supply
48 E Main St (19401-4915)
PHONE...............................610 233-3300
James Lovett, *COO*
Michael Cohen, *Branch Mgr*
EMP: 10
SALES (corp-wide): 12.6MM **Privately Held**
SIC: 2834 5122 Pharmaceutical preparations; pharmaceuticals
PA: Myers Drugstore, Inc.
    328 Dekalb St
    Norristown PA 19401
    610 272-8660

(G-12692)
NEWTERRA INC
2650 Eisenhower Ave 100a (19403-2337)
PHONE...............................610 631-7700
Joseph Strogus, *Branch Mgr*
EMP: 5 **Privately Held**
WEB: www.cranenv.com
SIC: 3589 Water treatment equipment, industrial
HQ: Newterra Inc.
    2248 Meridian Blvd Ste H
    Minden NV 89423
    800 420-4056

(G-12693)
NORCOM SYSTEMS INC
1055 W Germantown Pike # 4 (19403-3912)
PHONE...............................610 592-0167
John Newman, *President*
John W Newman, *President*
Christopher Aubertin, *General Mgr*
Everett Keech, *Treasurer*
Milana Isakov, *Info Tech Mgr*
EMP: 18
SALES (est): 2.1MM **Privately Held**
WEB: www.norcomsystemsinc.com
SIC: 2834 Pharmaceutical preparations

(G-12694)
NORFAB CORPORATION
1310 Stanbridge St (19401-5308)
P.O. Box 830 (19404-0830)
PHONE...............................610 275-7270
John W Weber Jr, *President*
Richard C Howard, *Admin Sec*
▲ EMP: 30
SQ FT: 50,000
SALES (est): 7.7MM **Privately Held**
SIC: 2211 Shirting fabrics, cotton

(G-12695)
NUWAVE TECHNOLOGIES INC
1221 Quarry Hall Rd (19403-4543)
PHONE...............................610 584-8428
Damian Coccio, *President*
EMP: 5 EST: 1996
SQ FT: 2,200
SALES: 600K **Privately Held**
SIC: 8711 3699 Consulting engineer; electrical equipment & supplies

(G-12696)
OAKS INDUSTRIAL SUPPLY INC
1055 W Germantown Pike # 3 (19403-3912)
P.O. Box 831, Oaks (19456-0831)
PHONE...............................610 539-7008
J Peter Leneweaver, *President*
Robert B Derbyshire, *Vice Pres*
EMP: 4

SQ FT: 2,700
SALES (est): 580.9K **Privately Held**
SIC: 2299 Oakum

(G-12697)
ODONNELL METAL FABRICATORS
315 W Germantown Pike (19403-4227)
PHONE...............................610 279-8810
Michael O'Donnell, *President*
Linda M O'Donnell, *Corp Secy*
Jason Rosen, *Office Mgr*
EMP: 10
SQ FT: 10,000
SALES (est): 2MM **Privately Held**
WEB: www.odonnelltruck.com
SIC: 3564 5051 3556 3444 Exhaust fans: industrial or commercial; metals service centers & offices; food products machinery; sheet metalwork; partitions & fixtures, except wood

(G-12698)
OMNIPRESS INC
2562 Industry Ln (19403-3908)
PHONE...............................610 631-2171
Edie Stanley, *President*
EMP: 5 EST: 2008
SQ FT: 2,000
SALES (est): 540K **Privately Held**
SIC: 2759 Commercial printing

(G-12699)
ON TRACK ENTERPRISES INC
Also Called: Clear Gear
1219 W Main St (19401-4332)
P.O. Box 149, Royersford (19468-0149)
PHONE...............................610 277-4995
Gary Ackerman, *President*
Steve Tracanna, *Vice Pres*
Bryan Covey, *Accounts Exec*
Ray Terwilliger, *General Counsel*
EMP: 11 EST: 2010
SALES (est): 1.5MM **Privately Held**
SIC: 2842 Sanitation preparations, disinfectants & deodorants; sanitation preparations

(G-12700)
PARK & PARK NORRISTOWN INC
409 W Main St (19401-4613)
PHONE...............................267 346-0932
Michael Park, *President*
EMP: 4
SALES (est): 337.8K **Privately Held**
SIC: 5231 3231 Glass; doors, glass: made from purchased glass

(G-12701)
PDIR INC
2101 Potshop Ln (19403-3931)
PHONE...............................215 794-5011
EMP: 10
SQ FT: 2,000
SALES: 1.5MM **Privately Held**
SIC: 3823 A Wholesaler And Broker For Process Control Equipment And Instrumentation Fl Measurement

(G-12702)
PENN FABRICATION LLC
220 E Washington St D (19401-5009)
PHONE...............................610 292-1980
Jerry Cerruci, *Mng Member*
EMP: 10
SQ FT: 10,000
SALES (est): 549.8K **Privately Held**
SIC: 3449 7692 3713 Bars, concrete reinforcing; fabricated steel; welding repair; truck bodies & parts

(G-12703)
PLUROGEN THERAPEUTICS LLC
2495 Gen Armistead Ave (19403-3685)
PHONE...............................610 539-3670
Neal G Koller, *CEO*
George T Rodeheaver, *Ch of Bd*
EMP: 3
SALES (est): 360.9K **Privately Held**
SIC: 2834 Pharmaceutical preparations

(G-12704)
POSITRAN MANUFACTURING INC
Also Called: P M I
800 E Main St (19401-4104)
PHONE.................................610 277-0500
Larry Keeney, *President*
Les Gambacorta, *Opers Staff*
Joseph R Uhl, *Treasurer*
Stephanie Mack, *Receptionist*
▲ **EMP:** 60
SQ FT: 45,000
SALES (est): 11.9MM **Privately Held**
WEB: www.positranmfg.com
SIC: 3672 Circuit boards, television & radio printed

(G-12705)
REVEL CAPEWELL INC
303 W Oak St (19401-3755)
PHONE.................................610 272-8075
Noel Boltuch, *Principal*
EMP: 3
SALES (est): 225.5K **Privately Held**
SIC: 3471 Plating & polishing

(G-12706)
ROCKWELL AUTOMATION INC
2650 Eisenhower Ave 108b (19403-2314)
PHONE.................................610 650-6840
Dave Hayes, *Branch Mgr*
EMP: 30 **Publicly Held**
SIC: 3625 Motor control accessories, including overload relays
PA: Rockwell Automation, Inc.
1201 S 2nd St
Milwaukee WI 53204

(G-12707)
SAFETY RAIL SOURCE LLC
2570 Blvd Of The Gen 20 (19403)
PHONE.................................610 539-9535
Jan C Vanning, *Mng Member*
Harold Swindell,
EMP: 5
SQ FT: 1,000
SALES (est): 2.7MM **Privately Held**
WEB: www.safetyrailsource.com
SIC: 3446 Railings, prefabricated metal

(G-12708)
SAMSON PAPER CO INC
2554 Industry Ln Ste 300 (19403-3930)
PHONE.................................610 630-9090
Sherry Cainordway, *President*
Sherry Cain-Ordway, *President*
Cindy Serratore, *Vice Pres*
Cynthia Serretore, *Vice Pres*
Robert E Cain, *Shareholder*
EMP: 20 **EST:** 1930
SQ FT: 18,000
SALES (est): 3.1MM **Privately Held**
SIC: 2754 5112 Business form & card printing, gravure; stationers, commercial

(G-12709)
SANFELICE WLDG FABRICATION LLC
620 W Washington St (19401-4531)
PHONE.................................610 337-4125
Paul Sanfelice,
EMP: 8
SALES (est): 1.6MM **Privately Held**
SIC: 7692 Welding repair

(G-12710)
SEARCH LIVE TODAY LLC
530 Waller Way (19403-3544)
PHONE.................................610 805-7734
Justin Caterbone, *CEO*
EMP: 3
SALES: 25K **Privately Held**
SIC: 7372 7375 Application computer software; on-line data base information retrieval

(G-12711)
SECURE COMPONENTS LLC
1000 E Main St (19401-4108)
PHONE.................................610 551-3475
Todd Kramer, *CEO*
Stephan Halper, *COO*
Ryan Brown, *Senior Buyer*
Andy Cho, *Senior Buyer*
Jesse Howarth, *Buyer*
EMP: 12
SQ FT: 4,000
SALES: 4MM **Privately Held**
SIC: 3674 3672 3452 Semiconductors & related devices; circuit boards, television & radio printed; bolts, nuts, rivets & washers

(G-12712)
SHETH INTERNATIONAL INC
2844 Highview Dr (19403-4700)
PHONE.................................610 584-8670
Bipin K Sheth, *President*
Nilesh K Sheth, *Treasurer*
Rita B Sheth, *Admin Sec*
Sanjay Sheth, *Admin Sec*
▲ **EMP:** 3
SQ FT: 600
SALES (est): 482K **Privately Held**
SIC: 5099 2673 Timber products, rough; plastic bags: made from purchased materials

(G-12713)
SHREE SWAMI NARAYAN CORP
Also Called: Dunkin' Donuts
1882 Markley St (19401-2904)
PHONE.................................610 272-8404
Vipul Patel, *President*
EMP: 20
SALES: 1.8MM **Privately Held**
SIC: 5461 5812 2051 Doughnuts; eating places; doughnuts, except frozen

(G-12714)
SPRING HEALTH PRODUCTS INC
705 General Washington Av (19403-3682)
PHONE.................................610 630-8024
Alexanden Lieb, *President*
Judy Lieb, *Vice Pres*
Jolie Lieb, *Sales Staff*
EMP: 10
SQ FT: 4,000
SALES (est): 953.1K **Privately Held**
WEB: www.springhealthproducts.com
SIC: 3843 Dental equipment

(G-12715)
SUNSATIONAL SIGNS WIN TINTING
234 W Johnson Hwy (19401-3031)
PHONE.................................610 277-4344
George A Amann, *Owner*
Midge Di Joseph, *Manager*
EMP: 6
SALES: 360K **Privately Held**
WEB: www.sunsationalsigns.com
SIC: 1799 3993 2759 Glass tinting, architectural or automotive; signs & advertising specialties; screen printing

(G-12716)
TECH EQUIPMENT SALES INC
Also Called: T E S I
1200 Markley St (19401-3233)
P.O. Box 69, Bridgeport (19405-0069)
PHONE.................................610 279-0370
Joseph T Meere Jr, *President*
Joseph Meere, *Engineer*
EMP: 20
SQ FT: 30,000
SALES (est): 1.1MM **Privately Held**
WEB: www.tech-equip.com
SIC: 5045 5734 3821 Computer peripheral equipment; computer peripheral equipment; laboratory apparatus & furniture

(G-12717)
TECHNOLOGY DEVELOPMENT CORP (PA)
1055 W Germantown Pike (19403-3912)
PHONE.................................610 631-5043
John Newman, *President*
EMP: 10
SQ FT: 12,000
SALES (est): 4.4MM **Privately Held**
SIC: 3829 Testing equipment: abrasion, shearing strength, etc.

(G-12718)
THREE BROTHERS PUBLISHING LLC
579 E Lafayette St (19401-5166)
PHONE.................................412 656-3905
John Russo, *Mng Member*
Joseph Grasso Jr,
Michael Grasso,
EMP: 3
SQ FT: 10,000
SALES (est): 141.3K **Privately Held**
SIC: 2731 Books: publishing & printing

(G-12719)
TITAN GROUP LTD
Also Called: Kidsbrigade
2566 Industry Ln (19403-3908)
PHONE.................................610 631-0831
Barton Nydish, *President*
Sandy Nydish, *Controller*
EMP: 40
SQ FT: 60,000
SALES (est): 2.8MM **Privately Held**
SIC: 3111 5139 Shoe leather; shoes

(G-12720)
TRAVAINI PUMPS USA INC
530 Foundry Rd (19403-3902)
PHONE.................................757 988-3930
Costantino Serpagli, *President*
Terri Madrid, *Vice Pres*
Sheri Sommers, *Sales Staff*
Jennifer Isaksen, *Manager*
▲ **EMP:** 40
SQ FT: 60,000
SALES (est): 17.9MM **Privately Held**
WEB: www.travaini.com
SIC: 5084 3563 3561 Pumps & pumping equipment; compressors, except air conditioning; vacuum (air extraction) systems, industrial; pumps & pumping equipment
HQ: Pompetravaini Spa
Via Per Turbigo 44
Castano Primo MI 20022
033 188-9000

(G-12721)
TRICOR INDUSTRIES INC
636 Markley St (19401-3704)
P.O. Box 978 (19404-0978)
PHONE.................................610 265-1111
Donald Morelli, *President*
Tony Villano, *Treasurer*
EMP: 10 **EST:** 1982
SQ FT: 10,000
SALES (est): 1MM **Privately Held**
WEB: www.tricorindustries.com
SIC: 3493 3496 Steel springs, except wire; miscellaneous fabricated wire products

(G-12722)
VIA VENETO ITALIAN ICE INC
2564 Industry Ln Ste 100 (19403-3952)
PHONE.................................610 630-3355
Domenico Stabile, *President*
Vito Parisi, *Vice Pres*
Natale Stabile, *Treasurer*
EMP: 5
SQ FT: 12,000
SALES (est): 555.6K **Privately Held**
WEB: www.viavenetoice.com
SIC: 2024 Ices, flavored (frozen dessert)

(G-12723)
WAYNE AUTOMATION CORPORATION
605 General Wash Ave (19403-3695)
PHONE.................................610 630-8900
Joseph Bachman Jr, *CEO*
Jay Bachman, *Vice Pres*
Joseph Bachman III, *Vice Pres*
David Didomenico, *Vice Pres*
Roy Reifsnyder, *CFO*
EMP: 60
SQ FT: 25,000
SALES (est): 20.9MM **Privately Held**
WEB: www.wayneautomation.com
SIC: 3565 Packaging machinery

(G-12724)
WOOD SPECIALTY COMPANY INC
2606 Mann Rd (19403-1331)
PHONE.................................610 539-6384
Steve Slaski, *President*
EMP: 10 **EST:** 1942
SQ FT: 15,000
SALES (est): 1.3MM **Privately Held**
WEB: www.woodspecialty.com
SIC: 3555 2426 Printing trades machinery; blocks, wood: engravers'; frames for upholstered furniture, wood

(G-12725)
WORKZONE LLC
16 W Township Line Rd (19401-1559)
PHONE.................................610 275-9861
Drew Moyer, *Engineer*
Allan Kalish,
Nicole Martin, *Admin Asst*
EMP: 10
SALES (est): 210.4K **Privately Held**
WEB: www.trichys.com
SIC: 7372 Prepackaged software

North Apollo
Armstrong County

(G-12726)
EAGLE DISPLAYS LLC
2112 River Rd (15673)
P.O. Box 876 (15673-0876)
PHONE.................................724 335-8900
Rick Rhoads, *President*
Luann Rhoads, *Office Mgr*
EMP: 15
SALES (est): 990K **Privately Held**
SIC: 3469 3999 2434 Kitchen fixtures & equipment: metal, except cast aluminum; advertising display products; wood kitchen cabinets

North Bend
Clinton County

(G-12727)
THOMPSON LOGGING AND TRCKG INC
Also Called: LPT Trucking
Po Box 264 (17760-0264)
P.O. Box 264
PHONE.................................570 923-2590
Lee Thompson, *President*
EMP: 20
SALES: 1MM **Privately Held**
SIC: 3537 4213 1795 1794 Truck trailers, used in plants, docks, terminals, etc.; trucking, except local; wrecking & demolition work; excavation work

(G-12728)
W T STOREY INC
96 Little Italy Rd (17760-9592)
PHONE.................................570 923-2400
Sue Cannon, *Branch Mgr*
Tracy L Embick, *Manager*
EMP: 10
SALES (corp-wide): 4.6MM **Privately Held**
WEB: www.wtstorey.com
SIC: 3613 Switchgear & switchboard apparatus
PA: W T Storey Inc
720 Hickory Rd
Dalmatia PA
570 758-2000

North East
Erie County

(G-12729)
ARROWHEAD WINE CELLARS INC
12073 E Main Rd (16428-3641)
PHONE.................................814 725-5509
Nicholas C Mobilia, *CEO*

GEOGRAPHIC

Kathy Mobilia, *Vice Pres*
Nikki Cole, *Executive Asst*
EMP: 10
SQ FT: 10,000
SALES (est): 1.1MM **Privately Held**
WEB: www.arrowheadwine.com
SIC: 2084 Wines

(G-12730)
ARUNDEL CELLARS INC
Also Called: Arundel Cellars & Brewing Co
11727 E Main Rd (16428-3635)
PHONE..................................814 725-1079
Lauri Boettcher, *President*
Marc Boettcher, *Vice Pres*
Evan Cboettcher, *Treasurer*
Adam Cschwindt, *Admin Sec*
EMP: 15
SQ FT: 5,000
SALES: 1MM **Privately Held**
SIC: 2084 Wines, brandy & brandy spirits

(G-12731)
BAY VALLEY FOODS LLC
11160 Parkway Dr (16428-6512)
P.O. Box 472 (16428-0472)
PHONE..................................814 725-9617
William Lewis,
▲ **EMP:** 125
SQ FT: 55,000
SALES (est): 30.8MM
SALES (corp-wide): 5.8B **Publicly Held**
WEB: www.ncpusa.com
SIC: 2035 Seasonings & sauces, except
tomato & dry; dressings, salad: raw &
cooked (except dry mixes)
PA: Treehouse Foods, Inc.
2021 Spring Rd Ste 600
Oak Brook IL 60523
708 483-1300

(G-12732)
BETTER BAKED FOODS LLC
(DH)
56 Smedley St (16428-1632)
PHONE..................................814 725-8778
Joseph Pacinelli, *President*
Brad Harrison, *Vice Pres*
Greg C Leone, *Plant Mgr*
Lane Neff, *Maint Spvr*
John Shifler, *Purch Mgr*
EMP: 300
SQ FT: 200,000
SALES (est): 125.3MM
SALES (corp-wide): 5.3B **Privately Held**
WEB: www.betterbaked.com
SIC: 2051 Bread, cake & related products
HQ: Schwan's Ne Foods, Llc
115 W College Dr
Marshall MN 56258
507 532-3274

(G-12733)
BOSTWICK ENTERPRISES INC
Also Called: Heritage Wine Cellars
12162 E Main Rd (16428-3644)
PHONE..................................814 725-8015
Matthew Bostwick, *President*
Joshua Bostwick, *Vice Pres*
EMP: 10
SQ FT: 4,037
SALES (est): 916.1K **Privately Held**
SIC: 2084 Wine cellars, bonded: engaged
in blending wines; wines

(G-12734)
C W S INC
Also Called: Galway Pumps
11828 Old Lake Rd (16428-3342)
PHONE..................................800 800-7867
Pat Sheridan, *Vice Pres*
EMP: 4
SQ FT: 4,000
SALES (est): 628.8K **Privately Held**
WEB: www.galwaypumps.com
SIC: 3561 Industrial pumps & parts

(G-12735)
CLIFFSTAR LLC
Also Called: Cliffstar North East
63 Wall St (16428-1128)
PHONE..................................814 725-3801
Bill Wroblawski, *Manager*
EMP: 27
SQ FT: 250,000

SALES (corp-wide): 58.5K **Privately Held**
SIC: 2033 2037 Fruit juices: fresh; fruit
juices
HQ: Cliffstar Llc
1 Cliffstar Dr
Dunkirk NY 14048
716 366-6100

(G-12736)
COURTYARD WINERIES LLC
10021 W Main Rd (16428-2851)
PHONE..................................814 725-0236
James Stover, *Owner*
EMP: 5
SALES (est): 570.9K **Privately Held**
SIC: 2084 Wines

(G-12737)
DAVID A BIERIG
Also Called: Bierig Sailmakers
11092 Freeport Ln (16428-3006)
PHONE..................................814 459-8001
David A Bierig, *Owner*
EMP: 3
SQ FT: 5,000
SALES: 300K **Privately Held**
SIC: 2394 Sails: made from purchased
materials

(G-12738)
DAVID LEE DESIGNS
Also Called: David Lee Furniture and Access
107 Clay St Ste 1 (16428-1527)
PHONE..................................814 725-4289
David Thornton, *Owner*
EMP: 17
SQ FT: 10,000
SALES (est): 2MM **Privately Held**
SIC: 2511 Wood household furniture

(G-12739)
ELECTRIC MATERIALS
COMPANY (HQ)
Also Called: Temco
50 S Washington St (16428-1599)
PHONE..................................814 725-9621
Rebecca Ramsdell, *President*
Anthony Newara, *QC Mgr*
▲ **EMP:** 128 **EST:** 1915
SQ FT: 400,000
SALES (est): 115.8MM
SALES (corp-wide): 0 **Privately Held**
WEB: www.elecmat.com
SIC: 3351 3463 3613 3341 Extruded
shapes, copper & copper alloy; rolled or
drawn shapes: copper & copper alloy;
nonferrous forgings; switchgear &
switchgear accessories; bus bar struc-
tures; secondary nonferrous metals; pri-
mary copper
PA: United Stars, Inc.
1546 Henry Ave
Beloit WI 53511
608 368-4625

(G-12740)
EPC POWDER
MANUFACTURING INC
101 Loomis St (16428-1510)
PHONE..................................814 725-2012
Brian Coutts, *President*
Dan Magruder, *Regl Sales Mgr*
▲ **EMP:** 3
SALES (est): 607.5K **Privately Held**
SIC: 3399 Powder, metal

(G-12741)
ERISCO INDUSTRIES INC
9565 New Rd (16428-5719)
PHONE..................................814 459-2720
Edward A Zacks, *Ch of Bd*
Philip H Zacks, *President*
Carol Zacks, *Admin Sec*
EMP: 62
SQ FT: 150,000
SALES (est): 10.3MM **Privately Held**
WEB: www.erisco-wire.com
SIC: 3496 3315 Miscellaneous fabricated
wire products; wire products, ferrous/iron:
made in wiredrawing plants

(G-12742)
EUREKA ELECTRICAL
PRODUCTS
79 Clay St (16428-1554)
P.O. Box 230 (16428-0230)
PHONE..................................814 725-9638
James Meehl, *President*
James R Meehl, *President*
Christine Murphy, *Treasurer*
EMP: 20 **EST:** 1960
SQ FT: 20,000
SALES (est): 3.5MM **Privately Held**
SIC: 3366 3369 3463 Copper foundries;
nonferrous foundries; nonferrous forgings

(G-12743)
F3 METALWORX INC (PA)
12069 E Main Rd (16428-3641)
P.O. Box 70 (16428-0070)
PHONE..................................814 725-8637
Richard M King, *President*
David G Heth, *Vice Pres*
Justin Buschman, *CFO*
Karen Kuehn, *Info Tech Dir*
Rich King, *Executive*
◆ **EMP:** 50
SQ FT: 150,000
SALES (est): 8.2MM **Privately Held**
WEB: www.costeffectivecoatings.com
SIC: 3479 Coating of metals with plastic or
resins

(G-12744)
GREENFIELD BASKET FACTORY
INC
11423 Wilson Rd (16428-6121)
PHONE..................................814 725-3419
David Foster, *CEO*
Rose Foster, *Corp Secy*
EMP: 20
SALES: 800K **Privately Held**
SIC: 2449 Wood containers

(G-12745)
GUYERS SUPERIOR WALLS
9391 W Main Rd (16428-2621)
PHONE..................................814 725-8575
Steve Charles Hunter, *Executive*
Peter J Shelp,
EMP: 140
SQ FT: 18,000
SALES (est): 9.6MM **Privately Held**
WEB: www.swscv.com
SIC: 3272 1521 Concrete products, pre-
cast; single-family housing construction

(G-12746)
HAINES PRINTING CO
10575 W Main Rd (16428-2223)
PHONE..................................814 725-1955
Jeff Haines, *President*
Stan Martin, *Consultant*
Dan Ruppert, *Consultant*
EMP: 7
SQ FT: 6,000
SALES (est): 1.4MM **Privately Held**
WEB: www.hainesprinting.com
SIC: 2759 Letterpress printing

(G-12747)
HARVESTMORE INC
10028 W Main Rd (16428-2852)
PHONE..................................814 725-5258
Terry W Allen, *CEO*
Julie Allen, *Admin Sec*
EMP: 10
SQ FT: 2,368
SALES (est): 200K **Privately Held**
SIC: 3523 Harvesters, fruit, vegetable, to-
bacco, etc.

(G-12748)
HERITAGE WINE CELLARS INC
12162 E Main Rd (16428-3644)
PHONE..................................814 725-8015
Robert Bostwick, *President*
Beverly A Bostwick, *Vice Pres*
Kenneth M Bostwick, *Treasurer*
Cathy Hoitink, *Office Mgr*
EMP: 15
SQ FT: 25,000
SALES (est): 1.5MM **Privately Held**
SIC: 2084 5182 5921 Wine cellars,
bonded: engaged in blending wines; wine;
wine

(G-12749)
LAKE ERIE REGIONAL CENTER
FOR
662 Cemetery Rd (16428-2999)
PHONE..................................814 725-4601
John Griggs, *Principal*
EMP: 3
SALES (est): 324.7K **Privately Held**
SIC: 2254 Underwear, knit

(G-12750)
LGE COACHWORKS INC
10190 W Main Rd (16428-2854)
PHONE..................................814 434-0856
Randy Galbreath, *President*
David Sacco, *Vice Pres*
Dan Rocky, *Marketing Staff*
▲ **EMP:** 7
SQ FT: 5,000
SALES: 2.2MM **Privately Held**
SIC: 3711 Bus & other large specialty vehi-
cle assembly

(G-12751)
MAZZA CHAUTAUQUA CELLARS
LLC (PA)
11580 Lake Rd (16428-3269)
PHONE..................................814 725-8695
Robert Mazza, *Mng Member*
EMP: 6
SALES (est): 2.4MM **Privately Held**
SIC: 2084 Wines

(G-12752)
MOBILIA FRUIT FARM INC
12073 E Main Rd (16428-3641)
PHONE..................................814 725-4077
Nick Mobilia, *President*
Kathleen Mobilia, *Vice Pres*
EMP: 10
SQ FT: 7,208
SALES (est): 684.9K **Privately Held**
SIC: 5431 2084 Fruit stands or markets;
wines

(G-12753)
NE FOODS INC
1640 Freeport Rd (16428-1963)
P.O. Box 349 (16428-0349)
PHONE..................................814 725-4835
Christopher R Miller, *President*
Richard Steele, *Senior VP*
EMP: 570
SALES (est): 65MM **Privately Held**
SIC: 2038 Pizza, frozen

(G-12754)
PAUL E SEYMOUR TOOL & DIE
LLC
11416 Wilson Rd (16428-6122)
PHONE..................................814 725-5170
Paul E Seymour, *Mng Member*
EMP: 16
SQ FT: 5,600
SALES: 2MM **Privately Held**
SIC: 3544 Special dies & tools

(G-12755)
RAE FOODS INC
Also Called: Nowinski Pierogies
8719 Windy Ln (16428-3897)
PHONE..................................716 326-7437
Rachelle McFeely, *President*
Beverly Braley, *Vice Pres*
EMP: 3
SQ FT: 15,000
SALES: 50K **Privately Held**
SIC: 2038 8099 Ethnic foods, frozen; nu-
trition services

(G-12756)
RIDG-U-RAK INC (PA)
120 S Lake St (16428-1232)
P.O. Box 150 (16428-0150)
PHONE..................................814 725-8751
John B Pellegrino Sr, *President*
Bob Grotkowski, *Regional Mgr*
Jay Stralo, *District Mgr*
David B Delancey, *Vice Pres*
Nels White, *Plant Mgr*
▼ **EMP:** 300 **EST:** 1942
SQ FT: 150,000

SALES (est): 76.3MM **Privately Held**
WEB: www.ridgurak.com
SIC: **2542** Racks, merchandise display or storage: except wood; shelving, office & store: except wood; pallet racks: except wood

(G-12757)
RIDG-U-RAK INC
4800 Loomis St (16428)
PHONE.....................................814 725-8751
John B Pellegrino Sr, *President*
EMP: 4
SALES (corp-wide): 76.3MM **Privately Held**
SIC: **2542** Partitions & fixtures, except wood
PA: Ridg-U-Rak Inc.
120 S Lake St
North East PA 16428
814 725-8751

(G-12758)
RIDG-U-RAK INC
12340 Gay Rd (16428-3576)
PHONE.....................................814 725-8751
John Pellegrino, *Branch Mgr*
EMP: 40
SQ FT: 7,822
SALES (corp-wide): 76.3MM **Privately Held**
WEB: www.ridgurak.com
SIC: **2542** Racks, merchandise display or storage: except wood; shelving, office & store: except wood; pallet racks: except wood
PA: Ridg-U-Rak Inc.
120 S Lake St
North East PA 16428
814 725-8751

(G-12759)
ROBERT MAZZA INC (PA)
Also Called: Mazza Vineyards
11815 Lake Rd (16428-3363)
PHONE.....................................814 725-8695
Robert Mazza, *President*
▲ EMP: 15
SQ FT: 10,000
SALES (est): 2.3MM **Privately Held**
WEB: www.mazzawines.com
SIC: **2084** Wines

(G-12760)
SAMUEL C RIZZO JR
Also Called: C C Printing
23 S Lake St (16428-1213)
PHONE.....................................814 725-3047
Samuel C Rizzo Jr, *Owner*
EMP: 4
SQ FT: 1,200
SALES: 100K **Privately Held**
SIC: **2752** Commercial printing, offset

(G-12761)
SPINWORKS LLC
10093 W Main Rd (16428-2851)
PHONE.....................................814 725-1188
Tom Briselden, *Mng Member*
Sharon Garwid, *Assistant*
EMP: 9
SQ FT: 750
SALES (est): 1.2MM **Privately Held**
WEB: www.spinworks.net
SIC: **3399** Powder, metal

(G-12762)
SPINWORKS INTERNATIONAL CORP
Also Called: Spin-Works
10093 W Main Rd (16428-2851)
P.O. Box 471 (16428-0471)
PHONE.....................................814 725-1188
Thomas Briselden, *President*
EMP: 20
SQ FT: 25,000
SALES (est): 2.4MM
SALES (corp-wide): 215.9MM **Privately Held**
SIC: **3433** Gas infrared heating units
HQ: Saint-Gobain Ceramics & Plastics, Inc.
750 E Swedesford Rd
Valley Forge PA 19482

(G-12763)
TREEHOUSE FOODS INC
11160 Parkway Dr (16428-6512)
PHONE.....................................814 725-5696
Mike Bartell, *Business Mgr*
Michael Massafra, *Business Mgr*
Michael Richter, *Business Mgr*
Larry Thomas, *Business Mgr*
Lisa Nicastri, *Counsel*
EMP: 5
SALES (corp-wide): 5.8B **Publicly Held**
SIC: **2035** Pickles, sauces & salad dressings
PA: Treehouse Foods, Inc.
2021 Spring Rd Ste 600
Oak Brook IL 60523
708 483-1300

(G-12764)
VINEYARD OIL & GAS COMPANY
10299 W Main Rd (16428-2855)
PHONE.....................................814 725-8742
Stephen B Millis, *President*
Jim Reynard, *Corp Secy*
James J Concilla, *Vice Pres*
Melissa D Eastman, *Vice Pres*
James M Reynard, *CFO*
EMP: 10
SQ FT: 2,853
SALES (est): 20.2MM **Privately Held**
WEB: www.vineyardoilandgas.com
SIC: **1382** 1311 Oil & gas exploration services; crude petroleum production

(G-12765)
W C H INC
10832 Lake Rd (16428-2965)
PHONE.....................................814 725-8431
Janeene Hesling, *President*
EMP: 6
SQ FT: 7,000
SALES: 750K **Privately Held**
SIC: **7692** Welding repair

(G-12766)
WELCH FOODS INC A COOPERATIVE
Also Called: North East Plant
139 S Lake St (16428-1299)
P.O. Box 471 (16428-0471)
PHONE.....................................814 725-4577
Gary Reese, *COO*
Bob Murray, *Maint Spvr*
Robert Murray, *Maint Spvr*
James Sprague, *Opers Staff*
Joe Emerick, *Human Res Mgr*
EMP: 475
SALES (corp-wide): 608.4MM **Privately Held**
WEB: www.welchs.com
SIC: **2033** 2087 Fruit juices: packaged in cans, jars, etc.; flavoring extracts & syrups
HQ: Welch Foods Inc., A Cooperative
300 Baker Ave Ste 101
Concord MA 01742
978 371-1000

North Huntingdon
Westmoreland County

(G-12767)
AMERICAN MFG & INTEGRATION LLC
1061 Main St (15642-7425)
PHONE.....................................724 861-2080
James Cullen, *President*
Bruce Newell, *General Mgr*
EMP: 15 EST: 2008
SALES (est): 1.9MM **Privately Held**
SIC: **3999** 3613 3679 Atomizers, toiletry; control panels, electric; harness assemblies for electronic use: wire or cable

(G-12768)
ASM PRODUCTS INC
10830 Glass St (15642-4380)
PHONE.....................................724 861-8026
Janet M Alfieri, *Principal*
EMP: 4
SALES (est): 472.6K **Privately Held**
SIC: **3541** Milling machines

(G-12769)
EXONE COMPANY (PA)
127 Industry Blvd (15642-3461)
PHONE.....................................724 863-9663
S Kent Rockwell, *Ch of Bd*
Hans J Sack, *President*
Brian W Smith, *CFO*
Rick Lucas, *CTO*
Joellen Lyons Dillon,
▲ EMP: 47
SQ FT: 67,886
SALES: 64.6MM **Publicly Held**
SIC: **3555** Printing trades machinery

(G-12770)
MJM ICES LLC
10101 Edgewood Ct (15642-5516)
PHONE.....................................412 401-4610
Michael Morrison, *Principal*
EMP: 7
SALES (est): 490.7K **Privately Held**
SIC: **2024** Ice cream & frozen desserts

North Versailles
Allegheny County

(G-12771)
ALPINE PACKAGING INC
4000 Crooked Run Rd (15137-2395)
PHONE.....................................412 664-4000
Dan I Lehigh, *President*
Katherine M Grunst, *Vice Pres*
Jill I Grunst, *Treasurer*
Jill D Grunst, *Admin Sec*
EMP: 46 EST: 1971
SQ FT: 45,000
SALES: 7.9MM
SALES (corp-wide): 7.6B **Privately Held**
WEB: www.alpinepackaging.com
SIC: **2754** 2673 Labels: gravure printing; plastic bags: made from purchased materials; cellophane bags, unprinted: made from purchased materials
HQ: Tuscarora, Inc.
203 Harrison St Se
Leesburg VA 20175
703 771-9300

(G-12772)
BOLTTECH MANNINGS INC (HQ)
501 Mosside Blvd (15137-2552)
PHONE.....................................724 872-4873
Jerry Jurkiewicz, *CEO*
Ed Komoski, *President*
Mark Reger, *Regional Mgr*
Brian Griffith, *District Mgr*
Jacob Shenesey, *Opers Mgr*
▲ EMP: 100
SQ FT: 19,200
SALES (est): 115.2MM
SALES (corp-wide): 460.4MM **Privately Held**
SIC: **3546** 5072 3599 7359 Power-driven handtools; power tools & accessories; machine & other job shop work; equipment rental & leasing; machine tool accessories; hand & edge tools
PA: Grey Mountain Partners, Llc
1470 Walnut St Ste 400
Boulder CO 80302
303 449-5692

(G-12773)
COPPER KETTLE FUDGE FACTORY
Also Called: Pitsburghfudge.com
355 Lincoln Hwy Ste 16 (15137-1683)
PHONE.....................................412 824-1233
Lisa M Kuiros, *President*
EMP: 10
SALES (est): 375.8K **Privately Held**
SIC: **2064** 7389 Fudge (candy); fund raising organizations

(G-12774)
FILLY FABRICATING INC
3916 Crooked Run Rd Ste A (15137-2356)
PHONE.....................................412 896-6452
Kory Kiczan, *President*
EMP: 3 EST: 2004
SQ FT: 5,600

SALES (est): 178.4K **Privately Held**
SIC: **3711** Mobile lounges (motor vehicle), assembly of

(G-12775)
G BESWICK ENTERPRISES INC
1719 Howell St (15137-2616)
PHONE.....................................412 829-3068
George Beswick, *President*
Tami Bradley Offc, *Manager*
EMP: 5
SQ FT: 16,500
SALES (est): 600K **Privately Held**
SIC: **7699** 3471 Compressor repair; finishing, metals or formed products

(G-12776)
GREAT VALLEY AUTOMOTIVE
1408 Greensburg Pike (15137-1614)
PHONE.....................................412 829-8904
Jim Cassidy, *Owner*
EMP: 3
SALES (est): 253.1K **Privately Held**
SIC: **3714** Transmissions, motor vehicle

(G-12777)
KICZAN MANUFACTURING INC
3916 Crooked Run Rd (15137-2356)
PHONE.....................................412 678-0980
Kenneth W Kiczan, *President*
Dale Jordan, *Project Mgr*
EMP: 35
SQ FT: 10,000
SALES (est): 8.7MM **Privately Held**
WEB: www.kiczanmfg.com
SIC: **3441** 3599 Fabricated structural metal; machine shop, jobbing & repair

(G-12778)
MAGDIC PRECISION TOOLING INC
1070 3rd St (15137-2057)
PHONE.....................................412 824-6661
Joseph Magdic, *President*
Joann Magdic, *Corp Secy*
EMP: 22
SQ FT: 10,000
SALES (est): 3.5MM **Privately Held**
WEB: www.magdicprecision.com
SIC: **3599** 3544 Machine shop, jobbing & repair; special dies, tools, jigs & fixtures

(G-12779)
MANNINGS USA INC
501 Mosside Blvd (15137-2552)
PHONE.....................................412 816-1264
Paul Dodsworth, *Branch Mgr*
EMP: 75
SALES (corp-wide): 17.8MM **Privately Held**
SIC: **3398** Metal heat treating
PA: Mannings, U.S.A., Inc.
200 Richards Ave
Dover NJ 07801
800 447-4473

(G-12780)
MANNINGS USA
501 Mosside Blvd (15137-2552)
PHONE.....................................863 619-8099
▲ EMP: 3 EST: 2010
SALES (est): 205K **Privately Held**
SIC: **3398** Metal Heat Treating

(G-12781)
MARTYS MUFFLER & WELD SHOP
Also Called: Marty's Welding Service
3433 5th Ave (15137-2319)
PHONE.....................................412 673-4141
Martin Antonelli Jr, *Owner*
Marin Antonelle Sr, *Owner*
EMP: 3
SQ FT: 1,792
SALES: 60K **Privately Held**
SIC: **7692** 1799 3444 Welding repair; welding on site; sheet metalwork

(G-12782)
RANCATORE & LAVENDER INC
Also Called: Minuteman Press
1727 Lincoln Hwy (15137-2509)
PHONE.....................................412 829-7456
Kimberly Rancatore, *President*
Bruce McKinney, *Owner*

Pat McKinney, *Owner*
EMP: 8
SQ FT: 2,000
SALES (est): 1.1MM **Privately Held**
WEB: www.minutemanpresspgh.com
SIC: 2752 Commercial printing, litho-
graphic

(G-12783)
VYNEX WINDOW SYSTEMS INC
1083 3rd St Ste 1 (15137-2067)
PHONE..................................412 681-3800
Gerald Mauro, *President*
Frederic A Mauro, *Corp Secy*
EMP: 14
SQ FT: 30,000
SALES (est): 1.8MM **Privately Held**
SIC: 2431 3442 Windows & window parts
& trim, wood; doors & door parts & trim,
wood; metal doors, sash & trim

North Wales
Montgomery County

(G-12784)
A V WEBER CO INC
101 Elm Ave Ste A (19454-3395)
PHONE..................................215 699-3527
Steven Weber, *President*
EMP: 9 **EST:** 1948
SQ FT: 33,000
SALES (est): 2.6MM **Privately Held**
WEB: www.avweber.com
SIC: 3496 3495 3469 Miscellaneous fab-
ricated wire products; wire springs;
stamping metal for the trade

(G-12785)
ACTAVIS PHARMA INC
1090 Horsham Rd (19454-1505)
PHONE..................................847 377-5508
Dragana Grujic, *Sales Staff*
Alex Pereyra, *Security Mgr*
Maria Gonzalez, *Manager*
Ernest Vella, *Manager*
Ray Paolazzi, *Director*
EMP: 18 **Privately Held**
SIC: 2834 Pharmaceutical preparations
HQ: Actavis Pharma, Inc.
400 Interpace Pkwy Ste A1
Parsippany NJ 07054
862 261-7000

(G-12786)
ACTAVIS PHARMA INC
1090 Horsham Rd (19454-1505)
PHONE..................................847 855-0812
Robert Walter, *Project Mgr*
Ed Grover, *Manager*
Mike Demelfi, *Info Tech Dir*
Michael Kovathana, *Telecomm Mgr*
Robert Mercado, *Analyst*
EMP: 103 **Privately Held**
WEB: www.watsonpharm.com
SIC: 2834 Pharmaceutical preparations
HQ: Actavis Pharma, Inc.
400 Interpace Pkwy Ste A1
Parsippany NJ 07054
862 261-7000

(G-12787)
ALDEN INDUSTRIES INC
1400 Welsh Rd (19454-1906)
P.O. Box 1053, Southampton (18966-0753)
PHONE..................................267 460-8904
Robert Mc Bride, *Vice Pres*
EMP: 8
SQ FT: 80,000
SALES (est): 1.4MM **Privately Held**
SIC: 2653 Boxes, corrugated: made from
purchased materials

(G-12788)
APOGEE LABS INC
210 S 3rd St (19454-2940)
PHONE..................................215 699-2060
Wayne J Klein, *President*
David Grebe, *President*
Nancy Aragon, *Supervisor*
Bob Weaver, *Technology*
James Evans, *Software Engr*
EMP: 20
SQ FT: 10,000

SALES (est): 4.3MM **Privately Held**
WEB: www.apogeelabs.com
SIC: 3679 Antennas, receiving; electronic
circuits

(G-12789)
ARCHITECTURAL MILLWORK ASSOC
327 S 5th St (19454-3001)
PHONE..................................215 699-0346
Gregory Lord, *Owner*
EMP: 3
SALES (est): 284K **Privately Held**
SIC: 2431 Millwork

(G-12790)
BARR LABORATORIES INC (HQ)
Also Called: Teva
1090 Horsham Rd (19454-1505)
PHONE..................................215 591-3000
William Marth, *CEO*
Christines Mundkur, *CEO*
Mike Bogda, *President*
Sigurd Kirk, *Senior VP*
Frederick J Killion, *Vice Pres*
◆ **EMP:** 170
SQ FT: 142,500
SALES (est): 2.2B
SALES (corp-wide): 18.8B **Privately Held**
WEB: www.barrlabs.com
SIC: 2834 Proprietary drug products
PA: Teva Pharmaceutical Industries Limited
5 Bazel
Petah Tikva 49510
392 672-67

(G-12791)
BARR LABORATORIES INC
1090 Horsham Rd (19454-1505)
PHONE..................................845 362-1100
Joe Were, *Manager*
Paul Morales, *Technology*
Keith Earle, *Associate Dir*
EMP: 173
SALES (corp-wide): 18.8B **Privately Held**
SIC: 2834 Pharmaceutical preparations
HQ: Barr Laboratories, Inc.
1090 Horsham Rd
North Wales PA 19454
215 591-3000

(G-12792)
BOSIO METAL SPECIALTIES INC
409 Industrial Dr (19454-4150)
PHONE..................................215 699-4100
John Bosio Jr, *President*
EMP: 18 **EST:** 1945
SQ FT: 16,000
SALES (est): 4.3MM **Privately Held**
WEB: www.bosiometalspecialties.com
SIC: 3312 Stainless steel

(G-12793)
BOUNDS WOOD PRODUCTS LTD
1076 Bethlehem Pike (19454)
PHONE..................................215 646-2122
Omar P Bounds III, *President*
EMP: 5
SQ FT: 7,200
SALES: 500K **Privately Held**
SIC: 2431 Millwork

(G-12794)
CARTON EDGE INTERNATIONAL INC (PA)
337 W Walnut St (19454-3322)
P.O. Box 1488 (19454-0488)
PHONE..................................215 699-8755
Jonathan Frank, *President*
Armin Frank, *Chairman*
John F Russo, *Corp Secy*
Paul G Markert, *Vice Pres*
Tracey Eckert, *Software Dev*
◆ **EMP:** 16 **EST:** 1978
SQ FT: 30,000
SALES (est): 2.5MM **Privately Held**
WEB: www.metaledge.com
SIC: 2653 3541 Boxes, solid fiber: made
from purchased materials; machine tools,
metal cutting type

(G-12795)
CIMA LABS INC (DH)
1090 Horsham Rd (19454-1505)
PHONE..................................763 488-4700
Derek Moe, *Vice Pres*
Sarma P Duddu, *Vice Pres*
EMP: 60
SQ FT: 75,000
SALES (est): 20.1MM
SALES (corp-wide): 18.8B **Privately Held**
WEB: www.cimalabs.com
SIC: 8734 2834 Testing laboratories; phar-
maceutical preparations
HQ: Cephalon, Inc.
41 Moores Rd
Malvern PA 19355
610 344-0200

(G-12796)
CIMA LABS INC
1090 Horsham Rd (19454-1505)
PHONE..................................763 315-4178
John Hontz, *Vice Pres*
EMP: 40
SALES (corp-wide): 18.8B **Privately Held**
WEB: www.cimalabs.com
SIC: 2834 Pharmaceutical preparations
HQ: Cima Labs Inc.
1090 Horsham Rd
North Wales PA 19454
763 488-4700

(G-12797)
DATUMRITE CORPORATION
206 Avondale Dr (19454-3972)
PHONE..................................215 407-4447
EMP: 10
SALES (est): 640K **Privately Held**
SIC: 7371 7372 Computer Programming
Svc Prepackaged Software Svc

(G-12798)
DEELY CUSTOM CABINETRY
240 Woodstream Dr (19454-2316)
PHONE..................................267 566-5704
Sean Deely, *Principal*
EMP: 3
SALES (est): 353.9K **Privately Held**
SIC: 2434 Wood kitchen cabinets

(G-12799)
EAST WEST COMPONENT INC
442 Industrial Dr (19454-4138)
PHONE..................................215 616-4414
Larry Roth, *President*
Steve Lavecchia, *Controller*
Tony Dagrosa, *Sales Executive*
Linda Puia, *Admin Asst*
▲ **EMP:** 5
SALES (est): 775.4K **Privately Held**
SIC: 3589 Commercial cooking & food-
warming equipment

(G-12800)
EXOTIC CAR GEAR INC
533 S Sumneytown Pike (19454-2646)
P.O. Box 355, Blue Bell (19422-0355)
PHONE..................................215 371-2855
David Schamerhorn, *President*
EMP: 6
SALES: 575K **Privately Held**
SIC: 3714 Motor vehicle parts & acces-
sories

(G-12801)
FILPRO CORPORATION
810 Dickerson Rd Ste B (19454-2369)
P.O. Box 374, West Point (19486-0374)
PHONE..................................215 699-4510
Richard Nelson, *President*
▲ **EMP:** 15
SQ FT: 14,000
SALES (est): 10.8MM **Privately Held**
WEB: www.filpro.com
SIC: 5085 3569 Filters, industrial; filters

(G-12802)
FLUID DYNAMICS INC
295 Dekalb Pike (19454-1806)
PHONE..................................215 699-8700
Allen B Apter, *President*
Michael Dowse, *Exec VP*
EMP: 22
SQ FT: 2,000

SALES (est): 3.9MM
SALES (corp-wide): 6.9B **Publicly Held**
WEB: www.dynablend.com
SIC: 3586 Measuring & dispensing pumps
HQ: Neptune Chemical Pump Company
1809 Century Ave Sw
Grand Rapids MI 49503
215 699-8700

(G-12803)
GEISSELE AUTOMATICS LLC
800 N Wales Rd (19454)
PHONE..................................610 272-2060
William Geissele, *CEO*
Elizabeth Pope, *General Mgr*
Frank Robinson, *Engineer*
Paul Rossi, *Design Engr*
James Clark, *Manager*
EMP: 12
SQ FT: 2,500
SALES (est): 3.7MM **Privately Held**
WEB: www.geissele.com
SIC: 3549 3812 3484 Metalworking ma-
chinery; defense systems & equipment;
small arms

(G-12804)
GOODS FROM WOODS
326 Washington Ave (19454-3429)
PHONE..................................215 699-6866
Fax: 215 628-2385
EMP: 3
SQ FT: 2,000
SALES (est): 280K **Privately Held**
SIC: 2431 7641 Mfg Millwork Reuphol-
stery/Furniture Repair

(G-12805)
GWYNEDD MANUFACTURING INC
800 N Wales Rd (19454)
P.O. Box 1369 (19454-0369)
PHONE..................................610 272-2060
William Geissele, *President*
Elizabeth Pope, *Accounting Mgr*
EMP: 41 **EST:** 2014
SQ FT: 70,000
SALES (est): 7.1MM **Privately Held**
SIC: 3484 Small arms

(G-12806)
I D TEK INC
297 Dekalb Pike (19454-1806)
PHONE..................................215 699-8888
Walter J Schaller, *President*
Joyce Schaller, *Vice Pres*
EMP: 20
SQ FT: 4,000
SALES (est): 2MM **Privately Held**
WEB: www.tekid.com
SIC: 3565 Labeling machines, industrial

(G-12807)
IVAX PHARMACEUTICALS LLC
1090 Horsham Rd (19454-1505)
PHONE..................................215 591-3000
Jeff Romero, *Engineer*
Dorothy Gerbounka, *Executive Asst*
EMP: 5
SALES (corp-wide): 18.8B **Privately Held**
SIC: 2834 Pharmaceutical preparations
HQ: Ivax Pharmaceuticals, Llc
74 Nw 176th St
Miami FL 33169

(G-12808)
JOSEPH NEDOREZOV
Also Called: Welding Technologies
504 Louise Ln (19454-2524)
PHONE..................................215 661-0600
Joseph Nedorezov, *Owner*
EMP: 4 **Privately Held**
SIC: 3548 8748 Welding apparatus; busi-
ness consulting
PA: Joseph Nedorezov
1365 Horseshoe Dr
Blue Bell PA 19422

(G-12809)
KEYSTONE PRECISION MACHINING
403 Elm Ave (19454-3333)
PHONE..................................215 699-5553
Robert Kurtz, *President*
Michael Sally, *Vice Pres*
EMP: 15

SQ FT: 8,000
SALES: 1.2MM **Privately Held**
WEB: www.keypremac.com
SIC: 3599 Machine shop, jobbing & repair

(G-12810)
KEYSTONE TECHNOLOGIES LLC (PA)
1390 Welsh Rd (19454-1900)
P.O. Box 246, Ambler (19002-0246)
PHONE................................215 283-2600
Frederick M Greenberg, *President*
Ira Greenberg, *COO*
Andrew Joseph, *Vice Pres*
David Pelak, *Regl Sales Mgr*
Mark Hood, *Sales Staff*
▲ EMP: 6
SALES (est): 2.5MM **Privately Held**
SIC: 3531 Ballast distributors

(G-12811)
L & L INDUSTRIAL CHEMICAL INC
115 Hemlock Dr (19454-1726)
P.O. Box 281, Montgomeryville (18936-0281)
PHONE................................215 368-7813
Robert Lindner, *President*
EMP: 2
SALES: 1MM **Privately Held**
SIC: 3089 Plastic containers, except foam

(G-12812)
LAURELL TECHNOLOGIES CORP
441 Industrial Dr (19454-4150)
PHONE................................215 699-7278
Kenneth Valeri, *President*
Sean O'Neill, *Vice Pres*
Debara Valeri, *Vice Pres*
Debra Valeri, *Vice Pres*
Chuck Ziegler, *Engineer*
▲ EMP: 14
SQ FT: 12,000
SALES (est): 3.1MM **Privately Held**
WEB: www.laurell.com
SIC: 3674 Wafers (semiconductor devices)

(G-12813)
MATRIX ATM
210 S Center St (19454)
PHONE................................215 661-2916
Rick Tibberino, *COO*
Vicki Tibberino, *Engineer*
EMP: 5
SALES (est): 624.3K **Privately Held**
SIC: 3578 Automatic teller machines (ATM)

(G-12814)
MERCK & CO INC
351 N Sumneytown Pike (19454-2536)
PHONE................................215 652-5000
Craig McKelvey, *Research*
Patrick Schneier, *Senior Engr*
Michele Pinkney, *Human Resources*
Robin Geller, *Director*
Patrick Jennings, *Director*
EMP: 99
SALES (corp-wide): 42.2B **Publicly Held**
SIC: 2834 Druggists' preparations (pharmaceuticals)
PA: Merck & Co., Inc.
2000 Galloping Hill Rd
Kenilworth NJ 07033
908 740-4000

(G-12815)
MERCK AND COMPANY INC
502 Louise Ln (19454-2531)
PHONE................................215 993-1616
EMP: 12
SALES (est): 1.9MM **Privately Held**
SIC: 2834 Pharmaceutical preparations

(G-12816)
MERCK SHARP & DOHME CORP
351 N Sumneytown Pike (19454-2505)
PHONE................................215 652-5000
Raymond Gilmartin, *Principal*
Dinesh Pethiyagoda, *Research*
Ralph May, *Marketing Staff*
Christiane L Arsever, *Rheumtlgy Spec*
Theresa Taylor, *Associate*
EMP: 120

SALES (corp-wide): 42.2B **Publicly Held**
SIC: 2834 Pharmaceutical preparations
HQ: Merck Sharp & Dohme Corp.
2000 Galloping Hill Rd
Kenilworth NJ 07033
908 740-4000

(G-12817)
MERCK SHARP & DOHME CORP
351 N Sumneytown Pike (19454-2505)
PHONE................................267 305-5000
Fran Casags, *Manager*
Paul Snyderman, *Director*
EMP: 200
SALES (corp-wide): 42.2B **Publicly Held**
SIC: 2834 Pharmaceutical preparations
HQ: Merck Sharp & Dohme Corp.
2000 Galloping Hill Rd
Kenilworth NJ 07033
908 740-4000

(G-12818)
MET-FIN CO INC
S 4th St & Railroad Ave (19454)
P.O. Box 1127 (19454-0127)
PHONE................................215 699-3505
Melvin Hemmerle, *Ch of Bd*
Gary Lukens, *President*
Carol Lukens, *Vice Pres*
EMP: 10 EST: 1960
SQ FT: 9,000
SALES (est): 1MM **Privately Held**
SIC: 3471 Electroplating & plating; electro-plating of metals or formed products

(G-12819)
MSP DISTRIBUTION SVCS C LLC
351 N Sumneytown Pike (19454-2505)
PHONE................................215 652-6160
Robert Rode,
EMP: 150
SALES (est): 13.2MM **Privately Held**
SIC: 2834 Pharmaceutical preparations

(G-12820)
MUELLER INDUSTRIES INC
Precision Tube
287 Wissahickon Ave (19454-4115)
PHONE................................215 699-5801
John Brower, *Manager*
EMP: 64
SALES (corp-wide): 2.5B **Publicly Held**
SIC: 3353 3357 3498 7538 Tubes, welded, aluminum; coaxial cable, nonferrous; fabricated pipe & fittings; general truck repair
PA: Mueller Industries, Inc.
150 Schilling Blvd # 100
Collierville TN 38017
901 753-3200

(G-12821)
OMNISPREAD COMMUNICATIONS INC
Also Called: Oci
809 Bethlehem Pike (19454)
PHONE................................215 654-9900
Wen Lin, *President*
EMP: 4
SQ FT: 2,000
SALES (est): 439.4K **Privately Held**
WEB: www.omnispread.com
SIC: 3661 5065 Fiber optics communications equipment; communication equipment

(G-12822)
P & H LUMBER MILLWORK CO INC
1616 Rose Ln (19454-3623)
PHONE................................215 699-9365
Peter J Bednarek, *President*
EMP: 32
SQ FT: 25,000
SALES (est): 2.2MM **Privately Held**
SIC: 2431 1751 Millwork; finish & trim carpentry

(G-12823)
PAINTED TRUFFLE
105 Guinness Ln (19454-1234)
PHONE................................215 996-0606
Sciascia Tom, *Owner*
EMP: 3
SALES (est): 211.3K **Privately Held**
SIC: 2066 Chocolate & cocoa products

(G-12824)
PETNET SOLUTIONS INC
398-406 Industrial Dr (19454)
PHONE................................865 218-2000
Kevin Young, *Branch Mgr*
EMP: 6
SALES (corp-wide): 95B **Privately Held**
SIC: 2835 Radioactive diagnostic substances
HQ: Petnet Solutions, Inc.
810 Innovation Dr
Knoxville TN 37932
865 218-2000

(G-12825)
PLUM MANUFACTURING CO INC
Also Called: Flextex
101 Colettes Ct (19454-2033)
PHONE................................215 520-2236
James H Plummer Jr, *CEO*
EMP: 5
SQ FT: 14,000
SALES (est): 580K **Privately Held**
WEB: www.flextex.com
SIC: 3053 2298 2241 Gaskets, packing & sealing devices; cordage & twine; narrow fabric mills

(G-12826)
PRECISION TUBE COMPANY INC
287 Wissahickon Ave (19454-4139)
PHONE................................215 699-5801
Greg Christopher, *CEO*
Michael Pfeiffenberger, *General Mgr*
John Gentile, *VP Sales*
Peter Matt, *Manager*
Jennifer James, *Technical Staff*
▼ EMP: 125
SQ FT: 166,000
SALES (est): 17.9MM **Privately Held**
SIC: 3351 3353 Tubing, copper & copper alloy; brass rolling & drawing; tubes, welded, aluminum

(G-12827)
RETROLINEAR INC
401 Elm Ave (19454-3333)
PHONE................................215 699-8000
Timothy Warneck, *President*
EMP: 5
SQ FT: 1,950
SALES (est): 608.1K **Privately Held**
SIC: 3679 Recording heads, speech & musical equipment

(G-12828)
STITCH U S A INC
436 Industrial Dr (19454-4138)
PHONE................................215 699-0123
Joel B Worster, *President*
Elizabeth Worster, *Admin Sec*
EMP: 10
SQ FT: 3,000
SALES (est): 894.7K **Privately Held**
WEB: www.stitchusa.net
SIC: 2395 Embroidery products, except schiffli machine; embroidery & art needlework

(G-12829)
SYNERGY INDUSTRIES LLC
407 Elm Ave (19454-3333)
PHONE................................215 699-4045
EMP: 10
SQ FT: 10,000
SALES: 1MM **Privately Held**
SIC: 3743 Mfg Railroad Equipment

(G-12830)
SYNERGY METAL SOLUTIONS INC
407 Elm Ave 120 (19454-3333)
PHONE................................215 699-7060
Daniel P Kelley, *CEO*
EMP: 3
SALES (est): 260.6K **Privately Held**
WEB: www.synergymetalsolutions.com
SIC: 3599 Machine shop, jobbing & repair

(G-12831)
TEK ID
297 Dekalb Pike (19454-1806)
PHONE................................215 699-8888
EMP: 16

SALES (est): 3.6MM **Privately Held**
SIC: 3565 Mfg Packaging Machinery

(G-12832)
TEVA PHARMACEUTICAL FIN CO LLC
1090 Horsham Rd (19454-1505)
PHONE................................215 591-3000
EMP: 7
SALES (est): 1.4MM **Privately Held**
SIC: 2834 Pharmaceutical preparations

(G-12833)
TEVA PHARMACEUTICAL FIN IV LLC
1090 Horsham Rd (19454-1505)
PHONE................................215 591-3000
Lindley Bley, *Auditor*
Patti Wurster, *Sales Staff*
Sharyn Albrecht, *Manager*
Susan Randall, *Manager*
Justin Wutti, *Manager*
EMP: 15
SALES (est): 1.3MM
SALES (corp-wide): 18.8B **Privately Held**
SIC: 2834 Pharmaceutical preparations
PA: Teva Pharmaceutical Industries Limited
5 Bazel
Petah Tikva 49510
392 672-67

(G-12834)
TEVA PHARMACEUTICALS USA INC (HQ)
Also Called: Teva North America
1090 Horsham Rd (19454-1505)
PHONE................................215 591-3000
Sigurdur Olafsson, *President*
Michael Fetell, *Vice Pres*
Deborah Griffin, *Vice Pres*
John Hassler, *Vice Pres*
Chaim Hurvitz, *Vice Pres*
◆ EMP: 350 EST: 1985
SQ FT: 130,000
SALES (est): 755.8MM
SALES (corp-wide): 18.8B **Privately Held**
WEB: www.lemmon.com
SIC: 2833 5122 2834 Medicinals & botanicals; penicillin: bulk, uncompounded; antibiotics; pharmaceuticals; penicillin preparations
PA: Teva Pharmaceutical Industries Limited
5 Bazel
Petah Tikva 49510
392 672-67

(G-12835)
TEVA PHARMACEUTICALS USA INC
Also Called: Finance Dept
1090 Horsham Rd (19454-1505)
PHONE................................215 591-3000
EMP: 91
SALES (corp-wide): 18.8B **Privately Held**
SIC: 2834 Pharmaceutical preparations
HQ: Teva Pharmaceuticals Usa, Inc.
1090 Horsham Rd
North Wales PA 19454
215 591-3000

(G-12836)
TEVA PHARMACEUTICALS USA INC
1090 Horsham Rd (19454-1505)
PHONE................................240 821-9000
Steven C Mayer, *CEO*
Houman Mesghali, *Associate Dir*
EMP: 5
SALES (corp-wide): 18.8B **Privately Held**
SIC: 2834 Pharmaceutical preparations
HQ: Teva Pharmaceuticals Usa, Inc.
1090 Horsham Rd
North Wales PA 19454
215 591-3000

(G-12837)
TRIUMPH CONTROLS LLC (HQ)
Also Called: Triumph Controls- North Wales
205 Church Rd (19454-4145)
PHONE................................215 699-4861
William Bernardo, *President*
Lisa McDermott, *Human Resources*
Bill Bernardo, *Info Tech Dir*
EMP: 178

▲ = Import ▼=Export
◆ =Import/Export

G E O G R A P H I C

SALES (est): 24.3MM **Publicly Held**
WEB: www.triumph-controls.com
SIC: 3812 Aircraft control instruments

(G-12838)
TSG FINISHING
1400 Welsh Rd (19454-1906)
PHONE...................................828 850-4381
EMP: 14
SALES (est): 2.7MM **Privately Held**
SIC: 3552 Textile machinery

(G-12839)
WATSON LABORATORIES INC
1090 Horsham Rd (19454-1505)
PHONE...................................951 493-5300
EMP: 3 **Privately Held**
SIC: 2834 Pharmaceutical preparations
HQ: Watson Laboratories, Inc.
400 Interpace Pkwy
Parsippany NJ 07054

(G-12840)
WESTROCK CP LLC
500 Church Rd (19454-4106)
PHONE...................................215 699-4444
Kevin Murphey, *Manager*
EMP: 16
SALES (corp-wide): 16.2B **Publicly Held**
WEB: www.smurfit-stone.com
SIC: 2631 Folding boxboard
HQ: Westrock Cp, Llc
1000 Abernathy Rd
Atlanta GA 30328

Northampton
Northampton County

(G-12841)
A CUT ABOVE LAWN CARE & LANDSP
4884 Circle Dr (18067-9308)
PHONE...................................484 239-6825
Tyler Tiuchty, *President*
EMP: 3
SALES: 185K **Privately Held**
SIC: 0781 3524 0782 Landscape services; snowblowers & throwers, residential; lawn services

(G-12842)
ALLERGAN INC
589 Coventry Ct (18067-1646)
PHONE...................................610 262-4844
Timothy Reigel, *Principal*
EMP: 4 **Privately Held**
WEB: www.allergan.com
SIC: 2834 Drugs acting on the central nervous system & sense organs
HQ: Allergan, Inc.
5 Giralda Farms
Madison NJ 07940
862 261-7000

(G-12843)
ANCHOR MACHINE INC
5432 Green Meadow Rd (18067-8918)
PHONE...................................610 261-4924
Thomas Werkheiser, *President*
Richard Werkheiser, *Vice Pres*
Emery Werkheiser Jr, *Treasurer*
Ann Grimshaw, *Admin Sec*
EMP: 25
SQ FT: 15,500
SALES: 2MM **Privately Held**
WEB: www.anchormachine.com
SIC: 3599 3544 Machine shop, jobbing & repair; special dies, tools, jigs & fixtures

(G-12844)
ATLAS MACHINING & WELDING INC
777 Smith Ln (18067-1500)
PHONE...................................610 262-1374
Harold Keeney, *CEO*
Lisa Keeney, *President*
Pat Keeney, *Treasurer*
▲ EMP: 50
SQ FT: 47,000
SALES (est): 10MM **Privately Held**
SIC: 3599 Machine shop, jobbing & repair

(G-12845)
BETHLEHEM HYDROGEN INC
600 Held Dr (18067-1152)
PHONE...................................610 762-1706
Thomas Joseph, *President*
EMP: 6
SQ FT: 27,000
SALES (est): 2MM **Privately Held**
SIC: 2813 3559 5084 Hydrogen; natural gas compressor station construction; cryogenic machinery, industrial; chemical process equipment

(G-12846)
BLUE MOUNTAIN PIGMENT
75 W 21st St Ste 3 (18067-1276)
PHONE...................................610 261-4963
John Kleppinger, *Owner*
EMP: 3 **Privately Held**
SIC: 2865 Color pigments, organic
PA: Blue Mountain Pigment
5031 Scheidys Rd
Schnecksville PA 18078

(G-12847)
BTI-COOPERMATICS INC
600 Held Dr (18067-1152)
PHONE...................................610 262-7700
Thomas Joseph, *President*
Ashik Hashim, *Director*
Anup Narayanan, *Director*
Manoj Thomas, *Director*
EMP: 7
SALES: 1.7MM **Privately Held**
SIC: 8711 3589 3585 Engineering services; swimming pool filter & water conditioning systems; heating equipment, complete

(G-12848)
CONTROL TEMP INSULATION LLC
7113 Goldcris Ln (18067-9747)
PHONE...................................610 393-0943
Paula Bitterman, *Principal*
EMP: 7
SALES (est): 778.4K **Privately Held**
SIC: 3292 Asbestos insulating materials

(G-12849)
EAGLE WOODWORKING LLC
1229 Main St (18067-1610)
PHONE...................................484 764-7275
Simone Lopes, *Principal*
EMP: 4
SALES (est): 226.6K **Privately Held**
SIC: 2431 Millwork

(G-12850)
FIRST REGIONAL COMPOST AUTH
6701 Weaversville Rd (18067-9047)
PHONE...................................610 262-1000
William J Bedics, *Director*
EMP: 3 EST: 2009
SALES (est): 369.4K **Privately Held**
SIC: 2875 Compost

(G-12851)
GREENSTAR ALLENTOWN LLC
Also Called: Greenstar Recycling-Allentown
799 Smith Ln (18067-1500)
P.O. Box 28 (18067-0028)
PHONE...................................610 262-6988
Marcelo Figueira, *CEO*
Brian Gaughan, *Senior VP*
Conor Roche, *Senior VP*
Robert Pickens, *Vice Pres*
EMP: 50
SQ FT: 1,500
SALES: 4.5MM
SALES (corp-wide): 14.9B **Publicly Held**
WEB: www.toddhellerinc.com
SIC: 4953 3229 3341 3231 Recycling, waste materials; glassware, industrial; secondary nonferrous metals; products of purchased glass
HQ: Greenstar Mid-America, Llc
1001 Fannin St Ste 4000
Houston TX 77002

(G-12852)
KAUFFMANS UPHOLSTERY INC
100 Main St (18067-1949)
PHONE...................................610 262-8298

Craig F Kauffman, *President*
EMP: 4
SQ FT: 1,800
SALES (est): 535.6K **Privately Held**
SIC: 2512 7641 Upholstered household furniture; reupholstery

(G-12853)
KELLER ENTERPRISES INC
507 Washington Ave (18067-1865)
PHONE...................................866 359-6828
Frank Keller Jr, *Branch Mgr*
EMP: 6
SALES (est): 786.7K
SALES (corp-wide): 7.3MM **Privately Held**
SIC: 3585 Heating equipment, complete
PA: Keller Enterprises Inc
1202 N Keller Dr
Effingham IL 62401
217 347-7777

(G-12854)
KOCH S CUSTOM WOODWORKING
3557 Howertown Rd (18067-9430)
PHONE...................................610 261-2607
Edward J Shellhammer, *Principal*
EMP: 4
SALES (est): 454.6K **Privately Held**
SIC: 2431 Millwork

(G-12855)
MILLWORK SPECIALTIES
159 W Laubach Ave (18067-1439)
PHONE...................................610 261-2878
Ted M Simmers, *Partner*
Henry Krouse, *Partner*
EMP: 5
SQ FT: 20,000
SALES: 400K **Privately Held**
SIC: 2431 Millwork

(G-12856)
NAZARETH PALLET CO INC
800 Held Dr (18067-1151)
PHONE...................................610 262-9799
George Frack Sr, *President*
Doris Frack, *Corp Secy*
▲ EMP: 38
SQ FT: 60,000
SALES (est): 8.3MM **Privately Held**
WEB: www.nazpallet.com
SIC: 2448 7699 Pallets, wood; pallet repair

(G-12857)
NEWSTECH PA LP
6 Horwith Dr (18067-9749)
PHONE...................................315 955-6710
Lars Dannberg, *CEO*
EMP: 3
SQ FT: 250,000
SALES (est): 404.9K **Privately Held**
SIC: 2611 Pulp manufactured from waste or recycled paper

(G-12858)
OSTERWALDER INC
1825 Franklin St Ste A (18067-1895)
PHONE...................................570 325-2500
Markus Eismann, *VP Opers*
▲ EMP: 3
SQ FT: 2,500
SALES (est): 344.8K **Privately Held**
WEB: www.osterwalder.com
SIC: 3465 Body parts, automobile: stamped metal
PA: Osterwalder Ag
Industriering 4
Lyss BE
323 871-400

(G-12859)
PENNSTAR LLC
Also Called: Scot Lubricants
6 Horwith Dr (18067-9749)
PHONE...................................484 275-7990
Timothy Fritz, *CEO*
EMP: 19 EST: 2010
SALES: 3.4MM
SALES (corp-wide): 59.1MM **Privately Held**
SIC: 2992 Lubricating oils

PA: Coolants Plus Inc.
2570 Van Hook Ave
Hamilton OH 45015
513 892-4000

(G-12860)
PRECISION MEDICAL INC
300 Held Dr (18067-1150)
PHONE...................................610 262-6090
Michael A Krupa, *President*
Clyde Shuman, *Vice Pres*
Jon Ondush, *Purchasing*
Joe Lutz, *Engineer*
Joseph Thomas, *Engineer*
▲ EMP: 104
SQ FT: 70,000
SALES (est): 27.5MM **Privately Held**
WEB: www.precisionmedical.com
SIC: 3829 Measuring & controlling devices

(G-12861)
SKRAPITS CONCRETE COMPANY (PA)
2650 Howertown Rd 3 (18067-8994)
PHONE...................................610 262-8830
John Skrapits, *President*
George Skrapits, *Vice Pres*
Geraldine Skrapits, *Treasurer*
Stephen Skrapits, *Admin Sec*
EMP: 4
SALES: 1.2MM **Privately Held**
SIC: 3273 Ready-mixed concrete

(G-12862)
TERRY L HANDWERK (PA)
Also Called: Handwerks Welding & Fabg
1522 Lincoln Ave (18067-1630)
PHONE...................................610 262-0986
Terry L Handwerk, *Owner*
EMP: 6
SALES (est): 438.5K **Privately Held**
SIC: 7692 Welding repair

Northern Cambria
Cambria County

(G-12863)
STARFIRE CORPORATION
617 Philadelphia Ave (15714-1631)
PHONE...................................814 948-5164
Vincent Terrizzi Sr, *Manager*
EMP: 4
SALES (corp-wide): 1MM **Privately Held**
WEB: www.starfirecorporation.com
SIC: 2899 Fireworks
PA: Starfire Corporation
682 Cole Rd
Carrolltown PA 15722
814 948-5164

Northpoint
Indiana County

(G-12864)
JORDANS BEAR DEN
112 Ewing Rd (15763-9610)
PHONE...................................814 938-4081
Connie Jordan, *Partner*
Tim Jordan, *Partner*
EMP: 6
SALES (est): 434.9K **Privately Held**
SIC: 2273 7699 Carpets & rugs; taxidermists

Northumberland
Northumberland County

(G-12865)
BOYER MACHINE
465 Duke St (17857-1825)
PHONE...................................570 473-1212
Ronald S Boyer Jr, *Owner*
EMP: 5
SALES (est): 312.8K **Privately Held**
WEB: www.boyermachineandmold.com
SIC: 3089 7699 Injection molding of plastics; industrial machinery & equipment repair

(G-12866)
CLUB COIN BOARDS INC
Also Called: Susquehanna Trl
616 Susquehanna Trl (17857-8513)
PHONE...................................570 473-0429
Craig Keller, *President*
Steve Kratzer, *Vice Pres*
EMP: 3
SQ FT: 5,000
SALES (est): 535.6K **Privately Held**
SIC: 2675 Cardboard cut-outs, panels &
foundations: die-cut

(G-12867)
FURMAN FOODS INC
Also Called: Furmano Foods
770 Cannery Rd (17857-8615)
P.O. Box 500 (17857-0500)
PHONE...................................570 473-3516
David N Geise, *CEO*
Chad Geise, *President*
Kermit K Kohl, *Vice Pres*
Bob Vanderhook, *Vice Pres*
Ted R Hancock, *CFO*
◆ EMP: 250 EST: 1921
SQ FT: 600,000
SALES (est): 79.8MM **Privately Held**
WEB: www.furmanos.com
SIC: 2033 Vegetables: packaged in cans,
jars, etc.

(G-12868)
KEYSTONE FORGING COMPANY
215 Duke St (17857-1838)
P.O. Box 269 (17857-0269)
PHONE...................................570 473-3524
Fred Schluter Jr, *Ch of Bd*
Joseph Cipriani, *President*
Richard Strycharz, *Purch Agent*
Brian Hemrick, *Controller*
Norman Gessner, *Accountant*
▲ EMP: 105
SQ FT: 55,000
SALES (est): 34MM **Privately Held**
WEB: www.keystoneforging.com
SIC: 3462 3463 Iron & steel forgings; non-
ferrous forgings

(G-12869)
LERKO PRODUCTS
103 Terrace St (17857-8410)
PHONE...................................570 473-3501
Lee F Miller,
David Lipko,
EMP: 14
SQ FT: 3,500
SALES: 500K **Privately Held**
SIC: 2261 Screen printing of cotton broad-
woven fabrics

(G-12870)
MASONITE CORPORATION
980 Point Township Dr (17857-8886)
P.O. Box 112 (17857-0112)
PHONE...................................570 473-3557
Barry U Shovlin, *Vice Pres*
Steve Hackman, *Purch Agent*
Frank Lingenfelter, *Manager*
EMP: 190
SQ FT: 385,000
SALES (corp-wide): 2.1B **Publicly Held**
SIC: 2431 Doors, wood
HQ: Masonite Corporation
201 N Franklin St Ste 300
Tampa FL 33602
813 877-2726

(G-12871)
MAYBERRY HOSPITALITY LLC
Also Called: Hilltop The
143 King St (17857-1617)
PHONE...................................570 275-9292
Bob Dressler, *Owner*
EMP: 3
SALES (est): 184.9K **Privately Held**
SIC: 7299 2599 Banquet hall facilities; bar,
restaurant & cafeteria furniture

(G-12872)
MOHAWK FLUSH DOORS (DH)
980 Point Township Dr (17857-8886)
PHONE...................................570 473-3557
Gary Willow, *Principal*
Bill Freeman, *Plant Mgr*
▲ EMP: 29

SALES (est): 3.6MM
SALES (corp-wide): 2.1B **Publicly Held**
SIC: 2431 Doors & door parts & trim,
wood; door trim, wood; door frames,
wood; doors, wood
HQ: Masonite Corporation
201 N Franklin St Ste 300
Tampa FL 33602
813 877-2726

(G-12873)
PENNS CREEK RACEWAY PARK
185 16th St (17857-9402)
PHONE...................................570 473-9599
Dwayne Zimmerman, *Owner*
EMP: 3 EST: 2008
SALES (est): 250.6K **Privately Held**
SIC: 3644 Raceways

(G-12874)
QUALITY PRINT SHOP INC
123 Duke St (17857-1910)
PHONE...................................570 473-1122
Laurie Weller, *CEO*
Carl Weller, *President*
EMP: 3 EST: 1933
SQ FT: 2,600
SALES (est): 332.5K **Privately Held**
SIC: 2752 2759 Commercial printing, off-
set; letterpress printing

(G-12875)
RIVER RUN FOODS INC
50 Blue HI (17857-8666)
PHONE...................................570 701-1192
Peter Dartley, *President*
Roger Hoffman, *COO*
Keith Palmer, *Vice Pres*
Sheldon Ganis, *Treasurer*
Michele Wetzel, *Controller*
▲ EMP: 24
SQ FT: 30,000
SALES: 1MM **Privately Held**
WEB: www.riverrunfoods.com
SIC: 2033 Canned fruits & specialties

(G-12876)
STRONG INDUSTRIES INC (PA)
Also Called: Strong Pools
3204 Point Township Dr (17857-8866)
P.O. Box 108 (17857-0108)
PHONE...................................570 275-2700
Wade Spicer, *President*
Joseph Carlin, *CFO*
◆ EMP: 225
SQ FT: 140,000
SALES: 40MM **Privately Held**
WEB: www.strong9.com
SIC: 3999 Hot tubs

(G-12877)
SYNERGY HEALTH SYSTEMS INC
173 Pint Twnship Dr Ste 2 (17857)
P.O. Box 298 (17857-0298)
PHONE...................................570 473-7506
Amanda Kessler, *Owner*
EMP: 22 EST: 1997
SQ FT: 3,600
SALES (est): 1.8MM **Privately Held**
WEB: www.synergyhealthsystems.com
SIC: 8748 2834 Business consulting;
pharmaceutical preparations

Norvelt
Westmoreland County

(G-12878)
ELECTRO-GLASS PRODUCTS INC
3936 Rte 981 (15674)
P.O. Box 157, Mammoth (15664-0157)
PHONE...................................724 423-5000
James Schmidt, *President*
Wendy R Koch, *Corp Secy*
Donald Shirer, *Vice Pres*
Kevin Tamblyn, *Vice Pres*
David Worst, *Maint Spvr*
EMP: 50
SQ FT: 40,000

SALES (est): 9.4MM **Privately Held**
WEB: www.electro-glassprod.com
SIC: 3229 3264 3548 3423 Insulators,
electrical: glass; porcelain electrical supplies; welding apparatus; hand & edge
tools; products of purchased glass

(G-12879)
UNION APPAREL INC
Main St (15674)
PHONE...................................724 423-4900
Michael Borg, *President*
Leo Borg, *Vice Pres*
◆ EMP: 550
SQ FT: 85,000
SALES (est): 30.6MM **Privately Held**
SIC: 2311 2337 Tailored dress & sport
coats: men's & boys'; women's & misses'
suits & coats

Norwood
Delaware County

(G-12880)
HARRIS GRAPHICS & DETAILING
122 Chester Pike (19074-1702)
PHONE...................................610 532-0209
Edward Harris, *Owner*
Diane Harris, *Owner*
EMP: 3
SALES (est): 161.4K **Privately Held**
SIC: 3993 7542 Signs & advertising spe-
cialties; carwashes

Nottingham
Chester County

(G-12881)
BROWN BROTHERS DRILLING INC
497 Kirks Mill Rd (19362-9013)
PHONE...................................717 548-2500
Larry Brown, *President*
Maurice Brown Jr, *Vice Pres*
Mark Brown, *Treasurer*
EMP: 4
SALES (est): 480K **Privately Held**
SIC: 1381 Drilling oil & gas wells

(G-12882)
HERR FOODS INCORPORATED (PA)
20 Herr Dr (19362-9788)
P.O. Box 300 (19362-0300)
PHONE...................................610 932-9330
James M Herr, *Ch of Bd*
Edwin Herr, *President*
Dana Hill, *District Mgr*
Dean Kinney, *District Mgr*
Mario Rivera, *District Mgr*
◆ EMP: 700
SQ FT: 250,000
SALES (est): 436.1MM **Privately Held**
WEB: www.herrs.com
SIC: 2096 Potato chips & other potato-
based snacks

(G-12883)
HERR FOODS INCORPORATED
Also Called: Herr's Potato Chip Factory
273 Old Baltimore Pike (19362-9102)
P.O. Box 300 (19362-0300)
PHONE...................................610 932-9330
Gary Bishop, *Branch Mgr*
EMP: 1300
SALES (corp-wide): 436.1MM **Privately Held**
WEB: www.herrs.com
SIC: 2096 Potato chips & other potato-
based snacks
PA: Herr Foods Incorporated
20 Herr Dr
Nottingham PA 19362
610 932-9330

(G-12884)
OXFORD CABINETRY LLC
209 Glen Roy Rd (19362-9764)
PHONE...................................610 932-3793

Labere Harnish,
Laverne Harnish,
EMP: 4 EST: 2013
SALES (est): 332.3K **Privately Held**
SIC: 2434 Wood kitchen cabinets

(G-12885)
STATE LINE FENCING
161 Stoney Ln (19362-9170)
PHONE...................................610 932-9352
Jonathan Esh, *Principal*
EMP: 4
SALES (est): 345.8K **Privately Held**
SIC: 3949 Fencing equipment (sporting
goods)

Noxen
Wyoming County

(G-12886)
WHISTLE PIG PUMPKIN PATCH
3369 Sr 29 S (18636-7777)
PHONE...................................570 298-0962
Joel Field, *Principal*
EMP: 3
SALES (est): 202.8K **Privately Held**
SIC: 3999 Whistles

Oakdale
Allegheny County

(G-12887)
ABSOLUTE ACSTIC NOISE CTRL LLC
800 Imperial Indus Pkwy (15071-3877)
PHONE...................................304 670-0095
EMP: 11 **Privately Held**
SIC: 3822 Auto controls regulating residntl
& coml environmt & applncs
PA: Absolute Acoustic Noise Control, Llc
3208 Fm 920
Weatherford TX 76088

(G-12888)
ALLEGHENY TECHNOLOGIES INC
Also Called: Allegheny Technologies ...
1001 Robb Hill Rd (15071-3200)
PHONE...................................724 224-1000
Kevin Ceraso, *Vice Pres*
Justin Frantz, *Buyer*
Bob McHugh, *Branch Mgr*
Jeff Stark, *Analyst*
EMP: 7 **Publicly Held**
SIC: 3312 Stainless steel
PA: Allegheny Technologies Incorporated
1000 Six Ppg Pl
Pittsburgh PA 15222

(G-12889)
AMERICAN HIGH PRFMCE SEALS INC
Also Called: American High Prfmce Seals
408 High Tech Dr (15071-3912)
PHONE...................................412 788-8815
Harald Kofler, *President*
John Gudac, *Sales Engr*
Jake Timon, *Sales Engr*
Lennie Andresky, *Admin Asst*
▲ EMP: 13
SALES (est): 2.4MM **Privately Held**
WEB: www.ahpseals.com
SIC: 3053 Gaskets & sealing devices

(G-12890)
AMERICAN ROBOT CORPORATION
305 High Tech Dr (15071-3911)
PHONE...................................724 695-9000
Peyton Collins, *President*
EMP: 8
SQ FT: 3,500
SALES (est): 1.5MM **Privately Held**
WEB: www.americanrobot.com
SIC: 3569 Robots, assembly line: industrial
& commercial

▲ = Import ▼=Export
◆ =Import/Export

(G-12891)
ATI POWDER METALS
1001 Robb Hill Rd (15071-3200)
PHONE..........................412 923-2670
James D Beckman, *Principal*
EMP: 18
SALES (est): 3.3MM **Privately Held**
SIC: 3312 Blast furnaces & steel mills

(G-12892)
ATI POWDER METALS LLC
ATI Specialty Materials
1001 Robb Hill Rd (15071-3200)
PHONE..........................412 923-2670
David Robbins, *Branch Mgr*
EMP: 60 **Publicly Held**
WEB: www.crucible.com
SIC: 3312 Stainless steel
HQ: Ati Powder Metals Llc
1000 Six Ppg Pl
Pittsburgh PA 15222

(G-12893)
ATLANTIS TECHNOLOGIES LLC
308 High Tech Dr (15071-3911)
PHONE..........................724 695-2900
David Descutner, *President*
EMP: 7
SQ FT: 6,000
SALES (est): 1.5MM **Privately Held**
WEB: www.atlantisllc.com
SIC: 3586 5074 Measuring & dispensing
pumps; plumbing fittings & supplies

(G-12894)
**BEST FEEDS & FARM SUPPLIES
INC (PA)**
Also Called: Joy Dog Food
106 Seminary Ave (15071-9755)
PHONE..........................724 693-9417
Russell N Kohser II, *President*
Joseph D Mc Hugh, *Vice Pres*
Robert Gueldner, *Treasurer*
EMP: 112 EST: 1945
SALES (est): 6.5MM **Privately Held**
SIC: 2047 5191 5083 Dog food; feed;
lawn & garden machinery & equipment

(G-12895)
CARNEGIE PRINTING COMPANY
7425 Steubenville Pike (15071-9311)
PHONE..........................412 788-4399
Carole Stewart, *CEO*
Jeff Stewart, *Principal*
John Stewart, *Principal*
EMP: 5 EST: 1855
SQ FT: 6,500
SALES (est): 861.7K **Privately Held**
SIC: 2752 Lithographic Commercial Print-
ing

(G-12896)
CHROMA GRAPHICS
1200 Mckee Rd (15071-3206)
PHONE..........................724 693-9050
Margret Walter Buchko, *Partner*
Joseph R Buchko, *Partner*
EMP: 5
SQ FT: 3,600
SALES (est): 604.7K **Privately Held**
SIC: 2759 2752 2754 7389 Screen print-
ing; commercial printing, lithographic;
commercial printing, gravure; laminating
service

(G-12897)
CLA INDUSTRIES INC
Also Called: Palladino Martial Arts
1358 Poplar St (15071)
P.O. Box 12 (15071-0012)
PHONE..........................724 858-7112
David Palladino, *Principal*
EMP: 3
SALES (est): 200K **Privately Held**
SIC: 3999 Manufacturing industries

(G-12898)
EXCLUSIVE SUPPLEMENTS INC
Also Called: Biorhythm
1231 Elm Dr (15071-1412)
PHONE..........................412 787-2770
Anthony Razzano, *Ch of Bd*
Mark Mangieri, *President*
EMP: 15
SQ FT: 8,500

SALES (est): 2.7MM **Privately Held**
SIC: 2023 5149 Mfg Dry/Evaporated Dairy
Products Whol Groceries

(G-12899)
**FROSTED FANTASIA CUPCAKES
LLC**
1309 Rebecca Ct (15071-1051)
PHONE..........................724 601-9440
EMP: 4
SALES (est): 176K **Privately Held**
SIC: 2051 Bread, cake & related products

(G-12900)
HAYCARB USA INC
Also Called: Haymark
100 Willow Ave (15071-1325)
P.O. Box 130430, Spring TX (77393-0430)
PHONE..........................281 292-8678
Mohan Pandithage, *President*
Neal Megonnell, *Senior VP*
Yapa Pathirathna, *Vice Pres*
▲ EMP: 4
SQ FT: 28,000
SALES: 9MM
SALES (corp-wide): 2.2MM **Privately
Held**
WEB: www.haymarket.com.au
SIC: 5159 2819 Fibers, vegetable; char-
coal (carbon), activated
HQ: Haycarb Plc
Hayley Building No. 400
Colombo 10
112 677-364

(G-12901)
**HENNEMUTH METAL
FABRICATORS**
101 N Branch Rd (15071-1506)
PHONE..........................724 693-9605
Craig R Hennemuth, *Owner*
EMP: 5
SALES (corp-wide): 902.6K **Privately
Held**
SIC: 3444 Ducts, sheet metal
PA: Hennemuth Metal Fabricators
255 W State St
Oakdale PA 15071
724 693-9605

(G-12902)
**HENNEMUTH METAL
FABRICATORS (PA)**
255 W State St (15071-1323)
PHONE..........................724 693-9605
Craig R Hennemuth, *Owner*
EMP: 6 EST: 1954
SQ FT: 23,500
SALES (est): 902.6K **Privately Held**
SIC: 3444 5075 Ducts, sheet metal; warm
air heating equipment & supplies

(G-12903)
HOSCH COMPANY LP (HQ)
1002 International Dr (15071-9226)
PHONE..........................724 695-3002
Hans Otto Schwarze, *Partner*
Hugh W Nevin Jr, *Partner*
▲ EMP: 30 EST: 1982
SALES: 4MM
SALES (corp-wide): 11.1MM **Privately
Held**
WEB: www.hoschusa.com
SIC: 3545 3537 3535 Machine tool ac-
cessories; industrial trucks & tractors; belt
conveyor systems, general industrial use
PA: Hosch Fordertechnik Gesellschaft Mit
Beschrankter Haftung
Am Stadion 36
Recklinghausen 45659
236 158-980

(G-12904)
**IMPERIAL DOUGH COMPANY
INC**
103a International Dr (15071-3907)
PHONE..........................724 695-3625
Daniel W Liwosz, *President*
Margaret A Liwosz, *Admin Sec*
EMP: 5
SALES (est): 631.7K **Privately Held**
WEB: www.imperialdough.com
SIC: 2041 Pizza dough, prepared

(G-12905)
LEE ENGRAVING SERVICES INC
318 Virginia Dr (15071-9450)
PHONE..........................412 788-4224
Lea Lester, *Owner*
EMP: 6
SALES (est): 24K **Privately Held**
SIC: 2759 3479 Engraving; engraving jew-
elry silverware, or metal

(G-12906)
MARG INC (DH)
Also Called: Tigg Corporation
1 Willow Ave (15071-1341)
PHONE..........................724 703-3020
Georgiana Riley, *President*
Anthony Mazzoni, *Vice Pres*
Doug Murray, *Plant Mgr*
Amy Ware, *Controller*
Brian Slanchik, *Accountant*
◆ EMP: 15 EST: 1977
SQ FT: 3,000
SALES (est): 11MM
SALES (corp-wide): 116.9MM **Privately
Held**
WEB: www.tigg.com
SIC: 3564 3589 3823 3443 Blowers &
fans; sewage & water treatment equip-
ment; chromatographs, industrial process
type; boiler shop products: boilers,
smokestacks, steel tanks
HQ: The Spencer Turbine Company
600 Day Hill Rd
Windsor CT 06095
860 688-8361

(G-12907)
MOBILITY AND ACCESS INC
1003 International Dr (15071-9226)
PHONE..........................724 695-1590
Werner Frank, *President*
EMP: 4
SALES (est): 158.6K **Privately Held**
SIC: 3843 Enamels, dentists'

(G-12908)
NEW CENTURY ENERGY INC
1851 North Rd (15071)
PHONE..........................724 693-9266
Ron Corbi, *President*
EMP: 8
SALES (est): 1.2MM **Privately Held**
SIC: 1311 Crude petroleum & natural gas
production

(G-12909)
**PRION MANUFACTURING CO
INC**
1 Prion Dr (15071-3645)
PHONE..........................724 693-0200
Vicki L Prion Jr, *Principal*
▼ EMP: 30 EST: 1965
SQ FT: 30,000
SALES (est): 5.8MM **Privately Held**
WEB: www.prionmfg.com
SIC: 3599 Machine shop, jobbing & repair

(G-12910)
RON MULKERRIN
Also Called: Mulkerrin Burial Vaults
401 Cottonwood Dr (15071-1113)
PHONE..........................724 693-8920
Ron Mulkerrin, *Owner*
EMP: 3
SALES (est): 233.8K **Privately Held**
SIC: 3272 Burial vaults, concrete or pre-
cast terrazzo

(G-12911)
SENSIBLE COMPONENTS LLC
Also Called: Jit Silicones Plus
5 Industrial Park Dr (15071-1288)
PHONE..........................855 548-7587
William Sharpsteen, *President*
George Staudacher,
EMP: 15
SQ FT: 20,000
SALES: 1MM **Privately Held**
SIC: 2992 2891 3535 Lubricating oils &
greases; adhesives & sealants; convey-
ors & conveying equipment

(G-12912)
WRIGHT LINEAR PUMP INC
103 International Dr (15071-3907)
PHONE..........................724 695-0800
Carol L Wright, *Principal*
EMP: 8 EST: 2010
SALES (est): 703.5K **Privately Held**
SIC: 3841 Surgical & medical instruments

Oakmont
Allegheny County

(G-12913)
ABB INC
201 Ann St B (15139-2008)
P.O. Box 91601, Raleigh NC (27675-1601)
PHONE..........................724 295-6000
Rich Stitt, *Engineer*
David Dfrimpter, *Manager*
EMP: 60
SALES (corp-wide): 34.3B **Privately Held**
WEB: www.elsterelectricity.com
SIC: 3823 Industrial instrmnts msrmnt dis-
play/control process variable
HQ: Abb Inc.
305 Gregson Dr
Cary NC 27511

(G-12914)
**CHELSEA BUILDING PRODUCTS
(DH)**
565 Cedar Way (15139-2049)
PHONE..........................412 826-8077
Pete Dewil, *CEO*
Terry Abels, *VP Sales*
Scott Cyphert, *Info Tech Mgr*
Paul Pacelli, *Technology*
Steve Shean, *Technical Staff*
▲ EMP: 200
SQ FT: 200,000
SALES (est): 36.2MM
SALES (corp-wide): 366MM **Privately
Held**
WEB: www.chelseabuildingproducts.com
SIC: 3089 Molding primary plastic; plastic
hardware & building products
HQ: Aluplast Gmbh
Auf Der Breit 2
Karlsruhe 76227
721 471-710

(G-12915)
CHI SIGNS & DESIGNS INC
387 Plum St (15139-1824)
PHONE..........................412 517-8691
Seff Desabato, *President*
Francesca M Desabato, *Principal*
Heather Sneddon, *Business Dir*
EMP: 3
SALES (est): 329.5K **Privately Held**
SIC: 3993 Signs & advertising specialties

(G-12916)
DENTE PITTSBURGH INC
Also Called: Dente Classic and Exotic Stone
201a Ann St (15139-2008)
PHONE..........................412 828-1772
Lynn Campbell, *President*
Elizabeth Baker, *Vice Pres*
EMP: 6
SALES (est): 848.7K
SALES (corp-wide): 5.7MM **Privately
Held**
SIC: 3281 5032 Curbing, granite or stone;
building stone
PA: Dente Trading Co., Inc.
30 Canfield Rd
Cedar Grove NJ 07009
973 857-4050

(G-12917)
**GOODIE BAR ICE-CREAM CO
INC**
828 3rd St (15139-1938)
PHONE..........................412 828-2840
Robert Czegan, *Principal*
EMP: 5
SALES (est): 157.8K **Privately Held**
SIC: 2024 Ice cream, bulk

(G-12918)
GREAT OAK ENERGY INC
637 Allegheny Ave (15139-2003)
P.O. Box 445 (15139-0445)
PHONE....................................412 828-2900
Terry Holt, *President*
Edward Klammer, *Vice Pres*
EMP: 8
SALES (est): 923.2K **Privately Held**
SIC: 1389 8742 Oil field services; gas field services; management consulting services

(G-12919)
LEWIS LUMBER & SUPPLY CO INC
364 Plum St (15139-1825)
PHONE....................................412 828-3810
Hans Wycich, *President*
EMP: 8
SQ FT: 15,000
SALES: 750K **Privately Held**
SIC: 2421 Lumber: rough, sawed or planed

(G-12920)
LIFESTYLE EVOLUTION INC (PA)
Also Called: Nugo Nutrition
520 2nd St (15139-2025)
PHONE....................................412 828-4115
David Levine, *President*
Keith Rohrlick, *Treasurer*
Steven Smith, *Admin Sec*
EMP: 10
SALES (est): 2MM **Privately Held**
WEB: www.nugonutrition.com
SIC: 2064 2066 Granola & muesli, bars & clusters; breakfast bars; chocolate bars, solid

(G-12921)
OLIVE OAKMONT OIL COMPANY
640 Allegheny River Blvd (15139-1539)
PHONE....................................412 435-6912
EMP: 3
SALES (est): 91.3K **Privately Held**
SIC: 2079 Olive oil

(G-12922)
PARKIN CHEMICAL CORPORATION
516 Allegheny River Blvd (15139-1617)
P.O. Box 108 (15139-0108)
PHONE....................................412 828-7355
Peter Parkin, *President*
Linda S Parkin, *Corp Secy*
EMP: 3
SQ FT: 1,500
SALES (est): 317.8K **Privately Held**
WEB: www.parkinchemical.com
SIC: 2899 Acid resist for etching; metal treating compounds

(G-12923)
PAUL WILLIAM BOYLE
Also Called: Faux Arts Galleries
610 Allegheny River Blvd (15139-1552)
P.O. Box 626, Gibsonia (15044-0626)
PHONE....................................412 828-0883
Fax: 412 828-2708
EMP: 5
SQ FT: 6,000
SALES (est): 363.8K **Privately Held**
SIC: 5947 3999 7389 Ret & Mfg Novelties And Decorating For Special Events

(G-12924)
PRECISION GRIT ETCHING & ENGRV
Also Called: Pge
930 3rd St (15139-1940)
P.O. Box 15 (15139-0015)
PHONE....................................412 828-5790
Thomas Dapra, *President*
EMP: 4
SQ FT: 5,000
SALES: 355K **Privately Held**
WEB: www.cnc-industrial-engraving.com
SIC: 3479 7389 Etching & engraving; engraving service

(G-12925)
R W PEFFERLE INC
91 Pennsylvania Ave (15139-1995)
P.O. Box 111228, Pittsburgh (15238-0628)
PHONE....................................724 265-2764
Ralph W Pefferle, *President*
William R Pefferle, *Vice Pres*
Ruth Pefferle, *Admin Sec*
EMP: 4
SQ FT: 1,500
SALES: 450K **Privately Held**
SIC: 3086 5199 Packaging & shipping materials, foamed plastic; packaging materials

(G-12926)
TEXAS KEYSTONE INC (PA)
333 Allegheny Ave Ste 201 (15139-2072)
PHONE....................................412 435-6555
Robert F Kozel, *President*
Frank W Kozel, *Chairman*
Todd F Kozel, *Vice Pres*
David F Kozel, *Treasurer*
EMP: 25
SQ FT: 13,000
SALES (est): 3MM **Privately Held**
SIC: 1381 Drilling oil & gas wells

(G-12927)
THERMO-TWIN INDUSTRIES INC (PA)
1155 Allegheny Ave (15139-1905)
PHONE....................................412 826-1000
Toll Free: 888   -
Paul M Brown II, *CEO*
Paul W Boyle, *Vice Pres*
Paul Boyle, *Vice Pres*
James Bunting, *Treasurer*
Brian Carricato, *Sales Staff*
EMP: 154
SQ FT: 150,000
SALES (est): 23.6MM **Privately Held**
WEB: www.thermotwin.com
SIC: 3442 1751 3231 3211 Storm doors or windows, metal; window & door (prefabricated) installation; products of purchased glass; flat glass; millwork

(G-12928)
TOMANETTI FOOD PRODUCTS INC
Also Called: Tomanetti Pizza
625 Allegheny Ave (15139-2003)
PHONE....................................412 828-3040
George Michel, *President*
Tammy Carroll, *Persnl Dir*
Chris Presutti, *Sales Mgr*
EMP: 30
SALES (est): 5MM **Privately Held**
WEB: www.tomanetti.com
SIC: 2041 Pizza dough, prepared

(G-12929)
TOUCHTOWN INC
931 3rd St Ste 100 (15139-1963)
PHONE....................................412 826-0460
Ted Teele, *CEO*
Jeff Pepper, *Corp Secy*
EMP: 30
SQ FT: 8,000
SALES (est): 4.4MM **Privately Held**
WEB: www.ericksonresident.com
SIC: 7372 Business oriented computer software
HQ: U.S. Hospitality Publishers, Inc.
2926 Kraft Dr
Nashville TN 37204
800 467-1218

Oaks
Montgomery County

(G-12930)
4 LESS FURNITURE AND RUGS LLC
122 Mill Rd (19456)
P.O. Box 393 (19456-0393)
PHONE....................................610 650-4000
Tom Kashi, *President*
▲ **EMP:** 13
SALES (est): 2.1MM **Privately Held**
SIC: 2511 Wood household furniture

(G-12931)
AEGIS TECHNOLOGIES INC
98 Highland Ave (19456)
PHONE....................................610 676-0300
Raymond H Jensen, *President*
Erik T Jensen, *Exec VP*
EMP: 14
SQ FT: 5,000
SALES (est): 3MM **Privately Held**
SIC: 2679 Pipes & fittings, fiber: made from purchased material

(G-12932)
DUNES POINT CAPITAL
98 Highland Ave (19456)
PHONE....................................610 666-1225
David Fix, *President*
EMP: 4 **EST:** 2015
SALES (est): 162.7K **Privately Held**
SIC: 3443 Industrial vessels, tanks & containers

(G-12933)
INSTA-MOLD PRODUCTS INC
640 Hollow Rd (19456)
P.O. Box 439 (19456-0439)
PHONE....................................610 935-7270
Richard Gersh, *President*
Todd Gersh, *Vice Pres*
EMP: 10 **EST:** 1991
SQ FT: 11,000
SALES (est): 1.2MM **Privately Held**
SIC: 2821 Silicone resins

(G-12934)
MAHOGANY AND MORE INC
1620 East Dr (19456)
PHONE....................................610 666-6500
Lam Tran, *President*
◆ **EMP:** 10
SALES (est): 3.6MM **Privately Held**
SIC: 2521 Wood office furniture

(G-12935)
PARTNERS PRESS INC
98 Highland Ave 18 (19456)
P.O. Box 628 (19456-0628)
PHONE....................................610 666-7960
J Scanlin, *President*
Paul Scanlin, *Vice Pres*
EMP: 19
SQ FT: 28,000
SALES (est): 3.7MM **Privately Held**
WEB: www.partners-press.com
SIC: 2752 2791 2789 Commercial printing, offset; typesetting; bookbinding & related work

(G-12936)
RAPID RECYCLING INC (HQ)
5 Brower Ave (19456)
P.O. Box 907 (19456-0907)
PHONE....................................610 650-0737
Vincent Catagnus, *President*
Louis Spera, *Manager*
▼ **EMP:** 56
SQ FT: 65,000
SALES (est): 29.1MM
SALES (corp-wide): 119.6MM **Privately Held**
WEB: www.rapidrecycling.com
SIC: 4953 7389 2611 Recycling, waste materials; document & office record destruction; pulp mills
PA: A. J. Catagnus Inc.
1299 W James St
Norristown PA 19401
610 275-5328

(G-12937)
UPPER PROVIDENCE TOWNSHIP
1286 Clack Rock Rd (19456)
PHONE....................................610 933-8179
U Mark Freeman, *Principal*
EMP: 18
SALES: 15K **Privately Held**
SIC: 3131 Mfg Footwear Cut Stock

(G-12938)
WEST COLLECTION
1 Freedom Valley Dr (19456-9989)
PHONE....................................570 762-8844
EMP: 3

SALES (est): 140K **Privately Held**
SIC: 3999 Mfg Misc Products

Ohiopyle
Fayette County

(G-12939)
OHIOPYLE PRINTS INC
410 Dinner Bell Rd (15470-1002)
PHONE....................................724 329-4652
Fred Wright, *President*
Kim Baker, *Vice Pres*
Trina Lowry, *CFO*
Laurie Crosby, *Natl Sales Mgr*
Brenda Livengood, *Cust Mgr*
▲ **EMP:** 112
SQ FT: 40,000
SALES (est): 16.5MM **Privately Held**
WEB: www.ohiopyleprints.com
SIC: 2396 Screen printing on fabric articles

Oil City
Venango County

(G-12940)
BARON DEVELOPMENT COMPANY
207 Maple Ave (16301)
PHONE....................................814 676-8703
John Boyle, *Owner*
Margaret Boyle, *Corp Secy*
EMP: 3
SALES (est): 210K **Privately Held**
SIC: 1311 1531 Crude petroleum production; condominium developers

(G-12941)
BARRETTS CUSTOM WROUGHT IRON
2237 Horsecreek Rd (16301-4107)
PHONE....................................814 676-4575
Edward J Barrett, *Owner*
EMP: 3
SQ FT: 2,100
SALES (est): 60.3K **Privately Held**
SIC: 7692 3446 Welding repair; railings, bannisters, guards, etc.: made from metal pipe

(G-12942)
BLACK KNIGHT INDUSTRIES INC
382 State Route 227 (16301-5742)
PHONE....................................814 676-3474
Dale A Black, *President*
▲ **EMP:** 3 **EST:** 2010
SALES (est): 778K **Privately Held**
SIC: 5084 3949 Fish processing machinery, equipment & supplies; fishing equipment; hooks, fishing; rods & rod parts, fishing

(G-12943)
CONSOLIDATED CONTAINER CO LP
Also Called: Consolidated Containers
15 Mineral St (16301-3244)
PHONE....................................814 676-5671
Douglas Conley, *Plant Mgr*
Doc Kirkland, *Plant Mgr*
Brendan Bowman, *Manager*
EMP: 45
SALES (corp-wide): 14B **Publicly Held**
SIC: 3089 Plastic containers, except foam
HQ: Consolidated Container Company Lp
2500 Windy Ridge Pkwy Se # 1400
Atlanta GA 30339
678 742-4600

(G-12944)
DERRICK PUBLISHING COMPANY (PA)
Also Called: Venango Newspaper
1510 W 1st St (16301-3299)
P.O. Box 928 (16301-0928)
PHONE....................................814 676-7444
Patrick Boyle, *President*
Ned Powart, *Principal*
E Michael Boyle, *Vice Pres*
William Lutz, *Vice Pres*

EMP: 30 EST: 1882
SQ FT: 36,000
SALES (est): 14.5MM **Privately Held**
SIC: 2711 Commercial printing & newspaper publishing combined

(G-12945)
G O CARLSON INC
Also Called: Ellectralloy Division
675 Colbert Ave (16301-2288)
PHONE.....................814 678-4100
Tracy Rudolph, *Manager*
EMP: 25
SALES (corp-wide): 56.2MM **Privately Held**
WEB: www.gocarlson.com
SIC: 3356 3313 Nickel & nickel alloy: rolling, drawing or extruding; electrometallurgical products
PA: G. O. Carlson, Inc.
175 Main St
Oil City PA 16301
814 678-4100

(G-12946)
GOC PROPERTY HOLDINGS LLC
175 Main St (16301-1038)
PHONE.....................814 678-4127
Tracy Rudolph, *Mng Member*
EMP: 19 EST: 2008
SALES (est): **Privately Held**
SIC: 6719 3312 Investment holding companies, except banks; stainless steel

(G-12947)
HONDELS MACHINE SHOP
2222 Horsecreek Rd (16301-4108)
PHONE.....................814 677-7768
Floyd Hondel, *Owner*
James R Hondel, *Treasurer*
EMP: 3
SQ FT: 5,000
SALES: 200K **Privately Held**
SIC: 3599 Machine shop, jobbing & repair

(G-12948)
KAPP ALLOY & WIRE INC
1 Klein St (16301-1029)
P.O. Box 1188 (16301-0688)
PHONE.....................814 676-0613
Jonathan Crawford, *CEO*
EMP: 13
SQ FT: 50,000
SALES (est): 2.7MM **Privately Held**
WEB: www.kappalloy.com
SIC: 3356 Solder: wire, bar, acid core, & rosin core

(G-12949)
KLAPEC EXCAVATING INC
201 Deer Run Trl (16301-3711)
PHONE.....................814 678-3478
David Klapec, *President*
Christopher Klapec, *Principal*
Nicholas Klapec, *Principal*
EMP: 4
SALES (est): 450.4K **Privately Held**
SIC: 1389 Excavating slush pits & cellars

(G-12950)
KRAFT CONCRETE PRODUCTS INC
304 Duncomb St (16301-1411)
P.O. Box 957 (16301-0957)
PHONE.....................814 677-3019
Fax: 814 676-1342
EMP: 26
SQ FT: 500
SALES (est): 2.5MM **Privately Held**
SIC: 3273 5032 Mfg Ready Mixed Concrete & Whol Concrete Blocks

(G-12951)
LINEMAN & SONS
447 Mcpherson Rd (16301-4621)
PHONE.....................814 677-7215
Bryan Lineman, *Owner*
Bryan Lineman, *Owner*
EMP: 4
SALES: 900K **Privately Held**
SIC: 3449 Bars, concrete reinforcing: fabricated steel

(G-12952)
MERISOL ANTIOXIDANTS LLC
292 State Route 8 (16301-5626)
PHONE.....................814 677-2028

Stephen Mastalski, *Owner*
Stephen A Mastalski, *Vice Pres*
Joseph McFadden, *Cust Svc Dir*
EMP: 20
SALES (est): 3.6MM **Privately Held**
SIC: 2869 Industrial organic chemicals

(G-12953)
NEW HEGEDUS ALUMINUM CO INC
Also Called: Hegedus Aluminum Industries
312 State Route 428 (16301-4732)
P.O. Box 1067 (16301-0567)
PHONE.....................814 676-5635
Glenn Davis, *President*
Jena Rhoads, *Vice Pres*
David Zacherl, *Manager*
EMP: 48
SALES (est): 10.4MM **Privately Held**
WEB: www.hegedus.com
SIC: 3365 Aluminum & aluminum-based alloy castings

(G-12954)
PIONEER ENERGY PRODUCTS LLC
Also Called: P E P R O
671 Colbert Ave (16301-2288)
P.O. Box 1061, Franklin (16323-5061)
PHONE.....................814 676-5688
Kelly Lander, *President*
Victor H Garmong, *Opers Staff*
Todd Plowman, *CFO*
Jeffrey Potter,
EMP: 17 EST: 1998
SQ FT: 100,000
SALES: 3.6MM **Privately Held**
SIC: 3444 Metal housings, enclosures, casings & other containers

(G-12955)
PRECISION TL & DIE MFG CO INC
651 N Seneca St (16301-1157)
PHONE.....................814 676-1864
Ezzetta R Malek, *President*
Frank Malek Jr, *Senior VP*
EMP: 15
SQ FT: 13,300
SALES (est): 1.3MM **Privately Held**
SIC: 3599 Custom machinery

(G-12956)
PRECISION TOOL & DIE CO INC
651 N Seneca St (16301-1198)
PHONE.....................814 676-1864
Ludwig Ganze, *President*
William Kluck, *CFO*
Kenneth Dundon, *Admin Sec*
▼ EMP: 24
SQ FT: 18,000
SALES: 1.8MM **Privately Held**
WEB: www.precisiontool-oilcity.com
SIC: 3599 Machine shop, jobbing & repair

(G-12957)
SASOL CHEMICALS (USA) LLC
292 State Route 8 (16301-5626)
PHONE.....................814 677-2028
EMP: 186
SALES (corp-wide): 20.7B **Privately Held**
SIC: 2869 Alcohols, industrial: denatured (non-beverage)
HQ: Sasol Chemicals (Usa) Llc
12120 Wickchester Ln
Houston TX 77079
281 588-3000

(G-12958)
TITAN BOARDS INC
Also Called: Pennswood Manufacturing
1798 State Route 157 (16301-4340)
P.O. Box 1181 (16301-0681)
PHONE.....................814 516-1899
David Mears, *President*
Joseph McDonald, *Vice Pres*
EMP: 7
SQ FT: 9,000
SALES (est): 623.5K **Privately Held**
SIC: 3949 Skateboards

(G-12959)
WEBCO INDUSTRIES INC
Also Called: Oil City Tube Div
363 Seneca St (16301-1311)
PHONE.....................814 678-1325
Randy Watson, *Vice Pres*
Scott Emrick, *Manager*
Tina Banner, *Director*
Kyle Herron, *Maintence Staff*
EMP: 160
SALES (corp-wide): 393.9MM **Privately Held**
WEB: www.webcoindustries.com
SIC: 3317 Steel pipe & tubes
PA: Webco Industries, Inc.
9101 W 21st St
Sand Springs OK 74063
918 245-2211

Olanta
Clearfield County

(G-12960)
GASBARRE PRODUCTS INC
McKee Carbide Tool Divison
159 Mckee Rd (16863-8229)
PHONE.....................814 236-3108
Rob Edwards, *Manager*
Scott Kalgren, *Manager*
EMP: 28
SQ FT: 18,000
SALES (corp-wide): 40MM **Privately Held**
WEB: www.gasbarre.com
SIC: 3542 3545 3544 Presses: forming, stamping, punching, sizing (machine tools); machine tool accessories; special dies, tools, jigs & fixtures
PA: Gasbarre Products, Inc.
590 Division St
Du Bois PA 15801
814 371-3015

(G-12961)
ROBBINS LOGGING & LUMBER
2365 Zion Rd (16863-8618)
PHONE.....................814 236-3384
Lynn Robbins, *Owner*
EMP: 13
SQ FT: 5,000
SALES (est): 1.1MM **Privately Held**
SIC: 2411 2421 2426 Logging camps & contractors; sawmills & planing mills, general; hardwood dimension & flooring mills

---

Old Forge
Lackawanna County

(G-12962)
AGOSTINI BAKERY INC
1216 S Main St (18518-2304)
PHONE.....................570 457-2021
Bob Agostini, *President*
Sam Agostini, *Vice Pres*
EMP: 23 EST: 1923
SALES: 500K **Privately Held**
SIC: 2051 5461 Breads, rolls & buns; bread, all types (white, wheat, rye, etc): fresh or frozen; bakeries

(G-12963)
DIGITAL PRINT & DESIGN INC
536 Fallon St (18518-1909)
PHONE.....................570 347-6001
Bernard P Andreoli, *President*
Scott W Ballard, *Vice Pres*
EMP: 4
SALES (est): 581.8K **Privately Held**
WEB: www.digitalprintanddesign.com
SIC: 2752 Commercial printing, offset

(G-12964)
FETCHEN SHEET METAL INC
329 S Main St Rear (18518-1676)
PHONE.....................570 457-3560
Ed Fetchen, *President*
EMP: 20
SQ FT: 7,000
SALES (est): 3.8MM **Privately Held**
WEB: www.fetchenhvac.com
SIC: 3444 Sheet metalwork

(G-12965)
GOLDEN BROTHERS INC (PA)
Also Called: Golden Technologies
401 Bridge St (18518-2323)
PHONE.....................570 457-0867
Robert Golden, *President*
Richard J Golden, *Vice Pres*
Fred Kiwak, *Treasurer*
Helen Golden, *Admin Sec*
◆ EMP: 129
SQ FT: 125,000
SALES (est): 60.7MM **Privately Held**
SIC: 2512 5021 3842 5023 Chairs: upholstered on wood frames; living room furniture: upholstered on wood frames; beds; wheelchairs; home furnishings

(G-12966)
GOLDEN TECHNOLOGIES INC
401 Bridge St (18518-2323)
PHONE.....................570 451-7477
EMP: 6
SALES (est): 272.6K **Privately Held**
SIC: 2512 Mfg Upholstered Household Furniture

(G-12967)
KEYSTONE PRINTED SPC CO LLC
1001 Moosic Rd Ste 1 (18518-2085)
PHONE.....................570 457-8334
John L McInerney,
Robert Bernaski,
EMP: 150
SQ FT: 80,000
SALES (est): 11.8MM **Privately Held**
WEB: www.keystoneprint.com
SIC: 7389 2752 2791 2759 Packaging & labeling services; commercial printing, lithographic; typesetting; commercial printing

(G-12968)
M E ENTERPRISE SERVICES INC
Also Called: Main Technologies
325 Bridge St (18518-2321)
P.O. Box 380, Taylor (18517-0380)
PHONE.....................570 457-5221
George Colburn, *President*
Michelle Richards, *Office Mgr*
EMP: 22
SALES: 1MM **Privately Held**
SIC: 3441 Fabricated structural metal

(G-12969)
MAIN ENGINES & SERVICE CENTER
Also Called: Main Engine Builders & Svc Ctr
325 Bridge St (18518-2321)
P.O. Box 380, Taylor (18517-0380)
PHONE.....................570 457-7081
Geogre Colburn, *Owner*
EMP: 3
SALES (est): 208.2K **Privately Held**
SIC: 3599 Machine shop, jobbing & repair

(G-12970)
MCCLURE ENTERPRISES INC (PA)
Also Called: Ashley Ant-Skid Aggregates Div
3 E Mcclure St (18518-1813)
P.O. Box 3775, Scranton (18505-0775)
PHONE.....................570 562-1180
Betty Domiano, *President*
David Domiano, *Treasurer*
EMP: 4
SQ FT: 300
SALES: 500K **Privately Held**
SIC: 1429 5032 6552 Igneous rock, crushed & broken-quarrying; aggregate; subdividers & developers

(G-12971)
NORTHEASTERN ENVELOPE COMPANY (PA)
2 Maxson Dr (18518-2065)
PHONE.....................800 233-4285
Terrence Burke, *President*
Eileen Burke, *Corp Secy*
Rose Fofi, *COO*
James F Ferrario Jr, *Vice Pres*
Shirley Ferrario, *Vice Pres*
◆ EMP: 100 EST: 1953
SQ FT: 18,000

GEOGRAPHIC

SALES (est): 18.9MM **Privately Held**
WEB: www.northeasternenvelope.com
SIC: **5943** 2677 5112 2752 Office forms
& supplies; envelopes; envelopes; commercial printing, offset

(G-12972)
OLD TOWN WOODWORKING INC
209 Dunn Ave (18518-1805)
PHONE..................................570 562-2117
David Verdetto, *President*
EMP: 6
SALES (est): 829.3K **Privately Held**
SIC: **2431** Millwork

(G-12973)
OPI HOLDINGS INC
1001 Moosic Rd Ste 1 (18518-2085)
PHONE..................................610 857-2000
EMP: 50 EST: 1919
SQ FT: 67,441
SALES (est): 6.8MM **Privately Held**
SIC: **2657** 2652 3089 Folding paperboard
boxes; setup paperboard boxes; thermo-
formed finished plastic products

(G-12974)
PENNSYLVANIA BEDDING INC
Also Called: King Koil Sleep Products
301 1st St (18518-2067)
P.O. Box 88, Taylor (18517-0088)
PHONE..................................570 457-0933
David H Adler, *CEO*
▲ EMP: 50 EST: 1906
SQ FT: 81,000
SALES (est): 9.8MM **Privately Held**
SIC: **2515** Mattresses, containing felt, foam
rubber, urethane, etc.; box springs, as-
sembled

(G-12975)
TOPPS COMPANY INC
1001 Moosic Rd (18518-2085)
P.O. Box 5013, Scranton (18505-5013)
PHONE..................................570 471-7649
EMP: 3
SALES (est): 198.4K **Privately Held**
SIC: **2064** Candy & other confectionery
products

(G-12976)
TORQUATO DRILLING ACC INC
533 S Main St (18518-1559)
PHONE..................................570 457-8565
Anthony Torquato, *President*
EMP: 3
SQ FT: 1,800
SALES (est): 728K **Privately Held**
SIC: **3533** Drilling tools for gas, oil or water
wells

(G-12977)
W M ABENE CO
Also Called: Panel Prints
1001 Moosic Rd Ste 2 (18518-2085)
PHONE..................................570 457-8334
John Mc Inerney, *President*
Robert Bernasky, *Vice Pres*
Robert Bernaski, *CFO*
Brad Coleman, *CIO*
EMP: 3
SALES: 27MM **Privately Held**
SIC: **2752** Commercial printing, offset

Oley
Berks County

(G-12978)
DOUBLE D SHEET METAL INC
196 Main St (19547-8704)
PHONE..................................610 987-3733
Dennis M Davies, *President*
Joyce A Davies, *Corp Secy*
EMP: 7
SALES: 75K **Privately Held**
SIC: **1761** 3444 Architectural sheet metal
work; sheet metalwork

(G-12979)
LADYFINGERS SEWING STUDIO
6375 Oley Turnpike Rd (19547-8942)
PHONE..................................610 689-0068

Gail Kessler, *Owner*
EMP: 3 EST: 1994
SQ FT: 3,200
SALES (est): 318.8K **Privately Held**
WEB: www.ladyfingerssewing.com
SIC: **2381** 5722 Fabric dress & work
gloves; sewing machines

(G-12980)
REPPERTS CANDY
2708 W Philadelphia Ave (19547-8929)
PHONE..................................610 689-9200
Larry Schell, *President*
Jean Schell, *Vice Pres*
EMP: 18
SQ FT: 12,000
SALES (est): 2.4MM **Privately Held**
WEB: www.reppertscandy.com
SIC: **2064** 5441 Candy & other confec-
tionery products; candy

(G-12981)
WENTZEL FABRICATION INC
52 Legion Dr (19547-8780)
P.O. Box 16 (19547-0016)
PHONE..................................610 987-6909
M Christopher Wentzel, *President*
EMP: 15 EST: 1947
SQ FT: 3,000
SALES (est): 2.1MM **Privately Held**
WEB: www.wentzelfabrication.com
SIC: **3089** Plastic hardware & building
products

(G-12982)
Z WELDCO
24 Covered Bridge Rd (19547-8931)
PHONE..................................610 689-8773
Gregory Zook, *President*
Sharon Zook, *Admin Sec*
EMP: 4 EST: 1992
SALES (est): 583.2K **Privately Held**
SIC: **7692** 7699 Automotive welding; farm
machinery repair

Olyphant
Lackawanna County

(G-12983)
ADVANCED PRECISION PDTS LLC
Also Called: Advanced Metals Machining
1159 Mid Valley Dr (18447-2606)
PHONE..................................570 487-2830
Sherri Sable, *Production*
David Chiocchi, *CFO*
George Rando, *Controller*
Kim Daniels, *Accounts Mgr*
Bob Gupko, *Sales Staff*
EMP: 24
SQ FT: 15,000
SALES: 2.5MM **Privately Held**
SIC: **3599** Machine shop, jobbing & repair

(G-12984)
ATLANTIC VEAL AND LAMB INC
Also Called: Atlantic Veal & Lamb
218 Hull Ave (18447-1418)
PHONE..................................570 489-4781
Ken Thomas, *Manager*
EMP: 25
SALES (corp-wide): 130.9MM **Privately Held**
SIC: **2011** Veal from meat slaughtered on site
PA: Atlantic Veal And Lamb, Inc.
275 Morgan Ave
Brooklyn NY 11211
718 599-6400

(G-12985)
C & S WOOD PRODUCTS INC
944 Underwood Rd (18447-2613)
P.O. Box 192 (18447-0192)
PHONE..................................570 489-8633
Joseph Barbuti, *President*
EMP: 25
SQ FT: 30,000
SALES (est): 3.2MM **Privately Held**
SIC: **2448** 2441 Pallets, wood; skids,
wood; boxes, wood

(G-12986)
CINRAM MANUFACTURING INC
1400 E Lackawanna St (18448-0999)
PHONE..................................570 383-3291
Dave Rubenstein, *President*
▲ EMP: 6836 EST: 1978
SQ FT: 1,030,000
SALES (est): 228.8MM **Privately Held**
WEB: www.weamfg.com
SIC: **3652** Phonograph record blanks;
magnetic tape (audio): prerecorded; com-
pact laser discs, prerecorded

(G-12987)
COFFEE AND TEA EXCHANGE CORP
406 Lackawanna Ave (18447-1524)
PHONE..................................570 445-8778
Syed Shaukat, *Principal*
EMP: 4 EST: 2017
SALES (est): 127.7K **Privately Held**
SIC: **2095** Roasted coffee

(G-12988)
DESAVINO & SONS INC
1003 Underwood Rd (18447-2135)
PHONE..................................570 383-3988
Leonard Desavino, *President*
Pat Desavino, *Corp Secy*
Mario Desavino, *Vice Pres*
Jason Matisko, *Sales Staff*
EMP: 42
SQ FT: 12,000
SALES (est): 7.1MM **Privately Held**
WEB: www.desavino.com
SIC: **2541** 5031 1799 2821 Table or
counter tops, plastic laminated; kitchen
cabinets; counter top installation; plastics
materials & resins

(G-12989)
ENTERPRISE FASHIONS
116 Grant St (18447-1410)
PHONE..................................570 489-1863
Fax: 570 489-9511
EMP: 4
SQ FT: 7,200
SALES: 200K **Privately Held**
SIC: **2326** 5699 Mfg Men's/Boy's Work
Clothing Ret Misc Apparel/Accessories

(G-12990)
FANGIO ENTERPRISES INC (PA)
Also Called: Fangio Lighting
905 Stanton Rd (18447-2617)
PHONE..................................570 383-1030
Marty Fangio, *President*
▲ EMP: 23 EST: 1978
SQ FT: 30,000
SALES (est): 4.6MM **Privately Held**
WEB: www.fangiolighting.com
SIC: **3641** 5023 Electric lamps & parts for
generalized applications; lamps: floor,
boudoir, desk

(G-12991)
GET IT RIGHT TAPE COMPANY INC
Also Called: Converter Pressure Sensitive
1118 Mid Valley Dr (18447-2607)
PHONE..................................570 383-6960
Walter Kulick, *President*
EMP: 4
SQ FT: 28,000
SALES (est): 516.6K **Privately Held**
SIC: **2241** Electric insulating tapes &
braids, except plastic

(G-12992)
HAS-MOR INDUSTRIES INC
503 Maplewood Dr (18447-1121)
P.O. Box 111, Dunmore (18512-0111)
PHONE..................................570 383-0185
Giles Morgan, *President*
EMP: 12
SQ FT: 30,000
SALES (est): 1.6MM **Privately Held**
WEB: www.has-mor.com
SIC: **3053** 5085 Gaskets, all materials;
packing, industrial

(G-12993)
MAGNUM SCREENING
214 Jackson St (18447-1628)
PHONE..................................570 489-2902

Joseph R Paciotti, *Owner*
EMP: 8
SQ FT: 3,500
SALES: 250K **Privately Held**
SIC: **2396** Screen printing on fabric articles

(G-12994)
NAJAFI COMPANIES LLC
Olyphant Division
1400 E Lackawanna St (18448-0999)
PHONE..................................570 383-3291
Steve Brown, *Branch Mgr*
EMP: 5 **Privately Held**
SIC: **3652** Pre-recorded records & tapes
PA: Najafi Companies, Llc
2525 E Camelback Rd
Phoenix AZ 85016

(G-12995)
NORTHEAST GEOTECHNICAL SUP LLC
1505 E Lackawanna St # 3 (18447-2600)
P.O. Box 474, Clarks Summit (18411-0474)
PHONE..................................570 307-1283
Tom Miller, *Regl Sales Mgr*
Warren Acker, *Mng Member*
▼ EMP: 3
SQ FT: 8,000
SALES (est): 400K **Privately Held**
WEB: www.northeastgeotech.com
SIC: **3532** Drills, bits & similar equipment

(G-12996)
PRIME CONTRACT PKG SVCS CORP
299 Main St Fl 2 (18447-2326)
PHONE..................................570 876-2300
Robert Arvonio, *President*
EMP: 30
SALES (est): 2.4MM **Privately Held**
SIC: **3053** Packing materials

(G-12997)
RJF ENTERPRISES INC
905 Stanton Rd (18447-2617)
PHONE..................................570 383-1030
Martin Fangio, *President*
EMP: 18
SQ FT: 21,000
SALES: 1.3MM **Privately Held**
SIC: **3645** Table lamps

(G-12998)
SAINT-GOBAIN CERAMICS PLAS INC
Also Called: ABC
1401 E Lackawanna St (18447-2152)
PHONE..................................570 383-3261
Brian Shaffer, *Branch Mgr*
EMP: 34
SALES (corp-wide): 215.9MM **Privately Held**
WEB: www.sgceramics.com
SIC: **3297** Nonclay refractories
HQ: Saint-Gobain Ceramics & Plastics, Inc.
750 E Swedesford Rd
Valley Forge PA 19482

(G-12999)
SKM INDUSTRIES INC (PA)
1012 Underwood Rd (18447-2160)
P.O. Box 278 (18447-0278)
PHONE..................................570 383-3062
Shanta Syal, *President*
▲ EMP: 10
SQ FT: 1,200
SALES: 4.8MM **Privately Held**
WEB: www.skmindustries.com
SIC: **3951** 2899 Markers, soft tip (felt, fab-
ric, plastic, etc.); correction fluid

(G-13000)
SMOKE TOWN LLC
594 Burke Byp Ste C (18447-1800)
PHONE..................................570 383-7833
Bonnie Borgna, *Principal*
EMP: 3 EST: 2008
SALES (est): 285K **Privately Held**
SIC: **3999** Cigarette & cigar products & ac-
cessories

(G-13001)
TECHNICOLOR HM ENTRMT SVCS INC
1400 E Lackawanna St (18448-0999)
PHONE....................................570 383-3291
EMP: 15
SALES (corp-wide): 62.9MM Privately Held
SIC: 3652 Pre-recorded records & tapes
HQ: Technicolor Home Entertainment Services, Inc.
3233 Mission Oaks Blvd
Camarillo CA 93012

(G-13002)
UNITED FENCE SUPPLY COMPANY
1105 Mid Valley Dr (18447-2606)
PHONE....................................570 307-0782
Al Fanella, President
EMP: 3
SQ FT: 3,500
SALES: 1.5MM Privately Held
WEB: www.unitedfencesupply.com
SIC: 3089 5051 3448 5039 Fences, gates & accessories: plastic; rails & accessories; docks: prefabricated metal; wire fence, gates & accessories

(G-13003)
WARNER MUSIC INC
1400 E Lackawanna St (18448-0999)
PHONE....................................570 383-3291
Joseph Kroll, Principal
EMP: 60 Privately Held
SIC: 3652 Phonograph records, prerecorded
HQ: Warner Music Inc.
1633 Broadway Fl 11
New York NY 10019

Ono
Lebanon County

(G-13004)
ONO INDUSTRIES INC (PA)
Rr 22 Box W (17077)
PHONE....................................717 865-6619
Carmine Petrozziello Sr, Ch of Bd
Carmine L Petrozziello Jr, President
Annette Petrozziello, Vice Pres
Annette Ewanyk, Treasurer
Suzanne Kania, Admin Sec
EMP: 25
SQ FT: 25,000
SALES (est): 5MM Privately Held
WEB: www.onoindustries.thomasnet.com
SIC: 3089 3084 3082 2821 Extruded finished plastic products; plastics pipe; unsupported plastics profile shapes; plastics materials & resins; broadwoven fabric mills, manmade

Orangeville
Columbia County

(G-13005)
DEIHL VAULT & PRECAST INC
1786 State Route 254 (17859-9213)
PHONE....................................570 458-6466
Michael R Deihl, President
EMP: 15
SQ FT: 15,000
SALES (est): 1.6MM Privately Held
WEB: www.deihlprecast.com
SIC: 3272 Burial vaults, concrete or precast terrazzo

Orbisonia
Huntingdon County

(G-13006)
HORSEPOWER WOOD PRODUCTS
Hwy Contract Rt 60 (17243)
PHONE....................................814 447-5662
Raymond H Morgan, Partner

Clyde J Cisney, Partner
EMP: 4
SALES (est): 400K Privately Held
SIC: 2421 Sawmills & planing mills, general

(G-13007)
ORBISONIA ROCKHILL JOINT
843 Elliot St Ste 1 (17243-9689)
P.O. Box 346 (17243-0346)
PHONE....................................814 447-5414
Bonnie Rose, Chairman
EMP: 3
SALES (est): 724.2K Privately Held
SIC: 3589 Sewage & water treatment equipment

Orefield
Lehigh County

(G-13008)
ASSOCIATED SPECIALTY CO
Also Called: Associated Specialties
3551 Route 309 (18069-2002)
PHONE....................................610 395-9172
George Allerton, Owner
V Laudenslager, Sales Staff
EMP: 10
SALES (est): 499.1K Privately Held
SIC: 3612 5063 Power transformers, electric; electrical apparatus & equipment

(G-13009)
CHARLES HARDY
Also Called: Competitive Edge Dynamics USA
2908 Betz Ct (18069-2800)
PHONE....................................610 366-9752
Charles Hardy, Owner
Rich Mitstifer, Opers Staff
▲ EMP: 8
SALES: 950K Privately Held
SIC: 3949 Shooting equipment & supplies, general

(G-13010)
CONSYST INC
1610 Applewood Dr (18069-9548)
PHONE....................................610 398-0752
Joe Nemeth, President
Theresa Nemeth, Treasurer
EMP: 3
SALES: 120K Privately Held
SIC: 8711 3571 Consulting engineer; electronic computers

(G-13011)
E F LAUDENSLAGER INC
Also Called: Honeywell Authorized Dealer
3545 Route 309 (18069-2002)
PHONE....................................610 395-1582
Stephen Laudenslager, President
EMP: 13
SQ FT: 3,000
SALES (est): 2.1MM Privately Held
WEB: www.eflaudenslager.com
SIC: 1711 1321 Heating & air conditioning contractors; ventilation & duct work contractor; propane (natural) production

(G-13012)
INTERNTNAL DEF SYSTEMS USA LLC
Also Called: IDS USA
2867 Post Rd (18069-2838)
PHONE....................................610 973-2228
EMP: 4
SQ FT: 8,000
SALES: 80K Privately Held
SIC: 3711 8299 8249 8748 Mfg Motor Vehicle Bodies School/Educational Svcs Vocational School Business Consulting Svcs

(G-13013)
JAINDLS INCORPORATED
3150 Coffeetown Rd (18069-2599)
PHONE....................................610 395-3333
David Jaindl, President
EMP: 100 EST: 1960
SQ FT: 51,000
SALES: 11MM Privately Held
SIC: 2015 Turkey, processed

(G-13014)
LONGS WATER TECHNOL
State Rt 309 (18069)
PHONE....................................610 398-3737
Scott Warwicik, Manager
EMP: 4
SALES (est): 297.1K Privately Held
SIC: 3589 Water treatment equipment, industrial

(G-13015)
THEOTEK CORPORATION
5934 Armstrong St (18069-2246)
PHONE....................................610 336-9191
Stephanie Economy, President
EMP: 10
SALES (est): 581.1K Privately Held
SIC: 3648 Lighting equipment

(G-13016)
VALLEY INSTANT PRINTING
2291 Bobby Ct (18069-9540)
PHONE....................................610 439-4122
Ed Conti, Owner
EMP: 5 EST: 1974
SQ FT: 4,000
SALES (est): 416.3K Privately Held
WEB: www.valleyinstantprinting.com
SIC: 2752 Lithographing on metal

Oreland
Montgomery County

(G-13017)
ANDERSON WELDING & SONS LLC
100 Ehrenpfort Ave (19075-1784)
PHONE....................................215 886-1726
Robert Anderson,
Clint Anderson,
EMP: 6
SQ FT: 2,600
SALES (est): 630K Privately Held
WEB: www.steelandironwork.com
SIC: 7692 1799 1791 Welding repair; ornamental metal work; structural steel erection

(G-13018)
CARDINAL PRECISION COMPANY
222 Roesch Ave Unit 24 (19075-1716)
PHONE....................................215 885-2050
Anthony Hartman, Co-Owner
Dennis Veasey, Co-Owner
EMP: 5
SQ FT: 2,000
SALES: 600K Privately Held
WEB: www.cardinalprecision.com
SIC: 3599 Machine shop, jobbing & repair

(G-13019)
CENTIFY LLC
204 Allison Rd (19075-1928)
PHONE....................................215 421-8375
Alet Aetcely, Mng Member
EMP: 13
SALES: 1MM Privately Held
SIC: 7372 Application computer software

(G-13020)
CHAPEL HILL MFG CO
1807 Walnut Ave (19075-1528)
P.O. Box 208 (19075-0208)
PHONE....................................215 884-3614
John Seeburger, President
John Robert Seeburger, Vice Pres
Robert Seeburger, Vice Pres
▲ EMP: 10
SQ FT: 7,600
SALES (est): 1.7MM Privately Held
WEB: www.chapelhillmfg.com
SIC: 2295 5084 5021 2257 Tubing, textile: varnished; safety equipment; office furniture; weft knit fabric mills; broadwoven fabric mills, manmade

(G-13021)
GRIFFITH POTTERY HOUSE INC
Also Called: Griffith Advertising
100 Lorraine Ave (19075-1799)
PHONE....................................215 887-2222

Kevin Griffith, President
EMP: 5 EST: 1944
SQ FT: 10,000
SALES (est): 704.5K Privately Held
WEB: www.gphprint.com
SIC: 2754 2759 2395 Promotional printing, gravure; screen printing; engraving; embroidery products, except schiffli machine

(G-13022)
INSPYR APPAREL CO LLC
1206 Susan Cir (19075-1939)
PHONE....................................267 784-3036
EMP: 3
SALES (est): 88.6K Privately Held
SIC: 2252 Socks

(G-13023)
IRISH EDITION
1506 Walnut Ave (19075-1714)
PHONE....................................215 836-4900
Anthony R Byrne, Owner
Deirdre Byrne, Advt Staff
EMP: 5
SALES (est): 237K Privately Held
WEB: www.irishedition.com
SIC: 2711 Newspapers: publishing only, not printed on site

(G-13024)
ISAAC STEPHENS & ASSOC INC
214 Paper Mill Rd (19075-2109)
PHONE....................................215 576-5414
Ron Jackson, President
Barbara Orloff, CFO
EMP: 3
SALES: 127K Privately Held
WEB: www.isa-assoc.com
SIC: 5531 3559 5013 Ret Auto/Home Supplies Mfg Misc Industry Machinery Whol Auto Parts/Supplies

(G-13025)
JAMISON BSMNT WTERPROOFING INC
150 Roesch Ave (19075-1715)
PHONE....................................215 885-2424
Frank Jamison, President
EMP: 5
SQ FT: 800
SALES (est): 530.7K Privately Held
SIC: 3272 Areaways, basement window: concrete

(G-13026)
PAUL ERIVAN
Also Called: Erivan Dairies
105 Allison Rd (19075-1808)
PHONE....................................215 887-2009
Paul Fereshetian, Manager
EMP: 4 Privately Held
SIC: 2026 2024 Yogurt; ice cream, bulk
PA: Paul Erivan
1984 Audubon Dr
Dresher PA

(G-13027)
PHILADELPHIA CARBIDE CO INC
1451 Anderson Ave (19075-1722)
PHONE....................................215 885-0770
Dean S De Carlo, President
Edna De Carlo, Corp Secy
EMP: 6 EST: 1958
SQ FT: 6,000
SALES: 1MM Privately Held
SIC: 3544 Special dies & tools

(G-13028)
PRECISION GLASS PRODUCTS CO
143 Montgomery Ave (19075-1810)
P.O. Box 147 (19075-0147)
PHONE....................................215 885-0145
Michael J Serianni, President
Gerald M Serianni, Shareholder
EMP: 12
SQ FT: 11,000
SALES (est): 178.4K Privately Held
WEB: www.pgpcompany.com
SIC: 3679 3231 Quartz crystals, for electronic application; products of purchased glass

GEOGRAPHIC

(G-13029)
SMART POTATO LLC
512 Marks Rd (19075-2341)
PHONE...................................215 380-5050
James Murray, *Co-Owner*
Emily Murray, *Co-Owner*
EMP: 3
SALES (est): 162.6K **Privately Held**
SIC: 3944 7389 Games, toys & children's
vehicles;

(G-13030)
SPECTROCELL INC
Also Called: Precision Glass
143 Montgomery Ave (19075-1810)
P.O. Box 147 (19075-0147)
PHONE...................................215 572-7605
Michael J Serianni, *President*
Gerald M Serianni, *Vice Pres*
EMP: 11
SQ FT: 11,000
SALES (est): 1.7MM **Privately Held**
WEB: www.spectrocell.com
SIC: 3211 Transparent optical glass, ex-
cept lenses

(G-13031)
TRICOUNTY PRINTERS LTD
222 Roesch Ave (19075-1700)
P.O. Box 180 (19075-0180)
PHONE...................................215 886-3737
Mark Strasburg, *President*
EMP: 7 **EST:** 1963
SQ FT: 3,600
SALES (est): 1.1MM **Privately Held**
SIC: 2752 Commercial printing, offset

Orrstown
Franklin County

(G-13032)
JEM PALLETS
11742 Weaver Rd (17244-9737)
PHONE...................................717 532-5304
Israel Stoltzfus, *Owner*
EMP: 7
SQ FT: 8,256
SALES (est): 816.5K **Privately Held**
SIC: 2653 Pallets, corrugated: made from
purchased materials

(G-13033)
JOHNSON SAWMILL LOGGING
10441 Tim Rd (17244-9727)
PHONE...................................717 532-7784
Donald Johnson, *Principal*
EMP: 3
SALES (est): 224.4K **Privately Held**
SIC: 2411 Logging

(G-13034)
MOUNTAIN MAN DEER PROCESSING
10125 Mountain Rd (17244-9413)
PHONE...................................717 532-7295
Byron Magee, *Principal*
EMP: 3
SALES (est): 249.8K **Privately Held**
SIC: 2011 Meat packing plants

(G-13035)
STOLTZFUS CUSTOM WELDING
11738 Weaver Rd (17244-9737)
PHONE...................................717 477-8200
Paul Stoltzfus, *Principal*
EMP: 5
SALES (est): 256.7K **Privately Held**
SIC: 7692 Welding repair

Orrtanna
Adams County

(G-13036)
KNOUSE FOODS COOPERATIVE INC
Apple Canning Division
1505 Orrtanna Rd (17353-9446)
PHONE...................................717 642-8291
Mike Binkley, *Manager*
EMP: 250

SALES (corp-wide): 281.7MM **Privately
Held**
SIC: 2033 Fruits: packaged in cans, jars,
etc.
PA: Knouse Foods Cooperative, Inc.
800 Pach Glen Idaville Rd
Peach Glen PA 17375
717 677-8181

(G-13037)
SHANKS PORTABLE SAWMILLS
540 Buchanan Valley Rd (17353-9543)
PHONE...................................717 334-0352
Ronald Shank, *Principal*
EMP: 3 **EST:** 2001
SALES (est): 238.3K **Privately Held**
SIC: 2421 Sawmills & planing mills, gen-
eral

Orwigsburg
Schuylkill County

(G-13038)
AMERICAN MACHINE LLC
206 N Washington St (17961-1914)
PHONE...................................215 674-4886
Dennis Jessup, *Owner*
▲ **EMP:** 3
SALES (est): 260K **Privately Held**
SIC: 3599 Machine shop, jobbing & repair

(G-13039)
ATKINSON INDUSTRIES INC
Lincoln Ave (17961)
P.O. Box 126 (17961-0126)
PHONE...................................570 366-2114
Gary Atkinson, *President*
Truman L Atkinson, *Vice Pres*
Janis Atkinson, *Treasurer*
EMP: 6 **EST:** 1953
SQ FT: 12,000
SALES (est): 334.7K **Privately Held**
SIC: 3479 3444 Painting, coating & hot
dipping; sheet metalwork

(G-13040)
BARTUSH SIGNS INC
302 N Washington St Apt A (17961-1962)
PHONE...................................570 366-2311
Felix E Bartush Jr, *President*
Jerry Frewald, *Vice Pres*
Christopher Bartush, *Treasurer*
Sherry M Bartush, *Admin Sec*
EMP: 40 **EST:** 1946
SQ FT: 44,000
SALES (est): 7.4MM **Privately Held**
WEB: www.bartush.com
SIC: 3993 Neon signs

(G-13041)
CYANIDE VS XANERIA
124 N Washington St (17961-1912)
PHONE...................................570 968-4522
EMP: 3
SALES (est): 92.9K **Privately Held**
SIC: 2819 Cyanides

(G-13042)
ENVIRONMENTAL MATERIALS LLC
Also Called: Environmental Stoneworks
98 Pheasant Run Rd (17961-9084)
PHONE...................................570 366-6460
Thomas Downey, *Branch Mgr*
EMP: 250
SALES (corp-wide): 2B **Publicly Held**
SIC: 3281 Stone, quarrying & processing
of own stone products
HQ: Environmental Materials, Llc
7306 S Alton Way Ste B
Centennial CO 80112
303 309-6610

(G-13043)
ENVIRONMENTAL STONEWORKS LLC (PA)
98 Pheasant Run Rd (17961-9084)
PHONE...................................570 366-6460
Tom Downey,
Tom Downy,
EMP: 25 **EST:** 1975
SALES (est): 10MM **Privately Held**
SIC: 3281 Granite, cut & shaped

(G-13044)
HETRAN-B INC
70 Pinedale Industrial Rd (17961-9078)
PHONE...................................570 366-1411
Russell Blyler Jr, *President*
Clinton Blyler, *Vice Pres*
EMP: 6
SALES (est): 126.3K
SALES (corp-wide): 12.7MM **Privately
Held**
SIC: 3599 3441 Machine shop, jobbing &
repair; fabricated structural metal
PA: Big B Manufacturing, Inc.
17 Municipal Rd
Klingerstown PA 17941
570 648-2084

(G-13045)
INTERLOCK INDUSTRIES INC
Also Called: Middlesales Manufacturing
29 Pinedale Industrial Rd (17961-9082)
PHONE...................................570 366-2020
John Fenstermacher, *Manager*
EMP: 60
SALES (corp-wide): 390.6MM **Privately
Held**
WEB: www.metalsales.us.com
SIC: 3444 Roof deck, sheet metal
PA: Interlock Industries, Inc.
545 S 3rd St Ste 310
Louisville KY 40202
502 569-2007

(G-13046)
JOHN EPPLER MACHINE WORKS
206 N Washington St (17961-1914)
PHONE...................................215 624-3400
Helen Schnabl, *President*
Martin J Schnabl, *Vice Pres*
John Eppler, *CFO*
Matt Stehm, *Technology*
EMP: 24 **EST:** 1885
SQ FT: 32,000
SALES: 1.5MM **Privately Held**
WEB: www.johneppler.com
SIC: 3554 5084 Paper industries machin-
ery; industrial machinery & equipment

(G-13047)
KEPNER-SCOTT SHOE CO
Also Called: CARPENTER
209 N Liberty St (17961-1805)
P.O. Box 247 (17961-0247)
PHONE...................................570 366-0229
Steven Zimmerman, *President*
Susan Murphy, *Vice Pres*
▲ **EMP:** 20 **EST:** 1888
SQ FT: 12,000
SALES: 1.1MM **Privately Held**
SIC: 3149 Children's footwear, except ath-
letic

(G-13048)
MAE-EITEL INC
97 Pinedale Industrial Rd (17961-9082)
PHONE...................................570 366-0585
Norm Walker, *President*
Hughes Mike, *Purch Mgr*
Cangialosi Jeff, *Purchasing*
Scott Donaldson, *VP Sales*
◆ **EMP:** 53
SALES (est): 10.4MM **Privately Held**
SIC: 3549 Metalworking machinery

(G-13049)
METAL SALES MANUFACTURING CORP
29 Pinedale Industrial Rd (17961-9082)
PHONE...................................570 366-2020
Don Fenstermacher, *Sales/Mktg Mgr*
Cameron McPherson, *Manager*
EMP: 30
SALES (corp-wide): 390.6MM **Privately
Held**
SIC: 3444 3448 Roof deck, sheet metal;
prefabricated metal buildings
HQ: Metal Sales Manufacturing Corporation
545 S 3rd St Ste 200
Louisville KY 40202
502 855-4300

(G-13050)
MONUMENT SIGN MFG LLC
804 N Warren St (17961-1314)
PHONE...................................570 366-9505
Troy C Schneider, *Principal*
EMP: 5
SALES (est): 406.6K **Privately Held**
SIC: 3993 Electric signs

(G-13051)
S R SLOAN INC
87 Pinedale Industrial Rd (17961-9082)
PHONE...................................570 366-8934
S Sloan, *Branch Mgr*
EMP: 23
SALES (corp-wide): 16.9MM **Privately
Held**
SIC: 2439 Trusses, except roof: laminated
lumber
PA: S. R. Sloan, Inc.
8111 Halsey Rd
Whitesboro NY 13492
315 736-7730

(G-13052)
SHALMET CORPORATION (HQ)
116 Pinedale Indus Rd (17961-9079)
PHONE...................................570 366-1414
Robert J Torcolini, *CEO*
EMP: 165
SQ FT: 110,000
SALES: 23MM
SALES (corp-wide): 2.1B **Publicly Held**
SIC: 3471 3316 Polishing, metals or
formed products; finishing, metals or
formed products; cold finishing of steel
shapes
PA: Carpenter Technology Corporation
1735 Market St Fl 15
Philadelphia PA 19103
610 208-2000

(G-13053)
SUMMIT CONTRACTING SVCS INC
1329 Red Dale Rd (17961-9463)
PHONE...................................570 943-2232
Guy Fidler, *President*
EMP: 3 **EST:** 1990
SALES: 100K **Privately Held**
SIC: 1731 3441 8711 Electronic controls
installation; fabricated structural metal;
machine tool design

(G-13054)
VISCONTI GARMENT HANGERS INC (PA)
1140 Centre Tpke Ste A (17961-9058)
P.O. Box 54 (17961-0054)
PHONE...................................570 366-7745
Steve Palvick, *President*
Carl Ziegmont, *Controller*
Stephen Pavlick, *VP Sales*
▲ **EMP:** 4
SALES (est): 584.4K **Privately Held**
WEB: www.viscontihangers.com
SIC: 2499 Garment hangers, wood

Osceola Mills
Clearfield County

(G-13055)
INNODYN LLC
156 Nearhoof Ln (16666-1726)
P.O. Box 97 (16666-0097)
PHONE...................................814 339-7328
Gregory Grose, *CEO*
Deborah Nearhoof, *Corp Secy*
Charles Nearhoof Sr, *Vice Pres*
Charles F Nearhoof Jr,
EMP: 6
SALES (est): 568.9K **Privately Held**
WEB: www.innodyn.com
SIC: 3724 Aircraft engines & engine parts

(G-13056)
NEARHOOF MACHINE INC
Also Called: Mid-State Electric
156 Nearhoof Ln (16666-1726)
P.O. Box 127 (16666-0127)
PHONE...................................814 339-6621
Charles F Nearhoof Sr, *President*
EMP: 7

SALES (est): 1.2MM **Privately Held**
SIC: 7699 3568 5063 7694 Industrial machinery & equipment repair; bearings, bushings & blocks; shafts, flexible; generators; motors, electric; motor repair services; motors & generators

(G-13057)
SEZ SEW STITCHING INC
105 Elizabeth St (16666-1405)
PHONE..................................814 339-6734
Greg Dufour, *President*
EMP: 12
SALES (est): 1.5MM **Privately Held**
SIC: 5136 2396 2395 Men's & boys' clothing; screen printing on fabric articles; embroidery & art needlework

Ottsville
Bucks County

(G-13058)
AFFORDABLE HOME FUEL LLC
89 Oak Grove Rd (18942-1749)
P.O. Box 578 (18942-0578)
PHONE..................................610 847-0972
Robert J Fuller, *Principal*
EMP: 7
SALES (est): 553.2K **Privately Held**
SIC: 2869 Fuels

(G-13059)
BENTON ELEVATOR
3567 Spruce Hill Rd # 18942 (18942-1544)
P.O. Box 772, Plumsteadville (18949-0772)
PHONE..................................215 795-0650
Kenneth Denton, *President*
EMP: 4
SALES (est): 330K **Privately Held**
SIC: 3534 Elevators & equipment

(G-13060)
BROWN & LOUNSBERRY INC
8490 Easton Rd (18942-9624)
P.O. Box 496 (18942-0496)
PHONE..................................610 847-2242
Dwayne Brown, *President*
Douglass Brown, *Vice Pres*
EMP: 4
SQ FT: 5,000
SALES (est): 343.2K **Privately Held**
SIC: 2411 Logging camps & contractors

(G-13061)
CARTER HANDCRAFTED FURNITURE
7541 Easton Rd (18942-9721)
PHONE..................................610 847-2101
Mark Carter, *President*
EMP: 5
SQ FT: 13,000
SALES (est): 723.5K **Privately Held**
SIC: 2511 5712 Wood household furniture; furniture stores

(G-13062)
HANSON AGGREGATES BMC INC
262 Quarry Rd (18942-9693)
PHONE..................................610 847-5211
Bob Melani, *Manager*
EMP: 9
SALES (corp-wide): 20.6B **Privately Held**
SIC: 3273 Ready-mixed concrete
HQ: Hanson Aggregates Bmc, Inc.
852 Swamp Rd
Penns Park PA
215 598-3152

(G-13063)
JONES MACHINE RACING PRODUCTS
72 Annawanda Rd (18942-9702)
PHONE..................................610 847-2028
Charles E Jones, *President*
Elise Jones, *Vice Pres*
EMP: 6
SQ FT: 7,500
SALES (est): 1.1MM **Privately Held**
WEB: www.jonesracingproducts.com
SIC: 3714 Motor vehicle engines & parts

(G-13064)
KETTLE CREEK CORPORATION
Also Called: Windsor Barrel Works
33 Sunset Dr (18942-9714)
P.O. Box 446 (18942-0446)
PHONE..................................800 527-7848
Bonnie Haas, *President*
Philip Haas, *Vice Pres*
EMP: 5
SQ FT: 1,500
SALES (est): 784.4K **Privately Held**
WEB: www.kettlecreek.com
SIC: 2531 Public building & related furniture

(G-13065)
LAMPIRE BIOLOGICAL LABS INC (PA)
3599 Farm School Rd (18942-1536)
P.O. Box 270, Pipersville (18947-0270)
PHONE..................................215 795-2838
Gregory F Krug, *President*
Kristen Day, *President*
Meredith Krug, *Admin Sec*
EMP: 30
SALES (est): 17.4MM **Privately Held**
WEB: www.lampire.com
SIC: 3841 2833 Diagnostic apparatus, medical; antibiotics

(G-13066)
LOMED INC
553 Geigel Hill Rd (18942-9795)
PHONE..................................800 477-0239
Dennis Bonner MD, *Principal*
EMP: 4
SALES (est): 156.7K **Privately Held**
SIC: 2834 Pharmaceutical preparations

(G-13067)
MARBLE SOURCE INC
87 Brownstone Rd (18942-9637)
PHONE..................................610 847-5694
Kevin Givnin, *President*
Janet Givnin, *Vice Pres*
EMP: 7
SQ FT: 7,200
SALES (est): 840.2K **Privately Held**
WEB: www.marblesource.com
SIC: 3281 Marble, building: cut & shaped; granite, cut & shaped

(G-13068)
VCW ENTERPRISES INC (DH)
210 Durham Rd (18942-1723)
PHONE..................................610 847-5112
Vernon Wehrung, *President*
James Loew, *Treasurer*
EMP: 85 EST: 1946
SQ FT: 25,000
SALES (est): 27MM
SALES (corp-wide): 29.7B **Privately Held**
WEB: www.modcon.com
SIC: 5211 5074 3272 5031 Lumber & other building materials; plumbing & hydronic heating supplies; septic tanks, concrete; steps, prefabricated concrete; manhole covers or frames, concrete; lumber, plywood & millwork; fabricated plate work (boiler shop); concrete block & brick
HQ: Oldcastle Infrastructure, Inc.
1002 15th St Sw Ste 110
Auburn WA 98001
253 833-2777

(G-13069)
WEHRUNGS SPECIALTY WOODS
8422 Rte 611 (18942)
P.O. Box 550 (18942-0550)
PHONE..................................610 847-6002
Vernon Wehrung, *Owner*
EMP: 60
SALES (est): 5.1MM **Privately Held**
WEB: www.specialtywoods.net
SIC: 2435 Hardwood plywood, prefinished

Oxford
Chester County

(G-13070)
5 STAR PLUS INC
716 Little Elk Creek Rd (19363-4304)
P.O. Box 530, Nottingham (19362-0530)
PHONE..................................610 470-9187
James M Stevenson III, *President*
John Stevenson, *Manager*
EMP: 4
SQ FT: 1,250
SALES (est): 402.3K **Privately Held**
WEB: www.5starplusinc.net
SIC: 3523 Sprayers & spraying machines, agricultural

(G-13071)
AMCS GROUP INC
119 S 5th St (19363-1770)
PHONE..................................610 932-4006
Jimmy Martin, *CEO*
EMP: 26 **Privately Held**
SIC: 7372 Prepackaged software
PA: Amcs Nominees Limited
Fanningstown
Limerick

(G-13072)
BOG TURTLE BREWERY LLC
145 Schoolview Ln (19363-2002)
PHONE..................................484 758-0416
John Topmiller, *General Mgr*
Christopher Davis, *Finance Dir*
EMP: 6
SALES (est): 385.7K **Privately Held**
SIC: 3556 Brewers' & maltsters' machinery

(G-13073)
BROWN MACHINE CO INC
125 Limestone Rd (19363-1229)
PHONE..................................610 932-3359
Gerald D Brown, *President*
Tom Taylor, *Instructor*
EMP: 4 EST: 1950
SALES (est): 200K **Privately Held**
SIC: 3599 3444 Machine shop, jobbing & repair; sheet metalwork

(G-13074)
CDS ANALYTICAL LLC
465 Limestone Rd (19363-1235)
P.O. Box 277 (19363-0277)
PHONE..................................610 932-3636
Ke Hu, *President*
Melinda Delp, *Opers Mgr*
Jim Byrd, *Safety Mgr*
Stephen Wesson, *Sales Mgr*
Gary Deger, *Chief Mktg Ofcr*
EMP: 2
SQ FT: 12,000
SALES (est): 4.6MM **Privately Held**
WEB: www.cdsanalytical.com
SIC: 3826 Analytical optical instruments
PA: Labtech Inc.
114 South St
Hopkinton MA 01748
508 435-5500

(G-13075)
COASTAL TREATED PRODUCTS CO
Also Called: Forest Resources
385 Waterway Rd (19363-2418)
PHONE..................................610 932-5100
Chip Moran, *Principal*
EMP: 20
SALES (est): 3.2MM **Privately Held**
SIC: 2411 Logging

(G-13076)
CONFISEURS INC
Also Called: Swiss Chocolatier, The
461 Limestone Rd (19363-1235)
PHONE..................................610 932-2706
Albert A Lauber, *President*
▲ EMP: 25
SQ FT: 6,000
SALES: 800K **Privately Held**
SIC: 2066 5149 5441 Chocolate; chocolate; candy, nut & confectionery stores

(G-13077)
DAISY MAE PRTG & DESIGN LLC
119 S 3rd St Ste 1 (19363-1771)
P.O. Box 44 (19363-0044)
PHONE..................................610 467-1989
EMP: 3
SALES (est): 80.6K **Privately Held**
SIC: 2759 Commercial printing

(G-13078)
DELL SUNNY FOODS LLC
135 N 5th St (19363-1502)
PHONE..................................610 932-5164
Gary Caligiuri, *President*
Dee Hughes, *Safety Mgr*
Lori Telegery, *Controller*
Bonnie Walleigh, *Admin Asst*
◆ EMP: 75
SALES: 11.3MM **Privately Held**
WEB: www.sunnydell.com
SIC: 2033 5148 Canned fruits & specialties; vegetables, fresh

(G-13079)
FLOWERS BAKING CO OXFORD INC
700 Lincoln St (19363-1529)
PHONE..................................610 932-2147
Carl Watts, *President*
Charles P Pizzi, *President*
Eugene P Malinowski, *Corp Secy*
Paul D Ridder, *Vice Pres*
◆ EMP: 40
SQ FT: 200,000
SALES (est): 8.2MM
SALES (corp-wide): 3.9B **Publicly Held**
WEB: www.tastykake.com
SIC: 2051 2052 Bakery: wholesale or wholesale/retail combined; cakes, bakery: except frozen; pies, bakery: except frozen; doughnuts, except frozen; cookies & crackers; cookies; pretzels
PA: Flowers Foods, Inc.
1919 Flowers Cir
Thomasville GA 31757
229 226-9110

(G-13080)
HARRIS WOODWORKING
120 Oxford St (19363-1246)
P.O. Box 113 (19363-0113)
PHONE..................................610 932-2646
Charles Harris, *Principal*
EMP: 5
SALES (est): 461.5K **Privately Held**
SIC: 2431 Millwork

(G-13081)
HOOVER TREATED WOOD PDTS INC
385 Waterway Rd (19363-2418)
PHONE..................................800 220-6046
Rick Farnsam, *Branch Mgr*
EMP: 7
SALES (corp-wide): 2.7B **Publicly Held**
WEB: www.coastallumbercompany.com
SIC: 2491 5031 Structural lumber & timber, treated wood; lumber: rough, dressed & finished
HQ: Hoover Treated Wood Products, Inc.
154 Wire Rd
Thomson GA 30824
706 595-5058

(G-13082)
HOWETTS CUSTOM SCREEN PRINTING
113 S 3rd St (19363-1703)
PHONE..................................610 932-3697
Scott Gold III, *President*
Dan Greer, *Vice Pres*
Gary Ham, *Treasurer*
EMP: 5
SQ FT: 2,160
SALES: 500K **Privately Held**
SIC: 2759 Screen printing

(G-13083)
HYPONEX CORPORATION
Also Called: Scotts- Hyponex
311 Reedville Rd (19363-2505)
PHONE..................................610 932-4200
Jim Witter, *Branch Mgr*
EMP: 75

SALES (corp-wide): 2.6B **Publicly Held**
SIC: 2873 Fertilizers: natural (organic), except compost
HQ: Hyponex Corporation
14111 Scottslawn Rd
Marysville OH 43040
937 644-0011

(G-13084)
OUTBACK TRADING COMPANY LTD
39 S 3rd St Ste 1 (19363-1689)
P.O. Box 87 (19363-0087)
PHONE...................................610 932-5314
Patricia Hazzard, *President*
Wilson King, *President*
Louis G Argyris, *Treasurer*
Louis Argyris, *Treasurer*
Winter Paxson, *Sales Mgr*
▲ EMP: 20
SQ FT: 80,000
SALES (est): 2.8MM **Privately Held**
WEB: www.outbacktrading.com
SIC: 2353 2329 2339 Hats & caps; men's & boys' leather, wool & down-filled outerwear; women's & misses' jackets & coats, except sportswear

(G-13085)
OXFORD AREA SEWER AUTHORITY
14 S 3rd St (19363-1601)
P.O. Box 379 (19363-0379)
PHONE...................................610 932-3493
W Kepler, *Vice Chairman*
Kathy Orcutt, *Sls & Mktg Exec*
Patrick Hughes, *Treasurer*
Edward A Lennex, *Exec Dir*
John Schaible, *Admin Sec*
EMP: 6
SALES (est): 833.6K **Privately Held**
SIC: 3589 Sewer cleaning equipment, power

(G-13086)
OXFORD MARKET PLACE INC
Also Called: Forever Christmas
180 Limestone Rd (19363-1229)
PHONE...................................610 998-9080
William Lewis, *President*
Laura Lewis, *Admin Sec*
EMP: 3
SALES: 200K **Privately Held**
SIC: 2273 Carpets & rugs

(G-13087)
PENN SAUNA CORP (PA)
Also Called: Baltic Leisure
601 Lincoln St (19363-1523)
P.O. Box 530 (19363-0530)
PHONE...................................610 932-5700
Thomas Smithson, *President*
Christine M Smithson, *Admin Sec*
◆ EMP: 34
SQ FT: 32,200
SALES (est): 6.5MM **Privately Held**
WEB: www.balticleisure.com
SIC: 2452 2084 0254 5999 Sauna rooms, prefabricated, wood; wine cellars, bonded: engaged in blending wines; poultry hatcheries; sauna equipment & supplies; fitness equipment & supplies; spa equipment & supplies

(G-13088)
ROBERT TRATE HOGG CBINETMAKERS
Also Called: Hogg, Robert Treate Cab Mkr Sp
5650 Homeville Rd (19363-1014)
PHONE...................................717 529-2522
William Dillon, *President*
Gail Dillon, *Treasurer*
Sheila Hoffmeier, *Manager*
EMP: 9
SQ FT: 15,000
SALES: 650K **Privately Held**
WEB: www.rthogg.com
SIC: 5947 2511 2531 2522 Gift shop; wood household furniture; public building & related furniture; office furniture, except wood; wood office furniture

(G-13089)
SCALE WATCHER NORTH AMER INC
345 Lincoln St (19363-1500)
PHONE...................................610 932-6888
Jan P De Baat Doelman, *President*
▲ EMP: 4
SQ FT: 4,500
SALES (est): 665.3K **Privately Held**
WEB: www.scalewatcher.com
SIC: 3589 Sewage & water treatment equipment

(G-13090)
SEITZ TECH LLC
1041 Hickory Hill Rd (19363-4218)
PHONE...................................610 268-2228
John R Seitz, *Principal*
EMP: 3
SALES (est): 408.3K **Privately Held**
SIC: 3841 Surgical & medical instruments

(G-13091)
SHELTONS PALLET COMPANY
102 Oaks Rd (19363-4014)
PHONE...................................610 932-3182
Charles Shelton, *Owner*
EMP: 30
SALES (est): 3.7MM **Privately Held**
SIC: 2448 Pallets, wood

(G-13092)
SMOKER MANUFACTURING
415 Jackson School Rd (19363-1265)
PHONE...................................717 529-6915
Isreal Smoker, *Owner*
Katie Smoker, *Co-Owner*
EMP: 6
SALES (est): 234.2K **Privately Held**
SIC: 7692 Welding repair

(G-13093)
THG/PARADIGM HEALTH INTL INC
Also Called: Thg Health Products
54 N 4th St (19363-1548)
PHONE...................................610 998-1080
Edward Harshaw, *President*
EMP: 5
SQ FT: 3,000
SALES (est): 814.4K **Privately Held**
WEB: www.eternallyfit.com
SIC: 2833 5122 Drugs & herbs: grading, grinding & milling; drugs & drug proprietaries

---

Palm
Montgomery County

(G-13094)
ELDERHORST BELLS INC
875 Gravel Pike (18070-1115)
PHONE...................................215 679-3264
Michael Elderhorst, *President*
Jay Scales, *Corp Secy*
EMP: 4
SQ FT: 5,000
SALES: 410.4K **Privately Held**
WEB: www.elderhorstbells.com
SIC: 3873 7699 3931 Watches, clocks, watchcases & parts; musical instrument repair services; carillon bells

(G-13095)
MICROPROCESS TECHNOLGIES LLC
1862 Tollgate Rd Unit D (18070-1228)
PHONE...................................570 778-0925
Charles Brown,
EMP: 6
SQ FT: 16,000
SALES: 500K **Privately Held**
WEB: www.microprocesstech.com
SIC: 3559 Semiconductor manufacturing machinery

(G-13096)
OPTOTECH OPTICAL MACHINERY INC
1862 Tollgate Rd (18070-1228)
PHONE...................................215 679-2091
Roland Mandler, *President*

Heidi Hofke, *Treasurer*
▲ EMP: 15
SQ FT: 5,000
SALES (est): 1.9MM
SALES (corp-wide): 1.2B **Privately Held**
WEB: www.optotech.de
SIC: 3829 Measuring & controlling devices
HQ: Optotech Optikmaschinen Gmbh
Lobstedter Str. 74
Jena 07749
641 982-030

(G-13097)
ZUKAY LIVE FOODS LLC
1904 Tollgate Rd (18070-1220)
P.O. Box 514, Elverson (19520-0514)
PHONE...................................610 286-3077
Scott Grzybek, *Mng Member*
William Moore,
EMP: 7
SQ FT: 5,000
SALES (est): 794.1K **Privately Held**
SIC: 2099 2035 Sauces: gravy, dressing & dip mixes; pickles, sauces & salad dressings

---

Palmer
Northampton County

(G-13098)
INNOVATIVE DESIGNS & PUBG (PA)
Also Called: Idp Association Management
3245 Freemansburg Ave (18045-7118)
PHONE...................................610 923-8000
Paul Prass, *President*
Pamela Deller, *Publisher*
Jobey Marlowe, *Vice Pres*
Lisa Prass, *Vice Pres*
Bob McKinney, *Accounts Mgr*
EMP: 25
SQ FT: 7,000
SALES: 3MM **Privately Held**
WEB: www.idpcreative.com
SIC: 2721 7336 Periodicals: publishing & printing; commercial art & graphic design

---

Palmerton
Carbon County

(G-13099)
ALLIANCE SAND CO INC
Also Called: Alliance Sand Company Office
415 Golf Rd (18071-5748)
PHONE...................................610 826-2248
Chad Shupp, *Manager*
EMP: 10
SALES (corp-wide): 1.8MM **Privately Held**
WEB: www.allpoconos.com
SIC: 1442 Construction Sand/Gravel
PA: Alliance Sand Co Inc
51 Tannery Rd
Somerville NJ 08876
908 534-4116

(G-13100)
AMPAL INC (HQ)
2115 Little Gap Rd (18071-5109)
PHONE...................................610 826-7020
K Clive Ramsey, *President*
Barry Anschutz, *Vice Pres*
John Askeland, *Vice Pres*
Rhonda Kasler, *Vice Pres*
Barry Schmutter, *Controller*
◆ EMP: 2 EST: 1966
SQ FT: 1,200
SALES (est): 9.2MM
SALES (corp-wide): 11.6MM **Privately Held**
WEB: www.ampal.net
SIC: 3399 Powder, metal
PA: United States Metal Powders Incorporated
K Clive Ramsey Bldg
Palmerton PA 18071
908 782-5454

(G-13101)
AMPAL INC
2125 Little Gap Rd (18071-5109)
PHONE...................................610 826-7020
John Askeland, *Vice Pres*
EMP: 27
SALES (corp-wide): 10.5MM **Privately Held**
WEB: www.ampal.net
SIC: 3399 Aluminum atomized powder
HQ: Ampal Inc.
2115 Little Gap Rd
Palmerton PA 18071
610 826-7020

(G-13102)
ARCHITECTURAL POLYMERS INC
Also Called: Poly Creations
1220 Little Gap Rd (18071-5028)
PHONE...................................610 824-3322
Marshall G Walters, *President*
Rick Fasching, *General Mgr*
Mark Digiamberdini, *Vice Pres*
Gil Waters, *Controller*
Kevin Schrock, *Regl Sales Mgr*
EMP: 25
SQ FT: 15,000
SALES (est): 5.7MM **Privately Held**
WEB: www.architecturalpolymers.com
SIC: 3272 Concrete products

(G-13103)
CLAUDES CREAMERY
289 Delaware Ave (18071-1812)
PHONE...................................610 826-2663
Ashley Southard, *Branch Mgr*
EMP: 9 EST: 2011
SALES (est): 460K **Privately Held**
SIC: 2052 Cones, ice cream

(G-13104)
EDWARD A SHELLY VMD
2695 Little Gap Rd (18071-5119)
PHONE...................................610 826-2793
Edward A Shelly, *Principal*
EMP: 3 EST: 2001
SALES (est): 176.9K **Privately Held**
SIC: 2834 Veterinary pharmaceutical preparations

(G-13105)
FRONTI FABRICATIONS INC
1145a Little Gap Rd (18071)
PHONE...................................610 900-6160
Joseph A Fronti Jr, *President*
Lisa L Fronti, *Treasurer*
EMP: 9
SQ FT: 17,000
SALES (est): 2.9MM **Privately Held**
SIC: 3441 Fabricated structural metal

(G-13106)
G AND H CONTRACTING INC
Also Called: G & H Contracting
316 Columbia Ave (18071-1602)
PHONE...................................610 826-7542
David R Silfies, *President*
Denise Silfies, *Treasurer*
EMP: 4
SALES (est): 476.9K **Privately Held**
SIC: 1521 1741 3281 New construction, single-family houses; masonry & other stonework; furniture, cut stone

(G-13107)
HORSEHEAD CORPORATION
Also Called: Zinc Corporation America Div
900 Delaware Ave (18071-2008)
PHONE...................................610 826-2111
Robert J Endres, *Branch Mgr*
EMP: 30 **Privately Held**
WEB: www.horseheadcorp.com
SIC: 3339 Lead & zinc
HQ: American Zinc Recycling Corp.
4955 Steubenville Pike # 405
Pittsburgh PA 15205
724 774-1020

(G-13108)
LEHIGH GAP SEAMLESS GUTTER LLC
380 Sand Quarry Rd Ste 1 (18071-5758)
PHONE...................................610 824-4888
Andy Pisulak,

EMP: 3
SALES (est): 251.2K **Privately Held**
SIC: 1761 3444 Gutter & downspout contractor; gutters, sheet metal

(G-13109)
LIBRA THREE INC
2235 Little Gap Rd (18071-5111)
PHONE..........................610 217-9992
Thomas F Kilcommons III, *President*
Christopher Kilcommons, *Vice Pres*
EMP: 4
SQ FT: 10,000
SALES: 500K **Privately Held**
SIC: 3565 Packaging machinery

(G-13110)
PENCOR SERVICES INC (PA)
Also Called: Times News, The
613 3rd Street Palmerton (18071)
P.O. Box 215 (18071-0215)
PHONE..........................610 826-2115
David Masenheimer, *President*
Avii Masenheimer, *President*
Styles S Butz, *Vice Pres*
Fred Masenheimer, *Vice Pres*
Johnathan Slanina, *Vice Pres*
EMP: 25
SQ FT: 2,000
SALES (est): 108.7MM **Privately Held**
WEB: www.pennspeak.com
SIC: 2711 7371 4813 4841 Newspapers: publishing only, not printed on site; custom computer programming communications; local & long distance telephone communications; cable television services

(G-13111)
SIKORSKY CONCRETE PRODUCT LLC
760 Little Gap Rd (18071-5018)
PHONE..........................610 826-3676
Pete Sikorsky, *Manager*
EMP: 5
SQ FT: 3,100
SALES: 1MM **Privately Held**
SIC: 3273 Ready-mixed concrete

(G-13112)
UNIMOVE LLC
1145c Little Gap Rd (18071-5050)
P.O. Box 1894, Goodlettsville TN (37070-1894)
PHONE..........................610 826-7855
Bob Shannon, *Managing Dir*
EMP: 8
SALES (est): 1.1MM **Privately Held**
SIC: 3535 Bulk handling conveyor systems

(G-13113)
UNITED STTES METAL POWDERS INC (PA)
Also Called: Royal Powdered Metals
K Clive Ramsey Bldg (18071)
PHONE..........................908 782-5454
K Clive Ramsey, *President*
Vincent J Vaccaro, *Vice Pres*
Joao Baptiste Dos Santos, *Purch Mgr*
▲ **EMP:** 18
SQ FT: 100,000
SALES (est): 11.6MM **Privately Held**
SIC: 3399 Powder, metal; brads: aluminum, brass or other nonferrous metal or wire; nails: aluminum, brass or other nonferrous metal or wire

(G-13114)
VICJAH CORPORATION
Also Called: Vics Time
450 Delaware Ave (18071-1909)
P.O. Box 75 (18071-0075)
PHONE..........................610 826-7475
Chris Jahelka, *President*
EMP: 7
SQ FT: 40,000
SALES: 690K **Privately Held**
WEB: www.vicstime.com
SIC: 2542 2522 3499 Racks, merchandise display or storage: except wood; cabinets, office: except wood; file drawer frames: except wood; aerosol valves, metal

---

Palmyra
Lebanon County

(G-13115)
AMERICAN MACHINE CO
435 N Lingle Ave (17078-9219)
PHONE..........................717 533-5678
Richard Eckert, *Owner*
EMP: 4
SALES (est): 240K **Privately Held**
SIC: 3469 7692 Machine parts, stamped or pressed metal; welding repair

(G-13116)
ARADIANT CORPORATION
101 N Harrison St (17078-1826)
PHONE..........................717 838-7220
Joseph T Burgio, *President*
Suzanne M Burgio, *President*
EMP: 8
SALES (est): 860.8K **Privately Held**
WEB: www.aradiant.biz
SIC: 8748 3555 Business consulting; printing trades machinery

(G-13117)
ASK FOODS INC (PA)
77 N Hetrick Ave (17078-1529)
P.O. Box 388 (17078-0388)
PHONE..........................717 838-6356
Wendie Dimatteo Holsinger, *CEO*
Robert B Di Matteo, *President*
Athalene J Di Matteo, *Vice Pres*
Steve Ortiz, *Purch Mgr*
Nancy Dundore, *Purch Agent*
EMP: 220 **EST:** 1947
SQ FT: 86,000
SALES (est): 59.6MM **Privately Held**
SIC: 2038 2099 Soups, frozen; salads, fresh or refrigerated

(G-13118)
ASK FOODS INC
140 N Locust St (17078-1695)
PHONE..........................717 838-6356
Dottie Engle, *Branch Mgr*
EMP: 40
SALES (corp-wide): 59.6MM **Privately Held**
SIC: 2038 2099 2035 2032 Soups, frozen; salads, fresh or refrigerated; pickles, sauces & salad dressings; canned specialties; sausages & other prepared meats
PA: Ask Foods, Inc.
77 N Hetrick Ave
Palmyra PA 17078
717 838-6356

(G-13119)
CURRY FLOUR MILLS INC
338 N Railroad St (17078-1327)
PHONE..........................717 838-2421
Ronald D Seavers, *President*
Darryl Seavers, *Treasurer*
Jody Seavers, *Admin Sec*
EMP: 14 **EST:** 1880
SQ FT: 12,000
SALES (est): 1.3MM **Privately Held**
WEB: www.curryflour.com
SIC: 2041 Flour mills, cereal (except rice)

(G-13120)
DECHERT DYNAMICS CORPORATION
713 W Main St (17078-1500)
P.O. Box 272 (17078-0272)
PHONE..........................717 838-1326
Arthur Arnold Jr, *President*
Larry Blouch, *Vice Pres*
Jim Speck, *Purch Mgr*
Susan Pankake, *Controller*
EMP: 28
SQ FT: 40,000
SALES (est): 2MM **Privately Held**
SIC: 3599 Machine shop, jobbing & repair

(G-13121)
DECHERTS MACHINE SHOP INC
713 W Main St (17078-1513)
P.O. Box 272 (17078-0272)
PHONE..........................717 838-1326
William Herr, *President*

Arthur Arnold Jr, *Vice Pres*
Bruce Miller, *Vice Pres*
EMP: 37 **EST:** 1946
SQ FT: 46,000
SALES (est): 4.1MM **Privately Held**
WEB: www.decherts.com
SIC: 3599 7692 3545 Machine shop, jobbing & repair; welding repair; machine tool accessories

(G-13122)
EARLYS BODY MACHINE & WELDING
917 N Forge Rd (17078-8408)
PHONE..........................717 838-1663
Henry J Early Jr, *Owner*
EMP: 5
SQ FT: 400
SALES (est): 220K **Privately Held**
SIC: 3441 Fabricated structural metal

(G-13123)
GALLAGHER PRINTING INC
601 W Main St Ste 3 (17078-1540)
PHONE..........................717 838-1527
Robert A Gallagher, *President*
Shirley H Gallagher, *Corp Secy*
Shirley Gallagher, *Treasurer*
EMP: 6
SQ FT: 5,000
SALES (est): 500K **Privately Held**
SIC: 2752 Commercial printing, offset

(G-13124)
GENERAL MILLS INC
350 N Lingle Ave (17078-9207)
PHONE..........................717 838-7600
Tim Carricato, *General Mgr*
Rob Morris, *Manager*
EMP: 20
SALES (corp-wide): 15.7B **Publicly Held**
WEB: www.generalmills.com
SIC: 2043 2041 Rice: prepared as cereal breakfast food; flour mixes
PA: General Mills, Inc.
1 General Mills Blvd
Minneapolis MN 55426
763 764-7600

(G-13125)
GREG SPEECE
Also Called: Gs Design
24 N Chestnut St Ste 4 (17078-1745)
P.O. Box 48 (17078-0048)
PHONE..........................717 838-8365
Greg Speece, *Owner*
EMP: 5
SQ FT: 800
SALES (est): 264.8K **Privately Held**
SIC: 7336 2759 5199 Graphic arts & related design; screen printing; art goods

(G-13126)
J & J SPECIALTIES OF PA
101 N Harrison St (17078-1826)
PHONE..........................717 838-7220
Joseph T Burgio, *President*
Suzanne M Burgio, *Vice Pres*
EMP: 16
SQ FT: 4,500
SALES (est): 2MM **Privately Held**
SIC: 3555 Printing trades machinery

(G-13127)
NK GRAPHICS INC
18 W Main St (17078-1627)
PHONE..........................717 838-8324
John Kristich, *President*
EMP: 7
SALES (est): 802.3K **Privately Held**
WEB: www.nk-graphics.com
SIC: 2396 2759 Screen printing on fabric articles; commercial printing

(G-13128)
PALMYRA BOLOGNA COMPANY (PA)
Also Called: Seltzer's Smokehouse Meats
230 N College St (17078-1697)
P.O. Box 111 (17078-0111)
PHONE..........................717 838-6336
Craig Seltzer, *President*
Peter A Stanilla Jr, *Corp Secy*
Pete Stanilla, *CFO*
Perry Smith, *Mktg Dir*
Bob Hartman, *Director*

EMP: 47 **EST:** 1902
SQ FT: 35,000
SALES: 14MM **Privately Held**
WEB: www.seltzerslebanonbologna.com
SIC: 2013 Bologna from purchased meat

(G-13129)
PHILADLPHIA MXING SLUTIONS LTD (HQ)
1221 E Main St (17078-9506)
P.O. Box 8500-2180, Philadelphia (19178-0001)
PHONE..........................717 832-2800
Larry Heck, *President*
Sean Roussel, *General Mgr*
Chris Stanton, *General Mgr*
Jeff Bradley, *Regional Mgr*
John Dillon, *Regionai Mgr*
◆ **EMP:** 100
SALES (est): 34.9MM
SALES (corp-wide): 153MM **Privately Held**
SIC: 3589 Water treatment equipment, industrial
PA: American Manufacturing Corporation
555 Croton Rd Ste 200
King Of Prussia PA 19406
610 962-3770

(G-13130)
PURCELL COMPANY
6021 Colebrook Rd (17078-8985)
P.O. Box 440, Hershey (17033-0440)
PHONE..........................717 838-5611
Milton Purcell, *President*
Keith Kobel, *Corp Secy*
Richard I Purcell, *Vice Pres*
EMP: 32
SQ FT: 40,000
SALES (est): 6.1MM **Privately Held**
SIC: 3599 3556 Custom machinery; confectionery machinery

(G-13131)
STERLING MACHINE TECH INC
220 Kreider Rd (17078-8980)
PHONE..........................717 838-1234
Gina V Herr, *President*
Randy Herr, *Vice Pres*
EMP: 35
SQ FT: 30,000
SALES (est): 6.6MM **Privately Held**
SIC: 3599 Machine shop, jobbing & repair

(G-13132)
SUE N DOUG INC
1218 E Main St (17078-9505)
PHONE..........................717 838-6341
Douglas Eiserman, *President*
EMP: 4
SALES (est): 288.3K **Privately Held**
SIC: 3949 Bowling alleys & accessories

(G-13133)
TELLUS THREE SIXTY
603 E Main St (17078-1834)
PHONE..........................717 628-1866
EMP: 20
SALES (est): 1.2MM **Privately Held**
SIC: 2426 Carvings, furniture: wood

Paoli
Chester County

(G-13134)
AMERICAN SOLDER & FLUX CO INC
28 Industrial Blvd (19301-1602)
PHONE..........................610 647-2375
James McBride, *President*
Michael Haynes, *Vice Pres*
EMP: 15 **EST:** 1967
SQ FT: 16,000
SALES (est): 1MM **Privately Held**
SIC: 2899 Mfg Chemical Preparations

(G-13135)
AMERICAN SOLDER & FLUX CO INC
28 Industrial Blvd (19301-1602)
PHONE..........................610 647-3575
James F McBride, *President*
EMP: 4

SALES (est): 330K **Privately Held**
SIC: 2899 Chemical preparations

(G-13136)
BRANSON ULTRASONICS CORP
136 W Lancaster Ave (19301-1786)
PHONE..................................610 251-9776
EMP: 41
SALES (corp-wide): 17.4B **Publicly Held**
WEB: www.bransonic.com
SIC: 3699 3548 3541 Cleaning equipment, ultrasonic, except medical & dental; welding apparatus; machine tools, metal cutting type
HQ: Branson Ultrasonics Corporation
41 Eagle Rd Ste 1
Danbury CT 06810
203 796-0400

(G-13137)
DECAL SPECIALTIES INC
37 Industrial Blvd Ste D (19301-1600)
PHONE..................................610 644-9200
John Andrews, *Principal*
▲ EMP: 3 EST: 2008
SALES (est): 229.1K **Privately Held**
SIC: 3577 Printers & plotters

(G-13138)
DEPUY SYNTHES INC
1690 Russell Rd (19301-1222)
PHONE..................................610 647-9700
Hansjoerg Wyss, *CEO*
Roderick McMillan, *Materials Mgr*
EMP: 287
SALES (corp-wide): 81.5B **Publicly Held**
SIC: 3842 3841 Surgical appliances & supplies; surgical & medical instruments
HQ: Depuy Synthes, Inc.
700 Orthopaedic Dr
Warsaw IN 46582

(G-13139)
DOLPHIN GROUP
537 Foxwood Ln (19301-2040)
PHONE..................................610 640-7513
Donna Cozzens, *Owner*
EMP: 3
SALES (est): 90K **Privately Held**
SIC: 2834 Pharmaceutical preparations

(G-13140)
FORCE INDUSTRIES INC
Also Called: American Solder and Flux
28 Industrial Blvd (19301-1602)
PHONE..................................610 647-3575
James F McBride, *President*
Michael Haynes, *Vice Pres*
Mike Haynes, *Business Dir*
▼ EMP: 15 EST: 1910
SQ FT: 16,000
SALES: 3MM **Privately Held**
WEB: www.force-industries.com
SIC: 2899 Fluxes: brazing, soldering, galvanizing & welding

(G-13141)
GRAND FINALE DESSERTS
442 Hilltop Rd (19301-1213)
PHONE..................................610 864-3824
Christin Friel, *Principal*
EMP: 4
SALES (est): 222K **Privately Held**
SIC: 2051 Bakery: wholesale or wholesale/retail combined

(G-13142)
KARDEX SYSTEMS INC (DH)
25 Industrial Blvd (19301-1601)
PHONE..................................610 296-9730
Ronald J Miller, *Chairman*
Christina Dube, *Marketing Staff*
▲ EMP: 3
SQ FT: 360,000
SALES (est): 4.9MM
SALES (corp-wide): 426MM **Privately Held**
WEB: www.kardex.com
SIC: 2542 Cabinets: show, display or storage: except wood; shelving, office & store: except wood
HQ: Kardex Remstar, Llc
41 Eisenhower Dr
Westbrook ME 04092
207 854-1861

(G-13143)
KESTONE DIGITAL PRESS
37 Industrial Blvd Ste A (19301-1600)
PHONE..................................484 318-7017
Madeline Christenson, *Owner*
EMP: 30
SALES (est): 2MM **Privately Held**
WEB: www.kdpress.com
SIC: 2752 Commercial printing, offset

(G-13144)
O & B COMMUNICATIONS
3 Paoli Plz Ste 1a (19301-1365)
PHONE..................................610 647-8585
Michael Bradley, *President*
Steven Osborne, *President*
EMP: 5
SALES (est): 588K **Privately Held**
SIC: 2721 Magazines: publishing only, not printed on site

(G-13145)
PAOLI PRINT & COPY INC
45 E Lancaster Ave (19301-1419)
PHONE..................................610 644-7471
Robert Graves, *President*
Chris Lackro, *Vice Pres*
EMP: 3
SALES (est): 444.3K **Privately Held**
WEB: www.paoliprint.com
SIC: 2752 Commercial printing, offset

(G-13146)
PENN SAUNA CORP
Also Called: Baltic Leisure
1604 E Lancaster Ave (19301-1506)
PHONE..................................610 932-5700
Mike Lombardi, *Branch Mgr*
EMP: 20
SALES (corp-wide): 6.5MM **Privately Held**
WEB: www.balticleisure.com
SIC: 2452 2084 5999 5091 Sauna rooms, prefabricated, wood; wine cellars, bonded: engaged in blending wines; sauna equipment & supplies; fitness equipment & supplies; spa equipment & supplies
PA: Penn Sauna Corp.
601 Lincoln St
Oxford PA 19363
610 932-5700

(G-13147)
PERENNIAL PLEASURES LLC
1604 E Lancaster Ave (19301-1506)
PHONE..................................484 318-8376
Martha L Naylor,
Hope D Hoffman,
EMP: 7
SQ FT: 2,100
SALES: 600K **Privately Held**
WEB: www.perennialpleasures.net
SIC: 2395 5712 Decorative & novelty stitching, for the trade; outdoor & garden furniture

(G-13148)
REAL AUTOMOTIVE PC INC
73 Chestnut Rd (19301-1502)
PHONE..................................609 876-7450
Stan Fischman, *President*
EMP: 3
SALES (est): 238.6K **Privately Held**
SIC: 3571 Electronic computers

(G-13149)
SUBURBAN AUDIOLOGY BALANCE CTR
11 Industrial Blvd # 102 (19301-1632)
PHONE..................................610 647-3710
Andrew Macielinski, *Director*
EMP: 6
SALES (est): 385.6K **Privately Held**
SIC: 5999 3842 8049 Hearing aids; hearing aids; audiologist

(G-13150)
TCG DOCUMENT SOLUTIONS LLC
Also Called: JPK Secure Healthcare Solution
16 Industrial Blvd (19301-1609)
PHONE..................................610 356-4700
EMP: 23

SALES (corp-wide): 3.1MM **Privately Held**
SIC: 2752 Commercial printing, lithographic
PA: Tcg Document Solutions, Llc
447 Veit Rd
Huntingdon Valley PA 19006
215 957-0600

(G-13151)
WHIRLED PEACE INC
111 E Lancaster Ave (19301-1421)
P.O. Box 68 (19301-0068)
PHONE..................................484 318-7735
Jesse Frank, *Owner*
EMP: 7
SALES (est): 509.6K **Privately Held**
SIC: 2026 Yogurt

Paradise
Lancaster County

(G-13152)
ALLAN MYERS INC
47 Mcilvaine Rd (17562-9604)
PHONE..................................717 442-4191
Jim Boulinger, *Manager*
EMP: 30
SALES (corp-wide): 751MM **Privately Held**
SIC: 1429 1422 Boulder, crushed & broken-quarrying; crushed & broken limestone
PA: Allan Myers, Inc
1805 Berks Rd
Worcester PA 19490
610 222-8800

(G-13153)
BARN YARD LLC
3351 Lincoln Hwy E (17562-9613)
PHONE..................................717 314-9667
Daniel Allgyer, *Partner*
Jonathan Allgyer, *Partner*
Samuel K Stoltzfus, *Partner*
EMP: 5
SQ FT: 220
SALES (est): 732.3K **Privately Held**
SIC: 2452 Prefabricated buildings, wood

(G-13154)
BELMONT FABRICS LLC
14 S Belmont Rd (17562-9642)
PHONE..................................717 768-0077
Samuel S Stoltzfus,
▲ EMP: 15
SQ FT: 15,000
SALES (est): 3.3MM **Privately Held**
SIC: 5131 5949 2392 Piece goods & other fabrics; fabric stores piece goods; sheets, fabric: made from purchased materials

(G-13155)
CREEKHILL CABINETRY
261 S Kinzer Rd (17562-9790)
PHONE..................................717 656-7438
Daniel Stoltzfus, *Owner*
EMP: 5
SALES (est): 200.2K **Privately Held**
SIC: 2434 Wood kitchen cabinets

(G-13156)
E H BEILER SAWMILL LLC
442 S Vintage Rd (17562-9734)
PHONE..................................610 593-5989
Elam Beiler, *Partner*
EMP: 14
SQ FT: 400
SALES (est): 1.4MM **Privately Held**
SIC: 2421 Sawmills & planing mills, general

(G-13157)
FOREST HILL WOODWORKING
1985 Mine Rd (17562-9726)
PHONE..................................717 806-0193
Ben Zook, *Principal*
EMP: 4
SALES (est): 353.2K **Privately Held**
SIC: 2431 Millwork

(G-13158)
FOREST RIDGE WOODWORKING
1733 Jack Russell Run (17562-9675)
PHONE..................................717 442-3191
John David Zook, *Principal*
EMP: 3
SALES (est): 300K **Privately Held**
SIC: 2431 Millwork

(G-13159)
FORK CREEK CABINS LLC
3351 Lincoln Hwy E (17562-9613)
PHONE..................................717 442-1902
Daniel Allgyer,
EMP: 13 EST: 2009
SALES (est): 616.3K **Privately Held**
SIC: 7011 3448 Tourist camps, cabins, cottages & courts; garages, portable: prefabricated metal

(G-13160)
JFS WELDING
4 Quarry Rd (17562-9400)
PHONE..................................717 687-6554
Ivan King, *Owner*
EMP: 4
SALES (est): 500K **Privately Held**
SIC: 7692 Welding repair

(G-13161)
KITCHENVIEW CUSTOM CABINETS
37 Mount Pleasant Rd (17562-9780)
PHONE..................................717 687-6740
Samuel Herschberger, *Owner*
EMP: 4
SQ FT: 1,367
SALES (est): 305K **Privately Held**
SIC: 2434 Wood kitchen cabinets

(G-13162)
LAPP LUMBER CO
1640 Mine Rd (17562-9744)
PHONE..................................717 442-4116
Jacob R Lapp, *President*
Melvin Lapp, *Corp Secy*
Jim Lapp, *Manager*
EMP: 20 EST: 1956
SQ FT: 15,000
SALES (est): 3MM **Privately Held**
WEB: www.lapplumber.com
SIC: 2421 Lumber: rough, sawed or planed

(G-13163)
UNIQUE WOOD CREATION LLC
609 Strasburg Rd (17562-9702)
PHONE..................................717 687-8843
Jacob Beiler, *Owner*
EMP: 4
SALES: 130K **Privately Held**
SIC: 3553 1751 Woodworking machinery; cabinet & finish carpentry

(G-13164)
UNIQUE WOOD CREATION LLC
609 Strasburg Rd (17562-9702)
PHONE..................................717 687-7900
Jacob Beiler Jr,
Aaron Briler,
EMP: 5
SALES: 480K **Privately Held**
SIC: 2511 3553 1751 Wood household furniture; woodworking machinery; cabinet & finish carpentry

---

Parker
Armstrong County

(G-13165)
GREAT LAKES FRAMING LLC
Also Called: Universal Forest Products
116 N River Ave (16049-8768)
PHONE..................................724 399-0220
Brent Ellenberger, *Principal*
EMP: 5
SALES (est): 444K
SALES (corp-wide): 4.4B **Publicly Held**
SIC: 2491 Wood preserving

PA: Universal Forest Products, Inc.
2801 E Beltline Ave Ne
Grand Rapids MI 49525
616 364-6161

(G-13166)
UFP EASTERN DIVISION INC
116 N River Ave (16049-8768)
PHONE...............................724 399-2992
EMP: 9
SALES (corp-wide): 4.4B Publicly Held
SIC: 2421 Building & structural materials,
wood
HQ: Ufp Eastern Division, Inc.
2801 E Beltline Ave Ne
Grand Rapids MI 49525
616 364-6161

(G-13167)
UFP PARKER LLC
116 N River Ave (16049-8768)
PHONE...............................724 399-2992
Laurie Mnnany, Principal
EMP: 9
SALES (est): 1.3MM
SALES (corp-wide): 4.4B Publicly Held
SIC: 2421 Sawmills & planing mills, general
PA: Universal Forest Products, Inc.
2801 E Beltline Ave Ne
Grand Rapids MI 49525
616 364-6161

Parker Ford
Chester County

(G-13168)
EP HENRY CORPORATION
16 Anderson Rd (19457)
PHONE...............................610 495-8533
Jack Lindberg, Superintendent
EMP: 50
SALES (corp-wide): 27.8MM Privately
Held
WEB: www.ephenry.com
SIC: 3271 3281 5211 3272 Concrete
block & brick; paving blocks, cut stone;
masonry materials & supplies; concrete
products, precast
PA: E.P. Henry Corporation
201 Park Ave
Woodbury NJ 08096
856 845-6200

(G-13169)
MACKISSIC INC
1189 Old Schuylkill Rd (19457)
P.O. Box 111 (19457-0111)
PHONE...............................610 495-7181
Richard Dhein, President
Michael Smollock, Vice Pres
Michael R Gleeson, Treasurer
Sharon Rumler, Human Res Mgr
L A Krupnick, Admin Sec
▼ EMP: 30 EST: 1947
SQ FT: 55,500
SALES (est): 7.2MM Privately Held
WEB: www.mackissic.com
SIC: 3524 Lawn & garden equipment

(G-13170)
WEST DAIRY INC
Also Called: Valley Vending
2492 Schuylkill Rd (19457)
P.O. Box 439 (19457-0439)
PHONE...............................610 495-0100
Cheryl West, President
EMP: 50
SALES (est): 8.9MM Privately Held
SIC: 3581 Automatic vending machines

Parkesburg
Chester County

(G-13171)
AMERICAN ROLL SUPPLIERS INC
186 Compass Rd (19365-2128)
PHONE...............................610 857-2988
Karen Ruppert, President
William J Price Sr, Vice Pres

EMP: 5
SQ FT: 12,000
SALES (est): 727.7K Privately Held
SIC: 3441 3444 Fabricated structural
metal; furnace casings, sheet metal

(G-13172)
BRANDYWINE QUARRY INC
151 N Church St (19365-1105)
PHONE...............................610 857-4200
Lynn Hanaway, President
EMP: 5
SQ FT: 600
SALES (est): 330K Privately Held
SIC: 3281 Stone, quarrying & processing
of own stone products

(G-13173)
DISTINCTIVE OUTDOOR SPACES LLC
101 Everett Ct (19365-2186)
P.O. Box 431, Downingtown (19335-0431)
PHONE...............................484 718-5050
Ray Moran, Mng Member
EMP: 11
SALES: 1MM Privately Held
SIC: 0781 3271 Landscape services;
blocks, concrete: landscape or retaining
wall

(G-13174)
E D WOODWORKS
215 Harry Rd (19365-1824)
PHONE...............................610 857-1465
Eli Dienner, Owner
EMP: 4
SALES (est): 206.1K Privately Held
SIC: 2499 Kitchen, bathroom & household
ware: wood; fencing, docks & other outdoor wood structural products

(G-13175)
HIGH ENERGY CORP
Lower Valley Rd (19365)
P.O. Box 308 (19365-0308)
PHONE...............................610 593-2800
George Georgopoulas, President
◆ EMP: 26 EST: 1950
SQ FT: 40,000
SALES: 5.7MM
SALES (corp-wide): 924.5MM Privately
Held
WEB: www.highenergycorp.com
SIC: 3629 3675 Capacitors & condensers;
electronic capacitors
HQ: Indel, Inc.
10 Indel Ave
Rancocas NJ 08073
609 267-9000

(G-13176)
JAN LEW TEXTILE CORP
Also Called: Comfort Care Textiles
102d Shamrock Ln (19365-2148)
PHONE...............................610 857-8050
Lewis Janicola, Principal
EMP: 60
SALES (est): 2.9MM
SALES (corp-wide): 11.9MM Privately
Held
SIC: 2399 Hand woven & crocheted products
PA: Jan Lew Textile Corp
368 Veterans Memorial Hwy # 5
Commack NY 11725
631 543-0531

(G-13177)
JONATHANS WOODCRAFT
6649 N Moscow Rd (19365-1813)
PHONE...............................610 857-1359
Jonathan Stoltzfus, Partner
EMP: 7
SQ FT: 20,000
SALES: 1MM Privately Held
SIC: 2511 Lawn furniture: wood; juvenile
furniture: wood

(G-13178)
JPMW PARTNERS LLC
Also Called: Northeast Specialty Packaging
3127 Lower Valley Rd (19365-9617)
PHONE...............................484 888-8558
Warren E Callaway,
EMP: 6

SALES (est): 367.3K Privately Held
SIC: 2041 Flour & other grain mill products

(G-13179)
MEGA ENTERPRISES INC
Also Called: Johnston Auto Body
37 E Highland Rd (19365-9550)
PHONE...............................610 380-0255
EMP: 4
SQ FT: 5,000
SALES (est): 654.5K Privately Held
SIC: 3559 Mfg Specialty Tools For Auto
Body Repair

(G-13180)
METAL FABRICATING CO
5425 W Lincoln Hwy (19365-1786)
PHONE...............................717 442-4729
Gus Shank, Owner
EMP: 4 EST: 1946
SQ FT: 11,250
SALES (est): 458.3K Privately Held
SIC: 3469 Metal stampings

(G-13181)
PATIOVA LLC
6649 N Moscow Rd (19365-1813)
PHONE...............................610 857-1359
Jason Smoker, General Mgr
Samuel Stoltzfus, Mng Member
Alex Smoker, Manager
EMP: 9
SALES (est): 351.5K Privately Held
SIC: 2421 Outdoor wood structural products

(G-13182)
PILLSBURY COMPANY LLC
Lower Valley Rd Rr 2 (19365)
P.O. Box 6a
PHONE...............................610 593-5133
EMP: 52
SALES (corp-wide): 17.9B Publicly Held
SIC: 2041 Mfg Flour/Grain Mill Prooducts
HQ: The Pillsbury Company Llc
1 General Mills Blvd
Minneapolis MN 55426

(G-13183)
VICTORY PARKESBURG
3127 Lower Valley Rd (19365-9617)
PHONE...............................610 574-4000
EMP: 3 EST: 2017
SALES (est): 185K Privately Held
SIC: 2082 Malt beverages

(G-13184)
WATERLOO STRUCTURES
3898 W Lincoln Hwy (19365-1773)
PHONE...............................610 857-2170
Paul D Zook, Partner
Marvin Zook, Partner
EMP: 3
SQ FT: 6,688
SALES (est): 340K Privately Held
WEB: www.waterloostructures.net
SIC: 2452 Prefabricated buildings, wood

(G-13185)
WAYNE ABEL REPAIRS
1934 Valley Rd (19365-2139)
PHONE...............................610 857-1708
Wayne Able, President
EMP: 4
SALES (est): 277.9K Privately Held
SIC: 3711 Motor vehicles & car bodies

Parryville
Carbon County

(G-13186)
ROCK HILL MATERIALS COMPANY
Rr 248 (18244)
P.O. Box 160 (18244-0160)
PHONE...............................610 852-2314
Dana Pico, Opers-Prdtn-Mfg
EMP: 8
SALES (est): 569K
SALES (corp-wide): 7.5MM Privately
Held
SIC: 3273 Ready-mixed concrete

PA: Rock Hill Materials Company
339 School St Ste 3
Catasauqua PA 18032
610 264-5586

Patton
Cambria County

(G-13187)
B & S BEVERAGE L L C
614 5th Ave (16668)
PHONE...............................814 674-2223
Justin Bender, Principal
EMP: 4
SALES (est): 195.4K Privately Held
SIC: 2082 Beer (alcoholic beverage)

(G-13188)
GEORGE SKEBECK
Also Called: George Skebeck Construction
146 Sugar Ln (16668-6020)
PHONE...............................814 674-8169
George Skebeck, Owner
EMP: 3
SALES (est): 189.8K Privately Held
SIC: 1542 1241 1522 Nonresidential construction; coal mining services; residential
construction

(G-13189)
ROCK RUN RECREATION AREA
1228 Saint Lawrence Rd (16668-8701)
PHONE...............................814 674-6026
Joe Lacue, President
Mike Kutruff, Office Mgr
EMP: 3
SALES (est): 189K Privately Held
SIC: 3799 7033 All terrain vehicles (ATV);
trailer parks & campsites

Paxinos
Northumberland County

(G-13190)
NATIONAL TICKET COMPANY (PA)
5562 Snydertown Rd (17860-7536)
P.O. Box 547, Shamokin (17872-0547)
PHONE...............................570 672-2900
Edward A Ludes, President
Todd Hauch, President
Edward Ludes, VP Prdtn
Chris Hager, Production
Patrick Carter, Accounts Exec
▼ EMP: 110 EST: 1905
SQ FT: 75,000
SALES (est): 30.7MM Privately Held
WEB: www.nationalticket.com
SIC: 2791 2752 2789 2759 Typesetting;
tickets, lithographed; coupons, lithographed; tags, lithographed; bookbinding
& related work; commercial printing

(G-13191)
NOVIPAX LLC
1123 W Valley Ave (17860)
P.O. Box 4 (17860-0004)
PHONE...............................570 644-0314
Skip Dressler, Branch Mgr
EMP: 32
SALES (corp-wide): 2.4B Privately Held
WEB: www.cryovac.com
SIC: 3086 Padding, foamed plastic
HQ: Novipax Llc
2215 York Rd Ste 504
Oak Brook IL 60523
630 686-2735

(G-13192)
QUIKRETE COMPANIES INC
3 Industrial Park 9 (17860)
PHONE...............................570 672-1063
Matt Osterlund, Sales Executive
Kevin Fick, Executive
EMP: 35 Privately Held
WEB: www.quikrete.com
SIC: 3272 Dry mixture concrete
HQ: The Quikrete Companies Llc
5 Concourse Pkwy Ste 1900
Atlanta GA 30328
404 634-9100

G
E
O
G
R
A
P
H
I
C

(G-13193)
SHAMROCK METERED CONCRETE INC
Also Called: Shamrock Concrete
129 Rose Dr (17860)
P.O. Box 166 (17860-0166)
PHONE..................................570 672-3223
Gary G Swank, *President*
EMP: 4
SQ FT: 276
SALES: 500K **Privately Held**
SIC: 3273 Ready-mixed concrete

(G-13194)
US WEB CONVERTING MCHY CORP
Also Called: U.S.webcon
138 Miles Rd (17860-9620)
P.O. Box 158, Catawissa (17820-0158)
PHONE..................................570 644-1401
Terry Ekope, *President*
Girard Fgretener, *Treasurer*
EMP: 19
SALES (est): 4.3MM **Privately Held**
SIC: 3826 Laser scientific & engineering instruments

Peach Bottom
Lancaster County

(G-13195)
ALLAN MYERS MANAGEMENT INC
219 Quarry Rd (17563-9405)
PHONE..................................717 548-2191
Brad Robinson, *Manager*
EMP: 15
SALES (corp-wide): 14.6MM **Privately Held**
WEB: www.dmstoltzfus.com
SIC: 1422 Limestones, ground
PA: Allan Myers Management, Inc.
330 Quarry Rd
Leola PA 17540
717 656-2411

(G-13196)
BLACK BEAR STRUCTURES INC (PA)
1865 Lancaster Pike (17563-9413)
PHONE..................................717 824-0983
Roy Zook, *President*
EMP: 25
SQ FT: 10,000
SALES (est): 2.5MM **Privately Held**
WEB: www.blackbearstructures.com
SIC: 2452 Prefabricated buildings, wood

(G-13197)
GUY SEXTON TIMBER MGMT
1148 Pilgrims Pathway (17563-9665)
PHONE..................................717 548-3422
Guy Sexton, *Owner*
EMP: 3
SALES (est): 99.3K **Privately Held**
SIC: 2411 Logging

(G-13198)
H&K GROUP INC
Penn/MD Materials
303 Quarry Rd (17563-9739)
PHONE..................................717 548-2147
Johnnie Haines, *Manager*
Tim Zimmerman, *Manager*
EMP: 13
SALES (corp-wide): 71.6MM **Privately Held**
WEB: www.hkgroup.com
SIC: 1411 Limestone, dimension-quarrying
PA: H&K Group, Inc.
2052 Lucon Rd
Skippack PA 19474
610 584-8500

(G-13199)
HILLSIDE HORSE SEW-IT
345 Little Britain Rd S (17563-9755)
PHONE..................................717 548-2293
Abner G Stoltzsus Jr, *Owner*
EMP: 9
SALES: 175K **Privately Held**
SIC: 2399 Horse blankets

(G-13200)
PEACH BOTTOM TRANSPORT LLC
2663 Robert Fulton Hwy (17563-9750)
PHONE..................................717 278-8055
Jordan A Skipper, *Owner*
EMP: 2
SALES: 175MM **Privately Held**
SIC: 2873 Fertilizers: natural (organic), except compost

(G-13201)
ROCKSOLID INSTALLATION INC
2030 Robert Fulton Hwy (17563-9629)
PHONE..................................717 548-8700
Mike Brackbill, *President*
EMP: 6
SALES (est): 869.1K **Privately Held**
SIC: 3559 Stone working machinery

(G-13202)
TINDALL VIRGIN TIMBERS CLNL WD
700 Nottingham Rd (17563-9783)
PHONE..................................717 548-2435
Rick Tindall, *President*
Kleat Tindall, *Vice Pres*
Wendy Sanders, *Office Mgr*
EMP: 3
SALES (est): 372.2K **Privately Held**
WEB: www.tindallstimbers.com
SIC: 2426 Parquet flooring, hardwood

(G-13203)
WAKEFIELD DAIRY LLC
125 Warfel Rd (17563-9518)
PHONE..................................717 548-2179
Sam Fisher, *President*
Henr R Lapp, *Treasurer*
Isaac B Stoltzfus, *Admin Sec*
EMP: 3
SQ FT: 4,500
SALES: 65K **Privately Held**
SIC: 2022 Processed cheese

(G-13204)
WAKEFIELD STEEL & WELDING LLC
Also Called: Wakefield Steel and Welding
1989 Lancaster Pike (17563-9609)
PHONE..................................717 548-2172
Jeffery Spencer, *Managing Prtnr*
Arthur Devoe,
EMP: 50
SALES (est): 1.4MM **Privately Held**
SIC: 7692 Welding repair

Peach Glen
Adams County

(G-13205)
KNOUSE FOODS COOPERATIVE INC (PA)
800 Pach Glen Idaville Rd (17375-0001)
PHONE..................................717 677-8181
Kenneth E Guise Jr, *President*
Thomas M Denisco, *Vice Pres*
Richard W Esser, *Vice Pres*
Emery C Etter Jr, *Vice Pres*
Eugene Kelly, *Vice Pres*
◆ **EMP:** 400
SALES: 281.7MM **Privately Held**
WEB: www.knouse.com
SIC: 2033 Fruits: packaged in cans, jars, etc.; fruit juices: packaged in cans, jars, etc.; fruit pie mixes & fillings: packaged in cans, jars, etc.; apple sauce: packaged in cans, jars, etc.

Peckville
Lackawanna County

(G-13206)
AUDIOLOGY & HEARING AID CENTER
1339 Main St Apt 4 (18452-2038)
PHONE..................................570 383-0500
David A Wadas, *Branch Mgr*
EMP: 4

SALES (corp-wide): 600.4K **Privately Held**
SIC: 3829 Measuring & controlling devices
PA: Audiology & Hearing Aid Center Of Wilkes Barre
34 S Main St Ste 19
Wilkes Barre PA 18701
570 822-6122

(G-13207)
CHOCOLATE CREATIONS
1520 Pennsylvania Ave (18452-2052)
PHONE..................................570 383-9931
Frank Mazzarella, *Owner*
Debbie Mazzarella, *Co-Owner*
EMP: 5
SALES (est): 434.5K **Privately Held**
SIC: 2066 Chocolate

(G-13208)
EQUIPMENT TECHNOLOGY INC (PA)
Also Called: E.T.I.
410 Cemetery St (18452-2206)
PHONE..................................570 489-8651
Ruslon J Smith, *President*
Miriam H Smith, *Treasurer*
David Smith, *Sales Mgr*
EMP: 8
SQ FT: 6,000
SALES (est): 1.7MM **Privately Held**
SIC: 3569 3599 Assembly machines, non-metalworking; machine shop, jobbing & repair

(G-13209)
GENERAL MACHINE & MFG CO
50 Pine St (18452-2220)
PHONE..................................570 383-0990
Dan Lamorte, *Owner*
EMP: 3
SALES: 92K **Privately Held**
SIC: 3544 3433 Special dies, tools, jigs & fixtures; burners, furnaces, boilers & stokers

Pen Argyl
Northampton County

(G-13210)
B J TOY COMPANY INC
Also Called: B J Toy Manufacturing Company
504 W Applegate Ave (18072-1403)
P.O. Box 58 (18072-0058)
PHONE..................................610 863-9191
Robert Antonioli, *President*
Roxann Nasatka, *Director*
▲ **EMP:** 18
SQ FT: 66,000
SALES (est): 3.3MM **Privately Held**
SIC: 3942 Stuffed toys, including animals

(G-13211)
BERKHEIMER REALTY COMPANY INC
1883 Jury Rd (18072-9652)
PHONE..................................610 588-0965
John Berkheimer, *President*
Henry Sandt, *Corp Secy*
EMP: 5
SQ FT: 1,500
SALES (est): 668.9K **Privately Held**
SALES (corp-wide): 39.8MM **Privately Held**
WEB: www.hab-inc.com
SIC: 3281 Blackboards, slate
PA: H. A. Berkheimer, Inc.
50 N 7th St
Bangor PA 18013
610 588-0965

(G-13212)
CREATIVE MANAGEMENT SVCS LLC
Also Called: Mc Square
521 W Babbitt Ave (18072-1459)
PHONE..................................610 863-1900
Mike Vant Hoogt, *Manager*
EMP: 50

SALES (corp-wide): 87.5MM **Privately Held**
SIC: 2653 3993 Display items, corrugated: made from purchased materials; signs & advertising specialties
PA: Creative Management Services, Llc
3 Alpine Ct
Chestnut Ridge NY 10977
845 578-1651

(G-13213)
DALLY SLATE COMPANY INC
500 Railroad Ave (18072)
PHONE..................................610 863-4172
John Dally Jr, *President*
EMP: 55
SALES (est): 5.2MM **Privately Held**
SIC: 3281 3229 2952 2541 Blackboards, slate; pressed & blown glass; asphalt felts & coatings; wood partitions & fixtures; hardwood veneer & plywood

(G-13214)
MONOCACY FABS INC (PA)
1122 Browntown Rd (18072-9409)
P.O. Box 475, Bethlehem (18016-0475)
PHONE..................................610 866-7311
Michael Poole, *President*
Jean Shipley, *Corp Secy*
Randolph Reinhardt, *Vice Pres*
Russell Schoenberger, *VP Mfg*
Robert Schoenberger, *Shareholder*
EMP: 55
SALES (est): 7.6MM **Privately Held**
SIC: 3441 Fabricated structural metal

(G-13215)
REAL ENGLISH FOODS INC
Also Called: Mr.pastie
10 E Bell Ave (18072-1512)
PHONE..................................610 863-9091
Linda Werkeister, *Manager*
EMP: 7
SQ FT: 5,243
SALES (corp-wide): 200K **Privately Held**
WEB: www.seniorsquare.com
SIC: 2038 Frozen specialties
PA: Real English Foods Inc
2753 Folkstone Rd
Columbus OH
614 459-3727

(G-13216)
SCOTTYS FASHION OF LEHIGHTON (PA)
315 W Pennsylvania Ave (18072-2025)
PHONE..................................610 377-3032
Neil Scott, *President*
Tighe Scott, *Vice Pres*
Amelia Scott, *Admin Sec*
▼ **EMP:** 4
SQ FT: 20,000
SALES (est): 5MM **Privately Held**
WEB: www.scottysfashions.com
SIC: 2329 Field jackets, military; bathing suits & swimwear: men's & boys'

(G-13217)
SLATE BELT PRINTERS INC
115 W Pennsylvania Ave (18072-2004)
P.O. Box 88 (18072-0088)
PHONE..................................610 863-6752
Peter Gheller, *President*
EMP: 5
SQ FT: 8,800
SALES (est): 400K **Privately Held**
SIC: 2752 Commercial printing, offset

(G-13218)
SOUL CUSTOMS METAL WORKS
320 W Main St (18072-1955)
PHONE..................................610 881-4300
David Baker, *Owner*
EMP: 4 **EST:** 2004
SQ FT: 6,000
SALES: 55K **Privately Held**
SIC: 7692 3441 Welding repair; fabricated structural metal

(G-13219)
TECHO-BLOC (NE) CORP
852 W Pennsylvania Ave (18072-2017)
PHONE..................................610 863-2300
EMP: 3 **EST:** 2013
SALES (est): 176.4K **Privately Held**
SIC: 3272 Concrete products

(G-13220)
TECHO-BLOC CORP (PA)
852 W Pennsylvania Ave (18072-2017)
PHONE..........................610 863-2300
Charles Ciccarello, *President*
Mike Nadeau, *COO*
Ambrogio Dipilato, *Vice Pres*
Nancy Larocca, *Vice Pres*
Ira Vosper, *Opers Mgr*
▲ **EMP:** 112
SALES (est): 38.6MM **Privately Held**
WEB: www.techo-bloc.com
SIC: 3271 Paving blocks, concrete; brick, concrete

Penfield
Clearfield County

(G-13221)
AWF LOGGING
1905 Hoovertown Rd (15849-6317)
PHONE..........................814 577-5070
Andrew Fiedor, *Owner*
EMP: 3 **EST:** 2012
SALES (est): 256.2K **Privately Held**
SIC: 2411 Logging

(G-13222)
NORTH STAR AGGREGATES INC
Rr 255 Box N (15849)
P.O. Box 51 (15849-0051)
PHONE..........................814 637-5599
Michael Buhler, *President*
EMP: 5
SALES: 500K **Privately Held**
SIC: 1442 Construction sand & gravel

(G-13223)
SKY HAVEN COAL INC
5510 State Park Rd (15849-4116)
PHONE..........................814 765-1665
Joseph A Owens, *President*
Gayle Ross, *Admin Sec*
Alberta Owens, *Asst Sec*
EMP: 120
SQ FT: 5,000
SALES (est): 13.1MM **Privately Held**
SIC: 1221 Strip mining, bituminous

(G-13224)
VALLEY MACHINE AND TOOL CO
48 Mill Run Rd (15849-6826)
PHONE..........................814 637-5621
David Moorhouse, *Owner*
EMP: 7
SQ FT: 2,100
SALES (est): 623.7K **Privately Held**
SIC: 3599 Machine shop, jobbing & repair

(G-13225)
WARRIOR ENERGY SERVICES CORP
10865 Bennetts Valley Hwy (15849-5401)
PHONE..........................814 637-5191
EMP: 15 **Publicly Held**
SIC: 1389 Oil field services
HQ: Warrior Energy Services Corporation
5801 Highway 90 E
Broussard LA 70518
662 329-1047

Penn
Westmoreland County

(G-13226)
A B N A INC
Also Called: Style-Rite Industries
100 Penn Ave (15675)
PHONE..........................724 527-2866
Robert Arendas, *President*
EMP: 35
SQ FT: 25,000
SALES: 5MM **Privately Held**
WEB: www.aabn.com
SIC: 3446 Architectural metalwork

(G-13227)
RAIL TRANSIT PRODUCTS INC
901 S Railroad St (15675-9228)
PHONE..........................724 527-2386
Gaynell Lerew, *President*
Richard Lerew, *Vice Pres*
James Osman, *Engineer*
David Pcsolar, *Engineer*
Pedro Delgado, *Treasurer*
EMP: 3
SQ FT: 600
SALES (est): 550K **Privately Held**
WEB: www.railtransit.com
SIC: 8711 3743 Consulting engineer; locomotives & parts

Penn Run
Indiana County

(G-13228)
JJ KENNEDY INC
8690 Route 422 Hwy E (15765-7316)
PHONE..........................724 357-9696
J Kennedy, *Principal*
EMP: 6
SALES (corp-wide): 10.8MM **Privately Held**
SIC: 3273 Ready-mixed concrete
PA: J.J Kennedy Inc
1790 Route 588
Fombell PA 16123
724 452-6260

(G-13229)
MOHNEY FABRICATING & MFG LLC
Also Called: B & R Welding & Fabricating
320 Chestnut Ridge Rd (15765-7917)
PHONE..........................724 349-6136
Doug Mohney, *CEO*
EMP: 3
SALES (est): 121K **Privately Held**
SIC: 3441 7692 Fabricated structural metal; welding repair

(G-13230)
PARAGON DEVELOPMENT CORP
4748 Route 403 Hwy N (15765-6634)
PHONE..........................724 254-1551
Gwendolyn Gresko, *President*
Edward Ratay Jr, *Vice Pres*
EMP: 10
SQ FT: 8,000
SALES (est): 985K **Privately Held**
SIC: 3021 Rubber & plastics footwear

(G-13231)
PENN RUN QUARRY SPRUCE MINE
590 Spruce Grove Rd (15765-6940)
PHONE..........................724 465-0272
Andy Cramer, *Partner*
EMP: 18 **EST:** 2007
SALES (est): 1.4MM **Privately Held**
SIC: 1423 Diorite, crushed & broken-quarrying

Penn Valley
Montgomery County

(G-13232)
A MESSINGER ARCH
1640 Oakwood Dr Apt W319 (19072-1042)
PHONE..........................610 896-7227
Alexander Messinger, *Owner*
EMP: 5
SALES (est): 229.3K **Privately Held**
SIC: 7336 3271 Art design services; architectural concrete: block, split, fluted, screen, etc.

(G-13233)
ACCURATE DIE WRKS OF PHLDLPHIA
954 Mcgomnery Ave Ste 3 (19072)
PHONE..........................610 667-9200
Allan Dranoff, *President*
Erwin Dranoff, *Vice Pres*

Minerva Dranoff, *Admin Sec*
EMP: 18
SQ FT: 5,000
SALES (est): 1.4MM **Privately Held**
SIC: 3554 Die cutting & stamping machinery, paper converting

(G-13234)
CITY SUBURBAN NEWS
857 Montgomery Ave Fl 2 (19072-1541)
P.O. Box 17, Bala Cynwyd (19004-0017)
PHONE..........................610 667-6623
Robert Klein, *Owner*
EMP: 4
SALES (est): 168.4K **Privately Held**
SIC: 2711 Commercial printing & newspaper publishing combined

(G-13235)
FAST SIGNS OF WYNNEWOOD
Also Called: Fastsigns
921 Montgomery Ave (19072-1501)
PHONE..........................484 278-4839
Louis Silverman, *Owner*
EMP: 3
SALES (est): 259.1K **Privately Held**
SIC: 3993 Signs & advertising specialties

(G-13236)
GSI
627 Moreno Rd (19072-1618)
PHONE..........................610 667-4271
George Koerner, *Principal*
EMP: 3
SALES (est): 155.6K **Privately Held**
SIC: 3699 Laser systems & equipment

(G-13237)
MARILYN COHEN DESIGNS
Also Called: Beadazzle
1121 Hillcrest Rd (19072-1223)
PHONE..........................610 664-6219
Marilyn Cohen, *Owner*
EMP: 6
SALES (est): 402.9K **Privately Held**
SIC: 3911 Jewelry, precious metal

Penndel
Bucks County

(G-13238)
ALL AMERICAN INSTALLS
422 Madison Ave (19047-7546)
PHONE..........................215 888-0046
Michael Caputo, *Owner*
EMP: 4
SALES: 950K **Privately Held**
SIC: 3651 Household audio & video equipment

(G-13239)
LANGHORNE CARPET COMPANY INC
201 W Lincoln Hwy (19047-5199)
P.O. Box 7175 (19047-7175)
PHONE..........................215 757-5155
William H Morrow, *President*
Winnifred K Morrow, *Exec VP*
William T Morrow, *Treasurer*
▲ **EMP:** 35 **EST:** 1948
SQ FT: 59,000
SALES (est): 6MM **Privately Held**
WEB: www.langhornecarpets.com
SIC: 2273 Wilton carpets; rugs, machine woven

(G-13240)
PENNSBURY ENTERPRISES INC
569 Hulmeville Ave Ste B (19047-5274)
PHONE..........................215 741-5960
Al Eggert, *President*
▲ **EMP:** 10
SQ FT: 7,500
SALES: 1.1MM **Privately Held**
WEB: www.pennsburyenterprises.com
SIC: 3949 Sporting & athletic goods

(G-13241)
PYCO LLC
600 E Lincoln Hwy (19047-2905)
PHONE..........................215 757-3704
Richard A Dovidio, *Sales Executive*
EMP: 3

SALES (est): 182.3K **Privately Held**
SIC: 3823 Thermocouples, industrial process type

(G-13242)
YOUTH SERVICES AGENCY
Also Called: Youth Services of Bucks County
120 Bellevue Ave (19047-5256)
PHONE..........................215 752-7050
Roger Dawson, *Owner*
EMP: 15
SQ FT: 2,988 **Privately Held**
SIC: 1389 Oil/Gas Field Services
PA: Youth Services Agency
79 Act Ln
Jim Thorpe PA 18229

Penns Park
Bucks County

(G-13243)
PROOFREADERS LLC
842 Durham Rd Ste 427 (18943-6000)
PHONE..........................215 295-9400
Lulu Murphy,
EMP: 5
SALES: 80K **Privately Held**
SIC: 2731 Books: publishing only

Pennsburg
Montgomery County

(G-13244)
BG INDUSTRIES LLC
1510 View Rd (18073-1725)
PHONE..........................267 374-8565
Brian Godshall, *Principal*
EMP: 3 **EST:** 2011
SALES (est): 148.2K **Privately Held**
SIC: 3999 Barber & beauty shop equipment

(G-13245)
BLESS PRECISION TOOL INC
601 Montgomery Ave (18073-1515)
PHONE..........................215 536-7836
Howard P Bless, *President*
Joan Nelson, *Office Mgr*
EMP: 20
SQ FT: 4,500
SALES (est): 3.6MM **Privately Held**
WEB: www.blessprecision.com
SIC: 3599 Machine shop, jobbing & repair

(G-13246)
CAMPANIA INTERNATIONAL INC
Also Called: Campania Imports
2452 Quakertown Rd # 100 (18073-1008)
PHONE..........................215 541-4627
Glenn Appel, *President*
Ichard M Horowitz, *Vice Pres*
Richard Frederick, *Treasurer*
Amy A Fox, *Admin Sec*
EMP: 83
SALES (est): 39.4MM
SALES (corp-wide): 353.3MM **Privately Held**
SIC: 5261 3269 Lawn ornaments; art & ornamental ware, pottery; figures: pottery, china, earthenware & stoneware
PA: R.A.F. Industries, Inc.
165 Township Line Rd # 2100
Jenkintown PA 19046
215 572-0738

(G-13247)
CROWN PRECIOUS METALS
859 Main St (18073-1601)
PHONE..........................267 923-5263
EMP: 6 **EST:** 2011
SALES (est): 547.6K **Privately Held**
SIC: 3339 Precious metals

(G-13248)
GERYVILLE EYE ASSOCIATES PC
430 Pottstown Ave (18073-1423)
PHONE..........................215 679-3500
Steven Eiss, *President*

EMP: 10
SQ FT: 2,800
SALES (est): 355.7K **Privately Held**
SIC: 8042 3851 Offices & clinics of optometrists; eyeglasses, lenses & frames

(G-13249)
IRVING K DOREMUS JR
Also Called: Doremus Kitchens
2025 Ziegler Rd (18073-2556)
PHONE...................................215 679-6653
Irving K Doremus Jr, *Owner*
Barry Doremus, *Plant Mgr*
EMP: 9 **EST:** 1965
SALES (est): 892.4K **Privately Held**
WEB: www.doremuskitchens.com
SIC: 2434 Wood kitchen cabinets

(G-13250)
MEMORY MAKERS LTD
2528 Quakertown Rd (18073-1010)
PHONE...................................215 679-3636
Christine R Werhkeiser, *President*
Pauline Schuler, *Corp Secy*
Richard Schuler, *Vice Pres*
▲ **EMP:** 24
SALES (est): 3.3MM **Privately Held**
SIC: 2759 Commercial printing

(G-13251)
N3 OCEANIC INC
Also Called: RES-Q
404 Main St (18073-1502)
PHONE...................................215 541-1073
Fred Pello, *President*
EMP: 30
SQ FT: 4,000
SALES: 9.2MM **Privately Held**
WEB: www.n3inc.com
SIC: 2869 Fatty acid esters, aminos, etc.

(G-13252)
PRECISION FILTRATION PDTS INC
Also Called: P F P
3770 Layfield Rd (18073-1950)
P.O. Box 218 (18073-0218)
PHONE...................................215 679-6645
Robert E Pepe Jr, *President*
Matt Glass, *Opers Mgr*
Sean Hogan, *Engineer*
John Ward, *Design Engr*
Allen Allison, *Controller*
EMP: 25
SQ FT: 9,000
SALES (est): 15.6MM **Privately Held**
WEB: www.precisionfiltration.com
SIC: 5085 3564 Filters, industrial; filters, air; furnaces, air conditioning equipment, etc.

(G-13253)
QUAD/GRAPHICS INC
2512 Quakertown Rd (18073-1010)
PHONE...................................215 541-2729
Sylvester Nelson, *Branch Mgr*
EMP: 404
SALES (corp-wide): 4.1B **Publicly Held**
SIC: 2752 2754 2721 Commercial printing, offset; commercial printing, gravure; magazines: publishing & printing
PA: Quad/Graphics Inc.
    N61w23044 Harrys Way
    Sussex WI 53089
    414 566-6000

(G-13254)
R A S INDUSTRIES INC
2452 Quakertown Rd # 100 (18073-1008)
PHONE...................................215 541-4627
Robert Fox, *President*
Anthony Cilio, *Vice Pres*
Joseph Cilio, *Vice Pres*
Peter C Cilio, *Vice Pres*
▲ **EMP:** 45
SALES (est): 5.9MM **Privately Held**
SIC: 5032 3269 3272 Plastering materials; pottery cooking & kitchen articles; concrete products

(G-13255)
RED HILL GRINDING WHEEL CORP
335 Dotts St (18073-1340)
PHONE...................................215 679-7964
Richard Caserta, *President*

Emma Jane Caserta, *Admin Sec*
◆ **EMP:** 23 **EST:** 1947
SQ FT: 35,000
SALES (est): 3.4MM **Privately Held**
SIC: 3291 Abrasive wheels & grindstones, not artificial

(G-13256)
REED SIGN COMPANY
1050 Main St (18073-1636)
PHONE...................................215 679-5066
Edward Reed, *Partner*
Edward T Reed, *Partner*
Robert Reed, *Partner*
Ronald Reed, *Partner*
EMP: 13
SQ FT: 8,000
SALES (est): 1.8MM **Privately Held**
WEB: www.reedsign.com
SIC: 3993 Electric signs

(G-13257)
T D LANDIS AIR FLOW DESIGN
3232 Hillegass Rd (18073-2215)
PHONE...................................215 679-4395
Tom D Landis, *Owner*
EMP: 8
SALES (est): 481.3K **Privately Held**
SIC: 3444 Ducts, sheet metal

(G-13258)
TWISTED TMBER DEADWOOD LOG INC
521 W 5th St (18073-1406)
PHONE...................................215 541-4140
Lee T Rumford, *Principal*
EMP: 3 **EST:** 2008
SALES (est): 161.6K **Privately Held**
SIC: 2411 Logging

(G-13259)
UPPER PERK ROBOTICS
1005 Jodie Ct (18073-1216)
PHONE...................................215 541-1654
EMP: 3
SALES (est): 205.5K **Privately Held**
SIC: 3131 Mfg Footwear Cut Stock

(G-13260)
UPPER PERK SHOPPERS GUIDE INC
878 Main St (18073-1602)
P.O. Box 443, Red Hill (18076-0443)
PHONE...................................215 679-4133
Paul Verna, *President*
Cathleen Verna, *Corp Secy*
EMP: 4
SQ FT: 800
SALES (est): 465K **Privately Held**
SIC: 2741 Guides: publishing only, not printed on site

(G-13261)
UPPER PERK SPORTSWEAR INC
343 Main St (18073-1315)
PHONE...................................215 541-3211
Martin Feldbruegge, *CEO*
EMP: 3 **EST:** 2000
SQ FT: 1,200
SALES (est): 252.4K **Privately Held**
WEB: www.upsportswear.com
SIC: 3949 5999 2759 7389 Team sports equipment; trophies & plaques; screen printing; embroidering of advertising on shirts, etc.

Pennsdale
Lycoming County

(G-13262)
DYNAMIC SURFC APPLICATIONS LTD
373 Village Rd (17756-7869)
PHONE...................................570 546-6041
Mike Stachowicz,
◆ **EMP:** 40
SALES (est): 9.2MM **Privately Held**
WEB: www.dsa-ltd.com
SIC: 3441 Expansion joints (structural shapes), iron or steel

Pennsylvania Furnace
Centre County

(G-13263)
HYDROFLOW PENNSYLVANIA LLC
4020 Tadpole Rd (16865-9568)
PHONE...................................814 643-7135
Matthew Berrena,
EMP: 3 **EST:** 2017
SALES (est): 122K **Privately Held**
SIC: 3589 Sewage & water treatment equipment

(G-13264)
SAM MANNINO ENTERPRISES LLC
Also Called: Lifestyle Furniture USA
191 Anaconda Dr Ste 100 (16865-9443)
PHONE...................................814 692-4100
Theodore Mannino, *Mng Member*
EMP: 21
SQ FT: 10,000
SALES (est): 1.8MM **Privately Held**
SIC: 2514 Metal household furniture

Perkasie
Bucks County

(G-13265)
ADVANCED PLASTIX INJECTION MOL
2819 Creek Rd (18944-3846)
PHONE...................................215 453-7808
Lawrence P Campbell, *President*
EMP: 11
SQ FT: 5,000
SALES: 1MM **Privately Held**
WEB: www.advancedplastix.com
SIC: 3544 Forms (molds), for foundry & plastics working machinery

(G-13266)
AQUA ENTERPRISES
311 Wyckford Dr (18944-1260)
PHONE...................................215 257-2231
Bill Poust, *Owner*
EMP: 13
SALES (est): 671.6K **Privately Held**
SIC: 1731 3365 Safety & security specialization; machinery castings, aluminum

(G-13267)
AVOX INC
Also Called: Avox Technologies
118 S 2nd St (18944-1603)
PHONE...................................267 404-2676
Raymond Bryant, *President*
Eileen Bryant, *Admin Sec*
EMP: 6
SQ FT: 2,000
SALES (est): 500K **Privately Held**
WEB: www.avoxtechnologies.com
SIC: 3825 5065 Instruments to measure electricity; electronic parts & equipment

(G-13268)
BSM ENTERPRISES COMPANY INC
311 Wyckford Dr (18944-1260)
PHONE...................................215 257-2231
William Poust, *President*
EMP: 15
SALES: 100K **Privately Held**
SIC: 3728 Military aircraft equipment & armament

(G-13269)
BUCKS COUNTY ALPACAS LLC
2736 Bedminster Rd (18944-4044)
PHONE...................................215 795-2453
Lawrence Giordano, *Principal*
EMP: 3
SALES (est): 261.9K **Privately Held**
SIC: 2231 Alpacas, mohair: woven

(G-13270)
CARSON HELICOPTERS INC
952 Blooming Glen Rd (18944-2999)
PHONE...................................215 249-3535
Franklin Carson, *President*
Clayton Carson, *Vice Pres*
Terril Zeigler Carson, *Vice Pres*
Rod Manogue, *Production*
Tammy Henderson, *CFO*
EMP: 65 **EST:** 1958
SQ FT: 158,700
SALES (est): 20.1MM **Privately Held**
WEB: www.carsonservices.com
SIC: 3728 Aircraft parts & equipment

(G-13271)
DARIA METAL FABRICATORS INC
1507 W Park Ave (18944-2148)
PHONE...................................215 453-2110
Ronald Herd Jr, *CEO*
Ronald J Herd, *Vice Pres*
Tara Grace, *Office Mgr*
▲ **EMP:** 35
SQ FT: 31,000
SALES: 5MM **Privately Held**
WEB: www.orbitmfg.com
SIC: 3444 Sheet metal specialties, not stamped

(G-13272)
DAVIS FEED OF BUCKS COUNTY
140 N 7th St (18944-1413)
P.O. Box 252 (18944-0252)
PHONE...................................215 257-2966
Allan Davis, *Owner*
EMP: 6 **EST:** 1926
SQ FT: 24,000
SALES (est): 354.4K **Privately Held**
SIC: 2048 5999 5191 Prepared feeds; feed & farm supply; animal feeds

(G-13273)
DIANE A WALTERS
615 Redwing Rd (18944-3129)
PHONE...................................215 453-0890
Diane Walters, *President*
EMP: 3
SALES (est): 120.9K **Privately Held**
SIC: 3451 Screw machine products

(G-13274)
DIVERSE SALES COMPANY INC
Also Called: DSC Label
311 Wyckford Dr (18944-1260)
P.O. Box 52, Sellersville (18960-0052)
PHONE...................................215 317-1815
Mark Poust, *President*
EMP: 4
SALES (est): 301.8K **Privately Held**
SIC: 3714 Motor vehicle parts & accessories

(G-13275)
DRAPER DBS INC
1803 N 5th St (18944-2212)
PHONE...................................215 257-3833
William Draper, *President*
Karin Trexler, *Manager*
Michael Tobin, *Supervisor*
Christine Berninger, *Technology*
EMP: 28
SALES (est): 5.4MM **Privately Held**
WEB: www.draperdbs.com
SIC: 3429 Cabinet hardware

(G-13276)
ERIC AND CHRISTOPHER LLC
410 E Walnut St Ste 5 (18944-1683)
PHONE...................................215 257-2400
Eric Fausnacht, *Mng Member*
Christopher Kline, *Mng Member*
EMP: 12
SALES (est): 1.2MM **Privately Held**
SIC: 2759 7389 5136 5023 Screen printing; sewing contractor; shirts, men's & boys'; pillowcases

(G-13277)
FROX (PA)
17 N 7th St (18944-1410)
PHONE...................................215 822-9011
Jill Strickland, *Owner*
EMP: 6

SALES (est): 1.3MM **Privately Held**
WEB: www.frox.com
SIC: 2339 Women's & misses' outerwear

(G-13278)
HART MCHNCL-LCTRCAL CONTRS INC
1200 N Ridge Rd (18944-2221)
PHONE..................................215 257-1666
Richard W Hart Jr, *President*
Nicole Hart, *Corp Secy*
Michael Tamburino, *Project Mgr*
Jeff Hart, *Mfg Staff*
EMP: 40
SQ FT: 10,400
SALES (est): 9.2MM **Privately Held**
WEB: www.hartmechanical.com
SIC: 3499 1799 Fire- or burglary-resistive products; welding on site; insulation of pipes & boilers

(G-13279)
HOLISTIC HORSE INC
84 Irish Meetinghouse Rd (18944-4204)
P.O. Box 2616, Palm City FL (34991-2616)
PHONE..................................215 249-1965
Stacey P Small, *President*
EMP: 3
SALES (est): 227K **Privately Held**
SIC: 2721 8041 Periodicals; offices & clinics of chiropractors

(G-13280)
K & K PRECISION ENTERPRISES
6109 Haring Rd (18944-4303)
PHONE..................................215 364-4120
Ken Doak, *President*
EMP: 10
SQ FT: 4,000
SALES (est): 1.2MM **Privately Held**
SIC: 3599 Machine shop, jobbing & repair

(G-13281)
L S WIMMER MACHINE CO INC
115 Ridge Ave (18944-1123)
PHONE..................................215 257-3006
Lee S Wimmer, *President*
EMP: 10
SQ FT: 6,000
SALES (est): 1.6MM **Privately Held**
SIC: 3599 Machine shop, jobbing & repair

(G-13282)
LABELCRAFT PRESS INC
304 S 4th St (18944-1822)
P.O. Box 194 (18944-0194)
PHONE..................................215 257-6368
Charles C Schmell, *President*
EMP: 4 EST: 1984
SQ FT: 2,000
SALES: 400K **Privately Held**
SIC: 2752 2759 Commercial printing, offset; letterpress printing

(G-13283)
LENAPE TOOLING INC
7 E Walnut St (18944-1631)
PHONE..................................215 257-0431
Mark Ford, *President*
Willliam Scheetz, *Admin Sec*
EMP: 11
SALES (est): 1.6MM **Privately Held**
SIC: 3365 Aluminum & aluminum-based alloy castings

(G-13284)
MERVINE CORP
Also Called: Lenape Castings
7 E Walnut St (18944-1631)
PHONE..................................215 257-0431
Michael Mervine, *President*
EMP: 12
SQ FT: 30,000
SALES (est): 1MM **Privately Held**
SIC: 3544 7699 Industrial molds; industrial equipment services

(G-13285)
MY BIBLICAL PERCEPTION LLC
2304 Applewood Ct (18944-5445)
PHONE..................................267 450-9655
Dawn Dean,
EMP: 5
SALES (est): 265.5K **Privately Held**
SIC: 5961 2741 ;

(G-13286)
NORTH PENN INDUSTRIES CORP
Also Called: North Penn Machine Works
410 E Walnut St Ste 7 (18944-1683)
PHONE..................................215 453-9775
Naomi Gutlman, *President*
EMP: 4
SQ FT: 3,300
SALES (est): 482K **Privately Held**
SIC: 3599 Machine shop, jobbing & repair

(G-13287)
PERKASIE CONTAINER CORPORATION
801 Pine St (18944-1354)
P.O. Box 171 (18944-0171)
PHONE..................................215 257-3683
E William Virtue, *President*
Bradley Virtue, *Vice Pres*
EMP: 12 EST: 1965
SQ FT: 15,500
SALES: 2MM **Privately Held**
SIC: 2653 Boxes, corrugated: made from purchased materials

(G-13288)
PERKASIE INDUSTRIES CORP
499 Constitution Ave (18944-1249)
P.O. Box 179 (18944-0179)
PHONE..................................215 257-6581
Hubert Hassinger, *CEO*
Adam Krisko, *Vice Pres*
Doug Hassinger, *Treasurer*
Jon Hendler, *Admin Sec*
EMP: 60 EST: 1950
SQ FT: 167,000
SALES (est): 10.1MM **Privately Held**
SIC: 3646 3083 Fluorescent lighting fixtures, commercial; plastic finished products, laminated

(G-13289)
PHIL SKRZAT
Also Called: Windover Fabricators
311 N 8th St Ste 1 (18944-1121)
PHONE..................................215 257-8583
Phil Skrzat, *Owner*
EMP: 3
SALES (est): 412.8K **Privately Held**
SIC: 3599 7692 Machine shop, jobbing & repair; welding repair

(G-13290)
POWER ONE INC
532 W Market St (18944-1419)
PHONE..................................267 429-0374
Michael Lughran, *President*
Dr Alex Levran, *President*
Dave Wojciechowski, *Vice Pres*
EMP: 7
SALES (est): 1.4MM **Privately Held**
SIC: 3629 Power conversion units, a.c. to d.c.: static-electric; advertising agencies; alcoholic beverage making equipment & supplies; promotional printing, lithographic

(G-13291)
RACECHAIRS LLC
312 Harriet Dr (18944-2139)
PHONE..................................267 632-5003
Ronald Hansen Jr,
EMP: 5
SALES (est): 359.3K **Privately Held**
SIC: 2531 2522 2514 Vehicle furniture; stadium furniture; office furniture, except wood; household furniture: upholstered on metal frames

(G-13292)
SHAWN HARR
Also Called: Masterpiece Kitchens
1831 Three Mile Run Rd (18944-2041)
PHONE..................................215 258-5434
Shawn Harr, *Owner*
EMP: 4
SALES (est): 457.9K **Privately Held**
SIC: 5712 2434 Cabinet work, custom; vanities, bathroom: wood

(G-13293)
SIGMA CONTROLS INC
217 S 5th St (18944-1315)
PHONE..................................215 257-3412

Les Souter, *President*
Joseph Gartner, *President*
Bob Popp, *Info Tech Mgr*
Janice Balliet, *Executive*
Gloria Gartner, *Admin Sec*
EMP: 10
SQ FT: 3,600
SALES (est): 1.7MM **Privately Held**
WEB: www.sigmacontrols.com
SIC: 3625 5084 Relays & industrial controls; industrial machinery & equipment

(G-13294)
SKY FUEL INC
501 Route 313 (18944-3788)
PHONE..................................215 257-5392
EMP: 3 EST: 2011
SALES (est): 206.9K **Privately Held**
SIC: 2869 Fuels

(G-13295)
SPECIALTY AUTOMATION INC
614 Hillcrest Dr (18944-2442)
PHONE..................................215 453-0817
Robert Ziegler, *President*
Jeffery Lapat, *Vice Pres*
EMP: 3 EST: 1999
SQ FT: 3,300
SALES (est): 430.6K **Privately Held**
WEB: www.specialtyautoinc.com
SIC: 3559 Frame straighteners, automobile (garage equipment)

(G-13296)
TMW PRODUCTS LLC
630 Broad St (18944-2806)
PHONE..................................215 997-9687
William Wampole, *Owner*
EMP: 6
SALES (est): 809.8K **Privately Held**
SIC: 2834 Pharmaceutical preparations

(G-13297)
VAN ETTEN JAMES
Also Called: James Van Etten Furn By Design
124 N 6th St (18944-1408)
PHONE..................................215 453-8228
James Van Etten, *Owner*
Jared Kulp, *General Mgr*
EMP: 6
SALES: 750K **Privately Held**
SIC: 2511 1751 Wood household furniture; cabinet & finish carpentry; cabinet building & installation

(G-13298)
WAYNE FUELING SYSTEMS
1000 E Walnut St (18944-5444)
PHONE..................................215 257-1046
EMP: 3 EST: 2014
SALES (est): 200.1K **Privately Held**
SIC: 2869 Fuels

Perkiomenville
Montgomery County

(G-13299)
ADELLO VINEYARD & WINERY LLC (PA)
21 Simmons Rd (18074-9799)
PHONE..................................610 754-0006
Domenic N Dellose,
EMP: 9
SALES (est): 1MM **Privately Held**
SIC: 2084 Wine cellars, bonded: engaged in blending wines; wines

(G-13300)
CENTECH INC
2190 Colflesh Rd (18074-9534)
PHONE..................................610 754-0720
James R Stafford, *President*
Fran Stafford, *Admin Sec*
EMP: 3
SALES: 700K **Privately Held**
WEB: www.centechwire.com
SIC: 3714 Automotive wiring harness sets

(G-13301)
HIGHWAY MATERIALS INC
Also Called: Perkiomenville Quarry
1128 Crusher Rd (18074-9303)
PHONE..................................215 234-4522

Steve Clapper, *Manager*
EMP: 25
SALES (corp-wide): 10.1MM **Privately Held**
WEB: www.highwaymaterials.com
SIC: 1429 5032 3531 2951 Trap rock, crushed & broken-quarrying; stone, crushed or broken; bituminous, cement & concrete related products & equipment; asphalt paving mixtures & blocks
PA: Highway Materials, Inc.
409 Stenton Ave
Flourtown PA 19031
610 832-8000

(G-13302)
IRVIN G TYSON & SON INC
6 Simmons Rd (18074-9756)
PHONE..................................610 754-0930
Kent D Tyson, *President*
Phillip W Tyson, *Corp Secy*
EMP: 4
SQ FT: 7,500
SALES: 452K **Privately Held**
SIC: 7694 5063 Electric motor repair; motors, electric

Perryopolis
Fayette County

(G-13303)
BULLSKIN TIPPLE COMPANY
2927 Pittsburgh Rd (15473-1005)
PHONE..................................724 628-7807
EMP: 6 EST: 2010
SALES (est): 326.4K **Privately Held**
SIC: 1221 Bituminous Coal/Lignite Surface Mining

(G-13304)
RUSS INDUSTRIAL SOLUTIONS LLC
3285 Pittsburgh Rd (15473)
P.O. Box 678 (15473-0678)
PHONE..................................724 736-2580
Eric Russell, *Mng Member*
EMP: 7
SALES (est): 2MM **Privately Held**
SIC: 3531 Construction machinery

Petrolia
Butler County

(G-13305)
INDSPEC CHEMICAL CORPORATION (HQ)
133 Main St (16050-9717)
P.O. Box 307 (16050-0307)
PHONE..................................724 756-2370
Mark Koppel, *President*
Dave Dorko, *Plant Mgr*
◆ EMP: 270
SALES (est): 82.7MM
SALES (corp-wide): 18.9B **Publicly Held**
WEB: www.indspec-chem.com
SIC: 2865 2819 Resorcinol; sodium & potassium compounds, exc. bleaches, alkalies, alum.; sodium sulfate, glauber's salt, salt cake; sodium sulfides
PA: Occidental Petroleum Corporation
5 Greenway Plz Ste 110
Houston TX 77046
713 215-7000

(G-13306)
LANXESS SOLUTIONS US INC
100 Sonneborn Ln (16050-1412)
P.O. Box 336 (16050-0336)
PHONE..................................724 756-2210
John Holloway, *Manager*
EMP: 200
SALES (corp-wide): 8.2B **Privately Held**
WEB: www.cromptoncorp.com
SIC: 2911 Petrolatums, nonmedicinal
HQ: Lanxess Solutions Us Inc.
2 Armstrong Rd Ste 101
Shelton CT 06484
203 573-2000

(G-13307)
SBN HOLDING LLC
100 Sonneborn Ln (16050-1412)
PHONE.................................724 756-2210
Mike Lopresti, *Director*
EMP: 6
SALES (est): 675.4K **Privately Held**
SIC: 2869 Industrial organic chemicals

(G-13308)
SONNEBORN LLC
100 Sonneborn Ln (16050-1412)
P.O. Box 933238, Atlanta GA (31193-3238)
PHONE.................................724 756-9337
John Holloway, *Branch Mgr*
Beth Hays, *Admin Asst*
EMP: 155
SALES (corp-wide): 17.7B **Publicly Held**
WEB: www.sonneborn.com
SIC: 2869 Industrial organic chemicals
HQ: Sonneborn, Llc
      600 Parsippany Rd Ste 100
      Parsippany NJ 07054

Phila
Philadelphia County

(G-13309)
CITYWIDE EXCLUSIVE
NEWSPPR INC
732 Federal St (19147-5113)
PHONE.................................215 467-8214
Joseph Russo, *Principal*
EMP: 4
SALES (est): 144.8K **Privately Held**
SIC: 2711 Newspapers

(G-13310)
CUTTING EDGE DOORS INC
3423 Melvale St (19134-6001)
PHONE.................................215 425-5921
Anthony Perpetua Jr, *President*
EMP: 4
SALES (est): 404.3K **Privately Held**
SIC: 3442 Metal doors; rolling doors for industrial buildings or warehouses, metal; louver doors, metal; screen doors, metal

(G-13311)
EZ SIGNS LLC
10016 Bridle Rd Fl 1 (19116-3602)
PHONE.................................866 349-5444
Igor Bykov, *Mng Member*
EMP: 3
SALES (est): 307.6K **Privately Held**
SIC: 3993 Signs & advertising specialties

(G-13312)
PST FUEL INC
413 Hendrix St (19116-2422)
PHONE.................................215 676-3545
Philip T Thomas, *President*
EMP: 3 EST: 2012
SALES (est): 257.6K **Privately Held**
SIC: 2869 Fuels

Philadelphia
Delaware County

(G-13313)
ACI TECHNOLOGIES INC
1 International Plz # 600 (19113-1510)
PHONE.................................610 362-1200
Alan J Criswell, *CEO*
Joe Stanislawczyk, *Project Mgr*
David Henry, *Manager*
Michael Czajkowski, *Director*
Susan Ward, *Admin Asst*
EMP: 50
SALES (est): 9.9MM **Privately Held**
SIC: 3672 Printed circuit boards

(G-13314)
ECOLAB INC
1 Scott Way (19113-1511)
PHONE.................................610 521-1072
EMP: 35
SALES (corp-wide): 13.8B **Publicly Held**
SIC: 2841 Mfg Soap/Other Detergents

PA: Ecolab Inc.
        1 Ecolab Pl
        Saint Paul MN 55102
        800 232-6522

(G-13315)
EMD MILLIPORE CORPORATION
1 International Plz # 300 (19113-1510)
PHONE.................................484 652-5600
Daniel Luna, *Sales Staff*
Heather Ahlborn, *Branch Mgr*
Scott Marriott, *Manager*
Doug Lehker, *Maintence Staff*
EMP: 317
SALES (corp-wide): 16.9B **Privately Held**
SIC: 3826 Liquid testing apparatus
HQ: Emd Millipore Corporation
      400 Summit Dr
      Burlington MA 01803
      781 533-6000

(G-13316)
JACOB HOLTZ COMPANY LLC
(PA)
10 Industrial Hwy Ste Ms6 (19113-2002)
PHONE.................................215 423-2800
William F Frame, *President*
James V Piraino, *Principal*
Richard M Horowitz, *Vice Pres*
Robert S Adelson, *Treasurer*
Chuck Lare, *Controller*
▲ **EMP:** 53 EST: 1949
SQ FT: 90,000
SALES (est): 8.6MM **Privately Held**
WEB: www.jacobholtz.com
SIC: 3469 3429 Metal stampings; furniture hardware

Philadelphia
Philadelphia County

(G-13317)
3D PRINTING SERVICE LLC
833 E Allegheny Ave (19134-2401)
P.O. Box 12725 (19134-0725)
PHONE.................................215 426-1510
Edward Dymowski Sr, *Principal*
Margaret Dymowski, *Co-Owner*
EMP: 5
SQ FT: 1,400
SALES (est): 400K **Privately Held**
SIC: 2752 Commercial printing, lithographic

(G-13318)
4 ELEMENTS OF LIFE LLC
2131 Fitzwater St (19146-1212)
PHONE.................................215 668-1643
Anthony West,
EMP: 3
SALES (est): 159K **Privately Held**
SIC: 2819 Mfg Industrial Inorganic Chemicals

(G-13319)
4 LIFE PROMOTIONS LLC
1210 E Palmer St (19125-3308)
PHONE.................................215 919-4985
Denise Petrella, *Mng Member*
EMP: 5
SALES (est): 482.2K **Privately Held**
SIC: 2396 2395 Screen printing on fabric articles; embroidery & art needlework

(G-13320)
549 INDUSTRIAL HOLDINGS INC
Also Called: Globe Canvas Products Company
5000 Paschall Ave (19143-5136)
PHONE.................................610 622-7211
Fax: 610 284-4323
EMP: 16
SQ FT: 16,000
SALES (est): 1.7MM
SALES (corp-wide): 17.1MM **Privately Held**
SIC: 2394 Mfg Canvas/Related Prdts
PA: D. C. Humphrys Co.
      5000 Paschall Ave
      Philadelphia PA 19143
      215 307-3363

(G-13321)
A & S MANUFACTURING CO
3246 Collins St (19134-3202)
P.O. Box 1282, Southeastern (19399-1282)
PHONE.................................888 651-6149
Steve Churchill, *Principal*
EMP: 11
SQ FT: 15,000
SALES (est): 4.1MM **Privately Held**
WEB: www.asmanufacturing.com
SIC: 3469 Metal stampings

(G-13322)
A & V WOODWORK CO
6525 Upland St (19142-1997)
PHONE.................................215 727-8832
John W Abatangelo, *President*
EMP: 10
SQ FT: 25,000
SALES (est): 1.2MM **Privately Held**
SIC: 2431 2541 Millwork; cabinets, except refrigerated: show, display, etc.: wood; shelving, office & store, wood; bar fixtures, wood

(G-13323)
A A A WELDING SERVICE INC
811 E Cayuga St (19124-3815)
PHONE.................................215 426-2240
Maurice Finnerty, *President*
John Finnerty, *Vice Pres*
EMP: 29
SQ FT: 35,000
SALES (est): 2.5MM **Privately Held**
WEB: www.aaawelding.org
SIC: 7692 Welding repair

(G-13324)
A C GENTRY INC
6631 Wyncote Ave (19138-2616)
P.O. Box 20665 (19138-0665)
PHONE.................................215 927-9948
John Green, *President*
EMP: 10
SALES (est): 1.3MM **Privately Held**
WEB: www.acgentry.com
SIC: 3444 1761 Sheet metalwork; roofing, siding & sheet metal work

(G-13325)
A C KISSLING COMPANY
574 Monastery Ave (19128-1624)
PHONE.................................215 423-4700
EMP: 12 EST: 1927
SQ FT: 10,000
SALES (est): 1.7MM **Privately Held**
SIC: 2092 Mfg Fresh/Frozen Packaged Fish

(G-13326)
A C SIGNS INC
1522 Alter St Ste 26 (19146-3104)
PHONE.................................215 465-0274
Maria Colavita, *President*
Angelo Colavita, *Treasurer*
▲ **EMP:** 4
SQ FT: 1,600
SALES (est): 343.9K **Privately Held**
SIC: 3993 Neon signs; signs, not made in custom sign painting shops

(G-13327)
A CUPCAKE WONDERLAND LLC
1620 Montrose St (19146-2012)
PHONE.................................267 324-5579
Lily Fischer, *Principal*
EMP: 4
SALES (est): 269K **Privately Held**
SIC: 2051 Bread, cake & related products

(G-13328)
A PLUS PRECIOUS METALS
6907 Torresdale Ave (19135-1905)
PHONE.................................215 821-3751
EMP: 3 EST: 2011
SALES (est): 415.4K **Privately Held**
SIC: 3339 Precious metals

(G-13329)
A WORD CONCEPTS INC
500 W Cheltenham Ave (19126-3044)
PHONE.................................215 924-2226
Joseph Kim, *President*
EMP: 6
SALES (est): 372.7K **Privately Held**
SIC: 2499 Engraved wood products

(G-13330)
A&J OPTICAL INC
8002 Frankford Ave (19136-2616)
PHONE.................................215 338-7645
Gerade E Bowden, *Admin Sec*
EMP: 3
SALES (est): 232.8K **Privately Held**
SIC: 3827 Optical instruments & lenses

(G-13331)
A-ONE ASPHALT PAVING
3716 Richmond St (19137-1414)
PHONE.................................215 658-1616
Thomas Stewart, *Owner*
EMP: 7
SALES (est): 400K **Privately Held**
SIC: 2951 Asphalt & asphaltic paving mixtures (not from refineries)

(G-13332)
AAPRYL LLC
1845 Walnut St Ste 800 (19103-4711)
PHONE.................................215 567-1100
David Andrade, *Mng Member*
EMP: 5
SALES (est): 100K **Privately Held**
SIC: 7371 7372 7389 Computer software systems analysis & design, custom; business oriented computer software; business services

(G-13333)
ABARDIA MEDIA
Also Called: Where Philadelphia
301 S 19th St Ste 1s (19103-2587)
PHONE.................................215 893-5100
Bethann Sands, *Principal*
EMP: 8
SALES (est): 559.3K **Privately Held**
SIC: 2759 Publication printing

(G-13334)
ABBEY COLOR INCORPORATED
Also Called: Abbey Products
400 E Tioga St (19134-1127)
PHONE.................................215 739-9960
Roger S Nielsen, *President*
Joe Fette, *Vice Pres*
Roseann Widmayer, *Sales Executive*
◆ **EMP:** 24 EST: 1968
SQ FT: 96,000
SALES (est): 6.7MM **Privately Held**
WEB: www.abbeycolor.com
SIC: 2865 Acid dyes, synthetic

(G-13335)
ABBI PRINT LLC
321 S 60th St (19143-1148)
P.O. Box 42109 (19101-2109)
PHONE.................................215 471-8801
Abdoulaye Coumbassa,
EMP: 5
SQ FT: 1,200
SALES (est): 684.1K **Privately Held**
SIC: 2752 Commercial printing, offset

(G-13336)
ABOVE RIM INTERNATIONAL
LLC
Also Called: Atr Int'l
1158 S 18th St (19146-2901)
PHONE.................................215 789-7893
Oliver J Adams, *Exec VP*
Jahi Ali Bey,
▼ **EMP:** 5
SALES (est): 357.9K **Privately Held**
SIC: 3446 7389 Grillwork, ornamental metal;

(G-13337)
ACC ACCOUNTING SOLUTIONS
INC
1800 Jfk Blvd Unit 300 (19103-7402)
PHONE.................................215 253-4738
EMP: 3
SALES (corp-wide): 847K **Privately Held**
SIC: 7372 Prepackaged Software Services
PA: Acc Accounting Solutions, Inc.
      535 Route 38 Ste 320
      Cherry Hill NJ 08002
      856 335-1010

GEOGRAPHIC

(G-13338)
ACCU-DECAL INC
5301 Tacony St Ste 201 (19137-2312)
PHONE.....................................215 535-0320
Kevin C Simmons, *President*
EMP: 7
SQ FT: 14,000
SALES (est): 1MM Privately Held
WEB: www.accudecal.com
SIC: 2759 Decals: printing; posters, including billboards: printing

(G-13339)
ACCUCORP PACKAGING INC
10101 Roosevelt Blvd (19154-2105)
PHONE.....................................215 673-3375
Leslie Leff, *President*
Jack Pipala, *Controller*
Ollie Selvi, *MIS Mgr*
▲ EMP: 120
SALES (est): 19.5MM Privately Held
SIC: 2834 Vitamin preparations

(G-13340)
ACME HEAT TREATING CO
4626 Hedge St (19124-3397)
PHONE.....................................215 743-8500
William Tisdale, *President*
EMP: 10 EST: 1955
SQ FT: 750
SALES (est): 1.6MM Privately Held
SIC: 3398 Brazing (hardening) of metal

(G-13341)
ACME MARKETS INC
6640 Oxford Ave (19111-4795)
PHONE.....................................215 725-9310
Greg Gallager, *Manager*
EMP: 165
SALES (corp-wide): 59.9B Privately Held
WEB: www.acmemarkets.com
SIC: 5411 2051 Supermarkets, chain;
bread, cake & related products
HQ: Acme Markets, Inc.
75 Valley Stream Pkwy # 100
Malvern PA 19355
610 889-4000

(G-13342)
ACORN COMPANY (PA)
4555 Tacony St (19124-4135)
PHONE.....................................215 743-6100
Rita Diantonio, *President*
▲ EMP: 16 EST: 1925
SQ FT: 25,000
SALES (est): 1.9MM Privately Held
SIC: 2752 Lithographing on metal; commercial printing, offset

(G-13343)
ADAMS GRAPHICS INC
211 N 13th St Fl 9 (19107-1608)
PHONE.....................................215 751-1114
David Adams, *President*
EMP: 7
SQ FT: 6,000
SALES (est): 1MM Privately Held
WEB: www.assemblage.com
SIC: 7336 2791 Graphic arts & related design; typographic composition, for the printing trade

(G-13344)
ADDISON BAKING COMPANY (PA)
Also Called: Moishe's Addison Bakery
10865 Bustleton Ave (19116-3301)
PHONE.....................................215 464-8055
Marvin Novick, *President*
Dorothy Novick, *Vice Pres*
Jim Novick, *Vice Pres*
EMP: 50 EST: 1960
SQ FT: 3,800
SALES (est): 3.2MM Privately Held
SIC: 5461 5149 2051 Retail Bakery Whol Groceries Mfg Bread/Related Prdts

(G-13345)
ADELPHIA STEEL EQP CO INC
6218 Gillespie St (19135-3215)
PHONE.....................................800 865-8211
Richard Berkenstock, *President*
Anthony F Visco Jr, *Chairman*
John J Vogel, *Vice Pres*
Richard Schnurpfiel, *Admin Sec*

EMP: 50 EST: 1934
SQ FT: 33,000
SALES (est): 7.3MM Privately Held
WEB: www.adelphiafurniture.com
SIC: 2522 2542 Office furniture, except wood; partitions & fixtures, except wood

(G-13346)
ADRENALATION INC
Also Called: Edas Premium Hard Candies
4900 N 20th St (19144-2402)
P.O. Box 48099 (19144-8099)
PHONE.....................................215 324-3412
Brian Berry, *President*
Andrew Adler, *Vice Pres*
Kevin Berry, *Treasurer*
EMP: 10 EST: 1957
SQ FT: 20,000
SALES: 1.4MM Privately Held
SIC: 2064 Lozenges, candy (non-medicated)

(G-13347)
ADVANCED SPORTS INC (DH)
Also Called: Advanced Sports International
10940 Dutton Rd (19154-3208)
PHONE.....................................215 824-3854
EMP: 70
SQ FT: 5,000
SALES (est): 15.7MM
SALES (corp-wide): 142.7MM Privately Held
SIC: 3751 Mfg Motorcycles/Bicycles
HQ: Advanced Sports Enterprises, Inc.
1 Performance Way
Chapel Hill NC 27517
919 933-9113

(G-13348)
ADVANCED VSR TECHNOLOGY
3615 Emerald St (19134-1503)
PHONE.....................................215 366-3315
Bruce Klauba, *President*
Ann Favarella, *CFO*
EMP: 4
SQ FT: 1,500
SALES (est): 491K Privately Held
SIC: 3599 8711 Custom machinery; mechanical engineering

(G-13349)
ADVANSIX INC
Also Called: Advansix Frankford Plant
2501 Margaret St (19137)
PHONE.....................................215 533-3000
Edward Koehler, *Engineer*
Bill Simmons, *Manager*
EMP: 216
SALES (corp-wide): 1.5B Publicly Held
SIC: 2821 5162 Plastics materials & resins; resins
PA: Advansix Inc.
300 Kimball Dr Ste 101
Parsippany NJ 07054
973 526-1800

(G-13350)
AECO INC
4923 Arendell Ave 25 (19114-4024)
PHONE.....................................215 335-2974
EMP: 6
SALES (est): 1.1MM Privately Held
SIC: 3471 Plating/Polishing Service

(G-13351)
AFCA COMPANY INC
Also Called: A A A Awning Company
2901 Hedley St (19137-1920)
PHONE.....................................215 425-2300
Len Dolkiewicz, *President*
Diane Dolkiewicz, *Corp Secy*
EMP: 20
SQ FT: 12,000
SALES (est): 1.7MM Privately Held
WEB: www.aaaawning.com
SIC: 3444 3089 Awnings, sheet metal; awnings, fiberglass & plastic combination

(G-13352)
AFFORDABLE SIGNS CO INC
Also Called: All State Signs
9986 Gantry Rd Ste 2 (19115-1002)
PHONE.....................................215 671-0646
Dmitry Kipervas, *President*
▲ EMP: 10
SQ FT: 3,800

SALES: 250K Privately Held
SIC: 3993 Electric signs

(G-13353)
AFRICAN CULTURAL ART FORUM LLC
221 S 52nd St (19139-4107)
PHONE.....................................215 476-0680
Sharif Abdur- Rahim,
Rashid Abdul- Samad,
EMP: 5
SALES (est): 510K Privately Held
SIC: 2899 Incense

(G-13354)
AGAS MFG INC
Also Called: A.G.A.S. Flags
2701 E Tioga St (19134-6123)
PHONE.....................................212 777-1178
Toll Free:.....................................866 -
Eli Salpeter, *President*
Ariel Davidson, *Corp Secy*
Eyal Greenberg, *Vice Pres*
Jordan Shalit, *Marketing Staff*
◆ EMP: 33
SQ FT: 30,000
SALES (est): 4.4MM Privately Held
WEB: www.agasmfg.com
SIC: 2399 Flags, fabric

(G-13355)
AGILESWITCH LLC
2002 Ludlow St Fl 2 (19103-3344)
PHONE.....................................484 483-3256
Rob Weber, *CEO*
Albert Charpentier, *CTO*
EMP: 15
SALES (est): 2.5MM Privately Held
SIC: 3612 Transformers, except electric

(G-13356)
AGROFRESH SOLUTIONS INC (PA)
510-530 Wlnut St Ste 1350 (19106)
PHONE.....................................267 317-9139
Jordi Ferre, *CEO*
Nance K Dicciani, *Ch of Bd*
Thomas Ermi, *Vice Pres*
Paul Nselel, *Vice Pres*
Peter Vriends, *Vice Pres*
EMP: 5
SQ FT: 11,200
SALES: 178.7MM Publicly Held
SIC: 2869 Industrial organic chemicals

(G-13357)
AGUSTAWESTLAND TILT-ROTOR LLC
Also Called: Agusta Westland
3076 Red Lion Rd (19114-1126)
PHONE.....................................215 281-1400
Vivian Berrios, *Principal*
EMP: 11
SALES (est): 1.7MM Privately Held
SIC: 3621 Rotors, for motors

(G-13358)
AGUSTWSTLAND PHILADELPHIA CORP (DH)
3050 Red Lion Rd (19114-1128)
PHONE.....................................215 281-1400
William Hunt, *CEO*
Robert J Budica, *President*
Louis Bartolotta, *Exec VP*
Giovanni Cecchelli, *Vice Pres*
Vincent Genovese, *Vice Pres*
◆ EMP: 90
SQ FT: 70,000
SALES (est): 114.8MM
SALES (corp-wide): 9.2B Privately Held
WEB: www.agustawestland.com
SIC: 3721 5088 Helicopters; aeronautical equipment & supplies
HQ: Agustawestland Spa
Via Sardegna 38/9-10
Roma RM
063 210-833

(G-13359)
AIRCON FILTER SALES & SVC CO
Also Called: Aircon Filter Manufacturing Co
441 Green St (19123-2810)
PHONE.....................................215 922-7727
Leon Schwartz, *President*

▲ EMP: 45
SQ FT: 33,000
SALES (est): 8.5MM Privately Held
SIC: 3564 Air cleaning systems

(G-13360)
AKAMARA THERAPEUTICS INC
3411 Chestnut St Apt 602 (19104-5521)
PHONE.....................................617 888-9191
Monideepa Roy, *CEO*
Shiladitya Sengupta, *President*
EMP: 3
SQ FT: 2,000
SALES (est): 123.2K Privately Held
SIC: 2834 Pharmaceutical preparations

(G-13361)
AL DIA NEWSPAPER INC
1835 Market St Ste 450 (19103-2939)
PHONE.....................................215 569-4666
Hernan Guaracao, *President*
EMP: 10 EST: 1983
SALES (est): 707.3K Privately Held
WEB: www.aldiainc.com
SIC: 2711 Newspapers, publishing & printing

(G-13362)
ALFRED ENVELOPE COMPANY INC
3536 N Mascher St (19140-4632)
P.O. Box 46849 (19160-6849)
PHONE.....................................215 739-1500
Owen A Comer, *President*
Linda S Comer, *Corp Secy*
EMP: 12
SQ FT: 22,500
SALES: 950K Privately Held
WEB: www.alfredenvelope.com
SIC: 2752 2675 Commercial printing, offset; folders, filing, die-cut: made from purchased materials

(G-13363)
ALFREDS VILLAGE BEVERAGE INC
Also Called: Alfred's Beverage
9218 Ashton Rd (19114-3408)
PHONE.....................................215 676-2537
Linda Giannone, *President*
Fred J Mayer, *Corp Secy*
EMP: 4
SQ FT: 1,800
SALES (est): 750K Privately Held
SIC: 5921 2086 Beer (packaged); bottled & canned soft drinks

(G-13364)
ALGORHYTHM DIAGNOSTICS LLC
1125 E Columbia Ave # 201 (19125-4222)
PHONE.....................................312 813-2959
Matthew Odell, *CEO*
EMP: 4
SALES (est): 98.3K Privately Held
SIC: 7372 Application computer software

(G-13365)
ALL STAR PEST SERVCIES LLC
4351 N Marshall St (19140-2317)
P.O. Box 46466 (19160-6466)
PHONE.....................................215 828-9099
EMP: 3 EST: 2009
SALES: 127K Privately Held
SIC: 2879 Pest Services

(G-13366)
ALLEGHENY IRON & METAL CO
2200 Adams Ave Rear (19124-4794)
PHONE.....................................215 743-7759
Charles Dolaway, *President*
Donald Dolaway, *Exec VP*
Harry K Dolaway, *Vice Pres*
EMP: 40
SQ FT: 80,000
SALES (est): 18.7MM Privately Held
SIC: 5093 4953 3341 3312 Ferrous metal scrap & waste; refuse systems; secondary nonferrous metals; blast furnaces & steel mills

(G-13367)
ALLEN L GEISER & SON INC
3237 Amber St Ste 2 (19134-3227)
PHONE.....................................215 426-0211

EMP: 12
SQ FT: 14,000
SALES (est): 1.1MM **Privately Held**
SIC: 2789 Bookbinding/Related Work

(G-13368)
ALLIANCE REMANUFACTURING INC
Also Called: Alliance Surface Technologies
620 E Erie Ave (19134-1209)
P.O. Box 1127, Willow Grove (19090-0827)
PHONE.................................215 291-4640
Roger Tarno, President
▲ EMP: 130
SQ FT: 43,000
SALES (est): 26.1MM **Privately Held**
WEB: www.alliancedet.com
SIC: 3593 3714 Fluid power cylinders & actuators; motor vehicle parts & accessories

(G-13369)
ALLIED TUBE & CONDUIT CORP
11350 Norcom Rd (19154-2399)
PHONE.................................215 676-6464
Steve Norvilas, Manager
EMP: 286
SQ FT: 40,000 **Publicly Held**
WEB: www.alliedtube.com
SIC: 4225 3694 3317 General warehousing; engine electrical equipment; steel pipe & tubes
HQ: Allied Tube & Conduit Corporation
16100 Lathrop Ave
Harvey IL 60426
708 339-1610

(G-13370)
ALM MEDIA LLC
Pennsylvania Law Weekly
1617 Jf Kennedy Blvd # 1750
(19103-1854)
PHONE.................................215 557-2300
David Umfer, Prdtn Dir
John Mason, Manager
Brian Harris, Info Tech Dir
EMP: 50
SALES (corp-wide): 176.1MM **Privately Held**
WEB: www.dailybusinessreview.com
SIC: 2754 2711 Commercial printing, gravure; newspapers
HQ: Alm Media, Llc
150 E 42nd St
New York NY 10017
212 457-9400

(G-13371)
ALMI GROUP INC
5419 N Mascher St (19120-2907)
PHONE.................................215 987-5768
Alexander Lev, President
EMP: 5
SALES (est): 282.7K **Privately Held**
SIC: 2038 Ethnic foods, frozen

(G-13372)
ALPHASOURCE INC
Also Called: Alphasrce Phldelphia Wiper Sup
4837-49 N Stenton Ave (19144)
P.O. Box 12250 (19144-0350)
PHONE.................................215 844-6470
Andrea U Bookbinder, President
Brian C Bookbinder, Treasurer
Margie Litton, Accounts Mgr
▲ EMP: 12
SQ FT: 67,000
SALES (est): 2.9MM **Privately Held**
WEB: www.alphasourceintl.com
SIC: 2299 5085 5093 Broadwoven fabrics: linen, jute, hemp & ramie; commercial containers; scrap & waste materials

(G-13373)
ALTOMARE PRECAST INC
Also Called: Altomare Construction
4300 Wissahickon Ave (19129-1298)
PHONE.................................215 225-8800
Phillip N Altomare, President
Michael Finn, Plant Mgr
John Giorgio, Project Mgr
Anthony Zeltner, Project Mgr
Mark Altomare, Opers Mgr
EMP: 13 EST: 1937
SQ FT: 10,000

SALES (est): 2.1MM **Privately Held**
SIC: 1623 3272 Manhole construction; concrete products; manhole covers or frames, concrete

(G-13374)
ALTUS GROUP INC
211 N 13th St Ste 802 (19107-1609)
P.O. Box 2630 (19130-0630)
PHONE.................................215 977-9900
David J Jefferys, President
Tamie Sortman, Vice Pres
EMP: 14
SQ FT: 4,500
SALES (est): 2MM **Privately Held**
WEB: www.altus-group.com
SIC: 7311 7336 2759 6411 Advertising agencies; graphic arts & related design; commercial printing; insurance agents, brokers & service

(G-13375)
AMBITION - THE FUEL FOR SCESS
1429 N 5th St (19122-3601)
PHONE.................................215 668-9561
Sean Reed, Principal
EMP: 4 EST: 2007
SALES (est): 242.3K **Privately Held**
SIC: 2869 Fuels

(G-13376)
AMCO BISCUIT DISTRIBUTORS INC (PA)
1717 S 26th St Ste 29 (19145-1700)
PHONE.................................215 467-8775
George Lutz, President
Candy Delrosey, Vice Pres
EMP: 10
SQ FT: 27,000
SALES (est): 1MM **Privately Held**
SIC: 2052 Biscuits, dry

(G-13377)
AMD GRAPHICS INC
Also Called: Print 'n Copy Center
10300 Drummond Rd Fl 2 (19154-3804)
PHONE.................................215 728-8600
Sherree Cobb, President
EMP: 6
SQ FT: 4,000
SALES (est): 950K **Privately Held**
SIC: 2752 Commercial printing, offset

(G-13378)
AMERICAN ASSOCIATION FOR CANCE
Also Called: Aacr
615 Chestnut St Fl 17 (19106-4406)
PHONE.................................215 440-9300
Margaret Foti, CEO
Micheal Stewart, President
CHI V Dang, Bd of Directors
EMP: 100
SQ FT: 49,000
SALES (est): 78.9MM **Privately Held**
SIC: 8621 2721 Health association; periodicals

(G-13379)
AMERICAN BIBLE SOCIETY (PA)
Also Called: ABS
101 N Indpdnc Mall E 8f (19106-2112)
PHONE.................................212 408-1200
Roy L Peterson, President
Robert L Briggs, Exec VP
Steve King, Exec VP
Julia A Oliver, CFO
Don P Cavanaugh, Admin Sec
◆ EMP: 145 EST: 1816
SQ FT: 120,000
SALES (est): 101.8MM **Privately Held**
SIC: 2731 8661 Books: publishing only; religious organizations

(G-13380)
AMERICAN CABLE COMPANY
1200 E Erie Ave (19124-5526)
P.O. Box 46827 (19160-6827)
PHONE.................................215 456-0700
Carlos M Gonzalez Jr, President
Matthew Tretter, Plant Mgr
Oleg Pogsky, Facilities Mgr
Sophio Shelia, Purch Agent
Thomas Duden, Asst Controller

▲ EMP: 59
SQ FT: 100,000
SALES: 8.6MM **Privately Held**
SIC: 3679 Harness assemblies for electronic use: wire or cable

(G-13381)
AMERICAN CABLE SYSTEMS LLC
1200 E Erie Ave (19124-5526)
PHONE.................................215 456-0700
Carlos Gonzalez Jr,
Carlos M Gonzalez,
EMP: 5
SALES (est): 621.9K **Privately Held**
SIC: 3714 Booster (jump-start) cables, automotive

(G-13382)
AMERICAN CALENDAR INC
2080 Wheatsheaf Ln 1a (19124-5031)
PHONE.................................215 743-3834
Rita Ciatonio, President
EMP: 16
SALES (est): 1.1MM
SALES (corp-wide): 1.9MM **Privately Held**
WEB: www.americancalendar.com
SIC: 5199 2759 2752 Advertising specialties; commercial printing; commercial printing, lithographic
PA: The Acorn Company
4555 Tacony St
Philadelphia PA 19124
215 743-6100

(G-13383)
AMERICAN CHIEF COMPANY
104 Tomlinson Rd (19116-3116)
PHONE.................................267 984-8852
Pogoretsky Anatoly, Owner
EMP: 3
SALES (est): 104.6K **Privately Held**
SIC: 2711 Newspapers

(G-13384)
AMERICAN CLLEGE PHYSICIANS INC (PA)
190 N Independence Mall W (19106-1554)
PHONE.................................215 351-2400
Darilyn Moyer, CEO
Yul D Ehnes MD, Ch of Bd
Thomas McCabe, Publisher
April Oeffler, General Mgr
Jennifer Kearney-Strouse, Editor
EMP: 300 EST: 1915
SQ FT: 322,000
SALES: 74.2MM **Privately Held**
WEB: www.ohacep.org
SIC: 8621 2721 Health association; trade journals: publishing only, not printed on site

(G-13385)
AMERICAN LAW INSTITUTE (PA)
Also Called: ALI-CLE
4025 Chestnut St Fl 5 (19104-3099)
PHONE.................................215 243-1600
Julie Scribner, CFO
Sarah Kuhn, Controller
Louis Moravec, Controller
Debbie Foley, Accounting Mgr
David Kicinski, Accountant
EMP: 83
SALES: 18.9MM **Privately Held**
SIC: 8621 2721 8111 2731 Medical field-related associations; magazines: publishing only, not printed on site; specialized law offices, attorneys; book publishing

(G-13386)
AMERICAN METAL & RUBBER INC
2545 N Broad St (19132-4014)
PHONE.................................215 225-3700
Harold Burgis, President
Julie Cepele, Exec Sec
▲ EMP: 15
SQ FT: 50,000
SALES: 2MM **Privately Held**
SIC: 3052 3399 Rubber & plastics hose & beltings; metal powders, pastes & flakes

(G-13387)
AMERICAN PAPER PRODUCTS OF PHI (PA)
Also Called: American Paper Tube Encore
2113 E Rush St 25 (19134-3910)
PHONE.................................215 739-5718
Ray Gerber, President
David Perelman, Treasurer
EMP: 3
SQ FT: 25,000
SALES (est): 7.1MM **Privately Held**
WEB: www.americanpaperproducts.com
SIC: 2655 Fiber shipping & mailing containers

(G-13388)
AMERICAN PROVEN PRODUCTS LLC
2000 S College Ave Ste 2 (19121-4812)
PHONE.................................215 876-5274
Vincent Curtis,
EMP: 3
SQ FT: 1,800
SALES (est): 172.9K **Privately Held**
SIC: 3841 Surgical & medical instruments

(G-13389)
ANALYTIC PLASTIC INC
8000 State Rd (19136-2909)
PHONE.................................215 638-7505
John Bobko, President
Hubert Pohl, Vice Pres
EMP: 30
SQ FT: 1,350
SALES: 2MM **Privately Held**
SIC: 3089 Plastic containers, except foam

(G-13390)
ANDORRA SALAD INC
8500 Henry Ave (19128-2111)
PHONE.................................215 482-5750
EMP: 3
SALES (est): 155.4K **Privately Held**
SIC: 2099 Salads, fresh or refrigerated

(G-13391)
ANDREW H LAWSON CO
2927 W Thompson St (19121-4547)
P.O. Box 308, Conshohocken (19428-0308)
PHONE.................................215 235-1609
Edward J Mitchell Sr, President
William F Wilson, Corp Secy
EMP: 6
SALES (est): 657.1K **Privately Held**
SIC: 2752 Lithographing on metal

(G-13392)
ANGEL COLON
Also Called: A C Rebuilders
4309 Rising Sun Ave (19140-2719)
P.O. Box 46676 (19160-6676)
PHONE.................................215 455-4000
Angel Colon, Owner
EMP: 4
SALES: 200K **Privately Held**
SIC: 3465 3714 Automotive stampings; motor vehicle parts & accessories

(G-13393)
ANITAS VEGAN KITCHEN
4500 Worth St Ste B101 (19124-3470)
PHONE.................................786 512-1428
Mauricio Mendez, Owner
EMP: 6
SQ FT: 2,000
SALES (est): 326.3K **Privately Held**
SIC: 2032 Ethnic foods: canned, jarred, etc.

(G-13394)
ANTHONY COCCO INC
529 Spring Garden St (19123-2820)
PHONE.................................215 629-4100
Anthony Cocco Jr, President
Richard Saltz, Treasurer
EMP: 7
SALES: 180K **Privately Held**
SIC: 7641 2512 Furniture refinishing; upholstered household furniture

(G-13395)
ANTHONY DS DAILY NUMBERS
2617 Lefevre St (19137-1730)
PHONE.................................215 537-0618

▲ = Import ▼=Export
◆ =Import/Export

Frank A Disalvo Jr, *Owner*
EMP: 4
SALES (est): 205.8K **Privately Held**
SIC: 2711 Newspapers, publishing & printing

(G-13396)
ANTONIO COLELLA CEMENT WORK
1414 Disston St (19111-4504)
PHONE...............................215 745-2951
Antonio Colella, *President*
EMP: 5
SALES (est): 453.8K **Privately Held**
SIC: 3241 Cement, hydraulic

(G-13397)
ANVIL IRON WORKS INC (PA)
1022 Washington Ave 26 (19147-3834)
PHONE...............................215 468-8300
William C Natoli III, *President*
EMP: 7 EST: 1952
SQ FT: 70,000
SALES (est): 882.9K **Privately Held**
SIC: 3446 3441 1791 Architectural metalwork; fabricated structural metal; iron work, structural

(G-13398)
APEX FOUNTAIN SALES INC
1140 N American St (19123-1514)
P.O. Box 51281 (19115-0281)
PHONE...............................215 627-4526
Abe Weinberg, *President*
Oren Weinberg, *Sales Associate*
EMP: 7
SQ FT: 20,000
SALES (est): 1.2MM **Privately Held**
SIC: 3585 Soda fountains, parts & accessories

(G-13399)
API TECHNOLOGIES CORP
Also Called: Spectrum Microwave
2707 Black Lake Pl (19154-1008)
PHONE...............................215 464-4000
Dick Soughworth, *Branch Mgr*
EMP: 9
SALES (corp-wide): 333.6MM **Privately Held**
SIC: 3677 Electronic transformers
HQ: Api Technologies Corp.
    400 Nickerson Rd Ste 1
    Marlborough MA 01752

(G-13400)
APPAREL MACHINERY & SUPPLY CO
1836 E Ontario St (19134-2098)
PHONE...............................215 634-2626
David Bachrach, *President*
Lee Boardman, *Vice Pres*
Maria Martinez, *Purchasing*
Sam Green, *CFO*
◆ EMP: 25
SQ FT: 103,000
SALES (est): 11.4MM **Privately Held**
WEB: www.apparelmachinery.com
SIC: 5084 5085 3582 Textile machinery & equipment; industrial supplies; commercial laundry equipment

(G-13401)
APR SUPPLY CO
462 N 4th St (19123-4126)
PHONE...............................215 592-1935
Joe Fernando, *Principal*
EMP: 6
SALES (corp-wide): 63MM **Privately Held**
SIC: 5074 3432 Plumbing fittings & supplies; plumbing fixture fittings & trim
PA: Apr Supply Co.
    749 Guilford St
    Lebanon PA 17046
    717 274-5999

(G-13402)
AR SCIENTIFIC INC (HQ)
1100 Orthodox St (19124-3168)
PHONE...............................215 288-6500
Richard Roberts, *CEO*
Dwight D Hanshew Jr, *Senior VP*
GP S Sachdeva, *Info Tech Mgr*
EMP: 7

SALES (est): 22.3MM
SALES (corp-wide): 1.1B **Privately Held**
SIC: 5122 2834 Pharmaceuticals; pharmaceutical preparations
PA: Sun Pharmaceutical Industries Limited
    Sun House, Plot No. 201 B/1, Western
    Express Highway,
    Mumbai MH 40006
    224 324-4324

(G-13403)
AR SCIENTIFIC INC
7722 Dungan Rd (19111-2733)
PHONE...............................215 807-1312
Jack Beattie, *Manager*
EMP: 3
SALES (corp-wide): 1.1B **Privately Held**
SIC: 5122 Drugs, proprietaries & sundries; pharmaceutical preparations
HQ: Ar Scientific, Inc.
    1100 Orthodox St
    Philadelphia PA 19124
    215 288-6500

(G-13404)
AR TART LLC
Also Called: Gentle Giant Brewing Co
8229 Germantown Ave Ste D (19118-3446)
PHONE...............................267 408-6507
Nick Gunderson, *Partner*
Lindsey Pete, *Partner*
EMP: 6 EST: 2015
SALES (est): 327.9K **Privately Held**
SIC: 2082 Malt beverages

(G-13405)
ARAMARK SERVICES INC
1101 Market St Ste 45 (19107-2988)
PHONE...............................800 999-8989
Kasey Schluterman, *Marketing Staff*
Nena Shomler, *Marketing Staff*
Tabitha Prestler, *Branch Mgr*
David Porrini, *Info Tech Mgr*
EMP: 11 **Publicly Held**
SIC: 2329 Men's & boys' sportswear & athletic clothing
HQ: Aramark Services, Inc.
    2400 Market St Ste 600
    Philadelphia PA 19103
    215 238-3000

(G-13406)
ARAMARK UNF CREER AP GROUP INC (DH)
1101 Market St Ste 45 (19107-2934)
PHONE...............................215 238-3000
Eric J Foss, *President*
Dale Hill, *General Mgr*
Chris Scherrer, *General Mgr*
Jeff Spencer, *General Mgr*
Stephen Donly, *Principal*
◆ EMP: 1300
SALES (est): 1.5B **Publicly Held**
SIC: 2337 2311 5699 5961 Uniforms, except athletic: women's, misses' & juniors'; men's & boys' uniforms; uniforms & work clothing; uniforms; work clothing; clothing, mail order (except women's); women's apparel, mail order; men's shoes; women's shoes; eating places
HQ: Aramark Services, Inc.
    2400 Market St Ste 600
    Philadelphia PA 19103
    215 238-3000

(G-13407)
ARBIL ENTERPRISES INC
Also Called: Allegra Print & Imaging
12285 Mcnulty Rd Ste 101 (19154-1210)
PHONE...............................215 969-0500
Michael Logan, *CEO*
Aileen Logan, *President*
EMP: 7
SQ FT: 1,600
SALES: 900K **Privately Held**
SIC: 2752 Commercial printing, offset

(G-13408)
ARCS DESIGN & PRINTING INC
211 N 9th St (19107-1832)
PHONE...............................215 238-1831
Yuk Ha Fung, *President*
Audrea Hung, *Shareholder*
EMP: 5 EST: 1996
SALES (est): 479.7K **Privately Held**
SIC: 2752 Commercial printing, offset

(G-13409)
ARCWEB TECHNOLOGIES LLC
234 Market St Fl 5 (19106-2870)
PHONE...............................800 846-7980
Christopher Cera, *President*
Joy Wittnebert, *Project Mgr*
Rob Gifford, *Accounts Exec*
EMP: 7 EST: 2011
SALES (est): 605.2K **Privately Held**
SIC: 7372 7373 7371 Application computer software; systems software development services; computer software writing services

(G-13410)
ARIBA INC
1500 Market St Fl 12 (19102-2152)
PHONE...............................215 246-3493
Bob Callan, *Manager*
EMP: 10
SALES (corp-wide): 28.2B **Privately Held**
WEB: www.ariba.com
SIC: 7372 Business oriented computer software
HQ: Ariba, Inc.
    3420 Hillview Ave Bldg 3
    Palo Alto CA 94304

(G-13411)
ARKWRIGHT LLC
11350 Norcom Rd (19154-2304)
PHONE...............................732 246-1506
Robert Curan, *Mng Member*
Hal Kanelsky,
EMP: 4
SALES (est): 2.4MM **Privately Held**
SIC: 2299 Towels & towelings, linen & linen-and-cotton mixtures

(G-13412)
ARMADANI INC
740 Sansom St Ste 204 (19106-3233)
PHONE...............................215 627-2601
Kevin Brosh, *President*
Steven Copening, *Treasurer*
EMP: 9
SALES (est): 624.8K **Privately Held**
SIC: 3911 Jewelry, precious metal

(G-13413)
ARTIES UNLIMITED LLC
Also Called: Artie's Waterice
6730 N Broad St (19126-2836)
PHONE...............................267 516-2575
Arthur Connor, *Mng Member*
EMP: 6
SQ FT: 75,000
SALES: 300K **Privately Held**
SIC: 2024 Ice cream & frozen desserts

(G-13414)
ARTISAN MOBILE INC
234 Market St Fl 4 (19106-2870)
P.O. Box 60505, King of Prussia (19406-0505)
PHONE...............................610 209-1959
Bob Moul, *CEO*
EMP: 10 EST: 2013
SALES (est): 1.2MM **Privately Held**
SIC: 7372 Application computer software

(G-13415)
ARTISAN SPECIALIST TECH
439 E High St (19144-1111)
P.O. Box 48069 (19144-8069)
PHONE...............................215 849-0509
James Brice, *Owner*
EMP: 5
SALES (est): 473.7K **Privately Held**
SIC: 3599 Mfg Industrial Machinery

(G-13416)
ARTLINE ORNAMENTAL IRON WORKS
4820 Yocum St (19143-4436)
PHONE...............................215 727-2923
Roosevelt Thompson, *Owner*
EMP: 4
SALES (est): 235.9K **Privately Held**
SIC: 3446 Architectural metalwork

(G-13417)
ARTY EMBROIDERY & DESIGN INC
3301 Frankford Ave (19134-3218)
PHONE...............................215 423-8114
Arty Suchodolski, *President*
EMP: 15
SQ FT: 4,000
SALES: 500K **Privately Held**
SIC: 2395 Embroidery products, except schiffli machine

(G-13418)
ASA BAKING CORP
2023 S Redfield St (19143-5902)
PHONE...............................267 535-1618
EMP: 4 EST: 2013
SALES (est): 157.1K **Privately Held**
SIC: 2051 Bread, cake & related products

(G-13419)
ASCENTIVE LLC
50 S 16th St Ste 3575 (19102-2568)
PHONE...............................215 395-8559
Adam Schran, *CEO*
EMP: 70
SALES (est): 5.3MM **Privately Held**
WEB: www.ascentive.com
SIC: 7372 7371 Prepackaged software; custom computer programming services

(G-13420)
ASHLAND LLC
Ashland Distribution
2801 Christopher Columbus (19148-5103)
PHONE...............................215 446-7900
Bob Detascule, *Manager*
EMP: 44
SQ FT: 42,875
SALES (corp-wide): 3.7B **Publicly Held**
WEB: www.ashland.com
SIC: 2821 Polyesters
HQ: Ashland Llc
    50 E Rivercenter Blvd # 1600
    Covington KY 41011
    859 815-3333

(G-13421)
ATLANTIC ALLIANCE PUBG CO
Also Called: Pinnacle Performace Group
318 Fitzwater St (19147-3204)
PHONE...............................267 319-1659
Mary L Hagy, *President*
Michael Hagy, *Admin Sec*
EMP: 5
SQ FT: 2,300
SALES (est): 335.1K **Privately Held**
SIC: 8742 2731 Marketing consulting services; book publishing

(G-13422)
ATLANTIC REFINING & MARKETING (DH)
1801 Market St (19103-1628)
PHONE...............................215 977-3000
Robert W Owens, *President*
Deborah M Fretz, *President*
S Blake Heinemann, *Vice Pres*
Paul A Mulholland, *Treasurer*
Elrich C Grener, *Admin Sec*
EMP: 225
SQ FT: 200,000
SALES (est): 49.8MM
SALES (corp-wide): 54B **Publicly Held**
SIC: 2911 5171 5541 5411 Petroleum refining; petroleum terminals; gasoline service stations; convenience stores, chain
HQ: Sunoco, Inc.
    3801 West Chester Pike
    Newtown Square PA 19073
    215 977-3000

(G-13423)
ATLAS ENERGY COMPANY LLC (HQ)
1845 Walnut St Ste 1000 (19103-4733)
PHONE...............................877 280-2857
Edward E Cohen, *President*
Brian Begley, *Vice Pres*
EMP: 39
SALES (est): 3.5MM
SALES (corp-wide): 9MM **Publicly Held**
SIC: 4922 1382 Natural gas transmission; oil & gas exploration services

PA: Atlas Energy Group, Llc
425 Houston St Ste 300
Fort Worth TX 76102
412 489-0006

(G-13424)
ATS-NEEDHAM LLC
Po Box 7501 (19101-7501)
P.O. Box 7247 (19170-0001)
PHONE..............................617 375-7500
James D Taiclet, *Ch of Bd*
EMP: 10
SALES (est): 358.9K **Publicly Held**
SIC: 4813 3663 ; radio broadcasting &
communications equipment
HQ: American Tower, L.P.
116 Huntington Ave # 1100
Boston MA 02116
617 375-7500

(G-13425)
AVANTEXT INC
30 S Bank St (19106-2811)
PHONE..............................610 796-2383
Kurt Schoenkopf, *President*
EMP: 25
SQ FT: 10,000
SALES: 6.5MM **Privately Held**
WEB: www.avantext.com
SIC: 5088 2741 Transportation equipment
& supplies; art copy: publishing & printing

(G-13426)
AVAX TECHNOLOGIES INC
Also Called: (A DEVELOPMENT STAGE
COMPANY)
2000 Hamilton St Ste 204 (19130-3847)
PHONE..............................215 241-9760
Adele Sommerfeld, *CEO*
John K A Prendergast PHD, *Ch of Bd*
Francois R Martelet MD, *President*
Andr S Crespo, *General Mgr*
Henry E Schea III, *Director*
EMP: 29
SQ FT: 11,900
SALES (est): 5.4MM **Privately Held**
WEB: www.avax-tech.com
SIC: 2836 Biological products, except diag-
nostic

(G-13427)
**AVID
RADIOPHARMACEUTICALS INC
(HQ)**
3711 Market St Fl 7 (19104-5533)
PHONE..............................215 298-0700
Daniel M Skovronsky, *CEO*
Richard Baron, *CFO*
Mark A Mintun, *Chief Mktg Ofcr*
EMP: 16
SALES (est): 3.9MM
SALES (corp-wide): 24.5B **Publicly Held**
WEB: www.avidrp.com
SIC: 2835 Blood derivative diagnostic
agents
PA: Eli Lilly And Company
Lilly Corporate Ctr
Indianapolis IN 46285
317 276-2000

(G-13428)
AWARD PRODUCTS INC
Also Called: Ampros Trophies
4830 N Front St (19120-4214)
PHONE..............................215 324-0414
Scott Borman, *President*
EMP: 25
SQ FT: 25,000
SALES (est): 2MM **Privately Held**
SIC: 3914 5999 Trophies; trophies &
plaques

(G-13429)
**AWESOME DUDES PRINTINGG
LLC**
1338 S 6th St (19147-5832)
PHONE..............................267 886-8492
Sean Doherty, *Principal*
EMP: 4
SALES (est): 374.7K **Privately Held**
SIC: 2752 Commercial printing, litho-
graphic

(G-13430)
AWWSUM INTERNET SERVICES
4227 Rhawn St (19136-2745)
PHONE..............................215 543-9078
Troy Pearsall, *Owner*
EMP: 3
SALES (est): 154.6K **Privately Held**
SIC: 2741 Miscellaneous publishing

(G-13431)
**AXALTA COATING SYSTEMS
LLC (HQ)**
2001 Market St Ste 3600 (19103-7105)
PHONE..............................215 255-4347
Robert Bryant, *CEO*
Luke Lu, *President*
Paul Thielsen, *District Mgr*
Michael A Cash, *Senior VP*
Michael F Finn, *Senior VP*
EMP: 120
SALES (est): 3.3B
SALES (corp-wide): 4.7B **Publicly Held**
SIC: 2851 Polyurethane coatings
PA: Axalta Coating Systems Ltd.
2001 Market St Ste 3600
Philadelphia PA 19103
855 547-1461

(G-13432)
**AXALTA COATING SYSTEMS IP
LLC**
2001 Market St Ste 3600 (19103-7105)
PHONE..............................855 547-1461
EMP: 4
SALES (est): 164K
SALES (corp-wide): 4.7B **Publicly Held**
SIC: 2851 Paints & allied products
PA: Axalta Coating Systems Ltd.
2001 Market St Ste 3600
Philadelphia PA 19103
855 547-1461

(G-13433)
**AXALTA COATING SYSTEMS
LTD (PA)**
Also Called: ELLIS PAINT COMPANY
2001 Market St Ste 3600 (19103-7105)
PHONE..............................855 547-1461
Robert Bryant, *CEO*
Charles W Shaver, *Ch of Bd*
Steven R Markevich, *Exec VP*
Michael A Cash, *Senior VP*
Robert Ferris, *Vice Pres*
EMP: 272
SALES (est): 4.7B **Publicly Held**
SIC: 2851 Paints & allied products

(G-13434)
AZUR PHARMA INC
1818 Market St (19103-3638)
PHONE..............................215 832-3750
David Brabazon, *President*
EMP: 6
SALES (est): 452.7K **Privately Held**
SIC: 2834 Pharmaceutical preparations

(G-13435)
B & B FOUNDRY INC
6101 Keystone St (19135-4292)
PHONE..............................215 333-7100
Gene Scarpa, *President*
EMP: 25 EST: 1920
SQ FT: 60,000
SALES (est): 5.2MM **Privately Held**
WEB: www.bbfoundry.com
SIC: 3321 3369 Gray iron castings; non-
ferrous foundries

(G-13436)
B & G FINISHING LLC
12417 Dunks Ferry Rd (19154-1922)
P.O. Box 63066 (19114-0866)
PHONE..............................267 229-2569
EMP: 3
SALES (est): 238.1K **Privately Held**
SIC: 3471 Plating & polishing

(G-13437)
B & G OPTICS INC
1320 Unity St (19124-3937)
PHONE..............................215 289-2480
William Hamburg, *President*
EMP: 50
SQ FT: 10,000

SALES (est): 5.5MM **Privately Held**
SIC: 3851 Eyeglasses, lenses & frames

(G-13438)
B K BARRIT CORP
Also Called: Bk Barrit
4011 G St (19124-5115)
P.O. Box 414, Valley Forge (19481-0414)
PHONE..............................267 345-1200
Bryson Kershner, *President*
EMP: 55 EST: 1959
SQ FT: 60,000
SALES (est): 5.6MM **Privately Held**
WEB: www.bkbarrit.com
SIC: 2521 5712 2512 Wood office furni-
ture; furniture stores; upholstered house-
hold furniture

(G-13439)
**B&B SALES CONSULTING CORP
INC**
2015 W Allegheny Ave (19132-1553)
PHONE..............................215 225-3200
EMP: 5
SALES (est): 173.6K **Privately Held**
SIC: 5149 2086 Beverages, except coffee
& tea; bottled & canned soft drinks

(G-13440)
BABY SPARKLES
4821 Unruh Ave (19135-2809)
PHONE..............................267 304-8787
Tamiera Harris,
EMP: 5
SALES (est): 225.3K **Privately Held**
SIC: 2361 Girls' & children's dresses,
blouses & shirts

(G-13441)
BAHDEEBAHDU
1522 N American St (19122-3811)
PHONE..............................215 627-5002
Warren Muller, *Owner*
Rj Thornburg, *Owner*
EMP: 5
SALES (est): 441.2K **Privately Held**
WEB: www.warrenmuller.com
SIC: 3645 7389 Residential lighting fix-
tures; interior designer

(G-13442)
BAINBRIDGE GROUP INC
Also Called: Famous Forth Street Cookies Co
4177 Ridge Ave (19129-1545)
PHONE..............................215 922-3274
David L Auspitz, *Chairman*
EMP: 11 EST: 1979
SQ FT: 1,800
SALES (est): 1.7MM **Privately Held**
WEB: www.famouscookies.com
SIC: 2052 Cookies

(G-13443)
BANGOR STEEL ERECTORS INC
Also Called: Disston Precision
6795 State Rd (19135-1528)
PHONE..............................215 338-1200
John C Lucid, *President*
John W Gabert, *CFO*
EMP: 20
SQ FT: 150,000
SALES: 3.5MM **Privately Held**
WEB: www.disstonprecision.com
SIC: 3312 Tool & die steel

(G-13444)
BAR BQ TOWN INC
7711 Ogontz Ave (19150-1818)
PHONE..............................215 549-9666
Seol Kim, *President*
EMP: 3
SALES (est): 160.9K **Privately Held**
SIC: 2091 Canned & cured fish & seafoods

(G-13445)
BARBARY
951 Frankford Ave (19125-4141)
PHONE..............................215 634-7400
EMP: 4
SALES (est): 206.8K **Privately Held**
SIC: 2869 Mfg Industrial Organic Chemi-
cals

(G-13446)
BARRYS LOBBY SHOP
399 Market St Ste 1 (19106-2138)
PHONE..............................215 925-1998
Barry Saunders, *President*
EMP: 10
SALES (est): 548.9K **Privately Held**
SIC: 2711 Newspapers

(G-13447)
BAW PLASTICS INC
7236 Charles St (19135-1004)
PHONE..............................215 333-6508
Robert Bauer, *Sales Staff*
EMP: 76
SALES (corp-wide): 32.4MM **Privately
Held**
SIC: 3089 Plastic processing
PA: Baw Plastics, Inc.
2148 Century Dr
Jefferson Hills PA 15025
412 384-3100

(G-13448)
BB AND CC INC (PA)
Also Called: Classic Brand Marketing
1821 E Sedgley Ave (19124-5619)
PHONE..............................215 288-7440
Barry Kratchman, *President*
EMP: 67
SALES (est): 8.2MM **Privately Held**
SIC: 2051 Cakes, pies & pastries

(G-13449)
BEARING PRODUCTS COMPANY
4567 Wayne Ave (19144-3643)
P.O. Box 1214, Bala Cynwyd (19004-5214)
PHONE..............................215 659-4768
Walter M Golaski, *President*
Alexandra B Golaski, *Vice Pres*
EMP: 10 EST: 1943
SQ FT: 40,000
SALES (est): 932.8K **Privately Held**
SIC: 3552 Knitting machines

(G-13450)
BECKER FASHION TECH LLC
Also Called: Beacon & Lively
123 Monroe St (19147-3411)
PHONE..............................215 776-2589
David Becker,
EMP: 5
SALES (est): 301.6K **Privately Held**
SIC: 3961 7389 Costume jewelry;

(G-13451)
BECOTTE DESIGN INC
9999 Global Rd (19115-1005)
PHONE..............................215 641-1257
Diane Becotte, *President*
EMP: 6
SALES (est): 600K **Privately Held**
SIC: 2752 Commercial printing, offset

(G-13452)
BELLA TURKA INC (PA)
Also Called: Bella Turka Jewelry
113 S 13th St (19107-4807)
PHONE..............................215 560-8733
Claire Pelino, *President*
Koray Avci, *Admin Sec*
EMP: 6
SALES (est): 1.2MM **Privately Held**
SIC: 3911 5944 Jewelry, precious metal;
jewelry, precious stones & precious met-
als

(G-13453)
BENNETT COMPOST
2901 W Hunting Park Ave (19129-1802)
PHONE..............................215 520-2406
Tim Bennett, *Principal*
EMP: 3
SALES (est): 335K **Privately Held**
SIC: 2875 Compost

(G-13454)
BENTECH INC
4135 N 5th St (19140-2613)
P.O. Box 46128 (19160-6128)
PHONE..............................215 223-9420
George Horrocks, *President*
Robert Benninghoff, *Vice Pres*
EMP: 35
SQ FT: 32,000

SALES (est): 2.6MM
SALES (corp-wide): 7.7MM **Privately Held**
WEB: www.bentechinc.com
SIC: 5085 2542 3498 Valves, pistons & fittings; partitions & fixtures, except wood; tube fabricating (contract bending & shaping)
PA: Philadelphia Pipe Bending Company Inc
4135 To 4165 N Fifth St
Philadelphia PA 19140
215 225-8955

(G-13455)
BENTLEY ROBE FACTORY INC
2246 N 52nd St (19131-2313)
PHONE..........................215 531-3862
Hobson R Reynolds, *President*
Shirley Thompson, *Corp Secy*
EMP: 5
SQ FT: 3,692
SALES (est): 541.3K **Privately Held**
SIC: 2384 5699 Robes & dressing gowns; caps & gowns (academic vestments)

(G-13456)
BERNARD SIGN CORPORATION
3325 Rorer St (19134-1729)
P.O. Box 29284 (19125-0984)
PHONE..........................215 425-1700
Robert Jaffe, *President*
EMP: 25 EST: 1938
SQ FT: 20,000
SALES (est): 2.9MM **Privately Held**
SIC: 3993 Signs, not made in custom sign painting shops

(G-13457)
BERNIES BEER & BEVERAGE INC
4291 Paul St (19124-4628)
PHONE..........................215 744-1946
Lawrence Bernstein, *Principal*
EMP: 4
SALES (est): 149.8K **Privately Held**
SIC: 2082 Beer (alcoholic beverage)

(G-13458)
BERWIND CONSUMER PRODUCTS LLC
1500 Market St Ste 3000w (19102-2107)
PHONE..........................215 563-2800
Bruce McKenney,
◆ EMP: 740
SALES (est): 40.8MM
SALES (corp-wide): 2.9B **Privately Held**
SIC: 2891 Adhesives, paste; adhesives, plastic; epoxy adhesives; glue
PA: Berwind Corporation
3000 Ctr Sq W 1500 Mkt St 1500 W
Philadelphia PA 19102
215 563-2800

(G-13459)
BIG 3 PACKAGING LLC (PA)
Also Called: Chemical Service Philadelphia
5039 Tomley St Ste B (19137)
PHONE..........................215 743-4201
Richard A Higgs, *CEO*
James Sullivan, *Vice Pres*
Nancy Garcia, *Info Tech Mgr*
EMP: 10
SQ FT: 100,000
SALES (est): 2.3MM **Privately Held**
WEB: www.dclsolutions.com
SIC: 2841 2842 Soap: granulated, liquid, cake, flaked or chip; specialty cleaning preparations

(G-13460)
BIKES & TRIKES FOR
2512 E Oakdale St (19125-2322)
PHONE..........................267 304-1534
Christopher Hartzag, *President*
Kevin Hartzag, *Vice Pres*
Terrance Sibley, *Treasurer*
EMP: 4
SALES (est): 230K **Privately Held**
SIC: 3751 Frames, motorcycle & bicycle

(G-13461)
BIO-NUCLEONICS INC (PA)
1600 Market St Ste 13200 (19103-7240)
PHONE..........................305 576-0996
Rosanne Satz, *President*

Eva Capps, *Principal*
Stanely Satz, *Security Dir*
EMP: 12
SQ FT: 9,899
SALES (est): 1.9MM **Privately Held**
WEB: www.bionucleonics.com
SIC: 2835 Radioactive diagnostic substances

(G-13462)
BIO-RAD LABORATORIES INC
1500 John F Kennedy Blvd # 800 (19102-1710)
PHONE..........................267 322-6931
Meryl Schorr, *Exec Dir*
EMP: 473
SALES (corp-wide): 2.2B **Publicly Held**
SIC: 3826 Analytical instruments
PA: Bio-Rad Laboratories, Inc.
1000 Alfred Nobel Dr
Hercules CA 94547
510 724-7000

(G-13463)
BIO-RAD LABORATORIES INC
2000 Market St Ste 1460 (19103-3212)
PHONE..........................267 322-6945
Gregory Banik, *General Mgr*
Rick Morris, *Opers Mgr*
John Baker, *Development*
Michael Ancone, *Controller*
Micheal Frey, *Sales Mgr*
EMP: 20
SALES (corp-wide): 2.2B **Publicly Held**
WEB: www.bio-rad.com
SIC: 3826 Analytical instruments
PA: Bio-Rad Laboratories, Inc.
1000 Alfred Nobel Dr
Hercules CA 94547
510 724-7000

(G-13464)
BIODETEGO LLC
3711 Market St Ste 800 (19104-5532)
PHONE..........................856 701-2453
David Zuzga, *CEO*
EMP: 3
SALES (est): 201.4K **Privately Held**
SIC: 2835 In vitro diagnostics

(G-13465)
BIOMEME INC
1015 Chestnut St Ste 1401 (19107-4300)
PHONE..........................267 519-9066
Max Perelman, *Principal*
Marc Dejohn, *Principal*
Jesse Vanwestrienen, *Principal*
Chris Cox, *Research*
Katelyn Gourley, *Office Mgr*
EMP: 19 EST: 2012
SQ FT: 4,500
SALES (est): 1.5MM **Privately Held**
SIC: 3841 3826 Diagnostic apparatus, medical; analytical instruments

(G-13466)
BIOREALIZE INC
3401 Grays Ferry Ave (19146-2701)
PHONE..........................610 216-5554
Orkan Telhan, *President*
Michael Hogan, *Treasurer*
Karen Hogan, *Admin Sec*
EMP: 6
SALES (est): 356K **Privately Held**
SIC: 2835 3821 8731 8071 Microbiology & virology diagnostic products; clinical laboratory instruments, except medical & dental; biological research; industrial laboratory, except testing; bacteriological laboratory

(G-13467)
BLACK & DECKER (US) INC
Also Called: Dewalt Industrial Tool
2715 S Front St Ste 5 (19148-4838)
PHONE..........................215 271-0402
Carlos Garcia, *Office Mgr*
EMP: 11
SALES (corp-wide): 13.9B **Publicly Held**
WEB: www.dewalt.com
SIC: 3546 7699 Power-driven handtools; power tool repair
HQ: Black & Decker (U.S.) Inc.
1000 Stanley Dr
New Britain CT 06053
860 225-5111

(G-13468)
BLAZING PASSION PUBL
8600 Provident St (19150-1608)
PHONE..........................215 247-2024
Scheryll Anderson, *Owner*
EMP: 4
SALES (est): 133.5K **Privately Held**
WEB: www.blazingpassion.com
SIC: 2741 Music books: publishing & printing

(G-13469)
BOATHOUSE ROW SPORTS LTD
Also Called: Boathouse Sports
425 E Hunting Park Ave (19124-6008)
PHONE..........................215 425-4300
Michael Zambelli, *President*
Katie McLaughlin, *Prdtn Mgr*
John B Kelly, *CFO*
Pat Connery, *Controller*
James Culyer, *Sales Staff*
▲ EMP: 214
SQ FT: 60,000
SALES (est): 31.2MM **Privately Held**
WEB: www.boathousesports.com
SIC: 2329 2339 Men's & boys' sportswear & athletic clothing; athletic clothing: women's, misses' & juniors'

(G-13470)
BOND PRODUCTS INC
4511 Wayne Ave (19144-3606)
PHONE..........................215 842-0200
Brian M Milnes, *President*
▲ EMP: 10 EST: 1947
SQ FT: 14,500
SALES (est): 1.3MM **Privately Held**
SIC: 2392 5131 5084 Linings, carpet: textile, except felt; piece goods & notions; narrow fabrics; tape, textile; binding, textile; textile machinery & equipment

(G-13471)
BONNIE KAISER
Also Called: Printing & Quick Copy
8799 Frankford Ave (19136-1433)
PHONE..........................215 331-6555
Bonnie Kaiser, *Owner*
EMP: 5
SQ FT: 2,100
SALES (est): 370.9K **Privately Held**
SIC: 2759 7331 2789 2752 Commercial printing; mailing service; bookbinding & related work; commercial printing, lithographic

(G-13472)
BORK INC
5301 N 2nd St Ste 3 (19120-3254)
PHONE..........................215 324-1155
Robert Anderson, *President*
Melinda Brassill, *Vice Pres*
EMP: 3
SALES (est): 251.6K **Privately Held**
SIC: 3444 Sheet metalwork

(G-13473)
BORNMANN MFG CO INC
3731 Old York Rd (19140-3714)
PHONE..........................215 228-5826
Robert Bornmann, *President*
Mary Ann Bornmann, *Corp Secy*
EMP: 8 EST: 1945
SQ FT: 6,000
SALES: 475K **Privately Held**
WEB: www.customradiatorcovers.com
SIC: 3537 2542 3444 Trucks: freight, baggage, etc.: industrial, except mining; dollies (hand or power trucks), industrial except mining; cabinets: show, display or storage: except wood; radiator shields or enclosures, sheet metal

(G-13474)
BOTTLING GROUP LLC
11701 Roosevelt Blvd (19154-2108)
PHONE..........................215 676-6400
Pancho Hall,
▲ EMP: 5
SALES (est): 492.6K
SALES (corp-wide): 64.6B **Publicly Held**
SIC: 2086 Bottled & canned soft drinks
PA: Pepsico, Inc.
700 Anderson Hill Rd
Purchase NY 10577
914 253-2000

(G-13475)
BPES BARR PUBLICATIO CO
824 N Stillman St (19130-1836)
PHONE..........................215 765-0383
Vilma Barr, *Principal*
EMP: 3
SALES (est): 140.4K **Privately Held**
SIC: 2741 Miscellaneous publishing

(G-13476)
BRAMANTE BIOSCIENCE LLC
2100 Christian St Apt A (19146-2514)
PHONE..........................860 634-0015
Faez Siddiqi, *CEO*
Christa Heyward, *COO*
Peter Clark,
EMP: 4 EST: 2017
SALES (est): 99K **Privately Held**
SIC: 2835 Blood derivative diagnostic agents

(G-13477)
BRANDS IMAGING LLC
521 Cecil B Moore Ave (19122-2928)
PHONE..........................215 279-7218
Brett Brand, *Owner*
EMP: 6
SALES (est): 481.8K **Privately Held**
SIC: 3993 Signs & advertising specialties

(G-13478)
BRASKEM AMERICA INC (HQ)
Also Called: Braskem Pp Americas
1735 Market St Fl 28 (19103-7534)
PHONE..........................215 841-3100
Bruce D Rubin, *CEO*
Laurence Kerrigan, *Superintendent*
Rachel Celiberti, *Vice Pres*
Alexandre Elias, *Vice Pres*
Srivatsan Iyer, *Vice Pres*
▲ EMP: 150
SQ FT: 100,000
SALES (est): 547.5MM **Privately Held**
SIC: 2821 2865 2869 Polypropylene resins; polyesters; acrylic resins; plasticizer/additive based plastic materials; cyclic crudes & intermediates; phenol, alkylated & cumene; aniline, nitrobenzene; diphenylamines; acetone, synthetic; alcohols, non-beverage

(G-13479)
BRIAN GINIEWSKI LLC
4500 Worth St (19124-3491)
PHONE..........................610 858-2821
Brian Giniewski, *Mng Member*
EMP: 5
SALES (est): 316K **Privately Held**
SIC: 3229 5719 5032 Tableware, glass or glass ceramic; pottery; tile, clay or other ceramic, excluding refractory

(G-13480)
BRIDGET MORRIS
Also Called: Bella Frte Bkbnding Ltterpress
2202 Alter St (19146-2800)
PHONE..........................215 828-9261
Bridget Morris, *Owner*
Rachel Brown, *General Mgr*
EMP: 3
SALES: 215K **Privately Held**
SIC: 2789 Bookbinding & related work

(G-13481)
BRIGHT SIGN CO INC
1215 Race St (19107-1692)
PHONE..........................215 563-9480
Louis A Cerino, *President*
Joyce Cerino, *Corp Secy*
Ralph Cerino, *Executive*
EMP: 7 EST: 1927
SQ FT: 5,830
SALES: 900K **Privately Held**
WEB: www.brightsignco.com
SIC: 3993 Signs, not made in custom sign painting shops; name plates: except engraved, etched, etc.: metal

(G-13482)
BRILLIANT INC
Also Called: Repro Center
1531 N 7th St (19147-6434)
PHONE..........................215 271-5041
Joyce Mak, *President*
Leslie Mak, *Vice Pres*
EMP: 4

SALES (est): 416.8K **Privately Held**
SIC: 2752 Commercial printing, lithographic

(G-13483)
BRINKMANN BROS INC
2617 Frankford Ave (19125-1411)
PHONE...................................215 739-4769
William Brinkmann, *President*
Arlinda Brinkmann, *Admin Sec*
EMP: 5
SQ FT: 1,500
SALES: 500K **Privately Held**
SIC: 3259 1761 Roofing tile, clay; roofing, siding & sheet metal work

(G-13484)
BRISTOL MILLWORK CO INC
4560 Tacony St (19124-4136)
PHONE...................................215 533-1921
Michael Baier, *President*
Maryellen Baier, *Vice Pres*
EMP: 10 EST: 1963
SQ FT: 15,000
SALES: 550K **Privately Held**
SIC: 2431 Millwork

(G-13485)
BRODERICK INDUSTRIES LLC
6101 Keystone St (19135-4219)
PHONE...................................215 409-5771
William Broderick, *President*
EMP: 6
SALES (est): 112.4K **Privately Held**
SIC: 3999 Manufacturing industries

(G-13486)
BRODYS WELDING AND MECH CONTRS
Also Called: Brodys Welding & Mech Contrs
2020 Orthodox St (19124-3439)
P.O. Box 23217 (19124-0217)
PHONE...................................215 941-7914
Kerry Brody, *President*
EMP: 8
SQ FT: 5,400
SALES (est): 621.1K **Privately Held**
SIC: 1799 1711 7692 Welding on site; mechanical contractor; welding repair

(G-13487)
BRYSI INC
233 S 33rd St (19104-3809)
PHONE...................................215 573-7918
Eun Ha Chung, *Principal*
EMP: 4 EST: 2010
SALES (est): 264.4K **Privately Held**
SIC: 3421 Table & food cutlery, including butchers'

(G-13488)
BUSHNELL ALVAH COMPANY
519 E Chelten Ave (19144-1202)
PHONE...................................215 842-9520
Art Bushnell, *President*
Rick Bushnell, *Vice Pres*
Bruce Walker, *Regl Sales Mgr*
EMP: 50 EST: 1876
SQ FT: 30,000
SALES (est): 11.3MM **Privately Held**
SIC: 2655 Containers, liquid tight fiber: from purchased material; tubes, mailing: made from purchased paper fiber

(G-13489)
BYRD ALLEY LLC
807 S Hancock St (19147-3440)
PHONE...................................215 669-0068
Jacqueline Rendeiro, *Project Mgr*
Gregory Jaspan,
EMP: 17
SQ FT: 2,400
SALES (est): 3.2MM **Privately Held**
SIC: 7374 7371 7372 Computer graphics service; computer software systems analysis & design, custom; application computer software

(G-13490)
C F MOORES CO INC
Also Called: Moore Bends
1123 Ivy Hill Rd (19150-1509)
PHONE...................................215 248-1250
David Neal, *President*
EMP: 10 EST: 1932
SQ FT: 45,000

SALES: 500K **Privately Held**
SIC: 3355 3351 Aluminum rolling & drawing; tubing, copper & copper alloy

(G-13491)
C SHARKEY KEYBOARD COVERS INC (PA)
9764 Redd Rambler Ter (19115-2929)
PHONE...................................215 969-8783
Ann Szylejko, *President*
Thomas Szylejko, *Vice Pres*
Daniel Szylejko, *Admin Sec*
EMP: 17 EST: 1972
SQ FT: 5,000
SALES (est): 1.5MM **Privately Held**
SIC: 3089 Injection molding of plastics

(G-13492)
C3 MEDIA LLC
Also Called: Philadelphia Business Services
442 Brown St (19123-2106)
PHONE...................................610 832-8077
Robert Reish, *CEO*
Kathleen Mahoney, *Office Mgr*
Patrick J Billings, *Admin Sec*
EMP: 32
SQ FT: 10,000
SALES (est): 3.4MM **Privately Held**
WEB: www.pbs.cc
SIC: 7334 7359 2752 2789 Photocopying & duplicating services; business machine & electronic equipment rental services; commercial printing, offset; binding & repair of books, magazines & pamphlets

(G-13493)
CABRUN INK PRODUCTS CORP
2020 Valetta St (19124-5074)
P.O. Box 4887 (19124-0887)
PHONE...................................215 533-2990
Kenneth L Reich, *President*
Joseph C Iannelli, *Vice Pres*
Melisa Reich, *Vice Pres*
Sharon Reich, *Treasurer*
Jean Reich, *Admin Sec*
EMP: 48
SQ FT: 20,500
SALES (est): 9.4MM **Privately Held**
SIC: 2893 5084 Printing ink; printing trades machinery, equipment & supplies

(G-13494)
CALEDONIAN DYE WORKS
3300 Emerald St (19134-2506)
P.O. Box 14842 (19134-0842)
PHONE...................................215 739-2322
Richard D Fitch, *President*
Kimberly Livingston, *Vice Pres*
▲ EMP: 26 EST: 1911
SQ FT: 32,000
SALES (est): 4.1MM **Privately Held**
SIC: 2269 Dyeing: raw stock yarn & narrow fabrics

(G-13495)
CAMDEN IRON & METAL INC
2600 Penrose Ave (19145-5902)
PHONE...................................215 952-1500
EMP: 5
SALES (corp-wide): 4.3B **Privately Held**
SIC: 3559 Recycling machinery
HQ: Camden Iron & Metal, Inc.
1500 S 6th St
Camden NJ 08104

(G-13496)
CAMPUS COPY CENTER (PA)
Also Called: Campus Shipping Center
3907 Walnut St (19104-3608)
PHONE...................................215 386-6410
Stanley Shapiro, *Owner*
Ron Shapiro, *Owner*
EMP: 16
SQ FT: 9,000
SALES (est): 1.7MM **Privately Held**
WEB: www.campuscopycenter.com
SIC: 2752 7334 Lithographing on metal; photocopying & duplicating services

(G-13497)
CANNON GRAPHICS INC
12301 Mcnulty Rd Unit L (19154-1034)
PHONE...................................215 676-5114
Jack Marco, *President*
Dan Mc Donald, *Treasurer*
EMP: 5

SQ FT: 4,500
SALES: 450K **Privately Held**
SIC: 2759 Commercial printing

(G-13498)
CANVAS AWNINGS INC
Also Called: Lockhart Gene Canvas Awnings
3029 Ruth St (19134-3115)
P.O. Box 26928 (19134-6928)
PHONE...................................215 423-1213
Prisilla Lockhart, *President*
Lin Lockhart, *Principal*
Jean Maslanik, *Treasurer*
EMP: 5
SQ FT: 3,500
SALES: 170K **Privately Held**
SIC: 2394 Awnings, fabric: made from purchased materials

(G-13499)
CAR FUEL 1 INC
914 Clinton St (19107-6108)
PHONE...................................215 545-2002
Louis Lanni, *President*
EMP: 3
SALES (est): 183.3K **Privately Held**
SIC: 2869 Fuels

(G-13500)
CARBONATOR RENTAL SERVICE INC
Also Called: Soda Rental Service
6500 Eastwick Ave (19142-3399)
P.O. Box 33327 (19142-0527)
PHONE...................................215 726-9100
Herbert Pincus, *Ch of Bd*
Andrew Pincus, *President*
Susan Pincus, *Treasurer*
Leatrice Pincus, *Admin Sec*
EMP: 32
SQ FT: 55,000
SALES (est): 6MM **Privately Held**
WEB: www.carbonatorrental.com
SIC: 7359 2087 Flavoring extracts & syrups; equipment rental & leasing

(G-13501)
CARDENAS OIL & VINEGAR TAPROOM
942 S 9th St (19147-3935)
PHONE...................................570 401-4718
Cardenas Laurissa, *Principal*
EMP: 5
SALES (est): 272.4K **Privately Held**
SIC: 2079 Olive oil

(G-13502)
CARDINAL HEALTH 407 INC
3001 Red Lion Rd Ste Ag (19114-1123)
PHONE...................................215 501-1210
Bill Mitchell, *President*
Robert Walter, *Chairman*
Steven J Magiera, *CFO*
Irina Vinokur, *Manager*
EMP: 1000
SQ FT: 40,000
SALES (est): 48.8MM
SALES (corp-wide): 136.8B **Publicly Held**
SIC: 7389 3086 3089 Packaging & labeling services; packaging & shipping materials, foamed plastic; thermoformed finished plastic products
PA: Cardinal Health, Inc.
7000 Cardinal Pl
Dublin OH 43017
614 757-5000

(G-13503)
CARDONE INDUSTRIES INC
5670 Rising Sun Ave (19120-2594)
PHONE...................................215 912-3000
Stephen Eichmann, *Principal*
EMP: 250
SALES (corp-wide): 1.6B **Privately Held**
WEB: www.cardone.com
SIC: 3714 Motor vehicle parts & accessories
PA: Cardone Industries, Inc
5501 Whitaker Ave
Philadelphia PA 19124
215 912-3000

(G-13504)
CARDONE INDUSTRIES INC (PA)
5501 Whitaker Ave (19124-1799)
PHONE...................................215 912-3000
Terry McCormack, *CEO*
Gowisnock Stanley, *President*
Sal Lo Dico, *Senior VP*
Marshall Hosel, *Senior VP*
Steve Feld, *Opers Staff*
◆ EMP: 450 EST: 1967
SQ FT: 1,600,000
SALES (est): 1.6B **Privately Held**
WEB: www.cardone.com
SIC: 3465 3714 Body parts, automobile: stamped metal; motor vehicle parts & accessories

(G-13505)
CARDONE INDUSTRIES INC
550 E Erie Ave (19134-1107)
PHONE...................................215 912-3000
EMP: 300
SALES (corp-wide): 1.6B **Privately Held**
SIC: 3714 Motor vehicle parts & accessories
PA: Cardone Industries, Inc
5501 Whitaker Ave
Philadelphia PA 19124
215 912-3000

(G-13506)
CARDONE INDUSTRIES INC
5660 Rising Sun Ave (19120-2511)
PHONE...................................215 912-3000
Greg Allander, *Manager*
EMP: 250
SALES (corp-wide): 1.6B **Privately Held**
WEB: www.cardone.com
SIC: 3714 Motor vehicle parts & accessories
PA: Cardone Industries, Inc
5501 Whitaker Ave
Philadelphia PA 19124
215 912-3000

(G-13507)
CARDONE INDUSTRIES INC
5501 Whitaker Ave (19124-1799)
PHONE...................................215 912-3000
Hank Mumma, *Branch Mgr*
EMP: 250
SALES (corp-wide): 1.6B **Privately Held**
WEB: www.cardone.com
SIC: 3714 Motor vehicle parts & accessories
PA: Cardone Industries, Inc
5501 Whitaker Ave
Philadelphia PA 19124
215 912-3000

(G-13508)
CARPENTER TECHNOLOGY CORP (PA)
1735 Market St Fl 15 (19103-7505)
P.O. Box 14662, Reading (19612-4662)
PHONE...................................610 208-2000
Gregory A Pratt, *Ch of Bd*
Tony R Thene, *President*
Bob Kemp, *General Mgr*
Stephen Cunningham, *Area Mgr*
James D Dee, *Vice Pres*
◆ EMP: 277
SALES: 2.1B **Publicly Held**
WEB: www.cartech.com
SIC: 3312 3443 3255 3316 Stainless steel; bar, rod & wire products; primary finished or semifinished shapes; tool & die steel; plate work for the nuclear industry; clay refractories; cold finishing of steel shapes; steel wire & related products

(G-13509)
CARROLLSISTERS
13421 Kelvin Ave (19116-1327)
PHONE...................................215 969-4688
Joan Elizabeth Carroll, *Owner*
Jennifer Carroll, *Co-Owner*
EMP: 38
SALES: 250K **Privately Held**
SIC: 5812 8742 2759 Caterers; restaurant & food services consultants; newspapers: printing

(G-13510)
CASE PAPER CO INC
499 E Tioga St (19134-1118)
PHONE...................................215 430-6400
EMP: 170
SALES (corp-wide): 237.1MM Privately Held
WEB: www.casepaper.com
SIC: 5111 2631 2621 Printing paper; paperboard mills; paper mills
PA: Case Paper Co., Inc.
500 Mamaroneck Ave Fl 2
Harrison NY 10528
914 899-3500

(G-13511)
CASTING HEADQUARTERS INC
Also Called: Maldonado T Norberto
740 Sansom St Ste 100 (19106-3233)
PHONE...................................215 922-2278
Ed Aguiar, President
Norberto Maldonado, Treasurer
EMP: 8
SQ FT: 1,500
SALES: 1.5MM Privately Held
SIC: 3911 Pins (jewelry), precious metal

(G-13512)
CASTOR PRINTING COMPANY INC
6376 Castor Ave 80 (19149-2756)
PHONE...................................215 535-1471
Barry Spector, President
Carol Spector, Corp Secy
EMP: 18 EST: 1975
SQ FT: 1,200
SALES (est): 2.4MM Privately Held
WEB: www.castorprinting.com
SIC: 2752 2791 2789 2759 Commercial printing, offset; typesetting; bookbinding & related work; commercial printing

(G-13513)
CATALENT CTS INC
10381 Decatur Rd (19154-3809)
PHONE...................................816 767-6013
Kristen Devito, Principal
EMP: 145 Publicly Held
SIC: 2834 Pharmaceutical preparations
HQ: Catalent Cts, Llc
10245 Hickman Mills Dr
Kansas City MO 64137

(G-13514)
CATALENT PHARMA SOLUTIONS INC
10381 Decatur Rd (19154-3809)
PHONE...................................215 637-3565
Kevin Robinson, Program Mgr
Chris Greco, Manager
Richard Roberts, Manager
EMP: 20 Publicly Held
SIC: 2834 Pharmaceutical preparations
HQ: Catalent Pharma Solutions, Inc.
14 Schoolhouse Rd
Somerset NJ 08873

(G-13515)
CATALENT PHARMA SOLUTIONS INC
3031 Red Lion Rd (19114-1123)
PHONE...................................215 613-3001
Thomas Fillis, Branch Mgr
EMP: 45 Publicly Held
SIC: 2834 Pharmaceutical preparations
HQ: Catalent Pharma Solutions, Inc.
14 Schoolhouse Rd
Somerset NJ 08873

(G-13516)
CAVA INTL MBL & GRAN INC
2000 Washington Ave (19146-2832)
PHONE...................................215 732-7800
Henry Mazzola, President
EMP: 30
SQ FT: 20,000
SALES (est): 2.6MM Privately Held
SIC: 6512 3441 3281 1411 Commercial & industrial building operation; fabricated structural metal; cut stone & stone products; dimension stone

(G-13517)
CDM HOLDINGS INC
Also Called: Crescent Designed Metals
5013 Grays Ave (19143-5812)
PHONE...................................215 724-8640
Joe Milani Jr, President
Christopher Milani, Vice Pres
EMP: 20
SALES (est): 4.4MM Privately Held
WEB: www.crescentmichaels.com
SIC: 3499 Aerosol valves, metal

(G-13518)
CELLUCAP MANUFACTURING CO (PA)
Also Called: Disco
4626 N 15th St (19140-1197)
PHONE...................................800 523-3814
Gilbert Wagenfeld, CEO
Jane Wagenfeldharris, President
Henry Wagebfeld, Vice Pres
Mark A Davis, Admin Sec
▲ EMP: 30 EST: 1954
SQ FT: 80,000
SALES (est): 25MM Privately Held
WEB: www.cellucap.com
SIC: 2676 Sanitary paper products

(G-13519)
CENTER CITY PRETZEL CO
816 Washington Ave (19147-4717)
PHONE...................................215 463-5664
Anthony Tonelli Jr, President
EMP: 10 EST: 1981
SALES (est): 620K Privately Held
WEB: www.littlebitofphilly.com
SIC: 2052 Pretzels

(G-13520)
CENTRAL CONCRETE SUPPLY COINC
118 W Clarkson Ave (19120-2926)
PHONE...................................215 927-4686
Bruce Sussman, Branch Mgr
EMP: 3
SALES (corp-wide): 1.5B Publicly Held
WEB: www.centralconcretegroup.com
SIC: 3273 Ready-mixed concrete
HQ: Central Concrete Supply Co.Inc.
755 Stockton Ave
San Jose CA 95126
408 293-6272

(G-13521)
CENTURY MOTORS INC
Also Called: Century Auto Parts
3101 S 61st St (19153-3588)
PHONE...................................215 724-8845
Gaetano Clemento, Principal
Tom Serno, Corp Secy
EMP: 5
SALES (est): 518.7K Privately Held
SIC: 3465 Body parts, automobile: stamped metal

(G-13522)
CHALMUR BAG LLC (PA)
4916 N 6th St (19120-3706)
PHONE...................................215 455-1360
Robert Woodard,
Patricia Lynn Danas,
Andrew Sacksteder,
EMP: 14
SQ FT: 15,000
SALES (est): 915.3K Privately Held
SIC: 2673 Cellophane bags, unprinted: made from purchased materials; plastic bags: made from purchased materials

(G-13523)
CHAMBORD ET CIE SARL
2633 Trenton Ave (19125-1837)
PHONE...................................215 425-9300
Claude Kistner, CEO
Norton Cooper, President
EMP: 30
SALES (est): 3.7MM Privately Held
SIC: 2085 Cordials, alcoholic

(G-13524)
CHANDLER-WHITE PUBLISHING CO
517 W Midvale Ave (19144-4617)
PHONE...................................312 907-3271
Alton Chandler, President

Ann Howell, Corp Secy
EMP: 3
SQ FT: 2,000
SALES (est): 174.7K Privately Held
WEB: www.chandlerwhitepub.com
SIC: 2731 2741 2791 Books: publishing only; miscellaneous publishing; typesetting

(G-13525)
CHANGO INC
1211 N 2nd St (19122-4501)
PHONE...................................215 634-0400
Mercedes Sanchez, President
Virginia Sanchez, Vice Pres
EMP: 4
SALES (est): 383.7K Privately Held
SIC: 1793 3211 Glass & glazing work; tempered glass; window glass, clear & colored

(G-13526)
CHARGEITSPOT LLC
111 S Independence Mall E (19106-2515)
PHONE...................................215 220-6600
Doug Baldasare, CEO
Robert Kay, Senior VP
Sheri Tate, Senior VP
Janelle Grace, Engineer
Ashwin Muthiah, Sales Staff
▲ EMP: 120
SALES (est): 2MM Privately Held
SIC: 3694 Battery charging alternators & generators

(G-13527)
CHARLES F MAY CO
Also Called: Wooden Nickel Sales
3245 Amber St Ste 5 (19134-3235)
PHONE...................................215 634-7257
Stephen Mc Nichol, Owner
EMP: 9 EST: 1934
SALES (est): 1MM Privately Held
SIC: 5136 2395 2269 Men's & boys' clothing; embroidery products, except schiffli machine; finishing plants

(G-13528)
CHARLES F WOODILL
Also Called: Phoenix Awning Company
5145 N 2nd St 47 (19120-3409)
PHONE...................................215 457-5858
Charles F Woodill, President
EMP: 3
SQ FT: 2,400
SALES (est): 408.6K Privately Held
SIC: 3444 5999 Awnings, sheet metal; awnings

(G-13529)
CHARLES JACQUIN ET CIE INC (PA)
2633 Trenton Ave (19125-1837)
PHONE...................................215 425-9300
Norton J Cooper, President
Robert Cooper, Vice Pres
Michael Allen, Treasurer
Mark Small, Admin Sec
▲ EMP: 80
SQ FT: 188,000
SALES (est): 19.7MM Privately Held
SIC: 2085 2084 Cordials, alcoholic; gin (alcoholic beverage); rye whiskey; vodka (alcoholic beverage); wines

(G-13530)
CHARLES JACQUIN ET CIE INC
Saint Dalfour Et Cie
2633 Trenton Ave (19125-1837)
PHONE...................................215 425-9300
Norton J Cooper, Branch Mgr
EMP: 15
SALES (corp-wide): 19.7MM Privately Held
SIC: 2099 Food preparations
PA: Charles Jacquin Et Cie., Inc.
2633 Trenton Ave
Philadelphia PA 19125
215 425-9300

(G-13531)
CHARLES RITTER INCORPORATED
3333 S 3rd St (19148-5602)
P.O. Box 37560 (19148-7560)
PHONE...................................215 320-5000

Samuel Ritter, President
David Giusti, Vice Pres
EMP: 140
SQ FT: 66,000
SALES (est): 32.3MM Privately Held
SIC: 2013 Sausages & other prepared meats; prepared beef products from purchased beef

(G-13532)
CHARLES W ROMANO CO
Also Called: Romano Service
2230 E Venango St (19134-2732)
PHONE...................................215 535-3800
Phill Fleming, President
EMP: 5
SQ FT: 3,000
SALES (est): 1.4MM Privately Held
SIC: 7694 5063 Electric motor repair; motors, electric

(G-13533)
CHARLESWORTH GROUP (USA) INC
325 Chestnut St Ste 510 (19106-2607)
PHONE...................................215 922-1611
Adrian T Stanley, CEO
EMP: 6
SALES (est): 374.8K Privately Held
SIC: 2731 Book publishing
PA: Charlesworth (Beijing) Information Service Co., Ltd.
12/F, Xiandai Baili Mansion, No.20, Dongsanhuan (S) Rd., Chaoyan
Beijing
105 869-6201

(G-13534)
CHATILLON SCALES TESTER CO
514 Knorr St (19111-4604)
PHONE...................................215 745-3304
Chuck Intrye, Principal
EMP: 3 EST: 2010
SALES (est): 208K Privately Held
SIC: 3821 Laboratory measuring apparatus

(G-13535)
CHAU FRESH DONUTS
5601 Market St (19139-3275)
PHONE...................................215 474-1533
N Fresh, Principal
EMP: 4
SALES (est): 253.5K Privately Held
SIC: 2051 Bread, cake & related products

(G-13536)
CHEFS DESIGN INC
6711 Vandike St (19135-2420)
PHONE...................................215 763-5252
Cort Wizorek, President
EMP: 5
SQ FT: 30,000
SALES (est): 695.3K Privately Held
WEB: www.chefsdesign.com
SIC: 3444 Metal housings, enclosures, casings & other containers

(G-13537)
CHELSEA PARTNERS INC
108 Arch St Ph 2 (19106-2279)
PHONE...................................215 603-7300
Tempa Berish, President
EMP: 35 EST: 2001
SALES (est): 2.5MM Privately Held
SIC: 8742 2754 7311 Marketing consulting services; business form & card printing, gravure; advertising agencies

(G-13538)
CHEMINOVA INC
1735 Market St (19103-7501)
P.O. Box 58549 (19102-8549)
PHONE...................................919 474-6600
Martin Petersen, President
▲ EMP: 4 EST: 2016
SALES (est): 131.8K Privately Held
SIC: 2899 Chemical preparations

(G-13539)
CHESTNUT HILL LOCAL
8434 Germantown Ave Ste 1 (19118-3386)
PHONE...................................215 248-8800
Harry Johnson, Manager

EMP: 20
SALES (est): 794.1K **Privately Held**
WEB: www.chestnuthilllocal.com
SIC: 2711 Newspapers: publishing only, not printed on site

(G-13540)
CHEU NOODLE BAR
255 S 10th St (19107-5777)
PHONE....................267 639-4136
Fergus Carey, *President*
EMP: 8
SALES (est): 618.1K **Privately Held**
SIC: 2098 Noodles (e.g. egg, plain & water), dry

(G-13541)
CHILD EVNGELISM FELLOWSHIP INC
4730 Chestnut St (19139-4613)
PHONE....................215 837-6324
Nathaniel Winslow, *Branch Mgr*
EMP: 41
SALES (corp-wide): 24.4MM **Privately Held**
SIC: 2752 Commercial printing, lithographic
PA: Child Evangelism Fellowship Incorporated
17482 Highway M
Warrenton MO 63383
636 456-4321

(G-13542)
CHRISTINI TECHNOLOGIES INC
Also Called: Christini Awd Mtcyc Mtn Bikes
611 N 2nd St (19123-3001)
PHONE....................215 351-9895
Steven Christini, *President*
David Christini, *CIO*
▲ **EMP:** 4
SQ FT: 5,000
SALES (est): 722.3K **Privately Held**
WEB: www.christini.com
SIC: 3751 Motorcycles & related parts

(G-13543)
CHRISTOPHER CO LTD
8701 Torresdale Ave Ste Q (19136-1521)
PHONE....................215 331-8290
CHI-Jiun Chen, *President*
▲ **EMP:** 5
SQ FT: 15,000
SALES (est): 600K **Privately Held**
WEB: www.christopherco.com
SIC: 2499 Picture frame molding, finished

(G-13544)
CIBO MEDIA GROUP LLC
1525 Locust St Ste 1201 (19102-3711)
PHONE....................215 732-6700
Joseph Marrone, *Mng Member*
EMP: 9
SQ FT: 1,948
SALES (est): 461.9K **Privately Held**
SIC: 2721 Magazines: publishing & printing

(G-13545)
CIR-CUT CORPORATION
4315 N 4th St (19140-2403)
PHONE....................215 324-1000
Carmen Dilello, *President*
EMP: 4 **EST:** 1954
SQ FT: 4,000
SALES (est): 880.3K **Privately Held**
SIC: 5085 3429 3544 Industrial supplies; manufactured hardware (general); metal fasteners; die sets for metal stamping (presses)

(G-13546)
CITI FUEL CONVENIENCE INC
6301 Dicks Ave (19142-3008)
PHONE....................215 724-2395
Paul Melletz, *Principal*
EMP: 10
SALES (est): 1MM **Privately Held**
SIC: 2869 Fuels

(G-13547)
CITY ENGRAVING & AWARDS LLC
1220 Walnut St (19107-5466)
P.O. Box 524, Maple Shade NJ (08052-0524)
PHONE....................215 731-0200
Jonathan Upfalow, *Principal*
EMP: 5
SALES (est): 480.9K **Privately Held**
SIC: 2759 3479 3993 3999 Card printing & engraving, except greeting; invitation & stationery printing & engraving; etching & engraving; letters for signs, metal; identification badges & insignia

(G-13548)
CLARIVATE ANALYTICS (US) LLC (DH)
Also Called: Endnote
1500 Spring Garden St # 400 (19130-4127)
PHONE....................215 386-0100
Mukhtar Ahmed, *President*
Chris Veator, *President*
Daniel Videtto, *President*
Hemant Gandhi, *Treasurer*
Freeto Helen, *Supervisor*
EMP: 600
SALES (est): 340.1MM
SALES (corp-wide): 328.1K **Privately Held**
WEB: www.endnote.com
SIC: 2741 7372 Miscellaneous publishing; prepackaged software
HQ: Camelot U.S. Acquisition Llc
1500 Spring Garden St 4th
Philadelphia PA 19130
215 386-0100

(G-13549)
CLEARKIN CHEMICAL CORP
Schiller & Allen Sts (19134)
PHONE....................215 426-7230
William J Clearkin, *President*
Robert Boland, *Vice Pres*
▼ **EMP:** 9 **EST:** 1941
SQ FT: 30,000
SALES (est): 891.9K **Privately Held**
SIC: 2851 Paints & allied products

(G-13550)
CLOTHES-PIN
2124 Spring St (19103-1002)
PHONE....................215 888-5784
Michael E Resnic, *Principal*
EMP: 4
SALES: 1K **Privately Held**
SIC: 3452 Pins

(G-13551)
CLP PUBLICATIONS INC
Also Called: Running Press Book Publishers
2300 Chestnut St Ste 200 (19103-4371)
PHONE....................215 567-5080
David Steinberg, *CEO*
Allan Struzinski, *COO*
Bill Riser, *CFO*
▲ **EMP:** 150
SQ FT: 10,000
SALES: 13.4MM
SALES (corp-wide): 156MM **Privately Held**
WEB: www.specialfavors.com
SIC: 2731 2791 Books: publishing only; typesetting
PA: Clp Pb, Llc
1290 Ave Of The Amrcas
New York NY 10104
212 340-8100

(G-13552)
CMA REFINISHING SOLUTIONS INC
1731 Tilghman St (19122-3113)
PHONE....................215 427-1141
Gregory Boccardo, *CEO*
EMP: 7
SALES (est): 677.6K **Privately Held**
SIC: 2869 Industrial organic chemicals

(G-13553)
CMI SYSTEMS
3601 Market St Unit 1605 (19104-5913)
P.O. Box 41809 (19101-1809)
PHONE....................215 596-0306
Osahon Emmanuel, *CEO*
EMP: 12
SALES (corp-wide): 1.1MM **Privately Held**
SIC: 1521 2392 5021 General remodeling, single-family houses; bridge sets, cloth & napkin: from purchased materials; household furniture
PA: Cmi Systems
5684 Bay St
Emeryville CA 94608
215 596-0306

(G-13554)
COATING & CONVERTING TECH CORP
Also Called: CCT
80 E Morris St (19148-1411)
PHONE....................215 271-0610
Robert Dempsey Jr, *President*
Roger Davis, *Plant Mgr*
John Carroll, *CFO*
Steve Reidenbach, *Manager*
Greg Cruciano, *Info Tech Mgr*
▲ **EMP:** 45
SQ FT: 77,000
SALES: 20MM **Privately Held**
WEB: www.ccttapes.com
SIC: 2671 Packaging paper & plastics film, coated & laminated

(G-13555)
COATING DEVELOPMENT GROUP INC
Schiller & Allen St (19134)
P.O. Box 14817 (19134-0817)
PHONE....................215 426-6216
Richard Greene, *President*
Mark Kochanowicz, *General Mgr*
Charles Robbins, *Vice Pres*
Joseph Lafountain, *Plant Mgr*
James Carpenter, *Treasurer*
EMP: 15
SQ FT: 27,000
SALES (est): 5.6MM **Privately Held**
WEB: www.cdgkonig.com
SIC: 2851 Lacquers, varnishes, enamels & other coatings

(G-13556)
COCA-COLA BTLG CO OF NY INC
725 E Erie Ave (19134-1294)
PHONE....................718 326-3334
David Prespitino, *Manager*
EMP: 116
SALES (corp-wide): 35.4B **Publicly Held**
SIC: 2086 Bottled & canned soft drinks
HQ: The Coca-Cola Bottling Company Of New York Inc
2500 Windy Ridge Pkwy Se
Atlanta GA 30339
770 989-3000

(G-13557)
COCCO BROS
2745 W Passyunk Ave (19145-4098)
PHONE....................215 334-3816
Carlo Cocco, *President*
Gabriel Cocco, *Corp Secy*
EMP: 25 **EST:** 1944
SQ FT: 7,000
SALES (est): 3.7MM **Privately Held**
SIC: 3842 Orthopedic appliances; prosthetic appliances; surgical appliances & supplies

(G-13558)
COGNITIVE OPRTONAL SYSTEMS LLC
3733 Spruce St Rm 408 (19104-6301)
PHONE....................908 672-4711
Jonas Cleveland,
Kostas Daniilidis,
EMP: 5
SALES (est): 290.1K **Privately Held**
SIC: 7372 Application computer software

(G-13559)
COILPLUS INC
Coilplus Pennsylvania
5135 Bleigh Ave (19136-4200)
PHONE....................215 331-5200
James Lehr, *Division Pres*
Mike Onody, *Plant Mgr*
Betty Chaput, *MIS Dir*
Betty Ghaput, *Info Tech Dir*
Margaret McRea, *Executive Asst*
EMP: 68
SALES (corp-wide): 71B **Privately Held**
WEB: www.coilpluspa.com
SIC: 3444 5051 Coal chutes, prefabricated sheet metal; steel
HQ: Coilplus, Inc.
6250 N River Rd Ste 6050
Rosemont IL 60018
847 384-3000

(G-13560)
COLMETAL INCORPORATED
944 W Tioga St (19140-4312)
PHONE....................215 225-1060
Fred Escobar, *President*
EMP: 5
SQ FT: 15,000
SALES (est): 719.6K **Privately Held**
SIC: 3444 7699 Flumes, sheet metal; industrial equipment cleaning

(G-13561)
COLUMBIA SILK DYEING COMPANY
1726 N Howard St (19122-3296)
PHONE....................215 739-2289
Craig S Garton, *President*
Curt Garton, *Treasurer*
▲ **EMP:** 20 **EST:** 1913
SQ FT: 45,000
SALES (est): 3MM **Privately Held**
SIC: 2262 2269 2261 Dyeing: manmade fiber & silk broadwoven fabrics; dyeing: raw stock yarn & narrow fabrics; finishing plants, cotton

(G-13562)
COMPASS RET DISPLAY GROUP INC
9250 Ashton Rd Unit 200 (19114-3498)
PHONE....................215 744-2787
Robert Smith, *Principal*
EMP: 3
SALES (est): 304.3K **Privately Held**
SIC: 2541 Store fixtures, wood

(G-13563)
COMPLETE HAND ASSEMBLY FINSHG
500 E Luzerne St (19124-4208)
PHONE....................215 634-7490
Peter B Sernoff, *CEO*
EMP: 30
SALES (est): 3.2MM **Privately Held**
SIC: 2789 2675 Bookbinding & related work; die-cut paper & board

(G-13564)
COMPORTO LLC
Also Called: Comporto Communications
1500 Market St Ste Cc1 (19102-2106)
PHONE....................215 595-6224
Bernadette Gaghan,
EMP: 3
SALES: 300K **Privately Held**
SIC: 2759 Commercial printing

(G-13565)
COMPOSING ROOM INC (PA)
Also Called: Crw Graphics
2001 Market St Ste 2500 (19103-7036)
PHONE....................215 310-5559
Harriet Weiss, *CEO*
Mark Weiss, *President*
Jon Conant, *General Mgr*
Elizabeth Lott, *Business Mgr*
Larry Weiss, *Corp Secy*
EMP: 4 **EST:** 1978
SALES (est): 30.6MM **Privately Held**
SIC: 2759 Screen printing

(G-13566)
COMPUDATA INC (PA)
2701 Commerce Way (19154-1087)
PHONE....................215 969-1000

▲ = Import ▼=Export
◆ =Import/Export

Steven Ciarciello, *President*
Angela Nadeau, *Exec VP*
Angela M Nadeau, *Vice Pres*
Angie Nadeau, *Treasurer*
EMP: 35
SQ FT: 30,000
SALES (est): 13.3MM **Privately Held**
WEB: www.compu.com
SIC: 7379 5045 7372 Computer related consulting services; computer software; prepackaged software

(G-13567)
COMPUTER COMPONENTS CORP
2751 Southampton Rd (19154-1205)
PHONE..................................215 676-7600
Nathu R Dandora, *President*
Michelle Cirelli, *Purch Agent*
Ilona Neal, *Purch Agent*
Rahul Dandora, *CFO*
Debra Beattie, *Technical Staff*
EMP: 95 **EST:** 1964
SQ FT: 75,000
SALES (est): 18.6MM **Privately Held**
SIC: 3444 Sheet metalwork

(G-13568)
CON-WALD CORP
Also Called: Cosolidated Drake Press
5050 Parkside Ave (19131)
PHONE..................................215 879-1400
Michael George, *President*
William Denenno, *Vice Pres*
Maureen Dobuski, *Vice Pres*
Joe Smith, *Vice Pres*
Dennis Fenstermaker, *Treasurer*
EMP: 38
SQ FT: 50,000
SALES: 7MM **Privately Held**
SIC: 2752 Commercial printing, lithographic

(G-13569)
CONANT CORPORATION
Also Called: Conant Printing & Copying
42 S 15th St Unit 905 (19102-2205)
PHONE..................................215 557-7466
Conant Scott Rogers, *President*
EMP: 15
SQ FT: 3,000
SALES (est): 2MM **Privately Held**
WEB: www.econant.com
SIC: 2752 Business form & card printing, lithographic

(G-13570)
CONNECTIFY INC
1429 Walnut St Fl 2 (19102-3210)
PHONE..................................215 854-8432
Alexander Gizis, *CEO*
Bhana Grover, *President*
▲ **EMP:** 12
SQ FT: 5,000
SALES (est): 1MM **Privately Held**
WEB: www.nomadio.net
SIC: 7372 Application computer software

(G-13571)
CONSOLIDATED PRINTING INC
Also Called: Consolidated/Drake Press
5050 Parkside Ave (19131-4751)
PHONE..................................215 879-1400
Michael George, *President*
William Denenno, *Vice Pres*
Maureen Dobuski, *Vice Pres*
Joe Smith, *Vice Pres*
Bill Tierno, *Plant Engr*
EMP: 20 **EST:** 1965
SQ FT: 50,000
SALES (est): 3.9MM **Privately Held**
WEB: www.condrake.com
SIC: 2752 3555 Business form & card printing, lithographic; collating machines for printing & bookbinding

(G-13572)
CONSUMER NETWORK INC
Also Called: Shopper Report, The
3624 Market St Ste 200s (19104-2616)
PHONE..................................215 235-2400
Mona Forman Doyle, *President*
EMP: 3
SALES: 499K **Privately Held**
SIC: 2731 Pamphlets: publishing only, not printed on site

(G-13573)
CONTRADO BBH HOLDINGS LLC
2929 Arch St Fl 27 (19104-2857)
PHONE..................................215 609-3400
R Emrich, *Principal*
EMP: 11
SALES (est): 396.9MM
SALES (corp-wide): 1.1B **Privately Held**
SIC: 3579 Envelope stuffing, sealing & addressing machines
PA: Versa Capital Management, Llc
2929 Arch St Ste 1650
Philadelphia PA 19104
215 609-3400

(G-13574)
CORONET BOOKS INC
311 Bainbridge St (19147-1543)
PHONE..................................215 925-2762
Ronald Smolin, *President*
EMP: 4
SQ FT: 1,350
SALES (est): 271.6K **Privately Held**
WEB: www.coronetbooks.com
SIC: 2731 Book publishing

(G-13575)
COUNTRY CLUB RESTAURANT
Also Called: Country CLB Rest Pastry Shops
1717 Cottman Ave (19111-3802)
PHONE..................................215 722-0500
Noel Perloff, *President*
Simone Perloff, *Vice Pres*
EMP: 100
SQ FT: 20,000
SALES (est): 2.9MM **Privately Held**
SIC: 5812 5461 2051 Restaurant, family: independent; bakeries; bread, cake & related products

(G-13576)
CPA OPERATIONS LLC
Also Called: Lensco
2917 Hedley St (19137-1920)
PHONE..................................215 743-6860
Kathleen Molyneaux, *President*
Kathleen Croddick Molyneaux, *President*
EMP: 5
SQ FT: 4,000
SALES (est): 520K **Privately Held**
SIC: 2842 Cleaning or polishing preparations

(G-13577)
CRAMCO INC (PA)
Also Called: Cramco Dinettes
2200 E Ann St (19134-4199)
PHONE..................................215 427-9500
Louis Cramer, *President*
Paul Cramer, *Vice Pres*
Vladimir Melnik, *QC Mgr*
Joan Cramer, *Treasurer*
Tracey McGurk, *Controller*
◆ **EMP:** 214
SQ FT: 200,000
SALES: 30.1MM **Privately Held**
WEB: www.cramco.net
SIC: 2511 2514 Dining room furniture: wood; metal household furniture

(G-13578)
CREATIVE CHARACTERS
990 Spring Garden St # 401 (19123-2606)
PHONE..................................215 923-2679
Marya Kaye, *President*
Brigid Kaye, *Vice Pres*
EMP: 5
SALES (est): 857K **Privately Held**
WEB: www.creativecharacters.com
SIC: 2752 7336 7331 8742 Commercial printing, offset; commercial art & graphic design; direct mail advertising services; marketing consulting services

(G-13579)
CREATIVE THOUGHT MEDIA LLC
2301 N 9th St Ste 310 (19133-1506)
P.O. Box 1449, Fort Washington (19034-8449)
PHONE..................................267 270-5147
Christina Johnson,
Christina Andrs Hpkns Johnson,
EMP: 3

SALES (est): 118.6K **Privately Held**
SIC: 7221 7313 3861 7812 Photographic studios, portrait; electronic media advertising representatives; motion picture film; television film production; commercials, television: tape or film

(G-13580)
CREATIVE TOUCH INC
Also Called: Display Design & Sales Co
11500 Roosevelt Blvd B (19116-3013)
PHONE..................................215 856-9177
Joseph Victor Jurciukonis, *President*
Robert Byrnes, *Corp Secy*
Donald Kasner, *Vice Pres*
Kara Person, *Project Mgr*
Ken Meyers, *Accounts Exec*
EMP: 30 **EST:** 1973
SQ FT: 85,000
SALES (est): 3.9MM **Privately Held**
WEB: www.displays4pop.com
SIC: 3999 Advertising display products

(G-13581)
CRG HOLDING INC
1845 Walnut St Ste 800 (19103-4711)
PHONE..................................215 569-9900
EMP: 3
SALES (corp-wide): 361.9MM **Publicly Held**
SIC: 2782 Albums
HQ: Crg Holding, Inc.
402 Bna Dr Ste 100
Nashville TN 37217
615 724-2900

(G-13582)
CRICKET COMMUNICATIONS LLC
930 Washington Ave (19147-3840)
PHONE..................................267 687-5949
EMP: 4
SALES (corp-wide): 170.7B **Publicly Held**
SIC: 7375 4812 3663 On-line data base information retrieval; cellular telephone services; radio & TV communications equipment
HQ: Cricket Communications, Llc
7337 Trade St
San Diego CA 92121
858 882-6000

(G-13583)
CRITICAL PATH PROJECT INC
2062 Lombard St (19146-1315)
PHONE..................................215 545-2212
Kiyoshi Kuromiya, *President*
EMP: 3
SALES: 200K **Privately Held**
SIC: 2741 5961 Newsletter publishing; catalog & mail-order houses

(G-13584)
CROWN AMERICAS LLC
1 Crown Way (19154-4501)
PHONE..................................215 698-5100
Tom Donnelly, *Principal*
EMP: 43
SALES (est): 7.8MM
SALES (corp-wide): 11.1B **Publicly Held**
WEB: www.crownholdings.net
SIC: 3411 Metal cans
PA: Crown Holdings Inc.
770 Township Line Rd # 100
Yardley PA 19067
215 698-5100

(G-13585)
CROWN BEVERAGE PACKAGING LLC
1 Crown Way (19154-4501)
PHONE..................................215 698-5100
John Conway, *President*
◆ **EMP:** 500
SALES (est): 48.3MM
SALES (corp-wide): 11.1B **Publicly Held**
WEB: www.crowncork.com
SIC: 3411 3466 Metal cans; crowns & closures
HQ: Crown Cork & Seal Usa, Inc.
770 Township Line Rd # 100
Yardley PA 19067
215 698-5100

(G-13586)
CROWN BOILER CO
Also Called: Crown Boilers
3633 I St (19134-1451)
P.O. Box 14818 (19134-0818)
PHONE..................................215 535-8900
Don Schwing, *President*
▲ **EMP:** 30 **EST:** 1953
SQ FT: 75,000
SALES (est): 6.5MM
SALES (corp-wide): 172.4MM **Publicly Held**
WEB: www.crownboiler.com
SIC: 5075 3585 3443 3433 Warm air heating & air conditioning; refrigeration & heating equipment; fabricated plate work (boiler shop); boilers, low-pressure heating: steam or hot water
PA: Burnham Holdings, Inc.
1241 Harrisburg Ave
Lancaster PA 17603
717 390-7800

(G-13587)
CROWN CORK & SEAL USA INC
3070 Red Lion Rd (19114-1130)
PHONE..................................215 698-5100
EMP: 3
SALES (corp-wide): 11.1B **Publicly Held**
SIC: 3411 Tin cans
HQ: Crown Cork & Seal Usa, Inc.
770 Township Line Rd # 100
Yardley PA 19067
215 698-5100

(G-13588)
CRYSTAL METAL PRODUCTS CO INC
2700 Castor Ave (19134-5598)
PHONE..................................215 423-2500
John Cristinzio, *President*
Michael Cristinzio Jr, *Vice Pres*
EMP: 20 **EST:** 1958
SQ FT: 25,000
SALES (est): 1.8MM **Privately Held**
WEB: www.crystalmetal.com
SIC: 3599 Machine shop, jobbing & repair

(G-13589)
CSS INTERNATIONAL CORPORATION
2061 E Glenwood Ave (19124-5674)
P.O. Box 19560 (19124-0060)
PHONE..................................215 533-6110
Vance Coulston, *President*
Eugene F Fijalkowski, *Vice Pres*
Gene Fijalkowski, *Vice Pres*
EMP: 12
SQ FT: 28,000
SALES (est): 2.8MM **Privately Held**
WEB: www.cssintl.com
SIC: 3999 3565 Custom pulverizing & grinding of plastic materials; packaging machinery

(G-13590)
CULPEPPER CORPORATION
1310 N 2nd St (19122-2504)
P.O. Box 37017 (19122-0717)
PHONE..................................215 425-6532
EMP: 40
SQ FT: 3,000
SALES (est): 2.2MM **Privately Held**
SIC: 1796 3341 Building Equipment Installation Secondary Nonferrous Metal Producer

(G-13591)
CURRENT HISTORY INC
4225 Main St (19127-1699)
PHONE..................................610 772-5709
Mark Redmond, *President*
EMP: 3 **EST:** 1914
SQ FT: 4,000
SALES: 460K **Privately Held**
WEB: www.currenthistory.com
SIC: 2721 Periodicals: publishing only

(G-13592)
CUSTOM BLENDS INC
9951 Global Rd (19115-1065)
PHONE..................................215 934-7080
Harvey Levitt, *President*
Julia Levitt, *Corp Secy*
EMP: 5 **EST:** 1889

SQ FT: 6,000
SALES: 1MM **Privately Held**
SIC: 2085 3589 2899 Distilled & blended liquors; water treatment equipment, industrial; water treating compounds

(G-13593)
CUSTOM CHILL INC
2751 Southampton Rd (19154-1205)
PHONE..................................215 676-7600
Nathu Dandora, *President*
Solomon Reznik, *Vice Pres*
Victor Reznik, *Mktg Dir*
EMP: 8
SALES: 1.2MM **Privately Held**
WEB: www.customchill.com
SIC: 3585 Refrigeration & heating equipment

(G-13594)
CUSTOM MANUFACTURED PRODUCTS
1100 W Indiana Ave (19133-1331)
PHONE..................................215 228-3830
Ruben Klugman, *President*
Marian Klugman, *President*
Samuel Klugman, *Vice Pres*
EMP: 36 **EST:** 1975
SQ FT: 53,000
SALES: 2MM **Privately Held**
WEB: www.powerbay.com
SIC: 3646 Commercial indusl & institutional electric lighting fixtures

(G-13595)
CUSTOM POLISHING AND FINISHING
8301 Torresdale Ave # 23 (19136-2911)
PHONE..................................215 331-0960
Mary Joan Maloney, *President*
Don Maloney Sr, *Vice Pres*
Donald Maloney Jr, *Vice Pres*
EMP: 4
SQ FT: 4,400
SALES: 290K **Privately Held**
WEB: www.dgmchrome.com
SIC: 3471 3479 Polishing, metals or formed products; finishing, metals or formed products; coating of metals & formed products

(G-13596)
CW THOMAS LLC
Also Called: C W Thomas
8000 State Rd (19136-2994)
PHONE..................................215 335-0200
Randy Altland, *Senior VP*
Bob Brennan, *VP Opers*
Rich Pomfret, *Opers Staff*
Marianne Wesley, *Purch Mgr*
Kimberly Gallo, *Human Resources*
EMP: 45
SQ FT: 70,000
SALES (est): 4.2MM **Privately Held**
WEB: www.cwthomas.com
SIC: 3089 2671 Thermoformed finished plastic products; plastic film, coated or laminated for packaging

(G-13597)
D & N ENTERPRISE INC
Also Called: Sign-A-Rama
238 Market St (19106-2816)
PHONE..................................215 238-9050
Neal Herzog, *President*
Donna Herzog, *Vice Pres*
EMP: 5
SALES: 700K **Privately Held**
WEB: www.signaramaccphila.com
SIC: 3993 Signs & advertising specialties

(G-13598)
D & S CLOTHING INC
176 W Loudon St Fl 2 (19120-4241)
PHONE..................................856 383-3794
Ki Chol Choe, *COO*
EMP: 5
SQ FT: 10,000
SALES (est): 314K **Privately Held**
SIC: 2311 2326 2329 2339 Men's & boys' uniforms; men's & boys' work clothing; work uniforms; men's & boys' sportswear & athletic clothing; athletic clothing: women's, misses' & juniors'

(G-13599)
D C HUMPHRYS CO
Also Called: Humphry's Textile Products
5000 Paschall Ave (19143-5136)
PHONE..................................215 307-3363
Ronald Nissenbaum, *President*
Fred Hoge, *Vice Pres*
Zak Nissenbaum, *Vice Pres*
◆ **EMP:** 65 **EST:** 1874
SQ FT: 82,000
SALES (est): 16.4MM **Privately Held**
WEB: www.humphrystextileproducts.com
SIC: 2393 2295 2394 Textile bags; coated fabrics, not rubberized; tarpaulins, fabric: made from purchased materials

(G-13600)
D L ELECTRONICS INC
6020 Palmetto St (19111-5797)
PHONE..................................215 742-2666
Caroline J Laschenski, *President*
Joseph Laschenski, *Vice Pres*
EMP: 19 **EST:** 1968
SQ FT: 10,000
SALES (est): 3.4MM **Privately Held**
SIC: 3679 7629 5065 Electronic circuits; electrical repair shops; electronic parts & equipment

(G-13601)
DACVAL LLC
7341 Tulip St Ste 101 (19136-4215)
PHONE..................................215 331-9600
Chuck Henry, *QA Dir*
David A Christian, *Mng Member*
Dominic J Durinzi,
EMP: 10
SQ FT: 5,000
SALES: 1MM **Privately Held**
SIC: 3545 Machine tool accessories

(G-13602)
DADDARIO & COMPANY INC
421 N 7th St (19123-3905)
PHONE..................................856 217-4954
Michael Daddario, *Branch Mgr*
EMP: 56
SALES (corp-wide): 193.1MM **Privately Held**
SIC: 3931 String instruments & parts
PA: D'addario & Company, Inc.
595 Smith St
Farmingdale NY 11735
631 439-3300

(G-13603)
DAEDAL GROUP INC
6136 Palmetto St 38 (19111-5730)
P.O. Box 205, Southampton (18966-0205)
PHONE..................................215 745-8718
John Watko, *President*
Michael Watko, *Vice Pres*
Wanda Watko, *Treasurer*
Susan Di Florio, *Admin Sec*
EMP: 7
SQ FT: 4,000
SALES (est): 836.7K **Privately Held**
WEB: www.daedalgroup.com
SIC: 2752 7336 Commercial printing, offset; chart & graph design; graphic arts & related design

(G-13604)
DAILY DOVE CARE LLC
1700 Market St Ste 1005 (19103-3920)
PHONE..................................215 316-5888
Fadwa Robinson, *CEO*
EMP: 3
SALES (est): 69.2K **Privately Held**
SIC: 2711 Newspapers, publishing & printing

(G-13605)
DATA TECH POS INC
702 N 3rd St Ste 100 (19123-2904)
PHONE..................................215 925-8888
Patrick White, *President*
EMP: 3
SQ FT: 1,800
SALES (est): 480K **Privately Held**
SIC: 3578 Point-of-sale devices

(G-13606)
DAVES AIRPORT SHUTTLE LLC
5915 Harbison Ave (19135-3946)
PHONE..................................215 288-1000

Gadi Berone, *President*
Rona Applebum, *Manager*
EMP: 3
SALES (est): 451.3K **Privately Held**
SIC: 3532 Shuttle cars, underground

(G-13607)
DAVID MICHAEL & CO INC (HQ)
Also Called: Tastepoint By Iff
10801 Decatur Rd (19154-3298)
PHONE..................................215 632-3100
Andreas Fibig, *CEO*
William Rosskam, *President*
Emilio Berardi, *President*
Steve A Rosskam, *Exec VP*
Diane Franzoni, *CFO*
▲ **EMP:** 92 **EST:** 1947
SQ FT: 66,000
SALES (est): 24.4MM
SALES (corp-wide): 3.9B **Publicly Held**
SIC: 2869 2087 Mfg Industrial Organic Chemicals Mfg Flavor Extracts/Syrup
PA: International Flavors & Fragrances Inc.
521 W 57th St
New York NY 10019
212 765-5500

(G-13608)
DAVID MICHAEL & CO INC
10801 Decatur Rd (19154-3298)
PHONE..................................909 887-3800
EMP: 10
SQ FT: 25,568
SALES (corp-wide): 3.4B **Publicly Held**
SIC: 2087 2869 Mfg Flavor Extracts/Syrup
HQ: David Michael & Co., Inc.
10801 Decatur Rd
Philadelphia PA 19154
215 632-3100

(G-13609)
DAVID MOSCINSKI
Also Called: Fabrications Costume Co
1632 S 2nd St (19148-1338)
PHONE..................................215 271-6193
David Moscinski, *Owner*
EMP: 3
SALES: 60K **Privately Held**
SIC: 2389 Costumes

(G-13610)
DAVID WEBER CO INC
Also Called: Weber Display & Packaging
3500 Richmond St (19134-6102)
PHONE..................................215 426-3500
James R Doherty, *President*
Patricia Doherty, *Corp Secy*
Chris O'Hearn, *Opers Mgr*
Dave De Rosa, *Opers Staff*
Bill Hodgson, *QC Mgr*
▲ **EMP:** 125
SQ FT: 125,000
SALES (est): 58.5MM **Privately Held**
SIC: 2653 3993 Boxes, corrugated: made from purchased materials; signs & advertising specialties

(G-13611)
DAVIS LAMP & SHADE INC
4550 Melrose St (19124-4116)
PHONE..................................215 426-2777
Michael Davis, *CEO*
EMP: 24 **EST:** 1946
SQ FT: 60,000
SALES (est): 918.7K **Privately Held**
SIC: 5947 3641 3645 Gift, novelty & souvenir shop; electric lamps; lamp & light shades

(G-13612)
DBAZA INC
3401 Market St Ste 201 (19104-3358)
P.O. Box 3513, Wilmington DE (19807-0513)
PHONE..................................412 681-1180
Sergey Sirotinin, *President*
EMP: 10 **EST:** 1997
SQ FT: 3,600
SALES (est): 732K **Privately Held**
WEB: www.dbaza.com
SIC: 7372 Educational computer software

(G-13613)
DECOPRO INC
300 E Godfrey Ave Ste 3 (19120-1646)
PHONE..................................215 939-7983

Louis Pollack, *President*
EMP: 5
SQ FT: 6,000
SALES (est): 537.1K **Privately Held**
SIC: 2391 Draperies, plastic & textile: from purchased materials

(G-13614)
DECORA INDUSTRIES INC (PA)
Also Called: Data Display Systems
14001 Townsend Rd (19154-1007)
PHONE..................................215 698-2600
Robert H Levitt, *President*
Theodore Liebman, *Vice Pres*
▲ **EMP:** 65
SQ FT: 38,000
SALES (est): 15MM **Privately Held**
WEB: www.datadisplaysystems.com
SIC: 3645 3993 3577 Residential lighting fixtures; electric signs; computer peripheral equipment

(G-13615)
DEF MEDICAL TECHNOLOGIES LLC
4040 Locust St (19104-3507)
PHONE..................................802 299-8457
Elsa Swanson, *Mng Member*
Forrest Miller,
EMP: 3
SALES (est): 117.4K **Privately Held**
SIC: 3842 Orthopedic appliances

(G-13616)
DEL REN ASSOC INC
3310 S 20th St (19145-5764)
PHONE..................................215 467-7000
John Pellak, *Principal*
EMP: 3
SALES (est): 242.5K **Privately Held**
SIC: 3446 Architectural metalwork

(G-13617)
DELAVAU LLC (HQ)
Also Called: Delavau Pharmaceutical Partner
10101 Roosevelt Blvd (19154-2105)
PHONE..................................215 671-1400
Jeff Billig, *Vice Pres*
Curt Pagano, *Vice Pres*
William Rhim, *Warehouse Mgr*
Jack Walter, *Opers Staff*
Gary Bolesta, *Research*
▲ **EMP:** 155
SQ FT: 235,000
SALES (est): 94MM **Privately Held**
WEB: www.delavau.com
SIC: 2834 Vitamin preparations

(G-13618)
DELKTECH SYSTEMS INC
1213 Vine St Ste 232 (19107-1111)
PHONE..................................267 341-8391
Harry Brown, *Principal*
EMP: 6
SALES (est): 490K **Privately Held**
SIC: 3661 Telephone & telegraph apparatus

(G-13619)
DENIM INC DIVISION
Also Called: Vision Denim, The
414 South St (19147-1535)
PHONE..................................215 627-1400
Moshe Hananel, *President*
EMP: 10
SQ FT: 3,000
SALES (est): 1.6MM **Privately Held**
SIC: 2211 Denims

(G-13620)
DESIGN DECORATORS
Also Called: Design Scapes
3076 Jasper St (19134-3147)
PHONE..................................215 634-8300
Sal Bonafino, *President*
Theresa Hearst,
▲ **EMP:** 35
SQ FT: 18,500
SALES: 4.3MM **Privately Held**
WEB: www.designscapes.net
SIC: 3699 5999 Christmas tree lighting sets, electric; Christmas tree ornaments, electric; Christmas lights & decorations

(G-13621)
DESIGNER FASHIONS PLUS
6100 City Ave Apt 512 (19131-1273)
PHONE..................................215 416-5062
Imani Farrington, *Principal*
EMP: 9
SALES: 440K **Privately Held**
SIC: 2331 Women's & misses' blouses &
shirts

(G-13622)
DESIGNS BY LAWRENCE INC
12301 Mcnulty Rd Ste A (19154-1000)
P.O. Box 61, Mechanicsville (18934-0061)
PHONE..................................215 698-4555
Michael F Giorgione, *President*
Ronald Levine, *Corp Secy*
▲ EMP: 30
SQ FT: 12,000
SALES (est): 4.4MM **Privately Held**
WEB: www.designsbylawrence.com
SIC: 3465 Tops, automobile: stamped
metal; moldings or trim, automobile:
stamped metal

(G-13623)
**DESMOND WHOLESALE DISTRS
INC**
270 Geiger Rd Bldg C (19115-1016)
PHONE..................................215 225-0300
Shirley Hartzell, *President*
Donald Hartzell, *Vice Pres*
William Hartzell, *Vice Pres*
EMP: 10 EST: 1955
SQ FT: 21,000
SALES (est): 1.8MM **Privately Held**
SIC: 5031 2541 Kitchen cabinets; wood
partitions & fixtures

(G-13624)
**DEVAL LIFE CYCLE SUPPORT
LLC**
7341 Tulip St (19136-4215)
PHONE..................................865 786-8675
Sam Thevanayagam, *CEO*
James Emerich, *Principal*
Andrew Hopper, *Principal*
EMP: 25
SQ FT: 40,000
SALES (est): 2.1MM
SALES (corp-wide): 3MM **Privately Held**
SIC: 3537 Dollies (hand or power trucks),
industrial except mining
PA: Parts Life Inc.
30 Twosome Dr Ste 1
Moorestown NJ 08057
856 786-8675

(G-13625)
DEVALTRONIX INC
7341 Tulip St (19136-4215)
PHONE..................................215 331-9600
Dominic Durinzi, *President*
Ronald Penska, *Vice Pres*
EMP: 13 EST: 1996
SQ FT: 40,000
SALES (est): 1MM **Privately Held**
SIC: 3993 3537 Electric signs; pallets,
metal

(G-13626)
DEVRA PARTY CORP
4343 G St Ste 1 (19124-4300)
PHONE..................................718 522-7421
Mendel Herschop, *President*
Rachel Hershkop, *Admin Sec*
EMP: 5
SALES (est): 610K **Privately Held**
SIC: 2679 5199 2621 Novelties, paper:
made from purchased material; novelties,
paper; paper mills

(G-13627)
DGM CUSTOM PLSG FINSG C
8301 Torresdale Ave # 23 (19136-2949)
PHONE..................................215 331-0960
Don Maloney, *Principal*
EMP: 5
SALES (est): 260K **Privately Held**
SIC: 3471 Finishing, metals or formed
products

(G-13628)
DIALOGUE INSTITUTE
Also Called: JOURNAL OF ECUMENICAL
STUDIES
1700 N Broad St Ste 315t (19121-3429)
PHONE..................................215 204-7520
Leonard Swidler, *President*
Julia Sheetz-Willard, *Opers Staff*
EMP: 5
SALES: 633.4K **Privately Held**
SIC: 2782 Ledger, inventory & account
books

(G-13629)
DIAMOND ROCK PRODUCTIONS
2101 Brandywine St # 200 (19130-3152)
P.O. Box 441, Zeeland MI (49464-0441)
PHONE..................................215 564-3401
Hugh O Brock, *Partner*
EMP: 3 EST: 1993
SALES (est): 273.4K **Privately Held**
WEB: www.harpist.com
SIC: 2721 Periodicals

(G-13630)
DIBRUNO BROS INC (PA)
1730 Chestnut St (19103-5120)
PHONE..................................215 665-9220
William Mignucci, *President*
Emilio Mignucci, *Vice Pres*
Rachelle Adams, *Bookkeeper*
Maria Crespo, *Office Mgr*
Amy Howe, *Manager*
▲ EMP: 9
SALES (est): 2MM **Privately Held**
SIC: 2022 5451 2011 Cheese, natural &
processed; cheese; bacon, slab & sliced
from meat slaughtered on site

(G-13631)
DIETZ & WATSON INC (PA)
Also Called: Black Bear Deli Meats
5701 Tacony St (19135-4394)
PHONE..................................800 333-1974
Louis Eni Jr, *CEO*
Christopher Eni, *COO*
Rich Wright, *Vice Pres*
Joe McMurtrie, *VP Opers*
Mike Bocchicchio, *Warehouse Mgr*
▲ EMP: 645 EST: 1939
SQ FT: 180,000
SALES (est): 234.7MM **Privately Held**
SIC: 2011 2013 Beef products from beef
slaughtered on site; pork products from
pork slaughtered on site; sausages &
other prepared meats

(G-13632)
DIM SUM & NOODLE
2000 Hamilton St (19130-3814)
PHONE..................................215 515-3992
EMP: 3 EST: 2016
SALES (est): 113.4K **Privately Held**
SIC: 2098 Noodles (e.g. egg, plain &
water), dry

(G-13633)
**DINARDO BROTHERS
MATERIAL INC**
Also Called: Metro Ready Mix and Supplies
4455 Castor Ave (19124-3849)
PHONE..................................215 535-4645
Anthony Dinardo, *President*
EMP: 5
SALES (est): 933.2K **Privately Held**
SIC: 3273 Ready-mixed concrete

(G-13634)
DIRECT DIGITAL MASTER INC
495 E Erie Ave (19134-1104)
PHONE..................................215 634-2235
Peter Choi, *President*
EMP: 4
SALES (est): 219.3K **Privately Held**
SIC: 3823 Digital displays of process vari-
ables
PA: All Americanlook, Inc.
495 E Erie Ave
Philadelphia PA 19134

(G-13635)
DISSTON PRECISION INC
6795 New State Rd (19135-1528)
PHONE..................................215 338-1200
Henry Disston, *Principal*

EMP: 4 EST: 2015
SALES: 87.9K **Privately Held**
SIC: 3531 Blades for graders, scrapers,
dozers & snow plows

(G-13636)
**DIVERSIFIED METAL PRODUCTS
CO**
2020 Frankford Ave (19125-1921)
PHONE..................................215 423-8877
William Oldfield, *President*
Marie Oldfield, *President*
Michael Chmielowski, *Manager*
EMP: 4
SQ FT: 6,500
SALES (est): 563.5K **Privately Held**
SIC: 3444 Sheet metalwork

(G-13637)
DOC PRINTING LLC
5156 Baynton St (19144-1758)
PHONE..................................267 702-6196
Charles White,
EMP: 5
SALES: 250K **Privately Held**
SIC: 5699 2262 Designers, apparel;
screen printing: manmade fiber & silk
broadwoven fabrics

(G-13638)
DOCK TOOL & MACHINE INC
Also Called: Milnor Auto Parts
5200 Unruh Ave Ste E1 (19135-2921)
PHONE..................................215 338-8989
Robert Foust, *President*
Robert Dock, *President*
EMP: 5
SALES (est): 443.3K **Privately Held**
SIC: 3545 3544 5015 Tools & accessories
for machine tools; special dies, tools, jigs
& fixtures; automotive parts & supplies,
used

(G-13639)
**DONATUCCI KITCHENS &
APPLS**
Also Called: Washington Fabricators
1901 Washington Ave (19146-2653)
PHONE..................................215 545-5755
Thomas F Donatucci Jr, *President*
Thomas F Donatucci III, *Vice Pres*
Robert C Donatucci, *Admin Sec*
EMP: 30
SQ FT: 40,000
SALES (est): 4.2MM **Privately Held**
WEB: www.customkitchens.com
SIC: 2434 5722 2541 Wood kitchen cabi-
nets; household appliance stores;
kitchens, complete (sinks, cabinets, etc.);
wood partitions & fixtures

(G-13640)
**DORLAND HEALTHCARE
INFORMATION (HQ)**
Also Called: Dorland Health Care Info
1500 Walnut St Ste 1000 (19102-3512)
PHONE..................................800 784-2332
Robert Graham, *President*
EMP: 6
SQ FT: 7,500
SALES (est): 1.5MM **Privately Held**
SIC: 2741 Directories: publishing & printing

(G-13641)
DOW CHEMICAL COMPANY
100 S Indpdnc Mall W Fl 5 (19106-2320)
PHONE..................................215 592-3000
Mary Ann Morrman, *Branch Mgr*
EMP: 4
SALES (corp-wide): 85.9B **Publicly Held**
SIC: 2819 2821 Industrial inorganic chem-
icals; plastics materials & resins
HQ: The Dow Chemical Company
2211 H H Dow Way
Midland MI 48642
989 636-1000

(G-13642)
DOYLE DESIGN
241 W Wyoming Ave (19140-1529)
PHONE..................................215 456-9745
John Doyle, *President*
EMP: 3
SQ FT: 4,000

SALES (est): 290K **Privately Held**
SIC: 2431 Woodwork, interior & ornamental

(G-13643)
DRD INC
4916 Merion Ave (19131-4611)
PHONE..................................215 879-1055
Dan Degidio, *Principal*
EMP: 3
SALES (est): 181.6K **Privately Held**
SIC: 3273 Ready-mixed concrete

(G-13644)
**DREAM WORLD
INTERNATIONAL INC**
10073 Sandmeyer Ln (19116-3501)
PHONE..................................215 320-0200
Ross Veltri, *President*
Michael Isaacson, *Corp Secy*
Peter C Lee, *Vice Pres*
▲ EMP: 7
SQ FT: 5,500
SALES (est): 1MM **Privately Held**
WEB: www.dreamworldintl.com
SIC: 2311 5136 Suits, men's & boys':
made from purchased materials; men's &
boys' clothing

(G-13645)
DREXEL BINDERY INC
3992 Rowena Dr (19114-2013)
PHONE..................................215 232-3808
Joseph C Passo, *President*
EMP: 10
SQ FT: 15,000
SALES (est): 867.1K **Privately Held**
WEB: www.drexelbindery.com
SIC: 2789 2752 Binding only: books, pam-
phlets, magazines, etc.; commercial print-
ing, lithographic

(G-13646)
DREXEL FOODS INC
1705 N American St (19122-3123)
PHONE..................................215 425-9900
Gary Kanellopoulos, *CEO*
Theodore Kanellopoulos, *President*
Michelle Rascher, *Opers Staff*
Kanellopoulos Evans, *Treasurer*
Evans Kanellopoulos, *Treasurer*
EMP: 35
SALES (est): 7MM **Privately Held**
WEB: www.drexelfoods.com
SIC: 2013 2015 2011 Sausages & other
prepared meats; poultry slaughtering &
processing; meat packing plants

(G-13647)
DREXEL UNIVERSITY
Also Called: Ties Magazine
3219 Arch St (19104-2711)
PHONE..................................215 590-8863
Catherine Connor, *Branch Mgr*
EMP: 6
SALES (corp-wide): 985.3MM **Privately
Held**
WEB: www.drexel.edu
SIC: 2721 8221 Periodicals; university
PA: Drexel University
3141 Chestnut St
Philadelphia PA 19104
215 895-2000

(G-13648)
DRIBAN BODY WORKS INC
8950 State Rd Ste 2 (19136-1601)
PHONE..................................215 468-6900
Richard Driban, *President*
EMP: 4 EST: 1911
SQ FT: 20,000
SALES (est): 550K **Privately Held**
SIC: 7532 3713 Lettering, automotive;
paint shop, automotive; exterior repair
services; truck bodies (motor vehicles)

(G-13649)
DUBOSE PRINTING & BUS SVCS
Also Called: Dubose Printing and Bus Svcs
7592a Haverford Ave (19151-2113)
PHONE..................................215 877-9071
Donna Du Bose Miller, *Owner*
EMP: 7
SQ FT: 1,900

SALES (est): 762.9K **Privately Held**
SIC: 2731 2741 2752 Books: publishing & printing; catalogs: publishing & printing; commercial printing; offset

(G-13650)
DURACART USA LLC
1300 Adams Ave (19124-4512)
PHONE..................................888 743-9957
Michael Dipietro, *Mng Member*
EMP: 7
SALES (est): 668.4K **Privately Held**
SIC: 3949 Carts, caddy

(G-13651)
DURALIFE INC
1255 Adams Ave Frnt (19124-3929)
PHONE..................................570 323-9743
Daniel Day, *President*
Timothy Ludgate, *Treasurer*
EMP: 25
SQ FT: 12,000
SALES (est): 3.3MM **Privately Held**
WEB: www.duralife-usa.com
SIC: 3842 Surgical appliances & supplies

(G-13652)
DUTCHER BROTHERS INC
134 S 8th St (19107-5124)
PHONE..................................215 922-4555
Madaline Bonfiglio, *President*
Peter Bonfiglio, *Vice Pres*
EMP: 3
SQ FT: 1,200
SALES: 400K **Privately Held**
SIC: 3911 7631 5094 Jewelry, precious metal; jewelry repair services; watches & parts

(G-13653)
E G EMILS AND SON INC
1344 N American St (19122-3804)
PHONE..................................215 763-3311
Ronald Ramstad, *President*
Emil Gontowski, *Vice Pres*
▲ **EMP:** 33
SQ FT: 20,000
SALES (est): 6.8MM **Privately Held**
WEB: www.emilsturkey.com
SIC: 2015 Turkey processing & slaughtering; chicken slaughtering & processing

(G-13654)
EAST ASIA NOODLE INC
212 N 11th St (19107-1729)
PHONE..................................215 923-6838
George W Yeps, *President*
Thomas Lee, *Corp Secy*
Henry W Wong, *Assistant VP*
Glenn J Mark, *Vice Pres*
Lam Toto, *Asst Treas*
EMP: 15
SQ FT: 4,000
SALES (est): 1.6MM **Privately Held**
WEB: www.thenoodlebox.net
SIC: 5149 2099 Pasta & rice; noodles, uncooked: packaged with other ingredients

(G-13655)
EAST COAST PARTNERS LLC
3225 N Smedley St (19140)
PHONE..................................215 207-9360
EMP: 56
SALES (est): 3.3MM **Privately Held**
SIC: 3711 Mfg Motor Vehicle/Car Bodies

(G-13656)
EAST FALLS BEVERAGE LLC
3343 445 Conrad St (19129)
PHONE..................................215 844-5600
EMP: 3
SALES (est): 75.3K **Privately Held**
SIC: 2082 Beer (alcoholic beverage)

(G-13657)
EBY GROUP LLC
Also Called: EBY Company
4300 H St (19124-4346)
PHONE..................................215 537-4700
Christopher Savine, *CEO*
Mitchell Solomon, *President*
Edward Morris, *General Mgr*
Dennis Savine, *Principal*
Dan Sisk, *Plant Mgr*
EMP: 28

SALES (est): 5.1MM **Privately Held**
SIC: 3678 3643 3679 5063 Electronic connectors; electric connectors; harness assemblies for electronic use: wire or cable; electronic wire & cable; automotive wiring harness sets

(G-13658)
ED JUPITER INC
614 S 4th St Ste 314 (19147-1664)
PHONE..................................888 367-6175
David Hundsness, *Principal*
Amy Pedigo Carmichael,
EMP: 10
SALES (est): 127.6K **Privately Held**
SIC: 7372 Educational computer software

(G-13659)
EDEN GREEN ENERGY INC
2405 Federal St (19146-2431)
PHONE..................................267 255-9462
Domenico Finocchiaro, *President*
EMP: 5
SALES (est): 739.7K **Privately Held**
SIC: 1389 Oil & gas field services

(G-13660)
EDENS TICKETING
115 Chestnut St (19106-3017)
PHONE..................................215 625-0314
Mike Eehan, *Manager*
EMP: 75
SALES (est): 4.9MM
SALES (corp-wide): 17MM **Privately Held**
SIC: 3743 Train cars & equipment, freight or passenger
PA: J. Edens Corporation
115 Chestnut St
Philadelphia PA 19106
215 625-0314

(G-13661)
EDWARD HECHT IMPORTERS INC
Also Called: Ehi Trading International
111 S Independence Mall E # 835 (19106-2511)
PHONE..................................215 925-5520
Saul L Hecht, *President*
Bill Zerega, *Traffic Mgr*
Craig Aaron, *CFO*
▲ **EMP:** 5
SQ FT: 1,700
SALES (est): 13.5MM **Privately Held**
WEB: www.edwardhecht.com
SIC: 5023 3499 5191 Decorative home furnishings & supplies; giftware, brass goods; greenhouse equipment & supplies

(G-13662)
EDWARD HENNESSY CO INC
3820 Pearson Ave (19114-2833)
PHONE..................................215 426-4154
EMP: 3
SQ FT: 8,000
SALES (est): 287.5K **Privately Held**
SIC: 2511 2519 Mfg Wood Household Furniture Mfg Household Furniture

(G-13663)
EG EMILS AND SON INC
1345 Germantown Ave (19122-4407)
PHONE..................................800 228-3645
Ronald Ramstad, *President*
EMP: 3
SALES (est): 254.9K **Privately Held**
SIC: 2015 Poultry slaughtering & processing

(G-13664)
EHMKE MANUFACTURING CO INC (PA)
4200 Macalester St (19124-6014)
PHONE..................................215 324-4200
Robert Rosania, *CEO*
Bob Rosania, *CEO*
Cliff Stokes, *COO*
S Clifford Stokes, *COO*
Brad Milnes, *Director*
▲ **EMP:** 95 **EST:** 1929
SQ FT: 50,000
SALES (est): 18.2MM **Privately Held**
WEB: www.ehmkemfg.com
SIC: 2394 Canvas covers & drop cloths

(G-13665)
ELEGANT FURNITURE & LIGHTING
Also Called: Elegant Lighting
500-550 E Erie Ave (19134)
P.O. Box 26829 (19134-6829)
PHONE..................................888 388-3390
Bin MAI, *President*
Ming Lu, *Admin Sec*
◆ **EMP:** 8
SALES (est): 3MM **Privately Held**
SIC: 5712 3646 Furniture stores; commercial indusl & institutional electric lighting fixtures

(G-13666)
ELEMENT GRANITE & QUARTZ
4800 Ashburner St (19136-2902)
PHONE..................................215 437-9368
EMP: 6
SALES (est): 914.1K **Privately Held**
SIC: 2819 Mfg Industrial Inorganic Chemicals

(G-13667)
ELEMENTAL 3 LLC
Also Called: Ethree
1701 Walnut St (19103-5235)
PHONE..................................267 217-3592
Anthony Bifano, *CEO*
EMP: 9
SQ FT: 1,000
SALES (est): 455.5K **Privately Held**
SIC: 7372 7371 6512 Educational computer software; computer software development & applications; property operation, retail establishment

(G-13668)
ELEMENTS OF LOVE
1051 Flanders Rd (19151-3013)
PHONE..................................267 262-9796
Delinda Green, *Principal*
EMP: 3
SALES (est): 161.5K **Privately Held**
SIC: 2819 Mfg Industrial Inorganic Chemicals

(G-13669)
ELSEVIER INC
1600 John F Kennedy Blvd # 1800 (19103-2398)
P.O. Box 7247-7969 (19170-0001)
PHONE..................................215 239-3441
EMP: 47
SALES (corp-wide): 9.7B **Privately Held**
SIC: 2741 Miscellaneous publishing
HQ: Elsevier Inc.
230 Park Ave Fl 8
New York NY 10169
212 989-5800

(G-13670)
ELSEVIER INC
1600 John F Kennedy Blvd # 1800 (19103-2398)
PHONE..................................215 239-3900
Darryl Spencer, *President*
Bill Olsen, *Manager*
EMP: 5
SALES (corp-wide): 9.7B **Privately Held**
WEB: www.elsevierfoundation.org
SIC: 2731 Book publishing
HQ: Elsevier Inc.
230 Park Ave Fl 8
New York NY 10169
212 989-5800

(G-13671)
ELSOL LATINO NEWSPAPER
198 W Chew Ave (19120-2465)
PHONE..................................215 424-1200
Ricardo Huartado, *Principal*
EMP: 3
SALES (est): 172.7K **Privately Held**
SIC: 2711 Newspapers: publishing only, not printed on site

(G-13672)
EMD PERFORMANCE MATERIALS CORP (HQ)
1200 Intrepid Ave Ste 3 (19112-1230)
PHONE..................................888 367-3275
Luiz G Vieira, *President*
Jeff Rokuskie, *Treasurer*

Paul Oconnor, *Asst Treas*
Octavio Diaz, *Financial Analy*
Billy Sharp, *Manager*
▲ **EMP:** 1
SALES (est): 204.8MM
SALES (corp-wide): 16.9B **Privately Held**
WEB: www.az-em.com
SIC: 2819 Industrial inorganic chemicals
PA: Merck Kg Auf Aktien
Frankfurter Str. 250
Darmstadt 64293
615 172-0

(G-13673)
EMERALD WINDOWS INC
2301 N 9th St (19133-1506)
P.O. Box 50207 (19132-6207)
PHONE..................................215 236-6767
James Cho, *President*
Ji Eun Cho, *Vice Pres*
▲ **EMP:** 10 **EST:** 1953
SQ FT: 42,000
SALES (est): 1.8MM **Privately Held**
WEB: www.emeraldwins.com
SIC: 3442 1751 Storm doors or windows, metal; window & door (prefabricated) installation

(G-13674)
ENERGIZE INC
5450 Wphickon Ave Ste C13 (19144)
PHONE..................................215 438-8342
Susan J Ellis, *President*
Kristen Floyd, *Treasurer*
Judy Wiater, *Director*
EMP: 3
SALES: 280K **Privately Held**
WEB: www.energizeinc.com
SIC: 2741 8742 Miscellaneous publishing; training & development consultant

(G-13675)
EPC INC
Also Called: Engineered Plastics
2180 Bennett Rd (19116-3022)
PHONE..................................215 464-1440
James J Carroll Jr, *President*
Francis Carroll, *Vice Pres*
EMP: 50 **EST:** 1967
SQ FT: 45,000
SALES (est): 9.2MM **Privately Held**
WEB: www.plastx.com
SIC: 3089 Injection molding of plastics

(G-13676)
EPOXTAL LLC
3401 Market St Ste 200 (19104-3358)
PHONE..................................908 376-9825
Chris Elsass, *President*
Andrei Akbasheu, *Principal*
Alessia Polemi, *Principal*
Jonathan Spanier, *Principal*
EMP: 4
SALES (est): 260K **Privately Held**
SIC: 3679 Microwave components

(G-13677)
ERECTOR SETS INC
4926 Benner St (19135-4214)
PHONE..................................215 289-1505
Brendan Kilroy, *President*
EMP: 4
SALES (est): 451.8K **Privately Held**
SIC: 1751 2499 Cabinet & finish carpentry; decorative wood & woodwork

(G-13678)
ERNEST HILL MACHINE CO INC
1434 Federal St (19146-3198)
PHONE..................................215 467-7750
Richard Hamburg, *President*
Dianne Hamburg, *Corp Secy*
EMP: 15
SQ FT: 8,500
SALES (est): 1.3MM **Privately Held**
SIC: 7389 3544 Grinding, precision: commercial or industrial; dies & die holders for metal cutting, forming, die casting

(G-13679)
ESOTERIX GENETIC LABS LLC
Integrated Genetics
833 Chestnut St Ste 1250 (19107-4419)
PHONE..................................215 351-2331
Stirling Puck, *Principal*
EMP: 40 **Publicly Held**

WEB: www.genzyme.com
SIC: 2835 In vitro & in vivo diagnostic substances
HQ: Esoterix Genetic Laboratories, Llc
3400 Computer Dr
Westborough MA 01581
508 389-6650

(G-13680)
ESSITY NORTH AMERICA INC (HQ)
Also Called: Tena
2929 Arch St Ste 2600 (19104-2863)
PHONE.............................610 499-3700
Sune Lundin, *President*
Kate Kunda, *Counsel*
James Carmichael, *Vice Pres*
Michael C Feenan, *Vice Pres*
Kevin Gorman, *Vice Pres*
▲ EMP: 150
SQ FT: 81,000
SALES (est): 2B
SALES (corp-wide): 7.6B **Privately Held**
WEB: www.sca.com
SIC: 2621 3086 2676 Towels, tissues & napkins: paper & stock; wrapping & packaging papers; packaging & shipping materials, foamed plastic; sanitary paper products
PA: Svenska Cellulosa Ab Sca
Skepparplatsen 1
Sundsvall 852 3
601 933-77

(G-13681)
ETERNITY FASHION INC
1410 Chestnut St (19102-2505)
PHONE.............................215 567-5571
Nira Jacobson, *President*
EMP: 5
SQ FT: 10,000
SALES (est): 686.9K **Privately Held**
SIC: 5621 3171 5661 Women's clothing stores; handbags, women's; women's shoes

(G-13682)
EUROPEAN & AMERICAN SAUSAGE CO
1242 S American St Ste 46 (19147)
PHONE.............................215 232-1716
Ilya Babenko, *President*
Daniil Babenko, *Vice Pres*
EMP: 5 EST: 1957
SQ FT: 10,000
SALES (est): 390.5K **Privately Held**
SIC: 2013 Sausages from purchased meat

(G-13683)
EVEREST DENTAL LLC
Also Called: Wolodymyr Zin, DDS
9892 Bustleton Ave # 302 (19115-2140)
PHONE.............................215 671-0188
Wolodymyr Zin,
EMP: 5
SALES (est): 587.6K **Privately Held**
SIC: 8021 3843 Dental clinic; enamels, dentists'

(G-13684)
EVERGREEN TANK SOLUTIONS INC
Also Called: Mobile Mini
4601 Pearce St (19137-1101)
PHONE.............................484 268-5168
Don Richard, *Branch Mgr*
EMP: 5
SALES (corp-wide): 593.2MM **Publicly Held**
SIC: 1791 3272 5084 Storage tanks, metal: erection; liquid catch basins, tanks & covers: concrete; tanks, storage
HQ: Evergreen Tank Solutions, Inc.
4646 E Van Buren St # 400
Phoenix AZ 85008
281 332-5170

(G-13685)
EXCEL MACHINE CO
6601 Marsden St (19135-2799)
PHONE.............................215 624-8600
James Barrett Jr, *President*
Carl Schuller, *Corp Secy*
EMP: 9
SQ FT: 5,000

SALES (est): 1.1MM **Privately Held**
SIC: 3599 Machine shop, jobbing & repair

(G-13686)
EXECUTIVE APPAREL INC
Also Called: Gourmet Restaurant Apparel
2150 Kubach Rd (19116-4203)
PHONE.............................215 464-5400
Donald Singer, *President*
Joe Nemanic, *Regl Sales Mgr*
Scott Kaplan, *Accounts Exec*
Robert Singer, *Admin Sec*
▲ EMP: 14
SQ FT: 30,000
SALES (est): 2.1MM **Privately Held**
WEB: www.executiveapparel.com
SIC: 2337 2326 Uniforms, except athletic: women's, misses' & juniors'; work uniforms

(G-13687)
EXHIBIT G LLC
Also Called: Fastsigns
1701 Welsh Rd (19115-3172)
PHONE.............................215 302-2260
Margo Scavone, *Owner*
EMP: 3
SALES (est): 255.6K **Privately Held**
SIC: 3993 Signs & advertising specialties

(G-13688)
EYELAND OPTICAL CORP (PA)
Also Called: Philadelphia Eyeglass Labs
1030 Arch St Ste 1 (19107-3011)
PHONE.............................215 368-1600
Craig Messinger, *President*
EMP: 55
SQ FT: 12,000
SALES (est): 5.2MM **Privately Held**
WEB: www.philadelphiaeyeglasslabs.com
SIC: 5995 3229 Opticians; pressed & blown glass

(G-13689)
F A DAVIS COMPANY (PA)
1915 Arch St (19103-1493)
PHONE.............................215 568-2270
Robert Craven Sr, *Ch of Bd*
Kobekt H Craven, *President*
Robert Craven Jr, *President*
Leigh Wells, *President*
Jacki Albertini, *Partner*
▲ EMP: 75 EST: 1879
SQ FT: 40,000
SALES (est): 22.9MM **Privately Held**
WEB: www.fadavis.com
SIC: 2731 Textbooks: publishing only, not printed on site

(G-13690)
F CREATIVE IMPRESSIONS INC
240 Lexington Ave (19124)
PHONE.............................215 743-7577
Richard P Freas, *President*
Gary Freas, *Vice Pres*
EMP: 9
SALES (est): 1.2MM **Privately Held**
SIC: 3993 2394 Signs & advertising specialties; awnings, fabric: made from purchased materials

(G-13691)
FAB DUBRUFAUT WOODWORKING
5635 Tulip St (19124-1626)
PHONE.............................215 533-4853
Sab Dubrufaut, *Owner*
EMP: 3
SQ FT: 4,000
SALES: 550K **Privately Held**
SIC: 2511 Wood household furniture

(G-13692)
FAMILY BUSINESS PUBLISHING CO
Also Called: Family Business Magazine
1845 Walnut St Ste 900 (19103-4710)
PHONE.............................215 567-3200
Milton L Rock, *President*
Charles E Fiero, *Partner*
Robert H Rock, *Partner*
EMP: 6
SALES (est): 600.6K **Privately Held**
WEB: www.familybusinessmagazine.com
SIC: 2711 Newspapers: publishing only, not printed on site

(G-13693)
FANTASY PRINTING SUPPLIES LLC
1243 Vine St (19107-1111)
PHONE.............................215 569-3744
Ken Tin, *Mng Member*
EMP: 4
SALES (est): 39.8K **Privately Held**
SIC: 2752 Commercial printing, lithographic

(G-13694)
FARM JOURNAL INC (PA)
Also Called: Farm Journal Media
1600 Market St Ste 1530 (19103-7235)
PHONE.............................215 557-8900
Andrew J Weber Jr, *Chairman*
Jessie Gunn, *Vice Pres*
Joseph Matthews, *Vice Pres*
Chuck Roth, *Opers Staff*
Megan Traub, *Sales Staff*
EMP: 30
SQ FT: 10,400
SALES (est): 51.2MM **Privately Held**
WEB: www.agweb.com
SIC: 2721 2741 7313 7375 Magazines: publishing only, not printed on site; newsletter publishing; radio, television, publisher representatives; data base information retrieval

(G-13695)
FEDERAL PRETZEL BAKING CO
636 Federal St (19147-4845)
PHONE.............................215 467-0505
Rich Bezila, *Manager*
EMP: 20
SALES (corp-wide): 1.2MM **Privately Held**
SIC: 5145 2099 2051 Pretzels; food preparations; bread, cake & related products
PA: Federal Pretzel Baking Co
300 Eagle Ct
Bridgeport NJ 08014
215 467-0505

(G-13696)
FEDEX OFFICE & PRINT SVCS INC
3535 Market St Ste 10b (19104-3386)
PHONE.............................215 386-5679
EMP: 5
SALES (corp-wide): 65.4B **Publicly Held**
WEB: www.kinkos.com
SIC: 7334 2791 2789 Photocopying & duplicating services; typesetting; bookbinding & related work
HQ: Fedex Office And Print Services, Inc.
7900 Legacy Dr
Plano TX 75024
800 463-3339

(G-13697)
FERMENTEC INC
301 S 19th St Apt 8f (19103-2581)
PHONE.............................203 809-8078
Alexander David, *CTO*
EMP: 3
SALES (est): 122K **Privately Held**
SIC: 3589 Service industry machinery

(G-13698)
FIBEMATICS INC
Also Called: Treco-Fibematics
3313 Stokley St (19140-4714)
PHONE.............................215 226-2672
Ivan Grossman, *President*
Paul Grossman, *President*
◆ EMP: 50
SQ FT: 200,000
SALES (est): 12.4MM **Privately Held**
WEB: www.fibemat.com
SIC: 2679 2392 Paper products, converted; household furnishings

(G-13699)
FIBERLAND INC
384 Tomlinson Pl (19116-3238)
PHONE.............................215 744-5446
Joy Abraham, *CEO*
Chandra Vyas, *President*
Kennady Kora, *Vice Pres*
EMP: 20

SALES (est): 1MM **Privately Held**
SIC: 2299 Preparing textile fibers for spinning (scouring & combing)

(G-13700)
FIBREFLEX PACKING & MFG CO
5101 Umbria St (19128-4345)
P.O. Box 4646 (19127-0646)
PHONE.............................215 482-1490
Joseph C Hofmann III, *President*
Thomas J Hofmann, *President*
Helen A Hofmann, *Admin Sec*
▼ EMP: 22
SQ FT: 35,000
SALES (est): 3.8MM **Privately Held**
WEB: www.fibreflex.com
SIC: 3053 Gasket materials

(G-13701)
FILIPPI BROS INC
7722 Winston Rd (19118-3531)
PHONE.............................215 247-5973
George Filippi, *President*
Sam Filippi, *Vice Pres*
Joseph D'Orazio, *Treasurer*
Ann Filippi, *Admin Sec*
EMP: 5 EST: 1946
SQ FT: 3,600
SALES (est): 648K **Privately Held**
SIC: 3446 Gates, ornamental metal

(G-13702)
FIORELLA WOODWORKING INC
20 E Herman St (19144-2040)
PHONE.............................215 843-5870
John Fiorella, *President*
Mike Fiorella, *Vice Pres*
Dan Fiorella, *Treasurer*
EMP: 3
SQ FT: 13,000
SALES (est): 427.5K **Privately Held**
WEB: www.watertown-ma.com
SIC: 2431 2434 Doors & door parts & trim, wood; wood kitchen cabinets

(G-13703)
FIS AVANTGARD LLC
Also Called: Sungard Availability Service
1500 Spring Garden St # 3 (19130-4067)
PHONE.............................215 413-4700
Eric Sullivan, *Branch Mgr*
EMP: 26
SALES (corp-wide): 8.4B **Publicly Held**
SIC: 7372 Business oriented computer software
HQ: Fis Avantgard Llc
680 E Swedesford Rd
Wayne PA 19087
800 468-7483

(G-13704)
FIS SG LLC
Also Called: Sungard
510 Walnut St Ste 900 (19106-3621)
PHONE.............................215 627-3800
EMP: 8
SALES (corp-wide): 9.1B **Publicly Held**
SIC: 7372 Prepackaged Software Services
HQ: Fis Sg, Llc
680 E Swedesford Rd
Wayne PA 19087

(G-13705)
FLUORO-PLASTICS INC
3601 G St (19134-1397)
PHONE.............................215 425-5500
C George Milner, *President*
Debbie Gray, *General Mgr*
C Siebert, *Vice Pres*
Rick Derosa, *Plant Mgr*
Donna Cross, *Human Resources*
▲ EMP: 14 EST: 1951
SQ FT: 48,800
SALES (est): 3.1MM **Privately Held**
WEB: www.fluoro-plastics.com
SIC: 3089 Molding primary plastic

(G-13706)
FLY MIX ENTERTAINMENT
942 Borbeck Ave (19111-2603)
PHONE.............................215 722-6287
Don Thanh Nguyen, *Owner*
EMP: 3
SALES (est): 245.8K **Privately Held**
SIC: 3273 Ready-mixed concrete

(G-13707)
FLYNN & OHARA UNIFORMS INC (PA)
10905 Dutton Rd (19154-3203)
PHONE..............................800 441-4122
Edward Flynn, *President*
Kathy Pietrzak, *District Mgr*
Edward O'Hara Jr, *Vice Pres*
Edward Ohara Jr, *Vice Pres*
James Natala, *Treasurer*
▲ EMP: 60
SQ FT: 54,000
SALES (est): 97.3MM **Privately Held**
WEB: www.flynnohara.com
SIC: 2337 2339 2311 Uniforms, except athletic: women's, misses' & juniors'; uniforms, athletic: women's, misses' & juniors'; men's & boys' uniforms

(G-13708)
FMC ASIA-PACIFIC INC (HQ)
2929 Walnut St (19104-5054)
PHONE..............................215 299-6000
Joseph Netherland, *President*
Stephanie Kushner, *Treasurer*
EMP: 4
SALES (est): 2.9MM
SALES (corp-wide): 4.7B **Publicly Held**
SIC: 2812 2879 2819 Soda ash, sodium carbonate (anhydrous); pesticides, agricultural or household; phosphates, except fertilizers: defluorinated & ammoniated
PA: Fmc Corporation
2929 Walnut St
Philadelphia PA 19104
215 299-6000

(G-13709)
FMC CORPORATION (PA)
2929 Walnut St (19104-5054)
PHONE..............................215 299-6000
Pierre R Brondeau, *Ch of Bd*
Mark A Douglas, *President*
Randy Young, *Business Mgr*
John Stillmun, *Counsel*
Andrea E Utecht, *Exec VP*
◆ EMP: 500 EST: 1928
SALES: 4.7B **Publicly Held**
WEB: www.fmc.com
SIC: 2812 2879 2869 Soda ash, sodium carbonate (anhydrous); agricultural chemicals; pesticides, agricultural or household; insecticides, agricultural or household; fungicides, herbicides; industrial organic chemicals

(G-13710)
FMC CORPORATION
1601 Market St Ste 910 (19103-2329)
PHONE..............................215 717-7500
Barbara Lichtman-Tayar, *Owner*
EMP: 5
SALES (corp-wide): 4.7B **Publicly Held**
SIC: 2812 Soda ash, sodium carbonate (anhydrous)
PA: Fmc Corporation
2929 Walnut St
Philadelphia PA 19104
215 299-6000

(G-13711)
FMC CORPORATION
FMC Biopolymer
1735 Market St Fl 14 (19103-7505)
PHONE..............................800 526-3649
Dan Fitzpatrick, *Project Mgr*
Kevin Farris, *Accounts Mgr*
Michael Smith, *Branch Mgr*
EMP: 400
SALES (corp-wide): 4.7B **Publicly Held**
SIC: 2812 2879 Alkalies & chlorine; agricultural chemicals
PA: Fmc Corporation
2929 Walnut St
Philadelphia PA 19104
215 299-6000

(G-13712)
FMC OVERSEAS LTD
1735 Market St Fl 14 (19103-7505)
PHONE..............................215 299-6000
Pierre R Brondeau, *Ch of Bd*
Antonio Crespo, *Technology*
Vincent Volpe, *Bd of Directors*
EMP: 3

SALES (est): 12.7K
SALES (corp-wide): 4.7B **Publicly Held**
WEB: www.fmc.com
SIC: 2869 Industrial organic chemicals
PA: Fmc Corporation
2929 Walnut St
Philadelphia PA 19104
215 299-6000

(G-13713)
FOR LENFEST INSTITUTE (PA)
1234 Market St Ste 1800 (19107-3704)
PHONE..............................215 854-5600
Burt Herman, *Director*
EMP: 3
SALES (est): 501K **Privately Held**
SIC: 8699 7372 Charitable organization; application computer software

(G-13714)
FOREIGN POLICY RESEARCH INST
1528 Walnut St Ste 610 (19102-3684)
PHONE..............................215 732-3774
Harvey Sicherman, *President*
Bruce Hooper, *Vice Chairman*
Alan H Luxenberg, *Vice Pres*
Charles Grace, *Treasurer*
Eileen Rosenau,
EMP: 50
SQ FT: 5,000
SALES: 2.6MM **Privately Held**
WEB: www.fpri.org
SIC: 8733 2721 7389 Research institute; trade journals: publishing only, not printed on site; lecture bureau

(G-13715)
FORMAN SIGN CO
10447 Drummond Rd (19154-3897)
PHONE..............................215 827-6500
Marty Jacobson, *President*
Barry Jacobson, *Vice Pres*
Erik Hersch, *Mktg Dir*
EMP: 35
SQ FT: 35,000
SALES (est): 5.6MM **Privately Held**
WEB: www.formansign.com
SIC: 3993 Neon signs; electric signs

(G-13716)
FOX WELDING SHOP INC
1801 W Sedgley Ave (19132-2110)
PHONE..............................215 225-3069
Albert Macchoine Jr, *President*
Lucille Paoli, *Corp Secy*
EMP: 5 EST: 1935
SQ FT: 20,000
SALES (est): 539.3K **Privately Held**
SIC: 7692 3469 Welding repair; metal stampings

(G-13717)
FP WOLL & COMPANY
10060 Sandmeyer Ln (19116-3502)
PHONE..............................215 934-5966
Frederick P Woll II, *President*
Stephen Woll, *Vice Pres*
Frederick Woll III, *Prdtn Mgr*
▲ EMP: 29 EST: 1907
SQ FT: 50,000
SALES (est): 4.6MM **Privately Held**
WEB: www.fpwollco.com
SIC: 2299 3081 3086 2823 Hair, curled: for upholstery, pillow & quilt filling; packing materials, plastic sheet; plastics foam products; cellulosic manmade fibers; plastics materials & resins; packaging paper & plastics film, coated & laminated

(G-13718)
FRANK J BUTCH CO INC
5629 Tulip St (19124-1695)
PHONE..............................215 322-7399
Frank J Butch, *President*
EMP: 15
SQ FT: 10,000
SALES (est): 1.3MM **Privately Held**
SIC: 3599 Machine shop, jobbing & repair

(G-13719)
FRANK J MAY CO INC
256 S 11th St (19107-6735)
PHONE..............................215 923-3165
Harry May, *President*
Frank May, *Vice Pres*

EMP: 3
SQ FT: 1,500
SALES (est): 292.8K **Privately Held**
SIC: 3843 7699 Dental hand instruments; dental instrument repair

(G-13720)
FRANKFORD CANDY LLC
9300 Ashton Rd Frnt (19114-3532)
PHONE..............................215 735-5200
Stuart Selarnick, *CEO*
Laurence Lang, *Finance*
Carolyn Videon, *Sales Staff*
Nathan Hoffman,
◆ EMP: 150
SQ FT: 512,000
SALES (est): 95MM **Privately Held**
SIC: 2066 Chocolate & cocoa products

(G-13721)
FRANKFORD PLATING INC
2505 Orthodox St (19137-1683)
PHONE..............................215 288-4518
Jonathon Barger, *President*
Jonathan Barger, *President*
EMP: 7 EST: 1956
SQ FT: 5,000
SALES (est): 859.2K **Privately Held**
SIC: 3471 Plating of metals or formed products; polishing, metals or formed products

(G-13722)
FRECKLED SAGE
3245 Amber St Ste 6 (19134-3235)
PHONE..............................610 888-2037
Anna Marino, *Principal*
EMP: 3
SALES (est): 230.8K **Privately Held**
SIC: 2295 Oilcloth

(G-13723)
FREESPIRITJEANSCOM INC
Also Called: Freespiritjeans Co
1735 Market St Ste 3750 (19103-7532)
P.O. Box 8174, Wilmington DE (19803-8174)
PHONE..............................302 319-9313
Maurice J Hall, *President*
Louise J Hall, *Vice Pres*
EMP: 5
SQ FT: 3,000
SALES (est): 220.7K **Privately Held**
SIC: 2325 Men's & boys' trousers & slacks

(G-13724)
FRESH MADE INC
810 Bleigh Ave (19111-3096)
PHONE..............................215 725-9013
Julie Smolyansky, *President*
Ilya Mandel, *President*
Edward Smolyansky, *Admin Sec*
EMP: 4
SALES (est): 641.1K
SALES (corp-wide): 118.8MM **Publicly Held**
WEB: www.freshmade.us
SIC: 2026 2021 Yogurt; creamery butter
PA: Lifeway Foods, Inc.
6431 Oakton St
Morton Grove IL 60053
847 967-1010

(G-13725)
FRETZ CORPORATION (PA)
4050 S 26th St Ste 100 (19112-1616)
PHONE..............................215 671-8300
Thomas J Dolan, *President*
Jim Dunleavy, *Vice Pres*
▲ EMP: 26 EST: 1932
SQ FT: 16,000
SALES (est): 6.8MM **Privately Held**
WEB: www.fretz.com
SIC: 3639 Major kitchen appliances, except refrigerators & stoves

(G-13726)
FRIENDLY ORGANIC LLC
821 N Hancock St (19123-3014)
PHONE..............................609 709-2924
Michael Coyne,
EMP: 3
SALES (est): 192.9K **Privately Held**
SIC: 2841 Soap & other detergents

(G-13727)
FRIENDS PUBLISHING CORP
Also Called: Friends Journal
1216 Arch St Ste 2a (19107-2835)
PHONE..............................215 563-8629
Susan Corsonfinnerty, *President*
Susan Corson Finnerty, *President*
Marianne D Lange, *Business Mgr*
Sara Waxman, *Advt Staff*
Gail Coyle, *Assoc Editor*
EMP: 10 EST: 1955
SQ FT: 5,700
SALES: 1.9MM **Privately Held**
SIC: 2741 Miscellaneous publishing

(G-13728)
FRONTIDA BIOPHARM INC
7722 Dungan Rd (19111-2733)
PHONE..............................215 288-6500
Tim Hanratty, *Principal*
EMP: 45
SALES (corp-wide): 39.5MM **Privately Held**
SIC: 2833 8731 2834 Medicinal chemicals; commercial physical research; pharmaceutical preparations
PA: Frontida Biopharm, Inc.
1100 Orthodox St
Philadelphia PA 19124
610 232-0112

(G-13729)
FRONTIDA BIOPHARM INC (PA)
1100 Orthodox St (19124-3168)
PHONE..............................610 232-0112
Song LI, *CEO*
Ronald Connolly, *COO*
Tony Liu, *Vice Pres*
Jane Wong, *Vice Pres*
Jim Scheirer, *VP Mfg*
EMP: 6
SALES (est): 39.5MM **Privately Held**
SIC: 2833 Medicinal chemicals

(G-13730)
FUEL
1917 E Passyunk Ave (19148-2248)
PHONE..............................215 468-3835
Rocco Cima, *Principal*
EMP: 4
SALES (est): 415.8K **Privately Held**
SIC: 2869 Fuels

(G-13731)
FUEL
1225 Walnut St (19107-4914)
PHONE..............................215 922-3835
EMP: 6
SALES (est): 707.3K **Privately Held**
SIC: 2869 Fuels

(G-13732)
FUEL ME GREEN LLC
1010 Race St Apt 6a (19107-2337)
PHONE..............................267 825-7193
EMP: 3
SALES (est): 169.7K **Privately Held**
SIC: 2869 Fuels

(G-13733)
FUEL RECHARGE YOURSELF INC 3
1650 Arch St (19103-2029)
PHONE..............................215 468-3835
Jeff Overton, *Principal*
EMP: 3
SALES (est): 260.1K **Privately Held**
SIC: 2869 Fuels

(G-13734)
FUN-TIME INTERNATIONAL INC
433 W Girard Ave (19123-1496)
PHONE..............................215 925-1450
Erik Lipson, *Owner*
Stephanie Shepard-Lipson, *Exec VP*
◆ EMP: 150
SQ FT: 3,565
SALES (est): 17.7MM **Privately Held**
WEB: www.Krazystraws.com
SIC: 3999 Novelties, bric-a-brac & hobby kits

(G-13735)
FUSION FIVE USA LLC
1735 Market St Ste 3750 (19103-7532)
PHONE..................................267 507-6127
Vashkar Chatterjee, *CEO*
EMP: 5
SALES (est): 245.5K **Privately Held**
SIC: 8748 2386 Telecommunications consultant; garments, leather

(G-13736)
FUTURA IDENTITIES INC
Also Called: Sign-A-Rama
6909 Frankford Ave (19135-1613)
PHONE..................................215 333-3337
Sami Uqureshi, *President*
EMP: 5
SALES (est): 736.5K **Privately Held**
SIC: 3993 Signs & advertising specialties

(G-13737)
G & F PRODUCTS INC
920 Levick St (19111-5422)
PHONE..................................215 781-6222
Sina Pan, *President*
EMP: 12
SALES (est): 413.3K **Privately Held**
SIC: 7218 3111 5072 Safety glove supply; glove leather; garden tools, hand

(G-13738)
G C CARL KLEMMER INC (PA)
4401 N Philip St (19140-2438)
PHONE..................................215 329-4100
Carl G C Klemmer Sr, *President*
Carl G C Klemmer Jr, *Vice Pres*
EMP: 3 **EST:** 1942
SQ FT: 7,500 **Privately Held**
SIC: 3599 Custom machinery; machine shop, jobbing & repair

(G-13739)
G J LITTLEWOOD & SON INC
Also Called: Dye Works
4045 Main St (19127-2111)
PHONE..................................215 483-3970
Wallace Littlewood, *Ch of Bd*
Richard Littlewood, *President*
D T Littlewood, *Vice Pres*
David T Littlewood, *Vice Pres*
▲ **EMP:** 20
SQ FT: 50,000
SALES (est): 3MM **Privately Held**
WEB: www.littlewooddyers.com
SIC: 2231 2262 2269 2261 Dyeing & finishing: wool or similar fibers; dyeing: manmade fiber & silk broadwoven fabrics; finishing plants; finishing plants, cotton

(G-13740)
GALAXY PRODUCTS
Also Called: Galaxy Silkscreening
317 Avon St (19116-3207)
PHONE..................................215 426-8640
Steven Kret, *Owner*
EMP: 4
SQ FT: 3,300
SALES (est): 184.4K **Privately Held**
SIC: 2759 Screen printing

(G-13741)
GAMEFREAKS101 INC
100 S Broad St Ste 623 (19110-1058)
PHONE..................................215 587-9787
Phyllis Powers, *President*
EMP: 6
SALES: 120K **Privately Held**
SIC: 7372 Home entertainment computer software

(G-13742)
GAMESA WIND PA LLC (DH)
1801 Market St Ste 2700 (19103-1609)
PHONE..................................215 665-9810
Elizabeth Golden, *Marketing Staff*
Jiddu Tapia,
▼ **EMP:** 19
SALES (est): 25MM
SALES (corp-wide): 95B **Privately Held**
SIC: 3621 Windmills, electric generating
HQ: Siemens Gamesa Renewable Energy Usa, Inc.
1150 Northbrook Dr # 300
Feasterville Trevose PA 19053
215 710-3100

(G-13743)
GANESH DONUTS INC
1113 Market St (19107-2901)
PHONE..................................215 351-9370
Sanjay Patel, *CEO*
EMP: 4
SALES (est): 144.7K **Privately Held**
SIC: 2051 Doughnuts, except frozen

(G-13744)
GARY N SNYDER
Also Called: Snyder Optical Co.
251 S 17th St (19103-6230)
PHONE..................................215 735-5656
Gary N Snyder, *Owner*
Dr Elmer A Snyder, *Partner*
EMP: 3 **EST:** 1937
SQ FT: 2,000
SALES (est): 325.3K **Privately Held**
SIC: 5995 3851 Eyeglasses, prescription; lens grinding, except prescription: ophthalmic

(G-13745)
GEHRET WIRE WORKS INC
437 N 11th St (19123-3701)
PHONE..................................215 236-3322
Constance Ebert, *President*
Robley J Ebert Jr, *Corp Secy*
Josephine G Ebert, *Vice Pres*
EMP: 7 **EST:** 1941
SQ FT: 20,000
SALES (est): 1.2MM **Privately Held**
SIC: 3496 Woven wire products

(G-13746)
GEM REFRIGERATOR CO (PA)
1339 Chestnut St Fl 16 (19107-3519)
PHONE..................................877 436-7374
Bruce Gruhler, *President*
John Greenwood, *Vice Pres*
Jeffery Steinberg, *Vice Pres*
EMP: 15 **EST:** 1939
SQ FT: 40,000
SALES (est): 9.7MM **Privately Held**
WEB: www.gemrefrigeratorcompany.com
SIC: 3585 5078 Refrigeration equipment, complete; cabinets, show & display, refrigerated; counters & counter display cases, refrigerated; display cases, refrigerated

(G-13747)
GEMINI BAKERY EQUIPMENT CO
9990 Gantry Rd (19115-1092)
PHONE..................................215 673-3520
Mark Rosenberg, *CEO*
Cindy Ng, *CFO*
Adam Herzig, *Admin Sec*
◆ **EMP:** 65 **EST:** 1972
SQ FT: 27,000
SALES (est): 17.4MM **Privately Held**
WEB: www.geminibe.com
SIC: 3556 Bakery machinery

(G-13748)
GEMS SERVICES INC
5856 Penn St (19149-3418)
PHONE..................................215 399-8932
Edward Barratt, *President*
EMP: 3
SALES (est): 174.5K **Privately Held**
SIC: 3496 Miscellaneous fabricated wire products

(G-13749)
GENERAL ELECTRIC COMPANY
1040 E Erie Ave (19124-5499)
PHONE..................................215 289-0400
Calvin Fritz, *Manager*
EMP: 70
SQ FT: 139,314
SALES (corp-wide): 121.6B **Publicly Held**
SIC: 7699 7694 7629 Industrial machinery & equipment repair; armature rewinding shops; electrical repair shops
PA: General Electric Company
41 Farnsworth St
Boston MA 02210
617 443-3000

(G-13750)
GENERAL PLASTICS INC
701 Kingston St (19134)
PHONE..................................215 423-8200
Robert Lavigne, *President*
EMP: 3
SALES: 250K **Privately Held**
SIC: 5084 3081 Plastic products machinery; packing materials, plastic sheet

(G-13751)
GENESIS ALKALI WYOMING LP
1735 Market St (19103-7501)
PHONE..................................215 299-6904
Edward T Flynn, *President*
EMP: 40 **Publicly Held**
SIC: 2812 Soda ash, sodium carbonate (anhydrous)
HQ: Genesis Alkali Wyoming, Lp
580 Westvaco Rd
Green River WY 82935
307 875-2580

(G-13752)
GENESIS ALKALI WYOMING LP
1735 Market St (19103-7501)
PHONE..................................215 845-4500
Edward T Flynn, *President*
Joe Calabrese, *Principal*
EMP: 55 **Publicly Held**
SIC: 2812 Soda ash, sodium carbonate (anhydrous); sodium bicarbonate; caustic soda, sodium hydroxide
HQ: Genesis Alkali Wyoming, Lp
580 Westvaco Rd
Green River WY 82935
307 875-2580

(G-13753)
GENESIS SPECIALTY ALKALI LLC (HQ)
Also Called: Tronox Specialty Alkali Corp
1735 Market St Fl 24 (19103-7516)
PHONE..................................215 845-4550
Edward T Flynn, *President*
Frederick A V On Ahrens, *Vice Pres*
Aaron Reichl, *Vice Pres*
Terry J Harding, *CFO*
Sanjay Gandhi, *VP Mktg*
EMP: 55
SALES (est): 6.3MM **Publicly Held**
SIC: 2812 Sodium bicarbonate; caustic soda, sodium hydroxide

(G-13754)
GENOA HEALTHCARE LLC
166 W Lehigh Ave (19133-3849)
PHONE..................................215 426-1007
Richard Sassano, *Principal*
EMP: 6
SALES (corp-wide): 226.2B **Publicly Held**
SIC: 2834 5122 5912 Pharmaceutical preparations; pharmaceuticals; drug stores & proprietary stores
HQ: Genoa Healthcare Llc
707 S Grady Way Ste 700
Renton WA 98057

(G-13755)
GEORGE T BISEL CO INC
710 S Washington Sq (19106-3591)
PHONE..................................215 922-5760
Franklin Jon Zuch, *President*
Anthony J Digioia, *Chief*
James L Betz Jr, *Vice Pres*
Paul Roberts,
EMP: 11
SQ FT: 15,000
SALES (est): 1.3MM **Privately Held**
WEB: www.bisel.com
SIC: 2731 Textbooks: publishing only, not printed on site

(G-13756)
GEORGE T FARAGHAN STUDIOS
940 N Delaware Ave Ste 2 (19123-3108)
PHONE..................................215 928-0499
EMP: 4
SQ FT: 12,000
SALES (est): 320K **Privately Held**
SIC: 7335 3861 Commercial Photography Mfg Photographic Equipment/Supplies

(G-13757)
GERALD MAIER
Also Called: Philly Designs
4332 Factory St (19124-3910)
PHONE..................................215 744-9999
Gerald Maier, *Owner*
EMP: 5
SALES: 300K **Privately Held**
SIC: 2521 Wood office furniture

(G-13758)
GERMANTOWN WELDING CO
25 E Price St (19144-2143)
PHONE..................................215 843-2643
Elizabeth Pohl, *President*
Richard Pohl, *Vice Pres*
EMP: 4
SQ FT: 8,100
SALES (est): 486.6K **Privately Held**
SIC: 7692 3599 Welding repair; machine shop, jobbing & repair

(G-13759)
GERSON ASSOCIATES PC (PA)
Also Called: University Services
2837 Southampton Rd (19154-1206)
PHONE..................................215 637-6800
Irvin M Gerson, *President*
Benjamin Gerson, *Treasurer*
EMP: 40
SQ FT: 8,500
SALES (est): 5.3MM **Privately Held**
SIC: 8099 2899 8734 Physical examination & testing services; ; forensic laboratory

(G-13760)
GH SILVER ASSET CORP
1100 Vine St Apt C5 (19107-1746)
PHONE..................................404 432-3707
Julie Wong, *CEO*
EMP: 5
SQ FT: 14,000
SALES (est): 201.8K **Privately Held**
SIC: 2541 Display fixtures, wood

(G-13761)
GIFT IS IN YOU LLC
13109 Bustleton Ave A17 (19116-1647)
PHONE..................................267 974-3376
Keith Newberry, *CEO*
EMP: 6
SALES: 100K **Privately Held**
SIC: 5947 2389 Gift shop; men's miscellaneous accessories

(G-13762)
GIL PREBELLI
Also Called: Prebelli Industries
10900 Dutton Rd (19154-3204)
PHONE..................................215 281-0300
Gil Prebelli, *Owner*
EMP: 14
SQ FT: 2,560
SALES (est): 2.8MM **Privately Held**
SIC: 3559 3544 Pharmaceutical machinery; special dies, tools, jigs & fixtures

(G-13763)
GILBERT PRINTING SERVICES
5635 Ridge Ave (19128-2764)
P.O. Box 26055 (19128-0055)
PHONE..................................215 483-7772
Jean Gilbert, *Owner*
Lisa Wiggins, *Office Mgr*
EMP: 6
SALES (est): 418.8K **Privately Held**
SIC: 2752 Commercial printing, lithographic

(G-13764)
GK INC (PA)
2914 N 16th St (19132-2225)
PHONE..................................215 223-7207
William Kowalchuk, *President*
Walter Cavalcanti, *Vice Pres*
EMP: 15 **EST:** 1923
SQ FT: 40,000
SALES (est): 2.1MM **Privately Held**
SIC: 2514 2522 Medicine cabinets & vanities: metal; office furniture, except wood

(G-13765)
GLASS U LLC (PA)
Also Called: Neu
4015 Chestnut St (19104-3019)
PHONE.................................855 687-7423
Daniel Fine, *CEO*
EMP: 10
SALES (est): 5.2MM **Privately Held**
SIC: 3993 Advertising novelties

(G-13766)
GLAXOSMITHKLINE LLC (DH)
Also Called: G S K
5 Crescent Dr (19112-1001)
PHONE.................................215 751-4000
Emma Walmsley, *CEO*
Jack Bailey, *President*
Tiffany Nardone, *President*
Simon Bicknell, *Senior VP*
Nick Hirons, *Senior VP*
◆ **EMP:** 3
SALES (est): 4.8B
SALES (corp-wide): 39.8B **Privately Held**
WEB: www.delks.com
SIC: 2834 5122 Pharmaceutical prepara-
tions; pharmaceuticals
HQ: Glaxosmithkline Holdings (Americas)
Inc.
1105 N Market St
Wilmington DE 19801
302 984-6932

(G-13767)
GLAXOSMITHKLINE PLC
Also Called: Glaxo Smith Kline
5 Crescent Dr (19112-1001)
PHONE.................................215 336-0824
Viehbacher Christopher, *Branch Mgr*
EMP: 31
SALES (corp-wide): 39.8B **Privately Held**
SIC: 2834 Pharmaceutical preparations
PA: Glaxosmithkline Plc
980 Great West Road
Brentford MIDDX TW8 9
208 047-5000

(G-13768)
**GLOBAL INDUS LTG
SOLUTIONS LLC**
12401 Mcnulty Rd (19154-1004)
PHONE.................................215 671-2029
Jay Goodman, *Mng Member*
EMP: 40
SQ FT: 25,000
SALES: 15MM
SALES (corp-wide): 111MM **Privately
Held**
WEB: www.westinghouselighting.com
SIC: 3646 Commercial indusl & institu-
tional electric lighting fixtures
PA: Westinghouse Lighting Corporation
12401 Mcnulty Rd
Philadelphia PA 19154
215 671-2000

(G-13769)
**GLOBAL INSTITUTE FOR STRGC
INV**
1127 N Orianna St (19123-1506)
PHONE.................................215 300-0907
Whitney White, *CEO*
EMP: 5 EST: 2012
SALES (est): 96.5K **Privately Held**
SIC: 7389 8621 2741 Advertising, promo-
tional & trade show services; fund raising
organizations; ; professional membership
organizations; business service newslet-
ters: publishing & printing

(G-13770)
**GLOBAL MEDICAL SOLUTIONS
INC (PA)**
1116 South St (19147-1915)
PHONE.................................215 440-7701
Richard Adelman, *President*
Jean Stoiberg, *Controller*
EMP: 9
SQ FT: 2,000
SALES (est): 930K **Privately Held**
WEB: www.globalmedicalsolutions.com
SIC: 5999 3842 Medical apparatus & sup-
plies; orthopedic appliances

(G-13771)
GLOBALSUBMIT INC
123 S Broad St Ste 1850 (19109-1032)
PHONE.................................215 253-7471
Rahul Mistry, *CEO*
Jason Rock, *Vice Pres*
Francesca Nanovic, *Opers Mgr*
John Marshall, *CFO*
Suzanne Damato, *Sales Staff*
EMP: 18
SQ FT: 6,000
SALES (est): 1.8MM **Privately Held**
WEB: www.globalsubmit.com
SIC: 7372 Business oriented computer
software

(G-13772)
GLOBE DYE WORKS
4500 Worth St (19124-3499)
PHONE.................................215 288-4554
Wilson Greenwood Jr, *President*
Jr W Greenwood, *Executive*
EMP: 50 EST: 1865
SQ FT: 156,000
SALES (est): 5.4MM **Privately Held**
SIC: 2211 2282 2281 Yarn-dyed fabrics,
cotton; winding yarn; yarn spinning mills

(G-13773)
**GLOBE METAL
MANUFACTURING CO**
2150 N 10th St (19122-1210)
P.O. Box 16456 (19122-0156)
PHONE.................................215 763-1024
David Polsky, *President*
Judith Brister, *Corp Secy*
EMP: 10 EST: 1918
SQ FT: 26,000
SALES (est): 1.4MM **Privately Held**
SIC: 3429 3469 Luggage hardware; metal
stampings

(G-13774)
GLONINGER BROTHERS INC
Also Called: Wilson, I L Company
176 W Loudon St (19120-4241)
PHONE.................................215 456-5100
David Gloninger, *President*
Andrew Gloninger, *Treasurer*
EMP: 4
SQ FT: 40,000
SALES (est): 267.7K **Privately Held**
SIC: 7389 2331 Cloth cutting, bolting or
winding; women's & misses' blouses &
shirts

(G-13775)
GOKAAF INTERNATIONAL INC
7029 Rutland St (19149-1717)
PHONE.................................267 343-3075
EMP: 5
SALES (est): 582.5K **Privately Held**
SIC: 5149 6798 7372 Whol Groceries
Real Estate Investment Trust Prepack-
aged Software Services

(G-13776)
GOLDEN PATH LLC
6514 Hasbrook Ave (19111-5210)
P.O. Box 394, Lansdale (19446-0394)
PHONE.................................215 290-1582
Jennifer Walker, *CFO*
EMP: 4
SALES (est): 170K **Privately Held**
SIC: 2035 Seasonings & sauces, except
tomato & dry

(G-13777)
GOOD LAD CO
Also Called: Pete's Partners
431 E Tioga St (19134-1118)
PHONE.................................215 739-0200
Peter J Sheintoch, *CEO*
Kenneth Sheintoch, *President*
Everett Sheintoch, *Vice Pres*
EMP: 400 EST: 1944
SQ FT: 300,000
SALES (est): 29.9MM **Privately Held**
SIC: 2369 Girls' & children's outerwear

(G-13778)
GRACE FILTER COMPANY INC
2251 Fraley St Ste 8 (19137-1824)
PHONE.................................610 664-5790
Jeff Gwein, *Vice Pres*

EMP: 7
SALES: 650K **Privately Held**
WEB: www.gracefilterco.com
SIC: 3569 Filters

(G-13779)
GRAHAM INTERNATIONAL INC
1528 Walnut St Ste 1601 (19102-3618)
PHONE.................................203 838-3355
Wendy Graham, *President*
Chira Adin, *Vice Pres*
▲ **EMP:** 13
SQ FT: 1,500
SALES (est): 1.5MM **Privately Held**
WEB: www.grahaminternational.com
SIC: 3199 Dog furnishings: collars,
leashes, muzzles, etc.: leather; straps,
leather

(G-13780)
GRAN ENTERPRISES
3609 N 5th St Fl 1 (19140-4525)
PHONE.................................215 634-2883
Felix Negron, *Partner*
Domingo Negron, *Partner*
EMP: 5 EST: 1979
SQ FT: 1,000
SALES (est): 600K **Privately Held**
SIC: 2752 2759 Commercial printing, off-
set; screen printing; letterpress printing

(G-13781)
GRANDSHARE LLC
2008 S 6th St (19148-2410)
P.O. Box 37163 (19148-7163)
PHONE.................................919 308-5115
Shannon Curtis, *CEO*
EMP: 3 EST: 2015
SALES (est): 98.2K **Privately Held**
SIC: 7371 2759 7389 Computer software
development & applications; commercial
printing;

(G-13782)
**GRAPHIC ARTS
INCORPORATED**
Also Called: G A
2867 E Allegheny Ave (19134-5903)
PHONE.................................215 382-5500
Colleen Binder, *President*
Barbara N Koontz, *President*
John Ciabattoni Jr, *Corp Secy*
Michael Koontz, *Corp Secy*
Doris N Binder, *Exec VP*
EMP: 20
SQ FT: 30,000
SALES (est): 4.2MM **Privately Held**
WEB: www.galitho.com
SIC: 2752 Commercial printing, offset

(G-13783)
GRATZ INDUSTRIES LLC
1108 Shackamaxon St (19125-4135)
PHONE.................................215 739-7373
Roberta Gratz,
Hugh Cosman,
David Rosencrans,
▲ **EMP:** 25
SQ FT: 15,000
SALES: 4MM **Privately Held**
WEB: www.gratzindustries.com
SIC: 3949 3446 Exercise equipment; ar-
chitectural metalwork

(G-13784)
GREENDESIGN LLC
8434 Germantown Ave (19118-3302)
PHONE.................................215 242-0700
EMP: 3
SALES (est): 292.2K **Privately Held**
SIC: 3826 Mfg Analytical Instruments

(G-13785)
GREENFIELD MFG CO INC
9800 Bustleton Ave (19115-2146)
PHONE.................................215 535-4141
Elliott Greenfield, *President*
Sandra Basickes, *Corp Secy*
Stanley Basickes, *Vice Pres*
Leah Basickes, *Treasurer*
▲ **EMP:** 19 EST: 1954
SQ FT: 50,000
SALES (est): 4.4MM **Privately Held**
SIC: 3432 Plumbing fixture fittings & trim

(G-13786)
GREENKEEPERS INC
2170 Bennett Rd Fl 1 (19116-3022)
PHONE.................................215 464-7540
Frank Carroll, *President*
James J Carroll Jr, *Corp Secy*
Matt Spinelli, *Vice Pres*
EMP: 5
SQ FT: 2,500
SALES (est): 430K **Privately Held**
WEB: www.gkspikes.com
SIC: 3149 Athletic shoes, except rubber or
plastic

(G-13787)
GREGG SHIRTMAKERS INC
Also Called: Hutspah Shirts
4830 N Front St (19120-4214)
PHONE.................................215 329-7700
Bernard Dunn, *President*
Jerome Dunn, *Vice Pres*
EMP: 6
SQ FT: 35,000
SALES (est): 460K **Privately Held**
SIC: 2329 Men's & boys' sportswear & ath-
letic clothing

(G-13788)
GRETZ MACHINE PRODUCTS
52 W Gowen Ave (19119-1645)
PHONE.................................215 247-2495
William Gretz, *President*
EMP: 3 EST: 1970
SQ FT: 10,000
SALES (est): 500K **Privately Held**
SIC: 3599 Machine shop, jobbing & repair

(G-13789)
GRIP-FLEX CORP
2245 E Ontario St (19134-2691)
PHONE.................................215 743-7492
Michael D Lowney, *President*
Jennifer Ramos, *General Mgr*
Jennifer Dauber, *CFO*
Jennifer Borah, *VP Sales*
EMP: 45 EST: 1955
SQ FT: 14,000
SALES (est): 4.5MM **Privately Held**
WEB: www.gripflexcorporation.com
SIC: 2396 Automotive trimmings, fabric

(G-13790)
GRYPHIN ELEMENTS LLC
5500 Wissahickon Ave A (19144-5653)
PHONE.................................215 694-7727
Nicholas Nehez, *Director*
EMP: 5
SALES (est): 302.4K **Privately Held**
SIC: 2851 Paints & allied products

(G-13791)
GUIDING TECHNOLOGIES CORP
1500 Jfk Blvd Ste 1825 (19102-1719)
PHONE.................................609 605-9273
Adrian Trevisan, *President*
John Nosek, *Development*
Tom Gradel, *Manager*
EMP: 8 EST: 2013
SALES (est): 387.9K **Privately Held**
SIC: 7372 Application computer software

(G-13792)
**GURPREET FUEL COMPANY
LLC**
536 W Roosevelt Blvd (19120-3704)
PHONE.................................215 493-6322
EMP: 3
SALES (est): 161.6K **Privately Held**
SIC: 2869 Fuels

(G-13793)
GURU TECHNOLOGIES INC
121 S Broad St Fl 11 (19107-4545)
PHONE.................................610 572-2086
Rick Nucci, *CEO*
Nicolas Schillagi, *Accounts Exec*
Cole Sherin, *Accounts Exec*
Sunny Manivannan, *VP Mktg*
EMP: 13
SALES (est): 483.1K **Privately Held**
SIC: 7372 Prepackaged software

(G-13794)
GWYNN-E-CO INC
2810 E Victoria St 28 (19134-6220)
PHONE..................................215 423-6400
Michael Gwynne, *President*
Patricia Gwynne, *Admin Sec*
EMP: 8 **EST:** 1971
SQ FT: 14,000
SALES: 500K **Privately Held**
SIC: 2426 Frames for upholstered furniture, wood

(G-13795)
HADCO ALUMINUM & METAL CORP PA
2811 Charter Rd (19154-2115)
PHONE..................................215 695-2705
Gerald Fishman, *CEO*
Jesse L Wiener, *President*
▲ **EMP:** 100
SALES (est): 10.2MM **Privately Held**
SIC: 3479 5051 Aluminum coating of metal products; aluminum bars, rods, ingots, sheets, pipes, plates, etc.

(G-13796)
HALF PLUS HALF INC ENTERPRISE
7800 Temple Rd (19150-2110)
PHONE..................................800 252-4545
Luke Harrs, *Principal*
Zumar Dubose, *Vice Pres*
EMP: 99
SQ FT: 250
SALES (est): 2.6MM **Privately Held**
SIC: 2051 Bakery: wholesale or wholesale/retail combined

(G-13797)
HALL-WOOLFORD WOOD TANK CO INC
5500 N Water St (19120-3093)
P.O. Box 2755 (19120-0755)
PHONE..................................215 329-9022
Scott Hochhauser, *President*
David Hochhauser, *Vice Pres*
EMP: 8 **EST:** 1854
SQ FT: 15,000
SALES (est): 1.3MM **Privately Held**
WEB: www.woodtank.com
SIC: 2449 Tanks, wood: coopered

(G-13798)
HALLELUJAH INK
2048 E Ann St (19134-3605)
PHONE..................................215 510-1152
Kurt Muller, *Owner*
Andrew Cutler, *Co-Owner*
EMP: 5
SALES (est): 139.9K **Privately Held**
SIC: 2051 7389 Bakery: wholesale or wholesale/retail combined;

(G-13799)
HAND IN HAND SOAP LLC
1646 S 12th St Ste 202 (19148-1053)
PHONE..................................267 714-4168
William Glaab, *Mng Member*
EMP: 4 **EST:** 2011
SALES (est): 484.8K **Privately Held**
SIC: 2841 Soap: granulated, liquid, cake, flaked or chip

(G-13800)
HANESBRANDS INC
1519 Franklin Mills Cir (19154-3132)
PHONE..................................336 519-8080
EMP: 6
SALES (corp-wide): 6.8B **Publicly Held**
SIC: 2211 Apparel & outerwear fabrics, cotton
PA: Hanesbrands Inc.
1000 E Hanes Mill Rd
Winston Salem NC 27105
336 519-8080

(G-13801)
HANGER PRSTHETCS & ORTHO INC
3015 Island Ave (19153-3015)
PHONE..................................215 365-1532
Ernie Gamaglia, *Branch Mgr*
EMP: 4
SQ FT: 1,000

SALES (corp-wide): 1B **Publicly Held**
SIC: 3842 Orthopedic appliances
HQ: Hanger Prosthetics & Orthotics, Inc.
10910 Domain Dr Ste 300
Austin TX 78758
512 777-3800

(G-13802)
HARI JAYANTI NEWS INC
230 S Broad St (19102-4121)
PHONE..................................215 546-1350
Kartik Patel, *Principal*
EMP: 4 **EST:** 2011
SALES (est): 243.7K **Privately Held**
SIC: 2711 Newspapers, publishing & printing

(G-13803)
HARMONIC RAYS MFG GROUP INC
1116 Buttonwood St Unit A (19123-3482)
PHONE..................................267 761-9558
Xiao Han, *President*
Rui Xu, *Vice Pres*
Yimin Zhou, *Bd of Directors*
▲ **EMP:** 4
SALES (est): 3.8MM **Privately Held**
SIC: 2392 5065 Household furnishings; electronic parts
PA: Ningbo Highland Import & Export Co.,Ltd.
12f,C15 Bldg R&D Park,No.37
Guanghua Road,High-Tech Industrial D
Ningbo
574 279-5230

(G-13804)
HARRISON CUSTOM CABINETS
Also Called: Harrison Manufacturing
125357 E Chelten Ave (19138)
PHONE..................................215 548-2450
M Thomas Harrison, *Owner*
Janis Harrison, *Corp Secy*
EMP: 4
SQ FT: 30,000
SALES (est): 408.9K **Privately Held**
SIC: 2434 2541 2511 Vanities, bathroom: wood; table or counter tops, plastic laminated; kitchen & dining room furniture

(G-13805)
HARRY J LAWALL & SON INC (PA)
8028 Frankford Ave (19136-2697)
PHONE..................................215 338-6611
Harry J Lawall Jr, *President*
Edward Moran, *Vice Pres*
David Duny, *Sls & Mktg Exec*
Sherry Troy, *Info Tech Mgr*
Wayne T Lawall, *Shareholder*
EMP: 110
SQ FT: 15,000
SALES (est): 16.8MM **Privately Held**
SIC: 3842 Limbs, artificial; orthopedic appliances

(G-13806)
HARVEY BELL
Also Called: Bell Floor Covering
1706 Frankford Ave (19125-2604)
PHONE..................................215 634-4900
Joseph Bell, *Branch Mgr*
EMP: 4
SQ FT: 15,552
SALES (corp-wide): 2MM **Privately Held**
WEB: www.harlynridge.com
SIC: 4225 5713 3253 General warehousing & storage; linoleum; carpets; floor tile, ceramic
PA: Bell Floor Llc
1050 N 2nd St
Philadelphia PA 19123
215 925-3089

(G-13807)
HEAD & THE HAND PRESS LLC
2312 Emerald St (19125-1504)
PHONE..................................856 562-8545
Robert Holtzman, *President*
EMP: 3
SALES (est): 211.5K **Privately Held**
SIC: 2741 Miscellaneous publishing

(G-13808)
HEALING ENVIRONMENTS INTL INC
7123 Cresheim Rd (19119-2430)
PHONE..................................215 758-2107
Joseph August, *President*
Jane London August, *Vice Pres*
EMP: 5
SALES (est): 182.5K **Privately Held**
WEB: www.bedscapes.com
SIC: 8748 3069 8249 Business consulting; medical & laboratory rubber sundries & related products; medical training services

(G-13809)
HEART MASTERS DIAGNSOSTICS LLC
413 E Allegheny Ave (19134-2322)
PHONE..................................267 503-3803
Dr Lipton Clarke, *CEO*
EMP: 4
SQ FT: 2,300
SALES (est): 170.7K **Privately Held**
SIC: 3829 Medical diagnostic systems, nuclear

(G-13810)
HECLYN PRECISION GEAR COMPANY
Also Called: Williamson Gear & Machine
1112 E Berks St (19125-3498)
PHONE..................................215 739-7094
David Rogers, *President*
Linda Rogers, *Shareholder*
EMP: 15 **EST:** 1947
SQ FT: 12,000
SALES (est): 1.3MM **Privately Held**
SIC: 3566 Speed changers, drives & gears

(G-13811)
HELCRIST LLC
4643 Paschall Ave (19143-4426)
PHONE..................................215 727-2050
Allen Heggs, *Mng Member*
EMP: 10 **EST:** 2014
SQ FT: 12,650
SALES (est): 552.1K **Privately Held**
SIC: 3441 Building components, structural steel

(G-13812)
HELENE BATOFF INTERIORS
7573 Haverford Ave (19151-2228)
PHONE..................................215 879-7727
Helene Batoff, *Owner*
EMP: 6
SALES (est): 602.7K **Privately Held**
SIC: 3199 7389 Desk sets, leather; interior designer; interior decorating

(G-13813)
HENDERSON BERNARD FURN ARDISON
150 Green Ln (19127-1290)
P.O. Box 29121 (19127-0121)
PHONE..................................215 930-0400
Bernard Henderson, *Owner*
EMP: 3
SQ FT: 2,700
SALES: 150K **Privately Held**
WEB: www.bernardhenderson.com
SIC: 2511 Wood household furniture

(G-13814)
HENRY H OTTENS MFG CO INC (HQ)
Also Called: Iff Ottens
7800 Holstein Ave (19153-3219)
PHONE..................................215 365-7800
George C Robinson III, *President*
Anthony Lomaistro, *Vice Pres*
Donna Horn, *Safety Mgr*
Greg Rowe, *Purch Mgr*
James Gray, *QA Dir*
◆ **EMP:** 79 **EST:** 1952
SQ FT: 80,000
SALES (est): 22.6MM
SALES (corp-wide): 3.9B **Publicly Held**
WEB: www.ottensflavors.com
SIC: 2087 Mfg Flavor Extracts/Syrup

PA: International Flavors & Fragrances Inc.
521 W 57th St
New York NY 10019
212 765-5500

(G-13815)
HENSHELL CORP
2922 N 19th St (19132-2196)
P.O. Box 46096 (19160-6096)
PHONE..................................215 225-7755
Sheldon E Gross, *President*
EMP: 25
SQ FT: 100,000
SALES (est): 3.8MM **Privately Held**
SIC: 3465 Automotive stampings

(G-13816)
HERB PENN CO LTD (PA)
Also Called: Nature's Wonderland
10601 Decatur Rd Ste 200 (19154-3212)
PHONE..................................215 632-6100
Ronald Betz, *President*
Bill Betz, *General Mgr*
Lydia Powell, *Editor*
Jane Betz, *Corp Secy*
William P Betz Jr, *CFO*
▲ **EMP:** 26 **EST:** 1924
SQ FT: 46,000
SALES: 3.5MM **Privately Held**
SIC: 2833 5961 2099 Medicinals & botanicals; catalog & mail-order houses; food preparations

(G-13817)
HERMAN IRON WORKS INC
1452 Grays Ferry Ave 54 (19143-4449)
PHONE..................................215 727-1127
Devin Click, *President*
Donna Click, *Corp Secy*
Douglas Click, *Vice Pres*
EMP: 3 **EST:** 1961
SQ FT: 2,000
SALES (est): 220.1K **Privately Held**
SIC: 3446 Architectural metalwork

(G-13818)
HERMETICS INC
6122 N 21st St (19138-2421)
P.O. Box 30261, Elkins Park (19027-0661)
PHONE..................................215 848-9522
Gerald Yarrow, *President*
EMP: 9 **EST:** 1961
SQ FT: 16,000
SALES (est): 1MM **Privately Held**
WEB: www.hermetics.com
SIC: 3585 Compressors for refrigeration & air conditioning equipment

(G-13819)
HERR FOODS INCORPORATED
2800 Comly Rd (19154-2106)
PHONE..................................215 934-7144
Brandon Hawes, *Manager*
EMP: 40
SALES (corp-wide): 436.1MM **Privately Held**
WEB: www.herrs.com
SIC: 2096 Potato chips & similar snacks
PA: Herr Foods Incorporated
20 Herr Dr
Nottingham PA 19362
610 932-9330

(G-13820)
HERR FOODS INCORPORATED
7548 Brewster Ave (19153-3207)
P.O. Box 33187 (19142-0187)
PHONE..................................215 492-5990
Butch Najmola, *Senior VP*
Butch Najmoli, *Manager*
EMP: 100
SQ FT: 15,067
SALES (corp-wide): 436.1MM **Privately Held**
WEB: www.herrs.com
SIC: 2096 Potato chips & similar snacks
PA: Herr Foods Incorporated
20 Herr Dr
Nottingham PA 19362
610 932-9330

(G-13821)
HERSH IMPORTS INC
721 Sansom St (19106-3202)
PHONE..................................215 627-1128
Hersh Waisbord, *President*

GEOGRAPHIC

EMP: 1
SALES: 1MM **Privately Held**
SIC: 3911 Jewelry, precious metal

(G-13822)
HIBACHI GRILL SUPREME BUFFET
2051 Cottman Ave (19149-1118)
PHONE...................................215 728-7222
EMP: 14
SALES (est): 314.6K **Privately Held**
SIC: 5812 2621 Buffet (eating places); bristols

(G-13823)
HIGHLAND TOOL & DIE COMPANY
2127 E Ann St (19134-4198)
PHONE...................................215 426-4116
Daniel Sywulak, *President*
Ann Sywulak, *Shareholder*
EMP: 5 EST: 1946
SQ FT: 11,000
SALES (est): 292.8K **Privately Held**
SIC: 3599 Machine shop, jobbing & repair

(G-13824)
HIGHLINE POLYCARBONATE LLC
2327 Lombard St (19146-1117)
P.O. Box 2086 (19103-0086)
PHONE...................................267 847-0056
Martyn Kelly,
▲ EMP: 2
SALES (est): 1.3MM **Privately Held**
SIC: 2821 Polycarbonate resins

(G-13825)
HILLOCK ANODIZING INC
5101 Comly St Ste 7 (19135-4391)
PHONE...................................215 535-8090
John Hillock Jr, *President*
Joseph M Hillock, *Vice Pres*
Chris Keenan, *Plant Mgr*
Melissa Murphy, *Purch Dir*
Steve Dungan, *Sales Mgr*
EMP: 33
SQ FT: 12,800
SALES: 8.2MM **Privately Held**
WEB: www.hillockanodizing.com
SIC: 3471 Anodizing (plating) of metals or formed products

(G-13826)
HILMARR RUBBER CO INC
2168 E Firth St 70 (19125-2224)
P.O. Box 3683 (19125-0683)
PHONE...................................215 426-3628
Mary Shlauter, *President*
EMP: 6 EST: 1952
SQ FT: 16,000
SALES: 100K **Privately Held**
SIC: 3069 Molded rubber products

(G-13827)
HINGS LAI FASHION
231 E Allegheny Ave (19134-2208)
PHONE...................................215 530-0348
George Chen, *Partner*
EMP: 20
SALES: 200K **Privately Held**
SIC: 2326 Men's & boys' work clothing

(G-13828)
HIS LIGHT KINGDOM LLC
5320 Webster St (19143-2629)
PHONE...................................267 777-3866
Shelton Taylor, *CEO*
Sydney Taylor, *COO*
EMP: 5
SQ FT: 500
SALES (est): 423K **Privately Held**
SIC: 3652 Pre-recorded records & tapes

(G-13829)
HISPANIC MEDIA LLC
2800 Tyson Ave (19149-1433)
PHONE...................................215 424-1200
Ricardo Hurtado, *Mng Member*
EMP: 20 EST: 1875
SALES (est): 2MM **Privately Held**
SIC: 2621 Catalog, magazine & newsprint papers

(G-13830)
HISTORICAL DOCUMENTS CO
Also Called: Historical Souvenirs
2555 Orthodox St (19137-1624)
PHONE...................................215 533-4500
Tom Manley, *President*
EMP: 7 EST: 1940
SQ FT: 10,000
SALES (est): 700K **Privately Held**
WEB: www.histdocs.com
SIC: 2621 8412 Parchment paper; museums & art galleries

(G-13831)
HMC ENTERPRISES LLC
Also Called: Howard McCray
831 E Cayuga St (19124-3815)
PHONE...................................215 464-6800
Jeff Ford, *Plant Mgr*
Brett Scott, *Opers Staff*
Diane Scott, *VP Mktg*
Will Bell, *Marketing Staff*
Christopher Scott,
▲ EMP: 50
SQ FT: 81,000
SALES (est): 17.8MM **Privately Held**
WEB: www.howardmccray.com
SIC: 3585 Refrigeration equipment, complete

(G-13832)
HONEYWELL INTERNATIONAL INC
2501 Margaret St (19137)
PHONE...................................215 533-3000
EMP: 708
SALES (corp-wide): 41.8B **Publicly Held**
SIC: 3724 3812 3585 2824 Turbines, aircraft type; research & development on aircraft engines & parts; aircraft control systems, electronic; cabin environment indicators; radar systems & equipment; aircraft flight instruments; air conditioning equipment, complete; heating equipment, complete; humidifiers & dehumidifiers; nylon fibers; polyester fibers; polyethylene resins
PA: Honeywell International Inc.
115 Tabor Rd
Morris Plains NJ 07950
973 455-2000

(G-13833)
HONEYWELL RESINS & CHEM LLC
4698 Bermuda St (19137-1139)
PHONE...................................215 533-3000
Bill Simmons, *Plant Mgr*
EMP: 200
SALES (corp-wide): 41.8B **Publicly Held**
SIC: 2899 2865 Chemical preparations; cyclic crudes & intermediates
HQ: Honeywell Resins & Chemicals Llc
905 E Randolph Rd Bldg 97
Hopewell VA 23860
804 541-5000

(G-13834)
HORSEY DARDEN ENTERPRISES LLC
Also Called: Scoop USA
1354 W Girard Ave (19123)
P.O. Box 14013 (19122-0013)
PHONE...................................215 309-3139
Sherri Darden,
EMP: 5
SALES: 250K **Privately Held**
SIC: 2711 7372 Newspapers; application computer software

(G-13835)
HOUSEHOLD METALS INC
645 E Erie Ave (19134-1208)
PHONE...................................215 634-2800
Noubar Yeremian, *President*
Razmig Yeremian, *Prdtn Mgr*
Roubina Yeremian, *Treasurer*
▲ EMP: 65
SQ FT: 139,000
SALES (est): 14MM **Privately Held**
WEB: www.hmidoors.com
SIC: 3442 Window & door frames; storm doors or windows, metal

(G-13836)
HOWARD DONUTS INC
Also Called: Dunkin' Donuts
2437 Aramingo Ave (19125-3707)
PHONE...................................215 634-7750
Allen Howard, *President*
EMP: 25
SALES (est): 1.2MM **Privately Held**
SIC: 5461 2051 Doughnuts; bread, cake & related products

(G-13837)
HP HOOD LLC
Penn Maid Crowley Foods
10975 Dutton Rd (19154-3203)
PHONE...................................215 637-2507
Mack Burns, *Purch Mgr*
Glenn Goenner, *Branch Mgr*
EMP: 115
SALES (corp-wide): 2.1B **Privately Held**
WEB: www.hphood.com
SIC: 2026 2022 Whipped topping, except frozen or dry mix; cream, whipped; half & half; cheese, natural & processed
PA: Hp Hood Llc
6 Kimball Ln Ste 400
Lynnfield MA 01940
617 887-8441

(G-13838)
HRI NETWORKS INC
170 S Independence Mall (19106)
PHONE...................................267 515-5880
Samuel Reeves, *CEO*
Christina Lee, *Opers Mgr*
EMP: 10
SQ FT: 8,000
SALES: 2MM **Privately Held**
SIC: 3669 3822 Emergency alarms; incinerator control systems, residential & commercial type

(G-13839)
HUB LLC (PA)
30 S 17th St Fl 14 (19103-4012)
PHONE...................................215 561-8090
Bill Decker, *Mng Member*
John New,
EMP: 9
SALES (est): 1.3MM **Privately Held**
SIC: 2395 Art needlework: made from purchased materials

(G-13840)
HUMANISTIC ROBOTICS INC
251 Saint Josephs Way (19106-3806)
PHONE...................................215 922-7803
Samuel Reeves, *President*
Joshua Koplin, *Vice Pres*
EMP: 3
SALES (est): 324.4K **Privately Held**
SIC: 3795 Tanks & tank components

(G-13841)
HUMANISTIC ROBOTICS INC
170 S Independence (19106)
PHONE...................................267 515-5880
Samuel Reeves, *President*
Joshua Koplin, *CTO*
EMP: 7
SQ FT: 5,300
SALES (est): 2.2MM **Privately Held**
SIC: 3795 Tanks, military, including factory rebuilding

(G-13842)
HUMANISTIC ROBOTICS INC
123 S Broad St Ste 2170 (19109-1022)
PHONE...................................267 515-5880
Josh Koplin, *Principal*
EMP: 3
SALES (est): 331.7K **Privately Held**
SIC: 3826 Environmental testing equipment

(G-13843)
HUNTER MUDLER INC
2638 W Gordon St (19132-4631)
PHONE...................................215 229-5470
Joseph Schurig, *President*
Edward Schurig Jr, *Treasurer*
EMP: 10 EST: 1875
SQ FT: 6,000
SALES (est): 790K **Privately Held**
SIC: 3931 7699 Pipes, organ; organ tuning & repair

(G-13844)
HUNTINGDON YARN MILLS INC
3114 E Thompson St (19134-5096)
PHONE...................................215 425-5656
Bob Birkenbach, *General Mgr*
EMP: 20
SQ FT: 10,350
SALES (corp-wide): 5.8MM **Privately Held**
SIC: 2299 Yarns, specialty & novelty
PA: Huntingdon Yarn Mills, Inc
3114 E Thompson St
Philadelphia PA 19134
215 425-5305

(G-13845)
I P GRAPHICS INC
Also Called: Innovation Prtg Communications
11601 Caroline Rd (19154-2116)
PHONE...................................215 673-2600
William Gates, *President*
John Cooley, *Corp Secy*
Robert Bradt, *Vice Pres*
EMP: 20
SALES (est): 2.3MM **Privately Held**
SIC: 2791 2796 Typesetting; platemaking services

(G-13846)
IDN GLOBAL INC
2815 Southampton Rd (19154-1206)
PHONE...................................215 698-8155
Matt Helms, *Branch Mgr*
EMP: 5
SALES (corp-wide): 23.1MM **Privately Held**
SIC: 3429 5087 Locks or lock sets; locksmith equipment & supplies
PA: Idn Global, Inc.
7330 W Montrose Ave
Norridge IL 60706
708 456-9600

(G-13847)
IGB TOOL & MACHINE INC
7363 Melrose St (19136-4208)
PHONE...................................215 338-1420
Istvan Budaji, *President*
Goran Budaji, *Vice Pres*
EMP: 3
SQ FT: 1,100
SALES (est): 750K **Privately Held**
SIC: 3469 Machine parts, stamped or pressed metal

(G-13848)
II-VI OPTICAL SYSTEMS INC
2710 Commerce Way (19154-1016)
PHONE...................................215 842-3675
Derek Rollins, *Manager*
EMP: 25
SQ FT: 44,000
SALES (corp-wide): 1.1B **Publicly Held**
SIC: 3827 Optical instruments & apparatus
HQ: Ii-Vi Optical Systems, Inc.
36570 Briggs Rd
Murrieta CA 92563
951 926-2994

(G-13849)
ILLADELPH GLASS INC
128 Leverington Ave (19127-2050)
PHONE...................................215 483-1801
Luca Falso, *President*
EMP: 7
SALES: 400K **Privately Held**
WEB: www.illadelphglass.com
SIC: 3231 Products of purchased glass

(G-13850)
IMAGE COMPONENTS INC
2502 Edgemont St (19125-4004)
P.O. Box 29323 (19125-0323)
PHONE...................................215 739-3599
Dennis Byrnes, *President*
EMP: 3
SQ FT: 12,000
SALES (est): 280K **Privately Held**
WEB: www.allbend.com
SIC: 3599 Machine & other job shop work; custom machinery

(G-13851)
IMPLANT RESEARCH CENTER
3401 Market St Ste 345 (19104-3319)
PHONE...................................215 571-4345

▲ = Import ▼=Export
◆ =Import/Export

GEOGRAPHIC

Steven M Kurtz, *Vice Pres*
EMP: 1
SALES (est): 3.5MM
SALES (corp-wide): 985.3MM **Privately Held**
SIC: 3842 3841 Trusses, orthopedic & surgical; surgical & medical instruments
PA: Drexel University
3141 Chestnut St
Philadelphia PA 19104
215 895-2000

(G-13852)
IMPRINTED PROMOTIONS
8529 Bustleton Ave (19152-1203)
PHONE..................215 342-7226
Helen Kravitz, *Owner*
EMP: 3
SALES: 150K **Privately Held**
SIC: 2759 Screen printing

(G-13853)
IMPRINTS UNLIMITED
4950 Parkside Ave Ste 400 (19131-4700)
PHONE..................215 879-9484
Jimmie W Sams, *President*
Monica Sams, *Treasurer*
EMP: 5
SALES (est): 1.1MM **Privately Held**
WEB: www.imprints-unlimited.com
SIC: 2759 Screen printing; business forms: printing

(G-13854)
INDUSTRIAL FOOD TRUCK LLC
5200 Grays Ave (19143-5817)
PHONE..................215 596-0010
Gary Koppelman, *Mng Member*
EMP: 10 **EST:** 2016
SALES (est): 412.2K **Privately Held**
SIC: 3711 Bus & other large specialty vehicle assembly

(G-13855)
INFRASCAN INC
3508 Market St Ste 128 (19104-3320)
PHONE..................215 387-6784
Baruh Ben Dor, *CEO*
Tony Groch, *Senior Engr*
Yosef Ben Dor, *VP Sls/Mktg*
Roy Bachrach, *VP Bus Dvlpt*
EMP: 4
SALES (est): 602K **Privately Held**
WEB: www.infrascan.com
SIC: 3841 Diagnostic apparatus, medical

(G-13856)
INKSEWN USA
128 Leverington Ave (19127-2050)
PHONE..................570 534-5199
Zachariah Jacobes, *President*
EMP: 12
SALES (est): 624.2K **Privately Held**
SIC: 2899 Ink or writing fluids

(G-13857)
INKSTER PRINTS
530 S 4th St 2 (19147-1684)
PHONE..................267 886-0021
Doug Wong, *Owner*
EMP: 7 **EST:** 2015
SALES (est): 331K **Privately Held**
SIC: 2759 Screen printing

(G-13858)
INNOTECH INDUSTRIES INC
3908 Frankford Ave (19124-4430)
PHONE..................215 533-6400
Warren Kaye, *President*
Harry Cann, *Vice Pres*
EMP: 27
SALES (est): 2MM **Privately Held**
SIC: 3714 3544 Mufflers (exhaust), motor vehicle; special dies, tools, jigs & fixtures

(G-13859)
INOLEX GROUP INC (PA)
2101 S Swanson St (19148-3404)
PHONE..................215 271-0800
Robert E Paganelli, *President*
Conrad A Plimpton, *Chairman*
▲ **EMP:** 100
SQ FT: 129,000
SALES (est): 44.2MM **Privately Held**
SIC: 2869 2821 Industrial organic chemicals; polyesters

(G-13860)
INSINGER MACHINE COMPANY
6245 State Rd (19135-2996)
PHONE..................215 624-4800
Antecedent N Available, *CEO*
Robert A Cantor, *CEO*
ARI B Cantor, *President*
David Begley, *Vice Pres*
Marie Lohwasser, *Human Res Dir*
▲ **EMP:** 60 **EST:** 1893
SQ FT: 60,000
SALES (est): 13.9MM **Privately Held**
WEB: www.insingermachine.com
SIC: 3589 3556 Dishwashing machines, commercial; potato peelers, electric

(G-13861)
INTEGRATED POWER SERVICES LLC
3240 S 78th St (19153-3288)
PHONE..................215 365-1500
Art Wolfe,
EMP: 23
SALES (est): 5.2MM **Privately Held**
SIC: 7694 Electric motor repair

(G-13862)
INTELLIDRIVES INC
8510 Bustleton Ave (19152-1204)
PHONE..................215 728-6804
Greg Kane, *President*
EMP: 15
SQ FT: 5,000
SALES (est): 2MM **Privately Held**
WEB: www.intellidrives.com
SIC: 3625 Motor control accessories, including overload relays

(G-13863)
INTERACTIVE WORLDWIDE CORP
7601 Edmund St (19136-3342)
PHONE..................906 370-7609
Vittoria Schutz, *President*
Victoria Baga, *Vice Pres*
Ed Friedman, *CFO*
EMP: 100
SQ FT: 250,000
SALES (est): 11.1MM **Privately Held**
SIC: 2541 Store & office display cases & fixtures

(G-13864)
INTERIOR CREATIONS INC
700 E Erie Ave Frnt Frnt (19134-1204)
PHONE..................215 425-9390
John Di Gregorio, *President*
EMP: 32
SQ FT: 47,000
SALES (est): 5.3MM **Privately Held**
WEB: www.interiorcreationsinc.com
SIC: 2541 2542 2522 Display fixtures, wood; partitions & fixtures, except wood; office furniture, except wood

(G-13865)
INTERNATIONAL CHEMICAL COMPANY
Also Called: H C Harding
2628 N Mascher St 48 (19133-3898)
PHONE..................215 739-2313
Michael Pelham, *President*
▼ **EMP:** 13 **EST:** 1906
SQ FT: 50,000
SALES (est): 4.4MM **Privately Held**
WEB: www.intlchemco.com
SIC: 2842 Cleaning or polishing preparations; rust removers

(G-13866)
INTERNATIONAL MFG CORP
712 Chestnut St Fl 3 (19106-3269)
PHONE..................215 925-7558
Charles Newman, *President*
EMP: 13
SQ FT: 5,000
SALES (est): 1.7MM **Privately Held**
SIC: 3911 Jewelry, precious metal

(G-13867)
INTERNATIONAL RAW MTLS LTD (PA)
Also Called: IRM
600 Chestnut St Ste 800 (19106-3413)
PHONE..................215 928-1010

William P Oneill Jr, *President*
Maria M V Gatmaitan, *Corp Secy*
Hunter B McMullin Jr, *Vice Pres*
◆ **EMP:** 26
SQ FT: 10,000
SALES (est): 20MM **Privately Held**
WEB: www.fertilizerworks.com
SIC: 2874 6221 2899 2875 Phosphatic fertilizers; commodity traders, contracts; chemical preparations; fertilizers, mixing only; industrial inorganic chemicals; nitrogenous fertilizers

(G-13868)
INTERNTNAL FLVORS FRGRNCES INC
Also Called: Otten Flavors
7800 Holstein Ave (19153-3219)
PHONE..................215 365-7800
EMP: 125
SALES (corp-wide): 3.9B **Publicly Held**
SIC: 2087 Food colorings
PA: International Flavors & Fragrances Inc.
521 W 57th St
New York NY 10019
212 765-5500

(G-13869)
INTERNTNAL FLVORS FRGRNCES INC
Also Called: Iff
12285 Mcnulty Rd (19154-1210)
PHONE..................215 365-7800
EMP: 5
SALES (corp-wide): 3.9B **Publicly Held**
SIC: 2869 Flavors or flavoring materials, synthetic; perfume materials, synthetic
PA: International Flavors & Fragrances Inc.
521 W 57th St
New York NY 10019
212 765-5500

(G-13870)
INTERNTNAL SOC OF NUROVIROLOGY
Merb 3500 Rm 740 (19140)
PHONE..................215 707-9788
Brian Wigdahl, *Chairman*
EMP: 3
SALES (est): 246.4K **Privately Held**
SIC: 2835 Microbiology & virology diagnostic products

(G-13871)
INTERNTONAL MAR OUTFITTING LLC
Also Called: IMO
321 S 17th St (19103-6726)
PHONE..................215 875-9911
Hardy Von Auenmueller,
Heinz Albinski,
Martin Sander,
EMP: 6
SALES (est): 480K **Privately Held**
SIC: 3731 1742 1751 Commercial cargo ships, building & repairing; commercial passenger ships, building & repairing; acoustical & insulation work; ship joinery

(G-13872)
IOP PUBLISHING INCORPORATED
Also Called: Institute of Physics Pubg
190 N Independence Mall W (19106-1554)
PHONE..................215 627-0880
Steven Moss, *President*
Anita Dallasta, *General Mgr*
Steve Moss, *COO*
Sharice Collins, *Vice Pres*
Curtis Zimmermann, *Sales Executive*
EMP: 18 **EST:** 1991
SQ FT: 19,000
SALES: 5.6MM
SALES (corp-wide): 84.3MM **Privately Held**
SIC: 2741 Technical manuals: publishing only, not printed on site
HQ: Iop Publishing Limited
Temple Circus, Temple Way
Bristol BS1 6
117 929-7481

(G-13873)
IPA SYSTEMS INC
2745 Amber St (19134-3924)
P.O. Box 26869 (19134-6869)
PHONE..................215 425-6607
Bruce T Grant, *President*
Warren Wolf, *Chairman*
▼ **EMP:** 12
SQ FT: 40,000
SALES (est): 3MM **Privately Held**
WEB: www.ipanex.com
SIC: 2899 Waterproofing compounds; concrete curing & hardening compounds

(G-13874)
IROKO INTERMEDIATE HOLDINGS
1 Crescent Dr Ste 400 (19112-1015)
PHONE..................267 546-3003
John F Vavricka, *President*
EMP: 5
SALES (est): 518.6K **Privately Held**
SIC: 2834 Pharmaceutical preparations

(G-13875)
IROKO PHARMACEUTICALS INC
1 Kew Pl 150 Rouse Blvd St 1 Kew Pla (19112)
PHONE..................267 546-3003
EMP: 5 **EST:** 2013
SALES (est): 110.5K **Privately Held**
SIC: 2834 Proprietary drug products

(G-13876)
IROKO PHARMACEUTICALS LLC (PA)
1 Kew Pl 150 Rouse Blvd St 1 Kew Pla (19112)
PHONE..................267 546-3003
Osagie Imasogie, *Ch of Bd*
Louis J Vollmer, *President*
John Vavricka, *President*
Robyn Aycock, *Business Mgr*
Kevin Bell, *Business Mgr*
▲ **EMP:** 108
SALES (est): 17.2MM **Privately Held**
SIC: 2834 Pharmaceutical preparations

(G-13877)
ISLAMIC COMMUNICATION NETWORK
2451 N 19th St (19132-4304)
P.O. Box 50714 (19132-6714)
PHONE..................215 227-0640
Waliyyuddin S Abdullah, *President*
Waliyyuddin S Abdul, *Chairman*
EMP: 3 **EST:** 1986
SALES (est): 187.5K **Privately Held**
SIC: 2711 7313 Commercial printing & newspaper publishing combined; magazine advertising representative

(G-13878)
ITT LLC
1 Crescent Dr Ste 304 (19112-1015)
PHONE..................215 218-7400
Steve Joseph, *Manager*
Ronald Romeike, *Manager*
EMP: 58
SALES (corp-wide): 2.7B **Publicly Held**
WEB: www.ittind.com
SIC: 3625 Control equipment, electric
HQ: Itt Llc
1133 Westchester Ave N-100
White Plains NY 10604
914 641-2000

(G-13879)
IVD LLC (HQ)
10101 Roosevelt Blvd (19154-2105)
PHONE..................949 664-5500
Ming Dai, *Mng Member*
Jialu Huang,
Chang Liang,
Chaohui Lou,
EMP: 6
SALES (est): 10.9MM **Privately Held**
SIC: 2834 Pharmaceutical preparations

(G-13880)
J & D JEWELERS INC
Also Called: D'Antonio-Klein Jewelers
726 Sansom St Ste 1 (19106-3245)
PHONE..................215 592-8956

John D Antonio, *President*
Dennis Klein, *Corp Secy*
EMP: 12 **EST:** 1974
SALES (est): 978.8K **Privately Held**
WEB: www.jdjewelers.com
SIC: 7631 5944 3911 Jewelry repair services; jewelry, precious stones & precious metals; jewel settings & mountings, precious metal

(G-13881)
J CARLTON JONES & ASSOCIATES
Also Called: Herald Products
4329 Paul St (19124-4035)
PHONE......................267 538-5009
Carlton G Jones, *President*
EMP: 7
SQ FT: 4,000
SALES (est): 721.6K **Privately Held**
SIC: 2759 2399 Screen printing; emblems, badges & insignia: from purchased materials

(G-13882)
J DAVIS PRINTING LLC
7109 Ridge Ave (19128-3277)
PHONE......................215 483-1006
John Davis, *CEO*
Rose Davis, *Office Mgr*
EMP: 3 **EST:** 1993
SQ FT: 900
SALES (est): 375.5K **Privately Held**
SIC: 2759 Commercial printing

(G-13883)
J F M PHILADELPHIA DONUT INC
Also Called: Dunkin' Donuts
9834 Bustleton Ave (19115-2146)
PHONE......................215 676-0700
Deepak Shah, *President*
EMP: 9
SALES (est): 411.3K **Privately Held**
SIC: 5461 2051 Doughnuts; doughnuts, except frozen

(G-13884)
J KINDERMAN & SONS INC
Also Called: Brite Star Manufacturing
2900 S 20th St Unit 1 (19145-4798)
PHONE......................215 271-7600
Judith Kinderman, *President*
Jerry Hamaday, *Purch Mgr*
Johnny Cox, *Natl Sales Mgr*
▲ **EMP:** 50 **EST:** 1896
SQ FT: 250,000
SALES (est): 21.3MM **Privately Held**
WEB: www.britestar.com
SIC: 5199 5999 3999 Christmas novelties; Christmas lights & decorations; tinsel

(G-13885)
J MEYER & SONS INC
4321 N 4th St (19140-2403)
PHONE......................215 324-4440
Paul Gawason, *Manager*
EMP: 16
SQ FT: 3,300
SALES (corp-wide): 20.7MM **Privately Held**
SIC: 3089 Coloring & finishing of plastic products
PA: J Meyer & Sons Inc
Jones Ave & Chestnut St
West Point PA 19486
215 699-7003

(G-13886)
J P CERINI TECHNOLOGIES INC
4600 N Fairhill St (19140-1418)
PHONE......................215 457-7337
Mary Cerini, *President*
EMP: 9
SQ FT: 15,584
SALES (est): 1.1MM **Privately Held**
SIC: 3471 Finishing, metals or formed products

(G-13887)
J P TEES INC
2930 Richmond St (19134-5706)
PHONE......................215 634-2348
Joseph F Petaccio III, *President*
Jayson Petaccio, *Vice Pres*
Margarette Petaccio, *Vice Pres*

EMP: 6
SQ FT: 5,000
SALES (est): 1MM **Privately Held**
WEB: www.jptees.com
SIC: 2261 Screen printing of cotton broadwoven fabrics

(G-13888)
JADE FASHION CORPORATION
Also Called: Jade Apparel
1017 Race St Fl 4 (19107-1826)
PHONE......................215 922-3953
Keo Luong, *CEO*
EMP: 4
SQ FT: 4,000
SALES (est): 565.7K **Privately Held**
SIC: 2339 Women's & misses' outerwear

(G-13889)
JAMAICA WAY LIMITED
2900 Island Ave Ste 2930 (19153-2028)
PHONE......................267 593-9724
Jane Henderson, *General Mgr*
EMP: 5
SALES (est): 252.7K **Privately Held**
SIC: 2099 Food preparations

(G-13890)
JAMES ABBOTT
Also Called: Abbott's Plating
2105 E Wishart St (19134-3844)
PHONE......................215 426-8070
James Abbott, *Owner*
▲ **EMP:** 15
SQ FT: 22,501
SALES (est): 1.1MM **Privately Held**
SIC: 3471 Plating & polishing

(G-13891)
JAWS INC
Also Called: All-Brite Metal Finishing
2148 E Tucker St (19125-1840)
PHONE......................215 423-2234
Carol Serotta, *President*
Howard Serotta, *Vice Pres*
EMP: 3
SQ FT: 15,000
SALES (est): 210.2K **Privately Held**
SIC: 3471 Anodizing (plating) of metals or formed products; polishing, metals or formed products

(G-13892)
JAZZ PHARMACEUTICALS
2005 Market St Fl 21 (19103-7042)
PHONE......................215 832-3750
Patricia Moore, *Vice Pres*
Enrique Antone, *Research*
Paul Marcotte, *Director*
Sokol Petushi, *Director*
Patricia Walsh, *Director*
EMP: 14 **Privately Held**
SIC: 2834 Pharmaceutical preparations
HQ: Jazz Pharmaceuticals (Eusa Pharma Usa), Inc.
1717 Langhorne Newtown Rd
Langhorne PA 19047

(G-13893)
JERITH MANUFACTURING LLC
14400 Mcnulty Rd (19154-1108)
PHONE......................215 676-4068
Bruce Schwartz, *President*
Sheila Schwartz, *Admin Sec*
▼ **EMP:** 75 **EST:** 1953
SQ FT: 444,000
SALES: 22.9MM
SALES (corp-wide): 9B **Privately Held**
WEB: www.jerith.com
SIC: 3446 3496 Fences or posts, ornamental iron or steel; miscellaneous fabricated wire products
HQ: Assa Abloy Inc.
110 Sargent Dr
New Haven CT 06511
203 624-5225

(G-13894)
JEROME W SINCLAIR
Also Called: We Care Screen Printing
888 N Lex St (19104-1353)
PHONE......................215 477-3996
Jerome Wesley, *Owner*
EMP: 4
SALES (est): 341.6K **Privately Held**
SIC: 2759 Screen printing

(G-13895)
JESSICA KINGSLEY PUBLISHERS
400 Market St Ste 400e (19106-2507)
PHONE......................215 922-1161
Robert Rooney, *President*
EMP: 5
SALES (est): 578.7K **Privately Held**
WEB: www.jkp.com
SIC: 2731 Books: publishing only

(G-13896)
JEWISH EXPONENT INC
Also Called: Jewish Publishing Group
2100 Arch St Fl 4 (19103-1300)
PHONE......................215 832-0700
David Alpher, *Division Mgr*
Liz Spikol, *Editor*
Joseph Kemp, *Production*
Taylor Orlin, *Accounts Exec*
EMP: 43 **EST:** 1887
SQ FT: 11,000
SALES (est): 6MM **Privately Held**
WEB: www.jewishexponent.com
SIC: 2711 2721 Newspapers: publishing only, not printed on site; magazines: publishing only, not printed on site

(G-13897)
JEWISH PUBLICATION SOC OF AMER
2100 Arch St Fl 2 (19103-1300)
PHONE......................215 832-0600
Carol Hupping, *Exec Dir*
Sarah Segal, *Director*
EMP: 15 **EST:** 1888
SQ FT: 5,000
SALES (est): 477.7K **Privately Held**
WEB: www.jewishpub.org
SIC: 2731 Books: publishing only

(G-13898)
JIBA LLC
Also Called: Penn Scale Manufacturing Co
1300 Adams Ave Ste 1 (19124-4512)
PHONE......................215 739-9644
Andreo Levin, *President*
Andrea Levin, *President*
Larry Biren, *Vice Pres*
Andrew Satek, *Treasurer*
Elissa Biren, *Admin Sec*
▲ **EMP:** 12 **EST:** 1923
SQ FT: 14,000
SALES (est): 2.3MM **Privately Held**
WEB: www.pennscale.com
SIC: 3596 3423 Scales & balances, except laboratory; hand & edge tools

(G-13899)
JIMMI NEWS
1234 Market St (19107-3721)
PHONE......................215 988-9095
Nehal Desai, *Principal*
EMP: 4 **EST:** 2010
SALES (est): 188.9K **Privately Held**
SIC: 2711 Newspapers, publishing & printing

(G-13900)
JOBOMAX GLOBAL LTD
1229 Chestnut St 153 (19107-4140)
PHONE......................215 253-3691
Mamady Doumbouya, *Managing Prtnr*
Robert Hornsby,
EMP: 3
SALES: 250K **Privately Held**
SIC: 3295 Minerals, ground or treated

(G-13901)
JOE BENTO CONSTRUCTION CO INC
806 Regina St (19116-2914)
PHONE......................215 969-1505
Jose R Bento, *President*
Christian M Bento, *Vice Pres*
Vanessa M Bento, *Treasurer*
Maria Bento, *Admin Sec*
EMP: 6
SALES: 950K **Privately Held**
SIC: 1081 7389 Overburden removal, metal mining;

(G-13902)
JOHN BEIRS STUDIO
Also Called: Jonas Home
225 Race St Fl 1 (19106-1964)
PHONE......................215 627-1410
EMP: 4
SALES (est): 243.4K **Privately Held**
SIC: 3231 5231 Mfg Products-Purchased Glass Ret Paint/Glass/Wallpaper

(G-13903)
JOHN J KELLEY ASSOCIATES LTD
1528 Walnut St Ste 1801 (19102-3612)
PHONE......................215 545-0939
John J Kelley, *President*
EMP: 5 **EST:** 1964
SQ FT: 2,000
SALES (est): 539.9K **Privately Held**
SIC: 3851 Eyes, glass & plastic

(G-13904)
JOHN O MACHINE CO
415 W Pike St (19140-3311)
PHONE......................215 228-1155
John Omeliantschuk, *Owner*
John O Meliantschuk, *Owner*
EMP: 6
SQ FT: 5,600
SALES (est): 363.9K **Privately Held**
WEB: www.shadoof.net
SIC: 3599 Machine shop, jobbing & repair

(G-13905)
JOHN SCHMIDT PRINTING CO
4721 Longshore Ave (19135-2319)
PHONE......................215 624-2945
EMP: 3
SALES (est): 150K **Privately Held**
SIC: 2759 Commercial Printing

(G-13906)
JOHN STORTZ AND SON INC
210 Vine St (19106-1213)
PHONE......................215 627-3855
John Stortz, *President*
Jeffrey Stortz, *Office Mgr*
◆ **EMP:** 6 **EST:** 1853
SQ FT: 20,000
SALES (est): 911.6K **Privately Held**
WEB: www.stortz.com
SIC: 3423 5085 Hand & edge tools; tools

(G-13907)
JOHN V POTERO ENTERPRISES INC
2100 Byberry Rd Ste 108 (19116-3026)
PHONE......................215 537-3320
Thomas J Potero, *President*
EMP: 5 **EST:** 1953
SQ FT: 12,000
SALES (est): 240K **Privately Held**
SIC: 3599 Machine shop, jobbing & repair

(G-13908)
JOHNS CSTM STAIRWAYS MLLWK CO
Also Called: Johns Custom Stairways & Mllwk
2115 S 8th St (19148-3133)
PHONE......................215 463-1211
John Tenaglia, *President*
EMP: 4 **EST:** 1970
SQ FT: 6,000
SALES (est): 470.3K **Privately Held**
SIC: 2431 Staircases & stairs, wood

(G-13909)
JOHNSON & JOHNSON
7050 Camp Hill Rd (19118)
PHONE......................215 273-7000
James Cash, *President*
Jean Eble, *President*
Michael English, *President*
Robert Guthrie, *President*
Stephen Lampkin, *President*
EMP: 1600
SALES (corp-wide): 81.5B **Publicly Held**
WEB: www.jnj.com
SIC: 3842 Surgical appliances & supplies
PA: Johnson & Johnson
1 Johnson And Johnson Plz
New Brunswick NJ 08933
732 524-0400

▲ = Import ▼=Export
◆ =Import/Export

(G-13910)
JOHNSON COMMUNICATIONS INC
Also Called: Westside Weekly
6253 Pine St (19143-1027)
P.O. Box 19437 (19143-0037)
PHONE..................................215 474-7411
Tyree Johnson, *President*
EMP: 3
SALES (est): 192.7K **Privately Held**
SIC: 2711 Newspapers: publishing only, not printed on site

(G-13911)
JOSEPH MIKSTAS
Also Called: K B D
2419 S 7th St 21 (19148-3812)
PHONE..................................215 271-2419
Joe Mikstas, *Owner*
EMP: 4
SQ FT: 2,500
SALES: 150K **Privately Held**
SIC: 5211 2434 2521 2431 Cabinets, kitchen; wood kitchen cabinets; wood office furniture; millwork

(G-13912)
JOWITT & RODGERS COMPANY (PA)
9400 State Rd (19114-3094)
PHONE..................................215 824-0401
Frederick S Rodgers, *President*
John Rodgers, *Vice Pres*
William Tonuci, *Treasurer*
Arnold D Rogers, *Admin Sec*
▲ **EMP:** 50
SQ FT: 30,000
SALES (est): 14.8MM **Privately Held**
WEB: www.jowittandrodgers.com
SIC: 3291 Abrasive wheels & grindstones, not artificial; wheels, abrasive

(G-13913)
JUICE MERCHANT
4330 Main St (19127-1421)
PHONE..................................215 483-8888
EMP: 6
SALES (est): 327.2K **Privately Held**
SIC: 2037 Fruit juices

(G-13914)
JUMPBUTTON STUDIO LLC
Also Called: Jbs
4738 Meridian St (19136-3311)
PHONE..................................267 407-7535
Nicodemus Madehdou, *CEO*
Matthew Auld, *Principal*
Kevin Ngo, *Principal*
Daniel Ostermiller, *COO*
EMP: 30
SALES (est): 811.4K **Privately Held**
SIC: 7372 3944 Home entertainment computer software; publishers' computer software; electronic games & toys

(G-13915)
JUST BORN INC
7701 State Rd (19136-3405)
PHONE..................................215 335-4500
David Goldenberg, *Branch Mgr*
EMP: 70
SQ FT: 112,500
SALES (est): 10.4MM
SALES (corp-wide): 170.4MM **Privately Held**
WEB: www.justborn.com
SIC: 2064 Chocolate candy, except solid chocolate
PA: Just Born, Inc.
1300 Stefko Blvd
Bethlehem PA 18017
610 867-7568

(G-13916)
JYOTI N STAND
Also Called: Miller News Stand
176 W Chelten Ave (19144-3302)
PHONE..................................215 843-5354
Anel Patell, *Owner*
EMP: 6
SALES (est): 218.2K **Privately Held**
SIC: 2711 Newspapers

(G-13917)
K & K PRECISION GRINDING CO
6795 State Rd Rear (19135-1594)
PHONE..................................215 333-1276
Joe Staszewski, *President*
Maurianne Staszewski, *Vice Pres*
EMP: 4 **EST:** 1950
SALES (est): 437K **Privately Held**
SIC: 3599 Grinding castings for the trade

(G-13918)
K-R-K PAVING LLC
6631 Gillespie St (19135-2716)
PHONE..................................267 602-7715
Kerry Stover,
Rashida Epps,
Kevin Stover,
EMP: 3
SALES (est): 252.8K **Privately Held**
SIC: 2951 7389 Asphalt paving mixtures & blocks;

(G-13919)
KADA ENERGY RESOURCES LLC
1441 S Bouvier St (19146-4724)
PHONE..................................215 839-9159
Kefi Nyame-Mensah, *Exec Dir*
EMP: 5 **EST:** 2013
SQ FT: 800
SALES: 290K **Privately Held**
SIC: 8711 5013 1389 Acoustical engineering; pumps, oil & gas; cementing oil & gas well casings

(G-13920)
KAJEVI SERVICES LLC
7229 Rising Sun Ave (19111-3926)
PHONE..................................215 722-0711
Betty L Gabilanes, *Owner*
EMP: 7
SQ FT: 1,200
SALES (est): 1MM **Privately Held**
SIC: 6411 3469 Insurance brokers; automobile license tags, stamped metal

(G-13921)
KAPLANS NEW MODEL BAKING CO
Also Called: Kaplan's New Model Gold Medal
901 N 3rd St (19123-2205)
PHONE..................................215 627-5288
Stan Silverman, *President*
Don Santman, *Vice Pres*
Jeff Soloman, *Vice Pres*
EMP: 22 **EST:** 1956
SQ FT: 15,000
SALES (est): 3.3MM **Privately Held**
SIC: 2051 Bread, all types (white, wheat, rye, etc); fresh or frozen; rolls, bread type: fresh or frozen

(G-13922)
KAREN WRIGLEY DR
Also Called: National Contact Lens
1919 Chestnut St Lbby 105 (19103-3456)
PHONE..................................215 563-8440
Karen Wrigley, *Owner*
EMP: 6 **EST:** 1978
SALES (est): 602.2K **Privately Held**
WEB: www.visionsource-wrigley.com
SIC: 8042 5995 3851 Specialized optometrists; optical goods stores; ophthalmic goods

(G-13923)
KATZ IMPORTS INC
723 Sansom St Fl 1 (19106-3200)
PHONE..................................215 238-0197
Todd Katz, *President*
Zachary Katz, *Business Mgr*
Howard Katz, *Corp Secy*
Stanley Katz, *Vice Pres*
EMP: 7
SQ FT: 9,612
SALES (est): 1.2MM **Privately Held**
SIC: 5094 3911 Jewelry; jewelry, precious metal

(G-13924)
KATZ MEDIA GROUP INC
Also Called: Katz Radio
1880 Jfk Blvd Ste 703 (19103-7400)
PHONE..................................215 567-5166
Terry Houston, *Manager*

EMP: 20 **Publicly Held**
WEB: www.ctvsales.com
SIC: 3663 Radio receiver networks
HQ: Katz Media Group, Inc.
125 W 55th St Fl 11
New York NY 10019

(G-13925)
KE CUSTOM PC MFG
3933 Germantown Ave (19140-3423)
P.O. Box 4498 (19140-0498)
PHONE..................................215 228-6437
Herbert Hauls, *Principal*
EMP: 3
SALES (est): 123.4K **Privately Held**
SIC: 3999 Manufacturing industries

(G-13926)
KENNEDY PRINTING CO INC
Also Called: Kpc Direct Mail
5534 Baltimore Ave (19143-3195)
PHONE..................................215 474-5150
James Kennedy Jr, *President*
Doris Smith, *Principal*
EMP: 19
SQ FT: 100,000
SALES (est): 3.2MM **Privately Held**
WEB: www.kennedyprinting.com
SIC: 2752 7331 Commercial printing, offset; mailing service

(G-13927)
KENTUCKY BERWIND LAND COMPANY (DH)
1500 Market St Ste 3000w (19102-2107)
PHONE..................................215 563-2800
Ryan Ronck, *President*
EMP: 5
SALES (est): 629.6K
SALES (corp-wide): 2.9B **Privately Held**
SIC: 1241 Mine preparation services

(G-13928)
KESSER BAKING CO
Also Called: NY Bagel Bakery
7555 Haverford Ave (19151-2227)
PHONE..................................215 878-8080
Bruce Meyer, *President*
Sarah Meyer, *Principal*
EMP: 15
SQ FT: 1,120
SALES (est): 1.2MM **Privately Held**
SIC: 2051 5461 Bakery: wholesale or wholesale/retail combined; bagels, fresh or frozen; bakeries

(G-13929)
KEVIN OBRIEN STUDIO INC
1412 S Broad St (19146-4808)
PHONE..................................215 923-6378
Kevin O'Brien, *President*
▲ **EMP:** 5
SQ FT: 3,000
SALES (est): 563.2K **Privately Held**
WEB: www.kevinobrienstudio.com
SIC: 2339 5137 7336 Scarves, hoods, headbands, etc.: women's; scarves, women's & children's; silk screen design

(G-13930)
KEYSTONE FLASHING CO
5119 N 2nd St Fl 1 (19120-3499)
PHONE..................................215 329-8500
Thomas N Spink Jr, *President*
Michael Spink, *Vice Pres*
EMP: 7 **EST:** 1938
SQ FT: 15,000
SALES (est): 1.1MM **Privately Held**
WEB: www.keystoneflashing.com
SIC: 3444 5051 Sheet metalwork; metals service centers & offices

(G-13931)
KEYSTONE PINE MACHINE INC CO
2130 E Somerset St (19134-3913)
PHONE..................................215 425-0605
Fax: 215 425-0192
EMP: 3 **EST:** 1967
SQ FT: 16,000
SALES (est): 170K **Privately Held**
SIC: 3599 Mfg Industrial Machinery

(G-13932)
KEYSTONE PRINTING INK CO (PA)
2700 Roberts Ave (19129-1294)
PHONE..................................215 228-8100
Robert B Chamness, *Ch of Bd*
Robert J Campbell Jr, *Corp Secy*
Philip J Chamness, *Exec VP*
EMP: 12 **EST:** 1928
SQ FT: 27,500
SALES (est): 2.8MM **Privately Held**
WEB: www.keystoneink.com
SIC: 2893 Printing ink

(G-13933)
KEYSTONE UNIFORM CAP LP
2251 Fraley St Ste 8 (19137-1824)
PHONE..................................215 821-3434
Harold Selvin, *Partner*
David Selbin, *Partner*
EMP: 45 **EST:** 1929
SQ FT: 16,000
SALES (est): 4.6MM **Privately Held**
WEB: www.keystoneuniformcap.com
SIC: 2353 2395 Uniform hats & caps; police hats & caps; chauffeurs' hats & caps, cloth; embroidery & art needlework

(G-13934)
KGM GAMING LLC
4250 Wissahickon Ave (19129-1215)
PHONE..................................215 430-0388
Lance Weiss, *President*
Jason Cohen, *Exec VP*
Jack McNamara, *Vice Pres*
Michael Bull, *Finance*
Curt Kugel, *Accounts Exec*
▲ **EMP:** 37
SQ FT: 2,000
SALES (est): 11.7MM **Privately Held**
WEB: www.kgmgaming.com
SIC: 2426 5099 Chair seats, hardwood; game machines, coin-operated

(G-13935)
KICKUP LLC
Also Called: Pedagology
31 N 2nd St 2 (19106-2214)
PHONE..................................610 256-1004
Jeremy Rogoff, *CEO*
Victoria Kinzig, *COO*
EMP: 4
SALES (est): 249.2K **Privately Held**
SIC: 7372 Application computer software

(G-13936)
KINETIC BUILDINGS LLC
4028 Filbert St (19104-2204)
PHONE..................................203 858-0813
Adam Regnier, *Principal*
EMP: 5
SALES (est): 163.4K **Privately Held**
SIC: 7372 Business oriented computer software

(G-13937)
KINETIC CERAMICS LLC
4050 S 26th St Ste 200 (19112-1616)
PHONE..................................510 264-2140
Robert Frantz, *President*
EMP: 14
SQ FT: 5,522
SALES (est): 2.3MM **Privately Held**
WEB: www.kineticceramics.com
SIC: 3679 Piezoelectric crystals

(G-13938)
KINGSBURY INC (PA)
10385 Drummond Rd (19154-3884)
PHONE..................................215 824-4000
Joseph C Hill, *Ch of Bd*
William R Strecker, *President*
Michael Brawley, *Vice Pres*
Mick McCann, *Vice Pres*
Jerry W Powers, *Vice Pres*
◆ **EMP:** 122
SQ FT: 120,000
SALES (est): 29MM **Privately Held**
SIC: 3568 Bearings, bushings & blocks

(G-13939)
KINGSBURY INC
Also Called: Messinger Bearings
10385 Drummond Rd (19154-3884)
PHONE..................................215 824-4000

EMP: 24
SALES (corp-wide): 29MM **Privately Held**
SIC: 3568 3562 Power transmission equipment; ball bearings & parts; roller bearings & parts
PA: Kingsbury, Inc.
   10385 Drummond Rd
   Philadelphia PA 19154
   215 824-4000

(G-13940)
KNOLL INC
130 N 18th St (19103-2768)
PHONE..................................215 988-1788
Bridgette Sabar, *Principal*
EMP: 50 **Publicly Held**
SIC: 2521 Panel systems & partitions (free-standing), office: wood
PA: Knoll, Inc.
   1235 Water St
   East Greenville PA 18041

(G-13941)
KOREN PUBLICATIONS
777-K Schwab Rd (19019)
PHONE..................................267 498-0071
Robert Esposito, *Principal*
EMP: 4
SALES (est): 296.6K **Privately Held**
SIC: 2721 Periodicals

(G-13942)
KREMERS URBAN PHARMACEUTICALS
13200 Townsend Rd (19154-1014)
PHONE..................................609 936-5940
EMP: 3
SALES (est): 182.9K **Privately Held**
SIC: 2834 Mfg Pharmaceutical Preparations

(G-13943)
KREMERS URBAN PHRMCUTICALS INC
13200 Townsend Rd (19154-1014)
PHONE..................................609 936-5940
EMP: 14
SALES (corp-wide): 542.4MM **Publicly Held**
SIC: 2834 Mfg Pharmaceutical Preparations
HQ: Kremers Urban Pharmaceuticals Inc.
   1101 C Ave W
   Seymour IN 47274
   812 523-5347

(G-13944)
KRENGEL QUAKER CITY CORP
Also Called: Quaker City Stamp & Stencil
12285 Mcnulty Rd Ste 103 (19154-1210)
PHONE..................................215 969-9800
John Collins Jr, *President*
EMP: 46
SQ FT: 6,200
SALES (est): 6.3MM
SALES (corp-wide): 10.3MM **Privately Held**
WEB: www.ams-stamps.com
SIC: 3953 Marking devices
PA: American Marking Systems Inc
   1015 Paulison Ave
   Clifton NJ 07011
   973 478-5600

(G-13945)
KRG ENTERPRISES INC
9901 Blue Grass Rd (19114-1013)
PHONE..................................215 708-2811
Kevin Gottlieb, *President*
Stevan P Gottlieb, *Corp Secy*
Maureen Gottlieb, *Vice Pres*
Andrew Rubenstein, *Vice Pres*
Gary Waldman, *Vice Pres*
▲ **EMP:** 125
SALES (est): 24.9MM **Privately Held**
WEB: www.krgenterprises.com
SIC: 2541 Store fixtures, wood

(G-13946)
KURZ-HASTINGS INC
10901 Dutton Rd (19154-3203)
PHONE..................................215 632-2300
Herbert Kurz, *Principal*
EMP: 7

SALES (est): 651.4K **Privately Held**
SIC: 3497 Metal foil & leaf

(G-13947)
KVAERNER PHILADELPHIA SHI
2100 Kitty Hawk Ave (19112-1895)
PHONE..................................215 875-2725
Ron J McAlear, *Principal*
EMP: 3 **EST:** 2013
SALES (est): 340.8K **Privately Held**
SIC: 3731 Shipbuilding & repairing

(G-13948)
L & L K INCORPORATED
Also Called: Keller-Charles of Philadelphia
2413 Federal St 27 (19146-2431)
P.O. Box 3993 (19146-0293)
PHONE..................................215 732-2614
Peggy Fields, *President*
Jim Katz, *Treasurer*
▲ **EMP:** 35 **EST:** 1945
SQ FT: 20,000
SALES (est): 4.9MM **Privately Held**
SIC: 5199 5023 3914 Gifts & novelties; home furnishings; silverware & plated ware

(G-13949)
L RAND INCORPORATED
2300 Pine St Apt 7 (19103-6467)
PHONE..................................215 490-8090
Leslie Wilderson, *Principal*
EMP: 3
SALES (est): 189.2K **Privately Held**
SIC: 3131 Rands

(G-13950)
LAGOS INC (PA)
Also Called: Lagos Design
441 N 5th St Fl 4 (19123-4010)
PHONE..................................215 925-1693
Chris Cullen, *CEO*
Steven Lagos, *President*
Joel Schecter, *Vice Pres*
Gina Dicicco, *Senior Buyer*
Stefanie Nagy, *QA Dir*
▲ **EMP:** 70
SQ FT: 40,000
SALES (est): 17.9MM **Privately Held**
WEB: www.lagos.com
SIC: 3911 Jewel settings & mountings, precious metal

(G-13951)
LANDES BIOSCIENCE INC
530 Walnut St Ste 850 (19106-3604)
PHONE..................................512 637-6050
Ronald Landes, *President*
Kimberly Mitchell, *Treasurer*
Cynthia Conomos, *Admin Sec*
EMP: 28
SALES (est): 1.9MM **Privately Held**
SIC: 2731 Books: publishing only

(G-13952)
LANNETT COMPANY INC (PA)
9000 State Rd (19136-1615)
PHONE..................................215 333-9000
Timothy C Crew, *CEO*
Patrick G Lepore, *Ch of Bd*
Maureen M Cavanaugh, *Senior VP*
Robert Ehlinger, *Vice Pres*
Zachary Hamm, *Project Mgr*
EMP: 277 **EST:** 1942
SQ FT: 31,000
SALES: 684.5MM **Publicly Held**
WEB: www.lannett.com
SIC: 2834 Pharmaceutical preparations

(G-13953)
LANNETT COMPANY INC
9001 Torresdale Ave (19136-1514)
PHONE..................................215 333-9000
Arthur Bedrosian, *President*
EMP: 100
SALES (corp-wide): 633.3MM **Publicly Held**
WEB: www.lannett.com
SIC: 2834 Pharmaceutical preparations
PA: Lannett Company, Inc.
   9000 State Rd
   Philadelphia PA 19136
   215 333-9000

(G-13954)
LANUM METAL PRODUCTS LLC
4100 N 16th St (19140-3008)
PHONE..................................215 329-5010
Helen Borrell,
Edward Borrell,
EMP: 4 **EST:** 1990
SALES (est): 330K **Privately Held**
WEB: www.lanummetal.com
SIC: 3544 3599 Special dies, tools, jigs & fixtures; special dies & tools; jigs & fixtures; machine shop, jobbing & repair

(G-13955)
LAP DISTRIBUTORS INC
3515 Amber St (19134-2707)
PHONE..................................215 744-4000
Paul Lapinson, *President*
EMP: 8 **EST:** 1966
SQ FT: 125,000
SALES (est): 1.5MM **Privately Held**
WEB: www.lapdistributors.com
SIC: 2679 5087 5112 Paper products, converted; janitors' supplies; stationery & office supplies

(G-13956)
LAPSLEY PRINTING INC
Also Called: Lapsley Print Shop
4612 Wellington St (19135-1234)
PHONE..................................215 332-7451
Mike Inglisa, *President*
Wayne Inglisa, *Vice Pres*
EMP: 3
SQ FT: 2,000
SALES (est): 471.9K **Privately Held**
SIC: 2752 Commercial printing, offset

(G-13957)
LARRY DARLING
Also Called: Rosie's Butterkins
10156 Ferndale St (19116-3659)
PHONE..................................215 677-1452
Larry Darling, *Owner*
EMP: 6
SALES (est): 246.1K **Privately Held**
SIC: 2051 Bread, cake & related products

(G-13958)
LARRY PAUL CASTING CO INC
720 Sansom St Fl 1 (19106-3210)
PHONE..................................215 928-1644
Larry Paul, *President*
Fred Paul, *Corp Secy*
Roseanne Paul, *Vice Pres*
EMP: 5
SALES (est): 748.4K **Privately Held**
WEB: www.lpcasting.com
SIC: 3911 Jewelry, precious metal

(G-13959)
LASERMATION INC
2629 N 15th St (19132-3904)
PHONE..................................215 228-7900
Joseph Molines, *President*
Margaret Molines, *Treasurer*
Charlene River, *Cust Mgr*
Doreen Parker, *Technology*
EMP: 28
SQ FT: 13,000
SALES (est): 3.3MM **Privately Held**
WEB: www.lasermation.com
SIC: 7389 3953 3471 Engraving service; marking devices; plating & polishing

(G-13960)
LAWRENCE R GILMAN LLC
Also Called: Larry Gilman
2417 Welsh Rd Ste 21-252 (19114-2213)
PHONE..................................215 432-2733
Lawrence R Gilman,
EMP: 3
SALES (est): 170K **Privately Held**
SIC: 5699 2253 T-shirts, custom printed; T-shirts & tops, knit

(G-13961)
LB FULL CIRCLE CANINE FITNESS
Also Called: Zoom Room
180 W Girard Ave (19123-1660)
PHONE..................................267 825-7375
Leigh McKinley, *Owner*
Marty McKinley, *Co-Owner*
EMP: 4 **EST:** 2013

SALES (est): 132.1K **Privately Held**
SIC: 7699 3199 Sewer cleaning & rodding; dog furnishings: collars, leashes, muzzles, etc.: leather

(G-13962)
LE GRAND ASSOC OF PITTSBURGH (PA)
Also Called: Legrand Associates
1601 Walnut St Ste 616 (19102-2904)
PHONE..................................215 496-1307
Joseph A Legrand Jr, *President*
David Legrand, *Corp Secy*
EMP: 7 **EST:** 1953
SALES (est): 925.9K **Privately Held**
SIC: 3851 Eyes, glass & plastic

(G-13963)
LEARJET INC
1500 Market St (19102-2100)
PHONE..................................215 246-3454
Alain Bellemare, *Branch Mgr*
EMP: 525
SALES (corp-wide): 16.2B **Privately Held**
SIC: 3721 Aircraft
HQ: Learjet Inc.
   1 Learjet Way
   Wichita KS 67209
   316 946-2000

(G-13964)
LEATEX CHEMICAL CO
2722 N Hancock St (19133-3597)
PHONE..................................215 739-2000
L Kevin McChesney, *President*
Brian McChesney, *Vice Pres*
EMP: 25 **EST:** 1922
SQ FT: 60,000
SALES (est): 5.9MM **Privately Held**
WEB: www.leatexcorp.com
SIC: 2843 Textile finishing agents; leather finishing agents

(G-13965)
LEGACY RESTORATION LLC
3237 Amber St (19134-3227)
PHONE..................................716 239-0695
Alex Pientka, *President*
EMP: 3
SALES (est): 143K **Privately Held**
SIC: 2431 Millwork

(G-13966)
LEONETTI FOOD DISTRIBUTORS INC
Also Called: Leonetti Frozen Food
5935 Woodland Ave (19143-5919)
PHONE..................................215 729-4200
Beth Di Pietro, *President*
Leroy Douglas, *Site Mgr*
Robert Ippaso, *Director*
EMP: 46
SQ FT: 36,000
SALES (est): 9.8MM **Privately Held**
WEB: www.leonettisfrozenfoods.com
SIC: 2099 2038 Food preparations; frozen specialties

(G-13967)
LIA DIAGNOSTICS INC
737 Bainbridge St (19147-2058)
PHONE..................................267 362-9670
Bethany Edwards, *CEO*
Sarah Rottenberg, *COO*
Frances Dimare, *Mktg Dir*
Anna Couturier, *Product Mgr*
EMP: 4
SQ FT: 5,000
SALES (est): 328.5K **Privately Held**
SIC: 2835 In vitro diagnostics

(G-13968)
LIBERTY BELL STEAK CO
3457 Janney St (19134-2607)
P.O. Box 12728 (19134-0728)
PHONE..................................215 537-4797
John Bellios, *President*
Joan Koltys, *Comptroller*
Paul Aylmer, *Sales Mgr*
Jonathan Vellios, *Manager*
EMP: 25
SALES (est): 8.3MM **Privately Held**
SIC: 5147 2013 Meats & meat products; sausages & other prepared meats

(G-13969)
LIBERTY COCA-COLA BEVS LLC (PA)
725 E Erie Ave (19134-1210)
PHONE...............................215 427-4500
Francis McGorry, *President*
Doug Herndon, *Vice Pres*
Robert J Jordan Jr, *Vice Pres*
Marie D Quintero-Johnson, *Vice Pres*
Sheri Preston, *CFO*
EMP: 16
SALES (est): 1.3B **Privately Held**
SIC: 2086 2087 Carbonated beverages, nonalcoholic; bottled & canned; soft drinks: packaged in cans, bottles, etc.; fruit drinks (less than 100% juice): packaged in cans, etc.; syrups, drink; concentrates, drink

(G-13970)
LIFETIME BATHTUB ENCLOSURES
2409 W Westmoreland St (19129-1309)
PHONE...............................215 228-2500
EMP: 17 EST: 1953
SQ FT: 34,000
SALES: 2MM **Privately Held**
SIC: 3231 Mfg Products-Purchased Glass

(G-13971)
LIMITLESS LONGEVITY LLC
1429 Walnut St Ste 1101 (19102-3205)
PHONE...............................215 279-8376
Charlie Seltzer,
EMP: 10
SALES (est): 1MM **Privately Held**
SIC: 2835 Microbiology & virology diagnostic products

(G-13972)
LIPPINCOTT WILLIAMS & WILKINS
530 Walnut St Fl 7 (19106-3607)
PHONE...............................215 521-8300
Joseph Bryant, *CEO*
EMP: 8
SALES (est): 506.5K **Privately Held**
SIC: 2731 Books: publishing only
PA: Lippincott Williams & Wilkins
Downsville Pike Rte
Hagerstown MD 21740

(G-13973)
LIVENT CORPORATION
2929 Walnut St (19104-5054)
PHONE...............................215 299-6000
Pierre R Brondeau, *Ch of Bd*
Paul W Graves, *President*
Thomas Schneberger, *COO*
Sara Ponessa, *Vice Pres*
Gilberto Antoniazzi, *CFO*
EMP: 750
SALES: 442.5MM
SALES (corp-wide): 4.7B **Publicly Held**
SIC: 2819 Lithium compounds, inorganic
PA: Fmc Corporation
2929 Walnut St
Philadelphia PA 19104
215 299-6000

(G-13974)
LONDON WREATH CO INC
2014 E Orleans St (19134-3615)
PHONE...............................215 739-6440
Ann Becker, *President*
EMP: 6
SQ FT: 15,000
SALES (est): 379.2K **Privately Held**
SIC: 3999 Flowers, artificial & preserved

(G-13975)
LONGEVITY PRMIER NTRACEUTICALS
325 Chestnut St Fl 8 (19106-2614)
PHONE...............................877 529-1118
Chuck Zhang, *President*
EMP: 50
SALES (est): 2.1MM **Privately Held**
SIC: 2833 Medicinals & botanicals

(G-13976)
LUNG HING NOODLE COMPANY INC
928 Ridge Ave (19107-1401)
PHONE...............................215 829-1988
Sheng-X Guo, *President*
EMP: 7
SALES (est): 449.2K **Privately Held**
SIC: 2099 Noodles, fried (Chinese)

(G-13977)
LUSCH FRAMES LLC
Also Called: Lusch Frames For Upholstering
1127 E Dunton St (19123-1702)
PHONE...............................215 739-6264
Steven Smarro, *Partner*
Louis C Smarro,
EMP: 3
SQ FT: 3,200
SALES: 200K **Privately Held**
SIC: 2512 Chairs: upholstered on wood frames

(G-13978)
LUXTECH LLC
325 Chestnut St Ste 1212 (19106-2612)
PHONE...............................888 340-4266
Sean Darras, *CEO*
Timothy O'Shaughnessy, *Production*
Jianchuan Tan, *Research*
Jeff Roeder, *Sales Staff*
Kevin Chu, *Technical Staff*
EMP: 10 EST: 2012
SALES (est): 3.9MM **Privately Held**
SIC: 3641 Electric lamps

(G-13979)
LYRRUS INC
Also Called: G-Vox
1080 N Delaware Ave Fl 8 (19125-4338)
PHONE...............................215 922-0880
Nathaniel Weiss, *President*
EMP: 40
SQ FT: 11,000
SALES (est): 2.8MM **Privately Held**
SIC: 3931 Synthesizers, music

(G-13980)
M & M DISPLAYS INC
Screen Craft Signs
3301 Maiden Ln (19145-1004)
PHONE...............................800 874-7171
Chris Mace, *President*
John Belfia, *Manager*
EMP: 14
SQ FT: 11,400
SALES (corp-wide): 9.1MM **Privately Held**
WEB: www.mmdisplays.com
SIC: 3993 Signs & advertising specialties
PA: M & M Displays, Inc.
7700 Brewster Ave
Philadelphia PA 19153
215 365-5200

(G-13981)
M P N INC (PA)
Also Called: Active Heavy-Duty Cooling Pdts
3675 Amber St (19134-2730)
PHONE...............................215 289-9480
Martin Newell Jr, *President*
Paul Luff, *Exec VP*
Dee McIntyre, *Purchasing*
Regina Newell, *Treasurer*
Dale Gordon, *Manager*
▲ EMP: 141
SQ FT: 66,000
SALES (est): 32.2MM **Privately Held**
WEB: www.activeradiator.com
SIC: 3714 Motor vehicle parts & accessories

(G-13982)
M S & M MANUFACTURING CO INC
7707 Dungan Rd (19111-2732)
P.O. Box 9565 (19124-0565)
PHONE...............................215 743-3930
Donald Reeder, *President*
EMP: 3
SQ FT: 4,000
SALES: 230K **Privately Held**
SIC: 3544 Industrial molds

(G-13983)
M3 MEDIA LLC
Also Called: M3 Printing
440 Brown St (19123-2106)
P.O. Box 31445 (19147-0745)
PHONE...............................215 463-6348
Barry Carr,
EMP: 15
SQ FT: 10,000
SALES (est): 2.4MM **Privately Held**
WEB: www.m3media.net
SIC: 2752 Commercial printing, offset

(G-13984)
MAC BEVERAGE INC
6120 Vine St (19139-1134)
PHONE...............................215 474-2024
Jay Hong, *President*
EMP: 5
SALES (est): 239.2K **Privately Held**
SIC: 2085 Ethyl alcohol for beverage purposes

(G-13985)
MAC MILLAN WILLIAM COMPANY
Also Called: Mac Millan Poultry
416 Vine St (19106-1127)
PHONE...............................215 627-3273
Robert Mac Millan, *President*
Madaline York, *Corp Secy*
EMP: 18
SQ FT: 5,000
SALES (est): 7MM **Privately Held**
SIC: 5144 2015 Poultry: live, dressed or frozen (unpackaged); poultry products; poultry, processed: fresh

(G-13986)
MAEVA USA INC
100 S Broad St Ste 1400a (19110-1005)
PHONE...............................215 461-2453
Charlie Humphrey, *President*
Luis Torres-Morente Concha, *Chairman*
▲ EMP: 5
SQ FT: 3,200
SALES: 15MM **Privately Held**
SIC: 2079 Olive oil

(G-13987)
MAGLIO BROS INC (PA)
Also Called: Maglio Sausage
3632 S 3rd St (19148-5382)
PHONE...............................215 465-3902
Anthony J Maglio, *President*
EMP: 60 EST: 1940
SQ FT: 15,000
SALES (est): 9.8MM **Privately Held**
WEB: www.magliosausage.com
SIC: 2013 Sausages from purchased meat

(G-13988)
MALONE & BLUNT INC
10300 Drummond Rd (19154-3804)
PHONE...............................215 563-1368
Daniel Doherty, *President*
EMP: 5
SQ FT: 2,000
SALES (est): 445.5K **Privately Held**
WEB: www.mbitype.com
SIC: 2791 7336 Photocomposition, for the printing trade; graphic arts & related design

(G-13989)
MANUFACTURED RUBBER PDTS CO
Also Called: Phillyrubber.com
4501 Tacony St (19124-4135)
PHONE...............................215 533-3600
Marie Hindman, *CEO*
Nancy M King, *President*
Juacqueline M Contrady, *Vice Pres*
Walter King, *Treasurer*
EMP: 15
SQ FT: 30,000
SALES (est): 2.5MM **Privately Held**
WEB: www.masterpak-usa.com
SIC: 3053 5085 Gaskets, all materials; rubber goods, mechanical

(G-13990)
MARATHON EMBROIDERY
719 S 7th St (19147-2123)
PHONE...............................215 627-8848
Cynthia Anastassiades, *President*
Cornelius Anastassiades,
Herman Shapiro,
EMP: 3
SALES (est): 196.7K **Privately Held**
WEB: www.marathonembroidery.com
SIC: 2395 Embroidery & art needlework

(G-13991)
MARATHON PRINTING INC
Also Called: Mail Center At Marathon Prtg
9 N 3rd St (19106-4591)
PHONE...............................215 238-1100
William M Shapiro, *President*
Meryl Eisman, *Manager*
E Gerald Riesenbach, *Admin Sec*
EMP: 14
SQ FT: 6,000
SALES (est): 2.6MM **Privately Held**
WEB: www.marathonprinting.com
SIC: 7336 7331 2752 Graphic arts & related design; mailing service; commercial printing, offset

(G-13992)
MARCO MANUFACTURING CO INC
1701 S 26th St 15 (19145-1700)
P.O. Box 11976 (19145-0276)
PHONE...............................215 463-2332
Anthony Simiriglio, *President*
Anthony Simiriglio Jr, *Vice Pres*
S Greenberg, *Treasurer*
Marie Simiriglio, *Treasurer*
▲ EMP: 40
SQ FT: 17,000
SALES (est): 6.9MM **Privately Held**
WEB: www.marcomanuf.com
SIC: 3469 3644 3643 3575 Metal stampings; terminal boards; current-carrying wiring devices; computer terminals; automotive & apparel trimmings

(G-13993)
MASCO COMMUNICATIONS INC
Also Called: Philadelphia Gay News
505 S 4th St (19147-1506)
PHONE...............................215 625-8501
Mark Segal, *President*
Rick Lombardo, *Publisher*
Sean Dorn, *Graphic Designe*
EMP: 14
SALES (est): 1MM **Privately Held**
WEB: www.epgn.com
SIC: 2711 Newspapers, publishing & printing

(G-13994)
MASTEROS HOMESTYLE FOODS INC
1511 Packer Ave (19145-4910)
PHONE...............................215 551-2530
Steven Mastero, *Principal*
EMP: 3
SALES (est): 117.5K **Privately Held**
SIC: 2099 Food preparations

(G-13995)
MATTHEW COLE INC
Also Called: Maternity Club
500 E Luzerne St Ste 1 (19124-4208)
PHONE...............................215 425-6606
Gary Weiss, *Manager*
EMP: 3
SALES (corp-wide): 1.2MM **Privately Held**
WEB: www.matthewcole.com
SIC: 2339 Maternity clothing
PA: Matthew Cole Inc
532 Newport Cir
Langhorne PA 19053
215 425-6606

(G-13996)
MAX LEVY AUTOGRAPH INC
2710 Commerce Way (19154-1016)
PHONE...............................215 842-3675
Donald Sedberry, *President*
Steven Seymour, *Project Mgr*
Rich Rosenfeld, *Human Resources*
EMP: 8
SALES (est): 349.1K **Privately Held**
SIC: 3542 Electroforming machines

(G-13997)
MAXIMAL ART INC
1606 S 8th St (19148-1254)
PHONE...................................484 840-0600
Robbin C Bellet, *President*
John Y Wind, *Vice Pres*
Alicia Nazario, *Purch Dir*
EMP: 4
SALES (est): 650.9K **Privately Held**
SIC: 3911 Jewelry, precious metal

(G-13998)
MBM INDUSTRIES INC
Also Called: Paper Preserve
4717 Stenton Ave (19144-3022)
PHONE...................................215 844-2490
Matthew Studner, *President*
Michael Studner, *CFO*
Jamie Wybar, *Administration*
▲ EMP: 20
SQ FT: 70,000
SALES: 5.2MM **Privately Held**
SIC: 2678 Stationery: made from purchased materials

(G-13999)
MCNEAR CHARLES & ASSOCIATES
1431 Dondill Pl (19122-3329)
PHONE...................................215 514-9431
Charles McNear, *Owner*
EMP: 5
SALES (est): 105.7K **Privately Held**
SIC: 2711 Newspapers

(G-14000)
MDG ASSOCIATES
Also Called: St Laurent Apartments
1865 Welsh Rd (19115-4764)
PHONE...................................215 969-6623
Samuel Gabriel, *Partner*
Dominic Cerruti, *Partner*
Victor De Maio, *Partner*
William Myles, *Partner*
EMP: 38
SALES (est): 1.8MM **Privately Held**
SIC: 6513 2752 2789 Apartment building operators; transfers, decalcomania or dry: lithographed; bookbinding & related work

(G-14001)
MDL LIGHTING LLC
2800 Comly Rd (19154-2106)
PHONE...................................267 968-3611
Michael Ginaldi, *President*
EMP: 20
SQ FT: 10,000
SALES (est): 821.6K **Privately Held**
SIC: 3648 Lighting equipment

(G-14002)
MECAER AVIATION GROUP INC
Also Called: Mag
9800 Ashton Rd Ste 1 (19114-1022)
PHONE...................................301 790-3645
Ed Pears, *President*
Grayson Barrows, *Sales Dir*
Lou Prudore, *Director*
EMP: 50 EST: 2008
SALES (est): 1.7MM **Privately Held**
SIC: 4581 3724 Aircraft maintenance & repair services; air scoops, aircraft

(G-14003)
MECHANICAL SAFETY EQUIPMENT
2070 Bennett Rd (19116-3020)
PHONE...................................215 676-7828
Meyer Ostrobrod, *President*
Jerome A Poole, *Vice Pres*
William L Curry, *Asst Sec*
▲ EMP: 30
SQ FT: 16,000
SALES (est): 3.6MM **Privately Held**
WEB: www.msecorporation.com
SIC: 3842 Personal safety equipment

(G-14004)
MEDCHIVE LLC
211 Brown St Unit 8 (19123-2277)
PHONE...................................215 688-7475
Olanrewaju Soremekun, *Principal*
EMP: 3

SALES (est): 136.3K **Privately Held**
SIC: 7371 7372 8748 Computer software development & applications; application computer software; business oriented computer software; systems analysis & engineering consulting services

(G-14005)
MEDICAL PRODUCTS LABS INC
9990 Global Rd (19115-1006)
P.O. Box 14366 (19115-0366)
PHONE...................................215 677-2700
Elliot Stone, *President*
Dave Waxler, *Vice Pres*
Bharat Patel, *VP Opers*
Darshil Patel, *Research*
Mark Sherr, *CFO*
▲ EMP: 185 EST: 1928
SQ FT: 140,000
SALES (est): 45MM **Privately Held**
WEB: www.medprodlab.com
SIC: 2834 Pharmaceutical preparations

(G-14006)
MEDSHIFTS INC
1500 Market St (19102-2100)
PHONE...................................856 834-0074
Albert Paramito, *CEO*
EMP: 5 EST: 2016
SALES (est): 133.6K **Privately Held**
SIC: 7372 7379 7373 Prepackaged Software Svc Computer Related Svcs Computer Systems Design

(G-14007)
MELRATH GASKET INC
1500 John F Kennedy Blvd # 200 (19102-1710)
P.O. Box 43099 (19129-3099)
PHONE...................................215 223-6000
Bruce Duffy, *President*
Marco Giubilato, *Vice Pres*
EMP: 55
SQ FT: 150,000
SALES (est): 8.5MM **Privately Held**
WEB: www.melrath.com
SIC: 3496 3053 Wire cloth & woven wire products; gaskets, all materials

(G-14008)
MENASHA PACKAGING COMPANY LLC
601 E Erie Ave (19134-1208)
PHONE...................................215 426-7110
EMP: 150
SALES (corp-wide): 1.7B **Privately Held**
WEB: www.menashapackaging.com
SIC: 2653 Boxes, corrugated: made from purchased materials; sheets, corrugated: made from purchased materials
HQ: Menasha Packaging Company, Llc
1645 Bergstrom Rd
Neenah WI 54956
920 751-1000

(G-14009)
MENASHA PACKAGING COMPANY LLC
601 E Erie Ave (19134-1208)
PHONE...................................215 426-7110
EMP: 6
SALES (corp-wide): 649MM **Privately Held**
SIC: 2653 Mfg Corrogated Boxes
HQ: Menasha Packaging Company, Llc
1645 Bergstrom Rd
Neenah WI 54956
920 751-1000

(G-14010)
MERRILL CORPORATION
2000 Market St Ste 760 (19103-3200)
PHONE...................................215 405-8443
Dorothy Potash, *Manager*
EMP: 10
SALES (corp-wide): 566.6MM **Privately Held**
WEB: www.merrillcorp.com
SIC: 2759 Commercial printing
PA: Merrill Corporation
1 Merrill Cir
Saint Paul MN 55108
651 646-4501

(G-14011)
MESHNET INC
Also Called: Suitable
206 N 22nd St Unit B (19103-1079)
PHONE...................................215 237-7712
Mark Visco Jr, *CEO*
EMP: 3 EST: 2015
SALES (est): 177.5K **Privately Held**
SIC: 7372 Prepackaged software

(G-14012)
METAL GROUP
740 E Vernon Rd (19119-1551)
PHONE...................................215 438-6156
EMP: 3
SALES (est): 212.4K **Privately Held**
SIC: 3399 Primary metal products

(G-14013)
METAL LIGHT MANUFACTURING
1100 W Indiana Ave (19133-1331)
PHONE...................................215 430-7200
Marion Klugman, *President*
EMP: 18
SQ FT: 50,000
SALES (est): 1.5MM **Privately Held**
SIC: 3646 Fluorescent lighting fixtures, commercial

(G-14014)
METRO CORP (HQ)
Also Called: Philadelphia Magazine
170 S Independence Mall (19106)
PHONE...................................215 564-7700
David Lipson Jr, *President*
D Herbert Lipson, *Chairman*
F B Waechter, *CFO*
Kenneth Artz, *Treasurer*
Margot Berg, *Director*
▼ EMP: 75
SQ FT: 22,126
SALES (est): 13.5MM **Privately Held**
WEB: www.elegantwedding.com
SIC: 2721 Magazines: publishing & printing; magazines: publishing only, not printed on site

(G-14015)
METRO CORP
Also Called: Philadelphia Magazine
170 S Independence Mall W # 200 (19106-3323)
PHONE...................................215 564-7700
Pam Ciccone, *Vice Pres*
EMP: 7 **Privately Held**
WEB: www.elegantwedding.com
SIC: 2721 Magazines: publishing & printing
HQ: Metro Corp.
170 S Independence Mall
Philadelphia PA 19106
215 564-7700

(G-14016)
METRO CORP HOLDINGS INC (PA)
Also Called: Metro Magazines
170 S Independence Mall W # 200 (19106-3323)
PHONE...................................215 564-7700
D Herbert Lipson, *Ch of Bd*
David Lipson Jr, *President*
F B Waechter, *Vice Pres*
EMP: 20
SQ FT: 22,000
SALES (est): 13.5MM **Privately Held**
WEB: www.phillymag.com
SIC: 2721 Magazines: publishing & printing

(G-14017)
METROWEEK CORP
Also Called: Philadelphia City Paper
1845 Walnut St Ste 900 (19103-4710)
PHONE...................................215 735-8444
Robert H Rock, *President*
Charles Fiero, *Treasurer*
EMP: 55 EST: 1957
SQ FT: 23,000
SALES (est): 3.4MM **Privately Held**
SIC: 2711 Operates As A Provider Of Newspaper Publishing And Printing
HQ: Sb New York, Inc.
120 Broadway
New York NY 10271
212 457-7790

(G-14018)
MGS04 CORPORATION
1700 Market St Ste 1105 (19103-3913)
PHONE...................................267 249-2372
Zacharia Ali, *Ch of Bd*
EMP: 5
SQ FT: 1,200
SALES (est): 380K **Privately Held**
SIC: 5047 3949 3842 Therapy equipment; sporting & athletic goods; whirlpool baths, hydrotherapy equipment

(G-14019)
MICFRALIP INC
Also Called: Michaels Glass Co
4625 Knorr St (19135-2238)
PHONE...................................215 338-3293
Bernice F Lipinski, *President*
EMP: 10 EST: 1977
SQ FT: 3,200
SALES (est): 1.2MM **Privately Held**
SIC: 7536 3231 1751 Automotive glass replacement shops; mirrors, truck & automobile: made from purchased glass; window & door (prefabricated) installation

(G-14020)
MICHAEL FURMAN PHOTOGRAPHY
Also Called: Coach Built Press
16 S 3rd St (19106-2701)
PHONE...................................215 925-4233
Michael Furman, *President*
▲ EMP: 9
SQ FT: 3,300
SALES: 730K **Privately Held**
WEB: www.michaelfurman.com
SIC: 2731 7335 Book publishing; photographic studio, commercial

(G-14021)
MICHAEL J DOYLE
Also Called: V Boxes
5918 Hammond Ave (19120-2011)
PHONE...................................215 587-1000
Michael J Doyle, *Owner*
EMP: 3
SALES (est): 184.7K **Privately Held**
SIC: 2652 Setup paperboard boxes

(G-14022)
MICHELS BAKERY INC
5698 Rising Sun Ave (19120-1698)
PHONE...................................215 742-3900
Jon Liss, *President*
Jon H Liss, *President*
Stanley C Walulek, *Vice Pres*
Kathy A Liss, *Admin Sec*
EMP: 130
SQ FT: 98,000
SALES (est): 30MM **Privately Held**
WEB: www.michelsbakery.com
SIC: 2051 Bread, cake & related products

(G-14023)
MILDER OFFICE INC (PA)
1901 S 9th St Ste 204 (19148-2366)
PHONE...................................215 717-7027
Jonas Milder, *President*
EMP: 7 EST: 1999
SQ FT: 5,000
SALES (est): 970.1K **Privately Held**
WEB: www.milderoffice.com
SIC: 2521 Bookcases, office: wood

(G-14024)
MINDY INC
2552 N 3rd St (19133-3041)
PHONE...................................215 739-0432
William Meckling, *President*
Lee Sunderland, *General Mgr*
Donald Shannon, *Treasurer*
EMP: 10
SQ FT: 20,000
SALES (est): 610K **Privately Held**
WEB: www.mindy.com
SIC: 2261 2262 Bleaching cotton broadwoven fabrics; dyeing cotton broadwoven fabrics; bleaching: manmade fiber & silk broadwoven fabrics; dyeing: manmade fiber & silk broadwoven fabrics

(G-14025)
MINUSNINE TECHNOLOGIES INC
2211 Christian St (19146-1718)
PHONE....................................215 704-9396
David Ruggieri, *CEO*
Jonathan Goodspeed, *Manager*
EMP: 3
SALES (est): 264.1K **Privately Held**
SIC: 2851 Paints & allied products

(G-14026)
MIO MECHANICAL CORPORATION
2020 Bennett Rd (19116-3020)
PHONE....................................215 613-8189
Mark Osterobrod, *President*
Elizebeth Osterobrod, *Admin Sec*
▲ **EMP:** 12 **EST:** 1981
SQ FT: 10,000
SALES (est): 1.8MM **Privately Held**
SIC: 3842 Personal safety equipment

(G-14027)
MIROGLYPHICS
5615 N Fairhill St (19120-2206)
PHONE....................................215 224-2486
Gerald A Colley, *President*
EMP: 4
SALES: 0 **Privately Held**
SIC: 2731 Book publishing

(G-14028)
MJS LLC
124 S 13th St (19107-4528)
PHONE....................................215 732-3501
EMP: 3
SALES (est): 181.4K **Privately Held**
SIC: 2672 Labels (unprinted), gummed: made from purchased materials

(G-14029)
MLR HOLDINGS LLC
1845 Walnut St Ste 900 (19103-4710)
PHONE....................................215 567-3200
Robert Auritt, *Principal*
EMP: 13 **EST:** 1998
SALES (est): 880K **Privately Held**
SIC: 2721 Magazines: publishing & printing

(G-14030)
MOBILE OUTFITTERS LLC (PA)
Also Called: Globalcomm Suppliers
3901b Main St Ste 106 (19127-2191)
PHONE....................................215 325-0747
Eric Griffin-Shelley, *President*
Dennis Odonnell, *Vice Pres*
▲ **EMP:** 10
SQ FT: 4,700
SALES (est): 2.5MM **Privately Held**
WEB: www.Clear-Coat.com
SIC: 3661 Telephones & telephone apparatus

(G-14031)
MOHAWK INDUSTRIES INC
2300 Chestnut St (19103-4331)
PHONE....................................215 977-2871
Katie Turner, *Branch Mgr*
EMP: 4
SALES (corp-wide): 9.9B **Publicly Held**
SIC: 7812 3253 Audio-visual program production; ceramic wall & floor tile
PA: Mohawk Industries, Inc.
160 S Industrial Blvd
Calhoun GA 30701
706 629-7721

(G-14032)
MOLTEC HEATING AND AC (PA)
120 Wharton St Ste 124 (19147-5424)
PHONE....................................215 755-2169
Pasquale Mollo, *Manager*
EMP: 10
SALES (est): 720K **Privately Held**
SIC: 1711 3444 Plumbing, heating, air-conditioning contractors; ducts, sheet metal

(G-14033)
MONARCH GLOBAL BRANDS INC (PA)
Also Called: Monarch Brands
11350 Norcom Rd (19154-2304)
PHONE....................................215 482-6100
Hal M Kanefsky, *President*
Joel Kanefsky, *Treasurer*
Albert Kanefsky, *Admin Sec*
◆ **EMP:** 60
SQ FT: 150,000
SALES (est): 17.2MM **Privately Held**
WEB: www.bestrags.com
SIC: 5999 5023 2394 2392 Cleaning equipment & supplies; towels; canvas & related products; household furnishings; broadwoven fabric mills, cotton

(G-14034)
MONDELEZ GLOBAL LLC
Also Called: Nabisco
12000 Roosevelt Blvd (19116-3001)
P.O. Box 6119 (19115-6119)
PHONE....................................215 673-4800
J Wilson, *Branch Mgr*
EMP: 24 **Publicly Held**
WEB: www.kraftfoods.com
SIC: 2052 Biscuits, dry
HQ: Mondelez Global Llc
3 N Pkwy Ste 300
Deerfield IL 60015
847 943-4000

(G-14035)
MONROE PRESS INC
4668 Canton St (19127-2001)
PHONE....................................215 778-7868
Tracy S Hardy, *President*
EMP: 4
SALES (est): 250K **Privately Held**
SIC: 2741 Miscellaneous publishing

(G-14036)
MOORE DESIGN INC
54 N 2nd St (19106-4505)
PHONE....................................215 627-3379
Steven Moore, *President*
EMP: 3
SALES: 500K **Privately Held**
WEB: www.mooredesign.com
SIC: 8712 3441 Architectural engineering; fabricated structural metal

(G-14037)
MOR SAW SERVICE CENTER INC
Also Called: National Carbide Saw Co
7353 State Rd (19136-4212)
PHONE....................................215 333-0441
Michael Santarone, *President*
EMP: 5
SQ FT: 6,000
SALES (est): 507.6K **Privately Held**
SIC: 3425 5251 7699 Saw blades & handsaws; hardware; knife, saw & tool sharpening & repair

(G-14038)
MORANTZ INC
Also Called: S Morantz, Inc
9984 Gantry Rd (19115-1076)
PHONE....................................215 969-0266
Lisa Morantz, *President*
Stanley Morantz, *President*
Heather Morantz, *Controller*
EMP: 6 **EST:** 1935
SQ FT: 12,000
SALES (est): 782.9K **Privately Held**
SIC: 2591 3589 2391 8748 Curtain & drapery rods, poles & fixtures; commercial cleaning equipment; draperies, plastic & textile: from purchased materials; business consulting; cleaning services

(G-14039)
MORRIS MILLWORK LLC
241 W Wyoming Ave (19140-1529)
PHONE....................................215 667-1889
David Morris, *Principal*
EMP: 4
SALES (est): 371K **Privately Held**
SIC: 2431 Millwork

(G-14040)
MOSAIC ENTERTAINMENT HOUSE
700 W Tabor Rd Ste 1 (19120-2727)
PHONE....................................215 353-1729
Armani Iman, *Director*
EMP: 52 **EST:** 2013
SQ FT: 10,000
SALES (est): 4.5MM **Privately Held**
SIC: 2731 Book music: publishing & printing

(G-14041)
MOSHES FOODS LLC
301 W Hunting Park Ave (19140-2625)
PHONE....................................215 291-8333
Moshe Malka, *President*
EMP: 7 **EST:** 2001
SALES (est): 564.4K **Privately Held**
SIC: 2099 Food preparations

(G-14042)
MOTIVOS LLC
220 Belgrade St (19125-4402)
P.O. Box 34391 (19101-4391)
PHONE....................................267 283-1733
Jenee Chizick, *Principal*
EMP: 3 **EST:** 2010
SALES (est): 231K **Privately Held**
SIC: 2721 Magazines: publishing only, not printed on site

(G-14043)
MRS RESSLERS FOOD PRODUCTS CO (PA)
Also Called: PCI
5501 Tabor Ave (19120-2127)
P.O. Box 47423 (19160-7423)
PHONE....................................215 744-4700
Joseph Israeli, *CEO*
David Israeli, *President*
Edith Ressler, *Corp Secy*
Michael Israeli, *Vice Pres*
Fred Burke, *Prdtn Mgr*
▲ **EMP:** 66 **EST:** 1954
SQ FT: 130,000
SALES: 63MM **Privately Held**
WEB: www.ressler.com
SIC: 2015 2013 Turkey, processed: cooked; chicken, processed: cooked; spreads, sandwich: poultry; corned beef from purchased meat; roast beef from purchased meat; spiced meats from purchased meat

(G-14044)
MULLER INC
2800 Grant Ave (19114-2302)
PHONE....................................215 676-7575
Sandy Muller, *President*
John Ashburn, *Area Mgr*
Patricia Iavarone, *Area Mgr*
Tim Jones, *Area Mgr*
Ed Odonnell, *Vice Pres*
▲ **EMP:** 156 **EST:** 1954
SQ FT: 200,000
SALES (est): 27.3MM **Privately Held**
WEB: www.mullerbev.com
SIC: 2082 5181 Beer (alcoholic beverage); beer & other fermented malt liquors

(G-14045)
MUSUMECI SANTO
Also Called: Sunrise Designs
1306 Jackson St (19148-2923)
P.O. Box 6422 (19145-0122)
PHONE....................................215 467-2158
Santo Musumeci, *Owner*
EMP: 5
SALES (est): 257.7K **Privately Held**
SIC: 3499 5021 Magnets, permanent: metallic; office furniture: filing units; chairs; advertising specialties

(G-14046)
MUTUAL INDUSTRIES NORTH INC (PA)
Also Called: Bilt-Rite Mastex
707 W Grange Ave Ste 1 (19120-2298)
PHONE....................................215 927-6000
Edmund Dunn, *CEO*
▲ **EMP:** 50
SQ FT: 105,000
SALES (est): 81.1MM **Privately Held**
WEB: www.mutualindustries.com
SIC: 3842 2221 Personal safety equipment; broadwoven fabric mills, manmade

(G-14047)
MUTUAL PHARMACEUTICAL CO INC (DH)
Also Called: Url Pharma
1100 Orthodox St (19124-3199)
PHONE....................................215 288-6500
Kurt R Nielsen, *Exec VP*
Donald L Evans, *Senior VP*
Gerald E Monigle, *Senior VP*
Scott Delancy, *Vice Pres*
Robert Dettery, *Vice Pres*
▲ **EMP:** 114
SQ FT: 111,000
SALES (est): 76.3MM
SALES (corp-wide): 1.1B **Privately Held**
SIC: 2834 Pharmaceutical preparations
HQ: Sun Pharmaceutical Industries, Inc.
270 Prospect Plains Rd
Cranbury NJ 08512
609 495-2800

(G-14048)
MUTUAL PHARMACEUTICAL CO INC
7722 Dungan Rd (19111-2779)
PHONE....................................215 807-1312
Craig Jacobsen, *Branch Mgr*
EMP: 6
SALES (corp-wide): 1.1B **Privately Held**
SIC: 2834 Pharmaceutical preparations
HQ: Mutual Pharmaceutical Company, Inc.
1100 Orthodox St
Philadelphia PA 19124
215 288-6500

(G-14049)
MYEXPOSOME INC
1024 Spruce St Apt A (19107-6281)
PHONE....................................610 668-0145
Marc Epstein, *CEO*
EMP: 4
SALES (est): 199.7K **Privately Held**
SIC: 3822 8731 8734 Hardware for environmental regulators; chemical laboratory, except testing; pollution testing; hazardous waste testing; water testing laboratory

(G-14050)
N BARSKY & SONS
Also Called: Barsky Diamonds
724 Sansom St (19106-3264)
PHONE....................................215 925-8639
Harold Barsky, *Owner*
Nathan Barsky, *Manager*
Rick Wool, *Manager*
EMP: 10
SQ FT: 4,000
SALES (est): 1.5MM **Privately Held**
SIC: 3911 5944 Bracelets, precious metal; rings, finger: precious metal; jewelry, precious stones & precious metals

(G-14051)
NAO INC (PA)
1284 E Sedgley Ave (19134-1590)
P.O. Box 820503 (19182-0503)
PHONE....................................215 743-5300
John F Straitz III, *President*
Nancy Tryens, *Principal*
John J Schwoerer Sr, *Vice Pres*
Henry Kramer, *Opers Mgr*
Andrew Tryens Jr, *CFO*
▼ **EMP:** 39
SQ FT: 45,000
SALES (est): 6.1MM **Privately Held**
WEB: www.nao.com
SIC: 3823 Combustion control instruments; controllers for process variables, all types

(G-14052)
NATIONAL AIROIL BURNER CO INC
1284 E Sedgley Ave (19134-1590)
PHONE....................................215 743-5300
John F Straitz III, *President*
Henry Kramer, *Opers Mgr*
Andrew Tryens Jr, *Treasurer*
John F Straitz Jr, *Shareholder*
Nancy S Tryens, *Admin Sec*
EMP: 3 **EST:** 1912
SQ FT: 45,000

SALES: 250K Privately Held
WEB: www.recaro-nao.com
SIC: 3823 Controllers for process variables, all types; combustion control instruments

(G-14053)
NATIONAL CHEMICAL LABS PA INC
401 N 10th St (19123-3893)
PHONE..................................215 922-1200
Harry Pollack, *President*
Samuel Pollack, *Treasurer*
◆ EMP: 108 EST: 1946
SQ FT: 365,000
SALES (est): 29.6MM Privately Held
SIC: 2842 2899 2841 Cleaning or polishing preparations; floor waxes; chemical preparations; soap & other detergents

(G-14054)
NATIONAL CTHLIC BTHICS CTR INC (PA)
Also Called: Ncbc
6399 Drexel Rd (19151-2511)
PHONE..................................215 877-2660
John Haas, *President*
Deacon J Hunter, *Exec VP*
EMP: 10
SQ FT: 11,976
SALES (est): 1.6MM Privately Held
WEB: www.ncbcenter.org
SIC: 2759 Publication printing

(G-14055)
NATIONAL PUBLISHING COMPANY
11311 Roosevelt Blvd (19154-2175)
P.O. Box 16234 (19114-0234)
PHONE..................................215 676-1863
James F Conway III, *President*
Rajeev Balakrishna, *Senior VP*
Peter M Folger, *Senior VP*
Joseph L Brennan, *Vice Pres*
Anthony F Caruso, *Vice Pres*
▲ EMP: 315 EST: 1863
SQ FT: 231,000
SALES (est): 32.6MM
SALES (corp-wide): 3.8B Publicly Held
SIC: 2731 2732 2789 Book publishing; books: printing & binding; bookbinding & related work
PA: Lsc Communications, Inc.
191 N Wacker Dr Ste 1400
Chicago IL 60606
773 272-9200

(G-14056)
NATIONAL REFRIGERANTS INC (PA)
Also Called: N R I
11401 Roosevelt Blvd (19154-2197)
P.O. Box 820103 (19182-0103)
PHONE..................................215 698-6620
John H Reilly Jr, *President*
John H Reilly III, *Vice Pres*
Hope V Nicholas, *Treasurer*
Carmen D Carosella V Pres-, *Admin Sec*
◆ EMP: 25
SQ FT: 5,000
SALES (est): 98.8MM Privately Held
WEB: www.refrigerants.com
SIC: 5078 3822 Refrigeration equipment & supplies; air conditioning & refrigeration controls

(G-14057)
NATIONWIDE RECYCLERS INC
1 Crown Way (19154-4501)
P.O. Box 63290 (19114-7290)
PHONE..................................215 698-5100
Ronald Thoma, *President*
Craig Calle, *Vice Pres*
EMP: 8
SALES (est): 1.2MM
SALES (corp-wide): 11.1B Publicly Held
WEB: www.crowncork.com
SIC: 3411 Metal cans
HQ: Crown Cork & Seal Usa, Inc.
770 Township Line Rd # 100
Yardley PA 19067
215 698-5100

(G-14058)
NATURE SOY LLC
713 N 10th St (19123-1902)
PHONE..................................215 765-3289
Yaqing Lu, *QC Mgr*
Sunfei Ye,
▲ EMP: 17
SQ FT: 17,500
SALES (est): 4.2MM Privately Held
WEB: www.naturesoy.com
SIC: 2075 5153 Soybean flour & grits; soybeans

(G-14059)
NAWALANY-FRANCIOTTI LLC
Also Called: Lipkin's Bakery
8013 Castor Ave (19152-2701)
PHONE..................................215 342-3005
Steven Nawalany,
Guerino Franciotti,
EMP: 15
SQ FT: 3,000
SALES (est): 1MM Privately Held
SIC: 2051 Cakes, bakery: except frozen

(G-14060)
NEAT COMPANY INC
Also Called: Neatreceipts
1500 Jf Kennedy Blvd # 700 (19102-1732)
PHONE..................................215 382-4283
Michael Crincoli, *President*
Mike Crincoli, *Vice Pres*
Rafi Spero, *Vice Pres*
Michelle Borowski, *Engineer*
Joseph Mauk, *Sales Staff*
EMP: 150
SALES (est): 29.6MM Privately Held
WEB: www.neatreceipts.com
SIC: 7371 7372 Computer software development; prepackaged software

(G-14061)
NEATSFOOT OIL REFINERIES CORP
2925 E Ontario St (19134-6003)
PHONE..................................215 739-1291
Alan S Berg, *CEO*
▼ EMP: 32 EST: 1873
SQ FT: 100,000
SALES (est): 4.8MM
SALES (corp-wide): 12MM Privately Held
SIC: 2077 Animal & marine fats & oils
PA: Nupro Industries Corporation
2925 E Ontario St
Philadelphia PA 19134
215 739-1291

(G-14062)
NEO LIGHTS HOLDINGS INC (PA)
700 Ramona Ave (19120-4600)
PHONE..................................215 831-7700
Alfred Heyer, *CEO*
EMP: 3
SALES (est): 46.3MM Privately Held
SIC: 3646 5063 Fluorescent lighting fixtures, commercial; electrical apparatus & equipment

(G-14063)
NEST
1301 Locust St (19107-5405)
PHONE..................................215 545-6378
Rob Nicol, *Principal*
EMP: 4
SALES (est): 322.2K Privately Held
SIC: 3949 Playground equipment

(G-14064)
NEUROFLOW INC
1635 Market St Ste 1600 (19103-2202)
PHONE..................................347 881-6306
Christopher Molaro, *CEO*
Adam Pardes, *Principal*
Wayne Tamarelli, *Principal*
EMP: 7 EST: 2016
SALES (est): 755.1K Privately Held
SIC: 7372 7389 Prepackaged software;

(G-14065)
NEUROKINE THERAPEUTICS LLC
3711 Market St Fl 8 (19104-5504)
PHONE..................................609 937-0409

Mark White, *CEO*
EMP: 3
SALES (est): 157.9K Privately Held
SIC: 2834 Drugs acting on the central nervous system & sense organs

(G-14066)
NEUXPOWER INC
1800 Jfk Blvd Ste 300 (19103-7402)
PHONE..................................267 238-3833
Michael Power, *CEO*
Loren Gartside, *Partner*
Paul Clerkin, *Marketing Staff*
EMP: 4
SALES (est): 208.7K
SALES (corp-wide): 792.5K Privately Held
SIC: 7372 Business oriented computer software
PA: Neuxpower Solutions Limited
Kemp House
London EC1V
208 068-2308

(G-14067)
NEW LIBERTY DISTILLERY
1431 N Cadwallader St (19122-3703)
PHONE..................................800 996-0595
Thomas Jensen, *Principal*
EMP: 3
SALES (est): 75.4K Privately Held
SIC: 2082 Malt beverages

(G-14068)
NEW STARS LLC
1603 N 5th St (19122-2907)
PHONE..................................215 962-4239
Thang Chau, *Owner*
▲ EMP: 6
SALES: 100K Privately Held
SIC: 2844 5021 Manicure preparations; chairs

(G-14069)
NEW VISIONS MAGAZINE (PA)
Also Called: Health Connection Center
530 S 2nd St Ste 106 (19147-2403)
P.O. Box 63716 (19147-7516)
PHONE..................................215 627-0102
Ann Khoury, *Owner*
▲ EMP: 11
SALES (est): 986.6K Privately Held
SIC: 2721 Magazines: publishing & printing

(G-14070)
NEWMAN & COMPANY INC
6101 Tacony St (19135-2998)
PHONE..................................215 333-8700
Bernard Newman, *Ch of Bd*
Fred Herman, *President*
Lee D Cohen, *CFO*
Jackie Issler, *Sales Staff*
Susan Paul, *Sales Associate*
◆ EMP: 150
SQ FT: 300,000
SALES (est): 53.1MM Privately Held
WEB: www.newmancompany.com
SIC: 2631 Paperboard mills

(G-14071)
NEWSPAPER GUILD OF PHILADELPHI
1329 Buttonwood St (19123-3609)
PHONE..................................215 928-0118
Dan Gross, *President*
EMP: 4
SALES (est): 273K Privately Held
SIC: 2711 Newspapers, publishing & printing

(G-14072)
NIAN-CRAE INC
2200 Benjamin Franklin Pk (19130-3739)
PHONE..................................732 545-5881
Nicki Newby, *President*
Bill Craelius, *Vice Pres*
EMP: 4
SALES: 300K Privately Held
WEB: www.niancrae.com
SIC: 3845 Electromedical apparatus; electrotherapeutic apparatus

(G-14073)
NICHOLS4NICKELS
6038 Master St (19151-4427)
PHONE..................................215 317-6717

Alfreda Williams-Nichols, *Principal*
EMP: 3
SALES (est): 203.9K Privately Held
SIC: 3356 Nickel

(G-14074)
NIGHTLIFE & CLOTHING CO
7415 Brockton Rd Unit 1 (19151-2911)
PHONE..................................718 415-6391
Jaree Cooper, *Mng Member*
Robert Wilkerson,
EMP: 4 EST: 2017
SALES: 50K Privately Held
SIC: 5621 2339 Ready-to-wear apparel, women's; women's & misses' outerwear

(G-14075)
NINE 2 FIVE CEO
806 Wynnewood Rd (19151-3451)
PHONE..................................919 729-2536
James Everett, *CEO*
EMP: 9
SALES (est): 267.6K Privately Held
SIC: 2731 7389 Textbooks: publishing & printing;

(G-14076)
NITROGEN (WAS DORLAND
1 S Broad St Fl 11 (19107-3426)
PHONE..................................215 928-2727
Jasper Sharon, *Principal*
EMP: 3
SALES (est): 149.1K Privately Held
SIC: 2813 Nitrogen

(G-14077)
NOOR FURNITURE INC
Also Called: Route One Furniture
6304 Roosevelt Blvd (19149-2931)
PHONE..................................215 533-0703
EMP: 3
SALES (est): 230K Privately Held
SIC: 2512 Mfg Upholstered Household Furniture

(G-14078)
NORMAN KIVITZ CO INC
Also Called: Celebrity Jewelry
731 Sansom St Fl 1 (19106-3294)
PHONE..................................215 922-3038
Norman Kivitz, *President*
Joyce Kivitz, *Corp Secy*
Mark Kivitz, *Vice Pres*
Wayne Kivitz, *Vice Pres*
EMP: 20 EST: 1947
SQ FT: 1,500
SALES (est): 2.6MM Privately Held
WEB: www.celebrityjewelry.com
SIC: 3911 Jewelry apparel

(G-14079)
NORTHEAST BUILDING PDTS CORP (HQ)
4280 Aramingo Ave (19124-5007)
PHONE..................................215 535-7110
Alan M Levin, *President*
Fran Levin, *Corp Secy*
Eric Gerstenbacher, *COO*
John Seiner, *CFO*
EMP: 117 EST: 1975
SQ FT: 165,000
SALES (est): 44.2MM
SALES (corp-wide): 1.1B Privately Held
WEB: www.nbpcorporation.com
SIC: 3442 2431 Storm doors or windows, metal; window frames, wood; doors & door parts & trim, wood
PA: Harvey Industries, Inc.
1400 Main St Fl 3
Waltham MA 02451
800 598-5400

(G-14080)
NORTHEAST BUILDING PDTS CORP
4926 Benner St (19135-4214)
PHONE..................................215 331-2400
Irwin Levin, *Branch Mgr*
EMP: 16
SALES (corp-wide): 43.8MM Privately Held
WEB: www.nbpcorporation.com
SIC: 3442 Casements, aluminum

PA: Northeast Building Products Corp.
4280 Aramingo Ave
Philadelphia PA 19124
215 535-7110

(G-14081)
NORTHEAST DISCOUNT PRINTING
Also Called: Northeast Print
2630 Welsh Rd Apt A3 (19152-1418)
PHONE....................................215 742-3111
Steve Peszlen, *Owner*
EMP: 4
SALES (est): 271.1K **Privately Held**
SIC: 2759 Screen printing

(G-14082)
NORTHEAST FENCE & IR WORKS INC
8451 Hegerman St (19136-1513)
PHONE....................................215 335-1681
Raymond Longstreath, *President*
EMP: 45
SQ FT: 55,000
SALES: 5MM **Privately Held**
WEB: www.northeastfence.com
SIC: 3496 1731 3315 1799 Miscellaneous fabricated wire products; electrical work; steel wire & related products; fence construction; ornamental metal work

(G-14083)
NORTHEAST GLASS CO
1913 Conwell Ave (19115-1729)
PHONE....................................267 991-0054
Lee Scornaienchi, *Owner*
EMP: 9
SQ FT: 15,000
SALES (est): 490K **Privately Held**
SIC: 3231 3442 Insulating glass: made from purchased glass; storm doors or windows, metal

(G-14084)
NORTHERN LIBERTY PRESS LLC
1223 N Mascher St 31 (19122-4616)
PHONE....................................215 634-3000
Ken Martz, *President*
EMP: 6
SALES (est): 716.1K **Privately Held**
WEB: www.northernlibertypress.com
SIC: 2752 Commercial printing, offset

(G-14085)
NOTARIES EQUIPMENT CO
2021 Arch St Fl 2 (19103-1401)
PHONE....................................215 563-8190
EMP: 15
SQ FT: 5,000
SALES (est): 644.6K
SALES (corp-wide): 2.4MM **Privately Held**
SIC: 3953 7389 Mfg Marking Devices Business Services
PA: M. Burr Keim Company
2021 Arch St Fl 2
Philadelphia PA 19103
215 563-8190

(G-14086)
NOVA GLOBAL INC
1518 Walnut St (19102-3419)
PHONE....................................619 822-2465
Jonas Barck, *Principal*
EMP: 10
SALES (est): 776.3K **Privately Held**
SIC: 2448 Wood pallets & skids

(G-14087)
NOVARTIS CORPORATION
1717 Arch St Fl 28 (19103-2820)
PHONE....................................215 255-4200
Heather McIntosh, *Branch Mgr*
EMP: 56
SALES (corp-wide): 49.1B **Privately Held**
WEB: www.novartis.com
SIC: 2834 Pharmaceutical preparations
HQ: Novartis Corporation
1 S Ridgedale Ave
East Hanover NJ 07936
212 307-1122

(G-14088)
NOVELLI INC
Also Called: Ritner Engraved Stationary
2011 Frankford Ave (19125-1920)
P.O. Box 86, Oreland (19075-0086)
PHONE....................................215 739-3538
Linda Novelli, *President*
Ferdinand Novelli, *Treasurer*
EMP: 19
SQ FT: 11,000
SALES (est): 1MM **Privately Held**
SIC: 2759 Stationery: printing

(G-14089)
NUTS & SUCH LTD
Also Called: Society Hill Snacks
8845 Torresdale Ave (19136-1510)
PHONE....................................215 708-8500
Ronna Schultz, *President*
EMP: 9
SQ FT: 5,000
SALES (est): 1.1MM **Privately Held**
WEB: www.societyhillsnacks.com
SIC: 2064 2052 Nuts, candy covered; cookies & crackers

(G-14090)
O S I SOFTWARE
1700 Market St Ste 2200 (19103-3925)
PHONE....................................215 606-0612
Pat Kennedy, *Owner*
EMP: 4
SALES (est): 269.6K **Privately Held**
WEB: www.osisoftware.com
SIC: 7372 Application computer software

(G-14091)
O2S LLC
1500 Spring Garden St (19130-4067)
PHONE....................................215 299-8500
Michael Yoh, *Principal*
EMP: 25
SALES (est): 1.9MM **Privately Held**
SIC: 3842 Surgical appliances & supplies

(G-14092)
OCEAN KING ENTERPRISES INC
7831 Bartram Ave (19153-3230)
PHONE....................................215 365-2500
Lee Aronson, *President*
Dan Dombrowski, *CFO*
Barbara Passaro, *Manager*
Gary Dunn, *Shareholder*
EMP: 120
SQ FT: 30,000
SALES (est): 1.1MM **Privately Held**
SIC: 2092 Fresh or frozen packaged fish

(G-14093)
OLD CITY PUBLISHING
Also Called: Norghern Liberty Press
628 N 2nd St (19123-3002)
PHONE....................................215 925-4390
Guy Griffiths, *President*
Ian Mellanby, *Director*
EMP: 10 EST: 1998
SQ FT: 3,000
SALES (est): 806.8K **Privately Held**
WEB: www.oldcitypublishing.com
SIC: 2741 Miscellaneous publishing

(G-14094)
OMEGA FENCE CO
5709 Whitby Ave (19143-4512)
PHONE....................................215 729-7474
Anthony Pollard, *Owner*
EMP: 3
SALES (est): 211.2K **Privately Held**
WEB: www.omegafence.com
SIC: 3315 1799 Fencing made in wire-drawing plants; special trade contractors

(G-14095)
ONCOCEUTICS INC
3675 Market St Ste 200 (19104-2897)
PHONE....................................678 897-0563
Wolfgang Oster, *CEO*
Josh Allen, *Vice Pres*
Joshua Allen, *Vice Pres*
Varun Prabhu, *Research*
Lee Schalop, *CFO*
EMP: 7
SALES (est): 3MM **Privately Held**
SIC: 2834 Pharmaceutical preparations

(G-14096)
ONEILL INDUSTRIES INC
5101 Comly St Ste 1 (19135-4317)
PHONE....................................215 533-2101
Robert J O'Neill, *President*
Joan B O'Neill, *Admin Sec*
EMP: 3
SQ FT: 18,000
SALES (est): 383.4K **Privately Held**
WEB: www.blendchem.com
SIC: 2841 Detergents, synthetic organic or inorganic alkaline; dishwashing compounds

(G-14097)
OOH LALA SALAD
1238 W Girard Ave (19123-1005)
PHONE....................................215 769-1006
EMP: 3 EST: 2014
SALES (est): 160.5K **Privately Held**
SIC: 2099 Salads, fresh or refrigerated

(G-14098)
OPERTECH BIO INC
5501 Old York Rd (19141-3018)
PHONE....................................215 456-8765
Scott Horvitz, *CEO*
EMP: 4
SALES (est): 250K **Privately Held**
SIC: 8731 2834 Commercial physical research; pharmaceutical preparations

(G-14099)
OPTIXTAL INC
1901 S 54th St (19143-5716)
PHONE....................................215 254-5225
Sagar Venkateswaran, *Principal*
EMP: 5
SALES (est): 100K **Privately Held**
SIC: 3675 Electronic capacitors

(G-14100)
OPTOFLUIDICS INC (PA)
Also Called: Halo Labs
3675 Market St Apt 1 (19104-5470)
PHONE....................................215 253-5777
Robert Hart, *CEO*
Robert Wicke, *CEO*
Joseph Keegan, *Ch of Bd*
David Ericson, *Ch of Bd*
Bernardo Cordovez, *President*
EMP: 11
SALES (est): 1.7MM **Privately Held**
SIC: 2834 Pharmaceutical preparations

(G-14101)
ORCHEM PUMPS INC
4434 Salmon St Ste 36 (19137-1607)
PHONE....................................215 743-6352
James T Beatty, *President*
Ralph Beatty, *Vice Pres*
EMP: 5
SQ FT: 2,000
SALES (est): 870.2K **Privately Held**
WEB: www.orchempumps.com
SIC: 3561 3559 Industrial pumps & parts; chemical machinery & equipment

(G-14102)
ORTHOPLI CORP
10061 Sandmeyer Ln (19116-3501)
PHONE....................................215 671-1000
William Tippy Sr, *President*
Patricia Tippy, *Corp Secy*
William Tippy Jr, *Vice Pres*
Gary Tippy, *VP Sales*
EMP: 44
SQ FT: 10,200
SALES (est): 6MM **Privately Held**
SIC: 3843 Orthodontic appliances

(G-14103)
OSHIKIRI CORPORATION AMERICA
10425 Drummond Rd (19154-3898)
PHONE....................................215 637-6005
Reona Oshikiri, *President*
Takashi Oshikiri, *President*
M Abe, *Treasurer*
Collette McCaleb, *Manager*
Shuichi Kobayashi, *Admin Sec*
▲ EMP: 12
SQ FT: 20,000
SALES (est): 3.7MM
SALES (corp-wide): 89.5MM **Privately Held**
WEB: www.oshikiri.com
SIC: 3556 Bakery machinery
PA: Osikiri Machinery Ltd.
4, Kiriharacho
Fujisawa KNG 252-0
466 446-011

(G-14104)
OSISOFT LLC
1700 Market St Ste 2200 (19103-3925)
PHONE....................................215 606-0700
Todd Pistorese, *CEO*
David Doll, *Project Mgr*
EMP: 13
SALES (corp-wide): 315.7MM **Privately Held**
SIC: 7372 Application computer software
PA: Osisoft, Llc
1600 Alvarado St
San Leandro CA 94577
510 297-5800

(G-14105)
OUTCAST STUDIOS LLC
2409 Cedar St 2417 (19125-3002)
P.O. Box 31560 (19147-0860)
PHONE....................................267 242-1332
Gregory Mangle, *President*
EMP: 6
SQ FT: 8,000
SALES: 300K **Privately Held**
SIC: 3299 Architectural sculptures: gypsum, clay, papier mache, etc.

(G-14106)
OXFORD CONSTRUCTION PA INC
1715 Rittenhouse Sq (19103-6109)
PHONE....................................215 809-2245
Jarred Yaron, *CEO*
EMP: 60
SALES: 30MM **Privately Held**
SIC: 1541 1389 1623 1522 Industrial buildings, new construction; construction, repair & dismantling services; communication line & transmission tower construction; hotel/motel & multi-family home construction; roofing, siding & sheet metal work; electrical work

(G-14107)
OXFORD DAILY LLC
5759 Oxford Ave (19149-3721)
PHONE....................................215 533-5656
Marc Hummel, *Owner*
EMP: 5
SALES (est): 221.5K **Privately Held**
SIC: 2711 Newspapers, publishing & printing

(G-14108)
P & S RAVIOLI CO (PA)
2001 S 26th St (19145-2523)
PHONE....................................215 465-8888
Secondo Digiacomo, *President*
Franco Digiacomo, *Finance Mgr*
EMP: 18 EST: 1965
SQ FT: 10,000
SALES (est): 3MM **Privately Held**
WEB: www.psravioli.com
SIC: 5499 2098 5142 Gourmet food stores; macaroni & spaghetti; packaged frozen goods

(G-14109)
P & S RAVIOLI CO
1722 W Oregon Ave (19145-4726)
PHONE....................................215 339-9929
Primo Jacomo, *President*
EMP: 4
SALES (corp-wide): 3MM **Privately Held**
WEB: www.psravioli.com
SIC: 2098 Macaroni & spaghetti
PA: P & S Ravioli Co.
2001 S 26th St
Philadelphia PA 19145
215 465-8888

(G-14110)
P & S SPORTSWEAR INC
176 W Loudon St (19120-4241)
PHONE....................................215 455-7133
Samantha Ung, *President*

John Ung, *Vice Pres*
EMP: 30
SALES: 1.1MM **Privately Held**
SIC: 5136 2329 2339 Men's & boys' clothing; men's & boys' sportswear & athletic clothing; women's & misses' outerwear

(G-14111)
PACKAGING COORDINATORS INC
Also Called: PCI Pharma Services
3001 Red Lion Rd (19114-1123)
PHONE..............................215 613-3600
William Mitchell, *President*
Mitch Blumenfeld, *COO*
Shad Sutherland, *Engineer*
Serge Dupuis, *CFO*
Mark Rose, *VP Finance*
EMP: 10
SALES (est): 3.9MM **Privately Held**
SIC: 5084 2834 Packaging machinery & equipment; druggists' preparations (pharmaceuticals)

(G-14112)
PACKER AVENUE FOODS INC
700 Packer Ave Ste R2 (19148-5302)
PHONE..............................215 271-0300
Rob Rubin, *President*
Randy Gilgore, *Vice Pres*
John Pelusi, *Vice Pres*
EMP: 15
SALES (est): 2.5MM **Privately Held**
SIC: 2099 Ready-to-eat meals, salads & sandwiches

(G-14113)
PACO WINDERS MFG LLC
2040 Bennett Rd (19116-3020)
PHONE..............................215 673-6265
Steven R Kiss, *President*
Edward Kiss, *Vice Pres*
Emil Kiss Jr, *Vice Pres*
Richard McGovern, *Treasurer*
EMP: 25 **EST:** 1955
SQ FT: 19,000
SALES (est): 5.2MM **Privately Held**
WEB: www.pacowinders.com
SIC: 3554 5084 3545 Paper industries machinery; industrial machinery & equipment; machine tool accessories

(G-14114)
PAEONIA ARTS & LITERATURE LLC
Also Called: Sunny's Music Studio
525 Wharton St (19147-5228)
PHONE..............................267 520-4572
Haitao Yan, *Director*
Jiayi Kang, *Bd of Directors*
EMP: 6
SALES (est): 257.4K **Privately Held**
SIC: 3999 8999 Framed artwork; commercial & literary writings

(G-14115)
PAPER RECOVERY SYSTEMS INC
3287 Chatham St (19134-4519)
PHONE..............................215 423-6624
Kenneth Fox, *Owner*
EMP: 3
SALES (est): 225.1K **Privately Held**
SIC: 2611 Pulp manufactured from waste or recycled paper

(G-14116)
PAPERIA
8521 Germantown Ave (19118-3316)
PHONE..............................215 247-8521
Martha Breslau, *Owner*
George Breslau, *Co-Owner*
EMP: 7
SQ FT: 2,992
SALES (est): 350K **Privately Held**
SIC: 2759 Invitation & stationery printing & engraving

(G-14117)
PAPPAJOHN WOODWORKING INC
4355 Orchard St (19124-4011)
PHONE..............................215 289-8625
Ian Pappajohn, *President*

Matthew Pappajohn, *Vice Pres*
EMP: 6
SQ FT: 13,500
SALES (est): 939.5K **Privately Held**
WEB: www.pappajohnwoodworking.com
SIC: 2431 Millwork

(G-14118)
PARABO PRESS LLC ○
4040 Locust St (19104-5439)
PHONE..............................484 843-1230
Sunny RAO, *Mng Member*
EMP: 7 **EST:** 2018
SALES (est): 248.7K **Privately Held**
SIC: 2759 7389 Business forms: printing; interior design services

(G-14119)
PARADE STRAPPING & BALING LLC
3300 Tulip St (19134-3205)
PHONE..............................215 537-9473
Edward Foy,
▲ **EMP:** 5
SALES (est): 594.3K **Privately Held**
SIC: 3317 Tubing, mechanical or hypodermic sizes: cold drawn stainless

(G-14120)
PARADISE PILLOW INC
2207 W Glenwood Ave (19132-4709)
PHONE..............................215 225-8700
Freddy Halfon, *President*
Ron Halfon, *Vice Pres*
▲ **EMP:** 40
SQ FT: 51,000
SALES (est): 5MM **Privately Held**
WEB: www.paradisepillow.com
SIC: 2392 Pillows, bed: made from purchased materials; bags, laundry: made from purchased materials

(G-14121)
PARAGON WELDING COMPANY INC
2134 E Lippincott St (19134-3815)
PHONE..............................215 634-7300
Mark Fairburn, *President*
EMP: 4
SQ FT: 3,000
SALES (est): 270K **Privately Held**
WEB: www.paragonwelding.com
SIC: 7692 Welding repair

(G-14122)
PARDEE RESOURCES COMPANY (PA)
1717 Arch St Ste 4010 (19103-2739)
PHONE..............................215 405-1260
Carleton P Erdman, *CEO*
William G Foulke, *Ch of Bd*
Matthew W Hall, *President*
Walter Stroud, *President*
Jeffery Allen, *Senior VP*
EMP: 12 **EST:** 1979
SQ FT: 5,400
SALES (est): 50.6MM **Privately Held**
SIC: 8741 1382 Business management; geological exploration, oil & gas field

(G-14123)
PATHFINDERS TRAVEL INC
Also Called: Pathfinders Travel Magazine
6325 Germantown Ave (19144-1907)
PHONE..............................215 438-2140
Weller Thomas, *President*
Pamela Thomas, *Chief*
EMP: 5
SQ FT: 5,000
SALES (est): 712.7K **Privately Held**
WEB: www.pathfinderstravel.com
SIC: 2721 4724 Magazines: publishing only, not printed on site; travel agencies

(G-14124)
PAUL DRY BOOKS INC
1700 Sansom St Ste 700 (19103-5214)
PHONE..............................215 231-9939
Paul Dry, *President*
EMP: 3
SALES (est): 167.9K **Privately Held**
WEB: www.pauldrybooks.com
SIC: 2741 Miscellaneous publishing

(G-14125)
PAUL MORELLI DESIGN INC
Also Called: Paul Morelli Studio
1118 Walnut St (19107-5513)
PHONE..............................215 922-7392
Paul Morelli, *President*
Robert Young, *Director*
▲ **EMP:** 15
SALES (est): 3.4MM **Privately Held**
SIC: 3911 Jewelry, precious metal

(G-14126)
PAYAL NEWS
1101 Market St (19107-2934)
PHONE..............................215 625-3699
EMP: 3
SALES (est): 111.3K **Privately Held**
SIC: 2711 Newspapers-Publishing/Printing

(G-14127)
PBG PHILADELPHIA 2120
Also Called: Pepsico
11701 Roosevelt Blvd (19154-2108)
PHONE..............................215 676-6401
Jeff Porter, *Principal*
Vicki Dougherty, *Vice Pres*
Stephen Brown, *Manager*
EMP: 31 **EST:** 2010
SALES (est): 7MM **Privately Held**
SIC: 2086 Carbonated soft drinks, bottled & canned

(G-14128)
PC NETWORK INC (PA)
Also Called: Pcn
1315 Walnut St Ste 1402 (19107-4720)
PHONE..............................267 236-0015
Katrin Hillner Antram, *President*
Charlotte Veazie, *General Mgr*
Stacy Winters, *Project Mgr*
Steven Goldfrad, *Accounting Mgr*
Karissa Kerns, *Hum Res Coord*
EMP: 60
SQ FT: 8,000
SALES (est): 12.5MM **Privately Held**
WEB: www.lanusa.com
SIC: 7371 7372 7373 7374 Computer software systems analysis & design, custom; prepackaged software; local area network (LAN) systems integrator; office computer automation systems integration; data processing & preparation; information retrieval services; computer facilities management

(G-14129)
PEI/GENESIS INC (PA)
Also Called: Pei Genesis International
2180 Hornig Rd Ste 2 (19116-4204)
PHONE..............................215 464-1410
Steven Fisher, *CEO*
Russell A Dorwart, *President*
Kim McLanigan, *Managing Dir*
Peter Christie, *Business Mgr*
Curt Rosenhoover, *Business Mgr*
▲ **EMP:** 102
SQ FT: 24,000
SALES (est): 307MM **Privately Held**
WEB: www.suresealconnections.com
SIC: 3678 3677 Electronic connectors; transformers power supply, electronic type

(G-14130)
PENN FISHING TACKLE MFG CO (DH)
Also Called: Penn Reel
3028 W Hunting Park Ave (19132-1192)
PHONE..............................215 227-1087
John Doerr, *CEO*
David Martin, *CEO*
Viola R Bird, *Vice Pres*
Robert Totte, *Vice Pres*
Ian Ashken, *Treasurer*
▲ **EMP:** 160 **EST:** 1950
SQ FT: 80,000
SALES (est): 16.2MM
SALES (corp-wide): 8.6B **Publicly Held**
SIC: 3949 5091 Reels, fishing; fishing equipment & supplies
HQ: Shakespeare Company, Llc
6111 Shakespeare Rd
Columbia SC 29223
803 754-7011

(G-14131)
PENN-CENTURY INC
7327 Bryan St (19119-1635)
PHONE..............................215 843-6540
Fax: 215 753-6541
EMP: 3
SALES (corp-wide): 2.5MM **Privately Held**
SIC: 3841 Mfg Surgical/Medical Instruments
PA: Penn-Century Inc
7670 Queen St
Glenside PA
215 233-0105

(G-14132)
PENNSYLVANIA INSTITUTE OF CPA (PA)
Also Called: Picpa
1801 Market St Fl 24 (19103-1628)
PHONE..............................215 496-9272
Epifanio De Jesus, *Technology*
Albert Trexler, *Director*
EMP: 45
SQ FT: 16,500
SALES: 5.7MM **Privately Held**
SIC: 8621 8721 2721 Accounting association; accounting, auditing & bookkeeping; periodicals

(G-14133)
PENNYPACK SUPPLY COMPANY (PA)
8047 Craig St (19136-2614)
PHONE..............................215 338-2200
Joe Galbally, *President*
Tim Galbally, *Vice Pres*
EMP: 7
SQ FT: 18,000
SALES (est): 2.2MM **Privately Held**
WEB: www.pennypacksupply.com
SIC: 5074 2499 Plumbing fittings & supplies; kitchen, bathroom & household ware: wood

(G-14134)
PEOPLEJOY INC
22 N 3rd St (19106-2113)
PHONE..............................267 603-7726
Emeka Oguh, *Owner*
EMP: 3
SALES (est): 78.2K **Privately Held**
SIC: 7372 Prepackaged software

(G-14135)
PEPSI-COLA METRO BTLG CO INC
3245 S 78th St (19153-3202)
PHONE..............................215 937-6102
Joe Burns, *Branch Mgr*
Wrenton Wright, *Manager*
EMP: 10
SQ FT: 39,200
SALES (corp-wide): 64.6B **Publicly Held**
WEB: www.joy-of-cola.com
SIC: 2086 4225 5149 Soft drinks: packaged in cans, bottles, etc.; general warehousing & storage; groceries & related products
HQ: Pepsi-Cola Metropolitan Bottling Company, Inc.
1111 Westchester Ave
White Plains NY 10604
914 767-6000

(G-14136)
PERAKIS FRAMES INC
18 S Bank St (19106-2804)
PHONE..............................215 627-7700
George Perakis, *President*
EMP: 4
SQ FT: 5,200
SALES (est): 357K **Privately Held**
SIC: 2499 Picture & mirror frames, wood

(G-14137)
PERFECTION FOODS COMPANY INC
3901 Old York Rd (19140-2098)
PHONE..............................215 455-5400
Hanh Tran, *President*
Roy Murray, *General Mgr*
Marvin Moldover, *Vice Pres*
Vickie Tran, *Vice Pres*
Vivian Tran, *Vice Pres*

▲ = Import ▼=Export
◆ =Import/Export

EMP: 100
SQ FT: 30,000
SALES (est): 22.1MM **Privately Held**
WEB: www.perfectionfoods.com
SIC: 2013 Sausages & other prepared meats

(G-14138)
PEROXYCHEM LLC (HQ)
1 Commerce Sq 2005 Mark (19103)
PHONE..................................267 422-2400
Bruce Lerner, *President*
Alberto Garibi, *Vice Pres*
Frank Flowers, *Project Mgr*
Tommy Napier, *Production*
Jennifer Jones, *Buyer*
◆ EMP: 40
SALES (est): 422.6MM **Privately Held**
SIC: 5169 2819 Chemicals & allied products; peroxides, hydrogen peroxide

(G-14139)
PETERS JAMES & SON INC
1934 N Front St 1936 (19122-2405)
PHONE..................................215 739-9500
Robert Smith, *President*
Robert Woodard, *Vice Pres*
EMP: 5 EST: 1944
SQ FT: 11,000
SALES (est): 1MM **Privately Held**
SIC: 3442 Shutters, door or window: metal; jalousies, metal

(G-14140)
PHILA LEGNDS OF JAZZ ORCHESTRA
1436 N 25th St (19121-3845)
PHONE..................................215 763-2819
Leon Mitchell, *Partner*
EMP: 17
SALES (est): 957.3K **Privately Held**
SIC: 2759 Commercial printing

(G-14141)
PHILADELPHIA ANIMAL HEALTH LLC
3401 Grays Ferry Ave (19146-2701)
PHONE..................................215 573-4503
Matthew Wilson, *Principal*
EMP: 3
SQ FT: 1,000
SALES (est): 123.2K **Privately Held**
SIC: 2834 Veterinary pharmaceutical preparations

(G-14142)
PHILADELPHIA BEER WORKS INC
Also Called: Manayunk Brewing Company
4120 Main St (19127-1651)
PHONE..................................215 482-8220
Harry Renner, *President*
Paris Rose, *Sales Mgr*
Kristen Moran, *Marketing Mgr*
EMP: 110
SQ FT: 8,000
SALES (est): 438.5K **Privately Held**
SIC: 2083 5812 2082 Malt; American restaurant; malt beverages

(G-14143)
PHILADELPHIA CHROME
3945 N Reese St (19140-3320)
PHONE..................................267 988-5834
Juan Gonzalez, *Principal*
EMP: 3
SALES (est): 126.4K **Privately Held**
SIC: 3471 Electroplating of metals or formed products

(G-14144)
PHILADELPHIA ENERGY SOLUTIONS (PA)
Also Called: Joint Venture Between
1735 Market St Fl 11 (19103-7535)
PHONE..................................267 238-4300
Mark J Smith, *CEO*
Thomas Scargle, *President*
John McShane, *Exec VP*
V Steve Herzog, *Senior VP*
Nithianathan Thaver, *Senior VP*
EMP: 104
SALES (est): 357.8MM **Privately Held**
SIC: 2911 Petroleum refining

(G-14145)
PHILADELPHIA ENERGY SOLUTIONS
3144 W Passyunk Ave (19145-5208)
PHONE..................................215 339-1200
Philip Rinaldi, *Branch Mgr*
EMP: 600
SALES (corp-wide): 350.5MM **Privately Held**
SIC: 2911 Petroleum refining
PA: Philadelphia Energy Solutions Refining And Marketing Llc
1735 Market St Fl 11
Philadelphia PA 19103
267 238-4300

(G-14146)
PHILADELPHIA INSTRS & CONTRLS
4401 N 6th St (19140-2319)
PHONE..................................215 329-8828
Eric Engelhardt, *President*
Robert Engelhardt, *Vice Pres*
John L Schwartz III, *Vice Pres*
EMP: 17 EST: 1905
SALES (est): 2.3MM **Privately Held**
WEB: www.philadelphiainstrument.com
SIC: 3823 3822 Thermometers, filled system: industrial process type; thermostats, except built-in

(G-14147)
PHILADELPHIA MEDIA NETWORK PBC (PA)
Also Called: Philadelphia Inquirer
801 Market St Ste 300 (19107-3183)
P.O. Box 8263 (19101-8263)
PHONE..................................215 854-2000
Terry Egger, *CEO*
H F Gerry Lenfest, *Chairman*
Andy Harrison, *CFO*
Taiwo Sokan, *Hum Res Coord*
Bob Ford, *Accounts Exec*
EMP: 80
SALES (est): 297.5MM **Privately Held**
SIC: 2711 Newspapers, publishing & printing

(G-14148)
PHILADELPHIA PHOTO ARTS CENTER
Also Called: PPAC
1400 N American St # 103 (19122-3838)
PHONE..................................215 232-5678
Sarah Stolsa, *CEO*
EMP: 6
SALES (est): 692K **Privately Held**
SIC: 8699 2752 7221 Charitable organization; commercial printing, lithographic; school photographer

(G-14149)
PHILADELPHIA PIPE BENDING CO (PA)
Also Called: Bentech
4135 To 4165 N Fifth St (19140)
P.O. Box 46128 (19160-6128)
PHONE..................................215 225-8955
George Horrocks II, *President*
Robert Benninghoff, *Vice Pres*
Vasyl Ishchenko, *Engineer*
Joseph Reese, *Manager*
Jeffrey Fox, *Admin Sec*
EMP: 42 EST: 1906
SQ FT: 50,000
SALES (est): 7.7MM **Privately Held**
WEB: www.philapipebend.com
SIC: 3498 3312 3351 7692 Coils, pipe: fabricated from purchased pipe; blast furnaces & steel mills; bands, copper & copper alloy; welding repair; sheet metalwork; fabricated structural metal

(G-14150)
PHILADELPHIA POULTRY INC
346 N Front St (19106-1302)
PHONE..................................215 574-0343
Ernie Dellapia, *President*
Antony Dellapia, *Vice Pres*
EMP: 30
SQ FT: 7,000
SALES: 5MM **Privately Held**
SIC: 2015 5144 Chicken, processed: frozen; poultry products

(G-14151)
PHILADELPHIA PROVISION CO
Also Called: Czerw's Phila Provision Co
3370 Tilton St (19134-6018)
PHONE..................................215 423-1707
Dennis Czerw, *Partner*
EMP: 3
SQ FT: 4,500
SALES (est): 191.7K **Privately Held**
SIC: 2013 Smoked meats from purchased meat

(G-14152)
PHILADELPHIA PUBLIC RECORD
1323 S Broad St (19147-4943)
PHONE..................................215 755-2000
Jim Tayoun, *President*
EMP: 10
SALES (est): 507.5K **Privately Held**
WEB: www.phillyrecord.com
SIC: 2711 Newspapers

(G-14153)
PHILADELPHIA RUST PROOF CO (PA)
2086 E Willard St (19134-3240)
PHONE..................................215 425-3000
Thomas J Vezzosi Jr, *President*
David Vezzosi, *Manager*
Ruth Vezzosi, *Admin Sec*
EMP: 15 EST: 1923
SQ FT: 42,000
SALES (est): 1.8MM **Privately Held**
WEB: www.philarustproof.com
SIC: 3471 Electroplating of metals or formed products

(G-14154)
PHILADELPHIA SHIP REPAIR LLC
5195 S 19th St (19112-1710)
PHONE..................................215 339-1026
Nicholas Lamparelli, *General Mgr*
Edward Snyder,
EMP: 10
SALES (est): 1.5MM **Privately Held**
WEB: www.atlanticmarine.com
SIC: 3731 Shipbuilding & repairing
PA: Northeast Ship Repair, Inc.
32a Drydock Ave
Boston MA 02210

(G-14155)
PHILADELPHIA SOFT PRETZELS
4315 N 3rd St (19140-2401)
PHONE..................................215 324-4315
Joseph Sidorick, *President*
Jeanne Sidorick, *Corp Secy*
EMP: 30
SQ FT: 10,000
SALES (est): 4.2MM **Privately Held**
WEB: www.philasoftpretzels.net
SIC: 2052 5461 5149 2051 Pretzels; pretzels; groceries & related products; bread, cake & related products

(G-14156)
PHILADELPHIA STYLE MAG LLC
141 League St (19147-4224)
PHONE..................................215 468-6670
Dana Spain-Smith, *COO*
Shannon Grotzinger, *Research*
Nichole Maurer, *Administration*
EMP: 18
SQ FT: 9,000
SALES (est): 1.7MM
SALES (corp-wide): 41MM **Privately Held**
WEB: www.phillystylemag.com
SIC: 2721 Magazines: publishing & printing
HQ: Niche Media Holdings, Llc
257 Park Ave S Fl 5
New York NY 10010
702 990-2500

(G-14157)
PHILADELPHIA SUN GROUP INC
Also Called: Philadelphia Sunday Sun
6661 Germantown Ave (19119-2251)
PHONE..................................215 848-7864
J Wyatt Mondesire, *President*
Harriet Garret, *Manager*
EMP: 10

SALES (est): 773K **Privately Held**
SIC: 2711 Newspapers, publishing & printing

(G-14158)
PHILADELPHIA TRIBUNE COMPANY
520 S 16th St (19146-1565)
PHONE..................................215 893-5356
Walter Livingston, *Ch of Bd*
Robert W Bogle, *President*
Bertha Godfrey, *Vice Pres*
John Holmes, *CFO*
Floyd Alston, *Treasurer*
EMP: 70 EST: 1884
SQ FT: 15,000
SALES (est): 4.7MM **Privately Held**
WEB: www.phila-tribune.com
SIC: 2711 Newspapers-Publishing/Printing

(G-14159)
PHILADELPHIA WINDOW WASHERS
1202 Ripley St (19111-2642)
PHONE..................................215 742-3875
Diane Cairns, *Principal*
EMP: 3
SALES (est): 157.2K **Privately Held**
SIC: 3452 Washers

(G-14160)
PHILADELPHIA WOODWORKS LLC
4901 Umbria St Ste C (19128-4539)
PHONE..................................267 331-5880
Michael Vogel, *Principal*
EMP: 4
SALES (est): 559.6K **Privately Held**
SIC: 2431 Millwork

(G-14161)
PHILADLPHIA ENRGY SLUTIONS LLC (PA)
3144 W Passyunk Ave (19145-5208)
PHONE..................................267 238-4300
Philip Rinaldi, *CEO*
Gregory Gatta, *COO*
Thomas Scargle, *Exec VP*
James Rens, *CFO*
John McShane, *General Counsel*
▲ EMP: 214
SALES (est): 725.9MM **Privately Held**
SIC: 2911 Petroleum refining

(G-14162)
PHILADLPHIA MEDIA HOLDINGS LLC
400 N Broad St (19130-4015)
PHONE..................................215 854-2000
EMP: 11
SALES (est): 605K **Privately Held**
SIC: 2711 Newspapers-Publishing/Printing

(G-14163)
PHILADLPHIA MTAL RSRCE RCOVERY
2200 E Somerset St (19134-3900)
PHONE..................................215 423-4800
Eric Bell, *Owner*
EMP: 20
SALES: 12MM **Privately Held**
SIC: 3443 5093 Metal parts; metal scrap & waste materials

(G-14164)
PHILADLPHIA PR-COKED STEAK INC
4001 N American St (19140-2604)
PHONE..................................215 426-4949
Nicholas Karamatsoukas, *President*
Stavros Kalisperis, *Corp Secy*
EMP: 40
SALES (est): 7.5MM
SALES (corp-wide): 40B **Publicly Held**
SIC: 2013 Beef stew from purchased meat
HQ: Original Philly Holdings, Inc.
31 Trailwood Dr
Southampton PA 18966
215 423-3333

(G-14165)
PHILADLPHIA TRAMRAIL ENTPS INC (PA)
2207 E Ontario St (19134-2615)
PHONE..................................215 743-4359
R J Riethmiller Jr, *Ch of Bd*
Michael Savage, *Vice Pres*
Calvin Mingione, *Engineer*
Jim Buccella, *Treasurer*
Lee McLaughlin, *Manager*
▼ EMP: 190
SQ FT: 110,000
SALES (est): 68.2MM **Privately Held**
SIC: 3589 3569 Garbage disposers & compactors, commercial; baling machines, for scrap metal, paper or similar material

(G-14166)
PHILARX PHARMACY INC (PA)
2102 S Broad St (19145-3960)
PHONE..................................267 324-5231
EMP: 9
SALES (est): 2MM **Privately Held**
SIC: 2834 Mfg Pharmaceutical Preparations

(G-14167)
PHILDELPHIA-NEWSPAPERS-LLC (PA)
Also Called: Philadelphia Inquirer
801 Market St Ste 300 (19107-3183)
PHONE..................................215 854-2000
Terrance Egger, *CEO*
Brian Tierney, *CEO*
Gerry Lenfest, *Ch of Bd*
Alfred Lubrano, *President*
Frederick B Mott, *President*
▲ EMP: 2000
SQ FT: 300,000
SALES (est): 232.9MM **Privately Held**
WEB: www.philly.com
SIC: 2711 Commercial printing & newspaper publishing combined

(G-14168)
PHILLY BANNER EXPRESS LLC
236 E Hunting Park Ave (19124-6003)
PHONE..................................267 385-5451
Curtis King, *Manager*
EMP: 4
SALES (est): 472.2K **Privately Held**
SIC: 2752 Commercial printing, lithographic

(G-14169)
PHILLY PRETZEL FACTORY (PA)
7368 Frankford Ave (19136-3829)
PHONE..................................215 962-5593
Dan N Dizio III, *President*
David Bee, *Research*
EMP: 30
SALES (est): 12.4MM **Privately Held**
SIC: 5461 2052 6794 Pretzels; pretzels; franchises, selling or licensing

(G-14170)
PHOENIX LITHOGRAPHING CORP
Also Called: Innovation Prtg Communications
11601 Caroline Rd (19154-2116)
PHONE..................................215 969-4600
Hallie Satz, *Branch Mgr*
EMP: 85
SALES (corp-wide): 105MM **Privately Held**
SIC: 2752 Commercial printing, offset
PA: Phoenix Lithographing Corp
11631 Caroline Rd Ste A
Philadelphia PA 19154
215 698-9000

(G-14171)
PHOENIX LITHOGRAPHING CORP (PA)
11631 Caroline Rd Ste A (19154-2116)
PHONE..................................215 698-9000
Magdy Maximos, *CEO*
Dave Carpenter, *President*
Barry Green, *Chairman*
Jay Adams, *Vice Pres*
Stacy Harris, *Vice Pres*
EMP: 172
SQ FT: 85,000

(G-14172)
PHOTO PROCESS SCREEN MFG CO
179 W Berks St (19122-2394)
PHONE..................................215 426-5473
Salvatore Oteri, *President*
EMP: 10 EST: 1945
SQ FT: 40,000
SALES (est): 1.2MM **Privately Held**
WEB: www.ppsilkscreen.com
SIC: 3861 2759 Screens, projection; screen printing

(G-14173)
PHRESH PRINTS INK LLC
2825 N 22nd St (19132-2626)
PHONE..................................267 687-7483
Nasir Yard, *Principal*
EMP: 3 EST: 2015
SALES (est): 101.5K **Privately Held**
SIC: 2752 Commercial printing, lithographic

(G-14174)
PHUFAR
6190 Ridge Ave (19128-2628)
PHONE..................................215 483-0487
Ronald Metzger, *Principal*
EMP: 3
SALES (est): 192K **Privately Held**
SIC: 3842 Abdominal supporters, braces & trusses

(G-14175)
PICWELL INC
2200 Arch St Ste 1a (19103-1352)
PHONE..................................215 563-0976
Matthew Sydney, *CEO*
EMP: 12
SALES (est): 1.4MM **Privately Held**
SIC: 7372 Prepackaged software

(G-14176)
PIERI CREATIONS LLC
100 W Oxford St (19122-3927)
PHONE..................................215 634-4000
Aron D Paneth,
◆ EMP: 40
SQ FT: 125,000
SALES (est): 5.3MM **Privately Held**
WEB: www.piericreations.net
SIC: 3646 3645 Commercial indusl & institutional electric lighting fixtures; lamp & light shades

(G-14177)
PIK-A-BOO PHOTOS LLC
6344 N 8th St Apt G7 (19126-3755)
PHONE..................................267 334-6379
Terrance Jackson, *President*
EMP: 5
SALES (est): 206.8K **Privately Held**
SIC: 2752 Commercial printing, offset

(G-14178)
PINE VALLEY SUPPLY CORPORATION
225 Geiger Rd Fl 2 (19115-1072)
PHONE..................................215 676-8100
Ed Barbano, *President*
Allen Supowitz, *Corp Secy*
Jack Bachmann, *Vice Pres*
EMP: 3
SQ FT: 12,000
SALES (est): 417.1K **Privately Held**
WEB: www.pinevalleysupply.com
SIC: 2875 5191 Fertilizers, mixing only; fertilizers & agricultural chemicals; fertilizer & fertilizer materials; grass seed

(G-14179)
PITA PITA LLC
1932 Liacouras Walk (19122-6027)
PHONE..................................267 440-7482
Amin Yousef,
Anwar Albarouki,
EMP: 6
SALES: 500K **Privately Held**
SIC: 5812 7372 Indian/Pakistan restaurant; application computer software

(G-14180)
PITNEY BOWES INC
2000 Hamilton St Ste C01 (19130-4123)
PHONE..................................215 751-9800
Lauren Loeffler, *General Mgr*
EMP: 175
SALES (corp-wide): 3.5B **Publicly Held**
SIC: 3579 7359 Postage meters; business machine & electronic equipment rental services
PA: Pitney Bowes Inc.
3001 Summer St Ste 3
Stamford CT 06905
203 356-5000

(G-14181)
PLANTARIUM LIVING ENVIROM
5101 Cottman Ave (19135-1516)
PHONE..................................215 338-2008
EMP: 3
SALES (est): 281.4K **Privately Held**
SIC: 3999 Mfg Misc Products

(G-14182)
PLASTIC COMPONENTS INC
1526 N American St (19122-3811)
P.O. Box 3799 (19125-0799)
PHONE..................................215 235-5550
Barnett Liss, *President*
EMP: 11
SQ FT: 8,000
SALES: 3.5MM **Privately Held**
SIC: 3089 Blister or bubble formed packaging, plastic; plastic containers, except cases; cases, plastic

(G-14183)
PLASTICONCENTRATES INC (PA)
4548 Market St (19139-3610)
PHONE..................................215 243-4143
Ed Tucker, *President*
EMP: 4
SQ FT: 12,000
SALES (est): 669.8K **Privately Held**
SIC: 3089 Extruded finished plastic products

(G-14184)
POLAR MANUFACTURING CO INC
2046 Castor Ave (19134-2132)
PHONE..................................215 535-6940
Brad Karasik, *President*
Howie Anderson, *Opers Mgr*
▲ EMP: 15 EST: 1912
SQ FT: 20,000
SALES (est): 3.5MM **Privately Held**
WEB: www.the-polar.com
SIC: 3199 Desk sets, leather; novelties, leather

(G-14185)
POLICYMAP INC (HQ)
Also Called: Policymap, LLC
1315 Walnut St Ste 1500 (19107-4715)
PHONE..................................866 923-6277
Maggie McCullough, *President*
Joel Rodriguez, *Web Dvlpr*
Tom Love, *Director*
Bernard Langer, *Analyst*
EMP: 9
SQ FT: 1,000
SALES: 2.9MM
SALES (corp-wide): 34.8MM **Privately Held**
SIC: 7372 7374 7371 Prepackaged software; data processing & preparation; data processing service; custom computer programming services
PA: The Reinvestment Fund Inc
1700 Market St Fl 19
Philadelphia PA 19103
215 574-5800

(G-14186)
POLLYODD
1908 E Passyunk Ave (19148-2221)
PHONE..................................215 271-1161
EMP: 3
SALES (est): 146.5K **Privately Held**
SIC: 2085 Distilled & blended liquors

(G-14187)
POLY SAT INC
Also Called: Vexcon
7240 State Rd (19135-1412)
PHONE..................................215 332-7700
Darryl Manuel, *President*
Sharan Murray, *Bookkeeper*
EMP: 25 EST: 1988
SQ FT: 75,000
SALES: 600K **Privately Held**
SIC: 2899 2821 Concrete curing & hardening compounds; acrylic resins

(G-14188)
POMCO GRAPHICS INC
4411-27 Whitaker Ave (19120)
PHONE..................................215 455-9500
Frank Wlodarczyk, *Principal*
EMP: 14
SALES (est): 1.7MM **Privately Held**
SIC: 2752 Commercial printing, lithographic

(G-14189)
PORT RICHMAN HOLDINGS LLC
2701 E Tioga St (19134-6123)
PHONE..................................212 777-1178
Elisabeth Benson,
Eyal Greenberg,
Eli Salpeter,
EMP: 5
SQ FT: 10,000
SALES (est): 156.7K **Privately Held**
SIC: 2399 7359 3069 Banners, pennants & flags; work zone traffic equipment (flags, cones, barrels, etc.); balloons, advertising & toy: rubber

(G-14190)
PORT RICHMOND MILLWORK
2909 Salmon St (19134)
PHONE..................................215 423-4803
Joanne Florkowski, *President*
Tom Florkowski, *Admin Sec*
EMP: 4
SALES (est): 289.7K **Privately Held**
SIC: 2431 Millwork

(G-14191)
PORT RICHMOND TOOL & DIE INC
2839 E Tioga St (19134-6119)
PHONE..................................215 426-2287
Eric Tottser, *President*
Jim Dipaolo, *Vice Pres*
EMP: 10
SQ FT: 15,000
SALES (est): 1MM **Privately Held**
WEB: www.portrichmondtool.com
SIC: 3544 Special dies & tools

(G-14192)
PORTICO PRINTING LLC
1310 Sansom St (19107-4526)
PHONE..................................215 717-5151
Richard Lee,
EMP: 6
SALES (est): 861.4K **Privately Held**
SIC: 2752 Commercial printing, offset

(G-14193)
PPG INDUSTRIES INC
Also Called: PPG Pittsburgh Paints
444 N 2nd St (19123-4210)
PHONE..................................215 873-8940
EMP: 6
SALES (corp-wide): 15.3B **Publicly Held**
SIC: 2851 Paints & allied products
PA: Ppg Industries, Inc.
1 Ppg Pl
Pittsburgh PA 15272
412 434-3131

(G-14194)
PRACTICOM
604 S Washington Sq # 2002 (19106-4118)
PHONE..................................267 979-5446
David Sun,
EMP: 3
SALES (est): 154.3K **Privately Held**
SIC: 3646 Commercial indusl & institutional electric lighting fixtures

▲ = Import ▼=Export
◆ =Import/Export

(G-14195)
PRAIRIE DOG TECH LLC
1500 John F Kennedy Blvd (19102-1710)
PHONE..........................215 558-4975
David Bassion, *Mng Member*
EMP: 3
SALES (est): 103K **Privately Held**
SIC: 7372 Prepackaged software

(G-14196)
PREMIER DENTAL PRODUCTS CO INC
Premier Medical Manufacturing
10090 Sandmeyer Ln (19116-3502)
PHONE..........................215 676-9090
William Frezel, *Principal*
EMP: 45
SQ FT: 3,500
SALES (corp-wide): 25.4MM **Privately Held**
WEB: www.premusa.com
SIC: 3843 3841 Dental tools; surgical & medical instruments
PA: Premier Dental Products Company
1710 Romano Dr
Plymouth Meeting PA 19462
610 239-6000

(G-14197)
PREMIER FENCE & IRON WORKS INC
5856 Penn St (19149-3418)
PHONE..........................267 567-2078
Steven Barratt, *President*
EMP: 5
SALES (est): 347.9K **Privately Held**
SIC: 1799 3312 Fence construction; fence posts, iron & steel

(G-14198)
PRESTO DYECHEM CO INC
Also Called: A&D Dyestuffs
60 N Front St (19106-2219)
PHONE..........................215 627-1863
Peter H Ellison, *Vice Pres*
Peter Ellison, *Vice Pres*
Helen C Ellison, *Admin Sec*
EMP: 3
SQ FT: 2,500
SALES (est): 330.4K **Privately Held**
WEB: www.prestodye.com
SIC: 2865 Cyclic crudes & intermediates

(G-14199)
PRETZELWORKS INC
5331 Oxford Ave (19124-1123)
PHONE..........................215 288-4002
Samuel Naselsky, *President*
Mike Naselsky, *Treasurer*
EMP: 100
SALES (est): 9.5MM **Privately Held**
SIC: 2053 5142 Frozen bakery products, except bread; packaged frozen goods

(G-14200)
PRICELESS TIMES
3538 Cottman Ave (19149-1606)
PHONE..........................267 538-5723
EMP: 3
SALES (est): 94.9K **Privately Held**
SIC: 2711 Newspapers

(G-14201)
PRINT AND SEW INC
10960 Dutton Rd Ste B (19154-3216)
PHONE..........................215 281-3909
Jim Miller, *President*
EMP: 6
SALES (est): 188.4K **Privately Held**
SIC: 2759 Screen printing

(G-14202)
PRINTFLY CORPORATION (PA)
2727 Commerce Way (19154-1011)
PHONE..........................800 620-1233
Jordan Nemeroff, *President*
Michael Nemeroff, *Vice Pres*
Dennis Abrams, *Opers Staff*
Alexis Nemeroff, *Admin Sec*
EMP: 23 EST: 2002
SALES (est): 42.2MM **Privately Held**
SIC: 2759 Screen printing

(G-14203)
PRINTFRESH STUDIO LLC
2930 Jasper St Unit 408 (19134-3532)
PHONE..........................215 426-1661
Leo Voloshin, *CEO*
Katie Hill, *Consultant*
Amy Voloshin,
EMP: 37
SQ FT: 3,400
SALES: 2.9MM **Privately Held**
SIC: 7389 7372 Design services; application computer software

(G-14204)
PRIVATE ZONE PRODUCTIONS CORP (PA)
Also Called: Pzp
1601 Cherry St 130016th (19102-1320)
PHONE..........................267 592-5447
Darryl L Brown, *CEO*
EMP: 4
SALES (est): 305.7K **Privately Held**
SIC: 3652 6531 2731 Compact laser discs, prerecorded; real estate agent, residential; book publishing

(G-14205)
PROFESSIONAL ELECTRONIC COMPON
Also Called: Peca
100 S Broad St Ste 707 (19110-1061)
P.O. Box 224, Bensalem (19020-0224)
PHONE..........................215 245-1550
EMP: 6
SQ FT: 11,000
SALES (est): 1MM **Privately Held**
SIC: 3663 3357 Manufactures Radio & Tv Communication Equipment

(G-14206)
PROFRESH INTERNATIONAL CORP
4900 S Broad St Ste Ll00 (19112-1313)
PHONE..........................800 610-5110
Dr Jon Richter, *President*
Leslie S Fisher, *Vice Pres*
Ted Tannenbaum, *Opers Mgr*
EMP: 10
SALES (est): 1.6MM **Privately Held**
SIC: 2844 5122 Oral preparations; mouthwashes; drugs, proprietaries & sundries

(G-14207)
PROGRESSIVE COMPUTER SVCS INC
Also Called: Pcs Technologies
4250 Wissahickon Ave (19129-1215)
PHONE..........................215 226-2220
Howard J Weiss, *Ch of Bd*
Martin Becker, *President*
Chandra Allred, *COO*
Chandra Kasakevich, *COO*
Sal Meloni, *Vice Pres*
▲ EMP: 31
SQ FT: 20,000
SALES (est): 5.7MM **Privately Held**
WEB: www.pcstechnologies.com
SIC: 5045 7378 3572 7371 Computers; computer maintenance & repair; computer tape drives & components; computer software development

(G-14208)
PROJECT ONE INC
3230 Market St Ste 410 (19104)
PHONE..........................267 901-7906
Mansoor Siddiqui, *CEO*
EMP: 3
SALES (est): 71.1K **Privately Held**
SIC: 7372 Educational computer software

(G-14209)
PROPERTY PRESERVERS
7126 Vandike St (19135-1317)
PHONE..........................267 975-3990
EMP: 3
SALES (est): 193.7K **Privately Held**
SIC: 2491 Wood preserving

(G-14210)
PROPORTAL LLC
124 Chestnut St (19106-3009)
PHONE..........................215 923-7100
Wade H Alexander III,
EMP: 3

SALES: 250K **Privately Held**
WEB: www.proportal.org
SIC: 7372 7379 Utility computer software; computer related consulting services

(G-14211)
PRUFTECHNIK INC
7821 Bartram Ave Ste 3 (19153-3233)
PHONE..........................844 242-6296
Florian Buder, *CEO*
Sebastian Busch, *President*
Timothy English, *Managing Dir*
EMP: 29 EST: 2016
SALES (est): 1.6MM
SALES (corp-wide): 97.4MM **Privately Held**
SIC: 3829 1389 7699 7629 Kinematic test & measuring equipment; vibration meters, analyzers & calibrators; testing, measuring, surveying & analysis services; industrial machinery & equipment repair; electrical measuring instrument repair & calibration
PA: Pruftechnik Dieter Busch Ag
Oskar-Messter-Str. 19-21
Ismaning 85737
899 961-60

(G-14212)
PRUFTECHNIK SERVICE INC
7821 Bartram Ave Ste 3 (19153-3233)
PHONE..........................856 401-3095
Sebastian Busch, *President*
◆ EMP: 27
SQ FT: 25,000
SALES: 3.2MM
SALES (corp-wide): 97.4MM **Privately Held**
SIC: 3829 1389 7699 Kinematic test & measuring equipment; testing, measuring, surveying & analysis services; industrial machinery & equipment repair
PA: Pruftechnik Dieter Busch Ag
Oskar-Messter-Str. 19-21
Ismaning 85737
899 961-60

(G-14213)
PS & QS INC
820 South St (19147-2025)
PHONE..........................215 592-0888
John W Erdley, *President*
Shane J Erdley, *Treasurer*
Rick Cao, *Creative Dir*
EMP: 5
SALES (est): 360K **Privately Held**
SIC: 2329 Men's & boys' sportswear & athletic clothing

(G-14214)
PSG CONTROLS INC
11401 Roosevelt Blvd (19154-2102)
PHONE..........................215 257-3621
John H Reilly Jr, *CEO*
Chad Billmyer, *Purch Mgr*
Jack Turner, *Chief Engr*
Jennifer Hartshorne, *Human Res Dir*
Greg Hicks, *Manager*
◆ EMP: 60
SQ FT: 28,000
SALES (est): 9.2MM **Privately Held**
WEB: www.psgcontrols.com
SIC: 3822 3823 Temperature controls, automatic; temperature measurement instruments, industrial; temperature instruments; industrial process type

(G-14215)
PTR BALER AND COMPACTOR CO
2207 E Ontario St (19134-2615)
PHONE..........................215 533-5100
Robert J Riethmiller Jr, *Ch of Bd*
Michael Savage, *President*
Garry L Fudala, *Vice Pres*
Eric Riethmiller, *Vice Pres*
Bobby Walker, *Plant Mgr*
◆ EMP: 175 EST: 1907
SQ FT: 150,000

SALES (est): 63.2MM
SALES (corp-wide): 68.2MM **Privately Held**
WEB: www.ptrco.com
SIC: 3569 3589 Baling machines, for scrap metal, paper or similar material; garbage disposers & compactors, commercial
PA: Philadelphia Tramrail Enterprises, Inc.
2207 E Ontario St
Philadelphia PA 19134
215 743-4359

(G-14216)
PUBLIC IMAGE PRINTING INC
11972 Dumont Rd (19116-2321)
PHONE..........................215 677-4088
Mark Nathans, *President*
EMP: 7
SQ FT: 2,000
SALES (est): 564.8K **Privately Held**
SIC: 2752 2791 Commercial printing, lithographic; typesetting

(G-14217)
PURE FISHING AMERICA INC
3028 W Hunting Park Ave (19132-1121)
PHONE..........................215 229-9415
▲ EMP: 4
SALES (est): 318.1K **Privately Held**
SIC: 3949 Fishing tackle, general

(G-14218)
PUROLITE CORPORATION
Also Called: Purolite Company
3620 G St (19134-1321)
PHONE..........................610 668-9090
John Carroll, *Branch Mgr*
EMP: 120
SQ FT: 145,000
SALES (corp-wide): 312MM **Privately Held**
WEB: www.puroliteusa.com
SIC: 2821 Plastics materials & resins
PA: Purolite Corporation
150 Monument Rd Ste 202
Bala Cynwyd PA 19004
610 668-9090

(G-14219)
QUALITY HEALTH AND LIFE INC
Also Called: Qohal
2927 N Stillman St (19132-1910)
PHONE..........................866 547-8447
Michael Allen Jr, *President*
Keena Allen, *Treasurer*
Mylayjah Allen, *Bd of Directors*
Zariah Davis, *Bd of Directors*
Carmen Diggs, *Bd of Directors*
EMP: 5
SALES (est): 278K **Privately Held**
SIC: 2834 Pills, pharmaceutical

(G-14220)
QUALITY PENN PRODUCTS INC
2015 W Allegheny Ave (19132-1553)
P.O. Box 3636 (19125-0636)
PHONE..........................215 430-0117
Frank L Rouco, *President*
EMP: 9
SQ FT: 60,000
SALES (est): 1MM **Privately Held**
WEB: www.qualitypenn.com
SIC: 2448 Pallets, wood

(G-14221)
QUIRK PRODUCTIONS INC
Also Called: Quirk Books
215 Church St Ste 1 (19106-4518)
PHONE..........................215 627-3581
David Borgenicht, *President*
Rick Chillot, *Editor*
Paul Stevens, *Editor*
Mary Wilson, *Manager*
▲ EMP: 18
SQ FT: 7,500
SALES (est): 2.9MM **Privately Held**
WEB: www.quirkproductions.com
SIC: 2731 Books: publishing only

(G-14222)
R & H JEWELERS
740 Sansom St Ste 402 (19106-3235)
PHONE..........................215 928-1240
Charles Rosenblum, *President*
EMP: 4

SALES (est): 243.1K **Privately Held**
SIC: 3479 Engraving jewelry silverware, or
metal

(G-14223)
R & M SHIP TECH USA INC (DH)
4619 S Broad St (19112-1202)
PHONE....................................352 403-8365
Thomas Grunwald, *President*
Michael E Zeller, *Admin Sec*
EMP: 12
SALES (est): 8.2MM
SALES (corp-wide): 123.9K **Privately
Held**
SIC: 3441 Fabricated structural metal
HQ: R & M International Gmbh
Schellerdamm 22-24
Hamburg 21079
407 524-440

(G-14224)
R G B BUSINESS TECH SOLUTIONS
7948 Oxford Ave (19111-2225)
PHONE....................................215 745-3646
Joe Pagano, *President*
Sue Pagano, *President*
Joseph G Pagano, *Vice Pres*
EMP: 5
SQ FT: 100,000
SALES (est): 510.7K **Privately Held**
WEB: www.rgbvideo.com
SIC: 5999 3812 Audio-visual equipment &
supplies; search & detection systems &
instruments

(G-14225)
R R DONNELLEY & SONS COMPANY
Also Called: Baum Printing Company
9985 Gantry Rd (19115-1001)
PHONE....................................215 671-9500
Mike Shirakawa, *Manager*
EMP: 200
SQ FT: 52,752
SALES (corp-wide): 6.8B **Publicly Held**
WEB: www.rrdonnelley.com
SIC: 2752 2796 2791 2789 Commercial
printing, offset; platemaking services;
typesetting; bookbinding & related work;
commercial printing
PA: R. R. Donnelley & Sons Company
35 W Wacker Dr Ste 3650
Chicago IL 60601
312 326-8000

(G-14226)
R R DONNELLEY & SONS COMPANY
Also Called: R R Donnelley
2 Logan Sq Ste 1800 (19103-2722)
PHONE....................................215 564-3220
Mariott Annapoly, *Manager*
EMP: 35
SALES (corp-wide): 6.8B **Publicly Held**
WEB: www.rrdonnelley.com
SIC: 2759 Screen printing
PA: R. R. Donnelley & Sons Company
35 W Wacker Dr Ste 3650
Chicago IL 60601
312 326-8000

(G-14227)
R SCHEINERT & SON INC
10092 Sandmeyer Ln (19116-3580)
PHONE....................................215 673-9800
Doris M Scheinert, *President*
Denise Scheinert, *Vice Pres*
Sheree Miller, *Controller*
EMP: 21
SQ FT: 24,000
SALES (est): 4.1MM **Privately Held**
SIC: 7629 7694 5063 Generator repair;
electric motor repair; generators

(G-14228)
R W HARTNETT COMPANY
2055 Bennett Rd (19116-3019)
PHONE....................................215 969-9190
Joan F Ackley, *CEO*
Andrea Boyce, *President*
Keith Boyce, *Vice Pres*
EMP: 24 EST: 1880

SALES (est): 12.6MM **Privately Held**
WEB: www.rwhartnett.com
SIC: 3555 Printing trades machinery

(G-14229)
R WAY GASKET & SUPPLY COMPANY
1950 E Sedgley Ave (19124-5658)
PHONE....................................215 743-1650
Charles J Killian Sr, *President*
EMP: 12 EST: 1978
SQ FT: 10,000
SALES (est): 1.7MM **Privately Held**
SIC: 3053 Gaskets, all materials

(G-14230)
R&M AMERICAN MARINE PDTS INC
2100 Kitty Hawk Ave (19112-1808)
PHONE....................................352 345-4866
▲ EMP: 10
SALES (est): 760K **Privately Held**
SIC: 3441 Mfg Structural Metal Fabrication

(G-14231)
READY FOOD PRODUCTS INC
10975 Dutton Rd (19154-3203)
PHONE....................................215 824-2800
Glenn Goenner, *President*
EMP: 115
SALES (est): 10.7MM
SALES (corp-wide): 2.1B **Privately Held**
WEB: www.crowleyfoods.com
SIC: 2026 Whipped topping, except frozen
or dry mix; cream, whipped; half & half
HQ: Crowley Foods, Inc.
93 Pennsylvania Ave
Binghamton NY 13903
800 637-0019

(G-14232)
RECCARE INCORPORATED
923 E Ellet St (19150-3506)
PHONE....................................215 886-0880
Lynda L Mitchell, *President*
Thomas D Mitchell, *Admin Sec*
EMP: 38
SALES (est): 4.4MM **Privately Held**
SIC: 3845 Electrotherapeutic apparatus

(G-14233)
RECON PUBLICATIONS
431 W Rittenhouse St (19144-3801)
PHONE....................................215 843-4256
Chris Robinson, *Owner*
EMP: 3
SALES (est): 131.2K **Privately Held**
SIC: 2741 Miscellaneous publishing

(G-14234)
RECOVERY NETWORKS INC
4747 S Broad St Ste 232 (19112-1327)
PHONE....................................215 809-1300
Thomas Dugan, *President*
EMP: 9
SALES (est): 830K **Privately Held**
SIC: 7372 Business oriented computer
software

(G-14235)
RED ASSOCIATES
605 Allengrove St (19120-2105)
PHONE....................................215 722-4895
Ronald Engler, *Owner*
EMP: 6
SALES (est): 360K **Privately Held**
SIC: 3861 Developers, photographic (not
made in chemical plants)

(G-14236)
RED BANDANA CO (PA)
Also Called: Ed London Wreath Co
3801 Castor Ave (19124-5611)
PHONE....................................215 744-3144
Janet Barag, *President*
EMP: 14
SQ FT: 40,000
SALES (est): 1.9MM **Privately Held**
SIC: 3999 5193 Flowers, artificial & pre-
served; flowers & florists' supplies

(G-14237)
RED FLAG MEDIA INC
1032 Arch St Fl 3 (19107-3018)
PHONE....................................215 625-9850

Alex Mulcahy, *President*
Andrea Leerman, *Opers Staff*
Andrew Bonazelli, *Manager*
Trevor Tivenan, *Executive*
Mark Evans,
EMP: 2
SALES (est): 1.5MM **Privately Held**
WEB: www.redflagmedia.com
SIC: 2721 Magazines: publishing only, not
printed on site

(G-14238)
REGENCY TYPOGRAPHIC SVCS INC
Also Called: Regency Infographics
2867 E Allegheny Ave (19134-5903)
PHONE....................................215 425-8810
David Kahn, *President*
John Caibuttoni, *CFO*
EMP: 12
SQ FT: 20,000
SALES (est): 1MM **Privately Held**
WEB: www.reginfo.com
SIC: 2741 2791 Miscellaneous publishing;
typesetting

(G-14239)
RELIANCE PARAGON PAPER BOX
2070 Wheatsheaf Ln (19124-5041)
PHONE....................................215 743-1231
Benjamin Chatzkel, *Principal*
EMP: 3 EST: 2010
SALES (est): 181.1K **Privately Held**
SIC: 2652 Setup paperboard boxes

(G-14240)
RENAPTYS VACCINES LLC
113 W Chestnut Hill Ave # 9 (19118-3701)
PHONE....................................917 620-2256
Paul Bolno, *Principal*
EMP: 7
SALES (est): 495.7K **Privately Held**
SIC: 2836 Bacterial vaccines

(G-14241)
RESTORATIVE CARE AMERICA INC
Also Called: L'Nard
27 N 3rd St (19106-4507)
PHONE....................................215 592-8880
Mark Turnbull, *Manager*
EMP: 9
SALES (corp-wide): 18.9MM **Privately
Held**
WEB: www.rcai.com
SIC: 3842 Orthopedic appliances
PA: Restorative Care Of America Incorpo-
rated
12221 33rd St N
Saint Petersburg FL 33716
727 573-1595

(G-14242)
REVIEW PUBLISHING LTD PARTNR (PA)
Also Called: SW Philadelphia Review
1617 Jfk Blvd Ste 1005 (19103-1825)
PHONE....................................215 563-7400
Anthony A Clifton, *Partner*
Anastasia Barbalios, *Editor*
Amy Stoller, *Sales Staff*
EMP: 95
SQ FT: 9,000
SALES (est): 4.2MM **Privately Held**
WEB: www.reviewpublishing.com
SIC: 2711 Newspapers, publishing & print-
ing

(G-14243)
RHOADS INDUSTRIES INC
5100 S 16th St (19112-1713)
P.O. Box 40, Huntingdon Valley (19006-
0040)
PHONE....................................267 728-6544
Daniel J Rhoads Jr, *Principal*
EMP: 40
SALES (est): 4.1MM **Privately Held**
SIC: 3731 Shipbuilding & repairing
PA: Rhoads Industries, Inc.
1900 Kitty Hawk Ave
Philadelphia PA 19112

(G-14244)
RHOADS INDUSTRIES INC (PA)
Also Called: Rhoads Marine Industries
1900 Kitty Hawk Ave (19112-1806)
PHONE....................................267 728-6300
Daniel I Rhoads Jr, *President*
William North, *Senior VP*
Phillip Disciullo, *Project Mgr*
Janice Gibbon, *Opers Staff*
Bill Fell, *CFO*
EMP: 100
SQ FT: 300,000
SALES (est): 58.3MM **Privately Held**
SIC: 1761 3731 3599 1799 Sheet metal-
work; shipbuilding & repairing; hose, flexi-
ble metallic; rigging & scaffolding

(G-14245)
RICH-ART SIGN CO INC
Also Called: Richart Graphics
1305 Vine St (19107-1012)
PHONE....................................215 922-1539
Richard Antner, *President*
Mark Spindler, *Controller*
Wanda Burnett, *Office Mgr*
Janice Antner, *Admin Sec*
Tim Korba, *Technician*
EMP: 9
SQ FT: 8,500
SALES (est): 1MM **Privately Held**
WEB: www.richartgraphics.com
SIC: 7336 7384 3993 Silk screen design;
photofinish laboratories; advertising art-
work

(G-14246)
RICHARD J MCMENAMIN INC
11000 Roosevelt Blvd (19116-3961)
PHONE....................................215 673-1200
Richard McMenamin, *Principal*
EMP: 3
SALES (est): 277.3K **Privately Held**
SIC: 2836 Vaccines & other immunizing
products

(G-14247)
RICHARDSAPEX INC (PA)
4202 Main St 24 (19127-1698)
PHONE....................................215 487-1100
Andrew Richards, *President*
Ronald E Higgins, *Vice Pres*
Ronald Reich, *Vice Pres*
David Richards, *Vice Pres*
Darbi Storti, *Buyer*
◆ EMP: 45
SQ FT: 105,000
SALES: 439.3K **Privately Held**
WEB: www.richardsapex.com
SIC: 2992 2842 Oils & greases, blending
& compounding; specialty cleaning prepa-
rations

(G-14248)
RICHARDSON PAINT CO INC
4821 Garden St (19137-2297)
PHONE....................................215 535-4500
James W Richardson Sr, *President*
David P Richardson, *Corp Secy*
Kenneth B Richardson, *Vice Pres*
EMP: 15 EST: 1949
SQ FT: 30,000
SALES (est): 2.4MM **Privately Held**
SIC: 2851 Paints & allied products

(G-14249)
RICOCHET MANUFACTURING CORP
4700 Wissahickon Ave # 112 (19144-4248)
P.O. Box 112 (19105-0112)
PHONE....................................888 462-1999
Peter Askey, *President*
Kathleen McDeromtt, *Admin Sec*
EMP: 40
SQ FT: 30,000
SALES (est): 1.1MM **Privately Held**
WEB: www.ricochet-gear.com
SIC: 3842 Clothing, fire resistant & protec-
tive

(G-14250)
RIDGWAYS INC
3751 Island Ave Ste 200 (19153-3237)
PHONE....................................215 735-8055
Gerry Burns, *CEO*
EMP: 20

GEOGRAPHIC

SALES (est): 2.9MM
SALES (corp-wide): 400.7MM **Publicly Held**
WEB: www.ridgwaysrms.com
SIC: 7334 2791 2789 2759 Photocopying & duplicating services; typesetting; bookbinding & related work; commercial printing; offset & photolithographic printing; engineers' equipment & supplies
HQ: Arc Document Solutions, Llc
6300 Gulfton St
Houston TX 77081
713 988-9200

(G-14251)
RITTENHOUSE INSTANT PRESS
1811 Sansom St (19103-4904)
PHONE..................................215 854-0505
John Stankovics, *President*
EMP: 4
SALES (est): 576.7K **Privately Held**
SIC: 2752 7334 Commercial printing, offset; photocopying & duplicating services

(G-14252)
RIVERSIDE MATERIALS INC
2870 E Allegheny Ave # 1 (19134-5995)
PHONE..................................215 426-7299
James J Anderson, *President*
Sharon Raffo, *Bookkeeper*
EMP: 13
SQ FT: 5,000
SALES (est): 4.8MM **Privately Held**
SIC: 2951 Asphalt & asphaltic paving mixtures (not from refineries)

(G-14253)
RJJ MOBILE LLC
5815 Wayne Ave (19144-3315)
P.O. Box 25, Flourtown (19031-0025)
PHONE..................................215 796-1935
Bob Bauer,
Jason Klotkowski,
John Thain,
EMP: 10
SALES (est): 547.1K **Privately Held**
SIC: 2052 Cones, ice cream

(G-14254)
ROBERT I OLDFIELD
Also Called: Ernamatic Tool & Die Co
4717 Duffield St (19124-2707)
PHONE..................................215 533-5860
Robert I Oldfield, *Owner*
EMP: 3 **EST:** 1935
SQ FT: 3,500
SALES (est): 219.9K **Privately Held**
SIC: 3544 Special dies, tools, jigs & fixtures

(G-14255)
ROBOTIC SERVICES INC (PA)
Also Called: Aerial Applications
3401 Grays Ferry Ave (19146-2701)
PHONE..................................215 550-1823
Joseph Sullivan, *CEO*
Jeff Brooks, *Chief Mktg Ofcr*
Nathan Sullivan, *CTO*
EMP: 8
SALES (est): 689.2K **Privately Held**
SIC: 7372 Business oriented computer software

(G-14256)
ROCKPETZ VENTURES LLC
Also Called: Ltlprints.com
34 N Front St Lowr Level (19106-2287)
PHONE..................................610 608-2788
Kendall Schoenrock, *Mng Member*
EMP: 8
SQ FT: 15,000
SALES (est): 498.3K **Privately Held**
SIC: 2759 Poster & decal printing & engraving

(G-14257)
ROHM AND HAAS CHEMICALS LLC
100 S Indpdnc Mall W Fl 5 (19106-2320)
PHONE..................................215 592-3696
John Waele, *Branch Mgr*
EMP: 5
SALES (corp-wide): 85.9B **Publicly Held**
SIC: 2899 Chemical preparations

HQ: Rohm And Haas Chemicals Llc
400 Arcola Rd
Collegeville PA 19426

(G-14258)
ROHMAX ADDITIVES GMBH LLC
Also Called: Rohmax USA
100 N Independence Mall W (19106-1521)
PHONE..................................215 706-5800
EMP: 20
SALES (est): 1.6MM **Privately Held**
SIC: 2911 Mfg Petroleum Additives

(G-14259)
ROMA ALUMINUM CO INC
Also Called: Roma Therm Window Systems Plus
1924 Washington Ave (19146-2831)
PHONE..................................215 545-5700
Jacob A Gulli, *President*
EMP: 15
SQ FT: 26,000
SALES: 1.1MM **Privately Held**
SIC: 3231 3442 5031 Products of purchased glass; storm doors or windows, metal; door frames, all materials

(G-14260)
ROSSI BROTHERS CABINET MAKERS
Also Called: Rossi Bros
1805 N Howard St (19122-2445)
PHONE..................................215 426-9960
Victor Rossi, *President*
EMP: 11 **EST:** 1957
SQ FT: 15,000
SALES (est): 1.3MM **Privately Held**
SIC: 2434 Wood kitchen cabinets

(G-14261)
RSC WORLDWIDE (US) INC
3711 Market St Ste 800 (19104-5532)
PHONE..................................215 966-6206
Wynne Beaumont, *Principal*
David James, *Director*
EMP: 3
SALES (est): 168.5K **Privately Held**
SIC: 2721 Periodicals

(G-14262)
RUBERTONES CASTING DIVISION
740 Sansom St Ste 306 (19106-3234)
PHONE..................................215 922-1314
William Desimone, *Principal*
EMP: 6
SALES (est): 754.4K **Privately Held**
SIC: 3911 Jewelry, precious metal

(G-14263)
RUCKUS WIRELESS INC
2 Logan Sq Ste 1810 (19103-2727)
PHONE..................................215 209-6160
EMP: 3
SALES (corp-wide): 6.6B **Privately Held**
SIC: 3661 Telephone & telegraph apparatus
HQ: Ruckus Wireless, Inc.
350 W Java Dr
Sunnyvale CA 94089
650 265-4200

(G-14264)
RUNWAY LIQUIDATION LLC
Also Called: Bcbg
1925 Chestnut St (19103-3534)
PHONE..................................401 351-4994
EMP: 3
SALES (corp-wide): 885.4MM **Privately Held**
SIC: 2335 Women's, juniors' & misses' dresses
HQ: Runway Liquidation, Llc
2761 Fruitland Ave
Vernon CA 90058
323 589-2224

(G-14265)
RUSCOMB TOOL & MACHINE CO INC
600 W Ruscomb St (19120-3761)
PHONE..................................215 455-1301
Carl Schmollinger Jr, *President*
Richard T Schmollinger, *Vice Pres*
EMP: 6 **EST:** 1939

SQ FT: 2,000
SALES (est): 660K **Privately Held**
SIC: 3599 Machine shop, jobbing & repair

(G-14266)
RUSH ORDER TEES
2727 Commerce Way (19154-1011)
PHONE..................................215 677-9200
Jordan Nemeroff, *Principal*
Tom Gaydos, *Vice Pres*
Ben Larue, *CTO*
EMP: 3 **EST:** 2016
SALES (est): 330.1K **Privately Held**
SIC: 2759 Screen printing

(G-14267)
RUSSO MACHINE WORKS
3341 D St (19134-1733)
PHONE..................................215 634-1630
Salvatore Russo, *Owner*
Salavatore Russo, *Owner*
EMP: 4
SQ FT: 3,600
SALES (est): 276.5K **Privately Held**
SIC: 3599 Machine shop, jobbing & repair

(G-14268)
RYAN FOSTER INC
7118 Germantown Ave (19119-1837)
PHONE..................................215 769-0118
EMP: 5
SALES: 185K **Privately Held**
SIC: 3999 7231 Mfg Misc Products Beauty Shop

(G-14269)
S & H HARDWARE & SUPPLY CO (PA)
6700 Castor Ave (19149-2103)
PHONE..................................215 745-9375
Stuart Stern, *President*
Harold Stern, *Principal*
Herbert Paul Stern, *Vice Pres*
Barbara Stern, *Admin Sec*
EMP: 19
SQ FT: 12,000
SALES (est): 5.3MM **Privately Held**
SIC: 5251 3993 5072 Tools; signs & advertising specialties; hardware

(G-14270)
S DROCCO UPHOLSTERY
Also Called: D'Rocco & Sons
7217 Montour St (19111-4016)
PHONE..................................215 745-2869
EMP: 7
SALES (est): 310K **Privately Held**
SIC: 7641 2512 Reupholstery/Furniture Repair Mfg Upholstered Household Furniture

(G-14271)
S G BUSINESS SERVICES INC
Also Called: Replica I
35 S 18th St (19103-4138)
PHONE..................................215 567-7107
Ratna Nambuuri, *President*
EMP: 7 **EST:** 1973
SQ FT: 1,600
SALES: 793K **Privately Held**
SIC: 7334 2752 2791 2789 Photocopying & duplicating services; commercial printing, lithographic; typesetting; bookbinding & related work

(G-14272)
S J A CONSTRUCTION INC
Also Called: S J A Concrete
3600 S 26th St (19145-5203)
PHONE..................................856 985-3400
Robert Root, *Manager*
EMP: 25
SALES (est): 4MM **Privately Held**
SIC: 3273 Ready-mixed concrete
PA: S J A Construction, Inc.
925 Route 73 N Ste A
Marlton NJ 08053

(G-14273)
S MORANTZ INC
9984 Gantry Rd (19115-1076)
PHONE..................................215 969-0266
Stan Morantz, *President*
Lisa Morantz, *Vice Pres*
EMP: 56
SQ FT: 12,000

SALES (est): 8MM **Privately Held**
SIC: 3589 3555 3552 3541 Commercial cleaning equipment; printing trades machinery; textile machinery; machine tools, metal cutting type; drapery hardware & blinds & shades; curtains & draperies

(G-14274)
S&P GLOBAL INC
2001 Market St (19103-7044)
PHONE..................................215 430-6000
Edith Douie, *Branch Mgr*
EMP: 149
SALES (corp-wide): 6.2B **Publicly Held**
SIC: 2731 Books: publishing only
PA: S&P Global Inc.
55 Water St
New York NY 10041
212 438-1000

(G-14275)
SAFE PAC PASTEURIZATION LLC
2712 Grays Ferry Ave (19146-3801)
PHONE..................................267 324-5631
G Giordano, *Mng Member*
▲ **EMP:** 15
SALES (est): 2MM **Privately Held**
SIC: 2086 Pasteurized & mineral waters, bottled & canned

(G-14276)
SANDYS NAIL
3726 Midvale Ave (19129-1715)
PHONE..................................215 848-0299
Chuong Thach, *Owner*
EMP: 3
SALES (est): 221.1K **Privately Held**
SIC: 2844 Manicure preparations

(G-14277)
SANGUIS LLC
3711 Market St Ste 800 (19104-5532)
PHONE..................................267 228-7502
Divyansh Agarwal, *CEO*
Prateek Agarwal,
Daniel Zhang,
EMP: 4
SALES (est): 162.8K **Privately Held**
SIC: 3826 Blood testing apparatus

(G-14278)
SANSOM QUILTING & EMB CO
511 Spring Garden St (19123-2820)
PHONE..................................215 627-6990
Milton Tarshish, *President*
Susan Greenberg, *Vice Pres*
EMP: 15 **EST:** 1947
SALES (est): 910K **Privately Held**
SIC: 2395 Quilting & quilting supplies

(G-14279)
SANSOM STREET SOFT PRETZEL FAC
1532 Sansom St (19102-2822)
PHONE..................................215 569-3988
Michael Gabbepp, *Partner*
EMP: 4 **EST:** 2001
SALES (est): 300.3K **Privately Held**
SIC: 2052 Pretzels

(G-14280)
SANTEES LOVE
5353 Akron St (19124-1219)
PHONE..................................215 821-9679
Sharena Williams, *Owner*
EMP: 4 **EST:** 2016
SALES (est): 114.6K **Privately Held**
SIC: 2759 Screen printing

(G-14281)
SAPOR FOOD GROUP LLC
Also Called: Simply Good Jars
30 N 41st St Ste 570 (19104-2590)
PHONE..................................267 714-4382
Jared Cannon, *CEO*
EMP: 14 **EST:** 2016
SALES: 233.3K **Privately Held**
SIC: 3581 Automatic vending machines

(G-14282)
SATURNALIAN N Y A
1811 S 2nd St (19148-1915)
PHONE..................................215 271-9181
EMP: 3

SQ FT: 4,550
SALES (est): 134.4K **Privately Held**
SIC: 2099 Food preparations

(G-14283)
SB DISTRIBUTION CENTER INC
30 S 15th St Graham Bldg (19102)
PHONE...................................215 717-2600
Eric Mayberry, *President*
Robert Patterson, *Vice Pres*
Oskar Bjorner, *CFO*
EMP: 4
SALES (est): 211.3K **Privately Held**
SIC: 2741 Miscellaneous publishing
PA: Seabay Media Holdings Llc
120 Broadway Fl 6
New York NY 10271

(G-14284)
SB NEW YORK INC
30 S 15th St Fl 14 (19102-4806)
PHONE...................................215 717-2600
Mike Greger, *Manager*
EMP: 26 **Privately Held**
SIC: 2711 Newspapers, publishing & printing
HQ: Sb New York, Inc.
120 Broadway
New York NY 10271
212 457-7790

(G-14285)
SCOOPERMAN WATER ICE INC
4603 Conshohocken Ave (19131-1513)
PHONE...................................267 623-8494
Gail Moore, *Principal*
EMP: 8
SALES (est): 95.9K **Privately Held**
SIC: 5812 2052 Snow cone stand; cones, ice cream

(G-14286)
SCOOPERMARKET INC
Also Called: Chelsea Plating Co
920 Pine St (19107-6128)
PHONE...................................215 925-1132
David Kieserman, *President*
EMP: 3
SQ FT: 6,000
SALES (est): 352.1K **Privately Held**
WEB: www.chelseaplating.com
SIC: 3471 Polishing, metals or formed products

(G-14287)
SCORECAST MEDICAL LLC
123 S Broad St Ste 1830 (19109-1026)
PHONE...................................877 475-1001
Gary Poole, *Mng Member*
EMP: 9
SALES: 3MM **Privately Held**
SIC: 7372 Application computer software

(G-14288)
SCREAM GRAPHIX INC
230 Nauldo Rd (19154-4332)
PHONE...................................215 638-3900
J Patrick Daly, *President*
Pat Daly, *Principal*
EMP: 6
SALES (est): 623.2K **Privately Held**
WEB: www.scrmx.com
SIC: 2759 2396 Commercial printing; automotive & apparel trimmings

(G-14289)
SCRIBE INC (PA)
842 S 2nd St (19147-3430)
PHONE...................................215 336-5094
David Rech, *President*
Abigail Parker, *Editor*
S L Bowden, *Vice Pres*
Michael Miller, *Prdtn Mgr*
Lori Dillard, *Opers Staff*
EMP: 5
SALES (est): 6.7MM **Privately Held**
WEB: www.scribenet.com
SIC: 7374 7371 2731 Computer processing services; computer software writing services; book publishing

(G-14290)
SCULLIN GROUP INC
2005 Market St Ste 3120 (19103-7001)
PHONE...................................215 640-3330
Frank E Scullin, *President*

Colleen Daniel, *General Mgr*
Alicia Thorpe, *Manager*
EMP: 4
SQ FT: 750
SALES (est): 345.7K **Privately Held**
WEB: www.scullingroup.com
SIC: 2759 Financial note & certificate printing & engraving

(G-14291)
SEAK INC
604 W York St (19133-2117)
PHONE...................................215 288-7209
Eng Seak, *President*
EMP: 3
SALES (est): 120.5K **Privately Held**
SIC: 2721 Periodicals

(G-14292)
SEARER SOLUTIONS INC
1315 Walnut St Ste 815 (19107-4708)
PHONE...................................302 475-6944
Michael Searer, *President*
EMP: 4
SALES (est): 420K **Privately Held**
WEB: www.searer.com
SIC: 7372 Application computer software

(G-14293)
SELECT MEDICAL SYSTEMS INC
Also Called: Km Custom Pack
1800 W Indiana Ave (19132-1603)
PHONE...................................215 207-9003
Edward J McLaughlin, *President*
Melissa McLaughlin, *Vice Pres*
▲ EMP: 12
SQ FT: 71,000
SALES (est): 1.5MM **Privately Held**
SIC: 2841 7389 Soap & other detergents; packaging & labeling services

(G-14294)
SERVICE DIE CUTNG & PACKG CORP
3250 Boudinot St (19134-1707)
P.O. Box 26866 (19134-6866)
PHONE...................................215 739-8809
Stanley Kuntz, *President*
Kathie Lehrich, *Corp Secy*
Jason Kuntz, *Vice Pres*
EMP: 10 EST: 1963
SQ FT: 37,000
SALES (est): 1.9MM **Privately Held**
WEB: www.servicedc.com
SIC: 2653 2657 Boxes, corrugated: made from purchased materials; display items, corrugated: made from purchased materials; folding paperboard boxes

(G-14295)
SH QUINTS SONS COMPANY (PA)
3725 Castor Ave (19124-5609)
PHONE...................................215 533-1988
Eric Sandberg, *President*
Harry Feby, *General Mgr*
Frank Smith, *Facilities Mgr*
Marianne Nichols, *Manager*
EMP: 17 EST: 1849
SQ FT: 30,000
SALES (est): 2.2MM **Privately Held**
WEB: www.quintco.com
SIC: 3555 3953 Printing plates; stencils, painting & marking; pads, inking & stamping

(G-14296)
SHANE CANDY CO
Also Called: Shane Candies
110 Market St (19106-3006)
PHONE...................................215 922-1048
Barry P Shane, *Owner*
EMP: 17 EST: 1892
SQ FT: 4,600
SALES: 450K **Privately Held**
WEB: www.shanecandies.com
SIC: 2064 5441 Candy & other confectionery products; candy, nut & confectionery stores

(G-14297)
SHAREDXPERTISE MEDIA LLC
123 S Broad St Ste 1930 (19109-1026)
PHONE...................................215 606-9520

Elliot H Clark,
EMP: 14
SALES (est): 1.1MM **Privately Held**
SIC: 2721 Magazines: publishing & printing

(G-14298)
SHARP COATINGS
Also Called: Crescent Paint Co
162 E Courtland St (19120-4441)
PHONE...................................215 324-8500
Barry E Krieger, *President*
Renee Krieger, *Vice Pres*
Bruce C Krieger, *Admin Sec*
EMP: 19
SQ FT: 43,672
SALES: 1.2MM **Privately Held**
SIC: 3089 Plastic containers, except foam; plastic kitchenware, tableware & houseware; plastic hardware & building products

(G-14299)
SHEET METAL WKRS LOCAL UN 19
1301 S Columbus Blvd (19147-5505)
PHONE...................................215 952-1999
Gary Masino, *President*
EMP: 3
SALES: 8.9MM **Privately Held**
SIC: 8631 3444 Labor union; sheet metalwork

(G-14300)
SHEINMAN PROVISION CO INC
4192 Viola St 96 (19104-1028)
PHONE...................................305 592-0300
Stan Rultenberg, *President*
EMP: 22 EST: 1922
SQ FT: 3,500
SALES (est): 1.9MM **Privately Held**
SIC: 2013 Corned beef from purchased meat; roast beef from purchased meat; frankfurters from purchased meat

(G-14301)
SHELTER STRUCTURES INC
2043 Locust St Fl 2b (19103-5662)
PHONE...................................267 239-5906
Patricia Smail, *President*
Charles Smail, *Vice Pres*
EMP: 5
SQ FT: 1,200
SALES (est): 2.9MM **Privately Held**
WEB: www.shelterstructures.com
SIC: 3448 Buildings, portable: prefabricated metal

(G-14302)
SHEREEN FUEL INC
9998 Frankford Ave (19114-1928)
PHONE...................................215 632-2160
Tszieal Singh, *Principal*
EMP: 2
SALES (est): 220.4K **Privately Held**
SIC: 2869 Fuels

(G-14303)
SIEMENS GAMESA RENEWABLE
1801 Market St Ste 2700 (19103-1609)
PHONE...................................215 665-9810
Glenn Smith,
EMP: 5
SALES (corp-wide): 95B **Privately Held**
SIC: 3621 Windmills, electric generating
HQ: Siemens Gamesa Renewable Energy Usa, Inc.
1150 Northbrook Dr # 300
Feasterville Trevose PA 19053
215 710-3100

(G-14304)
SIGN MAKER INC
Also Called: Sign-A-Rama
6909 Frankford Ave (19135-1613)
PHONE...................................215 676-6711
William Vivona, *Owner*
EMP: 3
SALES: 130K **Privately Held**
SIC: 3993 Signs, not made in custom sign painting shops

(G-14305)
SILARX PHARMACEUTICALS INC
13200 Townsend Rd (19154-1014)
PHONE...................................845 225-1500
EMP: 3
SALES (corp-wide): 684.5MM **Publicly Held**
SIC: 2834 Pharmaceutical preparations
HQ: Silarx Pharmaceuticals, Inc
1033 Stoneleigh Ave
Carmel NY 10512
845 352-4020

(G-14306)
SILBER BRUSH MANUFACTURING CO
1342 E Montgomery Ave (19125-2702)
PHONE...................................215 634-4063
Robert Buraczyk, *President*
EMP: 3 EST: 1929
SQ FT: 4,600
SALES (est): 267.9K **Privately Held**
SIC: 3991 Brushes, household or industrial

(G-14307)
SIMKAR LLC (HQ)
700 Ramona Ave (19120-4600)
PHONE...................................215 831-7700
David Coyne, *Vice Pres*
Rich Elles, *Senior Buyer*
Bob Ashworth, *Controller*
Ken Bopf, *VP Sales*
Jeffrey Hirsch, *Sales Staff*
◆ EMP: 189 EST: 1952
SQ FT: 200,000
SALES (est): 46.3MM **Privately Held**
WEB: www.simkar.com
SIC: 3646 5063 Fluorescent lighting fixtures, commercial; electrical apparatus & equipment
PA: Neo Lights Holdings, Inc.
700 Ramona Ave
Philadelphia PA 19120
215 831-7700

(G-14308)
SIMONS BROS COMPANY
2424 E Sergeant St (19125-3115)
PHONE...................................215 426-9901
Henry N Keyser Sr, *President*
Mary Keyser, *Admin Sec*
EMP: 17
SQ FT: 8,000
SALES (est): 2MM **Privately Held**
WEB: www.simonsbrothers.com
SIC: 3911 5944 Jewelry, precious metal; jewelry stores

(G-14309)
SINNOTT INDUSTRIES INC
2060 Bennett Rd (19116-3096)
PHONE...................................215 677-7793
Thomas Sinnott, *President*
Richard Gagliana, *General Mgr*
EMP: 6
SQ FT: 15,000
SALES (est): 954.4K **Privately Held**
SIC: 3317 Steel pipe & tubes

(G-14310)
SIP BULLETIN LLC
1920 S 23rd St (19145-2601)
PHONE...................................267 235-3359
Chunhua Jin, *Principal*
EMP: 3
SALES (est): 125.2K **Privately Held**
SIC: 2711 Newspapers, publishing & printing

(G-14311)
SIR SPEEDY INC
7573 Haverford Ave (19151-2228)
PHONE...................................215 877-8888
Marvin Lerner, *Branch Mgr*
EMP: 10
SALES (corp-wide): 5.6MM **Privately Held**
SIC: 2752 Commercial printing, lithographic
HQ: Sir Speedy, Inc.
26722 Plaza
Mission Viejo CA 92691
949 348-5000

▲ = Import ▼=Export
◆ =Import/Export

(G-14312)
SIRE PRESS LLC
3237 Amber St Ste 2 (19134-3227)
PHONE..................................267 909-9233
Chris Romano, *Principal*
EMP: 4 **EST:** 2008
SALES (est): 284.9K **Privately Held**
SIC: 2741 Miscellaneous publishing

(G-14313)
SIU KING
Also Called: Tung Yee Restaurant Supply
1024 Buttonwood St (19123-3703)
PHONE..................................215 769-9863
King Siu, *Owner*
EMP: 15
SALES (est): 1.1MM **Privately Held**
SIC: 2599 3441 Restaurant furniture,
wood or metal; fabricated structural metal

(G-14314)
SKYLINE BEAUTY SUPPLY INC
505 Washington Ave (19147-4027)
PHONE..................................215 468-1888
Vincent Nguyen, *President*
EMP: 3
SQ FT: 3,000
SALES (est): 420.5K **Privately Held**
WEB: www.skylinebeautysupply.com
SIC: 2844 Manicure preparations

(G-14315)
SKYROC LLC
122 N Lambert St (19103-1107)
PHONE..................................215 840-5466
Timothy Dugan, *CEO*
EMP: 4
SALES (est): 141.6K **Privately Held**
SIC: 7372 7389 Educational computer
software;

(G-14316)
SMITHKLINE BEECHAM CORPORATION
1 Franklin Sq (19106-1509)
PHONE..................................215 751-4000
Howard Marsh, *President*
EMP: 3
SALES (est): 638.5K
SALES (corp-wide): 39.8B **Privately Held**
SIC: 2834 Pharmaceutical preparations
HQ: Glaxosmithkline Llc
5 Crescent Dr
Philadelphia PA 19112
215 751-4000

(G-14317)
SMK & SON INC
Also Called: Beer Stop
4252 Rising Sun Ave (19140-2633)
PHONE..................................215 455-7867
Michael Tan, *President*
EMP: 4
SQ FT: 12,000
SALES (est): 340K **Privately Held**
SIC: 2082 5921 Beer (alcoholic beverage); beer (packaged)

(G-14318)
SNAP KITCHEN 3 LLC
1901 Callowhill St (19130-4150)
PHONE..................................215 845-0001
EMP: 6
SALES (corp-wide): 106.6MM **Privately Held**
SIC: 2099 Food preparations
PA: Snap Kitchen 3, Llc
9330 United Dr Ste 100
Austin TX 78758
512 428-4000

(G-14319)
SNB PUBLISHING INC
9908 Roosevelt Blvd (19115-1705)
PHONE..................................215 464-2500
Svitlana Shkuro, *President*
Natalia Simonova, *Vice Pres*
EMP: 5
SALES (est): 440K **Privately Held**
SIC: 2721 Magazines: publishing & printing

(G-14320)
SOCIETY FOR INDUSTRIAL & APPLI (PA)
Also Called: S I A M
3600 Market St Fl 6 (19104-2669)
PHONE..................................215 382-9800
Nicholas Higham, *President*
Bridget Ahad, *Vice Pres*
Melannie Aquino, *Vice Pres*
Travaughn Bain, *Vice Pres*
Frankie Camacho, *Vice Pres*
EMP: 69
SQ FT: 20,000
SALES: 12.5MM **Privately Held**
SIC: 2731 8621 2721 Book publishing;
education & teacher association; periodicals

(G-14321)
SOFTBOSS CORP (PA)
Also Called: Safeguard Systems
1735 Market St Ste A459 (19103-7501)
PHONE..................................215 563-7488
Nathan Wenograd, *President*
EMP: 8
SALES (est): 942.2K **Privately Held**
WEB: www.safeguardsystemsusa.com
SIC: 7389 7372 Fire extinguisher servicing; prepackaged software

(G-14322)
SOFTSTUF INC
333 Bainbridge St Fl 2 (19147-1542)
P.O. Box 40245 (19106-0245)
PHONE..................................215 627-8850
Maria Rothweiler, *President*
EMP: 4
SQ FT: 2,000
SALES (est): 468.2K **Privately Held**
WEB: www.softstuf.com
SIC: 7372 Application computer software

(G-14323)
SOLO SOUNDZ LLC
1714 N 61st St (19151-3923)
PHONE..................................610 931-8448
Tylill Black,
EMP: 3
SALES (est): 85.7K **Privately Held**
SIC: 2741 7371 ; computer software development & applications

(G-14324)
SOLTRACE INC
Also Called: Tracey
910 Fairmount Ave 950 (19123-1913)
PHONE..................................215 765-5700
James Trachtenberg, *President*
Dominic Costanzo, *Vice Pres*
EMP: 22
SQ FT: 25,000
SALES (est): 1.8MM **Privately Held**
WEB: www.soltrace.com
SIC: 2511 Wood household furniture

(G-14325)
SOUTHERN GRAPHIC SYSTEMS LLC
2781 Roberts Ave (19129-1218)
PHONE..................................215 843-2243
Anthony Maginnis, *Manager*
EMP: 110
SALES (corp-wide): 272.7MM **Privately Held**
SIC: 3555 Printing plates
HQ: Southern Graphic Systems, Llc
626 W Main St Ste 500
Louisville KY 40202
502 637-5443

(G-14326)
SPACE 1026
1026 Arch St (19107-3002)
PHONE..................................215 574-7630
Janet Kissinger, *Principal*
EMP: 4 **EST:** 1988
SALES (est): 302.4K **Privately Held**
SIC: 3949 Skateboards

(G-14327)
SPARK THERAPEUTICS INC (PA)
3737 Market St Ste 1300 (19104-5543)
PHONE..................................888 772-7560
Jeffrey D Marrazzo, *CEO*
Steven Altschuler, *Ch of Bd*
Katherine A High, *President*
John Furey, *COO*
Nakia Vance, *COO*
EMP: 136
SQ FT: 6,500
SALES: 64.7MM **Publicly Held**
SIC: 2836 Biological products, except diagnostic

(G-14328)
SPARKS CUSTOM RETAIL LLC (DH)
2828 Charter Rd (19154-2111)
PHONE..................................215 602-8100
Scott Tarte, *CEO*
David Sudjian, *President*
Jeff Harrow, *Chairman*
Jeffery Buttson, *Vice Pres*
Mike Ellery, *Vice Pres*
◆ **EMP:** 34
SQ FT: 60,000
SALES (est): 24.4MM **Privately Held**
WEB: www.dmsfixtures.com
SIC: 2542 Office & store showcases & display fixtures

(G-14329)
SPARKS EXHBITS ENVRNMENTS CORP (DH)
2828 Charter Rd (19154-2111)
PHONE..................................215 676-1100
Jeff K Harrow, *Ch of Bd*
Scott Tarte, *President*
Breana Dang, *Business Mgr*
Cregg Cannon, *Vice Pres*
Kristy Elisano, *Vice Pres*
▲ **EMP:** 78
SQ FT: 260,000
SALES (est): 24.3MM **Privately Held**
SIC: 3999 7389 Advertising display products; trade show arrangement

(G-14330)
SPARKS EXHIBITS HOLDING CORP (HQ)
2828 Charter Rd (19154-2111)
PHONE..................................215 676-1100
Scott Tarte, *CEO*
Gail Hummel, *COO*
Robert Ginsburg, *Senior VP*
Bill Cembor, *Project Mgr*
Barry Walton, *Manager*
◆ **EMP:** 4
SQ FT: 500
SALES (est): 70.4MM **Privately Held**
SIC: 2653 Corrugated & solid fiber boxes

(G-14331)
SPD ELECTRICAL SYSTEMS INC
Also Called: L-3 SPD Electrical Systems
13500 Roosevelt Blvd (19116-4201)
PHONE..................................215 698-6426
J C Wilcox, *President*
EMP: 480
SALES (est): 94.1MM
SALES (corp-wide): 10.2B **Publicly Held**
WEB: www.powercontrolsystemsgroup.com
SIC: 3612 3699 3613 Transformers, except electric; electrical equipment & supplies; switchgear & switchboard apparatus
PA: L3 Technologies, Inc.
600 3rd Ave Fl 34
New York NY 10016
212 697-1111

(G-14332)
SPECIALTY RETAIL FABRICATORS (PA)
901 N Penn St Apt P402 (19123-3121)
PHONE..................................215 477-5977
John Morrow, *President*
EMP: 10
SQ FT: 9,000
SALES: 550K **Privately Held**
WEB: www.kioskcartbuilders.com
SIC: 3441 1542 Building components, structural steel; commercial & office building, new construction; commercial & office buildings, renovation & repair

(G-14333)
SPECTRUM MICROWAVE INC
Also Called: API Technologies Corp
2707 Black Lake Pl (19154-1008)
PHONE..................................215 464-0586
Dick Soughworth, *CEO*
Walter Witt, *Manager*
EMP: 78
SQ FT: 19,950
SALES (corp-wide): 333.6MM **Privately Held**
WEB: www.spectrummicrowave.com
SIC: 3679 3625 3613 3825 Microwave components; switches, electronic applications; circuit breakers, air; instruments to measure electricity; household audio & video equipment; current-carrying wiring devices
HQ: Spectrum Microwave, Inc.
8061 Avonia Rd
Fairview PA 16415
814 474-4300

(G-14334)
SPENCER INDUSTRIES INC
80 Red Lion Rd (19115-1011)
PHONE..................................215 634-2700
Steven Glickman, *President*
EMP: 11
SQ FT: 16,000
SALES (est): 1.2MM **Privately Held**
SIC: 2759 3993 Engraving; letters for signs, metal

(G-14335)
SPRINGER ADIS US LLC
400 Market St Ste 700 (19106-2532)
PHONE..................................215 574-2201
Patty Goldstein, *Opers Staff*
Tom Lee, *Finance*
Nadine Lemmens, *Director*
EMP: 5
SALES (corp-wide): 1.7B **Privately Held**
SIC: 2721 2731 Trade journals: publishing only, not printed on site; magazines: publishing only, not printed on site; books: publishing only
HQ: Springer Adis Us, Llc
233 Spring St Fl 6
New York NY 10013
212 460-1500

(G-14336)
SRC ELASTOMERICS INC (PA)
Also Called: Stockwell Elastomerics
4749 Tolbut St (19136-1512)
PHONE..................................215 335-2049
William B Stockwell, *President*
Paul Gannon, *Vice Pres*
Margaret Robinson, *Purch Mgr*
Tom Jeffords, *Engineer*
Sandra Ratcliffe, *Treasurer*
◆ **EMP:** 80 **EST:** 1919
SQ FT: 47,373
SALES: 19.4MM **Privately Held**
SIC: 2822 2824 3069 Silicone rubbers; elastomeric fibers; sheeting, rubber or rubberized fabric; weather strip, sponge rubber; tape, pressure sensitive: rubber

(G-14337)
SSM INDUSTRIES INC
Also Called: S SM
5238 Comly St (19135-4315)
PHONE..................................215 288-7777
Ron Schnell, *Branch Mgr*
EMP: 80
SQ FT: 28,800
SALES (corp-wide): 79.4MM **Privately Held**
SIC: 3444 Sheet metalwork
PA: Ssm Industries, Inc.
3401 Grand Ave
Pittsburgh PA 15225
412 777-5100

(G-14338)
ST BENJAMINS BREWING CO
1710 N 5th St (19122-2909)
PHONE..................................215 232-4305
Tim Patton, *Office Mgr*
EMP: 13
SALES (est): 1.8MM **Privately Held**
SIC: 2082 Malt beverages

(G-14339)
STAGESTEP INC
Also Called: Aeson Flooring
4701 Bath St Ste 46b (19137-2311)
PHONE..................................267 672-2900
F Randolph Swartz, *President*
▲ EMP: 15
SQ FT: 9,500
SALES (est): 2.2MM **Privately Held**
WEB: www.stagestep.com
SIC: 3999 7331 Theatrical scenery; direct
mail advertising services

(G-14340)
STAINLESS STEEL SERVICES INC
4330 Sepviva St (19124-4126)
PHONE..................................215 831-1471
Albert D Stewart III, *President*
▲ EMP: 11
SQ FT: 15,000
SALES (est): 1.5MM **Privately Held**
SIC: 3471 Polishing, metals or formed
products

(G-14341)
STATEMENT WALLS LLC
Also Called: Statementwalls.com
1045 W Glenwood Ave (19133-1805)
PHONE..................................267 266-0869
Daniel Montanez, *CEO*
Alissa Thomas, *Exec VP*
EMP: 3
SQ FT: 17,000
SALES (est): 151.2K **Privately Held**
SIC: 2396 2621 5231 3952 Fabric print-
ing & stamping; poster & art papers;
paint, glass & wallpaper; frames for
artists' canvases

(G-14342)
STATIONARY ENGRAVERS INC
2011 Frankford Ave (19125-1920)
P.O. Box 86, Oreland (19075-0086)
PHONE..................................215 739-3538
Kimberly Davis, *President*
EMP: 10
SALES (est): 891.9K **Privately Held**
WEB: www.stationeryengravers.com
SIC: 2759 Engraving

(G-14343)
STEINS PASCO BATTERY STARTER
Also Called: Steins Generator & Starter Svc
10069 Sandmeyer Ln (19116-3501)
PHONE..................................215 969-6900
Scott Herman,
EMP: 5
SQ FT: 15,000
SALES (est): 256.3K **Privately Held**
SIC: 3694 5063 5013 Battery charging al-
ternators & generators; motor controls,
starters & relays: electric; automotive bat-
teries

(G-14344)
STEL LIFE INC
1 S Broad St Ste 1010 (19107-3427)
PHONE..................................610 724-3688
Siddharth Kandan, *CEO*
Carlos Roque, *Principal*
EMP: 4
SALES (est): 214.9K **Privately Held**
SIC: 3823 Fluidic devices, circuits & sys-
tems for process control

(G-14345)
STEPHANIE MCCLAIN
Also Called: Scorpion Signs
600 Hermitage St (19128-2604)
PHONE..................................267 820-9273
Stephanie McClain, *Owner*
EMP: 5
SALES (est): 301.2K **Privately Held**
SIC: 3993 Electric signs; letters for signs,
metal; signs, not made in custom sign
painting shops

(G-14346)
STERIS CORPORATION
1725 N 6th St (19122-2912)
PHONE..................................215 763-8200
Walter M Rosebrough, *Principal*
Laurie Brlas, *Principal*

Renato G Tamaro, *Treasurer*
J Adam Zangerle, *Admin Sec*
EMP: 3
SALES (est): 115.3K **Privately Held**
SIC: 3842 Surgical appliances & supplies

(G-14347)
STERLING PAPER COMPANY
2155 Castor Ave (19134-2799)
PHONE..................................215 744-5350
Martin E Stein, *President*
Suzanne Faigen, *Vice Pres*
EMP: 60
SQ FT: 325,000
SALES (est): 10.8MM **Privately Held**
SIC: 3086 2631 2657 Plastics foam prod-
ucts; paperboard mills; food containers,
folding: made from purchased material

(G-14348)
STEVENSON-COOPER INC
1039 W Venango St (19140-4391)
PHONE..................................215 223-2600
Dennis Cooper, *President*
Shirley Cooper, *Admin Sec*
▼ EMP: 7 EST: 1863
SQ FT: 25,000
SALES (est): 1.3MM **Privately Held**
WEB: www.stevensoncooper.com
SIC: 2992 2999 Oils & greases, blending
& compounding; waxes, petroleum: not
produced in petroleum refineries

(G-14349)
STONE MILL RUG CO
1250 Adams Ave Ste 2 (19124-3992)
P.O. Box 21940 (19124-0940)
PHONE..................................215 744-2331
William Ford, *Partner*
Bob Ford, *Partner*
EMP: 4 EST: 1962
SQ FT: 4,000
SALES (est): 479.4K **Privately Held**
SIC: 2273 Rugs, braided & hooked

(G-14350)
STRASSHEIM GRPHIC DSIGN & PRES
1500 Spring Garden St (19130-4067)
PHONE..................................215 525-5134
Rachel E Strassheim, *President*
EMP: 14
SALES (est): 1.5MM **Privately Held**
SIC: 2741 Miscellaneous publishing

(G-14351)
STRATEGIC DEFENSE UNIT LLC
3460 Joyce St (19134-2622)
PHONE..................................267 591-0725
EMP: 3
SALES (est): 164K **Privately Held**
SIC: 3812 Defense systems & equipment

(G-14352)
STRETCH DEVICES INC
3401 I St Ste 1 (19134-1469)
PHONE..................................215 739-3000
Don Newman, *President*
Andrew Kelly, *Controller*
Andy Kelly, *Controller*
Ximena Pena, *Sales Staff*
Wende Standefer, *Sales Staff*
◆ EMP: 30
SQ FT: 33,000
SALES (est): 6.7MM **Privately Held**
WEB: www.stretchdevices.com
SIC: 3829 3552 Measuring & controlling
devices; frames, doubling & twisting, tex-
tile machinery

(G-14353)
SUN CHEMICAL CORPORATION
General Printing Ink Division
3301 W Hunting Park Ave (19132-1884)
PHONE..................................215 223-8220
Reginald McCray, *Purch Mgr*
Doddit Debourke, *Manager*
Paul Haigh, *Manager*
EMP: 100
SQ FT: 20,000
SALES (corp-wide): 7.1B **Privately Held**
WEB: www.sunchemical.com
SIC: 2893 Printing ink

HQ: Sun Chemical Corporation
35 Waterview Blvd Ste 100
Parsippany NJ 07054
973 404-6000

(G-14354)
SUN CHEMICAL CORPORATION
Also Called: Graphic Fine Color
3301 W Hunting Park Ave (19132-1884)
PHONE..................................215 223-8220
Robert Peters, *Manager*
EMP: 80
SALES (corp-wide): 7.1B **Privately Held**
WEB: www.sunchemical.com
SIC: 2893 Printing ink
HQ: Sun Chemical Corporation
35 Waterview Blvd Ste 100
Parsippany NJ 07054
973 404-6000

(G-14355)
SUN KEE TOFU FOOD CO
Also Called: Sunkee Tofu
448 N 12th St (19123-3718)
PHONE..................................215 625-3818
Fax: 215 351-8629
▲ EMP: 5 EST: 1991
SQ FT: 5,000
SALES (est): 500K **Privately Held**
SIC: 2099 Manufacture Tofu

(G-14356)
SUNOCO (R&M) LLC
3144 W Passyunk Ave (19145-5208)
PHONE..................................215 339-2000
V S Herzog, *Opers Mgr*
Ginci Kelly, *Branch Mgr*
EMP: 33
SALES (corp-wide): 54B **Publicly Held**
WEB: www.mvoil.com
SIC: 3559 2951 Petroleum refinery equip-
ment; asphalt paving mixtures & blocks
HQ: Sunoco (R&M), Llc
3801 West Chester Pike
Newtown Square PA 19073
215 977-3000

(G-14357)
SUPERFIT INC
211 N 13th St Fl 9 (19107-1608)
PHONE..................................215 391-4380
Gena Alulis, *CEO*
Eric Alulis, *President*
▲ EMP: 12
SQ FT: 7,000
SALES (est): 1.2MM **Privately Held**
WEB: www.superfitinc.com
SIC: 3911 Rings, finger: precious metal

(G-14358)
SUPERIOR PASTA COMPANY INC
Also Called: 9th Street Management Com-
pany
905 Christian St Fl 1 (19147-3807)
PHONE..................................215 627-3306
Cheryl Lomano, *President*
Joe Lomano, *Admin Sec*
EMP: 8
SALES (est): 796.9K **Privately Held**
WEB: www.superiorpasta.com
SIC: 2099 2098 Pasta, uncooked: pack-
aged with other ingredients; macaroni &
spaghetti; pasta & rice; health & dietetic
food stores; spaghetti & other pasta
sauce: packaged in cans, jars, etc.

(G-14359)
SUPPORT MCRCOMPUTERS ASSOC INC
Also Called: S.O.M.A.
1819 John F Kennedy Blvd # 460
(19103-1733)
PHONE..................................215 496-0303
Ed Blumenthal, *President*
Carol Blumenthal, *Vice Pres*
Barbara Bailine, *Admin Sec*
EMP: 18
SQ FT: 4,000

SALES (est): 4.3MM **Privately Held**
WEB: www.somacomputer.com
SIC: 7378 3577 7373 Computer & data
processing equipment repair/mainte-
nance; computer peripheral equipment repair & maintenance; printers & plotters;
systems integration services; computer
system selling services

(G-14360)
SUPRA OFFICE SOLUTIONS INC
5070 Parkside Ave # 3200 (19131-4750)
P.O. Box 201, Bala Cynwyd (19004-0201)
PHONE..................................267 275-8888
Charles Carter, *President*
Lin Thomas, *Chairman*
Ismail Shahid, *VP Finance*
EMP: 8
SALES (est): 4MM **Privately Held**
SIC: 2621 5045 5112 5021 Offset paper;
printers, computer; stationery & office
supplies; office supplies; office furniture

(G-14361)
SUPREME TRADING LTD
431 E Tioga St Fl 3 (19134-1118)
PHONE..................................215 739-2237
Josephine Chan, *President*
Ken Sheintoch, *Vice Pres*
▲ EMP: 24
SALES (est): 497.9K **Privately Held**
SIC: 2269 2389 Cloth mending, for the
trade; men's miscellaneous accessories

(G-14362)
SURE FOLD CO INC
600 E Erie Ave Bldg 4 (19134-1209)
PHONE..................................215 634-7480
Michael Duffy, *President*
EMP: 17
SQ FT: 21,000
SALES: 1.5MM **Privately Held**
SIC: 2269 Linen fabrics: dyeing, finishing &
printing

(G-14363)
SWEET ROLL STUDIO LLC
504 N 39th St Unit 1 (19104-4602)
PHONE..................................209 559-8219
Jasmine Marcial,
Travis Chandler,
Timothy Day,
EMP: 3
SALES (est): 149.9K **Privately Held**
SIC: 7372 Prepackaged software

(G-14364)
T A E LTD
Also Called: Active Edge
233 Church St (19106-4514)
PHONE..................................215 925-7860
Evan Sharps, *President*
Bonnie Sharps, *Vice Pres*
EMP: 5 EST: 1977
SQ FT: 2,000
SALES (est): 900K **Privately Held**
WEB: www.theactiveedge.com
SIC: 5137 2339 Sportswear, women's &
children's; women's & misses' athletic
clothing & sportswear

(G-14365)
T&T BUTTAS LLC
6616 N 20th St (19138-3117)
PHONE..................................833 251-1357
Taija Price,
EMP: 3
SALES (est): 59.2K **Privately Held**
SIC: 5963 5999 2844 2841 Cosmetic
sales, house-to-house; toilet preparations;
toilet preparations; soap & other deter-
gents

(G-14366)
TABA LABELS COMPANY
210 W Mentor St (19120-4115)
PHONE..................................215 455-9977
Tamer Babadagli, *Owner*
EMP: 5
SQ FT: 2,000
SALES (est): 290K **Privately Held**
SIC: 2679 2671 Labels, paper: made from
purchased material; packaging paper &
plastics film, coated & laminated

(G-14367)
TACTILE DESIGN GROUP LLC
Also Called: Tactile Group, The
109 S 13th St Ste 3n (19107-4846)
PHONE..................................215 732-2311
Marc Coleman, *CEO*
Jim Kiley-Zufelt, *Vice Pres*
Jim Zufelt, *Vice Pres*
Kevin Yonn, *Info Tech Mgr*
EMP: 10
SALES: 130K **Privately Held**
WEB: www.tactiledesigngroup.com
SIC: 5045 7371 7372 Computers; periph-
erals & software; custom computer pro-
gramming services; application computer
software

(G-14368)
TAFISCO INC
Also Called: Ready Aim Fire
7932 State Rd (19136-3408)
PHONE..................................215 493-3167
Debbie Osifat, *President*
EMP: 3
SALES (est): 204.2K **Privately Held**
SIC: 3273 Ready-mixed concrete

(G-14369)
TAL TECHNOLOGIES INC
Also Called: Taltech
2101 Brandywine St # 102 (19130-3152)
PHONE..................................215 496-0222
Thomas Lutz, *President*
Susan Rogers, *Vice Pres*
Mike Owen, *Sales Staff*
EMP: 25
SALES (est): 2.2MM **Privately Held**
WEB: www.taltech.com
SIC: 7372 7371 Application computer soft-
ware; custom computer programming
services

(G-14370)
TAN CLOTHING CO INC
1017 Race St Ste 3 (19107-1826)
PHONE..................................215 625-2536
Zhihong Tan, *President*
Zhi-Hong Tan, *President*
EMP: 20
SQ FT: 4,000
SALES (est): 1MM **Privately Held**
SIC: 2335 2339 2337 2325 Dresses,
paper: cut & sewn; slacks: women's,
misses' & juniors'; skirts, separate:
women's, misses' & juniors'; men's &
boys' trousers & slacks

(G-14371)
**TARGA PIPELINE OPER PARTNR
LP (DH)**
Also Called: Atlas Pipeline Oper Partnr LP
1845 Walnut St (19103-4708)
PHONE..................................412 489-0006
Edward Cohen, *CEO*
Sean McGrath, *CFO*
EMP: 5
SALES (est): 399.7MM **Publicly Held**
SIC: 1311 Crude petroleum & natural gas
production
HQ: Targa Pipeline Partners Lp
1000 Commerce Dr Ste 400
Pittsburgh PA 15275
877 950-7473

(G-14372)
**TARGA PIPELINE PARTNERS GP
LLC**
Also Called: Atlas Pipeline Partners GP LLC
1845 Walnut St Ste 1000 (19103-4733)
PHONE..................................215 546-5005
Joe Bob Perkins, *CEO*
Patrick McDonie, *President*
Jeffrey McParland, *President*
Robert Karlovich III, *CFO*
Gerald Shrader, *General Counsel*
EMP: 91
SALES (est): 3.3MM **Publicly Held**
SIC: 1311 Crude petroleum & natural gas
production
HQ: Targa Resources Partners Lp
1000 Louisiana St # 4300
Houston TX 77002

(G-14373)
TARSA THERAPEUTICS INC
8 Penn Ctr 1628 John F (19103)
PHONE..................................267 273-7940
David Brand, *President*
James Gilligan, *Principal*
Nicholas A Labella Jr, *Vice Pres*
George R Maurer, *Vice Pres*
EMP: 11
SALES (est): 2MM **Privately Held**
SIC: 2834 Solutions, pharmaceutical

(G-14374)
TASTY BAKING COMPANY (HQ)
Also Called: Tasty Kake
4300 S 26th St (19112-1608)
PHONE..................................215 221-8500
Charles P Pizzi, *President*
Robert V Brown, *Exec VP*
Paul D Ridder, *Vice Pres*
Eugene P Malinowski, *Treasurer*
Laurence Weilheimer, *Admin Sec*
▲ EMP: 40 EST: 1914
SALES (est): 252.4MM
SALES (corp-wide): 3.9B **Publicly Held**
WEB: www.tastykake.com
SIC: 2051 2052 Cakes, pies & pastries;
cakes, bakery: except frozen; pies, bak-
ery: except frozen; doughnuts, except
frozen; bakery products, dry; cookies;
pretzels
PA: Flowers Foods, Inc.
1919 Flowers Cir
Thomasville GA 31757
229 226-9110

(G-14375)
TASTY BAKING COMPANY
4300 S 26th St (19112-1608)
PHONE..................................215 221-8500
Scott Secor, *Manager*
EMP: 595
SALES (corp-wide): 3.9B **Publicly Held**
SIC: 2051 2052 Cakes, pies & pastries;
cakes, bakery: except frozen; pies, bak-
ery: except frozen; doughnuts, except
frozen; bakery products, dry; cookies;
pretzels
HQ: Tasty Baking Company
4300 S 26th St
Philadelphia PA 19112
215 221-8500

(G-14376)
TASTY TWISTERS INC
5002 Umbria St (19128-4347)
PHONE..................................215 487-7828
Athena Louca, *President*
Loucas Louca, *Vice Pres*
Betsy Econome, *Treasurer*
Laura Econome, *Admin Sec*
EMP: 5
SALES: 850K **Privately Held**
SIC: 5145 2052 Pretzels; pretzels

(G-14377)
**TAYLOR & FRANCIS GROUP
LLC**
Also Called: Journals
530 Walnut St Ste 850 (19106-3604)
PHONE..................................215 625-8900
Lisa Bouam, *Advt Staff*
Kevin Bradley, *Branch Mgr*
Jean Charroin, *Director*
Florence Lesavre, *Director*
EMP: 75
SALES (corp-wide): 2.3B **Privately Held**
SIC: 2741 Miscellaneous publishing
HQ: Taylor & Francis Group, Llc
6000 Broken Sound Pkwy Nw # 300
Boca Raton FL 33487
561 994-0555

(G-14378)
TAYLOR & FRANCIS INC (DH)
Also Called: International Publications Svc
530 Walnut St Ste 850 (19106-3604)
PHONE..................................215 625-8900
Kevin Bradley, *CEO*
Leonardo Cuellar, *Marketing Staff*
Veronica Sydnor, *Manager*
▼ EMP: 60

SALES (est): 23.7MM
SALES (corp-wide): 2.3B **Privately Held**
WEB: www.taylorandfrancis.com
SIC: 5192 2731 2741 Books; textbooks:
publishing only, not printed on site; mis-
cellaneous publishing

(G-14379)
TECHNICALLY MEDIA INC
601 Walnut St Ste 1200 (19106-3323)
PHONE..................................215 821-8745
Christopher Wink, *CEO*
Jeanette Lloyd, *Marketing Mgr*
EMP: 9
SALES (est): 395.1K **Privately Held**
SIC: 2711 Newspapers, publishing & print-
ing

(G-14380)
TELESIS THERAPEUTICS LLC
3711 Market St Ste 800 (19104-5532)
PHONE..................................215 848-4773
Maurice T Hampton, *Chairman*
EMP: 3 EST: 2015
SQ FT: 35,000
SALES (est): 172K **Privately Held**
SIC: 2834 Pharmaceutical preparations

(G-14381)
TERMINI BROTHERS INC (PA)
Also Called: Termini Brothers Bakery
1523 S 8th St 25 (19147-6401)
PHONE..................................215 334-1816
Vincent Termini, *President*
Barbara Termini, *Corp Secy*
Joseph Termini, *Vice Pres*
EMP: 25
SQ FT: 14,000
SALES (est): 4.7MM **Privately Held**
WEB: www.termini.com
SIC: 2051 5961 Bakery: wholesale or
wholesale/retail combined; pastries, e.g.
danish: except frozen; food, mail order

(G-14382)
TERRAIN MERCHANDISING LLC
5000 S Broad St (19112-1402)
PHONE..................................310 709-8784
Brooks Carroll, *General Mgr*
Brooks McKinley, *General Mgr*
Vito Romano, *General Mgr*
Amay Smith, *General Mgr*
Kristen Comley, *Principal*
▲ EMP: 10 EST: 2007
SALES (est): 1.9MM **Privately Held**
SIC: 3524 5719 Lawn & garden equip-
ment; kitchenware

(G-14383)
THACKRAY INC
2071 Byberry Rd (19116-3015)
PHONE..................................800 245-4387
James F Thackray, *Principal*
EMP: 4
SALES (est): 298K **Privately Held**
SIC: 3625 Crane & hoist controls, including
metal mill

(G-14384)
THATS TRUE MEDIA LLC
744 South St Ste 40 (19147-2023)
PHONE..................................215 437-3292
Khalif M Townes,
EMP: 8
SALES (est): 323.6K **Privately Held**
SIC: 2741

(G-14385)
**THD CONTRACTING SERVICE
LLC**
1921 N 54th St (19131-3239)
PHONE..................................215 626-1548
Luke Cawley, *President*
Ian Groves, *Principal*
Upton Peart-Cawley, *Principal*
EMP: 3
SALES (est): 122K **Privately Held**
SIC: 3585 1711 7623 Refrigeration &
heating equipment; refrigeration contrac-
tor; refrigeration service & repair

(G-14386)
THE M & A JOURNAL INC
1008 Spruce St Apt 2r (19107-6021)
PHONE..................................215 238-0506
John Close, *President*

EMP: 4
SALES (est): 307.5K **Privately Held**
WEB: www.themandajournal.com
SIC: 2711 8111 Commercial printing &
newspaper publishing combined; legal
services

(G-14387)
**THERMO FISHER SCIENTIFIC
INC**
1601 Cherry St Ste 1200 (19102-1305)
PHONE..................................215 964-6020
Chris Neitz, *Finance Dir*
Jo Webber, *Branch Mgr*
Joy Ricco, *Manager*
Bryan Inagaki, *Director*
Trish Meek, *Director*
EMP: 110
SALES (corp-wide): 24.3B **Publicly Held**
WEB: www.thermo.com
SIC: 3826 Analytical instruments
PA: Thermo Fisher Scientific Inc.
168 3rd Ave
Waltham MA 02451
781 622-1000

(G-14388)
THOMAS NAY LLC
3332 Red Lion Rd (19114-1211)
PHONE..................................215 613-8367
Thomas Nay, *President*
EMP: 10
SQ FT: 1,000
SALES: 400K **Privately Held**
SIC: 0781 3524 7211 Landscape serv-
ices; snowblowers & throwers, residential;
power laundries, family & commercial

(G-14389)
TIME MAN JR CORPORATION
5253 Roosevelt Blvd (19124-1720)
PHONE..................................856 244-1485
Jerome Brown, *Principal*
EMP: 96
SALES (est): 8MM **Privately Held**
SIC: 3571 Electronic computers

(G-14390)
TIMS PRINTING INC
148 W Ashdale St (19120-3408)
PHONE..................................215 208-0699
Timothy Gauthney, *President*
EMP: 5
SALES (est): 350K **Privately Held**
SIC: 2731 Pamphlets: publishing & printing

(G-14391)
**TITANIUM BRKG SOLUTIONS
LLC**
1003 W Duncannon Ave (19141-4023)
PHONE..................................267 506-6642
Alan Broadus,
EMP: 7 EST: 2010
SALES (est): 580K **Privately Held**
SIC: 3356 Titanium

(G-14392)
TJ COPE INC
Also Called: Atkore International
11500 Norcom Rd (19154-2303)
PHONE..................................215 961-2570
Charles E Humphreys, *President*
Brad McGee, *Senior VP*
David Fitzpatrick, *CFO*
◆ EMP: 65
SQ FT: 82,000
SALES (est): 16.1MM **Publicly Held**
WEB: www.alliedtube.com
SIC: 3499 Ladders, portable: metal
HQ: Allied Tube & Conduit Corporation
16100 Lathrop Ave
Harvey IL 60426
708 339-1610

(G-14393)
TMW ASSOCIATES INC
7352 Melrose St (19136-4209)
PHONE..................................215 624-3940
Thomas Walsh, *President*
EMP: 4
SQ FT: 3,000
SALES (est): 621.9K **Privately Held**
SIC: 5023 2591 Window covering parts &
accessories; drapery hardware & blinds &
shades

(G-14394)
TODAYS GRAPHICS INC
Also Called: TGI
4848 Island Ave (19153-3703)
PHONE.................................215 634-6200
John J Glacken Jr, *President*
Richard Elfreth, *Exec VP*
Scott Elfreth, *Exec VP*
Tony Erwin, *Project Mgr*
Bill Thompson, *Prdtn Mgr*
EMP: 55 EST: 1978
SQ FT: 40,000
SALES: 10MM **Privately Held**
WEB: www.tginc.com
SIC: 2752 Commercial printing, offset

(G-14395)
TOP OF LINE AUTO SVC II LLC
919 S 53rd St (19143-4107)
PHONE.................................215 727-6958
EMP: 4 EST: 2012
SALES: 249.3K **Privately Held**
SIC: 3531 Automobile wrecker hoists

(G-14396)
TOP SHOP
1220 Wolf St (19148-2910)
PHONE.................................610 622-6101
Ralph Smith, *President*
Rose Marie Smith, *Corp Secy*
EMP: 5
SQ FT: 12,500
SALES: 600K **Privately Held**
SIC: 2599 2541 2511 2431 Factory furni-
ture & fixtures; wood partitions & fixtures;
showcases, except refrigerated: wood;
wood household furniture; millwork

(G-14397)
TORGEMAN GABI
42 S 11th St (19107-3624)
PHONE.................................215 563-0882
Gabi Torgeman, *Owner*
EMP: 4
SALES: 100K **Privately Held**
SIC: 2386 Coats & jackets, leather &
sheep-lined

(G-14398)
TORRESDALE PHARMACY
3998 Red Lion Rd Ste 105 (19114-1439)
PHONE.................................215 612-5400
Donald Cooper, *Principal*
EMP: 6
SALES (est): 571.8K **Privately Held**
SIC: 2834 Druggists' preparations (phar-
maceuticals)

(G-14399)
TOTAL PLASTICS INC
Also Called: Everything Plastics
444 N 2nd St (19123-4210)
PHONE.................................877 677-8872
Kim Chap, *Branch Mgr*
EMP: 5
SALES (corp-wide): 869.1MM **Privately
Held**
SIC: 5162 3083 Plastics sheets & rods;
thermoplastic laminates: rods, tubes,
plates & sheet
HQ: Total Plastics Resources Llc
2810 N Burdick St Ste A
Kalamazoo MI 49004
269 344-0009

(G-14400)
TOWERVIEW HEALTH INC
2001 Market St Ste 2500 (19103-7036)
PHONE.................................715 771-9831
Rahul Jain, *CEO*
EMP: 8
SALES (est): 754.2K **Privately Held**
SIC: 3821 Laboratory apparatus & furniture

(G-14401)
**TOXICITY ASSSSORS GLOBL PA
LLC**
5070 Parkside Ave # 2103 (19131-4747)
PHONE.................................215 921-6972
Augustine Agyekum,
Kerryn Agyekum,
EMP: 6
SALES (est): 510K **Privately Held**
SIC: 2899 8071 ; testing laboratories

(G-14402)
TRAN HOANG
Also Called: 5th Street Live Poultry
4938 N 5th St (19120-3810)
PHONE.................................215 833-0923
Hoang Tran, *Principal*
EMP: 3
SALES (est): 121.5K **Privately Held**
SIC: 2015 Poultry slaughtering & process-
ing

(G-14403)
TRBZ INK LLC
2435 N Park Ave Ste 100 (19132-4009)
PHONE.................................267 918-2242
Audra Jeffers, *Managing Dir*
Carey King, *Finance*
EMP: 5 EST: 2013
SQ FT: 1,000
SALES (est): 265.8K **Privately Held**
SIC: 2261 2396 5961 Screen printing of
cotton broadwoven fabrics; screen print-
ing on fabric articles;

(G-14404)
TRE-RAY CASES INC
Also Called: Philly Case Co
2409 S Water St (19148-4134)
PHONE.................................215 551-6811
Maryann Barbati, *CEO*
Vincent Barbati, *President*
EMP: 10
SALES: 950K **Privately Held**
WEB: www.phillycase.com
SIC: 3161 Cases, carrying

(G-14405)
TRECO INCORPORATED
Also Called: Treco-Fibematics
3313 Stokley St (19140-4714)
PHONE.................................215 226-0908
Ivan S Grossman, *President*
EMP: 10
SQ FT: 168,000
SALES (est): 1.9MM **Privately Held**
WEB: www.trecofibematics.com
SIC: 2679 Paper products, converted

(G-14406)
TRENT INC
201 Leverington Ave (19127-1295)
PHONE.................................215 482-5000
L J Silverthorn, *Ch of Bd*
Frances Koenig, *President*
Janey Barett, *Corp Secy*
Patricia A Flocco, *Vice Pres*
EMP: 15 EST: 1927
SQ FT: 42,000
SALES: 1.1MM **Privately Held**
WEB: www.trentheat.com
SIC: 3567 Heating units & devices, indus-
trial: electric

(G-14407)
TRI STATE GOLF INC
2421 S Philip St (19148-4016)
P.O. Box 37214 (19148-7214)
PHONE.................................215 200-7000
Joseph Burkhardt, *President*
Clare Burkhardt, *Vice Pres*
EMP: 5
SALES: 63K **Privately Held**
SIC: 2721 Magazines: publishing only, not
printed on site

(G-14408)
**TRI-STATE DOOR AND
HARDWARE**
Also Called: Doors Unlimited
318 W Hunting Park Ave (19140-2626)
PHONE.................................215 455-2100
J Gary Fromm, *President*
Mike Kutys, *Vice Pres*
Carol Fromm, *Admin Sec*
EMP: 9
SQ FT: 70,000
SALES: 810K **Privately Held**
WEB: www.doors1.com
SIC: 3442 5211 Metal doors; doors, storm:
wood or metal

(G-14409)
TRIAXIAL STRUCTURES INC
507 E Roumfort Rd (19119-1035)
PHONE.................................215 248-0380
Richard M Dow, *Principal*
EMP: 3
SALES (est): 197.1K **Privately Held**
SIC: 3676 Electronic resistors

(G-14410)
TRIDEX TECHNOLOGY LTD
4125 Whitaker Ave (19124-4239)
PHONE.................................484 388-5000
Daniel Stern, *President*
Thomas Travia, *Director*
Tom Travia, *Director*
EMP: 13
SALES (est): 2.7MM **Privately Held**
SIC: 3699 Electrical equipment & supplies

(G-14411)
TRIOMI INC
1317 S 10th St (19147-5618)
PHONE.................................215 756-2771
Michael Battaglia, *CEO*
EMP: 3
SALES (est): 117.4K **Privately Held**
SIC: 3845 Electrocardiographs

(G-14412)
TRIPLE PLAY SPORTS
827 S 9th St (19147-2822)
PHONE.................................215 923-5466
Frank Larosa, *Owner*
Frank M Larosa, *Owner*
Dewey Larosa, *Co-Owner*
EMP: 10 EST: 1971
SQ FT: 4,000
SALES (est): 732.5K **Privately Held**
WEB: www.tripleplaysports.com
SIC: 7299 2759 Stitching, custom; com-
mercial printing

(G-14413)
TRUSTEES OF THE UNIV OF PA
Also Called: Pennsylvania Gazette
3533 Locust Walk (19104-6226)
PHONE.................................215 898-5555
John Prendergast, *Manager*
EMP: 5
SALES (corp-wide): 9.1MM **Privately
Held**
WEB: www.med.upenn.edu
SIC: 2711 8221 Newspapers; university
PA: The Trustees Of The University Of
Pennsylvania
3451 Walnut St Rm 440a
Philadelphia PA 19104
215 898-5000

(G-14414)
TURBO SOFTWARE LLC
5450 Wissahickon Ave 553b (19144-5221)
PHONE.................................215 490-6806
Ibidapo Lawal,
EMP: 3
SALES (est): 135.8K **Privately Held**
SIC: 7372 Utility computer software

(G-14415)
TWENTY61 LLC
Also Called: Shopmuse
812 S Saint Bernard St # 3 (19143-3309)
PHONE.................................215 370-7076
David Salkin,
EMP: 4 EST: 2015
SALES (est): 92.7K **Privately Held**
SIC: 5961 7372 General merchandise,
mail order; application computer software

(G-14416)
UE LIFESCIENCES INC
3711 Market St (19104-5504)
PHONE.................................631 980-8340
Mihir Shah, *President*
Matthew Campisi, *Vice Pres*
▼ EMP: 3
SALES: 200K **Privately Held**
SIC: 3841 7389 Surgical & medical instru-
ments;

(G-14417)
UMOJA ERECTORS LLC
926 N 19th St (19130-1537)
PHONE.................................215 235-7662
Alburn H Brown,
EMP: 3
SALES (est): 623.3K **Privately Held**
SIC: 3531 Construction machinery

(G-14418)
UNI-PRO INC (PA)
Also Called: Universal Fire Protection
7330 Tulip St (19136-4216)
PHONE.................................610 668-9191
Paul Seidel, *President*
EMP: 18
SALES (est): 3.5MM **Privately Held**
WEB: www.uni-pro.com
SIC: 3441 5099 Fabricated structural
metal; safety equipment & supplies

(G-14419)
UNIFLEX HOLDINGS INC
2900 Grant Ave (19114-2310)
PHONE.................................516 932-2000
Andy Wilson, *CEO*
Robert Cunningham, *Vice Pres*
Rick Gettlin, *CFO*
EMP: 20
SQ FT: 44,000
SALES (est): 3.3MM
SALES (corp-wide): 96.2MM **Privately
Held**
WEB: www.uniflexbags.com
SIC: 2673 2674 2672 Plastic & pliofilm
bags; bags: uncoated paper & multiwall;
coated & laminated paper
HQ: Uniflex Holdings, Llc
1600 Caleds Ext Ste 135
Hauppauge NY 11788

(G-14420)
**UNITED COLOR
MANUFACTURING INC**
Also Called: Plant
2940 E Tioga St (19134-6106)
PHONE.................................215 423-2527
Kevin McClellan, *Manager*
EMP: 14
SQ FT: 15,000
SALES (corp-wide): 7.9MM **Privately
Held**
SIC: 2865 Color pigments, organic
PA: United Color Manufacturing, Inc.
660 Newtown Yardley Rd # 205
Newtown PA 18940
215 860-2165

(G-14421)
UNITED METAL TRADERS INC
5240 Comly St (19135-4386)
P.O. Box 8938 (19135-0938)
PHONE.................................215 288-6555
David Ingber, *President*
Steven Ingber, *Vice Pres*
Rosalind Ingber, *Admin Sec*
EMP: 25
SQ FT: 50,000
SALES (est): 5.8MM **Privately Held**
WEB: www.unitedmetaltraders.com
SIC: 5093 4953 3341 Ferrous metal
scrap & waste; nonferrous metals scrap;
refuse systems; secondary nonferrous
metals

(G-14422)
**UNITED RESEARCH LABS INC
(DH)**
Also Called: Url Distribution
1100 Orthodox St (19124-3168)
PHONE.................................215 535-7460
Richard H Roberts, *President*
Brendan Magrab, *President*
Kurt Nielsen, *Exec VP*
Dwight D Hanshew Jr, *Senior VP*
Gregory K Hayer, *Senior VP*
EMP: 29
SALES (est): 5.7MM
SALES (corp-wide): 1.1B **Privately Held**
SIC: 2834 Mfg Pharmaceutical Prepara-
tions
HQ: Url Pharma, Inc
1100 Orthodox St
Philadelphia PA 19124
215 288-6500

(G-14423)
UNITED STATES DEPT OF NAVY
Also Called: Naval Foundry Propeller Center
1701 Kitty Hawk Ave (19112-1805)
PHONE.................................215 897-3537
Bruce Bucari, *Engineer*
EMP: 150 **Publicly Held**
SIC: 3366 Copper foundries

▲ = Import ▼=Export
◆ =Import/Export

HQ: United States Department Of The Navy
1200 Navy Pentagon
Washington DC 20350

(G-14424)
UNITED THEATRICAL SERVICES
16 E Hartwell Ln (19118-3419)
PHONE.....................................215 242-2134
Lawrence J Fitzkee, *President*
Patricia Fitzkee, *Corp Secy*
EMP: 8
SALES (est): 162.5K **Privately Held**
SIC: 7922 3599 3531 Scenery rental, theatrical; custom machinery; winches

(G-14425)
UNIVERSAL AWNINGS & SIGNS INC
3119 Boudinot St (19134-2316)
PHONE.....................................215 634-7150
Moises Perez Hernandez, *Owner*
EMP: 3
SALES (est): 545.5K **Privately Held**
SIC: 5039 3993 Awnings; signs & advertising specialties

(G-14426)
UNIVERSAL FLUIDS INC
3010 E Ontario St (19134-6308)
PHONE.....................................267 639-2238
Albert Junkets, *President*
EMP: 3 EST: 2010
SALES (est): 310.4K **Privately Held**
SIC: 3492 Fluid power valves & hose fittings

(G-14427)
UNIVERSAL TRANSFERS INC
3800 Jasper St (19124-5536)
PHONE.....................................215 744-6227
Kim Pathemore, *President*
John Mc Clay, *Vice Pres*
William Royer, *Vice Pres*
Kelly Taylor, *Vice Pres*
EMP: 20 EST: 1997
SQ FT: 16,000
SALES: 1MM **Privately Held**
SIC: 2752 Transfers, decalcomania or dry; lithographed

(G-14428)
UNIVERSITY CITY REVIEW INC
Also Called: Weekly Press
3927 Walnut St Fl 3 (19104)
PHONE.....................................215 222-2846
Robert Christian, *President*
EMP: 8
SALES (est): 460K **Privately Held**
WEB: www.weeklypress.com
SIC: 2711 Newspapers

(G-14429)
UNIVERSITY COPY SERVICE INC
5070 Parkside Ave Unit 66 (19131-4750)
PHONE.....................................215 898-5574
Larry Mapp Sr, *President*
Luerell D Mapp, *Vice Pres*
EMP: 9
SQ FT: 1,800
SALES (est): 1.4MM **Privately Held**
WEB: www.ucscopy.com
SIC: 2752 7334 2791 2789 Commercial printing, offset; photocopying & duplicating services; typesetting; bookbinding & related work

(G-14430)
UNLOCKED ENTERTAINMENT TECH
1735 Market St Ste 3750 (19103-7532)
PHONE.....................................267 507-6028
Vernon Mears, *President*
EMP: 6 EST: 2000
SALES (est): 310.8K **Privately Held**
SIC: 7372 Educational computer software

(G-14431)
URBAN OUTFITTERS WHOLESALE INC (HQ)
5000 S Broad St (19112-1495)
PHONE.....................................215 454-5500
Richard A Hayne, *President*
Freeman M Zausner, *COO*
Glen T Senk, *Vice Pres*

Frank J Conforti, *CFO*
Eric Artz, *Treasurer*
EMP: 6 EST: 1987
SALES (est): 5.9MM
SALES (corp-wide): 3.9B **Publicly Held**
SIC: 5139 2329 3089 Shoes; bathing suits & swimwear: men's & boys'; plastic kitchenware, tableware & houseware
PA: Urban Outfitters, Inc.
5000 S Broad St
Philadelphia PA 19112
215 454-5500

(G-14432)
URBAN TEES INC DBA SOHO G
2741 E Country Club Rd (19131-2831)
PHONE.....................................646 295-8923
EMP: 3
SALES (est): 114.4K **Privately Held**
SIC: 2759 Screen printing

(G-14433)
URL PHARMA INC (HQ)
1100 Orthodox St (19124-3168)
PHONE.....................................215 288-6500
Richard Roberts, *President*
Dr Kurt Nielsen, *Exec VP*
Greg Jordan, *Opers Staff*
Richard Kremer MD, *Finance*
Dorothy Fitzgerald, *Manager*
EMP: 32
SQ FT: 175,000
SALES (est): 37.9MM
SALES (corp-wide): 1.1B **Privately Held**
SIC: 2834 5122 Pharmaceutical preparations; pharmaceuticals
PA: Sun Pharmaceutical Industries Limited
Sun House, Plot No. 201 B/1, Western
Express Highway,
Mumbai MH 40006
224 324-4324

(G-14434)
US BOILER
3633 I St (19134-1451)
PHONE.....................................215 535-8900
Larry Steingard, *President*
EMP: 3
SALES (est): 136.7K **Privately Held**
SIC: 5722 5075 3585 Air conditioning room units, self-contained; warm air heating equipment & supplies; heating equipment, complete

(G-14435)
US CUSTOM WIRING LLC
1501 N 18th St (19121-4212)
PHONE.....................................856 905-0250
Randolph Smith, *Principal*
EMP: 3
SALES (est): 224.7K **Privately Held**
SIC: 3357 Aluminum wire & cable

(G-14436)
VALDEZ FOODS INC
1815 N 2nd St (19122-2305)
PHONE.....................................215 634-6106
Perfecto Valdez Jr, *President*
Juanito Valdez, *Treasurer*
Dorothy Matteucci, *Admin Sec*
EMP: 12 EST: 1936
SQ FT: 3,600
SALES (est): 1.2MM **Privately Held**
SIC: 2032 Chinese foods: packaged in cans, jars, etc.

(G-14437)
VANS INC
1455 Franklin Mills Cir (19154-3131)
PHONE.....................................215 632-2481
Vanessa Vega, *Branch Mgr*
EMP: 10
SALES (corp-wide): 11.8B **Publicly Held**
SIC: 3021 Canvas shoes, rubber soled
HQ: Vans, Inc.
1588 S Coast Dr
Costa Mesa CA 92626
855 909-8267

(G-14438)
VANZEL INC
2900 N 18th St (19132-2122)
PHONE.....................................215 223-1000
Norman Fischell, *President*
Bart Kline, *Vice Pres*
Marc Fischell, *Admin Sec*

▲ EMP: 9 EST: 1950
SALES (est): 1MM **Privately Held**
SIC: 3599 5084 8711 Custom machinery; industrial machinery & equipment; mechanical engineering

(G-14439)
VENTURA FOODS LLC
650 W Sedgley Ave (19140-5528)
PHONE.....................................215 223-8700
Earnest Albert, *President*
EMP: 7 **Privately Held**
WEB: www.venturafoods.com
SIC: 2035 Dressings, salad: raw & cooked (except dry mixes)
PA: Ventura Foods, Llc
40 Pointe Dr
Brea CA 92821

(G-14440)
VENUS VIDEO
6301 Passyunk Ave (19153-3511)
PHONE.....................................215 937-1545
Bob Strong, *President*
EMP: 4
SALES (est): 204K **Privately Held**
SIC: 5994 5731 7372 News dealers & newsstands; video recorders, players, disc players & accessories; prepackaged software

(G-14441)
VERIZON PENNSYLVANIA INC
4860 W Jefferson St (19131-4785)
PHONE.....................................215 879-7898
Malik Waliyyudin, *Manager*
EMP: 68
SALES (corp-wide): 130.8B **Publicly Held**
SIC: 4813 8721 2741 1731 Local telephone communications; billing & bookkeeping service; directories, telephone: publishing only, not printed on site; voice, data & video wiring contractor; telecommunication equipment repair (except telephones)
HQ: Verizon Pennsylvania Llc
1717 Arch St Lbby 3
Philadelphia PA 19103
212 395-1000

(G-14442)
VESUVIUS U S A CORPORATION
8701 Torresdale Ave (19136-1521)
P.O. Box 39255 (19136-0255)
PHONE.....................................215 708-7404
Amel Polosi, *Manager*
EMP: 3
SALES (corp-wide): 2.2B **Privately Held**
WEB: www.vesuvius.com
SIC: 3297 Nonclay refractories
HQ: Vesuvius U S A Corporation
1404 Newton Dr
Champaign IL 61822
217 351-5000

(G-14443)
VEXCON CHEMICALS INC
7240 State Rd (19135-1412)
PHONE.....................................215 332-7709
Darryl Manuel, *President*
Clifford Platt, *Vice Pres*
John Breska, *Sales Staff*
Bonnie Burkholder, *Sales Staff*
◆ EMP: 20
SQ FT: 75,000
SALES (est): 4.4MM **Privately Held**
WEB: www.vexcon.com
SIC: 2819 2851 Industrial inorganic chemicals; paints & allied products

(G-14444)
VEYKO DESIGN INC
1600 N Amrcn St Phldlphia Philadelphia (19122)
PHONE.....................................215 928-1349
Richard Goloveyko, *President*
Lisa Neely, *Vice Pres*
Helen Goldblatt, *Manager*
EMP: 7
SQ FT: 28,000
SALES (est): 1.3MM **Privately Held**
WEB: www.veyko.com
SIC: 1799 3499 Ornamental metal work; metal household articles

(G-14445)
VIC AUTO TECH PLACE
10100 Bustleton Ave (19116-3704)
PHONE.....................................215 969-2083
Natalie Zarashenka, *Principal*
Natalie Darashenka, *Principal*
EMP: 3
SALES (est): 194.3K **Privately Held**
SIC: 7538 3469 General automotive repair shops; automobile license tags, stamped metal

(G-14446)
VICTOR SUN CTRL OF PHLADELPHIA
4101 G St (19124-5117)
PHONE.....................................215 743-0800
Suzanne B Patrizi, *President*
Marianne Patrizi, *Corp Secy*
Donna Patrizi, *Treasurer*
EMP: 30 EST: 1958
SQ FT: 33,000
SALES (est): 4.8MM **Privately Held**
WEB: www.victorsun.com
SIC: 3442 3354 Storm doors or windows, metal; aluminum extruded products

(G-14447)
VINCENT GIORDANO CORP
Also Called: Vincent Giordano Prosciutto
2600 Washington Ave (19146-3834)
PHONE.....................................215 467-6629
Guy Giordano, *President*
Bruce Belack, *Vice Pres*
John McVey, *Vice Pres*
▲ EMP: 85
SQ FT: 50,000
SALES (est): 57.7MM **Privately Held**
WEB: www.vgiordano.com
SIC: 2013 Roast beef from purchased meat; corned beef from purchased meat; pastrami from purchased meat

(G-14448)
VIP TECH LLC
2900 Hedley St (19137)
PHONE.....................................267 582-1554
Steven Guadalupe, *Owner*
EMP: 4
SQ FT: 3,500
SALES (est): 167.3K **Privately Held**
WEB: www.hostwithvip.com
SIC: 7373 3571 7389 7371 Turnkey vendors, computer systems; electronic computers; design services; software programming applications

(G-14449)
VIRGO INVESTMENT LLC
Also Called: Minuteman Press
1717 S Broad St (19148-1527)
PHONE.....................................215 339-1596
Jude Arijaje,
EMP: 10
SALES (est): 2.1MM **Privately Held**
SIC: 2752 Commercial printing, lithographic

(G-14450)
VIRIDOR GLOBAL
733 Winton St (19148-3255)
PHONE.....................................202 360-1617
EMP: 3
SALES (est): 160.3K **Privately Held**
SIC: 2673 Mfg Bags-Plastic/Coated Paper

(G-14451)
VISION GRINDING & TOOL CO
4572 Ditman St (19124-3453)
PHONE.....................................215 744-5069
Kenneth Oettinger, *Owner*
EMP: 5
SQ FT: 3,000
SALES (est): 356.9K **Privately Held**
SIC: 3599 Machine shop, jobbing & repair

(G-14452)
VISION OPTICS
2658 Germantown Ave (19133-1619)
PHONE.....................................267 639-5773
EMP: 3
SALES (est): 267K **Privately Held**
SIC: 3827 Optical instruments & lenses

(G-14453)
VITALTRAX LLC
3401 Market St Ste 200 (19104-3358)
PHONE..................................610 864-0211
Zikria Syed, *CEO*
Paul Elisii, *CFO*
EMP: 8
SALES (est): 225.2K Privately Held
SIC: 7372 Business oriented computer software

(G-14454)
VITOLS TOOL & MACHINE CORP
10082 Sandmeyer Ln (19116-3502)
PHONE..................................215 464-8240
Robert Vitols, *President*
Ingrid Stemme, *Vice Pres*
Valda Amoroso, *Admin Sec*
Debbie Cassidy, *Admin Sec*
EMP: 35 EST: 1962
SQ FT: 60,000
SALES (est): 7MM Privately Held
WEB: www.vitolsgroup.com
SIC: 3599 Machine shop, jobbing & repair

(G-14455)
VOICESTAR INC
1315 Walnut St Ste 1532 (19107-4724)
PHONE..................................267 514-0000
Todd Lieberman, *CEO*
ARI Jacoby, *President*
Max Sobol, *COO*
EMP: 14
SQ FT: 250
SALES (est): 1.7MM
SALES (corp-wide): 85.2MM Publicly Held
WEB: www.voicestar.com
SIC: 3661 PBX equipment, manual or automatic
PA: Marchex, Inc.
　520 Pike St Ste 2000
　Seattle WA 98101
　206 331-3300

(G-14456)
WADE TECHNOLOGY INCORPORATED
Also Called: Ls Zittle Company
445 N 11th St (19123-3722)
PHONE..................................215 765-2478
James Wade, *President*
EMP: 4 EST: 1919
SQ FT: 2,787
SALES (est): 230K Privately Held
WEB: www.waderowland.com
SIC: 3471 Electroplating & plating

(G-14457)
WAKEFERN FOOD CORP
Also Called: Shoprite of Oxford & Levick
6301 Oxford Ave (19111-5366)
PHONE..................................215 744-9500
Frank Goodwin, *Manager*
EMP: 100
SALES (corp-wide): 7.6B Privately Held
SIC: 5411 5912 2051 Supermarkets, chain; drug stores & proprietary stores; bread, cake & related products
PA: Wakefern Food Corp.
　5000 Riverside Dr
　Keasbey NJ 08832
　908 527-3300

(G-14458)
WARREN INDUSTRIES INCORPORATED (PA)
Also Called: Warren Knight Instr Co Div
2045 Bennett Rd (19116-3090)
PHONE..................................215 464-9300
John H Warren III, *President*
Ed Markowski, *Technology*
Margaret Rudzinski, *Admin Asst*
EMP: 7
SQ FT: 13,500
SALES (est): 2.5MM Privately Held
WEB: www.nasurvey.com
SIC: 3829 Meteorological instruments

(G-14459)
WARREN INDUSTRIES INCORPORATED
North American Survey Sup Co
2045 Bennett Rd (19116-3090)
PHONE..................................215 969-5011

Bob Marron, *General Mgr*
John Warren, *Branch Mgr*
EMP: 15
SALES (corp-wide): 2.5MM Privately Held
WEB: www.nasurvey.com
SIC: 3829 Meteorological instruments
PA: Warren Industries, Incorporated
　2045 Bennett Rd
　Philadelphia PA 19116
　215 464-9300

(G-14460)
WARRIOR FASHIONS INC
513 South St Frnt (19147-1656)
PHONE..................................215 925-7905
Sage Werbock, *Manager*
EMP: 3
SALES (corp-wide): 988.5K Privately Held
SIC: 2253 Knit outerwear mills
PA: Warrior Fashions Inc
　6714 Bustleton Ave
　Philadelphia PA 19149
　215 332-4141

(G-14461)
WARRIOR WIPER WRAPS LLC
3608 Woodhaven Rd Apt 1 (19154-2637)
PHONE..................................720 577-9499
Fredrick Williams, *Principal*
EMP: 4
SALES (est): 213.3K Privately Held
SIC: 2396 Automotive & apparel trimmings

(G-14462)
WAUSAU PAPER CORP (DH)
2929 Arch St Ste 2600 (19104-2863)
PHONE..................................866 722-8675
Donald E Lewis, *President*
Kevin S Gorman, *Vice Pres*
Dumitrache Martinez, *VP Finance*
EMP: 58 EST: 2015
SALES: 352MM
SALES (corp-wide): 7.6B Privately Held
WEB: www.wausaupaper.com
SIC: 2621 Towels, tissues & napkins: paper & stock
HQ: Essity Professional Hygiene North America Llc
　984 Winchester Rd
　Neenah WI 54956
　920 727-3770

(G-14463)
WAYNE MILLS COMPANY INC (HQ)
130 W Berkley St (19144-3691)
PHONE..................................215 842-2134
Martin Heilman Jr, *President*
Laura Diamond, *Corp Secy*
Wayne Heilman, *Vice Pres*
Roland Brubaker, *Prdtn Mgr*
Jim Jones, *Prdtn Mgr*
▲ EMP: 60 EST: 1910
SQ FT: 80,000
SALES: 10.4MM
SALES (corp-wide): 20.4MM Privately Held
WEB: www.waynemills.com
SIC: 2241 Narrow fabric mills
PA: Wayne Industries, Inc.
　1105 N Market St Ste 1300
　Wilmington DE 19801
　302 478-6160

(G-14464)
WELDSALE COMPANY LLC
2151 Dreer St (19125-1918)
PHONE..................................215 739-7474
J Cletus Cunningham, *Principal*
Cletus J Cunningham, *Principal*
Paul D Cunningham,
▲ EMP: 7
SQ FT: 3,200
SALES (est): 1.2MM Privately Held
WEB: www.outdoors.com
SIC: 3548 Welding & cutting apparatus & accessories

(G-14465)
WERTHER PARTNERS LLC (PA)
9990 Global Rd (19115-1006)
PHONE..................................215 677-5200
Daniel Werther, *CEO*
EMP: 4

SALES (est): 1.9MM Privately Held
SIC: 2064 Candy & other confectionery products

(G-14466)
WESTINGHOUSE LIGHTING CORP (PA)
Also Called: Angelo Brothers Co
12401 Mcnulty Rd (19154-1004)
PHONE..................................215 671-2000
Stanley Angelo Jr, *Ch of Bd*
Raymond Angelo, *President*
John Angelo, *Exec VP*
Leonard Dubas, *Vice Pres*
Steven Isaacman, *Treasurer*
▲ EMP: 100
SQ FT: 235,000
SALES (est): 111MM Privately Held
WEB: www.westinghouselighting.com
SIC: 5063 3641 3645 Lighting fixtures; lighting fittings & accessories; electric lamps; residential lighting fixtures

(G-14467)
WESTON COMMERCIAL GROUP INC
6020 Spruce St (19139-3738)
PHONE..................................215 717-9675
Patricia Hayes, *CEO*
Brandon Weston, *President*
EMP: 5 EST: 2012
SALES: 400K Privately Held
SIC: 3999 7389 Soap dispensers;

(G-14468)
WESTROCK CP LLC
5000 Flat Rock Rd (19127-2004)
PHONE..................................215 984-7000
Mark Prestileo, *Manager*
EMP: 117
SALES (corp-wide): 16.2B Publicly Held
WEB: www.smurfit-stone.com
SIC: 2631 Paperboard mills
HQ: Westrock Cp, Llc
　1000 Abernathy Rd
　Atlanta GA 30328

(G-14469)
WESTWAY FEED PRODUCTS LLC
Also Called: Westway Terminal Company
2900 E Allegheny Ave (19134-6394)
PHONE..................................215 425-3707
Manny Delia, *General Mgr*
EMP: 10
SALES (corp-wide): 8.1B Privately Held
WEB: www.westway.com
SIC: 2048 Prepared feeds
HQ: Westway Feed Products Llc
　365 Canal St Ste 2929
　New Orleans LA 70130
　504 934-1850

(G-14470)
WESWORLD FABRICATIONS INC
3441 Old York Rd (19140-5324)
PHONE..................................215 455-5015
Charles Barnett, *President*
Olga Barnett, *Vice Pres*
EMP: 4
SALES (est): 582K Privately Held
SIC: 3441 Fabricated structural metal

(G-14471)
WFC & C INC
Also Called: Lore's Chocolate
34 S 7th St (19106-2317)
PHONE..................................215 627-3233
John A Walter Jr, *President*
Claudette Walter, *Corp Secy*
John A Walter Sr, *Vice Pres*
EMP: 15
SQ FT: 1,900
SALES (est): 1.2MM Privately Held
WEB: www.loreschocolates.com
SIC: 5441 2064 2066 Candy; candy & other confectionery products; chocolate & cocoa products

(G-14472)
WHARTON SCHOOL UNIV OF PA
Knowledge Wharton
3620 Locust Walk Rm 305 (19104-6302)
PHONE..................................215 746-7846
Mukul Pandya, *Exec Dir*

EMP: 133
SALES (corp-wide): 5.9MM Privately Held
SIC: 2741
PA: The Wharton School University Of Pennsylvania
　3819 Chestnut St Ste 300
　Philadelphia PA 19104
　215 746-4626

(G-14473)
WHISPERING LEAF INC
5835 Stockton Rd (19138-1901)
PHONE..................................267 437-2991
Pearl Fisher, *Principal*
EMP: 20
SALES (est): 734.1K Privately Held
WEB: www.whisperingleaf.com
SIC: 2731 Book publishing

(G-14474)
WILLIAM J LABB SONS INC
Also Called: Labb Machine
4617 Milnor St (19137-1112)
PHONE..................................215 289-3450
Bill Wallace, *Vice Pres*
Janet Welsh, *Office Mgr*
Olga Wallace, *Executive*
EMP: 24 EST: 1940
SQ FT: 10,000
SALES (est): 4.4MM Privately Held
WEB: www.labbmachine.com
SIC: 3599 Machine shop, jobbing & repair

(G-14475)
WILLIAM PLANGE
Also Called: AJW Jamaican and American Food
4507 N Broad St Unit 1 (19140-1215)
PHONE..................................215 303-0069
William Plange, *Owner*
Jason Plange, *Co-Owner*
EMP: 3
SALES (est): 65K Privately Held
SIC: 5812 2099 American restaurant; spices, including grinding

(G-14476)
WILLIAMSON COSTUME COMPANY
Also Called: Pierre's Costumes
211 N 3rd St (19106-1901)
PHONE..................................215 925-7121
Toll Free:..................................888 -
Richard Williamson, *President*
Jennifer Valosen, *General Mgr*
EMP: 10
SQ FT: 10,000
SALES (est): 913.7K Privately Held
WEB: www.costumers.com
SIC: 5699 2389 Costumes, masquerade or theatrical; wigs, toupees & wiglets; masquerade costumes; theatrical costumes

(G-14477)
WILLIER ELC MTR REPR CO INC
Also Called: Penn Electric Motor Company
3080 Emerald St (19134-3145)
PHONE..................................215 426-9920
Tom Maguire, *Manager*
EMP: 8
SALES (corp-wide): 9.7MM Privately Held
WEB: www.willierelectric.com
SIC: 7694 7699 5063 Electric motor repair; aircraft flight instrument repair; motors, electric
PA: Willier Electric Motor Repair Co., Inc.
　1 Linden Ave
　Gibbsboro NJ 08026
　856 627-3535

(G-14478)
WILLOW TERRACE
1 Penn Blvd (19144-1476)
PHONE..................................215 951-8500
Jody Gross, *Principal*
Alex Ringkamp, *Administration*
EMP: 5
SALES (est): 621.9K Privately Held
SIC: 1389 Oil consultants

▲ = Import ▼=Export
◆ =Import/Export

(G-14479)
WINDLE MECH SOLUTIONS INC
Also Called: Excel
6601 Marsden St (19135-2725)
PHONE..........................215 624-8600
Peter M Windle, *President*
EMP: 8
SALES (est): 1.1MM **Privately Held**
SIC: 3469 Machine parts, stamped or pressed metal

(G-14480)
WISSAHICKON BREWING COMPANY
7524 Lawn St (19128-4129)
PHONE..........................267 239-6596
Timothy Gill, *President*
EMP: 4 EST: 2015
SALES (est): 187K **Privately Held**
SIC: 2082 Near beer

(G-14481)
WM C HALDEMAN
4713 N Broad St (19141-2105)
PHONE..........................215 324-2400
William C Haldeman, *Owner*
EMP: 7
SALES (est): 443.8K **Privately Held**
SIC: 3469 Automobile license tags, stamped metal

(G-14482)
WOLTERS KLUWER HEALTH INC (DH)
Also Called: Lippincott Williams & Wilkin
2001 Market St Ste 5 (19103-7044)
PHONE..........................215 521-8300
Diana L Nole, *CEO*
Robert Becker, *President*
Bruce C Lenz, *Corp Secy*
Richard J Parker, *Vice Pres*
Sheralynn J Sloan, *Train & Dev Mgr*
▲ EMP: 250
SALES (est): 167.7MM
SALES (corp-wide): 5.2B **Privately Held**
WEB: www.lww.com
SIC: 2721 2731 2741 7372 Trade journals: publishing only, not printed on site; books: publishing only; miscellaneous publishing; prepackaged software; business consulting
HQ: Wolters Kluwer United States Inc.
2700 Lake Cook Rd
Riverwoods IL 60015
847 580-5000

(G-14483)
WOOD MACHINERY MFRS AMER
Also Called: Wmma
100 N 20th St Fl 4 (19103-1462)
PHONE..........................215 564-3484
Kenneth R Hutton, *Exec VP*
EMP: 4
SALES (est): 950K **Privately Held**
SIC: 3553 Woodworking machinery

(G-14484)
WOOD MOULDING AND MILLWORK
316 W Hunting Park Ave (19140-2626)
PHONE..........................215 324-8400
Malcolm Pascal, *President*
David Pascal, *Vice Pres*
Richard Solomon, *Vice Pres*
▲ EMP: 10
SALES (est): 1.6MM **Privately Held**
SIC: 2431 Moldings, wood: unfinished & prefinished

(G-14485)
WOODCRAFT PRODUCTS CO INC (PA)
241 W Wyoming Ave (19140-1529)
PHONE..........................215 329-2793
Andrew Jacoby Jr, *President*
Eda Jacoby, *Shareholder*
▲ EMP: 10 EST: 1947
SQ FT: 650,000
SALES (est): 2.3MM **Privately Held**
WEB: www.woodcraftproducts.com
SIC: 2426 Frames for upholstered furniture, wood

(G-14486)
WOODCRAFT PRODUCTS CO INC
4057 G St (19124-5115)
PHONE..........................215 426-6123
Andrew Jacoby, *Branch Mgr*
EMP: 10
SALES (est): 1.6MM
SALES (corp-wide): 2.3MM **Privately Held**
WEB: www.woodcraftproducts.com
SIC: 2426 Frames for upholstered furniture, wood
PA: Woodcraft Products Co Inc
241 W Wyoming Ave
Philadelphia PA 19140
215 329-2793

(G-14487)
WORLD MANUFACTURING INC
3000 C St (19134-2909)
PHONE..........................215 426-0500
Joseph D Sisti Jr, *CEO*
Joseph Sisti III, *Principal*
David Aydelotte, *Vice Pres*
EMP: 40
SQ FT: 90,000
SALES (est): 4.6MM **Privately Held**
SIC: 3999 Advertising display products

(G-14488)
WORLD POETRY INC
Also Called: AMERICAN POETRY REVIEW, THE
1906 Rittenhouse Sq (19103-5735)
PHONE..........................215 309-3722
Stephen Berg, *President*
David Bonanno, *Corp Secy*
Arthur Vogelsang, *Vice Pres*
EMP: 4
SALES (est): 142.2K **Privately Held**
WEB: www.aprweb.org
SIC: 2721 Magazines: publishing only, not printed on site

(G-14489)
WORLDWIDE FABRICATING LTD (PA)
Also Called: Worldwide Window Fashions
171 E Hunting Park Ave (19124-6002)
P.O. Box 46945 (19160-6945)
PHONE..........................215 455-2266
Andy Yuen, *President*
Robert Caplan, *Vice Pres*
David Carpinella, *Sales Staff*
▲ EMP: 60 EST: 1995
SQ FT: 23,000
SALES (est): 10.8MM **Privately Held**
WEB: www.worldwidewindowfashions.com
SIC: 2591 Window blinds

(G-14490)
WRIGHT APPELLATE SERVICES LLC
1015 Chestnut St Ste 517 (19107-4305)
PHONE..........................215 733-9870
Frederick W Wright, *President*
EMP: 5
SALES (est): 423.2K **Privately Held**
WEB: www.wrightappellate.com
SIC: 2759 Commercial printing

(G-14491)
WUXI APPTEC INC
4000 S 26th St (19112-1613)
PHONE..........................215 334-1380
EMP: 4 **Privately Held**
SIC: 2834 Pharmaceutical preparations
HQ: Wuxi Apptec, Inc.
2540 Executive Dr
Saint Paul MN 55120
651 675-2000

(G-14492)
WUXI APPTEC INC
4701 League Island Blvd (19112-1220)
PHONE..........................215 218-5500
Felix Hsu, *Senior VP*
Sylvester Williams III, *Director*
EMP: 99 EST: 2009
SALES (est): 5.5MM **Privately Held**
SIC: 2836 Biological products, except diagnostic

(G-14493)
WWB HOLDINGS LLC
Also Called: Phillyvoice.com
1431 Walnut St (19102)
PHONE..........................267 519-4500
Lexie Norcross, *Managing Dir*
L Norcross, *Exec Dir*
EMP: 30
SQ FT: 5,000
SALES (est): 745.2K **Privately Held**
SIC: 2711 Newspapers, publishing & printing

(G-14494)
XRAY EYEWEAR
215 S Broad St Ste 203 (19107-5313)
PHONE..........................215 545-3361
Maia Nechemia, *CEO*
EMP: 6
SALES (est): 236.5K **Privately Held**
SIC: 3851 Ophthalmic goods

(G-14495)
XSER COATINGS LLC
3711 Spring Garden St (19104-2353)
PHONE..........................732 754-9887
John Braddock, *Mng Member*
EMP: 4
SALES: 1.2MM **Privately Held**
SIC: 3479 Etching & engraving

(G-14496)
XYNATECH MFG CO (PA)
Also Called: National Metalcrafters
1405 E Oxford St (19125-4421)
PHONE..........................215 423-0804
James T Redd, *President*
Peirson Kang, *Vice Pres*
EMP: 11 EST: 1950
SQ FT: 20,000
SALES (est): 1.5MM **Privately Held**
SIC: 3599 Machine shop, jobbing & repair

(G-14497)
Y H NEWSPAPER INC
1531 Locust St (19102-3721)
PHONE..........................215 546-0372
Chun H Won, *Principal*
EMP: 3
SALES (est): 167.6K **Privately Held**
SIC: 2711 Newspapers

(G-14498)
YARMOUTH CONSTRUCTION
4938 N 11th St (19141-3506)
PHONE..........................267 592-1432
Sheldon Bullock, *CEO*
David Bullock, *Vice Pres*
EMP: 4
SALES (est): 154.7K **Privately Held**
SIC: 3088 1771 1799 7692 Plastics plumbing fixtures; exterior concrete stucco contractor; coating, caulking & weather, water & fireproofing; automotive welding

(G-14499)
YBC HOLDINGS INC (PA)
500 Spring Garden St (19123-2833)
PHONE..........................215 634-2600
Thomas Kehoe, *President*
Nancy Barton, *Corp Secy*
Trevor Prichett, *COO*
William Barton, *Vice Pres*
Chris Hancq, *Opers Staff*
▲ EMP: 15
SALES (est): 4.5MM **Privately Held**
SIC: 2082 Beer (alcoholic beverage)

(G-14500)
YINGLI GREEN ENRGY AMRICAS INC
Also Called: Yingli Solar
2 Logan Sq Ste 1900 (19103-2602)
PHONE..........................212 609-4909
Cindy Hu, *CEO*
Liansheng Miao, *Chairman*
Andrew Christian, *Controller*
▲ EMP: 10
SALES (est): 2.3MM **Privately Held**
SIC: 3674 Solar cells

HQ: Baoding Tianwei Yingli New Energy Resources Co., Ltd.
No.3399, North Chaoyang Avenue, Gaokai Dist.
Baoding 07105
312 892-9778

(G-14501)
YOH INDUSTRIAL LLC
1500 Spring Garden St # 500 (19130-4067)
PHONE..........................215 656-2650
William Yoh, *Chairman*
EMP: 37 EST: 2012
SALES (est): 3.4MM **Privately Held**
SIC: 3599 Industrial machinery

(G-14502)
YOUNG AND BROTHERS CONSTUCTION
5952 Warrington Ave (19143-5218)
PHONE..........................215 852-5398
Dion Young, *Owner*
EMP: 3
SALES (est): 70K **Privately Held**
SIC: 3271 Concrete block & brick

(G-14503)
Z WOOD PRODUCTS CO INC
400 W Glenwood Ave (19140-5619)
PHONE..........................215 423-9891
Ernest Zagranichny, *President*
▲ EMP: 23
SQ FT: 75,000
SALES (est): 10.6MM **Privately Held**
SIC: 5031 2515 Lumber: rough, dressed & finished; box springs, assembled

(G-14504)
ZENTIS NORTH AMERICA LLC (HQ)
1741 Tomlinson Rd (19116-3847)
PHONE..........................215 676-3900
Brian Fox, *Branch Mgr*
◆ EMP: 100
SALES: 300MM
SALES (corp-wide): 789.1MM **Privately Held**
SIC: 2033 Canned fruits & specialties
PA: Zentis Gmbh & Co. Kg
Julicher Str. 177
Aachen 52070
241 476-00

(G-14505)
ZITNER CANDY CORP
3120 N 17th St (19132-2395)
PHONE..........................215 229-4990
Evan Prochniak, *Ch of Bd*
EMP: 25 EST: 1913
SQ FT: 125,000
SALES (est): 7MM **Privately Held**
SIC: 2064 Chocolate candy, except solid chocolate; fruit, chocolate covered (except dates)

(G-14506)
ZYNNIE BAKES
211 Mercer St (19125-3207)
PHONE..........................610 905-6283
EMP: 4
SALES (est): 210.5K **Privately Held**
SIC: 2051 Bread, cake & related products

Philipsburg
Centre County

(G-14507)
ADVANCED POWDER PRODUCTS INC
Also Called: A P P
301 Enterprise Dr (16866-3174)
PHONE..........................814 342-5898
Donald F Heaney, *President*
Tracy Potter, *Vice Pres*
EMP: 12
SQ FT: 5,000
SALES: 5MM **Privately Held**
WEB: www.advancedpowderproducts.com
SIC: 2899 Chemical preparations

(G-14508)
APEX HYDRAULIC & MACHINE INC
2859 Phlpsburg Bigler Hwy (16866-8124)
PHONE..................................814 342-1010
Adrian Powell, *President*
EMP: 12 EST: 1996
SQ FT: 20,000
SALES (est): 2.3MM **Privately Held**
WEB: www.apexhydraulic.com
SIC: 3569 5084 Bridge or gate machinery, hydraulic; industrial machinery & equipment

(G-14509)
BEST SOLUTIONS MED SYSTEMS LLC
516 Henrietta St (16866-2618)
PHONE..................................814 577-4184
David L Wilson, *Principal*
EMP: 4
SALES (est): 358K **Privately Held**
SIC: 3844 X-ray apparatus & tubes

(G-14510)
DIAMONDBACK AUTOMOTIVE ACC INC
Also Called: Diamondback Truck Covers
354 Enterprise Dr (16866-3174)
PHONE..................................800 935-4002
Ethan Wendle, *CEO*
Matthew Chverchko, *COO*
Ben Eltz, *Finance*
▲ EMP: 45
SALES (est): 2MM **Privately Held**
WEB: www.diamondbackcovers.com
SIC: 3714 Motor vehicle parts & accessories

(G-14511)
DOUGLAS EXPLOSIVES INC
2052 Phlpsburg Bigler Hwy (16866-8116)
PHONE..................................814 342-0782
Douglas Burnsworth, *President*
EMP: 30
SQ FT: 960
SALES (est): 6.6MM **Privately Held**
WEB: www.douglasdrillservices.com
SIC: 5169 2892 Explosives; explosives

(G-14512)
DRUCKER COMPANY INTL INC
168 Bradford Dr (16866)
PHONE..................................814 342-6210
Kenneth J Moscone, *President*
Kathleen Moscone, *Vice Pres*
Dennis Kennedy, *CFO*
▲ EMP: 23
SALES (est): 7.8MM **Privately Held**
WEB: www.druckerco.com
SIC: 3569 Centrifuges, industrial

(G-14513)
DRUCKER COMPANY LLC
Also Called: Qbc Dianostics
200 Shady Ln Ste 170 (16866-1986)
PHONE..................................814 692-7661
Ken Moscone, *President*
Craig Stout, *Vice Pres*
Melissa Ball, *Sales Staff*
Michael Weaver, *Admin Sec*
▲ EMP: 76 EST: 2004
SQ FT: 35,000
SALES: 21MM
SALES (corp-wide): 297MM **Privately Held**
SIC: 3821 Centrifuges, laboratory
PA: Madison Industries Holdings Llc
500 W Madison St Ste 3890
Chicago IL 60661
312 277-0156

(G-14514)
G-O-METRIC INCORPORATED
415 N 2nd St (16866-2103)
PHONE..................................814 376-6940
Aaron Teel, *President*
Jill Teel, *Vice Pres*
EMP: 9
SQ FT: 1,200
SALES: 1.1MM **Privately Held**
SIC: 3564 Filters, air: furnaces, air conditioning equipment, etc.

(G-14515)
GRAUCH ENTERPRISES INC
1878 Port Matilda Hwy (16866-3128)
PHONE..................................814 342-7320
Fred Grauch, *President*
EMP: 12
SQ FT: 11,000
SALES: 1MM **Privately Held**
WEB: www.grauch.com
SIC: 3599 Machine shop, jobbing & repair

(G-14516)
JUNIOR COAL CONTRACTING INC
2330 Six Mile Rd (16866-8203)
PHONE..................................814 342-2012
George Cowfer, *President*
Rise Cowfer, *Admin Sec*
EMP: 35
SALES (est): 4.4MM **Privately Held**
SIC: 1221 Bituminous coal surface mining

(G-14517)
KING COAL SALES INC (PA)
602 N Centre St (16866-1512)
P.O. Box 712 (16866-0712)
PHONE..................................814 342-6610
John A Decker, *President*
Tim Decker, *Vice Pres*
Timothy A Decker, *Vice Pres*
Joyce Kanour, *Admin Sec*
EMP: 20
SQ FT: 1,296
SALES: 8MM **Privately Held**
WEB: www.kingcoalsales.com
SIC: 5052 1221 Coal; strip mining, bituminous

(G-14518)
KONECRANES INC
200 Shady Ln Ste 150 (16866-1986)
PHONE..................................814 237-2663
Dee Rohrer, *Manager*
EMP: 14
SALES (corp-wide): 3.7B **Privately Held**
WEB: www.kciusa.com
SIC: 3536 Cranes, industrial plant
HQ: Konecranes, Inc.
4401 Gateway Blvd
Springfield OH 45502

(G-14519)
LEE INDUSTRIES INC
Also Called: Fluid Transfer
50 W Pine St (16866-2430)
P.O. Box 688 (16866-0688)
PHONE..................................814 342-0460
Robert W Montler, *President*
Joshua Montler, *Vice Pres*
Greg Wharton, *Vice Pres*
Jim Demchak, *Research*
Michael Dogal, *Engineer*
◆ EMP: 225 EST: 1927
SQ FT: 105,000
SALES (est): 63.5MM **Privately Held**
WEB: www.leeind.com
SIC: 3556 3559 3531 3494 Food products machinery; pharmaceutical machinery; chemical machinery & equipment; construction machinery; valves & pipe fittings; fabricated plate work (boiler shop); steel investment foundries

(G-14520)
NATIONAL FURNITURE ASSOC INC (PA)
Also Called: National Furniture Wholesaler
219 N Front St (16866-1605)
P.O. Box 707, State College (16804-0707)
PHONE..................................814 342-2007
Brian Mannino, *President*
Joseph Mannino, *Corp Secy*
Brandi McGarvey, *Exec VP*
▲ EMP: 6
SQ FT: 40,000
SALES (est): 1.3MM **Privately Held**
SIC: 2392 5021 Household furnishings; furniture

(G-14521)
NORTHSIDE MANUFACTURING INC
Also Called: Charles Navasky Co.
300 Shady Ln (16866-1944)
P.O. Box 728 (16866-0728)
PHONE..................................814 342-4638
Charles L Navasky, *President*
Jaye Navasky, *Vice Pres*
EMP: 50
SALES (est): 2.2MM **Privately Held**
SIC: 7389 2311 Cloth cutting, bolting or winding; men's & boys' suits & coats

(G-14522)
OLENICKS PRTG & PHOTOGRAPHY SP
122 N Front St Fl 1 (16866-1604)
PHONE..................................814 342-2853
James Olenick, *Owner*
EMP: 3
SALES: 150K **Privately Held**
SIC: 2752 2759 Commercial printing, offset; letterpress printing

(G-14523)
ORGANIC CLIMBING LLC
256 Enterprise Dr (16866-3173)
PHONE..................................651 245-1079
Josh Helke, *Principal*
EMP: 5
SALES (est): 287.6K **Privately Held**
SIC: 7032 2394 2392 Recreational camps; canvas & related products; laundry, garment & storage bags

(G-14524)
PHILIPSBURG JOURNAL
216 E Presqueisle St (16866-1641)
PHONE..................................814 342-1320
Phillip A Coy, *President*
EMP: 3
SALES (est): 120.5K **Privately Held**
SIC: 2711 Newspapers, publishing & printing

(G-14525)
REICHDRILL LLC
99 Troy Hawk Run Hwy (16866-8269)
P.O. Box 361 (16866-0361)
PHONE..................................814 342-5500
Patrick J Garrity, *Vice Pres*
James Hopkins, *Project Mgr*
Richard Pearce, *Engineer*
◆ EMP: 60
SQ FT: 50,000
SALES (est): 30.5MM **Privately Held**
SIC: 3532 3533 3339 Drills & drilling equipment, mining (except oil & gas); drilling tools for gas, oil or water wells; primary nonferrous metals

(G-14526)
SAUPP SIGNS CO LLC
220 New Liberty Rd (16866-8521)
PHONE..................................814 342-2100
Dillon Saupp Jr,
Robert Saupp,
EMP: 9
SALES: 150K **Privately Held**
SIC: 7312 3993 Billboard advertising; signs & advertising specialties

---

Phoenixville
Chester County

(G-14527)
AMERICAN ENGINEERS GROUP LLC
1220 Valley Forge Rd # 4 (19460-2676)
PHONE..................................484 920-8010
Vijay Gupta, *CEO*
Brent Basom, *Exec VP*
Joseph Nardella, *Vice Pres*
Andrew Parker, *Vice Pres*
Craig Welfer, *Vice Pres*
EMP: 4

SALES (est): 475.7K **Privately Held**
SIC: 8711 1389 8713 8748 Consulting engineer; civil engineering; construction & civil engineering; testing, measuring, surveying & analysis services; surveying services; environmental consultant; testing laboratories;

(G-14528)
AMERICAN INKS & COATINGS CORP
330 Pawlings Rd (19460-2683)
PHONE..................................610 933-5848
Jerry Moszley, *President*
Jerry Mosley, *President*
Mitch Baker, *Vice Pres*
William P Rimel III, *Vice Pres*
Rob Raeke, *Treasurer*
EMP: 95 EST: 1928
SQ FT: 66,000
SALES (est): 20.8MM
SALES (corp-wide): 21.6MM **Privately Held**
SIC: 2899 2851 2893 Chemical preparations; paints & allied products; gravure ink
PA: Mosley Holdings, Inc.
101a S Oak St
Sheridan AR 72150
870 942-2662

(G-14529)
BAYTER TECHNOLOGIES INC
30 Thayer Way (19460-6111)
PHONE..................................610 948-7447
Don Waasdorp, *President*
Herman Kessler, *Corp Secy*
Page Waasdorp, *Vice Pres*
EMP: 7
SALES: 350K **Privately Held**
SIC: 7389 3672 3841 Design services; printed circuit boards; medical instruments & equipment, blood & bone work

(G-14530)
BEE POSITIVE FOUNDATION
Also Called: Bee Positive Honey
497 Schuylkill Rd (19460-1894)
PHONE..................................484 302-8234
Issac Brown, *Principal*
Corrine Poulsen, *Co-Owner*
Jessica Vine, *Bookkeeper*
Thomas Beveridge,
EMP: 4 EST: 2015
SALES (est): 117.7K **Privately Held**
SIC: 0279 2099 8399 3999 Apiary (bee & honey farm); honey, strained & bottled; community development groups; honeycomb foundations (beekeepers' supplies)

(G-14531)
BENTLEY GRPHIC CMMNCATIONS INC (PA)
751 Pike Springs Rd (19460-4743)
PHONE..................................610 933-7400
James Bentley, *President*
Peter Korpel, *Vice Pres*
Annie Bentley, *Treasurer*
Sandra J Bronson, *Admin Sec*
EMP: 50
SQ FT: 10,000
SALES (est): 5.3MM **Privately Held**
SIC: 7336 2752 2791 Graphic arts & related design; commercial printing, lithographic; typesetting

(G-14532)
BILCARE INC
300 Kimberton Rd Ste 110 (19460-2114)
PHONE..................................610 935-4300
Mohan H Bhandari, *CEO*
Mohan Bhandari, *Managing Dir*
Walter Stroeder, *COO*
Karl Wiesler, *CFO*
Amy Hinton, *Human Res Mgr*
EMP: 160
SQ FT: 72,000
SALES (est): 569.9K
SALES (corp-wide): 39.4MM **Privately Held**
WEB: www.bilcare.com
SIC: 2834 5122 Pharmaceutical preparations; drugs, proprietaries & sundries

2019 Harris Pennsylvania
Manufacturers Directory

▲ = Import ▼=Export
◆ =Import/Export

PA: Bilcare Limited
601, B Wing, 6th Floor, Icc Trade
Tower, 403 - A
Pune MH 41101
203 025-7700

(G-14533)
BLACK ROCK FABRICATION LLC
485 Freemont St (19460-3159)
PHONE...................................610 212-3528
EMP: 4
SALES (est): 423.9K **Privately Held**
SIC: 3441 Fabricated structural metal;
wiredrawing & fabricating machinery &
equipment, ex. die

(G-14534)
BLUE SKY INTERNATIONAL INC
534 Brighton Way (19460-5718)
PHONE...................................610 306-1234
Henry A Julicher, *President*
Christopher Wright, *General Mgr*
Margit Julicher, *Principal*
EMP: 3
SALES: 1.1MM **Privately Held**
SIC: 3949 1799 Sporting & athletic goods;
athletic & recreation facilities construction

(G-14535)
BLUEBIRD DISTILLING LLC
100 Bridge St (19460-3492)
PHONE...................................610 933-7827
Jared Adkins, *Principal*
EMP: 11
SALES (est): 1.6MM **Privately Held**
SIC: 2085 Distilled & blended liquors

(G-14536)
BOEHRINGER LABORATORIES INC
300 Thoms Dr Ste 14 (19460-6117)
PHONE...................................610 278-0900
John R Boehringer, *President*
Carol Boehringer, *Corp Secy*
EMP: 30
SQ FT: 30,000
SALES (est): 5.7MM **Privately Held**
WEB: www.boehringerlabs.com
SIC: 3841 3845 3842 Surgical & medical
instruments; electromedical equipment;
surgical appliances & supplies

(G-14537)
BOEHRINGER LABORATORIES LLC
300 Thoms Dr (19460-6117)
PHONE...................................610 278-0900
John Karpowicz, *President*
David Rumbaugh, *CFO*
EMP: 35
SALES (est): 1.7MM **Privately Held**
SIC: 3841 Surgical & medical instruments

(G-14538)
BOEHRINGER WOUND SYSTEMS LLC
300 Thoms Dr Ste 14 (19460-6117)
PHONE...................................610 278-0900
David Rumbaugh, *CFO*
EMP: 30
SQ FT: 33,000
SALES (est): 3.1MM **Privately Held**
SIC: 3841 Surgical & medical instruments

(G-14539)
CDPRINTEXPRESS LLC
2208 Periwinkle Ct (19460-4857)
PHONE...................................610 450-6176
EMP: 3
SALES (est): 175.3K **Privately Held**
SIC: 3826 Thermal analysis instruments,
laboratory type

(G-14540)
COLONIAL ELECTRIC SUPPLY INC
41 2nd Ave (19460-3670)
PHONE...................................610 935-2493
EMP: 5
SALES (est): 115K **Privately Held**
SIC: 4911 3699 Electric services; electri-
cal equipment & supplies

(G-14541)
DAME DESIGN LLC
710 Wheatland St Ste 107 (19460-3988)
PHONE...................................610 458-3290
Alison Dame,
Lenora Dame,
EMP: 6
SQ FT: 2,500
SALES: 1.1MM **Privately Held**
SIC: 2392 Household furnishings

(G-14542)
DANCO PRECISION INC (PA)
601 Wheatland St (19460-3353)
P.O. Box 448 (19460-0448)
PHONE...................................610 933-8981
Nicholas B Fagan, *President*
John Krizmanich, *Vice Pres*
Rodney Danco Jr, *CFO*
Veronica Gormley, *Admin Sec*
EMP: 10
SQ FT: 43,000
SALES (est): 6.9MM **Privately Held**
WEB: www.dancoprecision.com
SIC: 3469 3544 3621 3677 Metal stamp-
ings; special dies & tools; motors & gen-
erators; electronic coils, transformers &
other inductors; electronic circuits

(G-14543)
DANCO PRECISION INC
354 Walnut St (19460-3548)
PHONE...................................610 933-1090
Nicholas Fagan, *President*
EMP: 44
SALES (corp-wide): 6.9MM **Privately Held**
WEB: www.dancoprecision.com
SIC: 3544 3469 3679 Special dies &
tools; metal stampings; electronic circuits
PA: Danco Precision, Inc.
601 Wheatland St
Phoenixville PA 19460
610 933-8981

(G-14544)
DANCO PRECISION INC
Also Called: Warehouse
Morgan St (19460)
P.O. Box 448 (19460-0448)
PHONE...................................610 933-8981
Nicholas Fagan, *President*
EMP: 20
SQ FT: 18,218
SALES (est): 1.4MM
SALES (corp-wide): 6.9MM **Privately Held**
WEB: www.dancoprecision.com
SIC: 3544 Special dies & tools
PA: Danco Precision, Inc.
601 Wheatland St
Phoenixville PA 19460
610 933-8981

(G-14545)
DINE-GLOW DBLO FD SVC FELS LLC
765 Pike Springs Rd (19460-4743)
PHONE...................................800 526-7583
Dominic D'Ambro Jr, *CEO*
EMP: 32
SALES (est): 9.5MM **Privately Held**
SIC: 3645 3999 Table lamps; candles

(G-14546)
EASTERN DIE CUTTING & FINSHG
1000 Township Line Rd # 5 (19460-2269)
PHONE...................................610 917-9765
Scott Rowland, *President*
EMP: 10
SQ FT: 4,000
SALES (est): 1.4MM **Privately Held**
SIC: 2752 Commercial printing, offset

(G-14547)
ELECTRO-OPTICAL SYSTEMS INC
1288 Valley Forge Rd # 49 (19460-2687)
PHONE...................................610 935-5838
William H Pinkston, *President*
EMP: 16
SQ FT: 6,000
SALES (est): 2.1MM **Privately Held**
WEB: www.eosystems.com
SIC: 3559 8731 Optical lens machinery;
engineering laboratory, except testing

(G-14548)
EPIC LITHO
751 Pike Springs Rd (19460-4743)
PHONE...................................610 933-7400
Jeff Pintof, *Principal*
John Gebhardt, *Controller*
EMP: 20
SALES (est): 4.3MM **Privately Held**
SIC: 2752 Commercial printing, offset

(G-14549)
FAST SHELTER INC
659 S 2nd Ave (19460-2541)
PHONE...................................610 415-0225
Dave Norris, *President*
EMP: 9
SQ FT: 3,000
SALES: 500K **Privately Held**
SIC: 3069 Balloons, advertising & toy: rub-
ber

(G-14550)
FASTSIGNS
257 Schuylkill Rd (19460-1879)
PHONE...................................610 296-0400
Kevin Mengel, *Owner*
EMP: 6
SALES (est): 301.7K **Privately Held**
SIC: 3993 Signs & advertising specialties

(G-14551)
GRAPHIC PACKAGING INTL LLC
Also Called: Altivity Packaging
1035 Longford Rd (19460-1205)
PHONE...................................610 935-4000
Jim Jackmore, *Plant Mgr*
Wayne Nonamaker, *Plant Mgr*
Pat Bucci, *Purch Agent*
Diane Kampia, *Buyer*
Darlene Holloway, *Branch Mgr*
EMP: 155 **Publicly Held**
SIC: 2657 Folding paperboard boxes
HQ: Graphic Packaging International, Llc
1500 Riveredge Pkwy # 100
Atlanta GA 30328

(G-14552)
GRAPHIC PACKAGING INTL LLC
1035 Longford Rd (19460-1205)
PHONE...................................610 725-9840
Dotti Asbert, *Manager*
EMP: 409 **Publicly Held**
SIC: 2631 Paperboard mills
HQ: Graphic Packaging International, Llc
1500 Riveredge Pkwy # 100
Atlanta GA 30328

(G-14553)
INNOVTIVE PRINT MDIA GROUP INC (PA)
Also Called: Safeguard By Innovative
500 Schell Ln (19460-1190)
PHONE...................................610 489-4800
Bob Fisher, *President*
Robert A Fisher, *President*
Jordan Hartline, *Opers Staff*
Barbara Mims, *Accounts Mgr*
EMP: 55
SQ FT: 62,000
SALES (est): 14.4MM **Privately Held**
WEB: www.innoprint.com
SIC: 7374 7389 2754 Computer graphics
service; brokers, contract services; com-
mercial printing, gravure

(G-14554)
INSTRUMENTAL ASSOCIATES
1220 Valley Forge Rd # 28 (19460-2676)
PHONE...................................610 992-3300
John Ciarrochi, *Principal*
EMP: 7
SALES (est): 572.9K **Privately Held**
WEB: www.instrumentationassoc.com
SIC: 3845 Audiological equipment, elec-
tromedical

(G-14555)
KB WOODCRAFT INC
Also Called: Finish Carpenter
128 Jackson St (19460-3559)
PHONE...................................502 533-2773
Edward Baird, *President*
EMP: 3
SALES (est): 150.4K **Privately Held**
SIC: 2511 2431 3553 Wood household
furniture; woodwork, interior & ornamen-
tal; furniture makers' machinery, wood-
working

(G-14556)
KESTREL GROWTH BRANDS INC
Also Called: Singing Dog Vanilla
1041 W Bridge St Ste 100 (19460-4326)
PHONE...................................484 932-8447
William Wiedmann, *Vice Pres*
EMP: 4 **Privately Held**
SIC: 2099 Seasonings & spices
PA: Kestrel Growth Brands, Inc.
255 Wallis St Ste 1
Eugene OR 97402

(G-14557)
KING TESTER CORPORATION
300 Schell Ln Ste 308 (19460-1187)
PHONE...................................610 279-6010
Ana C Borgersen, *President*
Barbara C Borgersen, *President*
Meredith Betts, *Marketing Staff*
Lula A Borgersen, *Admin Sec*
EMP: 10
SQ FT: 7,500
SALES (est): 2.2MM **Privately Held**
WEB: www.kingtester.com
SIC: 3829 Hardness testing equipment

(G-14558)
KING TESTER CORPORATION
308 Schell Ln (19460-1180)
PHONE...................................610 279-6010
James Knight, *Owner*
EMP: 12
SALES (est): 2.1MM **Privately Held**
SIC: 3829 Measuring & controlling devices

(G-14559)
LE JO ENTERPRISES INCORPORATED
Also Called: Dine-A-Heat
765 Pike Springs Rd (19460-4743)
PHONE...................................484 921-9000
Dominic Dambro Sr, *President*
Dominic D'Ambro Jr, *Vice Pres*
▲ **EMP:** 35
SQ FT: 67,000
SALES (est): 13.5MM **Privately Held**
SIC: 3646 3556 Commercial indusl & insti-
tutional electric lighting fixtures; slicers,
commercial, food

(G-14560)
MCAVOY BRICK COMPANY
75 Mcavoy Ln (19460-2613)
P.O. Box 468 (19460-0468)
PHONE...................................610 933-2932
Creighton H McAvoy, *President*
Stephen R McAvoy, *Treasurer*
H B Halladay, *Admin Sec*
EMP: 3
SALES (est): 118.4K **Privately Held**
SIC: 3251 3281 5211 Paving brick, clay;
cut stone & stone products; masonry ma-
terials & supplies

(G-14561)
MILLSTAT LLC
26 Ridge Rd (19460-1933)
P.O. Box 145, Wayne (19087-0145)
PHONE...................................610 783-0181
Stu Miller, *Sales Staff*
Stuart Miller,
EMP: 15
SALES (est): 433.6K **Privately Held**
SIC: 3699 Security control equipment &
systems

(G-14562)
MONTCO PACKAGING CO INC
400 Taylor St (19460-3040)
P.O. Box 90 (19460-0090)
PHONE...................................610 935-9545
Russell W Montalbano, *President*
Michael Delladonna, *Vice Pres*
▲ **EMP:** 6 **EST:** 2001
SQ FT: 100,000

SALES (est): 5MM **Privately Held**
WEB: www.montcopackaging.com
SIC: 2653 Boxes, corrugated: made from purchased materials

(G-14563)
MONTGOMERY PRODUCTS LTD
Also Called: Box King Products
30 S 2nd Ave (19460-3673)
PHONE..................................610 933-2500
Martin M Berman, *Ch of Bd*
Lillian Berman, *Vice Ch Bd*
Gary Berman, *President*
Ira Berman, *Admin Sec*
EMP: 25
SALES (est): 5.1MM **Privately Held**
WEB: www.boxking.com
SIC: 2653 7373 Boxes, corrugated: made from purchased materials; systems engineering, computer related

(G-14564)
NATAWILL INDUSTRIES LLC
1118 Almond Dr (19460-5917)
P.O. Box 350 (19460-0350)
PHONE..................................610 574-8226
William Illingworth, *Principal*
Bill Illingworth, *Opers Staff*
EMP: 3
SALES (est): 197.3K **Privately Held**
SIC: 3999 Manufacturing industries

(G-14565)
OTTINGER MACHINE CO INC
1138 Spring City Rd (19460-1827)
PHONE..................................610 933-2101
Robert Ottinger, *President*
Christine E Ottinger, *Corp Secy*
Wallace Ottinger, *Vice Pres*
Wayne Ottinger, *Vice Pres*
EMP: 8 **EST:** 1934
SQ FT: 2,000
SALES (est): 1.4MM **Privately Held**
WEB: www.ottingermachine.com
SIC: 3532 Grinders, stone: stationary; pulverizers (stationary), stone

(G-14566)
PETNOVATIONS INC
1100 Schell Ln Ste 101 (19460-6129)
PHONE..................................610 994-2103
Steven Yampolsky, *President*
▲ **EMP:** 20
SALES (est): 2.3MM **Privately Held**
SIC: 3999 Pet supplies

(G-14567)
PHILLY FADES INC
200 Bridge St (19460-3470)
PHONE..................................678 672-9727
David Fields, *President*
EMP: 8 **EST:** 2017
SALES (est): 235K **Privately Held**
SIC: 3999 Barber & beauty shop equipment

(G-14568)
PHOENIX CABINETRY INC
98 Highland Ave (19460-6138)
PHONE..................................484 831-5741
Matt Suntermier, *President*
John Angeloni, *Project Mgr*
EMP: 7
SALES (est): 1MM **Privately Held**
SIC: 2434 Wood kitchen cabinets

(G-14569)
PHOENIX PRINTERS INC
665 Nutt Rd (19460-3347)
PHONE..................................610 427-3069
Thomas McIntyre, *President*
Carl Kubitz, *Treasurer*
EMP: 8
SQ FT: 3,500
SALES (est): 1MM **Privately Held**
SIC: 2759 Commercial printing

(G-14570)
PRINT CITY GRAPHICS INC
680 Hollow Rd Ste 3 (19460-1146)
PHONE..................................610 495-5524
Thomas Freece, *President*
EMP: 7
SQ FT: 5,000

SALES (est): 1MM **Privately Held**
WEB: www.printcitygraphics.com
SIC: 2759 7331 Promotional printing; mailing service

(G-14571)
PRINTING CONSULTING INC
Also Called: PCI
200 Lincoln Ave Ste 105 (19460-3582)
P.O. Box 461, Valley Forge (19481-0461)
PHONE..................................610 933-9311
William E Lampe, *President*
EMP: 4
SALES (est): 228.4K **Privately Held**
SIC: 2721 8742 Periodicals; marketing consulting services

(G-14572)
PRO DYNE CORPORATION
136 Green Tree Rd Ste 100 (19460)
PHONE..................................610 789-0606
John A Lerro Sr, *President*
Chris Lerro, *Vice Pres*
Lisamarie Lerro, *Manager*
▲ **EMP:** 4
SALES (est): 705.3K **Privately Held**
WEB: www.prodynecorp.com
SIC: 3443 5084 Heat exchangers, condensers & components; materials handling machinery

(G-14573)
R & G GORR ENTERPRISES INC
Also Called: Lafayette Supply
1000 Schell Ln (19460-6121)
PHONE..................................610 356-8500
Robert C Gorr, *President*
EMP: 8
SQ FT: 15,000
SALES (est): 3MM **Privately Held**
WEB: www.lafpak.com
SIC: 5085 2671 Industrial supplies; packaging paper & plastics film, coated & laminated

(G-14574)
RMS OMEGA TECH GROUPING
406 Westridge Dr (19460-3389)
PHONE..................................610 917-0472
Michelle Berry, *Principal*
EMP: 3
SALES (est): 180.7K **Privately Held**
SIC: 3577 Bar code (magnetic ink) printers

(G-14575)
ROWLAND PRINTING INC
Also Called: Rowland Group
751 Pike Springs Rd (19460-4743)
PHONE..................................610 933-7400
James Rowland, *President*
Andrew Hoffman, *Shareholder*
▲ **EMP:** 44
SQ FT: 29,550
SALES (est): 11.6MM **Privately Held**
WEB: www.rowlandprint.com
SIC: 2752 2791 2789 2396 Commercial printing, offset; typesetting; bookbinding & related work; automotive & apparel trimmings

(G-14576)
ROYERSFORD FNDRY & MCH CO INC
Also Called: BARD MFG CO
835 Township Line Rd (19460-1828)
P.O. Box 190, Royersford (19468-0190)
PHONE..................................610 935-7200
Kurt Deisher, *President*
Robert Bellowoar, *Admin Sec*
EMP: 25
SQ FT: 57,000
SALES (est): 4.1MM **Privately Held**
WEB: www.royersford.com
SIC: 3599 3562 3568 Machine shop, jobbing & repair; ball & roller bearings; pillow blocks with plain bearings

(G-14577)
RSS OPTOMETRY LLC
Also Called: All About Eyes
523 Kimberton Rd Ste 11c (19460-4744)
PHONE..................................610 933-2177
Robert S Susan,
EMP: 4

SALES (est): 353.9K **Privately Held**
SIC: 8042 5995 3851 Specialized optometrists; contact lenses, prescription; eyeglasses, lenses & frames

(G-14578)
SAND CASTLE WINERY
236 Bridge St (19460-3495)
PHONE..................................484 924-9530
EMP: 4
SALES (corp-wide): 2.6MM **Privately Held**
SIC: 2084 Wines
PA: Sand Castle Winery
755 River Rd
Erwinna PA 18920
610 294-9181

(G-14579)
STEIMER AND CO INC
157 E 7 Stars Rd (19460-4773)
PHONE..................................610 933-7450
John F Steimer Jr, *President*
James A Steimer, *Vice Pres*
EMP: 10
SQ FT: 10,000
SALES (est): 1.9MM **Privately Held**
SIC: 3549 3699 Assembly machines, including robotic; electrical welding equipment

(G-14580)
STONE EDGE TECHNOLOGIES INC
1100 Schell Ln Ste 104 (19460-6129)
PHONE..................................484 927-4804
Bernard Stone, *President*
John Seaner, *Vice Pres*
EMP: 5
SALES (est): 388.3K **Privately Held**
SIC: 7372 Prepackaged software
HQ: Monsoon, Inc.
733 Sw 2nd Ave Ste 215
Portland OR 97204
503 239-1055

(G-14581)
SUPERIOR VALUE BEVERAGE CO
Also Called: Superior Value Beverage Center
701 Wheatland St (19460-3336)
P.O. Box 547 (19460-0547)
PHONE..................................610 935-3111
Tom Mirabile Jr, *President*
EMP: 6
SALES (est): 383.8K **Privately Held**
SIC: 5963 5999 2086 5921 Bottled water delivery; ice; bottled & canned soft drinks; beer (packaged); salt, edible

(G-14582)
T C B DISPLAYS INC (PA)
200 Lincoln Ave Ste 200 # 200 (19460-3234)
PHONE..................................610 983-0500
John Benson, *CEO*
Edward Lacey, *Exec VP*
EMP: 22
SQ FT: 22,000
SALES (est): 1.9MM **Privately Held**
SIC: 7336 3993 2542 Art design services; signs & advertising specialties; partitions & fixtures, except wood

(G-14583)
VALLEY FORGE INSTRUMENT CO
210 Buckwalter Rd (19460-2350)
PHONE..................................610 933-1806
Galloway Morris, *President*
Branin Boyd, *Treasurer*
Thomas R Kellogg, *Admin Sec*
EMP: 7
SALES (est): 731.7K **Privately Held**
SIC: 3625 Industrial controls: push button, selector switches, pilot

(G-14584)
XPRESS ENERGY
383 Schuylkill Rd (19460-1899)
P.O. Box 444 (19460-0444)
PHONE..................................610 935-9200
John Wilcox, *Opers Mgr*
EMP: 10

SALES (est): 295.6K **Privately Held**
SIC: 4911 2711 Electric services; newspapers

Picture Rocks
Lycoming County

(G-14585)
LEWIS LUMBER PRODUCTS INC
30 S Main St (17762)
P.O. Box 356 (17762-0356)
PHONE..................................570 584-6167
Keith Atherholt, *President*
Kelly Hill, *Business Mgr*
Marc Lewis, *Corp Secy*
Melvin Lewis, *Vice Pres*
Harry Jones, *Sales Mgr*
EMP: 55
SQ FT: 100,000
SALES (est): 9.1MM **Privately Held**
WEB: www.lewislp.com
SIC: 2426 2431 Flooring, hardwood; moldings & baseboards, ornamental & trim

---

Pillow
Dauphin County

(G-14586)
OPTILUMEN INC
167 Market St (17080)
P.O. Box 3 (17080-0003)
PHONE..................................717 547-5417
John Henninger, *President*
David Henninger, *Vice Pres*
Bruce Amerman, *CFO*
Bonnie Walker, *Director*
Vanessa Shipe, *Admin Sec*
▲ **EMP:** 6 **EST:** 2014
SQ FT: 10,000
SALES (est): 8.3MM **Privately Held**
SIC: 3671 Light sensing & emitting tubes

Pine Forge
Berks County

(G-14587)
DELVANIA INDUS FABRICATION INC
1535 Manatawny St (19548)
P.O. Box 334 (19548-0334)
PHONE..................................732 417-0333
William Demott, *President*
EMP: 3
SALES (est): 197.1K **Privately Held**
SIC: 3441 Building components, structural steel

(G-14588)
EAST COAST THREADING COMPANY
1520 Manatawny Rd (19548)
P.O. Box 347 (19548-0347)
PHONE..................................610 970-9933
Rick Kitchell, *President*
EMP: 4 **EST:** 2008
SALES (est): 700K **Privately Held**
SIC: 3452 Bolts, nuts, rivets & washers

Pine Grove
Schuylkill County

(G-14589)
ALPHA OMEGA MACHINE SHOP
992 Mountain Rd (17963-8046)
PHONE..................................570 573-4610
Jerry Zimmerman, *Partner*
Mike Keefer, *Partner*
EMP: 3
SALES (est): 145.7K **Privately Held**
SIC: 3599 Machine & other job shop work; propellers, ship & boat: machined

(G-14590)
CUSTOM EXTRUDERS INC
80 Roberts Rd (17963-9146)
P.O. Box 346 (17963-0346)
PHONE..................................570 345-6600
Bernard J Kulkaski, *President*
EMP: 3
SALES (est): 220.2K **Privately Held**
SIC: 3089 Injection molded finished plastic products

(G-14591)
D&R LOGGING
49 Trumbo Rd (17963-8861)
PHONE..................................570 345-4632
Carl R Bohr, *Principal*
EMP: 3
SALES (est): 284.1K **Privately Held**
SIC: 2411 Logging camps & contractors

(G-14592)
EMIL RARICK FUEL DELIVERY
250 Tremont Rd Side (17963-8776)
PHONE..................................570 345-8584
Emil Rarick, *Principal*
EMP: 6 **EST:** 2010
SALES (est): 937.4K **Privately Held**
SIC: 2869 Fuels

(G-14593)
EMILY J HIGH
60 Martins Rd (17963-8216)
PHONE..................................570 345-6268
Emily J High, *Principal*
EMP: 3
SALES (est): 267.1K **Privately Held**
SIC: 2421 Sawdust & shavings

(G-14594)
JOYCE STAIR CORP
Also Called: Stair Pak Products Co
23 Roberts Rd (17963-9150)
P.O. Box 186 (17963-0186)
PHONE..................................570 345-8000
Richard M Joyce Jr, *President*
Sandra M Joyce, *Treasurer*
EMP: 8 **EST:** 1948
SQ FT: 25,000
SALES (est): 1.3MM **Privately Held**
WEB: www.stairpak.com
SIC: 2431 Staircases & stairs, wood

(G-14595)
KT ZIMMERMAN LUMBER & LOGGING
21 Zimmerman Ln (17963-8676)
PHONE..................................570 345-2542
Kevin Zimmerman, *Principal*
EMP: 3
SALES (est): 323.7K **Privately Held**
SIC: 2411 Logging

(G-14596)
KUTZ FARM EQUIPMENT INC
Also Called: Pennsylvania Intl Trlr
72 Kutz Rd (17963-9097)
PHONE..................................570 345-4882
Gerald Kutz, *President*
▲ **EMP:** 4
SALES (est): 617.3K **Privately Held**
SIC: 3799 5999 Trailers & trailer equipment; farm equipment & supplies

(G-14597)
LEAR CORPORATION
141 Wideawake St (17963-1211)
P.O. Box 248 (17963-0248)
PHONE..................................570 345-6725
Russell Olt, *Purch Mgr*
Allen Margerum, *Buyer*
Brian Maroney, *Manager*
Ann Yazujian, *Athletic Dir*
EMP: 300
SALES (corp-wide): 21.1B **Publicly Held**
SIC: 3714 Motor vehicle parts & accessories
PA: Lear Corporation
21557 Telegraph Rd
Southfield MI 48033
248 447-1500

(G-14598)
LEAR CORPORATION
Also Called: Guildford Performance Textiles
1 Penn Dye St (17963-9106)
PHONE..................................570 345-2611
Mark Peiffer, *Manager*
EMP: 3
SALES (corp-wide): 21.1B **Publicly Held**
SIC: 2241 Lacings, textile
PA: Lear Corporation
21557 Telegraph Rd
Southfield MI 48033
248 447-1500

(G-14599)
MERIDIAN PRECISION INC
80 Roberts Rd (17963-9146)
P.O. Box 206 (17963-0206)
PHONE..................................570 345-6600
Bernard Kulkaski, *President*
Roxanne Dohner, *Manager*
EMP: 27
SQ FT: 50,000
SALES: 2MM **Privately Held**
SIC: 3089 Extruded finished plastic products; plastic processing

(G-14600)
MOEN INCORPORATED
12 Roberts Rd (17963-9146)
PHONE..................................570 345-8021
Todd Dinger, *Engineer*
Melanie McCormick, *Human Resources*
Jim Sepulveda, *Sales Staff*
Don Nelson, *Branch Mgr*
EMP: 13
SALES (corp-wide): 5.4B **Publicly Held**
SIC: 5074 3432 Plumbing fittings & supplies; plumbing fixture fittings & trim
HQ: Moen Incorporated
25300 Al Moen Dr
North Olmsted OH 44070
440 962-2000

(G-14601)
PARADIGM LABS INC
7 Roberts Rd (17963-9150)
P.O. Box 138 (17963-0138)
PHONE..................................570 345-2600
Terry Maier, *President*
Brendan Maier, *Vice Pres*
Mark A Maier, *Vice Pres*
Bobbi Maier, *Admin Sec*
EMP: 11
SQ FT: 16,000
SALES (est): 3.1MM **Privately Held**
WEB: www.paradigmlabs.com
SIC: 2899 Chemical preparations

(G-14602)
PINE GROVE MNFCTURED HOMES INC
2 Pleasant Valley Rd (17963-9563)
P.O. Box 88 (17963-0088)
PHONE..................................570 345-2011
Wayne A Fanelli, *CEO*
Salvatore J Fanelli, *Chairman*
Lee Fanelli, *Vice Pres*
Robert V Fanelli, *Vice Pres*
Joseph Gallagher, *CFO*
EMP: 100 **EST:** 1982
SQ FT: 125,000
SALES (est): 9.7MM **Privately Held**
WEB: www.pinegrovehomes.com
SIC: 2451 Mobile homes, except recreational

(G-14603)
PLEASANT VALLEY HOMES INC
Also Called: Pleasant Valley Modular Homes
100 Hammersmith Dr (17963-5000)
P.O. Box 88 (17963-0088)
PHONE..................................570 345-2011
Wayne Fanelli, *President*
Lee Fanelli, *Vice Pres*
Kevin Nickler, *Vice Pres*
Rob Miller, *Prdtn Mgr*
Earl Teter, *Mfg Staff*
EMP: 150
SALES (est): 32.3MM **Privately Held**
SIC: 2451 2452 Mobile homes, except recreational; modular homes, prefabricated, wood

(G-14604)
R & J TROPHY
36 S Tulpehocken St (17963-1135)
PHONE..................................570 345-2277
Doris M Frantz, *Owner*
EMP: 4
SQ FT: 140
SALES (est): 311.9K **Privately Held**
SIC: 7336 3914 Silk screen design; trophies, plated (all metals)

(G-14605)
SOLAR INNOVATIONS INC
31 Roberts Rd (17963-9150)
PHONE..................................570 915-1500
Gregory A Header, *President*
Darren E Coder, *Vice Pres*
Stacey L Header, *CFO*
◆ **EMP:** 175
SQ FT: 300,000
SALES: 26MM **Privately Held**
WEB: www.solarinnovations.com
SIC: 3442 3448 Window & door frames; storm doors or windows, metal; greenhouses: prefabricated metal; sunrooms, prefabricated metal; screen enclosures

(G-14606)
TSS INDUSTRIES INC
404 Oak Grove Rd (17963-8722)
PHONE..................................717 821-6570
Christine Schaeffer, *President*
EMP: 4
SALES (est): 250K **Privately Held**
SIC: 3589 Commercial cooking & food-warming equipment

(G-14607)
WHITES MACHINE INC
114 Covered Bridge Rd (17963-8100)
PHONE..................................570 345-1142
Dennis White, *President*
Dean White, *Vice Pres*
EMP: 4
SALES (est): 450K **Privately Held**
SIC: 3599 Machine shop, jobbing & repair

(G-14608)
WOOD RACING PRODUCTS LLC
146 Nut Grove Rd (17963-9172)
PHONE..................................717 454-7003
Mark Wood, *
EMP: 7 **EST:** 2017
SALES (est): 551.9K **Privately Held**
SIC: 3711 Chassis, motor vehicle

(G-14609)
ZERBE MANUFACTURING
245 Sweet Arrow Lake Rd (17963-9384)
PHONE..................................570 640-1528
EMP: 3
SALES (est): 132.9K **Privately Held**
SIC: 3999 Manufacturing industries

Pipersville
Bucks County

(G-14610)
ALBERTS JENNINGS
6184 Easton Rd (18947-1024)
PHONE..................................215 766-2852
Bill Jennings, *Owner*
EMP: 3 **EST:** 2017
SALES (est): 89.6K **Privately Held**
SIC: 3599 Industrial machinery

(G-14611)
BAUM PRECISION MACHINING INC
5136 Applebutter Rd (18947-1029)
PHONE..................................215 766-3066
William E Baum, *CEO*
Aaron Baum, *President*
Jo Joel Baum, *Vice Pres*
Jason Bogert, *Foreman/Supr*
Nick Vasile, *Opers Staff*
EMP: 43
SQ FT: 18,000
SALES: 2MM **Privately Held**
SIC: 3599 Machine shop, jobbing & repair

(G-14612)
BUCKS CNTY BREWING DISTLG LLC
31 Appletree Ln (18947-1083)
PHONE..................................215 766-7711
Andrew Knechel, *Principal*
EMP: 4
SALES (est): 176.1K **Privately Held**
SIC: 2082 Beer (alcoholic beverage)

(G-14613)
COMPRESSED AIR SYSTEMS INC
14 Appletree Ln (18947-1083)
P.O. Box 567, Buckingham (18912-0567)
PHONE..................................215 340-1307
Robert W Miller, *President*
EMP: 6
SALES: 1.8MM **Publicly Held**
WEB: www.compressedairpa.com
SIC: 5084 3563 Safety equipment; air & gas compressors
PA: Rev Group, Inc.
111 E Kilbourn Ave # 2600
Milwaukee WI 53202

(G-14614)
ELECTROLINE CORP
Also Called: Jenny Tools
6182 Easton Rd (18947-1024)
PHONE..................................215 766-2229
Robert Erbrick, *President*
Pam Erbrick, *Corp Secy*
Joseph E Erbrick, *Vice Pres*
EMP: 23 **EST:** 1973
SQ FT: 27,500
SALES (est): 2.6MM **Privately Held**
WEB: www.jennytools.com
SIC: 3423 3089 3678 3545 Hand & edge tools; injection molding of plastics; electronic connectors; machine tool accessories

(G-14615)
FIRST STATE SHEET METAL INC
6263 Kellers Church Rd (18947-1807)
PHONE..................................302 521-1609
Stephen Worth, *Principal*
EMP: 8
SALES (est): 939.3K **Privately Held**
SIC: 3444 Sheet metalwork

(G-14616)
FREEDOM MILLWORK CORP
5110 Applebutter Rd (18947-1029)
PHONE..................................215 642-2213
John Burke, *President*
EMP: 3 **EST:** 2014
SALES (est): 238.3K **Privately Held**
SIC: 2431 Millwork

(G-14617)
K & J MAGNETICS INC
18 Appletree Ln (18947-1083)
PHONE..................................215 766-8055
Kevin Stayer, *President*
▲ **EMP:** 21
SQ FT: 16,000
SALES (est): 3.1MM **Privately Held**
WEB: www.kjmagnetics.com
SIC: 3499 Magnets, permanent: metallic

(G-14618)
PH TOOL LLC (PA)
Also Called: PH Tool Reference Standards
6021 Easton Rd (18947-1827)
PHONE..................................267 203-1600
Phil Herman Jr, *President*
Philip R Herman Sr, *Vice Pres*
Philip R Herman Jr, *Vice Pres*
EMP: 39
SQ FT: 20,700
SALES (est): 9.2MM **Privately Held**
WEB: www.phtool.com
SIC: 3829 Measuring & controlling devices

(G-14619)
RWB SPECIAL SERVICES CORP
Also Called: R&M International
6250 Kellers Church Rd (18947-1020)
PHONE..................................215 766-4800
Robert Ball, *President*
Jason B Sanders, *Vice Pres*
Mark Weatherhead, *Treasurer*
▲ **EMP:** 15

SQ FT: 35,000
SALES (est): 3.9MM **Privately Held**
SIC: 5023 3089 Kitchenware; kitchenware, plastic; novelties, plastic

(G-14620)
TECHNICAL VISION INC
74 Stagecoach Rd (18947-1648)
PHONE.................................215 205-6084
Lorraine Keller, *CEO*
Sergey Naumovsky, *Principal*
EMP: 11
SALES (est): 1.2MM **Privately Held**
SIC: 3845 Electromedical equipment

Pitman
Schuylkill County

(G-14621)
CHRISTIANSBRUNN DIE FMLIES DER
75 Grove Rd (17964-9141)
PHONE.................................570 425-2548
Roger W Mervine, *Principal*
EMP: 3 EST: 2008
SALES: 18.2K **Privately Held**
SIC: 3544 Special dies & tools

(G-14622)
CK CONSTRUCTION & INDUS INC (PA)
308 Valley Rd (17964-9103)
PHONE.................................570 286-4128
Diane Maurer, *President*
June Maurer, *Vice Pres*
▼ EMP: 3 EST: 1962
SALES (est): 955.7K **Privately Held**
WEB: www.titanabrasive.com
SIC: 3589 5084 Sandblasting equipment; industrial machinery & equipment

Pittsburgh
Allegheny County

(G-14623)
101 CAMEO APPEARANCES LLC
Also Called: 101 Mobility of Pittsburgh
770 Vista Park Dr (15205-1214)
PHONE.................................412 787-7981
Gregory Slepecki,
EMP: 4
SALES (est): 517.8K **Privately Held**
SIC: 5047 7352 3799 Medical & hospital equipment; medical equipment rental; trailers & trailer equipment

(G-14624)
2124 BREWING COMPANY LLC
Also Called: Aurochs Brewing Company
8321 Ohio River Blvd (15202-1451)
PHONE.................................724 260-8737
Ryan Bove, *President*
EMP: 3
SALES (est): 261.6K **Privately Held**
SIC: 2082 Beer (alcoholic beverage)

(G-14625)
2820 ASSOCIATES INC
Also Called: I Design
2820 Smallman St Ste 2 (15222-4727)
PHONE.................................412 471-2525
Bruce Berman, *President*
Yale Berman, *Manager*
EMP: 3
SQ FT: 3,200
SALES (est): 252K **Privately Held**
SIC: 2511 8999 7389 Wood household furniture; sculptor's studio; interior decorating

(G-14626)
43RD ST INC
Also Called: 43rd St Concrete
1 43rd St (15201-3109)
PHONE.................................412 682-4090
Robert L Yeske, *President*
EMP: 22 EST: 1974
SQ FT: 125,452

SALES (est): 2.8MM **Privately Held**
WEB: www.43rdstreetconcrete.com
SIC: 3273 5032 Ready-mixed concrete; concrete building products

(G-14627)
A & P SUPPORT INC
525 William Penn Pl (15219-1707)
PHONE.................................570 265-9157
Christopher Allen, *Principal*
Herky Pollock, *Exec VP*
Ira Glasser, *CFO*
EMP: 51
SALES: 8MM **Privately Held**
SIC: 7359 1389 Equipment rental & leasing; oil field services

(G-14628)
A A A ENGRAVING
1042 5th Ave (15219-6229)
PHONE.................................412 281-7756
Daniel Petruzzi, *Owner*
EMP: 7
SQ FT: 1,800
SALES: 350K **Privately Held**
SIC: 7389 5999 3479 3229 Engraving service; trophies & plaques; engraving jewelry silverware, or metal; glassware, art or decorative; invitation & stationery printing & engraving; carved & turned wood

(G-14629)
A E FALGIANI ICE CO INC
3639 Poplar Ave (15234-2149)
PHONE.................................412 344-7538
Bruce Falgiani, *President*
Gladys R Falgiani, *Vice Pres*
EMP: 6
SQ FT: 3,500
SALES: 500K **Privately Held**
SIC: 2097 Ice cubes

(G-14630)
A M PARTS INC
Also Called: Johnson Contrls Authorized Dlr
3470 Babcock Blvd (15237-2454)
PHONE.................................412 367-8040
Mark Reidmiller, *Manager*
EMP: 4
SALES (corp-wide): 16.1MM **Privately Held**
WEB: www.amparts.com
SIC: 3585 5075 Heating & air conditioning combination units; warm air heating & air conditioning
PA: A M Parts, Inc.
    1548 Pennsylvania Ave
    Monaca PA 15061
    724 775-8041

(G-14631)
AAA BUSINESS SOLUTIONS LLC
500 Glass Rd (15205-9407)
PHONE.................................412 787-3333
Frank N Fera,
EMP: 4
SALES: 50K **Privately Held**
SIC: 2522 Office furniture, except wood

(G-14632)
ABARTA OIL & GAS CO INC (DH)
Also Called: Abarta Energy
200 Alpha Dr (15238-2906)
PHONE.................................412 963-6226
James A Taylor, *President*
Charles Hanlon, *Corp Secy*
John J Emmerling, *Vice Pres*
Charles Huczko, *Controller*
Andrea Mankey, *Executive*
EMP: 20
SALES (est): 13.9MM
SALES (corp-wide): 361.4MM **Privately Held**
SIC: 1382 Oil & gas exploration services
HQ: Wilmington Trust Sp Services
    1105 N Market St Ste 1300
    Wilmington DE 19801
    302 427-7650

(G-14633)
ABB INC
Also Called: Automtion Tech Analytical Pdts
575 Epsilon Dr Ste 1 (15238-2812)
PHONE.................................412 963-7530
Robert Seidelson, *Branch Mgr*
EMP: 11
SALES (corp-wide): 34.3B **Privately Held**
WEB: www.elsterelectricity.com
SIC: 3511 Turbines & turbine generator sets
HQ: Abb Inc.
    305 Gregson Dr
    Cary NC 27511

(G-14634)
ABBOUD SAMAR
Also Called: South Hills Printing
704 Brookline Blvd (15226-2176)
PHONE.................................412 343-6899
Samar Abboud, *Owner*
EMP: 4
SALES (est): 240K **Privately Held**
SIC: 2752 Commercial printing, lithographic

(G-14635)
ABILILIFE INC
100 S Commons Ste 102 (15212-5359)
PHONE.................................443 326-6395
Courtney Williamson, *CEO*
EMP: 3
SQ FT: 2,000
SALES (est): 210.8K **Privately Held**
SIC: 3999 Manufacturing industries

(G-14636)
ABT LLC
Also Called: A B T
500 Fountain St (15238)
P.O. Box 111329 (15238-0729)
PHONE.................................412 826-8002
John G Baver, *President*
George Zech, *Vice Pres*
James Zech, *Plant Mgr*
Al Caprara, *Director*
▲ EMP: 48
SALES (est): 12.3MM **Privately Held**
WEB: www.abt-mfg.com
SIC: 3443 3498 3444 3317 Fabricated plate work (boiler shop); fabricated pipe & fittings; sheet metalwork; steel pipe & tubes

(G-14637)
ACCEL SIGN GROUP INC
5600 Harrison St (15201-2335)
PHONE.................................412 781-7735
Curtis Sutton, *President*
Mark Wood, *General Mgr*
Jack Harnick, *Vice Pres*
Bill Whitehead, *Vice Pres*
Susan Hance, *Office Mgr*
EMP: 10
SQ FT: 1,600
SALES (est): 1.3MM **Privately Held**
SIC: 3993 Electric signs

(G-14638)
ACCURATE CONTROL & DESIGN CO
2948 Meadowvue Dr (15227-4038)
PHONE.................................412 884-3723
John W Mainarich, *President*
Linda Mainarich, *Corp Secy*
EMP: 4 EST: 1968
SQ FT: 1,300
SALES (est): 322.7K **Privately Held**
SIC: 3613 Control panels, electric

(G-14639)
ACE BINDERY CORPORATION
2323 Main St (15215-2812)
P.O. Box 7861 (15215-0861)
PHONE.................................412 784-3669
Elizabeth Tiani, *President*
Michael Tiani, *Vice Pres*
John Tiani, *Treasurer*
Rose Tiani, *Admin Sec*
EMP: 28
SQ FT: 29,000
SALES (est): 2.9MM **Privately Held**
SIC: 2789 Binding only: books, pamphlets, magazines, etc.

(G-14640)
ACHIEVA (HQ)
Also Called: ACHIEVA SUPPORT
711 Bingham St (15203-1007)
PHONE.................................412 995-5000
Marsha S Blanco, *CEO*
Gary K Horner, *Exec VP*
Shayne Roos, *Vice Pres*
Maria Smith, *Vice Pres*
Marte Novak, *Plant Mgr*
EMP: 100
SQ FT: 40,000
SALES: 2.7MM
SALES (corp-wide): 5.5MM **Privately Held**
SIC: 8331 7373 3643 2653 Sheltered workshop; computer systems analysis & design; current-carrying wiring devices; corrugated & solid fiber boxes; wood pallets & skids; nailed wood boxes & shook
PA: Achieva
    711 Bingham St
    Pittsburgh PA 15203
    412 995-5000

(G-14641)
ACHIEVA
Also Called: Parkway Industries
711 Bingham St 1 (15203-1007)
PHONE.................................412 391-4660
Marte Novak, *Manager*
EMP: 10
SALES (corp-wide): 5.5MM **Privately Held**
SIC: 2652 8331 2653 Setup paperboard boxes; job training services; corrugated & solid fiber boxes
HQ: Achieva
    711 Bingham St
    Pittsburgh PA 15203
    412 995-5000

(G-14642)
ACME METALS CO
3000 Grand Ave Ste 2 (15225-1614)
PHONE.................................412 331-4301
Jack Peters, *President*
Leslie Mazzarini, *Admin Sec*
EMP: 9
SQ FT: 10,500
SALES (est): 1.8MM **Privately Held**
WEB: www.acmemetals.com
SIC: 3441 Fabricated structural metal

(G-14643)
ACME ROOFING AND HEATING INC
1610 Noblestown Rd (15205-3613)
PHONE.................................412 921-8218
Martin Sanders, *President*
EMP: 4 EST: 1935
SQ FT: 2,500
SALES (est): 810K **Privately Held**
SIC: 3444 Sheet metal specialties, not stamped

(G-14644)
ACME STAMPING WIRE FORMING CO
201 Corliss St (15220-4813)
PHONE.................................412 771-5720
Donald L Moody, *President*
EMP: 22 EST: 1901
SQ FT: 65,000
SALES (est): 4.3MM **Privately Held**
SIC: 3469 3496 Machine parts, stamped or pressed metal; clips & fasteners, made from purchased wire

(G-14645)
ACTAIRE INC
1227 Prospect Rd (15227-1428)
PHONE.................................412 851-1040
Robert Defalle, *President*
Martha Defalle, *Vice Pres*
EMP: 6
SALES (est): 1.2MM **Privately Held**
SIC: 3491 Industrial valves

(G-14646)
ACTIVEBLU CORPORATION
4638 Centre Ave (15213-1556)
PHONE.................................412 490-1929
Raghu Arunachalam, *CEO*
Kent McElhattan, *Ch of Bd*

▲ = Import ▼ =Export
◆ =Import/Export

EMP: 3
SALES (est): 146.7K **Privately Held**
SIC: 3663 Mobile communication equipment

(G-14647)
ACUTRONIC COMPANY (PA)
700 Waterfront Dr (15222-4742)
PHONE..................................412 926-1200
Mark A Tatkow, *President*
Carl Hockenberry, *Vice Pres*
Bennett S Roland, *Treasurer*
Lisa R Pitell, *Admin Sec*
EMP: 2
SALES (est): 12.4MM **Privately Held**
SIC: 3812 3999 Aircraft/aerospace flight instruments & guidance systems; atomizers, toiletry

(G-14648)
ACUTRONIC USA INC
700 Waterfront Dr (15222-4742)
PHONE..................................412 926-1200
Mark Tatkow, *CEO*
Thomas W Jung, *Owner*
Keith Andrew, *General Mgr*
Jennie Lee, *General Mgr*
Robert Sanders, *General Mgr*
EMP: 1
SQ FT: 11,783
SALES (est): 12.4MM
SALES (corp-wide): 12.4MM **Privately Held**
SIC: 3812 3999 Aircraft/aerospace flight instruments & guidance systems; atomizers, toiletry
PA: The Acutronic Company
700 Waterfront Dr
Pittsburgh PA 15222
412 926-1200

(G-14649)
AD-ART SIGN CO
1380 Frey Rd (15235-4059)
PHONE..................................412 373-0960
Richard Crawford, *Owner*
EMP: 5
SQ FT: 1,560
SALES (est): 80K **Privately Held**
SIC: 3993 2759 3953 2396 Signs & advertising specialties; screen printing; marking devices; automotive & apparel trimmings

(G-14650)
ADVANCE SIGN COMPANY LLC
Also Called: Advance Signs & Awnings
1010 Saw Mill Run Blvd (15226-1109)
PHONE..................................412 481-6990
Anthony Dejoseph,
EMP: 22
SALES (est): 3.6MM **Privately Held**
WEB: www.advancesignco.com
SIC: 5999 3993 7389 3953 Awnings; signs & advertising specialties; lettering & sign painting services; marking devices

(G-14651)
ADVANCED CONTROLS INC
700 River Ave Ste 520 (15212-5907)
PHONE..................................412 322-0991
Vikram Rawal, *President*
EMP: 12
SALES (est): 2.2MM **Privately Held**
WEB: www.aciscada.com
SIC: 3829 Measuring & controlling devices

(G-14652)
ADVANCED ELECTROCIRCUITS CORP
750 Trumbull Dr (15205-4363)
PHONE..................................412 278-5200
Bharat Monpara, *President*
Vithal G Diora, *Treasurer*
EMP: 22
SQ FT: 40,000
SALES (est): 3.5MM **Privately Held**
WEB: www.aecpcb.com
SIC: 3672 Printed circuit boards

(G-14653)
ADVISION SIGNS INC
4735 Campbells Run Rd (15205-1317)
PHONE..................................412 788-8440
Michael Zilner, *President*
Cindy Zilner, *Vice Pres*

EMP: 10
SQ FT: 25,000
SALES (est): 960K **Privately Held**
WEB: www.advisionsigns.com
SIC: 3993 7336 Signs, not made in custom sign painting shops; commercial art & graphic design

(G-14654)
AEO MANAGEMENT CO (HQ)
Also Called: American Eagle Outfitters
77 Hot Metal St (15203-2382)
PHONE..................................412 432-3300
Jay Schottenstein, *CEO*
Chad Keefer, *Engineer*
Justin Chenetski, *Mktg Dir*
Scott Kramer, *Business Anlyst*
John Galla, *Manager*
▲ EMP: 12
SALES (est): 1.8MM **Publicly Held**
SIC: 7999 2339 2389 Outfitters, recreation; women's & misses' accessories; men's miscellaneous accessories

(G-14655)
AEROTECH INC (PA)
101 Zeta Dr (15238-2897)
PHONE..................................412 963-7470
Mark A Botos, *President*
Suzanne Gilkey, *General Mgr*
Brian Fink, *Vice Pres*
Bob Novotnak, *Vice Pres*
Dave Holmes, *Mfg Mgr*
◆ EMP: 294 EST: 1969
SQ FT: 180,000
SALES (est): 84.5MM **Privately Held**
WEB: www.aerotech.com
SIC: 3825 3699 Galvanometers; meters, power factor & phase angle; electrical equipment & supplies

(G-14656)
AGENT DYNAMICS INC
300 S Dallas Ave (15208-2628)
PHONE..................................412 441-4604
Katia Sycara, *President*
EMP: 3
SALES (est): 280K **Privately Held**
SIC: 3695 Computer software tape & disks: blank, rigid & floppy

(G-14657)
AII ACQUISITION LLC (DH)
1000 Six Ppg Pl (15222)
PHONE..................................412 394-2800
L Patrick Hassey, *CEO*
Terry Dunlap, *Principal*
Jon D Walton, *Principal*
Robert S Park, *Treasurer*
EMP: 9 EST: 1906
SQ FT: 44,000
SALES (est): 4.3MM **Publicly Held**
WEB: www.alleghenyludlum.com
SIC: 3312 Stainless steel; tool & die steel
HQ: Allegheny Ludlum, Llc
1000 Six Ppg Pl
Pittsburgh PA 15222
412 394-2800

(G-14658)
AIR-SCENT INTERNATIONAL
290a Alpha Dr (15238-2906)
PHONE..................................412 252-2000
Arnold Zlotnik, *President*
Neal White, *Purch Mgr*
Lisa Vasko, *Sales Mgr*
Ray Czapko, *Marketing Staff*
▼ EMP: 55
SQ FT: 100,000
SALES (est): 8.6MM **Privately Held**
WEB: www.airscent.com
SIC: 2842 3699 Deodorants, nonpersonal; electrical equipment & supplies

(G-14659)
ALAN PEPPER DESIGNS
827 S Trenton Ave (15221-3451)
PHONE..................................412 244-9299
Alan R Pepper, *Owner*
EMP: 4
SALES (est): 313.8K **Privately Held**
SIC: 2431 2434 5712 2511 Planing mill, millwork; wood kitchen cabinets; cabinet work, custom; wood household furniture

(G-14660)
ALCOA BUSINESS PARK LLC (HQ)
201 Isabella St Ste 500 (15212-5858)
PHONE..................................412 553-4545
Mark Stiffler, *CEO*
EMP: 3
SALES (est): 450.1K
SALES (corp-wide): 13.4B **Publicly Held**
SIC: 3355 Aluminum rolling & drawing
PA: Alcoa Corporation
201 Isabella St Ste 500
Pittsburgh PA 15212
412 315-2900

(G-14661)
ALCOA CORPORATION
1590 Omega Dr (15205-5004)
PHONE..................................412 553-4001
Gary Acinapura, *Principal*
EMP: 4
SALES (corp-wide): 13.4B **Publicly Held**
SIC: 3355 3363 3297 2819 Aluminum rolling & drawing; aluminum die-castings; alumina fused refractories; bauxite, refined
PA: Alcoa Corporation
201 Isabella St Ste 500
Pittsburgh PA 15212
412 315-2900

(G-14662)
ALCOA CORPORATION (PA)
201 Isabella St Ste 500 (15212-5858)
PHONE..................................412 315-2900
Michael G Morris, *Ch of Bd*
Roy C Harvey, *President*
Garret J Dixon, *President*
Michael A Parker, *President*
Timothy D Reyes, *President*
EMP: 50
SALES: 13.4B **Publicly Held**
SIC: 3355 3363 3297 2819 Aluminum rolling & drawing; aluminum die-castings; alumina fused refractories; bauxite, refined

(G-14663)
ALCOA REMEDIATION MGT LLC
201 Isabella St Ste 500 (15212-5858)
PHONE..................................412 553-4545
Mark Stiffler, *CEO*
EMP: 3
SALES (est): 60.4K
SALES (corp-wide): 13.4B **Publicly Held**
SIC: 3355 Aluminum rolling & drawing
PA: Alcoa Corporation
201 Isabella St Ste 500
Pittsburgh PA 15212
412 315-2900

(G-14664)
ALCOA SOUTH CAROLINA INC
201 Isabella St Ste 500 (15212-5858)
PHONE..................................412 553-4545
Mark Stiffler, *CEO*
EMP: 6 EST: 1982
SALES (est): 105.7K
SALES (corp-wide): 13.4B **Publicly Held**
SIC: 3355 Aluminum rolling & drawing
PA: Alcoa Corporation
201 Isabella St Ste 500
Pittsburgh PA 15212
412 315-2900

(G-14665)
ALCOA TECHNICAL CENTER LLC (HQ)
201 Isabella St Ste 500 (15212-5858)
PHONE..................................412 553-4545
Benjamin D Kahrs, *CEO*
EMP: 6
SALES (est): 561.2K
SALES (corp-wide): 13.4B **Publicly Held**
SIC: 3355 Aluminum rolling & drawing
PA: Alcoa Corporation
201 Isabella St Ste 500
Pittsburgh PA 15212
412 315-2900

(G-14666)
ALCOA USA CORP (HQ)
201 Isabella St Ste 500 (15212-5858)
PHONE..................................212 518-5400
Roy C Harvey, *CEO*

EMP: 1 EST: 2016
SALES (est): 45.1MM
SALES (corp-wide): 13.4B **Publicly Held**
SIC: 3334 3353 1099 Primary aluminum; aluminum sheet & strip; bauxite mining
PA: Alcoa Corporation
201 Isabella St Ste 500
Pittsburgh PA 15212
412 315-2900

(G-14667)
ALCOA USA CORP
201 Isabella St Ste 500 (15212-5858)
PHONE..................................412 553-4545
EMP: 4
SALES (corp-wide): 13.4B **Publicly Held**
SIC: 3334 Primary aluminum
HQ: Alcoa Usa Corp.
201 Isabella St Ste 500
Pittsburgh PA 15212
212 518-5400

(G-14668)
ALCOA WARRICK LLC (HQ)
201 Isabella St Ste 500 (15212-5858)
PHONE..................................412 553-4545
Benjamin Kahrs, *CEO*
Mark Steinkamp, *Project Engr*
EMP: 11
SALES (est): 10.5MM
SALES (corp-wide): 13.4B **Publicly Held**
SIC: 3355 Aluminum rolling & drawing
PA: Alcoa Corporation
201 Isabella St Ste 500
Pittsburgh PA 15212
412 315-2900

(G-14669)
ALCOA WENATCHEE LLC (HQ)
201 Isabella St Ste 500 (15212-5858)
PHONE..................................412 553-4545
Louis Langlois, *CEO*
▲ EMP: 4 EST: 2016
SALES (est): 21.4MM
SALES (corp-wide): 13.4B **Publicly Held**
SIC: 3355 Aluminum rolling & drawing
PA: Alcoa Corporation
201 Isabella St Ste 500
Pittsburgh PA 15212
412 315-2900

(G-14670)
ALCOA WORLD ALUMINA LLC (HQ)
201 Isabella St Ste 500 (15212-5858)
P.O. Box 1780 (15230-1780)
PHONE..................................412 315-2900
Bill Oplinger, *Principal*
Tomas Mar Sigurdsson, *COO*
Max Laun, *Counsel*
Lisa Balcer, *Exec VP*
Michael Winternheimer, *Maint Spvr*
◆ EMP: 20
SALES (est): 1.3B
SALES (corp-wide): 1.6B **Privately Held**
SIC: 1099 1081 4911 Bauxite mining; metal mining services; electric services
PA: Halco (Mining) Inc.
323 N Shore Dr
Pittsburgh PA 15212
412 235-0265

(G-14671)
ALEX AND ANI LLC
5505 Walnut St (15232-2311)
PHONE..................................412 742-4968
EMP: 7 **Privately Held**
SIC: 5137 3911 Women's & children's clothing; jewelry, precious metal
PA: Alex And Ani, Llc
2000 Chapel View Blvd # 360
Cranston RI 02920

(G-14672)
ALEX AND ANI LLC
1000 Ross Park Mall Dr (15237-3875)
PHONE..................................412 367-1362
Alexander Davison, *Owner*
EMP: 3 **Privately Held**
SIC: 5137 3911 2389 Women's & children's outerwear; jewelry apparel; men's miscellaneous accessories
PA: Alex And Ani, Llc
2000 Chapel View Blvd # 360
Cranston RI 02920

(G-14673)
ALL ADS UP
Also Called: SCHUMAN PARTNERS DBA
2606 Brownsville Rd (15227-2099)
PHONE..................................412 881-4114
Eric Schuman, *Owner*
Eric M Schuman, *Owner*
EMP: 4
SQ FT: 2,000
SALES: 300K **Privately Held**
SIC: 2261 Screen printing of cotton broadwoven fabrics

(G-14674)
ALL AMERICAN SWEATS INC (PA)
Also Called: All American Embroidery
15 Robinhood Rd (15220-3013)
PHONE..................................412 922-8999
Louis J Fani, *President*
Margaret Fani, *Corp Secy*
EMP: 12
SALES: 400K **Privately Held**
SIC: 2399 5699 Hand woven & crocheted products; sports apparel

(G-14675)
ALL PRO EMBROIDERY INC
4854 Streets Run Rd (15236-1237)
PHONE..................................412 942-0735
Gary Rohm, *CEO*
Matt Rohm, *President*
EMP: 15
SALES: 370K **Privately Held**
WEB: www.allproembroidery.com
SIC: 2395 Embroidery products, except schiffli machine

(G-14676)
ALLEGHENY ALLOYS
1700 N Highland Rd # 208 (15241-1375)
PHONE..................................412 833-9733
Brendan Breen, *Principal*
▲ **EMP:** 8
SALES (est): 1.2MM **Privately Held**
SIC: 2819 Mfg Industrial Inorganic Chemicals

(G-14677)
ALLEGHENY DISTILLING LLC
3212 Smallman St (15201-1427)
PHONE..................................412 709-6480
EMP: 6
SALES (est): 585.3K **Privately Held**
SIC: 2085 Distilled & blended liquors

(G-14678)
ALLEGHENY FABG & SUPS INC
Also Called: Allegheny Group, The
208 Woodland Rd (15238-3301)
PHONE..................................412 828-3320
Fax: 412 828-3325
EMP: 4
SQ FT: 8,500
SALES (est): 790K **Privately Held**
SIC: 5021 3559 5085 7378 Whol Furniture Mfg Misc Industry Mach Whol Industrial Supplies Computer Maint/Repair Whol Med/Hospital Equip

(G-14679)
ALLEGHENY LUDLUM LLC (DH)
Also Called: ATI Allegheny Ludlum
1000 Six Ppg Pl (15222)
P.O. Box 981305, El Paso TX (79998-1305)
PHONE..................................412 394-2800
Richard J Harshman, *President*
Robert Arnold, *President*
Danny L Greenfield, *Vice Pres*
Dale G Reid, *Vice Pres*
Jeff Thompson, *Vice Pres*
▼ **EMP:** 500 **EST:** 1938
SALES (est): 3.1B **Publicly Held**
WEB: www.alleghenyludlum.com
SIC: 3312 Stainless steel; sheet or strip, steel, cold-rolled: own hot-rolled
HQ: Ati Operating Holdings, Llc
1000 Six Ppg Pl
Pittsburgh PA 15222
412 394-2800

(G-14680)
ALLEGHENY LUDLUM LLC
Also Called: ATI Allegheny Ludlum
6 Ppg Pl Ste 1000 (15222-5428)
PHONE..................................724 773-2700
Robert Bozzone, *Ch of Bd*
Gerard Johnson, *General Mgr*
Carlos Carmona-Torres, *Business Mgr*
Terry Hartford, *Vice Pres*
Jeff Schussler, *Manager*
EMP: 65 **Publicly Held**
WEB: www.alleghenyludlum.com
SIC: 3312 Stainless steel
HQ: Allegheny Ludlum, Llc
1000 Six Ppg Pl
Pittsburgh PA 15222
412 394-2800

(G-14681)
ALLEGHENY METALS & MINERALS (PA)
733 Washington Rd Ste 2 (15228-2022)
PHONE..................................412 344-9900
Nadine Bognar, *Corp Secy*
Cynthia Bognar, *Exec VP*
Edwin J Bognar, *Exec VP*
EMP: 6 **EST:** 1963
SALES (est): 867K **Privately Held**
SIC: 1446 Industrial sand

(G-14682)
ALLEGHENY TECHNOLOGIES INC (PA)
Also Called: ATI
1000 Six Ppg Pl (15222)
PHONE..................................412 394-2800
Richard J Harshman, *Ch of Bd*
Robert S Wetherbee, *President*
John D Sims, *Exec VP*
Kevin B Kramer, *Senior VP*
Scott Minder, *Vice Pres*
EMP: 100
SALES: 4B **Publicly Held**
WEB: www.allegifenytechnologies.com
SIC: 3312 3339 3545 Stainless steel; primary nonferrous metals; machine tool accessories

(G-14683)
ALLEGRA PRINT & IMAGING
18 W Steuben St (15205-2602)
PHONE..................................412 922-0422
Mike Phlips, *Owner*
David Barringer, *Vice Pres*
Lisa Cusick, *Accounts Mgr*
Christine Mondin, *Admin Asst*
EMP: 10
SQ FT: 10,500
SALES (est): 1.7MM **Privately Held**
SIC: 2752 Commercial printing, offset

(G-14684)
ALLEN GAUGE & TOOL COMPANY
Also Called: Famco Manufacturing Div
421 N Braddock Ave (15208-2514)
P.O. Box 8647 (15221-0647)
PHONE..................................412 241-6410
Charles H Allen Jr, *President*
R Robert Allen, *Vice Pres*
EMP: 28
SQ FT: 28,000
SALES (est): 5.5MM **Privately Held**
SIC: 3823 3556 3545 Pressure gauges, dial & digital; sausage stuffers; machine tool accessories

(G-14685)
ALLIED MILLWORK OF PITTSBURGH
Also Called: Allied Millwork of P G H
3206 Penn Ave (15201-1423)
PHONE..................................412 471-9229
Charles Stein, *Owner*
EMP: 5 **EST:** 1951
SQ FT: 4,200
SALES (est): 455.3K **Privately Held**
WEB: www.alliedmillworkofpittsburgh.com
SIC: 2431 Window frames, wood

(G-14686)
ALPHA AROMATICS INC
Also Called: Airscent International
294 Alpha Dr (15238-2906)
PHONE..................................412 252-1012
Arnold Zlotnik, *President*
Tim George, *Vice Pres*
Roger Howell, *Vice Pres*
Jonas Neilson, *Marketing Staff*
Laura Boosinger, *Executive Asst*
◆ **EMP:** 68 **EST:** 1966
SALES (est): 56.5MM **Privately Held**
WEB: www.homefresheners.com
SIC: 5162 2844 5169 5999 Plastics basic shapes; toilet preparations; chemicals & allied products; toiletries, cosmetics & perfumes

(G-14687)
ALPHA SCREEN GRAPHICS INC
1200 Muriel St (15203-1127)
PHONE..................................412 431-9000
Jack Schmidt, *President*
Mark Johnson, *Corp Secy*
EMP: 7
SQ FT: 14,000
SALES (est): 918K **Privately Held**
WEB: www.alphasgx.com
SIC: 7336 7389 2759 Graphic arts & related design; laminating service; screen printing

(G-14688)
ALPINE METAL TECH N AMER INC
4853 Campbells Run Rd (15205-1323)
PHONE..................................412 787-2832
Justin Willott, *President*
Brian Glaser, *Manager*
▲ **EMP:** 30
SQ FT: 20,000
SALES (est): 6.7MM **Privately Held**
WEB: www.gega.com
SIC: 3547 Steel rolling machinery

(G-14689)
ALSTOM GRID LLC
Also Called: Cegelec Automation
610 Epsilon Dr (15238-2808)
PHONE..................................412 967-0765
Ron Dorrian, *Manager*
EMP: 54
SALES (corp-wide): 121.6B **Publicly Held**
SIC: 3612 8711 Autotransformers, electric (power transformers); power transformers, electric; electrical or electronic engineering
HQ: Alstom Grid Llc
130 3rd St Nw
Canton OH 44702
330 452-8428

(G-14690)
ALSTON MACHINE COMPANY INC
2 Commerce Dr (15239-1778)
PHONE..................................412 795-1000
Ruth Ann Craft, *President*
Robert Craft, *General Mgr*
Peter Nejak, *Vice Pres*
Elaine Conte, *Treasurer*
Bill Chapla, *Manager*
EMP: 20 **EST:** 1930
SQ FT: 10,000
SALES (est): 1.9MM **Privately Held**
SIC: 3599 3544 Machine shop, jobbing & repair; special dies, tools, jigs & fixtures

(G-14691)
ALTAMIRA INSTRUMENTS INC
149 Delta Dr Ste 200 (15238-2805)
PHONE..................................412 963-6385
Helena Santos, *CEO*
Brook March, *President*
Sharon Kiesel, *Office Mgr*
Bill Chandler, *Prgrmr*
Grace Morin, *Director*
EMP: 12
SQ FT: 6,800
SALES (est): 3.3MM
SALES (corp-wide): 8.4MM **Publicly Held**
WEB: www.altamirainstruments.com
SIC: 3826 Analytical instruments

PA: Scientific Industries, Inc.
80 Orville Dr Ste 102
Bohemia NY 11716
631 567-4700

(G-14692)
ALTAMIRA LTD
517 Mcneilly Rd (15226-2503)
PHONE..................................800 343-1066
Joseph Kramer, *Mng Member*
EMP: 3
SALES: 599.1K **Privately Held**
WEB: www.altamiraltd.com
SIC: 5047 3842 7389 7352 Medical equipment & supplies; surgical appliances & supplies; ; medical equipment rental

(G-14693)
ALTUS REFRACTORIES LLC
303 Murrays Ln (15234-2354)
P.O. Box 25, Cabot (16023-0025)
PHONE..................................412 430-0138
Jessica Fernandez, *Officer*
Bud Roenigk,
◆ **EMP:** 3
SALES: 1.3MM **Privately Held**
SIC: 3255 7389 Castable refractories, clay;

(G-14694)
ALUMAGRAPHICS INC
Also Called: Creative Case Works
214 Parkway View Dr (15205-1404)
PHONE..................................412 787-7594
Brian Pfeiffer, *President*
Drew Pfeiffer, *General Mgr*
EMP: 20
SALES (est): 4.2MM **Privately Held**
WEB: www.alumainc.com
SIC: 2679 Tags, paper (unprinted): made from purchased paper

(G-14695)
ALUMAX LLC (HQ)
201 Isabella St (15212-5872)
PHONE..................................412 553-4545
Russel W Porter Jr, *President*
William B Plummer, *Treasurer*
John Hopkins, *Manager*
Donna C Dabney, *Admin Sec*
EMP: 120
SALES (est): 1.2B
SALES (corp-wide): 14B **Publicly Held**
SIC: 3334 3353 3354 3449 Primary aluminum; aluminum sheet, plate & foil; coils, sheet aluminum; plates, aluminum; foil, aluminum; aluminum extruded products; miscellaneous metalwork; curtain wall, metal; store fronts, prefabricated, metal; storm doors or windows, metal; architectural metalwork; ornamental metalwork
PA: Arconic Inc.
390 Park Ave Fl 12
New York NY 10022
212 836-2758

(G-14696)
ALUMINUM COMPANY OF AMERICA
201 Isabella St (15212-5872)
PHONE..................................412 553-4545
John Kenna, *CEO*
EMP: 5
SALES (est): 123.3K
SALES (corp-wide): 13.4B **Publicly Held**
SIC: 3355 Aluminum rolling & drawing
PA: Alcoa Corporation
201 Isabella St Ste 500
Pittsburgh PA 15212
412 315-2900

(G-14697)
ALUNG TECHNOLOGIES INC (PA)
2500 Jane St Ste 1 (15203-2216)
PHONE..................................412 697-3370
Pete Decomo, *Ch of Bd*
Nicholas Kuhn, *President*
Joe Argyros, *Senior VP*
Frank Falcione, *Vice Pres*
Scott Morley, *Vice Pres*
EMP: 26
SALES (est): 3.8MM **Privately Held**
WEB: www.alung.com
SIC: 3845 Electromedical equipment

(G-14698)
AMC INC
Also Called: Ann Gregory For The Bride
2975 W Liberty Ave (15216-2543)
PHONE....................412 531-3160
Gregory Cherico, *President*
Ann Gregory, *Treasurer*
EMP: 6
SQ FT: 4,000
SALES (est): 559.7K **Privately Held**
SIC: 2335 5137 5621 5699 Wedding
gowns & dresses; dresses; bridal shops;
ready-to-wear apparel, women's; formal
wear

(G-14699)
**AMERICAN ADVENTURE
SPORTS**
1217 S Braddock Ave (15218-1239)
PHONE....................724 205-6450
EMP: 3
SALES (est): 213.9K **Privately Held**
SIC: 3949 Camping equipment & supplies

(G-14700)
AMERICAN BANK PRINTERS
600 Chatham Park Dr (15220-2410)
PHONE....................412 566-6737
David J Bummer, *Principal*
▲ **EMP:** 4
SALES (est): 295.8K **Privately Held**
SIC: 2752 Commercial printing, litho-
graphic

(G-14701)
**AMERICAN BEVERAGE
CORPORATION**
100 Papercraft Park (15238-3200)
PHONE....................412 828-9020
EMP: 5
SALES (corp-wide): 1.3B **Privately Held**
SIC: 2033 Fruits & fruit products in cans,
jars, etc.
HQ: American Beverage Corporation
1 Daily Way
Verona PA 15147
412 828-9020

(G-14702)
**AMERICAN ECONOMIC
ASSOCIATION**
Also Called: Journal of Economic Literature
2403 Sidney St Ste 260 (15203-5118)
PHONE....................412 432-2300
Edda Leithner, *Admin Asst*
EMP: 10
SALES (est): 830.7K
SALES (corp-wide): 11.1MM **Privately
Held**
SIC: 2721 Trade journals: publishing &
printing
PA: The American Economic Association
2014 Broadway Ste 305
Nashville TN 37203
615 322-2595

(G-14703)
**AMERICAN MADE SYSTEMS
INC**
Also Called: American Made Liner Systems
2600 Neville Rd (15225-1404)
PHONE....................412 771-3300
Mark A Chiarelli, *President*
Caroline Larocco, *COO*
Jason Williams, *Sales Staff*
Mike Weir, *Admin Sec*
EMP: 7 **EST:** 2010
SQ FT: 14,000
SALES (est): 1.4MM **Privately Held**
SIC: 3443 Liners/lining

(G-14704)
**AMERICAN PRINTING CO &
PDTS**
Also Called: American Printing Company
5406 Guarino Rd (15217-1919)
P.O. Box 81023 (15217-0523)
PHONE....................412 422-3488
Natalie Schneir, *Partner*
Don Millmaster, *Partner*
EMP: 6
SALES: 1.7MM **Privately Held**
SIC: 5112 2759 Business forms; office
supplies; promotional printing

(G-14705)
**AMERICAN REFINING GROUP
INC**
55 Alpha Dr W Ste 3 (15238-1419)
PHONE....................412 826-3014
Jeannine Schoenecker, *President*
Martin Greenberg, *Technology*
EMP: 13
SALES (corp-wide): 194.1MM **Privately
Held**
WEB: www.amref.com
SIC: 2911 Petroleum refining
PA: American Refining Group, Inc.
77 N Kendall Ave
Bradford PA 16701
814 368-1200

(G-14706)
**AMERICAN SENSORS
CORPORATION**
557 Long Rd (15235-4330)
PHONE....................412 242-5903
Francois Reizine, *President*
Janet Reizine, *Admin Sec*
EMP: 10
SQ FT: 11,000
SALES (est): 1.4MM **Privately Held**
WEB: www.americansensors.com
SIC: 3625 Control equipment, electric

(G-14707)
AMERICAN STRESS TECH INC
540 Alpha Dr (15238-2912)
PHONE....................412 784-8400
Robert M Fix, *President*
Stephen Kendrish, *President*
Wade Gubbels, *Engineer*
James Thomas, *Engineer*
Joseph Pannell, *Sales Engr*
EMP: 10 **EST:** 1983
SQ FT: 5,100
SALES (est): 2.5MM
SALES (corp-wide): 2.8MM **Privately
Held**
WEB: www.astresstech.com
SIC: 3829 Measuring & controlling devices
HQ: Stresstech Oy
Tikkutehtaantie 1
Vaajakoski 40800
143 330-00

(G-14708)
**AMERICAN ZINC RECYCLING
CORP (HQ)**
4955 Steubenville Pike # 405
(15205-9604)
PHONE....................724 774-1020
Wayne Isaacs, *President*
Rob Williamson, *General Mgr*
Mike Griffin, *COO*
Tim Basilone, *Vice Pres*
Al Lewis, *Safety Mgr*
◆ **EMP:** 30
SQ FT: 6,000
SALES (est): 145MM **Privately Held**
WEB: www.horseheadcorp.com
SIC: 3339 3629 Zinc smelting (primary),
including zinc residue; mercury arc recti-
fiers (electrical apparatus)

(G-14709)
**AMERICAN ZINC RECYCLING
LLC (PA)**
4955 Steubenville Pike (15205-9619)
PHONE....................724 773-2203
Wayne Isaacs, *Ch of Bd*
Michael Griffin, *COO*
Ali Alavi, *Senior VP*
Gary R Whitaker, *Vice Pres*
Marcelino Rodriguez, *CFO*
EMP: 35
SALES: 414.9MM **Privately Held**
WEB: www.zinccorp.com
SIC: 3339 Zinc refining (primary), including
slabs & dust

(G-14710)
**AMG RESOURCES
CORPORATION (HQ)**
2 Robinson Plz Ste 350 (15205-1045)
PHONE....................412 777-7300
Allan M Goldstein, *CEO*
Jimi Dipietro, *General Mgr*
Joe Joyce, *District Mgr*
Ronald R Zorn, *COO*

Eric Goldstein, *Exec VP*
◆ **EMP:** 25
SQ FT: 175,000
SALES (est): 57.6MM
SALES (corp-wide): 64.4MM **Privately
Held**
SIC: 3312 3341 5093 Billets, steel;
detinning of cans & scrap; metal scrap &
waste materials
PA: Amg Industries Corporation
2 Robinson Plz Ste 350
Pittsburgh PA 15205
412 777-7300

(G-14711)
ANGLE FOODS LLC
3100 Penn Ave (15201-1442)
P.O. Box 71, Callery (16024-0071)
PHONE....................724 900-0908
Dough Mariani,
Kurt Angle,
David Hawk,
EMP: 7
SALES: 400K **Privately Held**
SIC: 2099 Food preparations

(G-14712)
ANSEN CORPORATION
720 Trumbull Dr (15205-4363)
PHONE....................315 393-3573
EMP: 5
SALES (est): 455.9K **Privately Held**
SIC: 3672 Printed circuit boards

(G-14713)
ANSOFT LLC (HQ)
225 W Station Square Dr # 200
(15219-1179)
PHONE....................412 261-3200
James Cashman, *CEO*
Maria Shields, *CFO*
Torsten Fichtner, *Sales Staff*
EMP: 8
SQ FT: 28,000
SALES (est): 20.7MM
SALES (corp-wide): 1.2B **Publicly Held**
WEB: www.ansoft.com
SIC: 7372 Prepackaged software
PA: Ansys, Inc.
2600 Ansys Dr
Canonsburg PA 15317
884 462-6797

(G-14714)
**APTECH COMPUTER SYSTEMS
INC**
135 Delta Dr (15238-2805)
PHONE....................412 963-7440
Jay S Troutman, *President*
CAM Troutman, *Vice Pres*
Jill Wilder, *Vice Pres*
Betty Barberich, *Accounting Mgr*
Kimberly A Sieminski, *Sales Associate*
EMP: 20
SALES (est): 2.3MM **Privately Held**
WEB: www.aptech-inc.com
SIC: 7372 Business oriented computer
software

(G-14715)
AQUION ENERGY INC
32 39th St (15201-3205)
PHONE....................412 904-6400
Scott A Pearson, *CEO*
Steve Vassallo, *Principal*
Bill Wiberg, *Principal*
John Connolly, *CFO*
◆ **EMP:** 130 **EST:** 2008
SALES (est): 43.2MM **Privately Held**
SIC: 3691 Storage batteries

(G-14716)
**ARCELRMTTAL TBLAR PDTS
USA LLC (DH)**
4 Gateway Ctr (15222)
PHONE....................419 342-1200
Jerome Granboulan, *CEO*
William Chisholm, *President*
Robert Nuttall, *Treasurer*
Tom Lally, *Accountant*
Robert Parker, *Human Res Dir*
▼ **EMP:** 30
SQ FT: 15,000

SALES (est): 242MM
SALES (corp-wide): 9.1B **Privately Held**
SIC: 3317 Tubes, seamless steel; tubes,
wrought: welded or lock joint
HQ: Arcelormittal Dofasco G.P.
1330 Burlington St E
Hamilton ON L8N 3
905 548-7200

(G-14717)
**ARCHITECTURAL SIGN
ASSOCIATES**
300 Mount Lebanon Blvd 201a
(15234-1537)
P.O. Box 24596 (15234-4596)
PHONE....................412 563-5657
Gary Katz, *President*
Michael Kaplan, *Manager*
EMP: 12
SALES (est): 1.2MM **Privately Held**
SIC: 3993 Signs, not made in custom sign
painting shops

(G-14718)
ARCONIC INC
201 Isabella St Ste 200 (15212-5872)
PHONE....................412 553-4545
David Milbourne, *Vice Pres*
Melissa Miller, *Vice Pres*
Dennis Apon, *Project Mgr*
Ben Hernton, *Project Mgr*
Matthew Holland, *Safety Mgr*
EMP: 137
SALES (corp-wide): 14B **Publicly Held**
SIC: 3353 Aluminum sheet, plate & foil
PA: Arconic Inc.
390 Park Ave Fl 12
New York NY 10022
212 836-2758

(G-14719)
**ARCONIC MEXICO HOLDINGS
LLC**
201 Isabella St (15212-5872)
PHONE....................412 553-4545
Ernesto Zedillo, *Director*
EMP: 9001
SALES (est): 228.8MM
SALES (corp-wide): 14B **Publicly Held**
SIC: 3334 Primary aluminum
PA: Arconic Inc.
390 Park Ave Fl 12
New York NY 10022
212 836-2758

(G-14720)
ARDENT RESOURCES INC
61 Mcmurray Rd Ste 204 (15241-1633)
P.O. Box 12740 (15241-0740)
PHONE....................412 854-1193
David Copley, *President*
Christopher Robinson, *Vice Pres*
EMP: 6
SALES (est): 1MM **Privately Held**
WEB: www.ardentresources.com
SIC: 1311 1381 Natural gas production;
drilling oil & gas wells

(G-14721)
ARIBA INC
210 6th Ave Fl 25 (15222-2602)
PHONE....................412 644-0160
Jennifer Sinatra, *Partner*
Kent Parker, *COO*
Sandra Simmons, *Project Mgr*
Jason Brown, *Sales Executive*
Derrick Berad, *Manager*
EMP: 100
SALES (corp-wide): 28.2B **Privately Held**
WEB: www.ariba.com
SIC: 7372 Business oriented computer
software
HQ: Ariba, Inc.
3420 Hillview Ave Bldg 3
Palo Alto CA 94304

(G-14722)
ARIN TECHNOLOGIES INC
24 Terminal Way Ste 324 (15219-1209)
PHONE....................412 877-2877
Pradyumna Kulkarni, *CEO*
Mark Imgrund, *Vice Pres*
EMP: 7
SALES (est): 325.5K **Privately Held**
SIC: 3812 Distance measuring equipment;
inertial guidance systems

(G-14723)
ARLANXEO USA HOLDINGS CORP (DH)
111 Ridc Park West Dr (15275-1112)
PHONE...................................412 809-1000
Antonis Papadourakis, *President*
EMP: 1 EST: 2016
SALES (est): 86.5MM
SALES (corp-wide): 388.2MM **Privately Held**
SIC: 2821 2824 Elastomers, nonvulcaniz-able (plastics); elastomeric fibers
HQ: Arlanxeo Holding B.V.
Stationsplein 8
Maastricht
467 020-700

(G-14724)
ARLANXEO USA LLC (DH)
111 Ridc Park West Dr (15275-1112)
PHONE...................................412 809-1000
Antonis Papadourakis, *President*
EMP: 350
SALES (est): 86.5MM
SALES (corp-wide): 388.2MM **Privately Held**
SIC: 2821 2824 Elastomers, nonvulcaniz-able (plastics); elastomeric fibers
HQ: Arlanxeo Usa Holdings Corp.
111 Ridc Park West Dr
Pittsburgh PA 15275
412 809-1000

(G-14725)
ARMIN IRONWORKS INC
1800 Preble Ave (15233-2242)
PHONE...................................412 322-1622
Aldo Deciantis, *President*
EMP: 9
SQ FT: 6,500
SALES (est): 1.4MM **Privately Held**
SIC: 3441 3446 1799 Fabricated struc-tural metal; fire escapes, metal; ornamen-tal metal work

(G-14726)
ARMSTRONG PRECISION MFG LLC
1370 Old Frport Rd Ste 3b (15238)
PHONE...................................412 449-0160
William R German, *Principal*
EMP: 3
SALES (est): 225.7K **Privately Held**
SIC: 3999 Manufacturing industries

(G-14727)
ARTISTAGRAPHICS INC
2148 Ardmore Blvd (15221-4824)
PHONE...................................412 271-3252
Karen Horanic, *President*
Martin Hako, *Manager*
EMP: 12
SQ FT: 2,600
SALES (est): 990K **Privately Held**
WEB: www.artistagraphics.com
SIC: 7336 2759 2395 Graphic arts & re-lated design; invitation & stationery print-ing & engraving; embroidery products, except schiffli machine

(G-14728)
ASSURED POLYGRAPH SERVICES INC
3242 Babcock Blvd (15237-2827)
PHONE...................................412 492-9980
William E Barrett, *President*
EMP: 4
SALES (est): 412.3K **Privately Held**
SIC: 3829 Polygraph devices

(G-14729)
ASTROBOTIC TECHNOLOGY INC
2515 Liberty Ave (15222-4613)
PHONE...................................412 682-3282
John Thornton, *CEO*
William Whittaker, *Ch of Bd*
Dan Hendrickson, *Vice Pres*
Andrew Horchler, *Research*
Kerry Snyder, *Software Engr*
EMP: 15
SQ FT: 8,800

SALES (est): 1.2MM **Privately Held**
SIC: 3761 8711 Guided missiles & space vehicles, research & development; engi-neering services

(G-14730)
ATALANTI POLYMER INC
1016 Constance St (15212-5037)
PHONE...................................412 321-7411
Alex Vagias, *President*
Elizabeth Vagias, *Corp Secy*
EMP: 7
SALES (est): 363K **Privately Held**
SIC: 3089 Injection molding of plastics; plastic processing

(G-14731)
ATI OPERATING HOLDINGS LLC (DH)
1000 Six Ppg Pl (15222)
PHONE...................................412 394-2800
Richard J Harshman, *CEO*
Dylan Bates, *COO*
Sheila Denman, *Senior VP*
Christopher SL Pussey, *Vice Pres*
John Egofske, *CFO*
EMP: 9
SALES (est): 5.1B **Publicly Held**
SIC: 3462 Iron & steel forgings
HQ: A T I Funding Corporation
801 N West St Fl 2
Wilmington DE 19801
302 656-8937

(G-14732)
ATI POWDER METALS LLC (DH)
1000 Six Ppg Pl (15222)
PHONE...................................412 394-2800
Richard J Harshman, *CEO*
L Patrick Hassey, *President*
Brian Drummond, *Principal*
JD Walton, *Principal*
Gary Van Dyke, *Exec VP*
EMP: 72
SALES (est): 15.9MM **Publicly Held**
SIC: 3356 3312 3316 3339 Zirconium; ti-tanium; nickel; blast furnaces & steel mills; cold finishing of steel shapes; pri-mary nonferrous metals; nonferrous foundries
HQ: Tdy Industries, Llc
1000 Six Ppg Pl
Pittsburgh PA 15222
412 394-2896

(G-14733)
ATLAS GROWTH PARTNERS LP
1000 Commerce Dr Ste 400 (15275-1033)
PHONE...................................412 489-0006
EMP: 156
SALES (est): 4MM **Publicly Held**
SIC: 1382 Oil & gas exploration services
HQ: Targa Energy, L.P.
1000 Commerce Dr Ste 400
Pittsburgh PA 15275

(G-14734)
ATLAS RESOURCES LLC (DH)
Also Called: Atlas Energy Resources
1000 Commerce Dr Ste 510 (15275-1033)
PHONE...................................800 251-0171
Freddie M Kotek, *President*
Frank P Carolas, *Exec VP*
Jefferey C Simmons, *Exec VP*
Michael L Staines, *Senior VP*
Clint Duty, *Vice Pres*
EMP: 14
SQ FT: 24,000
SALES: 7MM
SALES (corp-wide): 9MM **Publicly Held**
SIC: 1311 Crude petroleum & natural gas
HQ: Titan Energy, Llc
425 Houston St Ste 300
Fort Worth TX 76102
817 698-8000

(G-14735)
ATLAS RSRCES SERIES 28-2010 LP
Park Pl Corp Ctr One 1000 Corporate Cen-ter (15275)
PHONE...................................412 489-0006
Edward E Cohen, *Principal*
EMP: 3 EST: 2012
SALES (est): 164.6K **Privately Held**
SIC: 1311 Crude petroleum & natural gas

(G-14736)
ATLS PRODUCTION COMPANY LLC
1000 Commerce Dr Ste 400 (15275-1033)
PHONE...................................412 489-0006
Jonathan Cohen, *CEO*
Matthew Jones, *President*
Mark Scheumacher, *COO*
Daniel Herz, *Senior VP*
Sean McGrath, *CFO*
EMP: 208
SALES (est): 4.9MM **Publicly Held**
SIC: 1382 2911 Oil & gas exploration serv-ices; oils; fuel
HQ: Targa Energy, L.P.
1000 Commerce Dr Ste 400
Pittsburgh PA 15275

(G-14737)
ATRP SOLUTIONS INC
855 William Pitt Way (15238-1334)
PHONE...................................412 735-4799
Patrick McCarthy, *CEO*
EMP: 8
SQ FT: 1,200
SALES (est): 468K
SALES (corp-wide): 109.1MM **Privately Held**
SIC: 2821 Plastics materials & resins
PA: Pilot Chemical Company Of Ohio
2744 E Kemper Rd
Cincinnati OH 45241
513 326-0600

(G-14738)
AUL COMPANY JACK
4687 Cook Ave (15236-1921)
PHONE...................................412 882-1836
Jack Aul, *Principal*
EMP: 4
SALES (est): 324.2K **Privately Held**
SIC: 3949 Sporting & athletic goods

(G-14739)
AURORA ELECTRICAL & DATA SVCS
2740 Smallman St Ste 600 (15222-4744)
PHONE...................................412 255-4060
Antonia Dallier, *Principal*
EMP: 8
SALES: 500K **Privately Held**
SIC: 1542 3577 5063 Commercial & of-fice building, new construction; data con-version equipment, media-to-media: computer; boxes & fittings, electrical

(G-14740)
AURORA INTERNATIONAL COAT
20 Grant Ave (15223-1883)
PHONE...................................412 782-2984
Beth Sarver, *Owner*
EMP: 13
SALES (est): 2MM **Privately Held**
SIC: 2851 Shellac (protective coating)

(G-14741)
AUTOGRAPH SIGNS INC
508 Rodi Rd (15235-4522)
PHONE...................................412 371-2877
Jeff Goodwill, *President*
EMP: 5
SALES (est): 594.5K **Privately Held**
SIC: 3993 Signs & advertising specialties

(G-14742)
AVATAR DATA PUBG SOLUTIONS
1815 Crafton Blvd (15205-3149)
PHONE...................................412 921-7747
Coletta Perry, *Owner*
EMP: 5
SALES: 435K **Privately Held**
WEB: www.avatardps.com
SIC: 7372 Publishers' computer software

(G-14743)
AVC SOLUTIONS LLC
2511 Sarah St (15203-2249)
PHONE...................................412 737-8945
Mark Anderson, *Mng Member*
EMP: 5

SALES (est): 100K **Privately Held**
SIC: 1389 6531 8742 Construction, repair & dismantling services; real estate agents & managers; construction project man-agement consultant

(G-14744)
AXIALL LLC
11 Stanwix St Ste 1900 (15222-1312)
PHONE...................................412 515-8149
Tim Mann, *Mng Member*
◆ EMP: 1000
SALES (est): 15.4MM **Privately Held**
SIC: 2899 Chemical preparations

(G-14745)
B & L MANUFACTURING CORP
Also Called: Straits Door Co
5629 Harrison St (15201-2334)
P.O. Box 40187 (15201-0187)
PHONE...................................412 784-9400
Mark S Lascher, *President*
Donald Lascher, *Chairman*
Michael A Bauer, *Vice Pres*
Raymond T Bauer, *Admin Sec*
EMP: 15
SQ FT: 30,000
SALES (est): 1.6MM **Privately Held**
SIC: 2431 3442 Doors, wood; metal doors

(G-14746)
BABCOCK LUMBER COMPANY
905 Old Hickory Rd (15243-1113)
PHONE...................................814 239-2281
Jim Dailey, *General Mgr*
Joe Campbell, *Manager*
EMP: 9
SALES (corp-wide): 5.5MM **Privately Held**
WEB: www.babcocklumber.com
SIC: 2426 5031 Lumber, hardwood dimen-sion; lumber, plywood & millwork
PA: Babcock Lumber Company
2220 Palmer St
Pittsburgh PA 15218
412 310-6291

(G-14747)
BACHARACH INSTRUMENTS LTD
625 Alpha Dr (15238-2819)
PHONE...................................724 334-5000
Paul Zito, *Principal*
EMP: 11
SALES (est): 1.3MM **Privately Held**
SIC: 3841 Surgical & medical instruments

(G-14748)
BADIN BUSINESS PARK LLC (HQ)
201 Isabella St (15212-5872)
PHONE...................................412 553-4545
Mark Stiffler, *CEO*
EMP: 3 EST: 2016
SALES (est): 450.1K
SALES (corp-wide): 1.7B **Privately Held**
SIC: 3355 Aluminum rolling & drawing
PA: Halco (Mining) Inc.
323 N Shore Dr
Pittsburgh PA 15212
412 235-0265

(G-14749)
BAI PRINTING
615 Plum Industrial Park (15239-2924)
PHONE...................................412 400-5555
Lucy Garrighan, *Owner*
John Zill, *Manager*
EMP: 3 EST: 1999
SALES (est): 172.6K **Privately Held**
SIC: 2752 Commercial printing, litho-graphic

(G-14750)
BAYER CORPORATION (HQ)
100 Bayer Rd Bldg 14 (15205-9741)
P.O. Box 135 (15230-0135)
PHONE...................................412 777-2000
Klaus H Risse, *President*
Patrick Lockwood-Taylor, *President*
Bruce Benda, *Principal*
Kurt De Ruwe, *COO*
Melvyn A Silver, *Vice Pres*
◆ EMP: 1900

SALES (est): 3.1B
SALES (corp-wide): 45.3B **Privately Held**
SIC: **2821** 2879 2819 2834 Polypropylene resins; pesticides, agricultural or household; industrial inorganic chemicals; pharmaceutical preparations; surgical & medical instruments
PA: Bayer Ag
Kaiser-Wilhelm-Allee 1
Leverkusen 51373
214 301-

(G-14751)
BAYER CROPSCIENCE HOLDING INC
100 Bayer Rd (15205-9707)
PHONE..................................412 777-2000
Franky Pauwels, *Vice Pres*
EMP: 4
SALES (est): 581K
SALES (corp-wide): 45.3B **Privately Held**
SIC: **2821** Polypropylene resins
HQ: Bayer Corporation
100 Bayer Rd Bldg 14
Pittsburgh PA 15205
412 777-2000

(G-14752)
BAYER CROPSCIENCE LP
100 Bayer Rd (15205-9707)
P.O. Box 98 (15230-0098)
PHONE..................................412 777-2000
Dana Kush, *Sales Staff*
Eddie Obrien, *Sales Staff*
Philip Blake, *Branch Mgr*
Dan Holleran, *IT/INT Sup*
Lori Compano, *Executive Asst*
EMP: 78
SALES (corp-wide): 71.7B **Privately Held**
SIC: **2879** Fungicides, herbicides
HQ: Bayer Cropscience Lp
2 Tw Alexander Dr
Durham NC 27709
919 549-2000

(G-14753)
BAYER DATA CENTER PITTSBURGH
810 Parish St (15220-3405)
PHONE..................................412 920-2950
Heidi Leep, *Manager*
EMP: 5
SALES (est): 363.9K **Privately Held**
SIC: **2834** Pharmaceutical preparations

(G-14754)
BAYER HEALTHCARE LLC
100 Bayer Rd (15205-9707)
PHONE..................................412 777-2000
George Paniagua, *President*
Stephan Gutsche, *Project Mgr*
Gueth Braddock, *Sales Staff*
Tom Dinn, *Sales Staff*
Doug Jones, *Sales Staff*
EMP: 134
SALES (corp-wide): 45.3B **Privately Held**
SIC: **2834** Pharmaceutical preparations
HQ: Bayer Healthcare Llc
100 Bayer Blvd
Whippany NJ 07981
862 404-3000

(G-14755)
BAYER INTL TRADE SVCS CORP
100 Bayer Rd Bldg 4 (15205-9707)
PHONE..................................412 777-2000
EMP: 4
SALES (est): 295.1K
SALES (corp-wide): 45.3B **Privately Held**
SIC: **2821** Polypropylene resins
HQ: Bayer Corporation
100 Bayer Rd Bldg 14
Pittsburgh PA 15205
412 777-2000

(G-14756)
BAYER MEDICAL CARE INC
Also Called: Bayer Healthcare
625 Alpha Dr (15238-2819)
PHONE..................................412 767-2400
Bradley Adams, *Engineer*
Andy Deutsch, *Engineer*
Sharon Standish, *Sr Project Mgr*
John P Friel, *Manager*
Jody Lobert, *Manager*
EMP: 57

SALES (corp-wide): 45.3B **Privately Held**
WEB: www.medrad.com
SIC: **3841** Surgical & medical instruments
HQ: Bayer Medical Care Inc.
1 Bayer Dr
Indianola PA 15051
724 940-6800

(G-14757)
BAYHILL DEFENSE LLC
221 Paulson Ave (15206-3229)
PHONE..................................412 877-9372
Biney Dhillon, *CEO*
Andrew Taglianetti, *President*
Kristopher Nagy, *Vice Pres*
EMP: 5
SALES (est): 300.2K **Privately Held**
SIC: **3812** Defense systems & equipment

(G-14758)
BEARING SERVICE COMPANY PA (PA)
630 Alpha Dr (15238-2802)
P.O. Box 371733 (15250-7733)
PHONE..................................412 963-7710
William J Banks, *President*
Carolyn Matta, *General Mgr*
Jacob W Banks, *Chairman*
Dan Nichiforel, *Vice Pres*
John Schoessel, *Vice Pres*
▲ EMP: 85
SQ FT: 88,000
SALES (est): 51.8MM **Privately Held**
WEB: www.bearing-service.com
SIC: **3562** 5085 Ball bearings & parts; bearings

(G-14759)
BEITLER-MCKEE OPTICAL COMPANY
160 S 22nd St (15203-2090)
PHONE..................................412 381-7953
W Daniel Driscoll, *Ch of Bd*
Clarke Lauffer, *Regional Mgr*
Diane Kimble, *Sales Staff*
Mike Klaphake, *Manager*
Peter Pugliese, *Manager*
EMP: 1
SQ FT: 25,000
SALES (est): 12.2MM
SALES (corp-wide): 283.5MM **Privately Held**
WEB: www.beitlermckee.com
SIC: **3851** 5048 Eyeglasses, lenses & frames; ophthalmic goods
HQ: Essilor Laboratories Of America Holding Co., Inc.
13555 N Stemmons Fwy
Dallas TX 75234
214 496-4141

(G-14760)
BEL AIRE FOODS INC
530 Camp Horne Rd (15237-1199)
PHONE..................................412 364-7277
Kenneth Kalb, *President*
Margaret Sling, *Treasurer*
EMP: 40 EST: 1961
SALES (est): 4.4MM **Privately Held**
SIC: **2037** 2033 Potato products, quick frozen & cold pack; vegetables, quick frozen & cold pack, excl. potato products; canned fruits & specialties

(G-14761)
BELTONE CORPORATION
1000 Robinson Center Dr (15205-4828)
PHONE..................................412 490-4902
EMP: 4
SALES (corp-wide): 1.6B **Privately Held**
SIC: **3842** Hearing aids
HQ: Beltone Corporation
2601 Patriot Blvd
Glenview IL 60026
847 832-3300

(G-14762)
BENSHAW INC (HQ)
615 Alpha Dr (15238-2819)
PHONE..................................412 968-0100
Mark J Gliebe, *CEO*
Glenn E Tynan, *Vice Pres*
Francis X Livingston, *Treasurer*
David J Linton, *Admin Sec*
◆ EMP: 80

SALES (est): 4.6MM
SALES (corp-wide): 3.6B **Publicly Held**
WEB: www.benshawexpress.com
SIC: **3625** Motor starters & controllers, electric
PA: Regal Beloit Corporation
200 State St
Beloit WI 53511
608 364-8800

(G-14763)
BERKMAN JOHN A DISPLAY SLS INC
Also Called: Creative Marketing Associates
5715 Beacon St Apt 318 (15217-2080)
PHONE..................................412 421-0201
John A Berkman, *President*
EMP: 3 EST: 1996
SQ FT: 8,000
SALES: 11MM **Privately Held**
WEB: www.creativemarketingassoc.com
SIC: **2541** Store fixtures, wood

(G-14764)
BEST MEDICAL INTERNATIONAL INC
Best Nomos
1 Best Dr (15202-1706)
PHONE..................................412 312-6700
Michael Ryan, *Manager*
EMP: 64
SALES (corp-wide): 41.3MM **Privately Held**
WEB: www.best-medical.com
SIC: **7372** 7371 3841 2834 Prepackaged software; custom computer programming services; surgical & medical instruments; drugs acting on the respiratory system
HQ: Best Medical International, Inc.
7643 Fullerton Rd
Springfield VA 22153
703 451-2378

(G-14765)
BEST-MADE SHOES
5143 Liberty Ave (15224-2217)
PHONE..................................412 621-9363
Eugene Rosen, *Owner*
▲ EMP: 4
SQ FT: 1,200
SALES (est): 388.3K **Privately Held**
WEB: www.bestmadeshoes.com
SIC: **5661** 3143 Shoes, orthopedic; orthopedic shoes, men's

(G-14766)
BIMBO BAKERIES USA INC
Also Called: C P C Baking Group
780 Pine Valley Dr Ste D (15239-2892)
PHONE..................................724 733-2332
Larry Tataro, *Branch Mgr*
EMP: 12 **Privately Held**
WEB: www.gwbakeries.com
SIC: **2051** Bakery: wholesale or wholesale/retail combined
HQ: Bimbo Bakeries Usa, Inc
255 Business Center Dr # 200
Horsham PA 19044
215 347-5500

(G-14767)
BIRDBRAIN TECHNOLOGIES LLC
544 Miltenberger St (15219-5971)
PHONE..................................412 216-5833
Allison Mora, *Marketing Staff*
Sarah Gremba, *Manager*
Tom Lauwers, *Info Tech Mgr*
Ashley Durham, *Media Spec*
Kelsey Derringer, *Coordinator*
▲ EMP: 5
SALES (est): 575.1K **Privately Held**
SIC: **3577** Computer peripheral equipment

(G-14768)
BISHOP METALS INCORPORATED
422 Hays Ave (15210-2206)
PHONE..................................412 481-5501
Arthur C Bishop Jr, *President*
Betsy Schoedel, *Corp Secy*
EMP: 17
SQ FT: 10,200

SALES (est): 2.3MM **Privately Held**
WEB: www.bishopmetals.com
SIC: **2542** Cabinets: show, display or storage: except wood; counters or counter display cases: except wood; fixtures, store: except wood

(G-14769)
BISS NUSS INC
2600 Boyce Plaza Rd # 141 (15241-3949)
PHONE..................................412 221-1200
Richard Bible, *Manager*
Jennifer Calfee, *Admin Asst*
EMP: 6
SALES (corp-wide): 7.9MM **Privately Held**
WEB: www.bissnuss.com
SIC: **3589** Water treatment equipment, industrial
PA: Biss Nuss, Inc.
Olde Crthuse Bldg Ste 260
Canfield OH 44406
330 533-5531

(G-14770)
BITTNER DISTRIBUTORS COMPANY
26th & Smallman Sts (15222)
PHONE..................................412 261-8000
John Bittner, *President*
Clarence Bittner, *Vice Pres*
Ken Wise, *Admin Sec*
EMP: 5
SALES (est): 400K **Privately Held**
SIC: **2434** Wood kitchen cabinets

(G-14771)
BLIND AND VISION REHAB (PA)
1816 Locust St (15219-5920)
PHONE..................................412 368-4400
Erika Abrogast, *President*
Leslie Montgomery, *Vice Pres*
Sally Taylor, *Vice Pres*
Sara Taylor, *CFO*
EMP: 60 EST: 1959
SQ FT: 65,000
SALES: 4.3MM **Privately Held**
WEB: www.pghvis.com
SIC: **8211** 8331 3991 3993 Public vocational/technical school; school for physically handicapped; vocational high school; job training & vocational rehabilitation services; brooms & brushes; signs & advertising specialties; men's & boys' work clothing

(G-14772)
BLIND DOCTORS
506 Seavey Rd (15209-1840)
P.O. Box 307, Ingomar (15127-0307)
PHONE..................................412 822-8580
John Duddy, *Owner*
EMP: 3
SALES (est): 307.4K **Privately Held**
SIC: **2591** Drapery hardware & blinds & shades

(G-14773)
BLOOM ENGINEERING COMPANY INC (HQ)
5460 Horning Rd (15236-2822)
PHONE..................................412 653-3500
Robert F Green, *President*
Christopher Armitage, *President*
Frank Beichner, *Vice Pres*
Charles G Drago, *Vice Pres*
David B Schalles, *Vice Pres*
▲ EMP: 12 EST: 1934
SQ FT: 145,000
SALES: 18MM
SALES (corp-wide): 421.6K **Privately Held**
WEB: www.bloomeng.com
SIC: **3433** 3255 3296 Burners, furnaces, boilers & stokers; gas-oil burners, combination; oil burners, domestic or industrial; fire clay blocks, bricks, tile or special shapes; mineral wool
PA: Sterling Industries Limited
South Building
Aylesbury BUCKS HP19
129 648-0210

(G-14774)
BLOOM REFRACTORY PRODUCTS LLC
5460 Curry Rd (15236-2822)
PHONE...................................412 653-3500
Robert Green, *Mng Member*
Charles Drago,
▲ EMP: 6
SQ FT: 50,000
SALES: 1.5MM Privately Held
SIC: 3255 Clay refractories

(G-14775)
BMI REFRACTORY SERVICES INC (HQ)
250 Parkwest Dr (15275-1002)
PHONE...................................412 429-1800
Gary Novak, *President*
Yves Nokerman, *Vice Pres*
Barry Salsi, *Project Engr*
John W Ehlman, *Treasurer*
Donald M Satina, *Admin Sec*
▲ EMP: 8
SALES (est): 20MM
SALES (corp-wide): 2.2B Privately Held
SIC: 3255 Glasshouse refractories
PA: Vesuvius Plc
165 Fleet Street
London EC4A
207 822-0000

(G-14776)
BNP MEDIA INC
1910 Cochran Rd Ste 450 (15220-1203)
PHONE...................................412 531-3370
Doug Glenn, *Principal*
EMP: 29
SALES (corp-wide): 158.1MM Privately Held
SIC: 2741 Miscellaneous publishing
PA: Bnp Media, Inc.
2401 W Big Beaver Rd # 700
Troy MI 48084
248 362-3700

(G-14777)
BNP MEDIA INC
Also Called: Industrial Heating Magazine
1910 Cochran Rd Ste 450 (15220-1203)
PHONE...................................412 531-3370
Doug Glenn, *Principal*
EMP: 9
SALES (corp-wide): 158.1MM Privately Held
SIC: 2721 Trade journals: publishing only, not printed on site
PA: Bnp Media, Inc.
2401 W Big Beaver Rd # 700
Troy MI 48084
248 362-3700

(G-14778)
BOBS DINER ENTERPRISES INC
1870 Painters Run Rd (15241-3114)
PHONE...................................412 221-7474
Bob Marshall, *Owner*
EMP: 11
SALES (est): 271.7K Privately Held
SIC: 5812 2024 Diner; ice cream & frozen desserts

(G-14779)
BOGNAR AND COMPANY INC (PA)
733 Washington Rd Ste 500 (15228-2022)
PHONE...................................412 344-9900
Nadine E Bognar, *CEO*
Edwin J Bognar Jr, *President*
▲ EMP: 1
SALES (est): 7.1MM Privately Held
SIC: 1221 Strip mining, bituminous

(G-14780)
BOKE INVESTMENT COMPANY (HQ)
12 Federal St Ste 320 (15212-5753)
PHONE...................................412 321-4252
Maysa Habelrih, *CEO*
EMP: 3000
SALES (est): 412MM
SALES (corp-wide): 1.7B Privately Held
SIC: 1099 Metal Ore Mining

PA: Halco (Mining) Inc.
323 N Shore Dr
Pittsburgh PA 15212
412 235-0265

(G-14781)
BOMBARDIER TRANSPORTATION
1400 Lebanon Church Rd (15236-1455)
PHONE...................................412 655-0325
Lindsey Hal, *Branch Mgr*
EMP: 17
SALES (corp-wide): 16.2B Privately Held
SIC: 3721 Aircraft
HQ: Bombardier Transportation (Holdings) Usa Inc.
1501 Lebanon Church Rd
Pittsburgh PA 15236
412 655-5700

(G-14782)
BOMBARDIER TRANSPORTATION (HQ)
Also Called: Bombardier Trnsp Systems
1501 Lebanon Church Rd (15236-1491)
P.O. Box 12299 (15231-0299)
PHONE...................................412 655-5700
Lutz Bertling, *President*
Richard Bradeen, *Senior VP*
ME Daniel Desjardin, *Senior VP*
John Paul Macdonald, *Senior VP*
Tomas Bjorkman, *Vice Pres*
◆ EMP: 948
SQ FT: 135,000
SALES (est): 675.5MM
SALES (corp-wide): 16.2B Privately Held
SIC: 3743 3315 3823 Interurban cars & car equipment; steel wire & related products; industrial instrmnts msrmnt display/control process variable
PA: Bombardier Inc
800 Boul Rene-Levesque O 29e Etage
Montreal QC H3B 1
514 861-9481

(G-14783)
BONES AND ALL LLC
6888 Hamilton Ave Rear (15208-1715)
PHONE...................................216 870-7177
Zachary Kruszynski,
EMP: 3 EST: 2014
SALES: 200K Privately Held
SIC: 2511 Wood household furniture

(G-14784)
BONURA JR CABINETS BY BILL
7940 Saltsburg Rd (15239-1900)
PHONE...................................412 793-6790
EMP: 3
SALES (est): 278.7K Privately Held
SIC: 3993 Signs & advertising specialties

(G-14785)
BOP LAND SERVICES LP
2547 Washington Rd # 720 (15241-2557)
PHONE...................................724 747-1594
Elizabeth Slozat, *Partner*
Kristen Buchanan, *Partner*
Bennett Wood, *Partner*
Joyce Wood, *Partner*
EMP: 19
SQ FT: 4,238
SALES (est): 1.2MM Privately Held
SIC: 1382 Aerial geophysical exploration oil & gas

(G-14786)
BOSS CONTROLS LLC
4117 Liberty Ave (15224-1446)
PHONE...................................724 396-8131
Gregory Puschnigg, *CEO*
EMP: 6 EST: 2012
SALES (est): 652.8K Privately Held
SIC: 3822 Auto controls regulating residntl & coml environmt & applncs

(G-14787)
BOWSER PONTIAC INC
Also Called: Bowser Pntc-Sbr-Suzu Oldsmbile
Lewis Run Rd & Rr 51 (15236)
P.O. Box 10019 (15236-6019)
PHONE...................................412 469-2100
Gary K Bowser, *President*
EMP: 180
SQ FT: 35,000

SALES (est): 52MM Privately Held
WEB: www.powerofbowser.com
SIC: 5511 3711 7538 5521 Automobiles, new & used; motor vehicles & car bodies; general automotive repair shops; used car dealers

(G-14788)
BPI INC (PA)
Also Called: B P I
612 S Trenton Ave (15221-3475)
PHONE...................................412 371-8554
Joseph Quigley, *President*
Richard A Baxter, *President*
Tony Ciccozzi, *Accountant*
Willy Wiltrout, *Manager*
Patricia Quigley, *Admin Sec*
▲ EMP: 12
SQ FT: 3,000
SALES (est): 20.5MM Privately Held
WEB: www.bpiminerals.com
SIC: 2899 Oxidizers, inorganic

(G-14789)
BRAD FOOTE GEAR WORKS INC
Also Called: Pittsburgh Gear Company
5100 Neville Rd (15225-1401)
PHONE...................................412 264-1428
Rich Baker, *Branch Mgr*
EMP: 40 Publicly Held
WEB: www.bradfoote.com
SIC: 3566 3536 3462 3441 Gears, power transmission, except automotive; hoists, cranes & monorails; iron & steel forgings; fabricated structural metal
HQ: Brad Foote Gear Works, Inc.
3250 S Central Ave
Cicero IL 60804
708 298-1100

(G-14790)
BRASKEM AMERICA INC
550 Technology Dr (15219-3111)
PHONE...................................412 208-8100
Chris Vaccaro, *Branch Mgr*
Ruben Migone, *Technical Staff*
EMP: 40 Privately Held
WEB: www.sunocoinc.com
SIC: 2821 2865 2869 Polypropylene resins; polyesters; acrylic resins; plasticizer/additive based plastic materials; cyclic crudes & intermediates; phenol, alkylated & cumene; aniline, nitrobenzene; diphenylamines; acetone, synthetic; alcohols, non-beverage
HQ: Braskem America, Inc.
1735 Market St Fl 28
Philadelphia PA 19103
215 841-3100

(G-14791)
BRENTANO CONCRETE CONNECTION
Also Called: Brentano's Concrete Connection
518 Rodi Rd Ste 520 (15235-4522)
PHONE...................................412 731-8485
Robert Colligan, *President*
Patricia Colligan, *Corp Secy*
EMP: 3 EST: 1947
SALES (est): 421.1K Privately Held
WEB: www.brentanostone.com
SIC: 3272 Concrete products

(G-14792)
BRIGHTON RESOURCES INC
5851 Ellsworth Ave Ste 1 (15232-1707)
P.O. Box 41063 (15202-0063)
PHONE...................................412 661-1025
Brendan McCarthy, *CEO*
Mike Moran, *President*
EMP: 2
SALES (est): 3.6MM Privately Held
SIC: 1382 Oil & gas exploration services

(G-14793)
BROCK ASSOCIATES LLC
180 Bilmar Dr Ste 2 (15205-4602)
PHONE...................................412 919-0690
Allen Brock, *Principal*
EMP: 17 EST: 2012
SALES (est): 13.1MM Privately Held
SIC: 5051 3448 Nonferrous metal sheets, bars, rods, etc.; panels for prefabricated metal buildings

(G-14794)
BROOKLINE FABRICS CO INC
5750 Baum Blvd (15206-3793)
PHONE...................................412 665-4925
Leonard Lachina, *President*
EMP: 25
SALES (est): 2.4MM Privately Held
WEB: www.brooklinefabrics.com
SIC: 5023 2392 2391 Draperies; household furnishings; curtains & draperies

(G-14795)
BRUTIS ENTERPRISES INC
Also Called: Level-Lok
105 S 12th St (15203-1225)
PHONE...................................412 431-5440
Bradley Bruback, *President*
David Bruback, *Treasurer*
▲ EMP: 5 EST: 1982
SALES: 120K Privately Held
WEB: www.level-lok.com
SIC: 3949 5941 Hunting equipment; hunting equipment

(G-14796)
BUCKLEY ASSOCIATES INC
636 Alpha Dr (15238-2893)
P.O. Box 111344 (15238-0744)
PHONE...................................412 963-7070
Harry W Buckley, *President*
M Bart Buckley, *Vice Pres*
EMP: 5 EST: 1952
SQ FT: 8,000
SALES: 3MM Privately Held
SIC: 1241 Coal mining services

(G-14797)
BURRELL SCIENTIFIC LLC
300 Parkway View Dr (15205-1406)
PHONE...................................412 747-2111
Walter Rausch, *President*
Kathy Vargo, *Sales Associate*
Aimee Speca, *Office Mgr*
▼ EMP: 10
SQ FT: 12,000
SALES (est): 4MM Privately Held
SIC: 3821 5047 Laboratory apparatus, except heating & measuring; medical equipment & supplies

(G-14798)
BWHIP MAGAZINE LLC
2439 Lyzell St (15214-3316)
PHONE...................................412 607-3963
Lisa Epps,
Kelly Morrissey,
EMP: 6
SQ FT: 13,000
SALES (est): 501K Privately Held
SIC: 2721 Magazines: publishing & printing

(G-14799)
CAFF CO
Also Called: Custom Aluminum Frame Fabg
370 Vista Park Dr (15205-1265)
PHONE...................................412 787-1761
John D Weaver Jr, *Owner*
Steve Weaver, *Purch Mgr*
Tom Haller, *Director*
EMP: 9
SQ FT: 13,000
SALES (est): 945.5K Privately Held
WEB: www.caffcompany.com
SIC: 3442 Window & door frames

(G-14800)
CALDWELLS WINDOWARE INC
166 Wabash St (15220-5404)
PHONE...................................412 922-1132
Gregory Gensler, *President*
Terrance Gensler, *Vice Pres*
Erik Gensler, *Project Mgr*
Joyce Nowak, *Project Mgr*
Raymond Gensler, *Treasurer*
EMP: 40 EST: 1954
SQ FT: 15,000
SALES: 5.5MM Privately Held
WEB: www.caldwells.com
SIC: 2591 2391 Drapery hardware & blinds & shades; curtains & draperies

(G-14801)
CALGON CARBON CORPORATION
200 Neville Rd Unit 1 (15225-1620)
PHONE.................................412 771-4050
Dean Qualas, *Manager*
EMP: 73
SALES (corp-wide): 5.3B **Privately Held**
WEB: www.calgoncarbon.com
SIC: 2819 Industrial inorganic chemicals
HQ: Calgon Carbon Corporation
3000 Gsk Dr
Moon Township PA 15108
412 787-6700

(G-14802)
CALGON CARBON CORPORATION
4301 Neville Rd (15225-1429)
PHONE.................................412 269-4188
Bill Oconnor, *Branch Mgr*
EMP: 10
SALES (corp-wide): 5.3B **Privately Held**
WEB: www.calgoncarbon.com
SIC: 2819 Industrial inorganic chemicals
HQ: Calgon Carbon Corporation
3000 Gsk Dr
Moon Township PA 15108
412 787-6700

(G-14803)
CALGON CARBON CORPORATION
500 Calgon Carbon Dr (15205-1124)
P.O. Box 717 (15230-0717)
PHONE.................................412 787-6700
EMP: 350
SALES (corp-wide): 555.1MM **Publicly Held**
SIC: 2819 7699 3589 3564 Mfg Indstl Inorgan Chem Repair Services Mfg Svc Industry Mach Mfg Blowers/Fans
PA: Calgon Carbon Corporation
3000 Gsk Dr
Moon Township PA 15108
412 787-6700

(G-14804)
CALGON CARBON CORPORATION
Also Called: Equipment & Assembly Plant
4301 Grand Ave (15225-1527)
PHONE.................................412 269-4000
David Drzemiecki, *General Mgr*
Paul Fabian, *Senior Mgr*
Dorothy Frank, *Admin Sec*
EMP: 10
SALES (corp-wide): 5.3B **Privately Held**
SIC: 3524 4953 Lawn & garden equipment; recycling, waste materials
HQ: Calgon Carbon Corporation
3000 Gsk Dr
Moon Township PA 15108
412 787-6700

(G-14805)
CALLERY SR JOHN
Also Called: Pittsburgh Advertising Spc Co
1515 Potomac Ave (15216-2109)
PHONE.................................412 344-9010
John Callery Sr, *Owner*
EMP: 3
SALES (est): 350K **Privately Held**
SIC: 5199 2395 Advertising specialties; embroidery & art needlework; decorative & novelty stitching, for the trade

(G-14806)
CAPSEN ROBOTICS INC
4638 Centre Ave (15213-1556)
PHONE.................................203 218-0204
Jared Glover, *CEO*
Mark Schnepf, *CTO*
EMP: 5
SQ FT: 100
SALES (est): 413.8K **Privately Held**
SIC: 3575 3577 Computer terminals; computer peripheral equipment

(G-14807)
CAR GAZETTE CO
450 Dawson Ave (15202-3212)
PHONE.................................412 951-5572
EMP: 3

SALES (est): 109.3K **Privately Held**
SIC: 2711 Newspapers

(G-14808)
CARDIACASSIST INC
Also Called: Tandemheart
620 Alpha Dr (15238-2836)
PHONE.................................412 963-8883
John Marous, *CEO*
Travis Deschamps, *COO*
Gary Bastin, *Opers Staff*
Jeffrey Stuckley, *Mfg Staff*
James Chastek, *Engineer*
EMP: 41
SQ FT: 16,000
SALES (est): 9.7MM
SALES (corp-wide): 1B **Privately Held**
WEB: www.cardiacassist.com
SIC: 3841 Surgical instruments & apparatus
PA: Livanova Plc
20 Eastbourne Terrace
London W2 6L
203 786-5275

(G-14809)
CARDINAL RESOURCES INC
201 Penn Center Blvd # 400 (15235-5441)
PHONE.................................412 374-0989
Kevin Jones, *President*
Adam Kassab, *CFO*
Chrissy McGaughey, *Executive Asst*
▼ EMP: 6
SALES: 1.9MM **Privately Held**
SIC: 3589 8711 8748 Water treatment equipment, industrial; engineering services; environmental consultant

(G-14810)
CARDINAL RESOURCES LLC
201 Penn Center Blvd # 400 (15235-5441)
PHONE.................................412 374-0989
Kevin Jones, *President*
Barbara Jones, *Exec VP*
EMP: 8
SQ FT: 7,500
SALES (est): 1.2MM **Privately Held**
SIC: 8711 3589 Engineering services; water treatment equipment, industrial

(G-14811)
CARDO SYSTEMS INC
1204 Parkway View Dr (15205-1403)
PHONE.................................412 788-4533
Abraham Glezerman, *Ch of Bd*
Kimberly Pitcock, *Accounting Mgr*
Mati Sachs, *Sales Staff*
▲ EMP: 32
SALES (est): 11.2MM **Privately Held**
SIC: 3661 Headsets, telephone

(G-14812)
CARIKS CUSTOM DECOR
Also Called: Carik's Signs
2523 Brownsville Rd (15210-4561)
PHONE.................................412 882-1511
Francis J Carik, *Owner*
Francis Carik, *Owner*
EMP: 7
SQ FT: 8,000
SALES: 200K **Privately Held**
SIC: 7389 3993 2679 Lettering & sign painting services; letters for signs, metal; signs, not made in custom sign painting shops; wallboard, decorated: made from purchased material

(G-14813)
CARLINI BROTHERS CO (PA)
701 Hazelwood Ave (15217-2898)
PHONE.................................412 421-9301
Orie Carlini, *President*
Richard Carlini, *Vice Pres*
EMP: 7
SQ FT: 8,000
SALES: 600K **Privately Held**
SIC: 3281 Monuments, cut stone (not finishing or lettering only)

(G-14814)
CARMEUSE LIME INC (DH)
Also Called: Carmeuse Natural Chemicals
11 Stanwix St Fl 21 (15222-1327)
PHONE.................................412 995-5500
Yves Willems, *CEO*
Felicia Reid, *General Mgr*

Jack Fahler, *Vice Pres*
Guss Grimsley, *Vice Pres*
Bob Roden, *Vice Pres*
▲ EMP: 95
SALES (est): 3.8B **Privately Held**
WEB: www.carmeusegroup.com
SIC: 1422 3274 Crushed & broken limestone; lime
HQ: Carmeuse
Rue Du Chateau 13a
Andenne 5300
858 301-20

(G-14815)
CARMEUSE LIME & STONE INC
3600 Neville Rd (15225-1416)
PHONE.................................412 777-0724
James Derby, *General Mgr*
Tony Pallotta, *Corp Comm Staff*
Marc Crab, *Manager*
Casey Schulz, *Manager*
EMP: 18 **Privately Held**
SIC: 1422 Crushed & broken limestone
HQ: Carmeuse Lime & Stone, Inc.
11 Stanwix St Fl 21
Pittsburgh PA 15222
412 995-5500

(G-14816)
CARMEUSE LIME & STONE INC (DH)
11 Stanwix St Fl 21 (15222-1327)
PHONE.................................412 995-5500
Thomas A Buck, *President*
Yves Willems, *COO*
Jessica Holcomb, *Counsel*
Jack Fahler, *Vice Pres*
Paul Tunnicliffe, *Vice Pres*
◆ EMP: 188
SQ FT: 30,000
SALES (est): 1.6B **Privately Held**
WEB: www.dravo.com
SIC: 1422 Crushed & broken limestone
HQ: Carmeuse Lime, Inc.
11 Stanwix St Fl 21
Pittsburgh PA 15222
412 995-5500

(G-14817)
CARNEGIE LEARNING INC
501 Grant St Ste 1075 (15219-4447)
PHONE.................................412 690-2442
Barry Malkin, *CEO*
Dawn Lesick, *Controller*
EMP: 113 EST: 1997
SQ FT: 20,000
SALES (est): 24.6MM
SALES (corp-wide): 660.6MM **Privately Held**
WEB: www.carnegielearning.com
SIC: 2741 7372 5999 Miscellaneous publishing; educational computer software; educational aids & electronic training materials
HQ: Apollo Education Group, Inc.
4025 S Riverpoint Pkwy
Phoenix AZ 85040
480 966-5394

(G-14818)
CARNEGIE MELLON UNIVERSITY
Also Called: Tartan News, The
5000 4th Ave Ste 314 (15213)
P.O. Box 1017 (15230-1017)
PHONE.................................412 268-2111
Brad Yankiver, *Chief*
Cindy Griffiths, *Business Mgr*
John Goodenough, *Engineer*
Steve Audia, *Info Tech Dir*
Mark Adamson, *Sr Ntwrk Engine*
EMP: 30
SALES (corp-wide): 1.3B **Privately Held**
WEB: www.cmu.edu
SIC: 8221 2711 University; newspapers
PA: Carnegie Mellon University
5000 Forbes Ave
Pittsburgh PA 15213
412 268-2000

(G-14819)
CARNEGIE ROBOTICS LLC
Also Called: Crl
4501 Hatfield St (15201-3023)
PHONE.................................412 251-0321
Stephen Diantonio, *President*

Brian Beyer, *President*
Kenneth Carmichael, *President*
Jeffrey Fullerton, *Opers Staff*
Justin Marini, *Engineer*
EMP: 67
SQ FT: 29,000
SALES (est): 12.2MM **Privately Held**
SIC: 3625 Control equipment, electric

(G-14820)
CARNEGIE SPEECH LLC
2425 Sidney St (15203-2116)
PHONE.................................412 471-1234
Angela Kennedy, *CEO*
EMP: 10
SALES (est): 221.8K **Privately Held**
SIC: 7372 Educational computer software

(G-14821)
CARPENTER CONNECTION INC
901 Killarney Dr (15234-2624)
PHONE.................................412 881-3900
Robert Buechel, *President*
Betty Jo Buechel, *Corp Secy*
Aaron Buechel, *Vice Pres*
◆ EMP: 35
SQ FT: 140,694
SALES (est): 6.2MM **Privately Held**
WEB: www.carpconn.com
SIC: 3577 Graphic displays, except graphic terminals

(G-14822)
CARSON PUBLISHING INC
506 Mcknight Park Dr 506a (15237-6535)
PHONE.................................412 548-3798
Kevin Gordon, *President*
EMP: 4 EST: 2010
SALES (est): 199K **Privately Held**
SIC: 2741 Miscellaneous publishing

(G-14823)
CARSON STREET COMMONS
2529 E Carson St (15203-2186)
PHONE.................................412 431-1183
Cyndi Jonov, *Manager*
EMP: 7
SALES (est): 955.2K **Privately Held**
SIC: 2441 Flats, wood: greenhouse

(G-14824)
CASA LUKER USA INC
71 Mcmurray Rd Ste 104 (15241-1634)
PHONE.................................412 854-9012
Camilo Romero, *President*
Francisco Gomez, *Vice Pres*
James Kilmer, *CFO*
Manuel De La Pena, *Admin Sec*
EMP: 5
SALES (est): 139.9K **Privately Held**
SIC: 2066 Baking chocolate

(G-14825)
CASTGRABBER LLC
6507 Wilkins Ave Ste 212 (15217-1305)
PHONE.................................412 362-6802
EMP: 15
SALES (est): 1MM **Privately Held**
SIC: 3651 Household audio & video equipment

(G-14826)
CASTLE CHEESE INC
525 William Penn Pl Fl 28 (15219-1728)
PHONE.................................724 368-3022
George L Myrter, *President*
Michelle Sabol, *Vice Pres*
▲ EMP: 25
SQ FT: 55,000
SALES (est): 5MM **Privately Held**
WEB: www.castlecheeseinc.com
SIC: 2022 2099 Cheese, natural & processed; food preparations

(G-14827)
CATALYST CROSSROADS LLC
210 Bower Hill Rd Rear (15228-1419)
PHONE.................................412 969-2733
Ryan Arthur Harold Smith, *Principal*
EMP: 3
SALES (est): 280K **Privately Held**
SIC: 7372 8049 8322 Educational computer software; nutrition specialist; ; multiservice center

(G-14828)
CATALYST ENERGY INC
424 S 27th St (15203-2379)
PHONE..................................412 325-4350
Paul Ryan Rodgers, *CEO*
Frank J Dignazio, *Vice Pres*
Douglas Edward Jones, *Vice Pres*
Ashley Bridge, *Accountant*
Donna Silverman, *Technology*
EMP: 40
SQ FT: 19,200
SALES (est): 12.5MM **Privately Held**
WEB: www.catalystenergyinc.com
SIC: 1381 Drilling oil & gas wells

(G-14829)
CBMM NORTH AMERICA INC
1000 Omega Dr Ste 1110 (15205-5001)
PHONE..................................412 221-7008
Jose Decamargo, *President*
Lisa Jones, *Principal*
Harry Stuart, *Vice Pres*
Jeff Tither, *Treasurer*
Debra Babin, *Admin Sec*
▲ **EMP:** 6
SALES (est): 1.2MM **Privately Held**
SIC: 1081 Metal mining exploration & development services
HQ: Companhia Brasileira De Metalurgia E
Mineracao.
Estr. Corrego Da Mata S/No
Araxa MG 38183

(G-14830)
CCL RESTORATION LLC
310 N Linden Ave (15208-2317)
PHONE..................................412 926-6156
Carmen Jordan, *Principal*
EMP: 5
SALES: 100K **Privately Held**
SIC: 3589 Service industry machinery

(G-14831)
CCN AMERICA LP
300 Penn Center Blvd # 505 (15235-5511)
PHONE..................................412 349-6300
Jeffrey Palmer, *President*
Thomas J Pollack, *Vice Pres*
David J Giannangeli, *Business Dir*
EMP: 5
SALES (est): 1.1MM **Privately Held**
WEB: www.coordinatedcarenetwork.com
SIC: 8641 2834 Civic social & fraternal associations; solutions, pharmaceutical

(G-14832)
CCR ELECTRONICS
311 Old Clairton Rd (15236-4334)
PHONE..................................317 469-4855
Barbara Holt, *Branch Mgr*
EMP: 3
SALES (corp-wide): 904.2K **Privately Held**
SIC: 3559 Electronic component making machinery
PA: Ccr Electronics
8425 Wdfld Xing Blvd # 100
Indianapolis IN 46240
317 469-4855

(G-14833)
CELLOMICS INC
Also Called: Thermo Scientific
100 Technology Dr Ste 100 # 100
(15219-3138)
PHONE..................................412 770-2500
Seth Hoogasian, *President*
Rick Salisbury, *Director*
EMP: 3 **EST:** 2011
SALES (est): 512.7K **Privately Held**
SIC: 2821 Thermoplastic materials

(G-14834)
CELSENSE INC
603 Stanwix St Ste 390 (15222-1423)
PHONE..................................412 263-2870
Charles F O'Hanlon, *CEO*
EMP: 4
SALES (est): 492.8K **Privately Held**
WEB: www.celsense.com
SIC: 2835 In vitro & in vivo diagnostic substances

(G-14835)
CERNOSTICS INC
1401 Forbes Ave Ste 302 (15219-5152)
PHONE..................................412 315-7359
EMP: 3
SALES (est): 360K **Privately Held**
SIC: 2835 Mfg Diagnostic Substances

(G-14836)
CH JAMES G THORNTON
25 Sheila Ct (15227-1221)
PHONE..................................412 207-2153
Jim Thornton, *Principal*
EMP: 3 **EST:** 2010
SALES (est): 186.8K **Privately Held**
SIC: 2834 Pharmaceutical preparations

(G-14837)
CHASE CORPORATION
201 Zeta Dr (15238-2813)
PHONE..................................412 963-6285
Stephen F Hiler, *Branch Mgr*
EMP: 12
SALES (corp-wide): 252.5MM **Publicly Held**
SIC: 3479 Etching & engraving
PA: Chase Corporation
295 University Ave
Westwood MA 02090
781 332-0700

(G-14838)
CHASE CORPORATION
201 Zeta Dr (15238-2813)
PHONE..................................412 828-5470
Dave Stephens, *Manager*
EMP: 5
SALES (corp-wide): 252.5MM **Publicly Held**
SIC: 2952 Asphalt felts & coatings
PA: Chase Corporation
295 University Ave
Westwood MA 02090
781 332-0700

(G-14839)
CHASE CORPORATION
201 Zeta Dr (15238-2813)
PHONE..................................412 828-1500
Steve Priester, *Engineer*
Adam Chase, *Branch Mgr*
EMP: 12
SALES (corp-wide): 252.5MM **Publicly Held**
SIC: 3644 Insulators & insulation materials, electrical
PA: Chase Corporation
295 University Ave
Westwood MA 02090
781 332-0700

(G-14840)
CHASE CORPORATION
Fluid Polymers
201 Zeta Dr (15238-2813)
PHONE..................................412 828-1500
Greg Pelagio, *Branch Mgr*
EMP: 37
SQ FT: 42,000
SALES (corp-wide): 252.5MM **Publicly Held**
WEB: www.chasecorp.com
SIC: 2821 2899 2851 2241 Plastics materials & resins; chemical preparations; paints & allied products; narrow fabric mills
PA: Chase Corporation
295 University Ave
Westwood MA 02090
781 332-0700

(G-14841)
CHASE INDUSTRIES INC
1370 Old Frport Rd Ste 3b (15238)
PHONE..................................412 449-0160
William German, *President*
EMP: 15 **EST:** 2007
SALES (est): 2.1MM **Privately Held**
SIC: 3441 Fabricated structural metal

(G-14842)
CHEETAH TECHNOLOGIES LP
Also Called: V-Factor Technologies
381 Mansfield Ave Ste 500 (15220-2754)
PHONE..................................412 928-7707
Stephen John, *Partner*

Steven Wright, *Manager*
EMP: 5
SALES (est): 1.1MM **Privately Held**
SIC: 3663 Cable television equipment

(G-14843)
CHEM IMAGE BIO THREAT LLC
7301 Penn Ave (15208-2528)
PHONE..................................412 241-7335
Patrick Treado, *President*
EMP: 32
SQ FT: 12,000
SALES (est): 3.2MM **Privately Held**
WEB: www.chemimage.com
SIC: 3826 Analytical instruments
PA: Chemimage Corporation
7301 Penn Ave
Pittsburgh PA 15208

(G-14844)
CHEMDAQ INC
300 Business Center Dr # 330
(15205-1335)
PHONE..................................412 787-0202
David M Hilliker, *President*
Bob Cornelia, *President*
Burke Davis, *Regl Sales Mgr*
Scott Pinney, *Regl Sales Mgr*
Richard Warburton, *CTO*
EMP: 14
SQ FT: 4,800
SALES (est): 3.2MM **Privately Held**
WEB: www.chemdaq.com
SIC: 3829 Measuring & controlling devices

(G-14845)
**CHEMIMAGE CORPORATION
(PA)**
7301 Penn Ave (15208-2528)
PHONE..................................412 241-7335
Patrick Treado, *CEO*
Mark C Brooks, *CFO*
Carey Treado, *Treasurer*
James Michael, *Director*
Christopher James, *Assistant*
EMP: 50
SQ FT: 4,000
SALES (est): 9.5MM **Privately Held**
WEB: www.chemimage.com
SIC: 3826 Analytical instruments

(G-14846)
**CHEMIMAGE FILTER TECH LLC
(PA)**
7301 Penn Ave (15208-2528)
PHONE..................................412 241-7335
John Belechak,
EMP: 47
SALES (est): 4.6MM **Privately Held**
SIC: 3826 Analytical instruments

(G-14847)
**CHESTERFIELD SPECIAL
CYLINDERS**
Also Called: Hydratron
55 Old Clairton Rd 205 (15236-3904)
PHONE..................................832 252-1082
Phil Sanders, *President*
Ian Brownhill, *Vice Pres*
◆ **EMP:** 50
SQ FT: 3,000
SALES (est): 10.2MM
SALES (corp-wide): 49.3MM **Privately Held**
SIC: 3561 Pumps & pumping equipment
HQ: Hydratron Limited
Unit A1
Altrincham WA14
161 928-6221

(G-14848)
**CHOICE GRANITE AND MARBLE
LLC**
803 Geyer Rd Ste 1 (15212-1155)
PHONE..................................412 821-3900
David Griffith, *Owner*
Kelsey Sowers, *Exec VP*
▲ **EMP:** 8
SQ FT: 15,000
SALES (est): 1.7MM **Privately Held**
SIC: 5039 3281 Structural assemblies, prefabricated: non-wood; granite, cut & shaped

(G-14849)
CHRIS CANDIES INC
1557 Spring Garden Ave (15212-3632)
PHONE..................................412 322-9400
Timothy Rogers, *President*
Karl Lex, *Plant Supt*
Jared Sutara, *QC Mgr*
Don Green, *Controller*
Mark Davis, *Accountant*
▲ **EMP:** 50 **EST:** 1947
SQ FT: 32,000
SALES (est): 10.4MM
SALES (corp-wide): 11MM **Privately Held**
WEB: www.chriscandies.com
SIC: 2064 Candy & other confectionery products
PA: G W Resources, Inc.
20 Stanwix St Ste 620
Pittsburgh PA 15222
412 261-3488

(G-14850)
CHROMALOX INC (HQ)
Also Called: Ogden
103 Gamma Dr Ste 2 (15238-2981)
PHONE..................................412 967-3800
Scott Dysert, *CEO*
Tony Castor, *President*
Steve Brian, *Chairman*
Robert Mihalco, *Vice Pres*
Kyle Hooper, *Opers Spvr*
◆ **EMP:** 80
SALES (est): 420.6MM
SALES (corp-wide): 1.3B **Privately Held**
WEB: www.chromalox.com
SIC: 3567 Heating units & devices, industrial: electric
PA: Spirax-Sarco Engineering Plc
Charlton House
Cheltenham GLOS GL53
124 252-1361

(G-14851)
**CIANFLONE SCIENTIFIC LLC
(PA)**
Also Called: Tensitron
135 Industry Dr (15275-1015)
PHONE..................................412 787-3600
Doug Hart, *President*
Mark Gorman, *Mng Member*
Chris Randazzo,
EMP: 7
SQ FT: 4,500
SALES: 1.2MM **Privately Held**
SIC: 3826 3829 3545 Spectrographs; gauging instruments, thickness ultrasonic; calipers & dividers

(G-14852)
CIMA TECHNOLOGY INC
480 Davidson Rd (15239-1749)
PHONE..................................724 733-2627
Jashwant K Sharma, *President*
Harold Boone, *CTO*
Carina Navarro, *Technology*
▲ **EMP:** 15
SQ FT: 6,000
SALES (est): 3MM **Privately Held**
SIC: 3851 Ophthalmic goods

(G-14853)
CITIZEN
535 Citizens Way (15202-3122)
PHONE..................................412 766-6679
Connie Rankin, *Owner*
EMP: 15
SQ FT: 468
SALES: 100K **Privately Held**
SIC: 2711 Newspapers: publishing only, not printed on site; newspapers, publishing & printing

(G-14854)
CITY OF PITTSBURGH
Also Called: Engineering & Cnstr Dept
414 Grant St Ste 301 (15219-2419)
PHONE..................................412 255-2883
Patrick Hassett, *Manager*
EMP: 33 **Privately Held**
WEB: www.conservatory.org
SIC: 1389 9199 Construction, repair & dismantling services; general government administration;

PA: City Of Pittsburgh
414 Grant St
Pittsburgh PA 15219
412 255-2640

(G-14855)
CITY OF PITTSBURGH
Also Called: General Services Fleet MGT
414 Grant St Ste 502 (15219-2419)
PHONE..............................412 255-2330
Scott Kunka, *Director*
EMP: 25 **Privately Held**
WEB: www.conservatory.org
SIC: 9621 3559 ; automotive mainte-
nance equipment
PA: City Of Pittsburgh
414 Grant St
Pittsburgh PA 15219
412 255-2640

(G-14856)
CIVIC MAPPER LLC
2014 Lacrosse St (15218-1826)
PHONE..............................315 729-7869
Emily Mercurio, *President*
Christian Gass, *Vice Pres*
Matthew Mercurio, *Vice Pres*
EMP: 3
SALES (est): 114.8K **Privately Held**
SIC: 1382 7389 8713 8731 Aerial geo-
physical exploration oil & gas; photogram-
matic mapping; ; ; natural resource
research; environmental research

(G-14857)
CLARK DECO MOLDINGS INC
1127 Washington Blvd (15206-3321)
PHONE..............................412 363-9602
Devon Clark Sr, *President*
Dave Shoop, *Manager*
EMP: 3
SQ FT: 1,000
SALES (est): 567K **Privately Held**
WEB: www.cdmcabinethardware.com
SIC: 3429 Cabinet hardware

(G-14858)
CLASSROOM SALON LLC
461 Melwood Ave (15213-1135)
PHONE..............................412 621-6287
Tommy Wang, *CEO*
EMP: 4 **EST:** 2014
SALES (est): 116K **Privately Held**
SIC: 7372 Educational computer software

(G-14859)
CLEARCOUNT MED SOLUTIONS INC
101 Bellevue Rd Ste 300 (15229-2132)
PHONE..............................412 931-7233
David Palmer, *President*
David Haffner, *CFO*
Steve Fleck, *CTO*
Gautam Gandhi, *Admin Sec*
EMP: 19
SALES (est): 2.8MM **Privately Held**
WEB: www.clearcount.com
SIC: 3842 7352 Mfg Surgical
Appliances/Supplies Medical Equipment
Rental

(G-14860)
CLICKCADENCE LLC
425 1st Ave Fl 1 (15219-1321)
PHONE..............................412 434-4911
Michael Dickey,
EMP: 6
SQ FT: 6,000
SALES: 1MM **Privately Held**
WEB: www.clickcadence.com
SIC: 3829 Instrument board gauges, auto-
motive: computerized

(G-14861)
CLOCKWISE TEES
400 N Lexington St (15208-2561)
PHONE..............................412 727-1602
EMP: 3
SALES (est): 403.8K **Privately Held**
SIC: 2759 Screen printing

(G-14862)
CLOSET-TIER (PA)
Also Called: Edlyn's Closet-Tier
2811 Shady Ave (15217-2740)
PHONE..............................412 421-7838

Edward M Margolis, *Partner*
Carolyn G Margolis, *Partner*
EMP: 3
SALES: 143K **Privately Held**
WEB: www.closettier.com
SIC: 5719 2431 Closet organizers &
shelving units; millwork

(G-14863)
CMU ROBOTICS
10 40th St (15201-3209)
PHONE..............................412 681-6900
Alonzo Kelly, *Principal*
Vu Nguyen, *Teacher*
EMP: 4
SALES (est): 411.8K **Privately Held**
SIC: 3625 Relays & industrial controls

(G-14864)
COCA- COLA
2747 Race St (15235-3630)
PHONE..............................412 726-1482
Michele Niehl, *Principal*
EMP: 3
SALES (est): 83K **Privately Held**
SIC: 2086 Soft drinks: packaged in cans,
bottles, etc.

(G-14865)
COGNITION THERAPEUTICS INC
2403 Sidney St Ste 261 (15203-5118)
PHONE..............................412 481-2210
Kenneth I Moch, *President*
Anthony Giordano, *President*
Franz Hefti, *Chairman*
Susan Catalano, *Director*
EMP: 3
SQ FT: 1,200
SALES (est): 749.2K **Privately Held**
WEB: www.cogrx.com
SIC: 2834 5122 Druggists' preparations
(pharmaceuticals); pharmaceuticals

(G-14866)
COGNOS CORPORATION
Also Called: COGNOS CORPORATION
4 Penn Ctr W Ste 210 (15276-0117)
PHONE..............................412 490-9804
Fax: 412 490-9807
EMP: 4
SALES (corp-wide): 81.7B **Publicly Held**
SIC: 7372 Prepackaged Software Services
HQ: Cognos, Llc
5 Technology Park Dr
Westford MA 01886
781 229-6600

(G-14867)
COMBUSTION SERVICE & EQP CO
Also Called: CS&e
2016 Babcock Blvd (15209-1398)
PHONE..............................412 821-8900
Ray Bauer, *President*
Tim Rider, *Project Mgr*
Barbara Geisler, *Mfg Staff*
Jackie Stack, *Purch Agent*
Shawn Dawson, *Engineer*
EMP: 72
SQ FT: 5,000
SALES (est): 52.6MM **Privately Held**
WEB: www.csande.net
SIC: 5074 1711 3443 3433 Heating
equipment (hydronic); plumbing, heating,
air-conditioning contractors; fabricated
plate work (boiler shop); heating equip-
ment, except electric

(G-14868)
COMDOC INC
900 Parish St Ste 100 (15220-3425)
PHONE..............................800 321-1009
Stuart Wise, *Vice Pres*
EMP: 75
SALES (corp-wide): 9.8B **Publicly Held**
SIC: 3577 5044 Computer peripheral
equipment; office equipment
HQ: Comdoc, Inc.
3458 Massillon Rd
Uniontown OH 44685
330 896-2346

(G-14869)
COMMONWEALTH PRESS LLC
2020 Carey Way (15203-2003)
PHONE..............................412 431-4207
Daniel Wayne Rugh,
Mark Bogacki, *Graphic Designe*
Shannon Kathleen Rugh,
EMP: 8 **EST:** 2009
SALES (est): 786.2K **Privately Held**
SIC: 2741 Miscellaneous publishing

(G-14870)
COMPAGNIE DES BXITES DE GUINEE
323 N Shore Dr Ste 510 (15212-5364)
PHONE..............................412 235-0279
Patrick Dielen, *Treasurer*
Joseph Denardis, *Manager*
Souleymane Traore, *Director*
Karifa Conde, *Admin Sec*
EMP: 3000
SQ FT: 3,000
SALES: 412MM
SALES (corp-wide): 1.7B **Privately Held**
SIC: 1099 Bauxite mining
HQ: Boke Investment Company
12 Federal St Ste 320
Pittsburgh PA 15212
412 321-4252

(G-14871)
COMPONENTONE ENTERPRISES LLC
201 S Highland Ave Fl 3 (15206-3970)
PHONE..............................412 681-4343
Martin De San Martin, *CFO*
Larry Krueger, *Sales Dir*
Leanne Lappe, *Marketing Mgr*
Eve Turzillo, *Comms Mgr*
John Juback, *Manager*
EMP: 70
SQ FT: 10,500
SALES (est): 8.2MM **Privately Held**
WEB: www.componentone.com
SIC: 7371 7372 Computer software devel-
opment; prepackaged software
HQ: Grapecity Inc.
3-1-4, Murasakiyama, Izumi-Ku
Sendai MYG 981-3
227 778-210

(G-14872)
CONROY FOODS INC
100 Chapel Harbor Dr # 2 (15238-4163)
PHONE..............................412 781-0977
James Conroy, *President*
William Conroy, *Vice Pres*
Dan Elston, *QC Mgr*
Leslee Conroy, *Treasurer*
Stacey Wolkiewicz, *Sales Staff*
▼ **EMP:** 15
SALES (est): 3.5MM **Privately Held**
WEB: www.conroyfoods.com
SIC: 2035 Dressings, salad: raw & cooked
(except dry mixes); spreads, sandwich:
salad dressing base

(G-14873)
CONTROL DESIGN INC (PA)
211 Ridc Park West Dr (15275-1003)
PHONE..............................412 788-2280
Bill Harrington, *President*
William G Harrington, *Principal*
Barbara Giblock, *Vice Pres*
William J Small, *Vice Pres*
William Small, *Vice Pres*
▼ **EMP:** 43
SQ FT: 30,000
SALES (est): 7.1MM **Privately Held**
WEB: www.controldesigninc.com
SIC: 3613 3823 3625 Control panels,
electric; industrial instrmnts msrmnt dis-
play/control process variable; relays & in-
dustrial controls

(G-14874)
COOPERHEAT MQS PROJ
4525 Campbells Run Rd (15205-1313)
PHONE..............................412 787-8690
John Olasz, *Principal*
EMP: 4 **EST:** 2010
SALES (est): 373.7K **Privately Held**
SIC: 3398 Metal heat treating

(G-14875)
COPPERS INC
436 7th Ave (15219-1826)
PHONE..............................412 233-2137
Steve Lish, *Manager*
EMP: 49
SALES (est): 5.2MM **Privately Held**
WEB: www.coppers.com
SIC: 2865 2911 Tar, coal tar & related
chemicals; petroleum refining

(G-14876)
CORE LABORATORIES LP
3915 Saw Mill Run Blvd (15227-2605)
PHONE..............................412 884-9250
Tom Hogya, *Branch Mgr*
EMP: 12
SALES (corp-wide): 659.8MM **Privately
Held**
SIC: 1382 Oil & gas exploration services
HQ: Core Laboratories Lp
6316 Windfern Rd
Houston TX 77040

(G-14877)
COSTAR BREWING INC
919 N Saint Clair St (15206-2133)
PHONE..............................412 401-8433
Kenneth Hanna, *CEO*
EMP: 3
SALES (est): 182.7K **Privately Held**
SIC: 2082 Beer (alcoholic beverage)

(G-14878)
COTTON BUREAU
110 Torrens St (15206-4138)
PHONE..............................412 573-9041
EMP: 12
SALES (est): 2.1MM **Privately Held**
SIC: 2759 Screen printing

(G-14879)
COUNTRY BARNS OF PITTSBURGH
1606 Bingham St 1 (15203-1531)
PHONE..............................412 221-1630
Leonoor Mastboom Zehner, *Owner*
EMP: 7
SALES (est): 497K **Privately Held**
WEB: www.countrybarnsofpittsburgh.com
SIC: 2511 Storage chests, household:
wood

(G-14880)
COUNTRY CUPBOARD COOKIES LT
947 Old Frankstown Rd G (15239-2509)
PHONE..............................724 325-3045
Daniel Wittig, *Partner*
Judy Wittig, *Partner*
EMP: 8
SALES (est): 125K **Privately Held**
WEB: www.countrycupboardcookies.com
SIC: 2051 Bread, cake & related products

(G-14881)
COVERS ALL CANVAS PRODUCTS
5171 Brownsville Rd (15236-2644)
PHONE..............................412 653-6010
Ellis A Stokes Jr, *President*
Marilyn S Stokes, *Vice Pres*
EMP: 8 **EST:** 1993
SQ FT: 5,600
SALES (est): 1MM **Privately Held**
WEB: www.coversallcanvas.com
SIC: 2393 2394 5131 5039 Canvas
bags; tarpaulins, fabric: made from pur-
chased materials; textiles, woven;
awnings

(G-14882)
COVESTRO LLC (DH)
1 Covestro Cir (15205-9723)
PHONE..............................412 413-2000
Jerry Maccleary, *CEO*
Haakan Jonsson, *President*
Richard Aldrich, *Business Mgr*
Scott Baker, *Vice Pres*
Mark Morrison, *Vice Pres*
◆ **EMP:** 900

G E O G R A P H I C

SALES (est): 3B
SALES (corp-wide): 16.7B **Privately Held**
WEB: www.bayerus.com
SIC: 2891 2821 Adhesives & sealants;
polyurethane resins; elastomers, nonvul-
canizable (plastics); polycarbonate resins
HQ: Covestro Deutschland Ag
Kaiser-Wilhelm-Allee 60
Leverkusen 51373
214 600-9200

(G-14883)
COVIA HOLDINGS
CORPORATION
3810 S Water St (15203-2375)
PHONE..................................412 431-4777
Mark Bannon, *Branch Mgr*
EMP: 6
SALES (corp-wide): 136.2MM **Publicly
Held**
WEB: www.unimin.com
SIC: 1481 Nonmetallic mineral services
HQ: Covia Holdings Corporation
3 Summit Park Dr Ste 700
Independence OH 44131
440 214-3284

(G-14884)
CP FOOD STORES INC (PA)
2610 Lindenwood Dr (15241-2508)
PHONE..................................412 831-7777
Joe Labriola, *President*
Alberta Labriola, *Vice Pres*
EMP: 10
SQ FT: 6,000
SALES (est): 1.7MM **Privately Held**
SIC: 5147 2013 Meats & meat products;
sausages & other prepared meats

(G-14885)
CRAFT PRODUCTS CO INC
2014b Babcock Blvd (15209-1354)
PHONE..................................412 821-8102
John Baum, *President*
Barbara Baum, *Treasurer*
EMP: 9
SQ FT: 12,000
SALES (est): 1.6MM **Privately Held**
WEB: www.craftprod.com
SIC: 2819 3589 2869 Industrial inorganic
chemicals; water treatment equipment, in-
dustrial; industrial organic chemicals

(G-14886)
CREATIVE NONFICTION
FOUNDATION
5119 Coral St (15224-1727)
PHONE..................................412 688-0304
Lee Gutkind, *President*
Patricia Park, *Treasurer*
EMP: 5
SALES: 656K **Privately Held**
WEB: www.leegutkind.com
SIC: 2731 2741 Books: publishing only;
miscellaneous publishing

(G-14887)
CROMIE MACHINE TOOL CO INC
(PA)
4800 Harrison St (15201-2721)
P.O. Box 40140 (15201-0140)
PHONE..................................724 385-0729
David Clinton Cromie, *President*
Melody Tlowey, *Admin Sec*
▲ EMP: 13 EST: 1961
SQ FT: 8,000
SALES (est): 1.6MM **Privately Held**
SIC: 3599 Machine shop, jobbing & repair

(G-14888)
CROWN MOLDING
2603 Old Washington Rd (15241-2540)
PHONE..................................412 779-9209
Michael Wittlin, *Principal*
EMP: 6
SALES (est): 532.7K **Privately Held**
SIC: 3089 Molding primary plastic

(G-14889)
CRYSTALPLEX CORPORATION
1816 Parkway View Dr (15205-1422)
PHONE..................................412 787-1525
Matt Bootman, *CEO*
EMP: 3

SALES (est): 300.1K **Privately Held**
SIC: 3559 5065 Semiconductor manufacturing machinery; semiconductor devices

(G-14890)
CS-B2 INVESTMENTS INC
Also Called: AlphaGraphics 514
814 Penn Ave (15222-3610)
PHONE..................................412 261-1300
Clara Meehan, *President*
Ali Bittner, *Marketing Staff*
EMP: 23 EST: 1999
SALES (est): 4.2MM **Privately Held**
SIC: 2752 7334 Commercial printing, off-
set; photocopying & duplicating services

(G-14891)
CSE CORPORATION
825 Plum Industrial Park (15239-2939)
PHONE..................................724 733-2247
Fax: 724 856-9203
EMP: 50
SALES (corp-wide): 37.7MM **Privately
Held**
SIC: 3625 Mfg Relays/Industrial Controls
PA: Cse Corporation
1001 Corporate Ln
Export PA 15632
412 856-9200

(G-14892)
CUMBERLAND FARMS INC
Also Called: Gulf
2620 Neville Rd (15225-1404)
PHONE..................................412 331-4419
Gary Kaneb, *President*
James White, *Principal*
EMP: 3
SALES (corp-wide): 1.5B **Privately Held**
SIC: 5541 1311 Filling stations, gasoline;
crude petroleum production
PA: Cumberland Farms, Inc.
165 Flanders Rd
Westborough MA 01581
508 270-1400

(G-14893)
CUMMINS INC
3 Alpha Dr (15238-2943)
PHONE..................................412 820-0330
William McKee, *Branch Mgr*
EMP: 27
SALES (corp-wide): 23.7B **Publicly Held**
WEB: www.bridgewaypower.com
SIC: 3519 Internal combustion engines
PA: Cummins Inc.
500 Jackson St
Columbus IN 47201
812 377-5000

(G-14894)
CUSTOM MFG & INDUS SVCS
LLC
4821 Harrison St (15201-2720)
PHONE..................................412 621-2982
Charles Bosiljevac,
EMP: 8
SALES (est): 1.5MM **Privately Held**
SIC: 3441 3599 3449 3547 Fabricated
structural metal; custom machinery;
crankshafts & camshafts, machining;
bars, concrete reinforcing: fabricated
steel; steel rolling machinery

(G-14895)
CUSTOM PRINTED GRAPHICS
INC (PA)
2933 Mary St (15203-2562)
PHONE..................................412 881-8208
Kenneth Ennis, *President*
Catherine Ennis, *Corp Secy*
Larry Ennis, *Vice Pres*
EMP: 25 EST: 1933
SQ FT: 30,000
SALES: 2.1MM **Privately Held**
WEB: www.customprintedgraphics.com
SIC: 2396 Screen printing on fabric articles

(G-14896)
CUSTOMIZED ENVMTL
SYSTEMS
Also Called: C E S, In
3930 Old William Penn Hwy # 302
(15235-4848)
PHONE..................................412 380-2311

Joseph Wilson, *President*
William Evans, *Vice Pres*
Peggy Dummar Williams, *Vice Pres*
EMP: 5
SQ FT: 2,500
SALES: 53K **Privately Held**
SIC: 3677 Filtration devices, electronic

(G-14897)
CUTTING EDGE EMBROIDERY
INC
681 Union Avenue Ext (15229-1421)
PHONE..................................412 732-9990
Mario Nazareth, *President*
EMP: 4 EST: 2000
SALES (est): 378.7K **Privately Held**
WEB: www.cuttingedgeembroidery.com
SIC: 2395 Embroidery & art needlework

(G-14898)
CUTTING EDGE KNIVES INC
1728 Berkwood Dr (15243-1514)
PHONE..................................412 279-9350
Lorraine Talleto, *President*
EMP: 50
SALES (est): 5.1MM **Privately Held**
SIC: 3423 Knives, agricultural or industrial

(G-14899)
CYMATICS LABORATORIES
CORP
425 N Craig St Ste 200 (15213-1154)
P.O. Box 8117 (15217-0117)
PHONE..................................412 578-0280
David F Guillou, *CEO*
EMP: 5
SALES (est): 652.6K **Privately Held**
SIC: 3674 Semiconductors & related de-
vices

(G-14900)
D & D MACHINE
5 Newland Ln (15209-2005)
PHONE..................................412 821-3725
Dennis Petrick, *Partner*
EMP: 3 EST: 1997
SALES (est): 345.5K **Privately Held**
SIC: 3541 Machine tool replacement & re-
pair parts, metal cutting types

(G-14901)
D I FURNACE LLC
100 Sandusky St (15212-5822)
PHONE..................................412 231-1200
▲ EMP: 3
SALES (est): 244K
SALES (corp-wide): 4.7B **Privately Held**
SIC: 3312 Blast Furnace-Steel Works
PA: Siemag Weiss Gmbh & Co. Kg
Wiesenstr. 30
Hilchenbach 57271
273 329-0

(G-14902)
DACAR INDUSTRIES (PA)
Also Called: Dacar Chemical Company
1007 Mccartney St (15220-5442)
PHONE..................................412 921-3620
James R Datesh, *President*
EMP: 9 EST: 1931
SQ FT: 10,000
SALES (est): 1.8MM **Privately Held**
SIC: 2899 Rust resisting compounds;
water treating compounds

(G-14903)
DALMO OPTICAL
CORPORATION (PA)
Also Called: Dalmo Optical Center
5831 Forbes Ave (15217-1601)
PHONE..................................412 521-2100
Morris Grossman, *President*
Ruth B Grossman, *Admin Sec*
EMP: 8 EST: 1960
SALES (est): 2.3MM **Privately Held**
SIC: 5995 3851 Contact lenses, prescrip-
tion; lens grinding, except prescription:
ophthalmic

(G-14904)
DALMO OPTICAL
CORPORATION
950 Greentree Rd 202 (15220-3314)
PHONE..................................412 937-1112
Sophia Taylor, *President*

EMP: 4
SALES (corp-wide): 2.3MM **Privately
Held**
SIC: 5995 3851 Contact lenses, prescrip-
tion; lens grinding, except prescription:
ophthalmic
PA: Dalmo Optical Corporation
5831 Forbes Ave
Pittsburgh PA 15217
412 521-2100

(G-14905)
DANIELS ELECTRIC SERVICE
329 Ohio St (15209-2721)
PHONE..................................412 821-2594
Alex G Daniels, *Owner*
EMP: 3
SQ FT: 3,750
SALES: 216K **Privately Held**
SIC: 7694 Electric motor repair

(G-14906)
DASCO INC
Also Called: Wbe
3001 Grand Ave (15225-1603)
PHONE..................................412 771-4140
Marsha Diehl, *President*
EMP: 7
SQ FT: 300
SALES (est): 1.6MM **Privately Held**
WEB: www.dasco.com
SIC: 1711 3441 Mechanical contractor;
fabricated structural metal

(G-14907)
DAVID I HELFER INC
717 Liberty Ave Ste 312 (15222-3510)
PHONE..................................412 281-6734
Ira Helfer, *President*
EMP: 4 EST: 1936
SQ FT: 5,500
SALES: 400K **Privately Held**
WEB: www.davidihelfer.com
SIC: 7631 3915 Jewelry repair services;
jewelers' materials & lapidary work

(G-14908)
DAVIDSON SUPPLY CO INC
4721 Mcknight Rd Ste 1 (15237-3415)
PHONE..................................412 635-2671
Joe Davidson, *President*
EMP: 4
SALES (est): 200.6K **Privately Held**
SIC: 2844 5099 Cosmetic preparations;
durable goods

(G-14909)
DAWAR TECHNOLOGIES INC
Also Called: Dawar Touch
1016 N Lincoln Ave (15233-2132)
PHONE..................................412 322-9900
Dennis Fitzgerald, *President*
Albert F Dombrowski, *Chairman*
Mike Robrecht, *Vice Pres*
Chang Cao, *Engineer*
Kevin Kozlowski, *Engineer*
▲ EMP: 50 EST: 1925
SQ FT: 47,000
SALES: 25MM **Privately Held**
SIC: 3577 Computer peripheral equipment

(G-14910)
DBMOTION INC
600 Grant St Ste 22017 (15219-2702)
PHONE..................................412 605-1952
Yuval Ofek, *CEO*
Peter McClennen, *President*
EMP: 18
SALES (est): 1.3MM
SALES (corp-wide): 1.7B **Publicly Held**
SIC: 7372 Business oriented computer
software
HQ: Dbmotion Ltd
77
Beer Sheba 84709
862 068-88

(G-14911)
DBMTION INC
600 Grant St Ste 22017 (15219-2702)
PHONE..................................412 605-1952
EMP: 3
SALES (est): 160.7K **Privately Held**
SIC: 3845 Mfg Electromedical Equipment

2019 Harris Pennsylvania
Manufacturers Directory
▲ = Import ▼=Export
◆ =Import/Export

G
E
O
G
R
A
P
H
I
C

(G-14912)
DE MARCO WASTE DUMPSTER SVC
229 Amanda Ave (15210-2149)
PHONE....................................412 904-4260
EMP: 3
SALES (est): 160.2K Privately Held
SIC: 3443 Dumpsters, garbage

(G-14913)
DE NORA WATER TECHNOLOGIES INC
1000 Cliffmine Rd (15275-1022)
PHONE....................................412 494-4077
EMP: 9 Privately Held
SIC: 3589 Water treatment equipment, industrial
HQ: De Nora Water Technologies, Inc.
3000 Advance Ln
Colmar PA 18915
215 997-4000

(G-14914)
DE NORA WATER TECHNOLOGIES INC
Also Called: Severn Trent Services
1000 Cliffmine Rd Ste 600 (15275-1029)
PHONE....................................412 788-8300
Joe Bonneza, Manager
EMP: 28 Privately Held
SIC: 3589 Water treatment equipment, industrial
HQ: De Nora Water Technologies, Inc.
3000 Advance Ln
Colmar PA 18915
215 997-4000

(G-14915)
DEFAULT SERVICING INC
4 Penn Ctr W (15276-0107)
PHONE....................................502 968-1400
Tom Huddleston, President
EMP: 5
SALES (est): 284.1K Privately Held
SIC: 1389 Roustabout service

(G-14916)
DEL ELECTRONIC CO
1060 Saw Mill Run Blvd (15220-5310)
PHONE....................................412 787-1177
Ludwig Delmastro, President
EMP: 6
SALES (est): 781.5K Privately Held
SIC: 3613 Control panels, electric

(G-14917)
DEL MONTE FOODS INC
375 N Shore Dr Ste 500 (15212-5836)
PHONE....................................412 222-2200
Rick Wolford, CEO
James Burgbacher, Manager
John Fusco, Manager
Sunshine Due, Info Tech Mgr
EMP: 141
SALES (corp-wide): 2.2B Privately Held
SIC: 2033 Canned fruits & specialties
HQ: Del Monte Foods, Inc.
3003 Oak Rd Ste 600
Walnut Creek CA 94597
925 949-2772

(G-14918)
DERRICK PUBLISHING COMPANY
Also Called: Michael Boyle
200 Mcknight Park Dr (15237-6507)
P.O. Box 236 (15230-0236)
PHONE....................................412 364-8202
Derrick Thomas, Branch Mgr
EMP: 25
SALES (corp-wide): 14.5MM Privately Held
SIC: 2711 Newspapers: publishing only, not printed on site
PA: Derrick Publishing Company
1510 W 1st St
Oil City PA 16301
814 676-7444

(G-14919)
DETROIT SWITCH INC
1025 Beaver Ave Ste 9 (15233-2397)
PHONE....................................412 322-9144
Gregory A Stein, President
Robert A Stein, Treasurer

Walter F Ruffer, Asst Treas
Richard Stein, Admin Sec
▲ EMP: 35 EST: 1917
SQ FT: 60,000
SALES (est): 6.9MM Privately Held
SIC: 3613 2431 Switches, electric power except snap, push button, etc.; windows, wood

(G-14920)
DEVON ENERGY CORPORATION
9805 Mcknight Rd (15237-6008)
PHONE....................................412 366-7474
Knox Young, Manager
EMP: 10
SALES (corp-wide): 10.7B Publicly Held
WEB: www.dvn.com
SIC: 1311 Crude petroleum production
PA: Devon Energy Corporation
333 W Sheridan Ave
Oklahoma City OK 73102
405 235-3611

(G-14921)
DIABETIC PASTRY CHEF INC
1438 Old Meadow Rd (15241-3408)
PHONE....................................412 260-6468
Stacey Harris, President
EMP: 3 EST: 2011
SALES (est): 172.4K Privately Held
SIC: 2099 Food preparations

(G-14922)
DIAMOND WIRE SPRING COMPANY
1901 Babcock Blvd (15209-1399)
PHONE....................................412 821-2703
Christopher Fazio, General Mgr
Karl A Schnack, General Mgr
Domenic Digiulio, Prdtn Mgr
J Haley, Marketing Mgr
Becky Bernarding, Manager
EMP: 50
SALES (corp-wide): 15.8MM Privately Held
WEB: www.diamondwire.com
SIC: 3495 Wire springs
PA: Diamond Wire Spring Company Inc
1479 Glenn Ave
Glenshaw PA 15116
412 684-1201

(G-14923)
DIELECTRIC SOLUTIONS LLC
192 Devonwood Dr (15241-2237)
PHONE....................................724 543-2333
Todd Kadar,
▲ EMP: 25
SALES (est): 3.5MM Privately Held
SIC: 3229 Glassware, industrial

(G-14924)
DINNEEN & SON INC
7838 Kelly St (15208-2035)
PHONE....................................412 241-2727
Robert Dinneen, President
EMP: 6
SQ FT: 9,000
SALES (est): 502.5K Privately Held
SIC: 2434 Wood kitchen cabinets

(G-14925)
DIRECT MAIL SERVICE INC
939 W North Ave (15233-1605)
PHONE....................................412 471-6300
Raymond Fragale, Ch of Bd
Martha Rudge, Cust Mgr
Darci Saunders, Accounts Exec
EMP: 60 EST: 1919
SQ FT: 50,000
SALES (est): 6.6MM Privately Held
WEB: www.dirmailserv.com
SIC: 2789 7331 2759 2752 Trade binding services; direct mail advertising services; commercial printing; commercial printing, lithographic

(G-14926)
DIRT RAG MAGAZINE
3483 Saxonburg Blvd (15238-1179)
PHONE....................................412 767-9910
Maurice Tierney, Owner
Mike Cushionbury, Editor
Trina Haynes, Sales Mgr
Eric McKeegan, Advt Staff
EMP: 7

SALES (est): 843.5K Privately Held
WEB: www.dirtragmag.com
SIC: 2721 5941 Magazines: publishing only, not printed on site; sporting goods & bicycle shops

(G-14927)
DJQUESNE BOTTLING COMPANY
2555 Washington Rd (15241-2574)
PHONE....................................412 831-2779
EMP: 3
SALES (est): 168.1K Privately Held
SIC: 2086 Bottled & canned soft drinks

(G-14928)
DMI LOCKSMITH INC
439 Wood St (15222-1829)
PHONE....................................412 232-3000
EMP: 4
SALES (est): 219.7K Privately Held
SIC: 3172 Key cases

(G-14929)
DMS COMPUTER SERVICES INC
91 Fort Couch Rd (15241-1033)
PHONE....................................412 835-3570
David Schweitzer, President
EMP: 6
SALES (est): 953K Privately Held
WEB: www.dmscomputerservices.com
SIC: 7372 Operating systems computer software

(G-14930)
DONALD CAMPBELL
Also Called: Campbell Machine & Fabricating
3262 Clements Rd (15239-2106)
PHONE....................................412 793-6068
Donald L Campbell, Owner
EMP: 4
SALES: 220K Privately Held
SIC: 3599 7692 3444 Machine shop, jobbing & repair; welding repair; sheet metalwork

(G-14931)
DONUT SHACK
13041 Frankstown Rd (15235-1952)
PHONE....................................412 793-4222
Guy Pratillo, Owner
EMP: 3
SALES (est): 111.6K Privately Held
SIC: 5461 2051 Doughnuts; doughnuts, except frozen

(G-14932)
DOOR GUARD INC
809 Parkway View Dr (15205-1416)
PHONE....................................724 695-8936
Briane Hartley, President
EMP: 6
SALES (est): 250K Privately Held
WEB: www.doorguardinc.com
SIC: 3534 Elevators & equipment

(G-14933)
DORAN & ASSOCIATES INC
200 Roessler Rd (15220-1037)
PHONE....................................412 344-5200
Weldon C Doran, Principal
Lois W Doran, Corp Secy
Bradley R Teets, VP Finance
Diana Doran Graham, Asst Sec
EMP: 5 EST: 1975
SQ FT: 10,000
SALES (est): 481.1K Privately Held
SIC: 1382 Oil & gas exploration services

(G-14934)
DORRANCE PUBLISHING CO INC
585 Alpha Dr Ste 103 (15238-2911)
PHONE....................................800 788-7654
David Zeolla, President
Elizabeth House, Managing Dir
Sean Irwin, Sales Staff
EMP: 45
SQ FT: 9,000
SALES: 5MM Privately Held
WEB: www.dorrancebookstore.com
SIC: 2741 5942 2731 Miscellaneous publishing; book stores; book publishing

(G-14935)
DOUGLAS LABORATORIES
600 Boyce Rd (15205-9742)
PHONE....................................412 494-0122
L Douglas Lioon, Partner
Jeffrey Lioon, Partner
EMP: 42
SQ FT: 35,000
SALES (est): 5.9MM Privately Held
SIC: 2833 5122 Vitamins, natural or synthetic: bulk, uncompounded; vitamins & minerals

(G-14936)
DQE COMMUNICATIONS LLC (DH)
424 S 27th St Ste 220 (15203-2388)
PHONE....................................412 393-1033
Jim Morozzi, President
James W Morozzi, President
Steven Balogh, Admin Asst
Mark Daday,
Kelly Pasterick,
EMP: 9
SALES (est): 2.7MM Privately Held
WEB: www.dqecom.com
SIC: 3229 7371 7372 Fiber optics strands; custom computer programming services; computer software development & applications; business oriented computer software
HQ: Duquesne Light Holdings, Inc.
411 7th Ave Ste 3
Pittsburgh PA 15219
412 393-6000

(G-14937)
DRINDUSTRIES
1320 Renton Rd (15239-1532)
PHONE....................................412 704-5840
EMP: 6
SALES (est): 634.9K Privately Held
SIC: 3999 Manufacturing industries

(G-14938)
DSI UNDERGROUND SYSTEMS INC
258 Kappa Dr (15238-2818)
PHONE....................................740 432-7302
EMP: 60 Privately Held
SIC: 3532 Mfg Mining Machinery
HQ: Dsi Underground Systems, Inc.
9786 S Prosperity Rd
West Jordan UT 84081
801 973-7169

(G-14939)
DUALSUN INTERNATIONAL INC
Also Called: Rainbow Mills
5539 Fair Oaks St (15217-1060)
PHONE....................................412 421-7934
Stanley Klein, President
◆ EMP: 7
SQ FT: 5,500
SALES: 3MM Privately Held
SIC: 2231 5137 5136 Dyeing & finishing: wool or similar fibers; sweaters, women's & children's; sweaters, men's & boys'

(G-14940)
DUCT SHOP USA INC
625 Plum Industrial Park (15239-2924)
PHONE....................................412 231-2330
Jay Graham, President
Jeff Gram, President
EMP: 5
SALES (est): 462.3K Privately Held
SIC: 3444 Sheet metalwork

(G-14941)
DUCTWORKS INC
Also Called: Greensburg Location
625 Plum Industrial Park (15239-2924)
PHONE....................................412 231-2330
Brent Hoak, Foreman/Supr
EMP: 3 Privately Held
SIC: 3444 Sheet metalwork
PA: The Ductworks Inc
350 Northgate Dr
Warrendale PA

(G-14942)
DUN RITE WINDOW AND DOOR
718 Main St (15215-2202)
P.O. Box 7866 (15215-0866)
PHONE....................................412 781-8200
Dino Trasatti, *Owner*
EMP: 4
SQ FT: 7,500
SALES (est): 407.7K **Privately Held**
SIC: 3442 1521 Storm doors or windows, metal; general remodeling, single-family houses

(G-14943)
DUNCAN LAND & ENERGY INC
147 Noble Ave Ste 100 (15205-2871)
PHONE....................................412 922-0135
Guy Trulli, *President*
Bradlee W Tebbs, *Vice Pres*
EMP: 4 EST: 2001
SALES (est): 372.6K **Privately Held**
SIC: 1382 Oil & gas exploration services

(G-14944)
DUQUESNE MINE SUPPLY COMPANY
Also Called: Dukane Mining Products
2 Cross St (15209-2080)
PHONE....................................412 821-2100
David L Genter, *President*
David C Genter, *President*
Ann Genter, *Treasurer*
▼ EMP: 5 EST: 1919
SQ FT: 53,000
SALES: 900K **Privately Held**
SIC: 1081 3613 1241 Metal mining services; switchgear & switchboard apparatus; coal mining services

(G-14945)
DUQUESNE UNIV OF HOLY SPIRIT
Also Called: Duquesne University Press
600 Forbes Ave (15219-3016)
PHONE....................................412 396-6610
Susan Wadsworth-Booth, *Director*
EMP: 1
SALES (corp-wide): 287.4MM **Privately Held**
WEB: www.duq.edu
SIC: 2731 8221 Book publishing; university
PA: Duquesne University Of The Holy Spirit
600 Forbes Ave
Pittsburgh PA 15219
412 396-6000

(G-14946)
DYKEMA RUBBER BAND
4075 Windgap Ave Bldg 5 (15204-1048)
PHONE....................................412 771-1955
Joe Venda, *President*
EMP: 6 EST: 2011
SALES (est): 827.7K **Privately Held**
SIC: 3069 Rubber bands

(G-14947)
DYNAMIC DIES INC
3251 Old Frankstown Rd E (15239-2902)
PHONE....................................724 325-1514
Daniel Obrien, *Manager*
Rob Bruno, *Supervisor*
Bud Bigley, *Info Tech Mgr*
Dave Richardson, *Director*
EMP: 25
SALES (corp-wide): 26.9MM **Privately Held**
WEB: www.dynamicdies.com
SIC: 3544 2796 Dies, steel rule; platemaking services
PA: Dynamic Dies, Inc.
1705 Commerce Rd
Holland OH 43528
419 865-0249

(G-14948)
DYNAVOX INC
Also Called: Boardmaker
2100 Wharton St Ste 400 (15203-1945)
PHONE....................................412 381-4883
Roger C Holstein, *Ch of Bd*
Michelle H Wilver, *President*
Raymond J Merk, *CFO*
Robert E Cunningham, *Officer*
EMP: 274

SQ FT: 36,000
SALES: 64.9MM **Privately Held**
SIC: 7372 Application computer software

(G-14949)
E D I ENVIRO-DRILL INC
5000 Steubenville Pike (15205-9650)
PHONE....................................412 788-1046
Larry Moore, *President*
EMP: 12
SALES (est): 459.8K **Privately Held**
SIC: 1081 1799 Metal mining services; special trade contractors

(G-14950)
E E ZIMMERMAN COMPANY (HQ)
1370 Old Frport Rd Ste 2a (15238)
P.O. Box 111254 (15238-0654)
PHONE....................................412 963-0949
E E Zimmerman II, *President*
EMP: 10
SQ FT: 2,000
SALES (est): 5.8MM
SALES (corp-wide): 6.2MM **Privately Held**
WEB: www.eezimmermanco.com
SIC: 5169 2899 2851 2842 Industrial chemicals; chemical preparations; paints & allied products; specialty cleaning, polishes & sanitation goods

(G-14951)
E O S GROUP INC
18 Oakhurst Cir (15215-1652)
PHONE....................................412 781-6023
Imre Kerenyi, *President*
EMP: 5
SALES (est): 767.4K **Privately Held**
SIC: 3827 Optical instruments & lenses

(G-14952)
EAGLE SPINCO INC
1 Ppg Pl (15272-0001)
PHONE....................................412 434-3131
Steven Beach, *President*
EMP: 3
SALES (est): 266K **Publicly Held**
SIC: 2821 Plastics materials & resins
HQ: Axiall Corporation
1000 Abernathy Rd # 1200
Atlanta GA 30328
304 455-2200

(G-14953)
EARNEST INDUSTRIES INC
Also Called: Team Laminates Co
1013 Spring Garden Ave (15212-4222)
PHONE....................................412 323-1911
John Earnest, *President*
Melissa Earnest, *Vice Pres*
EMP: 8 EST: 1972
SQ FT: 10,000
SALES (est): 1.4MM **Privately Held**
WEB: www.teamlaminates.com
SIC: 2541 Table or counter tops, plastic laminated

(G-14954)
EARTHWARE CORPORATION
100 Oak Way (15228)
PHONE....................................412 563-1920
Matthew R Graham, *President*
EMP: 3
SALES (est): 176K **Privately Held**
SIC: 7372 Prepackaged software

(G-14955)
EAST END BREWING COMPANY INC
6923 Susquehanna St (15208-1724)
PHONE....................................412 361-2848
Julie Smith, *Manager*
EMP: 10
SALES (est): 75.2K **Privately Held**
WEB: www.eastendbrewing.com
SIC: 2082 Malt beverages

(G-14956)
EAST PENN MANUFACTURING CO
4 Commerce Dr (15239-1778)
PHONE....................................412 793-0283
Pharon Metzgar, *Branch Mgr*
EMP: 14

SALES (corp-wide): 2.5B **Privately Held**
WEB: www.eastpenn-deka.com
SIC: 3691 Lead acid batteries (storage batteries)
PA: East Penn Manufacturing Co.
102 Deka Rd
Lyon Station PA 19536
610 682-6361

(G-14957)
EAST WEST MANUFACTURING A
3849 Willow Ave (15234-1850)
PHONE....................................412 207-7385
EMP: 14 EST: 2011
SALES (est): 2.3MM **Privately Held**
SIC: 3999 Manufacturing industries

(G-14958)
ECO PRODUCT GROUP LLC
5700 Corporate Dr Ste 455 (15237-5851)
PHONE....................................412 364-1792
Thomas Davis, *Mng Member*
EMP: 3
SALES (est): 397.1K **Privately Held**
SIC: 2339 Women's & misses' athletic clothing & sportswear

(G-14959)
ECO SOLUTION DISTRIBUTING LLC
2275 Swallow Hill Rd (15220-1656)
PHONE....................................724 941-4140
Joshua Herzing, *President*
James Smith, *Vice Pres*
EMP: 10
SALES (est): 8.2MM **Privately Held**
SIC: 5169 2841 Calcium chloride; glycerin, crude or refined: from fats

(G-14960)
EJ BOGNAR INCORPORATED (PA)
Also Called: Carb-Rite
733 Washington Rd Fl 5 (15228-2022)
PHONE....................................412 344-9900
Nadine E Bognar, *President*
▲ EMP: 3 EST: 1939
SALES (est): 8MM **Privately Held**
WEB: www.ejbognar.com
SIC: 1459 1442 Fire clay mining; common sand mining

(G-14961)
EL MILAGRO
1542 Beechview Ave (15216-3379)
PHONE....................................412 668-2627
EMP: 3
SALES (est): 130.6K **Privately Held**
SIC: 2099 Tortillas, fresh or refrigerated

(G-14962)
ELECTRICAL DESIGN DEVELOPM
Also Called: Teddico
1104 Parkway View Dr (15205-1425)
PHONE....................................412 747-4970
Lawrence Newmaster Jr, *President*
Greg Edwards, *Opers Mgr*
Brandy Spingola, *Admin Sec*
▲ EMP: 5
SQ FT: 5,000
SALES (est): 1MM **Privately Held**
SIC: 3644 Outlet boxes (electric wiring devices); switch boxes, electric

(G-14963)
ELEMENTS HOME ACCENTS LLC
1010 Greenfield Ave (15217-2945)
PHONE....................................412 521-0724
Phillip Mackes, *Principal*
EMP: 3
SALES (est): 90K **Privately Held**
SIC: 2819 Mfg Industrial Inorganic Chemicals

(G-14964)
ELROY TURPENTINE COMPANY (PA)
1370 Old Frport Rd Ste 2a (15238)
PHONE....................................412 963-0949
E E Zimmerman II, *President*
EMP: 8 EST: 1956

SALES (est): 1.2MM **Privately Held**
SIC: 2911 Solvents

(G-14965)
ELSTER AMERICAN METER CO LLC
1725 Washington Rd (15241-1207)
PHONE....................................412 833-2550
Russ Schrey, *General Mgr*
EMP: 3
SALES (corp-wide): 41.8B **Publicly Held**
SIC: 3824 Integrating & totalizing meters for gas & liquids
HQ: Elster American Meter Company, Llc
208 S Rogers Ln
Raleigh NC 27610
800 338-4800

(G-14966)
EM-BED-IT & CO INC
128 Green Commons Dr (15243-1470)
PHONE....................................412 781-8585
John A Pizzuto, *President*
Elaine Pizzuto, *Vice Pres*
Stephen Sobina, *Vice Pres*
EMP: 10
SQ FT: 6,200
SALES (est): 1.5MM **Privately Held**
WEB: www.embeditinc.com
SIC: 3089 2821 Novelties, plastic; plastics materials & resins

(G-14967)
EMBEDDED ENERGY TECHNOLOGY LLC
1936 5th Ave (15219-5544)
PHONE....................................412 254-3381
Philip Johns,
EMP: 6 EST: 2011
SALES: 500K **Privately Held**
SIC: 3829 Thermometers & temperature sensors

(G-14968)
EMBROIDERY ETC INC
42 Terminal Way (15219-1209)
PHONE....................................412 381-6884
Dorene Nelson, *President*
EMP: 4 EST: 1997
SALES (est): 337.3K **Privately Held**
SIC: 2395 Embroidery products, except schiffli machine; embroidery & art needlework

(G-14969)
EMBROIDERY SYSTEMS INC
523 Dorseyville Rd (15238-1651)
PHONE....................................412 967-9271
Guillermo Romero, *President*
EMP: 4
SALES (est): 140.5K **Privately Held**
SIC: 7372 Operating systems computer software

(G-14970)
EMERALD ART GLASS INC
2300 Josephine St (15203-2435)
PHONE....................................412 381-2274
Kim Zielinski, *President*
Robert J Zielinski, *Vice Pres*
EMP: 15
SALES (est): 2.2MM **Privately Held**
WEB: www.emeraldartglass.com
SIC: 5231 5023 3231 3211 Glass; glassware; products of purchased glass; flat glass

(G-14971)
EMERSON PROCESS MANAGEMENT (DH)
200 Beta Dr (15238-2918)
P.O. Box 270659, Saint Louis MO (63127-0659)
PHONE....................................412 963-4000
Robert Yeager, *President*
Denis Lawlor, *Vice Pres*
Steven Schilling, *Vice Pres*
Gary Woodward, *Purch Mgr*
Michael Durbin, *Engineer*
◆ EMP: 600

▲ = Import ▼=Export
◆ =Import/Export

SALES (est): 330.1MM
SALES (corp-wide): 17.4B **Publicly Held**
WEB:
www.emersonprocesspowerwater.com
SIC: 3823 5063 Industrial instrmnts
msrmnt display/control process variable;
generators

(G-14972)
EMP SALES ASSOCIATES INC
1445 Beulah Rd (15235-5002)
P.O. Box 17290 (15235-0290)
PHONE.................................412 731-9899
Florence W Palmieri, *President*
Edward M Palmieri, *Owner*
EMP: 3
SALES (est): 280K **Privately Held**
SIC: 2759 Commercial printing

(G-14973)
ENDOLOGIX INC
5831 Alder St (15232-1901)
PHONE.................................412 661-5877
EMP: 3
SALES (est): 118.5K **Privately Held**
SIC: 3841 Surgical & medical instruments

(G-14974)
ENERGY CONTROL SYSTEMS INC
100 Hafner Ave Ste 1 (15223-2225)
PHONE.................................412 781-8500
James Royston, *President*
Mark Royston, *Vice Pres*
Mitch Kennedy, *Controller*
Louis G Royston Jr, *Admin Sec*
EMP: 20
SQ FT: 6,500
SALES (est): 5.1MM **Privately Held**
WEB: www.ecsi4gas.com
SIC: 3441 Joists, open web steel: long-
span series; floor posts, adjustable: metal

(G-14975)
ENERGY CONVERSION TECHNOLOGY
206 Locust Ln (15241-1344)
PHONE.................................412 835-0191
Jobst W Seehausen, *President*
Barbara Seehausen, *Vice Pres*
EMP: 3
SQ FT: 500
SALES (est): 300K **Privately Held**
SIC: 3443 8733 Heat exchangers: coolers
(after, inter), condensers, etc.; scientific
research agency

(G-14976)
ENERGY INNOVATION CTR INST INC
1435 Bedford Ave (15219-3675)
PHONE.................................412 894-9800
Richard Diclaudio, *President*
EMP: 5
SQ FT: 35,000
SALES (est): 2.6MM **Privately Held**
SIC: 3086 Insulation or cushioning mate-
rial, foamed plastic

(G-14977)
ENRICO BISCOTTI COMPANY
2022 Penn Ave (15222-4418)
PHONE.................................412 281-2602
Larry Lagattuta, *President*
EMP: 5
SQ FT: 2,000
SALES (est): 558.7K **Privately Held**
WEB: www.enricobiscotti.com
SIC: 2051 Bakery: wholesale or whole-
sale/retail combined

(G-14978)
ENVIRONMENTAL INC
1000 Six Ppg Pl (15222)
PHONE.................................412 394-2800
Rj Harshman, *Principal*
EMP: 4
SALES (est): 164.6K **Publicly Held**
SIC: 3462 Iron & steel forgings
HQ: Tdy Holdings, Llc
1403 Foulk Rd Ste 200
Wilmington DE 19803
302 254-4172

(G-14979)
ENVIRONMENTAL AIR INC
1100 Mccartney St (15220-4625)
PHONE.................................412 922-8988
Paul N Neil, *President*
EMP: 30
SQ FT: 10,000
SALES: 5.9MM **Privately Held**
SIC: 3444 1711 Ducts, sheet metal;
plumbing, heating, air-conditioning con-
tractors

(G-14980)
EPI OF CLEVELAND INC (HQ)
1844 Ardmore Blvd (15221-4470)
PHONE.................................330 468-2872
Otto W Abraham, *Ch of Bd*
David Ventura, *President*
Robert Knazak, *Vice Pres*
James Rubino, *CFO*
EMP: 55
SQ FT: 2,500
SALES (est): 7.3MM
SALES (corp-wide): 15.9MM **Privately Held**
WEB: www.engineeredproducts.com
SIC: 3446 5051 Railings, bannisters,
guards, etc.: made from metal pipe; open
flooring & grating for construction; metals
service centers & offices
PA: Engineered Products, Inc.
200 Jones St
Verona PA 15147
412 423-4000

(G-14981)
EQT CORPORATION (PA)
625 Liberty Ave Ste 1700 (15222-3114)
PHONE.................................412 553-5700
James E Rohr, *Ch of Bd*
Robert J McNally, *President*
Gary E Gould, *COO*
Erin R Centofanti, *Exec VP*
Donald M Jenkins, *Exec VP*
EMP: 188 EST: 1888
SALES: 4.5B **Publicly Held**
WEB: www.eqt.com
SIC: 1311 Crude petroleum production

(G-14982)
EQT CORPORATION
Equitable Gas Company
625 Liberty Ave Ste 1700 (15222-3114)
P.O. Box 23535 (15222-6535)
PHONE.................................412 395-2080
Randall Crawford, *President*
Michael Butcher, *Vice Pres*
Patrick O'Brien, *Vice Pres*
Charlene Petrelli, *Vice Pres*
John Mackin, *Opers Staff*
EMP: 4
SALES (corp-wide): 4.5B **Publicly Held**
WEB: www.eqt.com
SIC: 1321 Natural gas liquids
PA: Eqt Corporation
625 Liberty Ave Ste 1700
Pittsburgh PA 15222
412 553-5700

(G-14983)
EQUIPMENT & CONTRLS AFRICA INC
Also Called: E & C Africa
1721 Cochran Rd (15220-1000)
PHONE.................................412 489-3000
Ritchie L Tabachnick, *President*
Dennis Petronko, *Corp Secy*
Beth Depretis, *CFO*
▼ EMP: 150
SALES (est): 49MM **Privately Held**
SIC: 2911 Oils, fuel

(G-14984)
ERIE SAND & GRAVEL CO INC (DH)
Also Called: Carmeuse Lime & Stone
11 Stanwix St Fl 21 (15222-1327)
PHONE.................................412 995-5500
Thomas A Buck, *President*
Jack Fahler, *Vice Pres*
Paul Tunnicliffe, *Vice Pres*
Kevin White, *Vice Pres*
Caroll Laufmann, *VP Engrg*
▲ EMP: 31 EST: 1888

SALES (est): 13.7MM **Privately Held**
SIC: 1422 Crushed & broken limestone
HQ: Norton Oglebay Company
11 Stanwix St Fl 21
Pittsburgh PA 15222
412 995-5500

(G-14985)
ERIKS NA LLC (DH)
Also Called: Eriks North America
650 Washington Rd Ste 500 (15228-2714)
PHONE.................................412 787-2400
Shawn Courtney, *Mng Member*
EMP: 35
SALES: 700MM **Privately Held**
SIC: 3491 Industrial valves
HQ: Eriks N.V.
Mariaplaats 21
Utrecht 3511
303 690-100

(G-14986)
ESTHERS SWEET SHOP INC
1814 Brownsville Rd (15210-3908)
PHONE.................................412 884-4224
Esther Wolfson, *President*
Robert Wolfson, *Vice Pres*
EMP: 7
SQ FT: 800
SALES: 288.9K **Privately Held**
WEB: www.esthersaweetshop.com
SIC: 2064 5145 5441 Candy & other con-
fectionery products; candy; candy

(G-14987)
ETI CLOSECO
2014a Babcock Blvd (15209-1354)
PHONE.................................412 822-8250
Charles Wbanas, *President*
Fredrick R Kim, *Principal*
Michael Abaverso, *Vice Pres*
Donna Mkim, *Admin Sec*
EMP: 9
SQ FT: 10,000
SALES (est): 1.8MM **Privately Held**
WEB: www.elcontech.com
SIC: 7373 3999 Systems integration serv-
ices; atomizers, toiletry

(G-14988)
EUREKA FOUNDRY CO
4 Shadow Ln (15238-2117)
PHONE.................................412 963-7881
EMP: 3
SALES (est): 220.6K **Privately Held**
SIC: 3325 Steel Foundries, Nec, Nsk

(G-14989)
EVERPOWER WIND HOLDINGS INC (DH)
1251 Waterfront Pl Fl 3 (15222-4228)
PHONE.................................412 253-9400
James Spencer, *CEO*
Andrew Golembeski, *Exec VP*
Charlie Williams, *CFO*
Larissa Zorn, *Accountant*
Bonnie Miller, *Manager*
EMP: 24
SQ FT: 8,000
SALES (est): 11.8MM
SALES (corp-wide): 352.2K **Privately Held**
SIC: 3511 8711 Turbines & turbine gener-
ator sets; energy conservation engineer-
ing
HQ: Terra Firma Capital Partners Limited
2 More London Riverside
London SE1 2
207 015-9500

(G-14990)
EVOQUA WATER TECHNOLOGIES CORP (PA)
210 6th Ave Ste 3300 (15222-2603)
PHONE.................................724 772-0044
Martin Lamb, *Ch of Bd*
Ronald C Keating, *President*
Herve Fages, *President*
Vincent Grieco, *Exec VP*
Jim Kohosek, *Exec VP*
EMP: 63
SQ FT: 60,000
SALES: 1.3B **Publicly Held**
SIC: 3589 Water treatment equipment, in-
dustrial

(G-14991)
EWT HOLDINGS III CORP (PA)
210 6th Ave Ste 3300 (15222-2603)
PHONE.................................724 772-0044
Ronald C Keating, *President*
EMP: 4
SALES (est): 52.4MM **Privately Held**
SIC: 3589 Sewage & water treatment
equipment

(G-14992)
EXCEL SIGNWORKS
132 23rd St (15215-2815)
PHONE.................................412 337-2966
EMP: 3
SALES (est): 203.4K **Privately Held**
SIC: 3993 Signs & advertising specialties

(G-14993)
EXEDYNE MANUFACTURING SERVICES
1527 Forestview Dr (15234-1007)
PHONE.................................724 651-5100
Matt Mawhinney, *Owner*
EMP: 5
SALES (est): 268.6K **Privately Held**
SIC: 3599 Machine shop, jobbing & repair

(G-14994)
EXPRESS PRESS INC
334 Penn Center Blvd (15235-5509)
PHONE.................................412 824-1000
Rosemary Burns, *CEO*
Robert L Burns, *Vice Pres*
Robert Burns, *Vice Pres*
EMP: 6
SQ FT: 5,500
SALES (est): 915.5K **Privately Held**
SIC: 2752 Commercial printing, offset

(G-14995)
EXTECH/EXTERIOR TECH INC
200 Bridge St (15223-2211)
PHONE.................................412 781-0991
William P Voegele Jr, *President*
Francis Coholich, *Vice Pres*
Thomas Day, *Vice Pres*
Voegele M Christine, *Treasurer*
Christine Voegele, *Admin Sec*
▲ EMP: 50
SQ FT: 65,000
SALES (est): 13MM **Privately Held**
WEB: www.extech-voegele.com
SIC: 3442 3444 Sash, door or window:
metal; skylights, sheet metal
PA: Voegele Company, Inc.
200 Bridge St
Pittsburgh PA 15223
412 781-0940

(G-14996)
EXTREL CMS LLC
575 Epsilon Dr Ste 2 (15238-2812)
PHONE.................................412 963-7530
Zbigniew Krieger, *Vice Pres*
Robin Moore, *Purch Mgr*
Luke Kephart, *Mng Member*
Brian Regel, *Manager*
Jian WEI, *Manager*
EMP: 35
SQ FT: 18,000
SALES (est): 9.7MM **Privately Held**
WEB: www.extrel.com
SIC: 3826 Mass spectrometers

(G-14997)
EYENAVISION INC
1501 Reedsdale St Ste 203 (15233-2350)
PHONE.................................412 456-2736
David Zewe, *Ch of Bd*
Joseph Zewe, *President*
Casey Cloonan, *Sales Staff*
Rae Hamm, *Mktg Coord*
Caitlin Northup, *Director*
▲ EMP: 10
SALES (est): 1.2MM **Privately Held**
SIC: 3841 Eye examining instruments &
apparatus

(G-14998)
F FERRATO FOODS COMPANY
Also Called: Ferrato Fine Foods
203 Boggs Ave (15211-2015)
P.O. Box 6026 (15211-0026)
PHONE.................................412 431-1479

G E O G R A P H I C

Robert Ferrato, *President*
Aldo Ferrato, *Corp Secy*
Teresa Ferrato, *Vice Pres*
EMP: 6
SQ FT: 4,000
SALES (est): 400K **Privately Held**
SIC: 2099 Bread crumbs, not made in bakeries

(G-14999)
F R INDUSTRIES INC
557 Long Rd (15235-4395)
PHONE..............................412 242-5903
Francois Reizine, *President*
Janet M Reizine, *Vice Pres*
EMP: 10
SQ FT: 11,000
SALES (est): 1.2MM **Privately Held**
WEB: www.iniflex.com
SIC: 3499 3443 Barricades, metal; jackets, metal; industrial: metal plate

(G-15000)
F TINKER AND SONS COMPANY
Also Called: Vacuumet Div, The
5665 Butler St (15201-2340)
PHONE..............................412 781-3553
Regis Synan, *President*
Fynan Ridges, *President*
Diane L Synan, *Admin Sec*
EMP: 23 **EST:** 1916
SQ FT: 10,000
SALES (est): 4.3MM **Privately Held**
SIC: 3545 3643 3541 3423 Shear knives; current-carrying wiring devices; machine tools, metal cutting type; hand & edge tools; metal heat treating

(G-15001)
F/K INDUSTRIES INC
506 Elaine Dr (15236-2419)
PHONE..............................412 655-4982
Carole L Farrell, *President*
Sarah L Keslar, *Treasurer*
EMP: 6
SALES (est): 610K **Privately Held**
SIC: 1222 Bituminous Coal-Underground Mining

(G-15002)
FAB UNIVERSAL CORP (PA)
5001 Baum Blvd Ste 770 (15213-1856)
PHONE..............................412 621-0902
Zhang Hongcheng, *Ch of Bd*
Christopher J Spencer, *President*
John Busshaus, *CFO*
EMP: 15
SQ FT: 3,100
SALES (est): 19.8MM **Privately Held**
WEB: www.wizzardsoftware.com
SIC: 7372 5735 5942 5994 Prepackaged software; compact discs; book stores; magazine stand; compact discs; software programming applications

(G-15003)
FACTORY UNLOCKED LLC
720 E Lacock St (15212-5900)
PHONE..............................724 882-9940
Bernie Lynch, *Founder*
EMP: 5 **EST:** 2017
SALES (est): 220.5K **Privately Held**
SIC: 3999 Manufacturing industries

(G-15004)
FARNSWORTH GOWNS AND FNRL SUPS
1806 Brownsville Rd (15210-3908)
PHONE..............................412 881-4696
George T Orsega, *Owner*
EMP: 7
SQ FT: 5,000
SALES (est): 920K **Privately Held**
WEB: www.farnsworthgowns.com
SIC: 2339 5087 Women's & misses' outerwear; funeral directors' equipment & supplies

(G-15005)
FARO TECHNOLOGIES INC
1216 Colescott St (15205-3808)
PHONE..............................412 559-7737
Carr Christopher, *Branch Mgr*
EMP: 3

SALES (corp-wide): 403.6MM **Publicly Held**
SIC: 3699 Laser systems & equipment
PA: Faro Technologies, Inc.
250 Technology Park
Lake Mary FL 32746
407 333-9911

(G-15006)
FASSINGER PRODUCTS & ENGRAVING
3526 Willow Ave (15234-2224)
PHONE..............................412 563-6226
Dennis Fassinger, *Owner*
EMP: 3
SALES (est): 220K **Privately Held**
SIC: 3993 Signs & advertising specialties

(G-15007)
FCLZ HOLDINGS INC
240 Vista Park Dr (15205-1204)
PHONE..............................412 788-4991
Ken Karmazyn, *President*
EMP: 11
SQ FT: 7,500
SALES (est): 1.1MM **Privately Held**
SIC: 3699 Door opening & closing devices, electrical

(G-15008)
FEDEX CORPORATION
5996 Penn Cir S Ste D-102 (15206)
PHONE..............................412 441-2379
Fax: 412 441-2413
EMP: 4
SALES (corp-wide): 47.4B **Publicly Held**
SIC: 2752 Lithographic Commercial Printing
PA: Fedex Corporation
942 Shady Grove Rd S
Memphis TN 38120
901 818-7500

(G-15009)
FEDEX OFFICE & PRINT SVCS INC
215 Summit Park Dr (15275-1203)
PHONE..............................412 788-0552
Jeffrey Novak, *Regional Mgr*
EMP: 15
SALES (corp-wide): 65.4B **Publicly Held**
WEB: www.kinkos.com
SIC: 7334 2791 2789 2759 Photocopying & duplicating services; typesetting; bookbinding & related work; commercial printing; coated & laminated paper
HQ: Fedex Office And Print Services, Inc.
7900 Legacy Dr
Plano TX 75024
800 463-3339

(G-15010)
FEDEX OFFICE & PRINT SVCS INC
Also Called: Fedex Office Print & Ship
1720 Washington Rd (15241-1208)
PHONE..............................412 835-4005
EMP: 22
SALES (corp-wide): 65.4B **Publicly Held**
WEB: www.kinkos.com
SIC: 7334 2791 2672 Photocopying & duplicating services; typesetting; coated & laminated paper
HQ: Fedex Office And Print Services, Inc.
7900 Legacy Dr
Plano TX 75024
800 463-3339

(G-15011)
FEDEX OFFICE & PRINT SVCS INC
4771 Mcknight Rd (15237-3424)
PHONE..............................412 366-9750
EMP: 16
SALES (corp-wide): 65.4B **Publicly Held**
WEB: www.kinkos.com
SIC: 7334 2791 2789 2759 Photocopying & duplicating services; typesetting; bookbinding & related work; commercial printing; lettering & sign painting services; facsimile transmission services
HQ: Fedex Office And Print Services, Inc.
7900 Legacy Dr
Plano TX 75024
800 463-3339

(G-15012)
FENNER DUNLOP AMERICAS LLC
1400 Omega Dr (15205-5007)
PHONE..............................412 249-0692
Charles Felix, *Branch Mgr*
EMP: 119
SALES (corp-wide): 855.1MM **Privately Held**
SIC: 2399 Belting & belt products
HQ: Fenner Dunlop Americas, Llc
1000 Omega Dr Ste 1400
Pittsburgh PA 15205

(G-15013)
FENNER DUNLOP AMERICAS LLC (HQ)
Also Called: Fenner Dunlop Engineered
1000 Omega Dr Ste 1400 (15205-5001)
PHONE..............................412 249-0700
Al Bonneau, *Senior VP*
Dan Wilson, *Opers Mgr*
Randy Haley, *Prdtn Mgr*
Erik Tanner, *Foreman/Supr*
Bill Fleming, *Opers Staff*
◆ **EMP:** 230
SQ FT: 300,000
SALES (est): 205.2MM
SALES (corp-wide): 855.1MM **Privately Held**
SIC: 3496 Conveyor belts
PA: Fenner Group Holdings Limited
Unit 5, Hesslewood Office Park
Hessle N HUMBS HU13
148 262-6500

(G-15014)
FERRARI IMPORTING COMPANY
Also Called: Gamma Technologies
200 Waterfront Dr (15222-4737)
PHONE..............................412 323-0335
Harry Ferrari, *President*
Ray Harrington, *Vice Pres*
Velma Ferrari, *Admin Sec*
◆ **EMP:** 48
SQ FT: 37,000
SALES (est): 6.5MM **Privately Held**
WEB: www.froghairfishing.com
SIC: 3949 5091 Tennis equipment & supplies; rackets & frames: tennis, badminton, squash, lacrosse, etc; strings, tennis racket; sporting & recreation goods

(G-15015)
FERRO CORPORATION
60 Greenway Dr (15204-2521)
P.O. Box 519, Washington (15301-0519)
PHONE..............................412 331-3550
Cliff Ruderer, *Manager*
EMP: 36
SALES (corp-wide): 1.6B **Publicly Held**
WEB: www.ferro.com
SIC: 2816 Inorganic pigments
PA: Ferro Corporation
6060 Parkland Blvd # 250
Mayfield Heights OH 44124
216 875-5600

(G-15016)
FIDELITY FLIGHT SIMULATION INC
Also Called: F2si
1815 Parkway View Dr (15205-1422)
PHONE..............................412 321-3280
Graham Hodgetts, *President*
Ronald Kostosky, *General Mgr*
Geoffrey Barefoot, *Exec VP*
Malik McClellan, *Project Mgr*
Jeremy Dwyer, *Research*
EMP: 10
SQ FT: 6,000
SALES (est): 6.8MM **Privately Held**
WEB: www.flightmotion.com
SIC: 3699 Flight simulators (training aids), electronic

(G-15017)
FIFTYONE K LLC
4885 Mcknight Rd Ste 308a (15237-3400)
PHONE..............................908 222-8780
Hans Zolet, *President*
Wendy Hall, *Opers Staff*
EMP: 3 **EST:** 2013

SALES (est): 135.4K **Privately Held**
SIC: 7372 7389 Application computer software;

(G-15018)
FIRST RSPNSE LTG SOLUTIONS LLC
3424 Babcock Blvd (15237-2402)
PHONE..............................412 585-6220
Robert M Stone, *President*
EMP: 4 **EST:** 2016
SALES (est): 125.1K **Privately Held**
SIC: 3999 Manufacturing industries

(G-15019)
FISHER SCIENTIFIC COMPANY LLC (HQ)
300 Industry Dr (15275-1001)
PHONE..............................724 517-1500
Marc Casper, *CEO*
Joseph Bernardo, *President*
Daniel F Pantano, *President*
Jeffrey Jochims, *Co-President*
Robert Forte, *Vice Pres*
▲ **EMP:** 500
SALES (est): 1.4B
SALES (corp-wide): 24.3B **Publicly Held**
WEB: www.fishersci.com
SIC: 5049 5169 3821 3826 Laboratory equipment, except medical or dental; scientific instruments; analytical instruments; chemicals & allied products; laboratory equipment: fume hoods, distillation racks, etc.; worktables, laboratory; analytical instruments; microscopes, electron & proton; laboratory chemicals, organic; industrial inorganic chemicals
PA: Thermo Fisher Scientific Inc.
168 3rd Ave
Waltham MA 02451
781 622-1000

(G-15020)
FIVES N AMERCN COMBUSTN INC
526 E Bruceton Rd Ste 101 (15236-4577)
PHONE..............................412 655-0101
Jack Cochenour, *General Mgr*
EMP: 5
SALES (corp-wide): 4.5MM **Privately Held**
SIC: 5084 3823 Industrial machinery & equipment; combustion control instruments
HQ: Fives North American Combustion, Inc.
4455 E 71st St
Cleveland OH 44105
216 271-6000

(G-15021)
FLIR SYSTEMS INC
2240 William Pitt Way (15238-1358)
PHONE..............................412 423-2100
Keith Lejeune, *CEO*
Stan Warner, *Manager*
EMP: 117
SALES (corp-wide): 1.7B **Publicly Held**
SIC: 3826 Infrared analytical instruments; thermal analysis instruments, laboratory type
PA: Flir Systems, Inc.
27700 Sw Parkway Ave
Wilsonville OR 97070
503 498-3547

(G-15022)
FLUOROUS TECHNOLOGIES INC
815 Copeland Way (15232-2217)
PHONE..............................267 225-5384
Philip Yeske, *President*
EMP: 15 **EST:** 2000
SALES (est): 1.5MM **Privately Held**
WEB: www.fluorous.com
SIC: 2869 Industrial organic chemicals

(G-15023)
FOERSTER INSTRUMENTS INC (HQ)
140 Industry Dr (15275-1028)
PHONE..............................412 788-8976
Tommie Nilson, *President*
Wesley Kelly, *Engineer*
Bob Maggs, *Engineer*
Mark Stepic, *Engineer*

▲ = Import ▼=Export
◆ =Import/Export

Thomas Watterson, *Sales Staff*
▲ **EMP:** 50 **EST:** 1978
SQ FT: 26,000
SALES (est): 10.2MM
SALES (corp-wide): 60.6MM **Privately Held**
WEB: www.foerstergroup.com
SIC: 3826 5065 3829 3825 Analytical instruments; electronic parts & equipment; measuring & controlling devices; instruments to measure electricity
PA: Institut Dr. Foerster Gmbh & Co. Kg
In Laisen 70
Reutlingen 72766
712 114-00

(G-15024)
FORALLSECURE INC
3710 Forbes Ave Fl 3 (15213-3409)
PHONE............................412 256-8809
David Brumley, *CEO*
Athanasios Avgerinos, *Shareholder*
Alexandre Rebert, *Shareholder*
EMP: 18
SALES (est): 614.3K **Privately Held**
SIC: 7371 7372 7373 7379 Computer software systems analysis & design, custom; computer software development & applications; application computer software; systems software development services; ;

(G-15025)
FOREST DEVICES INC
544 Miltenberger St (15219-5971)
PHONE............................724 612-1504
Matt Kesinger, *General Mgr*
Daniel Willis, *Principal*
Matthew Kesinger, *Principal*
Carmelo Montalvo, *Opers Staff*
EMP: 6
SALES (est): 187K **Privately Held**
SIC: 3845 Electromedical equipment

(G-15026)
FORMS AND SURFACES INC (PA)
Also Called: Vivid Glass
30 Pine St (15223-1919)
PHONE............................412 781-9003
Jeffrey M Stork, *President*
Bob Hoey, *Vice Pres*
Ed Baker, *Project Mgr*
Theresa Ortiz-Palsa, *Project Mgr*
Christian Shaffer, *Project Mgr*
◆ **EMP:** 550
SQ FT: 100,000
SALES (est): 161.5MM **Privately Held**
WEB: www.forms-surfaces.com
SIC: 3446 Architectural metalwork

(G-15027)
FORREST STEEL CORPORATION
1000 Baldwin Rd (15207-1934)
PHONE............................412 884-5533
Gary Hecht, *President*
Jeanne E Hecht, *Admin Sec*
EMP: 17 **EST:** 1957
SQ FT: 27,500
SALES (est): 4.4MM **Privately Held**
WEB: www.forreststeel.com
SIC: 3441 Fabricated structural metal

(G-15028)
FORUM INC
Also Called: Forum Lighting
100 Chapel Harbor Dr # 1 (15238-4162)
PHONE............................412 781-5970
Jonathan Garret, *President*
Nick Brahm, *Engineer*
Ryan Alm, *Design Engr*
Julie McElhattan, *Controller*
Paula Garret, *Shareholder*
EMP: 64
SQ FT: 78,000
SALES (est): 16.2MM **Privately Held**
WEB: www.forumlighting.com
SIC: 3646 Fluorescent lighting fixtures, commercial

(G-15029)
FRAME OUTLET INC
2314 Forest Dr (15235-4932)
PHONE............................412 351-7283
George D Ratliff, *President*

Jean Ratliff, *Corp Secy*
EMP: 3
SQ FT: 4,000
SALES (est): 349K **Privately Held**
SIC: 2499 5999 Picture & mirror frames, wood; picture frames, ready made

(G-15030)
FRANCIS J NOWALK
Also Called: Nowalk Lighting
4017 Liberty Ave (15224-1442)
PHONE............................412 687-4017
Francis J Nowalk, *Owner*
EMP: 6
SQ FT: 37,000
SALES (est): 691.6K **Privately Held**
SIC: 3645 3471 2514 5719 Residential lighting fixtures; polishing, metals or formed products; metal household furniture; lighting fixtures; sheet metalwork

(G-15031)
FRANK BRYAN INC
100 S 3rd St (15219-1128)
PHONE............................412 431-2700
Thomas Bryan Jr, *Branch Mgr*
EMP: 12
SALES (corp-wide): 17.5MM **Privately Held**
SIC: 3273 Ready-mixed concrete
PA: Frank Bryan, Inc.
1263 Chartiers Ave
Mc Kees Rocks PA 15136
412 331-1630

(G-15032)
FRANK CALANDRA INC (PA)
Also Called: JM Steel
258 Kappa Dr (15238-2818)
P.O. Box 111253 (15238-0653)
PHONE............................412 963-9071
John M Calandra, *President*
Barbara Zimmers, *Managing Dir*
James A Ceresa, *Exec VP*
Matthew Brock, *Vice Pres*
Frank Calandra Jr, *Vice Pres*
◆ **EMP:** 50 **EST:** 1922
SQ FT: 23,500
SALES (est): 571.6MM **Privately Held**
WEB: www.jennmar.com
SIC: 1241 Preparing shafts or tunnels, anthracite mining; preparing shafts or tunnels, bituminous or lignite mining

(G-15033)
FRANK CUSTOM STAINLESS INC
131 Cherry St (15223-2242)
PHONE............................412 784-0300
Frank Muto, *President*
Joanne Muto, *Admin Sec*
EMP: 7
SQ FT: 5,500
SALES (est): 945.9K **Privately Held**
SIC: 3469 Kitchen fixtures & equipment: metal, except cast aluminum

(G-15034)
FRANK MANCE PLATING SERVICE
2823 Penn Ave (15222-4713)
PHONE............................412 281-5748
Thomas J Mance, *Owner*
EMP: 3
SQ FT: 1,875
SALES (est): 202.9K **Privately Held**
WEB: www.frankmanceplatingservice.com
SIC: 3471 Electroplating of metals or formed products

(G-15035)
FREDIANI PRINTING COMPANY
Also Called: Unione Italian Newspaper
1719 Liberty Ave (15222-4397)
PHONE............................412 281-8533
Lawrence Frediani, *Partner*
Robert M Frediani, *Partner*
EMP: 7
SQ FT: 10,000
SALES: 500K **Privately Held**
SIC: 2711 Commercial printing & newspaper publishing combined

(G-15036)
FREDS SIGNS
22 Spruce St (15202-2104)
PHONE............................412 741-3153
Frederick Ruprecht, *Owner*
EMP: 3
SALES (est): 306.9K **Privately Held**
SIC: 3993 7389 Signs, not made in custom sign painting shops; lettering & sign painting services

(G-15037)
FRESH FOOD MANUFACTURING CO
101 Kappa Dr (15238-2809)
PHONE............................412 963-6200
David S Shapira, *President*
Lucot John, *Vice Pres*
Phillip W Oliveri, *Treasurer*
Mark I Minnaugh, *Admin Sec*
EMP: 705
SALES (est): 66.7MM
SALES (corp-wide): 6.9B **Privately Held**
SIC: 2099 Food preparations
PA: Giant Eagle, Inc.
101 Kappa Dr
Pittsburgh PA 15238
800 362-8899

(G-15038)
FRESHTEMP LLC
6739 Reynolds St (15206-4511)
PHONE............................844 370-1782
Jeff Rieger, *CEO*
EMP: 6
SALES (est): 152.6K
SALES (corp-wide): 228.3MM **Publicly Held**
SIC: 3823 Temperature measurement instruments, industrial
PA: Digi International Inc.
9350 Excelsior Blvd
Hopkins MN 55343
952 912-3444

(G-15039)
G & S METAL PRODUCTS INC
173 Pinchtown Rd (15236-1132)
PHONE............................412 462-7000
Robert Schuster, *President*
EMP: 8
SQ FT: 2,500
SALES (est): 1.1MM **Privately Held**
SIC: 3444 3442 Awnings & canopies; screen & storm doors & windows

(G-15040)
GANESCO INCORPORATED
2624 Thorntree Dr (15241-2966)
PHONE............................931 284-9033
Nancy Nunley, *President*
EMP: 5
SALES: 75K **Privately Held**
SIC: 8299 7372 Educational service, non-degree granting: continuing educ.; business oriented computer software; educational computer software

(G-15041)
GATEWAY NEWSPAPERS
460 Rodi Rd (15235-4547)
PHONE............................412 856-7400
Kim Palmiero, *Principal*
EMP: 5
SALES (est): 244K **Privately Held**
SIC: 2711 Newspapers, publishing & printing

(G-15042)
GATEWAY PAINT & CHEMICAL CO
2929 Smallman St (15201-1587)
PHONE............................412 261-6642
Harold Blumenfeld, *President*
Cheryl Blumenfeld, *Vice Pres*
EMP: 20 **EST:** 1953
SQ FT: 30,000
SALES (est): 4.3MM **Privately Held**
SIC: 2851 2952 Paints & paint additives; coating compounds, tar

(G-15043)
GENE SANES & ASSOCIATES
Also Called: Sanes, Gene Upholstery
1645 Penn Ave (15222-4322)
PHONE............................412 471-8224
Gene Sanes, *Principal*
EMP: 34
SQ FT: 11,000
SALES: 2.2MM **Privately Held**
SIC: 5949 7641 2519 Fabric, remnants; reupholstery; household furniture, except wood or metal: upholstered

(G-15044)
GENERAL DYNAMICS CORPORATION
2730 Sidney St Ste 310 (15203-5137)
PHONE............................412 432-2200
Ajmal Khan, *Engineer*
Scott Potter, *Engineer*
Dan Joyce, *Branch Mgr*
Andy Gillespie, *Security Mgr*
James Straub, *Software Engr*
EMP: 44
SALES (corp-wide): 36.1B **Publicly Held**
SIC: 3731 Combat vessels, building & repairing; submarines, building & repairing
PA: General Dynamics Corporation
2941 Frview Pk Dr Ste 100
Falls Church VA 22042
703 876-3000

(G-15045)
GENERAL DYNAMICS MISSION
2730 Sidney St Ste 310 (15203-5137)
PHONE............................412 488-8605
Matthew Gaston, *Manager*
Darren Siegel, *Software Engr*
EMP: 30
SALES (corp-wide): 36.1B **Publicly Held**
SIC: 3571 Electronic computers
HQ: General Dynamics Mission Systems, Inc.
12450 Fair Lakes Cir # 200
Fairfax VA 22033
703 263-2800

(G-15046)
GENERAL NUTRITION CENTERS INC (DH)
Also Called: GNC
300 6th Ave Fl 2 (15222-2511)
PHONE............................412 288-4600
Curt Larrimer, *Senior VP*
Michael Locke, *Senior VP*
Evan Pagonis, *Opers Staff*
Kelly Eyler, *Manager*
Nancy Herscoe, *Manager*
EMP: 500
SQ FT: 253,000
SALES (est): 3B **Publicly Held**
SIC: 5499 2023 Health foods; dietary supplements, dairy & non-dairy based
HQ: Gnc Corporation
300 6th Ave Fl 2
Pittsburgh PA 15222
412 288-4600

(G-15047)
GENILOGIX LLC
800 Waterfront Dr Ste 1 (15222-4755)
PHONE............................412 444-0554
Melvin Maxwell, *Mng Member*
Nate Stuyvesant,
EMP: 50
SALES (est): 3.5MM
SALES (corp-wide): 19B **Publicly Held**
WEB: www.genilogix.com
SIC: 7372 Application computer software
PA: Avnet, Inc.
2211 S 47th St
Phoenix AZ 85034
480 643-2000

(G-15048)
GET HIP INC
R.J Casey Industrial Park (15233)
PHONE............................412 231-4766
Gregg Kostelich, *President*
William Von Hagen, *Vice Pres*
Michael Joseph Kastelic, *Admin Sec*
EMP: 9
SQ FT: 2,000

SALES (est): 868.1K **Privately Held**
WEB: www.gethip.com
SIC: 5099 2782 Phonograph records;
record albums

(G-15049)
GEYER & SON INC
316 Poplargrove St (15210-3916)
PHONE...............................412 431-5231
Joseph Geyer, *President*
Sharon L Antonucci, *Admin Sec*
EMP: 18 EST: 2006
SQ FT: 300
SALES: 1.5MM **Privately Held**
SIC: 1389 Haulage, oil field

(G-15050)
GLAXOSMITHKLINE LLC
5547 Bartlett St (15217-1529)
PHONE...............................412 398-2600
EMP: 26
SALES (corp-wide): 39.8B **Privately Held**
SIC: 2834 Pharmaceutical preparations
HQ: Glaxosmithkline Llc
5 Crescent Dr
Philadelphia PA 19112
215 751-4000

(G-15051)
GLENFIELD SUPPLY COMPANY INC
Also Called: Glenfield Manufacturing
1935 Main St (15215-2714)
PHONE...............................412 781-8188
Helen L Crooks, *President*
William H Crooks Jr, *Admin Sec*
EMP: 6 EST: 1966
SQ FT: 2,700
SALES (est): 1MM **Privately Held**
SIC: 3315 3493 3469 Steel wire & related
products; flat springs, sheet or strip stock;
stamping metal for the trade

(G-15052)
GLOBAL EPP INC
7038 Front River Rd (15225-1151)
PHONE...............................412 580-4780
Andreas Nellner, *President*
Bernd Nussdorfer, *Corp Secy*
Stephan Peiffer, *Vice Pres*
▲ EMP: 6
SALES (est): 630.3K **Privately Held**
SIC: 3083 Thermoplastic laminates: rods,
tubes, plates & sheet

(G-15053)
GLOBE ELECTRIC COMPANY INC
200 23rd St (15215-2897)
PHONE...............................412 781-2671
Bill Connor, *President*
William P Connor, *President*
Jan Bennett, *Principal*
Mike Bosio, *Principal*
Chris Connor, *Principal*
▲ EMP: 26 EST: 1923
SQ FT: 11,200
SALES (est): 7.9MM **Privately Held**
WEB: www.globeelectric.com
SIC: 7694 5063 Electric motor repair; mo-
tors, electric

(G-15054)
GNC CORPORATION (DH)
300 6th Ave Fl 2 (15222-2528)
PHONE...............................412 288-4600
Joseph M Fortunato, *President*
Donna Wright, *Regional Mgr*
Guru Ramanathan, *Senior VP*
Dennis Magulick, *Vice Pres*
Jill McElhinny, *Vice Pres*
EMP: 4
SALES (est): 3B **Publicly Held**
SIC: 5499 2023 6719 Health & dietetic
food stores; dietary supplements, dairy &
non-dairy based; investment holding com-
panies, except banks
HQ: Gnc Parent Llc
300 6th Ave Fl 2
Pittsburgh PA 15222
412 288-4600

(G-15055)
GNC PARENT LLC (HQ)
300 6th Ave Fl 2 (15222-2528)
PHONE...............................412 288-4600

Robert F Moran,
EMP: 4 EST: 2006
SALES (est): 3B **Publicly Held**
SIC: 5499 2023 6719 Health & dietetic
food stores; dietary supplements, dairy &
non-dairy based; investment holding companies, except banks

(G-15056)
GOLD MEDAL PRODUCTS CO
Also Called: Gold Metal Pittsburgh
519 Parkway View Dr (15205-1410)
PHONE...............................412 787-1030
Greg Cramer, *Branch Mgr*
EMP: 5
SQ FT: 6,000
SALES (corp-wide): 129.8MM **Privately Held**
WEB: www.gmpopcorn.com
SIC: 3556 5113 5145 Food products ma-
chinery; industrial & personal service
paper; confectionery
PA: Gold Medal Products Co.
10700 Medallion Dr
Cincinnati OH 45241
513 769-7676

(G-15057)
GOLDEN BONE PET RESORT INC
6890 5th Ave (15208-2307)
PHONE...............................412 661-7001
David Anderson, *President*
EMP: 20
SQ FT: 7,000
SALES (est): 700K **Privately Held**
WEB: www.goldenbonepetresort.com
SIC: 0752 5999 3999 Boarding services,
kennels; grooming services, pet & animal
specialties; pet supplies; pet supplies

(G-15058)
GRAPHICS 22 SIGNS INC
5212 Lytle St (15207-1874)
PHONE...............................412 422-1125
Jennifer Panian, *President*
Geoff Panian, *Vice Pres*
EMP: 10
SQ FT: 5,000
SALES: 1MM **Privately Held**
WEB: www.graphics22signs.com
SIC: 3993 7532 Signs, not made in cus-
tom sign painting shops; truck painting &
lettering

(G-15059)
GRAY BRIDGE SOFTWARE INC
2353 Westgate Dr (15237-1623)
PHONE...............................412 401-1045
Frederick Gohh, *President*
EMP: 5
SALES (est): 183.9K **Privately Held**
SIC: 7372 Prepackaged software

(G-15060)
GREAT DAY IMPROVEMENTS LLC
4777 Streets Run Rd Ste 2 (15236-1200)
PHONE...............................412 304-0089
Tony Schipani, *Manager*
EMP: 25 **Privately Held**
WEB: www.patioenc.com
SIC: 5712 3448 Furniture stores; prefabri-
cated metal buildings
HQ: Great Day Improvements, Llc
700 Highland Rd E
Macedonia OH 44056

(G-15061)
GREATER PITTS SPECIALITY
Also Called: Gpsa
1610 Babcock Blvd (15209-1604)
PHONE...............................412 821-5976
Brian Klaas, *President*
EMP: 7
SQ FT: 10,000
SALES (est): 1MM **Privately Held**
SIC: 2261 Screen printing of cotton broad-
woven fabrics

(G-15062)
GREEN TREE TIMES
420 Sulgrave Rd (15211-1422)
P.O. Box 60142 (15211-0142)
PHONE...............................412 481-7830
Peg Stewart, *Owner*

EMP: 7 EST: 1994
SALES (est): 189.3K **Privately Held**
WEB: www.hometownpittsburgh.com
SIC: 2711 Commercial printing & newspa-
per publishing combined

(G-15063)
GREENHOUSE WINERY
3825 Saw Mill Run Blvd (15227-2603)
PHONE...............................412 892-9017
EMP: 4
SALES (est): 272.1K
SALES (corp-wide): 164.9K **Privately Held**
SIC: 2084 Wines
PA: Greenhouse Winery
10828 Guffey Rillton Rd
Rillton PA 15678
724 446-5000

(G-15064)
GREENTREE PRINTING INC
Also Called: Greentree Printing and Signs
2351 Noblestown Rd Ste 10 (15205-4138)
PHONE...............................412 921-5570
Lynn Gross, *President*
EMP: 15
SQ FT: 2,000
SALES (est): 2.5MM **Privately Held**
WEB: www.greentreeprinting.com
SIC: 2752 Commercial printing, offset

(G-15065)
GROLL ORNAMENTAL IR WORKS LLC
1201 Becks Run Rd (15210-3113)
PHONE...............................412 431-4444
Mark Groll, *Owner*
EMP: 6
SQ FT: 5,000
SALES: 550K **Privately Held**
SIC: 3446 Architectural metalwork

(G-15066)
GROUND 34 LLC
6024 Broad St Fl 2 (15206-3010)
PHONE...............................914 299-7212
Akhil Aniff,
EMP: 5
SALES (est): 117.2K **Privately Held**
SIC: 7372 7389 Prepackaged software;

(G-15067)
GUPTA PERMOLD CORPORATION
234 Lott Rd (15235-4025)
PHONE...............................412 793-3511
Lakshmi P Gupta, *President*
David Smith, *Sales Engr*
◆ EMP: 180
SQ FT: 55,000
SALES (est): 46.4MM **Privately Held**
WEB: www.guptapermold.com
SIC: 3365 3621 3743 2448 Machinery
castings, aluminum; motors & generators;
interurban cars & car equipment; wood
pallets & skids; electrical equipment &
supplies; nonferrous foundries

(G-15068)
GUYASUTA PRINTING CO
807 Main St (15215-2209)
PHONE...............................412 782-0112
Carl R Leya, *Owner*
EMP: 7 EST: 1887
SQ FT: 5,000
SALES (est): 834.1K **Privately Held**
SIC: 2759 2752 Letterpress printing; com-
mercial printing, offset

(G-15069)
H & H WHOLESALE LLC
3251 Old Frankstown Rd D (15239-2902)
PHONE...............................724 733-8338
Kevin Homel,
EMP: 4
SQ FT: 2,800
SALES (est): 406.2K **Privately Held**
WEB: www.hhweb.com
SIC: 5092 3479 Hobby supplies; engrav-
ing jewelry silverware, or metal

(G-15070)
H H SEIFERTH ASSOCIATES INC
Also Called: Seiferth Signs
2800 Smallman St (15222-4722)
PHONE...............................412 281-4983
Angelo J Marotto, *President*
Theresa Marotto Piccolomini, *Corp Secy*
Marlene Marotto, *Vice Pres*
EMP: 8 EST: 1890
SALES (est): 1.5MM **Privately Held**
WEB: www.seiferthsigns.com
SIC: 3993 Signs, not made in custom sign
painting shops

(G-15071)
H J HEINZ COMPANY LP (DH)
Also Called: Heinz North America
357 6th Ave (15222-2530)
P.O. Box 57 (15230-0057)
PHONE...............................412 237-5757
Robert James Meier, *CEO*
Jeffrey P Berger, *President*
◆ EMP: 200
SALES (est): 86.5MM
SALES (corp-wide): 26.2B **Publicly Held**
SIC: 2038 Frozen specialties
HQ: Kraft Heinz Foods Company
1 Ppg Pl Ste 3200
Pittsburgh PA 15222
412 456-5700

(G-15072)
H J HEINZ COMPANY BRANDS LLC
1 Ppg Pl (15222-5415)
PHONE...............................412 456-5700
William Goode, *Vice Pres*
EMP: 3
SALES (est): 68.6K
SALES (corp-wide): 26.2B **Publicly Held**
SIC: 2037 Frozen fruits & vegetables
PA: The Kraft Heinz Company
1 Ppg Pl Fl 34
Pittsburgh PA 15222
412 456-5700

(G-15073)
H P GAZZAM MACHINE COMPANY
3200 Penn Ave (15201-1423)
PHONE...............................412 471-6647
William J Wetzel, *President*
Bob K Kramer, *Manager*
Robert Kremer, *Manager*
EMP: 4 EST: 1906
SALES (est): 488.9K **Privately Held**
SIC: 3599 Machine shop, jobbing & repair

(G-15074)
HALCO (MINING) INC (PA)
323 N Shore Dr (15212-5319)
PHONE...............................412 235-0265
Maysa Habelrih, *President*
Robert St Pierre, *Treasurer*
William Taxay, *Admin Sec*
EMP: 2400
SQ FT: 12,200
SALES (est): 1.7B **Privately Held**
SIC: 1099 Bauxite mining

(G-15075)
HAMILTON L FISHER L C
2000 Park Ln (15275-1114)
PHONE...............................412 490-8300
Dan Quinn, *Opers Staff*
Anthony H Smith, *Treasurer*
EMP: 3 EST: 2012
SALES (est): 179.4K **Privately Held**
SIC: 3821 Laboratory apparatus & furniture

(G-15076)
HAMMAKER EAST (HQ)
285 Kappa Dr Ste 300 (15238-2814)
PHONE...............................412 221-7300
Matt Johnson, *Principal*
EMP: 20
SQ FT: 4,000
SALES (est): 13.1MM
SALES (corp-wide): 195.6MM **Privately Held**
SIC: 2951 Asphalt & asphaltic paving mix-
tures (not from refineries)

GEOGRAPHIC

PA: Russell Standard Corporation
285 Kappa Dr Ste 300
Pittsburgh PA 15238
412 449-0700

(G-15077)
HAMMAKER EAST EMULSIONS LLC
285 Kappa Dr Ste 300 (15238-2814)
PHONE..............................412 449-0700
EMP: 30
SALES (est): 2.3MM
SALES (corp-wide): 195.6MM **Privately Held**
SIC: 2951 Asphalt paving mixtures & blocks
PA: Russell Standard Corporation
285 Kappa Dr Ste 300
Pittsburgh PA 15238
412 449-0700

(G-15078)
HAMMOND PRESS INC
Also Called: New Kensington Green Sheet
404 North Ave (15209-2334)
P.O. Box 58167 (15209-0167)
PHONE..............................412 821-4100
Michael Hammond, *President*
Eleanor Hammond, *Sr Corp Ofcr*
James M Hammond Sr, *Vice Pres*
EMP: 30 **EST:** 1899
SQ FT: 18,000
SALES (est): 4.9MM **Privately Held**
SIC: 2752 2711 Commercial printing, lithographic; newspapers

(G-15079)
HANEL STORAGE SYSTEMS
121 Industry Dr (15275-1015)
PHONE..............................412 788-0509
Joachim Hanel, *Partner*
Michael Hanel, *Partner*
Glen Nelson, *Regional Mgr*
Scott Katzenell, *Controller*
Michael Fanning, *Natl Sales Mgr*
▲ **EMP:** 26
SQ FT: 10,000
SALES (est): 4.9MM **Privately Held**
WEB: www.hanel.us
SIC: 3599 5084 1796 7699 Custom machinery; materials handling machinery; machinery installation; industrial machinery & equipment repair; office furniture

(G-15080)
HANSON READY MIX INC
2220 2nd Ave (15219-3107)
PHONE..............................412 431-6001
Brian Montarti, *Manager*
EMP: 30
SALES (corp-wide): 20.6B **Privately Held**
SIC: 3273 Ready-mixed concrete
HQ: Hanson Ready Mix, Inc.
3251 Bath Pike
Nazareth PA 18064

(G-15081)
HAPPY BAKING CO
5 Bayard Rd (15213-1955)
PHONE..............................412 621-4020
Jocheyn Walker, *CEO*
William Lerch, *CFO*
EMP: 5
SALES (est): 183.2K **Privately Held**
SIC: 2053 Frozen bakery products, except bread

(G-15082)
HARPER PRINTING SERVICE
2640 Library Rd (15234-3107)
PHONE..............................412 884-2666
Franc Radzo, *Partner*
Adam Calabrese, *Partner*
Marc A Simon, *Partner*
EMP: 3 **EST:** 1955
SQ FT: 1,500
SALES (est): 300K **Privately Held**
SIC: 2752 2791 2789 Commercial printing, offset; typesetting; bookbinding & related work

(G-15083)
HARVIL INC
Also Called: Martin Burial Vault Co
1029 Mccartney St (15220-5406)
PHONE..............................412 682-1500

Harvey Klein, *President*
Phil Cox, *Vice Pres*
EMP: 20
SQ FT: 10,000
SALES (est): 2.4MM **Privately Held**
SIC: 3272 Burial vaults, concrete or precast terrazzo

(G-15084)
HDS MARKETING INC
Also Called: Promostitch
633 Napor Blvd (15205-6501)
PHONE..............................412 279-1600
Howard Schwartz, *CEO*
Martin Bohinski, *President*
Dave Dawson, *Partner*
Ashley Kraszewski, *Partner*
Andy Landsman, *Partner*
▲ **EMP:** 21
SQ FT: 6,500
SALES (est): 13.3MM **Privately Held**
WEB: www.hdsmarketing.com
SIC: 5199 2759 8742 Advertising specialties; commercial printing; management consulting services

(G-15085)
HEALTHSTRATICA LLC
315 Pasadena Dr S (15215-1915)
PHONE..............................412 956-1000
Donald Taylor, *CEO*
EMP: 5 **EST:** 2014
SALES (est): 256.9K **Privately Held**
SIC: 7372 Application computer software

(G-15086)
HEALTHY HOME RESOURCES
227 N Neville St (15213-1307)
PHONE..............................412 431-4449
John Gallo, *Exec Dir*
EMP: 15
SALES (est): 207.2K **Privately Held**
WEB: www.lm.com
SIC: 3822 Auto controls regulating residntl & coml environmt & applncs

(G-15087)
HEINTZ STORAGE CENTER
161 Rochester Rd (15229-1333)
PHONE..............................412 931-3444
John Heintz, *Partner*
Joe Heintz, *Partner*
Ray Heintz, *Partner*
EMP: 3
SALES (est): 205.7K **Privately Held**
SIC: 3448 Prefabricated metal buildings

(G-15088)
HEINZ FROZEN FOOD COMPANY
357 6th Ave (15222-2539)
PHONE..............................412 237-5700
William R Johnson, *CEO*
Neil Harrison, *President*
Charles C White, *Vice Pres*
John C Crowe, *Treasurer*
▼ **EMP:** 2602
SQ FT: 81,000
SALES (est): 228.8MM
SALES (corp-wide): 26.2B **Publicly Held**
WEB: www.heinz.com
SIC: 2038 2037 8741 Frozen specialties; potato products, quick frozen & cold pack; vegetables, quick frozen & cold pack, excl. potato products; management services
HQ: Kraft Heinz Foods Company
1 Ppg Pl Ste 3200
Pittsburgh PA 15222
412 456-5700

(G-15089)
HELM & HAHN CO INC
1738 N Highland Rd 105b (15241-1200)
PHONE..............................412 854-4367
Fred K Hahn III, *President*
EMP: 6 **EST:** 1952
SALES (est): 600K **Privately Held**
SIC: 3911 Pearl jewelry, natural or cultured

(G-15090)
HERALD NEWSPAPERS COMPANY INC
402 Loop St (15215-3225)
PHONE..............................412 782-2121
Richard Scaiffe, *Owner*

EMP: 100
SALES (corp-wide): 5.5B **Privately Held**
WEB: www.post-standard.com
SIC: 2711 Newspapers: publishing only, not printed on site
HQ: The Herald Newspapers Company Inc
220 S Warren St
Syracuse NY 13202
315 470-0011

(G-15091)
HERITAGE INDUSTRIES INC
600 Fountain St (15238-3421)
P.O. Box 111434 (15238-0834)
PHONE..............................412 435-0091
John Baver, *President*
Georgr Zech, *Treasurer*
EMP: 6
SALES (est): 1MM **Privately Held**
WEB: www.heritageindustries.net
SIC: 3446 Fences or posts, ornamental iron or steel

(G-15092)
HERKYS FOOD PRODUCTS INC
4507 Minerva St (15224-1813)
P.O. Box 90056 (15224-0456)
PHONE..............................412 683-8511
Robert Weinstein, *President*
Phyllis Weinstein, *Corp Secy*
Michelle Roper, *Vice Pres*
EMP: 20
SQ FT: 2,000
SALES (est): 2MM **Privately Held**
WEB: www.herkys.com
SIC: 5421 5146 2092 Fish & seafood markets; seafoods; prepared fish or other seafood cakes & sticks

(G-15093)
HERRMANN PRINTING & LITHO INC
Also Called: Herrmann Unlimited
1709 Douglas Dr (15221-1109)
PHONE..............................412 243-4100
Eugene V Herrmann Jr, *President*
Rodney A Herrmann Jr, *President*
Rodney A Herrmann Sr, *Corp Secy*
Larry Hermann, *Vice Pres*
Larry Herrmann, *Vice Pres*
EMP: 30 **EST:** 1955
SQ FT: 20,000
SALES (est): 300K **Privately Held**
WEB: www.herrmannprinting.com
SIC: 2752 2791 Commercial printing, offset; typesetting

(G-15094)
HILDEN ENTERPRISES INC (PA)
Also Called: American Whl Thermographers
1377 Mclaughlin Run Rd (15241-3101)
P.O. Box 12750 (15241-0750)
PHONE..............................412 257-8459
Robert O Hilden, *President*
Eric Hilden, *Vice Pres*
EMP: 30
SQ FT: 6,500
SALES (est): 3.5MM **Privately Held**
SIC: 2759 Thermography

(G-15095)
HINKEL-HOFMANN SUPPLY CO INC
1910 Cochran Rd Ste 110 (15220-1273)
PHONE..............................412 231-3131
EMP: 20
SQ FT: 150,000
SALES (est): 3MM **Privately Held**
SIC: 3442 5023 5033 Mfg Metal Doors/Sash/Trim Whol Homefurnishings Whol Roofing/Siding/Insulation

(G-15096)
HITACHI RAIL STS USA INC (DH)
Also Called: Ansaldo STS Usa, Inc.
1000 Technology Dr (15219-3120)
P.O. Box 420 (15230-0420)
PHONE..............................412 688-2400
Jason White, *CEO*
Joseph Pozza, *President*
Luca Meregalli, *Managing Dir*
Michele Golda, *Vice Pres*
Grazia Guazzi, *Vice Pres*
◆ **EMP:** 500
SQ FT: 175,000

SALES (est): 313.4MM
SALES (corp-wide): 87.9B **Privately Held**
SIC: 3669 Railroad signaling devices, electric
HQ: Hitachi Rail Sts Spa
Via Paolo Mantovani 3/5
Genova GE 16151
010 643-8836

(G-15097)
HOFFMAN-KANE DISTRIBUTORS INC (PA)
1143 Cochrans Mill Rd (15236-3666)
PHONE..............................412 653-6886
Robert Kane, *President*
Fay Kane, *Treasurer*
Tom Styperk, *Sales Mgr*
Tim Kane, *Sales Engr*
Kevin Midgley, *Sales Engr*
▲ **EMP:** 12
SQ FT: 10,500
SALES (est): 5.2MM **Privately Held**
WEB: www.hoffman-kane.com
SIC: 5085 3599 Seals, industrial; machine & other job shop work

(G-15098)
HOMEWOOD ENERGY SERVICES CORP
820 Washington Blvd (15206-4140)
PHONE..............................256 882-2796
Barry L Degroot, *President*
Kevin Monaco, *Vice Pres*
Diane M Hulings, *Shareholder*
John Mikach, *Shareholder*
Jim Kirk, *Admin Sec*
EMP: 7
SQ FT: 40,000
SALES (est): 630K **Privately Held**
SIC: 3699 Electrical equipment & supplies

(G-15099)
HOMEWOOD PRODUCTS CORPORATION
820 Washington Blvd (15206-4140)
PHONE..............................412 665-2700
Barry Degroot, *President*
Chuck Altopiedi, *Marketing Staff*
James T Kirk, *Admin Sec*
John Mikach, *Admin Sec*
EMP: 30
SQ FT: 40,000
SALES (est): 7.8MM **Privately Held**
SIC: 3621 3823 3625 3462 Motors & generators; industrial instrmnts msrmnt display/control process variable; motor controls & accessories; iron & steel forgings; switchgear & switchboard apparatus

(G-15100)
HORTY SPRINGER & MATTERN
4614 5th Ave Ste 200 (15213-3663)
PHONE..............................412 687-7677
John Horty, *President*
Barbara Blackmond, *Vice Pres*
Linda Haddad, *Vice Pres*
Daniel Mulholland III, *Vice Pres*
Kayleigh Mellas, *Marketing Staff*
EMP: 50
SQ FT: 13,000
SALES (est): 7MM **Privately Held**
SIC: 8111 2721 General practice law office; periodicals: publishing only

(G-15101)
HOSMER SUPPLY COMPANY INC
384 Old Curry Hollow Rd (15236-4692)
PHONE..............................412 892-2525
John J Pust, *President*
Shirley Pust, *Corp Secy*
EMP: 10
SQ FT: 2,500
SALES (est): 1.4MM **Privately Held**
SIC: 3273 Ready-mixed concrete

(G-15102)
HOWMET CASTINGS & SERVICES INC
201 Isabella St (15212-5872)
PHONE..............................973 361-2310
Daniel Hornstein, *Bd of Directors*
EMP: 11
SALES (est): 2MM **Privately Held**
SIC: 3363 Aluminum die-castings

(G-15103)
HP INC
651 Holiday Dr Ste 5 (15220-2740)
PHONE.....................412 928-4978
Peter Bruening, *Branch Mgr*
EMP: 12
SALES (corp-wide): 58.4B Publicly Held
WEB: www.3com.com
SIC: 3571 Personal computers (microcomputers)
PA: Hp Inc.
1501 Page Mill Rd
Palo Alto CA 94304
650 857-1501

(G-15104)
HPKD INC
1029 Mccartney St (15220-5406)
PHONE.....................412 922-7600
Kevin Pintar, *President*
EMP: 25
SALES (est): 3MM Privately Held
SIC: 3272 Concrete products

(G-15105)
HUNT STAINED GLASS STUDIOS
1756 W Carson St (15219-1036)
PHONE.....................412 391-1796
Nicholas Parrendo, *President*
David Parrendo, *Admin Sec*
EMP: 8 EST: 1890
SALES (est): 680K Privately Held
SIC: 3231 Silvered glass: made from purchased glass; leaded glass

(G-15106)
HUSTON NATIONAL PRINTING CO
Also Called: National Printing Company
209 Bausman St (15210-2009)
PHONE.....................412 431-5335
Ron Huston, *CEO*
Megan Huston, *President*
Beverly Huston, *Admin Sec*
EMP: 5 EST: 1929
SQ FT: 10,750
SALES (est): 700.9K Privately Held
WEB: www.national-printing.com
SIC: 2752 Letters, circular or form: lithographed; commercial printing, offset; color lithography

(G-15107)
HVL LLC
112 Technology Dr Ste 100 (15275-1067)
PHONE.....................412 494-9600
EMP: 49
SALES (est): 10MM Privately Held
SIC: 3634 3822 Fans, exhaust & ventilating, electric: household; fan control, temperature responsive

(G-15108)
HYPROCA NUTRITION USA INC
Also Called: Kabrita
71 Mcmurray Rd Ste 104 (15241-1634)
PHONE.....................416 565-4364
Carolyn Ansley, *CEO*
James Kilmer, *Vice Pres*
EMP: 12
SALES: 8MM Privately Held
SIC: 2026 Yogurt
HQ: Ausnutria Operations B.V.
Dokter Van Deenweg 150 4e
Verdieping
Zwolle 8025
881 163-600

(G-15109)
I OPTICAL CITY
1225 Brownsville Rd (15210-3677)
PHONE.....................412 881-3090
Kimberly Camesi, *Principal*
EMP: 3 EST: 2015
SALES (est): 158.7K Privately Held
SIC: 3827 Optical instruments & lenses

(G-15110)
IAM ROBOTICS LLC
31 Newgate Rd (15202-1001)
PHONE.....................412 636-7425
Thomas Galluzzo, *CEO*
EMP: 3

SALES (est): 323.8K Privately Held
SIC: 3569 Robots, assembly line: industrial & commercial

(G-15111)
IC MECHANICS INC
425 N Craig St Ste 500 (15213-1154)
PHONE.....................412 682-5560
EMP: 12 EST: 2001
SQ FT: 5,000
SALES (est): 1MM Privately Held
SIC: 3825 Mfg Electrical Measuring Instruments

(G-15112)
ICB ACQUISITIONS LLC
Also Called: Iron City Brewing Company
3340 Liberty Ave (15201-1321)
PHONE.....................412 682-7400
Brian Walsh, *President*
Robert Pyle, *CFO*
EMP: 19
SQ FT: 6,000
SALES (est): 3.9MM Privately Held
SIC: 2082 Beer (alcoholic beverage)

(G-15113)
IDEAL AEROSMITH INC
232 Alpha Dr (15238-2906)
PHONE.....................412 963-1495
Craig Woolheater, *President*
Gary Kleven, *Engineer*
Dennis Whitehead, *Sales Staff*
Mark Orait, *Branch Mgr*
EMP: 25
SALES (corp-wide): 29.1MM Privately Held
WEB: www.ideal-aerosmith.com
SIC: 8734 3826 3545 3494 Testing laboratories; analytical instruments; machine tool accessories; valves & pipe fittings; aircraft & motor vehicle measurement equipment
PA: Ideal Aerosmith, Inc.
3001 S Washington St
Grand Forks ND 58201
701 757-3400

(G-15114)
IKAN INDUSTRIES INC
905 Powers Run Rd (15238-2611)
PHONE.....................412 670-6026
Neal Ofiesh, *Principal*
EMP: 3
SALES (est): 145.1K Privately Held
SIC: 3999 Manufacturing industries

(G-15115)
IMPOSTERS LLC
Also Called: One Brilliant
12 Brilliant Ave (15215-3136)
PHONE.....................412 781-3443
Erica Miller,
EMP: 3
SALES (est): 332.3K Privately Held
SIC: 5621 2389 Boutiques; women's specialty clothing stores; men's miscellaneous accessories

(G-15116)
IMPRESSION TECHNOLOGY INC
Also Called: Imtech
2987 Babcock Blvd 201 (15237-3234)
P.O. Box 101633 (15237-8633)
PHONE.....................412 318-4437
Fax: 412 939-9414
EMP: 9 EST: 1981
SQ FT: 600
SALES (est): 1.6MM Privately Held
SIC: 3955 Mfg Coated Film For Computer Ribbons

(G-15117)
INDOCARB AC LLC
651 Holiday Dr Ste 300 (15220-2740)
PHONE.....................412 928-4970
Suji Santhoshkumar, *Mng Member*
Santhoshkumar Madhavan,
EMP: 6
SQ FT: 1,000
SALES (est): 7.5MM Privately Held
SIC: 2819 Charcoal (carbon), activated

(G-15118)
INDSPEC CHEMICAL CORPORATION
1010 William Pitt Way (15238-1336)
PHONE.....................412 826-3666
Tom Volek, *Manager*
EMP: 20
SALES (corp-wide): 18.9B Publicly Held
WEB: www.indspec-chem.com
SIC: 2819 Industrial inorganic chemicals
HQ: Indspec Chemical Corporation
133 Main St
Petrolia PA 16050
724 756-2370

(G-15119)
INDUSTRIAL MACHINE WORKS INC
Also Called: Penn Chrome
Grant St (15219-2213)
PHONE.....................412 782-5055
Alan Sarver, *CEO*
Jack Sarver, *Corp Secy*
Cindy Papalia, *Vice Pres*
Cynthia Papalia, *Vice Pres*
EMP: 40
SQ FT: 67,000
SALES (est): 4.5MM Privately Held
SIC: 3471 3599 Chromium plating of metals or formed products; grinding castings for the trade

(G-15120)
INDUSTRIAL SCIENTIFIC CORP (HQ)
1 Life Way (15205-7500)
PHONE.....................412 788-4353
Justin McElhattan, *President*
Bob Comer, *District Mgr*
Ilene Grimm, *District Mgr*
James Scelfo, *District Mgr*
Kevin Williams, *District Mgr*
▲ EMP: 500
SQ FT: 52,000
SALES (est): 164.3MM
SALES (corp-wide): 6.4B Publicly Held
WEB: www.indsci.com
SIC: 3829 Gas detectors
PA: Fortive Corporation
6920 Seaway Blvd
Everett WA 98203
425 446-5000

(G-15121)
INDUSTRIAL SYSTEMS & CONTROLS
317 S Main St (15220-5511)
PHONE.....................412 638-4977
James J Yeschenko, *President*
Ede Yeschenko, *Vice Pres*
EMP: 6
SQ FT: 30,000
SALES (est): 1MM Privately Held
SIC: 3613 1731 3625 3585 Control panels, electric; electronic controls installation; relays & industrial controls; refrigeration & heating equipment; heating equipment, except electric; plumbing, heating, air-conditioning contractors

(G-15122)
INDUSTRIAL SYSTEMS & PROCESS C
Also Called: Industrial Services and Pdts
1058 Larchdale Dr (15243-1835)
PHONE.....................412 279-4750
Paul Kiswardy, *President*
Jacklyn Gabel, *Vice Pres*
EMP: 8
SQ FT: 800
SALES (est): 905.6K Privately Held
SIC: 2911 Petroleum refining

(G-15123)
INDUSTRY WEAPON INC
900 Parish St (15220-3425)
PHONE.....................877 344-8450
David Wible, *CEO*
Brian Pullman, *Business Mgr*
Craig Hanna, *COO*
Matthew Polaski, *Production*
Sandy Weber, *Controller*
EMP: 41
SALES (est): 7.7MM Privately Held
SIC: 7372 Application computer software

(G-15124)
INFORMING DESIGN INC
216 Green St (15221-3236)
P.O. Box 81058 (15217-0558)
PHONE.....................412 465-0047
Robert Firth, *President*
Yelena Lamm, *Art Dir*
EMP: 4
SALES (est): 318.3K Privately Held
WEB: www.informingdesign.com
SIC: 7336 2741 Chart & graph design; miscellaneous publishing

(G-15125)
INGMAR MEDICAL LTD
5940 Baum Blvd Ste 6 (15206-3845)
PHONE.....................412 441-8228
Stefan Frembgen, *President*
Frank Mulley, *Purchasing*
Katherine Burdelski, *QC Mgr*
Susan Petersen, *Marketing Mgr*
EMP: 5
SALES (est): 1.1MM Privately Held
WEB: www.ingmarmed.com
SIC: 3841 Surgical & medical instruments

(G-15126)
INNOFOODS USA INC
Also Called: Marion's Kitchen
71 Mcmurray Rd Ste 104 (15241-1634)
PHONE.....................412 854-9012
Thristin Burns, *CEO*
Tim Stainlay, *CEO*
James Kilmer, *President*
EMP: 3
SALES: 2.8MM Privately Held
SIC: 2098 5149 2099 Macaroni & spaghetti; cooking oils & shortenings; sauces; seasonings & spices; seasonings: dry mixes
PA: Innofoods International Limited
Rm 901 Hermes Coml Ctr
Tsim Sha Tsui KLN

(G-15127)
INNOVATIVE DESIGNS INC (PA)
124 Cherry St (15223-2243)
PHONE.....................412 799-0350
Joseph Riccelli, *Ch of Bd*
EMP: 5
SQ FT: 15,000
SALES: 249.6K Publicly Held
WEB: www.idigear.com
SIC: 2326 2399 2329 Industrial garments, men's & boys'; jackets, overall & work; sleeping bags; hunting coats & vests, men's; bathing suits & swimwear: men's & boys'

(G-15128)
INNOVATIVE DESIGNS INC
124 Cherry St (15223-2243)
PHONE.....................412 799-0350
Greg Domian, *Manager*
EMP: 7
SALES (corp-wide): 249.6K Publicly Held
WEB: www.idigear.com
SIC: 3949 Sporting & athletic goods
PA: Innovative Designs, Inc.
124 Cherry St
Pittsburgh PA 15223
412 799-0350

(G-15129)
INSERVIO3 LLC
650 Smithfield St # 1810 (15222-3918)
PHONE.....................310 343-3486
Joe Bernal, *Manager*
EMP: 9
SALES (corp-wide): 3MM Privately Held
SIC: 2621 Book, bond & printing papers
PA: Inservio3 Llc
865 S Figueroa St Ste 103
Los Angeles CA 90017
213 439-9656

(G-15130)
INSTITUTE PROF ENVMTL PRACTICE
Also Called: I P E P
600 Forbes Ave (15219-3016)
PHONE.....................412 396-1703
Diana Kobus, *Director*
EMP: 3

▲ = Import ▼=Export
◆ =Import/Export

SALES: 108.5K **Privately Held**
SIC: 3822 Auto controls regulating residntl & coml environmt & applncs

(G-15131)
INTEGRITAS INC (DH)
40 24th St Fl 5 (15222-4657)
PHONE...........................800 411-6281
R Edwin Stroupe Jr, *President*
Mary Price, *Vice Pres*
EMP: 8
SQ FT: 2,457
SALES (est): 2.2MM
SALES (corp-wide): 2.4B **Publicly Held**
WEB: www.integritas.com
SIC: 7372 Business oriented computer software
HQ: Net Health Systems, Inc.
40 24th St Fl 1
Pittsburgh PA 15222
800 411-6281

(G-15132)
INTELIGISTICS INC
410 William Pitt Way (15238-1330)
PHONE...........................412 826-0379
Raul Mandava, *President*
Alexander McCredie, *Vice Pres*
Gopal Mandava, *Info Tech Mgr*
EMP: 6
SQ FT: 2,000
SALES (est): 680K **Privately Held**
WEB: www.inteligistics.com
SIC: 3825 Radio frequency measuring equipment

(G-15133)
INTERPHASE MATERIALS INC
370 William Pitt Way (15238-1329)
PHONE...........................814 282-8119
Noah Snyder, *CEO*
Kasey Catt, *Officer*
EMP: 3
SALES (est): 203.7K **Privately Held**
SIC: 2869 High purity grade chemicals, organic

(G-15134)
INTERSTATE EQUIPMENT CORP
929 Park Ave (15234-2177)
PHONE...........................412 563-5556
Joseph Vogel, *President*
EMP: 6 EST: 1937
SQ FT: 4,800
SALES (est): 2.1MM **Privately Held**
WEB: www.go-iec.com
SIC: 3441 3536 Fabricated structural metal; monorail systems

(G-15135)
INVITATIONS PLUS
1406 S Negley Ave (15217-1206)
PHONE...........................412 421-7778
Yvonne Stein, *Principal*
EMP: 3
SALES (est): 224.9K **Privately Held**
SIC: 2759 Invitations: printing

(G-15136)
IRON LUNG LLC
4609 Liberty Ave (15224-1922)
PHONE...........................412 291-8928
EMP: 3 EST: 2015
SALES (est): 126.9K **Privately Held**
SIC: 3842 Iron lungs

(G-15137)
IRONWOOD LEARNING LLC
101 Brilliant Ave 200 (15215-3119)
PHONE...........................412 784-1384
James I Mitnick, *CEO*
EMP: 7
SALES (est): 650K **Privately Held**
SIC: 7372 Business oriented computer software; application computer software

(G-15138)
IRP GROUP INC
726 Trumbull Dr (15205-4363)
PHONE...........................412 276-6400
Frank Kelly Jr, *Ch of Bd*
Michael Kerestes, *President*
David W Schnupp, *Treasurer*
EMP: 70
SQ FT: 70,000

SALES (est): 48.1MM **Privately Held**
WEB: www.irpgroup.com
SIC: 5085 3053 Rubber goods, mechanical; gaskets; gaskets, packing & sealing devices

(G-15139)
J & AK INC
5350 Campbells Run Rd (15205-9738)
PHONE...........................412 787-9750
Joseph Kleynjans, *President*
EMP: 60
SQ FT: 50,000
SALES (est): 6.3MM **Privately Held**
WEB: www.tmi-pvc.com
SIC: 3625 5074 3537 Control equipment, electric; pipes & fittings, plastic; loading docks: portable, adjustable & hydraulic

(G-15140)
J B KREIDER CO INC
Also Called: Kreider Printing
1800 Columbus Ave Ste 37 (15233-2247)
PHONE...........................412 246-0343
Michael Paranzino, *President*
EMP: 11
SQ FT: 13,000
SALES: 2.1MM **Privately Held**
WEB: www.jbkreider.com
SIC: 2759 Commercial printing

(G-15141)
J D PRINTING INC
1811 Route 286 (15239-2894)
PHONE...........................724 327-0006
Joseph Di Francesca, *President*
Dorothy Di Francesca, *Vice Pres*
EMP: 4
SQ FT: 5,000
SALES (est): 499.4K **Privately Held**
SIC: 2752 2759 7334 Commercial printing, offset; letterpress printing; photocopying & duplicating services

(G-15142)
J HARRIS & SONS CO (PA)
50 26th St (15222-4634)
PHONE...........................412 391-5532
Jack Harris, *President*
Craig Harris, *CFO*
▼ EMP: 30
SQ FT: 92,000
SALES (est): 10.4MM **Privately Held**
WEB: www.usalampshade.com
SIC: 3999 Shades, lamp or candle

(G-15143)
J K MILLER CORP
80 Wabash St (15220-5420)
PHONE...........................412 922-5070
Curt Bowen, *President*
EMP: 35 EST: 1959
SQ FT: 10,056
SALES (est): 2.8MM **Privately Held**
WEB: www.jkmiller.com
SIC: 3679 Quartz crystals, for electronic application

(G-15144)
JARCANDLESTORECOM
1316 Hillsdale Ave (15216-2502)
PHONE...........................412 758-8855
Debra A McCardle, *Owner*
EMP: 3
SALES: 15K **Privately Held**
SIC: 3999 Candles

(G-15145)
JATCO MACHINE & TOOL CO INC
4429 Ohio River Blvd (15202-3528)
PHONE...........................412 761-4344
Richard De Salle, *President*
Edward Sikora, *Corp Secy*
Nate Thomas, *Engineer*
EMP: 20
SQ FT: 6,500
SALES (est): 3.2MM **Privately Held**
WEB: www.jatcomold.com
SIC: 3544 Industrial molds

(G-15146)
JAY DESIGN INC
4603 Butler St (15201-2906)
PHONE...........................412 683-1184
James J Bernard, *President*
William Stanhope, *Vice Pres*

EMP: 5
SALES (est): 770.8K **Privately Held**
WEB: www.jaydesign.com
SIC: 2841 Soap: granulated, liquid, cake, flaked or chip

(G-15147)
JEFFERSON MEMORIAL PARK INC (PA)
Also Called: L & M Lawn Care
401 Curry Hollow Rd (15236-4636)
PHONE...........................412 655-4500
Harry Neel, *Ch of Bd*
Dagny Neel Fitzpatrick, *Vice Pres*
David Middlemiss, *Vice Pres*
Aleksandra Slavkovic, *Treasurer*
Paul J Gitnik, *Admin Sec*
EMP: 42
SQ FT: 5,400
SALES (est): 32.3MM **Privately Held**
WEB: www.jeffersonmemorial.biz
SIC: 6553 3272 Cemeteries, real estate operation; burial vaults, concrete or precast terrazzo

(G-15148)
JEM INDUSTRIES LLC
14 Sedgwick St (15209-2724)
PHONE...........................412 818-2606
Jacquelynn Michalik,
EMP: 6
SALES (est): 110K **Privately Held**
SIC: 6531 2951 Real estate agents & managers; asphalt paving mixtures & blocks

(G-15149)
JENNMAR CORP OF WEST VIRGINIA (HQ)
Also Called: Keystone Bolt
258 Kappa Dr (15238-2818)
P.O. Box 111253 (15238-0653)
PHONE...........................412 963-9071
Frank Calandra Jr, *President*
John M Calandra, *Vice Pres*
James Ceresa, *Vice Pres*
Jeff Reeves, *Sales Mgr*
EMP: 34
SQ FT: 23,500
SALES (est): 11MM
SALES (corp-wide): 571.6MM **Privately Held**
SIC: 3452 Bolts, metal
PA: Calandra Frank Inc
258 Kappa Dr
Pittsburgh PA 15238
412 963-9071

(G-15150)
JENNMAR OF KENTUCKY INC (HQ)
258 Kappa Dr (15238-2818)
P.O. Box 11253 (15238-0253)
PHONE...........................412 963-9071
Frank Calandra Jr, *President*
James Ceresa, *Exec VP*
John M Calandra, *Vice Pres*
▲ EMP: 43
SQ FT: 23,500
SALES (est): 10.2MM
SALES (corp-wide): 571.6MM **Privately Held**
SIC: 3532 Mining machinery
PA: Calandra Frank Inc
258 Kappa Dr
Pittsburgh PA 15238
412 963-9071

(G-15151)
JENNMAR OF PENNSYLVANIA LLC (HQ)
258 Kappa Dr (15238-2818)
P.O. Box 111253 (15238-0653)
PHONE...........................412 963-9071
Michael Calandra, *President*
Robert Wise, *COO*
◆ EMP: 40
SQ FT: 23,500
SALES (est): 231.8MM
SALES (corp-wide): 571.6MM **Privately Held**
SIC: 3532 Mining machinery

PA: Calandra Frank Inc
258 Kappa Dr
Pittsburgh PA 15238
412 963-9071

(G-15152)
JERSEY CHROME PLATING CO
144 46th St (15201-2996)
PHONE...........................412 681-7044
James Jersey, *President*
EMP: 14
SQ FT: 25,000
SALES (est): 1.6MM **Privately Held**
WEB: www.jerseychrome.com
SIC: 3471 Chromium plating of metals or formed products; buffing for the trade

(G-15153)
JEWISH CHRONICLE
5915 Beacon St (15217-2005)
PHONE...........................412 687-1000
Barbara Befferman, *Principal*
EMP: 7 EST: 2011
SALES (est): 404.3K **Privately Held**
SIC: 2711 Newspapers: publishing only, not printed on site

(G-15154)
JL CABINET COMPANY
128 Brookview Ln (15237-3202)
PHONE...........................412 931-8580
Lori Thomas, *Principal*
EMP: 4 EST: 2010
SALES (est): 351.2K **Privately Held**
SIC: 2434 Wood kitchen cabinets

(G-15155)
JOHN KEGGES JR
Also Called: Kegges Cabinets
4845 Harrison St Rear (15201-2720)
PHONE...........................412 821-5535
John Kegges Jr, *Owner*
Marcy Kegges, *Corp Secy*
EMP: 6 EST: 1956
SQ FT: 6,250
SALES: 540K **Privately Held**
SIC: 2434 Wood kitchen cabinets

(G-15156)
JOYCE INC
38 Southern Ave Ste 1 (15211-1928)
PHONE...........................206 937-4633
Kevin Joyce, *President*
EMP: 2
SALES (est): 1MM **Privately Held**
WEB: www.joycemcandrews.com
SIC: 2323 Men's & boys' neckties & bow ties

(G-15157)
JS LITTLE PUBLICATION
2120 Greentree Rd Apt 310 (15220-1409)
PHONE...........................412 343-5288
James R Martorella Jr, *Owner*
EMP: 5
SALES: 325K **Privately Held**
SIC: 2752 2721 Commercial printing, offset; periodicals: publishing only

(G-15158)
JULINE-TITANS LLC
32 39th St (15201-3205)
PHONE...........................412 352-4744
Joe Allbaugh,
EMP: 15 EST: 2017
SALES (est): 1.1MM **Privately Held**
SIC: 3691 Storage batteries

(G-15159)
K & I SHEET METAL INC
2010 Chapman St (15215-2711)
P.O. Box 7848 (15215-0848)
PHONE...........................412 781-8111
Irene Kotchey, *President*
Paul Kotchey, *President*
Debbie Kotchey, *Vice Pres*
Kenneth Kotchey, *Vice Pres*
EMP: 34
SQ FT: 14,000
SALES (est): 8.4MM **Privately Held**
WEB: www.kisheetmetal.com
SIC: 3444 1711 Ducts, sheet metal; ventilation & duct work contractor

(G-15160)
K S MANUFACTURING CO LP (PA)
4561 Peoples Rd (15237-3198)
PHONE....................................412 931-5365
Anthony M Katic, *Managing Prtnr*
Janet Katic, *Partner*
Michael Katic, *Partner*
▲ **EMP:** 14
SQ FT: 13,000
SALES: 1.6MM **Privately Held**
SIC: 2541 Sink tops, plastic laminated

(G-15161)
KASUNICK WELDING & FABG CO INC
Also Called: King Airline Tooling Co
1476 Spring Garden Ave (15212-3778)
PHONE....................................412 321-2722
Kenneth F Kasunick, *President*
EMP: 13
SQ FT: 15,000
SALES (est): 2.4MM **Privately Held**
SIC: 3312 Stainless steel

(G-15162)
KAWNEER COMPANY INC
201 Isabella St (15212-5872)
PHONE....................................570 784-8000
Robert Holcombe, *Branch Mgr*
EMP: 76
SALES (corp-wide): 14B **Publicly Held**
WEB: www.kawneer.com
SIC: 3446 Architectural metalwork
HQ: Kawneer Company, Inc.
555 Guthridge Ct
Norcross GA 30092
770 449-5555

(G-15163)
KELLEY
5999 Baptist Rd (15236-3337)
PHONE....................................412 833-4559
EMP: 4
SALES (est): 272.1K **Privately Held**
SIC: 2024 Ice cream & frozen desserts

(G-15164)
KELLNER MILLWORK CO INC
6301 Butler St (15201-2123)
PHONE....................................412 784-1414
Ron B D'Alessandro, *President*
EMP: 4 **EST:** 1957
SQ FT: 12,000
SALES (est): 455K **Privately Held**
SIC: 2431 Door shutters, wood

(G-15165)
KELLOGGS SNACKS
3 Penn Ctr W Ste 120 (15276-0112)
PHONE....................................412 787-1183
EMP: 3
SALES (est): 148.7K **Privately Held**
SIC: 2052 Cookies

(G-15166)
KELLY CUSTOM FURN & CABINETRY
5239 Butler St (15201-2621)
PHONE....................................412 781-3997
Joseph Kelly, *Owner*
EMP: 3
SALES (est): 270K **Privately Held**
WEB: www.kellyfurniture.com
SIC: 2434 Wood kitchen cabinets

(G-15167)
KELLY DRY ICE
590 Jacks Run Rd (15202-4006)
PHONE....................................412 766-1555
Edward V Kelly Jr, *Owner*
EMP: 9 **EST:** 1930
SQ FT: 5,000
SALES (est): 1.1MM **Privately Held**
SIC: 2097 Manufactured ice

(G-15168)
KENAI ASSOCIATES INC
5248 Becky Dr (15236-2621)
PHONE....................................412 655-2079
Scott Browne, *President*
Edward Browne, *Vice Pres*
EMP: 5 **EST:** 1991

SALES (est): 605.6K **Privately Held**
SIC: 3823 Computer interface equipment for industrial process control

(G-15169)
KENNAMETAL INC (PA)
600 Grant St Ste 5100 (15219-2706)
PHONE....................................412 248-8000
Lawrence W Stranghoener, *Ch of Bd*
Christopher Rossi, *President*
Alexander Broetz, *President*
Peter A Dragich, *President*
Peter Dragich, *President*
▲ **EMP:** 750 **EST:** 1938
SALES: 2.3B **Publicly Held**
WEB: www.kennametal.com
SIC: 3532 3531 3313 3399 Mining machinery; bits, except oil & gas field tools, rock; auger mining equipment; construction machinery attachments; blades for graders, scrapers, dozers & snow plows; snow plow attachments; screeds & screeding machines; electrometallurgical products; tungsten carbide powder; metal powders, pastes & flakes; cutting tools for machine tools

(G-15170)
KENNEBEC INC
2140 Greentree Rd (15220-1405)
PHONE....................................412 278-2040
Daniela Birkelbach, *President*
Ronald Birkelbach, *Vice Pres*
EMP: 4
SQ FT: 1,100
SALES: 365.3K **Privately Held**
WEB: www.kennebec-inc.com
SIC: 7372 Prepackaged software

(G-15171)
KENNEDY FUELS INC
223 4th Ave Ste 400 (15222-1713)
PHONE....................................412 721-7404
Albert M Hvostal, *President*
Lori F Hvostal, *Treasurer*
EMP: 4
SALES (est): 350K **Privately Held**
SIC: 3731 Drilling & production platforms, floating (oil & gas)

(G-15172)
KER COMMUNICATIONS
6520 Ventura Dr (15236-3650)
PHONE....................................412 310-1973
Joe Biden, *Principal*
EMP: 5
SALES (est): 309.4K **Privately Held**
SIC: 2741 7371 7379 8742 ; computer software development; ; marketing consulting services

(G-15173)
KEROTEST INDUSTRIES INC (PA)
5500 2nd Ave (15207-1807)
PHONE....................................412 521-4200
Larry R Lenarz, *Ch of Bd*
Bernard P Hilterman Jr, *Corp Secy*
Brian Snyder, *Engineer*
Justin Moidel, *Design Engr*
Kassandra Morgavo, *Human Res Mgr*
▲ **EMP:** 40
SQ FT: 60,000
SALES (est): 15MM **Privately Held**
SIC: 3494 3089 Valves & pipe fittings; fittings for pipe, plastic

(G-15174)
KEROTEST MANUFACTURING CORP (HQ)
5500 2nd Ave (15207-1807)
PHONE....................................412 521-4200
Robert G Visalli, *Ch of Bd*
David Frederick, *President*
Mark Sewell, *President*
Bernard P Hilterman Jr, *Corp Secy*
Bernie Hilterman, *Vice Pres*
▲ **EMP:** 37
SQ FT: 100,000
SALES (est): 14.5MM
SALES (corp-wide): 15MM **Privately Held**
WEB: www.kerotest.com
SIC: 3494 3089 Valves & pipe fittings; fittings for pipe, plastic

PA: Kerotest Industries, Inc.
5500 2nd Ave
Pittsburgh PA 15207
412 521-4200

(G-15175)
KEYSTONE CONTAINMENT CONTRS LP
250 Bilmar Dr (15205-4601)
PHONE....................................412 921-2070
Ted Maloney, *Partner*
Shawn Simmons, *Business Mgr*
Justin Pernell, *Opers Spvr*
Jill Blackburn, *Office Admin*
Jenny Units, *Administration*
EMP: 11 **EST:** 2011
SALES (est): 2.9MM **Privately Held**
SIC: 3561 Pumps, oil well & field

(G-15176)
KEYSTONE SPRING SERVICE INC (PA)
112 35th St (15201-1920)
PHONE....................................412 621-4800
Greg Valant, *President*
Edward A Valant Jr, *Vice Pres*
Jason E Valant, *Treasurer*
Ed Valant, *Executive*
EMP: 50
SQ FT: 26,000
SALES (est): 14MM **Privately Held**
SIC: 5013 5531 3493 7539 Springs, shock absorbers & struts; automotive parts; steel springs, except wire; automotive brake lining, installation

(G-15177)
KILLEEN PRINTING CO
Also Called: A Killeen Union Printing
537 E Carson St (15203-1020)
PHONE....................................412 381-4090
Brian Mixon, *Owner*
EMP: 5
SQ FT: 7,000
SALES (est): 290K **Privately Held**
SIC: 2752 2759 2791 2789 Commercial printing, offset; letterpress printing; typesetting; bookbinding & related work

(G-15178)
KINETIGEAR LLC
7800 Susquehanna St (15208-2118)
PHONE....................................412 810-0049
Justin D Johnson,
EMP: 3
SQ FT: 10,000
SALES (est): 317.4K **Privately Held**
SIC: 3541 Machine tools, metal cutting type

(G-15179)
KNOWLEDGE IN A NUT SHELL INC
1420 Centre Ave Apt 2213 (15219-3535)
PHONE....................................412 765-2020
Charles Reichblum, *President*
EMP: 5
SALES (est): 325K **Privately Held**
WEB: www.knowledgeinanutshell.com
SIC: 2731 Books: publishing only

(G-15180)
KOBOLD INSTRUMENTS INC
1801 Parkway View Dr (15205-1422)
PHONE....................................412 490-4806
Klaus J Kobold, *President*
Peter Barna, *General Mgr*
Robert McFabben, *Plant Mgr*
Eric Stofan, *Technical Mgr*
Glen Curry, *Chief Mktg Ofcr*
▲ **EMP:** 20
SQ FT: 10,000
SALES (est): 4.8MM **Privately Held**
WEB: www.koboldusa.com
SIC: 3492 5085 Control valves, fluid power: hydraulic & pneumatic; valves & fittings

(G-15181)
KOCKS PITTSBURGH CORPORATION
504 Mcknight Park Dr (15237-6535)
PHONE....................................412 367-4174
Sergio A Filippini, *President*
Glyn Ellis, *General Mgr*

Greg Decesare, *Finance Mgr*
▲ **EMP:** 8
SQ FT: 2,000
SALES (est): 1.2MM
SALES (corp-wide): 25.9MM **Privately Held**
WEB: www.kockspittsburgh.com
SIC: 3547 Rolling mill machinery
PA: Friedrich Kocks Gmbh & Co. Kg
Neustr. 69
Hilden 40721
210 379-00

(G-15182)
KONTRON AMERICA INCORPORATED
750 Holiday Dr Ste 560 (15220-2797)
PHONE....................................412 921-3322
EMP: 10
SALES (corp-wide): 407.2MM **Privately Held**
SIC: 3674 5045 Computers, peripherals & software; solid state electronic devices
HQ: Kontron America, Incorporated
9477 Waples St Ste 150
San Diego CA 92121
858 677-0877

(G-15183)
KOP-COAT INC (DH)
Also Called: Marine Division
3040 William Pitt Way (15238-1359)
PHONE....................................412 227-2426
Richard Kelly, *President*
Dawn Ludgate, *Vice Pres*
Gerald Nessenson, *Vice Pres*
Hans Ward, *Vice Pres*
Suzanne L Meyer, *Controller*
◆ **EMP:** 12
SALES (est): 30.1MM
SALES (corp-wide): 5.3B **Publicly Held**
WEB: www.kop-coat.com
SIC: 2851 Marine paints; varnishes; wood stains
HQ: Republic Powdered Metals, Inc.
2628 Pearl Rd
Medina OH 44256
330 225-3192

(G-15184)
KOP-COAT INC
Also Called: R & D Lab
3020 William Pitt Way (15238-1359)
PHONE....................................412 826-3387
Charles Go Pauli, *President*
EMP: 15
SALES (corp-wide): 5.3B **Publicly Held**
WEB: www.kop-coat.com
SIC: 2851 Paints & allied products
HQ: Kop-Coat, Inc.
3040 William Pitt Way
Pittsburgh PA 15238
412 227-2426

(G-15185)
KOPPERS ASIA LLC
436 7th Ave (15219-1826)
PHONE....................................412 227-2001
EMP: 87
SALES (est): 114.2K
SALES (corp-wide): 1.5B **Publicly Held**
SIC: 2865 Mfg Cyclic Crudes/Intermediates/Dyes
PA: Koppers Holdings Inc.
436 7th Ave
Pittsburgh PA 15219
412 227-2001

(G-15186)
KOPPERS CONCRETE PRODUCTS INC
436 7th Ave (15219-1826)
PHONE....................................412 227-2001
Leroy M Ball, *CEO*
EMP: 3 **EST:** 2015
SALES (est): 116.3K
SALES (corp-wide): 1.7B **Publicly Held**
SIC: 2865 Cyclic crudes, coal tar
PA: Koppers Holdings Inc.
436 7th Ave
Pittsburgh PA 15219
412 227-2001

▲ = Import ▼=Export
◆ =Import/Export

(G-15187)
KOPPERS HOLDINGS INC (PA)
436 7th Ave (15219-1826)
PHONE..................................412 227-2001
Stephen R Tritch, *Ch of Bd*
Leroy M Ball Jr, *President*
Steven R Lacy, *Senior VP*
Stephen C Reeder, *Vice Pres*
Phil Sturos, *Project Engr*
EMP: 139
SALES: 1.7B **Publicly Held**
SIC: 2865 2491 2895 3312 Cyclic crudes, coal tar; poles, posts & pilings: treated wood; carbon black; coke produced in chemical recovery coke ovens; coke oven products (chemical recovery); chemical preparations

(G-15188)
KOPPERS INC (HQ)
436 7th Ave (15219-1826)
PHONE..................................412 227-2001
Leroy M Ball Jr, *President*
Robert Dashevsky, *President*
Stephanie Apostolou, *Counsel*
Stephen C Kifer, *Counsel*
Paul A Goydan, *Senior VP*
◆ **EMP:** 139
SQ FT: 60,000
SALES (est): 731.3MM
SALES (corp-wide): 1.7B **Publicly Held**
WEB: www.koppers.com
SIC: 2865 2491 3312 2899 Cyclic crudes, coal tar; poles, posts & pilings: treated wood; coke produced in chemical recovery coke ovens; coke oven products (chemical recovery); oils & essential oils
PA: Koppers Holdings Inc.
436 7th Ave
Pittsburgh PA 15219
412 227-2001

(G-15189)
KOPPERS INDUSTRIES INC
Koppers RR & Utility Pdts Div
436 7th Ave Ste 2026 (15219-1800)
PHONE..................................412 227-2001
Jim Healey, *Manager*
EMP: 25
SQ FT: 18,150
SALES (corp-wide): 1.7B **Publicly Held**
WEB: www.koppers.com
SIC: 2491 2411 Poles, posts & pilings: treated wood; railroad cross bridges & switch ties, treated wood; railroad crossties, treated wood; logging
HQ: Koppers Industries Of Delaware Inc.
436 7th Ave Ste 2026
Pittsburgh PA 15219

(G-15190)
KOPPERS INDUSTRIES INC
Also Called: Koppers Technical Center
1005 William Pitt Way (15238-1336)
PHONE..................................412 826-3970
Carl Mueller, *Engineer*
Stacey McKinney, *Enginr/R&D Mgr*
EMP: 20
SALES (corp-wide): 1.7B **Publicly Held**
WEB: www.koppers.com
SIC: 8734 2491 Testing laboratories; wood preserving
HQ: Koppers Industries Of Delaware Inc.
436 7th Ave Ste 2026
Pittsburgh PA 15219

(G-15191)
KOPPERS INDUSTRIES DEL INC (DH)
Also Called: K S A
436 7th Ave Ste 2026 (15219-1800)
PHONE..................................412 227-2001
Walter W Turner, *CEO*
Bill Pilesi, *General Mgr*
Leroy M Ball Jr, *Vice Pres*
Dana Kinsey, *Executive Asst*
◆ **EMP:** 2
SQ FT: 800
SALES (est): 17.9MM
SALES (corp-wide): 1.7B **Publicly Held**
SIC: 2421 3272 Railroad ties, sawed; ties, railroad: concrete
HQ: Koppers Inc.
436 7th Ave
Pittsburgh PA 15219
412 227-2001

(G-15192)
KOPPERS PERFORMANCE CHEM INC
436 7th Ave (15219-1826)
PHONE..................................412 227-2001
Walter Turner, *CEO*
EMP: 5
SALES (corp-wide): 1.7B **Publicly Held**
SIC: 2491 Preserving (creosoting) of wood
HQ: Koppers Performance Chemicals Inc.
1016 Everee Inn Rd
Griffin GA 30224
770 228-8434

(G-15193)
KOPPERS UTILITY INDUS PDTS INC
707 Grant St Ste 2307 (15219-1945)
PHONE..................................412 620-6238
EMP: 63
SALES (corp-wide): 166.8MM **Privately Held**
SIC: 2411 Wooden bolts, hewn
PA: Koppers Utility And Industrial Products Inc.
860 Cannon Bridge Rd
Orangeburg SC 29115
803 534-7467

(G-15194)
KORYAK CONSULTING INC
2003 Kinvara Dr (15237-3801)
PHONE..................................412 364-6600
Suresh Ramanathan, *President*
Deepa Pattuswami, *General Mgr*
Janet Ramanathan, *Human Res Mgr*
Dilip Kuchipudi, *CTO*
Murugan Kannan, *Technology*
EMP: 25
SALES (est): 2.8MM **Privately Held**
WEB: www.koryak.com
SIC: 7373 7372 8742 Computer integrated systems design; prepackaged software; management information systems consultant

(G-15195)
KOS & ASSOCIATES INC
Also Called: PeopleSoft
Mc Knight Park Dr Ste 203 (15237)
PHONE..................................412 367-7444
Thomas P Kos, *President*
Patricia A Kos, *Corp Secy*
EMP: 12
SQ FT: 1,500
SALES (est): 1MM **Privately Held**
SIC: 7371 7372 Computer software systems analysis & design, custom; business oriented computer software

(G-15196)
KRAFT HEINZ COMPANY (PA)
1 Ppg Pl Fl 34 (15222-5400)
P.O. Box 57 (15230-0057)
PHONE..................................412 456-5700
Bernardo Hees, *CEO*
Alexandre Behring, *Ch of Bd*
John T Cahill, *Vice Ch Bd*
Nina Barton, *President*
Paulo Basilio, *President*
EMP: 277
SALES: 26.2B **Publicly Held**
SIC: 2033 2038 2032 2098 Tomato sauce: packaged in cans, jars, etc.; frozen specialties; baby foods, including meats: packaged in cans, jars, etc.; bean sprouts: packaged in cans, jars, etc.; soups, except seafood: packaged in cans, jars, etc.; macaroni & spaghetti

(G-15197)
KRAFT HEINZ FOODS COMPANY (HQ)
1 Ppg Pl Fl 34 (15222-5400)
PHONE..................................412 456-5700
Bernardo Hees, *CEO*
Theodore N Bobby, *Exec VP*
Edward J McMenamin, *Senior VP*
Paulo Basilio, *CFO*
Dan Shaw, *General Counsel*
▼ **EMP:** 155 **EST:** 1869

SALES (est): 11.2B
SALES (corp-wide): 26.2B **Publicly Held**
SIC: 2022 2032 2033 2038 Cheese spreads, dips, pastes & other cheese products; baby foods, including meats: packaged in cans, jars, etc.; bean sprouts: packaged in cans, jars, etc.; soups, except seafood: packaged in cans, jars, etc.; tomato sauce: packaged in cans, jars, etc.; frozen specialties; macaroni & spaghetti
PA: The Kraft Heinz Company
1 Ppg Pl Fl 34
Pittsburgh PA 15222
412 456-5700

(G-15198)
KRAFT HEINZ FOODS COMPANY
1062 Progress St (15212-5964)
P.O. Box 57 (15230-0057)
PHONE..................................412 237-5757
Jason Roth, *Manager*
EMP: 25
SALES (corp-wide): 26.2B **Publicly Held**
SIC: 2033 Canned fruits & specialties
HQ: Kraft Heinz Foods Company
1 Ppg Pl Fl 34
Pittsburgh PA 15222
412 456-5700

(G-15199)
KRAFT HEINZ FOODS COMPANY
H.j Heinz Company Foundation
1062 Progress St (15212-5964)
P.O. Box 57 (15230-0057)
PHONE..................................412 456-5773
Fax: 412 456-7859
EMP: 16
SALES (corp-wide): 26.2B **Publicly Held**
SIC: 2033 Mfg Canned Fruits/Vegetables
HQ: Kraft Heinz Foods Company
1 Ppg Pl Ste 3200
Pittsburgh PA 15222
412 456-5700

(G-15200)
KREIDER DIGITAL COMMUNICATIONS
2100 Babcock Blvd (15209-1357)
PHONE..................................412 446-2784
Jerry Johnson, *Partner*
EMP: 3
SALES (est): 437.9K **Privately Held**
SIC: 2752 Commercial printing, lithographic

(G-15201)
KROHMALYS PRINTING CO
Also Called: Fastsigns
7425 Washington Ave (15218-2574)
PHONE..................................412 271-4234
Robert Krohmaly, *Owner*
EMP: 4
SQ FT: 3,000
SALES (est): 404.7K **Privately Held**
SIC: 3993 2752 Signs & advertising specialties; commercial printing, lithographic

(G-15202)
KRYSTAL BIOTECH INC
2100 Wharton St Ste 701 (15203-1973)
PHONE..................................412 586-5830
Krish S Krishnan, *Ch of Bd*
Suma M Krishnan, *COO*
Pooja Agarwal, *Vice Pres*
Antony A Riley, *CFO*
EMP: 37
SQ FT: 25,000
SALES (est): 1.4MM **Privately Held**
SIC: 2836 2834 Biological products, except diagnostic; pharmaceutical preparations

(G-15203)
KUSS ENTERPRISES LLC
3608 Spring Garden Rd (15212-1144)
PHONE..................................412 583-0206
Mark Kuss, *President*
EMP: 4
SALES: 200K **Privately Held**
SIC: 3272 Grease traps, concrete

(G-15204)
KUTZ FABRICATING INC
4000 Windgap Ave (15204-1032)
PHONE..................................412 771-4161

Thomas Green, *President*
Nancy Green, *Vice Pres*
EMP: 15
SQ FT: 18,000
SALES (est): 3.4MM **Privately Held**
SIC: 3441 Building components, structural steel

(G-15205)
L & M MACHINE INC
947 Old Frankstown Rd (15239-2509)
PHONE..................................724 733-2283
Ronald Winters, *President*
EMP: 4
SQ FT: 2,400
SALES (est): 510K **Privately Held**
SIC: 3599 Machine shop, jobbing & repair

(G-15206)
L A WELTE INC
Also Called: Welte Roofing
535 Mcneilly Rd (15226-2503)
PHONE..................................412 341-9400
Patrick J McGonigle Jr, *President*
Doris Mc Gonigle, *Office Mgr*
EMP: 3
SALES (est): 3.2MM **Privately Held**
WEB: www.welteroofing.com
SIC: 1761 3531 Roofing contractor; sheet metalwork; roofing equipment

(G-15207)
L B FOSTER COMPANY (PA)
Also Called: Lbfoster
415 Holiday Dr Ste 1 (15220-2793)
P.O. Box 2806 (15230-2806)
PHONE..................................412 928-3400
Lee B Foster II, *Ch of Bd*
Robert P Bauer, *President*
Patrick J Guinee, *Senior VP*
John F Kasel, *Senior VP*
Brian H Kelly, *Senior VP*
EMP: 80 **EST:** 1902
SALES: 626.9MM **Publicly Held**
WEB: www.lbfoster.com
SIC: 3312 3272 3317 Railroad crossings, steel or iron; structural shapes & pilings, steel; ties, railroad: concrete; concrete products, precast; steel pipe & tubes

(G-15208)
L G GRAPHICS INC
Also Called: Instant Impressions & More
1886 Shaw Ave (15217-1728)
PHONE..................................412 421-6330
Lynne A Gottesman, *President*
Esther Gottesman, *Corp Secy*
Debra Ritt, *Vice Pres*
EMP: 10
SQ FT: 3,000
SALES (est): 1MM **Privately Held**
SIC: 2752 2791 Commercial printing, offset; typesetting

(G-15209)
L3 TECHNOLOGIES INC
Integrated Optical Systems
615 Epsilon Dr (15238-2807)
PHONE..................................412 967-7700
Dave Wessing, *General Mgr*
EMP: 150
SALES (corp-wide): 10.2B **Publicly Held**
SIC: 3827 3812 Cinetheodolites; search & navigation equipment
PA: L3 Technologies, Inc.
600 3rd Ave Fl 34
New York NY 10016
212 697-1111

(G-15210)
LA GOURMANDINE LLC
4605 Butler St (15201-2906)
PHONE..................................412 682-2210
Lisanne Lorin-Moreau,
EMP: 6 **Privately Held**
SIC: 2051 Bakery: wholesale or wholesale/retail combined; biscuits, baked: baking powder & raised; bread, all types (white, wheat, rye, etc): fresh or frozen
PA: La Gourmandine, Llc
5013 2nd Ave
Hazelwood PA 15207

(G-15211)
LA GOURMANDINE LLC
300 Cochran Rd (15228-1232)
PHONE............................412 200-7969
Lisanne Lorin-Moreau,
EMP: 8
SALES (est): 401.9K Privately Held
SIC: 2051 Bakery: wholesale or whole-sale/retail combined
PA: La Gourmandine, Llc
5013 2nd Ave
Hazelwood PA 15207

(G-15212)
LA PRIMA EXPRESSO CO (PA)
20th And Smallman (15222)
PHONE............................412 565-7070
Samuel Patti, CEO
EMP: 8
SALES (est): 533.9K Privately Held
SIC: 5812 2095 Coffee shop; coffee roasting (except by wholesale grocers)

(G-15213)
LA SALLE PRODUCTS INC
Also Called: Pro Knitwear
1250 Brookline Blvd (15226-2302)
PHONE............................412 488-1585
Timothy X Feeney, President
EMP: 19
SQ FT: 15,000
SALES (est): 1.6MM Privately Held
WEB: www.proknitwear.com
SIC: 2329 5136 Men's & boys' sportswear & athletic clothing; sportswear, men's & boys'

(G-15214)
LABRIOLA SAUSAGE CO
Also Called: Labriola Joseph Sausage Co
2614 Penn Ave (15222-4622)
PHONE............................412 281-5966
Alberta Labriola, Owner
EMP: 4
SALES (est): 258.2K Privately Held
SIC: 2013 Sausages from purchased meat

(G-15215)
LACHINA DRAPERY COMPANY INC
5750 Baum Blvd Ste 1 (15206-3793)
PHONE............................412 665-4900
Margaret Lachina, Corp Secy
Giovonni Lachina, Vice Pres
Leonard J Lachina, Vice Pres
EMP: 30 EST: 1959
SALES (est): 3.1MM Privately Held
WEB: www.factorypricing.com
SIC: 5713 5131 2211 Floor tile; drapery material, woven; draperies & drapery fabrics, cotton

(G-15216)
LAFARGE NORTH AMERICA INC
4810 Buttermilk Hollow Rd (15122-1106)
PHONE............................412 461-1163
Tim Neel, Principal
EMP: 28
SALES (corp-wide): 26.4B Privately Held
SIC: 3241 Cement, hydraulic
HQ: Lafarge North America Inc.
8700 W Bryn Mawr Ave
Chicago IL 60631
773 372-1000

(G-15217)
LAMBERT-JONES RUBBER CO
319 Butler St Ste 1 (15223-2199)
PHONE............................412 781-8100
Albert L Genter II, Owner
EMP: 4 EST: 1956
SQ FT: 2,500
SALES (est): 611.7K Privately Held
WEB: www.lambertjonesrubber.com
SIC: 5085 3083 3069 Rubber goods, mechanical; laminated plastics plate & sheet; sheeting, rubber or rubberized fabric

(G-15218)
LANE CONSTRUCTION CORPORATION
290 Bilmar Dr (15205-4601)
PHONE............................412 838-0251
Skip Wetmore, Manager
EMP: 100
SALES (corp-wide): 61.8K Privately Held
WEB: www.laneconstruct.com
SIC: 1611 1442 Highway & street paving contractor; construction sand & gravel
HQ: The Lane Construction Corporation
90 Fieldstone Ct
Cheshire CT 06410
203 235-3351

(G-15219)
LANXESS CORPORATION (DH)
111 Ridc Park West Dr (15275-1112)
PHONE............................800 526-9377
Antonis Papadourakis, President
Pieter Bouwer, General Mgr
Philipp Omlor, Business Mgr
George Shackil, VP Mfg
Nicolas Vetter, Plant Mgr
◆ EMP: 750
SALES (est): 1.4B
SALES (corp-wide): 8.2B Privately Held
SIC: 2821 2822 2816 2819 Plastics materials & resins; plasticizer/additive based plastic materials; synthetic rubber; butadiene rubbers; inorganic pigments; industrial inorganic chemicals; amines, acids, salts, esters
HQ: Lanxess Deutschland Gmbh
Kennedyplatz 1
Koln 50679
221 888-50

(G-15220)
LASERTEK TNER CRTRDGE RCHRGING
315 Unity Center Rd (15239-1317)
PHONE............................412 244-9505
Pamela Frantangelo, President
Mario Fratangelo, Vice Pres
EMP: 7
SQ FT: 4,500
SALES (est): 650K Privately Held
SIC: 3861 7378 5734 Toners, prepared photographic (not made in chemical plants); computer maintenance & repair; computer & software stores

(G-15221)
LAUREL MOUNTAIN PRODUCTION LLC
Also Called: Laurel Mountain Energy
61 Mcmurray Rd Ste 300 (15241-1633)
PHONE............................412 595-8700
David Nicklas, President
Keri Brunk, Manager
EMP: 4
SALES (est): 298.8K Privately Held
SIC: 1311 Crude petroleum production

(G-15222)
LEANFM TECHNOLOGIES INC
100 S Commons (15212-5359)
PHONE............................412 818-5167
Ehud Hershkovich, CEO
Burcu Akinci, Principal
Xuesong Liu, Principal
EMP: 3
SALES (est): 60.3K Privately Held
SIC: 7371 7372 Computer software systems analysis & design, custom; application computer software

(G-15223)
LEGAL SIFTER INC
1251 Waterfront Pl # 200 (15222-4227)
PHONE............................724 221-7438
Kevin Miller, CEO
Eben Adams, Vice Pres
Karin Gregory, Vice Pres
Sean Rollman, Vice Pres
Maggie Frey, Director
EMP: 7
SALES (est): 240.6K Privately Held
SIC: 7371 7372 Computer software development & applications; computer software development; application computer software; business oriented computer software

(G-15224)
LEON MILLER & COMPANY LTD
800 Penn Ave Ste 700 (15222-3615)
PHONE............................412 281-8498
Fredric Miller, President
EMP: 10 EST: 1912
SQ FT: 4,200

SALES (est): 1.2MM Privately Held
SIC: 3911 Jewelry, precious metal

(G-15225)
LETTERPRESS SHOP
R J Casey Industial Park (15233)
PHONE............................412 231-2282
Paul Adametz, Owner
EMP: 5
SALES (est): 557.5K Privately Held
SIC: 2759 Letterpress & screen printing; screen printing; embossing on paper

(G-15226)
LEVINE DESIGN INCORPORATED
Also Called: Levine & Co, Robert T
401 Amberson Ave Apt 103 (15232-1455)
PHONE............................412 288-0220
Robert T Levine, President
EMP: 8
SQ FT: 2,400
SALES (est): 1MM Privately Held
WEB: www.levinedesign.net
SIC: 3911 Jewelry, precious metal

(G-15227)
LEVROIL LLC (PA)
855 Lindsay Rd (15242)
P.O. Box 16503 (15242-1003)
PHONE............................412 722-9849
Christopher M Leverich, Mng Member
EMP: 6
SALES (est): 923.7K Privately Held
WEB: www.levroil.com
SIC: 2992 Lubricating oils & greases

(G-15228)
LIBERTY WELDING CO
1235 Washington Blvd (15206-3323)
PHONE............................412 661-1776
William Ferrari, President
Judy Ferrari, Vice Pres
EMP: 3
SQ FT: 3,000
SALES (est): 200K Privately Held
SIC: 3599 7692 7538 3443 Machine shop, jobbing & repair; automotive welding; general automotive repair shops; fabricated plate work (boiler shop)

(G-15229)
LIBRA SCALE
Also Called: Howe Scale
1601 Marys Ave Ste 6 (15215-2637)
PHONE............................412 782-0611
Deborah O' Malley, President
George O'Malley, Vice Pres
George O' Malley, Vice Pres
EMP: 6
SALES (est): 589.4K Privately Held
SIC: 3596 Weighing machines & apparatus

(G-15230)
LIGHTING ACCENTS INC
3946 Oswald St (15212-1757)
PHONE............................412 761-5000
Irwin Kotovsky, Vice Pres
Tom Pontzloff, Controller
▲ EMP: 40 EST: 1998
SALES (est): 2.3MM Privately Held
SIC: 3648 3646 3645 Lighting equipment; commercial indusl & institutional electric lighting fixtures; residential lighting fixtures

(G-15231)
LIGHTING BY LED LLC
105 Berwyn Rd (15237-2803)
PHONE............................412 600-3132
Michael Scotto, President
▲ EMP: 11
SALES (est): 1MM Privately Held
SIC: 3648 Lighting equipment

(G-15232)
LINCOLN FABRICATING CO INC
1920 Lincoln Rd (15235-1199)
PHONE............................412 361-2400
Frank C Perriello, CEO
Frank A Perriello, President
EMP: 25
SQ FT: 52,500
SALES (est): 6.1MM Privately Held
SIC: 3441 Fabricated structural metal

(G-15233)
LINETT CO INC
390 Fountain St (15238-3467)
PHONE............................412 826-8531
Fred I Schwartz, President
Melvin Solomon, Vice Pres
EMP: 140 EST: 1946
SQ FT: 247,000
SALES (est): 19.3MM Privately Held
WEB: www.tri-arc.com
SIC: 3499 Strapping, metal; ladders, portable: metal

(G-15234)
LIPELLA PHARMACEUTICALS INC
400 N Lexington St # 103 (15208-2561)
PHONE............................412 901-0315
Jonathan H Kaufman, President
EMP: 11
SQ FT: 3,000
SALES (est): 1.4MM Privately Held
SIC: 2834 Pharmaceutical preparations

(G-15235)
LIQUID ION SOLUTIONS LLC
1816 Parkway View Dr (15205-1422)
PHONE............................412 275-0919
Hunaid Nulwala, CEO
David Luebke,
EMP: 4
SALES (est): 329.1K Privately Held
SIC: 2869 Laboratory chemicals, organic

(G-15236)
LIQUID X PRINTED METALS INC
252 Parkwest Dr (15275-1002)
PHONE............................412 426-3521
Richard McCullough, President
Bill Babe, Marketing Staff
EMP: 6
SALES (est): 1MM Privately Held
SIC: 2893 Printing ink

(G-15237)
LITTLE EARTH PRODUCTIONS INC
2400 Josephine St Ste 1 (15203-2446)
PHONE............................412 471-0909
Robert Brandegee, CEO
Ava D Demarco, President
▲ EMP: 32
SQ FT: 30,000
SALES (est): 5.7MM Privately Held
WEB: www.littlearth.com
SIC: 2339 Women's & misses' accessories

(G-15238)
LOUIS BERKMAN COMPANY (PA)
Also Called: Meyer Products
600 Grant St Ste 3230 (15219-2704)
PHONE............................740 283-3722
Raphael J Omerza, Principal
Robert A Paul, Chairman
◆ EMP: 20
SQ FT: 3,000
SALES (est): 75MM Privately Held
WEB: www.meyerproducts.com
SIC: 3711 5085 Snow plows (motor vehicles), assembly of; industrial supplies

(G-15239)
LSC ACQUISTION COMPANY INC
Also Called: Lsc Company
100 Herman Dr (15239-1744)
PHONE............................412 795-6400
Robert L Baiz, President
▲ EMP: 41
SQ FT: 30,000
SALES (est): 6.5MM Privately Held
WEB: www.lsccompany.com
SIC: 3451 Screw machine products

(G-15240)
LUNCHERA LLC
5930 Walnut St Apt C3 (15232-2067)
PHONE............................787 607-8914
Eric Crespo, CEO
EMP: 33
SALES: 230K Privately Held
SIC: 7372 4213 7389 Business oriented computer software; automobiles, transport & delivery;

(G-15241)
LUSON DRUMS LLC
5328 Forbes Ave (15217-1104)
PHONE...................................412 867-9404
Carson Cashman, *CEO*
EMP: 3
SALES (est): 103.6K **Privately Held**
SIC: 3931 Drums, parts & accessories
(musical instruments)

(G-15242)
LUSTRA-LINE INC
Also Called: Warren Associates
2901 Brighton Rd (15212-2609)
PHONE...................................412 766-5757
Kurt Gottschalk, *President*
Leslie I Gottschalk, *Treasurer*
▲ EMP: 25
SQ FT: 30,000
SALES (est): 3.7MM **Privately Held**
WEB: www.warrenassociates.us
SIC: 7384 3844 Photofinishing laboratory;
X-ray apparatus & tubes

(G-15243)
**LUX ORNAMENTAL IRON
WORKS INC**
1815 S 18th St (15203-1629)
PHONE...................................412 481-5677
Robert Riccardi, *President*
Frank Riccardi, *Treasurer*
EMP: 8 EST: 1957
SQ FT: 3,600
SALES (est): 1.1MM **Privately Held**
SIC: 3446 Ornamental metalwork

(G-15244)
**M CIBRONE & SONS BAKERY
INC**
Also Called: Cibrone B & Sons Bakery
1231 Grove Rd (15234-2310)
PHONE...................................412 885-6200
James Cibrone, *President*
Irene Cibrone, *Admin Sec*
EMP: 25 EST: 1956
SQ FT: 8,000
SALES (est): 3.6MM **Privately Held**
SIC: 2051 2052 Bakery: wholesale or
wholesale/retail combined; cookies &
crackers

(G-15245)
**MACHINERY & INDUSTRIAL EQP
CO**
1850 Chapman St (15215-2708)
PHONE...................................412 781-8053
John T Howat Jr, *President*
EMP: 4
SQ FT: 11,000
SALES (est): 245K **Privately Held**
SIC: 3398 Metal heat treating

(G-15246)
MADERA CABINETS
13035 Frankstown Rd (15235-1952)
PHONE...................................412 793-5850
Marty Madera, *Owner*
EMP: 10
SQ FT: 6,500
SALES (est): 330K **Privately Held**
SIC: 3993 7319 Signs & advertising spe-
cialties; display advertising service

(G-15247)
MAGNA GRAPHICS INC
369 Coltart Ave (15213-3907)
PHONE...................................412 687-0500
Barry Rudski, *President*
Lilian Rudski, *Admin Sec*
EMP: 6 EST: 1979
SQ FT: 2,000
SALES (est): 682K **Privately Held**
WEB: www.magnagraphic.com
SIC: 2752 7334 Commercial printing, litho-
graphic; photocopying & duplicating serv-
ices

(G-15248)
MAIDEN FORMATS INC
Also Called: Cold Comp
91 Green Glen Dr (15227-4115)
PHONE...................................412 884-4716
Denise Maiden, *President*
EMP: 5
SQ FT: 2,800

SALES: 500K **Privately Held**
SIC: 2621 7336 Printing paper; commercial art & graphic design

(G-15249)
MAMAUX SUPPLY CO
1700 S Canal St (15215-2640)
PHONE...................................412 782-3456
Anthony Arcuri, *President*
Frank L Lodovico, *Vice Pres*
EMP: 16 EST: 1960
SQ FT: 5,000
SALES (est): 2.1MM **Privately Held**
WEB: www.mamauxsupply.com
SIC: 2231 2394 Broadwoven fabric mills,
wool; canvas & related products

(G-15250)
**MARC EDWARD BRANDS INC
(PA)**
Also Called: Edward Marc Chocolatier
55 38th St (15201-3203)
PHONE...................................412 380-0888
Donna Edwards, *President*
Gary Neff, *Principal*
Christian Edwards, *Co-CEO*
Dana Edwards Manatos, *Co-CEO*
Mark Edwards, *COO*
▼ EMP: 80
SQ FT: 50,000
SALES (est): 24.2MM **Privately Held**
WEB: www.chocolatecelebrations.com
SIC: 2064 3999 5441 Candy & other con-
fectionery products; coin-operated
amusement machines; candy, nut & con-
fectionery stores

(G-15251)
MARCELLUS SHALE COALITION
24 Summit Park Dr Ste 200 (15275-1104)
PHONE...................................412 706-5160
Marc A Levine, *Principal*
EMP: 12
SALES (est): 5.5MM **Privately Held**
SIC: 2813 Industrial gases

(G-15252)
**MARCUS J WHOLESALERS
INC**
Also Called: J Marcus Company
1728 Smallman St (15222-4310)
PHONE...................................412 261-3315
Jack Marcus, *President*
David Haber, *Vice Pres*
Benjamin Haber, *Accounts Mgr*
Pam Haber, *Accounts Mgr*
Marshall Neft, *Manager*
▲ EMP: 15
SQ FT: 57,000
SALES (est): 3.7MM **Privately Held**
SIC: 3171 5023 5092 5136 Women's
handbags & purses; home furnishings;
toys; men's & boys' sportswear & work
clothing; sporting & recreation goods;
women's & children's sportswear & swim-
suits

(G-15253)
MARCUS UPPE INC
Also Called: Clicks Professional Copy Svc
411 7th Ave Ste 350 (15219-1921)
PHONE...................................412 261-4233
Cory Renallo, *Manager*
EMP: 25 **Privately Held**
SIC: 3555 Copy holders, printers'
PA: Marcus Uppe Inc.
320 Fort Duquesne Blvd # 300
Pittsburgh PA 15222

(G-15254)
MARCUS UPPE INC (PA)
Also Called: Clicks Document Management
320 Fort Duquesne Blvd # 300
(15222-1102)
PHONE...................................412 391-1218
Timothy Moulton, *President*
EMP: 7
SALES (est): 15.1MM **Privately Held**
SIC: 2759 Commercial printing

(G-15255)
MARKOVITZ ENTERPRISES INC
Quality Rolls
1207 Muriel St (15203-1126)
P.O. Box 360 (15122-0360)
PHONE...................................412 381-2305

Brad Hood, *Controller*
Jim Walter, *Branch Mgr*
EMP: 200
SALES (corp-wide): 12.8MM **Privately
Held**
WEB: www.badgerind.com
SIC: 3312 Blast furnaces & steel mills
PA: Markovitz Enterprises, Inc.
100 Badger Dr
Zelienople PA 16063
724 452-4500

(G-15256)
MARSH LABORATORIES INC
2437 Waverly St (15218-2626)
PHONE...................................412 271-3060
David A Lampe, *President*
EMP: 11
SQ FT: 10,000
SALES (est): 2.1MM **Privately Held**
SIC: 2891 Sealing compounds, synthetic
rubber or plastic; adhesives, plastic

(G-15257)
MARSHALL WOODWORKS LTD
Also Called: Marshall Wood Works
1500 Spring Garden Ave (15212-3633)
PHONE...................................412 321-1685
Robert Spehar, *President*
EMP: 10
SQ FT: 5,000
SALES (est): 900K **Privately Held**
SIC: 2431 5944 Doors, wood; staircases &
stairs, wood; moldings, wood: unfinished
& prefinished; woodwork, interior & orna-
mental; jewelry stores

(G-15258)
MARSTRAND INDUSTRIES INC
12 Rutgers Rd (15205-2566)
P.O. Box 44089 (15205-0289)
PHONE...................................412 921-1511
Jack Marshall Jr, *CEO*
Lee Marshall, *President*
Terry Marshall, *Vice Pres*
Bob Usnick, *Engineer*
Thomas P Marshall, *Shareholder*
EMP: 52
SQ FT: 58,000
SALES (est): 11.6MM **Privately Held**
WEB: www.marstrand-industries.com
SIC: 3441 Fabricated structural metal

(G-15259)
**MARTEK POWER LASER DRIVE
LLC**
620 William Pitt Way (15238-1332)
PHONE...................................805 383-5548
Mike Innab,
EMP: 67 EST: 1976
SQ FT: 22,000
SALES (est): 8.7MM **Privately Held**
WEB: www.laserdrive.com
SIC: 3679 Power supplies, all types: static

(G-15260)
MARVEL MARKING PRODUCTS
3000 Jane St (15203-2392)
P.O. Box 427, Saxonburg (16056-0427)
PHONE...................................412 381-0700
Ludwig Riedl, *Principal*
Karl Kwolek, *VP Prdtn*
EMP: 15
SQ FT: 7,500
SALES (est): 2.1MM **Privately Held**
WEB: www.marvelmarking.com
SIC: 3953 Embossing seals & hand
stamps; stencils, painting & marking

(G-15261)
MASTRO ICE INC
835 Herron Ave (15219-3933)
PHONE...................................412 681-4423
Michael Mastro, *President*
Joe Mastro, *Vice Pres*
EMP: 6
SQ FT: 13,000
SALES (est): 721.2K **Privately Held**
WEB: www.mastroice.com
SIC: 2097 5999 5078 Manufactured ice;
ice; ice making machines

(G-15262)
MATRIX SOLUTIONS LLC
1 Allegheny Sq Ste 500 (15212-5307)
PHONE...................................412 697-3000

Curt Emerick, *VP Opers*
Gary Diven, *Mng Member*
Sandy Gardner, *Consultant*
Chuck Lewis, *Technical Staff*
Michael Collins, *Sr Software Eng*
EMP: 25
SQ FT: 7,300
SALES (est): 3.4MM **Privately Held**
WEB: www.matrixplus.com
SIC: 7372 Business oriented computer
software

(G-15263)
MATT MACHINE & MFG INC
820 Unity Center Rd (15239-1439)
PHONE...................................412 793-6020
Micheal Jezek, *President*
Michael Jezek, *President*
Rudolph Jezek, *General Mgr*
Tom Boozer, *Foreman/Supr*
Robin Jezek, *Treasurer*
EMP: 25
SQ FT: 6,000
SALES (est): 4.5MM **Privately Held**
WEB: www.mattmachine.com
SIC: 3599 3841 3829 Machine shop, job-
bing & repair; surgical & medical instru-
ments; measuring & controlling devices

(G-15264)
**MATTHEWS INTERNATIONAL
CORP (PA)**
2 N Shore Ctr Ste 200 (15212-5851)
PHONE...................................412 442-8200
John D Turner, *Ch of Bd*
Joseph C Bartolacci, *President*
Steven D Gackenbach, *President*
Paul F Rahill, *President*
John Parham, *Regional Mgr*
◆ EMP: 50 EST: 1850
SALES: 1.6B **Publicly Held**
SIC: 3366 1542 3569 3995 Bronze
foundry; mausoleum construction; cre-
mating ovens; burial caskets; marking de-
vices; platemaking services

(G-15265)
**MATTHEWS INTERNATIONAL
CORP**
Marking Products Division
6515 Penn Ave (15206-4482)
PHONE...................................412 665-2500
Liz Churchill, *Vice Pres*
Kathi Jaros, *Purchasing*
Louis Serventi, *Controller*
Steve Jupena, *Sales Staff*
Brain Dunn, *Branch Mgr*
EMP: 100
SALES (corp-wide): 1.5B **Publicly Held**
WEB: www.matthewsmarking.com
SIC: 3953 3577 3555 3549 Marking de-
vices; computer peripheral equipment;
printing trades machinery; metalworking
machinery
PA: Matthews International Corporation
2 N Shore Ctr Ste 200
Pittsburgh PA 15212
412 442-8200

(G-15266)
**MATTHEWS INTERNATIONAL
CORP**
Matthews Bronze Division
1315 W Liberty Ave (15226-1040)
PHONE...................................412 571-5500
Dave Hewitt, *President*
David Merrill, *Regional Mgr*
Jim Myers, *QC Mgr*
Ralph Schwartzmiller, *Engineer*
Tom Bevan, *Manager*
EMP: 310
SALES (corp-wide): 1.5B **Publicly Held**
SIC: 3366 1799 3993 3953 Bronze
foundry; ornamental metal work; signs &
advertising specialties; marking devices;
aluminum extruded products; cut stone &
stone products
PA: Matthews International Corporation
2 N Shore Ctr Ste 200
Pittsburgh PA 15212
412 442-8200

(G-15267)
MATTHEWS INTERNATIONAL CORP
Marking Products Division
101 Fairview Ave (15238-1943)
PHONE....................................412 665-2500
Fax: 412 365-2341
EMP: 65
SALES (corp-wide): 1.4B Publicly Held
SIC: 3953 Marking Devices, Nsk
PA: Matthews International Corporation
2 N Shore Ctr Ste 200
Pittsburgh PA 15212
412 442-8200

(G-15268)
MC GEAR CO INC
969 Route 910 (15238-1259)
PHONE....................................412 767-5502
Patrick McClelland, President
EMP: 4
SQ FT: 4,000
SALES: 229K Privately Held
SIC: 3599 Machine shop, jobbing & repair

(G-15269)
MCCONWAY & TORLEY LLC (HQ)
109 48th St (15201-2755)
PHONE....................................412 622-0494
Pat Wallace, President
Randall Schudalla, General Mgr
Scott Mautino, VP Opers
Brenda Lewis, Accounts Mgr
Debbie Hall, Cust Mgr
◆ EMP: 20 EST: 2006
SQ FT: 10,000
SALES (est): 21.3MM
SALES (corp-wide): 1.4B Publicly Held
WEB: www.mcconway.com
SIC: 3325 Steel foundries
PA: Arcosa, Inc.
500 N Akard St
Dallas TX 75201
972 942-6500

(G-15270)
MCKNIGHT SURGICAL INC
Also Called: McArdle Surgical
2171 Babcock Blvd (15209-1344)
PHONE....................................412 821-9000
Dan Corcoran, President
Kris Corcoran, Admin Sec
EMP: 4
SQ FT: 3,000
SALES (est): 360K Privately Held
SIC: 5999 5047 3999 Medical apparatus & supplies; technical aids for the handi-capped; hospital equipment & furniture; wheelchair lifts

(G-15271)
MECCO
1153 Southvale Rd (15237-4240)
PHONE....................................412 548-3549
EMP: 3
SALES (est): 23.9K Privately Held
SIC: 3577 Bar code (magnetic ink) printers

(G-15272)
MEDCONTROL TECHNOLOGIES LLC
6617 Jackson St (15206-1763)
PHONE....................................508 479-8109
David Jasnos, Principal
EMP: 3
SALES (est): 193.3K Privately Held
SIC: 3841 Surgical & medical instruments

(G-15273)
MEDRAD INCORPORATED OHARA
271 Kappa Dr (15238-2817)
PHONE....................................412 967-9700
EMP: 3 EST: 2007
SALES (est): 255.4K Privately Held
SIC: 3841 Mfg Surgical/Medical Instruments

(G-15274)
MEECO MANUFACTURING TARGE
5905 Brownsville Rd (15236-3507)
PHONE....................................412 653-1323

EMP: 3
SALES (est): 152.5K Privately Held
SIC: 3999 Manufacturing industries

(G-15275)
MEGATOR CORPORATION
1721 Main St (15215-2611)
PHONE....................................412 963-9200
Gregory Kasper, President
▲ EMP: 8 EST: 1957
SQ FT: 5,000
SALES (est): 2MM Privately Held
WEB: www.megator.com
SIC: 3561 5084 Pumps, oil well & field; in-dustrial machinery & equipment

(G-15276)
MEOW MIX COMPANY (DH)
375 N Shore Dr (15212-5866)
PHONE....................................412 222-2200
Richard C Thompson, President
Richard Kasser, CFO
Henry Atlas, Admin Sec
EMP: 45
SALES (est): 9.6MM
SALES (corp-wide): 7.3B Publicly Held
WEB: www.meowmix.com
SIC: 2047 Cat food
HQ: Big Heart Pet Brands, Inc.
1 Maritime Plz Fl 2
San Francisco CA 94111
415 247-3000

(G-15277)
MERCER VALVE CO INC
1616 Parkway View Dr (15205-1409)
PHONE....................................412 859-0300
Dick Taylor, President
Tina Hawkins, Manager
Terry Smith, Manager
EMP: 3
SALES (corp-wide): 46.3MM Privately Held
SIC: 3592 Valves
PA: Mercer Valve Co., Inc.
9609 Nw 4th St
Oklahoma City OK 73127
405 470-5213

(G-15278)
MERCURIOS MULBERRY CREAMERY
5523 Walnut St (15232-2350)
PHONE....................................412 621-6220
Linda Mercurio, Owner
Anna Mercurio, Co-Owner
Michael Mercurio, Co-Owner
EMP: 10
SALES (est): 739.3K Privately Held
SIC: 2024 Ice cream, bulk

(G-15279)
METAL BULLETIN HOLDINGS LLC
1 Gateway Ctr Ste 1375 (15222)
PHONE....................................412 765-2580
David Brooks, Senior VP
EMP: 11
SALES (corp-wide): 497.5MM Privately Held
WEB: www.amm.com
SIC: 2711 Newspapers
HQ: Metal Bulletin Holdings Llc
1120 Ave Of The Americas
New York NY 10036
212 213-6202

(G-15280)
METALTECH
2400 2nd Ave (15219-3116)
PHONE....................................412 464-5000
G Watts Humphrey Jr, Ch of Bd
Edwin H Gott Jr, General Ptnr
Robert W Riordan, General Ptnr
EMP: 90
SQ FT: 90,000
SALES (est): 11.5MM Privately Held
SIC: 3479 Galvanizing of iron, steel or end-formed products

(G-15281)
METRO BUILDING SERVICES
379 Rockhill Rd (15243-1458)
PHONE....................................412 221-1284
Steve Beggarly, Owner
EMP: 4

SALES (est): 201.4K Privately Held
SIC: 3589 Commercial cleaning equipment

(G-15282)
MG DEVELOPMENT AMERICA INC
187 36th St (15201-1955)
PHONE....................................412 288-9959
Danielle Spozarski, Director
EMP: 6
SALES (est): 298K Privately Held
SIC: 3845 Audiological equipment, elec-tromedical

(G-15283)
MGTF PAPER COMPANY LLC
650 Smithfield St # 2200 (15222-3900)
PHONE....................................412 316-3342
Michael Frischling,
EMP: 39
SALES: 4.2MM Privately Held
SIC: 2711 Newspapers

(G-15284)
MICHAEL S CWALINA
Also Called: Printing Services Unlimited
250 Mount Lebanon Blvd # 322
(15234-1252)
P.O. Box 71, Bethel Park (15102-0071)
PHONE....................................412 341-1606
Michael S Cwalina, Owner
EMP: 3
SALES (est): 297.8K Privately Held
SIC: 2752 Commercial printing, litho-graphic

(G-15285)
MICROGENICS
2000 Park Ln (15275-1114)
PHONE....................................412 490-8365
Seth Hoogasian, Principal
EMP: 3
SALES (est): 169.7K Privately Held
SIC: 2834 Dermatologicals

(G-15286)
MICROSOFT CORPORATION
30 Isabella St Ste 2 (15212-5862)
PHONE....................................412 323-6700
Joe Corey, Partner
Daniel Rim, Program Mgr
Tom Merrow, Manager
David Norsen, Manager
Ron Stom, Consultant
EMP: 35
SALES (corp-wide): 110.3B Publicly Held
WEB: www.microsoft.com
SIC: 7372 Application computer software
PA: Microsoft Corporation
1 Microsoft Way
Redmond WA 98052
425 882-8080

(G-15287)
MILAN ENERGY LLC
106 Isabella St (15212-5841)
PHONE....................................724 933-0140
Ron J Kiecana, Mng Member
EMP: 1 EST: 2013
SALES: 5.4MM
SALES (corp-wide): 9.9MM Privately Held
SIC: 3621 Frequency converters (electric generators)
PA: Img Midstream Llc
106 Isabella St
Pittsburgh PA 15212
877 260-1339

(G-15288)
MILLCRAFT INDUSTRIES INC
222 5th Ave (15222-2726)
PHONE....................................412 281-7675
EMP: 105
SALES (corp-wide): 30.7MM Privately Held
SIC: 3999 Barber & beauty shop equip-ment
PA: Millcraft Industries, Inc.
95 W Beau St Ste 600
Washington PA 15301
724 229-8800

(G-15289)
MILLER PROCESS COATINGMILLER
309 S Main St (15215-2134)
PHONE....................................724 274-5880
William J Miller, Principal
EMP: 7
SALES (est): 685K Privately Held
SIC: 2759 Commercial printing

(G-15290)
MINDFUL BREWING COMPANY LLC
3759 Library Rd (15234-2232)
PHONE....................................412 965-8428
EMP: 3
SALES (est): 68.6K Privately Held
SIC: 2082 5812 Malt beverages; eating places

(G-15291)
MINDMATRIX INC
Also Called: Mind Matrix
2403 Sidney St Ste 150 (15203-5130)
PHONE....................................412 381-0230
Harbinder Khera, President
Shawn Becket, Business Mgr
Narndra Bhat, Exec VP
Shawn Spensley, Sales Dir
Eric Weber, Sales Staff
EMP: 14
SQ FT: 3,000
SALES (est): 1.9MM Privately Held
SIC: 7372 Business oriented computer software

(G-15292)
MINE VISION SYSTEMS INC
5877 Commerce St Ste 118 (15206-3835)
PHONE....................................412 626-7461
Paul Lucey, CEO
Barry Henderson, COO
John Irvin, CFO
EMP: 4 EST: 2015
SALES (est): 173K Privately Held
SIC: 1081 Metal mining services

(G-15293)
MINTON HOLDINGS LLC
Also Called: UPS
1525 Park Manor Blvd (15205-4805)
PHONE....................................412 787-5912
Robert Kennedy, Owner
EMP: 5
SQ FT: 2,100
SALES (est): 472.9K Privately Held
SIC: 7389 3953 7221 2621 Mailbox rental & related service; seal presses, no-tary & hand; passport photographer; print-ing paper; photocopy machines

(G-15294)
MINUTEMAN PRESS
1963 Wharton Sq (15203-1883)
PHONE....................................412 621-7456
Eric Stinelli, Owner
Beth Stinelli, Co-Owner
EMP: 3 EST: 1981
SQ FT: 1,400
SALES (est): 272.3K Privately Held
SIC: 2752 2789 Commercial printing, off-set; bookbinding & related work

(G-15295)
MINUTEMAN PRESS SOUTH HILLS
Also Called: Ajb Productions
74 Markham Dr (15228-1057)
PHONE....................................412 531-0809
Andy J Booth, President
Andrew J Booth, Owner
Susan Giegel, Sales Staff
Darren Kennedy, Graphic Designe
EMP: 3
SALES: 330K Privately Held
WEB: www.ajbproductions.com
SIC: 2752 Commercial printing, offset

(G-15296)
MOAI TECHNOLOGIES INC (PA)
100 1st Ave Ste 1101 (15222-1518)
P.O. Box 1283, Wexford (15090-1283)
PHONE....................................412 454-5550
Ramesh Mehta, CEO
Mike Nelson, Ch of Bd

Ravi Ghai, *Vice Pres*
Michael J Kulmoski Jr, *CFO*
John Satterfield, *Info Tech Dir*
EMP: 26
SQ FT: 10,000
SALES (est): 14MM **Privately Held**
WEB: www.moai.com
SIC: 7372 Business oriented computer software

(G-15297)
MOBIUS ACQUISITION LLC (HQ)
1000 Mcknight Park Dr (15237-6514)
PHONE.................................412 281-7000
Lodovico C De Visconti,
EMP: 2
SALES (est): 4.6MM **Privately Held**
SIC: 7372 7371 Prepackaged software; custom computer programming services

(G-15298)
MODERN REPRODUCTIONS INC
127 Mckean St (15219-1190)
PHONE.................................412 488-7700
Ruth Winkowski, *President*
Lawrence P Winkowski, *President*
James Winkowski, *Vice Pres*
EMP: 14 **EST:** 1963
SQ FT: 20,000
SALES: 1.2MM **Privately Held**
WEB: www.modernrepro.com
SIC: 2752 7336 2759 2672 Commercial printing, offset; commercial art & graphic design; commercial printing; coated & laminated paper

(G-15299)
MODULAR INTERNATIONAL INC
3941 California Ave (15212-1610)
PHONE.................................412 734-9000
Irwin Kotovsky, *President*
Gary Heyl, *Opers Mgr*
Tony Onofrio, *Natl Sales Mgr*
▲ **EMP:** 30
SALES (est): 6.3MM **Privately Held**
WEB: www.modularinternational.com
SIC: 3646 Commercial indusl & institutional electric lighting fixtures

(G-15300)
MONROE SCALE COMPANY INC
424 Regency Dr (15239-1712)
P.O. Box 14175 (15239-0175)
PHONE.................................412 793-8134
William D Monroe Jr, *President*
Stephen Monroe, *Corp Secy*
John J Monroe, *Vice Pres*
EMP: 3
SALES (est): 506.9K **Privately Held**
SIC: 3596 1771 Scales & balances, except laboratory; concrete work

(G-15301)
MONTAUK ENERGY HOLDINGS LLC
680 Andersen Dr Ste 100 (15220-2759)
PHONE.................................412 747-8700
David Herrman,
EMP: 68
SQ FT: 2,000
SALES (est): 6.1MM **Privately Held**
SIC: 1311 Crude petroleum & natural gas

(G-15302)
MORRIS PRINTING COMPANY
5220 Elmwood Dr (15227-3630)
PHONE.................................412 881-8626
Sandra Morris, *Owner*
EMP: 4
SALES (est): 25.6K **Privately Held**
WEB: www.morrismotorsports.com
SIC: 2752 Commercial printing, offset

(G-15303)
MOSEBACH MANUFACTURING COMPANY
1417 Mclaughlin Run Rd # 2 (15241-3158)
PHONE.................................412 220-0200
Gordon Denny, *President*
Gordon P Denny, *President*
William R Elliott, *Vice Pres*
S D Sowell, *Treasurer*
▲ **EMP:** 59 **EST:** 1920
SQ FT: 32,000

SALES (est): 16.3MM
SALES (corp-wide): 1.2MM **Privately Held**
WEB: www.mosebachresistors.com
SIC: 3634 Heaters, space electric
HQ: Telema Spa
Via Luigi Bernardo Salvoni 60
Piacenza PC 29122
052 355-7226

(G-15304)
MOTHER NATURE CORPORATION
200 Carriage Blvd (15239-3601)
PHONE.................................412 798-3911
EMP: 3
SALES (est): 73.4K **Privately Held**
SIC: 7389 7372 Trade show arrangement; application computer software

(G-15305)
MOUNT LEBANON MUNICIPALITY
Also Called: Mount Lebanon Magazine
710 Washington Rd Ste 1 (15228-2018)
PHONE.................................412 343-3400
Steven Feller, *Manager*
EMP: 7 **Privately Held**
WEB: www.mtlebanonlibrary.org
SIC: 2721 Magazines: publishing only, not printed on site
PA: Municipality Of Mount Lebanon
710 Washington Rd Ste 1
Pittsburgh PA 15228
412 343-3745

(G-15306)
MR SMOOTHIE (PA)
1000 Ross Park Mall Dr Vc13
(15237-3872)
PHONE.................................412 630-9065
Jorge Cedillo, *Owner*
EMP: 6
SALES (est): 765K **Privately Held**
SIC: 2037 Fruit juices

(G-15307)
MULTILINGUAL COMMUNICATIONS
Also Called: McC
3603 Bates St (15213-4103)
P.O. Box 7164 (15213-0164)
PHONE.................................412 621-7450
Charles Kostecki, *President*
Annette Slezak, *Vice Pres*
EMP: 6 **EST:** 1973
SQ FT: 2,400
SALES (est): 600K **Privately Held**
WEB: www.mccworld.com
SIC: 7389 2791 Translation services; typesetting

(G-15308)
MULTIMEDIA TRAINING SYSTEMS
370 Broadmoor Ave (15228-2584)
PHONE.................................412 341-2185
David Coffaro, *President*
Bernadette Kozlowski, *Office Mgr*
EMP: 5
SALES (est): 457.5K **Privately Held**
SIC: 7372 8748 Educational computer software; business consulting

(G-15309)
MULTISORB TECH INTL LLC
6422 Monitor St (15217-2722)
PHONE.................................412 521-3685
Rick Cellich, *Principal*
EMP: 3 **Privately Held**
SIC: 2819 Industrial inorganic chemicals
PA: Multisorb Technologies International, Llc
325 Harlem Rd
Buffalo NY 14224

(G-15310)
MUNICIPAL FIRE EQUIPMENT INC
1038 Perry Hwy Ste 201 (15237-2122)
PHONE.................................412 366-8180
Ronald Mc Kee, *President*
Karen Mc Kee, *Corp Secy*
Dan Tschippert, *Vice Pres*
EMP: 4

SQ FT: 2,500
SALES (est): 439K **Privately Held**
SIC: 5099 3569 Safety equipment & supplies; firefighting apparatus & related equipment

(G-15311)
MUNROE INCORPORATED (HQ)
1820 N Franklin St (15233-2253)
PHONE.................................412 231-0600
Philip F Muck, *Ch of Bd*
Stephen E Zemba, *Vice Pres*
▲ **EMP:** 51 **EST:** 1835
SQ FT: 10,000
SALES: 13.8MM
SALES (corp-wide): 59.1MM **Privately Held**
SIC: 3443 3634 3444 Boiler & boiler shop work; electric housewares & fans; sheet metalwork
PA: Woodings Industrial Corporation
218 Clay Ave
Mars PA 16046
724 625-3131

(G-15312)
MURSLACK WELDING INC
484 Lowries Run Rd 2 (15237-1231)
PHONE.................................412 364-5554
David A Murslack, *President*
Mary Ellen Murslack, *Vice Pres*
EMP: 5
SQ FT: 1,600
SALES (est): 428.7K **Privately Held**
SIC: 7692 1799 Welding repair; welding on site

(G-15313)
MZP KILN SERVICES INC
201 Penn Center Blvd (15235-5435)
PHONE.................................412 825-5100
Marek Kolibal, *President*
Jakub Kolar, *Director*
David Velek, *Admin Sec*
▲ **EMP:** 7
SQ FT: 100
SALES (est): 947.4K **Privately Held**
SIC: 3531 Construction machinery

(G-15314)
N H MORGAN INC
Also Called: Print Craft Studio
3241 W Liberty Ave Ste 1 (15216-2369)
PHONE.................................412 561-1046
Howard Secher, *President*
EMP: 4
SQ FT: 2,700
SALES (est): 360K **Privately Held**
SIC: 2759 2752 Promotional printing; fashion plates, lithographed

(G-15315)
N3ZN KEYS LLC
74 Green Meadow Ct (15239-1459)
PHONE.................................412 389-7797
Anthony C Baleno, *Principal*
EMP: 3
SALES (est): 331.1K **Privately Held**
SIC: 3429 Keys, locks & related hardware

(G-15316)
NACAH TECH LLC
37 Mcmurray Rd Ste 203 (15241-1632)
PHONE.................................412 833-0687
Robert Keibler,
Valerie Keibler,
EMP: 6
SALES: 1.5MM **Privately Held**
WEB: www.nacahtech.com
SIC: 3433 8711 Burners, furnaces, boilers & stokers; consulting engineer

(G-15317)
NALCO COMPANY LLC
Also Called: Nalco Chemical
650 Trumbull Dr (15205-4361)
PHONE.................................412 278-8600
Frank Hervert, *Branch Mgr*
Joseph Koehler, *Executive*
EMP: 30
SALES (corp-wide): 14.6B **Publicly Held**
WEB: www.nalco.com
SIC: 3589 Water treatment equipment, industrial

HQ: Nalco Company Llc
1601 W Diehl Rd
Naperville IL 60563
630 305-1000

(G-15318)
NANOGRIPTECH INC
91 43rd St Ste 240 (15201-3161)
PHONE.................................412 224-2136
Metin Sitti,
EMP: 4
SALES (est): 530.7K **Privately Held**
SIC: 2891 Adhesives & sealants

(G-15319)
NARTAK MEDIA GROUP
2275 Swallow Hill Rd # 100 (15220-1656)
PHONE.................................412 276-4000
Arnold Green, *Owner*
EMP: 17
SALES (est): 2.3MM **Privately Held**
SIC: 2791 Typesetting

(G-15320)
NASCENT ENERGY SYSTEMS LLC
712 Filbert St Apt 2 (15232-2404)
PHONE.................................203 722-1101
Keith Heyde, *CEO*
Emile Fares, *Principal*
John Lake, *Principal*
EMP: 3
SALES (est): 125.9K **Privately Held**
SIC: 3743 Railroad equipment, except locomotives

(G-15321)
NATIONAL ARTIFICIAL LIMB CO
5740 Baum Blvd Ste 1 (15206-3775)
PHONE.................................412 608-9910
Mark Kalas, *President*
EMP: 4
SQ FT: 12,000
SALES: 130K **Privately Held**
SIC: 3842 Limbs, artificial; braces, elastic; braces, orthopedic

(G-15322)
NATIONAL WOODWORKS LLC
4075 Windgap Ave Bldg 20 (15204-1007)
P.O. Box 38781 (15238-8781)
PHONE.................................412 431-7071
Linda M Rice, *Mng Member*
Russell Rice,
EMP: 9
SALES (est): 1.9MM **Privately Held**
SIC: 2431 Millwork

(G-15323)
NEEDLE AND PIN
3271 W Liberty Ave (15216-2319)
PHONE.................................412 207-9724
EMP: 3 **EST:** 2017
SALES (est): 240.7K **Privately Held**
SIC: 3452 Pins

(G-15324)
NEIGHBORHOOD PUBLICATIONS INC
Also Called: South Pittsburgh Reporter, The
813 E Warrington Ave (15210-1559)
P.O. Box 4285 (15203-0285)
PHONE.................................412 481-0266
Tom Smith,
EMP: 3
SALES: 120K **Privately Held**
SIC: 2711 Newspapers: publishing only, not printed on site

(G-15325)
NEMA USA INC (PA)
2535 Washington Rd # 1121 (15241-2592)
PHONE.................................412 678-9541
Beyham Nakiboglu, *President*
Abdulah Nakiboglu, *Vice Pres*
Serdar Ayman, *Admin Sec*
EMP: 23
SALES (est): 1.2MM **Privately Held**
SIC: 2011 Meat packing plants

(G-15326)
NEON DOCTOR LLC
4658 Cook Ave (15236-1922)
PHONE.................................412 885-7075
David Bates,

G
E
O
G
R
A
P
H
I
C

EMP: 3
SALES (est): 215.3K **Privately Held**
SIC: 3993 Neon signs

(G-15327)
NEPTUNE-BENSON INC (DH)
210 6th Ave Ste 3300 (15222-2603)
PHONE..................................724 772-0044
Kenneth Rodi, *CEO*
EMP: 3
SALES (est): 6.1MM
SALES (corp-wide): 1.3B **Publicly Held**
SIC: 3589 Water treatment equipment, industrial
HQ: Evoqua Water Technologies Llc
210 6th Ave Ste 3300
Pittsburgh PA 15222
724 772-0044

(G-15328)
NETBEEZ INC
5124b Penn Ave (15224-1616)
PHONE..................................412 465-0638
Stefano Gridelli, *CEO*
Panagiotis Vouzis, *COO*
Panayiotis Neophytou, *Chief Engr*
EMP: 3 **EST:** 2013
SALES (est): 280.5K **Privately Held**
SIC: 7372 7371 Business oriented computer software; computer software development

(G-15329)
NEURO KINETICS INC
Also Called: N K I
128 Gamma Dr (15238-2920)
PHONE..................................412 963-6649
J H Schroeder, *President*
Brian Sullivan, *COO*
Hans Werner, *Vice Pres*
Richard Mosovsky, *Opers Staff*
Paul Mayercik, *Design Engr*
EMP: 13
SQ FT: 4,800
SALES (est): 2.5MM **Privately Held**
WEB: www.neurokinetics.com
SIC: 3841 Diagnostic apparatus, medical

(G-15330)
NEURONTRVNTNAL THRAPEUTICS INC
Also Called: Neurointerventions
2403 Sidney St Ste 200 (15203-2168)
PHONE..................................412 726-3111
Michele Migliuolo, *President*
EMP: 5
SALES (est): 419.8K **Privately Held**
SIC: 3841 Surgical & medical instruments

(G-15331)
NEVILLE GALVANIZING INC
3005 Grand Ave (15225-1603)
PHONE..................................412 771-9799
David Geisler, *President*
EMP: 25 **EST:** 1977
SQ FT: 10,000
SALES (est): 2.3MM **Privately Held**
SIC: 3479 Galvanizing of iron, steel or end-formed products

(G-15332)
NEVILLE GRATING LLC
3001 Grand Ave (15225-1603)
PHONE..................................412 771-6973
David Geisler,
EMP: 6
SALES (est): 245.2K **Privately Held**
SIC: 3446 3449 Gratings, tread: fabricated metal; lath, expanded metal

(G-15333)
NEW PITTSBURGH COURIER PUBG CO
315 E Carson St (15219-1202)
PHONE..................................412 481-8302
Rod Doss, *Publisher*
EMP: 19
SQ FT: 2,200
SALES (est): 1.1MM **Privately Held**
WEB: www.newpittsburghcourier.com
SIC: 2711 Newspapers: publishing only, not printed on site

(G-15334)
NEW PRECISION TECHNOLOGY INC
7800 Susquehanna St (15208-2118)
P.O. Box 81956 (15217-0956)
PHONE..................................412 596-5948
Axel Vanbriesen, *President*
EMP: 5
SALES: 100K **Privately Held**
SIC: 3559 Robots, molding & forming plastics

(G-15335)
NEXT GENERATION FILTRATION
3000 Mcknight East Dr (15237-6422)
PHONE..................................412 548-1659
Pete Canovali, *Partner*
EMP: 5
SALES (est): 682.8K **Privately Held**
SIC: 3569 Filters

(G-15336)
NEXUS INC
810 Penn Ave Ste 700 (15222-3614)
PHONE..................................412 391-2444
Stephen Delano, *President*
Diane Delano, *President*
Dale Riether, *Admin Sec*
EMP: 6
SQ FT: 1,600
SALES (est): 803.6K **Privately Held**
SIC: 3911 Jewelry, precious metal

(G-15337)
NICHOLAS WOHLFARTH
Also Called: Turtle Creek Sportswear
1370 Frey Rd (15235-4059)
PHONE..................................412 373-6811
Nicholas Wohlfarth, *Owner*
EMP: 15
SQ FT: 5,100
SALES (est): 1.3MM **Privately Held**
WEB: www.eturtlecreek.com
SIC: 2395 2759 Embroidery products, except schiffli machine; screen printing

(G-15338)
NICHOLS WELDING SERVICE INC
1309 Washington Blvd (15206-1801)
PHONE..................................412 362-8855
Joseph D Nichols III, *President*
EMP: 3
SQ FT: 8,000
SALES (est): 397.2K **Privately Held**
SIC: 1791 7692 Structural steel erection; welding repair

(G-15339)
NICK CHARLES KRAVITCH (PA)
Also Called: Kravitch Machine Co
3706 Rebecca St (15234-2337)
PHONE..................................412 341-7265
Nick Charles Kravitch, *Owner*
EMP: 1 **EST:** 1965
SQ FT: 12,500
SALES (est): 1.8MM **Privately Held**
SIC: 5084 3599 Hydraulic systems equipment & supplies; machine shop, jobbing & repair

(G-15340)
NICK CHARLES KRAVITCH
Also Called: Kravitch Machine
50 Mcneilly Rd (15226-2608)
PHONE..................................412 882-6262
Nick Kravitch, *Manager*
EMP: 4
SALES (corp-wide): 1.8MM **Privately Held**
SIC: 3599 3594 3568 3494 Machine shop, jobbing & repair; fluid power pumps & motors; power transmission equipment; valves & pipe fittings; fluid power valves & hose fittings; bolts, nuts, rivets & washers
PA: Nick Charles Kravitch
3706 Rebecca St
Pittsburgh PA 15234
412 341-7265

(G-15341)
NICKEL COBALT BATTERY LLC
2364 Eldridge St (15217-2306)
PHONE..................................412 567-6828
Anna Berkovich, *Principal*

EMP: 5
SQ FT: 1,800
SALES (est): 374.1K **Privately Held**
SIC: 3625 Truck controls, industrial battery

(G-15342)
NMB SIGNS INC
Also Called: Fastsigns
2831 Banksville Rd (15216-2815)
PHONE..................................412 344-5700
Barbara Belle, *President*
Norman Belle, *Corp Secy*
Sylvia Belle, *Vice Pres*
Christie Gardner, *Sales Staff*
EMP: 14
SQ FT: 4,000
SALES: 1.5MM **Privately Held**
WEB: www.nmbtz.com
SIC: 2759 7389 5999 3993 Commercial printing; lettering & sign painting services; banners, flags, decals & posters; signs, not made in custom sign painting shops

(G-15343)
NOFTZ SHEET METAL INC
2737 Penn Ave (15222-4711)
PHONE..................................412 471-1983
Toll Free:..................................888 -
Kenneth I Noftz, *President*
Ken Noftz, *President*
Lori J Noftz, *Corp Secy*
Wayne Noftz, *Vice Pres*
EMP: 20 **EST:** 1948
SQ FT: 58,000
SALES (est): 4.8MM **Privately Held**
WEB: www.noftz.com
SIC: 3444 Ducts, sheet metal

(G-15344)
NORMANDY INDUSTRIES INC (PA)
Also Called: Normandy Products
1150 Freeport Rd (15238-3104)
P.O. Box 446, Oakmont (15139-0446)
PHONE..................................412 826-1825
Robert L Americus, *President*
Lanny Seed, *Vice Pres*
EMP: 8 **EST:** 1947
SQ FT: 3,000
SALES (est): 12.5MM **Privately Held**
SIC: 3089 Fittings for pipe, plastic

(G-15345)
NORMANDY PRODUCTS COMPANY (HQ)
1150 Freeport Rd (15238-3104)
P.O. Box 446, Oakmont (15139-0446)
PHONE..................................412 826-1825
Robert L Americus, *President*
Scott Americus, *Vice Pres*
Lanny Seed, *Vice Pres*
Brian Jodkin, *Technology*
EMP: 8
SQ FT: 3,000
SALES (est): 6.6MM
SALES (corp-wide): 12.5MM **Privately Held**
WEB: www.normandyproducts.com
SIC: 3089 Fittings for pipe, plastic
PA: Normandy Industries, Inc.
1150 Freeport Rd
Pittsburgh PA 15238
412 826-1825

(G-15346)
NORTH AMERICAN DISPLAY
300 Camp Horne Rd (15202-1627)
PHONE..................................412 209-9988
Jeffrey Bouvy, *Principal*
EMP: 3
SALES (est): 291.5K **Privately Held**
SIC: 3993 Signs & advertising specialties

(G-15347)
NORTON OGLEBAY COMPANY (DH)
Also Called: Carmeuse Lime & Stone
11 Stanwix St Fl 21 (15222-1327)
PHONE..................................412 995-5500
Thomas A Buck, *President*
Jeffrey S Gray, *Vice Pres*
Bruce Routhieaux, *Vice Pres*
Paul Tunnicliffe, *Vice Pres*
Kevin White, *Vice Pres*
◆ **EMP:** 14 **EST:** 1854

SQ FT: 45,000
SALES (est): 58.4MM **Privately Held**
WEB: www.oglebaynorton.com
SIC: 1422 4432 4491 1446 Crushed & broken limestone; freight transportation on the Great Lakes; docks, piers & terminals; silica sand mining; perlite mining; pumice mining; iron ores
HQ: Carmeuse Lime & Stone, Inc.
11 Stanwix St Fl 21
Pittsburgh PA 15222
412 995-5500

(G-15348)
NORTON OGLEBAY SPECIALTY MNRL
Also Called: Carmeuse Lime & Stone
11 Stanwix St Fl 21 (15222-1327)
PHONE..................................412 995-5500
Thomas A Buck, *President*
Jack Fahler, *Vice Pres*
Paul Tunnicliffe, *Vice Pres*
Kevin White, *Vice Pres*
Caroll Laufmann, *VP Engrg*
EMP: 59
SALES (est): 174.2K **Privately Held**
SIC: 1422 Crushed & broken limestone
HQ: Norton Oglebay Company
11 Stanwix St Fl 21
Pittsburgh PA 15222
412 995-5500

(G-15349)
NOVA AURORA CORP
Also Called: Professional Health Pdts S W
781 Station St (15235)
PHONE..................................817 467-7567
Hersch Petrocelly, *President*
EMP: 3
SALES (est): 300K **Privately Held**
SIC: 2834 Vitamin, nutrient & hematinic preparations for human use

(G-15350)
NURELM INC
128 N Highland Ave # 201 (15206-3051)
P.O. Box 5549 (15206-0549)
PHONE..................................724 430-0490
Sami M Shaaban, *CEO*
Mona McGraw, *President*
Jeff Stuncard, *Manager*
EMP: 10
SQ FT: 12,000
SALES (est): 743.9K **Privately Held**
WEB: www.nurelm.com
SIC: 7372 Business oriented computer software

(G-15351)
NUTRICIA MFG USA INC
300 6th Ave (15222-2514)
PHONE..................................412 288-4600
EMP: 4
SALES (est): 601.1K **Publicly Held**
SIC: 3999 Manufacturing industries
PA: Gnc Holdings, Inc.
300 6th Ave Fl 2
Pittsburgh PA 15222

(G-15352)
O-N MINERALS CHEMSTONE COMPANY (DH)
Also Called: Carmeuse Lime & Stone
11 Stanwix St Fl 21 (15222-1327)
PHONE..................................412 995-5500
Thomas A Buck, *President*
Jack Fahler, *Vice Pres*
Paul Tunnicliffe, *Vice Pres*
Kevin White, *Vice Pres*
Caroll Laufmann, *VP Engrg*
▲ **EMP:** 172
SQ FT: 10,000
SALES (est): 125.4MM **Privately Held**
SIC: 1422 Crushed & broken limestone
HQ: O-N Minerals Company (Ohio)
11 Stanwix St Fl 21
Pittsburgh PA 15222
412 995-5500

(G-15353)
O-N MINERALS COMPANY (OHIO) (DH)
Also Called: Carmeuse Lime & Stone
11 Stanwix St Fl 21 (15222-1327)
PHONE..................................412 995-5500

Thomas A Buck, *President*
Jack Fahler, *Vice Pres*
Paul Tunnicliffe, *Vice Pres*
Kevin White, *Vice Pres*
Caroll Laufmann, *VP Engrg*
EMP: 7 **EST:** 2012
SALES (est): 128.3MM **Privately Held**
SIC: 1422 Crushed & broken limestone
HQ: Carmeuse Lime & Stone, Inc.
11 Stanwix St Fl 21
Pittsburgh PA 15222
412 995-5500

(G-15354)
O-N MINERALS LUTTRELL COMPANY (DH)
Also Called: Carmeuse Lime & Stone
11 Stanwix St Fl 21 (15222-1327)
PHONE....................................412 995-5500
Thomas A Buck, *President*
Jack Fahler, *Vice Pres*
Paul Tunnicliffe, *Vice Pres*
Kevin White, *Vice Pres*
Caroll Laufmann, *VP Engrg*
EMP: 11
SALES (est): 2.9MM **Privately Held**
SIC: 1422 Crushed & broken limestone
HQ: O-N Minerals Company (Ohio)
11 Stanwix St Fl 21
Pittsburgh PA 15222
412 995-5500

(G-15355)
O-N MINERALS MICHIGAN COMPANY (DH)
Also Called: Carmeuse Lime & Stone
11 Stanwix St Fl 21 (15222-1327)
PHONE....................................412 995-5500
Thomas A Buck, *President*
Jack Fahler, *Vice Pres*
Paul Tunnicliffe, *Vice Pres*
Kevin White, *Vice Pres*
Caroll Laufmann, *VP Engrg*
▲ **EMP:** 9
SALES (est): 3.7MM **Privately Held**
SIC: 1422 Crushed & broken limestone
HQ: Norton Oglebay Company
11 Stanwix St Fl 21
Pittsburgh PA 15222
412 995-5500

(G-15356)
O-N MINERALS PORTAGE CO LLC
Also Called: Carmeuse Lime & Stone
11 Stanwix St Fl 21 (15222-1327)
PHONE....................................412 995-5500
Thomas A Buck, *President*
Jack Fahler, *Vice Pres*
Paul Tunnicliffe, *Vice Pres*
Kevin White, *Vice Pres*
Caroll Laufmann, *VP Engrg*
EMP: 87
SALES (est): 3.1MM **Privately Held**
SIC: 1422 Crushed & broken limestone
HQ: Norton Oglebay Company
11 Stanwix St Fl 21
Pittsburgh PA 15222
412 995-5500

(G-15357)
OERLIKON MANAGEMENT USA INC
615 Epsilon Dr (15238-2807)
PHONE....................................412 967-7016
Cindy Racioppo, *Principal*
EMP: 12
SALES (est): 1.6MM
SALES (corp-wide): 2.6B **Privately Held**
SIC: 3433 Solar heaters & collectors
PA: Oc Oerlikon Corporation Ag, Pfaffikon
Churerstrasse 120
PfAffikon SZ 8808
583 609-696

(G-15358)
OHM- LABS INC
611 E Carson St (15203-1021)
PHONE....................................412 431-0640
Jay E Klevens, *President*
EMP: 12
SALES (est): 1.8MM **Privately Held**
WEB: www.ohm-labs.com
SIC: 3825 Instruments to measure electricity

(G-15359)
ONEILS CUSTOM CAB & DESIGN
5233 Gertrude St (15207-1771)
PHONE....................................412 422-4723
Mary Beth Doyle, *President*
Bill O'Neil, *CFO*
EMP: 10
SQ FT: 15,000
SALES: 400K **Privately Held**
SIC: 2599 7389 5712 1751 Cabinets, factory; design services; design, commercial & industrial; cabinet work, custom; cabinet building & installation

(G-15360)
ONLYBOTH INC
1110 S Negley Ave (15217-1048)
PHONE....................................412 303-8798
Raul Valdes-Perez, *CEO*
Andre Lessa, *CTO*
EMP: 3
SALES: 20K
SALES (corp-wide): 358.8K **Privately Held**
SIC: 7372 7389 Business oriented computer software;
PA: Valdes Capital Investments Llc
1110 S Negley Ave
Pittsburgh PA 15217
412 303-8798

(G-15361)
OPTIMIZED MARKETS INC
830 Amberson Ave (15232-2129)
PHONE....................................412 654-5994
Tuomas Sandholm, *President*
EMP: 5 **EST:** 2012
SALES (est): 253.3K **Privately Held**
SIC: 7372 Application computer software

(G-15362)
OPTIMUS TECHNOLOGIES INC
6901 Lynn Way (15208-2438)
PHONE....................................412 727-8228
Roger Byford, *COO*
Ian Winner, *Business Anlyst*
Colin Huwyler,
EMP: 10
SALES (est): 593.1K **Privately Held**
SIC: 3519 Internal combustion engines

(G-15363)
OREGON METALLURGICAL LLC (DH)
Also Called: ATI Albany Operations
1000 Six Ppg Pl (15222)
P.O. Box 460, Albany OR (97321-0460)
PHONE....................................541 967-9000
Jack W Shilling, *President*
John Sims, *Principal*
L Davis, *Principal*
Jon Walton, *Admin Sec*
Patrick J Decourcy,
▲ **EMP:** 10 **EST:** 1956
SALES (est): 12.8MM **Publicly Held**
WEB: www.h2membrane.com
SIC: 3356 3339 3369 Titanium; titanium & titanium alloy bars, sheets, strip, etc.; titanium metal, sponge & granules; titanium castings, except die-casting
HQ: Ati Operating Holdings, Llc
1000 Six Ppg Pl
Pittsburgh PA 15222
412 394-2800

(G-15364)
ORKIST LLC
322 N Shore Dr (15212-5875)
PHONE....................................412 346-8316
Cornita Pinchinat,
EMP: 3
SALES (est): 71.3K **Privately Held**
SIC: 7371 7372 Computer software systems analysis & design, custom; computer software writers, freelance; computer software development; educational computer software; home entertainment computer software

(G-15365)
OTOOLE PLASTIC SURGERY DR
5830 Ellsworth Ave # 300 (15232-1778)
PHONE....................................412 345-1615
James Otoole, *Principal*

EMP: 3 **EST:** 2014
SALES (est): 222.8K **Privately Held**
SIC: 2821 Plastics materials & resins

(G-15366)
P J ELECTRONICS INC
575 Davidson Rd (15239-1735)
PHONE....................................412 793-3912
Peter Mlynar, *President*
EMP: 7
SQ FT: 60,000
SALES (est): 1.3MM **Privately Held**
WEB: www.pjelectronics.com
SIC: 3829 5065 Testing equipment: abrasion, shearing strength, etc.; electronic parts & equipment

(G-15367)
PADDYCAKE BAKERY
4763 Liberty Ave (15224-2039)
PHONE....................................412 621-4477
Patrick Connolly, *Owner*
EMP: 39
SQ FT: 4,800
SALES (est): 1.3MM **Privately Held**
WEB: www.paddycakebakery.net
SIC: 5461 2052 2051 Cakes; cookies & crackers; bread, cake & related products

(G-15368)
PANNIER CORPORATION (PA)
207 Sandusky St (15212-5854)
PHONE....................................412 323-4900
John E Visconti, *President*
Robert Barker, *Superintendent*
Scott Heddaeus, *Co-President*
Jeffrey K Heddaeus Sr, *Vice Pres*
Howard Langston, *Purch Mgr*
▲ **EMP:** 15
SQ FT: 16,000
SALES (est): 17.9MM **Privately Held**
WEB: www.pannier.com
SIC: 3577 3542 3993 3549 Bar code (magnetic ink) printers; marking machines; signs, not made in custom sign painting shops; metalworking machinery; printing dies, rubber or plastic, for marking machines

(G-15369)
PARKER INDUSTRIES INC
Also Called: Parker Plastics
3585 Valley Dr (15234-2018)
PHONE....................................412 561-6902
Bette Blake Parker, *President*
Diane Moore, *Vice Pres*
Ken Murin, *Plant Mgr*
▲ **EMP:** 25
SQ FT: 22,000
SALES (est): 6.9MM **Privately Held**
SIC: 3089 3544 Injection molded finished plastic products; special dies, tools, jigs & fixtures

(G-15370)
PARMA SAUSAGE PRODUCTS INC
1734 Penn Ave (15222-4385)
PHONE....................................412 261-2532
Rina Edwards, *President*
Rita Spinabelli, *Vice Pres*
Darren Schumacher, *Sales Mgr*
EMP: 11 **EST:** 1955
SQ FT: 15,000
SALES (est): 1.4MM **Privately Held**
WEB: www.parmasausage.com
SIC: 2013 Sausages from purchased meat

(G-15371)
PAUL G BENEDUM JR
Also Called: Benedum Interests
223 4th Ave Ste 1500 (15222-1720)
PHONE....................................412 288-0280
Paul G Benedum Jr, *Owner*
EMP: 8
SQ FT: 3,500
SALES (est): 299.7K **Privately Held**
SIC: 1382 Oil & gas exploration services

(G-15372)
PECA LABS INC
4424 Penn Ave Ste 201 (15224-1338)
PHONE....................................412 589-9847
Douglas Bernstein, *CEO*
Steven Quinterno, *COO*
Arush Kalra, *Security Dir*

EMP: 5
SQ FT: 1,500
SALES (est): 245.7K **Privately Held**
SIC: 3841 Diagnostic apparatus, medical

(G-15373)
PENN A CASTER LOFT OFFICES
3030 Penn Ave (15201-1521)
PHONE....................................412 471-3285
Jeremy Kronman, *Exec VP*
Nathan Brindle, *Associate*
EMP: 3
SALES (est): 191.2K **Privately Held**
SIC: 3562 Casters

(G-15374)
PENNSYLVANIA AMERICAN WATER -
380 Becks Run Rd (15210-4366)
PHONE....................................412 884-5113
Tom Trok, *Principal*
EMP: 59
SALES (est): 7.2MM
SALES (corp-wide): 3.4B **Publicly Held**
SIC: 3589 Water purification equipment, household type
HQ: Pennsylvania - American Water Company
800 W Hershey Park Dr
Hershey PA 17033
717 533-5000

(G-15375)
PENNSYLVANIA BREWING COMPANY
Also Called: Penn Brewery
800 Vinial St Ste 1 (15212-5152)
PHONE....................................412 237-9400
Sandra Cindrich, *CEO*
Gene Mangrum, *General Mgr*
Stuart Nyman, *CFO*
Linda Nyman, *Mktg Dir*
▲ **EMP:** 38
SQ FT: 18,000
SALES (est): 2.4MM
SALES (corp-wide): 5.6MM **Privately Held**
WEB: www.pennbrew.com
SIC: 5813 2082 Tavern (drinking places); beer (alcoholic beverage)
PA: Birchmere Capital Management Llc
5000 Stonewood Dr Ste 220
Wexford PA 15090
724 940-2300

(G-15376)
PEPPERS PERFORMANCE EYEWARE
3001 Pulawski Way (15219-3725)
PHONE....................................412 688-8555
Daniel Thorn, *President*
Steven Pepper, *President*
◆ **EMP:** 22
SQ FT: 12,000
SALES (est): 3.8MM **Privately Held**
SIC: 3851 Ophthalmic goods

(G-15377)
PER MIDSTREAM LLC
1000 Commerce Dr Ste 400 (15275-1033)
PHONE....................................412 275-3200
Gregory D Muse, *President*
Robert Crissinger, *General Mgr*
Richard D Weber, *Principal*
John M Johnston, *Exec VP*
S Casey Bowers, *Senior VP*
EMP: 32 **EST:** 2014
SALES (est): 4.8MM **Privately Held**
SIC: 1382 Oil & gas exploration services

(G-15378)
PERFECT STRIDE LTD
1857 Tilton Dr (15241-2636)
PHONE....................................412 221-1722
Linda Benning, *Partner*
James M Benning, *Partner*
EMP: 3
SALES (est): 398.7K **Privately Held**
SIC: 3365 Aluminum & aluminum-based alloy castings

(G-15379)

PERROTTE WOOD FINISHING CO
19 35th St (15201-1917)
PHONE................................412 322-2592
Richard T Perrotte, *President*
Frank J Perrotte, *Vice Pres*
Gary Perrotte, *Admin Sec*
EMP: 7
SQ FT: 30,000
SALES: 2.1MM **Privately Held**
SIC: 2491 Millwork, treated wood

(G-15380)

PHOENIXX INTL RESOURCES INC
111 Delafield Rd (15215-3203)
PHONE................................412 782-7060
Brian P Helsel, *President*
Paul Helsel, *Principal*
Margueriete L Helsel, *Treasurer*
Patricia D Helsel, *Admin Sec*
EMP: 6 EST: 1990
SQ FT: 2,500
SALES (est): 381.3K
SALES (corp-wide): 1.9MM **Privately Held**
SIC: 3291 Abrasive metal & steel products
PA: Phoenixx, L.P.
111 Delafield Rd
Pittsburgh PA 15215
412 782-7060

(G-15381)

PIPES SKATE PARK
215 Obey St (15205-3434)
PHONE................................724 327-4247
William R Esch, *Owner*
Sander Esch, *Co-Owner*
EMP: 5
SALES: 100K **Privately Held**
SIC: 3949 Skates & parts, roller

(G-15382)

PITCAL INC
600 Grant St Ste 3214 (15219-2713)
PHONE................................412 433-1121
Thomas Usher, *Ch of Bd*
Charles A Corry, *Ch of Bd*
EMP: 3
SALES (est): 266K
SALES (corp-wide): 14.1B **Publicly Held**
SIC: 3429 Crab traps, steel
PA: United States Steel Corp
600 Grant St Ste 468
Pittsburgh PA 15219
412 433-1121

(G-15383)

PITNEY BOWES INC
800 Vinial St Ste B201 (15212-5152)
PHONE................................412 689-6639
Sally Sweep, *Branch Mgr*
EMP: 36
SALES (corp-wide): 3.5B **Publicly Held**
SIC: 3579 Mailing machines
PA: Pitney Bowes Inc.
3001 Summer St Ste 3
Stamford CT 06905
203 356-5000

(G-15384)

PITT OIL SERVICE INC
3498 Grand Ave (15225-1508)
PHONE................................412 771-6950
Richard E Langston Jr, *President*
Nancy C Langston Jr, *President*
Tom Langston, *President*
EMP: 3
SQ FT: 3,300
SALES (est): 340K **Privately Held**
SIC: 2992 4212 Lubricating oils; local trucking, without storage

(G-15385)

PITTS DOGGN IT LLC
260 Atwood St (15213-4286)
PHONE................................412 687-1440
Rahul Chovata, *Principal*
EMP: 4 EST: 2011
SALES (est): 265.1K **Privately Held**
SIC: 2087 Beverage bases

(G-15386)

PITTSBURGH ALUMINUM CO LLC
Also Called: Pittsburgh Window & Door
100 Evergreen Ave (15209-2351)
PHONE................................724 452-5900
Thomas M Conroy, *Mng Member*
James Conroy,
EMP: 12 EST: 1956
SQ FT: 6,000
SALES: 1.2MM **Privately Held**
WEB: www.pghwindowdoor.com
SIC: 1751 3442 3211 Window & door installation & erection; screens, window, metal; insulating glass, sealed units

(G-15387)

PITTSBURGH BINDING
2538 Mission St (15203-2444)
PHONE................................412 481-8108
Richard G Mirarchi, *Principal*
EMP: 36
SQ FT: 20,000
SALES (est): 3.8MM **Privately Held**
SIC: 2789 Binding only: books, pamphlets, magazines, etc.

(G-15388)

PITTSBURGH BREWING COMPANY
Also Called: Keystone Brewers
3340 Liberty Ave (15201-1394)
PHONE................................412 682-7400
Clifford Forrest, *President*
▲ **EMP:** 263
SALES (est): 32.5MM **Privately Held**
WEB: www.pittsburghbrewingco.com
SIC: 2082 Beer (alcoholic beverage); ale (alcoholic beverage)

(G-15389)

PITTSBURGH BUSINESS TIMES
45 S 23rd St (15203-2120)
PHONE................................412 481-6397
Allen Robertson, *Publisher*
Howard Burns, *Editor*
Douglas Fruehling, *Editor*
Laurie Lawrence, *Editor*
Ethan Lott, *Engineer*
EMP: 1
SALES (est): 2.5MM
SALES (corp-wide): 1.4B **Privately Held**
WEB: www.pittsburghbusinesstimes.com
SIC: 2711 2741 2721 Newspapers: publishing only, not printed on site; miscellaneous publishing; periodicals
HQ: American City Business Journals, Inc.
120 W Morehead St Ste 400
Charlotte NC 28202
704 973-1000

(G-15390)

PITTSBURGH CATHOLIC PUBG ASSOC
135 1st Ave Ste 200 (15222-1529)
PHONE................................412 471-1252
Kenneth Urish, *CEO*
Rita Ferki-Joyce, *President*
Eric Schorr, *Vice Pres*
EMP: 15
SQ FT: 3,750
SALES: 1.2MM **Privately Held**
WEB: www.pghcatholic.com
SIC: 2711 8661 Newspapers: publishing only, not printed on site; religious organizations

(G-15391)

PITTSBURGH CITY PAPER INC
650 Smithfield St # 2200 (15222-3925)
PHONE................................412 316-3342
Michael Fresling, *President*
Bill O'Driscoll, *Editor*
Kevin Shepherd, *Opers Staff*
Katy Jennings, *Sales Staff*
Deanna Krymowski, *Mktg Dir*
EMP: 32
SALES (est): 3.1MM **Privately Held**
SIC: 2711 Newspapers

(G-15392)

PITTSBURGH CORNING LLC (HQ)
800 Presque Isle Dr (15239-2799)
PHONE................................724 327-6100

James R Kane, *President*
Victor Delgado, *Engineer*
◆ **EMP:** 490
SQ FT: 45,000
SALES (est): 168.6MM **Publicly Held**
WEB: www.pcfoamglas.com
SIC: 3229 Pressed & blown glass

(G-15393)

PITTSBURGH DIGITAL
2530 Josephine St (15203-2458)
PHONE................................412 431-6008
Michael Mecca, *CEO*
EMP: 3
SALES (est): 246.5K **Privately Held**
WEB: www.pittsburghdigital.com
SIC: 7372 Prepackaged software

(G-15394)

PITTSBURGH DISTILLING CO LLC
Also Called: Wigle Whiskey
2401 Smallman St (15222-4673)
PHONE................................412 224-2827
Mark Meyer, *Mng Member*
EMP: 60
SQ FT: 1,200
SALES (est): 6.4MM **Privately Held**
SIC: 2085 Distilled & blended liquors

(G-15395)

PITTSBURGH FABRICATION MCH INC
3000 Grand Ave Ste 2 (15225-1614)
PHONE................................412 771-1400
Robert Drawl, *President*
Jan Drawl, *Corp Secy*
EMP: 20
SQ FT: 75,000
SALES (est): 3.9MM **Privately Held**
WEB: www.levyindustrial.com
SIC: 3441 Fabricated structural metal

(G-15396)

PITTSBURGH FILE & BOX CO
51 S 14th St (15203-1567)
PHONE................................412 431-5465
James Hess, *Owner*
EMP: 3 EST: 1926
SQ FT: 6,000
SALES: 500K **Privately Held**
SIC: 2652 2653 Filing boxes, paperboard: made from purchased materials; boxes, solid fiber: made from purchased materials

(G-15397)

PITTSBURGH FLATROLL COMPANY
1200 Reedsdale St Ste 3 (15233-2109)
PHONE................................412 237-2260
Michael Farrell, *President*
Tom Lomasney, *Vice Pres*
EMP: 5
SQ FT: 87,000
SALES (est): 750.1K **Privately Held**
SIC: 3312 3341 Blast furnaces & steel mills; secondary nonferrous metals

(G-15398)

PITTSBURGH GLASS WORKS LLC (HQ)
Also Called: Pgw
30 Isabella St Ste 500 (15212-5864)
PHONE................................412 995-6500
Joe Stas, *CEO*
Todd Fencak, *Vice Pres*
Ian Rogers, *VP Mfg*
Bruce Miller, *Project Mgr*
Tim Stauffer, *Export Mgr*
◆ **EMP:** 100
SALES (est): 1.4B **Privately Held**
WEB: www.pgwglass.com
SIC: 3211 5013 Flat glass; automobile glass

(G-15399)

PITTSBURGH JEWISH PUBLICATION
Also Called: Jewish Chronicle
5915 Beacon St (15217-2005)
PHONE................................412 687-1000
Barbara Befferman, *CEO*
Stephen Fienberg, *President*
EMP: 16

SQ FT: 3,000
SALES: 673.3K **Privately Held**
WEB: www.pittchron.com
SIC: 2711 8661 Newspapers, publishing & printing; religious organizations

(G-15400)

PITTSBURGH MAGAZINE
4802 5th Ave (15213-2942)
PHONE................................412 622-1360
George L Miles, *Principal*
EMP: 13
SALES (est): 966.2K **Privately Held**
SIC: 2721 Magazines: publishing only, not printed on site

(G-15401)

PITTSBURGH METAL PROCESSING CO
1850 Chapman St (15215-2708)
PHONE................................412 781-8053
Dorthy A Howat, *President*
EMP: 10 EST: 1944
SALES (est): 1.4MM **Privately Held**
WEB: www.pmpco.com
SIC: 3398 Metal heat treating

(G-15402)

PITTSBURGH MOBILE CONCRETE INC
1933 Babcock Blvd (15209-1303)
PHONE................................412 486-0186
Russell Zelich, *President*
EMP: 10 EST: 2009
SALES (est): 1.2MM **Privately Held**
SIC: 5099 3272 Durable goods; concrete products

(G-15403)

PITTSBURGH PHOTON STUDIO LLC
393 Vanadium Rd (15243-1427)
PHONE................................724 263-6502
EMP: 3
SALES (est): 137.2K **Privately Held**
SIC: 3661 Fiber optics communications equipment

(G-15404)

PITTSBURGH PRECISION
Also Called: Pptp
100 Herman Dr (15239-1744)
PHONE................................412 712-1111
Craig Neal, *President*
William Lobodinsky, *QC Mgr*
Ivan Doverspike,
▼ **EMP:** 29
SQ FT: 30,000
SALES (est): 10.5MM **Privately Held**
SIC: 3451 Screw machine products

(G-15405)

PITTSBURGH PROFESSIONAL MAGAZI
1885 Tilton Dr (15241-2636)
PHONE................................412 221-2992
Michael Yablonski, *Principal*
EMP: 3
SALES (est): 188.2K **Privately Held**
SIC: 2721 Magazines: publishing only, not printed on site

(G-15406)

PITTSBURGH PRTG SOLUTIONS LLC
1020 Timber Ridge Dr (15239-1640)
PHONE................................412 977-2026
Gary L Hill, *Principal*
EMP: 6
SALES (est): 731.5K **Privately Held**
SIC: 2759 Commercial printing

(G-15407)

PITTSBURGH SPECIAL-T DAIRY LLC (HQ)
1614 Brownsville Rd (15210-3986)
PHONE................................412 881-1409
Carl Colteryahn III, *President*
EMP: 50 EST: 1919
SQ FT: 10,000

G E O G R A P H I C

SALES (est): 43.4MM
SALES (corp-wide): 73.6MM **Privately Held**
WEB: www.colteryahndairy.com
SIC: 2026 5143 Fluid milk; milk & cream, fluid
PA: Turner Dairy Farms, Inc.
1049 Jefferson Rd
Pittsburgh PA 15235
412 372-7155

(G-15408)
PITTSBURGH SPICE SEASONING CO
Also Called: Pittsburgh Casing Co
1235 Clairhaven St (15205-3621)
PHONE..................................412 288-5036
Robert Rondinelli, *President*
Greg Mancini, *Vice Pres*
EMP: 8
SQ FT: 6,000
SALES (est): 958.8K **Privately Held**
WEB: www.pghspice.com
SIC: 5499 5149 2013 Spices & herbs; spices & seasonings; sausage casings, natural

(G-15409)
PITTSBURGH STAINED GL STUDIO
Also Called: Pittsburgh Stained GL Studios
160 Warden St (15220-5419)
PHONE..................................412 921-2500
John D Weaver Jr, *President*
Evelyn Weaver, *Treasurer*
EMP: 12
SQ FT: 5,000
SALES (est): 1.3MM **Privately Held**
SIC: 3231 1793 Stained glass: made from purchased glass; glass & glazing work

(G-15410)
PITTSBURGH TECHNOLOGY COUNCIL
2000 Tech Dr Ste 100 (15219)
PHONE..................................412 687-2700
Audrey Russo, *President*
Audrey Russel, *President*
Bryan Bowman, *Corp Comm Staff*
Heidi Huck, *Advt Staff*
EMP: 40
SQ FT: 7,000
SALES (est): 2.9MM **Privately Held**
SIC: 8611 2741 2721 Trade associations; miscellaneous publishing; periodicals

(G-15411)
PITTSBURGH TROPHY COMPANY INC
3225 Penn Ave (15201-1422)
PHONE..................................412 261-4376
Keith Nellis, *President*
Anna McCullough, *Graphic Designe*
EMP: 6
SQ FT: 2,000
SALES (est): 916.3K **Privately Held**
WEB: www.pittsburghtrophy.com
SIC: 5999 3914 Trophies & plaques; trophies

(G-15412)
PITTSBURGH WINERY
2815 Penn Ave (15222-4713)
PHONE..................................412 566-1000
Tim Gaber, *Owner*
EMP: 5
SALES (est): 330.3K **Privately Held**
SIC: 2084 Wines

(G-15413)
PITTSBURGH WOOL CO INC
2401 Smallman St (15222-4673)
PHONE..................................412 642-0606
Jeff Kumer, *President*
EMP: 5
SQ FT: 100,000
SALES (est): 439.5K **Privately Held**
SIC: 3999 Wool pulling

(G-15414)
PKT TECHNOLOGIES
114 Technology Dr (15275)
PHONE..................................412 494-5600
Alan Hayes, *President*
EMP: 22

SALES: 2.5MM **Privately Held**
SIC: 3569 Liquid automation machinery & equipment

(G-15415)
PLANTSCAPE INC (PA)
Also Called: MALL SILKS
3101 Liberty Ave (15201-1400)
PHONE..................................412 281-6352
Carole Horowitz, *President*
Cindy Urbach, *Vice Pres*
Thomas Horowitz, *Admin Sec*
EMP: 65
SQ FT: 65,000
SALES: 5.6MM **Privately Held**
WEB: www.plantscapeinc.com
SIC: 3999 0781 5992 0782 Artificial trees & flowers; horticulture services; plants, potted; lawn & garden services

(G-15416)
PLATYPUS LLC
2010 Smallman St (15222-4428)
PHONE..................................412 979-4629
Paul Scerri, *General Mgr*
Paul Cherry,
EMP: 6 EST: 2012
SALES (est): 468.2K **Privately Held**
SIC: 3535 Robotic conveyors

(G-15417)
PNC EQUITY PARTNERS LP (PA)
620 Liberty Ave (15222-2722)
PHONE..................................412 914-0175
David McL Hillman, *Partner*
Wali Bacdayan, *Partner*
Peter V Del Presto, *Partner*
John C Glover, *Partner*
◆ EMP: 13
SALES (est): 24.9MM **Privately Held**
SIC: 3589 3851 Water treatment equipment, industrial; sewage treatment equipment; ophthalmic goods

(G-15418)
POIESIS INFORMATICS INC
1710 Murray Ave Ste 1 (15217-1687)
PHONE..................................412 327-8766
Duncan James, *President*
Claudine Martin, *President*
EMP: 5
SALES (est): 228.8K **Privately Held**
SIC: 7372 Prepackaged software

(G-15419)
POLYCYCLE INDUSTRIAL PDTS INC
5501 Campbells Run Rd (15205-1025)
PHONE..................................412 747-1101
Terry Aarnio, *CEO*
Larry Macioce, *President*
▼ EMP: 25
SALES (est): 4.8MM
SALES (corp-wide): 599.5MM **Privately Held**
WEB: www.polycycle.com
SIC: 3089 Plastic & fiberglass tanks; plastic processing
HQ: Vigor Works Llc
9700 Se Lawnfield Rd
Clackamas OR 97015
503 653-6300

(G-15420)
PORT PITTSBURGH DISTILLERY LLC
1330 Akehurst Rd (15220-2549)
PHONE..................................412 294-8071
EMP: 3 EST: 2015
SALES (est): 151K **Privately Held**
SIC: 2085 Distilled & blended liquors

(G-15421)
POTOMAC BAKERY INC
1419 Potomac Ave (15216-2689)
PHONE..................................412 531-5066
Bob Tate, *President*
Lynda Tate, *Treasurer*
EMP: 20 EST: 1927
SQ FT: 1,350
SALES (est): 957.5K **Privately Held**
SIC: 5461 2051 Bread; pastries; cookies; bakery: wholesale or wholesale/retail combined

(G-15422)
POWERCAST CORPORATION
620 Alpha Dr Ste 1 (15238-2836)
PHONE..................................412 455-5800
Charles Goetz, *CEO*
Eric Biel, *Engineer*
Daniel Harrist, *Engineer*
Carrie Carlino, *VP Sales*
Charles Greene, *CTO*
EMP: 6
SALES (est): 1.4MM **Privately Held**
SIC: 3679 8711 Attenuators; engineering services

(G-15423)
POWERTRACK INTERNATIONAL LLC (PA)
Also Called: Texas Hose Products
4605 Campbells Run Rd (15205-1315)
PHONE..................................412 787-4444
Andrew Kuron, *President*
Alfred G Lunz, *Vice Pres*
▲ EMP: 31 EST: 1974
SQ FT: 21,000
SALES (est): 30.3MM **Privately Held**
SIC: 5085 3492 3429 3052 Hose, belting & packing; fluid power valves & hose fittings; manufactured hardware (general); rubber & plastics hose & beltings

(G-15424)
POWERTRACK INTERNATIONAL LLC
4625 Campbells Run Rd (15205-1315)
PHONE..................................412 787-4444
Mary Hampton, *Principal*
EMP: 4
SALES (corp-wide): 30.3MM **Privately Held**
SIC: 5085 3492 Hose, belting & packing; hose & tube fittings & assemblies, hydraulic/pneumatic
PA: Powertrack International, Llc
4605 Campbells Run Rd
Pittsburgh PA 15205
412 787-4444

(G-15425)
PPG INDUSTRIES INC (PA)
1 Ppg Pl (15272-0001)
PHONE..................................412 434-3131
Michael H McGarry, *Ch of Bd*
Johnny Chiou, *General Mgr*
Scott Haynes, *Regional Mgr*
Glenn E Bost II, *Senior VP*
Anne M Foulkes, *Senior VP*
EMP: 1400 EST: 1883
SALES: 15.3B **Publicly Held**
WEB: www.ppg.com
SIC: 2851 3211 3231 3229 Paints & allied products; paints & paint additives; coating, air curing; lacquers, varnishes, enamels & other coatings; flat glass; strengthened or reinforced glass; windshields, glass: made from purchased glass; glass fiber products; fiber optics strands; alkalies & chlorine; chlorine, compressed or liquefied; caustic soda, sodium hydroxide; plastics materials & resins

(G-15426)
PPG INDUSTRIES INC
1 Ppg Pl (15272-0001)
PHONE..................................412 434-4463
Michael Tutolo, *Branch Mgr*
EMP: 14
SQ FT: 30,000
SALES (corp-wide): 15.3B **Publicly Held**
SIC: 2851 Paints & allied products
PA: Ppg Industries, Inc.
1 Ppg Pl
Pittsburgh PA 15272
412 434-3131

(G-15427)
PPG INDUSTRIES FOUNDATION
1 Ppg Pl (15272-0001)
PHONE..................................412 434-3131
Lynne Schmidt, *Director*
EMP: 3
SQ FT: 1,000
SALES: 5.9MM **Privately Held**
SIC: 2851 Paints & allied products

(G-15428)
PRANTLS OF SHADYSIDE LLC
Also Called: Prantl's Bakery
5100 5th Ave Apt 311 (15232-2185)
PHONE..................................412 621-2092
Lara Bruhn, *Mng Member*
Annette Mich,
EMP: 13
SQ FT: 1,080
SALES: 1.3MM **Privately Held**
SIC: 5461 2051 Cakes; bread, cake & related products

(G-15429)
PRAXAIR DISTRIBUTION INC
28 Mccandless Ave (15201-2632)
PHONE..................................412 781-6273
Terry Peyton, *Manager*
EMP: 17 **Privately Held**
SIC: 5084 5999 2813 Welding machinery & equipment; welding supplies; carbon dioxide
HQ: Praxair Distribution, Inc.
10 Riverview Dr
Danbury CT 06810
203 837-2000

(G-15430)
PRC - DESOTO INTERNATIONAL INC
1 Ppg Pl (15272-0001)
PHONE..................................412 434-3131
Barry N Gillespie, *CEO*
EMP: 6
SALES (est): 835.5K
SALES (corp-wide): 15.3B **Publicly Held**
SIC: 2891 Sealants
PA: Ppg Industries, Inc.
1 Ppg Pl
Pittsburgh PA 15272
412 434-3131

(G-15431)
PRCO AMERICA INC
8150 Perry Hwy Ste 105 (15237-5232)
P.O. Box 30, Glenshaw (15116-0030)
PHONE..................................412 837-2798
▲ EMP: 12 EST: 2008
SALES (est): 1.1MM **Privately Held**
SIC: 1081 Metal mining services

(G-15432)
PRECISION SIGN & AWNING
1021 5th Ave (15219)
PHONE..................................412 281-0330
Mark Bertenthal, *President*
Goldie Bertenthal, *Vice Pres*
David Bertenthal, *Treasurer*
EMP: 9
SALES: 925K **Privately Held**
SIC: 3993 5199 Signs, not made in custom sign painting shops; advertising specialties

(G-15433)
PRECISION TECHNOLOGY ASSOC INC
Also Called: T.F.campbell Co.
1203 Edgebrook Ave (15226-1453)
PHONE..................................412 881-8006
Gina J Ladefian, *President*
EMP: 3 EST: 2003
SALES (est): 220.4K **Privately Held**
SIC: 3822 3585 Auto controls regulating residntl & coml environmt & applncs; parts for heating, cooling & refrigerating equipment

(G-15434)
PRESS CRAFT PRINTERS INC
532 California Ave 34 (15202-2453)
PHONE..................................412 761-8200
Bill Miller, *President*
EMP: 4
SQ FT: 3,000
SALES (est): 618K **Privately Held**
SIC: 2752 2759 Commercial printing, offset; letterpress printing

(G-15435)
PRESSURE CHEMICAL CO
3419 Smallman St (15201-1997)
PHONE..................................412 682-5882
John Pannucci, *CEO*
Brandon Ritchie, *Project Mgr*

Stephen Smith, *QC Mgr*
Rebecca Ostrzeniec, *Marketing Staff*
Mark Buraczewski, *Project Leader*
▲ **EMP**: 46 **EST**: 1964
SQ FT: 39,000
SALES: 15MM **Privately Held**
WEB: www.presschem.com
SIC: 2899 2819 Chemical preparations; nonmetallic compounds

(G-15436)
PRESSURE WATER SYSTEMS OF PA
130 Amabell St (15211-1402)
PHONE...................................412 668-0878
Michael Fritch, *Principal*
EMP: 6
SALES (est): 799.5K **Privately Held**
SIC: 3452 Washers

(G-15437)
PRETZEL SHOP
2316 E Carson St (15203-2110)
PHONE...................................412 431-2574
Catherine Bowen, *Owner*
EMP: 10
SALES (est): 490K **Privately Held**
SIC: 2052 5461 Pretzels; pretzels

(G-15438)
PRIME RIBBON INC (PA)
Also Called: Ribbon Renu
1239 Woodland Ave (15212-2633)
PHONE...................................412 761-4470
Adelbert J Tarasovich, *President*
EMP: 4
SALES (est): 450.1K **Privately Held**
WEB: www.primeinkjets.com
SIC: 3955 5112 Ribbons, inked: typewriter, adding machine, register, etc.; print cartridges for laser & other computer printers; stationery & office supplies

(G-15439)
PRINT ESCAPE LLC
5886 Hobart St (15217-2110)
P.O. Box 8230 (15217-0230)
PHONE...................................888 524-8690
EMP: 4 **EST**: 2016
SALES (est): 101.5K **Privately Held**
SIC: 2752 Commercial printing, lithographic

(G-15440)
PRINT TECH WESTERN PA (PA)
250 Alpha Dr (15238-2906)
PHONE...................................412 963-1500
Rod McMahon, *President*
Mike Graham, *Vice Pres*
Michael Diana, *Accounting Mgr*
Bruce Gleason, *Accounts Mgr*
Eric Pursh, *Accounts Mgr*
EMP: 22
SQ FT: 15,000
SALES: 7.8MM **Privately Held**
WEB: www.printtechofwpa.com
SIC: 2752 7334 2791 Commercial printing, offset; photocopying & duplicating services; typesetting

(G-15441)
PRINT TECH WESTERN PA
250 Alpha Dr (15238-2906)
PHONE...................................412 963-1500
Rick Baker, *Manager*
EMP: 12
SALES (corp-wide): 7.8MM **Privately Held**
WEB: www.printtechofwpa.com
SIC: 2759 Commercial printing
PA: Print Tech Of Western Pennsylvania
250 Alpha Dr
Pittsburgh PA 15238
412 963-1500

(G-15442)
PRINTBIZ LLC
4611 W Lawnview Ave (15227-1125)
PHONE...................................412 881-3318
Kathleen McPaul,
EMP: 4
SALES: 300K **Privately Held**
WEB: www.printbizpittsburgh.com
SIC: 2752 Commercial printing, lithographic

(G-15443)
PRINTDROPPER INC
945 Vista Park Dr (15205-1201)
PHONE...................................412 657-6170
Oliver Said, *Principal*
Jay Stipetic, *Principal*
EMP: 17
SQ FT: 9,759
SALES (est): 452.9K **Privately Held**
SIC: 2396 Fabric printing & stamping

(G-15444)
PRINTEX LLC
201 N Braddock Ave (15208-2598)
PHONE...................................412 371-6667
Thomas Hoburg, *President*
EMP: 5 **EST**: 2015
SQ FT: 2,200
SALES (est): 332.5K **Privately Held**
SIC: 2396 Screen printing on fabric articles

(G-15445)
PRINTING POST LLC
3458 Babcock Blvd Ste 2 (15237-2445)
PHONE...................................412 367-7468
Neil Deluca,
Allan A Deluca,
EMP: 4
SQ FT: 1,400
SALES (est): 450K **Privately Held**
WEB: www.theprintingpost.net
SIC: 2752 7311 Commercial printing, offset; advertising agencies

(G-15446)
PRINTWORX INC
Also Called: Envelope Worx
159 Cemetery Ln (15237-2719)
PHONE...................................412 939-6004
Walter Lang Jr, *President*
James Tate, *Vice Pres*
EMP: 6
SALES (est): 536.8K **Privately Held**
SIC: 2759 Commercial printing

(G-15447)
PRISM FIBER OPTICS INC
4514 Plummer St (15201-3032)
PHONE...................................412 802-0750
Bill Miller, *President*
Pete Luxton, *Vice Pres*
EMP: 3
SALES (est): 259.3K **Privately Held**
WEB: www.prismfiberoptics.com
SIC: 3993 Neon signs

(G-15448)
PRISMA INC
790 Holiday Dr Ste 11 (15220-2750)
PHONE...................................412 503-4006
Anthony Sciorilli, *President*
Mike Sullivan, *Corp Secy*
Edward J Chiodo, *Vice Pres*
EMP: 25
SQ FT: 3,500
SALES (est): 1.6MM **Privately Held**
SIC: 2741 Miscellaneous publishing

(G-15449)
PRISMATIC CONSULTING LLC
Also Called: Owl Testing Software
1484 Washington Rd (15228-1633)
PHONE...................................412 915-9072
Chris Dalessandri, *Mng Member*
Irwin Hurst,
EMP: 5
SALES (est): 425.8K **Privately Held**
WEB: www.prismaticconsulting.com
SIC: 7372 Prepackaged software

(G-15450)
PRO THERMAL INC
Also Called: Hinkle & Co
114 Lamar Rd (15241-1547)
P.O. Box 714, Bridgeville (15017-0714)
PHONE...................................412 203-1588
Timothy Biery, *Principal*
EMP: 4
SQ FT: 1,500
SALES (est): 541.3K **Privately Held**
SIC: 3443 Heat exchangers, condensers & components

(G-15451)
PROCESS INSTRUMENTS INC
615 E Carson St (15203-1021)
PHONE...................................412 431-4600
Tom Santacroce, *President*
Karl Klevens, *President*
Dale Robertson, *Corp Secy*
Jason Furlong, *Manager*
EMP: 23
SQ FT: 10,000
SALES (est): 4.6MM **Privately Held**
WEB: www.procinst.com
SIC: 7699 3825 3829 3822 Caliper, gauge & other machinists' instrument repair; lab standards, electric: resistance, inductance, capacitance; measuring & controlling devices; auto controls regulating residntl & coml environmt & applncs; relays & industrial controls; temperature measurement instruments, industrial

(G-15452)
PROCESS REPRODUCTIONS INC
939 W North Ave (15233-1605)
PHONE...................................412 321-3120
Paul J Neugebauer, *President*
Stephen Neugebauer, *Vice Pres*
Gary Kascur, *Sales Staff*
EMP: 27
SQ FT: 25,000
SALES (est): 4.8MM **Privately Held**
WEB: www.processreproductions.com
SIC: 2752 Commercial printing, offset

(G-15453)
PROMINENT FLUID CONTROLS INC (HQ)
136 Industry Dr (15275-1014)
PHONE...................................412 787-2484
Victor Dulger, *President*
Sandy Chu, *Vice Pres*
Kevin Pointer, *Engineer*
Brian Rodgers, *Project Engr*
Fran Perfett, *Treasurer*
▲ **EMP**: 36
SQ FT: 22,000
SALES (est): 13.4MM
SALES (corp-wide): 410.5MM **Privately Held**
SIC: 3824 3613 3825 Fluid meters & counting devices; switchgear & switchboard apparatus; meters: electric, pocket, portable, panelboard, etc.
PA: Prominent Gmbh
Im Schuhmachergewann 5-11
Heidelberg 69123
622 184-20

(G-15454)
PROMOTE ME PRINTING
134 Ridgewood Rd (15237-4050)
PHONE...................................412 486-2504
Maria Shepard, *Principal*
EMP: 3 **EST**: 2009
SALES (est): 234.9K **Privately Held**
SIC: 2759 Commercial printing

(G-15455)
PUBLICSOURCE
6300 5th Ave (15232-2922)
PHONE...................................412 315-0264
Halle Stockton, *Editor*
Mila Sanina, *Exec Dir*
EMP: 6
SALES (est): 298.6K **Privately Held**
SIC: 2711 Newspapers

(G-15456)
PURBLU BEVERAGES INC
1 Oxford Ctr Ste 820 (15219-1400)
PHONE...................................412 281-9808
Benjamin Lewis, *President*
EMP: 6
SQ FT: 1,800
SALES (est): 390K **Privately Held**
SIC: 2082 Malt beverage products

(G-15457)
PURE SCREENPRINTING INC
428 Bingham St (15203-1002)
PHONE...................................412 246-2048
Henry Panza, *Principal*
EMP: 3

SALES (est): 202.4K **Privately Held**
SIC: 2759 Screen printing

(G-15458)
PVS STEEL SERVICES INC
Fster Plz Ste 7661 (15220)
PHONE...................................412 929-0177
Jonathan S Taub, *Principal*
EMP: 175
SALES (corp-wide): 628.6MM **Privately Held**
SIC: 4953 2816 Recycling, waste materials; iron oxide pigments (ochers, siennas, umbers)
HQ: Pvs Steel Services, Inc.
1111 State Road 149
Burns Harbor IN 46304
313 921-1200

(G-15459)
QUALITY AGGREGATES INC (PA)
4955 Steubenville Pike (15205-9619)
P.O. Box 112700 (15241-0300)
PHONE...................................412 777-6704
Joseph Aloe, *President*
Gary Musto, *Vice Pres*
Michele Greene, *Treasurer*
Michelle Greene, *Treasurer*
Kathryn A Cashman, *Admin Sec*
EMP: 10
SQ FT: 4,000
SALES (est): 16.6MM **Privately Held**
WEB: www.aquascape-env.com
SIC: 1221 Bituminous coal & lignite-surface mining

(G-15460)
QUALITY CONCRETE INC
Also Called: Here Own By Bryan Materials
1051 Mccartney St (15220-5406)
PHONE...................................412 922-0200
Matt Bryan, *President*
Thomas Bryan, *Admin Sec*
EMP: 8 **EST**: 1977
SQ FT: 3,000
SALES: 3MM **Privately Held**
SIC: 3273 3272 Ready-mixed concrete; concrete products, precast

(G-15461)
QUANTUM ONE
2 Hot Metal St Ste 135 (15203-2348)
PHONE...................................412 432-5234
EMP: 11
SALES (est): 1.2MM **Privately Held**
SIC: 3572 Computer storage devices

(G-15462)
QUESTA PETROLEUM COMPANY
1580 Mclaughlin Run Rd (15241-3100)
P.O. Box 12863 (15241-0863)
PHONE...................................412 220-9210
Donald D Funnell, *President*
EMP: 7
SQ FT: 1,200
SALES (est): 682.5K **Privately Held**
SIC: 1311 Natural gas production

(G-15463)
R L HOLLIDAY COMPANY INC (PA)
525 Mcneilly Rd (15226-2503)
PHONE...................................412 561-7620
Richard L Holliday, *President*
EMP: 8
SQ FT: 3,000
SALES (est): 1.4MM **Privately Held**
WEB: www.rlholliday.com
SIC: 3829 Measuring & controlling devices

(G-15464)
R&N MANUFACTURING LLC
3500 Neville Rd (15225-1412)
PHONE...................................412 778-4103
EMP: 25
SALES (est): 3.5MM **Privately Held**
SIC: 3441 Building components, structural steel

(G-15465)
RADIO PARTS COMPANY
Also Called: Camrpc Electronics
650 Alpha Dr (15238-2802)
PHONE..............................412 963-6202
Arie Segall, *CEO*
Roslyn Segall, *Corp Secy*
Lynda Persson, *Vice Pres*
Benjamin Segall, *Vice Pres*
Herschel Segall, *CFO*
▲ EMP: 29
SQ FT: 20,000
SALES (est): 21.5MM **Privately Held**
WEB: www.camrpc.com
SIC: 5065 3999 Electronic parts; barber & beauty shop equipment

(G-15466)
RAFF PRINTING INC
2201 Mary St (15203-2222)
P.O. Box 42365 (15203-0365)
PHONE..............................412 431-4044
Fred C Aheimer, *President*
Fred Aheimer Jr, *Vice Pres*
Ron Yeckel, *Vice Pres*
Kim Yeckel, *Treasurer*
EMP: 90 EST: 1940
SQ FT: 28,000
SALES (est): 15.7MM **Privately Held**
WEB: www.raffprinting.com
SIC: 2752 2791 2789 Commercial printing, offset; typesetting; bookbinding & related work

(G-15467)
RANDALL INDUSTRIES LLC
1801 Centre Ave Ste 300 (15219-4376)
PHONE..............................412 281-6901
Jim Terwoord, *Principal*
EMP: 3
SALES (est): 411.9K **Privately Held**
SIC: 3999 Manufacturing industries

(G-15468)
RAPID TPC LLC
6945 Lynn Way (15208-2438)
PHONE..............................412 450-0482
David Herring, *Principal*
Mark Jreissaty, *Principal*
Benjamin Charley, *Mng Member*
EMP: 10
SALES (est): 396K **Privately Held**
SIC: 3083 Thermoplastic laminates: rods, tubes, plates & sheet; airplanes, toy; surgical & medical instruments

(G-15469)
RAYMOND DUNN
109 Seville Ave (15214-1029)
PHONE..............................412 734-2135
Raymond Dunn, *COO*
EMP: 3 EST: 2016
SALES (est): 103K **Privately Held**
SIC: 3052 Rubber & plastics hose & beltings

(G-15470)
RAZZY FRESH FRZ YOGURT FORBES
3533 Forbes Ave (15213-3306)
PHONE..............................412 586-5270
James X Chen, *Principal*
EMP: 4 EST: 2010
SALES (est): 276K **Privately Held**
SIC: 2026 Yogurt

(G-15471)
RBS IMPEX INC
717 Liberty Ave Ste 414 (15222-3510)
P.O. Box 13430 (15243-0430)
PHONE..............................412 566-2488
R Bharat Shah, *President*
EMP: 4
SQ FT: 800
SALES (est): 499.5K **Privately Held**
SIC: 3911 5094 Jewelry, precious metal; precious stones (gems); diamonds (gems)

(G-15472)
RE2 INC
4925 Harrison St (15201-2722)
PHONE..............................412 681-6382
Jorgen Pedersen, *President*
Jessica Pedersen, *COO*

Keith Gunnett, *Vice Pres*
Douglas Peters, *Vice Pres*
Carolyn Lehecka, *Project Mgr*
EMP: 22
SQ FT: 1,200
SALES (est): 4.2MM **Privately Held**
WEB: www.resquared.com
SIC: 8711 3812 8731 Engineering services; search & navigation equipment; commercial physical research

(G-15473)
RED SQUARE CORP
1722 Murray Ave Fl 2 (15217-1604)
PHONE..............................412 422-8631
Michael Kwadrat, *President*
Yulia Mostovoi, *Manager*
◆ EMP: 5
SALES (est): 1.4MM **Privately Held**
SIC: 2421 Building & structural materials, wood

(G-15474)
REDSTAR IRONWORKS LLC
2 Sedgwick St (15209-2724)
PHONE..............................412 821-3630
Peter Lambert, *Mng Member*
EMP: 9
SQ FT: 10,000
SALES (est): 500K **Privately Held**
WEB: www.redstarironworks.com
SIC: 3446 Ornamental metalwork

(G-15475)
REECON NORTH AMERICA LLC
Also Called: Thermablaster
2515 Liberty Ave (15222-4613)
PHONE..............................412 850-8001
David Brand,
▲ EMP: 7
SQ FT: 2,500
SALES (est): 1.4MM **Privately Held**
WEB: www.thermablaster.com
SIC: 3272 3699 Fireplace & chimney material: concrete; fireplace logs, electric

(G-15476)
REED & WITTING COMPANY
2900 Sassafras Way (15201-1547)
PHONE..............................412 682-1000
Edward J Cyphers, *President*
Jill Cyphers, *Corp Secy*
EMP: 40 EST: 1900
SQ FT: 20,000
SALES (est): 7.5MM **Privately Held**
WEB: www.reed-witting.com
SIC: 2752 2789 2759 2672 Commercial printing, offset; bookbinding & related work; commercial printing; coated & laminated paper

(G-15477)
REFINED OUTOOR LVNG ENVIRNMNTS
2130 Reis Run Rd (15237-1445)
PHONE..............................412 635-8440
Edward Bayer, *Principal*
EMP: 5
SALES (est): 523.2K **Privately Held**
SIC: 3271 Landscape counseling & planning

(G-15478)
RENERVA LLC
217 Vine St (15218-1340)
PHONE..............................412 841-7966
Lorenzo Soletti, *Mng Member*
EMP: 6 EST: 2017
SALES (est): 80.5K **Privately Held**
SIC: 3841 7389 Surgical & medical instruments;

(G-15479)
RESCO GROUP INC
1 Robinson Plz 300 (15205-1021)
PHONE..............................412 494-4491
William K Brown, *President*
EMP: 12
SALES (est): 1.4MM
SALES (corp-wide): 210.1MM **Privately Held**
SIC: 3297 3255 1455 Cement: high temperature, refractory (nonclay); clay refractories; kaolin & ball clay

PA: Resco Products, Inc.
6600 Steubenville Pike # 1
Pittsburgh PA 15205
888 283-5505

(G-15480)
RESOURCE DYNAMICS INCORPORATED
1549 Field Club Dr (15237-1525)
PHONE..............................412 369-7760
A J Kyriazis, *President*
Rochelle Kyriazis, *Vice Pres*
EMP: 2
SALES: 1MM **Privately Held**
SIC: 2064 Candy & other confectionery products

(G-15481)
REYNA FOODS INC
2031 Penn Ave Ste 3 (15222-4456)
P.O. Box 407, Cadogan (16212-0407)
PHONE..............................412 904-1242
Nick Dicio, *President*
Tony Dicio, *General Mgr*
EMP: 6
SQ FT: 4,000
SALES: 590K **Privately Held**
SIC: 5411 2096 Grocery stores; tortilla chips

(G-15482)
REYNOLDS METALS COMPANY LLC
Also Called: Alcoa
573 Audubon Ave (15228-2601)
PHONE..............................412 343-5020
Steven N Triano, *Manager*
EMP: 10
SALES (corp-wide): 13.4B **Publicly Held**
SIC: 3411 Aluminum cans
HQ: Reynolds Metals Company, Llc
390 Park Ave
New York NY 10022
212 518-5400

(G-15483)
REYNOLDS PRESTO PRODUCTS INC
Reynolds Consumer Products Co
201 Isabella St (15212-5872)
P.O. Box 535602 (15253-5602)
PHONE..............................866 254-3310
Gino Mangione, *Vice Pres*
EMP: 310
SALES (corp-wide): 1MM **Privately Held**
SIC: 2671 2673 3842 Plastic film, coated or laminated for packaging; food storage & frozen food bags, plastic; swabs, sanitary cotton
HQ: Reynolds Presto Products Inc.
670 N Perkins St
Appleton WI 54914
800 558-3525

(G-15484)
RICHARD RIBERICH
Also Called: Custom Wood Products
1027 Wilkins Ave (15221-4769)
PHONE..............................412 271-8427
Richard Riberich, *Owner*
EMP: 4
SALES (est): 410K **Privately Held**
SIC: 2541 1751 2521 2517 Cabinets, lockers & shelving; cabinet & finish carpentry; wood office furniture; wood television & radio cabinets; wood kitchen cabinets

(G-15485)
RICKS QUICK PRINTING INC
Also Called: Banksville Express
2239 Banksville Rd (15216-3111)
PHONE..............................412 571-0333
Richard Ozanick, *President*
EMP: 21
SQ FT: 10,500
SALES (est): 2.9MM **Privately Held**
WEB: www.banksvilleexpress.com
SIC: 2759 7334 2791 2789 Commercial printing; photocopying & duplicating services; typesetting; bookbinding & related work; commercial printing, lithographic

(G-15486)
RIN TIN TIM INC
1172 Jefferson Heights Rd (15235-4737)
PHONE..............................412 403-5378
Timothy J Townsend, *Principal*
EMP: 4
SALES (est): 347.1K **Privately Held**
SIC: 3356 Tin

(G-15487)
RISCO INDUSTRIES INC
971 Route 910 (15238-1259)
PHONE..............................412 767-0349
Richard J Schubert Jr, *President*
Beverly Schubert, *Admin Sec*
EMP: 4
SALES: 215.1K **Privately Held**
SIC: 3541 Screw machines, automatic

(G-15488)
RIVERBEND FOODS LLC
1080 River Ave (15212-5995)
PHONE..............................412 442-6989
Tom Lavan, *CEO*
Michelle Byrd, *Accountant*
EMP: 500
SALES: 250MM **Privately Held**
SIC: 2032 Baby foods, including meats: packaged in cans, jars, etc.

(G-15489)
RIZZO & SONS INDUSTRIAL SVC CO
9965 Rte 221 Hwy (15229)
PHONE..............................814 948-5381
John Rizzo, *President*
Deborah Letso, *Corp Secy*
Mike Rizzo, *Vice Pres*
EMP: 25
SQ FT: 5,000
SALES (est): 2.6MM **Privately Held**
SIC: 1731 1542 7692 1541 Electric power systems contractors; electronic controls installation; commercial & office buildings, renovation & repair; specialized public building contractors; welding repair; steel building construction; plumbing, heating, air-conditioning contractors

(G-15490)
RJW HIRED HANDS INC
505 Mcneilly Rd Ste 1 (15226-2563)
PHONE..............................412 341-1477
Robert Walther, *President*
EMP: 10
SALES (est): 973.2K **Privately Held**
SIC: 2721 Periodicals

(G-15491)
ROACH & ASSOCIATES INC
615 Washington Rd Ste 404 (15228-1932)
PHONE..............................412 344-9310
William Roach, *President*
Cathy Cortazzo, *Bd of Directors*
EMP: 6
SQ FT: 1,000
SALES (est): 747.5K **Privately Held**
WEB: www.roachassoc.com
SIC: 1389 Oil consultants

(G-15492)
ROADSIDE PA LLC
5747 Interboro Ave (15207-2227)
PHONE..............................412 464-1452
Robert Williams, *Principal*
EMP: 3
SALES (est): 302.6K **Privately Held**
SIC: 3711 Wreckers (tow truck), assembly of

(G-15493)
ROBANCO
415 Mower Dr (15239-1709)
PHONE..............................412 795-7444
Robert T Bannon, *Owner*
Robert Bannon, *Owner*
EMP: 3
SALES: 100K **Privately Held**
WEB: www.roban.com
SIC: 2759 5136 5137 Screen printing; sportswear, men's & boys'; sportswear, women's & children's

GEOGRAPHIC

(G-15494)
ROBERTA WEISSBURG LEATHERS (PA)
5415 Walnut St (15232-2231)
PHONE..............................412 681-8188
Roberta Weissburg, *Owner*
EMP: 5
SQ FT: 800
SALES (est): 1.4MM **Privately Held**
WEB: www.robertaweissburgleathers.com
SIC: 5699 5621 3199 Leather garments; boutiques; leather garments

(G-15495)
ROCKWELL VENTURE CAPITAL (PA)
960 Penn Ave Ste 800 (15222-3821)
PHONE..............................412 281-4620
S Kent Rockwell, *President*
Philip T Warman, *Vice Pres*
Judy Zsiros, *Treasurer*
◆ **EMP:** 3
SALES (est): 23.2MM **Privately Held**
SIC: 2491 Mine props, treated wood; poles & pole crossarms, treated wood; posts, treated wood; railroad cross-ties, treated wood

(G-15496)
ROSE A RUPP
Also Called: Christman Awning Company
4328 Butler St Rear (15201-3010)
PHONE..............................412 622-6827
Rose A Rupp, *Owner*
EMP: 3 **EST:** 1893
SQ FT: 5,000
SALES (est): 235.7K **Privately Held**
SIC: 5999 2394 Awnings; awnings, fabric: made from purchased materials

(G-15497)
ROSEMOUNT INC
3 Robinson Plz Ste 330 (15205-1018)
PHONE..............................412 788-1160
Doug Taylor, *Manager*
EMP: 10
SALES (corp-wide): 17.4B **Publicly Held**
WEB: www.rosemount.com
SIC: 3823 Manometers, industrial process type
HQ: Rosemount Inc.
8200 Market Blvd
Chanhassen MN 55317
952 906-8888

(G-15498)
ROTHMAN AWNING CO INC
44 W Elizabeth St (15207-1816)
PHONE..............................412 589-9974
Bobby Dudley, *CEO*
Sandra Johns, *President*
Linda Dudley, *Corp Secy*
William Eisel, *COO*
Paul Dudley, *Vice Pres*
EMP: 13 **EST:** 1915
SQ FT: 8,000
SALES (est): 1.6MM **Privately Held**
SIC: 2394 1799 Awnings, fabric: made from purchased materials; awning installation

(G-15499)
ROUGH STONE SOFTWARE LLC
200 Fleet St Ste 1200 (15220-2929)
PHONE..............................412 444-5295
Henry Gnad, *Co-Founder*
EMP: 9
SALES (est): 1MM **Privately Held**
SIC: 7372 Prepackaged software

(G-15500)
RR DONNELLEY & SONS COMPANY
218 N Braddock Ave (15208-2511)
PHONE..............................412 241-8200
Jim Ford, *Vice Pres*
EMP: 161
SALES (corp-wide): 6.8B **Publicly Held**
SIC: 2759 Commercial printing
PA: R. R. Donnelley & Sons Company
35 W Wacker Dr Ste 3650
Chicago IL 60601
312 326-8000

(G-15501)
RR DONNELLEY & SONS COMPANY
Also Called: R R Donnelley Financial
210 6th Ave Ste 3600 (15222-2602)
P.O. Box 6766 (15212-0766)
PHONE..............................412 281-7401
Barbara Kachurik, *Human Res Dir*
Joseph Bundick, *Persnl Mgr*
EMP: 60
SALES (corp-wide): 6.8B **Publicly Held**
WEB: www.rrdonnelley.com
SIC: 2752 2791 Commercial printing, lithographic; typesetting
PA: R. R. Donnelley & Sons Company
35 W Wacker Dr Ste 3650
Chicago IL 60601
312 326-8000

(G-15502)
RUBBER ROLLS INC (PA)
726 Trumbull Dr (15205-4363)
P.O. Box 398, Meadow Lands (15347-0398)
PHONE..............................412 276-6400
Frank J Kelly Jr, *CEO*
Michael C Kerestes, *President*
Mike Kerestes, *President*
David W Schnupp, *Corp Secy*
EMP: 33 **EST:** 1956
SQ FT: 40,000
SALES (est): 10.3MM **Privately Held**
SIC: 3069 Rolls, solid or covered rubber

(G-15503)
RUSSELL ROLLS INC
2217 Preble Ave (15233-1198)
PHONE..............................412 321-6623
John Russell, *President*
Yvonne Hosac Russell, *Corp Secy*
EMP: 5 **EST:** 1964
SQ FT: 14,000
SALES (est): 521.6K **Privately Held**
WEB: www.russellrolls.com
SIC: 3441 Building components, structural steel

(G-15504)
RUSSELL STANDARD CORPORATION (PA)
Also Called: Hammaker East
285 Kappa Dr Ste 300 (15238-2814)
PHONE..............................412 449-0700
James R Johnson, *CEO*
Mathew W Johnson, *President*
George E Leach, *CFO*
EMP: 11
SQ FT: 25,000
SALES (est): 195.6MM **Privately Held**
WEB: www.russellstandard.com
SIC: 1611 2951 Highway & street paving contractor; resurfacing contractor; concrete, bituminous; road materials, bituminous (not from refineries)

(G-15505)
SAC INDUSTRIES INC
Also Called: Sac Manufacturing
137 Industry Dr (15275-1015)
Rural Route 1285, Coraopolis (15108)
PHONE..............................412 787-7500
Samuel A Colosimo Jr, *President*
EMP: 13
SQ FT: 10,000
SALES (est): 2.1MM **Privately Held**
SIC: 3462 7692 3441 Iron & steel forgings; welding repair; fabricated structural metal

(G-15506)
SAFETY SLING COMPANY INC
919 Fulton St (15233-2091)
P.O. Box 6461 (15212-0461)
PHONE..............................412 231-6684
Tom Talkowski, *President*
Rick Talkowski, *Vice Pres*
Ted Talkowski, *Shareholder*
EMP: 13
SQ FT: 22,000
SALES (est): 2.4MM **Privately Held**
WEB: www.safetysling.com
SIC: 2298 5085 5072 3496 Slings, rope; rope, except wire rope; hardware; wire chain

(G-15507)
SALES MARKETING GROUP INC
300 Cedar Ridge Dr # 310 (15205-1159)
PHONE..............................412 928-0422
Robert L Smith, *President*
Dudley McDonough, *President*
Derrick Martin, *Sales Staff*
Wes Staud, *Sales Staff*
Jerry Brown, *Sales Associate*
EMP: 7
SALES (est): 851.9K **Privately Held**
WEB: www.smgpittsburgh.com
SIC: 3699 5063 Electrical equipment & supplies; electrical apparatus & equipment

(G-15508)
SALT FCTRY BY SNOW ICE MGT INC
2220 Palmer St (15218-2603)
PHONE..............................412 321-7669
EMP: 3
SALES (est): 90K **Privately Held**
SIC: 2899 Salt

(G-15509)
SAMIR CORP
200 Lothrop St (15213-2536)
PHONE..............................412 647-6000
Saba Samir, *Principal*
Samir Saba, *Director*
EMP: 5 **EST:** 2011
SALES (est): 377.5K **Privately Held**
SIC: 3845 Electrocardiographs

(G-15510)
SAMUEL SON & CO (USA) INC
Frontier Stl A Div Samuel Son
4990 Grand Ave (15225-1324)
PHONE..............................412 865-4444
John Matig, *President*
EMP: 50
SALES (corp-wide): 1.8B **Privately Held**
SIC: 3624 Carbon specialties for electrical use; electric carbons; electrodes, thermal & electrolytic uses: carbon, graphite
HQ: Samuel, Son & Co. (Usa) Inc.
1401 Davey Rd Ste 300
Woodridge IL 60517
630 783-8900

(G-15511)
SAPLING PRESS
4618 Friendship Ave (15224-1506)
PHONE..............................412 681-1003
Lisa Cairns-Krowinski, *Principal*
EMP: 4 **EST:** 2008
SALES (est): 288.1K **Privately Held**
SIC: 2741 Miscellaneous publishing

(G-15512)
SAUCY NOODLE
300 Munt Lbnon Blvd Ste 5 (15234)
PHONE..............................412 440-0432
Ralph Cerminara, *Principal*
EMP: 4
SALES (est): 207.8K **Privately Held**
SIC: 2098 Noodles (e.g. egg, plain & water), dry

(G-15513)
SAUER INDUSTRIES INC (PA)
30 51st St (15201-2708)
PHONE..............................412 687-4100
William N Steitz Sr, *President*
Sharon M Turchick, *Admin Sec*
EMP: 3 **EST:** 1876
SQ FT: 3,200
SALES (est): 2.8MM **Privately Held**
SIC: 3625 Relays & industrial controls

(G-15514)
SAUEREISEN INC
160 Gamma Dr (15238-2920)
PHONE..............................412 963-0303
J Eric Sauereisen, *President*
C Karl Sauereisen, *Vice Pres*
◆ **EMP:** 30 **EST:** 1899
SQ FT: 75,000
SALES (est): 6.4MM **Privately Held**
WEB: www.sauereisen.com
SIC: 3297 2891 2851 2899 Cement: high temperature, refractory (nonclay); adhesives & sealants; paints & allied products; chemical preparations

(G-15515)
SCHAFFNER MANUFACTURING CO (PA)
21 Herron Ave (15202-1798)
PHONE..............................412 761-9902
James Schaffner, *CEO*
Jeffrey Debski, *President*
William Schaffner, *President*
Paul Schaffner II, *Vice Pres*
Paul E Schaffner, *Vice Pres*
◆ **EMP:** 90 **EST:** 1946
SQ FT: 98,000
SALES (est): 22.2MM **Privately Held**
WEB: www.schaffnermfg.com
SIC: 3291 3469 2842 Wheels, abrasive; buffing or polishing wheels, abrasive or nonabrasive; abrasive buffs, bricks, cloth, paper, stones, etc.; metal stampings; specialty cleaning, polishes & sanitation goods

(G-15516)
SCHNEIDERS DAIRY INC (HQ)
726 Frank St (15227-1299)
PHONE..............................412 881-3525
William Schneider, *President*
Kenneth Schneider, *Corp Secy*
Edward Schneider, *Vice Pres*
Paul L Schneider, *Vice Pres*
Paul Schneider Jr, *Controller*
EMP: 150 **EST:** 1935
SQ FT: 60,000
SALES (est): 70.7MM
SALES (corp-wide): 33.2MM **Privately Held**
WEB: www.schneidersdairy.com
SIC: 2086 2026 Iced tea & fruit drinks, bottled & canned; fluid milk
PA: Schneider's Dairy Holdings, Inc.
726 Frank St
Pittsburgh PA 15227
412 881-3525

(G-15517)
SCHNEIDERS DAIRY HOLDINGS INC (PA)
Also Called: Schneider Dairy
726 Frank St (15227-1210)
PHONE..............................412 881-3525
William Schneider Jr, *General Mgr*
Paul Schneider, *Controller*
EMP: 375 **EST:** 1935
SQ FT: 60,000
SALES (est): 33.2MM **Privately Held**
SIC: 2026 Dips, sour cream based

(G-15518)
SEAGATE TECHNOLOGY LLC
1251 Waterfront Pl Fl 1 (15222-4227)
PHONE..............................412 918-7000
Mark Kryder, *Branch Mgr*
EMP: 240 **Privately Held**
SIC: 3572 Disk drives, computer
HQ: Seagate Technology Llc
10200 S De Anza Blvd
Cupertino CA 95014
408 658-1000

(G-15519)
SEBASTIAN MANAGEMENT LLC
1016 Greentree Rd Ste 102 (15220-3125)
P.O. Box 8, Rural Ridge (15075-0008)
PHONE..............................412 203-1273
Prabhu R Deshetty, *General Mgr*
EMP: 65
SALES (est): 1.7MM **Privately Held**
SIC: 1241 Coal mining services

(G-15520)
SEEGRID CORPORATION
216 Ridc Park West Dr (15275-1002)
PHONE..............................412 379-4500
James Rock, *CEO*
David Heilman, *President*
Jeff Christensen, *Vice Pres*
William Detemple, *Controller*
David Scheffrahn, *Sales Staff*
▲ **EMP:** 60 **EST:** 2014
SALES: 6MM **Privately Held**
SIC: 3549 Assembly machines, including robotic

(G-15521)
SELAH PUBLSHNG CO INC
4055 Cloverlea St (15227-3443)
P.O. Box 98066 (15227-0466)
PHONE................................412 886-1020
David P Schaap, *President*
Susan Hermance Sedak, *Vice Pres*
Alfred V Sedak, *Admin Sec*
EMP: 7
SQ FT: 1,400
SALES (est): 69K **Privately Held**
WEB: www.selahpub.com
SIC: 2741 8661 Music, sheet: publishing &
printing; religious organizations

(G-15522)
SEMI-MOUNTS INC
1618 Murdoch Rd (15217-1127)
PHONE................................412 422-7988
David Mc Rae, *President*
Art Keele, *Exec VP*
EMP: 3
SALES (est): 250K **Privately Held**
SIC: 3911 Jewelry, precious metal

(G-15523)
**SENECA RESOURCES
COMPANY LLC**
5800 Corporate Dr Ste 300 (15237-7098)
PHONE................................412 548-2500
Chris Trejchel, *Counsel*
Lee Kennemuth, *Foreman/Supr*
Seneca Resources, *Branch Mgr*
Robert Boulware, *Manager*
Julianne Heins, *Director*
EMP: 56
SALES (corp-wide): 1.5B **Publicly Held**
SIC: 1382 Oil & gas exploration services
HQ: Seneca Resources Company, Llc
1201 La St Ste 2600
Houston TX 77002
713 654-2600

(G-15524)
SENSUS USA INC
1501 Ardmore Blvd (15221-4451)
PHONE................................724 430-3956
Barry Seneri, *Exec VP*
Todd Kendall, *Manager*
Michael Gaston, *Director*
EMP: 200 **Publicly Held**
WEB: www.sensus.com
SIC: 3824 3491 3363 2891 Gas meters,
domestic & large capacity: industrial;
water meters; industrial valves; aluminum
die-castings; sealants
HQ: Sensus Usa Inc.
8601 Six Forks Rd Ste 700
Raleigh NC 27615
919 845-4000

(G-15525)
SENTAGE CORPORATION
Also Called: Dsg Pittsburgh
600 Old Clairton Rd (15236-4313)
PHONE................................412 431-3353
Lee A Weir, *General Mgr*
Glen Turnbull, *Branch Mgr*
EMP: 80
SALES (corp-wide): 81MM **Privately
Held**
WEB: www.dentalservices.net
SIC: 8072 3843 Dental laboratories; den-
tal equipment & supplies
PA: Sentage Corporation
146 2nd St N Ste 202
Saint Petersburg FL 33701
727 502-2069

(G-15526)
SHADY ACRES SADDLERY INC
595 Dorseyville Rd (15238-1524)
PHONE................................412 963-9454
Audrey Sico, *President*
EMP: 3 EST: 1973
SALES: 500K **Privately Held**
SIC: 3199 5941 Saddles or parts; saddlery
& equestrian equipment

(G-15527)
SHAMMY SOLUTIONS
344 Pennoak Dr (15235-3056)
PHONE................................412 871-0939
EMP: 3 EST: 2011

SALES (est): 141.3K **Privately Held**
SIC: 3471 Cleaning & descaling metal
products

(G-15528)
SHARED FINANCIAL SERVICES
Also Called: Barta
200 Alpha Dr (15238-2906)
PHONE................................412 968-1178
John F Bitzer III, *President*
EMP: 30 EST: 1997
SALES (est): 3.8MM **Privately Held**
WEB: www.barta.com
SIC: 2086 Carbonated beverages, nonal-
coholic: bottled & canned

(G-15529)
SHEMCO CORP
100 Skylark Cir (15234-1018)
PHONE................................412 831-6022
Jerome E Scherer Jr, *President*
Trish Cabello, *Treasurer*
EMP: 12
SALES (est): 930K **Privately Held**
WEB: www.usedprintequip.com
SIC: 2752 Commercial printing, offset

(G-15530)
SHENANGO GROUP INC
200 Neville Rd Ste 8 (15225-1694)
PHONE................................412 771-4400
Andrew Aloe, *President*
EMP: 175
SALES (est): 19.8MM **Privately Held**
SIC: 3312 Coke produced in chemical re-
covery coke ovens; coke oven products
(chemical recovery)

(G-15531)
SHENANGO INCORPORATED
200 Neville Rd Unit 5 (15225-1694)
PHONE................................412 771-4400
Andrew Aloe, *President*
Charles D Gress, *Vice Pres*
G Robert Muhl, *Vice Pres*
Kenneth I Kubacki, *Treasurer*
Charles E Ellison, *Admin Sec*
EMP: 175
SQ FT: 300,000
SALES (est): 57.2MM **Publicly Held**
WEB: www.shencoke.com
SIC: 3312 Coke produced in chemical re-
covery coke ovens; coke oven products
(chemical recovery)
PA: Dte Energy Company
1 Energy Plz
Detroit MI 48226

(G-15532)
SHERWOOD VALVE LLC (HQ)
100 Business Center Dr # 400
(15205-1329)
PHONE................................724 225-8000
Doug Murdock, *President*
Robert Leichliter, *Mfg Spvr*
Steve Greenberg, *Engineer*
Joseph Lacek, *Design Engr*
Rich Lutz, *Controller*
◆ EMP: 107
SQ FT: 106,000
SALES (est): 35MM
SALES (corp-wide): 2.5B **Publicly Held**
WEB: www.sherwoodvalve.com
SIC: 3491 Automatic regulating & control
valves; compressed gas cylinder valves;
gas valves & parts, industrial; pressure
valves & regulators, industrial
PA: Mueller Industries, Inc.
150 Schilling Blvd # 100
Collierville TN 38017
901 753-3200

(G-15533)
**SHIELDS EMBROIDERY BY
DESIGN**
4156 Library Rd Ste 2 (15234-1349)
PHONE................................412 531-2321
Joann Shields, *CEO*
Mike Shields, *President*
Kevin Shields, *Vice Pres*
EMP: 10
SQ FT: 1,800
SALES (est): 649.3K **Privately Held**
SIC: 2395 Embroidery products, except
schiffli machine

(G-15534)
SHORE CORPORATION
Also Called: Shore Chemical Co
2917 Spruce Way (15201-1530)
PHONE................................412 471-3330
Holly W Sphar Jr, *Ch of Bd*
Stuart G Hammerschm, *President*
Hillary Kern, *Business Mgr*
Stuart Hammerschm, *Vice Pres*
Robert A Walde, *Vice Pres*
EMP: 17
SQ FT: 40,000
SALES (est): 4.7MM **Privately Held**
WEB: www.shorechemical.com
SIC: 2842 Specialty cleaning preparations;
sweeping compounds, oil or water ab-
sorbent, clay or sawdust; industrial plant
disinfectants or deodorants

(G-15535)
SHS DRINKS US LLC
71 Mcmurray Rd Ste 104 (15241-1634)
PHONE................................412 854-9012
David McNulty, *President*
EMP: 3
SALES: 100K **Privately Held**
SIC: 2086 Bottled & canned soft drinks

(G-15536)
SIC MARKING USA INC
137 Delta Dr (15238-2805)
PHONE................................412 487-1165
Peter Bickel, *General Mgr*
Laurie Barcaskey, *Finance*
EMP: 7
SALES (est): 1.6MM
SALES (corp-wide): 27.5MM **Privately
Held**
SIC: 3953 Marking devices
PA: Sic Marking
Zone D Amenagement Concerte Bel
Air
Pommiers 69480

(G-15537)
SIERRA MEDIA SERVICES INC
2 Robinson Plz Ste 300 (15205-1017)
PHONE................................412 722-1701
Bruce Freshwater, *CEO*
Aaron Brown, *Senior VP*
Michael Giles, *Senior VP*
EMP: 3 EST: 2012
SALES (est): 234.9K **Privately Held**
SIC: 3663 Television broadcasting & com-
munications equipment

(G-15538)
SIMPLE TREAT BAKERY
4734 Liberty Ave (15224-2051)
PHONE................................412 681-0303
Sherman Weinstein, *President*
Richard Minder, *Corp Secy*
Greg Meitus, *Vice Pres*
EMP: 10
SALES (est): 520K **Privately Held**
SIC: 2051 Bread, cake & related products

(G-15539)
SIMPLY AUTOMATED LLC
190a Industry Dr (15275-1014)
PHONE................................412 343-0348
EMP: 7
SALES (est): 1.2MM **Privately Held**
SIC: 3651 Household audio & video equip-
ment

(G-15540)
**SIMULATION LIVE FIRE
TRAINING**
4853 Campbells Run Rd (15205-1323)
PHONE................................412 787-2832
Justin Willott, *President*
EMP: 3
SALES (est): 146.7K
SALES (corp-wide): 1B **Privately Held**
SIC: 3699 Flight simulators (training aids),
electronic
HQ: Alpine Metal Tech Uk Limited
Suite G-H The Maltsters
Burton-On-Trent STAFFS DE14

(G-15541)
SINFULLY SWEET
10114 Saltsburg Rd (15239-2133)
PHONE................................412 523-1887

Cindy Foreback, *Owner*
EMP: 3
SALES (est): 134.9K **Privately Held**
SIC: 2024 Ice cream, bulk

(G-15542)
SIR SPEEDY 7108 INC
Also Called: Sir Speedy Printing and Mktg
4573 Campbells Run Rd (15205-1313)
PHONE................................412 787-9898
Cynthia Johnston, *President*
Michael Mc Cready, *Vice Pres*
Mike McCready, *Vice Pres*
EMP: 12
SQ FT: 8,000
SALES (est): 1.8MM **Privately Held**
WEB: www.sirspeedy7108.com
SIC: 2752 7334 7331 5999 Commercial
printing, lithographic; photocopying & du-
plicating services; direct mail advertising
services; banners, flags, decals &
posters; signs & advertising specialties

(G-15543)
SIR SPEEDY PRINTING CENTER
369 Coltart Ave (15213-3907)
PHONE................................412 687-0500
Barry M Zwibel, *Owner*
Cathy Beckett, *Manager*
EMP: 7
SQ FT: 1,600
SALES (est): 611.2K **Privately Held**
SIC: 2752 Commercial printing, offset

(G-15544)
SIS SOFTWARE LLC
4955 Steubenville Pike (15205-9619)
PHONE................................888 844-6599
Dan Franklin, *Managing Prtnr*
EMP: 3
SALES (corp-wide): 6.1MM **Privately
Held**
SIC: 7372 Prepackaged software
PA: Sis Software, Llc
3700 Crestwood Pkwy Nw # 1050
Duluth GA 30096
678 380-2267

(G-15545)
SLAVIA PRINTING CO INC
157 Mcneilly Rd (15226-2624)
PHONE................................412 343-4444
Dale Blazek, *President*
EMP: 8 EST: 1918
SQ FT: 10,000
SALES (est): 1.3MM **Privately Held**
WEB: www.slaviaprinting.com
SIC: 2752 2789 2759 Commercial print-
ing, offset; bookbinding & related work;
commercial printing

(G-15546)
SMART SYSTEMS INC
R.J Casey Industrial Park (15233)
PHONE................................412 323-2128
Cynthia Crawbuck, *CEO*
James Burchell, *President*
John Burchell, *Vice Pres*
Edward Moss, *Vice Pres*
EMP: 6
SQ FT: 10,000
SALES (est): 946.3K **Privately Held**
WEB: www.smartsystemsinc.net
SIC: 3993 5162 3089 Signs & advertising
specialties; plastics products; plastic pro-
cessing

(G-15547)
**SMART SYSTEMS
ENTERPRISES INC**
1800 Preble Ave (15233-2242)
PHONE................................412 323-2128
Keith Fitzpatrick, *President*
EMP: 5
SALES: 500K **Privately Held**
SIC: 3999 7389 Manufacturing industries;
business services

(G-15548)
SMARTOPS CORPORATION (PA)
Also Called: Smart Ops
1251 Waterfront Pl # 301 (15222-4227)
PHONE................................412 231-0115
Sridhar Tayur, *President*
Martin Barkman, *President*
Lars M Barkman, *Vice Pres*

Arthur Brohinsky, *Admin Sec*
Edwin Lange,
EMP: 28
SQ FT: 3,861
SALES (est): 8.6MM **Privately Held**
WEB: www.smartops.com
SIC: 7372 8742 Application computer software; management consulting services

(G-15549)
SMARTSHAKE
307 Cola St (15203-1302)
PHONE..................................724 396-7947
Emily Mains, *Sales Mgr*
▲ **EMP:** 12 **EST:** 2009
SALES (est): 973.8K **Privately Held**
SIC: 3089 5113 Cups, plastic, except foam; cups, disposable plastic & paper

(G-15550)
SMITH MICRO SOFTWARE INC (PA)
5800 Corporate Dr Ste 500 (15237-7000)
PHONE..................................412 837-5300
William W Smith Jr, *Ch of Bd*
Marco Leal Goncalves, *Vice Pres*
Charles B Messman, *Vice Pres*
Kenneth Shebek, *Vice Pres*
David P Sperling, *Vice Pres*
EMP: 148
SQ FT: 24,688
SALES: 26.2MM **Publicly Held**
WEB: www.smithmicro.com
SIC: 7372 Business oriented computer software

(G-15551)
SMS DEMAG INC
100 Sandusky St (15212-5822)
PHONE..................................412 231-1200
Bill Emling, *Vice Pres*
Steve Winger, *Vice Pres*
Bob Bixby, *Project Dir*
Ron Lewis, *Controller*
Christopher Kahler, *Manager*
EMP: 4 **EST:** 2007
SALES (est): 214.9K **Privately Held**
SIC: 3312 Blast furnaces & steel mills

(G-15552)
SMS GROUP INC (DH)
100 Sandusky St (15212-5822)
PHONE..................................412 231-1200
Doug Dunworth, *CEO*
Pino Tese, *President*
Robert Bixby, *Vice Pres*
Bill Emling, *Vice Pres*
Judi Berrick, *Project Mgr*
EMP: 200
SALES (est): 98.1MM
SALES (corp-wide): 96.1K **Privately Held**
SIC: 3569 7539 3547 3542 Assembly machines, non-metalworking; machine shop, automotive; rod mills (rolling mill equipment); finishing equipment, rolling mill; extruding machines (machine tools), metal
HQ: Sms Gmbh
Eduard-Schloemann-Str. 4
Dusseldorf 40237
211 881-0

(G-15553)
SOLID STEEL BUILDINGS INC
1 Forestwood Dr Ste 101 (15237-1216)
PHONE..................................800 377-6543
Michael Masula, *President*
Michael A Masula, *Vice Pres*
EMP: 10
SALES: 4.2MM **Privately Held**
SIC: 3441 1771 1794 Fabricated structural metal; concrete work; excavation work; excavation & grading, building construction

(G-15554)
SOLVAY
2180 William Pitt Way (15238-1357)
PHONE..................................412 423-2030
Andrew W Hannah, *President*
Robert Kumps, *COO*
James A Dietz, *Vice Pres*
Glenn Thompson, *Vice Pres*
Sara Grayson, *Purch Mgr*
EMP: 72
SQ FT: 35,000

SALES (est): 11.6MM
SALES (corp-wide): 10MM **Privately Held**
WEB: www.plextronics.com
SIC: 3577 Magnetic ink recognition devices
PA: Solvay
Rue De Ransbeek 310
Bruxelles 1120
226 421-11

(G-15555)
SOLVAY USA INC
2180 William Pitt Way (15238-1357)
PHONE..................................609 860-4000
EMP: 131
SALES (corp-wide): 10MM **Privately Held**
SIC: 2819 Alkali metals: lithium, cesium, francium, rubidium
HQ: Solvay Usa Inc.
504 Carnegie Ctr
Princeton NJ 08540
609 860-4000

(G-15556)
SONGBIRD SANCTUARY LLC
1234 Oak Hill Dr (15239-1262)
PHONE..................................412 780-1270
Janet L Bronder, *Principal*
EMP: 3
SALES (est): 157.5K **Privately Held**
SIC: 2048 Bird food, prepared

(G-15557)
SONOCO PRTECTIVE SOLUTIONS INC
7218 Church Ave (15202-1847)
PHONE..................................800 377-2692
EMP: 4
SALES (corp-wide): 5.3B **Publicly Held**
SIC: 3086 Insulation or cushioning material, foamed plastic
HQ: Sonoco Protective Solutions, Inc.
1 N 2nd St
Hartsville SC 29550
843 383-7000

(G-15558)
SONOCO PRTECTIVE SOLUTIONS INC
7218 Church Ave (15202-1847)
PHONE..................................412 415-1462
Chris Marsh, *Manager*
EMP: 38
SALES (corp-wide): 5.3B **Publicly Held**
WEB: www.tuscarora.com
SIC: 3086 3089 Packaging & shipping materials, foamed plastic; molding primary plastic
HQ: Sonoco Protective Solutions, Inc.
1 N 2nd St
Hartsville SC 29550
843 383-7000

(G-15559)
SONOCO PRTECTIVE SOLUTIONS INC
7218 Church Ave (15202-1847)
PHONE..................................412 415-3784
John Yackey, *Manager*
EMP: 40
SALES (corp-wide): 5.3B **Publicly Held**
WEB: www.tuscarora.com
SIC: 2679 3086 Building, insulating & packaging paperboard; packaging & shipping materials, foamed plastic
HQ: Sonoco Protective Solutions, Inc.
1 N 2nd St
Hartsville SC 29550
843 383-7000

(G-15560)
SOROKA SALES INC
138 S 25th St (15203-2262)
PHONE..................................412 381-7700
EMP: 30 **EST:** 1948
SQ FT: 8,000
SALES (est): 2.2MM **Privately Held**
SIC: 2493 2821 Mfg Fiber Wall Plaques

(G-15561)
SOSNIAK OPTICIANS (PA)
Also Called: Group Optical
208 5th Ave (15222-2701)
PHONE..................................412 281-9199
Allen Sosniak, *Owner*
EMP: 3
SQ FT: 1,100
SALES (est): 314.2K **Privately Held**
SIC: 3851 5995 Lens grinding, except prescription: ophthalmic; opticians

(G-15562)
SOUR JUNKIE LLC
921 Clarissa St (15219-5705)
PHONE..................................412 612-6860
Pierre Wynn,
EMP: 3 **EST:** 2017
SALES (est): 121.3K **Privately Held**
SIC: 3652 Pre-recorded records & tapes

(G-15563)
SOUTH POLE MAGNETICS
225 Waldorf St (15214-1925)
PHONE..................................412 537-5625
EMP: 3
SALES (est): 190K **Privately Held**
SIC: 3497 Metal Foil And Leaf

(G-15564)
SOUTHSIDE HOLDINGS INC
Also Called: Technology Publishing Company
1501 Reedsdale St # 2008 (15233-2341)
PHONE..................................412 431-8300
Brion Palmer, *President*
Howard Booker, *Publisher*
Candace Hicks, *Sales Mgr*
Brian Naccarelli, *Senior Editor*
Ande Thomas, *Associate*
EMP: 35
SQ FT: 8,900
SALES: 50MM **Privately Held**
WEB: www.paintsquare.com
SIC: 2731 2721 7372 Books: publishing only; magazines: publishing only, not printed on site; application computer software

(G-15565)
SOVEREIGN SERVICES INC
Also Called: Allegheny Recycled Products
4201 Grand Ave (15225-1524)
PHONE..................................412 331-6704
William E Biedenbach, *Ch of Bd*
John M Cory III, *President*
Chris Biedenbach, *Admin Sec*
EMP: 40
SQ FT: 20,000
SALES (est): 7.3MM **Privately Held**
SIC: 2448 Pallets, wood

(G-15566)
SPANG & COMPANY (PA)
Also Called: Spang Power Electronics
110 Delta Dr (15238-2806)
PHONE..................................412 963-9363
Frank E Rath Jr, *Ch of Bd*
Robert K Smith, *President*
Lynne S Ellis, *Vice Pres*
Michael J Reilly, *Vice Pres*
◆ **EMP:** 200 **EST:** 1894
SALES (est): 103.9MM **Privately Held**
SIC: 3672 3944 3612 3613 Printed circuit boards; games, toys & children's vehicles; power transformers, electric; panelboards & distribution boards, electric; blast furnaces & steel mills

(G-15567)
SPANG & COMPANY
Magnetics Div
110 Delta Dr (15238-2806)
P.O. Box 11422 (15238-0422)
PHONE..................................412 963-9363
Joseph Huth Jr, *President*
James D Miller, *President*
Robert K Smith, *Division Pres*
C R Donsch, *Plant Mgr*
EMP: 150
SALES (corp-wide): 103.9MM **Privately Held**
WEB: www.spangpower.com
SIC: 3679 5065 Cores, magnetic; electronic parts & equipment

PA: Spang & Company
110 Delta Dr
Pittsburgh PA 15238
412 963-9363

(G-15568)
SPECIAL T ELECTRONIC LLC
9329 Doral Dr (15237-4805)
P.O. Box 906, Wexford (15090-0906)
PHONE..................................412 635-4997
Kathy Madeya, *Owner*
EMP: 3
SALES: 150K **Privately Held**
SIC: 3829 7389 Medical diagnostic systems, nuclear;

(G-15569)
SPECIALIZED DESANDERS USA INC
24 Summit Park Dr (15275-1104)
PHONE..................................412 535-3396
Lonnie L Johnson, *Chairman*
EMP: 3 **EST:** 2014
SALES (est): 176.2K **Privately Held**
SIC: 3533 Gas field machinery & equipment

(G-15570)
SPECTRAGENETICS INC
2403 Sidney St Ste 255 (15203-2194)
PHONE..................................412 488-9350
G Reid Asbury, *CEO*
Mary Anne Jarvik, *President*
Juan Herrero, *Vice Pres*
EMP: 6
SALES: 500K **Privately Held**
WEB: www.spectragenetics.com
SIC: 2836 5912 Biological products, except diagnostic; drug stores

(G-15571)
SPORTS IMAGES INTERNATIONAL
1725 Washington Rd # 200 (15241-1207)
PHONE..................................412 851-1610
Robert C Brandt III, *President*
EMP: 3 **EST:** 1997
SQ FT: 1,200
SALES (est): 257.2K **Privately Held**
SIC: 2741 Art copy & poster publishing

(G-15572)
SSW INTERNATIONAL INC (HQ)
Also Called: Magnetics International, Inc.
661 Andersen Dr Ste 7 (15220-2700)
PHONE..................................412 922-9100
Walter Sieckman, *President*
Paul Songer, *Chairman*
Satish Wadhawan, *Exec VP*
Michael Sieckmann, *Vice Pres*
▲ **EMP:** 22
SQ FT: 50,000
SALES (est): 4.8MM
SALES (corp-wide): 42.4MM **Privately Held**
WEB: www.issi-amrox-usa.com
SIC: 2819 3399 Inorganic acids, except nitric & phosphoric; iron, powdered
PA: International Steel Services, Inc.
661 Andersen Dr Ste 7
Pittsburgh PA 15220
412 922-9100

(G-15573)
ST CROIX ALUMINA LLC
201 Isabella St (15212-5872)
PHONE..................................412 553-4545
Benjamin D Kahrs, *CEO*
EMP: 3
SALES (est): 63.4K
SALES (corp-wide): 1.7B **Privately Held**
SIC: 3355 Aluminum rolling & drawing
PA: Halco (Mining) Inc.
323 N Shore Dr
Pittsburgh PA 15212
412 235-0265

(G-15574)
STAGNOS BAKERY INC
Also Called: Stagno Italian Accent
1747 Chislett St (15206-1129)
PHONE..................................412 361-2093
EMP: 6

SALES (corp-wide): 4.2MM **Privately Held**
SIC: 2051 5461 Mfg Bread/Related Products Retail Bakery
PA: Stagno's Bakery Inc
233 Auburn St
East Liberty PA 15206
412 441-3485

(G-15575)
STANDARD & CUSTOM LLC
6901 Lynn Way (15208-2438)
PHONE..................................412 345-7901
Jaeeun Chung,
EMP: 7
SALES: 400K **Privately Held**
SIC: 3446 Architectural metalwork

(G-15576)
STANDARD CAR TRUCK COMPANY
Barber Spring Company
1 Mccandless Ave (15201-2631)
PHONE..................................412 782-7300
David Jablonowski, *Manager*
EMP: 55
SALES (corp-wide): 4.3B **Publicly Held**
SIC: 3743 3493 Freight cars & equipment; steel springs, except wire
HQ: Standard Car Truck Company Inc
6400 Shafer Ct Ste 450
Rosemont IL 60018
847 692-6050

(G-15577)
STANLEY ACCESS TECH LLC
Also Called: Stanley Security Solutions
135 Plum Industrial Park (15239-2911)
P.O. Box 371595 (15250-7595)
PHONE..................................800 722-2377
EMP: 33
SALES (corp-wide): 13.9B **Publicly Held**
SIC: 2431 Doors & door parts & trim, wood
HQ: Stanley Access Technologies Llc
65 Scott Swamp Rd
Farmington CT 06032

(G-15578)
STARKIST CO (DH)
225 N Shore Dr Ste 400 (15212-5860)
PHONE..................................412 323-7400
Sam HWI Lee, *President*
Namjung Kim, *COO*
Stephen Hodge, *Senior VP*
C Thomas Hyun, *Senior VP*
Patrick M Moody, *Senior VP*
◆ EMP: 60
SALES (est): 23.1MM
SALES (corp-wide): 83.5MM **Privately Held**
WEB: www.starkist.com/
SIC: 2091 Canned & cured fish & seafoods
HQ: Dongwon Industries Co., Ltd.
7/F Dongwon Industries Bldg.
Seoul 06775
822 589-3764

(G-15579)
STATEASY
111 N Whitfield St (15206)
PHONE..................................412 437-8287
Michael Ressler, *Principal*
EMP: 6
SALES (est): 351.1K **Privately Held**
SIC: 3949 Sporting & athletic goods

(G-15580)
STEEL CONSULTING SERVICES LLC
58 Ridge Rd (15221-4622)
PHONE..................................412 727-6645
Anthony Mologne,
EMP: 3
SQ FT: 1,400
SALES (est): 6.5MM **Privately Held**
SIC: 8742 3317 Management consulting services; steel pipe & tubes

(G-15581)
STELLA-JONES CORPORATION (DH)
1000 Cliffmine Rd Ste 500 (15275-1040)
PHONE..................................412 325-0202
Brian McManus, *President*
Doug Fox, *Senior VP*

Marla Eichenbaum, *Vice Pres*
George Labelle, *Vice Pres*
Eric Vachon, *CFO*
◆ EMP: 36
SALES (est): 212.1MM
SALES (corp-wide): 250.7K **Privately Held**
SIC: 2491 Railroad cross bridges & switch ties, treated wood
HQ: Stella-Jones Inc
3100 Boul De La Cote-Vertu Bureau 300
Saint-Laurent QC H4R 2
514 934-8666

(G-15582)
STELLA-JONES US HOLDING CORP (DH)
603 Stanwix St (15222-1425)
PHONE..................................304 372-2211
Brian McManus, *CEO*
Eric Vachon, *Senior VP*
Marla Eichenbaum, *Vice Pres*
Gordon Murray, *Vice Pres*
▼ EMP: 24
SQ FT: 5,000
SALES (est): 91.5MM
SALES (corp-wide): 250.7K **Privately Held**
WEB: www.bpbcorp.com
SIC: 2491 Wood preserving
HQ: Stella-Jones Inc
3100 Boul De La Cote-Vertu Bureau 300
Saint-Laurent QC H4R 2
514 934-8666

(G-15583)
STEVE SCHWARTZ ASSOCIATES INC
1700 Forbes Ave (15219-5834)
PHONE..................................412 765-3400
Steven Schwartz, *President*
EMP: 41
SQ FT: 7,000
SALES (est): 5.6MM **Privately Held**
WEB: www.ssapgh.com
SIC: 5112 5199 3993 2761 Business forms; advertising specialties; signs & advertising specialties; manifold business forms

(G-15584)
STIMPLE AND WARD COMPANY (PA)
3400 Babcock Blvd (15237-2473)
PHONE..................................412 364-5200
Raymond Love, *President*
Thomas Love, *Corp Secy*
▲ EMP: 31 EST: 1898
SQ FT: 25,000
SALES (est): 10.6MM **Privately Held**
WEB: www.swcoils.com
SIC: 5051 3677 Copper products; electronic coils, transformers & other inductors

(G-15585)
STITCHES EMBROIDERY INC
1600 Marys Ave (15215-2614)
PHONE..................................412 781-7046
Cynthia Kearney, *President*
Keith Kearney, *Vice Pres*
Brian Kearney, *Treasurer*
EMP: 35
SQ FT: 6,000
SALES: 2MM **Privately Held**
SIC: 2395 Art goods for embroidering, stamped: purchased materials; embroidery & art needlework

(G-15586)
STX INDUSTRIES
245 Amboy St (15224-1705)
PHONE..................................412 513-6689
Mycol Santucci, *Principal*
EMP: 5
SALES (est): 150.7K **Privately Held**
SIC: 3999 Manufacturing industries

(G-15587)
SUNFLOWER GRAPHICS
337 Rochester Rd (15237-1731)
PHONE..................................412 369-7769
George Pazin, *Owner*

EMP: 4
SQ FT: 3,000
SALES: 250K **Privately Held**
WEB: www.sunflowergraphics.com
SIC: 2759 Screen printing

(G-15588)
SUPERIOR FORGE & STEEL CORP
1207 Muriel St (15203-1126)
PHONE..................................412 431-8250
Rick Roberts, *VP Engrg*
James C Markovitz, *Branch Mgr*
Kenneth Wheeler, *Supervisor*
Mike Bartz, *Webmaster*
EMP: 60
SALES (corp-wide): 26MM **Privately Held**
SIC: 3312 3316 Sheet or strip, steel, cold-rolled: own hot-rolled; cold finishing of steel shapes
PA: Superior Forge & Steel Corporation
1820 Mcclain Rd
Lima OH 45804
419 222-4412

(G-15589)
SUPERIOR WINDOW MFG INC
7903 Saltsburg Rd (15239-1923)
PHONE..................................412 793-3500
Lou Lagrotteria, *President*
Robert Sigurelli, *Vice Pres*
Joseph Lagrotteria, *Treasurer*
Lou Lagroeria, *Executive*
EMP: 10
SQ FT: 3,900
SALES (est): 1.5MM **Privately Held**
WEB: www.superiorwindowpgh.com
SIC: 3089 5211 1761 1521 Windows, plastic; door & window products; siding contractor; patio & deck construction & repair

(G-15590)
SURCO PRODUCTS INC
Also Called: Surco Portable Sanitation Pdts
292 Alpha Dr (15238-2906)
PHONE..................................412 252-7000
Arnold Zlotnik, *President*
▼ EMP: 15 EST: 1946
SQ FT: 45,000
SALES (est): 1.4MM **Privately Held**
WEB: www.surcopt.com
SIC: 2844 Toilet preparations

(G-15591)
SUREFLOW CORPORATION
3 Mcduff Industrial Park (15238)
P.O. Box 111274 (15238-0674)
PHONE..................................412 828-5900
Greg Winokur, *President*
▲ EMP: 15
SQ FT: 5,000
SALES (est): 1.2MM **Privately Held**
SIC: 3545 Tools & accessories for machine tools

(G-15592)
SURTREAT HOLDING LLC (PA)
437 Grant St Ste 1210 (15219-6101)
PHONE..................................412 281-1202
Robert A Walde, *Mng Member*
EMP: 3
SQ FT: 2,000
SALES (est): 1.1MM **Privately Held**
SIC: 1771 5169 3479 Concrete work; concrete additives; painting, coating & hot dipping

(G-15593)
SWAROVSKI NORTH AMERICA LTD
301 S Hills Vlg Spc 1045a (15241-1400)
PHONE..................................412 833-3708
Roxanne Hammer, *Branch Mgr*
EMP: 7
SALES (corp-wide): 3.7B **Privately Held**
SIC: 3961 5632 Costume jewelry; costume jewelry
HQ: Swarovski North America Limited
1 Kenney Dr
Cranston RI 02920
401 463-6400

(G-15594)
T P SCHWARTZ INC
Also Called: Schwartz Technical Plastics
7038 Front River Rd (15225-1151)
PHONE..................................724 266-7045
Bernd Nussdorfer, *President*
▲ EMP: 4
SALES (est): 690.2K
SALES (corp-wide): 2.1B **Privately Held**
SIC: 2821 Plastics materials & resins
HQ: Rochling Industrial Xanten Gmbh
Hagdornstr. 3
Xanten 46509
280 176-0

(G-15595)
TAMIS CORPORATION
10700 Frankstown Rd # 105 (15235-3050)
PHONE..................................412 241-7161
Murray C Bilby, *President*
Ron Jadara, *Opers Mgr*
Deana Davies, *Train & Dev Mgr*
Tom Gallagher, *Marketing Staff*
EMP: 18
SQ FT: 5,000
SALES (est): 5.8MM **Privately Held**
WEB: www.blockader.com
SIC: 3499 5099 Barricades, metal; safety equipment & supplies

(G-15596)
TANGENT RAIL CORPORATION (DH)
603 Stanwix St Ste 1000 (15222-1423)
PHONE..................................412 325-0202
William Donley, *President*
James Kenner, *Vice Pres*
▲ EMP: 9
SALES (est): 33.1MM
SALES (corp-wide): 250.7K **Privately Held**
SIC: 2865 2952 2951 2911 Cyclic crudes & intermediates; asphalt felts & coatings; asphalt paving mixtures & blocks; petroleum refining; wood preserving; railroad & subway construction

(G-15597)
TANGENT RAIL PRODUCTS INC (DH)
101 W Station Square Dr # 600 (15219-1196)
PHONE..................................412 325-0202
William Donley, *President*
Richard Cullinan, *Vice Pres*
Mike Sylvester, *Vice Pres*
James Kenner, *Admin Sec*
EMP: 12
SALES (est): 17.7MM
SALES (corp-wide): 250.7K **Privately Held**
SIC: 2491 2865 Wood preserving; tar
HQ: Tangent Rail Corporation
603 Stanwix St Ste 1000
Pittsburgh PA 15222
412 325-0202

(G-15598)
TARGA ENERGY LP (HQ)
Also Called: Atlas Energy, L.P.
1000 Commerce Dr Ste 400 (15275-1033)
PHONE..................................412 489-0006
Edward E Cohen, *President*
Atlas Energy GP, *General Ptnr*
Sean P McGrath, *CFO*
EMP: 19
SALES (est): 17.2MM **Publicly Held**
SIC: 1311 4922 Crude petroleum & natural gas; natural gas transmission

(G-15599)
TAYLOR COMMUNICATIONS INC
209 9th St Ste 700 (15222-3509)
PHONE..................................412 594-2800
Nancy Sterling, *Branch Mgr*
EMP: 7
SALES (corp-wide): 3.2B **Privately Held**
SIC: 2759 Commercial printing
HQ: Taylor Communications, Inc.
1725 Roe Crest Dr
North Mankato MN 56003
507 625-2828

(G-15600)
TDY INDUSTRIES LLC (DH)
Also Called: ATI Specialty Materials
1000 Six Ppg Pl (15222)
PHONE....................................412 394-2896
Richard J Harshman, *CEO*
L Patrick Hassey, *President*
Robert S Wetherbee, *President*
Richard Harshman, *Exec VP*
Dale G Reid, *Exec VP*
◆ EMP: 100
SALES (est): 1.3B Publicly Held
WEB: www.allvac.com
SIC: 3356 3312 3316 3339 Zirconium; titanium; nickel; blast furnaces & steel mills; cold finishing of steel shapes; primary nonferrous metals; nonferrous foundries
HQ: Tdy Holdings, Llc
1403 Foulk Rd Ste 200
Wilmington DE 19803
302 254-4172

(G-15601)
TECH SUPPORT SCREEN P
1441 Meteor Cir Ste 2 (15241)
PHONE....................................412 697-0171
Linda Redeker, *Controller*
William E Redeker, *Mng Member*
▲ EMP: 22
SALES (est): 4.9MM Privately Held
SIC: 2752 Commercial printing, offset

(G-15602)
TECHNOSYSTEMS SERVICE CORP
Also Called: Copies For Less
804 Penn Ave (15222-3610)
PHONE....................................412 288-2525
Scott Whitmore, *Manager*
EMP: 10
SALES (corp-wide): 39MM Privately Held
WEB: www.cflprinters.com
SIC: 2759 Commercial printing
HQ: Technosystems Service Corp
217 9th St
Pittsburgh PA 15222
412 288-1300

(G-15603)
TECHS INDUSTRIES INC
Also Called: Galvtech
300 Mifflin Rd (15207-1910)
PHONE....................................412 464-5000
Dave Dinardo, *Branch Mgr*
EMP: 20 Publicly Held
SIC: 3479 Galvanizing of iron, steel or end-formed products
HQ: The Techs Industries Inc
2400 2nd Ave
Pittsburgh PA 15219
412 464-5000

(G-15604)
TECHS INDUSTRIES INC (HQ)
Also Called: Techs, The
2400 2nd Ave (15219-3116)
PHONE....................................412 464-5000
Richard P Teets, *President*
Tom Logan, *Vice Pres*
Mark D Millett, *Vice Pres*
Bill Soldano, *Vice Pres*
Allen Gore, *Safety Mgr*
▲ EMP: 179
SALES (est): 52.2MM Publicly Held
WEB: www.thetechs.com
SIC: 3479 Galvanizing of iron, steel or end-formed products

(G-15605)
TELETRIX CORP
2000 Golden Mile Hwy C (15239-2814)
PHONE....................................412 798-3636
Michael E Podobnik, *President*
EMP: 9
SQ FT: 5,000
SALES (est): 1.1MM Privately Held
WEB: www.teletrix.com
SIC: 3829 Surveying instruments & accessories

(G-15606)
TEXAS CES INC
2 Penn Ctr W Ste 227 (15276-0113)
PHONE....................................412 490-9200
EMP: 291
SALES (corp-wide): 1B Privately Held
SIC: 1389 Oil/Gas Field Services
PA: Texas Ces, Inc.
3333 Ih 35 N Bldg F
Gainesville TX 76240
940 668-5100

(G-15607)
TG MARCIS WIRE DESIGNS LLC
50 26th St (15222-4634)
PHONE....................................412 391-5532
Jack Harris, *Mng Member*
EMP: 4
SALES (est): 344.2K
SALES (corp-wide): 10.4MM Privately Held
WEB: www.usalampshade.com
SIC: 3496 Lamp frames, wire
PA: J. Harris & Sons Co.
50 26th St
Pittsburgh PA 15222
412 391-5532

(G-15608)
THALES TRANSPORT & SEC INC (HQ)
5500 Corporate Dr Ste 500 (15237-5852)
PHONE....................................412 366-8814
John Brohm, *President*
Jean Pierre Forestier, *Vice Pres*
▲ EMP: 23
SALES (est): 4.5MM
SALES (corp-wide): 305.4MM Privately Held
WEB: www.alcatelusa.com
SIC: 3661 Telephone & telegraph apparatus
PA: Thales
Carpe Diem Esplanade Nord Tour Aig
Courbevoie 92400
157 778-000

(G-15609)
THAR PHARMACEUTICALS INC (DH)
150 Gamma Dr (15238-2904)
PHONE....................................412 963-6800
Raymond K Houck, *President*
Ira K D, *Officer*
Mazen Hanna PHD, *Officer*
EMP: 28
SALES (est): 1MM
SALES (corp-wide): 1.5B Privately Held
SIC: 2834 Pharmaceutical preparations
HQ: Grunenthal Gmbh
Zieglerstr. 6
Aachen 52078
241 569-0

(G-15610)
THAR PROCESS INC
150 Gamma Dr (15238-2904)
PHONE....................................412 968-9180
Lalit Chordia, *CEO*
Todd Palcic, *President*
▲ EMP: 3
SALES (est): 800.4K Privately Held
SIC: 3823 Industrial instrmnts msrmnt display/control process variable

(G-15611)
THERMO FISHER SCIENTIFIC INC
600 Business Center Dr (15205-1334)
PHONE....................................412 490-8000
EMP: 3
SALES (corp-wide): 24.3B Publicly Held
SIC: 3826 Analytical instruments
PA: Thermo Fisher Scientific Inc.
168 3rd Ave
Waltham MA 02451
781 622-1000

(G-15612)
THERMO FISHER SCIENTIFIC INC
100 Technology Dr Ste 100 # 100 (15219-3138)
PHONE....................................412 770-2326
Mike Ducar, *Manager*
EMP: 307
SALES (corp-wide): 24.3B Publicly Held
WEB: www.thermo.com
SIC: 3826 Analytical instruments

PA: Thermo Fisher Scientific Inc.
168 3rd Ave
Waltham MA 02451
781 622-1000

(G-15613)
THERMO FISHER SCIENTIFIC INC
Also Called: Fisher Safety
300 Industry Dr (15275-1001)
PHONE....................................412 490-8300
Kimberly Resnick, *Regional Mgr*
Bob Forte, *Senior VP*
Lori Crozier, *Vice Pres*
Jeff Gleason, *Vice Pres*
Robert Lozano, *Vice Pres*
EMP: 3500
SALES (corp-wide): 24.3B Publicly Held
SIC: 3826 Analytical instruments
PA: Thermo Fisher Scientific Inc.
168 3rd Ave
Waltham MA 02451
781 622-1000

(G-15614)
THERMO FISHER SCIENTIFIC INC
600 Business Center Dr (15205-1334)
PHONE....................................412 490-8000
Michael Guz, *IT/INT Sup*
EMP: 54
SALES (est): 33.2MM Privately Held
SIC: 3826 Analytical instruments

(G-15615)
THERMO SHANDON INC (HQ)
Also Called: Lerner Laboratories
171 Industry Dr (15275-1015)
PHONE....................................412 788-1133
Mark J Zinsky, *President*
Marijn Dekkers, *COO*
Stephen Sheehan, *Senior VP*
Jeff Brant, *Vice Pres*
Michael Bono, *CFO*
▲ EMP: 2
SQ FT: 70,000
SALES (est): 4.7MM
SALES (corp-wide): 24.3B Publicly Held
SIC: 3821 5049 3826 3825 Laboratory equipment: fume hoods, distillation racks, etc.; laboratory equipment, except medical or dental; analytical instruments; instruments to measure electricity; industrial organic chemicals; industrial inorganic chemicals
PA: Thermo Fisher Scientific Inc.
168 3rd Ave
Waltham MA 02451
781 622-1000

(G-15616)
THOROUGHCARE INC ✪
100 S Commons Ste 102 (15212-5359)
PHONE....................................412 737-7332
Dan Godla, *President*
EMP: 8 EST: 2018
SALES (est): 187.5K Privately Held
SIC: 7372 Prepackaged software

(G-15617)
THREAD INTERNATIONAL PBC INC
7800 Susquehanna St (15208-2118)
PHONE....................................814 876-9999
Ian Rosenberger, *CEO*
Lee Kimball, *COO*
Jenna Knapp, *Opers Staff*
Caroline Smith, *Pub Rel Mgr*
Kelsey Halling, *Director*
EMP: 8
SALES (est): 465.6K Privately Held
SIC: 2299 5093 Textile mill waste & remnant processing; scrap & waste materials

(G-15618)
THREE RIVERS CONFECTIONS LLC
Also Called: Fudgiewudgie
3530 Smallman St (15201)
PHONE....................................412 402-0388
Richard Condie, *President*
Phin Stubbs, *Chairman*
James Chandler, *CFO*
Carol Schmid, *Admin Sec*
Rob Solomon,
EMP: 60
SQ FT: 35,000
SALES (est): 15.5MM Privately Held
SIC: 2064 Candy & other confectionery products

(G-15619)
THREE RIVERS MOTHERS MILK BANK
3127 Penn Ave (15201-1421)
PHONE....................................412 281-4400
Beverly Brozanski, *Director*
Nilima Karamchandani, *Director*
EMP: 10 EST: 2015
SALES (est): 458.2K Privately Held
SIC: 2026 8399 Fluid milk; health systems agency

(G-15620)
THREE RIVERS OPTICAL COMPANY
260 Bilmar Dr (15205-4601)
PHONE....................................412 928-2020
William Seibert, *President*
Madolin Seibert, *Vice Pres*
Mary Ann, *Sales Mgr*
Tiffany Ernst, *Manager*
EMP: 75 EST: 1969
SQ FT: 3,000
SALES (est): 13.7MM Privately Held
WEB: www.threeriversoptical.com
SIC: 3827 3851 3229 3211 Lenses, optical: all types except ophthalmic; ophthalmic goods; pressed & blown glass; flat glass

(G-15621)
THREE RIVERS ORTHOTICS PRSTHTI
305 Overdale Rd (15221-4435)
PHONE....................................412 371-2318
EMP: 3
SALES (est): 191.6K Privately Held
SIC: 3842 Orthopedic appliances

(G-15622)
THRUWAYS DOOR SYSTEMS INC
400 Poplar St (15223-2221)
PHONE....................................412 781-4030
Dale Lichy, *President*
Barbara Lichy, *Vice Pres*
EMP: 12
SQ FT: 20,000
SALES: 800K Privately Held
SIC: 3442 5211 Rolling doors for industrial buildings or warehouses, metal; lumber & other building materials

(G-15623)
THYSSENKRUPP ELEVATOR CORP
539 Rochester Rd (15237-1747)
PHONE....................................412 364-2624
Christopher A Fisher, *Manager*
EMP: 45
SALES (corp-wide): 39.8B Privately Held
WEB: www.tyssenkrupp.com
SIC: 7699 3999 1796 Elevators: inspection, service & repair; wheelchair lifts; elevator installation & conversion
HQ: Thyssenkrupp Elevator Corporation
11605 Haynes Bridge Rd # 650
Alpharetta GA 30009
678 319-3240

(G-15624)
TI OREGON INC (DH)
1000 Six Ppg Pl (15222)
PHONE....................................412 394-2800
Richard J Harshman, *President*
EMP: 5
SALES (est): 963.1K Publicly Held
SIC: 3312 3339 3545 Stainless steel; primary nonferrous metals; machine tool accessories
HQ: Oregon Metallurgical, Llc
1000 Six Ppg Pl
Pittsburgh PA 15222
541 967-9000

(G-15625)
TITAN ROBOTICS INC
2516 Jane St (15203-2216)
PHONE....................................724 986-6737

▲ = Import ▼=Export
◆ =Import/Export

Stuart Lawrence, *CEO*
Charlene Bach, *CFO*
EMP: 3
SALES (est): 281.4K **Privately Held**
SIC: 3728 7389 Research & dev by
manuf., aircraft parts & auxiliary equip;

(G-15626)
TITAN TECHNOLOGIES INC (PA)
2543 Washington Rd # 900 (15241-2513)
PHONE..........................888 671-6649
EMP: 7
SQ FT: 2,800
SALES (est): 2.5MM **Privately Held**
SIC: 7371 7372 7379 Custom Computer
Programing Prepackaged Software Serv-
ices Computer Related Services

(G-15627)
TITUSVILLE ENTERPRISES INC (PA)
Also Called: Titusville Fabricators
700 Blaw Ave Ste 300 (15238-3216)
P.O. Box 111296 (15238-0696)
PHONE..........................412 826-8140
Ronald D Flach, *President*
Dennis Bernotas, *Vice Pres*
EMP: 8
SQ FT: 2,000
SALES (est): 9.1MM **Privately Held**
SIC: 3312 Bar, rod & wire products

(G-15628)
TMI INTERNATIONAL LLC (DH)
5350 Campbells Run Rd (15205-9738)
PHONE..........................412 787-9750
Patrick McMullen, *CFO*
▲ **EMP:** 57
SQ FT: 30,000
SALES (est): 23.5MM
SALES (corp-wide): 6.3B **Privately Held**
SIC: 2821 Polyvinyl chloride resins (PVC)
HQ: Tmi Holdco, Inc.
5350 Campbells Run Rd
Pittsburgh PA 15205
412 787-9750

(G-15629)
TMS INTERNATIONAL LLC
516 Delwar Rd (15236-1352)
PHONE..........................412 885-3600
Debbie Zawatski, *Purchasing*
Tammy Jakowski, *Manager*
Keith Miller, *Systems Mgr*
EMP: 50 **Privately Held**
WEB: www.tubecity.com
SIC: 5093 3341 Nonferrous metals scrap;
secondary nonferrous metals
HQ: Tms International, Llc
12 Monongahela Ave
Glassport PA 15045
412 678-6141

(G-15630)
TOBII DYNAVOX LLC (HQ)
2100 Wharton St Ste 400 (15203-1942)
PHONE..........................412 381-4883
Tara Rudnicki, *President*
Robert Cunningham, *President*
Anthony Pavlik, *President*
Frederick Ruben, *Corp Secy*
John Leydig, *Buyer*
▲ **EMP:** 150
SQ FT: 11,000
SALES (est): 40.3MM **Privately Held**
WEB: www.dynavoxtech.com
SIC: 3679 Recording heads, speech & mu-
sical equipment

(G-15631)
TOM JAMES COMPANY
412-414 Strawberry Way (15219)
PHONE..........................412 642-2797
EMP: 11
SALES (corp-wide): 618.7MM **Privately Held**
SIC: 2311 Mfg Men's/Boy's Suits/Coats
PA: Tom James Company
263 Seaboard Ln
Franklin TN 37067
615 771-1122

(G-15632)
TOMAYKO GROUP LLC (PA)
2403 Sidney St Ste 220 (15203-5119)
PHONE..........................412 481-0600

Valerie Wilt, *Finance*
Donald Ashton, *Human Res Dir*
John Tomayko, *Mng Member*
EMP: 16
SALES (est): 3.1MM **Privately Held**
SIC: 2834 8741 7361 Pharmaceutical
preparations; management services; em-
ployment agencies

(G-15633)
TOTAL SYSTEMS TECHNOLOGY INC (PA)
Also Called: TST
65 Terence Dr (15236-4198)
PHONE..........................412 653-7690
Charles Piscatelli, *President*
Thomas Sullivan, *General Mgr*
Bonnie Piscatelli, *Corp Secy*
EMP: 11
SQ FT: 16,000
SALES (est): 6.3MM **Privately Held**
WEB: www.tst.com
SIC: 2821 2842 3479 2899 Polytetrafluo-
roethylene resins (teflon); waxes for
wood, leather & other materials; specialty
cleaning preparations; coating of metals
with plastic or resins; chemical prepara-
tions; paints & allied products

(G-15634)
TP (OLD) LLC
Also Called: Tcp Printing Company
2403 Sidney St Ste 500 (15203-2167)
P.O. Box 4295 (15203-0295)
PHONE..........................412 488-1600
Gregg Bozzi, *President*
EMP: 40
SALES (est): 8.1MM **Privately Held**
SIC: 2752 Commercial printing, litho-
graphic

(G-15635)
TRANE US INC
400 Business Center Dr # 1 (15205-1337)
PHONE..........................412 747-3000
Steve Wey, *Branch Mgr*
EMP: 100 **Privately Held**
SIC: 3585 Refrigeration & heating equip-
ment
HQ: Trane U.S. Inc.
3600 Pammel Creek Rd
La Crosse WI 54601
608 787-2000

(G-15636)
TRANE US INC
Also Called: Pittsburgh Trane Parts Center
3042 New Beaver Ave (15233-1029)
PHONE..........................412 394-9021
Brian Sellew, *Manager*
EMP: 14 **Privately Held**
SIC: 3585 Refrigeration & heating equip-
ment
HQ: Trane U.S. Inc.
3600 Pammel Creek Rd
La Crosse WI 54601
608 787-2000

(G-15637)
TRANE US INC
2501 Smallman St (15222-4699)
PHONE..........................412 963-9021
Dean Howell, *Branch Mgr*
EMP: 8 **Privately Held**
SIC: 3585 Refrigeration & heating equip-
ment
HQ: Trane U.S. Inc.
3600 Pammel Creek Rd
La Crosse WI 54601
608 787-2000

(G-15638)
TRANS ENERGY INC (HQ)
625 Liberty Ave Ste 1790 (15222-3111)
PHONE..........................304 684-7053
David E Schlosser Jr, *President*
Brett Greene, *Vice Pres*
Daniel A Greenblatt, *Treasurer*
Nicole H King Yohe, *Admin Sec*
EMP: 11
SQ FT: 4,400

SALES: 12.4MM
SALES (corp-wide): 4.5B **Publicly Held**
WEB: www.transenergy.com
SIC: 1311 1382 1321 Crude petroleum &
natural gas production; oil & gas explo-
ration services; natural gas liquids
PA: Eqt Corporation
625 Liberty Ave Ste 1700
Pittsburgh PA 15222
412 553-5700

(G-15639)
TRANS-TECH TECHNOLOGIES INC
3247 Old Frankstown Rd C (15239-2916)
PHONE..........................724 327-6600
Savnaat Nagpaul, *President*
EMP: 3
SQ FT: 2,400
SALES: 1MM **Privately Held**
WEB: www.electricalweb.com
SIC: 3646 5063 Commercial indusl & insti-
tutional electric lighting fixtures; lighting
fixtures, commercial & industrial

(G-15640)
TRANSTAR INDUSTRIES INC
6550 Hamilton Ave (15206-4128)
PHONE..........................412 441-7353
Mark Famine, *Branch Mgr*
EMP: 9 **Privately Held**
SIC: 3999 Barber & beauty shop equip-
ment
HQ: Transtar Industries Llc
7350 Young Dr
Cleveland OH 44146
440 232-5100

(G-15641)
TREASURES INC
2180 Noblestown Rd (15205-3804)
PHONE..........................412 920-5421
John E Connelly, *CEO*
Regis McGrady, *President*
EMP: 6
SALES (est): 450K **Privately Held**
WEB: www.treasuresinc.com
SIC: 3961 Rosaries & small religious arti-
cles, except precious metal

(G-15642)
TRENCH SHORING SERVICES
1200 Neville Rd (15225-1609)
PHONE..........................412 331-8118
Ken Taytas, *Manager*
EMP: 6
SALES (corp-wide): 14.6MM **Privately Held**
SIC: 5082 3531 1799 General construc-
tion machinery & equipment; road con-
struction & maintenance machinery;
shoring & underpinning work
PA: Trench Shoring Services Of Jack-
sonville, Inc
6770 E 56th Ave
Commerce City CO 80022
303 287-2248

(G-15643)
TRESCO PAVING CORPORATION (PA)
415 Unity Center Rd (15239-3409)
P.O. Box 14004 (15239-0004)
PHONE..........................412 793-0651
Sonny Tresco, *President*
Salvatore Tresco, *President*
Diane Tresco, *Corp Secy*
Vincent Tresco, *Vice Pres*
EMP: 3
SQ FT: 2,000
SALES (est): 6.2MM **Privately Held**
SIC: 1611 2911 Surfacing & paving; as-
phalt or asphaltic materials, made in re-
fineries

(G-15644)
TRI STATE FILTER MFG CO
744 Edmond St (15224-2003)
PHONE..........................412 621-8491
Gloria Ledonne, *President*
Robert Ledonne, *Vice Pres*
EMP: 5 EST: 1937
SQ FT: 6,000
SALES: 175K **Privately Held**
SIC: 3564 Filters, air: furnaces, air condi-
tioning equipment, etc.

(G-15645)
TRI-AD LITHO INC
1385 Frey Rd (15235-4099)
PHONE..........................412 795-3110
John Novosel, *President*
EMP: 11
SQ FT: 7,200
SALES (est): 2.1MM **Privately Held**
WEB: www.triadlitho.com
SIC: 2752 Commercial printing, offset

(G-15646)
TRI-RIVERS ELECTRIC INC
35 W Prospect Ave (15205-2240)
PHONE..........................412 290-6525
Sandra Mdurkin, *President*
EMP: 7
SALES (est): 51.8K **Privately Held**
SIC: 3699 Electrical work

(G-15647)
TRI-STATE REPROGRAPHICS INC
2934 Smallman St (15201-1523)
PHONE..........................412 281-3538
George R Marshall, *President*
EMP: 12
SQ FT: 5,000
SALES (est): 1.3MM **Privately Held**
SIC: 7334 2759 Blueprinting service; com-
mercial printing

(G-15648)
TRIANGLE POSTER AND PRTG CO
2119 Robinson Blvd (15221-1562)
PHONE..........................412 371-0774
Alan Rosenberg, *President*
EMP: 10
SQ FT: 10,000
SALES (est): 860K **Privately Held**
SIC: 2759 Commercial printing

(G-15649)
TRINITY MINING SERVICES INC
Also Called: Diversified Wear Products
109 48th St (15201-2755)
PHONE..........................412 605-0612
Jim Lester, *Principal*
Lauren Wright, *Buyer*
Anita King, *Credit Mgr*
Sam McCullough, *Human Resources*
▲ **EMP:** 9
SQ FT: 900
SALES (est): 1MM
SALES (corp-wide): 2.5B **Publicly Held**
WEB: www.trin.net
SIC: 3499 Machine bases, metal
PA: Trinity Industries, Inc.
2525 N Stemmons Fwy
Dallas TX 75207
214 631-4420

(G-15650)
TRINITY SUP & INSTALLATION LLC
288a Corliss St (15220-4814)
PHONE..........................412 331-3044
Richard Berteotti, *Mng Member*
William Maceikis,
Amy Macklin,
EMP: 10
SQ FT: 16,000
SALES (est): 2.6MM **Privately Held**
SIC: 5033 5031 2434 Roofing, siding &
insulation; doors & windows; wood
kitchen cabinets

(G-15651)
TRIPLE TROPHY PRODUCTS INC
1102 N Canal St Ste E (15215-2444)
PHONE..........................412 781-8801
Fax: 412 781-4072
EMP: 4
SQ FT: 3,000
SALES (est): 284.9K **Privately Held**
SIC: 3949 Mfg Sporting/Athletic Goods

(G-15652)
TRIREME ENERGY DEVELOPMENT LLC
1251 Waterfront Pl Fl 3 (15222-4228)
PHONE..........................412 253-9400

James A Spencer, *CEO*
Michael Current, *CFO*
EMP: 60
SQ FT: 16,088
SALES (est): 2MM **Privately Held**
SIC: 3511 Turbines & turbine generator sets & parts

(G-15653)
TRISTATE BLUE PRINTING INC
Also Called: Tri-State Blueprinting
2934 Smallman St (15201-1523)
PHONE....................412 281-3538
George Marshall, *President*
EMP: 25
SALES (est): 2MM **Privately Held**
WEB: www.tsrepro.com
SIC: 2752 Commercial printing, offset

(G-15654)
TRIUMPH SALES INC
51 Bridge St Ste 100 (15223-2222)
PHONE....................412 781-0950
Richard Bruno, *President*
Anthony Bruno, *Vice Pres*
EMP: 8
SALES (est): 1MM **Privately Held**
SIC: 3432 5074 Plumbing fixture fittings & trim; plumbing fittings & supplies

(G-15655)
TRUFOOD MFG INC
106 Gamma Dr (15238-2985)
PHONE....................412 963-6600
EMP: 371
SALES (corp-wide): 206.1MM **Privately Held**
SIC: 2066 Chocolate
PA: Trufood Mfg., Inc.
610 Alpha Dr
Pittsburgh PA 15238
412 963-2330

(G-15656)
TRUFOOD MFG INC (PA)
610 Alpha Dr (15238-2802)
PHONE....................412 963-2330
Peter S Tsudis, *President*
George S Tsudis, *Vice Pres*
▲ **EMP:** 229
SQ FT: 155,000
SALES (est): 206.1MM **Privately Held**
SIC: 2066 2064 Chocolate; candy & other confectionery products; breakfast bars

(G-15657)
TRUGEN3 LLC
733 Wshington Rd Ste 211 (15228)
PHONE....................412 668-3831
Micheal Lioon, *Mng Member*
EMP: 3
SALES (est): 316K **Privately Held**
SIC: 2023 5122 Dietary supplements, dairy & non-dairy based; vitamins & minerals

(G-15658)
TRUST FRANKLIN PRESS CO
516 Bingham St (15203-1004)
PHONE....................412 481-6442
Gary Friedman, *President*
Bozicevich Gibby, *Foreman/Supr*
EMP: 15 EST: 1947
SQ FT: 8,000
SALES (est): 2.5MM **Privately Held**
WEB: www.trust-franklinpress.com
SIC: 2752 Commercial printing, offset

(G-15659)
TSB GROUP LLC
Also Called: Sweet Tammy's Bakery
2119 Murray Ave (15217-2105)
PHONE....................412 224-2306
Tamara Berkowitz,
Daniel Berkowitz,
EMP: 6 EST: 2006
SQ FT: 1,000
SALES (est): 675.3K **Privately Held**
SIC: 2051 Cakes, pies & pastries

(G-15660)
TUMACS CORP (PA)
50 Terence Dr (15236-4199)
PHONE....................412 653-1188
Robert Mc Call, *President*
Robert McCall, *President*

Scott McCall, *Treasurer*
EMP: 30
SQ FT: 5,000
SALES (est): 3.6MM **Privately Held**
SIC: 2394 Tarpaulins, fabric: made from purchased materials

(G-15661)
TURNER DAIRY FARMS INC (PA)
1049 Jefferson Rd (15235-4700)
PHONE....................412 372-7155
Charles H Turner Jr, *President*
Mike Agate, *Buyer*
Catherine Turner, *Human Res Dir*
Walter M Turner, *VP Sales*
Debby Lilac, *Sales Staff*
EMP: 93 EST: 1930
SQ FT: 15,000
SALES (est): 73.6MM **Privately Held**
SIC: 2022 2026 5451 2024 Processed cheese; milk processing (pasteurizing, homogenizing, bottling); dairy products stores; ice cream & frozen desserts; creamery butter; dairy farms

(G-15662)
TURNITIN LLC
160 N Craig St (15213-2716)
PHONE....................724 272-7250
Chris Caren, *President*
EMP: 6
SALES (corp-wide): 5.5B **Privately Held**
SIC: 7372 Educational computer software
HQ: Turnitin, Llc
2101 Webster St Ste 1800
Oakland CA 94612
866 816-5046

(G-15663)
TYPECRAFT PRESS INC
2403 Sidney St 500 (15203-2167)
P.O. Box 4295 (15203-0295)
PHONE....................412 488-1600
John A Major, *President*
Greg Bozzi, *President*
Richard G Major, *Vice Pres*
Edward J Major, *Treasurer*
Bernard A Klein, *Admin Sec*
EMP: 30
SALES (est): 4.6MM
SALES (corp-wide): 20MM **Privately Held**
WEB: www.typecraftpress.com
SIC: 2752 2791 2789 2759 Commercial printing, offset; typesetting; bookbinding & related work; commercial printing
HQ: Pemcor Printing Company, Llc
330 Eden Rd
Lancaster PA 17601
717 898-1555

(G-15664)
TYSON FOODS INC
1344 Greystone Dr (15241-3259)
PHONE....................412 257-3224
Mark Neice, *Principal*
EMP: 277
SALES (corp-wide): 40B **Publicly Held**
SIC: 2011 Meat packing plants
PA: Tyson Foods, Inc.
2200 W Don Tyson Pkwy
Springdale AR 72762
479 290-4000

(G-15665)
U SQUARED INTERACTIVE LLC
339 6th Ave Ste 1100 (15222-2507)
PHONE....................214 770-7437
Derrick Stratman,
EMP: 3 EST: 2011
SALES (est): 132.2K **Privately Held**
SIC: 7372 Application computer software

(G-15666)
UBER ATC
Also Called: Uber Advance Technologies Ctr
91 43rd St Ste 220 (15201-3161)
PHONE....................412 587-2986
EMP: 7
SALES (est): 91K **Privately Held**
SIC: 7372 Application computer software

(G-15667)
UKANI BROTHERS ENTERPRISE
2900 Banksville Rd (15216-2717)
PHONE....................412 269-0499

Bharet Ukani, *CEO*
EMP: 4
SALES (est): 483.3K **Privately Held**
SIC: 3578 Automatic teller machines (ATM)

(G-15668)
UNA BIOLOGICALS LLC
4322 Butler St (15201-3010)
PHONE....................412 889-9746
Jessica Graves,
EMP: 6
SALES: 98K **Privately Held**
SIC: 2844 Toilet preparations

(G-15669)
UNION MIN CO OF ALLEGHENY CNTY
Also Called: Kingston Brick Co
31 Moffett St (15243)
PHONE....................412 344-9900
N E Talovic, *Corp Secy*
EMP: 20
SALES (est): 2.3MM **Privately Held**
SIC: 5085 3255 Refractory material; clay refractories

(G-15670)
UNION ORTHOTICS PROSTHETICS CO
Also Called: Union Orthotics Prosthetics Co
5704 Brownsville Rd (15236-3504)
PHONE....................412 943-1950
Greg Reich, *Manager*
EMP: 6
SALES (corp-wide): 8MM **Privately Held**
WEB: www.unionoandp.com
SIC: 3842 5999 Limbs, artificial; braces, orthopedic; artificial limbs
PA: Union Orthotics & Prosthetics Co.
3424 Liberty Ave
Pittsburgh PA
412 622-2020

(G-15671)
UNION ORTHOTICS PROSTHETICS CO
6301 Northumberland St (15217-1360)
PHONE....................412 621-2698
John Wilson, *Manager*
EMP: 45
SALES (corp-wide): 8MM **Privately Held**
WEB: www.unionoandp.com
SIC: 3842 5999 Limbs, artificial; braces, orthopedic; artificial limbs
PA: Union Orthotics & Prosthetics Co.
3424 Liberty Ave
Pittsburgh PA
412 622-2020

(G-15672)
UNION SWITCH AND SIGNAL
68 Renova St (15207-1856)
PHONE....................412 688-2400
EMP: 5
SALES (est): 572.2K **Privately Held**
SIC: 3679 Electronic switches

(G-15673)
UNIPACK INC (PA)
Also Called: US PHARMACEUTICALS
3253 Old Frankstown Rd (15239-2940)
PHONE....................724 733-7381
Harilal Patel, *President*
Dinesh Patel, *Vice Pres*
Jimeet Patel, *Programmer Anys*
Jimit Patel, *Director*
Ranjan Patel, *Director*
▲ **EMP:** 4
SQ FT: 16,000
SALES: 6.5MM **Privately Held**
WEB: www.unipackinc.com
SIC: 2834 2844 Powders, pharmaceutical; solutions, pharmaceutical; toilet preparations

(G-15674)
UNITED OIL COMPANY CORP
1800 N Franklin St (15233-2295)
PHONE....................412 231-1269
Lane Feick, *President*
EMP: 10 EST: 1906
SQ FT: 30,000

SALES (est): 2.6MM **Privately Held**
WEB: www.unitedoil.com
SIC: 2992 5169 Lubricating oils; chemicals & allied products

(G-15675)
UNITED STATES PRODUCTS CO
Also Called: Lap-O-Valve
518 Melwood Ave (15213-1194)
PHONE....................412 621-2130
Leland C Brown Jr, *President*
Joann Tierney, *Manager*
EMP: 7
SQ FT: 15,000
SALES: 800K **Privately Held**
WEB: www.us-products.com
SIC: 3291 Abrasive products

(G-15676)
UNITED STATES STEEL CORP
Also Called: USS Irvin Works Plant
1268 Camp Hollow Rd (15122)
PHONE....................412 433-1121
David Lohr, *Manager*
EMP: 3367
SALES (corp-wide): 14.1B **Publicly Held**
SIC: 3325 Steel foundries
PA: United States Steel Corp
600 Grant St Ste 468
Pittsburgh PA 15219
412 433-1121

(G-15677)
UNITED STATES STEEL CORP (PA)
600 Grant St Ste 468 (15219-2805)
P.O. Box 267 (15230-0267)
PHONE....................412 433-1121
David S Sutherland, *Ch of Bd*
David B Burritt, *President*
James E Bruno, *President*
James Warren, *Division Mgr*
Amy Smith-Yoder, *General Mgr*
◆ **EMP:** 277
SALES: 14.1B **Publicly Held**
WEB: www.uss.com
SIC: 3312 3317 3356 Blast furnaces & steel mills; plate, steel; sheet or strip, steel, cold-rolled: own hot-rolled; chemicals & other products derived from coking; steel pipe & tubes; tin

(G-15678)
UNITED STATES STEEL CORP
U. S. Steel Tubular
600 Grant St Ste 468 (15219-2805)
PHONE....................412 433-1121
EMP: 235
SALES (corp-wide): 14.1B **Publicly Held**
SIC: 3312 Plate, steel
PA: United States Steel Corp
600 Grant St Ste 468
Pittsburgh PA 15219
412 433-1121

(G-15679)
UNITED STATES STEEL CORP
1509 Muriel St (15203-1535)
PHONE....................412 433-1419
Carl Downer, *Vice Pres*
Don Wright, *Administration*
James Stewart, *Analyst*
EMP: 235
SALES (corp-wide): 14.1B **Publicly Held**
SIC: 3312 Blast furnaces & steel mills
PA: United States Steel Corp
600 Grant St Ste 468
Pittsburgh PA 15219
412 433-1121

(G-15680)
UNITI TITANIUM LLC
400 Industry Dr Ste 220 (15275-1042)
PHONE....................412 424-0440
Andy Duan, *General Mgr*
Michael Metz, *Mng Member*
◆ **EMP:** 20
SALES (est): 10.7MM **Privately Held**
WEB: www.unitititanium.com
SIC: 3356 Titanium

(G-15681)
UNITY MARBLE AND GRANITE INC
3201 Universal Rd (15235-2506)
PHONE....................412 793-4220

John Carlino, *President*
EMP: 6
SQ FT: 3,000
SALES: 700K **Privately Held**
SIC: 3281 5032 1799 1743 Marble, building: cut & shaped; granite, cut & shaped; marble building stone; counter top installation; tile installation, ceramic

(G-15682)
UNIVERSITY OF PITTSBURGH
Also Called: University of Pittsburgh Press
3400 4th Ave Fl 5 Eurka B Flr 5 (15260)
PHONE..................412 383-2456
Peter Croft, *Director*
EMP: 15
SALES (corp-wide): 2.2B **Privately Held**
WEB: www.pitt.edu
SIC: 2731 8221 Books: publishing only; university
PA: University Of Pittsburgh
4200 5th Ave
Pittsburgh PA 15260
412 624-4141

(G-15683)
UNIVERSITY OF PITTSBURGH
Also Called: Pitt News
434 William Pitt Un (15260)
PHONE..................412 648-7980
Annie Tubbs, *Principal*
EMP: 115
SALES (corp-wide): 2.2B **Privately Held**
WEB: www.pitt.edu
SIC: 2711 8221 Newspapers; university
PA: University Of Pittsburgh
4200 5th Ave
Pittsburgh PA 15260
412 624-4141

(G-15684)
UNIVERSITY PITTSBURGH MED CTR
200 Lothrop St (15213-2536)
PHONE..................412 647-8762
EMP: 14
SALES (corp-wide): 12.8B **Privately Held**
SIC: 2834 Medicines, capsuled or ampuled
PA: Upmc
200 Lothrop St
Pittsburgh PA 15213
412 647-8762

(G-15685)
URGENT DENTURE REPAIR LLC
1201 Broughton Rd (15236-3451)
PHONE..................412 714-8157
Nick Carrington, *Mng Member*
Wakike Jones,
EMP: 3
SALES (est): 200K **Privately Held**
SIC: 3843 8021 Dental equipment & supplies; dental clinic

(G-15686)
URSUS MEDICAL LLC
100 Sandune Dr (15239-2716)
PHONE..................412 779-4016
Thomas Hayes, *CEO*
EMP: 3
SALES (est): 152.6K **Privately Held**
SIC: 3845 Electromedical equipment

(G-15687)
US STEEL HOLDINGS INC
600 Grant St Fl 1 (15219-2750)
PHONE..................412 433-1121
EMP: 1
SALES (est): 1.6MM
SALES (corp-wide): 14.1B **Publicly Held**
SIC: 3317 3356 3312 Steel pipe & tubes; tin; plate, steel
PA: United States Steel Corp
600 Grant St Ste 468
Pittsburgh PA 15219
412 433-1121

(G-15688)
V L H INC (DH)
Also Called: H V L
600 Boyce Rd (15205-9742)
PHONE..................800 245-4440
L Douglas Liioon, *President*
Harry E Vernacchio, *President*
▲ EMP: 340
SQ FT: 75,000

SALES (est): 94.1MM
SALES (corp-wide): 90.8B **Privately Held**
SIC: 2833 5122 2834 Vitamins, natural or synthetic; drugs, uncompounded; drugs, proprietaries & sundries; pharmaceutical preparations
HQ: Atrium Innovations Inc
3500 Boul De Maisonneuve O Bureau 2405
Westmount QC H3Z 3
514 205-6240

(G-15689)
VCI COATINGS LLC
437 Grant St Ste 1210 (15219-6101)
PHONE..................412 281-1202
Robert Walde, *Mng Member*
EMP: 3
SALES (est): 110.8K
SALES (corp-wide): 1.1MM **Privately Held**
SIC: 1771 5169 3479 Concrete work; concrete additives; painting, coating & hot dipping
PA: Surtreat Holding, L.L.C.
437 Grant St Ste 1210
Pittsburgh PA 15219
412 281-1202

(G-15690)
VELOCITY ROBOTICS
100 S Commons Ste 102 (15212-5359)
PHONE..................412 254-3011
Brad Kriel, *CEO*
EMP: 5 EST: 2014
SALES: 75K **Privately Held**
SIC: 3546 Power-driven handtools

(G-15691)
VENTASIA INC
6108 Howe St (15206-4242)
PHONE..................412 661-6600
Faith Bennett, *President*
EMP: 3
SALES (est): 258.9K **Privately Held**
SIC: 2721 Magazines: publishing only, not printed on site

(G-15692)
VERICHEM INC
Also Called: Lanxess
3499 Grand Ave (15225-1507)
PHONE..................412 331-2616
V James Gregory, *President*
Theodore W Zierden, *Vice Pres*
David Jaszcar, *Marketing Staff*
Charles Hrelec, *Manager*
▼ EMP: 20
SALES (est): 4.7MM
SALES (corp-wide): 8.2B **Privately Held**
WEB: www.verichem.com
SIC: 2865 Cyclic crudes & intermediates
HQ: Lanxess Corporation
111 Ridc Park West Dr
Pittsburgh PA 15275
800 526-9377

(G-15693)
VERTICAL ACCESS SOLUTIONS LLC (DH)
4465 Campbells Run Rd (15205-1311)
PHONE..................412 787-9102
Chris Altmeyer, *President*
EMP: 6
SALES: 26.8MM **Privately Held**
SIC: 2591 Blinds vertical
HQ: Enterprise Industrial Group Llc
4465 Campbells Run Rd
Pittsburgh PA 15205
717 399-5272

(G-15694)
VESUVIUS U S A CORPORATION
250 Parkwest Dr (15275-1002)
PHONE..................412 276-1750
Paul Edwards, *Production*
Dave Phillips, *Sales Mgr*
Lou Sebastian, *Manager*
Russ Pinzone, *Director*
EMP: 150
SALES (corp-wide): 2.2B **Privately Held**
WEB: www.vesuvius.com
SIC: 3297 Graphite refractories: carbon bond or ceramic bond

HQ: Vesuvius U S A Corporation
1404 Newton Dr
Champaign IL 61822
217 351-5000

(G-15695)
VESUVIUS U S A CORPORATION
4604 Campbells Run Rd (15205-1316)
PHONE..................419 986-5126
Jim Stendera, *General Mgr*
EMP: 28
SALES (corp-wide): 2.2B **Privately Held**
WEB: www.vesuvius.com
SIC: 3297 Commercial Nonphysical Research
HQ: Vesuvius U S A Corporation
1404 Newton Dr
Champaign IL 61822
217 351-5000

(G-15696)
VESUVIUS U S A CORPORATION
4604 Campbells Run Rd (15205-1316)
PHONE..................412 788-4441
Duane Debastiani, *Research*
Phil Rahn, *Accounts Mgr*
Maribeth Mulkerrin, *Office Mgr*
Don Mikulan, *Supervisor*
EMP: 55
SALES (corp-wide): 2.2B **Privately Held**
WEB: www.vesuvius.com
SIC: 3297 Nonclay refractories
HQ: Vesuvius U S A Corporation
1404 Newton Dr
Champaign IL 61822
217 351-5000

(G-15697)
VESUVIUS U S A CORPORATION
250 Parkwest Dr (15275-1002)
PHONE..................412 429-1800
John McDonough, *Chairman*
EMP: 10
SALES (corp-wide): 2.2B **Privately Held**
WEB: www.vesuvius.com
SIC: 3264 Porcelain electrical supplies
HQ: Vesuvius U S A Corporation
1404 Newton Dr
Champaign IL 61822
217 351-5000

(G-15698)
VIKING WOODWORKING LLC
201 E Carson St (15219-1105)
PHONE..................412 381-5171
EMP: 3
SALES: 350K **Privately Held**
SIC: 2434 Mfg Wood Kitchen Cabinets

(G-15699)
VISTA RESOURCES INC (PA)
Also Called: Vista Mercer County
61 Mcmurray Rd Ste 300 (15241-1633)
PHONE..................412 833-8884
Clark R Nicklas, *CEO*
David M Nicklas, *President*
Arlene Cassidy, *Vice Pres*
Thomas R Michael, *Vice Pres*
EMP: 1
SQ FT: 900
SALES (est): 4.6MM **Privately Held**
SIC: 1381 Drilling oil & gas wells

(G-15700)
VIVINO SELECTIONS INC
24 Woodville Ave 2 (15220-5416)
PHONE..................412 920-1336
Richard Francis, *President*
EMP: 4
SALES (est): 158.7K **Privately Held**
SIC: 2084 5182 Wines; bottling wines & liquors

(G-15701)
VOCI TECHNOLOGIES INCORPORATED
6301 Forbes Ave Ste 120 (15217-1725)
P.O. Box 1668, Herndon VA (20172-1668)
PHONE..................412 621-9310
Michael Coney, *CEO*
Anthony Gadient, *President*
Wayne Ramprashad, *COO*
Rob Rutenbar, *Vice Pres*
Tim Wallick, *Vice Pres*
EMP: 10

SALES (est): 2.1MM **Privately Held**
WEB: www.vocitec.com
SIC: 3571 Electronic computers

(G-15702)
VOCOLLECT INC (DH)
703 Rodi Rd (15235-4558)
PHONE..................412 829-8145
Joe Pajer, *President*
James Dilella, *President*
Laurence R Sweeney, *Senior VP*
Robert I Driessnack, *Vice Pres*
Steven M Barto, *CFO*
EMP: 250
SQ FT: 60,000
SALES (est): 119.7MM
SALES (corp-wide): 41.8B **Publicly Held**
WEB: www.vocollect.com
SIC: 3577 3571 7372 Encoders, computer peripheral equipment; electronic computers; application computer software

(G-15703)
VOCOLLECT HEALTHCARE SYSTEMS
701 Rodi Rd Ste 102 (15235-4559)
PHONE..................412 829-8145
Jim Rock, *President*
EMP: 30
SALES (est): 3.5MM
SALES (corp-wide): 41.8B **Publicly Held**
SIC: 3577 Computer peripheral equipment
HQ: Vocollect, Inc.
703 Rodi Rd
Pittsburgh PA 15235
412 829-8145

(G-15704)
VODKA BRANDS CORP
Also Called: Blue Diamond Vodka
554 33rd St (15201-1412)
PHONE..................412 681-7777
Mark Lucero, *President*
EMP: 5
SALES: 150K **Privately Held**
SIC: 2085 Vodka (alcoholic beverage)

(G-15705)
VOEGELE COMPANY INC (PA)
200 Bridge St (15223-2215)
P.O. Box 9543 (15223-0543)
PHONE..................412 781-0940
William P Voegele Jr, *President*
Francis Coholich, *Vice Pres*
Christine Voegele, *Admin Sec*
EMP: 33 EST: 1943
SQ FT: 70,000
SALES (est): 13MM **Privately Held**
WEB: www.extech-voegele.com
SIC: 1761 3442 3444 Roofing contractor; sheet metalwork; siding contractor; sash, door or window: metal; skylights, sheet metal

(G-15706)
W W PATTERSON COMPANY
870 Riversea Rd (15233-1677)
PHONE..................412 322-2012
David B Grapes, *President*
Kristie Ruston, *Controller*
▲ EMP: 20
SQ FT: 22,000
SALES (est): 4.5MM **Privately Held**
WEB: www.winches.com
SIC: 3429 Marine hardware

(G-15707)
WATERS CORPORATION
307 23rd Street Ext (15215)
PHONE..................412 967-5665
ABB Extrel, *Branch Mgr*
EMP: 12 **Publicly Held**
SIC: 3826 Analytical instruments
PA: Waters Corporation
34 Maple St
Milford MA 01757

(G-15708)
WELDED SHTMTL SPECIALTY CO
745 Greenway Dr (15204-2553)
PHONE..................412 331-3534
Frank Mehalov, *President*
William B Wintermatel Jr, *Corp Secy*
EMP: 8

SALES (est): 1.2MM **Privately Held**
SIC: 3444 Sheet metal specialties, not stamped

(G-15709)
WEST PENN EAR NOSE AND THROAT
Also Called: Sonus-USA
4815 Liberty Ave Ste 443 (15224-2156)
PHONE..................................412 621-2656
John Straka Lpn, *Owner*
EMP: 3
SALES (est): 319.5K **Privately Held**
SIC: 3842 Hearing aids

(G-15710)
WESTINGHOUSE ELECTRIC CO LLC
Also Called: Wec
1332 Beulah Rd (15235-5068)
PHONE..................................412 256-1085
Michael Blanciak, *Research*
EMP: 60 **Privately Held**
SIC: 3829 8711 3823 2819 Measuring & controlling devices; electrical or electronic engineering; energy conservation engineering; professional engineer; industrial instrmnts msrmnt display/control process variable; industrial inorganic chemicals
HQ: Westinghouse Electric Company Llc
1000 Westinghouse Dr
Cranberry Township PA 16066
412 374-2020

(G-15711)
WESTINGHOUSE ELECTRIC COMPANY (HQ)
20 Stanwix St (15222-4802)
PHONE..................................866 442-7873
Jose E Gutierrez, *President*
David Howell, *President*
Luc Van Hulle, *President*
Mark Marano, *COO*
Dan Sumner, *CFO*
EMP: 44
SALES (est): 44.3MM **Privately Held**
SIC: 3829 Measuring & controlling devices

(G-15712)
WESTMORELAND MACHINE & ELC CO
Also Called: Driveline Service Pittsburgh
5212 Butler St (15201-2622)
PHONE..................................412 784-1991
Philip D Rodgers Jr, *President*
EMP: 3
SQ FT: 7,500
SALES (est): 373.5K **Privately Held**
WEB: www.westadmat.biz
SIC: 3714 Drive shafts, motor vehicle; axles, motor vehicle

(G-15713)
WG PRODUCTS PITTSBURGH LLC
8031 Saltsburg Rd (15239)
PHONE..................................412 795-7177
Joe Brentzel, *Mng Member*
EMP: 7
SALES: 700K **Privately Held**
SIC: 3621 Power generators

(G-15714)
WHEMCO - STEEL CASTINGS INC (DH)
5 Hot Metal St Ste 300 (15203-2351)
PHONE..................................412 390-2700
Charles R Novelli, *President*
Robert J Peterson, *Vice Pres*
Carl Maskiewicz, *Treasurer*
▼ EMP: 60
SALES (est): 23.1MM
SALES (corp-wide): 568.1MM **Privately Held**
SIC: 3325 Alloy steel castings, except investment
HQ: Whemco Inc.
5 Hot Metal St Ste 300
Pittsburgh PA 15203
412 390-2700

(G-15715)
WHEMCO INC (HQ)
5 Hot Metal St Ste 300 (15203-2351)
PHONE..................................412 390-2700
Charles Novelli, *President*
John Shapaka, *General Mgr*
Kevin Marsden, *Vice Pres*
Carl Maskiewicz, *Vice Pres*
Robert J Peterson, *Vice Pres*
▼ EMP: 27
SQ FT: 8,500
SALES (est): 201MM
SALES (corp-wide): 574.3MM **Privately Held**
WEB: www.whemco.com
SIC: 3312 3462 3731 3325 Blast furnaces & steel mills; iron & steel forgings; shipbuilding & repairing; alloy steel castings, except investment; fabricated structural metal; nonferrous foundries
PA: Park Corporation
6200 Riverside Dr
Cleveland OH 44135
216 267-4870

(G-15716)
WHIRL PUBLISHING
Also Called: Whirl Magazine
2549 Penn Ave Ste 2 (15222-7601)
PHONE..................................412 431-7888
Jack Tumpson, *Owner*
Christine Tumpson, *Chief*
EMP: 17
SALES (est): 2MM **Privately Held**
SIC: 2721 Magazines: publishing only, not printed on site

(G-15717)
WILLIAM PENN PRINTING COMPANY
1800 Preble Ave (15233-2242)
PHONE..................................412 322-3660
Ed Mathews, *CEO*
Grant Matthews, *President*
EMP: 5
SQ FT: 1,500
SALES (est): 815.6K **Privately Held**
SIC: 2752 Commercial printing, offset

(G-15718)
WILSON & MC CRACKEN INC
5255 Butler St (15201-2624)
PHONE..................................412 784-1772
Vicki Mc Cracken, *President*
Gerald Wilson, *Treasurer*
Pam Wilson, *Admin Sec*
EMP: 4
SQ FT: 6,000
SALES: 200K **Privately Held**
SIC: 8712 2431 2499 5031 Architectural engineering; millwork; decorative wood & woodwork; millwork

(G-15719)
WINDSTAX INC
Also Called: Windstax Wind Power Systems
155 Plum Industrial Park (15239-2911)
PHONE..................................412 235-7907
Ronald Gdovic, *CEO*
Mark Goyke, *Opers Mgr*
EMP: 6
SALES (est): 1.2MM **Privately Held**
SIC: 3511 Turbines & turbine generator sets

(G-15720)
WINERY AT WILCOX INC
1940 Sttlers Ridge Ctr Dr (15205-1444)
PHONE..................................412 490-9590
Mike Williams, *Branch Mgr*
EMP: 5
SALES (est): 206.1K **Privately Held**
SIC: 2084 Wines
PA: The Winery At Wilcox Inc
1867 Mefferts Run Rd
Wilcox PA 15870

(G-15721)
WMPM LLC
Also Called: Pittsburgh Magazine
600 Waterfront Dr Ste 100 (15222-4795)
PHONE..................................303 662-5231
Colleen Mote, *Accounts Mgr*
Betsy Benson, *Branch Mgr*
EMP: 20 **Privately Held**
SIC: 2721 Periodicals

PA: Wmpm, Llc
1780 S Bellaire St # 505
Denver CO 80222

(G-15722)
WMS METALS - WELDING ALLOYS
1501 Reedsdale St (15233-2341)
PHONE..................................412 231-3811
EMP: 4 **EST**: 2016
SALES (est): 109.9K **Privately Held**
SIC: 3331 Bars (primary), copper

(G-15723)
WOMBAT SECURITY TECH INC (HQ)
3030 Penn Ave Fl 2 (15201-1521)
PHONE..................................412 621-1484
Joseph Ferrara, *President*
Rob Atherton, *President*
Bill Hallett, *Partner*
Kurt Wescoe, *Vice Pres*
Keith Bartlett, *QA Dir*
EMP: 47
SALES (est): 15.1MM
SALES (corp-wide): 716.9MM **Publicly Held**
SIC: 7372 Business oriented computer software
PA: Proofpoint, Inc.
892 Ross Dr
Sunnyvale CA 94089
408 517-4710

(G-15724)
WOV INC
111 Ryan Ct Ste 200 (15205-1310)
PHONE..................................412 261-3791
Gary Cindrich, *President*
Corey Little, *Vice Pres*
Stuart C Nyman, *Treasurer*
Nicole Milojevic, *Human Res Dir*
Rachel Graham, *Sales Staff*
EMP: 60
SQ FT: 15,000
SALES (est): 7.5MM **Privately Held**
WEB: www.virtualofficeware.net
SIC: 7372 Prepackaged software

(G-15725)
X-DECO LLC
633 Napor Blvd (15205-6501)
PHONE..................................412 257-9755
Ryan Niggel, *President*
Jason Preffer, *Prdtn Mgr*
EMP: 14 **EST**: 2004
SALES (est): 992.4K **Privately Held**
SIC: 2395 2759 Embroidery products, except schiffli machine; screen printing

(G-15726)
XEROX CORPORATION
8 Penn Ctr W Ste 200 (15276-0111)
PHONE..................................412 506-4000
William Walter, *Principal*
Joe Profeta, *Vice Pres*
EMP: 225
SALES (corp-wide): 9.8B **Publicly Held**
WEB: www.xerox.com
SIC: 3861 3577 7629 7378 Photocopy machines; computer peripheral equipment; business machine repair, electric; computer peripheral equipment repair & maintenance; fine paper; equipment & vehicle finance leasing companies
PA: Xerox Corporation
201 Merritt 7
Norwalk CT 06851
203 968-3000

(G-15727)
XPOGO LLC
1256 Franklin Ave (15221-3067)
PHONE..................................717 650-5232
Nicholas Ryan, *Mng Member*
EMP: 5
SQ FT: 300
SALES: 533.8K **Privately Held**
SIC: 3949 Sporting & athletic goods

(G-15728)
Y&Q HOME PLUS LLC
1739 Liberty Ave (15222-4302)
PHONE..................................412 642-6708
Raymond Wu, *Manager*
▲ EMP: 4

SALES (est): 390K **Privately Held**
SIC: 5712 2434 Cabinets, except custom made: kitchen; wood kitchen cabinets

(G-15729)
YESCO PITTSBURGH INC
1290 Western Ave (15233-2028)
PHONE..................................330 747-8593
Lee Derose, *President*
Tina McCoy, *Manager*
EMP: 5
SALES (est): 216K **Privately Held**
SIC: 3612 Distribution transformers, electric

(G-15730)
YOUNG FACE
651 Holiday Dr (15220-2740)
PHONE..................................412 928-2676
Mark Battaline, *Owner*
EMP: 3 **EST**: 2007
SALES (est): 119.8K **Privately Held**
SIC: 2741 Miscellaneous publishing

(G-15731)
YOURE PUTTING ME ON INC
Also Called: Home Town Sports
275 Curry Hollow Rd (15236-4631)
PHONE..................................412 655-9666
Linda C Meyer, *President*
Frances Meyer, *Corp Secy*
EMP: 20
SQ FT: 3,500
SALES: 2.2MM **Privately Held**
SIC: 2261 5611 5621 Screen printing of cotton broadwoven fabrics; clothing accessories: men's & boys'; women's clothing stores

(G-15732)
ZAMA PETROLEUM INC
225 Ross St Ste 4 (15219-2024)
PHONE..................................360 321-6160
Robert Windecker, *President*
EMP: 3 **EST**: 1981
SQ FT: 800
SALES (est): 282.2K **Privately Held**
SIC: 1311 Crude petroleum production

(G-15733)
ZIA-TECH GEAR MFG INC
2131 N Charles St (15214-3714)
PHONE..................................412 321-0770
Walter Ziatech, *President*
EMP: 5
SALES (est): 892.7K **Privately Held**
SIC: 3566 Gears, power transmission, except automotive

(G-15734)
ZOLL MANUFACTURING CORPORATION (PA)
121 Gamma Dr (15238-2919)
PHONE..................................412 968-3333
Wayne Toy, *Mng Member*
EMP: 77
SALES (est): 18.3MM **Privately Held**
SIC: 3845 Electromedical equipment

(G-15735)
ZOLL MEDICAL CORPORATION
121 Gamma Dr (15238-2919)
PHONE..................................800 543-3267
Marc Balsam, *Senior Buyer*
Earl Izydore, *Engineer*
Wayne Simon, *Marketing Mgr*
Horst Esser, *Marketing Staff*
Luke Patsey, *Manager*
EMP: 10
SALES (corp-wide): 19.1B **Privately Held**
SIC: 3845 Defibrillator
HQ: Zoll Medical Corporation
269 Mill Rd
Chelmsford MA 01824
978 421-9655

(G-15736)
ZOLL SERVICES LLC
121 Gamma Dr (15238-2919)
PHONE..................................412 968-3333
Marshal Linder, *President*
Pat Eastman, *Vice Pres*
Reno Fiolic, *Vice Pres*
Mike Hardy, *Vice Pres*
Thomas E Kaib, *Vice Pres*
EMP: 800

SQ FT: 137,400
SALES (est): 228.8MM
SALES (corp-wide): 19.1B **Privately Held**
WEB: www.lifecor.com
SIC: 3845 Ultrasonic scanning devices, medical
HQ: Zoll Medical Corporation
269 Mill Rd
Chelmsford MA 01824
978 421-9655

(G-15737)
ZOTTOLA STEEL CORPORATION
900 Washington Blvd (15206-4142)
PHONE..............................412 362-5577
Frances Donatelli, *Principal*
EMP: 8
SALES (corp-wide): 3.1MM **Privately Held**
SIC: 3441 Fabricated structural metal
PA: Zottola Steel Corporation
1401 Frey Rd
Pittsburgh PA
412 856-7540

Pittsfield
Warren County

(G-15738)
BROKENSTRAW GRAVEL CO INC
Rr 6 (16340)
PHONE..............................814 563-7911
Dan Hawbaker, *President*
EMP: 5
SQ FT: 320
SALES: 247K **Privately Held**
SIC: 1442 Gravel mining

(G-15739)
TORPEDO SPECIALTY WIRE INC
Rr 2 (16340)
PHONE..............................814 563-7505
Andy Kleinert, *Manager*
EMP: 20
SALES (corp-wide): 11.2MM **Privately Held**
WEB: www.torpedowire.com
SIC: 3496 3643 3471 3357 Miscellaneous fabricated wire products; current-carrying wiring devices; plating & polishing; nonferrous wiredrawing & insulating; nonferrous rolling & drawing; aluminum rolling & drawing
PA: Torpedo Specialty Wire, Inc.
1115 Instrument Dr
Rocky Mount NC 27804
252 977-3900

Pittston
Luzerne County

(G-15740)
100 THOMPSON STREET LLC
100 Thompson St (18640-1437)
PHONE..............................866 654-2676
Kevin Nelson, *Principal*
EMP: 3
SALES (est): 165.6K **Privately Held**
SIC: 3089 Injection molding of plastics

(G-15741)
ACTON TECHNOLOGIES INC
100 Thompson St (18640-1437)
P.O. Box 726 (18640-0726)
PHONE..............................570 654-0612
Terence Neville, *President*
Liam Neville, *Project Mgr*
Steve Marsh, *Manager*
▲ **EMP:** 58
SQ FT: 34,000
SALES (est): 16.7MM **Privately Held**
WEB: www.actontech.com
SIC: 3081 2843 Unsupported plastics film & sheet; surface active agents

(G-15742)
BARHILL MANUFACTURING CORP
396 S Township Blvd (18640-3420)
PHONE..............................570 655-2005
Joseph A Panella Jr, *President*
Brian Hilaire, *COO*
Dr Edward Filippone, *Vice Pres*
▲ **EMP:** 20
SQ FT: 17,000
SALES (est): 1.3MM **Privately Held**
WEB: www.barhill.com
SIC: 3999 Plaques, picture, laminated; novelties, bric-a-brac & hobby kits

(G-15743)
BIMBO BAKERIES USA INC
1186 Sathers Dr (18640-9542)
PHONE..............................570 654-4668
Regis Huray, *Manager*
EMP: 65 **Privately Held**
SIC: 2051 Bread, all types (white, wheat, rye, etc): fresh or frozen
HQ: Bimbo Bakeries Usa, Inc
255 Business Center Dr # 200
Horsham PA 19044
215 347-5500

(G-15744)
CASCADES TISSUE GROUP - PA INC (HQ)
901 Sathers Dr (18640-9589)
PHONE..............................570 388-4307
Joanne Besanto, *Controller*
◆ **EMP:** 147
SALES (est): 54.4MM
SALES (corp-wide): 3.3B **Privately Held**
WEB: www.cascades.com
SIC: 2621 Paper mills
PA: Cascades Inc
404 Boul Marie-Victorin
Kingsey Falls QC J0A 1
819 363-5100

(G-15745)
CLARCOR AIR FILTRATION PDTS
1001 Sathers Dr (18640-9573)
PHONE..............................570 602-6274
EMP: 66
SALES (corp-wide): 1.4B **Publicly Held**
SIC: 3564 Blowers And Fans
HQ: Clarcor Air Filtration Products, Inc
100 River Ridge Cir
Jeffersonville IN 47130
502 969-2304

(G-15746)
CORNING INCORPORATED
160 Research Dr (18640-6142)
PHONE..............................570 883-9005
Chris Louca, *Project Mgr*
Pfeiffer Jeff, *Engineer*
EMP: 51
SALES (corp-wide): 11.2B **Publicly Held**
SIC: 3229 Scientific glassware
PA: Corning Incorporated
1 Riverfront Plz
Corning NY 14831
607 974-9000

(G-15747)
CREATIVE ENGNRED SOLUTIONS INC
1 Freeport Rd (18640-9513)
PHONE..............................570 655-3399
Thomas K Wilhelm, *President*
Thomas Pavlick, *Engineer*
EMP: 8
SQ FT: 2,000
SALES (est): 1.7MM **Privately Held**
SIC: 3694 Engine electrical equipment

(G-15748)
DEADSOLID SIMULATIONS INC
1192 Sathers Dr (18640-9542)
PHONE..............................570 655-6500
Charles J Cheskiewicz, *President*
EMP: 18
SQ FT: 16,500

SALES: 2MM **Privately Held**
WEB: www.deadsolidgolf.com
SIC: 3949 7371 5091 Driving ranges, golf, electronic; computer software development; golf & skiing equipment & supplies

(G-15749)
EMBROIDERY FACTORY INC
137 Market St (18640-2559)
PHONE..............................570 654-7640
Richard Herman, *President*
Linda Herman, *Vice Pres*
EMP: 7
SALES (est): 490K **Privately Held**
SIC: 2395 7299 Emblems, embroidered; stitching, custom

(G-15750)
FIESELER NEON SIGN CO
28 Industrial Dr (18640-6122)
P.O. Box 699, Wilkes Barre (18703-0699)
PHONE..............................570 655-2976
Deborah J Dourand, *President*
James G Dourand, *Vice Pres*
EMP: 6 **EST:** 1947
SQ FT: 11,000
SALES (est): 832.6K **Privately Held**
WEB: www.fieselerneonsigns.com
SIC: 3993 Neon signs; electric signs

(G-15751)
FLONTECH USA LLC
100 Thompson St (18640-1437)
PHONE..............................866 654-2676
Terence Neville, *President*
Douglas Lane, *Finance Mgr*
Mark Marinko, *Manager*
▲ **EMP:** 37
SALES (est): 10.5MM **Privately Held**
WEB: www.flontechusa.com
SIC: 3089 Injection molding of plastics

(G-15752)
GC ENTERPRISES LLC
Also Called: North East Print Supplies
457 N Main St (18640-2183)
PHONE..............................570 655-5543
Carmen Pitarra,
Kimberly M Pitarra,
EMP: 4
SQ FT: 1,500
SALES (est): 577.4K **Privately Held**
SIC: 5943 5712 3575 7359 Office forms & supplies; office furniture; keyboards, computer, office machine; office machine rental, except computers

(G-15753)
GOOD HEALTH NATURAL PDTS INC
162 Commerce Rd (18640-9585)
PHONE..............................570 655-0823
EMP: 5
SALES (corp-wide): 589.6MM **Privately Held**
SIC: 2096 2841 Mfg Potato Chips/Snacks Mfg Soap/Other Detergents
HQ: Good Health Natural Products, Inc.
115 Pomona Dr
Greensboro NC 17331

(G-15754)
GREINER PACKAGING CORP
225 Enterprise Way (18640-5035)
PHONE..............................570 602-3900
David Kirkland, *CEO*
Karen Nocito, *Finance*
Jeff Brennan, *Sales Dir*
Stephen Patterson, *Info Tech Mgr*
▲ **EMP:** 10
SALES (est): 3.4MM
SALES (corp-wide): 1.5B **Privately Held**
SIC: 3089 2671 3086 Battery cases, plastic or plastic combination; plastic film, coated or laminated for packaging; packaging & shipping materials, foamed plastic
PA: Greiner Ag
Greiner StraBe 70
KremsmUnster 4550
758 372-5160

(G-15755)
HEALEY WELDING CO INC
3 Cemetery St (18640-3001)
PHONE..............................570 655-9437
William Healey Sr, *President*
William Healey Jr, *Vice Pres*
Andrew Healey, *Treasurer*
EMP: 5
SQ FT: 1,000
SALES (est): 463.7K **Privately Held**
SIC: 7692 Welding repair

(G-15756)
IMMUNOTEK BIO CENTERS LLC
1838 N Township Blvd (18640-3550)
PHONE..............................570 300-7940
William Woods, *Manager*
EMP: 21
SALES (corp-wide): 27MM **Privately Held**
SIC: 2836 Blood derivatives
PA: Immunotek Bio Centers, L.L.C.
5750 Johnston St Ste 302
Lafayette LA 70503
337 500-1175

(G-15757)
INTERSTATE BUILDING MTLS INC
3000 N Township Blvd (18640-3554)
PHONE..............................570 655-8496
Mike Di Marco, *Manager*
EMP: 74
SALES (corp-wide): 15.7MM **Privately Held**
WEB: www.interstatebldg.com
SIC: 3089 Window frames & sash, plastic; windows, plastic
PA: Interstate Building Materials, Inc.
3000 N Township Blvd
Pittston PA 18640
570 655-2811

(G-15758)
INTERSTATE BUILDING MTLS INC (PA)
Also Called: Interstate Window & Door Co
3000 N Township Blvd (18640-3554)
P.O. Box 708 (18640-0708)
PHONE..............................570 655-2811
Joseph J Pupa Jr, *Ch of Bd*
Joseph J Pupa III, *President*
Tony Pirrella, *General Mgr*
Don Montini, *Vice Pres*
Ron Dovman, *Purch Mgr*
▼ **EMP:** 35
SQ FT: 35,000
SALES (est): 15.7MM **Privately Held**
WEB: www.interstatebldg.com
SIC: 3089 5031 5032 5033 Window frames & sash, plastic; windows, plastic; lumber, plywood & millwork; brick, stone & related material; roofing, siding & insulation; glass construction materials; doors, sliding; ceiling systems & products

(G-15759)
ISLAND FRAGRANCES INC
1129 Sunset Dr (18640-3780)
PHONE..............................570 793-1680
Brian L Barr, *President*
Brian Barr, *President*
Marisse Barr, *Vice Pres*
EMP: 20
SQ FT: 1,550
SALES: 3MM **Privately Held**
SIC: 2842 Cleaning or polishing preparations

(G-15760)
LASCO FITTINGS INC
500 Keystone Ave (18640-6151)
PHONE..............................570 301-1170
Jack Novitski, *Branch Mgr*
EMP: 10
SALES (corp-wide): 3.1B **Privately Held**
SIC: 3494 Valves & pipe fittings
HQ: Lasco Fittings, Inc.
414 Morgan St
Brownsville TN 38012
800 776-2756

(G-15761)
LATONA MINING LLC
620 S Main St (18640-3219)
PHONE..................................570 654-3525
Joseph Latona,
Charles Latona,
EMP: 15
SALES (est): 1.3MM Privately Held
SIC: 1081 Metal mining services

(G-15762)
LESJOFORS SPRINGS AMERICA INC
250 Research Dr (18640-6143)
PHONE..................................800 551-0298
Brandy Davies, CFO
Simon Taylor, Sales Mgr
◆ EMP: 36
SQ FT: 30,000
SALES (est): 12.6MM
SALES (corp-wide): 470.6MM Privately Held
SIC: 3493 3495 Steel springs, except wire; mechanical springs, precision
HQ: Lesjofors Ab
Kopmannagatan 2
Karlstad 652 2
541 377-50

(G-15763)
LETICA CORPORATION
2 Commerce Rd (18640-9508)
PHONE..................................570 654-2451
Joe Santucci, Manager
Kevin Wykoff, Info Tech Mgr
Rita Ziobro, Admin Sec
EMP: 98 Privately Held
WEB: www.letica.com
SIC: 3089 Plastic containers, except foam
HQ: Letica Corporation
52585 Dequindre Rd
Rochester Hills MI 48307
248 652-0557

(G-15764)
LETICA CORPORATION
Maui Cup Division
20 Commerce Rd (18640-9508)
PHONE..................................570 883-0299
Mark Siderowicz, Branch Mgr
Raymond Gerlach, Maintence Staff
John Teixeira, Maintence Staff
EMP: 211 Privately Held
WEB: www.letica.com
SIC: 2656 Cups, paper: made from purchased material
HQ: Letica Corporation
52585 Dequindre Rd
Rochester Hills MI 48307
248 652-0557

(G-15765)
LINDE CORPORATION
118 Armstrong Rd (18640-9628)
PHONE..................................570 299-5700
Scott F Linde, President
Christopher Langel, Vice Pres
Robert Hessling, Treasurer
Robert N McGraw, Admin Sec
EMP: 250
SQ FT: 5,000
SALES: 31.3MM Privately Held
WEB: www.lindeco.com
SIC: 1623 1389 Underground utilities contractor; oil field services; gas field services

(G-15766)
MECHANICAL SERVICE COMPANY
1145 Oak St (18640-3726)
PHONE..................................570 654-2445
David Fusco, President
EMP: 15
SALES (est): 2.4MM Privately Held
SIC: 7699 3621 Industrial equipment services; motors & generators

(G-15767)
MILAZZO INDUSTRIES INC (PA)
Also Called: Lake Shore Charcoal
1609 River Rd (18640-1399)
PHONE..................................570 722-0522
Joseph Milazzo, President
Elizabeth Milazzo, Corp Secy

John Wesolowski, Senior VP
Nichols Zapoticky, Finance Mgr
John Richie, Manager
EMP: 28
SQ FT: 150,000
SALES (est): 8.2MM Privately Held
WEB: www.milazzoindustries.com
SIC: 2842 2861 2819 2899 Window cleaning preparations; charcoal, except activated; calcium chloride & hypochlorite; chemical preparations

(G-15768)
MONDLAK PRINTERY
Also Called: Brier Hill Press
5 Ambrose St (18640-1405)
PHONE..................................570 654-9871
Gerald Mondlak, Owner
EMP: 3
SQ FT: 3,600
SALES: 150K Privately Held
SIC: 2752 Commercial printing, offset

(G-15769)
NATURES WAY PRWTER SYSTEMS INC
164 Commerce Rd (18640-9585)
PHONE..................................570 655-7755
Leonard Insalaco, President
Prashant Shitut, President
John Lomonaco, Prdtn Mgr
David Solovey, Mfg Staff
Joseph Lapchak, CFO
EMP: 60
SALES (est): 15.3MM Privately Held
WEB: www.nwpinc.com
SIC: 2086 Water, pasteurized: packaged in cans, bottles, etc.

(G-15770)
NATURES WAY PURE WATER
900 Sathers Dr (18640-9588)
PHONE..................................800 407-7873
Prashant Shitut, CEO
EMP: 5
SALES (est): 268.1K Privately Held
SIC: 2086 Pasteurized & mineral waters, bottled & canned

(G-15771)
NORTHEAST FABRICATORS INC
490 N Main St Ste 101 (18640-2100)
PHONE..................................570 883-0936
Santo Insalaco Jr, President
EMP: 9
SQ FT: 2,000
SALES (est): 781.9K Privately Held
SIC: 2541 7349 Store fixtures, wood; building maintenance, except repairs

(G-15772)
P & S PALLET INC
40 Tompkins St (18640-1129)
PHONE..................................570 655-4628
Ronald L Penn, Vice Pres
EMP: 3 EST: 2009
SALES (est): 139.6K Privately Held
SIC: 2448 Pallets, wood

(G-15773)
PENNSY SUPPLY INC
300 Armstrong Rd (18640-9672)
PHONE..................................570 654-3462
Paul Sebolka, Principal
EMP: 15
SALES (corp-wide): 29.7B Privately Held
WEB: www.pennsysupply.com
SIC: 3273 Ready-mixed concrete
HQ: Pennsy Supply, Inc.
1001 Paxton St
Harrisburg PA 17104
717 233-4511

(G-15774)
PEPSI-COLA BTLG CO OF SCRANTON
290 Research Dr (18640-6143)
PHONE..................................570 344-1159
Audrey Eisenstat, President
EMP: 74
SQ FT: 20,000
SALES (est): 6.8MM Privately Held
SIC: 2086 Soft drinks: packaged in cans, bottles, etc.; carbonated soft drinks, bottled & canned

(G-15775)
PEPSI-COLA METRO BTLG CO INC
290 Research Dr (18640-6143)
PHONE..................................570 344-1159
Mark Cooke, Manager
EMP: 70
SALES (corp-wide): 64.6B Publicly Held
WEB: www.joy-of-cola.com
SIC: 5149 2086 Soft drinks; carbonated beverages, nonalcoholic: bottled & canned
HQ: Pepsi-Cola Metropolitan Bottling Company, Inc.
1111 Westchester Ave
White Plains NY 10604
914 767-6000

(G-15776)
PITTSTON LUMBER & MFG CO
234 N Main St (18640-2199)
PHONE..................................570 654-3328
Joseph Chairge Jr, President
EMP: 20
SQ FT: 100,000
SALES: 8.3MM Privately Held
SIC: 5211 2431 2421 Lumber products; millwork; sawmills & planing mills, general

(G-15777)
POCONO TRANSCRETE INCORPORATED
160 Brown Rd (18640-3723)
PHONE..................................570 655-9166
Margaret Chaya, Branch Mgr
EMP: 5
SALES (corp-wide): 5.2MM Privately Held
SIC: 5211 3273 Cement; ready-mixed concrete
PA: Pocono Transcrete Incorporated
179 Burger Rd
Blakeslee PA 18610
570 646-2662

(G-15778)
PRAXAIR DISTRIBUTION INC
114 Brown Rd (18640-3723)
PHONE..................................570 655-3721
Christi Lewis, Branch Mgr
EMP: 4 Privately Held
SIC: 2813 5984 Oxygen, compressed or liquefied; liquefied petroleum gas dealers
HQ: Praxair Distribution, Inc.
10 Riverview Dr
Danbury CT 06810
203 837-2000

(G-15779)
PRIDE MOBILITY PRODUCTS CORP
401 York Ave (18642-2025)
PHONE..................................570 655-5574
Scott S Meuser, President
Seth Johnson, Administration
EMP: 20
SALES (corp-wide): 293MM Privately Held
SIC: 3842 Orthopedic appliances
PA: Pride Mobility Products Corp
182 Susquehanna Ave
Exeter PA 18643
570 655-5574

(G-15780)
QUIETFLEX MANUFACTURING
220 Research Dr (18640-6143)
PHONE..................................570 883-9019
EMP: 11
SALES (est): 1.2MM Privately Held
SIC: 3999 Manufacturing industries

(G-15781)
R J REYNOLDS TOBACCO COMPANY
420 N Main St (18640-2114)
P.O. Box 612 (18640-0612)
PHONE..................................570 654-0770
Nate Bender, Branch Mgr
EMP: 20
SALES (corp-wide): 26.8B Privately Held
WEB: www.carolinagroup.com
SIC: 3999 5993 Tobacco pipes, pipestems & bits; tobacco stores & stands

HQ: R. J. Reynolds Tobacco Company
401 N Main St
Winston Salem NC 27101
336 741-5000

(G-15782)
ROCHESTER COCA COLA BOTTLING (DH)
Also Called: Coca-Cola
300 Oak St (18640-3719)
PHONE..................................570 655-2874
Roger D Williams, President
Michael B Melnic, Treasurer
Arthur F Flaherty, Admin Sec
EMP: 22 EST: 1906
SQ FT: 1,000
SALES (est): 149.5MM
SALES (corp-wide): 35.4B Publicly Held
SIC: 2086 5962 Soft drinks: packaged in cans, bottles, etc.; merchandising machine operators
HQ: Coca-Cola Refreshments Usa, Inc.
2500 Windy Ridge Pkwy Se
Atlanta GA 30339
770 989-3000

(G-15783)
TRI-OUR BRANDS
Also Called: Janoski Gus
400 Pollock Dr (18640-3164)
PHONE..................................570 655-1512
Gus Janoski, Owner
EMP: 6
SQ FT: 12,800
SALES: 450K Privately Held
SIC: 2013 2015 Frozen meats from purchased meat; poultry slaughtering & processing

(G-15784)
WEPCO INC (PA)
101 Armstrong Rd (18640-9640)
PHONE..................................570 368-8184
Christopher Paulsen, CEO
Edward Lstrayhorn, President
Bob Kern, Principal
Frank Trigan, Principal
Sam Arfanella, Senior VP
EMP: 47
SQ FT: 11,000
SALES (est): 26MM Privately Held
WEB: www.wepcoinc.com
SIC: 5084 3559 Materials handling machinery; foundry machinery & equipment

Plains
Luzerne County

(G-15785)
HUDSON ANTHRACITE INC
220 S River St Ste 1 (18705-1101)
PHONE..................................570 823-0531
Angelo Alfano, President
EMP: 4
SALES (est): 625.8K Privately Held
SIC: 1231 Anthracite mining

(G-15786)
MIDVALE PAPER BOX COMPANY (HQ)
19 Bailey St (18705-1907)
PHONE..................................570 824-3577
David Frank, President
◆ EMP: 11
SQ FT: 300,000
SALES (est): 2.3MM Privately Held
WEB: www.midvalebox.com
SIC: 2657 5113 Folding paperboard boxes; boxes, paperboard & disposable plastic
PA: Xomox Corporation
19 Bailey St
Wilkes Barre PA 18705
570 824-3577

(G-15787)
NEW ENTERPRISE STONE LIME INC
Also Called: Pioneer Aggregates
220 S River St Ste 1 (18705-1101)
PHONE..................................570 823-0531
EMP: 50

▲ = Import ▼=Export
◆ =Import/Export

SALES (corp-wide): 651.9MM **Privately Held**
SIC: 1221 4212 Bituminous coal surface mining; draying, local: without storage
PA: New Enterprise Stone & Lime Co., Inc.
3912 Brumbaugh Rd
New Enterprise PA 16664
814 224-6883

(G-15788)
RIVERVIEW ORTHOTICS
220 S River St Ste 2 (18705-1101)
PHONE....................................570 270-6231
Donald Dixon, *CEO*
Mike Mattingly, *Principal*
Timothy Nutgrass, *Principal*
Jeanette Sgonina, *Principal*
David Sickles, *Principal*
EMP: 7
SALES (est): 543.6K **Privately Held**
SIC: 5999 3842 Orthopedic & prosthesis applications; limbs, artificial; orthopedic appliances; braces, orthopedic

(G-15789)
SUPERIOR PACKAGING INC (PA)
19 Bailey St (18705-1907)
PHONE....................................570 824-3577
David Frank, *President*
EMP: 11 EST: 1950
SQ FT: 100,000
SALES (est): 3.8MM **Privately Held**
WEB: www.superiorpackaginginc.com
SIC: 2631 2673 2675 2674 Boxboard; plastic bags: made from purchased materials; die-cut paper & board; bags: uncoated paper & multiwall; folding paperboard boxes; setup paperboard boxes

(G-15790)
WILKES-BARRE MATERIALS LLC
130 Ridgewood Rd (18702)
PHONE....................................570 829-1181
Paul R Ober, *Mng Member*
EMP: 20 EST: 2005
SALES (est): 522.4K
SALES (corp-wide): 22MM **Privately Held**
WEB: www.amerasphalt.com
SIC: 2951 Asphalt & asphaltic paving mixtures (not from refineries)
PA: American Asphalt Paving Co.
500 Chase Rd
Shavertown PA 18708
570 696-1181

Pleasant Gap
Centre County

(G-15791)
BREONS INC A CLOSE CORPORATION
330 S Main St (16823-3518)
PHONE....................................814 359-3182
Mark Breon, *President*
Jay A Breon, *Corp Secy*
Roy Breon, *Vice Pres*
EMP: 6
SQ FT: 1,000
SALES (est): 966.2K **Privately Held**
WEB: www.breons.com
SIC: 5999 7694 3599 Motors, electric; electric motor repair; machine shop, jobbing & repair

(G-15792)
GLENN O HAWBAKER INC
Also Called: Central Valley Aggregates
118 Bedrock Ln (16823-7515)
PHONE....................................814 359-3411
Michael Hawbaker, *Branch Mgr*
EMP: 40
SALES (corp-wide): 300MM **Privately Held**
WEB: www.goh-inc.com
SIC: 1771 5032 2951 1611 Blacktop (asphalt) work; stone, crushed or broken; asphalt paving mixtures & blocks; highway & street construction; quarry tile, clay

PA: Glenn O. Hawbaker, Inc.
1952 Waddle Rd Ste 203
State College PA 16803
814 237-1444

(G-15793)
HAPPY VALLEY BLENDED PDTS LLC
660 Axemann Rd (16823-8101)
PHONE....................................814 548-7090
Barry L Gensimore,
EMP: 15
SALES (est): 1.6MM **Privately Held**
SIC: 3241 Natural cement

(G-15794)
MAXWELL TRUCK & EQUIPMENT LLC
689 E College Ave (16823-7544)
PHONE....................................814 359-2672
Edward Maxwell, *CEO*
Dan Smith,
EMP: 3
SALES (est): 727.6K **Privately Held**
SIC: 3713 5084 Truck bodies & parts; industrial machinery & equipment

(G-15795)
NOVOSEL INSTRUMENT SHOP INC
264 Commerce St (16823-7423)
PHONE....................................814 359-2249
Robert Novosel, *President*
Janet Novosel, *Vice Pres*
EMP: 14
SALES: 80K **Privately Held**
WEB: www.nismachining.com
SIC: 3599 Machine shop, jobbing & repair

Pleasant Unity
Westmoreland County

(G-15796)
JIM CONRATH
Also Called: Hard Metal Tooling
2136 Route 130 (15676)
PHONE....................................724 423-6363
Jim Conrath, *Owner*
EMP: 10
SQ FT: 800
SALES (est): 82.2K **Privately Held**
SIC: 3599 Machine shop, jobbing & repair

Pleasantville
Venango County

(G-15797)
BELDEN & BLAKE CORPORATION
22811 Titusville Rd (16341-1729)
PHONE....................................814 589-7091
Barry Lay, *Branch Mgr*
EMP: 12 **Privately Held**
WEB: www.beldenblake.com
SIC: 1311 1389 4922 5082 Crude petroleum production; natural gas production; oil field services; natural gas transmission; oil field equipment; oil & gas exploration services
HQ: Belden & Blake Corporation
1001 Fannin St Ste 800
Houston TX 77002
713 659-3500

(G-15798)
COLONIAL MACHINE COMPANY INC
140 W State St (16341-9788)
P.O. Box 359 (16341-0359)
PHONE....................................814 589-7033
Barry W Mallory, *President*
Karen M Mallory, *Vice Pres*
EMP: 30
SQ FT: 85,000
SALES (est): 6.7MM **Privately Held**
WEB: www.thecolonialmachinecompany.com
SIC: 3498 Fabricated pipe & fittings

(G-15799)
COOKS MACHINE WORK
17283 Bugtown Rd (16341-1703)
PHONE....................................814 589-5141
Charlotte Cook, *Owner*
EMP: 5
SQ FT: 4,000
SALES (est): 432.2K **Privately Held**
SIC: 3544 3441 Special dies, tools, jigs & fixtures; fabricated structural metal

(G-15800)
DEVONIAN RESOURCES INC
15566 Tionesta Rd (16341)
PHONE....................................814 589-7061
S G Thompson, *President*
Stanley Thompson, *Vice Pres*
EMP: 20
SALES (est): 3.6MM **Privately Held**
SIC: 1311 Natural gas production

(G-15801)
EAGLE LINE CORPORATION
Shamburg St (16341)
PHONE....................................814 589-7724
Marion Hoovler, *President*
David Swanson, *Corp Secy*
EMP: 12
SQ FT: 2,100
SALES (est): 678.9K **Privately Held**
SIC: 1381 1311 Directional drilling oil & gas wells; crude petroleum production

(G-15802)
IMOD OIL PRODUCTION LLC
15852 Pleasant Valley Dr (16341-2718)
PHONE....................................814 589-7539
Virginia Beck, *Principal*
EMP: 3
SALES (est): 215.5K **Privately Held**
SIC: 1311 Crude petroleum & natural gas production

(G-15803)
S & T SUPPLY CO
Also Called: S & T Service & Supply
15267 Tionesta Rd (16341-2817)
PHONE....................................814 589-7025
Harold R Jackson, *Partner*
Robert Greenhouse, *Partner*
EMP: 12
SALES (est): 1.2MM **Privately Held**
SIC: 1381 Service well drilling

(G-15804)
SPECIALTY MACHINE & HYDRAULIC
1736 Shreve Rd (16341)
P.O. Box 287 (16341-0287)
PHONE....................................814 589-7381
James Olson, *President*
Debbie Waddell, *Corp Secy*
Margaret Olson, *Vice Pres*
EMP: 6
SALES (est): 583K **Privately Held**
SIC: 7699 3599 Hydraulic equipment repair; machine shop, jobbing & repair

(G-15805)
VAN HAMPTON GAS & OIL INC
15566 Tionesta Rd (16341-2828)
PHONE....................................814 589-7061
Stanley R Thompson, *President*
EMP: 11
SQ FT: 1,200
SALES (est): 476.6K **Privately Held**
SIC: 1311 Crude petroleum production; natural gas production

Plumsteadville
Bucks County

(G-15806)
AIRGAS USA LLC
6141 Easton Rd (18949)
PHONE....................................215 766-8860
Steve Dziak, *President*
EMP: 3
SALES (corp-wide): 125.9MM **Privately Held**
SIC: 2911 5084 2813 Petroleum refining; materials handling machinery; industrial gases

HQ: Airgas Usa, Llc
259 N Radnor Chester Rd # 100
Radnor PA 19087
610 687-5253

(G-15807)
CUSTOM ELEVATOR MFG CO INC
5191 Stump Rd (18949)
PHONE....................................215 766-3380
Kennith Herrmann, *CEO*
Gary Herrmann, *Vice Pres*
Walter Herrmann, *Vice Pres*
Larry Keifer, *Prdtn Mgr*
Scott Geiger, *Engineer*
▲ EMP: 35
SQ FT: 60,000
SALES (est): 9.1MM **Privately Held**
WEB: www.customelevatorinc.com
SIC: 3534 Elevators & moving stairways

(G-15808)
CUSTOM PARTICLE REDUCTION INC
5189 Stump Rd (18949)
P.O. Box 479 (18949-0479)
PHONE....................................215 766-9791
Dennis Rice, *President*
Raymond Patridge, *Treasurer*
Dale Cotton, *Admin Sec*
▲ EMP: 11
SQ FT: 30,000
SALES (est): 690K **Privately Held**
SIC: 2099 Almond pastes

(G-15809)
ED CINI ENTERPRISES INC
Also Called: Cini Garment Sales Co
5611 Deer Path Rd (18949)
P.O. Box 635 (18949-0635)
PHONE....................................215 432-3855
Edgar Cini, *President*
EMP: 6
SQ FT: 1,200
SALES: 300K **Privately Held**
SIC: 2211 2759 Press cloth; screen printing

(G-15810)
KEENAN AND MEIER LLC
5191 Stump Rd (18949)
P.O. Box 690 (18949-0690)
PHONE....................................215 766-3010
Paul Keenan, *Mng Member*
Scott Meier,
EMP: 6
SQ FT: 6,800
SALES (est): 125.9K **Privately Held**
WEB: www.kmdampers.com
SIC: 3822 Damper operators: pneumatic, thermostatic, electric

(G-15811)
MALMARK INCORPORATED
Also Called: Malmark Bellcraftsmen
5712 Easton Rd (18949)
P.O. Box 1200 (18949-1200)
PHONE....................................215 766-7200
Timothy Schuback, *President*
Willard Markey, *Treasurer*
Jacob H Malta, *Admin Sec*
Adam Galpin, *Administration*
EMP: 36 EST: 1973
SQ FT: 45,000
SALES (est): 5MM **Privately Held**
WEB: www.malmark.com
SIC: 3931 Bells (musical instruments); chimes & parts (musical instruments)

(G-15812)
N F C INDUSTRIES INC (PA)
Also Called: School Bus Parts
6124 Potters Ln (18949)
PHONE....................................215 766-8890
Lawrence Brown, *President*
Emanuel Mendelsohn, *Vice Pres*
▲ EMP: 38
SQ FT: 33,000
SALES (est): 12.7MM **Privately Held**
WEB: www.schoolbusparts.com
SIC: 5013 3714 2399 Truck parts & accessories; exhaust systems & parts, motor vehicle; seat covers, automobile

(G-15813)
SCALETRON INDUSTRIES LTD
53 Apple Tree Ln (18949)
P.O. Box 365 (18949-0365)
PHONE..............................215 766-2670
Edward Dougherty, *President*
Jennifer Cochran, *Purch Mgr*
Nancy J Dougherty, *Admin Sec*
EMP: 10
SQ FT: 3,500
SALES (est): 2.4MM **Privately Held**
WEB: www.scaletronscales.com
SIC: 3596 Industrial scales

(G-15814)
TINICUM RESEARCH COMPANY
67 Appletree Ln (18949)
PHONE..............................215 766-7277
Stuart Louden, *Opers-Prdtn-Mfg*
EMP: 12
SALES (est): 1.2MM
SALES (corp-wide): 1.6MM **Privately Held**
SIC: 2789 Paper cutting
PA: Tinicum Research Company
17 Roaring Rocks Rd
Erwinna PA 18920
610 294-9390

Plymouth
Luzerne County

(G-15815)
ATWATER INC
Also Called: Atwater Self Storage
627 W Main St (18651-2806)
PHONE..............................570 779-9568
Elmo J Begliomini, *President*
David Begliomini, *Vice Pres*
John Tinner, *Treasurer*
EMP: 55
SQ FT: 100,000
SALES (est): 5.6MM **Privately Held**
SIC: 2282 2823 Nylon yarn: throwing, twisting, winding or spooling; polyester filament yarn: throwing, twisting, winding, etc.; cellulosic manmade fibers

(G-15816)
CUSTOM LININGS SPRAY ON BED
112 Narrows Rd (18651-3222)
PHONE..............................570 779-4609
Paul Furtak, *Principal*
EMP: 3
SALES (est): 375.3K **Privately Held**
SIC: 3523 Sprayers & spraying machines, agricultural

(G-15817)
FIBERTEL INC
576 W Main St (18651-2820)
PHONE..............................570 714-7189
Aaron Littzi, *President*
Marie Littzi, *President*
Al Littzi, *Vice Pres*
Michael Dorunda, *Project Mgr*
EMP: 13 EST: 2000
SQ FT: 1,575
SALES (est): 2.3MM **Privately Held**
SIC: 1731 3229 Fiber optic cable installation; fiber optics strands

(G-15818)
FLEET DECAL & GRAPHICS INC
Also Called: Brand Graphic Solutions
30 E Main St (18651-3017)
P.O. Box 157 (18651-0157)
PHONE..............................570 779-4343
Edward Vnuk, *President*
Mark Vnuk, *Vice Pres*
Brian Vnuk, *Treasurer*
Edward Vnuk Jr, *Admin Sec*
Matthew Rizzo, *Graphic Designe*
EMP: 15
SQ FT: 20,000
SALES (est): 2.8MM **Privately Held**
WEB: www.fleetdecal.com
SIC: 2759 3993 Decals: printing; signs & advertising specialties

(G-15819)
GLEN CARBONIC GAS CO
665 E Main St (18651-3203)
P.O. Box 650 (18651-0650)
PHONE..............................570 779-1226
Michael Duda Jr, *Partner*
John Duda Jr, *Partner*
EMP: 10
SALES (est): 1.3MM **Privately Held**
SIC: 2086 2813 Soft drinks: packaged in cans, bottles, etc.; carbon dioxide

(G-15820)
PLYMOUTH GRAPHICS INC
411 W Main St (18651-2907)
PHONE..............................570 779-9645
Daniel Morris, *President*
EMP: 4 EST: 1975
SQ FT: 3,000
SALES: 370K **Privately Held**
WEB: www.plymouthgraphics.com
SIC: 2759 7336 Screen printing; commercial art & graphic design

(G-15821)
SHAWNEE READY MIX CON & ASP CO (PA)
715 E Main St (18651-3205)
P.O. Box 9 (18651-0009)
PHONE..............................570 779-9586
George Schall, *President*
James Eric Schall, *President*
Judith Schall, *Corp Secy*
EMP: 24 EST: 1947
SQ FT: 1,000
SALES (est): 3.3MM **Privately Held**
SIC: 3273 Ready-mixed concrete

(G-15822)
UNIVERSAL PIONEERS LLC
67 Nottingham St (18651-2004)
PHONE..............................570 239-3950
John P Carson, *President*
EMP: 8
SALES (est): 446.5K **Privately Held**
SIC: 3541 6221 Electrical discharge erosion machines; commodity brokers, contracts

(G-15823)
WEBB COMMUNICATIONS INC
Also Called: Bayard Printing Group
1719 W Main St (18651)
PHONE..............................570 326-7634
Jason Aben, *Vice Pres*
EMP: 26 **Privately Held**
SIC: 2711 2752 7331 Commercial printing & newspaper publishing combined; commercial printing, lithographic; direct mail advertising services
PA: Webb Communications, Inc.
1 Maynard St
Williamsport PA 17701

(G-15824)
WEBB COMMUNICATIONS INC
Also Called: Bayard
301 W Main St (18651-2906)
PHONE..............................570 326-7634
Mark P Lunberg, *Manager*
EMP: 30 **Privately Held**
SIC: 2752 2789 2791 Commercial printing, lithographic; bookbinding & related work; typesetting
PA: Webb Communications, Inc.
1 Maynard St
Williamsport PA 17701

(G-15825)
WEBB COMMUNICATIONS INC
Also Called: Bayard Printing
180 W Main St (18651-2901)
P.O. Box 190 (18651-0190)
PHONE..............................570 779-9543
Rebecca Aben, *CEO*
Carolyn Aben, *Sales Dir*
EMP: 12 **Privately Held**
WEB: www.unigraphic.com
SIC: 2752 Commercial printing, offset
PA: Webb Communications, Inc.
1 Maynard St
Williamsport PA 17701

Plymouth Meeting
Montgomery County

(G-15826)
ACTIVESTRATEGY INC
620 W Germantown Pike (19462-1068)
PHONE..............................484 690-0700
Jack Steele, *CEO*
Jeff Bunting, *President*
Carolyn Peters, *Controller*
Alan Stahura, *Director*
Laurie Steele, *Director*
EMP: 48
SQ FT: 14,100
SALES (est): 4.6MM **Privately Held**
WEB: www.activestrategy.com
SIC: 7372 Prepackaged software

(G-15827)
ADVANCED MCRO CMPT SPECIALISTS
5100 Campus Dr Ste 140 (19462-1147)
PHONE..............................215 773-9700
Catherine Shimkus, *President*
EMP: 9 EST: 2015
SALES (est): 251.7K **Privately Held**
SIC: 3825 7373 Instruments to measure electricity; computer integrated systems design

(G-15828)
AEC SERVICES COMPANY LLC
525 Plymouth Rd Ste 320 (19462-1640)
PHONE..............................610 246-6470
Thomas Halloran,
Booth Halloran,
Jeremy Howard,
EMP: 4
SALES: 500K **Privately Held**
SIC: 1381 Drilling oil & gas wells

(G-15829)
ALENCON SYSTEMS INC
5150 Campus Dr (19462-1123)
PHONE..............................610 825-7094
Oleg Fishman, *CEO*
Ulrich Kw Schwabe, *Director*
EMP: 5
SALES (est): 592.5K
SALES (corp-wide): 924.5MM **Privately Held**
SIC: 3629 Inverters, nonrotating: electrical
HQ: indel, Inc.
10 Indel Ave
Rancocas NJ 08073
609 267-9000

(G-15830)
AMERICAN EXPLORATION COMPANY (PA)
525 Plymouth Rd Ste 320 (19462-1640)
PHONE..............................610 940-4015
Thomas Halloran, *President*
Tim Matthews, *Exec VP*
Tim Matthews, *Vice Pres*
Claire Kramer, *Office Mgr*
Booth Halloran, *Manager*
EMP: 60
SQ FT: 1,500
SALES: 5MM **Privately Held**
WEB: www.americanjourneys.org
SIC: 4212 1389 Local trucking, without storage; oil field services

(G-15831)
AMREP CORPORATION (PA)
Also Called: AXR HOLDINGS
620 W Germantown Pike # 175
(19462-2219)
PHONE..............................609 487-0905
Edward B Cloues II, *Ch of Bd*
Christopher V Vitale, *President*
James M McMonagle, *CFO*
EMP: 12 EST: 1961
SQ FT: 2,400
SALES: 40.1MM **Publicly Held**
WEB: www.amrepcorp.com
SIC: 6552 5192 2732 7389 Land subdividers & developers, residential; books, periodicals & newspapers; pamphlets: printing only, not published on site; subscription fulfillment services: magazine, newspaper, etc.

(G-15832)
ATHENA CONTROLS INC
5145 Campus Dr Ste 1 (19462-1195)
PHONE..............................610 828-2490
Robert S Schlegel, *President*
Mark Novack, *Research*
Tom Kachline, *Engineer*
Samuel James, *Treasurer*
Carol Dicesare, *Cust Mgr*
▲ **EMP:** 60
SQ FT: 24,000
SALES (est): 13.5MM
SALES (corp-wide): 924.5MM **Privately Held**
WEB: www.athenacontrols.com
SIC: 3823 Industrial instrmnts msrmnt display/control process variable
HQ: Indel, Inc.
10 Indel Ave
Rancocas NJ 08073
609 267-9000

(G-15833)
BENDINGER INC
4110 Butler Pike Ste A101 (19462-1547)
PHONE..............................484 342-3522
Virginia Wischhusen, *President*
◆ **EMP:** 5
SALES (est): 866K **Privately Held**
SIC: 2339 Neckwear & ties: women's, misses' & juniors'

(G-15834)
BLEACHER CREATURES LLC
527 Plymouth Rd Ste 407 (19462-1641)
P.O. Box 333, Blue Bell (19422-0333)
PHONE..............................484 534-2398
Matthew Hoffman,
Ed Strauss,
▲ **EMP:** 6 EST: 2011
SALES (est): 1.1MM **Privately Held**
WEB: www.bleachercreaturetoys.com
SIC: 3944 Games, toys & children's vehicles

(G-15835)
BRAEBURN PHARMACEUTICALS INC
450 Plymouth Rd Ste 400 (19462-1644)
PHONE..............................609 751-5375
Seth Harrison, *Ch of Bd*
Michael M Derkacz, *President*
Frank E Young, *Exec VP*
Craig C Brown, *Senior VP*
Susan Franks, *Senior VP*
EMP: 59 EST: 2012
SQ FT: 4,636
SALES: 25K **Privately Held**
SIC: 2834 Drugs acting on the central nervous system & sense organs

(G-15836)
BUSINESS WIRE INC
2250 Hickory Rd Ste 410 (19462-1037)
PHONE..............................610 617-9560
Catherine Bolton, *Branch Mgr*
EMP: 4
SALES (corp-wide): 225.3B **Publicly Held**
SIC: 3315 Steel wire & related products
HQ: Business Wire, Inc.
101 California St # 2000
San Francisco CA 94111
415 986-4422

(G-15837)
C S FULLER INC
Also Called: Johnson Contrls Authorized Dlr
400 Stenton Ave Ste 104 (19462-1204)
PHONE..............................610 941-9225
Clark Fuller, *President*
EMP: 3 EST: 1997
SQ FT: 450
SALES (est): 478.1K **Privately Held**
SIC: 3822 5075 Auto controls regulating residntl & coml environmt & applncs; warm air heating & air conditioning

(G-15838)
CARRIER CORPORATION
4110 Butler Pike Ste A104 (19462-1547)
PHONE..............................610 834-1717
Pete Acquavella, *Manager*
Joseph Smith, *Supervisor*
EMP: 45

▲ = Import ▼=Export
◆ =Import/Export

SALES (corp-wide): 66.5B **Publicly Held**
WEB: www.carrier.com
SIC: 3585 Air conditioning units, complete: domestic or industrial; refrigeration equipment, complete
HQ: Carrier Corporation
13995 Pasteur Blvd
Palm Beach Gardens FL 33418
800 379-6484

(G-15839)
COMMONWEALTH DRILLING COMPANY
525 Plymouth Rd Ste 320 (19462-1640)
PHONE....................610 940-4015
Thomas F Halloran, *President*
Tim Matthews, *Senior VP*
James Howard, *Vice Pres*
Tommy Lingenfelter, *Project Mgr*
EMP: 5
SALES (est): 580K **Privately Held**
SIC: 1381 Drilling oil & gas wells

(G-15840)
CSS INDUSTRIES INC (PA)
450 Plymouth Rd Ste 300 (19462-1644)
PHONE....................610 729-3959
Rebecca C Matthias, *Ch of Bd*
Christopher J Munyan, *President*
Carey B Edwards, *Exec VP*
Cara L Farley, *Exec VP*
William G Kiesling, *Exec VP*
EMP: 196
SALES: 361.9MM **Publicly Held**
WEB: www.cssindustries.com
SIC: 2771 2679 2389 2396 Greeting cards; gift wrap & novelties, paper; gift wrap, paper: made from purchased material; costumes; ribbons & bows, cut & sewed; tissue paper; dyes & pigments

(G-15841)
DAL-TILE CORPORATION
5105 Campus Dr (19462-1199)
PHONE....................484 530-9066
Steve Stevens, *Manager*
EMP: 11
SALES (corp-wide): 9.9B **Publicly Held**
WEB: www.mohawk.com
SIC: 3253 5032 Ceramic wall & floor tile; marble building stone
HQ: Dal-Tile Corporation
7834 C F Hawn Fwy
Dallas TX 75217
214 398-1411

(G-15842)
EXPENSEWATCH INC
620 W Germantown Pike (19462-1068)
PHONE....................610 397-0532
Bill Vergantino, *President*
EMP: 18
SQ FT: 2,397
SALES (est): 2.8MM
SALES (corp-wide): 35.5MM **Privately Held**
WEB: www.expensewatch.com
SIC: 7372 Business oriented computer software
HQ: Nexonia Technologies Inc
2 St Clair Ave E Suite 750
Toronto ON M4T 2
416 480-0688

(G-15843)
F&T APPAREL LLC (HQ)
Also Called: Fishman & Tobin
4000 Chemical Rd Ste 500 (19462-1713)
P.O. Box 3514, Allentown (18106-0514)
PHONE....................646 839-7000
Mario Lerias, *Vice Pres*
Charles Tarragano, *Vice Pres*
Harry Ciaccio, *VP Opers*
Nick Vetere, *Plant Mgr*
Ramon Rodriguez, *Prdtn Mgr*
◆ **EMP:** 100 **EST:** 1914
SALES (est): 155.8MM
SALES (corp-wide): 164MM **Publicly Held**
WEB: www.fishmantobin.com
SIC: 2311 2321 2325 Suits, men's & boys': made from purchased materials; men's & boys' sports & polo shirts; men's & boys' dress slacks & shorts

PA: Centric Brands Inc.
350 5th Ave Fl 6
New York NY 10118
646 582-6000

(G-15844)
F&T APPAREL LLC
Also Called: Fishman and Tobin
4000 Chemical Rd Ste 500 (19462-1713)
P.O. Box 3514, Allentown (18106-0514)
PHONE....................610 828-8400
Bernard Fishman, *President*
Jenny Vitale, *Vice Pres*
Phyllis Owens, *Human Res Mgr*
Debbie Livezey, *Manager*
Rhonda Weisberg, *Manager*
EMP: 100
SALES (corp-wide): 164MM **Publicly Held**
SIC: 2311 Men's & boys' suits & coats
HQ: F&T Apparel Llc
4000 Chemical Rd Ste 500
Plymouth Meeting PA 19462
646 839-7000

(G-15845)
HARMONY BIOSCIENCES LLC
630 W Germantown Pike (19462-1075)
PHONE....................847 715-0500
Bob Repella,
EMP: 25
SQ FT: 15,000
SALES (est): 1.2MM **Privately Held**
SIC: 2834 Pituitary gland pharmaceutical preparations

(G-15846)
HIGHWAY MATERIALS INC
500 Stenton Ave (19462)
PHONE....................610 828-4300
Eric Friend, *General Mgr*
EMP: 22
SQ FT: 2,115
SALES (corp-wide): 10.1MM **Privately Held**
WEB: www.highwaymaterials.com
SIC: 3274 1411 5032 Lime; dimension stone; paving materials
PA: Highway Materials, Inc.
409 Stenton Ave
Flourtown PA 19031
610 832-8000

(G-15847)
HOLLYFRONTIER CORPORATION
660 W Germantown Pike # 1 (19462-1111)
PHONE....................800 456-4786
Patrick J Gribbin, *Branch Mgr*
Karissa Mooney, *Manager*
EMP: 7
SALES (corp-wide): 17.7B **Publicly Held**
SIC: 2911 Petroleum refining
PA: Hollyfrontier Corporation
2828 N Harwood St # 1300
Dallas TX 75201
214 871-3555

(G-15848)
HOLLYFRONTIER CORPORATION
Also Called: Hollyfrntier Lubr Spcalty Pdts
401 Plymouth Rd Ste 350 (19462-1653)
PHONE....................800 395-2786
Jim Borthwick, *Manager*
Susan Campbell, *Analyst*
EMP: 6
SALES (corp-wide): 17.7B **Publicly Held**
SIC: 2899 Corrosion preventive lubricant
PA: Hollyfrontier Corporation
2828 N Harwood St # 1300
Dallas TX 75201
214 871-3555

(G-15849)
HOWDEN COMPRESSORS INC
1850 Gravers Rd Ste 2 (19462-2837)
PHONE....................610 313-9800
Jim Fairbairn, *President*
Darryl Halter, *Vice Pres*
Charles Bauer, *Engineer*
Clark Okemute, *Engineer*
Robert Stuart, *Engineer*
▲ **EMP:** 10 **EST:** 1998
SQ FT: 15,000

SALES (est): 2.2MM
SALES (corp-wide): 3.6B **Publicly Held**
WEB: www.howdencompressors.com
SIC: 3563 Air & gas compressors
PA: Colfax Corporation
420 Natl Bus Pkwy Ste 500
Annapolis Junction MD 20701
301 323-9000

(G-15850)
ILERA HEALTHCARE LLC (PA)
420 Plymouth Rd (19462-1608)
PHONE....................610 440-8443
Lisa Gray, *Mng Member*
EMP: 9 **EST:** 2016
SALES (est): 2.6MM **Privately Held**
SIC: 5999 2833 5499 0139 ; drugs & herbs: grading, grinding & milling; spices & herbs; herb or spice farm

(G-15851)
INFORMATION BUILDERS INC
620 W Germantown Pike # 410 (19462-1061)
PHONE....................610 940-0790
Jack Stover, *Manager*
EMP: 15
SALES (corp-wide): 262.6MM **Privately Held**
WEB: www.informationbuilders.com
SIC: 7372 Operating systems computer software
PA: Information Builders, Inc.
2 Penn Plz Fl 28
New York NY 10121
212 736-4433

(G-15852)
INSTECH LABORATORIES INC
Also Called: Instech Solomon
450 Gravers Rd Ste 100 (19462-1720)
PHONE....................610 941-0132
Michael H Loughnane, *President*
Tony Baldini, *President*
Julia Solo, *General Mgr*
Kenneth Cook, *Vice Pres*
Paul Loughnane, *Vice Pres*
EMP: 20
SQ FT: 14,000
SALES: 8.5MM **Privately Held**
WEB: www.instechlabs.com
SIC: 3561 3826 Pumps & pumping equipment; analytical instruments

(G-15853)
INTEGRATED SECURTY & COMMUNCTN
Also Called: Integrated SEC Communications
4110 Butler Pike Ste B100 (19462-1547)
PHONE....................610 397-0988
Mike Thomas, *CEO*
Linda Weems, *Purch Agent*
John Pichola, *CFO*
Kevin Comerford, *Sales Staff*
Tim Kelly, *Marketing Staff*
EMP: 50
SALES (est): 14.7MM **Privately Held**
SIC: 3699 Security devices

(G-15854)
LITHIUM TECHNOLOGY CORPORATION
5115 Campus Dr (19462-1129)
PHONE....................888 776-0942
EMP: 3
SALES (est): 117.6K **Privately Held**
SIC: 3691 Storage batteries

(G-15855)
MARKEL CORP
435 School Ln (19462-2744)
PHONE....................610 272-8960
Jon Kirchner, *CEO*
Kim Reynolds, *President*
Warren G Mang, *Chairman*
Robert Jerman, *Vice Pres*
Charles Marino, *Vice Pres*
▲ **EMP:** 150 **EST:** 1922
SQ FT: 160,000

SALES (est): 32.4MM **Privately Held**
WEB: www.markelcorporation.com
SIC: 3082 3357 3714 3496 Tubes, unsupported plastic; nonferrous wiredrawing & insulating; motor vehicle parts & accessories; miscellaneous fabricated wire products; steel wire & related products; laminated plastics plate & sheet

(G-15856)
MEDICAPTURE INC (PA)
2250 Hickory Rd Ste 200 (19462-2225)
PHONE....................610 238-0700
Michael Bishop, *President*
Mark Panetta, *CFO*
Kevin Miller, *Accounts Mgr*
Ben Stluka, *Sales Staff*
Louann Fare, *Manager*
EMP: 10
SQ FT: 4,000
SALES: 7MM **Privately Held**
SIC: 3841 Surgical & medical instruments

(G-15857)
MOTOROLA MOBILITY LLC
450 Plymouth Rd Ste 102 (19462-1644)
PHONE....................610 238-0109
EMP: 3
SALES (corp-wide): 43B **Privately Held**
SIC: 3663 Radio & TV communications equipment
HQ: Motorola Mobility Llc
222 Merchandise Mart Plz # 1800
Chicago IL 60654

(G-15858)
MOVAD LLC
5166 Campus Dr (19462-1123)
PHONE....................215 638-2679
Joan K McCloskey, *President*
EMP: 12
SQ FT: 5,000
SALES: 1.3MM **Privately Held**
SIC: 2752 2791 2796 7334 Commercial printing, offset; typesetting; platemaking services; photocopying & duplicating services; commercial printing; bookbinding & related work

(G-15859)
NELSONS CREAMERY LLC
Also Called: Nelson's Ice Cream
600 W Germantown Pike (19462-1046)
PHONE....................610 948-3000
Jay Vigdor, *President*
David Nelson, *Vice Pres*
Robert Nice, *Vice Pres*
EMP: 22
SALES (est): 1.4MM **Privately Held**
SIC: 2024 Ice cream & frozen desserts

(G-15860)
NORTH AMERICAN ARMS INC (PA)
600 W Germantown Pike # 4 (19462-1046)
PHONE....................610 940-1668
Sandy Chisholm, *President*
▲ **EMP:** 1
SQ FT: 25,000
SALES (est): 2.5MM **Privately Held**
WEB: www.naaminis.com
SIC: 3484 Small arms

(G-15861)
NRF US INC (PA)
105 E Germantown Pike (19462-1506)
PHONE....................814 947-1378
Sean Givnish, *Sales Mgr*
EMP: 8
SALES (est): 3MM **Privately Held**
SIC: 3714 3443 3053 Radiators & radiator shells & cores, motor vehicle; air coolers, metal plate; packing: steam engines, pipe joints, air compressors, etc.

(G-15862)
P H A FINANCE INC
Also Called: Hj Financial Group
1000 Germantown Pike E3 (19462-2480)
PHONE....................610 272-4700
EMP: 33
SALES (est): 2.3MM **Privately Held**
SIC: 2741 8721 Misc Publishing Accounting/Auditing/Bookkeeping

(G-15863)
PERFECTDATA CORPORATION (PA)
1323 Conshohocken Rd (19462-2707)
P.O. Box 748, Norristown (19404-0748)
PHONE...................................800 973-7332
Andrew B Bastian, *President*
William Bastian, *Vice Pres*
D Geer, *CFO*
EMP: 2
SALES (est): 3.5MM **Privately Held**
SIC: 5169 2842 Aerosols; specialty cleaning preparations

(G-15864)
PLASTIC LUMBER YARD LLC
227 Isabella St (19462-2717)
PHONE...................................610 277-3900
Cristene Pisano, *Principal*
Mark Siemon, *Mng Member*
◆ **EMP:** 5
SALES (est): 1.4MM **Privately Held**
WEB: www.plasticlumberyard.com
SIC: 2899 5162 Plastic wood; plastics materials & basic shapes

(G-15865)
PREMIER DENTAL PRODUCTS CO (PA)
Also Called: Premier Medical Products
1710 Romano Dr (19462-2822)
PHONE...................................610 239-6000
Julie Charlestein, *President*
Asad Tanvir, *General Mgr*
Gary Charlestein, *Chairman*
Morton Charlestein, *Chairman*
Steven Hayman, *COO*
▲ **EMP:** 50 **EST:** 1913
SQ FT: 34,350
SALES (est): 25.4MM **Privately Held**
WEB: www.premusa.com
SIC: 5047 3843 3841 Dental equipment & supplies; medical equipment & supplies; dental equipment & supplies; dental equipment; dental hand instruments; surgical & medical instruments

(G-15866)
QDP INC
4110 Butler Pike Ste F101 (19462-1547)
PHONE...................................610 828-2324
Stewart McDlhone, *President*
Stewart McElhone, *President*
Jon Murray, *Vice Pres*
EMP: 18
SQ FT: 7,000
SALES (est): 5.6MM **Privately Held**
WEB: www.qdpusa.com
SIC: 3462 3469 Iron & steel forgings; metal stampings

(G-15867)
REHA TECHNOLOGY USA INC
5209 Militia Hill Rd # 102 (19462-1216)
PHONE...................................267 419-8690
Don Labowsky, *Vice Pres*
EMP: 3
SALES (est): 393.9K **Privately Held**
SIC: 3845 Electrotherapeutic apparatus

(G-15868)
ROBAR INDUSTRIES INC (PA)
Also Called: Item Publications
1000 Germantown Pike F2 (19462-2486)
PHONE...................................484 688-0300
Robert D Goldblum, *President*
Leonard M Levin, *Vice Pres*
Barbara F Goldblum, *Admin Sec*
EMP: 5
SQ FT: 2,500
SALES (est): 1.1MM **Privately Held**
SIC: 2741 8748 2731 Technical manual & paper publishing; systems engineering consultant, ex. computer or professional; book publishing

(G-15869)
SEWING EQUIPMENT CO INC
3030 Warrior Rd (19462-2323)
PHONE...................................610 825-2581
EMP: 6 **EST:** 1956
SALES (est): 704.2K **Privately Held**
SIC: 3639 Mfg Household Appliances

(G-15870)
SIEMENS MED SOLUTIONS USA INC
Also Called: Ultrasound Division
5168 Campus Dr (19462-1123)
PHONE...................................610 834-1220
Art Schenck, *Vice Pres*
EMP: 25
SALES (corp-wide): 95B **Privately Held**
SIC: 3841 Medical instruments & equipment, blood & bone work
HQ: Siemens Medical Solutions Usa, Inc.
40 Liberty Blvd
Malvern PA 19355
888 826-9702

(G-15871)
SIMPLICITY CREATIVE CORP
450 Plymouth Rd Ste 300 (19462-1644)
PHONE...................................800 653-7301
EMP: 3
SALES (est): 107.4K
SALES (corp-wide): 361.9MM **Publicly Held**
SIC: 2741 Miscellaneous publishing
PA: Css Industries, Inc.
450 Plymouth Rd Ste 300
Plymouth Meeting PA 19462
610 729-3959

(G-15872)
SPRAY PRODUCTS CORPORATION (PA)
1323 Conshohocken Rd (19462-2707)
P.O. Box 737, Norristown (19404-0737)
PHONE...................................610 277-1010
Andrew Bastian, *President*
Douglas Geer, *CFO*
William Bastian, *Admin Sec*
◆ **EMP:** 72
SQ FT: 50,000
SALES (est): 25.9MM **Privately Held**
SIC: 2899 2813 2851 Chemical preparations; industrial gases; paints & allied products

(G-15873)
SPRING LOCK SCAFFOLDING EQP CO
Also Called: Crown Scaffolding
901 Artis Rd (19462-1267)
PHONE...................................215 426-5727
Ernest Rapoport, *President*
Jeffrey Rapoport, *Corp Secy*
Mitchell Rapoport, *Vice Pres*
Randy Rapoport, *Vice Pres*
Paula Rapoport, *Shareholder*
EMP: 6
SQ FT: 21,000
SALES (est): 729K **Privately Held**
SIC: 3446 7359 Scaffolds, mobile or stationary: metal; equipment rental & leasing

(G-15874)
STAYCHILLED USA LLC
13 Laurence Pl (19462-1919)
PHONE...................................215 284-6018
Bruce Mullen, *Mng Member*
EMP: 3
SALES (est): 178.1K **Privately Held**
SIC: 3085 Plastics bottles

(G-15875)
SYMBOL TECHNOLOGIES LLC
450 Plymouth Rd Ste 202 (19462-1659)
PHONE...................................610 834-8900
Marianne McKeown, *Manager*
EMP: 12
SALES (corp-wide): 4.2B **Publicly Held**
WEB: www.symbol.com
SIC: 3577 3663 5045 Magnetic ink & optical scanning devices; optical scanning devices; magnetic ink recognition devices; radio broadcasting & communications equipment; computers
HQ: Symbol Technologies, Llc
1 Zebra Plz
Holtsville NY 11742
631 737-6851

(G-15876)
THOMAS CATANESE & CO
324 Knoll Rd (19462-7110)
PHONE...................................610 277-6230
Thomas Catanese, *President*

Carol Marie Catanese, *Vice Pres*
▲ **EMP:** 5
SALES (est): 266.2K **Privately Held**
WEB: www.thomascatanese.com
SIC: 2679 Gift wrap & novelties, paper

(G-15877)
VAN EERDEN COATINGS COMPANY
60 Flourtown Rd (19462-1205)
PHONE...................................484 368-3073
Glenn Vaneereden, *President*
EMP: 5
SALES (est): 508K **Privately Held**
SIC: 2796 Engraving platemaking services

(G-15878)
VGX PHARMACEUTICALS LLC (HQ)
660 W Germantown Pike # 110 (19462-1111)
PHONE...................................215 542-5912
Joseph Kim, *CEO*
Kevin Rassas, *Vice Pres*
Gene Kim, *CFO*
Yuerong Ronni Wen, *Accountant*
EMP: 20 **EST:** 2000
SALES (est): 2.3MM **Publicly Held**
SIC: 2834 Pharmaceutical preparations

(G-15879)
WATERS CORPORATION
5205 Militia Hill Rd # 100 (19462-1216)
PHONE...................................484 344-5404
Eric Henning, *Manager*
EMP: 5 **Publicly Held**
SIC: 3826 Chromatographic equipment, laboratory type
PA: Waters Corporation
34 Maple St
Milford MA 01757

Pocono Lake
Monroe County

(G-15880)
H&K GROUP INC
Also Called: Jamico Materials
Hc 87 Box 282 (18347)
PHONE...................................570 646-3324
Dave Moyer, *Manager*
Bob Dudzinski, *MIS Dir*
EMP: 150
SALES (corp-wide): 71.6MM **Privately Held**
WEB: www.hkgroup.com
SIC: 1422 Lime rock, ground
PA: H&K Group, Inc.
2052 Lucon Rd
Skippack PA 19474
610 584-8500

Pocono Pines
Monroe County

(G-15881)
HUTTON METALCRAFTS INC
Also Called: Light By Hutton
1812 Route 940 Bldg 1 (18350-7744)
PHONE...................................570 646-7778
Thomas R Hutton, *President*
EMP: 5
SALES: 250K **Privately Held**
WEB: www.copperlamps.com
SIC: 3499 5947 3645 Giftware, copper goods; gift shop; residential lighting fixtures

(G-15882)
NAUGHTON ENERGY CORPORATION
1898 Route 940 (18350-7744)
P.O. Box 709 (18350-0709)
PHONE...................................570 646-0422
Mariette Naughton, *President*
Sean Naughton, *Vice Pres*
EMP: 17
SQ FT: 3,200

SALES: 16.4MM **Privately Held**
WEB: www.naughtonenergy.com
SIC: 5052 2869 5172 Coal; hydraulic fluids, synthetic base; lubricating oils & greases

(G-15883)
PRINTING CRAFTSMEN INC
Also Called: This Week In Poconos Magazine
112 Print Shop Rd (18350)
PHONE...................................570 646-2121
Edwin R Miller, *President*
EMP: 15 **EST:** 1932
SQ FT: 6,000
SALES (est): 169.9K **Privately Held**
WEB: www.thisweek.net
SIC: 2752 2721 Commercial printing, lithographic; magazines: publishing & printing

(G-15884)
SEAN NAUGHTON
Also Called: S&N Energy
Rr 940 (18350)
P.O. Box 709 (18350-0709)
PHONE...................................570 646-0422
Sean Naughton, *President*
EMP: 3
SALES: 500K **Privately Held**
SIC: 2992 5989 Lubricating oils & greases; fuel dealers

Pocono Summit
Monroe County

(G-15885)
ARDENT MILLS LLC
258 Harvest Ln (18346-7841)
PHONE...................................570 839-8322
John Covad, *Manager*
EMP: 40
SALES (corp-wide): 543.9MM **Privately Held**
WEB: www.horizonmilling.com
SIC: 2041 2075 Flour & other grain mill products; soybean oil, cake or meal
PA: Ardent Mills, Llc
1875 Lawrence St Ste 1400
Denver CO 80202
800 851-9618

Point Marion
Fayette County

(G-15886)
MICHAEL N SULLENBERGER
126 Penn St (15474-1234)
PHONE...................................724 725-5285
Michael N Sullenberger, *Owner*
EMP: 4
SALES (est): 330.5K **Privately Held**
SIC: 3429 Manufactured hardware (general)

Point Pleasant
Bucks County

(G-15887)
M DOBRON & SONS INC
7273 Ferry Rd (18950)
PHONE...................................215 297-5331
William Dobron Jr, *President*
Mary Francis Dobron, *Admin Sec*
EMP: 6 **EST:** 1918
SQ FT: 3,096
SALES (est): 554.2K **Privately Held**
SIC: 1794 3496 Excavation & grading, building construction; miscellaneous fabricated wire products

(G-15888)
TIFFANY TIFFANY DESIGNERS INC
27 Cafferty Rd (18950-2004)
P.O. Box 575 (18950-0575)
PHONE...................................215 297-0550
Barbara Tiffany, *President*
Robert Tiffany, *Vice Pres*
EMP: 5

SQ FT: 3,000
SALES (est): 275K **Privately Held**
SIC: 2512 Upholstered household furniture

Polk
Venango County

(G-15889)
TIME MACHINE INC (PA)
Also Called: Skinner Power Systems
1746 Pittsburgh Rd (16342-5322)
PHONE................................814 432-5281
Jeffrey P Latchaw, *President*
Jason Trippe, *General Mgr*
Todd Latchaw, *Corp Secy*
Michael Latchaw, *Vice Pres*
Dave Seyler, *CFO*
EMP: 56
SQ FT: 36,000
SALES (est): 11.5MM **Privately Held**
WEB: www.tmctools.com
SIC: 3599 3541 Machine shop, jobbing &
repair; machine tools, metal cutting type

Pomeroy
Chester County

(G-15890)
KEYSTONE DEHORNER
49 Chestnut St (19367)
PHONE................................610 857-9728
Terry L Franciscus, *Owner*
EMP: 3
SQ FT: 1,500
SALES: 250K **Privately Held**
SIC: 3523 Clippers, for animal use: hand
or electric

Port Allegany
Mckean County

(G-15891)
ARDAGH GLASS INC
1 Glass Pl (16743-1154)
PHONE................................814 642-2521
Ed Stewart, *Manager*
EMP: 21
SALES (corp-wide): 242.1K **Privately
Held**
WEB: www.sgcontainers.com
SIC: 3231 Products of purchased glass
HQ: Ardagh Glass Inc.
10194 Crosspoint Blvd
Indianapolis IN 46256

(G-15892)
COX MACHINING INC
479 Combs Creek Rd (16743-3109)
PHONE................................814 642-5009
Charles Cox, *President*
Lynn Cox, *Admin Sec*
EMP: 3
SQ FT: 2,000
SALES (est): 363K **Privately Held**
SIC: 3599 Machine shop, jobbing & repair

(G-15893)
D E ERRICK CORPORATION
24843 Route 6 (16743-2517)
PHONE................................814 642-2589
David E Errick, *President*
Marl Errick, *Info Tech Dir*
Patricia Errick, *Admin Sec*
EMP: 15
SQ FT: 16,000
SALES: 2MM **Privately Held**
WEB: www.de-errick.com
SIC: 4731 3053 Freight transportation
arrangement; gaskets, packing & sealing
devices

(G-15894)
LAPPS LOGGING
92 Volney St (16743-1060)
P.O. Box 142 (16743-0142)
PHONE................................814 642-7949
Mark Lapp, *Principal*
EMP: 3

SALES (est): 251.1K **Privately Held**
SIC: 2411 Logging

(G-15895)
TAYLOR LOGGING
36 E Vine St (16743-1054)
PHONE................................814 642-2788
EMP: 3
SALES (est): 251.1K **Privately Held**
SIC: 2411 Logging

(G-15896)
VERALLIA
1 Glass Pl (16743-1154)
PHONE................................814 642-2521
EMP: 3
SALES (est): 178.7K **Privately Held**
SIC: 3221 Glass containers

Port Carbon
Schuylkill County

(G-15897)
JOE KUPERAVAGE
Also Called: Kuperavage Coal Company
916 Park Ave (17965-1211)
PHONE................................570 622-8080
Joseph A Kuperavage, *Partner*
Robert Kuperavage, *Partner*
EMP: 14 **EST:** 1975
SALES (est): 947K **Privately Held**
SIC: 1231 Strip mining, anthracite

(G-15898)
K & K COAL COMPANY
133 Valley Furnace Ave (17965-1215)
PHONE................................570 622-0220
Bernard Kuperavage, *Partner*
David Kuperavage, *Partner*
EMP: 5
SALES (est): 406.3K **Privately Held**
SIC: 1231 Strip mining, anthracite

(G-15899)
**PENN EQUIPMENT
CORPORATION**
15 Main St (17965-1607)
P.O. Box 8 (17965-0008)
PHONE................................570 622-9933
Anthony Blaschak Jr, *President*
Charles Wezner, *Treasurer*
Stephen Blaschak, *Asst Treas*
Lawrence F Keba, *Admin Sec*
John Blaschak Jr, *Asst Sec*
EMP: 20 **EST:** 1930
SQ FT: 30,000
SALES (est): 3.4MM **Privately Held**
SIC: 3599 7699 Machine shop, jobbing &
repair; industrial machinery & equipment
repair

(G-15900)
PUSHCART USA INC
104 Pottsville St (17965-1513)
PHONE................................570 622-2479
Robert Scifo, *CEO*
EMP: 4 **EST:** 2015
SQ FT: 20,000
SALES (est): 206.4K **Privately Held**
SIC: 3799 Mfg Transportation Equipment

Port Matilda
Centre County

(G-15901)
BECKS PAVING
50 Peggy Cir (16870-8719)
PHONE................................814 692-7797
Charles Becks, *Owner*
EMP: 3 **EST:** 2000
SALES: 100K **Privately Held**
SIC: 2951 Asphalt paving mixtures &
blocks

(G-15902)
**MP MACHINERY AND TESTING
LLC**
260 Pantops Parade (16870-7032)
PHONE................................814 234-8860
Michael P Manahan,

EMP: 7
SALES (est): 520K **Privately Held**
SIC: 3829 Measuring & controlling devices

(G-15903)
MR SPOUTING
Also Called: Adams Construction
301 S Main St (16870)
P.O. Box 492 (16870-0492)
PHONE................................814 692-4880
Bob Adams, *Owner*
Karen Adams, *Co-Owner*
EMP: 9
SALES (est): 520K **Privately Held**
SIC: 3089 Spouting, plastic & glass fiber
reinforced

(G-15904)
PRICE LUMBER COMPANY
Meeks Ln (16870)
PHONE................................814 231-0260
John Price, *Owner*
EMP: 7
SQ FT: 60,000
SALES (est): 350K **Privately Held**
SIC: 2421 Furniture dimension stock, soft-
wood

(G-15905)
QBC DIAGNOSTICS LLC
168 Bradford Dr (16870-1024)
PHONE................................814 342-6210
Kenneth J Moscone, *CEO*
Craig Stout, *Vice Pres*
▲ **EMP:** 200
SQ FT: 13,000
SALES (est): 28.2MM **Privately Held**
WEB: www.qbcdiagnostics.com
SIC: 3841 Surgical & medical instruments

(G-15906)
SKYTOP MACHINE & TOOL INC
1263 Skytop Mountain Rd (16870-7719)
PHONE................................814 234-3430
Barbara Corl, *President*
Carolyn Kottwitz, *Vice Pres*
EMP: 5
SQ FT: 7,038
SALES (est): 888.6K **Privately Held**
WEB: www.skytopmachine.com
SIC: 3599 Machine shop, jobbing & repair

(G-15907)
TURTLE MOON GARDENS
303 Lower Julian Pike (16870-7513)
PHONE................................814 639-0287
Denise Defluri, *Owner*
EMP: 3
SALES (est): 272.1K **Privately Held**
SIC: 2911 5999 5169 Aromatic chemical
products; cosmetics; aromatic chemicals

(G-15908)
**ZEIGLERS PACKING AND
CRATING (PA)**
938 Meeks Ln (16870-7009)
PHONE................................814 238-4021
B Arlene Lightner-Rowe, *President*
Marian Kaller, *Manager*
EMP: 1 **EST:** 1961
SALES (est): 1MM **Privately Held**
WEB: www.zeiglerspacking.com
SIC: 5099 2449 Containers: glass, metal
or plastic; shipping cases & drums, wood:
wirebound & plywood

Port Royal
Juniata County

(G-15909)
BLUE VALLEY INDUSTRIES INC
304 N Third St (17082)
P.O. Box 5, Mexico (17056-0005)
PHONE................................717 436-8266
H Wayne Haubert, *President*
Martin E Druckemiller Jr, *Vice Pres*
▼ **EMP:** 8
SALES (est): 1.4MM **Privately Held**
WEB: www.bluevalleyind.com
SIC: 3559 3441 Recycling machinery; fab-
ricated structural metal

(G-15910)
KRISHNA PROTECTS COWS INC
534 Gita Nagari Rd (17082-7263)
PHONE................................717 527-4101
Ashik Raval, *Director*
Parijata Munien, *Director*
▲ **EMP:** 5
SALES: 275.6K **Privately Held**
SIC: 3556 Pasteurizing equipment, dairy
machinery

Port Trevorton
Snyder County

(G-15911)
**CUSTOM BEDFRAME
PRODUCTS**
49 Summer Breeze Ln (17864-9566)
PHONE................................570 539-8770
Delmar Staufer, *Principal*
Jeremy Martin, *Principal*
EMP: 16
SQ FT: 15,000
SALES (est): 6.6MM **Privately Held**
SIC: 2515 Mattresses & bedsprings

(G-15912)
CUSTOM BINS PALLET MFG
64 Summer Breeze Ln (17864-9568)
PHONE................................570 539-4158
EMP: 4 **EST:** 2010
SALES (est): 250K **Privately Held**
SIC: 2448 Mfg Wood Pallets/Skids

(G-15913)
HOME WOODWORK
180 Flanders Rd (17864-9371)
PHONE................................570 295-2185
Nevin EBY, *Owner*
EMP: 4
SALES (est): 180K **Privately Held**
WEB: www.homewoodwork.com
SIC: 2521 Wood office chairs, benches &
stools

(G-15914)
JBS WOODWORK SHOP
631 Lumber Hill Rd (17864-9541)
PHONE................................570 374-4883
Jonathan Brubaker, *Partner*
Kenneth Horst, *Partner*
Merle Zimmerman, *Partner*
EMP: 10
SQ FT: 12,000
SALES (est): 2.7MM **Privately Held**
SIC: 2515 Foundations & platforms

(G-15915)
STAUFFER FRAMES
460 Lumber Hill Rd (17864-9379)
PHONE................................570 374-7100
Lester Stauffer, *Partner*
Anthony Auker, *Partner*
Roy Brubaker, *Partner*
Benjamin Martin, *Partner*
Larry Martin, *Partner*
EMP: 20
SQ FT: 13,500
SALES: 9.6MM **Privately Held**
SIC: 2515 Mattresses & bedsprings

(G-15916)
**WINDVIEW TRUCK & TRLR
REPR LLC**
94 Windview Ln (17864-9573)
PHONE................................570 374-8077
Evan Curtis,
EMP: 4
SQ FT: 5,600
SALES (est): 320K **Privately Held**
SIC: 3715 Truck trailers

Portage
Cambria County

(G-15917)
GERMANTOWN WINERY LLC
3586 Frankstown Rd (15946-8108)
PHONE................................814 241-8458
EMP: 5 **EST:** 2013

SALES (est): 254.3K Privately Held
SIC: 2084 Wines

(G-15918)
LEMAN MACHINE COMPANY
1049 S Railroad Ave (15946-1554)
P.O. Box 269 (15946-0269)
PHONE....................................814 736-9696
Stuart E Leman, *President*
John W Gilbert, *Corp Secy*
Troy Gilbert, *Vice Pres*
EMP: 30 EST: 1929
SQ FT: 36,000
SALES (est): 3.5MM Privately Held
WEB: www.lemanmachine.com
SIC: 3441 3599 3547 3532 Fabricated
structural metal; machine shop, jobbing &
repair; rolling mill machinery; mining ma-
chinery; sheet metalwork

(G-15919)
MARTINDALE LUMBER CO INC
1047 Puritan Rd (15946-8402)
PHONE....................................814 736-3032
Donald R Mc Cabe, *President*
Raymond Mc Cabe, *Vice Pres*
Charles J Jubina, *Treasurer*
Francis Mc Cabe, *Admin Sec*
EMP: 22
SQ FT: 11,700
SALES (est): 1.7MM Privately Held
SIC: 2421 Lumber: rough, sawed or
planed; kiln drying of lumber

(G-15920)
SAY-CORE INC
132 Block Rd (15946-6905)
PHONE....................................814 736-8018
Barry Saylor, *Principal*
▲ EMP: 100 EST: 2001
SQ FT: 35,000
SALES (est): 18.8MM Privately Held
WEB: www.saycore.com
SIC: 3272 Concrete products, precast

(G-15921)
SHOJOBERRY MAGAZINE
805 Sherman St (15946-1836)
PHONE....................................814 736-3210
Garrett Boast, *Principal*
EMP: 3
SALES (est): 191.9K Privately Held
SIC: 2721 Periodicals

(G-15922)
STARPRINT PUBLICATIONS INC
(PA)
722 Dulancey Dr (15946-6902)
P.O. Box 216 (15946-0216)
PHONE....................................814 736-9666
Eugene Stepp, *President*
Susan Stepp, *Treasurer*
Gloria Stepp, *Admin Sec*
◆ EMP: 30 EST: 1951
SQ FT: 32,000
SALES: 4.2MM Privately Held
SIC: 2752 Commercial printing, offset

Portersville
Butler County

(G-15923)
ADAMS MFG CORP (DH)
109 W Park Rd (16051-2209)
PHONE....................................800 237-8287
Tom Lombardo, *CEO*
Marci Wheeler, *General Mgr*
David George, *Human Res Mgr*
Vincent Cannistra, *Natl Sales Mgr*
Ted Oczypok, *Natl Sales Mgr*
▼ EMP: 20
SQ FT: 60,000
SALES (est): 43.3MM Privately Held
WEB: www.adamsmfg.com
SIC: 3089 Plastic hardware & building
products
HQ: Keter Plastic Ltd
1 Sapir
Herzliya 46852
524 641-266

(G-15924)
ALUMINUM & CARBON PLUS
INC
2207 Erie Hwy (16051)
PHONE....................................724 368-9200
Jeannie Kruidenier, *President*
John Fecko, *President*
Jeannie S Kruidenier, *President*
Jean Kruiderier, *Vice Pres*
Lewis Patricia, *Vice Pres*
EMP: 3
SALES (est): 716.9K Privately Held
SIC: 3354 3624 Aluminum extruded prod-
ucts; carbon & graphite products

(G-15925)
APSS INC
Also Called: Automation Parts Sales & Svc
120 Fisher Rd (16051-1204)
PHONE....................................724 368-3001
Richard Montgomery, *President*
Matthew Teich, *Vice Pres*
Russell Hendrickson, *Admin Sec*
EMP: 10
SALES (est): 820K Privately Held
SIC: 3569 Liquid automation machinery &
equipment

(G-15926)
CABLE HARDWOODS INC
4401 State Route 488 (16051-3815)
P.O. Box 293 (16051-0293)
PHONE....................................724 452-5927
Jeffrey L Cable, *President*
Kim Cable, *Treasurer*
EMP: 12
SALES (est): 1.3MM Privately Held
SIC: 2411 Logging

(G-15927)
FRUEHAUF MANUFACTURING
2069 New Castle Rd (16051-1207)
PHONE....................................412 771-4200
Welling Fruehauf,
EMP: 7
SALES (est): 899.9K Privately Held
SIC: 3599 Machine shop, jobbing & repair

(G-15928)
JJ KENNEDY INC
120 Fisher Rd (16051-1204)
PHONE....................................724 368-8660
James Rader, *Manager*
EMP: 5
SALES (corp-wide): 10.8MM Privately
Held
WEB: www.jjkennedy.com
SIC: 3273 Ready-mixed concrete
PA: J.J. Kennedy Inc
1790 Route 588
Fombell PA 16123
724 452-6260

(G-15929)
KESTNER WOOD PRODUCTS
INC
330 Levis Rd (16051-1914)
P.O. Box 318 (16051-0318)
PHONE....................................724 368-3605
Bruce Kestner, *President*
Jan Kestner, *Owner*
▲ EMP: 6 EST: 1974
SQ FT: 3,760
SALES (est): 831K Privately Held
SIC: 2431 Moldings, wood: unfinished &
prefinished

(G-15930)
LAVEINGS MOBILITY
368 Heinz Camp Rd (16051-3906)
PHONE....................................724 368-9417
Michael Laveing, *Owner*
EMP: 3
SALES (est): 170K Privately Held
SIC: 3842 7532 Wheelchairs; customizing
services, non-factory basis

(G-15931)
M J M INDUSTRIES
1 Good Pl Ste A (16051-2329)
PHONE....................................724 368-8400
Michael Roberts, *Owner*
EMP: 3
SQ FT: 6,500

SALES (est): 750K Privately Held
SIC: 3471 3479 Cleaning & descaling
metal products; coating of metals &
formed products

(G-15932)
MEYER MACHINE COMPANY
INC
2647 Perry Hwy (16051-6329)
PHONE....................................724 368-3711
Joseph Meyer, *President*
EMP: 6
SALES (est): 828.6K Privately Held
SIC: 3599 Machine shop, jobbing & repair

(G-15933)
MONTGMRYS ATOMTN PARTS
SLS SVC
100 Fisher Rd (16051-1204)
PHONE....................................724 368-3001
Richard Montgomery, *Partner*
EMP: 4
SALES (est): 950K Privately Held
SIC: 3559 Special industry machinery

(G-15934)
OLDE RECIPE FOODS INC
120 Adams Ln (16051-2419)
P.O. Box 8457, New Castle (16107-8457)
PHONE....................................724 654-5779
Rodney Firmi, *President*
David Dugan, *Vice Pres*
EMP: 4
SALES (est): 372.9K Privately Held
WEB: www.deluxesausage.com
SIC: 2013 Sausages from purchased meat

(G-15935)
QUALITY AGGREGATES INC
552 Many Springs Farm Rd (16051-5310)
PHONE....................................724 924-2198
Craig Myers, *Manager*
EMP: 27
SALES (est): 821.9K Privately Held
WEB: www.aquascape-env.com
SIC: 1221 Bituminous coal & lignite-sur-
face mining
PA: Quality Aggregates Inc.
4955 Steubenville Pike # 245
Pittsburgh PA 15205

(G-15936)
SHOOK SPECIALTY WELDING
INC
3968 State Route 488 (16051-3724)
PHONE....................................724 368-8419
Joseph Shook, *President*
Samantha Shook, *Treasurer*
EMP: 11
SQ FT: 11,250
SALES (est): 1.6MM Privately Held
SIC: 3599 Machine shop, jobbing & repair

(G-15937)
TATE JONES INC
2069 New Castle Rd (16051-1207)
PHONE....................................412 771-4200
Welling Fruehaus, *President*
Welling Fruehauf, *Finance*
Johnny Fernandez, *Sales Staff*
EMP: 6
SQ FT: 15,000
SALES (est): 1.3MM Privately Held
WEB: www.tate-jones.com
SIC: 3567 Industrial furnaces & ovens

Portland
Northampton County

(G-15938)
AMERICAN PRCSION
MACHINING LLC
106 State St (18351-7023)
P.O. Box 133 (18351-0133)
PHONE....................................484 632-9449
John Vallance,
EMP: 5
SQ FT: 4,000
SALES (est): 617.5K Privately Held
SIC: 3599 Machine & other job shop work

(G-15939)
DUCKLOE FREDERICK AND
BROS
513 Delaware Ave (18351)
P.O. Box 427 (18351-0427)
PHONE....................................570 897-6172
Frederick B Duckloe Jr, *President*
Barbara Duckloe Townsend, *Corp Secy*
EMP: 18
SQ FT: 30,000
SALES (est): 2.9MM Privately Held
SIC: 5712 2511 2531 2521 Beds & ac-
cessories; wood household furniture;
chairs, household, except upholstered:
wood; public building & related furniture;
wood office furniture; partitions & fixtures,
except wood

(G-15940)
ULTRA-POLY CORPORATION
(PA)
102 Demi Rd (18351)
P.O. Box 330 (18351-0330)
PHONE....................................570 897-7500
Alan La Fiura, *President*
John McCullam, *Vice Pres*
▲ EMP: 46 EST: 1974
SQ FT: 150,000
SALES (est): 12.4MM Privately Held
WEB: www.ultra-poly.com
SIC: 2821 3087 Polyethylene resins; cus-
tom compound purchased resins

Pottstown
Chester County

(G-15941)
AECO SERVICE INC
Also Called: Art Engraving
1214 Grandview Cir (19465-7728)
PHONE....................................610 372-0561
Lynne K Moyer, *President*
Lawrence Beckner Jr, *Admin Sec*
EMP: 4 EST: 1922
SQ FT: 4,800
SALES (est): 516.6K Privately Held
WEB: www.artengraving.com
SIC: 2796 5999 Photoengraving plates,
linecuts or halftones; art, picture frames &
decorations

(G-15942)
AMERICAN WASTE DIGEST
CORP (PA)
1345 Thomas Oakes Dr (19465-7275)
PHONE....................................610 326-9480
Carasue B Moody, *President*
Charles G Moody III, *President*
EMP: 6
SQ FT: 1,250
SALES (est): 743K Privately Held
WEB: www.americanwastedigest.com
SIC: 2721 Magazines: publishing only, not
printed on site

(G-15943)
ARK IDEAZ INC
Also Called: Ismystuffreal.com
1198 Chestershire Pl (19465-9600)
PHONE....................................610 246-9106
Randy Feldman, *President*
EMP: 5
SALES (est): 242.3K Privately Held
SIC: 7371 7372 Computer software sys-
tems analysis & design, custom; applica-
tion computer software

(G-15944)
ATLAS FLASHER & SUPPLY CO
INC
2046 Pottstown Pike (19465-8670)
PHONE....................................610 469-2602
Karen Brown, *CEO*
EMP: 30
SALES (est): 2.4MM Privately Held
SIC: 3669 Transportation signaling devices

(G-15945)
BRANDYWINE BRANCH
DISTILLERS
247 Bishop Rd (19465-8252)
PHONE....................................610 326-8151

▲ = Import ▼=Export
◆ =Import/Export

Riannon Walsh, *Principal*
EMP: 4
SALES (est): 230.4K **Privately Held**
SIC: 2085 Distilled & blended liquors

(G-15946)
CHESTER COUNTY SPORTS PRODUCTS
38 Glocker Way (19465-9655)
PHONE..................................610 327-4843
Morrison Donald, *Owner*
EMP: 4
SALES (est): 354.1K **Privately Held**
SIC: 3949 Sporting & athletic goods

(G-15947)
H&K GROUP INC
Reading Site Contractor
392 N Sanatoga Rd (19465)
PHONE..................................610 705-0500
Neal Rotenberger, *Superintendent*
William Hollander, *Manager*
Keith Martin, *Manager*
EMP: 110
SALES (corp-wide): 71.6MM **Privately Held**
WEB: www.hkgroup.com
SIC: 2951 1411 1611 5032 Asphalt & asphaltic paving mixtures (not from refineries); dimension stone; highway & street paving contractor; paving materials
PA: H&K Group, Inc.
2052 Lucon Rd
Skippack PA 19474
610 584-8500

(G-15948)
HYVAC PRODUCTS INC (PA)
1265 Ridge Rd (19465-8705)
P.O. Box 389, Phoenixville (19460-0389)
PHONE..................................484 901-4100
Theodore Morgan, *Ch of Bd*
Jeff Morgan, *President*
▲ **EMP:** 11
SQ FT: 10,000
SALES (est): 1.3MM **Privately Held**
WEB: www.hyvac.com
SIC: 3821 5084 Vacuum pumps, laboratory; pumps & pumping equipment

(G-15949)
IRONSTONE CREAMERY
3500 Coventryville Rd (19465-8540)
PHONE..................................610 952-2748
Jeffrey Stetler, *President*
EMP: 5
SALES (est): 218.5K **Privately Held**
SIC: 2021 Creamery butter

(G-15950)
KLT GROUP INC
557 Kulp Rd (19465-8102)
PHONE..................................215 525-0902
Michael E Gdowik, *Principal*
EMP: 3
SALES (est): 525.9K **Privately Held**
SIC: 3599 Machine shop, jobbing & repair

(G-15951)
L & M CONSTRUCTION
498 Lower Fricks Lock Rd (19465-7904)
PHONE..................................610 326-9970
Larry Schweitz, *Partner*
EMP: 3
SALES (est): 233.1K **Privately Held**
SIC: 3531 Bituminous, cement & concrete related products & equipment

(G-15952)
LAY MACHINE AND TOOL INC
1751 Pottstown Pike (19465-8676)
P.O. Box 1203 (19464-0879)
PHONE..................................610 469-0928
Lester Yoder, *President*
Patricia Yoder, *Corp Secy*
EMP: 3
SQ FT: 5,000
SALES (est): 75K **Privately Held**
SIC: 3549 Metalworking machinery

(G-15953)
LIFEWEAR INC (PA)
1280 Laurelwood Rd (19465-7463)
PHONE..................................610 327-9938
Richard Bartman, *President*
Elizabeth Bartman, *Vice Pres*

EMP: 2
SQ FT: 10,000
SALES: 2MM **Privately Held**
WEB: www.lifewear.net
SIC: 2253 T-shirts & tops, knit

(G-15954)
LIN KAY ASSOCIATES INC
2132 Robin Ln (19465-8609)
PHONE..................................610 469-6833
Linda Kay Burston, *Owner*
Raymond Burston, *Vice Pres*
EMP: 3
SALES (est): 398.5K **Privately Held**
SIC: 3823 Industrial flow & liquid measuring instruments

(G-15955)
NEPTUNE PUMP MANUFACTURING CO
1265 Ridge Rd (19465-8705)
P.O. Box 389, Phoenixville (19460-0389)
PHONE..................................484 901-4100
Jeff Morgan, *Owner*
EMP: 5
SQ FT: 20,000
SALES (est): 820.9K
SALES (corp-wide): 1.3MM **Privately Held**
WEB: www.hyvac.com
SIC: 3561 Industrial pumps & parts
PA: Hyvac Products, Inc.
1265 Ridge Rd
Pottstown PA 19465
484 901-4100

(G-15956)
QUILTING STONE HOUSE
30 Hershey Dr (19465-8137)
PHONE..................................610 495-8762
Lisa Calle, *Principal*
EMP: 3
SALES (est): 170.9K **Privately Held**
SIC: 2221 Textile mills, broadwoven: silk & manmade, also glass

(G-15957)
WILLIAM A MODDREL
Also Called: W M Machine Tool
888 Scholl Rd (19465-7271)
PHONE..................................610 327-8296
William A Moddrel, *Owner*
Ellen Moddrel, *Co-Owner*
EMP: 3 **EST:** 1973
SQ FT: 1,500
SALES: 250K **Privately Held**
WEB: www.wmmachinetool.com
SIC: 3599 Machine shop, jobbing & repair

(G-15958)
WOODEN NICKELS LLC
117 Hillside Ln (19465-8583)
PHONE..................................484 408-4901
Joseph Piazza, *Principal*
EMP: 3
SALES (est): 234.8K **Privately Held**
SIC: 3356 Nickel

Pottstown
Montgomery County

(G-15959)
A G SOURCE INC
2029 Orlando Rd (19464-2349)
PHONE..................................484 459-9292
Alfred Giordano, *Branch Mgr*
EMP: 10 **Privately Held**
SIC: 3599 Machine shop, jobbing & repair
PA: A. G. Source, Inc.
11 Pinewood Dr
Downingtown PA 19335

(G-15960)
ADIDAS NORTH AMERICA INC
Also Called: Adidas Outlet Store Pottstown
18 W Lightcap Rd Ste 789 (19464-7816)
PHONE..................................610 327-9565
EMP: 15
SALES (corp-wide): 25B **Privately Held**
SIC: 2329 Athletic (warmup, sweat & jogging) suits: men's & boys'; men's & boys' athletic uniforms; knickers, dress (separate): men's & boys'

HQ: Adidas North America, Inc.
3449 N Anchor St Ste 500
Portland OR 97217
971 234-2300

(G-15961)
AGAPE PRECISION MFG LLC
320 Circle Of Progress Dr # 108 (19464-3800)
PHONE..................................484 704-2601
Michael Wolfe, *Opers Staff*
Dana Wolfe, *Mng Member*
Patricia Haraburda, *Mng Member*
EMP: 35
SALES: 3.5MM **Privately Held**
SIC: 3444 3599 Sheet metalwork; machine & other job shop work; machine shop, jobbing & repair

(G-15962)
AMBIT SWITCH
504 Walnut St (19464-5626)
PHONE..................................610 705-9695
Monica Henderson, *Principal*
EMP: 3
SALES (est): 198.3K **Privately Held**
SIC: 3679 Electronic switches

(G-15963)
AMERICAN KEG COMPANY LLC
31 Robinson St (19464-6439)
PHONE..................................484 524-8251
Richard Pentley, *Mng Member*
EMP: 28
SQ FT: 32,000
SALES: 7MM **Privately Held**
SIC: 3411 5084 Beer cans, metal; alcoholic beverage making equipment & supplies

(G-15964)
AMERICAN METAL FINISHERS INC
1346 Farmington Ave (19464-1848)
PHONE..................................610 323-1394
Carl L Heft, *President*
Deborah Heft, *Vice Pres*
EMP: 14 **EST:** 1946
SQ FT: 12,800
SALES (est): 2.2MM **Privately Held**
SIC: 3599 3479 3469 3471 Machine shop, jobbing & repair; painting of metal products; stamping metal for the trade; polishing, metals or formed products

(G-15965)
BASSETT INDUSTRIES INC
2119 Sanatoga Station Rd (19464-3275)
PHONE..................................610 327-1200
David Milks, *President*
Bret Milks, *Engineer*
Sharon Milks, *Treasurer*
Lee Gajewski, *Sales Mgr*
Doug Fox, *Sales Staff*
▲ **EMP:** 49
SQ FT: 33,000
SALES (est): 13.3MM **Privately Held**
WEB: www.bassettinc.com
SIC: 3499 5051 Fire- or burglary-resistive products; steel

(G-15966)
BERKS-MONT NEWSPAPERS INC
Also Called: Hamburg Item
24 N Hanover St (19464-5410)
PHONE..................................610 683-7343
James Webb, *President*
EMP: 10 **EST:** 1887
SQ FT: 2,700
SALES (est): 518.4K **Privately Held**
SIC: 2711 2759 Commercial printing & newspaper publishing combined; letterpress printing

(G-15967)
BESTWELD INC
40 Robinson St (19464-6440)
PHONE..................................610 718-9700
Rod Bayard, *President*
William Oscar, *Vice Pres*
▲ **EMP:** 40
SALES (est): 8.9MM **Privately Held**
WEB: www.bestweld.com
SIC: 3599 3548 Machine shop, jobbing & repair; welding apparatus

(G-15968)
BRAMLEY MACHINERY CORPORATION
824 Spruce St (19464-4218)
P.O. Box 842 (19464-0842)
PHONE..................................610 326-2500
EMP: 10
SQ FT: 800
SALES (est): 1.1MM **Privately Held**
SIC: 3531 Mfg Construction Machinery

(G-15969)
CAMPBELLS CUSTOM WOODWORKS LLC
62 Lemon St (19464-6744)
PHONE..................................484 300-4175
EMP: 4
SALES (est): 87.1K **Privately Held**
SIC: 2431 Millwork

(G-15970)
CLARK INDUSTRIAL SUPPLY INC
301 W High St (19464-6313)
PHONE..................................610 705-3333
David F Clark Jr, *President*
David Clark Jr, *President*
EMP: 12 **EST:** 1972
SQ FT: 2,400
SALES (est): 2.7MM **Privately Held**
WEB: www.clarkindustrialsupply.com
SIC: 3599 5085 Hose, flexible metallic; industrial supplies

(G-15971)
CODY COMPUTER SERVICES INC
1005 E High St (19464-4907)
PHONE..................................610 326-7476
David Heffner, *President*
Frances Heffner, *Treasurer*
Frances N Heffner, *Shareholder*
EMP: 30 **EST:** 1979
SQ FT: 5,000
SALES (est): 4.4MM **Privately Held**
WEB: www.codysystems.com
SIC: 7372 Educational computer software

(G-15972)
COLUMBIA BOILER COMPANY
Also Called: Columbia Heating Supply Co
390 Old Reading Pike (19464-2753)
PHONE..................................610 323-9200
Thomas A Meade, *Manager*
EMP: 35
SALES (corp-wide): 60.3MM **Privately Held**
SIC: 3433 5074 Boilers, low-pressure heating: steam or hot water; heating equipment (hydronic)
HQ: Columbia Boiler Company
390 Old Reading Pike
Stowe PA 19464
610 323-2700

(G-15973)
CONESTOGA USA INC
300 Old Reading Pike # 3 (19464-3772)
P.O. Box 3052 (19464-0955)
PHONE..................................610 327-2882
George M Gent, *President*
George R Gent, *Vice Pres*
EMP: 4
SQ FT: 3,000
SALES (est): 684.8K **Privately Held**
WEB: www.conestogausa.com
SIC: 3644 5063 3594 Electric conduits & fittings; electrical fittings & construction materials; pumps, hydraulic power transfer

(G-15974)
CONTINENTAL CONCRETE PDTS INC
1 S Grosstown Rd (19464-3763)
PHONE..................................610 327-3700
Warren J Constantine Jr, *President*
EMP: 40
SQ FT: 27,000
SALES: 5MM **Privately Held**
SIC: 3272 Concrete products, precast

(G-15975)
CONTRAST METALWORKS LLC
301 S Keim St (19464-6051)
PHONE....................................484 624-5542
Justin Rosenberger,
EMP: 4 **EST:** 2009
SALES (est): 879.4K **Privately Held**
SIC: 3449 Bars, concrete reinforcing: fabricated steel

(G-15976)
COONEY MANUFACTURING CO LLC
313 Circle Of Progress Dr (19464-3811)
PHONE....................................610 272-2100
Marion Cooney, *Mng Member*
EMP: 4
SALES (est): 324.5K **Privately Held**
SIC: 3498 3443 Fabricated pipe & fittings; tanks, lined: metal plate

(G-15977)
CRP INC
191 S Keim St (19464-6046)
P.O. Box 42 (19464-0042)
PHONE....................................610 970-7663
Richard Marsh, *President*
Mary Marsh, *Vice Pres*
EMP: 5
SQ FT: 5,000
SALES: 400K **Privately Held**
SIC: 3317 Tubes, seamless steel

(G-15978)
DANA AUTO SYSTEMS GROUP LLC
1040 Center Ave (19464-5802)
PHONE....................................610 323-4200
Roger Wood, *CEO*
Tim Farney, *Vice Pres*
EMP: 300
SQ FT: 550,000
SALES (est): 22.7MM **Publicly Held**
SIC: 3714 Motor vehicle parts & accessories
HQ: Dana Automotive Systems Group, Llc
3939 Technology Dr
Maumee OH 43537

(G-15979)
DANA DRIVESHAFT PRODUCTS LLC
Also Called: Dana Light Vehicle Driveline
1040 Center Ave (19464-5802)
PHONE....................................610 323-4200
Diana Gulotta, *Human Res Dir*
Pat Samboski, *Branch Mgr*
EMP: 400 **Publicly Held**
SIC: 3714 3568 Universal joints, motor vehicle; bearings, motor vehicle; power transmission equipment
HQ: Dana Driveshaft Products, Llc
3939 Technology Dr
Maumee OH 43537

(G-15980)
DAVID C WEIGLE
800 Heritage Dr Ste 811 (19464-9220)
PHONE....................................610 327-1616
David C Weigle, *Principal*
EMP: 4
SALES (est): 412.7K **Privately Held**
SIC: 3843 Enamels, dentists'

(G-15981)
DAYCO INC
325 Circle Of Progress Dr (19464-3811)
PHONE....................................610 326-4500
Rowland A Love Sr, *President*
Rowland Love Jr, *Vice Pres*
Barbara Love, *Treasurer*
Tamara Baro, *Admin Sec*
EMP: 5
SQ FT: 100,000
SALES (est): 1.5MM **Privately Held**
SIC: 5074 3567 Heating equipment & panels, solar; heating units & devices, industrial: electric

(G-15982)
DIKEN MACHINE INC
133 Possum Hollow Rd (19464-3409)
P.O. Box 5071, Limerick (19468-0971)
PHONE....................................610 495-9995
Kenneth Borzillo, *President*

EMP: 9
SQ FT: 6,000
SALES (est): 1.1MM **Privately Held**
SIC: 3599 Machine shop, jobbing & repair

(G-15983)
DIMEC RAIL SERVICE
Also Called: A Stuckeye
191 S Keim St Ste 212 (19464-6047)
PHONE....................................844 362-9221
Jennifer Welsh, *General Mgr*
EMP: 30 **EST:** 2015
SALES (est): 2.1MM **Privately Held**
SIC: 2411 Rails, fence: round or split

(G-15984)
EAGLE MICROSYSTEMS
366 Circle Of Progress Dr (19464-3810)
PHONE....................................610 323-2250
Michael Smith, *Owner*
EMP: 8
SQ FT: 500
SALES (est): 978.1K **Privately Held**
WEB: www.eaglemicrosystems.com
SIC: 3599 Custom machinery

(G-15985)
EDWARD H QUAY WELDING SPC
Also Called: H Edward Quay Welding
948 Commerce Dr (19464-1876)
PHONE....................................610 326-8050
H Edward Quay, *President*
Bob Overdorf, *Supervisor*
EMP: 5
SQ FT: 7,000
SALES: 450K **Privately Held**
WEB: www.edquay.com
SIC: 7692 3711 Automotive welding; motor vehicles & car bodies

(G-15986)
EMPEROR AQUATICS INC
940 Crimson Ln (19464-2900)
PHONE....................................610 970-0440
Stephen Zimmer, *President*
Don Conwell, *Corp Secy*
EMP: 17
SQ FT: 7,883
SALES (est): 1.9MM **Privately Held**
WEB: www.emperoraquatics.com
SIC: 3089 Aquarium accessories, plastic

(G-15987)
ETHAN HORWITZ CABINET MAK
383 Circle Of Progress Dr (19464-3811)
PHONE....................................610 948-4889
Ethan Horwitz, *Principal*
EMP: 8
SALES (est): 1MM **Privately Held**
SIC: 2434 Wood kitchen cabinets

(G-15988)
FORCE AMERICA INC
105 Jones Blvd 106 (19464-3464)
PHONE....................................610 495-4590
Steven Loessler, *Manager*
Josh Kerlin, *Manager*
EMP: 7
SALES (corp-wide): 141.7MM **Privately Held**
WEB: www.forceamerica.com
SIC: 5084 3568 Hydraulic systems equipment & supplies; drives, chains & sprockets
PA: Force America Inc.
501 Cliff Rd E Ste 100
Burnsville MN 55337
952 707-1300

(G-15989)
FULL-ON FILTERS
517 W Vine St (19464-6832)
PHONE....................................610 970-4701
Brian Wampole, *Owner*
▼ **EMP:** 7
SALES (est): 250K **Privately Held**
WEB: www.fullonfilters.com
SIC: 5085 5569 3589 3564 Filters, industrial; filters; commercial cleaning equipment; filters, air: furnaces, air conditioning equipment, etc.

(G-15990)
GEEMACHER LLC
331 Circle Of Progress Dr (19464-3811)
PHONE....................................484 524-8251

John Giannopoullas, *Manager*
▲ **EMP:** 3
SALES (est): 1.2MM **Privately Held**
SIC: 3312 Stainless steel

(G-15991)
GLENS DUMPSTER SERVICE LLC
1613 W High St (19464-3758)
PHONE....................................202 521-1493
Glen Shovelton, *President*
EMP: 3 **EST:** 2014
SALES (est): 187.5K **Privately Held**
SIC: 3443 Dumpsters, garbage

(G-15992)
GTR INDUSTRIES INCORPORATED
2113 Sanatoga Station Rd (19464-3275)
PHONE....................................610 705-5900
Richard T Girard, *President*
Robert Girard, *Exec VP*
EMP: 30
SQ FT: 35,000
SALES (est): 3.8MM **Privately Held**
SIC: 3083 Thermosetting laminates: rods, tubes, plates & sheet

(G-15993)
GUDEBROD INC
274 Shoemaker Rd (19464-6434)
PHONE....................................610 327-4050
Edward F John, *Ch of Bd*
William E Le Grande Jr, *President*
Edward D Le Grande, *Vice Pres*
Steve Gorsky, *CFO*
William E Le Grand III, *Treasurer*
▲ **EMP:** 180 **EST:** 1897
SQ FT: 150,000
SALES (est): 2.4MM **Privately Held**
WEB: www.gudebrod.com
SIC: 2824 2298 3843 Organic fibers, non-cellulosic; fishing lines, nets, seines: made in cordage or twine mills; dental equipment & supplies

(G-15994)
HAMBURG AREA ITEM
24 N Hanover St (19464-5410)
PHONE....................................610 367-6041
EMP: 3
SALES (est): 111K **Privately Held**
SIC: 2711 Newspapers-Publishing/Printing

(G-15995)
HAMMOND GROUP INC
Also Called: Hammond Lead Product
10 S Grosstown Rd (19464-3764)
PHONE....................................610 327-1400
Sudhir Patel, *Branch Mgr*
EMP: 28
SQ FT: 1,904
SALES (corp-wide): 31.8MM **Privately Held**
WEB: www.hmndgroup.com
SIC: 2816 5051 3356 3339 Lead pigments: white lead, lead oxides, lead sulfate; lead; nonferrous rolling & drawing; primary nonferrous metals
PA: Hammond Group, Inc.
1414 Field St Bldg B
Hammond IN 46320
219 931-9360

(G-15996)
HANESBRANDS INC
18 W Lightcap Rd Ste 1153 (19464-7838)
PHONE....................................610 970-5767
Michelle Romig, *Manager*
EMP: 9
SALES (corp-wide): 6.8B **Publicly Held**
WEB: www.hanesbrands.com
SIC: 2253 2342 T-shirts & tops, knit; bras, girdles & allied garments
PA: Hanesbrands Inc.
1000 E Hanes Mill Rd
Winston Salem NC 27105
336 519-8080

(G-15997)
HARTSTRINGS LLC
18 W Lightcap Rd Ste 723 (19464-7816)
PHONE....................................610 326-8221
EMP: 4
SALES (est): 284.2K **Privately Held**
SIC: 3643 Mfg Conductive Wiring Devices

(G-15998)
HAYES INDUSTRIES INC
41 Robinson St A (19464-6439)
PHONE....................................484 624-5314
Christopher Hayes, *President*
Carol Hayes, *Vice Pres*
▼ **EMP:** 6
SALES (est): 912.7K **Privately Held**
SIC: 3599 1799 1796 Machine shop, jobbing & repair; rigging & scaffolding; machine moving & rigging

(G-15999)
HUMPHRYS FLAG COMPANY INC
374 Laurel St (19464-5933)
PHONE....................................215 922-0510
Tim O'Conner, *Opers-Prdtn-Mfg*
EMP: 30
SQ FT: 9,194
SALES (corp-wide): 2.8MM **Privately Held**
WEB: www.humphrysflags.com
SIC: 2399 5999 Banners, pennants & flags; banners, flags, decals & posters
PA: Humphrys Flag Company, Inc.
238 Arch St
Philadelphia PA
215 922-0510

(G-16000)
ILSEMANN CORP
398 Circle Of Progrepa Dr (19464)
PHONE....................................610 323-4143
Stephan Ilsemann, *President*
▲ **EMP:** 4
SALES (est): 474K **Privately Held**
SIC: 3559 Robots, molding & forming plastics

(G-16001)
IMPERIAL SPECIALTY INC
1153 Sembling Ave (19464-5845)
P.O. Box 635 (19464-0635)
PHONE....................................610 323-4531
Petronella Savage, *President*
Michelle Paules, *Controller*
William McBride, *Admin Sec*
EMP: 18 **EST:** 1952
SQ FT: 17,000
SALES: 2.1MM **Privately Held**
WEB: www.imperialspecialty.com
SIC: 3451 Screw machine products

(G-16002)
INNOCHEM INC
400 Old Reading Pike B202 (19464-3781)
P.O. Box 3056 (19464-0955)
PHONE....................................610 323-0730
Sarah Chen, *President*
Johnson Chen, *Vice Pres*
◆ **EMP:** 3
SQ FT: 8,500
SALES (est): 524.7K **Privately Held**
WEB: www.innochem.com
SIC: 2834 Pharmaceutical preparations

(G-16003)
J D R FIXTURES INC
264 Shoemaker Rd (19464-6434)
PHONE....................................610 323-6599
James Shaughnessy, *President*
Steve Diachynsky, *Sr Project Mgr*
EMP: 35
SQ FT: 25,000
SALES (est): 6.1MM **Privately Held**
WEB: www.jdrfixtures.com
SIC: 2541 2431 Store fixtures, wood; millwork

(G-16004)
JACOB PATTERN WORKS INC
Also Called: Jacob Casting Division
449 Old Reading Pike (19464-3729)
PHONE....................................610 326-1100
Kenneth C Jacob Jr, *President*
James E Jacob, *Vice Pres*
EMP: 10 **EST:** 1944
SQ FT: 46,000
SALES (est): 1.4MM **Privately Held**
SIC: 3365 3543 Aluminum & aluminum-based alloy castings; industrial patterns

(G-16005)
JAY-ELL INDUSTRIES INC
Also Called: J L Machine & Tool
815 South St (19464-6019)
PHONE..................................610 326-0921
Joseph Voytilla, *President*
EMP: 16
SALES: 1.5MM **Privately Held**
SIC: 3544 3559 Special dies & tools; pharmaceutical machinery

(G-16006)
JRT CALIBRATION SERVICES INC
581b W High St (19464)
PHONE..................................610 327-9610
Ted Rubel, *President*
Steve Fowls, *Vice Pres*
Harold Harbison, *Vice Pres*
EMP: 5
SQ FT: 17,000
SALES (est): 418.8K **Privately Held**
SIC: 3821 8734 Calibration tapes for physical testing machines; calibration & certification; radiation laboratories

(G-16007)
KENDRED F HUNT (PA)
Also Called: K D & T Metals
471 N Charlotte St (19464-5376)
PHONE..................................610 327-4131
Kendred F Hunt, *Owner*
EMP: 4
SALES: 300K **Privately Held**
SIC: 3444 Sheet metalwork

(G-16008)
KONECRANES INC
371 Circle Of Progress Dr (19464-3811)
PHONE..................................610 321-2900
Scott Eddinger, *Branch Mgr*
EMP: 30
SALES (corp-wide): 3.7B **Privately Held**
WEB: www.kciusa.com
SIC: 3536 7699 Cranes, industrial plant; industrial machinery & equipment repair
HQ: Konecranes, Inc.
4401 Gateway Blvd
Springfield OH 45502

(G-16009)
LATICRETE INTERNATIONAL INC
412 Laurel St (19464-5950)
PHONE..................................610 326-9970
EMP: 4
SALES (est): 395.8K **Privately Held**
SIC: 2891 Adhesives & sealants

(G-16010)
LEGEND SPINE LLC
300 Old Reading Pike 3a (19464-3772)
PHONE..................................267 566-3273
Will Duffield, *COO*
Edward Karpowicz, *Vice Pres*
Chris Waganer, *Chief Mktg Ofcr*
Steve Marinelli, *Mng Member*
EMP: 7
SALES: 1MM **Privately Held**
SIC: 3841 Surgical & medical instruments

(G-16011)
LIFEWEAR INC
284 N Hanover St (19464-5300)
PHONE..................................610 327-2884
David Bartman, *President*
EMP: 24 **Privately Held**
WEB: www.lifewear.net
SIC: 2253 5137 5136 2331 T-shirts & tops, knit; women's & children's clothing; men's & boys' clothing; women's & misses' blouses & shirts; men's & boys' furnishings
PA: Lifewear, Inc.
1280 Laurelwood Rd
Pottstown PA 19465

(G-16012)
MACNIFICENT PAGES
Also Called: Route 422 Buisness Advisor
155 E High St Ste 360 (19464-5428)
P.O. Box 334 (19464-0334)
PHONE..................................610 323-6253
William Haley, *Owner*
EMP: 3

SALES (est): 116.7K **Privately Held**
SIC: 2741 Business service newsletters: publishing & printing

(G-16013)
MAGIC SLEEPER INC (PA)
Also Called: Magic Sleeper Bedding Co
125 E 4th St (19464-5217)
P.O. Box 994 (19464-0859)
PHONE..................................610 327-2322
Marco Santos, *President*
M Elizabeth Santos, *Principal*
EMP: 13
SQ FT: 25,000
SALES (est): 1.6MM **Privately Held**
WEB: www.magicsleeper.com
SIC: 2515 Mattresses, innerspring or box spring; box springs, assembled

(G-16014)
MANATAWNY STILL WORKS
320 Circle Of Progress Dr (19464-3800)
PHONE..................................484 624-8271
Paul Czachor, *Principal*
EMP: 4
SALES (est): 236.9K **Privately Held**
SIC: 2085 Distilled & blended liquors

(G-16015)
MARIO DINARDO JR CUSTOM WD WKG
103 Lightcap Rd (19464-3433)
PHONE..................................610 495-7010
Mario Dinardo Jr, *President*
Cheryl Dinardo, *Vice Pres*
EMP: 25
SQ FT: 14,500
SALES (est): 4.6MM **Privately Held**
SIC: 2434 2431 5031 Wood kitchen cabinets; millwork; kitchen cabinets

(G-16016)
MARTIN RAWDIN OD (PA)
1630 E High St Bldg 4 (19464-3244)
PHONE..................................610 323-8007
Martin Rawdin Od, *Owner*
EMP: 4
SALES (est): 396K **Privately Held**
WEB: www.mailup.net
SIC: 8042 3827 Optometrist's Office Mfg Optical Instruments/Lenses

(G-16017)
MASTER WATER CONDITIONING CORP
224 Shoemaker Rd (19464-6422)
PHONE..................................610 323-8358
Maurice E Kurtz, *President*
Lisa Clark, *Prdtn Mgr*
Helen Kurtz, *Treasurer*
Jay Holman, *Sales Staff*
Jason Moyer, *Sales Staff*
EMP: 17
SQ FT: 11,500
SALES (est): 3.9MM **Privately Held**
WEB: www.masterwater.com
SIC: 3589 Water purification equipment, household type; water filters & softeners, household type

(G-16018)
MERIT MANUFACTURING CORP
319 Circle Of Progress Dr (19464-3811)
P.O. Box 510, Waynesboro (17268-0510)
PHONE..................................610 327-4000
Raymond H Jensen, *President*
Theodore R Jensen, *Exec VP*
George Constantine, *CFO*
EMP: 76
SQ FT: 50,000
SALES (est): 7.7MM **Privately Held**
WEB: www.meritmfg.com
SIC: 3494 Pipe fittings

(G-16019)
MICRO-COAX INC (HQ)
206 Jones Blvd (19464-3465)
PHONE..................................610 495-4438
Drew Freed, *CEO*
EMP: 200 **EST:** 1999
SQ FT: 90,000

SALES (est): 39.4MM
SALES (corp-wide): 4.4B **Publicly Held**
WEB: www.micro-coax.com
SIC: 3679 3677 3663 3612 Microwave components; electronic coils, transformers & other inductors; radio & TV communications equipment; transformers, except electric; blowers & fans; nonferrous wiredrawing & insulating
PA: Carlisle Companies Incorporated
16430 N Scottsdale Rd # 400
Scottsdale AZ 85254
480 781-5000

(G-16020)
NATIONAL EMBROIDERY
429 E Moyer Rd (19464-1019)
PHONE..................................610 323-4400
Lynn L Guglielmo, *Owner*
Lynn Guglielmo, *Owner*
EMP: 3
SALES (est): 84K **Privately Held**
SIC: 2395 Embroidery products, except schiffli machine; embroidery & art needlework

(G-16021)
NEAPCO COMPONENTS LLC (DH)
740 Queen St (19464-6008)
P.O. Box 399 (19464-0399)
PHONE..................................610 323-6000
Kenneth L Hopkins, *CEO*
Keith Sanford, *President*
Gerald Coster, *COO*
▲ **EMP:** 50
SQ FT: 250,000
SALES (est): 601.4MM
SALES (corp-wide): 2.9B **Privately Held**
WEB: www.neapco.com
SIC: 3714 3568 Transmission housings or parts, motor vehicle; motor vehicle transmissions, drive assemblies & parts; power transmission equipment

(G-16022)
OCCIDENTAL CHEMICAL CORP
375 Armand Hammer Blvd (19464-5090)
PHONE..................................610 327-4145
John W Lessig, *Branch Mgr*
EMP: 12
SALES (corp-wide): 18.9B **Publicly Held**
WEB: www.oxychem.com
SIC: 2812 2874 2869 2821 Alkalies & chlorine; phosphatic fertilizers; industrial organic chemicals; plastics materials & resins; industrial inorganic chemicals; prepared feeds
HQ: Occidental Chemical Corporation
14555 Dallas Pkwy Ste 400
Dallas TX 75254
972 404-3800

(G-16023)
ONSITE STERILIZATION LLC
1200 E High St Ste 306 (19464-4938)
P.O. Box 837, Valley Forge (19482-0837)
PHONE..................................484 624-8566
Samuel Blanchard, *President*
Robert W Lewis, *Mng Member*
EMP: 6
SQ FT: 5,000
SALES (est): 849.6K **Privately Held**
WEB: www.askonsite.com
SIC: 3841 Medical instruments & equipment, blood & bone work

(G-16024)
ORBIT SOFTWARE INC
424 King St (19464-5610)
PHONE..................................484 941-0820
Sonia Mastros, *President*
George Mastros, *Vice Pres*
Daisy Oliveras, *Admin Asst*
EMP: 10
SQ FT: 1,800
SALES (est): 1.2MM **Privately Held**
WEB: www.orbitsoftware.net
SIC: 7372 Prepackaged software

(G-16025)
PALLADINO MTAL FABRICATION INC (PA)
337 W High St (19464-6313)
PHONE..................................610 323-9439
William Palladino, *President*

EMP: 7
SQ FT: 6,500
SALES: 850K **Privately Held**
WEB: www.pmfinc.com
SIC: 3441 3444 Fabricated structural metal; sheet metalwork

(G-16026)
PATRIOT KUTZTOWN AREA
24 N Hanover St (19464-5410)
PHONE..................................610 367-6041
EMP: 3
SALES (est): 101.3K **Privately Held**
SIC: 2711 Newspapers-Publishing/Printing

(G-16027)
PEERLESS PUBLICATIONS INC (HQ)
Also Called: Pottstown Mercury, The
24 N Hanover St (19464-5410)
PHONE..................................610 323-3000
Bob Gelmick, *President*
EMP: 171 **EST:** 1902
SQ FT: 9,000
SALES (est): 10.3MM
SALES (corp-wide): 661.2MM **Privately Held**
WEB: www.journalregister.com
SIC: 2711 Commercial printing & newspaper publishing combined; newspapers, publishing & printing
PA: Journal Register Company
5 Hanover Sq Fl 25
New York NY 10004
212 257-7212

(G-16028)
PEERLESS PUBLICATIONS INC
Also Called: The Penny Pincher
21 N Hanover St (19464-5485)
PHONE..................................610 970-3210
Isabella Mest, *Manager*
EMP: 14
SALES (corp-wide): 661.2MM **Privately Held**
SIC: 2711 Newspapers, publishing & printing
HQ: Peerless Publications, Inc
24 N Hanover St
Pottstown PA 19464
610 323-3000

(G-16029)
PERMABOND LLC
Also Called: Permabond Engrg Adhesives
14 Robinson St (19464-6440)
PHONE..................................732 868-1372
Amy Sutryn, *VP Opers*
EMP: 8
SQ FT: 9,999
SALES (corp-wide): 3.6MM **Privately Held**
WEB: www.permabond.com
SIC: 2891 Adhesives & sealants
PA: Permabond Llc
223 Churchill Ave
Somerset NJ 08873
610 323-5003

(G-16030)
PHOENIX COACH WORKS INC
39 Sheridan Ln (19464-3402)
PHONE..................................610 495-2266
Joseph J Skupski Jr, *President*
EMP: 8
SQ FT: 22,500
SALES (est): 1.2MM **Privately Held**
WEB: www.phoenixcoachworks.com
SIC: 3715 Trailers or vans for transporting horses

(G-16031)
PHOENIX COMBUSTION INC
15 Airport Rd (19464-3425)
P.O. Box 771 (19464-0771)
PHONE..................................610 495-5800
Gregory Ludwig, *President*
Albert Walker, *Director*
EMP: 10
SQ FT: 5,000
SALES (est): 704K **Privately Held**
SIC: 8711 3823 Machine tool design; combustion control instruments

(G-16032)
POSITIVELY PASTA
115 E High St (19464-5428)
PHONE.................................484 945-1007
Christopher Foster, *Owner*
EMP: 6
SALES (est): 483.3K **Privately Held**
SIC: 2099 5141 5411 Pasta, uncooked:
packaged with other ingredients; gro-
ceries, general line; grocery stores, inde-
pendent

(G-16033)
**POTTSGROVE METAL
FINISHERS**
1533 W High St (19464-6846)
PHONE.................................610 323-7004
Vincent A Savarese, *President*
Robert L Savarese, *Corp Secy*
EMP: 12 **EST:** 1910
SQ FT: 12,000
SALES (est): 920K **Privately Held**
SIC: 3471 Electroplating of metals or
formed products

(G-16034)
**POTTSTOWN TRAP ROCK
QUARRIES (PA)**
Also Called: Ptr Paving
394 S Sanatoga Rd (19464-3148)
PHONE.................................610 326-4843
Scott B Haines, *President*
John R Kibblehouse Jr, *Corp Secy*
Christian H Budenz, *Vice Pres*
H Christian Budenz, *Vice Pres*
James T Haines, *Vice Pres*
EMP: 18 **EST:** 1958
SQ FT: 1,500
SALES: 10MM **Privately Held**
SIC: 3281 1411 2951 1611 Stone, quar-
rying & processing of own stone products;
dimension stone; asphalt & asphaltic
paving mixtures (not from refineries);
highway & street paving contractor

(G-16035)
**PRECISION POLYMER
PRODUCTS INC**
815 South St (19464-6019)
PHONE.................................610 326-0921
Joseph Voytilla, *President*
Rich Molinaro, *CFO*
◆ **EMP:** 125
SQ FT: 53,000
SALES (est): 24.9MM **Privately Held**
WEB: www.precisionpolymer.com
SIC: 3089 Injection molding of plastics

(G-16036)
PREMAX TOOL MACHINE INC
76 Robinson St (19464-6440)
PHONE.................................610 326-3860
Bob Schickling, *President*
EMP: 5
SQ FT: 2,000
SALES (est): 1.1MM **Privately Held**
SIC: 3599 Machine shop, jobbing & repair

(G-16037)
PRO TOOL INDUSTRIES INC
337 W High St (19464-6313)
PHONE.................................484 945-5001
Jane Hollenbach, *President*
Mark Scheifley, *Vice Pres*
EMP: 12
SQ FT: 6,000
SALES: 1MM **Privately Held**
SIC: 3423 Hand & edge tools

(G-16038)
**RAY-GUARD INTERNATIONAL
LTD (PA)**
280 N Hanover St (19464)
PHONE.................................215 543-3849
Richard Kritschil, *CEO*
EMP: 7
SQ FT: 8,500
SALES (est): 570.3K **Privately Held**
SIC: 3442 3443 3441 3271 Metal doors;
plate work for the nuclear industry; nu-
clear shielding, metal plate; fabricated
structural metal; blocks, concrete: radia-
tion-proof; concrete block masonry laying

(G-16039)
RELAY SHOE COMPANY LLC
Also Called: Rockport
18 W Lightcap Rd (19464-7806)
PHONE.................................610 970-6450
EMP: 4
SALES (corp-wide): 191.9MM **Privately
Held**
SIC: 3143 Shoe stores
HQ: The Relay Shoe Company Llc
1220 Washington St
Newton MA 02465
617 213-6100

(G-16040)
RIXIE PAPER PRODUCTS INC
10 Quinter St (19464-6514)
PHONE.................................610 323-9220
Smytty Thomas, *President*
Bill Janda, *Plant Mgr*
EMP: 11
SALES (est): 1.1MM **Privately Held**
SIC: 2631 Paperboard mills

(G-16041)
**ROCKLAND
IMMUNOCHEMICALS INC**
321 Jones Blvd (19464-3468)
P.O. Box 5199, Royersford (19468-0900)
PHONE.................................484 791-3823
Natalie Joy Cappel, *Ch of Bd*
James Fendrick, *Vice Pres*
EMP: 75
SQ FT: 75,000
SALES (est): 16.1MM **Privately Held**
WEB: www.rockland-inc.com
SIC: 2836 Veterinary biological products;
serums; plasmas

(G-16042)
SANATOGA WATER COND INC
80 N Charlotte St (19464-5569)
PHONE.................................610 326-9803
John Theisen, *President*
Jessica Shaner, *Office Mgr*
Steve Knott, *Technician*
EMP: 5
SALES (est): 590K **Privately Held**
SIC: 3589 Water treatment equipment, in-
dustrial

(G-16043)
SCEPTER SIGNS INC
Also Called: Scepter Signs and Electric
431 W Vine St (19464-6830)
PHONE.................................610 326-7446
John J Bergandino, *President*
Donald C Mace, *Vice Pres*
Margaret A Bergandino, *Treasurer*
EMP: 9
SALES (est): 1.4MM **Privately Held**
WEB: www.sceptersigns.com
SIC: 3993 Electric signs

(G-16044)
**SCHUYLKILL VLY SPT TRAPPE
CTR**
118 Industrial Dr Ste 1 (19464-3462)
PHONE.................................877 711-8100
Randall R Ruch, *CEO*
Justin Risko, *Sales Staff*
EMP: 14
SQ FT: 17,000
SALES (est): 3.3MM
SALES (corp-wide): 118.6MM **Privately
Held**
WEB: www.svsports.com
SIC: 5091 5941 2396 2395 Sporting &
recreation goods; sporting goods & bicy-
cle shops; automotive & apparel trim-
mings; pleating & stitching
PA: Schuylkill Valley Sports, Inc.
118 Industrial Dr Ste 1
Pottstown PA 19464
610 495-8813

(G-16045)
**SFC GLOBAL SUPPLY CHAIN
INC**
255 South St (19464-5984)
PHONE.................................610 327-5074
Stephan Boyer, *Branch Mgr*
EMP: 251
SALES (corp-wide): 5.3B **Privately Held**
SIC: 2038 Frozen specialties

HQ: Sfc Global Supply Chain, Inc.
115 W College Dr
Marshall MN 56258
507 532-3274

(G-16046)
SIMMS ABRASIVES
122 E 4th St (19464-5218)
PHONE.................................610 327-1877
Glenn Simms, *President*
Laurie Simms, *Vice Pres*
EMP: 3
SQ FT: 4,000
SALES (est): 470K **Privately Held**
SIC: 5085 3471 Abrasives; electroplating
& plating

(G-16047)
SMALES PRINTERY INC
785 N Charlotte St (19464-4631)
PHONE.................................610 323-7775
David Scot Smale, *President*
Harold L Smale, *Vice Pres*
Kelly Smale, *Admin Sec*
EMP: 5 **EST:** 1973
SQ FT: 7,000
SALES (est): 250K **Privately Held**
SIC: 2752 2759 Commercial printing, off-
set; letterpress printing

(G-16048)
**SOLAR LAUNDRY & DRY
CLEANING**
1503 W High St (19464-6846)
PHONE.................................610 323-2121
Jules Colker, *Owner*
EMP: 3
SALES (est): 265.9K **Privately Held**
SIC: 3589 Servicing machines, except dry
cleaning, laundry: coin-oper.

(G-16049)
SONOCO PRODUCTS COMPANY
Sonoco Consumer Products
10 Quinter St (19464-6514)
PHONE.................................610 323-9221
Lee Burj, *Manager*
EMP: 25
SALES (corp-wide): 5.3B **Publicly Held**
WEB: www.sonoco.com
SIC: 2653 3221 2392 Corrugated & solid
fiber boxes; glass containers; household
furnishings
PA: Sonoco Products Company
1 N 2nd St
Hartsville SC 29550
843 383-7000

(G-16050)
**SPECIALTY CHEMICAL
SYSTEMS INC**
Also Called: Hectrio
243 Shoemaker Rd (19464-6433)
PHONE.................................610 323-2716
Hyman Gillman, *President*
George Hresko, *Plant Mgr*
Barbara Myers, *Bookkeeper*
▲ **EMP:** 16
SQ FT: 35,000
SALES (est): 3.9MM **Privately Held**
SIC: 2819 5169 Industrial inorganic chem-
icals; chemicals & allied products

(G-16051)
**STEALTH COMPOSITES INC
(PA)**
313 Johnson St (19464-5241)
PHONE.................................215 919-7584
John Dice, *President*
EMP: 4
SALES (est): 445.2K **Privately Held**
SIC: 2655 Cans, composite: foil-fiber &
other: from purchased fiber

(G-16052)
**SUPERIOR METAL PRODUCTS
CO**
116 Berks St (19464-6302)
P.O. Box 595 (19464-0595)
PHONE.................................610 326-0607
Robert Boarman, *President*
David Mercer, *Vice Pres*
Nancy B McCarthy, *Treasurer*
Bethany Dimaggio, *Controller*
EMP: 30 **EST:** 1958

SQ FT: 55,000
SALES (est): 5.1MM **Privately Held**
WEB: www.superiormetalproductsco.com
SIC: 3444 Sheet metalwork

(G-16053)
**SUPERIOR SURGICAL LTD
LBLTY CO**
321 Jones Blvd Ste 112 (19464-3468)
PHONE.................................877 669-7646
Daniel Cusack,
◆ **EMP:** 5
SALES (est): 355.4K **Privately Held**
SIC: 3841 Surgical & medical instruments

(G-16054)
THEORY LLC
18 W Lightcap Rd Ste 425 (19464-7810)
PHONE.................................610 326-5040
EMP: 84
SALES (corp-wide): 19.1B **Privately Held**
SIC: 2337 Suits: women's, misses' & jun-
iors'
HQ: Theory Llc
38 Gansevoort St
New York NY 10014
212 300-0800

(G-16055)
TOPOS MONDIAL CORP (PA)
600 Queen St (19464-6031)
PHONE.................................610 970-2270
Michael A Morabito Jr, *President*
Damian Morabito, *President*
John Eanes, *Foreman/Supr*
Ondrej Nikel, *Engineer*
Frank Merlino, *Controller*
◆ **EMP:** 28 **EST:** 1956
SQ FT: 300,000
SALES (est): 4.5MM **Privately Held**
WEB: www.toposmondial.com
SIC: 7694 5046 Rebuilding motors, except
automotive; bakery equipment & supplies

(G-16056)
TRI COUNTY RECORD
24 N Hanover St (19464-5410)
PHONE.................................610 970-3218
Robert Jelenic, *CEO*
EMP: 3
SALES (est): 98.1K **Privately Held**
SIC: 2711 Newspapers, publishing & print-
ing

(G-16057)
**TRI COUNTY TRANSIT SERVICE
INC**
110 Industrial Pkwy (19464-3485)
PHONE.................................610 495-5640
Clifford Kingsley, *President*
EMP: 80 **EST:** 1933
SALES (est): 15.9MM **Privately Held**
SIC: 3829 Transits, surveyors'

(G-16058)
**TRI STATE KITCHENS AND
BATHS**
139 Possum Hollow Rd (19464)
EMP: 12
SALES (est): 460.6K **Privately Held**
SIC: 2514 Mfg Metal Household Furniture

(G-16059)
TRIAD TRUCK EQUIPMENT
3380 W Ridge Pike (19464-3431)
PHONE.................................484 614-7349
Dawn L Southern, *President*
Gerald Southern, *President*
Richard Tornetto, *Corp Secy*
Frank Lambardo, *Vice Pres*
EMP: 8
SQ FT: 15,000
SALES (est): 2.4MM **Privately Held**
WEB: www.triadtruck.com
SIC: 5013 3713 7539 Truck parts & ac-
cessories; trailer parts & accessories;
dump truck bodies; trailer repair

(G-16060)
TRITON SIGNS INCORPORATED
133a Possum Hollow Rd (19464-3409)
PHONE.................................610 495-4747
John Yakscoe, *President*
Brandon O'Connor, *Assistant VP*
Ruth Anne Yakscoe, *Admin Sec*

▲ = Import ▼=Export
◆ =Import/Export

EMP: 3
SALES (est): 243.6K **Privately Held**
WEB: www.tritonsigns.com
SIC: 3993 Signs & advertising specialties

(G-16061)
ULTRAFLEX SYSTEMS INC
237 South St Ste 200 (19464-5984)
PHONE..................................610 906-1410
Mark De Harde, *President*
Brad Shirk, *COO*
James Lovely, *Purchasing*
Taffy Bowman,
EMP: 40
SQ FT: 7,500
SALES (est): 3.2MM **Privately Held**
SIC: 5047 3842 Medical equipment & supplies; orthopedic appliances; prosthetic appliances

(G-16062)
UNIVERSAL MCH CO POTTSTOWN INC
Also Called: Universal Machine & Engrg
645 Old Reading Pike (19464-3733)
PHONE..................................610 323-1810
Richard M Francis, *President*
Robert Francis, *President*
Rick Kelley, *Sales Engr*
Dave Cornelison, *Sales Staff*
Dave Burdan, *Manager*
EMP: 75 EST: 1946
SQ FT: 30,000
SALES (est): 16.8MM **Privately Held**
WEB: www.umc-oscar.com
SIC: 8711 3599 7692 3549 Mechanical engineering; machine & other job shop work; welding repair; metalworking machinery

(G-16063)
US AXLE INC
275 Shoemaker Rd (19464-6433)
PHONE..................................610 323-3800
Ernie Inmon, *President*
Mike Glanski, *Engineer*
Ken Krauss, *Engineer*
Pat Solley, *Engineer*
Matt Inmon, *Development*
▼ EMP: 53
SQ FT: 53,000
SALES (est): 14.1MM **Privately Held**
WEB: www.usaxle.com
SIC: 3714 3599 Motor vehicle parts & accessories; machine shop, jobbing & repair

(G-16064)
VALTECH CORPORATION (PA)
2113 Sanatoga Station Rd (19464-3275)
PHONE..................................610 705-5900
Richard T Girard, *President*
Kelley Towson, *Purchasing*
Malcolm Kok, *Regl Sales Mgr*
Robert T Girard, *Admin Sec*
▲ EMP: 30
SQ FT: 35,000
SALES (est): 7.2MM **Privately Held**
WEB: www.valtechcorp.com
SIC: 2819 3089 Industrial inorganic chemicals; extruded finished plastic products

(G-16065)
VF OUTDOOR LLC
18 W Lightcap Rd Ste 599 (19464-7820)
PHONE..................................610 327-1734
EMP: 4
SALES (corp-wide): 11.8B **Publicly Held**
SIC: 3143 Men's footwear, except athletic
HQ: Vf Outdoor, Llc
2701 Harbor Bay Pkwy
Alameda CA 94502
510 618-3500

(G-16066)
VF OUTDOOR LLC
18 W Lightcap Rd (19464-7806)
PHONE..................................610 323-6575
EMP: 4
SALES (corp-wide): 11.8B **Publicly Held**
SIC: 2329 Men's & boys' leather, wool & down-filled outerwear
HQ: Vf Outdoor, Llc
2701 Harbor Bay Pkwy
Alameda CA 94502
510 618-3500

(G-16067)
VIDEORAY LLC
212 E High St Ste 201 (19464-5596)
PHONE..................................610 458-3000
Scott Bentley, *President*
John Vestri, *Opers Staff*
Kevin McMonagle, *Research*
Cesar Hernandez, *Electrical Engi*
Tom Glebas, *CFO*
EMP: 33
SQ FT: 3,679
SALES (est): 11.3MM **Privately Held**
WEB: www.videoray.com
SIC: 3699 5941 Underwater sound equipment; sporting goods & bicycle shops

(G-16068)
VIDEOTEK INC
243 Shoemaker Rd (19464-6433)
PHONE..................................610 327-2292
Philip G Steyaert, *President*
Richard Hollowbush, *Admin Sec*
▲ EMP: 130
SQ FT: 40,000
SALES (est): 18.3MM **Privately Held**
WEB: www.videotek.com
SIC: 3829 3663 3651 3621 Measuring & controlling devices; radio & TV communications equipment; household audio & video equipment; motors & generators; switchgear & switchboard apparatus; computer peripheral equipment

(G-16069)
VILLANOVA CHEESE SHOP INC
Also Called: Betts Food Products
181 Ppaum Hollow Rd Ste A (19464)
PHONE..................................610 495-8343
John Fissinger, *President*
EMP: 14 EST: 1962
SQ FT: 4,000
SALES (est): 2.2MM **Privately Held**
SIC: 2026 2022 Fermented & cultured milk products; cheese, natural & processed

(G-16070)
WATSON MCDANIEL COMPANY (HQ)
428 Jones Blvd (19464-3469)
PHONE..................................610 495-5131
Robert Hickey, *President*
Frederick R Picut, *President*
Joe Cerjak, *Business Mgr*
Joe Prindible, *Business Mgr*
Russell Picut, *Vice Pres*
◆ EMP: 40 EST: 1878
SQ FT: 21,000
SALES (est): 31MM **Privately Held**
WEB: www.watsonmcdaniel.com
SIC: 3498 3494 3491 Fabricated pipe & fittings; valves & pipe fittings; steam traps

(G-16071)
WD SERVICES INC
300 Old Reading Pike # 10 (19464-3772)
PHONE..................................610 970-7946
William D Dukes, *President*
William Dukes, *General Mgr*
EMP: 7
SQ FT: 3,000
SALES (est): 630K **Privately Held**
WEB: www.wdserv.com
SIC: 3444 Booths, spray: prefabricated sheet metal

Pottsville
Schuylkill County

(G-16072)
ALPHA MILLS CORPORATION
70 Argo Rd (17901-9247)
PHONE..................................570 385-2400
Michael Hoffert, *Manager*
EMP: 58
SALES (corp-wide): 8.4MM **Privately Held**
SIC: 2254 2253 2341 2369 Underwear, knit; knit outerwear mills; shirts (outerwear), knit; women's & children's underwear; girls' & children's outerwear; women's & misses' outerwear

PA: Alpha Mills Corporation
122 S Margaretta St
Schuylkill Haven PA 17972
570 385-1791

(G-16073)
ATLANTIC TRACK & TURNOUT CO
Warehouse
St Clair Business Park (17901)
P.O. Box 360 (17901-0360)
PHONE..................................570 429-1462
Gary Lileck, *Manager*
EMP: 30
SQ FT: 20,000
SALES (corp-wide): 89.8MM **Privately Held**
WEB: www.atlantictrack.com
SIC: 4225 4226 3312 General warehousing; special warehousing & storage; blast furnaces & steel mills
PA: Atlantic Track & Turnout Co.
400 Broadacres Dr Ste 415
Bloomfield NJ 07003
973 748-5885

(G-16074)
BUZZY INC (PA)
121 Progress Ave Ste 300 (17901-2993)
PHONE..................................570 621-2883
Cornelius Wurth, *CEO*
▲ EMP: 13
SQ FT: 2,000
SALES (est): 3MM **Privately Held**
WEB: www.buzzyseeds.com
SIC: 3999 5193 Plants, artificial & preserved; plants, potted

(G-16075)
D G YUENGLING AND SON INC (PA)
Also Called: Yuengling Brewing
5th & Mahantongo Sts (17901)
PHONE..................................570 622-4141
Richard L Yuengling Jr, *President*
Dick Yuengling, *President*
James Buehler, *Principal*
Joe Frinzi, *Principal*
Carl Runicman, *Principal*
▲ EMP: 40 EST: 1829
SQ FT: 36,000
SALES (est): 60.4MM **Privately Held**
SIC: 2082 Beer (alcoholic beverage); ale (alcoholic beverage); porter (alcoholic beverage)

(G-16076)
D G YUENGLING AND SON INC
Also Called: Yuengling Brewing
310 Mill Creek Ave (17901-8692)
P.O. Box 1243 (17901-7243)
PHONE..................................570 622-0153
Darriell Carter, *Sales Staff*
Mike Brennan, *Manager*
Chris Calender, *Manager*
Mike Carvalho, *Manager*
Charlie Trepcos, *Director*
EMP: 50
SALES (est): 16.4MM
SALES (corp-wide): 60.4MM **Privately Held**
SIC: 2082 Beer (alcoholic beverage)
PA: D. G. Yuengling And Son, Incorporated
5th & Mahantongo Sts
Pottsville PA 17901
570 622-4141

(G-16077)
DR CONTROLS INC
353 E Railroad St (17901-1247)
P.O. Box 491, Frackville (17931-0491)
PHONE..................................570 622-7109
Daniel Demansky, *President*
Diane Rau, *Admin Sec*
EMP: 3
SALES: 550K **Privately Held**
SIC: 3613 Control panels, electric

(G-16078)
ENVIRNMNTAL PROTECTION PA DEPT
Also Called: Anthrcite Non-Coal Mine Safety
5 W Laurel Blvd (17901-2522)
PHONE..................................570 621-3139
Troy Wolfgang, *Manager*

EMP: 12 **Privately Held**
SIC: 1481 9511 Mine & quarry services, nonmetallic minerals; air, water & solid waste management
HQ: Pennsylvania Dept Of Environmental Protection
400 Market St
Harrisburg PA 17101
717 783-2300

(G-16079)
GALE MINING CO
1441 Oak Rd (17901-3323)
PHONE..................................570 622-2524
Job Suender, *Principal*
EMP: 8 EST: 1989
SALES (est): 953.2K **Privately Held**
SIC: 1241 5052 Coal mining services; coal & other minerals & ores

(G-16080)
HONEYWELL INTERNATIONAL INC
98 Westwood Rd (17901-1834)
PHONE..................................570 621-6000
James Terry, *Manager*
EMP: 300
SALES (corp-wide): 41.8B **Publicly Held**
WEB: www.honeywell.com
SIC: 3089 3081 2221 Extruded finished plastic products; unsupported plastics film & sheet; broadwoven fabric mills, manmade
PA: Honeywell International Inc.
115 Tabor Rd
Morris Plains NJ 07950
973 455-2000

(G-16081)
INDEPENDENT HOSE CO
16 Sunshine St (17901-8687)
PHONE..................................570 544-9528
James Obrien, *Principal*
EMP: 3
SALES (est): 220.5K **Privately Held**
SIC: 3492 Electrohydraulic servo valves, metal

(G-16082)
J H ZERBEY NEWSPAPERS INC
111 Mahantongo St (17901-3071)
PHONE..................................570 622-3456
Henry NYCE, *Publisher*
Everly Lorli, *Principal*
Leroy Boyer, *Editor*
Lori Everly, *Human Res Dir*
Aimee Eckley, *Mktg Dir*
EMP: 14 EST: 2010
SALES (est): 635.3K **Privately Held**
SIC: 2711 Newspapers, publishing & printing

(G-16083)
J R M MACHINERY INC
14 Coal Ln (17901-8310)
PHONE..................................570 544-9505
John Minder, *President*
EMP: 5
SQ FT: 2,560
SALES (est): 551.8K **Privately Held**
SIC: 3599 Machine shop, jobbing & repair

(G-16084)
JELD-WEN INC
Also Called: Jeld-Wen Doors
1162 Keystone Blvd (17901-9055)
PHONE..................................570 628-5317
Rick Michaels, *Branch Mgr*
EMP: 1000 **Publicly Held**
WEB: www.jeld-wen.com
SIC: 2431 Doors, wood
HQ: Jeld-Wen, Inc.
2645 Silver Crescent Dr
Charlotte NC 28273
800 535-3936

(G-16085)
KELLY LINE INC
Also Called: Kelly Printing Co
500 S Centre St (17901-3512)
P.O. Box 1265 (17901-7265)
PHONE..................................570 527-6822
Ronald M Kelly, *President*
John C Kelly Jr, *Vice Pres*
EMP: 14
SQ FT: 15,100

G
E
O
G
R
A
P
H
I
C

SALES (est): 1.8MM **Privately Held**
WEB: www.kellyline.com
SIC: 3944 2752 5199 2759 Bingo boards (games); commercial printing, offset; novelties, paper; advertising specialties; envelopes: printing; invitations: printing; letterpress printing

(G-16086)
KEYSTONE PRINTING CO
11 W Savory St (17901-3945)
PHONE...............................570 622-4377
Thomas Valle, *President*
EMP: 12
SALES (est): 679.5K **Privately Held**
SIC: 2752 Commercial printing, lithographic

(G-16087)
KOPENITZ LUMBER CO
89 Woodside Rd (17901-8343)
PHONE...............................570 544-2131
Michael Kopenitz, *Owner*
EMP: 4
SQ FT: 3,000
SALES (est): 180K **Privately Held**
SIC: 2448 Pallets, wood

(G-16088)
MICHELS HEARING AID CENTER (PA)
459 N Claude A Lord Blvd (17901-2705)
PHONE...............................570 622-9151
Nick Michel, *Owner*
EMP: 3
SALES (est): 314.2K **Privately Held**
SIC: 3842 5999 Hearing aids; alarm & safety equipment stores

(G-16089)
MYSTIC SCREEN PRINTING AND EMB
1108 S Centre St (17901-8401)
PHONE...............................570 628-3520
Jill Felty, *Partner*
Robin Beaver, *Partner*
EMP: 14
SQ FT: 100,000
SALES: 600K **Privately Held**
WEB: www.mysticscreenprinting.com
SIC: 2759 Screen printing

(G-16090)
OAK SPRING ENTERPRISES INC
130 W Bacon St (17901-3912)
PHONE...............................570 622-2001
Robert Stahl, *President*
EMP: 12
SQ FT: 10,000
SALES (est): 2.1MM **Privately Held**
WEB: www.costasfoodsinc.com
SIC: 2064 Candy & other confectionery products

(G-16091)
POTTSVILLE FUEL STOP INC
1471 Route 61 Hwy N (17901-8664)
PHONE...............................570 429-2970
Jan Colna, *Director*
EMP: 8 EST: 2010
SALES (est): 1MM **Privately Held**
SIC: 2869 Fuels

(G-16092)
POTTSVILLE REPUBLICAN INC (PA)
Also Called: Republican Herald
111 Mahantongo St (17901-3071)
P.O. Box 209 (17901-0209)
PHONE...............................570 622-3456
Henry NYCE, *Principal*
David McKeown, *Editor*
Brian Smith, *Editor*
Tina Tym, *Editor*
Leslie Wagner, *Sales Staff*
▲ EMP: 33 EST: 1929
SALES (est): 5.5MM **Privately Held**
WEB: www.pottsville.com
SIC: 2711 Commercial printing & newspaper publishing combined

(G-16093)
READING ANTHRACITE COMPANY (PA)
200 Mahantongo St (17901-3011)
P.O. Box 1200 (17901-7200)
PHONE...............................570 622-5150
Brian Rich, *President*
Mark Pishock, *Vice Pres*
John W Rich, *Vice Pres*
Rick Muntone, *Safety Mgr*
Joseph Kelly, *Engineer*
▲ EMP: 20 EST: 1920
SQ FT: 10,000
SALES (est): 6.7MM **Privately Held**
WEB: www.readinganthracite.com
SIC: 1231 Strip mining, anthracite; preparation plants, anthracite; recovery of anthracite from culm banks

(G-16094)
READING FRACTURE INC
200 Mahantongo St (17901-3011)
P.O. Box 1200 (17901-7200)
PHONE...............................570 628-2308
Brian Rich, *President*
John Rampolla, *CFO*
John W Rich Jr, *Shareholder*
Michael J Rich, *Shareholder*
Bonnie Ryan, *Shareholder*
EMP: 3
SQ FT: 15,000
SALES (est): 141.9K **Privately Held**
SIC: 1241 Coal mining exploration & test boring

(G-16095)
ROBERT J QUINN JR
146 W Savory St (17901-3948)
PHONE...............................570 622-4420
Robert J Quinn Jr, *Owner*
EMP: 4 EST: 1964
SQ FT: 25,000
SALES (est): 351.7K **Privately Held**
SIC: 3273 Ready-mixed concrete

(G-16096)
RUBBERMAID COMMERCIAL PDTS LLC
1400 Laurel Blvd (17901-1427)
PHONE...............................570 622-7715
George Derosa, *Manager*
EMP: 10
SALES (corp-wide): 8.6B **Publicly Held**
SIC: 3089 3643 Plastic containers, except foam; lamp sockets & receptacles (electric wiring devices)
HQ: Rubbermaid Commercial Products Llc
3124 Valley Ave
Winchester VA 22601
800 347-9800

(G-16097)
SEIDERS PRINTING CO INC
110 E Arch St (17901-2907)
PHONE...............................570 622-0570
Richard Setlock, *Owner*
Raymond J Caravan, *Owner*
EMP: 9
SALES (est): 712.5K **Privately Held**
WEB: www.schuylkillchamber.com
SIC: 2759 2752 Letterpress printing; commercial printing, offset

(G-16098)
SUMMIT PACKAGING LLC (PA)
200 Mahantongo St (17901-3011)
P.O. Box 1200 (17901-7200)
PHONE...............................570 622-5150
EMP: 7
SALES (est): 566.3K **Privately Held**
SIC: 1241 Coal mining services

(G-16099)
TOR INDUSTRIES INC
Also Called: Eastern Press Div
2067 W Market St (17901-1905)
PHONE...............................570 622-7370
Richard J Torpey, *President*
EMP: 7 EST: 1919
SQ FT: 3,000
SALES (est): 1MM **Privately Held**
WEB: www.schuylkillprint.com
SIC: 2752 2759 2761 Commercial printing, offset; letterpress printing; manifold business forms

(G-16100)
TREDEGAR CORPORATION
Also Called: Tredegar Film Products
30 S Maple Ave (17901-8946)
PHONE...............................570 544-7600
Delroy Elissett, *Branch Mgr*
EMP: 180
SALES (corp-wide): 1.1B **Publicly Held**
WEB: www.tredegar.com
SIC: 3354 3081 2671 Aluminum extruded products; unsupported plastics film & sheet; plastic film, coated or laminated for packaging
PA: Tredegar Corporation
1100 Boulders Pkwy # 200
North Chesterfield VA 23225
804 330-1000

(G-16101)
WALCO FABRICATING INC
501 W Bacon St (17901-3917)
P.O. Box 792 (17901-0792)
PHONE...............................570 628-4523
Josephine Walacavage, *President*
Ann Marie Adams, *Office Mgr*
EMP: 18
SQ FT: 72,000
SALES: 1.5MM **Privately Held**
SIC: 2542 Racks, merchandise display or storage: except wood

(G-16102)
WILLIAM A FRASER INC
Also Called: G J Bear Company
442 N C A Lord Blvd 3/4 (17901-2706)
PHONE...............................570 622-7347
Brad Bear, *Manager*
EMP: 6
SALES (corp-wide): 59.8MM **Privately Held**
SIC: 5044 2752 Office equipment; commercial printing, offset
PA: William A. Fraser Inc.
320 Penn Ave
Reading PA 19611
610 378-0101

(G-16103)
WORLD RESOURCES COMPANY
170 Walnut Ln (17901-8559)
PHONE...............................570 622-4747
Ken Riegel, *Vice Pres*
Colleen Bartley, *Accountant*
Shannon Witman, *Technology*
EMP: 41
SQ FT: 14,000
SALES (corp-wide): 34.6MM **Privately Held**
WEB: www.worldresourcescompany.com
SIC: 3399 Metal fasteners
PA: World Resources Company
8113 W Sherman St
Tolleson AZ 85353
703 734-9800

Presto
Allegheny County

(G-16104)
MT LEBANON AWNING & TENT CO
Also Called: Mt Lebanon Awning
5309 Thoms Run Rd (15142-1113)
P.O. Box 27 (15142-0027)
PHONE...............................412 221-2233
Robert Campbell, *President*
Linda Campbell, *Admin Sec*
EMP: 20
SQ FT: 11,000
SALES (est): 2.1MM **Privately Held**
WEB: www.mtlebanonawning.com
SIC: 2394 1799 2396 Awnings, fabric: made from purchased materials; awning installation; automotive & apparel trimmings

---

Preston Park
Wayne County

(G-16105)
POROSKY LUMBER COMPANY INC
1903 Crosstown Hwy (18455-1026)
P.O. Box 174 (18455-0174)
PHONE...............................570 798-2326
Theodore W Porosky, *President*
Kate Porosky, *Corp Secy*
EMP: 18
SALES (est): 3MM **Privately Held**
SIC: 2421 Sawmills & planing mills, general

Primos
Delaware County

(G-16106)
ACTION SPORTSWEAR INC
30 Bunting Ln (19018-2040)
P.O. Box 486, Chester Heights (19017-0486)
PHONE...............................610 623-1820
George L Patti, *President*
EMP: 15
SQ FT: 60,000
SALES (est): 990K **Privately Held**
WEB: www.actionsportswear.biz
SIC: 2396 Screen printing on fabric articles

(G-16107)
AMERICAN PROCESS LETTERING INC
Also Called: Ampro Sportswear
30 Bunting Ln (19018-2040)
P.O. Box 251, Clifton Heights (19018-0251)
PHONE...............................610 623-9000
Geoffrey Traub, *President*
Stephanie Shea, *COO*
Gary B Huddell, *Vice Pres*
Stephen Ironside, *Prdtn Mgr*
Tom Weber, *Prdtn Mgr*
▲ EMP: 170
SQ FT: 85,000
SALES (est): 25.1MM **Privately Held**
SIC: 2396 Screen printing on fabric articles

(G-16108)
GELATERIA
550 S Oak Ave (19018-2916)
PHONE...............................484 466-4228
EMP: 3 EST: 2015
SALES (est): 113.2K **Privately Held**
SIC: 2024 Ice cream & frozen desserts

Prompton
Wayne County

(G-16109)
ALDENVILLE LOG AND LUMBERINC
936 Creek Dr (18456-6007)
P.O. Box 28 (18456-0028)
PHONE...............................570 785-3141
Daniel Droppa, *Principal*
EMP: 5
SALES: 311.9K **Privately Held**
SIC: 5211 2421 Planing mill products & lumber; sawmills & planing mills, general

(G-16110)
SUNNYS SWEEPING SERVICE INC
948 Creek Dr (18456-6007)
PHONE...............................570 785-5564
Tina Danchak, *President*
Michael Danchak, *Admin Sec*
EMP: 5
SALES: 250K **Privately Held**
SIC: 3524 Grass catchers, lawn mower

GEOGRAPHIC

Prospect
Butler County

(G-16111)
CLASSIC METAL
311 Perry St (16052-3159)
PHONE...................724 991-2659
EMP: 3 EST: 2017
SALES (est): 151.3K Privately Held
SIC: 3471 Plating & polishing

(G-16112)
SLATER ELECTRIC & SONS
1115 New Castle Rd (16052-3117)
P.O. Box 449 (16052-0449)
PHONE...................724 306-1060
Gavon Slater, Principal
EMP: 4 EST: 2008
SALES (est): 578.3K Privately Held
SIC: 3699 Electrical work

(G-16113)
**SPECIALITY PRECAST
COMPANY**
830 Unionville Rd (16052-2126)
PHONE...................724 865-9255
Al Grady, President
Dave Atlmire, Treasurer
Trent Greenewalt, Admin Sec
EMP: 7
SALES (est): 660K Privately Held
WEB: www.specialtyprecast.com
SIC: 3531 Construction machinery

Prospect Park
Delaware County

(G-16114)
**GAR-REN TOOL & MACHINE CO
INC**
705 Chester Pike (19076-1597)
PHONE...................610 534-1897
Robert R Dent, President
Norma Dent, Vice Pres
EMP: 12
SALES (est): 1.9MM Privately Held
SIC: 3599 Machine shop, jobbing & repair

(G-16115)
HARBOR BAY GROUP INC
Also Called: Mr. Shrinkwrap
660 13th Ave Ste 4 (19076-1219)
PHONE...................610 566-5290
Kevin Comerford, President
EMP: 4 EST: 2013
SALES (est): 757.4K Privately Held
SIC: 7389 5199 2671 Packaging & labeling services; packaging materials; plastic film, coated or laminated for packaging

(G-16116)
**LIBERTY VHCL LTG & SAFETY
SUP**
700 Moore Industrial Park (19076-1217)
PHONE...................610 356-5320
Ralph Wike, Principal
EMP: 9
SALES (est): 346K Privately Held
SIC: 3647 Vehicular lighting equipment

(G-16117)
PHILADELPHIA REGALIA CO
529 Chester Pike Ste B (19076-1419)
PHONE...................610 237-9757
Helena T Yockey, Owner
EMP: 5
SQ FT: 2,400
SALES (est): 200K Privately Held
SIC: 3999 Identification badges & insignia

(G-16118)
R&S VENTURES LLC
Also Called: Synergy Print Design
1015 Lincoln Ave (19076-1308)
PHONE...................610 532-2950
Russell Watkins, Partner
EMP: 8
SALES (est): 590.3K Privately Held
SIC: 2759 Screen printing

(G-16119)
S B I INC
Also Called: Sew Be It
528 9th Ave (19076-1401)
PHONE...................610 595-3300
Marc Vasaturo, President
Fred Brennan, Vice Pres
Anthony Sulpizio, Admin Sec
EMP: 3
SQ FT: 3,000
SALES (est): 210K Privately Held
WEB: www.sbidesign.com
SIC: 2395 Embroidery products, except schiffli machine

(G-16120)
SNAKABLE INC
709 16th Ave Fl 2 (19076-1005)
P.O. Box 322 (19076-0322)
PHONE...................347 449-3378
Wes Goulbourne, President
EMP: 3 EST: 2014
SALES (est): 24K Privately Held
SIC: 3679 7389 Antennas, receiving;

(G-16121)
SYNERGY PRINT DESIGN LLC
1015 Lincoln Ave (19076-1308)
PHONE...................610 532-2950
Jesse Wyatt, Mng Member
EMP: 5
SQ FT: 1,700
SALES (est): 601.3K Privately Held
SIC: 2759 5941 Screen printing; sporting goods & bicycle shops

Prosperity
Washington County

(G-16122)
BARNHARTS HONDA SUZUKI
883 Washington Rd (15329-1657)
PHONE...................724 627-5819
Victoria Barnhart, Owner
EMP: 10 EST: 1968
SQ FT: 5,000
SALES (est): 1.2MM Privately Held
WEB: www.gpbarnharts.com
SIC: 3751 5521 Motorcycles & related parts; gears, motorcycle & bicycle; automobiles, used cars only

Pulaski
Lawrence County

(G-16123)
ELLIS MACHINE
303 N Street Ext (16143)
PHONE...................724 657-4519
Dale Ellis, Owner
Bill Weaver, Manager
EMP: 3
SALES: 65K Privately Held
SIC: 3312 7629 Pipes & tubes; business machine repair, electric

(G-16124)
LANE ENTERPRISES INC
8271 Mercer St (16143-4798)
PHONE...................724 652-7747
Jerry A Saylor, Branch Mgr
EMP: 20
SALES (corp-wide): 70.5MM Privately Held
WEB: www.lanepipe.com
SIC: 3444 Sheet metalwork
PA: Lane Enterprises, Inc.
3905 Hartzdale Dr Ste 514
Camp Hill PA 17011
717 761-8175

(G-16125)
**MITCHELTREE BROS LOGGING
& LBR**
8485 Mercer St (16143-4709)
P.O. Box 332 (16143-0332)
PHONE...................724 598-7885
L Kent Mitcheltree, President
Darrell Mitcheltree, Treasurer
EMP: 7

SALES (est): 1.1MM Privately Held
SIC: 2411 2426 Logging camps & contractors; hardwood dimension & flooring mills

(G-16126)
R G STEEL CORP
8301 Mercer St (16143-4707)
P.O. Box 356 (16143-0356)
PHONE...................724 656-1722
Richard H Price, CEO
David Price, President
Richard Price, Director
EMP: 21
SQ FT: 20,000
SALES (est): 9.5MM Privately Held
WEB: www.rgsteel.com
SIC: 3441 5051 Fabricated structural metal; steel

Punxsutawney
Jefferson County

(G-16127)
**ACME MACHINE & WELDING CO
LLC**
46 Anchor Inn Rd (15767)
P.O. Box 1099 (15767-0899)
PHONE...................814 938-6702
David Harvey, Opers Mgr
Terry Stewart, Manager
Chad Smith, Info Tech Dir
Sylvia Kalynchuk, Info Tech Mgr
Jolene McFarland, Technology
▲ EMP: 78
SALES (est): 19.1MM Privately Held
SIC: 3599 Machine shop, jobbing & repair

(G-16128)
**BFG MANUFACTURING
SERVICES INC (PA)**
701 Martha St (15767-1838)
P.O. Box 1065 (15767-0865)
PHONE...................814 938-9164
Jeffrey D Grube, President
EMP: 70
SALES (est): 12.6MM Privately Held
SIC: 3471 Electroplating of metals or formed products

(G-16129)
BURKE & SONS INC (PA)
110 Gaskill Ave (15767-2208)
PHONE...................814 938-7303
Robert Burke, President
John Burke, Vice Pres
Myron Smouse, Prdtn Mgr
Bill Burke, Treasurer
William Burke, Treasurer
EMP: 30
SQ FT: 20,000
SALES (est): 1.8MM Privately Held
WEB: www.burke-sons.com
SIC: 2431 5211 Window frames, wood; doors, storm: wood or metal; windows, storm: wood or metal

(G-16130)
CUSTOM MACHINED SPC INC
1356 N Main St (15767-2689)
PHONE...................814 938-1031
David A Szymanski, President
EMP: 4
SALES (est): 632.7K Privately Held
SIC: 3599 Machine shop, jobbing & repair

(G-16131)
CYB MACHINING INC
130 Brown Bridge Dr (15767-3504)
PHONE...................814 938-8133
Bob Yenek, President
Rebecca Fisher, Admin Sec
EMP: 3
SALES: 500K Privately Held
SIC: 3599 Machine shop, jobbing & repair

(G-16132)
D LUTHER TRUCKING
199 Jackson Run Rd (15767-4447)
PHONE...................814 952-2136
David J Luther, Owner
EMP: 3
SALES (est): 189.1K Privately Held
SIC: 2411 Logging

(G-16133)
**DE LIMITED FAMILY
PARTNERSHIP**
1406 N Main St (15767-2646)
PHONE...................814 938-0800
Wilbert Carney, Partner
Mike Mc Means, Partner
EMP: 10
SQ FT: 6,400
SALES (est): 1.2MM Privately Held
SIC: 6552 1321 1311 Subdividers & developers; natural gasoline production; natural gas production

(G-16134)
DEAN BARRETT
Also Called: Barrett's Machine
630 Mill Rd (15767-4638)
PHONE...................814 427-2586
Dean Barrett, Owner
EMP: 5
SALES (est): 400K Privately Held
SIC: 3599 Machine & other job shop work

(G-16135)
DYNO NOBEL INC
1132 Robertsville Rd (15767-3533)
PHONE...................814 938-2035
Keith Neal, Principal
EMP: 28 Privately Held
SIC: 2892 Explosives
HQ: Dyno Nobel Inc.
2795 E Cottonwood Pkwy # 500
Salt Lake City UT 84121
801 364-4800

(G-16136)
**EASTERN AMERICAN ENERGY
CORP**
Also Called: Early Corp of American Gas
725 Snyder Hill Rd (15767-2860)
PHONE...................814 938-9000
Allan Elikin, Manager
EMP: 13 Privately Held
WEB: www.eca-eaec.com
SIC: 1382 Oil & gas exploration services
HQ: Eastern American Energy Corp
500 Corporate Lndg
Charleston WV 25311
304 925-6100

(G-16137)
EXPLORATIONS INC
9590 Route 536 (15767-6601)
PHONE...................814 365-2105
Richard Shirey, President
EMP: 3 EST: 2009
SALES (est): 381.4K Privately Held
SIC: 1382 Oil & gas exploration services

(G-16138)
FEMCO HOLDINGS LLC (PA)
754 S Main Street Ext (15767-7943)
P.O. Box 17 (15767-0017)
PHONE...................906 576-0418
Dan Rondeau, President
Randy Lacrosse, President
EMP: 29
SALES (est): 7.2MM Privately Held
SIC: 3599 6719 Machine shop, jobbing & repair; investment holding companies, except banks

(G-16139)
**FEMCO MACHINE COMPANY
LLC (PA)**
754 S Main Street Ext (15767-7943)
PHONE...................814 938-9763
Dan Rondeau, President
Jim Pyle, Vice Pres
◆ EMP: 150
SQ FT: 200,000
SALES (est): 35.9MM Privately Held
WEB: www.femcomach.com
SIC: 3599 7629 Machine shop, jobbing & repair; electrical repair shops

(G-16140)
FRANKENSTEINS
113 Shields Ave (15767-1530)
PHONE...................814 938-2571
Francis Matts, Owner
Roxy Matts, Co-Owner
EMP: 6

SALES (est): 193.5K **Privately Held**
SIC: 5812 2082 Eating Place Mfg Malt
Beverages

(G-16141)
G-S HYDRAULICS INC
406 G And S Rd (15767-6413)
PHONE................................814 938-2862
Eugene F Smith, *President*
Kimberly Schaffron, *Corp Secy*
Brian Smith, *Vice Pres*
EMP: 11
SALES (est): 806.8K **Privately Held**
SIC: 7692 7699 5084 Welding repair; in-
dustrial machinery & equipment repair;
hydraulic systems equipment & supplies

(G-16142)
GRAPE FIBERGLASS INC
Also Called: Grape Fiberglass Products
100 Sutton St (15767-1427)
PHONE................................814 938-8118
Randy Grape, *President*
Esther Grape, *President*
EMP: 12
SALES (est): 1.5MM **Privately Held**
SIC: 3443 3088 Industrial vessels, tanks &
containers; plastics plumbing fixtures

(G-16143)
HOFFMAN DIAMOND
PRODUCTS INC
121 Cedar St (15767-2104)
PHONE................................814 938-7600
Steve Palovchik, *CEO*
Andrew S Labowsky, *Corp Secy*
Michael J Labowsky, *Vice Pres*
Robert Ehn, *CFO*
EMP: 48
SQ FT: 40,000
SALES (est): 7.6MM **Privately Held**
WEB: www.hoffmandiamond.com
SIC: 3425 3532 5084 Saw blades &
handsaws; bits, except oil & gas field
tools, rock; machine tools & metalworking
machinery; drilling bits

(G-16144)
HOT JAMS DJ SERVICE
200 Horatio St (15767-1806)
PHONE................................814 246-8144
Arthur Reed, *Principal*
EMP: 3 EST: 2017
SALES (est): 112.7K **Privately Held**
SIC: 2033 Jams, jellies & preserves: pack-
aged in cans, jars, etc.

(G-16145)
JOHN L MARY D SHAFFER
186 Route 410 (15767-8706)
PHONE................................814 427-2894
John L Shaffer, *Owner*
EMP: 6
SALES (est): 283.5K **Privately Held**
SIC: 3799 All terrain vehicles (ATV)

(G-16146)
KRIEBEL GAS INC
193 Yoder Rd (15767-8012)
PHONE................................814 938-2010
Gary Kriebel, *Owner*
EMP: 3
SALES (est): 208K
SALES (corp-wide): 8.6MM **Privately**
Held
SIC: 1381 1311 Drilling oil & gas wells;
natural gas production
PA: Kriebel Gas, Inc.
633 Mayfield Rd
Clarion PA 16214
814 226-4160

(G-16147)
LILYS LLC
535 E Mahoning St (15767-2126)
PHONE................................814 938-9419
Lil Cameron, *Owner*
EMP: 5
SALES (est): 402.4K **Privately Held**
SIC: 3411 Food & beverage containers

(G-16148)
NAC CARBON PRODUCTS INC
Elk Run Ave (15767)
P.O. Box 436 (15767-0436)
PHONE................................814 938-7450

Franklin C Schoch, *President*
Robert Bennett, *General Mgr*
Bob Bennett, *General Mgr*
Kathleen L Schoch, *Corp Secy*
Bob Froberg, *Vice Pres*
EMP: 35
SQ FT: 87,549
SALES (est): 5.4MM **Privately Held**
WEB: www.naccarbon.com
SIC: 3624 3823 Carbon & graphite prod-
ucts; industrial instrmnts msrmnt
display/control process variable

(G-16149)
NAC JOINT VENTURE PIPLINE
314 Elk Run Ave (15767-1622)
P.O. Box 436 (15767-0436)
PHONE................................814 938-7450
Jospeh Renwick, *Partner*
William Hanes, *Partner*
EMP: 55
SALES (est): 3.5MM **Privately Held**
SIC: 3624 Carbon & graphite products

(G-16150)
NATIONAL OILWELL VARCO
INC
Also Called: Star Iron Works
257 Caroline St (15767-4276)
PHONE................................814 427-2555
Frank Stockdale, *Branch Mgr*
EMP: 76
SALES (corp-wide): 8.4B **Publicly Held**
SIC: 5084 3533 Petroleum industry ma-
chinery; oil field machinery & equipment
PA: National Oilwell Varco, Inc.
7909 Parkwood Circle Dr
Houston TX 77036
713 346-7500

(G-16151)
NORTEK GLOBAL HVAC LLC
Also Called: Thermal-Gard
400 N Walnut St (15767-1368)
PHONE................................814 938-1408
Elmer Matillo, *Controller*
EMP: 253
SALES (corp-wide): 2.7B **Privately Held**
WEB: www.norflx.com
SIC: 3585 5023 3442 Heating & air condi-
tioning combination units; parts for heat-
ing, cooling & refrigerating equipment;
window shades; storm doors or windows,
metal
HQ: Nortek Global Hvac, Llc
8000 Phoenix Pkwy
O Fallon MO 63368
636 561-7300

(G-16152)
P & N COAL CO INC (PA)
240 W Mahoning St (15767-1919)
PHONE................................814 938-7660
George D Prushnok, *Ch of Bd*
John P Prushnok, *President*
Andrew Nelson, *Corp Secy*
David Prushnok, *Vice Pres*
Ken Stossel, *Opers Mgr*
EMP: 20
SQ FT: 2,800
SALES (est): 14.5MM **Privately Held**
SIC: 1221 Strip mining, bituminous

(G-16153)
PLATING UNLIMITED LLC
201 Rockland Ave (15767-2427)
PHONE................................814 952-3135
Michael Weaver,
EMP: 3
SALES (est): 91.3K **Privately Held**
SIC: 3471 Plating of metals or formed
products

(G-16154)
PROFORM POWDERED METALS
INC
700 Martha St (15767-1838)
P.O. Box 500 (15767-0500)
PHONE................................814 938-7411
Gerald Duffell, *President*
Michael Armanini, *Vice Pres*
Karen Duffell, *Vice Pres*
Jerry Dueffell, *Financial Exec*
EMP: 25
SQ FT: 80,000

SALES (est): 5.6MM **Privately Held**
WEB: www.proformpowderedmetals.com
SIC: 3499 3568 3562 3366 Friction material, made from powdered metal; power
transmission equipment; ball & roller
bearings; copper foundries

(G-16155)
PUNXSUTAWNEY FINSHG
WORKS INC
Also Called: Zinc Plating Specialists
701 Martha St (15767-1838)
P.O. Box 1065 (15767-0865)
PHONE................................814 938-9164
Jeffrey Grube, *President*
EMP: 105
SQ FT: 100,000
SALES (est): 10.2MM **Privately Held**
SIC: 3471 3479 Electroplating of metals or
formed products; aluminum coating of
metal products

(G-16156)
PUNXSUTAWNEY TILE & GLASS
INC
Also Called: Punxsutawney Glass Tile
220 Lane Ave (15767-2119)
PHONE................................814 938-4200
John W Triggs, *CEO*
EMP: 16
SALES (est): 1.8MM **Privately Held**
SIC: 3229 Pressed & blown glass

(G-16157)
QUALITY GEAR & MACHINE INC
Also Called: High Tech Machine
188 Blose Rd (15767-8420)
PHONE................................814 938-5552
Elizabeth Smail, *CEO*
Robert Ober, *President*
Michael Renwick, *General Mgr*
EMP: 10
SQ FT: 6,000
SALES (est): 3.8MM
SALES (corp-wide): 65MM **Publicly Held**
WEB: www.pfina.com
SIC: 3599 Machine shop, jobbing & repair
PA: P & F Industries, Inc.
445 Broadhollow Rd # 100
Melville NY 11747
631 694-9800

(G-16158)
R & S MACHINE INC
7707 Porter Rd (15767-5923)
PHONE................................814 938-7540
William Rugh, *President*
Tim Burkett, *Vice Pres*
EMP: 15
SALES (est): 1.9MM **Privately Held**
WEB: www.rsmachine.com
SIC: 3599 Machine shop, jobbing & repair

(G-16159)
ROCK RUN ENTERPRISES LLC
264 Sunny Acres Ln (15767-3746)
PHONE................................814 938-8778
Lancelott Joseph Casaday, *Principal*
EMP: 4
SALES (est): 547.1K **Privately Held**
SIC: 1381 Drilling oil & gas wells

(G-16160)
SALLACK WELL SERVICES INC
304 Hidden Hollow Ln (15767-3354)
P.O. Box 637 (15767-0637)
PHONE................................814 938-8179
Marc A Sallack, *President*
EMP: 3
SALES (est): 579.1K **Privately Held**
SIC: 1381 Service well drilling

(G-16161)
SANDYS FASHION JEWELRY
LLC
400 Sutton St Apt 4 (15767-1417)
PHONE................................814 938-4356
Frank J Blagdan,
Marion Blagdan,
Sandra Schickling,
Nick Terranova,
EMP: 5 EST: 2009
SALES: 250K **Privately Held**
SIC: 3961 Costume jewelry

(G-16162)
SCHETLER LUMBER - SAWMILL
3727 Route 410 (15767-8950)
PHONE................................814 590-9592
Andrew Schetler, *Principal*
EMP: 3
SALES (est): 150K **Privately Held**
SIC: 2421 Sawmills & planing mills, gen-
eral

(G-16163)
SPIRIT PUBLISHING COMPANY
Also Called: Horizon Publication
510 Pine St (15767-1404)
PHONE................................814 938-8740
Mary Judie Troute, *President*
EMP: 30
SALES (est): 1.6MM **Privately Held**
WEB: www.clintonnc.com
SIC: 2711 Newspapers

(G-16164)
STELLO FOODS INC
551 E Mahoning St (15767-2126)
P.O. Box 413 (15767-0413)
PHONE................................814 938-8764
Nickki L Stello, *President*
Richard Weaver, *Assistant VP*
James Stello, *Vice Pres*
Jamie Stello Fezell, *Treasurer*
David Daughenbaugh, *Admin Sec*
▲ EMP: 24
SQ FT: 53,000
SALES (est): 4.9MM **Privately Held**
WEB: www.stellofoods.com
SIC: 2035 5149 Pickles, sauces & salad
dressings; groceries & related products

(G-16165)
UNIVERSAL WELL SERVICES
INC
324 Meter St (15767-1843)
PHONE................................814 938-5327
Alex States, *Engineer*
Doug Valkosky, *Branch Mgr*
EMP: 7
SALES (corp-wide): 3.3B **Publicly Held**
SIC: 1381 Drilling oil & gas wells
HQ: Universal Well Services, Inc.
13549 S Mosiertown Rd
Meadville PA 16335
814 337-1983

(G-16166)
UNIVERSAL WELL SERVICES
INC
114 Universal Dr (15767-7940)
PHONE................................814 938-2051
Neil Boyer, *Sales Engr*
Jim Hickox, *Manager*
Shawn Houck, *Manager*
Brian Fletcher, *Supervisor*
EMP: 44
SALES (corp-wide): 3.3B **Publicly Held**
WEB: www.univwell.com
SIC: 1389 Hydraulic fracturing wells
HQ: Universal Well Services, Inc.
13549 S Mosiertown Rd
Meadville PA 16335
814 337-1983

Quakertown
Bucks County

(G-16167)
AGC FLAT GLASS NORTH AMER
INC
480 California Rd (18951-2408)
PHONE................................215 538-9424
Patrick Thompson, *Manager*
EMP: 50
SALES (corp-wide): 13.5B **Privately Held**
SIC: 3231 3211 Safety glass: made from
purchased glass; tempered glass
HQ: Agc Flat Glass North America, Inc.
11175 Cicero Dr Ste 400
Alpharetta GA 30022
404 446-4200

▲ = Import ▼=Export
◆ =Import/Export

(G-16168)
AL MARWA LLC
670 E Cherry Rd (18951-4500)
PHONE................................215 536-6050
Levent Demirgil,
EMP: 7 **EST:** 2001
SALES (est): 823.1K **Privately Held**
WEB: www.almarwa.com
SIC: 2011 Meat packing plants

(G-16169)
ASSOCIATED RUBBER INC
115 S 6th St (18951-1555)
P.O. Box 520 (18951-0520)
PHONE................................215 536-2800
John Oldt, *President*
Gary Scott, *Vice Pres*
EMP: 45 **EST:** 1940
SQ FT: 45,000
SALES (est): 7.5MM **Privately Held**
SIC: 3069 Molded rubber products

(G-16170)
AVERY DENNISON
CORPORATION
35 Penn Am Dr (18951-2434)
PHONE................................215 536-9000
Jim Adams, *Manager*
Valerie Fox, *Personnel Assit*
EMP: 75
SQ FT: 1,200
SALES (corp-wide): 7.1B **Publicly Held**
WEB: www.avery.com
SIC: 2672 2621 Adhesive papers, labels
or tapes: from purchased material; paper
mills
PA: Avery Dennison Corporation
207 N Goode Ave Ste 500
Glendale CA 91203
626 304-2000

(G-16171)
B & W MACHINE WORKS INC
550 California Rd Ste 8 (18951-2428)
PHONE................................215 529-2990
Joanne K Trumbauer, *President*
David Trumbauer, *Vice Pres*
EMP: 6
SQ FT: 2,000
SALES (est): 780.2K **Privately Held**
SIC: 3599 Machine shop, jobbing & repair

(G-16172)
BEVERLY HALL CO
Also Called: Philosophical Publishing Co
5966 Clymer Rd (18951-3275)
P.O. Box 220 (18951-0220)
PHONE................................215 536-7048
William Kracht, *President*
Betty Jo Benner, *Treasurer*
EMP: 20
SQ FT: 1,000
SALES (est): 2.1MM **Privately Held**
WEB: www.soul.org
SIC: 2731 8661 Books: publishing only;
religious organizations

(G-16173)
BLASTCO
1505 N West End Blvd (18951-4156)
PHONE................................215 529-7100
Richard Cuce, *Owner*
EMP: 5
SQ FT: 9,000
SALES (est): 450K **Privately Held**
SIC: 3471 1721 Sand blasting of metal
parts; industrial painting

(G-16174)
BODYBUILDERS BODYWASH
LLC
128 Woodview Dr (18951-2289)
PHONE................................954 682-8191
Seth Alan Lowell,
EMP: 3
SALES: 30K **Privately Held**
SIC: 2844 Toilet preparations

(G-16175)
BUCKS COUNTY FUR
PRODUCTS INC
220 N Ambler St (18951-1354)
P.O. Box 204 (18951-0204)
PHONE................................215 536-6614
Thomas Kline, *President*

EMP: 3
SQ FT: 4,000
SALES (est): 200K **Privately Held**
SIC: 3999 Fur stripping

(G-16176)
C & B IRON INC
100 Richlandtown Pike (18951-2500)
PHONE................................215 536-7162
Donald Bickley, *President*
EMP: 9
SALES (est): 117.1K **Privately Held**
SIC: 3446 Fire escapes, metal; railings,
bannisters, guards, etc.: made from metal
pipe; ornamental metalwork

(G-16177)
CENTRAL MACHINE CO INC
27 S 4th St (18951-1394)
P.O. Box 567 (18951-0567)
PHONE................................215 536-5071
Robert Druckenmiller, *President*
Marietta Druckenmiller, *Vice Pres*
EMP: 12
SQ FT: 3,200
SALES (est): 1.9MM **Privately Held**
SIC: 3599 Machine shop, jobbing & repair

(G-16178)
CIDER PRESS WOODWORKS
LLC
585 Old Bethlehem Rd (18951-5503)
PHONE................................215 804-1100
Molly Hanisch, *Vice Pres*
Tadd Kehler, *Project Mgr*
Jim Shirer, *Manager*
EMP: 4 **EST:** 2013
SALES (est): 522.7K **Privately Held**
SIC: 2431 Millwork

(G-16179)
CIDER PRESS WOODWORKS
LLC
2320 Trumbauersville Rd (18951-2281)
PHONE................................215 804-0880
Brad Sullivan,
EMP: 3
SALES (est): 152K **Privately Held**
SIC: 2741 Miscellaneous publishing

(G-16180)
CLEVELAND STEEL CONTAINER
CORP
350 E Mill St (18951-1325)
PHONE................................215 536-4477
Joe Kelly, *Branch Mgr*
EMP: 35
SQ FT: 50,000
SALES (corp-wide): 131.9MM **Privately
Held**
SIC: 3412 Metal barrels, drums & pails
PA: Cleveland Steel Container Corporation
30310 Emerald Valley Pkwy
Solon OH 44139
440 349-8000

(G-16181)
CRITIC PUBLICATIONS INC
Also Called: Audio Critic, The
1380 Masi Dr (18951-5221)
PHONE................................215 536-8884
Peter Aczel, *President*
EMP: 5
SALES (est): 240.4K **Privately Held**
SIC: 2721 Magazines: publishing & printing

(G-16182)
D-ELECTRIC INC
2070 Quaker Pointe Dr (18951-2163)
PHONE................................215 529-6020
Edward K Forster, *President*
Mark Steven, *Corp Secy*
EMP: 19
SQ FT: 25,000
SALES (est): 5.9MM **Privately Held**
WEB: www.d-electric.com
SIC: 5065 7694 7699 Electronic parts &
equipment; electric motor repair; industrial
equipment services

(G-16183)
DAYS COMMUNICATION INC
1208 Juniper St (18951-1520)
PHONE................................215 538-1240
David Yaw, *President*

EMP: 5
SQ FT: 840
SALES (corp-wide): 605K **Privately Held**
WEB: www.policeandsecuritynews.com
SIC: 2721 Magazines: publishing & printing
PA: Days Communication Inc
2965 Allentown Rd
Quakertown PA 18951
215 362-2233

(G-16184)
DEMCO ENTERPRISES INC
Also Called: Demco Automation
300 Commerce Dr (18951-3728)
PHONE................................888 419-3343
Maund R Stephen, *President*
Steven Werley, *Mfg Staff*
David Ritchie, *Engineer*
Peter Stepanoff, *Engineer*
Jean Lachman, *Office Mgr*
EMP: 18
SQ FT: 35,000
SALES (est): 5.7MM **Privately Held**
WEB: www.demcowedge.com
SIC: 3535 8711 3699 7373 Conveyors &
conveying equipment; engineering serv-
ices; electrical equipment & supplies; sys-
tems software development services;
robots, assembly line: industrial & com-
mercial; custom machinery

(G-16185)
DEWITT FAB WELDING CO
271 Scholls School Rd (18951-5313)
PHONE................................215 538-9477
Mark T Dewitt, *Owner*
EMP: 4
SALES (est): 270.6K **Privately Held**
SIC: 7692 Welding repair

(G-16186)
DHL MACHINE CO INC (PA)
Also Called: Dhl Machine
2450 Milford Square Pike (18951-2233)
PHONE................................215 536-3591
Dave Kirk, *President*
Ronald Datesman, *Vice Pres*
Kevin Hoffman, *Purch Mgr*
Joe Fasti, *Controller*
Bill Franks, *Executive*
EMP: 22 **EST:** 1957
SQ FT: 25,000
SALES (est): 5.6MM **Privately Held**
WEB: www.dhlmachine.com
SIC: 3599 7692 3443 Machine shop, job-
bing & repair; welding repair; fabricated
plate work (boiler shop)

(G-16187)
EISENHOWER TOOL INC
120 Pacific Dr (18951-3605)
PHONE................................215 538-9381
Bruce Eisenhower, *President*
Kathy Eisenhower, *Treasurer*
EMP: 15
SQ FT: 16,000
SALES (est): 1MM **Privately Held**
SIC: 3569 Filters

(G-16188)
ERGOGENIC TECHNOLOGY INC
533 Junction Ln (18951-2549)
PHONE................................215 766-8545
Paul E Richard, *President*
EMP: 25
SALES (est): 2MM **Privately Held**
SIC: 2522 Office furniture, except wood

(G-16189)
ERGONOMIC MFG GROUP INC
591 Union Rd (18951-4811)
P.O. Box 1627, Skippack (19474-1627)
PHONE................................800 223-6430
Timothy Burns, *President*
Edward Burns, *Manager*
▼ **EMP:** 6
SALES (est): 210.5K **Privately Held**
SIC: 3565 Packaging machinery

(G-16190)
ESTEN LUMBER PRODUCTS INC
2015 Trumbauersville Rd (18951-2266)
PHONE................................215 536-4976
Scott Moyer, *CEO*
Kimberly Moyer, *Project Mgr*
Barbara Moyer, *Bookkeeper*

EMP: 5 **EST:** 1969
SQ FT: 5,500
SALES (est): 897.3K **Privately Held**
SIC: 2448 Pallets, wood

(G-16191)
EVOLUTION GUN WORKS INC
Also Called: Egw
52 Belmont Ave (18951-1347)
PHONE................................215 538-1012
George Smith, *President*
EMP: 18
SQ FT: 22,000
SALES (est): 3.9MM **Privately Held**
WEB: www.egw-guns.com
SIC: 3489 7699 Guns or gun parts, over
30 mm.; gun services; gun parts made to
individual order; gunsmith shop

(G-16192)
FABRIC DEVELOPMENT INC
1217 W Mill St (18951-1127)
PHONE................................215 536-1420
Piyush A Shah, *President*
▲ **EMP:** 112 **EST:** 1971
SQ FT: 80,000
SALES (est): 35MM
SALES (corp-wide): 3.6B **Privately Held**
WEB: www.fabricdevelopment.com
SIC: 2221 Specialty broadwoven fabrics,
including twisted weaves
HQ: Kordsa Teknik Tekstil Anonim Sirketi
No:90 Alikahya Fatih Mahalelsi
Kocaeli 41310
262 316-7000

(G-16193)
FIBEROPTICSCOM
1919 Sycamore Dr (18951-6037)
PHONE................................215 499-8959
EMP: 3 **EST:** 2013
SALES (est): 212.5K **Privately Held**
SIC: 2834 Pharmaceutical preparations

(G-16194)
FMR INDUSTRIES INC
Also Called: Fmr Powder Coatings
130 Penn Am Dr (18951-2403)
PHONE................................215 536-2222
Andrew W Ford, *President*
John Wasserman, *Vice Pres*
EMP: 5
SQ FT: 15,000
SALES: 1MM **Privately Held**
SIC: 3479 Coating of metals & formed
products

(G-16195)
FRONTIER WOOD PRODUCTS
INC
500 E Pumping Station Rd (18951-2422)
PHONE................................215 538-2330
James Mc Andrew, *President*
Barbara Mc Andrew, *Vice Pres*
▲ **EMP:** 32
SALES: 3.6MM **Privately Held**
SIC: 5191 2421 Fertilizers & agricultural
chemicals; sawmills & planing mills, gen-
eral

(G-16196)
GEORGIA-PACIFIC LLC
3000 Am Dr (18951-3812)
PHONE................................215 538-7549
EMP: 23
SALES (corp-wide): 42.4B **Privately Held**
SIC: 2621 Paper mills
HQ: Georgia-Pacific Llc
133 Peachtree St Nw
Atlanta GA 30303
404 652-4000

(G-16197)
GLUNZ & JENSEN INC
500 Commerce Dr (18951-3730)
PHONE................................574 272-9950
Kent Deal, *General Mgr*
◆ **EMP:** 45
SQ FT: 19,000
SALES (est): 6.6MM
SALES (corp-wide): 36.6MM **Privately
Held**
WEB: www.glunz-jensen.com
SIC: 3861 Processing equipment, photo-
graphic

PA: Glunz & Jensen Holding A/S
Lindholm Havnevej 29
Nyborg 5800
576 881-81

(G-16198)
GLUNZ & JENSEN K&F INC
Also Called: K & F Printing Systems Intl
500 Commerce Dr (18951-3730)
PHONE....................................267 227-3493
Thomas Kocsis, *CEO*
Alex Kocsis, *Ch of Bd*
Joseph Bella, *President*
Michelle Kocsis, *Admin Sec*
◆ **EMP:** 110
SQ FT: 90,000
SALES (est): 14.6MM
SALES (corp-wide): 36.6MM **Privately Held**
SIC: 3555 Printing trades machinery
PA: Glunz & Jensen Holding A/S
Lindholm Havnevej 29
Nyborg 5800
576 881-81

(G-16199)
HAWKINS METAL
2020 Emerson Dr (18951-2295)
PHONE....................................215 538-9668
Robert Hawkins, *Partner*
Walter Hawkins, *Partner*
EMP: 5
SQ FT: 2,400
SALES (est): 500K **Privately Held**
SIC: 3599 3444 Machine shop, jobbing & repair; sheet metalwork

(G-16200)
HORIZON SIGNS LLC
1520 Allentown Rd (18951-3790)
PHONE....................................215 538-2600
Kevan Price, *Owner*
EMP: 10
SQ FT: 9,000
SALES: 900K **Privately Held**
SIC: 3993 Electric signs

(G-16201)
INNOVATIVE FINISHERS INC
130 Penn Am Dr (18951-2403)
P.O. Box 207, Richlandtown (18955-0207)
PHONE....................................215 536-2222
Jeffrey J Mullen, *Principal*
EMP: 7
SALES (est): 867.8K **Privately Held**
SIC: 2851 Shellac (protective coating)

(G-16202)
INSACO INCORPORATED
1365 Canary Rd (18951-3880)
P.O. Box 9006 (18951-9006)
PHONE....................................215 536-3500
David M Haines, *Ch of Bd*
Robert A Haines, *President*
Nadine C Haines, *CFO*
Nadine Haines, *CFO*
Susan H Zaharchuk, *Admin Sec*
EMP: 75 **EST:** 1948
SQ FT: 45,000
SALES (est): 17.9MM **Privately Held**
WEB: www.insaco.com
SIC: 3827 3471 3264 Optical elements & assemblies, except ophthalmic; plating & polishing; porcelain electrical supplies

(G-16203)
JC WOODWORKING INC (PA)
2150 Rosedale Rd (18951-4033)
PHONE....................................215 651-2049
EMP: 5
SALES (est): 1.7MM **Privately Held**
SIC: 2431 Millwork

(G-16204)
JEREMIAH JUNCTION INC
2410 Milford Square Pike (18951-2233)
PHONE....................................215 529-6430
Fax: 215 529-6434
▲ **EMP:** 5
SQ FT: 2,000
SALES (est): 585.2K **Privately Held**
SIC: 2731 Book Publisher

(G-16205)
JOHN PROSOCK MACHINE INC
2250 Trumbauersville Rd (18951-2317)
PHONE....................................215 804-0321
John Prosock, *President*
Diane H Horne, *Purch Mgr*
EMP: 39
SQ FT: 7,500
SALES (est): 6.8MM **Privately Held**
WEB: www.jprosock.com
SIC: 3599 Machine shop, jobbing & repair

(G-16206)
KNAUSS INC
625 E Broad St (18951-1713)
PHONE....................................215 536-4220
Donald T Knauss, *President*
E William Knauss, *Vice Pres*
Linda Tufft, *Director*
Donald O Merkel, *Admin Sec*
EMP: 58 **EST:** 1978
SQ FT: 1,000
SALES (est): 4.1MM **Privately Held**
SIC: 2013 Beef, dried: from purchased meat

(G-16207)
KWIK GOAL LTD
140 Pacific Dr (18951-3608)
PHONE....................................800 531-4252
Vincent C Caruso, *CEO*
Anthony Caruso, *President*
Ardie McCue, *Facilities Mgr*
Peter Noneman, *Site Mgr*
Doug Propst, *Finance*
◆ **EMP:** 60
SQ FT: 36,000
SALES: 33.2MM **Privately Held**
WEB: www.kwikgoal.com
SIC: 5091 3949 Sporting & recreation goods; soccer equipment & supplies

(G-16208)
LANCER SYSTEMS LP
2800 Milford Square Pike (18951-6004)
P.O. Box 62864, Baltimore MD (21264-2864)
PHONE....................................610 973-2600
Michael Delfiner, *Partner*
Kenneth Stanley, *Partner*
Debbie Nast, *General Mgr*
Angela Pennington, *Sales Staff*
Maria Deose, *Sales Associate*
▲ **EMP:** 40
SQ FT: 75,000
SALES (est): 10.3MM **Privately Held**
WEB: www.lancer-systems.com
SIC: 3089 3357 3484 3624 Plastic processing; communication wire; rifles or rifle parts, 30 mm. & below; fibers, carbon & graphite

(G-16209)
LAWRENCE SCHIFF SILK MILLS INC
Thermco Products
1409 W Broad St (18951-1109)
PHONE....................................215 536-5460
EMP: 15
SALES (corp-wide): 43.4MM **Privately Held**
SIC: 2269 2262 2261 Finishing Plants, Nec, Nsk
PA: Lawrence Schiff Silk Mills Inc.
590 California Rd
Quakertown PA 18951
215 538-2880

(G-16210)
LEPKO J D FINISHING
118 N Hellertown Ave (18951-1317)
PHONE....................................215 538-9717
Joseph Lepko, *Principal*
EMP: 8
SQ FT: 42,220
SALES (est): 580K **Privately Held**
SIC: 1721 3471 Residential painting; finishing, metals or formed products

(G-16211)
MANCINCI METAL SPECIALTY INC
2015 Grant Rd (18951-4019)
P.O. Box 207, Spinnerstown (18968-0207)
PHONE....................................215 529-5800
Arnold Mancinci, *President*
Anthony Mancinci, *Vice Pres*
Teresa Mancinci, *Admin Sec*
EMP: 3
SALES (est): 280K **Privately Held**
SIC: 3441 Fabricated structural metal

(G-16212)
MARQUEE GRAPHX LLC
243 W Broad St (18951-1232)
P.O. Box 656 (18951-0656)
PHONE....................................215 538-2992
Cynthia M Johnston,
EMP: 3
SALES: 75K **Privately Held**
SIC: 2759 Commercial printing

(G-16213)
MASTERMIX INC
1800 Shale Rd (18951-1910)
PHONE....................................610 346-8723
Robert Zisko, *President*
Raymond Duh, *Vice Pres*
EMP: 3
SQ FT: 10,000
SALES: 750K **Privately Held**
WEB: www.mastermix.com
SIC: 2875 Potting soil, mixed

(G-16214)
MCADOO & ALLEN INC
Also Called: Quaker Color Div
201 S Hellertown Ave (18951-1768)
P.O. Box 219 (18951-0219)
PHONE....................................215 536-3520
Kenneth F Brown, *President*
Philip Simak, *Vice Pres*
Phillip Simak, *Purch Agent*
Sue Barlow, *CFO*
Susan O Barlow, *Treasurer*
◆ **EMP:** 50
SQ FT: 171,127
SALES (est): 17MM **Privately Held**
WEB: www.quakercolor.com
SIC: 3111 2816 2851 5169 Hides: tanning, currying & finishing; inorganic pigments; paints & allied products; chemicals & allied products

(G-16215)
MEDICAL CREATIVE TECHNOLOGIES
2404 Milford Square Pike (18951-2233)
PHONE....................................267 347-4436
Robert Rambo, *President*
Linda Rambo, *Principal*
EMP: 4
SQ FT: 5,500
SALES (est): 360K **Privately Held**
SIC: 3841 Surgical & medical instruments

(G-16216)
MICKELSON MFG INDS INC
550 California Rd Ste 5 (18951-2428)
PHONE....................................215 529-5442
Fax: 215 529-5443
EMP: 7
SQ FT: 6,000
SALES (est): 570K **Privately Held**
SIC: 3599 Mfg Jobbing & Repair Machines

(G-16217)
MIDNIGHT OIL EXPRESS
203 N Ambler St (18951-1353)
PHONE....................................215 933-9690
Harry A Brown Jr, *Principal*
EMP: 3
SALES (est): 109K **Privately Held**
SIC: 1311 Crude petroleum & natural gas

(G-16218)
MILFORD ENTERPRISES INC (PA)
450 Commerce Dr (18951-3729)
PHONE....................................215 538-2778
Gary L Fetterman, *President*
Jane Raeder, *COO*
Jeffrey Adkins, *Vice Pres*
James F Dougherty, *Vice Pres*
Randall Hrabina, *Vice Pres*
▲ **EMP:** 95
SQ FT: 125,000
SALES (est): 22.7MM **Privately Held**
WEB: www.milfordenterprisesinc.com
SIC: 2541 Store fixtures, wood; store & office display cases & fixtures

(G-16219)
MILFORD SPORTSWEAR INC
2023 Emerson Dr (18951-2295)
PHONE....................................215 529-9316
Paul Owens, *President*
EMP: 4
SALES (est): 360K **Privately Held**
SIC: 2261 Screen printing of cotton broad-woven fabrics

(G-16220)
MILLENNIUM MANUFACTURING INC
130d Penn Am Dr (18951-2435)
PHONE....................................215 536-3006
David B Fricke, *CEO*
Peter A Vogel, *Vice Pres*
David Fricke, *Site Mgr*
EMP: 10
SQ FT: 5,000
SALES (est): 2.3MM **Privately Held**
SIC: 3599 Machine shop, jobbing & repair

(G-16221)
MINUTEMAN PRESS
39 Trumbauersville Rd (18951-2603)
PHONE....................................215 538-2200
Anton Ringenary, *Owner*
EMP: 5
SQ FT: 1,600
SALES (est): 723.1K **Privately Held**
SIC: 2752 7311 Commercial printing, offset; advertising agencies

(G-16222)
NATIONAL SCIENTIFIC COMPANY
205 E Paletown Rd (18951-2830)
P.O. Box 498 (18951-0498)
PHONE....................................215 536-2577
Dorothy M Drechsel, *President*
Norman H Drechsel, *Vice Pres*
EMP: 6 **EST:** 1949
SQ FT: 7,500
SALES (est): 1MM **Privately Held**
WEB: www.natl-scientific.com
SIC: 3679 3231 Quartz crystals, for electronic application; medical & laboratory glassware: made from purchased glass

(G-16223)
NEENAH NORTHEAST LLC
45 N 4th St (18951-1239)
PHONE....................................215 536-4600
Robert Mc Daniel, *Engng Exec*
Mike Wright, *Manager*
EMP: 150
SALES (corp-wide): 1B **Publicly Held**
SIC: 2631 2672 2679 Pressboard; coated & laminated paper; paper products, converted
HQ: Neenah Northeast, Llc
70 Front St
West Springfield MA 01089
413 533-0699

(G-16224)
NOVATECH LLC (PA)
1720 Molasses Way (18951-3360)
PHONE....................................484 812-6000
Volker Oakey, *CEO*
Aubrey Zey, *Vice Pres*
Buz Zey, *President*
Vincent V Horvath, *Vice Pres*
Gunther Oakey, *Admin Sec*
EMP: 150
SQ FT: 38,000
SALES (est): 44.6MM **Privately Held**
WEB: www.novatech-llc.com
SIC: 3822 3625 7372 Auto controls regulating residntl & coml environmt & applncs; control equipment, electric; prepackaged software

(G-16225)
OLD TIME GAMES INC
1915 Fawn Ln (18951-2695)
PHONE....................................215 538-5422
Plummer Dunkle, *President*
Paul Thenstedt, *Vice Pres*
David S Carlson, *Treasurer*
EMP: 3
SALES (est): 136.6K **Privately Held**
SIC: 3944 Games, toys & children's vehicles

(G-16226)
PANEL TECHNOLOGIES INC
550 California Rd Ste 2 (18951-2428)
PHONE...................215 538-7055
David Soltysiak, *President*
Ed Schmitt, *Treasurer*
EMP: 8
SQ FT: 2,000
SALES: 250K **Privately Held**
WEB: www.panel-tech.com
SIC: 3089 3444 3355 3083 Panels, building: plastic; sheet metalwork; aluminum rolling & drawing; laminated plastics plate & sheet

(G-16227)
PARTICLE SIZE TECHNOLOGY INC
1930 Kumry Rd (18951-3712)
PHONE...................215 529-9771
James Perry Jr, *President*
Jerry Jeffers, *Plant Mgr*
▲ EMP: 25
SQ FT: 55,000
SALES (est): 10MM **Privately Held**
WEB: www.particlesizetech.com
SIC: 3399 Metal powders, pastes & flakes

(G-16228)
PHASETEK INC
550 California Rd Ste 11 (18951-2428)
PHONE...................215 536-6648
Kurt Gorman, *President*
Robin Nelson, *Corp Secy*
Matthew Nelson, *Manager*
EMP: 5
SQ FT: 5,500
SALES (est): 941K **Privately Held**
WEB: www.phasetek.com
SIC: 3663 Radio broadcasting & communications equipment

(G-16229)
PLASTIC DIP MOLDINGS INC (PA)
Also Called: Insulboot Division
2345 Milford Square Pike (18951-2232)
P.O. Box 450, Plumsteadville (18949-0450)
PHONE...................215 766-2020
Graeme Houston, *CEO*
Ian D Macknight, *President*
Emilee Brill, *Train & Dev Mgr*
Jon Macknight, *Sales Staff*
Shawn Ranspot, *VP Mktg*
▲ EMP: 25
SQ FT: 15,000
SALES (est): 4.4MM **Privately Held**
WEB: www.plasticdipmoldings.com
SIC: 3089 3479 2821 Molding primary plastic; coating of metals with plastic or resins; polyvinyl chloride resins (PVC)

(G-16230)
POMA GL SPECIALTY WINDOWS INC
480 California Rd (18951-2408)
PHONE...................215 538-9424
Patrick Thompsons, *Branch Mgr*
EMP: 70
SALES (corp-wide): 13.5B **Privately Held**
SIC: 3211 Insulating glass, sealed units
HQ: Poma Glass & Specialty Windows Inc.
11175 Cicero Dr Ste 400
Alpharetta GA 30022
404 446-4200

(G-16231)
POWDERSIZE LLC
20 Pacific Dr (18951-3601)
PHONE...................215 536-5605
Guido Driesen, *CEO*
Wayne Sigler, *President*
Thomas Higley, *Vice Pres*
▲ EMP: 42
SQ FT: 100,000
SALES: 10MM **Privately Held**
SIC: 3821 Particle size reduction apparatus, laboratory
HQ: Capsugel Holdings Us, Inc.
412 Mount Kemble Ave 200c
Morristown NJ 07960

(G-16232)
PRECISION FINISHING INC (PA)
1800 Am Dr (18951-2114)
PHONE...................215 257-6862
John Bell, *CEO*
Jeff Bell, *President*
J Jeffrey Bell, *President*
Thom Bell, *Vice Pres*
William Walker, *Vice Pres*
▼ EMP: 30 EST: 1951
SQ FT: 25,000
SALES (est): 5.3MM **Privately Held**
WEB: www.precisionfinishinginc.com
SIC: 3471 3398 3291 2841 Finishing, metals or formed products; metal heat treating; abrasive products; soap & other detergents

(G-16233)
PRECISION PRODUCTS LTD
2365 Milford Square Pike (18951-2232)
PHONE...................215 538-1795
Fred G Diehl, *President*
EMP: 20 EST: 1978
SQ FT: 12,800
SALES (est): 1MM **Privately Held**
SIC: 3599 Machine shop, jobbing & repair

(G-16234)
PRODEX INC
Also Called: Dynagherm Boiler
43 E Cherry Rd (18951-4302)
PHONE...................215 536-4078
Kerry Moyer, *Manager*
EMP: 3
SALES (corp-wide): 1.5MM **Privately Held**
SIC: 3443 Tanks, standard or custom fabricated: metal plate
PA: Prodex, Inc.
436 Adams St Rear
Red Hill PA 18076
215 679-2405

(G-16235)
PULSE TECHNOLOGIES INC
2000 Am Dr (18951-3811)
PHONE...................267 733-0200
Joseph C Rosato Jr, *CEO*
Frank E Henofer, *Co-President*
Robert S Walsh, *Co-President*
Darlene Erdman, *Buyer*
Mark Manginam, *Treasurer*
▲ EMP: 250
SQ FT: 70,000
SALES: 50MM **Privately Held**
WEB: www.pulsetechinc.com
SIC: 3841 Surgical & medical instruments

(G-16236)
PUMP-WAREHOUSE CO INC
Also Called: CDF Industries
359 New St Ste 2 (18951-1781)
PHONE...................215 536-0500
Charles A McMurtrie, *President*
EMP: 26 EST: 1996
SALES (est): 5.6MM **Privately Held**
SIC: 3589 Car washing machinery

(G-16237)
QUAKER HARDWOODS COMPANY
992 E Cherry Rd (18951-4502)
PHONE...................215 538-0401
Brian Devery, *Owner*
▲ EMP: 2
SQ FT: 7,500
SALES: 1MM **Privately Held**
WEB: www.woodfloor.com
SIC: 2421 Sawmills & planing mills, general

(G-16238)
QUAKER SAFETY PRODUCTS CORP
1121 Richland Commrce Dr A (18951-2518)
PHONE...................215 536-2991
Alan D Dorrell, *President*
EMP: 50
SQ FT: 48,000
SALES (est): 12.5MM **Privately Held**
WEB: www.quakersafety.com
SIC: 3842 Clothing, fire resistant & protective

(G-16239)
QUANTUM GLOBAL TECH LLC (HQ)
Also Called: Quantumclean
1900 Am Dr Ste 200 (18951-6403)
P.O. Box 1000, Dublin (18917-1000)
PHONE...................215 892-9300
Scott Nicholas, *CEO*
David Zuck, *COO*
Dave Zuck, *Vice Pres*
Stan Webb, *Opers Mgr*
Dinesh Sharda, *Prdtn Mgr*
▲ EMP: 105
SALES (est): 44.7MM
SALES (corp-wide): 1.1B **Publicly Held**
WEB: www.quantumclean.com
SIC: 2842 Specialty cleaning preparations
PA: Ultra Clean Holdings, Inc.
26462 Corporate Ave
Hayward CA 94545
510 576-4400

(G-16240)
R E B INC (PA)
Also Called: Lee's Hoagie House
228 S West End Blvd (18951-1143)
PHONE...................215 538-7875
Ron Berlin, *Principal*
Elisa Berlin, *Admin Sec*
EMP: 6
SQ FT: 1,800
SALES: 300K **Privately Held**
SIC: 3713 Stake, platform truck bodies

(G-16241)
REO & SONS FUELS LLC
690 Mine Rd (18951-1875)
PHONE...................267 374-6400
Robert E Osipower, *Principal*
EMP: 5
SALES (est): 473.2K **Privately Held**
SIC: 2869 Fuels

(G-16242)
ROSELON INDUSTRIES INC (PA)
Also Called: Spinlon Industries
35 S 5th St (18951-1723)
PHONE...................215 536-3275
Robert R Adams, *President*
Bonnie Connors, *Vice Pres*
Thayer R Adams, *Admin Sec*
▲ EMP: 90 EST: 1923
SQ FT: 100,000
SALES (est): 37.3MM **Privately Held**
SIC: 2282 2284 2281 Textured yarn; thread mills; yarn spinning mills

(G-16243)
SARIK CORPORATION
Also Called: Creative Structures
420 Station Rd Ste 3 (18951-6300)
PHONE...................215 538-2269
Robert L Simmons, *President*
EMP: 9
SALES (est): 910K **Privately Held**
WEB: www.creativeconservatories.com
SIC: 2452 3231 Prefabricated wood buildings; insulating glass: made from purchased glass

(G-16244)
SCOTTS COMPANY LLC
2385 John Fries Hwy (18951-6005)
PHONE...................215 538-0191
Austin Wismer, *Branch Mgr*
EMP: 5
SALES (corp-wide): 2.6B **Publicly Held**
WEB: www.scottscompany.com
SIC: 2873 Fertilizers: natural (organic), except compost
HQ: The Scotts Company Llc
14111 Scottslawn Rd
Marysville OH 43040
937 644-0011

(G-16245)
SECANT GROUP LLC
195 Oneill Rd (18951-4211)
PHONE...................215 538-9601
Jeff Robertson, *President*
EMP: 10
SALES (corp-wide): 855.1MM **Privately Held**
SIC: 2299 Batting, wadding, padding & fillings

HQ: The Secant Group Llc
551 E Church Ave
Telford PA 18969
877 774-2835

(G-16246)
SPECTRODYNE INC
2036 Emerson Dr 577 (18951-2295)
PHONE...................215 804-1044
Howard Stross, *President*
EMP: 10
SALES (est): 1.1MM **Privately Held**
SIC: 3823 8734 Industrial instrmnts msrmnt display/control process variable; testing laboratories

(G-16247)
SUPERIOR CABINET COMPANY
2075 Baumans Rd (18951-2123)
PHONE...................215 536-5228
Dave Sterapy, *Owner*
EMP: 5
SQ FT: 4,100
SALES (est): 335.2K **Privately Held**
SIC: 2541 2522 2542 2434 Table or counter tops, plastic laminated; cabinets, office: except wood; partitions & fixtures, except wood; wood kitchen cabinets

(G-16248)
TAPESTRATION
1395 Doylestown Pike (18951-4926)
PHONE...................215 536-0977
Frank Agostino, *Owner*
EMP: 3
SQ FT: 2,800
SALES: 30K **Privately Held**
SIC: 7641 2657 2241 Reupholstery; folding paperboard boxes; narrow fabric mills

(G-16249)
TEXTEMP LLC
Also Called: Tuff Temp
3788 Sterner Mill Rd (18951-3202)
PHONE...................215 322-9670
EMP: 11
SALES (est): 1.1MM **Privately Held**
SIC: 2241 Manmade fiber narrow woven fabrics

(G-16250)
THA INC
Also Called: Thomas Hontz Associates
121 Park Ave (18951-1631)
PHONE...................215 804-0220
Thomas Hontz, *President*
Mitchell Eisen, *Vice Pres*
EMP: 30
SQ FT: 40,000
SALES (est): 4.7MM **Privately Held**
WEB: www.thafurniture.com
SIC: 2521 Wood office furniture

(G-16251)
THERMOCOUPLE TECHNOLOGIES INC
350 New St (18951-1736)
PHONE...................215 529-9394
EMP: 3
SALES (est): 97.2K **Privately Held**
SIC: 3823 Industrial instrmnts msrmnt display/control process variable

(G-16252)
THERMOCOUPLE TECHNOLOGY LLC
Also Called: T-TEC
350 New St (18951-1736)
PHONE...................215 529-9394
Giovanna McKinney,
Michael McKinney,
EMP: 20
SQ FT: 10,000
SALES (est): 3.4MM **Privately Held**
WEB: www.tteconline.com
SIC: 3829 3823 Thermometers & temperature sensors; thermocouples; temperature measurement instruments, industrial; resistance thermometers & bulbs, industrial process type; temperature instruments: industrial process type; thermocouples, industrial process type

(G-16253)
UNAMI RIDGE WINERY
2144 Kumry Rd (18951-3780)
PHONE..................................215 804-5445
James E Jenks Jr, *Principal*
EMP: 3 EST: 2009
SALES (est): 138.9K **Privately Held**
SIC: 2084 Wines

(G-16254)
VACU-BRAZE INC
2200 Kumry Rd (18951-3781)
PHONE..................................215 453-0414
Ralph Puerta, *President*
Jacquelene Puerta, *Vice Pres*
EMP: 18
SALES: 1.5MM **Privately Held**
SIC: 3398 Brazing (hardening) of metal

(G-16255)
VALLEY PRECISION LLC
195 Penn Am Dr (18951-2434)
PHONE..................................215 536-0676
John Seligman, *Sales Mgr*
Lou Conway, *Mng Member*
Brian Mannley,
EMP: 17
SQ FT: 30,000
SALES (est): 3.1MM **Privately Held**
WEB: www.valleyprecisioninc.com
SIC: 3599 Machine shop, jobbing & repair

(G-16256)
VENDORS 1ST CHOICE INC
2455 Willow Stream Dr (18951-6024)
PHONE..................................215 804-1011
B John Hens, *President*
EMP: 8
SQ FT: 30,000
SALES (est): 1.2MM **Privately Held**
SIC: 5087 3581 Vending machines & sup-
　plies; automatic vending machines

(G-16257)
VERTECH INTERNATIONAL INC
420 Station Rd (18951-6300)
PHONE..................................215 529-0300
Raj Verma, *President*
Ambi Verma, *Treasurer*
▲ EMP: 25
SQ FT: 57,000
SALES (est): 4.8MM **Privately Held**
WEB: www.vertechinternational.com
SIC: 3469 3444 Machine parts, stamped
　or pressed metal; sheet metal specialties,
　not stamped

(G-16258)
VIEW THRU TECHNOLOGIES INC
1765 Walnut Ln (18951-2046)
PHONE..................................215 703-0950
Michele Brienza, *Principal*
Ryan Newman, *Manager*
EMP: 15 EST: 1999
SQ FT: 6,000
SALES (est): 3.4MM **Privately Held**
WEB: www.viewthru.net
SIC: 3827 Optical elements & assemblies,
　except ophthalmic

(G-16259)
WILBOS INC
Also Called: Proper Brewing Company, The
117 W Broad St (18951-1291)
PHONE..................................267 490-5168
Brian Wilson, *Owner*
Kris Wilson, *Owner*
EMP: 4
SALES (est): 285.7K **Privately Held**
SIC: 2082 5813 5812 7299 Beer (alco-
　holic beverage); bar (drinking places);
　eating places; banquet hall facilities

(G-16260)
WILSEY TOOL COMPANY INC
140 Penn Am Dr (18951-2435)
P.O. Box 699 (18951-0699)
PHONE..................................215 538-0800
Timothy W Wilsey, *President*
William Wilsey, *Chairman*
Michael A Wilsey, *Vice Pres*
Patricia A Mitchell, *CFO*
EMP: 65
SQ FT: 25,000

SALES (est): 11.1MM **Privately Held**
WEB: www.wilseytool.com
SIC: 3599 Electrical discharge machining
　(EDM); machine & other job shop work

(G-16261)
YES TOWELS INC (PA)
1139 Red Barn Ln (18951-2443)
PHONE..................................215 538-5230
Manu Patel, *CEO*
Jagdish Malhotra, *President*
▲ EMP: 2
SQ FT: 1,500
SALES: 1MM **Privately Held**
SIC: 5046 2211 Hotel equipment & sup-
　plies; towels & toweling, cotton

Quarryville
Lancaster County

(G-16262)
B & S WOODCRAFT
501 Furnace Rd (17566-9422)
PHONE..................................717 786-8154
Ben Stalsfus, *Partner*
EMP: 5
SALES (est): 425.1K **Privately Held**
SIC: 2511 Wood household furniture

(G-16263)
B N S WOODCRAFTS
722 Tress Rd (17566)
PHONE..................................717 284-1035
Benjamin Stoltzfus, *Owner*
EMP: 7
SALES (est): 550K **Privately Held**
SIC: 3423 Edge tools for woodworking:
　augers, bits, gimlets, etc.

(G-16264)
BEILER SAWMILL
Also Called: Beiler Elam Sawmill
921 Lancaster Pike (17566-9746)
PHONE..................................717 284-5271
Elam Beiler, *Owner*
EMP: 6
SALES: 1.2MM **Privately Held**
SIC: 2421 Sawmills & planing mills, gen-
　eral

(G-16265)
BELLVIEW LAWN FURNITURE
87a Quarry Rd (17566-9455)
PHONE..................................717 786-1286
Abner Glick, *Principal*
EMP: 5
SQ FT: 6,000
SALES (est): 180K **Privately Held**
SIC: 3949 Playground equipment

(G-16266)
BUCK COMPANY INC
897 Lancaster Pike (17566-9738)
PHONE..................................717 284-4114
Dick McMinn, *President*
EMP: 6
SALES (corp-wide): 282.2MM **Privately Held**
WEB: www.buckcompany.com
SIC: 3322 3366 3365 3321 Malleable
　iron foundries; copper foundries; alu-
　minum foundries; gray & ductile iron
　foundries
HQ: Buck Company, Inc.
　897 Lancaster Pike
　Quarryville PA 17566
　717 284-4114

(G-16267)
COUNTRY VALUE WOODWORKS LLC
2302 Beaver Valley Pike (17566)
PHONE..................................717 786-7949
Elam Esh, *Exec Dir*
EMP: 40
SQ FT: 34,000
SALES (est): 4.6MM **Privately Held**
SIC: 2511 Wood household furniture

(G-16268)
DAILY GRIND QUARRYVILLE
221 W 4th St (17566-1122)
PHONE..................................717 786-0615

Andrew Morgan, *Owner*
EMP: 3
SALES (est): 307.3K **Privately Held**
SIC: 3599 Grinding castings for the trade

(G-16269)
FERGUSON AND HASSLER INC
Also Called: Fh
100 Townsedge Dr (17566-1300)
PHONE..................................717 786-7301
James Hassler, *President*
Thurston A Hassler, *President*
George W Hassler II, *Corp Secy*
Timothy K Hassler, *Corp Secy*
George W Hassler III, *Vice Pres*
EMP: 200
SQ FT: 45,000
SALES (est): 24MM **Privately Held**
WEB: www.fergusonhassler.com
SIC: 5411 2051 5399 Supermarkets;
　bread, cake & related products; country
　general stores

(G-16270)
FREY GROUP LLC
372 Puseyville Rd (17566-9501)
PHONE..................................717 786-2146
Ernst Frey II,
Karl Frey,
EMP: 10
SALES (est): 1.8MM **Privately Held**
SIC: 2499 Mulch or sawdust products,
　wood
PA: Coast Of Maine Organic Products, Inc.
　145 Newbury St Fl 3
　Portland ME 04101

(G-16271)
GREENTREE MACHINE WORKS
113a Greentree Rd (17566-9463)
PHONE..................................717 786-4047
Amos Beiler, *Owner*
EMP: 3
SALES (est): 150K **Privately Held**
SIC: 3599 3561 Machine shop, jobbing &
　repair; pumps, domestic: water or sump

(G-16272)
GROFFS PRINTING COMPANY
22 E State St Frnt (17566-1277)
PHONE..................................717 786-1511
EMP: 5
SALES (est): 375.6K **Privately Held**
SIC: 2752 Commercial printing, litho-
　graphic

(G-16273)
LAPPS PALLET REPAIR LLC
Also Called: Lapp's Pallet Repair
1315 Georgetown Rd (17566-9469)
PHONE..................................717 806-5348
Isaac Lapp, *Mng Member*
EMP: 15
SQ FT: 40,000
SALES: 9MM **Privately Held**
SIC: 2448 Pallets, wood

(G-16274)
NOLTPAK LLC
319 Conowingo Rd (17566-9119)
PHONE..................................717 725-9862
Chad Nolt, *Prdtn Mgr*
Gary Nolt, *Mng Member*
EMP: 6
SQ FT: 1,500
SALES: 1MM **Privately Held**
SIC: 5149 2095 Coffee & tea; instant cof-
　fee

(G-16275)
OAK RIDGE LOGGING LLC
3166 White Oak Rd (17566-9387)
PHONE..................................717 687-8168
Brent A Landis, *Owner*
EMP: 3
SALES (est): 258.2K **Privately Held**
SIC: 2411 Logging

(G-16276)
PETER SHEIMS COW MATTRESS
972 Dry Wells Rd (17566-9301)
PHONE..................................717 786-2918
Merrill Nolt, *Owner*
EMP: 3

SALES: 1.5MM **Privately Held**
SIC: 2392 Mattress pads

(G-16277)
PIECES BY PALLETS LLC
210 S Lime St (17566-9306)
PHONE..................................717 872-7238
EMP: 3
SALES (est): 119.9K **Privately Held**
SIC: 2448 Wood pallets & skids

(G-16278)
S FREY PALLETS
984 Buck Heights Rd (17566-9708)
PHONE..................................717 284-9937
Adolf E Frey, *Principal*
EMP: 4
SALES (est): 442.1K **Privately Held**
SIC: 2448 Pallets, wood

(G-16279)
SANER ARCHITECTURE MILLWORK
310 Park Ave (17566-9232)
PHONE..................................717 786-2014
Trent Saner, *President*
Martha Saner, *Admin Sec*
EMP: 8
SALES: 600K **Privately Held**
SIC: 2431 5211 Millwork; lumber & other
　building materials; insulation material,
　building

(G-16280)
STEEL SYSTEMS INSTALLATION INC
175 N Lime St (17566-9227)
P.O. Box 307 (17566-0307)
PHONE..................................717 786-1264
Richard D Welch, *President*
Craig V Gartzke, *Admin Sec*
▼ EMP: 40
SQ FT: 18,000
SALES (est): 16.3MM **Privately Held**
SIC: 3535 3537 3532 Belt conveyor sys-
　tems, general industrial use; hoppers, end
　dump; mining machinery

(G-16281)
STOLTZFUS JOHN
Also Called: John's Custom Gluing
918 Valley Rd (17566-9451)
PHONE..................................717 786-2481
John Stoltzfus, *Owner*
EMP: 3
SALES (est): 253.3K **Privately Held**
SIC: 2511 Wood household furniture

(G-16282)
STONER INCORPORATED (PA)
1070 Robert Fulton Hwy (17566-9617)
P.O. Box 65 (17566-0065)
PHONE..................................717 786-7355
Robert L Ecklin Jr, *President*
John Findley, *Mfg Dir*
Jonathan Crothers, *Research*
Quinn Houser, *Research*
Lottie Stoner, *Treasurer*
◆ EMP: 10
SQ FT: 36,500
SALES (est): 15.6MM **Privately Held**
WEB: www.spinmax.com
SIC: 2842 Cleaning or polishing prepara-
　tions

(G-16283)
STONY HILL WOODWORKS
332 Stony Hill Rd (17566-9361)
PHONE..................................717 786-8358
Stephen Beiler, *Principal*
EMP: 3
SALES (est): 77.2K **Privately Held**
SIC: 2511 Wood bedroom furniture

(G-16284)
WOOD FABRICATORS INC
938 Lancaster Pike (17566-9746)
PHONE..................................717 284-4849
David Nickle, *President*
Marie Nickle, *Vice Pres*
EMP: 15
SQ FT: 16,000

2019 Harris Pennsylvania
Manufacturers Directory

▲ = Import ▼=Export
◆ =Import/Export

SALES (est): 2.2MM **Privately Held**
SIC: 2439 5031 5211 Trusses, wooden
roof; paneling, wood; wallboard (composition) & paneling

Radnor
Delaware County

(G-16285)
ADAPT PHARMA INC
100 W Matsonford Rd # 4 (19087-4558)
PHONE...................................844 232-7811
Seamus Mulligan, *CEO*
Matthew Ruth, *Ch Credit Ofcr*
EMP: 13
SALES (est): 493.4K **Privately Held**
SIC: 2834 Pharmaceutical preparations

(G-16286)
AVANTOR INC (HQ)
100 W Matsonford Rd # 1 (19087-4558)
PHONE...................................610 386-1700
Michael Stubblefield, *President*
James M Kalinovich, *Treasurer*
EMP: 11 **EST:** 2016
SALES (est): 5B **Privately Held**
SIC: 2819 Industrial inorganic chemicals

(G-16287)
**AVANTOR PERFORMANCE
MTLS LLC (DH)**
100 W Matsonford Rd (19087-4558)
PHONE...................................610 573-2600
Michael Stubblefield, *CEO*
Rajiv L Gupta, *Ch of Bd*
Bjorn Hofman, *COO*
Helen Evans, *Exec VP*
Devashish Ohri, *Exec VP*
◆ **EMP:** 120 **EST:** 1904
SALES (est): 543.6MM **Privately Held**
WEB: www.avantormaterials.com
SIC: 2819 Chemicals, high purity: refined
from technical grade
HQ: Avantor Performance Materials Hold-
ings, Llc
100 W Matsonford Rd # 1
Radnor PA 19087
610 573-2600

(G-16288)
**AVANTOR PRFMCE MTLS
HLDNGS LLC (DH)**
100 W Matsonford Rd # 1 (19087-4558)
PHONE...................................610 573-2600
Rajiv L Gupta, *Ch of Bd*
Ashish K Kulkarni, *Exec VP*
Jamie Ethier, *Vice Pres*
Michael Baranski, *Buyer*
Damon Debusk, *QC Mgr*
EMP: 1
SALES (est): 543.6MM **Privately Held**
SIC: 2819 Industrial inorganic chemicals
HQ: Avantor, Inc.
100 W Matsonford Rd # 1
Radnor PA 19087
610 386-1700

(G-16289)
**BACKE DIGITAL BRAND
MARKETING**
100 W Matsonford Rd (19087-4558)
PHONE...................................610 947-6922
John Backe, *CEO*
Malcolm Brown, *Senior VP*
Boyd Maits, *Senior VP*
Zeke Kisling, *Vice Pres*
Mike O'Hara, *Vice Pres*
EMP: 17
SALES (est): 3.2MM **Privately Held**
SIC: 3823 Digital displays of process vari-
ables

(G-16290)
**CATERPILLAR URS
STOREROOM (PA)**
100 W Matsonford Rd (19087-4558)
PHONE...................................610 293-5576
Larry Newhart, *Chairman*
EMP: 12 **EST:** 2013
SALES (est): 2.8MM **Privately Held**
SIC: 3531 Construction machinery

(G-16291)
**CLEARFIELD OHIO HOLDINGS
INC (PA)**
Radnor Corp Ctr Bdg5 40 (19087)
PHONE...................................610 293-0410
Robert C Bumpus, *President*
Charles Pavalko Jr, *Exec VP*
EMP: 7
SQ FT: 3,000
SALES (est): 11.4MM **Privately Held**
SIC: 1389 Gas field services

(G-16292)
CREPERIE BECHAMEL LLC
11 Louella Ct (19087-3527)
PHONE...................................610 964-9700
Patrick Yasaitis, *Principal*
EMP: 5
SALES (est): 428.8K **Privately Held**
SIC: 2024 Ice cream & frozen desserts

(G-16293)
DITA EXCHANGE INC
150 N Radnor Chester Rd (19087-5252)
PHONE...................................267 327-4889
Kent Sorensen, *CEO*
EMP: 22
SALES (est): 1.2MM
SALES (corp-wide): 893.1K **Privately
Held**
SIC: 7372 7389 Business oriented com-
puter software;
PA: Dita Exchange Aps Under Konkurs
Abogade 15
Aarhus 8200
515 530-05

(G-16294)
IBERDROLA RENEWABLE (PA)
100 W Matsonford Rd (19087-4558)
PHONE...................................610 254-9800
Martin Mugica, *President*
EMP: 14
SALES (est): 10.4MM **Privately Held**
SIC: 3621 Windmills, electric generating

(G-16295)
**MARINUS PHARMACEUTICALS
INC (PA)**
100 W Matsonford Rd 3-304 (19087-4551)
PHONE...................................267 440-4200
Christopher M Cashman, *Ch of Bd*
Scott Braunstein, *Chairman*
Edward F Smith, *CFO*
Lorianne Masuoka, *Chief Mktg Ofcr*
EMP: 16
SQ FT: 8,500
SALES (est): 2.1MM **Publicly Held**
WEB: www.marinuspharma.com
SIC: 2834 Pharmaceutical preparations

(G-16296)
MITO BIOPHARM
170 N Radnor Chester Rd # 350
(19087-5280)
PHONE...................................215 767-9700
H Joseph Reiser, *Principal*
EMP: 3 **EST:** 2015
SALES (est): 174K **Privately Held**
SIC: 2834 Pharmaceutical preparations

(G-16297)
PREFERRED PROPPANTS LLC
100 W Matsonford Rd # 101 (19087-4558)
PHONE...................................610 834-1969
Michael O Neill,
EMP: 12 **EST:** 2012
SALES (est): 4.7MM **Privately Held**
SIC: 1382 Oil & gas exploration services

(G-16298)
PREFERRED SANDS LLC (PA)
100 W Matsonford Rd # 1 (19087-4569)
PHONE...................................610 834-1969
Michael O Neill, *CEO*
Christian Rheault, *President*
Mike Balitsaris, *Exec VP*
Tj Doyle, *Exec VP*
Kevin Traynor, *Exec VP*
EMP: 57
SALES (est): 671.8MM **Privately Held**
SIC: 1442 Sand mining

(G-16299)
QUINTIQ INC
Also Called: Dassault Systemes Americas
201 King Of Prussia Rd # 500
(19087-5151)
PHONE...................................610 964-8111
Victor Allis, *CEO*
David Kenneson, *General Mgr*
Eric Wuest, *Business Mgr*
Arjen Heeres, *COO*
Sara Gifford, *Vice Pres*
EMP: 62
SQ FT: 28,720
SALES (est): 12.2MM
SALES (corp-wide): 1.8B **Privately Held**
WEB: www.quintiq.com
SIC: 7372 Application computer software
HQ: Dassault Systemes B.V.
Utopialaan 25
's-Hertogenbosch
738 226-710

(G-16300)
RELX INC
201 King Of Prussia Rd (19087-5147)
PHONE...................................610 964-4516
Greg Sheremet, *Principal*
EMP: 49
SALES (corp-wide): 9.7B **Privately Held**
WEB: www.lexis-nexis.com
SIC: 2721 Magazines: publishing only, not
printed on site
HQ: Relx Inc.
230 Park Ave Ste 700
New York NY 10169
212 309-8100

(G-16301)
**SAFEGUARD SCIENTIFICS INC
(PA)**
170 N Radnor Chester Rd # 200
(19087-5279)
PHONE...................................610 293-0600
Robert J Rosenthal, *Ch of Bd*
Brian J Sisko, *President*
Brian Sisko, *COO*
Mark A Herndon, *CFO*
John Roberts, *Bd of Directors*
EMP: 33 **EST:** 1953
SQ FT: 15,600
SALES (est): 18.3MM **Publicly Held**
WEB: www.safeguard.com
SIC: 6799 7372 3841 Venture capital
companies; prepackaged software; diag-
nostic apparatus, medical

(G-16302)
SKANTRA DIAGNOSTICS INC
825 Hollow Rd (19087-2805)
PHONE...................................215 990-0381
Laura Spain, *General Counsel*
EMP: 5
SALES (est): 305.9K **Privately Held**
SIC: 3829 Measuring & controlling devices

(G-16303)
TV GUIDE MAGAZINE LLC
100 W Matsonford Rd Ste 1 (19087-4565)
P.O. Box 750, Wayne (19087)
PHONE...................................212 852-7500
Damian Holbrook, *Branch Mgr*
EMP: 23
SALES (corp-wide): 99.5MM **Privately
Held**
SIC: 2721 Television schedules: publishing
& printing
HQ: Tv Guide Magazine, Llc
50 Rockefeller Plz Fl 14
New York NY 10020

(G-16304)
VWR CORPORATION (DH)
Radnor Corp Ctr 1 200 (19087)
PHONE...................................610 386-1700
Michael Stubblefield, *CEO*
Nils Clausnitzer MD, *President*
Mark T McLoughlin, *President*
Bjorn Hofman, *COO*
Scott K Baker, *Counsel*
EMP: 157
SQ FT: 150,000

SALES: 4.5B **Privately Held**
SIC: 2869 2819 3821 5047 Industrial organic chemicals; chemicals, reagent
grade: refined from technical grade; laboratory apparatus & furniture; medical
laboratory equipment
HQ: Avantor, Inc.
100 W Matsonford Rd # 1
Radnor PA 19087
610 386-1700

Rankin
Allegheny County

(G-16305)
**EPIC METALS CORPORATION
(PA)**
Also Called: Space U Rent
11 Talbot Ave (15104-1106)
PHONE...................................412 351-3913
Donald H Landis, *President*
David F Landis, *Vice Pres*
Dave Mancosh, *Vice Pres*
David A Mancosh Jr, *Vice Pres*
Steve Potts, *Vice Pres*
◆ **EMP:** 70
SQ FT: 70,000
SALES (est): 21MM **Privately Held**
WEB: www.epicmetals.com
SIC: 3444 3448 3296 Flooring, cellular
steel; roof deck, sheet metal; prefabri-
cated metal buildings; mineral wool

Ransom
Lackawanna County

(G-16306)
**CASCADES TISSUE GROUP - PA
INC**
1 Main St (18653)
PHONE...................................570 388-6161
Ovyes Lamount, *Manager*
EMP: 16
SALES (corp-wide): 3.3B **Privately Held**
SIC: 2621 Sanitary tissue paper
HQ: Cascades Tissue Group - Pennsylva-
nia Inc.
901 Sathers Dr
Pittston PA 18640
570 388-4307

Reading
Berks County

(G-16307)
A T V BAKERY INC
36 S 3rd St (19602-1045)
PHONE...................................610 374-5577
Joseph Alber, *President*
Bradley O Albert, *Vice Pres*
Claudia Ferko, *CFO*
EMP: 47 **EST:** 1941
SQ FT: 31,500
SALES (est): 7.7MM **Privately Held**
WEB: www.atvbakery.com
SIC: 2051 Bread, all types (white, wheat,
rye, etc): fresh or frozen; rolls, bread type:
fresh or frozen

(G-16308)
A WBROWN AWNING
443 Buttonwood St (19601-3223)
PHONE...................................610 372-2908
George W Brown, *Owner*
EMP: 4
SALES: 150K **Privately Held**
SIC: 2394 Awnings, fabric: made from pur-
chased materials

(G-16309)
**ACRYSYSTEMS LABORATORIES
INC**
Also Called: Acrylabs
101 N Prospect St (19606-1407)
PHONE...................................610 273-1355
Mitchell Weinberger, *President*
Barry Lucas, *Vice Pres*
Richard Clawson, *Sales Staff*

Ray Fitzgerald, *Sales Staff*
Richard Barney, *Marketing Staff*
▼ **EMP:** 4
SQ FT: 4,200
SALES (est): 810K **Privately Held**
WEB: www.acrylabs.com
SIC: 2851 Undercoatings, paint

(G-16310)
AD-NET SERVICES INCORPORATED
1301 Allegheny Ave (19601-1703)
PHONE..................610 374-4200
Carl Harter, *President*
EMP: 15
SQ FT: 14,000
SALES (est): 2.3MM **Privately Held**
WEB: www.ad-netservices.com
SIC: 2752 Commercial printing, offset

(G-16311)
ADVANCE STORES COMPANY INC
Also Called: Advance Auto Parts
3409 N 5th Street Hwy (19605-2428)
PHONE..................610 939-0120
Hector Perez, *General Mgr*
EMP: 20
SALES (corp-wide): 9.3B **Publicly Held**
SIC: 5531 3714 7549 3825 Automobile & truck equipment & parts; wipers, windshield, motor vehicle; inspection & diagnostic service, automotive; battery testers, electrical
HQ: Advance Stores Company Incorporated
　　5008 Airport Rd Nw
　　Roanoke VA 24012
　　540 362-4911

(G-16312)
ADVANCED PLASMA SOLUTIONS
200 Sherwood Dr (19606-9100)
PHONE..................267 679-4077
Igor Shanis, *Managing Prtnr*
Roman Fedorovsky, *Officer*
EMP: 5
SALES (est): 390K **Privately Held**
SIC: 3674 Thermoelectric devices, solid state

(G-16313)
AI CONTROL SYSTEMS INC
90 Water St (19605-1210)
PHONE..................610 921-9670
Thomas Albright, *President*
EMP: 10
SQ FT: 15,000
SALES: 1.5MM **Privately Held**
WEB: www.aicontrols.com
SIC: 3613 Control panels, electric

(G-16314)
AKZO NOBEL COATINGS INC
150 Columbia Ave (19601-1748)
PHONE..................610 372-3600
Doug Holmberg, *President*
Ron Tomko, *Human Res Mgr*
EMP: 41
SALES (corp-wide): 11.3B **Privately Held**
SIC: 2851 5198 2821 Paints: oil or alkyd vehicle or water thinned; lacquer: bases, dopes, thinner; varnishes; paints; plastics materials & resins
HQ: Akzo Nobel Coatings Inc.
　　8220 Mohawk Dr
　　Strongsville OH 44136
　　440 297-5100

(G-16315)
AKZO NOBEL INC
150 Columbia Ave (19601-1748)
PHONE..................312 544-7000
Anthony Carrozza, *QC Mgr*
Rob Akker, *Manager*
Jan Reeuwijk, *Manager*
Fiona Hebdige, *Supervisor*
Brandelyn Rightnour, *Info Tech Mgr*
EMP: 9
SALES (corp-wide): 11.3B **Privately Held**
SIC: 2869 Industrial organic chemicals

HQ: Akzo Nobel Inc.
　　525 W Van Buren St Fl 16
　　Chicago IL 60607
　　312 544-7000

(G-16316)
ALCON MANUFACTURING LTD
Also Called: Alcon Precision Device
714 Columbia Ave (19608-1405)
PHONE..................610 670-3500
Rick Paterson, *Vice Pres*
Jackie Mendes, *Technology*
Dianna Noll, *Admin Asst*
EMP: 600
SQ FT: 42,181
SALES (corp-wide): 49.1B **Privately Held**
SIC: 3841 Surgical & medical instruments
HQ: Alcon Manufacturing, Ltd.
　　6201 South Fwy
　　Fort Worth TX 76134
　　817 293-0450

(G-16317)
ALCON RESEARCH LTD
Also Called: Precision Devices Facility
714 Columbia Ave (19608-1405)
PHONE..................610 670-3500
Peter Bliudzius, *Facilities Mgr*
John Leschner, *Production*
Dan Brickner, *Engineer*
Larry D Krebs, *Engineer*
David Rowe, *Engineer*
EMP: 500
SALES (corp-wide): 49.1B **Privately Held**
WEB: www.alconlabs.com
SIC: 3841 8733 Ophthalmic instruments & apparatus; research institute
HQ: Alcon Research, Llc
　　6201 South Fwy
　　Fort Worth TX 76134
　　817 551-4555

(G-16318)
ALLOY FABRICATION INC
1700 N 10th St (19604-1503)
P.O. Box 15045 (19612-5045)
PHONE..................610 921-9212
George Stuck Jr, *President*
Dennis Shueman, *Vice Pres*
EMP: 6
SQ FT: 17,000
SALES (est): 994.7K **Privately Held**
SIC: 3443 Fabricated plate work (boiler shop)

(G-16319)
AMERICAN FUTURE SYSTEMS INC
Also Called: Progressive Bus Publications
220 N Park Rd Bldg 5-2 (19610-2945)
PHONE..................610 375-8012
Bob Pirock, *Manager*
EMP: 50
SALES (corp-wide): 134.8MM **Privately Held**
WEB: www.pbp.com
SIC: 2741 2721 Newsletter publishing; periodicals
PA: American Future Systems, Inc.
　　370 Technology Dr
　　Malvern PA 19355
　　610 695-8600

(G-16320)
AMERICAN POLARIZERS INC
Also Called: API
141 S 7th St Ste 1 (19602-1697)
PHONE..................610 373-5177
Nicholas K Bentley, *CEO*
Jeffrey Snyder, *President*
Dave Bottiglieri, *Manager*
Mary F Lorah, *Executive*
EMP: 25 **EST:** 1950
SQ FT: 20,000
SALES: 4MM **Privately Held**
WEB: www.apioptics.com
SIC: 3827 Optical elements & assemblies, except ophthalmic
PA: Shadowfax Inc
　　141 S 7th St
　　Reading PA 19602
　　610 373-5177

(G-16321)
AMMERAAL BELTECH MODULAR INC
500 Brentwood Dr (19611-2015)
PHONE..................610 372-1800
Bo Danielsen, *President*
Paul Erik Damkjaer, *Chairman*
Christopher Amargo, *Engineer*
Bare Baldwin, *Sales Staff*
Lene Jrgensen, *Office Mgr*
▲ **EMP:** 33
SQ FT: 31,000
SALES (est): 5.9MM
SALES (corp-wide): 242.1K **Privately Held**
WEB: www.unichains.com
SIC: 3089 Hardware, plastic
HQ: Ammeraal Beltech Holding B.V.
　　Comeniusstraat 8
　　Alkmaar 1817
　　725 751-212

(G-16322)
ANGIOTECH PHARMACEUTICALS INC
1100 Berkshire Blvd # 308 (19610-1221)
PHONE..................610 404-1000
Kathleen Ferrara, *Senior VP*
EMP: 7 **EST:** 2016
SALES (est): 661.3K **Privately Held**
SIC: 2834 Pharmaceutical preparations

(G-16323)
ARROW INTERNATIONAL INC
1001 Hill Ave (19610-2017)
PHONE..................610 655-8522
Carl Botterbusch, *Branch Mgr*
EMP: 235
SALES (corp-wide): 2.1B **Publicly Held**
WEB: www.arrowintl.com
SIC: 3841 Catheters
HQ: Arrow International, Inc.
　　550 E Swedesford Rd # 400
　　Wayne PA 19087
　　610 225-6800

(G-16324)
ARROW INTERNATIONAL INC
2400 Bernville Rd (19605-9606)
P.O. Box 12, Durham NC (27702-0012)
PHONE..................610 378-0131
EMP: 235
SALES (corp-wide): 2.1B **Publicly Held**
WEB: www.arrowintl.com
SIC: 3841 Catheters
HQ: Arrow International, Inc.
　　550 E Swedesford Rd # 400
　　Wayne PA 19087
　　610 225-6800

(G-16325)
ATLAS COPCO COMPRESSORS LLC
260 Corporate Dr (19605-3339)
PHONE..................610 916-4002
Chris Fetting, *Manager*
EMP: 21
SALES (corp-wide): 13.8B **Privately Held**
WEB: www.atlascopco.com
SIC: 3563 Air & gas compressors
HQ: Atlas Copco Compressors Llc
　　300 Technology
　　Rock Hill SC 29730
　　866 472-1015

(G-16326)
AUSTIN HARDWARE
1001 Rockland St (19604-1520)
PHONE..................610 921-2723
EMP: 25
SALES (est): 1.6MM **Privately Held**
SIC: 3429 Mfg Hardware

(G-16327)
BARBETT INDUSTRIES INC
226 Cedar St (19601-3119)
PHONE..................610 372-2872
Frank J Loos Sr, *President*
Joe Loos, *Technology*
◆ **EMP:** 19 **EST:** 1979
SQ FT: 20,000
SALES: 1MM **Privately Held**
SIC: 2241 Bindings, textile

(G-16328)
BARCO INDUSTRIES INC
1020 Macarthur Rd (19605-9404)
PHONE..................610 374-3117
John E Rodgers, *CEO*
John Guers, *President*
Bob Harron, *Human Res Mgr*
Lisa Baer, *Cust Mgr*
Jim Halye, *Maintence Staff*
◆ **EMP:** 21
SQ FT: 45,000
SALES (est): 3.7MM **Privately Held**
WEB: www.pulaskitool.com
SIC: 3423 3469 3429 Hammers (hand tools); masons' hand tools; axes & hatchets; metal stampings; manufactured hardware (general)

(G-16329)
BERKS DIGITAL INC
2620 Hampden Blvd (19604-1011)
PHONE..................610 929-1200
Elaine Brown, *President*
Gary Brown, *Vice Pres*
EMP: 5
SQ FT: 3,500
SALES (est): 671.3K **Privately Held**
SIC: 2752 Commercial printing, offset

(G-16330)
BERKS ENGINEERING COMPANY
Reading Automatic Machine Div
1078 Stinson Dr (19605-9440)
PHONE..................610 926-4146
Joseph Codi, *Owner*
EMP: 23
SQ FT: 23,810
SALES (corp-wide): 6.6MM **Privately Held**
WEB: www.brownengco.com
SIC: 3599 Custom machinery
PA: Berks Engineering Company
　　1078 Stinson Dr
　　Reading PA
　　610 926-4146

(G-16331)
BERKS PRECISION MACHINE CORP
31 Catherine St Ste 1 (19607-1894)
PHONE..................610 603-0948
Jacob C Ruth, *President*
Charles Nydegger, *Corp Secy*
EMP: 4 **EST:** 1957
SQ FT: 10,000
SALES (est): 543.3K **Privately Held**
SIC: 3599 Machine shop, jobbing & repair

(G-16332)
BIMBO BAKERIES USA INC
Also Called: Maier's Bakery
640 Park Ave (19611-1926)
PHONE..................610 478-9369
Teresa Lambert, *Principal*
Gary Dunkelberger, *Manager*
EMP: 3 **Privately Held**
SIC: 2051 Bread, cake & related products
HQ: Bimbo Bakeries Usa, Inc
　　255 Business Center Dr # 200
　　Horsham PA 19044
　　215 347-5500

(G-16333)
BIMBO BAKERIES USA INC
Also Called: Stroehmann Bakeries 75
4432 Pottsville Pike (19605-1214)
PHONE..................610 921-2715
Michael Gustantino, *Branch Mgr*
EMP: 20 **Privately Held**
SIC: 2051 Bread, cake & related products
HQ: Bimbo Bakeries Usa, Inc
　　255 Business Center Dr # 200
　　Horsham PA 19044
　　215 347-5500

(G-16334)
BIRCHCRAFT KITCHENS INC (PA)
425 Richmond St (19605-3065)
PHONE..................610 375-4391
Elmer Martin, *President*
Timothy Howe, *Vice Pres*
EMP: 36
SQ FT: 20,000

▲ = Import ▼=Export
◆ =Import/Export

SALES (est): 4.8MM **Privately Held**
WEB: www.birchcraftkitchens.com
SIC: **2434** Wood kitchen cabinets

(G-16335)
BLANSKI ENERGY MANAGEMENT INC
1835 Pear St (19601-1216)
PHONE...................................610 373-5273
James Blanski, *President*
Matthew Blanski, *Vice Pres*
James Campbell, *Manager*
Bob Ganter, *Manager*
Phil Smith, *Comp Tech*
EMP: 45
SQ FT: 10,000
SALES (est): 6.3MM **Privately Held**
SIC: **1761** 1711 ·3444 Sheet metalwork; mechanical contractor; warm air heating & air conditioning contractor; ventilation & duct work contractor; sheet metalwork

(G-16336)
BRENTWOOD INDUSTRIES INC (PA)
Also Called: Brentwood Plastics Inc
500 Spring Ridge Dr (19610-1069)
P.O. Box 605 (19603-0605)
PHONE...................................610 374-5109
Peter Rye, *President*
Clinton McCorkle, *Vice Pres*
Peter Pellicano, *Treasurer*
Rita Rye, *Admin Sec*
◆ EMP: 150
SQ FT: 210,000
SALES (est): 194.6MM **Privately Held**
WEB: www.brentw.com
SIC: **3089** Molding primary plastic

(G-16337)
BULK CHEMICALS INC (PA)
1074 Stinson Dr (19605-9440)
PHONE...................................610 926-4128
Charles R Ike, *President*
Harry Adams, *General Mgr*
Percy A Satoris III, *Chairman*
Jose Rivera, *Vice Pres*
Tim Fudge, *Electrical Engi*
▲ EMP: 40 EST: 1974
SALES (est): 10.2MM **Privately Held**
SIC: **2819** Phosphates, except fertilizers: defluorinated & ammoniated

(G-16338)
BYRNE ENTERPRISES INC (PA)
Also Called: Budget Print Center
916 Bedford Ave (19607-2360)
PHONE...................................610 670-0767
James Byrne, *President*
Agnes G Byrne, *Corp Secy*
EMP: 4
SQ FT: 4,000
SALES (est): 566.7K **Privately Held**
WEB: www.budgetprintcenters.com
SIC: **2752** 7334 5943 Commercial printing, offset; photocopying & duplicating services; office forms & supplies

(G-16339)
C STRUNK INC
Also Called: Strunk Concrete Blocks
128 Green Valley Rd (19608-9742)
PHONE...................................610 678-1960
Carl P Strunk Jr, *President*
Stephen Strunk, *Vice Pres*
EMP: 8 EST: 1945
SQ FT: 3,500
SALES (est): 1.2MM **Privately Held**
SIC: **3271** Blocks, concrete or cinder: standard

(G-16340)
CAMBRIDGE-LEE HOLDINGS INC (HQ)
86 Tube Dr (19605-9274)
PHONE...................................610 926-4141
EMP: 15
SALES (est): 395.2MM **Privately Held**
SIC: **5051** 3351 5084 Steel; copper; aluminum bars, rods, ingots, sheets, pipes, plates, etc.; tubing, copper & copper alloy; machine tools & metalworking machinery

(G-16341)
CAMBRIDGE-LEE INDUSTRIES LLC (DH)
86 Tube Dr Plant 4 4 Plant (19605)
PHONE...................................610 926-4141
Dan Erck, *CEO*
David Spadafora, *Vice Pres*
Lynn Achey, *Plant Mgr*
Sara Aulestia, *Buyer*
Evelyn Walter, *Purchasing*
◆ EMP: 210 EST: 2004
SQ FT: 600,000
SALES (est): 54.8MM **Privately Held**
WEB: www.united-copper.com
SIC: **3351** 5051 Tubing, copper & copper alloy; steel; copper; aluminum bars, rods, ingots, sheets, pipes, plates, etc.
HQ: Iusa Wire, Inc.
74 Tube Dr
Reading PA 19605
610 926-4141

(G-16342)
CAN CORPORATION AMERICA INC
3723 Pottsville Pike (19605-1721)
PHONE...................................610 921-3460
Troy Toaldo, *Branch Mgr*
EMP: 24
SALES (corp-wide): 53.8MM **Privately Held**
SIC: **3411** Metal cans
PA: Can Corporation Of America, Inc.
326 June Ave
Blandon PA 19510
610 926-3044

(G-16343)
CARPENTER TECHNOLOGY CORP
2120 Centre Ave (19605-2818)
PHONE...................................610 208-2000
EMP: 4
SALES (corp-wide): 2.1B **Publicly Held**
SIC: **3312** Stainless steel; bar, rod & wire products; primary finished or semifinished shapes; tool & die steel
PA: Carpenter Technology Corporation
1735 Market St Fl 15
Philadelphia PA 19103
610 208-2000

(G-16344)
CARPENTER TECHNOLOGY CORP
101 Bern St (19601-1203)
P.O. Box 14662 (19612-4662)
PHONE...................................610 208-2000
James D Dee, *Vice Pres*
Robert Carnes, *Branch Mgr*
EMP: 33
SALES (corp-wide): 2.1B **Publicly Held**
SIC: **3312** Tool & die steel & alloys
PA: Carpenter Technology Corporation
1735 Market St Fl 15
Philadelphia PA 19103
610 208-2000

(G-16345)
CHIMA INC (PA)
1149 Bern Rd (19610-2060)
P.O. Box 6236 (19610-0236)
PHONE...................................610 372-6508
Douglas Heydt Jr, *President*
Douglas Heydt Sr, *President*
Alison Wilkins, *Shareholder*
EMP: 22
SQ FT: 10,000
SALES (est): 3.1MM **Privately Held**
WEB: www.chima.com
SIC: **2281** 3965 Knitting yarn, spun; pins & needles

(G-16346)
CLOVER FARMS DAIRY COMPANY (PA)
Also Called: Farmers Co-Op
3300 Pottsville Pike (19605)
P.O. Box 14627 (19612-4627)
PHONE...................................610 921-9111
Richard L Hartman, *President*
John B Rothenberger, *Corp Secy*
G R Rothenberger, *Vice Pres*
Ralph Reider, *Sales Mgr*
Dean Gibbel, *Director*

EMP: 285 EST: 1937
SALES (est): 68MM **Privately Held**
WEB: www.cloverfarms.com
SIC: **2086** 2033 2026 Iced tea & fruit drinks, bottled & canned; canned fruits & specialties; milk processing (pasteurizing, homogenizing, bottling)

(G-16347)
CLOVER FARMS TRANSPORTATION CO
3300 Pottsville Pike (19612)
P.O. Box 14627 (19612-4627)
PHONE...................................610 921-9111
Rodney L Speicher, *Principal*
Mike Davis, *QC Mgr*
EMP: 8
SALES (est): 971.6K **Privately Held**
SIC: **2026** Fluid milk

(G-16348)
CO OPTICS INC
1802 Papermill Rd (19610-1100)
PHONE...................................610 478-1884
Thomas Souders, *President*
Barbara Reisch, *Administration*
EMP: 4
SALES (est): 280K **Privately Held**
SIC: **3827** Optical instruments & lenses

(G-16349)
COCA-COLA BTLG CO POTTSVILLE
243 Snyder Rd (19605-9248)
PHONE...................................570 622-6991
Robert A Crosswell, *President*
Mary Jo Crosswell, *Vice Pres*
EMP: 32 EST: 1946
SQ FT: 23,000
SALES (est): 7MM **Privately Held**
SIC: **2086** Bottled & canned soft drinks

(G-16350)
COLUMBIAN CUTLERY COMPANY INC
440 Laurel St (19602-2643)
P.O. Box 123 (19603-0123)
PHONE...................................610 374-5762
George G Dougherty, *Ch of Bd*
Gholam R Ahmadi, *President*
Joyce M Germann, *Admin Sec*
EMP: 8 EST: 1895
SALES: 464.6K **Privately Held**
SIC: **3421** Scissors, shears, clippers, snips & similar tools

(G-16351)
COTTAGE COMMUNICATIONS INC
718 N Church Rd (19608-9723)
PHONE...................................610 678-7473
Randal Fegley, *President*
Constance Fegley, *Vice Pres*
EMP: 3
SALES: 80K **Privately Held**
SIC: **2731** Book publishing

(G-16352)
CRAFT-MAID KITCHEN INC
Also Called: Craft-Maid Custom Kitchens
501 S 9th St Bldg C (19602-2524)
PHONE...................................610 376-8686
Stuart B Zager, *President*
Gerald Goldberg, *Corp Secy*
Jerry Goldberg, *Corp Secy*
Stuart Quger, *Vice Pres*
Harold Massey, *Accountant*
▲ EMP: 50
SQ FT: 40,000
SALES (est): 8.6MM **Privately Held**
WEB: www.craft-maid.com
SIC: **2541** 2434 Wood partitions & fixtures; wood kitchen cabinets

(G-16353)
CRAIGG MANUFACTURING CORP
700 Henry Cir (19608-1507)
P.O. Box 901, Adamstown (19501-0901)
PHONE...................................610 678-8200
Gene Schlegel, *President*
Gene Schlegle, *Human Res Mgr*
EMP: 6
SQ FT: 9,000

SALES: 750K **Privately Held**
WEB: www.craigg.com
SIC: **3321** Manhole covers, metal

(G-16354)
CRONAN SHEET METAL INC
141 Schiller St (19601-2713)
PHONE...................................610 375-9230
James Cronan, *President*
EMP: 7 EST: 1959
SQ FT: 8,000
SALES (est): 1.3MM **Privately Held**
WEB: www.cronansheetmetal.com
SIC: **3444** Sheet metalwork

(G-16355)
CROSSROADS BEVERAGE GROUP LLC
1055 Crossroads Blvd (19605-9778)
P.O. Box 1029, Silver Springs FL (34489-1029)
PHONE...................................352 509-3127
Kyle Snyder, *Manager*
Cane E Richmond,
EMP: 5
SQ FT: 324,000
SALES (est): 1.3MM **Privately Held**
SIC: **2086** Mineral water, carbonated: packaged in cans, bottles, etc.

(G-16356)
CRYOVAC INC
4275 Reading Crest Ave (19605-1130)
PHONE...................................610 926-7500
John Larkin, *Branch Mgr*
EMP: 134
SALES (corp-wide): 4.7B **Publicly Held**
WEB: www.cryovac.com
SIC: **3086** Packaging & shipping materials, foamed plastic
HQ: Cryovac, Inc.
2415 Cascade Pointe Blvd
Charlotte NC 28208
980 430-7000

(G-16357)
CRYOVAC INC
1002 Patriot Pkwy (19605-2874)
PHONE...................................610 929-9190
EMP: 10
SALES (corp-wide): 4.7B **Publicly Held**
SIC: **3086** Packaging & shipping materials, foamed plastic
HQ: Cryovac, Inc.
2415 Cascade Pointe Blvd
Charlotte NC 28208
980 430-7000

(G-16358)
CURRY PRINTING & COPY
712 Corporate Dr (19605-1151)
PHONE...................................610 373-2890
Larry Lucas, *Owner*
EMP: 9
SALES (est): 818.4K **Privately Held**
WEB: www.currycandoit.com
SIC: **2752** 7334 Commercial printing, offset; photocopying & duplicating services

(G-16359)
CUSTOM PROCESSING SERVICES INC (PA)
2 Birchmont Dr Ste 3 (19606-3075)
PHONE...................................610 779-7001
Gregory J Shemanski, *President*
Jeff Klinger, *Vice Pres*
Jeffrey A Klinger, *Vice Pres*
William Lavelle, *Vice Pres*
Scott Lehr, *Plant Supt*
EMP: 30
SQ FT: 67,000
SALES (est): 11.6MM **Privately Held**
SIC: **3497** Magnesium & magnesium-base alloy foil

(G-16360)
DAVE ZERBE STUDIO
Also Called: David Zerbe
1135 N 5th St (19601-1810)
PHONE...................................610 376-0379
David Zerbe, *Owner*
EMP: 5
SQ FT: 6,000

SALES (est): 399.8K **Privately Held**
SIC: 7221 2752 7299 7335 Photographer, still or video; photo-offset printing; computer photography or portrait; commercial photography; picture framing, custom

(G-16361)
DIETRICHS MILK PRODUCTS LLC (HQ)
100 Mckinley Ave (19605-2117)
PHONE....................................610 929-5736
Thomas W Dietrich,
EMP: 90
SQ FT: 66,000
SALES (est): 8.4MM
SALES (corp-wide): 20.4MM **Privately Held**
SIC: 2023 2026 Dried nonfat milk; fluid milk

(G-16362)
DIGIORGIO MUSHROOM CORP (PA)
Also Called: Giorgio Foods
1161 Park Rd (19605)
P.O. Box 96, Temple (19560-0096)
PHONE....................................610 926-2139
Peter F Giorgi, *President*
Philip M Impink, *Corp Secy*
John Majaewski, *Vice Pres*
▲ **EMP:** 282 **EST:** 1960
SQ FT: 220,000
SALES (est): 40.6MM **Privately Held**
WEB: www.giorgimush.com
SIC: 2033 5148 2037 6512 Mushrooms: packaged in cans, jars, etc.; vegetables, fresh; vegetables, quick frozen & cold pack, excl. potato products; commercial & industrial building operation

(G-16363)
DIMENSIONS
1801 N 12th St (19604-1527)
PHONE....................................610 939-9900
Bruce H Bossidy, *President*
Keith Derr, *Vice Pres*
▲ **EMP:** 6
SALES (est): 916.8K **Privately Held**
SIC: 3944 Craft & hobby kits & sets

(G-16364)
DOR-MAE INDUSTRIES INC
4001 Reading Crest Ave (19605-1155)
P.O. Box 13069 (19612-3069)
PHONE....................................610 929-5003
Mitzi J Reitnouer, *President*
Pam Houck, *Vice Pres*
EMP: 46
SQ FT: 130,000
SALES (est): 9.5MM **Privately Held**
SIC: 3599 Machine shop, jobbing & repair

(G-16365)
DOW CHEMICAL COMPANY
3 Commerce Dr (19607-9780)
PHONE....................................610 775-6640
EMP: 120
SALES (corp-wide): 85.9B **Publicly Held**
SIC: 2819 2821 Industrial inorganic chemicals; plastics materials & resins
HQ: The Dow Chemical Company
2211 H H Dow Way
Midland MI 48642
989 636-1000

(G-16366)
DURYEA TECHNOLOGIES INC
1060 Old Bernville Rd # 300 (19605-9601)
PHONE....................................610 939-0480
Daniel J Sodomsky, *President*
Michael Sharer, *Vice Pres*
Tom Tessier, *CFO*
▼ **EMP:** 8
SQ FT: 5,000
SALES (est): 2.1MM **Privately Held**
WEB: www.ecycle.com
SIC: 3621 3699 Motors, electric; electric sound equipment

(G-16367)
DYNAFLO INC
10 Vanguard Dr Ste 20 (19606-3763)
PHONE....................................610 200-8017
William T Fleming, *President*
EMP: 5 **EST:** 1997

SALES (est): 589.9K **Privately Held**
WEB: www.dynaflopumps.com
SIC: 3563 3561 Air & gas compressors; pumps & pumping equipment

(G-16368)
EAST PENN MANUFACTURING CO
1002 Patriot Pkwy (19605-2874)
PHONE....................................610 929-4920
EMP: 6
SALES (corp-wide): 2.5B **Privately Held**
SIC: 3694 Battery cable wiring sets for internal combustion engines
PA: East Penn Manufacturing Co.
102 Deka Rd
Lyon Station PA 19536
610 682-6361

(G-16369)
EASTERN SLEEP PRODUCTS COMPANY
Also Called: Symbol Mattress
71 Vanguard Dr (19606-3765)
PHONE....................................610 582-7228
Doug Wilcox, *Business Mgr*
Tara Bissell, *Personnel Assist*
EMP: 45
SQ FT: 27,600
SALES (corp-wide): 118.7MM **Privately Held**
WEB: www.symbolmattress.com
SIC: 2515 Mattresses, innerspring or box spring
PA: Eastern Sleep Products Company
4901 Fitzhugh Ave
Richmond VA 23230
804 254-1711

(G-16370)
ELBECO INCORPORATED (PA)
4418 Pottsville Pike (19605-1214)
P.O. Box 13099 (19612-3099)
PHONE....................................610 921-0651
David L Lurio, *President*
David R Adams, *Vice Pres*
Rickie Brightbill, *Treasurer*
Douglas M Lurio, *Admin Sec*
◆ **EMP:** 53 **EST:** 1907
SQ FT: 75,200
SALES (est): 63.6MM **Privately Held**
WEB: www.elbeco.com
SIC: 2321 2326 Uniform shirts: made from purchased materials; work pants; jackets, overall & work

(G-16371)
ELEC CONST JT
20 Morgan Dr (19608-1753)
PHONE....................................610 777-3150
Randy Keifer, *Principal*
EMP: 8
SALES (est): 701.1K **Privately Held**
SIC: 3643 Current-carrying wiring devices

(G-16372)
ELGE PRECISION MACHINING INC
Also Called: Elge Spark Wheel Co
360 Blair Ave (19601-1908)
PHONE....................................610 376-5458
Hermann R Pfisterer, *President*
Robert S Pfisterer, *Vice Pres*
EMP: 15 **EST:** 1946
SQ FT: 15,000
SALES (est): 2.7MM **Privately Held**
WEB: www.elgeprecision.com
SIC: 3451 3423 3291 Screw machine products; hand & edge tools; abrasive products

(G-16373)
ENCHANTED ACRES FARM GROUP LLC
200 N 8th St Ste 500 (19601-4129)
PHONE....................................877 707-3833
EMP: 6
SALES (est): 766.6K **Privately Held**
SIC: 3565 Bottling & canning machinery

(G-16374)
ENCOMPASS HEALTH CORPORATION
Also Called: HealthSouth
1025 Berkshire Blvd # 500 (19610-1281)
PHONE....................................610 478-8797
James Ziner, *Manager*
EMP: 16
SQ FT: 7,678
SALES (corp-wide): 4.2B **Publicly Held**
WEB: www.healthsouth.com
SIC: 3829 Medical diagnostic systems, nuclear
PA: Encompass Health Corporation
9001 Liberty Pkwy
Birmingham AL 35242
205 967-7116

(G-16375)
ENERSYS (PA)
2366 Bernville Rd (19605-9457)
P.O. Box 14145 (19612-4145)
PHONE....................................610 208-1991
Arthur T Katsaros, *Ch of Bd*
David M Shaffer, *President*
Holger P Aschk, *President*
Myles Jones, *President*
Jeffrey W Long, *President*
◆ **EMP:** 200
SALES: 2.5B **Publicly Held**
WEB: www.enersys.com
SIC: 3691 3699 5063 Lead acid batteries (storage batteries); electrical equipment & supplies; electrical apparatus & equipment

(G-16376)
ENERSYS CAPITAL INC (HQ)
2366 Bernville Rd (19605-9457)
PHONE....................................610 208-1991
John Craig, *Ch of Bd*
EMP: 10
SQ FT: 109,000
SALES (est): 20.2MM
SALES (corp-wide): 2.5B **Publicly Held**
SIC: 3691 Lead acid batteries (storage batteries)
PA: Enersys
2366 Bernville Rd
Reading PA 19605
610 208-1991

(G-16377)
ENERSYS DELAWARE INC (HQ)
2366 Bernville Rd (19605-9457)
P.O. Box 14145 (19612-4145)
PHONE....................................214 324-8990
Richard W Zuidema, *Exec VP*
Michael J Schmidtlein, *Vice Pres*
Thomas L Oneill, *Treasurer*
Joseph G Lewis, *Admin Sec*
▲ **EMP:** 276
SALES (est): 1.2B
SALES (corp-wide): 2.5B **Publicly Held**
SIC: 3691 5063 Lead acid batteries (storage batteries); electrical apparatus & equipment
PA: Enersys
2366 Bernville Rd
Reading PA 19605
610 208-1991

(G-16378)
EQUINE SPECIALTY FEED CO
122 W Lancaster Ave (19607-1881)
PHONE....................................610 796-5670
EMP: 15
SALES (est): 956.8K **Privately Held**
SIC: 5191 2048 Animal feeds; prepared feeds

(G-16379)
ERGON ASPHALT & EMULSIONS INC
3847 Pottsville Pike (19605-1723)
PHONE....................................610 921-0271
EMP: 4
SALES (est): 430K **Privately Held**
SIC: 5032 2911 Asphalt mixture; asphalt or asphaltic materials, made in refineries

(G-16380)
ESF ENTERPRISE LLC
35 Queen St (19608-1137)
PHONE....................................610 334-2615

Daniel Shaffer, *President*
EMP: 5
SALES (est): 348.6K **Privately Held**
SIC: 2899 Chemical preparations

(G-16381)
EVRAZ INC NA
1290 Broadcasting Rd (19610-3203)
PHONE....................................610 743-5970
EMP: 700
SALES (corp-wide): 10.8B **Privately Held**
SIC: 3312 Blast furnaces & steel mills
HQ: Evraz Inc. Na
200 E Randolph St # 7800
Chicago IL 60601
312 533-3555

(G-16382)
EXIDE CORPORATION SMELTER
300 Spring Valley Rd (19605)
PHONE....................................610 921-4003
Tim Harris, *Manager*
EMP: 14
SALES (est): 3.8MM **Privately Held**
SIC: 3691 Batteries, rechargeable

(G-16383)
EXIDE TECHNOLOGIES
Exide Marketing Services
3000 Montrose Ave (19605-2751)
PHONE....................................610 921-4055
Jim Miller, *Branch Mgr*
EMP: 25
SALES (corp-wide): 2.4B **Privately Held**
WEB: www.exideworld.com
SIC: 5013 3629 Automotive batteries; battery chargers, rectifying or nonrotating
PA: Exide Technologies
13000 Deerfield Pkwy # 200
Milton GA 30004
678 566-9000

(G-16384)
F M BROWNS SONS INCORPORATED (PA)
205 Woodrow Ave (19608-1402)
P.O. Box 2116 (19608-0116)
PHONE....................................800 334-8816
Franklin M Brown Jr, *President*
Thomas E Brown, *Vice Pres*
Chris Gockley, *Warehouse Mgr*
Carl A Brown, *Treasurer*
Julie McKechnie, *Human Resources*
◆ **EMP:** 90
SQ FT: 35,000
SALES (est): 57.1MM **Privately Held**
WEB: www.fmbrown.com
SIC: 2041 0723 2048 5191 Flour; crop preparation services for market; bird food, prepared; feed

(G-16385)
FIDELITY TECHNOLOGIES CORP (PA)
2501 Kutztown Rd (19605-2961)
PHONE....................................610 929-3330
Jack D Gulati, *CEO*
Charles I Gulati, *Vice Pres*
Mark Dicocco, *Opers Staff*
David Nordschow, *Opers Staff*
Alexander Cubby, *Engineer*
▲ **EMP:** 110
SQ FT: 77,000
SALES (est): 49.2MM **Privately Held**
WEB: www.fidelitytech.com
SIC: 3663 Radio & TV communications equipment

(G-16386)
FUTERNAL ORDER POLICE LODGE
Also Called: Reading City Police Department
815 Washington St (19601-3615)
PHONE....................................610 655-6116
Barry Ranbo, *President*
Frank Deweski, *Chief*
EMP: 4
SALES (est): 120K **Privately Held**
SIC: 2389 Apparel & accessories

(G-16387)
G & M CO INC
1250 Roosevelt Ave (19606-1352)
P.O. Box 4009 (19606-0409)
PHONE....................................610 779-7812

William T Markle Jr, *President*
Lee High, *Admin Sec*
EMP: 18
SQ FT: 25,000
SALES: 3.5MM **Privately Held**
WEB: www.gandmco.com
SIC: 3469 3599 3544 Metal stampings; machine shop, jobbing & repair; special dies, tools, jigs & fixtures

(G-16388)
GAI-TRONICS CORPORATION (HQ)
3030 Kutztown Rd (19605-2617)
PHONE..................................610 777-1374
Rodd R Ruland, *President*
Bruce Held, *Managing Dir*
Carrie Brynan, *Vice Pres*
Wayne A Cable, *Vice Pres*
Bret Hatt, *Vice Pres*
◆ **EMP:** 240
SQ FT: 105,858
SALES (est): 71.4MM
SALES (corp-wide): 4.4B **Publicly Held**
WEB: www.gaitronics.com
SIC: 3661 3663 Telephones & telephone apparatus; radio & TV communications equipment
PA: Hubbell Incorporated
40 Waterview Dr
Shelton CT 06484
475 882-4000

(G-16389)
GARDA CL TECHNICAL SVCS INC
Also Called: A T I Systems A Garda Company
500 Corporate Dr Bldg 5 (19605-1149)
PHONE..................................610 926-7400
Jeanne Weidner, *Branch Mgr*
EMP: 100 **Privately Held**
WEB: www.gocashlink.com
SIC: 7381 4513 3578 Armored car services; security guard service; air courier services; coin counters; change making machines
HQ: Garda Cl Technical Services, Inc.
700 S Federal Hwy Ste 300
Boca Raton FL 33432

(G-16390)
GENERAL POLYMERIC CORPORATION
Also Called: Genpore
1136 Morgantown Rd (19607-9522)
P.O. Box 380 (19607-0380)
PHONE..................................610 374-5171
Joseph E Ferri, *President*
Pt Sreekumar, *Managing Dir*
Rose M Ferri, *Corp Secy*
Joe Borelli, *Vice Pres*
Ryan Cannon, *Engineer*
▲ **EMP:** 62
SQ FT: 115,000
SALES (est): 16.7MM **Privately Held**
WEB: www.genpore.com
SIC: 2821 2992 Plastics materials & resins; lubricating oils & greases

(G-16391)
GIORGIO FOODS INC (HQ)
1161 Park Rd (19605)
P.O. Box 96, Temple (19560-0096)
PHONE..................................610 926-2139
John Majaewski, *President*
Philip M Impink, *Corp Secy*
Ginaro Quaglia, *Vice Pres*
▲ **EMP:** 151 **EST:** 1960
SQ FT: 220,000
SALES (est): 92.4MM
SALES (corp-wide): 40.6MM **Privately Held**
WEB: www.giorgiofoods.com
SIC: 2033 2037 5148 2038 Mushrooms: packaged in cans, jars, etc.; vegetables, quick frozen & cold pack, excl. potato products; vegetables, fresh; frozen specialties
PA: Digiorgio Mushroom Corp.
1161 Park Rd
Reading PA 19605
610 926-2139

(G-16392)
GLAXOSMITHKLINE LLC
42 Golfview Ln (19606-9598)
PHONE..................................610 779-4774
EMP: 27
SALES (corp-wide): 36.5B **Privately Held**
SIC: 2834 Mfg Pharmaceuticals
HQ: Glaxosmithkline Llc
5 Crescent Dr
Philadelphia PA 19112
215 751-4000

(G-16393)
GLEN-GERY CORPORATION (DH)
Also Called: Glen Gery Brick
1166 Spring St (19610-1721)
P.O. Box 7001 (19610-6001)
PHONE..................................610 374-4011
Steve Matsick, *Ch of Bd*
Melissa Hepner, *Sales Staff*
Jeff Patterson, *Sales Staff*
Denise Smith, *Marketing Staff*
Chris Brophy, *Manager*
▲ **EMP:** 50
SQ FT: 30,000
SALES (est): 238MM
SALES (corp-wide): 1.2MM **Privately Held**
WEB: www.glengerybrick.com
SIC: 3251 Brick clay: common face, glazed, vitrified or hollow

(G-16394)
GODIVA CHOCOLATIER INC
650 E Neversink Rd (19606-3061)
PHONE..................................610 779-3797
Eileen Sandor, *Buyer*
Don Carlson, *QC Mgr*
Stephanie Shearer, *Hum Res Coord*
John A Kessler, *Personnel*
Robert J Smith, *Marketing Staff*
EMP: 500
SQ FT: 154,167 **Privately Held**
WEB: www.godiva.com
SIC: 2064 2066 Candy & other confectionery products; chocolate
HQ: Godiva Chocolatier, Inc.
333 W 34th St Fl 6
New York NY 10001
212 984-5900

(G-16395)
GORDEN INC (PA)
201 Inspiration Blvd # 400 (19607-9561)
PHONE..................................610 644-4476
William Gorden, *President*
Doris B Gorden, *Treasurer*
EMP: 3
SALES (est): 544.6K **Privately Held**
WEB: www.gorden.org
SIC: 6531 3679 5099 Real estate managers; electronic circuits; musical instruments parts & accessories

(G-16396)
GRAFIKA COMMERCIAL PRTG INC
710 Johnston St (19608-1437)
P.O. Box 2153 (19608-0153)
PHONE..................................610 678-8630
Bernard J Elzer Jr, *President*
Bernard J Elzer III, *COO*
Bernie Elzer, *COO*
Robert Zedaker, *CFO*
Kory Luginbuhl, *Accounts Mgr*
EMP: 258
SQ FT: 125,000
SALES (est): 47.3MM **Privately Held**
WEB: www.grafikaprint.com
SIC: 2752 2789 2672 2396 Commercial printing, offset; bookbinding & related work; coated & laminated paper; automotive & apparel trimmings; screen printing

(G-16397)
GUY HREZIK
Also Called: Exeter Printing
3209 Oley Turnpike Rd (19606-2369)
P.O. Box 4431 (19606-0131)
PHONE..................................610 779-7609
Guy Hrezik, *Owner*
EMP: 4
SQ FT: 3,000

SALES (est): 363K **Privately Held**
SIC: 2752 2791 2789 Commercial printing, lithographic; typesetting; bookbinding & related work

(G-16398)
HANNAHOES PALLETS & SKIDS
Also Called: Hannahoe Pallets
39 Riverside Dr (19605-9275)
PHONE..................................610 926-4699
Stacy Hanahoe, *President*
Michael Polley, *Vice Pres*
EMP: 17
SQ FT: 6,000
SALES (est): 2.1MM **Privately Held**
SIC: 2448 Pallets, wood; pallets, wood & wood with metal

(G-16399)
HAWKE AEROSPACE HOLDINGS LLC
128 W Apron Dr (19605-9403)
PHONE..................................610 372-5141
EMP: 17
SALES (corp-wide): 15MM **Privately Held**
SIC: 3999 Barber & beauty shop equipment
PA: Hawke Aerospace Holdings, Llc
189a Twin County Rd
Morgantown PA 19543
610 372-5191

(G-16400)
HENSON COMPANY INC
Also Called: Brute Group
8 Corporate Blvd (19608-8942)
PHONE..................................800 486-2788
Butler Glen, *CEO*
Purnell John, *President*
▲ **EMP:** 60
SQ FT: 16,500
SALES (est): 8.5MM **Privately Held**
WEB: www.brute.com
SIC: 2329 5091 2339 Men's & boys' athletic uniforms; athletic (warmup, sweat & jogging) suits: men's & boys'; sporting & recreation goods; women's & misses' outerwear

(G-16401)
HESS EMBROIDERY & UNIFORMS LLC
694 Reading Ave (19611-1010)
PHONE..................................610 816-5234
Linda Beam, *Mng Member*
EMP: 5
SALES (est): 631.6K **Privately Held**
SIC: 2395 Embroidery products, except schiffli machine; embroidery & art needlework

(G-16402)
HEYCO METALS INC (PA)
1069 Stinson Dr (19605-9464)
PHONE..................................610 926-4131
Michael P Jemison, *President*
Michael S Jemison, *Chairman*
Bill Barry, *Vice Pres*
Jhon Lamastra, *Vice Pres*
Ken Ritter, *CFO*
▲ **EMP:** 80
SQ FT: 110,000
SALES (est): 21.7MM **Privately Held**
WEB: www.heyco-metals.com
SIC: 3351 3366 3341 3331 Rolled or drawn shapes: copper & copper alloy; bronze rolling & drawing; brass rolling & drawing; copper foundries; secondary nonferrous metals; primary copper

(G-16403)
HOFMANN INDUSTRIES INC
3145 Shillington Rd (19608-1606)
PHONE..................................610 678-8051
Bernard M Hofmann, *Ch of Bd*
Stephen P Owens, *President*
Jeffrey C Hills, *Vice Pres*
John J Masley, *Vice Pres*
J P Owens, *Vice Pres*
▲ **EMP:** 275 **EST:** 1952
SQ FT: 315,400

SALES (est): 67.8MM **Privately Held**
WEB: www.hofmann.com
SIC: 3317 3498 3471 3479 Tubes, wrought: welded or lock joint; fabricated pipe & fittings; plating & polishing; coating of metals & formed products

(G-16404)
HORIZON SOFTWARE SOLUTIONS
223 Knott 6th St (19601)
PHONE..................................610 225-0989
Venkat Tandra, *Owner*
Rajendra Marpu, *Co-Owner*
EMP: 5
SALES: 500K **Privately Held**
SIC: 7372 Prepackaged software

(G-16405)
HYDROJET SERVICES INC
450 Gateway Dr (19601-2641)
PHONE..................................610 375-7500
Catharine Rado, *President*
Michael Rado, *Exec VP*
Jeremy Johnson, *Vice Pres*
Nelson H Long, *Treasurer*
EMP: 35
SQ FT: 35,000
SALES (est): 8.1MM **Privately Held**
WEB: www.hydrojet.com
SIC: 3599 Machine shop, jobbing & repair

(G-16406)
IFS INDUSTRIES INC (PA)
400 Orton Ave (19603)
P.O. Box 1053 (19603-1053)
PHONE..................................610 378-1381
Jack Chambers, *President*
Eric Delong, *Exec VP*
Patrick H Donahue, *Vice Pres*
Blair Philips, *CFO*
◆ **EMP:** 200
SQ FT: 27,800
SALES (est): 135MM **Privately Held**
WEB: www.ifscos.com
SIC: 2899 Chemical preparations

(G-16407)
INDUSTRIAL METAL PLATING INC
153 Wagner Ln (19601-1158)
PHONE..................................610 374-5107
Gregory J Maack, *President*
Webster Canning, *Vice Pres*
Gregory A Maack, *Treasurer*
Marjorie T Grube, *Admin Sec*
EMP: 100 **EST:** 1959
SQ FT: 40,000
SALES (est): 15.9MM **Privately Held**
WEB: www.indmp.com
SIC: 3471 Anodizing (plating) of metals or formed products

(G-16408)
INTERSTATE CONT BRUNSWICK LLC
100 Grace St (19611-1977)
PHONE..................................610 208-9300
Charles Feghali, *President*
Antoine N Frem, *Principal*
Ramez Skaff, *Admin Sec*
▲ **EMP:** 45 **EST:** 1948
SQ FT: 80,000
SALES (est): 8.6MM
SALES (corp-wide): 8B **Privately Held**
WEB: www.indevcogroup.com
SIC: 2653 Boxes, corrugated: made from purchased materials
HQ: Interstate Resources, Inc.
1300 Wilson Blvd Ste 1075
Arlington VA 22209
703 243-3355

(G-16409)
INTERSTATE CONT READING LLC
100 Grace St (19611-1977)
PHONE..................................800 822-2002
Tony Frem, *CEO*
Jim Morgan, *COO*
Pierre Khattar, *CFO*
▲ **EMP:** 240
SQ FT: 180,000

SALES (est): 186.6K
SALES (corp-wide): 8B Privately Held
SIC: 5113 2653 Boxes & containers; boxes, solid fiber: made from purchased materials
HQ: Interstate Resources, Inc.
1300 Wilson Blvd Ste 1075
Arlington VA 22209
703 243-3355

(G-16410)
IUSA WIRE INC (DH)
74 Tube Dr (19605)
PHONE..................................610 926-4141
Andrea Sunk, President
Carlos Peralta, Chairman
EMP: 8
SALES (est): 60.9MM Privately Held
SIC: 3351 5051 Tubing, copper & copper alloy; piling, iron & steel

(G-16411)
J BENSON CORP (PA)
Also Called: Campbell Companies
2201 Reading Ave (19609-2051)
PHONE..................................610 678-2692
J Benson Campbell, President
Alton P Haney, Vice Pres
EMP: 8 EST: 1945
SQ FT: 30,000
SALES (est): 26.4MM Privately Held
SIC: 5162 3083 3082 3081 Plastics products; laminated plastics plate & sheet; unsupported plastics profile shapes; unsupported plastics film & sheet

(G-16412)
JACK OREILLY TUXEDOS (PA)
Also Called: Tuxedos By Jack O'Reilly
1501 Rockland St (19604-1408)
PHONE..................................610 929-9409
John O'Reilly, Owner
Jim O'Reilly, Manager
EMP: 5 EST: 1952
SALES (est): 407.4K Privately Held
SIC: 7299 2311 Tuxedo rental; tuxedos: made from purchased materials

(G-16413)
JDH PACIFIC INC
4201 Pottsville Pike (19605-1219)
PHONE..................................562 926-8088
EMP: 43
SALES (corp-wide): 33.4MM Privately Held
SIC: 3321 Gray iron castings
PA: Jdh Pacific, Inc.
14821 Artesia Blvd
La Mirada CA 90638
562 926-8088

(G-16414)
JET PLATE INC
1840 Cotton St (19606-1713)
PHONE..................................610 373-6600
Guy A Weaver, President
Jack K Weaver, Admin Sec
EMP: 10
SQ FT: 5,000
SALES (est): 940K Privately Held
SIC: 3559 Electroplating machinery & equipment

(G-16415)
JOE GIGLIOTTI & SONS ORNAMENT
1530 Lancaster Ave Rear (19607-1560)
PHONE..................................610 775-3532
Larry Goldberg, President
EMP: 12
SALES (est): 1.3MM Privately Held
SIC: 3442 Metal doors, sash & trim

(G-16416)
JPMS MANUFACTURING LLC
237 Buttonwood St (19601-2950)
PHONE..................................610 373-1007
James Martrave, General Mgr
▲ EMP: 33
SALES (est): 6.3MM
SALES (corp-wide): 136.7MM Privately Held
SIC: 2844 Hair coloring preparations

PA: John Paul Mitchell Systems
20705 Centre Pointe Pkwy
Santa Clarita CA 91350
310 248-3888

(G-16417)
K & L WOODWORKING INC
440 N 4th St (19601-2847)
PHONE..................................610 372-0738
Perry Riegel, President
Kevin Hartman, Vice Pres
Brian Heinrich, Supervisor
EMP: 30
SQ FT: 35,000
SALES (est): 5.1MM Privately Held
WEB: www.klwood.com
SIC: 2431 Millwork

(G-16418)
KAPP ADVERTISING SERVICES INC
Also Called: Greater Reading Merchandiser
4239 Penn Ave Ste 11 (19608-1373)
PHONE..................................610 670-2595
Lewis Kahl, Manager
EMP: 20
SALES (est): 1.2MM
SALES (corp-wide): 10.8MM Privately Held
WEB: www.themerchandiser.com
SIC: 2741 Guides: publishing & printing; shopping news: publishing & printing
PA: Kapp Advertising Service, Inc.
100 E Cumberland St
Lebanon PA 17042
717 270-2742

(G-16419)
KEYSTONE ABRASIVES CO
621 Hiesters Ln (19605-3049)
PHONE..................................610 939-1060
Stephen Burns, President
Ted Mullens, Vice Pres
Ted Mullins, Vice Pres
EMP: 15 EST: 1996
SQ FT: 90,000
SALES (est): 1.9MM Privately Held
WEB: www.keystoneabrasives.com
SIC: 3291 5085 Coated abrasive products; abrasives

(G-16420)
KEYSTONE CONTAINERS INC
4201 Pottsville Pike # 2 (19605-1219)
PHONE..................................603 888-1315
EMP: 83
SALES (est): 6.2MM Privately Held
SIC: 3089 Plastic containers, except foam
PA: Carr Management, Inc.
1 Tara Blvd Ste 303
Nashua NH 03062

(G-16421)
KEYSTONE SFTWR SOLUTIONS INC
844 Centre Ave (19601-2550)
PHONE..................................610 685-2111
William Delgado, President
Tina Kercher, Corp Secy
Sam Wandzilak, Vice Pres
EMP: 8
SQ FT: 1,000
SALES (est): 543.8K Privately Held
WEB: www.keystonesoftware.com
SIC: 7379 7372 Computer related consulting services; prepackaged software

(G-16422)
KMN PACKAGING INC
Also Called: Kmn Associates
1610 Meadowlark Rd (19610-2821)
PHONE..................................610 376-3606
EMP: 3
SALES (est): 234.4K Privately Held
SIC: 2621 Paper Mill

(G-16423)
KREITZ WLDG & FABRICATION INC
788 Fritztown Rd (19608-1597)
PHONE..................................610 678-6010
Donald Kreitz Sr, President
Marian Kreitz, Admin Sec
EMP: 10 EST: 1970
SQ FT: 16,000

SALES (est): 2MM Privately Held
WEB: www.daveely.com
SIC: 3441 Structural Metal Fabrication

(G-16424)
L & H SIGNS INC
425 N 3rd St (19601-2812)
PHONE..................................610 374-2748
Chkisivphlk W Heinly, President
Christopher W Heinly, Corp Secy
Matt Robinson, VP Opers
Corey Woodman, Project Mgr
Jennifer Stitzer, Purch Mgr
EMP: 37
SQ FT: 50,000
SALES (est): 7.4MM Privately Held
WEB: www.lhsigns.com
SIC: 3993 Electric signs

(G-16425)
L A DRAPERIES INC
Also Called: L A Card and Gift
101 Newport Ave (19611-1853)
PHONE..................................610 375-2224
Linda I Dentala, President
EMP: 5
SQ FT: 9,500
SALES (est): 332.9K Privately Held
SIC: 5714 2391 5947 Draperies; draperies, plastic & textile: from purchased materials; gift, novelty & souvenir shop; greeting cards

(G-16426)
LAKELAND INDUSTRIES INC
5 Dutch Ct Ste C (19608-8987)
PHONE..................................610 775-0505
EMP: 4
SALES (corp-wide): 95.9MM Publicly Held
SIC: 2389 3842 Disposable garments & accessories; personal safety equipment; clothing, fire resistant & protective; gloves, safety
PA: Lakeland Industries, Inc.
3555 Vtrans Mem Hwy Ste C
Ronkonkoma NY 11779
631 981-9700

(G-16427)
LAURELDALE TOOL CO INC
3215 Holtry St (19605-2549)
PHONE..................................610 929-5406
Anna May Reedy, President
John Reedy III, Corp Secy
Mark Reedy, Vice Pres
EMP: 4 EST: 1963
SQ FT: 2,000
SALES: 200K Privately Held
SIC: 3544 Special dies & tools

(G-16428)
LEICO MANUFACTURING CORP
981 River Rd (19601-2039)
PHONE..................................610 376-8288
John Leimgruber, President
EMP: 4 EST: 1966
SALES (est): 434.5K Privately Held
SIC: 3599 Machine shop, jobbing & repair

(G-16429)
LINBOB LLC
Also Called: Sign-A-Rama
82 Commerce Dr (19610-3313)
PHONE..................................610 375-7446
Robert Myers, Partner
Linda Myers, Partner
EMP: 4
SALES (est): 406.5K Privately Held
SIC: 3993 Signs & advertising specialties

(G-16430)
LINCOLN INDUSTRIAL CHEMICAL CO
Also Called: The Lincoln Company
600 S 9th St (19602-2506)
P.O. Box 381 (19603-0381)
PHONE..................................610 375-4596
Thomas R Ziemer, President
EMP: 10
SQ FT: 72,000
SALES (est): 1.1MM Privately Held
WEB: www.thelincolncompany.com
SIC: 2841 2842 Detergents, synthetic organic or inorganic alkaline; polishing preparations & related products

(G-16431)
LITTLE PARTNERS INC
501 S 9th St (19602-2524)
PHONE..................................318 220-7005
Carol Gamble, President
▲ EMP: 3
SALES (est): 270K Privately Held
WEB: www.littlepartners.com
SIC: 2511 2514 5999 Children's wood furniture; juvenile furniture: wood; camp furniture: wood; juvenile furniture, household: metal; children's furniture

(G-16432)
LMT CORP OF PENNSYLVANIA
Also Called: Great Socks
205 E Bellevue Ave (19605-1733)
PHONE..................................610 921-3926
Jeff Tarnoff, President
▲ EMP: 26
SALES (est): 8.7MM
SALES (corp-wide): 28.2MM Privately Held
SIC: 2211 Broadwoven fabric mills, cotton
PA: Great Socks, Llc
7001 N Park Dr
Pennsauken NJ 08109
856 964-9700

(G-16433)
LONE STAR WESTERN BEEF INC
115 Little Rock Rd (19605-2750)
PHONE..................................484 509-2093
EMP: 5
SALES (est): 331.4K Privately Held
SIC: 2011 Beef products from beef slaughtered on site

(G-16434)
LOUISE GRACE PUBLISHING
2368 High St (19605-2829)
PHONE..................................610 781-6874
Carol Clouse, Principal
EMP: 4
SALES (est): 170.6K Privately Held
SIC: 2741 Miscellaneous publishing

(G-16435)
M B MUMMA INC
503 Penn St Ste 2 (19601-3462)
P.O. Box 64, Wernersville (19565-0064)
PHONE..................................610 372-6962
Michael Mumma, President
Andrea Stahl, Manager
EMP: 8
SQ FT: 3,000
SALES (est): 748.1K Privately Held
WEB: www.mbmumma.com
SIC: 3911 Jewelry, precious metal

(G-16436)
M J STRANKO INC
2413 Hampden Blvd (19604-1006)
PHONE..................................610 929-8080
Michael Stranko, President
Michele P Stranko, CFO
EMP: 4
SQ FT: 2,000
SALES: 400K Privately Held
SIC: 3297 Cement: high temperature, refractory (nonclay)

(G-16437)
MARANDO INDUSTRIES INC
90 Water St (19605-1210)
PHONE..................................610 621-2536
Richard Marando, President
Rich Marando, Sales Staff
EMP: 5
SALES: 1.5MM Privately Held
SIC: 7699 3569 3599 5084 Industrial machinery & equipment repair; lubrication machinery, automatic; custom machinery; metalworking machinery; mechanical engineering

(G-16438)
MARTINS POTATO CHIPS INC
7 Morgan Dr (19608-1754)
PHONE..................................610 777-3643
Kenneth Potter, President
EMP: 9

▲ = Import ▼ =Export
◆ =Import/Export

SALES (corp-wide): 47.3MM **Privately Held**
WEB: www.martinschips.com
SIC: 2096 Potato chips & similar snacks
PA: Martin's Potato Chips, Inc.
5847 Lincoln Hwy W
Thomasville PA 17364
717 792-3065

(G-16439)
MASS INDUSTRIAL CONTROL
19 Woodrow Ave (19608-1117)
PHONE.................................610 678-8228
Gurmeet Singh, *President*
Colleen Singh, *Vice Pres*
George Tattetshell, *Sales Staff*
EMP: 9
SQ FT: 3,000
SALES (est): 1.7MM **Privately Held**
WEB: www.massindustrial.com
SIC: 3625 Relays & industrial controls

(G-16440)
MBR INC
720 Laurel St (19602-2718)
P.O. Box 184, New Ringgold (17960-0184)
PHONE.................................570 386-8820
EMP: 4
SALES (est): 355.6K **Privately Held**
SIC: 3271 Brick, concrete

(G-16441)
METALSA SA DE CV
1100 Weiser St (19601-1461)
P.O. Box 13459 (19612-3459)
PHONE.................................610 371-7000
Perry Landis, *Branch Mgr*
EMP: 208 **Privately Held**
SIC: 8744 3713 Facilities support services; truck & bus bodies
HQ: Metalsa, S.A. De C.V.
Km. 16.5 Carr. Miguel Aleman
Apodaca N.L. 66600

(G-16442)
MICROSEMI CORP
2136 N 13th St Ste D (19604-1213)
PHONE.................................610 929-7142
George Terefenko, *Director*
Greg Jones, *Director*
EMP: 25
SALES (est): 2.2MM **Privately Held**
SIC: 3674 Semiconductors & related devices

(G-16443)
MIFFLIN VALLEY INC
Also Called: Mifflin Valley Reflective AP
31 S Sterley St (19607-1845)
PHONE.................................610 775-0505
Michael J Gallen, *President*
Donna Gallen, *CFO*
EMP: 35
SQ FT: 24,000
SALES (est): 3.4MM **Privately Held**
WEB: www.mifflinvalley.com
SIC: 3842 2326 Clothing, fire resistant & protective; men's & boys' work clothing

(G-16444)
MILROY ENTERPRISES INC
Also Called: Graffius Burial Vault Co
100 Park Ave (19608-1328)
PHONE.................................610 678-4537
Sandra Graffius, *CEO*
Kelly Pellicano, *President*
Peter Pellicano, *Vice Pres*
EMP: 30
SQ FT: 10,000
SALES (est): 4.4MM **Privately Held**
SIC: 3272 5999 Burial vaults, concrete or precast terrazzo; monuments, finished to custom order

(G-16445)
MISCO PRODUCTS CORPORATION
1048 Stinson Dr (19605-9440)
PHONE.................................610 926-4106
Steven Gable, *President*
Benjamin Gable, *Corp Secy*
Jeffrey Gable, *Vice Pres*
Madeline Gable, *Treasurer*
EMP: 80 EST: 1882
SQ FT: 125,000

SALES (est): 24.4MM **Privately Held**
WEB: www.miscoprod.com
SIC: 2842 2841 Floor waxes; detergents, synthetic organic or inorganic alkaline; soap: granulated, liquid, cake, flaked or chip

(G-16446)
MITSUBISHI CHEMICAL ADVNCD MTR (DH)
2120 Fairmont Ave (19605-3041)
PHONE.................................610 320-6600
EMP: 9
SALES (est): 85.2MM **Privately Held**
SIC: 2821 Stock shapes, plastic
HQ: Mitsubishi Chemical Advanced Materials Composites Ag
Hardstrasse 5
Lenzburg AG 5600
628 858-150

(G-16447)
MOBILE VIDEO DEVICES INC
Also Called: Mvd
156 Madison Ave (19605-2962)
PHONE.................................610 921-5720
Darryl Spangler, *President*
EMP: 3
SALES (est): 332K **Privately Held**
WEB: www.mobilevideodevices.com
SIC: 8742 3651 Distribution channels consultant; household video equipment

(G-16448)
MOORE PERFORMANCE PWR PDTS LLC
1199 Ashbourne Dr (19605-3225)
PHONE.................................610 507-2344
Richard I Moore, *President*
EMP: 4
SALES (est): 304.6K **Privately Held**
SIC: 3694 Engine electrical equipment

(G-16449)
MOUNTAINVIEW GRAPHICS
201 E Bellevue Ave (19605-1733)
PHONE.................................610 939-1471
Mike Shugar, *Owner*
EMP: 3 EST: 1996
SALES: 50K **Privately Held**
SIC: 2261 Screen printing of cotton broadwoven fabrics

(G-16450)
MPM HOLDINGS INC
7 Bristol Ct (19610-1805)
PHONE.................................610 678-8131
Mark Diefenderfer, *President*
Michael J Widel, *Vice Pres*
Peter E Mullenberg, *Admin Sec*
EMP: 26
SALES (est): 5MM **Privately Held**
WEB: www.lynxnet.com
SIC: 7372 5045 7378 Business oriented computer software; computer software; computer maintenance & repair

(G-16451)
MYERS CANNING CO
3721 Pottsville Pike (19605-1721)
P.O. Box 276, Temple (19560-0276)
PHONE.................................610 929-8644
Julio Savini, *President*
Ezio F De Santis, *Exec VP*
▲ EMP: 140
SQ FT: 52,000
SALES (est): 11MM
SALES (corp-wide): 40.6MM **Privately Held**
WEB: www.giorgiofoods.com
SIC: 2033 Mushrooms: packaged in cans, jars, etc.
HQ: Giorgio Foods, Inc.
1161 Park Rd
Reading PA 19605
610 926-2139

(G-16452)
NAVISTAR INC
1200 Brdcstg Rd Ste 102 (19610)
PHONE.................................610 375-4230
Chris Randalo, *Branch Mgr*
Bonnie Arentz, *Administration*
EMP: 290

SALES (corp-wide): 10.2B **Publicly Held**
WEB: www.internationaldelivers.com
SIC: 3519 Internal combustion engines
HQ: Navistar, Inc.
2701 Navistar Dr
Lisle IL 60532
331 332-5000

(G-16453)
NEENAH NORTHEAST LLC
220 Corporate Dr (19605-1146)
PHONE.................................610 926-1996
Vincent McFadden, *Sales/Mktg Mgr*
EMP: 44
SALES (corp-wide): 1B **Publicly Held**
SIC: 2631 2672 Pressboard; coated & laminated paper
HQ: Neenah Northeast, Llc
70 Front St
West Springfield MA 01089
413 533-0699

(G-16454)
NEW ENTERPRISE STONE LIME INC
1119 Snyder Rd (19609-1100)
PHONE.................................610 678-1913
Paul I Detwiler Jr, *Ch of Bd*
EMP: 30
SALES (corp-wide): 651.9MM **Privately Held**
SIC: 1611 2951 Highway & street construction; asphalt & asphaltic paving mixtures (not from refineries)
PA: New Enterprise Stone & Lime Co., Inc.
3912 Brumbaugh Rd
New Enterprise PA 16664
814 224-6883

(G-16455)
NEW YORK BAGELRY
2720 Penn Ave (19609-1528)
PHONE.................................610 678-6420
Joe Bilino, *Manager*
EMP: 3
SALES (est): 317.5K **Privately Held**
SIC: 5411 3556 Delicatessens; ovens, bakery

(G-16456)
NICHOLAS SHEA CO INC
3353 Perkiomen Ave (19606-2737)
PHONE.................................610 296-9036
Joseph Nicholas, *President*
EMP: 9
SALES (est): 995.7K **Privately Held**
SIC: 5091 2421 Sporting & recreation goods; outdoor wood structural products

(G-16457)
NORTHEAST SPRING INC
506 S 5th St (19602-2610)
PHONE.................................610 374-8508
John O'Leary, *President*
Keith Whitfield, *Mfg Mgr*
EMP: 27
SQ FT: 26,000
SALES (est): 6.2MM **Privately Held**
SIC: 3495 Wire springs

(G-16458)
ONA CORPORATION
400 Orton Ave (19603)
P.O. Box 1053 (19603-1053)
PHONE.................................610 378-1381
Jeff Prater, *Managing Dir*
Michael Kawaja, *Principal*
Patrick H Donahue Sr, *Vice Pres*
EMP: 200
SQ FT: 27,800
SALES (est): 19.3MM **Privately Held**
SIC: 3255 3297 Foundry refractories, clay; nonclay refractories

(G-16459)
OPTIMUM CONTROLS CORPORATION
Also Called: Honeywell Authorized Dealer
1044 Macarthur Rd (19605-9404)
P.O. Box 14174 (19612-4174)
PHONE.................................610 375-0990
Michael P Galiyano, *President*
Mark J Galiyano, *Vice Pres*
Pete Lutz, *Foreman/Supr*
Terry Campbell, *Engineer*
Frank Riotto, *Project Engr*

EMP: 82
SALES (est): 22.2MM **Privately Held**
WEB: www.optimumcontrols.com
SIC: 3822 3825 3625 7629 Building services monitoring controls, automatic; digital test equipment, electronic & electrical circuits; relays & industrial controls; electronic equipment repair

(G-16460)
OSCAR DANIELS & COMPANY INC
Also Called: Pennsylvania Wiping Mtl Co
35 Queen St (19608-1137)
P.O. Box 15074 (19612-5074)
PHONE.................................610 678-8144
Pamela Daniels, *President*
Jason Daniels, *Vice Pres*
Melissa Glassmire, *Vice Pres*
▲ EMP: 18 EST: 1922
SQ FT: 37,000
SALES (est): 1.2MM **Privately Held**
WEB: www.pawipers.com
SIC: 2299 5093 2842 2211 Fibers, textile: recovery from textile mill waste or rags; scrap & waste materials; specialty cleaning, polishes & sanitation goods; broadwoven fabric mills, cotton

(G-16461)
P & R UNITED WELDING AND FABG
Also Called: Rossi Welding Co
316 Franklin St 322 (19602-1018)
PHONE.................................610 375-9928
Larry Pergola, *President*
EMP: 15
SQ FT: 15,000
SALES (est): 2.5MM **Privately Held**
SIC: 3498 7692 Pipe sections fabricated from purchased pipe; welding repair

(G-16462)
PACKAGING CORPORATION AMERICA
Also Called: Pca/Reading 389
173 Tuckerton Rd (19605-1135)
PHONE.................................610 916-3200
Kelly Cashatt, *Controller*
Bob Hood, *Branch Mgr*
Craig Beswick, *Supervisor*
EMP: 50
SALES (corp-wide): 7B **Publicly Held**
SIC: 2653 Boxes, corrugated: made from purchased materials
PA: Packaging Corporation Of America
1 N Field Ct
Lake Forest IL 60045
847 482-3000

(G-16463)
PAGODA PRODUCTS INC
Also Called: Pagoda Industries
777 Commerce St (19608-1308)
P.O. Box 38, Kutztown (19530-0038)
PHONE.................................610 678-8096
David Weaver, *President*
R Oxanne Weaver, *Vice Pres*
EMP: 3
SQ FT: 6,000
SALES (est): 419.8K **Privately Held**
SIC: 2841 Detergents, synthetic organic or inorganic alkaline

(G-16464)
PALACE FOODS INC
100 Cleveland Ave (19605-2112)
PHONE.................................610 775-9947
Joe McGee, *President*
EMP: 10
SALES: 90K **Privately Held**
SIC: 2099 Food preparations

(G-16465)
PARKER-HANNIFIN CORPORATION
Also Called: Precision Rebuilding Division
1018 Stinson Dr (19605-9440)
PHONE.................................610 926-1115
Daniel D Packer, *Human Res Mgr*
Mark Kritz, *Manager*
EMP: 19
SALES (corp-wide): 14.3B **Publicly Held**
WEB: www.parker.com
SIC: 3599 Machine shop, jobbing & repair

PA: Parker-Hannifin Corporation
6035 Parkland Blvd
Cleveland OH 44124
216 896-3000

(G-16466)
PARTS TO YOUR DOOR LP
800 Corporate Dr (19605-1152)
P.O. Box 249, Bally (19503-0249)
PHONE.................................610 916-5380
Randall J Towers, *Partner*
Peter J Morgan, *Partner*
EMP: 4
SALES (est): 449K **Privately Held**
SIC: 3585 Heating & air conditioning combination units

(G-16467)
PENN IRON WORKS INC
700 Old Fritztown Rd (19608-9149)
PHONE.................................610 777-7656
Stylianos A Philippides, *President*
David H Roland, *Vice Pres*
Raymond C Schlegel, *Admin Sec*
◆ **EMP:** 30 **EST:** 1914
SQ FT: 53,000
SALES: 6.4MM **Privately Held**
WEB: www.penniron.com
SIC: 3443 Tanks, standard or custom fabricated: metal plate

(G-16468)
PERFORMANCE SPORTS APPAREL INC
Also Called: Medalist
2607 Keiser Blvd Ste 205 (19610-3326)
PHONE.................................508 384-8036
Rolf D Schmidt, *Ch of Bd*
David Ferguson, *President*
▲ **EMP:** 20
SQ FT: 35,000
SALES (est): 2.1MM **Privately Held**
WEB: www.medalist.com
SIC: 2329 Men's & boys' sportswear & athletic clothing; men's & boys' athletic uniforms

(G-16469)
PERMANENT SIGN & DISPLAY
1141 Penn Ave Rear (19610-2023)
PHONE.................................610 736-3222
Tom Cursher, *President*
EMP: 4 **EST:** 2000
SALES (est): 195.6K **Privately Held**
SIC: 3993 Electric signs

(G-16470)
PHOENIX FORGE GROUP LLC (PA)
Also Called: Capitol Manufacturing Division
1020 Macarthur Rd (19605-9404)
PHONE.................................800 234-8665
Stephanie McKibigan, *CFO*
Melanie Venable, *Sales Mgr*
John Rodgers,
EMP: 10 **EST:** 1997
SALES (est): 156.1MM **Privately Held**
SIC: 3462 Iron & steel forgings

(G-16471)
POHL RAILROAD MTLS CORP LLC
5662 Leesport Ave (19605-9704)
P.O. Box 13038 (19612-3038)
PHONE.................................610 916-7645
Christopher A Storck,
EMP: 4
SQ FT: 10,000
SALES (est): 409.4K **Privately Held**
SIC: 4011 3531 Interurban railways; railroad related equipment

(G-16472)
POLYFAB CORPORATION
Also Called: Reading Plastic Machining & FA
94 Dries Rd 222a (19605-9225)
P.O. Box 10, Temple (19560-0010)
PHONE.................................610 926-3245
Thomas Funk, *President*
Thomas C Funk, *Principal*
Timothy Long, *VP Sales*
EMP: 22
SQ FT: 3,500
SALES (est): 5.4MM **Privately Held**
WEB: www.readingplastic.com
SIC: 3089 Plastic hardware & building products

(G-16473)
PPG INDUSTRIES INC
2001 Centre Ave (19605-2816)
PHONE.................................888 774-1010
EMP: 4
SALES (corp-wide): 15.3B **Publicly Held**
SIC: 2851 Paints & allied products
PA: Ppg Industries, Inc.
1 Ppg Pl
Pittsburgh PA 15272
412 434-3131

(G-16474)
PRATT ROCK SOLID DISPLAYS LLC
184 Tuckerton Rd (19605-1136)
PHONE.................................610 929-4800
Tom Petroni, *Vice Pres*
Christopher Bull, *Admin Sec*
EMP: 22
SQ FT: 42,000
SALES (est): 5.3MM **Privately Held**
WEB: www.rksolid.com
SIC: 2653 Display items, solid fiber: made from purchased materials

(G-16475)
PRAXAIR DISTRIBUTION INC
1800 N 11th St (19604-1507)
P.O. Box 12977 (19612-2977)
PHONE.................................610 921-9230
Chris Olszewski, *Principal*
EMP: 25 **Privately Held**
SIC: 2813 Industrial gases
HQ: Praxair Distribution, Inc.
10 Riverview Dr
Danbury CT 06810
203 837-2000

(G-16476)
PROGRESS RAIL SERVICES CORP
211 Emerald Ave (19606-1449)
PHONE.................................610 779-2039
Ted Wickert, *Manager*
EMP: 44
SALES (corp-wide): 54.7B **Publicly Held**
WEB: www.progressrail.com
SIC: 4789 3312 7389 Railroad maintenance & repair services; railroad car repair; structural & rail mill products; metal cutting services
HQ: Progress Rail Services Corporation
1600 Progress Dr
Albertville AL 35950
256 593-1260

(G-16477)
Q D F INC
Also Called: Sir Speedy
2530 Penn Ave (19609-1540)
PHONE.................................610 670-2090
Joe De Marte, *President*
Diana Demarte, *Vice Pres*
EMP: 4
SALES (est): 517.9K **Privately Held**
WEB: www.qdf.com
SIC: 2752 Commercial printing, lithographic

(G-16478)
QUAKER MAID MEATS INC
610 Morgantown Rd (19611-2012)
P.O. Box 350 (19607-0350)
PHONE.................................610 376-1500
Stanley Szortyka, *CEO*
S Sergei Szortyka, *President*
Paula Szortyka, *Corp Secy*
P Nancy Rubin, *Vice Pres*
Andrew Sims, *CFO*
▲ **EMP:** 162 **EST:** 1960
SQ FT: 50,000
SALES (est): 42.4MM **Privately Held**
WEB: www.quakermaidmeats.com
SIC: 2013 Frozen meats from purchased meat

(G-16479)
QUAKER MAID MEATS INC
521 Carroll St (19611-2010)
PHONE.................................610 376-1500
EMP: 20
SALES (corp-wide): 40.1MM **Privately Held**
SIC: 2013 Operates As A Manufacturer Of Frozen Portioned Meat Products From Purchased Meat
PA: Quaker Maid Meats Inc.
521 Carroll St
Reading PA 19611
610 376-1500

(G-16480)
QUALITY LASER ALTERNATIVES
1615 Crowder Ave (19607-2909)
PHONE.................................610 373-0788
Daniel Kranis Jr, *Partner*
Vincent A Denunzio, *Partner*
EMP: 4
SALES (est): 352.6K **Privately Held**
SIC: 2759 Laser printing

(G-16481)
QUANTAM SOFTWARE SOLUTIONS
Also Called: Quantum Business Services
4228 Saint Lawrence Ave B (19606-2894)
PHONE.................................610 373-4770
John A Yergey, *President*
EMP: 7
SQ FT: 1,500
SALES: 750K **Privately Held**
WEB: www.quantumss.com
SIC: 7372 Prepackaged software

(G-16482)
R A EGAN SIGN & AWNG CO INC
1100 Berkshire Blvd (19610-1221)
PHONE.................................610 777-3795
Robert A Egan, *President*
Denise Rowe, *Accountant*
Michelle Weaver, *Sales Staff*
▲ **EMP:** 15
SQ FT: 22,000
SALES (est): 3.1MM **Privately Held**
WEB: www.egansign.com
SIC: 3444 3993 Awnings & canopies; signs & advertising specialties

(G-16483)
R M PALMER COMPANY
40 Dennis Dr (19606-3761)
P.O. Box 1723 (19603-1723)
PHONE.................................610 582-5551
Edward Ray, *Principal*
EMP: 40
SALES (corp-wide): 110.2MM **Privately Held**
SIC: 2066 2064 Chocolate candy, solid; chocolate candy, except solid chocolate
PA: R. M. Palmer Company
77 S 2nd Ave
Reading PA 19611
610 372-8971

(G-16484)
RASER INDUSTRIES INC
1630 N 9th St Ste 1 (19604-1760)
PHONE.................................610 320-5130
Gary Raser Jr, *President*
EMP: 19
SQ FT: 45,000
SALES (est): 5.5MM **Privately Held**
WEB: www.rasersteel.com
SIC: 3325 7692 Steel foundries; welding repair

(G-16485)
READING BOX COMPANY INC
250 Blair Ave (19601-1906)
PHONE.................................610 374-2080
Brent Atkins, *President*
EMP: 10 **EST:** 1921
SQ FT: 9,000
SALES (est): 1.7MM **Privately Held**
SIC: 2441 Boxes, wood

(G-16486)
READING COML HEAT TREATING CO
320 Greenwich St (19601-2821)
PHONE.................................610 376-3994
Lee Wentzel Jr, *President*
Christine Wentzel, *Admin Sec*
EMP: 6
SQ FT: 4,000
SALES (est): 750K **Privately Held**
SIC: 3398 Metal heat treating

(G-16487)
READING DRAFT BIRCH CO
614 Gregg Ave (19611-1624)
PHONE.................................610 372-2565
Fred Gaul, *President*
EMP: 3
SALES (est): 224.5K **Privately Held**
SIC: 2086 Bottled & canned soft drinks

(G-16488)
READING EAGLE COMPANY (PA)
Also Called: Reading Eagle Press
345 Penn St (19601-4029)
PHONE.................................610 371-5000
Shawn P Moliatu, *CEO*
William S Flippin, *Ch of Bd*
Peter D Barbey, *President*
James C Flippin, *Vice Pres*
Michael J Mizak Jr, *CFO*
EMP: 25
SQ FT: 100,000
SALES (est): 77MM **Privately Held**
WEB: www.readingeagle.com
SIC: 2711 2752 Commercial printing & newspaper publishing combined; commercial printing, offset

(G-16489)
READING EAGLE COMPANY
Also Called: Reading Eagle Press
340 Court St (19601)
PHONE.................................610 371-5180
Keith Frits, *Manager*
EMP: 20
SALES (corp-wide): 77MM **Privately Held**
WEB: www.readingeagle.com
SIC: 2711 Newspapers, publishing & printing
PA: Reading Eagle Company
345 Penn St
Reading PA 19601
610 371-5000

(G-16490)
READING ELECTRIC MOTOR SVC INC
80 Witman Rd (19605-1225)
PHONE.................................610 929-5777
Richard L Bashore, *President*
Jerry Frasso, *Project Mgr*
Craig Koyste, *Sales Staff*
Rich Polityka, *Manager*
Chris Bashore, *CTO*
▲ **EMP:** 65
SQ FT: 40,000
SALES (est): 15.8MM **Privately Held**
WEB: www.readingelectric.com
SIC: 3694 Engine electrical equipment

(G-16491)
READING SODA WORKS & CARBONIC
614 Gregg Ave (19611-1624)
PHONE.................................610 372-2565
Lisa Conner, *President*
EMP: 5
SALES (est): 272.6K **Privately Held**
SIC: 2086 Carbonated beverages, nonalcoholic: bottled & canned

(G-16492)
READING THERMAL SYSTEMS INC
7 Corporate Blvd (19608-8942)
PHONE.................................610 678-5890
Terry E Groff, *Chairman*
EMP: 4
SALES (est): 563.8K **Privately Held**
WEB: www.readingthermal.com
SIC: 3826 Instruments measuring thermal properties

(G-16493)
READING TRUCK BODY LLC (HQ)
Also Called: ABC
201 Hancock Blvd (19611)
P.O. Box 650 (19607-0650)
PHONE.................................610 775-3301
Mark Robinson, *CEO*

Dan Perlman, *CEO*
Scott Caldwell, *Vice Pres*
Bob Shangraw, *CFO*
Harry Schank, *VP Human Res*
◆ **EMP:** 168
SQ FT: 250,000
SALES (est): 62.7MM
SALES (corp-wide): 1.2B **Privately Held**
WEB: www.readingbody.com
SIC: 3713 3792 3469 Utility truck bodies; truck bodies & parts; travel trailers & campers; metal stampings
PA: J. B. Poindexter & Co., Inc
600 Travis St Ste 200
Houston TX 77002
713 655-9800

(G-16494)
REDNERS MARKETS INC
4870 Penn Ave (19608-8601)
PHONE...................................610 678-2900
Jeff Lingsey, *Manager*
EMP: 150
SALES (corp-wide): 838.7MM **Privately Held**
WEB: www.rednersmarkets.com
SIC: 5411 2051 Supermarkets, chain; convenience stores, chain; bread, cake & related products
PA: Redner's Markets, Inc.
3 Quarry Rd
Reading PA 19605
610 926-3700

(G-16495)
REID S TANNERY
2052 Lucon Rd (19605)
PHONE...................................610 929-4403
Debbie Rahmer, *Business Mgr*
EMP: 4 **EST:** 2009
SALES (est): 183.5K **Privately Held**
SIC: 2395 Embroidery products, except schiffli machine

(G-16496)
REMCON PLASTICS INC
208 Chestnut St (19602-1809)
PHONE...................................610 376-2666
Peter J Connors, *President*
Rich Maguire, *Vice Pres*
Alexandria Hamn, *Purch Agent*
Christine Kahn, *Director*
Doren Connors, *Admin Sec*
◆ **EMP:** 79
SQ FT: 78,000
SALES (est): 22.5MM **Privately Held**
WEB: www.remcon.com
SIC: 3089 Molding primary plastic; injection molding of plastics

(G-16497)
RICHARD J SUMMONS SCULPTURE
172 Mail Route Rd (19608-9012)
PHONE...................................610 223-9013
Richard Summons, *Owner*
EMP: 5 **EST:** 2008
SALES (est): 318.7K **Privately Held**
SIC: 3443 7389 Tanks, standard or custom fabricated: metal plate; interior designer

(G-16498)
RIECKS LETTER SERVICE INC
Also Called: Rieck's Printing
101 S 1st Ave (19611-1221)
PHONE...................................610 375-8581
Steven R Post, *President*
EMP: 15
SQ FT: 7,500
SALES (est): 2MM **Privately Held**
WEB: www.rieckssprinting.com
SIC: 2752 2759 Commercial printing, offset; letterpress printing

(G-16499)
RIECKS PUBLISHING
101 S 1st Ave (19611-1221)
PHONE...................................610 685-1222
Steven R Post, *President*
EMP: 4 **EST:** 2013
SALES (est): 182.3K **Privately Held**
SIC: 2741 Miscellaneous publishing

(G-16500)
RLC ELECTRONIC SYSTEMS INC
10 Corporate Blvd (19608-8942)
PHONE...................................610 898-4902
Richard Kundrat, *President*
Ken Altschuler, *Engineer*
Randy Mauger, *Engineer*
Bob Koch, *Controller*
Russ Abraham, *Manager*
▲ **EMP:** 20
SQ FT: 30,000
SALES (est): 4.9MM **Privately Held**
WEB: www.rlcsystems.com
SIC: 3825 8711 Analyzers for testing electrical characteristics; engineering services

(G-16501)
ROBERT W TURNER
Also Called: Turner Knit Products
425 Carsonia Ave (19606-1508)
PHONE...................................610 372-8863
EMP: 8
SQ FT: 12,500
SALES (est): 821.3K **Privately Held**
SIC: 5131 2257 Whol Piece Goods/Notions Weft Knit Fabric Mill

(G-16502)
ROCHESTER COCA COLA BOTTLING
Coca-Cola
243 Snyder Rd (19605-9248)
PHONE...................................610 916-3996
Doug Degroff, *Manager*
EMP: 75
SQ FT: 83,550
SALES (corp-wide): 35.4B **Publicly Held**
SIC: 2086 Bottled & canned soft drinks
HQ: Rochester Coca Cola Bottling Corp
300 Oak St
Pittston PA 18640
570 655-2874

(G-16503)
ROEBERG ENTERPRISES INC (PA)
Also Called: National Uniforms
1700 Fairview St (19606-2621)
PHONE...................................800 523-8197
Michael Roeberg, *President*
Richard Roeberg, *Vice Pres*
EMP: 42 **EST:** 1932
SQ FT: 30,000
SALES (est): 3.7MM **Privately Held**
WEB: www.nationalcleaners.com
SIC: 2326 2329 2389 2339 Work uniforms; medical & hospital uniforms, men's; windbreakers: men's, youths' & boys'; men's miscellaneous accessories; uniforms & vestments; sportswear, women's

(G-16504)
ROSE CORPORATION (PA)
Also Called: TRC Services
401 N 8th St (19601-4107)
P.O. Box 15208 (19612-5208)
PHONE...................................610 376-5004
Brian Higgins, *President*
Tom Mc Devitt, *General Mgr*
Tom McDevitt, *General Mgr*
Cynthia Bruno, *Vice Pres*
Rosemary Bruno, *Vice Pres*
EMP: 70
SQ FT: 150,000
SALES (est): 40.5MM **Privately Held**
WEB: www.therosecorp.com
SIC: 5075 3599 5051 3312 Machine shop, jobbing & repair; iron & steel (ferrous) products; welding repair; fabricated structural metal

(G-16505)
ROSE CORPORATION
Also Called: Mark Metal Division
2100 Adams St (19605-3002)
P.O. Box 12586 (19612-2586)
PHONE...................................610 921-9647
John Maillie, *Manager*
EMP: 13
SQ FT: 6,693

SALES (corp-wide): 40.5MM **Privately Held**
WEB: www.therosecorp.com
SIC: 3316 Cold finishing of steel shapes
PA: Rose Corporation
401 N 8th St
Reading PA 19601
610 376-5004

(G-16506)
RUNWELL SOLUTIONS INC
575 Van Reed Rd (19610-1769)
PHONE...................................610 376-7773
Jesse P Jepsen, *President*
Damien Malcolm, *Manager*
EMP: 17
SQ FT: 2,400
SALES (est): 6.6MM **Privately Held**
WEB: www.wyodata.com
SIC: 5045 7379 7372 Computers, peripherals & software; computer related consulting services; business oriented computer software

(G-16507)
SAFC BIOSCIENCES INC
5 Dutch Ct (19608-8987)
PHONE...................................610 750-8801
Brian Hart, *Principal*
EMP: 5
SALES (est): 383.3K **Privately Held**
SIC: 2836 Biological products, except diagnostic

(G-16508)
SCHUBERT CUSTOM CABINETRY INC (PA)
Also Called: Schubert's Cabinet Shop
39 Moss St (19601-3605)
PHONE...................................610 372-5559
Eba Schubert, *President*
Mike Horner, *Vice Pres*
Margret Schubert Cascino, *Admin Sec*
EMP: 4
SQ FT: 7,000
SALES: 600K **Privately Held**
SIC: 2434 2541 2517 Wood kitchen cabinets; wood partitions & fixtures; wood television & radio cabinets

(G-16509)
SEALED AIR CORPORATION
4275 Reading Crest Ave (19605-1130)
PHONE...................................610 926-7517
Brian Blackford, *Manager*
EMP: 8
SALES (corp-wide): 4.7B **Publicly Held**
SIC: 2673 2671 3087 3086 Plastic & pliofilm bags; packaging paper & plastics film, coated & laminated; custom compound purchased resins; plastics foam products; plastic processing
PA: Sealed Air Corporation
2415 Cascade Pointe Blvd
Charlotte NC 28208
980 221-3235

(G-16510)
SEALED AIR CORPORATION
Paper Mill Div
450 Riverfront Dr (19602-2600)
PHONE...................................610 375-4281
Michael Feeney, *General Mgr*
EMP: 35
SQ FT: 71,454
SALES (corp-wide): 4.7B **Publicly Held**
WEB: www.sealedair.com
SIC: 3086 2621 Packaging & shipping materials, foamed plastic; paper mills
PA: Sealed Air Corporation
2415 Cascade Pointe Blvd
Charlotte NC 28208
980 221-3235

(G-16511)
SENSITRON ASSOCIATES INC
223 Seidel St (19606-2896)
P.O. Box 4184 (19606-0584)
PHONE...................................610 779-0939
Michael Rutkowski, *President*
Anthony Maryniak, *Vice Pres*
EMP: 3
SALES (est): 407.1K **Privately Held**
WEB: www.sensitron-associates.com
SIC: 3823 Analyzers, industrial process type

(G-16512)
SENSORYEFFECTS INC
61 Vanguard Dr (19606-3765)
PHONE...................................610 582-2170
Thomas Dietrich, *President*
EMP: 5
SALES (corp-wide): 643.6MM **Publicly Held**
SIC: 2087 Extracts, flavoring
HQ: Sensoryeffects, Inc.
13723 Rverport Dr Ste 201
Maryland Heights MO 63043

(G-16513)
SFS GROUP USA INC
Also Called: Mfg Plant-Shipping
41 Dennis Dr (19606-3778)
PHONE...................................610 376-5751
B Hess, *Principal*
Carl Lutz, *Vice Pres*
EMP: 75
SQ FT: 54,768
SALES (corp-wide): 1.6B **Privately Held**
SIC: 3452 Screws, metal; washers, metal
HQ: Sfs Group Usa, Inc.
1045 Spring St
Wyomissing PA 19610
610 376-5751

(G-16514)
SGL LLC
796 Fritztown Rd (19608-1522)
P.O. Box 2193 (19608-0193)
PHONE...................................610 670-4040
Peter Hoffman, *Principal*
▲ **EMP:** 40
SQ FT: 10,000
SALES (est): 6.7MM
SALES (corp-wide): 1.2B **Privately Held**
WEB: www.sglcarbon.de
SIC: 3624 Carbon & graphite products
PA: Sgl Carbon Se
Sohleinstr. 8
Wiesbaden 65201
611 602-90

(G-16515)
SHADOWFAX INC (PA)
141 S 7th St (19602-1620)
PHONE...................................610 373-5177
Nicholas K Bentley, *CEO*
Mary Lorah, *Manager*
Mark Mayhew, *Manager*
H Anderson Ellsworth, *Admin Sec*
William Whiting, *Admin Sec*
▲ **EMP:** 21
SQ FT: 20,000
SALES: 4MM **Privately Held**
WEB: www.apioptics.com
SIC: 3827 Optical elements & assemblies, except ophthalmic

(G-16516)
SHEERLUND PRODUCTS LLC
740 Corporate Dr (19605-1151)
PHONE...................................484 248-2650
Steve Prenatt, *President*
Frank Owsiany, *Purchasing*
▲ **EMP:** 12
SALES (est): 1.9MM **Privately Held**
WEB: www.sheerlundproducts.com
SIC: 5199 3552 Christmas trees, including artificial; shearing machinery

(G-16517)
SHIVKANTA CORPORATION
1905 N 5th Street Hwy (19605-2801)
PHONE...................................610 376-3515
Vasant Patel, *President*
EMP: 5
SALES (est): 302.9K **Privately Held**
SIC: 2051 Bread, cake & related products

(G-16518)
SIEMENS INDUSTRY INC
4201 Pottsville Pike (19605-1219)
PHONE...................................610 921-3135
EMP: 10
SALES (corp-wide): 96B **Privately Held**
SIC: 3613 Mfg Switchgear/Switchboards
HQ: Siemens Industry, Inc.
1000 Deerfield Pkwy
Buffalo Grove IL 60089
847 215-1000

GEOGRAPHIC

(G-16519)
SKIAS CHUCK WLDG & FABRICATORS
322 Blair Ave (19601-1908)
PHONE...................................610 375-0912
Charles Skias, *Owner*
EMP: 4
SQ FT: 2,400
SALES: 350K **Privately Held**
SIC: 1799 3441 7692 Welding on site;
fabricated structural metal; welding repair

(G-16520)
SPECIALTY DESIGN & MFG CO INC
Also Called: Special T Design & Mfg Co
2000 Friedensburg Rd (19606-9357)
P.O. Box 4039 (19606-0439)
PHONE...................................610 779-1357
Craig A Knabb, *President*
Albert A Knabb, *Vice Pres*
EMP: 50 EST: 1967
SQ FT: 53,000
SALES (est): 8.3MM
SALES (corp-wide): 3.8MM **Privately Held**
WEB: www.specialtydesign.com
SIC: 3599 3549 3544 Machine shop, job-
bing & repair; custom machinery; metal-
working machinery; special dies, tools,
jigs & fixtures
PA: Specialty Holdings Corp
2000 Friedensburg Rd
Reading PA 19606
610 779-1357

(G-16521)
SPECIALTY HOLDINGS CORP (PA)
2000 Friedensburg Rd (19606-9357)
P.O. Box 4039 (19606-0439)
PHONE...................................610 779-1357
Craig Knabb, *President*
Albert Knabb, *Vice Pres*
EMP: 50
SQ FT: 50,000
SALES (est): 3.8MM **Privately Held**
SIC: 3599 3549 Machine shop, jobbing &
repair; custom machinery; metalworking
machinery

(G-16522)
SPECTRUM SOFTWARE INNOVATIONS
4 Saint Andrews Ct (19606-9445)
PHONE...................................610 779-6974
Brenda Millar, *Mng Member*
Seth Greenstein, *Mng Member*
Tony Narasco, *Mng Member*
EMP: 3
SALES (est): 154.6K **Privately Held**
SIC: 7372 Prepackaged software

(G-16523)
SPRING VALLEY MILLWORK INC
108 S Hull St (19608-1128)
P.O. Box 2118 (19608-0118)
PHONE...................................610 927-0144
Greg Longburger, *President*
Antonio Grande, *Vice Pres*
EMP: 25 EST: 2001
SQ FT: 20,000
SALES (est): 3.9MM **Privately Held**
SIC: 2431 Staircases & stairs, wood

(G-16524)
STANDARD OFFSET PRTG CO INC (PA)
Also Called: Calloway Network
433 Pearl St (19602-2621)
P.O. Box 1059 (19603-1059)
PHONE...................................610 375-6174
Scott Vaughn, *CEO*
Dennis Becker, *Vice Pres*
Bob Mellinger, *Plant Mgr*
Andrea Keller, *Project Mgr*
David Weaver, *Prdtn Mgr*
EMP: 75 EST: 1895
SQ FT: 75,000
SALES (est): 20.8MM **Privately Held**
WEB: www.standardoffset.com
SIC: 2752 Commercial printing, offset

(G-16525)
STEEL FABRICATORS LLC
1530 Lancaster Ave Rear (19607-1560)
PHONE...................................610 775-3532
Alexander Gigliotti, *Principal*
EMP: 5
SALES (est): 379.7K **Privately Held**
SIC: 3441 Fabricated structural metal

(G-16526)
STRATEGIC REPORTS INC
2645 Perkiomen Ave (19606-2001)
PHONE...................................610 370-5640
Tom Nordhoy, *President*
Jennifer Pascuzzi, *Business Mgr*
Leena Samant, *COO*
John Cochrane, *Project Dir*
Naoufal Elkrami, *Accounts Exec*
EMP: 3
SALES (est): 388K **Privately Held**
SIC: 2721 Statistical reports (periodicals):
publishing & printing

(G-16527)
STUDIO 8
832 Franklin St (19602-1146)
PHONE...................................610 372-7065
John Lord, *Owner*
EMP: 3 EST: 1972
SQ FT: 2,800
SALES (est): 130K **Privately Held**
SIC: 3231 1793 Leaded glass; glass &
glazing work

(G-16528)
SUMMIT STEEL & MFG INC
Also Called: Summit Storage Solutions
1005 Patriot Pkwy (19605-2874)
P.O. Box 14295 (19612-4295)
PHONE...................................610 921-1119
Gary L Romig, *Principal*
Angel Lyle, *Purch Mgr*
Jean Shalters, *Purch Agent*
Ron Billet, *Buyer*
Mike Missimer, *Buyer*
◆ EMP: 70
SQ FT: 150,000
SALES (est): 2.5MM **Privately Held**
WEB: www.summitsteelinc.com
SIC: 3317 Steel pipe & tubes

(G-16529)
SUNSHINE SCREEN PRINT
2411 Lasalle Dr (19609-1216)
PHONE...................................610 678-9034
John Chelius, *Principal*
EMP: 3
SALES (est): 228.6K **Privately Held**
SIC: 2752 Commercial printing, litho-
graphic

(G-16530)
SURGICAL INSTITUTE READING LP
2752 Century Blvd (19610-3345)
PHONE...................................610 378-8800
Deborah Beissel, *CEO*
EMP: 1
SALES: 46.2MM **Privately Held**
SIC: 8062 3842 General medical & surgi-
cal hospitals; autoclaves, hospital & surgi-
cal

(G-16531)
SUSAN BECKER
Also Called: Jersey Ink
1601 N 9th St Apt 1 (19604-1763)
PHONE...................................610 378-7844
Susan Becker, *Principal*
EMP: 3
SALES (est): 230.5K **Privately Held**
SIC: 2759 Screen printing

(G-16532)
SWEETHEARTS BRIDAL FORMALWEAR
4631 Penn Ave Ste 2 (19608-9701)
PHONE...................................610 750-5087
Kemp Elizabeth, *Owner*
EMP: 5
SALES (est): 411K **Privately Held**
SIC: 2335 Wedding gowns & dresses

(G-16533)
T G FAUST INC
544 Minor St (19602-2722)
P.O. Box 947 (19607-0947)
PHONE...................................610 375-8549
Thomas G Faust, *President*
Karen Lysczek, *Treasurer*
EMP: 15
SQ FT: 15,000
SALES (est): 2.7MM **Privately Held**
WEB: www.tgfaust.com
SIC: 3842 Bulletproof vests

(G-16534)
TEK PRODUCTS & SERVICES INC
530 Crestmont St (19611-2051)
PHONE...................................610 376-0690
Gary Naegle, *President*
Donald Lykens, *Vice Pres*
EMP: 10
SQ FT: 6,000
SALES (est): 1.1MM **Privately Held**
WEB: www.tekproductsinc.com
SIC: 2893 Printing ink

(G-16535)
TERMACO USA INC
171 Tuckerton Rd (19605-1135)
PHONE...................................610 916-2600
Roger Breton, *President*
EMP: 20 EST: 2008
SALES (est): 4.4MM
SALES (corp-wide): 51MM **Privately Held**
SIC: 3446 Ornamental metalwork
PA: Termaco Ltee
325 Boul Industriel
Saint-Jean-Sur-Richelieu QC J3B 7
450 346-6871

(G-16536)
TERRE TROPHY CO
Also Called: Ormsbees Pro Shop
965 New Holland Rd (19607-1646)
PHONE...................................610 777-2050
Frank Lepera Jr, *Partner*
Terre Lepera, *Partner*
EMP: 5
SQ FT: 6,000
SALES (est): 393.8K **Privately Held**
WEB: www.ormsbeesproshop.com
SIC: 5999 5941 3993 Trophies & plaques;
bowling equipment & supplies; signs &
advertising specialties

(G-16537)
THREEWAY PATTERN ENTERPRISES
3144 Marion St (19605-2746)
PHONE...................................610 929-2889
David Hunter, *President*
EMP: 5
SQ FT: 2,500
SALES: 250K **Privately Held**
SIC: 3543 Industrial patterns

(G-16538)
THRESHOLD RHBLITATION SVCS INC (PA)
Also Called: BERKS PERSONNEL NET-
WORK
1000 Lancaster Ave (19607-1610)
PHONE...................................610 777-7691
Ronald L Williams, *President*
Gregory Portner, *Treasurer*
Robert Ganter, *Finance*
Gary McMullen, *Finance*
Nancy Campling, *Director*
▲ EMP: 280 EST: 1965
SQ FT: 40,000
SALES: 14.7MM **Privately Held**
SIC: 8322 7361 2499 7389 Rehabilitation
services; employment agencies; spools,
reels & pulleys: wood; reels, plywood;
spools, wood; microfilm recording & de-
veloping service; data entry service;
men's & boys' work clothing

(G-16539)
TIMAC AGRO USA INC
153 Angstadt Ln (19607)
P.O. Box 888 (19607-0888)
PHONE...................................610 375-7272
Marc Bouvry, *CEO*

Phillppe J Morin, *President*
Alain Fortier, *Corp Secy*
Lori Greene,
▲ EMP: 44
SALES: 25MM
SALES (corp-wide): 14MM **Privately Held**
SIC: 5191 2873 Fertilizer & fertilizer mate-
rials; nitrogenous fertilizers
HQ: Timac Agro International
27 Avenue Franklin Roosevelt
Saint Malo 35400
299 206-520

(G-16540)
TMS INTERNATIONAL LLC
101 Bern St (19601-1203)
PHONE...................................610 208-3293
Steve Hoffman, *Branch Mgr*
EMP: 5 **Privately Held**
SIC: 3312 Blast furnaces & steel mills
HQ: Tms International, Llc
12 Monongahela Ave
Glassport PA 15045
412 678-6141

(G-16541)
TODD LENGLE & CO INC
50 S Brobst St (19607-2646)
P.O. Box 81 (19607-0081)
PHONE...................................610 777-0731
Todd Lengle, *President*
EMP: 20
SQ FT: 3,000
SALES: 400K **Privately Held**
SIC: 2394 2221 2591 2396 Awnings, fab-
ric: made from purchased materials;
draperies & drapery fabrics, manmade
fiber & silk; venetian blinds; window
shades; screen printing on fabric articles

(G-16542)
TODD WEIKEL
Also Called: Weikel's Sportswear
3100 Saint Lawrence Ave (19606-2828)
PHONE...................................610 779-5508
Todd Weikel, *Owner*
EMP: 5
SQ FT: 14,000
SALES (est): 656.2K **Privately Held**
SIC: 2396 5699 3499 3199 Screen print-
ing on fabric articles; customized clothing
& apparel; novelties & giftware, including
trophies; novelties, leather; novelties,
paper: made from purchased material;
novelties, plastic

(G-16543)
TOM HESTER HIESTERS HO RACEWAY
256 Old Lancaster Pike (19607-2371)
PHONE...................................610 796-0490
Tom Hiester, *Principal*
EMP: 3
SALES (est): 271.5K **Privately Held**
SIC: 3644 Raceways

(G-16544)
TOM STURGIS PRETZELS INC
2267 Lancaster Pike (19607-2498)
PHONE...................................610 775-0335
Thomas Sturgis, *CEO*
Bkul I Sturgis, *President*
Becky Schmaldienst, *General Mgr*
Barbara A Sturgis, *Vice Pres*
Lou Moyer, *Plant Mgr*
▲ EMP: 30 EST: 1970
SQ FT: 74,000
SALES (est): 6MM **Privately Held**
WEB: www.tomsturgispretzels.com
SIC: 2052 Pretzels

(G-16545)
TOWN SQUARE SOFTWARE LLC
24 Club Ln (19607-3302)
PHONE...................................610 374-7900
Jan Orcutt, *Principal*
EMP: 3
SALES (est): 187.4K **Privately Held**
SIC: 7372 Prepackaged software

(G-16546)
TRAY-PAK CORPORATION (PA)
4216 Reading Crest Ave (19605)
PHONE...................................888 926-1777

Scott Myers, *President*
Kenneth R Ritter, *Admin Sec*
▲ **EMP:** 129
SQ FT: 90,000
SALES (est): 59.3MM **Privately Held**
WEB: www.traypak.com
SIC: 3089 Trays, plastic

(G-16547)
TRAY-PAK CORPORATION
251 Tuckerton Rd (19605-1154)
PHONE.................................484 509-0046
EMP: 171
SALES (corp-wide): 59.3MM **Privately
Held**
SIC: 3089 Tubs, plastic (containers)
PA: Tray-Pak Corporation
4216 Reading Crest Ave
Reading PA 19605
888 926-1777

(G-16548)
TRI STATE SCALES LLC
28 Basket Rd (19606-9332)
PHONE.................................610 779-5361
Charles Millard, *Principal*
EMP: 3
SALES (est): 290.6K **Privately Held**
SIC: 3596 Counting scales

(G-16549)
TRI-STATE WELDING CORP
126 Carpenter St (19602-1614)
PHONE.................................610 374-0321
Carmen De Angelis, *President*
Carmen F De Angelis Jr, *President*
EMP: 6 **EST:** 1971
SQ FT: 2,700
SALES (est): 215.2K **Privately Held**
SIC: 7692 Welding repair

(G-16550)
TRICORN INC
Also Called: Hydro Dynamics
333 Trout Ln (19607-2423)
P.O. Box 796 (19607-0796)
PHONE.................................610 777-6823
Thomas Dobson, *President*
EMP: 4
SQ FT: 15,000
SALES (est): 839.5K **Privately Held**
WEB: www.hydro-dynamics.com
SIC: 2899 Water treating compounds

(G-16551)
TSI ASSOCIATES INC (PA)
1031g Macarthur Rd (19605-9402)
PHONE.................................610 375-4371
Todd B Thorp, *President*
James J Bria, *Vice Pres*
George T Hutchison, *Treasurer*
▲ **EMP:** 17
SQ FT: 5,000
SALES (est): 2.2MM **Privately Held**
SIC: 2752 4225 8741 Business forms,
lithographed; general warehousing; man-
agement services

(G-16552)
UNIQUE DESSERTS INC
Also Called: Unique Desserts By Anne Louise
530 Grape St (19611-1020)
PHONE.................................610 372-7879
Anne Louise Reinert, *President*
Michael Reinert, *Vice Pres*
Mary Louise Hutchinson, *Treasurer*
Robert Hutchinson, *Admin Sec*
EMP: 5
SALES (est): 420.1K **Privately Held**
SIC: 2051 2052 Bakery: wholesale or
wholesale/retail combined; cakes, bakery:
except frozen; pies, bakery: except
frozen; cookies

(G-16553)
UNIQUE PRETZEL BAKERY INC
215 E Bellevue Ave (19605-1729)
PHONE.................................610 929-3172
William Spannuth, *President*
Roseanne Rothenberger, *Vice Pres*
EMP: 24
SQ FT: 7,000
SALES (est): 5.4MM **Privately Held**
SIC: 2052 5145 5461 2099 Pretzels;
pretzels; pretzels; food preparations

(G-16554)
UNITED CORRSTACK LLC
Also Called: Ds Smith - Reading Mill
720 Laurel St (19602-2718)
PHONE.................................610 374-3000
Antoine N Frem,
Ramez Skaff,
▲ **EMP:** 75
SQ FT: 314,000
SALES (est): 55.9MM
SALES (corp-wide): 8B **Privately Held**
WEB: www.unitedcorrstack.com
SIC: 2631 Corrugating medium
HQ: Interstate Resources, Inc.
1300 Wilson Blvd Ste 1075
Arlington VA 22209
703 243-3355

(G-16555)
**UNIVERSAL PEN & PENCIL CO
INC (PA)**
Also Called: O K Automation
776 Fritztown Rd (19608-1522)
P.O. Box 2146 (19608-0146)
PHONE.................................610 670-4720
Harvey Glantz, *President*
John Mihalasky, *Treasurer*
EMP: 6 **EST:** 1925
SQ FT: 7,500
SALES (est): 783.8K **Privately Held**
SIC: 3951 5112 3544 Ball point pens &
parts; pencils & pencil parts, mechanical;
pens &/or pencils; special dies, tools, jigs
& fixtures

(G-16556)
UNIVERSITY RIFLE CLUB INC
590 Schoffers Rd (19606-9150)
PHONE.................................610 927-1810
Robert McCoy, *President*
Glen Huls, *Corp Secy*
EMP: 5
SQ FT: 135
SALES (est): 77K **Privately Held**
SIC: 3949 Targets, archery & rifle shooting

(G-16557)
UNLIMITED MOBILITY
39-5 Mint Tier Ct (19606-3923)
PHONE.................................484 620-9587
Robert J Luminella, *Owner*
◆ **EMP:** 4
SALES (est): 230K **Privately Held**
SIC: 3534 Elevators & moving stairways

(G-16558)
VAI POMINI INC
Also Called: Ashlow
4201 Pottsville Pike (19605-1219)
PHONE.................................610 921-9101
Fax: 610 921-1480
EMP: 10
SALES (corp-wide): 96B **Privately Held**
SIC: 3312 Blast Furnace-Steel Works
HQ: Vai Pomini Inc.
501 Technology Dr
Canonsburg PA 15317
724 514-8280

(G-16559)
VAN MAANEN ALBERT
706 Wayne Ave (19611-1409)
PHONE.................................610 373-7292
EMP: 5
SALES (est): 210K **Privately Held**
SIC: 2095 Mfg Roasted Coffee

(G-16560)
**VOSSLOH TRACK MATERIAL
INC (HQ)**
5662a Leesport Ave (19605-9704)
PHONE.................................610 926-5400
Eliseo Bandala, *CEO*
Robert Ryland, *President*
Mike Carlo, *COO*
Martin Neumann, *CFO*
▲ **EMP:** 75
SQ FT: 45,000
SALES (est): 40.6MM
SALES (corp-wide): 990.2MM **Privately
Held**
SIC: 5051 3743 Rails & accessories; track
spikes; railroad equipment

PA: Vossloh Ag
Vosslohstr. 4
Werdohl 58791
239 252-0

(G-16561)
W L FEGLEY & SON INC
2701 Perkiomen Ave (19606-2201)
P.O. Box 25550, Scottsdale AZ (85255-
0109)
PHONE.................................610 779-0277
EMP: 5
SQ FT: 8,000
SALES (est): 400K **Privately Held**
SIC: 2752 2759 Offset & Letterpress Print-
ing

(G-16562)
**WEIDENHAMMER SYSTEMS
CORP (PA)**
935 Berkshire Blvd (19610-1229)
PHONE.................................610 378-1149
John Weidenhammer, *President*
Nadine B Weidenhammer, *Corp Secy*
Frank W Heins, *Exec VP*
Curtis Johnson III, *Vice Pres*
Jane M Lewis, *Vice Pres*
EMP: 90
SQ FT: 15,040
SALES: 40MM **Privately Held**
WEB: www.hammer.net
SIC: 7372 5045 Prepackaged software;
computer peripheral equipment

(G-16563)
**WELDING & THERMAL
TECHNOLOGIES**
44 Woodrow Ave (19608-1118)
PHONE.................................610 678-4847
Francis A Butkus, *President*
Merrie Butkus, *Corp Secy*
EMP: 3 **EST:** 1964
SALES (est): 100K **Privately Held**
SIC: 7692 Welding repair

(G-16564)
WER CORPORATION (PA)
Also Called: Aluminum Alloys
4601 Penn Ave (19608-9707)
P.O. Box 2197 (19608-0197)
PHONE.................................610 678-8023
William E Rita, *President*
Lori J Rita, *Vice Pres*
Timothy Moore, *CFO*
EMP: 105 **EST:** 1952
SQ FT: 160,000
SALES (est): 25.4MM **Privately Held**
WEB: www.aluminumalloysinc.com
SIC: 3365 3599 3369 Aluminum & alu-
minum-based alloy castings; machine
shop, jobbing & repair; nonferrous
foundries

(G-16565)
WILLIAM KLEIN SIGNS INC
938 Walnut St (19601-3625)
PHONE.................................610 374-5371
William J Klein, *President*
William J Klein III, *Treasurer*
EMP: 4
SQ FT: 2,800
SALES (est): 230K **Privately Held**
SIC: 7389 3993 Sign painting & lettering
shop; signs & advertising specialties

(G-16566)
**WILLIAMS METALFINISHING
INC**
870 Commerce St (19608-1347)
P.O. Box 2029 (19608-0029)
PHONE.................................610 670-1077
Robert A Williams, *CEO*
Lee A Williams, *President*
Mitch Werner, *General Mgr*
Kim R Williams, *Vice Pres*
Betty Jane Williams, *Shareholder*
EMP: 64
SQ FT: 65,000
SALES (est): 8MM **Privately Held**
WEB: www.polishers.com
SIC: 3471 Polishing, metals or formed
products

(G-16567)
**WINDSOR SERVICE TRUCKING
CORP**
2415 Kutztown Rd (19605-2960)
PHONE.................................610 929-0716
Scott Haines, *President*
Rodney Kline, *General Mgr*
Levan Hoover, *Accountant*
EMP: 150
SQ FT: 10,000
SALES (est): 12.8MM
SALES (corp-wide): 71.6MM **Privately
Held**
WEB: www.hkgroup.com
SIC: 4213 2951 Trucking, except local; as-
phalt paving mixtures & blocks
PA: H&K Group, Inc.
2052 Lucon Rd
Skippack PA 19474
610 584-8500

(G-16568)
WIXONS BAKERY INC
332 S Wyomissing Ave (19607-2551)
P.O. Box 204, Mohnton (19540-0204)
PHONE.................................610 777-6056
Gerald Wixon, *President*
Matthew Wixon, *Partner*
Michael Wixon, *Partner*
EMP: 13
SQ FT: 5,000
SALES (est): 1.8MM **Privately Held**
SIC: 2051 Mfg Bread/Related Products

(G-16569)
**WORLD ELEC SLS & SVC INC
(PA)**
3000 Kutztown Rd (19605-2617)
PHONE.................................610 939-9800
Joseph A Rado Jr, *President*
John Morelli, *CFO*
Roy Harrison, *Treasurer*
Elaine Rado, *Admin Sec*
▲ **EMP:** 107
SQ FT: 83,000
SALES (est): 22.8MM **Privately Held**
WEB: www.worldsway.com
SIC: 3672 Wiring boards

(G-16570)
WORLD MOTORSPORTS INC
3000 Kutztown Rd (19605-2617)
PHONE.................................610 929-1982
J Christian Rado, *President*
EMP: 7
SALES (est): 750.9K **Privately Held**
SIC: 3714 Motor vehicle parts & acces-
sories

(G-16571)
YUASA BATTERY INC
2901 Montrose Ave (19605-2752)
P.O. Box 70838, Philadelphia (19176-5838)
PHONE.................................610 929-5781
Hitoshi Ohta, *CEO*
Donn McMillan, *President*
Keith Ordemann, *President*
Patrick Hojnacki, *Senior VP*
Michael Ehlerman, *Vice Pres*
◆ **EMP:** 265
SQ FT: 190,000
SALES: 64.7MM
SALES (corp-wide): 3.8B **Privately Held**
WEB: www.yuasabatteries.com
SIC: 3692 Primary batteries, dry & wet
PA: Gs Yuasa Corporation
1, Inobabacho, Kisshoinnishinosho,
Minami-Ku
Kyoto KYO 601-8
753 121-211

(G-16572)
ZIP-NET INC
801 William Ln (19604-1523)
PHONE.................................610 939-9762
Andrew Wicklow, *President*
Anna Norton, *Treasurer*
▲ **EMP:** 40
SQ FT: 30,000
SALES (est): 6.1MM **Privately Held**
WEB: www.zip-net.com
SIC: 2241 Elastic webbing

Reading Station
Berks County

(G-16573)
READING PLASTIC PRODUCTS INC
101 Elm St (19606-2837)
PHONE..................................610 779-3128
Delbert Long, *President*
Donna Long, *Vice Pres*
EMP: 5
SQ FT: 5,000
SALES: 250K **Privately Held**
SIC: 3089 Injection molding of plastics

Reamstown
Lancaster County

(G-16574)
BOOSE ALUMINUM FOUNDRY CO INC
77 N Reamstown Rd (17567)
P.O. Box 261 (17567-0261)
PHONE..................................717 336-5581
Roger Boose, *President*
Joseph Boose, *Vice Pres*
Don Varnea, *Plant Mgr*
Richard Good, *Production*
Doug Siegrist, *CFO*
▲ **EMP:** 125 **EST:** 1946
SQ FT: 87,000
SALES (est): 34.7MM **Privately Held**
WEB: www.boosealum.com
SIC: 3365 Aluminum & aluminum-based alloy castings

(G-16575)
COCALICO BIOLOGICALS INC
449 Stevens Rd (17567)
P.O. Box 265 (17567-0265)
PHONE..................................717 336-1990
EMP: 38
SQ FT: 4,800
SALES (est): 6.9MM **Privately Held**
SIC: 2836 Mfg Biological Products

(G-16576)
DORMAKABA USA INC (HQ)
100 Dorma Dr (17567)
P.O. Box Ac (17567-0411)
PHONE..................................717 336-3881
Michael Kincaid, *President*
David Ledesma, *Vice Pres*
Loren Rakich, *Vice Pres*
Scott Folfas, *Prdtn Mgr*
Bernard Brinker, *CFO*
◆ **EMP:** 150
SQ FT: 150,000
SALES (est): 299.4MM
SALES (corp-wide): 2.5B **Privately Held**
WEB: www.dorma-usa.com
SIC: 3429 Builders' hardware
PA: Dormakaba Holding Ag
Hofwisenstrasse 24
RUmlang ZH 8153
448 189-011

Rebersburg
Centre County

(G-16577)
A & L PAINT CO LLC
112 4 Wheel Dr Ste 2 (16872-9412)
PHONE..................................814 349-8064
Amos Yoder, *Mng Member*
Jonathan Zook,
EMP: 6
SQ FT: 6,000
SALES: 600K **Privately Held**
SIC: 2851 5231 Paints & allied products; paint

(G-16578)
CENTRE PALLETS LLC
118 Pallet Dr (16872)
PHONE..................................814 349-8693
Louis J Peachey, *Mng Member*

EMP: 17
SALES (est): 2.2MM **Privately Held**
SIC: 2448 Pallets, wood & wood with metal

(G-16579)
WOODSIDE GLUEING
210 Back Rd (16872-9203)
PHONE..................................814 349-5646
EMP: 3
SALES (est): 274.7K **Privately Held**
SIC: 2426 Flooring, hardwood

Red Hill
Montgomery County

(G-16580)
CORONA CORPORATION
Also Called: Edison
820 Main St (18076-1321)
PHONE..................................215 679-9538
Keith Manser, *President*
Ashton D Gerlach, *President*
EMP: 10
SQ FT: 27,500
SALES: 4.1MM **Privately Held**
WEB: www.coronacorporation.com
SIC: 3469 3053 Stamping metal for the trade; gaskets & sealing devices

(G-16581)
GANNETT STLLITE INFO NTWRK INC
Also Called: Town & Country Newspaper
501 Graber Aly (18076-1300)
P.O. Box 462 (18076-0462)
PHONE..................................215 679-9561
Larry Roader, *Systems Mgr*
EMP: 7
SALES (corp-wide): 2.9B **Publicly Held**
WEB: www.usatoday.com
SIC: 2711 Newspapers: publishing only, not printed on site
HQ: Gannett Satellite Information Network, Llc
7950 Jones Branch Dr
Mc Lean VA 22102
703 854-6000

(G-16582)
HELIX INC
436 Adams St (18076-1228)
P.O. Box 288 (18076-0288)
PHONE..................................215 679-7924
William Fogel, *President*
Paula Fogel, *Corp Secy*
Keith Pearson, *Purch Mgr*
EMP: 10 **EST:** 1958
SQ FT: 12,500
SALES (est): 1MM **Privately Held**
SIC: 3599 3451 Machine shop, jobbing & repair; screw machine products

(G-16583)
MUTUAL INDUSTRIES NORTH INC
Also Called: Columbia Tape Mfg Div
625 Washington St (18076-1113)
P.O. Box 91 (18076-0091)
PHONE..................................215 679-7682
Bonnie Mawer, *General Mgr*
EMP: 65
SALES (corp-wide): 81.1MM **Privately Held**
WEB: www.mutualindustries.com
SIC: 2241 5131 Tie tapes, woven or braided; piece goods & other fabrics
PA: Mutual Industries North, Inc.
707 W Grange Ave Ste 1
Philadelphia PA 19120
215 927-6000

(G-16584)
PRODEX INC (PA)
Also Called: Dynatherm Boiler Mfg
436 Adams St Rear (18076-1228)
P.O. Box 14 (18076-0014)
PHONE..................................215 679-2405
Gary Hellerman, *President*
Michael Hellerman, *Vice Pres*
Richard Hellerman, *Vice Pres*
Earl H Hellerman Jr, *CFO*
Earl Hellerman, *CFO*
EMP: 10 **EST:** 1960

SQ FT: 22,000
SALES (est): 1.5MM **Privately Held**
SIC: 3441 Fabricated structural metal

(G-16585)
THOMAS & MULLER SYSTEMS LTD
80 Gravel Pike (18076-1423)
P.O. Box 25 (18076-0025)
PHONE..................................215 541-1961
Thomas Folger Jr, *President*
Brian Halteman, *Project Mgr*
EMP: 8
SQ FT: 3,000
SALES (est): 1.7MM **Privately Held**
WEB: www.thomasandmuller.com
SIC: 3535 Conveyors & conveying equipment

Red Lion
York County

(G-16586)
ABEX INDUSTRIES
1 Vulcan Ln (17356-1562)
PHONE..................................717 246-2611
A S Thompson, *Owner*
EMP: 7
SQ FT: 3,750
SALES (est): 1MM **Privately Held**
SIC: 3441 Fabricated structural metal

(G-16587)
APEX URETHANE MILLWORKS LLC
105 Church Ln (17356-1129)
PHONE..................................717 246-1948
Earnest Dining, *Mng Member*
▼ **EMP:** 39
SALES (est): 5.7MM **Privately Held**
SIC: 3089 3442 Injection molded finished plastic products; louvers, shutters, jalousies & similar items

(G-16588)
ARDENT MILLS LLC
Also Called: Conagra Redline
321 Taylor Ave (17356-2211)
PHONE..................................717 244-4559
David Clark, *Branch Mgr*
EMP: 8
SALES (corp-wide): 543.9MM **Privately Held**
WEB: www.conagra.com
SIC: 2041 Flour: blended, prepared or self-rising
PA: Ardent Mills, Llc
1875 Lawrence St Ste 1400
Denver CO 80202
800 851-9618

(G-16589)
ATLANTIC GLASS ETCHING INC
Also Called: York Glass Etching
450 Sterling Dr (17356-9508)
PHONE..................................717 244-7045
EMP: 7
SQ FT: 5,000
SALES (est): 627.3K **Privately Held**
SIC: 3231 Mfg Products-Purchased Glass

(G-16590)
BATTERY BUILDERS INC
Also Called: Mto Battery
237 N Church Ln (17356-1101)
PHONE..................................717 751-2705
Jason Abel, *President*
▲ **EMP:** 3
SALES (est): 537.5K **Privately Held**
SIC: 3692 Primary batteries, dry & wet

(G-16591)
CREATION CABINETRY & SIGN CO
3265 Cape Horn Rd (17356-9074)
PHONE..................................717 246-3386
James Pilachowski, *Owner*
EMP: 3
SALES: 100K **Privately Held**
SIC: 3993 5712 Signs, not made in custom sign painting shops; customized furniture & cabinets

(G-16592)
CROUSES PALLET SERVICE
100 Redco Ave (17356-1436)
PHONE..................................717 577-9012
EMP: 3
SALES (est): 152.7K **Privately Held**
SIC: 2448 Pallets, wood

(G-16593)
D E GEMILL INC
10174 Chapel Church Rd (17356-7711)
PHONE..................................717 755-9794
Dave E Gemill, *President*
Cary Gordon, *Vice Pres*
Ashley Hamme, *Mktg Dir*
EMP: 24
SQ FT: 12,000
SALES: 2.7MM **Privately Held**
WEB: www.degemill.com
SIC: 1799 2499 Parking lot maintenance; signboards, wood

(G-16594)
FAMILY HEIR-LOOM WEAVERS INC
775 Meadowview Dr (17356-8608)
PHONE..................................717 246-2431
Patrick Kline, *President*
Carole Kline, *Corp Secy*
Kelly Kline, *Admin Sec*
EMP: 10
SQ FT: 6,000
SALES (est): 1.3MM **Privately Held**
WEB: www.familyheirloomweavers.com
SIC: 2281 Yarn spinning mills

(G-16595)
FRANKS MARBLE & GRANITE LLC
125 Householder Ave (17356-2004)
PHONE..................................717 244-2685
Frank Pantano,
Carmela Pantano,
▲ **EMP:** 9
SALES (est): 1.1MM **Privately Held**
WEB: www.franksgranite.com
SIC: 3281 Granite, cut & shaped

(G-16596)
GENERAL DYNAMICS OTS PA INC
200 E High St (17356-1426)
PHONE..................................717 244-4551
Tu Dam, *Human Res Mgr*
Daniel Mc Kenwick, *Director*
EMP: 106
SQ FT: 2,670
SALES (corp-wide): 36.1B **Publicly Held**
SIC: 3483 Ammunition, except for small arms
HQ: General Dynamics Ots (Pennsylvania), Inc.
200 E High St
Red Lion PA 17356
717 246-8208

(G-16597)
GENERAL DYNAMICS OTS PA INC (DH)
200 E High St (17356-1426)
PHONE..................................717 246-8208
Michael Wilson, *President*
Jason Fye, *President*
▲ **EMP:** 8
SALES (est): 30.3MM
SALES (corp-wide): 36.1B **Publicly Held**
SIC: 3483 Ammunition, except for small arms
HQ: General Dynamics Ordnance And Tactical Systems, Inc.
11399 16th Ct N Ste 200
Saint Petersburg FL 33716
727 578-8100

(G-16598)
GENIE ELECTRONICS CO INC
3090 Cape Horn Rd (17356-9068)
PHONE..................................717 244-1099
B Robert Snyder, *CEO*
William R Snyder, *President*
Holly Seace, *Vice Pres*
Lori A Noga, *Treasurer*
EMP: 60 **EST:** 1972
SQ FT: 24,000

▲ = Import ▼=Export
◆ =Import/Export

SALES (est): 21.4MM **Privately Held**
WEB: www.securityfence.com
SIC: **1799** 5039 3446 5065 Fence construction; wire fence, gates & accessories; flagpoles, metal; electronic parts & equipment; management services; printed circuit boards

(G-16599)
GENIE ELECTRONICS CO INC (PA)
3090 Cape Horn Rd (17356-9068)
PHONE.....................717 244-1099
Robert Snyder, *CEO*
Tom Harbaugh, *President*
William R Snyder, *President*
Holly Seace, *Vice Pres*
Lori A Noga, *Treasurer*
EMP: 140
SALES (est): 2MM **Privately Held**
SIC: **1799** 5039 3446 5065 Fence construction; wire fence, gates & accessories; flagpoles, metal; electronic parts & equipment; management services; printed circuit boards

(G-16600)
HESS S ORNAMENTAL IRON
1754 Raub Rd (17356)
PHONE.....................717 927-9160
Lori Hess, *President*
EMP: 10
SALES (est): 1.6MM **Privately Held**
SIC: **3446** Railings, bannisters, guards, etc.: made from metal pipe

(G-16601)
INFINITE QUEST CABINETRY CORP
560 Boundary Ave (17356-1939)
PHONE.....................301 222-3592
Amanda Bahari, *President*
EMP: 4
SALES (est): 786.9K **Privately Held**
SIC: **5031** 5712 2434 2499 Kitchen cabinets; customized furniture & cabinets; wood kitchen cabinets; vanities, bathroom: wood; woodenware, kitchen & household; carvings, furniture: wood; wood office furniture

(G-16602)
JOHN M ROHRBAUGH CO INC
237 N Church Ln (17356-1101)
P.O. Box 325 (17356-0325)
PHONE.....................717 244-2895
Terry L Rohrbaugh, *President*
Debra Rohrbaugh, *Corp Secy*
EMP: 6 EST: 1946
SQ FT: 18,000
SALES (est): 579.7K **Privately Held**
SIC: **2426** 2499 Frames for upholstered furniture, wood; laundry products, wood

(G-16603)
KRAEMER PROPERTIES INC
1 Vulcan Ln Ste 1 # 1 (17356-1563)
PHONE.....................717 246-0208
Brian Weaver, *Manager*
EMP: 6
SALES (corp-wide): 6.3MM **Privately Held**
WEB: www.luminer.com
SIC: **2672** Labels (unprinted), gummed: made from purchased materials
PA: Kraemer Properties, Inc.
1925 Swarthmore Ave Ste 1
Lakewood NJ 08701
732 886-6557

(G-16604)
LEVERWOOD MACHINE WORKS INC
Also Called: Leverwood Knife
100 Redco Ave Ste D (17356-1436)
PHONE.....................717 246-4105
Patrick Lever, *President*
Jody Alwood, *Vice Pres*
EMP: 10
SQ FT: 40,000
SALES: 1MM **Privately Held**
WEB: www.leverwood.com
SIC: **3545** Machine knives, metalworking

(G-16605)
LION INDUSTRIAL KNIFE CO INC
107 E High St (17356-1409)
PHONE.....................717 244-8195
John Morton, *President*
EMP: 5
SALES (est): 470K **Privately Held**
SIC: **3423** 7699 Knives, agricultural or industrial; knife, saw & tool sharpening & repair

(G-16606)
M B GRAPHICS
608 Nottingham Way (17356-9232)
PHONE.....................717 246-9000
Jason Martin, *Owner*
EMP: 3
SQ FT: 15,000
SALES: 780K **Privately Held**
SIC: **2672** Labels (unprinted), gummed: made from purchased materials

(G-16607)
MARSHMALLOWMBA
35 East Ave (17356-2201)
PHONE.....................703 340-7157
Amy Hughes, *Partner*
Sandra Stegman, *Partner*
EMP: 3
SALES (est): 100.5K **Privately Held**
SIC: **2064** Chewing candy, not chewing gum

(G-16608)
MAS-FAB INC
Also Called: Formit Steel Co
775 Lombard Rd (17356-8226)
P.O. Box 285 (17356-0285)
PHONE.....................717 244-4561
Richard R Massey II, *President*
Peter Ronky, *Exec VP*
Ray Ruth, *Vice Pres*
Donna Massey, *Treasurer*
EMP: 45
SQ FT: 35,000
SALES (est): 14.3MM **Privately Held**
WEB: www.formit.com
SIC: **3441** Fabricated structural metal

(G-16609)
MICRO-FUSION LLC
536 Boundary Ave (17356-1906)
PHONE.....................717 244-4648
James Bucher, *Principal*
EMP: 4 EST: 2009
SALES (est): 347.6K **Privately Held**
SIC: **3842** Welders' hoods

(G-16610)
NUPAK PRINTING LLC
177 E Walnut St (17356-2523)
P.O. Box 128 (17356-0128)
PHONE.....................717 244-4041
Scott Drawbaugh, *Mfg Dir*
Sherry Smith,
◆ EMP: 60 EST: 1929
SQ FT: 100,000
SALES (est): 11.4MM
SALES (corp-wide): 70.4MM **Privately Held**
WEB: www.nupakprinting.com
SIC: **3672** 2675 Printed circuit boards; die-cut paper & board
PA: Specialty Finance And Consulting Corporation
5541 Gulf Of Mexico Dr
Longboat Key FL 34228
717 246-1661

(G-16611)
PRECISION CARBIDE TOOLING INC
267 Cherry St Western (17356-1597)
PHONE.....................717 244-4771
Harry A Lohss Jr, *President*
EMP: 7 EST: 1963
SQ FT: 6,000
SALES (est): 908.1K **Privately Held**
SIC: **3545** 7699 Cutting tools for machine tools; knife, saw & tool sharpening & repair

(G-16612)
S & S PRECISION TOOL INC
380 Boxwood Rd (17356-8348)
PHONE.....................717 244-1600
John Shanbarger, *President*
EMP: 6
SQ FT: 3,012
SALES (est): 825K **Privately Held**
SIC: **3599** Machine shop, jobbing & repair

(G-16613)
SPECIALTY INDUSTRIES INC (HQ)
175 E Walnut St (17356-2523)
P.O. Box 330 (17356-0330)
PHONE.....................717 246-1661
Carl W Cheek, *President*
John Forrey Jr, *President*
Steve Overmiller, *Plant Mgr*
Kim Snyder, *Safety Mgr*
John Diventi, *CFO*
▲ EMP: 130 EST: 1972
SQ FT: 191,000
SALES (est): 30.5MM
SALES (corp-wide): 70.4MM **Privately Held**
WEB: www.westreetindustries.com
SIC: **2653** 2679 Sheets, corrugated: made from purchased materials; boxes, corrugated: made from purchased materials; paper products, converted
PA: Specialty Finance And Consulting Corporation
5541 Gulf Of Mexico Dr
Longboat Key FL 34228
717 246-1661

(G-16614)
SPECILTY MTALLURGICAL PDTS INC
Also Called: S M P
25 Pleasant Ave (17356-2012)
PHONE.....................717 246-0385
James B Clark, *President*
▲ EMP: 10
SQ FT: 6,000
SALES (est): 1.7MM **Privately Held**
SIC: **3399** 3354 3341 Powder, metal; aluminum extruded products; secondary nonferrous metals

(G-16615)
STEVEN LAUCKS
Also Called: Stone House Logistics
675 Blouse Rd (17356-8445)
PHONE.....................717 244-6310
Steven Laucks, *Owner*
EMP: 1
SALES: 1MM **Privately Held**
SIC: **3545** Tools & accessories for machine tools

(G-16616)
TATE ACCESS FLOORS INC
Also Called: Access Floor Division
52 Spring Bale Rd (17356)
PHONE.....................717 244-4071
Russel Shiels, *President*
Jeff Horn, *Controller*
Ed Blazeck, *Exec Dir*
EMP: 150 **Privately Held**
WEB: www.tateaccessfloors.com
SIC: **3469** Stamping metal for the trade
HQ: Tate Access Floors, Inc.
7510 Montevideo Rd
Jessup MD 20794
410 799-4200

(G-16617)
TATE ACCESS FLOORS INC
52 Springvale Rd (17356-8337)
PHONE.....................717 244-4071
Ed Blazek, *Manager*
EMP: 200 **Privately Held**
WEB: www.tateaccessfloors.com
SIC: **3275** 3444 Gypsum products; sheet metalwork
HQ: Tate Access Floors, Inc.
7510 Montevideo Rd
Jessup MD 20794
410 799-4200

(G-16618)
TYSON
440 Steinfelt Rd (17356-8224)
PHONE.....................717 755-4782
Linda Tyson, *Principal*
EMP: 3
SALES (est): 162.7K **Privately Held**
SIC: **2011** Meat packing plants

Reeders
Monroe County

(G-16619)
J J C L INC
6 Mountain Rd (18352)
P.O. Box 186 (18352-0186)
PHONE.....................570 619-7347
James A Fallenstein, *President*
EMP: 9
SALES (est): 1.8MM **Privately Held**
WEB: www.jjcl.net
SIC: **2873** Fertilizers: natural (organic), except compost

Reedsville
Mifflin County

(G-16620)
ALLTRISTA PLASTICS CORPORATION
Also Called: Jarden Plastic Solutions
20 Setar Way (17084-8634)
PHONE.....................717 667-2131
Kevin D Bower, *President*
▼ EMP: 33
SALES (est): 7.1MM **Privately Held**
SIC: **3089** Injection molding of plastics

(G-16621)
AUTO ACCESSORIES AMERICA INC
Also Called: Corvette America
100 Classic Car Dr (17084-8851)
PHONE.....................717 667-3004
Daniel J Lekander, *CEO*
David E Hall, *President*
John T Weaver, *Vice Pres*
John Weaver, *Vice Pres*
Karen Burke, *Purch Mgr*
▲ EMP: 110
SQ FT: 55,000
SALES (est): 36.6MM **Privately Held**
WEB: www.corvetteamerica.com
SIC: **5013** 2396 3714 Automotive supplies & parts; automotive trimmings, fabric; motor vehicle parts & accessories

(G-16622)
BIG VALLEY BEVERAGE INC
8 Apple Ln (17084-9413)
PHONE.....................717 667-1414
Diana Adair, *President*
Diane Lingle, *President*
EMP: 3
SALES (est): 217.8K **Privately Held**
SIC: **2082** Malt liquors

(G-16623)
HI-TECH NUTRACEUTICALS LLC (PA)
5135 Old Us Highway 322 (17084-8840)
P.O. Box 55 (17084-0055)
PHONE.....................717 667-2142
Jared Wheat, *Principal*
▲ EMP: 24
SALES (est): 4.4MM **Privately Held**
SIC: **2023** 7389 Dietary supplements, dairy & non-dairy based; labeling bottles, cans, cartons, etc.

(G-16624)
JARDEN CORPORATION
Also Called: Jarden Plastic Solution
20 Plastics Ave (17084)
PHONE.....................717 667-2131
Steve Parrish, *Branch Mgr*
EMP: 179
SALES (corp-wide): 8.6B **Publicly Held**
WEB: www.jarden.com
SIC: **3089** Plastic containers, except foam

HQ: Jarden Llc
221 River St
Hoboken NJ 07030

(G-16625)
JOHN J PEACHEY
Also Called: Peaches Wood Products
209 Sawmill Rd (17084-9346)
PHONE.................................717 667-9373
John J Peachey, *Owner*
Mike Hoffman, *Manager*
EMP: 10
SALES (est): 856.5K **Privately Held**
SIC: 2431 Millwork

(G-16626)
PHILIPS ULTRASOUND INC
Phillips Ultrasound
1 Echo Dr (17084-8603)
PHONE.................................717 667-5000
Tracey Peters, *Manager*
EMP: 28
SALES (corp-wide): 20.9B **Privately Held**
SIC: 3845 Electromedical equipment
HQ: Philips Ultrasound, Inc.
22100 Bothell Everett Hwy
Bothell WA 98021
800 982-2011

(G-16627)
S&K PALLET LLC
684 Old Three Cent Ln (17084-9464)
PHONE.................................717 667-0001
Steven Yoder, *Partner*
EMP: 3
SALES (est): 228.4K **Privately Held**
SIC: 2448 Pallets, wood & wood with metal

(G-16628)
TIP TOP RESOURCES LLC (PA)
Also Called: Go2products
837 Green Ln (17084-9352)
PHONE.................................407 818-6937
Scott Mogel, *Mng Member*
Mark L Yoder, *Manager*
EMP: 3 **EST:** 2013
SQ FT: 20,000
SALES (est): 453.5K **Privately Held**
SIC: 8748 2841 Business consulting; soap & other detergents

(G-16629)
UNIPAR INC
130 Royal St (17084-9783)
PHONE.................................717 667-3354
Robert D Parks, *President*
James R Parks, *Vice Pres*
▲ **EMP:** 49
SQ FT: 54,000
SALES (est): 7.6MM **Privately Held**
WEB: www.uniparplastics.com
SIC: 3089 Molding primary plastic

Reinholds
Lancaster County

(G-16630)
CANDLSETCETERA CANDLES ACC LLC
Also Called: Candlesetcetera.com
550 Golf Rd (17569-9043)
PHONE.................................610 507-7830
Penny Spratling,
Nigel Spratling,
▼ **EMP:** 4
SQ FT: 1,200
SALES (est): 325.6K **Privately Held**
SIC: 3999 Candles

(G-16631)
FILTER SHINE INC
80 W Main St (17569-9513)
P.O. Box 202, Denver (17517-0202)
PHONE.................................866 977-4463
EMP: 4
SALES (est): 671.5K **Privately Held**
SIC: 3569 Mfg General Industrial Machinery

(G-16632)
HORSTS HANDPAINTING
1070 W Swartzville Rd (17569-9405)
PHONE.................................717 336-7098

Howard Horst, *President*
EMP: 3
SALES (est): 200K **Privately Held**
SIC: 3993 Signs & advertising specialties

(G-16633)
JAYCO GRAFIX INC
16 Buck Run (17569-9003)
PHONE.................................610 678-2640
James A Adams, *President*
Leo F D, *Editor*
James Crane, *Vice Pres*
EMP: 51
SQ FT: 30,000
SALES: 7MM **Privately Held**
WEB: www.westlawngraphic.com
SIC: 7311 2752 2741 7334 Advertising agencies; commercial printing, offset; miscellaneous publishing; photocopying & duplicating services; motion picture & video production; commercial printing

(G-16634)
KEYSTONE NITEWEAR CO INC (PA)
Also Called: Kool Dri Rainwear
550 W Route 897 (17569-9800)
PHONE.................................717 336-7534
Earl M Myers, *President*
▲ **EMP:** 20 **EST:** 1932
SQ FT: 40,000
SALES (est): 2.1MM **Privately Held**
WEB: www.kooldrirainwear.com
SIC: 2385 5136 Raincoats, except vulcanized rubber: purchased materials; men's & boys' clothing

(G-16635)
LANCASTER MAID CABINETS INC
45 Lincoln Ave (17569-9590)
PHONE.................................717 336-0111
Larry Binkley, *CEO*
EMP: 10
SQ FT: 16,000
SALES (est): 1.8MM **Privately Held**
WEB: www.lancastermaid.com
SIC: 5211 2434 Cabinets, kitchen; bathroom fixtures, equipment & supplies; vanities, bathroom: wood

(G-16636)
PREMIER SPOUTING DESIGN LLC
50 Willow St (17569-9332)
PHONE.................................717 336-1205
Jason Rivers, *Mng Member*
EMP: 5
SALES: 150K **Privately Held**
SIC: 3089 Spouting, plastic & glass fiber reinforced

(G-16637)
W & W WELDING INC
530a Swamp Church Rd (17569-9419)
PHONE.................................717 336-4314
Clifford Walter, *President*
EMP: 4
SALES: 200K **Privately Held**
SIC: 7692 1799 Welding repair; welding on site

Renfrew
Butler County

(G-16638)
CHARLES STECKMAN
Also Called: Steckman, C K Memorials
1009 Evans City Rd (16053-8401)
PHONE.................................724 789-7066
Charles Steckman, *Owner*
EMP: 3
SQ FT: 4,000
SALES: 300K **Privately Held**
WEB: www.rocks2art.com
SIC: 3281 5021 3993 2541 Granite, cut & shaped; outdoor & lawn furniture; signs & advertising specialties; wood partitions & fixtures

(G-16639)
FREYS RESEARCH INC (PA)
Also Called: Carbinite Metal Coatings
463 Brownsdale Rd 1 (16053-8803)
PHONE.................................724 586-5659
Robert Freyvogle, *President*
Lauren Busch, *Sales Staff*
Andrew Towns, *Marketing Staff*
EMP: 4
SALES (est): 839.7K **Privately Held**
WEB: www.carbinite.com
SIC: 3479 Etching & engraving

(G-16640)
JAMES MCATEE
Also Called: J E M Manufacturing
101 Eckstein Dr (16053-8315)
PHONE.................................724 789-9078
James McAtee, *Owner*
Kristen McAtee, *Corp Secy*
EMP: 3
SALES (est): 250.3K **Privately Held**
SIC: 3599 3444 Machine shop, jobbing & repair; sheet metalwork

(G-16641)
NELMARK ELECTRIC INC
335 Beacon Rd (16053-9406)
PHONE.................................724 290-0314
Mark Cukovich, *President*
EMP: 4
SALES: 100K **Privately Held**
SIC: 3495 Wire springs

(G-16642)
SHEDIO LOGGING & LUMBER (PA)
114 Silver Dr (16053-9648)
PHONE.................................724 794-1321
John P Shedio Jr, *Owner*
EMP: 9
SALES: 1.1MM **Privately Held**
SIC: 2421 Sawmills & planing mills, general

(G-16643)
VIKING VEE INC
Also Called: Viking-Spirit Trailers
839 Evans City Rd (16053-9205)
PHONE.................................724 789-9194
Greg Whittenberger, *President*
Harold W Whittenberger, *Corp Secy*
EMP: 7
SQ FT: 6,000
SALES: 800K **Privately Held**
WEB: www.vikingtrailer.com
SIC: 3715 7539 Truck trailers; trailer repair

(G-16644)
XTO ENERGY INC
230 Hicks Rd (16053-9708)
PHONE.................................540 772-3220
Joshua Abbott, *Supervisor*
EMP: 71
SALES (corp-wide): 290.2B **Publicly Held**
SIC: 1311 Crude petroleum production
HQ: Xto Energy Inc.
22777 Sprngwoods Vlg Pkwy
Spring TX 77389

Reno
Venango County

(G-16645)
BUSINESS APPLICATIONS LTD
Also Called: Precision Plastic Balls
805 Walnut St (16343)
P.O. Box 425 (16343-0425)
PHONE.................................814 677-7056
George E Tarr II, *President*
▲ **EMP:** 3 **EST:** 2000
SALES: 50K **Privately Held**
WEB: www.precisionplasticballs.com
SIC: 3069 Balls, rubber

(G-16646)
LIBERTY ELECTRONICS
191 Howard St (16343)
PHONE.................................814 676-0600
John Dumot, *President*
EMP: 275

SALES (est): 22MM **Privately Held**
SIC: 3679 Mfg Electronic Components

(G-16647)
METALIFE INDUSTRIES INC
141 Mong Way (16343)
P.O. Box 53 (16343-0053)
PHONE.................................814 676-5661
Robert Kockler, *President*
Andrew Kockler, *Vice Pres*
Robert Jacoby, *Sales Staff*
EMP: 10 **EST:** 1964
SQ FT: 2,400
SALES (est): 1.5MM **Privately Held**
WEB: www.metalifeind.com
SIC: 3471 Electroplating of metals or formed products

(G-16648)
VENANGO MACHINE PRODUCTS INC
702 Walnut St (16343)
P.O. Box 427 (16343-0427)
PHONE.................................814 676-5741
Donald Jones, *President*
Bonnie Rodgers, *Corp Secy*
Duane Jones, *Vice Pres*
EMP: 15
SQ FT: 6,300
SALES (est): 2MM **Privately Held**
SIC: 3599 Machine shop, jobbing & repair

Renovo
Clinton County

(G-16649)
RENOVO RAIL INDUSTRIES LLC (PA)
504 Erie Ave (17764-1018)
PHONE.................................570 923-2093
Gene Sockman, *Mng Member*
Randy Bibey,
EMP: 3
SALES (est): 1.6MM **Privately Held**
SIC: 3743 4789 Railroad car rebuilding; sleeping cars, railroad; railroad car repair

(G-16650)
SMITH LUMBER CO
12476 Renovo Rd (17764-1333)
PHONE.................................570 923-0188
Barbara Riddles, *Partner*
Robert E Probst Jr, *Partner*
EMP: 10
SALES: 800K **Privately Held**
SIC: 2411 Pole cutting contractors

(G-16651)
UNITRAC RAILROAD MATERIALS INC
100 Industrial Park Rd (17764)
PHONE.................................570 923-1514
EMP: 4
SALES (corp-wide): 168.9MM **Privately Held**
SIC: 5088 3312 Whol Transportation Equipment Blast Furnace-Steel Works
HQ: Unitrac Railroad Materials, Inc.
2715 Byington Solway Rd
Knoxville TN 37931
865 693-9063

Republic
Fayette County

(G-16652)
B W E LTD
Legion St (15475)
PHONE.................................724 246-0470
Jannetta Moscovits, *Partner*
Paul Moscovits, *Partner*
EMP: 20
SALES: 1MM **Privately Held**
WEB: www.bwe.co.uk
SIC: 2671 5169 Plastic film, coated or laminated for packaging; explosives

Revere
Bucks County

(G-16653)
M L SCOTT & SONS
8537 Easton Rd (18953)
P.O. Box 3 (18953-0003)
PHONE..............................610 847-5671
Marianne L Scott, *Partner*
Eric J Scott, *Partner*
EMP: 4
SALES: 175K **Privately Held**
SIC: 3599 1522 Machine shop, jobbing & repair; hotel/motel & multi-family home renovation & remodeling

Rew
Mckean County

(G-16654)
NORTHERN TIER INC
24 Northland Rd (16744-1402)
PHONE..............................814 465-2299
David Grady, *President*
EMP: 8
SQ FT: 3,200
SALES (est): 800K **Privately Held**
SIC: 1389 Gas field services

Reynoldsville
Jefferson County

(G-16655)
BUY PHOTO STOCK LOWES DIGITA
57 Yellow Brick Rd (15851-1085)
PHONE..............................814 954-0273
EMP: 4
SALES (est): 185.9K **Privately Held**
SIC: 2741 Miscellaneous publishing

(G-16656)
CACTUS WELLHEAD LLC
194 Aviation Way (15851-8188)
PHONE..............................814 308-0344
EMP: 9
SALES (corp-wide): 544.1MM **Publicly Held**
SIC: 3533 Oil & gas drilling rigs & equipment
HQ: Cactus Wellhead, Llc
920 Mmrial Cy Way Ste 300
Houston TX 77024

(G-16657)
INTERNATIONAL CARTRIDGE CORP
Also Called: ICC Ammo
2273 Route 310 (15851-2429)
PHONE..............................814 938-6820
David Smith, *President*
Ryan Forsythe, *General Mgr*
Alexander Krot, *Vice Pres*
Louise Smith, *Treasurer*
Joy Krot, *Admin Sec*
◆ EMP: 15
SQ FT: 10,000
SALES: 3MM **Privately Held**
WEB: www.iccammo.com
SIC: 3482 5099 Small arms ammunition; firearms & ammunition, except sporting

(G-16658)
NC INDUSTRIES INC (PA)
Also Called: Niagara Cutter
150 S 5th St (15851-8930)
PHONE..............................248 528-5200
Roger D Bollier, *Ch of Bd*
Sherwood L Bollier, *Vice Pres*
Jeff Bush, *Engineer*
Jason Stiver, *Engineer*
William C Szabo, *Treasurer*
EMP: 15
SQ FT: 8,500

SALES (est): 63.3MM **Privately Held**
SIC: 3545 3479 5084 Cutting tools for machine tools; coating of metals & formed products; machine tools & accessories

(G-16659)
NIAGARA CUTTER PA INC
150 S 5th St (15851-8999)
P.O. Box 279 (15851-0279)
PHONE..............................814 653-8211
Sherwood L Bollier, *CEO*
Roger D Bollier, *Vice Pres*
EMP: 50
SALES (est): 6.7MM
SALES (corp-wide): 63.3MM **Privately Held**
SIC: 3545 Cutting tools for machine tools
PA: Nc Industries, Inc.
150 S 5th St
Reynoldsville PA 15851
248 528-5200

(G-16660)
PAULA KESWICK
Also Called: Cherish Creamery
2771 Paradise Rd (15851-8621)
PHONE..............................574 298-2022
Paula Keswick, *Owner*
EMP: 3
SALES (est): 185.7K **Privately Held**
SIC: 2021 Creamery butter

(G-16661)
R AND C LOGGING
1964 Shale Pit Rd (15851-2042)
PHONE..............................814 590-4422
Raymond Coblentz, *Principal*
EMP: 3
SALES (est): 209.9K **Privately Held**
SIC: 2411 Logging

(G-16662)
RALPH MCCLURE
Also Called: G & M Sales
1500 Mcdaniel Dr (15851)
PHONE..............................610 738-1440
Ralph E McClure, *Principal*
Kimberly Guthrie, *Principal*
Dave Myers, *Sales Staff*
EMP: 6
SALES (est): 248.7K **Privately Held**
SIC: 3354 Aluminum extruded products

(G-16663)
REYNOLDSVILLE CASKET COMPANY (HQ)
560 Myrtle St (15851-8928)
P.O. Box 68 (15851-0068)
PHONE..............................814 653-9666
Wayne Jackson, *President*
Lloyd Deible, *Vice Pres*
John Bean, *Treasurer*
Robert Hanak, *Admin Sec*
EMP: 3
SQ FT: 60,000
SALES (est): 5.9MM
SALES (corp-wide): 1.5B **Publicly Held**
WEB: www.reynoldsvillecasket.com
SIC: 3995 Burial caskets
PA: Matthews International Corporation
2 N Shore Ctr Ste 200
Pittsburgh PA 15212
412 442-8200

(G-16664)
SINTERGY INC
2130 Indl Blvd (15851)
PHONE..............................814 653-9640
Ricky Young, *President*
Jason Emery, *Vice Pres*
Daryl Almendarez, *QC Mgr*
Doug Grieneisen, *Sales Mgr*
Steve Miller, *Admin Sec*
EMP: 15
SQ FT: 6,000
SALES (est): 2.7MM **Privately Held**
WEB: www.sintergy.net
SIC: 3599 Machine shop, jobbing & repair

(G-16665)
SMITH LOGGING
887 Sterrett Rd (15851-7553)
PHONE..............................814 371-2698
EMP: 3 EST: 2010
SALES (est): 272.7K **Privately Held**
SIC: 2411 Logging

(G-16666)
STAAR DISTRIBUTING LLC (PA)
560 Myrtle St (15851-8928)
PHONE..............................814 612-2115
Ben Lovingood, *Project Mgr*
Ed Ward, *Project Mgr*
William Young, *Mktg Dir*
Todd Gordon, *Administration*
EMP: 88
SALES (est): 27.3MM **Privately Held**
SIC: 3441 1771 1389 3443 Building components, structural steel; concrete repair; building oil & gas well foundations on site; industrial vessels, tanks & containers

(G-16667)
UTILITIES & INDUSTRIES INC (HQ)
1995 Reynoldsville (15851)
PHONE..............................814 653-8269
George Roseman, *President*
Robert J Perry, *Vice Pres*
Rich Filer, *Prdtn Mgr*
Cheryl Scott, *Admin Sec*
EMP: 70
SALES (est): 5.6MM
SALES (corp-wide): 22MM **Privately Held**
SIC: 7699 3824 Industrial equipment services; fluid meters & counting devices
PA: Brookville Glove Manufacturing Company, Inc.
98 Service Center Rd B
Brookville PA 15825
814 849-7324

Rheems
Lancaster County

(G-16668)
WENGER CORPORATE SERVICES LLC
101 W Harrisburg Ave (17570)
P.O. Box 26 (17570-0026)
PHONE..............................800 692-6008
EMP: 3
SALES (est): 221.9K **Privately Held**
SIC: 2048 Prepared feeds

Rices Landing
Greene County

(G-16669)
FERNCLIFF MEAT PROCESSING
276 Ferncliff Rd (15357-1173)
PHONE..............................724 592-6042
EMP: 6
SALES (est): 413.3K **Privately Held**
SIC: 2011 Meat packing plants

(G-16670)
NEXGEN INDUSTRIAL SERVICES INC
Also Called: Nexgen Industrial Contractors
125 Long St (15357-1130)
PHONE..............................724 592-5133
Don Lemley, *President*
Dean Stanley, *Corp Secy*
Marsha Presock, *Office Mgr*
EMP: 38
SALES (est): 9.9MM **Privately Held**
SIC: 1081 Metal mining services

(G-16671)
PIONEER DRILLING SERVICES LTD
1083 N 88 Rd (15357)
PHONE..............................724 592-6707
Seldon Gus Miller, *Division Mgr*
EMP: 6
SALES (corp-wide): 590.1MM **Publicly Held**
SIC: 1381 Drilling oil & gas wells
HQ: Pioneer Drilling Services, Ltd.
1250 Ne Loop 410 Ste 1000
San Antonio TX 78209
210 828-7689

Richboro
Bucks County

(G-16672)
ADVANCED PLASMA SOLUTIONS INC
24 Purdue Dr (18954-1246)
PHONE..............................484 568-4942
Pavel Kovtunenko, *President*
EMP: 10 EST: 2014
SALES (est): 1.4MM **Privately Held**
SIC: 2836 Plasmas

(G-16673)
ADVANCED TECHNOLOGY LABS INC (PA)
Also Called: A T L
12 E Georgianna Dr (18954-1314)
PHONE..............................215 355-8111
Kenneth S Fertner, *President*
Catherine M Butler, *Treasurer*
EMP: 260
SQ FT: 5,000
SALES (est): 16.2MM **Privately Held**
WEB: www.atllabs.com
SIC: 7373 8731 3672 Turnkey vendors, computer systems; electronic research; printed circuit boards

(G-16674)
DIGITAL SIGN ID CORPORATION
Also Called: Dsid
853 2nd Street Pike A111 (18954-1082)
PHONE..............................800 407-9188
Brandon Edgerton, *CEO*
Richard Brock, *COO*
EMP: 6
SALES (est): 7.4K **Privately Held**
SIC: 3993 Signs & advertising specialties

(G-16675)
HORIZON ELECTRIC LIGHTING LLC
998 2nd Street Pike (18954-1527)
PHONE..............................267 288-5353
EMP: 4
SALES (est): 473.6K **Privately Held**
SIC: 3699 Electrical work

(G-16676)
MR PRINTER INC
855 Bustleton Pike (18954-1355)
PHONE..............................215 354-5533
Donald E Walterick, *President*
Sarah Ann Walterick, *Corp Secy*
EMP: 4
SALES (est): 44.2K **Privately Held**
SIC: 2752 Commercial printing, lithographic

(G-16677)
PHARMCTCAL STFFING SLTONS INC
130 Almshouse Rd (18954-1100)
PHONE..............................215 322-5392
Rachpal Malhotra, *Principal*
EMP: 3 EST: 2016
SALES (est): 87.1K **Privately Held**
SIC: 2834 Pharmaceutical preparations

(G-16678)
WEBCO INC
7 Legacy Oaks Dr (18954-1066)
PHONE..............................215 942-9366
Louis Garber, *President*
Victoria Garber, *Vice Pres*
EMP: 10
SQ FT: 10,000
SALES: 650K **Privately Held**
SIC: 3599 Machine shop, jobbing & repair

GEOGRAPHIC

Richfield
Juniata County

(G-16679)
HOFFMAN BROTHERS LUMBER INC
118 Sand Valley Rd (17086-9600)
PHONE..................................717 694-3340
Delbert Hoffman, *President*
Jeffrey Hoffman, *Vice Pres*
Corey R Hoffman, *Treasurer*
Audrey Hoffman, *Admin Sec*
EMP: 17
SQ FT: 4,000
SALES (est): 2.6MM **Privately Held**
SIC: 2421 Lumber: rough, sawed or planed

(G-16680)
HORSTCRAFT MILLWORKS LLC
272 Mill Rd (17086-9147)
PHONE..................................717 694-9222
Marlin J Horst, *Mng Member*
Jason L Horst,
EMP: 9
SALES (est): 1.3MM **Privately Held**
SIC: 2431 2426 Millwork; lumber, hardwood dimension

(G-16681)
QUAKER VALLEY SPECIALTIES
Also Called: Mountain Meadows Cheese Mfrs
2383 Quaker Run Rd (17086-8578)
PHONE..................................717 694-3999
Glenn Wenger, *Owner*
EMP: 4
SALES (est): 300K **Privately Held**
SIC: 2434 Wood kitchen cabinets

(G-16682)
S&S CUSTOM SAWING
31 Saw Mill Ln (17086-9633)
P.O. Box 1 (17086-0001)
PHONE..................................717 694-3248
Mark Strawser, *Partner*
EMP: 3 **EST:** 1994
SALES (est): 181.1K **Privately Held**
SIC: 2421 Sawmills & planing mills, general

Richland
Lebanon County

(G-16683)
BROWN SIGNS INC
190 Millardsville Rd (17087-9709)
PHONE..................................717 866-2669
David Binner, *President*
Patricia Binner, *Admin Sec*
EMP: 4
SQ FT: 3,000
SALES (est): 398.5K **Privately Held**
SIC: 3993 7532 Electric signs; truck painting & lettering

(G-16684)
CORETEC PLASTICS INC
308 Poplar St (17087-9715)
PHONE..................................717 866-7472
James S Anglin, *CEO*
Loretta Mathias, *Vice Pres*
Randolph Holmes, *Admin Sec*
EMP: 13
SALES (est): 1.4MM **Privately Held**
SIC: 3089 Extruded finished plastic products

(G-16685)
DELSTAR TECHNOLOGIES INC
308 Poplar St (17087-9715)
PHONE..................................717 866-7472
Pamela Duca, *President*
EMP: 9 **EST:** 2017
SALES (est): 1.3MM **Privately Held**
SIC: 3081 Unsupported plastics film & sheet

(G-16686)
DELSTAR TECHNOLOGIES INC
Also Called: Coretec
308 Poplar St (17087-9715)
PHONE..................................717 866-7472
Loreta Mathias, *Principal*
EMP: 25 **Publicly Held**
SIC: 3089 Injection molding of plastics
HQ: Delstar Technologies, Inc.
601 Industrial Rd
Middletown DE 19709
302 378-8888

(G-16687)
FARGO ASSEMBLY OF PA INC
Also Called: Richland Manufacturing
Apple & Curtis St (17087)
P.O. Box 126 (17087-0126)
PHONE..................................717 866-5800
Bruce Hensley, *Branch Mgr*
EMP: 165 **Privately Held**
WEB: www.dillblox.com
SIC: 3679 3699 Harness assemblies for electronic use: wire or cable; electrical equipment & supplies
PA: Fargo Assembly Of Pa, Inc.
800 W Washington St
Norristown PA 19401

(G-16688)
OCELLO INC
300 Poplar St (17087-9715)
P.O. Box 609 (17087-0609)
PHONE..................................717 866-5778
Charles Haddad, *President*
Jeffrey Haddad, *Corp Secy*
Afifie Haddad, *Vice Pres*
EMP: 185 **EST:** 1976
SQ FT: 50,000
SALES (est): 9.5MM **Privately Held**
SIC: 2321 2341 Sport shirts, men's & boys': from purchased materials; women's & children's undergarments

(G-16689)
RIGIDPLY RAFTERS INC
701 E Linden St (17087-9720)
PHONE..................................717 866-6581
Arthur Shirk, *President*
Ken Guffey, *General Mgr*
Steve Shirk, *Principal*
Vernon Shirk, *Principal*
Marlin Horst, *Corp Secy*
EMP: 110 **EST:** 1949
SQ FT: 200,000
SALES (est): 29.4MM **Privately Held**
SIC: 2439 Trusses, except roof: laminated lumber; trusses, wooden roof

Richlandtown
Bucks County

(G-16690)
RICHARD BARINGER
Also Called: Springfield Meat Co
1868 California Rd (18955-1100)
PHONE..................................610 346-7661
Richard Baringer, *Owner*
EMP: 6
SQ FT: 4,800
SALES (est): 490K **Privately Held**
SIC: 2011 5421 Meat by-products from meat slaughtered on site; meat markets, including freezer provisioners

Ridgway
Elk County

(G-16691)
ADVANTAGE METAL POWDERS INC
44 Spleen Rd (15853-6262)
PHONE..................................814 772-5363
John Brennen, *President*
Stephen Aul, *President*
Wilfred Brennen Jr, *Corp Secy*
John Gabler, *Vice Pres*
Marie Aul, *Treasurer*
EMP: 12
SQ FT: 22,000
SALES (est): 2.3MM **Privately Held**
SIC: 3399 Powder, metal

(G-16692)
ALLEGHENY BLENDING TECH INC
143 Maine Ln (15853-5115)
P.O. Box 103 (15853-0103)
PHONE..................................814 772-9279
Paul A Reed, *President*
▲ **EMP:** 4 **EST:** 1997
SQ FT: 40,000
SALES (est): 2.9MM **Privately Held**
WEB: www.abtblending.com
SIC: 3399 Metal powders, pastes & flakes

(G-16693)
ALPHA PRECISION GROUP LLC (PA)
95 Mason Run Rd (15853-6901)
PHONE..................................814 773-3191
Joanne Ryan, *President*
Robert Hathorn, *CFO*
EMP: 4
SALES (est): 16.9MM **Privately Held**
SIC: 3399 Powder, metal

(G-16694)
ALPHA SINTERED METALS LLC (DH)
Also Called: Asm
95 Mason Run Rd (15853-6901)
PHONE..................................814 773-3191
Joanne Ryan, *President*
Robert Hathorn, *Vice Pres*
John Holohan, *Treasurer*
Tammy Decker, *Admin Sec*
EMP: 189
SQ FT: 100,000
SALES (est): 49.2MM **Privately Held**
SIC: 6726 3399 Investment offices; powder, metal

(G-16695)
ARC METALS CORPORATION (DH)
224 River Rd Ste 9 (15853-2138)
P.O. Box 372 (15853-0372)
PHONE..................................814 776-2116
Mark Vosacek, *Vice Pres*
Joann Donachy, *Purch Mgr*
Ed Ritz, *Treasurer*
◆ **EMP:** 4
SQ FT: 45,000
SALES (est): 7.3MM
SALES (corp-wide): 2.7B **Privately Held**
WEB: www.arcmetals.com
SIC: 4953 3399 Recycling, waste materials; powder, metal
HQ: Hoeganaes Corporation
1001 Taylors Ln
Cinnaminson NJ 08077
856 303-0366

(G-16696)
ARETE QIS LLC
103 Bridge St (15853-7605)
PHONE..................................814 781-1194
David Vanslander Jr, *President*
Carl Loeffler, *Vice Pres*
Matthew Rupprecht, *CFO*
Pam Samick, *Accountant*
Dennis P Schatz, *Accountant*
EMP: 65 **EST:** 2007
SQ FT: 55,000
SALES (est): 2.5MM **Privately Held**
SIC: 7389 2842 Inspection & testing services; rust removers

(G-16697)
BLUEWATER THERMAL SERVICES
337 N Broad St (15853-2103)
PHONE..................................814 772-8474
Jeffrey D Hemmer, *Principal*
EMP: 4
SALES (est): 302.3K **Privately Held**
SIC: 3398 Metal heat treating

(G-16698)
BUDDY BOY WINERY
29 N Broad St (15853-1001)
PHONE..................................814 772-3751
EMP: 5

SALES (est): 168.2K **Privately Held**
SIC: 5921 5181 2084 Liquor stores; beer & ale; wines, brandy & brandy spirits

(G-16699)
CLARION SINTERED METALS INC
Also Called: C S M
3472 Montmorenci Rd (15853-7110)
PHONE..................................814 773-3124
Howard Peterson, *President*
Mark Hoffman, *Project Mgr*
James Hess, *Engineer*
Shelley Glatt, *Manager*
Pam Ott, *Supervisor*
▼ **EMP:** 287
SQ FT: 120,000
SALES (est): 39.1MM **Privately Held**
SIC: 3399 Powder, metal

(G-16700)
CMSJLP LLC
Also Called: Quality Components
103 Bridge St (15853-7605)
PHONE..................................814 834-2817
Judson Porter Jr, *President*
EMP: 15
SALES (est): 1.9MM **Privately Held**
SIC: 3629 Capacitors, fixed or variable

(G-16701)
CONTINUOUS METAL TECH INC
439 W Main St (15853-1527)
PHONE..................................814 772-9274
Timothy Smith, *President*
Tiffany Mecca, *Admin Mgr*
EMP: 46
SQ FT: 32,000
SALES (est): 9.7MM **Privately Held**
WEB: www.powdered-metal.com
SIC: 3399 Powder, metal

(G-16702)
D & K MACHINE COMPANY INC
23514 Route 949 (15853-2546)
PHONE..................................814 328-2382
Carl Dixon, *President*
Rhonda Dixon, *Corp Secy*
EMP: 6
SQ FT: 6,000
SALES (est): 943.2K **Privately Held**
SIC: 3599 Machine shop, jobbing & repair

(G-16703)
DAGUS MACHINING INC
138 Station St (15853-7666)
PHONE..................................814 834-3491
Jaquelyn Bobenrieth, *President*
Anthony Bobenrieth, *Shareholder*
EMP: 3
SQ FT: 2,520
SALES (est): 319.7K **Privately Held**
SIC: 3599 Machine shop, jobbing & repair

(G-16704)
DISCHEM INC
17295 Boot Jack Rd Ste A (15853-6325)
P.O. Box 267 (15853-0267)
PHONE..................................814 772-6603
Andrew M Thompson, *President*
Andrew Thompson, *Director*
Patrick C Thompson, *Admin Sec*
EMP: 3
SALES: 1MM **Privately Held**
WEB: www.discheminc.com
SIC: 2819 Industrial inorganic chemicals

(G-16705)
DIVERSIFIED COATINGS INC
Also Called: Allegheny Coatings
224 River Rd (15853-2138)
P.O. Box 186 (15853-0186)
PHONE..................................814 772-3850
Steve Quinn, *President*
Craig Reuscher, *Corp Secy*
Bethany Ford, *Engineer*
Cindy Roselli, *Finance*
Leonid Frayman, *Sales Mgr*
EMP: 190
SQ FT: 11,000
SALES (est): 22.9MM **Privately Held**
WEB: www.alleghenycoatings.com
SIC: 3479 Coating of metals & formed products

(G-16706)
EAGLE BIO DIESEL INC
111 Metoxet St (15853-1938)
PHONE..................................814 773-3133
Dan Howard, *President*
Dan Diiulio, *Vice Pres*
John Shuey, *Treasurer*
EMP: 20 **EST:** 2008
SALES (est): 2MM **Privately Held**
SIC: 2911 Petroleum refining

(G-16707)
ENGINEERED PRESSED MATERIALS
1 Grant Rd (15853-1403)
PHONE..................................814 772-6127
Richard Philips, *Owner*
Pricilla Philips, *Co-Owner*
EMP: 5
SALES (est): 424.3K **Privately Held**
SIC: 2899 3399 Metal treating compounds; aluminum atomized powder

(G-16708)
FAIRVIEW COAL CO INC
324 Allenhurst Ave (15853-1132)
PHONE..................................814 776-1158
Margaret Buhler, *President*
EMP: 3
SQ FT: 800
SALES (est): 254.3K **Privately Held**
SIC: 1221 Bituminous coal & lignite-surface mining

(G-16709)
FORMFAST POWDER MTL TECH LLC
2190 Montmorenci Rd (15853-6960)
PHONE..................................814 201-5292
Blaise Bornisch, *CEO*
Jayson Sedor, *Director*
EMP: 3
SQ FT: 15,000
SALES (est): 169.3K **Privately Held**
SIC: 3399 Iron, powdered

(G-16710)
GOSNELL LOGGING
6484 Grant Rd (15853-5734)
PHONE..................................814 776-2038
Patricia Gosnell, *Owner*
EMP: 4 **EST:** 1992
SALES (est): 236.4K **Privately Held**
SIC: 2411 Logging camps & contractors

(G-16711)
INTECH P/M STAINLESS INC
Also Called: Intect Metals
7028 Ridgway St Marys Rd (15853-6562)
PHONE..................................814 776-6150
David J Hanlin, *President*
Ken Hanford, *Manager*
EMP: 30
SQ FT: 14,000
SALES (est): 4.5MM **Privately Held**
WEB: www.intechpm.com
SIC: 3399 Powder, metal

(G-16712)
ION TECHNOLOGIES INC
324 Servidea Dr (15853-6340)
P.O. Box 110 (15853-0110)
PHONE..................................814 772-0440
Anthony Viglione, *President*
EMP: 14
SQ FT: 10,000
SALES (est): 1.6MM **Privately Held**
WEB: www.iontechnologies.com
SIC: 3471 Plating of metals or formed products

(G-16713)
J & S GRINDING CO INC
224 River Rd (15853-2138)
P.O. Box 338 (15853-0338)
PHONE..................................814 776-1113
Shelley Schneider, *President*
EMP: 15
SQ FT: 33,000
SALES (est): 1.9MM **Privately Held**
SIC: 3599 Grinding castings for the trade

(G-16714)
JOB LOGGING INC
3915 Montmorenci Rd (15853-7119)
PHONE..................................814 772-0513
Justin O Buehler, *Principal*
EMP: 3
SALES (est): 285.1K **Privately Held**
SIC: 2411 Logging camps & contractors

(G-16715)
JOHN L LUCHS LOGGING
Also Called: Luchs John L Logging
508 Olson St (15853-9792)
PHONE..................................814 772-5767
John L Luchs, *President*
EMP: 3
SALES (est): 206.8K **Privately Held**
SIC: 7389 2421 2426 2411 Artists' agents & brokers; sawmills & planing mills, general; hardwood dimension & flooring mills; logging camps & contractors

(G-16716)
METAL POWDER PRODUCTS LLC
Mpp Ridgway Division
310 Tanner St (15853-2160)
P.O. Box 520, Saint Marys (15857-0520)
PHONE..................................814 776-2141
John Mosco, *Manager*
EMP: 110
SALES (corp-wide): 185.3MM **Privately Held**
WEB: www.metalpowder.com
SIC: 3399 Powder, metal
PA: Metal Powder Products, Llc
16855 Suthpark Dr Ste 100
Westfield IN 46074
317 805-3764

(G-16717)
METALDYNE SINTERED RIDGWAY LLC
Also Called: Ridgway Mfg Facility
1149 Rocky Rd (15853-6427)
PHONE..................................814 776-1141
Thomas Anato, *Mng Member*
◆ **EMP:** 90
SQ FT: 170,000
SALES (est): 71.3MM
SALES (corp-wide): 7.2B **Publicly Held**
SIC: 3399 3441 3462 Powder, metal; fabricated structural metal; automotive & internal combustion engine forgings
HQ: Metaldyne Sinterforged Products, Llc
3100 N State Highway 3
North Vernon IN 47265

(G-16718)
MOUNTAIN-VALLEY SERVICES LLC
6584 Ridgway St Marys Rd (15853-6552)
P.O. Box 553 (15853-0553)
PHONE..................................814 594-3167
EMP: 4
SALES (est): 193.2K **Privately Held**
SIC: 0781 3271 1741 Landscape services; blocks, concrete: landscape or retaining wall; foundation & retaining wall construction; retaining wall construction

(G-16719)
NOCO DISTRIBUTION LLC
20 Gillis Ave (15853-1604)
PHONE..................................866 946-3927
Bobby Lewis, *Principal*
EMP: 5 **Privately Held**
SIC: 5172 2992 Petroleum products; lubricating oils & greases
HQ: Noco Distribution, Llc
2440 Sheridan Dr
Tonawanda NY 14150
800 500-6626

(G-16720)
NORTHERN POWDERED METALS INC
439b W Main St (15853-1527)
PHONE..................................814 772-0882
David Chittester, *President*
EMP: 7
SQ FT: 7,000

SALES (est): 955.9K **Privately Held**
WEB: www.northernpowderedmetals.com
SIC: 3399 Metal powders, pastes & flakes

(G-16721)
O ALPINE PRESSED METALS INC
Also Called: Metal Powder Pdts Ridgway Div
310 Tanner St (15853-2160)
PHONE..................................814 776-2141
Elliot Archer, *President*
EMP: 94
SQ FT: 60,000
SALES (est): 11.9MM
SALES (corp-wide): 185.3MM **Privately Held**
WEB: www.metalpowder.com
SIC: 3399 Powder, metal
PA: Metal Powder Products, Llc
16855 Suthpark Dr Ste 100
Westfield IN 46074
317 805-3764

(G-16722)
OLIO FRESCA OLIVE OIL COMPANY
217 Irving Ave (15853-1809)
PHONE..................................585 820-8400
Lawrence Pitoni, *Principal*
EMP: 3 **EST:** 2010
SALES (est): 253.3K **Privately Held**
SIC: 2079 Olive oil

(G-16723)
PARKER MACHINE COMPANY
1 Grant Rd (15853-1403)
P.O. Box 377 (15853-0377)
PHONE..................................814 772-0135
Edward Parker, *Owner*
Lisa Parker, *Principal*
EMP: 5
SQ FT: 4,000
SALES: 500K **Privately Held**
SIC: 3599 Machine shop, jobbing or repair

(G-16724)
PC SYSTEMS INC
Also Called: P C S
288 Servidea Dr (15853-6337)
P.O. Box C (15853-0308)
PHONE..................................814 772-6359
Anthony Viglione, *President*
Charlie Steger, *Corp Secy*
Joseph R Depanfilis, *Vice Pres*
Joseph Uhmov, *Vice Pres*
▲ **EMP:** 44
SQ FT: 23,000
SALES: 5.9MM **Privately Held**
WEB: www.pcsridgway.com
SIC: 3643 Current-carrying wiring devices

(G-16725)
PUMP STATION RIDGWAY
Also Called: Ridgway Waterworks
12230 Waterworks Rd (15853)
PHONE..................................814 772-3251
Paul McCurdy, *General Mgr*
EMP: 3
SALES (est): 341.7K **Privately Held**
SIC: 3561 7389 Pumps, domestic: water or sump; business services

(G-16726)
REDMONDS READY MIX INC
Johnsonburg Rd (15853)
PHONE..................................814 776-1437
Amy Vonarx, *President*
Ed Heiberger, *Vice Pres*
EMP: 7
SQ FT: 10,000
SALES (est): 717.8K **Privately Held**
SIC: 3273 Ready-mixed concrete

(G-16727)
RIDGWAY POWDERED METALS INC
6931 Ridgway St Marys Rd (15853-7703)
P.O. Box 398 (15853-0398)
PHONE..................................814 772-5551
Edward Pangersis, *President*
Brian Delhunty, *Production*
Jim Paladino, *Engineer*
Brittany Gnan, *Manager*
EMP: 29
SQ FT: 33,000

SALES (est): 3.9MM **Privately Held**
WEB: www.ridgwaypm.com
SIC: 3399 Powder, metal

(G-16728)
RIDGWAY RECORD
325 Main St Ste A (15853-8099)
PHONE..................................814 773-3161
Joe Piccirillo, *Manager*
EMP: 5
SALES (est): 242.3K **Privately Held**
SIC: 2711 Newspapers: publishing only, not printed on site

(G-16729)
SECONDARY DEVELOPMENT & RES
Also Called: S D & R
219 Servidea Dr (15853-6337)
PHONE..................................814 772-3882
Sam Bennett, *President*
Rod Shaffer, *Vice Pres*
Doug Shaffer, *Treasurer*
EMP: 38
SQ FT: 12,000
SALES: 2.5MM **Privately Held**
SIC: 3599 Machine shop, jobbing & repair

(G-16730)
ST MARYS PRESSED METALS INC
2 Bark St (15853-2146)
PHONE..................................814 772-7455
Arthur Aiello Jr, *President*
James Aiello, *Vice Pres*
EMP: 30
SQ FT: 20,000
SALES: 1.9MM **Privately Held**
WEB: www.smpm.com
SIC: 3399 3568 3462 3452 Powder, metal; power transmission equipment; iron & steel forgings; bolts, nuts, rivets & washers

(G-16731)
SUSQUHNNA WIRE ROPE RGGING INC
112 South St (15853-2009)
PHONE..................................814 772-4766
Kimberly V Hacht, *President*
Charles W Jaques, *Treasurer*
EMP: 9
SALES (est): 1.3MM **Privately Held**
SIC: 3315 Steel wire & related products

(G-16732)
TORY TOOL INC
6955 Ridgeway St Marys Rd (15853-6559)
PHONE..................................814 772-5439
James Lewis, *Manager*
EMP: 20
SALES (corp-wide): 3.1MM **Privately Held**
SIC: 3599 3544 Machine & other job shop work; special dies, tools, jigs & fixtures
PA: Tory Tool Inc
1906 Bucktail Rd
Saint Marys PA 15857
814 772-5439

Ridley Park
Delaware County

(G-16733)
APPLICATION CONSULTANTS INC
Also Called: Appcon
119 W Chester Pike (19078-1902)
PHONE..................................610 521-1529
Garry Reinhard, *President*
EMP: 16
SQ FT: 2,500
SALES (est): 3MM **Privately Held**
WEB: www.appcon4.com
SIC: 7371 3577 Computer software development; input/output equipment, computer

(G-16734)
BOEING COMPANY
300 Industrial Hwy (19078-1140)
PHONE..................................610 591-1978

GEOGRAPHIC

Timothy Terry, *Production*
Michael Houser, *Project Engr*
Joseph Toriello, *Manager*
EMP: 5
SALES (corp-wide): 101.1B **Publicly Held**
SIC: 3721 Airplanes, fixed or rotary wing
PA: The Boeing Company
100 N Riverside Plz
Chicago IL 60606
312 544-2000

(G-16735)
BOEING COMPANY
Stewart Ave Rr 291 (19078)
P.O. Box 16858, Philadelphia (19142-0858)
PHONE....................................610 591-2121
James Morris, *Vice Pres*
Dan Lichtner, *Engineer*
EMP: 6
SALES (corp-wide): 101.1B **Publicly Held**
SIC: 3721 Helicopters
PA: The Boeing Company
100 N Riverside Plz
Chicago IL 60606
312 544-2000

(G-16736)
BOEING COMPANY
1 S Stewart Ave (19078-1002)
PHONE....................................610 591-2121
Dan Schepperd, *Purch Agent*
Neil Berkowitz, *Engineer*
Tom Hughes, *Engineer*
Robert Kaplan, *Engineer*
Martin Lohr, *Engineer*
EMP: 450
SALES (corp-wide): 101.1B **Publicly Held**
SIC: 3721 Helicopters
PA: The Boeing Company
100 N Riverside Plz
Chicago IL 60606
312 544-2000

(G-16737)
BOEING COMPANY
Stewart Ave Rr 291 (19078)
PHONE....................................610 591-2121
William Delany, *Branch Mgr*
EMP: 996
SALES (corp-wide): 101.1B **Publicly Held**
SIC: 3721 Airplanes, fixed or rotary wing
PA: The Boeing Company
100 N Riverside Plz
Chicago IL 60606
312 544-2000

(G-16738)
C-THRU PRODUCTS INC
400 W Chester Pike (19078-1522)
P.O. Box 8635, Collingswood NJ (08108-8635)
PHONE....................................610 586-1130
Hilda Needleman, *President*
EMP: 20
SQ FT: 7,000
SALES (est): 3.1MM **Privately Held**
SIC: 3083 Laminated plastics plate & sheet

(G-16739)
IT TAKES A VILLAGE TO FEED (PA)
112 Kearney Pl (19078-2500)
PHONE....................................888 702-9610
Mark Wainwright, *President*
Theresa Wainwright, *Vice Pres*
EMP: 8
SALES (est): 348.5K **Privately Held**
SIC: 8351 8748 2099 8399 Preschool center; head start center, except in conjunction with school; testing service, educational or personnel; ready-to-eat meals, salads & sandwiches; community development groups

(G-16740)
PRIDE GROUP INC
Also Called: Pride Garden Products
500 W Sellers Ave (19078-1126)
PHONE....................................484 540-8059
Ravi Rajagopalan, *President*
Chase Kruer, *Vice Pres*
Juliana Rogenski, *Opers Mgr*

Danielle Thompson, *Human Res Mgr*
◆ **EMP:** 30
SALES (est): 3.1MM **Privately Held**
WEB: www.thepridegroup.com
SIC: 3524 Lawn & garden equipment

(G-16741)
PRIDE GROUP INC
Also Called: Pride Garden Products
500 W Sellers Ave (19078-1126)
PHONE....................................484 540-8059
▲ **EMP:** 10
SQ FT: 28,000
SALES: 5.4MM **Privately Held**
SIC: 3524 Mfg Lawn/Garden Equipment

(G-16742)
TAIF INC
20 E Sellers Ave (19078-2207)
PHONE....................................610 534-0669
Nina Kimmel, *Branch Mgr*
EMP: 11
SALES (corp-wide): 3.5MM **Privately Held**
SIC: 2032 Italian foods: packaged in cans, jars, etc.
PA: Taif, Inc
600 Kaiser Dr Ste A
Folcroft PA 19032
610 522-0122

Riegelsville
Bucks County

(G-16743)
AMD GROUP INC
2502 Slifer Valley Rd (18077-9507)
PHONE....................................610 972-4491
Andrew S Allen, *CEO*
EMP: 6 **EST:** 2011
SALES (est): 580.3K **Privately Held**
SIC: 2431 7389 Millwork;

(G-16744)
CLEARARMOR SOLUTIONS CORP
519 Easton Rd (18077-7203)
P.O. Box 647 (18077-0647)
PHONE....................................610 816-0101
Walt Szablowski, *Ch of Bd*
Walter Szablowski, *Ch of Bd*
Bruce Hafner, *President*
Jessica Diaz, *COO*
Paula Aulisi, *CFO*
EMP: 5
SALES (est): 156.6K **Privately Held**
SIC: 7371 7372 7373 Software programming applications; application computer software; business oriented computer software

(G-16745)
JOHNSON BROS MACHINE
231 Red Bridge Rd (18077)
P.O. Box 477 (18077-0477)
PHONE....................................610 749-2313
Dick Johnson, *Partner*
Dan Johnson, *Partner*
EMP: 5
SALES (est): 240.4K **Privately Held**
SIC: 3599 Machine shop, jobbing & repair

Rillton
Westmoreland County

(G-16746)
HERWIN INC
2995 Clay Pike (15678-2707)
P.O. Box 152 (15678-0152)
PHONE....................................724 446-2000
Harry E Smith, *Principal*
▲ **EMP:** 4
SALES (est): 491.4K **Privately Held**
SIC: 3444 Guard rails, highway: sheet metal

(G-16747)
HOLT LE GRINDING SERVICE
Maple St (15678)
P.O. Box 452 (15678-0452)
PHONE....................................724 864-6865
James Holt, *Principal*
EMP: 10
SALES (est): 1.1MM **Privately Held**
SIC: 3599 Grinding castings for the trade

(G-16748)
L E HOLT GRINDING SERVICE INC
452 Maple St (15678)
PHONE....................................724 446-0977
James H Holt, *President*
EMP: 8
SQ FT: 10,000
SALES (est): 400K **Privately Held**
SIC: 3999 Custom pulverizing & grinding of plastic materials

Rimersburg
Clarion County

(G-16749)
DAVIS COOKIE COMPANY
256 Baker St (16248-3302)
P.O. Box 430 (16248-0430)
PHONE....................................814 473-3125
Dana Davis, *President*
Daniel Davis, *Corp Secy*
Donn Davis, *Shareholder*
EMP: 64
SQ FT: 44,000
SALES (est): 10.4MM **Privately Held**
WEB: www.daviscookie.com
SIC: 2052 Cookies

(G-16750)
MAPLE GROVE ENTERPRISES INC
1873 Flick Rd (16248-6415)
PHONE....................................814 473-6272
Richard Radiker, *CEO*
R Heber Radiker, *President*
Casey Bliss, *Vice Pres*
Becky Radiker, *Treasurer*
EMP: 4
SALES (est): 380K **Privately Held**
WEB: www.maplegroveenterprises.com
SIC: 1311 Natural gas production

Ringgold
Jefferson County

(G-16751)
J R RESOURCES L P
18 J R Resources Dr (15770-8346)
PHONE....................................814 365-5821
James Doverspike, *Partner*
Eric Doverspike, *Partner*
Randy Doverspike, *Partner*
EMP: 7 **EST:** 1975
SQ FT: 7,100
SALES (est): 1.2MM **Privately Held**
SIC: 1311 6512 Natural gas production; commercial & industrial building operation

---

Ringtown
Schuylkill County

(G-16752)
BERRY GLOBAL INC
75 W Main St (17967-9537)
P.O. Box 260 (17967-0260)
PHONE....................................570 889-3131
Tom George, *Branch Mgr*
EMP: 300 **Publicly Held**
WEB: www.6sens.com
SIC: 3089 Clothes hangers, plastic
HQ: Berry Global, Inc.
101 Oakley St
Evansville IN 47710
812 424-2904

(G-16753)
GENERAL WELDING & MACHINE CO
Bridge St (17967)
P.O. Box 255 (17967-0255)
PHONE....................................570 889-3776
George V Roulin, *Owner*
EMP: 4
SQ FT: 4,000
SALES (est): 190K **Privately Held**
SIC: 3544 7692 Welding positioners (jigs); welding repair

(G-16754)
JELD-WEN INC
Also Called: Jeld-Wen Windows
700 W Main St (17967-9449)
P.O. Box 259 (17967-0259)
PHONE....................................570 889-3173
Joseph D Tomtishen, *Manager*
EMP: 250 **Publicly Held**
SIC: 2431 Window frames, wood
HQ: Jeld-Wen, Inc.
2645 Silver Crescent Dr
Charlotte NC 28273
800 535-3936

(G-16755)
NORDIC TOOL & DIE CO
76 Main Blvd (17967-9687)
PHONE....................................570 889-5650
Peter Damgaard, *Owner*
EMP: 5 **EST:** 1981
SQ FT: 3,000
SALES: 50K **Privately Held**
SIC: 3544 Special dies & tools

(G-16756)
RINGTOWN WILBERT VAULT WORKS
Also Called: Ringtown Concrete Products
710 W Main St (17967-9449)
P.O. Box 215 (17967-0215)
PHONE....................................570 889-3153
Noel D Brouse, *CEO*
Jeff Brouse, *President*
EMP: 15
SQ FT: 23,600
SALES (est): 2.2MM **Privately Held**
SIC: 3272 Septic tanks, concrete; burial vaults, concrete or precast terrazzo

---

Riverside
Northumberland County

(G-16757)
CHEROKEE PHARMACEUTICALS LLC
100 Ave C (17868)
P.O. Box 367 (17868-0367)
PHONE....................................570 271-4195
Justin Noll,
◆ **EMP:** 425
SALES (est): 142.1MM **Privately Held**
SIC: 2834 Pharmaceutical preparations

(G-16758)
PRWT SERVICES INC
100 Avenue C (17868)
PHONE....................................570 275-2220
Tom McCaubbins, *Manager*
EMP: 100
SALES (corp-wide): 166.3MM **Privately Held**
WEB: www.prwt.com
SIC: 2833 2899 Organic medicinal chemicals: bulk, uncompounded; inorganic medicinal chemicals: bulk, uncompounded; botanical products, medicinal: ground, graded or milled; chemical preparations
PA: Prwt Services, Inc.
1835 Market St Ste 800
Philadelphia PA 19103
215 563-7698

▲ = Import ▼=Export
◆ =Import/Export

Rixford
Mckean County

(G-16759)
MAGEE AND MAGEE INC
1441 Looker Mountain Trl (16745-1403)
PHONE.................................814 966-3623
Dale Magee, *Principal*
EMP: 10
SALES (est): 569.9K **Privately Held**
SIC: 1389 Oil & gas field services

Roaring Brook Twp
Lackawanna County

(G-16760)
STEINMETZ INC
Also Called: Steinmetz Polymers
660 Spencer Rd (18444-7784)
P.O. Box 393, Moscow (18444-0393)
PHONE.................................570 842-6161
Michael Steinmetz, *President*
EMP: 50 **EST:** 1967
SQ FT: 23,500
SALES (est): 6.8MM **Privately Held**
WEB: www.steinmetz.com
SIC: 2821 3089 3544 Polyurethane
resins; injection molded finished plastic
products; special dies, tools, jigs & fix-
tures

Roaring Spring
Blair County

(G-16761)
APPVION OPERATIONS INC
100 Paper Mill Rd (16673-1480)
PHONE.................................814 224-2131
Anthony Fago, *Branch Mgr*
EMP: 500
SALES (corp-wide): 6.3B **Publicly Held**
WEB: www.appletonpapers.com
SIC: 2621 2672 Business form paper;
coated & laminated paper
HQ: Appvion Operations, Inc.
825 E Wisconsin Ave
Appleton WI 54911
920 734-9841

(G-16762)
CANDLES IN COVE
624 Locust St (16673-1730)
PHONE.................................518 368-3381
EMP: 3
SALES (est): 63.9K **Privately Held**
SIC: 3999 Candles

(G-16763)
COUNTRY WOODCRAFTS
345 Windy Acres Ln (16673-9033)
PHONE.................................814 793-4417
Charles Sweigart, *Owner*
EMP: 4
SALES (est): 449.2K **Privately Held**
SIC: 2541 Cabinets, lockers & shelving

(G-16764)
EDGEMATE INC (PA)
213 Smith Transport Rd (16673-2248)
P.O. Box 72 (16673-0072)
PHONE.................................814 224-5717
Harry K Benjamin, *President*
Whitney Emeigh, *Opers Staff*
Adam Lardieri, *Buyer*
Paula Cherico, *Asst Controller*
Scott Hileman, *Marketing Staff*
▲ **EMP:** 150
SQ FT: 90,000
SALES (est): 21.1MM **Privately Held**
WEB: www.edgemate.com
SIC: 2435 Veneer stock, hardwood

(G-16765)
MACINNIS GROUP LLC
Also Called: Pennstress
8180 Woodbury Pike (16673-8103)
P.O. Box 597, Hollidaysburg (16648-0597)
PHONE.................................814 695-2016

James Vanburen, *President*
Gregory J Gorman, *Senior VP*
Greg Gorman, *Software Dev*
EMP: 64
SQ FT: 250,000
SALES: 20MM **Privately Held**
SIC: 3272 Concrete products, precast

(G-16766)
**NEW ENTERPRISE STONE LIME
INC**
Also Called: Newcrete Products
301 Plum Creek Rd (16673-1163)
P.O. Box 77, New Enterprise (16664-0077)
PHONE.................................814 224-2121
Dexter Fowler, *Manager*
EMP: 150
SALES (corp-wide): 651.9MM **Privately
Held**
WEB: www.nesl.com
SIC: 1611 2951 3273 3272 General con-
tractor, highway & street construction;
concrete, bituminous; ready-mixed con-
crete; concrete products; construction
sand & gravel
PA: New Enterprise Stone & Lime Co., Inc.
3912 Brumbaugh Rd
New Enterprise PA 16664
814 224-6883

(G-16767)
**RENAISSANCE NUTRITION INC
(PA)**
339 Frederick Rd (16673-8340)
P.O. Box 229 (16673-0229)
PHONE.................................814 793-2113
Craig R Brown, *President*
Rebecca L Brown, *Corp Secy*
EMP: 30
SQ FT: 5,000
SALES (est): 19.1MM **Privately Held**
SIC: 5191 2048 Animal feeds; prepared
feeds

(G-16768)
**ROARING SPRING BLANK
BOOK CO (PA)**
Also Called: Roaring Spring Paper Products
740 Spang St (16673-1924)
PHONE.................................814 224-2306
Daniel B Hoover, *President*
Robert J Allen, *Vice Pres*
David M Riccitelli, *Administration*
◆ **EMP:** 300 **EST:** 1887
SQ FT: 46,000
SALES (est): 96.8MM **Privately Held**
WEB: www.roaringspring.com
SIC: 2678 5149 2653 7389 Tablets &
pads, book & writing: from purchased ma-
terials; notebooks: made from purchased
paper; mineral or spring water bottling;
boxes, corrugated: made from purchased
materials; coffee service

(G-16769)
**ROARING SPRING BLANK
BOOK CO**
Also Called: Spring Cove Container
301 Cove Lane Rd (16673-1619)
P.O. Box 12 (16673-0012)
PHONE.................................814 224-2222
John Sneed, *Manager*
EMP: 35
SALES (corp-wide): 96.8MM **Privately
Held**
WEB: www.roaringspring.com
SIC: 2653 Corrugated & solid fiber boxes
PA: Roaring Spring Blank Book Company
740 Spang St
Roaring Spring PA 16673
814 224-2306

(G-16770)
ROARING SPRING WATER
420 Water St (16673-1928)
P.O. Box 97 (16673-0097)
PHONE.................................814 942-9844
Dan Hoover,
Scott Hoover,
EMP: 4
SALES (est): 267.4K **Privately Held**
SIC: 2086 5078 Mineral water, carbon-
ated: packaged in cans, bottles, etc.;
drinking water coolers, mechanical

(G-16771)
SPRING TOOL & DIE CO INC
408 E Main St (16673-1304)
PHONE.................................814 224-5173
Vincent Heaton, *President*
Fredda K Heaton, *Corp Secy*
Lesa Pressel,
EMP: 7
SQ FT: 2,800
SALES (est): 486.8K **Privately Held**
SIC: 3599 3544 Grinding castings for the
trade; special dies & tools

Robesonia
Berks County

(G-16772)
ADELPHI KITCHENS INC
Also Called: Whitebrier
E Penn Ave Freeman St (19551)
P.O. Box 10 (19551-0010)
PHONE.................................610 693-3101
William P Yatron, *President*
Stratton D Yatron, *Corp Secy*
John C Conlon Jr, *Vice Pres*
George H Pyle, *Vice Pres*
Nicholas H Yatron, *Vice Pres*
EMP: 115
SQ FT: 160,000
SALES (est): 18.4MM **Privately Held**
WEB: www.adelphikitchens.com
SIC: 2434 Wood kitchen cabinets

(G-16773)
FUSION COATINGS INC
932 W Penn Ave (19551-9520)
P.O. Box 224 (19551-0224)
PHONE.................................610 693-5886
Douglas G Jones, *President*
Douglas Jones, *President*
Patrick Jones, *Treasurer*
EMP: 45
SQ FT: 35,000
SALES (est): 6.5MM **Privately Held**
WEB: www.fusioncoatingsinc.com
SIC: 3479 Coating of metals with plastic or
resins

(G-16774)
GO TELL IT INC
Also Called: Atlantic Novelties
350 N Church St Rear Offc (19551-9708)
PHONE.................................212 769-3220
Nathan Harkrader, *CEO*
Richard Pearlman, *President*
EMP: 3
SQ FT: 5,000
SALES: 800K **Privately Held**
SIC: 5961 2262 Catalog & mail-order
houses; screen printing: manmade fiber &
silk broadwoven fabrics

(G-16775)
GRAPHITE MACHINING INC
70 E Meadow Ave (19551-9655)
PHONE.................................610 682-0080
Frank Schoch, *Principal*
Kevin Wanner, *Plant Mgr*
EMP: 3
SALES (corp-wide): 17.8MM **Privately
Held**
SIC: 3599 Machine shop, jobbing & repair
PA: Graphite Machining, Inc.
240 N Main St
Topton PA 19562
610 682-0080

(G-16776)
**HIGH PRINTING & GRAPHICS
INC**
231 E Penn Ave (19551-1529)
P.O. Box 36 (19551-0036)
PHONE.................................610 693-5399
Jay L High, *President*
Starlette A High, *Treasurer*
EMP: 6
SALES (est): 600K **Privately Held**
SIC: 2759 Commercial printing

(G-16777)
READING ALLOYS INC
220 Old West Penn Ave (19551-8904)
P.O. Box 53 (19551-0053)
PHONE.................................610 693-5822
H I McGavisk, *President*
Brian Higgins, *Vice Pres*
Graham P Walker, *Vice Pres*
Debbie Folk, *Purchasing*
Todd Bartashus, *Engineer*
◆ **EMP:** 125 **EST:** 1953
SQ FT: 140,000
SALES: 100MM
WEB: www.readingalloys.com
SIC: 3313 3341 Ferroalloys; alloys, addi-
tive, except copper: not made in blast fur-
naces; secondary nonferrous metals
PA: Ametek, Inc.
1100 Cassatt Rd
Berwyn PA 19312
610 647-2121

(G-16778)
**READING BAKERY SYSTEMS
INC (PA)**
380 Old West Penn Ave (19551-8903)
PHONE.................................610 693-5816
Joseph Zaleski, *President*
Roseann Reinhold, *Principal*
E Terry Groff, *Chairman*
Chip Czulada, *Vice Pres*
Travis Getz, *Vice Pres*
◆ **EMP:** 100
SQ FT: 50,000
SALES (est): 20.4MM **Privately Held**
SIC: 3556 Food products machinery

(G-16779)
SONOCO PRODUCTS COMPANY
30 W Meadow Ave (19551-1701)
PHONE.................................610 693-5804
Scott Grenawalt, *Manager*
EMP: 50
SQ FT: 75,000
SALES (corp-wide): 5.3B **Publicly Held**
WEB: www.sonoco.com
SIC: 2655 Fiber cans, drums & similar
products
PA: Sonoco Products Company
1 N 2nd St
Hartsville SC 29550
843 383-7000

(G-16780)
WESTERLY INCORPORATED
17 E Meadow Ave (19551-9623)
PHONE.................................610 693-8866
David L Thun, *Ch of Bd*
James Burton, *President*
Paul Kozloff, *Admin Sec*
▲ **EMP:** 46
SQ FT: 86,000
SALES (est): 8.2MM **Privately Held**
WEB: www.magnatech-int.com
SIC: 3552 3549 Braiding machines, tex-
tile; metalworking machinery

Rochester
Beaver County

(G-16781)
**ALKALI BEAVER PRODUCTS
(PA)**
Also Called: Beaver Valley Bowl
25 New York Ave (15074-1938)
PHONE.................................724 709-7857
Harold W Davidson, *Partner*
William Allen, *Vice Pres*
Bette Davidson, *Treasurer*
EMP: 7
SQ FT: 40,000
SALES (est): 848.3K **Privately Held**
SIC: 2842 7933 Degreasing solvent;
cleaning or polishing preparations; ten pin
center

(G-16782)
**ATI PRECISION FINISHING LLC
(DH)**
Also Called: ATI Rome Metals
499 Delaware Ave (15074-2419)
PHONE.................................724 775-1664

Harry Turic, *President*
▲ EMP: 40
SQ FT: 40,000
SALES (est): 9.5MM Publicly Held
WEB: www.romemetals.com
SIC: 3471 Finishing, metals or formed products
HQ: Allegheny Ludlum, Llc
1000 Six Ppg Pl
Pittsburgh PA 15222
412 394-2800

(G-16783)
CHARLES A HENDERSON PRTG SVC
101 Brighton Ave (15074-2293)
PHONE.................................724 775-2623
Domenic Leone, *Owner*
Candy Ragozzino, *Corp Secy*
EMP: 6
SQ FT: 9,000
SALES: 400K Privately Held
SIC: 2752 2759 Commercial printing, offset; letterpress printing

(G-16784)
DEANGELIS BROS INC
Also Called: De Angelis Donut Shop
202 Pleasant St (15074)
PHONE.................................724 775-1641
Thomas De Angelis, *President*
Richard De Angelis, *Vice Pres*
EMP: 46
SQ FT: 1,755
SALES (est): 1.3MM Privately Held
SIC: 5461 2051 Doughnuts; bread, cake & related products

(G-16785)
ENVIROTROL INC
670 Pennsylvania Ave (15074-1644)
P.O. Box 61, Sewickley (15143-0061)
PHONE.................................412 741-2030
Robert Roodman, *President*
Carl W Tobias, *Vice Pres*
Keith G Tobias, *Vice Pres*
Renee Tobias, *Shareholder*
▲ EMP: 25 EST: 1970
SQ FT: 1,500
SALES (est): 3.6MM
SALES (corp-wide): 1.3B Publicly Held
SIC: 2819 Charcoal (carbon), activated
HQ: Evoqua Water Technologies Llc
210 6th Ave Ste 3300
Pittsburgh PA 15222
724 772-0044

(G-16786)
INNOVATIVE CUSTOM CABINETRY
118 Snyder Dr (15074-2706)
PHONE.................................724 624-0164
Gary W Leasure, *President*
EMP: 4
SALES (est): 261.3K Privately Held
SIC: 2434 Wood kitchen cabinets

(G-16787)
PITTSBRGH TUBULAR SHAFTING INC (PA)
Also Called: P T S
Cleveland St Kentucky Ave (15074)
P.O. Box 146 (15074-0146)
PHONE.................................724 774-7212
Mark Jackson, *Ch of Bd*
Gregory A Keriotis, *President*
Robert A Wolfe Jr, *Vice Pres*
Lynn Murphy, *Treasurer*
John Baumgard, *Admin Sec*
▼ EMP: 22
SQ FT: 105,000
SALES: 3.5MM Privately Held
WEB: www.ptsco.com
SIC: 3498 3568 Tube fabricating (contract bending & shaping); power transmission equipment

(G-16788)
PITTSBRGH TUBULAR SHAFTING INC
611 Connecticut Ave (15074-1625)
P.O. Box 149 (15074-0149)
PHONE.................................724 774-7212
Lynn Murphy, *Manager*
EMP: 4

SQ FT: 59,000
SALES: 314.1K
SALES (corp-wide): 3.5MM Privately Held
WEB: www.ptsco.com
SIC: 3498 Tube fabricating (contract bending & shaping)
PA: Pittsburgh Tubular Shafting, Inc.
Cleveland St Kentucky Ave
Rochester PA 15074
724 774-7212

(G-16789)
Q-CAST INC
630 New York Ave (15074-1618)
P.O. Box 230 (15074-0230)
PHONE.................................724 728-7440
Les Finney, *President*
Helen Finney, *Treasurer*
EMP: 23
SQ FT: 13,000
SALES (est): 4.5MM Privately Held
SIC: 3089 3069 Molding primary plastic; custom compounding of rubber materials

Rochester Mills
Indiana County

(G-16790)
R&R MACHINE INC
1440 Watering Trough Rd (15771-7338)
PHONE.................................724 286-9507
Rusty Brubaker, *Chairman*
EMP: 4 EST: 1982
SALES (est): 453.5K Privately Held
SIC: 3599 Machine & other job shop work

Rockledge
Montgomery County

(G-16791)
KOREAN PHILA TIME INC
103 Township Line Rd 2a (19046-5127)
PHONE.................................215 663-2400
Jessy Kang, *Owner*
▲ EMP: 10
SALES (est): 663K Privately Held
SIC: 2711 Newspapers

Rockwood
Somerset County

(G-16792)
ROCKWOOD MANUFACTURING COMPANY
300 Main St (15557-1023)
P.O. Box 79 (15557-0079)
PHONE.................................814 926-2026
William V Gurzenda, *President*
Kent Dykstra, *Vice Pres*
Kirk R Sherbine, *Vice Pres*
David M Ambrosini, *Treasurer*
Jeffrey A Mereschuk, *Admin Sec*
▲ EMP: 120 EST: 1946
SQ FT: 50,000
SALES (est): 51.3MM Privately Held
WEB: www.rockwoodmfg.com
SIC: 3354 3429 Aluminum extruded products; builders' hardware

(G-16793)
SVONAVEC INC
Also Called: New Centervill
2555 New Centerville Rd (15557-7425)
PHONE.................................814 926-2815
David Svonavec, *President*
EMP: 5
SALES (corp-wide): 10.9MM Privately Held
SIC: 1442 Construction sand & gravel
PA: Svonavec, Inc.
150 W Union St Ste 201
Somerset PA
814 445-7324

(G-16794)
WILLIAM RICHTER LUMBER
367 Fox Rd (15557-6428)
PHONE.................................814 926-4608
William Richter, *Owner*
EMP: 8
SALES (est): 384.3K Privately Held
SIC: 2421 Sawmills & planing mills, general

Rogersville
Greene County

(G-16795)
DAVID JONATHAN WDWKG & MFG CO
3250 Golden Oaks Rd (15359-1502)
PHONE.................................724 499-5225
Jonathan David, *Owner*
EMP: 3
SQ FT: 12,000
SALES: 200K Privately Held
SIC: 2434 2521 Wood kitchen cabinets; cabinets, office: wood

Rome
Bradford County

(G-16796)
COUNTRY KEEPSAKES
5232 Route 467 (18837-7970)
PHONE.................................570 744-2246
David Salitrynski Etal, *Owner*
EMP: 3
SALES (est): 377.1K Privately Held
SIC: 2261 Preshrinking cotton fabrics

(G-16797)
DAVID M OLEY
Also Called: Northeast Wood Products
Rr 1 Box 285 (18837)
PHONE.................................570 247-5599
David M Oley, *Owner*
David Oley, *Owner*
EMP: 10
SQ FT: 30,000
SALES (est): 860K Privately Held
WEB: www.northeastwoodproducts.com
SIC: 5031 2431 Lumber, plywood & millwork; woodwork, interior & ornamental

(G-16798)
DAVID TRUNK
486 West Rd (18837-8521)
PHONE.................................570 247-2012
David Trunk, *Principal*
EMP: 5
SALES (est): 493.8K Privately Held
SIC: 3161 Trunks

(G-16799)
HARMONY HILL FORESTRY
1441 Harmony Hill Rd (18837-7802)
PHONE.................................570 247-2676
Jim Alexander Jr, *Principal*
EMP: 3
SALES (est): 274K Privately Held
SIC: 2421 Sawmills & planing mills, general

(G-16800)
MSK INDUSTRIES LLC
232 Rocky Top Ln (18837-8210)
PHONE.................................570 485-4908
Michael Kelley, *President*
EMP: 3 EST: 2016
SALES (est): 231K Privately Held
SIC: 3999 Manufacturing industries

(G-16801)
PRIMITIVE COUNTRY TOLE
185 Edsell Rd (18837-8093)
PHONE.................................570 247-2719
Carol Wolstencroft, *Owner*
EMP: 3
SALES (est): 202.1K Privately Held
SIC: 3143 Men's footwear, except athletic

Ronks
Lancaster County

(G-16802)
AIMEE & DARIAS DOLL OUTLET
2682 Lincoln Hwy E Ste A (17572-9797)
PHONE.................................717 687-8118
Brenda Schaffer, *Owner*
EMP: 3
SALES (est): 180.2K Privately Held
WEB: www.dolloutlet.com
SIC: 3942 Dolls & stuffed toys

(G-16803)
BEECHDALE FRAMES
2856 Lincoln Hwy E (17572-9799)
PHONE.................................717 288-2723
Allen Miller, *Owner*
EMP: 3
SALES (est): 274.6K Privately Held
SIC: 5712 5023 2499 0191 Furniture stores; home furnishings; rulers & yardsticks, wood; general farms, primarily crop

(G-16804)
BEILERS MANUFACTURING & SUPPLY (PA)
3025 Harvest Dr (17572-9756)
PHONE.................................717 768-0174
Chris B Beiler, *Owner*
▲ EMP: 4 EST: 1968
SQ FT: 10,000
SALES (est): 1.5MM Privately Held
SIC: 2399 5191 Horse harnesses & riding crops, etc.: non-leather; harness equipment

(G-16805)
CEDAR RIDGE MANUFACTURING LLC
255 Mascot Rd (17572-9715)
PHONE.................................717 656-0404
Joseph B Glick,
▲ EMP: 4
SQ FT: 4,000
SALES: 525K Privately Held
SIC: 3315 Fence gates posts & fittings: steel

(G-16806)
FARMCO MANUFACTURING LP
2937 Irishtown Rd (17572)
PHONE.................................717 768-7769
Michael Beiler, *Partner*
EMP: 8
SQ FT: 18,000
SALES (est): 990K Privately Held
SIC: 3523 Trailers & wagons, farm; cattle feeding, handling & watering equipment

(G-16807)
FUEL DOCTOR INC
85 Tucker Dr (17572-9545)
PHONE.................................904 521-9889
Thomas Schumm, *Principal*
EMP: 4
SALES (est): 239.5K Privately Held
SIC: 2869 Fuels

(G-16808)
JOHNATHAN STOLTZFUS
Also Called: Harvest Structures
3104 Harvest Dr (17572-9752)
PHONE.................................717 768-7922
Jonathan A Stoltzfus, *Owner*
EMP: 6
SQ FT: 5,000
SALES (est): 480K Privately Held
SIC: 3448 Farm & utility buildings

(G-16809)
KAUFFMANTREATSCOM LLC
Also Called: Amishtastes
33 S Weavertown Rd (17572-9708)
PHONE.................................717 715-6409
EMP: 3
SALES (est): 152.7K Privately Held
SIC: 2087 Beverage bases

(G-16810)
LANE CHERRY MANUFACTURING
2849 Lincoln Hwy E (17572-9609)
PHONE..................................717 687-9059
Joseph S Fisher, *Partner*
Levy Fisher, *Partner*
EMP: 4
SALES (est): 418.6K **Privately Held**
SIC: 3524 Lawn & garden equipment

(G-16811)
MID ATLNTIC STL FBRICATION LLC
14 N Ronks Rd (17572-9602)
PHONE..................................717 687-0292
Matthew McClarigan, *CFO*
EMP: 5
SALES (est): 921.7K **Privately Held**
SIC: 3441 Fabricated structural metal

(G-16812)
PEIFER WELDING INC
Also Called: Peifer Welding Water Jet Cutng
715 Georgetown Rd (17572-9524)
PHONE..................................717 687-7581
Craig A Peifer, *President*
James K Keener, *Treasurer*
EMP: 6 EST: 1965
SQ FT: 3,640
SALES (est): 975.7K **Privately Held**
SIC: 3446 Railings, bannisters, guards, etc.: made from metal pipe; stairs, stair-cases, stair treads: prefabricated metal

(G-16813)
SCHAEFER PAINT COMPANY
Also Called: Schafco Packaging Co
730 Georgetown Rd (17572-9524)
P.O. Box 338, Strasburg (17579-0338)
PHONE..................................717 687-7017
Kimmel Schaefer, *President*
Caroline Schaefer, *Corp Secy*
Anthony Schaefer, *Vice Pres*
EMP: 15 EST: 1946
SQ FT: 12,800
SALES (est): 1.7MM **Privately Held**
WEB: www.schafco.com
SIC: 7389 2851 Packaging & labeling services; paints & allied products

(G-16814)
SCHAEFER PYROTECHNICS INC
Also Called: Schaefer Fireworks
376 Hartman Bridge Rd (17572-9513)
P.O. Box 100, Strasburg (17579-0100)
PHONE..................................717 687-0647
Kimmel R Schaefer Jr, *President*
Rana Schaefer, *Vice Pres*
▲ EMP: 4
SALES (est): 577.8K **Privately Held**
WEB: www.schaeferfireworks.com
SIC: 2899 5092 Fireworks; fireworks

(G-16815)
SMOKERS SPORTS STORE
Also Called: Smokers Sports
247 Gap Rd Ste B (17572-9539)
P.O. Box 123, Strasburg (17579-0123)
PHONE..................................717 687-9445
Marlon R Smoker, *Owner*
EMP: 3
SQ FT: 1,200
SALES (est): 178.5K **Privately Held**
SIC: 3949 Sporting & athletic goods

(G-16816)
STOLTZFUS WOODTURNING
264 Paradise Ln (17572-9510)
PHONE..................................717 687-8237
Henry J Stoltzfus, *Partner*
Jacob Blank, *Partner*
▲ EMP: 4
SQ FT: 8,000
SALES (est): 523K **Privately Held**
SIC: 2431 Millwork

Roscoe
Washington County

(G-16817)
INTERSTATE PAPER SUPPLY CO INC
Also Called: Ipsco
103 Good St (15477)
PHONE..................................724 938-2218
Bart R Raitano, *President*
Bill Angelo, *Vice Pres*
Dean Zelenski, *Sales Staff*
Ed Raitano, *Shareholder*
Larry Booze, *Representative*
EMP: 100
SQ FT: 100,000
SALES (est): 27.3MM **Privately Held**
WEB: www.ipscoinc.com
SIC: 2679 3086 2671 Paper products, converted; plastics foam products; packaging paper & plastics film, coated & laminated

Rose Valley
Delaware County

(G-16818)
LYNN PARKER ASSOCIATES LLC
14 Forest View Rd (19086-6721)
PHONE..................................561 406-6472
Jerald Lynn Parker,
▲ EMP: 6
SQ FT: 4,000
SALES (est): 1.1MM **Privately Held**
SIC: 3714 Motor vehicle parts & accessories

Roseto
Northampton County

(G-16819)
DANTE DEFRANCO PRINTING
4 Dante St (18013-1249)
PHONE..................................610 588-7300
Dante Defranco, *Owner*
EMP: 20
SALES (est): 1.1MM **Privately Held**
SIC: 2261 Screen printing of cotton broad-woven fabrics

(G-16820)
E S S PACKAGING MACHINERY
305 Roseto Ave (18013-1345)
PHONE..................................610 588-8579
James Enman Sr, *President*
James Enman Jr, *Vice Pres*
▲ EMP: 6 EST: 1998
SQ FT: 3,000
SALES (est): 809.5K **Privately Held**
WEB: www.esspack.com
SIC: 3565 Packaging machinery

(G-16821)
PENNSYLVANIA AVENUE SPORTS
405 Pennsylvania Ave (18013-1125)
PHONE..................................610 533-4133
Philip Stambaugh, *Owner*
EMP: 3
SALES (est): 120K **Privately Held**
SIC: 3949 Sporting & athletic goods

(G-16822)
ROBERT BATH
Also Called: Ledonne Brothers Bakery
314 Garibaldi Ave (18013-1353)
PHONE..................................610 588-0423
Robert Bath, *Owner*
EMP: 4
SQ FT: 4,372
SALES (est): 124.2K **Privately Held**
SIC: 5461 5812 2051 Bakeries; pizza restaurants; bread, cake & related products

Rossiter
Indiana County

(G-16823)
MCKEE DRILLING
770 Bonner Rd (15772-8822)
PHONE..................................814 427-2444
Delbert McKee, *Partner*
Howard McKee, *Partner*
Corona McKee, *Manager*
EMP: 5
SALES (est): 410K **Privately Held**
SIC: 1241 Coal mining services

Rossville
York County

(G-16824)
RICHARD E KRALL INC
60 Yeager Rd (17358)
P.O. Box 59 (17358-0059)
PHONE..................................717 432-4179
Barbara Krall, *President*
EMP: 21
SALES (est): 2MM **Privately Held**
SIC: 3531 1794 Construction machinery; excavation work

Rostraver Township
Fayette County

(G-16825)
EVIVE STATION LLC
236 Finley Rd Ste 20 (15012-3811)
PHONE..................................724 972-6421
▲ EMP: 7
SALES (est): 1MM **Privately Held**
SIC: 3581 Automatic Vending Machines

(G-16826)
EXIDE TECHNOLOGIES
236 Finley Rd Ste 15 (15012-3811)
PHONE..................................304 345-5616
George Hurman, *Manager*
EMP: 5
SALES (corp-wide): 2.4B **Privately Held**
WEB: www.exideworld.com
SIC: 3691 5063 5013 3629 Lead acid batteries (storage batteries); electrical apparatus & equipment; motor vehicle supplies & new parts; battery chargers, rectifying or nonrotating
PA: Exide Technologies
13000 Deerfield Pkwy # 200
Milton GA 30004
678 566-9000

(G-16827)
LESLEH PRECISION INC
Also Called: LPI
430 Jonathan Willey Rd (15012-2958)
PHONE..................................724 823-0901
Ronald Helsel, *Principal*
Denise Helsel, *Treasurer*
Donna Beitler, *Office Mgr*
EMP: 38
SQ FT: 10,000
SALES (est): 8.3MM **Privately Held**
WEB: www.lesleh.com
SIC: 3484 3621 Guns (firearms) or gun parts, 30 mm. & below; generating apparatus & parts, electrical

(G-16828)
NCM BARGE MAINTENCE
1231 Rostraver Rd (15012-4502)
PHONE..................................724 469-0083
Mario Greco, *Owner*
EMP: 10
SALES (est): 397.1K **Privately Held**
SIC: 3731 Barges, building & repairing

(G-16829)
PARKER PRECISION MOLDING INC
129 Landmark Ln (15012-6815)
P.O. Box 744, Belle Vernon (15012-0744)
PHONE..................................724 930-8099
Blake Parker, *President*
Linda Parker, *Corp Secy*
EMP: 24
SQ FT: 15,000
SALES (est): 5.5MM **Privately Held**
SIC: 3089 Injection molding of plastics

(G-16830)
SNYDERS-LANCE INC
230 Finley Rd (15012)
PHONE..................................724 929-6270
Ryan Miller, *Branch Mgr*
EMP: 282
SALES (corp-wide): 8.6B **Publicly Held**
SIC: 2052 Cookies
HQ: Snyder's-Lance, Inc.
13515 Balntyn Corp Pl
Charlotte NC 28277
704 554-1421

(G-16831)
TRAILGATE TAILGATE SYSTEMS
1012 Fells Church Rd (15012-4701)
PHONE..................................724 321-6558
Rick Haskins, *President*
Steve Bowers, *Vice Pres*
Sandra Haskins, *Admin Sec*
EMP: 3
SALES (est): 100K **Privately Held**
WEB: www.trailgatetailgates.com
SIC: 3446 Gates, ornamental metal

(G-16832)
VINOSKI WINERY LLC
333 Castle Dr (15012-4331)
PHONE..................................724 872-3333
EMP: 3
SQ FT: 10,000
SALES (est): 136K **Privately Held**
SIC: 2084 Wines

Roulette
Potter County

(G-16833)
C & S LUMBER COMPANY INC
398 Main St (16746-2026)
P.O. Box 221 (16746-0221)
PHONE..................................814 544-7544
Jonathan Sherry, *President*
EMP: 4
SALES (est): 818.4K **Privately Held**
SIC: 2421 Sawmills & planing mills, general

(G-16834)
C A ELLIOT LUMBER CO INC
Also Called: Elliott Lumber Company
200 Main St (16746-2008)
P.O. Box 272 (16746-0272)
PHONE..................................814 544-7523
Kurt P Elliott, *President*
Kenneth S Elliott, *President*
EMP: 20 EST: 1950
SALES (est): 2.9MM **Privately Held**
SIC: 2426 Furniture squares, hardwood; rounds or rungs, furniture: hardwood

Rouseville
Venango County

(G-16835)
ASELS CABINET COMPANY
Rouseville Rd Rr 8 (16344)
P.O. Box 346 (16344-0346)
PHONE..................................814 677-3063
William Schettler, *Partner*
Thomas P Schettler, *Partner*
EMP: 5
SALES: 550K **Privately Held**
SIC: 2431 1799 2434 Millwork; kitchen cabinet installation; vanities, bathroom: wood

(G-16836)
GOC PROPERTY HOLDINGS LLC
61 Main St (16344-3209)
P.O. Box 337 (16344-0337)
PHONE..................................814 678-4193
Mark Kimmel, *General Mgr*
EMP: 9 EST: 2012

G E O G R A P H I C

SQ FT: 5,000
SALES: 500K **Privately Held**
SIC: 3398 Metal heat treating

(G-16837)
JUDY RAYMOND CORPORATION
Also Called: Betts Machine Shop
10 Myers St (16344)
P.O. Box 335 (16344-0335)
PHONE.............................814 677-4058
Raymond Judy, *President*
Kenneth Davis, *Vice Pres*
EMP: 7 **EST:** 1949
SQ FT: 1,300
SALES (est): 600K **Privately Held**
SIC: 3599 Machine shop, jobbing & repair

Roxbury
Franklin County

(G-16838)
HOLTRYS LLC
Also Called: Www.deutzboyz.com
10948 Roxbury Rd (17251-7000)
P.O. Box 11 (17251-0011)
PHONE.............................717 532-7261
Mae Holtry,
Luke Holtry,
EMP: 4
SQ FT: 13,000
SALES: 520K **Privately Held**
SIC: 5083 7699 3621 5999 Tractors, agricultural; farm machinery repair; generator sets: gasoline, diesel or dual-fuel; engines & parts, air-cooled; engines & parts, diesel; engines, used

Royersford
Montgomery County

(G-16839)
ACCOUNTABLE SOFTWARE INC
70 Buckwalter Rd Ste 226 (19468-1846)
PHONE.............................610 983-3100
David Haabestad, *CEO*
Marci Haabestad, *COO*
EMP: 20
SQ FT: 8,600
SALES (est): 1.2MM **Privately Held**
WEB: www.accountable.com
SIC: 7372 Prepackaged software

(G-16840)
ACCUMETRICS LIMITED
134 Adams St (19468-2232)
PHONE.............................610 948-0181
Paul W Pitcher, *President*
Gerry Colden, *Mfg Staff*
Diane Brunner, *Production*
Paul Bobinsky, *QC Mgr*
Steven Fuller, *Engineer*
▼ **EMP:** 30
SQ FT: 10,000
SALES (est): 7.6MM **Privately Held**
SIC: 3317 3498 Tubing, mechanical or hypodermic sizes: cold drawn stainless; fabricated pipe & fittings

(G-16841)
ALUMINUM ATHLETIC EQUIPMENT CO
Also Called: A A E
1000 Enterprise Dr (19468-1298)
PHONE.............................610 825-6565
Timothy Driscoll, *President*
Patricia Driscoll, *Vice Pres*
Timothy W Driscoll, *Treasurer*
Mark Jasse, *Admin Sec*
Diana C Mascaro, *Admin Sec*
▼ **EMP:** 35
SQ FT: 40,000
SALES (est): 5.6MM **Privately Held**
WEB: www.aaesports.com
SIC: 3949 Track & field athletic equipment

(G-16842)
AMT PUMP COMPANY
Also Called: A M T
400 Spring St (19468-2519)
PHONE.............................610 948-3800
Keith Bearde, *President*

Robert Kirkendall, *Senior VP*
Samuel Marcus, *Vice Pres*
Brenda Feairhelle, *Controller*
Michael Mikita, *Sales Mgr*
▲ **EMP:** 38 **EST:** 1987
SQ FT: 75,000
SALES (est): 17.5MM
SALES (corp-wide): 414.3MM **Publicly Held**
WEB: www.amtpump.com
SIC: 3561 Industrial pumps & parts
PA: Gorman-Rupp Company
600 S Airport Rd
Mansfield OH 44903
419 755-1011

(G-16843)
ARALEZ PHARMACEUTICALS MGT INC
Also Called: Aralez Management
70 Bayhill Cir (19468-1638)
PHONE.............................609 917-9330
Adrian Adams, *CEO*
EMP: 5
SALES (est): 149.1K
SALES (corp-wide): 71.6MM **Privately Held**
SIC: 2834 Pharmaceutical preparations
PA: Old Api Wind-Down Ltd
7100 West Credit Ave Suite 101
Mississauga ON L5N 0
905 876-1118

(G-16844)
ARALEZ PHARMACEUTICALS R&D INC
Also Called: Aralez R&D
70 Bayhill Cir (19468-1638)
PHONE.............................609 917-9330
Adrian Adams, *CEO*
EMP: 3 **EST:** 2016
SALES (est): 140.7K
SALES (corp-wide): 71.6MM **Privately Held**
SIC: 2834 Pharmaceutical preparations
PA: Old Api Wind-Down Ltd
7100 West Credit Ave Suite 101
Mississauga ON L5N 0
905 876-1118

(G-16845)
ARALEZ PHARMACEUTICALS US INC
70 Bayhill Cir (19468-1638)
PHONE.............................609 917-9330
Andrew Koven, *Director*
EMP: 11
SALES (est): 3MM **Privately Held**
SIC: 2834 Pharmaceutical preparations

(G-16846)
BECTON DICKINSON AND COMPANY
Also Called: B D Medical Systems-Injection
10 Galie Way (19468-3302)
PHONE.............................610 948-3492
Martin Shields, *Branch Mgr*
EMP: 5
SALES (corp-wide): 15.9B **Publicly Held**
SIC: 2834 Pharmaceutical preparations
PA: Becton, Dickinson And Company
1 Becton Dr
Franklin Lakes NJ 07417
201 847-6800

(G-16847)
CRANECO LLC
490 1st Ave (19468-2247)
PHONE.............................610 948-1400
William H Miller, *Principal*
EMP: 6 **EST:** 2008
SALES (est): 917.7K **Privately Held**
SIC: 3531 3537 Tractors, construction; industrial trucks & tractors

(G-16848)
CREATIVE KINK LLC
12 Char Mar Ln (19468-2625)
PHONE.............................610 506-9809
John Barthle, *Mng Member*
EMP: 3
SALES: 43K **Privately Held**
SIC: 2499 7389 Decorative wood & woodwork;

(G-16849)
EMERSON ELECTRIC CO
410 W Linfield Trappe Rd # 200
(19468-4295)
PHONE.............................610 569-4023
Jenny Alvaro, *Branch Mgr*
EMP: 23
SALES (corp-wide): 17.4B **Publicly Held**
SIC: 3823 Industrial instrmnts msrmnt display/control process variable
PA: Emerson Electric Co.
8000 West Florissant Ave
Saint Louis MO 63136
314 553-2000

(G-16850)
GLAXOSMITHKLINE LLC
129 Buckwalter Rd (19468-2729)
PHONE.............................610 917-4085
EMP: 26
SALES (corp-wide): 39.8B **Privately Held**
SIC: 2834 Pharmaceutical preparations
HQ: Glaxosmithkline Llc
5 Crescent Dr
Philadelphia PA 19112
215 751-4000

(G-16851)
HIG CAPITAL LLC
Also Called: Teleflex Marine
640 N Lewis Rd (19468-1228)
PHONE.............................610 495-7011
George Bradley, *Sales/Mktg Mgr*
EMP: 120 **Privately Held**
WEB: www.teleflex.com
SIC: 3625 3731 3519 3714 Marine & navy auxiliary controls; marine rigging; marine engines; motor vehicle parts & accessories; manufactured hardware (general); steel wire & related products
HQ: H.I.G. Capital, L.L.C.
1450 Brickell Ave Fl 31
Miami FL 33131
305 379-2322

(G-16852)
I F H INDUSTRIES INC
Also Called: 1fh Industries
522 Chestnut St (19468-2022)
PHONE.............................215 699-9344
Glen Reese, *President*
EMP: 8
SQ FT: 2,500
SALES: 500K **Privately Held**
SIC: 3823 Thermocouples, industrial process type

(G-16853)
JANSSEN BIOTECH INC
184 Bayberry Dr (19468-1244)
PHONE.............................610 651-7200
Robert Studt, *Principal*
EMP: 74
SALES (corp-wide): 81.5B **Publicly Held**
SIC: 2834 Pharmaceutical preparations
HQ: Janssen Biotech, Inc.
800 Ridgeview Dr
Horsham PA 19044
610 651-6000

(G-16854)
KALIL PRINTING INC
241 Vaughn Rd (19468-1567)
PHONE.............................610 948-9330
Walter M Kalil, *President*
Joseph D Kalil, *Vice Pres*
Patsy Kalil, *Vice Pres*
Michael A Kalil Sr, *Treasurer*
Michelle A Kalil, *Admin Sec*
EMP: 32
SQ FT: 10,500
SALES (est): 5.2MM **Privately Held**
WEB: www.kalilsprinting.com
SIC: 2752 2759 Commercial printing, offset; commercial printing

(G-16855)
KRONOS INCORPORATED
2704 Noble Way (19468-1359)
PHONE.............................610 567-2127
EMP: 35
SALES (corp-wide): 1.1B **Privately Held**
WEB: www.kronos.com
SIC: 7372 Prepackaged software

HQ: Kronos Incorporated
900 Chelmsford St # 312
Lowell MA 01851
978 250-9800

(G-16856)
KRUPPKO INC
Also Called: Rental World
44 W Ridge Pike (19468-1712)
PHONE.............................610 489-2334
Harold Kodikian, *President*
Mike Nase, *Vice Pres*
Mark Labonte, *Asst Mgr*
EMP: 12
SQ FT: 2,862
SALES: 648.8K **Privately Held**
SIC: 3993 Signs & advertising specialties

(G-16857)
LAFAYETTE WELDING INC
Also Called: Plow Shop At Lafayette Welding
64 W Ridge Pike (19468-1700)
PHONE.............................610 489-3529
John T Mellon, *Treasurer*
EMP: 8
SQ FT: 5,000
SALES (est): 1.8MM **Privately Held**
SIC: 3441 7389 Fabricated structural metal; crane & aerial lift service

(G-16858)
MEDIMMUNE
104 Rosemont Ln (19468-3234)
PHONE.............................240 751-5625
EMP: 3
SALES (est): 141.3K **Privately Held**
SIC: 2834 Pharmaceutical preparations

(G-16859)
PENNERGY SOLUTIONS LLC
7 Buckwalter Cir (19468-2733)
PHONE.............................484 393-1539
Richard Colasanti, *Mng Member*
Robert Lowry,
EMP: 6
SALES: 200K **Privately Held**
SIC: 3585 8711 7389 Refrigeration & heating equipment; engineering services;

(G-16860)
PENNSYLVANIA INSERT CORP
490 1st Ave (19468-2247)
P.O. Box 199, Spring City (19475-0199)
PHONE.............................610 474-0112
Jennifer Kawar, *President*
Arthur C Miller, *Chairman*
Buddy Frederick, *Plant Mgr*
Kyle Stahl, *Sales Staff*
Hank Droneburg, *Director*
EMP: 14
SQ FT: 9,000
SALES (est): 3.1MM **Privately Held**
WEB: www.pennsylvaniainsert.com
SIC: 3449 3089 Miscellaneous metalwork; thermoformed finished plastic products

(G-16861)
POLISH THIS INC
3006 Gateway Dr (19468-1355)
PHONE.............................484 269-9450
Jeffrey Goodhart, *Principal*
Jeffrey G Goodhart, *Purch Mgr*
EMP: 5
SALES (est): 513.5K **Privately Held**
SIC: 3471 Polishing, metals or formed products

(G-16862)
ROBBIE HOLLAND
Also Called: Robbie Holland Welding
44 Church Rd (19468-1010)
PHONE.............................610 495-5441
Robbie Holland, *Owner*
EMP: 4
SALES (est): 210K **Privately Held**
SIC: 7692 1711 Welding repair; mechanical contractor

(G-16863)
ROYERSFORD SPRING CO
Also Called: Royco Logistics
98 Main St (19468-2296)
PHONE.............................610 948-4440
Samantha Canestro, *President*
Edward T Claghorn, *President*
Frederic S Claghorn Jr, *Admin Sec*

▲ **EMP:** 15 **EST:** 1898
SQ FT: 62,500
SALES (est): 6.7MM **Privately Held**
SIC: 3495 4225 Wire springs; general warehousing & storage

(G-16864)
SIGNATURE GALLERY
50 1st Ave (19468-2239)
PHONE..................................610 792-5399
Sherrie Schoen, *Owner*
Edward Schoen, *Owner*
EMP: 8
SQ FT: 4,000
SALES (est): 300K **Privately Held**
WEB: www.signaturegallery.com
SIC: 5712 2511 1751 Customized furniture & cabinets; wood household furniture; cabinet & finish carpentry

(G-16865)
SPECIALTY EXTRUSION INC
135 1st Ave (19468-2200)
PHONE..................................610 792-3800
Thomas Yip, *Managing Prtnr*
EMP: 3
SQ FT: 8,500
SALES: 500K **Privately Held**
WEB: www.specialtyextrusioninc.com
SIC: 3081 Unsupported plastics film & sheet

(G-16866)
STICKMAN BREWS
326 N Lewis Rd (19468-1509)
PHONE..................................484 938-5900
James M Buckman, *Manager*
EMP: 8
SALES (est): 110.5K **Privately Held**
SIC: 2082 Malt beverages

(G-16867)
TELEFLEX INCORPORATED
640 N Lewis Rd (19468-1233)
PHONE..................................610 495-7011
Melissa Buttry, *Asst Controller*
D Dr Stephen Klask, *Director*
Jeffrey Graves, *Bd of Directors*
EMP: 150
SALES (corp-wide): 2.1B **Publicly Held**
WEB: www.teleflex.com
SIC: 3625 Relays & industrial controls
PA: Teleflex Incorporated
550 E Swedesford Rd # 400
Wayne PA 19087
610 225-6800

(G-16868)
THERMAL ENGRG INTL USA INC
155 S Limerick Rd 200 (19468-1603)
PHONE..................................610 948-5400
EMP: 35
SALES (corp-wide): 627.7MM **Privately Held**
SIC: 3443 Mfg Fabricated Plate Wrk Mfg Elec Housewares/Fans
HQ: Thermal Engineering International (Usa) Inc.
10375 Slusher Dr
Santa Fe Springs CA 90703
323 726-0641

(G-16869)
WINTERTHUR WENDT USA INC
Also Called: Wendt Dunnington Company
546 Enterprise Dr (19468-1288)
PHONE..................................610 495-2850
Mary Beth Martino, *President*
Daniel E Herzo, *President*
Bruce Dunnington, *Vice Pres*
▲ **EMP:** 150
SQ FT: 50,000
SALES (est): 18.9MM
SALES (corp-wide): 32.7B **Publicly Held**
WEB: www.wdi.wendtgroup.com
SIC: 3291 5084 3545 Abrasive products; industrial machinery & equipment; machine tool accessories
PA: 3m Company
3m Center
Saint Paul MN 55144
651 733-1110

Ruffs Dale
Westmoreland County

(G-16870)
ASSURED TOLL & GAUGE INC
184 Gressly Rd (15679-1463)
PHONE..................................724 722-3410
Sheryl Heid, *President*
EMP: 5
SALES (est): 533.1K **Privately Held**
SIC: 3599 Machine shop, jobbing & repair

(G-16871)
CARBIGRIND INC
186 Waltz Mill Rd (15679-1126)
PHONE..................................724 722-3536
David L Mencer, *President*
EMP: 3 **EST:** 1998
SALES (est): 368.9K **Privately Held**
WEB: www.carbigrindinc.com
SIC: 3544 Special dies & tools

(G-16872)
GERALD KING LUMBER CO INC
1720 State Route 981 (15679-1176)
PHONE..................................724 887-3688
Gerald King, *President*
Donna King, *Corp Secy*
Gregory King, *Vice Pres*
Pamela King, *Manager*
Pamala King, *Admin Sec*
EMP: 13 **EST:** 1965
SQ FT: 3,000
SALES (est): 1.7MM **Privately Held**
SIC: 2421 Sawmills & planing mills, general

(G-16873)
J L SCREEN PRINTING
Rr 31 (15679)
PHONE..................................724 696-5630
Joanne Moyer, *Owner*
EMP: 3
SQ FT: 5,000
SALES: 500K **Privately Held**
WEB: www.jlscreen.com
SIC: 3993 2759 Signs, not made in custom sign painting shops; screen printing

(G-16874)
MENASHA PACKAGING COMPANY LLC
567 Waltz Mill Rd (15679-1217)
PHONE..................................800 245-2486
EMP: 200
SALES (corp-wide): 1.7B **Privately Held**
WEB: www.menashapackaging.com
SIC: 2653 Corrugated & solid fiber boxes
HQ: Menasha Packaging Company, Llc
1645 Bergstrom Rd
Neenah WI 54956
920 751-1000

(G-16875)
REYNOLDS MACHINE CO INC
229 Potoka Mine Rd (15679-1507)
PHONE..................................724 925-1982
Wayne H Reynolds, *President*
Patty Reynolds, *Vice Pres*
Greg Reynolds, *Manager*
EMP: 6
SQ FT: 2,340
SALES: 900K **Privately Held**
SIC: 3599 Machine shop, jobbing & repair

Rural Valley
Armstrong County

(G-16876)
BLACK HAWK MINING INC
221 Creek Rd (16249-2303)
PHONE..................................724 783-6433
Michael McCullough, *President*
EMP: 25
SQ FT: 800
SALES: 1.6MM **Privately Held**
SIC: 1222 1221 Bituminous coal-underground mining; auger mining, bituminous

---

(G-16877)
US ENERGY
145 Valley Rd (16249-2517)
P.O. Box 237 (16249-0237)
PHONE..................................724 783-7532
Michael Boyer, *Principal*
EMP: 7
SALES (est): 412.7K **Privately Held**
SIC: 3541 Drilling & boring machines

(G-16878)
US ENERGY EXPL CORP
Also Called: U.S. Energy Exploration Group
145 Valley Rd (16249)
P.O. Box 237 (16249-0237)
PHONE..................................724 783-7624
Dennis C Boyer, *President*
EMP: 5
SALES (est): 1.5MM **Privately Held**
SIC: 1381 1382 Drilling oil & gas wells; oil & gas exploration services

---

Rushland
Bucks County

(G-16879)
MILLER AND SON PAVING INC
Also Called: Miller Quarries
887 Mill Creek Rd (18956)
PHONE..................................215 598-7801
Joseph Johnson, *Manager*
Duane Johnson, *Manager*
EMP: 13
SQ FT: 2,012
SALES (est): 784.8K
SALES (corp-wide): 7.2MM **Privately Held**
WEB: www.millersonpaving.com
SIC: 1771 1422 Concrete work; crushed & broken limestone
PA: Miller And Son Paving, Inc.
1371 W Street Rd
Warminster PA
215 675-0111

Russell
Warren County

(G-16880)
ELECTRIC PEPPER COMPANY LLC
1716 Akeley Rd (16345-4406)
PHONE..................................812 340-4321
Dj Steinberg, *Mng Member*
EMP: 4
SALES: 200K **Privately Held**
SIC: 1731 2033 Electrical work; chili sauce, tomato: packaged in cans, jars, etc.

(G-16881)
LARIMER & NORTON INC
2 Cable Hollow Rd (16345)
PHONE..................................814 757-4532
Jeff Eckman, *Manager*
EMP: 17
SALES (corp-wide): 96.3MM **Privately Held**
WEB: www.larimerlounge.com
SIC: 3949 2421 Baseball equipment & supplies, general; sawmills & planing mills, general
HQ: Larimer & Norton, Inc.
800 W Main St
Louisville KY 40202
502 585-5226

(G-16882)
WAYNE LAWSON
Also Called: Lawson Pallet Co
110 Creek Rd (16345)
P.O. Box 57 (16345-0057)
PHONE..................................814 757-8424
Wayne Lawson, *Owner*
EMP: 6
SQ FT: 8,000
SALES: 300K **Privately Held**
WEB: www.waynelawson.com
SIC: 2448 2441 Pallets, wood; nailed wood boxes & shook

Russellton
Allegheny County

(G-16883)
CARO BROTHERS INC
1 Main St (15076-9701)
P.O. Box 1 (15076-0001)
PHONE..................................724 265-1538
EMP: 15
SQ FT: 10,000
SALES (est): 1.9MM **Privately Held**
SIC: 5531 3599 Ret Automotive Supplies & Parts & Machine Shop

(G-16884)
PITTSBURGH ANODIZING CO
Also Called: Rooster Anodizing
41 Blue Rd (15076)
PHONE..................................724 265-5110
Eleanor Windows, *President*
Eric M Windows, *Corp Secy*
Howard Windows Jr, *Vice Pres*
Keith Domiano, *Financial Exec*
Timothy Horneman, *Manager*
EMP: 28
SQ FT: 5,000
SALES (est): 3.6MM **Privately Held**
WEB: www.pghanodizing.com
SIC: 3471 Anodizing (plating) of metals or formed products

Rydal
Montgomery County

(G-16885)
GLOBAL MACHINE AND MAINT LLC
Also Called: G M M
1131 Delene Rd (19046-3018)
PHONE..................................215 356-3077
Donald Spitko, *Mng Member*
EMP: 3 **EST:** 2011
SQ FT: 20,000
SALES (est): 349.4K **Privately Held**
SIC: 3559 Semiconductor manufacturing machinery

(G-16886)
PHARMA ACUMEN LLC
947 Frog Hollow Rd (19046-2402)
PHONE..................................215 885-1029
Brian Bamberger, *Principal*
EMP: 4
SALES (est): 309.2K **Privately Held**
SIC: 2834 Pharmaceutical preparations

(G-16887)
TS MCCORRY HEATING AND COOLING
1035 Kipling Rd (19046-3339)
PHONE..................................215 379-2800
EMP: 3
SALES (est): 160K **Privately Held**
SIC: 3585 Mfg Refrigeration/Heating Equipment

S Abingtn Twp
Lackawanna County

(G-16888)
ACKER DRILL CO INC
710 Shady Lane Rd (18411-9149)
P.O. Box 830, Scranton (18501-0830)
PHONE..................................570 586-2061
Wyane Wise, *President*
Mike Dicindio, *Vice Pres*
Bill Kearney, *Traffic Mgr*
Joseph Accardi, *Sales Staff*
Matt Pisanchyn, *Sales Staff*
◆ **EMP:** 28
SQ FT: 47,778
SALES (est): 10MM **Privately Held**
WEB: www.ackerdrill.com
SIC: 3532 3545 5084 Drills, core; drilling machine attachments & accessories; drilling equipment, excluding bits; drilling bits

---

(G-16889)
AMERICAN PLUME FANCY
FEATHER (PA)
11 Skyline Dr E Ste 2 (18411-9388)
PHONE.................................570 586-8400
Anthony Trento Jr, *President*
Elizabeth Trento, *Admin Sec*
▲ EMP: 17
SQ FT: 15,000
SALES (est): 1.3MM **Privately Held**
WEB: www.americanplume.com
SIC: 3999 Feathers & feather products

(G-16890)
CAMPUS CREAMERY LLC
1150 Northern Blvd (18411-2222)
PHONE.................................570 351-1738
EMP: 3 EST: 2010
SALES (est): 110.8K **Privately Held**
SIC: 2021 Creamery butter

(G-16891)
CHRYSLER ENCPSULATED
SEALS INC
11 Skyline Dr E Ste 1 (18411-9388)
PHONE.................................570 319-1694
EMP: 40
SALES (est): 4.9MM **Privately Held**
SIC: 2891 Mfg Adhesives/Sealants

(G-16892)
CIRCLE MANUFACTURING
COMPANY
995 Griffin Pond Rd (18411-9214)
PHONE.................................570 585-2139
EMP: 3
SALES (est): 464.3K **Privately Held**
SIC: 3999 Manufacturing industries

(G-16893)
COMPLETE FLUID CONTROL
INC
9 Skyline Dr E Ste 2 (18411-8751)
PHONE.................................570 382-3376
Michael Beamish, *CEO*
Larry L Mostoller, *President*
EMP: 25 EST: 2011
SQ FT: 2,100
SALES: 52MM **Privately Held**
SIC: 1389 7389 Construction, repair & dis-
mantling services; water softener service

(G-16894)
CREATIVE DESIGN &
MACHINING
Also Called: C D M I
969 Griffin Pond Rd (18411-9214)
P.O. Box 773, Clarks Summit (18411-0773)
PHONE.................................570 587-3077
William P Toman, *President*
Lori A Zielinski, *Treasurer*
Lori Bogaski, *Accounts Exec*
EMP: 26
SQ FT: 21,500
SALES (est): 7.4MM **Privately Held**
WEB: www.cdmi.cc
SIC: 3599 7692 Machine shop, jobbing &
repair; welding repair

(G-16895)
ELECAST INC
937 Griffin Pond Rd (18411-9214)
P.O. Box 234, Waverly (18471-0234)
PHONE.................................570 587-5105
David Wessell, *President*
Daniel J Churla, *Vice Pres*
EMP: 14
SQ FT: 20,000
SALES (est): 600K **Privately Held**
SIC: 3369 Machinery castings, nonferrous:
ex. alum., copper, die, etc.

(G-16896)
FLOWSERVE CORPORATION
942 Griffin Pond Rd (18411-9214)
P.O. Box 3055, Scranton (18505-3055)
PHONE.................................570 451-2200
Joe Ruddy, *Safety Dir*
Tom Hollenbeck, *Buyer*
John Skordos, *Sales Engr*
Robert Davis, *Manager*
EMP: 67
SALES (corp-wide): 3.8B **Publicly Held**
SIC: 3561 Industrial pumps & parts

PA: Flowserve Corporation
5215 N Oconnor Blvd Connor
Irving TX 75039
972 443-6500

(G-16897)
HEATED HUNTS
515 Leach St (18411-8973)
PHONE.................................570 575-5080
Jonathan Kalasinski, *Principal*
EMP: 4 EST: 2016
SALES (est): 390K **Privately Held**
SIC: 3949 Sporting & athletic goods

(G-16898)
RONCO MACHINE INC
11 Skyline Dr E Ste 3&4 (18411-9388)
PHONE.................................570 319-1832
Brad Reeves, *President*
EMP: 10
SALES (est): 311.4K **Privately Held**
SIC: 3999 Manufacturing industries

(G-16899)
SANDVIK INC
Sandvik Materials Technology
982 Griffin Pond Rd (18411-9214)
PHONE.................................570 585-7500
David Richard, *Human Res Mgr*
Helen Recipko, *Sales Staff*
Peter Frosini, *Branch Mgr*
Keith Hottle, *Manager*
Philip Thornton, *Manager*
EMP: 350
SALES (corp-wide): 10.7B **Privately Held**
SIC: 3312 Blast furnaces & steel mills
HQ: Sandvik, Inc.
17-02 Nevins Rd
Fair Lawn NJ 07410
201 794-5000

(G-16900)
VALMET INC
987 Griffin Pond Rd (18411-9214)
PHONE.................................570 587-5111
Dave Dimello, *Manager*
EMP: 100
SQ FT: 77,000
SALES (corp-wide): 3.7B **Privately Held**
WEB: www.metso.com
SIC: 3069 7699 3061 Rolls, solid or cov-
ered rubber; professional instrument re-
pair services; mechanical rubber goods
HQ: Valmet, Inc.
2425 Commerce Ave Ste 100
Duluth GA 30096
770 263-7863

(G-16901)
VALMET INC
987 Griffin Pond Rd (18411-9214)
P.O. Box 155, Clarks Summit (18411-0155)
PHONE.................................570 587-5111
EMP: 48 **Privately Held**
SIC: 3069 Mfg Fabricated Rubber Prod-
ucts
HQ: Valmet, Inc.
2425 Commerce Ave Ste 100
Duluth GA 30096
770 263-7863

(G-16902)
VAULT CLOTHING STORE INC
335 Bailey St (18411-8968)
PHONE.................................570 780-8240
Frank Letoski, *Principal*
EMP: 3 EST: 2008
SALES (est): 188.1K **Privately Held**
SIC: 3272 Burial vaults, concrete or pre-
cast terrazzo

(G-16903)
WESEL MANUFACTURING
COMPANY
710 Layton Rd (18411-9309)
PHONE.................................570 586-8978
John R Thomas, *Ch of Bd*
Russell Cammer Jr, *President*
EMP: 20
SQ FT: 33,000
SALES: 2MM **Privately Held**
WEB: www.weselmfg.en.busytrade.com
SIC: 3549 3542 5084 Metalworking ma-
chinery; machine tools, metal forming
type; machine tools & metalworking ma-
chinery

Sadsburyville
Chester County

(G-16904)
BLACK WALNUT WINERY (PA)
3000 E Lincoln Hwy (19369)
PHONE.................................610 857-5566
Lance Castle, *President*
EMP: 7 EST: 2008
SALES (est): 607.3K **Privately Held**
SIC: 2084 Wines

(G-16905)
MANUFCTRING TECHNICAL
SVCS INC
Also Called: MTS Forge
Greenbelt Dr (19369)
P.O. Box 309 (19369-0309)
PHONE.................................610 857-3500
Stephen Carr, *President*
Edward Waddell, *Vice Pres*
EMP: 6
SQ FT: 12,000
SALES (est): 1MM **Privately Held**
WEB: www.mtsforge.com
SIC: 3312 Blast furnaces & steel mills

(G-16906)
R S MACHINE & TOOL INC
Valley E Industrial Park (19369)
P.O. Box 238 (19369-0238)
PHONE.................................610 857-1644
Robert G Silvernail, *President*
EMP: 5
SQ FT: 4,000
SALES (est): 525.5K **Privately Held**
SIC: 3599 Machine shop, jobbing & repair

Saegertown
Crawford County

(G-16907)
ASSOCIATED TOOL & MACHINE
19817 Bertram Dr (16433-5405)
PHONE.................................814 783-0083
Scott Smith, *Owner*
EMP: 5
SALES (est): 474.7K **Privately Held**
SIC: 3544 Special dies, tools, jigs & fix-
tures

(G-16908)
BYLER RELISH HOUSE LLC
18258 Leimbach Rd (16433-6816)
PHONE.................................814 763-6510
Urie A Byler, *Mng Member*
EMP: 7
SALES (est): 440.3K **Privately Held**
SIC: 2035 Relishes, vinegar

(G-16909)
CELLCON PLASTICS INC
17763 State Highway 198 (16433-3635)
P.O. Box 728 (16433-0728)
PHONE.................................814 763-2195
Marilyn Hillburn, *CEO*
EMP: 15
SALES (est): 881.7K **Privately Held**
SIC: 3089 Plastic processing

(G-16910)
CENTURY BUILDINGS
17067 Townhouse Rd (16433-3847)
PHONE.................................814 336-1446
Russ Williams, *Owner*
Beverly Williams, *Co-Owner*
EMP: 6
SALES: 500K **Privately Held**
SIC: 3448 1542 Prefabricated metal build-
ings; nonresidential construction

(G-16911)
CLASSIC TOOL INC
236 Grant St (16433-7623)
P.O. Box 967 (16433-0967)
PHONE.................................814 763-4805
Joseph Lawrence, *President*
Charles Lawrence, *Admin Sec*
EMP: 6

SALES (est): 638.7K **Privately Held**
SIC: 3312 Tool & die steel & alloys

(G-16912)
DIMENSION CARBIDE
25320 State St (16433-7428)
PHONE.................................814 789-2102
James Spaulding, *Partner*
Gregory Allen, *Partner*
EMP: 5
SQ FT: 1,200
SALES (est): 586.1K **Privately Held**
SIC: 3599 Machine shop, jobbing & repair

(G-16913)
FAME MANUFACTURING INC
(PA)
Also Called: Saegertown Hardware
329 Mill St (16433)
PHONE.................................814 763-5645
Richard Bidwell, *President*
Mark Simchak, *Corp Secy*
Daniel Bidwell, *Vice Pres*
EMP: 15
SQ FT: 15,000
SALES (est): 5.7MM **Privately Held**
SIC: 5561 3792 5251 Campers (pickup
coaches) for mounting on trucks; travel
trailers: automobile, new & used; travel
trailers & campers; hardware

(G-16914)
FISHER & LUDLOW INC
607 Erie St (16433-5001)
P.O. Box 909 (16433-0909)
PHONE.................................814 763-5914
Landahl Thomas, *Branch Mgr*
EMP: 9
SALES (corp-wide): 25B **Publicly Held**
SIC: 3446 Gratings, open steel flooring
HQ: Fisher & Ludlow Inc.
2000 Corporate Dr Ste 400
Wexford PA 15090

(G-16915)
GREENLEAF CORPORATION
(PA)
18695 Greenleaf Dr (16433-4429)
P.O. Box 1040 (16433-1040)
PHONE.................................814 763-2915
Walter J Greenleaf Jr, *Ch of Bd*
James M Greenleaf, *Ch of Bd*
Bernie McConnell, *Exec VP*
Keith Taylor, *VP Mfg*
Elizabeth Jemetz, *QC Mgr*
▲ EMP: 311 EST: 1945
SALES (est): 102.7MM **Privately Held**
WEB: www.greenleafcorporation.com
SIC: 3545 3541 Cutting tools for machine
tools; machine tools, metal cutting type

(G-16916)
HAEMER/WRIGHT TOOL & DIE
INC
19990 State Highway 198 (16433-5048)
P.O. Box 291 (16433-0291)
PHONE.................................814 763-6076
Brad Wright, *President*
Mark Haemer, *Vice Pres*
EMP: 20
SQ FT: 8,500
SALES (est): 2.2MM **Privately Held**
SIC: 3089 3544 Plastic processing; spe-
cial dies, tools, jigs & fixtures

(G-16917)
HIGHPOINT TOOL & MACHINE
INC
Also Called: Highpoint Tool and Machine
17380 State Highway 198 (16433-3628)
P.O. Box 641 (16433-0641)
PHONE.................................814 763-5453
John J Kolcun, *President*
Carol L Kolcun, *Vice Pres*
Barbara J Kolcun, *Treasurer*
EMP: 35
SQ FT: 13,000
SALES (est): 7.3MM **Privately Held**
SIC: 3599 Machine shop, jobbing & repair

(G-16918)
HYDE SPECIAL TOOLS
16380 State Highway 86 (16433-6138)
PHONE.................................814 763-4140
Lon Hyde, *Owner*

EMP: 4
SQ FT: 6,000
SALES: 2MM **Privately Held**
SIC: 3544 Special dies, tools, jigs & fixtures

(G-16919)
JAMES A SCHULTZ
Also Called: Schultz Industries
18879 Schultz Dr (16433-5419)
P.O. Box 23 (16433-0023)
PHONE..............................814 763-5561
James A Schultz, *Owner*
James S Schultz, *Owner*
James Schultz, *Owner*
EMP: 10
SQ FT: 8,000
SALES: 300K **Privately Held**
WEB: www.schultzindustries.com
SIC: 7692 1796 Welding repair; installing
    building equipment

(G-16920)
JOHN W CZECH
Also Called: Czeck Tool
17741 Brookhouser Rd (16433-3621)
PHONE..............................814 763-4470
John W Czech, *Owner*
Travis Czech, *Manager*
EMP: 20
SALES (est): 3.4MM **Privately Held**
SIC: 3312 3544 Tool & die steel & alloys;
    special dies, tools, jigs & fixtures

(G-16921)
LASER TOOL INC
17763 State Highway 198 (16433-3635)
P.O. Box 728 (16433-0728)
PHONE..............................814 763-2032
Christopeher M Minnis, *President*
Todd Costello, *Project Mgr*
Gregory Styborski, *Manager*
EMP: 28
SQ FT: 28,000
SALES (est): 4.5MM **Privately Held**
WEB: www.laser-tool.com
SIC: 3544 Special dies & tools

(G-16922)
LON HYDE
Also Called: Hyde Special Tools
16380 State Highway 86 (16433-6138)
PHONE..............................814 763-4140
Lon Hyde, *Owner*
EMP: 4
SQ FT: 3,000
SALES: 250K **Privately Held**
SIC: 3599 Machine shop, jobbing & repair

(G-16923)
LORD CORPORATION
Chemical Products Division
601 South St (16433-5050)
P.O. Box 1050 (16433-1050)
PHONE..............................814 763-2345
Ron Miller, *Plant Mgr*
Charles Garrity, *Plant Mgr*
Chuck Smith, *Facilities Mgr*
Joe Boughton, *Purchasing*
David Jacobs, *QC Dir*
EMP: 156
SALES (corp-wide): 1B **Privately Held**
WEB: www.lordcorp.com
SIC: 2899 2891 2851 Chemical preparations; adhesives; paints & allied products
PA: Lord Corporation
    111 Lord Dr
    Cary NC 27511
    919 468-5979

(G-16924)
**MACLEAN SAEGERTOWN LLC
(DH)**
Also Called: Mvs Saegertown
1 Crawford St (16433-5006)
P.O. Box 828 (16433-0828)
PHONE..............................814 763-2655
Duncan Maclean, *Mng Member*
Sharon Dunn, *Mng Member*
John Cox, *Manager*
Tracy Pituch, *Manager*
▼ EMP: 9

SALES (est): 3.9MM
SALES (corp-wide): 1.3B **Privately Held**
SIC: 3532 3498 3714 3965 Bits, except
    oil & gas field tools, rock; couplings; pipe:
    fabricated from purchased pipe; motor ve-
    hicle parts & accessories; fasteners
HQ: Maclean-Fogg Component Solutions,
    L.L.C
    1000 Allanson Rd
    Mundelein IL 60060
    248 853-2525

(G-16925)
**MAJR PRODUCTS
CORPORATION**
780 South St (16433-5046)
PHONE..............................814 763-3211
Donald Hester Jr, *President*
Mark Stoner, *Vice Pres*
Brian Hester, *Sales Staff*
Autumn Shoaf, *Sales Staff*
▲ EMP: 15
SQ FT: 20,000
SALES (est): 2.9MM **Privately Held**
WEB: www.majr.com
SIC: 3679 Electronic circuits

(G-16926)
NORTHWEST TOOL & DIE INC
22973 Cannon Hollow Rd (16433-6507)
PHONE..............................814 763-5087
Wayne Bogardus Jr, *President*
EMP: 15
SQ FT: 15,000
SALES: 1.5MM **Privately Held**
SIC: 3544 Special dies & tools

(G-16927)
PRICE TOOL INC
514 Broad St (16433)
PHONE..............................814 763-4410
Craig Price, *President*
Edward Price, *Vice Pres*
EMP: 10 EST: 2001
SALES: 980K **Privately Held**
SIC: 3545 Machine tool accessories

(G-16928)
PROGRESS FOR INDUSTRY INC
201 Grant St (16433-7624)
PHONE..............................814 763-3707
Gary Mc Bride, *President*
Don Mc Bride, *Treasurer*
Jean Bianco, *Manager*
Wilhemina Mc Bride, *Admin Sec*
EMP: 10 EST: 1982
SQ FT: 8,000
SALES: 1MM **Privately Held**
WEB: www.pfiinc.com
SIC: 3471 Electroplating of metals or
    formed products

(G-16929)
**PROSTHETIC CAD-CAM TECH
INC**
21150 Peters Rd (16433-5736)
PHONE..............................814 763-1151
Donald Smith, *Principal*
EMP: 3 EST: 2010
SALES (est): 224.7K **Privately Held**
SIC: 3842 Prosthetic appliances; orthope-
    dic appliances

(G-16930)
PTC-IN-LIQUIDATION INC
606 Erie St (16433-5002)
PHONE..............................814 763-2000
Thomas M Kapusta, *President*
Deborah Kapusta, *Corp Secy*
EMP: 40
SQ FT: 12,000
SALES (est): 4.4MM
SALES (corp-wide): 1.3B **Privately Held**
WEB: www.proformtool.com
SIC: 3544 Industrial molds
PA: Mac Lean-Fogg Company
    1000 Allanson Rd
    Mundelein IL 60060
    847 566-0010

(G-16931)
**REISINGERS PRECISION POLSG
LLC**
19881 S Mosiertown Rd (16433-3137)
PHONE..............................814 763-2226

Roger Reisinger, *Principal*
EMP: 3
SALES (est): 155.1K **Privately Held**
SIC: 3471 Polishing, metals or formed
    products

(G-16932)
**SAEGERTOWN
MANUFACTURING CORP**
Also Called: SMC
1 Crawford St (16433-5006)
P.O. Box 828 (16433-0828)
PHONE..............................814 763-2655
Desmond J McDonald, *President*
Chalmer Jordan, *Chairman*
Nancy C Lewis, *Corp Secy*
EMP: 150 EST: 1964
SQ FT: 140,000
SALES: 23.1MM
SALES (corp-wide): 1.3B **Privately Held**
SIC: 3532 3498 3714 3545 Bits, except
    oil & gas field tools, rock; couplings; pipe:
    fabricated from purchased pipe; motor ve-
    hicle parts & accessories; machine tool
    accessories; bolts, nuts, rivets & washers;
    cold finishing of steel shapes
PA: Mac Lean-Fogg Company
    1000 Allanson Rd
    Mundelein IL 60060
    847 566-0010

(G-16933)
SHORTS TOOL & MFG INC
18927 Reservoir Rd (16433-4547)
P.O. Box 648 (16433-0648)
PHONE..............................814 763-2401
Kevin Shorts, *President*
Jason Tomcho, *General Mgr*
EMP: 22 EST: 2001
SQ FT: 8,000
SALES: 2.5MM **Privately Held**
SIC: 3089 Molding primary plastic; injec-
    tion molding of plastics

(G-16934)
SIGNS BY RENEE
16520 State Highway 198 (16433-3314)
PHONE..............................814 763-4206
Renee Bowersox, *Owner*
Cristy Bowersox, *Admin Sec*
EMP: 3
SALES: 150K **Privately Held**
SIC: 3993 Signs & advertising specialties

(G-16935)
VAULT SERVICES
22237 Stull Rd (16433-5837)
PHONE..............................814 282-8143
EMP: 3
SALES (est): 275.3K **Privately Held**
SIC: 3272 Burial vaults, concrete or pre-
    cast terrazzo

Saint Benedict
Cambria County

(G-16936)
CAMBRIA WELDING & FABG INC
196 Shop Rd (15773)
PHONE..............................814 948-5072
Cynthia Cunningham, *President*
EMP: 7
SQ FT: 7,000
SALES (est): 1MM **Privately Held**
SIC: 7692 1799 Welding repair; welding
    on site

Saint Clair
Schuylkill County

(G-16937)
E A QUIRIN MACHINE SHOP INC
W Hancock (17970)
PHONE..............................570 429-0590
Edmund P Quirin, *President*
Elizabeth Corby, *Admin Sec*
EMP: 45 EST: 1932
SQ FT: 25,000
SALES (est): 5.7MM **Privately Held**
SIC: 3363 Aluminum die-castings

(G-16938)
POLYFLO INC
2 Tension Way St (17970)
P.O. Box 309 (17970-0309)
PHONE..............................570 429-2340
Michael Yaworsky, *President*
Richelle Yaworsky, *Office Mgr*
▲ EMP: 25
SALES (est): 4.2MM **Privately Held**
WEB: www.polyfloinc.com
SIC: 3089 Injection molding of plastics

(G-16939)
REIDLER DECAL CORPORATION
264 Industrial Park Rd (17970)
PHONE..............................800 628-7770
Edward Reidler, *President*
Barry Frey, *Vice Pres*
Randall Reidler, *Vice Pres*
Melody Wagner, *Treasurer*
Richard C Reidler, *Shareholder*
EMP: 50 EST: 1926
SQ FT: 51,000
SALES (est): 14.5MM **Privately Held**
WEB: www.reidlerdecal.com
SIC: 2752 3993 Decals, lithographed;
    signs & advertising specialties

(G-16940)
ROBERT D RENNICK
2 Overlook Dr (17970-1300)
PHONE..............................570 429-0784
EMP: 3
SALES (est): 119.9K **Privately Held**
SIC: 2448 Wood pallets & skids

(G-16941)
**SPECTOR MANUFACTURING
INC**
Also Called: Spec-TEC
158 Industrial Park Rd (17970)
PHONE..............................570 429-2510
Jerry Blecker, *President*
Saul Spector, *President*
◆ EMP: 43
SQ FT: 110,000
SALES (est): 12.1MM **Privately Held**
SIC: 3715 Semitrailers for truck tractors;
    trailer bodies

(G-16942)
**TENSION ENVELOPE
CORPORATION**
1 Tension Way (17970)
P.O. Box 127 (17970-0127)
PHONE..............................570 429-1444
Doug Bush, *Manager*
EMP: 45
SQ FT: 37,000
SALES (corp-wide): 234MM **Privately
Held**
WEB: www.tension.com
SIC: 2677 Envelopes
PA: Tension Envelope Corporation
    819 E 19th St
    Kansas City MO 64108
    816 471-3800

Saint Marys
Elk County

(G-16943)
ABBOTT FURNACE COMPANY
1068 Trout Run Rd (15857-3146)
P.O. Box 967 (15857-0967)
PHONE..............................814 781-6355
Thomas Jesberger, *President*
Jeffrey Marzella, *Vice Pres*
EMP: 75
SQ FT: 50,000
SALES (est): 17.7MM **Privately Held**
WEB: www.abbottfurnace.com
SIC: 3625 3567 Industrial controls: push
    button, selector switches, pilot; industrial
    furnaces & ovens

(G-16944)
**ABSOLUTE POWDER COATING
LLC**
202 Grotzinger Rd (15857-3180)
P.O. Box 838 (15857-0838)
PHONE..............................814 781-1160

Mike Geiser, *General Mgr*
Audra Geiser,
EMP: 4
SQ FT: 7,500
SALES (est): 544.1K **Privately Held**
SIC: 3479 Coating of metals & formed products

(G-16945)
ACCU-CHEK MACHINING INC
37 Accu Chek Dr (15857-2201)
PHONE..................................814 834-2342
Ernest Kronenwetter, *President*
David Fox, *Treasurer*
EMP: 16
SQ FT: 7,000
SALES (est): 1.4MM **Privately Held**
SIC: 3599 Machine shop, jobbing & repair

(G-16946)
AGRIPOWER MFG & SVCS INC
230 State St (15857-1628)
PHONE..................................814 781-1009
James Eabcock, *President*
Anthony Chan, *Treasurer*
EMP: 3
SALES: 189K
SALES (corp-wide): 1.8MM **Privately Held**
SIC: 3511 Turbines & turbine generator sets
PA: Agripower, Inc.
46 Deepdale Dr
Great Neck NY 11021
516 829-2000

(G-16947)
AMPHENOL CORPORATION
Amphenol Advanced Sensors
967 Windfall Rd (15857-3333)
PHONE..................................814 834-9140
Charlene Juhasz, *Materials Mgr*
Rick Morrow, *Buyer*
Matt Schwabenbauer, *Treasurer*
Lori McCoy, *Sales Staff*
Joe Zilka, *Sales Staff*
EMP: 7
SALES (corp-wide): 8.2B **Publicly Held**
SIC: 3829 Measuring & controlling devices
PA: Amphenol Corporation
358 Hall Ave
Wallingford CT 06492
203 265-8900

(G-16948)
AMPHENOL THERMOMETRICS INC (HQ)
Also Called: GE Sensing & Inspection Tech
967 Windfall Rd (15857-3333)
PHONE..................................814 834-9140
Brian Palmer, *CEO*
John Carter, *President*
Monica A Oconnor, *Vice Pres*
Angie Fabiano, *Buyer*
Nelson Schaffner, *Engineer*
▲ **EMP:** 190
SQ FT: 80,000
SALES (est): 109.3MM
SALES (corp-wide): 8.2B **Publicly Held**
SIC: 3823 Thermistors, industrial process type
PA: Amphenol Corporation
358 Hall Ave
Wallingford CT 06492
203 265-8900

(G-16949)
ASMAC INC
338 West Creek Rd (15857-3349)
PHONE..................................814 781-3358
Don Fritz, *President*
EMP: 35
SALES (est): 4.5MM **Privately Held**
SIC: 3599 Machine shop, jobbing & repair

(G-16950)
AYRSHIRE DAIRY
Also Called: Uhl's Ayrshire Dairy
347 Old Kersey Rd (15857)
PHONE..................................814 781-1978
James Uhl, *Partner*
Gertrude Uhl Hippchen, *Partner*
Gretude Hippchen, *Partner*
Charles Uhl, *Partner*
EMP: 10
SQ FT: 750

SALES (est): 608.2K **Privately Held**
SIC: 0241 2026 5411 5541 Milk production; milk processing (pasteurizing, homogenizing, bottling); convenience stores; filling stations, gasoline

(G-16951)
C I HAYES INC
Also Called: Sinterite Products
310 State St (15857-2648)
PHONE..................................814 834-2200
Steve Smith, *President*
Julie Stebick, *Mktg Coord*
▲ **EMP:** 47
SALES (est): 11.3MM **Privately Held**
SIC: 3567 3549 3542 Industrial furnaces & ovens; metalworking machinery; machine tools, metal forming type

(G-16952)
CARBON CITY PRODUCTS INC
Also Called: C C P
150 Ford Rd (15857-2931)
P.O. Box 520 (15857-0520)
PHONE..................................814 834-2886
Arlan J Clayton, *Ch of Bd*
Michael P Risdon, *CFO*
EMP: 80 EST: 1956
SQ FT: 56,000
SALES (est): 11MM
SALES (corp-wide): 185.3MM **Privately Held**
SIC: 3399 Powder, metal
PA: Metal Powder Products, Llc
16855 Suthpark Dr Ste 100
Westfield IN 46074
317 805-3764

(G-16953)
CATALUS CORPORATION (PA)
286 Piper Rd (15857-3099)
PHONE..................................814 781-7004
Stephen J Lanzel, *President*
Richard Smith, *Principal*
Gary Millsop, *Treasurer*
John Challingsworth, *VP Sales*
Dave Parsons, *VP Sales*
EMP: 13
SALES (est): 10.4MM **Privately Held**
SIC: 3399 Powder, metal

(G-16954)
CLEAR CREEK INDUSTRIES INC
85 Stackpole St (15857-1473)
PHONE..................................814 834-9880
Jason Ryan, *President*
EMP: 18 EST: 2013
SALES (est): 394.9K **Privately Held**
SIC: 2514 Metal lawn & garden furniture

(G-16955)
CNHI LLC
Daily Press
245 Brusselles St (15857-1501)
PHONE..................................814 781-1596
Wayne Bauer, *General Mgr*
Jim Bauer, *Treasurer*
James Mulcahy, *Loan Officer*
Jill Golden, *Advt Staff*
Laura Evers, *Manager*
EMP: 25 **Privately Held**
WEB: www.clintonnc.com
SIC: 2711 Newspapers, publishing & printing
HQ: Cnhi, Llc
445 Dexter Ave
Montgomery AL 36104

(G-16956)
COMTEC MFG INC
1012 Delaum Rd (15857-3360)
P.O. Box 940 (15857-0940)
PHONE..................................814 834-9300
David L Delullo Jr, *President*
Donna Wendel, *Treasurer*
EMP: 60
SQ FT: 44,100
SALES (est): 8.8MM **Privately Held**
WEB: www.comtecmfg.com
SIC: 3499 Friction material, made from powdered metal

(G-16957)
CONTACT TECHNOLOGIES INC
229 West Creek Rd (15857-3309)
PHONE..................................814 834-9000

Robert Dayton, *President*
Gary Butcher, *COO*
▲ **EMP:** 156
SQ FT: 39,000
SALES (est): 41.4MM **Privately Held**
WEB: www.contactechnologies.com
SIC: 3643 Contacts, electrical

(G-16958)
CUSTOM INDUSTRIAL PROCESSING
336 State St (15857-2648)
PHONE..................................814 834-1883
Stephen J Lanzel, *President*
Paul A Baumgratz, *Vice Pres*
Matt Hillebrand, *Manager*
EMP: 18 EST: 1976
SQ FT: 11,200
SALES (est): 1.7MM **Privately Held**
WEB: www.ciprocessing.com
SIC: 3471 Electroplating of metals or formed products

(G-16959)
CUSTOM SINTERED SPECIALTIES
199 Ceramic St (15857-2217)
P.O. Box 190 (15857-0190)
PHONE..................................814 834-5154
Joseph D Szymanski, *President*
Nancy J Szymanski, *Vice Pres*
David A Szymanski, *Treasurer*
Jesse J Szymanski, *Admin Sec*
EMP: 3
SALES (est): 282.3K **Privately Held**
SIC: 3299 Ceramic fiber

(G-16960)
D A D FABRICATION AND WELDING
1009 Delaum Rd (15857-3359)
PHONE..................................814 781-1886
David Piccolo, *President*
Daniel Lechien, *Vice Pres*
EMP: 6
SALES (est): 614K **Privately Held**
SIC: 1799 3441 Welding on site; fabricated structural metal

(G-16961)
DAVES PRO SHOP INC
83 Erie Ave (15857-1408)
PHONE..................................814 834-6116
Gary E Hoffman, *President*
Kim Hoffman, *Treasurer*
EMP: 10 EST: 1964
SQ FT: 6,500
SALES (est): 1MM **Privately Held**
WEB: www.davesproshop.com
SIC: 2396 5941 Screen printing on fabric articles; sporting goods & bicycle shops

(G-16962)
DIETECH TOOL & DIE INC
425 W Theresia Rd (15857-2719)
PHONE..................................814 834-2779
Michael P Roberts, *President*
Ginny Roberts, *Corp Secy*
EMP: 13
SQ FT: 9,000
SALES (est): 1.7MM **Privately Held**
SIC: 3544 Special dies & tools

(G-16963)
DOMINION POWDERED METALS
266 Battery St (15857-2204)
PHONE..................................814 598-4684
EMP: 4
SALES (est): 588.9K **Privately Held**
SIC: 3399 Primary metal products

(G-16964)
DUBROOK INC
875 Theresia St (15857)
PHONE..................................814 834-3111
Jenny Brem, *Manager*
EMP: 12
SALES (corp-wide): 9.1MM **Privately Held**
WEB: www.dubrook.com
SIC: 3273 Ready-mixed concrete
PA: Dubrook, Inc.
40 Hoover Ave
Du Bois PA 15801
814 371-3113

(G-16965)
E-CARBON AMERICA LLC
806 Theresia St (15857-1831)
PHONE..................................814 834-7777
Paul Casper,
EMP: 16
SALES (est): 3.2MM **Privately Held**
SIC: 3624 Electric carbons

(G-16966)
EASTERN SINTERED ALLOYS INC
126 Access Rd (15857-3396)
PHONE..................................814 834-1216
John Sterbank, *President*
Ashok Sethi, *Corp Secy*
Arthur Hillebrand, *Vice Pres*
Dennis G Lindberg, *Vice Pres*
EMP: 275
SQ FT: 27,000
SALES (est): 53.9MM **Privately Held**
SIC: 3399 Powder, metal

(G-16967)
EASTERN TOOL STEEL SERVICE INC
1045 Delaum Rd (15857-3359)
P.O. Box 857 (15857-0857)
PHONE..................................814 834-7224
Mark Mohney, *President*
Timothy Mohney, *Vice Pres*
Clifford Mohney, *Treasurer*
EMP: 6
SQ FT: 5,000
SALES (est): 1.2MM **Privately Held**
WEB: www.easterntoolsteel.com
SIC: 5051 3312 Copper products; tool & die steel & alloys

(G-16968)
ELK COUNTY HEAT TREATERS INC
316 Battery St (15857-2209)
PHONE..................................814 834-0056
Steve Reusher, *President*
Benjamin Vrobel, *General Mgr*
EMP: 16
SQ FT: 12,000
SALES (est): 2.7MM **Privately Held**
SIC: 3398 Metal heat treating

(G-16969)
ELK COUNTY MACHINING
Also Called: Elk County Designing
177 West Creek Rd (15857-3307)
PHONE..................................814 781-3502
Jim Buttery, *President*
John Buttery, *Vice Pres*
EMP: 9
SALES (est): 430K **Privately Held**
SIC: 3599 3552 Machine shop, jobbing & repair; dyeing, drying & finishing machinery & equipment

(G-16970)
ELK COUNTY TOOL & DIE INC
1020 Graphite Rd (15857-3150)
P.O. Box 835 (15857-0835)
PHONE..................................814 834-1434
Mark J Sicheri, *President*
Kenneth A Sicheri, *Corp Secy*
David J Gleixiner, *Vice Pres*
▲ **EMP:** 30
SQ FT: 5,200
SALES (est): 2.7MM **Privately Held**
WEB: www.elkcountytool.com
SIC: 3544 Special dies, tools, jigs & fixtures

(G-16971)
ELK METALS INC
266 Battery St (15857-2204)
PHONE..................................814 834-4959
Kenneth J Mattivi, *President*
Joan Deprater, *Corp Secy*
Howard Gradl, *Vice Pres*
EMP: 10
SQ FT: 34,400
SALES (est): 1.9MM **Privately Held**
SIC: 3399 Powder, metal

(G-16972)
ENGINEERED PRESSED MATERIALS
Also Called: E P M
348 Center St (15857-1134)
PHONE...................................814 834-3189
Richard J Phillips, *Owner*
EMP: 5
SALES (est): 464.6K Privately Held
SIC: 3399 8711 5084 Powder, metal; designing: ship, boat, machine & product; metalworking machinery

(G-16973)
ENHANCED SINTERED PRODUCTS INC
74 Pm St (15857-2242)
P.O. Box 330 (15857-0330)
PHONE...................................814 834-2470
Joseph Lecker, *CEO*
EMP: 7
SALES (est): 1MM Privately Held
SIC: 3449 Miscellaneous metalwork

(G-16974)
FLORIO TOOLING INC
Also Called: Florio Tooling Co
1103 Aumadel Rd (15857-3367)
PHONE...................................814 781-3973
Daniel R Florio, *President*
Donna Florio, *Corp Secy*
EMP: 6 EST: 1976
SQ FT: 3,500
SALES (est): 835.6K Privately Held
SIC: 3599 3544 Machine shop, jobbing & repair; special dies & tools

(G-16975)
GASBARRE PRODUCTS INC
Sinterite Furnace Division
310 State St (15857-2648)
PHONE...................................814 834-2200
Steve Smith, *President*
Mark Saline, *General Mgr*
EMP: 34
SQ FT: 30,000
SALES (corp-wide): 40MM Privately Held
WEB: www.gasbarre.com
SIC: 3567 3549 3542 Industrial furnaces & ovens; metalworking machinery; machine tools, metal forming type
PA: Gasbarre Products, Inc.
590 Division St
Du Bois PA 15801
814 371-3015

(G-16976)
GE INFRASTRUCTURE SENSING INC
967 Windfall Rd (15857-3333)
PHONE...................................814 834-5506
James Preshak, *Manager*
EMP: 301
SALES (corp-wide): 121.6B Publicly Held
SIC: 3823 Moisture meters, industrial process type
HQ: Ge Infrastructure Sensing, Llc
1100 Technology Park Dr # 100
Billerica MA 01821
978 437-1000

(G-16977)
GERG TOOL & DIE INC
Also Called: B & B Tool & Die, Subsidiary
356 West Creek Rd (15857-3340)
PHONE...................................814 834-3888
Anthony Gerg, *CEO*
Michael J Gerg, *President*
EMP: 31
SQ FT: 40,000
SALES (est): 3.4MM Privately Held
SIC: 5251 3599 Tools; machine shop, jobbing & repair

(G-16978)
GLOBAL METAL PRODUCTS INC
230 Stackpole St (15857-1418)
PHONE...................................814 834-2214
Yi Yao, *CEO*
Roger J Smith, *President*
Roger Smith, *Manager*
▲ EMP: 7

SALES: 750K Privately Held
WEB: www.globalmetalproducts.com
SIC: 3399 Powder, metal

(G-16979)
GRAFTECH USA LLC
Also Called: Graphite Electrode Mfg Fcilty
800 Theresia St (15857-1831)
PHONE...................................814 781-2478
David R Jardini, *Mng Member*
Nathan Milikowsky,
▲ EMP: 160
SALES (est): 40.5MM
SALES (corp-wide): 8.5B Publicly Held
WEB: www.cgelectrodes.com
SIC: 3624 3823 3567 Carbon & graphite products; industrial instrmnts msrmnt display/control process variable; industrial furnaces & ovens
HQ: Graftech International Ltd.
982 Keynote Cir Ste 6
Brooklyn Heights OH 44131

(G-16980)
HORIZON TECHNOLOGY INC
293 Battery St (15857-2206)
PHONE...................................814 834-4004
Eric Wolfe, *President*
Kenneth Wolfe, *Corp Secy*
Cathy Cuneo, *QC Mgr*
Ken Wolfe, *Treasurer*
Jennifer Thorwart, *Sales Mgr*
EMP: 23
SQ FT: 15,300
SALES (est): 5.9MM Privately Held
SIC: 3499 Fire- or burglary-resistive products

(G-16981)
INNOVATIVE SINTERED METALS INC
1037 Delaum Rd (15857-3359)
PHONE...................................814 781-1033
John Dippold III, *President*
David Bobby, *Vice Pres*
Darla Pollino, *QC Mgr*
EMP: 20
SQ FT: 15,000
SALES (est): 2.6MM Privately Held
WEB: www.innovativesintered.com
SIC: 3499 Friction material, made from powdered metal

(G-16982)
JET METALS INC
412 Grotzinger Rd (15857-3183)
P.O. Box 907 (15857-0907)
PHONE...................................814 781-7399
Jim Buehler, *President*
▲ EMP: 12 EST: 2001
SQ FT: 30,000
SALES (est): 1.6MM Privately Held
SIC: 3399 Powder, metal

(G-16983)
KEVRO PRECISION COMPONENTS INC
1273 Brusselles St (15857-1915)
PHONE...................................814 834-5387
Rodney Anderson, *President*
Kevin Gnan, *Vice Pres*
EMP: 4
SQ FT: 2,000
SALES: 500K Privately Held
SIC: 3451 Screw machine products

(G-16984)
KEYSTONE POWDERED METAL CO (DH)
251 State St (15857-1658)
PHONE...................................814 781-1591
Richard T Maxstadt, *President*
Pete Imbrogno, *General Mgr*
Stephen Feidler, *Opers Staff*
Dave Leithner, *Production*
Cindy Klein, *Buyer*
▲ EMP: 375 EST: 1927
SQ FT: 551,371
SALES (est): 30.2MM
SALES (corp-wide): 28.9B Privately Held
SIC: 3499 5051 Friction material, made from powdered metal; tubing, metal; ferrous metals; stampings, metal

HQ: Sumitomo Electric U.S.A. Holdings, Inc.
600 5th Ave Fl 18
New York NY 10020
212 490-6610

(G-16985)
KEYSTONE POWDERED METAL CO
Thermistor Division
967 Windfall Rd (15857-3333)
PHONE...................................814 834-9140
EMP: 250
SALES (corp-wide): 28.9B Privately Held
SIC: 3823 Thermistors, industrial process type
HQ: Keystone Powdered Metal Co
251 State St
Saint Marys PA 15857
814 781-1591

(G-16986)
KRECKEL ENTERPRISES INC
1044 Windfall Rd (15857-3336)
PHONE...................................814 834-1874
Lavern Kreckel III, *President*
EMP: 10
SALES (est): 1.2MM Privately Held
SIC: 3469 Machine parts, stamped or pressed metal

(G-16987)
MATHESON TRI-GAS INC
203 West Creek Rd (15857-3373)
PHONE...................................814 781-6990
EMP: 13 Privately Held
SIC: 5084 2813 Welding machinery & equipment; safety equipment; nitrogen
HQ: Matheson Tri-Gas, Inc.
150 Allen Rd Ste 302
Basking Ridge NJ 07920
908 991-9200

(G-16988)
MERSEN USA BN CORP
215 Stackpole St (15857-1401)
P.O. Box 360217, Pittsburgh (15251-6217)
PHONE...................................814 781-1234
Jose Ruiz, *General Mgr*
Susan Fledderman, *General Mgr*
Steve Fritz, *Purch Mgr*
Mike Lang, *Engineer*
Diane Nash, *Human Res Mgr*
EMP: 200
SALES (corp-wide): 2MM Privately Held
SIC: 3624 Carbon & graphite products
HQ: Mersen Usa Ptt Corp.
400 Myrtle Ave
Boonton NJ 07005
973 334-0700

(G-16989)
MERSEN USA ST MARYS-PA CORP (HQ)
215 Stackpole St (15857-1401)
PHONE...................................814 781-1234
Christophe Boomier, *President*
Ronald Braund, *Mktg Dir*
◆ EMP: 60
SALES (est): 34.2MM
SALES (corp-wide): 2MM Privately Held
SIC: 3624 Carbon & graphite products
PA: Mersen
Tour Eqho La Defense
Puteaux 92800
146 915-400

(G-16990)
MERSEN USA ST MARYS-PA CORP
Graphite Materials Division
215 Stackpole St (15857-1401)
PHONE...................................814 781-1234
Edward Stumpff, *Branch Mgr*
EMP: 160
SALES (corp-wide): 2MM Privately Held
WEB: www.carbonebrush.com
SIC: 3624 3399 3264 Carbon & graphite products; metal powders, pastes & flakes; porcelain electrical supplies
HQ: Mersen Usa St. Marys-Pa Corp.
215 Stackpole St
Saint Marys PA 15857
814 781-1234

(G-16991)
METAL POWDER PRODUCTS LLC
Also Called: Mpp Ford Road Division
150 Ford Rd (15857-2931)
P.O. Box 520 (15857-0520)
PHONE...................................814 834-2886
Paul Vavala, *Principal*
Emily Swanson, *Hum Res Coord*
EMP: 80
SALES (corp-wide): 185.3MM Privately Held
WEB: www.metalpowder.com
SIC: 3399 3469 Aluminum atomized powder; machine parts, stamped or pressed metal
PA: Metal Powder Products, Llc
16855 Suthpark Dr Ste 100
Westfield IN 46074
317 805-3764

(G-16992)
METAL POWDER PRODUCTS LLC
Also Called: Mpp Washington Street Division
879 Washington St (15857-3644)
P.O. Box 520 (15857-0520)
PHONE...................................814 834-7261
Paul Vavala, *Principal*
EMP: 150
SALES (corp-wide): 185.3MM Privately Held
WEB: www.metalpowder.com
SIC: 3399 3568 3714 Powder, metal; power transmission equipment; bearings, motor vehicle
PA: Metal Powder Products, Llc
16855 Suthpark Dr Ste 100
Westfield IN 46074
317 805-3764

(G-16993)
METALDYNE SNTERFORGED PDTS LLC
Also Called: St. Marys Mfg Facility
197 West Creek Rd (15857-3339)
PHONE...................................814 834-1222
Thomas A Amato, *CEO*
Mark Blaufuss, *CFO*
▲ EMP: 5050
SALES (est): 14.9MM
SALES (corp-wide): 7.2B Publicly Held
SIC: 3714 Motor vehicle parts & accessories
PA: American Axle & Manufacturing Holdings, Inc.
1 Dauch Dr
Detroit MI 48211
313 758-2000

(G-16994)
METCO INDUSTRIES INC
1241 Brusselles St (15857-1999)
PHONE...................................814 781-3630
Richard A Buchheit, *President*
Dick Buchheit, *President*
Jeff Herzing, *Facilities Mgr*
Toni Zettle, *Production*
Jim Wimer, *QC Dir*
▲ EMP: 97 EST: 1981
SQ FT: 47,000
SALES (est): 22.9MM Privately Held
WEB: www.metcopm.com
SIC: 3399 Powder, metal

(G-16995)
MICHAEL MEYER PALLETS
1022 S Michael St (15857-3003)
PHONE...................................814 781-1107
Michael Meyer, *Owner*
EMP: 3
SQ FT: 768
SALES (est): 325.4K Privately Held
SIC: 2448 Pallets, wood

(G-16996)
MILLER MACHINE SHOP INC
1030 Brusselles St Ste C (15857-1850)
PHONE...................................814 834-2114
William R Miller, *President*
Barbara Miller, *Admin Sec*
EMP: 6
SQ FT: 3,000
SALES: 285K Privately Held
SIC: 3599 Machine shop, jobbing & repair

(G-16997)
MILLION DOLLAR MACHINING INC
930 S Saint Marys St (15857-2829)
PHONE..................................814 834-9224
Thomas E Lewis Jr, *President*
Jeffrey T Lewis, *Admin Sec*
EMP: 5
SQ FT: 5,800
SALES (est): 580.8K **Privately Held**
SIC: 3599 Machine shop, jobbing & repair

(G-16998)
MORGAN ADVANCED MTLS TECH INC (DH)
Also Called: Morgan AM&t
441 Hall Ave (15857-1400)
PHONE..................................814 781-1573
John Stang, *CEO*
Don Klas, *President*
Susan Georgino, *Vice Pres*
Lance Mohney, *Engineer*
Eric Catalone, *Design Engr*
▲ EMP: 160
SQ FT: 280,000
SALES (est): 96.9MM
SALES (corp-wide): 1.3B **Privately Held**
SIC: 3624 3291 3592 3568 Carbon & graphite products; silicon carbide abrasive; carburetors, pistons, rings, valves; power transmission equipment; porcelain electrical supplies; gaskets, packing & sealing devices
HQ: Morganite Industries Inc.
4000 Westchase Blvd # 170
Raleigh NC 27607
919 821-1253

(G-16999)
OSRAM SYLVANIA INC
Also Called: General Lighting Division
835 Washington St (15857-3697)
PHONE..................................814 834-1800
Chris Sconzo, *Manager*
EMP: 221
SALES (corp-wide): 4.7B **Privately Held**
WEB: www.sylvania.com
SIC: 3641 Lamps, incandescent filament, electric
HQ: Osram Sylvania Inc
200 Ballardvale St # 305
Wilmington MA 01887
978 570-3000

(G-17000)
OSRAM SYLVANIA INC
Electronic Components & Mtls
835 Washington St (15857-3697)
PHONE..................................717 854-3499
John Salerno, *Manager*
EMP: 290
SALES (corp-wide): 4.7B **Privately Held**
WEB: www.sylvania.com
SIC: 3641 3469 Electric lamps; metal stampings
HQ: Osram Sylvania Inc
200 Ballardvale St # 305
Wilmington MA 01887
978 570-3000

(G-17001)
P/M NATIONAL INC
201 Grotzinger Rd (15857-3180)
PHONE..................................814 781-1960
Tom Fleming, *President*
Ted Weisner, *Corp Secy*
Julia Tomaski, *QC Mgr*
Karen Horning, *Cust Mgr*
Joe Fleming, *Sales Staff*
EMP: 33
SQ FT: 15,000
SALES (est): 3.9MM **Privately Held**
SIC: 3399 Powder, metal

(G-17002)
PENN PALLET INC (PA)
675 Fillmore Rd (15857-3227)
P.O. Box 8 (15857-0008)
PHONE..................................814 834-1700
Daniel Cunningham, *President*
Dora J Cunningham, *Corp Secy*
John Cunningham, *Vice Pres*
EMP: 65
SQ FT: 35,000

SALES (est): 11.3MM **Privately Held**
WEB: www.pennpallet.com
SIC: 2448 Pallets, wood; pallets, wood & wood with metal

(G-17003)
PENN-ELKCO INC
1017 Delaum Rd (15857-3359)
PHONE..................................814 834-4304
Elizabeth Cotter, *President*
Jerry Cotter, *Vice Pres*
John G Cotter, *Treasurer*
EMP: 17
SQ FT: 18,000
SALES (est): 1.5MM **Privately Held**
WEB: www.pespring.com
SIC: 3495 3496 3469 Wire springs; miscellaneous fabricated wire products; metal stampings

(G-17004)
PENNSYLVANIA POWDERED MTLS INC
1066 Trout Run Rd (15857-3146)
PHONE..................................814 834-9565
Dan A Geci, *CEO*
Christine A Geci, *CEO*
Dan Geci, *President*
George Heigel, *Vice Pres*
Charles Cunningham, *Treasurer*
EMP: 21
SQ FT: 16,250
SALES (est): 4.4MM **Privately Held**
WEB: www.papowderedmetals.com
SIC: 3399 Powder, metal

(G-17005)
PEPSI-COLA METRO BTLG CO INC
854 S Saint Marys St (15857-2831)
PHONE..................................814 834-5700
Vinny Adamo, *Manager*
EMP: 50
SALES (corp-wide): 64.6B **Publicly Held**
WEB: www.joy-of-cola.com
SIC: 5149 2086 Soft drinks; bottled & canned soft drinks
HQ: Pepsi-Cola Metropolitan Bottling Company, Inc.
1111 Westchester Ave
White Plains NY 10604
914 767-6000

(G-17006)
PHAZTECH INC
40 S Saint Marys St (15857-1667)
P.O. Box 174 (15857-0174)
PHONE..................................814 834-3262
Carl E Pfeufer, *President*
EMP: 20
SQ FT: 12,000
SALES (est): 2.9MM **Privately Held**
WEB: www.phaztech.com
SIC: 3544 Special dies & tools

(G-17007)
PIHT LLC
Also Called: Bluewater Thermal Solutions
118 Access Rd (15857-3370)
PHONE..................................814 781-6262
Michael C Wellham, *CEO*
Keith Beasley, *CFO*
James D Hedman, *Director*
Jeffrey D Hemmer, *Director*
John Pyle, *Director*
EMP: 65
SQ FT: 48,500
SALES (est): 12.8MM **Privately Held**
SIC: 3398 Metal heat treating
HQ: Bwt Llc
201 Brookfield Pkwy
Greenville SC 29607

(G-17008)
POWDER METAL PRODUCTS INC
879 Washington St (15857-3644)
P.O. Box 520 (15857-0520)
PHONE..................................814 834-7261
James M Schloder Jr, *Ch of Bd*
William Kelly, *President*
Christine Stebick, *Corp Secy*
Steve Patrick, *Sr Exec VP*
Gerald L Schloder, *Director*
EMP: 150 EST: 1947

SQ FT: 110,000
SALES: 15MM **Privately Held**
SIC: 3399 Powder, metal

(G-17009)
PRINTING PLUS+ INC (PA)
Also Called: Furniture Connection, The
207 Stackpole St Ste 1 (15857-1449)
PHONE..................................814 834-1000
David Doyle, *President*
EMP: 14
SQ FT: 15,000
SALES (est): 1.5MM **Privately Held**
SIC: 2752 5712 Commercial printing, offset; office furniture

(G-17010)
PRO PRINTING & OFFICE LLC
969 Brusselles St (15857-1804)
PHONE..................................814 834-3006
EMP: 3
SALES (est): 200.2K **Privately Held**
SIC: 2759 Commercial printing

(G-17011)
QUALA-DIE INC
1250 Brusselles St (15857-1902)
PHONE..................................814 781-6280
Dennis P Schatz, *President*
Tom Dorsey, *General Mgr*
Richard Schatz, *Corp Secy*
Leo Gregori, *Engineer*
Kenneth Levenduski, *Sales Staff*
EMP: 90
SQ FT: 45,000
SALES (est): 14.6MM **Privately Held**
WEB: www.quala-die.com
SIC: 3599 Machine shop, jobbing & repair

(G-17012)
QUALITY METAL COATINGS INC
122 Access Rd (15857-3370)
PHONE..................................814 781-6161
Joe Handwerger, *President*
EMP: 4
SALES (est): 507.5K **Privately Held**
SIC: 3479 3399 3471 Coating of metals & formed products; powder, metal; plating & polishing

(G-17013)
QUALITY TOOL & DIE ENTERPRISES
967 Cherry Hill Rd (15857-3065)
PHONE..................................814 834-2384
Mark Bankovic, *President*
Mary Lee Bankovic, *Corp Secy*
EMP: 7
SQ FT: 3,600
SALES: 200K **Privately Held**
SIC: 3423 3544 Hand & edge tools; special dies, tools, jigs & fixtures

(G-17014)
SEEL TOOL & DIE INC
421 N Michael St (15857-1189)
PHONE..................................814 834-4561
Denny Andres, *President*
EMP: 5 EST: 1936
SQ FT: 6,000
SALES: 450K **Privately Held**
SIC: 3599 Machine shop, jobbing & repair

(G-17015)
ST MARYS BOX COMPANY
109 Jeep Rd (15857-2915)
P.O. Box 910 (15857-0910)
PHONE..................................814 834-3819
William W Pistner, *President*
Tom Pistner, *Sales Executive*
Karen Yonker, *Manager*
EMP: 45 EST: 1954
SALES: 9.7MM **Privately Held**
SIC: 2631 2653 Paperboard mills; boxes, corrugated: made from purchased materials

(G-17016)
ST MARYS CARBON CO INC (PA)
259 Eberl St (15857-1696)
PHONE..................................814 781-7333
Michael A Lanzel, *President*
Robert Wortman, *Business Mgr*
Michael J Emmert, *Vice Pres*

James Slay, *Vice Pres*
Bill Agosti, *Engineer*
▲ EMP: 150 EST: 1939
SQ FT: 118,000
SALES (est): 29.1MM **Privately Held**
WEB: www.stmaryscarbon.com
SIC: 3643 3366 3053 3624 Current-carrying wiring devices; copper foundries; gaskets, packing & sealing devices; brushes & brush stock contacts, electric

(G-17017)
ST MARYS CARBON CO INC
SMC Powder Metallurgy Division
259 Eberl St (15857-1696)
PHONE..................................814 781-7333
John Challingsworth, *Marketing Staff*
EMP: 100
SALES (corp-wide): 29.1MM **Privately Held**
WEB: www.stmaryscarbon.com
SIC: 3399 Metal powders, pastes & flakes
PA: St. Marys Carbon Co., Inc.
259 Eberl St
Saint Marys PA 15857
814 781-7333

(G-17018)
ST MARYS CARBON CO INC
259 Eberl St (15857-1696)
PHONE..................................814 781-7333
Tom Anzinger, *Branch Mgr*
EMP: 75
SALES (corp-wide): 29.1MM **Privately Held**
WEB: www.stmaryscarbon.com
SIC: 3399 3624 Powder, metal; brush blocks, carbon or molded graphite
PA: St. Marys Carbon Co., Inc.
259 Eberl St
Saint Marys PA 15857
814 781-7333

(G-17019)
ST MARYS METAL FINISHING INC
1057 Trout Run Rd (15857-3197)
PHONE..................................814 834-6500
Joseph Benninger, *President*
EMP: 9
SQ FT: 10,000
SALES: 1.5MM **Privately Held**
SIC: 3471 Electroplating of metals or formed products

(G-17020)
ST MARYS SPRING CO
630 Lehner Ave (15857-1814)
PHONE..................................814 834-2460
Adam Bailey, *Owner*
EMP: 5 EST: 1946
SQ FT: 4,500
SALES: 300K **Privately Held**
WEB: www.stmarysspring.com
SIC: 3495 Wire springs

(G-17021)
ST MARYS TOOL & DIE CO INC
1003 Trout Run Rd (15857-3124)
P.O. Box 14 (15857-0014)
PHONE..................................814 834-7420
Jim Smith, *President*
James Smith, *Vice Pres*
Joe Neubert, *Engineer*
EMP: 30
SQ FT: 8,200
SALES (est): 1MM **Privately Held**
WEB: www.stmarystool.com
SIC: 3544 Special dies & tools

(G-17022)
THERMISTORS UNLIMITED INC
1028 Graphite Rd (15857-3150)
P.O. Box 49 (15857-0049)
PHONE..................................814 781-5920
Gregory Stauffer, *President*
EMP: 7
SQ FT: 6,000
SALES: 400K **Privately Held**
SIC: 3676 Thermistors, except temperature sensors

(G-17023)
TORY TOOL INC (PA)
1906 Bucktail Rd (15857-3224)
PHONE..................................814 772-5439

▲ = Import ▼=Export
◆ =Import/Export

James Lewis, *President*
Jim Lewis, *President*
Robin Jasper, *Vice Pres*
Christine Lewis, *Treasurer*
EMP: 34
SALES (est): 3.1MM **Privately Held**
SIC: 3599 3544 Machine & other job shop work; special dies, tools, jigs & fixtures

(G-17024)
TROUT RUN SECONDARY
1105 Monroe Rd (15857-3235)
PHONE..................................814 834-0075
Randy Gyer, *Partner*
Doug Cheatle, *Partner*
EMP: 6
SALES (est): 733.6K **Privately Held**
SIC: 3599 Machine shop, jobbing & repair

(G-17025)
ULTRAMET HEAT TREATING INC
258 Church St (15857-1010)
PHONE..................................814 781-7215
Dale E Bille, *Principal*
EMP: 4
SALES (est): 275.9K **Privately Held**
SIC: 3398 Metal heat treating

(G-17026)
US RESISTOR INC
1016 Delaum Rd (15857-3360)
PHONE..................................814 834-9369
Thomas Cotter, *President*
Charles Ehrensberger, *Admin Sec*
▲ **EMP:** 8
SALES: 1MM
SALES (corp-wide): 29.1MM **Privately Held**
WEB: www.usresistor.com
SIC: 3676 Electronic resistors
PA: St. Marys Carbon Co., Inc.
    259 Eberl St
    Saint Marys PA 15857
    814 781-7333

(G-17027)
VOLLMER TAR & CHIP INC
Also Called: Vollmer Tar and Chip Asp Pav
1069 Trout Run Rd (15857-3124)
PHONE..................................814 834-1332
Glenn Vollmer, *President*
Angela Leithner, *Corp Secy*
EMP: 3
SALES: 100K **Privately Held**
SIC: 3531 Construction machinery

(G-17028)
W & H MACHINE SHOP CO LLC
1051 Trout Run Rd (15857-3124)
PHONE..................................814 834-6258
EMP: 11
SALES (est): 797.5K **Privately Held**
SIC: 3599 Mfg Industrial Machinery

(G-17029)
W & H MACHINE SHOP INC
1051 Trout Run Rd (15857-3124)
PHONE..................................814 834-6258
Marc Carpin, *President*
Richard M Meyer, *Vice Pres*
EMP: 13
SQ FT: 5,600
SALES (est): 1.7MM **Privately Held**
SIC: 3599 Custom machinery

(G-17030)
WITTMANS PURE MAPLE SYRUP LLC
214 N Saint Marys St (15857-1238)
PHONE..................................814 781-7523
Julie Wittman, *Principal*
EMP: 3 **EST:** 2014
SALES (est): 180.3K **Privately Held**
SIC: 2099 Maple syrup

(G-17031)
WORTMAN CONTROLS INC
207 Stackpole St (15857-1449)
PHONE..................................814 834-1299
Daniel Wortman, *President*
EMP: 7 **EST:** 2013
SALES (est): 1MM **Privately Held**
SIC: 3823 Industrial process control instruments

Saint Michael
Cambria County

(G-17032)
SAMCO INC
Rr 869 (15951)
P.O. Box 116 (15951-0116)
PHONE..................................814 495-4632
James Schrader, *President*
EMP: 7
SQ FT: 20,000
SALES (est): 1.2MM **Privately Held**
SIC: 3713 Truck bodies (motor vehicles)

Saint Peters
Chester County

(G-17033)
BALLOON FLIGHTS DAILY
490 Hopewell Rd (19470)
PHONE..................................610 469-0782
EMP: 3
SALES (est): 117.3K **Privately Held**
SIC: 2711 Newspapers, publishing & printing

(G-17034)
GLASSLIGHT INC
3611 Saint Peters Rd (19470)
P.O. Box 310 (19470-0310)
PHONE..................................610 469-9066
Joel Bless, *President*
Candice L Bless, *Vice Pres*
EMP: 5
SALES: 275K **Privately Held**
WEB: www.glasslightstudio.com
SIC: 3645 5719 Residential lighting fixtures; lighting fixtures

(G-17035)
STORED ENERGY CONCEPTS INC
3250b St Peters Rd (19470)
P.O. Box 387 (19470-0387)
PHONE..................................610 469-6543
Richard Lisowski, *President*
Elizabeth Lisowski, *Treasurer*
EMP: 13
SALES (est): 2.5MM **Privately Held**
WEB: www.storedenergyconcepts.com
SIC: 3548 Mfg Welding Apparatus

Saint Thomas
Franklin County

(G-17036)
APPLE WAY CSTM STAIRS RAILING
9523 Lincoln Way W (17252-9710)
PHONE..................................717 369-0502
Samuel Armstrong, *Owner*
EMP: 25
SALES (est): 701.5K **Privately Held**
SIC: 2431 Staircases, stairs & railings

(G-17037)
APX INDUSTRIAL COATINGS INC
9473 Lincoln Way W (17252-9710)
PHONE..................................717 369-0037
Andrew V Papoutsis, *President*
Michael S Snyder, *Treasurer*
EMP: 25
SQ FT: 300
SALES (est): 3.1MM
SALES (corp-wide): 7.9MM **Privately Held**
WEB: www.apx-enclosures.com
SIC: 3479 Coating of metals & formed products
PA: Apx Enclosures, Inc.
    200 Oregon St
    Mercersburg PA 17236
    717 328-9399

(G-17038)
BEAVER CREEK AVIARY
942 Loudon Rd (17252-9752)
PHONE..................................717 369-9983
Gary Mong, *Principal*
EMP: 3
SALES (est): 227.6K **Privately Held**
SIC: 3999 Pet supplies

(G-17039)
EXTREME MANUFACTURING INC
9230 Mountain Brook Rd (17252-9778)
PHONE..................................717 369-0044
Lamar S Lehman, *President*
Judy Kanner, *Assistant*
EMP: 12
SALES (est): 3.5MM **Privately Held**
SIC: 3449 Bars, concrete reinforcing: fabricated steel

(G-17040)
MOUNTAIN BROOK INDUSTRIAL COAT
9226 Mountain Brook Rd (17252-9778)
PHONE..................................717 369-4040
Brian E Wise, *Principal*
EMP: 6
SALES (est): 953.1K **Privately Held**
SIC: 2952 Coating compounds, tar

(G-17041)
ST THOMAS DEVELOPMENT INC
8153b Lincoln Way W (17252-9776)
PHONE..................................717 369-3030
EMP: 3
SALES (est): 131K **Privately Held**
SIC: 2951 Asphalt paving mixtures & blocks

(G-17042)
SVM2 PHARMA INC
4495 Lincoln Way W (17252-9679)
PHONE..................................717 369-4636
Krishna Koneru, *Manager*
EMP: 4
SALES (est): 393.9K **Privately Held**
SIC: 2834 Pharmaceutical preparations

Salina
Westmoreland County

(G-17043)
JOHNSON PATTERN & MACHINE SHOP
46 Stewart St (15680)
P.O. Box 129 (15680-0129)
PHONE..................................724 697-4079
Dennis B Johnson, *Owner*
EMP: 3
SQ FT: 1,500
SALES: 200K **Privately Held**
SIC: 3544 3543 Industrial molds; industrial patterns

Salisbury
Somerset County

(G-17044)
BRENNEMANS MAPLE SYRUP & EQP
572 Oak Dale Rd (15558-2314)
PHONE..................................814 941-8974
Harry Brenneman, *Owner*
EMP: 3 **EST:** 1998
SALES (est): 153.1K **Privately Held**
SIC: 2099 Maple syrup

(G-17045)
SAM BEACHY & SONS
381 Niverton Rd (15558-2406)
PHONE..................................814 662-2220
Willis Sommers, *Owner*
EMP: 3
SALES: 230K **Privately Held**
SIC: 1794 2033 5261 Excavation work; fruit butters: packaged in cans, jars, etc.; lawn & garden equipment

(G-17046)
TALL PINES DISTILLERY LLC
9224 Mason Dixon Hwy (15558-2007)
PHONE..................................814 442-2245
EMP: 3
SALES (est): 189.4K **Privately Held**
SIC: 2085 Distilled & blended liquors

Salix
Cambria County

(G-17047)
EVERYTHING ICE INC (PA)
115 School St (15952)
P.O. Box 250 (15952-0250)
PHONE..................................814 244-5477
John Burley, *President*
Tim Elgin, *Treasurer*
▲ **EMP:** 35
SQ FT: 35,000
SALES (est): 12.8MM **Privately Held**
WEB: www.everything-ice.com
SIC: 1629 3585 Athletic & recreation facilities construction; air conditioning condensers & condensing units

(G-17048)
SALIX CABINETRY INC
307 Bellwood Dr (15952-9113)
PHONE..................................814 266-4181
Scott Good, *President*
EMP: 8
SQ FT: 1,000
SALES: 2MM **Privately Held**
SIC: 2434 Wood kitchen cabinets

Salona
Clinton County

(G-17049)
HANSON AGGREGATES PA LLC
Rr 477 (17767)
PHONE..................................570 726-4511
Barry Davis, *Superintendent*
EMP: 6
SALES (corp-wide): 20.6B **Privately Held**
SIC: 1442 1446 Gravel mining; silica sand mining
HQ: Hanson Aggregates Pennsylvania, Llc
    7660 Imperial Way
    Allentown PA 18195
    610 366-4626

Saltsburg
Indiana County

(G-17050)
AMERICAN ORNAMENTAL IRON CORP
2484 Elders Ridge Rd (15681-3028)
PHONE..................................724 639-8684
Wayne R Smith, *President*
Anita Hadden, *Principal*
Alexander D Shashur, *Vice Pres*
John Shawley, *Treasurer*
Brent A Smith, *Treasurer*
EMP: 12 **EST:** 2002
SQ FT: 10,000
SALES (est): 2.5MM **Privately Held**
WEB: www.americanoic.com
SIC: 3446 Fences or posts, ornamental iron or steel

(G-17051)
HOOVERS STONE QUARRY LLC
3497 State Route 981 (15681-1491)
PHONE..................................724 639-9813
Timothy Hoover, *Mng Member*
EMP: 12
SALES (est): 875.2K **Privately Held**
SIC: 1422 Crushed & broken limestone

(G-17052)
NORMA PENNSYLVANIA INC
Also Called: Breeze Industrial Products
3582 Tunnelton Rd (15681-3305)
PHONE..................................724 639-3571
Werner Deggim, *CEO*

Tim Jones, *President*
Mike Russel, *President*
Durg Kumar, *Corp Secy*
John Stephenson, *COO*
▲ **EMP:** 320
SALES (est): 119.7MM
SALES (corp-wide): 1.2B **Privately Held**
WEB: www.breezeclamps.com
SIC: 3429 Clamps & couplings, hose
HQ: Norma Group Holding Gmbh
Edisonstr. 4
Maintal 63477
618 140-30

(G-17053)
STRAIGHTLINE SAW MILL INC
207 Lucky Ln (15681-4247)
PHONE.................................724 639-3090
James M Wilson, *Principal*
EMP: 3 **EST:** 2010
SALES (est): 229.2K **Privately Held**
SIC: 2421 Sawmills & planing mills, general

Salunga
Lancaster County

(G-17054)
LUTECH INC
127 W Main St Ste B (17538-1159)
PHONE.................................717 898-9150
Robert Lukwoski, *President*
Dana Costello, *Treasurer*
EMP: 4
SQ FT: 5,000
SALES (est): 432.6K **Privately Held**
WEB: www.eplwoodcoating.com
SIC: 2891 Adhesives

(G-17055)
ORTHO DEPOT LLC
Also Called: Ops
127 W Main St (17538-1159)
PHONE.................................800 992-9999
Robert Lukowski,
▲ **EMP:** 4
SALES (est): 491.3K **Privately Held**
WEB: www.orthodepot.net
SIC: 3842 Surgical appliances & supplies

(G-17056)
SUSQUEHANNA TIMES &
MAGAZINE
Also Called: Old News
3 W Brandt Blvd (17538-1105)
PHONE.................................717 898-9207
Richard Bromer, *President*
Kathy McCarty, *Manager*
EMP: 3
SALES: 190K **Privately Held**
SIC: 2721 Magazines: publishing only, not printed on site

(G-17057)
SUSQUHNNA VLY
WOODCRAFTERS INC
131 W Main St (17538-1128)
PHONE.................................717 898-7564
Jose Gonzalez, *President*
Rick Boyer, *Vice Pres*
David Gonzalez, *Vice Pres*
▲ **EMP:** 23
SQ FT: 24,000
SALES (est): 3MM **Privately Held**
SIC: 2434 Wood kitchen cabinets

Sanatoga
Montgomery County

(G-17058)
PRECISION GLASS
TECHNOLOGIES
3110 W Ridge Pike (19464-3426)
PHONE.................................610 323-2825
Arthur Mengel, *President*
Clyde Mock, *Marketing Staff*
EMP: 4

SALES (est): 431.8K
SALES (corp-wide): 11.9MM **Publicly Held**
WEB: www.videodisplay.com
SIC: 3827 Optical instruments & apparatus
PA: Video Display Corporation
1868 Tucker Industrial Rd
Tucker GA 30084
770 938-2080

Sandy Lake
Mercer County

(G-17059)
FERGIES BAIT & TACKLE
857 Georgetown Rd (16145-2525)
PHONE.................................724 253-3655
Robert Mohra, *Partner*
John Klescz, *Partner*
EMP: 5
SQ FT: 1,600
SALES (est): 405.9K **Privately Held**
SIC: 3949 Buckets, fish & bait

(G-17060)
FLEXOSPAN STEEL BUILDINGS
INC
253 Railroad St (16145)
P.O. Box 515 (16145-0515)
PHONE.................................724 376-7221
Lauri L Frederick, *President*
Laurel H McQuiston Mclallen, *Vice Pres*
Lou Ann Miller, *Treasurer*
Lou Miller, *Controller*
Nancy Lewis, *Sales Staff*
EMP: 60 **EST:** 1971
SQ FT: 267,000
SALES: 18.2MM **Privately Held**
WEB: www.flexospan.com
SIC: 3448 3444 Prefabricated metal buildings; siding, sheet metal; sheet metal specialties, not stamped; metal roofing & roof drainage equipment

(G-17061)
PRODUCTION PLUS STEEL INC
21 A Pine Tree Dr (16145)
P.O. Box 713 (16145-0713)
PHONE.................................724 376-3634
David McCartney, *President*
David E Mc Cartney, *President*
EMP: 6
SQ FT: 2,500
SALES (est): 453.5K **Privately Held**
SIC: 7692 Welding repair

(G-17062)
SPANG & COMPANY
Also Called: Spang Power Electronic
5241 Lake St (16145)
P.O. Box 457 (16145-0457)
PHONE.................................724 376-7515
Timothy Lindey, *Branch Mgr*
EMP: 23
SALES (corp-wide): 103.9MM **Privately Held**
SIC: 3695 3677 3699 3625 Magnetic & optical recording media; electronic transformers; electrical equipment & supplies; relays & industrial controls; transformers, except electric
PA: Spang & Company
110 Delta Dr
Pittsburgh PA 15238
412 963-9363

(G-17063)
VISTA CUSTOM MILLWORK INC
Also Called: VCM Salvage
4843 Sndy Lk Grenville Rd (16145)
P.O. Box 621 (16145-0621)
PHONE.................................724 376-4093
Jeremy Kline, *President*
Greg Burns, *Treasurer*
Robert Hovis, *Admin Sec*
EMP: 13
SQ FT: 9,500
SALES (est): 1.2MM **Privately Held**
SIC: 5211 3442 Lumber & other building materials; metal doors, sash & trim

Sarver
Butler County

(G-17064)
AMERICAN METALS & MFG CO
200 Obringer Ln (16055-9670)
P.O. Box 41 (16055-0041)
PHONE.................................724 934-8866
Frank Ll, *Owner*
Celia Jia, *Owner*
EMP: 5
SALES (est): 694K **Privately Held**
SIC: 3444 Sheet metalwork

(G-17065)
ASSOCIATED CERAMICS &
TECH (PA)
400 N Pike Rd (16055-1109)
PHONE.................................724 353-1585
Raymond C Lassinger, *President*
Jeffrey Lassinger, *Vice Pres*
Terry L Lassinger, *Treasurer*
Patty Ann Kanterman, *Admin Sec*
▲ **EMP:** 60 **EST:** 1966
SQ FT: 37,000
SALES (est): 8.5MM **Privately Held**
WEB: www.associatedceramics.com
SIC: 3264 3829 3354 3291 Insulators, electrical: porcelain; measuring & controlling devices; aluminum extruded products; abrasive products

(G-17066)
CID ASSOCIATES INC
730 Ekastown Rd (16055-9724)
PHONE.................................724 353-0300
Scott Docherty, *President*
Casey S Docherty, *Treasurer*
Marlene J Docherty, *Shareholder*
▲ **EMP:** 50
SQ FT: 40,000
SALES (est): 15.9MM **Privately Held**
WEB: www.cidbldgs.com
SIC: 3441 3448 3446 3444 Building components, structural steel; prefabricated metal components; architectural metalwork; sheet metalwork

(G-17067)
CONTRAIL SYSTEMS INC
199 Parker Rd (16055-9554)
PHONE.................................724 353-1127
David Parkhill, *President*
EMP: 10
SALES (est): 809.2K **Privately Held**
SIC: 3663 5084 Receiver-transmitter units (transceiver); controlling instruments & accessories

(G-17068)
DYNAMIC CERAMICS INC
265 N Pike Rd (16055-9209)
PHONE.................................724 353-9527
Daryl Beer, *President*
Leona Beer, *Corp Secy*
Terry Beer, *Vice Pres*
Darla Beer, *Office Mgr*
▼ **EMP:** 38
SQ FT: 4,000
SALES (est): 5MM **Privately Held**
SIC: 3264 Insulators, electrical: porcelain

(G-17069)
FASHION OPTICAL INC
228 Buffalo Plz (16055-8302)
PHONE.................................724 339-4595
Darcy Caliguri, *President*
EMP: 3
SALES (est): 398.4K **Privately Held**
WEB: www.lbfashionoptical.com
SIC: 3851 5995 Ophthalmic goods; opticians

(G-17070)
GOURMET VINEGARS BY LINDA
LU
116 Orchard Dr (16055-9529)
PHONE.................................724 353-2026
Nancy Hagins, *Principal*
EMP: 3
SALES (est): 145.4K **Privately Held**
SIC: 2099 Vinegar

(G-17071)
HARSCO MINERALS PA LLC
Also Called: Excell Cement Technologies
357 N Pike Rd 9 (16055-8633)
PHONE.................................724 352-0066
Wayne Hursen, *Branch Mgr*
EMP: 4
SALES (corp-wide): 1.6B **Publicly Held**
SIC: 3341 Secondary nonferrous metals
HQ: Harsco Minerals Pa Llc
359 N Pike Rd
Sarver PA 16055

(G-17072)
HEI-WAY LLC
290 N Pike Rd (16055-9735)
PHONE.................................724 353-2700
David D Heilman, *Administration*
EMP: 12
SALES (est): 2.2MM **Privately Held**
SIC: 2951 Asphalt paving mixtures & blocks

(G-17073)
HEILMAN PAVEMENT
SPECIALTIES
290 N Pike Rd (16055-9735)
PHONE.................................724 353-2700
William B Heilman Jr, *President*
Glenn H Heilman, *Vice Pres*
EMP: 6 **EST:** 1955
SALES (est): 850K **Privately Held**
WEB: www.hei-way.com
SIC: 2951 1611 Asphalt paving mixtures & blocks; highway & street paving contractor

(G-17074)
OBERG INDUSTRIES INC
Also Called: Oberg Arizona
275 N Pike Rd (16055-9209)
PHONE.................................724 353-9700
Julie Silsby, *Branch Mgr*
EMP: 102
SQ FT: 90,170
SALES (corp-wide): 265.3MM **Privately Held**
SIC: 3469 Stamping metal for the trade
PA: Oberg Industries, Inc.
2301 Silverville Rd
Freeport PA 16229
724 295-2121

(G-17075)
OBERG INDUSTRIES INC
Also Called: Oberg Stamping & Tech Center
275 N Pike Rd (16055-9209)
PHONE.................................724 353-9700
Scott Adams, *Branch Mgr*
EMP: 101
SALES (corp-wide): 265.3MM **Privately Held**
SIC: 3469 3544 Stamping metal for the trade; special dies, tools, jigs & fixtures
PA: Oberg Industries, Inc.
2301 Silverville Rd
Freeport PA 16229
724 295-2121

(G-17076)
OBERG INDUSTRIES INC
Also Called: Oberg Sarver
275 N Pike Rd (16055-9209)
PHONE.................................724 353-9700
EMP: 101
SALES (corp-wide): 265.3MM **Privately Held**
SIC: 3545 Machine tool attachments & accessories
PA: Oberg Industries, Inc.
2301 Silverville Rd
Freeport PA 16229
724 295-2121

(G-17077)
OEM SHADES INC
141 Singleton Rd (16055-9639)
PHONE.................................724 763-3600
Sanford Crossman, *President*
Ralph Herman, *Vice Pres*
Frank Wolfe, *Treasurer*
▲ **EMP:** 30
SQ FT: 30,000
SALES (est): 5MM **Privately Held**
WEB: www.oemshades.com
SIC: 2591 Blinds vertical; window blinds

(G-17078)
PENN UNITED TECHNOLOGIES INC
Also Called: Parker-Majestic Div
300 N Pike Rd (16055-9737)
P.O. Box 399, Saxonburg (16056-0399)
PHONE...................................724 431-2482
Jim Shilander, *Branch Mgr*
EMP: 25
SALES (corp-wide): 147.3MM **Privately Held**
WEB: www.pennunited.com
SIC: 3544 3545 3541 Special dies & tools; machine tool accessories; machine tools, metal cutting type
PA: Penn United Technologies, Inc.
799 N Pike Rd
Cabot PA 16023
724 352-1507

(G-17079)
SARVER HARDWARE CO INC
551 S Pike Rd (16055-9203)
PHONE...................................724 295-5131
Michael J Broniszewski, *President*
EMP: 9
SALES (est): 1.2MM **Privately Held**
SIC: 2851 Paints & allied products

Sassamansville
Montgomery County

(G-17080)
BAUMAN FAMILY
116 Hoffmansville Rd (19472)
PHONE...................................610 754-7251
Harvey J Bauman, *Partner*
Kathleen Bauman, *Partner*
John Bauman, *Engineer*
EMP: 10
SQ FT: 7,000
SALES (est): 978.6K **Privately Held**
WEB: www.baumanfamily.com
SIC: 2033 Fruit butters: packaged in cans, jars, etc.

Saxonburg
Butler County

(G-17081)
BAYER MEDICAL CARE INC
150 Victory Rd (16056-9772)
PHONE...................................724 360-7600
Robert Lucas, *Branch Mgr*
EMP: 57
SALES (corp-wide): 45.3B **Privately Held**
SIC: 3841 Surgical & medical instruments
HQ: Bayer Medical Care Inc.
1 Bayer Dr
Indianola PA 15051
724 940-6800

(G-17082)
CYGNUS MANUFACTURING CO LLC
491 Chantler Dr (16056-9721)
PHONE...................................724 352-8000
John Mahol, *CEO*
Craig Harding, *Chairman*
Carlo Crisci, *COO*
Carolyn Crouse, *Vice Pres*
Jodi Ricketts, *Vice Pres*
▲ **EMP:** 150 **EST:** 1964
SQ FT: 100,000
SALES (est): 26.6MM **Privately Held**
WEB: www.cmc-usa.com
SIC: 3599 3845 Custom machinery; CAT scanner (Computerized Axial Tomography) apparatus

(G-17083)
DAVE FINE MEAT PACKER INC
Butler Rd (16056)
PHONE...................................724 352-1537
EMP: 5
SQ FT: 5,400
SALES (est): 365.2K **Privately Held**
SIC: 2011 Meat Packing Plant

(G-17084)
DAVIS MACHINE INC
967 Saxonburg Blvd (16056-2317)
PHONE...................................724 265-2266
Shawn Davis, *President*
Orvis Davis III, *Corp Secy*
Ron Davis, *Vice Pres*
EMP: 5
SQ FT: 1,200
SALES (est): 764K **Privately Held**
WEB: www.davismmi.com
SIC: 3599 Machine shop, jobbing & repair

(G-17085)
DU-CO CERAMICS COMPANY (PA)
155 S Rebecca St (16056-9514)
P.O. Box 568 (16056-0568)
PHONE...................................724 352-1511
Lora C Rothen, *CEO*
Thomas W Arbanas, *President*
Kyle Knapp, *General Mgr*
Michael P Crytzer, *Engineer*
EMP: 210 **EST:** 1949
SQ FT: 200,000
SALES (est): 29.9MM **Privately Held**
WEB: www.du-co.com
SIC: 3264 Porcelain electrical supplies

(G-17086)
ENDICOTT INTERCONNECT TECH
Also Called: Ei Detection & Imaging
373 Saxonburg Blvd (16056-9430)
PHONE...................................724 352-6315
Rick Smith, *General Mgr*
EMP: 4
SALES (est): 409.7K **Privately Held**
SIC: 3844 X-ray apparatus & tubes

(G-17087)
GAVEN INDUSTRIES INC
6655 N Noah Dr (16056-9719)
PHONE...................................724 352-8100
John J Gaviglia, *President*
Joel Kohler, *Project Mgr*
Jason Rivera, *Marketing Staff*
Karen P Gaviglia, *Admin Sec*
EMP: 32
SQ FT: 15,000
SALES (est): 10.1MM **Privately Held**
WEB: www.gavenindustries.com
SIC: 3499 Magnetic shields, metal

(G-17088)
II-VI INCORPORATED (PA)
375 Saxonburg Blvd (16056-9499)
PHONE...................................724 352-4455
Francis J Kramer, *Ch of Bd*
Vincent D Mattera Jr, *President*
Tom Neff, *General Mgr*
Gary A Kapusta, *COO*
John Almquist, *Vice Pres*
▲ **EMP:** 500 **EST:** 1971
SQ FT: 230,000
SALES: 1.1B **Publicly Held**
WEB: www.ii-vi.com
SIC: 3229 3674 3699 3827 Optical glass; fiber optics strands; semiconductors & related devices; laser welding, drilling & cutting equipment; optical elements & assemblies, except ophthalmic

(G-17089)
II-VI LASER ENTERPRISE INC
375 Saxonburg Blvd (16056-9499)
PHONE...................................724 352-4455
Francis J Kramer, *President*
Craig A Creaturo, *Corp Secy*
EMP: 20 **EST:** 2013
SALES (est): 2MM
SALES (corp-wide): 1.1B **Publicly Held**
SIC: 3674 Semiconductors & related devices
PA: Ii-Vi Incorporated
375 Saxonburg Blvd
Saxonburg PA 16056
724 352-4455

(G-17090)
JOHN W THROWER INC (PA)
409 Saxonburg Blvd (16056-9451)
PHONE...................................724 352-9421
John W Thrower Sr, *President*
Diana Christy, *Corp Secy*

John W Thrower Jr, *Vice Pres*
EMP: 7 **EST:** 1959
SQ FT: 8,000
SALES (est): 1.1MM **Privately Held**
SIC: 3273 Ready-mixed concrete

(G-17091)
KINGSLY COMPRESSION INC (PA)
3750 S Noah Dr (16056-9703)
P.O. Box 819, Mars (16046-0819)
PHONE...................................724 524-1840
Jeffrey B Sable, *President*
EMP: 20
SQ FT: 20,600
SALES (est): 5MM **Privately Held**
WEB: www.kinglycompression.com
SIC: 3563 7359 5084 6513 Air & gas compressors; equipment rental & leasing; compressors, except air conditioning; apartment building operators; dwelling operators, except apartments

(G-17092)
PENN UNITED TECHNOLOGIES INC
Also Called: Penn United Carbide
196 Alwine Rd (16056-8606)
P.O. Box 399 (16056-0399)
PHONE...................................724 352-5151
Bill Jones, *President*
Gary Weightman, *Manager*
EMP: 150
SALES (corp-wide): 147.3MM **Privately Held**
WEB: www.pennunited.com
SIC: 3544 Special dies & tools
PA: Penn United Technologies, Inc.
799 N Pike Rd
Cabot PA 16023
724 352-1507

(G-17093)
QUANTUM ENGINEERED PDTS INC
438 Saxonburg Blvd (16056-9407)
PHONE...................................724 352-5100
Steven Kozora, *President*
Margaret M Yucas, *Corp Secy*
Mike Albert, *Vice Pres*
Margaret Yucas, *Controller*
▲ **EMP:** 21
SQ FT: 13,000
SALES (est): 5.7MM **Privately Held**
WEB: www.quantumforming.com
SIC: 3559 Glass making machinery: blowing, molding, forming, etc.

(G-17094)
RONALD D JONES FINANCIAL SVC
101 Alwine Rd Ste 210 (16056-8604)
PHONE...................................724 352-5020
Ronald Jones, *Principal*
EMP: 3
SALES (est): 88.5K **Privately Held**
SIC: 2721 Periodicals

(G-17095)
SPRENG MACHINE CO INC
190 Pittsburgh St (16056-9562)
PHONE...................................724 352-9467
Henry H Spreng, *President*
EMP: 12 **EST:** 1959
SQ FT: 1,800
SALES (est): 1.6MM **Privately Held**
SIC: 3599 Machine shop, jobbing & repair

(G-17096)
TGB I LLC
220 S Noah Dr (16056-9702)
PHONE...................................724 431-3090
EMP: 179
SALES (corp-wide): 84.4MM **Privately Held**
SIC: 3699 Mfg Electrical Equipment/Supplies
PA: Tgb I, Llc
471 Dutchtown Rd
Butler PA 16002
724 586-6005

(G-17097)
THOMA MEAT MARKET INC
748 Dinnerbell Rd (16056-9348)
P.O. Box 261 (16056-0261)
PHONE...................................724 352-2020
Brian Thoma, *President*
Timothy Thoma, *Partner*
Kimberly Thoma, *Corp Secy*
Tim Thoma, *Vice Pres*
EMP: 25
SALES: 2MM **Privately Held**
SIC: 2011 5411 5421 5147 Meat packing plants; grocery stores, independent; meat markets, including freezer provisioners; meats & meat products

(G-17098)
TOPHOLE DRILLING LLC
2900 S Noah Dr (16056-9728)
PHONE...................................724 272-1932
Chad Linamen, *President*
EMP: 15
SALES: 2MM **Privately Held**
SIC: 1381 1629 Service well drilling; caisson drilling

Saxton
Bedford County

(G-17099)
BROADTOP BULLETIN
900 6th St (16678-1008)
PHONE...................................814 635-2851
John Baughman, *Owner*
EMP: 3 **EST:** 1947
SQ FT: 900
SALES (est): 135.2K **Privately Held**
SIC: 2711 Newspapers, publishing & printing; newspapers: publishing only, not printed on site

(G-17100)
BRODE LUMBER INC
20188 Little Valley Rd (16678-7810)
PHONE...................................814 635-3436
Randy O Brode, *President*
Robert D Brode, *Vice Pres*
Arnold Brode, *Treasurer*
EMP: 13
SALES: 2MM **Privately Held**
SIC: 2421 Lumber: rough, sawed or planed

(G-17101)
HAMILTON HIGH HEAT INC
1951 Lytle Ln (16678-7840)
PHONE...................................814 635-4131
Donald G Hamilton, *CEO*
Christopher M Hamilton, *Corp Secy*
EMP: 5
SALES (est): 497.9K **Privately Held**
SIC: 3535 Conveyors & conveying equipment

(G-17102)
MCCAHANS PHARMACY INC
813 Lower Main St (16678-1139)
PHONE...................................814 635-2911
Steve McAhan, *President*
EMP: 8 **EST:** 1971
SALES (est): 809.5K **Privately Held**
SIC: 2834 Pharmaceutical preparations

Saylorsburg
Monroe County

(G-17103)
BLUE RIDGE DISTILLERY LLC
239 Blue Ridge Rd (18353-8131)
PHONE...................................610 895-4205
EMP: 5
SALES (est): 397K **Privately Held**
SIC: 2085 Distilled & blended liquors

(G-17104)
COPY CORNER INC
Also Called: Copy Corner, The
Old Rte 115 Mxvlle Vly Rd (18353)
P.O. Box 940 (18353-0940)
PHONE...................................570 992-4769
Holly Schneebeli, *President*

William Schneebeli, *Vice Pres*
EMP: 3
SQ FT: 2,160
SALES (est): 200K **Privately Held**
SIC: 7334 2759 2791 4822 Photocopying & duplicating services; commercial printing; typesetting; facsimile transmission services

(G-17105)
LONGEVITY COATINGS
221 Evergreen Ct (18353-9363)
PHONE..................................610 871-1427
Mark Purington, *Principal*
EMP: 5
SALES (est): 672.4K **Privately Held**
SIC: 3479 Coating of metals & formed products

(G-17106)
SAYLORSBURG STL FBRICATORS INC
Also Called: Saylorsburg Metal Works
1281 Princess Run Rd (18353-7802)
PHONE..................................610 381-4444
Thomas Bartholomew, *Principal*
Darlene Bartholemew, *Principal*
EMP: 3
SQ FT: 1,800
SALES (est): 24.5K **Privately Held**
SIC: 3441 Fabricated structural metal

(G-17107)
SILVER VLY DRLG & BLASTG INC
Rr 4 (18353-9804)
P.O. Box 506 (18353-0506)
PHONE..................................570 992-1125
Ed Wean Jr, *President*
Mike Chopek, *Office Mgr*
EMP: 6
SALES (est): 432.2K **Privately Held**
SIC: 1381 1629 Drilling oil & gas wells; blasting contractor, except building demolition

(G-17108)
SORRENTI ORCHARDS INC
Also Called: Cherry Valley Vinyrd & Winery
130 Lower Cherry Vly Rd (18353-8325)
PHONE..................................570 992-2255
Mary Sorrenti, *President*
Nick Sorrenti, *Vice Pres*
Pam Saldibar, *Manager*
EMP: 4
SQ FT: 10,000
SALES (est): 524.7K **Privately Held**
WEB: www.cherryvalleyvineyards.com
SIC: 2084 5812 Wines; wine cellars, bonded: engaged in blending wines; Italian restaurant

Sayre
Bradford County

(G-17109)
AJAX XRAY INC
Also Called: Foundry Division
150 Bradford St (18840-1802)
P.O. Box 98 (18840-0098)
PHONE..................................570 888-6605
Nancy Brittain, *President*
William H McCreary, *Admin Sec*
EMP: 35 **EST:** 1959
SQ FT: 200,000
SALES: 2.5MM **Privately Held**
SIC: 3365 Aluminum foundries

(G-17110)
AVERY DENNISON CORPORATION
1 Wilcox St (18840-2929)
PHONE..................................570 888-6641
David Osiecki, *Vice Pres*
Ped Pnkard, *Plant Mgr*
EMP: 75
SALES (corp-wide): 7.1B **Publicly Held**
WEB: www.avery.com
SIC: 2672 Coated paper, except photographic, carbon or abrasive

PA: Avery Dennison Corporation
207 N Goode Ave Ste 500
Glendale CA 91203
626 304-2000

(G-17111)
BIBLE LIGHTHOUSE INC
Also Called: Bible Lighthouse Book Store
518 N Keystone Ave (18840-2944)
P.O. Box 99 (18840-0099)
PHONE..................................570 888-6615
William Northwood, *Chairman*
Kenneth R Pope, *Treasurer*
Shirley Dimmick, *Admin Sec*
EMP: 4 **EST:** 1950
SQ FT: 8,400
SALES: 32.1K **Privately Held**
SIC: 5942 7922 2721 Books, religious; radio producers; periodicals: publishing & printing

(G-17112)
BIMBO BAKERIES
901 N Elmer Ave (18840-1835)
PHONE..................................570 888-2289
Ray Smith, *Vice Pres*
EMP: 8
SALES (est): 906.4K **Privately Held**
SIC: 2051 Bread, cake & related products

(G-17113)
CAMCO MANUFACTURING INC
317 S Thomas Ave (18840-2129)
PHONE..................................570 731-4109
Richard Arnold, *President*
Sam Goble, *Vice Pres*
Edward Gorman, *CFO*
Mike Gorman, *CFO*
EMP: 50
SQ FT: 75,000
SALES (est): 11.4MM **Privately Held**
SIC: 3469 Machine parts, stamped or pressed metal

(G-17114)
GARY MURELLE
Also Called: Murrelle, Joe Press
109 S Elmer Ave (18840-2005)
PHONE..................................570 888-7006
Gary Murrelle, *Owner*
EMP: 7
SQ FT: 1,440
SALES: 450K **Privately Held**
SIC: 2752 2759 2791 Lithographing on metal; business forms, lithographed; commercial printing; typesetting

(G-17115)
GREAT PLAINS OILFLD RENTL LLC
40 Lamoka Rd (18840-9404)
PHONE..................................570 882-7700
EMP: 4
SALES (corp-wide): 3.3B **Publicly Held**
SIC: 1381 Drilling oil & gas wells
HQ: Great Plains Oilfield Rental, L.L.C.
777 Nw 63rd St
Oklahoma City OK 73116
405 608-7777

(G-17116)
HOUSE OF WINGS FOODS LLC
102 Bradford St (18840)
PHONE..................................570 627-6116
Bradley Wilson, *Co-Owner*
Henry Fratarcangeli, *Co-Owner*
Karen Fratarcangeli, *Co-Owner*
Jennifer Wilson, *Co-Owner*
EMP: 4 **EST:** 2014
SQ FT: 4,800
SALES (est): 120K **Privately Held**
SIC: 2033 Barbecue sauce: packaged in cans, jars, etc.

(G-17117)
KURTS MAKING WHOOPIE
122 S Hopkins St (18840-1329)
PHONE..................................570 888-9102
Kurt Priester, *Principal*
EMP: 4 **EST:** 2012
SALES (est): 204.7K **Privately Held**
SIC: 2051 Bread, cake & related products

(G-17118)
LEPRINO FOODS COMPANY
217 Yanuzzi Dr (18840-2618)
PHONE..................................570 888-9658
Jim Laprino, *Principal*
George Conrad, *Supervisor*
EMP: 238
SALES (corp-wide): 1.8B **Privately Held**
SIC: 2022 Natural cheese
PA: Leprino Foods Company
1830 W 38th Ave
Denver CO 80211
303 480-2600

(G-17119)
MURRELLE PRINTING CO INC
Also Called: Bradford County Law Jurnl The
206 S Keystone Ave (18840-1322)
PHONE..................................570 888-2244
Ian Clare, *President*
Beverley Clare, *Corp Secy*
Sue Wright, *Bookkeeper*
EMP: 14
SQ FT: 7,000
SALES (est): 1.7MM **Privately Held**
WEB: www.clareprint.com
SIC: 2732 2791 2752 Books: printing only; pamphlets: printing & binding, not published on site; typesetting; commercial printing, lithographic

(G-17120)
NC INDUSTRIES ANTIQ AUTO PARTS
301 S Thomas Ave (18840-2129)
P.O. Box 254 (18840-0254)
PHONE..................................570 888-6216
Kevin Brown, *Partner*
Bob Petruschak, *Partner*
EMP: 3
SQ FT: 5,000
SALES: 200K **Privately Held**
SIC: 3714 Motor vehicle parts & accessories

(G-17121)
RYNONE MANUFACTURING CORP (PA)
N Thomas Ave (18840)
P.O. Box 128 (18840-0128)
PHONE..................................570 888-5272
Richard T Rynone, *President*
George Ingrassia, *Project Mgr*
Jim Rieker, *Human Resources*
Frank Coolbaugh, *Manager*
◆ **EMP:** 127
SQ FT: 102,000
SALES (est): 34.9MM **Privately Held**
WEB: www.rynone.com
SIC: 3281 2493 2541 2511 Table tops, marble; particleboard, plastic laminated; cabinets, except refrigerated: show, display, etc.: wood; wood household furniture; wood kitchen cabinets

(G-17122)
SAMPLE NEWS GROUP LLC
Also Called: Morning Times
201 N Lehigh Ave (18840-2246)
PHONE..................................570 888-9643
Kelly Lubison, *Branch Mgr*
EMP: 28
SALES (corp-wide): 8MM **Privately Held**
SIC: 2711 Newspapers, publishing & printing
PA: Sample News Group, L.L.C.
28 W South St
Corry PA 16407
814 665-8291

(G-17123)
TOPS MARKETS LLC
Also Called: Tops Friendly Markets 650
1006 N Elmira St (18840)
PHONE..................................570 882-9188
Rick Emerson, *Manager*
EMP: 135
SALES (corp-wide): 2.5B **Privately Held**
WEB: www.topsmarkets.com
SIC: 5411 2051 5992 5421 Supermarkets, chain; bread, cake & related products; florists; meat & fish markets; bakeries

HQ: Tops Markets, Llc
6363 Main St
Williamsville NY 14221
716 635-5000

Scenery Hill
Washington County

(G-17124)
ASCO ENTERPRISES INC
1684 E National Pike (15360-1019)
PHONE..................................724 945-5525
Ed Gaussa, *President*
Neil Gaussa, *Vice Pres*
EMP: 6 **EST:** 1999
SQ FT: 9,000
SALES (est): 1.3MM **Privately Held**
WEB: www.ascotrucks.com
SIC: 3713 Automobile wrecker truck bodies

(G-17125)
REDSTONE INTERNATIONAL INC
1200 E National Pike (15360-1005)
PHONE..................................724 439-1500
Richard Walton, *CEO*
Heath Kefover, *President*
EMP: 56 **EST:** 2012
SQ FT: 2,000
SALES (est): 13.8MM **Privately Held**
SIC: 1741 2491 Foundation & retaining wall construction; foundation building; piles, foundation & marine construction: treated wood

(G-17126)
TEST BORING SERVICES INC
140 Mong Rd (15360-1720)
PHONE..................................724 267-4649
Jeffrey C Selvoski, *President*
Paula Selvoski, *Treasurer*
EMP: 10
SALES (est): 1.6MM **Privately Held**
WEB: www.testboring.com
SIC: 1481 Test boring for nonmetallic minerals

(G-17127)
WESTERWALD CORP OF AMERICA
Also Called: Westerwald Pottery
40 Pottery Ln (15360-1700)
PHONE..................................724 945-6000
Phil Schaltenbrand, *President*
EMP: 9
SQ FT: 1,300
SALES (est): 1MM **Privately Held**
WEB: www.westerwaldpottery.com
SIC: 3269 Figures: pottery, china, earthenware & stoneware

Schaefferstown
Lebanon County

(G-17128)
KOCH INDUSTRIES INC
Rr 501 Box South (17088)
P.O. Box 486 (17088-0486)
PHONE..................................717 949-3469
Mike Schaefer, *Manager*
EMP: 4
SALES (corp-wide): 42.4B **Privately Held**
WEB: www.kochind.com
SIC: 2879 Agricultural disinfectants; defoliants; fungicides, herbicides
PA: Koch Industries, Inc.
4111 E 37th St N
Wichita KS 67220
316 828-5500

(G-17129)
PLAIN N FANCY KITCHENS INC (PA)
Also Called: Plain & Fancy Custom Cabinetry
2550 Stiegel Pike (17088)
P.O. Box 519 (17088-0519)
PHONE..................................717 949-6571
George Hachey, *Principal*
Nicholas Achey, *Vice Pres*
Loretta L Achey, *Treasurer*

▲ = Import ▼ = Export
◆ = Import/Export

Shane Achey, *Manager*
Jody Stoever, *Admin Sec*
▲ **EMP:** 138
SQ FT: 160,000
SALES (est): 26.8MM **Privately Held**
WEB: www.plain-n-fancykitchens.com
SIC: 2434 5211 5031 5021 Wood kitchen cabinets; lumber & other building materials; lumber, plywood & millwork; furniture

(G-17130)
PRACTICAL MACHINE SOLUTIONS
300 E Main St (17088)
P.O. Box 313 (17088-0313)
PHONE.............................717 949-3345
Jason Davis, *President*
▲ **EMP:** 3
SALES: 260K **Privately Held**
SIC: 3599 Machine shop, jobbing & repair

(G-17131)
TARGET TOOL INC
450 W Main St (17088)
P.O. Box 538 (17088-0538)
PHONE.............................717 949-2407
Mark Albright, *President*
Don Carpenter, *Vice Pres*
EMP: 3
SQ FT: 1,500
SALES: 150K **Privately Held**
SIC: 3544 Special dies, tools, jigs & fixtures

Schellsburg
Bedford County

(G-17132)
J&J CARRIERS INC
754 Winegardner Rd (15559-8041)
PHONE.............................814 285-0217
John Ling, *Principal*
EMP: 3
SALES: 200K **Privately Held**
SIC: 3537 Trucks, tractors, loaders, carriers & similar equipment

(G-17133)
KEYSTONE TEST SOLUTIONS INC
2164 Lincoln Hwy (15559-7516)
PHONE.............................814 733-4490
Howard H Bush, *President*
EMP: 3
SALES (est): 185K **Privately Held**
SIC: 3679 Electronic circuits

(G-17134)
LAMENS FURNITURE
145 Sugar Camp Rd (15559-1707)
PHONE.............................814 733-4537
Roger Lamens, *Owner*
EMP: 4
SALES: 350K **Privately Held**
SIC: 2511 Stools, household: wood; dining room furniture: wood

(G-17135)
RIDGE WOODWORKING
329 Ferguson Rd (15559-8940)
PHONE.............................814 839-0151
J Leroy Summy, *Owner*
Dave Summy, *Owner*
Allen Summy, *Co-Owner*
EMP: 3 **EST:** 1998
SALES (est): 157.3K **Privately Held**
WEB: www.ridgewoodworking.com
SIC: 2499 Decorative wood & woodwork

Schenley
Armstrong County

(G-17136)
SPARK TECHNOLOGIES INC
150 Railroad St (15682)
P.O. Box 84 (15682-0084)
PHONE.............................724 295-3860
Janie Bertieri, *Ch of Bd*
Dennis Smail, *President*
Patricia Smail, *Manager*

EMP: 14
SQ FT: 28,000
SALES (est): 1.5MM **Privately Held**
WEB: www.spark-tech.com
SIC: 3544 Special dies & tools

Schnecksville
Lehigh County

(G-17137)
COBALT COMPUTERS INC
5960 Waterfowl Rd (18078-3232)
PHONE.............................610 395-3771
Paul Mazzucco, *President*
EMP: 10
SQ FT: 30,000
SALES (est): 1.2MM **Privately Held**
WEB: www.cobaltcomputers.com
SIC: 3571 Electronic computers

(G-17138)
DALLAS MACHINE INC
4410 Park View Dr (18078-2550)
PHONE.............................610 799-2800
James Dalla Palu, *President*
Brian Pollitt, *General Mgr*
Dan Diehl, *COO*
Stephen Ehasz, *Plant Mgr*
Donna Simock, *Manager*
EMP: 40
SQ FT: 15,000
SALES: 5.5MM **Privately Held**
WEB: www.dallamachine.com
SIC: 3469 7692 Machine parts, stamped or pressed metal; welding repair

(G-17139)
ELEMENT 27 INC
Also Called: Cobalt Computers
5960 Waterfowl Rd (18078-3232)
PHONE.............................610 502-2727
EMP: 3
SQ FT: 5,000
SALES (est): 2.9MM **Privately Held**
SIC: 5045 3571 Whol Computers/Peripherals Mfg Electronic Computers

(G-17140)
EVERGREEN GROUP INC
4460 Bachman Dr (18078-2246)
P.O. Box 3071, Landers CA (92285-0071)
PHONE.............................610 799-2263
Craig Edwards, *President*
EMP: 4
SQ FT: 400
SALES: 30K **Privately Held**
WEB: www.evergreengrp.com
SIC: 3571 Personal computers (microcomputers)

(G-17141)
LIBERTY BELL BEVERAGES
4041 Route 309 Unit 2 (18078-2578)
PHONE.............................610 799-6600
Lee Goldstein, *Owner*
EMP: 6
SALES (est): 428.5K **Privately Held**
SIC: 2086 Bottled & canned soft drinks

(G-17142)
PEACHTREE CITY FOAMCRAFT INC
4215 Independence Dr (18078-2591)
PHONE.............................610 769-0661
Michael A Fetter, *Principal*
EMP: 4
SQ FT: 10,000 **Privately Held**
SIC: 3993 Signs & advertising specialties
PA: Peachtree City Foamcraft, Inc.
386 Senoia Rd
Tyrone GA

(G-17143)
SEA MAR TACKLE CO INC
4440 Spring Hill Dr (18078-2543)
PHONE.............................610 769-0755
Eric Mistler, *President*
Maria Mistler, *Corp Secy*
▲ **EMP:** 7
SQ FT: 4,000
SALES (est): 1.2MM **Privately Held**
SIC: 5091 3949 Fishing tackle; fishing equipment

(G-17144)
SWAGELOK COMPANY
Also Called: Swagelok Allentown
4245 Independence Dr (18078-2591)
PHONE.............................610 799-9001
Taylor Vincent, *Marketing Staff*
Kayla Mjaatvedt, *Branch Mgr*
Rob McNamara, *Manager*
EMP: 5
SALES (corp-wide): 940.1MM **Privately Held**
SIC: 3494 Valves & pipe fittings
PA: Swagelok Company
29500 Solon Rd
Solon OH 44139
440 248-4600

Schuylkill Haven
Schuylkill County

(G-17145)
ALPHA MILLS CORPORATION (PA)
Also Called: Hi-LI Company Division
122 S Margaretta St (17972-1694)
PHONE.............................570 385-1791
Richard D Biever, *President*
Barton R Biever Jr, *Vice Pres*
Timothy Shadler, *CFO*
Josh Biever, *Admin Sec*
▲ **EMP:** 60 **EST:** 1936
SQ FT: 65,000
SALES: 8.4MM **Privately Held**
WEB: www.alphamillsnyc.com
SIC: 2254 2253 2369 2341 Underwear, knit; knit outerwear mills; girls' & children's outerwear; women's & children's underwear; women's & misses' outerwear; men's & boys' sportswear & athletic clothing

(G-17146)
ALPHA MILLS CORPORATION
301 S Margaretta St (17972-1609)
PHONE.............................570 385-1791
EMP: 29
SALES (corp-wide): 8.4MM **Privately Held**
SIC: 2254 2253 2369 Underwear, knit; knit outerwear mills; girls' & children's outerwear
PA: Alpha Mills Corporation
122 S Margaretta St
Schuylkill Haven PA 17972
570 385-1791

(G-17147)
ARIELA AND ASSOCIATES INTL LLC
301 S Margaretta St (17972-1609)
PHONE.............................570 385-8340
Michael Belovesick, *Manager*
EMP: 7
SALES (est): 1.3MM
SALES (corp-wide): 28.8MM **Privately Held**
WEB: www.ariela-alpha.com
SIC: 2341 Women's & children's undergarments
PA: Ariela And Associates International Llc
1359 Broadway Fl 21
New York NY 10018
212 683-4131

(G-17148)
AXIOM INC
Also Called: Axiom Hydraulics
200 Willow St (17972-1134)
P.O. Box 41 (17972-0041)
PHONE.............................570 385-1944
Kevin Steinmetz, *President*
Kent Steinmetz, *General Mgr*
Janet Steinmetz, *Corp Secy*
Karl Steinmetz, *Vice Pres*
EMP: 12
SQ FT: 6,000
SALES (est): 1.8MM **Privately Held**
SIC: 3469 3599 Machine parts, stamped or pressed metal; machine shop, jobbing & repair

(G-17149)
BROWNS MILL FARM LLC
21 Grist Mill Rd (17972-8525)
PHONE.............................570 345-3153
Jean Herring,
John Brommer,
EMP: 5
SALES (est): 320.9K **Privately Held**
SIC: 2015 Egg processing

(G-17150)
CALL NEWSPAPERS INC (PA)
Also Called: South Schuylkill Prtg & Pubg
960 E Main St (17972-9752)
P.O. Box 178 (17972-0178)
PHONE.............................570 385-3120
Bill V Knecht, *President*
EMP: 15
SALES (est): 2.6MM **Privately Held**
SIC: 2711 2759 2752 Newspapers, publishing & printing; letterpress & screen printing; commercial printing, lithographic

(G-17151)
CARDINAL SYSTEMS INC
Also Called: Quaker Plastics
250 Route 61 S (17972-9708)
PHONE.............................570 385-4733
Warren H Bradley, *Ch of Bd*
Timothy Hawkins, *President*
Walter Bradley, *President*
Richard Steele, *General Mgr*
John Barnetsky, *Vice Pres*
▲ **EMP:** 40 **EST:** 1978
SQ FT: 100,000
SALES (est): 14.3MM **Privately Held**
SIC: 3589 3949 3444 Swimming pool filter & water conditioning systems; sporting & athletic goods; sheet metalwork

(G-17152)
CHOOSE BLACKSTONE LLC
285 Blue Mountain Rd (17972-9031)
PHONE.............................570 754-7800
Joseph H Schoffstall,
EMP: 3 **EST:** 2012
SALES (est): 256.3K **Privately Held**
SIC: 2952 Asphalt felts & coatings

(G-17153)
DEAN TRANSPORATION INC
110 Manheim Rd (17972-9705)
PHONE.............................570 385-1884
Brian Quick, *Principal*
Joan Stevensky, *Buyer*
John Koinski, *Engineer*
Brenda Haag, *Human Res Dir*
EMP: 3 **EST:** 2008
SALES (est): 259.3K **Privately Held**
SIC: 2026 Fluid milk

(G-17154)
DIVISION OF THERMO DYNAMICS
155 Route 61 S (17972-1000)
PHONE.............................570 385-0731
John R Mease Jr, *President*
David Mease, *VP Admin*
Jim Becker, *VP Mfg*
James Meade, *Treasurer*
EMP: 230
SQ FT: 60,000
SALES (est): 20.1MM
SALES (corp-wide): 60.3MM **Privately Held**
WEB: www.thermodynamicsboiler.com
SIC: 3433 Oil burners, domestic or industrial
PA: Vari Corporation
155 Route 61 S
Schuylkill Haven PA 17972
570 385-0731

(G-17155)
EBINGER IRON WORKS INC
38 Keystoker Ln (17972-9774)
P.O. Box 251 (17972-0251)
PHONE.............................570 385-3460
Bill Miller, *President*
Robert Ebinger, *Vice Pres*
Mary Ebinger, *Treasurer*
Elaine Miller, *Admin Sec*
M Elaine Miller, *Admin Sec*
EMP: 30
SQ FT: 40,000

SALES (est): 7.2MM **Privately Held**
WEB: www.ebingeriron.com
SIC: 3446 Stairs, staircases, stair treads: prefabricated metal; railings, bannisters, guards, etc.: made from metal pipe

(G-17156)
ELEMENT 1 LLC
950 E Main St (17972-9720)
PHONE..................................570 593-8177
Amy Gherghel, *Principal*
EMP: 3
SALES (est): 152.7K **Privately Held**
SIC: 2819 Mfg Industrial Inorganic Chemicals

(G-17157)
GARDINIER ASSOCIATES INC
Also Called: Ethel Maid
202 E Liberty St (17972-1706)
P.O. Box 211 (17972-0211)
PHONE..................................570 385-2721
Richard Gardinier, *President*
Denise Gardinier, *Corp Secy*
EMP: 50 EST: 1931
SQ FT: 17,000
SALES (est): 5MM **Privately Held**
WEB: www.ethelmaid.com
SIC: 2389 Burial garments

(G-17158)
HECLA MACHINERY & EQUIPMENT CO
401 Route 61 S (17972-9725)
P.O. Box 559 (17972-0559)
PHONE..................................570 385-4783
Gene Gangloff, *President*
EMP: 17
SQ FT: 10,000
SALES (est): 1.2MM **Privately Held**
SIC: 4213 1231 Heavy hauling; anthracite mining

(G-17159)
HESS READY MIX INC
2 Coal St (17972)
P.O. Box 115 (17972-0115)
PHONE..................................570 385-0300
George I Hess, *President*
Walter Faux, *Corp Secy*
EMP: 11
SALES (est): 1.5MM **Privately Held**
SIC: 3273 Ready-mixed concrete

(G-17160)
J A & W A HESS INC
Also Called: Hess Readi-Mix
Coal St (17972)
P.O. Box 115 (17972-0115)
PHONE..................................570 385-0300
George C Hess, *Manager*
EMP: 12
SALES (corp-wide): 3.3MM **Privately Held**
SIC: 3273 Ready-mixed concrete
PA: J. A. & W. A. Hess, Inc.
10 Hess Rd
Hazleton PA 18202
570 454-3731

(G-17161)
M&Q HOLDINGS LLC (PA)
3 Earl Ave (17972-8961)
PHONE..................................570 385-4991
Michael Schmal, *President*
EMP: 11
SALES (est): 94.8MM **Privately Held**
SIC: 3089 6719 Plastic processing; investment holding companies, except banks

(G-17162)
MAMMOTH MATERIALS
44 Keystoker Ln (17972-9774)
PHONE..................................570 385-4232
John Melochick, *Partner*
Lester Krasno, *Partner*
EMP: 3
SALES (est): 376K **Privately Held**
WEB: www.mammothmaterials.com
SIC: 1231 1429 Strip mining, anthracite; igneous rock, crushed & broken-quarrying

(G-17163)
PENNSY SUPPLY INC
2225 Fair Rd (17972-9393)
PHONE..................................570 754-7508

Mark Rivera, *Superintendent*
EMP: 10
SALES (corp-wide): 29.7B **Privately Held**
SIC: 1429 1442 Trap rock, crushed & broken-quarrying; construction sand & gravel
HQ: Pennsy Supply, Inc.
1001 Paxton St
Harrisburg PA 17104
717 233-4511

(G-17164)
PRYSMIAN CBLES SYSTEMS USA LLC
1 Tamaqua Blvd (17972-1133)
PHONE..................................570 385-4381
Bob Cavorsi, *Vice Pres*
EMP: 67
SALES (corp-wide): 1.3B **Privately Held**
SIC: 3643 3357 Current-carrying wiring devices; coaxial cable, nonferrous; communication wire
HQ: Prysmian Cables And Systems Usa, Llc
4 Tesseneer Dr
Highland Heights KY 41076
859 572-8000

(G-17165)
RECYCLED PALLETS
224 Blue Mountain Rd (17972-9030)
PHONE..................................717 754-3114
EMP: 4
SALES (est): 268K **Privately Held**
SIC: 2448 Mfg Wood Pallets/Skids

(G-17166)
SAN-FAB CO INC
319 Saint Charles St (17972-1922)
PHONE..................................570 385-2551
Merlin Sandler, *CEO*
Stephen Sandler, *President*
EMP: 3 EST: 1978
SQ FT: 6,000
SALES (est): 440.9K **Privately Held**
SIC: 3429 Metal fasteners

(G-17167)
TDC MANUFACTURING INC
155 Route 61 S (17972-1000)
P.O. Box 325 (17972-0325)
PHONE..................................570 385-0731
James F Meade, *President*
EMP: 12
SALES (est): 2.2MM **Privately Held**
SIC: 3433 Heating equipment, except electric

(G-17168)
TOKARICK PRINTING SERVICES
419 Hess St (17972-1117)
PHONE..................................570 385-4639
Dave Tokarick, *Owner*
EMP: 15
SALES (est): 787K **Privately Held**
SIC: 2759 Commercial printing

(G-17169)
VARI CORPORATION (PA)
Also Called: Columbia Boiler Co
155 Route 61 S (17972-1000)
PHONE..................................570 385-0731
John J Meade Jr, *President*
James Meade, *Corp Secy*
Thomas A Meade Sr, *Vice Pres*
EMP: 3
SALES (est): 60.3MM **Privately Held**
WEB: www.columbiaboiler.com
SIC: 3433 3443 3444 Heating equipment, except electric; fabricated plate work (boiler shop); sheet metalwork

(G-17170)
VISTA FUELS LLC
Also Called: Fast Fill
356 Center Ave (17972-1008)
PHONE..................................570 385-7274
Amanda Yeich, *Manager*
EMP: 7
SALES (corp-wide): 3.1MM **Privately Held**
SIC: 2869 Fuels
PA: Vista Fuels Llc
2083 W Penn Pike Ste 16
Andreas PA 18211
570 386-2248

(G-17171)
WALTER B STALLER INC
106 Tennis Ave (17972-1927)
PHONE..................................570 385-5386
Betty Stevenosky, *President*
EMP: 5 EST: 1954
SQ FT: 3,840
SALES (est): 434.9K **Privately Held**
SIC: 1761 1711 3444 Roofing/Siding Contr Plumbing/Heat/Ac Contr Mfg Sheet Metalwork

Schwenksville
Montgomery County

(G-17172)
ALDON FOOD CORPORATION
Also Called: Don's Food Products
4461 Township Line Rd (19473-2148)
PHONE..................................484 991-1000
Victor Skloff, *President*
Thomas Marshall, *General Mgr*
Albert Chickelero, *Vice Pres*
Mike Melvin, *Opers Staff*
EMP: 50
SQ FT: 30,384
SALES (est): 12.3MM **Privately Held**
WEB: www.donssalads.com
SIC: 2099 Salads, fresh or refrigerated

(G-17173)
ATLANTIC PRTG GRPHIC CMMNCTONS
2019 Lucon Rd (19473-2013)
PHONE..................................610 584-2060
Scott Jones, *Owner*
Andy Camp,
EMP: 5
SQ FT: 7,500
SALES (est): 365.7K **Privately Held**
SIC: 2752 7336 Commercial printing, lithographic; graphic arts & related design

(G-17174)
BARNSIDE MULCH AND COMPOST
991 Haldeman Rd (19473-2106)
PHONE..................................610 287-8880
Nancy J Larkin, *Owner*
EMP: 3 EST: 2014
SALES (est): 326.2K **Privately Held**
SIC: 2875 Compost

(G-17175)
DARK STAR ALPACAS LLC
443 Mayberry Rd (19473-1830)
PHONE..................................610 235-6638
EMP: 5
SALES (est): 426.6K **Privately Held**
SIC: 2231 Alpacas, mohair: woven

(G-17176)
GIUNTAS FINE WOODWORKING
107 Yerger Rd (19473-1717)
PHONE..................................610 287-1749
Brad Thomas, *Principal*
EMP: 4 EST: 2007
SALES (est): 406.1K **Privately Held**
SIC: 2431 Woodwork, interior & ornamental

(G-17177)
J D LOHR WOODWORKING INC
242 N Limerick Rd (19473-1611)
PHONE..................................610 287-7802
Jeffrey D Lohr, *President*
EMP: 3
SQ FT: 3,346
SALES (est): 262.8K **Privately Held**
WEB: www.jdlohrwood.com
SIC: 2511 Wood household furniture

(G-17178)
KOAXIS INC
2081 Lucon Rd (19473-2013)
PHONE..................................610 222-0154
Henry P Bowen, *President*
Kevin Brown, *Controller*
EMP: 25
SQ FT: 12,000

SALES (est): 4.1MM **Privately Held**
WEB: www.koaxis.com
SIC: 3678 Electronic connectors

(G-17179)
TEECO ASSOCIATES INC
Also Called: Laser Wizard
63 Tanglewood Dr (19473-2601)
PHONE..................................610 539-4708
Willard Teets, *President*
Jeffrey Teets, *Vice Pres*
Lucille Teets, *Vice Pres*
EMP: 27
SQ FT: 30,000
SALES (est): 1.7MM **Privately Held**
SIC: 7699 3829 7378 Printing trades machinery & equipment repair; measuring & controlling devices; computer maintenance & repair

(G-17180)
TRANS ATLANTIC PUBLICATIONS
Also Called: Coronet Books
33 Ashley Dr (19473-2613)
PHONE..................................215 925-2762
Ronald Smolin, *President*
Jeff Goldstein, *Vice Pres*
EMP: 3
SALES (est): 297.1K **Privately Held**
WEB: www.transatlanticpub.com
SIC: 2759 Publication printing

Sciota
Monroe County

(G-17181)
IDAC CORPORATION
207 Johnson Ct Ste B (18354)
P.O. Box 522 (18354-0522)
PHONE..................................570 534-4400
Brian Hockendury, *Manager*
EMP: 6 **Privately Held**
SIC: 3561 Pumps & pumping equipment
PA: Idac Corporation
316 Windsor Way
Stroudsburg PA

Scotland
Franklin County

(G-17182)
PURPLE DECK MEDIA INC
3583 Scotland Rd (17254-1200)
P.O. Box 177 (17254-0177)
PHONE..................................717 884-9529
James Sulfare Jr, *President*
Nathan J Neil, *COO*
Daniel L Shope, *CTO*
EMP: 3
SALES (est): 218.4K **Privately Held**
SIC: 7372 Business oriented computer software

Scott Township
Lackawanna County

(G-17183)
CATHOLIC GOLDEN AGE INC
50 Pegula Ln (18447-7847)
PHONE..................................570 586-1091
Gerald Dino, *President*
Rev George Billy, *Corp Secy*
James Kluass, *Vice Pres*
Leonard Verrastro, *Treasurer*
EMP: 10
SQ FT: 1,000
SALES (est): 193.8K **Privately Held**
SIC: 8322 2721 8661 Senior citizens' center or association; magazines: publishing only, not printed on site; religious organizations

▲ = Import ▼=Export
◆ =Import/Export

(G-17184)
LABORATORY CONTROL SYSTEMS INC
Also Called: L C S
91 Quinton Rd (18447-7523)
PHONE...................................570 487-2490
Stephen J Davis, *President*
EMP: 5
SQ FT: 2,500
SALES: 1.6MM **Privately Held**
WEB: www.labcontrols.com
SIC: 3679 Electronic circuits

(G-17185)
MAIOLATESI WINE CELLAR
210 Green Grove Rd (18447-7604)
PHONE...................................570 254-9977
Sal Maiolatesi, *Branch Mgr*
EMP: 7
SALES (est): 588.9K
SALES (corp-wide): 112.1K **Privately Held**
SIC: 2084 Wines
PA: Maiolatesi Wine Cellar
1106 Texas Palmyra Hwy
Honesdale PA

(G-17186)
MONTDALE FARM DAIRY
453 Montdale Rd (18447)
PHONE...................................570 254-6511
William A Popovich, *Owner*
EMP: 9 **EST:** 1937
SQ FT: 10,000
SALES (est): 540.2K **Privately Held**
SIC: 2026 Milk processing (pasteurizing, homogenizing, bottling)

(G-17187)
PRECISION SHEET METAL LLC
1226 Heart Lake Rd (18433-3229)
PHONE...................................570 254-6670
EMP: 6
SALES (est): 758.6K **Privately Held**
SIC: 3444 Sheet metalwork

(G-17188)
PROCESS TECH & PACKG LLC
102 Life Science Dr (18447-7778)
PHONE...................................570 587-8326
Craig Godfrey, *President*
Edward E Kausmeyer, *Corp Secy*
W Michael Godfrey, *Vice Pres*
Krissy Dougherty, *Research*
Peter Rafalko, *Engineer*
▲ **EMP:** 120
SQ FT: 50,000
SALES (est): 60.6MM
SALES (corp-wide): 791.8MM **Privately Held**
WEB: www.protechandpack.com
SIC: 2844 Cosmetic preparations
PA: Kolmar Korea Co., Ltd.
12-11 Deokgogae-Gil, Jeonui-Myeon
Sejong 30004
822 348-5037

Scottdale
Westmoreland County

(G-17189)
AMDEX METALLIZING INC
2 Church St (15683)
P.O. Box 381 (15683-0381)
PHONE...................................724 887-4977
Niles L Stauffer, *President*
Larry Stauffer, *Vice Pres*
EMP: 6
SQ FT: 56,000
SALES (est): 665.3K **Privately Held**
SIC: 3479 2851 2816 Enameling, including porcelain, of metal products; coating of metals & formed products; paints & allied products; inorganic pigments

(G-17190)
DURALOY TECHNOLOGIES INC (HQ)
120 Bridge St (15683-1748)
PHONE...................................724 887-5100
Vincent Schiavoni, *President*
Dale Smodic, *General Mgr*
Rick Kauffman, *Vice Pres*

Roman Pankiw, *Vice Pres*
Alberto Jablonski, *Engineer*
EMP: 101
SQ FT: 286,000
SALES: 35MM
SALES (corp-wide): 574.3MM **Privately Held**
WEB: www.duraloy.com
SIC: 3325 3441 3369 Alloy steel castings, except investment; fabricated structural metal; nonferrous foundries
PA: Park Corporation
6200 Riverside Dr
Cleveland OH 44135
216 267-4870

(G-17191)
EUTSEY LUMBER CO INC
Star Rte (15683)
PHONE...................................724 887-8404
Christopher Eutsey, *President*
Dale Eutsey, *Corp Secy*
Harold Eutsey Jr, *Vice Pres*
EMP: 12
SALES (est): 1.7MM **Privately Held**
SIC: 2421 5211 Lumber: rough, sawed or planed; planing mill products & lumber

(G-17192)
GENEVA ROTH INTERNATIONAL LLC
3 Moyer Ave (15683-2142)
PHONE...................................724 887-8771
Philip J Indovina, *Principal*
EMP: 3
SALES (est): 241.3K **Privately Held**
SIC: 3339 Precious metals

(G-17193)
INDEPENDENT-OBSERVER (PA)
Also Called: Laurel Group Newspapers
228 Pittsburgh St (15683-1735)
PHONE...................................724 887-7400
Joseph F Soforic, *President*
Richard Scaife, *Principal*
Richard Zahrobsky, *Vice Pres*
EMP: 44 **EST:** 1963
SQ FT: 40,000
SALES (est): 4.3MM **Privately Held**
WEB: www.laurelgrouponline.com
SIC: 2711 2752 Newspapers, publishing & printing; commercial printing, offset

(G-17194)
KEN-CO COMPANY INC
Also Called: Kenco Fabricating
1009 Water St (15683-7754)
PHONE...................................724 887-7070
Paul Kendi Jr, *President*
Robert Kendi, *Vice Pres*
Mary Giroux, *Treasurer*
EMP: 30
SQ FT: 20,000
SALES (est): 4.9MM **Privately Held**
SIC: 3713 7699 Specialty motor vehicle bodies; industrial truck repair

(G-17195)
MLP STEEL LLC (PA)
Also Called: Fayette Steel Division
18 Mount Pleasant Rd (15683-1208)
PHONE...................................724 887-8100
R Jeffrey Pfeifer, *President*
James Philipkosky, *Chairman*
Robert Mannella, *Vice Pres*
EMP: 30
SALES (est): 13.9MM **Privately Held**
SIC: 3315 Steel wire & related products

(G-17196)
MYERS CABINET CO
312 Mount Pleasant Rd (15683-1213)
PHONE...................................724 887-4070
William L Myers, *Partner*
Thomas D Myers, *Partner*
EMP: 3
SALES (est): 351.5K **Privately Held**
SIC: 5712 2434 Cabinet work, custom; wood kitchen cabinets

(G-17197)
NATIONAL HYDRAULICS INC
1000 Water St (15683-7753)
P.O. Box 20 (15683-0020)
PHONE...................................724 887-3850
Frank Brush, *Branch Mgr*

EMP: 6
SALES (corp-wide): 12.1MM **Privately Held**
WEB: www.nationalhydraulicinc.com
SIC: 5261 7699 3599 Hydroponic equipment & supplies; hydraulic equipment repair; machine shop, jobbing & repair
PA: National Hydraulics, Inc.
1558 Mt Plsant Connell Rd
Mount Pleasant PA 15666
724 547-9222

(G-17198)
RANGE RSURCES - APPALACHIA LLC
Also Called: Range Operating Co
156 Mill Ln (15683-2622)
PHONE...................................724 887-5715
Doug Bargerscock, *Manager*
EMP: 10
SALES (corp-wide): 3.2B **Publicly Held**
WEB: www.gl-energy.com
SIC: 1382 Oil & gas exploration services
HQ: Range Resources - Appalachia, Llc.
3000 Town Center Blvd
Canonsburg PA 15317
724 743-6700

(G-17199)
RE UPTEGRAFF MFG CO LLC
120 Uptegraff Dr (15683-1736)
P.O. Box 182 (15683-0182)
PHONE...................................724 887-7700
Carmen Irwing, *Purchasing*
Shunli LI,
▲ **EMP:** 51 **EST:** 1924
SQ FT: 80,000
SALES (est): 14MM **Privately Held**
WEB: www.uptegraff.com
SIC: 3612 Power transformers, electric
PA: Jiangsu Shenda Electric Co., Ltd.
No.8, Zone B Avenue, Fucheng Industrial Park, Funing County
Yancheng

(G-17200)
SENSOR CORPORATION
303 Scottdale Ave (15683-1239)
PHONE...................................724 887-4080
George Mordwinkin, *President*
Nina Mordwinkin, *Admin Sec*
EMP: 5
SQ FT: 3,000
SALES (est): 380K **Privately Held**
SIC: 7389 3679 3825 3823 Inspection & testing services; electronic circuits; instruments to measure electricity; industrial instrmnts msrmnt display/control process variable; current-carrying wiring devices; relays & industrial controls

(G-17201)
SKOVIRA MACHINE COMPANY
146 Catalina Farm Rd (15683-7724)
PHONE...................................724 887-4896
Michael Skovira, *Bd of Directors*
Thomas Skovira, *Bd of Directors*
EMP: 15 **EST:** 1951
SQ FT: 12,000
SALES: 3.5MM **Privately Held**
WEB: www.skoviramachine.com
SIC: 3599 Machine shop, jobbing & repair

(G-17202)
SUMMERILL TUBE CORPORATION
220 Franklin St (15683)
PHONE...................................724 887-9700
Joseph Handrahan, *President*
Duane Maietta, *COO*
Randy Pavlinich, *CFO*
Michael Yukevich, *Admin Sec*
▲ **EMP:** 60
SQ FT: 3,000
SALES (est): 21.7MM **Privately Held**
SIC: 3317 Welded pipe & tubes

(G-17203)
UNITED TECHNOLOGIES CORP
303 Mount Pleasant Rd (15683-1212)
PHONE...................................800 227-7437
James Schultheis, *Branch Mgr*
EMP: 268
SALES (corp-wide): 66.5B **Publicly Held**
SIC: 3585 Refrigeration & heating equipment

PA: United Technologies Corporation
10 Farm Springs Rd
Farmington CT 06032
860 728-7000

Scranton
Lackawanna County

(G-17204)
A&A BEVERAGES WAREHOUSE
949 Adams Ave (18510-1003)
PHONE...................................570 344-0024
Dawn Schoefield, *Manager*
EMP: 11
SALES (est): 986.2K **Privately Held**
SIC: 2086 5921 5499 Bottled & canned soft drinks; beer (packaged); beverage stores

(G-17205)
ABBOTT LABORATORIES
3271 Greenwood Ave (18505-3510)
PHONE...................................570 347-0319
EMP: 3
SALES (est): 92.3K **Privately Held**
SIC: 2834 Pharmaceutical preparations

(G-17206)
ADVANCED TEX COMPOSITES INC
700 E Parker St (18509-1016)
PHONE...................................570 207-7000
Paul Bocchino, *President*
Michael Chekan, *VP Sales*
John Post, *Shareholder*
EMP: 26
SQ FT: 55,000
SALES (est): 4.1MM **Privately Held**
WEB: www.advtextile.com
SIC: 2221 Manmade & synthetic broadwoven fabrics; glass & fiberglass broadwoven fabrics

(G-17207)
ALL - AMERICAN TROPHY COMPANY
Also Called: Ace Trophy Co
1415 Capouse Ave (18509-2375)
PHONE...................................570 342-2613
James P Boles, *Owner*
EMP: 3
SQ FT: 3,000
SALES (est): 140K **Privately Held**
SIC: 3499 5999 Trophies, metal, except silver; trophies & plaques

(G-17208)
ANDREW BILLETS & SON INC
1105 Capouse Ave (18509-2730)
PHONE...................................570 207-7253
Scott Billets, *President*
EMP: 5 **EST:** 1955
SQ FT: 15,000
SALES (est): 740.6K **Privately Held**
SIC: 3713 7538 Truck bodies (motor vehicles); general truck repair

(G-17209)
ASTRO APPAREL INC (PA)
Also Called: Bensol Trousers
300 Brook St Ste 2 (18505-2494)
P.O. Box 3627 (18505-0627)
PHONE...................................570 346-1700
Jim Alperin, *CEO*
James L Alperin, *President*
Irwin Alperin, *Vice Pres*
James Pusateri, *Vice Pres*
Ronald Daniels, *CFO*
▲ **EMP:** 50
SQ FT: 150,000
SALES (est): 9.1MM **Privately Held**
SIC: 2325 4225 Trousers, dress (separate): men's, youths' & boys'; general warehousing

(G-17210)
AZEK BUILDING PRODUCTS INC (DH)
888 N Keyser Ave (18504-9723)
PHONE...................................877 275-2935
James Keisling, *CEO*
Scott C Harrison, *Vice Pres*
▼ **EMP:** 40

SALES (est): 44MM
SALES (corp-wide): 958.4MM Publicly Held
WEB: www.azek.com
SIC: 3081 3086 3441 Polyvinyl film & sheet; plastics foam products; building components, structural steel
HQ: Cpg International Llc
1330 W Fulton St Ste 350
Chicago IL 60607
570 558-8000

(G-17211)
BEVILACQUA SHEET METAL INC
916 Capouse Ave (18509-2932)
PHONE...................................570 558-0397
Mike Bevilacqua, *Principal*
EMP: 8
SALES (est): 612K Privately Held
SIC: 1761 3444 5722 5999 Sheet metalwork; sheet metal specialties, not stamped; household appliance stores; plumbing & heating supplies

(G-17212)
BIRCH CUTTING CORPORATION
Birch Street & Crown Ave (18510)
PHONE...................................570 343-7477
David Dickstein, *President*
EMP: 31
SALES (est): 2.4MM Privately Held
SIC: 2353 Hats, caps & millinery

(G-17213)
BYRNE CANDLE CO INC
1200 Remington Ave (18505-1511)
PHONE...................................570 346-4070
Paul G Byrne, *President*
William L Byrne III, *Treasurer*
EMP: 25
SQ FT: 25,000
SALES (est): 2.2MM Privately Held
SIC: 3999 Candles

(G-17214)
CALVIN TAYLOR CORPORATION
101 Pittston Ave Ste 2 (18505-1150)
PHONE...................................570 983-2288
Michele L Roberston, *President*
EMP: 50
SALES (est): 5.1MM Privately Held
SIC: 2253 Pants, slacks or trousers, knit

(G-17215)
CATHOLIC LIGHT PUBLISHING CO
330 Wyoming Ave 208 (18503-1224)
PHONE...................................570 207-2229
William Genello, *Manager*
Eileen Manley, *Manager*
Kevin McDonnell, *Manager*
EMP: 4
SALES (est): 230.8K Privately Held
SIC: 2711 Newspapers, publishing & printing; newspapers: publishing only, not printed on site

(G-17216)
CATHOLIC SCL SVCS OF SCRANTON (PA)
Also Called: Diocese of Scranton, The
516 Fig St (18505-1753)
PHONE...................................570 207-2283
Joseph C Bambera, *Principal*
EMP: 100 EST: 1877
SQ FT: 25,000
SALES (est): 77.2MM Privately Held
WEB: www.catholiccharities-cc.org
SIC: 8661 2711 8211 8322 Catholic Church; newspapers: publishing only, not printed on site; seminary; Catholic elementary & secondary schools; youth center; cemetery association

(G-17217)
COMPRESSION POLYMERS
888 N Keyser Ave (18504-9723)
PHONE...................................570 558-8000
Jeffrey Keisling, *Principal*
EMP: 3
SALES (est): 215.2K Privately Held
SIC: 3081 Plastic film & sheet

(G-17218)
CONCRETE STEP UNITS INC
3102 N Main Ave (18508-1434)
P.O. Box 645, Chinchilla (18410-0645)
PHONE...................................570 343-2458
Nancy Luciane, *Corp Secy*
Nancy Luciani, *Corp Secy*
EMP: 26
SQ FT: 13,000
SALES: 2MM Privately Held
WEB: www.concretestep.com
SIC: 3272 3446 Steps, prefabricated concrete; septic tanks, concrete; railings, prefabricated metal

(G-17219)
COPITECH ASSOCIATES
336 Adams Ave (18503-1604)
PHONE...................................570 963-1391
Joseph Prcybylski, *Partner*
Joseph Ryzner, *Partner*
EMP: 7
SQ FT: 2,000
SALES (est): 750K Privately Held
SIC: 3861 3661 5999 5734 Photocopy machines; facsimile equipment; photocopy machines; facsimile equipment; modems, monitors, terminals & disk drives: computers

(G-17220)
COURTSIDE DOCUMENT SVCS INC
408 Spruce St Apt 1 (18503-1857)
PHONE...................................570 969-2991
Andrew McDonald, *President*
EMP: 4
SALES (est): 581K Privately Held
SIC: 2752 Commercial printing, lithographic

(G-17221)
CPG INTERNATIONAL HOLDINGS LP
888 N Keyser Ave (18504-9723)
PHONE...................................570 558-8000
Eric K Jungbluth, *CEO*
Jason Grommon, *President*
Don Wharton, *Principal*
Andy Vander Woude, *Principal*
Jim Gross, *Vice Pres*
EMP: 695
SALES (est): 34.7MM Privately Held
SIC: 3081 Plastic film & sheet; film base, cellulose acetate or nitrocellulose plastic

(G-17222)
CPG INTERNATIONAL I INC (DH)
801 E Corey St (18505-3523)
PHONE...................................570 346-8797
Eric K Jungbluth, *CEO*
Eric Colborn, *Production*
Tim Norman, *IT/INT Sup*
Andrew Gadomski, *Director*
Gil Garcia, *Director*
EMP: 0
SALES (est): 1.9MM
SALES (corp-wide): 958.4MM Publicly Held
SIC: 6719 2821 3081 3086 Personal holding companies, except banks; polyvinyl chloride resins (PVC); polyvinyl film & sheet; plastics foam products
HQ: Cpg International Llc
1330 W Fulton St Ste 350
Chicago IL 60607
570 558-8000

(G-17223)
CPG INTERNATIONAL LLC
Comtec Industries
801 Corey Ave (18505)
PHONE...................................570 348-0997
Delbert Keisling, *Principal*
EMP: 10
SALES (corp-wide): 958.4MM Publicly Held
WEB: www.cpg-vycom.com
SIC: 3081 2542 3251 Unsupported plastics film & sheet; partitions & fixtures, except wood; partition tile, clay
HQ: Cpg International Llc
1330 W Fulton St Ste 350
Chicago IL 60607
570 558-8000

(G-17224)
CPG INTERNATIONAL LLC
888 N Keyser Ave (18504-9723)
PHONE...................................570 558-8000
Eric Jungbluth, *Owner*
Rob Pazzaglia, *Director*
EMP: 5
SALES (corp-wide): 958.4MM Publicly Held
SIC: 3272 3089 Building materials, except block or brick: concrete; plastic hardware & building products; prefabricated plastic buildings
HQ: Cpg International Llc
1330 W Fulton St Ste 350
Chicago IL 60607
570 558-8000

(G-17225)
CPI SCRANTON INC
Also Called: Compression Polymers
801 E Corey St (18505-3523)
PHONE...................................570 558-8000
Scott Harrison, *CEO*
Don Wharton, *President*
James G Keisling, *Treasurer*
EMP: 350
SQ FT: 1,000,000
SALES (est): 49.1MM
SALES (corp-wide): 3.1B Privately Held
WEB: www.aeainvestors.com
SIC: 3081 Unsupported plastics film & sheet
PA: Aea Investors Lp
666 5th Ave Fl 36
New York NY 10103
212 644-5900

(G-17226)
CUSTOM DESIGNS & MFG CO
Also Called: Contempri Kitchens
40 Poplar St (18509-2622)
PHONE...................................570 207-4432
Alex Tarapchak III, *President*
EMP: 20
SQ FT: 50,000
SALES (est): 2.3MM Privately Held
WEB: www.quakermaid.com
SIC: 2434 2541 Wood kitchen cabinets; wood partitions & fixtures

(G-17227)
DANAKEN DESIGNS INC
949 Adams Ave (18510-1003)
PHONE...................................570 445-9797
Kevin Jenkins, *CEO*
EMP: 13 EST: 2010
SQ FT: 74,000
SALES (est): 1.6MM Privately Held
SIC: 2631 7389 Cardboard; design services

(G-17228)
DAVID ELLIOT POULTRY FARM INC
300 Breck St (18505-1602)
PHONE...................................570 344-6348
Shlomo Fink, *President*
Moshe Fink, *COO*
EMP: 110
SQ FT: 28,000
SALES (est): 10MM Privately Held
SIC: 0251 2015 Broiler, fryer & roaster chickens; chicken slaughtering & processing

(G-17229)
DUPLI CRAFT PRINTING INC
Also Called: Dupli-Craft Printing
1000 W Market St (18508-1243)
PHONE...................................570 344-8980
J Brian Mc Goff, *President*
Joseph J McGoff Sr, *Treasurer*
EMP: 5
SQ FT: 2,500
SALES (est): 656.9K Privately Held
SIC: 2752 Commercial printing, offset

(G-17230)
EARLY MORNING DONUTS CORP
Also Called: Krispy Kreme
511 Moosic St (18505-1409)
PHONE...................................570 961-5150
Marybeth Stenaro, *President*

EMP: 4
SALES (corp-wide): 3.5MM Privately Held
SIC: 5461 2051 Doughnuts; bread, cake & related products
PA: Early Morning Donuts Corp
511 Moosic St
Scranton PA 18505
570 961-5150

(G-17231)
EASTERN MILLWORK LTD
108 E Elm St (18505-1530)
PHONE...................................570 344-7128
Mathew Born, *Partner*
Jeff Kubasti, *Partner*
Steven Penneypacker, *Partner*
Douglas Traumbauer, *Partner*
Joseph Wynsek, *Partner*
EMP: 5
SALES (est): 500K Privately Held
SIC: 3429 Cabinet hardware

(G-17232)
ELECTRIC CITY BASEBALL & SOFT
501 Wyoming Ave (18509-3013)
PHONE...................................570 955-0471
Paul McGloin, *Principal*
EMP: 3 EST: 2012
SALES (est): 105.5K Privately Held
SIC: 8299 3699 Schools & educational service; electrical equipment & supplies

(G-17233)
ELECTRIC CITY YOGA
1120 Moosic St (18505-2106)
P.O. Box 20019 (18502-0019)
PHONE...................................570 558-9642
EMP: 3 EST: 2015
SALES (est): 51K Privately Held
SIC: 7999 3699 1731 Yoga instruction; electrical equipment & supplies; electrical work

(G-17234)
EMBROIDER SMITH
1021 Lookout Dr (18504-9519)
PHONE...................................570 961-8781
Nancy Smith, *Owner*
Bob Smith, *Co-Owner*
EMP: 3
SALES (est): 207.1K Privately Held
SIC: 2395 Embroidery & art needlework

(G-17235)
ENTERPRISE MACHINE AND TOOL CO
229 Marion St (18509-2260)
PHONE...................................570 969-2587
Mike Klos Jr, *President*
Robert E Young, *Treasurer*
EMP: 6
SQ FT: 7,000
SALES (est): 847.4K Privately Held
SIC: 3599 Machine shop, jobbing & repair

(G-17236)
EZ GARMENT PRINTING INC
501 Wyoming Ave (18509-3013)
PHONE...................................570 703-0961
Paul Ezeiansky, *CEO*
EMP: 5 EST: 2013
SALES (est): 285.2K Privately Held
SIC: 2759 Screen printing

(G-17237)
GENERAL DYNAMICS CORPORATION
156 Cedar Ave (18505-1138)
PHONE...................................570 340-1136
Eric Shultz, *Branch Mgr*
James Nayavich, *Info Tech Mgr*
EMP: 19
SALES (corp-wide): 36.1B Publicly Held
SIC: 3489 Ordnance & accessories
PA: General Dynamics Corporation
2941 Frview Pk Dr Ste 100
Falls Church VA 22042
703 876-3000

(G-17238)
GENERAL DYNAMICS OTS PA INC
Scranton Div
156 Cedar Ave (18505-1138)
PHONE..................................570 342-7801
Jim Nayavich, *Technology*
James J Flaherty, *Systems Staff*
EMP: 106
SQ FT: 500,000
SALES (corp-wide): 36.1B **Publicly Held**
SIC: 3769 3568 3545 3483 Casings, missiles & missile components: storage; power transmission equipment; machine tool accessories; ammunition, except for small arms; nonferrous forgings; iron & steel forgings
HQ: General Dynamics Ots (Pennsylvania), Inc.
200 E High St
Red Lion PA 17356
717 246-8208

(G-17239)
GERRITYS SUPER MARKET INC
Also Called: Gerrity Markets
320 Meadow Ave (18505-2138)
PHONE..................................570 961-9030
Jack Archer, *Branch Mgr*
EMP: 95
SALES (corp-wide): 169.7MM **Privately Held**
WEB: www.gerritygifts.com
SIC: 5411 5812 2051 Grocery stores, independent; eating places; bread, cake & related products
PA: Gerrity's Super Market, Inc.
950 N South Rd Ste 5
Scranton PA 18504
570 342-4144

(G-17240)
GODINO WEST MTN STONE QUAR
Also Called: Godinos West Mtn Stone Quar
703 Newton Rd (18504-1017)
PHONE..................................570 342-4340
Theresa Godino-Gurnani, *Owner*
EMP: 5
SALES: 250K **Privately Held**
SIC: 1411 Sandstone, dimension-quarrying

(G-17241)
HOUGHTON CHEMICAL CORPORATION
705 Davis St (18505-3505)
PHONE..................................800 777-2466
EMP: 7
SALES (corp-wide): 35.1MM **Privately Held**
WEB: www.houghton.com
SIC: 5169 2899 2842 Organic chemicals, synthetic; antifreeze compounds; specialty cleaning, polishes & sanitation goods
PA: Houghton Chemical Corporation
52 Cambridge St
Allston MA 02134
617 254-1010

(G-17242)
ICY BITES INC
Also Called: Cold Stone Creamery
2603 Stafford Ave (18505-3608)
PHONE..................................570 558-5558
Kevin Olsen, *Principal*
EMP: 4
SALES (est): 26.7K **Privately Held**
SIC: 2053 Frozen bakery products, except bread

(G-17243)
IMPERIAL BAKERY
416 S Hyde Park Ave (18504-2225)
PHONE..................................570 343-4537
Carol Bernardini, *Owner*
EMP: 4
SQ FT: 3,000
SALES (est): 200K **Privately Held**
SIC: 2051 Bakery: wholesale or wholesale/retail combined

(G-17244)
INERT PRODUCTS LLC
100 Powderly Ct (18504-1888)
PHONE..................................570 341-3751
Dean Klipple, *Exec VP*
Bridgette Nealon, *Bookkeeper*
Richard F Carrick, *Sales Staff*
Robert Rozzi, *Mng Member*
◆ EMP: 15
SALES: 3.5MM **Privately Held**
WEB: www.inertproducts.com
SIC: 3999 5999 Education aids, devices & supplies; educational aids & electronic training materials

(G-17245)
J & R WIRE INC
943 Sanderson Ave (18509-2603)
PHONE..................................570 342-3193
Joe Grizzanti Sr, *President*
Robert L Carter, *Treasurer*
▲ EMP: 10
SQ FT: 5,040
SALES: 800K **Privately Held**
SIC: 3496 Lamp frames, wire

(G-17246)
JACOBSON HAT CO INC (PA)
Also Called: J Hats
1301 Ridge Row (18510-2251)
P.O. Box 1429 (18501-1429)
PHONE..................................570 342-7887
Howard Jacobson, *President*
Estelle Chunca, *Superintendent*
Claire Jacobson, *Principal*
Jeffrey Jacobson, *Vice Pres*
David Dickstein, *Treasurer*
◆ EMP: 58 EST: 1931
SQ FT: 80,000
SALES (est): 10.8MM **Privately Held**
WEB: www.jhats.com
SIC: 2679 2353 Hats, paper novelties: made from purchased paper; hats, caps & millinery

(G-17247)
JAMES SAKS
Also Called: Design Print
731 Saginaw St (18505-3628)
PHONE..................................570 343-8150
James Saks, *Owner*
EMP: 5
SQ FT: 600
SALES (est): 381.9K **Privately Held**
SIC: 2752 2791 Commercial printing, offset; typesetting

(G-17248)
JUJAMA INC
600 Jefferson Ave (18510-1622)
PHONE..................................570 209-7670
Nadia Deley, *President*
Robert W Naismith, *Chairman*
EMP: 20 EST: 2009
SALES (est): 1.4MM **Privately Held**
SIC: 7372 Application computer software

(G-17249)
K DIAMOND INCORPORATED
900 Battle St (18508-2556)
PHONE..................................570 346-4684
David L Kirtland, *President*
Susan Tully, *Admin Sec*
EMP: 30 EST: 1955
SQ FT: 80,000
SALES (est): 5.3MM **Privately Held**
SIC: 4953 4212 2611 Recycling, waste materials; local trucking, without storage; pulp mills

(G-17250)
KEVINS WHOLESALE LLC
Also Called: Kevins Worldwide
710 Capouse Ave (18509-3120)
PHONE..................................570 344-9055
Larry Tinkelman, *Ch of Bd*
Kevin Tinkelman, *President*
Scott Tinkelman, *Exec VP*
Scott Vogelmeier, *Vice Pres*
Debbie Boedeker, *Sales Staff*
▲ EMP: 82
SQ FT: 85,000

SALES (est): 11.5MM **Privately Held**
WEB: www.kevins.biz
SIC: 2395 7389 5199 Emblems, embroidered; buttonhole making, except fur, for the trade; advertising, promotional & trade show services; badges

(G-17251)
KEYSTONE CON BLOCK SUP CO INC (PA)
600 Glenn St (18509-2213)
PHONE..................................570 346-7701
Paul J Galdieri, *President*
Gayle Mc Laughlin, *Corp Secy*
Richard Galdieri, *Vice Pres*
Robert A Galdieri, *Vice Pres*
EMP: 25 EST: 1926
SQ FT: 65,000
SALES: 6MM **Privately Held**
WEB: www.keystone-block.com
SIC: 3271 Blocks, concrete or cinder: standard

(G-17252)
KOROTEO INVESTMENTS INC
Also Called: Fastsigns
205 Scrnton Crbondale Hwy (18508-1111)
PHONE..................................570 342-4422
Alvaro Arnal, *President*
Mary Jo Arnal, *Treasurer*
EMP: 8
SQ FT: 1,500
SALES (est): 1.1MM **Privately Held**
SIC: 3993 Signs & advertising specialties

(G-17253)
LACKAWANNA PRINTING CO
902 Capouse Ave (18509-2932)
PHONE..................................570 342-0528
Aldo Vagnetti, *Owner*
EMP: 6
SALES (est): 350K **Privately Held**
SIC: 2752 Commercial printing, offset

(G-17254)
LEONARDS AUTO TAG SERVICE
635 Luzerne St Ste 4 (18504-2657)
PHONE..................................570 693-0122
Steven Celenski, *Branch Mgr*
EMP: 3 **Privately Held**
SIC: 2679 Tags & labels, paper
PA: Leonard's Auto Tag Service
295 Susquehanna Ave
Wyoming PA 18644

(G-17255)
LIQUOR CONTROL BOARD PA
Also Called: Wine & Spirits Shoppe 3502
1512 Scrnton Crbndale Hwy (18508-1136)
PHONE..................................570 383-5248
Glenn Mikolaezyk, *Manager*
EMP: 5 **Privately Held**
SIC: 2084 9651 5921 Wines; alcoholic beverage control board, government; ; wine; hard liquor
HQ: Pennsylvania Liquor Control Board
406 Nw Office Bldg 910
Harrisburg PA 17124
717 783-7637

(G-17256)
LOMMA INVESTMENTS
Also Called: Lomma Investments Citrus Div
305 Cherry St (18505-1505)
PHONE..................................570 346-5555
Ralph J Lomma, *Owner*
EMP: 25 EST: 1955
SQ FT: 5,000
SALES (est): 737.2K **Privately Held**
SIC: 6512 6513 3949 Commercial & industrial building operation; apartment building operators; sporting & athletic goods

(G-17257)
MAC SIGN SYSTEMS INC
232 S Sherman Ave (18504-2390)
PHONE..................................570 347-7446
Kevin McDonough, *President*
EMP: 15
SALES: 1.5MM **Privately Held**
WEB: www.macsigns.com
SIC: 3993 Electric signs

(G-17258)
MAID-RITE SPECIALTY FOODS LLC
151 Cedar Ave (18505-1139)
PHONE..................................570 346-3572
Donald Bernstein, *President*
Brenda Samsell, *Opers Mgr*
EMP: 15
SALES (corp-wide): 20.1MM **Privately Held**
WEB: www.maidritesteak.com
SIC: 5812 2013 Sandwiches & submarines shop; frozen meats from purchased meat
PA: Maid-Rite Specialty Foods, Llc
105 Keystone Indus Park
Dunmore PA 18512
570 343-4748

(G-17259)
MICROBIOLOGY LAB CO
300 Mulberry St (18503-1225)
PHONE..................................570 800-5795
Hassan Namdari, *Principal*
EMP: 3 EST: 2016
SALES (est): 224.5K **Privately Held**
SIC: 2835 Microbiology & virology diagnostic products

(G-17260)
MSP CORPORATION
Also Called: Corner News
1055 Blair Ave (18508-2303)
PHONE..................................570 344-7670
EMP: 4
SALES (est): 234.7K **Privately Held**
SIC: 2711 Newspapers, publishing & printing

(G-17261)
MULDOON WINDOW DOOR & AWNING
1230 Sanderson Ave (18509-2611)
PHONE..................................570 347-9453
Joe Benova, *President*
Doug Kniese, *Vice Pres*
EMP: 3 EST: 1954
SQ FT: 24,000
SALES: 500K **Privately Held**
SIC: 2431 3442 5033 5039 Awnings, wood; storm doors or windows, metal; siding, except wood; awnings

(G-17262)
MURAZZI PROVISION CO
1262 Providence Rd (18508-2229)
PHONE..................................570 344-2285
Hugo Murazzi, *President*
Angelo Murazzi, *Vice Pres*
EMP: 10 EST: 1934
SQ FT: 13,600
SALES (est): 1.2MM **Privately Held**
SIC: 2013 5149 5143 Sausages & other prepared meats; specialty food items; cheese

(G-17263)
NAMMO POCAL INC (PA)
100 Electric St (18509-1804)
PHONE..................................570 961-1999
Poju Zabludowicz, *Ch of Bd*
Vince Fedele, *President*
Anne Koniszewski, *Treasurer*
▲ EMP: 40
SQ FT: 30,000
SALES (est): 14.2MM **Privately Held**
WEB: www.pocal.com
SIC: 3483 Mortar shells, over 30 mm.

(G-17264)
NATIONAL BAKERY INC (PA)
1100 Capouse Ave (18509-2799)
PHONE..................................570 343-1609
Anthony Vitaletti III, *President*
Enrico Vitaletti, *Vice Pres*
Dale Long, *Sales/Mktg Mgr*
EMP: 44 EST: 1946
SQ FT: 18,000
SALES (est): 2.2MM **Privately Held**
SIC: 5461 2051 5149 Bakeries; bread, cake & related products; groceries & related products

(G-17265)
NOBLE BIOMATERIALS INC (PA)
300 Palm St (18505-1618)
PHONE................570 955-1800
Jeff B Keane, *CEO*
Joel Furey, *President*
Guy Grubel, *President*
James F Walsh, *CFO*
Gregory Gianforcaro,
▲ **EMP:** 64
SQ FT: 65,000
SALES (est): 22.5MM **Privately Held**
SIC: 2299 Broadwoven fabrics: linen, jute, hemp & ramie

(G-17266)
NORTH AMERICAN MFG CO
1074 Barring Ave (18508-2501)
PHONE................570 348-1163
Joe Shea, *President*
Marvin Pearl, *Vice Pres*
▲ **EMP:** 50
SQ FT: 60,000
SALES (est): 14.6MM **Privately Held**
SIC: 3444 5084 Mail (post office) collection or storage boxes, sheet metal; sewing machines, industrial

(G-17267)
NORTH END ELECTRIC SERVICE INC
Also Called: Tristate Golf Carts
1225 N Keyser Ave (18504-9732)
PHONE................570 342-6740
Cale Hendricks, *President*
Cody Hendricks, *Vice Pres*
▲ **EMP:** 26
SQ FT: 6,000
SALES (est): 7.4MM **Privately Held**
SIC: 7694 5084 Electric motor repair; compressors, except air conditioning

(G-17268)
OLYMPIA CHIMNEY SUPPLY INC
600 Sanders St Ste 2 (18505-3400)
PHONE................570 496-8890
William Kozlansky, *President*
Christopher Hoffman, *Vice Pres*
Richard Grzyboski, *Manager*
▲ **EMP:** 70
SQ FT: 138,000
SALES (est): 28.9MM **Privately Held**
WEB: www.olympicchimney.com
SIC: 3312 Stainless steel

(G-17269)
PALLET CONNECTION
120 N Van Buren Ave (18504-3436)
PHONE................570 963-1432
William Vigillant, *Owner*
EMP: 4
SALES (est): 270.8K **Privately Held**
SIC: 2448 Pallets, wood & wood with metal

(G-17270)
PARTRIDGE WIRTH COMPANY INC
523 Wyoming Ave (18509-3088)
PHONE................570 344-8514
William A Gnall, *President*
Robin Gnall, *Vice Pres*
David Gnall, *Treasurer*
Debbie Gnall, *Admin Sec*
EMP: 10 **EST:** 1972
SALES (est): 1.1MM **Privately Held**
SIC: 2752 Commercial printing, offset

(G-17271)
PENN SHADECRAFTERS INC
941 Sanderson Ave (18509-2603)
PHONE................570 342-3193
Stephen Carter, *President*
▲ **EMP:** 34 **EST:** 1974
SQ FT: 24,000
SALES: 1MM **Privately Held**
WEB: www.pennminerals.com
SIC: 3999 3645 Shades, lamp or candle; residential lighting fixtures

(G-17272)
PITTSTON BAKING CO INC
Also Called: Chiampi's Bakery
2646 Pittston Ave (18505-3218)
PHONE................570 343-2102
Frank Alu, *President*

Carmen Alu, *Vice Pres*
Joseph Alu, *Treasurer*
Joanne Alu, *Admin Sec*
EMP: 7
SQ FT: 2,400
SALES (est): 715.1K **Privately Held**
SIC: 2051 Bakery: wholesale or wholesale/retail combined

(G-17273)
POCONO SCREEN SUPPLY LLC
908 E Elm St (18505-2463)
PHONE................570 253-6375
Neil Wicker, *Mng Member*
▲ **EMP:** 5
SALES: 800K **Privately Held**
SIC: 3861 Printing frames, photographic

(G-17274)
PRECISION POLYMER PROCESSORS
2400 Stafford Ave Ste 700 (18505-3692)
P.O. Box 315, Carbondale (18407-0315)
PHONE................570 344-9916
John Parenta, *Principal*
Gentex Corp, *Principal*
EMP: 15
SQ FT: 3,000
SALES (est): 1.1MM **Privately Held**
SIC: 3081 Plastic film & sheet

(G-17275)
PRINT FACTORY
1807 Luzerne St Unit 1 (18504-2393)
PHONE................570 961-2111
Sandra Galdieri, *Partner*
Denise Hines, *Partner*
EMP: 3
SALES (est): 226.4K **Privately Held**
SIC: 2759 Screen printing

(G-17276)
QUADRANT HOLDING INC
900 N South Rd (18504-1412)
PHONE................570 558-6000
Andre Fischbach, *Branch Mgr*
Michael Ruane, *Assistant*
EMP: 127
SQ FT: 95,000 **Privately Held**
WEB: www.quadrantepp.com
SIC: 3089 3082 Stock shapes, plastic
HQ: Mitsubishi Chemical Advanced Materials Inc.
2120 Fairmont Ave
Reading PA 19605
610 320-6600

(G-17277)
QUAKERMAID CABINETS INC
Also Called: Quarkermaid
40 Poplar St (18509-2622)
PHONE................570 207-4432
Alexander Tarapchak III, *President*
EMP: 35
SQ FT: 20,000
SALES (est): 3.5MM **Privately Held**
SIC: 2599 Cabinets, factory

(G-17278)
RED GRAVEL PARTNERS LLC
Also Called: PostNet
219 N Main St (18504)
PHONE................570 445-3553
Matthew Keisling, *Mng Member*
James Keeler,
Sarah Snyder,
EMP: 4
SQ FT: 1,700
SALES: 150K **Privately Held**
SIC: 2752 Commercial printing, lithographic

(G-17279)
ROSCIOLIS BAKERY
716 Court St (18508-2209)
PHONE................570 961-1151
Richard Roscioli, *Owner*
EMP: 5
SALES (est): 277.5K **Privately Held**
SIC: 2051 Bakery: wholesale or wholesale/retail combined

(G-17280)
S & L MOTORS INC
Also Called: S&L Motor Service
200 S 7th Ave (18505-1037)
PHONE................570 342-9718
William J Lewis, *President*
EMP: 4 **EST:** 1934
SALES: 400K **Privately Held**
SIC: 7538 3599 3621 Engine rebuilding: automotive; machine shop, jobbing & repair; motors & generators

(G-17281)
S K P COMPANY
710 E Mountain Rd (18505-2665)
PHONE................570 344-0561
Darwin Shoener, *Owner*
Pushkar Bagmar, *Partner*
Sandeep Jain, *Partner*
EMP: 3
SQ FT: 6,500
SALES (est): 323.9K **Privately Held**
SIC: 3559 7699 Refinery, chemical processing & similar machinery; industrial equipment services

(G-17282)
S SCHIFF RESTAURANT SVC INC
Also Called: Schiff's Cash & Carry
3410 N Main Ave (18508-1439)
PHONE................570 343-1294
Mark Reese, *President*
Dave Pitcavage, *Vice Pres*
David Pitcavage, *Vice Pres*
EMP: 125
SQ FT: 30,000
SALES (est): 67.6MM **Privately Held**
SIC: 5141 5147 2013 2011 Groceries, general line; meats, fresh; sausages & other prepared meats; meat packing plants

(G-17283)
SAUQUOIT INDUSTRIES LLC
300 Palm St (18505-1618)
PHONE................570 348-2751
Jeffery B Keane, *CEO*
James F Walsh, *CFO*
▼ **EMP:** 100 **EST:** 1870
SQ FT: 60,000
SALES (est): 16MM **Privately Held**
WEB: www.sauquoit.com
SIC: 2284 2221 Thread from manmade fibers; specialty broadwoven fabrics, including twisted weaves
PA: Noble Biomaterials, Inc.
300 Palm St
Scranton PA 18505

(G-17284)
SCHOOL COLORS INC
507 New York St (18509-2433)
PHONE................570 561-2632
Cheryl Gnoinski, *President*
EMP: 8
SALES (est): 305.8K **Privately Held**
SIC: 2759 Screen printing

(G-17285)
SCRANTON GRINDER & HARDWARE
1020 Hemlock St (18505-2116)
PHONE................570 344-2520
Joseph Ferrari, *Owner*
EMP: 20 **EST:** 1921
SQ FT: 15,000
SALES: 800K **Privately Held**
SIC: 3599 5251 5261 7699 Machine shop, jobbing & repair; builders' hardware; lawnmowers & tractors; garden supplies & tools; lawn mower repair shop

(G-17286)
SCRANTON MATERIALS LLC
819 Newton Rd (18504-1019)
PHONE................570 961-8586
EMP: 10
SALES (est): 1.3MM **Privately Held**
SIC: 3281 Stone, quarrying & processing of own stone products

(G-17287)
SCRANTON PRODUCTS INC
801 E Corey St (18505-3523)
PHONE................570 558-8000
Eric K Jungbluth, *CEO*
Delbert Keisling, *President*
Don Wharton, *Principal*
Robert Donlon, *Vice Pres*
Scott Harrison, *CFO*
▼ **EMP:** 150 **EST:** 2001
SALES (est): 58.4MM
SALES (corp-wide): 958.4MM **Publicly Held**
SIC: 2542 Partitions & fixtures, except wood
HQ: Cpg International Llc
1330 W Fulton St Ste 350
Chicago IL 60607
570 558-8000

(G-17288)
SCRANTON SHEET METAL INC
240 E Elm St Unit 2 (18505-4651)
PHONE................570 342-2904
Marco Richione, *President*
Teri Richione, *Financial Exec*
Brenda Rosencrans, *Office Mgr*
EMP: 25
SQ FT: 15,000
SALES (est): 4.1MM **Privately Held**
WEB: www.scrantonsheetmetal.com
SIC: 1711 7692 3444 Warm air heating & air conditioning contractor; ventilation & duct work contractor; welding repair; sheet metalwork

(G-17289)
SCRANTON TIMES-TRIBUNE
149 Penn Ave Ste 1 (18503-2094)
PHONE................570 348-9100
EMP: 12
SALES (est): 857.1K **Privately Held**
SIC: 2711 Newspapers

(G-17290)
SENIOR CRAFTSMENS SHOP
232 Wyoming Ave (18503-1408)
PHONE................570 344-7089
Nancy Post, *President*
Cheryl Burrier, *Exec Dir*
Veronica Sedlisky, *Administration*
EMP: 3
SALES (est): 203.4K **Privately Held**
SIC: 3944 Craft & hobby kits & sets

(G-17291)
SIMPLEX INDUSTRIES INC (PA)
1 Simplex Dr (18504-1400)
PHONE................570 346-5113
Patrick A Fricchione, *President*
Patrick J Fricchione, *Vice Pres*
Marie Fricchione, *Treasurer*
Marie R Fricchione, *Treasurer*
Patrick I Fricchione, *Admin Sec*
EMP: 120
SQ FT: 65,000
SALES (est): 45.4MM **Privately Held**
WEB: www.simplexhomes.com
SIC: 2451 Mobile homes

(G-17292)
SPENCER INDUSTRIES INC
1014-1016 Sanderson Ave (18509)
PHONE................570 969-9931
Stanley Bednarz, *Branch Mgr*
EMP: 3
SALES (corp-wide): 4.8MM **Privately Held**
WEB: www.spencerindinc.com
SIC: 2298 Wire rope centers
PA: Spencer Industries, Inc.
80 Holmes St
Belleville NJ 07109
973 751-2200

(G-17293)
STANDARD IRON WORKS
Also Called: Siw
990 N South Rd Ste 1 (18504-1498)
PHONE................570 347-2058
Paul J Dennebaum Jr, *President*
Mark P Dennebaum, *Vice Pres*
P J Dennebaum Sr, *Admin Sec*
Lynn Mensel, *Admin Sec*
EMP: 35
SQ FT: 70,000

SALES (est): 11.7MM **Privately Held**
WEB: www.standardiron.com
SIC: 3312 3441 3446 3713 Hot-rolled iron & steel products; fabricated structural metal; architectural metalwork; car carrier bodies

(G-17294)
STRAZ
Also Called: Mr Kotula
1006 Pittston Ave (18505-4109)
PHONE................................570 344-1513
Edmond Kotula, *Director*
EMP: 5
SALES (est): 304K **Privately Held**
WEB: www.pnu.org
SIC: 2759 Commercial printing

(G-17295)
SUPERIOR TROPHY & ENGRAVING CO
965 Providence Rd (18508-2540)
PHONE................................570 343-4087
Gerard Welby, *President*
EMP: 5 **EST:** 1952
SQ FT: 10,700
SALES (est): 280K **Privately Held**
SIC: 3914 5999 Trophies; trophies & plaques

(G-17296)
SUPERIOR WELDING CO
870 Providence Rd (18508-2595)
PHONE................................570 344-4212
John Oakes, *Owner*
EMP: 3 **EST:** 1925
SQ FT: 5,148
SALES (est): 155.6K **Privately Held**
SIC: 7692 Welding repair

(G-17297)
THE SCRANTON TIMES L P
Also Called: Production Department
149 Scranton Times Bldg (18503-2094)
PHONE..............,.............570 348-9146
John McAndrew, *Manager*
EMP: 85
SALES (corp-wide): 114.5MM **Privately Held**
WEB: www.scrantontimesefcu.com
SIC: 2711 4832 2741 Newspapers, publishing & printing; radio broadcasting stations; miscellaneous publishing
PA: The Scranton Times L P
149 Penn Ave Ste 1
Scranton PA 18503
570 348-9100

(G-17298)
THE SCRANTON TIMES L P (PA)
Also Called: City Paper of Baltimore
149 Penn Ave Ste 1 (18503-2094)
PHONE................................570 348-9100
Charles Schillinger, *Managing Prtnr*
Edward J Lynett Jr, *Partner*
Cecelia Lynett Haggerty, *Partner*
George V Lynett, *Partner*
Lynda Mulligan Lynett, *Partner*
EMP: 250
SQ FT: 70,000
SALES (est): 114.5MM **Privately Held**
WEB: www.scrantontimesefcu.com
SIC: 2711 4832 Newspapers, publishing & printing; radio broadcasting stations

(G-17299)
THE SCRANTON TIMES L P
Also Called: City Paper
149 Penn Ave Ofc C (18503-2056)
PHONE................................410 523-2300
EMP: 50
SALES (corp-wide): 114.5MM **Privately Held**
SIC: 2711 4832 Newspapers-Publishing/Printing Radio Broadcast Station
PA: The Scranton Times L P
149 Penn Ave Ste 1
Scranton PA 18503
570 348-9100

(G-17300)
THERMOLITE INC
950 N South Rd Ste 3 (18504-1430)
PHONE................................570 969-1957
John P Mesko, *President*

Joseph R Mesko, *Treasurer*
George E Mesko, *Admin Sec*
EMP: 40
SQ FT: 50,000
SALES (est): 5.1MM **Privately Held**
WEB: www.thermoliteinc.com
SIC: 3211 5032 3442 5211 Insulating glass, sealed units; brick, stone & related material; screen & storm doors & windows; door & window products; doors & windows

(G-17301)
THIRD DIMENSION SPC LLC
Also Called: Third Dimension Graphics Group
856 Capouse Ave (18509-3124)
PHONE................................570 969-0623
Tim Morgan,
EMP: 4
SQ FT: 1,500
SALES (est): 385K **Privately Held**
WEB: www.34print.com
SIC: 2759 2791 2789 2752 Thermography; typesetting; bookbinding & related work; commercial printing, offset

(G-17302)
TIMES PARTNER LLC
149 Penn Ave (18503)
PHONE................................570 348-9100
EMP: 3
SALES (est): 119.2K **Privately Held**
SIC: 2711 Newspapers, publishing & printing

(G-17303)
TIMES SHAMROCK NEWSPAPER GROUP
149 Penn Ave (18503-2055)
PHONE................................570 348-9100
Scott Lynett, *Partner*
Matthwe Hagderty, *Partner*
Bobby Lynett, *Partner*
George Lynett Jr, *Partner*
Kevin Fitzgerald, *Chief Engr*
EMP: 8
SALES (est): 274.4K **Privately Held**
SIC: 2711 Newspapers, publishing & printing

(G-17304)
TJAWS LLC
Also Called: Jaworski Sign Company
913 S Main Ave (18504-2748)
PHONE................................570 344-2117
Margaret Jaworski, *Principal*
EMP: 3
SALES (est): 133.8K **Privately Held**
SIC: 3993 Signs & advertising specialties

(G-17305)
TOPPS COMPANY INC
Also Called: Topps Chewing Gum
50 Poplar St (18509-2602)
PHONE................................570 346-5874
Tom Shermanski, *Plant Mgr*
Bob Logan, *Manager*
Dale Horvath, *Manager*
EMP: 85 **Privately Held**
SIC: 2064 Lollipops & other hard candy
HQ: The Topps Company Inc
1 Whitehall St Fl 4
New York NY 10004
212 376-0300

(G-17306)
TRIBORO BANNER
149 Penn Ave (18503-2055)
PHONE................................570 348-9185
John Christmas, *Owner*
EMP: 8 **EST:** 1970
SQ FT: 2,000
SALES (est): 258.4K **Privately Held**
WEB: www.triborobanner.com
SIC: 2711 Newspapers: publishing only, not printed on site

(G-17307)
TWANDA PRINTING
Also Called: Tocono Shopper
149 Penn Ave (18503-2055)
PHONE................................570 421-4800
David Barry, *Manager*
EMP: 4

SALES (est): 180.2K **Privately Held**
SIC: 2711 Newspapers, publishing & printing

(G-17308)
UNITED GILSONITE LABORATORIES (PA)
Also Called: U G L
1396 Jefferson Ave (18509-2415)
P.O. Box 70 (18501-0070)
PHONE................................570 344-1202
James Tate, *CEO*
Tim Weems, *General Mgr*
Donald R Mancuso, *Corp Secy*
Robert Connolly, *Vice Pres*
Joe Johnson, *Vice Pres*
▲ **EMP:** 80 **EST:** 1932
SQ FT: 300,000
SALES: 56.2MM **Privately Held**
WEB: www.ugl.com
SIC: 2851 2891 Varnishes; wood stains; paints & paint additives; caulking compounds

(G-17309)
VAULT CLOTHING STORE
721 Scrnton Crbondale Hwy (18508-1121)
PHONE................................570 871-4135
Tracylynn Bannon, *Principal*
EMP: 5
SALES (est): 368.6K **Privately Held**
SIC: 3272 Burial vaults, concrete or pre-cast terrazzo

(G-17310)
VMF INC
415 Walnut St (18509-2712)
PHONE................................570 575-0997
John M Van Fleet, *President*
Shirley Van Fleet, *Treasurer*
EMP: 20
SQ FT: 16,000
SALES (est): 2.4MM **Privately Held**
WEB: www.vmfinc.com
SIC: 2542 3559 3441 Racks, merchandise display or storage: except wood; garment racks: except wood; degreasing machines, automotive & industrial; metal finishing equipment for plating, etc.; building components, structural steel

(G-17311)
WALSH SHEET METAL INC
818 Meadow Ave (18505-2534)
PHONE................................570 344-3495
Donald Walsh Sr, *President*
Jeffrey Walsh, *Treasurer*
Leonard Walsh, *Admin Sec*
EMP: 7
SQ FT: 1,600
SALES (est): 757.3K **Privately Held**
SIC: 1711 3444 Ventilation & duct work contractor; sheet metal specialties, not stamped

(G-17312)
WHISKEY DICKS
308 N Washington Ave (18503-1502)
PHONE................................570 342-9824
Gregory Evans, *Principal*
EMP: 5
SALES (est): 627.7K **Privately Held**
SIC: 3577 Bar code (magnetic ink) printers

(G-17313)
WIDMER SIGN COMPANY INC
2209 Amelia Ave (18509-1353)
PHONE................................570 343-0319
Todd Collins, *President*
EMP: 9
SQ FT: 30,000
SALES (est): 1.1MM **Privately Held**
WEB: www.widmersign.com
SIC: 3993 Neon signs; electric signs; displays & cutouts, window & lobby

(G-17314)
WILLIAM KLEINBERGER & SONS (PA)
217 Reese St Rear (18508-1448)
PHONE................................570 347-9331
Bruce Kleinberger, *President*
Bernard Kleinberger, *Treasurer*
EMP: 20 **EST:** 1920
SALES (est): 2.9MM **Privately Held**
SIC: 2035 Pickles, vinegar

(G-17315)
WILLIAM KLEINBERGER & SONS
1039 Quincy Ave (18510-1121)
PHONE................................570 347-9331
Bruce Kleinberger, *President*
Bernard Kleinberger, *Principal*
EMP: 20
SALES (corp-wide): 2.9MM **Privately Held**
SIC: 2035 Pickles, sauces & salad dressings
PA: William Kleinberger & Sons Inc
217 Reese St Rear
Scranton PA 18508
570 347-9331

Secane
Delaware County

(G-17316)
21ST CNTURY MDIA NWSPAPERS LLC
500 Mildred Ave (19018-2914)
PHONE................................610 622-4186
EMP: 3
SALES (est): 83.8K **Privately Held**
SIC: 2711 Newspapers-Publishing/Printing

(G-17317)
KONTROL AUTOMATION INC (PA)
528 Mildred Ave (19018-2914)
P.O. Box 483, Primos Secane (19018-0483)
PHONE................................610 284-4106
Edward Sharretts, *President*
EMP: 3
SALES (est): 1.1MM **Privately Held**
WEB: www.kontrolauto.com
SIC: 3823 Controllers for process variables, all types

(G-17318)
LIME SPORTSWEAR
164 S Bishop Ave (19018-2016)
PHONE................................484 461-7000
Thomas A Healy, *Owner*
EMP: 15
SQ FT: 12,000
SALES: 1.5MM **Privately Held**
SIC: 2759 Screen printing

(G-17319)
PIONEER MACHINE & TOOLING LLC
515 Mildred Ave (19018-2915)
PHONE................................610 623-3908
Yong Choe, *Owner*
Jim Choe, *Prdtn Mgr*
EMP: 16
SQ FT: 14,000
SALES (est): 2.9MM **Privately Held**
WEB: www.garneaux.com
SIC: 3599 Machine shop, jobbing & repair

Selinsgrove
Snyder County

(G-17320)
ASP SERVICES INC (PA)
10 Lisalyn Rd (17870-8650)
PHONE................................570 374-5333
Kirk B Johnson, *President*
Mark A Johnson, *Corp Secy*
EMP: 21
SQ FT: 20,000
SALES (est): 3.3MM **Privately Held**
WEB: www.aspservicesinc.com
SIC: 3441 Fabricated structural metal

(G-17321)
BENIGNAS CREEK VINEYARD WINE
1 Susquehanna Vly Mall Dr (17870-1271)
PHONE................................570 374-4750
Rick Masser, *Owner*
Mike Masser, *Co-Owner*
EMP: 5 **EST:** 2007

SALES (est): 215.9K **Privately Held**
SIC: 2084 Wines

(G-17322)
BIO-DIVERSITY LLC
2585 Route 522 (17870-8893)
PHONE..................................570 884-3057
John Schrey, *Manager*
EMP: 13
SALES (est): 1.7MM **Privately Held**
SIC: 2448 Wood pallets & skids

(G-17323)
DINOSAW INC
81 Universal Rd (17870-8630)
PHONE..................................570 374-5531
Jim Preussre, *Manager*
EMP: 13
SALES (corp-wide): 3.9MM **Privately Held**
WEB: www.dinosaw.com
SIC: 3425 5085 Saw blades & handsaws; industrial tools
PA: Dinosaw, Inc.
340 Power Ave
Hudson NY 12534
518 828-9942

(G-17324)
EMPIRE KOSHER POULTRY INC
Also Called: K & L Feeds
2243 Route 522 (17870-8731)
PHONE..................................570 374-0501
Michael Shutt, *Mill Mgr*
Mike Watkins, *Manager*
EMP: 26 **Publicly Held**
WEB: www.empirekosher.com
SIC: 2015 Chicken, processed
HQ: Empire Kosher Poultry, Inc.
Chicken Plant Rd
Mifflintown PA 17059
717 436-5921

(G-17325)
EMS SURGICAL LP
801 N Old Trl (17870-7811)
P.O. Box 3619, Fort Myers FL (33918-3619)
PHONE..................................570 374-0569
Edna Stuck, *Partner*
Troy Stuck, *Manager*
EMP: 15
SALES: 1.9MM **Privately Held**
SIC: 2211 Broadwoven fabric mills, cotton

(G-17326)
ICON LGACY CSTM MDLAR HMES LLC
246 Sand Hill Rd (17870-8370)
PHONE..................................570 374-3280
Kevin Hicks, *President*
Jonathan Aungst, *Engineer*
Joseph R Maiolo, *Treasurer*
Connie Nipple, *Admin Sec*
EMP: 45
SALES (est): 9.6MM **Privately Held**
SIC: 2452 Modular homes, prefabricated, wood

(G-17327)
INK SPOT PRINTING
6821 Park Rd (17870-7624)
PHONE..................................570 743-7979
Scott Tanner, *Owner*
EMP: 3
SQ FT: 900
SALES (est): 261.8K **Privately Held**
SIC: 2752 2759 Commercial printing, offset; letterpress printing

(G-17328)
KEN-TEX CORP
Also Called: Parent Company Is Selmax
599 S High St (17870-1311)
P.O. Box 149 (17870-0149)
PHONE..................................570 374-4476
EMP: 20 EST: 1976
SQ FT: 4,000
SALES (est): 2.5MM
SALES (corp-wide): 3.1MM **Privately Held**
SIC: 3544 3552 Mfg Molds Tools Dies & Parts For Textile Machines

PA: Selmax Corp.
599 S High St
Selinsgrove PA 17870
570 374-2833

(G-17329)
KERRICO CORPORATION
2254 Route 522 (17870-8732)
PHONE..................................570 374-9831
Robert Kerris Jr, *President*
Micheal Gill, *General Mgr*
Darlene Snyder, *Manager*
EMP: 35 EST: 1978
SQ FT: 15,800
SALES (est): 3.6MM **Privately Held**
SIC: 3281 Marble, building: cut & shaped; bathroom fixtures, cut stone; table tops, marble

(G-17330)
MARLIN A INCH
Also Called: Penn Valley Printing Company
201 W Pine St (17870-1550)
PHONE..................................570 374-1106
Fax: 570 374-7254
EMP: 4 EST: 1965
SQ FT: 3,200
SALES (est): 240K **Privately Held**
SIC: 2752 2759 Offset Printing

(G-17331)
MIDDLEBURG YARN PROCESSING CO
909 Orange St (17870-1729)
PHONE..................................570 374-1284
Howard Reece, *President*
EMP: 70
SALES (corp-wide): 9.9MM **Privately Held**
SIC: 2282 2284 2281 Throwing yarn; thread mills; yarn spinning mills
PA: Middleburg Yarn Processing Co Inc
375 Diamond Bridge Ave
Hawthorne NJ 07506
973 238-1800

(G-17332)
RIVERVIEW ORTHTICS PROSTHETICS
Also Called: Susquehanna Valley Prosthetics
2 Atrium Ct Ste B (17870-9019)
P.O. Box 243, Shamokin Dam (17876-0243)
PHONE..................................570 743-1414
Donald Dixon, *President*
Vicki Preston, *Business Mgr*
Keith Senn, *CFO*
Michael Mattingly, *Director*
Timothy Nutgrass, *Director*
EMP: 5 EST: 2015
SQ FT: 1,500
SALES (est): 319.5K **Privately Held**
SIC: 3842 Limbs, artificial; braces, orthopedic

(G-17333)
SELINSGROVE INSTNL CSEWORK LLC
Also Called: Wood-Metal Industries
100 E Sherman St (17870-2021)
PHONE..................................570 374-1176
Scott Groce, *Plant Mgr*
Travis Martin, *Manager*
EMP: 40
SALES (est): 3.8MM **Privately Held**
SIC: 2521 Wood office furniture

(G-17334)
SELMAX CORP
599 S High St (17870-1311)
P.O. Box 149 (17870-0149)
PHONE..................................570 374-2833
Paul Koster, *CEO*
Alicia Shaffer, *Office Mgr*
EMP: 21 EST: 1971
SQ FT: 16,000
SALES (est): 4.5MM **Privately Held**
SIC: 3089 Injection molding of plastics

(G-17335)
SNYDER COUNTY AUTOMOTIVE INC
Also Called: NAPA Auto Parts
808 N Market St (17870-2010)
PHONE..................................570 374-2072

Micheal Schlenker, *President*
Steve Beeler, *General Mgr*
Joseph T Brennan, *Corp Secy*
M G Schwartz, *Vice Pres*
EMP: 8 EST: 1966
SALES (est): 1MM **Privately Held**
SIC: 5531 3599 5013 Automotive parts; machine shop, jobbing & repair; automotive supplies & parts

(G-17336)
STOP N GO SIGNS
18 Lenker Ave (17870-9109)
PHONE..................................570 374-3939
Corey Kappen, *Owner*
EMP: 4
SALES (est): 208.9K **Privately Held**
WEB: www.stopngosigns.com
SIC: 3993 Signs, not made in custom sign painting shops

(G-17337)
SUSQUEHANNA VALLEY PROSTHETICS
2 Atrium Ct Ste B (17870-9019)
PHONE..................................570 743-1414
Frank Dominick, *President*
EMP: 10
SALES (est): 1MM **Privately Held**
SIC: 3842 5047 Orthopedic appliances; medical & hospital equipment

(G-17338)
WOOD-MODE INCORPORATED
Also Called: Woode Mode
100 E Sherman St (17870-2021)
PHONE..................................570 374-1176
Harold Persing, *Purchasing*
Scott Groce, *Branch Mgr*
EMP: 30
SALES (corp-wide): 1B **Privately Held**
WEB: www.wood-mode.com
SIC: 2541 2521 2434 Mfg Wood Partitions/Fixtures Mfg Wood Office Furniture Mfg Wood Kitchen Cabinets
PA: Wood-Mode, Incorporated
1 Second St
Kreamer PA 17833
570 374-2711

Sellersville
Bucks County

(G-17339)
AMERICAN SAFETY CLOTHING INC
30 E Park Ave (18960-2705)
PHONE..................................215 257-7667
Barry L Clymer, *President*
EMP: 30
SQ FT: 15,000
SALES (est): 6.6MM **Privately Held**
SIC: 3842 Surgical appliances & supplies

(G-17340)
ANNAMAET PET FOODS INC
41 Daniels Rd (18960-1019)
P.O. Box 151 (18960-0151)
PHONE..................................215 453-0381
Robert Downey, *President*
Mary Downey, *Vice Pres*
Linda Reszneki, *Sales Staff*
▲ EMP: 3
SALES (est): 358.5K **Privately Held**
WEB: www.annamaet.com
SIC: 2047 Dog food

(G-17341)
BUX MONT AWARDS (PA)
Also Called: Bux-Mont Awards and Engrv Svcs
225 N Main St (18960-2331)
PHONE..................................215 257-5432
Gregory Bencsik, *President*
EMP: 7
SALES: 125K **Privately Held**
WEB: www.promopros.com
SIC: 7389 3993 Engraving service; signs & advertising specialties

(G-17342)
D DIETRICH ASSOCIATES INC
9 Blue Rock Dr (18960-1949)
P.O. Box 218, Perkasie (18944-0218)
PHONE..................................215 258-1071
Wayne Dietrich, *President*
EMP: 5 EST: 1973
SALES (est): 530K **Privately Held**
WEB: www.dsurveys.com
SIC: 8748 2721 Publishing consultant; statistical reports (periodicals): publishing only

(G-17343)
DAVES BOAT REPAIR LLC
3 Ridge Valley Rd (18960-1125)
PHONE..................................215 453-6904
David L Klinger, *Principal*
EMP: 3
SALES (est): 323.2K **Privately Held**
SIC: 3732 Boat building & repairing

(G-17344)
DETWILER TOOL CO
720 Ridge Rd (18960-1340)
PHONE..................................215 257-5770
Lloyd Detwiler, *President*
EMP: 5
SQ FT: 5,500
SALES (est): 603.9K **Privately Held**
SIC: 3544 Special dies & tools; dies & die holders for metal cutting, forming, die casting; industrial molds

(G-17345)
DIAMOND TRPCL HARDWOODS INTL (PA)
220 N Main St (18960-2332)
P.O. Box 122 (18960-0122)
PHONE..................................215 257-2556
Kevin Yardley, *President*
John Yardley, *CFO*
Fred Ramos, *Treasurer*
◆ EMP: 6
SQ FT: 6,800
SALES (est): 6.3MM **Privately Held**
WEB: www.diamondtropicalhardwoods.com
SIC: 2511 5047 5031 5021 Wood lawn & garden furniture; medical & hospital equipment; lumber, plywood & millwork; furniture

(G-17346)
FEDEGARI TECHNOLOGIES INC
1228 Bethlehem Pike (18960-1448)
PHONE..................................215 453-0400
Ronal J Sacco, *President*
Anna Ramaioli, *Project Mgr*
Parris Dattilo, *Opers Staff*
Riccardo Boatti, *QC Mgr*
Franco Grugni, *Engineer*
EMP: 18 EST: 2007
SALES (est): 2.5MM
SALES (corp-wide): 63MM **Privately Held**
SIC: 3821 Sterilizers
PA: Fedegari Autoclavi Spa
Strada Statale 235 Di Orzinuovi
Albuzzano PV 27010
038 243-4111

(G-17347)
FEDEGARI TECHNOLOGIES INC
1228 Bethlehem Pike (18960-1448)
PHONE..................................215 453-2180
Giuseppe Fedegari, *President*
Paolo Fedegari, *Vice Pres*
▲ EMP: 14
SQ FT: 9,500
SALES: 5.4MM **Privately Held**
SIC: 3821 Sterilizers

(G-17348)
G&W PA LABORATORIES LLC (HQ)
650 Cathill Rd (18960-1512)
PHONE..................................215 799-5333
Ronald Greenblatt, *Mng Member*
Aaron Greenblatt, *Mng Member*
EMP: 250
SALES: 50MM
SALES (corp-wide): 241.2MM **Privately Held**
SIC: 2834 Pharmaceutical preparations

PA: G & W Laboratories, Inc.
301 Helen St
South Plainfield NJ 07080
908 753-2000

(G-17349)
HENKEL CORP
20 Bricks Way (18960-2900)
PHONE..................................267 424-5645
EMP: 3
SALES (est): 197.6K **Privately Held**
SIC: 2869 Industrial organic chemicals

(G-17350)
JAY WELLER
Also Called: Weller Wood Works
119 3 Mile Run Rd (18960-1821)
PHONE..................................215 257-4859
Jay Weller, Owner
EMP: 3
SALES: 250K **Privately Held**
SIC: 2499 3944 Handles, poles, dowels &
stakes: wood; games, toys & children's
vehicles

(G-17351)
JC WOODWORKING INC
98 Tower Rd (18960-3120)
PHONE..................................215 651-2049
EMP: 15
SALES (corp-wide): 1.7MM **Privately
Held**
SIC: 2431 Millwork
PA: J.C. Woodworking, Inc.
2150 Rosedale Rd
Quakertown PA 18951
215 651-2049

(G-17352)
JM FABRICATIONS LLC
220 N Main St B (18960-2332)
PHONE..................................267 354-1741
Jim McKeone Jr, Principal
EMP: 4
SALES (est): 198.2K **Privately Held**
SIC: 3441 Fabricated structural metal

(G-17353)
LADIE & FRIENDS INC
Also Called: Lizzie High Collection
220 N Main St (18960-2332)
PHONE..................................215 453-8200
Barbara K Wisber, President
Peter F Wisber Jr, Treasurer
April Sherry, Receptionist
EMP: 5
SQ FT: 15,000
SALES (est): 696.9K **Privately Held**
WEB: www.lizziehigh.com
SIC: 3942 5945 Dolls, except stuffed toy
animals; dolls & accessories

(G-17354)
NACEVILLE MATERIALS JV
2001 Ridge Rd (18960-3055)
PHONE..................................215 453-8933
Bob Miller, Owner
Darren Landis, Manager
EMP: 13
SALES (est): 2.2MM
SALES (corp-wide): 2.6MM **Privately
Held**
SIC: 3273 Ready-mixed concrete
PA: Naceville Materials J.V.
350 S Main St Ste 207
Doylestown PA 18901
267 880-2422

(G-17355)
**NORTH PENN POLISHING AND
PLTG**
40 W Park Ave (18960-2540)
P.O. Box 370 (18960-0370)
PHONE..................................215 257-4945
Douglas Imbody, President
Guillaume Gignac, Vice Pres
EMP: 39 **EST:** 1947
SQ FT: 50,000
SALES (est): 4.1MM **Privately Held**
WEB: www.npplating.com
SIC: 3471 Plating of metals or formed
products

(G-17356)
PARKSIDE GRAPHICS INC
Also Called: Becker's Printing
160 E Walnut St (18960-2425)
PHONE..................................215 453-1123
Dennis Becker, President
EMP: 4
SALES (est): 340K **Privately Held**
WEB: www.parksidegraphics.com
SIC: 2752 7336 Commercial printing, litho-
graphic; commercial art & graphic design

(G-17357)
PLASTI-COAT CORP
3225 State Rd (18960-1655)
PHONE..................................475 235-2761
Robert Mitchell, President
Gary Santoro, Vice Pres
▲ **EMP:** 25
SQ FT: 50,000
SALES (est): 3.6MM **Privately Held**
WEB: www.plasti-coat.com
SIC: 2821 Polyvinyl chloride resins (PVC);
molding compounds, plastics

(G-17358)
SELL-IT
Also Called: It Sell
1214 Ridge Rd (18960-1350)
PHONE..................................215 453-8937
Peter Tascarella, Owner
EMP: 4
SQ FT: 2,500
SALES (est): 150.8K **Privately Held**
SIC: 2711 5521 Newspapers: publishing
only, not printed on site; used car dealers

(G-17359)
**TEVA PHARMACEUTICALS USA
INC**
650 Cathill Rd (18960-1512)
PHONE..................................215 591-3000
Frank Raffaele, Materials Mgr
Martin Haring, QA Mgr
Seetha Murthy, Research
Eric Klingaman, Engineer
Melanie Nano, Engineer
EMP: 106
SALES (corp-wide): 18.8B **Privately Held**
WEB: www.lemmon.com
SIC: 2834 Pharmaceutical preparations
HQ: Teva Pharmaceuticals Usa, Inc.
1090 Horsham Rd
North Wales PA 19454
215 591-3000

(G-17360)
TOHICKON CORP (PA)
Also Called: Tohickon Glass Eyes
60 Noble St (18960-2310)
P.O. Box 15, Erwinna (18920-0015)
PHONE..................................267 450-5020
Barbara Murray, President
Jessie N Alfaro, Vice Pres
Antonio R Alfaro, Director
▲ **EMP:** 2
SQ FT: 2,500
SALES (est): 3.8MM **Privately Held**
WEB: www.tohickonglasseyes.com
SIC: 3851 3231 Eyes, glass & plastic;
products of purchased glass

(G-17361)
U S PLASTIC COATINGS CORP
3225 State Rd (18960-1655)
PHONE..................................215 257-5300
Scott Ketterer, President
▲ **EMP:** 25
SQ FT: 22,000
SALES (est): 3MM **Privately Held**
SIC: 3479 3089 Painting, coating & hot
dipping; coating of metals & formed prod-
ucts; plastic processing; injection molding
of plastics; injection molded finished plas-
tic products

(G-17362)
**WISMER MACHINE COMPANY
INC**
1006 Old Bethlehem Pike (18960-1422)
PHONE..................................215 257-5081
Robert S Jones, President
Patricia Jones, Corp Secy
EMP: 7
SQ FT: 4,000

SALES: 1.3MM **Privately Held**
SIC: 3599 Machine shop, jobbing & repair

Seminole
Armstrong County

(G-17363)
RICHARD SHILLING JR
Also Called: Rich and Sons
209 Chestnut Ave (16253-1213)
PHONE..................................814 319-4326
Richard Shilling Jr, Owner
EMP: 5
SALES (est): 239.8K **Privately Held**
SIC: 3523 Greens mowing equipment

Seneca
Venango County

(G-17364)
BILL HARDS
Also Called: Hards Welding & Fabricating
231 Gilmore Dr (16346-2409)
PHONE..................................814 677-2460
Bill Hard, Owner
EMP: 14 **EST:** 1994
SQ FT: 8,000
SALES (est): 2MM **Privately Held**
SIC: 3599 1799 Machine shop, jobbing &
repair; welding on site

(G-17365)
CABINET STORE
3272 State Route 257 (16346-2532)
PHONE..................................814 677-5522
Tom Schettler, President
William Schettler, Vice Pres
Kathleen Schettler, Treasurer
Timberly Schettler, Admin Sec
EMP: 4
SALES: 400K **Privately Held**
SIC: 2434 Wood kitchen cabinets

(G-17366)
MATRIC GROUP LLC (PA)
2099 Hill City Rd (16346-3711)
PHONE..................................814 677-0716
Terry Havens-Turner, Corp Secy
Tod George, CFO
Richard E Turner Jr,
◆ **EMP:** 277
SQ FT: 80,000
SALES: 52MM **Privately Held**
WEB: www.matricgroup.com
SIC: 3672 3511 3663 3679 Printed circuit
boards; turbines & turbine generator sets;
radio & TV communications equipment;
electronic switches; electronic computers;
assembly machines, non-metalworking

(G-17367)
QRS MUSIC INC (PA)
Also Called: Q-R-S Music Rolls
269 Quaker Dr (16346-2419)
P.O. Box 110280, Naples FL (34108-0105)
PHONE..................................239 597-5888
Tom Dolan, President
▲ **EMP:** 6
SQ FT: 11,913
SALES (est): 10.6MM **Publicly Held**
SIC: 3931 5736 Music rolls, perforated;
piano parts & materials; pianos, all types:
vertical, grand, spinet, player, etc.; key-
board instruments

(G-17368)
**QRS MUSIC TECHNOLOGIES
INC (HQ)**
Also Called: Story & Clark Piano's
269 Quaker Dr (16346-2419)
PHONE..................................814 676-6683
Richard A Dolan, Ch of Bd
Thomas A Dolan, President
Ann A Jones, CFO
Lori Clutter, Regl Sales Mgr
Tim Omiatek, Manager
▲ **EMP:** 8 **EST:** 1990
SQ FT: 4,000

SALES (est): 2.5MM
SALES (corp-wide): 10.6MM **Publicly
Held**
WEB: www.qrsmusic.com
SIC: 3931 5736 Music rolls, perforated;
piano parts & materials; pianos, all types:
vertical, grand, spinet, player, etc.; key-
board instruments; pianos
PA: Qrs Music Inc.
269 Quaker Dr
Seneca PA 16346
239 597-5888

(G-17369)
SCHAKE INDUSTRIES INC
3467 State Route 257 (16346-2927)
P.O. Box 564 (16346-0564)
PHONE..................................814 677-9333
Bob Baker, CEO
Mark Kline, President
Steven Schake, Principal
Kerby Elliott, Engineer
▲ **EMP:** 20
SQ FT: 20,000
SALES: 3.5MM **Privately Held**
WEB: www.schakeinc.com
SIC: 3549 3535 3471 3479 Assembly
machines, including robotic; conveyors &
conveying equipment; plating & polishing;
coating of metals & formed products; stor-
age tanks, metal; erection

(G-17370)
VENANGO COUNTY NOTARY
3537 State Rt 357 (16346)
PHONE..................................814 677-2216
Ed Caton, Principal
EMP: 5
SALES (est): 397.9K **Privately Held**
SIC: 3469 Automobile license tags,
stamped metal

(G-17371)
**VENANGO TRAINING & DEV CTR
INC (PA)**
Also Called: Venango Innovative Services
239 Quaker Dr (16346-2417)
P.O. Box 289 (16346-0289)
PHONE..................................814 676-5755
Susanna Giesey, Manager
Colleen Stuart, Exec Dir
EMP: 56
SQ FT: 28,800
SALES: 4MM **Privately Held**
WEB: www.vtdc.org
SIC: 8331 2789 Vocational training
agency; bookbinding & related work

(G-17372)
WINDURANCE
2099 Hill City Rd (16346-3711)
PHONE..................................814 678-1318
George Karg, Principal
EMP: 5
SALES (est): 598K **Privately Held**
SIC: 3621 Windmills, electric generating

(G-17373)
WORLD OF WHEELS INC
2572 State Route 257 (16346-2120)
PHONE..................................814 676-5721
Robert J Felmlee, President
Gertrude K Vandermaak, Admin Sec
EMP: 12 **EST:** 1981
SQ FT: 12,500
SALES (est): 3MM **Privately Held**
WEB: www.worldofwheels6.com
SIC: 5571 3799 3621 Motorcycles; all ter-
rain vehicles (ATV); motors & generators

Seven Fields
Butler County

(G-17374)
**BRUSTERS OLD FASHIONED
ICE CRE**
510 Northpointe Cir (16046-7868)
PHONE..................................724 772-9999
Mark Neely, Principal
EMP: 4

SALES (est): 217K **Privately Held**
SIC: **2024** 5143 5812 Ice cream & frozen desserts; frozen dairy desserts; ice cream stands or dairy bars

(G-17375)
KINKISHARYO USA INC
2100 Garden Dr Ste 201 (16046-7870)
PHONE.................................724 778-0100
John Pekarcik, *Manager*
EMP: 4
SALES (est): 181.6K **Privately Held**
SIC: **3743** Train cars & equipment, freight or passenger

(G-17376)
MICHELIN NORTH AMERICA INC
100 Northpointe Cir (16046-7851)
PHONE.................................301 641-0121
Tony McNeill, *Branch Mgr*
EMP: 402
SALES (corp-wide): 1B **Privately Held**
WEB: www.michelin-us.com
SIC: **3011** Tires & inner tubes
HQ: Michelin North America, Inc.
1 Parkway S
Greenville SC 29615
864 458-5000

Seven Valleys
York County

(G-17377)
DIVERSIFIED TRAFFIC PDTS INC
Also Called: Mercury Electronics
3846 Green Valley Rd (17360-8608)
P.O. Box 248 (17360-0248)
PHONE.................................717 428-0222
Gary M Hayers, *President*
Gary M Hayes, *President*
Sue Houck, *Materials Mgr*
John Hunt, *Electrical Engi*
Gregory M Myers, *CFO*
▲ EMP: 220
SQ FT: 27,000
SALES (est): 43.4MM **Privately Held**
WEB: www.mercuryelectronics.com
SIC: **3679** 5063 5046 3357 Harness assemblies for electronic use: wire or cable; signaling equipment, electrical; signs, electrical; nonferrous wiredrawing & insulating

(G-17378)
EFFECTIVE PLAN INC
47 Cherry St (17360-8955)
PHONE.................................717 428-6190
Isaac Dvory, *President*
EMP: 5
SALES (est): 532K **Privately Held**
SIC: **2253** 5699 T-shirts & tops, knit; shirts, custom made

(G-17379)
HANDYGAS CORPORATION (PA)
7927 Player Blvd (17360-9173)
PHONE.................................717 428-2506
Donald Smith, *CEO*
Michael A Smith, *President*
Phyllis Smith, *Treasurer*
EMP: 7
SALES: 150K **Privately Held**
WEB: www.handygascorp.com
SIC: **5172** 3559 Gases, liquefied petroleum (propane); refinery, chemical processing & similar machinery

(G-17380)
SPECIALTY TSTG & DEV CO INC
21 Church St (17360-8713)
P.O. Box 296 (17360-0296)
PHONE.................................717 428-0186
Frank Leaman, *CEO*
Diane Gibble, *President*
EMP: 8
SALES (est): 250K **Privately Held**
SIC: **3826** 7389 Coulometric analyzers, except industrial process type;

Seward
Westmoreland County

(G-17381)
ENVIRNMNTAL ENRGY SLUTIONS LLC
10027 Route 403 Hwy S (15954-8925)
PHONE.................................814 446-5625
Bryan Force, *Managing Prtnr*
EMP: 8
SQ FT: 10,000
SALES (est): 930K **Privately Held**
SIC: **3713** Utility truck bodies

(G-17382)
MILLWORK SOLUTIONS INC
450 Route 711 Hwy (15954-8620)
PHONE.................................814 446-4009
Anthony Gangi, *President*
John W Mundy, *President*
EMP: 20
SQ FT: 22,000
SALES (est): 2.4MM **Privately Held**
WEB: www.millworksolutions.com
SIC: **2431** 2541 2521 2434 Millwork; wood partitions & fixtures; wood office furniture; wood kitchen cabinets

Sewickley
Allegheny County

(G-17383)
BADEN STEELBAR & BOLT CORP
852 Big Sewickley Crk R (15143-8652)
P.O. Box 414 (15143-0414)
PHONE.................................724 266-3003
Mark Holzbach, *President*
EMP: 16
SQ FT: 15,000
SALES (est): 3.7MM **Privately Held**
WEB: www.badensteel.com
SIC: **5072** 3452 Bolts; bolts, metal

(G-17384)
CARTRIDGE SPECIALIST
111 Linda Vista Rd (15143-9523)
PHONE.................................412 741-4442
George W Logan, *Owner*
EMP: 5
SALES (est): 240K **Privately Held**
SIC: **3955** 7378 Print cartridges for laser & other computer printers; computer maintenance & repair

(G-17385)
CROUSE RUN VENTURES INC
706 Timber Ln (15143-8959)
PHONE.................................412 491-5738
John Cain, *CEO*
EMP: 3
SALES (est): 124.5K **Privately Held**
SIC: **3499** Fabricated metal products

(G-17386)
ESMARK INC (PA)
100 Hazel Ln Ste 300 (15143-1249)
PHONE.................................412 259-8868
James P Bouchard, *CEO*
J Gregory Pilewicz, *President*
Stephen W Powers, *Exec VP*
Karl F Csensich, *CFO*
Michael P Diclemente, *Treasurer*
EMP: 18
SALES (est): 249.1MM **Privately Held**
SIC: **1382** 3324 Oil & gas exploration services; steel investment foundries

(G-17387)
ESMARK INDUSTRIAL GROUP LLC (HQ)
100 Hazel Ln Ste 300 (15143-1249)
PHONE.................................412 259-8868
David A Luptak, *CEO*
EMP: 11

SALES (est): 26.1MM
SALES (corp-wide): 249.1MM **Privately Held**
SIC: **3441** 5084 Fabricated structural metal; machine tools & metalworking machinery
PA: Esmark, Inc.
100 Hazel Ln Ste 300
Sewickley PA 15143
412 259-8868

(G-17388)
EVEOS CORPORATION
1888 Pioneer Dr (15143-8585)
PHONE.................................412 366-0159
Steven Radney, *CEO*
Evens Augustin, *CFO*
EMP: 3
SALES (est): 171.7K **Privately Held**
SIC: **3845** Electromedical equipment

(G-17389)
H-D ADVANCED MANUFACTURING CO (PA)
2200 Georgetown Dr # 300 (15143-8752)
PHONE.................................724 759-2850
Michael Vincent, *President*
Dale Mikus, *CFO*
EMP: 4
SALES (est): 59.4MM **Privately Held**
SIC: **3728** Gears, aircraft power transmission

(G-17390)
HAMAMATSU CORPORATION
2593 Wexford Bayne Rd # 305 (15143-8608)
PHONE.................................724 935-3600
Bill Burnip, *Manager*
Ellen Dugan, *Manager*
EMP: 6
SALES (corp-wide): 1.3B **Privately Held**
SIC: **3671** Photomultiplier tubes
HQ: Hamamatsu Corporation
360 Foothill Rd
Bridgewater NJ 08807
908 231-0960

(G-17391)
HG ENERGY LLC
2200 Georgetown Dr # 501 (15143-8752)
PHONE.................................724 935-8952
Jared Hall,
EMP: 6
SQ FT: 2,500
SALES (est): 784.1K **Privately Held**
SIC: **1382** Oil & gas exploration services

(G-17392)
HOEHL ASSOC
508 Grove St (15143-1233)
PHONE.................................412 741-4170
EMP: 4
SALES (est): 319.9K **Privately Held**
SIC: **3999** Mfg Misc Products

(G-17393)
HRP METALS INC
207 Overlook Dr Ste 8 (15143-2605)
PHONE.................................412 741-6781
Hasmukh Parekh, *President*
Abhishek Parekh, *Vice Pres*
EMP: 7
SQ FT: 5,000
SALES (est): 1.1MM **Privately Held**
WEB: www.komalherbals.com
SIC: **3399** Silver powder; flakes, metal

(G-17394)
INDEPENDENT CONCEPTS INC
109 Priscilla Dr (15143-8714)
PHONE.................................412 741-7903
Frederick J Kellinger, *President*
Richard Plum, *Principal*
Lawrence M Turner, *CFO*
Virginia Betz Kellinger, *Admin Sec*
EMP: 5
SQ FT: 225
SALES (est): 391.3K **Privately Held**
WEB: www.independentconcepts.com
SIC: **2843** Processing assistants

(G-17395)
INTERLOCKING DECK SYSTEMS INTE
Also Called: I D S I Fabrication Machining
921 Beaver St (15143-1747)
PHONE.................................412 682-3041
Alexander Simakas,
Ed Coholich,
EMP: 54
SQ FT: 120,000
SALES (est): 10MM **Privately Held**
SIC: **3441** 1622 Fabricated structural metal for bridges; bridge construction

(G-17396)
JETNET CORPORATION (PA)
505 North Dr (15143-2339)
PHONE.................................412 741-0100
Donald G Sartore, *President*
William L Sartore, *Vice Pres*
Craig Hartle, *Plant Mgr*
Michael A Spitznagle, *Treasurer*
Ron Howard, *Sales Executive*
◆ EMP: 76 EST: 1966
SALES (est): 15.3MM **Privately Held**
WEB: www.jetnetcorp.com
SIC: **3089** 2399 2393 2259 Thermoformed finished plastic products; hammocks & other net products; textile bags; meat bagging, knit; weft knit fabric mills; broadwoven fabric mills, manmade

(G-17397)
JKA INC (PA)
Also Called: Arnold Printed Communications
1718 Mount Nebo Rd (15143-8564)
PHONE.................................412 741-9288
Kristin Arnold, *President*
EMP: 11
SQ FT: 1,300
SALES (est): 3.3MM **Privately Held**
WEB: www.arnoldprint.com
SIC: **5112** 2752 Business forms; color lithography

(G-17398)
JKLM ENERGY LLC
2200 Georgetown Dr # 500 (15143-8750)
PHONE.................................561 826-3620
EMP: 3
SALES (est): 434.4K **Privately Held**
SIC: **1389** Oil field services

(G-17399)
LINDE GAS NORTH AMERICA LLC
Also Called: Lifegas
503 North Dr (15143-2339)
PHONE.................................412 741-6613
Mike Benscoter, *Branch Mgr*
EMP: 19 **Privately Held**
SIC: **2813** Nitrogen; oxygen, compressed or liquefied
PA: Linde Gas North America Llc
200 Somerset Corp Blvd # 7000
Bridgewater NJ 08807

(G-17400)
MCLAUGHLIN DISTILLERY
3799 Blackburn Rd (15143-8535)
PHONE.................................315 486-1372
Kim McLaughlin, *Principal*
EMP: 3
SALES (est): 68.6K **Privately Held**
SIC: **2082** Malt beverages

(G-17401)
OPTOTHERM INC
2591 Wexford Bayne Rd (15143-8676)
PHONE.................................724 940-7600
Richard Barton, *President*
Al Stricker, *General Mgr*
EMP: 8
SALES (est): 1.5MM **Privately Held**
WEB: www.optotherm.com
SIC: **3829** Measuring & controlling devices

(G-17402)
OSI INDUSTRIES
101 Sonie Dr (15143-8587)
PHONE.................................412 741-3630
EMP: 3
SALES (est): 106.8K **Privately Held**
SIC: **3999** Mfg Misc Products

(G-17403)
PITTSBURGH STAGE INC
2 South Ave (15143-2108)
PHONE..................................412 534-4500
Allen P Fowkes, *Principal*
Jake Poling, *Sales Staff*
David Seifert, *Director*
▲ EMP: 31
SQ FT: 35,000
SALES (est): 3.8MM Privately Held
WEB: www.pittsburghstage.com
SIC: 3999 5063 Stage hardware & equipment, except lighting; lighting fixtures, commercial & industrial

(G-17404)
PRO PAK CONTAINERS INC
103 Chateau Ct (15143-9569)
PHONE..................................412 741-0549
George Galoop, *President*
EMP: 4
SALES (est): 321.7K Privately Held
SIC: 2631 Container, packaging & boxboard

(G-17405)
PROFESSIONAL GRAPHIC CO
2260 Big Swckly Crk Rd (15143-8621)
PHONE..................................724 318-8530
Michael J Weinzierl, *President*
EMP: 30
SQ FT: 3,000
SALES (est): 7.4MM Privately Held
WEB: www.pgcinc.com
SIC: 5112 2752 7331 2796 Business forms; commercial printing, lithographic; mailing service; platemaking services; typesetting; commercial printing

(G-17406)
QUANTUM QUBE INC
2629 Syracuse Ct (15143-6520)
PHONE..................................412 767-0506
SAI Mandava, *President*
EMP: 3
SALES (est): 191.1K Privately Held
SIC: 3572 Computer storage devices

(G-17407)
RESPIRONICS INC
137 Gary Dr (15143-9549)
PHONE..................................724 733-5803
Jeffry Huth, *Engineer*
Greg Prevenslik, *Engineer*
Leverda Wallace, *Surgery Dir*
EMP: 164
SALES (corp-wide): 20.9B Privately Held
WEB: www.respironics.com
SIC: 3842 Surgical appliances & supplies
HQ: Respironics, Inc.
1001 Murry Ridge Ln
Murrysville PA 15668
724 387-5200

(G-17408)
SEWICKLEY CREEK GREENHOUSE
2639 Big Swckly Crk Rd (15143-8642)
PHONE..................................724 935-8500
Janet Helbling, *Principal*
EMP: 3
SQ FT: 500
SALES (est): 203.8K Privately Held
SIC: 5947 3448 Gift shop; greenhouses: prefabricated metal

(G-17409)
SEWICKLEY HERALD
504 Beaver St (15143-1753)
PHONE..................................412 324-1403
EMP: 3 EST: 2017
SALES (est): 116K Privately Held
SIC: 2711 Newspapers, publishing & printing

(G-17410)
SEWICKLEY VILLAGE FUEL AND SVC
590 Beaver St (15143-1779)
PHONE..................................412 741-9972
Edward Brosie, *Owner*
EMP: 3
SALES (est): 375.5K Privately Held
SIC: 2869 Fuels

(G-17411)
SOLAR TURBINES INCORPORATED
2200 Georgetown Dr # 601 (15143-8752)
PHONE..................................724 759-7800
John Hutchins, *Manager*
EMP: 89
SALES (corp-wide): 54.7B Publicly Held
WEB: www.esolar.cat.com
SIC: 3511 Gas turbine generator set units, complete
HQ: Solar Turbines Incorporated
2200 Pacific Hwy
San Diego CA 92101
619 544-5000

(G-17412)
SP ENVIRONMENTAL INC
1718 Mount Nebo Rd (15143-8564)
PHONE..................................724 935-1300
▲ EMP: 50
SALES (est): 4.5MM Privately Held
SIC: 3564 8711 Mfg Blowers/Fans Engineering Services

(G-17413)
STEMMETRY
1529 Brimfield Dr (15143-8538)
PHONE..................................678 770-6781
Kevin C Lei, *Principal*
EMP: 4
SALES (est): 182.5K Privately Held
SIC: 2833 Vitamins, natural or synthetic: bulk, uncompounded

(G-17414)
TAMINI TRANSFORMERS USA LLC
518 Broad St Ste 1 (15143-1708)
PHONE..................................412 534-4275
Gary Urso, *Mng Member*
EMP: 3
SALES (est): 408.8K Privately Held
SIC: 3612 Transformers, except electric

(G-17415)
WINE CONCRETE PRODUCTS INC
1000 Big Swckly Crk Rd (15143-8689)
PHONE..................................724 266-9500
Floyd Wine, *President*
EMP: 35
SALES (est): 5.7MM Privately Held
SIC: 3272 3273 Precast terrazo or concrete products; ready-mixed concrete

Shade Gap
Huntingdon County

(G-17416)
SHADE GAP FARM SUPPLIES
21963 Croghan Pike (17255-9215)
PHONE..................................814 259-3258
Mike Morgan, *Owner*
EMP: 3
SQ FT: 3,000
SALES (est): 275.4K Privately Held
SIC: 2048 5191 5251 Prepared feeds; animal feeds; hardware

(G-17417)
VALLEY MACHINE LTD
11210 Dlg Dr (17255-8811)
P.O. Box 62 (17255-0062)
PHONE..................................814 259-3624
David Gischel, *President*
EMP: 3
SQ FT: 1,800
SALES (est): 220K Privately Held
SIC: 3599 Machine shop, jobbing & repair

(G-17418)
WOOD MIZER (PA)
Also Called: Parsons Garage
22638 Croghan Pike (17255-9271)
PHONE..................................814 259-9976
Martin R Parsons, *Owner*
Lisa Parsons, *Principal*
Tyler Smith, *Accountant*
EMP: 3

SALES (est): 570.2K Privately Held
SIC: 2421 Sawmills & planing mills, general

(G-17419)
WOOD-MIZER HOLDINGS INC
Also Called: Wood-Mizer Resharp
22638 Croghan Pike (17255-9271)
PHONE..................................814 259-9976
Martin Parsons, *Manager*
EMP: 3
SALES (corp-wide): 127.3MM Privately Held
WEB: www.lastec.com
SIC: 2421 Sawmills & planing mills, general
PA: Wood-Mizer Holdings, Inc.
8180 W 10th St
Indianapolis IN 46214
317 271-1542

Shady Grove
Franklin County

(G-17420)
GROVE US LLC
Also Called: Manitowoc Crane Group
1565 Buchanan Trl E (17256)
P.O. Box 21 (17256-0021)
PHONE..................................717 597-8121
Dave Birkhauser, *Vice Pres*
Eric Spring, *Engineer*
Eric Etchart, *Mng Member*
Glen E Tellock,
Larry Weyers,
◆ EMP: 82 EST: 1998
SALES (est): 85.5MM
SALES (corp-wide): 1.8B Publicly Held
WEB: www.groveworldwide.com
SIC: 3531 3537 Cranes; platforms, cargo
HQ: Manitowoc Cranes, Llc
2401 S 30th St
Manitowoc WI 54220

(G-17421)
GROVE WORLDWIDE LLC
1565 Buchanan Trl E (17256)
PHONE..................................717 597-8121
Larry Weyers, *Mng Member*
◆ EMP: 74 EST: 1989
SALES (est): 43.8MM
SALES (corp-wide): 1.8B Publicly Held
WEB: www.grovecraneparts.com
SIC: 3536 Hoists, cranes & monorails
PA: The Manitowoc Company Inc
11270 W Park Pl Ste 1000
Milwaukee WI 53224
414 760-4600

(G-17422)
NATIONAL CRANE CORPORATION
1565 Buchanan Trl E (17256)
PHONE..................................717 597-8121
Ted J Urbanek, *President*
James Hansbrough, *Vice Pres*
◆ EMP: 9
SQ FT: 220,000
SALES (est): 5.1MM
SALES (corp-wide): 1.8B Publicly Held
WEB: www.cranecare.com
SIC: 3531 3536 Cranes; hoists, cranes & monorails
HQ: Manitowoc Cranes, Llc
2401 S 30th St
Manitowoc WI 54220

Shamokin
Northumberland County

(G-17423)
CLARKS FEED MILLS INC
19 Mountain Rd (17872-7518)
P.O. Box W (17872-0923)
PHONE..................................570 648-4351
Robert W Clark, *President*
Sue Clark Mansell, *Treasurer*
▲ EMP: 26
SQ FT: 40,000

SALES (est): 5.5MM Privately Held
SIC: 2048 Chicken feeds, prepared; poultry feeds; stock feeds, dry

(G-17424)
JENS FLOWERS & MORE
618 N 8th St (17872-5304)
PHONE..................................570 898-3176
Jennifer S Sandri, *Principal*
EMP: 3 EST: 2007
SALES (est): 200.4K Privately Held
SIC: 3269 Pottery products

(G-17425)
MARIONETTE COMPANY INC
401 S Pearl St (17872-6507)
PHONE..................................570 644-1936
Dennis Wellskie, *Plant Mgr*
EMP: 14
SALES (corp-wide): 25MM Privately Held
SIC: 2299 Coir yarns & roving
PA: The Marionette Company Inc
3003 Piedmont Rd Ne Fl 2
Atlanta GA 30305
404 995-8785

(G-17426)
NEWS ITEM CIN 5
707 N Rock St (17872-4930)
P.O. Box 587 (17872-0587)
PHONE..................................570 644-0891
Barbara Freeman, *Principal*
Andy Heintzelman, *Editor*
Tim Zyla, *Editor*
Aimee Eckley, *Director*
Bob Marciniak, *Director*
EMP: 15
SALES (est): 866.1K Privately Held
SIC: 2711 Newspapers, publishing & printing

(G-17427)
THE SCRANTON TIMES L P
Also Called: Shamokin News Item
707 N Rock St (17872-4930)
P.O. Box 587 (17872-0587)
PHONE..................................570 644-6397
EMP: 84
SALES (corp-wide): 114.5MM Privately Held
SIC: 2711 Newspapers, publishing & printing
PA: The Scranton Times L P
149 Penn Ave Ste 1
Scranton PA 18503
570 348-9100

Shamokin Dam
Snyder County

(G-17428)
SVPO INC
3120 N Old Trl (17876-9428)
PHONE..................................570 743-1414
Frank Dominic, *President*
Katie Marquez, *Vice Pres*
EMP: 10
SALES (est): 1MM Privately Held
SIC: 3842 Prosthetic appliances

(G-17429)
TRAUTMAN ASSOCIATES INC (PA)
Also Called: On Fire Promotions
2832 N Susquehanna Trl (17876-9109)
P.O. Box 489 (17876-0489)
PHONE..................................570 743-0430
Gregory H Trautman, *President*
Karen K Trautman, *Vice Pres*
EMP: 14
SQ FT: 3,000
SALES: 750K Privately Held
SIC: 5199 5999 2759 2679 Advertising specialties; trophies & plaques; screen printing; labels, paper: made from purchased material; embroidery products, except schiffli machine

Sharon
Mercer County

(G-17430)
CALVERT LUMBER COMPANY INC
139 W Budd St (16146-1697)
P.O. Box 677 (16146-0677)
PHONE..................................724 346-5553
Jerry Calvert, *President*
Deborah Calvert, *Treasurer*
Sharon Calvert, *Admin Sec*
EMP: 15 **EST:** 1943
SQ FT: 4,000
SALES (est): 3.7MM **Privately Held**
WEB: www.calvertlumberco.com
SIC: 5211 2499 Lumber & other building materials; fencing, docks & other outdoor wood structural products

(G-17431)
CROSSTEX INTERNATIONAL INC
534 Vine Ave (16146-2151)
PHONE..................................724 347-0400
Robert J Rabiea MD, *Vice Pres*
Bill French, *Branch Mgr*
EMP: 25
SALES (corp-wide): 871.9MM **Publicly Held**
WEB: www.crosstex.com
SIC: 3081 Polyethylene film
HQ: Crosstex International, Inc.
　10 Ranick Rd
　Hauppauge NY 11788
　631 582-6777

(G-17432)
DAFFINS INC (PA)
Also Called: Daffin's Candies
496 E State St (16146-2056)
PHONE..................................724 342-2892
Jean M Daffin, *President*
Diane Daffin, *Principal*
Connie Leon, *Marketing Mgr*
▲ **EMP:** 50
SQ FT: 11,000
SALES (est): 15MM **Privately Held**
WEB: www.daffins.com
SIC: 2064 5441 5947 Candy & other confectionery products; confectionery; greeting cards; gift shop

(G-17433)
FESSLER MACHINE COMPANY
800 N Water Ave (16146-4801)
P.O. Box 451 (16146-0451)
PHONE..................................724 346-0878
Terry Dudzenski, *Branch Mgr*
EMP: 40
SALES (corp-wide): 8.3MM **Privately Held**
WEB: www.fesslermachine.com
SIC: 3492 3593 3535 3547 Fluid power valves & hose fittings; fluid power cylinders, hydraulic or pneumatic; conveyors & conveying equipment; rolling mill machinery; valves & pipe fittings; iron & steel forgings
PA: Fessler Machine Company
　800 N Water Ave
　Sharon PA 16146
　412 367-3663

(G-17434)
FESSLER MACHINE COMPANY (PA)
800 N Water Ave (16146-4801)
PHONE..................................412 367-3663
C Edward Fessler III, *President*
Charles E Fessler Jr, *President*
Charles Fessler III, *Vice Pres*
Lawrence Lloyd, *Controller*
Doris Fessler, *Admin Sec*
EMP: 5
SQ FT: 2,000
SALES (est): 8.3MM **Privately Held**
WEB: www.fesslermachine.com
SIC: 3561 Cylinders, pump

(G-17435)
GRIMMS INC
Also Called: Grimm's Awnings
1017 Myrtle Pl (16146-3038)
P.O. Box 533 (16146-0533)
PHONE..................................724 346-4952
Jerry Grimm, *President*
Kim Hughes, *Vice Pres*
EMP: 9 **EST:** 1926
SQ FT: 2,000
SALES (est): 1MM **Privately Held**
WEB: www.grimmsinc.com
SIC: 2394 3444 7359 Awnings, fabric: made from purchased materials; tents: made from purchased materials; awnings, sheet metal; tent & tarpaulin rental

(G-17436)
HIGH VOLTAGE SOLUTIONS SLS INC
359 Vine Ave (16146-2183)
PHONE..................................412 523-0238
Keith Rypczyk, *President*
EMP: 3
SALES (est): 302.1K **Privately Held**
SIC: 3612 Transformers, except electric

(G-17437)
J & R BECK INC
Also Called: Sharon Commercial Printing
309 Penn Ave (16146-1534)
P.O. Box 681 (16146-0681)
PHONE..................................724 981-5220
Randall A Beck, *President*
Dana Catoline-Wasser, *Graphic Designe*
EMP: 12
SQ FT: 11,500
SALES (est): 1.2MM **Privately Held**
WEB: www.jrbeck.com
SIC: 2752 Commercial printing, offset

(G-17438)
MERCER CO
Also Called: Warren Scrap
200 Stewart Way (16146-1610)
P.O. Box 29, Girard OH (44420-0029)
PHONE..................................724 347-4534
Michael Clayman, *CEO*
Gary Clyman, *CEO*
David P Miller, *Ch of Bd*
Mike Diamond, *COO*
Fred B Knox, *Vice Pres*
EMP: 30
SQ FT: 12,000
SALES (est): 9MM **Privately Held**
SIC: 3312 Blast furnaces & steel mills
HQ: Liberty Iron & Metal Southwest, Llc
　2144 W Mcdowell Rd
　Phoenix AZ 85009
　602 254-2154

(G-17439)
NEVILLE ISLAND RR HOLDINGS INC
American Way (16146)
PHONE..................................724 981-4100
Wm S Hansen, *President*
Jack Rowland, *Treasurer*
EMP: 10
SALES (est): 1.5MM **Privately Held**
SIC: 3743 Railroad equipment

(G-17440)
NEWSPAPER HOLDING INC
Also Called: Sharon Herald
52 S Dock St (16146-1808)
P.O. Box 51 (16146-0051)
PHONE..................................724 981-6100
Sharon Sorg, *Branch Mgr*
Matt Der Meulen, *Info Tech Mgr*
EMP: 51
SQ FT: 6,500 **Privately Held**
WEB: www.clintonnc.com
SIC: 2711 Newspapers, publishing & printing
HQ: Newspaper Holding, Inc.
　425 Locust St
　Johnstown PA 15901
　814 532-5102

(G-17441)
NOISE SOLUTIONS (USA) INC
420 Vine Ave (16146-2149)
P.O. Box 650 (16146-0650)
PHONE..................................724 308-6901

Scott McDonald, *President*
EMP: 22
SALES (est): 4.1MM
SALES (corp-wide): 3.2MM **Privately Held**
SIC: 3625 1541 Noise control equipment; industrial buildings & warehouses; industrial buildings, new construction; prefabricated building erection, industrial; steel building construction
PA: Noise Solutions Inc
　3015 5 Ave Ne Unit 210
　Calgary AB T2A 6
　403 232-0916

(G-17442)
SHARON COATING LLC
277 N Sharpsville Ave (16146-2153)
PHONE..................................724 983-6464
Christopher H Lake, *President*
Bryan Murphy, *Foreman/Supr*
▲ **EMP:** 220
SQ FT: 245,000
SALES (est): 27.9MM **Privately Held**
WEB: www.winnersteel.com
SIC: 3479 3312 Galvanizing of iron, steel or end-formed products; blast furnaces & steel mills

(G-17443)
SPEC SCIENCES INC
758 Thornton St (16146-3576)
PHONE..................................607 972-3159
Craig Borawski, *Vice Pres*
Joseph Scott, *Vice Pres*
Patrick Scott, *Treasurer*
EMP: 3
SALES (est): 250K **Privately Held**
WEB: www.ultrasonic-alcohol.com
SIC: 3589 3699 3845 Commercial cleaning equipment; cleaning equipment, ultrasonic, except medical & dental; medical cleaning equipment, ultrasonic

(G-17444)
VICTOR PRINTING INC (PA)
1 Victor Way (16146)
PHONE..................................724 342-2106
Terence A Richards, *President*
William G Richards, *Vice Pres*
Kim Nanosky, *Marketing Mgr*
Larry Weiser, *Manager*
▲ **EMP:** 100
SQ FT: 70,000
SALES (est): 22.7MM **Privately Held**
WEB: www.victorptg.com
SIC: 2761 2752 Manifold business forms; commercial printing, lithographic

(G-17445)
WHEATLAND TUBE LLC
Also Called: Wheatland Tube Company
134 Mill St (16146-2118)
PHONE..................................724 981-5200
William Kerins, *Manager*
EMP: 100 **Privately Held**
SIC: 3317 3644 Pipes, seamless steel; electric conduits & fittings
HQ: Wheatland Tube, Llc
　700 S Dock St
　Sharon PA 16146
　800 257-8182

(G-17446)
WHEATLAND TUBE LLC
Also Called: Spw Warehouse
1169 N Sharpsville Ave (16146-2442)
PHONE..................................724 342-6851
Carol Pylypiw, *Manager*
EMP: 118 **Privately Held**
SIC: 3317 Pipes, seamless steel
HQ: Wheatland Tube, Llc
　700 S Dock St
　Sharon PA 16146
　800 257-8182

(G-17447)
WHITEHEAD EAGLE CORPORATION
191 N Sharpsville Ave (16146-2135)
PHONE..................................724 346-4280
Thomas Gilson, *President*
Charlene Gilson, *Vice Pres*
EMP: 5 **EST:** 1926
SQ FT: 5,200

SALES (est): 692.2K **Privately Held**
SIC: 2752 Commercial printing, offset

(G-17448)
WINNER INTERNATIONAL INC
Also Called: Club, The
32 W State St (16146-1302)
PHONE..................................724 981-1152
Karen Winner Sed, *CEO*
Gerald J Trontel, *President*
▲ **EMP:** 90
SQ FT: 22,000
SALES (est): 15.9MM **Privately Held**
SIC: 3429 Motor vehicle hardware

(G-17449)
WINTRONICS INC
191 Pitt St (16146-2104)
PHONE..................................724 981-5770
Ted Daigneault, *President*
Dan Chuey, *Director*
Steve Quillen, *Director*
▲ **EMP:** 50
SQ FT: 60,000
SALES (est): 10.7MM **Privately Held**
WEB: www.wintronicsinc.com
SIC: 3672 Printed circuit boards

(G-17450)
ZEKELMAN INDUSTRIES INC
Wheatland Tube Division
700 S Dock St (16146-1836)
PHONE..................................724 342-6851
Mark Magno, *Manager*
EMP: 118 **Privately Held**
SIC: 3317 Pipes, seamless steel
PA: Zekelman Industries, Inc.
　227 W Monroe St Ste 2600
　Chicago IL 60606

(G-17451)
ZEKELMAN INDUSTRIES INC
Also Called: Wheatland Tube
700 S Dock St (16146-1836)
PHONE..................................724 342-6851
Dolly Nickels, *Branch Mgr*
EMP: 77 **Privately Held**
SIC: 3317 Steel pipe & tubes
PA: Zekelman Industries, Inc.
　227 W Monroe St Ste 2600
　Chicago IL 60606

Sharon Hill
Delaware County

(G-17452)
ARCHWAY PRESS INC
825 Chester Pike (19079-1408)
PHONE..................................610 583-4004
John C Lannelli, *CEO*
Doris M Iannelli, *President*
Thomas A Gaffney, *Vice Pres*
Nanamarie Gaffney, *Treasurer*
Nina Marie Gaffney, *Admin Sec*
EMP: 10 **EST:** 1939
SQ FT: 15,000
SALES (est): 2MM **Privately Held**
WEB: www.archwaypress.com
SIC: 2752 Commercial printing, offset

(G-17453)
BIOMED HEALTHCARE INC (HQ)
Also Called: Soleo Health
950 Calcon Hook Rd Ste 19 (19079-1822)
PHONE..................................888 244-2340
Drew Walk, *CEO*
John Ginzler, *CFO*
EMP: 2 **EST:** 2008
SALES (est): 1.2MM
SALES (corp-wide): 42.3MM **Privately Held**
SIC: 2834 5912 Druggists' preparations (pharmaceuticals); drug stores & proprietary stores
PA: Soleo Health Holdings, Inc.
　950 Calcon Hook Rd Ste 19
　Sharon Hill PA 19079
　888 244-2340

(G-17454)
CAMDEN IRON & METAL LLC
3 Industrial Dr (19079-1106)
PHONE..................................610 532-1080

▲ = Import ▼=Export
◆ =Import/Export

EMP: 112
SALES (corp-wide): 47.5MM Privately
Held
SIC: 3312 Blast furnaces & steel mills
PA: Camden Iron & Metal, Llc
143 Harding Ave Ste 20
Bellmawr NJ 08031
856 969-7065

(G-17455)
CANTOL USA INC
Sharon Ct 105 Hnderson Dr (19079)
PHONE.....................................905 475-6141
Jay Brightman, *President*
Vincent Spragins, *Vice Pres*
EMP: 15
SQ FT: 23,000
SALES (est): 1.8MM Privately Held
SIC: 2819 Bleaching powder, lime bleach-
ing compounds

(G-17456)
DEVERSIGN
Also Called: Sign-A-Rama
1400 Chester Pike (19079-1906)
PHONE.....................................610 583-2312
Frank Devers, *President*
EMP: 9
SQ FT: 6,500
SALES: 725K Privately Held
SIC: 3993 Signs & advertising specialties

(G-17457)
DNH SPEAKERS INC
900 Calcon Hook Rd Ste 16 (19079-1820)
PHONE.....................................484 494-5790
Arne Johannessen, *President*
▲ EMP: 4
SALES (est): 555.8K Privately Held
SIC: 3651 Loudspeakers, electrodynamic
or magnetic

(G-17458)
LIFE TREE PHARMACY SVCS
LLC
800 Chester Pike (19079-1400)
PHONE.....................................610 522-2010
Mark Francis Taglianetti, *CEO*
EMP: 5 EST: 2014
SALES (est): 574.7K Privately Held
SIC: 2834 Pharmaceutical preparations

(G-17459)
POWER PRODUCTS INC
950 Calcon Hook Rd Ste 5 (19079-1822)
PHONE.....................................610 532-3880
Steven R Murphy, *President*
▲ EMP: 5 EST: 1964
SQ FT: 5,000
SALES: 280K Privately Held
SIC: 3679 3629 Rectifiers, electronic; bat-
tery chargers, rectifying or nonrotating

(G-17460)
SOLEO HEALTH HOLDINGS INC
(PA)
950 Calcon Hook Rd Ste 19 (19079-1822)
PHONE.....................................888 244-2340
Drew Walk, *CEO*
John Ginzler, *CFO*
EMP: 0
SALES (est): 42.3MM Privately Held
SIC: 6719 2834 5912 Investment holding
companies, except banks; druggists'
preparations (pharmaceuticals); drug
stores & proprietary stores

(G-17461)
SOLEO HEALTH INC (HQ)
950 Calcon Hook Rd Ste 19 (19079-1822)
PHONE.....................................888 244-2340
Drew Walk, *CEO*
Eric Krause, *Vice Pres*
John Ginzler, *CFO*
Jason Howard, *Director*
EMP: 87
SALES (est): 17.9MM
SALES (corp-wide): 42.3MM Privately
Held
SIC: 2834 5912 Druggists' preparations
(pharmaceuticals); drug stores & propri-
etary stores
PA: Soleo Health Holdings, Inc.
950 Calcon Hook Rd Ste 19
Sharon Hill PA 19079
888 244-2340

(G-17462)
STERIS BARRIER PDTS
SOLUTIONS
3000 Henderson Dr (19079-1036)
PHONE.....................................215 763-8200
James G Baxter, *President*
Harvey Kimmel, *Chairman*
Jeffrey Markowitz, *CFO*
Edward Cahill, *Treasurer*
Michael M Cone, *Admin Sec*
EMP: 75
SQ FT: 85,000
SALES (est): 22.8MM
SALES (corp-wide): 2.6B Privately Held
WEB: www.generaleconopak.com
SIC: 3842 Surgical appliances & supplies
HQ: Steris Corporation
5960 Heisley Rd
Mentor OH 44060
440 354-2600

(G-17463)
SUNSHINE BIOLOGIES INC
501 Elmwood Ave (19079-1014)
PHONE.....................................484 494-0818
Sadlier James, *President*
EMP: 20
SALES (est): 1MM Privately Held
SIC: 2834 Pharmaceutical preparations

(G-17464)
TECH MANUFACTURING
CORPORATION
801 Chester Pike (19079-1496)
P.O. Box 1003 (19079-0703)
PHONE.....................................610 586-0620
Erick Raak, *President*
Jake Raas, *President*
EMP: 25
SQ FT: 14,000
SALES (est): 4.5MM Privately Held
WEB: www.techmfg.com
SIC: 3444 Sheet metal specialties, not
stamped

(G-17465)
US CONCRETE INC
Also Called: Action Supply
1401 Calcon Hook Rd (19079-1102)
PHONE.....................................610 532-6290
EMP: 45
SALES (corp-wide): 1.5B Publicly Held
SIC: 5032 3273 Concrete mixtures; ready-
mixed concrete
PA: U.S. Concrete, Inc.
331 N Main St
Euless TX 76039
817 835-4105

(G-17466)
W ROSE INC
1300 Elmwood Ave (19079-2205)
PHONE.....................................610 583-4125
Ronald Meyer, *President*
EMP: 36 EST: 1798
SQ FT: 25,000
SALES (est): 4.5MM
SALES (corp-wide): 43.5MM Privately
Held
WEB: www.krafttool.com
SIC: 3423 Masons' hand tools
PA: Kraft Tool Company
8325 Hedge Lane Ter
Shawnee Mission KS 66227
913 422-4848

Sharpsburg
Allegheny County

(G-17467)
PARAGON AMERICA LLC
Also Called: Maxx-Flex
111 3rd St (15215-2002)
P.O. Box 397, Mars (16046-0397)
PHONE.....................................412 408-3447
Dan Diliberto,
Harry Klaus,
EMP: 11
SALES (est): 1MM Privately Held
SIC: 3052 3599 Rubber & plastics hose &
beltings; hose, flexible metallic

(G-17468)
SEARS CARPET AND UPHL
CARE INC
1601 Marys Ave Ste 10 (15215-2647)
PHONE.....................................412 821-5200
John Hassey, *President*
Mary Brisentine, *Treasurer*
Isaiah Halivni, *Admin Sec*
EMP: 4
SALES (est): 325.1K Privately Held
SIC: 2211 Upholstery, tapestry & wall cov-
erings: cotton

Sharpsville
Mercer County

(G-17469)
BARBERS CHEMICALS INC
950 W Main St (16150-2012)
P.O. Box 135 (16150-0135)
PHONE.....................................724 962-7886
Edward L Earnhardt III, *President*
Michelle Earnhardt, *Admin Sec*
EMP: 10
SQ FT: 11,500
SALES (est): 4.8MM Privately Held
WEB: www.barbchem.com
SIC: 5169 5999 2819 Industrial chemi-
cals; swimming pool chemicals, equip-
ment & supplies; industrial inorganic
chemicals

(G-17470)
CHAUTAUQUA MFG CORP
80 Canal St (16150-2201)
PHONE.....................................513 423-8840
Dave Dayton, *Principal*
EMP: 4
SALES (est): 246.2K Privately Held
SIC: 3089 Plastics products

(G-17471)
DEAN DAIRY PRODUCTS
COMPANY
Also Called: Dean Foods Company
1690 Oneida Ln (16150-9665)
PHONE.....................................724 962-7801
Gregg L Engles, *President*
Frank Crastina, *Vice Pres*
Dave Laitala, *Engineer*
Rod Petrosky, *Controller*
Doug Faber, *Financial Exec*
▲ EMP: 350
SQ FT: 45,000
SALES (est): 93.4MM Publicly Held
SIC: 2026 Milk processing (pasteurizing,
homogenizing, bottling)
HQ: Dean Holding Company
2711 N Haskell Ave
Dallas TX 75204
214 303-3400

(G-17472)
DEAN FOODS COMPANY
1858 Oneida Ln (16150-9638)
PHONE.....................................724 962-7801
Frank Chrastina, *Branch Mgr*
EMP: 87 Publicly Held
SIC: 2026 Milk processing (pasteurizing,
homogenizing, bottling)
PA: Dean Foods Company
2711 N Haskell Ave
Dallas TX 75204

(G-17473)
LIMPACH INDUSTRIES INC
Also Called: Johnson Industries
6774 Orangeville Rd (16150-8425)
P.O. Box 7, Orangeville OH (44453-0007)
PHONE.....................................724 646-4011
David Limpach, *President*
Deborah Limpach, *Admin Sec*
EMP: 19
SQ FT: 18,000
SALES (est): 3.2MM Privately Held
SIC: 2448 2441 2499 Pallets, wood; ship-
ping cases, wood: nailed or lock corner;
reels, plywood

(G-17474)
PRECISION RUNNERS LLC
140 W Shenango St B (16150-1126)
PHONE.....................................330 240-5988

Jason Longwell, *Owner*
EMP: 25
SALES (est): 2.7MM Privately Held
SIC: 3743 Tank freight cars & car equip-
ment

(G-17475)
SHARPSVILLE CONTAINER
CORP
600 W Main St (16150-2058)
PHONE.....................................724 962-1100
Don Zappa, *President*
James D Vantiem, *Admin Sec*
▲ EMP: 50
SQ FT: 110,000
SALES (est): 14.8MM Privately Held
WEB: www.sharpsvillecontainer.com
SIC: 3443 3089 Tanks, standard or cus-
tom fabricated: metal plate; plastic &
fiberglass tanks

(G-17476)
SUNRISE PUBLISHING &
DISTRG
7500 Seneca Rd (16150-8422)
PHONE.....................................724 946-9057
James Biros, *CEO*
Florance Biros, *Corp Secy*
EMP: 4
SALES (est): 173.8K Privately Held
SIC: 2731 Book publishing

(G-17477)
VALLEY SILK SCREENING INC
412 W Main St (16150-2054)
PHONE.....................................724 962-5255
Rocco A Piccirilli, *Owner*
Gary Piccirilli, *Finance*
EMP: 7
SQ FT: 4,000
SALES (est): 500K Privately Held
WEB: www.valleysilkscreening.com
SIC: 2262 Screen printing: manmade fiber
& silk broadwoven fabrics

Shavertown
Luzerne County

(G-17478)
AMERICAN ASPHALT PAVING
CO (PA)
500 Chase Rd (18708-9689)
PHONE.....................................570 696-1181
Bernard C Banks Jr, *President*
Ron Schreiver, *Exec VP*
Dave Silvon, *CFO*
Karen Banks, *Human Resources*
Brian C Banks, *Admin Sec*
▼ EMP: 105 EST: 1951
SQ FT: 11,500
SALES (est): 22MM Privately Held
WEB: www.amerasphalt.com
SIC: 2951 1611 1442 Asphalt & asphaltic
paving mixtures (not from refineries);
highway & street paving contractor; gen-
eral contractor, highway & street con-
struction; construction sand & gravel

(G-17479)
BACK MOUNTAIN CREAMERY
24 Carverton Rd (18708-1711)
PHONE.....................................570 855-3487
Carl J Peterlin, *Owner*
EMP: 4
SALES (est): 252.4K Privately Held
SIC: 2024 Ice cream, bulk

(G-17480)
DERNIER CREE INC
15 Genoa Ln (18708-9608)
PHONE.....................................917 287-7452
Neeru Khanna, *President*
◆ EMP: 3
SQ FT: 800
SALES: 2.5MM Privately Held
SIC: 5094 5122 3873 Jewelry & precious
stones; cosmetics, perfumes & hair prod-
ucts; watches, clocks, watchcases & parts

(G-17481)
WOODRUFF CORPORATION
1540 Huntsville Rd (18708-9335)
PHONE.....................................570 675-0890

J David Roskos, *President*
Joan B Roskos, *Vice Pres*
EMP: 3
SALES: 4MM **Privately Held**
SIC: 2448 2441 Pallets, wood; skids, wood; boxes, wood

Sheffield
Warren County

(G-17482)
HOLDEN PRECISION MACHINE
102 Horton Ave (16347)
PHONE..................................814 968-3833
Tom Holden, *Owner*
EMP: 4
SALES (est): 273K **Privately Held**
SIC: 3599 Machine shop, jobbing & repair

(G-17483)
SHEFFIELD CONTAINER CORP
311 Horton Ave (16347)
P.O. Box 578 (16347-0578)
PHONE..................................814 968-3287
Robert Sixt, *President*
Thomas Sixt, *President*
John Sixt, *Vice Pres*
Barbara Maines, *Treasurer*
James Sixt, *Admin Sec*
EMP: 40 EST: 1960
SQ FT: 100,000
SALES (est): 9.4MM **Privately Held**
SIC: 2631 2448 3496 2653 Corrugating medium; cargo containers, wood; miscellaneous fabricated wire products; corrugated & solid fiber boxes; nailed wood boxes & shook

Shelocta
Indiana County

(G-17484)
C&J ENERGY SERVICES INC
228 Lawton Rd (15774-7337)
PHONE..................................724 354-5225
Joe Zacharek, *Manager*
EMP: 70
SALES (corp-wide): 2.2B **Publicly Held**
SIC: 1389 Oil field services
PA: C&J Energy Services, Inc.
    3990 Rogerdale Rd
    Houston TX 77042
    713 325-6000

(G-17485)
DOMINION ENERGY TRANSM INC
Rte 156 Rr 3 Rt 156 (15774)
PHONE..................................724 354-3433
Kevin Miknis, *Branch Mgr*
EMP: 9
SALES (corp-wide): 13.3B **Publicly Held**
WEB: www.domres.com
SIC: 4922 1311 Natural gas transmission; crude petroleum & natural gas
HQ: Dominion Energy Transmission, Inc.
    120 Tredegar St
    Richmond VA 23219
    800 688-4673

(G-17486)
LLC ARMSTRONG POWER
2313 State Route 156 (15774-3005)
PHONE..................................724 354-5300
Herman Schopman,
EMP: 10
SALES (est): 2.7MM
SALES (corp-wide): 9.1B **Publicly Held**
SIC: 3621 Generating apparatus & parts, electrical
HQ: Vistra Intermediate Company Llc
    601 Travis St Ste 1400
    Houston TX 77002
    713 507-6400

(G-17487)
MARION CENTER SUPPLY INC
10680 Route 422 Hwy W (15774-7342)
PHONE..................................724 354-2143
Gary Riffer, *Manager*
EMP: 9

SALES (corp-wide): 2MM **Privately Held**
SIC: 3273 5211 Ready-mixed concrete; lumber & other building materials
PA: Marion Center Supply, Inc
    517 Church St
    Marion Center PA 15759
    724 397-5505

(G-17488)
ROSEBUD MINING COMPANY
4460 Mccreight Rd (15774-2037)
PHONE..................................724 354-4050
David Doney, *Manager*
EMP: 41
SALES (corp-wide): 605.3MM **Privately Held**
WEB: www.rosebudmining.com
SIC: 1222 1221 Bituminous coal-underground mining; bituminous coal & lignite-surface mining
PA: Rosebud Mining Company
    301 Market St
    Kittanning PA 16201
    724 545-6222

(G-17489)
TITAN WIRELINE SERVICE INC
717 State Route 210 (15774-2310)
P.O. Box 286, Elderton (15736-0286)
PHONE..................................724 354-2629
Fax: 724 354-4105
EMP: 11
SQ FT: 3,200
SALES (est): 1.1MM **Privately Held**
SIC: 1389 Perforating & Servicing Of Gas & Oil Wells

(G-17490)
WEST PENN ENERGY SERVICES LLC (PA)
865 State Route 210 (15774-2346)
PHONE..................................724 354-4118
Michael Zentz, *President*
Andrew Iezzi, *Vice Pres*
John M Sveda CPA, *CFO*
Kimberly Gallagher, *Admin Sec*
EMP: 115
SALES (est): 58.2MM **Privately Held**
WEB: www.wpes-pa.com
SIC: 1389 Oil field services

(G-17491)
WJM COAL CO INC
8955 Rte 422 W (15774)
P.O. Box 171 (15774-0171)
PHONE..................................724 354-2922
William J McIntire, *President*
EMP: 10
SALES (est): 1.6MM **Privately Held**
SIC: 1221 1241 Coal preparation plant, bituminous or lignite; coal mining services

Shenandoah
Schuylkill County

(G-17492)
ATEECO INC (PA)
Also Called: Mrs. T'S
600 E Centre St (17976-1825)
P.O. Box 606 (17976-0606)
PHONE..................................570 462-2745
Thomas F Twardzik, *President*
Leeann Smulligan, *General Mgr*
Mark Tarzwell, *COO*
Christopher S Dende, *Vice Pres*
Joe Donahoe, *Transptn Dir*
EMP: 40 EST: 1957
SQ FT: 60,000
SALES (est): 58MM **Privately Held**
WEB: www.ateeco.com
SIC: 2038 Ethnic foods, frozen

(G-17493)
CUSTOM DESIGN
144 Delaware Ave (17976-1221)
PHONE..................................570 462-0041
Vincent Madaffari, *Owner*
EMP: 3 EST: 1993
SALES (est): 160K **Privately Held**
SIC: 2759 Screen printing

(G-17494)
LEES ORNTAL GOURMET FOODS INC
99 E Washington St (17976-1766)
PHONE..................................570 462-9505
Ted Twardzik, *Principal*
▲ **EMP:** 20
SALES (est): 2.1MM **Privately Held**
SIC: 2038 Ethnic foods, frozen

(G-17495)
MARKO RADIATOR INC (PA)
725 W Coal St (17976-1415)
PHONE..................................570 462-2281
Ray Sachleben, *President*
Robert Decusky, *Vice Pres*
Arlene Sachleben, *Treasurer*
Anna Marie Decusky, *Admin Sec*
EMP: 17
SQ FT: 3,000
SALES (est): 2.6MM **Privately Held**
SIC: 7539 3714 Radiator repair shop, automotive; radiators & radiator shells & cores, motor vehicle

(G-17496)
SHENANDOAH WATER TRTMNT PLANT
Also Called: Municpl Athrty of the Brgh of Raven Run (17976)
P.O. Box 110 (17976-0110)
PHONE..................................570 462-4918
Dan Salvador, *Manager*
EMP: 3
SALES (est): 412.6K **Privately Held**
SIC: 3589 Water treatment equipment, industrial

(G-17497)
TRI-VET DESIGN FABRICATION LLC
301 E Washington St (17976-2646)
PHONE..................................570 462-4941
Joseph McDemus, *President*
Wesley Williams, *Vice Pres*
Richard McDemus, *Treasurer*
EMP: 12
SQ FT: 22,400
SALES (est): 2.2MM **Privately Held**
SIC: 2431 3441 3446 Staircases, stairs & railings; building components, structural steel; stairs, fire escapes, balconies, railings & ladders; gratings, open steel flooring; fences or posts, ornamental iron or steel

(G-17498)
TRI-WAY METALWORKERS INC
Also Called: Amity Carts
301 E Washington St (17976-2646)
PHONE..................................570 462-4941
John Brigs, *President*
John Matino, *Vice Pres*
Joseph McBemus, *Treasurer*
EMP: 28
SQ FT: 12,000
SALES (est): 2.1MM **Privately Held**
SIC: 3441 Building components, structural steel

Sheppton
Schuylkill County

(G-17499)
BIROS JOHN
Also Called: Biros Utilities
14 Schoolhouse Rd (18248)
P.O. Box 94 (18248-0094)
PHONE..................................570 384-3473
John Biros, *Owner*
Michael Biros, *Vice Pres*
◆ **EMP:** 10
SALES: 850K **Privately Held**
SIC: 3446 Stairs, staircases, stair treads: prefabricated metal

Shermans Dale
Perry County

(G-17500)
DGH KOI INC
5055 Spring Rd (17090-8317)
P.O. Box 120 (17090-0120)
PHONE..................................717 582-7749
Earl Henderson, *President*
EMP: 4
SALES (est): 244.4K
SALES (corp-wide): 1.2MM **Privately Held**
WEB: www.pachometer.com
SIC: 3841 Medical instruments & equipment, blood & bone work
PA: Dgh Technology Inc.
    110 Summit Dr Ste B
    Exton PA 19341
    610 594-9100

(G-17501)
RITTERS FUEL DELIVERY LLC
4335 Valley Rd (17090-8555)
PHONE..................................717 957-4477
John E Ritter, *Principal*
EMP: 3
SALES (est): 258.9K **Privately Held**
SIC: 2869 Fuels

Shickshinny
Luzerne County

(G-17502)
RONALD HINES
Also Called: Hines Water Pumps
75 Park Ridge Dr (18655-4323)
PHONE..................................570 256-3355
Ronald Hines, *Owner*
EMP: 3
SALES (est): 270K **Privately Held**
SIC: 5084 3589 Pumps & pumping equipment; sewage treatment equipment

Shillington
Berks County

(G-17503)
CITADELLE
400 Pennsylvania Ave (19607-1316)
PHONE..................................610 777-8844
Chris Golden, *Owner*
EMP: 3
SALES (est): 121.5K **Privately Held**
SIC: 2099 Maple syrup

Shinglehouse
Potter County

(G-17504)
BUCHER JJ PRODUCING CORP
2568 Bells Run Rd (16748-3030)
PHONE..................................814 697-6593
Joseph J Bucher, *President*
Mary Elizabeth Bucher, *Admin Sec*
EMP: 4
SALES (est): 550K **Privately Held**
SIC: 1311 Crude petroleum production

(G-17505)
CANFIELDS OUTDOOR PWR EQP INC
2932 Kings Run Rd (16748-3526)
PHONE..................................814 697-6233
Patrick M Canfield, *President*
EMP: 6
SALES (est): 113.3K **Privately Held**
SIC: 3053 Packing: steam engines, pipe joints, air compressors, etc.

(G-17506)
DONOVAN SCHOONOVER LUMBER CO
Academy St Ext (16748)
PHONE..................................814 697-7266

Brent Schoonover, *Partner*
George Donovan, *Partner*
EMP: 6
SQ FT: 10,000
SALES (est): 566.7K **Privately Held**
SIC: 2448 Wood pallets & skids

(G-17507)
GAS FIELD SPECIALISTS INC (PA)
2107 State Route 44 S (16748-4429)
P.O. Box 697 (16748-0697)
PHONE.....................................814 698-2122
Gregory West, *President*
John Hargrave, *Superintendent*
Bradley A West, *Vice Pres*
Jeffrey B West, *Vice Pres*
Rodney G West, *Vice Pres*
EMP: 75
SQ FT: 4,800
SALES: 44.6MM **Privately Held**
SIC: 1389 Oil field services; gas field services

(G-17508)
JJ BUCHER PRODUCING CORP
2568 Bells Run Rd (16748-3030)
PHONE.....................................814 697-6593
Gregory A Maxson, *Principal*
EMP: 3
SALES (est): 346.9K **Privately Held**
SIC: 1311 Crude petroleum & natural gas

(G-17509)
LISA LITTLE INC
Also Called: Wayne Concrete
262 Route 44 (16748-3620)
PHONE.....................................814 697-7500
Lisa A Stephen, *President*
EMP: 5
SALES (est): 520K **Privately Held**
WEB: www.lisalittle.com
SIC: 3273 5039 Ready-mixed concrete; septic tanks

(G-17510)
NORTONS BUILDING SUPPLY INC
112 Water St (16748)
P.O. Box 639 (16748-0639)
PHONE.....................................814 697-6351
Dale Norton, *President*
Phyllis Norton, *President*
EMP: 5 **EST:** 1936
SQ FT: 7,500
SALES (est): 820K **Privately Held**
SIC: 5211 3271 Lumber & other building materials; brick, concrete

(G-17511)
PLANTS AND GOODWIN INC
1034 Route 44 (16748-3406)
PHONE.....................................814 697-6330
Paul R Plants, *President*
Stephen D Plants, *Vice Pres*
Tonya Pack, *Admin Sec*
EMP: 21
SQ FT: 9,600
SALES (est): 6MM **Privately Held**
SIC: 1382 Oil & gas exploration services

(G-17512)
RAM FOREST PRODUCTS INC
Honeoye Rd (16748)
PHONE.....................................814 697-7185
Robert A Mallery, *President*
Paul Westburg, *Admin Sec*
◆ **EMP:** 90
SQ FT: 55,000
SALES: 2MM **Privately Held**
WEB: www.ram-forest.com
SIC: 2426 2421 5211 2435 Hardwood dimension & flooring mills; custom sawmill; lumber products; hardwood veneer & plywood

(G-17513)
SIMON OF BOLIVAR ENTERPRISES
1140 State Route 44 S (16748-4622)
PHONE.....................................814 697-7891
Jim Reynolds, *President*
EMP: 3
SALES (est): 75K **Privately Held**
SIC: 1381 Drilling oil & gas wells

(G-17514)
WAYNE CONCRETE INC
262 Route 44 (16748-3620)
PHONE.....................................814 697-7500
Wayne Stephn, *President*
EMP: 10
SQ FT: 2,500
SALES (est): 700K **Privately Held**
SIC: 3273 Ready-mixed concrete

Shippensburg
Cumberland County

(G-17515)
ARCHITECTURAL WOODSMITHS INC (PA)
Also Called: A.W.I.
40 Lurgan Ave (17257-1622)
P.O. Box 333 (17257-0333)
PHONE.....................................717 532-7700
Henry B Schan, *President*
Mark Wescott, *Admin Sec*
EMP: 65
SQ FT: 125,000
SALES (est): 7.4MM **Privately Held**
SIC: 2431 3446 2542 2541 Moldings & baseboards, ornamental & trim; architectural metalwork; partitions & fixtures, except wood; wood partitions & fixtures

(G-17516)
BEIDEL PRINTING HOUSE INC
63 W Burd St (17257-1259)
P.O. Box 708 (17257-0708)
PHONE.....................................717 532-5063
Trudy J Collier, *President*
Duane A Collier, *Admin Sec*
EMP: 20
SALES: 2.1MM **Privately Held**
SIC: 2752 2732 2731 7389 Commercial printing, offset; book printing; book publishing; packaging & labeling services

(G-17517)
BEISTLE COMPANY (PA)
1 Beistle Plz (17257-9684)
PHONE.....................................717 532-2131
H R Luhrs, *CEO*
Patricia D Lacy, *President*
Kenneth E Shoap, *Vice Pres*
Alan R Weist, *Vice Pres*
Doug Wilson, *VP Prdtn*
◆ **EMP:** 370
SQ FT: 75,000
SALES (est): 87.6MM **Privately Held**
WEB: www.beistle.com
SIC: 2679 3993 2675 2657 Novelties, paper: made from purchased material; signs & advertising specialties; die-cut paper & board; folding paperboard boxes; paperboard mills; paper mills

(G-17518)
BELTONE CORPORATION
341 Baltimore Rd (17257-9404)
PHONE.....................................717 300-7163
EMP: 5
SALES (corp-wide): 1.6B **Privately Held**
SIC: 3842 Hearing aids
HQ: Beltone Corporation
2601 Patriot Blvd
Glenview IL 60026
847 832-3300

(G-17519)
BLUE MTN A COMPRSR SVCS LLC
26 Jumper Rd (17257-9723)
PHONE.....................................717 423-5262
Thomas Yaukey, *Mng Member*
EMP: 6
SALES (est): 1.3MM **Privately Held**
SIC: 3563 Air & gas compressors

(G-17520)
BYERS LOGGING LLC
1275 Baltimore Rd (17257-9422)
PHONE.....................................717 530-5995
Philip Byers, *Principal*
EMP: 3 **EST:** 2014
SALES (est): 317K **Privately Held**
SIC: 2411 Logging

(G-17521)
CARGILL INCORPORATED
580 N Morris St (17257-1640)
PHONE.....................................717 530-7778
Rob Schaffer, *Branch Mgr*
EMP: 20
SALES (corp-wide): 114.7B **Privately Held**
WEB: www.cargill.com
SIC: 2048 Prepared feeds
PA: Cargill, Incorporated
15407 Mcginty Rd W
Wayzata MN 55391
952 742-7575

(G-17522)
CHRIS S SENSENIG
Also Called: Sensenig's Woodworking
1033 Ridge Rd (17257-9716)
PHONE.....................................717 423-5311
Chris S Sensenig, *Owner*
EMP: 4
SALES: 300K **Privately Held**
SIC: 2511 Wood household furniture

(G-17523)
COLLEGE TOWN INC (PA)
73 W Burd St (17257-1259)
P.O. Box 337 (17257-0337)
PHONE.....................................717 532-7354
Duaine A Collier, *President*
Edward Goodhart, *Treasurer*
Trudy J Collier, *Admin Sec*
EMP: 4 **EST:** 1971
SALES (est): 954.6K **Privately Held**
WEB: www.collegetown.com
SIC: 1711 6512 2752 Warm air heating & air conditioning contractor; nonresidential building operators; commercial printing, offset

(G-17524)
COLLEGE TOWN INC
17 W Burd St (17257-1223)
P.O. Box 337 (17257-0337)
PHONE.....................................717 532-3034
T Collier, *Branch Mgr*
EMP: 3
SALES (corp-wide): 954.6K **Privately Held**
WEB: www.collegetown.com
SIC: 1711 6512 2752 Warm air heating & air conditioning contractor; nonresidential building operators; commercial printing, offset
PA: College Town Inc.
73 W Burd St
Shippensburg PA 17257
717 532-7354

(G-17525)
CUMBERLAND VALLEY COOP ASSN
908 Mount Rock Rd (17257-7710)
P.O. Box 350 (17257-0350)
PHONE.....................................717 532-2197
Wayne Craig, *CEO*
Vernon Hearst, *President*
EMP: 32 **EST:** 1929
SQ FT: 2,000
SALES: 17.6MM **Privately Held**
WEB: www.cumberlandvalley.coop
SIC: 2048 2873 Poultry feeds; livestock feeds; nitrogenous fertilizers

(G-17526)
DESTINY IMAGE INC
167 Walnut Bottom Rd (17257-9698)
P.O. Box 310 (17257-0310)
PHONE.....................................717 532-3040
Donald Nori, *President*
Cathy Nori, *Vice Pres*
Kyle Loffelmacher, *Natl Sales Mgr*
Wil Brown, *Manager*
▲ **EMP:** 22 **EST:** 1989
SQ FT: 12,600
SALES: 3.8MM
SALES (corp-wide): 663.1K **Privately Held**
WEB: www.destinyimage.com
SIC: 2731 Book publishing
PA: Nori Medical Group
167 Walnut Bottom Rd
Shippensburg PA 17257
717 532-3040

(G-17527)
FORGING PARTS & MACHINING CO
150 Reading Rd (17257-1634)
PHONE.....................................717 530-8810
Shirley Crow, *President*
EMP: 25
SALES (est): 1.3MM **Privately Held**
SIC: 3599 Machine shop, jobbing & repair

(G-17528)
GABLERS BEVERAGE DISTRIBUTORS
29 N Seneca St (17257-1207)
PHONE.....................................717 532-2241
Steve Gabler, *President*
Adam Gabler, *President*
EMP: 5
SQ FT: 2,000
SALES: 1MM **Privately Held**
SIC: 2086 5149 5921 5182 Bottled & canned soft drinks; beverages, except coffee & tea; liquor stores; wine & distilled beverages; beer & ale

(G-17529)
GODFREYS CUSTOM PRINTING
253 Walnut St (17257-2019)
PHONE.....................................717 530-8818
Nancy Godfrey, *Owner*
Morgan Godfrey, *Co-Owner*
EMP: 4
SALES: 100K **Privately Held**
SIC: 2752 Commercial printing, offset

(G-17530)
GOOSE BROS INC
81 Walnut Bottom Rd (17257-9401)
PHONE.....................................717 477-0010
Mathew Ulmer, *General Mgr*
EMP: 3 **EST:** 2010
SALES (est): 149.7K **Privately Held**
SIC: 2024 Ice cream, bulk

(G-17531)
HARRISON HOUSE INC
Also Called: Harrison House Publishers
167 Walnut Bottom Rd (17257-9601)
PHONE.....................................918 523-5700
Keith Provance, *President*
Pat Harrison, *Corp Secy*
Jason Smith, *Finance Dir*
◆ **EMP:** 115
SALES (est): 7.5MM **Privately Held**
SIC: 2731 Books: publishing only

(G-17532)
INDUSTRIAL HARNESS COMPANY INC (PA)
100 Outlook Ln (17257-8130)
PHONE.....................................717 477-0100
Jeffrey A Lundeen, *President*
Carey Fullmer, *Plant Mgr*
Charlene Shields, *Purchasing*
Matthew Parker, *Engineer*
Patsy Wheeler, *Treasurer*
EMP: 60
SQ FT: 48,000
SALES (est): 9.2MM **Privately Held**
WEB: www.indharness.com
SIC: 3714 8711 3694 3357 Automotive wiring harness sets; engineering services; engine electrical equipment; nonferrous wiredrawing & insulating

(G-17533)
INGERSOLL-RAND CO
328 E Burd St (17257-1404)
PHONE.....................................717 530-1160
Rand Ingersoll, *Principal*
EMP: 3 **EST:** 1964
SALES (est): 259.6K **Privately Held**
SIC: 3131 Rands

(G-17534)
JLG INDUSTRIES INC
560 Walnut Bottom Rd (17257-9604)
PHONE.....................................717 530-9000
A Teclosky, *Branch Mgr*
EMP: 125
SALES (corp-wide): 7.7B **Publicly Held**
WEB: www.jlg.com
SIC: 3531 Aerial work platforms: hydraulic/elec. truck/carrier mounted

HQ: Jlg Industries, Inc.
　　1 J L G Dr
　　Mc Connellsburg PA 17233
　　717 485-5161

(G-17535)
KINETICS HYDRO INC
108 E Orange St (17257-1912)
PHONE...............................717 532-6016
Larry Gutshall, *President*
Bonnie Gutshall, *Admin Sec*
EMP: 5
SALES: 500K **Privately Held**
SIC: 3829 7699 Kinematic test & measuring equipment; industrial machinery & equipment repair

(G-17536)
KITTATINNY MANUFACTURING SVCS
Also Called: Kms
160 Reading Rd (17257-1634)
P.O. Box 39 (17257-0039)
PHONE...............................717 530-1242
Rick Fleming, *President*
Bob Rotz, *General Mgr*
Dave Coldsmith, *Sales Executive*
EMP: 19
SQ FT: 14,000
SALES (est): 3.2MM **Privately Held**
WEB: www.kittatinnymfg.com
SIC: 3599 7692 Machine shop, jobbing & repair; welding repair

(G-17537)
LANE ENTERPRISES INC
34 Strohm Rd (17257-9652)
PHONE...............................717 532-5959
Mark Dick, *Branch Mgr*
EMP: 25
SALES (corp-wide): 70.5MM **Privately Held**
WEB: www.lanepipe.com
SIC: 3444 Pipe, sheet metal
PA: Lane Enterprises, Inc.
　　3905 Hartzdale Dr Ste 514
　　Camp Hill PA 17011
　　717 761-8175

(G-17538)
MACHINE TL REBUILD SPECIALISTS
299 Shippensburg Rd (17257-8616)
PHONE...............................717 423-6073
Harry J Hedge Jr, *President*
Kathy L Hedge, *Corp Secy*
EMP: 5
SQ FT: 10,000
SALES (est): 652.2K **Privately Held**
SIC: 3541 3542 Machine tool replacement & repair parts, metal cutting types; rebuilt machine tools, metal forming types

(G-17539)
NEWBURG WOODCRAFTS (PA)
8915 Rowe Run Rd (17257-9339)
PHONE...............................717 530-8823
Royce Martin, *Managing Prtnr*
Thomas Martin, *Partner*
EMP: 7
SQ FT: 11,000
SALES: 1MM **Privately Held**
SIC: 2511 5712 Wood household furniture; furniture stores

(G-17540)
NEWS CHRONICLE CO INC (PA)
Also Called: Valley Times Star, The
1011 Ritner Hwy (17257-9777)
PHONE...............................717 532-4101
Kenneth E Wolfrom, *President*
Robert Riggs, *Exec VP*
Linda Wolfrom, *Vice Pres*
C Graydon Schlichter, *Treasurer*
EMP: 28
SQ FT: 6,000
SALES (est): 1.7MM **Privately Held**
SIC: 2711 2752 2721 2671 Newspapers, publishing & printing; commercial printing, offset; periodicals; packaging paper & plastics film, coated & laminated

(G-17541)
NICHE ELECTRONICS TECH INC
201 Dykeman Rd (17257-8700)
PHONE...............................717 532-6620

Joseph Augustine, *President*
Tony Casella, *Vice Pres*
Jim Riggs, *Vice Pres*
EMP: 25 **EST:** 1997
SQ FT: 16,000
SALES (est): 8.5MM **Privately Held**
WEB: www.nichelect.com
SIC: 3672 Printed circuit boards

(G-17542)
NORI MEDICAL GROUP (PA)
167 Walnut Bottom Rd (17257-9601)
PHONE...............................717 532-3040
Don Nori Sr, *Principal*
Jonathan Nori, *COO*
Eric Hockenberry, *IT/INT Sup*
Eileen Rockwell, *Graphic Designe*
EMP: 6 **EST:** 2015
SALES (est): 663.1K **Privately Held**
SIC: 2731 Book publishing

(G-17543)
R S MYERS WELDING
402 S Washington St (17257-2030)
PHONE...............................717 532-4714
Ray S Myers, *Owner*
EMP: 3 **EST:** 1950
SQ FT: 3,360
SALES (est): 173.5K **Privately Held**
SIC: 7692 7539 Automotive welding; radiator repair shop, automotive

(G-17544)
RIDGEVIEW FOREST PRODUCTS LLC
Also Called: Ridgeview Woodwork
550 Ridge Rd (17257-9764)
PHONE...............................717 423-6465
Timothy Shirk, *Mng Member*
EMP: 30
SQ FT: 50,000
SALES (est): 1.8MM **Privately Held**
SIC: 2431 Millwork

(G-17545)
ROSENBERRY SEPTIC TANK SERVICE
8885 Pineville Rd (17257-9391)
PHONE...............................717 532-4026
Larry Rosenberry, *Partner*
Larry Rossenburry, *Partner*
EMP: 6 **EST:** 1947
SQ FT: 1,200
SALES (est): 941.6K **Privately Held**
SIC: 3272 1711 Septic tanks, concrete; septic system construction

(G-17546)
SCHREIBER FOODS INC
208 Dykeman Rd (17257-8700)
PHONE...............................717 530-5000
Dave Pilgert, *Branch Mgr*
EMP: 150
SALES (corp-wide): 2.4B **Privately Held**
WEB: www.sficorp.com
SIC: 2022 Spreads, cheese
PA: Schreiber Foods, Inc.
　　400 N Washington St
　　Green Bay WI 54301
　　920 437-7601

(G-17547)
SHETRON MANUFACTURING LLC
Also Called: Shetron Trailer Sales
103 Hammond Rd (17257-9763)
PHONE...............................717 532-4400
Terry Shetron,
EMP: 6
SALES (est): 1.7MM **Privately Held**
SIC: 3715 Truck trailers

(G-17548)
SHETRON WLDG & FABRICATION INC
1100 Remmington Dr (17257-7908)
PHONE...............................717 776-4344
Ray Cullen, *President*
Kirk Naugle, *Vice Pres*
EMP: 40
SQ FT: 11,000
SALES (est): 5.9MM **Privately Held**
SIC: 3446 Railings, prefabricated metal

(G-17549)
SHIPPENSBURG PUMP CO INC
1 Schwenk Dr (17257)
P.O. Box 279 (17257-0279)
PHONE...............................717 532-7321
Duaine A Collier, *President*
EMP: 50
SALES (est): 27.7MM **Privately Held**
WEB: www.shipcopumps.com
SIC: 5084 3561 Pumps & pumping equipment; pumps & pumping equipment; industrial pumps & parts

(G-17550)
SHIRKS SAW MILL
2033 Ritner Hwy (17257-9554)
PHONE...............................717 776-7083
Ivan Shirk, *Principal*
EMP: 3
SALES (est): 208.1K **Privately Held**
SIC: 2421 Sawmills & planing mills, general

(G-17551)
TINICUM MAGNETICS INC
345 Baltimore Rd (17257-9404)
PHONE...............................717 530-2424
Stewart Cook, *President*
Brian Demnicki, *Vice Pres*
EMP: 10 **EST:** 2007
SALES: 500K **Privately Held**
SIC: 3677 Electronic coils, transformers & other inductors

(G-17552)
VALLEY QUARRIES INC
Also Called: Valley Transit Mix Div
472 Newville Rd (17257-9504)
PHONE...............................717 532-4161
Robert Commerer, *Manager*
EMP: 11
SQ FT: 1,404
SALES (corp-wide): 651.9MM **Privately Held**
WEB: www.valleyquarries.com
SIC: 3273 Ready-mixed concrete
HQ: Valley Quarries, Inc.
　　297 Quarry Rd
　　Chambersburg PA 17202
　　717 267-2244

(G-17553)
VALLEY QUARRIES INC
470 Newville Rd (17257-9504)
PHONE...............................717 532-4456
Joe Zimmerman, *CEO*
EMP: 17
SALES (corp-wide): 651.9MM **Privately Held**
WEB: www.valleyquarries.com
SIC: 1422 Limestones, ground
HQ: Valley Quarries, Inc.
　　297 Quarry Rd
　　Chambersburg PA 17202
　　717 267-2244

(G-17554)
WENGER FEEDS LLC
1122 Mount Rock Rd (17257-8764)
PHONE...............................717 367-1195
M M Wenger, *President*
J Michael Lutz, *Admin Sec*
EMP: 200
SALES (corp-wide): 111.1MM **Privately Held**
WEB: www.easternag.com
SIC: 2048 Poultry feeds
PA: Wenger Feeds, Llc
　　101 W Harrisburg Ave
　　Rheems PA 17570
　　717 367-1195

(G-17555)
WHITE MANE PUBLISHING CO INC
63 W Burd St (17257-1250)
P.O. Box 708 (17257-0708)
PHONE...............................717 532-2237
Martin Gordon, *President*
Duaine Collier, *Corp Secy*
EMP: 10
SQ FT: 6,400
SALES (est): 783.8K **Privately Held**
WEB: www.dreamprint.com
SIC: 2741 Miscellaneous publishing

Shippenville
Clarion County

(G-17556)
CLARION BATHWARE INC (PA)
44 Amsler Ave (16254-4802)
PHONE...............................814 226-5374
David Groner, *President*
Lee Wentling, *Senior VP*
▲ **EMP:** 120
SQ FT: 51,000
SALES (est): 20.8MM **Privately Held**
WEB: www.clarionbathware.com
SIC: 3431 3088 Bathroom fixtures, including sinks; tubs (bath, shower & laundry), plastic

(G-17557)
CLARION BOARDS LLC
143 Fiberboard Rd (16254)
P.O. Box 340 (16254-0340)
PHONE...............................814 226-0851
Jose Luiskofman, *President*
Jose Kofman, *Vice Pres*
◆ **EMP:** 125
SQ FT: 340,000
SALES: 47.7MM
SALES (corp-wide): 108.2MM **Privately Held**
SIC: 2431 2295 Panel work, wood; laminating of fabrics
HQ: Clarion Industries, Inc.
　　1 Kronsopan Way
　　Eastaboga AL 36260
　　256 741-8755

(G-17558)
CLARION INDUSTRIES LLC (PA)
Also Called: Clarion Boards
11120 Route 322 (16254-4932)
P.O. Box 340 (16254-0340)
PHONE...............................814 226-0851
Jim Confer, *Plant Mgr*
Derek Myers, *Supervisor*
Anthony Sturrus,
▲ **EMP:** 35
SALES (est): 14.8MM **Privately Held**
SIC: 2493 Reconstituted wood products

(G-17559)
CLARION LAMINATES LLC
301 Fiberboard Rd (16254)
PHONE...............................814 226-8032
Jose Kofman, *CEO*
▲ **EMP:** 100
SQ FT: 350,000
SALES (est): 20MM
SALES (corp-wide): 108.2MM **Privately Held**
SIC: 2431 2295 Panel work, wood; laminating of fabrics
HQ: Clarion Industries, Inc.
　　1 Kronsopan Way
　　Eastaboga AL 36260
　　256 741-8755

(G-17560)
DEER CREEK WINERY LLC
3333 Soap Fat Rd (16254-3031)
PHONE...............................814 354-7392
Denis Brooks, *Mng Member*
EMP: 51
SALES (est): 1.5MM **Privately Held**
SIC: 2084 5812 2024 Wines; coffee shop; ice cream & frozen desserts

(G-17561)
FULTON FOREST PRODUCTS
683 Fulton Rd (16254-1615)
PHONE...............................814 782-3448
Steven Fulton, *Partner*
Larry Fulton, *Partner*
EMP: 20
SQ FT: 840
SALES: 1.6MM **Privately Held**
SIC: 2421 2449 2431 2426 Lumber: rough, sawed or planed; wood containers; millwork; hardwood dimension & flooring mills; logging

GEOGRAPHIC

(G-17562)
JJ KENNEDY INC
19929 Paint Blvd (16254-4619)
PHONE..................................814 226-6320
Paul R Rader, *Branch Mgr*
EMP: 7
SALES (corp-wide): 10.8MM **Privately Held**
WEB: www.jjkennedy.com
SIC: 3273 Ready-mixed concrete
PA: J.J Kennedy Inc
1790 Route 588
Fombell PA 16123
724 452-6260

(G-17563)
RONNAS RUFF BARK TRUCKING INC
2928 Knight Town Rd (16254-2930)
PHONE..................................814 221-4410
Ronna Merryman, *President*
EMP: 6
SALES (est): 561.2K **Privately Held**
SIC: 2411 Skidding logs

(G-17564)
THOMAS E SIEGEL
Also Called: Briun Stone Plant
208 Woodland Rd (16254-8710)
PHONE..................................814 226-7421
Thomas E Siegel, *Owner*
EMP: 4
SALES (est): 220K **Privately Held**
SIC: 1422 Crushed & broken limestone

(G-17565)
UNIQUE FABRICATION LLC
19059 Paint Blvd Ste 2 (16254-4329)
P.O. Box 269, Strattanville (16258-0269)
PHONE..................................814 227-2627
Elliot Fabri,
EMP: 7
SALES (est): 1.5MM **Privately Held**
WEB: www.uniquefabrication.com
SIC: 3441 Fabricated structural metal

(G-17566)
VINYL GRAPHICS UNLIMITED
9912 Route 322 (16254-8742)
PHONE..................................814 226-7887
Gary Wiant, *Owner*
EMP: 3 EST: 1995
SQ FT: 13,000
SALES (est): 229.3K **Privately Held**
WEB: www.vinylgraphicsunl.com
SIC: 3993 Signs & advertising specialties

Shippingport
Beaver County

(G-17567)
NEW NGC INC
Also Called: Ngc Industries
168 Shippingport Hill Rd (15077-1000)
P.O. Box 346 (15077-0346)
PHONE..................................724 643-3440
Chuck Newell, *Manager*
EMP: 85
SALES (corp-wide): 685.8MM **Privately Held**
WEB: www.natgyp.com
SIC: 3275 Gypsum board
HQ: New Ngc, Inc.
2001 Rexford Rd
Charlotte NC 28211

Shiremanstown
Cumberland County

(G-17568)
BASS PALLETS LLC
311 Railroad Ave (17011)
PHONE..................................717 731-1091
Jeff Stoner, *President*
Owen Erdman, *Vice Pres*
EMP: 45
SALES (est): 4.3MM **Privately Held**
SIC: 2448 Pallets, wood

Shirleysburg
Huntingdon County

(G-17569)
BRUMBAUGH LUMBER LLC
16460 Croghan Pike (17260-9546)
PHONE..................................814 542-8880
Corey Brumbaugh,
Wesley Brumbaugh,
EMP: 9
SQ FT: 9,000
SALES (est): 1.3MM **Privately Held**
SIC: 2421 Sawmills & planing mills, general

Shoemakersville
Berks County

(G-17570)
GLEN-GERY CORPORATION
423 S Pottsville Pike (19555-9742)
PHONE..................................610 374-4011
Ricky McDavid, *Manager*
EMP: 78 **Privately Held**
WEB: www.glengerybrick.com
SIC: 3251 3255 Brick clay: common face, glazed, vitrified or hollow; clay refractories
HQ: Glen-Gery Corporation
1166 Spring St
Reading PA 19610
610 374-4011

(G-17571)
MASTERCRAFT WOODWORKING CO INC
681 Mohrsville Rd (19555-9714)
PHONE..................................610 926-1500
Susan Peters, *President*
EMP: 40
SQ FT: 20,000
SALES (est): 6.6MM **Privately Held**
SIC: 2542 Cabinets: show, display or storage: except wood

(G-17572)
MATERION BRUSH INC
230 Shoemakersville Rd (19555-9028)
PHONE..................................610 562-2211
EMP: 180
SQ FT: 29,829
SALES (corp-wide): 1.2B **Publicly Held**
WEB: www.brushwellman.com
SIC: 3339 3312 Beryllium metal; blast furnaces & steel mills
HQ: Materion Brush Inc.
6070 Parkland Blvd Ste 1
Mayfield Heights OH 44124
216 486-4200

(G-17573)
O-Z/GEDNEY CO INC
150 Birch Hill Rd (19555-9246)
PHONE..................................610 926-3645
EMP: 4
SALES (est): 177.3K **Privately Held**
SIC: 3369 Nonferrous foundries

(G-17574)
S P PRINTING
620 Franklin St (19555-1617)
PHONE..................................610 562-8551
Carl Leibensperger, *Owner*
June Leibensperger, *Admin Sec*
EMP: 3 EST: 1930
SQ FT: 2,550
SALES (est): 250K **Privately Held**
SIC: 2752 Commercial printing, offset

(G-17575)
SCREEN IMAGES INC
392a Five Locks Rd (19555-9630)
PHONE..................................610 926-3061
Richard Slegel, *President*
Kraig R Biehl, *Vice Pres*
EMP: 5
SQ FT: 8,000
SALES (est): 344.8K **Privately Held**
SIC: 2759 Screen printing

(G-17576)
TEX STYLES LLC
392 Five Locks Rd Ste 4 (19555-9643)
PHONE..................................610 562-4939
Kraig Biehl, *Partner*
Michelle Milliron, *Graphic Designe*
EMP: 5
SQ FT: 1,000
SALES: 600K **Privately Held**
SIC: 2759 Screen printing

(G-17577)
WOLFE DYE AND BLEACH WORKS INC
25 Ridge Rd (19555-8916)
PHONE..................................610 562-7639
Mark Nwolfe, *Principal*
John D Rampolla, *Treasurer*
EMP: 47 EST: 1902
SQ FT: 1,200
SALES (est): 10.2MM **Privately Held**
SIC: 2269 Dyeing: raw stock yarn & narrow fabrics

Shohola
Pike County

(G-17578)
COFLEX INC
851 Route 6 (18458-3509)
PHONE..................................570 296-2100
Edward Ryman, *President*
Geraldine Ryman, *Corp Secy*
EMP: 7
SQ FT: 4,500
SALES: 1.5MM **Privately Held**
WEB: www.coflexinc.com
SIC: 3613 Bus bar structures

(G-17579)
ROBINSON SAWMILL WORKS
450 Route 434 (18458-3809)
PHONE..................................570 559-7454
EMP: 3
SALES (est): 162.7K **Privately Held**
SIC: 2421 Sawmills & planing mills, general

(G-17580)
SPIRAL TOOL CORPORATION
Also Called: STC Industries
761 Route 6 (18458-3604)
PHONE..................................570 409-1331
Jean Mutzek, *CEO*
Fred Mutzek, *President*
Paul Mutzek, *Vice Pres*
EMP: 7
SQ FT: 5,000
SALES: 750K **Privately Held**
WEB: www.stcind.com
SIC: 3599 Machine shop, jobbing & repair

Shrewsbury
York County

(G-17581)
ASHLAND INDUSTRIAL SVCS LLC (PA)
Also Called: Ais
1 N Main St (17361-1321)
PHONE..................................717 347-5616
Debra Clasing,
Shawn Clasing,
EMP: 9
SQ FT: 3,000
SALES: 759.6K **Privately Held**
SIC: 7699 7389 3534 5084 Elevators: inspection, service & repair; inspection & testing services; elevators & moving stairways; elevators & equipment; elevators; safety training service

(G-17582)
EBER & WEIN INC
Also Called: Eber & Wein Publishing
595 S Main St (17361-1737)
P.O. Box 326 (17361-0326)
PHONE..................................717 759-8065
Rachel Mueck, *President*
EMP: 12 EST: 2009

SALES (est): 922.7K **Privately Held**
SIC: 2741 Miscellaneous publishing

(G-17583)
EYSTERS MACHINE SHOP INC
Also Called: Eysters Machine and Wire Pdts
50 W Clearview Dr (17361-1103)
PHONE..................................717 227-8400
Glenn R Eyster Jr, *President*
Wanda Eyster, *Vice Pres*
EMP: 31 EST: 1978
SQ FT: 86,000
SALES (est): 6.4MM **Privately Held**
SIC: 3496 3545 Miscellaneous fabricated wire products; tools & accessories for machine tools

(G-17584)
INGERSOLL-RAND COMPANY
16 Northbrook Ln (17361-1260)
PHONE..................................410 238-0542
Mottley Tom, *Manager*
EMP: 21 **Privately Held**
WEB: www.ingersoll-rand.com
SIC: 3563 3561 3429 Air & gas compressors; pumps & pumping equipment; furniture builders' & other household hardware; keys, locks & related hardware
HQ: Ingersoll-Rand Company
800 Beaty St Ste B
Davidson NC 28036
704 655-4000

(G-17585)
LZK MANUFACTURING INC
28 Onion Blvd (17361-1740)
PHONE..................................717 891-5792
Lisa Lazarek, *President*
EMP: 8
SALES: 1MM **Privately Held**
SIC: 3325 Steel foundries

(G-17586)
NEOSYSTEMSUSA INC
19 W Railroad Ave (17361-1535)
PHONE..................................717 586-5040
Gary Papas, *CEO*
EMP: 5
SALES (est): 260K **Privately Held**
SIC: 3444 Metal housings, enclosures, casings & other containers

(G-17587)
REHMEYER PRECISION MLLWK INC
6 Onion Blvd (17361-1740)
PHONE..................................717 235-0607
Bradley Rehmeyer, *President*
EMP: 10
SQ FT: 10,000
SALES (est): 1.1MM **Privately Held**
WEB: www.rehmeyerfloors.com
SIC: 2431 Millwork

(G-17588)
TE CONNECTIVITY CORPORATION
Also Called: Molded Products Division
50 W Clearview Dr (17361-1103)
PHONE..................................717 227-4400
Gary Owens, *Enginr/R&D Mgr*
EMP: 273
SALES (corp-wide): 13.1B **Privately Held**
WEB: www.raychem.com
SIC: 3643 Connectors & terminals for electrical devices
HQ: Te Connectivity Corporation
1050 Westlakes Dr
Berwyn PA 19312
610 893-9800

(G-17589)
TRENTON GROUP INC
Also Called: Shrewsbury Concrete Co
35 Constitution Ave (17361-1709)
P.O. Box 176 (17361-0176)
PHONE..................................717 235-3807
Ronald Albright, *General Mgr*
EMP: 8
SALES (corp-wide): 4MM **Privately Held**
WEB: www.hanoverconcrete.com
SIC: 3273 Ready-mixed concrete
PA: Trenton Group, Inc.
2000 Carlisle Pike
Hanover PA 17331
717 637-2288

Silver Spring
Lancaster County

(G-17590)
R J BRUNNER & COMPANY
3540 Marietta Ave (17575)
P.O. Box 46 (17575-0046)
PHONE..............................717 285-3534
Raymond J Brunner, *Owner*
EMP: 6
SALES: 250K **Privately Held**
SIC: 3931 Pipes, organ

Silverdale
Bucks County

(G-17591)
ENCHLOR INC
130 W Main St (18962)
PHONE..............................215 453-2533
Thane Tagg, *Principal*
EMP: 7
SALES (est): 4.4MM **Privately Held**
SIC: 2899 Water treating compounds

Simpson
Lackawanna County

(G-17592)
DOYLE & ROTH MFG CO INC
1 Morse Ave (18407-1122)
PHONE..............................570 282-5010
Joseph Twardzik, *District Mgr*
EMP: 40
SQ FT: 54,000
SALES (corp-wide): 12.6MM **Privately Held**
WEB: www.doyleroth.com
SIC: 3443 Heat exchangers: coolers (after, inter), condensers, etc.
PA: Doyle & Roth Manufacturing Co., Inc.
39 Broad St Ste 710
New York NY 10004
212 269-7840

(G-17593)
GENTEX CORPORATION (PA)
324 Main St (18407-1182)
P.O. Box 315, Carbondale (18407-0315)
PHONE..............................570 282-3550
Leonard P Frieder III, *President*
David Shoffner, *General Mgr*
Trevor Austin, *Editor*
Danny Mendoza, *Project Mgr*
Tom Yale, *Opers Staff*
▲ **EMP:** 415
SQ FT: 285,000
SALES (est): 143.3MM **Privately Held**
WEB: www.gentex.net
SIC: 8731 2295 3842 Commercial physical research; coated fabrics, not rubberized; helmets, space

Skippack
Montgomery County

(G-17594)
AMERICAN FUELS LLC
2052 Lucon Rd (19474)
P.O. Box 1467 (19474-1467)
PHONE..............................610 222-3569
Robert Self, *Principal*
EMP: 6 **EST:** 2010
SALES (est): 780.7K **Privately Held**
SIC: 2869 Fuels

(G-17595)
CHOWNS FABRICATION RIGGING INC
2053 Cressman Rd (19474)
P.O. Box 697 (19474-0697)
PHONE..............................610 584-0240
Kevin Chowns, *President*
Matthew Chowns, *Vice Pres*

Barbara Chowns, *Treasurer*
EMP: 100
SQ FT: 2,000
SALES (est): 20MM **Privately Held**
SIC: 1791 3441 Structural steel erection; fabricated structural metal

(G-17596)
FETTEROLF CORPORATION
2021 Cressman Rd (19474)
P.O. Box 103 (19474-0103)
PHONE..............................610 584-1500
Roderick Stanley, *CEO*
David Callaghan, *Vice Pres*
James W Williams IV, *Vice Pres*
Janet Adie, *Project Mgr*
Diane Hazlett, *Project Mgr*
◆ **EMP:** 53 **EST:** 1968
SQ FT: 30,000
SALES (est): 8.9MM
SALES (corp-wide): 4.7MM **Privately Held**
WEB: www.fetterolfvalves.com
SIC: 3491 Industrial valves
PA: Schuf Chemieventile Vertriebs Gmbh & Co. Kg
An Der Guldenmuhle 8-10
Eppstein 65817
619 857-1100

(G-17597)
H&K GROUP INC (PA)
Also Called: Locust Ridge Quarry
2052 Lucon Rd (19474)
P.O. Box 196 (19474-0196)
PHONE..............................610 584-8500
Scott Haines, *Ch of Bd*
John B Haines IV, *President*
John R Kibblehouse, *Corp Secy*
Jules Cattie, *Project Mgr*
Baird Garvin, *Project Mgr*
▲ **EMP:** 150
SQ FT: 40,000
SALES (est): 71.6MM **Privately Held**
WEB: www.hkgroup.com
SIC: 1794 1611 1422 2951 Excavation work; surfacing & paving; limestones, ground; asphalt paving mixtures & blocks

(G-17598)
HERITAGE FENCE & DECK LLC
3890 Skippack Pike (19474)
PHONE..............................610 476-0003
Christopher Caruso, *Principal*
EMP: 4 **EST:** 2017
SALES (est): 133.4K **Privately Held**
SIC: 1799 3089 3446 2411 Fence construction; fences, gates & accessories: plastic; railings, prefabricated metal; rails, fence: round or split

(G-17599)
HERITAGE FENCE COMPANY
Skippack Pike (19474)
PHONE..............................610 584-6710
Rick Ross, *Owner*
EMP: 10
SQ FT: 2,000
SALES: 1MM **Privately Held**
WEB: www.heritage-fence.com
SIC: 3446 5072 5211 3496 Fences or posts, ornamental iron or steel; builders' hardware; fencing; miscellaneous fabricated wire products

(G-17600)
MAR COR PURIFICATION INC (HQ)
4450 Township Line Rd (19474)
P.O. Box 1429 (19474-1429)
PHONE..............................800 633-3080
Curt Weitnauer, *President*
Andrew G Stitzinger, *Vice Pres*
Andy Stitzinger, *Vice Pres*
Mike Carlson, *Buyer*
Ryan Augustine, *Engineer*
▲ **EMP:** 250 **EST:** 1970
SQ FT: 20,000
SALES (est): 200MM
SALES (corp-wide): 871.9MM **Publicly Held**
WEB: www.marcorservices.com
SIC: 3569 3677 Filters; filtration devices, electronic

PA: Cantel Medical Corp.
150 Clove Rd Ste 36
Little Falls NJ 07424
973 890-7220

(G-17601)
NOVATECH INDUSTRIES INC
1221 Bridge Rd (19474)
PHONE..............................610 584-8996
John Smith, *President*
Philip Henderson, *Shareholder*
Joseph Rovito, *Shareholder*
EMP: 6
SALES (est): 610K **Privately Held**
WEB: www.novatech-industries.com
SIC: 3674 Solid state electronic devices

(G-17602)
PALMER INTERNATIONAL INC (PA)
2036 Lucon Rd (19474)
P.O. Box 315 (19474-0315)
PHONE..............................610 584-4241
Kevin Palmer, *President*
Derrick Crowe, *General Mgr*
Stephen T Palmer, *Vice Pres*
Mark Ragnauth, *Plant Mgr*
Sean Richardson, *Purch Agent*
◆ **EMP:** 47
SQ FT: 52,000
SALES (est): 16.4MM **Privately Held**
SIC: 2822 2865 Synthetic rubber; cyclic organic crudes

(G-17603)
PENCO PRODUCTS INC
2024 Cressman Rd (19474)
P.O. Box 378 (19474-0378)
PHONE..............................800 562-1000
Phil Krugler, *Principal*
Suzanne Moore, *Manager*
EMP: 7 **EST:** 2016
SALES (est): 101.4K **Privately Held**
SIC: 2711 Newspapers

Slatington
Lehigh County

(G-17604)
B & F GENERAL MACHINE INC
4875 Park Ave (18080-3142)
P.O. Box 206 (18080-0206)
PHONE..............................610 767-2448
Bob Faust, *President*
Michelle Faust, *Vice Pres*
EMP: 15
SQ FT: 12,000
SALES (est): 2.1MM **Privately Held**
SIC: 3599 Machine shop, jobbing & repair

(G-17605)
DORWARDS ELECTRIC CORP
450 W Church St (18080-1750)
PHONE..............................610 767-8148
Kevin Geist, *President*
EMP: 3
SALES (est): 482.8K **Privately Held**
SIC: 7694 Electric motor repair

(G-17606)
DREAMLIKE ENTERTAINMENT
2122 Mountain Rd (18080-3543)
PHONE..............................610 392-5614
Robert W Deibert Jr, *Principal*
EMP: 5
SALES (est): 255.5K **Privately Held**
SIC: 7372 Prepackaged software

(G-17607)
IDENTITY GROUP
4 N Walnut St (18080-1547)
PHONE..............................610 767-4700
Malcom Gieske, *Owner*
▲ **EMP:** 3 **EST:** 1992
SQ FT: 2,600
SALES (est): 470.5K **Privately Held**
WEB: www.identityaudio.com
SIC: 5065 2517 Sound equipment, electronic; stereo cabinets, wood

(G-17608)
L M ROBBINS CO (PA)
5757 Oakwood Ln (18080-3116)
P.O. Box 217, Neffs (18065-0217)
PHONE..............................610 760-8301
Andrew Brezak, *President*
David H Brink, *Sales Staff*
Maryann Schmoyer, *Admin Sec*
EMP: 11
SQ FT: 16,000
SALES (est): 8.5MM **Privately Held**
WEB: www.lmrobbins.com
SIC: 5084 3199 Conveyor systems; belting for machinery: solid, twisted, flat, etc.: leather

(G-17609)
N E D LLC
2225 Park Pl (18080-4074)
PHONE..............................610 442-1017
Nick Riccione, *Principal*
EMP: 3
SALES (est): 289.2K **Privately Held**
SIC: 3841 Surgical & medical instruments

(G-17610)
NOVA MOLDING
8867 N Loop Rd (18080-3600)
PHONE..............................610 767-7858
Gregory Miller, *President*
Peter George, *Vice Pres*
EMP: 8
SALES (est): 871.8K **Privately Held**
SIC: 3442 Metal doors, sash & trim

(G-17611)
PENN BIG BED SLATE CO INC
8450 Brown St (18080-3583)
P.O. Box 184 (18080-0184)
PHONE..............................610 767-4601
Peter Papay Jr, *President*
Steven Papay, *Corp Secy*
EMP: 70
SQ FT: 1,200
SALES (est): 4.5MM **Privately Held**
WEB: www.pennbigbedslate.com
SIC: 3281 3949 3429 2952 Slate products; sporting & athletic goods; manufactured hardware (general); asphalt felts & coatings

(G-17612)
RELIABLE SIGN & STRIPING INC
301 Chestnut St (18080-1565)
PHONE..............................610 767-8090
Thomas Mengoni, *President*
Louise Mengoni, *Vice Pres*
EMP: 3
SALES (est): 500K **Privately Held**
SIC: 3993 Signs & advertising specialties

(G-17613)
SLATEDALE AGGREGATE MTLS INC
8452 Brown St (18080-3583)
P.O. Box 152 (18080-0152)
PHONE..............................610 767-4601
Peter J Papay Sr, *President*
Erik Eitner, *Treasurer*
EMP: 6 **EST:** 2007
SALES: 300K **Privately Held**
SIC: 1429 Crushed & broken stone

(G-17614)
SNYDER WELDING LLC
7747 Harbor Ct (18080-3656)
PHONE..............................610 657-4916
Terry Snyder, *President*
Natalie Snyder, *Vice Pres*
EMP: 6 **EST:** 2012
SQ FT: 1,800
SALES: 273K **Privately Held**
SIC: 7692 1799 Welding repair; welding on site

Sligo
Clarion County

(G-17615)
HALTEMANS HARDWOOD PRODUCTS
236 Halteman Ln (16255-3850)
PHONE..............................814 745-2519
Dale Halteman, *Partner*
Lester Hertzler, *Partner*
EMP: 5
SALES (est): 398.1K **Privately Held**
SIC: 2511 Chairs, household, except upholstered: wood

(G-17616)
SAYLORS FARM & WOOD PRODUCTS
17319 Route 68 (16255-4343)
PHONE..............................814 745-2306
John W Saylor, *Owner*
Mark Saylor, *Prdtn Mgr*
EMP: 10
SALES: 524K **Privately Held**
SIC: 2449 0171 0175 Fruit crates, wood: wirebound; strawberry farm; apple orchard

Slippery Rock
Butler County

(G-17617)
ALLEGHENY MINERAL CORPORATION
140 Arner Ln (16057-2802)
PHONE..............................724 794-6911
Tom Sanderson, *Manager*
EMP: 25
SALES (corp-wide): 790.5MM **Privately Held**
WEB: www.snydercos.com
SIC: 1411 Limestone & marble dimension stone
HQ: Allegheny Mineral Corporation
1 Glade Dr
Kittanning PA 16201
724 548-8101

(G-17618)
BOROUGH OF SLIPPERY ROCK
Also Called: Municipal Board
155 Branchton Rd (16057-2400)
P.O. Box 207 (16057-0207)
PHONE..............................724 794-3823
John Hines, *Manager*
EMP: 5 **Privately Held**
WEB: www.srboro.net
SIC: 2761 9111 Continuous forms, office & business; city & town managers' offices
PA: Borough Of Slippery Rock
306 E Water St Ste 1
Slippery Rock PA 16057

(G-17619)
DUNHUNTIN MACHINE SHOP INC
799 W Liberty Rd (16057-4715)
PHONE..............................724 794-5404
Eric Hoye, *President*
Samuel Hoye, *Vice Pres*
Susan Hoye, *Admin Sec*
EMP: 6
SQ FT: 4,200
SALES: 500K **Privately Held**
SIC: 3599 Machine shop, jobbing & repair

(G-17620)
M & M WELDING & FABRICATING
124 Smith Rd (16057-4628)
PHONE..............................724 794-2045
Christopher Mahood, *President*
Gale McClaine, *Vice Pres*
EMP: 5
SQ FT: 4,252

SALES (est): 302.5K **Privately Held**
SIC: 3443 7699 Tanks for tank trucks, metal plate; tanks, lined: metal plate; tanks, standard or custom fabricated: metal plate; tank repair

(G-17621)
MACHINING CENTER
Also Called: Metal Fence Supply
85 State Route 956 (16057-7015)
PHONE..............................724 530-7212
Paul Gajda, *Owner*
EMP: 4
SQ FT: 1,400
SALES (est): 321.6K **Privately Held**
SIC: 3599 5211 5039 7692 Machine shop, jobbing & repair; fencing; wire fence, gates & accessories; welding repair

(G-17622)
MINTEQ INTERNATIONAL INC
Zedmark Division of Minteq
395 Grove City Rd (16057-8508)
PHONE..............................724 794-3000
Ronnie Nanni, *Manager*
EMP: 50
SQ FT: 46,000 **Publicly Held**
WEB: www.minteq.com
SIC: 3297 3255 Nonclay refractories; clay refractories
HQ: Minteq International Inc.
35 Highland Ave
Bethlehem PA 18017

(G-17623)
MOVING OUT
118 And A Half Frnklin St (16057)
P.O. Box 97 (16057-0097)
PHONE..............................724 794-6831
Steven Pollock, *Owner*
EMP: 5
SALES (est): 260.1K **Privately Held**
SIC: 2711 Newspapers

(G-17624)
POLLOCK ADVERTISING
Also Called: Tri-County News
118 1/2 Franklin St (16057-1101)
PHONE..............................724 794-6857
Brian Pollock, *Owner*
EMP: 8
SQ FT: 6,500
SALES (est): 263.8K **Privately Held**
WEB: www.gfxadvertising.com
SIC: 2711 7336 Newspapers: publishing only, not printed on site; graphic arts & related design

(G-17625)
R W SIDLEY INC
715 New Castle Rd (16057-4219)
PHONE..............................724 794-4451
Robert Sidley, *President*
Dan Addicot, *Manager*
EMP: 25
SQ FT: 15,000
SALES (est): 2.3MM
SALES (corp-wide): 132.6MM **Privately Held**
WEB: www.rwsidleyinc.com
SIC: 3271 5032 3273 3272 Blocks, concrete or cinder: standard; sand, construction; gravel; ready-mixed concrete; concrete products
PA: R. W. Sidley Incorporated
436 Casement Ave
Painesville OH 44077
440 352-9343

(G-17626)
R W SIDLEY INCORPORATED
715 New Castle Rd (16057-4219)
PHONE..............................724 794-4451
Dan Addicott, *Manager*
EMP: 8
SALES (corp-wide): 132.6MM **Privately Held**
WEB: www.rwsidleyinc.com
SIC: 3273 Ready-mixed concrete
PA: R. W. Sidley Incorporated
436 Casement Ave
Painesville OH 44077
440 352-9343

(G-17627)
S & N INDUSTRIES LLC (PA)
871 New Castle Rd (16057-4227)
PHONE..............................724 406-0322
Marcia Pfab,
Nick Pfab,
Randy Pfab,
EMP: 3
SALES (est): 1.4MM **Privately Held**
SIC: 3444 Sheet metalwork

(G-17628)
TRAC FABRICATION INC
111 Arrowhead Dr Ste D (16057-2667)
PHONE..............................717 862-8722
David Kennedy,
Ben Ridenbaugh,
EMP: 7
SALES (est): 1.1MM **Privately Held**
SIC: 3842 Wheelchairs

(G-17629)
WHITEHALL SPECIALTIES
2850 Perry Hwy (16057-6308)
PHONE..............................724 368-3959
EMP: 5
SALES (est): 425.3K **Privately Held**
SIC: 2022 Cheese, natural & processed

Slovan
Washington County

(G-17630)
SUNNYSIDE SUPPLY INC
1830 Route 18 (15078)
P.O. Box 307 (15078-0307)
PHONE..............................724 947-9966
Dan Billman, *Principal*
Paul Battista, *Vice Pres*
Theresa Hrnciar, *Sales Staff*
Nikki McDivitt, *Sales Associate*
EMP: 7
SQ FT: 30,000
SALES (est): 1.9MM **Privately Held**
WEB: www.sunnysidesupply.com
SIC: 2821 5084 Polycarbonate resins; polyethylene resins; pumps & pumping equipment

(G-17631)
TESTA MACHINE COMPANY INC
28 Baird Ave (15078)
P.O. Box 416 (15078-0416)
PHONE..............................724 947-9397
Richard Lounder, *President*
Marty Santek, *Foreman/Supr*
Tom Euston, *Engineer*
Judy Lounder, *CFO*
Bongiorni Lee, *Human Resources*
EMP: 43
SQ FT: 40,000
SALES (est): 8.5MM **Privately Held**
WEB: www.testa-machine.com
SIC: 3599 3547 3532 Machine shop, jobbing & repair; rolling mill machinery; mining machinery

Smethport
Mckean County

(G-17632)
BACKUS COMPANY (PA)
411 W Water St (16749-1199)
PHONE..............................814 887-5705
William L Pierotti Jr, *Ch of Bd*
James M Pierotti, *President*
John W Pierotti, *Vice Pres*
EMP: 25 **EST:** 1906
SQ FT: 25,000
SALES (est): 2.6MM **Privately Held**
SIC: 3469 3544 3429 3421 Stamping metal for the trade; special dies & tools; manufactured hardware (general); cutlery

(G-17633)
CHEF SPECIALTIES INC
411 W Water St (16749-1199)
PHONE..............................814 887-5652
John W Pierotti, *Ch of Bd*
James M Pierotti, *Admin Sec*
▲ **EMP:** 20

SQ FT: 25,000
SALES (est): 2.4MM
SALES (corp-wide): 2.6MM **Privately Held**
WEB: www.chefspecialties.com
SIC: 2499 Woodenware, kitchen & household
PA: Backus Company
411 W Water St
Smethport PA 16749
814 887-5705

(G-17634)
DEAN CONSTRUCTION LLC
15884 Route 6 (16749-3846)
PHONE..............................814 887-8750
Craig Dean, *Co-Owner*
Cory Dean, *Co-Owner*
EMP: 5 **EST:** 2016
SALES (est): 204.5K **Privately Held**
SIC: 1629 0851 1389 1611 Land preparation construction; forestry services; grading oil & gas well foundations; highway & street construction; oil & gas exploration services

(G-17635)
JONI BRITTON LOGGING
232 Bloomster Holw (16749-2408)
PHONE..............................814 887-9920
Joni Britton, *Owner*
EMP: 3
SALES (est): 221.6K **Privately Held**
SIC: 2411 Logging camps & contractors

(G-17636)
PETRONORTH LTD
510 W Green St (16749-1124)
P.O. Box 742 (16749-0742)
PHONE..............................814 368-6992
CJ Duke, *Ch of Bd*
James R Young, *President*
John F Young, *Vice Pres*
Clarence H Steiner, *Treasurer*
EMP: 1
SALES: 1MM **Privately Held**
SIC: 1311 Natural gas production

(G-17637)
TODD SMITH LOGGING INC
120 W Green St (16749-1250)
PHONE..............................814 887-2183
Todd Smith, *President*
EMP: 8
SALES (est): 924.8K **Privately Held**
SIC: 2411 Logging camps & contractors

Smicksburg
Indiana County

(G-17638)
GREENTREE LUMBER
26 Wolf Rd (16256)
P.O. Box 126 (16256-0126)
PHONE..............................814 257-9878
David Dalessio, *Owner*
Tammy Dalessio, *Co-Owner*
EMP: 12
SALES (est): 1.1MM **Privately Held**
SIC: 2421 1542 Lumber: rough, sawed or planed; custom builders, non-residential

(G-17639)
ROBERT PEARCE & SONS
Also Called: Pearce Lumber Co
7416 Route 210 Hwy (16256-4412)
PHONE..............................724 286-9757
Tom Pearce, *Partner*
George Pearce, *Partner*
Kevin Pearce, *Partner*
EMP: 17
SQ FT: 50,000
SALES (est): 2.5MM **Privately Held**
WEB: www.robertpearce.net
SIC: 2421 Lumber: rough, sawed or planed; kiln drying of lumber

(G-17640)
WINDGATE VINEYARDS INC
1998 Hemlock Acres Rd (16256-2808)
PHONE..............................814 257-8797
Daniel Enerson, *President*
Tammy Delicio, *Office Mgr*

EMP: 20
SALES (est): 1.8MM Privately Held
WEB: www.windgatevineyards.com
SIC: 2084 Wines

Smithfield
Fayette County

(G-17641)
ARGON ST INC
90 Laurel View Dr (15478-1643)
PHONE..................724 564-4100
Jeff Brown, President
Kevin Godfrey, General Mgr
Mark Smith, Opers Mgr
EMP: 25
SQ FT: 60,000
SALES (est): 1MM
SALES (corp-wide): 101.1B Publicly Held
SIC: 3812 Search & detection systems & instruments
HQ: Argon St, Inc.
12701 Fair Lakes Cir # 800
Fairfax VA 22033
703 322-0881

(G-17642)
BERKLEY MEDICAL RESOURCES INC (PA)
700 Mountain View Dr (15478-8924)
PHONE..................724 564-5002
John R Berkley, President
Sherry Berkley, Corp Secy
Suzanne Herman, Manager
◆ EMP: 140
SQ FT: 290,000
SALES (est): 27.9MM Privately Held
WEB: www.berkleymedical.com
SIC: 3841 Surgical & medical instruments

(G-17643)
CALFRAC WELL SERVICES CORP
2001 Summit View Dr (15478-1646)
P.O. Box 279 (15478-0279)
PHONE..................724 564-5350
Joe Wilken, Branch Mgr
EMP: 234
SALES (corp-wide): 1.2B Privately Held
SIC: 1389 Oil field services
HQ: Calfrac Well Services Corp.
717 17th St Ste 1445
Denver CO 80202

(G-17644)
CARLISLE CONSTRUCTION MTLS LLC
2000 Summit View Dr (15478-1645)
PHONE..................724 564-5440
John Falkner, Manager
EMP: 130
SALES (corp-wide): 4.4B Publicly Held
SIC: 3086 Plastics foam products
HQ: Carlisle Construction Materials, Llc
1285 Ritner Hwy
Carlisle PA 17013

(G-17645)
CARLISLE CONSTRUCTION MTLS LLC
2000 Summit View Dr (15478-1645)
PHONE..................724 564-5440
Dave Gibson, Branch Mgr
EMP: 48
SALES (corp-wide): 4.4B Publicly Held
WEB: www.hpanels.com
SIC: 3086 Insulation or cushioning material, foamed plastic
HQ: Carlisle Construction Materials, Llc
1285 Ritner Hwy
Carlisle PA 17013

(G-17646)
CHARLES L SWENGLISH SONS COAL
83 Swenglish Ln (15478-1085)
PHONE..................724 437-3541
Charles C Swenglish, President
Carl Robin, Vice Pres
Curtis Swenglsih, Admin Sec
EMP: 6

SALES: 900K Privately Held
SIC: 1221 1794 Bituminous coal & lignite-surface mining; excavation work

(G-17647)
CHICOPEE INC
Also Called: Chicopee Specialty Products
700 Mountain View Dr (15478-8924)
PHONE..................800 835-2442
Dan Levi, Manager
EMP: 3 Publicly Held
SIC: 2297 Nonwoven fabrics
HQ: Chicopee, Inc.
9335 Harr Corn Pkwy Ste 3
Charlotte NC 28269

(G-17648)
FREY LUMBER COMPANY INC
2883 Morgantown Rd (15478-1722)
PHONE..................724 564-1888
James E Frey Sr, President
James E Frey Jr, Vice Pres
Cheryl A Frey, Property Mgr
Kristen Frey, Admin Sec
EMP: 22
SQ FT: 600
SALES (est): 3.1MM Privately Held
WEB: www.freylumber.com
SIC: 2421 Lumber: rough, sawed or planed

(G-17649)
FREY PALLET CORPORATION
2883 Morgantown Rd (15478-1722)
PHONE..................724 564-1888
James E Frey Sr, President
James Frey Jr, President
Kristen Frey, Admin Sec
EMP: 10
SALES: 600K Privately Held
SIC: 2448 Skids, wood & wood with metal

(G-17650)
GEROME MANUFACTURING CO INC
80 Laurel View Dr (15478-1643)
P.O. Box 1089, Uniontown (15401-1089)
PHONE..................724 438-8544
Joseph Putila, President
Henry Gerome, Vice Pres
Chris Ramage, QC Mgr
Kevin Firmani, Engineer
Fred Gantzhorn, Manager
▲ EMP: 83 EST: 1957
SQ FT: 150,000
SALES (est): 30.8MM Privately Held
WEB: www.geromemfg.com
SIC: 3444 3812 3699 3613 Sheet metal specialties, not stamped; magnetic field detection apparatus; electrical equipment & supplies; switchgear & switchboard apparatus; metal stampings; fabricated plate work (boiler shop)

(G-17651)
GRAPHTEK LLC
Also Called: Pennsylvania Carbon Products
219 Hope Rd (15478-1263)
PHONE..................724 564-9211
Joseph Skala, Branch Mgr
EMP: 15
SALES (corp-wide): 2.2MM Privately Held
WEB: www.graphtekllc.com
SIC: 3624 Carbon & graphite products
PA: Graphtek Llc
600 Academy Dr Ste 100
Northbrook IL 60062
847 279-1925

(G-17652)
KLONDIKE BLOCK MASNRY SUPS INC
Also Called: Klondike Block and Masonry Sup
331 Shoaf Rd (15478-1209)
PHONE..................724 439-3888
John Sexton, President
Don Myers, Vice Pres
EMP: 5 EST: 1980
SALES (est): 83.5K Privately Held
SIC: 3271 Blocks, concrete or cinder: standard

(G-17653)
MATTHEY JOHNSON INC
605 Mountain View Dr (15478-1648)
PHONE..................724 564-7200

Bob Weido, Branch Mgr
EMP: 15
SALES (corp-wide): 15B Privately Held
SIC: 3714 Exhaust systems & parts, motor vehicle
HQ: Matthey Johnson Inc
435 Devon Park Dr Ste 600
Wayne PA 19087
610 971-3000

(G-17654)
PENNSYLVANIA CARBON PDTS LLC
219 Hope Rd (15478-1263)
PHONE..................724 564-9211
Vlatimer Novahoski,
Joe Skala,
EMP: 6 EST: 2000
SALES (est): 550K Privately Held
SIC: 3295 Graphite, natural: ground, pulverized, refined or blended

(G-17655)
SUPERIOR CABINET CO
701 Old Frame Rd (15478-1177)
PHONE..................724 569-9581
Dean Marunyak, Owner
EMP: 7
SQ FT: 6,000
SALES: 600K Privately Held
WEB: www.superiorcabinet.com
SIC: 2541 2542 2434 Cabinets, lockers & shelving; partitions & fixtures, except wood; wood kitchen cabinets

(G-17656)
ZACHARY R MARELLA
1178 Walnut Hill Rd (15478-1044)
PHONE..................724 557-1671
Zachary Marella, Owner
EMP: 5
SALES (est): 369.8K Privately Held
SIC: 3499 Fire- or burglary-resistive products

(G-17657)
ZRM ENTERPRISES LLC
1178 Walnut Hill Rd (15478-1044)
PHONE..................724 437-3116
Zachary Marella, Principal
EMP: 16 EST: 2010
SQ FT: 16,000
SALES (est): 3.5MM Privately Held
SIC: 3599 Machine shop, jobbing & repair

Smithton
Westmoreland County

(G-17658)
BODRIE INC
Also Called: Minuteman Press
138 Flora St B (15479-1578)
PHONE..................724 836-3666
Tom Bosetti, President
EMP: 3
SQ FT: 8,000
SALES (est): 438.3K Privately Held
SIC: 2752 7334 Commercial printing, offset; photocopying & duplicating services

(G-17659)
COMPLETION SNUBBING SERVI
158 Painter Rd (15479-8722)
P.O. Box 1299, Gainesville TX (76241-1299)
PHONE..................940 668-5109
EMP: 4 EST: 2013
SALES (est): 295.5K Privately Held
SIC: 1389 Construction, repair & dismantling services

(G-17660)
ELIZABETH MILLING COMPANY LLC (PA)
Also Called: Pritts Feed & Supply
608 Center St (15479)
PHONE..................724 872-9404
Mike Adams, President
David Felgar, General Mgr
EMP: 11 EST: 1957
SQ FT: 6,000
SALES (est): 1.5MM Privately Held
SIC: 2899 Chemical preparations

(G-17661)
JONES BREWING COMPANY INC
Also Called: Stoney's Brewing Company
260 Second St (15479)
PHONE..................724 872-2337
Sandra Podlucky, President
EMP: 6
SQ FT: 100,000
SALES (est): 568.6K Privately Held
WEB: www.stoneysbeer.com
SIC: 2082 Beer (alcoholic beverage)

(G-17662)
SMITHTON RACEWAY LLC
425 Fitz Henry Rd (15479-8703)
PHONE..................724 797-1822
Adam J Skokut, Principal
EMP: 3
SALES (est): 197.7K Privately Held
SIC: 3644 Raceways

(G-17663)
TARGET DRILLING INC
Also Called: Td's
1112 Glacier Rd (15479-8766)
PHONE..................724 633-3927
Stephen Kravits, CEO
Don Williams, Treasurer
Jessica Gardner, Human Res Mgr
Tom Marshall, Manager
EMP: 27
SQ FT: 3,000
SALES (est): 15.7MM Privately Held
SIC: 1381 Directional drilling oil & gas wells

(G-17664)
WISE INTERVENTION SVCS USA INC
146 Painter Rd (15479-8722)
PHONE..................724 405-6660
Josh Thompson, President
Neil Bothwell, CFO
EMP: 73 EST: 2012
SQ FT: 17,000
SALES (est): 17.9MM
SALES (corp-wide): 9.5MM Privately Held
SIC: 3533 Oil field machinery & equipment
PA: Wise Intervention Services Inc
540 5 Ave Sw Unit 950
Calgary AB T2P 0
587 538-0586

Smock
Fayette County

(G-17665)
F DEFRANK& SON CUSTOM CABINETS
593 Industrial Park Rd (15480-1227)
PHONE..................724 430-1812
Roxann Defrank, CEO
Dominic Defrank, Vice Pres
EMP: 6
SQ FT: 5,000
SALES: 600K Privately Held
SIC: 2434 2439 Wood kitchen cabinets; structural wood members

(G-17666)
POLKABLA INDUSTRIES LLC
16 1st St (15480-2067)
P.O. Box 84 (15480-0084)
PHONE..................724 322-7740
Thomas Polkabla, Principal
EMP: 3
SALES (est): 291.9K Privately Held
SIC: 3999 Manufacturing industries

(G-17667)
SKC GULF COAST INC
75 Colonial Ave (15480-2051)
PHONE..................724 677-0340
Daniel L Guild, President
EMP: 7
SALES (corp-wide): 25.9MM Privately Held
SIC: 3569 Filters
HQ: Skc Gulf Coast, Inc.
17459 Village Green Dr
Jersey Village TX 77040
281 859-8050

Smoketown
Lancaster County

(G-17668)
SCHMITT ALUMINUM FOUNDRY INC
2485 Old Phladelphia Pike (17576)
P.O. Box 276 (17576-0276)
PHONE.................................717 299-5651
Raymond Hohenwarter, *President*
Raymond E Hohenwarter, *President*
David A Hohenwarter, *Vice Pres*
EMP: 12 EST: 1953
SALES (est): 1.8MM **Privately Held**
SIC: 3365 3369 Aluminum & aluminum-based alloy castings; zinc & zinc-base alloy castings, except die-castings

Snow Shoe
Centre County

(G-17669)
GP CABINETS LLC
604 S Moshannon Ave (16874-8601)
PHONE.................................814 933-8902
James Josefik,
EMP: 6
SALES (est): 491.8K **Privately Held**
SIC: 2434 Vanities, bathroom: wood

(G-17670)
R S CARLIN INC (PA)
Also Called: Carlin Coal Co
951 Fountain Rd (16874-8824)
PHONE.................................814 387-4190
Marilyn Spear, *President*
Ray J Carlin, *Vice Pres*
EMP: 10 **EST:** 1943
SALES (est): 1.7MM **Privately Held**
SIC: 1221 5983 Strip mining, bituminous; fuel oil dealers

(G-17671)
VESUVIUS U S A CORPORATION
895 Clarence Rd (16874)
P.O. Box 276 (16874-0276)
PHONE.................................814 387-6811
Neil Crilly, *Opers-Prdtn-Mfg*
EMP: 65
SQ FT: 86,000
SALES (corp-wide): 2.2B **Privately Held**
WEB: www.vesuvius.com
SIC: 3297 Graphite refractories: carbon bond or ceramic bond
HQ: Vesuvius U S A Corporation
1404 Newton Dr
Champaign IL 61822
217 351-5000

Somerset
Somerset County

(G-17672)
ABILENE BOOT CO INC
841 S Center Ave (15501-2823)
PHONE.................................814 445-6545
Rench P Humphries, *CEO*
Anil K Gupta, *Vice Pres*
Ross W Gupta, *Admin Sec*
▲ **EMP:** 45
SQ FT: 68,000
SALES (est): 6.6MM **Privately Held**
SIC: 3144 3143 Boots, canvas or leather: women's; boots, dress or casual: men's

(G-17673)
ANGERMEIER TOOL & DIE INC
2414 Glades Pike (15501-8518)
PHONE.................................814 445-2285
Alan Angermeier, *President*
Amy Angermeier, *Corp Secy*
EMP: 7
SQ FT: 5,600
SALES (est): 540K **Privately Held**
SIC: 3544 Special dies & tools

(G-17674)
ASSOCIATED WINDOWS
Also Called: AWC Mr Spouting
334 Emert Rd (15501-7117)
PHONE.................................814 445-9744
Daniel Emert, *Owner*
EMP: 4
SALES: 340K **Privately Held**
SIC: 3211 Window glass, clear & colored

(G-17675)
ATLAS PRINTING COMPANY
421 W Patriot St (15501-1500)
PHONE.................................814 445-2516
Cindy Breen, *Owner*
EMP: 5
SQ FT: 6,500
SALES: 415K **Privately Held**
SIC: 2752 Commercial printing, offset

(G-17676)
AUGUSTINE DIE & MOLD INC
492 Drum Ave (15501-3401)
PHONE.................................814 443-2390
Anthony Augustine Jr, *President*
Greg Good, *Vice Pres*
EMP: 15
SQ FT: 31,000
SALES (est): 3.2MM **Privately Held**
WEB: www.amoldinc.com
SIC: 3544 Industrial molds

(G-17677)
AUGUSTINE PLASTICS INC
492 Drum Ave (15501-3401)
PHONE.................................814 443-7428
Tony Augustine, *Owner*
▲ **EMP:** 23 **EST:** 1998
SALES (est): 321.6K **Privately Held**
SIC: 3089 Injection molding of plastics

(G-17678)
BAKERS LAWN ORNAMENTS
570 Berlin Plank Rd (15501-2413)
PHONE.................................814 445-7028
Michael D Baker, *Partner*
Valerie Baker, *Partner*
EMP: 18
SQ FT: 61,000
SALES (est): 1.1MM **Privately Held**
SIC: 3269 3231 5947 0181 Art & ornamental ware, pottery; ornamental glass: cut, engraved or otherwise decorated; gift shop; ornamental nursery products

(G-17679)
CHILD EVNGELISM FELLOWSHIP INC
571 Felgar Rd (15501-7208)
P.O. Box 403, Indiana (15701-0403)
PHONE.................................724 463-1600
Susan Crooks, *Exec Dir*
EMP: 41
SALES (corp-wide): 24.4MM **Privately Held**
SIC: 2752 Commercial printing, lithographic
PA: Child Evangelism Fellowship Incorporated
17482 Highway M
Warrenton MO 63383
636 456-4321

(G-17680)
CLARK H REAM LUMBER
221 Salem Ave (15501-7576)
PHONE.................................814 445-8185
Clark H Ream, *Owner*
Patricia Ream, *Officer*
EMP: 8 **EST:** 1933
SALES: 1MM **Privately Held**
SIC: 2421 2448 Sawmills & planing mills, general; pallets, wood

(G-17681)
COALVIEW RECOVERY GROUP LLC
1166 Village Rd (15501-4222)
PHONE.................................814 443-6454
EMP: 4
SALES (est): 411.9K **Privately Held**
SIC: 1221 Bituminous Coal/Lignite Surface Mining

(G-17682)
CUSTOM IRON WORKS WELDING
570 Berlin Plank Rd (15501-2413)
PHONE.................................814 444-1315
Shawn Gross, *President*
Michelle Zolla, *Admin Sec*
EMP: 11 **EST:** 2014
SQ FT: 10,000
SALES (est): 1.3MM **Privately Held**
SIC: 7692 1799 Welding repair; ornamental metal work

(G-17683)
DAILY AMERICAN (DH)
334 W Main St (15501-1502)
P.O. Box 638 (15501-0638)
PHONE.................................814 444-5900
Andy Bruns, *Principal*
Tom Koppenhofer, *Adv Mgr*
EMP: 22
SQ FT: 12,500
SALES (est): 3.2MM
SALES (corp-wide): 1B **Publicly Held**
WEB: www.dailyamerican.com
SIC: 2711 2721 Commercial printing & newspaper publishing combined; periodicals
HQ: Schurz Communications, Inc.
1301 E Douglas Rd Ste 200
Mishawaka IN 46545
574 247-7237

(G-17684)
DEVILBISS HEALTHCARE LLC (HQ)
100 Devilbiss Dr (15501-2125)
PHONE.................................814 443-4881
Rich Kocinski, *President*
Chandrajeet Singh, *General Mgr*
Joe Lewarski, *Vice Pres*
Mike Marcinek, *Vice Pres*
Brad Ritt, *Vice Pres*
◆ **EMP:** 273
SQ FT: 152,600
SALES: 100MM **Privately Held**
SIC: 3845 Electromedical equipment

(G-17685)
DIAMOND TECH GROUP INC
Also Called: Somerset Plastics
1012 S Center Ave (15501-2828)
PHONE.................................814 445-8953
Charles Crum Jr, *President*
Charles Crum Sr, *CFO*
EMP: 10
SQ FT: 35,000
SALES: 1.4MM **Privately Held**
WEB: www.dtginc.co
SIC: 3089 Injection molding of plastics

(G-17686)
E J BOGNAR INC
Also Called: Somerset Sand & Stone Co Div
182 Bando Rd (15501-4804)
PHONE.................................814 443-6000
Nadine Bognar, *Branch Mgr*
EMP: 12
SALES (corp-wide): 8MM **Privately Held**
WEB: www.ejbognar.com
SIC: 1459 Stoneware clay mining
PA: E.J. Bognar Incorporated
733 Washington Rd Fl 5
Pittsburgh PA 15228
412 344-9900

(G-17687)
EDGEWOOD WELDING & FABRICATION
842 S Edgewood Ave (15501-2614)
PHONE.................................814 445-7746
Brad Cole, *President*
Todd Eutin, *Corp Secy*
EMP: 14 **EST:** 1972
SQ FT: 14,000
SALES (est): 2.6MM **Privately Held**
WEB: www.weimersblacksmith.com
SIC: 7692 Welding repair

(G-17688)
FETTEROLF GROUP INC (HQ)
227 New Centerville Rd (15501-8755)
PHONE.................................814 443-4688
Donald Fetterolf, *Chairman*
Mitchell Fetterolf, *Vice Pres*
EMP: 6
SQ FT: 5,000
SALES (est): 11.1MM **Privately Held**
SIC: 3661 6331 Communication headgear, telephone; fire, marine & casualty insurance

(G-17689)
GLADES PIKE WINERY INC
2208 Glades Pike (15501-8516)
PHONE.................................814 445-3753
Steven Addleman, *President*
Liz Diesel, *General Mgr*
EMP: 10
SALES: 750K **Privately Held**
WEB: www.gladespikewinery.com
SIC: 2084 Wines

(G-17690)
GLOBAL INCORPORATED
Also Called: MFC Valve
160 Cannery Rd (15501-2804)
P.O. Box 24 (15501-0024)
PHONE.................................814 445-9671
Robert Kirst, *President*
Joseph D Kirst II, *Principal*
Jk Kirst, *Admin Sec*
EMP: 25 **EST:** 1965
SQ FT: 20,000
SALES (est): 4.5MM **Privately Held**
WEB: www.globalsfc.com
SIC: 3599 Machine shop, jobbing & repair

(G-17691)
GROSS BROS WLDG FBRICATION INC
1344 Berlin Plank Rd (15501-3726)
PHONE.................................814 443-1130
Shawn Gross, *President*
Michelle Zolla, *Principal*
Jamey Gross, *Vice Pres*
EMP: 9
SQ FT: 5,000
SALES: 1.2MM **Privately Held**
SIC: 7692 Welding repair

(G-17692)
GSP MARKETING INC
Also Called: G-S Products
322 Lavansville Rd (15501-8090)
PHONE.................................814 445-5866
Gerald F Martin, *President*
Stan Haines, *Regl Sales Mgr*
Dave Cote, *Sales Staff*
Steve Martin, *Manager*
Geni Witosky, *Admin Asst*
EMP: 50
SQ FT: 20,000
SALES (est): 11.1MM **Privately Held**
WEB: www.g-sproducts.com
SIC: 3713 Truck bodies (motor vehicles)

(G-17693)
JENNY PRODUCTS INC (PA)
850 N Pleasant Ave (15501-1069)
PHONE.................................814 445-3400
Peter Leiss, *President*
Jodell Antram, *General Mgr*
Daniel Leiss, *Vice Pres*
▲ **EMP:** 50
SQ FT: 52,000
SALES (est): 12MM **Privately Held**
WEB: www.jennyproductsinc.com
SIC: 3563 3589 Air & gas compressors; high pressure cleaning equipment

(G-17694)
K & H DIE AND MOLD INC
648 W Bakersville Edie Rd (15501-8937)
PHONE.................................814 445-9584
Donald W Kimmel, *President*
Lois Kimmel, *Vice Pres*
EMP: 4
SQ FT: 3,000
SALES: 500K **Privately Held**
SIC: 3089 Injection molding of plastics

(G-17695)
LEISS TOOL & DIE
801 N Pleasant Ave (15501-1092)
PHONE.................................814 444-1444
Peter Leiss, *Owner*
Thomas Samole, *Managing Prtnr*
▲ **EMP:** 140
SQ FT: 160,000

SALES: 18MM **Privately Held**
WEB: www.leiss.com
SIC: 3599 3441 3544 7692 Machine shop, jobbing & repair; fabricated structural metal; special dies & tools; welding repair; metal stampings; sheet metalwork

(G-17696)
LOUIS G SREDY
Also Called: La Rue Meat Processing
1908 Water Level Rd (15501-2902)
PHONE......................................814 445-7229
EMP: 9
SQ FT: 10,000
SALES (est): 310K **Privately Held**
SIC: 2011 0212 2013 Meat Packing Plant Beef Cattle-Except Feedlot Mfg Prepared Meats

(G-17697)
MOROCCO WELDING LLC
133 Morocco St (15501-8761)
PHONE......................................814 444-9353
John Morocco,
EMP: 14
SQ FT: 1,000
SALES (est): 3MM **Privately Held**
SIC: 1799 3599 Welding on site; machine & other job shop work

(G-17698)
NEW ENTERPRISE STONE LIME INC
Somerset Limestone Div
1100 S Edgewood Ave (15501-2624)
PHONE......................................814 443-6494
Keith Van Horn, *Engineer*
Eugene Barron, *Manager*
EMP: 50
SALES (corp-wide): 651.9MM **Privately Held**
SIC: 2951 3273 1422 3271 Concrete, bituminous; ready-mixed concrete; crushed & broken limestone; concrete block & brick
PA: New Enterprise Stone & Lime Co., Inc.
3912 Brumbaugh Rd
New Enterprise PA 16664
814 224-6883

(G-17699)
NORCORP INC
610 N Center Ave (15501-1024)
PHONE......................................814 445-2523
Ken Baker, *President*
EMP: 5
SQ FT: 3,800
SALES (est): 350K **Privately Held**
SIC: 2752 Commercial printing, offset

(G-17700)
PRECISION MILLWORK & CABINETRY
731 E Bakersville Edie Rd (15501-6578)
PHONE......................................814 445-9669
Bruce Eller, *President*
Kelly Eller, *Admin Sec*
EMP: 20
SALES (est): 1.5MM **Privately Held**
WEB: www.pm-cinc.com
SIC: 1751 2431 Cabinet building & installation; millwork

(G-17701)
PYLE MACHINE MANUFACTURING INC
343 Bromm Rd (15501-5110)
PHONE......................................814 443-3171
Lawrence E Pyle, *President*
EMP: 7 **EST:** 1978
SQ FT: 4,400
SALES (est): 1MM **Privately Held**
SIC: 3599 Machine shop, jobbing & repair

(G-17702)
QUANTUM LEAP ENGNERED PDTS LLC
330 High St (15501-1301)
PHONE......................................814 289-1476
Theodore V Harris, *Mng Member*
EMP: 4
SQ FT: 50,000
SALES: 40K **Privately Held**
SIC: 3792 Travel trailers & campers

(G-17703)
SAJ PUBLISHING
113 S Center Ave Ste 1 (15501-2063)
PHONE......................................814 445-9695
Glenn Kashurba, *Owner*
EMP: 5
SQ FT: 3,000
SALES (est): 155.6K **Privately Held**
WEB: www.sajpublishing.com
SIC: 2741 Business service newsletters: publishing & printing

(G-17704)
SFC VALVE CORPORATION
Also Called: Global / Sfc Valve
160 Cannery Rd (15501-2804)
P.O. Box 24 (15501-0024)
PHONE......................................814 445-9671
Robert H Kirst, *President*
Michael Toneff, *Vice Pres*
EMP: 51
SQ FT: 21,000
SALES (est): 12.2MM **Privately Held**
SIC: 3494 Steam fittings & specialties

(G-17705)
SHAFFER BLOCK AND CON PDTS INC
951 S Edgewood Ave (15501-2617)
PHONE......................................814 445-4414
Donald Shaffer, *President*
Joel Shaffer, *Vice Pres*
Mark Shaffer, *Admin Sec*
EMP: 20 **EST:** 1945
SQ FT: 25,000
SALES (est): 3.1MM **Privately Held**
WEB: www.shafferblock.com
SIC: 3273 5251 3271 3999 Ready-mixed concrete; hardware; blocks, concrete or cinder: standard; advertising curtains

(G-17706)
SOMERSET CONSOLIDATED INDS INC (PA)
Also Called: Somerset Foundry & Mch Co Div
809 S Edgewood Ave (15501-2615)
P.O. Box L, Callery (16024-0176)
PHONE......................................814 445-7927
Edward Byrnes, *Ch of Bd*
Greg Frick, *President*
EMP: 40
SQ FT: 30,000
SALES (est): 5.5MM **Privately Held**
SIC: 3321 Gray iron castings

(G-17707)
SOMERSET DOOR & COLUMN COMPANY
174 Sagamore St (15501-7700)
PHONE......................................814 444-9427
Roger Lemens, *General Mgr*
EMP: 11
SALES (est): 1MM **Privately Held**
WEB: www.somersetdoor.com
SIC: 2431 Doors, wood

(G-17708)
SOMERSET DOOR AND COLUMN CO
Also Called: SDC Building Center
1123 S Edgewood Ave (15501-2601)
P.O. Box 755 (15501-0755)
PHONE......................................814 445-9608
Dean Hottle, *President*
George Shafer, *Vice Pres*
Adams Ira R, *Treasurer*
Richard Adams, *Admin Sec*
EMP: 35 **EST:** 1906
SQ FT: 16,000
SALES (est): 4.9MM **Privately Held**
SIC: 2431 5211 3443 2435 Doors & door parts & trim, wood; lumber & other building materials; fabricated plate work (boiler shop); hardwood veneer & plywood; sawmills & planing mills, general

(G-17709)
SOMERSET WELDING & STEEL INC
Riggs Industries
422 Riggs Rd (15501-9350)
PHONE......................................814 444-7000
Joe Ladosky, *Partner*
David Spear, *General Mgr*

Richard Stouffer, *Store Mgr*
Gary Shaffer, *Engineer*
Bryan Cordell, *Credit Mgr*
EMP: 50
SALES (corp-wide): 119.8MM **Privately Held**
WEB: www.jjbodies.net
SIC: 5083 5072 3444 3441 Agricultural machinery & equipment; hardware; sheet metalwork; fabricated structural metal
HQ: Somerset Welding & Steel, Inc.
10558 Somerset Pike
Somerset PA 15501
814 443-2671

(G-17710)
SOMERSET WELDING & STEEL INC (HQ)
Also Called: J & J Truck Bodies and Trlrs
10558 Somerset Pike (15501-7352)
P.O. Box 97, Boswell (15531-0097)
PHONE......................................814 443-2671
S William Riggs, *President*
Michael Riggs, *Senior VP*
Gerald A Johnson, *Vice Pres*
Doug Garman, *Foreman/Supr*
Matt Matusko, *Foreman/Supr*
EMP: 150
SQ FT: 177,000
SALES: 52MM
SALES (corp-wide): 119.8MM **Privately Held**
WEB: www.jjbodies.net
SIC: 3713 3715 5531 5083 Dump truck bodies; truck trailers; automotive parts; farm & garden machinery
PA: Riggs Industries, Inc.
2478 Lincoln Hwy
Stoystown PA 15563
814 629-5621

(G-17711)
SOMERSET WELDING & STEEL INC
Also Called: J & J Truck Equipment
422 Riggs Rd (15501-9350)
PHONE......................................814 444-7000
Craig Hauger, *Manager*
EMP: 35
SALES (corp-wide): 119.8MM **Privately Held**
WEB: www.jjbodies.net
SIC: 5083 5072 3444 Farm & garden machinery; hardware; sheet metalwork
HQ: Somerset Welding & Steel, Inc.
10558 Somerset Pike
Somerset PA 15501
814 443-2671

(G-17712)
STOUT LUMBER COMPANY
Also Called: Stout Logging
246 Stout Ln (15501-6472)
PHONE......................................814 443-9920
Ronald Stout, *Partner*
Shirley Stout, *Partner*
EMP: 3
SALES (est): 260K **Privately Held**
SIC: 2411 Logging

(G-17713)
SULLIS WLDG & PIPE FITTING LLC
1217 Glades Pike (15501-5811)
PHONE......................................814 445-9147
Andy Sullivan, *Owner*
EMP: 3
SALES (est): 195K **Privately Held**
SIC: 7692 Welding repair

(G-17714)
TIMS ELECTRIC MOTOR REPAIR CO
220 S Ankeny Ave (15501-2099)
PHONE......................................814 445-5078
Tim Knupp, *Partner*
Robin Knupp, *Partner*
EMP: 3
SALES (est): 375.6K **Privately Held**
SIC: 7694 5999 Electric motor repair; motors, electric

(G-17715)
VCP MOBILITY INC
Also Called: Respiratory Products Division
100 Devilbiss Dr (15501-2125)
PHONE......................................814 443-4881
Raymond Dyer, *President*
EMP: 400
SQ FT: 160,000
SALES (corp-wide): 402.8MM **Privately Held**
SIC: 3842 3841 Respirators; surgical & medical instruments
HQ: Vcp Mobility, Inc.
6899 Winchester Cir # 200
Boulder CO 80301
303 218-4500

(G-17716)
WHEELER BROS INC
Also Called: Wheeler Brothers
501 Drum Ave (15501)
PHONE......................................814 443-3269
Chad Wheeler, *President*
EMP: 9
SALES (corp-wide): 697.2MM **Publicly Held**
SIC: 3714 Mfg Motor Vehicle Parts/Accessories
HQ: Wheeler Bros., Inc.
384 Drum Ave
Somerset PA 15501
814 443-7000

(G-17717)
WHEELER BROS INC (HQ)
Also Called: Wheeler Brothers
384 Drum Ave (15501-3400)
P.O. Box 737 (15501-0737)
PHONE......................................814 443-7000
Chad Wheeler, *President*
◆ **EMP:** 90
SQ FT: 22,000
SALES (est): 45.3MM
SALES (corp-wide): 697.2MM **Publicly Held**
WEB: www.teamwbi.com
SIC: 3714 5013 Acceleration equipment, motor vehicle; motor vehicle supplies & new parts; automotive supplies & parts; automotive supplies; automotive brakes
PA: Vse Corporation
6348 Walker Ln
Alexandria VA 22310
703 960-4600

(G-17718)
WOODBINE PROPERTIES (PA)
227 New Centerville Rd (15501-8755)
PHONE......................................814 443-4688
Mitch Fetterolf, *Partner*
Donald Fetterolf, *Partner*
EMP: 230
SQ FT: 10,000
SALES (est): 5MM **Privately Held**
SIC: 6512 6331 3661 Nonresidential building operators; fire, marine & casualty insurance; telephones & telephone apparatus; communication headgear, telephone

---

Souderton
Montgomery County

(G-17719)
A F MOYER INC
249 Allentown Rd (18964-2207)
P.O. Box 64395 (18964-0395)
PHONE......................................215 723-5555
EMP: 3
SALES (est): 323K **Privately Held**
SIC: 2077 Animal & marine fats & oils

(G-17720)
ADVANCED DESIGN AND CTRL CORP
Also Called: Advanced Equipment Sales
535 Hagey Rd (18964-2434)
PHONE......................................215 723-7200
Jeff Dietterich, *President*
Jill Dietterich, *Vice Pres*
EMP: 15
SQ FT: 10,000

▲ = Import ▼=Export
◆ =Import/Export

SALES (est): 5.1MM **Privately Held**
WEB: www.aesales.net
SIC: 3564 8711 Blowers & fans; engineering services

(G-17721)
ALMAC CENTRAL MANAGEMENT LLC
25 Fretz Rd (18964-2610)
PHONE...................................215 660-8500
Alan Armstrong, *CEO*
EMP: 113
SQ FT: 4,158
SALES (est): 12.2MM
SALES (corp-wide): 69.2K **Privately Held**
SIC: 8071 8748 2834 Testing laboratories; testing services; pharmaceutical preparations
HQ: Almac Group Incorporated
25 Fretz Rd
Souderton PA 18964

(G-17722)
ALMAC CLINICAL SERVICES LLC
Also Called: Almac Clinical Svcs
25 Fretz Rd (18964-2610)
PHONE...................................610 666-9500
Allen McClay, *President*
EMP: 12
SALES (corp-wide): 69.2K **Privately Held**
WEB: www.clinicaltrialservices.com
SIC: 2834 Pharmaceutical preparations
HQ: Almac Clinical Services Llc
25 Fretz Rd
Souderton PA 18964

(G-17723)
ALMAC GROUP INCORPORATED (DH)
25 Fretz Rd (18964-2610)
PHONE...................................215 660-8500
Alan Armstrong, *President*
David Downey, *President*
Ronald R Daukaus, *Business Mgr*
Scott Dickson, *Business Mgr*
Lisa Lloyd, *Business Mgr*
EMP: 1000
SALES (est): 731.4MM
SALES (corp-wide): 69.2K **Privately Held**
SIC: 2834 Pharmaceutical preparations
HQ: Almac Group Limited
Almac House 20 Seagoe Industrial Estate
Craigavon BT63
283 833-2200

(G-17724)
AMPLIFIER RESEARCH CORP (PA)
Also Called: AR Rf/Mcrowave Instrumentation
160 Schoolhouse Rd (18964-2412)
PHONE...................................215 723-8181
Donald Shepherd, *Ch of Bd*
Jim Maginn, *President*
Harry Parke, *CFO*
▲ **EMP:** 160
SQ FT: 75,000
SALES (est): 37.6MM **Privately Held**
WEB: www.amplifiers.com
SIC: 3663 Amplifiers, RF power & IF

(G-17725)
APPLIED CLINICAL CONCEPTS INC
25 Fretz Rd (18964-2610)
PHONE...................................215 660-8500
Alan Armstrong, *President*
Stephen Campbell, *Treasurer*
Colin Hayburn, *Admin Sec*
EMP: 3 **EST:** 1997
SALES (est): 177K
SALES (corp-wide): 69.2K **Privately Held**
SIC: 2834 Pharmaceutical preparations
HQ: Almac Group Incorporated
25 Fretz Rd
Souderton PA 18964

(G-17726)
BISHOP WOOD PRODUCTS INC
Also Called: Bishops Fencing & Outdoor Pdts
75 Schoolhouse Rd (18964-2602)
PHONE...................................215 723-6644
Michael Bishop, *President*
EMP: 11

SQ FT: 5,000
SALES (est): 2.6MM **Privately Held**
WEB: www.bishopwood.com
SIC: 5211 2448 2449 Millwork & lumber; pallets, wood; boxes, wood: wirebound

(G-17727)
BOILER ERECTION AND REPAIR CO
142 Schoolhouse Rd (18964-2412)
P.O. Box 36, Uwchland (19480-0036)
PHONE...................................215 721-7900
John H Carey Sr, *President*
EMP: 40 **EST:** 1941
SQ FT: 105,000
SALES (est): 3.2MM **Privately Held**
SIC: 1796 3498 Installing building equipment; pipe fittings, fabricated from purchased pipe

(G-17728)
BOYD MACHINE CO INC
36 E Cherry Ln (18964-1906)
P.O. Box 64156 (18964-0156)
PHONE...................................215 723-8941
Robert T Boyd, *President*
Harry Natalini, *Business Mgr*
Barbara Boyd, *Corp Secy*
EMP: 18 **EST:** 1966
SQ FT: 9,999
SALES (est): 3.1MM **Privately Held**
SIC: 3599 Machine shop, jobbing & repair

(G-17729)
CHESTER A ASHER INC (PA)
Also Called: Asher Chocolates
80 Wambold Rd (18964-2700)
PHONE...................................215 721-3000
David B Asher, *President*
Jeffrey S Asher, *Vice Pres*
John L Asher Jr, *Vice Pres*
Robert B Asher, *Vice Pres*
Ed Lomas, *Vice Pres*
▲ **EMP:** 120
SQ FT: 108,000
SALES (est): 23MM **Privately Held**
WEB: www.ashers.com
SIC: 2066 2064 Chocolate candy, solid; candy & other confectionery products

(G-17730)
COMMONWEALTH PRECAST INC
694 Forman Rd (18964-2407)
PHONE...................................215 721-6005
Timothy Smith, *President*
EMP: 11
SQ FT: 7,000
SALES (est): 1.2MM **Privately Held**
SIC: 3272 5211 Precast terrazo or concrete products; concrete products used to facilitate drainage; manhole covers or frames, concrete; masonry materials & supplies

(G-17731)
CRAFT-BILT MANUFACTURING CO
Also Called: Craftbilt
53 Soderton Hatfield Pike (18964-1913)
PHONE...................................215 721-7700
Andrew Stone, *President*
Richard Ball, *Accounts Mgr*
James Lazzaro, *Regl Sales Mgr*
Ruth Stone, *Admin Sec*
▲ **EMP:** 95 **EST:** 1946
SQ FT: 214,000
SALES (est): 23.6MM **Privately Held**
WEB: www.craftbilt.com
SIC: 3449 3442 3354 2394 Miscellaneous metalwork; metal doors, sash & trim; aluminum extruded products; canvas & related products; awnings, sheet metal

(G-17732)
ELECTRONIC ASSEMBLY CO INC
150 S Front St (18964-1575)
PHONE...................................215 799-0600
Robert J Harding, *President*
Margit Harding, *Vice Pres*
Richard Charfier, *Admin Sec*
EMP: 30 **EST:** 1994
SQ FT: 47,000

SALES (est): 3.3MM **Privately Held**
WEB: www.teacinc.com
SIC: 3679 Electronic circuits

(G-17733)
FIRST ARTICLE INC
150 S Front St Ste B (18964-1575)
PHONE...................................267 382-0761
Mark Matczak, *President*
Robert Tate, *Vice Pres*
EMP: 30 **EST:** 1987
SQ FT: 8,000
SALES (est): 3.1MM **Privately Held**
WEB:
www.firstarticleinspectionservices.com
SIC: 3599 Machine shop, jobbing & repair

(G-17734)
FLEXMOVE AMERICAS LLC
255 Schoolhouse Rd (18964-2430)
PHONE...................................267 203-8351
Lee Stratton, *Manager*
▲ **EMP:** 3 **EST:** 2015
SALES (est): 152.8K **Privately Held**
SIC: 3535 Conveyors & conveying equipment

(G-17735)
FRANCONIA PLASTICS CORP
675 Forman Rd (18964-2408)
PHONE...................................215 723-8926
Walter Koestel, *President*
EMP: 7
SQ FT: 12,400
SALES (est): 715K **Privately Held**
SIC: 3089 3544 Plastic hardware & building products; forms (molds), for foundry & plastics working machinery

(G-17736)
GEARMAKERS INC
704 Forman Rd (18964-2409)
PHONE...................................215 703-0390
Michael Potere, *President*
EMP: 10
SQ FT: 5,000
SALES: 2MM **Privately Held**
WEB: www.gearmakers.com
SIC: 3566 Speed changers, drives & gears

(G-17737)
GOULDEY WELDING & FABRICATIONS
84 Allentown Rd (18964-2201)
PHONE...................................215 721-9522
Bruce Gouldey, *President*
Diane Gouldey, *Vice Pres*
EMP: 20
SQ FT: 13,000
SALES (est): 2.3MM **Privately Held**
WEB: www.gouldey.com
SIC: 7692 3443 Welding repair; fabricated plate work (boiler shop)

(G-17738)
HABERLE STEEL INC (PA)
1946 E Cherry Ln Ste A (18964-1030)
PHONE...................................215 723-8848
Russell Haberle, *President*
Bill Quade, *Vice Pres*
◆ **EMP:** 58
SALES (est): 19.9MM **Privately Held**
WEB: www.haberlesteel.com
SIC: 3441 Fabricated structural metal

(G-17739)
HALKETT WOODWORKING INC
50 Schoolhouse Rd (18964-2612)
PHONE...................................215 721-9331
William G Halkett III, *President*
Sara Halkett, *Treasurer*
EMP: 20
SQ FT: 10,500
SALES: 2.5MM **Privately Held**
SIC: 2431 Woodwork, interior & ornamental

(G-17740)
HOFF INDUSTRIES LLC
362 Winslow Dr (18964-2192)
PHONE...................................215 516-9849
EMP: 3
SALES (est): 252.5K **Privately Held**
SIC: 3999 Manufacturing industries

(G-17741)
INDIAN VALLEY PRINTING CO INC
16 Harbor Pl (18964-1737)
PHONE...................................215 723-7884
Charles D Grasse, *President*
Norma Grasse, *Vice Pres*
EMP: 45 **EST:** 1960
SQ FT: 20,000
SALES (est): 5.2MM **Privately Held**
SIC: 2752 Commercial printing, offset

(G-17742)
IPSEN INC
1946 E Cherry Ln Ste B (18964-1030)
PHONE...................................215 723-8125
George Carter, *Branch Mgr*
EMP: 3
SALES (corp-wide): 229.3MM **Privately Held**
SIC: 3567 Industrial furnaces & ovens
HQ: Ipsen, Inc.
984 Ipsen Rd
Cherry Valley IL 61016
815 332-4941

(G-17743)
JBS PACKERLAND INC
741 Souder Rd (18964-2406)
PHONE...................................215 723-5559
John Cramer, *Purchasing*
EMP: 11
SALES (est): 2.3MM **Privately Held**
SIC: 2011 2013 Beef products from beef slaughtered on site; prepared beef products from purchased beef

(G-17744)
JBS SOUDERTON INC (HQ)
Also Called: Mopac
249 Allentown Rd (18964-2207)
P.O. Box 64395 (18964-0395)
PHONE...................................215 723-5555
Michael Bracella, *General Mgr*
Joshua Duckworth, *General Mgr*
Keith Fratrick, *Principal*
Nicholas C Renzi, *Principal*
Matthew Barnes, *Safety Mgr*
EMP: 1200
SQ FT: 504,000
SALES (est): 208.5MM **Publicly Held**
SIC: 2011 2077 2013 Beef products from beef slaughtered on site; cured meats from meat slaughtered on site; luncheon meat from meat slaughtered on site; meat by-products from meat slaughtered on site; animal & marine fats & oils; sausages & other prepared meats

(G-17745)
JDN BLOCK INC
Also Called: Landis Block & Concrete
711 N County Line Rd (18964-1180)
P.O. Box 64418 (18964-0418)
PHONE...................................215 723-5506
James Dewitt NYCE, *President*
Janet D NYCE, *Corp Secy*
Jarrod NYCE, *Vice Pres*
Justine Landis, *Controller*
Ray Tufano, *Maintence Staff*
▼ **EMP:** 50 **EST:** 1932
SQ FT: 10,800
SALES (est): 11.5MM **Privately Held**
WEB: www.landisbc.com
SIC: 5211 3271 Sand & gravel; lime & plaster; cement; blocks, concrete or cinder: standard

(G-17746)
JERICO BOLT CO
381 Moyer Rd (18964-2313)
PHONE...................................215 721-9567
EMP: 3 **EST:** 2001
SALES (est): 140K **Privately Held**
SIC: 3479 Coating/Engraving Service

(G-17747)
L R M INC
215 N Main St (18964-1605)
PHONE...................................215 721-4840
Mark Crawford, *President*
Ross Crawford, *Corp Secy*
Lewis Crawford, *Controller*
EMP: 5

GEOGRAPHIC

SALES: 1.8MM **Privately Held**
SIC: 5065 2819 Electronic parts & equipment; industrial inorganic chemicals

(G-17748)
LAWRENCE PRINTING SERVICE
28 N 3rd St (18964-1112)
PHONE...............................215 799-2332
Nancy Lawrence, *Principal*
EMP: 4
SALES (est): 311.2K **Privately Held**
WEB: www.lawrenceprintingservice.com
SIC: 2752 Commercial printing, offset

(G-17749)
LEIDYS INC (HQ)
266 W Cherry Ln (18964-2819)
P.O. Box 64257 (18964-0257)
PHONE...............................215 723-4606
James Vanstone, *President*
Thomas K Leidy, *Vice Pres*
Fred Winter, *Vice Pres*
Scott A Schanzenbach, *Treasurer*
Jerry Mc Millan, *Sales Executive*
EMP: 76
SQ FT: 80,000
SALES (est): 36.4MM
SALES (corp-wide): 77.5MM **Privately Held**
WEB: www.leidys.com
SIC: 2011 5147 Meat packing plants; meats, fresh
PA: All Holding Company Inc.
　382 Main St
　Harleysville PA 19438
　215 256-8818

(G-17750)
LETTERCO INC
108 Clarion Dr (18964-1052)
PHONE...............................215 721-9010
Dorothy Kapps-Slack, *President*
Carl Kapps, *Vice Pres*
Mark Kapps, *Admin Sec*
EMP: 7
SALES: 1MM **Privately Held**
WEB: www.letterco.com
SIC: 3993 Letters for signs, metal

(G-17751)
MAGAGNA ASSOCIATES INC
Also Called: Macorp Print Group
261 Schoolhouse Rd Ste 8 (18964-2431)
PHONE...............................610 213-2335
David C Magagna, *CEO*
EMP: 15
SQ FT: 10,000
SALES (est): 1.9MM **Privately Held**
WEB: www.4macorp.com
SIC: 5112 2754 Business forms; business forms: gravure printing

(G-17752)
MOUNTAIN VIEW RENDERING CO (PA)
249 Allentown Rd (18964-2207)
P.O. Box 64417 (18964-0417)
PHONE...............................215 723-5555
William G Morral, *Partner*
EMP: 21
SQ FT: 28,776
SALES (est): 3.4MM **Privately Held**
SIC: 2077 Rendering

(G-17753)
MOYER & SON INC (PA)
113 E Reliance Rd (18964-1308)
PHONE...............................215 799-2000
John Moyer, *President*
Lori Klinger, *Division Mgr*
Jon Clemmer, *Vice Pres*
David A Moyer, *Vice Pres*
David Moyer, *Vice Pres*
▼ EMP: 220
SQ FT: 30,000
SALES (est): 96.2MM **Privately Held**
WEB: www.purgrain.com
SIC: 5191 5983 2875 0782 Animal feeds; fuel oil dealers; fertilizers, mixing only; lawn care services; plumbing, heating, air-conditioning contractors

(G-17754)
MOYER SPECIALTY FOODS LLC
20 S 2nd St (18964-1505)
P.O. Box 64324 (18964-0324)
PHONE...............................215 703-0100
Randall Moyer, *President*
EMP: 10
SQ FT: 10,000
SALES (est): 1.1MM **Privately Held**
SIC: 2064 2068 2034 Candy & other confectionery products; nuts: dried, dehydrated, salted or roasted; dried & dehydrated fruits

(G-17755)
MULCH BARN
10 Schoolhouse Rd Ste 2 (18964-2608)
PHONE...............................215 703-0300
Keith Heavener, *Principal*
EMP: 3
SALES (est): 430.4K **Privately Held**
SIC: 3251 Brick & structural clay tile

(G-17756)
NCC AUTOMATED SYSTEMS INC
255 Schoolhouse Rd Ste 2 (18964-2430)
PHONE...............................215 721-1900
Kevin J Mauger, *President*
Robert Berry, *Materials Mgr*
Eddie Santiago, *Mfg Staff*
Randal Hughes, *Engineer*
Ron Rawa, *Engineer*
▲ EMP: 44
SQ FT: 45,000
SALES (est): 33.1MM **Privately Held**
WEB: www.nccas.com
SIC: 5084 3535 Materials handling machinery; conveyors & conveying equipment

(G-17757)
NOODLE 88
664 E Broad St (18964-1219)
PHONE...............................215 721-0888
EMP: 3
SALES (est): 116.3K **Privately Held**
SIC: 2098 Noodles (e.g. egg, plain & water), dry

(G-17758)
PACKAGING PROGRESSIONS INC
261 Schoolhouse Rd Ste 7 (18964-2431)
PHONE...............................610 489-9096
Larry Noel, *President*
Dante Pietrinferni, *Vice Pres*
EMP: 25
SQ FT: 23,000
SALES (est): 6.5MM **Privately Held**
WEB: www.pacproinc.com
SIC: 3556 3579 3565 5199 Food products machinery; perforators (office machines); packaging machinery; packaging materials

(G-17759)
PAK INNOVATIONS INC
206 Diamond St (18964-1603)
PHONE...............................215 723-0498
Thomas Kilmer, *President*
Susane Badoux, *Vice Pres*
Laure Wentz, *Vice Pres*
EMP: 3
SQ FT: 1,400
SALES (est): 500K **Privately Held**
SIC: 2821 Molding compounds, plastics

(G-17760)
PRAXAIR INC
2929 E Township Line Rd (18964-2527)
PHONE...............................215 721-9099
Stephen F Angel, *President*
Ricardo S Malfitano, *Vice Pres*
Dan Schafer, *Technical Mgr*
EMP: 4 EST: 1988
SALES (est): 210.5K **Privately Held**
SIC: 1321 4922 Natural gas liquids; natural gas transmission

(G-17761)
PURE FLOW WATER CO
101 W Broad St Ste A (18964-1875)
PHONE...............................215 723-0237
Steven Clemmer, *President*

EMP: 4
SQ FT: 10,000
SALES (est): 450K **Privately Held**
WEB: www.pureflowwater.com
SIC: 2086 5999 3589 Pasteurized & mineral waters, bottled & canned; water purification equipment; water filters & softeners, household type

(G-17762)
SELECT VEAL FEEDS INC (PA)
519 Allentown Rd (18964-2109)
PHONE...............................215 721-7131
Wayne A Marcho, *President*
Martha G Marcho, *Vice Pres*
EMP: 10
SALES (est): 1.8MM **Privately Held**
SIC: 2048 7389 Feed premixes;

(G-17763)
SHED-SHOP INCORPORATED
Also Called: Hoffmann Tool & Die
203 E Chestnut St 50 (18964-1166)
P.O. Box 64256 (18964-0256)
PHONE...............................215 723-4209
Sharon Doucet, *CEO*
William Doucet, *President*
Dave Fischer, *Opers Mgr*
EMP: 9 EST: 1966
SQ FT: 3,200
SALES (est): 900K **Privately Held**
SIC: 3599 Machine shop, jobbing & repair

(G-17764)
SHOEMAKER MFG SOLUTIONS INC
302 Leidy Rd (18964-1903)
PHONE...............................215 723-5567
J Harry Shoemaker, *President*
Linda Shoemaker, *Corp Secy*
EMP: 30
SQ FT: 11,000
SALES (est): 7.3MM **Privately Held**
SIC: 3441 3443 3452 3451 Fabricated structural metal; weldments; bolts, nuts, rivets & washers; screw machine products; pipe, sheet metal

(G-17765)
SOLAR ATMOSPHERES INC (PA)
1969 Clearview Rd (18964-1021)
PHONE...............................215 721-1502
William R Jones, *President*
Kevin Bekelja, *General Mgr*
Jamie Jones, *General Mgr*
Jamie A Jones, *Vice Pres*
Scott Jacoby, *CFO*
EMP: 52
SQ FT: 30,000
SALES (est): 27.5MM **Privately Held**
SIC: 3398 Metal heat treating

(G-17766)
SOLAR ATMOSPHERES MFG INC (PA)
Also Called: Solar Manufacturing
1983 Clearview Rd (18964-1021)
PHONE...............................267 384-5040
William R Jones, *CEO*
James Nagy, *President*
Robert Wilson, *President*
Wes Crouse, *Project Mgr*
Tom Smith, *Production*
EMP: 37
SQ FT: 60,000
SALES (est): 9.3MM **Privately Held**
WEB: www.solarmfg.com
SIC: 3567 Vacuum furnaces & ovens

(G-17767)
SYNATEK LP
737 Hagey Center Dr A (18964-2404)
PHONE...............................888 408-5433
Kenneth Clemmer, *Partner*
Nate Clemmer, *Partner*
Leah Gendron, *General Mgr*
Bruce Landis, *Purchasing*
Doug Cherry, *Sales Staff*
EMP: 51
SALES (est): 11.4MM **Privately Held**
WEB: www.synateksolutions.com
SIC: 2875 3523 Fertilizers, mixing only; turf & grounds equipment; turf equipment, commercial

(G-17768)
TOTAL EQUESTRIAN INC
Also Called: Custom Riding Apparel
38 Green St (18964-1702)
PHONE...............................215 721-1247
Nancy Gingrich, *CEO*
Kerry Gingrich, *Principal*
▲ EMP: 6
SALES (est): 813.6K **Privately Held**
SIC: 2329 2339 2399 Riding clothes:, men's, youths' & boys'; riding habits: women's, misses' & juniors'; horse & pet accessories, textile

---

South Canaan
Wayne County

(G-17769)
LOVESHAW CORPORATION
2206 Easton Tpke (18459)
P.O. Box 83 (18459-0083)
PHONE...............................570 937-4921
Valarie Lapinski, *President*
▼ EMP: 105 EST: 1961
SQ FT: 42,000
SALES (est): 23.5MM **Privately Held**
SIC: 3565 3577 5084 7699 Packaging machinery; printers, computer; packaging machinery & equipment; industrial equipment services

(G-17770)
SIGNODE INDUSTRIAL GROUP LLC
Loveshaw
2206 Easton Tpke (18459)
PHONE...............................570 937-4921
Doug Henry, *Manager*
EMP: 105
SALES (corp-wide): 11.1B **Publicly Held**
SIC: 3565 5084 7699 Packaging machinery; packaging machinery & equipment; industrial equipment services
HQ: Signode Industrial Group Llc
　3650 W Lake Ave
　Glenview IL 60026
　847 724-7500

(G-17771)
SIGNODE INDUSTRIAL GROUP LLC
2206 Easton Trpke (18459)
P.O. Box 83 (18459-0083)
PHONE...............................570 937-4921
EMP: 5
SALES (est): 435.1K
SALES (corp-wide): 11.1B **Publicly Held**
SIC: 3565 5084 Packaging machinery; packaging machinery & equipment
PA: Crown Holdings Inc.
　770 Township Line Rd # 100
　Yardley PA 19067
　215 698-5100

South Fork
Cambria County

(G-17772)
BLAIRSVILLE WILBERT BURIAL VLT
Cambria Wilbert Vault
530 Railroad St (15956)
PHONE...............................814 495-5921
Donnie Cumberledge, *Manager*
EMP: 15
SALES (corp-wide): 5MM **Privately Held**
SIC: 3272 Burial vaults, concrete or precast terrazzo
PA: Blairsville Wilbert Burial Vault Company Inc
　6 Decker St
　Blairsville PA 15717
　724 459-9677

(G-17773)
CONTINENTAL APPAREL CORP
Also Called: Gear 1
300 Grant St (15956-1333)
PHONE...............................814 495-4625
EMP: 5

▲ = Import ▼ =Export
◆ =Import/Export

SALES (est): 376.5K **Privately Held**
SIC: 2253 Mfg Women's Sportswear

(G-17774)
FAREL CORP
Also Called: Trim Line Foundations
300 Grant St (15956-1333)
PHONE..................................814 495-4625
Matthew Farel, *President*
Joe Farel, *President*
Mary Farel, *Vice Pres*
Barbara Slonac, *Controller*
EMP: 45 EST: 1959
SQ FT: 40,000
SALES (est): 7.2MM **Privately Held**
WEB: www.empireintimates.net
SIC: 2342 Brassieres; foundation gar-
ments, women's; girdles & panty girdles

(G-17775)
MASTER MACHINE CO INC
310 River St (15956-1349)
PHONE..................................814 495-4900
Joseph Barnouski, *President*
Tom Shero, *Treasurer*
EMP: 11
SALES (est): 1.6MM **Privately Held**
SIC: 3599 3441 3532 Machine shop, job-
bing & repair; fabricated structural metal;
mining machinery

(G-17776)
PROLINE COMPOSITES CORP
883 Ragers Hill Rd (15956-4039)
PHONE..................................814 536-8491
Curtis Turner, *President*
EMP: 4
SALES: 550K **Privately Held**
SIC: 2655 Cans, composite: foil-fiber &
other: from purchased fiber

(G-17777)
SOUTH FORK NEWS AGENCY
403 Main St (15956-1361)
PHONE..................................814 495-9394
Rodney Fye, *Owner*
EMP: 5
SQ FT: 2,500
SALES (est): 246.7K **Privately Held**
SIC: 2711 Newspapers, publishing & print-
ing

(G-17778)
**STINEMAN MANAGEMENT
CORP**
Also Called: Stineman Ribbon Company
128 Ribbon Ln (15956-4118)
PHONE..................................814 495-4686
Joanna Stineman, *President*
Carol Schroder, *Principal*
Jeffrey Stineman, *Vice Pres*
EMP: 40 EST: 1931
SALES (est): 4.2MM **Privately Held**
WEB: www.stineman.com
SIC: 2399 3499 2396 Emblems, badges
& insignia: from purchased materials; tro-
phies, metal, except silver; automotive &
apparel trimmings

South Gibson
Susquehanna County

(G-17779)
MATT KILMER FLAGSTONE LLC
13763 State Route 92 (18842-9791)
PHONE..................................570 756-2591
EMP: 5
SALES (est): 30K **Privately Held**
SIC: 3281 Flagstones

(G-17780)
ORDIE PRICE SAWMILL INC
7025 State Route 92 (18842-9750)
PHONE..................................570 222-3986
Ordie E Price Jr, *President*
Ordie E Price III, *Vice Pres*
Aline J Price, *Admin Sec*
▼ EMP: 10
SQ FT: 2,800
SALES (est): 1.3MM **Privately Held**
SIC: 2426 2421 Hardwood dimension &
flooring mills; kiln drying of lumber

South Park
Allegheny County

(G-17781)
DONNA STANTON
6365 Library Rd (15129-8502)
PHONE..................................412 561-2661
Donna Stanton, *Owner*
EMP: 3
SALES (est): 108.3K **Privately Held**
SIC: 2024 Ice cream & ice milk

(G-17782)
DYNAMIC BUSINESS SYSTEMS
6420 Pleasant St (15129-9717)
PHONE..................................800 782-2946
Roger D Oldaker, *Vice Pres*
Kathleen A Oldaker, *Treasurer*
Nancy Hickey, *Director*
EMP: 4
SALES (est): 320.4K **Privately Held**
SIC: 2754 Business form & card printing,
gravure

(G-17783)
**GENERAL ANESTHETIC
SERVICES**
1900 Sleepy Hollow Rd (15129-9111)
PHONE..................................412 851-4390
William Narey, *CEO*
Lynn Fisher, *Director*
EMP: 10
SQ FT: 4,650
SALES (est): 1.6MM **Privately Held**
WEB: www.general-anesthetic.com
SIC: 3841 Surgical & medical instruments

(G-17784)
LETTUCE TURNIP THE BEET
Also Called: Lettuce Turnip The Beet Csga
3008 Amy Dr (15129-9350)
PHONE..................................412 334-8631
Marissa Evarts, *Vice Pres*
David Hunt, *Vice Pres*
Jamie Christian, *Exec Dir*
EMP: 3
SALES (est): 92.5K **Privately Held**
SIC: 0721 2099 8742 7389 Crop planting
& protection; food preparations; planning
consultant;

(G-17785)
SOMNI SCIENTIFIC LLC
1900 Sleepy Hollow Rd (15129-9111)
PHONE..................................412 851-4390
Sharon Lunney, *Manager*
EMP: 10
SALES (est): 456.3K **Privately Held**
SIC: 3841 Surgical & medical instruments

(G-17786)
**UNITED COMMERCIAL SUPPLY
LLC**
Also Called: U C S
6348 Lib Rd Bldg 1 Ste 2 (15129)
PHONE..................................412 835-2690
David King, *Technology*
EMP: 9
SQ FT: 5,000
SALES (est): 1.9MM **Privately Held**
WEB: www.ucs-supply.com
SIC: 7389 7539 3429 5074 Personal
service agents, brokers & bureaus; elec-
trical services; manufactured hardware
(general); plumbing fittings & supplies;
hand tools; power tools & accessories

South Sterling
Wayne County

(G-17787)
GF EDWARDS INC
Also Called: Edwards Sand & Stone
Rr 191 (18460)
PHONE..................................570 676-3200
George F Edwards, *Manager*
EMP: 30

SALES (corp-wide): 4.6MM **Privately
Held**
SIC: 3273 5211 Ready-mixed concrete;
sand & gravel
PA: G.F. Edwards Inc.
204 State Route 435
Elmhurst Township PA 18444
570 842-8438

(G-17788)
STONE SILO FOODS INC
Rr 191 (18460)
PHONE..................................570 676-0809
James Struble, *Branch Mgr*
EMP: 3 **Privately Held**
SIC: 5146 2092 Fish & seafoods; fresh or
frozen packaged fish
PA: Stone Silo Foods, Inc.
1322 Main St
Gouldsboro PA

South Williamsport
Lycoming County

(G-17789)
A M SHEET METAL INC
Also Called: A M Metal Specialties
410 W 2nd Ave (17702-7299)
PHONE..................................570 322-5417
David L Danneker, *President*
Glen Burger, *General Mgr*
Stephen I Danneker, *Vice Pres*
Edward H Danneker, *Admin Sec*
EMP: 10
SQ FT: 12,000
SALES: 2.7MM **Privately Held**
WEB: www.am-metal.com
SIC: 3441 1761 3498 Fabricated struc-
tural metal; sheet metalwork; fabricated
pipe & fittings

(G-17790)
CERALN CORP (PA)
Also Called: Stratagem Consoles
110 Reynolds St (17702-7123)
PHONE..................................570 322-8400
Alfred Schainholz, *President*
Jeff Brechman, *Vice Pres*
Gary Newcomer, *Vice Pres*
John Burrows, *CFO*
EMP: 45
SQ FT: 100,000
SALES (est): 4.9MM **Privately Held**
WEB: www.woodtronics.com
SIC: 2521 2522 2531 Wood office desks
& tables; cabinets, office: wood; office
desks & tables: except wood; office cabi-
nets & filing drawers: except wood; public
building & related furniture

(G-17791)
HARVEY LEON
2117 Harvard Ave (17702-6964)
PHONE..................................570 337-2665
Harvey Leon, *Owner*
EMP: 3
SALES (est): 231.5K **Privately Held**
SIC: 2448 Wood pallets & skids

(G-17792)
HOYT INC
Also Called: Lycoming Bakery
220 Curtin St (17702-7247)
PHONE..................................570 326-9426
Jeff Hoyt, *President*
EMP: 10
SALES (est): 1.1MM **Privately Held**
SIC: 2051 Bakery: wholesale or whole-
sale/retail combined

(G-17793)
**UNDER PRESSURE
CONNECTIONS LLC**
825 Us Highway 15 (17702-8550)
PHONE..................................570 326-1117
Brandy Permen, *Principal*
EMP: 4
SALES (est): 90.5K **Privately Held**
SIC: 7349 3599 Building maintenance
services; machine & other job shop work

(G-17794)
YOUNGS TRUCK REPAIR LLC
44 Steinbacher Ln (17702-8622)
PHONE..................................570 329-3571
John Young,
EMP: 10
SQ FT: 15,000
SALES (est): 1MM **Privately Held**
SIC: 7538 7692 General truck repair;
welding repair

Southampton
Bucks County

(G-17795)
A&A MACHINE CO INC
1085 Industrial Blvd (18966-4006)
PHONE..................................215 355-8330
Andrew F Schlotter, *Owner*
Linda M Schlotter, *Admin Sec*
EMP: 20
SALES (est): 4.5MM **Privately Held**
WEB: www.aamachineco.com
SIC: 3599 Machine shop, jobbing & repair

(G-17796)
ADENINE SOLUTIONS INC
285 Wisteria Dr (18966-1417)
PHONE..................................267 684-6013
Dmitri Prozorov, *Principal*
EMP: 5
SALES (est): 274.5K **Privately Held**
SIC: 7371 7372 Computer software devel-
opment & applications; software program-
ming applications; prepackaged software;
business oriented computer software

(G-17797)
**ADVANCED CARBIDE TOOL
COMPANY (PA)**
1385 Industrial Blvd (18966-4012)
PHONE..................................267 960-1222
Ray Johnston, *President*
Thomas Bornemeier, *Vice Pres*
EMP: 18
SQ FT: 13,500
SALES (est): 3.2MM **Privately Held**
WEB: www.advancedcarbide.com
SIC: 3545 Cutting tools for machine tools

(G-17798)
ASAP PRINTING & COPYING INC
1300 Industrial Blvd # 100 (18966-4029)
PHONE..................................215 357-5033
Philip Sidkoff, *President*
EMP: 10
SQ FT: 5,600
SALES: 650K **Privately Held**
SIC: 2752 Commercial printing, offset

(G-17799)
BLUESTONE INC
170 Cherry Blossom Dr (18966-1091)
PHONE..................................215 364-1415
William Donaldson, *President*
Scott E Mueller, *General Mgr*
Scott Mueller, *Sales Staff*
EMP: 15
SALES (est): 3.3MM **Privately Held**
WEB: www.bluestonedrilling.com
SIC: 1411 Dimension stone

(G-17800)
**BRISTOL-MYERS SQUIBB
COMPANY**
139 Lark Dr (18966-1943)
PHONE..................................609 818-5513
John Stevenson, *Vice Pres*
Victoria Carey, *Manager*
Mike Saraceno, *Director*
EMP: 89
SALES (corp-wide): 22.5B **Publicly Held**
WEB: www.bms.com
SIC: 2834 Pharmaceutical preparations
PA: Bristol-Myers Squibb Company
430 E 29th St Fl 14
New York NY 10016
212 546-4000

(PA)=Parent Co (HQ)=Headquarters (DH)=Div Headquarters
✪ = New Business established in last 2 years

2019 Harris Pennsylvania
Manufacturers Directory

671

GEOGRAPHIC

(G-17801)
CENTRAL CONCRETE CO INC
1066 Gravel Hill Rd (18966-4509)
PHONE..................................215 953-9736
Jaime Costa, *President*
EMP: 27
SALES: 3MM Privately Held
SIC: 3273 Ready-mixed concrete

(G-17802)
CHALLENGER MANUFACTURING LTD
16 Cricket Dr (18966-2725)
PHONE..................................215 968-6004
Mike C Miller,
Lawrence Ousky,
EMP: 113
SQ FT: 135,000
SALES (est): 6.2MM Privately Held
SIC: 3648 Outdoor lighting equipment

(G-17803)
CHURCHVILLE MECH ASSOC LLC
1080 Industrial Blvd # 1 (18966-4001)
PHONE..................................267 231-5968
Daniel Ryan, *President*
EMP: 4
SALES (est): 878K Privately Held
SIC: 3559 Automotive maintenance equipment

(G-17804)
COMPUTER BOSS
1111 Street Rd Ste 205 (18966-4250)
PHONE..................................215 444-9393
Audrone Krinke, *Owner*
Dina Abbate, *Treasurer*
EMP: 5
SALES (est): 414.6K Privately Held
WEB: www.computer-boss.com
SIC: 7372 Prepackaged software

(G-17805)
CONTINENTAL-WIRT ELEC CORP (PA)
130 James Way (18966-3818)
PHONE..................................215 355-7080
Burton Lifson, *Ch of Bd*
Kalman Lifson, *President*
William F O'Shea Jr, *Vice Pres*
EMP: 200
SQ FT: 54,000
SALES (est): 34.5MM Privately Held
WEB: www.cwind.com
SIC: 3679 3678 Electronic switches; electronic connectors

(G-17806)
COPY SYSTEMS GROUP INC
Also Called: Budget Printing Center
1300 Industrial Blvd # 100 (18966-4029)
PHONE..................................215 355-2223
Eric Joseph, *President*
EMP: 3
SQ FT: 850
SALES (est): 250K Privately Held
SIC: 2791 7334 Typesetting; photocopying & duplicating services

(G-17807)
D & R MACHINE CO
1330 Industrial Blvd (18966-4013)
PHONE..................................215 526-2080
Paul Redante, *President*
Isabel Vala, *General Mgr*
Nelso Redante, *Shareholder*
EMP: 38
SQ FT: 41,000
SALES (est): 7.5MM Privately Held
WEB: www.drmachine.com
SIC: 3599 Machine shop, jobbing & repair

(G-17808)
DIGITAL COLOR GRAPHICS INC
Also Called: Paradigm Digital Color Graphics
105 James Way (18966-3860)
PHONE..................................215 942-7500
John Rosenthal, *President*
David Matez, *General Mgr*
Thomas Monteleone, *Vice Pres*
James Rosenthal, *Vice Pres*
Jim Rosenthal, *Vice Pres*
EMP: 40
SQ FT: 4,700

SALES (est): 8.3MM Privately Held
WEB: www.digital-color.com
SIC: 2759 2752 7336 Commercial printing; commercial printing, lithographic; commercial art & graphic design

(G-17809)
ENVIRONMENTAL TECTONICS CORP (PA)
Also Called: Etc
125 James Way (18966-3817)
PHONE..................................215 355-9100
William F Mitchell, *President*
Gene Davis, *President*
Robert L Laurent Jr, *President*
Bernhard H Ricter, *President*
Marco Van Wijngaarden, *President*
▲ EMP: 168
SQ FT: 92,000
SALES (est): 82.2MM Publicly Held
WEB: www.etc-turkey.com
SIC: 3728 3842 3826 3823 Aircraft training equipment; sterilizers, hospital & surgical; environmental testing equipment; industrial instrmnts msrmnt display/control process variable; surgical & medical instruments

(G-17810)
EXPRESS PRINTING
Also Called: Kenney Press
324 2nd Street Pike # 14 (18966-3849)
PHONE..................................215 357-7033
Bob Kenney, *President*
EMP: 4
SQ FT: 3,500
SALES (est): 546.2K Privately Held
SIC: 2752 Commercial printing, offset

(G-17811)
F B F INC
1145 Industrial Blvd (18966-4063)
PHONE..................................215 322-7110
Joseph Medvic Jr, *President*
Ben Wilson, *Vice Pres*
EMP: 35
SQ FT: 45,000
SALES (est): 7.5MM Privately Held
WEB: www.fbfinc.com
SIC: 3469 3544 Stamping metal for the trade; special dies, tools, jigs & fixtures

(G-17812)
F B F INDUSTRIES INC
1145 Industrial Blvd (18966-4063)
PHONE..................................215 322-7110
Joe Medvic, *President*
EMP: 90
SQ FT: 45,000
SALES (est): 10.2MM Privately Held
SIC: 3469 Stamping metal for the trade

(G-17813)
FRESH START VEND & COF SVC LLC
86 Green Valley Dr (18966-1614)
PHONE..................................215 322-8647
Patrick Donnelly, *Principal*
EMP: 5
SALES (est): 270.7K Privately Held
SIC: 2095 Coffee extracts

(G-17814)
GM HOME INC
Also Called: GM Homes of Florida Inc
1111 Street Rd Ste 304 (18966-4250)
PHONE..................................888 352-3442
Antonia Rodriguez, *Principal*
EMP: 3 EST: 2016
SALES (est): 95.9K Privately Held
SIC: 3716 Motor homes

(G-17815)
HANKS BEVERAGE COMPANY
969 Street Rd (18966-4728)
PHONE..................................215 396-2809
John Salvatore, *President*
William Dunman, *General Mgr*
Anthony J Salvatore, *Admin Sec*
EMP: 6
SQ FT: 3,200
SALES (est): 926.9K Privately Held
SIC: 2086 Carbonated beverages, nonalcoholic: bottled & canned

(G-17816)
HARRIS MANUFACTURING COMPANY (PA)
37 Rotterdam Rd E (18966-2318)
PHONE..................................609 393-3717
S David Harris, *President*
Nancy Harris, *President*
Leslie Donovan, *Vice Pres*
▲ EMP: 4 EST: 1972
SQ FT: 40,000
SALES (est): 6.5MM Privately Held
WEB: www.harrismanufacturingco.com
SIC: 2385 3069 Waterproof outerwear; clothing, vulcanized rubber or rubberized fabric

(G-17817)
HELIX SCIENTIFIC INC
129 Frog Hollow Rd (18966-1030)
PHONE..................................215 953-2072
Stephen Hoare, *President*
EMP: 4 EST: 1996
SALES (est): 319.6K Privately Held
SIC: 3089 Novelties, plastic

(G-17818)
HULLVAC PUMP CORP
95 Pine Run Dr (18966-2276)
PHONE..................................215 355-3995
Lewis W Hull, *President*
Stephen P Hull, *Admin Sec*
▲ EMP: 7
SQ FT: 4,000
SALES: 1MM Privately Held
WEB: www.hullvacpumps.com
SIC: 3625 Vacuum relays

(G-17819)
INDUSTRIAL ENTERPRISES INC (HQ)
Also Called: C-W Industries
130 James Way (18966-3818)
PHONE..................................215 355-7080
James Freeman, *President*
William Oshea Jr, *Vice Pres*
Carol De Thomas, *Purchasing*
Russ Rosenzweig, *CFO*
Martin Mikelburg, *Treasurer*
▲ EMP: 100 EST: 1961
SQ FT: 54,000
SALES (est): 16.9MM
SALES (corp-wide): 34.5MM Privately Held
WEB: www.industrialenterprises.com
SIC: 3679 3678 3643 3357 Electronic circuits; electronic connectors; current-carrying wiring devices; nonferrous wiredrawing & insulating
PA: Continental-Wirt Electronics Corporation
130 James Way
Southampton PA 18966
215 355-7080

(G-17820)
KEYSTONE CONTROLS COMPANY
130 James Way (18966-3818)
PHONE..................................215 355-7080
Kalman Lifson, *President*
EMP: 4
SALES (est): 5MM
SALES (corp-wide): 34.5MM Privately Held
WEB: www.cwind.com
SIC: 3679 3678 Switches, stepping; electronic connectors
PA: Continental-Wirt Electronics Corporation
130 James Way
Southampton PA 18966
215 355-7080

(G-17821)
KOVACS MANUFACTURING INC
Also Called: Kovacs Machine Co
67 Heather Rd (18966-1109)
PHONE..................................215 355-1985
Tomas Dobo, *President*
EMP: 12
SQ FT: 6,600
SALES (est): 1.6MM Privately Held
SIC: 3599 7692 Machine shop, jobbing & repair; welding repair

(G-17822)
LEGACY SERVICE USA LLC
95 James Way Ste 100 (18966-3847)
PHONE..................................215 675-7770
Tomas Kalkys,
EMP: 57 EST: 2011
SALES: 16.3MM Privately Held
SIC: 3444 Siding, sheet metal

(G-17823)
M & C SPECIALTIES CO
90 James Way (18966-3825)
PHONE..................................215 322-7441
Donald Rauch, *President*
Sevan Demirdogden, *President*
Daniel Cistone, *Corp Secy*
Mark W Croll, *Vice Pres*
Felix L Rodriguez Jr, *Treasurer*
▲ EMP: 400 EST: 1962
SQ FT: 65,000
SALES (est): 109.7MM
SALES (corp-wide): 14.7B Publicly Held
WEB: www.mcspecialties.com
SIC: 2672 Tape, pressure sensitive: made from purchased materials
PA: Illinois Tool Works Inc.
155 Harlem Ave
Glenview IL 60025
847 724-7500

(G-17824)
MAJESTIC CREATIONS INC
Also Called: Shvarts, Roman
31 Cottonwood Dr (18966-2831)
PHONE..................................215 968-5411
Roman Schwartz, *President*
EMP: 4
SQ FT: 2,500
SALES: 200K Privately Held
SIC: 3911 Jewelry, precious metal

(G-17825)
MDBEL INC
123 Hayhurst Ct (18966-2908)
PHONE..................................215 738-3383
Michael Belaga, *President*
EMP: 3
SALES: 100K Privately Held
SIC: 3679 Electronic circuits

(G-17826)
MELITTA USA INC
1394 Hiview Dr (18966-3557)
PHONE..................................215 355-5581
Michael Difebbo, *Branch Mgr*
EMP: 3
SALES (corp-wide): 1.8B Privately Held
SIC: 2095 Roasted coffee
HQ: Melitta Usa, Inc.
13925 58th St N
Clearwater FL 33760
727 535-2111

(G-17827)
NEWAGE INDUSTRIES INC
Also Called: Advantapure Division
145 James Way (18966-3817)
PHONE..................................215 526-2151
Kenneth Baker, *President*
David Schofield, *Warehouse Mgr*
Chris Boytim, *QC Dir*
Kyle Murphy, *Engineer*
John-Paul Deitz, *Project Engr*
▲ EMP: 135
SQ FT: 243,000
SALES: 45.8MM Privately Held
SIC: 3052 Rubber & plastics hose & beltings

(G-17828)
NORTHSTAR SALES
963 Street Rd 2 (18966-4728)
PHONE..................................215 364-5540
Bruno Zumbo, *Owner*
Tina Knowles, *Office Mgr*
EMP: 5
SALES (est): 370K Privately Held
WEB: www.northstarsales.com
SIC: 2656 Sanitary food containers

(G-17829)
ORIGINAL PHILLY HOLDINGS INC (HQ)
31 Trailwood Dr (18966-2198)
PHONE..................................215 423-3333

G
E
O
G
R
A
P
H
I
C

John Karamatsoukas, *President*
EMP: 200
SALES (corp-wide): 40B **Publicly Held**
SIC: 6719 5142 2013 Investment holding companies, except banks; meat, frozen: packaged; sausages & other prepared meats; beef stew from purchased meat
PA: Tyson Foods, Inc.
2200 W Don Tyson Pkwy
Springdale AR 72762
479 290-4000

(G-17830)
PLASMA SOURCE
649 2nd Street Pike Ste B (18966-3996)
PHONE.....................................215 942-6370
EMP: 3
SALES (est): 214.4K **Privately Held**
SIC: 2836 Mfg Biological Products

(G-17831)
PRINTING WORKS
975 Jaymor Rd Ste 2 (18966-3854)
PHONE.....................................215 357-5609
William Morrison Jr, *Principal*
EMP: 6
SALES (est): 776.1K **Privately Held**
SIC: 2752 Commercial printing, lithographic

(G-17832)
PUBLISHING OFFICE US GVERNMENT
Also Called: Philadlphia Reg Prtg Prcrement
928 Jaymor Rd Ste A190 (18966-3850)
PHONE.....................................215 364-6465
Cathy Miller, *Manager*
EMP: 5 **Publicly Held**
WEB: www.gpo.gov
SIC: 2741 9199 Technical manual & paper publishing; general government administration;
HQ: Publishing Office, Us Government
732 N Capitol St Nw
Washington DC 20401
202 512-0000

(G-17833)
R & R BRIGGS INC
1067 Churchville Rd (18966-4701)
PHONE.....................................215 357-3413
Robert Briggs Sr, *President*
Kathleen Briggs, *Treasurer*
EMP: 5
SALES (est): 614.2K **Privately Held**
SIC: 3589 5023 1752 Commercial cleaning equipment; carpets; carpet laying

(G-17834)
R C KLETZING INC
1325 Industrial Blvd # 1 (18966-4047)
PHONE.....................................215 357-1788
Arthur E Greisiger, *President*
Ruth Greisiger, *Corp Secy*
John Gresisger, *Vice Pres*
EMP: 6 **EST:** 1952
SQ FT: 10,000
SALES (est): 500K **Privately Held**
SIC: 3599 Machine shop, jobbing & repair

(G-17835)
ROSENAU BECK INC (PA)
1310 Industrial Blvd # 201 (18966-4030)
PHONE.....................................215 364-1714
Barry Richman, *CEO*
Thomas R Rosenau, *President*
▲ **EMP:** 23
SQ FT: 32,000
SALES (est): 2.5MM **Privately Held**
SIC: 2361 Dresses: girls', children's & infants'

(G-17836)
SCHILLER GROUNDS CARE INC
Mantis Manufacturing Div
1028 Street Rd (18966-4227)
PHONE.....................................215 355-9700
Robert Bell, *Branch Mgr*
EMP: 25
SALES (corp-wide): 37.7MM **Privately Held**
WEB: www.littlewonder.com
SIC: 3524 Lawn & garden equipment

PA: Schiller Grounds Care, Inc.
1028 Street Rd
Southampton PA 18966
215 357-5110

(G-17837)
STEVE GOLDBERG COMPANY
145 Meadowfield Dr (18966-3045)
PHONE.....................................215 322-0615
Lona Goldberg, *Partner*
Steve Goldberg, *Partner*
EMP: 5
SALES (est): 350K **Privately Held**
SIC: 2389 Men's miscellaneous accessories

(G-17838)
SUPERPAC INC
1220 Industrial Blvd (18966-4011)
P.O. Box 189 (18966-0189)
PHONE.....................................215 322-1010
Leon W Marchetti, *President*
Alice E Medleycott, *Corp Secy*
Mount Tom, *COO*
Andrew Lear, *Vice Pres*
Mary E Medleycott, *Vice Pres*
▲ **EMP:** 150 **EST:** 1963
SQ FT: 95,000
SALES (est): 60.9MM **Privately Held**
WEB: www.superpacinc.com
SIC: 2759 Flexographic printing

(G-17839)
SYNCOM SPECIALTY INC (PA)
16 Arbor Rd (18966-1008)
PHONE.....................................215 322-9708
John A Baurer Jr, *President*
John Bauer, *Sales Staff*
EMP: 2
SQ FT: 3,100
SALES (est): 1.9MM **Privately Held**
WEB: www.syncomspecialties.com
SIC: 3599 Machine shop, jobbing & repair

(G-17840)
THOMAS FETTERMAN INC
1680 Hillside Rd (18966-4514)
PHONE.....................................215 355-8849
Thomas Fetterman, *President*
Alan Fetterman, *Vice Pres*
James Fetterman, *Treasurer*
Brian Hartman, *Manager*
▲ **EMP:** 3
SALES (est): 250K **Privately Held**
WEB: www.fetterman-crutches.com
SIC: 3842 Surgical appliances & supplies

(G-17841)
TLR REDWOOD INC
Also Called: Rococo
265 2nd Street Pike (18966-3833)
PHONE.....................................215 322-1005
Richard Toll, *President*
EMP: 6 **EST:** 2010
SALES (est): 643.3K **Privately Held**
SIC: 2311 Men's & boys' suits & coats

(G-17842)
TOTTSER TOOL AND DIE SHOP INC (PA)
935 Jaymor Rd (18966-3819)
PHONE.....................................215 357-7600
Linda Macht, *President*
Bernard Reichart, *Vice Pres*
Tom Kneib, *Production*
Jim Sullivan, *CFO*
Stanley Silverstein, *Treasurer*
▲ **EMP:** 60 **EST:** 1958
SQ FT: 22,000
SALES (est): 11MM **Privately Held**
WEB: www.tottser.com
SIC: 3469 3544 Stamping metal for the trade; die sets for metal stamping (presses)

(G-17843)
TOTTSER TOOL AND DIE SHOP INC
Also Called: Tottser Tool & Manufacturing
935 Jaymor Rd (18966-3819)
PHONE.....................................215 357-7600
Linda Macht, *Manager*
EMP: 52
SQ FT: 26,240

SALES (corp-wide): 11MM **Privately Held**
WEB: www.tottser.com
SIC: 3469 3544 Metal stampings; special dies & tools
PA: Tottser Tool And Die Shop, Inc.
935 Jaymor Rd
Southampton PA 18966
215 357-7600

(G-17844)
TRU TEMP SENSORS INC
495 Morgan Ct (18966-2787)
PHONE.....................................215 396-1550
Terry Hale, *President*
EMP: 4
SQ FT: 2,000
SALES (est): 597.2K **Privately Held**
WEB: www.trutempsensors.com
SIC: 3823 3812 3357 Temperature measurement instruments, industrial; search & navigation equipment; nonferrous wire-drawing & insulating

(G-17845)
VEKTRON CORPORATION
83 Blaises Gate Dr (18966-1173)
PHONE.....................................215 354-0300
Scott Banks, *President*
Valary Kravets, *President*
▲ **EMP:** 3
SQ FT: 2,000
SALES (est): 389.2K **Privately Held**
WEB: www.vektroncorp.com
SIC: 3625 Relays & industrial controls

(G-17846)
WFC COMPANY INC (PA)
Also Called: Warminster Fiberglass
725 County Line Rd (18966)
P.O. Box 188 (18966-0188)
PHONE.....................................215 953-1260
John J Roley, *President*
Carl P Schmidt, *Corp Secy*
Glen A Ford, *Vice Pres*
Robert Carsley, *Shareholder*
John Freeman, *Shareholder*
▼ **EMP:** 60
SQ FT: 120,000
SALES (est): 18.3MM **Privately Held**
WEB: www.warminsterfiberglass.com
SIC: 3089 Molding primary plastic

Spartansburg
Crawford County

(G-17847)
CLEAR LAKE LUMBER INC (PA)
409 Main St (16434-1007)
P.O. Box 129 (16434-0129)
PHONE.....................................800 237-1191
Eric Bonnett, *President*
Scott Brown, *Vice Pres*
▼ **EMP:** 50
SQ FT: 1,000
SALES (est): 14.8MM **Privately Held**
WEB: www.clearlakelumber.com
SIC: 2421 5031 Lumber: rough, sawed or planed; lumber, plywood & millwork; lumber: rough, dressed & finished; millwork

(G-17848)
COASTAL FOREST RESOURCES CO
Spartywood Products
43647 Fairview Rd (16434-1627)
PHONE.....................................814 654-7111
Jay Reese, *Manager*
EMP: 5
SALES (corp-wide): 105.3MM **Privately Held**
SIC: 2421 Sawmills & planing mills, general
PA: Coastal Forest Resources Company
8007 Florida Georgia Hwy
Havana FL 32333
850 539-6432

(G-17849)
D & K LOGGING INC
1335 Cobb Rd (16434-5727)
PHONE.....................................814 663-0210
Douglas Puckly, *Principal*
EMP: 3

SALES (est): 262.2K **Privately Held**
SIC: 2411 Logging camps & contractors

(G-17850)
FIRTH MAPLE PRODUCTS INC
22418 Firth Rd (16434-3222)
PHONE.....................................814 654-7265
Troy Firth, *Owner*
Ron Weisenstein, *Info Tech Mgr*
▼ **EMP:** 11
SALES (est): 2.2MM **Privately Held**
WEB: www.firthmapleproducts.com
SIC: 2099 Maple syrup

(G-17851)
HAROLD GRAVES TRUCKING
45332 Sundback Rd (16434-4338)
PHONE.....................................814 654-7836
Harold Graves, *Owner*
EMP: 8 **EST:** 1967
SALES (est): 526.1K **Privately Held**
SIC: 2411 4212 Logging; lumber (log) trucking, local

(G-17852)
LOG HARD PREMIUM PELLETS INC
44939 Old Route 77 (16434-4439)
PHONE.....................................814 654-2100
EMP: 4
SALES (est): 424K **Privately Held**
SIC: 3433 Mfg Heating Equipment-Non-electric

(G-17853)
PENN-SYLVAN INTERNATIONAL INC (PA)
43647 Fairview Rd (16434-1627)
PHONE.....................................814 654-7111
Michael Reese, *President*
Jay Reese, *Vice Pres*
EMP: 10
SALES (est): 5.2MM **Privately Held**
WEB: www.salemhardwood.com
SIC: 2421 5031 Lumber: rough, sawed or planed; lumber: rough, dressed & finished

---

Spring Church
Armstrong County

(G-17854)
BRITT ENERGIES INC
2960 State Route 156 (15686-1043)
P.O. Box 515, Indiana (15701-0515)
PHONE.....................................724 465-9333
Christopher Evans, *President*
Stephanie Marshall, *Manager*
EMP: 7
SQ FT: 696,960
SALES: 270K **Privately Held**
SIC: 3281 Altars, cut stone

(G-17855)
BRITT RESOURCES INC
2960 State Route 156 (15686-1043)
PHONE.....................................724 465-9333
Christopher J Evans, *President*
EMP: 3 **EST:** 1996
SALES (est): 515.1K **Privately Held**
SIC: 1241 Coal mining services

Spring City
Chester County

(G-17856)
A C MILLER CONCRETE PDTS INC (PA)
31 E Bridge St (19475-1404)
P.O. Box 199 (19475-0199)
PHONE.....................................610 948-4600
David H Miller, *CEO*
John Rutkowski, *Ch of Bd*
Arthur C Miller, *Corp Secy*
Michael Buchan, *Vice Pres*
Steve Bonsall, *Prdtn Mgr*
▲ **EMP:** 105 **EST:** 1960
SQ FT: 500,000
SALES (est): 22MM **Privately Held**
WEB: www.acmiller.com
SIC: 3272 Concrete products, precast

(G-17857)
CINEMAPLEX TECHNOLOGIES CORP
238 Ridge Rd (19475-2228)
PHONE..................................610 935-8366
Brandon Hoishik, *President*
EMP: 4 **EST:** 1999
SQ FT: 2,500
SALES (est): 637.7K **Privately Held**
SIC: 3651 Household audio & video equipment

(G-17858)
GREAT VALLEY PUBLISHING CO
3801 Schuylkill Rd (19475-1554)
PHONE..................................610 948-7639
Fax: 610 948-4202
EMP: 40
SQ FT: 10,392
SALES (est): 3.2MM **Privately Held**
SIC: 2711 2741 Newspapers-Publishing/Printing Misc Publishing

(G-17859)
HONE ALONE INC
119 Alackness Rd (19475-2714)
PHONE..................................610 495-5832
Donald Kolb, *President*
EMP: 4
SALES (est): 387K **Privately Held**
SIC: 3541 Cylinder reboring machines

(G-17860)
HYDROMOTION INC
85 E Bridge St (19475-1404)
PHONE..................................610 948-4150
Mike Klute, *President*
▲ **EMP:** 87 **EST:** 1971
SQ FT: 55,000
SALES (est): 22.1MM
SALES (corp-wide): 40.1MM **Privately Held**
WEB: www.hydromotion.com
SIC: 3599 3621 3594 Machine shop, jobbing & repair; motors & generators; fluid power pumps & motors
HQ: Texas Hydraulics, Inc.
3410 Range Rd
Temple TX 76504
254 778-4701

(G-17861)
IRONSHORE MARINE LLC
1713 Sawmill Rd (19475-9532)
PHONE..................................484 941-3914
Monty Reeder,
EMP: 3 **EST:** 2017
SALES (est): 145.6K **Privately Held**
SIC: 3531 Marine related equipment

(G-17862)
JACK BURNLEY SON STAIR CONTRS
405 Reitnour Rd (19475-2707)
PHONE..................................610 948-4166
Tom Burnley, *President*
EMP: 40
SQ FT: 10,000
SALES: 800K **Privately Held**
SIC: 2431 Staircases & stairs, wood

(G-17863)
MONTCO ENTERPRISES LTD
500 S Main St (19475-2019)
PHONE..................................610 948-5316
▲ **EMP:** 25
SQ FT: 18,000
SALES (est): 3.7MM **Privately Held**
SIC: 3674 Mfg Semiconductors/Related Devices

(G-17864)
PROGRESSIVE MACHINING
473 Pughtown Rd (19475-3413)
PHONE..................................610 469-6204
Warren Mangan, *CEO*
EMP: 7 **EST:** 1965
SQ FT: 14,000
SALES (est): 623.9K **Privately Held**
SIC: 3599 Machine shop, jobbing & repair

(G-17865)
S & W RACE CARS COMPONENTS INC
11 Mennonite Church Rd (19475-1518)
PHONE..................................610 948-7303
Walter J Weney Jr, *Ch of Bd*
Scott Weney, *President*
Terri Weney, *Corp Secy*
John Burke, *Engineer*
Jill Canuso, *Mktg Dir*
EMP: 26
SQ FT: 28,000
SALES (est): 4.5MM **Privately Held**
WEB: www.swracecars.com
SIC: 7538 3711 5013 3714 General automotive repair shops; automobile assembly, including specialty automobiles; automotive supplies & parts; motor vehicle parts & accessories

(G-17866)
SECOND CENTURY MEDIA LLC
3801 Schuylkill Rd (19475-1554)
PHONE..................................610 948-9500
Mara Honicker,
EMP: 30
SALES (est): 652.4K **Privately Held**
SIC: 2741 Miscellaneous publishing

(G-17867)
SPRING CITY ELECTRICAL MFG CO (PA)
Also Called: Spring City Foundry Co
1 S Main St (19475-1858)
P.O. Box 19 (19475-0019)
PHONE..................................610 948-4000
Alan Brink, *President*
Charles D Lanyon, *Vice Pres*
Jim Madara, *Vice Pres*
Donald K Wiggins, *Vice Pres*
John Trego, *Safety Mgr*
◆ **EMP:** 102 **EST:** 1843
SQ FT: 75,000
SALES (est): 20.5MM **Privately Held**
WEB: www.springcity.com
SIC: 3648 3644 Outdoor lighting equipment; public lighting fixtures; street lighting fixtures; electric outlet, switch & fuse boxes; electric conduits & fittings

(G-17868)
SPRING CITY ELECTRICAL MFG CO
Hall & Main St (19475)
PHONE..................................610 948-4000
Alan Brink, *President*
EMP: 100
SALES (corp-wide): 20.5MM **Privately Held**
WEB: www.springcity.com
SIC: 3648 3644 Outdoor lighting equipment; public lighting fixtures; street lighting fixtures; electric outlet, switch & fuse boxes; electric conduits & fittings
PA: Spring City Electrical Manufacturing Co
1 S Main St
Spring City PA 19475
610 948-4000

(G-17869)
TRANS AMERICAN TOOL COMPANY
305 S Main St (19475-2016)
PHONE..................................610 948-4411
Gerald J Vespaziani, *President*
Elizabeth Vespaziani, *Vice Pres*
EMP: 5
SQ FT: 2,400
SALES (est): 639K **Privately Held**
SIC: 3599 Machine shop, jobbing & repair

(G-17870)
TRI BMS LLC (PA)
Also Called: R & M Equipment Company
501 S Main St Ste 106 (19475-2038)
P.O. Box 937, Royersford (19468-8056)
PHONE..................................610 495-9700
Mark T McAndrew, *Mng Member*
Arthur J Balzereit,
Kevin Smith,
▲ **EMP:** 30 **EST:** 1982
SQ FT: 27,000

SALES (est): 8.2MM **Privately Held**
WEB: www.ramequipment.com
SIC: 3564 Blowing fans: industrial or commercial

(G-17871)
VEPAR LLC
Also Called: Veteran Pallet Remanufacturing
900 W Bridge St (19475-2612)
P.O. Box 2376, Malvern (19355-0831)
PHONE..................................610 462-4545
John Grobe, *Principal*
EMP: 5 **EST:** 2013
SALES (est): 449K **Privately Held**
SIC: 2448 4212 4789 Wood pallets & skids; local trucking, without storage; pipeline terminal facilities, independently operated

(G-17872)
VERSITEX OF AMERICA LTD
3545 Schuylkill Rd (19475-1550)
PHONE..................................610 948-4442
Fax: 610 948-7310
EMP: 10
SQ FT: 10,000
SALES (est): 640K **Privately Held**
SIC: 3949 5091 5084
Manufactures/Wholesales Fishing & Rods Building Comp

Spring Glen
Schuylkill County

(G-17873)
KING LOGGING AND SAWMILL
200 Joss Ln (17978-9534)
PHONE..................................717 365-3341
Aquilla King, *Owner*
EMP: 5 **EST:** 1994
SALES (est): 569.1K **Privately Held**
SIC: 2421 Sawmills & planing mills, general

(G-17874)
WENGER FEEDS LLC
Rr 25 (17978)
PHONE..................................717 367-1195
M M Wenger, *Ch of Bd*
J Michael Lutz, *Admin Sec*
EMP: 35
SALES (corp-wide): 111.1MM **Privately Held**
WEB: www.easternag.com
SIC: 2048 Prepared feeds
PA: Wenger Feeds, Llc
101 W Harrisburg Ave
Rheems PA 17570
717 367-1195

Spring Grove
York County

(G-17875)
B & F TOOL & GEAR INC
2551 Pine Tree Rd (17362-8335)
PHONE..................................717 632-8977
William Fuss, *President*
Christine M Garrett, *President*
Dona Fuss, *Corp Secy*
William Heiser, *Treasurer*
EMP: 5
SQ FT: 20,000
SALES (est): 689.7K **Privately Held**
WEB: www.hanovergear.com
SIC: 3566 Gears, power transmission, except automotive

(G-17876)
CAPUTO BROTHERS CREAMERY LLC
6403 Pahagaco Rd (17362-8810)
PHONE..................................717 739-1087
Rynn Caputo, *Owner*
Mark Severn, *Sales Staff*
EMP: 8 **EST:** 2011
SALES (est): 304.8K **Privately Held**
SIC: 5451 2022 Cheese; cheese, natural & processed

(G-17877)
H & H GENERAL EXCAVATING CO (PA)
Also Called: H & H Construction
660 Old Hanover Rd (17362-8914)
P.O. Box 141 (17362-0141)
PHONE..................................717 225-4669
Michael A Hartman, *President*
Charles Hartman Jr, *Vice Pres*
Charles L Hartman, *Admin Sec*
EMP: 100
SQ FT: 2,500
SALES (est): 27.6MM **Privately Held**
SIC: 5193 1794 2421 Flowers & florists' supplies; excavation & grading, building construction; sawmills & planing mills, general

(G-17878)
HANOVER ICE CO INC
1904 Yingling Dr (17362-8967)
PHONE..................................717 637-9137
Paul E Jacobs, *President*
EMP: 5 **EST:** 1917
SQ FT: 10,000
SALES (est): 578K **Privately Held**
SIC: 2097 Manufactured ice

(G-17879)
MWI SERVICE
6182 Hill Top Dr E (17362-9131)
PHONE..................................717 578-2324
John Meador, *Principal*
EMP: 3
SALES (est): 174.8K **Privately Held**
SIC: 7692 Welding repair

(G-17880)
PIXELLE SPCIALTY SOLUTIONS LLC (PA)
228 S Main St (17362-1000)
PHONE..................................717 225-4711
Tim Hess, *President*
EMP: 3
SALES (est): 2.8MM **Privately Held**
SIC: 2621 Specialty or chemically treated papers

Spring House
Montgomery County

(G-17881)
ART GLASS SGO INC
Also Called: Sgo Designer Glass
909 Bethlehem Pike (19477)
P.O. Box 168 (19477-0168)
PHONE..................................215 884-8543
Paul Mamolou, *President*
Bill Hurley, *Vice Pres*
EMP: 4
SALES (est): 592.2K **Privately Held**
WEB: www.sgopa.com
SIC: 3231 Products of purchased glass

(G-17882)
JANSSEN RESEARCH & DEV LLC
Welsh And Mckean Rds (19477)
PHONE..................................215 628-5000
Gregory McKenzie, *Principal*
EMP: 228
SALES (corp-wide): 81.5B **Publicly Held**
WEB: www.jnjpharmarnd.com
SIC: 2834 Druggists' preparations (pharmaceuticals)
HQ: Janssen Research & Development, Llc
920 Us Highway 202
Raritan NJ 08869
908 704-4000

(G-17883)
SIEMENS INDUSTRY INC
Also Called: Siemens Energy
1201 Sumneytown Pike (19477)
PHONE..................................215 646-7400
Bob Flint, *Facilities Mgr*
EMP: 100
SALES (corp-wide): 95B **Privately Held**
WEB: www.sea.siemens.com
SIC: 3545 3823 Precision measuring tools; temperature instruments: industrial process type

HQ: Siemens Industry, Inc.
1000 Deerfield Pkwy
Buffalo Grove IL 60089
800 743-6367

Spring Mills
Centre County

(G-17884)
A M LOGGING LLC
4873 Penns Valley Rd (16875-8504)
P.O. Box 436, Millheim (16854-0436)
PHONE...............................814 349-8089
Mark Byler, *Principal*
EMP: 12
SALES (est): 1.2MM **Privately Held**
SIC: 2411 Logging camps & contractors

(G-17885)
BUFFALO BILLFOLD
711 Upper Georges Vly Rd (16875-8001)
PHONE...............................814 422-8955
Ronald H Snider, *Owner*
EMP: 9
SALES: 150K **Privately Held**
WEB: www.buffalobillfoldcompany.com
SIC: 3172 Leather money holders

(G-17886)
CALDER INDUSTRIES INC
187 Edgewood Ln (16875-8722)
PHONE...............................814 422-8026
James L Calder, *President*
Eileen L Calder, *Vice Pres*
EMP: 10
SALES (est): 2.5MM **Privately Held**
WEB: www.calderindustries.com
SIC: 3291 3545 Wheels, abrasive;
dressers, abrasive wheel: diamond point
or other; milling cutters

(G-17887)
COOKE TAVERN LTD
Also Called: Cooke Tavern Soups
4158 Penns Valley Rd (16875-8306)
PHONE...............................814 422-7687
Greg Williams, *President*
EMP: 5
SALES (est): 234.2K **Privately Held**
WEB: www.cooketavern.com
SIC: 5961 5813 2034 2099 Food, mail
order; tavern (drinking places); soups, de-
hydrated; food preparations

(G-17888)
K&J MACHINE SHOP
195 Sand Mountain Rd (16875-9038)
PHONE...............................814 364-1101
Kent Smith, *Principal*
EMP: 3
SALES (est): 247.2K **Privately Held**
SIC: 3599 Machine shop, jobbing & repair

(G-17889)
MILLHEIM SMALL ENGINE INC
4857 Penns Valley Rd (16875-8504)
PHONE...............................814 349-5007
Henry S Beiler, *President*
EMP: 7
SALES (est): 130.1K **Privately Held**
SIC: 3429 Manufactured hardware (gen-
eral)

(G-17890)
NORSE PADDLE CO
Also Called: Browns Tree Farm
121 Penn Field Ln (16875-7908)
PHONE...............................814 422-8844
Richard Brown, *Owner*
EMP: 3
SQ FT: 4,500
SALES: 90K **Privately Held**
SIC: 2499 Oars & paddles, wood

(G-17891)
OCTOBER 6 2011
Also Called: Rising Spring Meat Company
119 Cooper St (16875-8102)
PHONE...............................814 422-8810
John Young, *President*
EMP: 5
SALES (est): 249.9K **Privately Held**
SIC: 2011 Meat packing plants

(G-17892)
SEAY CUSTOM WOODWORKING
106 Windy Way (16875-8216)
PHONE...............................814 422-8986
Bill Seay, *Principal*
EMP: 4
SALES (est): 364.1K **Privately Held**
SIC: 2431 Millwork

(G-17893)
SPRING MILLS MANUFACTURING INC
1 Streamside Pl E (16875)
P.O. Box 85 (16875-0085)
PHONE...............................814 422-8892
William Abrams, *President*
EMP: 9
SQ FT: 25,000
SALES (est): 940.3K **Privately Held**
SIC: 2679 Tags & labels, paper

Springboro
Crawford County

(G-17894)
BORTNICK CONSTRUCTION INC (PA)
146 Beaver St (16435-5406)
P.O. Box 30 (16435-0030)
PHONE...............................814 587-6023
Marie F Bortnick, *President*
Russell Nelson, *General Mgr*
Doreen Nelson, *Treasurer*
EMP: 6
SQ FT: 26,000
SALES: 5MM **Privately Held**
SIC: 1796 3441 Millwright; fabricated
structural metal

(G-17895)
ERIE TOOL AND FORGE INC
25035 N Center Rd (16435-2605)
P.O. Box 277, Jefferson OH (44047-0277)
PHONE...............................814 587-2841
Robert Richardson, *President*
Gwynne Richardson, *Corp Secy*
Mary Lou Lenhardt, *Manager*
EMP: 25 EST: 1952
SQ FT: 20,000
SALES (est): 3.9MM **Privately Held**
WEB: www.erietoolandforge.com
SIC: 3462 Iron & steel forgings

(G-17896)
TOOL-RITE INC
14136 W Center Rd (16435-3412)
PHONE...............................814 587-3151
Palma G Leone, *CEO*
William F Leone, *President*
EMP: 7
SQ FT: 2,500
SALES (est): 650K **Privately Held**
SIC: 3089 Injection molding of plastics

Springdale
Allegheny County

(G-17897)
AMERICAN GAS LAMP WORKS LLC (PA)
101 Hoeveler St (15144-1711)
PHONE...............................724 274-7131
Dawn Jardini,
◆ EMP: 9
SQ FT: 5,000
SALES (est): 1.8MM **Privately Held**
WEB: www.gaslite.com
SIC: 3648 Gas lighting fixtures

(G-17898)
AMERICAN GAS LAMP WORKS LLC
Also Called: Gaslite America
101 Hoeveler St (15144-1711)
PHONE...............................724 274-7131
Wendy Stover, *Manager*
EMP: 11

SALES (corp-wide): 1.8MM **Privately Held**
WEB: www.gaslite.com
SIC: 3648 Gas lighting fixtures
PA: American Gas Lamp Works Llc
101 Hoeveler St
Springdale PA 15144
724 274-7131

(G-17899)
PPG INDUSTRIES INC
Also Called: P P G Coatings & Resins Group
125 Colfax St (15144-1506)
PHONE...............................724 274-7900
Joan Kunkle, *Branch Mgr*
EMP: 24
SALES (corp-wide): 15.3B **Publicly Held**
WEB: www.ppg.com
SIC: 2851 Paints & allied products
PA: Ppg Industries, Inc.
1 Ppg Pl
Pittsburgh PA 15272
412 434-3131

(G-17900)
R I LAMPUS COMPANY (PA)
816 R I Lampus Ave (15144)
PHONE...............................412 362-3800
Donald L Lampus Jr, *President*
Joe Vansovich, *President*
Tasha Thomas, *Sales Staff*
Thomas Dudley, *Manager*
Gail L Labik, *Executive*
▲ EMP: 180
SQ FT: 12,500
SALES: 43MM **Privately Held**
WEB: www.lampus.com
SIC: 3339 3271 3272 Silicon & chromium;
silicon refining (primary, over 99% pure);
silicon, epitaxial (silicon alloy); silicon,
pure; blocks, concrete or cinder: stan-
dard; paving blocks, concrete; concrete
products

(G-17901)
SPRINGDALE SPECIALTY PLAS INC
997 Sherosky Way (15144-1185)
P.O. Box 296, Creighton (15030-0296)
PHONE...............................724 274-4144
Robert L Ross, *Ch of Bd*
Mark Sever, *President*
EMP: 50
SALES (est): 4.2MM **Privately Held**
SIC: 3085 Plastics bottles

(G-17902)
STEVES REFACING
731 Pittsburgh St (15144-1561)
PHONE...............................724 274-4740
EMP: 4
SALES (est): 210K **Privately Held**
SIC: 3553 Mfg Woodworking Machinery

(G-17903)
TECKLANE MANUFACTURING INC (PA)
200 Hoeveler St (15144-1713)
P.O. Box 185 (15144-0185)
PHONE...............................724 274-9464
Thomas H Mentecki, *CEO*
Deborah J Beech, *Corp Secy*
Todd Mentecki, *Vice Pres*
EMP: 14
SQ FT: 20,000
SALES (est): 1.7MM **Privately Held**
WEB: www.tecklane.com
SIC: 3469 3599 Machine parts, stamped
or pressed metal; machine shop, jobbing
& repair

(G-17904)
UNITED REFINING COMPANY
13 Mellon (15144)
P.O. Box 121 (15144-0121)
PHONE...............................724 274-0885
Randall Beltrami, *Manager*
EMP: 5
SALES (corp-wide): 2.5B **Privately Held**
WEB: www.urc.com
SIC: 2841 Soap & other detergents
HQ: United Refining Company
15 Bradley St
Warren PA 16365
814 723-1500

(G-17905)
VIEW WORKS INC
944 Lincoln Ave (15144-1744)
PHONE...............................724 226-9773
Ernest D Gaston, *President*
EMP: 4
SALES (est): 270K **Privately Held**
WEB: www.viewworksinc.com
SIC: 3999 7319 Blocks, hat; display ad-
vertising service

Springfield
Delaware County

(G-17906)
ALFRED TROILO
434 Kennerly Rd (19064-2132)
PHONE...............................610 544-0115
Alfred Troilo, *Director*
EMP: 3
SALES (est): 173.8K **Privately Held**
SIC: 3577 Data conversion equipment,
media-to-media: computer

(G-17907)
ASERDIV INC (DH)
Also Called: Nri Data and Business Products
940 W Sproul Rd (19064-1255)
PHONE...............................800 966-7770
Philip M Lanctot Jr, *CEO*
Philip R Lanctot, *President*
EMP: 30
SQ FT: 23,000
SALES (est): 8.2MM
SALES (corp-wide): 1.8MM **Privately Held**
SIC: 5045 3955 3861 7379 Computer
software; carbon paper & inked ribbons;
photographic equipment & supplies; com-
puter related consulting services
HQ: Transcend United Technologies, Llc
1170 Devon Park Dr # 102
Wayne PA 19087
484 654-1500

(G-17908)
BUSINESS 21 PUBLISHING LLC
477 Baltimore Pike (19064-3810)
PHONE...............................484 479-2700
Stephen Meyer, *CEO*
Glenn Eckard, *President*
EMP: 65
SALES (est): 5.5MM **Privately Held**
WEB: www.b21pubs.com
SIC: 2731 Books: publishing only

(G-17909)
CALIFORNIA LINEAR DEVICES INC
750 W Sproul Rd (19064-4001)
PHONE...............................610 328-4000
Larry Colangelo, *CEO*
Ronald Noble, *President*
Joann Willhite, *CFO*
EMP: 12
SQ FT: 8,000
SALES (est): 1.3MM **Privately Held**
WEB: www.calinear.com
SIC: 3621 Motors & generators

(G-17910)
CHARLES ERNSTS SONS LLC
Also Called: Charles Ernst's Sons Imports
74 S Hillcrest Rd (19064-2441)
PHONE...............................267 237-1271
Robert Ernst, *Principal*
EMP: 3
SALES: 500K **Privately Held**
SIC: 2092 Fresh or frozen fish or seafood
chowders, soups & stews

(G-17911)
COVENTRY PEWTER INC
118 Lynbrooke Rd (19064-2412)
P.O. Box 171 (19064-0171)
PHONE...............................610 328-1557
John Boyer, *Principal*
EMP: 5
SALES (est): 303.5K **Privately Held**
WEB: www.coventrypewter.com
SIC: 3914 Pewter ware

(G-17912)
ERGON ASPHALT & EMULSIONS INC
153 Saxer Ave (19064-2421)
PHONE..................................484 471-3999
EMP: 4
SALES (corp-wide): 1B Privately Held
SIC: 2951 Asphalt paving mixtures & blocks
HQ: Ergon Asphalt & Emulsions Inc
2829 Lakeland Dr Ste 2000
Flowood MS 39232
601 933-3000

(G-17913)
F W B & SONS WELDING INC
206 N State Rd (19064-1333)
PHONE..................................610 543-0348
Frank Bendinelli, Principal
EMP: 5
SALES: 500K Privately Held
SIC: 7692 Welding repair

(G-17914)
FIRST SHELBURNE CORPORATION
Also Called: M & M Quick Print
162 Saxer Ave Ste 2 (19064-2336)
PHONE..................................610 544-8660
Lawrence J Milkowski, President
EMP: 3
SALES (est): 340.5K Privately Held
SIC: 2752 Commercial printing, offset

(G-17915)
GLOBAL MONITORING LLC
491 Baltimore Pike # 421 (19064-3810)
PHONE..................................610 604-0760
Stephen Sanislo,
EMP: 5
SALES (est): 606.2K Privately Held
SIC: 3663

(G-17916)
GLOBAL PASSIVE SAFETY SYSTEMS
761 W Sproul Rd Ste 208 (19064-1215)
PHONE..................................267 297-2340
Andrew Abrans,
▲ EMP: 3
SALES (est): 308.4K Privately Held
SIC: 3492 Hose & tube fittings & assemblies, hydraulic/pneumatic

(G-17917)
LUNACOR INC
616 Sheffield Dr (19064-2824)
PHONE..................................610 328-6150
Rory Mc Manus, President
EMP: 3
SALES: 250K Privately Held
SIC: 2731 7379 3861 Book publishing; ; motion picture film

(G-17918)
LUXOTTICA OF AMERICA INC
Also Called: Lenscrafters
910 E Woodland Ave Rear A (19064-3955)
PHONE..................................610 543-8622
Mary Lyons, Branch Mgr
EMP: 25
SALES (corp-wide): 283.5MM Privately Held
WEB: www.lenscrafters.com
SIC: 5995 3851 Eyeglasses, prescription; ophthalmic goods
HQ: Luxottica Of America Inc.
4000 Luxottica Pl
Mason OH 45040

(G-17919)
MOOG INC
Also Called: Moog Components Group
750 W Sproul Rd (19064-4001)
PHONE..................................610 328-4000
Karen Mitchell, Production
Dave McCaffrey, Purch Mgr
Anne Steltz, Purch Mgr
Regina Donnelly, Buyer
Guy Cortese, Engineer
EMP: 200

SALES (corp-wide): 2.7B Publicly Held
WEB: www.moog.com
SIC: 3674 3089 3812 3593 Infrared sensors, solid state; buoys & floats, plastic; search & navigation equipment; fluid power cylinders & actuators; computer peripheral equipment
PA: Moog Inc.
400 Jamison Rd
Elma NY 14059
716 652-2000

(G-17920)
PPG INDUSTRIES INC
160 Baltimore Pike (19064-3629)
PHONE..................................610 544-1925
EMP: 4
SALES (corp-wide): 15.3B Publicly Held
SIC: 2851 Paints & allied products
PA: Ppg Industries, Inc.
1 Ppg Pl
Pittsburgh PA 15272
412 434-3131

(G-17921)
PRINTCOMPASS LLC
451 Alliston Rd (19064-3225)
PHONE..................................610 541-6763
Barry Walsh,
EMP: 3 EST: 2015
SALES (est): 180.2K Privately Held
SIC: 2752 Commercial printing, lithographic

(G-17922)
SAJ PUBLISHING
100 Harned Dr (19064-1713)
P.O. Box 5178 (19064-5178)
PHONE..................................610 544-5484
Stephen Jones, Principal
EMP: 4
SALES (est): 203.1K Privately Held
SIC: 2741 Miscellaneous publishing

(G-17923)
SPRINGFIELD PASTA
Also Called: Napoletano Pasta
186 Saxer Ave (19064-2335)
PHONE..................................610 543-5687
Corrado Napoletano, Partner
Claude Napoletano, Vice Pres
EMP: 6
SQ FT: 3,800
SALES (est): 360K Privately Held
WEB: www.napoletanopasta.com
SIC: 2099 Pasta, uncooked: packaged with other ingredients

(G-17924)
VIKING IMPORTING CO
1260 E Wdlnd Ave Ste 15 (19064)
P.O. Box 253 (19064-0253)
PHONE..................................610 690-2900
Anthony Marcozzi, President
▲ EMP: 7
SALES (est): 413.9K Privately Held
SIC: 2621 Bank note paper

Springs
Somerset County

(G-17925)
KEYSTONE LIME COMPANY (PA)
1156 Christner Hollow Rd (15562)
P.O. Box 278 (15562-0278)
PHONE..................................814 662-2025
Melinda F Gibson, President
Melinda Walker, President
Lura M Folk, Vice Pres
Melinda Gibson, CFO
Kendra K Geiger, Treasurer
EMP: 30 EST: 1928
SQ FT: 1,500
SALES (est): 20.6MM Privately Held
SIC: 1611 1422 3274 Highway & street construction; crushed & broken limestone; agricultural lime

Springtown
Bucks County

(G-17926)
DYNACUT INC
Also Called: Platt Robert E Machine Pdts
3425 Funks Mill Rd (18081)
P.O. Box 156 (18081-0156)
PHONE..................................610 346-7386
Robert Platt II, President
Heather Young, Corp Secy
EMP: 3
SALES: 500K Privately Held
WEB: www.dynacut.com
SIC: 3545 3291 Cutting tools for machine tools; abrasive products

(G-17927)
LEE ANTENNA & LINE SERVICE INC
3050 Route 212 Springtown (18081)
P.O. Box 514 (18081-0514)
PHONE..................................610 346-7999
Bryan D Lee, President
Brian D Lee, President
Andrea Lee, Vice Pres
EMP: 14
SALES (est): 1MM Privately Held
SIC: 3441 1623 Tower sections, radio & television transmission; transmitting tower (telecommunication) construction

Springville
Susquehanna County

(G-17928)
DAYE-LICIOUS BAKING
487 Hunsinger Rd (18844-7786)
PHONE..................................570 965-2491
Jody Daye, Principal
EMP: 4
SALES (est): 228.2K Privately Held
SIC: 2051 Bread, cake & related products

(G-17929)
FINCH FLAGSTONE
1673 Sheldon Hill Rd (18844-7928)
PHONE..................................570 965-0982
Tim Finch, Partner
Sam Finch, Partner
EMP: 5
SALES: 220K Privately Held
SIC: 1221 Surface mining, bituminous

(G-17930)
JIM BORDEN
Also Called: Borden Accuracy
1325 Sheldon Hill Rd (18844-7924)
PHONE..................................570 965-2505
Jim Borden, Owner
EMP: 5
SQ FT: 6,000
SALES (est): 502.6K Privately Held
WEB: www.bordenrifles.com
SIC: 3489 5941 Rifles, recoiless; sporting goods & bicycle shops

(G-17931)
LOCHS MAPLE FIBER MILL INC
143 Cokely Rd (18844-7730)
PHONE..................................570 965-2679
EMP: 6
SALES (est): 402.8K Privately Held
SIC: 2099 Mfg Food Preparations

Sprng Brk Twp
Lackawanna County

(G-17932)
INTERNATIONAL UNION-ELEVATOR
16 Park St (18444-6361)
PHONE..................................570 842-5430
Saugust Whymeyer, General Mgr
EMP: 3

SALES (est): 444.4K Privately Held
SIC: 5153 3534 Grain elevators; elevators & equipment

(G-17933)
JUSTICK & JUSTICK INC
888 State Route 307 (18444-6452)
PHONE..................................570 840-0187
Martin K Justick Sr, President
Martin Justick Jr, Vice Pres
EMP: 2
SALES: 1MM Privately Held
SIC: 2411 Wooden logs

(G-17934)
TIMINSKI LOGGING CO
5 Timinski Rd (18444-6534)
PHONE..................................570 457-2641
Gerald Timinski, Owner
EMP: 4
SALES: 300K Privately Held
SIC: 2411 Logging camps & contractors

Stahlstown
Westmoreland County

(G-17935)
AMERIKOHL MINING INC
1384 State Route 711 (15687-1301)
PHONE..................................724 282-2339
Todd Fiedor, Branch Mgr
EMP: 35
SALES (est): 3.8MM
SALES (corp-wide): 28.4MM Privately Held
WEB: www.amerikohl.com
SIC: 1221 5052 Strip mining, bituminous; coal
PA: Amerikohl Mining, Inc.
202 Sunset Dr
Butler PA 16001
724 282-2339

(G-17936)
PATRIOT EXPLORATION
1384 State Route 711 (15687-1301)
PHONE..................................724 593-4427
John Stilley, Principal
EMP: 4
SALES (est): 410.6K Privately Held
SIC: 1381 Directional drilling oil & gas wells

(G-17937)
THERMO FISHER SCIENTIFIC INC
195 Shearer Ln (15687-1312)
PHONE..................................561 688-8725
EMP: 264
SALES (corp-wide): 24.3B Publicly Held
SIC: 3826 Analytical instruments
PA: Thermo Fisher Scientific Inc.
168 3rd Ave
Waltham MA 02451
781 622-1000

Star Junction
Fayette County

(G-17938)
TRILLI HOLDINGS INC
Also Called: Culligan
228 Church St (15482)
PHONE..................................724 736-8000
Arthur F Trilli Jr, President
William Trilli, Vice Pres
EMP: 6
SALES (est): 57.2K Privately Held
SIC: 5963 3589 3585 Bottled water delivery; water filters & softeners, household type; coolers, milk & water: electric

GEOGRAPHIC

State College
Centre County

(G-17939)
21ST CENTURY MEDIA NEWSPPR LLC
Also Called: Nittany Valley Offset
1015 Benner Pike (16801-7319)
PHONE..................................814 238-3071
Jody Lingle, *General Mgr*
Robert Butkins, *Branch Mgr*
Terry Wilkinson, *Info Tech Dir*
EMP: 50
SALES (corp-wide): 4.2B **Privately Held**
WEB: www.journalregister.com
SIC: 2752 2711 Commercial printing, lithographic; newspapers, publishing & printing
HQ: 21st Century Media Newspaper, Llc
600 Perry St
Trenton NJ 08618
215 504-4200

(G-17940)
AMCHEMTEQ INC (PA)
Also Called: Aci
2514 Shawn Cir (16801-7489)
PHONE..................................814 234-0123
Leela Venkat, *President*
Venkat Mani, *Treasurer*
EMP: 3
SQ FT: 500
SALES (est): 154K **Privately Held**
SIC: 2834 Pharmaceutical preparations

(G-17941)
API CRYPTEK INC (DH)
Also Called: Emcom
1900 W College Ave (16801-2723)
PHONE..................................908 546-3900
Robert Tavares, *CEO*
Eric Seeton, *CFO*
Sean Lyons, *Treasurer*
Pat Shoup, *VP Finance*
EMP: 13
SALES (est): 3.9MM
SALES (corp-wide): 333.6MM **Privately Held**
SIC: 7382 3699 7373 7371 Security systems services; security devices; computer integrated systems design; computer software development & applications

(G-17942)
ATOPTIX LLC
200 Innovation Blvd (16803-6602)
PHONE..................................814 808-7056
Perry Edwards,
Zhiwen Liu,
EMP: 4
SALES (est): 290.2K **Privately Held**
SIC: 3845 Laser systems & equipment, medical

(G-17943)
ATOTECH USA LLC
270 Walker Dr (16801-7097)
PHONE..................................814 238-0514
Don Houtz, *Production*
Greg Merritt, *Purch Mgr*
Terje Johnsen, *Manager*
John H Auman, *Manager*
Eve Powars-Bahr, *Manager*
EMP: 40
SALES (corp-wide): 8.4B **Publicly Held**
SIC: 2899 Chemical preparations
HQ: Atotech Usa, Llc
1750 Overview Dr
Rock Hill SC 29730

(G-17944)
B N I SOLUTIONS LLC
2820 E College Ave Ste B (16801-7548)
PHONE..................................814 237-4073
Scott Kimble, *Principal*
EMP: 3 EST: 2016
SALES (est): 173.2K **Privately Held**
SIC: 3661 Telephone & telegraph apparatus

(G-17945)
BIOMAGNETIC SOLUTIONS LLC
420 Amblewood Way (16803-1109)
PHONE..................................814 689-1801
Paul A Liberti,
Ted L Liberti,
EMP: 5
SALES (est): 429.4K **Privately Held**
SIC: 8731 2835 Commercial physical research; commercial physical research; in vitro diagnostics

(G-17946)
BLATEK INDUSTRIES INC
2820 E College Ave Ste F (16801-7548)
PHONE..................................814 231-2085
Stuart Blacker, *President*
Kevin Knarr, *Opers Mgr*
Chris Rishel, *QC Mgr*
Calvin Zimmerman, *Engineer*
Glenn Mactavish,
EMP: 63
SQ FT: 10,000
SALES (est): 13.8MM **Privately Held**
WEB: www.blatek.com
SIC: 3829 3679 Measuring & controlling devices; transducers, electrical

(G-17947)
BROADBAND NETWORKS INC (DH)
2820 E College Ave Ste B (16801-7548)
PHONE..................................814 237-4073
Mike Marett, *President*
Dennis F Coslo, *VP Mfg*
EMP: 70
SQ FT: 9,130
SALES (est): 6.2MM
SALES (corp-wide): 692MM **Privately Held**
WEB: www.bnisolutions.com
SIC: 3663 3661 3827 Radio & TV communications equipment; telephone & telegraph apparatus; optical instruments & lenses

(G-17948)
CANNON INSTRUMENT COMPANY
Also Called: Scientific Development Co
2139 High Tech Rd (16803-1733)
PHONE..................................814 353-8000
Charles Maggi, *President*
Kenneth O Henderson, *Vice Pres*
Dan Hook, *VP Mfg*
Richard Cassatt, *Prdtn Mgr*
Jennie Rogers, *Purch Agent*
EMP: 90
SQ FT: 35,000
SALES (est): 23.8MM
SALES (corp-wide): 97.4MM **Privately Held**
WEB: www.cannoninstrument.com
SIC: 3823 Industrial flow & liquid measuring instruments; industrial process control instruments; controllers for process variables, all types; thermal conductivity instruments, industrial process type
PA: Arthur H. Thomas Company
1654 High Hill Rd
Swedesboro NJ 08085
856 467-2000

(G-17949)
CENTRE OF WEB INC
Also Called: Centreweb
2026 Sandy Dr (16803-2515)
PHONE..................................814 235-9592
Duane R Champion, *President*
Bill Brackley, *Vice Pres*
John Stitzinger, *Treasurer*
John Balogh, *Admin Sec*
EMP: 9
SALES (est): 133.1K **Privately Held**
WEB: www.centreweb.com
SIC: 4813 7372 ; ; prepackaged software

(G-17950)
CHEMCUT CORPORATION
500-1 Science Park Rd (16803)
PHONE..................................814 272-2800
Rick Lies, *CEO*
Karl F Ketelhohn, *Vice Pres*
Dan Lamorte, *Vice Pres*
Kenneth A Slocumb, *Vice Pres*

Ken Gawryla, *Opers Mgr*
▼ EMP: 340 EST: 1980
SALES (est): 23.9MM **Privately Held**
SIC: 3559 3545 3999 Chemical machinery & equipment; precision measuring tools; atomizers, toiletry

(G-17951)
CHEMCUT HOLDINGS LLC
500-1 Science Park Rd (16803)
PHONE..................................814 272-2800
Richard Doherty, *Sales Mgr*
Richard Lies, *Mng Member*
◆ EMP: 95
SQ FT: 102,800
SALES (est): 24.5MM **Privately Held**
WEB: www.chemcut.net
SIC: 3559 Chemical machinery & equipment; brick making machinery

(G-17952)
COIL SPECIALTY CO INC
60 Decibel Rd Ste 108 (16801-7574)
PHONE..................................814 234-7044
Keith Krick, *President*
Dena Arnold, *Office Mgr*
Thomas P Hooley, *Shareholder*
EMP: 30 EST: 1957
SQ FT: 15,000
SALES (est): 3.9MM **Privately Held**
WEB: www.coilspecialty.com
SIC: 3677 5065 3621 3612 Coil windings, electronic; transformers power supply, electronic type; electronic parts & equipment; motors & generators; transformers, except electric; blowers & fans

(G-17953)
COLLEGIAN INC
Also Called: DAILY COLLEGIAN, THE
123 S Burrowes St Ste 200 (16801-3882)
PHONE..................................814 865-2531
Wayne Lowman, *General Mgr*
EMP: 21
SQ FT: 10,000
SALES: 908K **Privately Held**
WEB: www.collegian.com
SIC: 2711 5199 Newspapers: publishing only, not printed on site; advertising specialties

(G-17954)
COLLEGIATE FURNISHINGS INC (PA)
1199 E College Ave (16801-6868)
PHONE..................................814 234-1660
Thomas Meade, *President*
Linda Zellers, *Office Mgr*
Carol Meade, *Admin Sec*
▼ EMP: 29
SQ FT: 30,000
SALES (est): 2.7MM **Privately Held**
WEB: www.roomdoctor.com
SIC: 2511 5712 Unassembled or unfinished furniture, household: wood; furniture stores

(G-17955)
CONSTRUCTION TOOL SERVICE INC
2929 Stewart Dr A (16801-7565)
PHONE..................................814 231-3090
John Becker, *Sales Mgr*
Van Winter, *Manager*
EMP: 6
SALES (corp-wide): 12.7MM **Privately Held**
SIC: 3545 Drills (machine tool accessories)
PA: Construction Tool Service, Inc.
3500 Liberty Ave
Pittsburgh PA 15201
412 681-6673

(G-17956)
D&E COMMUNICATIONS LLC
441 Science Park Rd (16803-2217)
PHONE..................................814 238-0000
Troy Knecht, *Branch Mgr*
EMP: 50
SALES (corp-wide): 5.7B **Publicly Held**
WEB: www.decommunications.com
SIC: 3661 Telephones & telephone apparatus
HQ: D&E Communications, Llc
124 E Main St Fl 6
Ephrata PA 17522

(G-17957)
DAVID R ENGLEHART
220 Regent Ct Ste D (16801-7969)
PHONE..................................814 238-6734
David R Englehart, *Principal*
EMP: 6
SALES (est): 695.5K **Privately Held**
SIC: 3821 8021 Clinical laboratory instruments, except medical & dental; offices & clinics of dentists

(G-17958)
E-NANOMEDSYS LLC
746 E Mccormick Ave (16801-6525)
PHONE..................................917 734-1462
Vijay Varadan, *Director*
EMP: 4
SALES (est): 212.8K **Privately Held**
SIC: 2331 2321 3663 3679 T-shirts & tops, women's: made from purchased materials; sport shirts, men's & boys': from purchased materials; mobile communication equipment; electronic circuits; medical research, commercial

(G-17959)
ECLIPSE RESOURCES HOLDINGS LP
2121 Old Gatesburg Rd # 110 (16803-2290)
PHONE..................................814 308-9754
Benjamin W Hulburt, *Principal*
EMP: 227 EST: 2014
SALES (est): 5.1MM **Privately Held**
SIC: 1311 Crude petroleum & natural gas

(G-17960)
ECLIPSE RESOURCES I LP (HQ)
2121 Old Gatesburg Rd # 110 (16803-2290)
PHONE..................................814 308-9754
Benjamin W Hulburt, *CEO*
Bryan Moody, *President*
Matthew R Denezza, *Exec VP*
Christopher K Hulburt, *Exec VP*
Thomas S Liberatore, *Exec VP*
EMP: 15
SQ FT: 28,000
SALES (est): 134.4MM
SALES (corp-wide): 515.1MM **Publicly Held**
SIC: 1311 1382 Crude petroleum production; oil & gas exploration services
PA: Montage Resources Corporation
122 W John Carpenter Fwy
Irving TX 75039
469 444-1647

(G-17961)
ECLIPSE RESOURCES OPER LLC
2121 Old Gatesburg Rd # 110 (16803-2290)
PHONE..................................814 308-9731
Hulburt Benjamin W, *CEO*
Hulburt Christopher K, *Exec VP*
Liberatore Thomas S, *Exec VP*
Brian Panetta, *Vice Pres*
Matthew Denezza, *CFO*
EMP: 1
SALES (est): 1.5MM
SALES (corp-wide): 515.1MM **Publicly Held**
SIC: 1382 Geological exploration, oil & gas field
PA: Montage Resources Corporation
122 W John Carpenter Fwy
Irving TX 75039
469 444-1647

(G-17962)
ECLIPSE RESOURCES-PA LP
2121 Old Gatesburg Rd # 110 (16803-2290)
PHONE..................................814 409-7006
Christopher Hulburt, *Exec VP*
EMP: 15
SQ FT: 35,000
SALES: 10MM
SALES (corp-wide): 515.1MM **Publicly Held**
SIC: 1382 Oil & gas exploration services

PA: Montage Resources Corporation
122 W John Carpenter Fwy
Irving TX 75039
469 444-1647

(G-17963)
ENERGYCAP INC
2026 Sandy Dr (16803-2515)
PHONE.................................814 237-3744
Steven D Heinz, *CEO*
Ryan Ohlson, *COO*
Ryan Booz, *Vice Pres*
Adam Hegedus, *Vice Pres*
Chris Heinz, *Vice Pres*
EMP: 45
SQ FT: 10,980
SALES: 9.8MM **Privately Held**
WEB: www.energycap.com
SIC: 7372 Publishers' computer software

(G-17964)
FINISH LINE SCREEN PRTG INC
1869 Park Forest Ave (16803-1404)
PHONE.................................814 238-0122
Linda McGough, *President*
Linda Mc Gough, *Partner*
EMP: 8
SALES: 325K **Privately Held**
WEB: www.finishlinescreenprinting.com
SIC: 2262 Screen printing: manmade fiber
& silk broadwoven fabrics

(G-17965)
FIVE STAR GROUP INC
26 Cricklewood Cir (16803-2105)
PHONE.................................814 237-0241
S Ramachandran, *President*
Henry L Ritell, *Shareholder*
EMP: 6
SQ FT: 12,000
SALES (est): 465.9K **Privately Held**
SIC: 2869 Industrial organic chemicals

(G-17966)
FREEZE THAW CYCLES
109 S Allen St (16801-4737)
PHONE.................................814 272-0178
Corey Lev, *Principal*
EMP: 5
SALES (est): 564.8K **Privately Held**
SIC: 3751 7699 Bicycles & related parts;
motorcycle repair service

(G-17967)
GALLIMED SCIENCES INC
3500 E College Ave # 1000 (16801-7569)
PHONE.................................814 777-2973
Guy F Barbato, *President*
EMP: 6
SALES (est): 415.3K **Privately Held**
SIC: 2879 Agricultural chemicals

(G-17968)
GDA CORP
301 Science Park Rd # 112 (16803-2293)
PHONE.................................814 237-4060
Stephanie Hulina, *President*
Dmitry Verlyguin, *Vice Pres*
EMP: 10
SQ FT: 2,500
SALES (est): 1.3MM **Privately Held**
WEB: www.gdacorp.com
SIC: 3577 Computer peripheral equipment

(G-17969)
GENERAL DYNMICS STCOM TECH INC
60 Decibel Rd Ste 200 (16801-7574)
PHONE.................................814 238-2700
Victor Lanio, *Vice Pres*
Betty Glass, *Buyer*
Brian Reuss, *Branch Mgr*
Karen Kinsey, *Executive*
EMP: 120
SALES (corp-wide): 36.1B **Publicly Held**
WEB: www.tripointglobal.com
SIC: 3663 Antennas, transmitting & communications
HQ: General Dynamics Satcom Technologies, Inc.
1700 Cable Dr Ne
Conover NC 28613
704 462-7330

(G-17970)
GLENN O HAWBAKER INC (PA)
1952 Waddle Rd Ste 203 (16803-1649)
PHONE.................................814 237-1444
Daniel R Hawbaker, *President*
D Michael Hawbaker, *Vice Pres*
Patrick G Hawbaker, *Treasurer*
EMP: 75
SQ FT: 18,000
SALES: 300MM **Privately Held**
WEB: www.goh-inc.com
SIC: 2951 3281 1622 1794 Asphalt & asphaltic paving mixtures (not from refineries); stone, quarrying & processing of own stone products; bridge construction; excavation work; highway & street paving contractor; crushed & broken limestone

(G-17971)
HANSON READY MIX INC
123 Hawbaker Indus Dr (16803-2307)
PHONE.................................814 238-1781
Angie Hall, *Manager*
EMP: 12
SALES (corp-wide): 20.6B **Privately Held**
SIC: 3273 Ready-mixed concrete
HQ: Hanson Ready Mix, Inc.
3251 Bath Pike
Nazareth PA 18064

(G-17972)
HAPPY VALLEY COM
Also Called: Jack's 6 Pack Bottle Shop
1669 N Atherton St (16803-1417)
PHONE.................................814 238-8066
Jack Sapia, *Branch Mgr*
EMP: 5 **Privately Held**
SIC: 2086 Bottled & canned soft drinks
PA: Happy Valley Com
2160 Sandy Dr Ste D
State College PA 16803

(G-17973)
HAPPY VLY VINYRD & WINERY LLC
576 S Foxpointe Dr (16801-3300)
PHONE.................................814 308-8756
Elwin Stewart, *Mng Member*
Barbara Stewar, *Mng Member*
EMP: 3 **EST:** 2008
SALES (est): 208.9K **Privately Held**
SIC: 0762 2084 Vineyard management & maintenance services; wines

(G-17974)
HEIMER ENTERPRISES INC
Also Called: The Sign Factory
228 S Allen St (16801-4805)
PHONE.................................814 234-7446
Ralph Heimer, *President*
Richard Heimer, *Vice Pres*
Jeffrey Heimer MD, *Treasurer*
EMP: 5
SALES (est): 649.1K **Privately Held**
SIC: 3993 7389 Signs, not made in custom sign painting shops; laminating service

(G-17975)
HERLOCHER FOODS INC
415 E Calder Way (16801-5663)
PHONE.................................814 237-0134
Charles C Herlocher II, *President*
Tara Herlocher, *Principal*
EMP: 4
SQ FT: 3,000
SALES (est): 452.1K **Privately Held**
WEB: www.herlocherfoods.com
SIC: 2035 Mustard, prepared (wet)

(G-17976)
HOMELAND MFG SVCS INC
2591 Clyde Ave Ste 2 (16801-7560)
PHONE.................................814 862-9103
John Bonislawski Jr, *President*
EMP: 17
SQ FT: 7,000
SALES: 2.6MM **Privately Held**
SIC: 3569 3679 Robots, assembly line: industrial & commercial; electronic circuits

(G-17977)
INNOGREEN USA LLC
Also Called: Innogreen Group
200 Innovation Blvd # 257 (16803-6602)
PHONE.................................814 880-4493
David Jordan, *Managing Dir*
Mohammad Fatemi, *Mng Member*
EMP: 5
SALES (est): 352.1K **Privately Held**
SIC: 3646 Commercial indusl & institutional electric lighting fixtures

(G-17978)
ISLIP TRANSFORMER AND METAL CO
Also Called: API Technologies Corp
1900 W College Ave (16801-2723)
PHONE.................................814 272-2700
Judith Dubitsky, *President*
Bart Nachamie, *Principal*
EMP: 10
SQ FT: 5,200
SALES (est): 1.8MM
SALES (corp-wide): 333.6MM **Privately Held**
SIC: 3825 8711 Analog-digital converters, electronic instrumentation type; digital test equipment, electronic & electrical circuits; electrical or electronic engineering
HQ: Api Technologies Corp.
400 Nickerson Rd Ste 1
Marlborough MA 01752

(G-17979)
IWOM OUTERWEAR LLC
1981 Pine Hall Rd (16801-2435)
PHONE.................................814 272-5400
Allen M Potter, *Partner*
EMP: 6
SALES (est): 607.1K **Privately Held**
SIC: 2329 Hunting coats & vests, men's

(G-17980)
JMB SIGNS LLC
616 Old Farm Ln (16803-1223)
PHONE.................................814 933-9725
Richard Bugden, *Principal*
EMP: 3 **EST:** 2010
SALES (est): 264.2K **Privately Held**
SIC: 3993 Signs, not made in custom sign painting shops

(G-17981)
JOSTENS INC
Jostens Yearbook Prtg & Pubg
401 Science Park Rd (16803-2217)
PHONE.................................814 237-5771
Jim Crom, *Branch Mgr*
EMP: 400
SALES (corp-wide): 1.3B **Privately Held**
WEB: www.jostens.com
SIC: 3911 Rings, finger: precious metal
HQ: Jostens, Inc.
7760 France Ave S Ste 400
Minneapolis MN 55435
952 830-3300

(G-17982)
K B OFFSET PRINTING INC
3500 E College Ave # 1000 (16801-7569)
PHONE.................................814 238-8445
R J Caravan, *CEO*
William L Kocher Jr, *President*
William Kocher, *Vice Pres*
Ted Brown, *CFO*
Mark Weaver, *Cust Mgr*
EMP: 50 **EST:** 1973
SQ FT: 22,000
SALES (est): 11.9MM **Privately Held**
SIC: 2752 2791 2789 Commercial printing, offset; typesetting; bookbinding & related work

(G-17983)
KCF TECHNOLOGIES INC
336 S Fraser St (16801-4830)
PHONE.................................814 867-4097
Jeremy Frank, *President*
Gary Koopmann, *Principal*
Jacob Loverich, *Vice Pres*
Flavio Bombonato, *Engineer*
Dave Kraige, *Manager*
EMP: 12 **EST:** 2000

SALES (est): 2.5MM **Privately Held**
WEB: www.kcftech.com
SIC: 8711 7372 Consulting engineer; business oriented computer software

(G-17984)
KEYTRONICS INC
Also Called: Magnetics Div
1900 W College Ave (16801-2723)
PHONE.................................814 272-2700
Lazar Bel, *President*
EMP: 53
SALES (corp-wide): 333.6MM **Privately Held**
WEB: www.keytronics.com
SIC: 3674 Semiconductors & related devices
HQ: Keytronics, Inc.
8031 Avonia Rd
Fairview PA

(G-17985)
KING PRINTING AND PUBG INC
1305 W College Ave (16801-2712)
PHONE.................................814 238-2536
Thomas D King, *President*
Jana King, *Vice Pres*
EMP: 6
SQ FT: 4,000
SALES (est): 789.9K **Privately Held**
WEB: www.kingprintingonline.com
SIC: 2752 Commercial printing, offset

(G-17986)
LASER CENTER OF CENTRAL PA
428 Windmere Dr Ste 100 (16801-7644)
PHONE.................................814 867-1852
Katrina Heath, *Principal*
EMP: 4
SALES (est): 261.5K **Privately Held**
SIC: 3845 Laser systems & equipment, medical

(G-17987)
M G INDUSTRIES
1348 Benner Pike (16801-7393)
PHONE.................................814 238-5092
Trudi Fleck, *Principal*
EMP: 15
SALES (est): 237K **Privately Held**
SIC: 3999 Manufacturing industries

(G-17988)
MATREYA LLC
2178 High Tech Rd (16803-1734)
PHONE.................................814 355-1030
Robert Hufnagel, *Mng Member*
Amy Houtz, *Manager*
Gary C Walker, *Vice Pres*
EMP: 12
SQ FT: 3,000
SALES: 1MM **Privately Held**
WEB: www.matreya.com
SIC: 2911 Mineral waxes, natural

(G-17989)
METAL INTEGRITY INC
341 Airport Rd (16801-2702)
PHONE.................................814 234-7399
Adam Bergman, *Principal*
EMP: 23
SALES (corp-wide): 1.1MM **Privately Held**
SIC: 3599 Machine & other job shop work
PA: Metal Integrity, Inc.
47 N Scott St
Carbondale PA 18407
570 281-2303

(G-17990)
MICROMECHATRONICS INC
200 Innovation Blvd # 155 (16803-6602)
PHONE.................................814 861-5688
Alfredo Vazquez-Carazo, *President*
EMP: 5
SQ FT: 2,000
SALES: 1MM **Privately Held**
WEB: www.micromechatronicsinc.com
SIC: 3679 Electronic circuits

(G-17991)
MILLER WELDING SERVICE
1831 W College Ave (16801-2847)
PHONE.................................814 238-2950
Robert Miller Jr, *Owner*

▲ = Import ▼=Export
◆ =Import/Export

EMP: 5
SALES: 300K Privately Held
SIC: 7692 Welding repair

(G-17992)
MINITAB LLC (PA)
1829 Pine Hall Rd (16801-3008)
PHONE..................................814 238-3280
Barbara F Ryan, *President*
Steven Pincus, *Corp Secy*
Ryan Yearick, *Vice Pres*
Duane Long, *Research*
Jeremy Zerbe, *Engineer*
▼ EMP: 276
SQ FT: 141,000
SALES (est): 101.1MM Privately Held
WEB: www.minitab.com
SIC: 7372 Business oriented computer
software

(G-17993)
MMS TECHNOLOGIES LLC
Also Called: Microwave Measurement Systems
2597 Clyde Ave Ste 2 (16801-7555)
PHONE..................................814 238-2323
EMP: 3 EST: 2010
SALES (est): 180K Privately Held
SIC: 3825 Mfg Electrical Measuring Instruments

(G-17994)
MORGAN SIGNS INC (PA)
Also Called: Barash Group, The
403 S Allen St Ste 200 (16801-5253)
PHONE..................................814 238-5051
Marian Coppersmith Fredman, *Ch of Bd*
Richard E Hall, *President*
Aimee Aiello, *Business Mgr*
Nan R Barash, *Senior VP*
Elizabeth Ebersole, *Traffic Mgr*
EMP: 32
SQ FT: 5,000
SALES (est): 4.3MM Privately Held
WEB: www.accuwx.com
SIC: 7311 7312 2721 3993 Advertising
consultant; billboard advertising; magazines: publishing only, not printed on site;
signs & advertising specialties; miscellaneous publishing

(G-17995)
MOSAIC ENGINEERING INC
210 W Hamilton Ave # 290 (16801-5218)
PHONE..................................406 544-7902
David Cubanski, *President*
EMP: 4
SQ FT: 2,000
SALES: 750K Privately Held
WEB: www.mosaicengineering.com
SIC: 3861 8711 Cameras & related equipment; engineering services

(G-17996)
NEIDIGHS INC
Also Called: Centre Glass Co
1121 W College Ave (16801-2823)
PHONE..................................814 237-3985
Michael Sowko, *President*
Frances Sowko, *Admin Sec*
EMP: 13 EST: 1947
SQ FT: 16,400
SALES (est): 1.6MM Privately Held
WEB: www.centreglassco.com
SIC: 1793 5231 3231 Glass & glazing
work; glass; products of purchased glass

(G-17997)
NEWELL BRANDS INC
2568 Park Center Blvd (16801-3005)
PHONE..................................814 278-6771
Gerald Hanscom, *Branch Mgr*
EMP: 6
SALES (corp-wide): 8.6B Publicly Held
SIC: 5944 2759 Jewelry stores; publication printing
PA: Newell Brands Inc.
221 River St Ste 13
Hoboken NJ 07030
201 610-6600

(G-17998)
NITTANY EMB & DIGITIZING
153 S Allen St (16801-4752)
PHONE..................................814 359-0905
Dennis Rallis, *Manager*

EMP: 14
SALES (corp-wide): 2.2MM Privately
Held
WEB: www.nittanyembroidery.com
SIC: 5651 2395 2396 5947 Family clothing stores; embroidery & art needlework;
decorative & novelty stitching, for the
trade; screen printing on fabric articles;
gift shop; advertising specialties; screen
printing
PA: Nittany Embroidery & Digitizing
101 E Beaver Ave
State College PA 16801
814 234-1146

(G-17999)
NITTANY EXTRACTION TECH LLC
Also Called: Netco
149 W Fairmount Ave (16801-5204)
PHONE..................................814 571-4776
Martin Bradley, *President*
Timothy Hurley, *Vice Pres*
EMP: 4
SALES: 100K Privately Held
SIC: 3295 Minerals, ground or treated

(G-18000)
NITTANY PRINTING AND PUBG CO
Also Called: Centre Daily Times
3400 E College Ave (16801-7528)
PHONE..................................814 238-5000
Adrian Pratt, *President*
Nate Cobler, *Editor*
Matt Hymowitz, *Editor*
Lauren Muthler, *Editor*
Sarah Rafacz, *Editor*
EMP: 72
SQ FT: 39,600
SALES (est): 18.2MM
SALES (corp-wide): 807.2MM Publicly
Held
WEB: www.centredaily.com
SIC: 2711 2759 2752 2396 Commercial
printing & newspaper publishing combined; commercial printing; commercial
printing, lithographic; automotive & apparel trimmings
PA: The Mcclatchy Company
2100 Q St
Sacramento CA 95816
916 321-1844

(G-18001)
NOVASENTIS INC
200 Innovation Blvd # 237 (16803-6602)
PHONE..................................814 238-7400
Francois Jeanneau, *CEO*
Ralph Russo, *Ch of Bd*
Rick Ducharme, *Vice Pres*
John Jacobi, *Vice Pres*
SRI Peruvemba, *Vice Pres*
EMP: 10
SALES (est): 1.1MM Privately Held
SIC: 3625 Actuators, industrial

(G-18002)
NOVASENTIS INC
200 Innovation Blvd # 237 (16803-6602)
PHONE..................................814 238-7400
Ralph Russo, *Ch of Bd*
Francois Jeanneau, *President*
Michael Vestel, *CTO*
EMP: 15
SALES (est): 3.2MM Privately Held
SIC: 3699 Electrical equipment & supplies

(G-18003)
OBERON INC
1315 S Allen St Ste 410 (16801-5923)
PHONE..................................814 867-2312
Scott Thompson, *President*
Fred Thompson, *Chairman*
Andrew Krzewinski, *Design Engr*
Eric Schleyer, *Design Engr*
EMP: 12
SQ FT: 2,500
SALES (est): 2.8MM Privately Held
WEB: www.oberonwireless.com
SIC: 3577 5045 Computer peripheral
equipment; computer peripheral equipment

(G-18004)
OMEGA PIEZO TECHNOLOGIES INC
2591 Clyde Ave Ste 3 (16801-7560)
PHONE..................................814 861-4160
David Pickrell, *President*
Sarah Crymes, *Director*
Tracy Struble, *Admin Asst*
▲ EMP: 16
SQ FT: 10,000
SALES: 1.5MM Privately Held
WEB: www.omegapiezo.com
SIC: 3577 Computer peripheral equipment

(G-18005)
PHIBRO ANIMAL HEALTH CORP
3048 Research Dr (16801-2782)
PHONE..................................201 329-7300
Melissa Whitsel, *Manager*
EMP: 15
SALES (corp-wide): 764.2MM Publicly
Held
SIC: 2834 Pharmaceutical preparations
HQ: Phibro Animal Health Corporation
300 Frank W Burr Blvd
Teaneck NJ 07666
201 329-7300

(G-18006)
PLUMRIVER LLC (PA)
1257 E College Ave (16801-6810)
PHONE..................................781 577-9575
John R Marchione,
EMP: 11
SALES (est): 5.7MM Privately Held
WEB: www.plumriver.com
SIC: 7372 Business oriented computer
software

(G-18007)
POLYMER INSTRUMENTATION & C (PA)
Also Called: Polymics
2215 High Tech Rd (16803-1731)
PHONE..................................814 357-5860
Tim Hsu, *President*
Henry Shen, *Vice Pres*
Craig Praskovich, *Plant Mgr*
Emily W Chiang, *Treasurer*
Camma Rossman, *Manager*
▲ EMP: 45
SQ FT: 65,000
SALES (est): 8.6MM Privately Held
WEB: www.polymics.com
SIC: 3089 2821 8711 Injection molding of
plastics; plastics materials & resins; consulting engineer

(G-18008)
POND HOCKEY BREWING CO LLC
Also Called: Pond Hockey Brewing Company
508 Outer Dr (16801-7935)
PHONE..................................814 429-9846
Kyle Jordan,
EMP: 3
SQ FT: 400
SALES (est): 247.3K Privately Held
SIC: 3949 7999 Hockey equipment & supplies, general; sticks: hockey, lacrosse,
etc.; hockey instruction school

(G-18009)
PRAXAIR DISTRIBUTION INC
1348 Benner Pike (16801-7325)
PHONE..................................814 238-5092
Andrew Ripka, *Sales & Mktg St*
Trudi Fleck, *Director*
EMP: 10 Privately Held
SIC: 3548 5984 Welding & cutting apparatus & accessories; liquefied petroleum
gas dealers
HQ: Praxair Distribution, Inc.
10 Riverview Dr
Danbury CT 06810
203 837-2000

(G-18010)
PROCOPY INC (PA)
434 W Aaron Dr Ste 200 (16803-3074)
PHONE..................................814 231-1256
Matthew Vidic, *President*
Rick Fuller, *General Mgr*
Myles D Lilley, *Corp Secy*
Leslie Beyer, *Accountant*

EMP: 15
SALES (est): 1.8MM Privately Held
WEB: www.procopyonline.com
SIC: 7334 2752 Blueprinting service; commercial printing, lithographic

(G-18011)
QUANTUM VORTEX INC
200 Innovation Blvd # 254 (16803-6602)
PHONE..................................814 325-0148
Max Fomitchev Zamilov, *CEO*
EMP: 3
SALES (est): 293K Privately Held
SIC: 3572 Computer storage devices

(G-18012)
RAYTHEON COMPANY
302 Science Park Rd (16803-2201)
PHONE..................................814 278-2256
Randall Bowers, *Principal*
Jane Orsulak, *Principal*
Marty Fix, *Prdtn Mgr*
Sydney Seitz, *Engineer*
Andy Mazzara, *Manager*
EMP: 400
SALES (corp-wide): 27B Publicly Held
SIC: 3812 3663 3674 7371 Electronic
field detection apparatus (aeronautical);
airborne radio communications equipment; semiconductors & related devices;
custom computer programming services
PA: Raytheon Company
870 Winter St
Waltham MA 02451
781 522-3000

(G-18013)
RE GAS DEVELOPMENT LLC
366 Walker Dr (16801-7085)
PHONE..................................814 278-7267
Thomas C Stabley,
EMP: 28
SALES (est): 1.2MM Privately Held
SIC: 1382 Oil & gas exploration services
PA: Rex Energy Corporation
366 Walker Dr
State College PA 16801

(G-18014)
REX ENERGY CORPORATION (PA)
366 Walker Dr (16801-7085)
PHONE..................................814 278-7267
Thomas C Stabley, *CEO*
Lance T Shaner, *Ch of Bd*
Robert W Ovitz, *COO*
F Scott Hodges, *Senior VP*
Jennifer L McDonough, *Senior VP*
EMP: 54
SALES (est): 205.2MM Privately Held
SIC: 1311 Crude petroleum production

(G-18015)
REX ENERGY IV LLC
366 Walker Dr (16801-7085)
PHONE..................................814 278-7267
F Lynch, *Vice Pres*
EMP: 24
SALES (est): 2.3MM Privately Held
SIC: 1382 Oil & gas exploration services
PA: Rex Energy Corporation
366 Walker Dr
State College PA 16801

(G-18016)
REX ENERGY OPERATING CORP (HQ)
366 Walker Dr (16801-7085)
PHONE..................................814 278-7267
Thomas C Stabley, *CEO*
Benjamin Hulbert, *President*
Lance T Shaner, *President*
Jason Arnold, *Counsel*
F Scott Hodges, *Vice Pres*
EMP: 35
SALES (est): 80.4MM Privately Held
SIC: 1382 Oil & gas exploration services

(G-18017)
RTD EMBEDDED TECHNOLOGIES INC
103 Innovation Blvd (16803-6608)
PHONE..................................814 234-8087
Robert J Haris, *Ch of Bd*
Paul Haris, *President*

John E Hazel, *COO*
Gary Sellers, *Vice Pres*
Randy Meyers, *QA Dir*
EMP: 34
SQ FT: 22,000
SALES (est): 19.7MM **Privately Held**
SIC: 3577 7372 7373 3823 Computer peripheral equipment; application computer software; computer integrated systems design; industrial instrmnts msrmnt display/control process variable; semiconductors & related devices; switchgear & switchboard apparatus

(G-18018)
RUCKUS WIRELESS INC
270 Walker Dr (16801-7097)
PHONE..............................814 231-3710
Andy Krishak, *Principal*
EMP: 20
SALES (corp-wide): 6.6B **Privately Held**
SIC: 3661 3663 3357 Telephone & telegraph apparatus; radio & TV communications equipment; cable television equipment; television broadcasting & communications equipment; satellites, communications; fiber optic cable (insulated); coaxial cable, nonferrous
HQ: Ruckus Wireless, Inc.
350 W Java Dr
Sunnyvale CA 94089
650 265-4200

(G-18019)
SALIMETRICS LLC
101 Innovation Blvd # 302 (16803-6605)
PHONE..............................814 234-7748
Linda McCall, *Prdtn Mgr*
Pam Lehota, *Human Res Mgr*
Richard Supina,
Doug Granger,
Hans Schroeder,
EMP: 29 **EST:** 1998
SALES (est): 4.7MM **Privately Held**
WEB: www.salimetrics.com
SIC: 8734 2835 Testing laboratories; in vitro diagnostics

(G-18020)
SCHOOL GATE GUARDIAN INC
301 Science Park Rd # 123 (16803-2293)
PHONE..............................800 805-3808
Steve Ramsey, *Vice Pres*
Christopher L Keller, *Vice Pres*
Terence W Kirby, *Vice Pres*
EMP: 12
SQ FT: 4,000
SALES (est): 232.7K **Privately Held**
SIC: 8211 2542 Elementary & secondary schools; stands, merchandise display: except wood

(G-18021)
SCITECH ASSOC HOLDINGS INC
232 Woodland Dr (16803-3550)
PHONE..............................201 218-3777
Dr Paul Cutler, *CEO*
Daniel Cutler, *Controller*
EMP: 8
SALES: 950K **Privately Held**
SIC: 3674 Semiconductors & related devices

(G-18022)
SIEMENS PRODUCT LIFE MGMT SFTW
Also Called: Engineering Animation
100 Walker Dr (16801-7001)
PHONE..............................814 237-4999
Tony Deluca, *Manager*
EMP: 20
SALES (corp-wide): 95B **Privately Held**
WEB: www.ugs.com
SIC: 7372 Prepackaged software
HQ: Siemens Product Lifecycle Management Software Inc.
5800 Granite Pkwy Ste 600
Plano TX 75024
972 987-3000

(G-18023)
SIEMENS PRODUCT LIFE MGMT SFTW
330 Innovation Blvd # 202 (16803-6611)
PHONE..............................814 861-1651
William Conway, *Project Mgr*

EMP: 5
SALES (corp-wide): 95B **Privately Held**
SIC: 7372 Business oriented computer software
HQ: Siemens Product Lifecycle Management Software Inc.
5800 Granite Pkwy Ste 600
Plano TX 75024
972 987-3000

(G-18024)
SIGN STOP
426 S Atherton St (16801-4047)
PHONE..............................814 238-3338
Scott Stephenson, *Owner*
EMP: 3
SALES (est): 235.4K **Privately Held**
SIC: 3993 Signs & advertising specialties

(G-18025)
SIMPLR TECHNOLOGIES LLC
1754 Cambridge Dr (16803-3263)
PHONE..............................814 883-6463
James Wang, *Principal*
Jia LI, *Principal*
EMP: 3
SALES (est): 95.2K **Privately Held**
SIC: 7371 7372 Computer software development & applications; application computer software

(G-18026)
SMART FERTILIZER LLC
932 E Mccormick Ave (16801-6529)
PHONE..............................814 880-8873
Gordon L Kauffman III, *Principal*
EMP: 3
SALES (est): 197K **Privately Held**
SIC: 2873 Nitrogenous fertilizers

(G-18027)
SOAPHIES
244 E Calder Way (16801-4729)
P.O. Box 1382 (16804-1382)
PHONE..............................814 861-7627
Linda Pagani, *Partner*
EMP: 7
SALES (est): 544.2K **Privately Held**
WEB: www.soaphies.com
SIC: 2841 Soap & other detergents

(G-18028)
SOLID STATE CERAMICS INC
341 Science Park Rd # 105 (16803-2287)
PHONE..............................570 322-2700
Gareth Knowlesm, *CEO*
Steven Dynan, *President*
Cathy Bower, *Corp Secy*
EMP: 5
SQ FT: 400
SALES (est): 65.4K **Privately Held**
SIC: 3677 Transformers power supply, electronic type

(G-18029)
SOUND TECHNOLOGY INC (DH)
401 Science Park Rd (16803-2217)
PHONE..............................814 234-4377
Danny Pelache, *President*
Chad Burns, *Mfg Staff*
Kellyjo Sadley, *Buyer*
Joseph Conklin, *Engineer*
Kevin Dietz, *Engineer*
▲ **EMP:** 122
SQ FT: 9,000
SALES: 33.5MM
SALES (corp-wide): 486.3MM **Privately Held**
WEB: www.sti-ultrasound.com
SIC: 3679 Transducers, electrical; piezoelectric crystals
HQ: Analogic Corporation
8 Centennial Dr
Peabody MA 01960
978 326-4000

(G-18030)
SPECTRA INC
Also Called: Chase Collection, The
2625 Carolean Indus Dr (16801-7506)
PHONE..............................814 238-6332
Lawrence Roeshot, *President*
Rita Roeshot, *Corp Secy*
EMP: 49
SQ FT: 58,500

SALES (est): 10.9MM **Privately Held**
WEB: www.spectrawood.com
SIC: 2499 2521 2522 2511 Woodenware, kitchen & household; wood office furniture; tables, office: wood; cabinets, office: wood; filing cabinets (boxes), office: wood; office furniture, except wood; household furniture

(G-18031)
SPECTRUM CONTROL INC
Spectrum Control Technology
1900 W College Ave (16801-2723)
PHONE..............................814 272-2700
Tracy Shasfer, *Branch Mgr*
EMP: 240
SALES (corp-wide): 333.6MM **Privately Held**
SIC: 3677 Filtration devices, electronic
HQ: Spectrum Control, Inc.
8061 Avonia Rd
Fairview PA 16415
814 474-2207

(G-18032)
SPECTRUM CONTROL INC
Also Called: Spectrum Power MGT Systems
1900 W College Ave (16801-2723)
PHONE..............................814 272-2700
EMP: 24
SALES (corp-wide): 333.6MM **Privately Held**
SIC: 3677 Filtration devices, electronic
HQ: Spectrum Control, Inc.
8061 Avonia Rd
Fairview PA 16415
814 474-2207

(G-18033)
SPECTRUM MICROWAVE INC
Also Called: API Technologies Corp
1900 W College Ave (16801-2723)
PHONE..............................814 272-2700
Walt Gordon, *Branch Mgr*
EMP: 44
SALES (corp-wide): 333.6MM **Privately Held**
WEB: www.spectrummicrowave.com
SIC: 3679 3569 Microwave components; filters
HQ: Spectrum Microwave, Inc.
8061 Avonia Rd
Fairview PA 16415
814 474-4300

(G-18034)
STATE OF ART INC
2470 Fox Hill Rd (16803-1797)
PHONE..............................814 355-2714
Donald Hamer, *CEO*
Jamie Heddens, *President*
Robert I Hufnagel, *President*
Jim Eckstaedt, *Exec VP*
Dave Pensak, *Facilities Mgr*
▲ **EMP:** 114
SQ FT: 41,500
SALES: 17MM **Privately Held**
WEB: www.sotaworld.com
SIC: 3676 Electronic resistors

(G-18035)
TAKE SIX
100 W College Ave (16801-3838)
PHONE..............................814 237-4350
Mike Desmond, *Owner*
EMP: 4
SALES (est): 142.2K **Privately Held**
SIC: 2086 Bottled & canned soft drinks

(G-18036)
TELEDYNE DEFENSE ELEC LLC
Also Called: Teledyne Paradise Datacom
328 Innovation Blvd # 100 (16803-6609)
PHONE..............................814 238-3450
Richard Palilonis, *CEO*
Jim Jeffries, *Engineer*
EMP: 63
SALES (corp-wide): 2.9B **Publicly Held**
SIC: 7374 3663 3651 Data processing & preparation; radio & TV communications equipment; household audio & video equipment
HQ: Teledyne Defense Electronics, Llc
1274 Terra Bella Ave
Mountain View CA 94043
650 691-9800

(G-18037)
TELEDYNE INSTRUMENTS INC
Also Called: Teledyne Ssi
349 Science Park Rd (16803-2215)
PHONE..............................814 234-7311
EMP: 53
SALES (corp-wide): 2.9B **Publicly Held**
SIC: 3826 Chromatographic equipment, laboratory type
HQ: Teledyne Instruments, Inc.
1049 Camino Dos Rios
Thousand Oaks CA 91360
805 373-4545

(G-18038)
THEPRINTERSCOM INC
3500 E College Ave # 1000 (16801-7569)
PHONE..............................814 238-8445
Raymond J Caravan Jr, *President*
Robert Fulton, *Prdtn Mgr*
Randy Stahl, *Purch Mgr*
Darren Langenbach, *Info Tech Mgr*
Anne M Spak, *Executive*
EMP: 5
SQ FT: 5,000
SALES (est): 713.8K **Privately Held**
SIC: 2752 Commercial printing, lithographic

(G-18039)
TM SYSTEMS INC
Also Called: API Technologies
1900 W College Ave (16801-2723)
PHONE..............................814 272-2700
Thomas Mills, *President*
Irwin Shuldman, *Vice Pres*
▲ **EMP:** 18
SALES (est): 3.1MM
SALES (corp-wide): 333.6MM **Privately Held**
SIC: 3663 Radio & TV communications equipment
HQ: Api Technologies Corp.
400 Nickerson Rd Ste 1
Marlborough MA 01752

(G-18040)
TRS TECHNOLOGIES INC (HQ)
2820 E College Ave (16801-7548)
PHONE..............................814 238-7485
Wesley Hackenberger, *President*
Kari Quay, *Director*
Stuart N Blacker, *Admin Sec*
EMP: 45
SALES (est): 14.1MM
SALES (corp-wide): 399.1MM **Privately Held**
WEB: www.trstechnologies.com
SIC: 8711 3679 Engineering services; power supplies, all types: static
PA: Tayca Corporation
3-6-13, Kitahama, Chuo-Ku
Osaka OSK 541-0
662 086-400

(G-18041)
VIDEON CENTRAL INC
2171 Sandy Dr (16803-2283)
PHONE..............................814 235-1111
Todd Erdley, *CEO*
Tina Angellotti, *Buyer*
John Lynch, *Senior Engr*
Paul Brown, *CFO*
Joan Potter, *Human Res Mgr*
EMP: 63 **EST:** 1997
SQ FT: 16,000
SALES (est): 13.4MM **Privately Held**
WEB: www.videon-central.com
SIC: 3651 Household audio & video equipment

(G-18042)
X MATERIAL PROCESSING COMPANY
200 Innovation Blvd (16803-6602)
PHONE..............................717 968-8765
Matthew Woods, *Principal*
EMP: 3
SALES (est): 163.1K **Privately Held**
SIC: 3549 Metalworking machinery

(G-18043)
XACT METAL INC
200 Innovation Blvd # 257 (16803-6602)
PHONE..............................814 777-7727
Juan Mario, *CEO*

Matt Woods, *CTO*
EMP: 3
SALES (est): 140.9K **Privately Held**
SIC: 3549 Metalworking machinery

Steelton
Dauphin County

(G-18044)
ARCELORMITTAL STEELTON LLC
215 S Front St (17113-2538)
PHONE...............................717 986-2000
Lakshmi Niwas Mittal, *CEO*
Joseph Petravage, *Human Res Mgr*
▲ EMP: 640
SQ FT: 50,000
SALES (est): 129.2MM
SALES (corp-wide): 9.1B **Privately Held**
SIC: 3312 Structural & rail mill products; rails, steel or iron; blooms, steel
HQ: Arcelormittal Usa Llc
1 S Dearborn St Ste 1800
Chicago IL 60603
312 346-0300

(G-18045)
ARCELORMITTAL USA LLC
Also Called: Mittal Steel USA Steelton
215 S Front St (17113-2538)
PHONE...............................717 986-2887
Sharon Asche-Nichol, *Division Mgr*
George Downey, *Division Mgr*
Howard Koch, *Division Mgr*
James McCarthy, *Division Mgr*
Thomas Spurlock, *Division Mgr*
EMP: 600
SALES (corp-wide): 9.1B **Privately Held**
SIC: 3312 Blast furnaces & steel mills
HQ: Arcelormittal Usa Llc
1 S Dearborn St Ste 1800
Chicago IL 60603
312 346-0300

(G-18046)
DURA-BOND COATING INC
Also Called: Durabond Pipes
2716 S Front St (17113-3099)
PHONE...............................717 939-1079
George Keller, *Manager*
Dan Harvey, *Supervisor*
EMP: 101
SALES (corp-wide): 119.9MM **Privately Held**
WEB: www.durabond.com
SIC: 3479 Coating or wrapping steel pipe
HQ: Dura-Bond Coating, Inc.
2658 Puckety Dr
Export PA 15632
724 327-0782

(G-18047)
DURA-BOND PIPE LLC (DH)
2716 S Front St (17113-3099)
PHONE...............................717 986-1100
Wayne Norris, *President*
Josue Rivera, *Purch Mgr*
EMP: 80
SALES (est): 4.4MM
SALES (corp-wide): 119.9MM **Privately Held**
SIC: 3317 Steel pipe & tubes
HQ: Dura-Bond Coating, Inc.
2658 Puckety Dr
Export PA 15632
724 327-0782

Sterling
Wayne County

(G-18048)
BROWN BROTHERS LLP
Also Called: Brown Bro Stock Photography
100 Bortree Rd (18463)
PHONE...............................570 689-9688
Raymond A Collins, *Partner*
EMP: 5

SALES (est): 326.8K **Privately Held**
WEB: www.brownbrothersusa.com
SIC: 2741 7335 6794 Art copy: publishing & printing; commercial photography; patent owners & lessors

(G-18049)
EUREKA STONE QUARRY INC
Also Called: Sterling Division
Rr 196 (18463)
P.O. Box 26 (18463-0026)
PHONE...............................570 689-2901
Tony Eleckna, *Manager*
EMP: 5
SALES (corp-wide): 24.4MM **Privately Held**
SIC: 3281 5032 Stone, quarrying & processing of own stone products; stone, crushed or broken
PA: Eureka Stone Quarry, Inc.
Lower Stte Pickertown Rds
Chalfont PA 18914
215 822-0593

Stevens
Lancaster County

(G-18050)
F&F MACHINE WORKS
23 Blue Jay Dr (17578-9715)
PHONE...............................717 335-3008
Devin Fry, *Principal*
EMP: 3
SALES (est): 311.7K **Privately Held**
SIC: 3599 Machine shop, jobbing & repair

(G-18051)
GOOD
1247 N Reading Rd (17578-9703)
PHONE...............................717 271-2917
EMP: 3 EST: 2011
SALES (est): 265.3K **Privately Held**
SIC: 2759 Screen printing

(G-18052)
HEIRLOOM ENGRAVING LLC
179 E Church St (17578-9529)
PHONE...............................717 336-8451
Jason L Groff, *Principal*
EMP: 4
SALES (est): 219.3K **Privately Held**
SIC: 2435 2752 Hardwood veneer & plywood; commercial printing, lithographic

(G-18053)
INGHAMS REGROOVING SERVICE INC (PA)
Also Called: Ingham's Powder Coating
1860 N Reading Rd (17578-9311)
PHONE...............................717 336-8473
Kyle Ingham, *President*
Barb Ingham, *Admin Sec*
EMP: 23
SQ FT: 5,000
SALES (est): 605K **Privately Held**
WEB: www.inghamspowdercoating.com
SIC: 3479 Painting, coating & hot dipping

(G-18054)
JOHN F MARTIN & SONS LLC
Also Called: John F Martin & Sons
55 Lower Hillside Rd (17578-9787)
P.O. Box 137 (17578-0137)
PHONE...............................717 336-2804
Lester Martin,
Bernell Martin,
EMP: 250
SQ FT: 85,000
SALES (est): 20.4MM
SALES (corp-wide): 135MM **Privately Held**
SIC: 2013 0212 Bacon, side & sliced: from purchased meat; ham, smoked: from purchased meat; beef cattle except feedlots
PA: Martin Jf Family Corporation
55 Lower Hillside Rd
Stevens PA 17578
717 336-2804

(G-18055)
RISSLER CONVEYORS
1275 Indiantown Rd (17578-9729)
PHONE...............................717 336-2244

Leroy Weaver, *Owner*
EMP: 6
SQ FT: 7,000
SALES (est): 694.5K **Privately Held**
SIC: 3535 Conveyors & conveying equipment

(G-18056)
S W MACHINE
401 Stevens Rd (17578-9416)
PHONE...............................717 336-2699
Sid Walmer, *Owner*
EMP: 6
SQ FT: 2,500
SALES (est): 350K **Privately Held**
SIC: 3599 7699 Machine shop, jobbing & repair; custom machinery; farm machinery repair; textile roll covering

(G-18057)
W M S PHASE CONVERTERS
Also Called: Maxi Phase
187 E Church St (17578-9529)
PHONE...............................717 336-6566
David Witmer, *Owner*
EMP: 4
SALES (est): 276.4K **Privately Held**
WEB: www.maxiphase.com
SIC: 3621 Motors, electric

(G-18058)
WITMER MOTOR SERVICE
187 E Church St (17578-9529)
PHONE...............................717 336-2949
David Witmer, *Owner*
EMP: 3
SQ FT: 6,000
SALES (est): 697.1K **Privately Held**
SIC: 7694 5063 5999 Rewinding stators; electric motor repair; electrical apparatus & equipment; motors, electric; engine & motor equipment & supplies

Stevensville
Bradford County

(G-18059)
JOHNSON QUARRIES INC
Also Called: Johnson Jerry Flagstone Quarry
15962 Route 467 (18845-7812)
PHONE...............................570 744-1284
Jerry Johnson, *President*
EMP: 20
SALES (est): 6.2MM **Privately Held**
WEB: www.johnsonquarries.com
SIC: 1411 7389 Flagstone mining;

Stewartstown
York County

(G-18060)
DUBEL D H MILL & LUMBER CO
15979 Sawmill Rd (17363-7862)
PHONE...............................717 993-2566
David H Dubel, *Owner*
EMP: 9
SQ FT: 3,200
SALES (est): 580K **Privately Held**
SIC: 2421 Sawmills & planing mills, general

(G-18061)
ENDOSCOPIC LASER TECHNOLOGIES
20 W Pennsylvania Ave (17363-4146)
PHONE...............................443 205-9340
Michael Tabor, *Principal*
EMP: 3 EST: 2011
SALES (est): 188.9K **Privately Held**
SIC: 3845 Endoscopic equipment, electromedical

Stillwater
Columbia County

(G-18062)
VICTOR METALS
70 Mchenry St (17878-9440)
PHONE...............................570 925-2618
Victor Dumond, *Owner*
EMP: 5
SALES (est): 426.7K **Privately Held**
SIC: 3425 Saws, hand: metalworking or woodworking

Stockertown
Northampton County

(G-18063)
A & H SPORTSWEAR CO INC
110 Commerce Way (18083-7006)
P.O. Box 97 (18083-0097)
PHONE...............................610 759-9550
Bruce Waltman, *Manager*
EMP: 120
SALES (corp-wide): 21.4MM **Privately Held**
SIC: 5621 5641 2339 Women's sportswear; infants' wear; women's & misses' outerwear
PA: A & H Sportswear Co., Inc.
610 Uhler Rd
Easton PA 18040
484 373-3600

(G-18064)
BUZZI UNICEM USA INC
Also Called: Lonestar
501 Hercules Dr (18083-7009)
P.O. Box 69 (18083-0069)
PHONE...............................610 746-6222
Kal Stocker, *Principal*
EMP: 20
SALES (corp-wide): 287.7MM **Privately Held**
SIC: 3241 Masonry cement
HQ: Buzzi Unicem Usa Inc.
100 Brodhead Rd Ste 230
Bethlehem PA 18017
610 882-5000

(G-18065)
HERCULES CEMENT COMPANY LP
501 Hercules Dr (18083-7009)
P.O. Box 69 (18083-0069)
PHONE...............................610 759-6300
Massimo Toso, *Partner*
William S Collumbien, *Partner*
Thomas Hood, *Partner*
EMP: 134
SALES (est): 22.9MM
SALES (corp-wide): 287.7MM **Privately Held**
SIC: 3241 Portland cement
HQ: Rc Lonestar Inc.
100 Brodhead Rd Ste 230
Bethlehem PA 18017

(G-18066)
PRAXAIR INC
90 Commerce Way (18083-7050)
P.O. Box 400 (18083-0400)
PHONE...............................610 759-3923
Edward E Sheets, *Branch Mgr*
EMP: 67 **Privately Held**
SIC: 2813 Industrial gases
HQ: Praxair, Inc.
10 Riverview Dr
Danbury CT 06810
203 837-2000

(G-18067)
UFP STOCKERTOWN LLC
Also Called: Universal Forest Products
33 Rr 191 (18083)
PHONE...............................610 759-8536
EMP: 3

SALES (est): 77.5K
SALES (corp-wide): 3.2B **Publicly Held**
SIC: 2436 2491 2431 Mfg Softwd Ve-
neers/Plywd Wood Preserving Mfg Millwork
PA: Universal Forest Products, Inc.
2801 E Beltline Ave Ne
Grand Rapids MI 49525
616 364-6161

Stoneboro
Mercer County

(G-18068)
CUSTOMFOLD INC
926 Fredonia Rd (16153-2404)
P.O. Box 278 (16153-0278)
PHONE..................................724 376-8565
Walter W Claypool, *President*
Genie L Claypool, *Vice Pres*
EMP: 12
SQ FT: 16,000
SALES (est): 1.9MM **Privately Held**
WEB: www.customfold.com
SIC: 2542 Partitions for floor attachment,
prefabricated: except wood

(G-18069)
H & H MATERIALS INC
190 Canon Rd (16153-2022)
PHONE..................................724 376-2834
David Hoobler, *President*
Evan Hoobler, *Vice Pres*
EMP: 20 EST: 1979
SQ FT: 3,100
SALES: 2.9MM **Privately Held**
WEB: www.hhmaterialsinc.com
SIC: 1442 Construction sand mining;
gravel mining

(G-18070)
SUPREME - DSC DREDGE LLC
327 Billy Boyd Rd (16153-1701)
PHONE..................................724 376-4368
David Hobbler,
EMP: 4
SALES (est): 618.5K **Privately Held**
SIC: 3731 Dredges, building & repairing

(G-18071)
SUPREME MANUFACTURING
INC
327 Billy Boyd Rd (16153-1701)
PHONE..................................724 376-4110
Neil E Hoobler, *President*
Rudy Troples, *Foreman/Supr*
William Rose, *Controller*
Rose Will, *Controller*
EMP: 25
SQ FT: 28,200
SALES: 8MM **Privately Held**
WEB: www.suprememfg.com
SIC: 3441 Fabricated structural metal

Stowe
Montgomery County

(G-18072)
KESTREL SHUTTERS & DOORS
INC
Also Called: Diyshutters
9 E Race St (19464-6721)
PHONE..................................610 326-6679
Jim Lapic, *President*
John Lapic, *Vice Pres*
Debbie Thompson, *Office Mgr*
▼ EMP: 16
SQ FT: 9,000
SALES (est): 2.6MM **Privately Held**
WEB: www.diyshutters.com
SIC: 2431 3442 Doors & door parts & trim,
wood; door shutters, wood; louver doors,
wood; window shutters, wood; louvers,
shutters, jalousies & similar items

(G-18073)
UNIVERSAL CONCRETE PDTS
CORP (HQ)
400 Old Reading Pike A100 (19464-3781)
PHONE..................................610 323-0700

Donald Faust Jr, *President*
Shawn Lape, *Project Mgr*
Claire Williams, *Marketing Staff*
Daniel Gutierrez, *Manager*
Bill Hydock, *Manager*
EMP: 10
SQ FT: 5,000
SALES (est): 14.2MM
SALES (corp-wide): 25.9MM **Privately
Held**
SIC: 3272 Concrete products, precast
PA: Bodon Industries, Inc.
1513 Ben Franklin Hwy E
Douglassville PA 19518
610 323-0700

Stoystown
Somerset County

(G-18074)
CUSTOM ENTRYWAYS &
MILLWORK
2989 Whistler Rd (15563-8552)
PHONE..................................814 798-2500
Ed Harodetsky, *Owner*
EMP: 4
SQ FT: 5,000
SALES (est): 390.2K **Privately Held**
WEB: www.customentryways.com
SIC: 3442 1446 2431 Storm doors or win-
dows, metal; molding sand mining; porch
columns, wood

(G-18075)
DELWELD INDUSTRIES CORP
(PA)
149 Commerce Dr (15563-7892)
PHONE..................................814 535-2412
Joseph R Del Signore, *President*
Chris Delsignore, *Vice Pres*
John Farabaugh, *Opers Mgr*
Wendy Dillon, *Office Mgr*
EMP: 13
SQ FT: 105,000
SALES: 5MM **Privately Held**
WEB: www.antigo.com
SIC: 2514 Beds, including folding & cabi-
net, household: metal

(G-18076)
DONALD GREATHOUSE
2966 Whistler Rd (15563-8551)
PHONE..................................814 242-7624
Don Greathouse, *President*
EMP: 7
SALES (est): 631.9K **Privately Held**
SIC: 1241 Mine preparation services

(G-18077)
FIEG BROTHERS COAL (PA)
3070 Stoystown Rd (15563-8164)
PHONE..................................814 893-5270
Scott Fieg, *Partner*
Kevin Fieg, *Partner*
EMP: 12
SALES (est): 2.2MM **Privately Held**
SIC: 1221 Strip mining, bituminous

(G-18078)
GLOW MFG
2891 Whistler Rd (15563-8550)
PHONE..................................814 798-2215
Bob Miller, *Principal*
EMP: 3
SALES (est): 224K **Privately Held**
SIC: 3999 Manufacturing industries

(G-18079)
GM&S COAL CORP
5815 Penn Ave (15563-7858)
P.O. Box 99, Boswell (15531-0099)
PHONE..................................814 629-5661
EMP: 60
SQ FT: 2,000
SALES (est): 2.6MM **Privately Held**
SIC: 1221 1222 Bituminous Coal/Lignite
Surface Mining Bituminous Coal-Under-
ground Mining

(G-18080)
HIGHLAND TANK AND MFG CO
(PA)
1 Highland Rd (15563-6456)
P.O. Box 338 (15563-0338)
PHONE..................................814 893-5701
Michael Van Lenten, *President*
John W Jacob, *Vice Pres*
Ashley Hess, *Purch Agent*
Charles A Frey, *Treasurer*
Robert E Jacob, *Treasurer*
▼ EMP: 135 EST: 1946
SQ FT: 15,000
SALES (est): 24.3MM **Privately Held**
SIC: 3443 Tanks, standard or custom fabri-
cated: metal plate

(G-18081)
KERN BROTHERS LUMBER INC
3075 Whistler Rd (15563-8554)
P.O. Box 17 (15563-0017)
PHONE..................................814 893-5042
Gerald Kern, *President*
Robert Kern, *Vice Pres*
Terry Kern, *Treasurer*
Roxanne Kern, *Asst Treas*
Richard Kern, *Admin Sec*
EMP: 30
SQ FT: 20,000
SALES (est): 2.1MM **Privately Held**
SIC: 2421 Lumber: rough, sawed or planed

(G-18082)
LINCOLN CONTG & EQP CO INC
(HQ)
2478 Lincoln Hwy (15563-7821)
P.O. Box 96, Boswell (15531-0096)
PHONE..................................814 629-6641
Harold Walker, *President*
C Daniel Riggs, *Vice Pres*
Kevin Macy, *Safety Dir*
William B Friedline, *CFO*
David F Lowry, *Treasurer*
EMP: 60
SQ FT: 6,400
SALES: 27.7MM
SALES (corp-wide): 119.8MM **Privately
Held**
WEB: www.lincolncontracting.com
SIC: 7353 3441 1241 Heavy construction
equipment rental; fabricated structural
metal; mine preparation services
PA: Riggs Industries, Inc.
2478 Lincoln Hwy
Stoystown PA 15563
814 629-5621

(G-18083)
OAKS POULTRY CO INC
172 Folly Ln (15563-8561)
PHONE..................................814 798-3631
Kenneth E Blough, *President*
Janet Blough, *Treasurer*
EMP: 15 EST: 1947
SALES (est): 1.7MM **Privately Held**
SIC: 2015 5144 Poultry slaughtering &
processing; poultry, slaughtered &
dressed; poultry, processed: frozen; poul-
try & poultry products

(G-18084)
RICK WEYAND SIGNS
Also Called: Weyand Sign Company
4277 Lincoln Hwy (15563-8000)
PHONE..................................814 893-5524
Rick Weyand, *Owner*
EMP: 6
SQ FT: 5,000
SALES (est): 390K **Privately Held**
SIC: 3993 Signs & advertising specialties

(G-18085)
RIGGS INDUSTRIES INC (PA)
2478 Lincoln Hwy (15563-7821)
P.O. Box 86, Boswell (15531-0086)
PHONE..................................814 629-5621
William B Friedline, *President*
S William Riggs, *Vice Pres*
David F Lowry, *Treasurer*
Harold E Walker, *Shareholder*
C Daniel Riggs, *Admin Sec*
EMP: 15
SQ FT: 6,400

SALES: 119.8MM **Privately Held**
SIC: 3713 3441 Truck & bus bodies; fabricated structural metal

(G-18086)
ROLLOCK COMPANY (PA)
3179 Lincoln Hwy (15563-7919)
PHONE..................................814 893-6421
Tony Kordell, *President*
Chris Kordell, *Vice Pres*
EMP: 20
SQ FT: 8,000
SALES (est): 2.7MM **Privately Held**
SIC: 5093 3429 Whol Scrap/Waste Mate-
rial Mfg Hardware

(G-18087)
STOYSTOWN TANK & STEEL CO
235 Reading Mine Rd (15563-8183)
P.O. Box 239 (15563-0239)
PHONE..................................814 893-5133
Stephen Zufall, *President*
Clair Zufall, *Corp Secy*
John Kasnick, *Manager*
Rick Veres, *Manager*
Cindy Reiking, *Admin Asst*
EMP: 43 EST: 1956
SQ FT: 19,000
SALES (est): 8.4MM **Privately Held**
WEB: www.stoystowntank.com
SIC: 3443 Tanks, standard or custom fabri-
cated: metal plate; vessels, process or
storage (from boiler shops): metal plate

(G-18088)
WAMPUM HARDWARE CO
533 Old Lincoln Hwy (15563-6446)
PHONE..................................814 893-5470
John Platt, *Manager*
EMP: 18
SALES (corp-wide): 36.1MM **Privately
Held**
WEB: www.wampumhardware.com
SIC: 2893 Printing ink
PA: Wampum Hardware Co.
636 Paden Rd
New Galilee PA 16141
724 336-4501

(G-18089)
WEST POINT MINING CORP
2811 Lincoln Hwy (15563-7830)
P.O. Box 306, Mount Carmel (17851-0306)
PHONE..................................570 339-5259
Ed Smock, *President*
EMP: 33
SALES (est): 1.6MM **Privately Held**
SIC: 1231 Anthracite mining

Strasburg
Lancaster County

(G-18090)
LANCASTER FUELS
902 Strasburg Pike (17579-9621)
PHONE..................................717 687-5390
EMP: 3
SALES (est): 192.4K **Privately Held**
SIC: 2869 Mfg Industrial Organic Chemi-
cals

(G-18091)
M K CRAFTS
450 Walnut Run Rd (17579-9753)
PHONE..................................717 786-6080
Michael Beiler, *Owner*
EMP: 4
SALES (est): 325.3K **Privately Held**
SIC: 2499 Novelties, wood fiber

(G-18092)
MCCULLOUGH
MANUFACTURING INC
Also Called: McCullough Banner Company
27 Miller St (17579-1111)
PHONE..................................717 687-8784
James R Mc Cullough, *President*
Sharon A Mc Cullough, *Corp Secy*
EMP: 6
SQ FT: 6,500

▲ = Import ▼=Export
◆ =Import/Export

SALES (est): 666.9K **Privately Held**
WEB: www.mcbanner.com
SIC: 2394 Awnings, fabric: made from purchased materials

(G-18093)
STRASBURG LAWN STRUCTURES LLC
909 Strasburg Pike (17579-9653)
PHONE.................................717 687-8210
Benuel S King, *President*
EMP: 6
SALES (est): 322.1K **Privately Held**
SIC: 3949 7389 Playground equipment;

(G-18094)
STRASBURG PALLET CO INC
2940 White Oak Rd (17579-9428)
PHONE.................................717 687-8131
John S Beiler, *President*
Richard Spangler, *Treasurer*
EMP: 50
SQ FT: 25,000
SALES (est): 9.2MM **Privately Held**
SIC: 2448 2449 Pallets, wood; cargo containers, wood; wood containers

(G-18095)
TIGER ENTERPRISES INC
2052 White Oak Rd (17579-9412)
PHONE.................................717 786-5441
Thelma Webbere, *President*
Thelma J Webbere, *President*
EMP: 3
SALES: 50K **Privately Held**
WEB: www.tigerenterprises.com
SIC: 3471 4959 Cleaning & descaling metal products; environmental cleanup services

(G-18096)
TRUE FORM PLASTICS LLC
904c Strasburg Pike (17579-9621)
PHONE.................................717 875-4521
EMP: 3
SALES (est): 190.5K **Privately Held**
SIC: 2821 Plastics materials & resins

Strattanville
Clarion County

(G-18097)
HITCHCOCK E & R & SONS LBR INC
69 Hitchcock Ln (16258-2819)
PHONE.................................814 229-9402
Ernest A Hitchcock, *President*
Genevieve Hitchcock, *Corp Secy*
Dale Hitchcock, *Vice Pres*
EMP: 8
SQ FT: 2,600
SALES (est): 720K **Privately Held**
SIC: 2421 Sawmills & planing mills, general

(G-18098)
MILLCREEK METALS INC
58 Mcm Ln (16258-3202)
PHONE.................................814 764-3708
Joe Ferguson, *President*
Jim Christie, *Vice Pres*
EMP: 3
SQ FT: 5,000
SALES (est): 482.5K **Privately Held**
SIC: 3442 Storm doors or windows, metal

Strausstown
Berks County

(G-18099)
POST PRECISION CASTINGS INC
21 Walnut St (19559-7707)
P.O. Box A (19559-0100)
PHONE.................................610 488-1011
John R Post, *Principal*
Craig V Thompson, *Vice Pres*
Clarence Brossman, *Purch Mgr*
Sue Sholl, *Sales Staff*
▲ EMP: 125

SQ FT: 150,000
SALES (est): 29.6MM **Privately Held**
WEB: www.postprecision.com
SIC: 3324 Commercial investment castings, ferrous

(G-18100)
SICKAFUS SHEEPSKINS
Also Called: Pat Garrett Western Wear
Exit 19 Rr 78 (19559)
P.O. Box 1 (19559-0001)
PHONE.................................610 488-1782
Patrick Sickafus, *Owner*
▲ EMP: 20 EST: 1966
SQ FT: 45,000
SALES (est): 1.3MM **Privately Held**
SIC: 5699 2386 5136 Leather garments; garments, sheep-lined; leather & sheep lined clothing, men's & boys'

Stroudsburg
Monroe County

(G-18101)
7TH SOUL LLC
602 Thomas St (18360-2107)
PHONE.................................917 880-8423
Jonathan Bodt,
EMP: 3
SALES (est): 83.9K **Privately Held**
SIC: 3999 Manufacturing industries

(G-18102)
AMERICAN RIBBON MANUFACTURERS
925 Ann St (18360-1628)
PHONE.................................570 421-7470
Kenneth A Barthold, *Branch Mgr*
EMP: 20
SALES (corp-wide): 2.3MM **Privately Held**
WEB: www.americanribbon.com
SIC: 2241 5131 Rayon narrow fabrics; ribbons
PA: American Ribbon Manufacturers Inc
925 Ann St
Stroudsburg PA 18360
570 421-7470

(G-18103)
AMERICAN RIBBON MANUFACTURERS (PA)
Also Called: Cutting Sheet
925 Ann St (18360-1628)
PHONE.................................570 421-7470
Kenneth Barthold, *President*
Kenneth A Barthold, *President*
EMP: 20
SQ FT: 30,000
SALES (est): 2.3MM **Privately Held**
SIC: 2241 5131 5949 2396 Ribbons; ribbons; sewing, needlework & piece goods; automotive & apparel trimmings

(G-18104)
ARCH PARENT INC
205 Applegate Rd (18360-6502)
PHONE.................................570 534-6026
Dan Mulligan, *Branch Mgr*
EMP: 1904
SALES (corp-wide): 3B **Privately Held**
SIC: 2752 Commercial printing, lithographic
PA: Arch Parent Inc.
9 W 57th St Fl 31
New York NY 10019
212 796-8500

(G-18105)
ARTISANS OF THE ANVIL INC
40 N 2nd St (18360-2508)
PHONE.................................570 476-7950
Andrew Molinaro, *President*
EMP: 6 EST: 2000
SALES (est): 628.3K **Privately Held**
WEB: www.artisansoftheanvil.com
SIC: 3446 Stairs, staircases, stair treads: prefabricated metal

(G-18106)
ATLANTIC METAL INDUSTRIES LLC
2213 Shafer Rd (18360-7097)
PHONE.................................908 445-4299
Evan Weissglass, *Mng Member*
EMP: 5 EST: 2014
SQ FT: 200
SALES (est): 249.4K **Privately Held**
SIC: 3441 Fabricated structural metal

(G-18107)
BASE LAB TOOLS INC
140 N 2nd St Unit 3 (18360-2528)
PHONE.................................570 371-5710
John Myrick, *CEO*
Jenna Myrick, *Office Mgr*
EMP: 5 EST: 2015
SQ FT: 3,300
SALES (est): 585.9K **Privately Held**
SIC: 3821 Physics laboratory apparatus

(G-18108)
BIOSPECTRA INC (PA)
1474 Rockdale Ln (18360-7361)
PHONE.................................610 599-3400
Richard Mutchler, *President*
Joseph Mastrobattista, *Vice Pres*
▲ EMP: 65
SALES (est): 17.6MM **Privately Held**
WEB: www.biospectra.com
SIC: 2836 Biological products, except diagnostic

(G-18109)
CHARLES BESELER CO INC
2018 W Main St (18360)
PHONE.................................800 237-3537
Semmes Brightman, *Ch of Bd*
Hank Gasikowski, *Ch of Bd*
▼ EMP: 55
SQ FT: 200,000
SALES (est): 10.6MM **Privately Held**
WEB: www.beseler.com
SIC: 3861 5043 3565 2542 Photographic equipment & supplies; photographic equipment & supplies; packaging machinery; shelving, office & store: except wood; office cabinets & filing drawers: except wood

(G-18110)
CLAPPER LEON PLBG HTG WTR COND
425 Neyhart Rd (18360-8102)
PHONE.................................570 629-2833
Leon Clapper, *President*
Dorris Clapper, *Admin Sec*
EMP: 12
SALES (est): 1.5MM **Privately Held**
SIC: 1711 3589 Plumbing contractors; swimming pool filter & water conditioning systems

(G-18111)
CRAIG COLABAUGH GUNSMITH INC
Also Called: Cgi Products
4168 Gumm St (18360)
PHONE.................................570 992-4499
Craig Colabaugh, *President*
Jacqueline Colabaugh, *Treasurer*
▼ EMP: 3
SQ FT: 4,072
SALES: 175K **Privately Held**
SIC: 7699 3423 Gunsmith shop; gun parts made to individual order; tools or equipment for use with sporting arms

(G-18112)
CULTURENIK PUBLISHING INC
1901 W Main St (18360-1029)
PHONE.................................570 424-9848
▲ EMP: 9 EST: 2008
SALES (est): 1MM **Privately Held**
SIC: 2741 Misc Publishing

(G-18113)
D AND S ARTISTIC WDWKG LLC
1410 Spruce St Ste 116 (18360-2911)
PHONE.................................973 495-7008
EMP: 4
SALES (corp-wide): 628K **Privately Held**
SIC: 2431 Millwork

PA: D And S Artistic Woodworking Llc
144 Salzer Way
Henryville PA 18332
973 495-7008

(G-18114)
DOUBLE M PRODUCTIONS LLC
N 1st St Bldg 8 (18360)
P.O. Box 392 (18360-0392)
PHONE.................................570 476-8000
Michael Kohout, *Mng Member*
Scott Heiss,
EMP: 15 EST: 1996
SQ FT: 20,000
SALES (est): 1.9MM **Privately Held**
WEB: www.doublemproductions.net
SIC: 2262 5092 Screen printing: manmade fiber & silk broadwoven fabrics; toys

(G-18115)
EUREKA STONE QUARRY INC
2443 Bush Ln (18360)
PHONE.................................570 992-4444
Ed Bracht, *Manager*
EMP: 6
SALES (corp-wide): 24.4MM **Privately Held**
SIC: 3281 Stone, quarrying & processing of own stone products
PA: Eureka Stone Quarry, Inc.
Lower Stte Pickertown Rds
Chalfont PA 18914
215 822-0593

(G-18116)
EUREKA STONE QUARRY INC
300 Keiser Rd (18360-9442)
PHONE.................................570 992-4210
Ed Breck, *Branch Mgr*
EMP: 23
SALES (corp-wide): 24.4MM **Privately Held**
SIC: 5032 1422 Stone, crushed or broken; crushed & broken limestone
PA: Eureka Stone Quarry, Inc.
Lower Stte Pickertown Rds
Chalfont PA 18914
215 822-0593

(G-18117)
EXECUTIVE PRINT SOLUTIONS LLC
Also Called: Minuteman Press
1250 N 9th St Unit 101 (18360-7800)
PHONE.................................570 421-1437
Nathan Foeller,
EMP: 4
SQ FT: 2,400
SALES (est): 177K **Privately Held**
SIC: 2752 Commercial printing, offset

(G-18118)
EXPERT PROCESS SYSTEMS LLC
745 Main St Ste 202 (18360-2060)
PHONE.................................570 424-0581
EMP: 6 EST: 2010
SALES (est): 437.1K **Privately Held**
SIC: 3444 Mfg Sheet Metalwork

(G-18119)
FABRICATED COMPONENTS INC
2018 W Main St (18360-6549)
P.O. Box 431 (18360-0431)
PHONE.................................570 421-4110
Robert Deinarowicz Jr, *President*
John Possinger, *Vice Pres*
Peter Daley, *Purchasing*
▲ EMP: 52
SQ FT: 95,000
SALES: 7.4MM **Privately Held**
WEB: www.fabricatedcomponents.com
SIC: 3444 Sheet metal specialties, not stamped

(G-18120)
FINISH TECHNOLOGY INC
2044 W Main St (18360-6549)
PHONE.................................570 421-4110
Robert Deinarowicz Jr, *President*
EMP: 30

SALES (est): 1.6MM **Privately Held**
SIC: 3465 Body parts, automobile: stamped metal

(G-18121)
GREGORY W MOYER DEFIBRILLATO
819 Ann St (18360-1606)
PHONE..................................570 421-9993
Arthur L Zulick, *Principal*
EMP: 3
SALES: 144.4K **Privately Held**
SIC: 3845 Defibrillator

(G-18122)
HANSON AGGREGATES PA LLC
5804 Cherry Valley Rd (18360-6896)
PHONE..................................570 992-4951
John Serague, *Sales/Mktg Mgr*
EMP: 53
SALES (corp-wide): 20.6B **Privately Held**
SIC: 1442 2951 Gravel mining; asphalt paving mixtures & blocks
HQ: Hanson Aggregates Pennsylvania, Llc
7660 Imperial Way
Allentown PA 18195
610 366-4626

(G-18123)
HG SMITH WILBERT VAULT COMPANY
Also Called: Hg Smith Crematory
2120 N 5th St (18360-2802)
PHONE..................................570 420-9599
Sharon Possinger, *Owner*
EMP: 8
SALES (est): 1.4MM **Privately Held**
SIC: 3272 1794 Burial vaults, concrete or precast terrazzo; excavation work

(G-18124)
JENERAL MACHINE COMPANY
6070 Route 209 (18360-7191)
PHONE..................................610 837-5206
Ronald Urbanski, *President*
EMP: 5
SALES (est): 430.8K **Privately Held**
SIC: 3599 Machine shop, jobbing & repair

(G-18125)
LOCAL MEDIA GROUP INC
Also Called: Pocono Record
511 Lenox St (18360-1516)
PHONE..................................570 421-3000
Stan Gett, *Principal*
EMP: 200
SALES (corp-wide): 1.5B **Publicly Held**
WEB: www.ottaway.com
SIC: 2711 Newspapers: publishing only, not printed on site
HQ: Local Media Group, Inc.
40 Mulberry St
Middletown NY 10940
845 341-1100

(G-18126)
MAIN ST PRTG & COPY CTR INC
408 Main St Unit 1 (18360-2550)
PHONE..................................570 424-0800
Ron Bittenbenner, *President*
EMP: 5
SALES (est): 677.7K **Privately Held**
SIC: 2752 Commercial printing, offset

(G-18127)
MAIN ST STOP N GO
1650 W Main St (18360-1024)
PHONE..................................570 424-5505
Yi Zhang, *Owner*
EMP: 3
SALES (est): 237.8K **Privately Held**
SIC: 2911 Petroleum refining

(G-18128)
MARVEL MANUFACTURING COMPANY
40 N 2nd St (18360-2508)
PHONE..................................570 421-6221
Larry Struble, *General Mgr*
EMP: 4
SALES (corp-wide): 928.8K **Privately Held**
WEB: www.marvelmfg.com
SIC: 3829 Measuring & controlling devices

PA: Marvel Manufacturing Company
40 N 2nd St
Stroudsburg PA 18360
570 421-6221

(G-18129)
MARVEL MANUFACTURING COMPANY (PA)
40 N 2nd St (18360-2508)
PHONE..................................570 421-6221
Louis M Byron Jr, *President*
James S Fuller, *Principal*
EMP: 10
SQ FT: 10,000
SALES (est): 928.8K **Privately Held**
WEB: www.marvelmfg.com
SIC: 3829 Measuring & controlling devices

(G-18130)
MEGAPHASE LLC
122 Banner Rd (18360-6433)
PHONE..................................570 424-8400
William Pote III, *CEO*
David J Lutkins,
EMP: 43
SQ FT: 20,000
SALES: 8.8MM **Privately Held**
WEB: www.megaphase.com
SIC: 3678 Electronic connectors

(G-18131)
MOUNTAIN VLY MOLD SOLUTION LLC
515 Queen St (18360-2215)
PHONE..................................570 460-6592
David Keenhold,
EMP: 3
SALES (est): 206.8K **Privately Held**
SIC: 3544 Industrial molds

(G-18132)
MR ZS FOOD MART
1070 N 9th St (18360-1210)
PHONE..................................570 421-7070
Carl Di Grlando, *Principal*
Dan Lundon, *Vice Pres*
EMP: 4 **EST:** 1992
SALES (est): 318.1K **Privately Held**
SIC: 2051 5992 5421 Bread, cake & related products; florists; meat & fish markets

(G-18133)
NCN DATA NETWORKS LLC
586 Main St (18360-2004)
P.O. Box 945 (18360-0945)
PHONE..................................570 213-8300
Robert Johnstone, *Mng Member*
EMP: 4
SALES (est): 294.7K **Privately Held**
SIC: 3669 4813 4899 Emergency alarms; data telephone communications; data communication services

(G-18134)
POCONO INDUSTRIES INC
Hickory Valley Rd (18360)
PHONE..................................570 421-3889
Pete Lesoine, *President*
EMP: 3 **EST:** 1951
SALES (est): 254.3K **Privately Held**
SIC: 1442 Common sand mining; gravel mining

(G-18135)
POCONO LAND & HOMES MAGAZINE P
1929 N 5th St (18360-2707)
PHONE..................................570 424-1000
Larry Sebring, *Principal*
EMP: 3
SALES (est): 178.2K **Privately Held**
SIC: 2721 Magazines: publishing only, not printed on site

(G-18136)
POCONO PISTOL CLUB LLC
85 N 1st St (18360-2503)
PHONE..................................570 424-2940
Jere Dunkelberger, *Principal*
EMP: 7 **EST:** 2007
SALES (est): 918.9K **Privately Held**
SIC: 3482 Small arms ammunition

(G-18137)
R M FRANTZ INC
909 Mill Aly (18360-1610)
PHONE..................................570 421-3020
Paul R Frantz, *President*
Kim Frantz, *Admin Sec*
EMP: 6 **EST:** 1949
SQ FT: 5,000
SALES (est): 353.7K **Privately Held**
SIC: 1721 3589 Residential painting; wallcovering contractors; floor sanding machines, commercial

(G-18138)
REBTECH CORPORATION
140 N 2nd St (18360-2528)
PHONE..................................570 421-6616
Beatrice Balakonis, *President*
EMP: 10
SQ FT: 3,800
SALES: 500K **Privately Held**
SIC: 2821 Silicone resins

(G-18139)
RENEGADE WINERY LLC
600 Main St (18360-2051)
PHONE..................................570 664-6626
EMP: 3 **EST:** 2016
SALES (est): 68.6K **Privately Held**
SIC: 2084 Wines, brandy & brandy spirits

(G-18140)
RITTER GROUP USA INC
Also Called: Regasol
105 Fetherman Rd (18360-6792)
PHONE..................................570 517-5380
Michael Dipaolo, *President*
▲ **EMP:** 3
SQ FT: 3,000
SALES: 1MM **Privately Held**
SIC: 3433 5074 Solar heaters & collectors; heating equipment & panels, solar

(G-18141)
VENUS MACHINES & TOOL
64 N 3rd St (18360-2452)
PHONE..................................570 421-4564
Steven Ujvari, *Owner*
EMP: 4
SQ FT: 2,500
SALES (est): 381.3K **Privately Held**
SIC: 3545 Machine tool attachments & accessories

(G-18142)
WALTER S CUSTOM CABINETRY
1410 Spruce St (18360-2911)
PHONE..................................570 420-9800
Camille Bonanno, *Principal*
EMP: 4
SALES (est): 470.2K **Privately Held**
SIC: 2434 Wood kitchen cabinets

Stump Creek
Jefferson County

(G-18143)
KOSKO WOOD PRODUCTS INC
Rr 119 (15863)
P.O. Box 197 (15863-0197)
PHONE..................................814 427-2499
Dan Kosko, *President*
Micheal Kosko, *Vice Pres*
EMP: 6
SALES (est): 527.9K **Privately Held**
SIC: 2511 Wood household furniture

Sugar Grove
Warren County

(G-18144)
COLLINS DRILLING LLC
1050 Stillwater Rd (16350-4032)
P.O. Box 527 (16350-0527)
PHONE..................................814 489-3297
Mike Collins, *Mng Member*
EMP: 10
SQ FT: 3,250

SALES (est): 968.3K **Privately Held**
SIC: 1381 Directional drilling oil & gas wells; drilling water intake wells

(G-18145)
RHOADES LOGGING
781 White Rd (16350-6017)
PHONE..................................814 757-4711
Everett L Rhoades, *Principal*
EMP: 3
SALES (est): 184.7K **Privately Held**
SIC: 2411 Logging camps & contractors

(G-18146)
S & K SCOPE MOUNTS
70 Swede Hollow Rd (16350-1702)
PHONE..................................814 489-3091
Howard Labowski, *Owner*
EMP: 3
SALES (est): 257.8K **Privately Held**
WEB: www.scopemounts.com
SIC: 3484 Guns (firearms) or gun parts, 30 mm. & below

(G-18147)
SKYLON INC
12210 Jackson Run Rd (16350-4524)
P.O. Box 325 (16350-0325)
PHONE..................................814 489-3622
Diana C Elmquist, *President*
Scott A Elmquist, *Vice Pres*
Scott Elmquist, *Vice Pres*
Scott Kemery, *Manager*
EMP: 15
SQ FT: 7,700
SALES (est): 2.7MM **Privately Held**
WEB: www.skylonmold.com
SIC: 3599 3544 2759 Custom machinery; machine shop, jobbing & repair; special dies, tools, jigs & fixtures; commercial printing

(G-18148)
VERTICAL RESOURCES INC
Also Called: Vertical Energy
44 Valley Park Dr (16350-5232)
PHONE..................................814 489-3931
Stephen Ford, *President*
Cynthia Ford, *Vice Pres*
EMP: 15
SALES (est): 2.4MM **Privately Held**
SIC: 1381 Drilling oil & gas wells

Sugar Notch
Luzerne County

(G-18149)
CRAFT METAL PRODUCTS INC
1 Industrial Dr (18706-2137)
PHONE..................................570 829-2441
David Marich, *President*
EMP: 4
SQ FT: 5,000
SALES: 300K **Privately Held**
SIC: 3444 Sheet metalwork

Sugargrove
Warren County

(G-18150)
CURTIS AND SON OIL INC
Also Called: Curtis Well Service
Lander Rd (16350)
P.O. Box 367, Sugar Grove (16350-0367)
PHONE..................................814 489-7858
Jay Curtis, *President*
EMP: 9 **EST:** 1970
SALES (est): 1.1MM **Privately Held**
SIC: 1381 Drilling oil & gas wells

(G-18151)
CURTIS WELL SERVICE COMPANY
Also Called: Curtis and Sons Oil
Rr 957 (16350)
P.O. Box 367, Sugar Grove (16350-0367)
PHONE..................................814 489-7858
Jay Curtis, *President*
Darwin Curtis, *Vice Pres*
EMP: 10

SQ FT: 12,000
SALES (est): 1.1MM Privately Held
SIC: 1389 Hydraulic fracturing wells

Sugarloaf
Luzerne County

(G-18152)
BEN COOK RACING LTD
362 State Route 93 Hwy (18249)
P.O. Box 1006, Conyngham (18219-1006)
PHONE...............................570 788-4223
Ben Cook, *President*
Danny Cook, *Vice Pres*
Bill Cook, *Treasurer*
EMP: 3
SQ FT: 5,000
SALES: 170K Privately Held
SIC: 3711 Automobile assembly, including
specialty automobiles

(G-18153)
GLOBAL UTILITY STRUCTURES LLC
39 Aristocrat Cir (18249-3020)
P.O. Box 751, Conyngham (18219-0751)
PHONE...............................570 788-0826
Donna Jean Grant, *Mng Member*
Donna Grant, *Executive*
Lew Grant, *Executive*
Jaime Scatton,
EMP: 4
SALES (est): 236.2K Privately Held
SIC: 3441 8711 Tower sections, radio &
television transmission; engineering serv-
ices

Summerhill
Cambria County

(G-18154)
NEW GERMANY WOOD PRODUCTS INC
1444 New Germany Rd (15958-5307)
P.O. Box 349 (15958-0349)
PHONE...............................814 495-5923
Robert Long, *President*
Sharon Penatzer, *Corp Secy*
Jeffrey A Long, *Vice Pres*
EMP: 10 EST: 1966
SQ FT: 5,000
SALES: 1MM Privately Held
WEB: www.newgermanywoodproducts.com
SIC: 2426 Furniture dimension stock, hard-
wood

(G-18155)
SIMPLY BUSINESS LLC
1016 New Germany Rd (15958-5603)
PHONE...............................814 241-7113
EMP: 4
SALES (est): 353.6K Privately Held
SIC: 2752 Commercial printing, litho-
graphic

Summerville
Jefferson County

(G-18156)
ALTRAX
1557 Limestone Rd (15864-3819)
PHONE...............................814 379-3706
Brent Miller, *Partner*
Bradley Miller, *Partner*
Brian Miller, *Partner*
EMP: 4
SALES (est): 218.9K Privately Held
SIC: 6531 7692 3531 3443 Real estate
brokers & agents; welding repair; con-
struction machinery; fabricated plate work
(boiler shop); fabricated structural metal;
metal barrels, drums & pails

(G-18157)
CHARLES MACHINE INC
10037 Olean Trl (15864-3825)
PHONE...............................814 379-3706
Brian Miller, *President*

Bradley Miller, *Vice Pres*
Judy Miller, *Treasurer*
Brent Miller, *Admin Sec*
▲ EMP: 50
SQ FT: 50,000
SALES (est): 9.3MM Privately Held
SIC: 3599 3444 Machine shop, jobbing &
repair; sheet metalwork

(G-18158)
GLEN-GERY CORPORATION
Also Called: Glen-Gery Hanley Plant
12637 Harrison St (15864-6333)
P.O. Box 68 (15864-0068)
PHONE...............................814 856-2171
Terry Bullers, *Manager*
Cathy Rowles, *Manager*
EMP: 90 Privately Held
WEB: www.glengerybrick.com
SIC: 3251 3255 Structural clay tile; clay
refractories
HQ: Glen-Gery Corporation
1166 Spring St
Reading PA 19610
610 374-4011

Summit Hill
Carbon County

(G-18159)
CRAIG WALTERS (PA)
Also Called: Walters Monument Co
348 E White St (18250-1326)
P.O. Box 35 (18250-0035)
PHONE...............................570 645-3415
Craig Walters Sr, *Owner*
Lisa Stefinck, *Owner*
Lisa Stefanick, *Admin Sec*
EMP: 4
SQ FT: 10,000
SALES (est): 427.3K Privately Held
SIC: 5999 3272 3281 Monuments, fin-
ished to custom order; monuments &
grave markers, except terrazo; monument
or burial stone, cut & shaped

(G-18160)
ELK LIGHTING INC
101 W White St (18250-1120)
PHONE...............................800 613-3261
Sandy Zapata, *Branch Mgr*
EMP: 12
SALES (corp-wide): 5.7MM Privately
Held
SIC: 5063 3646 3645 Lighting fixtures,
commercial & industrial; commercial in-
dusl & institutional electric lighting fix-
tures; residential lighting fixtures
PA: Elk Lighting Inc
40 3rd St
Walnutport PA 18088
610 767-0511

Summit Station
Schuylkill County

(G-18161)
SUMMIT TRAILER SALES INC
1 Summit Plz (17979)
PHONE...............................570 754-3511
Chuck Pishock, *President*
Leo McKeown, *Vice Pres*
▼ EMP: 50
SQ FT: 5,000
SALES (est): 11.5MM Privately Held
WEB: www.summittrailer.com
SIC: 3715 Trailer bodies

Sunbury
Northumberland County

(G-18162)
AMERICAN LADY US MALE HAIR SLN
Also Called: American Lady Hair Care Center
12 N 5th St (17801-2310)
PHONE...............................570 286-7759
Wally Kerstetter, *Owner*

EMP: 5
SALES (est): 108.9K Privately Held
SIC: 7231 7299 3999 Unisex hair salons;
manicurist, pedicurist; tanning salon;
comb mountings

(G-18163)
ANTHRACITE INDUSTRIES INC
Also Called: Asbury Carbons
610 Anthracite Rd (17801)
P.O. Box 112 (17801-0112)
PHONE...............................570 286-2176
Timothy L Hendricks, *General Mgr*
EMP: 45
SALES (corp-wide): 126.7MM Privately
Held
SIC: 3295 3624 3494 3312 Minerals,
ground or treated; carbon & graphite
products; valves & pipe fittings; blast fur-
naces & steel mills; anthracite mining
HQ: Anthracite Industries, Inc.
405 Old Main St
Asbury NJ 08802
908 537-2155

(G-18164)
ASBURY CARBONS INC
216 E Haas Manor Rd (17801-5623)
P.O. Box 112 (17801-0112)
PHONE...............................570 286-9721
Robert Gilson, *Principal*
EMP: 3
SALES (est): 158.2K Privately Held
SIC: 3624 Carbon & graphite products

(G-18165)
BRUSH INDUSTRIES INC
301 Reagan St (17801-1200)
P.O. Box 638 (17801-0638)
PHONE...............................570 286-5611
Karen Nickolauson, *CEO*
Joseph Stenglein, *President*
EMP: 53 EST: 1951
SQ FT: 30,000
SALES (est): 10.3MM Privately Held
WEB: www.brushindustries.com
SIC: 3679 3599 Recording & playback
heads, magnetic; recording heads,
speech & musical equipment; machine
shop, jobbing & repair

(G-18166)
COMMUNITY NEWSPAPER GROUP LLC
Also Called: Danville News
200 Market St (17801-3402)
PHONE...............................570 275-3235
Gary Grossnan, *Branch Mgr*
EMP: 7 Privately Held
SIC: 2711 Newspapers: publishing only,
not printed on site
HQ: Community Newspaper Group, Llc
3500 Colonnade Pkwy # 600
Birmingham AL 35243

(G-18167)
COMMUNITY SERVICES GROUP INC
Also Called: Csg Bakery
330 N 2nd St (17801-1804)
PHONE...............................570 286-0111
Lon Deitrick, *Branch Mgr*
EMP: 45
SALES (corp-wide): 77.8MM Privately
Held
WEB: www.csgonline.org
SIC: 2051 Bread, cake & related products
PA: Community Services Group, Inc.
320 Highland Dr
Mountville PA 17554
717 285-7121

(G-18168)
E I T CORPORATION PHOENIX
Rr 61 (17801)
PHONE...............................570 286-7744
Hans Lawrence, *President*
Robert E Fatz, *Vice Pres*
▼ EMP: 10
SQ FT: 10,000
SALES (est): 1.5MM Privately Held
WEB: www.eit-corp.com
SIC: 3629 3692 Blasting machines, elec-
trical; dry cell batteries, single or multiple
cell

(G-18169)
FRESH ROASTED COFFEE LLC
200 N River Ave (17801-1820)
PHONE...............................570 743-9228
Andrew Oakes, *Mng Member*
EMP: 12
SALES: 3.5MM Privately Held
SIC: 2095 5812 3589 5149 Roasted cof-
fee; coffee shop; coffee brewing equip-
ment; coffee & tea

(G-18170)
GREAT COASTERS INTL INC (PA)
2627 State Route 890 (17801-8042)
PHONE...............................570 286-9330
Clair Hain Jr, *President*
Leeanne Hain, *Corp Secy*
▲ EMP: 15
SQ FT: 25,890
SALES (est): 5.3MM Privately Held
SIC: 7999 2499 Amusement ride; applica-
tors, wood

(G-18171)
LOLLIPOP HM HALTHCARE SVCS LLC
204 N Front St (17801-1810)
PHONE...............................570 286-9460
Laura Shrawder Miles, *Principal*
EMP: 3
SALES (est): 182.3K Privately Held
SIC: 2064 Lollipops & other hard candy

(G-18172)
SIMPLEX INDUSTRIES INC
1180 Line St (17801-1609)
PHONE...............................570 495-4333
EMP: 4
SALES (est): 243.4K
SALES (corp-wide): 45.4MM Privately
Held
SIC: 3999 Atomizers, toiletry
PA: Simplex Industries, Inc.
1 Simplex Dr
Scranton PA 18504
570 346-5113

(G-18173)
SUN-RE CHEESE CORP
178 Lenker Ave (17801-2902)
P.O. Box 52 (17801-0052)
PHONE...............................570 286-1511
Thomas Aiello Jr, *President*
EMP: 50
SQ FT: 56,000
SALES (est): 11.7MM Privately Held
SIC: 2022 Natural cheese

(G-18174)
SUNBURY CONTROLS INC
1030 Walnut St (17801-3231)
P.O. Box 433, Glenshaw (15116-0433)
PHONE...............................570 274-7847
Michelle Lsmyers, *President*
James Hsnyder, *Vice Pres*
Jesse Asmyers, *Admin Sec*
EMP: 5 EST: 2017
SALES (est): 237.9K Privately Held
SIC: 3491 Pressure valves & regulators,
industrial

(G-18175)
TIMBER SKATE SHOP
257 Market St (17801-3401)
P.O. Box 208 (17801-0208)
PHONE...............................570 492-6063
Jeremy Lauer, *Owner*
EMP: 3 EST: 2014
SQ FT: 2,500
SALES (est): 86.9K Privately Held
SIC: 5999 2759 Miscellaneous retail
stores; screen printing

(G-18176)
WHISPERING OAKS VINEYARD
1306 State Route 61 (17801-6157)
PHONE...............................570 495-4054
Ryan Bonney, *Manager*
EMP: 7
SALES (est): 526.4K Privately Held
SIC: 2084 Wines

(G-18177)
WIREROPE WORKS INC
880 S 2nd St (17801-3305)
PHONE................................570 286-0115
Rick Krex, *General Mgr*
Virgil Probasco, *Exec Dir*
EMP: 30
SALES: 1,000K Privately Held
SIC: 2298 Wire rope centers

Susquehanna
Susquehanna County

(G-18178)
CB EXCAVATING & LOGGING LLC
2108 Lakeview Rd (18847-7366)
PHONE................................570 756-2749
Charles Boman, *Principal*
EMP: 3 EST: 2011
SALES (est): 318.1K Privately Held
SIC: 2411 Logging camps & contractors

(G-18179)
CHILEWSKI FLAGSTONE
Lakeview Rd (18847)
P.O. Box 88 (18847-0088)
PHONE................................570 756-3096
C Thomas Chilewski Jr, *Owner*
EMP: 12
SALES (est): 710K Privately Held
SIC: 1411 Flagstone mining

(G-18180)
HARMONY FLAGSTONE LLC
21188 State Route 171 (18847-8081)
PHONE................................570 727-2077
Edward Greene III, *Principal*
EMP: 6
SALES (est): 486.1K Privately Held
SIC: 3281 Flagstones

(G-18181)
MARK GINGERELLA
Also Called: Mach-Dynamics
494 Main St (18847-7979)
PHONE................................570 213-5603
Mark Gingerella, *Owner*
EMP: 3
SQ FT: 3,000
SALES (est): 262.1K Privately Held
WEB: www.mach-dynamics.com
SIC: 2851 2899 Paints & allied products;
rifle bore cleaning compounds

(G-18182)
PREMIER BLUESTONE INC
Also Called: Endless Mountain Stone Co
5212 Brushville Rd (18847-8180)
PHONE................................570 465-7200
Robert A Coleman, *President*
EMP: 28
SQ FT: 2,000
SALES (est): 4.2MM Privately Held
WEB: www.endlessmountainstone.com
SIC: 3281 Flagstones

(G-18183)
SUSQUEHANNA TRANSCRIPT INC
36 Exchange St (18847-2610)
PHONE................................570 853-3134
Charles Ficarro, *President*
Rita Ficarro, *Corp Secy*
EMP: 3
SALES: 320K Privately Held
SIC: 2711 Newspapers: publishing only,
not printed on site

Sutersville
Westmoreland County

(G-18184)
NETMERCATUS LLC
Also Called: Mal Parts Financial
1784 Mars Hill Rd (15083-1380)
PHONE................................646 822-7900
EMP: 5
SALES (est): 370K Privately Held
SIC: 3724 Mfg Aircraft Engines/Parts

Swarthmore
Delaware County

(G-18185)
NEWS OF DELAWARE COUNTY
639 S Chester Rd (19081-2315)
PHONE................................610 583-4432
Richard Crowe, *Principal*
Karen Donehower, *Sales Associate*
EMP: 6
SALES (est): 228.2K Privately Held
SIC: 2711 Commercial printing & newspaper publishing combined; newspapers,
publishing & printing

(G-18186)
TITANIUM 40 LLC
539 Riverview Rd (19081-1021)
PHONE................................610 338-0446
Christine Donato, *Principal*
EMP: 4 EST: 2009
SALES (est): 441.8K Privately Held
SIC: 3356 Titanium

Sweet Valley
Luzerne County

(G-18187)
BRIAN O KEFFE
Also Called: Mooretown Sawmill & Supply
27 Scavone Ln (18656-2291)
PHONE................................570 477-3962
Brian O'Keefe, *Owner*
EMP: 4
SQ FT: 20,000
SALES: 3MM Privately Held
SIC: 2421 7699 2426 Lumber: rough,
sawed or planed; power tool repair; hardwood dimension & flooring mills

Swiftwater
Monroe County

(G-18188)
MCM VACCINE CO
1 Discovery Dr (18370-9100)
PHONE................................570 957-7187
Shawn Burrier, *Principal*
EMP: 3
SALES (est): 152.7K
SALES (corp-wide): 42.2B Publicly Held
SIC: 2836 Vaccines
PA: Merck & Co., Inc.
2000 Galloping Hill Rd
Kenilworth NJ 07033
908 740-4000

(G-18189)
POCONO POOL PRODUCTS INC
117 Carlton Rd (18370)
P.O. Box 727 (18370-0727)
PHONE................................570 839-9291
Tim Harrison, *Accounts Mgr*
Robin Homequist,
EMP: 50
SQ FT: 7,000
SALES (est): 4.6MM Privately Held
WEB: www.poolsourcedirect.com
SIC: 3949 5091 Swimming pools, plastic;
swimming pools, equipment & supplies

(G-18190)
SANOFI PASTEUR INC (HQ)
1 Discovery Dr (18370-9100)
PHONE................................570 839-7187
Damian A Braga, *President*
Jean Cappelli, *President*
Janet Voorhees, *General Mgr*
Dan Casey, *Vice Pres*
Erik Grau, *Vice Pres*
▲ EMP: 1500 EST: 1977
SQ FT: 6,000
SALES (est): 549.6MM Privately Held
WEB: www.immunizingpharmacist.com
SIC: 2836 Biological products, except diagnostic

Swissvale
Allegheny County

(G-18191)
COPY STOP INC
2013 Noble St (15218-2100)
P.O. Box 8298, Pittsburgh (15218-0298)
PHONE................................412 271-4444
Chuck Rotella, *President*
EMP: 5
SALES (est): 480K Privately Held
SIC: 2759 7334 Commercial printing; photocopying & duplicating services

(G-18192)
MCCLOY AWNING COMPANY
2029 Noble St (15218-2103)
P.O. Box 82609, Pittsburgh (15218-0609)
PHONE................................412 271-4044
Sandy McCloy, *President*
EMP: 15
SQ FT: 5,000
SALES (est): 1.1MM Privately Held
SIC: 2394 Awnings, fabric: made from purchased materials

(G-18193)
O K MCCLOYAWNINGS INC
2029 Noble St (15218-2103)
P.O. Box 82609, Pittsburgh (15218-0609)
PHONE................................412 271-4044
Sandy Mc Cloy, *President*
EMP: 15
SQ FT: 18,000
SALES (est): 1.2MM Privately Held
SIC: 2394 Awnings, fabric: made from purchased materials

Swoyersville
Luzerne County

(G-18194)
BAUT STUDIOS INC
1095 Main St (18704-1337)
PHONE................................570 288-1431
Conrad Baut, *President*
Harriett Baut, *Chairman*
Karen Klemm-Baut, *Treasurer*
Heide Cebrick, *Admin Sec*
EMP: 25 EST: 1927
SQ FT: 40,000
SALES (est): 2.6MM Privately Held
WEB: www.baut.com
SIC: 3231 3442 3446 2499 Stained
glass: made from purchased glass; metal
doors; sash, door or window: metal; architectural metalwork; decorative wood &
woodwork; fabricated structural metal; flat
glass

(G-18195)
BLUE RIBBON FARM DAIRY
1209 Main St (18704-1328)
PHONE................................570 763-5570
EMP: 4
SALES (est): 88.5K Privately Held
SIC: 5451 2024 Dairy products stores; ice
cream & frozen desserts

(G-18196)
COR-RITE INC
195 Slocum St (18704-2935)
PHONE................................570 287-1718
EMP: 11
SALES (est): 100K Privately Held
SIC: 2653 Mfg Corrugated Cartons Pads
Partitions

(G-18197)
CROFCHICK INC
Also Called: Owen St Bakers
90 Owen St (18704-4337)
PHONE................................570 287-3940
Robert F Crofchick, *President*
EMP: 4
SALES (est): 110.5K Privately Held
SIC: 2051 Cakes, bakery: except frozen

(G-18198)
S & G CORRUGATED PACKAGING INC
195 Slocum St (18704-2935)
PHONE................................570 287-1718
Allan Dunzello, *President*
Harold Sampson, *President*
EMP: 8
SALES (est): 1.9MM Privately Held
SIC: 2653 Boxes, corrugated: made from
purchased materials

(G-18199)
SHARPER EMBROIDERY INC
1081 Main St (18704-1308)
PHONE................................570 714-3617
Mike Harper, *President*
EMP: 3 EST: 2000
SALES (est): 271.7K Privately Held
WEB: www.sharperembroidery.com
SIC: 2395 Embroidery products, except
schiffli machine; embroidery & art needlework

(G-18200)
SUSQUEHANNA SERVICES LLC
1204 Main St (18704-1318)
PHONE................................570 288-5269
Arnie Little, *President*
John S Yarosz, *President*
EMP: 2
SALES (est): 1.1MM Privately Held
SIC: 1389 Mud service, oil field drilling

Sycamore
Greene County

(G-18201)
MORRIS TWNSHIP SPERVISORS BARN
Also Called: Supervisors' Barn
1317 Browns Creek Rd (15364-1302)
PHONE................................724 627-3096
Judy Moninger, *Corp Secy*
EMP: 4
SALES: 330K Privately Held
SIC: 3523 Barn, silo, poultry, dairy & livestock machinery

Sykesville
Jefferson County

(G-18202)
PREMIER GRAPHICS LLC
Also Called: Nupp Printing Company
5 E Main St (15865-1105)
PHONE................................814 894-2467
Pat Reasinger, *Mng Member*
EMP: 10
SQ FT: 8,000
SALES (est): 2MM Privately Held
WEB: www.nupp-printing.com
SIC: 2759 8742 Commercial printing; marketing consulting services

(G-18203)
SYMMCO INC
40 S Park St (15865-1199)
P.O. Box F (15865-0039)
PHONE................................814 894-2461
John A Mosco, *President*
John Bean, *Chairman*
Richard Mowrey, *Vice Pres*
Norman Flanders, *Prdtn Mgr*
Debbie McDonnell, *QA Dir*
EMP: 110
SQ FT: 74,000
SALES (est): 28.1MM
SALES (corp-wide): 29.7MM Privately
Held
WEB: www.symmco.com
SIC: 3399 3463 Metal powders, pastes &
flakes; powder, metal; bearing & bearing
race forgings, nonferrous
PA: Symmco Group, Inc.
40 S Park St
Sykesville PA 15865
814 894-2461

(G-18204)
SYMMCO GROUP INC (PA)
40 S Park St (15865-1199)
P.O. Box F (15865-0039)
PHONE...............................814 894-2461
John Bean, *Ch of Bd*
Alfred C Torretti, *President*
Richard Mowrey, *Treasurer*
Betty D Hoare, *Asst Sec*
EMP: 100
SQ FT: 90,000
SALES (est): 29.7MM **Privately Held**
SIC: 3399 Powder, metal

Tafton
Pike County

(G-18205)
STERLING FOREST PRODUCTS
136 Wenonah Rd (18464-9652)
PHONE...............................570 226-4233
Brian Williams, *Owner*
EMP: 4
SQ FT: 4,500
SALES: 750K **Privately Held**
SIC: 2421 Sawmills & planing mills, general

Talmage
Lancaster County

(G-18206)
BEILERS WOODWORKING
81 Locust St (17580)
PHONE...............................717 656-8956
Emanuel Beiler, *Partner*
Priscilla Beiler, *Partner*
EMP: 7
SQ FT: 5,000
SALES (est): 777.4K **Privately Held**
SIC: 2434 Wood kitchen cabinets

(G-18207)
MELVIN STOLTZFUS
Also Called: Stoltzfus Cabinet Shop
S State St (17580)
P.O. Box 22 (17580-0022)
PHONE...............................717 656-3520
Melvin Stoltzfus, *Owner*
EMP: 10
SQ FT: 5,000
SALES (est): 894.3K **Privately Held**
SIC: 2541 2434 Wood partitions & fixtures; vanities, bathroom: wood

Tamaqua
Schuylkill County

(G-18208)
AIR PRODUCTS AND CHEMICALS INC
357 Marian Ave (18252-4762)
PHONE...............................570 467-2981
Carl Molty, *Branch Mgr*
EMP: 300
SALES (corp-wide): 8.9B **Publicly Held**
WEB: www.airproducts.com
SIC: 2813 2899 Industrial gases; chemical preparations
PA: Air Products And Chemicals, Inc.
7201 Hamilton Blvd
Allentown PA 18195
610 481-4911

(G-18209)
COPPERHEAD CHEMICAL CO INC
120 River Rd (18252-5403)
PHONE...............................570 386-6123
Catherin McPhail, *President*
Mary Brooks, *Chairman*
Farooque Dawood, *Chairman*
Kaiya J Campbell, *Vice Pres*
Daniel Stigliano, *Vice Pres*
▼ **EMP:** 39
SQ FT: 93,612

SALES: 14.5MM **Privately Held**
WEB: www.copperheadchemical.com
SIC: 2892 2834 2844 Primary explosives, fuses & detonators; proprietary drug products; cosmetic preparations
PA: Cobra Investments Management Inc
103 Foulk Rd
Wilmington DE 19803
302 691-6333

(G-18210)
GELLNER INDUSTRIAL LLC (PA)
105 Tide Rd (18252-4331)
P.O. Box 208 (18252-0208)
PHONE...............................570 668-8800
Otto Gellner,
Robert Gellner,
Theresia Gellner,
▲ **EMP:** 31
SQ FT: 42,000
SALES (est): 6.1MM **Privately Held**
SIC: 2821 Plastics materials & resins

(G-18211)
GROUSE HUNT FARMS INC
458 Fairview St (18252-4718)
PHONE...............................570 573-2868
Paul Zukovich, *President*
Debra Zukovich, *Corp Secy*
Christopher Thompson, *Sales Staff*
EMP: 12
SALES: 1.2MM **Privately Held**
SIC: 2033 Vegetables: packaged in cans, jars, etc.; fruits: packaged in cans, jars, etc.

(G-18212)
HIGHWOOD USA LLC
87 Tide Rd (18252-4337)
PHONE...............................570 668-6113
John Quarmley, *President*
Danielle Hess, *Plant Mgr*
Alex Witiszin, *Engineer*
Adam Barilla, *Plant Engr*
Marsha Thomas, *Manager*
EMP: 48
SALES (est): 12.5MM **Privately Held**
WEB: www.highwoodusa.com
SIC: 3086 Plastics foam products

(G-18213)
KNF CORPORATION (PA)
734 W Penn Pike (18252-5672)
PHONE...............................570 386-3550
Mary Lou Kennedy, *President*
Philip J Carcara, *President*
Donald U Kennedy Sr, *Treasurer*
Lee Gordon, *Sales Staff*
Matt Lukash, *Director*
▲ **EMP:** 50
SQ FT: 26,000
SALES (est): 11.1MM **Privately Held**
SIC: 2821 3089 Nylon resins; injection molded finished plastic products

(G-18214)
KNF FLEXPAK CORPORATION
734 W Penn Pike (18252-5672)
PHONE...............................570 386-3550
Philip J Carcara, *President*
◆ **EMP:** 60
SQ FT: 26,000
SALES (est): 13.3MM **Privately Held**
WEB: www.knfcorporation.com
SIC: 2673 Plastic bags: made from purchased materials

(G-18215)
LEHIGH ANTHRACITE LP
1233 E Broad St (18252-2229)
PHONE...............................570 668-9060
▼ **EMP:** 6
SALES (est): 4.3MM **Privately Held**
SIC: 1311 Coal liquefaction

(G-18216)
LEHIGH ASPHALT PAV & CNSTR CO (DH)
1314 E Broad St (18252-2200)
P.O. Box 549 (18252-0549)
PHONE...............................570 668-2040
Jeffery J Frantz, *President*
Rachael R Mc Cool, *Corp Secy*
Jeffery Frantz, *Director*
EMP: 11 **EST:** 1954
SQ FT: 1,500

SALES (est): 8.7MM
SALES (corp-wide): 102.1MM **Privately Held**
SIC: 2951 1611 Asphalt & asphaltic paving mixtures (not from refineries); general contractor, highway & street construction

(G-18217)
LEIBYS ICHR LLC
848 W Penn Pike (18252-5658)
PHONE...............................570 778-0108
EMP: 3
SALES (est): 48.3K **Privately Held**
SIC: 5812 2024 2051 Restaurant, family: independent; American restaurant; ice cream & frozen desserts; pies, bakery: except frozen

(G-18218)
LEWISTOWN VALLEY ENTPS INC
Also Called: Koch's Turkey Farm
416 Valley Rd (18252-5115)
PHONE...............................570 668-2089
Lowell R Koch, *President*
Duane L Koch, *Vice Pres*
Pamela S Williams, *Vice Pres*
Beth K Argall, *Treasurer*
Barbara Hill, *Admin Sec*
EMP: 100
SQ FT: 8,000
SALES (est): 12.7MM **Privately Held**
WEB: www.kochsturkey.com
SIC: 0253 0191 2015 Turkey farm; general farms, primarily crop; chicken, processed: frozen

(G-18219)
LUXFER MAGTECH INC
1415 E Broad St (18252-2232)
PHONE...............................570 668-0001
Jim Gardella, *CEO*
EMP: 48
SALES (est): 4.4MM
SALES (corp-wide): 441.3MM **Privately Held**
SIC: 2819 3339 3274 Magnesium compounds or salts, inorganic; primary nonferrous metals; lime
PA: Luxfer Holdings Plc
Anchorage Gateway
Salford LANCS M50 3
161 300-0611

(G-18220)
MAGNESIUM ELEKTRON
1415 E Broad St (18252-2232)
PHONE...............................570 668-0001
Raymond G Harper, *President*
EMP: 11
SALES (est): 1.7MM **Privately Held**
SIC: 2819 Magnesium compounds or salts, inorganic

(G-18221)
NESTORS WELDING CO
Also Called: Nestor's Iron Works
431 E Broad St (18252-2136)
PHONE...............................570 668-3401
Robert Palumbo, *Owner*
EMP: 4
SQ FT: 25,000
SALES (est): 393.6K **Privately Held**
SIC: 3441 7692 1799 Fabricated structural metal; welding repair; welding on site

(G-18222)
NORTHEASTERN HYDRO-SEEDING INC
Also Called: Post Service
411 Claremont Ave (18252-4832)
PHONE...............................570 668-1108
Wayne Postupack, *President*
EMP: 3
SALES: 500K **Privately Held**
WEB: www.postservice.com
SIC: 3399 Reclaiming ferrous metals from clay

(G-18223)
PENCOR SERVICES INC
Also Called: Time's News, The
200 E Broad St (18252-2054)
PHONE...............................570 668-1250
Joseph Plasko, *Opers-Prdtn-Mfg*
EMP: 4

SALES (corp-wide): 108.7MM **Privately Held**
WEB: www.pennspeak.com
SIC: 2711 Newspapers: publishing only, not printed on site
PA: Pencor Services, Inc.
613 3rd Street Palmerton
Palmerton PA 18071
610 826-2115

(G-18224)
SILBERLINE HOLDING CO (PA)
130 Lincoln Dr (18252-4321)
P.O. Box B (18252-0420)
PHONE...............................570 668-6050
Lisa Peretz, *President*
John Kalinovich, *Vice Pres*
Frank Nataro, *Vice Pres*
Martin Fay, *Manager*
Thomas Schwarz, *Officer*
◆ **EMP:** 10
SALES (est): 2MM **Privately Held**
SIC: 2816 Metallic & mineral pigments

(G-18225)
SILBERLINE MFG CO INC (PA)
130 Lincoln Dr (18252-4321)
P.O. Box B (18252-0420)
PHONE...............................570 668-6050
Ernest Scheller Jr, *Ch of Bd*
Lisa J Scheller, *President*
Matthew Rudy, *Plant Supt*
Brian Newton, *Production*
Craig Keemer, *Research*
◆ **EMP:** 126 **EST:** 1945
SQ FT: 110,000
SALES (est): 113.8MM **Privately Held**
WEB: www.silberline.com
SIC: 2816 2819 Metallic & mineral pigments; industrial inorganic chemicals

(G-18226)
SOUTH TAMAQUA COAL POCKETS
804 W Penn Pike (18252-5658)
P.O. Box 161, Orefield (18069-0161)
PHONE...............................570 386-5445
William Keba, *President*
Mary Keba, *Director*
George Racho, *Director*
EMP: 12
SQ FT: 20,000
SALES: 16MM **Privately Held**
SIC: 1231 5989 Preparation plants, anthracite; coal

(G-18227)
SPARE TIME BOWLING
17 Tide Rd (18252-4337)
PHONE...............................570 668-3210
Bill Reese, *President*
EMP: 8
SALES (est): 511.6K **Privately Held**
SIC: 2599 Bowling establishment furniture

(G-18228)
STONE COUNTY SPECIALTIES INC
458 Fairview St (18252-4718)
PHONE...............................570 467-2850
Derek Zukovich, *President*
EMP: 3
SQ FT: 2,800
SALES: 976.2K **Privately Held**
SIC: 2099 5141 Food preparations; food brokers

(G-18229)
TAMAQUA TRUCK & TRAILER INC
794 W Penn Pike (18252-5656)
PHONE...............................570 386-5994
Robin Wood, *President*
Karen Wood, *Corp Secy*
EMP: 5
SALES: 750K **Privately Held**
WEB: www.tamaquatrucktrailer.com
SIC: 3713 7532 Dump truck bodies; body shop, trucks

(G-18230)
TRANS WESTERN POLYMERS INC
31 Progress Ave (18252-4333)
PHONE...............................570 668-5690

Kenny Brandmier, *Principal*
▲ EMP: 28 EST: 2008
SALES (est): 6.7MM Privately Held
SIC: 3089 Plastic processing

(G-18231)
VERSUM MATERIALS US LLC
357 Marian Ave (18252-4762)
PHONE...................................570 467-2981
Karl H Nolte III, *Branch Mgr*
EMP: 6
SALES (corp-wide): 1.1B Publicly Held
SIC: 2842 2891 3569 Ammonia, house-
hold; adhesives; gas producers, genera-
tors & other gas related equipment; gas
separators (machinery); separators for
steam, gas, vapor or air (machinery)
HQ: Versum Materials Us, Llc
8555 S River Pkwy
Tempe AZ 85284
602 282-1000

Tamiment
Pike County

(G-18232)
**BIG BROTHER HD LTD LBLTY
CO**
107 Oakenshield Dr (18371-9454)
PHONE...................................201 355-8166
Bassel Mallah,
Billy Mallah,
▲ EMP: 6
SQ FT: 1,000
SALES (est): 510K Privately Held
SIC: 3669 5731 5999 Burglar alarm appa-
ratus, electric; video cameras, recorders
& accessories; telephone equipment &
systems

(G-18233)
**HEALTHY ALTERNATIVE PET
DIETS**
1016 E Underhill Dr (18371)
PHONE...................................210 745-1493
Marsha E Burton,
Marsha Burton,
EMP: 4
SALES (est): 420K Privately Held
SIC: 2047 Dog & cat food

Tannersville
Monroe County

(G-18234)
BASKET WORKS INC
2951 Route 611 Ste 102 (18372-7927)
PHONE...................................516 367-9200
Brian Herr, *President*
Ellen Shield, *Vice Pres*
EMP: 6
SQ FT: 1,800
SALES (est): 340K Privately Held
SIC: 5947 2066 5199 Gift baskets; choco-
late candy, solid; gift baskets

(G-18235)
CRITICAL SYSTEMS LLC
2369 Route 715 (18372-9156)
P.O. Box 69, Pocono Summit (18346-0069)
PHONE...................................570 643-6903
Thomas White, *Mng Member*
EMP: 5
SALES: 1.2MM Privately Held
SIC: 3621 7389 Motors & generators;

(G-18236)
PRECISIAN INC
Merchants Plz 9 Rte 611 (18372)
P.O. Box 861 (18372-0861)
PHONE...................................610 861-0844
John F Fox, *Principal*
EMP: 3
SALES (est): 193.8K Privately Held
SIC: 3677 Electronic coils, transformers &
other inductors

(G-18237)
STAINED GLASS CREATIONS
2736 Route 611 (18372-7876)
PHONE...................................570 629-5070
Debra B Herman, *Partner*
Joan Smith, *Partner*
EMP: 5
SALES (est): 498.1K Privately Held
WEB: www.stainedglasscreation.com
SIC: 3231 5231 Stained glass: made from
purchased glass; glass, leaded or stained

Tarentum
Allegheny County

(G-18238)
**2000 F PROCESS HTG &
CONTRLS**
221 James E Wolfe St (15084-1711)
PHONE...................................724 224-2800
Don Antonice, *Owner*
EMP: 5
SALES (est): 694.1K Privately Held
SIC: 3823 Combustion control instruments

(G-18239)
CLARK CANDIES INC
621 E 1st Ave (15084-2005)
PHONE...................................724 226-0866
Robert Clark, *President*
EMP: 7
SQ FT: 3,600
SALES (est): 810.5K Privately Held
SIC: 2064 Chocolate candy, except solid
chocolate

(G-18240)
CYCLE SOURCE MAGAZINE
118 Dellenbaugh Rd (15084-3468)
PHONE...................................724 226-2867
Christopher Callen, *Owner*
EMP: 3 EST: 1997
SALES (est): 270.3K Privately Held
WEB: www.cyclesource.com
SIC: 2721 Periodicals

(G-18241)
DUNAY TOOL & DIE CO
2027 Bakerstown Rd (15084-2917)
PHONE...................................724 335-7972
Catherine Dunay, *President*
Robert Dunay, *Treasurer*
Richard Dunay, *Admin Sec*
EMP: 3 EST: 1960
SQ FT: 9,000
SALES (est): 431.2K Privately Held
SIC: 3544 Special dies & tools; industrial
molds

(G-18242)
ED FISH MACHING CO
Also Called: Fish Ed Machine
2627 Butler Logan Rd (15084-3707)
PHONE...................................724 224-0992
Edward L Fish, *Owner*
EMP: 8
SQ FT: 6,800
SALES (est): 1MM Privately Held
SIC: 3599 Machine shop, jobbing & repair

(G-18243)
**EVCO EMBOUCHURE
VISUALIZER CO**
120 Evco Ln (15084-3217)
P.O. Box 348 (15084-0348)
PHONE...................................724 224-4817
Erik Windows, *President*
Howard G Windows Jr, *Vice Pres*
Helen Windows, *Treasurer*
EMP: 8
SQ FT: 2,000
SALES: 430K Privately Held
SIC: 3441 Fabricated structural metal

(G-18244)
GRAY SIGN ADVERTISING
1300 Metz Rd (15084-3097)
PHONE...................................724 224-5008
Arden Verner Jr, *Owner*
EMP: 3
SQ FT: 3,200

SALES: 50K Privately Held
SIC: 3993 Electric signs

(G-18245)
HOLCIM (US) INC
445 Grantham St (15084-1321)
P.O. Box 44109, Pittsburgh (15205-0309)
PHONE...................................724 226-1449
David Nale, *Manager*
EMP: 5
SALES (corp-wide): 26.4B Privately Held
WEB: www.holcim.com/us
SIC: 3241 Portland cement
HQ: Holcim (Us) Inc.
8700 W Bryn Mawr Ave
Chicago IL 60631
773 372-1000

(G-18246)
SAM ANDREW
588 Meander Ln (15084-3378)
PHONE...................................724 224-5445
Sam Andrew, *Principal*
EMP: 3
SALES (est): 228.3K Privately Held
SIC: 3299 Architectural sculptures: gyp-
sum, clay, papier mache, etc.

(G-18247)
STACY LLOYD
Also Called: Lloyd Concrete Products
1612 Saxonburg Blvd (15084-2303)
P.O. Box 224, Curtisville (15032-0224)
PHONE...................................724 265-3445
Stacy Lloyd, *Owner*
EMP: 5
SQ FT: 6,000
SALES: 550K Privately Held
SIC: 3272 3273 Concrete products, pre-
cast; ready-mixed concrete

(G-18248)
TED VENESKY CO INC
5746 Bull Creek Rd (15084-3309)
PHONE...................................724 224-7992
Charles Venesky, *President*
EMP: 6 EST: 1976
SQ FT: 8,000
SALES: 100K Privately Held
SIC: 2441 5085 2448 Boxes, wood; in-
dustrial supplies; wood pallets & skids

(G-18249)
TRI-STATE PETROLEUM CORP
Also Called: Marathon Oil
100 E 7th Ave (15084-1511)
PHONE...................................724 226-0135
Kitty Petrak, *Branch Mgr*
EMP: 70
SALES (corp-wide): 200MM Privately
Held
SIC: 2911 Petroleum refining
PA: Tri-State Petroleum Corporation
2627 Vance Ave
Wheeling WV 26003
304 277-3232

(G-18250)
TRIB TOTAL MEDIA LLC
Also Called: Pittsburgh Tribune Review
210 Wood St (15084-1726)
PHONE...................................412 871-2301
Sandy Barancyk, *Principal*
EMP: 100
SALES (corp-wide): 157.2MM Privately
Held
SIC: 2711 Commercial printing & newspa-
per publishing combined; newspapers:
publishing only, not printed on site
PA: Trib Total Media, Llc
622 Cabin Hill Dr
Greensburg PA 15601
412 321-6460

(G-18251)
**TRIBUNE-REVIEW PUBLISHING
CO**
Also Called: Gateway Newspapers
210 Wood St (15084-1726)
PHONE...................................724 779-8742
Caroline Holland, *Principal*
EMP: 5
SALES (est): 142.7K Privately Held
SIC: 2711 Newspapers, publishing & print-
ing

(G-18252)
**UNITED BRONZE OF
PITTSBURGH**
344 W 6th Ave (15084-1304)
PHONE...................................724 226-8500
Claire Orringer, *President*
Robert Orringer, *Vice Pres*
EMP: 7 EST: 1918
SQ FT: 16,000
SALES (est): 1.2MM Privately Held
WEB: www.unitedbronzepgh.com
SIC: 3366 3365 Castings (except die):
bronze; castings (except die): brass; alu-
minum & aluminum-based alloy castings

(G-18253)
VERNERS PAINT CENTER INC
711 E 2nd Ave (15084-2003)
PHONE...................................724 224-7445
Arden H Verner Jr, *President*
EMP: 12
SQ FT: 8,000
SALES (est): 1.1MM Privately Held
SIC: 3993 Signs & advertising specialties

(G-18254)
WEEKLY SHOPPER (HQ)
Also Called: Pennysaver
210 Wood St (15084-1726)
PHONE...................................412 243-4215
Bill Weaver, *President*
Ron Wiederstein, *Vice Pres*
EMP: 100 EST: 1975
SQ FT: 13,000
SALES (est): 9.1MM
SALES (corp-wide): 37.2MM Privately
Held
WEB: www.weeklyshopper.com
SIC: 2711 Newspapers, publishing & print-
ing
PA: Gateway Publications
610 Beatty Rd Ste 2
Monroeville PA 15146
412 856-7400

(G-18255)
**WORLDWIDE REFRACTORIES
INC**
Sixth & Center Sts (15084)
P.O. Box 28 (15084-0028)
PHONE...................................724 224-8800
William K Brown, *President*
Richard Copp, *Vice Pres*
Dennis Peters, *Vice Pres*
Tim Powell, *CFO*
▲ EMP: 100
SQ FT: 165,000
SALES (est): 10.7MM
SALES (corp-wide): 216.3MM Privately
Held
WEB: www.wri-web.com
SIC: 3297 5085 3255 Brick refractories;
refractory material clay refractories
PA: Resco Products, Inc.
6600 Steubenville Pike # 1
Pittsburgh PA 15205
888 283-5505

Tatamy
Northampton County

(G-18256)
**CONSOLDATED STOR
COMPANIES INC (PA)**
Also Called: Equipto
225 Main St (18085-7059)
PHONE...................................610 253-2775
Robert Logemann, *CEO*
Helen Martin, *General Mgr*
Jeff Williams, *General Mgr*
Robert C Ammerman, *Corp Secy*
Ronnie Labar, *Prdtn Mgr*
EMP: 140
SQ FT: 2,000
SALES (est): 34.7MM Privately Held
WEB: www.equipto.com
SIC: 2542 Shelving, office & store: except
wood

(G-18257)
CONSOLDATED STOR COMPANIES INC
Also Called: Equipto
225 Main St (18085-7059)
P.O. Box 429 (18085-0429)
PHONE..................................610 253-2775
Jack Walters, *Branch Mgr*
Dennis Derr, *Manager*
EMP: 150
SQ FT: 190,000
SALES (corp-wide): 34.7MM **Privately Held**
WEB: www.equipto.com
SIC: 2542 Shelving, office & store: except wood; cabinets: show, display or storage: except wood
PA: Consolidated Storage Companies, Inc.
225 Main St
Tatamy PA 18085
610 253-2775

Taylor
Lackawanna County

(G-18258)
ARLINGTON INDUSTRIES INC
1 Stauffer Industrial Par (18517-9620)
PHONE..................................267 580-2620
Don Ambrose, *Natl Sales Mgr*
Greg Kenealy, *Branch Mgr*
EMP: 5
SALES (corp-wide): 225MM **Privately Held**
SIC: 3299 Images, small: gypsum, clay or papier mache
HQ: Arlington Industries, Inc.
1616 S Lakeside Dr
Waukegan IL 60085
847 689-2754

(G-18259)
JOHN L STOPAY LLC (PA)
Also Called: Stopay, Jon L Candies
354 N Main St (18517-1106)
PHONE..................................570 562-6541
Mark Young, *Owner*
Doug Young, *Co-Owner*
EMP: 7
SALES (est): 1.1MM **Privately Held**
SIC: 5441 2064 Candy; chocolate candy, except solid chocolate

(G-18260)
METKOTE LAMINATED PRODUCTS INC
1151 Union St (18517-1614)
PHONE..................................570 562-0107
Jay Weinstein, *CEO*
John Dormer, *President*
Michael Seigle, *Vice Pres*
EMP: 15
SQ FT: 25,000
SALES (est): 2.8MM **Privately Held**
WEB: www.metkote.com
SIC: 3399 Laminating steel

(G-18261)
SANOFI PASTEUR INC
50 Stauffer Industrial Pa (18517-9601)
PHONE..................................570 957-7187
Mike Fleming, *Branch Mgr*
EMP: 13 **Privately Held**
WEB: www.immunizingpharmacist.com
SIC: 2836 Biological products, except diagnostic
HQ: Sanofi Pasteur Inc.
1 Discovery Dr
Swiftwater PA 18370
570 839-7187

(G-18262)
TAYLOR CHEMICAL INC
Also Called: Polychemy
10 Stauffer Industrial Pa (18517-9601)
PHONE..................................570 562-7771
Tim Priest, *Manager*
EMP: 10
SQ FT: 10,000

SALES (est): 1.9MM **Privately Held**
WEB: www.snfinc.com
SIC: 2821 5169 Polymethyl methacrylate resins (plexiglass); chemicals & allied products
HQ: Snf Holding Company
1 Chemical Plant Rd
Riceboro GA 31323

(G-18263)
TAYLORED BUILDING SOLUTIONS
9 Stauffer Industrial Par (18517-9601)
PHONE..................................570 898-5361
Frank Briano, *Principal*
EMP: 4
SALES (est): 475.1K **Privately Held**
SIC: 8711 2451 Building construction consultant; mobile homes

(G-18264)
UNITED PARTNERS LTD
Also Called: Times Printing
27 Stauffer Industrial Pa (18517-9601)
PHONE..................................570 288-7603
EMP: 19
SALES (corp-wide): 2.6MM **Privately Held**
SIC: 2752 2791 Commercial printing, offset; typesetting
PA: United Partners, Ltd.
27 Stauffer Industrial Pa
Taylor PA 18517
570 283-0995

(G-18265)
UNITED PARTNERS LTD (PA)
Also Called: PDQ Print Center
27 Stauffer Industrial Pa (18517-9601)
PHONE..................................570 283-0995
David J Price, *President*
William F Gavigan, *Exec VP*
Norma White, *Admin Asst*
EMP: 7
SQ FT: 6,000
SALES (est): 2.6MM **Privately Held**
SIC: 3823 2752 Digital displays of process variables; commercial printing, offset

---

Telford
Montgomery County

(G-18266)
ACTIVE BRASS FOUNDRY INC
330 Progress Dr (18969-1143)
PHONE..................................215 257-6519
Arthur Nissen, *President*
Roslyn Nissen, *Corp Secy*
Jill Nissen, *Vice Pres*
EMP: 14 EST: 1958
SQ FT: 20,000
SALES (est): 1.9MM **Privately Held**
SIC: 3365 3366 Aluminum & aluminum-based alloy castings; castings (except die): brass

(G-18267)
AMPLIFIER SOLUTIONS CORP
Also Called: A S C
3009 Old State Rd (18969-1058)
PHONE..................................215 799-2561
Vince Nguyen, *President*
Brett Trump, *Manager*
EMP: 15
SQ FT: 2,500
SALES (est): 2.8MM **Privately Held**
SIC: 3663 Amplifiers, RF power & IF

(G-18268)
AXCENTRIA PHARMACEUTICAL LLC
306 Keystone Dr (18969-1117)
PHONE..................................215 453-5055
David Simpson, *VP Bus Dvlpt*
David Singh,
▲ EMP: 10
SQ FT: 30,000
SALES (est): 2.4MM **Privately Held**
SIC: 2834 Syrups, pharmaceutical; tablets, pharmaceutical

(G-18269)
CARL E REICHERT CORP
Also Called: Creative Forge
4120 Bethlehem Pike (18969-1127)
PHONE..................................215 723-9525
John Baldwin, *President*
Elmer Brunk, *Director*
EMP: 6
SQ FT: 2,500
SALES (est): 640K **Privately Held**
WEB: www.creativeforge.com
SIC: 3441 3446 Fabricated structural metal; architectural metalwork

(G-18270)
CASE DESIGN CORPORATION
333 School Ln (18969-2047)
PHONE..................................215 703-0130
Roger Ernst, *President*
Alan R Ernst, *Vice Pres*
Paul Lowman, *Vice Pres*
Margaret Lorenz, *Treasurer*
Alan Ernst, *Manager*
▲ EMP: 83 EST: 1920
SQ FT: 80,000
SALES (est): 4.1MM **Privately Held**
WEB: www.casedesigncorp.com
SIC: 3161 Cases, carrying

(G-18271)
CASE DESIGN CORPORATION
333 School Ln (18969-2047)
PHONE..................................800 847-4176
Fax: 215 703-0139
▲ EMP: 4
SALES (est): 114.1K **Privately Held**
SIC: 3161 Luggage

(G-18272)
CECO FILTERS INC (DH)
Also Called: Mefiag Filtration
700 Emlen Way (18969-1773)
PHONE..................................215 723-8155
Philip Detwirek, *Ch of Bd*
Matt Lee, *Director*
Hilary A Taub, *Admin Sec*
▲ EMP: 14 EST: 1974
SQ FT: 38,000
SALES (est): 3.1MM
SALES (corp-wide): 337.3MM **Publicly Held**
WEB: www.cecofilters.com
SIC: 3564 Filters, air: furnaces, air conditioning equipment, etc.
HQ: Ceco Group, Inc.
4625 Red Bank Rd Ste 200
Cincinnati OH 45227
513 458-2600

(G-18273)
CHANTELAU INC
3225 Meetinghouse Rd (18969-1061)
PHONE..................................215 723-1383
George Chantelau, *President*
EMP: 12
SQ FT: 10,700
SALES (est): 1.6MM **Privately Held**
WEB: www.chantelau.com
SIC: 3599 Machine shop, jobbing & repair

(G-18274)
CMW TECHNOLOGIES INC
Also Called: Cmw Stainless
841 Tech Dr (18969-1183)
PHONE..................................215 721-5824
Joseph Zero Jr, *CEO*
Joseph T Zero Sr, *Shareholder*
Barbara Vesay, *Admin Sec*
EMP: 15
SQ FT: 250,000
SALES (est): 1MM **Privately Held**
SIC: 3449 Bars, concrete reinforcing: fabricated steel

(G-18275)
COCKER-WEBER BRUSH CO
104 E Broad St (18969-1731)
P.O. Box 97 (18969-0097)
PHONE..................................215 723-3880
Lewis A Daniels Sr, *President*
EMP: 10 EST: 1892
SQ FT: 8,000
SALES: 559.9K **Privately Held**
SIC: 3991 Brushes, household or industrial

(G-18276)
CONTEMPRARY ARTISANS CABINETRY
1020 Revenue Dr (18969-1072)
PHONE..................................215 723-8803
Peter Hanson, *President*
Joe Walsh, *Project Mgr*
▼ EMP: 23
SALES (est): 3MM **Privately Held**
SIC: 2521 2434 2431 Cabinets, office: wood; wood kitchen cabinets; millwork

(G-18277)
CORNERSTONE AUTOMATION LLC
Also Called: KEYSTONE CHARGE
112 Moyer Rd (18969-1523)
PHONE..................................215 513-4111
Alan Ferrin, *Mng Member*
Valerie Ferrin,
EMP: 6
SQ FT: 260
SALES: 1.1MM **Privately Held**
SIC: 3829 Measuring & controlling devices

(G-18278)
COUNTRY CREEK WINERY
Also Called: Country Creek Winery Orchards
133 Cressman Rd (18969-1504)
PHONE..................................215 723-6516
Doug Killian, *Partner*
Donna Killian, *Partner*
Joy Klein, *Partner*
EMP: 3
SQ FT: 5,000
SALES (est): 205.1K **Privately Held**
SIC: 2084 Wines

(G-18279)
DALTON PAVILLIONS INC
3120 Commerce Dr (18969-1052)
PHONE..................................215 721-1492
James E Dalton, *President*
Glenn Dalton, *Treasurer*
Gerald Dalton, *Admin Sec*
EMP: 9 EST: 1970
SQ FT: 20,000
SALES (est): 1.2MM **Privately Held**
WEB: www.daltonpavilions.com
SIC: 2452 Prefabricated buildings, wood

(G-18280)
DATALOGIC USA INC
511 School House Rd (18969-1148)
PHONE..................................215 723-0981
Valentina Volta, *President*
Bradley Gruss, *Engineer*
Stuart Britland, *Accounts Mgr*
Chris Jones, *Accounts Mgr*
Jacques Glemaud, *Accounts Exec*
EMP: 260 **Privately Held**
SIC: 3577 Optical scanning devices; input/output equipment, computer
HQ: Datalogic Usa, Inc.
959 Terry St
Eugene OR 97402
541 683-5700

(G-18281)
DRAEGER INC
3135 Quarry Rd (18969-1042)
PHONE..................................215 721-5400
Michael Vintis, *Project Engr*
Vasudev Menon, *Controller*
Hirendra Chatterjee, *Sales Dir*
Markus Peter, *VP Mktg*
Ali Pourrad, *VP Mktg*
EMP: 17 **Privately Held**
SIC: 3841 Anesthesia apparatus
HQ: Draeger, Inc.
3135 Quarry Rd
Telford PA 18969
215 721-5400

(G-18282)
DRAEGER INC
3124 Commerce Dr (18969-1052)
PHONE..................................215 660-2252
Glenn Clark, *Principal*
EMP: 10 **Privately Held**
SIC: 3841 Anesthesia apparatus
HQ: Draeger, Inc.
3135 Quarry Rd
Telford PA 18969
215 721-5400

(G-18283)
DRAEGER MEDICAL SYSTEMS INC (DH)
3135 Quarry Rd (18969-1051)
PHONE...................................800 437-2437
Stefan Drager, *Ch of Bd*
Ruben Derderian, *President*
▲ EMP: 198
SQ FT: 80,000
SALES (est): 47.2MM Privately Held
SIC: 3841 Anesthesia apparatus
HQ: Draeger, Inc.
3135 Quarry Rd
Telford PA 18969
215 721-5400

(G-18284)
DREISTERN INC
801 Tech Dr (18969-1183)
PHONE...................................215 799-0220
Thomas Krueckels, *President*
Werner Wasmer, *Vice Pres*
Franz Liebler, *Engineer*
▲ EMP: 5
SQ FT: 3,500
SALES: 8.7MM
SALES (corp-wide): 45.3MM Privately
Held
WEB: www.dreistern.com
SIC: 3542 5051 Spinning, spline rolling &
winding machines; iron & steel (ferrous)
products
PA: Dreistern Gmbh & Co. Kg
Wiechser Str. 9
Schopfheim 79650
762 239-10

(G-18285)
DRILLMASTERS LLC
712 Ridge Rd (18969-1447)
P.O. Box 73, Tylersport (18971-0073)
PHONE...................................717 319-8657
Timothy Miller,
EMP: 4
SALES (est): 674.8K Privately Held
SIC: 1381 Service well drilling

(G-18286)
EAST COAST HOIST INC
105 Keystone Dr (18969-1013)
PHONE...................................215 646-2336
Ted Harrison, *President*
James Kehan, *Vice Pres*
▲ EMP: 99
SQ FT: 400
SALES (est): 24MM Privately Held
WEB: www.harrisonhoist.com
SIC: 3536 Hoists, cranes & monorails

(G-18287)
EMC GLOBAL TECHNOLOGIES INC (PA)
Also Called: E M C
1060 Revenue Dr (18969-1072)
PHONE...................................267 347-5100
Jay R Johnson, *President*
Eric A Cindrich, *Vice Pres*
EMP: 10
SQ FT: 16,000
SALES (est): 7MM Privately Held
WEB: www.emcgti.com
SIC: 3589 3599 3544 2448 Commercial
cleaning equipment; machine shop, job-
bing & repair; special dies, tools, jigs &
fixtures; wood pallets & skids

(G-18288)
EUREKA STONE QUARRY INC
451 E Reliance Rd (18969-1867)
P.O. Box 217, Southampton (18966-0217)
PHONE...................................215 723-9801
Joe Guld, *Manager*
EMP: 8
SQ FT: 6,000
SALES (corp-wide): 24.4MM Privately
Held
SIC: 3273 Ready-mixed concrete
PA: Eureka Stone Quarry, Inc.
Lower Stte Pickertown Rds
Chalfont PA 18914
215 822-0593

(G-18289)
FLUID ENERGY PROC & EQP CO (PA)
4300 Bethlehem Pike (18969-1131)
PHONE...................................215 721-8990
Patricia Stephanoff, *President*
Steven G Baxter, *Vice Pres*
W Rodzewich, *Engineer*
Nancy Malloy, *Accountant*
▲ EMP: 6 EST: 1955
SQ FT: 2,942
SALES (est): 16.4MM Privately Held
WEB: www.fluidenergype.com
SIC: 3599 3295 3559 Grinding castings
for the trade; minerals, ground or treated;
stone working machinery

(G-18290)
FRES-CO SYSTEMS USA INC (DH)
Also Called: Termalock
3005 State Rd (18969-1021)
PHONE...................................215 721-4600
Tullio Vigano, *President*
Lawrence Ashton, *Senior VP*
◆ EMP: 290
SQ FT: 200,000
SALES (est): 221.6MM
SALES (corp-wide): 177.9K Privately
Held
WEB: www.fresco.com
SIC: 5084 3565 2891 Packaging machin-
ery & equipment; packaging machinery;
adhesives & sealants
HQ: Goglio Spa
Via Andrea Solari 0010
Milano MI 20144
024 804-31

(G-18291)
GARY EDWARD SODEN
Also Called: Montgomery Cnty Womans
Newsppr
133 Winding Way (18969-2164)
PHONE...................................215 723-5964
Gary E Soden, *Owner*
EMP: 3
SALES (est): 115.9K Privately Held
SIC: 2711 Newspapers: publishing only,
not printed on site

(G-18292)
GEITZ MACHINE INC
4422 Bethlehem Pike (18969-1133)
PHONE...................................215 257-6752
Mark M Geitz, *President*
Barbara Geitz, *Vice Pres*
Marianne Geitz, *Admin Sec*
EMP: 8
SQ FT: 600
SALES (est): 1.2MM Privately Held
WEB: www.geitzmachine.com
SIC: 3599 Machine shop, jobbing & repair

(G-18293)
H D SAMPEY INC
115 S Main St (18969-1895)
PHONE...................................215 723-3471
Arlin Moyer, *President*
Donna Moyer, *Corp Secy*
EMP: 5 EST: 1928
SQ FT: 2,400
SALES (est): 715.6K Privately Held
SIC: 3555 3599 Printing trades machinery;
machine shop, jobbing & repair

(G-18294)
HPI PROCESSES INC
Also Called: H P I
1030 Revenue Dr (18969-1072)
PHONE...................................215 799-0450
Joseph Jacob, *President*
Mary Jacob, *Exec Dir*
EMP: 8
SQ FT: 41,502
SALES: 100K Privately Held
WEB: www.hpicleaningsystems.com
SIC: 5162 3443 Plastics materials; tanks,
lined: metal plate

(G-18295)
HYDRO INSTRUMENTS INC
600 Emlen Way (18969-1772)
PHONE...................................215 799-0980
John Messina, *President*

David Morgan, *Owner*
Gregory Sell, *Consultant*
Brad Snow, *Director*
▲ EMP: 20
SQ FT: 27,500
SALES (est): 3.4MM Privately Held
WEB: www.hydroinstruments.com
SIC: 3823 Water quality monitoring & con-
trol systems

(G-18296)
INNOVATIVE FINISHERS INC
871 Tech Dr (18969-1183)
PHONE...................................215 536-2222
EMP: 9
SALES (est): 1MM Privately Held
SIC: 3479 Coating of metals & formed
products

(G-18297)
J&M FLUIDICS INC
851 Tech Dr (18969-1183)
PHONE...................................888 539-1731
Jim Meiler, *President*
EMP: 9
SALES: 3MM Privately Held
SIC: 3585 Refrigeration & heating equip-
ment

(G-18298)
KDC ENGINEERING
500 Emlen Way (18969-1781)
PHONE...................................267 203-8487
Daniel Carlin, *Principal*
EMP: 3
SALES (est): 272.3K Privately Held
SIC: 3546 3545 3544 Power-driven hand-
tools; machine tool accessories; special
dies & tools

(G-18299)
KEYSTONE FINDINGS INC
Emlen Way (18969)
PHONE...................................215 723-4600
Richard Frederick, *President*
Kurt Morton, *Vice Pres*
EMP: 75
SQ FT: 28,000
SALES (est): 8.3MM Privately Held
WEB: www.keystonefindings.com
SIC: 3915 Jewelers' materials & lapidary
work

(G-18300)
KUTZNER MANUFACTURING INDS INC
3255 Meetinghouse Rd (18969-1061)
PHONE...................................215 721-1712
Paul Renninger, *President*
Carly Kuebler, *Info Tech Mgr*
EMP: 20
SALES (est): 838.8K Privately Held
SIC: 3444 7692 3599 Ducts, sheet metal;
automotive welding; crankshafts &
camshafts, machining

(G-18301)
M&M STONE CO
2840 Clymer Ave Ste 100 (18969-1000)
PHONE...................................215 723-1177
William G Carpenter, *Ch of Bd*
Brian L Carpenter, *President*
Regina S Carpenter, *Corp Secy*
Gary M Carpenter, *Vice Pres*
EMP: 60
SQ FT: 4,000
SALES (est): 8.4MM Privately Held
WEB: www.mmstone.net
SIC: 1411 2951 Dimension stone; asphalt
& asphaltic paving mixtures (not from re-
fineries)

(G-18302)
MERRILL Y LANDIS LTD
20 S 3rd St (18969-2001)
P.O. Box 249 (18969-0249)
PHONE...................................215 723-8177
Steven Landis, *CEO*
Linda Maiers, *Corp Secy*
EMP: 65
SQ FT: 75,000
SALES: 3MM Privately Held
WEB: www.mylltd.com
SIC: 2391 Curtains & draperies

(G-18303)
MET-PRO TECHNOLOGIES LLC
Keystone Filter Division
700 Emlen Way (18969-1773)
PHONE...................................215 822-1963
Sonja Haggert, *Vice Pres*
Robert Remick, *Prdtn Mgr*
EMP: 25
SALES (corp-wide): 337.3MM Publicly
Held
WEB: www.met-pro.com
SIC: 3569 5085 3564 Filters; industrial
supplies; blowers & fans
HQ: Met-Pro Technologies Llc
4625 Red Bank Rd
Cincinnati OH 45227
513 458-2600

(G-18304)
MET-PRO TECHNOLOGIES LLC
Fybroc Division
700 Emlen Way (18969-1773)
PHONE...................................215 723-4700
Jerry D'Alterio, *Manager*
EMP: 65
SQ FT: 8,000
SALES (corp-wide): 337.3MM Publicly
Held
WEB: www.met-pro.com
SIC: 3561 Pumps & pumping equipment
HQ: Met-Pro Technologies Llc
4625 Red Bank Rd
Cincinnati OH 45227
513 458-2600

(G-18305)
MET-PRO TECHNOLOGIES LLC
Also Called: Sethco
700 Emlen Way (18969-1773)
PHONE...................................215 723-8155
Gennaro Alterio, *Branch Mgr*
EMP: 52
SALES (corp-wide): 337.3MM Publicly
Held
SIC: 3564 Air cleaning systems
HQ: Met-Pro Technologies Llc
4625 Red Bank Rd
Cincinnati OH 45227
513 458-2600

(G-18306)
OLDCASTLE PRECAST INC
Also Called: Oldcastle Prcast Modular Group
200 Keystone Dr (18969-1115)
PHONE...................................215 257-8081
Michael Grapsy- Rotondo, *President*
Roxanne Grimmer, *General Mgr*
EMP: 150
SQ FT: 22,000
SALES (corp-wide): 29.7B Privately Held
WEB: www.oldcastle-precast.com
SIC: 3272 3448 3441 Concrete products,
precast; prefabricated metal buildings;
fabricated structural metal
HQ: Oldcastle Infrastructure, Inc.
1002 15th St Sw Ste 110
Auburn WA 98001
253 833-2777

(G-18307)
OLDCASTLE PRECAST INC
200 Keystone Dr (18969-1115)
P.O. Box 210 (18969-0210)
PHONE...................................215 257-2255
David Steeven, *President*
Charlie Umland, *Purch Mgr*
Keith Shirey, *Director*
EMP: 25
SALES (corp-wide): 29.7B Privately Held
WEB: www.oldcastle-precast.com
SIC: 3272 Precast terrazo or concrete
products
HQ: Oldcastle Infrastructure, Inc.
1002 15th St Sw Ste 110
Auburn WA 98001
253 833-2777

(G-18308)
PATRIOT ARMORY & COATINGS LLC
1000 Revenue Dr (18969-1072)
PHONE...................................215 723-7228
Darrin Baughman, *Principal*
EMP: 4 EST: 2014
SQ FT: 5,400

SALES (est): 252.7K **Privately Held**
SIC: 3479 Painting, coating & hot dipping

(G-18309)
PLANTATION CANDIES INC
4224 Bethlehem Pike (18969-1129)
PHONE..........................215 723-6810
Charles P Crawford Jr, *President*
John P Crawford, *Vice Pres*
EMP: 15
SQ FT: 25,000
SALES (est): 1.6MM **Privately Held**
WEB: www.plantationcandies.com
SIC: 2064 Nuts, candy covered

(G-18310)
PROBEE SAFETY LLC
320 N Main St (18969-1956)
PHONE..........................302 893-0258
Daniel Shirley, *CEO*
Robert McGurk, *COO*
EMP: 3
SALES (est): 139.9K **Privately Held**
SIC: 3669 7389 Signaling apparatus, electric;

(G-18311)
RAY DERSTINE
Also Called: Derstine's Custom Embroidery
76 Hunsberger Rd (18969-1510)
PHONE..........................215 723-6573
Ray Derstine, *Owner*
EMP: 4
SALES: 600K **Privately Held**
SIC: 2395 Embroidery products, except
schiffli machine

(G-18312)
SANAVITA MEDICAL LLC
551 E Church Ave (18969-1727)
PHONE..........................267 517-3220
EMP: 4
SALES (est): 126.1K **Privately Held**
SIC: 3829 Measuring & controlling devices

(G-18313)
SCOTT H PAYNE (PA)
Also Called: Payne Engineering Sales
26 Orchard Cir (18969-1852)
P.O. Box 389 (18969-0389)
PHONE..........................215 723-0510
H Scott Payne, *Owner*
EMP: 3
SALES (est): 240.9K **Privately Held**
SIC: 3053 5085 Gaskets & sealing devices; gaskets & seals

(G-18314)
SECANT GROUP LLC (DH)
551 E Church Ave (18969-1727)
PHONE..........................877 774-2835
Jeff Robertson, *President*
John Dottavio, *Vice Pres*
Jim Sokolas, *Mfg Mgr*
Bryan Parker, *Engineer*
Thomas Dertoucos, *CFO*
▲ **EMP:** 140 **EST:** 1975
SQ FT: 87,000
SALES (est): 24.4MM
SALES (corp-wide): 855.1MM **Privately
Held**
WEB: www.prodesco.com
SIC: 2299 Batting, wadding, padding & fillings

(G-18315)
**SHELLY ENTERPRISES -US LBM
LLC (DH)**
3110 Old State Rd (18969-1031)
PHONE..........................215 723-5108
P Gregory Shelly,
Willard Shelly,
EMP: 65
SALES (est): 64.6MM
SALES (corp-wide): 2B **Privately Held**
SIC: 5211 2431 2439 Lumber products;
millwork; trusses, except roof: laminated
lumber; trusses, wooden roof

(G-18316)
SOLAR TRANSFORMERS INC
Also Called: Magnetic Specialties
174 Keystone Dr (18969-1012)
PHONE..........................267 384-5231
William R Jones, *President*
Michael Afflerbach, *President*

Myrle E Jones, *Treasurer*
EMP: 14
SQ FT: 10,500
SALES (est): 3.3MM **Privately Held**
WEB: www.magspecinc.com
SIC: 3679 Electronic loads & power supplies

(G-18317)
SPECIALTY SNACKS INC
Also Called: Great American Popcorn Works
336 W Broad St (18969-1931)
PHONE..........................215 721-0414
Steve Fleischer, *President*
EMP: 5
SALES: 1MM **Privately Held**
SIC: 2064 Popcorn balls or other treated
popcorn products

(G-18318)
**SPECTRUM DEVICES
CORPORATION**
3009a Old State Rd (18969-1058)
PHONE..........................215 997-7870
Jere Hohmann, *President*
Jere W Hohmann, *President*
Benedict Caccavale, *General Mgr*
Ben Caccavale, *Vice Pres*
Robert Blake, *VP Sls/Mktg*
▼ **EMP:** 6
SQ FT: 5,000
SALES: 200K **Privately Held**
WEB: www.spectrumdevices.com
SIC: 3674 Semiconductors & related devices

(G-18319)
SPRINGER PUMPS LLC
861 Tech Dr (18969-1183)
P.O. Box 269 (18969-0269)
PHONE..........................484 949-2900
Rick Springer,
EMP: 12
SALES: 4MM **Privately Held**
SIC: 3561 Industrial pumps & parts

(G-18320)
STAIRWORKS INC
811 Tech Dr (18969-1183)
PHONE..........................215 703-0823
Wayne E Johnston, *President*
Doug Gehman, *Vice Pres*
Brian Lambert, *Admin Sec*
▲ **EMP:** 20
SQ FT: 22,500
SALES (est): 4.3MM **Privately Held**
SIC: 2431 Millwork

(G-18321)
STROBIC AIR CORPORATION
Also Called: Metpro Fybroc Division
700 Emlen Way (18969-1773)
PHONE..........................215 723-4700
Raymond Dehont, *President*
Gary Morgan, *Treasurer*
◆ **EMP:** 10
SQ FT: 60,000
SALES (est): 18.2MM
SALES (corp-wide): 29.6MM **Privately
Held**
WEB: www.strobicair.com
SIC: 3564 3822 3714 Blowers & fans;
auto controls regulating residntl & coml
environmt & applncs; motor vehicle parts
& accessories
PA: Cincinnati Fan & Ventilator Company,
Inc.
7697 Snider Rd
Mason OH 45040
513 573-1000

(G-18322)
**TENNETT MANUFACTURING
INC**
3205 Meetinghouse Rd (18969-1061)
PHONE..........................215 721-3803
Dale R Tennett, *President*
Elizabeth Tennett, *Manager*
EMP: 10
SQ FT: 7,000
SALES: 1.7MM **Privately Held**
WEB: www.tennettmfg.com
SIC: 3599 Machine shop, jobbing & repair

(G-18323)
TIGER PRINTING GROUP LLC
65 W Madison Ave (18969-2026)
PHONE..........................215 799-0500
Craig Lindsay,
Bruce Pedersen,
EMP: 25
SALES (est): 4.5MM **Privately Held**
WEB: www.tigerpg.com
SIC: 2752 Commercial printing, lithographic

(G-18324)
VMD MACHINE CO INC
4304 Bethlehem Pike (18969-1131)
PHONE..........................215 723-7782
Vinicio D'Allesio, *President*
EMP: 12
SQ FT: 4,200
SALES (est): 1.6MM **Privately Held**
SIC: 3491 Automatic regulating & control
valves; valves, automatic control

(G-18325)
**WARGO INTERIOR SYSTEMS
INC**
416 School House Rd 1 (18969-1145)
PHONE..........................215 723-6200
Paul K Fetch, *President*
Frank Genghini, *Vice Pres*
Jim Lynch, *CFO*
Timothy M Jeremeciz, *Treasurer*
EMP: 55
SQ FT: 22,200
SALES (est): 10.2MM **Privately Held**
WEB: www.wargointerior.com
SIC: 2452 1742 Prefabricated wood buildings; acoustical & ceiling work

---

Temple
Berks County

(G-18326)
COBRA ANCHORS CORP
504 Mount Laurel Ave (19560-1410)
PHONE..........................610 929-5764
Pierre McDuff, *President*
William Crossley, *Vice Pres*
Andre Jauron, *Vice Pres*
Richard Labelle, *Vice Pres*
▲ **EMP:** 65
SQ FT: 66,000
SALES (est): 13.1MM **Privately Held**
SIC: 3429 3462 3452 Manufactured hardware (general); iron & steel forgings;
bolts, nuts, rivets & washers

(G-18327)
DAVID SEIDEL
Also Called: Metal Service
4700 5th Street Hwy # 101 (19560-1457)
PHONE..........................610 921-8310
David A Seidel, *Owner*
EMP: 10
SQ FT: 25,000
SALES: 1.2MM **Privately Held**
WEB: www.davidseidel.com
SIC: 3441 3444 Fabricated structural
metal; sheet metalwork

(G-18328)
DOELLKEN- WOODTAPE INC
141 Beacon Hill Rd (19560-9404)
PHONE..........................610 929-1910
EMP: 6
SQ FT: 96,000
SALES (est): 637.6K **Privately Held**
SIC: 2431 2621 5031 Mfg Millwork Paper
Mill Whol Lumber/Plywood/Millwork

(G-18329)
FABRICON INC
Also Called: Trimmaster
4860 5th Street Hwy (19560-1406)
PHONE..........................610 921-0203
Carl Knutsen, *President*
William G Koch, *Corp Secy*
John Shubeck, *Controller*
EMP: 50
SQ FT: 66,000

SALES (est): 12.3MM **Privately Held**
WEB: www.trimmaster.com
SIC: 3441 3599 3444 Fabricated structural metal; machine shop, jobbing & repair; sheet metalwork

(G-18330)
**GARL MACHINE & FABRICATION
INC**
1000 Midway Ave (19560-1947)
PHONE..........................610 929-7886
Joseph Garl, *President*
Heather Garl, *Corp Secy*
EMP: 3
SQ FT: 4,700
SALES: 250K **Privately Held**
WEB: www.garlmachine.com
SIC: 3559 Frame straighteners, automobile
(garage equipment)

(G-18331)
K D HOME & GARDEN INC
Also Called: Fehl's Home & Garden
5369 Allentown Pike (19560-1257)
PHONE..........................610 929-5794
Robert D Fehl, *President*
Marcia Fehl, *Corp Secy*
Kurt Fehl, *Vice Pres*
Ron Hix, *Sales Mgr*
Scott Adams, *Associate*
EMP: 15
SQ FT: 26,200
SALES: 2.7MM **Privately Held**
WEB: www.fehls.com
SIC: 5712 5261 3089 Outdoor & garden
furniture; lawn & garden equipment; lawn
& garden supplies; fences, gates & accessories: plastic

(G-18332)
KINTECO INC
Also Called: Kinteco Screen Printing
4434 Kutztown Rd (19560-1841)
PHONE..........................610 921-1494
Karen Phillips, *President*
Mary Ocetnik, *Vice Pres*
Joseph Ocetnik Sr, *Treasurer*
EMP: 7
SQ FT: 2,400
SALES: 750K **Privately Held**
WEB: www.kinteco.com
SIC: 2396 5199 Screen printing on fabric
articles; advertising specialties

(G-18333)
MONTEREY MUSHROOMS INC
1108 Beaumont Ave (19560-1603)
PHONE..........................610 929-1961
Fax: 610 929-3288
EMP: 15
SALES (corp-wide): 815.5MM **Privately
Held**
SIC: 2034 Mfg Dehydrated Fruits/Vegetables
PA: Monterey Mushrooms, Inc.
260 Westgate Dr
Watsonville CA 95076
831 763-5300

(G-18334)
ONTELAUNEE FARMS INC
5379 Allentown Pike (19560-1257)
P.O. Box 219 (19560-0219)
PHONE..........................610 929-5753
Albert Gaspari, *CEO*
David A Carroll, *President*
Thomas Versagli, *Corp Secy*
John Majewski, *Vice Pres*
▲ **EMP:** 31
SALES (est): 6.9MM **Privately Held**
SIC: 2875 Compost

(G-18335)
**PHILADELPHIA SHUTTER
COMPANY**
4700 5th Street Hwy # 100 (19560-1460)
PHONE..........................610 685-2344
Jonathan Ebling, *President*
EMP: 3
SQ FT: 4,000
SALES (est): 607.5K **Privately Held**
WEB: www.philadelphiashutters.com
SIC: 2431 Blinds (shutters), wood

(G-18336)
SMITH-FREEMAN & ASSOCIATES
4900 Kutztown Rd Ste Frnt (19560-1594)
PHONE..................................610 929-5728
Lucille Freeman, *Partner*
Eleanor Smith, *Partner*
EMP: 14
SALES (est): 1MM Privately Held
SIC: 2721 Trade journals: publishing only, not printed on site

(G-18337)
SQUARE WHEEL INC
80 Irish Mountain Rd (19560-9770)
PHONE..................................610 921-8561
Joseph R Butchko, *President*
Olga M Butchko, *Vice Pres*
Mary Beth Butchko, *Manager*
EMP: 3
SALES (est): 296.9K Privately Held
WEB: www.trailertester.com
SIC: 3825 Test equipment for electronic & electric measurement

(G-18338)
STEWARTS FABRICATION INC
4927 Commerce St (19560-1623)
PHONE..................................610 921-1600
Russ Stewart, *President*
EMP: 4
SQ FT: 2,800
SALES: 200K Privately Held
SIC: 3444 Sheet metalwork

Terre Hill
Lancaster County

(G-18339)
TERRE HILL SILO COMPANY INC (PA)
Also Called: Terre Hill Concrete Products
485 Weaverland Valley Rd (17581)
PHONE..................................717 445-3100
A Eugene Martin Jr, *President*
Scott Burkhart, *Mfg Staff*
Dale Wiest, *Treasurer*
Dale Weiste, *Controller*
Ron Cozzone, *Credit Mgr*
EMP: 40
SQ FT: 30,000
SALES: 20MM Privately Held
WEB: www.terrehill.com
SIC: 3272 Concrete products, precast; tanks, concrete

(G-18340)
WOOD CREATIONS LLC
125 W Main St (17581)
P.O. Box 87 (17581-0087)
PHONE..................................717 445-7007
Robert Sauder,
Jay Sauder,
EMP: 3
SALES: 560K Privately Held
SIC: 2434 Wood kitchen cabinets

Thomasville
York County

(G-18341)
MARTINS POTATO CHIPS INC (PA)
5847 Lincoln Hwy W (17364-9796)
P.O. Box 28 (17364-0028)
PHONE..................................717 792-3065
Kenneth A Potter Jr, *President*
David J Potter, *Vice Pres*
Steven Fitz, *Treasurer*
▲ EMP: 150
SQ FT: 78,000
SALES (est): 47.3MM Privately Held
WEB: www.martinschips.com
SIC: 2096 5145 2099 Potato chips & other potato-based snacks; pretzels; food preparations

(G-18342)
PENNSY SUPPLY INC
Also Called: Oldcastle Industrial Minerals
550 S Biesecker Rd (17364-9699)
PHONE..................................717 792-2631
Don Shearer, *Manager*
EMP: 85
SALES (corp-wide): 29.7B Privately Held
SIC: 3273 Ready-mixed concrete
HQ: Pennsy Supply, Inc.
1001 Paxton St
Harrisburg PA 17104
717 233-4511

(G-18343)
WALNUT BURL WOODMILL
87 N Ridge Rd (17364-9260)
PHONE..................................717 259-8479
Jeff Weaver, *Owner*
EMP: 3
SALES (est): 210K Privately Held
SIC: 2434 Wood kitchen cabinets

(G-18344)
YORK BUILDING PRODUCTS CO INC
Also Called: Lincoln Stone
Rr 30 (17364)
P.O. Box 241 (17364-0241)
PHONE..................................717 792-9922
Eric Riddle, *Manager*
EMP: 15
SALES (corp-wide): 56.4MM Privately Held
SIC: 1422 Limestones, ground
PA: York Building Products Co., Inc.
950 Smile Way
York PA 17404
717 848-2831

(G-18345)
YORK BUILDING PRODUCTS CO INC
Also Called: Workrite Packaged Cement Pdts
5799 Lincoln Hwy W (17364-9506)
P.O. Box 206 (17364-0206)
PHONE..................................717 792-4700
Robert Stuwart, *Principal*
EMP: 10
SALES (corp-wide): 56.4MM Privately Held
SIC: 3271 Concrete block & brick
PA: York Building Products Co., Inc.
950 Smile Way
York PA 17404
717 848-2831

Thompson
Susquehanna County

(G-18346)
ROCK CREEK LUMBER
232 State Route 2036 (18465-9104)
PHONE..................................570 756-2909
Donald Twining, *Partner*
Anthony Price, *Partner*
EMP: 13 EST: 1991
SALES: 1.3MM Privately Held
SIC: 2421 Sawmills & planing mills, general

Thompsontown
Juniata County

(G-18347)
KLINGLER INCORPORATED
Also Called: Agronomy Center, The
12039 William Penn Hwy (17094-8647)
PHONE..................................717 535-5151
Richard Bucher, *President*
Ivonne Bucher, *Corp Secy*
EMP: 6
SQ FT: 3,500
SALES (est): 1MM Privately Held
WEB: www.klingler.net
SIC: 2875 Fertilizers, mixing only

(G-18348)
LOCUST RUN PALLET LLC
299 Jonestown Rd (17094-8545)
PHONE..................................717 535-5883
Emery Younder,
EMP: 16
SALES (est): 2.4MM Privately Held
SIC: 2448 Pallets, wood

(G-18349)
MARILYN STRAWSER BEAUTY SALON
Rr 1 (17094)
P.O. Box 1 (17094-0001)
PHONE..................................717 463-2804
Marilyn Strawser, *Owner*
EMP: 4
SALES (est): 185.4K Privately Held
SIC: 4226 3546 1711 5999 Special warehousing & storage; saws & sawing equipment; heating systems repair & maintenance; engine & motor equipment & supplies; engines, gasoline; beauty shops

(G-18350)
PANNEBAKER HOLDINGS INC
758 Johnstown Rd (17094)
P.O. Box 187 (17094-0187)
PHONE..................................717 463-3615
Matthew L Pannebaker, *President*
Paul T Pannebaker, *Corp Secy*
Bruce Nussbaum, *Sales Dir*
EMP: 80
SQ FT: 35,000
SALES (est): 10.6MM
SALES (corp-wide): 314.2MM Privately Held
WEB: www.teddwood.com
SIC: 2434 Wood kitchen cabinets
HQ: Executive Cabinetry, Llc
2838 Grandview Dr
Simpsonville SC 29680

(G-18351)
SENSENIG CHAIR SHOP
Rr 1 (17094)
PHONE..................................717 463-3480
Leonard E Sensenig, *Partner*
Jonathan Sensenig, *Partner*
Joseph Sensenig, *Partner*
Nathaniel Sensenig, *Partner*
Aaron Sensening, *Partner*
EMP: 4
SQ FT: 9,000
SALES (est): 220K Privately Held
SIC: 2511 Dining room furniture: wood

(G-18352)
TEDD WOOD LLC
758 Johnstown Rd (17094)
PHONE..................................717 463-3615
David Romeo, *CEO*
Matthew L Pannebaker, *President*
Doug Gano, *CFO*
EMP: 95 EST: 2013
SQ FT: 135,000
SALES: 14.8MM Privately Held
SIC: 2434 Wood kitchen cabinets

Thorndale
Chester County

(G-18353)
BRAMPTON ENTP & DESIGN LLC
332 Garden View Dr (19372-1171)
PHONE..................................484 678-4855
Derek Steinbach, *Principal*
EMP: 4
SALES (est): 359K Privately Held
SIC: 2431 Millwork

(G-18354)
CELLMYLIGHT INC
315 Municipal Dr (19372-1023)
P.O. Box 72573 (19372-0573)
PHONE..................................800 575-5913
John Lafferty, *CEO*
Jennifer Lafferty, *Vice Pres*
EMP: 3
SALES (est): 113.9K Privately Held
SIC: 3229 Lenses, lantern, flashlight, headlight, etc.: glass

Thornton
Delaware County

(G-18355)
SAVEMYPIXCOM INC
Also Called: New Hope Dealer Services
82 Stirrup Ln (19373-1068)
P.O. Box 165, Concordville (19331-0165)
PHONE..................................800 535-6299
Monica Messinger, *President*
Maxx Messinger, *Vice Pres*
EMP: 5
SALES: 350K Privately Held
SIC: 3993 7389 Signs & advertising specialties;

Three Springs
Huntingdon County

(G-18356)
SLATES SALVAGE
22380 Waterfall Rd (17264-8025)
PHONE..................................814 448-3218
David Slates Jr, *Owner*
EMP: 4
SALES (est): 374.4K Privately Held
SIC: 7389 3341 Salvaging of damaged merchandise, service only; secondary nonferrous metals

Throop
Lackawanna County

(G-18357)
CONCRETE TEXTURING LLC
Also Called: Concrete Texturing Tool & Sup
45 Underwood Rd (18512-1179)
PHONE..................................570 489-6025
Bart Sacco, *Owner*
EMP: 8
SALES (est): 2MM Privately Held
WEB: www.concrete-texturing.com
SIC: 5032 5072 3272 Concrete building products; hardware; concrete products

(G-18358)
ENRICO J FIORE
Also Called: Fiore Precision Machine
9 Esther St (18512-1441)
PHONE..................................570 489-8430
Enrico J Fiore, *Owner*
EMP: 6
SQ FT: 4,500
SALES (est): 446.7K Privately Held
SIC: 3599 7692 Mfg Industrial Machinery Welding Repair

(G-18359)
J & J PALLET CO INC
1000 Marshwood Rd (18512)
PHONE..................................570 489-7705
Joseph Wahl, *President*
John Bonadio, *Treasurer*
EMP: 25
SQ FT: 7,000
SALES (est): 1.6MM Privately Held
SIC: 7699 2499 2448 Pallet repair; mulch, wood & bark; pallets, wood

(G-18360)
SCRANTON CRAFTSMEN EXCVTG INC
930 Dunmore St (18512-1114)
P.O. Box 97, Dunmore (18512-0097)
PHONE..................................800 775-1479
P Frank Kozik, *President*
Jeff Rohckel, *Vice Pres*
EMP: 70
SQ FT: 30,000

SALES (est): 14MM **Privately Held**
WEB: www.scrantoncraftsmen.com
SIC: 3446 3273 3272 3443 Architectural metalwork; ready-mixed concrete; steps, prefabricated concrete; fabricated plate work (boiler shop); fabricated structural metal

(G-18361)
SCRANTON CRAFTSMEN INC
930 Dunmore St (18512-1114)
P.O. Box 97, Dunmore (18512-0097)
PHONE..................................570 347-5125
Paul F Kozik, *President*
Jeff Rohckel, *Vice Pres*
EMP: 55
SALES (est): 7.9MM **Privately Held**
SIC: 1711 5051 3446 5211 Septic system construction; steel; stairs, staircases, stair treads: prefabricated metal; masonry materials & supplies; ornamental metal work; ready-mixed concrete

(G-18362)
SQUARE TOOL AND DIE CORP INC
934 Sanderson St (18512-1497)
PHONE..................................570 489-8657
Charles Wardach Jr, *President*
Paul Wardach, *Treasurer*
EMP: 10
SQ FT: 5,000
SALES (est): 1.3MM **Privately Held**
SIC: 3599 3544 Machine shop, jobbing & repair; special dies, tools, jigs & fixtures

Tioga
Tioga County

(G-18363)
KLX ENERGY SERVICES LLC
18355 Route 287 (16946-8511)
PHONE..................................570 835-0149
Amin J Khoury, *Ch of Bd*
EMP: 3
SALES (corp-wide): 495.3MM **Publicly Held**
SIC: 1389 Fishing for tools, oil & gas field; gas field services
HQ: Klx Energy Services Llc
3040 Post Oak Blvd # 1500
Houston TX 77056
832 844-1015

(G-18364)
ROSE WILD INC
17288 Route 287 (16946-8500)
PHONE..................................570 835-4329
Stan Matthews, *Principal*
EMP: 3
SALES (est): 257.6K **Privately Held**
SIC: 3273 Ready-mixed concrete

(G-18365)
TY-PAK INC
Also Called: Tyoga Container
9 Fish St (16946-8847)
PHONE..................................570 835-5269
Charlie Frysinger, *President*
▲ **EMP:** 45
SQ FT: 10,000
SALES (est): 3.8MM **Privately Held**
WEB: www.tyogacontainer.com
SIC: 3086 5199 Packaging & shipping materials, foamed plastic; packaging materials
PA: Tyoga Container Company, Inc.
9 Fish St
Tioga PA 16946
570 835-5295

(G-18366)
TYOGA CONTAINER COMPANY INC (PA)
9 Fish St (16946-8847)
P.O. Box 517 (16946-0517)
PHONE..................................570 835-5295
Charlie W Frysinger, *President*
Larry V Grimaldi, *Vice Pres*
John Beiser, *Treasurer*
Ralph I Ruvolo, *VP Sales*
Mike Ruvolo, *Admin Sec*
▲ **EMP:** 42 **EST:** 1970

SQ FT: 105,000
SALES (est): 3.8MM **Privately Held**
SIC: 2653 Boxes, corrugated: made from purchased materials; sheets, corrugated: made from purchased materials; pads, corrugated: made from purchased materials; partitions, corrugated: made from purchased materials

(G-18367)
WAUPACA FOUNDRY INC
18986 Route 287 (16946-8815)
PHONE..................................570 724-5191
EMP: 103
SQ FT: 117,500
SALES (corp-wide): 87.9B **Privately Held**
SIC: 3465 3321 3559 Mfg Automotive Stampings Gray/Ductile Iron Foundry Mfg Misc Industry Machinery
HQ: Waupaca Foundry, Inc.
1955 Brunner Dr
Waupaca WI 54981
715 258-6611

(G-18368)
WAUPACA FOUNDRY INC
18986 Route 287 (16946-8815)
PHONE..................................570 827-3245
EMP: 255
SALES (corp-wide): 87.9B **Privately Held**
SIC: 3465 3321 3559 Body parts, automobile: stamped metal; ductile iron castings; automotive related machinery
HQ: Waupaca Foundry, Inc.
1955 Brunner Dr
Waupaca WI 54981
715 258-6611

Tionesta
Forest County

(G-18369)
ANDERSON FAMILY FARM INC
Also Called: Rals Run Ranch
15255 Route 66 (16353)
PHONE..................................814 463-0202
Carl Anderson, *President*
EMP: 10 **EST:** 2009
SALES (est): 380.7K **Privately Held**
SIC: 0721 1382 Tree orchards, cultivation of; oil & gas exploration services

(G-18370)
DIRECT ENERGY PRODUCTS INC
13649 Route 36 (16353)
P.O. Box 17 (16353-0017)
PHONE..................................216 255-7777
Joe Nader, *CEO*
EMP: 17
SQ FT: 6,500
SALES: 3MM **Privately Held**
SIC: 1382 4924 Oil & gas exploration services; natural gas distribution

(G-18371)
FOREST SCIENTIFIC CORPORATION
408 Emert Rd (16353-7206)
PHONE..................................814 463-5006
EMP: 9
SQ FT: 7,500
SALES (est): 1.6MM **Privately Held**
SIC: 3541 Mfg Machine Tools-Cutting

(G-18372)
J C K SERVICES
Hc 1 (16353)
PHONE..................................814 755-7772
Fax: 814 755-7772
EMP: 3
SALES: 160K **Privately Held**
SIC: 1389 Oil/Gas Field Services

(G-18373)
JM ENTERPRISE LLC
634 Elm St (16353-8804)
P.O. Box 442 (16353-0442)
PHONE..................................814 758-5998
Janey S Brown, *Principal*
EMP: 4 **EST:** 2009
SALES (est): 468.8K **Privately Held**
SIC: 1381 Drilling oil & gas wells

Tipton
Blair County

(G-18374)
DELGROSSO FOODS INC (PA)
632 Sauce Factory Dr (16684)
P.O. Box 337 (16684-0337)
PHONE..................................814 684-5880
Joseph Delgrosso, *President*
Bob Whiteford, *Plant Mgr*
James Mayall, *Opers Staff*
Lisa Pier, *Purch Mgr*
James A Delgrosso, *Treasurer*
▼ **EMP:** 85 **EST:** 1955
SQ FT: 135,000
SALES (est): 38.8MM **Privately Held**
SIC: 2033 Spaghetti & other pasta sauce: packaged in cans, jars, etc.; pizza sauce: packaged in cans, jars, etc.; tomato products: packaged in cans, jars, etc.

Titusville
Crawford County

(G-18375)
BAILLIE LUMBER CO LP
Lindsay Dry Kilns
45529 State Highway 27 The (16354-5727)
P.O. Box 292 (16354-0292)
PHONE..................................814 827-1877
Dewey Swift, *Opers-Prdtn-Mfg*
EMP: 77
SALES (corp-wide): 344.3MM **Privately Held**
WEB: www.baillie.com
SIC: 2421 Sawmills & planing mills, general
PA: Baillie Lumber Co., L.P.
4002 Legion Dr
Hamburg NY 14075
800 950-2850

(G-18376)
BLUEGILL GRAPHIX
318 N Franklin St (16354-2528)
PHONE..................................814 827-7003
Kathy Irwin, *Owner*
EMP: 4
SALES: 350K **Privately Held**
SIC: 2759 Screen printing

(G-18377)
CULVER HARDWOODS
13977 Windfall Rd (16354-5465)
PHONE..................................814 827-3202
Dan Culver, *Owner*
EMP: 3
SALES (est): 165.2K **Privately Held**
SIC: 2426 Lumber, hardwood dimension

(G-18378)
G O CARLSON INC
Also Called: Ellectralloy Division
2456 Petroleum Center Rd (16354-7240)
PHONE..................................814 678-4168
Edward Carlson, *Branch Mgr*
EMP: 42
SALES (corp-wide): 56.2MM **Privately Held**
SIC: 3356 Nickel & nickel alloy: rolling, drawing or extruding
PA: G. O. Carlson, Inc.
175 Main St
Oil City PA 16301
814 678-4100

(G-18379)
GRAND VALLEY MANUFACTURING CO (PA)
Also Called: G. V. M. Company
701 E Spring St Unit 8 (16354-7899)
P.O. Box 8 (16354-0008)
PHONE..................................814 728-8760
David B Ewing, *President*
Gary Shaffer, *Vice Pres*
Brian Warner, *Plant Supt*
Roger Warner, *Purch Mgr*
Frank Humes, *CFO*
▲ **EMP:** 55 **EST:** 1950

SQ FT: 90,000
SALES (est): 14.4MM **Privately Held**
WEB: www.gvmco.com
SIC: 3599 3441 Machine shop, jobbing & repair; fabricated structural metal

(G-18380)
HILL PRECISION MANUFACTURING
Also Called: Hill Tool and Die
10978 Skyline Dr (16354-1368)
PHONE..................................814 827-4333
Sue Hill, *President*
Ron Hill, *Vice Pres*
EMP: 4
SALES (est): 397K **Privately Held**
SIC: 3544 Special dies & tools

(G-18381)
HILLCREST TOOL & DIE INC
10978 Skyline Dr (16354-1368)
PHONE..................................814 827-1296
Rahn Hill, *President*
Dustin Mattocks, *Vice Pres*
Sue Hill, *Admin Sec*
EMP: 12
SQ FT: 5,000
SALES (est): 1.3MM **Privately Held**
SIC: 3469 Machine parts, stamped or pressed metal

(G-18382)
HOMERWOOD HARDWOOD FLOORING CO
Also Called: Armstrong Flooring
1026 Industrial Park (16354-1010)
PHONE..................................814 827-3855
Frank J Ready, *President*
Erik Christensen, *General Mgr*
Thomas J Waters, *Treasurer*
▲ **EMP:** 90
SQ FT: 60,000
SALES (est): 16.5MM
SALES (corp-wide): 728.2MM **Publicly Held**
WEB: www.homerwood.com
SIC: 2426 Flooring, hardwood
PA: Armstrong Flooring, Inc.
2500 Columbia Ave
Lancaster PA 17603
717 672-9611

(G-18383)
HOPKINS LOGGING
313 Davis Pl (16354-1871)
PHONE..................................814 827-1681
EMP: 3 **EST:** 2010
SALES (est): 160K **Privately Held**
SIC: 2411 Logging

(G-18384)
HORN TEXTILE INC
Also Called: Ribbon Factory Outlet
600 N Brown St (16354-1222)
PHONE..................................814 827-3606
David Steinbuhler, *President*
Chase Steinbuhler, *Vice Pres*
Jack Steinbuhler Jr, *Treasurer*
Peter Steinbuhler, *Treasurer*
Zach Steinbuhler, *Office Mgr*
▲ **EMP:** 30 **EST:** 1897
SQ FT: 70,000
SALES (est): 4.8MM **Privately Held**
WEB: www.horntextile.com
SIC: 2241 Trimmings, textile; webbing, braids & belting; cotton narrow fabrics; manmade fiber narrow woven fabrics

(G-18385)
INTERNATIONAL GROUP INC (DH)
Also Called: I G I
1007 E Spring St (16354-7826)
PHONE..................................814 827-4900
Kenneth Reucassel, *President*
W Ross Reucassel, *Principal*
◆ **EMP:** 30
SALES (est): 180.3MM **Privately Held**
SIC: 5169 2911 Waxes, except petroleum; oils, lubricating; petrolatums, nonmedicinal; paraffin wax
HQ: International Group, Inc, The
50 Salome Dr
Scarborough ON M1S 2
416 293-4151

(G-18386)
INTERNATIONAL WAXES INC
1007 E Spring St (16354-7826)
PHONE..............................814 827-3609
Stacy Log, *Manager*
EMP: 50 **Privately Held**
SIC: 2999 Waxes, petroleum: not produced in petroleum refineries
HQ: International Waxes, Inc.
45 Route 446
Smethport PA 16749
814 887-5501

(G-18387)
KEYSTONE HONING CORPORATION
11663 Mckinney Rd (16354-1008)
P.O. Box 187 (16354-0187)
PHONE..............................814 827-9641
Jeff Hadley, *CEO*
EMP: 62 **EST:** 1964
SQ FT: 55,000
SALES (est): 5.4MM **Privately Held**
SIC: 3599 Machine shop, jobbing & repair

(G-18388)
MARSH PLANING INC
Also Called: Marsh Planing Company
5034 State Route 8 (16354)
PHONE..............................814 827-9947
David Keith Zimmerman, *CEO*
EMP: 7 **EST:** 1971
SQ FT: 17,600
SALES: 500K **Privately Held**
SIC: 2431 2421 Planing mill, millwork; sawmills & planing mills, general

(G-18389)
OCP INC
Also Called: Oil Creek Plastics
45619 State Highway 27 (16354-5729)
P.O. Box 385 (16354-0385)
PHONE..............................814 827-3661
James I Osborne, *President*
Michael Pedensky, *Sales Staff*
Stacy Warner, *Office Mgr*
Clifford Kirvan, *CTO*
Ron Reeher, *Maintence Staff*
▲ **EMP:** 50
SQ FT: 91,000
SALES (est): 12MM **Privately Held**
WEB: www.oilcreek.com
SIC: 3084 2821 Plastics pipe; plastics materials & resins

(G-18390)
PRECISION PROFILES LLC
45727 State Highway 27 (16354-5835)
P.O. Box 324 (16354-0324)
PHONE..............................814 827-9887
Clifford R Hastings, *President*
Matthew J Lucco, *Principal*
Richard M Jardin, *Vice Pres*
P Kay Jardin, *Treasurer*
Loretta C Hastings, *Admin Sec*
EMP: 6
SQ FT: 3,200
SALES (est): 885.5K **Privately Held**
WEB: www.precision-profiles.com
SIC: 3599 Machine shop, jobbing & repair

(G-18391)
RICHARD J CLICKETT INC
Also Called: Clickett,
708 N Perry St (16354-1154)
PHONE..............................814 827-7548
Richard J Clickett, *President*
A Margaret Clickett, *Treasurer*
EMP: 32
SQ FT: 11,500
SALES: 778K **Privately Held**
SIC: 3679 1542 Voice controls; service station construction; commercial & office building, new construction; commercial & office buildings, renovation & repair

(G-18392)
RONALD COPELAND
Also Called: RC Machine
933 Meadville Rd (16354-6623)
PHONE..............................814 827-3968
Ronald Copeland, *Owner*
EMP: 4
SQ FT: 3,600
SALES: 400K **Privately Held**
SIC: 3599 Machine shop, jobbing & repair

(G-18393)
ROSER TECHNOLOGIES INC (PA)
Also Called: R T I
701 E Spring St Unit 3 (16354-7815)
PHONE..............................814 827-7717
Daniel J Roser, *Principal*
Daniel Roser, *Vice Pres*
▲ **EMP:** 97
SQ FT: 60,000
SALES (est): 28.5MM **Privately Held**
SIC: 3544 Industrial molds

(G-18394)
ROSER TECHNOLOGIES INC
347 E Industrial Dr (16354-7805)
PHONE..............................814 589-7031
EMP: 65
SALES (corp-wide): 28.5MM **Privately Held**
SIC: 3366 Bushings & bearings
PA: Roser Technologies, Inc.
701 E Spring St Unit 3
Titusville PA 16354
814 827-7717

(G-18395)
SHAFFER LOGGING
13955 State Highway 8 (16354-4309)
PHONE..............................814 827-1729
Robert P Shaffer, *Principal*
EMP: 3 **EST:** 2010
SALES (est): 182.8K **Privately Held**
SIC: 2411 Logging

(G-18396)
SMOKERS OUTLET
302 E Central Ave (16354-1907)
PHONE..............................814 827-1104
John Catsimatidis, *President*
EMP: 5
SALES (est): 306.4K
SALES (corp-wide): 2.5B **Privately Held**
SIC: 3556 Smokers, food processing equipment
HQ: United Refining Company Of Pennsylvania
15 Bradley St
Warren PA 16365
814 723-1500

(G-18397)
STEFFEES
Also Called: City Limits Ice Cream
4219 State Route 8 (16354-7559)
PHONE..............................814 827-4332
EMP: 11
SALES (est): 410K **Privately Held**
SIC: 2024 Mfg Ice Cream/Frozen Desert

(G-18398)
THERMA-FAB INC (PA)
109 W Central Ave (16354-1728)
P.O. Box 345 (16354-0345)
PHONE..............................814 827-9455
Clarence Prichard, *President*
Thomas Lombardi, *Vice Pres*
Peggy Hartman, *Office Mgr*
Mary Ann Hartman, *Manager*
▲ **EMP:** 4
SQ FT: 2,500
SALES (est): 961.3K **Privately Held**
WEB: www.thermafab.com
SIC: 3443 Fabricated plate work (boiler shop)

(G-18399)
TITUSVILLE DAIRY PRODUCTS CO
217 S Washington St (16354-1660)
P.O. Box 186 (16354-0186)
PHONE..............................814 827-1833
Charles Turner Jr, *President*
William Scheider Jr, *Vice Pres*
Bruce Reid, *Treasurer*
Craig Marburger, *Admin Sec*
James Nistrom, *Asst Sec*
EMP: 27
SQ FT: 30,000
SALES (est): 5.1MM **Privately Held**
SIC: 2024 5143 Ice cream & frozen desserts; frozen dairy desserts; milk cooling stations

(G-18400)
TITUSVILLE HERALD INC
Also Called: Titusville Herald
209 W Spring St (16354-1687)
PHONE..............................814 827-3634
Michael Sample, *Principal*
Donna Barrett, *Vice Pres*
EMP: 21 **EST:** 1865
SQ FT: 10,000
SALES (est): 1MM **Privately Held**
SIC: 2711 Commercial printing & newspaper publishing combined
HQ: Cnhi, Llc
445 Dexter Ave
Montgomery AL 36104

(G-18401)
TITUSVILLE LAUNDRY CENTER
117 Diamond St (16354-1846)
P.O. Box 109 (16354-0109)
PHONE..............................814 827-9127
Rick Shrout, *Owner*
Bruce Peterson, *Partner*
EMP: 3
SALES (est): 170.4K **Privately Held**
SIC: 2842 7216 Laundry cleaning preparations; drycleaning collecting & distributing agency

(G-18402)
UNIVERSAL STAINLESS& ALLOY
121 Caldwell St (16354-2055)
PHONE..............................814 827-9723
Stanley Peak, *General Mgr*
Jeff Clark, *Safety Mgr*
Charlie Swartzlander, *Purch Mgr*
Scott Barker, *QC Dir*
EMP: 51
SQ FT: 265,000 **Publicly Held**
SIC: 3325 3312 Steel foundries; blast furnaces & steel mills
PA: Universal Stainless & Alloy Products, Inc.
600 Mayer St
Bridgeville PA 15017

(G-18403)
WEABER INC
Also Called: Choice Wood
11117 Skyline Dr (16354-1375)
PHONE..............................814 827-4621
EMP: 50
SALES (corp-wide): 180.8MM **Privately Held**
SIC: 5211 2426 Lumber products; hardwood dimension & flooring mills
HQ: Weaber, Inc.
1231 Mount Wilson Rd
Lebanon PA 17042
717 867-2212

(G-18404)
WEYERHAEUSER COMPANY
Also Called: Northwest Hardwoods
10589 Campbell Rd (16354-5701)
PHONE..............................814 827-4621
Bret Johnson, *President*
David Hansen, *Manager*
EMP: 200
SALES (corp-wide): 7.4B **Publicly Held**
SIC: 2421 2431 2426 Lumber: rough, sawed or planed; millwork; hardwood dimension & flooring mills
PA: Weyerhaeuser Company
220 Occidental Ave S
Seattle WA 98104
206 539-3000

(G-18405)
WILSON HARDWOODS INC
10951 Johnson Rd (16354-4035)
PHONE..............................814 827-0277
Douglas Wilson, *Owner*
▼ **EMP:** 20
SALES (est): 3.8MM **Privately Held**
SIC: 2421 Lumber: rough, sawed or planed

Tobyhanna
Monroe County

(G-18406)
ABS AND APPLES
5111 Juliet Rd (18466-8244)
PHONE..............................646 847-8262
Deatra Cummings, *Principal*
EMP: 3 **EST:** 2016
SALES (est): 210K **Privately Held**
SIC: 3571 Personal computers (microcomputers)

(G-18407)
MENASHA PACKAGING COMPANY LLC
2086 Corporate Ctr Dr W (18466-7773)
PHONE..............................570 243-5512
Thomas Randell, *Branch Mgr*
EMP: 6
SALES (corp-wide): 1.7B **Privately Held**
SIC: 2653 Boxes, corrugated: made from purchased materials
HQ: Menasha Packaging Company, Llc
1645 Bergstrom Rd
Neenah WI 54956
920 751-1000

(G-18408)
RIGHT REASON TECHNOLOGIES LLC
430 Sterling Rd (18466-3906)
PHONE..............................570 234-0324
Peter Schmitt,
David Mehrtens,
Thomas Schmitt,
EMP: 15
SALES (est): 1.2MM **Privately Held**
WEB: www.rightreasontech.com
SIC: 3571 Electronic computers

Topton
Berks County

(G-18409)
ADVANCED CARBON TECH INC
220 N Main St Ste 4 (19562-1430)
PHONE..............................610 682-1086
Franklin C Schoch, *President*
Kathleen Schoch, *Corp Secy*
Dr Robert Froberg, *Vice Pres*
Frank Schoch, *Sales Executive*
▼ **EMP:** 13
SALES: 2.8MM **Privately Held**
WEB: www.advancedcarbon.com
SIC: 3599 Machine shop, jobbing & repair

(G-18410)
ADVANCED SYSTEMS TECHNOLOGIES
3 N Main St Fl 1 (19562-1517)
PHONE..............................610 682-0610
Terry Schartel, *President*
Christine A Belejo, *Vice Pres*
EMP: 5
SQ FT: 600
SALES: 350K **Privately Held**
WEB: www.advancedsystemstechnologies.com
SIC: 3625 Relays & industrial controls

(G-18411)
EAST PENN MANUFACTURING CO
50 W Jefferson St (19562-1432)
PHONE..............................610 682-6361
Graham Anderson, *President*
Jack Lesniewski, *Principal*
EMP: 14
SALES (corp-wide): 2.5B **Privately Held**
WEB: www.eastpenn-deka.com
SIC: 3691 Storage batteries
PA: East Penn Manufacturing Co.
102 Deka Rd
Lyon Station PA 19536
610 682-6361

(G-18412)
ELECTRO-SPACE
FABRICATORS INC
Also Called: E S F
300 W High St (19562-1420)
PHONE..............................610 682-7181
William I Straccia III, *President*
David Carbaugh, *Engineer*
Robert Sheetz, *Design Engr*
Jeffrey C Straccia, *Treasurer*
Mark Sismour, *VP Sales*
EMP: 90
SQ FT: 120,000
SALES (est): 21.1MM **Privately Held**
WEB: www.esfinc.com
SIC: 3444 Sheet metal specialties, not stamped

(G-18413)
GRAPHITE MACHINING INC (PA)
240 N Main St (19562-1419)
PHONE..............................610 682-0080
Franklin C Schoch, *President*
Timothy Bearss, *Vice Pres*
Erica L Schochshane, *Treasurer*
Paige Bearss, *Finance Mgr*
Ron Barshinger, *Technology*
▲ EMP: 33 EST: 1973
SQ FT: 60,000
SALES: 17.8MM **Privately Held**
WEB: www.graphitemachininginc.com
SIC: 3624 Carbon & graphite products

(G-18414)
NORTHEAST PRODUCTS &
SVCS INC
130 W High St (19562-1417)
PHONE..............................610 899-0286
Nina Bailey, *President*
EMP: 3
SALES (est): 295.8K **Privately Held**
SIC: 2499 2435 Fencing, docks & other outdoor wood structural products; panels, hardwood plywood

(G-18415)
ROCKLAND EMBROIDERY INC
125 Centre Ave (19562-1002)
PHONE..............................610 682-5042
David Schlier, *President*
David G Schlier, *President*
Kelly Eager, *Director*
Denise A Schlier, *Admin Sec*
EMP: 40
SQ FT: 19,000
SALES (est): 3.8MM **Privately Held**
WEB: www.rocklandembroidery.com
SIC: 2395 Embroidery products, except schiffli machine; embroidery & art needlework

(G-18416)
SPECIALTY MILLWORKS INC
(PA)
130 W High St (19562-1417)
PHONE..............................610 682-6334
Phil Roth, *President*
Mary Claire Roth, *Corp Secy*
EMP: 5 EST: 1978
SQ FT: 12,300
SALES (est): 2MM **Privately Held**
SIC: 5031 3842 5211 Millwork; supports: abdominal, ankle, arch, kneecap, etc.; millwork & lumber

---

Toughkenamon
Chester County

(G-18417)
CALIFORNIA MUSHROOM FARM
INC
1320 Newark Rd (19374-1034)
PHONE..............................805 642-3253
Charles Ciarrocchi, *CEO*
James Ciarrocchi, *Director*
▲ EMP: 330
SALES (est): 24.1MM **Privately Held**
SIC: 2033 Mushrooms: packaged in cans, jars, etc.

(G-18418)
DSI-LANG GEOTECH LLC
1263 Newark Rd (19374-1033)
PHONE..............................610 268-2221
Christopher Lang,
▲ EMP: 4
SALES (est): 643.2K **Privately Held**
WEB: www.dsi-lang.com
SIC: 3315 5051 Steel wire & related products; steel decking

(G-18419)
INTERNATIONAL PAPER
COMPANY
1270 Old Baltimore Park (19374)
P.O. Box 493 (19374-0493)
PHONE..............................610 268-5456
William Hower, *Branch Mgr*
EMP: 50
SALES (corp-wide): 23.3B **Publicly Held**
WEB: www.tin.com
SIC: 2653 Boxes, corrugated: made from purchased materials
PA: International Paper Company
6400 Poplar Ave
Memphis TN 38197
901 419-9000

(G-18420)
MODERN MUSHROOM FARMS
INC
1330 Newark Rd (19374-1034)
P.O. Box 340, Avondale (19311-0340)
PHONE..............................610 268-3535
Charles J Ciarrocchi Jr, *President*
Charles J Ciarrocchi Sr, *Treasurer*
Brett Bell, *Controller*
Jackie Lugo, *Executive*
James Ciarrocchi, *Admin Sec*
EMP: 500
SQ FT: 375,000
SALES (est): 95.3MM **Privately Held**
WEB: www.modernmush.com
SIC: 2099 0182 2033 Food preparations; mushrooms grown under cover; canned fruits & specialties

---

Towanda
Bradford County

(G-18421)
BLACK KNIGHT QUARRIES INC
293 Beacon Light Rd (18848-9298)
PHONE..............................570 265-8991
John Maloey, *President*
EMP: 4
SALES (est): 237.3K **Privately Held**
SIC: 1422 Limestones, ground

(G-18422)
C & G WILCOX ENGRV &
IMAGES
502 Main St (18848-1612)
PHONE..............................570 265-3621
Cindy Wilcox, *Partner*
Gary Wilcox, *Partner*
EMP: 4
SQ FT: 1,800
SALES (est): 390K **Privately Held**
SIC: 7389 3993 5944 5699 Engraving service; signs, not made in custom sign painting shops; jewelry stores; customized clothing & apparel

(G-18423)
DENNYS WELDING
Also Called: Debweld
207 N Main St (18848-1907)
P.O. Box 415, Wysox (18854-0415)
PHONE..............................570 265-8015
Denny Moran, *Owner*
EMP: 5
SALES (est): 259.8K **Privately Held**
SIC: 7692 Welding repair

(G-18424)
DUPONT SPECIALTY PDTS USA
LLC
Also Called: Dupont Elec & Communications
192 Patterson Blvd (18848-8208)
PHONE..............................570 265-6141
Tom Foreman, *Principal*

Eugene Weisbrod, *Area Mgr*
Bruce Marks, *Electrical Engi*
Thomas Kramer, *Manager*
Renee Arnold, *Manager*
EMP: 50
SALES (corp-wide): 85.9B **Publicly Held**
WEB: www.dupont.com
SIC: 2819 Industrial inorganic chemicals
HQ: Dupont Specialty Products Usa, Llc
2030 Dow Ctr
Midland MI 48674
989 636-1000

(G-18425)
EASTERN INDUSTRIES INC
6154 Leisure Dr (18848)
PHONE..............................570 265-9191
Lynn Lenox, *Opers-Prdtn-Mfg*
EMP: 39
SALES (corp-wide): 651.9MM **Privately Held**
SIC: 1442 2951 3271 3273 Construction sand mining; gravel mining; asphalt & asphaltic paving mixtures (not from refineries); blocks, concrete or cinder: standard; ready-mixed concrete
HQ: Eastern Industries, Inc.
3724 Crescent Ct W 200
Whitehall PA 18052
610 866-0932

(G-18426)
FRONTIER LLC
67 Campbell Rd (18848-8093)
PHONE..............................570 265-2500
Evan Schiebout, *Mng Member*
Thomas J Forbes, *Director*
EMP: 10 EST: 2015
SALES (est): 619.2K **Privately Held**
SIC: 3567 3552 7389 8711 Industrial furnaces & ovens; printing machinery, textile; design services; mechanical engineering; electroplating machinery & equipment

(G-18427)
GAMBAL PRINTING & DESIGN
1038 Golden Mile Rd (18848-9247)
P.O. Box 6 (18848-0006)
PHONE..............................570 265-8968
Michael Gambal, *Mng Member*
Dave Colton, *Graphic Designe*
EMP: 3
SALES (est): 293.3K **Privately Held**
WEB: www.coldwellpreferred.com
SIC: 2759 Screen printing

(G-18428)
GEXPRO
151 Liberty Ln (18848-5301)
PHONE..............................570 265-2420
EMP: 4 EST: 2014
SALES (est): 215.7K **Privately Held**
SIC: 5063 3699 3645 Whol Electrical Equipment Mfg Electrical Equipment/Supplies Mfg Residential Lighting Fixtures

(G-18429)
GLOBAL TUNGSTEN &
POWDERS CORP
Also Called: Gtp
1 Hawes St (18848-2134)
PHONE..............................570 268-5000
Hermann Walser, *CEO*
Karlheinz Wax, *President*
Eric Rowe, *Asst Treas*
◆ EMP: 500
SQ FT: 100,000
SALES (est): 328MM **Privately Held**
SIC: 3313 3291 Tungsten carbide powder; molybdenum silicon, not made in blast furnaces; tungsten carbide abrasive
HQ: Plansee Holding Ag
Metallwerk Plansee-StraBe 71
Reutte 6600
567 260-00

(G-18430)
HEP PENNSYLVANIA
GATHERING LLC
36 Fox Chase Dr (18848)
PHONE..............................210 298-2229
Ricky Smith, *Opers Staff*
EMP: 27 EST: 2015
SALES (est): 704.8K **Privately Held**
SIC: 1382 Oil & gas exploration services

(G-18431)
JELD-WEN INC
825 Shiner Rd (18848-9207)
PHONE..............................570 265-9121
Bob Andzulis, *Manager*
EMP: 250 **Publicly Held**
WEB: www.cmicompany.com
SIC: 2493 Hardboard, tempered
HQ: Jeld-Wen, Inc.
2645 Silver Crescent Dr
Charlotte NC 28273
800 535-3936

(G-18432)
METADYNE INC (PA)
Also Called: Towanda Metadyne
Fox Chase Dr (18848)
PHONE..............................570 265-6963
Raman L Daga, *Ch of Bd*
Amit Daga, *Vice Pres*
Cori Lasco, *Vice Pres*
Dave Reeder, *VP Opers*
Gangadharan S Raman, *Treasurer*
▲ EMP: 45
SQ FT: 60,000
SALES (est): 11.7MM **Privately Held**
WEB: www.towandametadyne.com
SIC: 3532 Drills, bits & similar equipment

(G-18433)
MOUNTAIN LAKE WINERY LLC
391 Bailey Rd (18848-8071)
PHONE..............................267 664-6343
EMP: 4
SALES (est): 212.3K **Privately Held**
SIC: 2084 Wines

(G-18434)
SUNDAY REVIEW
116 Main St Ste 5 (18848-1832)
PHONE..............................570 265-2151
Kelly Andrus, *Editor*
Dawn Hibbert, *Sales Staff*
Pam Hornung, *Advt Staff*
Sheila May, *Advt Staff*
Sue Rought, *Advt Staff*
EMP: 7 EST: 2016
SALES (est): 101.4K **Privately Held**
SIC: 2711 Newspapers, publishing & printing

(G-18435)
THE SCRANTON TIMES L P
Also Called: Farmer's Friend, The
116 N Main St (18848-1906)
PHONE..............................570 265-2151
George Lynett, *Owner*
EMP: 6
SALES (corp-wide): 114.5MM **Privately Held**
WEB: www.scrantontimesefcu.com
SIC: 2711 Newspapers, publishing & printing
PA: The Scranton Times L P
149 Penn Ave Ste 1
Scranton PA 18503
570 348-9100

(G-18436)
TOWANDA PRINTING CO INC
(PA)
116 N Main St (18848-1906)
P.O. Box 503 (18848-0503)
PHONE..............................570 265-2151
George V Lynett, *President*
David Barry, *General Mgr*
James Towner, *Vice Pres*
Edward J Lynett Jr, *Treasurer*
Joel Crayton, *Advt Staff*
EMP: 224 EST: 1879
SQ FT: 18,000
SALES (est): 12MM **Privately Held**
WEB: www.sundayreview.com
SIC: 2711 2741 2791 2752 Commercial printing & newspaper publishing combined; guides: publishing & printing; typesetting; commercial printing, lithographic

(G-18437)
WHITE REFRIGERATION INC
13838 Route 220 (18848-9126)
PHONE..............................570 265-7335
Ray White, *President*
EMP: 7

SALES: 1MM **Privately Held**
SIC: **1711** 3822 Refrigeration contractor;
air conditioning & refrigeration controls

Tower City
Schuylkill County

(G-18438)
JOLIETT COAL CO
837 E Grand Ave (17980-1217)
PHONE.................................717 647-9628
William R Reiner, *Partner*
Kay L Reiner, *Partner*
EMP: 3
SALES (est): 260K **Privately Held**
SIC: **1241** Coal mining services

(G-18439)
ORWIN LATHE & DOWEL
50 Snyder Ave (17980-1814)
PHONE.................................717 647-4397
Jay Alvin Snyder, *Partner*
Leslie Berkholder, *Partner*
David Snyder, *Partner*
Joel Snyder, *Partner*
EMP: 4
SALES: 250K **Privately Held**
SIC: **2431** Woodwork, interior & ornamental

(G-18440)
REINER ASSOCIATES INC
22 S Yohe St (17980-1713)
PHONE.................................717 647-7454
Larry Reiner, *President*
Rosemary Reiner, *Vice Pres*
EMP: 5
SALES (est): 350K **Privately Held**
SIC: **3544** 3643 Dies & die holders for
metal cutting, forming, die casting; current-carrying wiring devices

(G-18441)
STAUFFER WOOD PRODUCTS
221 Clarks Valley Rd (17980-9449)
PHONE.................................717 647-4372
Elvin K Stauffer, *Partner*
Bruce Stauffer, *Partner*
James Stauffer, *Partner*
Wayne Stauffer, *Partner*
EMP: 7
SQ FT: 7,125
SALES (est): 510K **Privately Held**
SIC: **2434** 2511 Wood kitchen cabinets;
wood household furniture

(G-18442)
TALLMAN SUPPLY COMPANY
114 E Church St (17980-9416)
PHONE.................................717 647-2123
Robert W Tallman, *President*
Suzanne Tallman, *Admin Sec*
EMP: 5
SQ FT: 20,000
SALES: 375K **Privately Held**
SIC: **5082** 5084 3532 Mining machinery &
equipment, except petroleum; general
construction machinery & equipment; industrial machinery & equipment; mining
machinery

(G-18443)
VALLEY PRECISION TL & TECH INC
20 Clarks Valley Rd (17980-9441)
PHONE.................................717 647-7550
Ronald Raudenbush, *President*
Larry Slingwine, *Vice Pres*
Tammy Smeltz, *Vice Pres*
Alice Raudenbush, *Treasurer*
Dione Sowers, *Info Tech Mgr*
EMP: 47
SQ FT: 15,000
SALES (est): 10.8MM **Privately Held**
SIC: **3355** 3678 Aluminum wire & cable;
electronic connectors

Townville
Crawford County

(G-18444)
BRIAN L DEWEY
Also Called: Diamond Tool & Die, Inc
33328 N Main St (16360-2718)
P.O. Box 184 (16360-0484)
PHONE.................................814 967-3246
Brian L Dewey, *President*
EMP: 8
SQ FT: 3,000
SALES: 500K **Privately Held**
SIC: **3544** Special dies, tools, jigs & fixtures

(G-18445)
JOHN HUNT LOGGING
33229 Terrill Rd (16360-1203)
PHONE.................................814 967-4464
EMP: 3
SALES (est): 130K **Privately Held**
SIC: **2411** Logging

(G-18446)
MERCER SPRING & WIRE LLC
15715 Mercer Rd (16360-1926)
PHONE.................................814 967-2545
Charles McWilliams,
EMP: 32
SALES: 3.2MM **Privately Held**
SIC: **3495** Wire springs

(G-18447)
STEADMAN TOOL & DIE INC
32883 State Highway 408 (16360-3113)
PHONE.................................814 967-4333
Ross Steadman, *President*
EMP: 7
SALES (est): 869.2K **Privately Held**
SIC: **3544** Special dies & tools

(G-18448)
TAYLOR TOOL INC
29914 State Highway 408 (16360-2304)
PHONE.................................814 967-4642
William Taylor, *President*
Kathy Taylor, *Corp Secy*
EMP: 4
SALES: 150K **Privately Held**
SIC: **3544** Special dies & tools

(G-18449)
UNION SPRING & MFG CORP
Mercer Spring & Wire Co Div
15715 Mercer Rd (16360-1926)
PHONE.................................814 967-2545
Jeff Dahl, *General Mgr*
Al V Guilder, *Plant Mgr*
EMP: 37
SALES (est): 2.3MM
SALES (corp-wide): 22.7MM **Privately Held**
WEB: www.pontotocspring.com
SIC: **5085** 3495 3493 Springs; wire
springs; torsion bar springs
PA: Union Spring & Manufacturing Corporation
4268 N Pike Ste 1
Monroeville PA 15146
412 843-5900

Trafford
Westmoreland County

(G-18450)
ABLE TOOL CO INC (PA)
13160 Route 993 (15085-9523)
PHONE.................................724 863-2508
Sandra Brammell, *President*
EMP: 25 EST: 1964
SQ FT: 10,600
SALES (est): 4MM **Privately Held**
WEB: www.abletool.us
SIC: **3599** Machine shop, jobbing & repair

(G-18451)
BIRRBATT PRINTING INC
421 Cavitt Ave (15085-1062)
PHONE.................................412 373-9047
Anthony Battle, *President*
Sharon Battle, *Vice Pres*
EMP: 7
SALES (est): 600K **Privately Held**
WEB: www.birrbattprinting.com
SIC: **2752** Commercial printing, offset

(G-18452)
BUCHANAN HAULING
1200 Commerce Cir (15085-2410)
PHONE.................................412 373-6760
Mike Wardzinski, *Manager*
EMP: 5
SALES: 330K **Privately Held**
SIC: **4213** 3524 Contract haulers; loaders
(garden tractor equipment)

(G-18453)
DELTA ANALYTICAL INSTRUMENTS
108 Saunders Station Rd (15085-9701)
PHONE.................................412 372-0739
EMP: 4
SQ FT: 8,000
SALES (est): 440K **Privately Held**
SIC: **3826** Commercial Laboratory

(G-18454)
EDWARDS SHERM CANDIES INC (PA)
509 Cavitt Ave (15085-1060)
PHONE.................................412 372-4331
David Golembeski, *President*
EMP: 22
SQ FT: 11,520
SALES: 724K **Privately Held**
WEB: www.shermedwardscandies.com
SIC: **2064** 5441 2066 Candy & other confectionery products; candy; chocolate &
cocoa products

(G-18455)
EXCEL SPORTSWEAR INC
15 Forbes Rd (15085-1201)
PHONE.................................412 856-7616
Patrick Tzanis, *Owner*
Cheryl Maust, *CFO*
Paul Waclo, *Sales Mgr*
Jeremy Geyer, *Marketing Staff*
Linda Tipton, *Office Mgr*
EMP: 70 EST: 2011
SALES (est): 7.3MM **Privately Held**
WEB: www.excelsportswear.com
SIC: **2759** Screen printing

(G-18456)
EXCL INC
Also Called: Excl Sportswear
15 Forbes Rd (15085-1201)
PHONE.................................412 856-7616
Patrick Tzanis, *President*
Mike Zanolli, *Vice Pres*
EMP: 30
SQ FT: 800
SALES (est): 3.9MM **Privately Held**
WEB: www.excltees.com
SIC: **5136** 3993 2396 Sportswear, men's
& boys'; signs & advertising specialties;
automotive & apparel trimmings

(G-18457)
HAMILL MANUFACTURING COMPANY
500 Pleasant Valley Rd (15085-2700)
PHONE.................................724 744-2131
Jeffrey S Kelly, *Ch of Bd*
Janis Herschkowitz, *President*
William B Kelly, *Chairman*
Bob McCracken, *Maint Spvr*
Thomas Moran, *Senior Buyer*
▲ EMP: 97 EST: 1952
SQ FT: 110,000
SALES: 24.1MM **Privately Held**
SIC: **3599** 3469 3444 Machine shop, jobbing & repair; welding repair; sheet metalwork

(G-18458)
METAL MENDERS LLC
230 Saunders Station Rd (15085-9708)
PHONE.................................412 580-8625
Daniel T Adamik, *Principal*
EMP: 3
SALES (est): 292.5K **Privately Held**
SIC: **3398** Metal heat treating

(G-18459)
MINNOTTE MANUFACTURING CORP
1000 Commerce Cir (15085-2411)
PHONE.................................412 373-5270
Clam Uram, *Branch Mgr*
EMP: 55
SALES (corp-wide): 47.1MM **Privately Held**
SIC: **3599** 3443 3441 Machine & other
job shop work; industrial vessels, tanks &
containers; fabricated structural metal for
ships
PA: Minnotte Manufacturing Corporation
Minnotte Sq
Pittsburgh PA 15220
412 922-2963

(G-18460)
PARKSIDE CREAMERY LLC
1 Forbes Rd (15085-1201)
PHONE.................................412 372-1110
EMP: 6
SALES (est): 204.7K **Privately Held**
SIC: **2024** Ice cream, packaged: molded,
on sticks, etc.

(G-18461)
WIRECO WORLDGROUP INC
Also Called: Wire Rope
2500 Commerce Cir (15085-2422)
PHONE.................................412 373-6122
Mark Dillner, *Branch Mgr*
EMP: 15 **Privately Held**
WEB: www.wrca.com
SIC: **3496** Woven wire products
HQ: Wireco Worldgroup Inc.
2400 W 75th St
Prairie Village KS 66208
816 270-4700

Trainer
Delaware County

(G-18462)
A & R IRON WORKS INC
21 Nealy Blvd Ste 2101 (19061-5330)
PHONE.................................610 497-8770
Guy Romero, *President*
Robin E Romero, *Vice Pres*
EMP: 12
SQ FT: 20,500
SALES (est): 3.3MM **Privately Held**
WEB: www.ariron.com
SIC: **3441** 1791 3443 3446 Fabricated
structural metal; structural steel erection;
fabricated plate work (boiler shop); architectural metalwork; rails, steel or iron

(G-18463)
MISTRAS GROUP INC
5 Nealy Blvd (19061-5312)
PHONE.................................610 497-0400
Sam Ternowchek, *Branch Mgr*
EMP: 20 **Publicly Held**
SIC: **3829** Measuring & controlling devices
PA: Mistras Group, Inc.
195 Clarksville Rd Ste 2
Princeton Junction NJ 08550

(G-18464)
MONROE ENERGY LLC (HQ)
4101 Post Rd (19061-5052)
PHONE.................................610 364-8000
Jeffrey Warmann, *President*
Rodney Smith, *Vice Pres*
Mike Mogar, *Safety Dir*
Donald Wasson, *Opers Mgr*
Chris Bullock, *Foreman/Supr*
▲ EMP: 445
SALES (est): 228.8MM
SALES (corp-wide): 44.4B **Publicly Held**
SIC: **2911** Petroleum refining
PA: Delta Air Lines, Inc.
1030 Delta Blvd
Atlanta GA 30354
404 715-2600

▲ = Import ▼=Export
◆ =Import/Export

Transfer
Mercer County

(G-18465)
GREENVILLE METALS INC
Also Called: PCC Forged Products
99 Crestview Drive Ext (16154-1709)
PHONE.................................724 509-1861
Joseph Snowden, *President*
Robert H Elwell, *Principal*
William D Larsson, *Vice Pres*
Geoffrey A Hawkes, *Treasurer*
Roger A Cooke, *Admin Sec*
◆ **EMP:** 83
SALES (est): 29.5MM
SALES (corp-wide): 225.3B **Publicly Held**
WEB: www.greenvillemetals.com
SIC: 3313 Alloys, additive, except copper: not made in blast furnaces
HQ: Sps Technologies, Llc
      301 Highland Ave
      Jenkintown PA 19046
      215 572-3000

Trappe
Montgomery County

(G-18466)
ACCELLENT
200 W 7th Ave (19426-2112)
PHONE.................................610 489-0300
Bruce Rogers, *Vice Pres*
EMP: 19
SALES (est): 2.1MM **Privately Held**
SIC: 3841 Surgical & medical instruments

(G-18467)
B O H I C A INC
Also Called: Print Copy Design Solutions
521 W Main St (19426-1923)
PHONE.................................610 489-4540
Justin Schlegel, *President*
EMP: 7
SQ FT: 2,175
SALES (est): 881.6K **Privately Held**
SIC: 7334 2752 Photocopying & duplicating services; commercial printing, offset

(G-18468)
EYE DESIGN LLC (PA)
220 W 5th Ave (19426-2106)
PHONE.................................610 409-1900
Richard Winig, *Partner*
Alan M Winig, *Partner*
EMP: 50
SALES (est): 15.8MM **Privately Held**
SIC: 7389 2521 3993 3821 Interior designer; wood office furniture; signs & advertising specialties; laboratory apparatus & furniture; store & office display cases & fixtures

(G-18469)
H B INSTRUMENT CO
102 W 7th Ave (19426-2150)
P.O. Box 26770, Collegeville (19426-0770)
PHONE.................................610 489-5500
Edward D Hiergesell, *President*
James R Robinson, *Vice Pres*
Leslie Knorr Gall, *CFO*
▲ **EMP:** 35
SQ FT: 30,000
SALES (est): 5MM **Privately Held**
WEB: www.hboriginals.com
SIC: 3823 3648 Industrial instrmnts msrmnt display/control process variable; street lighting fixtures

(G-18470)
HB INSTRMENT DIV BEL-ART PRODU
102 W 7th Ave (19426-2110)
PHONE.................................610 489-5500
EMP: 3
SALES (est): 329K **Privately Held**
SIC: 3821 Laboratory apparatus & furniture

(G-18471)
LAKE REGION MEDICAL INC
Also Called: Uniform Tubes Division
200 W 7th Ave (19426-2112)
PHONE.................................610 489-0300
Rachel Gilbreath, *Buyer*
Mark Broadley, *Research*
Brad Hart, *Branch Mgr*
Tom Shultz, *CIO*
Beth Morrisey, *Software Dev*
EMP: 187
SALES (corp-wide): 1.2B **Publicly Held**
SIC: 3841 Surgical & medical instruments
HQ: Lake Region Medical, Inc.
      100 Fordham Rd Ste 3
      Wilmington MA 01887

(G-18472)
RACKWARE INC
580 W Main St Ste D (19426-1940)
PHONE.................................408 430-5821
Steven Olson, *Principal*
EMP: 3
SALES (est): 201.6K **Privately Held**
SIC: 7372 Business oriented computer software
PA: Rackware, Inc.
      39355 California St
      Fremont CA 94538

(G-18473)
SPRING FORD CASTINGS INC
Also Called: W D Pattern Company
25 W 5th Ave (19426-2101)
PHONE.................................610 489-2600
Warren Mangan, *President*
EMP: 6 **EST:** 1958
SQ FT: 20,000
SALES (est): 980.6K **Privately Held**
SIC: 3543 Industrial patterns

(G-18474)
STAPF ENERGY SERVICES
5 Center Ave Ste A (19426-2055)
PHONE.................................610 831-1500
Michael Stapf, *President*
Alan Swenson, *VP Sales*
EMP: 3
SALES (est): 308K **Privately Held**
SIC: 3568 Power transmission equipment

(G-18475)
VANALSTINE MANUFACTURING CO
27 Cherry Ave (19426-2133)
PHONE.................................610 489-7670
Guy Van Alstine, *President*
EMP: 6
SQ FT: 2,100
SALES (est): 1MM **Privately Held**
WEB: www.vanalstinemfg.com
SIC: 3541 5531 Machine tools, metal cutting type; automotive & home supply stores

Treichlers
Northampton County

(G-18476)
ARDENT MILLS LLC
321 E Breadfruit Dr (18086)
P.O. Box 426 (18086-0426)
PHONE.................................972 660-9980
Travis Kapusta, *Branch Mgr*
EMP: 12
SALES (corp-wide): 543.9MM **Privately Held**
WEB: www.conagra.com
SIC: 2041 Flour
PA: Ardent Mills, Llc
      1875 Lawrence St Ste 1400
      Denver CO 80202
      800 851-9618

(G-18477)
NESTOR SYSTEMS INTERNATIONAL
4347 2nd St (18086)
PHONE.................................610 767-5000
Nestor Barolin, *President*
Glen Rex, *President*
Nestor E Barolin, *Principal*
Elizabeth Barolin, *Vice Pres*

Margaret Barolin, *Vice Pres*
EMP: 5
SQ FT: 3,700
SALES (est): 410K **Privately Held**
WEB: www.nestorsys.com
SIC: 3559 Optical lens machinery

Tremont
Schuylkill County

(G-18478)
B & B ANTHRACITE COAL
225 W Main St (17981-1711)
PHONE.................................570 695-3707
Rick Bender, *Partner*
Donald Bender, *Partner*
EMP: 5
SALES (est): 354.5K **Privately Held**
SIC: 1241 Mining services: anthracite

(G-18479)
B & B COAL COMPANY
320 Main St (17981-1310)
PHONE.................................570 695-3188
Joanne Schmidt, *Principal*
EMP: 5
SALES (est): 230K **Privately Held**
SIC: 1241 Coal mining services

(G-18480)
DAYTON SUPERIOR CORPORATION
55 N Pine St (17981-1410)
PHONE.................................570 695-3163
Harvey R Moore, *Opers-Prdtn-Mfg*
EMP: 94 **Publicly Held**
WEB: www.daytonsuperior.com
SIC: 3466 3531 3272 Closures, stamped metal; construction machinery; concrete products
HQ: Dayton Superior Corporation
      1125 Byers Rd
      Miamisburg OH 45342
      937 866-0711

(G-18481)
NATURAL SOIL PRODUCTS COMPANY
200 E Main St (17981-1837)
P.O. Box 283 (17981-0283)
PHONE.................................570 695-2211
Richard Valiga, *General Mgr*
EMP: 60
SALES (est): 8.6MM
SALES (corp-wide): 55.1MM **Privately Held**
WEB: www.tullyenvironmental.com
SIC: 2875 5191 Compost; farm supplies
PA: Tully Environmental Inc.
      12750 Northern Blvd
      Flushing NY 11368
      718 446-7000

(G-18482)
ORCHARD COAL COMPANY
214 Vaux Ave (17981-1420)
PHONE.................................570 695-2301
David Hinnelberger, *Partner*
Rick Grave, *Partner*
Mike Miller, *Partner*
EMP: 8 **EST:** 1992
SALES (est): 900K **Privately Held**
SIC: 1241 Coal mining services

(G-18483)
TUKES TEAROFF (PA)
57 E Main St (17981-1819)
PHONE.................................570 695-3171
Ray Matukewicz, *Owner*
EMP: 8
SQ FT: 6,800
SALES (est): 985.9K **Privately Held**
SIC: 2339 2396 2395 Sportswear, women's; automotive & apparel trimmings; pleating & stitching

(G-18484)
WEST END PRECISION
196 S Tremont St (17981-1622)
PHONE.................................570 695-3911
Jeff Ochs, *President*
William Ochs, *Vice Pres*
EMP: 6

SALES: 500K **Privately Held**
SIC: 3544 Special dies, tools, jigs & fixtures

Trevose
Bucks County

(G-18485)
AIRCLIC INC (HQ)
900 Northbrook Dr Ste 100 (19053-8432)
PHONE.................................215 504-0560
Michael Lee, *CEO*
Tim Bradley, *President*
Matthew Foroughi, *Vice Pres*
Cherryl Graham, *Vice Pres*
Jim Weger, *Senior Engr*
EMP: 59
SQ FT: 13,000
SALES (est): 15.7MM
SALES (corp-wide): 237.4MM **Privately Held**
WEB: www.airclic.com
SIC: 7372 Business oriented computer software; application computer software
PA: Descartes Systems Group Inc, The
      120 Randall Dr
      Waterloo ON N2V 1
      519 746-8110

(G-18486)
AMERICAN BANK NOTE COMPANY (HQ)
2520 Metropolitan Dr (19053-6738)
PHONE.................................215 396-8707
Joseph Caffarella, *President*
Larry Graves, *Vice Pres*
Steven Singer, *Vice Pres*
Joseph W Caffarella, *CFO*
Elaine Lazaridis, *Treasurer*
▲ **EMP:** 20 **EST:** 1878
SQ FT: 10,000
SALES (est): 68.5MM
SALES (corp-wide): 292.8MM **Privately Held**
SIC: 2752 2759 Commercial printing, offset; currency: engraved; security certificates: engraved; coupons: printing
PA: American Banknote Corporation
      1055 Washington Blvd Fl 6
      Stamford CT 06901
      203 941-4090

(G-18487)
BELDEN BRICK SALES & SVC INC
Also Called: Belden Tri-State Building Mtls
7 Neshaminy Interplex Dr # 117 (19053-6927)
PHONE.................................215 639-6561
Robert Turzilli Jr, *Branch Mgr*
EMP: 10
SALES (corp-wide): 8.1MM **Privately Held**
SIC: 5032 2421 Brick, stone & related material; building & structural materials, wood
HQ: Belden Brick Sales & Service, Inc.
      333 7th Ave Fl 5
      New York NY 10001
      212 686-3939

(G-18488)
BURLINGTON INSTR SLS ASSOC
4921 Carver Ave (19053-6251)
PHONE.................................215 322-8750
Dan McHugh, *President*
EMP: 5
SALES (est): 757.3K **Privately Held**
SIC: 5084 3823 Industrial machinery & equipment; temperature instruments: industrial process type

(G-18489)
C-FAB-1 INC
2820 Old Lincoln Hwy # 1 (19053-6828)
PHONE.................................215 331-2797
Greg Michalowski, *President*
Chris McGuckin, *Principal*
EMP: 8
SALES: 500K **Privately Held**
SIC: 3842 Braces, orthopedic; prosthetic appliances

(G-18490)
CORTENDO AB INC
900 Northbrook Dr Ste 200 (19053-8433)
PHONE..................................610 254-9200
Theodore Kozial, *COO*
Alexander Lindstom, *CFO*
EMP: 4
SALES: 353.9K **Privately Held**
SIC: 2834 Pharmaceutical preparations

(G-18491)
CREATIVE DESIGNS INTL LTD
2450 Metropolitan Dr (19053)
PHONE..................................215 953-2800
Michael Rinvler, *President*
▲ EMP: 70
SQ FT: 15,000
SALES (est): 7.5MM **Publicly Held**
WEB: www.cditoys.com
SIC: 3944 Games, toys & children's vehicles
PA: Jakks Pacific, Inc.
2951 28th St Ste 51
Santa Monica CA 90405

(G-18492)
DEANE CARBIDE PRODUCTS INC
2820 Momerton Rd Old Lincoln (19053)
PHONE..................................215 639-3333
Walter R Deane, *President*
Donald L Deane, *Corp Secy*
John S Deane, *Vice Pres*
EMP: 14
SALES (est): 1.2MM **Privately Held**
SIC: 3479 3545 Painting, coating & hot dipping; cutting tools for machine tools

(G-18493)
ENVOY LIGHTING INC
4 Neshaminy (19053)
PHONE..................................215 512-7000
Michael Katz, *President*
Micheal Katz, *President*
EMP: 8
SQ FT: 2,000
SALES (est): 1.5MM **Privately Held**
SIC: 3646 Commercial indusl & institutional electric lighting fixtures

(G-18494)
FRASER OPTICS LLC
210 Andrews Rd (19053-3428)
PHONE..................................215 443-5240
Luke Ritter, *Principal*
John Verdon, *CFO*
EMP: 40
SQ FT: 20,000
SALES (est): 4.1MM **Privately Held**
WEB: www.fraser-volpe.com
SIC: 3827 Telescopes: elbow, panoramic, sighting, fire control, etc.; binoculars; periscopes; gun sights, optical
PA: Fraser-Volpe Llc
210 Andrews Rd
Feasterville Trevose PA 19053

(G-18495)
GAMESA ENERGY USA INC
1150 Northbrook Dr # 150 (19053-8409)
PHONE..................................215 665-9810
Fernando F Vitales, *President*
Jose Calvo, *Principal*
EMP: 10
SALES (est): 1.1MM **Privately Held**
SIC: 3621 Windmills, electric generating

(G-18496)
GENERAL MACHINE PDTS KT LLC
Also Called: G M P
3111 Old Lincoln Hwy (19053-4996)
PHONE..................................215 357-5500
William Pfundt, *President*
Thmoas Klein Jr, *President*
Leah Klein Fox, *Vice Pres*
Kurt Owen, *Vice Pres*
Paul Richardson, *Purch Mgr*
◆ EMP: 100 EST: 1936
SQ FT: 1,000,000
SALES (est): 21MM
SALES (corp-wide): 328.2MM **Privately Held**
WEB: www.gmptools.com
SIC: 3531 Winches

(G-18497)
GLEEPET INC
1631 Loretta Ave Ste D (19053-7337)
PHONE..................................347 607-7850
Sufen Chen, *Admin Sec*
▲ EMP: 10
SALES (est): 655.9K **Privately Held**
SIC: 2511 Wood household furniture
PA: Jiangsu Suzhou Pet Cloth Art Co., Ltd.
No.659, Jinmen Rd.
Suzhou
512 653-2329

(G-18498)
HARBISON WALKER
4667 Somerton Rd (19053-6754)
PHONE..................................215 364-5555
Stephen Macinsky, *Manager*
EMP: 3
SALES (est): 299.2K **Privately Held**
SIC: 3255 Clay refractories

(G-18499)
INFACARE PHARMACEUTICAL CORP
8 Neshaminy Interplex Dr # 221 (19053-6980)
PHONE..................................267 515-5850
John R Post, *CEO*
E Ronald Goldfuss, *CFO*
Simon Tulloch, *Chief Mktg Ofcr*
EMP: 5
SALES (est): 1MM **Privately Held**
WEB: www.infacarepharm.com
SIC: 2834 Pharmaceutical preparations
PA: Mallinckrodt Public Limited Company
College Business & Technology Park
Cruiserath
Dublin 15

(G-18500)
LENOX INSTRUMENT CO INC
265 Andrews Rd (19053-3427)
PHONE..................................215 322-9990
John W Lang Jr, *President*
Paul Lang, *Vice Pres*
Terry Smith, *Engineer*
William Lang, *Admin Sec*
◆ EMP: 21 EST: 1978
SQ FT: 30,000
SALES: 3.2MM **Privately Held**
WEB: www.lenoxinst.com
SIC: 3827 3829 Periscopes; boroscopes; measuring & controlling devices

(G-18501)
MAINLINE ENVIRONMENTAL LLC
605 Elmwood Ave (19053-3308)
PHONE..................................215 651-6635
Frank Ferreiro, *Mng Member*
EMP: 4
SALES: 1MM **Privately Held**
SIC: 3822 Auto controls regulating residntl & coml environmt & applncs

(G-18502)
SCHUTTE KOERTING ACQUISION (PA)
2510 Metropolitan Dr (19053-6738)
PHONE..................................215 639-0900
Michael Pintozzi, *President*
Neil Hughes, *Vice Pres*
Robert Mayers, *Purch Mgr*
Bob Chirona, *Engineer*
Chris Pintozzi, *Engineer*
◆ EMP: 40
SQ FT: 40,000
SALES (est): 14.8MM **Privately Held**
WEB: www.s-k.com
SIC: 3559 3491 3443 3564 Refinery, chemical processing & similar machinery; petroleum refinery equipment; industrial valves; heat exchangers, condensers & components; dust or fume collecting equipment, industrial

(G-18503)
SCULPTZ INC (PA)
Also Called: Hci Direct
1150 Northbrook Dr # 300 (19053-8443)
PHONE..................................215 494-2900
Jean Vernor, *President*
Joe Toczydlowski, *Accounting Dir*
Anil Mathews, *Programmer Anys*
Marijke Bekaert, *Director*
Sue Dudek, *Director*
EMP: 22
SQ FT: 26,000
SALES (est): 18.1MM **Privately Held**
WEB: www.silkies.com
SIC: 2251 5961 2341 5122 Women's hosiery, except socks; catalog & mail-order houses; women's & children's underwear; drugs, proprietaries & sundries

(G-18504)
STRONGBRIDGE BIOPHARMA PLC (PA)
900 Northbrook Dr Ste 200 (19053-8433)
PHONE..................................610 254-9200
Matthew Pauls, *CEO*
John H Johnson, *Ch of Bd*
Brian Conner, *Vice Pres*
Jim Englund, *Vice Pres*
Steve Moloney, *Vice Pres*
EMP: 27
SQ FT: 22,069
SALES: 18MM **Publicly Held**
SIC: 2834 8731 Pharmaceutical preparations; medical research, commercial

(G-18505)
SUEZ WTS SYSTEMS USA INC (DH)
4636 Somerton Rd (19053-6742)
PHONE..................................781 359-7000
David L Calhoun, *President*
Heinrich Markhoff, *President*
Hong Shao, *General Mgr*
Jennifer Horrigan, *Counsel*
Catherine Winter, *Counsel*
◆ EMP: 300 EST: 1986
SQ FT: 134,000
SALES (est): 428.7MM
SALES (corp-wide): 94.7MM **Privately Held**
WEB: www.ionics.com
SIC: 3589 2086 4941 3559 Water purification equipment, household type; water filters & softeners, household type; water treatment equipment, industrial; water, pasteurized: packaged in cans, bottles, etc.; water supply; desalination equipment; water treating compounds; water quality monitoring & control systems
HQ: Suez Wts Usa, Inc.
4636 Somerton Rd
Trevose PA 19053
215 355-3300

(G-18506)
SUEZ WTS USA INC (HQ)
Also Called: Suez Water Tech & Solutions
4636 Somerton Rd (19053-6742)
PHONE..................................215 355-3300
William R Cook, *CEO*
Heiner Markhoff, *President*
Monica A Oconnor, *Treasurer*
R D Voncanon, *Treasurer*
Derick Swarr, *Accounts Exec*
◆ EMP: 600
SQ FT: 375,500
SALES (est): 1.3B
SALES (corp-wide): 94.7MM **Privately Held**
SIC: 2899 3826 5084 3823 Water treating compounds; water testing apparatus; pumps & pumping equipment; industrial instrmnts msrmnt display/control process variable
PA: Suez
Courbevoie Tour Cb 21
Courbevoie 92400
158 813-000

(G-18507)
THERMAL INSTRUMENT CO INC
217 Sterner Mill Rd (19053-6594)
PHONE..................................215 355-8400
Joseph E Curran, *President*
Mark Heinig, *Engineer*
Mary Jane Fiandra, *Manager*
Branin Boyd, *Admin Sec*
EMP: 15 EST: 1959
SQ FT: 11,000
SALES: 2MM **Privately Held**
WEB: www.thermalinstrument.com
SIC: 3823 Flow instruments, industrial process type

(G-18508)
VIDEO VISIONS INC (PA)
3600 Boundbrook Ave (19053-6202)
PHONE..................................215 942-6642
Mary Ellen Milanese, *President*
Ann Marie Milanese, *Admin Sec*
EMP: 13
SQ FT: 5,000
SALES (est): 4.1MM **Privately Held**
WEB: www.video-visions.com
SIC: 3663 5065 Television broadcasting & communications equipment; electronic parts & equipment

(G-18509)
ZERO TECHNOLOGIES LLC
Also Called: Zero Water
7 Neshaminy Interplex Dr # 116 (19053-6973)
PHONE..................................215 244-0823
Doug Kellam, *CEO*
Robert Thaler, *CFO*
Kevin Greczyn, *Accounting Mgr*
▲ EMP: 16
SQ FT: 3,000
SALES (est): 5.1MM **Privately Held**
SIC: 3589 Water filters & softeners, household type

Trexlertown
Lehigh County

(G-18510)
ELITE SWEETS INC (PA)
7150 Hamilton Blvd (18087-9725)
PHONE..................................610 391-1719
EMP: 10
SALES (est): 807.5K **Privately Held**
SIC: 2064 Candy & other confectionery products

(G-18511)
VALLEY BUSINESS SERVICES INC (PA)
Also Called: Express Business Center
6900 Hamilton Blvd # 285 (18087-9101)
PHONE..................................610 366-1970
Mustafa Jaffer, *President*
▼ EMP: 12 EST: 2002
SQ FT: 1,500
SALES (est): 1.9MM **Privately Held**
WEB: www.valleybusinessservices.com
SIC: 2732 2759 2752 Pamphlets: printing & binding, not published on site; promotional printing; advertising literature: printing; commercial printing, offset

---

Trout Run
Lycoming County

(G-18512)
CASCADE CORPORATION
1456 Kelly Rd (17771-8693)
PHONE..................................570 995-5099
R C Warren Jr, *President*
EMP: 123
SALES (corp-wide): 18.8B **Privately Held**
SIC: 3537 Lift trucks, industrial: fork, platform, straddle, etc.
HQ: Cascade Corporation
2201 Ne 201st Ave
Fairview OR 97024
503 669-6300

(G-18513)
COGAN WIND LLC
623 Taylor Rd (17771-8621)
PHONE..................................570 998-9554
John P Leatherman, *Mng Member*
EMP: 3 EST: 2010
SALES: 47.8K **Privately Held**
SIC: 1389 7389 Oil field services;

(G-18514)
HORN LINDA COLLECTIBLES & CO
8837 Rose Valley Rd (17771-8906)
PHONE.................................570 998-8401
Linda Horn, *Partner*
Regina A Latini, *Partner*
James Solomon, *Partner*
EMP: 3
SQ FT: 972
SALES (est): 120K **Privately Held**
SIC: 3269 Stationery articles, pottery

(G-18515)
JPW DESIGN & MANUFACTURING INC
6080 State Route 14 (17771-9087)
PHONE.................................570 995-5025
Michael Jameson, *President*
Mike Paternostro, *Vice Pres*
Tim Wagner, *Vice Pres*
EMP: 30
SQ FT: 9,000
SALES (est): 6MM **Privately Held**
SIC: 3567 Industrial furnaces & ovens

(G-18516)
ROSSS CUSTOM BUTCHERING
44 Ross Rd (17771-8608)
PHONE.................................570 634-3571
Nila Ross, *Owner*
EMP: 10
SALES (est): 10K **Privately Held**
SIC: 2011 Meat packing plants

Troy
Bradford County

(G-18517)
BRADCO PRINTERS INC
Also Called: Troy Gazette Register
11 Canton St (16947)
PHONE.................................570 297-3024
Thomas Pine, *President*
Kathy Close, *Vice Pres*
EMP: 3
SALES (est): 25K **Privately Held**
SIC: 2759 2752 Commercial printing; commercial printing, offset

(G-18518)
BRADFORD COUNTY SANITATION INC
Also Called: Bradford County Sanitation Svc
9 Canton St (16947)
P.O. Box 334 (16947-0334)
PHONE.................................570 673-3128
Crist Palmer, *President*
Rick Hoover, *Vice Pres*
Harriett J Hoover, *Treasurer*
EMP: 3
SALES (est): 311.5K **Privately Held**
SIC: 7699 2721 Septic tank cleaning service; periodicals

(G-18519)
CONTROL TECH USA LTD
22025 Route 14 (16947-8790)
PHONE.................................570 529-6011
Dale Watkins, *General Mgr*
EMP: 75
SALES (est): 8.5MM
SALES (corp-wide): 71.1MM **Privately Held**
SIC: 3822 Auto controls regulating residntl & coml environmt & applncs
PA: Control Tech 2011 Ltd
11001 78 Ave
Grande Prairie AB T8W 2
780 539-7114

(G-18520)
CUMMINGS VENEER PRODUCTS INC
23189 Rte 14 N (16947)
P.O. Box 203 (16947-0203)
PHONE.................................570 995-1892
Lee Cummings, *Ch of Bd*
Doug Cummings, *President*
▲ EMP: 9
SQ FT: 12,000

SALES: 1.2MM **Privately Held**
SIC: 2435 Hardwood veneer & plywood

(G-18521)
DALYRMPLE GRAVEL AND CONTRACTI
278 Elmira St (16947-1244)
PHONE.................................570 297-0340
EMP: 3
SALES (est): 79.9K **Privately Held**
SIC: 1442 Construction Sand/Gravel

(G-18522)
E-TECH INDUSTRIAL
1 Skyline Dr (16947)
P.O. Box 35 (16947-0035)
PHONE.................................570 297-1300
John Estep, *President*
EMP: 8
SQ FT: 3,500
SALES (est): 3MM **Privately Held**
SIC: 5085 3462 Industrial supplies; gear & chain forgings

(G-18523)
LEONA MEAT PLANT INC
1961 Leona Rd (16947-8591)
PHONE.................................570 297-3574
Charles Debach II, *President*
Charles De Bach II, *President*
Mike Debach, *Corp Secy*
Mike De Bach, *Treasurer*
EMP: 12 EST: 1963
SQ FT: 6,500
SALES (est): 888K **Privately Held**
SIC: 5421 2011 2013 Meat markets, including freezer provisioners; meat packing plants; sausages & other prepared meats

(G-18524)
OAK HILL VENEER INC
Also Called: Channel Veneer USA
23189 Rte 14 (16947)
P.O. Box 304 (16947-0304)
PHONE.................................570 297-4137
Lee P Cummings, *President*
Maria Diaz, *President*
Doug Cummings, *Vice Pres*
Jerry D Ross, *Opers Staff*
Roy Cummings Sr, *Treasurer*
◆ EMP: 52
SQ FT: 82,000
SALES (est): 9.2MM
SALES (corp-wide): 601K **Privately Held**
WEB: www.oakhillveneer.com
SIC: 2435 Veneer stock, hardwood
HQ: Comercial Losan Sl
Carretera Nacional 211 (Pol. Los Arcos Cr. Alcaliz), S/N
Caspe 50700
976 639-000

(G-18525)
PENN TROY MANUFACTURING INC
182 Railroad St (16947-1424)
P.O. Box 187 (16947-0187)
PHONE.................................570 297-2125
Mark Powers, *CEO*
Margaret Powers, *Admin Sec*
◆ EMP: 30
SQ FT: 50,000
SALES (est): 6.6MM **Privately Held**
SIC: 3491 Water works valves

(G-18526)
SHADES OF COUNTRY
5103 Route 6 (16947-9251)
PHONE.................................570 297-3327
Marie Bauman, *Principal*
EMP: 4
SALES (est): 328.8K **Privately Held**
SIC: 3089 Lamp bases & shades, plastic

(G-18527)
TNT DISPOSAL
Rr 3 (16947)
PHONE.................................570 297-0101
Tom Baldwin, *Principal*
EMP: 4
SALES (est): 320.5K **Privately Held**
SIC: 3089 Garbage containers, plastic

(G-18528)
TOWANDA PRINTING CO INC
Also Called: Troy Penny Saver
778 Canton St (16947-1449)
P.O. Box 342 (16947-0342)
PHONE.................................570 297-4158
Dave Berry, *General Mgr*
EMP: 3
SALES (corp-wide): 12MM **Privately Held**
WEB: www.sundayreview.com
SIC: 2711 Newspapers, publishing & printing
PA: Towanda Printing Co Inc
116 N Main St
Towanda PA 18848
570 265-2151

Trumbauersville
Bucks County

(G-18529)
B & J SHEET METAL INC
1535 Allentown Rd (18970)
P.O. Box 872 (18970-0872)
PHONE.................................215 538-9543
Jerry A Schmidt, *President*
EMP: 16 EST: 1971
SALES (est): 3.3MM **Privately Held**
SIC: 3556 3599 Smokers, food processing equipment; custom machinery

(G-18530)
BRACALENTE GLOBAL LTD
20 W Creamery Rd (18970)
P.O. Box 570 (18970-0570)
PHONE.................................215 536-3077
Ronald Bracalente, *President*
Scott Keaton, *CFO*
Paul Nevells, *Sales Mgr*
◆ EMP: 130 EST: 2005
SQ FT: 80,000
SALES: 10MM
SALES (corp-wide): 30.9MM **Privately Held**
SIC: 3448 Prefabricated metal buildings
PA: Bracalente's Manufacturing Co., Inc.
20 W Creamery Rd
Trumbauersville PA 18970
215 536-3077

(G-18531)
BRACALENTES MFG CO INC (PA)
Also Called: Bracalente Manufacturing Group
20 W Creamery Rd (18970)
P.O. Box 570 (18970-0570)
PHONE.................................215 536-3077
Thomas Bracalente, *Ch of Bd*
Ron Bracalente, *President*
Ken Kratz, *Vice Pres*
Richard Nast, *Prdtn Mgr*
Stephen Kemp, *Manager*
▲ EMP: 160
SQ FT: 65,000
SALES (est): 30.9MM **Privately Held**
WEB: www.bracalente.com
SIC: 3599 3451 Machine shop, jobbing & repair; screw machine products

(G-18532)
MIDNIGHT MADNESS DISTLG LLC
2300 Trumbauersville Rd (18970)
P.O. Box 116, Quakertown (18951-0116)
PHONE.................................215 268-6071
Anthony Lorubbio, *CEO*
Casey Parzych, *President*
EMP: 3
SQ FT: 500
SALES (est): 341.7K **Privately Held**
SIC: 2085 Distilled & blended liquors

Tunkhannock
Wyoming County

(G-18533)
CENTERMORELAND CONCRETE PDTS
12 Creamery Rd (18657-5861)
PHONE.................................570 333-4944
James G Sickler Sr, *Owner*
Jim Sickler Jr, *Manager*
Randy Sickler, *Manager*
EMP: 16 EST: 1963
SALES (est): 1.5MM **Privately Held**
SIC: 3272 Septic tanks, concrete

(G-18534)
CK STONE LLC
69 Vago Rd (18657-5712)
PHONE.................................570 903-5868
Cheri Schultz,
EMP: 4
SALES (est): 224.5K **Privately Held**
SIC: 1411 Bluestone, dimension-quarrying

(G-18535)
CUMMINS INC
24 Pine Ridge Rd (18657-5961)
PHONE.................................570 333-0360
EMP: 7
SALES (corp-wide): 23.7B **Publicly Held**
SIC: 5084 3519 Engines & parts, diesel; internal combustion engines
PA: Cummins Inc.
500 Jackson St
Columbus IN 47201
812 377-5000

(G-18536)
D J PRECISION INSTRUMENT CORP
Also Called: D. J. Mfg Co
149 Marcy Rd (18657-7114)
P.O. Box 676 (18657-0676)
PHONE.................................570 836-2229
Nicholas Aletras, *President*
Jan Aletras, *Admin Sec*
EMP: 12
SQ FT: 5,000
SALES (est): 700K **Privately Held**
WEB: www.janick.com
SIC: 3599 Machine shop, jobbing & repair

(G-18537)
DAVIS LATTEMANN INC
7 Stonier Rd (18657-6052)
PHONE.................................877 576-5885
Arthur Davis, *President*
▲ EMP: 6
SALES (est): 403.6K **Privately Held**
SIC: 3443 Heat exchangers, condensers & components

(G-18538)
DEER PARK LUMBER INC
3042 Sr 6 (18657-7797)
PHONE.................................570 836-1133
Ronald Andrews, *Principal*
Jack Monnoyer, *Purch Dir*
Paul Reining, *Buyer*
Matthew Andrews, *Treasurer*
Cindy Roberts, *Controller*
▼ EMP: 85
SQ FT: 50,000
SALES (est): 37MM **Privately Held**
WEB: www.deer-park-lumber.com
SIC: 5031 2421 2426 Lumber: rough, dressed & finished; sawmills & planing mills, general; kiln drying of lumber; hardwood dimension & flooring mills

(G-18539)
HORLACHER & SHERWOOD
108 Sr 92 S (18657-6930)
P.O. Box 179 (18657-0179)
PHONE.................................570 836-6298
Arthur Carpenter Jr, *Manager*
EMP: 7
SALES (corp-wide): 3MM **Privately Held**
WEB: www.skiddershop.com
SIC: 5082 1011 2411 Forestry equipment; iron ores; logging

PA: Horlacher & Sherwood
312 Mile Rd
Tunkhannock PA 18657
570 836-1116

(G-18540)
KEYSTONE TRUCK CAPS LLC
3444 Sr 6 (18657-7830)
PHONE....................570 836-4322
Glen Werkheiser, *Owner*
Aaron Werkheiser, *Mng Member*
EMP: 4
SQ FT: 2,100
SALES (est): 773.9K **Privately Held**
WEB: www.keystonecaps.com
SIC: 5561 3792 5015 Campers (pickup coaches) for mounting on trucks; pickup covers, canopies or caps; automotive accessories, used

(G-18541)
LAKE PAPER PRODUCTS INC
2722 Sr 6 (18657-7793)
P.O. Box 249, Lake Winola (18625-0249)
PHONE....................570 836-8815
Scott Kresge, *President*
Mark Manglaviti, *Vice Pres*
EMP: 32
SQ FT: 42,000
SALES (est): 6.5MM **Privately Held**
SIC: 2676 Toilet paper: made from purchased paper

(G-18542)
MCKENNAS WOODWORKING
88 Shupp Hill Rd (18657-5720)
PHONE....................570 836-3652
Bruce McKennas, *Principal*
EMP: 5
SALES (est): 516.1K **Privately Held**
SIC: 3995 Burial caskets

(G-18543)
MILLWOOD INC
5530 Sr 6 (18657-7900)
PHONE....................570 836-9280
David Shingler, *Branch Mgr*
EMP: 17 **Privately Held**
SIC: 3565 5084 Packaging machinery; packaging machinery & equipment
PA: Millwood, Inc.
3708 International Blvd
Vienna OH 44473

(G-18544)
MULLIGAN PRINTING CORPORATION
Also Called: Penny Saver
110 E Harrison St (18657-1140)
PHONE....................570 278-3271
Charles I Mulligan, *President*
Charles J Mulligan, *President*
Frank Mulligan, *Vice Pres*
EMP: 27
SALES (est): 1.7MM **Privately Held**
WEB: www.mulliganprinting.com
SIC: 2711 2752 Newspapers, publishing & printing; commercial printing, lithographic

(G-18545)
NUFEEDS INC
16 Sr 1006 (18657)
PHONE....................570 836-2866
David Williams, *Manager*
EMP: 8
SALES (est): 830.5K
SALES (corp-wide): 846.7K **Privately Held**
SIC: 2048 Prepared feeds
PA: Nufeeds Inc
200 Jackson St
Montrose PA 18801
570 278-3767

(G-18546)
OLD EPP INC
150 Lawson Ln (18657-7891)
PHONE....................570 430-9089
Bennie M Wharry, *Principal*
EMP: 3
SALES (corp-wide): 62.7MM **Privately Held**
SIC: 3083 Laminated plastics plate & sheet

HQ: Old Epp, Inc.
360 Epic Circle Dr
Fairmont WV 26554
304 534-3600

(G-18547)
PROCTER & GAMBLE COMPANY
Rr 87 Box S (18657)
PHONE....................570 833-5141
William Sims, *Manager*
EMP: 150
SALES (corp-wide): 66.8B **Publicly Held**
SIC: 2844 Deodorants, personal
PA: The Procter & Gamble Company
1 Procter And Gamble Plz
Cincinnati OH 45202
513 983-1100

(G-18548)
RECON ENTERPRISES
Also Called: Harry's Wood Shop
3971 Sr 6 (18657-7839)
PHONE....................570 836-1179
Gary Toczko, *Owner*
EMP: 5
SQ FT: 5,000
SALES (est): 800K **Privately Held**
SIC: 5712 2431 Unfinished furniture; millwork

(G-18549)
T & B LOGGING INC
530 E Avery Station Rd (18657-6034)
PHONE....................570 561-4847
Ted Brown, *Principal*
EMP: 3 **EST:** 2010
SALES (est): 265.6K **Privately Held**
SIC: 2411 Logging

(G-18550)
T-TOWN SHEDS & SUPPLY
100 Dymond Ter (18657-1734)
PHONE....................570 836-5686
Chris Jescavage, *Owner*
EMP: 3
SQ FT: 5,500
SALES (est): 210K **Privately Held**
SIC: 2452 5211 Prefabricated buildings, wood; prefabricated buildings; lumber products

(G-18551)
TUSCARORA ELECTRIC MFG CO
41 Hilltop Dr (18657-6605)
PHONE....................570 836-2101
Jean E Mieczkowski, *President*
Stanley R Mieczkowski, *Vice Pres*
EMP: 5
SALES (est): 646.3K **Privately Held**
SIC: 3564 3523 Ventilating fans: industrial or commercial; trailers & wagons, farm

(G-18552)
WILLIAMS FIELD SERVICES
310 Sr 29 N (18657-6817)
PHONE....................570 965-7643
EMP: 6
SALES (est): 95.9K **Privately Held**
SIC: 4925 1389 Gas production and/or distribution; oil & gas field services

(G-18553)
WYOMING COUNTY PRESS INC
Also Called: New Age Examiner
16 E Tioga St (18657-1506)
P.O. Box 59 (18657-0059)
PHONE....................570 348-9185
George V Lynett, *President*
James E Towner, *Principal*
Edward J Lynett Jr, *Admin Sec*
William R Lynett, *Asst Sec*
EMP: 10 **EST:** 1868
SQ FT: 1,800
SALES (est): 100K **Privately Held**
WEB: www.wyomingpa.com
SIC: 2711 Newspapers: publishing only, not printed on site

Turbotville
Northumberland County

(G-18554)
MUNCY INDUSTRIES LLC
5820 Susquehanna Trl (17772-8542)
P.O. Box 205, Muncy (17756-0205)
PHONE....................570 649-5188
Jason Fetter, *Vice Pres*
Alex Marconnet, *Engineer*
James R Fetter Jr,
EMP: 8
SQ FT: 2,000
SALES: 11.5MM **Privately Held**
SIC: 2298 Wire rope centers

(G-18555)
MUNCY MACHINE & TOOL CO INC
5820 Susquehanna Trl (17772-8542)
P.O. Box 205, Muncy (17756-0205)
PHONE....................570 649-5188
James R Fetter Jr, *President*
Jason K Fetter, *Vice Pres*
EMP: 25
SQ FT: 34,000
SALES (est): 3.9MM **Privately Held**
SIC: 3315 3599 Wire, ferrous/iron; machine & other job shop work

(G-18556)
NITE LITE SIGN CO
1359 Schuyler Rd (17772-8544)
PHONE....................570 649-5825
Ruth King, *Owner*
Tim King, *Owner*
EMP: 6
SALES (est): 200K **Privately Held**
SIC: 3993 Signs, not made in custom sign painting shops

(G-18557)
UPSON-WALTON COMPANY
5820 Susquehanna Trl (17772-8542)
P.O. Box 205, Muncy (17756-0205)
PHONE....................570 649-5188
Ophelia T Fetter, *President*
James R Fetter Jr, *CFO*
EMP: 6
SQ FT: 4,800
SALES (est): 2.8MM **Privately Held**
SIC: 3429 5085 Manufactured hardware (general); industrial supplies

---

Turtle Creek
Allegheny County

(G-18558)
ARMOLOY WESTERN PENNSYLVANIA
Also Called: Armoloy Western Pennsylvania
1231 Rodi Rd (15145-1038)
PHONE....................412 823-1030
Gregory E Glaner Sr, *President*
George F Glaner III, *Vice Pres*
Greg Glaner Jr, *Opers Mgr*
EMP: 13
SQ FT: 10,000
SALES (est): 2MM **Privately Held**
WEB: www.armoloy-wpa.com
SIC: 3479 Coating of metals & formed products

(G-18559)
BP STOP N GO
638 Brown Ave (15145-1138)
PHONE....................412 823-4500
EMP: 3
SALES (est): 271K **Privately Held**
SIC: 2911 Petroleum refining

(G-18560)
BRUSH AFTERMARKET N AMER INC
Also Called: Brush Aftermarket US
601 Braddock Ave (15145-2069)
PHONE....................412 829-7500
Chris Abbott, *CEO*
Michael Daly, *Finance Dir*
EMP: 14

SALES (est): 3.7MM **Privately Held**
SIC: 3621 7539 Motors & generators; brake services; alternators & generators, rebuilding & repair

(G-18561)
CASCADE ARCHITECTURAL PRODUCTS
132 George St (15145-1040)
PHONE....................412 824-9313
John Aiello Sr, *President*
John Aiello Jr, *Vice Pres*
EMP: 4
SALES (est): 310K **Privately Held**
SIC: 3211 Skylight glass

(G-18562)
CIRCADIANCE LLC
1300 Rodi Rd (15145-1095)
P.O. Box 17480, Pittsburgh (15235-0480)
PHONE....................724 858-2837
David G Groll, *CEO*
Tracy Singh, *Opers Staff*
Rich Lordo, *Engineer*
Donna Brozda, *Accountant*
Kathleen Groll, *Human Res Mgr*
EMP: 18 **EST:** 2006
SQ FT: 7,000
SALES: 1MM **Privately Held**
SIC: 3842 5047 Gas masks; industrial safety devices: first aid kits & masks

(G-18563)
CONICITY TECHNOLOGIES LLC
519 Braddock Ave (15145-2067)
PHONE....................412 601-1874
William Shaffer, *Owner*
EMP: 3 **EST:** 1999
SALES (est): 256.7K **Privately Held**
SIC: 3541 7389 Machine tools, metal cutting type; metal cutting services

(G-18564)
E H SCHWAB COMPANY
1281 Rodi Rd (15145-1038)
PHONE....................412 823-5003
Dale F Harrison, *President*
Diane V Harrison, *Corp Secy*
Neal Harrison, *Vice Pres*
Neal R Harrison, *Vice Pres*
Mark Whitney, *Prdtn Mgr*
EMP: 43 **EST:** 1929
SQ FT: 20,000
SALES (est): 9.3MM **Privately Held**
WEB: www.ehschwab.com
SIC: 3469 Spinning metal for the trade; stamping metal for the trade

(G-18565)
GENERATOR AND MTR SVCS PA LLC
Also Called: Brush G M S
601 Braddock Ave (15145-2073)
PHONE....................412 829-7500
Martyn Vaughan, *Principal*
Saul Seigel, *Treasurer*
Robert Leach, *Director*
Paula Orr, *Admin Sec*
◆ **EMP:** 65
SQ FT: 25,000
SALES (est): 14.4MM
SALES (corp-wide): 456.8K **Privately Held**
WEB: www.gmsinternational.com
SIC: 3621 Electric motor & generator parts
HQ: Brush Electrical Machines Limited
Nottingham Road
Loughborough LEICS LE11
150 961-1511

(G-18566)
NZK PLASTICS LLC
1210 Airbrake Ave (15145-1821)
P.O. Box 208 (15145-0208)
PHONE....................412 823-8630
Nick Karnavas,
▲ **EMP:** 4
SQ FT: 1,200
SALES (est): 360K **Privately Held**
SIC: 3089 Injection molding of plastics

GEOGRAPHIC

(G-18567)
PRECISION PARTS & MACHINE CO
510 Braddock Ave (15145-2074)
PHONE..............................412 824-9367
James R Kocis, *President*
W A Rugolsky, *Corp Secy*
EMP: 6
SQ FT: 9,000
SALES (est): 1.4MM **Privately Held**
SIC: 3599 Machine shop, jobbing & repair

(G-18568)
QUALITY DIE MAKERS INC
831 Oak Ave (15145-1768)
PHONE..............................724 325-1264
Todd E Zatezalo, *President*
Diane Zatezalo, *Corp Secy*
Donald Burt, *Shareholder*
Joseph W Latta, *Shareholder*
EMP: 20
SQ FT: 5,200
SALES: 250K **Privately Held**
SIC: 3544 3599 Extrusion dies; machine shop, jobbing & repair

(G-18569)
TAKTL LLC
503 Braddock Ave (15145-2066)
PHONE..............................412 486-1600
Barry Schnauber, *Prdtn Mgr*
Jamie Bolten, *Production*
Brian Knapp, *Accountant*
Steven Swartz, *Sr Project Mgr*
Jason Howell, *Manager*
▲ EMP: 128
SQ FT: 177,713
SALES (est): 20.7MM **Privately Held**
SIC: 3272 Panels & sections, prefabricated concrete

(G-18570)
TECHS INDUSTRIES INC
Also Called: Nextech
300 Braddock Ave (15145-2064)
PHONE..............................412 464-5000
Jack Forbes, *Vice Pres*
Bart Miller, *Vice Pres*
EMP: 17 **Publicly Held**
SIC: 3479 Galvanizing of iron, steel or end-formed products
HQ: The Techs Industries Inc
2400 2nd Ave
Pittsburgh PA 15219
412 464-5000

Turtlepoint
Mckean County

(G-18571)
GLENN O HAWBAKER INC
Also Called: Plant 7
1724 Champlin Hill Rd (16750-1212)
PHONE..............................814 642-7869
Mike Hall, *Branch Mgr*
EMP: 10
SALES (corp-wide): 300MM **Privately Held**
SIC: 3531 Asphalt plant, including gravel-mix type
PA: Glenn O. Hawbaker, Inc.
1952 Waddle Rd Ste 203
State College PA 16803
814 237-1444

Twin Rocks
Cambria County

(G-18572)
ROSEBUD MINING CO
776 Plank Rd (15960)
P.O. Box 267 (15960-0267)
PHONE..............................814 749-5208
EMP: 40
SALES (est): 1.2MM **Privately Held**
SIC: 1481 6211 Nonmetallic Mineral Services Security Broker/Dealer

---

Tylersburg
Clarion County

(G-18573)
FREDERICK DRILLING CO & SONS
18 Piper Ln (16361)
P.O. Box 66 (16361-0066)
PHONE..............................814 744-8581
Clyde Frederick, *President*
Rick Frederick, *Corp Secy*
Don Frederick, *Vice Pres*
EMP: 7
SQ FT: 5,400
SALES (est): 1.1MM **Privately Held**
SIC: 1311 1381 1781 Crude petroleum production; directional drilling oil & gas wells; water well servicing

---

Tylersport
Montgomery County

(G-18574)
BACHMAN DRAPERY STUDIO INC
20 Ridge Rd (18971)
P.O. Box 8 (18971-0008)
PHONE..............................215 257-8810
Barbara Bachman, *President*
Bruce Bachman, *Vice Pres*
Janice Beer, *Admin Sec*
EMP: 4
SQ FT: 3,100
SALES (est): 230K **Privately Held**
SIC: 2211 2221 5023 Draperies & drapery fabrics, cotton; draperies & drapery fabrics, manmade fiber & silk; home furnishings

---

Tyrone
Blair County

(G-18575)
ALBEMARLE CORPORATION
2858 Back Vail Rd (16686-8100)
PHONE..............................814 684-4310
Randy Anders, *Plant Mgr*
Jeff Dreibelbis, *Warehouse Mgr*
Robin Latchford, *Purch Agent*
Gary Donner, *Engineer*
Ivan Riggle, *Manager*
EMP: 170 **Publicly Held**
WEB: www.stabrom.com
SIC: 2869 2819 Industrial organic chemicals; industrial inorganic chemicals
PA: Albemarle Corporation
4250 Congress St Ste 900
Charlotte NC 28209

(G-18576)
ARCTIC STAR SLEDS
2842 Butternut Rd (16686-3501)
PHONE..............................814 684-3594
Johnn Molburg, *Principal*
EMP: 4
SALES (est): 256.2K **Privately Held**
WEB: www.arcticstarsleds.com
SIC: 3949 Sporting & athletic goods

(G-18577)
BOROUGH OF TYRONE
Also Called: Tyrone Bureau Water Department
1100 Logan Ave (16686-1624)
PHONE..............................814 684-5396
Ardean Latchford, *Superintendent*
EMP: 7 **Privately Held**
WEB: www.tyroneboropa.com
SIC: 3589 9111 Water treatment equipment, industrial; mayors' offices
PA: Borough Of Tyrone
1100 Logan Ave
Tyrone PA 16686
814 684-2110

(G-18578)
CCK INC
Also Called: Juniata Packing Co
Hc 220 (16686)
P.O. Box 276 (16686-0276)
PHONE..............................814 684-2270
Christian C Kunzler Jr, *President*
Christian C Kunzler III, *Exec VP*
John S Kunzler, *Vice Pres*
Robert Zigment, *Treasurer*
Marsha Pear, *Office Mgr*
EMP: 200
SQ FT: 46,000
SALES (est): 23.3MM
SALES (corp-wide): 117.4MM **Privately Held**
SIC: 2011 2013 Meat packing plants; sausages & other prepared meats
PA: Kunzler & Company, Inc.
652 Manor St
Lancaster PA 17603
717 299-6301

(G-18579)
CENTER HARDWOOD LLC
14082 S Eagle Valley Rd (16686-8123)
PHONE..............................814 684-3600
Melvin Reese Jr, *President*
Barb Shilbt, *Admin Sec*
EMP: 17
SALES (est): 7.2MM **Privately Held**
WEB: www.centerhardwood.com
SIC: 2421 2431 2426 Sawmills & planing mills, general; millwork; hardwood dimension & flooring mills

(G-18580)
CHICAGO RIVET & MACHINE CO
Tyrone Division
2728 Adams Ave (16686-8851)
P.O. Box 278 (16686-0278)
PHONE..............................814 684-2430
Diane Decker, *Purch Mgr*
Clay Oshell, *Buyer*
M P Sweitzer, *Branch Mgr*
George Bonsell, *Supervisor*
Tanya Harpster, *Technology*
EMP: 100
SALES (corp-wide): 37.1MM **Publicly Held**
WEB: www.chicagorivetsw.com
SIC: 3542 3452 Riveting machines; bolts, nuts, rivets & washers
PA: Chicago Rivet & Machine Co.
901 Frontenac Rd
Naperville IL 60563
630 357-8500

(G-18581)
DIXON TOOL & DIE INC
2500 Adams Ave (16686-8849)
P.O. Box 188 (16686-0188)
PHONE..............................814 684-0266
Bill Dixon Jr, *President*
Brenda Dixon, *Treasurer*
EMP: 19
SQ FT: 30,000
SALES: 1.2MM **Privately Held**
WEB: www.dixontool.net
SIC: 3544 Special dies & tools

(G-18582)
FORT DEARBORN COMPANY
13985 S Eagle Valley Rd (16686-7905)
PHONE..............................814 686-7656
EMP: 7
SALES (corp-wide): 117.3MM **Privately Held**
SIC: 2752 Commercial printing, lithographic
HQ: Fort Dearborn Company
1530 Morse Ave
Elk Grove Village IL 60007
847 357-9500

(G-18583)
FOWLERS LOGGING
309 Washington Ave (16686-1249)
PHONE..............................814 684-9883
Kathy Fowler, *Principal*
EMP: 3
SALES (est): 203.2K **Privately Held**
SIC: 2411 Logging camps & contractors

(G-18584)
JOHNSTON-MOREHOUSE-DICKEY CO
5582 E Pleasant Vly Blvd (16686-1279)
PHONE..............................814 684-0916
Scott Walters, *Branch Mgr*
EMP: 6
SALES (corp-wide): 33.8MM **Privately Held**
SIC: 2299 3089 5039 Narrow woven fabrics: linen, jute, hemp & ramie; plastic hardware & building products; netting, plastic; soil erosion control fabrics
PA: Johnston-Morehouse-Dickey Co Inc
5401 Progress Blvd
Bethel Park PA 15102
412 833-7100

(G-18585)
JOSEPH F BIDDLE PUBLISHING CO
Also Called: Daily Herald
1067 Pennsylvania Ave (16686-1513)
P.O. Box 246 (16686-0246)
PHONE..............................814 684-4000
Joan Cook, *Manager*
EMP: 6
SALES (corp-wide): 5.9MM **Privately Held**
SIC: 2711 Newspapers, publishing & printing
PA: Joseph F Biddle Publishing Co Inc
325 Penn St
Huntingdon PA
814 643-4040

(G-18586)
LIGHT TOOL AND MACHINE INC
108 Enterprise Dr (16686-8146)
PHONE..............................814 684-2755
Melvin Light, *President*
Nancy Light, *Vice Pres*
EMP: 11
SALES: 1.5MM **Privately Held**
SIC: 3599 7389 Machine shop, jobbing & repair;

(G-18587)
NEW ENTERPRISE STONE LIME INC
Also Called: Tryone Forge Limestone
1 Mile S Of Tyrone Rt 453 (16686)
PHONE..............................814 684-4905
Jeff Lindsey, *Manager*
EMP: 40
SQ FT: 1,200
SALES (corp-wide): 651.9MM **Privately Held**
WEB: www.nesl.com
SIC: 5032 1422 Limestone; crushed & broken limestone
PA: New Enterprise Stone & Lime Co., Inc.
3912 Brumbaugh Rd
New Enterprise PA 16664
814 224-6883

(G-18588)
P G RECYCLING INCORPORATED
155 Rossman Rd (16686-8553)
PHONE..............................814 696-6000
Peter Gati Jr, *President*
Suzanne Gati, *Vice Pres*
EMP: 15
SALES (est): 1.8MM **Privately Held**
SIC: 4212 2448 5093 Delivery service, vehicular; pallets, wood; skids, wood; plastics scrap

(G-18589)
PITTSBURGH GLASS WORKS LLC
Also Called: Works27
4408 E Pleasant Vly Blvd (16686-7029)
PHONE..............................814 684-2300
Eric Schramm, *Branch Mgr*
EMP: 295 **Privately Held**
SIC: 3231 Mirrors, truck & automobile: made from purchased glass
HQ: Pittsburgh Glass Works, Llc
30 Isabella St Ste 500
Pittsburgh PA 15212

(G-18590)
PRECISION DIMENSION INC
121 Cherry Ave (16686-1003)
PHONE..................................814 684-4150
Tim Brobeck, *President*
EMP: 15
SQ FT: 4,000
SALES (est): 2.2MM **Privately Held**
WEB: www.precisiondimension.com
SIC: 2434 Wood kitchen cabinets

(G-18591)
RAY BURIAL VAULT COMPANY INC
N3 N 3 Miles Rr 220 (16686)
P.O. Box 218 (16686-0218)
PHONE..................................814 684-0104
Matthew Ray, *President*
Anita Ray, *Admin Sec*
EMP: 14
SQ FT: 1,300
SALES (est): 1MM **Privately Held**
SIC: 3272 Burial vaults, concrete or pre-cast terrazzo; septic tanks, concrete

(G-18592)
RECLAMERE INC
905 Pennsylvania Ave (16686-1511)
PHONE..................................814 684-5505
Robert E Dornich, *President*
Joseph P Harford, *Vice Pres*
Angie S Keating, *Vice Pres*
EMP: 34
SQ FT: 10,000
SALES (est): 3.2MM **Privately Held**
WEB: www.reclamere.com
SIC: 7375 7379 3571 On-line data base information retrieval; computer related consulting services; electronic computers

(G-18593)
STOTT PUBLICATIONS INC
Also Called: Bellefonte Gazette
2314 Pennington Rd (16686-3247)
P.O. Box 129, Warriors Mark (16877-0129)
PHONE..................................814 632-6700
Fax: 814 632-6699
EMP: 5
SQ FT: 2,000
SALES (est): 240K **Privately Held**
SIC: 2711 2721 Newspapers-Publishing/Printing Periodicals-Publishing/Printing

(G-18594)
SUPERIOR LUMBER INC
2432 Ridge Rd (16686-3341)
P.O. Box 248 (16686-0248)
PHONE..................................814 684-3420
Ken Eier, *Principal*
EMP: 10 EST: 2004
SALES (est): 27.4K **Privately Held**
SIC: 2421 Lumber: rough, sawed or planed

(G-18595)
TEAM TEN LLC
Also Called: American Eagle Paper Mills
1600 Pennsylvania Ave (16686-1758)
PHONE..................................814 684-1610
Michael P Grimm, *President*
Ryan McChessney, *Business Mgr*
Scott Igoe, *COO*
Greg Bowen, *Vice Pres*
Betsy Patton, *Buyer*
◆ EMP: 270
SALES (est): 120MM **Privately Held**
WEB: www.aepaper.com
SIC: 2621 Uncoated paper

(G-18596)
TERRY D MILES
Also Called: Bald Eagle Precision
6096 Tyrone Pike (16686-9434)
PHONE..................................814 686-1997
Terry D Miles, *Owner*
EMP: 3
SALES: 118K **Privately Held**
SIC: 3599 7389 Machine shop, jobbing & repair;

Ulster
Bradford County

(G-18597)
ANTLER RIDGE WINERY (PA)
37 Antler Ridge Ln (18850-8455)
PHONE..................................570 247-7222
Stephen C Unis, *Principal*
EMP: 8
SALES (est): 870.5K **Privately Held**
SIC: 2084 Wines

(G-18598)
CDK PERFORATING LLC
Also Called: Nine Energy Service
75 Stowell Ln (18850-8444)
P.O. Box 240 (18850-0240)
PHONE..................................570 358-3250
Sue Frederick, *Manager*
EMP: 22
SALES (corp-wide): 827.1MM **Publicly Held**
SIC: 1389 Perforating well casings
HQ: Cdk Perforating, Llc
6500 West Fwy Ste 600
Fort Worth TX 76116
817 945-1051

(G-18599)
HOLDRENS PRECISION MACHINING
23931 Route 220 (18850-7721)
P.O. Box 307 (18850-0307)
PHONE..................................570 358-3377
Howard Holdren, *President*
Aaron Holdren, *Corp Secy*
Jessie Holdren, *Vice Pres*
EMP: 10
SALES: 730K **Privately Held**
SIC: 7699 3549 Machinery cleaning; metalworking machinery

Ulysses
Potter County

(G-18600)
CADY ENTERPRISES
1336 Fox Hill Rd (16948-9352)
PHONE..................................814 848-7408
Lonnie Cady, *Principal*
Ann Cady, *Office Admin*
EMP: 4
SALES (est): 336.9K **Privately Held**
SIC: 3291 Abrasive metal & steel products

(G-18601)
CARPENTER SHOP INC
2228 Sr 49 W (16948)
PHONE..................................814 848-7448
Calvin Horning, *President*
Mabel Horning, *Corp Secy*
EMP: 12
SQ FT: 2,400
SALES (est): 1.6MM **Privately Held**
SIC: 2431 Millwork

(G-18602)
GODS COUNTRY CREAMERY
439 Pushersiding Rd (16948-9394)
PHONE..................................814 848-7262
Melanie Bachman, *Owner*
EMP: 4
SALES (est): 274.7K **Privately Held**
SIC: 2022 Cheese, natural & processed

(G-18603)
J&B OUTDOOR CENTER
1600 White Knoll Rd (16948-9516)
PHONE..................................814 848-3838
Bart Bodo, *Principal*
EMP: 4
SALES (est): 321.3K **Privately Held**
SIC: 3799 Snowmobiles

(G-18604)
PA PELLETS LLC
958 State Route 49 W (16948-9364)
PHONE..................................814 848-9970
Jason Holmburg, *Branch Mgr*
EMP: 12

SALES (corp-wide): 22.1MM **Privately Held**
SIC: 2421 Fuelwood, from mill waste
HQ: Pa Pellets, Llc
1 Fischers Rd Ste 160
Pittsford NY 14534
814 848-9970

Union City
Erie County

(G-18605)
ALL-AMERICAN HOLDINGS LLC (PA)
217 Titusville Rd (16438-8601)
PHONE..................................814 438-7616
Rob Shuler,
▲ EMP: 130
SALES (est): 20.2MM **Privately Held**
SIC: 3052 Rubber & plastics hose & belt-ings

(G-18606)
CORY RESERVIOR TESTING INC
Also Called: Ram Instrumentation
16450 Route 8 (16438-9108)
P.O. Box 32 (16438-0032)
PHONE..................................814 438-2006
Mark A Miller, *President*
Tom Miller, *Vice Pres*
Karla Miller, *Admin Sec*
EMP: 7
SQ FT: 5,000
SALES (est): 1MM **Privately Held**
SIC: 1389 8711 Testing, measuring, surveying & analysis services; measurement of well flow rates, oil & gas; engineering services

(G-18607)
GREAT LAKES FINISHES LLC
7724 Route 97 (16438-7646)
PHONE..................................814 438-2518
Kevi Vanderhoof, *Manager*
Melanie Vanderhoof,
EMP: 6
SALES: 600K **Privately Held**
SIC: 3479 Painting, coating & hot dipping

(G-18608)
KILBANE WOOD CREATIONS
9 Putnam St (16438-1018)
PHONE..................................814 664-0563
EMP: 3
SALES (est): 147.1K **Privately Held**
SIC: 2431 Millwork

(G-18609)
MFG WATER TREAT PROD
55 4th Ave (16438-1247)
P.O. Box 458 (16438-0458)
PHONE..................................814 438-3959
Jerry Bender, *President*
Mike Sjostrom, *Sales Mgr*
EMP: 6
SALES (est): 463.9K **Privately Held**
WEB: www.mfgwtp.com
SIC: 3589 Sewage & water treatment equipment

(G-18610)
MOLDED FIBER GLASS COMPANIES
Mfg Union City Operations
55 4th Ave (16438-1293)
PHONE..................................814 438-3841
Dennis Vorse, *General Mgr*
Jerry Tromans, *Mfg Spvr*
Vicki Greer, *Purch Mgr*
Jerry Bender, *Branch Mgr*
Laurie Patterson, *Administration*
EMP: 250
SALES (corp-wide): 589.3MM **Privately Held**
WEB: www.moldedfiberglass.com
SIC: 3089 Molding primary plastic
PA: Molded Fiber Glass Companies
2925 Mfg Pl
Ashtabula OH 44004
440 997-5851

(G-18611)
PARKER SNAP-TITE QDV ASSEMBLY
74 S Main St (16438)
PHONE..................................814 438-3821
Rich Golonka, *Principal*
EMP: 99
SALES: 950K **Privately Held**
SIC: 3451 Screw machine products

(G-18612)
PARKER-HANNIFIN CORPORATION
Also Called: Snap Tite Qd & V
201 Titusville Rd (16438-8601)
PHONE..................................814 438-3821
Tim Shaffer, *Engineer*
Glenn McKinney, *Branch Mgr*
EMP: 79
SALES (corp-wide): 14.3B **Publicly Held**
SIC: 3594 Fluid power pumps & motors
PA: Parker-Hannifin Corporation
6035 Parkland Blvd
Cleveland OH 44124
216 896-3000

(G-18613)
WATERFORD SAND & GRAVEL CO
15871 Sturgis Rd (16438-8541)
PHONE..................................814 796-6250
Joan E Wurst, *President*
Randy Wurst, *Vice Pres*
Tracy Hamrick, *Manager*
EMP: 20
SQ FT: 2,219
SALES (est): 1.9MM **Privately Held**
SIC: 5032 1794 1442 Sand, construction; gravel; excavation work; construction sand & gravel

---

Uniontown
Fayette County

(G-18614)
AD STAR INC
Also Called: Weekenders
15 W Church St (15401-3418)
PHONE..................................724 439-5519
Jeff Rasco, *President*
Janis Rasco, *Corp Secy*
EMP: 14
SALES (est): 1.1MM **Privately Held**
WEB: www.adstarpublishing.com
SIC: 2741 7313 Shopping news: publishing only, not printed on site; newspaper advertising representative

(G-18615)
ANATOMICAL DESIGNS INC
383 Dixon Blvd (15401-3967)
PHONE..................................724 430-1470
Shandon Hime, *CEO*
Kim Thomas, *Principal*
EMP: 12
SALES (est): 1.8MM **Privately Held**
SIC: 3842 Surgical appliances & supplies

(G-18616)
ARCH MFG LLC
336 E Main St (15401-4349)
PHONE..................................724 438-5170
Greg Bauth, *Owner*
EMP: 8
SALES (est): 983.6K **Privately Held**
SIC: 3999 Manufacturing industries

(G-18617)
BERKLEY MEDICAL RESOURCES INC
Also Called: Berkeley Surgicals
49 Virginia Ave (15401-4929)
PHONE..................................724 438-3000
Dom Pommarello, *Manager*
EMP: 60 **Privately Held**
WEB: www.berkleymedical.com
SIC: 3841 Surgical & medical instruments
PA: Berkley Medical Resources, Inc.
700 Mountain View Dr
Smithfield PA 15478

▲ = Import ▼=Export
◆ =Import/Export

(G-18618)
BERKLEY SURGICAL CORPORATION
49 Virginia Ave (15401-4929)
PHONE.........................724 438-3000
John R Berkley, *President*
▲ EMP: 190 EST: 1996
SQ FT: 90,000
SALES (est): 27.9MM Privately Held
WEB: www.berkleymedical.com
SIC: 3841 Surgical instruments & apparatus
PA: Berkley Medical Resources, Inc.
700 Mountain View Dr
Smithfield PA 15478

(G-18619)
C&C BACKHOE SERVICE LLC
1345 W Penn Blvd (15401-2180)
PHONE.........................724 438-5283
Chris Kress, *Principal*
EMP: 4
SALES (est): 486.2K Privately Held
SIC: 3531 Backhoes

(G-18620)
CHRISTOPHER RESOURCES INC
682 W Main St (15401-2648)
PHONE.........................724 430-9610
Richard Filiaggi, *Principal*
EMP: 6
SALES (est): 558.1K Privately Held
SIC: 1241 Coal mining services

(G-18621)
COOLSPRING STONE SUPPLY INC
850 N Gallatin Avenue Ext (15401-2117)
P.O. Box 945 (15401-0945)
PHONE.........................724 437-8663
William Smoddy, *Branch Mgr*
EMP: 22 Privately Held
SIC: 1411 Dimension stone
PA: Coolspring Stone Supply, Inc.
1122 Jumonville Rd
Uniontown PA 15401

(G-18622)
COOLSPRING STONE SUPPLY INC (PA)
1122 Jumonville Rd (15401)
P.O. Box 1328 (15401-1328)
PHONE.........................724 437-5200
William R Snoddy Sr, *President*
William R Snoddy Jr, *Admin Sec*
EMP: 4
SQ FT: 3,000
SALES (est): 13.4MM Privately Held
SIC: 1411 5032 Limestone, dimension-quarrying; stone, crushed or broken

(G-18623)
DICK RUGHS AUTO PARTS INC
Also Called: Dick Rughs Aut PA & En REB
285 E Fayette St (15401-4352)
PHONE.........................724 438-3425
Richard Rugh Sr, *President*
Richard Rugh Jr, *Vice Pres*
EMP: 7
SQ FT: 5,000
SALES: 606K Privately Held
SIC: 5013 3599 Automotive supplies & parts; machine shop, jobbing & repair

(G-18624)
ELITE OIL FIELD SERVICES INC (PA)
99 E Main St Ste 1 (15401-3519)
PHONE.........................724 627-6060
Robert Hayden, *President*
Roger Grim, *General Mgr*
EMP: 3
SALES (est): 1.2MM Privately Held
SIC: 1389 Oil/Gas Field Services

(G-18625)
ES & SON OF UNION I
999 N Gallatin Avenue Ext (15401-2113)
PHONE.........................724 439-5589
Edward Smith, *Owner*
EMP: 7
SALES (est): 605.3K Privately Held
SIC: 3949 Sporting & athletic goods

(G-18626)
FASTSIGNS OF UNIONTOWN
140 Morgantown St (15401-4277)
PHONE.........................724 430-7446
EMP: 4
SALES (est): 246.3K Privately Held
SIC: 3993 Signs & advertising specialties

(G-18627)
FIKES DAIRY INC
47 W Craig St (15401-4735)
P.O. Box 1247 (15401-1247)
PHONE.........................724 437-7931
Joseph Carson, *Chairman*
Jame Carson, *Vice Pres*
George Wood, *Vice Pres*
EMP: 200 EST: 1922
SQ FT: 100,000
SALES: 24.5MM
SALES (corp-wide): 202.7MM Privately Held
WEB: www.uniteddairy.com
SIC: 2024 2026 Ice cream, packaged: molded, on sticks, etc.; milk processing (pasteurizing, homogenizing, bottling)
PA: United Dairy, Inc.
300 N 5th St
Martins Ferry OH 43935
740 633-1451

(G-18628)
GOLDEN EAGLE CONSTRUCTION CO (PA)
850 N Gallatin Avenue Ext (15401-2117)
P.O. Box 945 (15401-0945)
PHONE.........................724 437-6495
William R Snoddy Sr, *President*
John Dzurko, *Marketing Staff*
EMP: 20 EST: 1970
SQ FT: 5,000
SALES (est): 5.7MM Privately Held
SIC: 1611 2951 Highway & street paving contractor; paving mixtures

(G-18629)
HANGER PRSTHETCS & ORTHO INC
Also Called: Hanger Clinic
211 Easy St Ste 120 (15401-3129)
PHONE.........................724 438-4582
Sam Liang, *President*
EMP: 6
SALES (corp-wide): 1B Publicly Held
SIC: 8011 3842 Orthopedic physician; limbs, artificial
HQ: Hanger Prosthetics & Orthotics, Inc.
10910 Domain Dr Ste 300
Austin TX 78758
512 777-3800

(G-18630)
HIBBS AWNING COMPANY INC
63 E Fayette St (15401-3658)
PHONE.........................724 437-1494
Jack Cole, *President*
Diane Condulucci, *Admin Sec*
EMP: 6
SQ FT: 3,300
SALES (est): 665.5K Privately Held
SIC: 3444 2394 Awnings, sheet metal; awnings, fabric: made from purchased materials

(G-18631)
HRANEC SHEET METAL INC
763 Rte 21 (15401)
PHONE.........................724 437-2211
Steve A Hranec, *President*
Mike Sylvester, *Vice Pres*
Josh Tressler, *Vice Pres*
EMP: 135
SQ FT: 55,000
SALES: 24.8MM Privately Held
WEB: www.hranec.com
SIC: 1711 3444 Mechanical contractor; ducts, sheet metal

(G-18632)
KWIKTICKETSCOM INC
Also Called: Copycat Quick Print
109 S Mount Vernon Ave (15401-3246)
PHONE.........................724 438-7712
David Smith, *President*
EMP: 11
SQ FT: 4,500

SALES (est): 1.2MM Privately Held
WEB: www.kwiktickets.com
SIC: 7334 2752 Photocopying & duplicating services; commercial printing, lithographic

(G-18633)
L AND J EQUIPMENT CO INC
682 W Main St (15401-2648)
PHONE.........................724 437-5405
James Filiaggi Jr, *President*
Lawrence E Filiaggi, *Admin Sec*
EMP: 3
SQ FT: 800
SALES (est): 492.2K
SALES (corp-wide): 18.9MM Privately Held
SIC: 7353 1221 3281 Heavy construction equipment rental; strip mining, bituminous; stone, quarrying & processing of own stone products
PA: Filiaggi Holding Company Inc
682 W Main St
Uniontown PA

(G-18634)
LAUREL AGGREGATES INC
2480 Springhill Frnc Rd (15401)
PHONE.........................724 564-5099
Barry Fink, *President*
EMP: 50 EST: 2007
SALES (est): 3.6MM Privately Held
SIC: 5211 1422 Masonry materials & supplies; crushed & broken limestone

(G-18635)
LITTLE PRINTING CO INC (PA)
Also Called: Mark IV Office Supply
110 S Beeson Ave (15401-4266)
PHONE.........................724 437-4831
Kevin D Staub, *President*
Melanie Lancaster, *Corp Secy*
Joyce Staub, *Vice Pres*
Melanie Staubkanche, *Vice Pres*
EMP: 16 EST: 1933
SQ FT: 10,000
SALES (est): 3.6MM Privately Held
SIC: 5943 2752 5712 Office forms & supplies; commercial printing, offset; office furniture

(G-18636)
MACHINE FABG & WEIGHT EQP SP
Also Called: Machine Fabg & Weight Eqp S
267 Coolspring St (15401-4450)
P.O. Box 645 (15401-0645)
PHONE.........................724 439-1222
Edward Dutkewycz Jr, *Owner*
EMP: 5
SQ FT: 9,300
SALES (est): 583.7K Privately Held
SIC: 3599 Machine shop, jobbing & repair

(G-18637)
MAPLE MOUNTAIN INDUSTRIES INC
655 Pittsburgh Rd (15401-2215)
PHONE.........................724 439-1234
Ralph Woods, *Principal*
EMP: 12 Privately Held
WEB: www.maplemountain.com
SIC: 2512 Upholstered household furniture
PA: Maple Mountain Industries Inc
1820 Mulligan Hill Rd
New Florence PA 15944

(G-18638)
NICHOLAS MEYOKOVICH
Also Called: Nicholas Custom Interiors
62 Easy St (15401-3172)
PHONE.........................724 439-0955
Nicholas Meyokovich, *Owner*
EMP: 4
SQ FT: 1,024
SALES (est): 265K Privately Held
SIC: 2591 5719 5714 Window blinds; window furnishings; draperies

(G-18639)
SENSUS METERING SYSTEMS-NORTH
450 N Gallatin Ave (15401-2458)
P.O. Box 487 (15401-0487)
PHONE.........................724 439-7700

Dan W Harness, *President*
Brenda Del Signore, *Purch Mgr*
Terry Van Olst, *Engineer*
Carmen De Witt, *Director*
▲ EMP: 739
SQ FT: 271,000
SALES (est): 125.2MM Privately Held
SIC: 3824 Water meters

(G-18640)
SENSUS USA INC
Also Called: Sensus Metering Systems
450 N Gallatin Ave (15401-2458)
P.O. Box 487 (15401-0487)
PHONE.........................724 439-7700
Peter Mainz, *President*
Norm Berkshire, *Technical Mgr*
Jim Hitchcock, *Engineer*
Paula Albertson, *Manager*
Wendy Springer, *Manager*
EMP: 300 Publicly Held
WEB: www.sensus.com
SIC: 3824 Water meters
HQ: Sensus Usa Inc.
8601 Six Forks Rd Ste 700
Raleigh NC 27615
919 845-4000

(G-18641)
SEW SPECIAL
73 W Main St (15401-3341)
PHONE.........................724 438-1765
Donna Eicher, *Owner*
EMP: 4
SALES (est): 492.6K Privately Held
WEB: www.sew-special.biz
SIC: 7389 2395 5722 Sewing contractor; embroidery & art needlework; sewing machines

(G-18642)
SILBAUGH VAULT AND BURIAL SVC
4 Speedway Blvd (15401-6554)
P.O. Box 1434 (15401-1434)
PHONE.........................724 437-3002
Todd A Rice, *President*
Kerry Rice, *Corp Secy*
EMP: 6
SQ FT: 8,000
SALES (est): 390K Privately Held
SIC: 3272 7261 Burial vaults, concrete or precast terrazzo; crematory

(G-18643)
TSITOUCH INC
1 Millennium Dr 1 # 1 (15401-6408)
PHONE.........................802 874-0123
Gary Mundrake, *President*
Brianna Rust, *Buyer*
Thomas Broglio, *CFO*
Valerie Randolph, *Sales Staff*
EMP: 45
SQ FT: 23,000
SALES: 19MM Privately Held
SIC: 3577 Input/output equipment, computer

(G-18644)
UNIONTOWN NEWSPAPERS INC (HQ)
Also Called: Herald Standard
8 E Church St Ste 18 (15401-3563)
PHONE.........................724 439-7500
Gary K Shorts, *President*
Val J Laub, *Publisher*
Edward Birch, *Vice Pres*
Stanley M Ellis, *Vice Pres*
Sandra C Hardy, *Vice Pres*
EMP: 248
SQ FT: 39,000
SALES (est): 25.7MM
SALES (corp-wide): 207.2MM Privately Held
WEB: www.heraldstandard.com
SIC: 2711 Commercial printing & newspaper publishing combined; newspapers, publishing & printing
PA: Calkins Media Incorporated
8400 Bristol Pike
Levittown PA 19057
215 949-4000

(G-18645)
UNITED STATES STEEL CORP
Also Called: U. S. Steel
751 Mcclellandtown Rd (15401-5053)
PHONE...................................724 439-1116
Anthony Graciani, *Manager*
EMP: 50
SALES (corp-wide): 14.1B **Publicly Held**
SIC: 3312 Blast furnaces & steel mills
PA: United States Steel Corp
   600 Grant St Ste 468
   Pittsburgh PA 15219
   412 433-1121

(G-18646)
UPPER ROOM INC
Also Called: Upper Room Tees
311 Dixon Blvd (15401-3913)
PHONE...................................724 437-5815
EMP: 15
SQ FT: 4,000
SALES (est): 1.6MM **Privately Held**
SIC: 2759 3993 Commercial Printing Mfg
   Signs/Advertising Specialties

Unionville
Chester County

(G-18647)
CHARLES GINTY ASSOCIATES INC
Also Called: Ginty, Charles Cabinetmaker
Pennsylvania 82 (19375)
P.O. Box 321 (19375-0321)
PHONE...................................610 347-1101
Charles Ginty, *President*
Nina Ginty, *Vice Pres*
EMP: 6
SQ FT: 6,000
SALES (est): 635.7K **Privately Held**
SIC: 2511 7389 Wood household furniture;
   interior design services

(G-18648)
KINLOCH WOODWORKING LTD
Rr 82 (19375)
P.O. Box 461 (19375-0461)
PHONE...................................610 347-2070
D Douglas Mooberry, *President*
EMP: 8
SALES (est): 1MM **Privately Held**
WEB: www.kinlochwoodworking.com
SIC: 2511 Novelty furniture: wood

(G-18649)
SOUNDHORSE TECHNOLOGIES LLC
82 N Lanefield Rd (19375)
P.O. Box 689 (19375-0689)
PHONE...................................610 347-0453
William Kirkpatrick, *General Mgr*
Mary Hazzard, *Mng Member*
Robert Figafoof -Technical, *Director*
EMP: 5
SALES: 1MM **Privately Held**
WEB: www.soundhorse.com
SIC: 3462 Horseshoes

Unityville
Lycoming County

(G-18650)
EM1 SERVICES LLC
359 Clyde Rd (17774-9362)
PHONE...................................570 560-2561
Daniel Roberts, *Mng Member*
EMP: 15 EST: 2015
SALES: 1.1MM **Privately Held**
SIC: 1389 Gas field services; oil field services

University Park
Centre County

(G-18651)
BERKEY CREAMERY
119 Food Science Bldg (16802-2604)
PHONE...................................814 865-7535
Tom Palchak, *President*
EMP: 3
SALES (est): 234K **Privately Held**
SIC: 2024 Ice cream, bulk

(G-18652)
PENNSYLVANIA STATE UNIVERSITY
Also Called: Engineering Machining Ser
102 Engineering Unit E (16802-1432)
PHONE...................................814 865-4963
Jerry Anderson, *Director*
EMP: 8
SALES (corp-wide): 6.3B **Privately Held**
WEB: www.psu.edu
SIC: 3599 8221 Machine shop, jobbing &
   repair; university
PA: The Pennsylvania State University
   201 Old Main
   University Park PA 16802
   814 865-4700

(G-18653)
PENNSYLVANIA STATE UNIVERSITY
Also Called: American Ctr For Stdy of Dstnc
110 Rackley Bldg (16802-3202)
PHONE...................................814 863-3764
Michael G Moore, *Principal*
EMP: 4
SALES (corp-wide): 6.3B **Privately Held**
WEB: www.psu.edu
SIC: 2731 8221 Book publishing; university
PA: The Pennsylvania State University
   201 Old Main
   University Park PA 16802
   814 865-4700

(G-18654)
PENNSYLVANIA STATE UNIVERSITY
Penn State University Press
820 N University Dr (16802-1012)
PHONE...................................814 865-1327
Sanford Thatcher, *Branch Mgr*
EMP: 22
SALES (corp-wide): 6.3B **Privately Held**
WEB: www.psu.edu
SIC: 2731 2741 Book publishing; miscellaneous publishing
PA: The Pennsylvania State University
   201 Old Main
   University Park PA 16802
   814 865-4700

Upper Black Eddy
Bucks County

(G-18655)
LUCKS UPPER BUCKS GYM LLC
542 Cafferty Hill Rd (18972)
PHONE...................................610 847-2392
Donna Luck, *Principal*
EMP: 3
SALES (est): 187.9K **Privately Held**
SIC: 3131 Mfg Footwear Cut Stock

Upper Chichester
Delaware County

(G-18656)
ARCTIC GLACIER TEXAS INC
410 Bethel Ave (19014-3442)
PHONE...................................610 494-8200
EMP: 4
SALES (corp-wide): 2.4B **Publicly Held**
SIC: 2097 Manufactured ice

HQ: Arctic Glacier Texas Inc.
   130 E 42nd St
   Lubbock TX

(G-18657)
BURMANS MEDICAL SUPPLIES INC
Also Called: Burman's Apothecary
7 Creek Pkwy Ste 700 (19061-3100)
PHONE...................................610 876-6068
Chris Duphrayne, *Principal*
EMP: 13
SALES (est): 1.2MM **Privately Held**
WEB: www.burmansmedical.com
SIC: 5912 3843 5047 Proprietary (non-prescription medicine) stores; dental
   equipment & supplies; hospital equipment
   & supplies; oxygen therapy equipment
PA: Burman's Medical Supplies, Inc.
   210 Bridgewater Rd Ste 1
   Aston PA 19014

(G-18658)
CLEMENT COMMUNICATIONS INC (HQ)
3 Creek Pkwy (19061-3148)
P.O. Box 398, Buffalo NY (14240-0398)
PHONE...................................610 497-6800
George Y Clement II, *President*
Robert Gove, *Vice Pres*
▲ EMP: 53 EST: 1919
SQ FT: 36,000
SALES (est): 5.1MM
SALES (corp-wide): 1.1B **Publicly Held**
WEB: www.clement.com
SIC: 2731 Books: publishing & printing
PA: Brady Corporation
   6555 W Good Hope Rd
   Milwaukee WI 53223
   414 358-6600

(G-18659)
ELLIOTT MACHINE COMPANY
3345 Market St (19014-3430)
P.O. Box 2421, Aston (19014-0421)
PHONE...................................610 485-5345
Sofia Elliott, *President*
Steve Schrass, *Vice Pres*
EMP: 7 EST: 1951
SQ FT: 8,000
SALES: 750K **Privately Held**
SIC: 3599 7692 Machine shop, jobbing &
   repair; welding repair

(G-18660)
ENGINRED ARRSTING SYSTEMS CORP (DH)
Also Called: Zodiac Arresting Systems Amer
2550 Market St (19014-3426)
PHONE...................................610 494-8000
Craig H Scott, *President*
Richard Orner, *President*
Laura Sabetti, *General Mgr*
Peter Mahal, *Exec VP*
Eric Elison, *Vice Pres*
◆ EMP: 116 EST: 1937
SQ FT: 130,000
SALES (est): 25.5MM
SALES (corp-wide): 833.4MM **Privately Held**
WEB: www.arrestinggear.com
SIC: 3728 3829 3812 3462 Aircraft landing assemblies & brakes; measuring &
   controlling devices; search & navigation
   equipment; iron & steel forgings; seats,
   aircraft
HQ: Zodiac Us Corporation
   1747 State Route 34
   Wall Township NJ 07727
   732 681-3527

(G-18661)
FARMERS FROM ITALY FOODS LLC
8 Creek Pkwy Fl 2 (19061-3132)
PHONE...................................484 480-3836
Roberto Magello, *Mng Member*
Luigi Mantuano,
EMP: 2
SQ FT: 3,000
SALES: 3MM **Privately Held**
SIC: 2032 Italian foods: packaged in cans,
   jars, etc.

(G-18662)
GREIF INC
3033 Market St (19014-3436)
PHONE...................................610 485-8148
Bill Bell, *Engineer*
Thomas Coon, *Manager*
Patrick Norton, *Bd of Directors*
EMP: 70
SALES (corp-wide): 3.8B **Publicly Held**
WEB: www.greif.com
SIC: 2655 Drums, fiber: made from purchased material
PA: Greif, Inc.
   425 Winter Rd
   Delaware OH 43015
   740 549-6000

(G-18663)
HA HARPER SONS INC (PA)
2800 Chichester Ave (19061-3428)
PHONE...................................610 485-4776
Adele H Warner, *President*
Jennifer Scaramuzza, *Corp Secy*
E Blair Harper, *Vice Pres*
EMP: 4 EST: 1906
SQ FT: 5,000
SALES (est): 560.3K **Privately Held**
SIC: 2394 5719 Awnings, fabric: made
   from purchased materials; window
   shades

(G-18664)
HARTZELL MACHINE WORKS INC
3354 Market St (19014-3499)
PHONE...................................610 485-3502
Richard M Hartzell, *President*
Ida S Hartzell, *Vice Pres*
▲ EMP: 20 EST: 1937
SQ FT: 7,500
SALES (est): 3.5MM **Privately Held**
WEB: www.hartzellmachineworks.com
SIC: 3599 Machine shop, jobbing & repair

(G-18665)
INDUSTRIAL CONTROL & ELEC INC
4009 Market St Unit J (19014-3140)
PHONE...................................610 859-9272
Rich Misturak, *President*
Richard Misturak, *Chief Engr*
Sue Hammann, *Director*
EMP: 5
SQ FT: 4,500
SALES (est): 1MM **Privately Held**
SIC: 3823 8711 Industrial process control
   instruments; designing: ship, boat, machine & product

(G-18666)
KEBB INC
213 Meetinghouse Rd (19014-3353)
PHONE...................................610 859-0907
William Francis, *President*
Kenneth P Roark, *Treasurer*
EMP: 6
SQ FT: 4,500
SALES: 800K **Privately Held**
SIC: 3446 8712 Architectural metalwork;
   architectural services

(G-18667)
MARCOM GROUP LTD
20 Creek Pkwy (19061-3132)
PHONE...................................610 859-8989
Donald L Leonard Jr, *President*
Ann V Diersing, *Treasurer*
Jennifer Manning, *Manager*
EMP: 14
SQ FT: 11,500
SALES (est): 1.3MM **Privately Held**
WEB: www.marcomltd.com
SIC: 7812 8299 2741 Educational computer software; educational service, non-degree granting: continuing educ.;

(G-18668)
NEW HUDSON FACADES LLC (PA)
815 Columbia Ave (19061-3903)
PHONE...................................610 494-8100
Allen Cohen,
Michael Budd,
EMP: 101 EST: 2014

SALES (est): 101.4MM **Privately Held**
SIC: 3449 1741 1542 Curtain walls for buildings, steel; masonry & other stonework; commercial & office building contractors

(G-18669)
PENNSYLVANIA MACHINE WORKS INC (PA)
Also Called: Penn Forged
201 Bethel Ave (19014-3485)
PHONE..................................610 497-3300
Ronald C Lafferty, *CEO*
Joseph M Proi Jr, *President*
Dennis Lafferty, *Treasurer*
John W Lafferty Jr, *Treasurer*
Jason Joseph, *Sales Staff*
◆ **EMP: 225 EST:** 1931
SQ FT: 88,000
SALES (est): 35.9MM **Privately Held**
SIC: 3462 3498 5085 Iron & steel forgings; pipe fittings, fabricated from purchased pipe; industrial supplies

(G-18670)
PENTEC HEALTH INC
Also Called: Renal Ntrtn Intrathecal Pumps
4 Creek Pkwy (19061-3132)
PHONE..................................800 223-4376
EMP: 163
SALES (corp-wide): 110.5MM **Privately Held**
SIC: 2834 Pharmaceutical preparations
PA: Pentec Health, Inc.
50 Applied Card Way
Glen Mills PA 19342
610 494-8700

(G-18671)
PENTEC HEALTH INC
9 Creek Pkwy (19061-3148)
PHONE..................................610 494-8700
Barbara Knightly, *Branch Mgr*
EMP: 25
SALES (corp-wide): 110.5MM **Privately Held**
SIC: 8082 2834 Home health care services; druggists' preparations (pharmaceuticals)
PA: Pentec Health, Inc.
50 Applied Card Way
Glen Mills PA 19342
610 494-8700

(G-18672)
R J MACHINE CO INC
3353 Market St (19014-3430)
PHONE..................................610 494-8107
Robert Rossney, *President*
EMP: 7
SQ FT: 2,800
SALES (est): 690K **Privately Held**
WEB: www.rjmachine.com
SIC: 3599 5013 Machine shop, jobbing & repair; motor vehicle supplies & new parts

(G-18673)
THOMAS E FERRO
Also Called: Ferro Plumbing & Heating
2124 Vernon Ave (19061-3711)
PHONE..................................610 485-1356
Thomas E Ferro, *Owner*
John Ferro, *Co-Owner*
EMP: 9
SQ FT: 6,400
SALES (est): 1.8MM **Privately Held**
SIC: 2899 5983 Fuel treating compounds; igniter grains, boron potassium nitrate; fuel oil dealers

(G-18674)
TOTAL SCOPE INC
17 Creek Pkwy (19061-3148)
PHONE..................................484 490-2100
Ann Glavin, *CEO*
Ryan Gades, *Accounts Mgr*
David Deely, *Manager*
EMP: 45
SQ FT: 26,000
SALES (est): 6.5MM **Privately Held**
WEB: www.totalscopeinc.com
SIC: 7699 3843 3845 Medical equipment repair, non-electric; professional instrument repair services; electrical repair shops; electromedical equipment

(G-18675)
UFC AEROSPACE
18 Creek Pkwy (19061-3132)
PHONE..................................610 485-4704
Ray Mikell, *Principal*
EMP: 3
SALES (est): 218.9K **Privately Held**
SIC: 3812 Aircraft/aerospace flight instruments & guidance systems

(G-18676)
VISUALIZE DIGITIZED LLC
603 Taylor Ave (19061-4051)
PHONE..................................610 494-9504
EMP: 3 **EST:** 2012
SALES (est): 321.4K **Privately Held**
SIC: 3993 Signs & advertising specialties

Upper Darby
Delaware County

(G-18677)
ALLERGAN INC
423 Beverly Blvd (19082-3714)
PHONE..................................610 352-4992
Jamie Debow, *Manager*
EMP: 15 **Privately Held**
WEB: www.allergan.com
SIC: 2834 Drugs acting on the central nervous system & sense organs
HQ: Allergan, Inc.
5 Giralda Farms
Madison NJ 07940
862 261-7000

(G-18678)
AMARRIAGE ENTERTAINMENT LLC
444 Glendale Rd (19082-4918)
PHONE..................................267 973-5288
EMP: 15
SALES (est): 710K **Privately Held**
SIC: 2052 Mfg Cookies/Crackers

(G-18679)
AMERICAN BEER BEVERAGE LTD
770 Garrett Rd (19082-3811)
PHONE..................................610 352-2211
George Hionis, *Principal*
EMP: 4
SALES (est): 153.5K **Privately Held**
SIC: 2082 Beer (alcoholic beverage)

(G-18680)
AMIGO EXPRESS
7209 W Chester Pike (19082-1603)
PHONE..................................484 461-3135
Nancy Barros, *Principal*
EMP: 4
SALES (est): 221.4K **Privately Held**
SIC: 2741 Miscellaneous publishing

(G-18681)
ASTRA FOODS INC
6430 Market St (19082-3396)
PHONE..................................610 352-4400
Demosthenes Vasiliou, *President*
Spiros Poulimenos, *Treasurer*
EMP: 52
SALES (est): 22.5MM **Privately Held**
SIC: 2011 Meat packing plants

(G-18682)
ATKINS KAREEMAH
Also Called: Galbar Couture
6 S Cedar Ln (19082-2817)
PHONE..................................267 428-0019
Kareemah Atkins, *Owner*
EMP: 4
SALES (est): 49.2K **Privately Held**
SIC: 2339 Athletic clothing: women's, misses' & juniors'

(G-18683)
BROP TECH LLC
121 Normandy Rd (19082-4804)
PHONE..................................323 229-7390
Prince Kweh, *Principal*
EMP: 10
SALES (est): 390.1K **Privately Held**
SIC: 3357 7389 Communication wire;

(G-18684)
DAVENMARK INC
707 Long Ln (19082-5323)
PHONE..................................484 461-8683
Mark Wainwright, *President*
Herman Wood, *Vice Pres*
EMP: 15
SALES (est): 633.7K **Privately Held**
SIC: 5812 2038 8741 Caterers; ethnic foods, frozen; restaurant management

(G-18685)
DERCHER ENTERPRISES INC
Also Called: Gordon Laboratories
6801 Ludlow St (19082-2408)
PHONE..................................610 734-2011
Sue Ellen Dercher, *President*
David Dercher, *Vice Pres*
EMP: 27 **EST:** 1950
SQ FT: 25,000
SALES (est): 4.5MM **Privately Held**
SIC: 2834 Pharmaceutical preparations

(G-18686)
GRAMMECO INC
Also Called: Astra Distributors
6430 Market St (19082-3304)
PHONE..................................610 352-4400
Demostenes Vasiliou, *President*
Spiros Poulimenos, *Vice Pres*
▲ **EMP:** 110 **EST:** 1979
SQ FT: 35,000
SALES (est): 21.9MM **Privately Held**
WEB: www.astrafoods.com
SIC: 5143 5147 2011 5146 Cheese; meats & meat products; meat packing plants; fish, fresh

(G-18687)
IRISH NETWORK PHILADELPHIA
7 S Cedar Ln (19082-2836)
PHONE..................................215 690-1353
Siobhan Lyons, *President*
EMP: 3
SALES (est): 124.6K **Privately Held**
SIC: 2711 Newspapers, publishing & printing

(G-18688)
MAXWELL CANBY FUEL OIL CO
Also Called: Bell Fuel
8301 Lansdowne Ave (19082-5408)
PHONE..................................610 269-0288
Barry Radcliffe, *General Mgr*
EMP: 3
SALES (est): 280K **Privately Held**
SIC: 2911 Oils, fuel

(G-18689)
METRO NEWS GIFTS
6901 Market St (19082-1830)
PHONE..................................610 734-2262
EMP: 4
SALES (est): 182.2K **Privately Held**
SIC: 2711 Newspapers, publishing & printing

(G-18690)
MINIT RUBBER STAMPS
6425 Market St (19082-1824)
PHONE..................................610 352-8600
Amy Arya, *Partner*
Roger Arya, *Partner*
EMP: 5
SALES (est): 344.3K **Privately Held**
SIC: 2752 Lithographic Commercial Printing

(G-18691)
NEWSPAPER NETWORKS INC
8600 W Chester Pike # 206 (19082-2629)
PHONE..................................610 853-2121
EMP: 3
SALES (est): 142.4K **Privately Held**
SIC: 2711 Newspapers-Publishing/Printing

(G-18692)
SUPERIOR PRINTING & ENGRAVING
6425 Market St (19082-1824)
PHONE..................................610 352-1966
Amy Arya, *President*
EMP: 8
SQ FT: 2,500

SALES (est): 1.3MM **Privately Held**
SIC: 2759 Invitations: printing

(G-18693)
TK BEER INC
8794 W Chester Pike (19082-2631)
PHONE..................................610 446-2337
Sieu Kim Tang, *Principal*
EMP: 6
SALES (est): 486.7K **Privately Held**
SIC: 2082 Beer (alcoholic beverage)

(G-18694)
WEST PHARMACEUTICAL SVCS INC
8647 W Chester Pike (19082-1101)
PHONE..................................610 853-3200
Dave Cochel, *Manager*
EMP: 15
SALES (corp-wide): 1.7B **Publicly Held**
WEB: www.westpharma.com
SIC: 2834 Pharmaceutical preparations
PA: West Pharmaceutical Services, Inc.
530 Herman O West Dr
Exton PA 19341
610 594-2900

Upper Gwynedd
Montgomery County

(G-18695)
KEMKO INDUSTRIES INC
5105 Lilac Ct (19446-7621)
PHONE..................................267 613-8651
Naomi Berman, *President*
Theresa Booth, *Manager*
EMP: 6
SQ FT: 600
SALES (est): 500K **Privately Held**
WEB: www.adspecpromos.com
SIC: 5199 2759 Advertising specialties; commercial printing

Utica
Venango County

(G-18696)
GREG KISER
Also Called: Kiser Construction
1458 Frenchcreek Rd (16362-2016)
PHONE..................................814 425-1678
Greg Kiser, *Owner*
EMP: 3
SALES (est): 163.5K **Privately Held**
SIC: 3444 5051 Concrete forms, sheet metal; forms, concrete construction (steel)

Valencia
Butler County

(G-18697)
GIOVANNI DEMARCO
271 Glade Mills Rd (16059-3309)
PHONE..................................724 898-7239
Giovanni Demarco, *Principal*
EMP: 3
SALES (est): 308.4K **Privately Held**
SIC: 3273 Ready-mixed concrete

(G-18698)
HAMPTON CONCRETE PRODUCTS INC
1435 Pittsburgh Rd (16059-2429)
PHONE..................................724 443-7205
Virgil Knox, *President*
June Knox, *Corp Secy*
Mary Knox, *Vice Pres*
EMP: 10
SALES (est): 1.9MM **Privately Held**
WEB: www.hamptonconcrete.com
SIC: 3272 3446 3355 Steps, prefabricated concrete; stone, cast concrete; concrete products used to facilitate drainage; ornamental metalwork; rails, rolled & drawn, aluminum

GEOGRAPHIC

(G-18699)
MYSTIC LANES LLC
1318 Pittsburgh Rd (16059-1104)
PHONE...................................724 898-2960
David Greene, *Principal*
EMP: 4
SALES (est): 285.9K **Privately Held**
SIC: 3949 Bowling alleys & accessories

(G-18700)
PULVA CORPORATION
105 Industrial Dr W (16059-3321)
P.O. Box 427, Saxonburg (16056-0427)
PHONE...................................724 898-3000
Edward Ferree, *President*
Caroline Ferree, *Vice Pres*
Gayle Ferree, *Vice Pres*
Brian Dean, *Engineer*
Brad Gray, *Supervisor*
EMP: 50
SQ FT: 12,000
SALES (est): 14.3MM **Privately Held**
WEB: www.pulva.com
SIC: 3531 Hammer mills (rock & ore crushing machines), portable

(G-18701)
RUSSELL STANDARD CORPORATION
171 7th Ave (16059-1307)
P.O. Box 802, Mars (16046-0802)
PHONE...................................724 625-1505
Tim Mohney, *Manager*
EMP: 31
SALES (corp-wide): 195.6MM **Privately Held**
WEB: www.russellstandard.com
SIC: 2952 2951 1611 Asphalt felts & coatings; asphalt & asphaltic paving mixtures (not from refineries); surfacing & paving
PA: Russell Standard Corporation
285 Kappa Dr Ste 300
Pittsburgh PA 15238
412 449-0700

(G-18702)
STRUTZ FABRICATORS INC
440 Mars Valencia Rd (16059-1336)
P.O. Box 509, Mars (16046-0509)
PHONE...................................724 625-1501
Carl Strutz Jr, *President*
Frank Strutz, *Vice Pres*
John Zwigart, *Engineer*
EMP: 40 **EST:** 1973
SQ FT: 15,000
SALES (est): 7.1MM
SALES (corp-wide): 8.6MM **Privately Held**
SIC: 3552 Silk screens for textile industry
PA: Carl Strutz & Company Inc
440 Mars Valencia Rd
Mars PA 16046
724 625-1501

(G-18703)
TRI MAX MANUFACTURING CO INC
103 Mcfann Rd (16059-1917)
PHONE...................................724 898-1400
Jeffrey Haffely, *President*
EMP: 4
SQ FT: 3,500
SALES (est): 453.3K **Privately Held**
SIC: 3599 Machine shop, jobbing & repair

(G-18704)
VORTEQ COIL FINISHERS LLC
125 Mcfann Rd (16059-1917)
PHONE...................................724 898-1511
EMP: 11
SALES (corp-wide): 37.7MM **Privately Held**
SIC: 3479 Coating of metals & formed products
PA: Vorteq Coil Finishers, Llc
930 Armour Rd
Oconomowoc WI 53066
262 567-1112

(G-18705)
WISMARQ VALENCIA LLC
125 Mcfann Rd (16059-1917)
PHONE...................................724 898-1511
Jim Dockey, *CEO*
Jim Barr, *Safety Mgr*

EMP: 10 **EST:** 2010
SALES (est): 150K **Privately Held**
SIC: 3479 Coating of metals & formed products

Valier
Jefferson County

(G-18706)
VALIER COAL YARD
Cool Spring Rd (15780)
P.O. Box 343, Punxsutawney (15767-0343)
PHONE...................................814 938-5171
David Osikowicz, *President*
Jessica Perry, *Admin Sec*
EMP: 12
SALES (est): 940.2K **Privately Held**
SIC: 1221 Bituminous coal & lignite-surface mining

Valley Forge
Chester County

(G-18707)
GH HOLDINGS INC (DH)
Madison & Van Buren Ave (19482)
PHONE...................................610 666-4000
Paul De Vivo, *CEO*
Ali Ganjaei, *Admin Sec*
EMP: 2 **EST:** 2012
SALES (est): 615.1MM **Privately Held**
SIC: 2869 2992 Hydraulic fluids, synthetic base; lubricating oils & greases
HQ: Gulf Oil International Uk Limited
16 Charles The 2nd Street
London SW1Y
207 839-2402

(G-18708)
GRID COMPANY LLC
750 E Swedesford Rd (19482)
PHONE...................................610 341-7307
EMP: 25
SALES (est): 2.1MM **Privately Held**
SIC: 3325 Steel Foundry

(G-18709)
MID-ATLANTIC TECH PUBLICATIONS
10 Gay St (19481)
PHONE...................................610 783-6100
Jacob Fattal, *President*
Don Craig, *Sales Staff*
Walter Salm, *Manager*
EMP: 10
SQ FT: 2,500
SALES (est): 520K **Privately Held**
WEB: www.gim.net
SIC: 2711 Newspapers, publishing & printing

(G-18710)
PLUM ENTERPRISES INC
500 Freedom View Ln (19481)
PHONE...................................610 783-7377
Janice Carrington, *President*
Eric Carrington, *Mfg Dir*
EMP: 50
SALES (est): 4MM **Privately Held**
WEB: www.plument.com
SIC: 3842 Surgical appliances & supplies

(G-18711)
SAINT-GOBAIN CERAMICS PLAS INC (DH)
Also Called: Saint-Gobain Crystals
750 E Swedesford Rd (19482)
P.O. Box 15137, Worcester MA (01615-0137)
PHONE...................................508 795-5000
John J Sweeney III, *President*
M Shawn Puccio, *Vice Pres*
Timothy Feagans, *Admin Sec*
▲ **EMP:** 3000

SALES (est): 929.5MM
SALES (corp-wide): 215.9MM **Privately Held**
WEB: www.sgceramics.com
SIC: 2819 3679 3544 3297 Industrial inorganic chemicals; electronic crystals; special dies & tools; nonclay refractories
HQ: Saint-Gobain Abrasives, Inc.
1 New Bond St
Worcester MA 01606
508 795-5000

(G-18712)
SAINT-GOBAIN DELAWARE CORP (DH)
750 E Swedesford Rd (19482)
PHONE...................................610 341-7000
Jean F Phelizon, *President*
James F Harkins Jr, *Vice Pres*
◆ **EMP:** 4
SALES (est): 5.1B
SALES (corp-wide): 215.9MM **Privately Held**
SIC: 3291 3269 2891 3296 Abrasive products; laboratory & industrial pottery; adhesives & sealants; fiberglass insulation; plastics pipe; glass containers

(G-18713)
SAINT-GOBAIN VETROTEX AMER INC (DH)
20 Moores Rd (19482)
P.O. Box 860 (19482-0860)
PHONE...................................610 893-6000
David L Mascarin, *President*
Steven F Messmer, *Vice Pres*
John J Sweeney, *Treasurer*
Timothy L Feagans, *Admin Sec*
▲ **EMP:** 11
SQ FT: 2,500
SALES (est): 147.4MM
SALES (corp-wide): 215.9MM **Privately Held**
WEB: www.sgva.com
SIC: 3089 Spouting, plastic & glass fiber reinforced
HQ: Certainteed Corporation
20 Moores Rd
Malvern PA 19355
610 893-5000

(G-18714)
SCRIPTURE UNION
1485 Valley Forge Rd (19481)
P.O. Box 215 (19481-0215)
PHONE...................................610 935-2807
Whitney T Kuniholm, *President*
Roger Somsum, *President*
Richard Patterson, *Principal*
Dan Sheldon, *Vice Pres*
EMP: 14
SQ FT: 2,700
SALES: 1.9MM **Privately Held**
WEB: www.scriptureunion.gospelcom.net
SIC: 8661 2721 Religious organizations; periodicals: publishing only

(G-18715)
STREAMLINE ENERGY SERVICES LLC
1220 Valley Rd Ste 25 (19482)
PHONE...................................610 415-1220
John Smith, *Principal*
John K Smith,
EMP: 14 **EST:** 2012
SALES (est): 1.9MM **Privately Held**
SIC: 1794 1389 1611 Excavation & grading, building construction; oil & gas wells: building, repairing & dismantling; gravel or dirt road construction

Valley View
Schuylkill County

(G-18716)
PROTO FAB TECHNOLOGIES
924 W Maple St (17983-9733)
P.O. Box 172 (17983-0172)
PHONE...................................570 682-2000
Benjamin Machamer, *Owner*
EMP: 9
SQ FT: 15,000

SALES (est): 101K **Privately Held**
SIC: 3544 Special dies, tools, jigs & fixtures

(G-18717)
RAUSCH CREEK LAND LP (PA)
978 Gap St (17983-9749)
PHONE...................................570 682-4600
Robert Rivkin, *Partner*
EMP: 21
SQ FT: 2,000
SALES (est): 4.1MM **Privately Held**
SIC: 1221 Bituminous coal & lignite-surface mining

(G-18718)
THE SCRANTON TIMES L P
Also Called: Citizen Standard
104 W Main St (17983-9423)
P.O. Box 147 (17983-0147)
PHONE...................................570 682-9081
Henry NYCE, *Principal*
EMP: 4
SALES (corp-wide): 114.5MM **Privately Held**
WEB: www.scrantontimesefcu.com
SIC: 2711 Newspapers, publishing & printing
PA: The Scranton Times L P
149 Penn Ave Ste 1
Scranton PA 18503
570 348-9100

Vanderbilt
Fayette County

(G-18719)
201 DISTRIBUTING INC
206 Round Barn Rd (15486-1334)
PHONE...................................724 529-2320
Douglas White, *President*
Connie White, *Admin Sec*
EMP: 4
SQ FT: 2,368
SALES: 80K **Privately Held**
SIC: 3999 Pet supplies

(G-18720)
MILLER AND ROEBUCK INC
Also Called: Laurel Mountain Stone Works
256 Virgin Run Rd (15486-1138)
PHONE...................................724 398-3054
John E Roebuck, *President*
Shawn Miller, *Vice Pres*
EMP: 8
SALES (est): 944.7K **Privately Held**
SIC: 1411 Granite dimension stone

Vandergrift
Westmoreland County

(G-18721)
ALLEGHENY LUDLUM LLC
Also Called: ATI Allegheny Ludlum
130 Lincoln Ave (15690-1249)
PHONE...................................724 567-2001
Tom Trienski, *Facilities Mgr*
Tim Washko, *Facilities Mgr*
Russ Connor, *Manager*
Joe Dileo, *Manager*
Kevin Cerason, *Exec Dir*
EMP: 237 **Publicly Held**
WEB: www.alleghenyludlum.com
SIC: 3316 3471 Sheet, steel, cold-rolled: from purchased hot-rolled; plating & polishing
HQ: Allegheny Ludlum, Llc
1000 Six Ppg Pl
Pittsburgh PA 15222
412 394-2800

(G-18722)
ALLEGHENY LUDLUM LLC
Also Called: ATI Allegheny Ludlum
132 Lincoln Ave (15690-1249)
PHONE...................................724 567-2670
EMP: 10 **Publicly Held**
SIC: 3462 Iron & steel forgings

HQ: Allegheny Ludlum, Llc
1000 Six Ppg Pl
Pittsburgh PA 15222
412 394-2800

(G-18723)
COMPOSIDIE INC
Toolex Division
1159 Industrial Park Rd (15690-6050)
PHONE.................................724 845-8602
Dean Hoch, *Manager*
Dieter Hilss, *Systems Mgr*
EMP: 30
SALES (corp-wide): 60.5MM **Privately Held**
WEB: www.composidie.com
SIC: 3544 Special dies, tools, jigs & fixtures
PA: Composidie, Inc.
1295 Route 380
Apollo PA 15613
724 845-8602

(G-18724)
COOK VANDERGRIFT INC
1186 Montgomery Ln (15690-6065)
PHONE.................................724 845-8621
Louis Goode, *President*
Thomas Kardos, *Vice Pres*
Thomas Palko, *Vice Pres*
Adele Ameno, *Buyer*
Dustin Arabia, *Engineer*
EMP: 250
SQ FT: 38,500
SALES (est): 30.8MM
SALES (corp-wide): 1.1B **Privately Held**
WEB: www.cookvascular.com
SIC: 3841 Catheters
PA: Cook Group Incorporated
750 N Daniels Way
Bloomington IN 47404
812 339-2235

(G-18725)
ELECTROMAGNETIC LIBERATION
410 Harrison Ave (15690-1317)
PHONE.................................724 568-2869
Joe Rusak, *Owner*
EMP: 4
SALES (est): 233.6K **Privately Held**
SIC: 3674 Photoelectric magnetic devices

(G-18726)
F F FRICKANISCE IRON WORKS
1124 Airport Rd (15690-6072)
PHONE.................................724 568-2001
Warren F Frickanisce, *Owner*
EMP: 5
SQ FT: 4,000
SALES (est): 250K **Privately Held**
SIC: 7692 1791 3446 3444 Welding repair; iron work, structural; architectural metalwork; sheet metalwork; fabricated plate work (boiler shop); fabricated structural metal

(G-18727)
FRED FOUST
Also Called: F and L Medical Products Co
1129 Industrial Park Rd # 3 (15690-9646)
PHONE.................................724 845-7028
Fred Foust, *Partner*
EMP: 8
SQ FT: 6,500
SALES (est): 1.1MM **Privately Held**
WEB: www.fandlmedicalproducts.com
SIC: 3069 Medical & laboratory rubber sundries & related products

(G-18728)
FROSTY HOLLOW HARDWOODS
1127 Frosty Hollow Ln (15690-6041)
PHONE.................................724 568-2406
Jeff Knell, *Owner*
EMP: 3
SALES (est): 347.4K **Privately Held**
SIC: 2431 2421 Moldings, wood: unfinished & prefinished; sawmills & planing mills, general

(G-18729)
GRAVEL BAR INC
2274 River Rd (15690-2422)
PHONE.................................724 568-3518
James Espaniol, *President*
EMP: 3
SALES (est): 130.4K **Privately Held**
SIC: 1442 Construction sand & gravel

(G-18730)
JENSEN MACHINE CO INC
403 Jackson Ave (15690-1355)
PHONE.................................724 568-3787
Byron Maloney, *President*
Ruth Maloney, *Corp Secy*
Jason Maloney, *Vice Pres*
EMP: 7
SQ FT: 3,200
SALES: 400K **Privately Held**
WEB: www.jensensteamengines.com
SIC: 3451 Screw machine products

(G-18731)
KENSINGTON HPP INC
Also Called: Kensington High Prfmce Pdts
1136 Industrial Park Rd (15690-6049)
PHONE.................................866 318-6628
Chuck Wetmore, *CEO*
Donald Kilgore, *Prdtn Mgr*
Tami George, *Buyer*
John Barker, *CFO*
Brad Fennel, *Supervisor*
EMP: 47
SALES (est): 13.2MM **Privately Held**
SIC: 3442 Window & door frames

(G-18732)
LEGACY PRINTING AND PUBG CO
340 Chestnut St (15690-1406)
PHONE.................................724 567-5657
Gabriel Cole, *Owner*
EMP: 4
SALES (est): 382.5K **Privately Held**
SIC: 2752 Commercial printing, lithographic

(G-18733)
METAL SERVICE COMPANY INC (PA)
210 1st St (15690-1100)
PHONE.................................724 567-6500
Henery W Mc Laughlin III, *President*
Henry Mc Laughlin III, *President*
EMP: 13
SQ FT: 300,000
SALES (est): 4.7MM **Privately Held**
WEB: www.msicorporation.com
SIC: 3312 Blast furnaces & steel mills

(G-18734)
NATURES BEST CBD PA LLC
700 Hancock Ave (15690-1524)
PHONE.................................724 568-4657
Amy Bufalini, *CEO*
EMP: 3
SALES (est): 158.4K **Privately Held**
SIC: 3999

(G-18735)
PENNSYLVNIA PRECISION PDTS INC
309 Walnut St (15690-3401)
PHONE.................................724 568-4397
Terry Klingensmith, *President*
EMP: 7
SQ FT: 2,000
SALES: 1MM **Privately Held**
SIC: 3599 Machine shop, jobbing & repair

(G-18736)
UNCLE CHARLEYS SAUSAGE CO LLC
Also Called: Unclecharleyssausage.com
1135 Industrial Park Rd (15690-6050)
PHONE.................................724 845-3302
Len Caric, *President*
Charlie Gabriel, *Business Mgr*
Paul Beranek, *Marketing Staff*
Charles Armitage Sr, *Consultant*
Philip Conty, *Maintence Staff*
EMP: 49
SQ FT: 18,000
SALES (est): 9.7MM **Privately Held**
WEB: www.unclecharleyssausage.com
SIC: 2013 Sausages from purchased meat

(G-18737)
WALLACE MOVING & STORAGE
210 Washington Ave (15690-1206)
PHONE.................................724 568-2411
John C Wallace, *Owner*
EMP: 3
SALES (est): 198.2K **Privately Held**
SIC: 4212 4213 2511 Local trucking, without storage; contract haulers; wood household furniture

(G-18738)
WYSOCKI-COLE ENTERPRISES INC (PA)
Also Called: Leechburg Advance
143 Washington Ave (15690-1211)
PHONE.................................724 567-5656
Donald J Cole, *President*
Suzanne E Cole, *Corp Secy*
EMP: 20
SQ FT: 10,000
SALES (est): 1.2MM **Privately Held**
SIC: 2711 Job printing & newspaper publishing combined

Vandling
Susquehanna County

(G-18739)
SELECT TISSUE PENNSYLVANIA LLC
939 Main St (18421-1531)
PHONE.................................570 785-2000
Jamie Roffers, *Mng Member*
EMP: 45
SALES (est): 5.6MM
SALES (corp-wide): 12.6MM **Privately Held**
SIC: 2621 Paper mills
PA: Select Products Holdings Llc
1 Arnold Dr Unit 3
Huntington NY 11743
631 421-6000

Venango
Crawford County

(G-18740)
DOUTT TOOL INC
21879 Gravel Run Rd (16440-2648)
PHONE.................................814 398-2989
Robert A Melvin, *President*
EMP: 20
SQ FT: 5,000
SALES (est): 2.6MM **Privately Held**
WEB: www.doutttool.com
SIC: 3544 Special dies & tools

Venetia
Washington County

(G-18741)
BACK BAY INDUSTRIES INC
116 Sugar Camp Rd (15367-1034)
PHONE.................................724 941-5825
Douglas S Bacchiochi, *President*
EMP: 7
SALES: 350K **Privately Held**
SIC: 3399 Metal fasteners

(G-18742)
ELECTRICHP USA CORP
309 Merrifield Dr (15367-3001)
PHONE.................................724 678-5084
Adrian Lachance,
EMP: 20 EST: 2016
SALES (est): 951.5K **Privately Held**
SIC: 3533 Oil field machinery & equipment

(G-18743)
R Q I INC
Also Called: Bar & Cap System
807 E Mcmurray Rd Ste 202 (15367-2003)
PHONE.................................724 209-4100
Gregory K Orphall, *President*
Jack Perkins, *Admin Sec*
▼ **EMP:** 4

SQ FT: 2,500
SALES: 500K **Privately Held**
SIC: 3532 Crushing, pulverizing & screening equipment

(G-18744)
SONIC ENERGY SERVICES USA INC
405 Longleaf Dr (15367-2105)
PHONE.................................724 782-0560
EMP: 1
SALES: 1MM **Privately Held**
SIC: 1381 7389 Oil/Gas Well Drilling
PA: Sonic Energy Services Ltd
633 6 Ave Sw Suite 720
Calgary AB T2P 2
403 237-9823

Verona
Allegheny County

(G-18745)
AFFIVAL INC (DH)
Also Called: Affimex Code Wire
1967 Eastern Ave (15147-3936)
PHONE.................................412 826-9430
Tim Schwadron, *CEO*
Gary Spolarith, *President*
◆ **EMP:** 4
SQ FT: 85,000
SALES (est): 28.5MM **Privately Held**
WEB: www.affival.com
SIC: 3312 Wire products, steel or iron
HQ: Skw Stahl-Metallurgie Holding Gmbh
Prinzregentenstr. 68
Munchen 81675
895 998-9230

(G-18746)
AFFIVAL INC
1967 Eastern Ave (15147-3936)
PHONE.................................412 826-9430
Dave Poremba, *Branch Mgr*
EMP: 40 **Privately Held**
WEB: www.affival.com
SIC: 3312 Wire products, steel or iron
HQ: Affival Inc.
1967 Eastern Ave
Verona PA 15147
412 826-9430

(G-18747)
AMERICAN BEVERAGE CORPORATION (DH)
Also Called: ABC
1 Daily Way (15147-1135)
P.O. Box 644822, Pittsburgh (15264-4822)
PHONE.................................412 828-9020
Fhj Koffrie, *President*
Kevin McGahren-Clemens, *President*
Frans Eelkmanrooda, *Vice Pres*
Ken Janowitz, *Vice Pres*
Edward M Levy, *Treasurer*
◆ **EMP:** 243
SQ FT: 125,000
SALES (est): 215.2MM
SALES (corp-wide): 1.3B **Privately Held**
WEB: www.ambev.com
SIC: 2033 Fruits & fruit products in cans, jars, etc.
HQ: Harvest Hill Beverage Company
1 High Ridge Park Fl 2
Stamford CT 06905
203 914-1620

(G-18748)
B & R SPEED SHOP
Also Called: B & R Automotive
4859 Allegheny River Blvd (15147-1709)
PHONE.................................412 795-7022
Charles Dinunzio, *Owner*
Philip Kalebch, *Manager*
EMP: 6
SALES (est): 497.6K **Privately Held**
WEB: www.bandrspeedsupply.com
SIC: 3599 5531 Machine shop, jobbing & repair; automotive parts

(G-18749)
BON AIR PRODUCTS INC
147 Sandy Creek Rd (15147-1791)
PHONE.................................412 793-8600
Daniel Boni, *President*

EMP: 6 **EST:** 1959
SQ FT: 5,000
SALES (est): 1.3MM **Privately Held**
SIC: 5031 2499 1799 Doors; kitchen, bathroom & household ware: wood; window treatment installation

(G-18750)
BUNTING INC (PA)
20 River Rd (15147-1159)
PHONE.................................412 820-2200
Joseph Bunting, *President*
Mike Rourk, *Regional Mgr*
Joshua Bunting, *Corp Secy*
Andrew Bunting, *Vice Pres*
Donald Stiefvater, *Project Mgr*
EMP: 175 **EST:** 1869
SQ FT: 109,000
SALES (est): 25.1MM **Privately Held**
WEB: www.buntinginc.com
SIC: 3953 3993 Marking devices; signs & advertising specialties

(G-18751)
BUNTING GRAPHICS INC
20 River Rd (15147-1159)
PHONE.................................412 481-0445
Joseph P Bunting, *President*
Andrew Bunting, *Corp Secy*
Don Stiefvater, *Project Mgr*
Luke Mattocks, *Purch Dir*
Louis Irizarry, *Accountant*
▲ **EMP:** 180
SQ FT: 110,000
SALES (est): 35.9MM **Privately Held**
WEB: www.buntinggraphics.com
SIC: 3993 7336 Signs, not made in custom sign painting shops; commercial art & graphic design

(G-18752)
BUNTING STAMP COMPANY
20 River Rd (15147-1159)
PHONE.................................412 820-2200
Jody Bunting, *President*
Andrew Bunting, *Vice Pres*
EMP: 130
SQ FT: 110,000
SALES (est): 14MM **Privately Held**
SIC: 5099 3993 3953 Rubber stamps; signs & advertising specialties; marking devices

(G-18753)
CONCEPT ENGINEERING GROUP
15 Plum St Ste 3 (15147-2100)
PHONE.................................412 826-8800
Fax: 412 826-8601
EMP: 4
SQ FT: 3,000
SALES (est): 413.7K **Privately Held**
SIC: 8711 3531 Engineering Services Mfg Construction Machinery

(G-18754)
CONSOLIDATED CONTAINER CO LLC
Also Called: Double R Enterprises
601 Seldon Ave (15147-1434)
PHONE 412 828-1111
Doug Conley, *Plant Mgr*
Gene Allen, *Manager*
Michael Ostovich, *Manager*
EMP: 100
SALES (corp-wide): 14B **Publicly Held**
WEB: www.cccllc.com
SIC: 3089 3085 Pallets, plastic; plastics bottles
HQ: Consolidated Container Company, Llc
2500 Windy Ridge Pkwy Se # 1400
Atlanta GA 30339
678 742-4600

(G-18755)
DODSON BROS INC
164 Sandy Creek Rd (15147-1728)
PHONE..................................412 793-0600
William Dodson, *President*
Colleen Dodson, *Vice Pres*
EMP: 7 **EST:** 1966
SQ FT: 6,000
SALES: 300K **Privately Held**
SIC: 2434 Vanities, bathroom: wood

(G-18756)
KINCAID MANUFACTURING INC
201 Sandy Creek Rd (15147-1795)
PHONE.................................412 795-9811
John Mihm, *President*
Susan Mihm, *Corp Secy*
Frank Mihm, *Vice Pres*
John Andrew Mimh, *Vice Pres*
EMP: 8 **EST:** 1963
SQ FT: 18,000
SALES: 1MM **Privately Held**
SIC: 3441 3599 Fabricated structural metal; machine shop, jobbing & repair

(G-18757)
MERLOT TRPULIN SIDEKIT MFG INC
Also Called: Merlot Graphics
10 Plum St (15147-2162)
PHONE.................................412 828-7664
Lori A Merlot, *President*
▲ **EMP:** 20
SQ FT: 22,000
SALES (est): 2.3MM **Privately Held**
WEB: www.merlottarp.com
SIC: 2394 3713 5199 7538 Tarpaulins, fabric: made from purchased materials; truck bodies & parts; tarpaulins; general truck repair

(G-18758)
MRCKL CLOSECO INC
Also Called: Lamagna Cheese
1 Lamagna Dr (15147-1137)
P.O. Box 303 (15147-0303)
PHONE.................................412 828-6112
Michael Lamagna, *President*
Chris Lamagna, *Vice Pres*
Rudolph Lamagna Jr, *Vice Pres*
Justin Parry, *CFO*
Kirk Lamagna, *Treasurer*
EMP: 22
SQ FT: 40,000
SALES (est): 7MM **Privately Held**
WEB: www.lamagnacheese.com
SIC: 2022 Natural cheese

(G-18759)
NADINE CORPORATION
184 Sandy Creek Rd (15147-1796)
PHONE..................................412 795-5100
Gary R Ireland, *President*
Nancy Phillips, *Vice Pres*
Andrew Reese, *Engineer*
Joe Ireland, *Controller*
Richard L Phillips, *Admin Sec*
EMP: 20 **EST:** 1964
SQ FT: 20,000
SALES (est): 5.3MM **Privately Held**
WEB: www.nadinecorp.com
SIC: 3441 Fabricated structural metal

(G-18760)
PRINT & COPY CENTER INC
731 Allegheny River Blvd (15147-1301)
PHONE..................................412 828-2205
James O'Malley, *President*
Anne O'Malley, *Treasurer*
Larry Kosht, *Sales Staff*
Jim Baird, *Graphic Designe*
EMP: 10
SQ FT: 3,500
SALES (est): 2.1MM **Privately Held**
WEB: www.printcopycenter.com
SIC: 2752 Commercial printing, offset

(G-18761)
ROBROY INDUSTRIES INC (PA)
10 River Rd (15147-1159)
PHONE..................................412 828-2100
Peter McIlroy II, *Ch of Bd*
David Marshall, *President*
Craig Mitchell, *Vice Pres*
Mike Parsell, *Buyer*
Michael T Deane, *CFO*
▲ **EMP:** 12 **EST:** 1905
SQ FT: 5,000
SALES (est): 74MM **Privately Held**
SIC: 3644 3533 Noncurrent-carrying wiring services; oil & gas field machinery

(G-18762)
ROGERS & DETURCK PRINTING INC
467 Wildwood Ave Ste 1 (15147-1267)
PHONE..................................412 828-8868
Bruce Deturck, *President*
Ray Rogers, *Vice Pres*
EMP: 4
SQ FT: 2,000
SALES: 385K **Privately Held**
SIC: 2752 Commercial printing, lithographic

(G-18763)
T J CORPORATION
Also Called: Halco
723 E Railroad Ave (15147-1115)
PHONE..................................724 929-7300
Allen M Hoffman, *CEO*
Terri Greenberg, *President*
▲ **EMP:** 25
SALES (est): 1.5MM **Privately Held**
SIC: 2389 Costumes

(G-18764)
WILKINSBURG PENN JOINT WTR
7603 Tyler Rd (15147-1530)
PHONE..................................412 243-6254
Lou Ammon, *Lab Dir*
EMP: 90
SALES (est): 8MM **Privately Held**
SIC: 2899 Water treating compounds

Villanova
Delaware County

(G-18765)
BRYNAVON GROUP INC (PA)
2000 Montgomery Ave (19085-1738)
P.O. Box 160 (19085-0160)
PHONE..................................610 525-2102
George B Lemmon, *President*
EMP: 9 **EST:** 1977
SQ FT: 2,000
SALES: 30MM **Privately Held**
WEB: www.brynavon.com
SIC: 6799 3825 5961 Venture capital companies; test equipment for electronic & electrical circuits; catalog & mail-order houses

(G-18766)
EPILOGUE SYSTEMS LLC
190 Woodstock Rd (19085-1417)
P.O. Box 296 (19085-0296)
PHONE..................................281 249-5405
David Miller, *General Mgr*
Ulrich Weigelt, *Vice Pres*
Robert Moore, *VP Finance*
Robert E Brown Jr, *Mng Member*
Cameron Kelley, *Officer*
EMP: 5
SALES (est): 214.2K **Privately Held**
SIC: 7372 Business oriented computer software

(G-18767)
NORTON PULPSTONES INCORPORATED (PA)
604 Lindsay Cir (19085-1141)
PHONE..................................610 964-0544
William D Walker, *Co-President*
Ronald L Constein, *Co-President*
EMP: 10 **EST:** 2013
SALES (est): 1.1MM **Privately Held**
SIC: 3554 Pulp mill machinery

(G-18768)
ORGAN HISTORICAL SOCIETY
330 N Spring Mill Rd (19085-1737)
PHONE..................................804 353-9226
Dan Colburn, *Exec Dir*
EMP: 6
SQ FT: 1,500
SALES: 633K **Privately Held**
WEB: www.organsociety.org
SIC: 8699 2741 5961 Historical club; miscellaneous publishing; book & record clubs

---

Vintondale
Cambria County

(G-18769)
REMINGTON PALLETS & CRATES
1452 Pyer Rd (15961-8812)
PHONE..................................814 749-7557
Remington Rose, *Owner*
EMP: 4
SALES: 150K **Privately Held**
SIC: 2448 Pallets, wood & metal combination; cargo containers, wood & metal combination

---

Virginville
Berks County

(G-18770)
H & L CONCRETE
Also Called: H & L Concrete Service
470 Main St (19564)
PHONE..................................610 562-8273
Paul Yerk, *Owner*
Diana Carter, *Manager*
EMP: 11
SALES (est): 882.8K **Privately Held**
SIC: 3273 Ready-mixed concrete

Volant
Lawrence County

(G-18771)
COMANCHE MANUFACTURING INC
3049 State Route 208 (16156-4731)
PHONE..................................724 530-7278
David Duddy, *President*
EMP: 5
SQ FT: 100,000
SALES (est): 701.5K **Privately Held**
SIC: 3715 Truck trailers

(G-18772)
DEEMS LOGGING
223 Grange Hall Rd (16156-5325)
PHONE..................................724 657-7384
Jeff Deems, *Partner*
Joel Deems, *Partner*
Mark Deems, *Partner*
EMP: 3
SALES (est): 240K **Privately Held**
SIC: 2411 Logging camps & contractors

(G-18773)
ELLIOTT BROS STEEL COMPANY
356 George Washington Rd (16156-3408)
PHONE..................................724 658-5561
Thomas C Elliott, *President*
John Peluso, *Vice Pres*
▲ **EMP:** 40 **EST:** 1893
SQ FT: 37,000
SALES (est): 5.2MM **Privately Held**
SIC: 3312 3316 Blast furnaces & steel mills; strip steel, cold-rolled: from purchased hot-rolled

(G-18774)
GENESEE RIVER TRADING COMPANY
395 Brenneman Rd (16156-1205)
P.O. Box 126, New Wilmington (16142-0126)
PHONE..................................724 533-5354
Steve Trainor, *Owner*
EMP: 5
SALES (est): 240K **Privately Held**
WEB: www.geneseeriver.com
SIC: 2511 Wood household furniture

▲ = Import ▼=Export
◆ =Import/Export

(G-18775)
MAYBERRY SUPPLY COMPANY INC
Also Called: Mayberry Hardwoods
629 State Route 956 (16156-6809)
PHONE....................724 652-6008
EMP: 3
SALES (est): 596.5K Privately Held
SIC: 2421 Sawmill/Planing Mill

(G-18776)
PITTSBURGH BAKERY EQUIPMENT CO
1118 State Route 956 (16156-3534)
PHONE....................724 533-2158
Wayne E Bisbey, President
EMP: 5
SALES (est): 896.1K Privately Held
SIC: 3556 Bakery machinery

(G-18777)
SLIPPERY ROCK MATERIALS INC
704 Golf Course Rd (16156-5518)
PHONE....................724 530-7472
David Hoobler, President
Neil Hoobler, Admin Sec
EMP: 20
SQ FT: 1,000
SALES (est): 4MM Privately Held
SIC: 1442 Sand mining; gravel mining

(G-18778)
VOLANT ENTERPRISES LTD (PA)
Also Called: Volant Mills
550 Main St (16156-7020)
P.O. Box 238 (16156-0238)
PHONE....................724 533-2500
John Geidner, President
Karen Rodenstein, Vice Pres
EMP: 6
SQ FT: 6,000
SALES (est): 498K Privately Held
SIC: 2084 Wines

Wall
Allegheny County

(G-18779)
METAL PHOTO SERVICE INC
465 Wall Ave (15148-1355)
PHONE....................412 829-2992
Ken McCombs, President
Marlene McCombs, Vice Pres
Tara Saunders, Vice Pres
Drew McCaffrey, Admin Sec
Brian Jovan, Graphic Designe
EMP: 7 EST: 1954
SQ FT: 2,400
SALES (est): 1.1MM Privately Held
SIC: 2752 Commercial printing, offset

Wallingford
Delaware County

(G-18780)
ALCHEMET INC
202 Highland Ave (19086-6120)
PHONE....................610 566-5964
Jaydee W Miller, President
Katherine L Miller, Treasurer
Frederick Orthlieb, Shareholder
EMP: 3
SQ FT: 1,300
SALES (est): 467.6K Privately Held
SIC: 3443 Industrial vessels, tanks & containers

(G-18781)
B & Q TECHNICAL SERVICE INC
417 Karen Ln (19086-6925)
PHONE....................610 872-8428
Robert A Quinn, President
EMP: 3 EST: 1970
SALES: 160K Privately Held
SIC: 3829 Fatigue testing machines, industrial: mechanical; stress, strain & flaw detecting/measuring equipment

(G-18782)
COMPOST FILMS INC
307 W Brookhaven Rd (19086-6711)
PHONE....................215 668-3001
Claudio Kuhn, Principal
EMP: 3 EST: 2008
SALES (est): 233.5K Privately Held
SIC: 2875 Compost

(G-18783)
DAVID JEFFERYS LLC
Also Called: Altus Agency
1 Chester Rd (19086-6601)
PHONE....................215 977-9900
David Jefferys, CEO
EMP: 8 EST: 2008
SQ FT: 6,500
SALES (est): 283.6K Privately Held
SIC: 8999 2741 Communication services; miscellaneous publishing

(G-18784)
HIDENSEE INC
Also Called: Stownsee
203 Beaumont Dr (19086-6802)
P.O. Box 515, Media (19063-0515)
PHONE....................614 465-3375
Bonnie Breit, President
EMP: 4
SALES (est): 255.5K Privately Held
SIC: 3089 Boxes, plastic

(G-18785)
NIRAMAYA INC
212 Moore Rd (19086-6843)
PHONE....................267 799-2120
EMP: 3 EST: 2012
SALES (est): 170K Privately Held
SIC: 2833 Mfg Medicinal/Botanical Products

(G-18786)
OAK CREST INDUSTRIES INC
500 Oakcrest Ln (19086-6515)
PHONE....................610 246-9177
Lisa Foth, Principal
EMP: 3
SALES (est): 131.5K Privately Held
SIC: 3999 Manufacturing industries

(G-18787)
UNIQUE SYSTEMS INC
221 Stanford Dr (19086-6637)
PHONE....................610 499-1463
Randy Williams, President
Sarah Sykes, Vice Pres
Martha Williams, Treasurer
EMP: 4
SQ FT: 500
SALES (est): 200K Privately Held
SIC: 3669 Emergency alarms

Walnut Bottom
Cumberland County

(G-18788)
AGAR WELDING SERVICE & STL SUP
93 Firehouse Rd (17266-9761)
PHONE....................717 532-1000
Denise Agar, President
Donald Agar, Vice Pres
EMP: 23
SALES (est): 2.7MM Privately Held
SIC: 1799 5051 3441 Welding on site; steel; fabricated structural metal

(G-18789)
FEHL AWNING COMPANY INC
12 W Main St (17266-9702)
P.O. Box 24 (17266-0024)
PHONE....................717 776-3162
Thomas L Hovetter, President
EMP: 5
SALES (est): 610.5K Privately Held
SIC: 2394 5999 Awnings, fabric: made from purchased materials; awnings

Walnutport
Northampton County

(G-18790)
AMERICAN NICKELOID COMPANY
200 Spruce St (18088-1649)
PHONE....................610 767-3842
EMP: 3
SALES (est): 84.6K Privately Held
SIC: 3471 Plating & polishing

(G-18791)
ELK LIGHTING INC (PA)
40 3rd St (18088-1470)
PHONE....................610 767-0511
EMP: 5
SALES (est): 5.7MM Privately Held
SIC: 5063 3645 Lighting fixtures; residential lighting fixtures

(G-18792)
MONUMENTAL TOUCH
4557 Lehigh Dr (18088-9510)
PHONE....................484 226-7277
Michael Paff, Principal
EMP: 3
SALES (est): 209.6K Privately Held
SIC: 3272 Monuments & grave markers, except terrazo

(G-18793)
MR REBUILDABLES INC
4800 Lehigh Dr (18088-9461)
PHONE....................610 767-2100
Joe Disaverio, President
Joe Di Saverio, President
EMP: 5
SALES (est): 411.6K Privately Held
SIC: 3714 Radiators & radiator shells & cores, motor vehicle

(G-18794)
SZOKE IRON WORKS INC
1115 Riverview Dr (18088-9108)
PHONE....................610 760-9565
Randal L Szoke, President
EMP: 10
SQ FT: 4,200
SALES (est): 910K Privately Held
SIC: 3441 Building components, structural steel

Waltersburg
Fayette County

(G-18795)
PICCOLOMINI CONTRACTORS INC
Also Called: PCI
1790 Pittsburgh Rd (15488)
PHONE....................724 437-7946
John Piccolomini Jr, President
Louise Piccolomini, Corp Secy
John Piccolomini III, Vice Pres
EMP: 8
SALES (est): 1.5MM Privately Held
SIC: 1794 1221 Excavation & grading, building construction; strip mining, bituminous

Wampum
Lawrence County

(G-18796)
ALLIED RUBBER & RIGGING SUP CO
Rr 18 (16157)
PHONE....................724 535-7380
Dave Marki, Branch Mgr
EMP: 9
SALES (corp-wide): 3.1B Privately Held
SIC: 3052 5085 Rubber & plastics hose & beltings; hose, belting & packing
HQ: Allied Rubber & Rigging Supply Company
1655 Route 65
Ellwood City PA 16117
724 482-2965

(G-18797)
AMPTECH INC
1605 Old Route 18 9-26 (16157-3417)
PHONE....................724 843-7605
Robin Park, Branch Mgr
Bernie Pieczynski, Manager
EMP: 22
SALES (est): 2.4MM Privately Held
WEB: www.amptechinc.com
SIC: 3672 Printed circuit boards
PA: Amptech, Inc.
201 Glocheski Dr
Manistee MI 49660

(G-18798)
CEMEX CNSTR MTLS ATL LLC
Cem - Wampum Quarry
2001 Portland Park (16157-3913)
PHONE....................724 535-4311
Melony Lloyd, Branch Mgr
EMP: 164 Privately Held
SIC: 3241 1422 Cement, hydraulic; crushed & broken limestone
HQ: Cemex Construction Materials Atlantic, Llc
1501 Belvedere Rd
West Palm Beach FL 33406
561 833-5555

(G-18799)
DOREN INC
2313 State Route 18 (16157-2217)
PHONE....................724 535-4397
Donald L Lampus Jr, President
William R Stevens, Vice Pres
Gregg Boehler, Plant Mgr
▲ EMP: 13
SALES (est): 2.9MM Privately Held
WEB: www.doren.net
SIC: 3272 Concrete products

(G-18800)
FERRANTE UPHLSTRNG & CRPTNG
3384 State Route 18 (16157-3610)
PHONE....................724 535-8866
James L Ferrante, President
EMP: 13
SALES (est): 1.6MM Privately Held
WEB: www.ferranteinteriors.com
SIC: 1752 5713 2391 2512 Carpet laying; ceramic floor tile installation; linoleum installation; carpets; floor tile; linoleum; curtains & draperies; couches, sofas & davenports: upholstered on wood frames

(G-18801)
KERRY COAL COMPANY INC
309 Industrial Park Dr (16157-2209)
PHONE....................724 535-1311
EMP: 12
SALES (est): 1MM Privately Held
SIC: 1221 Bituminous Coal/Lignite Surface Mining

(G-18802)
MINES AND MEADOWS LLC
1307 Old Route 18 (16157-3407)
PHONE....................724 535-6026
Robert Svihra, Principal
EMP: 3
SALES (est): 319.9K Privately Held
SIC: 3599 Amusement park equipment

(G-18803)
OMNI PRECAST PRODUCTS INC
339 Industrial Park Dr (16157-2209)
PHONE....................724 316-1582
EMP: 5
SALES (est): 403K Privately Held
SIC: 3272 Precast terrazo or concrete products

(G-18804)
ROMAR TEXTILE CO INC
1605 Old Route 18 Unit 3 (16157-3417)
PHONE....................724 535-7787
Amy J Weinberg, President
Paul A Levinsohn, Vice Pres
▲ EMP: 150

GEOGRAPHIC

SQ FT: 52,000
SALES (est): 14.2MM **Privately Held**
SIC: 2211 2262 2261 Broadwoven fabric mills, cotton; finishing plants, manmade fiber & silk fabrics; finishing plants, cotton

(G-18805)
TITA MACHINE & TOOL INC
229 Industrial Park Dr (16157-2207)
P.O. Box 111, Koppel (16136-0111)
PHONE..................................724 535-4988
George Tita, *President*
Beverly Means, *Vice Pres*
Kenneth Shoaf, *Treasurer*
William Buzard, *Admin Sec*
EMP: 8 **EST:** 1947
SQ FT: 7,200
SALES: 1MM **Privately Held**
SIC: 3599 Machine shop, jobbing & repair

(G-18806)
UNIVERSAL REFRACTORIES INC (PA)
Also Called: Universal Specialties
915 Clyde St (16157-4403)
P.O. Box 97 (16157-0097)
PHONE..................................724 535-4374
Walter Sylvester, *President*
Thomas Sylvester, *Vice Pres*
Leroy Thompson, *Vice Pres*
Michael Sylvester, *Admin Sec*
Frank Yenca, *Admin Sec*
▲ **EMP:** 25
SQ FT: 100,000
SALES (est): 47.8MM **Privately Held**
SIC: 3255 3297 Castable refractories, clay; gunning mixes, nonclay

Wapwallopen
Luzerne County

(G-18807)
ANDREAS LUMBER INC
16 Sawmill Ln (18660-1242)
PHONE..................................570 379-3644
Carl Andreas, *President*
Caroline Andreas, *Vice Pres*
EMP: 8
SALES (est): 480K **Privately Held**
SIC: 2421 5211 Sawmills & planing mills, general; planing mill products & lumber

(G-18808)
PENNSY SUPPLY INC
51 Small Mountain Rd (18660-1644)
PHONE..................................570 868-6936
Dave Johnson, *Manager*
EMP: 50
SALES (corp-wide): 29.7B **Privately Held**
WEB: www.pennsysupply.com
SIC: 3273 Ready-mixed concrete
HQ: Pennsy Supply, Inc.
1001 Paxton St
Harrisburg PA 17104
717 233-4511

(G-18809)
SHEPHERD PRESS INC
437 S River St (18660-1028)
P.O. Box 24 (18660-0024)
PHONE..................................570 379-2015
Ted Tripp, *President*
Rick Irvin, *Prdtn Mgr*
Linda Riggall, *Marketing Staff*
EMP: 9
SALES (est): 882.4K **Privately Held**
WEB: www.shepherdpress.com
SIC: 2731 Books: publishing only

Warfordsburg
Fulton County

(G-18810)
B B EXPRESS
Also Called: Bb Express Welding
3771 Pleasant Grove Rd (17267-8822)
PHONE..................................717 573-2686
EMP: 4
SALES (est): 504K **Privately Held**
SIC: 3399 Mfg Primary Metal Products

(G-18811)
BLUEGRASS MATERIALS CO LLC
424 Pigeon Cove Rd (17267-8982)
PHONE..................................410 683-1250
EMP: 5 **Publicly Held**
SIC: 1411 Limestone, dimension-quarrying
HQ: Bluegrass Materials Company, Llc
200 W Forsyth St Ste 1200
Jacksonville FL 32202

(G-18812)
H B MELLOTT ESTATE INC
424 Pigeon Cove Rd (17267-8982)
PHONE..................................301 678-2050
Fax: 717 678-2012
EMP: 17 **EST:** 2009
SALES (est): 2MM **Privately Held**
SIC: 3281 Mfg Cut Stone/Products

(G-18813)
M & C LUMBER CO INC
4693 Great Cove Rd (17267-8540)
PHONE..................................717 573-2200
Mark A Mellot, *President*
Connie Mellot, *Corp Secy*
EMP: 6
SALES: 577.6K **Privately Held**
SIC: 2426 Lumber, hardwood dimension

Warminster
Bucks County

(G-18814)
A K U WIRE INC
1800 Mearns Rd Ste D (18974-1191)
PHONE..................................215 672-8071
Kathy Wetzel, *Principal*
EMP: 3
SALES (est): 281.9K **Privately Held**
SIC: 3599 Machine shop, jobbing & repair

(G-18815)
A LANDAU DIAMOND CO
Also Called: Landau, A Co
1811 Stout Dr (18974-1157)
P.O. Box 3416 (18974-0142)
PHONE..................................215 675-2700
Robert Sgro, *President*
Joan Sgro, *Corp Secy*
Louis A Sgro, *Vice Pres*
Louis Sgro, *Info Tech Mgr*
EMP: 6
SQ FT: 6,000
SALES (est): 839K **Privately Held**
WEB: www.alandau.net
SIC: 3545 Diamond cutting tools for turning, boring, burnishing, etc.

(G-18816)
A-1 RACING PRODUCTS INC
1927 Stout Dr Ste 2 (18974-3870)
PHONE..................................215 675-8442
Brad M Creighton, *President*
Joe Creighton, *Vice Pres*
EMP: 4
SQ FT: 3,500
SALES: 1MM **Privately Held**
WEB: www.a1racing.com
SIC: 3714 5531 Motor vehicle parts & accessories; automotive & home supply stores

(G-18817)
AA PLASMA LLC
32 Richard Rd (18974-1513)
PHONE..................................312 371-7947
Gary Nirenberg, *CEO*
EMP: 4 **EST:** 2017
SALES (est): 254.5K **Privately Held**
SIC: 2836 Plasmas

(G-18818)
ABB INC
Also Called: Process Automation
125 County Line Rd (18974-4974)
PHONE..................................215 674-6000
Dane Maisel, *General Mgr*
EMP: 250
SALES (corp-wide): 34.3B **Privately Held**
WEB: www.elsterelectricity.com
SIC: 3612 Transformers, except electric

HQ: Abb Inc.
305 Gregson Dr
Cary NC 27511

(G-18819)
ACCURATE COMPONENTS
48 Vincent Cir Ste B (18974-1538)
PHONE..................................215 442-1023
Rock Patel, *Principal*
EMP: 6
SALES (est): 621.1K **Privately Held**
SIC: 3999 Manufacturing industries

(G-18820)
ACCURATE MACHINE TECH INC
Also Called: Accurate Machine Technology
1800 Mearns Rd Ste L (18974-1191)
PHONE..................................267 885-7344
Darren Guthrie, *President*
EMP: 4
SALES (est): 305.3K **Privately Held**
SIC: 3599 Machine shop, jobbing & repair

(G-18821)
ADVANCED AVIONICS INC
607 Louis Dr Ste G (18974-2843)
PHONE..................................215 441-0449
Joesph McCandless, *President*
Donald Scott, *Principal*
Mr Lawrence Howarth, *Corp Secy*
EMP: 12
SQ FT: 1,000
SALES: 2.5MM **Privately Held**
WEB: www.advancedavionics.net
SIC: 3825 Test equipment for electronic & electrical circuits

(G-18822)
AFTERGLO LIGHTING CO INC
1825 Stout Dr (18974-1157)
PHONE..................................215 355-7942
Bonnie Fleming-Jacoby, *CEO*
Hal Luble, *Vice Pres*
EMP: 6 **EST:** 2014
SALES (est): 316.8K **Privately Held**
SIC: 3629 Power conversion units, a.c. to d.c.: static-electric

(G-18823)
AFTERPRINT SERVICES INC
1800 Mearns Rd Ste G (18974-1191)
PHONE..................................215 674-3082
David Anthony, *President*
EMP: 6
SQ FT: 1,800
SALES (est): 420K **Privately Held**
SIC: 2789 Binding only: books, pamphlets, magazines, etc.

(G-18824)
AGD PRODUCTS INC
952 Thomas Dr (18974-2883)
PHONE..................................215 682-9643
David Sayers, *President*
Mike Osilka, *Sales Staff*
◆ **EMP:** 6
SALES (est): 1.2MM **Privately Held**
WEB: www.agdproducts.com
SIC: 3089 Plastic containers, except foam

(G-18825)
AJ KANE INCORPORATED
92 Railroad Dr (18974-1454)
PHONE..................................215 953-5152
Thomas M Hull, *President*
Frank H Bastian, *Vice Pres*
EMP: 8
SALES (est): 1.4MM **Privately Held**
SIC: 3446 Stairs, fire escapes, balconies, railings & ladders

(G-18826)
ALTAIR EQUIPMENT COMPANY INC
335 Constance Dr (18974-2816)
PHONE..................................215 672-9000
Rick E Krager, *President*
Edward W Krager, *Vice Pres*
Tom Bigley, *Prdtn Mgr*
Joanne Badolato, *Info Tech Mgr*
Edward G Krager, *Admin Sec*
EMP: 20
SQ FT: 11,000

SALES (est): 5.6MM **Privately Held**
WEB: www.altairequipment.com
SIC: 3589 7359 Water treatment equipment, industrial; water purification equipment, household type; equipment rental & leasing

(G-18827)
AMERICAN BRCHURE CATALOGUE INC
Also Called: Americor Press
882 Louis Dr (18974-2819)
PHONE..................................215 259-1600
James Notte, *President*
Robert Dean, *CFO*
EMP: 49
SQ FT: 50,000
SALES (est): 7.6MM **Privately Held**
WEB: www.americorpress.com
SIC: 2752 2791 2759 3993 Commercial printing, offset; typesetting; commercial printing; signs & advertising specialties

(G-18828)
ARBUTUS BIOPHARMA CORPORATION
701 Veterans Cir (18974-3531)
PHONE..................................267 469-0914
Mark Murray, *CEO*
EMP: 13
SALES (corp-wide): 10.7MM **Privately Held**
SIC: 2834 Pharmaceutical preparations
PA: Arbutus Biopharma Corporation
8900 Glenlyon Pky Suite 100
Burnaby BC V5J 5
604 419-3200

(G-18829)
ARBUTUS BIOPHARMA INC
701 Veterans Cir (18974-3531)
PHONE..................................215 675-5921
Elizabeth Howard, *President*
EMP: 7
SALES (est): 1.4MM **Privately Held**
SIC: 2834 Pharmaceutical preparations

(G-18830)
ASTRA CORPORATION
21 Industrial Dr Ste B (18974-1470)
PHONE..................................215 674-3539
Dennis Mayorschoff, *President*
EMP: 3
SALES (est): 402K **Privately Held**
SIC: 3823 Pressure gauges, dial & digital

(G-18831)
ASTRO PRINTING SERVICES INC
Also Called: Astro Dynmc Print Graphic Svcs
882 Louis Dr (18974-2819)
PHONE..................................215 441-4444
Darrel Dundore, *President*
Brian Jamison, *Manager*
Scott Lang, *Director*
EMP: 11
SQ FT: 10,000
SALES: 2.4MM **Privately Held**
WEB: www.astro-printing.com
SIC: 2752 Commercial printing, offset

(G-18832)
AUTOMATIC FORECASTING SYSTEMS
Also Called: Auto B J
759 Ivyland Rd (18974-2223)
P.O. Box 563, Hatboro (19040-0563)
PHONE..................................215 675-0652
Elvy A Reilly, *President*
David P Reilly, *Treasurer*
EMP: 12
SALES: 900K **Privately Held**
WEB: www.autobox.com
SIC: 7379 7371 7372 Computer related consulting services; custom computer programming services; prepackaged software

(G-18833)
AZTEC MACHINERY COMPANY
960 Jacksonville Rd (18974-1719)
PHONE..................................215 672-2600
David Rattner, *President*
Harriet Rattner, *Admin Sec*
EMP: 45 **EST:** 1960

SQ FT: 45,000
SALES (est): 8.7MM **Privately Held**
SIC: 3552 3567 Textile machinery; driers
  & redriers, industrial process

(G-18834)
BAFCO INC
717 Mearns Rd (18974-2876)
P.O. Box 2428 (18974-0043)
PHONE..............................215 674-1700
James Hamtil, *President*
Ron Rietsma, *General Mgr*
Gary Seums, *Purch Mgr*
Ronald Jacoby, *Treasurer*
Tara Hughes, *Asst Controller*
▲ **EMP:** 30
SQ FT: 23,000
SALES (est): 13MM **Privately Held**
WEB: www.bafco.com
SIC: 3823 Industrial process measurement
  equipment

(G-18835)
BALTIMORE CORP (PA)
Also Called: Old York Road Publishing Co
905 Louis Dr (18974-2821)
PHONE..............................215 957-6200
Joann S Pitt, *President*
Charles A Pitt, *Vice Pres*
▼ **EMP:** 25
SQ FT: 12,000
SALES (est): 5.1MM **Privately Held**
WEB: www.oyrp.com
SIC: 2759 Publication printing

(G-18836)
BENNETT HEAT TRTING BRZING INC
82 Richard Rd (18974-1513)
PHONE..............................215 674-8120
John Di Trapano, *Manager*
EMP: 10
SALES (corp-wide): 6.4MM **Privately Held**
WEB: www.bennetheat.com
SIC: 3398 Brazing (hardening) of metal
PA: Bennett Heat Treating And Brazing Co.,
  Inc.
  690 Ferry St
  Newark NJ 07105
  973 589-0590

(G-18837)
BIG BOYZ INDUSTRIES INC
128 Railroad Dr (18974-1449)
PHONE..............................215 942-9971
Leonard Feldman, *CEO*
Terry Weisberg, *President*
Jennifer Frankel, *Corp Secy*
EMP: 9
SQ FT: 5,800
SALES (est): 1.1MM **Privately Held**
WEB: www.bariatricbeds.com
SIC: 2511 Bed frames, except water bed
  frames: wood

(G-18838)
BIGGS TOOL AND DIE INC
365 Patricia Dr (18974-2840)
PHONE..............................215 674-9911
Charles Biggs, *President*
EMP: 15 **EST:** 1978
SQ FT: 8,100
SALES (est): 3MM **Privately Held**
WEB: www.biggstd.com
SIC: 3599 3544 Machine shop, jobbing &
  repair; special dies, tools, jigs & fixtures

(G-18839)
BONEHEAD PERFORMANCE INC
1836 Stout Dr Ste 18 (18974-1198)
PHONE..............................215 674-8206
Chuck Steele, *President*
EMP: 14
SALES (est): 1.9MM **Privately Held**
WEB: www.boneheadperformance.com
SIC: 3479 5046 5531 7542 Coating of
  metals & formed products; commercial
  equipment; automotive & home supply
  stores; carwashes

(G-18840)
BP LUBRICANTS USA INC
775 Louis Dr (18974-2827)
PHONE..............................215 443-5220

Christ Herman, *Manager*
EMP: 75
SALES (corp-wide): 240.2B **Privately Held**
WEB: www.lubecon.com
SIC: 2992 Lubricating oils
HQ: Bp Lubricants Usa Inc.
  1500 Valley Rd
  Wayne NJ 07470
  973 633-2200

(G-18841)
BP LUBRICANTS USA INC
Also Called: Castrol H D L
1020 Louis Dr (18974-2822)
PHONE..............................215 674-5301
Ben Casole, *Manager*
EMP: 26
SALES (corp-wide): 240.2B **Privately Held**
SIC: 2992 Oils & greases, blending & compounding
HQ: Bp Lubricants Usa Inc.
  1500 Valley Rd
  Wayne NJ 07470
  973 633-2200

(G-18842)
BUCKS COUNTY SHUTTERS LLC
940 Thomas Dr (18974-2883)
PHONE..............................215 957-3333
Jamie Camarello, *Mng Member*
EMP: 12
SALES (est): 1.2MM **Privately Held**
SIC: 3442 Shutters, door or window: metal

(G-18843)
C P COMMERCIAL PRINTING INC (PA)
Also Called: C P Commerical Printing
2031 Stout Dr Ste 2 (18974-3860)
P.O. Box 550, Chalfont (18914-0550)
PHONE..............................215 675-7605
Patricia Hueber Boder, *President*
EMP: 6
SQ FT: 3,500
SALES (est): 1.7MM **Privately Held**
SIC: 2752 Commercial printing, offset

(G-18844)
CALTECH MANUFACTURING
109 Industrial Dr (18974-1434)
PHONE..............................215 322-2025
Sandra Callender, *Principal*
EMP: 12
SALES (est): 1.1MM **Privately Held**
SIC: 3999 Boutiquing: decorating gift items
  with sequins, fruit, etc.

(G-18845)
COLOR HOUSE COMPANY LTD
5 Charter Cir (18974-5805)
PHONE..............................215 322-4310
John P Shay, *President*
Joseph P Cusick, *Admin Sec*
EMP: 15
SQ FT: 10,000
SALES (est): 1.9MM **Privately Held**
WEB: www.cigar-accs.com
SIC: 2752 2796 Commercial printing, lithographic; lithographic plates, positives or
  negatives

(G-18846)
CONTROL DYNAMICS CORPORATION
960 Louis Dr (18974-2841)
PHONE..............................215 956-0700
Harvey A Shuhart Jr, *President*
Janet K Shuhart, *Vice Pres*
EMP: 7
SALES (est): 1MM **Privately Held**
WEB: www.cdcradio.com
SIC: 3625 3663 Relays & industrial controls; radio & TV communications equipment

(G-18847)
CONVERGING SCIENCES TECH INC
1403 Old Jacksonville Rd (18974-1219)
PHONE..............................215 626-5705
Robin Pettit, *President*
EMP: 4

SALES (est): 207.6K **Privately Held**
SIC: 3761 8731 7389 Space vehicles,
  complete; commercial physical research;

(G-18848)
CP PRECISION INC
1979 Stout Dr Unit 3 (18974-3871)
P.O. Box 2100 (18974-0010)
PHONE..............................267 364-0870
Paul Brady, *President*
Shaun Gordon, *Cust Mgr*
EMP: 3
SALES (est): 354.5K **Privately Held**
WEB: www.cpprecision.com
SIC: 3451 Screw machine products

(G-18849)
CP PRECISION INC
1979 Stout Dr Ste 3 (18974-3871)
PHONE..............................267 364-0870
Paul Brady, *Principal*
John Miller, *Engineer*
EMP: 3
SALES (est): 319.3K **Privately Held**
SIC: 7389 3423 Hand tool designers;
  hand & edge tools

(G-18850)
CRC INDUSTRIES INC
86 Railroad Dr (18974-1454)
PHONE..............................800 556-5074
Charlie Straub, *Principal*
EMP: 5
SALES (corp-wide): 2.9B **Privately Held**
SIC: 2992 2899 Lubricating oils &
  greases; chemical preparations
HQ: Crc Industries, Inc.
  800 Enterprise Rd Ste 101
  Horsham PA 19044
  215 674-4300

(G-18851)
CRC INDUSTRIES INC
Manufacturing and R&D Center
885 Louis Dr (18974-2869)
PHONE..............................215 441-4380
EMP: 7
SALES (corp-wide): 2.9B **Privately Held**
SIC: 5169 2992 Chemicals & allied products; lubricating oils
HQ: Crc Industries, Inc.
  800 Enterprise Rd Ste 101
  Horsham PA 19044
  215 674-4300

(G-18852)
CURRENT CIRCUITS INC
375 Ivyland Rd Ste 21 (18974-2235)
PHONE..............................215 444-9295
Manish Detroja, *Principal*
EMP: 3
SALES (est): 306.5K **Privately Held**
SIC: 3679 Electronic components

(G-18853)
CUSTOM WOOD CRAFTERS INC
135 Industrial Dr (18974-1434)
PHONE..............................215 357-6677
Wendy S Hudson, *President*
Steve Hudson, *Corp Secy*
EMP: 3
SQ FT: 3,500
SALES (est): 433.3K **Privately Held**
WEB: www.customwoodcrafters.com
SIC: 2541 Cabinets, except refrigerated:
  show, display, etc.: wood

(G-18854)
D K P -HARDY INC
2015 Stout Dr (18974-3859)
PHONE..............................215 441-0383
Norman L Monks, *Principal*
EMP: 3
SALES (est): 175.1K **Privately Held**
SIC: 2819 Carbides

(G-18855)
DDM NOVASTAR INC
212 Railroad Dr (18974-1447)
PHONE..............................610 337-3050
Ed Cicutti, *President*
Barb Kirkpatrick, *Vice Pres*
Robert Voigt, *Vice Pres*
▲ **EMP:** 30
SQ FT: 50,000

SALES (est): 5.2MM **Privately Held**
SIC: 3672 3559 Printed circuit boards;
  electronic component making machinery

(G-18856)
DELMAR ENTERPRISES INC
Also Called: Salem Supply Co
995 Louis Dr (18974-2821)
PHONE..............................215 674-4534
Andrew Conley, *CEO*
Andy Conly, *Vice Pres*
Sandra Yerkes, *Admin Sec*
EMP: 12
SALES (est): 3.4MM **Privately Held**
WEB: www.delmarent.com
SIC: 5084 3429 Food industry machinery;
  keys, locks & related hardware

(G-18857)
DESIGNED FOR FUN INC
1800 Mearns Rd Ste G (18974-1191)
P.O. Box 883, Doylestown (18901-0883)
PHONE..............................215 675-4718
Brett Haddaway, *President*
▲ **EMP:** 3
SQ FT: 1,800
SALES (est): 230K **Privately Held**
WEB: www.designedforfun.com
SIC: 3949 Playground equipment

(G-18858)
DIGITAL MACHINE COMPANY INC
1055 Louis Dr Ste B (18974-2823)
PHONE..............................215 672-6454
Gregory M Schmitt, *President*
Mark Dickson, *Corp Secy*
EMP: 23
SQ FT: 12,000
SALES (est): 2.4MM **Privately Held**
SIC: 3599 Machine shop, jobbing & repair

(G-18859)
DONALDSON COMPANY INC
85 Railroad Dr (18974-1478)
PHONE..............................215 396-8349
Mark Engel, *Branch Mgr*
EMP: 4
SALES (corp-wide): 2.7B **Publicly Held**
WEB: www.donaldson.com
SIC: 5075 2851 Dust collecting equipment; paints & allied products
PA: Donaldson Company, Inc.
  1400 W 94th St
  Minneapolis MN 55431
  952 887-3131

(G-18860)
DOUBLE H MANUFACTURING CORP
Also Called: Double H Plastics
2548 W 26th St (18974)
PHONE..............................215 674-4100
Joseph Harp, *President*
EMP: 70 **Privately Held**
WEB: www.doublehplastics.com
SIC: 3544 Special dies & tools
PA: Double H Manufacturing Corporation
  50 W Street Rd
  Warminster PA 18974

(G-18861)
DOUBLE H MANUFACTURING CORP (PA)
50 W Street Rd (18974-3203)
PHONE..............................215 674-4100
Joseph C Harp, *President*
EMP: 9
SALES (est): 9.5MM **Privately Held**
SIC: 3544 Special dies & tools

(G-18862)
DOUGLAS PHARMA US INC
1035 Louis Dr (18974-2823)
PHONE..............................267 317-2010
Kevin Connolley, *President*
Dr Raju Vegefna, *Senior VP*
EMP: 10
SQ FT: 12,000
SALES: 10MM
SALES (corp-wide): 1.3MM **Privately Held**
SIC: 8733 2834 Medical research; druggists' preparations (pharmaceuticals)

HQ: Douglas Pharmaceuticals Limited
Central Park Drive
Auckland 0610

(G-18863)
DREAMLINE
905 Louis Dr (18974-2821)
PHONE....................................215 957-1411
Morris Kastiyel, *Principal*
EMP: 6 **EST:** 2007
SALES (est): 678.9K **Privately Held**
SIC: 3444 Metal housings, enclosures, casings & other containers

(G-18864)
DVM MANUFACTURING LLC
315 W Street Rd (18974-3208)
PHONE....................................215 839-3425
Kelley Flynn, *Vice Pres*
EMP: 11 **EST:** 2014
SQ FT: 10,000
SALES (est): 4.1MM **Privately Held**
SIC: 3699 Electrical equipment & supplies

(G-18865)
DYNAMIC CONCEPTS MFG LLC
1836 Stout Dr Ste 8 (18974-1197)
PHONE....................................215 675-9006
Raymond Brettle, *Owner*
Neil H Miller, *Principal*
EMP: 3
SALES (est): 268.5K **Privately Held**
SIC: 3599 Machine shop, jobbing & repair

(G-18866)
EAGLE FAR EAST INC
Also Called: Eagle Stainless Container
816 Nina Way (18974-2833)
PHONE....................................215 957-9333
Charles Lin, *President*
Peter Lin, *Vice Pres*
Tara Dougherty, *Sales Mgr*
Dolores Lin, *Admin Sec*
◆ **EMP:** 20
SQ FT: 34,000
SALES: 3.3MM **Privately Held**
WEB: www.estainless.com
SIC: 3441 Expansion joints (structural shapes), iron or steel

(G-18867)
EAGLERISE E&E INC
320 Constance Dr Ste 1 (18974-2877)
PHONE....................................215 675-5953
Liangbin Lu, *President*
Tony Y Xu, *Treasurer*
Lucy Y Cheng, *Admin Sec*
▲ **EMP:** 14 **EST:** 2006
SALES (est): 2.3MM **Privately Held**
SIC: 3679 Electronic loads & power supplies; tube transformer assemblies used in firing electronic tubes
PA: Eaglerise Electric & Electronic (China) Co., Ltd.
No.A3, Guicheng Technology Park, Jianping Road, Nanhai District
Foshan 52820

(G-18868)
EASTERN GAUGE & REGULATOR
1825 Stout Dr (18974-1157)
PHONE....................................215 443-5192
Bruce Blackway, *President*
EMP: 15
SQ FT: 6,500
SALES (est): 1.4MM **Privately Held**
WEB: www.eicsolutionsinc.com
SIC: 3825 Meters: electric, pocket, portable, panelboard, etc.

(G-18869)
ECOBEE ADVANCED TECH LLC
1531 Meetinghouse Rd (18974-1031)
PHONE....................................609 474-0010
Yasushi Sasaki, *Managing Dir*
Yeol Seong
Seong Heun Cheon,
Yeol Chang Seong,
Jong Ho Woo,
EMP: 5 **EST:** 2014
SALES (est): 306.8K **Privately Held**
SIC: 3593 3519 3694 Fluid power cylinders & actuators; diesel, semi-diesel or duel-fuel engines, including marine; ignition apparatus & distributors

(G-18870)
EIC SOLUTIONS INC
700 Veterans Cir Ste 200 (18974-3532)
PHONE....................................215 443-5190
David Bates, *CEO*
Myra Hodgdon, *Office Mgr*
◆ **EMP:** 35 **EST:** 1988
SQ FT: 11,000
SALES (est): 7.9MM **Privately Held**
WEB: www.eicsolutionsinc.com
SIC: 3585 Air conditioning equipment, complete

(G-18871)
EMP INDUSTRIES INC
Also Called: Electrical Mechanical Products
153 Railroad Dr (18974-1448)
PHONE....................................215 357-5333
Ed Pentz, *President*
Rob Hughes, *Engineer*
Brian Pentz, *Engineer*
Dan Ralston, *Engineer*
Gabriella Pentz, *Administration*
EMP: 9
SQ FT: 10,500
SALES (est): 810K **Privately Held**
WEB: www.empindustries.com
SIC: 3559 3565 7629 3549 Semiconductor manufacturing machinery; pharmaceutical machinery; electronic component making machinery; packing & wrapping machinery; electrical repair shops; metalworking machinery; special dies, tools, jigs & fixtures; sheet metalwork

(G-18872)
ENEFLUX ARMTEK MAGNETICS INC
1775 Stout Dr Ste G (18974-3832)
PHONE....................................215 443-5303
Anthony Mantella, *President*
EMP: 4
SALES (corp-wide): 11.9MM **Privately Held**
WEB: www.eamagnetics.com
SIC: 5085 3264 Industrial supplies; magnets, permanent: ceramic or ferrite
HQ: Eneflux Armtek Magnetics, Inc.
6 Platinum Ct
Medford NY 11763
516 576-3434

(G-18873)
ENERSYS
375 Constance Dr (18974-2816)
PHONE....................................215 420-1000
EMP: 15
SALES (corp-wide): 2.5B **Publicly Held**
SIC: 3691 Lead acid batteries (storage batteries)
PA: Enersys
2366 Bernville Rd
Reading PA 19605
610 208-1991

(G-18874)
ESSEX ENGINEERING CORP
21 Industrial Dr Ste A (18974-1483)
PHONE....................................215 322-5880
Fax: 215 322-8368
EMP: 8
SQ FT: 6,000
SALES (est): 930K **Privately Held**
SIC: 3613 Mfg Instrument Panels

(G-18875)
EXHAUST TRACK INC (PA)
1011 Howard Rd (18974-2748)
PHONE....................................215 675-1021
Edward Pfeiffer, *President*
Joseph Mullelly, *Treasurer*
EMP: 4
SALES (est): 1.5MM **Privately Held**
SIC: 3564 Exhaust fans: industrial or commercial

(G-18876)
EXPRESSWAY PRINTING INC
1800 Mearns Rd Ste V (18974-1192)
PHONE....................................215 244-0233
Russell E Parker Jr, *President*
Kevin Parker, *Vice Pres*
EMP: 4
SQ FT: 1,800

SALES (est): 739.1K **Privately Held**
WEB: www.expresswayprinting.com
SIC: 2752 Commercial printing, offset

(G-18877)
FHRITP HOLDINGS LLC
309 Camars Dr (18974-3874)
PHONE....................................215 675-4590
David Walter, *Opers Mgr*
Mike Klesh,
EMP: 10
SALES (est): 1.9MM **Privately Held**
SIC: 3452 Screws, metal

(G-18878)
FINISH TECH CORP
184 Railroad Dr (18974-1449)
PHONE....................................215 396-8800
Dan Griffin, *Branch Mgr*
EMP: 15
SALES (corp-wide): 6MM **Privately Held**
SIC: 3083 Plastic finished products, laminated
PA: Finish Tech Corp
90 Industrial Dr
Warminster PA 18974
215 396-8800

(G-18879)
FINISH TECH CORP (PA)
Also Called: Red Strings Holographics
90 Industrial Dr (18974-1445)
PHONE....................................215 396-8800
Mahesh Dani, *President*
Renuka Dani, *Corp Secy*
Terry Carroll, *COO*
Jay Shah, *CFO*
▲ **EMP:** 30
SQ FT: 25,000
SALES: 6MM **Privately Held**
WEB: www.finishtechcorp.com
SIC: 3083 Plastic finished products, laminated

(G-18880)
FINISHING ASSOCIATES LLC
1119 Mearns Rd (18974-2215)
P.O. Box 40760, Lansing MI (48901-7960)
PHONE....................................517 371-2460
Richard T Lindgren, *President*
Donald Kevarka, *Admin Sec*
▲ **EMP:** 10
SALES (est): 2MM
SALES (corp-wide): 978.3MM **Privately Held**
SIC: 2231 Broadwoven fabric mills, wool
HQ: Sinto America, Inc.
3001 W Main St
Lansing MI 48917
517 371-2460

(G-18881)
FORANNE MANUFACTURING INC
83 Steam Whistle Dr (18974-1475)
PHONE....................................215 357-4650
Victor Gentile Jr, *President*
Anthony Gentile, *Vice Pres*
Michael Gentile, *VP Mfg*
EMP: 25
SQ FT: 11,000
SALES (est): 5MM **Privately Held**
WEB: www.foranne.com
SIC: 3599 3728 3841 Machine shop, jobbing & repair; aircraft parts & equipment; surgical & medical instruments

(G-18882)
FOX RUN HOLDINGS INC (PA)
Also Called: Fox Run Craftmen
1907 Stout Dr (18974-3869)
PHONE....................................215 675-7700
Lynn Nowicki, *President*
Bob Di Renzo, *CFO*
Govan Henry, *Accountant*
Jamie Rivero, *Human Res Mgr*
Orla Moloney, *Mktg Coord*
◆ **EMP:** 2
SQ FT: 100,000
SALES (est): 35.2MM **Privately Held**
WEB: www.foxruncraftsmen.com
SIC: 3499 5023 Metal household articles; kitchenware

(G-18883)
FRANKLIN INSTRUMENT CO INC
1187 Spencer Rd (18974-1331)
P.O. Box 161, Trexlertown (18087-0161)
PHONE....................................215 355-7942
Bonnie Fleming-Jacoby, *President*
Nancy S Ohara, *Vice Pres*
Ellis Funchess, *Treasurer*
◆ **EMP:** 10
SQ FT: 7,800
SALES (est): 1.1MM **Privately Held**
WEB: www.franklinclock.com
SIC: 3873 Watches, clocks, watchcases & parts

(G-18884)
G F GOODMAN & SON INC (PA)
2 Ivybrook Blvd (18974-1700)
P.O. Box 2909 (18974-0091)
PHONE....................................215 672-8810
William R Rumble, *President*
Harry Davis, *Vice Pres*
Robert R Seaner, *CFO*
Bill Davis, *Technology*
Steve Wilson, *Technology*
◆ **EMP:** 19 **EST:** 1922
SQ FT: 20,000
SALES (est): 2.7MM **Privately Held**
WEB: www.gfgoodman.com
SIC: 3541 Machine tools, metal cutting type

(G-18885)
GAMRY INSTRUMENTS INC
734 Louis Dr (18974-2829)
PHONE....................................215 682-9330
Gregory A Martinchek, *President*
Max Yaffe, *Chairman*
Cora Bahr, *Treasurer*
EMP: 23
SQ FT: 10,000
SALES (est): 5.7MM **Privately Held**
WEB: www.gamry.com
SIC: 3829 Measuring & controlling devices

(G-18886)
GEMEL PRECISION TOOL INC
31 Industrial Dr (18974-1499)
PHONE....................................215 355-2174
Klaus Gehlert, *President*
Hedwig Gehlert, *Corp Secy*
EMP: 30 **EST:** 1974
SQ FT: 2,500
SALES (est): 5.5MM **Privately Held**
WEB: www.gemel.com
SIC: 3469 3545 3496 Machine parts, stamped or pressed metal; machine tool accessories; miscellaneous fabricated wire products

(G-18887)
GERDING CORP
809 Nina Way (18974-2813)
PHONE....................................215 441-0900
William R Gerding, *President*
Lois B Gerding, *Corp Secy*
Todd A Gerding, *Vice Pres*
EMP: 3
SALES: 300K **Privately Held**
WEB: www.gerdingcorp.com
SIC: 3993 3999 Name plates: except engraved, etched, etc.: metal; plaques, picture, laminated

(G-18888)
GLOBAL CHEM FEED SOLUTIONS LLC
2015 Stout Dr (18974-3859)
PHONE....................................215 675-2777
Timothy Horrox, *Project Mgr*
Donald Crawford, *Sales Mgr*
Scott Wynn, *Regl Sales Mgr*
William J Herbert, *Marketing Staff*
Bill Herbert, *Marketing Staff*
▼ **EMP:** 29
SQ FT: 8,000
SALES: 4MM **Privately Held**
WEB: www.globalchem-feed.com
SIC: 3559 Chemical machinery & equipment

(G-18889)
GLOBE DATA SYSTEMS INC
Also Called: Globe Ticket
300 Constance Dr (18974-2815)
PHONE....................................215 443-7960

Ralph R Whitney, *Ch of Bd*
Robert Puleo, *President*
EMP: 72 **EST:** 1868
SQ FT: 53,000
SALES (est): 6.1MM **Privately Held**
WEB: www.globeticket.com
SIC: 2752 Tickets, lithographed
PA: Seneca Enterprises, Inc
  1642 Debence Dr
  Franklin PA 16323
  814 432-7890

(G-18890)
GOTTSCHO PRINTING SYSTEMS INC
740 Veterans Cir (18974-3531)
PHONE..................................267 387-3005
Aimee N Hasson, *President*
Kathryn A Smith, *Vice Pres*
James E Hasson, *Admin Sec*
EMP: 7 **EST:** 2009
SALES (est): 142K **Privately Held**
SIC: 3565 Packaging machinery
HQ: Hapa Ag
  Chriesbaumstrasse 4
  Volketswil ZH 8604
  433 993-256

(G-18891)
GRAPHIC COMMUNICATIONS INC
793 Nina Way (18974-2824)
PHONE..................................215 441-5335
Loretta Dymant, *President*
Bob Lawler, *Vice Pres*
Robert Lawler IV, *Vice Pres*
Rita Lawler, *Admin Sec*
EMP: 18 **EST:** 1974
SQ FT: 28,000
SALES (est): 3.4MM **Privately Held**
WEB: www.graphiccommunications.us
SIC: 2759 Labels & seals: printing

(G-18892)
GREIF INC
695 Louis Dr (18974-2825)
PHONE..................................215 956-9049
Christopher Weinrauch, *Plant Mgr*
Paul Heise, *Branch Mgr*
Dona Bergner, *Manager*
Chris Singer, *Maintence Staff*
EMP: 95
SALES (corp-wide): 3.8B **Publicly Held**
WEB: www.greif.com
SIC: 2655 Fiber cans, drums & similar
  products
PA: Greif, Inc.
  425 Winter Rd
  Delaware OH 43015
  740 549-6000

(G-18893)
HAVIS INC
40 Indian Dr (18974-1431)
PHONE..................................215 354-3280
Tim McElrory, *Owner*
Dean Wright, *Sales Executive*
EMP: 6
SALES (est): 568.3K **Privately Held**
SIC: 3089 Injection molding of plastics

(G-18894)
HERITAGE SCREEN PRINTING INC
331 York Rd (18974-4506)
PHONE..................................215 672-2382
Glenn McKee, *President*
Jesse Persico, *Sales Staff*
Steve McKee, *Branch Mgr*
EMP: 6
SALES (corp-wide): 363K **Privately Held**
SIC: 2396 2759 Screen printing on fabric
  articles; commercial printing
PA: Heritage Screen Printing Inc
  3625 Daviscilla 2
  Warrington PA 18976
  215 672-2382

(G-18895)
HORDIS DOORS INC
1250 Woodbrook Ln (18974-2329)
P.O. Box 2213 (18974-0022)
PHONE..................................215 957-9585
Karen Hordis, *President*
Bill Hordis, *Principal*

EMP: 3
SQ FT: 3,000
SALES: 300K **Privately Held**
SIC: 2431 7699 Doors, combination
  screen-storm, wood; door & window re-
  pair

(G-18896)
INDUS GRAPHICS INC
Also Called: Sir Speedy
445 York Rd (18974-4517)
P.O. Box 465 (18974-0547)
PHONE..................................215 443-7773
Dilip Namjoshi, *President*
Jim Swan, *Vice Pres*
EMP: 4
SQ FT: 3,500
SALES (est): 605.5K **Privately Held**
SIC: 2752 2791 2789 Commercial print-
  ing, offset; typesetting; bookbinding & re-
  lated work

(G-18897)
INDUSTRIAL ENTERPRISES INC
Also Called: Cw Industries
550 Davisville Rd (18974-5546)
PHONE..................................215 355-7080
Kalman Lifson, *President*
EMP: 95
SALES (corp-wide): 34.5MM **Privately Held**
WEB: www.industrialenterprises.com
SIC: 3679 Electronic circuits
HQ: Industrial Enterprises, Inc.
  130 James Way
  Southampton PA 18966
  215 355-7080

(G-18898)
INDUSTRIAL NAMEPLATE INC
29 Indian Dr (18974-1487)
PHONE..................................215 322-1111
J David Stitzer, *President*
EMP: 30
SQ FT: 20,000
SALES: 3MM **Privately Held**
WEB: www.industrialnameplate.com
SIC: 3479 2679 2759 2396 Name plates:
  engraved, etched, etc.; labels, paper:
  made from purchased material; commer-
  cial printing; automotive & apparel trim-
  mings

(G-18899)
INSTANT WEB INC
65 Steamboat Dr (18974-4857)
PHONE..................................952 474-0961
Pat Deck, *Principal*
EMP: 7
SALES (est): 866.7K **Privately Held**
SIC: 2752 Commercial printing, offset

(G-18900)
IVY GRAPHICS INC
29 Indian Dr (18974-1430)
PHONE..................................215 396-9446
J David Stitzer, *President*
John D Stitzer, *General Mgr*
EMP: 14
SALES (est): 1MM **Privately Held**
WEB: www.ivygraphics.biz
SIC: 2679 2759 3479 3999 Tags & la-
  bels, paper; letterpress & screen printing;
  name plates: engraved, etched, etc.;
  identification plates; name plates: except
  engraved, etched, etc.: metal

(G-18901)
JARMENS FASHION
1207 Wedgewood Dr (18974-2249)
PHONE..................................215 441-5242
Jarmen Eddy, *Owner*
EMP: 3
SALES (est): 201.9K **Privately Held**
SIC: 2331 Women's & misses' blouses &
  shirts

(G-18902)
JM AUTOMATION SERVICES
1800 Mearns Rd (18974-1100)
P.O. Box 128, Trumbauersville (18970-
0128)
PHONE..................................215 675-0125
Philip Murray, *Owner*
EMP: 5
SQ FT: 2,400

SALES (est): 665K **Privately Held**
SIC: 3569 Liquid automation machinery &
  equipment

(G-18903)
JOHNSON MARCH SYSTEMS INC
220 Railroad Dr (18974-1447)
PHONE..................................215 364-2500
Earl Grow, *President*
Thomas Connell, *President*
John Kreyenhagen, *Vice Pres*
Mike Gale, *Project Mgr*
Don Hess, *Project Engr*
▼ **EMP:** 50
SQ FT: 44,400
SALES (est): 16.6MM **Privately Held**
WEB: www.johnsonmarch.com
SIC: 3823 3561 3564 Industrial instrmnts
  msrmnt display/control process variable;
  pumps & pumping equipment; dust or
  fume collecting equipment, industrial

(G-18904)
KAMPUS KLOTHES INC
164 Railroad Dr (18974-1449)
PHONE..................................215 357-0892
Mary Gonsiewski, *President*
Thomas Gonsiewski, *Corp Secy*
Mike Gonsiewski, *Sales Mgr*
Jackie Horvath, *Sales Staff*
Joe Kaiser, *Sales Staff*
EMP: 32
SQ FT: 22,000
SALES: 6MM **Privately Held**
WEB: www.kampusklothes.com
SIC: 7336 2396 2395 Silk screen design;
  screen printing on fabric articles; embroi-
  dery products, except schiffli machine

(G-18905)
KNM MACHINE AND TOOL INC
Also Called: K N M
1800 Mearns Rd Ste H (18974-1191)
P.O. Box 504, Montgomeryville (18936-
0504)
PHONE..................................215 443-9660
Karl Miok, *President*
EMP: 3
SQ FT: 2,300
SALES: 350K **Privately Held**
SIC: 3599 Machine shop, jobbing & repair

(G-18906)
KRAUSS S E TOOL & DIE CO
Also Called: Krauss Tool & Die
1843 Stout Dr (18974-1157)
PHONE..................................215 957-1517
Siegfried Krauss, *Owner*
EMP: 4
SQ FT: 3,500
SALES: 250K **Privately Held**
SIC: 3544 Special dies, tools, jigs & fix-
  tures

(G-18907)
KUFEN ELECTRIC MOTORS INC
27 York Rd (18974-4501)
P.O. Box 417 (18974-0542)
PHONE..................................215 672-5250
John Finney, *President*
EMP: 6 **EST:** 1948
SQ FT: 2,700
SALES (est): 339.1K **Privately Held**
SIC: 7694 Electric motor repair

(G-18908)
KUFEN MOTOR AND PUMP TECH
27 York Rd (18974-4501)
P.O. Box 417 (18974-0542)
PHONE..................................215 672-5250
John L Finney, *President*
EMP: 5
SQ FT: 3,500
SALES (est): 994.5K **Privately Held**
SIC: 7694 7699 Electric motor repair;
  pumps & pumping equipment repair

(G-18909)
LAMINAR FLOW INC
102 Richard Rd (18974-1545)
P.O. Box 2427 (18974-0043)
PHONE..................................215 672-0232
Anthony M Diccianni, *President*
Eric Diccianni, *Vice Pres*

EMP: 52
SQ FT: 30,000
SALES (est): 11.9MM **Privately Held**
WEB: www.laminarflowinc.com
SIC: 3822 3564 3469 1761 Auto controls
  regulating residntl & coml environmt & ap-
  plncs; blowers & fans; metal stampings;
  sheet metalwork

(G-18910)
LAURENCE RONALD ENTPS INC
Also Called: Rle Millwork
300 Constance Dr (18974-2815)
PHONE..................................215 677-3801
Ronald L Perry, *President*
Andrew Gross, *Corp Secy*
EMP: 10
SALES (est): 1.7MM **Privately Held**
WEB: www.rlemillwork.com
SIC: 7389 2599 Aquarium design & main-
  tenance; factory furniture & fixtures

(G-18911)
LB BOHLE LLC
700 Veterans Cir Ste 100 (18974-3532)
PHONE..................................215 957-1240
Lorenz Bohle, *Managing Dir*
Martin Hack, *Vice Pres*
Michael Fazio, *Sales Mgr*
Fran Drzewicki, *Cust Mgr*
Lawrence Bohle,
▲ **EMP:** 11
SQ FT: 102,500
SALES (est): 2.8MM **Privately Held**
WEB: www.lbbohle.com
SIC: 3559 Pharmaceutical machinery

(G-18912)
LINK GROUP INC
Also Called: Tescor
341 Ivyland Rd (18974-2205)
PHONE..................................215 957-6061
Jeff Badger, *Branch Mgr*
EMP: 50
SALES (est): 1.7MM **Privately Held**
SIC: 3825 Test equipment for electronic &
  electric measurement
PA: Link Group, Inc.
  43855 Plymouth Oaks Blvd
  Plymouth MI 48170

(G-18913)
LOUIS NEIBAUER CO INC
Also Called: Neibauer Press
20 Industrial Dr (18974-1433)
PHONE..................................215 322-6200
Nathan Neibauer, *President*
Louis Neibauer, *Chairman*
Larry Neibauer, *Senior VP*
Lawrence J Neibauer, *Vice Pres*
Ethel Neibauer, *Asst Treas*
▲ **EMP:** 25
SQ FT: 20,000
SALES (est): 3.4MM **Privately Held**
WEB: www.neibauer.com
SIC: 2731 Books: publishing & printing;
  pamphlets: publishing & printing

(G-18914)
LUFTROL INC
550 Concord Rd (18974-5559)
PHONE..................................215 355-0532
Ernest Rocker, *President*
Sally H Rocker, *Admin Sec*
EMP: 8 **EST:** 1977
SALES (est): 750.1K **Privately Held**
SIC: 3564 Air purification equipment

(G-18915)
LYNN ELECTRONICS CORP
154 Railroad Dr (18974-1449)
PHONE..................................954 977-3800
Yvette Snelbaker, *Principal*
EMP: 4
SALES (corp-wide): 20MM **Privately Held**
WEB: www.lynnelec.com
SIC: 3679 3643 Harness assemblies for
  electronic use: wire or cable; connectors
  & terminals for electrical devices
PA: Lynn Electronics Corp.
  154 Railroad Dr
  Ivyland PA 18974
  215 355-8200

(G-18916)
MANOR HOUSE PUBLISHING CO INC
Also Called: Pool and Spa Living
880 Louis Dr (18974-2819)
PHONE...................................215 259-1700
Toll Free:.............................888　-
EMP: 12
SQ FT: 50,000
SALES (est): 940K **Privately Held**
SIC: 2721 Magazines: publishing & printing

(G-18917)
MANSCO PRODUCTS INC
34 Richard Rd (18974-1513)
PHONE...................................215 674-4395
Daniel L Mangle, *President*
▲ EMP: 5
SQ FT: 10,000
SALES (est): 1MM **Privately Held**
WEB: www.manscoproducts.com
SIC: 3823 Industrial instrmnts msrmnt display/control process variable

(G-18918)
MCBROTHERS INC
665 Mary St (18974-2803)
PHONE...................................215 675-3003
Patrick McCollum, *President*
EMP: 10
SALES (est): 1.5MM **Privately Held**
SIC: 3442 Garage doors, overhead: metal

(G-18919)
MCNULTY TOOL DIE
36 Vincent Cir Ste A (18974-1515)
PHONE...................................215 957-9900
Joseph P Mc Nulty, *Principal*
EMP: 5
SALES (est): 648.3K **Privately Held**
SIC: 3544 3599 Special dies & tools; machine shop, jobbing & repair

(G-18920)
MEDICAL PRECISION PLASTICS INC
447 Ivyland Rd (18974-2207)
P.O. Box 2851 (18974-0086)
PHONE...................................215 441-4800
David Bergeron, *President*
Michael Jacobson, *Vice Pres*
Andrea Bergeron, *CFO*
EMP: 19
SQ FT: 13,000
SALES (est): 3.3MM **Privately Held**
SIC: 3089 Extruded finished plastic products

(G-18921)
MEDL TOOL & DIE INC
1800 Mearns Rd Ste B (18974-1191)
PHONE...................................215 443-5457
Charlotte Medl, *President*
Christopher Medl, *Vice Pres*
EMP: 3
SQ FT: 1,600
SALES: 200K **Privately Held**
SIC: 3599 3544 Machine shop, jobbing & repair; special dies & tools

(G-18922)
MID-ATLANTIC CIRCUIT INC
1001 Pulinski Rd Ste B (18974-1539)
PHONE...................................215 672-8480
John Toutkoushian, *President*
Linda Toutkoushian, *Corp Secy*
▲ EMP: 10
SQ FT: 10,000
SALES (est): 1.6MM **Privately Held**
SIC: 3672 Circuit boards, television & radio printed

(G-18923)
MIGU PRESS INC (PA)
260 Ivyland Rd (18974-2204)
PHONE...................................215 957-9763
Pamela S Mirabile, *President*
Lisa Furry, *President*
Philip Mirabile, *Vice Pres*
Lawrence J Mirabile, *Treasurer*
Mark Witzigman, *Executive*
EMP: 25
SQ FT: 15,000
SALES (est): 3.9MM **Privately Held**
WEB: www.migupress.com
SIC: 2752 Commercial printing, offset

(G-18924)
MK PRECISION
Also Called: Colleen Klesh
1621 Mearns Rd Ste 206 (18974-1115)
PHONE...................................215 675-4590
EMP: 3 EST: 2006
SQ FT: 2,000
SALES: 305K **Privately Held**
SIC: 3541 Mfg Machine Tools-Cutting

(G-18925)
MRC ELECTRIC
145 Railroad Dr Ste C (18974-1460)
PHONE...................................267 988-4370
EMP: 4
SALES (est): 218K **Privately Held**
SIC: 3993 Signs & advertising specialties

(G-18926)
MYSTIC ASSEMBLY & DCTG CO
19 Vincent Cir (18974-1529)
PHONE...................................215 957-0280
Jerry Doyle, *President*
Brian Doyle, *Corp Secy*
Dave Doyle, *Vice Pres*
David M Doyle, *Vice Pres*
EMP: 30
SQ FT: 19,750
SALES: 2.7MM **Privately Held**
WEB: www.mysticassembly.com
SIC: 7389 3479 2759 2396 Packaging & labeling services; etching & engraving; screen printing; automotive & apparel trimmings

(G-18927)
N B GARBER INC
Also Called: Sunrise Technologies
1520 Campus Dr Ste H (18974-3967)
PHONE...................................267 387-6225
David Tyler, *President*
Natalie Tyler, *Vice Pres*
EMP: 6
SALES (est): 1.6MM **Privately Held**
WEB: www.nbgarber.com
SIC: 2842 Cleaning or polishing preparations

(G-18928)
NEIL M DAVIS
Also Called: Medicalabbreviations
605 Louis Dr Ste 508b (18974-2830)
PHONE...................................215 442-7430
Neil M Davis, *Owner*
EMP: 3
SQ FT: 2,000
SALES (est): 900K **Privately Held**
WEB: www.neilmdavis.com
SIC: 2731 Textbooks: publishing only, not printed on site

(G-18929)
NEU DYNAMICS CORP
Also Called: N D C
110 Steam Whistle Dr (18974-1452)
PHONE...................................215 355-2460
Kevin Hartsow, *President*
Fred Lening, *Opers Mgr*
Frank Tome, *Senior Engr*
Don Johnson, *VP Sales*
▲ EMP: 19
SQ FT: 11,000
SALES (est): 4.1MM **Privately Held**
WEB: www.neudynamics.com
SIC: 3544 Industrial molds; dies & die holders for metal cutting, forming, die casting

(G-18930)
NOTATIONS INC (PA)
Also Called: Notations Clothing Co
539 Jacksonville Rd (18974-4826)
PHONE...................................215 259-2000
Kurt Erman, *President*
Ric Lazarus, *Vice Pres*
Fred Trachtenberg, *Vice Pres*
Lisa Harm, *Production*
Michael Levine, *Purch Mgr*
▲ EMP: 150
SQ FT: 113,000
SALES (est): 44.8MM **Privately Held**
SIC: 2331 2339 Blouses, women's & juniors': made from purchased material; T-shirts & tops, women's: made from purchased materials; women's & misses' outerwear

(G-18931)
OLD YORK ROAD PRINTING LLC
905 Louis Dr (18974-2821)
PHONE...................................215 957-6200
David Harp,
EMP: 50 EST: 2012
SALES (est): 8.1MM **Privately Held**
SIC: 2752 Commercial printing, offset

(G-18932)
OP SCHUMAN & SONS INC
817 Nina Way (18974-2813)
PHONE...................................215 343-1530
William Tschuman, *President*
R Mark Schuman, *Vice Pres*
Jason Dalton, *Project Mgr*
EMP: 85
SALES (est): 20.6MM **Privately Held**
WEB: www.opschuman.com
SIC: 3552 3565 3829 Textile machinery; packaging machinery; tensile strength testing equipment

(G-18933)
ORBIT ADVANCED TECH INC
650 Louis Dr Ste 100 (18974-2845)
PHONE...................................215 674-5100
Per Iversen, *President*
William Campbell, *COO*
▲ EMP: 40
SQ FT: 18,000
SALES: 7.3MM
SALES (corp-wide): 16.5MM **Privately Held**
SIC: 3825 Instruments to measure electricity
HQ: Orbit/Fr, Inc.
650 Louis Dr Ste 100
Warminster PA 18974

(G-18934)
ORBIT/FR INC (HQ)
650 Louis Dr Ste 100 (18974-2845)
PHONE...................................215 674-5100
Per Iversen, *President*
John Aubin, *Vice Pres*
William Campbell, *Vice Pres*
Relland Winand, *CFO*
▲ EMP: 41
SQ FT: 18,000
SALES (est): 24.1MM
SALES (corp-wide): 16.5MM **Privately Held**
SIC: 3825 Instruments to measure electricity

(G-18935)
OSKIS WOODWORKS
31 Dorsett Cir (18974-2320)
PHONE...................................215 444-0523
Frank Orzehoski, *Principal*
EMP: 4
SALES (est): 222.3K **Privately Held**
SIC: 2431 Millwork

(G-18936)
PALACE INDUSTRIES
605 Louis Dr Ste 501c (18974-2830)
PHONE...................................215 442-5508
Neal Weinraub, *Principal*
EMP: 3
SALES (est): 262.7K **Privately Held**
SIC: 3999 Manufacturing industries

(G-18937)
PDC MACHINES INC
Also Called: Pressure Dynamic Consultants
1875 Stout Dr (18974-1157)
P.O. Box 2733 (18974-0074)
PHONE...................................215 443-9442
Syed M Afzal, *President*
Syed O Afzal, *Vice Pres*
Tom Greco, *Engineer*
Tom Phillips, *Engineer*
Syed Ahmed, *Project Engr*
▲ EMP: 52
SQ FT: 31,000

SALES (est): 13.6MM **Privately Held**
WEB: www.pdcmachines.com
SIC: 3545 3563 3566 3561 Scales, measuring (machinists' precision tools); air & gas compressors; speed changers, drives & gears; pumps & pumping equipment

(G-18938)
PEDCO-HILL INC
91 Steam Whistle Dr (18974-1451)
PHONE...................................215 942-5193
Newton Hill, *President*
EMP: 14
SQ FT: 8,000
SALES (est): 1.7MM **Privately Held**
SIC: 2759 Screen printing

(G-18939)
PENNSYLVANIA STATE UNIVERSITY
Also Called: Applied Research Lab
995 Newtown Rd (18974-2935)
PHONE...................................215 682-4000
Herbert L Seligman, *Director*
EMP: 45
SALES (corp-wide): 6.3B **Privately Held**
WEB: www.psu.edu
SIC: 3812 8733 Navigational systems & instruments; research institute
PA: The Pennsylvania State University
201 Old Main
University Park PA 16802
814 865-4700

(G-18940)
PHILADELPHIA MACARONI COMPANY
Conte Luna Foods Inc Division
40 Jacksonville Rd (18974-4804)
PHONE...................................215 441-5220
John Hagerty, *Plant Mgr*
EMP: 50
SALES (corp-wide): 59.1MM **Privately Held**
SIC: 2099 2098 Packaged combination products: pasta, rice & potato; macaroni & spaghetti
PA: Philadelphia Macaroni Company
760 S 11th St
Philadelphia PA 19147
215 923-3141

(G-18941)
PHOENIX CFB INC
971 Mearns Rd (18974-2811)
PHONE...................................215 957-0500
William Marsh, *Ch of Bd*
EMP: 7
SALES (est): 922K **Privately Held**
SIC: 2819 Carbides

(G-18942)
PHOENIX MOLD AND MACHINE LLC
42 Steam Whistle Dr (18974-1450)
PHONE...................................215 355-1985
Dennis Healy, *Mng Member*
Robert Healy, *Mng Member*
EMP: 4 EST: 2010
SALES: 90K **Privately Held**
SIC: 3544 Industrial molds

(G-18943)
PRECISION WOODWORKING & C
1365 Barness Dr (18974-1973)
P.O. Box 464, Hatboro (19040-0464)
PHONE...................................215 317-3533
Stethen Bonanni, *Owner*
EMP: 4
SALES: 150K **Privately Held**
SIC: 2499 Decorative wood & woodwork

(G-18944)
PRESCO SHEET METAL FABRICATORS
355 Constance Dr (18974-2816)
PHONE...................................215 672-7200
John Campbell, *Partner*
Richard Campbell, *Partner*
EMP: 8
SQ FT: 14,500
SALES (est): 447.6K **Privately Held**
SIC: 3444 Sheet metalwork

▲ = Import ▼ =Export
◆ =Import/Export

(G-18945)
PRESSURE INNOVATORS LLC
1800 Mearns Rd Bldg 4 (18974-1100)
PHONE..................................215 431-6520
Vince McCalley, *Chief Engr*
Joseph Derum,
EMP: 7 **EST:** 2014
SQ FT: 1,800
SALES: 1MM **Privately Held**
SIC: 3545 Machine tool accessories

(G-18946)
PRESSURE TECHNOLOGY INC
415 Patricia Dr (18974-2839)
PHONE..................................215 674-8844
Arnold Bowles, *President*
David Bowles, *Vice Pres*
EMP: 19
SQ FT: 8,500
SALES (est): 5.3MM **Privately Held**
WEB: www.pressuretechnology.com
SIC: 3398 Metal heat treating

(G-18947)
PRIETO MACHINE CO INC
1785 Stout Dr Ste D (18974-3863)
PHONE..................................215 675-6061
Robert Prieto, *President*
EMP: 18 **EST:** 1977
SQ FT: 4,200
SALES (est): 3MM **Privately Held**
SIC: 3599 Machine shop, jobbing & repair

(G-18948)
PRO CEL INC
39 Steam Whistle Dr (18974-1451)
PHONE..................................215 322-9883
Jay Colby, *President*
Donna Colby, *Vice Pres*
EMP: 4
SQ FT: 2,800
SALES: 500K **Privately Held**
SIC: 3544 7699 Industrial molds; industrial
equipment services

(G-18949)
QUAD TRON INC
303 Camars Dr (18974-3874)
PHONE..................................215 441-9303
James Miller, *President*
Richard H Moyer Jr, *Vice Pres*
EMP: 9
SQ FT: 10,000
SALES (est): 1.4MM **Privately Held**
SIC: 3674 Microcircuits, integrated (semi-
conductor)

(G-18950)
R AND R GLASS INC
30 Steam Whistle Dr (18974-1450)
PHONE..................................215 443-7010
Donald Poirier Jr, *President*
EMP: 3
SALES (est): 330K **Privately Held**
SIC: 3211 1799 Insulating glass, sealed
units; window treatment installation

(G-18951)
RELIABLE EQUIPMENT MFG CO
Also Called: Reliable Equipment Mfg
101 Steam Whistle Dr (18974-1453)
PHONE..................................215 357-7015
Norman Delan, *President*
John Zitkus, *Vice Pres*
EMP: 36
SQ FT: 6,000
SALES: 2.1MM **Privately Held**
SIC: 3423 3544 Soldering guns or tools,
hand: electric; forms (molds), for foundry
& plastics working machinery

(G-18952)
RENU LABS INC
1836 Stout Dr Ste 5 (18974-1197)
PHONE..................................215 675-5227
Gregg Hanson, *President*
Dr Leigh Hopkins, *Vice Pres*
Colleen Best, *Treasurer*
▲ **EMP:** 8
SQ FT: 3,000
SALES: 500K **Privately Held**
WEB: www.renulabs.com
SIC: 2844 Cosmetic preparations

(G-18953)
**RESOLVE TRNCHLESS
SLUTIONS INC**
Also Called: Resolve Rooter
216 W Bristol Rd Ste A (18974-1784)
PHONE..................................215 441-5544
Denise Carr, *President*
EMP: 4
SALES (est): 429.8K **Privately Held**
SIC: 1623 3822 1711 Water & sewer line
construction; air conditioning & refrigera-
tion controls; plumbing contractors

(G-18954)
**RETROLITE CORPORATION
AMERICA**
89 Steam Whistle Dr (18974-1451)
PHONE..................................215 443-9370
Richard Karton, *President*
Marlene Karton, *Admin Sec*
▲ **EMP:** 6
SQ FT: 9,000
SALES (est): 1.3MM **Privately Held**
WEB: www.retrolite.com
SIC: 3645 3646 3641 5063 Residential
lighting fixtures; ornamental lighting fix-
tures, commercial; electric lamps; lighting
fixtures; lighting fittings & accessories;
lighting fixtures, commercial & industrial;
lighting fixtures, residential

(G-18955)
**REVTUR WELDING COMPANY
LLC**
1836 Stout Dr Ste 9 (18974-1198)
PHONE..................................215 672-8233
Charles Revotskie, *Owner*
Germanie Revotskie, *Owner*
Paul Lowry, *Co-Owner*
EMP: 4
SQ FT: 2,500
SALES (est): 266.2K **Privately Held**
SIC: 7692 Welding repair

(G-18956)
RSR INDUSTRIES INC
315 W Street Rd (18974-3208)
PHONE..................................215 543-3350
Robert Schmidt, *President*
Rita Schmidt, *Vice Pres*
▲ **EMP:** 8
SQ FT: 3,300
SALES (est): 1.7MM **Privately Held**
WEB: www.rsrindustries.com
SIC: 3625 Control equipment, electric

(G-18957)
**S & G WATER CONDITIONING
INC**
525 York Rd (18974-4518)
P.O. Box 2868 (18974-0087)
PHONE..................................215 672-2030
James S Steele Jr, *President*
James Steele Sr, *Admin Sec*
EMP: 8 **EST:** 1959
SQ FT: 1,500
SALES: 750K **Privately Held**
WEB: www.sngwater.com
SIC: 3589 5078 5084 3823 Water treat-
ment equipment, industrial; refrigeration
equipment & supplies; industrial machin-
ery & equipment; industrial instrmnts
msrmnt display/control process variable;
dams, waterways, docks & other marine
construction

(G-18958)
S P INDUSTRIES INC
Also Called: Penntech - Sp Scientific
103 Steam Whistle Dr (18974-1453)
PHONE..................................215 396-2200
EMP: 34
SALES (corp-wide): 1.5B **Privately Held**
SIC: 3821 Laboratory apparatus & furniture
HQ: S P Industries, Inc.
935 Mearns Rd
Warminster PA 18974
215 672-7800

(G-18959)
S P INDUSTRIES INC (HQ)
Also Called: Sp Scientific
935 Mearns Rd (18974-2811)
PHONE..................................215 672-7800
Brian Larkin, *President*

Mary Seto, *General Mgr*
Brian Wright, *COO*
Ian Whitehall, *Exec VP*
Thomas Granger, *Project Mgr*
▲ **EMP:** 80
SQ FT: 62,000
SALES (est): 222.1MM
SALES (corp-wide): 1.5B **Privately Held**
WEB: www.virtis.com
SIC: 3826 3585 7699 3821 Instruments
measuring thermal properties; differential
thermal analysis instruments; refrigeration
& heating equipment; evaporative con-
densers, heat transfer equipment; indus-
trial machinery & equipment repair;
laboratory apparatus & furniture
PA: Harbour Group Ltd.
7733 Forsyth Blvd Fl 23
Saint Louis MO 63105
314 727-5550

(G-18960)
**SAFE-TEC CLINICAL PRODUCTS
LLC**
142 Railroad Dr (18974-5802)
P.O. Box 3243 (18974-0125)
PHONE..................................215 364-5582
Andy Ring, *President*
EMP: 5
SQ FT: 4,000
SALES (est): 861.9K **Privately Held**
SIC: 3841 Surgical & medical instruments

(G-18961)
SAPLING INC
670 Louis Dr (18974-2880)
PHONE..................................215 322-6063
Ilan Shemesh, *President*
Alan Folsom, *Research*
Robin Shemesh, *Treasurer*
Lauren Fisher, *Regl Sales Mgr*
David Gouck, *Regl Sales Mgr*
▲ **EMP:** 43
SQ FT: 4,000
SALES (est): 9.4MM **Privately Held**
WEB: www.sapling-inc.com
SIC: 3579 Time clocks & time recording
devices

(G-18962)
SCANMASTER
375 Lemon St (18974-4601)
PHONE..................................215 208-4732
Robert Dalfen, *Principal*
EMP: 3
SALES (est): 204.7K **Privately Held**
SIC: 3829 Measuring & controlling devices

(G-18963)
**SCHLOTTER PRECISION PDTS
INC (PA)**
40 Indian Dr (18974-1431)
PHONE..................................215 354-3280
Frank N Schlotter, *President*
Dean Wright, *Corp Secy*
EMP: 30 **EST:** 1978
SQ FT: 32,000
SALES (est): 3.4MM **Privately Held**
WEB: www.schlotterprecision.com
SIC: 3089 Hardware, plastic; injection
molding of plastics

(G-18964)
SEAFOOD ENTERPRISES LP
Also Called: Seafood America
645 Mearns Rd (18974-2805)
PHONE..................................215 672-2211
James Burke, *CEO*
Jim Burke, *Vice Pres*
Daniel Donnelly, *VP Opers*
Hope Kadesh, *Controller*
Edward Reim, *Maintence Staff*
EMP: 105
SQ FT: 30,000
SALES (est): 31.8MM **Privately Held**
WEB: www.seafoodamerica.com
SIC: 2092 Seafoods, fresh: prepared

(G-18965)
SMIT CORPORATION
103 Steam Whistle Dr (18974-1453)
PHONE..................................215 396-2200
Ger Smit, *CEO*
Vincent Smit, *Vice Pres*
Angela Tao, *Project Mgr*
▲ **EMP:** 34 **EST:** 1999

SALES (est): 7.7MM **Privately Held**
WEB: www.penntech-corp.com
SIC: 3565 Packaging machinery

(G-18966)
SMITH GROUP INC (PA)
816 Nina Way (18974-2833)
PHONE..................................215 957-7800
Richard S Smith, *President*
Michael Smith, *Vice Pres*
Burton Zaslow, *VP Mktg*
EMP: 35 **EST:** 1935
SQ FT: 29,000
SALES (est): 16.8MM **Privately Held**
SIC: 5169 5199 3624 Polyurethane prod-
ucts; packaging materials; carbon &
graphite products

(G-18967)
SONIC SYSTEMS INC
204 Railroad Dr (18974-1447)
PHONE..................................267 803-1964
Scott Nugent, *President*
Jerry Barlow, *Vice Pres*
Jane Nugent, *Admin Sec*
▲ **EMP:** 25
SQ FT: 24,000
SALES (est): 5.5MM **Privately Held**
WEB: www.sonicsystemsinc.com
SIC: 3699 3444 3841 Cleaning equip-
ment, ultrasonic, except medical & dental;
generators, ultrasonic; forming machine
work, sheet metal; ultrasonic medical
cleaning equipment

(G-18968)
SOUTHCO INC
Also Called: Southco Counterbalance Div FL
1025 Louis Dr (18974-2823)
PHONE..................................267 957-9260
Brian McNeill, *CEO*
EMP: 35
SALES (est): 1.7MM **Privately Held**
SIC: 3429 Keys, locks & related hardware

(G-18969)
SOUTHCO INC
Also Called: Southco Counterbalance
1025 Louis Dr (18974-2823)
PHONE..................................215 957-9260
EMP: 35
SALES (corp-wide): 681.3MM **Privately
Held**
SIC: 3545 Balancing machines (machine
tool accessories)
HQ: Southco, Inc.
210 N Brinton Lake Rd
Concordville PA 19331
610 459-4000

(G-18970)
**SOUTHCO CUNTERBALANCE
DIV - PA**
1025 Louis Dr (18974-2823)
PHONE..................................267 957-9260
Brian McNeill, *CEO*
EMP: 35
SALES (est): 1.5MM **Privately Held**
SIC: 3429 Keys, locks & related hardware

(G-18971)
SPECGAS INC
86 Vincent Cir (18974-1530)
PHONE..................................215 355-2405
Alfred Boehm, *CEO*
Tony Kozlowski, *CFO*
Thomas Snyder, *Admin Sec*
▼ **EMP:** 5 **EST:** 2001
SQ FT: 4,000
SALES (est): 700K **Privately Held**
WEB: www.specgasinc.com
SIC: 2813 5169 Industrial gases; industrial
gases

(G-18972)
**SPECIALTY VHCL SOLUTIONS
LLC**
Also Called: Manufacturing
1540 Campus Dr Ste B (18974-3970)
PHONE..................................609 882-1900
J Michael Burke, *CEO*
Karen Burke, *General Mgr*
Brian Tomchik, *Principal*
Michael Burke, *Manager*
◆ **EMP:** 25
SQ FT: 22,000

SALES (est): 4.9MM **Privately Held**
WEB: www.vehiclesolutionsnow.com
SIC: 3711 Bus & other large specialty vehicle assembly

(G-18973)
SPYWARE
227 York Rd (18974-4515)
PHONE......................................215 444-0405
Scott A Black, *Owner*
EMP: 12
SALES (est): 499.9K **Privately Held**
WEB: www.spywarespyshops.com
SIC: 8748 3663 Business consulting;

(G-18974)
SUBURBAN MARBLE LLC
1010 Pulinski Rd (18974-1522)
PHONE......................................215 734-9100
Simon Opie, *Controller*
EMP: 3
SALES (est): 158.5K **Privately Held**
SIC: 3281 Cut stone & stone products

(G-18975)
TASMAN PHARMA INC
1035 Louis Dr (18974-2823)
PHONE......................................267 317-2010
Raju Vegesna, *Treasurer*
EMP: 3
SQ FT: 12,000
SALES (est): 164.6K **Privately Held**
SIC: 2834 Solutions, pharmaceutical

(G-18976)
TECH MODEM CB COMCAST
55 Industrial Dr (18974-1444)
PHONE......................................267 288-5661
EMP: 5
SALES (est): 455.2K **Privately Held**
SIC: 3661 Modems

(G-18977)
TESCOR INC
341 Ivyland Rd (18974-2205)
PHONE......................................215 957-6061
Jacques Boudin, *President*
Margaret Boudin, *Corp Secy*
Charles Beaver, *Vice Pres*
Jeff Badger, *Engineer*
Peggy Boudin, *Treasurer*
◆ **EMP:** 48
SQ FT: 27,000
SALES (est): 14.6MM **Privately Held**
WEB: www.tescor-inc.com
SIC: 3826 Environmental testing equipment

(G-18978)
TETRATEC CORP
85 Railroad Dr (18974-1478)
PHONE......................................215 396-8349
Lisa Wagner, *Principal*
▲ **EMP:** 15
SALES (est): 1.1MM **Privately Held**
SIC: 2299 Textile goods

(G-18979)
TEXAN CORPORATION
355 Ivyland Rd (18974-2205)
PHONE......................................215 441-8967
Linda Pirkle, *President*
EMP: 30
SQ FT: 3,000
SALES (est): 3.7MM **Privately Held**
WEB: www.texancorp.com
SIC: 3823 8711 3585 Gas flow computers, industrial process type; consulting engineer; refrigeration & heating equipment

(G-18980)
THERM-OMEGA-TECH INC (PA)
353 Ivyland Rd (18974-2205)
PHONE......................................877 379-8258
James F Logue Jr, *President*
Bobby Jo, *Human Res Mgr*
Tim Hartung, *Manager*
John Cupp, *Technology*
▲ **EMP:** 74
SQ FT: 25,000

SALES: 19.5MM **Privately Held**
WEB: www.thermomegatech.com
SIC: 3822 3494 3491 Auto controls regulating residntl & coml environmt & applncs; valves & pipe fittings; automatic regulating & control valves

(G-18981)
THOMAS A LASKOWSKI
Also Called: High Fidelity Screen Printing
239 Madison Ave Ste D (18974-4864)
PHONE......................................215 957-1544
Thomas A Laskowski, *Owner*
EMP: 10
SQ FT: 1,600
SALES (est): 500K **Privately Held**
WEB: www.hifiscreen.com
SIC: 2759 2396 2395 Screen printing; automotive & apparel trimmings; pleating & stitching

(G-18982)
TIMOTHY EMIG
Also Called: Emig Machine and Tool
2031 Stout Dr Ste 4 (18974-3860)
PHONE......................................215 443-7810
Timothy Emig, *Owner*
EMP: 4
SQ FT: 2,200
SALES (est): 424.7K **Privately Held**
SIC: 3599 Machine shop, jobbing & repair

(G-18983)
TOASTMASTERS INTERNATIONAL
30 Remington Pl (18974-1272)
PHONE......................................215 355-4838
Jim Clapp, *Treasurer*
EMP: 25
SALES (corp-wide): 34.8MM **Privately Held**
WEB: www.d70toastmasters.org
SIC: 8299 2721 Educational service, non-degree granting: continuing educ.; magazines: publishing only, not printed on site
PA: Toastmasters International
    9127 S Jamaica St 400
    Englewood CO 80112
    949 858-8255

(G-18984)
TRI STAR PRECISION MFG
375 Ivyland Rd Ste 28 (18974-2235)
PHONE......................................215 443-8610
Victor Vala, *President*
Jim Goodwin, *Vice Pres*
EMP: 4 **EST:** 1998
SQ FT: 5,500
SALES (est): 481.9K **Privately Held**
SIC: 3599 Machine shop, jobbing & repair

(G-18985)
TRIBOLOGY SYSTEMS (PA)
239-K Madison Ave (18974-4806)
PHONE......................................610 466-7547
Lewis B Sibley, *President*
EMP: 3
SQ FT: 2,500
SALES: 450K **Privately Held**
WEB: www.tribologysystems.com
SIC: 3562 8731 Ball bearings & parts; industrial laboratory, except testing

(G-18986)
TRIDENT PLASTICS INC (PA)
1029 Pulinski Rd (18974-1531)
PHONE......................................215 443-7147
Ronald Cadic, *President*
William A Thomas, *Vice Pres*
Thyra Cadic, *Vice Pres*
EMP: 24
SQ FT: 15,000
SALES (est): 14MM **Privately Held**
WEB: www.tridentplastics.com
SIC: 5162 3541 Plastics products; plastics sheets & rods; machine tools, metal cutting type

(G-18987)
TUBRO COMPANY INC
30 Council Rock Dr (18974-1468)
PHONE......................................800 673-7887
Kevin Gift, *Principal*
James Wright, *Corp Secy*
H William Gift, *Vice Pres*
▲ **EMP:** 20

SQ FT: 10,000
SALES (est): 3.9MM **Privately Held**
WEB: www.tubro.com
SIC: 3089 Molding primary plastic; injection molding of plastics

(G-18988)
TWO M ELECTRIC INC
109 Camars Dr (18974-3875)
PHONE......................................215 530-9964
Kurt Meister, *Principal*
EMP: 10
SALES (est): 1.4MM **Privately Held**
SIC: 3699 Electrical work

(G-18989)
UGM PRECISION MACHINING INC
239-P Madison Ave Ste P (18974-4806)
PHONE......................................215 957-6175
John Urban, *President*
Ken Mueller, *Treasurer*
EMP: 6
SALES (est): 316.3K **Privately Held**
SIC: 3599 Machine shop, jobbing & repair

(G-18990)
ULTRA CHEM LLC
665a Catherine St (18974-2801)
PHONE......................................215 778-5967
Kurt Vonder Schmaz,
EMP: 6
SALES (est): 536.7K **Privately Held**
SIC: 2819 Chemicals, high purity: refined from technical grade

(G-18991)
UNITEX GROUP USA LLC
48 Vincent Cir Ste D (18974-1538)
PHONE......................................864 846-8700
Trevor Waycott, *CEO*
▲ **EMP:** 22
SALES (est): 5.6MM **Privately Held**
SIC: 2299 Linen fabrics

(G-18992)
USA ALL PRO AUTO SALON INC
869 W Street Rd Unit B (18974-3126)
PHONE......................................267 230-7442
Zaza Lobzhanidze, *President*
EMP: 3
SALES (est): 240.5K **Privately Held**
SIC: 3589 Car washing machinery

(G-18993)
VARSAL LLC
363 Ivyland Rd (18974-2205)
PHONE......................................215 957-5880
Jenny Zhang, *President*
Ping Xin Wang, *Principal*
◆ **EMP:** 224
SQ FT: 9,000
SALES (est): 33MM **Privately Held**
WEB: www.varsal.com
SIC: 5169 3297 3645 Chemicals & allied products; graphite refractories: carbon bond or ceramic bond; lamp & light shades

(G-18994)
VIANT WESTFIELD LLC
Also Called: Medplast Westfield, LLC
631 Catherine St (18974-2801)
PHONE......................................215 675-4653
Michelle Kallick, *President*
Eugene B Wolstenholme, *Vice Pres*
Jean Wolstenholme, *Treasurer*
Matthew Feil, *Personnel*
EMP: 80 **EST:** 1963
SQ FT: 3,200
SALES (est): 25.7K
SALES (corp-wide): 228.9MM **Privately Held**
SIC: 3089 3841 3544 Injection molding of plastics; surgical & medical instruments; special dies & tools
HQ: Medplast Engineered Products, Inc.
    405 W Geneva Dr
    Tempe AZ 85282

(G-18995)
VISCO
65 Richard Rd (18974-1512)
PHONE......................................215 420-7437
Vincent Visco, *President*
EMP: 3

SALES (est): 242.4K **Privately Held**
SIC: 3842 Wheelchairs

(G-18996)
VIVID PRODUCTS LLC
Also Called: Vivid Apparel
622 Mary St Ste 3-B (18974-2800)
P.O. Box 623, Richboro (18954-0623)
PHONE......................................215 394-0235
Richard Blum,
▲ **EMP:** 6
SALES (est): 1MM **Privately Held**
SIC: 2389 Men's miscellaneous accessories

(G-18997)
VOGEL CARTON LLC
670 Louis Dr (18974-2880)
PHONE......................................215 957-0612
Michael J Kane, *Mng Member*
EMP: 20 **EST:** 1971
SQ FT: 65,000
SALES (est): 5.2MM **Privately Held**
WEB: www.vogelcarton.com
SIC: 2631 2657 Folding boxboard; folding paperboard boxes

(G-18998)
VOLLMAN PERSHING H INC
Also Called: Automation Aides
301 Camars Dr (18974-3874)
PHONE......................................215 956-1971
Roland H Vollman, *President*
Donna Greenbarg, *Technology*
EMP: 6 **EST:** 1955
SQ FT: 3,000
SALES (est): 1.3MM **Privately Held**
WEB: www.autoaides.com
SIC: 3423 Hand & edge tools

(G-18999)
WELLS TECHNOLOGY INC
31 Commerce Dr (18974-1510)
PHONE......................................215 672-7000
Clayton M Wells, *President*
Phyllis A Wells, *Admin Sec*
EMP: 7
SQ FT: 18,000
SALES (est): 2.6MM **Privately Held**
WEB: www.wellstechnology.com
SIC: 5063 3625 Motors, electric; control equipment, electric

(G-19000)
WILMAND LABGLASS
935 Mearns Rd (18974-2811)
PHONE......................................215 672-7800
Allen Hundley, *Regional Mgr*
Ronald Dimaria, *CFO*
Eric Karatschmer, *CTO*
EMP: 3
SALES (est): 158.8K **Privately Held**
SIC: 3841 Surgical & medical instruments

(G-19001)
WINSTON INDUSTRIES INC
29 Richard Rd (18974-1512)
PHONE......................................215 394-8178
David Brown, *President*
Edward T Poehlmann, *Principal*
▲ **EMP:** 12 **EST:** 1950
SQ FT: 8,538
SALES (est): 1.9MM **Privately Held**
SIC: 3469 Metal stampings

(G-19002)
WISTEX II LLC
1730 Stout Dr Ste 1 (18974-3855)
PHONE......................................215 328-9100
Christina Pittaoulis,
EMP: 7
SQ FT: 1,800
SALES (est): 2.8MM **Privately Held**
WEB: www.swc-wistex.com
SIC: 5063 3699 7629 3823 Electrical supplies; electrical equipment & supplies; electrical equipment repair services; controllers for process variables, all types

(G-19003)
WORLD FLAVORS INC
76 Louise Dr (18974-1588)
PHONE......................................215 672-4400
Christine Hafner, *President*
Doris Holmquist, *Admin Sec*
◆ **EMP:** 84

SQ FT: 55,000
SALES (est): 16.9MM **Privately Held**
WEB: www.worldflavors.com
SIC: **2087** 2099 Flavoring extracts &
syrups; seasonings & spices

(G-19004)
WYCON MOLD & TOOL INC
1756 Stout Dr (18974-1152)
P.O. Box 2926 (18974-0093)
PHONE......................215 675-2945
William E Rau, *President*
Carol Rau, *Corp Secy*
EMP: 8
SALES (est): 1.5MM **Privately Held**
WEB: www.wyconmold.com
SIC: **3544** Special dies & tools; industrial
molds

(G-19005)
YUM YUM BAKE SHOPS INC
500 W Street Rd (18974-3213)
PHONE......................215 675-9874
Glen Conly, *President*
EMP: 5
SALES (est): 360K **Privately Held**
SIC: **2051** Doughnuts, except frozen

(G-19006)
Z-AXIS CONNECTOR COMPANY
345 Ivyland Rd (18974-2205)
P.O. Box 379, Jamison (18929-0379)
PHONE......................267 803-9000
George Glatts, *President*
EMP: 15
SQ FT: 5,000
SALES (est): 2.5MM **Privately Held**
WEB: www.z-axiscc.com
SIC: **3643** 3599 Connectors & terminals
for electrical devices; machine & other job
shop work

Warren
Warren County

(G-19007)
A D M WELDING & FABRICATION
37 Broadhead St (16365-3302)
PHONE......................814 723-7227
Mark Zawacki, *Partner*
Alex Zawacki, *Partner*
EMP: 8
SQ FT: 37,000
SALES (est): 1.7MM **Privately Held**
SIC: **7692** 3441 1623 Welding repair; fab-
ricated structural metal; water, sewer &
utility lines

(G-19008)
**ALLEGHENY VALVE &
COUPLING INC**
Also Called: Allegheny Coupling Company
419 W 3rd Ave (16365-2212)
P.O. Box 708 (16365-0708)
PHONE......................814 723-8150
Raymond V Heelan, *President*
Scott Colvin, *Business Mgr*
Cairn Biship, *Vice Pres*
Karen Bishop, *Vice Pres*
John Riel, *Supervisor*
EMP: 46
SQ FT: 2,000
SALES (est): 7.5MM **Privately Held**
WEB: www.alleghenycoupling.com
SIC: **3494** Valves & pipe fittings

(G-19009)
ALLIMAGE GRAPHICS LLC
900 4th Ave (16365-1888)
PHONE......................814 728-8650
David Hone, *Partner*
Lawrence Lareau, *Partner*
EMP: 5
SQ FT: 3,000
SALES (est): 250K **Privately Held**
SIC: **7336** 7389 3993 2754 Graphic arts
& related design; design services; signs,
not made in custom sign painting shops;
commercial printing, gravure

(G-19010)
AR TRUCKING
2072 Pennsylvania Ave W (16365-1960)
PHONE......................814 723-1245
Coralee Wenzel, *Principal*
EMP: 21
SALES (est): 1.7MM **Privately Held**
SIC: **1389** Gas field services

(G-19011)
**AUDIO VIDEO AUTOMATION
SEC INC**
Also Called: Avas
920 Pennsylvania Ave W (16365-1836)
PHONE......................814 313-1108
Joseph Albert Loranger III, *President*
Marlo Nowacki, *Project Mgr*
EMP: 7 EST: 2009
SQ FT: 2,600
SALES (est): 859.4K **Privately Held**
SIC: **1731** 3571 4822 5731 Sound equip-
ment specialization; electronic computers;
telegraph & other communications; radio,
television & electronic stores; custom
computer programming services; custom
computer programming services; com-
puter software writing services; software
programming applications

(G-19012)
**B & N TROPHIES & AWARDS
LLC**
318 Pennsylvania Ave E (16365-2786)
PHONE......................814 723-8130
Donald Thomas,
Noelle Hone,
EMP: 3
SQ FT: 800
SALES: 100K **Privately Held**
SIC: **3999** 2241 3499 Identification
badges & insignia; plaques, picture, lami-
nated; ribbons; novelties & giftware, in-
cluding trophies

(G-19013)
BETTS INDUSTRIES INC (PA)
1800 Pennsylvania Ave W (16365-1932)
P.O. Box 888 (16365-0888)
PHONE......................814 723-1250
Clifford Betts, *President*
Charles Bettsq, *President*
Rodney E Betts, *Chairman*
M Dennis Hedges Jr, *Corp Secy*
Charles A Betts, *Vice Pres*
▲ EMP: 250 EST: 1901
SQ FT: 205,000
SALES (est): 47.5MM **Privately Held**
SIC: **3494** 3321 3647 Valves & pipe fit-
tings; manhole covers, metal; vehicular
lighting equipment

(G-19014)
BOEKELOO INC
Also Called: G & R Machine Company
1501 Pennsylvania Ave W (16365-1925)
PHONE......................814 723-5950
Harry F Boekeloo, *President*
Dorothy L Boekeloo, *Vice Pres*
Ross Bevevino, *Office Mgr*
EMP: 10
SQ FT: 10,800
SALES: 400K **Privately Held**
SIC: **3599** Custom machinery; machine
shop, jobbing & repair

(G-19015)
**CARDINAL INDUSTRIAL
FINISHES**
4 Harmar St (16365)
PHONE......................814 723-0721
David Lawson, *Manager*
John Latimer, *Manager*
EMP: 7
SALES (corp-wide): 78.7MM **Privately
Held**
WEB: www.cardinalpaint.com
SIC: **2851** Paints & allied products
PA: Cardinal Industrial Finishes
1329 Potrero Ave
South El Monte CA 91733
626 444-9274

(G-19016)
CLASSIFIED ADVERTISING
205 Pennsylvania Ave W (16365-2412)
PHONE......................814 723-1400
Brett Torres, *Owner*
EMP: 3
SALES (est): 101.8K **Privately Held**
SIC: **2711** Newspapers, publishing & print-
ing

(G-19017)
CNE MACHINERY LTD
Also Called: C N C Auto Motion
4 E Harmar St (16365)
PHONE......................814 723-1685
Ted Verf, *President*
EMP: 5
SALES (est): 390K **Privately Held**
SIC: **3553** Woodworking machinery

(G-19018)
CONN & COMPANY LLC
11 S Marion St (16365-3117)
PHONE......................814 723-7980
Richard C Freeman, *President*
EMP: 5
SQ FT: 1,500
SALES: 1MM **Privately Held**
WEB: www.acme-metals.com
SIC: **7389** 3599 Design, commercial & in-
dustrial; machine & other job shop work

(G-19019)
DANZI ENERGY
422 Crescent Park (16365-2250)
PHONE......................814 723-8640
EMP: 4
SALES (est): 277.4K **Privately Held**
SIC: **3494** Mfg Valves/Pipe Fittings

(G-19020)
DAVIES & SONS LLC
3200 Conewango Ave (16365-8214)
PHONE......................814 723-7430
Alfred T Davies, *Owner*
EMP: 5
SQ FT: 15,000
SALES (est): 597.4K **Privately Held**
WEB: www.daviesandsons.com
SIC: **5261** 1311 5999 5251 Lawn & gar-
den equipment; natural gas production;
plumbing & heating supplies; builders'
hardware; truck rental & leasing, no driv-
ers

(G-19021)
DRINKWORKS CORPORATION
618 4th Ave (16365-4923)
P.O. Box 988 (16365-0988)
PHONE......................800 825-5575
Ben Ludwig, *President*
Andrew Sokolski, *Vice Pres*
Lincoln Sokolski, *Vice Pres*
Kevin Weigle, *CFO*
▲ EMP: 42
SALES (est): 304.1K
SALES (corp-wide): 45.9MM **Privately
Held**
SIC: **3089** Plastic kitchenware, tableware &
houseware
PA: Whirley Industries, Inc.
618 4th Ave
Warren PA 16365
814 723-7600

(G-19022)
EASYGO DRINKWARE LLC
618 4th Ave (16365-4923)
PHONE......................814 723-7600
EMP: 31
SALES (est): 1.6MM
SALES (corp-wide): 45.9MM **Privately
Held**
SIC: **3089** Tumblers, plastic
PA: Whirley Industries, Inc.
618 4th Ave
Warren PA 16365
814 723-7600

(G-19023)
**ELKHORN OPERATING
COMPANY**
Also Called: Elkhorn Propane
15470 Route 6 (16365-9669)
PHONE......................814 723-4390

Jeff Gazdak, *Principal*
Jeffrey Gazdake, *Manager*
EMP: 7
SALES (corp-wide): 52MM **Privately
Held**
SIC: **1311** Natural gas production
PA: Elkhorn Operating Company
4613 E 91st St
Tulsa OK 74137
918 492-4418

(G-19024)
EMC FINTECH
34 E Harmar St (16365-3398)
PHONE......................814 230-9157
EMP: 3
SALES (est): 102.2K **Privately Held**
SIC: **3572** Computer storage devices

(G-19025)
EMC TECHNOLOGY LLC
22 Drumcliffe Dr (16365-3516)
PHONE......................814 728-8857
Eric M Corey,
EMP: 7
SALES (est): 1.8MM **Privately Held**
SIC: **3585** Parts for heating, cooling & re-
frigerating equipment

(G-19026)
**FRANK D SUPPA LUMBER INC
(PA)**
740 Pleasant Dr (16365-3534)
PHONE......................814 723-7360
John P Suppa, *President*
EMP: 13
SALES (est): 827.6K **Privately Held**
SIC: **2421** 2426 Lumber: rough, sawed or
planed; hardwood dimension & flooring
mills

(G-19027)
**G G GREENE ENTERPRISES INC
(PA)**
21610 Route 6 (16365-7983)
P.O. Box 866 (16365-0866)
PHONE......................814 723-5700
Craig Greene, *President*
Donald Olson, *Corp Secy*
▼ EMP: 50
SQ FT: 300,000
SALES (est): 7.1MM **Privately Held**
SIC: **3469** 3489 3443 3482 Stamping
metal for the trade; ordnance & acces-
sories; industrial vessels, tanks & contain-
ers; small arms ammunition;
manufactured hardware (general)

(G-19028)
**GRAND VALLEY
MANUFACTURING CO**
1000 Pennsylvania Ave W (16365-1838)
PHONE......................814 728-8760
Duane Baker, *Manager*
EMP: 7
SALES (corp-wide): 14.4MM **Privately
Held**
WEB: www.gvmco.com
SIC: **3599** Machine shop, jobbing & repair
PA: Grand Valley Manufacturing Company
701 E Spring St Unit 8
Titusville PA 16354
814 728-8760

(G-19029)
**GREAT LAKES CUSTOM
GRAPHICS**
221 Pennsylvania Ave W (16365-2412)
PHONE......................814 723-0110
Scott Campbell, *President*
EMP: 8
SALES (est): 810.2K **Privately Held**
WEB: www.glcgcentral.com
SIC: **2395** Embroidery products, except
schiffli machine

(G-19030)
H&R BLOCK INC
Also Called: H & R Block
229 Pennsylvania Ave W A (16365-2430)
PHONE......................814 723-3001
Cathlyn Smith, *Manager*
EMP: 12

SALES (corp-wide): 3.1B **Publicly Held**
WEB: www.hrblock.com
SIC: 7291 6794 7372 Tax return preparation services; franchises, selling or licensing; application computer software
PA: H&R Block, Inc.
　　1 H&R Block Way
　　Kansas City MO 64105
　　816 854-3000

(G-19031)
HOUSE OF PRINTING
Also Called: Steppin' Out
716 Pennsylvania Ave E # 2　(16365-5908)
PHONE..................................814 723-3701
Richard Swick, *Owner*
EMP: 9
SQ FT: 5,000
SALES: 197K **Privately Held**
SIC: 2759 2752 Catalogs: printing; commercial printing, lithographic

(G-19032)
INSERT MOLDING TECH INC
36 Clark St　(16365-2524)
P.O. Box 396　(16365-0396)
PHONE..................................814 406-7033
John P Loranger, *President*
Theodore P Eldridge, *Vice Pres*
Ralph D Pasquino, *Admin Sec*
EMP: 50
SQ FT: 45,000
SALES (est): 6.5MM **Privately Held**
WEB: www.insertmoldingtech.com
SIC: 3089 Molding primary plastic

(G-19033)
INTERLECTRIC CORPORATION (HQ)
Also Called: Nesglo Products Division
1401 Lexington Ave　(16365-2849)
PHONE..................................814 723-6061
Steven Rothenberg, *President*
Joy Lim, *Senior VP*
Sandra Rothenberg, *Treasurer*
Lisa Marino, *Human Res Dir*
Joy Caumban-Lim, *Office Mgr*
▲ **EMP:** 119
SQ FT: 70,000
SALES: 11MM
SALES (corp-wide): 11.5MM **Privately Held**
WEB: www.interlectric.com
SIC: 3641 5063 Lamps, fluorescent, electric; electrical apparatus & equipment
PA: Intervestment Corporation
　　1401 Lexington Ave
　　Warren PA
　　814 726-2470

(G-19034)
JOHNNY APPLESEEDS INC
220 Hickory St　(16366-0002)
PHONE..................................800 546-4554
EMP: 3
SALES (corp-wide): 2B **Publicly Held**
SIC: 2335 Bridal & formal gowns
HQ: Johnny Appleseed's, Inc.
　　35 Village Rd Fl 4
　　Middleton MA 01949
　　978 922-2040

(G-19035)
KCS ENERGY INC
201 Wetmore St　(16365-2029)
P.O. Box 187　(16365-0187)
PHONE..................................814 723-4672
Thomas Moyer, *President*
EMP: 8
SALES (est): 1.9MM **Privately Held**
SIC: 1311 Crude petroleum & natural gas

(G-19036)
LARIMER & NORTON INC
1163 Scandia Rd　(16365-8439)
PHONE..................................814 723-1778
Jack Buckler, *Manager*
EMP: 17
SALES (corp-wide): 87.6MM **Privately Held**
WEB: www.larimerlounge.com
SIC: 3949 Baseball equipment & supplies, general

HQ: Larimer & Norton, Inc.
　　800 W Main St
　　Louisville KY 40202
　　502 585-5226

(G-19037)
LAWRENCE R MCGUIGAN
Also Called: Precision Plus Machine Shop
7 Hemlock St　(16365-3212)
PHONE..................................724 493-9175
Lawrence R McGuigan, *Owner*
EMP: 3
SALES: 10K **Privately Held**
SIC: 3569 Baling machines, for scrap metal, paper or similar material

(G-19038)
LORANGER INTERNATIONAL CORP (PA)
817 4th Ave　(16365-1801)
PHONE..................................814 723-2250
J Albert Loranger, *CEO*
Kirk Geary, *Executive*
Ariane Loranger, *Admin Sec*
EMP: 85
SQ FT: 56,000
SALES (est): 11.5MM **Privately Held**
SIC: 3825 3672 3678 3577 Instruments to measure electricity; printed circuit boards; electronic connectors; computer peripheral equipment; blowers & fans; manufactured hardware (general)

(G-19039)
MARK A KULKA
6 Mader Dr　(16365-4015)
PHONE..................................814 726-7331
Mark A Kulka, *Owner*
EMP: 3
SALES: 300K **Privately Held**
SIC: 2411 Logging

(G-19040)
NORTHWEST SYNERGY CORP
1438 Stone Hill Rd　(16365-5401)
PHONE..................................814 726-0543
Steven Rothenberg, *President*
Pamela Myers, *Vice Pres*
Sharon Myers, *Vice Pres*
Dr Sandra M Rothenberg, *Vice Pres*
Jennifer M Beckley, *Treasurer*
EMP: 3
SALES: 66K **Privately Held**
SIC: 1381 Drilling oil & gas wells

(G-19041)
OSRAM SYLVANIA INC
Also Called: Electronic Components & Mtls
816 Lexington Ave　(16365-2834)
PHONE..................................814 726-6600
Robert Bennis, *General Mgr*
EMP: 220
SALES (corp-wide): 4.7B **Privately Held**
WEB: www.sylvania.com
SIC: 3641 3714 3678 Electric lamps; motor vehicle parts & accessories; electronic connectors
HQ: Osram Sylvania Inc
　　200 Ballardvale St # 305
　　Wilmington MA 01887
　　978 570-3000

(G-19042)
PAPCO INC (PA)
213 W 3rd Ave Rm 304　(16365-2358)
P.O. Box 627　(16365-0627)
PHONE..................................814 726-2130
Jon A Petersen, *President*
Darryl E Pierce, *Corp Secy*
Daniel M Pierce, *Vice Pres*
EMP: 12
SQ FT: 1,400
SALES (est): 4.6MM **Privately Held**
SIC: 1311 1381 Natural gas production; drilling oil & gas wells

(G-19043)
PENNSYLVANIA GEN ENRGY CORP (PA)
Also Called: P G E
120 Market St　(16365-2510)
PHONE..................................814 723-3230
Douglas E Kuntz, *CEO*
Thomas H Henry, *President*
Tricia Durbin, *Vice Pres*
Charles W Kirkwood, *Vice Pres*

Tim Munksgard, *Purch Mgr*
EMP: 69
SQ FT: 14,000
SALES (est): 138.3MM **Privately Held**
WEB: www.penngeneralenergy.com
SIC: 1311 Crude petroleum production; natural gas production

(G-19044)
PETREX INC
2349 Dorcon Rd　(16365-9619)
P.O. Box 907　(16365-0907)
PHONE..................................814 723-2050
Daniel Gray, *President*
James R McBride, *Principal*
◆ **EMP:** 30
SQ FT: 30,000
SALES (est): 8MM
SALES (corp-wide): 6.8MM **Privately Held**
WEB: www.petrex.net
SIC: 3443 3444 Floating covers, metal plate; separators, industrial process: metal plate; sheet metalwork
PA: Warren Industries, Inc.
　　2349 Crescent Park Ext
　　Warren PA 16365
　　814 723-2050

(G-19045)
R C SOUTHWELL
59 Scientific Rd　(16365-3686)
PHONE..................................814 723-7182
Russell C Southwell, *Owner*
EMP: 3
SALES (est): 206.2K **Privately Held**
SIC: 1311 Crude petroleum & natural gas production

(G-19046)
RISTAU DRILLING CO
100 Kamp St　(16365-3560)
PHONE..................................814 723-4858
Rick Ristau, *Owner*
Andrea Ristau, *Co-Owner*
EMP: 9
SALES (est): 871.8K **Privately Held**
SIC: 1381 Drilling oil & gas wells

(G-19047)
SOUTHWELL OIL CO
381 Hillcrest Dr　(16365-1259)
PHONE..................................814 723-5178
William Southwell, *Owner*
EMP: 3
SALES (est): 210.1K **Privately Held**
SIC: 1381 Drilling oil & gas wells

(G-19048)
STURDEVANT SIGNS
20980 Route 6　(16365-7972)
PHONE..................................814 723-3361
Mike Ranst, *Owner*
EMP: 3 **EST:** 1957
SQ FT: 4,000
SALES: 400K **Privately Held**
SIC: 3993 Electric signs; signs, not made in custom sign painting shops

(G-19049)
SUPERIOR TIRE & RUBBER CORP (PA)
40 Scientific Rd　(16365-3686)
P.O. Box 308　(16365-0308)
PHONE..................................814 723-2370
Henri E Lemeur Jr, *Principal*
Paul J Blasco, *Vice Pres*
William T Lemeur, *Vice Pres*
Eric Lucks, *Purch Mgr*
Tim Rowles, *Technical Mgr*
◆ **EMP:** 179 **EST:** 1959
SQ FT: 45,000
SALES (est): 43.6MM **Privately Held**
WEB: www.superiortire.com
SIC: 3011 Tires, cushion or solid rubber

(G-19050)
SUPERIOR TIRE & RUBBER CORP
1818 Pennsylvania Ave W　(16365-1932)
P.O. Box 308　(16365-0308)
PHONE..................................814 723-2370
EMP: 57
SALES (corp-wide): 43.6MM **Privately Held**
SIC: 3011 Tires & inner tubes

PA: Superior Tire & Rubber Corp.
　　40 Scientific Rd
　　Warren PA 16365
　　814 723-2370

(G-19051)
TARGETED PET TREATS LLC
151 Struthers St　(16365-1956)
PHONE..................................814 406-7351
Gregory Austin, *President*
Nick Jackson, *Manager*
Mike Mortimer, *Manager*
EMP: 125
SALES (est): 20MM
SALES (corp-wide): 40.8MM **Privately Held**
SIC: 3999 Pet supplies
HQ: Pestell Pet Products Inc
　　141 Hamilton Rd Suite 794
　　New Hamburg ON N3A 2
　　519 662-2877

(G-19052)
TRIANGLE PETROLEUM INC
Also Called: North Warren BP
107 Jackson Run Rd　(16365-4669)
PHONE..................................908 380-2685
Baldev Singh, *President*
EMP: 5
SALES (est): 368.8K **Privately Held**
SIC: 1311 Crude petroleum & natural gas

(G-19053)
TURNING SOLUTIONS INC
34 E Harmar St Ste 3　(16365-3398)
PHONE..................................814 723-1134
Gloria Genberg, *President*
EMP: 10
SALES (est): 740K **Privately Held**
SIC: 3599 3451 3452 3491 Electrical discharge machining (EDM); screw machine products; bolts, nuts, rivets & washers; industrial valves; valves & pipe fittings

(G-19054)
UNITED REFINING INC (DH)
Also Called: United Refining Company
15 Bradley St　(16365-3299)
P.O. Box 780　(16365-0780)
PHONE..................................814 723-1500
John A Catsimatidis, *Ch of Bd*
Myron L Turfitt, *President*
Debbie Gath, *General Mgr*
Diane McCauley, *General Mgr*
David Dunn, *Regional Mgr*
▲ **EMP:** 100 **EST:** 1902
SQ FT: 16,500
SALES (est): 2B
SALES (corp-wide): 2.5B **Privately Held**
SIC: 2911 5541 5411 4612 Petroleum refining; gasoline service stations; convenience stores; crude petroleum pipelines
HQ: United Acquisition Corp.
　　802 N West St
　　Wilmington DE 19801
　　302 651-9856

(G-19055)
UNITED REFINING COMPANY (DH)
15 Bradley St　(16365-3299)
PHONE..................................814 723-1500
John A Catsimatidis, *Ch of Bd*
Myron L Turfitt, *President*
Ashton L Ditka, *Senior VP*
Frederick J Martin, *Vice Pres*
John R Wagner, *Vice Pres*
EMP: 201
SALES: 2B
SALES (corp-wide): 2.5B **Privately Held**
WEB: www.urc.com
SIC: 5541 5411 2911 Gasoline service stations; grocery stores; convenience stores; oils; fuel
HQ: United Refining, Inc.
　　15 Bradley St
　　Warren PA 16365
　　814 723-1500

(G-19056)
UNITED REFINING COMPANY
Also Called: Quick Field
2351 Market St　(16365-4674)
PHONE..................................814 723-6511
Curtis McGaugaty, *Manager*
EMP: 5

▲ = Import ▼=Export
◆ =Import/Export

SALES (corp-wide): 2.5B **Privately Held**
WEB: www.urc.com
SIC: 2911 Petroleum refining
HQ: United Refining Company
15 Bradley St
Warren PA 16365
814 723-1500

(G-19057)
WARREN ELECTRIC MOTOR SERVICE
900 Pennsylvania Ave W (16365-1836)
PHONE..................................814 723-2045
Kenneth Johnson, *Partner*
Laura Johnson, *Partner*
William R Johnson, *General Ptnr*
EMP: 3
SALES (est): 220K **Privately Held**
SIC: 7694 5063 Electric motor repair; motors, electric

(G-19058)
WARREN INDUSTRIAL SOLUTIONS
21890 Route 6 (16365-7950)
PHONE..................................814 728-8500
Joseph A Glotz, *Managing Prtnr*
Ralph J Dowd, *Managing Prtnr*
Joseph Glotz, *Managing Prtnr*
EMP: 10
SQ FT: 8,000
SALES (est): 1.6MM **Privately Held**
WEB: www.warrenindustrialsolutions.com
SIC: 3599 Machine shop, jobbing & repair

(G-19059)
WARREN INDUSTRIES INC (PA)
2349 Crescent Park Ext (16365-9619)
P.O. Box 1404 (16365-6404)
PHONE..................................814 723-2050
James R McBride, *President*
Mike McElravy, *Admin Sec*
▼ EMP: 34
SQ FT: 30,000
SALES (est): 6.8MM **Privately Held**
WEB: www.warrenindustries.com
SIC: 3443 Fabricated plate work (boiler shop)

(G-19060)
WARREN PLASTICS MFG
123 Elm St (16365-2809)
PHONE..................................814 726-9511
Tim Saporito, *Owner*
EMP: 5
SALES (est): 352K **Privately Held**
WEB: www.warrenplastics.com
SIC: 3089 Injection molding of plastics

(G-19061)
WARREN RAILCAR SERVICE INC
51 Railcar Rd (16365-7969)
P.O. Box 452, Russell (16345-0452)
PHONE..................................814 723-2500
Byron West, *Manager*
EMP: 16
SQ FT: 50,000
SALES (est): 2.4MM **Privately Held**
SIC: 3743 4789 Railroad car rebuilding; railroad car repair

(G-19062)
WARREN SHEET METAL INC
21 S Irvine St (16365-2899)
PHONE..................................814 726-5777
Jim Widrig, *President*
EMP: 4
SQ FT: 6,500
SALES: 410K **Privately Held**
SIC: 3441 Fabricated structural metal

(G-19063)
WARREN TIMES OBSERVER
205 Pennsylvania Ave W (16365-2412)
P.O. Box 188 (16365-0188)
PHONE..................................814 723-8200
John Elchert, *President*
Andy Close, *Editor*
Jon Sitler, *Editor*
Monica Keller, *Cust Mgr*
EMP: 30
SQ FT: 12,000

SALES (est): 2.2MM **Privately Held**
WEB: www.timesobserver.com
SIC: 2711 Newspapers, publishing & printing
HQ: The Ogden Newspapers Inc
1500 Main St
Wheeling WV 26003
304 233-0100

(G-19064)
WHIRLEY INDUSTRIES INC (PA)
Also Called: Whirley-Drinkworks
618 4th Ave (16365-4923)
PHONE..................................814 723-7600
Lincoln Sokolski, *President*
Gregory M Gross, *Vice Pres*
▲ EMP: 207 EST: 1966
SQ FT: 120,000
SALES (est): 45.9MM **Privately Held**
SIC: 3089 Plastic containers, except foam; cups, plastic, except foam

(G-19065)
WHIRLEY INDUSTRIES INC
Also Called: Whirley Drinkworks
140 W Harmar St (16365-2184)
P.O. Box 988 (16365-0988)
PHONE..................................814 723-7600
EMP: 5
SALES (est): 118.4K **Privately Held**
SIC: 3089 Plastic containers, except foam

(G-19066)
ZEHRCO-GIANCOLA COMPOSITES INC
36 Clark St (16365-2524)
PHONE..................................814 406-7033
EMP: 3
SALES (est): 232.8K **Privately Held**
SIC: 3089 Plastics products

Warrendale
Allegheny County

(G-19067)
AEO MANAGEMENT CO
150 Thorn Hill Rd (15086-7528)
PHONE..................................724 776-4857
Jay Schottenstein, *CEO*
EMP: 4 **Publicly Held**
SIC: 7999 2339 2389 Outfitters, recreation; women's & misses' accessories; men's miscellaneous accessories
HQ: Aeo Management Co.
77 Hot Metal St
Pittsburgh PA 15203

(G-19068)
ATLAS NEON SIGN CORP (PA)
230 Northgate Dr (15086-7593)
PHONE..................................724 935-2171
Fax: 724 935-8788
EMP: 7
SQ FT: 4,800
SALES (est): 1.2MM **Privately Held**
SIC: 3993 3089 Mfg Signs/Advertising Specialties Mfg Plastic Products

(G-19069)
BOLT WORKS INC
2150 Woodland Rd (15086-7536)
PHONE..................................724 776-7273
Richard P Norris, *President*
EMP: 14 EST: 1969
SQ FT: 10,000
SALES (est): 2.2MM **Privately Held**
WEB: www.fastenersunlimited.com
SIC: 3965 3599 Fasteners; machine & other job shop work

(G-19070)
CHICK WRKHOLDING SOLUTIONS INC
500 Keystone Dr (15086-7537)
PHONE..................................724 772-1644
Paul S Swann, *Principal*
Mike Olson, *Business Mgr*
Diane Alexander, *Opers Mgr*
Diane Stehle, *Purch Agent*
Amanda Sens, *Manager*
▲ EMP: 55

SALES (est): 11.9MM **Privately Held**
SIC: 3545 3429 Vises, machine (machine tool accessories); manufactured hardware (general)

(G-19071)
DERSE INC
422 Keystone Dr (15086-7567)
PHONE..................................724 772-4853
Michael Bradley, *General Mgr*
EMP: 75
SALES (est): 7MM
SALES (corp-wide): 111.9MM **Privately Held**
WEB: www.derse.com
SIC: 3993 7312 Displays & cutouts, window & lobby; outdoor advertising services
PA: Derse, Inc.
3800 W Canal St
Milwaukee WI 53208
414 257-2000

(G-19072)
DYMAX CORPORATION
110 Marshall Dr (15086-7554)
PHONE..................................800 296-4146
Irene Skolnick, *President*
Andy Bachmann, *Owner*
Greg Bachmann, *Chairman*
Dennis C Walczak, *Admin Sec*
▲ EMP: 40
SQ FT: 15,000
SALES (est): 9.8MM
SALES (corp-wide): 15.9B **Publicly Held**
WEB: www.site-rite.com
SIC: 3845 Ultrasonic medical equipment, except cleaning
HQ: Bard Access Systems, Inc.
605 N 5600 W
Salt Lake City UT 84116
801 522-5000

(G-19073)
FRESENIUS KABI USA INC
770 Commonwealth Dr (15086-7521)
PHONE..................................724 772-6900
John Maholtz, *Owner*
Matthew Varga, *Engineer*
EMP: 8
SALES (corp-wide): 38.3B **Privately Held**
SIC: 2834 Pharmaceutical preparations
HQ: Fresenius Kabi Usa, Inc.
3 Corporate Dr
Lake Zurich IL 60047
847 969-2700

(G-19074)
GANNETT CO INC
770 Commonwealth Dr Ste 1 (15086-7521)
PHONE..................................724 778-3388
Fax: 724 778-3338
EMP: 78
SALES (corp-wide): 5.3B **Publicly Held**
SIC: 2711 Newspapers-Publishing/Printing
PA: Gannett Co., Inc.
7950 Jones Branch Dr
Mc Lean VA 22102
703 854-6000

(G-19075)
GATAN INC
780 Commonwealth Dr (15086-7598)
PHONE..................................724 779-2572
Robert Deutsch, *Branch Mgr*
EMP: 100
SALES (corp-wide): 5.1B **Publicly Held**
SIC: 3826 3827 Analytical optical instruments; optical instruments & lenses
HQ: Gatan Inc.
5794 W Las Positas Blvd
Pleasanton CA 94588

(G-19076)
GEOSONICS INC (PA)
359 Northgate Dr Ste 200 (15086-7597)
PHONE..................................724 934-2900
D T Froedge, *President*
Jeffrey A Straw, *Vice Pres*
Jeffrey Straw, *Vice Pres*
John L Wright, *Vice Pres*
Marion B Henry, *CFO*
EMP: 15
SQ FT: 7,200

SALES (est): 5.5MM **Privately Held**
SIC: 3829 7699 8999 3825 Seismographs; professional instrument repair services; geological consultant; instruments to measure electricity

(G-19077)
GLYCOL TECHNOLOGIES INC
140 Commonwealth Dr (15086-7501)
PHONE..................................724 776-3554
Charles Logan, *President*
EMP: 5 EST: 2001
SALES (est): 1.6MM **Privately Held**
WEB: www.glycoltechnologies.com
SIC: 2869 Ethylene glycols

(G-19078)
GOSIGER INC
549a Keystone Dr (15086-7538)
PHONE..................................724 778-3220
Jerry Haas, *Sales Engr*
Gene Porter, *Sales Engr*
Dick Albert, *Branch Mgr*
Tim Stewart, *Manager*
EMP: 15
SALES (corp-wide): 140.8MM **Privately Held**
WEB: www.gosiger.com
SIC: 3599 Custom machinery
PA: Gosiger, Inc.
108 Mcdonough St
Dayton OH 45402
937 228-5174

(G-19079)
GRAPHIC PRODUCTS INC
320 Northgae Dr Ste B (15086)
PHONE..................................724 935-6600
Kenneth Young, *President*
Dawn Pustay, *Corp Secy*
Betty Young, *Vice Pres*
EMP: 5
SALES (est): 548.7K **Privately Held**
SIC: 2759 Commercial printing

(G-19080)
HEALTH CARE COUNCIL WESTERN PA (PA)
500 Commonwealth Dr (15086-7516)
PHONE..................................724 776-6400
Alvin J Harper, *President*
EMP: 11
SQ FT: 33,000
SALES: 4.2MM **Privately Held**
WEB: www.hcwp.org
SIC: 8621 2721 8611 Medical field-related associations; periodicals; business associations

(G-19081)
HEALTHCARE INFORMATION CORP
500 Commonwealth Dr (15086-7516)
PHONE..................................724 776-9411
Dr Iam Rawson, *President*
Donald J Seigle, *Exec VP*
Walter K Wayne, *VP Finance*
EMP: 18
SQ FT: 10,000
SALES: 118.2K
SALES (corp-wide): 4.2MM **Privately Held**
WEB: www.shhrpp.org
SIC: 2752 2721 Commercial printing, lithographic; periodicals
PA: Health Care Council Of Western Pennsylvania
500 Commonwealth Dr
Warrendale PA 15086
724 776-6400

(G-19082)
HUB PARKING TECHNOLOGY USA INC (PA)
Also Called: Hub USA
761 Commonwealth Dr # 204 (15086-7615)
PHONE..................................724 772-2400
John Lovell, *CEO*
EMP: 41
SALES (est): 12MM **Privately Held**
SIC: 1799 3559 Parking facility equipment & maintenance; parking facility equipment & supplies

(G-19083)
JOY GLOBAL UNDERGROUND MIN LLC (DH)
Also Called: Mining Joy Machinery
40 Pennwood Pl Ste 100 (15086-6526)
PHONE....................724 779-4500
Wayne Hunnell, *President*
Michael Sutherlin, *President*
Michael S Olsen, *Vice Pres*
John D Major, *Admin Sec*
Kenneth J Stark, *Admin Sec*
◆ **EMP:** 190
SQ FT: 82,750
SALES (est): 1.1B
SALES (corp-wide): 23.4B **Privately Held**
SIC: 3535 3532 Conveyors & conveying equipment; drills, bits & similar equipment
HQ: Komatsu Mining Corp.
100 E Wisconsin Ave # 2780
Milwaukee WI 53202
414 319-8500

(G-19084)
KADMON PHARMACEUTICALS LLC
119 Commonwealth Dr (15086-7503)
PHONE....................724 778-6100
Steven N Gordon, *Exec VP*
Adriann Sax, *Exec VP*
Zhenping Zhu, *Exec VP*
Lawrence K Cohen, *Senior VP*
Hamm Gary Conte, *Vice Pres*
▲ **EMP:** 95
SQ FT: 10,000
SALES (est): 20.1MM **Privately Held**
WEB: www.kadmon.com
SIC: 2834 Pharmaceutical preparations
PA: Kadmon Corporation, Llc
450 E 29th St Fl 5
New York NY 10016

(G-19085)
KRAFT HEINZ FOODS COMPANY
Also Called: Hj Heinz Innovation Center
1000 Ericsson Dr (15086-6508)
PHONE....................724 778-5700
Michael Parton, *Branch Mgr*
EMP: 262
SALES (corp-wide): 26.2B **Publicly Held**
SIC: 2033 Catsup: packaged in cans, jars, etc.
HQ: Kraft Heinz Foods Company
1 Ppg Pl Ste 3200
Pittsburgh PA 15222
412 456-5700

(G-19086)
KRONOS INCORPORATED
555 Keystone Dr (15086-7538)
PHONE....................724 772-2400
Dru Duffy, *Branch Mgr*
EMP: 36
SALES (corp-wide): 1.1B **Privately Held**
WEB: www.kronos.com
SIC: 7372 Business oriented computer software
HQ: Kronos Incorporated
900 Chelmsford St # 312
Lowell MA 01851
978 250-9800

(G-19087)
MAGEE PLASTICS COMPANY
303 Brush Creek Rd (15086-7595)
PHONE....................724 776-2220
Glen H Maus, *President*
Kelly S Magee, *Corp Secy*
Sheridan L Kelly, *COO*
Sean Magee, *Senior VP*
Charles W Story, *Vice Pres*
EMP: 84 **EST:** 1969
SQ FT: 100,000
SALES (est): 23.4MM **Privately Held**
WEB: www.mageeplastics.com
SIC: 3083 7389 3743 3728 Plastic finished products, laminated; design, commercial & industrial; railroad equipment; aircraft parts & equipment

(G-19088)
MITSUBISHI ELC PWR PDTS INC (DH)
Also Called: Meppi
530 Keystone Dr (15086-7537)
PHONE....................724 772-2555

Brian Herry, *President*
Ben Steiner, *President*
Kevin Beamer, *General Mgr*
Carla Collier, *General Mgr*
George Danbury, *General Mgr*
◆ **EMP:** 225
SALES (est): 286.7MM
SALES (corp-wide): 41.5B **Privately Held**
WEB: www.meppi.com
SIC: 3613 Power circuit breakers
HQ: Mitsubishi Electric Us Holdings, Inc.
5900 Katella Ave Ste A
Cypress CA 90630
714 220-2500

(G-19089)
MITSUBISHI ELC PWR PDTS INC
520 Keystone Dr (15086-7537)
PHONE....................724 778-5112
Diane Ziccarelli, *Sales Staff*
Jack Greaf, *Branch Mgr*
Takehiko Suga, *Director*
EMP: 7
SALES (corp-wide): 41.5B **Privately Held**
SIC: 3613 Power circuit breakers
HQ: Mitsubishi Electric Power Products, Inc.
530 Keystone Dr
Warrendale PA 15086
724 772-2555

(G-19090)
MW/TD INSPIRED LLC
Also Called: Performance Inspired Nutrition
750 Commonwealth Dr (15086-7521)
PHONE....................724 741-0473
Tom Dowd, *Mng Member*
EMP: 7
SALES (est): 4.9MM **Privately Held**
SIC: 2048 Mineral feed supplements

(G-19091)
PHILLIPS DRILLING COMPANY (DH)
190 Thorn Hill Rd (15086-7528)
PHONE....................724 479-1135
Bruce Wiegand, *CEO*
Samuel Fragale, *President*
David Grecco, *Vice Pres*
Steve Sickafuse, *Vice Pres*
Jeffrey Mallon, *CFO*
EMP: 17
SQ FT: 2,000
SALES (est): 7.6MM
SALES (corp-wide): 290.2B **Publicly Held**
WEB: www.lkdrillingcorp.com
SIC: 1381 Drilling oil & gas wells
HQ: Phillips Resources, Inc.
502 Keystone Dr
Warrendale PA
800 842-8091

(G-19092)
PHILLIPS EXPLORATION LLC
502 Keystone Dr (15086-7537)
PHONE....................724 772-3500
Jeff Mallon, *Manager*
EMP: 60
SALES (est): 1.7MM
SALES (corp-wide): 290.2B **Publicly Held**
SIC: 1311 Natural gas production
HQ: Phillips Resources, Inc.
502 Keystone Dr
Warrendale PA
800 842-8091

(G-19093)
PRINT AND GRAPHICS SCHOLRSHIP
301 Brush Creek Rd (15086-7529)
PHONE....................412 741-6860
Angela Pulkowski, *Principal*
EMP: 3
SALES (est): 1.2MM **Privately Held**
SIC: 2752 Commercial printing, offset

(G-19094)
PRINTING INDS AMER FOUNDATION
301 Brush Creek Rd (15086-7529)
PHONE....................412 741-6860
Michael Makin, *CEO*
Nicholas Stratigos, *CFO*

EMP: 12
SQ FT: 40,000
SALES: 2.4MM **Privately Held**
WEB: www.piagatf.org
SIC: 8733 2731 2721 Educational research agency; book publishing; periodicals

(G-19095)
RENAL SOLUTIONS INC (HQ)
Also Called: Sorbent
770 Commonwealth Dr (15086-7521)
PHONE....................724 772-6900
Pete Decomo, *CEO*
John Maholtz, *President*
Donald W Joseph, *Principal*
Mark Fawcett, *Treasurer*
Douglas Kott, *Admin Sec*
EMP: 39
SALES (est): 10.8MM
SALES (corp-wide): 18.9B **Privately Held**
WEB: www.renalsolutionsinc.com
SIC: 3845 Electromedical equipment
PA: Fresenius Medical Care Ag & Co. Kgaa
Else-Kroner-Str. 1
Bad Homburg 61352
617 260-90

(G-19096)
REPSOL OIL & GAS USA LLC
50 Pennwood Pl (15086-6512)
PHONE....................724 814-5300
James Odriscoll, *Principal*
Kevin Dunkle, *Accountant*
Robert Broen, *Manager*
Walter Hufford, *Manager*
Alissa Field, *Administration*
EMP: 5
SALES (corp-wide): 1.5B **Privately Held**
SIC: 1311 Natural gas production
HQ: Repsol Oil & Gas Usa, Llc
2455 Tech Forest Blvd
Spring TX 77381
832 442-1000

(G-19097)
SIEMENS INDUSTRY INC
181 Thorn Hill Rd (15086-7527)
PHONE....................724 772-0044
Kim Lukens, *Manager*
EMP: 35
SALES (corp-wide): 95B **Privately Held**
SIC: 3589 Sewage & water treatment equipment
HQ: Siemens Industry, Inc.
1000 Deerfield Pkwy
Buffalo Grove IL 60089
800 743-6367

(G-19098)
STRUCTURED MINING SYSTEMS INC
Also Called: Cervis
170 Thorn Hill Rd (15086-7528)
PHONE....................724 741-9000
Ronald Snyder, *President*
Kevin R Hadley, *Corp Secy*
Robert W Thomas Jr, *Vice Pres*
Ron Heasley, *Engineer*
Anthony M Di Tommaso, *Treasurer*
EMP: 30
SQ FT: 7,600
SALES (est): 6MM **Privately Held**
WEB: www.cervis.net
SIC: 8711 3663 Designing: ship, boat, machine & product; radio broadcasting & communications equipment

(G-19099)
TIGEREYE ENTERPRISE INC
100 Allegheny Dr Ste 100 # 100 (15086-7610)
PHONE....................724 443-7810
B Douglas Wright, *President*
Bruce A Wrght, *Vice Pres*
Ron Wallace, *Marketing Staff*
EMP: 3
SALES (est): 248.8K **Privately Held**
WEB: www.tigereyeenterprise.com
SIC: 3599 Mfg Of Flexible Devices

(G-19100)
WE-EF LIGHTING USA LLC
410 Keystone Dr (15086-7558)
PHONE....................724 742-0027
Benjamin Smith, *Engineer*

Kevin Rose, *Sales Staff*
David Nolfi,
▲ **EMP:** 6
SQ FT: 5,000
SALES (est): 1.5MM **Privately Held**
SIC: 3648 Lighting equipment

(G-19101)
WESCO DISTRIBUTION INC
Wesco Express
780 Commonwealth Dr (15086-7611)
PHONE....................724 772-5000
Gerald Blair, *Safety Mgr*
Pat Cote, *Manager*
Jeff Mandell, *Manager*
EMP: 15 **Publicly Held**
SIC: 5063 5085 3699 Electrical supplies; industrial supplies; electrical equipment & supplies
HQ: Wesco Distribution, Inc.
225 W Station Square Dr # 700
Pittsburgh PA 15219

(G-19102)
WESTINGHOUSE ELECTRIC CO LLC
5000 Ericsson Dr (15086-7523)
PHONE....................412 374-4252
Rebecca Witt, *Principal*
Timothy Ellis, *Vice Pres*
Louis Martin, *Project Mgr*
Marilyn Reeder, *Project Mgr*
Joshua Standridge, *Project Mgr*
EMP: 2030
SIC: 3829 Measuring & controlling devices
HQ: Westinghouse Electric Company Llc
1000 Westinghouse Dr
Cranberry Township PA 16066
412 374-2020

(G-19103)
XTO ENERGY INC
190 Thorn Hill Rd (15086-7528)
PHONE....................724 772-3500
Mike Linn, *Manager*
EMP: 59
SALES (corp-wide): 290.2B **Publicly Held**
SIC: 1311 Crude petroleum production
HQ: Xto Energy Inc.
22777 Sprngwoods Vlg Pkwy
Spring TX 77389

Warrington
Bucks County

(G-19104)
75 CABINETS LLC
646 Easton Rd (18976-2017)
PHONE....................215 343-7500
Derrick Simmons, *Principal*
Rachel Walsh, *Cust Mgr*
EMP: 4
SALES (est): 566.8K **Privately Held**
SIC: 2434 Wood kitchen cabinets

(G-19105)
A/S CUSTOM FURNITURE COMPANY
364 Valley Rd Ste C (18976-2510)
PHONE....................215 491-3100
W Roy Smith, *President*
Roy Smith Jr, *President*
Frank Perlman, *General Mgr*
Matthew Smith, *Director*
EMP: 24
SQ FT: 51,000
SALES (est): 4MM **Privately Held**
SIC: 2541 2499 2521 2522 Store & office display cases & fixtures; decorative wood & woodwork; wood office furniture; office furniture, except wood

(G-19106)
AAXIOS TECHNOLOGIES LLC
272 Titus Ave Ste 217 (18976-2437)
PHONE....................267 545-7400
EMP: 3
SALES (est): 236.8K **Privately Held**
SIC: 7371 7372 Computer software development & applications; operating systems computer software

(G-19107)
AMERIPAK
Also Called: Packaging Equipment Sales
2001 County Line Rd (18976-2486)
PHONE..............................215 343-1530
Donald Shelmire, *President*
Robert A Sterner, *Treasurer*
Phillip R Kelly, *Admin Sec*
EMP: 35
SALES (est): 744.8K **Privately Held**
SIC: 3565 3999 Packaging machinery; atomizers, toiletry

(G-19108)
APEX MANUFACTURING CO INC
1750 Costner Dr Ste B (18976-2500)
PHONE..............................215 343-4850
Chris Nagle, *President*
EMP: 8
SQ FT: 9,000
SALES (est): 830K **Privately Held**
WEB: www.apextrikes.com
SIC: 3441 Fabricated structural metal

(G-19109)
BENCHSMITH LLC
429 Easton Rd Ste B (18976-2447)
PHONE..............................215 491-1711
Bryan Paul, *President*
M Brian Paul, *President*
Tim Kroh, *Principal*
◆ EMP: 9
SQ FT: 8,000
SALES: 1.2MM **Privately Held**
WEB: www.benchsmith.com
SIC: 2511 Wood lawn & garden furniture; garden furniture: wood; porch furniture & swings: wood
HQ: W. Atlee Burpee Company
300 Park Ave
Warminster PA 18974
215 674-4900

(G-19110)
BOSTOCK COMPANY INC (PA)
Also Called: Snapcab
175 Titus Ave Ste 200 (18976-2467)
PHONE..............................215 343-7040
Glenn Bostock, *President*
Glen Bostock, *President*
Tom Bostock, *Project Mgr*
Cole Giordano, *Project Mgr*
Vince Luppino, *Research*
EMP: 23
SQ FT: 10,000
SALES (est): 5.3MM **Privately Held**
WEB: www.snapcabs.com
SIC: 5712 2517 1796 Customized furniture & cabinets; home entertainment unit cabinets, wood; elevator installation & conversion

(G-19111)
COMPRESSION COMPONENTS SVC LLC
364 Valley Rd Ste 100 (18976-2510)
PHONE..............................267 387-2000
Kim Berish, *Purchasing*
Dan Mallee, *Info Tech Mgr*
Fran Mallee,
▲ EMP: 14
SQ FT: 5,000
SALES: 4MM **Privately Held**
SIC: 3499 Tablets, bronze or other metal

(G-19112)
COUNTY LINE FENCE CO
2051 County Line Rd (18976-2416)
PHONE..............................215 343-5085
Daniel I Defebo, *President*
Chris Defebo, *General Mgr*
EMP: 15
SQ FT: 12,000
SALES (est): 2.2MM **Privately Held**
WEB: www.countylinefence.com
SIC: 1799 5039 3315 Fence construction; wire fence, gates & accessories; fencing made in wiredrawing plants

(G-19113)
COUPLER ENTERPRISES INC
Also Called: Innovative Pharmacy Services
125 Titus Ave Ste 200 (18976-2424)
PHONE..............................267 487-8982
Wayne Shafer, *President*
Jean Shafer, *Treasurer*

EMP: 6
SQ FT: 11,500
SALES (est): 723.2K **Privately Held**
SIC: 3081 Plastic film & sheet

(G-19114)
DIGITAL DIRECT TM INC
2445 Greensward N (18976-2061)
PHONE..............................215 491-1725
Manny Olivo, *President*
Elizabeth Greer, *Corp Secy*
EMP: 5
SALES (est): 300K **Privately Held**
SIC: 2759 Commercial printing

(G-19115)
DIRENZO INC
1426 Marielle Dr (18976-1385)
P.O. Box 518 (18976-0518)
PHONE..............................215 740-6166
Al Direnzo Jr, *President*
EMP: 5
SALES (est): 27.3K **Privately Held**
WEB: www.direnzo.com
SIC: 2084 Wines

(G-19116)
EDWARDS CO
2124 Wodock Ave (18976-2317)
PHONE..............................215 343-2133
Pam Edwards, *Owner*
EMP: 8 EST: 2000
SALES: 560K **Privately Held**
SIC: 3499 Metal household articles

(G-19117)
FCG INC
Also Called: Flexible Circuits
222 Valley Rd (18976-2520)
PHONE..............................215 343-4617
George Stollsteimer, *Ch of Bd*
David Stollsteimer, *President*
Jay Sergo, *Mfg Mgr*
Paul McDowell, *QC Mgr*
Roger Hartley, *Engineer*
▲ EMP: 155 EST: 1963
SQ FT: 52,000
SALES (est): 39.8MM **Privately Held**
WEB: www.flexiblecircuits.net
SIC: 3679 3861 Electronic circuits; graphic arts plates, sensitized

(G-19118)
GOTCHA COVERED PRETZELS LLC
2411 Continental Dr (18976-1743)
PHONE..............................215 253-3176
Patricia K Frendak, *Mng Member*
EMP: 4
SALES (est): 203.9K **Privately Held**
SIC: 2052 Pretzels

(G-19119)
GROSS MACHINE INC
1760 Costner Dr Ste 1 (18976-2571)
PHONE..............................215 491-7077
R Bruce Gross Sr, *Ch of Bd*
Bruce R Gross Jr, *President*
Brian Fellin, *Plant Mgr*
EMP: 15
SQ FT: 17,500
SALES (est): 2.5MM **Privately Held**
WEB: www.grossmachine.com
SIC: 3599 Machine shop, jobbing & repair

(G-19120)
HERITAGE SCREEN PRINTING INC (PA)
3625 Daviscilla 2 (18976)
PHONE..............................215 672-2382
Glenn McKee, *President*
EMP: 4
SALES (est): 363K **Privately Held**
SIC: 2759 Screen printing

(G-19121)
HPT PHARMA LLC
364 Valley Rd Unit 100 (18976-2521)
PHONE..............................215 792-0020
James Hasson, *Mng Member*
EMP: 15
SALES (est): 423.6K **Privately Held**
SIC: 3469 Machine parts, stamped or pressed metal

(G-19122)
JACOB GERGER & SONS INC
2546 Park Rd (18976-1706)
PHONE..............................215 491-4659
Jacob Gerger, *President*
EMP: 3 EST: 1903
SALES (est): 144.4K **Privately Held**
SIC: 3999 Manufacturing industries

(G-19123)
LUCIFER FURNACES INC
2048 Bunnell Rd (18976-2497)
PHONE..............................215 343-0411
Larry Jones, *President*
Salvatore Stea, *Vice Pres*
Jack Auerbach, *Engineer*
Robert Hauser, *Sales Mgr*
Dave Lachman, *Executive*
EMP: 16 EST: 1953
SQ FT: 15,000
SALES (est): 4.6MM **Privately Held**
WEB: www.luciferfurnaces.com
SIC: 3567 Heating units & devices, industrial: electric

(G-19124)
MARY HAIL RUBBER CO INC
803 Monaco Dr (18976-2223)
P.O. Box 236, Warminster (18974-0524)
PHONE..............................215 343-1955
Patricia Jones, *President*
William D Jones, *President*
EMP: 10
SQ FT: 1,200
SALES: 1.7MM **Privately Held**
WEB: www.hailmaryrubber.com
SIC: 3069 5169 Hard rubber products; gaskets; chemicals & allied products; sealants

(G-19125)
MEECO INC
250 Titus Ave (18976-2426)
PHONE..............................215 343-6600
Jerry Riddle, *Ch of Bd*
Lisa Bergson-Riddle, *President*
Borys Mychajliw, *Principal*
EMP: 20 EST: 1948
SQ FT: 20,000
SALES (est): 7.1MM **Privately Held**
WEB: www.meeco.com
SIC: 3823 Moisture meters, industrial process type

(G-19126)
METAL CRAFTERS INC
1409 Easton Rd Ste 1 (18976-2850)
PHONE..............................215 491-9925
Joe Ermigotti, *President*
EMP: 3
SQ FT: 1,500
SALES (est): 100K **Privately Held**
SIC: 3915 Gems, real & imitation: preparation for settings; jewel bearings, synthetic

(G-19127)
PETRILLOS APPLIANCE
1111 Easton Rd Ste 6 (18976-1845)
PHONE..............................215 491-9400
James Petrillo, *Manager*
EMP: 6
SALES (est): 476.4K
SALES (corp-wide): 1.1MM **Privately Held**
SIC: 3639 5064 Major kitchen appliances, except refrigerators & stoves; electrical appliances, television & radio
PA: Petrillo's Appliance
222 Bustleton Pike
Feasterville Trevose PA 19053
215 355-9400

(G-19128)
POLYSCIENCES INC (PA)
400 Valley Rd (18976-2590)
PHONE..............................215 343-6484
Michael H Ott, *President*
Ryan Ott, *President*
Andrew Ott, *Vice Pres*
▲ EMP: 209 EST: 1961
SQ FT: 50,000
SALES (est): 71.2MM **Privately Held**
WEB: www.polysciences.com
SIC: 2899 Chemical preparations

(G-19129)
POLYSCIENCES INC
1981 County Line Rd (18976-2511)
PHONE..............................215 520-9358
EMP: 6
SQ FT: 30,000
SALES (est): 495.2K
SALES (corp-wide): 71.2MM **Privately Held**
SIC: 2899 Chemical preparations
PA: Polysciences, Inc.
400 Valley Rd
Warrington PA 18976
215 343-6484

(G-19130)
REMCAL PRODUCTS CORPORATION
2068 Bunnell Rd (18976-2415)
PHONE..............................215 343-5500
Denise Pancari, *President*
Dave Doebler, *Prdtn Mgr*
Paul Wheeler, *Design Engr*
▲ EMP: 12
SQ FT: 5,000
SALES (est): 2.8MM **Privately Held**
WEB: www.remcal.com
SIC: 3578 3812 Calculating & accounting equipment; bank & turn indicators & components

(G-19131)
RESDEL CORPORATION
Also Called: Brebling Plastics
150 Franklin Dr (18976-2431)
PHONE..............................215 343-2400
Roselynn Calio, *Branch Mgr*
EMP: 5
SALES (corp-wide): 2.3MM **Privately Held**
SIC: 3082 Unsupported plastics profile shapes
PA: Resdel Corporation
Industrial Park
Rio Grande NJ 08242
609 886-1111

(G-19132)
ROCAL CORPORATION
Also Called: Rebling Plastics
150 Franklin Dr (18976-2431)
PHONE..............................215 343-2400
Nathaniel Bower, *President*
Nick Calio, *Principal*
John Gallagher, *Principal*
Mark Burg, *Business Mgr*
Roselynn Calio, *Corp Secy*
▲ EMP: 26 EST: 1962
SQ FT: 23,000
SALES (est): 5.9MM **Privately Held**
WEB: www.rebling.com
SIC: 3089 3678 Thermoformed finished plastic products; injection molding of plastics; electronic connectors

(G-19133)
SENCILLO SYSTEMS INC
966 Argyle Rd (18976-1604)
PHONE..............................610 340-2848
Tom Halley, *President*
EMP: 3
SQ FT: 3,000
SALES: 2MM **Privately Held**
SIC: 3594 Fluid power pumps

(G-19134)
SKY FUEL INC
318 Evening Walk Ln (18976-1663)
PHONE..............................215 343-3825
Jagtar Singh, *Principal*
EMP: 3
SALES (est): 238.6K **Privately Held**
SIC: 2869 Fuels

(G-19135)
TIGER OPTICS LLC
250 Titus Ave (18976-2426)
PHONE..............................215 343-6600
Lisa Bergson, *CEO*
Stacy Fowler, *Officer*
EMP: 15
SQ FT: 16,000
SALES (est): 3.6MM **Privately Held**
WEB: www.tigeroptics.com
SIC: 3826 Analytical instruments

(G-19136)
WARREN MACHINE CO INC
429 Easton Rd Ste A (18976-2447)
PHONE....................................215 491-5500
Henry Meil, *President*
Joan Meil, *Corp Secy*
EMP: 10
SQ FT: 8,500
SALES (est): 983.4K **Privately Held**
SIC: 3812 Navigational systems & instruments

(G-19137)
WARREN MACHINE TECHNOLOGY INC
429 Easton Rd Ste A (18976-2447)
PHONE....................................215 491-5500
Ed Palombo, *President*
Karen Palombo, *Corp Secy*
EMP: 5
SQ FT: 8,500
SALES (est): 1MM **Privately Held**
WEB: www.warren-machine.com
SIC: 3599 Machine shop, jobbing & repair

(G-19138)
WARRINGTON EQUIPMENT MFG CO
2051 Bunnell Rd (18976-2414)
PHONE....................................215 343-1714
Bill McDonald, *President*
EMP: 20
SQ FT: 80,000
SALES (est): 3.9MM
SALES (corp-wide): 3.6B **Publicly Held**
WEB: www.uhaul.com
SIC: 3713 3792 Truck bodies (motor vehicles); travel trailer chassis
HQ: U-Haul International, Inc.
2727 N Central Ave
Phoenix AZ 85004
602 263-6011

(G-19139)
WARRINGTON PASTRY SHOP
1380 Easton Rd Ste 3 (18976-1818)
PHONE....................................215 343-1946
Henry Stoughton, *Partner*
Fred Piechocki, *Partner*
EMP: 10
SQ FT: 1,000
SALES (est): 942.6K **Privately Held**
SIC: 2051 5461 Bakery: wholesale or wholesale/retail combined; cakes, bakery: except frozen; pies, bakery: except frozen; pastries, e.g. danish: except frozen; bread; cakes

(G-19140)
WINDTREE THERAPEUTICS INC (PA)
2600 Kelly Rd Ste 100 (18976-3652)
PHONE....................................215 488-9300
John R Leone, *Ch of Bd*
Craig Fraser, *President*
Kathryn A Cole, *Senior VP*
Steven G Simonson, *Senior VP*
Mary B Templeton, *Senior VP*
EMP: 58
SQ FT: 39,594
SALES: 1.4MM **Publicly Held**
WEB: www.discoverylabs.com
SIC: 2834 2836 Drugs acting on the respiratory system; biological products, except diagnostic

(G-19141)
WYSS-GALLIFENT CORPORATION
2123 Longview Rd (18976-1524)
PHONE....................................215 343-3974
EMP: 3
SALES: 480K **Privately Held**
SIC: 7699 3484 Repair Services Mfg Small Arms

Warriors Mark
Huntingdon County

(G-19142)
HELENA AGRI-ENTERPRISES LLC
2413 Pennington Rd (16877)
P.O. Box 131 (16877-0131)
PHONE....................................814 632-5177
EMP: 9
SALES (corp-wide): 70.7B **Privately Held**
SIC: 5191 2819 Chemicals, agricultural; seeds & bulbs; chemicals, high purity: refined from technical grade
HQ: Helena Agri-Enterprises, Llc
255 Schilling Blvd # 300
Collierville TN 38017
901 761-0050

Washington
Washington County

(G-19143)
A M E R INC
Also Called: Rush Archtectural Met Erectors
5 Commercial Dr (15301-1374)
PHONE....................................724 229-8020
Abbie Rush, *President*
Bryce Rush, *Project Mgr*
Matt Kress, *Manager*
EMP: 20
SALES (est): 5.1MM **Privately Held**
SIC: 3444 Roof deck, sheet metal

(G-19144)
ACRELORMITTAL US LLC
Also Called: Washington Steel Products
Woodland & Griffith Ave (15301)
PHONE....................................724 222-7769
Joe Kusic, *Principal*
EMP: 100
SALES (corp-wide): 9.1B **Privately Held**
SIC: 3312 Plate, steel
HQ: Arcelormittal Usa Llc
1 S Dearborn St Ste 1800
Chicago IL 60603
312 346-0300

(G-19145)
ADVANCED COIL INDUSTRIES
175 Plumpton Ave (15301-1948)
PHONE....................................724 225-1885
Robert Rohr, *President*
Robert Garrett, *Manager*
EMP: 10
SALES (est): 1.6MM **Privately Held**
SIC: 3083 Laminated plastics plate & sheet

(G-19146)
AMERICAN DATA LINK INC
124 W Maiden St (15301-4652)
PHONE....................................724 503-4290
Mindi S Harden, *President*
Michael J Harden, *Vice Pres*
Lynn Garner, *Director*
▲ EMP: 7
SQ FT: 80,000
SALES (est): 1.7MM **Privately Held**
SIC: 3357 5063 5251 Nonferrous wiredrawing & insulating; electrical apparatus & equipment; hardware

(G-19147)
AMERICAN FOODS INC
230 Oak Hill Dr (15301-3053)
PHONE....................................724 223-0820
Calvin Henry, *President*
Brian Henry, *Treasurer*
Janis Krawchyk, *Admin Sec*
EMP: 15
SALES (est): 1.9MM **Privately Held**
SIC: 2011 Meat packing plants

(G-19148)
AMERICAN PIPE AND SUPPLY LLC
124 W Maiden St (15301-4652)
PHONE....................................724 228-6360
Gary Garber, *Principal*
EMP: 6

SALES (est): 1.1MM **Privately Held**
SIC: 3494 3561 Valves & pipe fittings; pumps & pumping equipment

(G-19149)
AMERICAN WELL SERVICE LLC
1478 Jefferson Ave (15301-2118)
PHONE....................................724 206-9372
Amy Savage, *CEO*
EMP: 100
SALES (est): 7.7MM
SALES (corp-wide): 62.7MM **Privately Held**
SIC: 1389 Oil field services
HQ: Old Epp, Inc.
360 Epic Circle Dr
Fairmont WV 26554
304 534-3600

(G-19150)
ANGELOS INC
2109 N Franklin Dr (15301-5893)
PHONE....................................724 350-8715
Michael Passalacqua, *President*
Silvio M Passalacqua, *Shareholder*
EMP: 35
SQ FT: 8,450
SALES (est): 1.4MM **Privately Held**
WEB: www.angelosrestaurant.com
SIC: 5812 5813 2035 Italian restaurant; cocktail lounge; dressings, salad: raw & cooked (except dry mixes)

(G-19151)
AUDIA INTERNATIONAL INC (HQ)
450 Racetrack Rd (15301-8935)
P.O. Box 236 (15301-0236)
PHONE....................................724 228-1260
Robert Andy, *CEO*
William Stough, *CFO*
EMP: 19
SALES (est): 290.9MM **Privately Held**
SIC: 2821 Polypropylene resins; polyethylene resins
PA: Audia Group, Llc
450 Racetrack Rd
Washington PA 15301
724 228-1260

(G-19152)
BELDEN INC
2001 N Main St (15301-6155)
PHONE....................................724 228-7373
Carl M Bruckner, *Principal*
Russell Griffith, *Chief Engr*
Kurt Coffield, *Engineer*
Ed Koot, *Engineer*
Pat Glose, *Maintence Staff*
EMP: 80
SALES (corp-wide): 2.5B **Publicly Held**
SIC: 3357 Nonferrous wiredrawing & insulating
PA: Belden Inc.
1 N Brentwood Blvd Fl 15
Saint Louis MO 63105
314 854-8000

(G-19153)
BELDEN INC
West Penn Wire
2833 W Chestnut St (15301-2543)
P.O. Box 762 (15301-0762)
PHONE....................................724 222-7060
Dave Harden, *President*
Andy Oswald, *VP Sales*
Jeremy Lucovich, *Sales Mgr*
Sandra Davis, *Sales Staff*
Ron Leone, *Sales Staff*
EMP: 181
SALES (corp-wide): 2.5B **Publicly Held**
WEB: www.cdtc.com
SIC: 3357 3315 2851 Nonferrous wiredrawing & insulating; steel wire & related products; paints & allied products
PA: Belden Inc.
1 N Brentwood Blvd Fl 15
Saint Louis MO 63105
314 854-8000

(G-19154)
BENCHMARK ORTHOT & PROSTH INC (DH)
Also Called: Novacare Prosthetics Orthotics
351 W Beau St Ste A (15301-4663)
PHONE....................................724 825-4200

EMP: 2
SALES (est): 1.3MM **Privately Held**
SIC: 3842 Orthopedic appliances

(G-19155)
CDK PERFORATING LLC
125 Museum Rd (15301-6135)
PHONE....................................724 222-8900
Adam Malooney, *Regional Mgr*
EMP: 6
SALES (corp-wide): 827.1MM **Publicly Held**
SIC: 1389 Oil field services
HQ: Cdk Perforating, Llc
6500 West Fwy Ste 600
Fort Worth TX 76116
817 945-1051

(G-19156)
CITY OF WASHINGTON
Also Called: South Franklin Township Garage
25 Old Scales Rd (15301)
PHONE....................................724 225-4883
Demsay Moore, *Foreman/Supr*
EMP: 4 **Privately Held**
SIC: 3531 Road construction & maintenance machinery
PA: City Of Washington
55 W Maiden St
Washington PA 15301
724 223-4200

(G-19157)
CONFLOW INC
270 Meadowlands Blvd (15301-8903)
PHONE....................................724 746-0200
Michael Goddard, *President*
Karen McKinney, *Treasurer*
▲ EMP: 12
SQ FT: 9,500
SALES (est): 4.1MM
SALES (corp-wide): 14.3B **Publicly Held**
WEB: www.conflow.com
SIC: 5082 3823 Mining machinery & equipment, except petroleum; pressure measurement instruments, industrial
HQ: President Engineering Group Ltd
Unit 5, President Building
Sheffield S4 7U
114 224-0000

(G-19158)
CREATIVE PRINTING & GRAPHICS
1250 Washington Rd (15301-9641)
PHONE....................................724 222-8304
Marybelle Beachy, *President*
Harold Beachy, *Vice Pres*
EMP: 7
SQ FT: 7,800
SALES: 500K **Privately Held**
SIC: 2752 Commercial printing, offset

(G-19159)
CRILE CONSOLIDATED INDS INC
1086 Jolly School Rd (15301-8589)
PHONE....................................724 228-0880
Brian Crile, *President*
Christy L Crile, *Corp Secy*
Daniel W Crile, *Vice Pres*
EMP: 18
SQ FT: 12,000
SALES (est): 3.7MM **Privately Held**
SIC: 7699 3471 Hydraulic equipment repair; plating of metals or formed products

(G-19160)
CURTIS PHARMACEUTICAL SERVICE
36 Old Hickory Ridge Rd (15301-8613)
PHONE....................................724 223-1114
EMP: 15
SALES (est): 1.2MM **Privately Held**
SIC: 2834 Mfg Pharmaceutical Preparations

(G-19161)
CUSTOM TOOL & GRINDING INC
2131 W Chestnut St (15301-2643)
PHONE....................................724 223-1555
Kenneth F Stasiowski, *President*
Janis E Stasiowski, *Treasurer*
Pamela Sanders, *Admin Sec*

▲ = Import ▼ =Export
◆ =Import/Export

EMP: 16
SQ FT: 4,000
SALES (est): 1.7MM **Privately Held**
WEB: www.customtoolandgrinding.com
SIC: 3545 Machine tool accessories

(G-19162)
DAVAN MANUFACTURING INC
500 Crile Rd (15301-6116)
PHONE................................724 228-0115
Mark Van Istendael, *President*
Andy Blum, *Supervisor*
EMP: 15
SQ FT: 17,500
SALES (est): 2.4MM **Privately Held**
SIC: 3599 Machine shop, jobbing & repair

(G-19163)
DIAMOND FABRICATIONS INC (PA)
30 Stewart Ct (15301-8218)
PHONE................................724 228-8422
Nancy Conley, *President*
Thomas Conley, *Vice Pres*
EMP: 2
SALES: 1MM **Privately Held**
SIC: 3441 Fabricated structural metal

(G-19164)
DIVERSIFIED AIR SYSTEMS INC
269 Meadowlands Blvd (15301-8902)
PHONE................................724 873-0884
George Mega, *Manager*
EMP: 7
SALES (corp-wide): 13.5MM **Privately Held**
WEB: www.diversifiedair.com
SIC: 3563 Air & gas compressors including vacuum pumps
PA: Diversified Air Systems, Inc.
4760 Van Epps Rd
Brooklyn Heights OH 44131
216 741-1700

(G-19165)
DURITZAS ENTERPRISES INC (PA)
Also Called: Washington Shop N Save
125 W Beau St (15301-4401)
PHONE................................724 223-5494
Robert Duritza Sr, *President*
Elizabeth Duritza, *Corp Secy*
EMP: 135 EST: 1972
SALES (est): 31.2MM **Privately Held**
SIC: 5411 5992 2051 Supermarkets; florists; bread, cake & related products

(G-19166)
DYNAMIC CREATIONS SCREEN PRTG
600 W Chestnut St (15301-4622)
PHONE................................724 229-1157
Terri Bonazza, *Owner*
EMP: 3
SALES (est): 400.6K **Privately Held**
SIC: 2759 Screen printing

(G-19167)
EATON ELECTRIC HOLDINGS LLC
2800 N Main St (15301-6100)
PHONE................................724 228-7333
Olive Werace, *Branch Mgr*
EMP: 6 **Privately Held**
WEB: www.cooperus.com
SIC: 3646 Commercial indusl & institutional electric lighting fixtures
HQ: Eaton Electric Holdings Llc
1000 Eaton Blvd
Cleveland OH 44122
440 523-5000

(G-19168)
EMBROIDERY CONCEPTS
231 S College St (15301-5143)
PHONE................................724 225-3644
Kevin Booth, *Owner*
EMP: 5
SQ FT: 1,200
SALES (est): 80K **Privately Held**
WEB: www.1clickshirts.com
SIC: 2395 2759 Embroidery & art needlework; screen printing

(G-19169)
ENERSYS
80 Stewart Ave (15301-3751)
PHONE................................724 223-4255
Charlie Riggs, *Owner*
EMP: 88
SALES (corp-wide): 2.5B **Publicly Held**
SIC: 3691 Lead acid batteries (storage batteries)
PA: Enersys
2366 Bernville Rd
Reading PA 19605
610 208-1991

(G-19170)
ENSINGER INC
365 Meadowlands Blvd (15301-8900)
PHONE................................724 746-6050
W D Phillips, *President*
Lawrence C Resavage, *Vice Pres*
Robert Racchini, *Treasurer*
Hugh W Nevin Jr, *Admin Sec*
EMP: 3 EST: 1985
SALES (est): 3.6MM
SALES (corp-wide): 434.6MM **Privately Held**
SIC: 3089 Stock shapes, plastic; extruded finished plastic products
HQ: Ensinger Industries, Inc.
365 Meadowlands Blvd
Washington PA 15301
724 746-6050

(G-19171)
ENSINGER INDUSTRIES INC (DH)
365 Meadowlands Blvd (15301-8904)
PHONE................................724 746-6050
Warren J Phillips, *President*
Fred Nass, *Partner*
Roland Reber, *Managing Dir*
John Rizno, *Safety Mgr*
Stefan Schimmel, *Engineer*
▲ EMP: 90
SQ FT: 22,000
SALES (est): 164.5MM
SALES (corp-wide): 434.6MM **Privately Held**
SIC: 3089 Injection molding of plastics
HQ: Ensinger Gmbh
Rudolf-Diesel-Str. 8
Nufringen 71154
703 281-90

(G-19172)
FALCON PLASTICS INC
250 W Wylie Ave (15301-2287)
PHONE................................724 222-2620
Robert Delach, *President*
Angelo F Falconi, *Chairman*
Edward Morascyzk, *Corp Secy*
Austin Sechser, *Design Engr*
Sarah Perry, *Human Res Dir*
EMP: 95
SQ FT: 400,000
SALES (est): 13MM **Privately Held**
WEB: www.falconplastics.com
SIC: 3089 Blow molded finished plastic products; injection molding of plastics

(G-19173)
FALOSK CONTRACT MACHINE INC
169 Vaneal Rd (15301-9099)
PHONE................................724 228-0567
James J Falosk Jr, *President*
Matthew D Falosk, *Manager*
EMP: 3
SALES (est): 325K **Privately Held**
SIC: 3599 Machine shop, jobbing & repair

(G-19174)
FAMILY FARM CREAMERY
786 Western Ave (15301-8656)
PHONE................................412 418-2596
Nathan Holmes, *Owner*
EMP: 4
SALES (est): 159.2K **Privately Held**
SIC: 2026 Fluid milk

(G-19175)
FERRO COLOR & GLASS CORP (HQ)
Also Called: Drakenfeld Products
251 W Wylie Ave (15301-2276)
PHONE................................724 223-5900
◆ EMP: 300
SQ FT: 208,000
SALES (est): 70.7MM
SALES (corp-wide): 1.6B **Publicly Held**
SIC: 3231 Enameled glass
PA: Ferro Corporation
6060 Parkland Blvd # 250
Mayfield Heights OH 44124
216 875-5600

(G-19176)
FERRO CORPORATION
251 W Wylie Ave (15301-2276)
P.O. Box 519 (15301-0519)
PHONE................................724 207-2152
David Klimas, *Manager*
EMP: 200
SALES (corp-wide): 1.6B **Publicly Held**
WEB: www.ferro.com
SIC: 2816 Color pigments
PA: Ferro Corporation
6060 Parkland Blvd # 250
Mayfield Heights OH 44124
216 875-5600

(G-19177)
FRAZIER-SIMPLEX MACHINE CO
1720 N Main St (15301-6142)
PHONE................................724 222-5700
John Frazier, *President*
Nicole Frazier, *Vice Pres*
EMP: 25
SQ FT: 28,000
SALES (est): 4MM **Privately Held**
SIC: 3599 3441 7692 3567 Machine shop, jobbing & repair; fabricated structural metal; welding repair; industrial furnaces & ovens; metalworking machinery; machine tool accessories

(G-19178)
GAS N GO WASHINGTON
98 Murtland Ave (15301-3378)
PHONE................................724 228-2850
EMP: 4 EST: 2007
SALES (est): 416.9K **Privately Held**
SIC: 2869 Fuels

(G-19179)
GREENBANK ENERGY SOLUTIONS INC
Also Called: G E S I
185 Plumpton Ave (15301-1948)
PHONE................................724 229-4454
Brian Gallagher, *Chairman*
Howard Gregg, *Vice Pres*
Donald Halulko, *Vice Pres*
Steven McCaffery, *Vice Pres*
Andrew Lorenzi, *Officer*
EMP: 6
SALES (est): 954.9K
SALES (corp-wide): 14.1MM **Privately Held**
WEB: www.cbpengineering.com
SIC: 3829 Coal testing apparatus
PA: The Greenbank Group Inc
185 Plumpton Ave
Washington PA 15301
724 229-1180

(G-19180)
GREENBANK GROUP INC (PA)
185 Plumpton Ave (15301-1948)
PHONE................................724 229-1180
Brian Gallagher, *CEO*
Andrew Lorenzi, *Corp Secy*
Howard Gregg, *Vice Pres*
Donald Halulko, *Vice Pres*
Steven McCaffrey, *Vice Pres*
EMP: 7
SQ FT: 60,000
SALES (est): 14.1MM **Privately Held**
SIC: 3498 3829 6719 Coils, pipe: fabricated from purchased pipe; coal testing apparatus; public utility holding companies

(G-19181)
GREENETECH MFG CO INC
470 Crile Rd (15301-6114)
PHONE................................724 228-2400
Dan Levine, *President*
Tuffy Bennett, *General Mgr*
Larry A Levine, *Vice Pres*
▲ EMP: 28
SQ FT: 24,000
SALES: 5MM **Privately Held**
WEB: www.greenetechmfg.com
SIC: 3443 3599 Fabricated plate work (boiler shop); machine & other job shop work

(G-19182)
GRIMM MACHINE & MODEL
95 Statement St (15301-3144)
PHONE................................724 228-2133
Lawrence S Grimm, *Owner*
Lawerence Grimm, *Owner*
EMP: 4
SQ FT: 5,500
SALES: 150K **Privately Held**
SIC: 3599 7692 Machine shop, jobbing & repair; welding repair

(G-19183)
H & R NEON SERVICE INC
Also Called: H&R Signs
1942 Jefferson Ave (15301-1507)
PHONE................................724 222-6115
Robert J Masisak, *President*
EMP: 4
SQ FT: 2,900
SALES (est): 290K **Privately Held**
SIC: 3993 7629 Signs & advertising specialties; electrical repair shops

(G-19184)
HADDAD AND BROOKS INC (PA)
30 E Beau St Ste 700 (15301-4705)
PHONE................................724 228-8811
Jerry J Hopkins, *President*
James Cropp, *Vice Pres*
EMP: 3
SALES (est): 1MM **Privately Held**
SIC: 1382 Oil & gas exploration services

(G-19185)
INTEGRATED ENVMTL TECH INC
124 Edgewood Dr (15301-6466)
PHONE................................412 298-5845
Dean Heffernan, *President*
EMP: 5
SALES: 500K **Privately Held**
SIC: 3561 Pumps & pumping equipment

(G-19186)
INTEGRATED POWER SERVICES LLC
Also Called: Rockwell Automation
320 Reliance Dr (15301-6140)
PHONE................................724 225-2900
Dolin Gallgher, *Manager*
EMP: 18
SALES (corp-wide): 924.8MM **Privately Held**
WEB: www.integratedps.com
SIC: 7629 3599 7692 7699 Electrical repair shops; machine shop, jobbing & repair; welding repair; balancing service; motors, electric; motors & generators
HQ: Integrated Power Services Llc
3 Independence Pt Ste 100
Greenville SC 29615

(G-19187)
J M SMUCKER COMPANY
Also Called: JM Smuckers Foodservice
946 Manifold Rd (15301-9610)
PHONE................................724 228-6633
EMP: 10
SALES (corp-wide): 7.3B **Publicly Held**
SIC: 2033 Canned fruits & specialties
PA: The J M Smucker Company
1 Strawberry Ln
Orrville OH 44667
330 682-3000

(G-19188)
JESSOP STEEL LLC
500 Green St (15301-2398)
PHONE................................724 222-4000
Terry Dunlap, *Principal*

JD Walton, *Principal*
David R Cate, *Vice Pres*
EMP: 39 EST: 1901
SQ FT: 600,000
SALES (est): 374.8K **Publicly Held**
WEB: www.alleghenyludlum.com
SIC: 3312 Stainless steel
HQ: Aii Acquisition, Llc
　　1000 Six Ppg Pl
　　Pittsburgh PA 15222
　　412 394-2800

(G-19189)
JO JAN SPORTSEQUIP CO INC
W Pointe Dr Bldg 3 (15301)
PHONE......................724 225-5582
Robert Coyle, *President*
Joanne Coyle, *Treasurer*
EMP: 8
SQ FT: 7,000
SALES: 500K **Privately Held**
SIC: 3949 Archery equipment, general

(G-19190)
JOB-FAB INC
295 Meadow Ave (15301-4229)
P.O. Box 174 (15301-0174)
PHONE......................724 225-8225
James F O'Brien Jr, *President*
EMP: 8
SQ FT: 30,000
SALES (est): 1.5MM **Privately Held**
SIC: 3441 Building components, structural
steel

(G-19191)
KIMENSKI BURIAL VAULTS
1703 E Maiden St (15301-3112)
PHONE......................724 223-0364
Lisa Kimenski, *Owner*
David Kimenski, *Co-Owner*
EMP: 6
SALES (est): 369.2K **Privately Held**
SIC: 3272 Burial vaults, concrete or pre-
cast terrazzo

(G-19192)
KIMZEY CASING SERVICE LLC
1000 Sheffield St (15301-2362)
PHONE......................724 225-0529
EMP: 5
SALES (corp-wide): 47.9MM **Privately
Held**
SIC: 1389 Oil/Gas Field Services
PA: Kimzey Casing Service, Llc
　　3400 Quebec St Ste 3200
　　Denver CO 80207
　　303 248-3425

(G-19193)
**KNOWLEDGE MGT & TECH
CORP**
269 N Main St (15301-4361)
PHONE......................412 503-3657
Jason McCloy, *President*
EMP: 6
SALES: 140K **Privately Held**
SIC: 7372 Business oriented computer
software

(G-19194)
KRISPY KREME DOUGHNUTS
14 Trinity Point Dr (15301-2974)
PHONE......................724 228-1800
Rob Joseph, *Principal*
EMP: 8 EST: 2008
SALES (est): 221.6K **Privately Held**
SIC: 5461 2051 Doughnuts; doughnuts,
except frozen

(G-19195)
LAGONDA MACHINE LLC
2410 Park Ave (15301-8136)
PHONE......................724 222-2710
Donald L Greene, *President*
Cecilia J Greene, *Corp Secy*
EMP: 22 EST: 1975
SQ FT: 10,000
SALES (est): 5MM **Privately Held**
WEB: www.lagondamachine.com
SIC: 3599 Machine shop, jobbing & repair

(G-19196)
M & A COATINGS LLC
1508 Amity Ridge Rd (15301-6467)
PHONE......................724 267-2868

Matthew Loeffert,
EMP: 10 **EST:** 2015
SALES: 925K **Privately Held**
SIC: 3471 1721 Sand blasting of metal
parts; industrial painting

(G-19197)
M W GARY AND ASSOCIATES
470 Johnson Rd Ste 220 (15301-8944)
PHONE......................724 206-0071
Margaret Joyce, *Principal*
EMP: 3
SALES (est): 140K **Privately Held**
SIC: 1321 Natural gas liquids

(G-19198)
**MARKWEST HYDROCARBON
INC**
1084 Western Ave (15301)
PHONE......................724 514-4398
Noel Ryan, *Branch Mgr*
EMP: 20
SALES (corp-wide): 6.4B **Publicly Held**
SIC: 1321 4924 Fractionating natural gas
liquids; propane (natural) production;
isobutane (natural) production; butane
(natural) production; natural gas distribu-
tion
HQ: Markwest Hydrocarbon, L.L.C.
　　1515 Arapahoe St
　　Denver CO 80202
　　303 290-8700

(G-19199)
**MARKWEST LIBERTY
MIDSTREAM**
800 Western Ave (15301-8655)
PHONE......................724 514-4401
Andrew Schroeder, *President*
EMP: 75
SALES (est): 7.5MM
SALES (corp-wide): 6.4B **Publicly Held**
SIC: 4922 1389 1321 Pipelines, natural
gas; storage, natural gas; gas compress-
ing (natural gas) at the fields; processing
service, gas; fractionating natural gas liq-
uids
HQ: Markwest Energy Partners, L.P.
　　1515 Arapahoe St
　　Denver CO 80202
　　303 925-9200

(G-19200)
**MASS MACHINE &
FABRICATING CO**
595 Meadow Ave (15301-4263)
P.O. Box 453 (15301-0453)
PHONE......................724 225-1125
Daniel Mass, *President*
Dave Belford, *Corp Secy*
John Behun, *Vice Pres*
EMP: 10
SALES (est): 1.9MM **Privately Held**
SIC: 3441 Fabricated structural metal

(G-19201)
**MASTER WOODCRAFT
CORPORATION**
100 Stationvue (15301-6184)
PHONE......................724 225-5530
David Diesel, *President*
Robert J Kmick, *Vice Pres*
Larry Morgan, *VP Opers*
James H Sheehan Jr, *Treasurer*
James Sheehan, *Treasurer*
EMP: 25
SQ FT: 23,500
SALES: 3.5MM **Privately Held**
SIC: 2434 2431 1751 Wood kitchen cabi-
nets; millwork; cabinet & finish carpentry

(G-19202)
MICHELS CORPORATION
Also Called: Michels Pipeline
2155 Park Ave (15301-8160)
PHONE......................724 249-2065
Joe Searl, *Owner*
EMP: 6
SALES (corp-wide): 3.2B **Privately Held**
SIC: 1623 1381 1629 3498 Pipeline con-
struction; telephone & communication line
construction; drilling oil & gas wells; oil re-
finery construction; fabricated pipe & fit-
tings; excavation work

PA: Michels Corporation
　　817 Main St
　　Brownsville WI 53006
　　920 583-3132

(G-19203)
MIKES PACKING COMPANY
1600 Weirich Ave (15301-2471)
PHONE......................724 222-5476
Helen Provenzano, *Owner*
EMP: 10 **EST:** 1960
SQ FT: 3,200
SALES: 150K **Privately Held**
SIC: 5421 0751 2013 2011 Meat mar-
kets, including freezer provisioners;
slaughtering: custom livestock services;
sausages & other prepared meats; meat
packing plants

(G-19204)
MILLCRAFT CORPORATION
95 W Beau St Ste 600 (15301-6827)
PHONE......................724 743-3400
Jack B Piatt, *CEO*
EMP: 6
SALES (est): 604.4K
SALES (corp-wide): 30.7MM **Privately
Held**
WEB: www.millcraftindustries.com
SIC: 3312 6799 Chemicals & other prod-
ucts derived from coking; commodity in-
vestors
PA: Millcraft Industries, Inc.
　　95 W Beau St Ste 600
　　Washington PA 15301
　　724 229-8800

(G-19205)
**MILLCRAFT INDUSTRIES INC
(PA)**
95 W Beau St Ste 600 (15301-6827)
PHONE......................724 229-8800
Jack B Piatt, *Ch of Bd*
Charles D Boehm, *Corp Secy*
Lucas B Piatt, *COO*
Brandon Guy, *Project Mgr*
John Jones, *VP Bus Dvlpt*
EMP: 10 **EST:** 1971
SQ FT: 5,200
SALES (est): 34.1MM **Privately Held**
WEB: www.millcraftindustries.com
SIC: 7699 3312 6799 Industrial equip-
ment services; blast furnace & related
products; real estate investors, except
property operators

(G-19206)
MILLCRAFT SMS SERVICES LLC
750 Manifold Rd (15301-9606)
P.O. Box 587 (15301-0587)
PHONE......................724 222-5000
Michael Gorman, *Project Mgr*
Jack B Piatt, *Mng Member*
▲ **EMP:** 180
SALES (est): 8.1MM
SALES (corp-wide): 34.1MM **Privately
Held**
WEB: www.millcraftindustries.com
SIC: 7699 3312 Industrial equipment serv-
ices; blast furnace & related products
PA: Millcraft Industries, Inc.
　　95 W Beau St Ste 600
　　Washington PA 15301
　　724 229-8800

(G-19207)
**MINGO CREEK CRAFT
DISTILLERS**
68 W Maiden St (15301-6908)
PHONE......................724 503-4014
James H Hough, *Manager*
EMP: 4
SALES (est): 83K **Privately Held**
SIC: 2085 Distilled & blended liquors

(G-19208)
MOUNTS EQUIPMENT CO INC
Berry Rd (15301)
PHONE......................724 225-0460
Richard C Mounts II, *President*
EMP: 3
SQ FT: 1,500

SALES (est): 260K **Privately Held**
SIC: 1711 5075 3443 Warm air heating &
air conditioning contractor; refrigeration
contractor; warm air heating & air conditioning; ducting, metal plate

(G-19209)
**NATIONAL OILWELL VARCO
INC**
850 Wilmington St (15301-5434)
PHONE......................318 243-5910
EMP: 23
SALES (corp-wide): 8.4B **Publicly Held**
SIC: 3533 Oil & gas field machinery
PA: National Oilwell Varco, Inc.
　　7909 Parkwood Circle Dr
　　Houston TX 77036
　　713 346-7500

(G-19210)
**NETWORK PRODUCTS &
SERVICES**
Also Called: N P S
41 Stone Marker Dr (15301-2745)
PHONE......................724 229-0332
Keith Edge, *President*
EMP: 5 **EST:** 1998
SQ FT: 2,500
SALES: 400K **Privately Held**
SIC: 2298 Cable, fiber

(G-19211)
NORPLAS INDUSTRIES INC
292 E Maiden St (15301-4944)
PHONE......................724 705-7483
EMP: 4
SALES (corp-wide): 38.9B **Privately Held**
SIC: 3465 Automotive stampings
HQ: Norplas Industries Inc.
　　7825 Caple Blvd
　　Northwood OH 43619
　　419 662-3317

(G-19212)
**OBSERVER PUBLISHING
COMPANY (PA)**
Also Called: Observer-Reporter
122 S Main St (15301-4904)
PHONE......................724 222-2200
Thomas Northrop, *President*
William B Northrop, *Vice Pres*
EMP: 270 **EST:** 1808
SALES (est): 28.7MM **Privately Held**
WEB: www.observer-reporter.com
SIC: 2711 Newspapers, publishing & print-
ing

(G-19213)
OMCO CAST METALS INC
259 S College St (15301-5153)
PHONE......................724 222-7006
Larry Ross, *President*
EMP: 3
SQ FT: 60,000
SALES (est): 180K **Privately Held**
SIC: 3544 Industrial molds

(G-19214)
**PACIFIC PROCESS SYSTEMS
INC**
1385 Washington Rd # 105 (15301-9674)
PHONE......................724 993-4445
Alan George, *Principal*
EMP: 135 **Privately Held**
SIC: 1389 Oil field services
PA: Pacific Process Systems, Inc.
　　7401 Rosedale Hwy
　　Bakersfield CA 93308

(G-19215)
**PENN PRO MANUFACTURING
INC**
1561 Hillcrest St (15301-1229)
PHONE......................724 222-6450
EMP: 10
SQ FT: 30,000
SALES (est): 133.6K **Privately Held**
SIC: 2621 2299 3999 Mfr Insulation &
Bedding From Recycled Paper & Fiber
Fillers

▲ = Import ▼ =Export
◆ =Import/Export

(G-19216)
PLEIGER PLASTICS COMPANY
498 Crile Rd (15301-6114)
P.O. Box 1271 (15301-7271)
PHONE....................................724 228-2244
Ruth Pleiger-Kraft, *Partner*
Scott Crouse, *Opers Mgr*
Angela Skinner, *Purchasing*
Mary Jo Kennedy, *Controller*
Ron Beiersdorf, *Sales Mgr*
◆ EMP: 55
SQ FT: 16,800
SALES (est): 15.8MM Privately Held
WEB: www.pleiger.com
SIC: 3089 2821 Molding primary plastic;
plastics materials & resins

(G-19217)
PRECISION INDUSTRIES INC (PA)
Also Called: Precision-Marshall Steel Co
99 Berry Rd (15301-2700)
P.O. Box 711 (15301-0711)
PHONE....................................724 222-2100
Jack Milhollan, *President*
R Allen Koch, *Vice Pres*
Denise Slates, *Production*
Anna Maria Defilipp, *Finance*
Rena Moore, *Sales Executive*
▲ EMP: 65 EST: 1964
SQ FT: 80,000
SALES (est): 16.9MM Privately Held
WEB: www.pmsteel.com
SIC: 3316 Bars, steel, cold finished, from
purchased hot-rolled

(G-19218)
PRETZELS PLUS
1500 W Chestnut St # 266 (15301-5884)
PHONE....................................724 228-9785
Gemma Ross, *Owner*
Sharon Crow, *Co-Owner*
EMP: 6
SALES (est): 203.5K Privately Held
SIC: 5461 2052 Pretzels; pretzels

(G-19219)
PRIME PLASTICS INC
100 Detroit Ave (15301-3777)
PHONE....................................724 250-7172
George Retos, *President*
Dr Jacqueline Myers, *President*
Miles McGoff, *Principal*
Rudy Dinardo, *Vice Pres*
Nicholas Retos, *Vice Pres*
EMP: 20
SALES (est): 6.7MM Privately Held
WEB: www.primeplasticsinc.com
SIC: 3089 Injection molding of plastics

(G-19220)
R G JOHNSON COMPANY INC (PA)
25 S College St (15301-4879)
PHONE....................................724 222-6810
James E Leckie, *President*
Norman E McHolme, *Corp Secy*
Thomas G Crooks, *Vice Pres*
Murray Johnson, *Vice Pres*
Amy Carter, *Administration*
▲ EMP: 11
SQ FT: 1,600
SALES (est): 32.8MM Privately Held
WEB: www.rgjohsoninc.com
SIC: 1241 Preparing shafts or tunnels, bi-
tuminous or lignite mining

(G-19221)
R G JOHNSON COMPANY INC
75 Shady Ln (15301-2531)
PHONE....................................724 225-4969
EMP: 83
SALES (corp-wide): 40.5MM Privately
Held
SIC: 1241 Coal mining services
PA: R. G. Johnson Company, Inc.
25 S College St
Washington PA 15301
724 222-6810

(G-19222)
ROSS MOULD LLC (PA)
259 S College St (15301-5153)
PHONE....................................724 222-7006
Mark Ross,

Mary Kay Bails, *Administration*
Joann C Ross,
Laurence F Ross,
◆ EMP: 150
SQ FT: 60,000
SALES (est): 33.8MM Privately Held
SIC: 5032 3544 Tile, clay or other ce-
ramic, excluding refractory; industrial
molds

(G-19223)
ROSS SAND CASTING
259 S College St (15301-5153)
PHONE....................................724 222-7006
Dan REA, *Principal*
▲ EMP: 8
SALES (est): 938.1K Privately Held
SIC: 3321 Gray & ductile iron foundries

(G-19224)
RPM INDUSTRIES LLC
1660 Jefferson Ave (15301-1604)
PHONE....................................724 228-5130
John K Apostolides, *President*
Joshua Morgan, *Engineer*
George Horensky, *Senior Engr*
Mike Carman, *Prgrmr*
EMP: 49
SQ FT: 61,000
SALES (est): 14.3MM Privately Held
WEB: www.prelub.com
SIC: 3714 3625 Motor vehicle engines &
parts; relays & industrial controls

(G-19225)
SHANGRI-LA BEVERAGE LLC
1601 Park Ave (15301-5900)
PHONE....................................724 222-2222
Anthony F Gennaccaro,
EMP: 3
SQ FT: 800
SALES: 100K Privately Held
SIC: 2086 Tea, iced: packaged in cans,
bottles, etc.

(G-19226)
SMG-GLOBAL CIRCUITS INC (PA)
120 Stationvue (15301-6184)
PHONE....................................724 229-3200
Tulsi Sutaria, *President*
Dale Sutaria, *President*
Narsinbhai Ghelani, *Vice Pres*
Sureshbhai Golakiya, *Admin Sec*
▲ EMP: 40
SQ FT: 23,000
SALES: 6MM Privately Held
SIC: 3672 Circuit boards, television & radio
printed

(G-19227)
SPX CORPORATION
100 Commerce Dr 40 (15301-3772)
PHONE....................................724 746-4240
Bill Wilbert, *Branch Mgr*
EMP: 200
SALES (corp-wide): 1.5B Publicly Held
WEB: www.spx.com
SIC: 3443 Cooling towers, metal plate
PA: Spx Corporation
13320a Balntyn Corp Pl
Charlotte NC 28277
980 474-3700

(G-19228)
SSSI INC (PA)
Also Called: Songer Steel Services
2755a Park Ave (15301-8147)
PHONE....................................724 743-5815
Paul Songer, *CEO*
Paul J Songer, *CEO*
Joseph C Meneskie, *President*
Jo Stright, *Exec VP*
John P Songer, *Vice Pres*
EMP: 450
SQ FT: 3,000
SALES (est): 175.9MM Privately Held
WEB: www.songernet.com
SIC: 1611 3312 4925 General contractor;
highway & street construction; blast fur-
naces & steel mills; coke oven gas, pro-
duction & distribution

(G-19229)
STALLION OILFIELD SERVICES LTD
2699 Jefferson Ave (15301-1425)
PHONE....................................724 222-9059
Jeffery Pinkerton, *Branch Mgr*
EMP: 20 Privately Held
SIC: 1389 Oil field services
HQ: Stallion Oilfield Services Ltd.
950 Corbindale Rd Ste 400
Houston TX 77024
713 528-5544

(G-19230)
TAGS PROCESSING
320 Lynn Portal Rd (15301-8777)
PHONE....................................724 345-8279
Mark Tagart, *Owner*
EMP: 3 EST: 1991
SALES (est): 167K Privately Held
SIC: 2011 Meat packing plants

(G-19231)
TARRS CONCRETE & SUPPLIES
Also Called: Tarr's Ready Mix Concrete
45 Arden Rd (15301-8626)
PHONE....................................724 438-4114
John E Tarr Jr, *President*
Kathy Tarr, *Admin Sec*
EMP: 8 EST: 1959
SQ FT: 1,248
SALES (est): 1.7MM Privately Held
WEB: www.johnetarr.com
SIC: 3273 Ready-mixed concrete

(G-19232)
TITAN METAL & MACHINE CO INC
46 E Wheeling St (15301-4804)
PHONE....................................724 747-9528
Daniel Mass, *President*
EMP: 7
SQ FT: 8,000
SALES: 450K Privately Held
SIC: 3547 3532 3444 3494 Bar mills;
steel rolling machinery; mining machinery;
sheet metalwork; valves & pipe fittings;
welding repair

(G-19233)
UNION CITY NON-FERROUS INC
259 S College St (15301-5153)
PHONE....................................937 968-5460
Larry Ross, *President*
◆ EMP: 41 EST: 1946
SQ FT: 45,000
SALES (est): 4.3MM Privately Held
SIC: 3369 Nonferrous foundries

(G-19234)
UNITED INDUSTRIAL GROUP INC
290 Meadowlands Blvd (15301-8903)
PHONE....................................724 746-4700
William R Furdey, *President*
John Turek, *Sales Engr*
Terry Hayduk, *Office Mgr*
Terry Hayduk, *Office Mgr*
Chuck Lowden, *Supervisor*
EMP: 15 EST: 1953
SQ FT: 15,000
SALES (est): 7.6MM Privately Held
WEB: www.united-industrialgroup.com
SIC: 5063 7694 Motors, electric; rebuild-
ing motors, except automotive

(G-19235)
UNITED STATES HARDWARE MFG INC (PA)
79 Stewart Ave (15301-3750)
PHONE....................................724 222-5110
Richard Gubanish, *President*
Betty Gubanish, *Corp Secy*
EMP: 5
SQ FT: 15,000
SALES (est): 5.1MM Privately Held
WEB: www.americanhardwaremfg.com
SIC: 5072 2451 Hardware

(G-19236)
UPPER CASE LIVING
475 Mankey Rd (15301-6447)
PHONE....................................724 229-8190
EMP: 3 EST: 2010

SALES (est): 110K Privately Held
SIC: 3131 Mfg Footwear Cut Stock

(G-19237)
US CORRUGATED INC (PA)
95 W Beau St Ste 430 (15301-6833)
PHONE....................................724 345-2050
Dennis Mehiel, *CEO*
David Doherty, *CFO*
EMP: 24
SALES (est): 111.6MM Privately Held
SIC: 2653 Boxes, corrugated: made from
purchased materials

(G-19238)
WASHINGTON GREENE COUNTY BLIND
566 E Maiden St (15301-3720)
PHONE....................................724 228-0770
M Waychoff, *Exec Dir*
Meagan Waychoff, *Exec Dir*
EMP: 16
SALES: 697K Privately Held
SIC: 3069 Medical & laboratory rubber
sundries & related products

(G-19239)
WASHINGTON PENN MEXICO HOLDING
450 Racetrack Rd (15301-8935)
P.O. Box 236 (15301-0236)
PHONE....................................724 228-1260
EMP: 3 EST: 2016
SALES (est): 93.7K Privately Held
SIC: 3083 Laminated plastics plate & sheet

(G-19240)
WASHINGTON PENN PLASTIC CO INC (DH)
450 Racetrack Rd (15301-8935)
P.O. Box 236 (15301-0236)
PHONE....................................724 228-1260
Paul Cusolito, *President*
Martin Devine, *Opers Mgr*
Mark Ritchie, *Maint Spvr*
Adam Hovanec, *Engineer*
Scott Ward, *Engineer*
◆ EMP: 200 EST: 1965
SQ FT: 195,000
SALES (est): 198.6MM
SALES (corp-wide): 290.9MM Privately
Held
SIC: 3083 3087 Laminated plastics plate
& sheet; custom compound purchased
resins
HQ: Audia International, Inc.
450 Racetrack Rd
Washington PA 15301
724 228-1260

(G-19241)
WASHINGTON PENN PLASTIC CO INC
2080 N Main St (15301-6146)
PHONE....................................724 228-1260
Michael Kanzius, *Engineer*
Bruce Evans, *Marketing Staff*
Rob Andy, *Branch Mgr*
Bob Johnston, *Administration*
EMP: 6
SALES (corp-wide): 290.9MM Privately
Held
SIC: 3087 Custom compound purchased
resins
HQ: Washington Penn Plastic Co., Inc.
450 Racetrack Rd
Washington PA 15301
724 228-1260

(G-19242)
WASHINGTON PENN PLASTIC CO INC
V Bat Plastic Processing Div
1500 Weirich Ave (15301-2462)
P.O. Box 189 (15301-0189)
PHONE....................................724 206-2120
Steven Shoup, *Manager*
EMP: 46
SALES (corp-wide): 290.9MM Privately
Held
SIC: 2821 Plastics materials & resins
HQ: Washington Penn Plastic Co., Inc.
450 Racetrack Rd
Washington PA 15301
724 228-1260

(G-19243)
WASHINGTON ROTATING CONTROL
63 Springfield Ave (15301-5239)
P.O. Box 261 (15301-0261)
PHONE....................724 228-8889
Denise A Johnson, *President*
Joyce Mayernik, *President*
Albert F Calfo, *Vice Pres*
Joyce Johnston, *Treasurer*
EMP: 14
SQ FT: 18,000
SALES (est): 4MM **Privately Held**
WEB: www.washingtonrotating.com
SIC: 3545 5084 Drills (machine tool accessories); industrial machinery & equipment

(G-19244)
WEST POINT ACQUISITION LLC (DH)
Also Called: West Point Products
95 W Beau St Ste 400 (15301-6800)
PHONE....................724 222-2354
Tom Day Jr, *CEO*
William A Ferrari, *Vice Pres*
◆ EMP: 150 EST: 1972
SALES (est): 64.1MM
SALES (corp-wide): 702.5MM **Privately Held**
WEB: www.westpointproducts.com
SIC: 3955 Print cartridges for laser & other computer printers

(G-19245)
WHITMORE MANUFACTURING COMPANY
63 W Point Rd (15301-5453)
PHONE....................724 225-4151
EMP: 5
SALES (corp-wide): 35.1MM **Publicly Held**
SIC: 2992 Lubricating oils & greases
HQ: The Whitmore Manufacturing Company
930 Whitmore Dr
Rockwall TX 75087
972 771-1000

(G-19246)
WHITMORE MANUFACTURING COMPANY
Also Called: Deacon Industries
1 W Point Rd (15301-5453)
PHONE....................724 225-8008
Greg Brockner, *Director*
EMP: 15
SALES (corp-wide): 35.1MM **Publicly Held**
SIC: 2891 2992 Sealants; lubricating oils & greases
HQ: The Whitmore Manufacturing Company
930 Whitmore Dr
Rockwall TX 75087
972 771-1000

(G-19247)
WILSONS OUTDOOR SERVICES LLC
456 Craft Rd (15301)
PHONE....................724 503-4261
EMP: 30
SALES (est): 9MM **Privately Held**
SIC: 3537 Mfg Industrial Trucks/Tractors

(G-19248)
X-MARK/CDT INC
2001 N Main St (15301-6155)
PHONE....................724 228-7373
John S Stroup, *President*
Carl Bruckner, *General Mgr*
Kevin L Bloomfield, *Corp Secy*
Gray G Benoist, *Vice Pres*
Robert J Kastelic, *CFO*
▼ EMP: 3
SQ FT: 80,000
SALES (est): 685.1K
SALES (corp-wide): 2.5B **Publicly Held**
WEB: www.xmark-cdt.com
SIC: 3444 7692 3443 Sheet metalwork; welding repair; fabricated plate work (boiler shop)

PA: Belden Inc.
1 N Brentwood Blvd Fl 15
Saint Louis MO 63105
314 854-8000

(G-19249)
YESCO HANDYMAN SERVICES
Also Called: Yesco Hndyman Remodelling Svcs
1250 W Wylie Ave (15301-1636)
PHONE....................724 206-9541
Jim McClelland, *Owner*
EMP: 5
SALES (est): 493.9K **Privately Held**
SIC: 1521 3993 General remodeling, single-family houses; signs & advertising specialties

Washington Boro
Lancaster County

(G-19250)
KREIDERS MULCH
356 Penn St (17582-9762)
PHONE....................717 871-9177
Clyde E Kreider, *President*
EMP: 3
SALES (est): 340K **Privately Held**
SIC: 2082 Malt syrups

(G-19251)
MARVIN DALE SLAYMAKER
Also Called: Slaymaker Group
146 Penn St (17582-9704)
PHONE....................717 684-5050
Marvin Dale Slaymaker, *Owner*
EMP: 3
SALES (est): 150.7K **Privately Held**
SIC: 3621 3613 Electric motor & generator parts; control panels, electric

Washington Crossing
Bucks County

(G-19252)
BALDWIN PUBLISHING INC
1107 Tylrsvlle Rd Ste 101 (18977)
PHONE....................215 369-1369
Toni Donina, *President*
Hal Pitkow, *Treasurer*
Marinn Hersh, *Director*
EMP: 15
SALES (est): 608.4K **Privately Held**
SIC: 2741 Miscellaneous publishing

(G-19253)
BUCKS CNTY ARTESIAN WELL DRLG
1075 General Sullivan Rd (18977-1334)
PHONE....................215 493-1867
Leonard Stone, *President*
Patricia Stone, *Treasurer*
EMP: 16 EST: 1950
SQ FT: 17,500
SALES (est): 1.9MM **Privately Held**
SIC: 1381 1781 7699 7389 Service well drilling; geothermal drilling; pumps & pumping equipment repair; water softener service

(G-19254)
CLEAN CONCEPTS GROUP LLC
Also Called: Wheyclean
31 Beidler Dr (18977-1350)
P.O. Box 736 (18977-0736)
PHONE....................908 229-8812
Michael Wasyl, *Managing Prtnr*
Derick Hughes, *Managing Prtnr*
EMP: 3 EST: 2014
SALES: 15K **Privately Held**
SIC: 2841 Dishwashing compounds

(G-19255)
CROSSING VINEYARDS AND WINERY
1853 Wrightstown Rd (18977)
PHONE....................215 493-6500
Thomas Carroll, *President*
Chris Carroll, *Mktg Dir*
EMP: 20

SALES (est): 3.6MM **Privately Held**
SIC: 2084 Wines

(G-19256)
CYBERSCAN TECHNOLOGIES INC
17 Lookout Ln (18977-1137)
PHONE....................215 321-0447
Kurt Goszyk, *CEO*
Kurt A Goszyk, *CEO*
EMP: 5
SALES (est): 490K **Privately Held**
WEB: www.cyberscan.com
SIC: 3823 8731 Industrial instrmnts msrmnt display/control process variable; commercial physical research

(G-19257)
NITEBRITE LTD
1126 Taylorsville Rd (18977-1140)
PHONE....................215 493-9361
Mary Joy Webster, *Owner*
EMP: 6 EST: 2001
SALES (est): 343.9K **Privately Held**
SIC: 3648 Flashlights

(G-19258)
PHARMA REP TRAINING
34 Jonathan Way (18977-1036)
PHONE....................215 369-1719
Richard B Wathey, *Principal*
EMP: 4
SALES (est): 222.8K **Privately Held**
SIC: 2834 Pharmaceutical preparations

Waterford
Erie County

(G-19259)
AUTOMATED CONCEPTS TOOLING INC
14500 Willy Rd (16441-3746)
PHONE....................814 796-6302
Craig Hall, *CEO*
EMP: 13
SQ FT: 10,000
SALES (est): 1.6MM **Privately Held**
SIC: 3549 3599 Assembly machines, including robotic; machine & other job shop work

(G-19260)
BRENT A LINDBERG
Also Called: Lindberg Tool
2930 Old Meadville Rd (16441-3426)
PHONE....................814 796-9068
Brent A Lindberg, *Owner*
EMP: 4
SALES (est): 430.2K **Privately Held**
SIC: 3599 Machine shop, jobbing & repair

(G-19261)
DAVES WELDING SHOP
1389 Old State Rd (16441-3901)
PHONE....................814 796-6520
John Winkelbauer, *President*
EMP: 3 EST: 1978
SQ FT: 10,000
SALES: 333K **Privately Held**
SIC: 7692 Welding repair

(G-19262)
EXECUMOLD INC
1649 Lee Rd (16441-4119)
PHONE....................814 864-2535
Todd King, *President*
EMP: 27
SQ FT: 25,000
SALES (est): 3.4MM **Privately Held**
WEB: www.execumold.com
SIC: 2821 Molding compounds, plastics

(G-19263)
INDIAN HEAD TL CUTTER GRINDING
Also Called: Indian Head TI Cutter Grinding
802 Walnut St N (16441)
P.O. Box 1094 (16441-1094)
PHONE....................814 796-4954
Dan Huck, *President*
Marsha Huck, *Admin Sec*
EMP: 6

SQ FT: 2,400
SALES (est): 250K **Privately Held**
SIC: 7389 3599 Grinding, precision: commercial or industrial; machine shop, jobbing & repair

(G-19264)
LEASE MORE
2160 Elk Creek Rd (16441-8760)
PHONE....................814 796-4047
Robert Bestzina, *Partner*
EMP: 4
SALES (est): 261.3K **Privately Held**
WEB: www.leasemore.com
SIC: 7372 Business oriented computer software

(G-19265)
LEBOEUF INDUSTRIES INC
14960 Willy Rd (16441-3754)
PHONE....................814 796-9000
Sparkie Edwards, *President*
EMP: 15
SQ FT: 4,000
SALES (est): 587.9K **Privately Held**
WEB: www.leboeufindustriesinc.com
SIC: 7699 7694 Pumps & pumping equipment repair; electric motor repair

(G-19266)
MITCHELL HARDWOOD
13926 Flatts Rd (16441-4348)
PHONE....................814 796-4925
Rod Mitchell, *Partner*
Brian Mitchell, *Partner*
EMP: 5
SALES: 650K **Privately Held**
SIC: 2421 Sawmills & planing mills, general

(G-19267)
OCONNELL HARDWOOD INC
5636 Route 97 (16441-4414)
PHONE....................814 796-2297
Albert O'Connell, *CEO*
EMP: 20
SQ FT: 432
SALES (est): 2.4MM **Privately Held**
SIC: 2421 Lumber: rough, sawed or planed

(G-19268)
PROMACHINING AND TECHNOLOGY
627 Walnut St (16441)
PHONE....................814 796-3254
Scott Proctor, *Partner*
Ray Proctor, *Partner*
Tim Proctor, *Partner*
EMP: 10
SQ FT: 6,120
SALES (est): 1.3MM **Privately Held**
SIC: 3531 Construction machinery

(G-19269)
SHETLER LUMBER COMPANY INC
2850 Route 6 (16441-3702)
PHONE....................814 796-0303
Noah Shetler, *President*
▼ EMP: 20
SALES (est): 3MM **Privately Held**
WEB: www.shetler.com
SIC: 2411 2421 2426 Logging; sawmills & planing mills, general; hardwood dimension & flooring mills

(G-19270)
SUMMIT CONTROL PANELS
10190 Tiger Lily Ln (16441-9256)
PHONE....................814 431-4402
Earley Mary Kay, *Owner*
EMP: 4 EST: 2012
SALES (est): 453.4K **Privately Held**
SIC: 3829 Testers for checking hydraulic controls on aircraft

(G-19271)
SWISSAERO INC
802 Walnut St (16441)
P.O. Box 1210 (16441-1210)
PHONE....................814 796-4166
Robert Oberlander, *President*
Michael J Oberlander, *President*
EMP: 15 EST: 2008

SALES (est): 7.7MM **Privately Held**
SIC: 3599 3545 Machine shop, jobbing &
repair; machine tool accessories

(G-19272)
SYNERGISTIC SYSTEMS INC
2800 White Oak Dr (16441-3422)
PHONE..................................814 796-4217
Robert M Smith, *President*
Carol M Struchen, *Treasurer*
Dolores W Smith, *Admin Sec*
EMP: 4
SQ FT: 2,800
SALES (est): 290K **Privately Held**
SIC: 3625 Relays & industrial controls

Watsontown
Northumberland County

(G-19273)
ADVANCED METAL COATINGS INC
1200a Matthew St (17777-9400)
PHONE..................................570 538-1249
Chris Garman, *President*
Rick Whistler, *Corp Secy*
▲ EMP: 50
SQ FT: 130,000
SALES: 2.6MM **Privately Held**
SIC: 3479 3471 Coating of metals &
formed products; painting of metal prod-
ucts; electroplating of metals or formed
products; polishing, metals or formed
products

(G-19274)
GLEN-GERY CORPORATION
Also Called: Glen-Gery Brick Center
423 Susquehanna Trl (17777-8112)
PHONE..................................570 742-4721
Albert Cresswell, *Manager*
EMP: 5
SALES (corp-wide): 571K **Privately Held**
WEB: www.glengerybrick.com
SIC: 3251 Brick & structural clay tile
HQ: Glen-Gery Corporation
1166 Spring St
Reading PA 19610
610 374-4011

(G-19275)
HOEGANAES CORPORATION
4330 Paradise Rd (17777-8802)
PHONE..................................570 538-3587
James Tracewski, *Vice Pres*
Mike Conrad, *Plant Mgr*
Shelton Clisby, *Manager*
EMP: 29
SALES (corp-wide): 2.7B **Privately Held**
WEB: www.hoeganaes.com
SIC: 3399 Iron, powdered
HQ: Hoeganaes Corporation
1001 Taylors Ln
Cinnaminson NJ 08077
856 303-0366

(G-19276)
J & J CARBIDE TOOL CO INC
1199 Matthew St (17777-8069)
P.O. Box 54 (17777-0054)
PHONE..................................570 538-9283
Jesse Donald Jones, *President*
Cindy Gresh, *Manager*
Dan Obercors, *Manager*
EMP: 6
SALES (est): 857.2K **Privately Held**
SIC: 3545 Cutting tools for machine tools

(G-19277)
NU-TEC TOOLING CO
13115 State Route 405 (17777-8066)
P.O. Box 98 (17777-0098)
PHONE..................................570 538-2571
Larry Peterman, *President*
Robert Kear, *General Mgr*
Dale Peterman, *Vice Pres*
April West, *Admin Sec*
EMP: 12
SALES (est): 2.5MM **Privately Held**
SIC: 3423 Edge tools for woodworking:
augers, bits, gimlets, etc.

(G-19278)
OIL STATES ENERGY SERVICES LLC
449 E 8th St Bldg 11 (17777-8821)
PHONE..................................570 538-1623
Bart Shoemaker, *Area Mgr*
EMP: 100
SALES (corp-wide): 1B **Publicly Held**
SIC: 1389 Bailing, cleaning, swabbing &
treating of wells; bailing wells
HQ: Oil States Energy Services, L.L.C.
333 Clay St Ste 2100
Houston TX 77002
713 425-2400

(G-19279)
OTEX SPECIALTY NARROW FABRICS
204 E 7th St (17777-1147)
PHONE..................................570 538-5990
Alexis Mook, *Human Res Dir*
Lisa Grover, *Marketing Staff*
Melanie Chapman, *Manager*
Kevin Graham, *Director*
EMP: 10
SALES (corp-wide): 32.7MM **Privately Held**
SIC: 2241 Ribbons
PA: Otex Specialty Narrow Fabrics, Inc
4 Essex Ave Ste 403
Bernardsville NJ 07924
908 879-3636

(G-19280)
RENEWAL PROCESSING INC
10705 State Route 44 (17777-8294)
PHONE..................................570 838-3838
Mike Sensenig, *President*
Chris D Sensenig, *Vice Pres*
Ernest Schooley, *CFO*
EMP: 28
SQ FT: 50,000
SALES: 8.1MM **Privately Held**
SIC: 2048 Prepared feeds

(G-19281)
XYLEM WTR SLTONS ZLIENOPLE LLC
Also Called: Media Div
Glen Gery Rd Off 8th St (17777)
P.O. Box 128 (17777-0128)
PHONE..................................570 538-2260
Leonard Zukas, *Manager*
EMP: 8 **Publicly Held**
WEB: www.fbleopold.com
SIC: 1241 Coal mining services
HQ: Xylem Water Solutions Zelienople Llc
227 S Division St Ste 1
Zelienople PA 16063
724 452-6300

Wattsburg
Erie County

(G-19282)
RICK LEASURE
Also Called: High Point Tool & Die Company
11355 Backus Rd (16442-9747)
PHONE..................................814 739-9521
Rick Leasure, *Owner*
EMP: 9
SQ FT: 4,500
SALES (est): 1.2MM **Privately Held**
WEB: www.hparchery.com
SIC: 3089 Injection molding of plastics

(G-19283)
VENANGO MACHINE COMPANY INC
14118 Route 8 89 (16442-2924)
P.O. Box 239 (16442-0239)
PHONE..................................814 739-2211
David M Tullio, *President*
Thomas B Hagen, *Chairman*
James B Ohrn, *CFO*
Steven Gilbert, *Sales Mgr*
Nyla Vogel, *Sales Mgr*
EMP: 15 EST: 1954
SQ FT: 30,000

SALES: 4MM
SALES (corp-wide): 28MM **Privately Held**
WEB: www.venangomachine.com
SIC: 3599 Machine shop, jobbing & repair
PA: Custom Engineering Co.
2800 Mcclelland Ave
Erie PA 16510
814 898-1390

(G-19284)
WATTSBURG LUMBER CO LLC
9723 Jamestown St (16442-1101)
P.O. Box 215 (16442-0215)
PHONE..................................814 739-2770
Charles Zaborowski,
John Zaborowski,
Paul Zaborowski,
EMP: 7 EST: 1956
SQ FT: 3,400
SALES: 500K **Privately Held**
SIC: 2421 5211 Sawmills & planing mills,
general; lumber & other building materials

Waverly
Lackawanna County

(G-19285)
IN-TEC INC (PA)
1 Kennedy Creek Rd (18471)
PHONE..................................570 342-8464
Joseph O'Connor, *President*
Keith Williams, *Admin Sec*
EMP: 8
SQ FT: 3,000
SALES: 1MM **Privately Held**
WEB: www.intecweb.com
SIC: 7812 2731 Training motion picture
production; textbooks: publishing & print-
ing

Waymart
Wayne County

(G-19286)
DAVID TUTTLE
Also Called: Big Daddy D Trucking
391 Belmont Tpke (18472-6001)
PHONE..................................570 280-8441
David Tuttle, *Owner*
EMP: 3
SALES (est): 193.8K **Privately Held**
SIC: 3751 Motorcycles, bicycles & parts

(G-19287)
GUTENBERG INC
Also Called: Universal Publishing
677 Roosevelt Hwy Ste 2 (18472-3117)
P.O. Box 3900 (18472-3900)
PHONE..................................570 488-9820
Thomas Wasylyk, *President*
Josh Wasylyk, *Principal*
Jennifer Schweighofer, *Editor*
Larry Wildenstein, *Vice Pres*
EMP: 5
SALES (est): 542.5K **Privately Held**
WEB: www.upub.net
SIC: 2731 Books: publishing only

(G-19288)
NORTHEASTERN FOAM AND FIBER
Also Called: Northeast Contracting
Owego Tpke (18472)
P.O. Box 370 (18472-0370)
PHONE..................................570 488-6859
Felix V Vallone, *President*
EMP: 3
SALES (est): 150K **Privately Held**
SIC: 3086 Insulation or cushioning mate-
rial, foamed plastic

(G-19289)
QUANTUM MFG SERVICES INC
20 Anderson Ln (18472-6017)
PHONE..................................570 785-9716
Charles Anderson, *President*
Cathlene Anderson, *Vice Pres*
EMP: 4
SALES: 200K **Privately Held**
SIC: 3599 Machine shop, jobbing & repair

Wayne
Delaware County

(G-19290)
21ST CENTURY SOFTWARE TECH INC
940 W Valley Rd (19087-1832)
PHONE..................................610 341-9017
Rebecca Levesque, *President*
Danielle Dickie, *CFO*
Paul Eckert, *CTO*
Rose Guignard, *Admin Asst*
EMP: 28
SALES (est): 4MM **Privately Held**
WEB: www.21stCenturySoftware.com
SIC: 7371 7372 7379 Computer software
development; publishers' computer soft-
ware; computer related maintenance
services

(G-19291)
39 DESIGN COMPANY INC
Also Called: Baker The Sign Man
207b Highland Ave (19087-4745)
PHONE..................................215 563-1320
Nacine Supinsky, *President*
EMP: 6 EST: 1870
SQ FT: 3,600
SALES (est): 745.1K **Privately Held**
WEB: www.bakerthesignman.com
SIC: 3993 Signs, not made in custom sign
painting shops; electric signs; neon signs

(G-19292)
465 DEVON PARK DRIVE INC
465 Devon Park Dr (19087-1815)
PHONE..................................610 293-1330
John J Collins, *President*
Jack Collins, *Vice Pres*
EMP: 3
SALES (est): 260K **Privately Held**
SIC: 2621 Wallpaper (hanging paper)

(G-19293)
ACLARIS THERAPEUTICS INC (PA)
640 Lee Rd Ste 200 (19087-5600)
PHONE..................................484 324-7933
Stephen A Tullman, *Ch of Bd*
Neal Walker, *President*
Frank Ruffo, *CFO*
Stuart Shanler, *Security Dir*
Kamil Ali-Jackson,
EMP: 62
SQ FT: 33,019
SALES: 10MM **Publicly Held**
SIC: 2834 Dermatologicals

(G-19294)
AEVI GENOMIC MEDICINE INC (PA)
435 Devon Park Dr Ste 715 (19087-1946)
PHONE..................................610 254-4201
Sol J Barer, *Ch of Bd*
Michael F Cola, *President*
Brian D Piper, *CFO*
Garry A Neil, *Security Dir*
EMP: 17
SALES (est): 2.1MM **Publicly Held**
SIC: 8731 2834 Biotechnical research,
commercial; pharmaceutical preparations

(G-19295)
AFFIL DISTRIBUTORS
440 E Swedesford Rd # 1000
(19087-1820)
PHONE..................................610 977-3100
Bill Weisberg, *CEO*
Bob Jordan, *President*
Stan Haas, *COO*
Brian Carroll, *Vice Pres*
Neil Cohen, *Vice Pres*
EMP: 5
SALES (est): 1.3MM **Privately Held**
SIC: 7692 Federal Reserve Bank

(G-19296)
ALL-STEEL FABRICATORS CO INC
292 Sunset Rd (19087-2439)
PHONE..................................610 687-2267

Richard L Mc Cormick, *President*
Juliana T Mc Cormick, *Vice Pres*
EMP: 9
SQ FT: 18,000
SALES (est): 760K **Privately Held**
WEB: www.allsteelfabco.com
SIC: 3443 Fabricated plate work (boiler shop)

(G-19297)
AMG ALUMINUM NORTH AMERICA LLC (HQ)
435 Devon Park Dr Ste 200 (19087-1937)
PHONE....................................610 293-2501
Scott Charnoff, *Controller*
Richard Malliris,
James Bailey,
Ron Duckworth,
Thomas Formolo,
◆ **EMP:** 15
SALES (est): 23MM
SALES (corp-wide): 1B **Privately Held**
WEB: www.kballoys.com
SIC: 3355 3354 3365 3339 Aluminum rod & bar; aluminum ingot; aluminum extruded products; aluminum foundries; primary nonferrous metals
PA: Amg Advanced Metallurgical Group N.V.
Strawinskylaan 1343
Amsterdam 1077
207 147-140

(G-19298)
ANDERSON PRINTS LLC
465 Devon Park Dr (19087-1815)
PHONE....................................610 293-1330
John Collins,
EMP: 10
SALES (est): 1.3MM **Privately Held**
WEB: www.andersonprints.com
SIC: 2621 Wallpaper (hanging paper)

(G-19299)
ARGOSY CAPITAL GROUP LLC
Also Called: Argosy Private Equity
950 W Valley Rd Ste 2902 (19087-1845)
PHONE....................................610 971-9685
John Paul Kirwin III, *Partner*
Kirkgriswo Partner, *Principal*
EMP: 13 **EST:** 1998
SALES (est): 1.6MM **Privately Held**
SIC: 3053 Gasket materials

(G-19300)
ARGOSY INV PARTNERS IV LP (PA)
950 W Valley Rd Ste 2900 (19087-1845)
PHONE....................................610 971-9685
Kirk B Griswold, *Mng Member*
EMP: 10
SALES (est): 35.4MM **Privately Held**
SIC: 3053 Gasket materials

(G-19301)
ARGUS PRINTING
168 E Lancaster Ave (19087-4190)
PHONE....................................610 687-0411
Suzan McCauley, *President*
EMP: 3 **EST:** 1970
SQ FT: 1,200
SALES (est): 400K **Privately Held**
WEB: www.argusprinting.com
SIC: 2759 5113 Letterpress printing; industrial & personal service paper

(G-19302)
ARGUS PRINTING & COPY
168 E Lancaster Ave (19087-4190)
PHONE....................................610 687-0411
Susan M Mc Cauley, *President*
William Mc Cauley, *Vice Pres*
EMP: 5
SALES (est): 560K **Privately Held**
SIC: 2759 Commercial printing

(G-19303)
ARROW INTERNATIONAL INC (HQ)
Also Called: Teleflex
550 E Swedesford Rd # 400 (19087-1601)
P.O. Box 12888, Reading (19612-2888)
PHONE....................................610 225-6800
John E Gallagher, *President*
Catherine Gallagher, *Corp Secy*

Dennis P Gallagher, *Vice Pres*
Sherry Weist, *Buyer*
▲ **EMP:** 600
SQ FT: 165,000
SALES (est): 730.6MM
SALES (corp-wide): 2.1B **Publicly Held**
WEB: www.arrowintl.com
SIC: 3841 3844 Catheters; therapeutic X-ray apparatus & tubes
PA: Teleflex Incorporated
550 E Swedesford Rd # 400
Wayne PA 19087
610 225-6800

(G-19304)
BABY MATTERS LLC
153 Finn Ln (19087-4239)
PHONE....................................919 724-7087
Leslie Gudel Kemm,
▲ **EMP:** 7
SALES (est): 486.2K **Privately Held**
SIC: 2032 Baby foods, including meats: packaged in cans, jars, etc.

(G-19305)
BEYE LLC
Also Called: Beye.com
1008 Upper Gulph Rd (19087-2700)
PHONE....................................484 581-1840
David Cox, *Mng Member*
EMP: 4 **EST:** 2013
SALES (est): 70.8K **Privately Held**
SIC: 7812 2741 7313 Motion picture & video production; miscellaneous publishing; electronic media advertising representatives

(G-19306)
BILL ONEILL
46 Meadowbrook Rd (19087-2511)
PHONE....................................610 688-6135
Bill O'Neill, *President*
EMP: 3 **EST:** 2011
SALES (est): 125.8K **Privately Held**
SIC: 2711 Newspapers, publishing & printing

(G-19307)
BIONIX SAFETY TECHNOLOGIES
996 Old Eagle School Rd # 1118 (19087-1806)
PHONE....................................610 408-0555
Andrew Milligan, *Branch Mgr*
EMP: 8
SALES (est): 1.9MM
SALES (corp-wide): 12.1MM **Privately Held**
WEB: www.nst-usa.com
SIC: 3825 3826 5084 3829 Test equipment for electronic & electric measurement; analytical instruments; gas testing apparatus; industrial machinery & equipment; measuring & controlling devices
HQ: Bionix Safety Technologies, Ltd.
5154 Enterprise Blvd
Toledo OH 43612
419 727-0552

(G-19308)
BLUE GOLF COM
Also Called: Bluegolf
724 W Lancaster Ave # 220 (19087-2542)
PHONE....................................909 592-6411
Stacey Kohlbrenner, *Vice Pres*
Trevin Ray, *Accounts Mgr*
Shelley Durbanis, *Software Engr*
Angela Trexler, *Software Engr*
Roberta Winkler, *Software Engr*
EMP: 5
SALES (est): 819.6K **Privately Held**
WEB: www.bluegolf.com
SIC: 3695 Computer software tape & disks: blank, rigid & floppy

(G-19309)
BRYN MAWR COMMUNICATIONS LLC
1008 Upper Gulph Rd # 200 (19087-2700)
PHONE....................................610 687-0887
Rick Ehrlich, *Publisher*
Bill Carroll, *Editor*
Nick Hatsis, *Editor*
Steve Farrell, *Accounts Exec*
Rachel Kagan, *Producer*
EMP: 19

SALES (est): 3.4MM **Privately Held**
WEB: www.bmctoday.com
SIC: 2721 Magazines: publishing only, not printed on site

(G-19310)
BUSINESS 21 PUBLISHING LLC
435 Devon Park Dr Ste 510 (19087-1939)
PHONE....................................484 490-9205
Stephen Meyer, *Principal*
EMP: 4
SALES (est): 220.4K **Privately Held**
SIC: 2741 Miscellaneous publishing

(G-19311)
BUSINESS INTELLIGENCE INTL INC
Also Called: B I International
993 Old Eagle School Rd # 405 (19087-1710)
PHONE....................................484 688-8300
Richard Connelly, *President*
Roland Mosimann, *Managing Dir*
William E Tomassini, *Senior VP*
EMP: 50
SQ FT: 5,000
SALES (est): 7.2MM **Privately Held**
SIC: 5045 7372 Computer software; educational computer software

(G-19312)
CERTAINTEED GYPSUM MFG INC (DH)
750 E Swedesford Rd (19087-1633)
PHONE....................................813 286-3900
David Engelhardt, *President*
Don Moses, *President*
Kieth Campbell, *Vice Pres*
John Sweeney III, *Treasurer*
David Pugh, *Director*
EMP: 26
SALES (est): 79.3MM
SALES (corp-wide): 215.9MM **Privately Held**
SIC: 3568 3275 Joints & couplings; gypsum products

(G-19313)
CHESTNUT GROUP INC (PA)
Also Called: Atlantic Spring & Mfg Co Div
115 Bloomingdale Ave # 101 (19087-4086)
PHONE....................................610 688-3300
M Parker Blatchford, *Principal*
EMP: 8
SQ FT: 1,100
SALES (est): 34.2MM **Privately Held**
WEB: www.chestnutgroup.com
SIC: 3999 3451 3495 3469 Advertising display products; screw machine products; precision springs; metal stampings; military goods & regalia

(G-19314)
COOL BIO INC
Also Called: USA
1489 Lexington Ln (19087-1334)
PHONE....................................973 452-8309
Dawn Bell, *CEO*
EMP: 3
SALES (est): 181.7K **Privately Held**
SIC: 2834 Pharmaceutical preparations

(G-19315)
CROWN CORK SEAL
233 Plant Ave (19087-3519)
PHONE....................................610 687-2616
EMP: 3
SALES (est): 155K **Privately Held**
SIC: 3411 Metal cans

(G-19316)
CUTIX INC
585 E Swedes Rd Ste 200 (19080-0001)
PHONE....................................610 246-7518
Neal Walker, *President*
EMP: 4
SALES (est): 332.7K **Privately Held**
SIC: 2834 Pharmaceutical preparations

(G-19317)
DELCO TRADE SERVICES INC
235 Strafford Ave (19087-3227)
PHONE....................................610 659-9978
Albert Calvy Jr, *President*
EMP: 6

SQ FT: 6,500
SALES (est): 300K **Privately Held**
SIC: 2752 Commercial printing, offset

(G-19318)
DOOR STOP LTD
326 Overhill Rd (19087-3206)
PHONE....................................610 353-8707
EMP: 4
SALES (est): 332.3K **Privately Held**
SIC: 1751 2499 Carpentry Contractor Mfg Wood Products

(G-19319)
DORCHESTER PUBLISHING CO INC
Also Called: Leisure Books Division
100 W Matsonford Rd # 101 (19087-4558)
PHONE....................................212 725-8811
John Preibrch, *President*
Tim Deyoung, *Senior VP*
Tim De Young, *VP Mktg*
EMP: 21
SQ FT: 2,700
SALES (est): 1.6MM **Privately Held**
WEB: www.dorchesterpub.com
SIC: 2731 Books: publishing only

(G-19320)
DRUGDEV INC (PA)
Also Called: Incyte Chemicals
1170 Devon Park Dr # 300 (19087-2128)
PHONE....................................888 650-1860
Hugo Stephenson, *President*
Sean Melville, *President*
Stewart Mackie, *Vice Pres*
Sherry Miller, *Vice Pres*
Cameron Snider, *Vice Pres*
EMP: 19
SALES (est): 14.9MM **Privately Held**
SIC: 2834 Medicines, capsuled or ampuled

(G-19321)
E-FINITY DSTRBTED GNRATION LLC
161 Pennsylvania Ave (19087-3559)
PHONE....................................610 688-6212
Jeffrey Beiter,
Sandy Ohara,
EMP: 9
SALES (est): 2.3MM **Privately Held**
SIC: 3511 3585 5063 Turbines & turbine generator sets; heating & air conditioning combination units; electrical apparatus & equipment

(G-19322)
EGALET CORPORATION (PA)
600 Lee Rd Ste 100 (19087-5624)
PHONE....................................610 833-4200
Timothy P Walbert, *Ch of Bd*
Robert Radie, *President*
Mark Strobeck, *COO*
Wendy Niebler, *Vice Pres*
Stan Musial, *CFO*
EMP: 46 **EST:** 2013
SQ FT: 19,797
SALES: 30.3MM **Publicly Held**
SIC: 2834 Pharmaceutical preparations

(G-19323)
EGALET LTD
460 E Swedesford Rd (19087-1801)
PHONE....................................484 875-3095
Bob Radie, *CEO*
Stan Musial, *CFO*
EMP: 12
SALES (est): 3.8MM **Privately Held**
SIC: 2834 Pharmaceutical preparations

(G-19324)
EGALET US INC
600 Lee Rd Ste 100 (19087-5624)
PHONE....................................610 833-4200
Robert Radie, *CEO*
EMP: 11
SALES (est): 1.8MM
SALES (corp-wide): 30.3MM **Publicly Held**
SIC: 2834 Pharmaceutical preparations
PA: Egalet Corporation
600 Lee Rd Ste 100
Wayne PA 19087
610 833-4200

▲ = Import ▼ =Export
◆ =Import/Export

(G-19325)
ESCALON MEDICAL CORP (PA)
435 Devon Park Dr Ste 100 (19087-1942)
PHONE..............................610 688-6830
Richard J Depiano, *Ch of Bd*
Mark G Wallace, *COO*
EMP: 46
SQ FT: 3,954
SALES (est): 10.2MM **Privately Held**
SIC: 3841 2834 Surgical & medical instruments; pharmaceutical preparations

(G-19326)
EXIT STORE LLC
303 W Lancaster Ave # 138 (19087-3938)
PHONE..............................310 305-4646
Gary Glass,
William Lynch,
EMP: 9
SQ FT: 2,600
SALES (est): 880K **Privately Held**
WEB: www.theexitstore.com
SIC: 3646 Commercial indusl & institutional electric lighting fixtures

(G-19327)
F S CONVERGENT
460 E Swedesford Rd (19087-1801)
PHONE..............................484 581-7065
EMP: 4
SALES (est): 267.7K **Privately Held**
SIC: 3674 Semiconductors & related devices

(G-19328)
FEMMEPHRMA CNSMR HALTHCARE LLC
175 Strafford Ave Ste 275 (19087-3347)
PHONE..............................610 995-0801
Isidora Lans, *Manager*
Gerianne Dipiano,
EMP: 5
SALES (est): 467.4K **Privately Held**
SIC: 2834 Pharmaceutical preparations

(G-19329)
FIS AVANTGARD LLC (DH)
Also Called: Sungard
680 E Swedesford Rd (19087-1605)
PHONE..............................800 468-7483
Jl Alarcon, *General Mgr*
Alain Fraiberger,
Thomas McDugall,
Karen Mullane,
EMP: 42
SQ FT: 22,000
SALES (est): 55.5MM
SALES (corp-wide): 8.4B **Publicly Held**
SIC: 7372 7378 7379 Business oriented computer software; computer maintenance & repair; computer related consulting services
HQ: Fis Data Systems Inc.
200 Campus Dr
Collegeville PA 19426
484 582-2000

(G-19330)
FIS SG LLC (HQ)
Also Called: Sungard
680 E Swedesford Rd (19087-1605)
PHONE..............................484 582-5400
Russell P Fradin, *President*
Victoria E Silbey, *Senior VP*
Christopher P Breakiron, *Vice Pres*
Charles J Neral, *CFO*
Paul Gordon, *Accounts Exec*
EMP: 148
SALES: 2.8B
SALES (corp-wide): 8.4B **Publicly Held**
SIC: 7372 7374 Business oriented computer software; data processing & preparation
PA: Fidelity National Information Services, Inc.
601 Riverside Ave
Jacksonville FL 32204
904 438-6000

(G-19331)
FLAGS FOR ALL SEASONS INC
230 Orchard Way (19087-4806)
PHONE..............................610 688-4235
Jessica Packard, *President*
Ralph K Packard, *Corp Secy*
EMP: 7

SQ FT: 1,200
SALES (est): 394.6K **Privately Held**
SIC: 2399 5999 Flags, fabric; flags

(G-19332)
GL TRADE CAPITL MKTS SOLUTIONS (DH)
595 E Swedesford Rd 300 (19087-1615)
PHONE..............................484 530-4400
Farid A Naib, *CEO*
Philip F Bell, *CFO*
EMP: 80
SQ FT: 30,000
SALES (est): 10.6MM
SALES (corp-wide): 8.4B **Publicly Held**
WEB: www.fnx.com
SIC: 7371 7372 Computer software development; prepackaged software
HQ: Fis Financial Systems (France)
Sungard Global Trading
Paris 75002
153 400-000

(G-19333)
GLOBAL RUBBER LLC
303 W Lancaster Ave Frnt (19087-3955)
PHONE..............................610 878-9200
Mike Hovsepian, *Branch Mgr*
EMP: 5
SQ FT: 5,000
SALES (corp-wide): 8.8MM **Privately Held**
SIC: 3069 Floor coverings, rubber
PA: Global Rubber, Llc
1350 Venture Dr
Janesville WI 53546
608 754-9200

(G-19334)
H B FOWLER CO INC
Also Called: Fowler Equipment Market
250 Conestoga Rd (19087-4771)
PHONE..............................610 688-0567
Americo Taddeo, *President*
EMP: 3 **EST:** 1941
SQ FT: 1,200
SALES (est): 137.5K **Privately Held**
SIC: 2759 Screen printing

(G-19335)
HB FULLER COMPANY
547 Saint Davids Ave (19087-4432)
PHONE..............................610 688-1234
William Main, *Branch Mgr*
EMP: 47
SALES (corp-wide): 3B **Publicly Held**
WEB: www.hbfuller.com
SIC: 2891 Adhesives
PA: H.B. Fuller Company
1200 Willow Lake Blvd
Saint Paul MN 55110
651 236-5900

(G-19336)
HB TRADING LLC
37 Briar Rd (19087-2602)
P.O. Box 506, Uwchland (19480-0506)
PHONE..............................610 212-4565
Henry Brons,
▲ **EMP:** 1 **EST:** 2011
SALES: 1.5MM **Privately Held**
SIC: 2023 2759 7389 Dry, condensed, evaporated dairy products; currency: engraved;

(G-19337)
ICTV HOLDINGS INC (HQ)
489 Devon Park Dr Ste 315 (19087-1809)
PHONE..............................484 598-2300
Richard Ransom, *President*
EMP: 11
SQ FT: 2,726
SALES (est): 1.7MM
SALES (corp-wide): 31.4MM **Publicly Held**
SIC: 2834 3845 3699 6719 Laser systems & equipment, medical; laser systems & equipment; investment holding companies, except banks; emulsions, pharmaceutical
PA: Ictv Brands Inc.
489 Devon Park Dr Ste 306
Wayne PA 19087
484 598-2300

(G-19338)
INTACT VASCULAR INC
1285 Drummers Ln Ste 200 (19087-1572)
PHONE..............................484 253-1048
Bruce J Shook, *President*
Bryan A Claseman, *Vice Pres*
Joseph C Griffin, *Vice Pres*
Steve Mackinnon, *VP Sales*
Steve Combes, *Director*
EMP: 25 **EST:** 2012
SALES (est): 4.3MM **Privately Held**
SIC: 3841 Surgical & medical instruments

(G-19339)
INTERNATIONAL BUS MCHS CORP
Also Called: IBM
650 E Swedesford Rd # 200 (19087-1610)
PHONE..............................610 578-2017
Svetlana Gorodetsky, *Vice Pres*
Mark Michener, *Purchasing*
Tom Yezzi, *Sales Associate*
Steve Lautz, *Manager*
Robert Mowery, *Senior Mgr*
EMP: 923
SALES (corp-wide): 79.5B **Publicly Held**
WEB: www.ibm.com
SIC: 3571 7372 7378 3572 Electronic computers; prepackaged software; computer maintenance & repair; computer storage devices
PA: International Business Machines Corporation
1 New Orchard Rd Ste 1 # 1
Armonk NY 10504
914 499-1900

(G-19340)
ITS ONLY CUPCAKES LLC
90 Drummers Ln (19087-1515)
PHONE..............................717 421-6646
EMP: 4 **EST:** 2012
SALES (est): 154.5K **Privately Held**
SIC: 2051 Bread, cake & related products

(G-19341)
J F CHOBERT ASSOCIATES INC
112 Lemonton Way (19087-4665)
PHONE..............................610 431-2200
John F Chobert, *President*
Frank Kearney, *Corp Secy*
EMP: 8 **EST:** 1976
SALES (est): 1.5MM **Privately Held**
WEB: www.jfchobert.com
SIC: 2672 2679 Labels (unprinted), gummed: made from purchased materials; tags, paper (unprinted): made from purchased paper

(G-19342)
JSP INTERNATIONAL GROUP LTD (DH)
1285 Drummers Ln Ste 301 (19087-1572)
PHONE..............................610 651-8600
Rokurou Inoue, *President*
Carl W Moyer, *Vice Pres*
Daniel W Doyle, *CFO*
Zachary R Estrin, *Admin Sec*
EMP: 8
SALES (est): 81.6MM
SALES (corp-wide): 5.9B **Privately Held**
SIC: 2821 Polypropylene resins
HQ: Jsp Corporation
3-4-2, Marunouchi
Chiyoda-Ku TKY 100-0
362 126-300

(G-19343)
JSP INTERNATIONAL LLC (DH)
Also Called: Speciality Firms
1285 Drummers Ln Ste 301 (19087-1572)
PHONE..............................610 651-8600
Carl W Moyer, *President*
Richard C Alloway, *Vice Pres*
Zachary R Estrin, *Vice Pres*
Richard Bulley, *Treasurer*
Joe Landy, *Info Tech Dir*
▲ **EMP:** 18
SQ FT: 8,000
SALES: 80.3MM
SALES (corp-wide): 5.9B **Privately Held**
SIC: 2821 Polypropylene resins

(G-19344)
JSP RESINS LLC
1285 Drummers Ln Ste 301 (19087-1572)
PHONE..............................610 651-8600
Carl W Moyer, *President*
Richzrd C Alloway, *Vice Pres*
EMP: 10
SALES (est): 1.3MM
SALES (corp-wide): 5.9B **Privately Held**
SIC: 2821 Polypropylene resins
HQ: Jsp International Group Ltd.
1285 Drummers Ln Ste 301
Wayne PA 19087

(G-19345)
KB ALLOYS HOLDINGS LLC
435 Devon Park Dr Ste 200 (19087-1937)
PHONE..............................484 582-3520
Robert Longenecker, *Ch of Bd*
Richard Malliris, *President*
Andrew W Code, *Vice Pres*
Thomas Formolo, *Vice Pres*
Timothy Weaver, *Admin Sec*
◆ **EMP:** 15
SQ FT: 6,000
SALES (est): 1.4MM **Privately Held**
SIC: 3355 3354 3365 3339 Aluminum rod & bar; aluminum ingot; aluminum extruded products; aluminum foundries; primary nonferrous metals

(G-19346)
KENEXA LEARNING INC (DH)
650 E Swedesford Rd 2nd (19087-1610)
PHONE..............................610 971-9171
Steve Henkels, *President*
Troy A Kanter, *President*
Nooruddin Rudy S Karsan, *Principal*
EMP: 23
SALES (est): 9.9MM
SALES (corp-wide): 79.5B **Publicly Held**
WEB: www.outstart.com
SIC: 7372 7379 Business oriented computer software; computer related consulting services
HQ: Kenexa Corporation
650 E Swedesford Rd # 200
Wayne PA 19087
877 971-9171

(G-19347)
LED SAVING SOLUTIONS LLC (PA)
487 Devon Park Dr Ste 204 (19087-1808)
PHONE..............................484 588-5401
Charlie Szoradi,
EMP: 2
SALES (est): 2MM **Privately Held**
SIC: 3646 Commercial indusl & institutional electric lighting fixtures

(G-19348)
LIFEGUARD HEALTH NETWORKS INC
993 Old Eagle School Rd (19087-1710)
PHONE..............................484 584-4071
Martin Carty, *President*
Danielle Klein, *Vice Pres*
EMP: 11
SQ FT: 1,100
SALES (est): 488.4K **Privately Held**
SIC: 7372 Application computer software

(G-19349)
MAIN LINE PRINT SHOP INC
Also Called: Assocted Grphic Communications
25 West Ave (19087-3292)
PHONE..............................610 688-7782
Mike Libert, *President*
EMP: 4
SQ FT: 1,800
SALES (est): 564.9K **Privately Held**
SIC: 2752 Commercial printing, offset

(G-19350)
MATTHEY JOHNSON HOLDINGS INC (HQ)
435 Devon Park Dr Ste 600 (19087-1944)
PHONE..............................610 971-3000
Robert Talley, *President*
Edward Ravert, *Vice Pres*
Edward H Ravert Jr, *Vice Pres*
A J Trifiletti, *Vice Pres*
Mark Dietz, *Maint Spvr*

◆ **EMP:** 26
SQ FT: 15,000
SALES (est): 739.4MM
SALES (corp-wide): 19.7B **Privately Held**
SIC: 3341 3339 3356 2834 Platinum group metals, smelting & refining (secondary); gold smelting & refining (secondary); silver smelting & refining (secondary); platinum group metal refining (primary); gold refining (primary); silver refining (primary); precious metals; platinum group metals: rolling, drawing or extruding; gold & gold alloy: rolling, drawing or extruding; powders, pharmaceutical; metal powders, pastes & flakes; paste, metal; exhaust systems & parts, motor vehicle
PA: Johnson Matthey Plc
5th Floor, 25 Farringdon Street
London EC4A
207 269-8400

(G-19351)
MATTHEY JOHNSON INC (DH)
435 Devon Park Dr Ste 600 (19087-1944)
PHONE...................................610 971-3000
William Claus, *President*
Michael Gula, *General Mgr*
Tim Murray, *General Mgr*
Tim Stevenson, *Chairman*
E H Ravert Jr, *Vice Pres*
◆ **EMP:** 45 **EST:** 1909
SQ FT: 15,000
SALES (est): 702.1MM
SALES (corp-wide): 19.7B **Privately Held**
WEB: www.matthey.com
SIC: 3341 3339 3356 2834 Platinum group metals, smelting & refining (secondary); gold smelting & refining (secondary); silver smelting & refining (secondary); platinum group metal refining (primary); gold refining (primary); silver refining (primary); precious metals; platinum group metals: rolling, drawing or extruding; gold & gold alloy: rolling, drawing or extruding; silver & silver alloy: rolling, drawing or extruding; powders, pharmaceutical; metal powders, pastes & flakes; paste, metal; exhaust systems & parts, motor vehicle
HQ: Matthey Johnson Holdings Inc
435 Devon Park Dr Ste 600
Wayne PA 19087
610 971-3000

(G-19352)
MATTHEY JOHNSON INC
Also Called: Envirnmntal Catalysts Tech Div
436 Devon Park Dr (19087-1827)
PHONE...................................610 341-8300
Michael Cleare, *President*
Paul Johnson, *Research*
Robert Trevison, *Engineer*
Alan Myers, *Branch Mgr*
Ann Macchia, *Manager*
EMP: 400
SQ FT: 65,000
SALES (corp-wide): 19.7B **Privately Held**
SIC: 3999 3714 3564 Advertising curtains; motor vehicle parts & accessories; blowers & fans
HQ: Matthey Johnson Inc
435 Devon Park Dr Ste 600
Wayne PA 19087
610 971-3000

(G-19353)
MATTHEY JOHNSON INC
Emission Control Technologies
456 Devon Park Dr (19087-1816)
PHONE...................................610 341-8300
Dawn Sagaser, *Vice Pres*
William Burt, *Plant Mgr*
Tony Edwards, *Project Mgr*
Paul Smith, *Purch Agent*
Karen Wright, *Buyer*
EMP: 104

SALES (corp-wide): 19.7B **Privately Held**
SIC: 3812 3339 3356 2834 Light or heat emission operating apparatus; platinum group metal refining (primary); gold refining (primary); silver refining (primary); precious metals; platinum group metals: rolling, drawing or extruding; gold & gold alloy: rolling, drawing or extruding; silver & silver alloy: rolling, drawing or extruding; powders, pharmaceutical; platinum group metals, smelting & refining (secondary); gold smelting & refining (secondary); silver smelting & refining (secondary)
HQ: Matthey Johnson Inc
435 Devon Park Dr Ste 600
Wayne PA 19087
610 971-3000

(G-19354)
MEASUREMENT SPECIALTIES INC
460 E Swedesford Rd # 3005 (19087-1801)
PHONE...................................610 971-9893
Joseph Mallon, *Branch Mgr*
EMP: 4
SALES (corp-wide): 13.1B **Privately Held**
WEB: www.measurementspecialties.com
SIC: 3829 3596 Measuring & controlling devices; scales & balances, except laboratory
HQ: Measurement Specialties, Inc.
1000 Lucas Way
Hampton VA 23666
757 766-1500

(G-19355)
METALLURG INC (DH)
Also Called: AMG Advnced Mtllrgcal Group NV
435 Devon Park Dr Ste 200 (19087-1937)
PHONE...................................610 293-2501
Arthur R Spector, *Vice Ch Bd*
Eric E Jackson, *President*
Heinz Schimmelbusch, *Chairman*
Dennis Shea, *Vice Pres*
Amy E Ard, *CFO*
EMP: 3 **EST:** 1947
SQ FT: 13,800
SALES (est): 250.5MM
SALES (corp-wide): 1B **Privately Held**
WEB: www.metallurg.com
SIC: 3313 1081 Alloys, additive, except copper: not made in blast furnaces; ferrochromium; ferromolybdenum; ferrotitanium; metal mining services
HQ: Metallurg Holdings, Inc.
435 Devon Park Dr Ste 200
Wayne PA 19087
610 293-2501

(G-19356)
METALLURG HOLDINGS INC (HQ)
435 Devon Park Dr Ste 200 (19087-1937)
PHONE...................................610 293-2501
Heinz C Schimmelbusch, *President*
Arthur R Spector, *Treasurer*
EMP: 13
SALES (est): 250.5MM
SALES (corp-wide): 1B **Privately Held**
WEB: www.safeguardintl.com
SIC: 3313 1081 Alloys, additive, except copper: not made in blast furnaces; metal mining services
PA: Amg Advanced Metallurgical Group N.V.
Strawinskylaan 1343
Amsterdam 1077
207 147-140

(G-19357)
MINUTEMAN PRESS INTL INC
489 Devon Park Dr Ste 307 (19087-1809)
PHONE...................................610 902-0203
Robert G Emmett, *Vice Pres*
EMP: 3
SALES (corp-wide): 23.4MM **Privately Held**
SIC: 2752 Commercial printing, offset
PA: Minuteman Press International, Inc.
61 Executive Blvd
Farmingdale NY 11735
631 249-1370

(G-19358)
MUMPS AUDIOFAX INC
Also Called: Audiocare Systems
744 W Lancaster Ave # 250 (19087-2523)
PHONE...................................610 293-2160
Badra Berkane, *President*
Kelly Minissale, *General Mgr*
Michael McGrann, *Engineer*
Kristina Roberts, *Engineer*
Debra Lefin, *Manager*
EMP: 25
SALES (est): 2.7MM **Privately Held**
SIC: 7371 7372 Computer software development; application computer software

(G-19359)
NANOPACK INC
Also Called: Pack Nano
985 Old Eagle School Rd # 501 (19087-1712)
P.O. Box 1553, Southeastern (19399-1553)
PHONE...................................484 367-7015
Howard Kravitz, *President*
EMP: 7
SALES (est): 1.1MM **Privately Held**
SIC: 2671 Plastic film, coated or laminated for packaging

(G-19360)
NORTH AMRCN SPECIALTY PDTS LLC (DH)
993 Old Eagle School Rd (19087-1710)
PHONE...................................484 253-4545
Joseph Bondi, *Vice Pres*
EMP: 56 **EST:** 2013
SALES (est): 14.5MM **Publicly Held**
SIC: 2821 Plastics materials & resins

(G-19361)
ORAHEALTH INTERNATIONAL
407 E Lancaster Ave (19087-4202)
PHONE...................................610 971-9600
Sean Stubbs, *CEO*
Mike Levenstein, *Principal*
EMP: 3
SQ FT: 4,000
SALES: 8MM **Privately Held**
SIC: 3843 Dental materials; cement, dental

(G-19362)
PLAN MANAGEMENT CORPORATION
5 Radnor Corp Ctr Ste 450 (19087-4538)
PHONE...................................610 359-5870
Jonathan Miller, *President*
Elaina Thomas, *COO*
Christina Bastas, *Manager*
Lisa Klevence, *Director*
Chris Salica, *Director*
EMP: 10 **EST:** 1996
SALES: 1.1MM **Privately Held**
SIC: 7372 Business oriented computer software

(G-19363)
PREFERRED ROCKS LLC
100 W Matsonford Rd # 101 (19087-4558)
PHONE...................................484 684-1221
Mike O'Neill, *CEO*
EMP: 10
SALES (est): 850.5K **Privately Held**
SIC: 1081 Metal mining exploration & development services

(G-19364)
PREMIER MAGNESIA LLC (PA)
1275 Drummers Ln Ste 102 (19087-1571)
PHONE...................................610 828-6929
John Gehret, *CEO*
Mark Shand, *President*
Rick Wrenn Jr, *President*
Peter Ahl, *General Mgr*
Wolfgang Von Der Heyde, *General Mgr*
◆ **EMP:** 20
SALES (est): 60.2MM **Privately Held**
SIC: 3295 Minerals, ground or treated

(G-19365)
PROSOFT SOFTWARE INC
Also Called: Prosoft Clinical
996 Old Eagle School Rd # 1106 (19087-1806)
PHONE...................................484 580-8162
Dror Rom, *President*
Rebecca Scherzer, *Manager*

EMP: 13
SQ FT: 1,000
SALES (est): 2.4MM **Privately Held**
WEB: www.prosof.com
SIC: 3821 Clinical laboratory instruments, except medical & dental

(G-19366)
PURAGLOBE FLORIDA LLC (PA)
435 Devon Park Dr (19087-1935)
PHONE...................................813 247-1754
Matt Bulley,
EMP: 3
SALES (est): 675.8K **Privately Held**
SIC: 1389 Servicing oil & gas wells

(G-19367)
R R DONNELLEY & SONS COMPANY
Also Called: R R Donnelley
440 E Swedesford Rd # 480 (19087-1820)
PHONE...................................610 688-9090
Tasha Nilsen, *Manager*
EMP: 4
SALES (corp-wide): 6.8B **Publicly Held**
WEB: www.rrdonnelley.com
SIC: 2759 Commercial printing
PA: R. R. Donnelley & Sons Company
35 W Wacker Dr Ste 3650
Chicago IL 60601
312 326-8000

(G-19368)
RAPID LEARNING INSTITUTE
435 Devon Park Dr Ste 510 (19087-1939)
PHONE...................................877 792-2172
Stephen Meyer, *President*
Michael Boyette, *Vice Pres*
Andrew Elia, *Vice Pres*
Rob Krekstein, *VP Sales*
Brian McCallum, *VP Mktg*
EMP: 19
SALES (est): 2MM **Privately Held**
SIC: 7372 8299 Educational computer software; educational services

(G-19369)
REGENCY ENERGY PARTNERS LP
100 W Matsonford Rd 3-301 (19087-4556)
PHONE...................................610 687-8900
EMP: 6
SALES (corp-wide): 54B **Publicly Held**
SIC: 1311 Crude petroleum & natural gas
HQ: Regency Energy Partners Lp
8111 Westchester Dr # 600
Dallas TX 75225
214 750-1771

(G-19370)
ROVI CORPORATION
550 E Swedesford Rd # 350 (19087-1607)
PHONE...................................610 293-8561
EMP: 5
SALES (est): 457.4K **Privately Held**
SIC: 7372 Prepackaged software

(G-19371)
SHERWIN-WILLIAMS COMPANY
317 W Lancaster Ave (19087-3904)
PHONE...................................610 975-0126
Theresa Kramer, *Manager*
EMP: 6
SALES (corp-wide): 17.5B **Publicly Held**
WEB: www.sherwin.com
SIC: 5231 2851 5198 Paint; paints & allied products; paints
PA: The Sherwin-Williams Company
101 W Prospect Ave # 1020
Cleveland OH 44115
216 566-2000

(G-19372)
SPECTRASONICS INC
Also Called: Spectrasonics Imaging
440 Woodcrest Rd (19087-5413)
PHONE...................................610 964-9637
EMP: 6
SQ FT: 1,900
SALES: 600K **Privately Held**
SIC: 5047 3841 Whol Medical/Hospital Equipment Mfg Surgical/Medical Instruments

(G-19373)
STICKMAN BREWS
431 Woodhill Rd (19087-2224)
PHONE.....................................856 912-4372
EMP: 3
SALES (est): 75.4K Privately Held
SIC: 2082 Malt beverages

(G-19374)
SUNGARD AR FINANCING LLC
Also Called: Sungard Availability Services
680 E Swedesford Rd (19087-1605)
PHONE.....................................484 582-2000
Andrew A Stern, CEO
EMP: 3
SALES (est): 136.7K
SALES (corp-wide): 8.4B Publicly Held
SIC: 7371 7372 Software programming
   applications; business oriented computer
   software
HQ: Fis Data Systems Inc.
   200 Campus Dr
   Collegeville PA 19426
   484 582-2000

(G-19375)
SUNGARD CAPITAL CORP II (DH)
680 E Swedesford Rd (19087-1605)
PHONE.....................................484 582-2000
Glenn H Hutchins, Ch of Bd
Russell P Fradin, President
Christopher Breakiron, Vice Pres
Charles J Neral, CFO
Patricia K Cassidy, Officer
EMP: 11
SALES: 2.8B
SALES (corp-wide): 8.4B Publicly Held
SIC: 7372 7374 Prepackaged software;
   data processing & preparation

(G-19376)
SUNGARD HOLDCO LLC
680 E Swedesford Rd (19087-1605)
PHONE.....................................484 582-2000
Russell P Fradin, President
EMP: 12996
SALES (est): 98.4MM
SALES (corp-wide): 8.4B Publicly Held
SIC: 7372 7374 Prepackaged software;
   data processing & preparation
HQ: Sungard Holding Corp.
   680 E Swedesford Rd
   Wayne PA 19087
   888 332-2564

(G-19377)
SUNGARD HOLDING CORP (DH)
680 E Swedesford Rd (19087-1605)
PHONE.....................................888 332-2564
Russell P Fradin, President
Chris Breakiron, Principal
Regina Brab, Vice Pres
Marianne Brown, CFO
EMP: 4 EST: 2005
SALES: 111.1MM
SALES (corp-wide): 8.4B Publicly Held
SIC: 7372 7374 Prepackaged software;
   data processing & preparation

(G-19378)
TAYLOR COMMUNICATIONS INC
440 E Swedesford Rd # 3045
(19087-1820)
PHONE.....................................610 688-9090
Bruce Coppola, Branch Mgr
EMP: 6
SQ FT: 10,000
SALES (corp-wide): 3.2B Privately Held
WEB: www.stdreg.com
SIC: 2761 Manifold business forms
HQ: Taylor Communications, Inc.
   1725 Roe Crest Dr
   North Mankato MN 56003
   507 625-2828

(G-19379)
TECH-SEAL PRODUCTS INC ✪
460 E Swedesford Rd # 3000
(19087-1835)
PHONE.....................................847 805-6400
EMP: 3 EST: 2018
SALES (est): 222K Privately Held
SIC: 3069 Linings, vulcanizing rubber

(G-19380)
TECHNOLOGY DYNAMICS INC
489 Devon Park Dr Ste 318 (19087-1809)
PHONE.....................................888 988-3243
Marc A Martina, President
Greg McGinn, Principal
EMP: 4
SALES (est): 546.3K Privately Held
WEB: www.tech-dynamics.com
SIC: 7371 7372 7373 Computer software
   development & applications; prepackaged
   software; systems software development
   services

(G-19381)
TEKNI-PLEX INC (PA)
Also Called: Tekniplex Co
460 E Swedesford Rd # 3000
(19087-1835)
PHONE.....................................484 690-1520
Paul J Young, President
Glenn Fish, COO
Russell Hubbard, Vice Pres
John Seifert, CFO
Joan Centifonti, Controller
▲ EMP: 30 EST: 1994
SALES (est): 1.1B Privately Held
WEB: www.dolco.net
SIC: 2679 3462 3052 2672 Egg cartons,
   molded pulp: made from purchased mate-
   rial; pump & compressor forgings, ferrous;
   garden hose, plastic; cloth lined paper:
   made from purchased paper; coated
   paper, except photographic, carbon or
   abrasive; glazed paper, except photo-
   graphic, carbon or abrasive

(G-19382)
TELEFLEX INCORPORATED (PA)
550 E Swedesford Rd # 400 (19087-1607)
PHONE.....................................610 225-6800
Benson F Smith, Ch of Bd
Liam J Kelly, President
Demetrio Cadiente, Business Mgr
Cynthia Sharo, Counsel
Thomas A Kennedy, Senior VP
▲ EMP: 277 EST: 1943
SQ FT: 84,000
SALES: 2.1B Publicly Held
WEB: www.teleflex.com
SIC: 3841 3842 Surgical & medical instru-
   ments; surgical appliances & supplies

(G-19383)
TOOL TEC INC
Also Called: TTi Metals
900 W Valley Rd Ste 504 (19087-1848)
PHONE.....................................610 688-9086
Clayton Hardon, President
Tom Hardon, Sales Staff
Lisa Michell, Manager
Mike Zataveski, Manager
▲ EMP: 12
SQ FT: 5,500
SALES (est): 2.6MM Privately Held
WEB: www.tooltec.com
SIC: 3549 Metalworking machinery

(G-19384)
TRIDENT TPI HOLDINGS INC
460 E Swedesford Rd # 3000
(19087-1801)
PHONE.....................................484 690-1520
EMP: 2500
SALES (est): 49.2MM Privately Held
SIC: 2679 3462 3052 2672 Egg cartons,
   molded pulp: made from purchased material; pump & compressor forgings, ferrous;
   garden hose, plastic; cloth lined paper:
   made from purchased paper; coated
   paper, except photographic, carbon or
   abrasive; glazed paper, except photographic, carbon or abrasive

(G-19385)
TV GUIDE DISTRIBUTION INC
100 W Matsonford Rd Ste 1 (19087-4565)
PHONE.....................................610 293-8500
Richard Battista, President
Stephen H Kay, Vice Pres
Vince Ohanya, Vice Pres
Bedi Singh, Treasurer
EMP: 500
SALES (est): 42.1MM Privately Held
SIC: 2721 Television schedules: publishing
   & printing

(G-19386)
TWO PAPERDOLLS LLC
163 E Lancaster Ave (19087-3525)
PHONE.....................................610 293-4933
Vanessa D Kreckel,
EMP: 16
SQ FT: 6,000
SALES (est): 1.5MM Privately Held
WEB: www.twopaperdolls.com
SIC: 2759 Card printing & engraving, ex-
   cept greeting

(G-19387)
VELICEPT THERAPEUTICS INC
640 Lee Rd Ste 119 (19087-5600)
PHONE.....................................484 318-2988
James Walker, CEO
Douglas Gessl, CFO
EMP: 8
SALES (est): 340K Privately Held
SIC: 2834 Pharmaceutical preparations

(G-19388)
VIRTIC INDUSTRIES LLC
504 Woodland Ct (19087-3426)
PHONE.....................................610 246-9428
Andres Lebaudy, Partner
EMP: 3
SALES (est): 191.1K Privately Held
SIC: 3949 7389 Striking (punching) bags;

(G-19389)
WALLQUEST INC
465 Devon Park Dr (19087-1871)
PHONE.....................................610 293-1330
John Collins, President
Jack Collins, Vice Pres
John Ohara, Vice Pres
Carl Robinson, Director
Robert E Shields, Admin Sec
◆ EMP: 65
SQ FT: 96,000
SALES (est): 18.4MM Privately Held
SIC: 2679 2396 Wallpaper; fabric printing
   & stamping

(G-19390)
WAVERLY PARTNERS INC
175 Strafford Ave (19087-3317)
PHONE.....................................610 687-7867
Brian Kelly, President
Patrick Burke, Vice Pres
EMP: 152
SALES (est): 8.8MM Privately Held
SIC: 3469 3599 Metal stampings; machine
   shop, jobbing & repair

(G-19391)
WESTLAKE CHEMICAL PARTNERS LP
993 Old Eagle School Rd (19087-1710)
PHONE.....................................484 253-4545
EMP: 4 Publicly Held
SIC: 2869 Ethylene
HQ: Westlake Chemical Partners Lp
   2801 Post Oak Blvd # 600
   Houston TX 77056
   713 585-2900

(G-19392)
WHEELER ENTERPRISES INC
Also Called: ABS Print Management
175 Strafford Ave Ste 1 (19087-3340)
PHONE.....................................610 975-9230
Samuel Wheeler, President
Ellen Wheeler, Corp Secy
EMP: 3
SQ FT: 1,000
SALES (est): 513K Privately Held
WEB: www.absprint.com
SIC: 5112 2752 Business forms; commer-
   cial printing, lithographic

Waynesboro
Franklin County

(G-19393)
AAIM CONTROLS INC
11885 Mutual Dr (17268-8627)
PHONE.....................................717 765-9100
Arthur J Marshall, President
Emily Stuff, Purchasing
Darren Marshall, Electrical Engi

Teresa Izer, Administration
EMP: 12
SQ FT: 10,000
SALES (est): 2.9MM
SALES (corp-wide): 6.8B Privately Held
WEB: www.aaimcontrols.com
SIC: 8711 3625 Electrical or electronic en-
   gineering; control equipment, electric
HQ: Danfoss A/S
   Nordborgvej 81
   Nordborg 6430
   748 822-22

(G-19394)
AAXIS DISTRIBUTORS
8605 Anthony Hwy (17268-9710)
PHONE.....................................717 762-2947
Paul Mohn, Owner
EMP: 3 EST: 2014
SALES (est): 156.9K Privately Held
SIC: 3999 Manufacturing industries

(G-19395)
AJ PALLET LLC
Also Called: Shank Pallet Recyclers
300 Walnut St (17268-2045)
PHONE.....................................717 597-3545
Archie Jones, Mng Member
EMP: 40
SQ FT: 40,000
SALES (est): 360.7K Privately Held
SIC: 2448 Pallets, wood & wood with metal

(G-19396)
ANVIL INTERNATIONAL LLC
330 E 9th St (17268-2064)
PHONE.....................................717 762-9141
Cathy Minnich, Branch Mgr
EMP: 3
SALES (corp-wide): 4.8B Privately Held
SIC: 3498 Fabricated pipe & fittings
HQ: Anvil International, Llc
   2 Holland Way
   Exeter NH 03833
   603 418-2800

(G-19397)
APPALACHAIN GRILLS
146 Briar Ridge Dr (17268-1814)
PHONE.....................................717 762-3321
Randolph C Monn, Principal
EMP: 4
SALES: 526K Privately Held
SIC: 3631 Barbecues, grills & braziers
   (outdoor cooking)

(G-19398)
ARMACLAD INC
6806 Anthony Hwy (17268-9783)
P.O. Box 70 (17268-0070)
PHONE.....................................717 749-3141
EMP: 40
SQ FT: 117,000
SALES (est): 4MM Privately Held
SIC: 3442 Mfg Metal Doors/Sash/Trim

(G-19399)
BECK MANUFACTURING COMPANY (DH)
330 E 9th St (17268-2064)
P.O. Box 510 (17268-0510)
PHONE.....................................717 762-9141
Tom Fish, President
John Ashbaugh, Vice Pres
▲ EMP: 23
SALES (est): 39MM
SALES (corp-wide): 4.8B Privately Held
WEB: www.anvilint.com
SIC: 3498 Fabricated pipe & fittings
HQ: Anvil International, Llc
   2 Holland Way
   Exeter NH 03833
   603 418-2800

(G-19400)
BILTWOOD POWDER COATING LLC
217 N Franklin St (17268-1105)
PHONE.....................................717 655-5664
EMP: 4
SALES (est): 475.6K Privately Held
SIC: 3399 Powder, metal

GEOGRAPHIC

(G-19401)
BITREKPASUB INC (DH)
Also Called: Picoma Industries
330 E 9th St (17268-2064)
P.O. Box 510 (17268-0510)
PHONE...................................717 762-9141
John Ashbaugh, *General Mgr*
EMP: 77
SQ FT: 70,000
SALES (est): 30.8MM
SALES (corp-wide): 4.8B **Privately Held**
SIC: 3494 Pipe fittings; couplings,
except pressure & soil pipe; fabricated
pipe & fittings
HQ: Anvil International, Llc
2 Holland Way
Exeter NH 03833
603 418-2800

(G-19402)
BLUE RIDGE MTN COOKERY INC
Also Called: Brmc Fabrications
6806 Anthony Hwy (17268-9783)
P.O. Box 70 (17268-0070)
PHONE...................................717 762-1211
Nick Turano, *President*
EMP: 33 **EST:** 1998
SQ FT: 45,000
SALES (est): 8.1MM **Privately Held**
WEB: www.classiccookers.com
SIC: 3496 Grilles & grillework, woven wire

(G-19403)
BROWNS WELDING INC
2110a Market Square Blvd (17268-3800)
PHONE...................................717 762-6467
Samuel J Checote IV, *President*
Don Checote, *Treasurer*
EMP: 4
SQ FT: 3,400
SALES (est): 250K **Privately Held**
SIC: 7692 3498 Welding repair; fabricated
pipe & fittings

(G-19404)
CLEVER INC
Also Called: Clever Advertising and Prtg
809 S Potomac St (17268-2158)
PHONE...................................717 762-7508
Dale E Clever, *President*
Ann Clever, *Vice Pres*
Mike Clever, *Treasurer*
EMP: 3
SQ FT: 4,000
SALES (est): 456.2K **Privately Held**
SIC: 2752 5199 Commercial printing, off-
set; advertising specialties

(G-19405)
CORPORATE GRAPHICS INTL INC
101 E 9th St (17268-2200)
PHONE...................................800 247-2751
Kendra Eraithwaite, *General Mgr*
EMP: 15
SALES (corp-wide): 3.2B **Privately Held**
SIC: 2752 Commercial printing, offset
HQ: Corporate Graphics International, Inc.
1885 Northway Dr
North Mankato MN 56003
507 625-4400

(G-19406)
COUNTRY ACRES CIDER & PROD INC
6540 Wayne Hwy (17268-8600)
PHONE...................................717 263-9349
Mark Toigo, *President*
Laban Garber, *Vice Pres*
EMP: 6
SALES (est): 530K **Privately Held**
SIC: 2099 Cider, nonalcoholic

(G-19407)
D L GEORGE & SONS MFG INC
20 E 6th St Ste 201 (17268-9491)
PHONE...................................717 765-4700
David George, *President*
Christopher Hess, *General Mgr*
Phillip Vandeuren, *Vice Pres*
David L George, *Treasurer*
Cheryl Gochenauer, *Treasurer*
EMP: 74
SQ FT: 500,000

SALES: 5.8MM **Privately Held**
SIC: 3498 3599 3444 3443 Pipe fittings,
fabricated from purchased pipe; pipe sections fabricated from purchased pipe;
tube fabricating (contract bending & shaping); machine & other job shop work; machine shop, jobbing & repair; sheet
metalwork; fabricated plate work (boiler
shop); fabricated structural metal; laser
welding, drilling & cutting equipment

(G-19408)
DANIEL W BENEDICT
Also Called: Benedict Cabinetry
4574 Altenwald Rd (17268-8606)
PHONE...................................717 709-0149
Daniel W Benedict, *Owner*
EMP: 5
SALES (est): 300K **Privately Held**
SIC: 1751 2434 Finish & trim carpentry;
wood kitchen cabinets

(G-19409)
ERIC L SOCKS
4974 Orphanage Rd (17268-8538)
PHONE...................................717 762-7488
Eric L Socks, *Principal*
EMP: 4
SALES (est): 319.2K **Privately Held**
SIC: 2252 Socks

(G-19410)
H M W ENTERPRISES INC
207 N Franklin St (17268-1105)
P.O. Box 3597, Hagerstown MD (21742-
3597)
PHONE...................................717 765-4690
H Michael Wutz, *Ch of Bd*
Vernon Crampton, *Vice Pres*
EMP: 13 **EST:** 1965
SQ FT: 20,000
SALES (est): 3MM **Privately Held**
WEB: www.hmwent.com
SIC: 3823 3575 3577 3571 Computer in-
terface equipment for industrial process
control; computer terminals; computer pe-
ripheral equipment; electronic computers

(G-19411)
HOLLOWELL ALUMINUM
14471 Hollowell Church Rd (17268-9554)
PHONE...................................717 597-0826
Richard Martin, *Owner*
EMP: 3
SALES (est): 442.3K **Privately Held**
SIC: 3334 7699 Primary aluminum; metal
reshaping & replating services

(G-19412)
HOPEWELL MANUFACTURING INC
217 N Franklin St (17268-1105)
PHONE...................................717 593-9400
James McCleaf II, *President*
Jackie Woodcock, *Graphic Designe*
EMP: 6
SQ FT: 7,900
SALES (est): 964.4K **Privately Held**
SIC: 3354 7336 Shapes, extruded alu-
minum; commercial art & graphic design

(G-19413)
INNOVATIVE ADVERTISING & MKTG
12178 Country Club Rd (17268-9284)
PHONE...................................717 788-1385
Ronda Linck, *President*
EMP: 4
SALES (est): 360K **Privately Held**
SIC: 7311 2721 Advertising consultant;
magazines: publishing only, not printed on
site

(G-19414)
JOHNSON CONTROLS INC
100 Cumberland Valley Ave (17268-1206)
PHONE...................................717 765-2461
EMP: 94 **Privately Held**
SIC: 2531 Seats, automobile
HQ: Johnson Controls, Inc.
5757 N Green Bay Ave
Milwaukee WI 53209
414 524-1200

(G-19415)
LSI CONTROLS INC
Also Called: L S I Controls
11664 Orchard Rd (17268-9656)
PHONE...................................717 762-2191
Randy Holl, *CEO*
Walt Nuschke, *President*
Eric Holl, *Vice Pres*
Jack Scott, *Vice Pres*
Jason Bartholow, *Prdtn Mgr*
EMP: 6
SQ FT: 6,000
SALES: 1MM **Privately Held**
WEB: www.lsicontrols.com
SIC: 3823 8711 Industrial instrmnts
msrmnt display/control process variable;
consulting engineer

(G-19416)
MADISON INDS HOLDINGS LLC
Also Called: ATI Landis Threading Systems
360 S Church St (17268-2610)
PHONE...................................717 762-3151
Matthew Brown, *Branch Mgr*
EMP: 125
SALES (corp-wide): 297MM **Privately
Held**
SIC: 3541 3545 3498 3398 Machine
tools, metal cutting: exotic (explosive,
etc.); machine tool accessories; fabri-
cated pipe & fittings; metal heat treating
PA: Madison Industries Holdings Llc
500 W Madison St Ste 3890
Chicago IL 60661
312 277-0156

(G-19417)
MAGNUM CARBIDE LLC
225 E 9th St (17268-2063)
PHONE...................................717 762-7181
Michael C Mouton,
Sandra M Woodard,
▲ **EMP:** 9 **EST:** 2012
SALES (est): 1.1MM **Privately Held**
SIC: 3545 Cutting tools for machine tools

(G-19418)
MERCERSBURG PRINTING INC
Also Called: J & M Printing
114 Walnut St Ste 1 (17268-1668)
PHONE...................................717 762-8204
Karen Beaver, *Manager*
EMP: 3
SALES (corp-wide): 7.3MM **Privately
Held**
SIC: 2752 2759 Commercial printing, off-
set; letterpress printing
PA: Mercersburg Printing, Inc.
9964 Buchanan Trl W
Mercersburg PA 17236
717 328-3902

(G-19419)
NAVITOR INC
Navitor East
725 Clayton Ave (17268-2060)
PHONE...................................717 765-3121
Kendra Braithwrite, *General Mgr*
Vickie Seeger, *Human Res Mgr*
Robyn Stoops, *Info Tech Dir*
Eddie Lowman, *Associate*
EMP: 480
SALES (corp-wide): 3.2B **Privately Held**
WEB: www.labelworks.com
SIC: 2759 2796 2752 Invitations: printing;
stationery: printing; envelopes: printing;
platemaking services; commercial print-
ing, lithographic
HQ: Navitor, Inc.
1625 Roe Crest Dr
North Mankato MN 56003
507 625-2828

(G-19420)
OLYMPIAN ATHLETICS
55 W Main St (17268-1555)
PHONE...................................717 765-8615
Ronald Hartzok, *Partner*
Shirley Hartzok, *Partner*
EMP: 3
SQ FT: 1,200
SALES (est): 319.7K **Privately Held**
SIC: 3949 Sporting & athletic goods

(G-19421)
PACEMAKER PRESS PP&S INC
4999 Zane A Miller Dr (17268-9822)
P.O. Box 304, Arendtsville (17303-0304)
PHONE...................................301 696-9629
Matthew W Whitney, *President*
EMP: 50 **EST:** 1969
SQ FT: 33,000
SALES (est): 9.9MM **Privately Held**
WEB: www.pacepressinc.com
SIC: 2752 Commercial printing, litho-
graphic

(G-19422)
RECORD HERALD PUBLISHING CO (DH)
30 Walnut St (17268-1644)
P.O. Box 271 (17268-0271)
PHONE...................................717 762-2151
Denise Igram, *General Mgr*
Shawn Hardy, *Editor*
Scott Weaver, *Editor*
Jay Wetzel, *Prdtn Mgr*
Dawn Friedman, *Sales Staff*
EMP: 50 **EST:** 1847
SQ FT: 15,000
SALES (est): 4.2MM
SALES (corp-wide): 1.5B **Publicly Held**
WEB: www.therecordherald.com
SIC: 2711 2752 Commercial printing &
newspaper publishing combined; com-
mercial printing, lithographic
HQ: Gatehouse Media, Llc
175 Sullys Trl Fl 3
Pittsford NY 14534
585 598-0030

(G-19423)
RICHARD K MOHN
Also Called: Mohn's Lumber Mill
10375 Old Forge Rd (17268-8888)
PHONE...................................717 762-7646
Richard K Mohn, *Owner*
EMP: 5
SALES (est): 568.2K **Privately Held**
SIC: 2421 2426 Lumber: rough, sawed or
planed; railroad ties, sawed; hardwood di-
mension & flooring mills

(G-19424)
SOUDERS INDUSTRIES INC
Also Called: Sesco
6806 Anthony Hwy (17268-9783)
PHONE...................................717 271-4975
EMP: 30
SALES (corp-wide): 14.5MM **Privately
Held**
SIC: 3679 Harness assemblies for elec-
tronic use: wire or cable
PA: Souders Industries, Inc.
19 Ash St
Mont Alto PA 17237
717 749-3900

(G-19425)
TE CONNECTIVITY CORPORATION
627 N Grant St (17268-8654)
PHONE...................................717 762-9186
Scott Stein, *Branch Mgr*
EMP: 215
SALES (corp-wide): 13.1B **Privately Held**
WEB: www.raychem.com
SIC: 3625 3823 Switches, electronic appli-
cations; programmers, process type
HQ: Te Connectivity Corporation
1050 Westlakes Dr
Berwyn PA 19312
610 893-9800

(G-19426)
TE CONNECTIVITY CORPORATION
627 N Grant St (17268-8654)
PHONE...................................717 762-9186
EMP: 130
SALES (corp-wide): 12.2B **Privately Held**
SIC: 3312 3678 Manufactures Tooling
Component Partstool & Die
HQ: Te Connectivity Corporation
1050 Westlakes Dr
Berwyn PA 19312
610 893-9800

GEOGRAPHIC

(G-19427)
THORSENS PRECISION GRINDING
20 E 6th St Ste 216 (17268-2068)
PHONE...............................717 765-9090
Kelly Thorsen, *CEO*
EMP: 3
SALES (est): 341.5K **Privately Held**
SIC: 3599 Grinding castings for the trade

(G-19428)
THREE SOLES CORP
Also Called: James Shoe Store
76 W Main St Frnt (17268-1553)
PHONE...............................717 762-1945
Barbara Chanceller, *President*
EMP: 4
SQ FT: 1,200
SALES (est): 345.2K **Privately Held**
SIC: 5661 5999 2396 Shoes, orthopedic; trophies & plaques; screen printing on fabric articles

(G-19429)
VISION WAREHOUSING AND DIST
144 Cleveland Ave (17268-2646)
PHONE...............................717 762-5912
John Iser, *President*
Paul Hovis, *Vice Pres*
Richard Piper, *Treasurer*
Robert Rodgers, *Admin Sec*
EMP: 5 EST: 1900
SALES (est): 759.2K **Privately Held**
SIC: 4222 2097 Warehousing, cold storage or refrigerated; manufactured ice

(G-19430)
WILMER R EBY
Also Called: Sickley Hollow Sawyer
15640 Oak Rd (17268-9547)
PHONE...............................717 597-1090
Wilmer R EBY, *Owner*
EMP: 6 EST: 2010
SALES (est): 673.7K **Privately Held**
SIC: 2421 Sawmills & planing mills, general

(G-19431)
YORK INTERNATIONAL CORPORATION
100 C V Ave (17268)
PHONE...............................717 762-1440
Jim Furlong, *Manager*
EMP: 500 **Privately Held**
SIC: 3585 Refrigeration & heating equipment
HQ: York International Corporation
631 S Richland Ave
York PA 17403
717 771-7890

(G-19432)
YORK INTERNATIONAL CORPORATION
Jci Frick
100 Cumberland Valley Ave (17268-1206)
PHONE...............................717 762-2121
Ian McGavifk, *Manager*
EMP: 300 **Privately Held**
SIC: 3585 Refrigeration equipment, complete
HQ: York International Corporation
631 S Richland Ave
York PA 17403
717 771-7890

Waynesburg
Greene County

(G-19433)
BAILEYS STEEL & SUPPLY LLC
60 Moscow Rd (15370-2752)
PHONE...............................724 267-4648
Daniel E Bailey, *Mng Member*
EMP: 3
SALES (est): 1.2MM **Privately Held**
SIC: 5051 3449 3441 3429 Structural shapes, iron or steel; miscellaneous metalwork; fabricated structural metal; manufactured hardware (general); steel pipe & tubes; blast furnaces & steel mills

(G-19434)
BLOWOUT TOOLS INC
114 Baker Dr (15370-7012)
PHONE...............................724 627-0208
EMP: 14 **Publicly Held**
SIC: 3533 Mfg Oil/Gas Field Machinery
HQ: Blowout Tools, Inc.
2202 Oil Center Ct
Houston TX 77073
405 671-3800

(G-19435)
BURRELL MINING PRODUCTS INC
I 79 S Ext Kirby George (15370)
PHONE...............................724 966-5183
James Barbina, *Manager*
EMP: 14
SALES (corp-wide): 18.4MM **Privately Held**
SIC: 3271 Concrete block & brick
HQ: Burrell Mining Products, Inc.
2400 Leechburg Rd Ste 216
New Kensington PA 15068
724 339-2511

(G-19436)
CUMBERLAND COAL RESOURCES LP (DH)
158 Portal Rd (15370-2330)
P.O. Box 1020 (15370-3020)
PHONE...............................724 852-5845
Richard H Verheij, *CEO*
James Bryja, *Vice Pres*
▼ EMP: 40
SQ FT: 12,000
SALES (est): 72.9MM
SALES (corp-wide): 2B **Publicly Held**
SIC: 1222 Bituminous coal-underground mining
HQ: Alpha Natural Resources, Inc.
636 Shelby St Ste 1c
Bristol TN 37620
423 574-5100

(G-19437)
CUMBERLAND COAL RESOURCES LP
855 Kirby Rd (15370-3592)
PHONE...............................724 627-7500
Charles Zabrosky, *General Mgr*
EMP: 529
SALES (corp-wide): 2B **Publicly Held**
SIC: 1222 Bituminous coal-underground mining
HQ: Cumberland Coal Resources Lp
158 Portal Rd
Waynesburg PA 15370

(G-19438)
CUMBERLAND CONTURA LLC
158 Portal Rd (15370-2330)
P.O. Box 848, Bristol TN (37621-0848)
PHONE...............................724 627-7500
Kevin S Crutchfield, *CEO*
EMP: 9
SALES (est): 299K
SALES (corp-wide): 24.8MM **Privately Held**
SIC: 1222 Bituminous coal-underground mining
PA: Contura Energy Services, Llc
340 Martin Luth
Bristol TN 37620
423 573-0300

(G-19439)
DIRECT RESULTS BSP INC
Also Called: Greenesaver
185 Wade St (15370-8118)
PHONE...............................724 627-2040
Shelly Brown, *CEO*
Pam Blaker, *COO*
EMP: 15
SALES (est): 300K **Privately Held**
WEB: www.greenesaver.com
SIC: 3993 Signs & advertising specialties

(G-19440)
EMERALD COAL RESOURCES LP
Also Called: Emerald Mine
2071 Garards Fort Rd (15370-2491)
P.O. Box 1020 (15370-3020)
PHONE...............................724 627-7500

Jim Roberts, *Managing Prtnr*
James Bryja, *Partner*
Frank Wood, *Partner*
Pennsylvania Services Corporat, *General Ptnr*
▲ EMP: 571
SQ FT: 8,000
SALES (est): 47.1MM
SALES (corp-wide): 2B **Publicly Held**
WEB: www.emeraldmine.com
SIC: 1222 Underground mining, subbituminous
HQ: Alpha Natural Resources, Inc.
636 Shelby St Ste 1c
Bristol TN 37620
423 574-5100

(G-19441)
FRAME UP & GALLERY
126 N Maiden St (15370-1716)
PHONE...............................724 627-0552
John McCall, *Owner*
EMP: 3
SALES (est): 109.7K **Privately Held**
SIC: 2511 Bed frames, except water bed frames: wood

(G-19442)
GRAHAMS WELDING
1775 Oak Forest Rd (15370-7326)
PHONE...............................724 627-6082
Beverly Graham, *Owner*
EMP: 4
SALES (est): 176.1K **Privately Held**
SIC: 7692 Welding repair

(G-19443)
GREENE COUNTY DRILLING CO INC
155 Dark Hollow Rd (15370-2434)
PHONE...............................724 627-3393
Richard Pultorak, *President*
Carole Pultorak, *Vice Pres*
EMP: 5 EST: 1943
SALES: 67.5K **Privately Held**
SIC: 1389 Servicing oil & gas wells

(G-19444)
GREENE COUNTY GAS & OIL CO
155 Dark Hollow Rd (15370-2434)
PHONE...............................724 627-3393
Richard A Pultorak, *Partner*
Gary Bowers, *Partner*
EMP: 5
SALES (est): 336K **Privately Held**
SIC: 1381 Reworking oil & gas wells

(G-19445)
HOYS CONSTRUCTION COMPANY INC
Also Called: Hoy Redi-Mix
165 Rolling Meadows Rd (15370)
P.O. Box 957 (15370-0957)
PHONE...............................724 852-1112
Charles N Hoy, *President*
Robert Hoy, *Vice Pres*
EMP: 11 EST: 1971
SQ FT: 1,500
SALES (est): 1.8MM **Privately Held**
SIC: 3273 Ready-mixed concrete

(G-19446)
HYDRA SERVICE INC
500 Jefferson Rd (15370)
P.O. Box 88 (15370-0088)
PHONE...............................724 852-2423
James Camigiani, *President*
EMP: 6
SQ FT: 12,500
SALES (est): 1.1MM **Privately Held**
WEB: www.hydra-service.net
SIC: 7699 3599 Hydraulic equipment repair; custom machinery

(G-19447)
JEFFREY L ROBERTS
Also Called: Roberts Orthotics Prosthetics
107 E Oakland Ave (15370)
PHONE...............................724 627-4600
Jeffrey Roberts, *Owner*
EMP: 3 EST: 2000
SALES (est): 508K **Privately Held**
SIC: 3842 Prosthetic appliances

(G-19448)
MOUNTAINEER PUBLISHING
601 Pisgah Ridge Rd (15370-3875)
P.O. Box 646 (15370-0646)
PHONE...............................724 880-3753
Lisa Smith, *Principal*
EMP: 3
SQ FT: 650
SALES: 30K **Privately Held**
SIC: 2721 Periodicals: publishing & printing

(G-19449)
OBSERVER PUBLISHING COMPANY
32 S Church St Fl 1 (15370-1862)
PHONE...............................724 852-2602
Matt Miller, *Director*
EMP: 7
SALES (corp-wide): 28.7MM **Privately Held**
WEB: www.observer-reporter.com
SIC: 2711 Newspapers, publishing & printing
PA: Observer Publishing Company
122 S Main St
Washington PA 15301
724 222-2200

(G-19450)
OMEGA TRANSWORLD LTD
877 Garards Fort Rd (15370-6708)
P.O. Box 57, Garards Fort (15334-0057)
PHONE...............................724 966-5183
Tom Sullivan, *Principal*
EMP: 10
SALES (est): 307.4K **Privately Held**
SIC: 3272 Concrete products

(G-19451)
RHODES & HAMMERS PRINTING
54 S Church St (15370-1832)
P.O. Box 667 (15370-0667)
PHONE...............................724 852-1457
Jay Hammers, *President*
EMP: 7
SQ FT: 3,500
SALES (est): 607.1K **Privately Held**
SIC: 2752 Commercial printing, offset

(G-19452)
WAYNESBURG MILLING CO
387 S Washington St (15370-2199)
PHONE...............................724 627-6137
Donald Lindsay, *President*
Janice Blair Martin, *Corp Secy*
Jeanette Blair Lindsay, *Vice Pres*
EMP: 4
SALES: 500K **Privately Held**
SIC: 5191 2048 Feed; fertilizer & fertilizer materials; prepared feeds

---

Weatherly
Carbon County

(G-19453)
BRADFORD CLOCKS LIMITED
1080 Hudson Dr (18255-2820)
PHONE...............................570 427-4493
Dan Humenick, *President*
Leo L Humenick Jr, *Vice Pres*
▲ EMP: 11 EST: 1961
SQ FT: 17,000
SALES (est): 700K **Privately Held**
WEB: www.bradfordclocks.com
SIC: 2541 Cabinets, lockers & shelving

(G-19454)
KAMILA FARM LLC
174 Dulcey Rd (18255-3302)
PHONE...............................570 427-8318
James Dulcey,
EMP: 3
SALES (est): 107.4K **Privately Held**
SIC: 2086 Mineral water, carbonated: packaged in cans, bottles, etc.

(G-19455)
WEATHERLY CASTING AND MCH CO
300 Commerce St (18255-1200)
P.O. Box 21 (18255-0021)
PHONE..................................570 427-8611
Michael Leib, *President*
Mary Brown, *Principal*
Larry Palmer, *Plant Mgr*
Susan Rupert, *Purch Agent*
Michele Regan, *Treasurer*
▼ **EMP:** 82
SQ FT: 32,000
SALES (est): 18.8MM **Privately Held**
WEB: www.wecast.com
SIC: 3321 3543 3369 Gray iron castings;
ductile iron castings; industrial patterns;
nonferrous foundries

Webster
Westmoreland County

(G-19456)
CENTER MACHINE COMPANY
And 136 Rr 906 (15087)
PHONE..................................724 379-4066
James Palanza, *Owner*
EMP: 3
SQ FT: 5,000
SALES (est): 308.7K **Privately Held**
SIC: 3541 Machine tools, metal cutting
type

(G-19457)
ELITE TOOL COMPANY INC
First & Wall (15087)
PHONE..................................724 379-5800
James Guerrieri, *President*
EMP: 15
SQ FT: 6,500
SALES (est): 2.3MM **Privately Held**
SIC: 3599 Machine shop, jobbing & repair

Weedville
Elk County

(G-19458)
ELK RIVER LOGGING INC
3342 River Rd (15868-4616)
PHONE..................................814 787-4327
Curtis E Hahn, *Principal*
EMP: 6
SALES (est): 477.6K **Privately Held**
SIC: 2411 Logging

(G-19459)
SHAWN PAUL ZIMMERMAN KEVIN JOH
24670 Bennetts Valley Hwy (15868-2534)
PHONE..................................814 594-1371
Shawn P Zimmerman, *Owner*
EMP: 4
SALES (est): 271.7K **Privately Held**
SIC: 2084 Wines

(G-19460)
TODD A FORSYTHE
22949 Bennetts Valley Hwy (15868-2306)
PHONE..................................814 512-1457
Todd A Forsythe, *Principal*
EMP: 3
SALES (est): 285.3K **Privately Held**
SIC: 2411 Logging

Weissport
Carbon County

(G-19461)
TOP CIRCLE HOSIERY MILLS CO
329 Franklin St (18235-2703)
PHONE..................................610 379-0470
Jerry Zhao, *President*
Leon Song, *COO*
▲ **EMP:** 20
SQ FT: 26,000

SALES (est): 2.6MM **Privately Held**
WEB: www.topcircle.com
SIC: 2252 Socks

Wellsboro
Tioga County

(G-19462)
BAKWELL LLC
61 Bodine St (16901-8206)
PHONE..................................570 724-7067
Ward D Baker, *Owner*
EMP: 3
SALES (est): 161.5K **Privately Held**
SIC: 1311 Crude petroleum & natural gas

(G-19463)
GREAT LAKES WELLHEAD INC
81 Central Ave (16901-1836)
PHONE..................................570 723-8995
Larry Rein Hardt II, *Manager*
Kyle Fitzpatrick, *Manager*
EMP: 6
SALES (corp-wide): 4MM **Privately Held**
SIC: 1389 Oil field services
PA: Great Lakes Wellhead, Inc.
4243 S M 37
Grawn MI 49637
231 943-9100

(G-19464)
HAMPSONS FARM & GARDEN INC (PA)
Also Called: Agway
1 E Delmar Mdws (16901-7769)
PHONE..................................570 724-3012
Craig A Hampson, *CEO*
James L Hampson, *Treasurer*
EMP: 6
SALES (est): 2.7MM **Privately Held**
SIC: 5261 2048 Lawn & garden supplies;
livestock feeds

(G-19465)
HN AUTOMOTIVE INC
9728 Route 287 Ste 10 (16901-6717)
PHONE..................................570 724-5191
Garry Heatley, *Manager*
◆ **EMP:** 80
SALES (est): 10.7MM **Privately Held**
WEB: www.hnautomotive.com
SIC: 3559 Automotive related machinery

(G-19466)
INTELLIGENT DIRECT INC
10 1st St (16901-8167)
P.O. Box 119 (16901-0119)
PHONE..................................570 724-7355
Daniel Olasin, *President*
Jordan Foust, *Prdtn Mgr*
Jenn Frank, *Accounting Mgr*
Kyle Bower, *Accounts Mgr*
Ahin Chakraborty, *Accounts Mgr*
EMP: 37
SQ FT: 5,000
SALES (est): 3.7MM **Privately Held**
WEB: www.zipcodemaps.com
SIC: 2741 7375 Atlas, map & guide pub-
lishing; data base information retrieval

(G-19467)
JOHNSON MACHINE & PROD INC
70 Woodland Ave (16901-1930)
PHONE..................................570 724-2042
EMP: 7
SQ FT: 8,000
SALES: 391K **Privately Held**
SIC: 3999 3599 Barber & beauty shop
equipment; machine shop, jobbing & re-
pair

(G-19468)
JOKERS COAL & BUILDING SUPS (PA)
368 Tioga St (16901-6778)
PHONE..................................570 724-4912
James K Stager, *President*
Robert Baker, *Vice Pres*
Kelli Stager, *Treasurer*
EMP: 9 **EST:** 1926
SQ FT: 7,800

SALES (est): 742.4K **Privately Held**
SIC: 3271 5211 5989 Blocks, concrete or
cinder: standard; sand & gravel; brick;
concrete & cinder block; coal

(G-19469)
METALKRAFT INDUSTRIES INC
1944 Shumway Hill Rd (16901-6842)
P.O. Box 606 (16901-0606)
PHONE..................................570 724-6800
Aaron Singer, *President*
Ed Welfling, *Vice Pres*
Steve Macensky, *Purch Mgr*
Julie Sticklin, *Human Res Dir*
EMP: 47
SQ FT: 26,000
SALES (est): 10.8MM **Privately Held**
WEB: www.metalkraftpm.com
SIC: 3562 3469 3568 Ball bearings &
parts; machine parts, stamped or pressed
metal; drives, chains & sprockets

(G-19470)
MOSS MACHINE & DESIGN LLC
1121 Route 362 (16901-7214)
PHONE..................................570 724-9119
Steve Moss, *CEO*
EMP: 3
SALES: 250K **Privately Held**
SIC: 3599 Machine shop, jobbing & repair

(G-19471)
OSRAM SYLVANIA INC
1 Jackson St (16901-1797)
PHONE..................................570 724-8200
Robert Alspaugh, *Branch Mgr*
EMP: 300
SALES (corp-wide): 4.7B **Privately Held**
WEB: www.sylvania.com
SIC: 3641 3647 3646 3643 Electric
lamps; headlights (fixtures), vehicular;
commercial indusl & institutional electric
lighting fixtures; current-carrying wiring
devices; crucibles: graphite, magnesite,
chrome, silica, etc.; pressed & blown
glass
HQ: Osram Sylvania Inc
200 Ballardvale St # 305
Wilmington MA 01887
978 570-3000

(G-19472)
ROCKWELLS FEED FARM & PET SUP
1943 Shumway Hill Rd (16901-6841)
PHONE..................................877 797-4575
James H Rockwell, *President*
Charles H Rockwell, *Vice Pres*
Dauid G Rockwell, *Treasurer*
Philip C Rockwell, *Admin Sec*
EMP: 5
SALES (est): 408.2K
SALES (corp-wide): 3.8MM **Privately Held**
SIC: 2048 5999 Feeds from meat & from
meat & vegetable meals; feed & farm
supply
PA: H. Rockwell & Son Inc.
430 Troy St
Canton PA 17724
570 673-5148

(G-19473)
TIOGA PUBLISHING COMPANY (HQ)
Also Called: Wellfboro Gazette
25 East Ave Frnt Ste (16901-1620)
PHONE..................................570 724-2287
Larry Paerrotto, *President*
Cheryl Clarke, *Editor*
EMP: 28
SALES (est): 8.4MM **Privately Held**
SIC: 2711 2752 Commercial printing &
newspaper publishing combined; com-
mercial printing, offset

(G-19474)
WEIS MARKETS INC
11798 Route 6 (16901-6753)
PHONE..................................570 724-6364
Jeff Canyon, *Manager*
EMP: 115

SALES (corp-wide): 3.5B **Publicly Held**
WEB: www.weis.com
SIC: 5411 5912 2051 Supermarkets,
chain; drug stores & proprietary stores;
bread, cake & related products
PA: Weis Markets, Inc.
1000 S 2nd St
Sunbury PA 17801
570 286-4571

(G-19475)
WILD ASAPH OUTFITTERS
71 Main St (16901-1503)
PHONE..................................570 724-5155
Elizabeth Berkowitz, *Principal*
EMP: 4
SALES (est): 312.1K **Privately Held**
SIC: 3949 Sporting & athletic goods

Wellsville
York County

(G-19476)
AIRCOOLED RACING AND PARTS
1560 Old Mountain Rd (17365-9556)
PHONE..................................717 432-4116
Steve Limbert, *Owner*
EMP: 3 **EST:** 1978
SALES (est): 160K **Privately Held**
SIC: 3711 5531 Automobile assembly, in-
cluding specialty automobiles; automotive
& home supply stores

(G-19477)
BELJAN MANUFACTURING CORP
7675 Carlisle Rd (17365-9412)
PHONE..................................717 432-2891
Joseph Beljan, *President*
Jennifer Beljan, *Admin Sec*
EMP: 5
SQ FT: 5,600
SALES: 400K **Privately Held**
SIC: 3599 Machine shop, jobbing & repair

(G-19478)
KAMPEL ENTERPRISES INC
Also Called: Myers Sheet Metal Division
8930 Carlisle Rd (17365-9660)
P.O. Box 157 (17365-0157)
PHONE..................................717 432-9688
Thomas E Kampel, *President*
Christopher Kampel, *Vice Pres*
Dan Livingston, *Supervisor*
Mary A Maccluskie, *Info Tech Mgr*
Judy Kampel, *Director*
▼ **EMP:** 49
SQ FT: 63,000
SALES (est): 9.5MM **Privately Held**
WEB: www.kampelent.com
SIC: 2499 3444 Kitchen, bathroom &
household ware: wood; sheet metalwork

(G-19479)
KEN WEAVER MEATS INC
Also Called: WEAVERS OF WELLSVILLE
47 North St (17365-9636)
P.O. Box 66 (17365-0066)
PHONE..................................717 502-0118
Craig Weaver, *President*
Kimberly Weaver, *Admin Sec*
EMP: 30
SQ FT: 20,000
SALES: 50.3MM **Privately Held**
SIC: 2013 5147 5143 5421 Sausages
from purchased meat; bologna from pur-
chased meat; prepared pork products
from purchased pork; meats, fresh;
cheese; meat markets, including freezer
provisioners; cheese

Wendel
Westmoreland County

(G-19480)
FASSETT MFG CO
Wendel Herminie Rd (15691)
P.O. Box 34 (15691-0034)
PHONE..................................724 446-7870

Karen Fassett, *President*
James R Fassett Sr, *Vice Pres*
John R Fassett, *Vice Pres*
EMP: 7
SQ FT: 2,500
SALES (est): 1.5MM **Privately Held**
SIC: 3599 Machine shop, jobbing & repair

(G-19481)
HAMPTON CONTROLS INC (PA)
Also Called: Hampton Controls, Optics Div.
Wendel Rd (15691)
PHONE..................724 861-0150
Paul Nacin, *President*
EMP: 10
SQ FT: 13,000
SALES (est): 1.1MM **Privately Held**
WEB: www.hcitemp.com
SIC: 3625 3827 Control circuit relays, in-
dustrial; optical instruments & lenses

(G-19482)
SELECT DISMANTLING CORP
137 Sycamore St (15691)
P.O. Box 215 (15691-0215)
PHONE..................724 861-6004
Jimmy Cilvo, *CEO*
James D Celio, *President*
EMP: 15
SALES: 2MM **Privately Held**
SIC: 1389 1795 Construction, repair & dis-
mantling services; demolition, buildings &
other structures

Wernersville
Berks County

(G-19483)
ADMIXTURES INC (PA)
200 Furnace Rd (19565)
P.O. Box 225 (19565-0225)
PHONE..................610 775-0371
Jeffrey Behm, *President*
Robert P Behm, *Vice Pres*
Don Ford, *VP Sales*
EMP: 19 **EST:** 1957
SALES (est): 5MM **Privately Held**
WEB: www.admixtures.com
SIC: 5032 3531 Concrete mixtures; ma-
sons' materials; bituminous, cement &
concrete related products & equipment

(G-19484)
HARTMAN DESIGN INC
Also Called: Escort Lighting
51 N Elm St (19565-1209)
PHONE..................610 670-2517
Michael S Hartman, *President*
Vicki Cesar, *Director*
EMP: 4
SALES (est): 626.8K **Privately Held**
SIC: 3645 Residential lighting fixtures

(G-19485)
J & J CONSULTING CORP
Also Called: Stockwatch
421 N Church Rd (19565-1305)
PHONE..................610 678-6611
Janet Hildebrandt, *President*
John Hildebrandt, *Corp Secy*
EMP: 6
SALES: 500K **Privately Held**
WEB: www.stockwatch.com
SIC: 7372 Prepackaged software

(G-19486)
NOBILITY ALPACAS
99 Heffner Rd (19565-9760)
PHONE..................484 332-1499
Jeanne Noble, *Principal*
EMP: 3
SALES (est): 265K **Privately Held**
SIC: 2231 Alpacas, mohair: woven

(G-19487)
TRIMETRIC ENTERPRISES INC
Also Called: Trimetric Mold & Design
250 Holland St (19565-1625)
PHONE..................610 670-2099
Joe Soisson, *President*
Robert Woratyla, *Treasurer*
EMP: 8
SQ FT: 6,000

SALES (est): 1MM **Privately Held**
SIC: 3544 Industrial molds

Wescosville
Lehigh County

(G-19488)
**D R GAUMER METAL
FABRICATING**
589 Krocks Rd (18106)
PHONE..................610 395-5101
Douglas R Gaumer, *Owner*
EMP: 3
SQ FT: 1,200
SALES (est): 231.5K **Privately Held**
SIC: 7692 Welding repair

(G-19489)
EXPRESS SIGN OUTLET INC
4865 Hamilton Blvd 100 (18106-9705)
PHONE..................610 336-9636
Linda Depolo, *President*
EMP: 3
SALES (est): 273.6K **Privately Held**
SIC: 3993 Signs & advertising specialties

West Alexander
Washington County

(G-19490)
B AND N ELECTRONICS
240 Chambers Ridge Rd (15376-2270)
P.O. Box 506, Claysville (15323-0606)
PHONE..................724 484-0164
Bud Plants, *Owner*
EMP: 4
SALES (est): 210K **Privately Held**
WEB: www.bnelectronics.com
SIC: 3679 5731 Electronic circuits; anten-
nas, satellite dish

West Bridgewater
Beaver County

(G-19491)
**HANGER PRSTHETCS & ORTHO
INC**
500 Market St Ste 105 (15009-2998)
PHONE..................714 774-0637
EMP: 20
SALES (corp-wide): 762.8MM **Publicly
Held**
SIC: 3842 Surgical Appliances And Sup-
plies, Nsk
HQ: Hanger Prosthetics & Orthotics, Inc.
10910 Main Dr
Austin TX 78758
512 777-3800

West Chester
Chester County

(G-19492)
A STUART MORTON INC
Also Called: Sir Speedy
315 Westtown Rd Ste 11 (19382-4997)
PHONE..................610 692-1190
David Morton, *President*
A Stuart Morton, *Vice Pres*
Betty Morton, *Vice Pres*
Stuart Morton, *Vice Pres*
EMP: 13
SQ FT: 6,600
SALES: 1.4MM **Privately Held**
SIC: 2752 2791 7334 Commercial print-
ing, lithographic; typesetting, computer
controlled; photocopying & duplicating
services

(G-19493)
AAA HELLENIC MARBLE INC
301 E Market St (19382-2741)
PHONE..................610 344-7700
Thomas Gakis, *President*
Tasos Papadopoulos, *Treasurer*

▲ **EMP:** 35
SQ FT: 12,000
SALES (est): 6MM **Privately Held**
WEB: www.aaamarble.com
SIC: 3281 1743 5032 Building stone
products; marble installation, interior;
marble building stone

(G-19494)
ACCURATE TOOL CO INC
891 Fernhill Rd (19380-4282)
P.O. Box 226, Newtown Square (19073-
0226)
PHONE..................610 436-4500
Robert A Cocco, *President*
Eleanor Cocco, *Admin Sec*
EMP: 45 **EST:** 1963
SQ FT: 40,000
SALES (est): 10.5MM **Privately Held**
WEB: www.accuratetool.com
SIC: 3599 3545 3452 Machine shop, job-
bing & repair; machine tool attachments &
accessories; bolts, nuts, rivets & washers

(G-19495)
AIRGREEN LLC
515 Highland Rd (19380-1932)
PHONE..................610 209-8067
Andrew Mongar, *President*
EMP: 3
SALES (est): 232.4K **Privately Held**
SIC: 3585 Refrigeration & heating equip-
ment

(G-19496)
**ALLY HOME CARE LTD LBLTY
CO**
Also Called: Allyms
1554 Paoli Pike Ste 251 (19380-6123)
PHONE..................800 930-0587
Jason Rowinski, *Mng Member*
EMP: 3
SQ FT: 3,000
SALES (est): 71.1K **Privately Held**
SIC: 7372 Application computer software

(G-19497)
ALTUS PARTNERS LLC
Also Called: Altus Spine
1340 Enterprise Dr (19380-5960)
PHONE..................610 355-4156
Michael Wiggle Purchase, *Manager*
Michael Fitzgerald,
EMP: 20
SALES (est): 3.2MM **Privately Held**
SIC: 3842 3841 Surgical appliances &
supplies; implants, surgical; bone plates &
screws

(G-19498)
AMERICAN PRECISION INDS INC
Portescap
110 Westtown Rd Ste 101 (19382-4978)
PHONE..................610 235-5499
Manthan Patel, *QC Mgr*
Chris Schaefer, *Engineer*
Rishi Bhatenger, *Branch Mgr*
Sara Altman, *Executive*
EMP: 110
SALES (corp-wide): 6.4B **Publicly Held**
SIC: 3679 Electronic circuits
HQ: American Precision Industries Inc.
45 Hazelwood Dr
Amherst NY 14228
716 691-9100

(G-19499)
**ANNALEE WOOD PRODUCTS
INC**
Also Called: Thrifty Pallet Co
701 S Franklin St (19382-3729)
PHONE..................610 436-0142
William Sairvaira, *Manager*
EMP: 8
SALES (corp-wide): 1.5MM **Privately
Held**
SIC: 2448 Pallets, wood; cargo containers,
wood
PA: Annalee Wood Products, Inc.
789 Cedar Knoll Rd
Coatesville PA 19320
610 436-0142

(G-19500)
AP-O-GEE INDUSTRIES INC
Also Called: Apogee Industries
827 Lincoln Ave Unit 4-6 (19380-4472)
PHONE..................610 719-8010
David J Hayes, *President*
Elaine Hayes, *Admin Sec*
EMP: 14
SQ FT: 12,700
SALES (est): 2.2MM **Privately Held**
WEB: www.apogeeindustries.com
SIC: 2759 Labels & seals: printing; flexo-
graphic printing

(G-19501)
**ARMSTRONG ENGRG ASSOC
INC**
1101 W Strasburg Rd (19382-1932)
PHONE..................610 436-6080
Walter Kuchlak, *Branch Mgr*
EMP: 3
SALES (corp-wide): 10MM **Privately
Held**
SIC: 3567 3443 Industrial furnaces &
ovens; heat exchangers, plate type
PA: Armstrong Engineering Associates, Inc.
1845 W Strasburg Rd
Coatesville PA 19320
610 436-6080

(G-19502)
ASCENSION PUBLISHING LLC
20 Hagerty Blvd Ste 3 (19382-5910)
PHONE..................610 696-7795
Matthew L Pinto,
Jeffrey S Cavins,
EMP: 6
SALES (est): 642.6K **Privately Held**
SIC: 2731 Book publishing

(G-19503)
AUSKIN INC
Also Called: Biehn Printing
200 S Franklin St Ste 7 (19382-3498)
PHONE..................610 696-0234
EMP: 4
SQ FT: 2,700
SALES: 304K **Privately Held**
SIC: 2759 5943 Offset & Letterpress Print-
ing

(G-19504)
AVIDTOX INC
833 Lincoln Ave Unit 9 (19380-4471)
PHONE..................610 738-7938
Koon Pak, *President*
Andrew Mazar, *Director*
Ming Zhao, *Director*
EMP: 3
SALES (est): 135.6K **Privately Held**
SIC: 2835 In vivo diagnostics

(G-19505)
AVIOM INC
1157 Phoenixville Pike # 201 (19380-4254)
PHONE..................610 738-9005
Carl Bader, *President*
Carl V Bader, *President*
Thomas Costello, *Treasurer*
▲ **EMP:** 61
SQ FT: 9,000
SALES (est): 14.3MM **Privately Held**
WEB: www.aviom.com
SIC: 3651 Household audio equipment

(G-19506)
B & C CONTROLS INC
1155 Phoenixville Pike # 107 (19380-4285)
PHONE..................610 738-9204
Dean W Beebe, *CEO*
EMP: 15
SQ FT: 6,800
SALES (est): 2.6MM **Privately Held**
SIC: 3613 1731 Control panels, electric;
electronic controls installation

(G-19507)
BACON JAMS LLC
1554 Paoli Pike Ste 254 (19380-6123)
PHONE..................856 720-0255
Bruce Williams, *CEO*
EMP: 5 **EST:** 2013
SALES (est): 1.1MM **Privately Held**
SIC: 2099 7389 Food preparations;

(G-19508)

BAILLIE FABRICATING & WLDG INC
1109 Saunders Ct Ste 110 (19380-4213)
PHONE.................................610 701-5808
Stephen Baillie, *CEO*
EMP: 3
SALES (est): 552.1K **Privately Held**
WEB: www.bailliefab.com
SIC: 3441 Fabricated structural metal

(G-19509)

BELAR ELECTRONICS LAB INC
1140 Mcdermott Dr Ste 105 (19380-4043)
P.O. Box 76, Devon (19333-0076)
PHONE.................................610 687-5550
Arno M Meyer, *President*
Lynd Meyer, *Treasurer*
EMP: 23
SQ FT: 22,500
SALES (est): 4.1MM **Privately Held**
WEB: www.belar.com
SIC: 3663 Radio & TV communications equipment

(G-19510)

BERLIN STEEL CONSTRUCTION CO
Also Called: Berlin Steel Mid-Atlantic
501 Garfield Ave (19380-4436)
PHONE.................................610 240-8953
Carl Johnson, *President*
EMP: 16
SALES (corp-wide): 34.9MM **Privately Held**
WEB: www.berlinsteel.com
SIC: 3441 Fabricated structural metal
PA: The Berlin Steel Construction Company
76 Depot Rd
Kensington CT 06037
860 828-3531

(G-19511)

BLUE DOG PRINTING & DESIGN
Also Called: Designing Wright
1039 Andrew Dr (19380-4293)
PHONE.................................610 430-7992
Bill Friedman, *Owner*
Debbi Friedman, *Principal*
Jennifer Giunta, *Cust Mgr*
EMP: 4
SALES (est): 639.5K **Privately Held**
WEB: www.bluedogprintinginc.com
SIC: 2752 Commercial printing, lithographic

(G-19512)

BNP MEDIA INC
Also Called: Packaging Stratagies
600 Willowbrook Ln # 610 (19382-5565)
PHONE.................................610 436-4220
Peggy Georges, *Principal*
EMP: 11
SALES (corp-wide): 158.1MM **Privately Held**
SIC: 2721 Trade journals: publishing only, not printed on site
PA: Bnp Media, Inc.
2401 W Big Beaver Rd # 700
Troy MI 48084
248 362-3700

(G-19513)

BRANDYWINE PHARMACEUTICALS INC
600 W Strasburg Rd (19382-1955)
PHONE.................................800 647-0172
Brian Anderson, *President*
EMP: 12
SALES (est): 553.1K **Privately Held**
SIC: 2834 Pharmaceutical preparations

(G-19514)

BRANDYWINE WOODWORKS LLC
186 Bragg Hill Rd (19382-6714)
PHONE.................................610 793-7979
Seth Cavallari,
EMP: 4
SALES (est): 320.1K **Privately Held**
SIC: 2431 Millwork

(G-19515)

BROOKS GROUP AND ASSOC INC
16 E Market St (19382-3151)
PHONE.................................610 429-8990
Willis Brooks Jr, *President*
Mark D Cotterman, *Vice Pres*
Ryan Evans, *Vice Pres*
Ed Roberts, *Vice Pres*
EMP: 8
SALES (est): 974.7K **Privately Held**
SIC: 2731 Book publishing

(G-19516)

CALIBURN INC
7 N 5 Points Rd Ste 4 (19380-4777)
PHONE.................................610 429-9500
Andy Woods, *President*
Tish Molloy, *Vice Pres*
EMP: 3 EST: 1998
SALES (est): 250K **Privately Held**
WEB: www.caliburn-inc.com
SIC: 3695 Computer software tape & disks: blank, rigid & floppy

(G-19517)

CALLAHAN DAVID E POOL PLST INC
1198 Phoenixville Pike (19380-4216)
PHONE.................................610 429-4496
David E Callahan, *President*
Bonnie E Callahan, *Admin Sec*
EMP: 32 EST: 1979
SQ FT: 4,300
SALES (est): 2.1MM **Privately Held**
WEB: www.callahanpool.com
SIC: 1742 3272 1743 Plastering, plain or ornamental; copings, concrete; tile installation, ceramic

(G-19518)

CAPITAL COIL & AIR LLC
1544 Mcdaniel Dr (19380-7035)
PHONE.................................484 498-6880
Matt Jacobs, *President*
Dan Jacobs, *Vice Pres*
Robert Jacobs, *Vice Pres*
EMP: 3
SQ FT: 2,000
SALES (est): 250.3K **Privately Held**
SIC: 3585 3621 Air conditioning equipment, complete; coils, for electric motors or generators

(G-19519)

CAREY SCHUSTER LLC
Also Called: Yellow Goat Design
120 S Church St (19382-3255)
PHONE.................................610 431-2512
Carey Schuster,
EMP: 3 EST: 2013
SALES (est): 377.3K **Privately Held**
SIC: 7389 3646 Textile designers; chandeliers, commercial

(G-19520)

CELLCO PARTNERSHIP
Also Called: Verizon
966 S Matlack St (19382-7517)
PHONE.................................610 431-5800
Sandra Alshakhshri, *Branch Mgr*
EMP: 100
SALES (corp-wide): 130.8B **Publicly Held**
SIC: 2741 4812 1731 Miscellaneous publishing; radio telephone communication; electrical work
HQ: Cellco Partnership
1 Verizon Way
Basking Ridge NJ 07920

(G-19521)

CEPHALON INC
502 Brandywine Pkwy (19380-4276)
PHONE.................................610 738-6410
Vicky Conway, *Senior Mgr*
Francine Del Ricci, *Exec Dir*
Planz Paul, *Director*
Mark Ator, *Director*
EMP: 453
SALES (corp-wide): 18.8B **Privately Held**
SIC: 2834 Pharmaceutical preparations

HQ: Cephalon, Inc.
41 Moores Rd
Malvern PA 19355
610 344-0200

(G-19522)

CEPHALON CLINICAL PARTNERS LP
145 Brandywine Pkwy (19380-4249)
PHONE.................................610 883-5260
Valli Balassano, *Principal*
EMP: 4
SALES (est): 358K **Privately Held**
SIC: 2834 Pharmaceutical preparations

(G-19523)

CHEM SERVICE INC
660 Tower Ln (19380-1965)
P.O. Box 599 (19381-0599)
PHONE.................................610 692-3026
Lyle H Phifer, *President*
John Pullekines, *Prdtn Mgr*
Danielle Wardigo, *Accounting Mgr*
James Huang, *Manager*
Denise Simmers, *Manager*
EMP: 24
SQ FT: 11,500
SALES (est): 5.7MM **Privately Held**
WEB: www.mmchale.com
SIC: 2865 2869 2879 2819 Cyclic crudes & intermediates; industrial organic chemicals; agricultural chemicals; industrial inorganic chemicals

(G-19524)

CHIEF FIRE
1416 Phoenixville Pike (19380-1438)
PHONE.................................484 356-5316
EMP: 4
SALES (est): 545K **Privately Held**
SIC: 3429 Manufactured hardware (general)

(G-19525)

CHRISBER CORPORATION
705 E Union St (19382-4937)
P.O. Box 1209 (19380-0157)
PHONE.................................800 872-7436
Bernard Azorin, *President*
Christian Azorin, *Vice Pres*
Frank Sheldon, *Vice Pres*
EMP: 22
SQ FT: 22,400
SALES (est): 2.3MM **Privately Held**
WEB: www.rapidocolor.com
SIC: 2759 2791 2789 2752 Letterpress & screen printing; typesetting; bookbinding & related work; commercial printing, lithographic

(G-19526)

CMPRESSED A ZEKS SOLUTIONS LLC
1302 Goshen Pkwy (19380-5985)
PHONE.................................610 692-9100
Bob Fisher, *General Mgr*
Terry Webber, *Buyer*
Chris Decker, *Engineer*
Steve Bergh, *Marketing Mgr*
Chris Ursillo, *Manager*
EMP: 135 EST: 2006
SALES: 20MM **Privately Held**
SIC: 3563 Air & gas compressors

(G-19527)

COMMUNICATION AUTOMATION CORP
Also Called: C A C
1171 Mcdermott Dr (19380-4042)
PHONE.................................610 692-9526
John Sweeney, *President*
James E Bridges, *Treasurer*
EMP: 42
SQ FT: 38,000
SALES (est): 345.2K
SALES (corp-wide): 3.5MM **Privately Held**
WEB: www.cacdsp.com
SIC: 8731 7371 3672 Computer (hardware) development; computer software development; printed circuit boards
PA: Woodward Mccoach, Inc
1171 Mcdermott Dr
West Chester PA 19380
610 692-9526

(G-19528)

CONCENTRIC MACHINING GRINDING
510 E Barnard St Unit 29 (19382-3463)
PHONE.................................610 692-9450
Michael P Morris, *President*
Daniel L Broomal, *Admin Sec*
EMP: 3
SQ FT: 5,000
SALES: 593.2K **Privately Held**
WEB: www.concentricmachine.com
SIC: 3599 Machine shop, jobbing & repair

(G-19529)

CONREX PHARMACEUTICAL CORP
Also Called: Sesha Anti Oxdent Skin Therapy
1155 Phoenixvlle Pike 1 (19380)
PHONE.................................610 355-2454
Phyllis Hsieh, *President*
▲ EMP: 13
SQ FT: 8,000
SALES (est): 2.9MM **Privately Held**
WEB: www.seshaskin.com
SIC: 2844 Cosmetic preparations

(G-19530)

CORROSION TECHNOLOGY INC
125 Willowbrook Ln (19382-5571)
PHONE.................................610 429-1450
Jim Kent, *President*
Carol Max, *Opers Staff*
EMP: 4
SQ FT: 200
SALES (est): 759K **Privately Held**
SIC: 3589 Water treatment equipment, industrial

(G-19531)

DALECO RESOURCES CORPORATION
929 S High St Ste 174 (19382-5466)
PHONE.................................570 795-4347
Grant Lin, *Ch of Bd*
Gary J Novinskie, *President*
Richard A Thibault, *Vice Pres*
EMP: 4
SALES (est): 679.4K **Privately Held**
WEB: www.dalecoresources.com
SIC: 1382 1081 Geological exploration, oil & gas field; metal mining exploration & development services

(G-19532)

DANAHER CORPORATION
110 Westtown Rd (19382-4978)
PHONE.................................610 692-2700
Jimmy Rayford, *Principal*
EMP: 100
SALES (corp-wide): 19.8B **Publicly Held**
WEB: www.portescap.com
SIC: 3621 Motors, electric
PA: Danaher Corporation
2200 Penn Ave Nw Ste 800w
Washington DC 20037
202 828-0850

(G-19533)

DAVIS TROPHIES & SPORTS WEAR
Also Called: Davis Trophy & Sportswear
1004 Plumly Rd (19382-7559)
PHONE.................................610 455-0640
Donal S Wolf, *Owner*
EMP: 4
SQ FT: 1,200
SALES: 475K **Privately Held**
SIC: 5999 3993 3231 Trophies & plaques; signs & advertising specialties; products of purchased glass

(G-19534)

DELICIOUS BITE LLC
1128 Greenhill Rd (19380-4053)
PHONE.................................610 701-4213
Susana Cabrera, *President*
EMP: 10
SQ FT: 1,200
SALES (est): 600K **Privately Held**
SIC: 2099 2038 Ready-to-eat meals, salads & sandwiches; frozen specialties

(G-19535)
DENTAL CORP OF AMERICA
889 S Matlack St (19382-4971)
PHONE....................................610 344-7488
Don Taylor, *President*
EMP: 10 EST: 1978
SALES (est): 1.1MM **Privately Held**
WEB: www.dentalcorp.com
SIC: 5047 3843 Dentists' professional
supplies; dental laboratory equipment

(G-19536)
DEPUY SYNTHES INC
108 Willowbrook Ln (19382-5571)
PHONE....................................610 701-7078
Charlie Arnold, *Owner*
EMP: 287
SALES (corp-wide): 81.5B **Publicly Held**
SIC: 3842 Surgical appliances & supplies
HQ: Depuy Synthes, Inc.
700 Orthopaedic Dr
Warsaw IN 46582

(G-19537)
DEPUY SYNTHES INC
1303 Goshen Pkwy (19380-5986)
PHONE....................................610 738-4600
Joseph Frey, *Engineer*
Steve Dixon, *Manager*
EMP: 285
SALES (corp-wide): 81.5B **Publicly Held**
SIC: 3842 Surgical appliances & supplies
HQ: Depuy Synthes, Inc.
700 Orthopaedic Dr
Warsaw IN 46582

(G-19538)
DEPUY SYNTHES INC
1303 Goshen Pkwy (19380-5986)
PHONE....................................610 719-5000
EMP: 287
SALES (corp-wide): 81.5B **Publicly Held**
SIC: 3842 Surgical appliances & supplies
HQ: Depuy Synthes, Inc.
700 Orthopaedic Dr
Warsaw IN 46582

(G-19539)
**DEPUY SYNTHES PRODUCTS
INC**
1302 Wrights Ln E (19380-3417)
PHONE....................................610 719-5000
EMP: 9
SALES (est): 849K
SALES (corp-wide): 81.5B **Publicly Held**
SIC: 3841 Surgical & medical instruments
PA: Johnson & Johnson
1 Johnson And Johnson Plz
New Brunswick NJ 08933
732 524-0400

(G-19540)
DEPUY SYNTHES SALES INC
Depuy Synthes Biomaterials
1302 Wrights Ln E (19380-3417)
PHONE....................................610 719-5000
EMP: 6
SALES (corp-wide): 81.5B **Publicly Held**
SIC: 3841 Surgical & medical instruments
HQ: Depuy Synthes Sales Inc
325 Paramount Dr
Raynham MA 02767
508 880-8100

(G-19541)
DEPUY SYNTHES SALES INC
Also Called: Synthes Technical Center
1301 Goshen Pkwy (19380-5986)
PHONE....................................610 738-4600
EMP: 18
SALES (corp-wide): 81.5B **Publicly Held**
SIC: 3841 Surgical & medical instruments
HQ: Depuy Synthes Sales Inc
325 Paramount Dr
Raynham MA 02767
508 880-8100

(G-19542)
DISC HOUNDS LLC
323 E Gay St Ste 2 (19380-2777)
PHONE....................................610 696-8668
Heather Bird, *Office Mgr*
Michael Guerriero, *Mng Member*
EMP: 8
SQ FT: 5,000
SALES (est): 650K **Privately Held**
WEB: www.dischounds.com
SIC: 3652 Compact laser discs, prere-
corded

(G-19543)
DORADO SOLUTIONS INC
1185 Hampshire Pl (19382-8009)
P.O. Box 1501, Chandler AZ (85244-1501)
PHONE....................................480 216-1056
Wally Dodds, *President*
Mink Levoy, *Director*
EMP: 9
SALES: 3.5MM **Privately Held**
SIC: 7372 Prepackaged software

(G-19544)
DUMOND CHEMICALS INC (PA)
1475 Phnxvlle Pike Ste 18 (19380)
PHONE....................................609 655-7700
John Petroci, *President*
Erik Gertsen, *Vice Pres*
▼ EMP: 6
SQ FT: 2,000
SALES (est): 1.3MM **Privately Held**
WEB: www.dumondchemicals.com
SIC: 2851 Paint removers

(G-19545)
ECCO/GREGORY INC
1199 Mcdermott Dr (19380-4042)
P.O. Box 5210 (19380-0405)
PHONE....................................610 840-0390
William Gregory Jr, *President*
Robert A Trenner Jr, *Vice Pres*
Christopher Zee, *Sales Staff*
George M Hahn, *Admin Sec*
EMP: 22
SQ FT: 5,400
SALES (est): 7.4MM **Privately Held**
WEB: www.wagregory.com
SIC: 3567 3491 3569 Industrial furnaces
& ovens; pressure valves & regulators, in-
dustrial; filters

(G-19546)
**EDGMONT METALLIC PIGMENT
INC**
203 Garfield Ave (19380-4511)
P.O. Box 405, Bryn Mawr (19010-0405)
PHONE....................................610 429-1345
Dolores T Horsell, *President*
Janet Horsell, *Admin Sec*
EMP: 10 EST: 1971
SQ FT: 6,800
SALES (est): 1.5MM **Privately Held**
SIC: 3399 2816 Metal powders, pastes &
flakes; metallic & mineral pigments

(G-19547)
**EFFECTIVE SHIELDING
COMPANY**
Also Called: E S C O
817 Lincoln Ave (19380-4435)
PHONE....................................610 429-9449
Mark Brozyno, *President*
Steve Miller, *Vice Pres*
Mary D Miller, *Treasurer*
William Miller, *VP Finance*
Trisha Brozyno, *Admin Sec*
EMP: 12
SQ FT: 4,500
SALES (est): 1.9MM **Privately Held**
WEB: www.effshield.com
SIC: 3053 3679 Gaskets, packing & seal-
ing devices; electronic circuits

(G-19548)
EFFICIENT IP INC
Also Called: E I P
1 S Church St Ste 400 (19382-3228)
PHONE....................................888 228-4655
Mark Anthony, *CEO*
Chris Pyne, *President*
Lauren McAluney, *Research*
Nuwan Vitharana, *Engineer*
Kathleen Gabriel, *Finance*
EMP: 11
SQ FT: 10,000
SALES: 1.4MM
SALES (corp-wide): 5.6MM **Privately
Held**
SIC: 7371 7372 Computer software sys-
tems analysis & design, custom; operat-
ing systems computer software

PA: Efficient Ip Sas
Efficient Ip
La Garenne-Colombes 92250
156 836-811

(G-19549)
ELMARK SIGN & GRAPHICS INC
307 Westtown Rd Ste 1 (19382-4990)
PHONE....................................610 692-0525
Tim Long, *President*
Jeff Pinkerton, *Accounts Exec*
EMP: 11
SALES (est): 840K **Privately Held**
SIC: 7336 3993 Commercial art & graphic
design; signs & advertising specialties

(G-19550)
ELMARK SIGN & GRAPHICS INC
307 Westtown Rd Ste 1 (19382-4990)
PHONE....................................610 692-0525
Timothy R Long, *President*
EMP: 10
SALES (est): 442.1K **Privately Held**
SIC: 3993 Signs & advertising specialties

(G-19551)
EPS PRINTING SERVICES INC
1246 Upton Cir (19380-5869)
PHONE....................................610 701-6403
Bob Evans, *President*
Michelle Evans, *Admin Sec*
EMP: 8
SQ FT: 3,000
SALES (est): 1MM **Privately Held**
SIC: 2759 Screen printing

(G-19552)
ETHNIC GOURMET FOODS INC
Also Called: Thai Chef
700 Old Fern Hill Rd (19380-4274)
PHONE....................................610 692-2209
Paul Jaggi, *President*
Sangeeta Jaggi, *Vice Pres*
Harmeet S Sandhu, *Vice Pres*
▲ EMP: 25
SQ FT: 15,000
SALES (est): 2.2MM **Publicly Held**
WEB: www.hain-celestial.com
SIC: 5142 5812 2099 2038 Dinners,
frozen; eating places; food preparations;
frozen specialties
PA: The Hain Celestial Group Inc
1111 Marcus Ave Ste 100
New Hyde Park NY 11042

(G-19553)
**EVOLVE GUEST CONTROLS
LLC**
827 Lincoln Ave Unit 2 (19380-4472)
PHONE....................................855 750-9090
David Korcz, *Manager*
EMP: 15 **Privately Held**
SIC: 3822 7371 Auto controls regulating
residntl & coml environmt & applncs;
computer software development
PA: Evolve Guest Controls, Llc
16 S Maryland Ave
Port Washington NY 11050

(G-19554)
FEDOR FABRICATION INC
207 Carter Dr Ste A (19382-4506)
PHONE....................................610 431-7150
Mark Fedor, *President*
Michael Morrison, *Vice Pres*
Linda Fedor, *Treasurer*
EMP: 13
SALES: 1.3MM **Privately Held**
WEB: www.fedorfab.com
SIC: 2434 Wood kitchen cabinets

(G-19555)
**FIVES N AMERCN COMBUSTN
INC**
702 Mercers Mill Ln (19382-4100)
PHONE....................................610 996-8005
EMP: 43
SALES (corp-wide): 4.5MM **Privately
Held**
SIC: 3433 Heating equipment, except elec-
tric
HQ: Fives North American Combustion, Inc.
4455 E 71st St
Cleveland OH 44105
216 271-6000

(G-19556)
G S P SIGNS & BANNERS INC
Also Called: Goshen Sign Products
553 E Gay St (19380-2778)
PHONE....................................610 430-7000
David Siegel, *President*
Jeff Siegel, *Vice Pres*
EMP: 3
SQ FT: 1,500
SALES (est): 341.6K **Privately Held**
SIC: 3993 Signs, not made in custom sign
painting shops

(G-19557)
**GALAXY GLOBAL PRODUCTS
LLC (PA)**
820 Lincoln Ave (19380-4469)
PHONE....................................610 692-7400
Michael Boneck,
William Scott Mayer,
EMP: 6
SALES (est): 190.2MM **Privately Held**
SIC: 5064 3585 3564 Electrical appli-
ances, television & radio; refrigeration &
heating equipment; blowers & fans

(G-19558)
**HAAS CHEM MANAGMENT OF
MEXICO (DH)**
1646 W Chester Pike 4-6 (19382-7995)
PHONE....................................610 656-7454
Thaddeus Fortin, *CEO*
EMP: 13
SALES (est): 1.6MM **Publicly Held**
SIC: 2899 Metal treating compounds
HQ: Haas Group International, Llc
1475 Phoeni Pike Ste 101
West Chester PA 19380
484 564-4500

(G-19559)
HAAS GROUP
1475 Phoenixville Pike (19380-1437)
PHONE....................................484 564-4500
Thaddeus J Fortin, *CEO*
Jim Gutknecht,
EMP: 1300
SALES (est): 624MM **Publicly Held**
SIC: 8741 3369 Business management;
aerospace castings, nonferrous: except
aluminum
PA: Wesco Aircraft Holdings, Inc.
24911 Avenue Stanford
Valencia CA 91355

(G-19560)
HEALTHY PET FOODS INC
505 Legion Dr (19380-7202)
PHONE....................................610 918-4702
Michael F Gagliardi, *President*
▼ EMP: 4
SALES (est): 701.1K **Privately Held**
WEB: www.healthypetfoodsinc.com
SIC: 3999 7389 Pet supplies;

(G-19561)
HEPCO QUARRIES INC
820 E Washington St (19380-4542)
PHONE....................................484 844-5024
EMP: 3
SALES (est): 99.6K **Privately Held**
SIC: 1411 Granite dimension stone

(G-19562)
HOLLY METALS INC
892 Fernhill Rd (19380-4275)
PHONE....................................610 692-4989
Paul Sam, *President*
Glenda Sam, *Corp Secy*
EMP: 10 EST: 1964
SQ FT: 28,000
SALES: 860K **Privately Held**
SIC: 3444 Sheet metal specialties, not
stamped

(G-19563)
**HOPPER LAWN & LDSCP MGT
LLC**
Also Called: Froio's Lawn & Landscape
1306 Pottstown Pike (19380-1210)
P.O. Box 5282 (19380-0407)
PHONE....................................610 692-3879
Nicholas Froio, *President*
Daniel Froio, *Vice Pres*
EMP: 7

GEOGRAPHIC

SALES (est): 517.2K **Privately Held**
SIC: 3271 3645 7389 Blocks, concrete:
landscape or retaining wall; garden, patio,
walkway & yard lighting fixtures: electric;

(G-19564)
HOREB INC
927 Sage Rd (19382-7587)
P.O. Box 5170 (19380-0404)
PHONE...............................610 285-1917
Sharon Alexander, *CEO*
Pannir Alexander, *CFO*
EMP: 3
SALES: 84.4K **Privately Held**
SIC: 7371 5045 3571 Computer software
development; computer software; main-
frame computers

(G-19565)
HW MARSTON & CO
Also Called: Marston Records
206 Cheshire Cir (19380-6707)
PHONE...............................610 328-6669
H W Marston, *Principal*
EMP: 3
SALES (est): 219.8K **Privately Held**
SIC: 2782 Record albums

(G-19566)
IDRECO USA LTD
24 Hagerty Blvd Ste 9 (19382-7595)
PHONE...............................610 701-9944
Paolo Stafforini, *President*
Italo Chiodi, *Treasurer*
Roberto Lovato, *Manager*
William Runyan, *Manager*
Enrico Molina, *Technology*
EMP: 11
SQ FT: 4,400
SALES (est): 5.9MM **Privately Held**
WEB: www.idrecousa.com
SIC: 3589 3556 Water treatment equip-
ment, industrial; sugar plant machinery
HQ: Idreco Spa
Via Pietro Nenni 15
Voghera PV 27058
038 336-9052

(G-19567)
IMAGE NET VENTURES LLC
Also Called: Imagenet/Docstar
1140 Mcdermott Dr Ste 200 (19380-4043)
PHONE...............................610 240-0800
Marianne G Kriza,
T Leighton Forbes,
EMP: 29
SQ FT: 5,890
SALES: 701.2K **Privately Held**
SIC: 5999 7372 Business machines &
equipment; business oriented computer
software

(G-19568)
IMP INC
232 W Gay St (19380-2917)
PHONE...............................610 458-1533
EMP: 4
SALES (est): 102.4K **Privately Held**
SIC: 3471 Plating & polishing

(G-19569)
IMPAC TECHNOLOGY INC
967 S Matlack St (19382-7556)
PHONE...............................610 430-1400
James Freed, *CEO*
EMP: 24
SQ FT: 20,000
SALES (est): 2MM **Privately Held**
WEB: www.impacweb.com
SIC: 7371 7372 7373 7389 Custom com-
puter programming services; prepack-
aged software; computer integrated
systems design; telemarketing services

(G-19570)
INFINITE CONTROL SYSTEMS INC
Also Called: I C S
320 Turner Ln (19380-4538)
PHONE...............................610 696-8600
Bob Kunkle, *President*
Willard Bungard, *Corp Secy*
EMP: 6
SQ FT: 4,500
SALES: 2MM **Privately Held**
SIC: 3625 Relays & industrial controls

(G-19571)
INTERNET PROBATION AND
Also Called: Ippc Technologies
1562 Mcdaniel Dr (19380-6672)
P.O. Box 60144, King of Prussia (19406-
0144)
PHONE...............................610 701-8921
Judy Hogaboom, *President*
EMP: 7
SALES (est): 75K **Privately Held**
SIC: 3575 Computer terminals, monitors &
components

(G-19572)
INTERNTNAL LTHERS OF PHLDLPHIA
1073 Squire Cheney Dr (19382-8046)
PHONE...............................610 793-1140
Craig Eisenfelder, *President*
Gladys Eisenfelder, *Corp Secy*
EMP: 5
SALES (est): 615.6K **Privately Held**
WEB:
www.internationalleatherdirectory.com
SIC: 3111 5199 Leather processing;
leather, leather goods & furs

(G-19573)
IONX LLC
515 S Franklin St Ste 200 (19382-3725)
PHONE...............................484 653-2600
J Wories, *Mng Member*
EMP: 5
SALES (est): 725.7K
SALES (corp-wide): 2.4B **Privately Held**
SIC: 3743 Railroad equipment
HQ: Amsted Rail Company, Inc.
311 S Wacker Dr Ste 5300
Chicago IL 60606

(G-19574)
ITC SUPPLIES LLC
Also Called: Ink Toner Store
1043 Andrew Dr Ste B (19380-4293)
PHONE...............................610 430-1300
Scott Itc, *Sales Staff*
Stephanie Jia, *Mng Member*
▲ EMP: 4
SALES (est): 707.5K **Privately Held**
SIC: 5085 3955 3861 2865 Ink, printers';
print cartridges for laser & other computer
printers; toners, prepared photographic
(not made in chemical plants); color lakes
or toners

(G-19575)
J J CACCHIO ENTERPRISES
1515 W Chester Pike A6 (19382-7778)
P.O. Box 479, Westtown (19395-0479)
PHONE...............................610 399-9750
Joseph Cacchio, *President*
Amy Cacchio, *Vice Pres*
EMP: 4
SQ FT: 1,400
SALES (est): 517.6K **Privately Held**
SIC: 1731 3571 Electronic controls instal-
lation; electronic computers

(G-19576)
J M CALDWELL CO INC
322 Turner Ln (19380-4538)
PHONE...............................610 436-9997
James M Caldwell Jr, *President*
EMP: 3 EST: 1979
SQ FT: 4,030
SALES (est): 200K **Privately Held**
SIC: 3471 Polishing, metals or formed
products; finishing, metals or formed
products

(G-19577)
JESS MILLER MACHINE SHOP INC
325 Westtown Rd Ste 6 (19382-4999)
PHONE...............................610 692-2193
Jess B Miller, *Owner*
EMP: 3 EST: 1975
SQ FT: 4,000
SALES: 350K **Privately Held**
WEB: www.jessmillermachineshop.com
SIC: 3599 Machine shop, jobbing & repair

(G-19578)
KC-13 LLC
900 Airport Rd Ste 3b (19380-3416)
PHONE...............................484 887-8900
Joseph G Gerardi, *CFO*
EMP: 9
SQ FT: 6,000 **Privately Held**
SIC: 3841 Medical instruments & equip-
ment, blood & bone work
PA: Kc-13 Llc
505 Park Ave Fl 14
New York NY 10022

(G-19579)
KEEBAR ENTERPRISES INC
1514 Machinery Rd (19380-1541)
P.O. Box 416, Downingtown (19335-0416)
PHONE...............................610 873-0150
Steven Miller, *President*
EMP: 5
SQ FT: 6,500
SALES (est): 884K **Privately Held**
WEB: www.keebar.com
SIC: 2679 7389 5045 Labels, paper:
made from purchased material; labeling
bottles, cans, cartons, etc.; computers,
peripherals & software

(G-19580)
KEENAN CNSTR & EXCVTG INC
Also Called: Keenan Construction & Excvtg
171 Dilworthtown Rd (19382-8325)
PHONE...............................610 724-4157
Justin P Keenan, *President*
Patrick X Bresnan, *Vice Pres*
EMP: 4 EST: 2005
SQ FT: 300
SALES (est): 689.9K **Privately Held**
SIC: 3531 Plows: construction, excavating
& grading

(G-19581)
KIDDE FIRE PROTECTION INC (HQ)
Also Called: Kidde Fire Fighting
350 E Union St (19382-3450)
PHONE...............................610 363-1400
John Hargreaves, *President*
Holly O Paz, *Senior VP*
Dean Byrne, *Vice Pres*
Bill Langan, *Treasurer*
Jonathan Mahlowitz, *Admin Sec*
◆ EMP: 28
SALES (est): 300.2MM
SALES (corp-wide): 66.5B **Publicly Held**
SIC: 3669 3999 3823 Fire detection sys-
tems, electric; fire extinguishers, portable;
temperature instruments: industrial
process type
PA: United Technologies Corporation
10 Farm Springs Rd
Farmington CT 06032
860 728-7000

(G-19582)
KIMJOHN INDUSTRIES INC
Also Called: Tarod Roll Forming Div
905 Fernhill Rd (19380-4203)
PHONE...............................610 436-8600
Bradley B Evans, *President*
C Barry Buckley, *Admin Sec*
EMP: 10
SQ FT: 40,000
SALES (est): 744.8K **Privately Held**
SIC: 3469 Stamping metal for the trade

(G-19583)
KODABOW INC (PA)
1126 Greenhill Rd (19380-4053)
P.O. Box 5305 (19380-0407)
PHONE...............................484 947-5471
Charles Matasic, *President*
Charles Griste, *CFO*
EMP: 3
SALES (est): 354.3K **Privately Held**
SIC: 3949 Crossbows

(G-19584)
KRAFT HEINZ FOODS COMPANY
1247 Wrights Ln (19380-3438)
PHONE...............................610 430-1536
Jim Boyle, *Principal*
EMP: 12
SALES (corp-wide): 26.2B **Publicly Held**
SIC: 2038 Frozen specialties

HQ: Kraft Heinz Foods Company
1 Ppg Pl Ste 3200
Pittsburgh PA 15222
412 456-5700

(G-19585)
KYLES AUTO TAGS & INSURANCE (PA)
529 E Gay St (19380-2718)
PHONE...............................610 429-1447
Kyle Smith, *Owner*
▲ EMP: 6
SALES (est): 777K **Privately Held**
SIC: 3469 6311 Automobile license tags,
stamped metal; life insurance

(G-19586)
LARKIN C COMPANY INC
510 E Barnard St Unit D10 (19382-3902)
PHONE...............................610 696-9096
Christopher Larkin, *President*
Anne Larkin, *Vice Pres*
EMP: 3
SQ FT: 5,000
SALES (est): 524.1K **Privately Held**
SIC: 2431 2434 Millwork; wood kitchen
cabinets

(G-19587)
LASKO GROUP INC (PA)
820 Lincoln Ave (19380-4469)
PHONE...............................610 692-7400
Oscar Lasko, *President*
Edward Mc Assey, *Exec VP*
EMP: 100
SQ FT: 190,000
SALES (est): 147MM **Privately Held**
WEB: www.laskoproducts.com
SIC: 4789 3634 Railroad car repair; ceiling
fans

(G-19588)
LASKO PRODUCTS LLC (HQ)
Also Called: Galaxy Fans & Heaters
820 Lincoln Ave (19380-4469)
PHONE...............................610 692-7400
William Lasko, *President*
Oscar Lasko, *President*
Edward McAssey, *Vice Pres*
James Perella, *Vice Pres*
Yen Tsai, *CFO*
◆ EMP: 200 EST: 1906
SQ FT: 190,000
SALES (est): 190.2MM **Privately Held**
SIC: 3585 3564 Refrigeration & heating
equipment; blowers & fans

(G-19589)
LEAHMARLIN CORP
Also Called: C & D Fence Company
501 Hannum Ave (19380-2296)
P.O. Box 718, Unionville (19375-0718)
PHONE...............................610 692-7378
Bill Mullen, *President*
EMP: 8 EST: 1972
SQ FT: 18,000
SALES (est): 691.7K **Privately Held**
SIC: 2499 3496 5039 Fencing, wood;
fencing, made from purchased wire; wire
fence, gates & accessories

(G-19590)
LEDGER NEWSPAPERS
250 N Bradford Ave (19382-1912)
PHONE...............................610 444-6590
EMP: 3 EST: 2008
SALES (est): 170K **Privately Held**
SIC: 5994 2711 Ret News Dealer/News-
stand Newspapers-Publishing/Printing

(G-19591)
LEISURE GRAPHICS INC
808 Lauber Rd (19382-4810)
PHONE...............................610 692-9872
Tom Kukoda, *President*
Eileen Kukoda, *Corp Secy*
EMP: 6
SQ FT: 3,000
SALES (est): 586.6K **Privately Held**
WEB: www.leisuregraphics.com
SIC: 2759 Screen printing

(G-19592)
LENAPE FORGED PRODUCTS CORP
1334 Lenape Rd (19382-6893)
PHONE....................610 793-5090
John Willbur, *President*
Matthew Troutman, *General Mgr*
Kevin Shaw, *Vice Pres*
Sam Sgro, *Purch Mgr*
Earl Yarnall, *Engineer*
EMP: 60
SQ FT: 2,500
SALES (est): 11.8MM **Privately Held**
WEB: www.lenapeforge.com
SIC: 3462 Iron & steel forgings

(G-19593)
LIGHT MY FIBER LLC
882 S Matlack St Ste 109 (19382-4505)
PHONE....................888 428-4454
Chad Parnis, *CEO*
Jill Plouffe,
EMP: 5
SALES (est): 255.2K **Privately Held**
SIC: 3577 Optical scanning devices

(G-19594)
LINEN SAND SUPPLIES
15 Bolingbroke Rd (19382-8348)
PHONE....................610 399-8305
John Genovese, *Principal*
EMP: 3 **EST:** 2015
SALES (est): 79.9K **Privately Held**
SIC: 1442 Construction sand & gravel

(G-19595)
MARINE INFORMATION TECH LLC
Also Called: Selco Publications
104 Willowbrook Ln (19382-5571)
PHONE....................610 429-5180
Barry Beck,
Dean Morgantini,
▲ **EMP:** 6
SALES (est): 755.5K **Privately Held**
WEB: www.seloconline.com
SIC: 2759 Publication printing

(G-19596)
MARKET SERVICE CORP
1244 W Chester Pike # 402 (19382-5687)
P.O. Box 522, Malvern (19355-0522)
PHONE....................610 696-1884
John Salyers, *Principal*
EMP: 3
SALES: 2MM **Privately Held**
SIC: 3845 Ultrasonic medical equipment, except cleaning

(G-19597)
MARTIN LIMESTONE INC
Also Called: Construction Supply Center
820 E Washington St (19380-4542)
PHONE....................814 224-6837
Mark Arnold, *Manager*
EMP: 3
SALES (corp-wide): 651.9MM **Privately Held**
WEB: www.martinlimestone.com
SIC: 3273 Ready-mixed concrete
HQ: Martin Limestone, Inc.
3580 Division Hwy
East Earl PA 17519
717 335-4500

(G-19598)
MATTHEY JOHNSON INC
Also Called: Noble Metals
1401 King Rd (19380-1467)
PHONE....................610 648-8000
Daniel Peterson, *Engineer*
David Vincent, *Marketing Mgr*
Jim Malanga, *Branch Mgr*
Scott Kelly, *Info Tech Mgr*
EMP: 200
SQ FT: 75,000
SALES (corp-wide): 19.7B **Privately Held**
SIC: 3341 8711 3444 3339 Secondary nonferrous metals; engineering services; sheet metalwork; primary nonferrous metals
HQ: Matthey Johnson Inc
435 Devon Park Dr Ste 600
Wayne PA 19087
610 971-3000

(G-19599)
MATTHEY JOHNSON INC
Also Called: Gas Processing Tech Group
1397 King Rd (19380-1467)
PHONE....................610 232-1900
Jim Malanga, *Branch Mgr*
EMP: 30
SALES (corp-wide): 19.7B **Privately Held**
SIC: 3569 3823 Centrifugal purifiers; industrial process measurement equipment
HQ: Matthey Johnson Inc
435 Devon Park Dr Ste 600
Wayne PA 19087
610 971-3000

(G-19600)
MEDIA ROOMS INC
20 Hagerty Blvd Ste 5 (19382-5910)
PHONE....................610 719-8500
Robert Dzeozy, *President*
EMP: 7
SALES (est): 1MM **Privately Held**
WEB: www.mediaroomsinc.com
SIC: 3651 5099 Audio electronic systems; video & audio equipment

(G-19601)
METALLURGICAL PRODUCTS COMPANY
810 Lincoln Ave (19380-4406)
P.O. Box 598 (19381-0598)
PHONE....................610 696-6770
Michael Goodman, *President*
Jerome Cotzen, *CFO*
◆ **EMP:** 25 **EST:** 1909
SQ FT: 40,000
SALES (est): 7.4MM **Privately Held**
WEB: www.metprodco.com
SIC: 3364 3643 3341 2819 Copper & copper alloy die-castings; current-carrying wiring devices; secondary nonferrous metals; industrial inorganic chemicals

(G-19602)
MUSCLE GAUGE NUTRITION LLC
893 S Matlack St Ste 150 (19382-4507)
PHONE....................484 840-8006
Robert Reed, *CEO*
Osagie Osunde,
Christine Solari,
▲ **EMP:** 13 **EST:** 2009
SALES (est): 2.1MM **Privately Held**
SIC: 2833 5122 Vitamins, natural or synthetic: bulk, uncompounded; vitamins & minerals

(G-19603)
MWM GRAPHICS
Also Called: Elmark Graphics
307 Westtown Rd Ste 1 (19382-4990)
PHONE....................610 692-0525
Marjorie Wentz, *Owner*
EMP: 10
SALES (est): 805.4K **Privately Held**
SIC: 3993 Signs, not made in custom sign painting shops

(G-19604)
MXSTRATEGIES LLC
1003 Saber Rd (19382-8071)
PHONE....................610 241-2099
David Brown, *President*
EMP: 5
SALES (est): 337K **Privately Held**
SIC: 7372 8742 Business oriented computer software; industrial & labor consulting services

(G-19605)
N/S CORPORATION
Also Called: NS Corporation - Eastern Off
1230 Wrights Ln (19380-4252)
PHONE....................610 436-5552
Sam Dimaio, *Branch Mgr*
EMP: 3
SALES (corp-wide): 20MM **Privately Held**
WEB: www.nswash.com
SIC: 3589 Car washing machinery
PA: N/S Corporation
235 W Florence Ave
Inglewood CA 90301
310 412-7074

(G-19606)
NATIONAL FOAM INC (PA)
350 E Union St (19382-3450)
PHONE....................610 363-1400
Jack Hittson, *President*
Robert Nelson, *General Mgr*
▼ **EMP:** 65
SALES: 51.8MM **Privately Held**
SIC: 3052 3569 2899 5012 Fire hose, rubber; firefighting apparatus & related equipment; firefighting apparatus; foam charge mixtures; fire trucks

(G-19607)
NATIONAL FOAM INC
350 E Union St (19382-3450)
PHONE....................610 363-1400
Ronald Correia, *Branch Mgr*
EMP: 6
SALES (corp-wide): 51.8MM **Privately Held**
SIC: 3569 2899 Firefighting apparatus & related equipment; fire retardant chemicals
PA: National Foam, Inc.
350 E Union St
West Chester PA 19382
610 363-1400

(G-19608)
NU-ART GRAPHICS INC
899 Fernhill Rd Ste A (19380-4260)
PHONE....................610 436-4336
Raydeen Leek, *President*
EMP: 11
SQ FT: 12,000
SALES (est): 1.6MM **Privately Held**
WEB: www.nuartgraphics.com
SIC: 2759 Decals: printing; screen printing

(G-19609)
OBH ENTERPRISES LLC
205 Gypsie Ln (19380-1203)
PHONE....................610 436-0796
Suzanne Kirkland,
EMP: 3
SALES: 2K **Privately Held**
WEB: www.obhenterprises.com
SIC: 3089 Plastics products

(G-19610)
ON DEMAND PRINTING
1210 Nottingham Dr (19380-4074)
PHONE....................610 696-2258
Loretta Dagostiono, *President*
Mike Dagostiono, *Vice Pres*
EMP: 6
SALES: 330K **Privately Held**
SIC: 2759 Commercial printing

(G-19611)
ONEXIA BRASS INC
Also Called: Phoenix Lock Company
1220 American Blvd (19380-3445)
PHONE....................610 431-3271
Greg Selke, *President*
Anthony Selke, *CIO*
▼ **EMP:** 9
SALES (est): 832.3K **Privately Held**
SIC: 3429 Furniture hardware

(G-19612)
ORGANIZATION DESIGN & DEV INC
Also Called: Hrdq
827 Lincoln Ave Unit B-10 (19380-4472)
PHONE....................610 279-2202
Bradford Glaser, *President*
Rollin O Glaser, *Chairman*
Barbara Roadcap, *Exec VP*
Martin Delahoussaye, *Vice Pres*
Linda Short, *Vice Pres*
EMP: 21
SQ FT: 2,700
SALES (est): 2.5MM **Privately Held**
WEB: www.hrdq.com
SIC: 2731 8748 8742 Books: publishing only; educational consultant; training & development consultant

(G-19613)
OROURKE & SONS INC
992 S Bolmar St (19382-4906)
PHONE....................610 436-0932
Michael O'Rourke, *President*

Michael Orourke, *President*
Michael J Orourke, *Vice Pres*
Mike McDonald, *Purch Agent*
Clement Orourke, *Treasurer*
▲ **EMP:** 35
SQ FT: 6,000
SALES (est): 28.8MM **Privately Held**
WEB: www.orourkesteel.com
SIC: 5051 3443 Steel; fabricated plate work (boiler shop)

(G-19614)
OUT OF SITE STUMP REMOVAL LLC
27 Patrick Ave (19380-4852)
PHONE....................610 692-9907
Michael Cadden, *Mng Member*
EMP: 4
SALES (est): 306.6K **Privately Held**
SIC: 2411 Stumping for turpentine or powder manufacturing

(G-19615)
PAXSON LIGHTNING RODS INC
620 W Union St (19382-3335)
PHONE....................610 696-8290
Francis J Paxson III, *President*
EMP: 4
SALES (est): 421.7K **Privately Held**
WEB: www.paxsonlightningrods.com
SIC: 3643 Current-carrying wiring devices

(G-19616)
PERSONLYTICS LLC
763 Wesley Ct (19382-4985)
PHONE....................484 929-0853
Robert Cybulski, *Managing Prtnr*
Ralph Julius, *Managing Prtnr*
EMP: 4
SALES (est): 98.3K **Privately Held**
SIC: 7372 7389 Business oriented computer software;

(G-19617)
PICCOLO GROUP INC
1204 Waterford Rd (19380-5814)
PHONE....................610 738-7733
Bob Gallagher, *President*
EMP: 3
SALES (est): 320K **Privately Held**
WEB: www.piccologroup.com
SIC: 2821 Molding compounds, plastics

(G-19618)
POCOPSON INDUSTRIES INC
919 Pocopson Rd (19380-7043)
P.O. Box 391, Pocopson (19366-0391)
PHONE....................610 793-0344
Edward Marra, *CEO*
Paige Marra, *Corp Secy*
▲ **EMP:** 15
SQ FT: 5,633
SALES (est): 1.2MM **Privately Held**
WEB: www.timberworks.com
SIC: 1751 2439 Framing contractor; trusses, wooden roof

(G-19619)
PRI INTERNATIONAL INC
404 Price St (19382-3531)
PHONE....................610 436-8292
Vince Vitollo, *President*
EMP: 3
SALES: 500K **Privately Held**
WEB: www.hazmatship.com
SIC: 2741 8999 Technical papers: publishing only, not printed on site; chemical consultant

(G-19620)
PRINT SHOP INC
705 E Union St (19382-4937)
P.O. Box 1419 (19380-0023)
PHONE....................610 692-1810
Ron Barbato, *President*
Anne Anderko, *Manager*
EMP: 8
SQ FT: 12,000
SALES (est): 1.3MM **Privately Held**
WEB: www.theprintshopinc.com
SIC: 2752 Commercial printing, offset

(G-19621)
PROPER NUTRITION INC
439 S Bolmar St (19382-4933)
PHONE....................610 692-2060

Leonard C Giunta, *President*
Dee Eckert, *Corp Secy*
EMP: 3
SQ FT: 1,200
SALES (est): 321.9K
SALES (corp-wide): 401.6K **Privately Held**
WEB: www.propernutrition.com
SIC: 2023 Dietary supplements, dairy & non-dairy based
PA: Bio-Proteus Corporation, Inc
    11 S 11th St
    Reading PA 19602
    610 378-5441

(G-19622)
PROSIT LLC
Also Called: Prosit Print & Copy
1554 Paoli Pike (19380-6123)
PHONE.................................610 430-1470
Timothy Sharr, *Principal*
EMP: 6 **EST:** 2000
SALES (est): 802.7K **Privately Held**
SIC: 2759 Commercial printing

(G-19623)
PUMP SHOP INC
823 Lincoln Ave Ste 2 (19380-4433)
PHONE.................................610 431-6570
Michael J Weber, *President*
Gregory J Weber, *Vice Pres*
EMP: 4
SQ FT: 2,500
SALES (est): 799.9K **Privately Held**
WEB: www.pumpshop.com
SIC: 3561 5084 Pumps & pumping equipment; pumps & pumping equipment

(G-19624)
QUBE GLOBAL SOFTWARE AMERICAS
105 E Evans St (19380-2676)
PHONE.................................610 431-9080
Simon Dibble, *VP Opers*
EMP: 7
SALES (corp-wide): 151.1MM **Privately Held**
SIC: 7372 Prepackaged software
HQ: Qube Global Software Americas Ltd
    3 Westlakes
    Berwyn PA 19312

(G-19625)
R GRAPHICS INC
Also Called: Merit Press
1313 W Chester Pike (19382-6400)
PHONE.................................610 918-0373
Patricia Storlazzi, *President*
Richard Storlazzi, *Corp Secy*
Tracey Treat, *VP Sales*
EMP: 2
SQ FT: 10,000
SALES (est): 2.9MM **Privately Held**
SIC: 2759 2791 2752 Commercial printing; typesetting; commercial printing, lithographic

(G-19626)
R J EVERCREST POLYMERS INC
1234 Wrights Ln (19380-4252)
PHONE.................................610 647-1555
Rob Panetta, *CEO*
▲ **EMP:** 3
SALES (est): 1.1MM **Privately Held**
WEB: www.evercrestinc.com
SIC: 3089 Plastic processing
PA: Evercrest, Inc.
    1234 Wrights Ln
    West Chester PA 19380

(G-19627)
R R PANKRATZ INC
1241 Wrights Ln (19380-4252)
PHONE.................................610 696-1043
Richard R Pankratz, *President*
EMP: 5
SQ FT: 12,600
SALES (est): 796.6K **Privately Held**
SIC: 3565 Packaging machinery

(G-19628)
REBUS INC
595 Dilworthtown Rd (19382-8404)
PHONE.................................610 459-1597
James Steever, *President*

Mark Eisenhower, *Vice Pres*
Todd Eisenhower, *Shareholder*
▲ **EMP:** 25
SALES (est): 5.5MM **Privately Held**
WEB: www.rebusinc.net
SIC: 2816 Color pigments

(G-19629)
RHOTAU PHARMA SERVICES LLC
920 Sassafras Cir (19382-7589)
PHONE.................................484 437-2654
EMP: 4 **EST:** 2013
SALES (est): 297.5K **Privately Held**
SIC: 2834 Pharmaceutical preparations

(G-19630)
RJ EVERCRESTS INC
1234 Wrights Ln (19380-4252)
PHONE.................................610 431-4200
Robert Panetta, *President*
EMP: 4
SALES (est): 315.5K **Privately Held**
SIC: 3089 Plastic processing

(G-19631)
RLE SYSTEMS LLC
1155 Phoenixville Pike 104a (19380-4285)
PHONE.................................610 518-3751
Robert N Coomes, *Mng Member*
Linda Coomes, *Mng Member*
Robert Coomes,
▲ **EMP:** 7
SQ FT: 2,800
SALES: 1.5MM **Privately Held**
SIC: 3492 Control valves, fluid power: hydraulic & pneumatic

(G-19632)
RUSMAR INCORPORATED
216 Garfield Ave (19380-4512)
PHONE.................................610 436-4314
Brian McNamara, *President*
Andrew Peppel, *Vice Pres*
Jeffrey Yarnell, *Sales Mgr*
Theresa Lewis, *Office Mgr*
Jt Bielan, *Manager*
▲ **EMP:** 12
SQ FT: 18,000
SALES (est): 3.7MM **Privately Held**
WEB: www.rusmarinc.com
SIC: 2899 3559 Foam charge mixtures; chemical machinery & equipment

(G-19633)
S & H LTD
Also Called: Metropolitan Flag & Banner
620 Oakbourne Rd (19382-7508)
PHONE.................................215 426-2775
Robert Snyder, *President*
Thomas Healy, *Corp Secy*
Kelly Laughead, *Marketing Mgr*
Matthew Wang, *Graphic Designe*
▲ **EMP:** 9
SALES (est): 400K **Privately Held**
WEB: www.metflag.com
SIC: 2399 Banners, pennants & flags

(G-19634)
S & S SBSRFACE INVSTGTIONS INC
24 Hagerty Blvd Ste 11 (19382-7595)
PHONE.................................610 738-8762
Arthur Salvatore, *President*
EMP: 4
SALES: 600K **Privately Held**
SIC: 1381 1623 Service well drilling; water, sewer & utility lines

(G-19635)
SALUS SECURITY DEVICES LLC
459 Chambers Ln (19382-6949)
PHONE.................................610 388-6387
Benjamin Tomb,
EMP: 4
SALES (est): 376.1K **Privately Held**
SIC: 3699 Security devices

(G-19636)
SAMUELSON LEATHER LLC (PA)
638 Metro Ct (19380-1763)
PHONE.................................610 719-7391
Samuel Paul, *President*
Sumil Samuel, *Vice Pres*
EMP: 4

SQ FT: 300
SALES (est): 1.2MM **Privately Held**
SIC: 3199 5651 Leather garments; unisex clothing stores

(G-19637)
SARTOMER COMPANY DIVISON TOTAL
610 S Bolmar St (19382-3805)
PHONE.................................610 692-8401
Robert Ripchinski, *Principal*
Brian Cirillo, *Engineer*
Robert Costagliola, *Manager*
Bob Costagliola, *Director*
Ken Sweeney, *Executive*
◆ **EMP:** 23
SALES (est): 5MM **Privately Held**
SIC: 2821 2822 5169 Polymethyl methacrylate resins (plexiglass); acrylic rubbers, polyacrylate; chemicals & allied products

(G-19638)
SCHRAMM INC
800 E Virginia Ave Ste 3 (19380-4497)
PHONE.................................610 696-2500
Bobby Bryan, *CEO*
Craig Mayman, *President*
Sean Roach, *Vice Pres*
Fred P Slack, *Vice Pres*
Nathan Case, *Engineer*
◆ **EMP:** 132 **EST:** 1900
SQ FT: 250,000
SALES (est): 61.7MM **Privately Held**
WEB: www.schramminc.com
SIC: 3533 Water well drilling equipment; oil & gas drilling rigs & equipment

(G-19639)
SHUTTER TECH INC
1155 Phoenixville Pike # 105 (19380-4285)
PHONE.................................610 696-9322
Robert W Miller, *President*
EMP: 6
SQ FT: 7,500
SALES (est): 1.7MM **Privately Held**
WEB: www.shuttertech.com
SIC: 3089 5719 Shutters, plastic; window furnishings

(G-19640)
SIGNS BY TOMORROW
1609 Margo Ln (19380-6649)
PHONE.................................484 356-0707
Stewart Lunick, *President*
EMP: 4
SALES (est): 260K **Privately Held**
SIC: 3993 Signs & advertising specialties

(G-19641)
SNAPPER CANE LLC
1021 Hidden Hollow Ln (19380-3314)
PHONE.................................516 770-3569
Daniel Byrne,
▲ **EMP:** 4
SALES (est): 281.8K **Privately Held**
SIC: 3842 Canes, orthopedic

(G-19642)
SONOBOND ULTRASONICS INC
1191 Mcdermott Dr (19380-4042)
PHONE.................................610 696-4710
Janet Devine, *President*
Melissa Alleman, *Vice Pres*
Dennis Bell, *Treasurer*
EMP: 10
SQ FT: 15,000
SALES (est): 2.5MM
SALES (corp-wide): 924.5MM **Privately Held**
WEB: www.sonobondultrasonic.com
SIC: 3699 Welding machines & equipment, ultrasonic
HQ: Indel, Inc.
    10 Indel Ave
    Rancocas NJ 08073
    609 267-9000

(G-19643)
SPENCER GRAPHICS INC
Also Called: Marguerite Davison
711 Haines Mill Rd (19382-6911)
P.O. Box 649, Chadds Ford (19317-0611)
PHONE.................................610 793-2348
William Spencer, *President*
EMP: 3

SQ FT: 1,200
SALES (est): 433.7K **Privately Held**
WEB: www.sgiweb.com
SIC: 2752 7336 Commercial printing, lithographic; graphic arts & related design

(G-19644)
STINGFREE TECHNOLOGIES COMPANY
Also Called: Sting Free Company
1851 Huntsman Ln (19382-6962)
PHONE.................................610 444-2806
Richard F Rudinger, *CEO*
Robert A Vito, *President*
EMP: 5 **EST:** 2001
SALES: 10.1MM **Privately Held**
SIC: 3069 3949 3151 Grips or handles, rubber; soles, boot or shoe: rubber, composition or fiber; helmets, athletic; leather gloves & mittens

(G-19645)
STOLTZFUS TRAILER SALES INC
Also Called: Stoltzfus Rv's & Marine
1335 Wilmington Pike (19382-8217)
PHONE.................................610 399-0628
Earl Stoltzfus, *President*
Bob Cox, *General Mgr*
Robert Cox, *Vice Pres*
◆ **EMP:** 60
SQ FT: 36,000
SALES (est): 25.4MM **Privately Held**
WEB: www.stoltzfus-rec.com
SIC: 5551 5561 3732 Boat dealers; recreational vehicle dealers; boat building & repairing

(G-19646)
STRUCTURE PROBE INC
Also Called: S.P.I. Supplies
206 Garfield Ave (19380-4512)
P.O. Box 656 (19381-0656)
PHONE.................................610 436-5400
Violet Garber, *President*
Andrew W Blackwood, *Vice Pres*
Eugene Rodek, *Vice Pres*
Gene Rodek, *Vice Pres*
Carol A Storm, *Treasurer*
▲ **EMP:** 30 **EST:** 1970
SQ FT: 11,000
SALES (est): 7MM **Privately Held**
WEB: www.spisupplies.com
SIC: 3826 8731 Analytical optical instruments; engineering laboratory, except testing

(G-19647)
SUBTERRANEAN TECH INC
109 Ashton Way (19380-6919)
PHONE.................................610 517-0995
Whitney Jackson, *President*
EMP: 6
SALES: 600K **Privately Held**
SIC: 1389 Oil consultants

(G-19648)
SUBURBAN WATER TECHNOLOGY INC
Also Called: Ecowater Systems
300 E Evans St (19380-2739)
PHONE.................................610 696-1495
Randy Eddinger, *President*
EMP: 10
SALES (est): 898.7K **Privately Held**
SIC: 3823 Water quality monitoring & control systems

(G-19649)
SWEDENBORG FOUNDATION INC
320 N Church St (19380-3213)
PHONE.................................610 430-3222
Jonathan Rose, *President*
John Connolly, *Editor*
Alice Skinner, *Vice Pres*
Amy Acquarola, *Corp Comm Staff*
EMP: 6
SALES: 1.4MM **Privately Held**
WEB: www.swedenborg.com
SIC: 2731 8661 Books: publishing only; religious organizations

(G-19650)
SYNTHES INC (DH)
1302 Wrights Ln E (19380-3417)
PHONE..............................610 647-9700
Michel Orsinger, *President*
Tim Parker, *Regional Mgr*
Mark Pannenberg, *Exec VP*
Kurt Birchler, *Senior VP*
Tony Randazzo, *Vice Pres*
▲ EMP: 3
SALES (est): 1.4B
SALES (corp-wide): 81.5B **Publicly Held**
SIC: 3841 3842 6719 Surgical & medical instruments; surgical appliances & supplies; implants, surgical; investment holding companies, except banks

(G-19651)
SYNTHES SPINE INC
1380 Enterprise Dr (19380-5990)
PHONE..............................610 695-2424
EMP: 35
SALES (corp-wide): 71.3B **Publicly Held**
SIC: 3841 Mfg Surgical Instruments
HQ: Synthes Spine, Inc.
1302 Wrights Ln E
West Chester PA 19380
610 719-5000

(G-19652)
SYNTHES USA LLC (DH)
1302 Wrights Ln E (19380-3417)
PHONE..............................610 719-5000
Steven Murray, *President*
EMP: 3 EST: 2012
SALES (est): 49.6MM
SALES (corp-wide): 81.5B **Publicly Held**
SIC: 3842 Surgical appliances & supplies
HQ: Depuy Products Inc
700 Orthopaedic Dr
Warsaw IN 46582
574 267-8143

(G-19653)
SYNTHES USA PRODUCTS LLC
1302 Wrights Ln E (19380-3417)
PHONE..............................610 719-5000
Mary Schafer, *President*
Gary Reehl, *Project Mgr*
EMP: 8
SALES (est): 733.5K
SALES (corp-wide): 81.5B **Publicly Held**
SIC: 3841 Surgical & medical instruments
HQ: Medical Device Business Services, Inc.
700 Orthopaedic Dr
Warsaw IN 46582

(G-19654)
SYSTEMATICS INC
1025 Saunders Ln (19380-4217)
P.O. Box 2429 (19380-0125)
PHONE..............................610 696-9040
James L Conley, *President*
William C Jones, *Vice Pres*
Bill Jones, *Engineer*
James R Beltz, *Treasurer*
Mark Suska, *Manager*
▲ EMP: 60
SQ FT: 65,000
SALES (est): 10.8MM **Privately Held**
SIC: 3548 Gas welding equipment

(G-19655)
TAGGART PRINTING CORPORATION
323 S Matlack St (19382-3799)
PHONE..............................610 431-2500
J Michael Taggart Jr, *President*
Ruth Taggart, *Admin Sec*
EMP: 15
SQ FT: 12,000
SALES (est): 2.5MM **Privately Held**
WEB: www.taggartprinting.com
SIC: 2752 Commercial printing, offset

(G-19656)
TAYLOR RUN
795 Downingtown Pike (19380-1972)
PHONE..............................610 436-1369
Robert Baker, *Director*
EMP: 8 EST: 2008
SALES (est): 829.3K **Privately Held**
SIC: 3589 Water treatment equipment, industrial

(G-19657)
TEF - CAP INDUSTRIES INC
1155 Phoenixville Pike # 103 (19380-4285)
PHONE..............................610 692-2576
John Walls, *President*
Chris Walls, *Sales Staff*
EMP: 8
SQ FT: 2,800
SALES: 1.1MM **Privately Held**
WEB: www.tefcap.com
SIC: 3089 Closures, plastic

(G-19658)
TEVA BOPHARMACEUTICALS USA INC
145 Brandywine Pkwy (19380-4245)
PHONE..............................240 821-9000
Steven C Mayer, *CEO*
Derek Dunn, *Manager*
Weihua Wan, *Manager*
EMP: 72
SALES (est): 11.3MM **Privately Held**
WEB: www.cogenesys.com
SIC: 2834 Pharmaceutical preparations

(G-19659)
TEVA BRANDED PHRM PDTS R&D INC
145 Brandywine Pkwy (19380-4245)
PHONE..............................215 591-3000
Barbara Butler, *Director*
Meital Mendel, *Administration*
Mehran Yazdanian, *Products*
EMP: 61
SALES (corp-wide): 18.8B **Privately Held**
SIC: 2834 Penicillin preparations; drugs acting on the respiratory system; drugs acting on the cardiovascular system, except diagnostic
HQ: Teva Branded Pharmaceutical Products R&D, Inc.
41 Moores Rd
Malvern PA 19355
215 591-3000

(G-19660)
THE ADIRONDACK GROUP INC (PA)
Also Called: Fence Authority
100 Colonial Way (19382-6895)
PHONE..............................610 431-4343
John S Digiuseppe, *President*
Steven C Lauriello, *Vice Pres*
Robert Casterline, *Treasurer*
Gregg Neumann, *Controller*
▲ EMP: 30
SQ FT: 25,000
SALES (est): 6.9MM **Privately Held**
WEB: www.fenceauthority.com
SIC: 5211 5031 2499 1799 Fencing; fencing, wood; fencing, wood; fence construction

(G-19661)
THERMO ELECTRIC COMPANY INC (PA)
1193 Mcdermott Dr (19380-4042)
PHONE..............................610 692-7990
Richard R Rodelli, *President*
Pierre Emmanuel Lucq, *COO*
James Abboud, *Opers Mgr*
Lee Sitvarin, *Opers Mgr*
Phil Avallone, *Purch Mgr*
▲ EMP: 60 EST: 1941
SQ FT: 144,500
SALES (est): 42MM **Privately Held**
WEB: www.thermo-electric-direct.com
SIC: 3822 3111 3829 Temperature controls, automatic; accessory products, leather; thermometers & temperature sensors

(G-19662)
THERMO ELECTRIC PA INC
1193 Mcdermott Dr (19380-4042)
PHONE..............................610 692-7990
Richard R Rodelli, *CEO*
EMP: 100 EST: 2012
SQ FT: 25,000
SALES: 10MM
SALES (corp-wide): 42MM **Privately Held**
SIC: 3829 Thermometers & temperature sensors

PA: Thermo Electric Company Inc.
1193 Mcdermott Dr
West Chester PA 19380
610 692-7990

(G-19663)
TIN TECHNOLOGY AND REF LLC
905 Fernhill Rd (19380-4203)
PHONE..............................610 430-2225
Lee Morris, *Vice Pres*
Luke Etherington, *Vice Pres*
Peter Morris, *Vice Pres*
Tanya Dashkiwsky, *Controller*
Peter Ruth, *Manager*
▼ EMP: 7
SALES (est): 745.2K **Privately Held**
SIC: 2611 3339 Pulp mills, mechanical & recycling processing; tin refining (primary)

(G-19664)
TITANIUM WEALTH ADVISORS LLC
1217 W Chester Pike Ste A (19382-5658)
PHONE..............................610 429-1700
EMP: 3
SALES (est): 233K **Privately Held**
SIC: 3356 Titanium

(G-19665)
TLC REFRESHMENTS INC
Also Called: Polish Water Ice
797 Tree Ln (19380-2001)
PHONE..............................610 429-4124
Thomas Curyto, *President*
Corey Curyto, *Vice Pres*
EMP: 15
SALES (est): 1.8MM **Privately Held**
SIC: 2097 Block ice

(G-19666)
TORNIER INC ✪
801 Wagonwheel Ln (19380-2010)
PHONE..............................610 585-2111
EMP: 3 EST: 2018
SALES (est): 140.1K **Privately Held**
SIC: 3842 Implants, surgical

(G-19667)
TOTAL PTRCHEMICALS REF USA INC
Also Called: Cray Valley
610 S Bolmar St (19382-3797)
PHONE..............................610 692-8401
Robert Costagliola, *Branch Mgr*
EMP: 100
SALES (corp-wide): 8.4B **Publicly Held**
WEB: www.sartomer.com
SIC: 2911 2899 2869 Petroleum refining; chemical preparations; fuels
HQ: Total Petrochemicals & Refining Usa, Inc.
1201 La St Ste 1800
Houston TX 77002
713 483-5000

(G-19668)
TRANSWALL CORP
1220 Wilson Dr (19380-4231)
P.O. Box 1930 (19380-0147)
PHONE..............................610 429-1400
H Hayes Aikens, *Ch of Bd*
EMP: 85 EST: 1956
SALES (est): 11.2MM **Privately Held**
WEB: www.transwall.com
SIC: 2542 Partitions for floor attachment, prefabricated; except wood

(G-19669)
TRANSWALL OFFICE SYSTEMS INC
1220 Wilson Dr (19380-4231)
P.O. Box 1930 (19380-0147)
PHONE..............................610 429-1400
Shaun Mannix, *President*
Frank Lytle, *Vice Pres*
Jay Aikens, *Treasurer*
EMP: 49
SQ FT: 80,000
SALES (est): 10.1MM **Privately Held**
SIC: 2522 Panel systems & partitions, office: except wood

(G-19670)
UNIPAK INC
Also Called: Unipak Products Company
715 E Washington St (19380-4595)
PHONE..............................610 436-6600
Steve Frain, *Principal*
Theodore H Frain III, *Principal*
Teddy Frain, *Vice Pres*
Theodore H Frain IV, *Vice Pres*
Greg Nelms, *Controller*
EMP: 45 EST: 1912
SQ FT: 45,000
SALES (est): 12.8MM **Privately Held**
WEB: www.unipakinc.com
SIC: 2657 2652 2752 Folding paperboard boxes; setup paperboard boxes; commercial printing, lithographic

(G-19671)
VAN HEYNEKER FINE WOODWORKING
1005 Brintons Bridge Rd (19382-8111)
PHONE..............................610 388-1772
Van Heyneker, *Owner*
EMP: 4
SALES (est): 207.7K **Privately Held**
SIC: 1751 2499 Cabinet & finish carpentry; decorative wood & woodwork

(G-19672)
VANGUARD IDENTIFICATION
Also Called: Vanguard ID Systems
1210 American Blvd (19380-4268)
PHONE..............................610 719-0700
Richard O Warther, *President*
Josh Scott, *President*
Victor Murray, *Natl Sales Mgr*
Gabi Terrell, *Marketing Staff*
Alan Neves, *Manager*
EMP: 45
SQ FT: 7,200
SALES (est): 9.6MM **Privately Held**
WEB: www.vanguardid.com
SIC: 3577 3429 2671 Bar code (magnetic ink) printers; manufactured hardware (general); packaging paper & plastics film, coated & laminated

(G-19673)
VARINEL INC
929 S High St Ste 159 (19382-5466)
PHONE..............................610 256-3119
Vincent R Zurawski Jr PHD, *CEO*
EMP: 4
SALES: 180K **Privately Held**
SIC: 2834 Pharmaceutical preparations

(G-19674)
VERRICA PHARMACEUTICALS INC
10 N High St Fl 2 (19380-3014)
PHONE..............................484 453-3300
Paul B Manning, *Ch of Bd*
Ted White, *President*
Linda Palczuk, *COO*
Chris Degnan, *CFO*
Joe Bonaccorso, *Ch Credit Ofcr*
EMP: 16
SQ FT: 4,962
SALES (est): 248.4K **Privately Held**
SIC: 2834 Dermatologicals

(G-19675)
VTG TANKTAINER NORTH AMER INC
109 E Evans St Ste C (19380-2660)
PHONE..............................610 429-5440
Lars Schuster, *President*
Leon Van Bergen, *President*
Ulrich Schnoor, *Treasurer*
◆ EMP: 17
SQ FT: 3,600
SALES: 1.6MM **Privately Held**
SIC: 2899 Fuel tank or engine cleaning chemicals
HQ: Vtg Tanktainer Gmbh
Hammerbrookstr. 5
Hamburg 20097
402 805-90

(G-19676)
WESCHO COMPANY INC
924 S Concord Rd (19382-7537)
PHONE..............................610 436-5866
Joachim Nussbaumer, *President*

EMP: 20
SQ FT: 3,000
SALES (est): 2.2MM **Privately Held**
WEB: www.wescho.com
SIC: 2542 1799 Office & store showcases & display fixtures; home/office interiors finishing, furnishing & remodeling

(G-19677)
WIGGINS SHREDDING INC
Also Called: Shred Patrol
1301 W Chester Pike (19382-6420)
PHONE..............................610 692-8327
Brad Wiggins, *President*
EMP: 6
SQ FT: 22,000
SALES: 850K **Privately Held**
SIC: 3559 Ammunition & explosives, loading machinery

(G-19678)
WINDRIDGE DESIGN INC
Also Called: Windridge/Cheryl Nash
319 Westtown Rd Ste J (19382-4514)
PHONE..............................610 692-1919
Cheryl Nash, *President*
David Nash, *Corp Secy*
▲ **EMP:** 15
SQ FT: 5,000
SALES (est): 1.6MM **Privately Held**
SIC: 2339 7389 Women's & misses' athletic clothing & sportswear; apparel designers, commercial

(G-19679)
WIRE AND CABLE SPECIALTIES INC
Also Called: W C S
205 Carter Dr (19382-4973)
PHONE..............................610 692-7551
Jim N Clark, *President*
EMP: 40
SALES (corp-wide): 12.2MM **Privately Held**
WEB: www.wire-cablespecialties.com
SIC: 3496 Miscellaneous fabricated wire products
PA: Wire And Cable Specialties, Inc.
440 Highland Blvd
Coatesville PA 19320
610 466-6200

(G-19680)
WIRTHMORE PDTS & SVC CO INC
1330 Green Hill Ave (19380-3960)
PHONE..............................610 430-0300
James Christopher Smith, *President*
EMP: 3
SALES (est): 24K **Privately Held**
SIC: 3281 2493 Blackboards, slate; slate products; building board, except gypsum: hard pressed

(G-19681)
WOODWARD MCCOACH INC (PA)
1171 Mcdermott Dr (19380-4042)
PHONE..............................610 692-9526
Thomas Woodward, *CEO*
John Sweeney, *President*
Wayne Bullaughey, *Vice Pres*
David D McCoach, *Vice Pres*
James Bridges, *Admin Sec*
EMP: 18
SQ FT: 8,000
SALES (est): 3.5MM **Privately Held**
WEB: www.wmi.com
SIC: 3672 Printed circuit boards

(G-19682)
WYETH LLC
611 E Nields St (19382-3772)
PHONE..............................610 696-3100
Anthony Demarco, *President*
Guy St Pierre, *Supervisor*
EMP: 6
SALES (corp-wide): 53.6B **Publicly Held**
WEB: www.wyeth.com
SIC: 2834 Pharmaceutical preparations
HQ: Wyeth Llc
235 E 42nd St
New York NY 10017
212 733-2323

(G-19683)
XL PRECISION TECHNOLOGIES
19 Hagerty Blvd Ste C (19382-7572)
PHONE..............................610 696-6800
EMP: 11
SALES (est): 1.7MM **Privately Held**
SIC: 3599 Machine shop, jobbing & repair

West Conshohocken
Montgomery County

(G-19684)
ALUMINUM ATHLETIC EQUIPMENT CO
Also Called: Marzucco Enterprises
1000 Enterprises St (19428)
PHONE..............................610 825-6565
Timothy W Driscoll, *President*
Rita Marzucco, *Vice Pres*
EMP: 35
SQ FT: 30,000
SALES (est): 2MM **Privately Held**
SIC: 3949 Sporting & athletic goods

(G-19685)
ARG RESOURCES INC (PA)
100 Four Fls Ste 215 (19428)
PHONE..............................610 940-4420
John Trinkl, *CFO*
Harry H Halloran Jr, *Treasurer*
EMP: 45
SALES (est): 3.3MM **Privately Held**
WEB: www.arbgeowell.com
SIC: 1311 Crude petroleum & natural gas production

(G-19686)
BTG INTERNATIONAL INC (HQ)
300 Four Falls Corporate (19428)
PHONE..............................610 943-6000
Louise Makin, *CEO*
Simon Joseph, *General Mgr*
Darby C Kane, *Business Mgr*
Shannon McFarland, *Counsel*
Julia Anastas, *Vice Pres*
EMP: 53
SALES (est): 12.1MM **Privately Held**
SIC: 8731 2834 Medical research, commercial; solutions, pharmaceutical

West Decatur
Clearfield County

(G-19687)
ACTION CYCLE & ATV LLC
8081 Old Erie Pike (16878-8731)
PHONE..............................814 765-2578
Annett Lumadue, *President*
EMP: 9
SALES (est): 216.3K **Privately Held**
SIC: 7694 5571 Motor repair services; motorcycle parts & accessories

(G-19688)
HOLT PRECISION TOOL CO
1422 Wllaceton Bigler Hwy (16878-8836)
PHONE..............................814 342-3595
Tim Holt, *President*
EMP: 5
SQ FT: 1,720
SALES (est): 200K **Privately Held**
SIC: 3544 Special dies & tools

(G-19689)
NEW ENTERPRISE STONE LIME INC
1556 Clearfield St (16878-9203)
PHONE..............................814 342-7096
Paul Detwiler, *Manager*
EMP: 25
SALES (corp-wide): 651.9MM **Privately Held**
WEB: www.nesl.com
SIC: 1422 Crushed & broken limestone
PA: New Enterprise Stone & Lime Co., Inc.
3912 Brumbaugh Rd
New Enterprise PA 16664
814 224-6883

(G-19690)
RES COAL LLC
1128 3rd Level Rd (16878)
PHONE..............................814 765-0352
Allan Legrand, *Branch Mgr*
EMP: 64
SALES (corp-wide): 17.7MM **Privately Held**
SIC: 1241 Coal mining services
PA: Res Coal Llc
51 Airport Rd
Clearfield PA 16830
814 765-7525

(G-19691)
S & S LOGGS INC
2030 Eagle Eye Rd (16878-8010)
PHONE..............................814 339-7375
Jason Swatsworth, *Principal*
EMP: 3
SALES (est): 214K **Privately Held**
SIC: 2411 Logging

West Elizabeth
Allegheny County

(G-19692)
BJ REO INC
Also Called: Vincents Welding
Madison Ave (15088)
P.O. Box 345 (15088-0345)
PHONE..............................412 384-2161
Marie Olmsted, *President*
EMP: 22 **EST:** 1947
SQ FT: 12,000
SALES (est): 4.2MM **Privately Held**
SIC: 3498 Fabricated pipe & fittings

(G-19693)
CLAIRTON SLAG INC
Also Called: Winter Transfer Company
1000 Madison Ave (15088)
P.O. Box 532 (15088-0532)
PHONE..............................412 384-8420
Mark Schaefer, *President*
Robert Schaefer, *Vice Pres*
Bob Schaefer, *Materials Mgr*
EMP: 15
SQ FT: 8,000
SALES (est): 1.8MM **Privately Held**
WEB: www.csiriverterm.com
SIC: 4491 2951 Marine cargo handling; asphalt & asphaltic paving mixtures (not from refineries)

(G-19694)
DONALD PLANTS
Also Called: Shadlure Tackle
3067 Scotia Hollow Rd (15088)
P.O. Box 185 (15088-0185)
PHONE..............................412 384-5911
Donald Plants, *Owner*
EMP: 3
SALES (est): 190K **Privately Held**
SIC: 3949 5941 Fishing tackle, general; fishing equipment

(G-19695)
MON RIVER SUPPLY LLC
120 First St (15088)
P.O. Box 553 (15088-0553)
PHONE..............................412 382-7178
Brian Gunzenhauser,
EMP: 7
SALES (est): 1.2MM **Privately Held**
SIC: 3273 Ready-mixed concrete

(G-19696)
OLMSTED INC
Madison Ave (15088)
P.O. Box 572 (15088-0572)
PHONE..............................412 384-2161
Marie C Olmsted, *President*
Terry Heckert, *Manager*
EMP: 15
SQ FT: 10,000
SALES (est): 2.4MM **Privately Held**
WEB: www.olmsted.com
SIC: 3443 Fabricated plate work (boiler shop)

(G-19697)
SANYO CHEMICAL & RESINS LLC
2200 St Hwy 837 (15088)
P.O. Box 567 (15088-0567)
PHONE..............................412 384-5700
Camille Golock, *Finance Mgr*
Hiroshi Kishiai, *Mng Member*
Akiyoshi Kodera,
▲ **EMP:** 4
SQ FT: 7,500
SALES (est): 790.9K
SALES (corp-wide): 1.5B **Privately Held**
SIC: 2865 2893 Color lakes or toners; duplicating ink
PA: Sanyo Chemical Industries, Ltd.
11-1, Nomotocho, Ichinohashi, Higashiyama-Ku
Kyoto KYO 605-0
755 414-311

West Grove
Chester County

(G-19698)
COUNTRY HEIRLOOMS INC
3844 Gap Newport Pike (19390-9280)
PHONE..............................610 869-9550
John J Lamontagne, *President*
Ann Smith, *Vice Pres*
EMP: 6
SQ FT: 20,000
SALES (est): 717K **Privately Held**
WEB:
www.countryheirloomsquiltdesigns.com
SIC: 2511 Wood household furniture

(G-19699)
CUSTOM MACHINE & DESIGN INC
Also Called: Cmd
21 Commerce Blvd (19390-9185)
PHONE..............................610 932-4717
James D Price, *President*
William A Parker Jr, *Vice Pres*
EMP: 10
SQ FT: 10,000
SALES (est): 2.4MM **Privately Held**
WEB: www.cmdinc.biz
SIC: 3599 Machine shop, jobbing & repair

(G-19700)
HARMONY DESIGNS INC
129 E Harmony Rd (19390-1009)
PHONE..............................610 869-4234
Sherrill Franklin, *President*
EMP: 8
SQ FT: 1,200
SALES: 185K **Privately Held**
WEB: www.harmonydesigns.com
SIC: 2679 Gift wrap & novelties, paper; novelties, paper: made from purchased material

(G-19701)
JAMES KIRKPATRICK
Also Called: Kreutz Creek Vineyards
553 S Guernsey Rd (19390-9726)
PHONE..............................610 869-4412
Carroll Kirkpatrick, *President*
James Kirkpatrick, *Owner*
EMP: 52
SALES (est): 3.2MM **Privately Held**
WEB: www.kreutzcreekvineyards.com
SIC: 2084 0172 Wines; grapes

(G-19702)
MILLER EDGE INC (PA)
300 N Jennersville Rd (19390-9155)
P.O. Box 159 (19390-0159)
PHONE..............................610 869-4422
Bearge Miller, *President*
Ginny Miller, *Corp Secy*
Virginia D Miller, *Corp Secy*
Kathleen Bard, *COO*
Florence D Mohler, *Vice Pres*
▲ **EMP:** 65 **EST:** 1940
SQ FT: 60,000

SALES (est): 12.9MM **Privately Held**
WEB: www.milleredge.com
SIC: 3699 3812 3613 3496 Electrical
equipment & supplies; search & navigation equipment; switchgear & switchboard
apparatus; miscellaneous fabricated wire
products

(G-19703)
NUTRA-SOILS INC
324 E Baltimore Pike (19390)
PHONE..................................610 869-7645
EMP: 25
SALES (est): 3.7MM **Privately Held**
SIC: 2879 Mfg Agricultural Chemicals

(G-19704)
POWELL ELECTRO SYSTEMS LLC
5 Briar Dr (19390-9455)
PHONE..................................610 869-8393
William P Powell, *CEO*
EMP: 15
SQ FT: 18,000
SALES (est): 2.7MM **Privately Held**
WEB: www.electrosystems.com
SIC: 3052 3679 Plastic hose; harness as-
semblies for electronic use: wire or cable

(G-19705)
ROBERTSON MANUFACTURING INC
112 Woodland Ave (19390-1118)
PHONE..................................610 869-9600
Jack Hanlon, *President*
Katherine Reid, *Vice Pres*
EMP: 36
SQ FT: 22,500
SALES (est): 4.6MM **Privately Held**
SIC: 2394 Canvas & related products

West Hazleton
Luzerne County

(G-19706)
BEMIS COMPANY INC
Also Called: Bemis North America
20 Jaycee Dr (18202-1142)
PHONE..................................570 501-1400
Bob Caccese, *Manager*
EMP: 250
SALES (corp-wide): 4B **Publicly Held**
WEB: www.bemis.com
SIC: 2671 2673 Paper coated or lami-
nated for packaging; bags: plastic, lami-
nated & coated
PA: Bemis Company, Inc.
2301 Industrial Dr
Neenah WI 54956
920 527-5000

(G-19707)
BIMBO BAKERIES USA INC
350 Kiwanis Blvd (18202-1162)
PHONE..................................570 455-7691
John King, *Branch Mgr*
EMP: 14 **Privately Held**
SIC: 2051 Bread, cake & related products
HQ: Bimbo Bakeries Usa, Inc
255 Business Center Dr # 200
Horsham PA 19044
215 347-5500

(G-19708)
BIMBO BAKERIES USA INC
325 Kiwanis Blvd (18202-1163)
PHONE..................................570 455-2066
John King, *Manager*
EMP: 350 **Privately Held**
SIC: 2051 Bread, cake & related products
HQ: Bimbo Bakeries Usa, Inc
255 Business Center Dr # 200
Horsham PA 19044
215 347-5500

(G-19709)
FEDERAL BUSINESS PRODUCTS INC
150 Jaycee Dr (18202-1190)
PHONE..................................570 454-2451
Bill Shannon, *Production*
John Zola, *Manager*
EMP: 75

SALES (corp-wide): 20MM **Privately Held**
WEB: www.feddirect.com
SIC: 2761 2752 Manifold business forms;
commercial printing, lithographic
PA: Federal Business Products Inc
150 Clove Rd Ste 5
Little Falls NJ 07424
973 667-9800

(G-19710)
G WESTON BAKERIES
325 Kiwanis Blvd (18202-1163)
PHONE..................................570 455-2066
Gary Perrin, *Manager*
EMP: 8
SALES (est): 353.8K **Privately Held**
SIC: 2051 Bakery: wholesale or whole-
sale/retail combined

(G-19711)
GREIF INC
95 Jaycee Dr (18202-1143)
PHONE..................................570 459-9075
Kellie Clark, *Financial Exec*
Tammy Drumheller, *Accounts Mgr*
Dean Babcock, *Manager*
Janet Evans, *Technology*
EMP: 40
SALES (corp-wide): 3.8B **Publicly Held**
WEB: www.greif.com
SIC: 3089 Air mattresses, plastic
PA: Greif, Inc.
425 Winter Rd
Delaware OH 43015
740 549-6000

(G-19712)
HENKEL US OPERATIONS CORP
125 Jaycee Dr (18202-1145)
PHONE..................................570 455-9980
Keith Ahlbrandt, *Engineer*
Michael Williams, *Project Engr*
James Babula, *Manager*
EMP: 175
SALES (corp-wide): 22.7B **Privately Held**
WEB: www.dialcorp.com
SIC: 2841 Soap: granulated, liquid, cake,
flaked or chip
HQ: Henkel Us Operations Corporation
1 Henkel Way
Rocky Hill CT 06067
860 571-5100

(G-19713)
LDP INC (PA)
Also Called: Quest Systems & Technology
75 Kiwanis Blvd (18202-1157)
P.O. Box O, Hazleton (18201-0376)
PHONE..................................570 455-8511
Charles J Mason, *President*
Toni Kluck, *Business Mgr*
Charles J Mason Jr, *Corp Secy*
Joseph Koval, *Engineer*
Ron Angel, *Accounts Mgr*
EMP: 70
SQ FT: 30,000
SALES (est): 10.2MM **Privately Held**
WEB: www.leaderservices.com
SIC: 7372 4813 7373 Prepackaged soft-
ware; ; local area network (LAN) systems
integrator

(G-19714)
NEUROPEDIC LLC
115 Rotary Dr Ste 1 (18202-1218)
PHONE..................................570 501-7713
Antonio Nunez,
Gary Wells,
EMP: 15
SQ FT: 24,000
SALES (est): 1.9MM **Privately Held**
WEB: www.neuropedic.com
SIC: 2515 2392 Mattresses & foundations;
pillows, bed: made from purchased mate-
rials

(G-19715)
PREMIER INK SYSTEMS INC
103 Rotary Dr Ste 1 (18202-1193)
P.O. Box 2158, Hazleton (18201-1058)
PHONE..................................570 459-2300
Charles De Cosmo, *Branch Mgr*
EMP: 5

SALES (corp-wide): 16.5MM **Privately Held**
WEB: www.premierink.com
SIC: 2851 2899 Lacquers, varnishes,
enamels & other coatings; ink or writing
fluids
PA: Premier Ink Systems, Inc.
10420 N State St
Harrison OH 45030
513 367-2300

(G-19716)
THERMA-TEK RANGE CORP
115 Rotary Dr (18202-1218)
PHONE..................................570 455-3000
EMP: 37
SALES (corp-wide): 6.5MM **Privately Held**
SIC: 3639 Household Appliances, Nec, Nsk
PA: Therma-Tek Range Corp.
9121 Atlanta Ave Ste 331
Huntington Beach CA 92646

(G-19717)
VALMONT NEWMARK INC
Valmont Newmark-Hazelton
225 Kiwanis Blvd (18202-1161)
PHONE..................................570 454-8730
John Staconis, *Design Engr*
Paul O'Fallon, *Manager*
Tom Griffin, *Info Tech Mgr*
Gina T Corazza, *Executive*
EMP: 225
SALES (corp-wide): 2.7B **Publicly Held**
WEB: www.newmark.com
SIC: 3272 3317 Poles & posts, concrete;
steel pipe & tubes
HQ: Valmont Newmark, Inc.
2 Perimeter Park S 475w
Birmingham AL 35243
205 968-7200

(G-19718)
VICTORIAS CANDIES INC
Airport Hwy Rd Laurel (18201)
PHONE..................................570 455-6345
Paul Esposita, *Manager*
EMP: 6
SALES (corp-wide): 2MM **Privately Held**
WEB: www.victoriascandies.com
SIC: 2064 Candy & other confectionery
products
PA: Victoria's Candies Inc
51 N Laurel St Frnt
Hazleton PA 18201
570 455-6341

West Homestead
Allegheny County

(G-19719)
ABMECH ACQUISITIONS LLC
976 Forest Ave (15120-1113)
P.O. Box 713, Homestead (15120-5713)
PHONE..................................412 462-7440
Ben Ditson,
EMP: 28
SALES (est): 839.5K **Privately Held**
SIC: 3292 Asbestos products

(G-19720)
SIGN CREATORS INC
Also Called: Sign Crafters
345 Cherry St (15120-1148)
P.O. Box 276, Homestead (15120-0276)
PHONE..................................412 461-3567
Charles K Brandt, *CEO*
Matt Sedlak, *Production*
Karen Breitweiser, *Art Dir*
Star Hicks Brandt, *Admin Sec*
EMP: 5
SALES (est): 694.9K **Privately Held**
WEB: www.signcreators.com
SIC: 1799 2759 Sign installation & mainte-
nance; screen printing

West Middlesex
Mercer County

(G-19721)
AUTOSOFT INC
Also Called: Autosoft International
61 Executive Ct Ste 1 (16159-3070)
PHONE..................................800 473-4630
Bryce Veon, *Principal*
Chris Dukes, *Business Mgr*
Christopher Morris, *Senior VP*
John Schneider, *Senior VP*
Steve Gilbert, *Vice Pres*
EMP: 85
SQ FT: 30,000
SALES (est): 17.7MM **Privately Held**
WEB: www.autosoft-asi.com
SIC: 7372 Business oriented computer
software

(G-19722)
DAIRY FARMERS AMERICA INC
82 North St (16159-3474)
PHONE..................................724 946-8729
Max Shaw, *Branch Mgr*
EMP: 41
SALES (corp-wide): 14.6B **Privately Held**
SIC: 2022 2021 2023 2024 Natural
cheese; processed cheese; creamery butter; condensed milk; powdered milk; ice
cream & ice milk; dairy machinery &
equipment; milk processing (pasteurizing,
homogenizing, bottling)
PA: Dairy Farmers Of America, Inc.
1405 N 98th St
Kansas City KS 66111
816 801-6455

(G-19723)
DUNBAR ASPHALT PRODUCTS INC (HQ)
3766 New Castle Rd (16159-2830)
P.O. Box 477, Wheatland (16161-0477)
PHONE..................................724 528-9310
Brad J Berlin, *President*
EMP: 5
SQ FT: 1,500
SALES (est): 2.6MM
SALES (corp-wide): 1MM **Privately Held**
SIC: 2951 Asphalt paving mixtures &
blocks
PA: Integrated Construction Systems, Inc.
3766 New Castle Rd
West Middlesex PA 16159
724 528-9310

(G-19724)
EXTREME MACHINE AND FABG INC
2340 Quality Ln Ste 1 (16159-6310)
PHONE..................................724 342-4340
Richard D Wanchisn, *President*
Gerald Taafe Jr, *General Mgr*
▲ EMP: 85
SQ FT: 10,000
SALES (est): 16.1MM **Privately Held**
SIC: 3599 Machine shop, jobbing & repair

(G-19725)
GARRETTS FABRICATING
2646 Mrcer W Middlesex Rd (16159-3142)
PHONE..................................724 528-8193
Melissa Garrett, *Principal*
EMP: 3
SALES (est): 250.6K **Privately Held**
SIC: 2451 3351 3548 Mobile home
frames; copper rolling & drawing; welding
apparatus

(G-19726)
INTEGRATED CNSTR SYSTEMS INC (PA)
3766 New Castle Rd (16159-2830)
P.O. Box 233 (16159-0233)
PHONE..................................724 528-9310
Brad R Berlin, *President*
Doug Greene, *Vice Pres*
Pat Burke, *Treasurer*
Robert Bretz, *Admin Sec*
EMP: 15 EST: 1995
SQ FT: 1,500

SALES (est): 1MM **Privately Held**
SIC: 2951 6719 Asphalt paving mixtures & blocks; personal holding companies, except banks

(G-19727)
JONES PERFORMANCE PRODUCTS INC
1 Jones Way (16159)
P.O. Box 808 (16159-0808)
PHONE..................................724 528-3569
Dave Jones, *President*
Gary Antus, *Manager*
▲ EMP: 60
SQ FT: 75,000
SALES (est): 13.9MM **Privately Held**
WEB: www.jonesperformance.com
SIC: 3714 3713 Hoods, motor vehicle; truck & bus bodies

(G-19728)
REGENEX CORPORATION
1 New St (16159-3533)
P.O. Box 608 (16159-0608)
PHONE..................................724 528-5900
Daniel Berent, *President*
Barbara Berent, *Corp Secy*
Daniel J Berent, *Treasurer*
EMP: 75
SALES (est): 17.1MM **Privately Held**
WEB: www.regenex.com
SIC: 3089 3442 Plastic hardware & building products; metal doors, sash & trim

(G-19729)
RIISE INC
9 Carbaugh St (16159-4101)
P.O. Box 607 (16159-0607)
PHONE..................................724 528-3305
T Scott Campbell, *President*
Robert E Campbell, *Treasurer*
EMP: 4
SQ FT: 9,000
SALES (est): 2.6MM
SALES (corp-wide): 18.2MM **Privately Held**
WEB: www.riiseinc.com
SIC: 5051 3567 5084 8711 Steel; industrial furnaces & ovens; processing & packaging equipment; engineering services
PA: T. Bruce Sales, Inc.
9 Carbaugh St
West Middlesex PA 16159
724 528-9961

(G-19730)
T BRUCE CAMPBELL CNSTR CO INC
3658 New Castle Rd (16159)
PHONE..................................724 528-9944
T Scott Campbell, *President*
Robert Campbell, *Vice Pres*
Wayne Miller, *Vice Pres*
EMP: 200
SQ FT: 30,000
SALES (est): 34.8MM **Privately Held**
SIC: 3441 1541 Building components, structural steel; industrial buildings, new construction

(G-19731)
T BRUCE SALES INC (PA)
9 Carbaugh St (16159-4101)
P.O. Box 607 (16159-0607)
PHONE..................................724 528-9961
T Scott Campbell, *President*
Robert Campbell, *Vice Pres*
Christopher Stewart, *Info Tech Mgr*
▲ EMP: 70
SQ FT: 70,000
SALES (est): 18.2MM **Privately Held**
WEB: www.tbrucesales.com
SIC: 3441 3567 3547 3537 Fabricated structural metal; industrial furnaces & ovens; rolling mill machinery; industrial trucks & tractors; hoists, cranes & monorails; sheets, metal

(G-19732)
WILLARD BURIAL SERVICE INC
3955 New Cstl Rd Rr 18 (16159)
PHONE..................................724 528-9965
Glenda W Cunningham, *President*
Robert Cunningham, *Vice Pres*
William Cunningham Jr, *Treasurer*

EMP: 8
SQ FT: 5,400
SALES (est): 1.4MM **Privately Held**
SIC: 3272 5087 Burial vaults, concrete or precast terrazzo; service establishment equipment

(G-19733)
ZRILE BROTHERS PACKING INC
4129 Longview Rd (16159-3115)
P.O. Box 816 (16159-0816)
PHONE..................................724 528-9246
John J Zrile, *President*
Krste Zrile, *Vice Pres*
Marko Zrile, *Admin Sec*
EMP: 5
SQ FT: 1,400
SALES (est): 3.1MM **Privately Held**
SIC: 2011 Beef products from beef slaughtered on site

West Mifflin
Allegheny County

(G-19734)
ACTIVAIDED ORTHOTICS LLC
5012 Ball Ave (15122-1343)
PHONE..................................412 901-2658
Kelly Collier, *CEO*
EMP: 3
SALES (est): 255.4K **Privately Held**
SIC: 3842 Abdominal supporters, braces & trusses; braces, elastic; braces, orthopedic; elastic hosiery, orthopedic (support)

(G-19735)
ADVANCED PULTRUSIONS LLC
Also Called: Liberty Polyglas Pultrusions
1575 Lebanon School Rd (15122-3433)
PHONE..................................412 466-8611
David Griffith, *President*
Gayle Volz, *Controller*
Brian Morton, *Sales Associate*
Brian Falzarano, *Manager*
Dale Peters, *Information Mgr*
◆ EMP: 60
SALES (est): 22.8MM **Privately Held**
WEB: www.libertypultrusions.com
SIC: 3089 Molding primary plastic

(G-19736)
EPIC APPAREL LLC
217 Mellon St (15122-3956)
PHONE..................................412 350-9543
Lawrence Hill,
EMP: 4
SALES (est): 127.4K **Privately Held**
SIC: 2396 Screen printing on fabric articles

(G-19737)
ESPRESSO SOLUTIONS
1200 Lebanon Rd (15122-1083)
PHONE..................................412 326-0170
EMP: 4 EST: 2014
SALES (est): 236.4K **Privately Held**
SIC: 3589 Coffee brewing equipment

(G-19738)
FENTON HEAT TREATING INC
3605 Hmestead Duquesne Rd (15122-2912)
PHONE..................................412 466-3960
Charles Fenton Jr, *President*
Bernadine M Fenton, *Corp Secy*
EMP: 4 EST: 1973
SQ FT: 4,400
SALES: 450K **Privately Held**
WEB: www.fentonheattreating.com
SIC: 3398 1711 Metal heat treating; plumbing, heating, air-conditioning contractors

(G-19739)
GENERAL ELECTRIC COMPANY
4930 Buttermilk Hollow Rd (15122-1198)
PHONE..................................412 469-6080
John Anderson, *Opers-Prdtn-Mfg*
EMP: 70

SALES (corp-wide): 121.6B **Publicly Held**
SIC: 7629 7694 3462 Electrical equipment repair, high voltage; electrical household appliance repair; armature rewinding shops; iron & steel forgings
PA: General Electric Company
41 Farnsworth St
Boston MA 02210
617 443-3000

(G-19740)
HARBISONWALKER INTL INC
Technical Centre
1001 Pittsbrg Mckeesp Blv (15122-2898)
PHONE..................................412 469-3880
Dawn McIntyere, *Branch Mgr*
EMP: 50
SALES (corp-wide): 703.8MM **Privately Held**
WEB: www.hwr.com
SIC: 3255 Clay refractories
HQ: Harbisonwalker International, Inc.
1305 Cherrington Pkwy # 100
Moon Township PA 15108

(G-19741)
JOHNSONS PHARMACEUTICALS
Also Called: Johnson's Pharmacy
2000 Clairton Rd (15122-3006)
PHONE..................................412 655-2151
Larry Johnson, *Owner*
EMP: 14
SALES (est): 1.7MM **Privately Held**
SIC: 2834 Pharmaceutical preparations

(G-19742)
KEYWELL METALS LLC
890 Noble Dr (15122-1069)
PHONE..................................412 462-5555
Mike Matta, *Production*
Dave Campbell, *Opers-Prdtn-Mfg*
EMP: 17
SALES (corp-wide): 869.1MM **Privately Held**
SIC: 5093 3341 Ferrous metal scrap & waste; secondary nonferrous metals
HQ: Keywell Metals Llc
7808 W College Dr Ste 3ne
Palos Heights IL 60463
708 608-8020

(G-19743)
NRG TEXAS POWER LLC
2351 Century Dr (15122-2430)
PHONE..................................412 655-4134
EMP: 3 **Publicly Held**
SIC: 3621 Motors & generators
HQ: Nrg Texas Power Llc
1201 Fannin St
Houston TX 77002
713 537-3000

(G-19744)
SAYBOLT LP
1200 Lebanon Rd Ste 1 (15122-1057)
PHONE..................................412 464-7380
Brady Ruffner, *Manager*
EMP: 7
SALES (corp-wide): 659.8MM **Privately Held**
SIC: 1389 Testing, measuring, surveying & analysis services
HQ: Saybolt Lp
6316 Windfern Rd
Houston TX 77040
713 328-2673

(G-19745)
SCIULLO MACHINE SHOP & TOOL CO (PA)
1061 Kentucky Blue Dr (15122-3105)
PHONE..................................412 462-1604
Sam Sciullo, *CEO*
EMP: 4
SALES: 480.1K **Privately Held**
SIC: 3599 Machine shop, jobbing & repair

(G-19746)
UNITED STATES STEEL CORP
Also Called: Irvin Plant
1 Camp Hollow Rd (15122)
PHONE..................................412 675-7459
David Lorh, *Branch Mgr*
EMP: 130

SALES (corp-wide): 14.1B **Publicly Held**
SIC: 3312 3444 Blast furnaces & steel mills; sheet metalwork
PA: United States Steel Corp
600 Grant St Ste 468
Pittsburgh PA 15219
412 433-1121

(G-19747)
USV OPTICAL INC
Also Called: J C Penney Optical Center
3075 Clairton Rd Ste 100 (15123-0005)
PHONE..................................412 655-8311
Chris Harvey, *General Mgr*
EMP: 3
SALES (corp-wide): 792.2MM **Privately Held**
WEB: www.ntouchcomm.net
SIC: 5995 3851 Eyeglasses, prescription; ophthalmic goods
HQ: Usv Optical, Inc.
1 Harmon Dr Glen Oaks Par
Glendora NJ 08029

West Newton
Westmoreland County

(G-19748)
C PALMER MANUFACTURING INC
5 Palmers Rd (15089-2014)
PHONE..................................724 872-8200
John Palmieri, *President*
Kathryn Palmieri, *Vice Pres*
Kami Faulds, *Shareholder*
Philip Palmieri, *Shareholder*
Darcy Smouse, *Shareholder*
EMP: 10
SQ FT: 15,400
SALES: 934.6K **Privately Held**
WEB: www.cpalmermfg.com
SIC: 3363 3544 Aluminum die-castings; special dies & tools

(G-19749)
CAREER LFSTYLE ENHNCMENT JURNL
244 N 5th St (15089-1602)
PHONE..................................724 872-5344
Linda Tomich, *Principal*
EMP: 3
SALES (est): 132.3K **Privately Held**
SIC: 2711 Newspapers, publishing & printing

(G-19750)
CRAWFORD DZIGNES INC
Also Called: Crawford Designs
430 Turkeytown Rd (15089-1841)
P.O. Box 323 (15089-0323)
PHONE..................................724 872-4644
Terry Crawford, *President*
Darleen Crawford, *Corp Secy*
EMP: 8
SALES: 600K **Privately Held**
SIC: 7389 3993 2542 2434 Interior design services; signs & advertising specialties; partitions & fixtures, except wood; wood kitchen cabinets

(G-19751)
SCHMITT WALTER H AND ASSOC
Also Called: Therm-Coil Mfg Co
580 Plummer School Rd (15089-2033)
P.O. Box 326 (15089-0326)
PHONE..................................724 872-5007
Walter H Schmitt, *President*
Sara Schmitt, *Vice Pres*
Rheinhold Schmitt, *VP Mfg*
Clinton Schmitt, *Treasurer*
Betsy Sweeney, *Admin Sec*
EMP: 20
SQ FT: 10,000
SALES (est): 5.6MM **Privately Held**
WEB: www.thermcoil.com
SIC: 5074 3634 Plumbing & hydronic heating supplies; heating units, for electric appliances

---

GEOGRAPHIC

West Pittsburg
Lawrence County

(G-19752)
S & S PROCESSING INC
478 Beaver Rd (16160)
P.O. Box 373 (16160-0373)
PHONE...................................724 535-3110
Christopher S Collier, *President*
Byron Collier, *Vice Pres*
Laura L Flowers, *Treasurer*
EMP: 36
SQ FT: 7,500
SALES (est): 6.3MM **Privately Held**
WEB: www.ssprocessing.com
SIC: 2499 0181 2421 Mulch or sawdust products, wood; ornamental nursery products; sawmills & planing mills, general

West Pittston
Luzerne County

(G-19753)
ACUMARK INC
702 Exeter Ave (18643-1756)
P.O. Box 1000, Pittston (18640-5001)
PHONE...................................570 883-1800
Thomas A Joseph Sr, *President*
Thomas J Joseph Jr, *Vice Pres*
◆ **EMP:** 8
SQ FT: 30,000
SALES (est): 1.3MM **Privately Held**
WEB: www.acumarkdigital.com
SIC: 2752 7331 Commercial printing, offset; direct mail advertising services

(G-19754)
DONS MACHINE SHOP INC
777 Ash St (18643-1741)
PHONE...................................570 655-1950
Donald Eifert, *President*
Barbara D Eifert, *Vice Pres*
Donnie E Eifert, *Manager*
Maria Hartley, *Admin Sec*
Donald Eifert Sr, *Post Master*
EMP: 20
SQ FT: 5,000
SALES (est): 4.4MM **Privately Held**
WEB: www.donsmachine.com
SIC: 3599 Machine shop, jobbing & repair

(G-19755)
ELC MANUFACTURING
330 Philadelphia Ave (18643-2147)
PHONE...................................570 655-3060
Edward Chukinas Jr, *Owner*
EMP: 8
SQ FT: 13,000
SALES (est): 1MM **Privately Held**
SIC: 2431 1751 1521 Millwork; cabinet building & installation; new construction, single-family houses

(G-19756)
FINCH MANUFACTURING & TECH LLC
540 Montgomery Ave (18643-2120)
PHONE...................................570 655-2277
Rober Zinnen, *President*
Michael Brown, *General Mgr*
Michael Batyko, *Engineer*
John Martines, *CFO*
Scott Lowry, *VP Sales*
EMP: 30
SALES (est): 6.1MM **Privately Held**
SIC: 3599 Machine shop, jobbing & repair

(G-19757)
WARREN PRODUCTS INC
530 Exeter Ave (18643-1755)
PHONE...................................570 655-4596
Warren A Himmelwright, *President*
EMP: 4 **EST:** 1958
SQ FT: 32,000
SALES (est): 260.8K **Privately Held**
SIC: 2621 Wrapping & packaging papers

West Point
Montgomery County

(G-19758)
COLORCON INC (HQ)
420 Moyer Blvd (19486)
P.O. Box 24 (19486-0024)
PHONE...................................215 699-7733
Marti Hedman, *CEO*
John J Byrne Jr, *President*
David Cavacini, *Vice Pres*
Luciana Paganini, *Vice Pres*
DOT Barbera, *Opers Mgr*
◆ **EMP:** 350
SQ FT: 165,000
SALES (est): 432.6MM
SALES (corp-wide): 2.9B **Privately Held**
WEB: www.colorcon.com
SIC: 2834 Pharmaceutical preparations
PA: Berwind Corporation
3000 Ctr Sq W 1500 Mkt St 1500 W
Philadelphia PA 19102
215 563-2800

(G-19759)
J MEYER & SONS INC (PA)
Jones Ave & Chestnut St (19486)
PHONE...................................215 699-7003
Daniel Ginty, *President*
Brendan Ginty, *Plant Mgr*
Jane Ginty, *Treasurer*
EMP: 150 **EST:** 1888
SALES (est): 20.7MM **Privately Held**
SIC: 3087 Custom compound purchased resins

(G-19760)
MERCK SHARP & DOHME CORP
770 Sumneytown Pike (19486-8000)
PHONE...................................215 652-6777
Adam Kaufman, *General Mgr*
John Bradley, *Project Mgr*
Lisa Toback, *Mfg Spvr*
Diana Lewis, *Opers Staff*
William Moll, *Opers Staff*
EMP: 10
SALES (corp-wide): 42.2B **Publicly Held**
SIC: 2834 Pharmaceutical preparations
HQ: Merck Sharp & Dohme Corp.
2000 Galloping Hill Rd
Kenilworth NJ 07033
908 740-4000

(G-19761)
MERCK SHARP & DOHME CORP
770 Sumneytown Pike (19486-8000)
P.O. Box 4 (19486-0004)
PHONE...................................215 652-8368
Matthew Moyer, *Project Mgr*
Lisa Dugeau, *Branch Mgr*
Emily Pratt, *Supervisor*
Peihong Chen, *Technical Staff*
Veronica Mason, *Associate Dir*
EMP: 38
SALES (corp-wide): 42.2B **Publicly Held**
SIC: 2834 Pharmaceutical preparations
HQ: Merck Sharp & Dohme Corp.
2000 Galloping Hill Rd
Kenilworth NJ 07033
908 740-4000

(G-19762)
MERCK SHARP & DOHME CORP
770 Sumneytown Pike (19486-8000)
PHONE...................................215 631-5000
Jennifer Iannetta, *Principal*
Michele Lagler, *Executive Asst*
EMP: 120
SALES (corp-wide): 42.2B **Publicly Held**
SIC: 2836 5961 6411 2834 Biological products, except diagnostic; vaccines; veterinary biological products; catalog & mail-order houses; medical insurance claim processing, contract or fee basis; drugs acting on the central nervous system & sense organs
HQ: Merck Sharp & Dohme Corp.
2000 Galloping Hill Rd
Kenilworth NJ 07033
908 740-4000

(G-19763)
MERCK SHARP & DOHME CORP
770 Sumneytown Pike (19486-8000)
PHONE...................................215 652-5000
David Anstice, *Principal*
EMP: 500
SALES (corp-wide): 42.2B **Publicly Held**
SIC: 2834 Pharmaceutical preparations
HQ: Merck Sharp & Dohme Corp.
2000 Galloping Hill Rd
Kenilworth NJ 07033
908 740-4000

West Reading
Berks County

(G-19764)
ESTERLY CONCRETE CO INC
401 Elm St (19611-1143)
PHONE...................................610 376-2791
John Esterly, *President*
EMP: 13
SQ FT: 6,000
SALES (est): 2.2MM **Privately Held**
SIC: 3272 1771 Burial vaults, concrete or precast terrazzo; concrete work

West Salisbury
Somerset County

(G-19765)
WEST SALISBURY FNDRY MCH INC
700 Tub Mill Run Rd (15565-6512)
P.O. Box 541, Salisbury (15558-0541)
PHONE...................................814 662-2809
Bryan H Hay, *President*
Roy D Ashby, *Vice Pres*
EMP: 20 **EST:** 1982
SQ FT: 45,000
SALES (est): 4.3MM **Privately Held**
WEB: www.westsalisburyfoundry.com
SIC: 3321 Gray iron castings

West Springfield
Erie County

(G-19766)
AMERICAN EAGLE WINDMILLS LLC
13053 Ridge Rd (16443-9731)
PHONE...................................814 922-3180
Susan Weisenbach, *Mng Member*
EMP: 4
SALES (est): 450.3K **Privately Held**
SIC: 3621 Windmills, electric generating

(G-19767)
ELSIE A MUNDKOWSKY
14415 Ridge Rd (16443-1627)
PHONE...................................814 922-3072
Elsie A Mundkowsky, *Owner*
Brenda Boniger, *Administration*
EMP: 9
SQ FT: 6,300
SALES (est): 754.3K **Privately Held**
WEB: www.eamf.net
SIC: 3471 Plating & polishing

(G-19768)
FREELANDS FINE WOOD FINISHINGS
Also Called: Freeland's Fine Woodfinishings
14315 Underridge Rd (16443-9632)
PHONE...................................814 922-7101
Garth Freeland, *Owner*
Tammie Freeland, *Co-Owner*
EMP: 4
SALES: 200K **Privately Held**
SIC: 2434 Wood kitchen cabinets

West Sunbury
Butler County

(G-19769)
BLACKBIRD INDUSTRIES INC
Also Called: One Outboard
569 Mahood Rd (16061-2611)
PHONE...................................724 283-2537
Michael Demayo, *President*
▼ **EMP:** 11
SALES (est): 2.1MM **Privately Held**
SIC: 3732 Boat building & repairing

(G-19770)
HAUGH WOODWORKING
119 Oak Hill Rd (16061-1513)
PHONE...................................724 894-2205
James Haugh, *Owner*
EMP: 5
SALES (est): 382.2K **Privately Held**
SIC: 2434 Wood kitchen cabinets

(G-19771)
KEN HALL MACHINE SHOP INC
384 Thompsontown Rd (16061-2824)
PHONE...................................724 637-3273
Ken Hall, *President*
Judy Hall, *Vice Pres*
EMP: 3
SQ FT: 4,800
SALES: 175K **Privately Held**
SIC: 3599 Machine shop, jobbing & repair

(G-19772)
METAL PEDDLER INC
110 Miller School Ln (16061-2516)
PHONE...................................724 476-1061
Danielle Fannin, *Owner*
Jason Fannin, *Owner*
EMP: 5
SALES (est): 450K **Privately Held**
SIC: 3469 Metal stampings

West View
Allegheny County

(G-19773)
ARCHETYPE DESIGN STUDIO LLC
Also Called: Kitchen and Bath Concepts
176 Rochester Rd (15229-1334)
PHONE...................................412 369-2900
Thomas Trzcinski, *Principal*
▲ **EMP:** 9
SALES (est): 888.9K **Privately Held**
SIC: 3469 5211 Kitchen fixtures & equipment: metal, except cast aluminum; bathroom fixtures, equipment & supplies

(G-19774)
VIPER NETWORK SYSTEMS LLC
40 Center Ave (15229-1903)
PHONE...................................855 758-4737
Francesco Trama,
Dan Gynn,
Brian McGinty,
Gary McGuirk,
EMP: 5
SALES (est): 357.9K **Privately Held**
SIC: 7372 3571 Business oriented computer software; electronic computers

West Wyoming
Luzerne County

(G-19775)
ASHLEY MACHINE & TOOL CO
1450 1460 Shoemaker Ave (18644)
PHONE...................................570 287-0966
John J Mulhern Jr, *President*
Debby Bernardoni, *Accountant*
Matt Wafenski, *Human Res Dir*
▼ **EMP:** 40
SQ FT: 41,000
SALES: 7.4MM **Privately Held**
SIC: 3599 Machine shop, jobbing & repair

Westfield
Tioga County

(G-19776)
CV ANGLERS CLUB
354 Azelta Rd (16950)
PHONE..............................814 203-3861
Jason Stpeter, *Partner*
EMP: 5
SALES (est): 310K **Privately Held**
SIC: 2452 Farm & agricultural buildings, prefabricated wood

(G-19777)
ELECTRI-CORD MANUFACTURING CO (PA)
Also Called: CORD TEST
312 E Main St (16950-1609)
P.O. Box 167 (16950-0167)
PHONE..............................814 367-2265
Mitchell G Samuels, *President*
Tr Schilb, *President*
Hector Ramon, *Vice Pres*
Maurice Swede, *Materials Mgr*
Jamie Murray, *Senior Buyer*
▲ **EMP:** 115
SQ FT: 52,000
SALES (est): 36.9MM **Privately Held**
WEB: www.powercabling.com
SIC: 3699 Extension cords

(G-19778)
JACOBSONS FARM SYRUP CO
234 Cooper Rd (16950-8777)
PHONE..............................814 367-2880
Larry Foor, *President*
Terry Jacobson, *Treasurer*
EMP: 4
SALES (est): 92K **Privately Held**
SIC: 2099 Maple syrup

(G-19779)
L W GREEN FRAMES
1584 Alley Close Hill Rd (16950-8993)
PHONE..............................610 432-3726
Lawrence W Green, *Owner*
EMP: 3
SQ FT: 2,000
SALES (est): 209.2K **Privately Held**
SIC: 5023 2499 Frames & framing, picture & mirror; picture frame molding, finished

(G-19780)
MEDPLAST ENGINEERED PDTS INC
K & W Medical Specialties Div
115 Pritchard Hollow Rd (16950-1416)
PHONE..............................814 367-2246
Eugene Wolstenholme, *President*
Ralph Wolstenholme, *Info Tech Dir*
EMP: 80
SALES (corp-wide): 228.9MM **Privately Held**
SIC: 3841 Surgical & medical instruments
HQ: Medplast Engineered Products, Inc.
405 W Geneva Dr
Tempe AZ 85282

(G-19781)
SUNRISE MAPLE
Also Called: Michael Eldridge
5695 Route 349 (16950)
PHONE..............................814 628-3110
Timothy Eldridge, *Owner*
Michael Eldridge, *Owner*
EMP: 10
SALES (est): 250.8K **Privately Held**
SIC: 5149 2099 2035 Syrups, except for fountain use; maple syrup; dressings, salad: dry mixes; seasonings, meat sauces (except tomato & dry)

Westland
Washington County

(G-19782)
EDWIN RINGER
188 Dogwood St (15378)
P.O. Box 436 (15378-0436)
PHONE..............................724 746-3374
Edwin Ringer, *Owner*
Debra Ringer, *Co-Owner*
EMP: 5
SQ FT: 1,500
SALES (est): 760.4K **Privately Held**
SIC: 2261 2752 Screen printing of cotton broadwoven fabrics; commercial printing, lithographic

Westmoreland City
Westmoreland County

(G-19783)
A3-USA INC
1350 Biddle Ave (15692-1239)
PHONE..............................724 871-7170
Jens Sonntag, *Vice Pres*
EMP: 4
SALES: 1.3MM **Privately Held**
SIC: 3589 Water treatment equipment, industrial

(G-19784)
PEN DOR MANUFACTURING INC
1 Biddle Ave (15692)
P.O. Box 52 (15692-0052)
PHONE..............................724 863-7180
Paul Kolesar, *President*
EMP: 6
SQ FT: 8,500
SALES (est): 866.5K **Privately Held**
SIC: 3599 Machine shop, jobbing & repair

(G-19785)
SPECTRA HARDWARE INC
1150 First St (15692)
P.O. Box 368 (15692-0368)
PHONE..............................724 863-7527
Fax: 724 864-0348
EMP: 3
SQ FT: 17,000
SALES: 300K **Privately Held**
SIC: 7699 3821 5049 Mfg Laboratory Instrumentation Whol Laboratory Equipment & Laboratory Instrument Repair

Wexford
Allegheny County

(G-19786)
AMERICAN NATURAL RETAIL PA LLC
115 Vip Dr Ste 205 (15090-7906)
PHONE..............................212 359-4483
Benjamin Whitfield, *Exec VP*
EMP: 3 **EST:** 2012
SALES (est): 109.8K **Privately Held**
SIC: 2911 Oils, fuel

(G-19787)
APEX ENERGY LLC (PA)
6041 Wallace Road Ext # 100 (15090-7471)
PHONE..............................724 719-2611
Mark Rothenberg, *CEO*
Ed Long, *COO*
Chris Hess, *Vice Pres*
Broc Richardson, *CFO*
EMP: 12 **EST:** 2013
SALES (est): 28.9MM **Privately Held**
SIC: 1382 Oil & gas exploration services

(G-19788)
APEX ENERGY LLC
6041 Wallace Road Ext # 100 (15090-7471)
PHONE..............................724 719-2611
Mark Rothenberg, *CEO*
Ed Long, *COO*
Chris Hess, *Vice Pres*
Broc Richardson, *CFO*
EMP: 27
SALES: 1.1MM
SALES (corp-wide): 28.9MM **Privately Held**
SIC: 1311 Crude petroleum & natural gas

PA: Apex Energy, Llc
6041 Wallace Road Ext # 100
Wexford PA 15090
724 719-2611

(G-19789)
ARCHROCK SERVICES LP
3000 Stonewood Dr (15090-8317)
PHONE..............................724 935-7660
Matt Susy, *Branch Mgr*
EMP: 3 **Publicly Held**
SIC: 1389 Gas compressing (natural gas) at the fields
HQ: Archrock Services, L.P.
9807 Katy Fwy Ste 100
Houston TX 77024
281 836-8000

(G-19790)
ARSENAL RESOURCES ENERGY LLC
6031 Wallace Road Ext (15090-3400)
PHONE..............................724 940-1100
David Wood, *CEO*
Steve Bishop, *President*
EMP: 12
SALES (est): 651.2K **Privately Held**
SIC: 1321 Natural gas liquids

(G-19791)
ARSENAL RESOURCES LLC
6031 Wallace Road Ext # 300 (15090-3400)
PHONE..............................724 940-1100
Jon Farmer, *President*
Stacey Lucas, *Vice Pres*
Andrew Repine, *Finance*
Michael Lancaster, *Info Tech Dir*
EMP: 41
SALES (est): 44.4MM **Privately Held**
SIC: 1381 Drilling oil & gas wells

(G-19792)
BUSCH COMPANY
Also Called: Martec-A Division of Busch
10431 Perry Hwy Ste 210 (15090-9200)
PHONE..............................724 940-2326
Dick Perryman, *Vice Pres*
EMP: 16
SALES (est): 1.1MM **Privately Held**
SIC: 8748 3826 Environmental consultant; environmental testing equipment

(G-19793)
BXVIDEO SOLUTIONS LLC
12330 Perry Hwy Ste 101 (15090-8319)
PHONE..............................724 940-4190
David Breit, *Partner*
Dwight Dietrich, *Partner*
EMP: 8
SQ FT: 2,000
SALES (est): 1MM **Privately Held**
WEB: www.bxvideo.com
SIC: 3577 Data conversion equipment, media-to-media: computer

(G-19794)
CDL NUCLEAR TECHNOLOGIES INC
6400 Brooktree Ct Ste 320 (15090-9271)
PHONE..............................724 933-5570
Keith Loiselle, *President*
Lon Wilson, *General Mgr*
Carolyn Cannon, *Manager*
Ron Morosko, *Manager*
Michelle Markley, *Info Tech Mgr*
EMP: 25
SQ FT: 2,500
SALES (est): 8.8MM **Privately Held**
WEB: www.cdlmedical.com
SIC: 3829 Nuclear radiation & testing apparatus

(G-19795)
COEPTIS PHARMACEUTICALS INC
105 Bradford Rd Ste 420 (15090-6920)
PHONE..............................724 290-1183
David Mehalick, *CEO*
Christine Sheehy, *Vice Pres*
Daniel Yerace, *Vice Pres*
EMP: 3
SALES (est): 237.4K **Privately Held**
SIC: 2834 Pills, pharmaceutical

(G-19796)
COSMA USA LLC
229 Huckleberry Ct (15090-7523)
PHONE..............................412 551-0708
Ernest M Meyer, *Principal*
EMP: 3
SALES (est): 147.4K **Privately Held**
SIC: 3465 Tops, automobile: stamped metal

(G-19797)
CRU GROUP
2000 Corporate Dr Ste 410 (15090-7605)
PHONE..............................724 940-7100
Jim Southwood, *President*
Margarita Agapidou, *Business Mgr*
Glenn Cooney, *Opers Staff*
Sabine Kilgus, *Manager*
Sola Adebiyi, *Consultant*
EMP: 6
SALES (est): 512K **Privately Held**
WEB: www.commoditymetals.com
SIC: 1081 Metal mining services

(G-19798)
DORSO LLC
104 Bradford Rd (15090-8314)
PHONE..............................724 934-7710
Walter C Phillips,
EMP: 7
SALES (est): 1.4MM **Privately Held**
SIC: 1382 Oil & gas exploration services

(G-19799)
EXTERRAN ENERGY SOLUTIONS LP
12330 Perry Hwy Ste 220 (15090-8319)
PHONE..............................724 935-7660
Matt Susy, *Manager*
EMP: 100
SALES (corp-wide): 1.3B **Publicly Held**
SIC: 1389 Gas field services
HQ: Exterran Energy Solutions, L.P.
4444 Brittmoore Rd
Houston TX 77041
281 836-7000

(G-19800)
EXTREMITY IMAGING PARTNERS (PA)
4500 Brooktree Rd Ste 300 (15090-9289)
PHONE..............................724 493-7452
Calvin F Zontine, *CEO*
▲ **EMP:** 15
SALES (est): 2MM **Privately Held**
WEB: www.extremitymri.com
SIC: 3845 CAT scanner (Computerized Axial Tomography) apparatus

(G-19801)
FISHER & LUDLOW INC
2000 Corporate Dr Ste 400 (15090-7657)
PHONE..............................859 282-7767
Tony McHugh, *Manager*
EMP: 15
SALES (corp-wide): 25B **Publicly Held**
SIC: 3446 3499 5039 Elevator guide rails; aerosol valves, metal; architectural metalwork
HQ: Fisher & Ludlow Inc.
2000 Corporate Dr Ste 400
Wexford PA 15090

(G-19802)
FISHER & LUDLOW INC
2000 Corporate Dr Ste 400 (15090-7657)
PHONE..............................217 324-6106
Carl Orourke, *Plant Mgr*
Thomas Clinard, *Production*
Michelle Paulos, *Human Res Dir*
Carol Lee, *Data Proc Dir*
Carl O'Roake, *Systems Mgr*
EMP: 56 **Privately Held**
SIC: 3441 3446 Fabricated structural metal; architectural metalwork

(G-19803)
FISHER & LUDLOW INC (HQ)
2000 Corporate Dr Ste 400 (15090-7657)
PHONE..............................724 934-5320
Brian Rutter, *President*
Michael Fernie, *Vice Pres*
Jim Kowalchyk, *Treasurer*
Douglas Deighton, *Admin Sec*
EMP: 64

SQ FT: 6,500
SALES (est): 28.9MM
SALES (corp-wide): 25B **Publicly Held**
SIC: 3446 Gratings, open steel flooring
PA: Nucor Corporation
1915 Rexford Rd Ste 400
Charlotte NC 28211
704 366-7000

(G-19804)
FRAMES & MORE
100 Vip Dr Ste 104 (15090-6928)
PHONE....................................724 933-5557
Tim Payne, *Owner*
Allen Payne, *Owner*
EMP: 3
SALES (est): 134.7K **Privately Held**
SIC: 3999 3496 Framed artwork; lamp
frames, wire

(G-19805)
GCL INC (PA)
2559 Brandt School Rd # 201
(15090-7621)
PHONE....................................724 933-7260
Carol B Wochley, *President*
George R Wochley, *Vice Pres*
EMP: 4
SQ FT: 600
SALES (est): 4.8MM **Privately Held**
WEB: www.cambergroup.com
SIC: 3532 3441 3272 Mining machinery;
fabricated structural metal; precast ter-
razo or concrete products

(G-19806)
HOP MILLWORK INC
10539 Perry Hwy (15090-9530)
PHONE....................................724 934-3880
Craig Williams, *President*
Jay Stinger, *Manager*
EMP: 4
SALES: 500K **Privately Held**
SIC: 2431 Staircases & stairs, wood

(G-19807)
INNOVALGAE LLC
113 Rabold Dr (15090-8697)
PHONE....................................412 996-2556
Jeremiah Mpagazehe, *Principal*
Cecil Higgs, *Principal*
Philip Leduc,
EMP: 3 **Privately Held**
SIC: 2911 Oils, fuel

(G-19808)
INTELOMED INC
6041 Wallace Road Ext # 110
(15090-7471)
P.O. Box 784, Warrendale (15095-0784)
PHONE....................................412 536-7661
Jill F Schiaparelli, *President*
Marydel Brady, *Principal*
William Malloy, *Principal*
John Moran MD, *Principal*
Mark Rossi, *Principal*
EMP: 12
SALES (est): 1.8MM **Privately Held**
WEB: www.intelomed.com
SIC: 3841 Surgical & medical instruments

(G-19809)
JSKC LLC
Also Called: Wexford Beer
2602 Fountain Hills Dr (15090-7800)
PHONE....................................724 933-5575
Andrew Schomos,
Linda Schomos,
EMP: 7
SALES (est): 319.1K **Privately Held**
SIC: 2082 Malt liquors

(G-19810)
**MEDICAL DEVICE BUS SVCS
INC**
7500 Brooktree Ste 101 (15090-9285)
PHONE....................................724 933-0288
Doug Wray, *Manager*
EMP: 7
SALES (corp-wide): 81.5B **Publicly Held**
SIC: 3842 Surgical appliances & supplies
HQ: Medical Device Business Services,
Inc.
700 Orthopaedic Dr
Warsaw IN 46582

(G-19811)
MEDTRONIC USA INC
1603 Carmody Ct Ste 401 (15090)
PHONE....................................724 933-8100
Lalo Berezo, *Vice Pres*
EMP: 3 **Privately Held**
WEB: www.medtronic.com
SIC: 3841 Surgical & medical instruments
HQ: Medtronic Usa, Inc.
710 Medtronic Pkwy
Minneapolis MN 55432
763 514-4000

(G-19812)
MISTERPLEXI
10475 Perry Hwy Ste 105g (15090-9213)
PHONE....................................724 759-7500
Mark Miller, *Principal*
EMP: 4
SALES (est): 357.8K **Privately Held**
SIC: 3089 Plastics products

(G-19813)
N PGH IMAGING SPECIALISTS
6001 Stonewood Dr Ste 100 (15090-7380)
PHONE....................................724 935-6200
Frank Madonna, *President*
EMP: 12
SALES (est): 837.4K **Privately Held**
SIC: 3826 Magnetic resonance imaging
apparatus

(G-19814)
NARSA
Also Called: International Heat Transf Assn
3000 Village Run Rd # 103 (15090-6315)
PHONE....................................724 799-8415
Wayne Juchno, *Exec Dir*
EMP: 15
SALES (est): 1.1MM **Privately Held**
SIC: 3585 Evaporative condensers, heat
transfer equipment

(G-19815)
NEW BUSCH CO INC
Also Called: Busch International Division
10431 Perry Hwy Ste 210 (15090-9200)
PHONE....................................724 940-2326
William W Frank, *President*
EMP: 4 EST: 1952
SALES (est): 944.5K
SALES (corp-wide): 337.3MM **Publicly
Held**
WEB: www.busch-co.com
SIC: 3564 5075 Air purification equipment;
fans, heating & ventilation equipment
HQ: Ceco Filters, Inc.
700 Emlen Way
Telford PA 18969
215 723-8155

(G-19816)
**NORTHSTERN CNSLD ENRGY
PRTNERS**
2570 Matterhorn Dr (15090-7962)
PHONE....................................412 491-6660
Jon V Malis, *President*
EMP: 4
SALES (est): 972K **Privately Held**
SIC: 1381 Drilling oil & gas wells

(G-19817)
NUCOR GRATING
2000 Corporate Dr Ste 400 (15090-7657)
P.O. Box 1238 (15090-1238)
PHONE....................................724 934-5320
Tom Clinard, *President*
EMP: 4
SALES (est): 432.5K
SALES (corp-wide): 25B **Publicly Held**
SIC: 3446 Gratings, open steel flooring
HQ: Nucor Canada Inc
1455 Lakeshore Rd Suite 204n
Burlington ON L7S 2
905 634-6868

(G-19818)
OA SYSTEMS LLC
2559 Brandt School Rd # 102
(15090-7621)
PHONE....................................888 347-7950
Jhony Perez, *CEO*
EMP: 7
SQ FT: 900

SALES (est): 731.4K **Privately Held**
SIC: 7372 Educational computer software

(G-19819)
**PENGUIN LOGISTICS HOLDINGS
LLC**
4500 Brooktree Rd Ste 200 (15090-9289)
PHONE....................................724 772-9800
Robert Shawwer, *President*
Jared Stango, *CFO*
EMP: 5
SALES (est): 433K **Privately Held**
SIC: 3443 Industrial vessels, tanks & con-
tainers

(G-19820)
**PITTSBURGH BOLT COMPANY
LLC**
114 Vip Dr (15090-7913)
PHONE....................................724 935-6844
Michael Clay, *Mng Member*
EMP: 3
SALES (est): 150.3K **Privately Held**
SIC: 3452 Bolts, metal

(G-19821)
PIXEL INNOVATIONS INC
Also Called: Circuit Design Center, The
11676 Perry Hwy Ste 3202 (15090-7206)
PHONE....................................724 935-8366
David Ross, *President*
EMP: 5
SQ FT: 1,500
SALES (est): 520K **Privately Held**
WEB: www.pixelabs.com
SIC: 3577 Computer peripheral equipment

(G-19822)
PROFIT ENGINE LLC
5500 Brooktree Rd Ste 104 (15090-9260)
PHONE....................................412 848-8187
John Kachaylo,
EMP: 3
SALES (est): 71.1K **Privately Held**
SIC: 7372 Publishers' computer software

(G-19823)
PTC ALLIANCE CORP (HQ)
Also Called: Pittsburgh Tube Company
6051 Wallace Road Ext # 200
(15090-7386)
PHONE....................................412 299-7900
Peter Whiting, *President*
Cary Hart, *President*
William Allison, *Vice Pres*
Don Nelson, *Vice Pres*
Dave Sizemore, *Plant Mgr*
◆ EMP: 72 EST: 1924
SQ FT: 6,700
SALES (est): 21.2MM **Privately Held**
SIC: 3317 Tubing, mechanical or hypoder-
mic sizes: cold drawn stainless
PA: Black Diamond Capital Management,
L.L.C.
100 N Field Dr Ste 170
Lake Forest IL 60045
847 615-9000

(G-19824)
**PTC GROUP HOLDINGS CORP
(PA)**
6051 Wallace Road Ext # 2 (15090-7386)
PHONE....................................412 299-7900
Peter Whiting, *President*
Thomas W Crowley, *Vice Pres*
Patty Coleman, *Treasurer*
Mark Keefer, *Controller*
Martha Rogers, *Admin Sec*
◆ EMP: 20
SALES (est): 270.1MM **Privately Held**
SIC: 3317 Tubing, mechanical or hypoder-
mic sizes: cold drawn stainless

(G-19825)
PTC HOLDINGS I CORP
6051 Wallace Road Ext # 200
(15090-7386)
PHONE....................................412 299-7900
Peter Whiting, *CEO*
Thomas W Crowley, *CFO*
EMP: 7
SQ FT: 9,438
SALES (est): 987K **Privately Held**
SIC: 3317 Steel pipe & tubes

(G-19826)
PURE HOSPITALITY LLC
119 Neely School Rd (15090-7536)
PHONE....................................724 935-1515
EMP: 6 EST: 2009
SALES (est): 434.9K **Privately Held**
SIC: 3949 Mfg Sporting/Athletic Goods

(G-19827)
RIJUVEN CORP
10475 Perry Hwy Ste 104 (15090-9213)
PHONE....................................412 404-6292
Raj Kapoor MD, *President*
EMP: 9
SALES (est): 922K **Privately Held**
SIC: 3845 Electrocardiographs

(G-19828)
**RM BENNEY TECHNICAL SLS
INC**
207 Pine Creek Rd Ste 202 (15090-9229)
PHONE....................................724 935-0150
Cheryl Benney, *President*
Ronald Pasniewski, *Vice Pres*
Jo McMurtry, *Sales Staff*
EMP: 4
SQ FT: 1,200
SALES (est): 885.7K **Privately Held**
SIC: 5084 3564 Fans, industrial; blowers
& fans

(G-19829)
**STEPHEN GOULD
CORPORATION**
8000 Brooktree Rd Ste 110 (15090-9474)
PHONE....................................724 933-1400
Aaron Salko, *Office Mgr*
EMP: 7
SALES (corp-wide): 678.7MM **Privately
Held**
WEB: www.stephengould.com
SIC: 3086 Packaging & shipping materials,
foamed plastic
PA: Stephen Gould Corporation
35 S Jefferson Rd
Whippany NJ 07981
973 428-1500

(G-19830)
**SWANSON PUBLISHING
COMPANY INC**
Also Called: Northern Connection Magazine
6600 Brooktree Rd # 1600 (15090-9205)
P.O. Box 722 (15090-0722)
PHONE....................................724 940-2444
Marion Piotrowski, *President*
Stephen Piotrowski, *Treasurer*
Laura Piotrowski-Arno, *Marketing Staff*
Mary Simpson, *Marketing Staff*
Marisa Tomasic, *Marketing Staff*
EMP: 8
SALES (est): 13.3K **Privately Held**
SIC: 2741 Miscellaneous publishing

(G-19831)
UPS STORE INC
3000 Village Run Rd # 103 (15090-6315)
PHONE....................................724 934-1088
Ambrogio Nick, *Manager*
EMP: 3
SALES (est): 273.2K **Privately Held**
SIC: 7389 2621 7331 Mailbox rental & re-
lated service; packaging & labeling serv-
ices; printing paper; mailing service

(G-19832)
VIRTIX CONSULTING LLC
228 Fox Meadow Dr (15090-8672)
PHONE....................................412 440-4835
Leon Robinson, *President*
EMP: 4
SALES (est): 73.3K **Privately Held**
SIC: 7373 7379 7372 8742 Computer integrated systems design; computer related maintenance services; prepackaged
software; management consulting services; systems engineering consultant, ex.
computer or professional

(G-19833)
WEBB-MASON INC
12330 Perry Hwy Ste 240 (15090-8319)
PHONE....................................724 935-1770
Chris Berexa, *Manager*
EMP: 23

GEOGRAPHIC

SALES (corp-wide): 113.5MM **Privately
Held**
SIC: 2752 Business form & card printing,
lithographic
PA: Webb-Mason, Inc.
10830 Gilroy Rd
Hunt Valley MD 21031
410 785-1111

Wheatland
Mercer County

(G-19834)
AMERICAN CAP COMPANY LLC
15 Church St (16161)
P.O. Box 107 (16161-0107)
PHONE..................................724 981-4461
Todd Diehl, *COO*
Scott Slater, *Project Mgr*
Richard Moroco, *CFO*
Jessica Vavithes, *Controller*
Mary Hansley, *Sales Mgr*
◆ **EMP:** 55
SQ FT: 100,000
SALES (est): 15.7MM **Privately Held**
WEB: www.americap-mfg.com
SIC: 3491 3599 Compressed gas cylinder
valves; machine shop, jobbing & repair

(G-19835)
**CRONIMET SPCIALTY MTLS USA
INC (DH)**
40 Council Ave (16161)
P.O. Box 399 (16161-0399)
PHONE..................................724 347-2208
Frank Santoro, *CEO*
Rob Santoro, *Vice Pres*
Kevin Covell, *CFO*
EMP: 28
SALES (est): 8.5MM
SALES (corp-wide): 2.5B **Privately Held**
SIC: 5051 3479 Metals service centers &
offices; coating of metals & formed prod-
ucts
HQ: Cronimet Corporation
1 Pilarsky Way
Aliquippa PA 15001
724 375-5004

(G-19836)
**CUSTOM METAL INNOVATIONS
INC**
1 Church St Ext (16161)
P.O. Box 309 (16161-0309)
PHONE..................................724 965-3929
Tanis Rae Birch, *Principal*
EMP: 3
SALES (est): 83.9K **Privately Held**
SIC: 3999 Manufacturing industries

(G-19837)
**DUNBAR ASPHALT PRODUCTS
INC**
Ohio St (16161)
PHONE..................................724 346-3594
Doug Green, *Branch Mgr*
EMP: 3
SALES (corp-wide): 1MM **Privately Held**
SIC: 2951 Asphalt paving mixtures &
blocks
HQ: Dunbar Asphalt Products, Inc.
3766 New Castle Rd
West Middlesex PA 16159
724 528-9310

(G-19838)
**INDUSTRIAL MACHINE DESIGNS
INC**
30 Ohio St (16161)
P.O. Box 426 (16161-0426)
PHONE..................................724 981-2707
Robert R Sinibaldi Jr, *President*
Sherry Osmon, *Admin Sec*
EMP: 5
SALES: 370K **Privately Held**
SIC: 3549 Metalworking machinery

(G-19839)
OMEGA LOGGING INC
21 Council Ave (16161)
P.O. Box 524, West Middlesex (16159-
0524)
PHONE..................................724 342-5430
Patrick Ghovan, *Branch Mgr*
EMP: 10
SALES (corp-wide): 5MM **Privately Held**
WEB: www.omega-inc.biz
SIC: 2411 2421 Logging camps & contrac-
tors; sawmills & planing mills, general
PA: Omega Logging, Inc.
2550 State Line Rd
Hubbard OH 44425
330 534-0378

(G-19840)
PARAMOUNT GAMES INC
30 Mill St (16161)
P.O. Box 428 (16161-0428)
PHONE..................................800 282-5766
Paul Swartz, *President*
Farrah Multari, *Vice Pres*
Mark Batfista, *Director*
EMP: 85
SALES (est): 15.3MM **Privately Held**
WEB: www.paramountgames.com
SIC: 2759 Tickets: printing

(G-19841)
PM KALCO INC
Also Called: Kalco Metals
40 Council Ave (16161)
P.O. Box 399 (16161-0399)
PHONE..................................724 347-2208
Mark Spano, *Ch of Bd*
Gary Boigon, *President*
▼ **EMP:** 30
SQ FT: 8,000
SALES (est): 4.1MM
SALES (corp-wide): 32.8MM **Privately
Held**
WEB: www.kalcometals.com
SIC: 3312 Tool & die steel & alloys
PA: P.M. Recovery Inc.
106 Calvert St
Harrison NY 10528
914 835-1900

(G-19842)
PRO-MACHINE LLC
83 Main St (16161)
PHONE..................................724 342-9895
Paul Massey, *Partner*
EMP: 14 **EST:** 1966
SQ FT: 6,000
SALES (est): 1.9MM **Privately Held**
SIC: 3599 Machine shop, jobbing & repair

(G-19843)
**WHEATLAND STEEL
PROCESSING CO**
1700 Broadway Ave (16161)
P.O. Box 578 (16161-0578)
PHONE..................................724 981-4242
Timothy Jablon, *President*
David P Mac Harg Jr, *Vice Pres*
Robert Schnurr, *Vice Pres*
David P Mac Harg Sr, *Treasurer*
Corrie Paden, *Admin Sec*
EMP: 35
SQ FT: 27,000
SALES (est): 7.6MM **Privately Held**
WEB: www.wheatlandsteel.com
SIC: 3312 Sheet or strip, steel, cold-rolled:
own hot-rolled

White
Fayette County

(G-19844)
HEATHEN MFG
657 Spruce Hollow Rd (15490-1011)
PHONE..................................724 887-0337
Harry Fabian, *Principal*
EMP: 3
SALES (est): 128.8K **Privately Held**
SIC: 3999 Manufacturing industries

(G-19845)
KESLAR LUMBER CO
884 Buchanan Rd (15490-1000)
PHONE..................................724 455-3210
Senneth Keslar, *Partner*
Charles Keslar, *Partner*
EMP: 31
SQ FT: 20,000
SALES: 4MM **Privately Held**
SIC: 2421 5031 Lumber: rough, dressed &
finished; lumber: rough, sawed or planed

White Haven
Luzerne County

(G-19846)
ASONE TECHNOLOGIES INC
Also Called: Evolution Custom Coach
13 Berwick St (18661-1520)
PHONE..................................570 443-5700
Angelica Cherry, *President*
Frank Tavaris, *Vice Pres*
EMP: 20
SALES (est): 3.4MM **Privately Held**
WEB: www.evolutioncustomcoach.com
SIC: 3713 Bus bodies (motor vehicles)

(G-19847)
FUEL ON WHITEHAVEN LLC
601 Church St (18661-1008)
PHONE..................................570 443-8830
EMP: 3
SALES (est): 102.7K **Privately Held**
SIC: 2869 Fuels

(G-19848)
**FUELONE GAS CNVENIENCE
STR LLC**
601 Church St (18661-1008)
PHONE..................................570 443-8830
Harvey Morrison, *Principal*
EMP: 7
SALES (est): 984.4K **Privately Held**
SIC: 2869 Fuels

(G-19849)
JOURNAL NEWSPAPERS INC
Also Called: Journal Herald
211 Main St (18661-1406)
PHONE..................................570 443-9131
Seth Isenberg, *President*
Clara Holder, *Treasurer*
Ruth Isenberg, *Admin Sec*
EMP: 8
SQ FT: 850
SALES: 300K **Privately Held**
SIC: 2711 Newspapers: publishing only,
not printed on site; newspapers, publish-
ing & printing

(G-19850)
**POCONO MOUNTAIN
CREAMERY LLC**
501 Main St (18661-1513)
PHONE..................................570 443-9868
EMP: 5 **EST:** 2015
SALES (est): 212.7K **Privately Held**
SIC: 2021 Creamery butter

(G-19851)
PSC PUBLISHING
1220 Vine St (18661-4061)
PHONE..................................570 443-9749
Stephen Pompella, *Owner*
EMP: 20
SALES (est): 152.3K **Privately Held**
SIC: 2731 Book publishing

(G-19852)
RENEES COLD CUT HUT
103 Berwick St (18661-1501)
PHONE..................................570 215-0057
EMP: 4 **EST:** 2010
SALES (est): 334.6K **Privately Held**
SIC: 3421 Table & food cutlery, including
butchers'

White Oak
Allegheny County

(G-19853)
APTER INDUSTRIES INC
1224 Long Run Rd Ste 1 (15131-2036)
PHONE..................................412 672-9628
James Scott Apter, *President*
Joe Deluca, *Vice Pres*
Joseph Deluca, *Vice Pres*
Connie Roland, *Controller*
Wayne Ratesic, *Accounts Exec*
EMP: 15
SQ FT: 10,000
SALES (est): 3.9MM **Privately Held**
WEB: www.apterindustries.com
SIC: 2842 Cleaning or polishing prepara-
tions

(G-19854)
DEX MEDIA INC
1985 Lincoln Way Ste 23 (15131-2415)
PHONE..................................412 858-4800
EMP: 42
SALES (corp-wide): 1.8B **Privately Held**
SIC: 2741 Misc Publishing
PA: Dex Media, Inc.
2200 W Airfield Dr
Dfw Airport TX 75261
972 453-7000

(G-19855)
**HELPING HNDS FOR WNDED
VTERANS**
1641 Lincoln Way (15131-1719)
PHONE..................................724 600-4965
Andrew Pope, *Exec Dir*
EMP: 8
SALES: 10K **Privately Held**
SIC: 3531 Crushers, grinders & similar
equipment

(G-19856)
**MANNS SICKROOM SERVICE
INC (PA)**
Also Called: Manns Home Medical Products
1101 Lincoln Way (15131-1301)
PHONE..................................412 672-5680
David Manns, *President*
Walter E Manns Jr, *Vice Pres*
Eleanoke Manns, *Treasurer*
EMP: 24
SQ FT: 4,000
SALES (est): 2.5MM **Privately Held**
SIC: 2515 1796 5999 Chair beds; eleva-
tor installation & conversion; hospital
equipment & supplies

(G-19857)
PURE POWER
515 Mckee Rd (15131-2524)
PHONE..................................412 673-5285
Jordan Garbin, *Owner*
EMP: 4
SALES (est): 428K **Privately Held**
SIC: 3589 High pressure cleaning equip-
ment

(G-19858)
ROBERT W GASTEL JR
Also Called: Dorothy's Candies
1228 Long Run Rd (15131-2035)
PHONE..................................412 678-2723
Robert W Gastel Jr, *Owner*
EMP: 28
SQ FT: 13,000
SALES (est): 2.6MM **Privately Held**
WEB: www.dorothyscandies.com
SIC: 2064 5441 2066 Lozenges, candy
(non-medicated); candy; chocolate &
cocoa products

(G-19859)
WOLENSKI ENTERPRISES INC
Also Called: Tempus Transport
1415 Pittsbugh Rd (15131)
PHONE..................................205 307-9862
Michael N Wolenski, *President*
EMP: 24 **EST:** 2010
SQ FT: 25,000
SALES: 1.7MM **Privately Held**
SIC: 3537 Trucks: freight, baggage, etc.:
industrial, except mining

Whitehall
Lehigh County

(G-19860)
ADVANCED VALVE DESIGN INC
480 Mickley Rd (18052-6215)
PHONE................................610 435-8820
Robert Rhoades, *President*
▲ EMP: 18 EST: 1981
SQ FT: 20,000
SALES (est): 4MM Privately Held
WEB: www.advancedvalve.com
SIC: 3491 3822 Industrial valves; damper operators: pneumatic, thermostatic, electric

(G-19861)
AMERICAN FENCE INC
2738 Eberhart Rd (18052-3699)
PHONE................................610 437-1944
Harold Mante, *President*
EMP: 15
SQ FT: 2,000
SALES: 1.2MM Privately Held
SIC: 1799 5211 2399 5039 Fence construction; fencing; banners, pennants & flags; wire fence, gates & accessories; fences, gates, posts & flagpoles; patio & deck construction & repair

(G-19862)
ATLAS MATERIAL HANDLING INC
4167 S Church St (18052-2412)
PHONE................................610 262-0644
Harold Keeney, *President*
Pat Keeney, *Admin Sec*
EMP: 3
SALES (est): 301.2K Privately Held
WEB: www.atlasmw.com
SIC: 3599 Machine shop, jobbing & repair

(G-19863)
BRIDESBURG FOUNDRY COMPANY
901 Front St (18052-5905)
P.O. Box 269 (18052-0269)
PHONE................................610 266-0900
Vincent J Rivetti, *President*
Marlene E White, *Corp Secy*
Donna Frack, *Human Res Dir*
John Manini, *Sales Executive*
Carisa Druckenmiller, *Admin Asst*
EMP: 70 EST: 1914
SQ FT: 50,000
SALES (est): 14.5MM Privately Held
WEB: www.bridesburg.com
SIC: 3366 3365 Castings (except die): brass; castings (except die): bronze; aluminum & aluminum-based alloy castings

(G-19864)
CENTURY PACKAGING CO INC
5217 Kemmerer St (18052-1848)
PHONE................................610 262-8860
Gary Collina, *President*
Nido Collina, *Vice Pres*
Doug Collina, *Treasurer*
EMP: 25
SQ FT: 28,000
SALES (est): 5.4MM Privately Held
SIC: 2653 2671 2631 Boxes, corrugated: made from purchased materials; packaging paper & plastics film, coated & laminated; paperboard mills

(G-19865)
CHOICE PRECISION MACHINE INC
4380 Commerce Dr (18052-2506)
PHONE................................610 502-1111
Thomas Gunkel, *President*
Robin Gunkel, *Corp Secy*
EMP: 45
SQ FT: 48,000
SALES (est): 10.6MM Privately Held
WEB: www.choiceprecision.com
SIC: 3599 Machine shop, jobbing & repair

(G-19866)
CJ OPTICAL HOLDINGS LLC
Also Called: Pro Vision
201 Lehigh Valley Mall (18052-5719)
PHONE................................610 264-8537
PHI Nguyen, *Mng Member*
EMP: 15 EST: 2012
SQ FT: 2,500
SALES (est): 1.6MM Privately Held
SIC: 3827 8042 Optical instruments & lenses; offices & clinics of optometrists

(G-19867)
COMPUTER DESIGNS INC (HQ)
Also Called: Nelipak Healthcare Packaging
5235 W Coplay Rd (18052-2211)
PHONE................................610 261-2100
Scott A McKeever, *President*
EMP: 71
SQ FT: 42,000
SALES (est): 16.4MM
SALES (corp-wide): 29.8MM Privately Held
WEB: www.computer-designs.com
SIC: 3081 7372 Packing materials, plastic sheet; prepackaged software
PA: Nelipak Corporation
21 Amflex Dr
Cranston RI 02921
401 946-2699

(G-19868)
CORDOVA
3396 S 2nd St (18052-3535)
PHONE................................570 578-7413
Karla Cordova, *President*
EMP: 3
SALES (est): 130.8K Privately Held
SIC: 2051 Bread, cake & related products

(G-19869)
CRAIG SIDLECK
Also Called: Sidleck Welding & Fabricating
5988 Coplay Rd (18052-2243)
P.O. Box 232 (18052-0232)
PHONE................................610 261-9580
Craig Sidleck, *Owner*
EMP: 10
SALES (est): 900.1K Privately Held
SIC: 1799 3441 Welding on site; fabricated structural metal

(G-19870)
DIAMOND WEAR
116 7th St (18052-7110)
PHONE................................610 433-2680
D Diamandopoulos Jr, *Owner*
Dimitri Diamandopoulos Jr, *Owner*
EMP: 5
SALES (est): 140K Privately Held
SIC: 3949 Sporting & athletic goods

(G-19871)
DYNALENE INC (PA)
5250 W Coplay Rd (18052-2212)
PHONE................................610 262-9686
Daniel Loikits, *Ch of Bd*
Satish Mohapatra, *President*
Dave Arcury, *COO*
Melissa Adams, *Sales Staff*
Keith A Lutz, *Director*
EMP: 19 EST: 1997
SQ FT: 5,000
SALES: 7MM Privately Held
WEB: www.dynalene.com
SIC: 2899 7819 Antifreeze compounds; laboratory service, motion picture

(G-19872)
EAMCO CORP
5275 W Coplay Rd (18052-2211)
PHONE................................610 262-5731
John Myers, *President*
Joseph Fernandes Jr, *Vice Pres*
Chris Fernandes, *Marketing Staff*
EMP: 15
SQ FT: 22,500
SALES (est): 1.4MM Privately Held
WEB: www.eamco.net
SIC: 3599 Machine shop, jobbing & repair

(G-19873)
EASTERN INDUSTRIES INC (DH)
3724 Crescent Ct W 200 (18052-3446)
PHONE................................610 866-0932
Cyril C Dunmire Jr, *Ch of Bd*

Paul B Shannon, *Vice Ch Bd*
Snyder Kim, *President*
Paul I Detwiler III, *President*
Robert M Mc Cann, *Exec VP*
EMP: 425 EST: 1941
SQ FT: 25,000
SALES (est): 110.5MM
SALES (corp-wide): 651.9MM Privately Held
WEB: www.eastern-ind.com
SIC: 5032 3273 1611 Paving mixtures; ready-mixed concrete; highway & street paving contractor
HQ: Stabler Companies Inc.
635 Lucknow Rd
Harrisburg PA 17110
717 236-9307

(G-19874)
GOOCH THERMAL MFG INC
4631 S Church St (18052-2400)
PHONE................................610 285-2496
Kevin Guitas, *General Mgr*
▲ EMP: 10 EST: 2011
SALES (est): 1.3MM Privately Held
SIC: 3443 Heat exchangers, plate type

(G-19875)
HINES INDUSTRIES INC
Also Called: Zellner Welding
2820 Lehigh St (18052-3693)
PHONE................................610 264-1656
John A Hines, *President*
Karen Hines, *Vice Pres*
EMP: 5
SQ FT: 10,000
SALES: 1MM Privately Held
SIC: 1791 1799 7692 Iron work, structural; welding on site; welding repair

(G-19876)
ICY FEET INC
2629 Augusta Dr (18052-3837)
PHONE................................610 462-3887
Kenneth C Snyder, *President*
EMP: 4
SALES (est): 214.9K Privately Held
SIC: 2037 Fruits, quick frozen & cold pack (frozen)

(G-19877)
INDUSTRIAL SERVICES
2300 Eberhart Rd (18052-3606)
PHONE................................610 437-1453
Barry Butz, *Owner*
▲ EMP: 15
SALES (est): 2.9MM Privately Held
SIC: 3399 Flakes, metal

(G-19878)
JACK WILLIAMS TIRE CO INC
Also Called: Auto Addictions
2157 Macarthur Rd (18052-4519)
PHONE................................610 437-4651
EMP: 16
SALES (corp-wide): 247.3MM Privately Held
SIC: 5531 3714 3011 Automotive tires; motor vehicle wheels & parts; tires & inner tubes
PA: Jack Williams Tire Co., Inc.
700 Rocky Glen Rd
Avoca PA 18641
570 457-5000

(G-19879)
JANATICS USA INC
2004 Eberhart Rd (18052-3645)
PHONE................................610 443-2400
Tiarat Gaysin, *President*
EMP: 3 Privately Held
SIC: 6719 3822 Investment holding companies, except banks; pneumatic relays, air-conditioning type

(G-19880)
LAFARGE NORTH AMERICA INC
5160 Main St (18052-1827)
PHONE................................610 262-7831
David Johns, *Marketing Mgr*
Joe Berlucchi, *Marketing Staff*
Munzer Ghosh, *Branch Mgr*
Jim Hess, *Manager*
Michael Klenk, *Manager*
EMP: 100

SALES (corp-wide): 26.4B Privately Held
WEB: www.lafargenorthamerica.com
SIC: 3241 Portland cement
HQ: Lafarge North America Inc.
8700 W Bryn Mawr Ave
Chicago IL 60631
773 372-1000

(G-19881)
LEHIGH FABRICATION LLC
1139 Lehigh Ave Ste 500 (18052-5527)
PHONE................................908 791-4800
Erica Vandell,
Conti Group The,
EMP: 20
SALES (est): 1.9MM
SALES (corp-wide): 328MM Privately Held
SIC: 3272 Precast terrazo or concrete products
PA: Conti Enterprises, Inc.
2045 Lincoln Hwy
Edison NJ 08817
732 520-5000

(G-19882)
LEHIGH VALLEY VENOM BASBAL CLB
4556 Cairo Dr (18052-1011)
PHONE................................610 262-1750
Jeff Dobeck, *Principal*
EMP: 3
SALES (est): 189.3K Privately Held
SIC: 2836 Venoms

(G-19883)
LIGHTWEIGHT MANUFACTURING INC
Also Called: L W M
1139 Sumner Ave Ste 1 (18052-6941)
PHONE................................610 435-4720
Dirk Cos, *President*
▲ EMP: 15
SALES (est): 2.9MM Privately Held
WEB: www.lightweightmanufacturing.com
SIC: 2394 Canvas & related products

(G-19884)
M E INC
Also Called: Manufacturing Enterprises
133 Mickley Rd (18052-6205)
PHONE................................610 820-5250
Robert J Twardzik, *President*
EMP: 20
SQ FT: 5,600
SALES (est): 1.2MM Privately Held
SIC: 7389 8711 3599 Design, commercial & industrial; engineering services; machine shop, jobbing & repair

(G-19885)
PACE ENVIRONMENTAL
Also Called: Fd Pace
5240 W Coplay Rd (18052-2212)
PHONE................................610 262-3818
John Donnelly, *Partner*
EMP: 6
SALES (est): 495.9K Privately Held
SIC: 3829 Measuring & controlling devices

(G-19886)
PENNSYLVANIA STEEL COMPANY
1139 Lehigh Ave Ste 500 (18052-5527)
P.O. Box 285 (18052-0285)
PHONE................................610 432-4541
Stan Millard, *Principal*
EMP: 40
SALES (est): 6.5MM Privately Held
SIC: 3317 Steel pipe & tubes

(G-19887)
PROTICA INC (PA)
Also Called: Protica Research
1002 Macarthur Rd (18052)
PHONE................................610 832-2000
James F Duffy, *President*
▲ EMP: 29
SQ FT: 24,000
SALES (est): 6.1MM Privately Held
WEB: www.protica.com
SIC: 2099 Food preparations

(PA)=Parent Co (HQ)=Headquarters (DH)=Div Headquarters
✿ = New Business established in last 2 years

2019 Harris Pennsylvania
Manufacturers Directory

749

G E O G R A P H I C

(G-19888)
SAWCOM TECH INC
Also Called: STI
3676 Crescent Ct E (18052-3400)
PHONE..................................610 433-7900
David Y Shaw, *President*
EMP: 5
SQ FT: 7,500
SALES: 986.1K **Privately Held**
SIC: 8711 5065 3589 Engineering serv-
ices; electronic parts & equipment; com-
mercial cooking & foodwarming
equipment

(G-19889)
**SOUMAYA & SONS BAKERY
LLC**
264 Fullerton Ave (18052-6811)
PHONE..................................610 432-0405
Youssef Ballan, *Owner*
EMP: 5 EST: 1979
SQ FT: 3,000
SALES (est): 300K **Privately Held**
SIC: 5149 5461 2051 Bakery products;
bakeries; bread, cake & related products

(G-19890)
SWOPE & BARTHOLOMEW INC
925 Front St (18052-5905)
PHONE..................................610 264-2672
Thomas Bartholomew, *President*
EMP: 10 EST: 1944
SQ FT: 3,300
SALES (est): 1.2MM **Privately Held**
SIC: 3543 Foundry cores; foundry pattern-
making

(G-19891)
TIGER PC DEFENSE
502 Jefferson St (18052-5220)
PHONE..................................888 531-1530
EMP: 3 EST: 2017
SALES (est): 153K **Privately Held**
SIC: 3812 Defense systems & equipment

(G-19892)
VALLEY LITHO INC
504 Spruce St (18052-6437)
PHONE..................................610 437-5122
Thomas David, *President*
Danny David, *Manager*
EMP: 3
SQ FT: 2,500
SALES: 100K **Privately Held**
SIC: 2752 2759 Commercial printing, off-
set; letterpress printing

(G-19893)
**WARNER-CRIVELLARO
STAINED GLAS**
603 8th St (18052-5701)
PHONE..................................610 264-1100
Charles Warner, *President*
▲ EMP: 11
SQ FT: 14,000
SALES: 1.1MM **Privately Held**
SIC: 5231 5039 2731 Glass, leaded or
stained; interior flat glass: plate or win-
dow; books: publishing only; pamphlets:
publishing only, not printed on site

Whitney
Westmoreland County

(G-19894)
**LATROBE FOUNDRY MCH & SUP
CO**
120 Augusta Ln (15693)
P.O. Box 74 (15693-0074)
PHONE..................................724 423-4210
Darryl Musha, *Manager*
EMP: 10
SALES (corp-wide): 3.5MM **Privately
Held**
WEB: www.latrobefoundry.com
SIC: 3295 Foundry facings, ground or oth-
erwise treated
PA: Latrobe Foundry Machine & Supply Co
5655 State Route 981
Latrobe PA 15650
724 537-3341

Wiconisco
Dauphin County

(G-19895)
**KIMMELS COAL AND
PACKAGING INC**
401 Machamer Ave (17097)
PHONE..................................717 453-7151
Scott B Kimmel, *President*
Tamela E Kimmel, *Treasurer*
Tamela Kimmel, *Treasurer*
▼ EMP: 50
SQ FT: 8,300
SALES (est): 25MM **Privately Held**
WEB: www.kimmelcoal.com
SIC: 5052 5032 1422 1241 Coal; stone,
crushed or broken; crushed & broken
limestone; coal mining services

(G-19896)
MEDCO PROCESS INC (HQ)
Coaldale Rd (17097)
P.O. Box 105, Lykens (17048-0105)
PHONE..................................717 453-7298
Patrick J Savage, *President*
Donald E Nestor, *Treasurer*
Jo Ann M Twardzik, *Asst Treas*
Mary Nestor, *Admin Sec*
EMP: 5
SQ FT: 10,000
SALES (est): 1.2MM
SALES (corp-wide): 6MM **Privately Held**
SIC: 3541 Machine tools, metal cutting
type
PA: Reiff & Nestor Company
50 Reiff St W
Lykens PA 17048
717 453-7113

Wilcox
Elk County

(G-19897)
**CAMERON DIVERSIFIED PDTS
INC**
479 Buena Vista Hwy (15870-2715)
PHONE..................................814 929-5834
Edward Anderson, *President*
Mark Anderson, *Vice Pres*
Glenn Anderson, *Treasurer*
Lynn Anderson, *Admin Sec*
EMP: 30
SQ FT: 42,000
SALES (est): 4.1MM
SALES (corp-wide): 5.7MM **Privately
Held**
WEB: www.elcam.co.il
SIC: 3399 Powder, metal
PA: Elcam Tool & Die Inc
479 Buena Vista Hwy
Wilcox PA 15870
814 929-5831

(G-19898)
ELCAM TOOL & DIE INC (PA)
479 Buena Vista Hwy (15870-2715)
PHONE..................................814 929-5831
Edward Anderson, *President*
Mark Anderson, *Vice Pres*
Lynn Anderson, *Treasurer*
Glenn Anerson, *Treasurer*
EMP: 35
SQ FT: 45,000
SALES (est): 5.7MM **Privately Held**
WEB: www.elcam.co.il
SIC: 3399 3544 Powder, metal; special
dies, tools, jigs & fixtures

(G-19899)
**PRECISION CMPCTED
CMPNENTS LLC**
317 Buena Vista Hwy (15870-2709)
PHONE..................................814 929-5805
Hugh Dornisch, *President*
Jason Wensel, *Engineer*
Judy Yates, *Engineer*
Todd Alexander, *CFO*
Ernie Bertolasio, *Sales Mgr*
▲ EMP: 52

SALES (est): 10.7MM **Privately Held**
WEB: www.pccpm.com
SIC: 3399 Powder, metal
HQ: Alpha Sintered Metals, Llc
95 Mason Run Rd
Ridgway PA 15853
814 773-3191

(G-19900)
**SCOTT ZIMMERMAN LOGGING
INC**
59 East Branch Dam Rd (15870-5201)
PHONE..................................814 965-5070
Scott Zimmerman, *President*
EMP: 6
SALES (est): 494.6K **Privately Held**
SIC: 2411 Logging camps & contractors

(G-19901)
WINERY AT WILCOX INC (PA)
1867 Mefferts Run Rd (15870-7137)
PHONE..................................814 929-5598
Mike Williams, *President*
Jamie Williams, *Vice Pres*
EMP: 22
SQ FT: 8,000
SALES (est): 3MM **Privately Held**
WEB: www.wineryatwilcox.net
SIC: 2084 Wines

Wilkes Barre
Luzerne County

(G-19902)
A ALLAN INDUSTRIES INC
Allan Rd (18703)
P.O. Box 999 (18703-0999)
PHONE..................................570 826-0123
John Allan, *Corp Secy*
EMP: 20
SQ FT: 20,000
SALES (est): 3.9MM **Privately Held**
SIC: 5093 3341 Ferrous metal scrap &
waste; nonferrous metals scrap; second-
ary nonferrous metals

(G-19903)
**ADVERTSING OTSOURCING
SVCS LLC**
106 S Main St Fl 1 (18701-1624)
PHONE..................................570 793-2000
Laura Stark, *Marketing Staff*
James B Kelly, *Mng Member*
Kelly Berecin, *Manager*
Randy Russo, *Graphic Designe*
EMP: 20
SALES (est): 870K **Privately Held**
WEB: www.americanhelpdesk.com
SIC: 2711 Newspapers

(G-19904)
ALTEC INDUSTRIES INC
250 Laird St (18705-3821)
PHONE..................................570 822-3104
John Peterson, *General Mgr*
Chris Brzenchek, *Safety Mgr*
EMP: 200
SALES (corp-wide): 764.4MM **Privately
Held**
WEB: www.altec.com
SIC: 3531 3536 3713 3566 Derricks, ex-
cept oil & gas field; aerial work platforms:
hydraulic/elec. truck/carrier mounted;
cranes, overhead traveling; truck bodies
(motor vehicles); speed changers, drives
& gears; industrial trucks & tractors
HQ: Altec Industries, Inc.
210 Inverness Center Dr
Birmingham AL 35242
205 991-7733

(G-19905)
**AMERICAN STEEL CARPORTS
INC**
22 Ruddle St (18702-4310)
PHONE..................................570 825-8260
Onesimo Gobellan, *Manager*
EMP: 10
SALES (corp-wide): 22.7MM **Privately
Held**
SIC: 3448 Carports: prefabricated metal

PA: American Steel Carports, Inc.
457 N Brwy St
Joshua TX 76058
866 471-8761

(G-19906)
**AUDIOLOGY & HEARING AID
CENTER (PA)**
34 S Main St Ste 19 (18701-1723)
PHONE..................................570 822-6122
David A Wadas, *Owner*
▲ EMP: 5 EST: 1949
SQ FT: 500
SALES (est): 600.4K **Privately Held**
SIC: 3829 5999 7629 Testing equipment:
abrasion, shearing strength, etc.; hearing
aids; hearing aid repair

(G-19907)
AXELRAD LLC (PA)
152 N Pennsylvania Ave (18701-3604)
PHONE..................................570 714-3278
Stan Donnelly, *Principal*
Dave Maloney,
Matt Trievel,
EMP: 8
SQ FT: 20,000
SALES (est): 725.1K **Privately Held**
SIC: 2759 Screen printing; letterpress &
screen printing

(G-19908)
BELLA MACHINE INC
421 N Penna Ave Ste 1 (18702-4582)
PHONE..................................570 826-9127
Myron Bella, *President*
Ark Menater, *Treasurer*
EMP: 5
SALES (est): 751K **Privately Held**
WEB: www.bellamachine.com
SIC: 3549 Metalworking machinery

(G-19909)
CARBON SALES INC
Also Called: Anthrafilt
375 Johnson St (18702-7411)
PHONE..................................570 823-7664
Matthew Dewees, *President*
Mike Lavelle, *Sales Executive*
EMP: 30
SQ FT: 100,000
SALES (est): 7.2MM **Privately Held**
WEB: www.carbon-sales.com
SIC: 2819 Industrial inorganic chemicals

(G-19910)
CARLA BELLA ENT LLC
1 George Ave (18705-2511)
PHONE..................................570 704-0077
Charles Umphred,
EMP: 3
SALES (est): 245.9K **Privately Held**
SIC: 3999 Candles

(G-19911)
CCFFG INC
7 George Ave (18705-2511)
PHONE..................................570 270-3976
Frank Schiel, *President*
Carleen Schiel, *Vice Pres*
Fred Schiel, *Vice Pres*
Gary Schiel, *Vice Pres*
Connie Schiel, *Admin Sec*
EMP: 100
SALES (est): 8.4MM **Privately Held**
SIC: 5411 2051 Grocery stores, independ-
ent; bread, cake & related products

(G-19912)
CITIZENS VOICE
75 N Washington St (18701-3109)
PHONE..................................570 821-2000
Robert Manganiello, *Publisher*
Larry Holeva, *Editor*
Houston Patty, *Editor*
Heather Petrikonis, *Accounts Exec*
Stephanie Whitt, *Accounts Exec*
EMP: 300 EST: 1978
SQ FT: 37,000
SALES (est): 15.4MM **Privately Held**
WEB: www.citizensvoice.com
SIC: 2711 Commercial printing & newspa-
per publishing combined; newspapers,
publishing & printing

(G-19913)
CIVITAS MEDIA LLC
Also Called: Times Leader
90 E Market St (18701-3501)
PHONE.....................................570 829-7100
Richard Connor, *Publisher*
EMP: 9
SALES (corp-wide): 763.9MM **Privately Held**
SIC: 2711 Newspapers, publishing & printing
PA: Civitas Media, Llc
130 Harbour Place Dr # 300
Davidson NC 28036
704 897-6020

(G-19914)
CORCORAN PRINTING INC
641 N Pennsylvania Ave (18705-2421)
P.O. Box 201 (18703-0201)
PHONE.....................................570 822-1991
William T Corcoran, *President*
EMP: 15
SQ FT: 14,000
SALES (est): 2.6MM **Privately Held**
WEB: www.corcoranprinting.com
SIC: 2752 Commercial printing, lithographic

(G-19915)
CUSTOM SEATS INC
1212 Scott St (18705-3724)
PHONE.....................................570 602-7408
Thomas Dellamalva, *President*
EMP: 70
SQ FT: 12,000
SALES (est): 10.5MM **Privately Held**
WEB: www.customseatsinc.com
SIC: 2531 Seats, miscellaneous public conveyances

(G-19916)
DREAMSPRING INSTITUTE
Also Called: Dreamspring Institute , The
9 Hutson St (18702-4915)
PHONE.....................................570 829-1378
Chris Degraffenreid, *President*
EMP: 3
SALES (est): 135.7K **Privately Held**
SIC: 2741 Miscellaneous publishing

(G-19917)
ELKAY WEAVING CO INC
701 E Northampton St (18702-7515)
PHONE.....................................570 822-5371
Tom Claus, *Principal*
EMP: 5
SALES (corp-wide): 2.5MM **Privately Held**
SIC: 2281 Weaving yarn, spun
HQ: Elkay Weaving Co., Inc.
415 Delaware Ave
West Pittston PA
570 603-0432

(G-19918)
EMPIRE GLOVE INC
525 Scott St (18702-5607)
PHONE.....................................570 824-4400
Manzoor Hassan, *President*
EMP: 5 EST: 2011
SALES: 1MM **Privately Held**
SIC: 3111 Glove leather

(G-19919)
EZY PRODUCTS CO INC
530 Blackman St (18702-6034)
PHONE.....................................570 822-9600
Ed Sarieh, *President*
EMP: 8
SALES (est): 514.6K **Privately Held**
SIC: 3442 Garage doors, overhead: metal

(G-19920)
FASTSIGNS
763 Kidder St (18702-6910)
PHONE.....................................570 824-7446
Michelle Ledine, *Principal*
EMP: 3
SALES (est): 186.8K **Privately Held**
SIC: 3993 Signs & advertising specialties

(G-19921)
FENTIMANS NORTH AMERICA INC
76 Passan Dr (18702-7348)
PHONE.....................................877 326-3248
Craig James, *President*
Napoleon Veltri, *Vice Pres*
▲ EMP: 10
SALES (est): 365.1K **Privately Held**
SIC: 2086 Carbonated beverages, nonalcoholic: bottled & canned

(G-19922)
GREAT NORTHERN PRESS OF WILKES
173 Gilligan St (18702-4501)
PHONE.....................................570 822-3147
Larry N Llewellyn, *President*
EMP: 30
SQ FT: 85,000
SALES: 5MM **Privately Held**
SIC: 2752 2759 2677 Commercial printing, lithographic; laser printing; envelopes

(G-19923)
HANGER INC
176 S Wilkes Barre Blvd (18702-5029)
PHONE.....................................877 442-6437
Ronald Maholic, *Branch Mgr*
EMP: 14
SALES (corp-wide): 1B **Publicly Held**
SIC: 3842 Surgical appliances & supplies
PA: Hanger, Inc.
10910 Domain Dr Ste 300
Austin TX 78758
512 777-3800

(G-19924)
HARRISON ELECTRONIC SYSTEMS
Also Called: Harrison Systems
1167 N Washington St (18705-1855)
PHONE.....................................570 639-5695
Colin R Keefer, *Ch of Bd*
Karen Keefer, *President*
David J Keefer, *Director*
EMP: 17
SQ FT: 10,000
SALES (est): 1.4MM **Privately Held**
SIC: 3669 Burglar alarm apparatus, electric; sirens, electric: vehicle, marine, industrial & air raid

(G-19925)
HULLIHENS PRINTERY
45 Summit St (18704-2407)
PHONE.....................................570 288-6804
EMP: 3
SALES: 900K **Privately Held**
SIC: 2759 2752 Commercial Printing Lithographic Commercial Printing

(G-19926)
IDEAL SLEEVES INTL LLC
182 Courtright St (18702-1802)
PHONE.....................................570 823-8456
Robert Werner, *Manager*
James Dwyer,
▲ EMP: 10
SALES (est): 2.4MM
SALES (corp-wide): 18.8MM **Privately Held**
SIC: 5199 2671 Packaging materials; packaging paper & plastics film, coated & laminated
PA: R.B. Dwyer Co., Inc.
2891 E Miraloma Ave
Anaheim CA 92806
714 630-4391

(G-19927)
IMPRESSIONS MEDIA
Also Called: Times Leader Circulation
90 E Market St (18701-3501)
PHONE.....................................570 829-7140
Prashant Shitut, *President*
EMP: 200
SALES (est): 8.3MM **Privately Held**
WEB: www.timesleader.com
SIC: 2711 Newspapers, publishing & printing

(G-19928)
INNAVENTURE LLC
7 S Main St Ste 271 (18701-1732)
PHONE.....................................570 371-9390
James Abrams,
EMP: 4
SQ FT: 20,000
SALES (est): 156.7K **Privately Held**
SIC: 2869 High purity grade chemicals, organic

(G-19929)
INTERMETRO INDUSTRIES CORP (DH)
651 N Washington St (18705-1799)
PHONE.....................................570 825-2741
John Nackley, *President*
Becky Pokorny, *Credit Staff*
Valerie Madensky, *Marketing Staff*
Scott Burghart, *Manager*
Donald Fisher, *Manager*
◆ EMP: 400 EST: 1998
SQ FT: 40,000
SALES (est): 409.2MM **Privately Held**
WEB: www.metro.com
SIC: 2541 2542 Cabinets, lockers & shelving; partitions & fixtures, except wood
HQ: Ali Group North America Corporation
101 Corporate Woods Pkwy
Vernon Hills IL 60061
847 215-6565

(G-19930)
ITOH DENKI USA INC (HQ)
2 Great Valley Blvd (18706-5332)
PHONE.....................................570 820-8811
Richard R Kosik, *President*
Brad Bachle, *Engineer*
Lisa Sturmi, *Engineer*
Mike Baur, *Accounts Mgr*
Paul Kesner, *Accounts Mgr*
▲ EMP: 20
SQ FT: 27,000
SALES (est): 3.9MM
SALES (corp-wide): 76.1MM **Privately Held**
WEB: www.itohdenki.com
SIC: 3535 Pneumatic tube conveyor systems
PA: Itoh Denki Co., Ltd.
1146-2, Asazumacho
Kasai HYO 679-0
790 471-225

(G-19931)
J & H CONCRETE CO
84 Scott St (18702-4402)
PHONE.....................................570 824-3565
James W Smith, *President*
EMP: 20 EST: 1952
SQ FT: 1,800
SALES (est): 2.1MM **Privately Held**
SIC: 3273 1794 Ready-mixed concrete; excavation & grading, building construction

(G-19932)
JB MACHINE INC
398 N Pennsylvania Ave (18702-4415)
PHONE.....................................570 824-2003
James Erecinsky, *President*
EMP: 7
SALES (est): 810.1K **Privately Held**
SIC: 3599 Machine shop, jobbing & repair

(G-19933)
JEDDO-HIGHLAND COAL COMPANY (HQ)
46 Public Sq Ste 600 (18701-2609)
PHONE.....................................570 825-8700
James J Tedesco, *Ch of Bd*
Michelene Kennedy, *President*
Mary Ann Eggleston, *Vice Pres*
Daniel Kripplebauer, *QC Mgr*
▼ EMP: 9
SALES (est): 957.7K
SALES (corp-wide): 92.4MM **Privately Held**
SIC: 1231 Strip mining, anthracite
PA: Pagnotti Enterprises Inc
46 Public Sq Ste 600
Wilkes Barre PA 18701
570 825-8700

(G-19934)
JOEL MFG CO INC
Also Called: Joel Alan
219 S Washington St 221 (18701-2800)
PHONE.....................................570 822-1182
Lawrence Hollander, *President*
Ruth Hollander, *Corp Secy*
EMP: 3 EST: 1952
SQ FT: 20,000
SALES (est): 195.7K **Privately Held**
SIC: 2335 Women's, juniors' & misses' dresses

(G-19935)
KNIGHT RIDDER INC
15 N Main St (18701-2604)
PHONE.....................................570 829-7100
Richard L Connor, *President*
EMP: 3
SALES (est): 160.3K **Privately Held**
SIC: 2711 Newspapers

(G-19936)
LION BREWERY INC (PA)
Also Called: Gibbons Brewing Co
700 N Pennsylvania Ave (18705-2451)
PHONE.....................................570 823-8801
W Smulowitz, *CEO*
Charles Lawson Jr, *President*
W Ciolek, *Corp Secy*
Brian Mitchell, *Production*
Paul Lauer, *Engineer*
▲ EMP: 125 EST: 1905
SQ FT: 2,000
SALES (est): 32.2MM **Privately Held**
WEB: www.lionbrewery.com
SIC: 2082 2086 Beer (alcoholic beverage); ale (alcoholic beverage); porter (alcoholic beverage); malt liquors; soft drinks: packaged in cans, bottles, etc.

(G-19937)
LUZERNE OPTICAL LABORATORIES
180 N Wilkes Barre Blvd (18702-5341)
P.O. Box 998 (18773-0998)
PHONE.....................................570 822-3183
John Dougherty, *President*
Neil J Dougherty, *General Mgr*
Lorraine Dougherty, *CFO*
▲ EMP: 185 EST: 1973
SQ FT: 20,000
SALES (est): 35.3MM **Privately Held**
WEB: www.luzerneoptical.com
SIC: 3827 Optical instruments & lenses

(G-19938)
LUZERNE TRADING COMPANY INC
Also Called: Impecca USA
8 W Market St Ste 930 (18701-1801)
PHONE.....................................866 954-4440
John Bock, *President*
Miriam Friedman, *Marketing Staff*
Goldie Reese, *Admin Sec*
▲ EMP: 10 EST: 2007
SALES (est): 1.1MM **Privately Held**
SIC: 3651 Home entertainment equipment, electronic

(G-19939)
M B BEDDING CO
Also Called: General Foam Fabricators
526 S Main St Unit 1 (18701-2114)
P.O. Box 1301 (18703-1301)
PHONE.....................................570 822-2491
Murray Brown, *Partner*
Marilyn Shaffern, *Partner*
EMP: 6 EST: 1923
SQ FT: 30,000
SALES (est): 400K **Privately Held**
SIC: 7641 3069 2515 Reupholstery; foam rubber; mattresses & foundations

(G-19940)
MALLINCKRODT LLC
300 Laird St Ste C (18702-7027)
PHONE.....................................570 824-8980
Karen Pieszala, *Manager*
EMP: 12 **Privately Held**
WEB: www.mallinckrodt.com
SIC: 2834 Pharmaceutical preparations

HQ: Mallinckrodt Llc
675 Jmes S Mcdonnell Blvd
Hazelwood MO 63042
314 654-2000

(G-19941)
MARY J BACKAROO
107 Wyoming Valley Mall (18702-6812)
PHONE.............................570 819-4809
Mary J Backaroo, *Manager*
EMP: 20
SALES (est): 963.9K **Privately Held**
SIC: 2759 Commercial printing

(G-19942)
MEDICO INDUSTRIES INC (PA)
1500 Highway 315 Blvd (18702-7090)
PHONE.............................570 825-7711
Thomas A Medico, *President*
Ed Gray, *Parts Mgr*
Rich Yanalis, *Parts Mgr*
Pat Donnelly, *Engineer*
Lawrence Medico, *Treasurer*
◆ EMP: 148 EST: 1938
SQ FT: 127,000
SALES: 72.9MM **Privately Held**
SIC: 3489 5211 3795 3483 Artillery or ar-
tillery parts, over 30 mm.; electrical con-
struction materials; tanks & tank
components; ammunition, except for
small arms; iron & steel forgings

(G-19943)
METRO INTERNATIONAL CORP
651 N Washington St (18705-1707)
PHONE.............................570 825-2741
Louis T Alesi, *President*
EMP: 27
SALES (est): 2.4MM **Privately Held**
SIC: 3496 2542 3537 Miscellaneous fabricated wire products; shelving, made
from purchased wire; grocery carts, made
from purchased wire; cabinets: show, display or storage: except wood; dollies
(hand or power trucks), industrial except
mining
HQ: Intermetro Industries Corporation
651 N Washington St
Wilkes Barre PA 18705
570 825-2741

(G-19944)
MODERN PLASTICS CORP (PA)
152 Horton St (18702-3433)
P.O. Box 431, Stroudsburg (18360-0431)
PHONE.............................570 822-1124
Bernadette Murphy, *CEO*
Larry I Taren, *President*
Paul Taren, *Vice Pres*
Bernadette Cook, *Admin Sec*
EMP: 20 EST: 1971
SQ FT: 32,000
SALES (est): 3.4MM **Privately Held**
WEB: www.modernplastics.cc
SIC: 3089 Laminating of plastic; injection
molding of plastics

(G-19945)
MONDELEZ GLOBAL LLC
Also Called: Kraft Foods
50 New Commerce Blvd (18762-1400)
PHONE.............................570 820-1200
Vince Tassitano, *Branch Mgr*
Shantanu Agarwal, *Manager*
Michele Ley, *Manager*
Tracy Sanborn, *Manager*
Daniel Morgan, *Associate*
EMP: 520 **Publicly Held**
WEB: www.kraftfoods.com
SIC: 2022 2013 2095 2043 Processed
cheese; natural cheese; spreads, cheese;
dips, cheese-based; sausages & other
prepared meats; bacon, side & sliced:
from purchased meat; frankfurters from
purchased meat; luncheon meat from purchased meat; coffee roasting (except by
wholesale grocers); freeze-dried coffee;
instant coffee; cereal breakfast foods;
dressings, salad: raw & cooked (except
dry mixes); powders, drink
HQ: Mondelez Global Llc
3 N Pkwy Ste 300
Deerfield IL 60015
847 943-4000

(G-19946)
MOUNTAINTOP EAGLE INC
85 S Main Rd (18707-1961)
P.O. Box 10, Mountain Top (18707-0010)
PHONE.............................570 474-6397
Stephanie Grubert, *President*
Charles Grubert, *Corp Secy*
EMP: 6
SALES (est): 270K **Privately Held**
WEB: www.mteagle.com
SIC: 2711 Newspapers: publishing only,
not printed on site

(G-19947)
MR MOO COW LLC
1280 Highway 315 Blvd (18702-7002)
PHONE.............................570 235-1061
EMP: 3
SALES (est): 180.7K **Privately Held**
SIC: 2024 Ice cream, bulk

(G-19948)
NABISCO BRANDS INC
50 New Commerce Blvd (18762-1400)
PHONE.............................570 820-1669
Joe Bobeck, *Principal*
EMP: 8
SALES (est): 1.1MM **Privately Held**
SIC: 2052 Cookies & crackers

(G-19949)
NE FIBERS LLC
157 Passan Dr Bldng 2 2 Bldng (18702)
PHONE.............................570 445-2086
Jose Galvan, *Branch Mgr*
EMP: 48 EST: 2014
SALES (est): 11.5MM **Privately Held**
SIC: 2621 Building paper, insulation
HQ: Us Greenfiber, Llc
5500 77 Center Dr Ste 100
Charlotte NC 28217

(G-19950)
NEWTOWN MFG & BLDG SUP CORP (PA)
247 Old River Rd (18702-1616)
PHONE.............................570 825-3675
Carl Slocomb, *President*
Donald S Sennett Jr, *Vice Pres*
EMP: 85 EST: 1962
SQ FT: 53,000
SALES (est): 11MM **Privately Held**
SIC: 3089 2431 Plastic hardware & build-
ing products; windows & window parts &
trim, wood

(G-19951)
NORTHEAST ENERGY CO INC
254 Johnson St (18702-7435)
PHONE.............................570 823-1719
Michael A Corgan, *President*
EMP: 5
SQ FT: 2,000
SALES (est): 510K **Privately Held**
SIC: 1231 1794 Strip mining, anthracite;
excavation work

(G-19952)
OFFSET PAPERBACK
10 Passan Dr (18702-7321)
PHONE.............................570 602-1316
Nancy Lavan, *Principal*
EMP: 5 EST: 2011
SALES (est): 502.4K **Privately Held**
SIC: 7372 Publishers' computer software

(G-19953)
ONYX OPTICAL
113 S Washington St (18701-2904)
PHONE.............................570 951-7750
Ronald Avenia, *Principal*
EMP: 3 EST: 2013
SALES (est): 192.3K **Privately Held**
SIC: 3827 Mirrors, optical

(G-19954)
PAGNOTTI ENTERPRISES INC (PA)
46 Public Sq Ste 600 (18701-2609)
PHONE.............................570 825-8700
Charles E Parente, *CEO*
Michelene Kennedy, *President*
Mary Ann Eggleston, *Vice Pres*
David Swisher, *Vice Pres*
EMP: 25

SQ FT: 10,000
SALES (est): 92.4MM **Privately Held**
SIC: 6411 1231 4841 Insurance agents,
brokers & service; strip mining, anthracite;
cable television services

(G-19955)
PALACE FOODS INC (PA)
194 Mill St (18705-2622)
PHONE.............................610 939-0631
Rajavel Jagadesan, *President*
Erik Kneppman, *President*
EMP: 14
SQ FT: 10,000
SALES (est): 4.4MM **Privately Held**
SIC: 2099 Food preparations

(G-19956)
PIC MOBILE ADVERTISING LLC
550 Anderson St (18702-6157)
PHONE.............................570 208-1459
EMP: 4
SALES (est): 355.1K **Privately Held**
SIC: 2752 Lithographic Commercial Print-
ing

(G-19957)
PIZZA ASSOCIATES INCORPORATED
Also Called: Grotto Pizza Delivery
337 Wyoming Valley Mall (18702-6834)
PHONE.............................570 822-6600
Joseph Pagliante, *President*
Dominic Pulieri, *Treasurer*
Armand Mascioli, *Admin Sec*
EMP: 150
SQ FT: 8,500
SALES (est): 4.4MM **Privately Held**
WEB: www.grottopizzapa.com
SIC: 5812 2099 Pizzeria, independent;
food preparations

(G-19958)
POWER MECHANICAL CORP
Pethick Rd Rr 315 (18705)
P.O. Box 1048 (18703-1048)
PHONE.............................570 823-8824
Tara Wilson, *President*
EMP: 25
SQ FT: 17,000
SALES: 1.6MM **Privately Held**
WEB: www.powermechanical.com
SIC: 1711 3444 1761 Mechanical con-
tractor; sheet metalwork; roofing, siding &
sheet metal work

(G-19959)
PRECISION CASTPARTS CORP
Also Called: PCC Arostructures Wilkes-Barre
120 Hazle St (18702-4306)
P.O. Box 626 (18703-0626)
PHONE.............................570 825-4544
Ron Felix, *Branch Mgr*
EMP: 120
SALES (corp-wide): 225.3B **Publicly Held**
SIC: 3724 Aircraft engines & engine parts
HQ: Precision Castparts Corp.
4650 Sw Mcdam Ave Ste 300
Portland OR 97239
503 946-4800

(G-19960)
R & D PACKAGING PA INC
458 S Empire St Unit A (18702-6191)
PHONE.............................570 235-2310
Robert E Post, *President*
EMP: 5
SQ FT: 13,000
SALES (est): 390K **Privately Held**
SIC: 3241 Cement, hydraulic

(G-19961)
SANDLEX CORPORATION
84 Beekman St (18702-2136)
P.O. Box 832 (18703-0832)
PHONE.............................570 820-8568
Nicholas Marino Jr, *President*
EMP: 4
SALES (est): 340K **Privately Held**
SIC: 3499 Ladders, portable: metal

(G-19962)
SCHIEL INC
Also Called: Schiel's Family Market
30 Hanover St (18702-3618)
PHONE.............................570 970-4460
Frank Shiel, *President*
Carleen Schiel, *Vice Pres*
Fred Schiel, *Vice Pres*
Gary Schiel, *Treasurer*
Connie Schiel-Owca, *Admin Sec*
EMP: 110
SQ FT: 27,000
SALES: 12MM **Privately Held**
SIC: 5411 5812 2051 Grocery stores, in-
dependent; eating places; bread, cake &
related products

(G-19963)
SILVERBROOK ANTHRACITE INC
Also Called: Kassa Coal Co
1 Market St (18702-7105)
PHONE.............................570 654-3560
Vincent Kassa, *President*
Theodore Kassa, *Treasurer*
Cary Kassa, *Admin Sec*
EMP: 14 EST: 1956
SALES (est): 1.9MM **Privately Held**
SIC: 1231 Underground mining, anthracite

(G-19964)
SNACK SHACK
750 Wilkes Barre Townshp (18702-6126)
PHONE.............................570 270-2929
Candice Sarrell, *Owner*
EMP: 4
SALES (est): 278.8K **Privately Held**
SIC: 2024 Ice cream, bulk

(G-19965)
THE SCRANTON TIMES L P
Also Called: Citizens Voice
75 N Washington St (18701-3109)
PHONE.............................570 821-2095
Irene Williams, *Manager*
EMP: 140
SALES (corp-wide): 114.5MM **Privately Held**
WEB: www.scrantontimesefcu.com
SIC: 2711 Newspapers, publishing & print-
ing
PA: The Scranton Times L P
149 Penn Ave Ste 1
Scranton PA 18503
570 348-9100

(G-19966)
UNIFILT CORPORATION (PA)
Also Called: Suburbia Systems-Div
375 Johnson St (18702-7411)
P.O. Box 614, Ellwood City (16117-0614)
PHONE.............................717 823-0313
Matthew Dewees, *President*
Fedrick Dewees, *Treasurer*
Mary Anne Eggleston, *Admin Sec*
▼ EMP: 2
SALES (est): 1.6MM **Privately Held**
WEB: www.unifilt.com
SIC: 3677 5074 Filtration devices, elec-
tronic; water heaters & purification equip-
ment

(G-19967)
UNISON ENGINE COMPONENTS INC
Also Called: PCC Aerostructure
120 Hazle St (18702-4306)
PHONE.............................570 825-4544
Ron Felix, *Manager*
EMP: 150
SALES (corp-wide): 121.6B **Publicly Held**
SIC: 3724 8711 3812 3545 Aircraft en-
gines & engine parts; industrial engineers;
search & navigation equipment; precision
tools, machinists'
HQ: Unison Engine Components Inc.
333 S 3rd St
Terre Haute IN 47807

(G-19968)
WALLACE BROTHERS MFG CO
275 Mundy St Ste 103 (18702-6818)
PHONE.............................570 822-3808
Joseph J Wallace Jr, *Partner*

▲ = Import ▼=Export
◆ =Import/Export

Julia Wallace, *Partner*
EMP: 10 **EST:** 1958
SALES: 2.1MM **Privately Held**
SIC: 5094 3961 Diamonds (gems); rosaries & small religious articles, except precious metal

(G-19969)
WALSH TOOL COMPANY INC
33 Hanover St (18702-3617)
PHONE..............................570 823-1375
Joseph Wasilewski, *President*
Mary Barbara Wasilewski, *Corp Secy*
EMP: 7
SQ FT: 16,000
SALES: 729K **Privately Held**
SIC: 3599 7692 3544 3535 Machine shop, jobbing & repair; custom machinery; welding repair; special dies, tools, jigs & fixtures; conveyors & conveying equipment

(G-19970)
WEB PAINT INC
Also Called: Auto Graphix
152 Horton St (18702-3433)
PHONE..............................570 208-2528
Steven Taren, *President*
EMP: 10
SALES (est): 647.3K **Privately Held**
WEB: www.unixpapa.com
SIC: 3993 Signs & advertising specialties

(G-19971)
WEEKENDER
90 E Market St (18701-3501)
PHONE..............................570 831-7320
Rich Connor, *Owner*
EMP: 10
SALES (est): 310K **Privately Held**
SIC: 2711 Newspapers: publishing only, not printed on site

(G-19972)
WEST SIDE TOOL AND DIE COMPANY
93 John St (18702)
PHONE..............................570 331-7016
Christopher Boyd, *Owner*
Carl Boyd, *Co-Owner*
EMP: 4
SQ FT: 6,000
SALES (est): 369.8K **Privately Held**
SIC: 3599 Machine shop, jobbing & repair

(G-19973)
WET PAINT T SHIRTS INC
152 Horton St (18702-3433)
PHONE..............................570 822-2221
Steve Taren, *President*
EMP: 8
SQ FT: 5,000
SALES (est): 1MM **Privately Held**
WEB: www.wetpainttshirts.com/
SIC: 2253 5699 T-shirts & tops, knit; T-shirts, custom printed

(G-19974)
WHITEMAN TOWER INC
600 Baltimore Dr (18702-7901)
PHONE..............................800 748-3891
Andrew J Sordoni III, *Ch of Bd*
William B Sordoni, *President*
Charles E Parente, *Treasurer*
Edward J Conway Jr, *Controller*
Stephen Sordoni, *Admin Sec*
▼ **EMP:** 4
SQ FT: 40,000
SALES (est): 551.2K
SALES (corp-wide): 23.3B **Publicly Held**
WEB: www.centrallewmar.com
SIC: 3577 Paper tape (computer) equipment: punches, readers, etc.
PA: International Paper Company
6400 Poplar Ave
Memphis TN 38197
901 419-9000

(G-19975)
WILKES BARRE LAW & LIB ASSN
Also Called: LUZERNE COUNTY BAR ASSOCIATION
200 N River St Rm 23 (18711-1004)
PHONE..............................570 822-6712
Micheal I Butera, *President*

EMP: 3
SALES: 41.7K **Privately Held**
SIC: 8621 8231 2721 Bar association; law library; trade journals: publishing & printing

(G-19976)
WILKES-BARRE PUBLISHING CO
15 N Main St (18701-2604)
PHONE..............................570 829-7100
Richard L Connor, *CEO*
Mark Amendola, *CFO*
▲ **EMP:** 215 **EST:** 1907
SALES (est): 10MM
SALES (corp-wide): 763.9MM **Privately Held**
SIC: 2711 Newspapers: publishing only, not printed on site
HQ: Wilkes-Barre Publishing Company, Inc.
15 N Main St
Wilkes Barre PA 18701

(G-19977)
WILKES-BARRE PUBLISHING CO INC (HQ)
Also Called: Civitas Media
15 N Main St (18701-2604)
PHONE..............................570 829-7100
Prashant Shitut, *President*
Joe Butkiewicz, *Vice Pres*
Lisa Daris, *Vice Pres*
Denise Sellers, *Vice Pres*
Allison Uhrin, *Vice Pres*
▲ **EMP:** 2
SALES (est): 24.2MM
SALES (corp-wide): 763.9MM **Privately Held**
SIC: 2711 Newspapers
PA: Civitas Media, Llc
130 Harbour Place Dr # 300
Davidson NC 28036
704 897-6020

(G-19978)
WYMAN-GORDON PENNSYLVANIA LLC
Also Called: PCC Forged Products
1141 Highway 315 Blvd (18702-6928)
PHONE..............................570 474-3059
EMP: 11
SALES (corp-wide): 225.3B **Publicly Held**
SIC: 3491 3823 Gas valves & parts, industrial; automatic regulating & control valves; industrial process control instruments
HQ: Wyman-Gordon Pennsylvania, Llc
701 Crestwood Dr
Mountain Top PA 18707
570 474-6371

(G-19979)
WYOMING VLY PRSTHTIC ORTHOTICS
300 Avenue A (18704-1911)
PHONE..............................570 283-3835
Dante Molino, *Owner*
EMP: 4
SALES (est): 270K **Privately Held**
SIC: 3842 Limbs, artificial

(G-19980)
XOMOX CORPORATION (PA)
19 Bailey St (18705-1907)
PHONE..............................570 824-3577
David Frank, *President*
EMP: 1
SALES (est): 2.3MM **Privately Held**
SIC: 2657 Folding paperboard boxes

Wilkinsburg
Allegheny County

(G-19981)
TECHNIQUE ARCHITECTURAL PDTS
815 Penn Ave (15221-2324)
PHONE..............................412 241-1644
Raymond Appleby, *President*
EMP: 8
SQ FT: 10,000

SALES (est): 569.2K **Privately Held**
WEB: www.techniqueap.com
SIC: 3446 Architectural metalwork

Williamsburg
Blair County

(G-19982)
TRANSFER JUNCTION (PA)
442 Polecat Hollow Rd (16693-6410)
PHONE..............................814 942-4434
Martin Strogen, *Owner*
EMP: 8
SQ FT: 2,500
SALES (est): 796.5K **Privately Held**
SIC: 5699 2329 5941 Bathing suits; field jackets, military; soccer supplies

---

Williamsport
Lycoming County

(G-19983)
3-D CREATIVE SERVICES INC
3500 W 4th St (17701-4262)
PHONE..............................570 329-1111
Daniel B French, *President*
Travis Best, *Vice Pres*
EMP: 10
SQ FT: 13,000
SALES: 1.2MM **Privately Held**
WEB: www.3dcreativeservices.com
SIC: 2541 Display fixtures, wood

(G-19984)
ALERTONE SERVICES INC
24 W 4th St (17701-6206)
PHONE..............................570 321-5433
Paul Graafsma, *President*
▲ **EMP:** 19
SQ FT: 10,000
SALES (est): 2.9MM **Privately Held**
WEB: www.alert-1.com
SIC: 3669 Emergency alarms

(G-19985)
AMERICAN WELDING & GAS INC
100 Reading Ave (17701-4121)
PHONE..............................570 323-8400
Rick Malicky, *Manager*
EMP: 10
SALES (corp-wide): 191.1MM **Privately Held**
SIC: 5084 5169 2813 Welding machinery & equipment; industrial gases; oxygen; industrial gases
PA: American Welding & Gas, Inc.
4900 Falls Of Neuse Rd # 150
Raleigh NC 27609
918 573-2982

(G-19986)
ANADARKO PETROLEUM
2011 Lycoming Creek Rd (17701-1206)
PHONE..............................570 326-1535
EMP: 3 **EST:** 2014
SALES (est): 181.6K **Privately Held**
SIC: 5172 1382 Petroleum products; oil & gas exploration services

(G-19987)
ANADARKO PETROLEUM CORP
33 W 3rd St Ste 200 (17701-6523)
PHONE..............................570 323-4157
EMP: 14
SALES (est): 1.9MM **Privately Held**
SIC: 1311 Crude Petroleum/Natural Gas Production

(G-19988)
ANADARKO PETROLEUM CORPORATION
33 W 3rd St Ste 400 (17701-6532)
PHONE..............................570 323-4157
EMP: 6
SALES (corp-wide): 13.3B **Publicly Held**
SIC: 1311 Crude petroleum production

PA: Anadarko Petroleum Corporation
1201 Lake Robbins Dr
The Woodlands TX 77380
832 636-1000

(G-19989)
ARD OPERATING LLC
33 W 3rd St (17701-6523)
PHONE..............................570 979-1240
Stephanie Mitchell, *Supervisor*
EMP: 80
SALES (corp-wide): 42.7MM **Privately Held**
SIC: 1382 Oil & gas exploration services
PA: Ard Operating, Llc
500 Dallas St Ste 2700
Houston TX 77002
713 759-1155

(G-19990)
AVCO CORPORATION
Lycoming Engines
652 Oliver St (17701-4410)
PHONE..............................570 323-6181
Scott Witmer, *Branch Mgr*
EMP: 120
SALES (corp-wide): 13.9B **Publicly Held**
WEB: www.lycoming.textron.com
SIC: 3724 Aircraft engines & engine parts
HQ: Avco Corporation
40 Westminster St
Providence RI 02903

(G-19991)
AXEMAN-ANDERSON COMPANY
300 E Mountain Ave (17702-7722)
PHONE..............................570 326-9114
Peter H Axeman Sr, *President*
EMP: 25
SQ FT: 35,000
SALES (est): 4.3MM **Privately Held**
WEB: www.axeman-anderson.com
SIC: 3433 3443 Boilers, low-pressure heating: steam or hot water; fabricated plate work (boiler shop)

(G-19992)
BASTIAN TIRE SALES INC
Also Called: Bastian Tire and Auto
2940 Reach Rd (17701-4146)
PHONE..............................570 323-8651
Katherine Campbell, *Sales Staff*
Mike Bastian II, *Manager*
EMP: 33 **Privately Held**
WEB: www.bastiantire.com
SIC: 3011 7534 Retreading materials, tire; tire retreading & repair shops
HQ: Bastian Tire Sales, Inc.
430 Washington Blvd
Williamsport PA 17701
570 326-9181

(G-19993)
BIMBO BAKERIES USA INC
Also Called: Stroehmann Bakeries 20
3375 Lycoming Creek Rd (17701-1035)
PHONE..............................570 494-1191
Ann Young, *Branch Mgr*
EMP: 15 **Privately Held**
SIC: 2051 Bagels, fresh or frozen
HQ: Bimbo Bakeries Usa, Inc
255 Business Center Dr # 200
Horsham PA 19044
215 347-5500

(G-19994)
BRIGHT BANNERS
216 S Market St (17702-7320)
PHONE..............................570 326-3524
Kathryn Marcello, *President*
EMP: 6
SALES (est): 490.9K **Privately Held**
SIC: 5999 2211 5131 Banners; flags; table cover fabrics, cotton; flags & banners

(G-19995)
BRODART CO (PA)
Also Called: McNaughton Book Service
500 Arch St (17701-4471)
PHONE..............................570 326-2461
Joseph Largen, *President*
Franck Chenet, *Vice Pres*
Tim Gage, *Vice Pres*
Gretchen Herman, *Vice Pres*
Randall Mackenzie, *Vice Pres*

◆ **EMP:** 56
SQ FT: 339,000
SALES (est): 431.1MM **Privately Held**
WEB: www.brodart.com
SIC: 5192 5942 2752 2782 Books; book stores; commercial printing, lithographic; library binders, looseleaf; bookbinding & related work; public building & related furniture; school furniture; library furniture

(G-19996)
BUCK-A-LEW TOOLING MACHINING
2401 Reach Rd (17701-4193)
PHONE...............................570 321-0640
Fax: 570 321-0640
EMP: 20
SALES (est): 1.5MM **Privately Held**
SIC: 3599 Mfg Industrial Machinery

(G-19997)
CHARLES KOMAR & SONS INC
801 Foresman St (17701-4187)
PHONE...............................570 326-3741
Richard McKee, *President*
Paul Shreck, *President*
John Hauck, *Branch Mgr*
EMP: 150
SALES (corp-wide): 293.8MM **Privately Held**
SIC: 4225 8721 2341 General warehousing; accounting services, except auditing; women's & children's underwear
PA: Charles Komar & Sons, Inc.
90 Hudson St Fl 9
Jersey City NJ 07302
212 725-1500

(G-19998)
CLAPPER ENTERPRISES INC
Also Called: 21st Century Signs
701 1st St Ste 101 (17701-6146)
PHONE...............................570 368-3327
Ron Clapper, *President*
Dave Hornberger, *Manager*
EMP: 21
SQ FT: 33,000
SALES (est): 3MM **Privately Held**
WEB: www.21stcenturysigns.com
SIC: 3993 Electric signs

(G-19999)
CLARKS EXPERT SALES & SERVICE
1919 Lycoming Creek Rd (17701-1204)
PHONE...............................570 321-8206
Ronald L Clark, *Owner*
EMP: 7
SQ FT: 3,000
SALES (est): 450K **Privately Held**
SIC: 3545 Tools & accessories for machine tools

(G-20000)
CLARKSON CHEMICAL COMPANY INC
213 Main St (17702-7312)
PHONE...............................570 323-3631
Michael I Stuempfle, *President*
EMP: 6
SQ FT: 4,000
SALES: 1.2MM **Privately Held**
WEB: www.ccpcorp.com
SIC: 5087 2842 Janitors' supplies; sanitation preparations

(G-20001)
COUNTRY ACCENTS (PA)
Also Called: Pierce Pen Design Limited
615 Dunwoody Rd (17701-8353)
PHONE...............................570 478-4127
James Pallotas, *President*
EMP: 3
SALES (est): 389.5K **Privately Held**
WEB: www.piercedtin.com
SIC: 3446 3944 Architectural metalwork; craft & hobby kits & sets

(G-20002)
DANZER VENEER AMERICAS INC
240 N Reach Rd (17701-9101)
PHONE...............................570 322-4400
Michael Folmar, *VP Opers*
Timothy Ward, *Buyer*

Jennifer Jutte, *Controller*
Thomas Vester, *Sales Staff*
Zane Brown, *Sales Associate*
EMP: 85
SALES (corp-wide): 297.2MM **Privately Held**
SIC: 2435 Hardwood veneer & plywood
HQ: Danzer Veneer Americas, Inc.
119 A I D Dr
Darlington PA 16115

(G-20003)
DAVID R WEBB COMPANY INC
3100 Reach Rd (17701)
PHONE...............................570 322-7186
Vijay Reddy, *Vice Pres*
EMP: 200
SALES (corp-wide): 58MM **Privately Held**
WEB: www.davidrwebb.com
SIC: 5031 2499 Veneer; decorative wood & woodwork
HQ: David R. Webb Company, Inc.
206 S Holland St
Edinburgh IN 46124
812 526-2601

(G-20004)
DELTA GALIL USA INC
Also Called: Kickaway
1501 W 3rd St (17701-7814)
PHONE...............................570 326-2451
Paula Serafin, *Purch Mgr*
Bill Mull, *Manager*
EMP: 300
SQ FT: 213,000
SALES (corp-wide): 1.3B **Privately Held**
SIC: 2341 2369 Women's & children's undergarments; women's & children's nightwear; girls' & children's outerwear
HQ: Delta Galil Usa Inc.
1 Harmon Plz Fl 5
Secaucus NJ 07094
201 902-0055

(G-20005)
DIAMOND DRINKS INC
600 Railway St Unit 1 (17701-5362)
PHONE...............................570 326-2003
Anthony J Cenimo, *President*
Robert F Pierce, *Corp Secy*
Jessica Gehr, *Plant Mgr*
Robert Pierce, *Treasurer*
EMP: 75
SQ FT: 135,000
SALES: 6.6MM **Privately Held**
SIC: 3085 Plastics bottles

(G-20006)
DISCOVERY MACHINE INC
153 W 4th St Ste 1 (17701-6244)
PHONE...............................570 601-1966
Anna Griffith, *CEO*
Todd W Griffith, *President*
Jared Snyder, *Sr Software Eng*
Molly Bender, *Officer*
Molly Lusk, *Officer*
EMP: 16
SQ FT: 2,400
SALES (est): 2.5MM **Privately Held**
WEB: www.discoverymachine.com
SIC: 3812 Acceleration indicators & systems components, aerospace

(G-20007)
DR DAVIES PRODUCTS INC
Also Called: Tory Leather Co
1318 Commerce Park Dr (17701-5470)
PHONE...............................570 321-5423
Ronald Cimini, *President*
Rosalie Cimini, *Corp Secy*
EMP: 7
SALES (est): 930K **Privately Held**
SIC: 5191 3172 Equestrian equipment; personal leather goods

(G-20008)
E R KINLEY & SONS
131 W 4th St (17701-6110)
PHONE...............................570 323-6740
Gerald R Kinley, *Managing Prtnr*
William E Kinley, *Partner*
EMP: 8
SQ FT: 2,500

SALES (est): 1MM **Privately Held**
SIC: 5719 5063 3911 3915 Glassware; china; watch repair; jewelry repair services; jewelry, precious metal; gems, real & imitation: preparation for settings; jewelry, precious stones & precious metals

(G-20009)
EAGLE ROCK WINERY
414 W 4th St Apt 1 (17701-6150)
PHONE...............................570 567-7715
EMP: 4
SALES (est): 244.9K **Privately Held**
SIC: 2084 Wines

(G-20010)
ECM ENERGY SERVICES INC
130 Court St (17701-6545)
PHONE...............................888 659-2413
EMP: 26
SALES (corp-wide): 34.2MM **Privately Held**
SIC: 3572 Computer storage devices
PA: Ecm Energy Services, Inc.
460 Market St Ste 400
Williamsport PA 17701
888 523-9095

(G-20011)
EQUINOX LTD
1307 Park Ave Unit 14 (17701-4488)
PHONE...............................570 322-5900
Robert Cross, *President*
Nicole De Anda, *Manager*
▲ **EMP:** 25
SQ FT: 40,000
SALES (est): 9.1MM **Privately Held**
WEB: www.equinoxltd.com
SIC: 5091 2393 Camping equipment & supplies; textile bags

(G-20012)
FELCHAR MANUFACTURING CORP
2323 Reach Rd (17701-5579)
P.O. Box 3307 (17701-0307)
PHONE...............................607 723-4076
Jonathan Miller, *Principal*
Richard Pincofski, *VP Finance*
EMP: 2
SALES (est): 6.8MM
SALES (corp-wide): 304.9MM **Privately Held**
SIC: 3999 Mfg Misc Products
PA: Shop Vac Corporation
2323 Reach Rd
Williamsport PA 17701
570 326-0502

(G-20013)
FINK & STACKHOUSE INC (PA)
515 Princeton Avenue Ext (17701-9608)
PHONE...............................570 323-3475
Robert L Stackhouse, *President*
Barbara Wagner, *Admin Sec*
EMP: 5 **EST:** 1952
SALES (est): 898.3K **Privately Held**
SIC: 1459 4213 Clays (common) quarrying; heavy hauling

(G-20014)
FRITO-LAY NORTH AMERICA INC
220 N Reach Rd (17701-9101)
PHONE...............................570 323-6175
William Berg, *Safety Dir*
Ed Gengaro, *Manager*
Howard Stewart, *Maintence Staff*
EMP: 25
SQ FT: 30,000
SALES (corp-wide): 64.6B **Publicly Held**
WEB: www.fritolay.com
SIC: 2096 2099 2035 Potato chips & similar snacks; food preparations; pickles, sauces & salad dressings
HQ: Frito-Lay North America, Inc.
7701 Legacy Dr
Plano TX 75024

(G-20015)
G I ELECTRIC COMPANY
944 Sheridan St Rear (17701-3697)
PHONE...............................570 323-6147
David L Shollenberger, *President*
EMP: 5 **EST:** 1947
SQ FT: 1,720

SALES: 250K **Privately Held**
SIC: 7694 5063 Rebuilding motors, except automotive; rewinding stators; motor controls, starters & relays: electric

(G-20016)
GARLOCK SEALING TECH LLC
Also Called: Garlock Lubri Kup Division
208 Rose St (17701-5717)
P.O. Box 3066 (17701-0066)
PHONE...............................570 323-9409
Mike Wathers, *Branch Mgr*
EMP: 55
SQ FT: 17,000
SALES (corp-wide): 1.5B **Publicly Held**
SIC: 3053 Gaskets & sealing devices
HQ: Garlock Sealing Technologies Llc
1666 Division St
Palmyra NY 14522
315 597-4811

(G-20017)
GENERAL CABLE CORPORATION
409 Reighard Ave (17701-4171)
PHONE...............................570 321-7750
Gregory B Kenny, *President*
Brian Moriarty, *Vice Pres*
Frank Clark, *Engineer*
Ed Vanhorn, *Electrical Engi*
EMP: 250
SALES (corp-wide): 1.3B **Privately Held**
SIC: 3351 3355 3496 3357 Wire, copper & copper alloy; wire, aluminum: made in rolling mills; miscellaneous fabricated wire products; nonferrous wiredrawing & insulating
HQ: General Cable Corporation
4 Tesseneer Dr
Highland Heights KY 41076

(G-20018)
GLAMORISE FOUNDATIONS INC
Also Called: Maidwell-Glamorise
2729 Reach Rd (17701-9114)
PHONE...............................570 322-7806
George Sink, *Manager*
EMP: 230
SQ FT: 20,000
SALES (corp-wide): 35.6MM **Privately Held**
WEB: www.glamorise.com
SIC: 2342 2341 Foundation garments, women's; women's & children's underwear
PA: Glamorise Foundations, Inc.
135 Madison Ave Fl 3
New York NY 10016
212 684-5025

(G-20019)
GP METAL FABRICATION
1827 Liberty Dr (17701-1127)
PHONE...............................570 494-1002
Jeffry Hills, *Owner*
EMP: 7
SALES (est): 808K **Privately Held**
SIC: 3499 Fabricated metal products

(G-20020)
HANSON AGGREGATES PA LLC
3485 W 4th St (17701-4104)
PHONE...............................570 322-6737
Dave Baier, *Manager*
EMP: 15
SALES (corp-wide): 20.6B **Privately Held**
SIC: 2951 Asphalt & asphaltic paving mixtures (not from refineries)
HQ: Hanson Aggregates Pennsylvania, Llc
7660 Imperial Way
Allentown PA 18195
610 366-4626

(G-20021)
HERMANCE MACHINE COMPANY
Also Called: Rockler Woodworking Hardware
178 Campbell St (17701-5829)
PHONE...............................570 326-9156
Joseph Strouse, *Principal*
Claire Strouse, *Vice Pres*
Megan Powell, *Marketing Staff*
▲ **EMP:** 24

▲ = Import ▼ =Export
◆ =Import/Export

SALES (est): 6.4MM **Privately Held**
SIC: 3553 Woodworking machinery

(G-20022)
HIGH STEEL STRUCTURES LLC
3501 W 4th St (17701-4196)
PHONE.....................................570 326-9051
Jamie Gartley, *Plant Mgr*
Larry Beach, *Manager*
EMP: 12
SALES (corp-wide): 434.6MM **Privately Held**
SIC: 3441 Fabricated structural metal
HQ: High Steel Structures Llc
1915 Old Phladelphia Pike
Lancaster PA 17602

(G-20023)
HILSHER GRAPHICS FLP
1626 Riverside Dr (17702-7041)
PHONE.....................................570 326-9159
John Hilsher III, *Partner*
Sally Hilsher, *General Ptnr*
EMP: 18 EST: 1971
SQ FT: 28,000
SALES (est): 2.1MM **Privately Held**
WEB: www.hilsherprinting.com
SIC: 2759 Catalogs: printing; circulars:
printing; embossing on paper; engraving

(G-20024)
INDOOR SKY LLC
2401 Reach Rd (17701-4193)
PHONE.....................................570 220-1903
Paul Moulton, *President*
EMP: 4
SALES (est): 208.6K **Privately Held**
SIC: 2591 Drapery hardware & blinds &
shades

(G-20025)
INFLECTION ENERGY
49 E 4th St (17701-6355)
PHONE.....................................303 531-2343
EMP: 4
SALES (est): 386.5K **Privately Held**
SIC: 1311 Natural gas production

(G-20026)
J K J TOOL CO
2102 Marydale Ave (17701-1422)
P.O. Box 3065 (17701-0065)
PHONE.....................................570 322-1411
Lauren R Siegfried, *President*
Susan Mc Dermott, *Vice Pres*
EMP: 10 EST: 1947
SQ FT: 6,000
SALES: 300K **Privately Held**
SIC: 7699 3544 3545 Tool repair services;
dies & die holders for metal cutting, form-
ing, die casting; machine tool accessories

(G-20027)
JASPER STEEL FABRICATION INC
701 1st St Ste 101 (17701-6146)
PHONE.....................................570 329-3330
Timothy Jasper, *President*
EMP: 8
SQ FT: 10,000
SALES (est): 1.6MM **Privately Held**
WEB: www.jaspersteel.com
SIC: 3449 3441 Bars, concrete reinforc-
ing: fabricated steel; fabricated structural
metal for bridges

(G-20028)
JCM AUDIO INC
Also Called: Stereo Shoppe
900 Washington Blvd (17701-3632)
PHONE.....................................570 323-9014
Joseph C Myers, *President*
EMP: 7
SQ FT: 2,500
SALES (est): 1.2MM **Privately Held**
WEB: www.jcmaudio.com
SIC: 3651 7539 Household audio & video
equipment; automotive sound system
service & installation

(G-20029)
JEFF HILLS
Also Called: Guards Plus
1827 Liberty Dr (17701-1127)
PHONE.....................................570 322-4536
Jeff Hills, *Owner*

EMP: 5
SALES (est): 488.2K **Privately Held**
WEB: www.jeffhills.com
SIC: 3441 Fabricated structural metal

(G-20030)
JW ALUMINUM COMPANY
2475 Trenton Ave (17701-7904)
PHONE.....................................570 323-4430
Karen Howes, *Controller*
Jesse B Hackenberg, *Branch Mgr*
Martin Wingert, *Manager*
EMP: 126
SALES (corp-wide): 6.8B **Publicly Held**
SIC: 3353 3497 Coils, sheet aluminum;
metal foil & leaf
HQ: Jw Aluminum Company
435 Old Mount Holly Rd
Goose Creek SC 29445
843 572-1100

(G-20031)
KEYSTONE LEATHER DISTRS LLC
2100 Reach Rd Frnt (17701-8784)
P.O. Box 1 (17703-0001)
PHONE.....................................570 329-3780
Dave Murdock, *Co-Owner*
Dave Schall, *Co-Owner*
▲ EMP: 14
SQ FT: 12,000
SALES (est): 4.6MM **Privately Held**
SIC: 3131 Footwear cut stock

(G-20032)
KNITTLE & FREY AG-CENTER INC
2101 Sweeley Ave (17701-1138)
PHONE.....................................570 323-7554
Ronald R Wenning, *President*
Kristen A Wenning, *Corp Secy*
Ed Paulhamus,
EMP: 7
SQ FT: 12,000
SALES (est): 948.4K **Privately Held**
WEB: www.knittleandfrey.com
SIC: 5261 5999 2731 Fertilizer; feed &
farm supply; book publishing

(G-20033)
L3 ELECTRON DEVICES INC
Electron Devices Division
1035 Westminster Dr (17701-3911)
PHONE.....................................570 326-3561
Clayton McClain, *CEO*
Steve Shpock, *Engineer*
EMP: 150
SALES (corp-wide): 10.2B **Publicly Held**
SIC: 3663 3679 Radio broadcasting &
communications equipment; electronic
circuits
HQ: L3 Electron Devices, Inc.
3100 Lomita Blvd
Torrance CA 90505
310 517-6000

(G-20034)
LABELS BY PULIZZI INC
3325 Wahoo Dr (17701-9243)
PHONE.....................................570 326-1244
Charline M Pulizzi, *President*
Joseph V Pulizzi Jr, *Vice Pres*
Jamie Welshans, *Marketing Staff*
EMP: 50
SQ FT: 20,000
SALES (est): 10.4MM **Privately Held**
SIC: 2672 2752 2791 2789 Tape, pres-
sure sensitive: made from purchased ma-
terials; commercial printing, offset;
typesetting; bookbinding & related work;
commercial printing

(G-20035)
LONZA INC
3500 Trenton Ave (17701-7924)
PHONE.....................................570 321-3900
Pete Schug, *Mfg Staff*
Amanda Durland, *Production*
Josh Mensinger, *Engineer*
Ronald V De Feo, *Branch Mgr*
Matt Rebeck, *Manager*
EMP: 180

SALES (corp-wide): 5.1B **Privately Held**
WEB: www.riversidecap.com
SIC: 2843 2899 2819 Surface active
agents; chemical preparations; industrial
inorganic chemicals
HQ: Lonza Inc.
90 Boroline Rd Ste 1
Allendale NJ 07960
201 316-9200

(G-20036)
LOVELL STROUBLE INC
312 South St (17701-6044)
PHONE.....................................570 326-5561
Robert E Wenner, *President*
EMP: 7
SQ FT: 2,500
SALES: 500K **Privately Held**
SIC: 3599 Machine shop, jobbing & repair

(G-20037)
LUNDY WAREHOUSING INC
Also Called: LTI
25 W 3rd St Ste 504 (17701-6529)
PHONE.....................................570 327-4541
Don M Lundy, *President*
EMP: 3
SALES (est): 407.7K **Privately Held**
SIC: 3822 Air conditioning & refrigeration
controls

(G-20038)
LYCOMING SCREEN PRINTING CO
1 Maynard St (17701-5870)
PHONE.....................................570 326-3301
Howard E Morehart, *President*
EMP: 7 EST: 1946
SQ FT: 20,000
SALES (est): 578.8K **Privately Held**
SIC: 3555 2759 5085 Galleys or chases,
printers'; screen printing; industrial sup-
plies

(G-20039)
M & M SHEET METAL INC
Also Called: M & M Shtmtl & Fabricators
2104 Marydale Ave (17701-1479)
PHONE.....................................570 326-4655
Donald L Messner, *President*
EMP: 18 EST: 1979
SQ FT: 10,000
SALES: 2.2MM **Privately Held**
WEB: www.mandmsheetmetal.net
SIC: 3444 3564 Sheet metal specialties,
not stamped; dust or fume collecting
equipment, industrial

(G-20040)
MARC WILLIAMS GOLDSMITH INC (PA)
430 William St (17701-6109)
PHONE.....................................570 322-4248
Marc Williams, *President*
EMP: 8
SQ FT: 4,000
SALES: 900K **Privately Held**
SIC: 3911 5944 7631 Jewelry, precious
metal; jewelry, precious stones & precious
metals; jewelry repair services

(G-20041)
MICHAEL ANTHONY SALVATORI
Also Called: M A S Printing & Storage
116 Emery St (17701-5531)
PHONE.....................................570 326-9222
Michael Anthony Salvatori, *Owner*
EMP: 4
SQ FT: 2,000
SALES (est): 370.2K **Privately Held**
SIC: 2752 Commercial printing, offset; let-
ters, circular or form: lithographed

(G-20042)
MOONLIGHT GRAPHICS STUDIO
2310 Lycoming Creek Rd (17701-1157)
PHONE.....................................570 322-6570
Robert Williams, *Owner*
EMP: 7
SALES (est): 791K **Privately Held**
SIC: 2759 Screen printing

(G-20043)
MOUNTAIN TOP DISTILLERY
150 Bennardi Dev Rd (17702)
PHONE.....................................570 745-2227
Zimmerman Shawn, *Principal*
EMP: 7 EST: 2013
SALES (est): 488.9K **Privately Held**
SIC: 2084 Wines, brandy & brandy spirits

(G-20044)
MOUNTAINSIDE LOG HOMES
105 Mountainstone Ln (17702-8095)
PHONE.....................................570 745-2388
Ross Mahosky, *Principal*
EMP: 8
SALES (est): 1.2MM **Privately Held**
SIC: 2452 Log cabins, prefabricated, wood

(G-20045)
NEW BERN PBG PEPSI
1320 Dewey Ave (17701-1562)
PHONE.....................................570 320-3324
EMP: 4
SALES (est): 231.2K **Privately Held**
SIC: 2086 Soft drinks: packaged in cans,
bottles, etc.

(G-20046)
NEW LYCOMING BAKERY INC
220 Curtin St (17702-7247)
PHONE.....................................570 326-9426
Richard Callahan, *President*
EMP: 25
SQ FT: 10,800
SALES (est): 855.2K **Privately Held**
SIC: 5461 2051 Bread; bread, cake & re-
lated products

(G-20047)
NEWPARK MATS INTGRTED SVCS LLC
573 E 3rd St (17701-5316)
PHONE.....................................570 323-4970
Eric Haft, *Branch Mgr*
EMP: 10
SALES (corp-wide): 946.5MM **Publicly Held**
SIC: 1389 Construction, repair & disman-
tling services
HQ: Newpark Mats & Integrated Services
Llc
9320 Lkeside Blvd Ste 100
The Woodlands TX 77381
281 362-6800

(G-20048)
NIPPON PANEL INC
Also Called: American Beauty Panels
124 Reynolds St (17702-7160)
PHONE.....................................570 326-4258
Mervin Minnich, *President*
EMP: 3 EST: 1941
SALES: 100K **Privately Held**
SIC: 3999 Plaques, picture, laminated

(G-20049)
NORTECH ENERGY SOLUTIONS LLC
75 Palmer Industrial Rd (17701-8782)
PHONE.....................................570 323-3060
Lynda Livingston,
Chad Livingston,
EMP: 7
SALES: 545.1K **Privately Held**
SIC: 1389 Gas field services

(G-20050)
NORTH CENTRAL SIGHT SVCS INC
2121 Reach Rd (17701-5575)
P.O. Box 3292 (17701-0292)
PHONE.....................................570 323-9401
Robert Garrett, *President*
Laura Chilian, *Business Mgr*
Jamie Snyder, *Vice Pres*
Justin Waycaster CPA, *Accounting Mgr*
Cory Lehman, *Sales Staff*
EMP: 63
SQ FT: 36,000
SALES: 8.6MM **Privately Held**
WEB: www.ncsight.org
SIC: 8331 3572 Vocational rehabilitation
agency; computer storage devices

(G-20051)
NUWELD INC
2600 Reach Rd (17701-4119)
P.O. Box 3482 (17701-0482)
PHONE.....................................570 505-1500
Timothy Satterfield, *President*
Marilyn J Satterfield, *Treasurer*
EMP: 217 **EST:** 1997
SQ FT: 211,000
SALES (est): 27.1MM **Privately Held**
WEB: www.nu-weld.com
SIC: 7692 3441 Welding repair; fabricated
structural metal

(G-20052)
OPTICSCAMPCOM
422 Louisa St (17701-3223)
PHONE.....................................888 978-5330
EMP: 3
SALES (est): 222.3K **Privately Held**
SIC: 3827 Optical instruments & lenses

(G-20053)
**OVERHEAD DOOR
CORPORATION**
3200 Reach Rd (17701-4154)
P.O. Box 3555 (17701-0555)
PHONE.....................................570 326-7325
Thomas Rodden, *Branch Mgr*
EMP: 150
SALES (corp-wide): 3.6B **Privately Held**
WEB: www.overheaddoor.com
SIC: 2431 3442 Doors, wood; garage
doors, overhead: metal
HQ: Overhead Door Corporation
2501 S State Hwy 121 Ste
Lewisville TX 75067
469 549-7100

(G-20054)
PENN RECYCLING INC
2525 Trenton Ave (17701-7906)
P.O. Box 3514 (17701-0514)
PHONE.....................................570 326-9041
David Simon, *President*
Loy Johnson, *Vice Pres*
George McGarvey, *Buyer*
Kenneth Simon, *Treasurer*
Larry Simon, *Admin Sec*
EMP: 45
SQ FT: 8,000
SALES (est): 9.9MM **Privately Held**
WEB: www.pennrecycling.com
SIC: 4953 5093 3341 Recycling, waste
materials; metal scrap & waste materials;
secondary nonferrous metals

(G-20055)
**PENNRAM DIVERSIFIED MFG
CORP**
Also Called: Pennram Diversified Mfg
1315 W 3rd St (17701-7816)
P.O. Box 695 (17703-0695)
PHONE.....................................570 327-2802
Andrew C Hooker, *President*
Astra Reaser, *Office Mgr*
Karen Hooker, *Bd of Directors*
▼ **EMP:** 26
SQ FT: 32,000
SALES (est): 8.5MM **Privately Held**
WEB: www.pennram.com
SIC: 3567 3535 Incinerators, metal: do-
mestic or commercial; conveyors & con-
veying equipment

(G-20056)
**PEPSI-COLA METRO BTLG CO
INC**
1450 Dewey Ave (17701-1503)
P.O. Box 3157 (17701-0157)
PHONE.....................................570 326-9086
Jim Swope, *General Mgr*
Elaine Jessell, *Supervisor*
EMP: 100
SALES (corp-wide): 64.6B **Publicly Held**
WEB: www.joy-of-cola.com
SIC: 2086 Carbonated soft drinks, bottled
& canned
HQ: Pepsi-Cola Metropolitan Bottling Com-
pany, Inc.
1111 Westchester Ave
White Plains NY 10604
914 767-6000

(G-20057)
PHOENIX TRIM WORKS INC
2211 Reach Rd (17701-5577)
PHONE.....................................570 320-0322
Sean Gibbons, *Ch of Bd*
Joe Leavens, *President*
Frank Degray, *Shareholder*
Lisa Walsh Gibbons, *Shareholder*
EMP: 45 **EST:** 2000
SQ FT: 78,000
SALES (est): 6.6MM **Privately Held**
SIC: 2211 Decorative trim & specialty fab-
rics, including twist weave

(G-20058)
**PLASTIC DEVELOPMENT
COMPANY PA**
Also Called: PDC Spas
75 Palmer Industrial Rd (17701-8782)
P.O. Box 4007 (17701-0607)
PHONE.....................................800 451-1420
David Livingston Jr, *President*
Lynda M Livingston, *Vice Pres*
▼ **EMP:** 50
SQ FT: 45,000
SALES (est): 6.7MM **Privately Held**
WEB: www.pdcspas.com
SIC: 3999 3949 3088 Hot tubs; sporting &
athletic goods; plastics plumbing fixtures

(G-20059)
PMF INDUSTRIES INC
2601 Reach Rd (17701-4181)
P.O. Box 3186 (17701-0186)
PHONE.....................................570 323-9944
John Perrotto, *President*
Ann M Alsted, *Corp Secy*
Kenneth F Healy, *Vice Pres*
▲ **EMP:** 60 **EST:** 1961
SQ FT: 70,000
SALES (est): 20.7MM **Privately Held**
WEB: www.pmfind.com
SIC: 3444 Sheet metalwork

(G-20060)
PMT MACHINING INC
200 Fleming St (17702-7451)
PHONE.....................................570 329-0349
Thomas Lorson, *President*
EMP: 8
SQ FT: 7,200
SALES (est): 1MM **Privately Held**
SIC: 3599 Machine shop, jobbing & repair

(G-20061)
PNEU-DART INC
15223 State Route 87 (17701-9532)
PHONE.....................................570 323-2710
Blair D Soars, *President*
Abby Johnson, *Partner*
Melissa Klementovich, *Purchasing*
Kelly Lightbourn, *Human Res Dir*
Donna Emick, *Manager*
▼ **EMP:** 65
SQ FT: 17,000
SALES (est): 4.7MM **Privately Held**
SIC: 3841 3484 Veterinarians' instruments
& apparatus; small arms

(G-20062)
**PRECISION DRILLING OILFLD
SVCS**
2640 Reach Rd (17701-4119)
PHONE.....................................570 329-5100
Rick Weiskerger, *Principal*
EMP: 3
SALES (est): 459.6K **Privately Held**
SIC: 1381 Drilling oil & gas wells

(G-20063)
**PRIMUS TECHNOLOGIES CORP
(PA)**
2333 Reach Rd (17701-5579)
PHONE.....................................570 326-6591
Christopher Sullivan, *CEO*
Stephen Stone, *President*
Jeremiah W Sullivan, *Chairman*
Mike Brennan, *Buyer*
Katie Myers, *Buyer*
▲ **EMP:** 467
SQ FT: 160,000
SALES (est): 123.9MM **Privately Held**
WEB: www.primus-tech.com
SIC: 3672 Printed circuit boards

(G-20064)
PRINT SHOP
421 Washington Blvd Frnt (17701-5260)
PHONE.....................................570 327-9005
Michael Foster, *President*
Patrcia Foster, *Vice Pres*
EMP: 6
SALES (est): 490K **Privately Held**
SIC: 2752 Commercial printing, offset

(G-20065)
PRINTING MAS
116 Emery St (17701-5531)
PHONE.....................................570 326-9222
Michael Salvatori, *Principal*
EMP: 3
SALES (est): 243.5K **Privately Held**
SIC: 2752 Commercial printing, litho-
graphic

(G-20066)
QORTEK INC (PA)
1965 Lycoming Creek Rd # 205
(17701-1251)
PHONE.....................................570 322-2700
Gareth Knowles, *President*
Gregory Bower, *CTO*
EMP: 3
SQ FT: 4,000
SALES (est): 3.7MM **Privately Held**
WEB: www.qortek.com
SIC: 8711 3699 Electrical or electronic en-
gineering; electrical equipment & supplies

(G-20067)
**RADIANT STEEL PRODUCTS
COMPANY**
205 Locust St (17701-6017)
PHONE.....................................570 322-7828
Andree P Phillips, *President*
Richard L Fenstamaker, *General Mgr*
Richard Fenstamaker, *Vice Pres*
EMP: 15 **EST:** 1927
SQ FT: 44,000
SALES (est): 3.9MM **Privately Held**
WEB: www.radiantsteel.com
SIC: 3444 Sheet metal specialties, not
stamped

(G-20068)
REYNOLDS IRON WORKS INC
157 Palmer Industrial Rd (17701-8518)
PHONE.....................................570 323-4663
John Reynolds, *President*
Joseph H Reynolds, *Corp Secy*
James Reynolds, *Vice Pres*
EMP: 15
SQ FT: 28,840
SALES (est): 5MM **Privately Held**
WEB: www.reynoldsironworks.com
SIC: 3441 3446 Fabricated structural
metal; architectural metalwork

(G-20069)
ROBO CONSTRUCTION LLC
2700 Lycoming Creek Rd (17701-1025)
PHONE.....................................570 494-1028
Timothy Satterfield, *President*
EMP: 50
SALES (est): 1.3MM **Privately Held**
SIC: 1541 3441 Steel building con-
struction; factory construction; industrial
buildings, new construction; stadium con-
struction; fabricated structural metal for
bridges

(G-20070)
SCHNOCH CORPORATION
Also Called: Bullfrog Brewery
229 W 4th St 231 (17701-6112)
PHONE.....................................570 326-4700
Steven Koch, *President*
Bob Koch, *Purch Dir*
Harriet Koch, *Treasurer*
Barbara Whipple, *Admin Sec*
EMP: 30
SQ FT: 3,240
SALES (est): 1.1MM **Privately Held**
SIC: 5813 5812 2082 Bar (drinking
places); eating places; malt beverages

(G-20071)
SELECTRIM CORPORATION
Also Called: James Wood Company
140 Catawissa Ave (17701-4114)
P.O. Box 3547 (17701-0547)
PHONE.....................................570 326-3662
James Wood, *President*
Marc Annicelli, *Vice Pres*
EMP: 27
SQ FT: 22,000
SALES (est): 2.2MM **Privately Held**
WEB: www.selectrim.com
SIC: 2431 2511 Millwork; wood household
furniture

(G-20072)
SHOP VAC CORPORATION
Canton Manufacturing Division
2323 Reach Rd (17701-5579)
P.O. Box 97, Canton (17724-0097)
PHONE.....................................570 673-5145
Michael Dechamps, *Vice Pres*
Larry Tempesco, *VP Sales*
EMP: 300
SALES (corp-wide): 304.9MM **Privately
Held**
WEB: www.shopvac.com
SIC: 3089 Injection molded finished plastic
products; injection molding of plastics
PA: Shop Vac Corporation
2323 Reach Rd
Williamsport PA 17701
570 326-0502

(G-20073)
**SOVEREIGN MEDIA COMPANY
INC**
Also Called: Publishers Survey Associate
2406 Reach Rd (17701-4183)
PHONE.....................................570 322-7848
Mark Hintz, *Manager*
EMP: 20
SQ FT: 1,000 **Privately Held**
SIC: 2721 Magazines: publishing only, not
printed on site
PA: Sovereign Media Company, Inc
441 Carlisle Dr Ste C
Herndon VA

(G-20074)
**STAIMAN RECYCLING
CORPORATION (PA)**
201 Hepburn St (17701-6501)
P.O. Box 1235 (17703-1235)
PHONE.....................................717 646-0951
Richard P Staiman, *President*
Rick Palger, *CFO*
EMP: 52
SQ FT: 5,000
SALES (est): 61.1MM **Privately Held**
WEB: www.staimanrecycling.com
SIC: 5093 3341 2611 Ferrous metal scrap
& waste; secondary nonferrous metals;
pulp mills

(G-20075)
**STOPPER CONSTRUCTION CO
INC**
339 Washington Blvd (17701-5129)
P.O. Box 389, Montoursville (17754-0389)
PHONE.....................................570 322-5947
Benjamin Stopper Jr, *President*
EMP: 50
SQ FT: 25,000
SALES (est): 4.1MM **Privately Held**
SIC: 1611 2951 Highway & street paving
contractor; asphalt & asphaltic paving
mixtures (not from refineries)

(G-20076)
SUN-GAZETTE COMPANY
Also Called: Williamsport Sun-Gazette
252 W 4th St (17701-6133)
P.O. Box 728 (17703-0728)
PHONE.....................................570 326-1551
George Ogden Nutting, *President*
Tim Williams, *President*
L Janssen, *Editor*
Robert M Nutting, *Vice Pres*
William C Nutting, *Vice Pres*
EMP: 170 **EST:** 1870
SQ FT: 60,000

▲ = Import ▼=Export
◆ =Import/Export

SALES (est): 9MM **Privately Held**
WEB: www.sungazette.com
SIC: 2711 Commercial printing & newspaper publishing combined; newspapers, publishing & printing
HQ: The Ogden Newspapers Inc
1500 Main St
Wheeling WV 26003
304 233-0100

(G-20077)
SUNSET ICE CREAM
1849 Lycoming Creek Rd (17701-1523)
PHONE............................570 326-3902
John Fritz, *Owner*
EMP: 25
SALES (est): 150.9K **Privately Held**
SIC: 2024 5812 Ice cream, bulk; ice cream stands or dairy bars

(G-20078)
SUSCON INC
600 Railway St Unit 2 (17701-5363)
PHONE............................570 326-2003
Anthony Cenimo Jr, *President*
Robert Pierce, *Treasurer*
EMP: 85
SQ FT: 131,000
SALES: 4MM **Privately Held**
SIC: 3085 Plastics bottles

(G-20079)
SUSQUEHANNA GAMES & BINGO SUPS
Also Called: Susquehanna Sales
25 W 2nd Ave Ste 5 (17702-7381)
PHONE............................570 322-9941
Donald Gorasi, *Owner*
EMP: 3
SALES (est): 200K **Privately Held**
SIC: 3944 Games, toys & children's vehicles

(G-20080)
TECH GROUP NORTH AMERICA INC
2921 Reach Rd (17701-4177)
P.O. Box 7777 (17701-0977)
PHONE............................570 326-7673
David Lancer, *Manager*
EMP: 150
SQ FT: 80,750
SALES (corp-wide): 1.7B **Publicly Held**
SIC: 3089 Injection molding of plastics
HQ: Tech Group North America, Inc.
14677 N 74th St
Scottsdale AZ 85260
480 281-4500

(G-20081)
TEXTRON INC
Also Called: Textron Lycoming
652 Oliver St (17701-4410)
PHONE............................570 323-6181
Donald Wagner, *General Mgr*
Noel Nightingale, *Vice Pres*
EMP: 60
SALES (corp-wide): 13.9B **Publicly Held**
SIC: 3721 Aircraft
PA: Textron Inc.
40 Westminster St
Providence RI 02903
401 421-2800

(G-20082)
THE KEYSTONE FRICTION HINGE CO (PA)
520 Matthews Blvd (17702-7243)
P.O. Box 5087 (17702-0887)
PHONE............................570 321-0693
Edward J Hannan, *President*
Creighton Mac Gill, *Treasurer*
Thomas Humphris, *Shareholder*
Constance Taggart, *Shareholder*
Shirley Mac Gill, *Admin Sec*
▲ **EMP:** 110
SQ FT: 80,000
SALES (est): 25.3MM **Privately Held**
SIC: 3469 3429 Stamping metal for the trade; furniture hardware

(G-20083)
TIN CUP INC
972 2nd St (17701-5806)
PHONE............................570 322-1115

Brent Wilson, *Principal*
EMP: 4
SALES (est): 406.1K **Privately Held**
SIC: 3356 Tin

(G-20084)
TQ ELECTRONICS INC
1965 Lycoming Creek Rd # 205 (17701-1251)
PHONE............................570 320-1760
Jonathan Zook, *President*
EMP: 7
SQ FT: 25,000
SALES (est): 750.4K
SALES (corp-wide): 3.7MM **Privately Held**
SIC: 3679 Electronic circuits
PA: Qortek, Inc.
1965 Lycoming Creek Rd # 205
Williamsport PA 17701
570 322-2700

(G-20085)
TRANSCO RAILWAY PRODUCTS INC
2483 Trenron Ave (17701)
P.O. Box 4031 (17701-0631)
PHONE............................570 322-3411
Greg T Lucas, *Branch Mgr*
EMP: 36
SQ FT: 25,200
SALES (corp-wide): 96.7MM **Privately Held**
SIC: 7699 3743 Railroad car customizing; railroad equipment
HQ: Transco Railway Products Inc.
200 N La Salle St # 1550
Chicago IL 60601
312 427-2818

(G-20086)
UNIVERSAL WELL SERVICES INC
250 Arch St (17701-7810)
PHONE............................570 321-5302
John W Lundy, *Branch Mgr*
EMP: 10
SALES (corp-wide): 3.3B **Publicly Held**
SIC: 1382 Oil & gas exploration services
HQ: Universal Well Services, Inc.
13549 S Mosiertown Rd
Meadville PA 16335
814 337-1983

(G-20087)
UPSTATE NIAGARA COOP INC
Also Called: Valley Farm LLC
1860 E 3rd St (17701-3923)
PHONE............................570 326-2021
Larry Webster, *CEO*
EMP: 80
SALES (corp-wide): 893.9MM **Privately Held**
SIC: 2026 Fermented & cultured milk products
PA: Upstate Niagara Cooperative, Inc.
25 Anderson Rd
Buffalo NY 14225
716 892-3156

(G-20088)
VIVID PUBLISHING INC
924 Funston Ave Apt 1 (17701-4358)
P.O. Box 3174 (17701-0174)
PHONE............................570 567-7808
Larry Seaman, *President*
Linda Daugherty, *Vice Pres*
EMP: 5
SQ FT: 5,000
SALES: 500K **Privately Held**
WEB: www.streammaps.com
SIC: 2741 Miscellaneous publishing

(G-20089)
WEBB COMMUNICATIONS INC (PA)
Also Called: Bayard Printing Group
1 Maynard St (17701-5870)
PHONE............................570 326-7634
Mark P Lundberg, *President*
Nigel Emms, *Prdtn Mgr*
John Winder, *Safety Mgr*
Dave Lundberg, *CFO*
David Lundberg, *CFO*
EMP: 85

SQ FT: 58,000
SALES (est): 30.1MM **Privately Held**
WEB: www.printersandmailers.com
SIC: 2711 2752 7331 Newspapers; commercial printing, lithographic; direct mail advertising services

(G-20090)
WEBB WEEKLY
280 Kane St Ste 2 (17702-7166)
PHONE............................570 326-9322
James Webb, *Owner*
Steph Nordstrom, *Editor*
Ron Mingle, *Accounts Exec*
EMP: 10
SALES (est): 564.3K **Privately Held**
SIC: 2711 Newspapers: publishing only, not printed on site

(G-20091)
WHEELAND INC
Also Called: Home Service Beverage
419 5th Ave (17701-4720)
PHONE............................570 323-3237
Jessica Wheeland, *President*
EMP: 12
SQ FT: 7,200
SALES: 1.5MM **Privately Held**
WEB: www.wheeland.com
SIC: 5921 2097 5499 Beer (packaged); manufactured ice; soft drinks; water: distilled mineral or spring

(G-20092)
WILLAMSPORT DIES & CUTS INC
5 Hoover Rd (17701-9612)
PHONE............................570 323-8351
Robert J Hacker, *President*
EMP: 3
SQ FT: 4,000
SALES: 150K **Privately Held**
SIC: 3544 Dies, steel rule

(G-20093)
WILLIAMSPORT FOUNDRY CO INC
164 Maynard St (17701-5899)
PHONE............................570 323-6216
Walter W Doebler, *President*
Frank L Doebler, *Corp Secy*
Wilson K Doebler Sr, *Vice Pres*
EMP: 25
SQ FT: 20,000
SALES: 1MM **Privately Held**
SIC: 3321 3366 3365 Gray iron castings; brass foundry; aluminum & aluminum-based alloy castings

(G-20094)
WILLIAMSPORT ORTHOPEDIC
613 E 3rd St Ste 1 (17701-5374)
PHONE............................570 322-5277
Robert Pulizzi, *President*
Benjamin L Pulizzi, *Treasurer*
EMP: 5 EST: 1922
SQ FT: 4,800
SALES (est): 420K **Privately Held**
SIC: 3842 Orthopedic appliances; prosthetic appliances; surgical appliances & supplies; braces, orthopedic

(G-20095)
WILLIAMSPORT STEEL CONT CORP
360 Arch St (17701-7811)
PHONE............................570 323-9473
Mike Foglia, *President*
Anthony Foglia, *President*
Michael Foglia, *Treasurer*
▼ **EMP:** 35
SQ FT: 42,000
SALES (est): 6.4MM **Privately Held**
SIC: 3412 Metal barrels, drums & pails

(G-20096)
WIREROPE WORKS INC
100 Maynard St (17701-5809)
PHONE............................570 327-4229
Thomas M Saltsgiver, *President*
Virgil R Probasco, *Vice Pres*
Lamar M Richards, *Vice Pres*
Lamar J Richards, *Vice Pres*
Steve Maurer, *Maint Spvr*
◆ **EMP:** 412

SQ FT: 650,000
SALES (est): 135.1MM **Privately Held**
WEB: www.wwrope.com
SIC: 3496 2298 3315 Miscellaneous fabricated wire products; wire rope centers; wire, steel: insulated or armored

(G-20097)
WOLYNIEC CONSTRUCTION INC
Also Called: J & F Ready Mix
294 Freedom Rd (17701-8803)
P.O. Box 666 (17703-0666)
PHONE............................570 322-8634
James T Wolyniec Sr, *President*
Jack Hauser, *Superintendent*
James T Wolyniec Jr, *Treasurer*
Cynthia Mussina, *Manager*
EMP: 30 EST: 1961
SQ FT: 2,000
SALES (est): 5.9MM **Privately Held**
WEB: www.wolyniec.com
SIC: 1622 1623 3273 1771 Bridge construction; highway construction, elevated; sewer line construction; water main construction; ready-mixed concrete; concrete work

(G-20098)
WOODCRAFT INDUSTRIES
Also Called: Ego Construction
647 E 3rd St (17701-5318)
PHONE............................570 323-4458
Marvin Hurwitz, *Owner*
EMP: 8
SQ FT: 3,000
SALES (est): 456.9K **Privately Held**
SIC: 2434 Wood kitchen cabinets

(G-20099)
WOOL CONCRETE BLOCK
525 Poplar St (17701-5580)
PHONE............................570 322-1943
Fred Wool, *Partner*
Alfred E Wool, *Partner*
Samuel M Wool, *Partner*
EMP: 8 EST: 1946
SQ FT: 9,000
SALES (est): 940K **Privately Held**
SIC: 3271 Blocks, concrete or cinder: standard

(G-20100)
WORKCENTER
1100 Grampian Blvd (17701-1909)
PHONE............................570 320-7444
Kirby Smith, *President*
EMP: 35
SALES (est): 3MM **Privately Held**
SIC: 2834 Medicines, capsuled or ampuled

(G-20101)
WORTHINGTON TRAILERS LP
333 Rose St (17701-6095)
PHONE............................570 567-7921
Steve Mattie, *Managing Prtnr*
George Hutchinson, *Partner*
Daniel Mathers, *Partner*
Raymond Mattie, *Partner*
Chuck Williams, *General Mgr*
EMP: 10 EST: 2013
SALES (est): 2.5MM **Privately Held**
SIC: 5599 3715 3799 Utility trailers; truck trailers; semitrailers for truck tractors; trailers & trailer equipment; automobile trailer chassis

(G-20102)
WUNDIES
1501 W 3rd St (17701-7832)
PHONE............................570 322-7245
Steve Lockoff, *Principal*
EMP: 5
SALES (est): 590.3K **Privately Held**
SIC: 5137 5136 2341 2322 Underwear: women's, children's & infants'; underwear, men's & boys'; women's & children's underwear; men's & boys' underwear & nightwear

Williamstown
Dauphin County

(G-20103)
ROAD READY LLC
469 E Market St (17098-1541)
PHONE..................................717 647-7902
Gene Troutman, *Mng Member*
EMP: 3
SALES: 46K **Privately Held**
SIC: 3751 7389 Motorcycle accessories;

(G-20104)
ZEMCO TOOL & DIE INC
113 S West St (17098-1561)
PHONE..................................717 647-7151
John Zemaitis, *Principal*
Gary Scheib, *QC Mgr*
Karl Sierer, *Marketing Staff*
Tom Dunlop, *Manager*
James Zemaitis, *Manager*
EMP: 80
SALES (est): 12.5MM **Privately Held**
WEB: www.zemco.net
SIC: 3089 3599 3577 3544 Injection
molding of plastics; machine shop, job-
bing & repair; computer peripheral equip-
ment; special dies, tools, jigs & fixtures

Willow Grove
Montgomery County

(G-20105)
ACRO LABELS INC
2530 Wyandotte Rd (19090-1290)
P.O. Box 444, Abington (19001-0444)
PHONE..................................215 657-5366
Robert E Regan, *President*
EMP: 50 EST: 1976
SQ FT: 15,000
SALES (est): 10.8MM **Privately Held**
WEB: www.acrolabels.com
SIC: 2672 2759 2671 Labels (unprinted),
gummed: made from purchased materi-
als; commercial printing; packaging paper
& plastics film, coated & laminated

(G-20106)
ALBERT C PHY & SONS INC
2290 Wyandotte Rd (19090-1204)
PHONE..................................215 659-2125
Edward A Phy, *President*
Donald Phy, *Vice Pres*
EMP: 10 EST: 1952
SQ FT: 15,000
SALES (est): 1.3MM **Privately Held**
SIC: 3444 Sheet metal specialties, not
stamped

(G-20107)
ANNUITY VAULT
616 Easton Rd (19090-2513)
P.O. Box 499 (19090-0499)
PHONE..................................215 830-8666
Sal Di Nardo, *Principal*
EMP: 4 EST: 2010
SALES (est): 321.3K **Privately Held**
SIC: 3272 Burial vaults, concrete or pre-
cast terrazzo

(G-20108)
ARROW SUPPLY COMPANY INC
2517 Wyandotte Rd (19090-1219)
PHONE..................................773 863-8655
Bernard Rojas, *Principal*
EMP: 3
SALES (est): 140.4K **Privately Held**
SIC: 2099 Food preparations

(G-20109)
B P S COMMUNICATIONS INC
801 Easton Rd Ste 2 (19090-2024)
P.O. Box 340 (19090-0340)
PHONE..................................215 830-8467
Carol Memberg, *President*
Laslia Schaeffer, *Vice Pres*
Leslie Schaeffer, *Sales Staff*
EMP: 10 EST: 1956
SQ FT: 3,600

SALES (est): 870K **Privately Held**
SIC: 2752 2721 Commercial printing, offset; periodicals: publishing only

(G-20110)
CARRIER CLASS GREEN INFRAS
601 Davisville Rd Ste 210 (19090-1528)
PHONE..................................267 419-8496
James Innes,
EMP: 6
SALES (est): 721.1K **Privately Held**
SIC: 2531 Picnic tables or benches, park

(G-20111)
CENPREPAVANDCON
1926 Fleming Ave (19090-3019)
PHONE..................................215 778-6103
George Ceniviva, *Owner*
EMP: 8
SALES (est): 750.9K **Privately Held**
SIC: 3271 Paving blocks, concrete

(G-20112)
COACH INC
2500 W Mrland Rd Ste 2065 (19090)
PHONE..................................215 659-6158
EMP: 13
SALES (corp-wide): 4.1B **Publicly Held**
SIC: 3171 Mfg Women's Handbags/Purses
PA: Coach, Inc.
516 W 34th St Bsmt 5
New York NY 10001
212 594-1850

(G-20113)
DAILEY MANUFACTURING CO (PA)
700 Davisville Rd (19090-1516)
PHONE..................................215 659-0477
George Dailey Sr, *President*
George Dailey Jr, *Corp Secy*
EMP: 15 EST: 1959
SQ FT: 22,000
SALES (est): 1.8MM **Privately Held**
SIC: 3442 5031 5211 Storm doors or win-
dows, metal; doors; windows; doors,
storm: wood or metal; windows, storm:
wood or metal

(G-20114)
DECILOG INC
2500 Maryland Rd Ste 302 (19090-1224)
PHONE..................................215 657-0817
Robert Pusicz, *Manager*
EMP: 4
SALES (corp-wide): 10.1MM **Privately Held**
WEB: www.decilog.com
SIC: 8111 7372 Administrative & govern-
ment law; prepackaged software
PA: Decilog, Inc
555 Broadhollow Rd # 425
Melville NY 11747
631 694-4610

(G-20115)
EF PRECISION INC
2301 Computer Rd Ste A (19090-1779)
PHONE..................................215 784-0861
Ernest Farabella, *President*
Stuart Kellerman, *President*
Bud Tyler, *Exec VP*
Bill Penecale, *Vice Pres*
Jean Reed, *Materials Mgr*
EMP: 75
SQ FT: 60,000
SALES (est): 14.7MM **Privately Held**
SIC: 3599 Machine shop, jobbing & repair

(G-20116)
EVAPORATED COATINGS INC
2365 Maryland Rd (19090-1708)
PHONE..................................215 659-3080
Robert W Schaffer, *President*
J Frank Motson, *Vice Pres*
Stephen L Schaffer, *Vice Pres*
John J Walls, *Vice Pres*
Paul Mathis, *QC Mgr*
EMP: 49 EST: 1960
SQ FT: 14,800

SALES (est): 7.3MM **Privately Held**
WEB: www.evaporatedcoatings.com
SIC: 3479 3861 3827 3699 Painting,
coating & hot dipping; photographic
equipment & supplies; optical instruments
& lenses; electrical equipment & supplies;
electronic capacitors; paints & allied products

(G-20117)
FAST SIGNS OF WILLOW GROVE
Also Called: Fastsigns
707 Easton Rd (19090-2003)
PHONE..................................215 830-9960
Clint Ehlers, *President*
EMP: 5
SQ FT: 1,600
SALES (est): 353.7K **Privately Held**
SIC: 3993 Signs & advertising specialties

(G-20118)
GB BIOSCIENCES CORPORATION
3959 Welsh Rd 369 (19090-2900)
PHONE..................................713 453-7281
EMP: 6
SALES (est): 1.6MM **Privately Held**
SIC: 2819 Industrial inorganic chemicals

(G-20119)
GLAXOSMITHKLINE LLC
1440 Bernard Ave (19090-4206)
PHONE..................................610 962-7548
EMP: 26
SALES (corp-wide): 39.8B **Privately Held**
SIC: 2834 Pharmaceutical preparations
HQ: Glaxosmithkline Llc
5 Crescent Dr
Philadelphia PA 19112
215 751-4000

(G-20120)
HAJOCA CORPORATION
Also Called: Weinstein Sup - Willow Grove
3155 Terwood Rd (19090-1436)
PHONE..................................215 657-0700
Richard J Klau, *President*
Albert Brodsky, *Admin Mgr*
EMP: 5
SALES (corp-wide): 2.4B **Privately Held**
WEB: www.hajoca.com
SIC: 3432 5074 5078 Plumbing fixture fit-
tings & trim; plumbing & hydronic heating
supplies; refrigeration equipment & sup-
plies
PA: Hajoca Corporation
2001 Joshua Rd
Lafayette Hill PA 19444
610 649-1430

(G-20121)
JMG INC
Also Called: Beuerle, J Co
1851 Fairview Ave (19090-4113)
PHONE..................................215 659-4087
Michael Gushue, *President*
John Gushue, *Vice Pres*
EMP: 9
SQ FT: 10,000
SALES (est): 1.3MM **Privately Held**
SIC: 2653 2499 3567 3535 Boxes, solid
fiber: made from purchased materials;
spools, reels & pulleys: wood; industrial
furnaces & ovens; conveyors & conveying
equipment

(G-20122)
JOO YOUNG INC
1823 Davisville Rd Side A (19090-4119)
PHONE..................................267 298-0054
Hyuck Kwon, *President*
EMP: 3 EST: 2010
SALES (est): 146.9K **Privately Held**
SIC: 2099 Food preparations

(G-20123)
KEYSTONE SCRW CORP
535 Davisville Rd (19090-1599)
PHONE..................................215 657-7100
George F Hanny, *CEO*
David Marchetti, *Vice Pres*
David Roach, *Vice Pres*
James Lapp, *QC Dir*
Tom Todd, *Sales Associate*
◆ EMP: 55 EST: 1950

SQ FT: 42,000
SALES (est): 10.3MM **Privately Held**
WEB: www.keystonescrew.com
SIC: 3452 5063 5072 Screws, metal; riv-
ets, metal; wire & cable; screws; rivets

(G-20124)
KIRKLAND PRINTING INC
526 York Rd (19090-2626)
PHONE..................................215 706-2399
Donald F Kirkland, *President*
Kathleen Kirkland, *Corp Secy*
Eric Schada, *Vice Pres*
Scott Bailey, *Sales Staff*
Kristen Schada, *Sales Staff*
EMP: 7
SQ FT: 2,500
SALES (est): 1.2MM **Privately Held**
WEB: www.kirklandprinting.com
SIC: 7334 2752 7331 Photocopying & du-
plicating services; commercial printing,
offset; direct mail advertising services

(G-20125)
KLEIN ELECTRIC ADVERTISING INC
242 Duffield St (19090-2109)
PHONE..................................215 657-6984
Klein M Jacqueline, *President*
Robert C Klein, *Principal*
EMP: 11
SALES (est): 1.3MM **Privately Held**
SIC: 3993 Signs & advertising specialties

(G-20126)
KMZ ENTERPRISES LLC
Also Called: Specialty Glass Products
2885 Terwood Rd (19090-1434)
PHONE..................................215 659-8400
Kenneth J Zaborowski,
EMP: 25
SQ FT: 12,000
SALES (est): 3.1MM **Privately Held**
WEB: www.sgpinc.com
SIC: 3231 Products of purchased glass

(G-20127)
MENU WORLD INC
Also Called: Menu Mon.net
726 Fitzwatertown Rd # 9 (19090-1331)
PHONE..................................267 784-8515
Lisa Bordo, *President*
EMP: 4
SALES (est): 215.6K **Privately Held**
SIC: 2759 Commercial printing

(G-20128)
MODERN MANUFACTURING CO INC
680 Davisville Rd (19090-1586)
PHONE..................................215 659-4820
Stanley D Noreika, *President*
Connie Noreika, *Admin Sec*
Kathy Snyder, *Admin Sec*
EMP: 10 EST: 1946
SQ FT: 10,000
SALES (est): 840K **Privately Held**
SIC: 3546 Power-driven handtools

(G-20129)
MORGAN PRINTING COMPANY
2365 Wyandotte Rd (19090-1283)
PHONE..................................215 784-0966
David A Morgan, *Owner*
EMP: 7 EST: 1971
SQ FT: 10,000
SALES (est): 983.4K **Privately Held**
WEB: www.morganprintingcompany.com
SIC: 2752 Commercial printing, offset

(G-20130)
MYBIANI LLC
Also Called: Nydia Cake Nuggets
197 Fairhill St (19090-2639)
PHONE..................................267 253-1866
Lucianda Sowah,
EMP: 3
SALES (est): 147.2K **Privately Held**
SIC: 2038 Snacks, including onion rings,
cheese sticks, etc.

(G-20131)
OGONTZ CORPORATION (PA)
Also Called: Industrial Division
2835 Terwood Rd (19090-1434)
PHONE..................................215 657-4770
Thomas M Kenny, *Ch of Bd*
Vincent Pettinato, *COO*
F V Laurich, *Admin Sec*
EMP: 13 **EST:** 1954
SQ FT: 11,000
SALES (est): 2.8MM **Privately Held**
WEB: www.ogontz.com
SIC: 3491 3494 Industrial valves; steam
fittings & specialties

(G-20132)
PARAVANO COMPANY INC
2557 Wyandotte Rd Ste C (19090-1201)
PHONE..................................215 659-4600
Philip C Paravano Jr, *President*
EMP: 3 **EST:** 1921
SQ FT: 100
SALES: 225K **Privately Held**
WEB: www.paravano.com
SIC: 2752 2759 2754 Commercial print-
ing, offset; letterpress printing; invitations:
gravure printing; imprinting, gravure

(G-20133)
PEERLESS PAPER SPECIALTY
INC
349 York Rd Ste 2 (19090-2660)
P.O. Box 502 (19090-0502)
PHONE..................................215 657-3460
Theodore R Osuch, *President*
Constance H Osuch, *Corp Secy*
EMP: 5 **EST:** 1975
SALES: 4.5MM **Privately Held**
SIC: 2679 Labels, paper: made from pur-
chased material; tags, paper (unprinted):
made from purchased paper

(G-20134)
PHOTOMEDEX INC
2300 Computer Rd Ste G26 (19090-1755)
PHONE..................................215 619-3286
EMP: 3
SALES (est): 195.7K **Privately Held**
SIC: 2834 Mfg Pharmaceutical Prepara-
tions

(G-20135)
PHOTOMEDEX INC
2300 Computer Rd Ste G26 (19090-1755)
PHONE..................................215 619-3235
EMP: 12
SALES (est): 1.5MM **Privately Held**
SIC: 2834 Pharmaceutical preparations

(G-20136)
PRECISION ASSEMBLY INC
2301 Computer Rd (19090-1746)
PHONE..................................215 784-0861
Stuart Kellerman, *President*
Ernest Farabella, *Vice Pres*
Bud Tyler, *Vice Pres*
Barry Bennett, *Manager*
EMP: 40
SQ FT: 33,000
SALES (est): 10.1MM **Privately Held**
WEB: www.precisionassembly.com
SIC: 3569 3643 Assembly machines, non-
metalworking; current-carrying wiring de-
vices

(G-20137)
R & R EYEWEAR IMPORTS INC
311 W Moreland Rd (19090-3107)
PHONE..................................215 393-5895
Richard Rosoff, *President*
Chris Cranage, *Supervisor*
▲ **EMP:** 45
SALES (est): 6.3MM **Privately Held**
WEB: www.rreyewear.com
SIC: 3851 Frames & parts, eyeglass &
spectacle

(G-20138)
RADIANCY INC (DH)
2300 Computer Rd Ste G26 (19090-1755)
PHONE..................................845 398-1647
Dolev Rafaeli, *CEO*
Giora Fishman, *Vice Pres*
AVI Hanin, *Controller*
Megi Devolli, *Accountant*

Miki Van Soest, *Office Mgr*
▲ **EMP:** 10
SALES (est): 1.4MM
SALES (corp-wide): 31.4MM **Publicly**
Held
WEB: www.radiancy.com
SIC: 3845 Electromedical equipment
HQ: Ictv Holdings, Inc.
489 Devon Park Dr Ste 315
Wayne PA 19087
484 598-2300

(G-20139)
RUCH CARBIDE BURS INC
2750 Terwood Rd (19090-1428)
P.O. Box 252 (19090-0252)
PHONE..................................215 657-3660
Robert Ruch III, *President*
Karen Kurz, *Controller*
EMP: 22
SQ FT: 3,053
SALES (est): 2.9MM **Privately Held**
WEB: www.ruchcarbide.com
SIC: 7699 3599 3545 3541 Industrial ma-
chinery & equipment repair; grinding cast-
ings for the trade; machine tool
accessories; machine tools, metal cutting
type; hand & edge tools

(G-20140)
SCHEERER BEARING
CORPORATION (PA)
645 Davisville Rd (19090-1514)
P.O. Box 156, Horsham (19044-0156)
PHONE..................................215 443-5252
George Rymar, *President*
Daniel Hebling, *Mfg Mgr*
Leon Gorbonosov, *Purch Mgr*
Ryan Kennedy, *Engineer*
Fausto Mariazzi, *Engineer*
◆ **EMP:** 50 **EST:** 1963
SQ FT: 45,000
SALES (est): 12.6MM **Privately Held**
WEB: www.sbcbearing.com
SIC: 3562 3568 7699 Ball bearings &
parts; roller bearings & parts; power
transmission equipment; industrial ma-
chinery & equipment repair

(G-20141)
SIGN O RAMA INC
Also Called: Sign-A-Rama
215 Easton Rd (19090-3204)
PHONE..................................215 784-9494
Joan Schnitcher, *President*
Larry Schnitcher, *Vice Pres*
EMP: 4
SALES (est): 356.6K **Privately Held**
SIC: 3993 Signs & advertising specialties

(G-20142)
SILVINE INC
1843 Fairview Ave (19090-4113)
P.O. Box 1, Abington (19001-0001)
PHONE..................................215 657-2345
Norman Silver, *President*
Sharyn Brawns, *CFO*
▲ **EMP:** 32
SQ FT: 40,000
SALES (est): 5MM **Privately Held**
SIC: 5063 5085 3645 3644 Wire & cable;
rope, cord & thread; residential lighting
fixtures; noncurrent-carrying wiring serv-
ices

(G-20143)
SPADONE MACHINE INC
601 Davisville Rd (19090-1528)
P.O. Box 185, Horsham (19044-0185)
PHONE..................................215 396-8005
Aimee Hasson, *President*
EMP: 11
SALES (est): 1.8MM **Privately Held**
SIC: 3061 Mechanical rubber goods

(G-20144)
SUN LABORATORIES INC
319 Davisville Rd (19090-3330)
PHONE..................................215 659-1111
Hamid Tehrani, *President*
EMP: 20
SQ FT: 2,314
SALES (est): 2.6MM **Privately Held**
SIC: 2844 Cosmetic preparations

(G-20145)
SWAROVSKI RETAIL VENTURES
LTD
2500 W Moreland Rd (19090-4003)
PHONE..................................215 659-3649
Vince Fisher, *Manager*
EMP: 3
SALES (corp-wide): 3.7B **Privately Held**
SIC: 3961 Costume jewelry
HQ: Swarovski Retail Ventures Ltd.
1 Kenney Dr
Cranston RI 02920
401 463-6400

(G-20146)
TECHLINE TECHNOLOGIES INC
Also Called: MPS Techline of PA
668 Davisville Rd (19090-1515)
P.O. Box 879, Richboro (18954-0879)
PHONE..................................215 657-1909
Sandra Parry, *President*
David Parry, *Vice Pres*
▼ **EMP:** 23
SQ FT: 13,000
SALES: 4.5MM **Privately Held**
SIC: 3069 Custom compounding of rubber
materials

(G-20147)
VANDERSLICE MACHINE
COMPANY
2557a Wyandotte Rd Bldg A (19090-1209)
PHONE..................................215 659-0429
David Vanderslice, *President*
Karl Vanderslice, *Vice Pres*
EMP: 5
SQ FT: 4,000
SALES (est): 754.5K **Privately Held**
SIC: 3599 Machine shop, jobbing & repair

(G-20148)
WEINRICH BAKERY
Also Called: Weinrichs Bakery A Konditorei
55 Easton Rd (19090-3201)
PHONE..................................215 659-7062
Edward Weinrich, *President*
EMP: 20
SQ FT: 1,200
SALES (est): 995.3K **Privately Held**
WEB: www.weinrichbakery.com
SIC: 5461 2051 Cakes; bakery: wholesale
or wholesale/retail combined

(G-20149)
WILLIAM HENRY ORNA IR
WORKS
Also Called: Henry William Orna Ir Works
524 Davisville Rd (19090-1513)
PHONE..................................215 659-1887
William Henry, *Owner*
Bill Henry, *Foreman/Supr*
EMP: 5
SQ FT: 2,000
SALES (est): 200K **Privately Held**
WEB: www.ironworksonline.com
SIC: 3441 5712 3446 Fabricated struc-
tural metal; furniture stores; architectural
metalwork

(G-20150)
WILLOW GROVE AUTO TOP INC
43 York Rd (19090-3416)
PHONE..................................215 659-3276
Joe Dennin, *President*
EMP: 4
SQ FT: 4,752
SALES (est): 500K **Privately Held**
WEB: www.wgautotop.com
SIC: 7532 7539 2399 5063 Interior repair
services; tops (canvas or plastic), installa-
tion or repair: automotive; automotive
sound system service & installation; seat
covers, automobile; alarm systems

Willow Street
Lancaster County

(G-20151)
HERSHEY DIGITAL
234 Peach Bottom Rd (17584-9594)
PHONE..................................717 431-9602
EMP: 3

SALES (est): 184.8K **Privately Held**
SIC: 2066 Mfg Chocolate/Cocoa Products

(G-20152)
JOHN R ARMSTRONG
200 Radcliff Rd (17584-9799)
PHONE..................................717 464-3239
EMP: 3
SALES (est): 120K **Privately Held**
SIC: 3471 Plating/Polishing Service

(G-20153)
LANCASTER COUNTY WINERY
LTD
Also Called: Lancaster Country Winery
799 Rawlinsville Rd (17584-8700)
PHONE..................................717 464-3555
Suzanne Dickel, *President*
Todd Dickel, *Vice Pres*
EMP: 6 **EST:** 1972
SQ FT: 7,000
SALES: 100K **Privately Held**
WEB: www.lancastercountywinery.com
SIC: 0172 2084 Grapes; wines, brandy &
brandy spirits

(G-20154)
MELLINGER MANUFACTURING
CO INC
367 Millwood Rd (17584-9561)
PHONE..................................717 464-3318
Paul B Mellinger, *President*
Kenneth Mellinger, *President*
P Dale Mellinger, *Shareholder*
EMP: 10 **EST:** 1945
SQ FT: 20,000
SALES (est): 1.6MM **Privately Held**
SIC: 3444 3732 Forming machine work,
sheet metal; houseboats, building & re-
pairing

(G-20155)
RAYCO PROCESS SERVICES
INC
3551 Willow Street Pike N (17584-9720)
P.O. Box 330 (17584-0330)
PHONE..................................717 464-2572
Ray C Long, *President*
Karen D Long, *Corp Secy*
EMP: 8
SQ FT: 7,000
SALES: 1.1MM **Privately Held**
SIC: 3432 Plumbing fixture fittings & trim

(G-20156)
ROTATION DYNAMICS
CORPORATION
Also Called: Poly-Caster
2 Brooks Ave (17584-8966)
P.O. Box 275 (17584-0275)
PHONE..................................717 464-2724
Daryl Royal, *Branch Mgr*
EMP: 15
SALES (corp-wide): 164.4MM **Privately**
Held
SIC: 3555 Printing trades machinery
PA: Rotation Dynamics Corporation
1101 Windham Pkwy
Romeoville IL 60446
630 769-9255

(G-20157)
SA-FE WINDOWS INC
206 W Kendig Rd (17584-9514)
PHONE..................................717 464-9605
Ferid Brkic, *President*
Elvira Brkic, *Admin Sec*
▲ **EMP:** 10
SALES: 1.2MM **Privately Held**
SIC: 2431 Windows & window parts & trim,
wood

Wilmerding
Allegheny County

(G-20158)
ALLEGHENY PETROLEUM PDTS
CO (PA)
999 Airbrake Ave (15148-1064)
PHONE..................................412 829-1990
James L Kudis, *CEO*
Barbara Kudis, *President*

◆ **EMP:** 61
SQ FT: 100,000
SALES: 102MM **Privately Held**
WEB: www.oils.com
SIC: 2992 Oils & greases, blending & compounding; lubricating oils; cutting oils, blending: made from purchased materials

(G-20159)
AMERICAN WIRE RESEARCH INC
1005 Airbrake Ave (15148-1036)
PHONE..................................412 349-8431
Beau Barsotti, *President*
▲ **EMP:** 32 **EST:** 2013
SQ FT: 300,000
SALES: 1.5MM **Privately Held**
SIC: 3315 Steel wire & related products

(G-20160)
WABTEC CORPORATION (HQ)
Also Called: Wabtec Global Services
1001 Airbrake Ave (15148-1036)
PHONE..................................412 825-1000
Raymond T Betler, *President*
Robert J Brooks, *President*
John M Meister, *President*
R Mark Cox, *Senior VP*
Patrick D Dugan, *Senior VP*
◆ **EMP:** 300
SQ FT: 19,000
SALES (est): 1B
SALES (corp-wide): 4.3B **Publicly Held**
WEB: www.wabtecglobalservices.com
SIC: 3743 Railroad equipment
PA: Westinghouse Air Brake Technologies Corporation
1001 Airbrake Ave
Wilmerding PA 15148
412 825-1000

(G-20161)
WABTEC INVESTMENTS LIMITED LLC
1001 Airbrake Ave (15148-1036)
PHONE..................................412 825-1000
Albert J Neupaver, *Chairman*
EMP: 3 **EST:** 2015
SALES (est): 111.2K
SALES (corp-wide): 4.3B **Publicly Held**
SIC: 3743 Railroad equipment
PA: Westinghouse Air Brake Technologies Corporation
1001 Airbrake Ave
Wilmerding PA 15148
412 825-1000

(G-20162)
WATTS BROTHERS TOOL WORKS INC
760 Airbrake Ave (15148-1014)
P.O. Box 335 (15148-0335)
PHONE..................................412 823-7877
Richard Keller, *President*
EMP: 10 **EST:** 1919
SQ FT: 8,500
SALES: 900K **Privately Held**
SIC: 3532 Drills & drilling equipment, mining (except oil & gas)

(G-20163)
WESTINGHOUSE A BRAKE TECH CORP (PA)
Also Called: Wabtec
1001 Airbrake Ave (15148-1036)
PHONE..................................412 825-1000
Albert J Neupaver, *Ch of Bd*
Emilio A Fernandez, *Vice Ch Bd*
Raymond T Betler, *President*
David L Deninno, *Exec VP*
John A Mastalerz, *Senior VP*
▲ **EMP:** 400
SQ FT: 365,000
SALES: 4.3B **Publicly Held**
WEB: www.wabco-rail.com
SIC: 3743 Brakes, air & vacuum: railway; locomotives & parts; freight cars & equipment; rapid transit cars & equipment

---

Wind Gap
Northampton County

(G-20164)
ALL PALLET INC
198 W Mountain Rd (18091-9730)
PHONE..................................610 614-1905
James P Heisler, *President*
EMP: 120
SALES: 3.8MM **Privately Held**
SIC: 2448 Wood pallets & skids

(G-20165)
APS ADVANCE PRODUCTS & SVCS
316 N Broadway (18091-1296)
PHONE..................................610 863-0570
Victor Quinones, *Principal*
EMP: 4
SALES (est): 451.6K **Privately Held**
SIC: 3399 1799 Powder, metal; sandblasting of building exteriors

(G-20166)
BLUE MOUNTAIN LAWN SERVICE
Also Called: Blue Mountain Rock Drilling
1433 Church Rd (18091-9754)
PHONE..................................610 759-6979
David Costenbader, *President*
Michael Costenbader, *Corp Secy*
EMP: 6
SALES (est): 650K **Privately Held**
SIC: 3532 Drills (portable), rock

(G-20167)
BRD NOISE & VIBRATION CTRL INC (PA)
112 Fairview Ave (18091-1226)
P.O. Box 127 (18091-0127)
PHONE..................................610 863-6300
Kris Kollevoll, *President*
Tracey O'Gorman, *Materials Mgr*
Regina Landry, *Sales Staff*
Laura Riehl, *Sales Staff*
Mark Stephens, *Sales Staff*
EMP: 7
SQ FT: 5,500
SALES (est): 2.3MM **Privately Held**
WEB: www.brd-nonoise.com
SIC: 3086 3625 3469 3444 Insulation or cushioning material, foamed plastic; noise control equipment; metal stampings; sheet metalwork; mineral wool

(G-20168)
CONVERTER ACCESSORY CORP
Also Called: Cac
201 Alpha Rd (18091-1279)
P.O. Box 188 (18091-0188)
PHONE..................................610 863-6008
Jeffrey Damour, *President*
Cecily Archer, *Corp Secy*
Pamela Damour, *Vice Pres*
Pam Damour, *Purch Agent*
Jeff Damour, *Engineer*
EMP: 10
SQ FT: 11,000
SALES (est): 2.3MM **Privately Held**
WEB: www.con-res.com
SIC: 3568 3621 Power transmission equipment; motors & generators

(G-20169)
INNOVATIVE CONTROL SYSTEMS INC (PA)
Also Called: I C S
1349 Jacobsburg Rd (18091-9716)
PHONE..................................610 881-8000
Kevin W Detrick, *President*
Cindy Penchishen, *Corp Secy*
Brian Bath, *Exec VP*
Rob Deal, *Vice Pres*
Louis Huffman, *Prdtn Mgr*
▲ **EMP:** 110
SQ FT: 27,000
SALES: 42MM **Privately Held**
WEB: www.innovative-control.com
SIC: 3589 3612 Car washing machinery; control transformers

(G-20170)
KULP FOUNDRY INC
1349 Jacobsburg Rd (18091-9716)
PHONE..................................610 881-8093
Robert Houch, *President*
Olive Kulp, *Corp Secy*
EMP: 65
SQ FT: 6,500
SALES (est): 12.1MM **Privately Held**
WEB: www.kulpfoundry.com
SIC: 3321 3322 Gray iron castings; ductile iron castings; malleable iron foundries

(G-20171)
MENSCO INC
125 W West St Ste A (18091-1309)
PHONE..................................610 863-9233
Laurie Levits, *President*
Paul Levits, *Corp Secy*
▲ **EMP:** 7
SQ FT: 6,500
SALES: 225K **Privately Held**
SIC: 3599 Machine shop, jobbing & repair

(G-20172)
SIGN SHOP OF THE POCONOS INC
196 W Moorestown Rd (18091-9764)
PHONE..................................347 972-1775
Michael Gabriele, *Principal*
Tim Bennett, *Sales Staff*
EMP: 3
SALES (est): 332.4K **Privately Held**
SIC: 3993 Signs & advertising specialties

(G-20173)
SMARTERFUEL INC (PA)
591 Male Rd (18091-8503)
P.O. Box 66 (18091-0066)
PHONE..................................570 972-4727
David Dunham, *CEO*
Ken Knicolosi, *CFO*
EMP: 25
SQ FT: 25,000
SALES (est): 3MM **Privately Held**
SIC: 2869 Fuels

(G-20174)
TERMAC CORP
65 Constitution Ave (18091-1118)
PHONE..................................610 863-5356
Terrance Oreily, *CEO*
EMP: 6
SALES (est): 830.9K **Privately Held**
SIC: 3442 Rolling doors for industrial buildings or warehouses, metal

(G-20175)
WILLIAMS & SONS SLATE & TILE
6596 Sullivan Trl (18091-9798)
PHONE..................................610 863-4161
Anthony J Williams, *President*
William Williams, *Vice Pres*
▲ **EMP:** 23 **EST:** 1955
SQ FT: 8,600
SALES: 601.7K **Privately Held**
WEB: www.williamsslate.com
SIC: 3281 5032 Slate products; stone, crushed or broken; building stone

---

Wind Ridge
Greene County

(G-20176)
FINNEGAN GAS CORP
229 Finnegan Rd (15380-1212)
PHONE..................................724 428-3688
George R Finnegan, *President*
George Finnegan, *Principal*
EMP: 5
SALES: 300K **Privately Held**
SIC: 1321 Natural gas liquids production

Windber
Somerset County

(G-20177)
ALL-SIGN GRAPHICS & DESIGN
148 Minnow Creek Ln 1 (15963-9108)
PHONE..................................814 467-9995
Dawn Mihalko, *Owner*
EMP: 3 **EST:** 1997
SQ FT: 600
SALES (est): 160K **Privately Held**
SIC: 3993 Signs & advertising specialties

(G-20178)
BCL MANUFACTURING INC
161 Bello Dr (15963-7224)
PHONE..................................814 467-8225
William Sipko, *President*
Wayne R Tilley, *Vice Pres*
Lauree S Lapinsky, *Treasurer*
Michelle A Tokarsky, *Admin Sec*
EMP: 31
SQ FT: 20,000
SALES (est): 6.4MM **Privately Held**
WEB: www.bclmanufacturing.com
SIC: 3444 Sheet metalwork

(G-20179)
CONJELKO DAIRY & ICE SERVICE
Also Called: Conjelko's Ice Service
518 Graham Ave (15963-1323)
PHONE..................................814 467-9997
Gregory Conjelko, *President*
Robert Conjelko, *Principal*
EMP: 8
SQ FT: 1,750
SALES (est): 876.1K **Privately Held**
SIC: 2097 5451 5411 Manufactured ice; dairy products stores; grocery stores

(G-20180)
CURRENCY INC
1700 Somerset Ave (15963-1958)
PHONE..................................814 509-6157
Ronald Kuchera, *President*
William Kuchera, *Admin Sec*
EMP: 25
SQ FT: 77,000
SALES (est): 3.4MM **Privately Held**
SIC: 3679 3672 Harness assemblies for electronic use: wire or cable; printed circuit boards

(G-20181)
ESCO WINDBER
214 Railroad St (15963-1825)
PHONE..................................814 509-8927
Dave Kelley, *Owner*
EMP: 4
SALES (est): 343.6K **Privately Held**
SIC: 3535 Conveyors & conveying equipment

(G-20182)
HURDLES INC
640 Main St (15963-1021)
PHONE..................................814 467-8787
Robert Snyder, *Principal*
EMP: 5 **EST:** 2007
SALES (est): 456.4K **Privately Held**
SIC: 2599 Bar, restaurant & cafeteria furniture

(G-20183)
HWP FABRICATIONS
5013 Clear Shade Dr (15963-4620)
PHONE..................................814 487-5507
Marlin Plummer, *President*
EMP: 4
SALES (est): 538.6K **Privately Held**
SIC: 3441 Fabricated structural metal

(G-20184)
KEYSTONE AUTOMOTIVE INDS INC
320 Dobson St (15963-2506)
PHONE..................................814 467-5531
Larry Mihalick, *Manager*
EMP: 41

SALES (corp-wide): 11.8B **Publicly Held**
WEB: www.kool-vue.com
SIC: 3471 5013 Plating of metals or
  formed products; body repair or paint
  shop supplies, automotive
HQ: Keystone Automotive Industries, Inc.
  5846 Crossings Blvd
  Antioch TN 37013
  615 781-5200

(G-20185)
KIRKWOOD ELECTRIC
902 Wissinger Rd (15963-1002)
PHONE..................................814 467-7171
William F Kirkwood, *Principal*
EMP: 4 EST: 2009
SALES (est): 326K **Privately Held**
SIC: 3699 Electrical work

(G-20186)
KITRON HOLDING USA INC (HQ)
345 Pomroys Dr (15963-2425)
PHONE..................................814 467-9060
Hans Peter Thomassen, *President*
Israel Losada Salvador, *Chairman*
Cathrin Nylander, *Admin Sec*
EMP: 5
SQ FT: 10,000
SALES (est): 21.1MM **Privately Held**
SIC: 3679 Electronic circuits
PA: Kitron, Inc.
  160 Jari Dr Ste 160 # 160
  Johnstown PA 15904
  814 619-0523

(G-20187)
KITRON TECHNOLOGIES INC
345 Pomroys Dr (15963-2425)
PHONE..................................814 474-4300
Hans Peter Thomassen, *President*
Israel Losada Salvador, *Chairman*
Cathrin Nylander, *Admin Sec*
EMP: 110
SQ FT: 108,000
SALES (est): 21.1MM **Privately Held**
SIC: 3672 Printed circuit boards
HQ: Kitron Holding Usa Inc.
  345 Pomroys Dr
  Windber PA 15963

(G-20188)
LEE CONCRETE PRODUCTS
648 Seanor Rd (15963-7204)
PHONE..................................814 467-4470
Edward J Lee, *Owner*
EMP: 5
SALES (est): 597.5K **Privately Held**
SIC: 3272 Septic tanks, concrete

(G-20189)
MARC-SERVICE INC
Also Called: Honeywell Authorized Dealer
135 5th St Ste 3 (15963-1102)
PHONE..................................814 467-8611
Tom Naglic, *President*
Tim Naglic, *Vice Pres*
Julie Naglic, *Admin Sec*
EMP: 38
SQ FT: 8,000
SALES (est): 8MM **Privately Held**
SIC: 1711 3444 Warm air heating & air
  conditioning contractor; sheet metalwork

(G-20190)
NATIONAL HYBRID INC
Also Called: N H I
345 Pomroys Dr (15963-2425)
PHONE..................................814 467-9060
Steve Putles, *CEO*
Tom Mills, *President*
EMP: 100 EST: 1974
SQ FT: 30,000
SALES (est): 13.3MM
SALES (corp-wide): 333.6MM **Privately
Held**
WEB: www.nationalhybrid.com
SIC: 3674 3672 3571 Microcircuits, inte-
  grated (semiconductor); printed circuit
  boards; electronic computers
HQ: Api Technologies Corp.
  400 Nickerson Rd Ste 1
  Marlborough MA 01752

(G-20191)
PETRUNAK & COMPANY INC
Also Called: Petrunak Paving
819 Horner St (15963-2210)
PHONE..................................814 467-7860
Philip Petrunak, *President*
EMP: 20
SALES (est): 4.1MM **Privately Held**
SIC: 2951 Asphalt paving mixtures &
  blocks

(G-20192)
SENDEC CORP (DH)
Also Called: API Technologies
345 Pomroys Dr (15963-2425)
PHONE..................................585 425-3390
Kenton W Fiske, *President*
Tom Tette, *CFO*
▲ EMP: 140
SQ FT: 86,000
SALES (est): 14.1MM
SALES (corp-wide): 333.6MM **Privately
Held**
WEB: www.sendec.com
SIC: 3679 Electronic circuits

(G-20193)
TYGER CONSTRUCTION
217 Cameron Ct (15963-6648)
PHONE..................................814 467-9342
Robert Tyger, *Owner*
EMP: 4
SALES (est): 385K **Privately Held**
WEB: www.tygerleader.com
SIC: 2431 1761 1751 Windows & window
  parts & trim, wood; siding contractor; win-
  dow & door (prefabricated) installation

(G-20194)
**UNITED WLDG & FABRICATION
INC**
246 Seanor Rd (15963-7202)
PHONE..................................814 266-3598
Norma Mowery, *President*
EMP: 5
SALES (est): 378.1K **Privately Held**
SIC: 3441 Fabricated structural metal

Windsor
York County

(G-20195)
**ADOMIS INDUSTRIAL MCH
MAINT**
Also Called: Aimm
1812 Snyder Corner Rd (17366-8455)
PHONE..................................717 244-0716
Mary Adomis, *President*
EMP: 5
SALES (est): 340K **Privately Held**
SIC: 3462 Iron & steel forgings

(G-20196)
G&U SAND SVCS
50 3rd St (17366-9721)
PHONE..................................717 246-6724
Frank Collins, *Owner*
EMP: 5
SALES (est): 140K **Privately Held**
WEB: www.sandcontrolonline.com
SIC: 1446 Foundry sand mining

(G-20197)
**WISE ELECTRONIC SYSTEMS
INC**
1362 Craley Rd (17366-8960)
PHONE..................................717 244-0111
Fred W Wise, *President*
EMP: 4
SQ FT: 3,329
SALES: 500K **Privately Held**
SIC: 5063 3823 Switches, except elec-
  tronic; controllers for process variables,
  all types

Winfield
Union County

(G-20198)
CARGILL INCORPORATED
70 Agway Ln (17889-9131)
PHONE..................................570 524-4777
Brent Hackenburg, *Manager*
EMP: 8
SALES (corp-wide): 114.7B **Privately
Held**
WEB: www.cargill.com
SIC: 2048 Prepared feeds
PA: Cargill, Incorporated
  15407 Mcginty Rd W
  Wayzata MN 55391
  952 742-7575

(G-20199)
EASTERN INDUSTRIES INC
220 Park Rd (17889)
PHONE..................................570 524-2251
Bill Patton, *Manager*
EMP: 50
SALES (corp-wide): 651.9MM **Privately
Held**
WEB: www.eastern-ind.com
SIC: 5032 1611 2951 Paving mixtures;
  stone, crushed or broken; concrete & cin-
  der block; highway & street construction;
  asphalt paving mixtures & blocks
HQ: Eastern Industries, Inc.
  3724 Crescent Ct W 200
  Whitehall PA 18052
  610 866-0932

(G-20200)
EPHRAIM L KING
Also Called: Vision Design
636 Scholl Rd (17889-8831)
PHONE..................................570 837-9470
Ephraim L King, *Owner*
EMP: 6
SALES (est): 469.1K **Privately Held**
SIC: 3524 5261 0781 0782 Lawnmow-
  ers, residential: hand or power; lawnmow-
  ers & tractors; landscape services;
  landscape contractors

(G-20201)
GILSON BOARDS LLC
62 Mountain View Rd (17889-8805)
PHONE..................................570 798-9102
Nicholas Gilson, *CEO*
Austin Royer, *Prdtn Mgr*
Steve Blackman, *Opers Staff*
EMP: 15
SALES (est): 568.7K **Privately Held**
SIC: 3949 Winter sports equipment

(G-20202)
PENN CHEESE CORPORATION
7199 County Line Rd (17889-9266)
PHONE..................................570 524-7700
Ed Claus, *President*
Jonathan Weber, *General Mgr*
Fred Greenberg, *Admin Sec*
Lenore Spade, *Admin Asst*
EMP: 16
SQ FT: 20,300
SALES (est): 3MM **Privately Held**
WEB: www.penncheese.com
SIC: 2022 Natural cheese

(G-20203)
PENN DAIRY LLC
7199 County Line Rd (17889-9266)
PHONE..................................570 524-7700
Jon Weber, *General Mgr*
EMP: 4
SALES (est): 152.7K **Privately Held**
SIC: 2022 Natural cheese

(G-20204)
VETCH LLC
Also Called: Penn Cheese
7199 County Line Rd (17889-9266)
PHONE..................................570 524-7700
J Edward Clouse, *President*
Jonathan Weber,
EMP: 15
SQ FT: 22,000

SALES (est): 1.3MM **Privately Held**
SIC: 2022 Natural cheese

Womelsdorf
Berks County

(G-20205)
AMHERST CORPORATION
Also Called: Society Printers
80 Begonia Ct (19567-7007)
PHONE..................................610 589-1090
Jim Pearson, *Vice Pres*
EMP: 12
SQ FT: 5,500
SALES (est): 1.6MM **Privately Held**
SIC: 2752 Commercial printing, offset

(G-20206)
**DIEFFENBACHS POTATO CHIPS
INC**
51 Host Rd (19567-9421)
PHONE..................................610 589-2385
Nevin J Dieffenbach, *CEO*
Mike Marlowe, *COO*
Elam R Dieffenbach, *Admin Sec*
▼ EMP: 80
SQ FT: 65,000
SALES (est): 15.4MM **Privately Held**
WEB: www.dieffenbachs.com
SIC: 2096 Potato chips & other potato-
  based snacks

(G-20207)
LIME KILN AG LLC
37 Weiser Ln (19567-9767)
PHONE..................................610 589-4302
EMP: 3
SALES (est): 139.1K **Privately Held**
SIC: 3559 Kilns

(G-20208)
PROJECT ENTERPRISE
82 Deck Rd (19567-9400)
PHONE..................................717 933-9517
Auker Glenn, *Owner*
EMP: 3
SALES (est): 351K **Privately Held**
SIC: 2541 Cabinets, lockers & shelving

(G-20209)
**TREEHOUSE PRIVATE BRANDS
INC**
336 Hill Rd (19567-9200)
PHONE..................................610 589-4526
Bill Mallis, *Branch Mgr*
EMP: 8
SALES (corp-wide): 5.8B **Publicly Held**
SIC: 2043 Cereal breakfast foods
HQ: Treehouse Private Brands, Inc.
  800 Market St Ste 2600
  Saint Louis MO 63101

(G-20210)
WEAVER WOOD SPECIALTIES
36 Host Rd (19567-9420)
PHONE..................................610 589-5889
Larry Weaver, *Owner*
EMP: 3
SALES (est): 284.1K **Privately Held**
SIC: 2511 Wood household furniture

Woodland
Clearfield County

(G-20211)
FORCEY LUMBER CO INC
2020 Shiloh Rd (16881-8121)
PHONE..................................814 857-5002
Brant M Forcey, *President*
Yvonne Shaner, *Principal*
Annette Forcey, *Corp Secy*
Roff Forcey, *Vice Pres*
Ross Forcey, *Vice Pres*
▼ EMP: 23 EST: 1943
SQ FT: 10,000
SALES (est): 2.1MM **Privately Held**
WEB: www.forceylumber.com
SIC: 2421 5211 Kiln drying of lumber; lum-
  ber & other building materials

(G-20212)
IMPACT PRINTING AND
EMBROIDERY
4199 Clearfield Wdlnd Hwy (16881-9363)
PHONE...................................814 857-7246
Timothy Bates, *Principal*
EMP: 4 **EST:** 2010
SALES (est): 361.8K **Privately Held**
SIC: 2752 Commercial printing, litho-
graphic

(G-20213)
PENN PALLET INC
553 Independent Rd (16881-9356)
PHONE...................................814 857-2988
Robert Refalsky, *Branch Mgr*
EMP: 3
SALES (corp-wide): 11.3MM **Privately**
Held
SIC: 2448 Pallets, wood
PA: Penn Pallet, Inc.
675 Fillmore Rd
Saint Marys PA 15857
814 834-1700

(G-20214)
STONE & WOOD INC
Also Called: Lansberry Stone & Wood
Rr 2 (16881)
PHONE...................................814 857-7621
EMP: 9
SALES: 200K **Privately Held**
SIC: 5032 3541 Whol Fill Material And Mfg
Shearing And Delimbing Equipment

(G-20215)
WALKER LUMBER CO INC
148 Tipple Ln (16881)
P.O. Box 60 (16881-0060)
PHONE...................................814 857-7642
Nick Ince, *President*
EMP: 50
SQ FT: 3,560
SALES (est): 1MM **Privately Held**
SIC: 2421 2426 Kiln drying of lumber; fur-
niture stock & parts, hardwood

Woodlyn
Delaware County

(G-20216)
ACE SPORTS INC
Also Called: Net Synergy
90 Randall Ave Ste F (19094-1800)
PHONE...................................610 833-5513
John Pelligrino, *President*
Marc Watson, *Technology*
EMP: 75
SALES: 10MM **Privately Held**
WEB: www.acejerseys.com
SIC: 3949 Sporting & athletic goods

(G-20217)
ALIBERT INDUSTRIES INC
1925 Macdade Blvd Fl 1 (19094-2004)
PHONE...................................610 872-3900
Olive Alibert, *President*
EMP: 4 **EST:** 1959
SQ FT: 4,000
SALES (est): 441.2K **Privately Held**
SIC: 3599 Machine shop, jobbing & repair

(G-20218)
COLUMBIA RESEARCH LABS
INC
1925 Macdade Blvd (19094-2099)
PHONE...................................610 872-3900
Gian F Savona, *President*
Monica Bailey, *Marketing Staff*
Ken Sipple, *Admin Mgr*
◆ **EMP:** 32 **EST:** 1952
SQ FT: 20,000
SALES: 4.4MM **Privately Held**
WEB: www.columbiaresearchlab.com
SIC: 3825 3829 3823 3625 Transducers
for volts, amperes, watts, vars, frequency,
etc.; measuring & controlling devices; in-
dustrial instrmnts msrmnt display/control
process variable; relays & industrial con-
trols

(G-20219)
KENT STUDIOS
190 Fairview Rd (19094-1705)
PHONE...................................610 534-7777
Rob Hoffeeaer, *Owner*
EMP: 20
SALES (est): 1.4MM **Privately Held**
WEB: www.kentstudios.net
SIC: 3952 5199 Frames for artists' can-
vases; artists' materials

Woolrich
Clinton County

(G-20220)
WOOLRICH INC (DH)
2 Mill St (17779)
PHONE...................................570 769-6464
Arthur Rosenberg, *President*
Nick Brayton, *Vice Pres*
Sue Moshier, *Sales Mgr*
Bill Lilley, *Manager*
Conrad Schlesinger, *Manager*
▲ **EMP:** 199 **EST:** 1830
SQ FT: 16,000
SALES (est): 48.3MM **Privately Held**
WEB: www.woolrich.com
SIC: 2311 2329 2331 2337 Coats, tailored, men's & boys': from purchased materials; jackets, tailored suit-type: men's &
boys'; sweaters & sweater jackets: men's
& boys'; jackets (suede, leatherette, etc.),
sport: men's & boys'; vests (suede,
leatherette, etc.), sport: men's & boys';
shirts, women's & juniors': made from
purchased materials; blouses, women's &
juniors': made from purchased material;
women's & misses' suits & coats; jackets
& vests, except fur & leather: women's;
sport shirts, men's & boys': from purchased materials; flannel shirts, except
work: men's, youths' & boys'; wool broadwoven fabrics

(G-20221)
WOOLRICH INC
1 Mill St (17779)
PHONE...................................570 769-7401
Martin I Geisser, *Principal*
EMP: 9 **Privately Held**
SIC: 3643 Outlets, electric: convenience
HQ: Woolrich, Inc.
2 Mill St
Woolrich PA 17779
570 769-6464

Worcester
Chester County

(G-20222)
ALLAN MYERS MATERIALS INC
(HQ)
1805 Berks Rd (19355)
P.O. Box 98 (19490-0098)
PHONE...................................610 560-7900
Ross Myers, *CEO*
Dale R Wilson, *President*
Allan B Myers, *Vice Pres*
Denis P Moore, *Treasurer*
Teresa S Hasson, *Admin Sec*
EMP: 200 **EST:** 1953
SQ FT: 1,500
SALES (est): 317.6MM
SALES (corp-wide): 751MM **Privately**
Held
WEB: www.americaninfrastructure.com
SIC: 1422 Whiting mining, crushed & bro-
ken-quarrying
PA: Allan Myers, Inc
1805 Berks Rd
Worcester PA 19490
610 222-8800

Worcester
Montgomery County

(G-20223)
ALLAN A MYERS
1805 Berks Rd (19490)
P.O. Box 1340 (19490-1340)
PHONE...................................610 584-6020
Allan A Myers, *Principal*
EMP: 3
SALES (est): 119.4K **Privately Held**
SIC: 3799 Transportation equipment

(G-20224)
BOURNE GRAPHICS INC
2901 Skippack Park (19490)
P.O. Box 53 (19490-0053)
PHONE...................................610 584-6120
Richard Bourne, *President*
Wendy Bourne, *Corp Secy*
Wendi Bourne, *Treasurer*
EMP: 5
SALES: 300K **Privately Held**
WEB: www.bournegraphics.com
SIC: 2759 7336 8999 Screen printing;
commercial art & graphic design; artist

(G-20225)
PALMER INTERNATIONAL INC
2955 Skippack Pike (19490)
P.O. Box 350, Skippack (19474-0350)
PHONE...................................610 584-3204
Tom Stralkowski, *Branch Mgr*
EMP: 45
SALES (corp-wide): 16.4MM **Privately**
Held
SIC: 2822 Synthetic rubber
PA: Palmer International, Inc.
2036 Lucon Rd
Skippack PA 19474
610 584-4241

Worthington
Armstrong County

(G-20226)
AIR/TAK INC
107 W Main St (16262-2303)
PHONE...................................724 297-3416
Donald Burk, *President*
▲ **EMP:** 12
SQ FT: 20,000
SALES (est): 3.1MM **Privately Held**
WEB: www.airtak.com
SIC: 3567 3564 3585 Industrial furnaces
& ovens; blowers & fans; refrigeration
equipment, complete

(G-20227)
BAKER GAS INC
136 Baker Gas Dr (16262-3902)
P.O. Box 739 (16262-0739)
PHONE...................................724 297-3456
Ronald Baker, *President*
Michael Baker, *Vice Pres*
EMP: 13 **EST:** 1945
SALES (est): 3MM **Privately Held**
WEB: www.bakergas.com
SIC: 1311 Natural gas production

(G-20228)
BAUER COMPANY INC
119 Ruth Hill Rd (16262-4109)
PHONE...................................724 297-3200
David Snyder, *President*
James Held, *Sales Mgr*
EMP: 26
SALES (est): 3.7MM **Privately Held**
SIC: 3272 Concrete products

(G-20229)
COUNTRY FLAIR QUARTER
HORSES
214 Worthington S L Rd (16262-2830)
PHONE...................................724 822-8413
EMP: 3
SALES (est): 186.4K **Privately Held**
SIC: 3131 Quarters

(G-20230)
LOCKCRETE BAUER
119 Ruth Hill Rd (16262-4109)
PHONE...................................800 419-9255
Elmer Snyder, *President*
EMP: 3
SALES (est): 214.1K **Privately Held**
SIC: 3272 Concrete products, precast

(G-20231)
M & M LIME CO INC
215 Nichola Rd (16262-4303)
PHONE...................................724 297-3958
Kelli McGaughey, *President*
Scott McGaughey, *Vice Pres*
Tammy McGaughey, *Admin Sec*
EMP: 20 **EST:** 1958
SQ FT: 700
SALES (est): 2.5MM **Privately Held**
SIC: 1422 Crushed & broken limestone

(G-20232)
ROSUCO INC
1503 Butler Rd (16262-3917)
PHONE...................................724 297-5610
Gary Bowser, *President*
EMP: 9 **EST:** 1984
SALES: 800K **Privately Held**
WEB: www.rosuco.com
SIC: 3993 Displays & cutouts, window &
lobby

(G-20233)
SNOWTOP LLC
1 Moonlight Dr (16262-9730)
PHONE...................................724 297-5491
Daniel Lucovich, *Mng Member*
EMP: 13
SALES (est): 1.1MM **Privately Held**
WEB: www.snowtop.com
SIC: 2033 Mushrooms: packaged in cans,
jars, etc.

(G-20234)
STROBEL MACHINE INC
1442 Butler Rd (16262-3999)
PHONE...................................724 297-3441
Larry Strobel, *President*
Marilyn J Strobel, *Treasurer*
EMP: 13 **EST:** 1946
SQ FT: 14,000
SALES (est): 1.2MM **Privately Held**
WEB: www.strobelmachine.com
SIC: 3599 Machine shop, jobbing & repair

Wrightsville
York County

(G-20235)
COUNTY LINE QUARRY INC
740 S Front St (17368-9794)
P.O. Box 99 (17368-0099)
PHONE...................................717 252-1584
Ed Kline, *Branch Mgr*
EMP: 20
SALES (corp-wide): 9.3MM **Privately**
Held
SIC: 1422 3273 Crushed & broken lime-
stone; ready-mixed concrete
PA: County Line Quarry, Inc.
1750 Walton Rd
Blue Bell PA
610 832-8000

(G-20236)
DONSCO INC (PA)
Also Called: Registry For Excellence
124 N Front St (17368-1374)
PHONE...................................717 252-1561
Arthur K Mann, *President*
Arthur Mann Jr, *President*
Chris Buck, *Vice Pres*
Michael Day, *Vice Pres*
John Smeltzer, *Vice Pres*
▲ **EMP:** 375
SALES (est): 191.5MM **Privately Held**
WEB: www.donsco.com
SIC: 3398 3321 Metal heat treating; gray
iron castings

(G-20237)
HIGHWAY MATERIALS INC
740 S Front St (17368-9794)
PHONE..................................717 252-3636
Ben Burchard, *Purchasing*
Steve Bolger, *Controller*
Michael Landis, *Sales Staff*
Carl Miller, *Manager*
EMP: 4
SALES (corp-wide): 10.1MM **Privately Held**
WEB: www.highwaymaterials.com
SIC: **2951** 5032 Asphalt & asphaltic paving mixtures (not from refineries); paving materials
PA: Highway Materials, Inc.
409 Stenton Ave
Flourtown PA 19031
610 832-8000

(G-20238)
IMPERIAL EAGLE PRODUCTS INC
319 Cool Creek Rd (17368-9382)
P.O. Box 148, Columbia (17512-0148)
PHONE..................................717 252-1573
Heidi Nikolaus, *Office Mgr*
Gregory Nikolaus, *Mng Member*
EMP: 10
SALES (est): 1.7MM **Privately Held**
SIC: **2421** 6519 Custom sawmill; real property lessors

(G-20239)
J AND D CUSTOM STRINGS
118 Brook Ln (17368-1414)
PHONE..................................717 252-4078
Donna Loser, *Owner*
Jack Loser, *Co-Owner*
EMP: 13
SALES (est): 400K **Privately Held**
SIC: **3949** Archery equipment, general

(G-20240)
KAUFFMAN ELEC CONTRLS & CONTG
Also Called: Kauffman Controls
1058 Cool Creek Rd (17368-9126)
PHONE..................................717 252-3667
Kenneth A Kauffman, *President*
Timothy D Bricker, *Treasurer*
Elaine Kauffman, *Admin Sec*
EMP: 50
SQ FT: 10,000
SALES: 1.5MM **Privately Held**
WEB: www.krbmachinery.com
SIC: **3613** 3541 Control panels, electric; machine tools, metal cutting type

(G-20241)
LEHMAN SCIENTIFIC LLC
85 Surrey Dr (17368-9081)
PHONE..................................717 244-7540
Wade Lehman,
EMP: 3
SQ FT: 18,000
SALES (est): 310.7K **Privately Held**
SIC: **5049** 3825 Laboratory equipment, except medical or dental; test equipment for electronic & electric measurement

(G-20242)
MOON DANCER VINEYARDS & WINERY
1282 Klines Run Rd (17368-9120)
PHONE..................................717 252-9463
Jim Miller, *Principal*
EMP: 7
SALES (est): 778.4K **Privately Held**
SIC: **2084** Wines

(G-20243)
SCRITCHFIELD CONTROLS LLC
210 S 2nd St (17368-1514)
PHONE..................................717 887-5992
Randee Scritchfield,
Greg Scritchfield,
EMP: 3
SALES (est): 442.7K **Privately Held**
SIC: **3823** Temperature instruments: industrial process type

(G-20244)
STEWART WELDING & FABG INC
Also Called: Swf Industrial
6287 Lincoln Hwy (17368-9341)
PHONE..................................717 252-3948
Al Stewart, *President*
Robert Bretz, *Project Mgr*
Allen Edgell, *Project Mgr*
Tom Hanlon, *Project Mgr*
Ben Martin, *Project Mgr*
EMP: 89
SQ FT: 76,000
SALES (est): 37.7MM **Privately Held**
WEB: www.swfindustrial.com
SIC: **3444** 3441 Sheet metalwork; fabricated structural metal

---

Wyalusing
Bradford County

(G-20245)
BLUHMS GAS SALES INC
44340 Route 6 (18853-8921)
PHONE..................................570 746-2440
Keith Bluhm Sr, *President*
EMP: 10
SALES (est): 1.6MM **Privately Held**
SIC: **3714** Propane conversion equipment, motor vehicle

(G-20246)
BOB JOHNSON FLAGSTONE INC
3658 Old Stagecoach Rd (18853-8013)
PHONE..................................570 746-0907
Robert Johnson, *Principal*
EMP: 3
SALES (est): 196K **Privately Held**
SIC: **3281** Flagstones

(G-20247)
C C ALLIS & SONS INC
2 Miles E Of Rte 467 (18853)
PHONE..................................570 744-2631
Donald Allis, *President*
Raymond R Allis, *President*
Donald D Allis, *Vice Pres*
EMP: 35 EST: 1940
SQ FT: 3,600
SALES: 9.6MM **Privately Held**
SIC: **5211** 2421 Lumber products; sawmills & planing mills, general

(G-20248)
CARGILL MEAT SOLUTIONS CORP
1252 Route 706 (18853-9073)
P.O. Box 188 (18853-0188)
PHONE..................................570 746-3000
Andy Ripic, *Branch Mgr*
EMP: 1200
SALES (corp-wide): 114.7B **Privately Held**
WEB: www.excelmeats.com
SIC: **2011** 2013 Beef products from beef slaughtered on site; sausages & other prepared meats
HQ: Cargill Meat Solutions Corp
151 N Main St Ste 900
Wichita KS 67202
316 291-2500

(G-20249)
DIECI UNITED STATES LLC (PA)
40851 Route 6 (18853-9069)
P.O. Box 741 (18853-0741)
PHONE..................................724 215-7081
Tracy Keeney, *CEO*
Jorge Salas, *President*
EMP: 6 EST: 2016
SQ FT: 30,000
SALES: 5.3MM **Privately Held**
SIC: **3531** Construction machinery

(G-20250)
EDSELL & EDSELL LOGGING
285 Herrickville Rd (18853-7865)
PHONE..................................570 746-3203
Walter Edsell, *Principal*
EMP: 3 EST: 2011

SALES (est): 300.8K **Privately Held**
SIC: **2411** Logging

(G-20251)
EVERGREEN OILFLD SOLUTIONS LLC
42751 Route 6 (18853-8203)
PHONE..................................570 485-9998
David Patrick, *Mng Member*
Jeff Homer, *Mng Member*
EMP: 15
SALES (est): 1.5MM **Privately Held**
SIC: **1389** 7389 Oil & gas wells: building, repairing & dismantling;

(G-20252)
FENTON WELDING LLC
41166 Route 6 (18853-8197)
PHONE..................................570 746-9018
Daniel L Fenton, *President*
Gary Matson, *Engineer*
Chad Fenton,
EMP: 35
SQ FT: 2,000
SALES (est): 2MM **Privately Held**
SIC: **7692** 1794 Welding repair; excavation work

(G-20253)
GROVEDALE WINERY & VINYARD (PA)
119 Grovedale Ln (18853-8933)
PHONE..................................570 746-1400
Jeff Homer, *President*
Jonathan Homer, *Principal*
EMP: 4
SALES (est): 327.1K **Privately Held**
SIC: **2084** Wines

(G-20254)
MESTEK INC
Arrow United Industries Div
450 Riverside Dr (18853-8926)
PHONE..................................570 746-1888
Ken Wahlers, *Opers-Prdtn-Mfg*
Terry Cobb, *Sales Executive*
Andrew Lamb, *Technology*
EMP: 105
SALES (corp-wide): 669.8MM **Privately Held**
WEB: www.arrowunited.com
SIC: **3444** Sheet metalwork
PA: Mestek, Inc.
260 N Elm St
Westfield MA 01085
413 568-9571

(G-20255)
P & N PACKING INC
180 Rr 2 (18853)
PHONE..................................570 746-1974
Walter E Newton III, *President*
Doris Newton, *Treasurer*
Roger Hoey, *Manager*
Debbie Cobb, *Admin Sec*
EMP: 24
SQ FT: 15,000
SALES (est): 4.5MM **Privately Held**
SIC: **5147** 5421 2011 Meats, fresh; meat markets, including freezer provisioners; meat packing plants

(G-20256)
ROBERT JOHNSON
Lime Hill Rd (18853)
PHONE..................................570 746-1287
Robert Johnson, *Owner*
EMP: 6 EST: 1971
SALES (est): 440K **Privately Held**
SIC: **1411** Dimension stone

(G-20257)
ROCK STAR QUARRIES LLC
75 Johnson Hill Ln (18853-9023)
PHONE..................................570 721-1426
EMP: 4 EST: 2015
SALES (est): 373.9K **Privately Held**
SIC: **1422** Crushed & broken limestone

(G-20258)
ROCKET-COURIER NEWSPAPER
Also Called: Rocket Shopper
302 State St (18853)
PHONE..................................570 746-1217
W David Keeler, *Owner*

EMP: 15 EST: 1887
SQ FT: 2,800
SALES: 1MM **Privately Held**
SIC: **2711** 2752 Newspapers: publishing only, not printed on site; commercial printing, offset

(G-20259)
TONY BENNETT FLAGSTONE
Also Called: Lombardo Quarry
3657 Old Stagecoach Rd (18853-8012)
PHONE..................................570 746-6015
Kim Bennett, *Principal*
EMP: 4
SALES (est): 287K **Privately Held**
SIC: **3281** Flagstones

Wycombe
Bucks County

(G-20260)
INDUSTRIAL INSTRS & SUPS INC
865 Cherry Ln (18980)
P.O. Box 416, Southampton (18966-0416)
PHONE..................................215 396-0822
Christine Walter, *President*
Charles Walter, *Vice Pres*
EMP: 10
SALES (est): 2.4MM **Privately Held**
WEB: www.iisusa.com
SIC: **3823** 5961 3829 5046 Humidity instruments, industrial process type; catalog sales; hardness testing equipment; balances, excluding laboratory; sewage testing apparatus; digital test equipment, electronic & electrical circuits; battery testers, electrical

---

Wyncote
Montgomery County

(G-20261)
ATD-AMERICAN CO
135 Greenwood Ave (19095-1396)
PHONE..................................215 576-1000
Jerome M Zaslow, *Ch of Bd*
Robert Zaslow, *President*
Jonathan Zaslow, *Vice Pres*
Janet Zaslow-Wischnia, *Vice Pres*
Ken Spector, *Opers Staff*
◆ EMP: 35 EST: 1931
SQ FT: 32,000
SALES: 25.6MM **Privately Held**
WEB: www.atdgsa.com
SIC: **2299** Broadwoven fabrics: linen, jute, hemp & ramie

(G-20262)
E S SPECIALTY MANUFACTURING
Also Called: L B Taxin
8470 Limekiln Pike B814 (19095-2701)
P.O. Box 11289, Elkins Park (19027-0289)
PHONE..................................215 635-0973
Joel Taxin, *Owner*
EMP: 3
SALES (est): 170K **Privately Held**
SIC: **3432** 5047 Plumbing fixture fittings & trim; medical & hospital equipment

(G-20263)
GENE SZCZUREK S QUARTERLY P R
26 North Ave (19095-1206)
PHONE..................................215 887-7377
EMP: 3
SALES (est): 140K **Privately Held**
SIC: **2721** Periodicals-Publishing/Printing

(G-20264)
MACK INFORMATION SYSTEMS INC
25 South Ave (19095-1340)
PHONE..................................215 884-8123
N Kenneth Mc Kinney, *President*
Matthew Williams, *Corp Secy*
John Clifford, *Vice Pres*
EMP: 14
SQ FT: 5,000

GEOGRAPHIC

SALES (est): 1.3MM **Privately Held**
SIC: 3825 7373 Instruments to measure electricity; computer system selling services

(G-20265)
NIKAL IMAGING PRODUCTS IN
1108 Arboretum Rd (19095-2025)
PHONE...................................215 887-1319
Brenda Wright, *President*
EMP: 4
SALES (est): 137.2K **Privately Held**
SIC: 3299 Images, small: gypsum, clay or papier mache

(G-20266)
THOMASTON MANUFACTURING LLC (PA)
135 Greenwood Ave (19095-1325)
PHONE...................................215 576-6352
Jerome M Zaslow,
Eric Wischnia,
Arnold Zaslow,
Robert Zaslow,
Spencer Zaslow,
▲ EMP: 8
SALES (est): 9.2MM **Privately Held**
WEB: www.thomastonmills.com
SIC: 2221 Broadwoven fabric mills, manmade

Wynnewood
Montgomery County

(G-20267)
FEAST MAG LLC
Also Called: Spoonful Mag
1210 W Wynnewood Rd (19096-2206)
PHONE...................................484 343-5483
Kristina Pines, *President*
EMP: 12
SALES: 500K **Privately Held**
SIC: 2721 7389 Magazines: publishing & printing;

(G-20268)
HARVEY M STERN & CO
Also Called: Antique Lighting
431 Haverford Rd (19096-2437)
PHONE...................................610 649-1728
EMP: 5
SQ FT: 5,000
SALES (est): 300K **Privately Held**
SIC: 3471 Plating/Polishing Service

(G-20269)
IMPILO LLC
Also Called: Health Tree
307 Violet Ln (19096-1656)
PHONE...................................610 662-2867
Joshua Stein, *CEO*
EMP: 3
SALES (est): 63.5K **Privately Held**
SIC: 7371 7372 Computer software development & applications; application computer software

(G-20270)
JEFCO MANUFACTURING INC
Also Called: Jefco Awning Manufacturing
432 Owen Rd (19096-1807)
PHONE...................................215 334-3220
Jeffrey Kleger, *President*
EMP: 10 EST: 1950
SQ FT: 5,000
SALES (est): 1.6MM **Privately Held**
SIC: 3444 5031 2394 Awnings & canopies; doors & windows; awnings, fabric: made from purchased materials

(G-20271)
QUANOTECH INC
428 Ballytore Cir (19096-2354)
PHONE...................................610 658-0116
Jeffrey M Rosenberg, *President*
EMP: 5
SALES (est): 430K **Privately Held**
SIC: 3843 Dental equipment & supplies

(G-20272)
RIBONOVA INC
100 E Lancaster Ave R133 (19096-3450)
PHONE...................................610 801-2541

Nigel Webb, *President*
EMP: 4
SALES (est): 350K **Privately Held**
SIC: 2834 Pharmaceutical preparations

(G-20273)
UNITED AMMUNITION CONTAINER (PA)
101h Cherry Ln (19096-1208)
PHONE...................................610 658-0888
Jeffrey Perelman, *President*
Brian King, *Plant Mgr*
EMP: 1 EST: 1961
SALES (est): 4.9MM **Privately Held**
SIC: 2655 Ammunition cans or tubes, board laminated with metal foil

Wyoming
Luzerne County

(G-20274)
BHS ENERGY LLC
56 Deer Path Ln (18644-9218)
PHONE...................................570 696-3754
Bryan Reggie,
EMP: 3
SALES (est): 327.2K **Privately Held**
SIC: 3523 Farm machinery & equipment

(G-20275)
DIAMOND MANUFACTURING COMPANY (HQ)
243 W Eigth St (18644)
P.O. Box 4174 (18644-0174)
PHONE...................................570 693-0300
Charles D Flack Jr, *CEO*
Rusty Flack, *CEO*
Harold E Flack II, *President*
David L Simpson, *President*
Marty Bonetski, *General Mgr*
▲ EMP: 185
SQ FT: 100,000
SALES: 137.4MM
SALES (corp-wide): 11.5B **Publicly Held**
WEB: www.diamondman.com
SIC: 3469 3471 3479 3089 Perforated metal, stamped; cleaning, polishing & finishing; coating of metals & formed products; plastic processing
PA: Reliance Steel & Aluminum Co.
350 S Grand Ave Ste 5100
Los Angeles CA 90071
213 687-7700

(G-20276)
DIAMOND MANUFACTURING COMPANY
Diamond Consolidated Inds
243 W 8th St (18644-1699)
PHONE...................................570 693-0300
David L Simpson, *Manager*
EMP: 15
SALES (corp-wide): 11.5B **Publicly Held**
SIC: 3469 3471 3479 3089 Perforated metal, stamped; cleaning, polishing & finishing; coating of metals & formed products; plastic processing; local trucking, without storage; sheets, metal
HQ: Diamond Manufacturing Company
243 W Eigth St
Wyoming PA 18644
570 693-0300

(G-20277)
EXETER ARCHITECTURAL PRODUCTS (PA)
243 W 8th St (18644-1609)
PHONE...................................570 693-4220
Charles D Flack Jr, *Ch of Bd*
Harold E Flack II, *President*
Keith A Zinn, *CFO*
EMP: 14
SQ FT: 90,000
SALES (est): 1.1MM **Privately Held**
SIC: 3446 Architectural metalwork

(G-20278)
GRUNDY INDUSTRIES LLC
944 Shoemaker Ave (18644-1122)
PHONE...................................570 609-5487
EMP: 3 EST: 2015

SALES (est): 160.9K **Privately Held**
SIC: 3999 Manufacturing industries

(G-20279)
INDEPENDENT GRAPHICS INC
242 W 8th St (18644-1643)
P.O. Box 703, Pittston (18640-0703)
PHONE...................................570 609-5267
Louis Ciampi Jr, *President*
Jim Ciampi, *Cust Mgr*
Pam Cartwright, *Office Mgr*
Jeff Fusco, *Manager*
Murph Murphy, *Manager*
EMP: 30
SQ FT: 5,600
SALES (est): 5.9MM **Privately Held**
WEB: www.independentgraphics.com
SIC: 2752 Commercial printing, offset

(G-20280)
JAMES EAGEN SONS COMPANY
200 W 8th St (18644-1610)
P.O. Box 4097 (18644-0097)
PHONE...................................570 693-2100
James E Golden Jr, *President*
Marie T Golden, *Vice Pres*
EMP: 35
SQ FT: 55,000
SALES (est): 6MM **Privately Held**
WEB: www.jameseagen.com
SIC: 3535 Conveyors & conveying equipment

(G-20281)
KITCHEN EXPRESS INC
Also Called: Aaron Products
55 W 7th St (18644-1616)
PHONE...................................570 693-0285
John Mosca, *President*
EMP: 10
SQ FT: 10,000
SALES: 900K **Privately Held**
SIC: 5211 2434 Cabinets, kitchen; wood kitchen cabinets

(G-20282)
KITCHEN EXPRESS OF WYOMING
55 W 7th St (18644-1616)
PHONE...................................570 693-0285
John Mosca, *President*
EMP: 5
SQ FT: 12,000
SALES (est): 380K **Privately Held**
SIC: 2434 Wood kitchen cabinets

(G-20283)
PREBOLA ENTERPRISES INC
206 W 6th St (18644-1713)
PHONE...................................570 693-3036
Edward Prebola, *President*
EMP: 50
SQ FT: 21,500
SALES (est): 8.1MM **Privately Held**
SIC: 3544 Special dies, tools, jigs & fixtures

(G-20284)
SANTARELLI VIBRATED BLOCK LLC
Also Called: Santarelli Ready Mixed Con
966 Shoemaker Ave (18644-1122)
PHONE...................................570 693-2200
EMP: 15 EST: 1935
SQ FT: 10,000
SALES (est): 2.1MM **Privately Held**
SIC: 3271 3273 Mfg Concrete Block/Brick Mfg Ready-Mixed Concrete

(G-20285)
USM AEROSTRUCTURES CORP
Also Called: Usma
74 W 6th St (18644-1705)
PHONE...................................570 613-1234
Ernesto S Jurado, *President*
EMP: 50
SQ FT: 50,000
SALES (est): 9.6MM **Privately Held**
WEB: www.usmaero.net
SIC: 3728 3721 Aircraft parts & equipment; aircraft

Wyomissing
Berks County

(G-20286)
AMERICAN POWERNET MGT LP
45 Commerce Dr (19610-1038)
PHONE...................................610 372-8500
R S Helm, *Partner*
Greg Krajnik, *Vice Pres*
Jordan Dialectos, *Wholesale*
Linda Jablonski, *Manager*
EMP: 9
SALES (est): 2.5MM **Privately Held**
WEB: www.americanpowernet.com
SIC: 3612 4911 Power transformers, electric;

(G-20287)
R M PALMER COMPANY
800 Van Reed Rd (19610-1711)
P.O. Box 1723, Reading (19603-1723)
PHONE...................................610 374-5224
Robert Burkart, *Plant Mgr*
Bill Boczkowski, *Manager*
EMP: 218
SALES (corp-wide): 110.2MM **Privately Held**
WEB: www.rmpalmer.com
SIC: 2066 2064 Chocolate candy, solid; chocolate candy, except solid chocolate
PA: R. M. Palmer Company
77 S 2nd Ave
Reading PA 19611
610 372-8971

(G-20288)
SAVOR STREET FOODS INC (PA)
1 Park Plz (19610-1301)
P.O. Box 15053, Reading (19612-5053)
PHONE...................................610 320-7800
John J Mastromarino, *Vice Ch Bd*
Scott R Carpenter, *President*
Marcia Welch, *Corp Secy*
Roy Emery, *Vice Pres*
Joseph F Welch, *Treasurer*
▲ EMP: 50
SQ FT: 20,000
SALES (est): 93.3MM **Privately Held**
WEB: www.thepretzelstore.com
SIC: 2052 2096 2099 Pretzels; potato chips & other potato-based snacks; cheese curls & puffs; popcorn, already popped (except candy covered); corn chips & other corn-based snacks; food preparations

(G-20289)
SURGICAL SPECIALTIES CORP
1100 Berkshire Blvd # 308 (19610-1221)
PHONE...................................610 404-1000
EMP: 14
SALES (corp-wide): 278.3MM **Privately Held**
SIC: 3842 3841 Sutures, absorbable & non-absorbable; knives, surgical; needles, suture
HQ: Surgical Specialties Corporation
247 Station Dr Ste Ne1
Westwood MA 02090
781 751-1000

Wysox
Bradford County

(G-20290)
PICKERING WINERY
27697 Pennsylvania 187 (18854)
PHONE...................................570 247-7269
Jim Pickering, *Principal*
EMP: 4
SALES (est): 296.1K **Privately Held**
SIC: 2084 Wines

(G-20291)
WYSOX S&G INC
Also Called: Wysox Sand and Gravel
22448 Route 187 (18854)
PHONE...................................570 265-6760
Andrew Bishop, *President*

Donald Bishop, *Vice Pres*
EMP: 11
SALES (est): 1.4MM **Privately Held**
SIC: 3273 1442 Ready-mixed concrete;
construction sand & gravel

Yardley
Bucks County

(G-20292)
21ST CENTURY NEWSPAPERS INC
Lower Makefield Corporate (19067)
PHONE.................................215 504-4200
William J Higginson, *Principal*
EMP: 6 **EST:** 2012
SALES (est): 227.5K **Privately Held**
SIC: 2711 Newspapers

(G-20293)
ADVANCED SOFTWARE INC
301 Oxford Valley Rd (19067-7706)
PHONE.................................215 369-7800
Joseph Hentz, *President*
Julie Hentz, *Treasurer*
John Loeb, *Administration*
EMP: 12
SQ FT: 1,200
SALES (est): 1.3MM **Privately Held**
WEB: www.advantzware.com
SIC: 7372 5734 5045 Business oriented
computer software; computer software &
accessories; computers

(G-20294)
ALIEN FUEL INC
1220 Linden Ave (19067-7416)
PHONE.................................609 306-8592
Burton C Smith Jr, *Principal*
EMP: 4
SALES (est): 348.3K **Privately Held**
SIC: 2869 Fuels

(G-20295)
AMERICAN LYOPHILIZER INC
668 Stony Hill Rd (19067-4498)
PHONE.................................610 999-4151
William Rariden, *President*
▼ **EMP:** 14
SQ FT: 4,000
SALES (est): 930K **Privately Held**
WEB: www.freezedrying.com
SIC: 3821 Dryers, laboratory

(G-20296)
AQUAMED TECHNOLOGIES INC
1010 Stony Hill Rd # 200 (19067-5518)
PHONE.................................215 970-7194
EMP: 3
SALES (est): 254.5K **Privately Held**
SIC: 2834 Pharmaceutical preparations

(G-20297)
BMS INC (PA)
679 Deerpath Rd (19067-3006)
PHONE.................................609 883-5155
Vera Bongartz, *President*
EMP: 9
SQ FT: 22,000
SALES (est): 2.5MM **Privately Held**
SIC: 2899 5112 3861 Ink or writing fluids;
inked ribbons; photographic equipment &
supplies

(G-20298)
BRY MAR TROPHY INC
85 Makefield Rd Ste 13 (19067-5967)
PHONE.................................215 295-4053
Rita Chesley, *President*
EMP: 8 **EST:** 1957
SQ FT: 2,000
SALES (est): 959.4K **Privately Held**
WEB: www.brymartrophy.com
SIC: 3914 3999 5999 Trophies, plated (all
metals); plaques, picture, laminated; tro-
phies & plaques

(G-20299)
BUCKS SHIP & PRINT
25 S Main St Ste 6 (19067-1527)
PHONE.................................215 493-8100
Ramon Regaino, *Manager*
EMP: 6

SALES (est): 708.8K **Privately Held**
SIC: 2752 Commercial printing, offset

(G-20300)
CHARKIT CHEMICAL COMPANY LLC
301 Oxford Valley Rd (19067-7706)
PHONE.................................267 573-4062
EMP: 4
SALES (corp-wide): 141.7MM **Privately Held**
SIC: 2899 Chemical preparations
PA: Charkit Chemical Company, Llc
32 Haviland St Unit 1
Norwalk CT 06854
203 299-3220

(G-20301)
CRAMER PARTNERSHIP
Also Called: Cramer Bakery
26 E Afton Ave (19067-1414)
PHONE.................................215 378-6024
Thomas Cramer, *Partner*
EMP: 3
SQ FT: 12,086
SALES (est): 80.5K **Privately Held**
WEB: www.cramerbakery.com
SIC: 6512 2052 2051 Commercial & in-
dustrial building operation; cookies &
crackers; bread, cake & related products

(G-20302)
CROWN CORK & SEAL COMPANY INC
770 Township Line Rd # 100 (19067-4232)
PHONE.................................215 698-5100
Timothy J Donahue, *President*
William T Gallagher, *Senior VP*
Thomas A Kelly, *CFO*
Kevin C Clothier, *Treasurer*
Adam J Dickstein, *Admin Sec*
EMP: 4400
SALES (est): 177.2MM
SALES (corp-wide): 11.1B **Publicly Held**
SIC: 3411 Tin cans
PA: Crown Holdings Inc.
770 Township Line Rd # 100
Yardley PA 19067
215 698-5100

(G-20303)
CROWN CORK & SEAL USA INC (HQ)
770 Township Line Rd # 100 (19067-4232)
PHONE.................................215 698-5100
Djalma Novaes Jr, *President*
Michael J Rowley, *Counsel*
Alfred J Dermody, *Vice Pres*
Edward C Vesey, *Vice Pres*
Robert Lucas, *Plant Mgr*
◆ **EMP:** 375 **EST:** 1996
SALES (est): 1.8B
SALES (corp-wide): 11.1B **Publicly Held**
WEB: www.crowncork.com
SIC: 3466 3411 Crowns & closures; jar
tops & crowns, stamped metal; bottle
caps & tops, stamped metal; tin cans
PA: Crown Holdings Inc.
770 Township Line Rd # 100
Yardley PA 19067
215 698-5100

(G-20304)
CROWN HOLDINGS INC (PA)
770 Township Line Rd # 100 (19067-4232)
PHONE.................................215 698-5100
John W Conway, *Ch of Bd*
Timothy J Donahue, *President*
Gerard H Gifford, *COO*
William T Gallagher, *Senior VP*
David A Beaver, *Vice Pres*
◆ **EMP:** 172
SALES: 11.1B **Publicly Held**
WEB: www.crownholdings.net
SIC: 3411 3466 3499 Metal cans; tin
cans; aluminum cans; bottle caps & tops,
stamped metal; jar tops & crowns,
stamped metal; closures, stamped metal;
aerosol valves, metal

(G-20305)
CROWN INTL HOLDINGS INC (HQ)
770 Township Line Rd (19067-4219)
PHONE.................................215 698-5100

Timothy Donahue, *President*
Patrick Szmyt, *Principal*
EMP: 300
SQ FT: 50,000
SALES (est): 10.1MM
SALES (corp-wide): 11.1B **Publicly Held**
SIC: 3411 Metal cans
PA: Crown Holdings Inc.
770 Township Line Rd # 100
Yardley PA 19067
215 698-5100

(G-20306)
DHARINI LLC
1471 Hidden Pond Dr (19067-4494)
PHONE.................................215 595-3915
Mihir Vyas, *Mng Member*
EMP: 15
SALES (est): 639.5K **Privately Held**
SIC: 2051 7389 Doughnuts, except
frozen;

(G-20307)
DIGITAL FIRST MEDIA INC
Lower Makefield Corpor (19067)
PHONE.................................215 504-4200
William J Higginson, *Principal*
Jim Mitchell, *Sr Ntwrk Engine*
Jim Ackerman, *Director*
EMP: 8
SALES (est): 308.1K **Privately Held**
SIC: 2711 Newspapers

(G-20308)
DIRECT MARKETING PUBLISHERS
1304 University Dr (19067-2829)
PHONE.................................215 321-3068
Bernard A Goldberg, *President*
Sandra Goldberg, *CFO*
EMP: 2
SALES (est): 1MM **Privately Held**
WEB: www.dmpublishers.com
SIC: 2731 8748 Books: publishing only;
publishing consultant

(G-20309)
EURAND PHARMACEUTICALS INC
790 Township Line Rd (19067-4248)
PHONE.................................937 898-9669
Gearoid Faherty, *President*
EMP: 50
SALES (est): 3.9MM **Privately Held**
SIC: 2834 Pharmaceutical preparations

(G-20310)
EXIM STEEL & SHIPBROKING INC
1215 Knox Dr (19067-4423)
PHONE.................................215 369-9746
Nilkanth Trivedi, *President*
Priya Trivedi, *Corp Secy*
Priti Trivedi, *Treasurer*
◆ **EMP:** 5
SALES: 5MM **Privately Held**
SIC: 5051 3549 5093 3545 Steel; metal-
working machinery; scrap & waste materi-
als; machine tool accessories; stainless
steel

(G-20311)
FIBER OPTIC DESIGNS INC
1790 Yardley Langhorne Rd (19067-5523)
PHONE.................................215 321-9750
David Allen, *President*
EMP: 4
SALES (est): 383.2K **Privately Held**
SIC: 3699 Christmas tree lighting sets,
electric

(G-20312)
FX EXPRESS PUBLICATIONS INC
Also Called: Global Traveler
310 Floral Vale Blvd (19067-5525)
PHONE.................................267 364-5811
Francis X Gallagher, *President*
Kim Krol, *Editor*
Angelique Platas, *Marketing Staff*
Jan Hecht, *Senior Editor*
Fran Gallagher, *Officer*
EMP: 3

SALES (est): 380.8K **Privately Held**
SIC: 2721 Magazines: publishing only, not
printed on site

(G-20313)
GREENERWAYS LLC (PA)
668 Stony Hill Rd Ste 143 (19067-4498)
PHONE.................................215 280-7658
Jayme Bella, *CEO*
EMP: 10 **EST:** 2010
SALES (est): 2MM **Privately Held**
SIC: 2869 Industrial organic chemicals

(G-20314)
HERAEUS INCORPORATED (DH)
770 Township Line Rd # 300 (19067-4232)
PHONE.................................215 944-9981
Maike Schuh Klaeren, *President*
Thomas Lyons, *Treasurer*
Fred Salek, *Admin Sec*
◆ **EMP:** 8
SQ FT: 3,000
SALES (est): 434.1MM
SALES (corp-wide): 96.1K **Privately Held**
WEB: www.heraeuspm.com
SIC: 3399 3823 3339 3469 Paste, metal;
temperature measurement instruments,
industrial; precious metals; machine
parts, stamped or pressed metal
HQ: Heraeus Holding Gesellschaft Mit
Beschrankter Haftung
Heraeusstr. 12-14
Hanau 63450
618 135-0

(G-20315)
HERAEUS INCORPORATED
Materials Technology Division
770 Township Line Rd # 300 (19067-4232)
PHONE.................................480 961-9200
Michael Barthmoulous, *Principal*
EMP: 400
SQ FT: 49,606
SALES (corp-wide): 96.1K **Privately Held**
WEB: www.heraeuspm.com
SIC: 3469 3341 3339 Metal stampings;
secondary nonferrous metals; primary
nonferrous metals
HQ: Heraeus Incorporated
770 Township Line Rd # 300
Yardley PA 19067
215 944-9981

(G-20316)
HERAEUS PRCOUS MTLS N AMER LLC
Also Called: Heraeus Group
770 Township Line Rd (19067-4219)
PHONE.................................562 921-7464
Uve Kupka, *President*
Levon Fattal, *Engineer*
Kim Jessum, *General Counsel*
EMP: 6 **EST:** 2000
SALES (est): 82.7K **Privately Held**
SIC: 7372 Business oriented computer
software

(G-20317)
HERAEUS QUARTZ AMERICA LLC (DH)
770 Township Line Rd # 300 (19067-4232)
PHONE.................................512 703-9000
Arno Pitzen, *President*
Frederick Salek, *Admin Sec*
▲ **EMP:** 75
SALES (est): 16.6MM
SALES (corp-wide): 96.1K **Privately Held**
SIC: 3679 Quartz crystals, for electronic
application
HQ: Heraeus Holding Gesellschaft Mit
Beschrankter Haftung
Heraeusstr. 12-14
Hanau 63450
618 135-0

(G-20318)
HERAEUS QUARTZ AMERICA LLC
770 Township Line Rd # 300 (19067-4232)
PHONE.................................512 251-2027
Howard Savage, *Manager*
EMP: 7
SALES (corp-wide): 96.1K **Privately Held**
SIC: 3679 Quartz crystals, for electronic
application

HQ: Heraeus Quartz America Llc
770 Township Line Rd # 300
Yardley PA 19067
512 703-9000

(G-20319)
HERAEUS SENSOR TECH USA LLC
770 Township Line Rd # 300 (19067-4232)
PHONE.................................732 940-4400
David Molnar, *Partner*
▲ EMP: 6
SALES: 1,000K **Privately Held**
SIC: 3823 Industrial instrmnts msrmnt display/control process variable

(G-20320)
HOOTBOARD LLC
2 Spring Ln (19067-5401)
PHONE.................................610 844-2423
Satyajeet Shahade, *CEO*
EMP: 7 EST: 2014
SALES (est): 168K **Privately Held**
SIC: 7372 7389 Business oriented computer software;

(G-20321)
HPF LLC
Also Called: High Performance Formulas
2001 Makefield Rd (19067-3127)
PHONE.................................215 321-8170
Blaine Applegate,
EMP: 5
SQ FT: 4,000
SALES (est): 325.5K **Privately Held**
WEB: www.hpfonline.com
SIC: 2023 Dietary supplements, dairy & non-dairy based

(G-20322)
JAS PRECISION INC
355 Ramsey Rd (19067-4627)
PHONE.................................215 239-7299
John A Snedeker, *President*
Lisa Snedeker, *Treasurer*
EMP: 5
SALES (est): 300K **Privately Held**
SIC: 1731 3827 Fiber optic cable installation; optical instruments & apparatus

(G-20323)
LONG ISLAND PLLUTION STRIPPERS
Also Called: Lip Strippers
484 Franklin Cir (19067-7229)
PHONE.................................215 752-2709
David Adler, *President*
EMP: 3
SQ FT: 200
SALES (est): 250K **Privately Held**
SIC: 3829 Measuring & controlling devices

(G-20324)
LUXURY ELECTRONICS LLC
660 Bayberry Ln (19067-6337)
PHONE.................................215 847-0937
Matthew Farrell, *Mng Member*
EMP: 5
SALES (est): 117.2K **Privately Held**
SIC: 7372 7389 Application computer software;

(G-20325)
MICROSILVER WEAR LLC
593 Nottingham Dr (19067-3324)
PHONE.................................215 917-7203
Ignazio M Indiano, *Mng Member*
EMP: 3
SQ FT: 1,200
SALES: 250K **Privately Held**
SIC: 2297 2211 Nonwoven fabrics; sheets & sheetings, cotton

(G-20326)
MM USA HOLDINGS LLC (PA)
780 Township Line Rd (19067-4200)
PHONE.................................267 685-2300
William Goldberg, *CEO*
Amy Milkowski, *Editor*
Cindy Shaw, *Editor*
Earlene Biggs, *Vice Pres*
Paul Miller, *Vice Pres*
EMP: 475
SQ FT: 106,500

SALES (est): 441MM **Privately Held**
WEB: www.medimedia.com
SIC: 2741 8732 Miscellaneous publishing; market analysis or research

(G-20327)
MORRIS MILLWORK LLC
82 Sutphin Pnes (19067-3460)
PHONE.................................215 736-0708
Dorothy Rosh, *Principal*
EMP: 4
SALES (est): 483.6K **Privately Held**
SIC: 2431 Millwork

(G-20328)
NEURODX DEVELOPMENT LLC
115 E Ferry Rd (19067-1020)
PHONE.................................609 865-4426
Frederick J Fritz,
EMP: 4
SALES (est): 347.2K **Privately Held**
SIC: 3841 Surgical & medical instruments

(G-20329)
NITROGEN
800 Township Line Rd (19067-4237)
PHONE.................................440 208-7474
EMP: 3
SALES (est): 123.2K **Privately Held**
SIC: 2813 Mfg Industrial Gases

(G-20330)
OPTINOSE INC (PA)
1020 Stony Hill Rd # 300 (19067-5539)
PHONE.................................267 364-3500
Peter K Miller, *CEO*
Larry G Pickering, *Ch of Bd*
Ramy A Mahmoud, *President*
Michele Janis, *Vice Pres*
Keith A Goldan, *CFO*
EMP: 6 EST: 2000
SQ FT: 20,500
SALES: 7MM **Publicly Held**
SIC: 2834 Pharmaceutical preparations

(G-20331)
PENNGEAR LLC
2305 Waterford Rd (19067-5433)
P.O. Box 727, Washington Crossing (18977-0727)
PHONE.................................215 968-2403
Craig Stranahan,
EMP: 5 EST: 2016
SALES: 500K **Privately Held**
SIC: 3566 7389 Speed changers, drives & gears;

(G-20332)
PERFORMANCE ADDITIVES LLC
33 S Delaware Ave Ste 204 (19067-1524)
PHONE.................................215 321-4388
Arthur Van Nostrand, *Mng Member*
Thomas Saloon,
▲ EMP: 15
SQ FT: 3,000
SALES: 30MM **Privately Held**
WEB: www.performance-additives.com
SIC: 2821 Plastics materials & resins

(G-20333)
PRIME PACKAGING LLC (PA)
Also Called: Kollman Label and Packg Group
1000 Garey Dr (19067-4561)
PHONE.................................215 499-0446
Kevin Kollman, *President*
EMP: 70
SALES (est): 3.6MM **Privately Held**
SIC: 2759 2671 Flexographic printing; packaging paper & plastics film, coated & laminated

(G-20334)
PRINT2FINISH LLC
835 Hudson Dr (19067-4319)
PHONE.................................215 369-5494
Larry Macko,
◆ EMP: 4
SALES (est): 470.3K **Privately Held**
SIC: 2752 Commercial printing, offset

(G-20335)
PRINTWEARONLINE
510 Heritage Oak Dr (19067-5623)
PHONE.................................267 987-6118
EMP: 3

SALES (est): 200.7K **Privately Held**
SIC: 2752 Commercial printing, lithographic

(G-20336)
ROYAL KARINA AIR SERVICE INC
504 Aspen Woods Dr (19067-6340)
PHONE.................................215 321-3981
Robert L Cherry, *President*
Gail Cherry, *Vice Pres*
EMP: 5
SALES: 500K **Privately Held**
SIC: 3699 Flight simulators (training aids), electronic

(G-20337)
RPW GROUP INC
503 Jenny Dr (19067-5615)
PHONE.................................215 493-7456
Robert Williams, *President*
Judith Ann Williams, *Corp Secy*
EMP: 28
SALES (est): 3MM **Privately Held**
WEB: www.rpwgroup.com
SIC: 7336 3086 Package design; packaging & shipping materials, foamed plastic

(G-20338)
SANDVIK PUBG INTERACTIVE INC
9 South Dr (19067-3101)
PHONE.................................203 205-0188
Anna M Hladchuk, *President*
EMP: 44 **Privately Held**
SIC: 2741 Miscellaneous publishing
PA: Sandvik Publishing Interactive, Inc.
83 Wooster Hts Ste 208
Danbury CT 06810

(G-20339)
SIGMA BIOLOGICS INC
24203 Cornerstone Dr (19067-7948)
PHONE.................................215 741-1523
Ramesh G Shah, *President*
Daksha Shah, *Vice Pres*
EMP: 5
SALES: 100K **Privately Held**
WEB: www.sigmabiologics.com
SIC: 2836 Biological products, except diagnostic

(G-20340)
SPECIALTY PHRM PDTS LLC
1 Harlow Ct (19067-2716)
PHONE.................................215 321-5836
Ronald S Harland,
EMP: 10
SALES (est): 1MM **Privately Held**
SIC: 2834 Pharmaceutical preparations

(G-20341)
STAINLESS DISTRIBUTORS INC
1215 Knox Dr (19067-4423)
PHONE.................................215 369-9746
Nilkanth Trivedi, *President*
EMP: 5
SQ FT: 3,700
SALES: 4MM **Privately Held**
SIC: 3462 5051 Flange, valve & pipe fitting forgings, ferrous; forgings, ferrous; bars, metal; tubing, metal

(G-20342)
SYMPHONY BREWING SYSTEMS LLC
173 N Main St (19067-1321)
PHONE.................................215 493-0430
Donald James Kyle, *Principal*
EMP: 3 EST: 2011
SALES (est): 130.3K **Privately Held**
SIC: 2082 Malt beverages

(G-20343)
T FOSTER & CO INC
7 W Afton Ave (19067-1419)
P.O. Box 488 (19067-8488)
PHONE.................................215 493-1044
Timothy Foster, *President*
Rhiannon Davis, *Store Mgr*
Suzanne Foster, *Sales Staff*
EMP: 7
SQ FT: 1,200

SALES (est): 879.7K **Privately Held**
WEB: www.tfosterjewelers.com
SIC: 5944 5094 3911 Jewelry, precious stones & precious metals; jewelry; jewel settings & mountings, precious metal

(G-20344)
ULTRA-MOLD CORPORATION
301 Oxford Valley Rd 504a (19067-7711)
PHONE.................................215 493-9840
Fax: 215 493-1440
EMP: 3
SQ FT: 1,000
SALES: 473K **Privately Held**
SIC: 3089 Mfg Plastic Products

(G-20345)
WOOD HOLLOW CRAFTS LLC
561 Gordon Dr (19067-3803)
PHONE.................................215 428-0870
Susan Salyer, *Mng Member*
Darren Salyer,
Dennis Salyer,
Joshua Salyer,
EMP: 4
SALES (est): 284.8K **Privately Held**
WEB: www.woodhollowcrafts.net
SIC: 3944 Craft & hobby kits & sets

(G-20346)
YARDLEY PRODUCTS LLC
Also Called: Yardley Products Corp.
10 W College Ave (19067-1517)
P.O. Box 357 (19067-8357)
PHONE.................................215 493-2700
Ken Grady, *President*
Tim Bailey, *Co-President*
EMP: 20
SALES (est): 3.9MM
SALES (corp-wide): 282.2MM **Privately Held**
WEB: www.yardleyproducts.com
SIC: 3429 3541 Metal fasteners; machine tools, metal cutting type
HQ: Dixon Valve & Coupling Company, Llc
800 High St
Chestertown MD 21620

(G-20347)
ZIAMATIC CORP (PA)
Also Called: Zico Safety Products
10 W College Ave (19067-1592)
P.O. Box 337 (19067-8337)
PHONE.................................215 493-2777
Mike Ziaylek, *President*
Mike Adams, *Vice Pres*
Ronald Larue, *Vice Pres*
Joan Ziaylek, *CFO*
Joan E Ziaylek, *Treasurer*
▼ EMP: 33 EST: 1960
SQ FT: 50,000
SALES (est): 8.8MM **Privately Held**
WEB: www.ziamatic.com
SIC: 3569 3647 Firefighting apparatus & related equipment; firefighting apparatus; boat & ship lighting fixtures

Yatesboro
Armstrong County

(G-20348)
RANGE RSURCES - APPALACHIA LLC
Also Called: Range Operating Company
150 4th Ave N (16263)
PHONE.................................724 783-7144
Denton Barret, *Manager*
EMP: 25
SALES (corp-wide): 3.2B **Publicly Held**
WEB: www.gl-energy.com
SIC: 1382 Oil & gas exploration services
HQ: Range Resources - Appalachia, Llc.
3000 Town Center Blvd
Canonsburg PA 15317
724 743-6700

Yatesville
Luzerne County

(G-20349)
VILIMIA INC (PA)
Also Called: Adhesives & Chemicals
131 Brown Rd (18640-3722)
PHONE.................................570 654-6735
William Fischer, *President*
EMP: 12
SQ FT: 24,000
SALES (est): 2.9MM **Privately Held**
WEB: www.adhesivesandchemicals.com
SIC: 2891 Adhesives

Yeadon
Delaware County

(G-20350)
1732 MEATS LLC
6250 Baltimore Ave (19050-2700)
PHONE.................................267 879-7214
ARI Miller, *Principal*
EMP: 3
SALES (est): 182.5K **Privately Held**
SIC: 2011 Bacon, slab & sliced from meat slaughtered on site

(G-20351)
BRYN HILL INDUSTRIES INC
407 Industrial Park Dr (19050-3010)
PHONE.................................610 623-4005
Leslie R Archard, *President*
Deborah L Archard, *Corp Secy*
Deborah Young, *Web Dvlpr*
EMP: 20
SQ FT: 16,000
SALES (est): 5.7MM **Privately Held**
SIC: 3086 Packaging & shipping materials, foamed plastic

(G-20352)
DELAWARE TOOL & MACHINE CO
Also Called: Dti
544 Industrial Park Dr (19050-3032)
PHONE.................................610 259-1810
Kevin T Yum, *CEO*
Bryan Yum, *President*
Rick Giordano, *General Mgr*
EMP: 23
SQ FT: 30,000
SALES (est): 1.7MM **Privately Held**
SIC: 3599 3769 Machine shop, jobbing & repair; guided missile & space vehicle parts & auxiliary equipment

(G-20353)
DIGITAL IMPACT LLC
451 Penn St (19050-3016)
P.O. Box 5324, Lansdowne (19050-9324)
PHONE.................................610 623-1269
Robert A Mormile, *Managing Prtnr*
EMP: 4
SALES (est): 584K **Privately Held**
SIC: 2752 Commercial printing, offset

(G-20354)
HYDROL CHEMICAL COMPANY INC
520 Commerce Dr (19050-3076)
PHONE.................................610 622-3603
H F Haabestad Jr, *President*
Harold F Haabestad Jr, *President*
Michael Martin, *Sales Staff*
EMP: 15 EST: 1929
SQ FT: 12,000
SALES (est): 2.5MM **Privately Held**
WEB: www.hydrolchemical.com
SIC: 2869 2899 Embalming fluids; chemical preparations

(G-20355)
MARTINO SIGNS INC (PA)
453 Penn St (19050-3016)
PHONE.................................610 622-7446
David Martino, *President*
EMP: 10
SALES (est): 1.3MM **Privately Held**
SIC: 3993 Signs & advertising specialties

(G-20356)
UNION PACKAGING LLC
6250 Baltimore Ave Ste 1 (19050-2700)
PHONE.................................610 572-7265
Mike Pearson, *President*
▲ EMP: 56
SQ FT: 105,000
SALES (est): 12.1MM **Privately Held**
SIC: 2657 8742 4225 8741 Folding paperboard boxes; marketing consulting services; general warehousing & storage; management services

Yeagertown
Mifflin County

(G-20357)
MOLEK BROTHERS
250 High Dump Rd (17099-9414)
P.O. Box 444 (17099-0444)
PHONE.................................717 248-8032
Jeffrey Molek, *Partner*
Tom Molek, *Administration*
EMP: 3
SALES (est): 300.7K **Privately Held**
SIC: 3312 3639 Rods, iron & steel: made in steel mills; trash compactors, household

Yoe
York County

(G-20358)
ARCHETYPE FRAMELESS GLASS CO
180 S Orchard St (17313-1000)
PHONE.................................717 244-5240
Paul J Weber, *President*
Todd E Stahl, *Vice Pres*
Karen Fackler, *Sales Staff*
EMP: 8 EST: 1999
SQ FT: 10,000
SALES (est): 1.1MM **Privately Held**
WEB: www.archetypeglass.com
SIC: 3231 Decorated glassware: chipped, engraved, etched, etc.

(G-20359)
CUSTOM MOLDS PLASTIC
165 S Orchard St (17313-1009)
PHONE.................................717 417-5639
EMP: 3
SALES (est): 207.4K **Privately Held**
SIC: 3089 Injection molding of plastics

(G-20360)
EPIC PICKLES LLC
165b S Orchard St (17313-1009)
PHONE.................................717 487-1323
Robert Seufert, *Mng Member*
EMP: 4
SALES (est): 251.4K **Privately Held**
SIC: 2035 Pickled fruits & vegetables

York
York County

(G-20361)
A/C SERVICE AND REPAIR INC
5166 Commerce Dr (17408-9510)
PHONE.................................717 792-3492
Robert Ross, *President*
EMP: 22
SQ FT: 22,000
SALES (est): 7.8MM **Privately Held**
WEB: www.acserviceandrepair.com
SIC: 5085 7699 3491 Valves & fittings; valve repair, industrial; industrial valves

(G-20362)
AARON ENTERPRISES INC
300 Cloverleaf Rd (17406-6028)
PHONE.................................717 854-2641
Vincent Trice, *President*
Kathleen Arice, *Vice Pres*
Darrin Smith, *Safety Mgr*
Bob McDowell, *Engineer*
Johnathan Seibert, *Engineer*
▲ EMP: 151
SQ FT: 50,000

EMP: 74
SALES (est): 5.4MM **Privately Held**
SIC: 3541 1799 Drilling & boring machines; boring for building construction

(G-20363)
ACCENT METALS INC
3675 Sandhurst Dr (17406-7927)
PHONE.................................717 699-5676
Steven Feldman, *President*
Michael Marino, *Vice Pres*
EMP: 15
SALES (est): 3.4MM **Privately Held**
SIC: 3471 5051 Polishing, metals or formed products; metals service centers & offices

(G-20364)
ACCENT METALS INC
3675 Sandhurst Dr (17406-7927)
PHONE.................................717 699-5676
Fax: 717 815-1676
EMP: 6
SALES (corp-wide): 3.4MM **Privately Held**
SIC: 5051 3471 Dist / Polish Metal Products
PA: Accent Metals Inc
75 Jackson Ave
Syosset NY 17406
800 633-1787

(G-20365)
ACCO MTL HDLG SOLUTIONS INC (DH)
76 Acco Dr (17402-4668)
P.O. Box 792 (17405-0792)
PHONE.................................800 967-7333
Jim Coughlin, *CEO*
Alan Hopes, *District Mgr*
Greg Logan, *District Mgr*
Andrew Roy, *District Mgr*
Shirley Cohen, *Buyer*
▲ EMP: 95
SALES (est): 13.4MM **Privately Held**
SIC: 3536 3449 3537 Hoists, cranes & monorails; miscellaneous metalwork; industrial trucks & tractors
HQ: Fki Industries Inc.
2801 Dawson Rd
Tulsa OK 74110
918 834-4611

(G-20366)
ADEPT CORPORATION
4601 N Susquehanna Trl (17406-8496)
PHONE.................................800 451-2254
David Williamson, *President*
Walter E Gropp, *Chairman*
Norma Hoover, *Corp Secy*
Glenn McKinley, *Project Mgr*
Kathy Bailey, *Mfg Staff*
▲ EMP: 68 EST: 1966
SQ FT: 62,000
SALES (est): 13MM **Privately Held**
WEB: www.adeptcorp.com
SIC: 3083 3469 3599 Plastic finished products, laminated; metal stampings; custom machinery

(G-20367)
ADLAMCO INC
1189 Smallbrook Ln (17403-3411)
PHONE.................................717 292-1577
Peter J McQuaid, *President*
▲ EMP: 3
SQ FT: 1,456
SALES (est): 500K **Privately Held**
SIC: 2891 Adhesives

(G-20368)
ADVANCED INDUSTRIAL SVCS INC
3250 N Susquehanna Trl (17406-9754)
PHONE.................................717 764-9811
James Heinrichs, *President*
Jim Heinrichs, *VP Opers*
Jim Hess, *Project Mgr*
Paul Senft, *Project Mgr*
Ken Smith, *Project Mgr*
▲ EMP: 151
SQ FT: 50,000

SALES (est): 25.8MM **Publicly Held**
WEB: www.ais-york.com
SIC: 1796 4212 3441 Machine moving & rigging; machinery installation; heavy machinery transport, local; fabricated structural metal
PA: Cemtrex, Inc.
3030 47th Ave
Long Island City NY 11101

(G-20369)
ADVANCED LASER PRINTER S
Also Called: Alps
40 Aberdeen Rd (17406-7912)
P.O. Box 156, Emigsville (17318-0156)
PHONE.................................717 764-3272
Steve McKibben, *President*
Donald Risser, *Vice Pres*
EMP: 9
SQ FT: 1,500
SALES (est): 1.5MM **Privately Held**
WEB: www.alpslaser.com
SIC: 3661 Facsimile equipment

(G-20370)
AIR DYNMICS INDUS SYSTEMS CORP
180 Roosevelt Ave (17401-3333)
PHONE.................................717 854-4050
Daniel Lehman, *President*
▲ EMP: 17
SQ FT: 23,300
SALES (est): 3.3MM **Privately Held**
WEB: www.airdynamics.net
SIC: 3564 5084 Filters, air: furnaces, air conditioning equipment, etc.; industrial machinery & equipment

(G-20371)
AMERICAN COLLOID COMPANY
600 Lincoln St (17401-3317)
PHONE.................................717 845-3077
Raymond Arpin, *Branch Mgr*
EMP: 35
SQ FT: 36,982 **Publicly Held**
WEB: www.colloid.com
SIC: 1459 2899 Bentonite mining; chemical preparations
HQ: American Colloid Company
2870 Forbs Ave
Hoffman Estates IL 60192

(G-20372)
AMERICAN CONE VALVE INC
5166 Commerce Dr (17408-9510)
PHONE.................................717 792-3492
Robert Ross, *President*
EMP: 19
SQ FT: 15,000
SALES (est): 541.2K **Privately Held**
SIC: 7699 5085 3491 Valve repair, industrial; valves & fittings; industrial valves

(G-20373)
AMERICAN COOLING TECH INC
715 Willow Springs Ln (17406-8434)
PHONE.................................717 767-2775
Janes R Schreiber, *President*
John R Lucas, *Vice Pres*
▲ EMP: 16
SQ FT: 20,000
SALES (est): 8.1MM **Privately Held**
WEB: www.americancoolingtechnology.com
SIC: 3585 Air conditioning, motor vehicle; automotive air conditioners

(G-20374)
AMERICAN HYDRO CORPORATION
135 Stonewood Rd (17402-9356)
P.O. Box 3628 (17402-0136)
PHONE.................................717 755-5300
Alan Roth, *President*
Terry Smith, *Administration*
▲ EMP: 166
SQ FT: 121,500
SALES (est): 46.8MM
SALES (corp-wide): 5.8B **Privately Held**
WEB: www.ahydro.com
SIC: 3511 1796 Hydraulic turbines; power generating equipment installation
HQ: Wartsila Holding, Inc.
11710 N Gessner Rd Ste A
Houston TX 77064
281 233-6200

(G-20375)
AMERICAN PRODUCTS INC (PA)
Also Called: API
45 Leigh Dr (17406-8474)
PHONE.................................717 767-6510
John I Eltringham, President
Christopher H Tillotson, Vice Pres
David Wentz, Safety Mgr
Melissa Smith, Purchasing
Kenneth A Palovitz, Admin Sec
EMP: 98
SQ FT: 50,000
SALES (est): 25.7MM Privately Held
WEB: www.americanproductsinc.com
SIC: 3679 2675 Electronic circuits; card-
board cut-outs, panels & foundations: die-
cut

(G-20376)
**AMZ MANUFACTURING
CORPORATION**
100 Boxwood Ln (17402-9305)
PHONE.................................717 751-2714
Jason Graves, Manager
EMP: 30 Privately Held
SIC: 3471 Electroplating of metals or
formed products
PA: Amz Manufacturing Corporation
2206 Pennsylvania Ave
York PA 17404

(G-20377)
**AMZ MANUFACTURING
CORPORATION (PA)**
2206 Pennsylvania Ave (17404-1790)
PHONE.................................717 848-2565
Jeffrey L Adams, Principal
EMP: 15
SQ FT: 30,000
SALES (est): 5.4MM Privately Held
WEB: www.amzmfg.com
SIC: 3471 Electroplating of metals or
formed products

(G-20378)
**ANSTADT PRINTING
CORPORATION**
Also Called: Anstadt Communications
3300 Farmtrail Rd (17406-5614)
PHONE.................................717 767-6891
Matthew R Doran, President
Ann E Anstadt, Vice Pres
Jennifer E Doran, Admin Sec
EMP: 24
SQ FT: 20,000
SALES (est): 4.9MM Privately Held
WEB: www.anstadt.com
SIC: 2752 2759 Commercial printing, off-
set; commercial printing; letterpress print-
ing

(G-20379)
ANSTINES CANDY BOX
Also Called: Anstines Home Made Candy
1901 S Queen St (17403-4715)
PHONE.................................717 854-9269
Anna L Currier, Owner
Anna Currier, Technology
EMP: 3
SQ FT: 624
SALES (est): 192K Privately Held
WEB: www.anstinescandy.com
SIC: 2064 Candy & other confectionery
products

(G-20380)
APPLIED CONTROLS INC
144 Roosevelt Ave Ste 400 (17401-3333)
PHONE.................................717 854-2889
Rick Gehring, Manager
EMP: 28
SALES (corp-wide): 55.2MM Privately
Held
WEB: www.appliedc.com
SIC: 3829 Measuring & controlling devices
PA: Applied Controls, Inc.
47 General Warren Blvd
Malvern PA 19355
610 695-4628

(G-20381)
APPLIED MAGNETICS LAB INC
Also Called: A M L
401 Manor St (17401-2110)
PHONE.................................717 430-2774

Drew Wildonger, President
▲ EMP: 6
SQ FT: 14,000
SALES (est): 1.1MM Privately Held
SIC: 3812 3821 Magnetic field detection
apparatus; laboratory apparatus & furni-
ture

(G-20382)
APX YORK SHEET METAL INC
Also Called: York Sheet Metal
255 Church Rd (17406-9731)
PHONE.................................717 767-2704
Andrew V Papoutsis, President
Daniel J Burchstead, Principal
Michael S Snyder, Treasurer
Ron Van Saghi, Manager
Jamie L Papoutsis, Admin Sec
EMP: 45 EST: 2009
SQ FT: 60,000
SALES (est): 13.4MM Privately Held
WEB: www.yorksheet.com
SIC: 3444 Sheet metalwork

(G-20383)
APX-SEETECH SYSTEMS INC
95 Willow Springs Cir (17406-8428)
PHONE.................................717 751-6445
Andy Mularerin, President
Andrew Papuotsis, Principal
EMP: 5
SALES (est): 178.7K Privately Held
SIC: 3496 5084 Conveyor belts; conveyor
systems

(G-20384)
ARBUTUS ELECTRONICS INC
600 Farmbrook Ln (17406-5641)
PHONE.................................717 764-3565
Gary Shoemaker, President
Christine A Leber, Vice Pres
EMP: 15
SQ FT: 7,000
SALES: 1MM Privately Held
SIC: 3625 3822 Relays & industrial con-
trols; auto controls regulating residntl &
coml environmt & applncs

(G-20385)
ARDENT MILLS LLC
2800 Black Bridge Rd (17406-9703)
PHONE.................................717 846-7773
EMP: 32
SALES (corp-wide): 543.9MM Privately
Held
SIC: 2041 Flour & other grain mill products
PA: Ardent Mills, Llc
1875 Lawrence St Ste 1400
Denver CO 80202
800 851-9618

(G-20386)
**ARMARK AUTHENTICATION
TECH LLC**
3400 Farmtrail Rd (17406-5618)
PHONE.................................717 767-4651
EMP: 4
SQ FT: 10,000
SALES (est): 330.6K
SALES (corp-wide): 118MM Privately
Held
SIC: 3999 Mfg Identification Tags Except
Paper
PA: Adhesives Research, Inc.
400 Seaks Run Rd
Glen Rock PA 17327
717 235-7979

(G-20387)
**ASHCOMBE PRODUCTS
COMPANY INC**
1065 Box Hill Ln (17403-5910)
PHONE.................................717 848-1271
John Thornton, President
EMP: 5
SALES (est): 300K Privately Held
SIC: 3499 3545 Aerosol valves, metal;
drills (machine tool accessories)

(G-20388)
**ASSOCIATION TEST
PUBLISHERS**
2995 Round Hill Rd (17402-4143)
PHONE.................................717 755-9747
Lauren Scheib, Principal

EMP: 5 EST: 2007
SALES (est): 470.4K Privately Held
SIC: 8621 2721 Medical field-related as-
sociations; periodicals

(G-20389)
ATHLETIC LETTERING INC
2860 Eastern Blvd (17402-2908)
PHONE.................................717 840-6373
Jeffrey Folkenroth, President
Vicki Mead, Admin Sec
EMP: 10
SQ FT: 10,000
SALES (est): 800K Privately Held
WEB: www.athletic-lettering.com
SIC: 7389 5091 3993 5094 Lettering
service; athletic goods; signs & advertis-
ing specialties; trophies

(G-20390)
**ATLAS RUBBER STAMP &
PRINTING**
3755 E Market St Ste 5 (17402-5200)
P.O. Box 3216 (17402-0216)
PHONE.................................717 755-3882
Lowell Sipe Sr, President
EMP: 8 EST: 1972
SQ FT: 2,400
SALES (est): 500K Privately Held
WEB: www.atlasrubberstamp.com
SIC: 2752 3953 Commercial printing, off-
set; embossing seals & hand stamps

(G-20391)
ATR MAGNETICS LLC
385 Emig Rd Ste A (17406-9741)
PHONE.................................717 718-8008
Mike Spitz, Managing Prtnr
Tracy Doten,
Tracy Ann Doten,
EMP: 5
SALES (est): 460K Privately Held
WEB: www.nothingsoundsliketape.com
SIC: 3652 Magnetic tape (audio): prere-
corded

(G-20392)
**AUTOCARE SERVICE CENTER
INC**
450 Loucks Rd (17404-1724)
PHONE.................................717 854-0242
Larry A Ebersole, President
Debra L Bryant, Corp Secy
EMP: 8
SALES (est): 964.9K Privately Held
SIC: 3714 Motor vehicle parts & acces-
sories

(G-20393)
**AUTOMATIC MACHINING MFG
CO INC (PA)**
Also Called: Ammac
3405 Board Rd (17406-8409)
PHONE.................................717 767-4448
Jesse Booth, President
J T Halegans, President
John W Albright, Vice Pres
Marie Martin, QC Mgr
John Albright II, Treasurer
EMP: 30 EST: 1983
SQ FT: 24,000
SALES (est): 4.7MM Privately Held
WEB: www.ammacinc.com
SIC: 3451 3452 Screw machine products;
bolts, nuts, rivets & washers

(G-20394)
B & D ADVERTISING INC
333 E 7th Ave Ste 1 (17404-2144)
P.O. Box 709 (17405-0709)
PHONE.................................717 852-6950
Robert B McCreary, President
EMP: 90
SALES (est): 3.1MM Privately Held
WEB: www.bdadvertising.com
SIC: 2389 7311 Costumes; advertising
agencies

(G-20395)
B & D MACHINE SHOP
808 W Mason Ave (17401-3692)
PHONE.................................717 843-0312
Donna Ilgenfritz, Owner
EMP: 4
SQ FT: 3,200

SALES: 500K Privately Held
WEB: www.stamplerauctions.com
SIC: 3599 Machine shop, jobbing & repair

(G-20396)
B & W METAL WORKS INC
635 Hay St (17403-1379)
PHONE.................................717 848-1077
Fax: 717 848-1078
EMP: 9
SALES (est): 720K Privately Held
SIC: 7692 Welding Repair

(G-20397)
**BAE SYSTEMS LAND
ARMAMENTS LP**
Ground Systems Division
1100 Bairs Rd (17408-8975)
P.O. Box 15512 (17405-1512)
PHONE.................................717 225-8000
Dale Wenrich, General Mgr
Adam Zarfoss, Vice Pres
Jim Schell, Project Mgr
Cathy Zerbe, Project Mgr
Craig Herr, Senior Buyer
EMP: 56
SALES (corp-wide): 24.2B Privately Held
WEB: www.udlp.com
SIC: 3795 8711 3812 Tanks & tank com-
ponents; engineering services; search &
navigation equipment
HQ: Bae Systems Land & Armaments L.P.
2000 15th Nw Fl 11 Flr 11
Arlington VA 22201
703 907-8250

(G-20398)
BAILEY LEASING INC
Also Called: Bailey Coach
55 S Fayette St Ste 1 (17404-5537)
P.O. Box 367, Spring Grove (17362-0367)
PHONE.................................717 718-0490
John W Bailey, President
Jane L Bailey, Corp Secy
Rodney L Seachrist, Vice Pres
EMP: 54
SQ FT: 20,000
SALES (est): 9.2MM Privately Held
SIC: 3792 4111 Trailer coaches, automo-
bile; airport transportation

(G-20399)
BAKER HYDRO INCORPORATED
3490 Board Rd (17406-8478)
PHONE.................................717 764-8581
Donald H Weir, Chairman
Robert E Seitz, Treasurer
Wentworth D Vedder, Admin Sec
EMP: 9
SALES (est): 831.9K
SALES (corp-wide): 124MM Privately
Held
SIC: 3842 Whirlpool baths, hydrotherapy
equipment
PA: Wexco Incorporated
3490 Board Rd
York PA 17406
717 764-8585

(G-20400)
BAREFOOT PELLET COMPANY
Rr 14 Box North (17315)
P.O. Box 96, Troy (16947-0096)
PHONE.................................570 297-4771
Roy W Cummings Jr, President
Mike Davison, Plant Mgr
▲ EMP: 3
SALES (est): 611.7K Privately Held
WEB: www.barefootpellet.com
SIC: 3532 Pellet mills (mining machinery)

(G-20401)
**BEECHER & MYERS COMPANY
INC**
5176 Commerce Dr (17408-9510)
PHONE.................................717 292-3031
Gary Beecher, President
Blaine Feeser, Vice Pres
EMP: 18
SQ FT: 40,000
SALES (est): 3.3MM Privately Held
WEB: www.beecherandmyers.com
SIC: 2491 Wood products, creosoted

▲ = Import ▼=Export
◆ =Import/Export

(G-20402)
BETTER WORLD SPIRITS INC
131 E Philadelphia St (17401-2437)
PHONE..................................717 758-9346
Wade Keech, *President*
EMP: 1
SALES: 1MM **Privately Held**
SIC: **2082** Beer (alcoholic beverage)

(G-20403)
BICKELS SNACK FOODS INC (HQ)
1120 Zinns Quarry Rd (17404-3533)
P.O. Box 2427 (17405-2427)
PHONE..................................800 233-1933
John A Warehime, *President*
Jeffery Warehime, *General Mgr*
Pietro D Giraffa Jr, *Vice Pres*
Steven E Robertson, *Vice Pres*
Gary T Knisely, *Admin Sec*
▲ EMP: 25
SALES (est): 65.9MM
SALES (corp-wide): 292MM **Publicly Held**
SIC: **2096 2052** Potato chips & similar snacks; pretzels
PA: Hanover Foods Corporation
1486 York St
Hanover PA 17331
717 632-6000

(G-20404)
BICKELS SNACK FOODS INC
1000 W College Ave (17404-3537)
P.O. Box 334, Hanover (17331-0334)
PHONE..................................717 843-0738
Ed Beckle, *President*
EMP: 77
SALES (corp-wide): 292MM **Publicly Held**
SIC: **2099 2096** Food preparations; potato chips & similar snacks
HQ: Bickel's Snack Foods, Inc.
1120 Zinns Quarry Rd
York PA 17404
800 233-1933

(G-20405)
BILLET INDUSTRIES INC
247 Campbell Rd (17402-8635)
PHONE..................................717 840-0280
Troy Billet, *President*
Keith D Billet, *Treasurer*
Keith Billet, *Treasurer*
Gloria Lauer, *Admin Sec*
EMP: 25
SQ FT: 36,000
SALES (est): 5.2MM **Privately Held**
WEB: www.billet-industries.com
SIC: **3599 3544** Machine shop, jobbing & repair; special dies, tools, jigs & fixtures

(G-20406)
BIMBO BAKERIES USA INC
Also Called: Maier's Bakery
1851 Loucks Rd (17408-9708)
PHONE..................................800 222-7495
Jim Carter, *Manager*
EMP: 31 **Privately Held**
SIC: **2051 5461** Bakery: wholesale or wholesale/retail combined; bakeries
HQ: Bimbo Bakeries Usa, Inc
255 Business Center Dr # 200
Horsham PA 19044
215 347-5500

(G-20407)
BIMBO BAKERIES USA INC
3670 Sandhurst Dr Ste A (17406-7939)
PHONE..................................717 764-9999
EMP: 157 **Privately Held**
SIC: **2051** Bread, cake & related products
HQ: Bimbo Bakeries Usa, Inc
255 Business Center Dr # 200
Horsham PA 19044
215 347-5500

(G-20408)
BITUMINOUS PAV MTLS YORK INC (PA)
1300 Zinns Quarry Rd (17404-3553)
PHONE..................................717 843-4573
Barbara Sindicich, *President*
Richard Sindicich, *Vice Pres*
Susanne Sindicich, *Treasurer*
Mark Sindicich, *Admin Sec*
EMP: 5 EST: 1963
SQ FT: 750
SALES (est): 1.1MM **Privately Held**
SIC: **2951** Concrete, bituminous

(G-20409)
BLACK & DECKER (US) INC
2201 Industrial Hwy (17402-2224)
PHONE..................................717 755-3441
David Bresin, *Manager*
EMP: 8
SALES (corp-wide): 13.9B **Publicly Held**
WEB: www.dewalt.com
SIC: **3546** Power-driven handtools
HQ: Black & Decker (U.S.) Inc.
1000 Stanley Dr
New Britain CT 06053
860 225-5111

(G-20410)
BLACK BEAR STRUCTURES INC
1213 Hanover Rd (17408-6219)
PHONE..................................717 225-0377
Fax: 717 225-0387
EMP: 3
SALES (corp-wide): 2.8MM **Privately Held**
SIC: **1521 2452** Single-Family House Construction Mfg Prefabricated Wood Buildings
PA: Black Bear Structures, Inc.
1865 Lancaster Pike
Peach Bottom PA 17563
717 548-2937

(G-20411)
BOXWOOD MANUFACTURING CORP
100 Boxwood Ln (17402-9305)
PHONE..................................717 751-2712
Jeffrey Adams, *Principal*
EMP: 3
SALES (est): 212.7K **Privately Held**
SIC: **3999** Manufacturing industries

(G-20412)
BRENTEK INTERNATIONAL INC
1249 Ridgewood Rd (17406-1754)
P.O. Box 217, Shade Gap (17255-0217)
PHONE..................................814 259-3333
Brian Breneman, *President*
EMP: 6
SQ FT: 1,500
SALES (est): 590K **Privately Held**
SIC: **3625** Relays & industrial controls

(G-20413)
BREWERS OUTLET
Also Called: Colletti
409 E Philadelphia St (17403-1614)
PHONE..................................717 848-5250
Rosario Colletti, *President*
EMP: 8
SALES: 2.7MM **Privately Held**
SIC: **5181 2082** Beer & other fermented malt liquors; malt beverages

(G-20414)
BREWSKEES OF SHILOH
2010 Carlisle Rd (17408-4033)
PHONE..................................717 764-2994
Chad Wagner, *Principal*
EMP: 4
SALES (est): 225.7K **Privately Held**
SIC: **2082** Beer (alcoholic beverage)

(G-20415)
C P CONVERTERS INC (HQ)
Also Called: C-P Flexible Packaging
15 Grumbacher Rd (17406-8421)
PHONE..................................717 764-1193
Anthony Vaudo, *President*
Ryan Smith, *Safety Dir*
Thomas Sperlazzo, *Project Mgr*
John Beard, *Warehouse Mgr*
Brian Michalski, *Maint Spvr*
▲ EMP: 78 EST: 1958
SQ FT: 105,000
SALES (est): 101MM
SALES (corp-wide): 757.8MM **Privately Held**
WEB: www.cpconverters.com
SIC: **2891 7389 2821 2823** Adhesives & sealants; laminating service; plastics materials & resins; cellulosic manmade fibers; flexographic printing
PA: First Atlantic Capital, Ltd.
477 Madison Ave Ste 330
New York NY 10022
212 207-0300

(G-20416)
C T E INC
30 Willow Springs Cir (17406-8428)
PHONE..................................717 767-6636
John F Wohlin, *President*
▲ EMP: 45
SQ FT: 28,000
SALES (est): 10.5MM **Privately Held**
WEB: www.cte-inc.com
SIC: **3469 3544** Stamping metal for the trade; special dies, tools, jigs & fixtures

(G-20417)
CAPWAY SYSTEMS INC
725 Vogelsong Rd (17404-1765)
PHONE..................................717 843-0003
Frank Achterberg, *President*
Keith Schoff, *Vice Pres*
Dan Crabill, *Prdtn Mgr*
James Gaver, *Mfg Staff*
Jeff McDonnell, *Engineer*
▲ EMP: 44
SQ FT: 25,000
SALES (est): 17.9MM
SALES (corp-wide): 183.7K **Privately Held**
WEB: www.capwayusa.com
SIC: **3535** Conveyors & conveying equipment
HQ: Conway Holding B.V.
Mijllerweg 16
Lunteren
655 338-576

(G-20418)
CARAUSTAR INDUSTRIES INC
Also Called: Protect-A-Board
2510 N George St (17406-3110)
PHONE..................................717 846-4559
John Bailey, *Manager*
EMP: 10
SALES (corp-wide): 3.8B **Publicly Held**
WEB: www.caraustar.com
SIC: **2655** Fiber cans, drums & similar products
HQ: Caraustar Industries, Inc.
5000 Austell Powder Sprin
Austell GA 30106
770 948-3101

(G-20419)
CARTRIDGE WORLD YORK
1805 Loucks Rd Ste 100 (17408-7903)
PHONE..................................717 699-4465
David Mazurek, *Partner*
Pat Byrne, *Partner*
EMP: 7
SALES (est): 1MM **Privately Held**
SIC: **3951** Cartridges, refill: ball point pens

(G-20420)
CASKEY PRINTING INC (PA)
850 Vogelsong Rd (17404-1379)
PHONE..................................717 764-4500
Gregory S Caskey, *President*
Margo Caskey, *Vice Pres*
Tony Rife, *Admin Sec*
EMP: 48
SQ FT: 24,000
SALES (est): 5.2MM **Privately Held**
WEB: www.caskeyprinting.com
SIC: **2752** Commercial printing, offset

(G-20421)
CATERPILLAR INC
600 Memory Ln (17402-2234)
P.O. Box 787 (17405-0787)
PHONE..................................717 751-5123
Luke Robinson, *Engineer*
John Pfeffer, *Branch Mgr*
EMP: 347
SQ FT: 500,000
SALES (corp-wide): 54.7B **Publicly Held**
WEB: www.cat.com
SIC: **3531** Excavators: cable, clamshell, crane, derrick, dragline, etc.
PA: Caterpillar Inc.
510 Lake Cook Rd Ste 100
Deerfield IL 60015
224 551-4000

(G-20422)
CBF SYSTEMS
3100 Farmtrail Rd (17406-5625)
PHONE..................................717 793-2941
EMP: 12
SALES (est): 2.7MM **Privately Held**
SIC: **3535** Conveyors & conveying equipment

(G-20423)
CHARLES R KELLEY
Also Called: Fremor Orchards Custom Mchs
1295 Christensen Rd (17402-9510)
P.O. Box 20833 (17402-0184)
PHONE..................................717 840-0181
EMP: 5
SQ FT: 47,000
SALES (est): 122.3K **Privately Held**
SIC: **0251 3443** Chicken Farm Mfg Fabricated Plate Work

(G-20424)
CHARTER DURA-BAR INC
Also Called: Dura-Bar Services Div
90 Grumbacher Rd (17406-8420)
P.O. Box 217, Mequon WI (53092-0217)
PHONE..................................717 779-0807
Tim Hauri, *Manager*
EMP: 15
SALES (corp-wide): 754.3MM **Privately Held**
WEB: www.wellsmanufacturing.com
SIC: **3321 5051** Gray iron castings; ductile iron castings; steel
HQ: Charter Dura-Bar, Inc.
2100 W Lake Shore Dr
Woodstock IL 60098
815 338-3900

(G-20425)
CHLOE TEXTILES INCORPORATED
135 N George St Ste 203 (17401-1134)
P.O. Box 7607 (17404-0607)
PHONE..................................717 848-2800
Chloe Eichelberger, *President*
Ron Rhoads, *Exec VP*
EMP: 90
SQ FT: 180,000
SALES (est): 5.7MM **Privately Held**
SIC: **2257 2231 2261** Dyeing & finishing circular knit fabrics; dyeing & finishing: wool or similar fibers; finishing plants, cotton

(G-20426)
CHURCH & DWIGHT CO INC
5197 Commerce Dr (17408-9511)
PHONE..................................717 781-8800
Ashish Mallick, *Principal*
EMP: 54
SALES (corp-wide): 4.1B **Publicly Held**
SIC: **2842** Specialty cleaning preparations
PA: Church & Dwight Co., Inc.
500 Charles Ewing Blvd
Ewing NJ 08628
609 806-1200

(G-20427)
CLINTON INDUSTRIES INC
525 E Market St (17403-1619)
PHONE..................................717 848-2391
Robert C Bohn, *President*
◆ EMP: 25
SQ FT: 9,600
SALES (est): 7.7MM **Privately Held**
WEB: www.clinton-ind.com
SIC: **3841** Surgical & medical instruments

(G-20428)
COLEMAN CABLE LLC
160 S Hartman St (17403-1853)
PHONE..................................717 845-5100
Daniel Delph, *Branch Mgr*
EMP: 44

SALES (corp-wide): 2.3B **Privately Held**
SIC: 3357 Nonferrous wiredrawing & insulating
HQ: Coleman Cable, Llc
1 Overlook Pt
Lincolnshire IL 60069
847 672-2300

(G-20429)
COMPOSIDIE INC
30 Willow Springs Cir (17406-8428)
PHONE.................................717 764-2233
EMP: 82
SALES (corp-wide): 34MM **Privately Held**
SIC: 3544 Mfg Dies/Tools/Jigs/Fixtures
PA: Composidie, Inc.
1295 State Route 380
Apollo PA 15613
724 727-3466

(G-20430)
COMPOUND TECHNOLOGY INC
609 E King St (17403-1721)
PHONE.................................717 845-8646
Fred Fay II, President
Jeeferey Hammel, Admin Sec
EMP: 4
SQ FT: 2,000
SALES: 4.9MM **Privately Held**
SIC: 2819 Industrial inorganic chemicals

(G-20431)
CONAGRA BRANDS INC
2800 Black Bridge Rd (17406-9704)
PHONE.................................717 846-7773
Sean Gager, Branch Mgr
EMP: 17
SALES (corp-wide): 7.9B **Publicly Held**
WEB: www.conagra.com
SIC: 2041 Flour & other grain mill products
PA: Conagra Brands, Inc.
222 Merchandise Mart Plz
Chicago IL 60654
312 549-5000

(G-20432)
CONCEPTS
1150 N Sherman St Ste 600 (17402-2135)
PHONE.................................717 600-2964
Diane Wolf, Owner
EMP: 3
SALES (est): 186.3K **Privately Held**
SIC: 2759 Laser printing

(G-20433)
CONDUCTIVE TECHNOLOGIES INC (PA)
935 Borom Rd (17404-1382)
PHONE.................................717 764-6931
Richard Eagle, President
Tina Fleisher, Purch Mgr
Joseph Bevilacqua, Controller
Rich Ryan, Sales Staff
EMP: 97 EST: 2000
SQ FT: 100,000
SALES (est): 29.1MM **Privately Held**
WEB: www.conductivetech.com
SIC: 3674 3679 Radiation sensors; electronic switches

(G-20434)
CONSOLDTED SCRAP RESOURCES INC (PA)
Also Called: C S R
120 Hokes Mill Rd (17404-5505)
P.O. Box 7520 (17404-0520)
PHONE.................................717 843-0931
Richard Abrams, Ch of Bd
Marty Fogle, Senior VP
EMP: 14 EST: 1897
SQ FT: 38,000
SALES (est): 33MM **Privately Held**
SIC: 5093 3341 Junk & scrap; nonferrous metals scrap; secondary nonferrous metals

(G-20435)
CONSOLDTED SCRAP RESOURCES INC
600 E Princess St (17403-2422)
P.O. Box 389 (17405-0389)
PHONE.................................717 843-0660
Eric Berman, General Mgr
EMP: 29

SQ FT: 1,500
SALES (corp-wide): 33MM **Privately Held**
SIC: 5093 3569 Ferrous metal scrap & waste; baling machines, for scrap metal, paper or similar material
PA: Consolidated Scrap Resources, Inc.
120 Hokes Mill Rd
York PA 17404
717 843-0931

(G-20436)
CONSOLDTED SCRAP RESOURCES INC
530 Vander Ave (17403-2806)
P.O. Box 389 (17405-0389)
PHONE.................................717 843-0931
Bryan Wagaman, Manager
EMP: 4
SALES (corp-wide): 33MM **Privately Held**
SIC: 5093 3341 Metal scrap & waste materials; secondary nonferrous metals
PA: Consolidated Scrap Resources, Inc.
120 Hokes Mill Rd
York PA 17404
717 843-0931

(G-20437)
CONSOLIDATED CONT HOLDINGS LLC
15 Lightner Rd (17404-1610)
PHONE.................................717 854-3454
Doc Kirkland, Branch Mgr
EMP: 91
SALES (corp-wide): 1.6B **Privately Held**
SIC: 3089 Plastic containers, except foam
PA: Consolidated Container Holdings Llc
2500 Windy Ridge Pkwy Se
Atlanta GA 30339
678 742-4600

(G-20438)
CONSOLIDATED CONTAINER CO LLC
15 Lightner Rd (17404-1610)
PHONE.................................610 869-4021
Jeff Greene, CEO
James Kane, QC Mgr
EMP: 28
SALES (est): 4MM **Privately Held**
SIC: 3089 Food casings, plastic; plastic containers, except foam

(G-20439)
CSL PLASMA INC
2430 Eastern Blvd (17402-2901)
PHONE.................................717 767-2348
Brandi Boyles, Branch Mgr
EMP: 5 **Privately Held**
SIC: 2836 Plasmas
HQ: Csl Plasma Inc.
900 Broken Sound Pkwy Nw # 4
Boca Raton FL 33487
561 981-3700

(G-20440)
D & M WELDING CO INC
1550 Trolley Rd (17408-4313)
PHONE.................................717 767-9353
Mark Wagman, President
Brad Wagman, Vice Pres
Chris Wagman, Vice Pres
Teri Perry, Treasurer
EMP: 21
SALES: 4.5MM **Privately Held**
WEB: www.dmwelding.com
SIC: 7692 3499 Brazing; fire- or burglary-resistive products

(G-20441)
D F STAUFFER BISCUIT CO INC (DH)
360 S Belmont St (17403-2616)
P.O. Box 12002 (17402-0672)
PHONE.................................717 815-4600
Shun Yoshioka, President
James L Wilson, COO
Jim Wilson, COO
Peggy Harmon, Project Mgr
Rick Druck, Engineer
▲ EMP: 500 EST: 1950
SQ FT: 259,000

SALES (est): 162.2MM **Privately Held**
WEB: www.stauffers.net
SIC: 2052 Cookies; crackers, dry
HQ: Meiji Co., Ltd.
2-2-1, Kyobashi
Chuo-Ku TKY 104-0
332 730-700

(G-20442)
D L CARMODY HOLDINGS LLC
Also Called: Acco Material Hdlg Solutions
76 Acco Dr (17402-4668)
P.O. Box 792 (17405-0792)
PHONE.................................717 741-4863
Daniel Carmody, President
Lonnie Staley, Traffic Mgr
Thomas Bluett, Engineer
John Peiffer, Engineer
Stuart Pinkerton, Design Engr
◆ EMP: 165
SQ FT: 107
SALES (est): 34.3MM **Privately Held**
SIC: 3536 Hoists, cranes & monorails

(G-20443)
DALLCO INDUSTRIES INC (PA)
463 S Albemarle St (17403-2554)
P.O. Box 2727 (17405-2727)
PHONE.................................717 854-7875
Douglas A Dallmeyer, President
David Haverstock, Vice Pres
Steve Lauer, Admin Sec
Kathy Reed, Asst Sec
EMP: 30 EST: 1923
SQ FT: 300,000
SALES (est): 20.3MM **Privately Held**
WEB: www.dallco.com
SIC: 2392 2339 2331 2341 Cushions & pillows; slacks: women's, misses' & juniors'; shorts (outerwear): women's, misses' & juniors'; T-shirts & tops, women's: made from purchased materials; nightgowns & negligees: women's & children's

(G-20444)
DANSKIN
305 N State St (17403-1316)
PHONE.................................717 747-3051
Michelle Barnhart, Principal
▲ EMP: 10 EST: 2008
SALES (est): 939.5K **Privately Held**
SIC: 2339 Women's & misses' outerwear

(G-20445)
DAWN FOOD PRODUCTS INC
Original Knaub Delicious Cakes
3701 Concord Rd (17402-9101)
PHONE.................................717 840-0044
John Hertel, Safety Mgr
John Duda, Facilities Mgr
Jack Mahon, Sales Dir
David Koff, Accounts Mgr
Sid Williams, Manager
EMP: 235
SALES (corp-wide): 1.6B **Privately Held**
WEB: www.dawnfoods.com
SIC: 2053 2051 2038 Cakes, bakery: frozen; bread, cake & related products; frozen specialties
HQ: Dawn Food Products, Inc.
3333 Sargent Rd
Jackson MI 49201

(G-20446)
DEBBIE DENGLER
4845 Fake Rd (17406-6127)
PHONE.................................717 755-5226
EMP: 3 EST: 2016
SALES (est): 135.6K **Privately Held**
SIC: 2813 Neon

(G-20447)
DELL PERRY FARMS
Also Called: Perrydell Farm Dairy
90 Indian Rock Dam Rd (17403-5201)
PHONE.................................717 741-3485
Tom Perry, Partner
Greg Perry, Partner
EMP: 26
SALES (est): 3.5MM **Privately Held**
SIC: 0241 2026 Milk production; fluid milk

(G-20448)
DENTSPLY HOLDING COMPANY
221 W Philadelphia St # 60 (17401-2991)
PHONE.................................717 845-7511
Bret W Wise, CEO
Delia Hill, Human Res Mgr
Paula Caya, Director
EMP: 33
SALES (est): 17.8MM
SALES (corp-wide): 3.9B **Publicly Held**
SIC: 3844 3275 3843 X-ray apparatus & tubes; X-ray generators; radiographic X-ray apparatus & tubes; gypsum products; impression material, dental
PA: Dentsply Sirona Inc.
221 W Philadelphia St
York PA 17401
717 845-7511

(G-20449)
DENTSPLY INTERNATIONAL INC
Dentsply Professional
1301 Smile Way (17404-1785)
PHONE.................................717 767-8500
Ken Guaragno, Engineer
Kevin Lint, Engineer
Ray Woodyard, Engineer
Steve Cornelius, Branch Mgr
Charles Ebbert, Manager
EMP: 100
SQ FT: 17,436
SALES (corp-wide): 3.9B **Publicly Held**
WEB: www.dentsply.com
SIC: 3843 Dental equipment & supplies
PA: Dentsply Sirona Inc.
221 W Philadelphia St
York PA 17401
717 845-7511

(G-20450)
DENTSPLY INTERNATIONAL INC
500 W College Ave (17401-3866)
P.O. Box 2845 (17405-2845)
PHONE.................................717 487-0100
Brian Addison, Treasurer
Goldblatt Bruce, Sales Executive
Lee Peck, Marketing Staff
Kyle Muse, Manager
EMP: 100
SALES (corp-wide): 3.9B **Publicly Held**
WEB: www.dentsply.com
SIC: 3843 Dental equipment & supplies
PA: Dentsply Sirona Inc.
221 W Philadelphia St
York PA 17401
717 845-7511

(G-20451)
DENTSPLY LLC
Also Called: Dentsply Rinn
1301 Smile Way (17404-1785)
PHONE.................................800 323-0970
Thomas Heusing, Natl Sales Mgr
EMP: 87
SALES (est): 12MM
SALES (corp-wide): 3.9B **Publicly Held**
WEB: www.dentsply.com
SIC: 3843 3844 Dental equipment & supplies; X-ray apparatus & tubes
PA: Dentsply Sirona Inc.
221 W Philadelphia St
York PA 17401
717 845-7511

(G-20452)
DENTSPLY NORTH AMERICA LLC
221 W Philadelphia St (17401-2991)
P.O. Box 2558 (17405-2558)
PHONE.................................717 849-4229
Mark A Thierer, CEO
EMP: 7
SALES (est): 401.9K
SALES (corp-wide): 3.9B **Publicly Held**
SIC: 3843 Dental equipment & supplies
PA: Dentsply Sirona Inc.
221 W Philadelphia St
York PA 17401
717 845-7511

(G-20453)
DENTSPLY SIRONA INC
Dentsply Pharmaceutical
1301 Smile Way (17404-1785)
PHONE.................................717 699-4100
Rollie McSherry, Branch Mgr

▲ = Import ▼=Export
◆ =Import/Export

EMP: 30
SALES (corp-wide): 3.9B Publicly Held
SIC: 3843 Dental equipment & supplies
PA: Dentsply Sirona Inc.
221 W Philadelphia St
York PA 17401
717 845-7511

(G-20454)
DENTSPLY SIRONA INC (PA)
221 W Philadelphia St (17401-2991)
PHONE....................717 845-7511
Donald M Casey Jr, CEO
Eric K Brandt, Ch of Bd
Keith J Ebling, Exec VP
Markus Boehringer, Senior VP
Dominique P Legros, Senior VP
◆ EMP: 600
SALES: 3.9B Publicly Held
WEB: www.dentsply.com
SIC: 3843 Impression material, dental

(G-20455)
DENTSPLY SIRONA INC
Dentsply Prosthetics
470 W College Ave (17401-3810)
PHONE....................717 845-7511
Thomas Cole, Vice Pres
Bob Size, Vice Pres
Melody Lherisson, Sales Staff
Steve Jenson, Manager
Joshua Bylotas, Manager
EMP: 10
SALES (corp-wide): 3.9B Publicly Held
WEB: www.dentsply.com
SIC: 3843 5047 Teeth, artificial (not made
in dental laboratories); dental equipment
& supplies
PA: Dentsply Sirona Inc.
221 W Philadelphia St
York PA 17401
717 845-7511

(G-20456)
DOUCETTE INDUSTRIES INC
20 Leigh Dr (17406-8474)
PHONE....................717 845-8746
John E Lebo, President
Steven M Wand, Vice Pres
Falenski M Stanley, Treasurer
Philippe Doucette, Admin Sec
▼ EMP: 42
SQ FT: 15,000
SALES (est): 9MM Privately Held
WEB: www.doucetteindustries.com
SIC: 3443 Fabricated plate work (boiler
shop)

(G-20457)
DREUMEX USA INC
3445 Board Rd (17406-8409)
PHONE....................717 767-6881
Jan-Chris Heeger, President
Stijn Grielen, Corp Secy
Jeffrey Strickler, Vice Pres
Scott Hermes, Natl Sales Mgr
Karen Hansen, VP Mktg
▲ EMP: 20
SQ FT: 44,000
SALES (est): 6MM Privately Held
SIC: 2842 2841 5169 Cleaning or polish-
ing preparations; soap: granulated, liquid,
cake, flaked or chip; chemicals & allied
products
HQ: Dreumex B.V.
Dommelstraat 1
Oss 5347
412 406-506

(G-20458)
DSC2 INC
Also Called: Dixie Seating Company
586 Campbell Rd (17402-3335)
PHONE....................980 223-2270
David Jacobs, President
EMP: 18
SALES (est): 527.1K Privately Held
SIC: 2512 2521 2426 Upholstered house-
hold furniture; wood office furniture; furni-
ture stock & parts, hardwood

(G-20459)
EAGLE MFG & DESIGN CORP
1245 W Princess St (17404-3524)
PHONE....................717 848-9767
Paul L Bender, President

Donald E Sipe, Corp Secy
EMP: 20
SQ FT: 28,000
SALES (est): 3.2MM Privately Held
WEB: www.eagleboards.com
SIC: 3571 Electronic computers

(G-20460)
**EAST YORK DIAGNOSTIC
CENTER**
2250 E Market St (17402-2857)
PHONE....................717 851-1850
Ron Cerrvy, President
Ron Cernarvy, Manager
EMP: 4
SALES (est): 285.2K Privately Held
SIC: 2835 In vitro & in vivo diagnostic sub-
stances

(G-20461)
EASY LINER LLC
1069 Kings Mill Rd (17403-3482)
PHONE....................717 825-7962
Leke OSI, Mng Member
Andrew Chettle,
▲ EMP: 5
SQ FT: 5,000
SALES (est): 1.5MM
SALES (corp-wide): 528.5K Privately
Held
SIC: 3589 Sewage treatment equipment
PA: Project Building Company Limited
57 Glengall Road
London SE15
207 277-8878

(G-20462)
**EATON ELECTRIC HOLDINGS
LLC**
3990 E Market St (17402-2769)
PHONE....................717 755-2933
Terry Bires, Plant Mgr
Donald Frey, Mfg Mgr
Vera Verbitsky, Branch Mgr
EMP: 85 Privately Held
WEB: www.cooperus.com
SIC: 3546 3462 Power-driven handtools;
iron & steel forgings
HQ: Eaton Electric Holdings Llc
1000 Eaton Blvd
Cleveland OH 44122
440 523-5000

(G-20463)
EDAPTIVE SYSTEMS LLC
1246 Greensprings Dr (17402-8826)
PHONE....................717 718-1230
Shawn Reardon, Owner
Frank Zemrose, Senior VP
Melinda Plaugher, Vice Pres
Amanda Throckmorton, Corp Comm Staff
Dawn Loughborough, Sr Project Mgr
EMP: 4
SALES (corp-wide): 1.9B Publicly Held
SIC: 7372 Prepackaged software
HQ: Edaptive Systems, Llc
400 Red Brook Blvd # 220
Owings Mills MD 21117
410 327-3366

(G-20464)
EHB LOGISITICS INC
40 Willow Springs Cir (17406-8428)
PHONE....................717 764-5800
Marie E Sweet, President
Edward Brothers, Principal
EMP: 15
SALES (est): 2.4MM Privately Held
SIC: 3715 4789 Truck trailers; cargo load-
ing & unloading services

(G-20465)
EL SERRANO INC
Also Called: Sucursal Espana
3410 E Market St Ste E (17402-2629)
PHONE....................717 397-6191
Manuel J Torres, President
EMP: 3
SALES (est): 123.1K Privately Held
SIC: 2084 Wines

(G-20466)
**ELECTRO-PLATERS OF YORK
INC**
100 B Lane York St 1 (17402)
PHONE....................717 751-2712
David Sollenberger, President
Rose Walter, Corp Secy
Terry L Miller, Vice Pres
EMP: 11
SALES (est): 750K Privately Held
SIC: 3471 Electroplating of metals or
formed products

(G-20467)
**ELECTRONIC MFG SVCS
GROUP INC**
Also Called: Emsg
951 Monocacy Rd (17404-1615)
PHONE....................717 764-0002
Douglas J Hamp, President
Douglas I Hamp, President
Douglas R Boyer, Corp Secy
Alex Hamp, Vice Pres
Rocky Turnbaugh, VP Opers
EMP: 80
SQ FT: 20,000
SALES: 12MM Privately Held
WEB: www.emsginc.com
SIC: 3672 Printed circuit boards

(G-20468)
**ENGDAHL MANUFACTURING
INC**
190 Carlisle Ave (17401-3237)
PHONE....................717 854-7114
Robert Ehlenbeck, President
James Ehgdahl, President
Ellen Ehlenbeck, Treasurer
EMP: 5
SALES (est): 440K Privately Held
WEB: www.engdahlmfg.com
SIC: 3544 Special dies & tools

(G-20469)
EPEX SOFT PETALS
984 Loucks Rd (17404-2274)
PHONE....................717 848-8488
Gene Smith, Owner
EMP: 12
SALES (est): 450K Privately Held
SIC: 2052 Pretzels

(G-20470)
EPY INDUSTRIES INC
100 Boxwood Ln Ste 2 (17402-9305)
PHONE....................717 751-2712
Jeffery Adams, President
EMP: 10
SALES (est): 1MM Privately Held
SIC: 3471 Electroplating of metals or
formed products; finishing, metals or
formed products

(G-20471)
**ETTCO TOOL & MACHINE CO
INC**
1600 6th Ave Ste 114 (17403-2627)
P.O. Box 5744, Rockford IL (61125-0744)
PHONE....................717 792-1417
Patricia M Grayson, Ch of Bd
Natalie Nichols, President
John Crist, Vice Pres
Richard Parks, Treasurer
EMP: 14
SQ FT: 67,000
SALES: 1.7MM Privately Held
WEB: www.ettco.com
SIC: 3541 Machine tool replacement & re-
pair parts, metal cutting types

(G-20472)
EVAPCO ALCOIL INC
3627 Sandhurst Dr (17406-7927)
PHONE....................717 347-7500
John J Calkins, President
EMP: 29
SALES (est): 2.6MM
SALES (corp-wide): 384.1MM Privately
Held
SIC: 3585 3353 Refrigeration & heating
equipment; coils, sheet aluminum
PA: Evapco, Inc.
5151 Allendale Ln
Taneytown MD 21787
410 756-2600

(G-20473)
EXACT MACHINE SERVICE INC
144 Roosevelt Ave (17401-3333)
PHONE....................717 848-2121
Thomas J Cassidy, President
Nicole Cassidy, General Mgr
Eric Quesenderry, Vice Pres
EMP: 5
SQ FT: 3,000
SALES (est): 1MM Privately Held
WEB: www.exactmachineservice.com
SIC: 3541 Machine tool replacement & re-
pair parts, metal cutting types

(G-20474)
FABBCO STEEL INC
101 Mundis Race Rd (17406-9723)
PHONE....................717 792-4904
Dennis Fritz, President
Lynn Anderson, Vice Pres
Fern Bressler, CFO
EMP: 22
SQ FT: 36,000
SALES (est): 8.5MM Privately Held
WEB: www.fabbcosteel.com
SIC: 3441 Building components, structural
steel

(G-20475)
**FASTSIGNS INTERNATIONAL
INC**
2801 E Market St (17402-2406)
PHONE....................717 840-6400
John Toy, Owner
EMP: 3
SALES (corp-wide): 27.1MM Privately
Held
SIC: 3993 Signs & advertising specialties
PA: Fastsigns International, Inc.
2542 Highlander Way
Carrollton TX 75006
888 285-5935

(G-20476)
FB SHOEMAKER LLC
Also Called: UPS Store, The
2159 White St Ste 3 (17404-4948)
PHONE....................717 852-8029
Fred B Shoemaker, Mng Member
EMP: 4
SQ FT: 1,800
SALES (est): 376.2K Privately Held
SIC: 7389 2752 Mailbox rental & related
service; artists' agents & brokers; inspec-
tion & testing services; commercial print-
ing, lithographic

(G-20477)
FEC TECHNOLOGIES INC
700 Willow Springs Ln (17406-8434)
PHONE....................717 764-5959
Darren Lepage, President
Frederick R Lepage, President
Jeffrey Anderson, Vice Pres
John Mackinder, Vice Pres
Harry Block, Admin Sec
EMP: 45
SQ FT: 32,000
SALES (est): 5.8MM Privately Held
SIC: 8711 3613 3444 7371 Engineering
Services Mfg Switchgear/Boards Mfg
Sheet Metalwork Computer Programming
Svc Mfg Process Cntrl Instr

(G-20478)
**FEDERAL-MOGUL
MOTORPARTS LLC**
20 Leo Ln (17406-9122)
PHONE....................717 430-5021
EMP: 4
SALES (corp-wide): 11.7B Publicly Held
SIC: 3462 Iron & steel forgings
HQ: Federal-Mogul Motorparts Llc
27300 W 11 Mile Rd # 101
Southfield MI 48034
248 354-7700

(G-20479)
**FEDERAL-MOGUL
MOTORPARTS LLC**
20 Leo Ln (17406-9122)
P.O. Box 981469 (17406)
PHONE....................717 430-5021
EMP: 3

GEOGRAPHIC

SALES (corp-wide): 11.7B **Publicly Held**
SIC: 3559 Degreasing machines, automotive & industrial
HQ: Federal-Mogul Motorparts Llc
27300 W 11 Mile Rd # 101
Southfield MI 48034
248 354-7700

(G-20480)
FICORE INCORPORATED
Also Called: Reprint Management Services
3650 W Market St (17404-5813)
PHONE...................................717 735-9740
G Michael Biggerstaff, *President*
Roxanne L Edwards, *Vice Pres*
James T Lewis, *Vice Pres*
EMP: 50
SQ FT: 25,000
SALES (est): 3.8MM **Privately Held**
WEB: www.reprintbuyer.com
SIC: 2741 Miscellaneous publishing

(G-20481)
FIRST LEVEL INC
3109 Espresso Way (17406-6040)
PHONE...................................717 266-2450
Carol J Homsy, *President*
Rick Herbst, *Facilities Mgr*
Maria Heisler, *Opers Staff*
Mukesh Patel, *Project Engr*
Vicki Coppersmith, *Admin Asst*
EMP: 13
SQ FT: 5,500
SALES: 850K **Privately Held**
WEB: www.firstlevel.org
SIC: 3674 Semiconductors & related devices

(G-20482)
FITZKEES CANDIES INC
2352 S Queen St (17402-4939)
PHONE...................................717 741-1031
Robert L Fitzkee, *President*
Gloria Ann Carter, *Admin Sec*
EMP: 19 EST: 1933
SQ FT: 3,000
SALES (est): 2.8MM **Privately Held**
SIC: 2064 5441 Candy & other confectionery products; candy

(G-20483)
FLINCHBAUGH ENGINEERING INC
4387 Run Way (17406-8054)
PHONE...................................717 755-1900
Michael D Lehman, *President*
James D Flinchbaugh, *Chairman*
John Eifert, *Engineer*
Michael E Deppen, *Treasurer*
Tom Frauman, *Marketing Staff*
◆ EMP: 200
SQ FT: 20,000
SALES (est): 51.5MM **Privately Held**
WEB: www.fei-york.com
SIC: 3599 Machine shop, jobbing & repair

(G-20484)
FORM TOOL TECHNOLOGY INC (PA)
Also Called: Form Tech
5174 Commerce Dr (17408-9510)
PHONE...................................717 792-3626
Michael M Robbins, *President*
Brooks Boland, *Principal*
Beth Flory, *Principal*
Roxanne Robbins, *Vice Pres*
EMP: 20
SQ FT: 16,000
SALES (est): 3.1MM **Privately Held**
WEB: www.formtooltech.com
SIC: 3545 5085 Cutting tools for machine tools; tools

(G-20485)
FORMIT METAL FABRICATORS LLC
101 Mundis Race Rd (17406-9723)
PHONE...................................717 650-2895
Dennis Fritz, *General Mgr*
EMP: 8
SALES (est): 2.2MM **Privately Held**
SIC: 3441 Fabricated structural metal

(G-20486)
FORSYTHE MARKETING
Also Called: Performa Forsythe Marketing
2575 Hepplewhite Dr (17404-1215)
PHONE...................................717 764-9863
Sue Forsythe, *Owner*
Paul Forsythe, *Owner*
EMP: 4
SALES (est): 260K **Privately Held**
WEB: www.forsythemkt.com
SIC: 2759 Promotional printing

(G-20487)
FOX POOL LANCASTER INC (HQ)
Also Called: Fabcote
3490 Board Rd (17406-8478)
PHONE...................................717 718-1977
Jeffery Kurtz, *CEO*
Robert E Seitz, *President*
Donald E Dahowski, *Vice Pres*
Jeffery C Kurth, *Vice Pres*
EMP: 60
SQ FT: 175,000
SALES: 6.6MM
SALES (corp-wide): 124MM **Privately Held**
SIC: 3949 5047 5091 Swimming pools, plastic; medical equipment & supplies; swimming pools, equipment & supplies
PA: Wexco Incorporated
3490 Board Rd
York PA 17406
717 764-8585

(G-20488)
FRITO-LAY NORTH AMERICA INC
3553 Gillespie Dr (17404-5803)
PHONE...................................717 792-2611
Janice Gross, *Human Res Mgr*
Danielle Shultz, *Personnel Assit*
Jeff Green, *Maintnce Staff*
EMP: 300
SALES (corp-wide): 64.6B **Publicly Held**
WEB: www.fritolay.com
SIC: 2096 Potato chips & similar snacks
HQ: Frito-Lay North America, Inc.
7701 Legacy Dr
Plano TX 75024

(G-20489)
GAMLET INC
1750 Toronita St (17402-1923)
P.O. Box 7658 (17404-0658)
PHONE...................................717 852-9200
David F Cutright, *CEO*
Scott Cutright, *President*
Chad Kenny, *Safety Mgr*
Kimberly March, *CFO*
Kim March, *Controller*
EMP: 64 EST: 1965
SALES: 9.2MM **Privately Held**
WEB: www.gamlet.com
SIC: 3444 3699 Metal housings, enclosures, casings & other containers; electrical equipment & supplies

(G-20490)
GARRETT PRECISION LLC
55 S Fayette St Ste 4 (17404-5537)
P.O. Box 7302 (17404-0302)
PHONE...................................717 779-1384
EMP: 7
SALES (est): 1.4MM **Privately Held**
SIC: 3823 Industrial process measurement equipment

(G-20491)
GARTH GROFT
Also Called: Microcomputer Task Group
2164 Southbrook Dr (17403-4951)
PHONE...................................717 819-9479
Garth Groft, *Owner*
EMP: 3
SALES (est): 173.5K **Privately Held**
WEB: www.mctg.com
SIC: 7371 7372 Computer software systems analysis & design, custom; prepackaged software

(G-20492)
GAUMER TOOL MACHINE CO INC
230 Industrial Rd (17406-8424)
PHONE...................................717 266-0273
Benjamin Gaumer, *CEO*
EMP: 20
SQ FT: 10,500
SALES (est): 1.4MM **Privately Held**
SIC: 3599 Machine shop, jobbing & repair

(G-20493)
GEA SYSTEMS NORTH AMERICA LLC
3475 Board Rd (17406-8414)
PHONE...................................717 767-6411
Ronald Eberhard, *CEO*
EMP: 210
SALES (corp-wide): 5.5B **Privately Held**
SIC: 3585 Refrigeration & heating equipment
HQ: Gea Systems North America Llc
9165 Rumsey Rd
Columbia MD 21045
410 772-5792

(G-20494)
GENERAL MACHINE WORKS INC
515 E Prospect St (17403-2406)
P.O. Box 546 (17405-0546)
PHONE...................................717 848-2713
Robert F Davis, *CEO*
EMP: 10 EST: 1905
SALES (est): 2.2MM **Privately Held**
SIC: 3599 Machine shop, jobbing & repair

(G-20495)
GENERAL REGULATOR CORP
Also Called: Accudriv
517 E Prospect St (17403-2406)
P.O. Box 546 (17405-0546)
PHONE...................................717 848-5960
Robert Davis, *CEO*
Donald Swartz, *President*
EMP: 20 EST: 1908
SQ FT: 50,000
SALES (est): 2.6MM **Privately Held**
WEB: www.generalregulator.com
SIC: 3599 3823 Machine shop, jobbing & repair; combustion control instruments

(G-20496)
GENIE ELECTRONICS CO INC
1087 Valley View Rd (17406-6310)
PHONE...................................717 840-6999
Robert J Owen, *Branch Mgr*
EMP: 25
SALES (corp-wide): 2MM **Privately Held**
WEB: www.securityfence.com
SIC: 3672 3679 Printed circuit boards; harness assemblies for electronic use: wire or cable
PA: Genie Electronics Co., Inc.
3090 Cape Horn Rd
Red Lion PA 17356
717 244-1099

(G-20497)
GERDAU AMERISTEEL US INC
2870 Eastern Blvd (17402-2908)
PHONE...................................717 751-6898
Ameristeel Gerdau, *Branch Mgr*
EMP: 232 **Privately Held**
SIC: 3312 Blast furnaces & steel mills
HQ: Gerdau Ameristeel Us Inc.
4221 W Boy Scout Blvd # 600
Tampa FL 33607
813 286-8383

(G-20498)
GERDAU AMERISTEEL US INC
1700 7th Ave (17403-2645)
PHONE...................................717 846-7865
Tom Doyle, *Branch Mgr*
EMP: 100 **Privately Held**
SIC: 3449 Bars, concrete reinforcing: fabricated steel
HQ: Gerdau Ameristeel Us Inc.
4221 W Boy Scout Blvd # 600
Tampa FL 33607
813 286-8383

(G-20499)
GGS INFORMATION SERVICES INC (PA)
Also Called: G G S
3265 Farmtrail Rd (17406-5602)
PHONE...................................717 764-2222
Paul V Kilker, *President*
Rita A Hoover, *Vice Pres*
Lloyd D Kendall, *Vice Pres*
EMP: 210 EST: 1988
SQ FT: 34,000
SALES (est): 56.1MM **Privately Held**
WEB: www.ggsinc.com
SIC: 2796 2741 2791 8711 Color separations for printing; catalogs: publishing only, not printed on site; technical manuals: publishing only, not printed on site; photocomposition, for the printing trade; engineering services; personal service agents, brokers & bureaus; custom computer programming services

(G-20500)
GLATFELTER HOLDINGS LLC
96 S George St Ste 500 (17401-1434)
PHONE...................................717 225-2772
Dante C Parrini, *CEO*
EMP: 3 EST: 2015
SALES (est): 84.3K
SALES (corp-wide): 866.2MM **Publicly Held**
SIC: 2621 Paper mills
PA: P. H. Glatfelter Company
96 S George St Ste 520
York PA 17401
717 225-4711

(G-20501)
GLAXOSMITHKLINE CONSUMER
105 Willow Springs Ln (17406-8511)
PHONE...................................717 268-0110
Dennis Kovacevich, *Branch Mgr*
EMP: 98
SALES (corp-wide): 39.8B **Privately Held**
SIC: 2834 Pharmaceutical preparations
HQ: Glaxosmithkline Consumer Healthcare, L.P.
184 Libery Corner Rd
Warren NJ 07059

(G-20502)
GLAXOSMITHKLINE LLC
105 Willow Springs Ln (17406-8511)
PHONE...................................717 268-0319
Greg M Cauley, *Branch Mgr*
EMP: 8
SALES (corp-wide): 39.8B **Privately Held**
SIC: 2834 Pharmaceutical preparations
HQ: Glaxosmithkline Llc
5 Crescent Dr
Philadelphia PA 19112
215 751-4000

(G-20503)
GLEN-GERY CORPORATION
Also Called: Glen-Gery Brick Center
1090 E Boundary Ave (17403-2920)
P.O. Box 2903 (17405)
PHONE...................................717 854-8802
Michael Lighty, *Principal*
EMP: 78
SALES (corp-wide): 1.2MM **Privately Held**
SIC: 3251 Brick clay: common face, glazed, vitrified or hollow
HQ: Glen-Gery Corporation
1166 Spring St
Reading PA 19610
610 374-4011

(G-20504)
GLEN-GERY CORPORATION
Glen-Gery York Plant
1090 E Boundary Ave (17403-2920)
PHONE...................................717 848-2589
Michael Lighty, *Manager*
EMP: 100
SALES (corp-wide): 571K **Privately Held**
WEB: www.glengerybrick.com
SIC: 3251 3255 Brick clay: common face, glazed, vitrified or hollow; clay refractories
HQ: Glen-Gery Corporation
1166 Spring St
Reading PA 19610
610 374-4011

(G-20505)
GPC CAPITAL CORP II
2401 Pleasant Valley Rd (17402-9600)
PHONE..................................717 849-8500
Philip R Yates, *Ch of Bd*
Roger M Prevot, *President*
Jay W Hereford, *Vice Pres*
John E Hamilton, *CFO*
EMP: 4100
SQ FT: 395,500
SALES (est): 150.6MM
SALES (corp-wide): 1MM **Privately Held**
SIC: 3089 Blow molded finished plastic
products; extruded finished plastic products

HQ: Graham Packaging Holdings Co
700 Indian Springs Dr # 100
Lancaster PA 17601
717 849-8500

(G-20506)
**GRAHAM ARCHITECTURAL
PDTS CORP (PA)**
1551 Mount Rose Ave (17403-2909)
PHONE..................................717 849-8100
William Kerlin, *Ch of Bd*
Brian Hurley, *President*
Georges Thiret, *President*
Michael Derosa, *Vice Pres*
Dennis Kelly, *Vice Pres*
▲ **EMP:** 265
SQ FT: 170,000
SALES (est): 103.1MM **Privately Held**
WEB: www.grahamwindows.com
SIC: 3442 Screen & storm doors & windows

(G-20507)
**GRAHAM ENGINEERING
CORPORATION**
1203 Eden Rd (17402-1965)
P.O. Box 12003 (17402-0673)
PHONE..................................717 848-3755
David Schroeder, *CEO*
Wolfgang Liebertz, *President*
Dave Yenor, *Vice Pres*
Keith Foor, *Buyer*
Wayne Leidy, *VP Engrg*
◆ **EMP:** 175 EST: 1960
SALES (est): 62.5MM **Privately Held**
SIC: 3559 Plastics working machinery

(G-20508)
**GRAHAM PACKAGING CO
EUROPE LLC**
Also Called: Liquid Container
2401 Pleasant Valley Rd # 2 (17402-9600)
PHONE..................................209 572-5187
Tom Fponder, *Manager*
EMP: 44
SALES (corp-wide): 1MM **Privately Held**
WEB: www.liquidcontainer.com
SIC: 3089 Plastic containers, except foam
HQ: Graham Packaging Company Europe
Llc
2401 Pleasant Valley Rd # 2
York PA 17402

(G-20509)
**GRAHAM PACKAGING
COMPANY LP**
500 Windsor St (17403-1046)
P.O. Box 2618 (17405-2618)
PHONE..................................717 849-8700
Stephen Weiss, *Manager*
Jeff Brown, *Executive*
Richard Roberts, *Maintence Staff*
EMP: 35
SALES (corp-wide): 1MM **Privately Held**
WEB: www.grahampackaging.com
SIC: 3089 3085 Plastic containers, except
foam; plastics bottles
HQ: Graham Packaging Company, L.P.
700 Indian Springs Dr # 100
Lancaster PA 17601
717 849-8500

(G-20510)
**GRAHAM PACKAGING
COMPANY LP**
2401 Pleasant Valley Rd # 99
(17402-9600)
PHONE..................................717 849-1800
Cathy Blackner, *Human Res Mgr*
EMP: 40

SALES (corp-wide): 1MM **Privately Held**
WEB: www.grahampackaging.com
SIC: 3089 Blow molded finished plastic
products; plastic containers, except foam
HQ: Graham Packaging Company, L.P.
700 Indian Springs Dr # 100
Lancaster PA 17601
717 849-8500

(G-20511)
**GRAHAM PACKAGING
COMPANY LP**
2401 Pleasant Valley Rd # 2 (17402-9600)
PHONE..................................717 849-8500
Mike McClure, *Manager*
EMP: 21
SALES (corp-wide): 1MM **Privately Held**
WEB: www.grahampackaging.com
SIC: 3089 3085 2992 Plastic containers,
except foam; plastics bottles; lubricating
oils & greases
HQ: Graham Packaging Company, L.P.
700 Indian Springs Dr # 100
Lancaster PA 17601
717 849-8500

(G-20512)
**GRAHAM RECYCLING
COMPANY LP**
505 Windsor St (17403-1054)
PHONE..................................717 852-7744
John Hamilton, *Partner*
Philip R Yates, *General Ptnr*
EMP: 80 EST: 1990
SALES (est): 7.1MM
SALES (corp-wide): 1MM **Privately Held**
WEB: www.grahampackaging.com
SIC: 4953 2821 Recycling, waste materials; plastics materials & resins
HQ: Graham Packaging Company, L.P.
700 Indian Springs Dr # 100
Lancaster PA 17601
717 849-8500

(G-20513)
GRAMMATON RESEARCH LLC
1005 Cherimoya St (17404-8302)
PHONE..................................410 703-9237
Rebekah Mellen,
EMP: 3
SALES (est): 150K **Privately Held**
SIC: 7379 7372 7389 Computer related
consulting services; prepackaged software;

(G-20514)
**GRID ELC & SOLAR SOLUTIONS
LLC**
320 Loucks Rd Ste 202 (17404-1752)
PHONE..................................717 885-5249
EMP: 3
SALES (est): 117.6K **Privately Held**
SIC: 3699 Electrical equipment & supplies

(G-20515)
GROWMARK FS LLC
980 Loucks Mill Rd (17402-1973)
PHONE..................................717 854-3818
Linda Grim, *Branch Mgr*
EMP: 10
SALES (corp-wide): 7.2B **Privately Held**
WEB: www.growmarkfs.com
SIC: 2874 0721 Phosphatic fertilizers;
crop planting & protection
HQ: Growmark Fs, Llc
308 Ne Front St
Milford DE 19963
302 422-3002

(G-20516)
GTY INC
2075 Loucks Rd (17408-9704)
PHONE..................................717 764-8969
Carl Vizzi, *President*
Stan Thomas, *Corp Secy*
Bob Henniman, *Vice Pres*
▲ **EMP:** 56
SALES (est): 8.3MM **Privately Held**
SIC: 2621 Wallpaper (hanging paper)

(G-20517)
GUILDCRAFT INC
401 S Sherman St (17403-2492)
PHONE..................................717 854-3888
Lisa Elfner, *President*

Scott Dephtereos, *Vice Pres*
Craig Elfner, *Treasurer*
EMP: 12
SQ FT: 53,000
SALES (est): 1.3MM **Privately Held**
WEB: www.guildcraftfurniture.com
SIC: 2519 5712 5199 2671 Household
furniture, except wood or metal: upholstered; furniture stores; packaging materials; packaging paper & plastics film,
coated & laminated; upholstered household furniture

(G-20518)
H & H CASTINGS INC
4300 Lincoln Hwy (17406-8022)
PHONE..................................717 751-0064
Kenneth Haugh, *President*
Rodney E Haugh, *Vice Pres*
Ellen Stickles, *Human Res Mgr*
EMP: 75
SQ FT: 88,000
SALES (est): 18.7MM **Privately Held**
WEB: www.hhcast.com
SIC: 3365 Aluminum foundries

(G-20519)
**HAAS ARCHITECTURAL MLLWK
INC**
3750 E Market St (17402-2765)
PHONE..................................717 840-4227
Randy Haas, *President*
EMP: 30
SALES (est): 5MM **Privately Held**
SIC: 2431 Millwork

(G-20520)
**HANGER PRSTHETCS & ORTHO
INC**
Also Called: Zielke Orthotics & Prosthetics
1603 Rodney Rd (17408-9106)
PHONE..................................717 767-6667
Donald Zielke, *Manager*
EMP: 6
SALES (corp-wide): 1B **Publicly Held**
SIC: 3842 Orthopedic appliances
HQ: Hanger Prosthetics & Orthotics, Inc.
10910 Domain Dr Ste 300
Austin TX 78758
512 777-3800

(G-20521)
**HANOVER FOODS
CORPORATION**
Also Called: Bickels Potato Chips
1000 W College Ave (17404-3537)
P.O. Box 2427 (17405-2427)
PHONE..................................717 665-2002
EMP: 200
SALES (corp-wide): 675.2MM **Publicly
Held**
SIC: 2096 Mfg Potato Chips
PA: Hanover Foods Corporation
1486 York St
Hanover PA 17331
717 632-6000

(G-20522)
**HANOVER FOODS
CORPORATION**
Also Called: Bickle Snack Foods
1120 Zinns Quarry Rd (17404-3533)
PHONE..................................717 843-0738
Jeff Warehime, *General Mgr*
EMP: 10
SALES (corp-wide): 292MM **Publicly
Held**
WEB: www.hanoverfoods.com
SIC: 2033 Tomato products: packaged in
cans, jars, etc.
PA: Hanover Foods Corporation
1486 York St
Hanover PA 17331
717 632-6000

(G-20523)
HISTORIC YORK INC
25 N Duke St Ste 102 (17401-1800)
PHONE..................................717 843-0320
Michael Stebbins, *President*
Melinda Higgins, *Exec Dir*
EMP: 6

SALES: 111.2K **Privately Held**
WEB: www.campsecurity.com
SIC: 5932 5211 3564 1711 Antiques;
lumber & other building materials; filters,
air: furnaces, air conditioning equipment,
etc.; boiler & furnace contractors; ice
making machines

(G-20524)
**HOLLINGER TCHNCAL
PBLCTONS INC**
2550 Kingston Rd Ste 221 (17402-3733)
P.O. Box 7292 (17404-0292)
PHONE..................................717 755-8800
Schawn Dobson, *President*
EMP: 4
SQ FT: 1,500
SALES (est): 270.8K **Privately Held**
WEB: www.holltechpubs.com
SIC: 2741 7336 Technical manuals: publishing only, not printed on site; commercial art & graphic design

(G-20525)
**HOMER OPTICAL COMPANY
INC**
Also Called: Homer Optics
60 Hokes Mill Rd (17404-5503)
PHONE..................................717 843-1822
Kenn White, *Manager*
EMP: 12
SALES (corp-wide): 283.5MM **Privately
Held**
SIC: 3851 Ophthalmic goods
HQ: Homer Optical Company, Inc.
2401 Linden Ln
Silver Spring MD 20910
301 585-9060

(G-20526)
**HONEYWELL INTERNATIONAL
INC**
525 E Market St (17403-1619)
P.O. Box 934 (17405-0934)
PHONE..................................717 771-8100
Fax: 717 771-8165
EMP: 160
SALES (corp-wide): 40.3B **Publicly Held**
SIC: 3625 Mfg Relays/Industrial Controls
PA: Honeywell International Inc.
115 Tabor Ave
Morris Plains NJ 07950
973 455-2000

(G-20527)
**HONEYWELL INTERNATIONAL
INC**
383 Holyoke Dr (17402-5013)
PHONE..................................717 741-3799
EMP: 673
SALES (corp-wide): 41.8B **Publicly Held**
SIC: 3724 Aircraft engines & engine parts
PA: Honeywell International Inc.
115 Tabor Rd
Morris Plains NJ 07950
973 455-2000

(G-20528)
**HOOVER DESIGN &
MANUFACTURING**
1410 Harley Davidson Dr (17402-1506)
PHONE..................................717 767-9555
Richard Hoover, *President*
Rick Miller, *General Mgr*
Kathleen Hoover, *Admin Sec*
EMP: 8
SQ FT: 6,600
SALES (est): 1MM **Privately Held**
SIC: 3599 Custom machinery

(G-20529)
HOWE WOOD PRODUCTS INC
3107 Espresso Way (17406-6040)
PHONE..................................717 266-9855
Mike Howe, *President*
Susan J Howe, *Admin Sec*
▲ **EMP:** 12
SQ FT: 13,000
SALES (est): 1.5MM **Privately Held**
WEB: www.howewoodproducts.com
SIC: 2436 2449 2448 Plywood, softwood;
rectangular boxes & crates, wood; containers, plywood & veneer wood; skids,
wood

(G-20530)
HR PHARMACEUTICALS INC
2600 Eastern Blvd Ste 201 (17402-2916)
PHONE....................................877 302-1110
Jon P Wiesman, *CEO*
Leeanna M Wiesman, *Corp Secy*
Ryan Dohm, *COO*
Robert L Waltz Jr, *Vice Pres*
Corey Righter, *Opers Mgr*
▼ EMP: 20
SQ FT: 4,200
SALES (est): 3.8MM **Privately Held**
SIC: 2834 Pharmaceutical preparations

(G-20531)
HUGHES NETWORK SYSTEMS LLC
2115 Bannister St (17404-4803)
PHONE....................................717 792-2987
EMP: 32 **Publicly Held**
SIC: 3663 Space satellite communications equipment
HQ: Hughes Network Systems, Llc
11717 Exploration Ln
Germantown MD 20876
301 428-5500

(G-20532)
HYDRO PARTNERS LLC
1800 W King St (17404-5643)
PHONE....................................717 825-1332
Kem Hostler, *Mng Member*
EMP: 4
SALES (est): 250K **Privately Held**
SIC: 3612 Transformers, except electric

(G-20533)
ID TECHNOLOGY LLC
391 Greendale Rd (17403-4638)
PHONE....................................717 848-3875
EMP: 30
SALES (corp-wide): 599.3MM **Privately Held**
SIC: 2759 3953 3565 5084 Commercial printing; marking devices; labeling machines, industrial; industrial machinery & equipment
HQ: Id Technology Llc
5051 N Sylvania Ave
Fort Worth TX 76137
817 626-7779

(G-20534)
IMAGINEERED SIGNS & DISPLAY
1890 W Market St Ste 1 (17404-5400)
PHONE....................................717 846-6114
Tod Klunk, *President*
David L Klunk, *Vice Pres*
Mary Klunk, *Treasurer*
EMP: 9 EST: 1972
SQ FT: 23,000
SALES (est): 1.1MM **Privately Held**
WEB: www.imagineeredsigns.biz
SIC: 3993 Signs & advertising specialties

(G-20535)
IMPRESSIVE SIGNS INC
351 N East St (17403-1260)
PHONE....................................717 848-9305
Mike Montgomery, *President*
Lisa Montgomery, *Vice Pres*
EMP: 9
SALES (est): 1MM **Privately Held**
WEB: www.impressivesigns.com
SIC: 3993 7532 Signs, not made in custom sign painting shops; truck painting & lettering

(G-20536)
INDUSTRIAL POLSG & GRINDING
390 N Eberts Ln (17403-1139)
PHONE....................................717 854-9001
Scot Thomas, *President*
Jeff Raynes, *Vice Pres*
Lance Thomas, *Treasurer*
EMP: 53
SQ FT: 25,000
SALES (est): 8MM **Privately Held**
WEB: www.ipgyork.com
SIC: 3449 3471 Miscellaneous metalwork; plating & polishing

(G-20537)
INK RE PHILL
1833 Shawan Ln (17406-6610)
PHONE....................................717 840-0835
Philip Serros, *Owner*
EMP: 4
SALES (est): 181.1K **Privately Held**
SIC: 2893 Lithographic ink

(G-20538)
IWM INTERNATIONAL LLC
408 E Philadelphia St (17403)
PHONE....................................800 323-5585
John Caley, *Branch Mgr*
EMP: 3
SALES (corp-wide): 380MM **Privately Held**
SIC: 3315 Wire & fabricated wire products
HQ: Iwm International, Llc
500 E Middle St
Hanover PA 17331
717 637-3795

(G-20539)
J WALKER & ASSOCIATES LLC
3521 Thunderhill Rd (17402-4441)
PHONE....................................717 755-7142
Jackie Walker, *Principal*
EMP: 3 EST: 2007
SALES (est): 181.7K **Privately Held**
SIC: 3842 Walkers

(G-20540)
JAMIES COURTSIDE SPT & SPIRITS
18 S Belmont St (17403-1915)
PHONE....................................717 757-7689
Harry Craley, *Owner*
EMP: 20
SQ FT: 528
SALES (est): 1.7MM **Privately Held**
SIC: 2599 Bar, restaurant & cafeteria furniture

(G-20541)
JLS AUTOMATION LLC
20 Innovation Dr (17402-2777)
PHONE....................................717 505-3800
Craig A Souser, *President*
Craig Wolfe, *Vice Pres*
Frank Weinstein, *Purchasing*
Mark Ewing, *VP Sls/Mktg*
Eric Olson, *CFO*
EMP: 27
SQ FT: 42,000
SALES (est): 8.5MM **Privately Held**
WEB: www.jlsouser.com
SIC: 8711 3625 3565 3555 Engineering services; relays & industrial controls; packaging machinery; printing trades machinery

(G-20542)
JOHNSON CONTROLS INC
631 S Richland Ave (17403-3486)
PHONE....................................717 771-7890
Anwar Hassan, *Vice Pres*
EMP: 3 **Privately Held**
SIC: 3714 Motor vehicle parts & accessories
HQ: Johnson Controls, Inc.
5757 N Green Bay Ave
Milwaukee WI 53209
414 524-1200

(G-20543)
JOHNSON CONTROLS INC
631 S Richland Ave (17403-3486)
PHONE....................................717 771-7890
EMP: 99 **Privately Held**
SIC: 3585 Refrigeration & heating equipment
HQ: Johnson Controls, Inc.
5757 N Green Bay Ave
Milwaukee WI 53209
414 524-1200

(G-20544)
JOHNSON CONTROLS INC
1499 E Philadelphia St (17403-1232)
PHONE....................................717 815-4200
EMP: 94 **Privately Held**
SIC: 2531 Seats, automobile

HQ: Johnson Controls, Inc.
5757 N Green Bay Ave
Milwaukee WI 53209
414 524-1200

(G-20545)
JRKN INDUSTRIES LLC
2765 Pilgrim Rd (17406-2360)
PHONE....................................717 324-3996
Kim A Krout, *Owner*
EMP: 3
SALES (est): 181.6K **Privately Held**
SIC: 3999 Manufacturing industries

(G-20546)
K S TOOLING INC
535 Willow Springs Ln (17406-8427)
PHONE....................................717 764-5817
Kenneth E Sweigart, *President*
Patti Sweigart, *Vice Pres*
Jim Flaim, *Manager*
EMP: 45
SQ FT: 50,000
SALES (est): 10MM **Privately Held**
WEB: www.kstooling.com
SIC: 3544 Dies & die holders for metal cutting, forming, die casting

(G-20547)
KARMA INDUSTRIAL SERVICES LLC
275 Herman St (17404-3420)
PHONE....................................717 814-7101
EMP: 3
SALES (est): 430.1K **Privately Held**
SIC: 3625 Crane & hoist controls, including metal mill

(G-20548)
KBA NORTH AMERICA INC (HQ)
Also Called: Web Press Div
3900 E Market St (17402-2776)
PHONE....................................717 505-1150
Scott R Smith, *President*
Gerrit Zwergel, *Vice Pres*
EMP: 179
SQ FT: 206,000
SALES (est): 12.5MM
SALES (corp-wide): 1.4B **Privately Held**
WEB: www.kbavt.com
SIC: 3555 Printing trades machinery
PA: Koenig & Bauer Ag
Friedrich-Koenig-Str. 4
Wurzburg 97080
931 909-0

(G-20549)
KEENER COATINGS INC
3711 Board Rd (17406-8425)
P.O. Box 335, Emigsville (17318-0335)
PHONE....................................717 764-9412
Dean Keener, *President*
Cris Keener, *Vice Pres*
Terry Keener, *Treasurer*
Jodi Hamberger, *Admin Sec*
EMP: 20
SQ FT: 52,000
SALES (est): 2.4MM **Privately Held**
SIC: 3479 Coating of metals & formed products

(G-20550)
KELTROL ENTERPRISES INC
140 Rose Ct (17406-8411)
PHONE....................................717 764-5940
Thomas O Troxell, *President*
EMP: 8 EST: 1976
SALES (est): 1.3MM **Privately Held**
WEB: www.keltrol.com
SIC: 3089 Plastic containers, except foam

(G-20551)
KERMITOOL LIQUIDATION COMPANY
401 Manor St (17401-2110)
PHONE....................................717 846-8665
Kermit S Hoke, *President*
Bryan Wickard, *Supervisor*
Beverly Hoke, *Admin Sec*
EMP: 18
SQ FT: 4,000
SALES (est): 4.3MM **Privately Held**
WEB: www.kermitool.com
SIC: 3545 Cutting tools for machine tools

(G-20552)
KEYSTONE AUTOMOTIVE INDS INC
275a Cross Farm Ln (17406-6201)
PHONE....................................717 843-8927
Ed Rodemyer, *Manager*
EMP: 10
SALES (corp-wide): 11.8B **Publicly Held**
WEB: www.kool-vue.com
SIC: 5013 3714 Automotive supplies & parts; bumpers & bumperettes, motor vehicle
HQ: Keystone Automotive Industries, Inc.
5846 Crossings Blvd
Antioch TN 37013
615 781-5200

(G-20553)
KEYSTONE ELECTRONICS INC
2315 S Queen St (17402-4938)
PHONE....................................717 747-5900
Kathy Hartwigsen, *President*
Dan Hartwigsen, *Manager*
EMP: 29
SQ FT: 25,000
SALES (est): 5MM **Privately Held**
SIC: 3672 3679 Printed circuit boards; harness assemblies for electronic use: wire or cable

(G-20554)
KINSLEY CONSTRUCTION INC
Also Called: Kinsley Concrete
629 Loucks Mill Rd (17403-1010)
PHONE....................................717 846-6711
Chris Kinsley, *President*
EMP: 30
SALES (corp-wide): 753.2MM **Privately Held**
WEB: www.rkinsley.com
SIC: 3273 1771 Ready-mixed concrete; concrete work
PA: Kinsley Construction, Inc.
2700 Water St
York PA 17403
717 741-3841

(G-20555)
KKR & CO LP
Acco Material Hdlg Solutions
76 Acco Dr (17402-4668)
P.O. Box 792 (17405-0792)
PHONE....................................717 741-4863
Daniel Carmody, *President*
Jeffrey Smith, *Director*
EMP: 135 **Publicly Held**
WEB: www.fkiinc.com
SIC: 3536 Cranes & monorail systems; hoists
PA: Kkr & Co. Inc.
9 W 57th St Ste 4200
New York NY 10019

(G-20556)
KLINGE CORPORATION (PA)
Also Called: Reefer Parts
4075 E Market St (17402-5123)
PHONE....................................717 840-4500
Allan Klinge, *President*
Henrik Klinge, *Chairman*
Tom Baldwin, *Prdtn Mgr*
Matthew Grove, *Foreman/Supr*
Steve Miller, *Purch Mgr*
◆ EMP: 75
SQ FT: 140,000
SALES (est): 3.4MM **Privately Held**
SIC: 3585 3621 Refrigeration equipment, complete; power generators

(G-20557)
KLOECKNER METALS CORPORATION
420 Memory Ln (17402-2204)
P.O. Box 20218 (17402-0165)
PHONE....................................717 755-1923
Frank King, *Manager*
EMP: 100
SALES (corp-wide): 7.7B **Privately Held**
WEB: www.macsteelusa.com
SIC: 5051 3444 3441 3316 Steel; sheet metalwork; fabricated structural metal; cold finishing of steel shapes
HQ: Kloeckner Metals Corporation
500 Colonial Center Pkwy # 500
Roswell GA 30076

▲ = Import ▼=Export
◆ =Import/Export

(G-20558)
KOTTCAMP SHEET METAL
145 Roosevelt Ave (17401-3332)
P.O. Box 426 (17405-0426)
PHONE..............................717 845-7616
Tom McKee, *President*
Brian Small, *Vice Pres*
Mary McKee, *Admin Sec*
EMP: 22 **EST:** 1979
SQ FT: 42,000
SALES (est): 4.6MM **Privately Held**
SIC: 3444 7692 3585 3564 Sheet metal-
work; welding repair; refrigeration & heat-
ing equipment; blowers & fans; heating
equipment, except electric

(G-20559)
KRAFT HOME SOLUTIONS LLC
352 Westwood Dr (17404-9177)
PHONE..............................717 819-2690
EMP: 3 **EST:** 2016
SALES (est): 117K **Privately Held**
SIC: 2022 Mfg Cheese

(G-20560)
**KROSAKI MGNSITA
RFRCTORIES LLC**
425 S Salem Church Rd (17408-5955)
PHONE..............................717 793-5536
Junichi Yamawaki,
Yohsuke Shimazaki,
EMP: 42
SQ FT: 27,000
SALES: 32MM **Privately Held**
SIC: 3297 Cement: high temperature, re-
fractory (nonclay)

(G-20561)
KS KRAFTS
2923 Balsa St (17404-8483)
PHONE..............................717 764-7033
Kay Bischof, *Principal*
EMP: 3
SALES (est): 130.5K **Privately Held**
SIC: 2022 Mfg Cheese

(G-20562)
LAUCKS AND SPAULDING INC
Also Called: Continental Signs
350 S Albemarle St (17403-2534)
PHONE..............................717 845-3312
Andrea Laucks, *President*
Mark Laucks, *Vice Pres*
EMP: 15
SQ FT: 10,450
SALES (est): 2.2MM **Privately Held**
WEB: www.continentalsigns.net
SIC: 3993 Neon signs

(G-20563)
**LBLOCK TRANSPORTATION
INC**
362 W Princess St (17401-3836)
PHONE..............................347 533-0943
Pedro Cabrera, *President*
EMP: 6
SALES (est): 82.5K **Privately Held**
SIC: 7539 3799 Automotive repair shops;
transportation equipment

(G-20564)
LEGACY VULCAN LLC
Also Called: Vulcan Materials
322 N Baker Rd (17408-5802)
PHONE..............................717 792-6996
David Statum, *Manager*
Justin Burrage, *Manager*
EMP: 9 **Publicly Held**
WEB: www.vulcanmaterials.com
SIC: 1422 Crushed & broken limestone
HQ: Legacy Vulcan, Llc
1200 Urban Center Dr
Vestavia AL 35242
205 298-3000

(G-20565)
LEHIGH CEMENT COMPANY LLC
200 Hokes Mill Rd (17404-5540)
PHONE..............................717 843-0811
Gary Gerber, *Buyer*
Curvin Hersh, *Branch Mgr*
EMP: 72

SALES (corp-wide): 20.6B **Privately Held**
WEB: www.lehighcement.com
SIC: 3297 Cement refractories; ce-
ment, hydraulic
HQ: Lehigh Cement Company Llc
300 E John Carpenter Fwy
Irving TX 75062
877 534-4442

(G-20566)
LINDSTROM MACHINE SHOP
1420 Orange St Rear (17404-3229)
P.O. Box 7636 (17404-0636)
PHONE..............................717 848-2983
Alan Lindstrom, *President*
Chris Limdstrom, *Principal*
Rose Lindstrom, *Corp Secy*
EMP: 5 **EST:** 1950
SQ FT: 2,000
SALES (est): 765.2K **Privately Held**
WEB: www.lindstrommachine.com
SIC: 3599 Machine shop, jobbing & repair

(G-20567)
LUBE CENTER
1195 Loucks Rd (17404-2203)
PHONE..............................717 848-4885
Randall Simpson, *Owner*
EMP: 3
SALES (est): 21.7K **Privately Held**
SIC: 2992 Lubricating oils

(G-20568)
LUMBER AND THINGS INC
1850 Lemon St (17404-5586)
PHONE..............................717 848-1622
EMP: 4
SALES (est): 286K **Privately Held**
SIC: 2448 Pallets, wood

(G-20569)
LWB HOLDING COMPANY
Lwb Refractories
425 S Salem Church Rd (17408-5955)
PHONE..............................717 792-3611
EMP: 250 **Privately Held**
SIC: 3297 3255 Mfg Nonclay Refractories
Mfg Clay Refractories
HQ: Lwb Holding Company
425 S Salem Church Rd
York PA 17408
717 792-3611

(G-20570)
LWB HOLDING COMPANY (HQ)
425 S Salem Church Rd (17408-5955)
PHONE..............................717 792-3611
Paul A Dydek, *Vice Pres*
Kelly L Myers, *Admin Sec*
Monte L Miller, *Asst Sec*
◆ **EMP:** 4
SALES (est): 55.4MM
SALES (corp-wide): 179.8K **Privately
Held**
SIC: 1422 3297 Dolomite, crushed & bro-
ken-quarrying; dolomite or dolomite-mag-
nesite brick & shapes
PA: Rearden G Holdings Eins Gmbh
Dolomitstr. 10
Hagen
210 389-50

(G-20571)
M AND M PALLET LLC
1601 W King St Ste 1 (17404-5644)
PHONE..............................717 845-4039
Hunter Lamparter,
Chris Lamparter,
EMP: 11
SQ FT: 2,500
SALES: 600K **Privately Held**
SIC: 2448 5085 Pallets, wood; boxes,
crates, etc., other than paper

(G-20572)
**MAGNESITA REFRACTORIES
COMPANY (DH)**
Also Called: Lwb Refractories Co
425 S Salem Church Rd (17408-5955)
P.O. Box 7708 (17404-0708)
PHONE..............................717 792-3611
Justin M Bucks, *President*
Al Ginter, *General Mgr*
Craig Powell, *Vice Pres*
Giovanni Tancredo, *Vice Pres*
Wayne Eyster, *Project Mgr*

◆ **EMP:** 360 **EST:** 1941
SALES (est): 149.3MM **Privately Held**
WEB: www.magnesita.com
SIC: 3297 3274 1422 Dolomite or
dolomite-magnesite brick & shapes; lime;
dolomite, crushed & broken-quarrying

(G-20573)
**MAGNESITA REFRACTORIES
COMPANY**
2580 W Philadelphia St (17404-5737)
PHONE..............................717 792-4216
Tim Harren, *Manager*
EMP: 280 **Privately Held**
SIC: 3297 3274 1422 Dolomite or
dolomite-magnesite brick & shapes; lime;
dolomite, crushed & broken-quarrying
HQ: Magnesita Refractories Company
425 S Salem Church Rd
York PA 17408
717 792-3611

(G-20574)
**MAGNESITA REFRACTORIES
COMPANY**
Also Called: Baker Refractories
425 S Salem Church Rd (17408-5955)
PHONE..............................717 792-3611
Lee Hogue, *Accounts Mgr*
Larry Schultz, *Branch Mgr*
EMP: 200 **Privately Held**
SIC: 3297 3274 3255 2875 Dolomite or
dolomite-magnesite brick & shapes; lime;
clay refractories; fertilizers, mixing only;
stone, quarrying & processing of own
stone products
HQ: Magnesita Refractories Company
425 S Salem Church Rd
York PA 17408
717 792-3611

(G-20575)
MAGNUS GROUP INC
Also Called: Progressive Information Tech
2013 Mount Zion Rd (17406-9758)
PHONE..............................717 764-5908
Richard B Schiding, *CEO*
Jim Zito, *President*
David Nelson, *CFO*
Suzanne Mescan, *Admin Sec*
EMP: 30
SQ FT: 27,000
SALES (est): 3.5MM **Privately Held**
WEB: www.vasont.com
SIC: 2791 7336 7371 Typesetting, com-
puter controlled; commercial art & graphic
design; computer software development
& applications

(G-20576)
MANCHESTER INDUSTRIES INC
10 Grumbacher Rd (17406-8417)
PHONE..............................717 764-1161
Gerald Roger, *Owner*
EMP: 14
SALES (est): 1.3MM **Privately Held**
SIC: 3999 Manufacturing industries

(G-20577)
MANCHESTER TOWNSHIP
Also Called: Pump Station 2
3200 Farmtrail Rd (17406-5699)
PHONE..............................717 779-0297
David Raver, *Manager*
EMP: 3 **Privately Held**
SIC: 3561 Pumps & pumping equipment
PA: Manchester Township
3200 Farmtrail Rd
York PA 17406
717 764-4646

(G-20578)
MAPLE DONUTS INC (PA)
3455 E Market St (17402-2696)
PHONE..............................717 757-7826
Charles F Burnside, *President*
Ralph E Wooten, *Vice Pres*
Susan M Burnside, *Treasurer*
Damian Burnside, *Sales Dir*
Mark Fisher, *Manager*
EMP: 165 **EST:** 1946
SQ FT: 12,000
SALES (est): 83.9MM **Privately Held**
WEB: www.mapledonuts.com
SIC: 2051 5461 Doughnuts, except
frozen; bakeries

(G-20579)
MAPLE DONUTS INC
970 Loucks Rd Ste A (17404-2273)
PHONE..............................717 843-4276
Charles Burnside, *Owner*
EMP: 12
SALES (corp-wide): 83.9MM **Privately
Held**
WEB: www.mapledonuts.com
SIC: 2051 Bread, cake & related products
PA: Maple Donuts, Inc.
3455 E Market St
York PA 17402
717 757-7826

(G-20580)
MAPLE PRESS COMPANY (PA)
Also Called: Maple-Vail
480 Willow Springs Ln (17406-6047)
P.O. Box 2695 (17405-2695)
PHONE..............................717 764-5911
James S Wisotzkey, *CEO*
John U Wisotzkey, *Ch of Bd*
Joan Myers Verdier, *Credit Mgr*
▲ **EMP:** 250 **EST:** 1903
SQ FT: 200,000
SALES (est): 182MM **Privately Held**
WEB: www.maple-vail.com
SIC: 2732 2791 2789 2752 Books: print-
ing & binding; photocomposition, for the
printing trade; bookbinding & related
work; commercial printing, lithographic

(G-20581)
**MARINE TECH WIRE AND
CABLE INC**
631 S Richland Ave (17403-3445)
P.O. Box 7309 (17404-0309)
PHONE..............................717 854-1992
Mark Lindsay, *President*
Kosta Kontanis, *General Mgr*
Constantine Kontanis, *Treasurer*
Lynda Bollinger, *Manager*
Jeff Vail, *Manager*
EMP: 25
SQ FT: 35,000
SALES (est): 7.2MM **Privately Held**
WEB: www.marinetechwire.com
SIC: 3357 Nonferrous wiredrawing & insu-
lating

(G-20582)
MASTER TOOL AND MOLD INC
4075 E Market St Ste 30 (17402-5123)
PHONE..............................717 757-3671
Frederick A Stermer, *President*
Farrell Flinchbaugh, *Opers Staff*
EMP: 19
SQ FT: 25,000
SALES (est): 1.3MM **Privately Held**
WEB: www.mtmyork.com
SIC: 3544 Industrial molds; forms (molds),
for foundry & plastics working machinery

(G-20583)
**MATRIX PUBLISHING SERVICES
INC**
36 N Highland Ave (17404-5306)
PHONE..............................717 764-9673
Doug Ward, *President*
Julia Quickel, *Corp Secy*
EMP: 18
SQ FT: 1,500
SALES: 1.7MM **Privately Held**
WEB: www.matrixpublishing.com
SIC: 4226 2791 Document & office
records storage; typesetting

(G-20584)
**MATTHEWS INTERNATIONAL
CORP**
2880 Black Bridge Rd (17406-9703)
PHONE..............................717 854-9566
Brian Kendig, *Manager*
EMP: 9
SALES (corp-wide): 1.5B **Publicly Held**
SIC: 3366 Copper foundries
PA: Matthews International Corporation
2 N Shore Ctr Ste 200
Pittsburgh PA 15212
412 442-8200

(PA)=Parent Co (HQ)=Headquarters (DH)=Div Headquarters
✪ = New Business established in last 2 years

2019 Harris Pennsylvania
Manufacturers Directory

775

GEOGRAPHIC

(G-20585)
MEIGHEN JINJOU
Also Called: Gem Boutique
1243 E Market St Frnt (17403-1279)
PHONE...............................717 846-5600
Jinjou Meighen, *Owner*
EMP: 4
SALES (est): 244.3K **Privately Held**
SIC: 3911 3914 3915 5094 Jewelry, precious metal; silverware & plated ware; jewelers' materials & lapidary work; jewelry; jewelry stores

(G-20586)
MELINESSENCE LLC
1875 Church Rd (17408-1507)
PHONE...............................717 668-3730
EMP: 4 EST: 2013
SALES (est): 340.9K **Privately Held**
SIC: 2844 Toilet preparations

(G-20587)
MENASHA PACKAGING COMPANY LLC
30 Grumbacher Rd (17406-8420)
PHONE...............................800 477-8746
Tim Castor, *General Mgr*
EMP: 100
SALES (corp-wide): 1.7B **Privately Held**
SIC: 2653 Boxes, corrugated: made from purchased materials
HQ: Menasha Packaging Company, Llc
1645 Bergstrom Rd
Neenah WI 54956
920 751-1000

(G-20588)
MENASHA PACKAGING COMPANY LLC
3301 Barwood Rd (17406)
PHONE...............................800 477-8746
Chris Spinelli, *Manager*
EMP: 50
SALES (corp-wide): 1.7B **Privately Held**
WEB: www.strine.com
SIC: 2653 2657 Boxes, corrugated: made from purchased materials; folding paperboard boxes
HQ: Menasha Packaging Company, Llc
1645 Bergstrom Rd
Neenah WI 54956
920 751-1000

(G-20589)
METABLOC INC
Also Called: Applied Electronics
120 Rose Ct (17406-8410)
PHONE...............................717 764-4937
Deborah Henry, *President*
EMP: 5 EST: 1957
SQ FT: 7,200
SALES (est): 686.1K **Privately Held**
WEB: www.metabloc.com
SIC: 3669 Metal detectors

(G-20590)
METSO MINERALS INDUSTRIES INC
2715 Pleasant Valley Rd (17402-9604)
PHONE...............................717 843-8671
David Smith, *Vice Pres*
Hugh Benedict, *Engineer*
Robert Hendrix, *Engineer*
Darla Landis, *Engineer*
Frank Weaver, *Engineer*
EMP: 300
SALES (corp-wide): 3.1B **Privately Held**
SIC: 3321 Ductile iron castings
HQ: Metso Minerals Industries, Inc.
20965 Crossroads Cir
Waukesha WI 53186
262 717-2500

(G-20591)
METSO MINERALS INDUSTRIES INC
Also Called: Bulk Material Handling
2715 Pleasant Valley Rd (17402-9604)
P.O. Box 15043 (17405-7043)
PHONE...............................717 843-8671
William Marsella, *President*
Mike McCoy, *Vice Pres*
Scott Snyder, *Vice Pres*
Jennifer Okin, *Buyer*
Angela Rock, *Buyer*

EMP: 150
SQ FT: 70,000
SALES (est): 3.1B **Privately Held**
WEB: www.metsominerals.com
SIC: 2621 Paper mills
HQ: Metso Minerals Industries, Inc.
20965 Crossroads Cir
Waukesha WI 53186
262 717-2500

(G-20592)
MI-KEE-TRO METAL MFG INC
460 Grim Ln Ste 2 (17406-7949)
PHONE...............................717 764-9090
Tabatha Musso, *Corp Secy*
Frank Kottcamp, *Shareholder*
Ken Brown, *Shareholder*
Kurt Russel, *Shareholder*
Mike Sunday, *Shareholder*
EMP: 53
SQ FT: 18,000
SALES (est): 14.9MM **Privately Held**
WEB: www.mi-kee-tro.com
SIC: 3444 Sheet metalwork

(G-20593)
MICHAEL P HOOVER COMPANY INC
Also Called: Michael P Hoover Excavating
3775 Starview Dr (17402-4370)
PHONE...............................717 757-7842
Michael P Hoover, *President*
EMP: 8 EST: 1924
SQ FT: 8,000
SALES: 800K **Privately Held**
SIC: 3272 Burial vaults, concrete or precast terrazzo

(G-20594)
MICROCUT INC
1758 S Queen St (17403-4642)
PHONE...............................717 848-4150
John Mader, *President*
Steve Nagorny, *President*
D Charles Porter, *Vice Pres*
EMP: 6
SQ FT: 8,000
SALES (est): 1.4MM **Privately Held**
WEB: www.microcut.com
SIC: 3599 Electrical discharge machining (EDM)

(G-20595)
MICROTRAC INC
3230 N Susquehanna Trl (17406-9716)
PHONE...............................717 843-4433
Phil Plantz, *Principal*
EMP: 13
SALES (est): 2.3MM **Privately Held**
SIC: 3826 Analytical instruments

(G-20596)
MICROTRAC INC
3230 N Susquehanna Trl (17406-9716)
PHONE...............................717 843-4433
Jeff Hoke, *Manager*
EMP: 12
SALES (corp-wide): 1.4B **Privately Held**
WEB: www.microtrac.com
SIC: 3826 Analytical instruments
HQ: Microtrac, Inc.
215 Keystone Dr
Montgomeryville PA 18936
215 619-9920

(G-20597)
MIDLANTIC PALLET LLC
35 N Marshall St (17402-2317)
PHONE...............................717 266-0300
Peter B Snyder, *Principal*
EMP: 11
SALES (est): 1.7MM **Privately Held**
SIC: 2448 Wood pallets & skids

(G-20598)
MILITARY AND COML FAS CORP (PA)
11 Grumbacher Rd (17406-8417)
PHONE...............................717 767-6856
Craig Siewert, *President*
David Kin, *Corp Secy*
Ron Kin, *Vice Pres*
Ronald Kin, *Vice Pres*
Deborah Walls, *Production*
▲ EMP: 63
SQ FT: 35,000

SALES (est): 34.4MM **Privately Held**
WEB: www.mcfcorp.com
SIC: 5085 5072 3452 Fasteners, industrial: nuts, bolts, screws, etc.; hardware; bolts, nuts, rivets & washers

(G-20599)
MITCHCO INC
Also Called: Rudy Art Glass Studio
15 E Philadelphia St (17401-1124)
PHONE...............................717 843-3345
Stephen Mitchell, *President*
Rosina Mitchell, *Corp Secy*
▲ EMP: 25
SQ FT: 40,000
SALES (est): 2.9MM **Privately Held**
WEB: www.rudyglass.com
SIC: 3231 Art glass: made from purchased glass; stained glass: made from purchased glass

(G-20600)
MITRE WRIGHT INC
160 E 9th Ave (17404-2147)
PHONE...............................717 812-1000
Todd Salony, *Vice Pres*
EMP: 26
SQ FT: 7,000
SALES (est): 3.5MM **Privately Held**
SIC: 2541 Store & office display cases & fixtures

(G-20601)
MK SOLUTIONS INC
75 Acco Dr Ste A-3 (17402-4656)
PHONE...............................860 760-0438
Markus Flory, *President*
Rachel Davis, *Manager*
EMP: 5
SALES (est): 156.7K **Privately Held**
SIC: 8231 7382 3581 Libraries; security systems services; automatic vending machines

(G-20602)
MKT METAL MANUFACTURING
460 Grim Ln Ste 2 (17406-7949)
PHONE...............................717 764-9090
Ken Brown, *CEO*
EMP: 140 EST: 2013
SALES (est): 376.6K **Privately Held**
SIC: 3441 Fabricated structural metal

(G-20603)
MOREHOUSE INSTRUMENT COMPANY
1742 6th Ave (17403-2643)
PHONE...............................717 843-0081
Henry Zumbrun, *President*
Harry Zumbrun, *President*
Bill Lane, *Engineer*
John Shafto, *Marketing Staff*
Becky Pinto, *Office Admin*
▼ EMP: 16
SQ FT: 7,500
SALES: 3MM **Privately Held**
WEB: www.mhforce.com
SIC: 3825 3821 Instruments to measure electricity; laboratory equipment: fume hoods, distillation racks, etc.

(G-20604)
MORRISON CONSULTING INC
Also Called: Access411
190 Canal Road Ext (17406-8470)
PHONE...............................717 268-8201
William F Morrison III, *President*
Eric Johnson, *Vice Pres*
Karen Morrison, *Manager*
Steve Horn, *Systs Prg Mgr*
EMP: 22
SALES (est): 3.6MM **Privately Held**
SIC: 7372 Application computer software

(G-20605)
MOTOR TECHNOLOGY INC
515 Willow Springs Ln (17406-8427)
PHONE...............................717 266-4045
Thomas I Ryan, *President*
Lisa Flaharty, *Vice Pres*
Kim Flaheraty, *Vice Pres*
Kirk E Ryan, *Vice Pres*
Del Dooley, *Mfg Staff*
EMP: 93
SQ FT: 65,000

SALES: 15.7MM **Privately Held**
WEB: www.motortechnologyinc.com
SIC: 7694 5063 5065 Electric motor repair; motors, electric; generators; electronic parts

(G-20606)
MUDHOOK BREWING COMPANY LLC
34 N Cherry Ln (17401-5306)
PHONE...............................717 747-3605
Jeffrey G Lau, *Principal*
Linda Lau, *Principal*
Kate Wheeler, *Principal*
Tim Wheeler, *Principal*
EMP: 10 EST: 2010
SALES (est): 164.6K **Privately Held**
SIC: 5812 5813 2082 American restaurant; bar (drinking places); malt beverages; beer (alcoholic beverage)

(G-20607)
MULTI-COLOR CORPORATION
405 Willow Springs Ln (17406-6047)
PHONE...............................717 266-9675
John P McKernan, *Branch Mgr*
EMP: 60
SALES (corp-wide): 1.3B **Publicly Held**
SIC: 2752 Commercial printing, lithographic
PA: Multi-Color Corporation
4053 Clough Woods Dr
Batavia OH 45103
513 381-1480

(G-20608)
MUNDORF SIGN CO
29 Overbrook Ave (17404-3417)
P.O. Box 7225 (17404-0225)
PHONE...............................717 854-3071
Raymond Mundorf, *Partner*
Sandra Mundorf, *Partner*
EMP: 3
SALES (est): 325.4K **Privately Held**
SIC: 7389 3993 Lettering service; sign painting & lettering shop; signs & advertising specialties; neon signs

(G-20609)
NASS INC
501 E King St (17403-1773)
P.O. Box 1988 (17405-1988)
PHONE...............................717 846-3685
John F Enright III, *President*
EMP: 4
SQ FT: 40,000
SALES (est): 512.6K **Privately Held**
WEB: www.nass.net
SIC: 3567 Incinerators, metal: domestic or commercial

(G-20610)
NEILLYS FOOD LLC
75 Acco Dr Ste A-12 (17402-4656)
PHONE...............................717 428-6431
Albert Ndjee, *President*
Julie Ndjee, *Vice Pres*
▲ EMP: 17
SQ FT: 12,000
SALES: 2MM **Privately Held**
SIC: 2099 Food preparations

(G-20611)
NEW STANDARD CORPORATION (PA)
74 Commerce Way (17406-8038)
PHONE...............................717 757-9450
Morton F Zifferer Jr, *CEO*
Dave Meckley, *President*
Mike Lofties, *Business Mgr*
Todd Musso, *COO*
Elizabeth Goodwater, *Vice Pres*
▲ EMP: 100 EST: 1909
SQ FT: 75,000
SALES (est): 130.8MM **Privately Held**
WEB: www.newstandard.com
SIC: 3469 3465 Stamping metal for the trade; automotive stampings

(G-20612)
NU-U LASER CENTER
1600 6th Ave Ste 117 (17403-2627)
PHONE...............................717 718-7880
Lori Eichelberger, *Principal*
EMP: 4

SALES (est): 226.2K **Privately Held**
SIC: **3845** Laser systems & equipment, medical

(G-20613)
NUTS ABOUT GRANOLA LLC
9 W Philadelphia St (17401-5309)
PHONE.....................717 814-9648
Sarah Lanthier, *CEO*
Evan Himes, *COO*
Evan Matthew Himes, *Opers Mgr*
EMP: 3
SALES: 300K **Privately Held**
SIC: **2064** Chocolate candy, except solid chocolate

(G-20614)
O LAND LAKES
365 Emig Rd (17406-9741)
PHONE.....................717 845-8076
Mark McCaslin, *President*
EMP: 10
SALES (est): 345.5K
SALES (corp-wide): 10.4B **Privately Held**
SIC: **5411 5143 2099** Grocery stores; dairy products, except dried or canned; food preparations
PA: Land O'lakes, Inc.
   4001 Lexington Ave N
   Arden Hills MN 55126
   651 375-2222

(G-20615)
P H GLATFELTER COMPANY (PA)
96 S George St Ste 520 (17401-1434)
PHONE.....................717 225-4711
Dante C Parrini, *Ch of Bd*
Christopher W Astley, *President*
Timothy R Hess, *President*
Martin Rapp, *President*
Kent K Matsumoto, *Vice Pres*
EMP: 1100 EST: 1864
SALES: 866.2MM **Publicly Held**
WEB: www.glatfelter.com
SIC: **2621** Book paper; copy paper; envelope paper; filter paper

(G-20616)
PACE RESOURCES INC (PA)
140 E Market St Fl 2 (17401-1219)
P.O. Box 15055 (17405-7055)
PHONE.....................717 852-1300
William Dannehl, *President*
Russell E Horn Jr, *President*
Russell E Horn Sr, *Founder*
Brian Funkhouser, *Vice Pres*
Hal G McClure, *CFO*
EMP: 25
SQ FT: 8,000
SALES (est): 100.1MM **Privately Held**
WEB: www.pace-resources.com
SIC: **2752 5049 7334 2789** Commercial printing, offset; drafting supplies; photocopying & duplicating services; bookbinding & related work

(G-20617)
PALLETS UNLIMITED INC
1721 Eberts Ln (17406-1732)
PHONE.....................717 755-3691
Douglas L Clemens, *Principal*
EMP: 4 EST: 2008
SALES (est): 309.6K **Privately Held**
SIC: **2448** Pallets, wood & wood with metal

(G-20618)
PANACHE PLUS
403 W Market St (17401-3803)
PHONE.....................717 812-8999
Tina Jamison, *Principal*
EMP: 3
SALES (est): 224.9K **Privately Held**
SIC: **3999** Barber & beauty shop equipment

(G-20619)
PCXPERT COMPANY INC
1370 Sven Vlleys Rd Ste 2 (17408)
PHONE.....................717 792-0005
Brian Buchanan, *President*
EMP: 4
SQ FT: 1,000

SALES (est): 405.3K **Privately Held**
SIC: **7372 7629 5734** Application computer software; electrical repair shops; electronic equipment repair; personal computers

(G-20620)
PENN KLEEN EX-ITS INC (PA)
2607 W Market St (17404-5538)
P.O. Box 4601, Harrisburg (17111-0601)
PHONE.....................717 792-3608
Daison R Shouck, *President*
Barry Nauss, *Principal*
Carolyn S Nauss, *Treasurer*
Melinda A Shouck, *Admin Sec*
EMP: 4
SQ FT: 6,000
SALES (est): 405.6K **Privately Held**
SIC: **2842** Specialty cleaning preparations

(G-20621)
PENNSYLVANIA PERLITE CORP YORK
125 Stonewood Rd (17402-9356)
PHONE.....................717 755-6206
Ron Mundis, *Plant Mgr*
William Runkle, *Manager*
EMP: 5
SALES (corp-wide): 2.7MM **Privately Held**
WEB: www.pennperlite.com
SIC: **3297** Nonclay refractories
PA: Pennsylvania Perlite Corp Of York
   1428 Mauch Chunk Rd
   Bethlehem PA 18018
   610 868-0992

(G-20622)
PENNY PRESS OF YORK INC
53 S Adams St Ste 1 (17404-5464)
PHONE.....................717 843-4078
Wade Glosser, *President*
Coral Glosser, *Vice Pres*
Mike Bingham, *Sales Mgr*
Meleah Miller, *Graphic Designe*
EMP: 5 EST: 1972
SALES (est): 810.8K **Privately Held**
WEB: www.penny-press.com
SIC: **2752** Commercial printing, offset

(G-20623)
PEPSI CO INC
Also Called: Pepsico
3553 Gillespie Dr (17404-5803)
PHONE.....................717 792-2935
Steve Pfeiffenberger, *Principal*
EMP: 3
SALES (est): 188.8K **Privately Held**
SIC: **2086** Carbonated soft drinks, bottled & canned

(G-20624)
PERFORM GROUP LLC (PA)
Also Called: Curtain Call Costumes
333 E 7th Ave Ste 2 (17404-2144)
P.O. Box 20879 (17402-0184)
PHONE.....................717 852-6950
Karen Frey, *Buyer*
Mike Higgins, *Engineer*
Jolynn McDowell, *Accountant*
Jane Deamer, *Marketing Mgr*
Jim Staub, *Program Mgr*
▲ EMP: 360
SQ FT: 122,000
SALES (est): 40.2MM **Privately Held**
WEB: www.performgroupllc.com
SIC: **2389 2339** Costumes; leotards: women's, misses' & juniors'; bathing suits: women's, misses' & juniors'

(G-20625)
PERFORM GROUP LLC
Also Called: Perform Group Mfg
5130 E Prospect Rd (17406-8639)
PHONE.....................717 252-1578
Mike Robertson, *Principal*
EMP: 220
SALES (est): 14.9MM
SALES (corp-wide): 40.2MM **Privately Held**
SIC: **2389 2339** Costumes; women's & misses' outerwear
PA: Perform Group, Llc
   333 E 7th Ave Ste 2
   York PA 17404
   717 852-6950

(G-20626)
PFALTZGRAFF FACTORY STORES INC (HQ)
140 E Market St (17401-1219)
PHONE.....................717 848-5500
Marsha M Everton, *President*
Clair Bange, *President*
Peter P Brubaker, *Vice Pres*
John L Finlayson, *Vice Pres*
Craig W Bremer, *Admin Sec*
▲ EMP: 400
SQ FT: 20,000
SALES (est): 92.6MM
SALES (corp-wide): 704.5MM **Publicly Held**
WEB: www.pfz.com
SIC: **3269 5719** Stoneware pottery products; kitchenware
PA: Lifetime Brands, Inc.
   1000 Stewart Ave
   Garden City NY 11530
   516 683-6000

(G-20627)
PHILIP COOKE
Also Called: Triple C Motor Accessories
1900 Orange St (17404-5228)
PHONE.....................717 854-4081
Fax: 717 854-6706
◆ EMP: 3
SQ FT: 4,500
SALES (est): 170K **Privately Held**
SIC: **3711 5531** Mfg Motor Vehicle/Car Bodies Ret Auto/Home Supplies

(G-20628)
PLASTIC FABRICATORS INC
1450 W College Ave (17404-5608)
PHONE.....................717 843-4222
Joseph H Frantz, *President*
Cindy Strickler, *Corp Secy*
William C Frantz, *Vice Pres*
Greg Wood, *Info Tech Mgr*
EMP: 12 EST: 1968
SQ FT: 26,000
SALES (est): 2.1MM **Privately Held**
WEB: www.plasticfabinc.com
SIC: **3089** Thermoformed finished plastic products; plastic processing

(G-20629)
POFF SHEET METAL INC
736 Vander Ave (17403-2810)
PHONE.....................717 845-9622
Steven Poff, *President*
EMP: 6
SQ FT: 18,000
SALES (est): 620K **Privately Held**
SIC: **3444** Sheet metal specialties, not stamped

(G-20630)
POINT BLANK DEFENSE LLC
2956 Woodshead Ter (17403-9751)
PHONE.....................717 801-2632
Gary Smith, *Principal*
EMP: 3
SALES (est): 164K **Privately Held**
SIC: **3812** Defense systems & equipment

(G-20631)
POLY LITE WINDSHIELD REPR SUPS
1952 Stanton St (17404-5348)
PHONE.....................717 845-1596
Keith J Surdich, *President*
EMP: 6
SQ FT: 2,100
SALES: 750K **Privately Held**
WEB: www.poly-lite.com
SIC: **2821 5013** Plastics materials & resins; automotive supplies

(G-20632)
POOLPAK INC
3491 Industrial Hwy (17402-9051)
PHONE.....................717 757-2648
Patrick Reynolds, *President*
Kenneth W Cooper, *Corp Secy*
John III Goodrich, *Vice Pres*
EMP: 95
SALES (est): 20MM **Privately Held**
SIC: **3585** Heat pumps, electric; humidifiers & dehumidifiers

(G-20633)
POOLPAK LLC
3491 Industrial Hwy (17402-9051)
P.O. Box 3331 (17402-0331)
PHONE.....................717 757-2648
Robert Paley, *President*
EMP: 7
SALES (est): 128.8K
SALES (corp-wide): 297MM **Privately Held**
SIC: **3585** Heating & air conditioning combination units
HQ: Specified Air Solutions Llc
   1250 William St
   Buffalo NY 14206
   716 852-4400

(G-20634)
POWDER CITY LLC
408 Willeta Ct (17402-8249)
PHONE.....................717 745-4795
Nathan Smeltzer, *CEO*
EMP: 10
SALES (est): 376.7K **Privately Held**
SIC: **2023** Dietary supplements, dairy & non-dairy based

(G-20635)
POWDER COATING SPECIALISTS LLC
40 Leigh Dr (17406-5648)
PHONE.....................717 968-1479
EMP: 3
SALES (est): 271K **Privately Held**
SIC: **3559** Metal finishing equipment for plating, etc.

(G-20636)
PRE-MACH INC
4365 Run Way (17406-8005)
PHONE.....................717 757-5685
Barry L Klinedinst, *President*
Bryan L Klinedinst, *General Mgr*
Bryan Klinedinst, *Opers Staff*
Jason Sharp, *Purchasing*
Carol Klinedinst, *Admin Sec*
EMP: 28 EST: 1969
SQ FT: 38,000
SALES: 5.3MM **Privately Held**
WEB: www.pre-mach.com
SIC: **3599** Machine shop, jobbing & repair

(G-20637)
PRECISION COMPONENTS GROUP LLC
500 Lincoln St (17401-3367)
P.O. Box 15101 (17405-7101)
PHONE.....................717 848-1126
Jonathan Ferree, *Project Engr*
Gary Butler,
John Frieling,
EMP: 219
SALES (est): 34MM **Privately Held**
SIC: **3443** Fabricated plate work (boiler shop)

(G-20638)
PRECISION CSTM COMPONENTS LLC
500 Lincoln St (17401-3367)
P.O. Box 15101 (17405-7101)
PHONE.....................717 848-1126
Gary C Butler, *CEO*
Robert Bingman, *General Mgr*
Earl Newman, *Business Mgr*
Mike Billet, *Vice Pres*
James Stouch, *Vice Pres*
▲ EMP: 280
SQ FT: 350,000
SALES (est): 116.7MM **Privately Held**
WEB: www.pcc-york.com
SIC: **3443 3699** Fabricated plate work (boiler shop); high-energy particle physics equipment

(G-20639)
PRINT HAPPY LLC
Also Called: Computer Part and Technologies
1805 Loucks Rd Ste 100 (17408-7903)
PHONE.....................717 699-4465
Caren Mazurek, *Mng Member*
EMP: 3

SALES (est): 274.9K **Privately Held**
SIC: 5112 2893 7378 Office filing supplies; printing ink; computer maintenance & repair

(G-20640)
PRINT-O-STAT INC (HQ)
1011 W Market St (17404-3411)
P.O. Box 15046 (17405-7046)
PHONE...................................717 812-9476
Silvia H Dugan, *President*
Randy Byrd, *Vice Pres*
Russell E Horn III, *Vice Pres*
Hal McClure, *CFO*
Russell E Horn Jr, *Treasurer*
EMP: 40 **EST:** 1954
SQ FT: 17,000
SALES (est): 35MM
SALES (corp-wide): 100.1MM **Privately Held**
WEB: www.digitalblueprinting.com
SIC: 2752 5049 7334 2789 Commercial printing, offset; photolithographic printing; drafting supplies; engineers' equipment & supplies; photocopying & duplicating services; bookbinding & related work
PA: Pace Resources, Inc.
140 E Market St Fl 2
York PA 17401
717 852-1300

(G-20641)
PRINTING EXPRESS INC
3460 Industrial Hwy (17402-9050)
P.O. Box 20849 (17402-0184)
PHONE...................................717 600-1111
Rick Armitage, *President*
Patricia Whitehurst, *Treasurer*
EMP: 9 **EST:** 1975
SQ FT: 4,400
SALES: 650K **Privately Held**
WEB: www.theprintingexpress.com
SIC: 2752 Commercial printing, offset

(G-20642)
PRO PALLET PARTNERS
460 Chestnut Ln (17403-4549)
PHONE...................................717 741-2418
Mark Schaffer, *Principal*
EMP: 4
SALES (est): 317.9K **Privately Held**
SIC: 2448 Pallets, wood & wood with metal

(G-20643)
PROCONVEYOR LLC
251 Herman St (17404-3420)
PHONE...................................717 887-5897
Brady Stearn,
EMP: 9
SALES (est): 568.7K **Privately Held**
SIC: 3535 Robotic conveyors

(G-20644)
PRODUCT DESIGN AND DEVELOPMENT (PA)
2603 Keyway Dr (17402-4712)
PHONE...................................717 741-4844
Troy Fregm, *President*
Michael S Brezler, *President*
Larry Mitzel, *Corp Secy*
EMP: 35
SQ FT: 26,000
SALES (est): 5.3MM **Privately Held**
SIC: 3545 8711 Machine tool accessories; engineering services

(G-20645)
PROMOTION CENTRE INC
Also Called: Exhibits By Promotion Centre
701 Hay St (17403-1360)
PHONE...................................717 843-1582
Robert A Stitt, *President*
Jacqueline Stitt, *Exec VP*
Julie Malloy, *Executive*
EMP: 22
SQ FT: 110,000
SALES (est): 2.4MM **Privately Held**
WEB: www.exhibitsbypromo.com
SIC: 7389 3993 2542 Exhibit construction by industrial contractors; signs & advertising specialties; partitions & fixtures, except wood

(G-20646)
PROTECH POWDER COATINGS INC
939 Monocacy Rd (17404-1615)
PHONE...................................717 767-6996
Alan Hartman, *Technical Staff*
James Abrial, *Maintence Staff*
EMP: 23 **Privately Held**
SIC: 2851 Paints & allied products
PA: Protech Powder Coatings, Inc.
21 Audrey Pl
Fairfield NJ 07004

(G-20647)
PROTECH POWDER COATINGS INC
939 Monocacy Rd (17404-1615)
PHONE...................................814 899-7628
Pete Froess, *Manager*
EMP: 14 **Privately Held**
SIC: 2851 Lacquers, varnishes, enamels & other coatings
PA: Protech Powder Coatings, Inc.
21 Audrey Pl
Fairfield NJ 07004

(G-20648)
PT INDUSTRIES INC
807 Arbor Ln (17406-7060)
PHONE...................................717 755-1679
Ricky L Poff, *President*
EMP: 10
SALES (est): 650K **Privately Held**
SIC: 3599 Machine shop, jobbing & repair

(G-20649)
R & R COMPONENTS INC
76 Bowman Rd (17408-8793)
PHONE...................................717 792-4641
Bradford J Ream, *President*
Barry Ream, *Vice Pres*
Sean T Ream, *Vice Pres*
Ryan J Ream, *Treasurer*
Ryan Ream, *Treasurer*
EMP: 185
SQ FT: 110,000
SALES (est): 35.3MM **Privately Held**
WEB: www.rrcomponents.com
SIC: 2439 Trusses, wooden roof

(G-20650)
R H FINK INC
3945 N Susquehanna Trl (17404-8406)
PHONE...................................717 266-1054
Tim Diamond, *President*
Karen Diamond, *Vice Pres*
▲ **EMP:** 15 **EST:** 2004
SALES (est): 1.7MM **Privately Held**
SIC: 3599 Machine shop, jobbing & repair

(G-20651)
RBNA FLUID EXCHANGE INC
10 Innovation Dr (17402-2777)
P.O. Box 3099 (17402-0099)
PHONE...................................717 840-0678
Max Dull, *General Mgr*
◆ **EMP:** 37
SQ FT: 70,700
SALES (est): 11.9MM
SALES (corp-wide): 336.4K **Privately Held**
WEB: www.rtitech.com
SIC: 3559 Automotive related machinery; automotive maintenance equipment
HQ: Mahle Aftermarket Inc.
23030 Mahle Dr
Farmington MI 48335

(G-20652)
READCO KURIMOTO LLC
460 Grim Ln (17406-7949)
PHONE...................................717 848-2801
David Sieglitz, *President*
Dana Grim, *Corp Secy*
▲ **EMP:** 21
SQ FT: 30,000
SALES (est): 5.3MM **Privately Held**
SIC: 3549 Metalworking machinery

(G-20653)
REAM PRINTING CO INC
515 Farmbrook Ln (17406-5611)
P.O. Box 2891 (17405-2891)
PHONE...................................717 764-5663
Jim Ream, *President*

Jean Ream, *Treasurer*
EMP: 21
SQ FT: 12,500
SALES (est): 3.1MM **Privately Held**
SIC: 2759 2752 Screen printing; commercial printing, lithographic

(G-20654)
REBECCA WILSON LTD LBLTY CO
Also Called: Rj Foods
2159 White St Ste 3 (17404-4948)
PHONE...................................973 670-7089
Michael A Wilson, *CEO*
Rebecca Wilson, *COO*
EMP: 3
SALES (est): 469.1K **Privately Held**
SIC: 5063 5141 2092 Electrical apparatus & equipment; food brokers; prepared fish or other seafood cakes & sticks; seafood cakes, frozen; seafoods, frozen: prepared

(G-20655)
RECYCLING TECH INTL LLC
76 Acco Dr (17402-4668)
PHONE...................................717 633-9008
Timothy Leighty,
▲ **EMP:** 41
SQ FT: 86,000
SALES (est): 6MM
SALES (corp-wide): 51.5MM **Privately Held**
WEB: www.rtillc.com
SIC: 3069 Hard rubber & molded rubber products
PA: Ecore International Inc.
715 Fountain Ave
Lancaster PA 17601
717 295-3400

(G-20656)
RED LION MANUFACTURING INC
Also Called: Zero Restriction
20 Willow Springs Cir (17406-8428)
PHONE...................................717 767-6511
Chris Heyn, *CEO*
Gary A Tolton, *President*
Gregg Chopskie, *Treasurer*
Michael Balter, *Accountant*
▲ **EMP:** 104
SALES (est): 7.4MM **Privately Held**
WEB: www.zerorestriction.com
SIC: 2385 3151 2381 2339 Waterproof outerwear; leather gloves & mittens; fabric dress & work gloves; women's & misses' outerwear
PA: Summit Golf Brands, Inc.
4 Corporate Dr Ste 388
Shelton CT 06484

(G-20657)
REH HOLDINGS INC (PA)
150 S Sumner St (17404-5451)
PHONE...................................717 843-0021
Basil A Shorb III, *CEO*
Robert E Hirschman, *Ch of Bd*
William J Shorb, *President*
Constance H Shorb, *Admin Sec*
EMP: 4
SQ FT: 3,000
SALES (est): 78.7MM **Privately Held**
SIC: 1611 3444 3479 Guardrail construction, highways; guard rails, highway: sheet metal; hot dip coating of metals or formed products

(G-20658)
RG INDUSTRIES INC
Also Called: RG Group
15 Flour Mill Rd (17406-9786)
PHONE...................................717 849-0345
Dave Hoke, *Project Engr*
Ed Stum, *Branch Mgr*
Bob Sherick, *Webmaster*
EMP: 30
SALES (corp-wide): 44.2MM **Privately Held**
WEB: www.rg-group.com
SIC: 3585 3714 3593 3498 Refrigeration & heating equipment; motor vehicle parts & accessories; fluid power cylinders & actuators; fabricated pipe & fittings; fabricated plate work (boiler shop)

PA: Rg Industries, Inc.
650 N State St
York PA 17403
717 846-9300

(G-20659)
ROCKWELL AUTOMATION INC
390 Saint Charles Way (17402-4647)
PHONE...................................717 747-8240
Diane Cadrin, *Branch Mgr*
EMP: 12 **Publicly Held**
SIC: 3625 Electric controls & control accessories, industrial
PA: Rockwell Automation, Inc.
1201 S 2nd St
Milwaukee WI 53204

(G-20660)
RONAL TOOL COMPANY INC
99 Hokes Mill Rd (17404-5502)
PHONE...................................717 741-0880
Tj Andrew Krebs, *President*
Joyce Johnson, *Purch Agent*
EMP: 12
SQ FT: 5,800
SALES (est): 1.8MM **Privately Held**
WEB: www.ronal.com
SIC: 3544 3545 3423 3398 Special dies & tools; machine tool accessories; hand & edge tools; metal heat treating

(G-20661)
RUTTER BROS DAIRY INC (PA)
Also Called: Rutter's Dairy
2100 N George St (17404-1815)
PHONE...................................717 848-9827
Todd Rutter, *President*
Randi Sheeler, *District Mgr*
Leo E Rutter, *Vice Pres*
Terry Hayostek, *Controller*
Ronald Afflebach, *VP Human Res*
EMP: 119
SQ FT: 100,000
SALES (est): 23.2MM **Privately Held**
SIC: 2026 Milk processing (pasteurizing, homogenizing, bottling)

(G-20662)
S M E FOODS LLC
Also Called: Big John's Beef Jerky
70 Aberdeen Rd (17406-7912)
PHONE...................................717 852-8515
Bill Lenzer, *Mng Member*
Renee Lenzer, *Mng Member*
EMP: 4
SALES (est): 356.2K **Privately Held**
WEB: www.bigjohnsbeefjerky.com
SIC: 2013 Snack sticks, including jerky: from purchased meat

(G-20663)
SALMON PILLOWMAKERS
2076 Church Rd (17408-4012)
PHONE...................................717 767-4978
Carol Salmon, *Owner*
EMP: 5
SQ FT: 2,700
SALES (est): 210K **Privately Held**
SIC: 2392 Pillows, bed: made from purchased materials

(G-20664)
SENTINEL CONNECTOR SYSTEMS INC
1953 Stanton St (17404-5358)
PHONE...................................717 843-4240
Robert J Brennan, *President*
Justin S Wagner, *Vice Pres*
Steve Baker, *CFO*
Rod Brandstedter, *CFO*
Jim Lawrence, *Director*
▲ **EMP:** 35
SQ FT: 45,000
SALES: 15MM **Privately Held**
WEB: www.sentinelconn.com
SIC: 3678 Electronic connectors

(G-20665)
SENTINEL HOLDING INC
Also Called: Sentinel Connector System
1953 Stanton St (17404-5358)
PHONE...................................717 843-4240
Robert Brennan, *President*
Rod Brandstedter, *CFO*
▲ **EMP:** 33
SQ FT: 50,000

▲ = Import ▼=Export
◆ =Import/Export

SALES: 15MM **Privately Held**
SIC: 3678 Electronic connectors

(G-20666)
SENTRY FIRE PROTECTION INC
277 Rose Ave (17401-2132)
PHONE.....................717 843-4973
Joel A Warner, *CEO*
Paul Cunningham, *Admin Sec*
EMP: 19
SALES (est): 4.1MM **Privately Held**
SIC: 3498 1711 Fabricated pipe & fittings; fire sprinkler system installation

(G-20667)
SHARP & WILY LLC ✪
1012 Smallbrook Ln (17403-3410)
PHONE.....................717 893-2970
Kevin Helson, *Mng Member*
EMP: 3 EST: 2018
SALES: 3.3K **Privately Held**
SIC: 2844 Toilet preparations

(G-20668)
SIGNS BY TOMORROW
2260 Industrial Hwy (17402-2202)
PHONE.....................717 757-4909
Robert Kaun, *Mng Member*
EMP: 7
SALES (est): 745.8K **Privately Held**
SIC: 3993 Signs & advertising specialties

(G-20669)
SLOTHOWER MACHINE SHOP LLC
1700 Toronita St (17402-1994)
PHONE.....................717 846-3409
Tim Howard, *President*
Rebekkah Pawelczyk, *Info Tech Mgr*
EMP: 15 EST: 1953
SQ FT: 6,400
SALES (est): 2.6MM **Privately Held**
SIC: 3599 Machine shop, jobbing & repair

(G-20670)
SMT MANUFACTURING GROUP LLC
60 S Prospect St Ste 100 (17406-1433)
PHONE.....................717 767-4900
Mark Gingalewski,
Joseph Rago,
EMP: 50
SQ FT: 13,900
SALES: 4.5MM **Privately Held**
WEB: www.smt-llc.com
SIC: 3679 Electronic circuits

(G-20671)
SODIUM SYSTEMS LLC
1100 N Hartley St Ste 300 (17404-2868)
PHONE.....................800 821-8962
Shawn Hall, *Principal*
EMP: 14
SQ FT: 3,500
SALES (est): 417.1K **Privately Held**
SIC: 7389 8071 3843 5047 Personal service agents, brokers & bureaus; X-ray laboratory, including dental; dental equipment & supplies; dental equipment; dental equipment & supplies

(G-20672)
SONOCO DISPLAY & PACKAGING LLC
200 Boxwood Ln (17402-9302)
PHONE.....................717 757-2683
Larry Burgman, *Manager*
Chuck Prowell, *Director*
EMP: 123
SALES (corp-wide): 5.3B **Publicly Held**
SIC: 2653 3412 Boxes, corrugated: made from purchased materials; sheets, corrugated: made from purchased materials; metal barrels, drums & pails
HQ: Sonoco Display & Packaging, Llc
555 Aureole St
Winston Salem NC 27107

(G-20673)
SOURIAU USA INC
150 Farm Ln Ste 100 (17402-4992)
PHONE.....................717 718-8810
Rob Hanes, *President*
EMP: 11

SALES (corp-wide): 3.8B **Publicly Held**
SIC: 3643 Current-carrying wiring devices
HQ: Souriau Usa, Inc.
1750 Commerce Way
Paso Robles CA 93446
805 238-2840

(G-20674)
SOUTHWIRE COMPANY LLC
1500 Bartlett Dr (17406-6144)
PHONE.....................717 266-2004
Michael Wilson, *Owner*
EMP: 18
SALES (corp-wide): 2.3B **Privately Held**
WEB: www.southwire.com
SIC: 3355 3351 Aluminum rolling & drawing; copper rolling & drawing
PA: Southwire Company, Llc
1 Southwire Dr
Carrollton GA 30119
770 832-4242

(G-20675)
SPARKS BELTING COMPANY INC
66 Leigh Dr (17406-8474)
PHONE.....................717 767-1490
David Englehard, *Regional Mgr*
EMP: 3
SALES (corp-wide): 541.6MM **Privately Held**
SIC: 3535 Conveyors & conveying equipment
HQ: Sparks Belting Company, Inc.
3800 Stahl Dr Se
Grand Rapids MI 49546

(G-20676)
SPECIALTY EMULSIONS INC
1194 Zinns Quarry Rd (17404-3533)
PHONE.....................717 849-5020
Richard E Campbell, *President*
Adrian F Berger, *Vice Pres*
Brandon Staub, *Director*
EMP: 3 EST: 2004
SALES (est): 620.7K **Privately Held**
SIC: 2951 Asphalt paving mixtures & blocks

(G-20677)
SPX COOLING TECHNOLOGIES INC
Also Called: Marley Cooling Technologies
1670 Toronita St (17402-1921)
PHONE.....................717 845-4830
Paul Phouttasinh, *Manager*
EMP: 24
SALES (corp-wide): 1.5B **Publicly Held**
WEB: www.cts.spx.com
SIC: 3443 Fabricated plate work (boiler shop)
HQ: Spx Cooling Technologies, Inc.
7401 W 129th St
Overland Park KS 66213
913 664-7400

(G-20678)
SRD DESIGN CORP
207 S Sumner St Frnt (17404-5441)
PHONE.....................717 699-0005
Stephen Duttera, *President*
Scott Sturner, *Vice Pres*
Joann Duttera, *Treasurer*
▼ EMP: 8
SQ FT: 13,000
SALES (est): 1.1MM **Privately Held**
WEB: www.sternerduttera.com
SIC: 3541 Machine tools, metal cutting type

(G-20679)
STANDARD CONCRETE PRODUCTS CO
Also Called: Pro Hardware 12923
700 N Sherman St (17402-2128)
PHONE.....................717 843-8074
George F Parthmer, *President*
John Anthony, *Vice Pres*
Rosemary Jackson, *Vice Pres*
Kitty Karr, *Vice Pres*
Keith Knapp, *Vice Pres*
EMP: 30
SQ FT: 6,000

SALES (est): 5.7MM **Privately Held**
WEB: www.standardconcreteproducts.com
SIC: 3271 5211 3272 5251 Blocks, concrete or cinder: standard; lumber & other building materials; concrete products; hardware

(G-20680)
STEVE JONES
Also Called: Jones Manufacturing
948 Elm St (17403-2506)
PHONE.....................717 845-7700
Steven Jones, *Owner*
EMP: 9 EST: 1994
SQ FT: 15,000
SALES (est): 900.9K **Privately Held**
SIC: 3599 Machine shop, jobbing & repair

(G-20681)
STONYBROOK SHOOTING SUPPLIES
3755 E Market St Ste 18 (17402-5200)
PHONE.....................717 757-1088
John Sheurman, *President*
EMP: 4
SALES (est): 300K **Privately Held**
SIC: 3949 Sporting & athletic goods

(G-20682)
SURTECH INDUSTRIES INC
915 Borom Rd (17404-1382)
PHONE.....................717 767-6808
David Gotwald, *CEO*
Terrence M Spisak, *President*
Jeffrey Brown, *Treasurer*
Margaret Gotwald, *Admin Sec*
EMP: 35
SQ FT: 66,500
SALES (est): 5.9MM **Privately Held**
WEB: www.surtech-ind.com
SIC: 3479 3471 Coating of metals & formed products; finishing, metals or formed products

(G-20683)
T-BIRD MCHNING FABRICATION LLC
Also Called: L&S Tool and Machine
710 Willow Springs Ln (17406-8434)
PHONE.....................717 384-8362
Robert Macdiarmid,
EMP: 10
SALES (est): 2.1MM **Privately Held**
SIC: 3545 Machine tool accessories

(G-20684)
TAYLOR COMMUNICATIONS INC
121 Mount Zion Rd (17402-8985)
PHONE.....................717 755-1051
Troy Warner, *Opers Mgr*
Tim Hyer, *Branch Mgr*
EMP: 79
SQ FT: 1,799
SALES (corp-wide): 3.2B **Privately Held**
SIC: 2759 Commercial printing
HQ: Taylor Communications, Inc.
1725 Roe Crest Dr
North Mankato MN 56003
507 625-2828

(G-20685)
TEKGARD INC
3390 Farmtrail Rd (17406-5614)
PHONE.....................717 854-0005
G L Cramer Jr, *President*
Michael Bahn, *Vice Pres*
EMP: 60
SQ FT: 92,000
SALES (est): 13.9MM **Privately Held**
WEB: www.tekgard.com
SIC: 3585 Refrigeration & heating equipment

(G-20686)
TEXAS-NEW MXICO NEWSPAPERS LLC
Also Called: Mediaonepa
1891 Loucks Rd (17408-9708)
PHONE.....................717 767-3554
Jared Bean, *President*
Rich Canazaro, *Advt Staff*
EMP: 65
SALES (est): 950K **Privately Held**
SIC: 2711 Newspapers

(G-20687)
TEXTBOOK LLC
1911 E Market St (17402-2838)
PHONE.....................717 779-7101
Jesse Daugherty, *Principal*
EMP: 6
SALES (est): 185.3K **Privately Held**
SIC: 2741 Internet Publishing And Broadcasting

(G-20688)
THREE M TOOL AND DIE CORP (PA)
1038 Elm St (17403-2596)
PHONE.....................717 854-6379
Austin Hunt, *President*
Suzette Chismar, *Sales Staff*
Sara Hunt, *Admin Sec*
◆ EMP: 12 EST: 1946
SQ FT: 17,000
SALES (est): 2.9MM **Privately Held**
WEB: www.threemtool.com
SIC: 3423 3315 Hand & edge tools; steel wire & related products

(G-20689)
TKD MFG INC
3945 N Susquehanna Trl (17404-8406)
PHONE.....................717 266-3156
Jonathan Diamond, *Principal*
▲ EMP: 16
SALES (est): 2MM **Privately Held**
SIC: 3999 Manufacturing industries

(G-20690)
TOOLING DYNAMICS LLC
905 Vogelsong Rd (17404-1378)
PHONE.....................717 764-8873
Tyson Berkey, *Opers Mgr*
Jeff Noll, *Materials Mgr*
Larry Wildasin, *Safety Mgr*
John Wilson, *Opers Staff*
Nicole Updike, *Buyer*
◆ EMP: 140
SQ FT: 60,000
SALES (est): 30.2MM **Privately Held**
WEB: www.toolingdynamics.com
SIC: 3469 3544 Stamping metal for the trade; special dies, tools, jigs & fixtures

(G-20691)
TRI- MED LABORATORIES INC
2159 White St Ste 3 (17404-4948)
PHONE.....................732 249-6363
EMP: 20
SQ FT: 10,000
SALES (est): 3.7MM **Privately Held**
SIC: 2834 Mfg Pharmaceutical Preparations

(G-20692)
TRIANGLE PRINTING COMPANY INC
Also Called: Triangle Printing & Packg Co
1000 E Boundary Ave (17403-2981)
P.O. Box 1782 (17405-1782)
PHONE.....................717 854-1521
Colby Wiesman, *President*
Guy Wilcomb, *Exec VP*
C Michael Dohm, *Vice Pres*
Michael Burd, *Mktg Dir*
Ginger Levi,
EMP: 50
SQ FT: 45,000
SALES (est): 9.3MM **Privately Held**
WEB: www.triangle-printing.com
SIC: 7336 2752 Package design; commercial printing, lithographic

(G-20693)
TWO TOYS INC
Also Called: Fastsigns
2801 E Market St (17402-2406)
PHONE.....................717 840-6400
John Toy, *President*
EMP: 9
SALES (est): 1MM **Privately Held**
SIC: 3993 3669 Signs & advertising specialties; visual communication systems

(G-20694)
UNITED COOLAIR CORPORATION
491 E Princess St (17403-2417)
PHONE.....................717 845-8685

Neil R Tucker, *President*
Joe Garner, *Safety Mgr*
Kirill Ogdanets, *Engineer*
Rodney Johnson, *Treasurer*
Rich Pierse, *Sales Mgr*
EMP: 104
SQ FT: 75,000
SALES: 20MM **Privately Held**
SIC: 1711 3585 Warm air heating & air conditioning contractor; air conditioning units, complete: domestic or industrial

(G-20695)
USA OPTICAL INC (PA)
2553 E Market St (17402-2403)
PHONE......................717 757-5632
Lillie E McHale, *President*
Kit Crable, *Manager*
Candy Whorley, *Manager*
EMP: 11
SQ FT: 1,550
SALES (est): 2.3MM **Privately Held**
WEB: www.usaopticalinc.com
SIC: 3229 Optical glass

(G-20696)
V R MACHINE CO INC
257a N Duke St (17401-2458)
PHONE......................717 846-9203
T Richard De Ribert, *President*
EMP: 15 **EST:** 1968
SQ FT: 10,000
SALES (est): 2.7MM **Privately Held**
WEB: www.vrmachineco.com
SIC: 3451 Screw machine products

(G-20697)
VENTWELL INC
78 Willow Springs Cir (17406-8428)
PHONE......................717 683-1477
EMP: 3
SALES (est): 228.4K **Privately Held**
SIC: 3563 Air & gas compressors

(G-20698)
VOITH DIGITAL SOLUTIONS INC
Also Called: Voith It Solutions Inc.
760 E Berlin Rd (17408-8701)
PHONE......................717 792-7000
Darryl Stevenson, *President*
Stuart Coulson, *Vice Pres*
Nick Vu, *Engineer*
Rene Habets, *Treasurer*
Christopher Hageman, *Info Tech Mgr*
EMP: 18
SALES (est): 3.9MM
SALES (corp-wide): 177.9K **Privately Held**
SIC: 3566 Speed changers, drives & gears
HQ: Voith Gmbh & Co. Kgaa
St.-Poltener-Str. 43
Heidenheim An Der Brenz 89522
732 137-0

(G-20699)
VOITH HYDRO INC (DH)
760 E Berlin Rd (17408-8701)
P.O. Box 15022 (17405-7022)
PHONE......................717 792-7000
Robert J Gallo, *President*
Jeremy Smith, *General Mgr*
Daniel Hollenbach, *Regional Mgr*
Stanley J Kocon, *COO*
Joshua Christensen, *Counsel*
▲ **EMP:** 441
SQ FT: 48,000
SALES (est): 126.1MM
SALES (corp-wide): 177.9K **Privately Held**
SIC: 3511 7699 Hydraulic turbines; hydraulic equipment repair
HQ: Voith Gmbh & Co. Kgaa
St.-Poltener-Str. 43
Heidenheim An Der Brenz 89522
732 137-0

(G-20700)
VOITH PAPER FABRIC AND ROLL SY (DH)
760 E Berlin Rd (17408-8701)
PHONE......................717 792-7000
David Barefield, *President*
◆ **EMP:** 148 **EST:** 1973
SQ FT: 10,000

SALES (est): 17.6MM
SALES (corp-wide): 177.9K **Privately Held**
SIC: 3496 Fourdrinier wire cloth
HQ: Voith Paper Inc.
2200 N Roemer Rd
Appleton WI 54911
920 731-0769

(G-20701)
W R MEADOWS INC
Also Called: W R Meadows of Pennsylvannia
2150 Monroe St (17404-5568)
PHONE......................717 792-2627
EMP: 20
SALES (corp-wide): 120.1MM **Privately Held**
WEB: www.wrmeadows.com
SIC: 5032 3272 2899 Brick, stone & related material; concrete products; chemical preparations
PA: W. R. Meadows, Inc.
300 Industrial Dr
Hampshire IL 60140
847 214-2100

(G-20702)
WAGMAN METAL PRODUCTS INC
400 S Albemarle St (17403-2514)
PHONE......................717 854-2120
George F Wagman III, *President*
Joe Mazur, *Financial Exec*
▲ **EMP:** 35 **EST:** 1963
SQ FT: 65,000
SALES (est): 9.1MM **Privately Held**
WEB: www.wagmanmetal.com
SIC: 3531 Blades for graders, scrapers, dozers & snow plows

(G-20703)
WALMAN OPTICAL COMPANY
150 Rose Ct (17406-8410)
P.O. Box 575, Emigsville (17318-0575)
PHONE......................717 767-5193
Robert Foard, *QC Mgr*
Bob Foard, *Branch Mgr*
EMP: 22
SALES (corp-wide): 404.2MM **Privately Held**
SIC: 3851 5048 Eyeglasses, lenses & frames; contact lenses; lens coating, ophthalmic; optometric equipment & supplies; frames, ophthalmic
PA: The Walman Optical Company
801 12th Ave N Ste 1
Minneapolis MN 55411
612 520-6000

(G-20704)
WAYNECO INC
800 Hanover Rd (17408-6200)
PHONE......................717 225-4413
Wayne M Meyer, *President*
Ann Meyer, *Corp Secy*
Todd Meyer, *Vice Pres*
EMP: 55 **EST:** 1961
SQ FT: 65,000
SALES (est): 6.3MM **Privately Held**
WEB: www.wayneco.inc.com
SIC: 2511 2434 Wood household furniture; vanities, bathroom: wood

(G-20705)
WEDJ/THREE CS INC
491 E Princess St (17403-2417)
P.O. Box 2423 (17405-2423)
PHONE......................717 845-8685
Neil Tucker, *President*
George Cooper, *Vice Pres*
George E Mac Donald, *Admin Sec*
EMP: 90
SQ FT: 75,000
SALES (est): 9.9MM **Privately Held**
WEB: www.unitedcoolair.com
SIC: 3585 3443 Refrigeration & heating equipment; parts for heating, cooling & refrigerating equipment; fabricated plate work (boiler shop)

(G-20706)
WELDON MACHINE TOOL INC
Also Called: Weldon Solutions
425 E Berlin Rd (17408-8810)
PHONE......................717 846-4000
Travis Gentzler, *President*

Barry Eckard, *Vice Pres*
Denny Rowe, *Director*
EMP: 41
SQ FT: 40,000
SALES: 14MM **Privately Held**
WEB: www.weldonsolutions.com
SIC: 3541 3535 Grinding machines, metalworking; lathes, metal cutting & polishing; conveyors & conveying equipment

(G-20707)
WELLM DYNA MACH AND ASSE INC
706 Willow Springs Ln (17406-8434)
PHONE......................717 764-8855
Jim Mahoney, *CEO*
Danette Miro, *President*
Dennis Goulden, *General Mgr*
EMP: 23
SALES (est): 5.1MM **Privately Held**
SIC: 3593 Fluid power cylinders & actuators

(G-20708)
WESTFALIA TECHNOLOGIES INC
3655 Sandhurst Dr (17406-7927)
PHONE......................717 764-1115
Dan Labell, *President*
Jon Schultz, *President*
Caio Seabra, *COO*
Caio Sebra, *COO*
Gary Frank, *Vice Pres*
▲ **EMP:** 85
SQ FT: 43,000
SALES (est): 39.9MM **Privately Held**
WEB: www.westfaliausa.com
SIC: 3535 Conveyors & conveying equipment

(G-20709)
WESTROCK CP LLC
Also Called: Containerboard & Paper Div
423 Kings Mill Rd (17401)
P.O. Box 26998, Jacksonville FL (32226-6998)
PHONE......................904 751-6400
Green Long, *Branch Mgr*
EMP: 174
SQ FT: 100,000
SALES (corp-wide): 16.2B **Publicly Held**
WEB: www.smurfit-stone.com
SIC: 2631 Corrugating medium
HQ: Westrock Cp, Llc
1000 Abernathy Rd
Atlanta GA 30328

(G-20710)
WEXCO INCORPORATED (PA)
3490 Board Rd (17406-8478)
PHONE......................717 764-8585
Jeffrey Kurth, *President*
Linda Luckenbaugh, *Vice Pres*
John Schrenk, *Vice Pres*
Robert E Seitz, *Treasurer*
Lisa Crone, *Technology*
EMP: 6
SALES (est): 124MM **Privately Held**
SIC: 3089 3949 3999 5091 Extruded finished plastic products; swimming pools, plastic; hot tubs; watersports equipment & supplies; vinyl film & sheet

(G-20711)
WINFOSOFT INC
910 S George St (17403-3708)
PHONE......................717 226-1299
David Myers, *President*
Jim Prevatte, *Principal*
Larry King, *Vice Pres*
John Ross, *CFO*
Chapin Fay, *Accounts Exec*
EMP: 30
SALES (est): 3.2MM **Privately Held**
SIC: 7372 Business oriented computer software

(G-20712)
WINTERCORP LLC
847 Galtee Ct (17402-9267)
PHONE......................717 848-3425
EMP: 4
SALES (est): 272.9K **Privately Held**
SIC: 3599 7389 3444 Mfg Industrial Machinery Business Services At Non-Commercial Site Mfg Sheet Metalwork

(G-20713)
WINTERS PERFORMANCE PDTS INC
1580 Trolley Rd (17408-4313)
PHONE......................717 764-9844
Vaughn Winter, *President*
Madeline Winter, *Treasurer*
▲ **EMP:** 46 **EST:** 1951
SALES (est): 13.1MM **Privately Held**
WEB: www.wintersperformance.com
SIC: 3714 Transmissions, motor vehicle

(G-20714)
WIRE MESH PRODUCTS INC (PA)
501 E King St Ste 1 (17403-1773)
P.O. Box 1988 (17405-1988)
PHONE......................717 848-3620
Richard D Riva II, *President*
Dustin Carl, *Vice Pres*
◆ **EMP:** 50
SQ FT: 50,000
SALES (est): 6.6MM **Privately Held**
WEB: www.wire-mesh.com
SIC: 3496 Miscellaneous fabricated wire products

(G-20715)
WISE PRINTING CO INC
2449 S Queen St Rear Rear (17402-5078)
PHONE......................717 741-2751
Harry Overlander, *President*
Gary Reachard, *Partner*
EMP: 5 **EST:** 1957
SQ FT: 1,200
SALES (est): 510K **Privately Held**
WEB: www.wiseprinting.com
SIC: 2752 2759 Commercial printing, offset; letterpress printing

(G-20716)
WOLF PRINTING
Also Called: Wolf Printing & Copy Center
1200 Haines Rd (17402-8864)
PHONE......................717 755-1560
Barry Wolf, *Partner*
Brian Wolf, *Partner*
Greg Wolf, *Partner*
EMP: 6
SALES: 400K **Privately Held**
WEB: www.wolfprinting.com
SIC: 2752 7334 Commercial printing, offset; photocopying & duplicating services

(G-20717)
WOLFE TOOL & MACHINE COMPANY
210 Lafayette St (17401-2108)
P.O. Box 2586 (17405-2586)
PHONE......................717 848-6375
Keith Wolfe, *President*
Lisa Wolfe, *Corp Secy*
EMP: 13
SQ FT: 18,000
SALES: 1.2MM **Privately Held**
SIC: 3544 3599 7629 Special dies & tools; machine shop, jobbing & repair; electrical repair shops

(G-20718)
WOLFGANG OPERATIONS LLC (PA)
Also Called: Wolfgang Candy Company
50 E 4th Ave (17404-2507)
PHONE......................717 843-5536
Michael Stillman, *CEO*
Samuel Miller, *President*
Brad McGlaughlin, *Vice Pres*
Bruce Limpert, *CFO*
EMP: 60
SQ FT: 65,000
SALES (est): 30.4MM **Privately Held**
SIC: 2064 Candy & other confectionery products

(G-20719)
WOLFGANG OPERATIONS LLC
122 North St (17403-9403)
PHONE......................717 843-5536
Samuel Miller, *President*
EMP: 40
SALES (corp-wide): 30.4MM **Privately Held**
SIC: 2064 Candy & other confectionery products

▲ = Import ▼=Export
◆ =Import/Export

PA: Wolfgang Operations, Llc
50 E 4th Ave
York PA 17404
717 843-5536

(G-20720)
WOODY ASSOCIATES INC
844 E South St (17403-2849)
PHONE....................................717 843-3975
Harry Reinke, *President*
Kerrie A Reinke, *Vice Pres*
Kerrie Reinke, *Vice Pres*
Steven Ziolkowski, *Engineer*
▲ **EMP:** 10 **EST:** 1954
SQ FT: 6,600
SALES: 1.8MM **Privately Held**
WEB: www.woody-decorators.com
SIC: 3556 Chocolate processing machinery

(G-20721)
XCELL AUTOMATION INC
20 Innovation Dr (17402-2777)
P.O. Box 21487 (17402-0187)
PHONE....................................717 755-6800
Brian Micciche, *President*
Bill Duncan, *Vice Pres*
William D Duncan, *Vice Pres*
Pete Kostic, *Vice Pres*
▲ **EMP:** 52
SQ FT: 100,000
SALES (est): 17.4MM **Privately Held**
SIC: 3569 5074 3548 Assembly machines, non-metalworking; heating equipment & panels, solar; soldering equipment, except hand soldering irons

(G-20722)
Y T & A INC
Also Called: York Tent & Awning
7 E 7th Ave (17404-2101)
PHONE....................................717 854-3806
John Musti, *President*
EMP: 15
SQ FT: 4,500
SALES (est): 1.8MM **Privately Held**
SIC: 7699 2394 Awning repair shop; tent repair shop; awnings, fabric: made from purchased materials

(G-20723)
YGS GROUP INC (PA)
3650 W Market St (17404-5813)
PHONE....................................717 505-9701
James Kell, *CEO*
Margaret Littman, *Editor*
Ashley Reid, *Editor*
Yvonne Desalle, *Vice Pres*
Paula Oleary, *Vice Pres*
EMP: 68
SALES (est): 22.2MM **Privately Held**
WEB: www.theygsgroup.com
SIC: 2754 8742 7336 2721 Publication printing, gravure; management consulting services; commercial art & graphic design; graphic arts & related design; periodicals; custom computer programming services

(G-20724)
YGS GROUP INC
3650 W Market St (17404-5813)
PHONE....................................425 251-5005
James Kell, *CEO*
EMP: 4
SALES (est): 327.9K
SALES (corp-wide): 22.2MM **Privately Held**
SIC: 2754 7336 Commercial printing, gravure; commercial art & graphic design
PA: The Ygs Group Inc
3650 W Market St
York PA 17404
717 505-9701

(G-20725)
YGS WEST LLC
3650 W Market St (17404-5813)
PHONE....................................425 251-5005
Alan Myers, *Accounts Mgr*
Robert Glass, *Accounts Exec*
Tina Meyer, *Accounts Exec*
Frank Tate, *Technology*
Ray Carter, *Technical Staff*
EMP: 30

SALES (est): 7.3MM **Privately Held**
SIC: 2752 Commercial printing, offset

(G-20726)
YORK BUILDING PRODUCTS CO INC (PA)
950 Smile Way (17404-1725)
PHONE....................................717 848-2831
Robert Stewart Jr, *President*
Gary Stewart, *Vice Pres*
Terrence Stewart, *Treasurer*
Carol Gilbert, *Admin Sec*
▲ **EMP:** 50 **EST:** 1957
SQ FT: 15,000
SALES (est): 56.4MM **Privately Held**
SIC: 3271 1442 3281 2951 Blocks, concrete or cinder: standard; construction sand mining; limestone, cut & shaped; concrete, bituminous; crushed & broken limestone

(G-20727)
YORK BUILDING PRODUCTS CO INC
915 Loucks Mill Rd (17402-1936)
PHONE....................................717 845-5333
Jo Warner, *Manager*
EMP: 21
SALES (corp-wide): 56.4MM **Privately Held**
SIC: 3271 Concrete block & brick
PA: York Building Products Co., Inc.
950 Smile Way
York PA 17404
717 848-2831

(G-20728)
YORK BUILDING PRODUCTS CO INC
Also Called: Mason Dixon Sand and Gravel
950 Smile Way Ste A (17404-1725)
PHONE....................................717 324-2379
EMP: 5
SALES (corp-wide): 56.4MM **Privately Held**
SIC: 3271 Blocks, concrete or cinder: standard
PA: York Building Products Co., Inc.
950 Smile Way
York PA 17404
717 848-2831

(G-20729)
YORK BUILDING PRODUCTS CO INC
Also Called: Lintel Plant
900 N Hartley St (17404-2865)
PHONE....................................717 764-5996
Dave Stewart, *President*
EMP: 26
SALES (corp-wide): 56.4MM **Privately Held**
WEB: www.yorkbuilding.com
SIC: 3272 Concrete products
PA: York Building Products Co., Inc.
950 Smile Way
York PA 17404
717 848-2831

(G-20730)
YORK BUILDING PRODUCTS CO INC
542 N West St (17404-3149)
P.O. Box 241, Thomasville (17364-0241)
PHONE....................................717 792-1200
Dennis Hoffman, *Manager*
EMP: 15
SALES (corp-wide): 56.4MM **Privately Held**
SIC: 3271 Concrete block & brick
PA: York Building Products Co., Inc.
950 Smile Way
York PA 17404
717 848-2831

(G-20731)
YORK CASKET COMPANY
Also Called: York Products
2880 Black Bridge Rd (17406-9703)
PHONE....................................717 854-9566
Scott Wright, *President*
Jay Keech, *Supervisor*
▼ **EMP:** 450

SALES (est): 53.9MM
SALES (corp-wide): 1.6B **Publicly Held**
WEB: www.yorkcasketcompany.com
SIC: 3995 Burial caskets
HQ: The York Group Inc
2 N Shore Ctr
Pittsburgh PA 15212
412 995-1600

(G-20732)
YORK CONCRETE COMPANY
400 Girard Ave (17403-2483)
PHONE....................................717 843-8746
Frederick L Miller, *President*
Lois A Miller, *President*
Anne N Miller-Thomas, *Treasurer*
EMP: 15 **EST:** 1929
SQ FT: 500
SALES (est): 1.5MM **Privately Held**
SIC: 3273 Ready-mixed concrete

(G-20733)
YORK CONTAINER COMPANY
138 Mount Zion Rd (17402-8985)
P.O. Box 3008 (17402-0008)
PHONE....................................717 757-7611
Dennis E Willman, *CEO*
Charles S Wolf Jr, *President*
Charles S Wolf, *Vice Pres*
William C Ludwig, *CFO*
Brent Ames, *Sales Staff*
◆ **EMP:** 240
SQ FT: 260,000
SALES (est): 79.2MM **Privately Held**
WEB: www.yorkcontainer.com
SIC: 2653 Boxes, corrugated: made from purchased materials

(G-20734)
YORK CORRUGATING COMPANY (PA)
120 S Adams St (17404-5454)
P.O. Box 1192 (17405-1192)
PHONE....................................717 845-3512
Kim P Raub, *President*
T R Miller, *Vice Pres*
Thomas R Miller, *Vice Pres*
Miller T R, *Vice Pres*
Hovis J E, *Admin Sec*
EMP: 87 **EST:** 1900
SQ FT: 190,000
SALES (est): 20MM **Privately Held**
WEB: www.yorkcorrugating.com
SIC: 3469 3465 5074 Metal stampings; automotive stampings; body parts, automobile: stamped metal; fenders, automobile: stamped or pressed metal; boilers, hot water heating

(G-20735)
YORK COUNTY WOMENS JOURNAL
545 Quaker Dr (17402-4141)
PHONE....................................717 634-1658
EMP: 3
SALES (est): 72.6K **Privately Held**
SIC: 2711 Newspapers, publishing & printing

(G-20736)
YORK DAILY RECORD SUNDAY NEWS
1891 Loucks Rd (17408-9708)
PHONE....................................717 771-2000
Fred Uffelman, *Principal*
Jared Bean, *Adv Dir*
EMP: 13
SALES (est): 893.1K **Privately Held**
SIC: 2711 4212 7311 Newspapers, publishing & printing; local trucking, without storage; advertising agencies

(G-20737)
YORK ELECTRO-MECHANICAL CORP
120 Rose Ct (17406-8410)
PHONE....................................717 764-5262
Deborah King, *CEO*
William Latchaw, *President*
Brady Bentz, *Corp Secy*
Troy Hull, *Vice Pres*
EMP: 38
SQ FT: 35,000

SALES (est): 6.9MM **Privately Held**
WEB: www.yorkelectro.com
SIC: 3599 Machine shop, jobbing & repair

(G-20738)
YORK GRAPHIC SERVICES CO
Also Called: Ygs Group, The
3650 W Market St (17404-5813)
PHONE....................................717 505-9701
James M Kell, *CEO*
Brad Altman, *President*
Jack Davidson, *Vice Pres*
Tom Grentz, *CFO*
Charles Calta, *VP Sales*
EMP: 141
SQ FT: 40,000
SALES (est): 22.5MM **Privately Held**
WEB: www.theygsgroup.com
SIC: 2721 2759 Periodicals: publishing only; commercial printing; publication printing

(G-20739)
YORK ICE CO INC
Also Called: GOOD TIME ICE
281 Kings Mill Rd (17401-2158)
PHONE....................................717 848-2639
Edward Neuman Jr, *President*
David R Neuman, *Vice Pres*
Elizabeth Snyder, *Admin Sec*
EMP: 36
SQ FT: 50,000
SALES (est): 4.6MM **Privately Held**
WEB: www.yorkskate.com
SIC: 2097 Manufactured ice

(G-20740)
YORK IMPERIAL PLASTICS INC
718 Country Rd (17403-9425)
PHONE....................................717 428-3939
Dennis A Paules, *CEO*
Sharon Bucher, *Admin Sec*
▲ **EMP:** 40
SQ FT: 45,000
SALES (est): 14.6MM **Privately Held**
WEB: www.yorkimperial.com
SIC: 3089 Injection molding of plastics

(G-20741)
YORK INDUSTRIAL TOOL INC
491 Maryland Ave (17404-2819)
PHONE....................................717 200-1149
EMP: 30 **EST:** 1965
SQ FT: 20,000
SALES (est): 320.5K **Privately Held**
SIC: 3599 Mfg Industrial Machinery

(G-20742)
YORK INDUSTRIES INC
706 Willow Springs Ln (17406-6044)
PHONE....................................717 764-8855
Thomas Nazmack, *CEO*
Michael Nazmack, *Ch of Bd*
Dennis Golden, *President*
Mark Keller, *Treasurer*
▲ **EMP:** 46
SQ FT: 61,000
SALES (est): 8.8MM **Privately Held**
WEB: www.yorkind.com
SIC: 3593 3594 3492 3769 Fluid power actuators, hydraulic or pneumatic; fluid power cylinders, hydraulic or pneumatic; fluid power pumps; control valves, fluid power: hydraulic & pneumatic; guided missile & space vehicle parts & auxiliary equipment

(G-20743)
YORK INTEGRA PA INC
3670 Concord Rd (17402-8629)
PHONE....................................717 840-3438
EMP: 3 **EST:** 2012
SALES (est): 280.8K **Privately Held**
SIC: 3841 Surgical & medical instruments

(G-20744)
YORK INTERNATIONAL CORPORATION
1499 E Philadelphia St (17403-1232)
PHONE....................................717 815-4200
Larry Weist, *Manager*
EMP: 250 **Privately Held**
SIC: 3585 Air conditioning units, complete: domestic or industrial

HQ: York International Corporation
631 S Richland Ave
York PA 17403
717 771-7890

(G-20745)
YORK INTERNATIONAL CORPORATION (DH)
631 S Richland Ave (17403-3445)
PHONE..................717 771-7890
C David Myers, *President*
Jane B Davis, *Vice Pres*
Jerome Okarma, *Vice Pres*
Stephen Roell, *Treasurer*
Derek T Faulkner, *Asst Sec*
◆ **EMP:** 1200
SQ FT: 1,500,000
SALES (est): 2.1B **Privately Held**
SIC: 3585 Air conditioning units, complete: domestic or industrial
HQ: Johnson Controls, Inc.
5757 N Green Bay Ave
Milwaukee WI 53209
414 524-1200

(G-20746)
YORK NEWSPAPER COMPANY
1891 Loucks Rd (17408-9708)
PHONE..................717 767-6397
Sara Glines, *President*
Buckner News Alliance, *Partner*
Edward Magee, *Vice Pres*
EMP: 300
SQ FT: 80,000
SALES (est): 13.2MM **Privately Held**
SIC: 2711 2752 Newspapers, publishing & printing; color lithography

(G-20747)
YORK NEWSPAPERS INC
Also Called: York Sunday News, The
1891 Loucks Rd (17408-9708)
PHONE..................717 767-6397
Richard B Scudder, *Ch of Bd*
W Dean Singleton, *Vice Chairman*
EMP: 60 **EST:** 1876
SALES (est): 21.5MM
SALES (corp-wide): 4.2B **Privately Held**
WEB: www.heathersbridal.com
SIC: 2752 Publication printing, lithographic
HQ: Medianews Group, Inc.
101 W Colfax Ave Ste 1100
Denver CO 80202

(G-20748)
YORK P-B TRUSS INC
3487 N Susquehanna Trl (17406-7904)
PHONE..................717 779-0327
Robert Ream, *President*
Larry R Haas, *Vice Pres*
Susan Green, *Marketing Staff*
Harry Reynolds, *Admin Sec*
EMP: 25 **EST:** 1997
SQ FT: 24,000
SALES (est): 4.9MM **Privately Held**
WEB: www.yorkpbtruss.com
SIC: 2439 5199 Trusses, except roof: laminated lumber; trusses, wooden roof; wood carvings

(G-20749)
YORK PRECISION
706 Willow Springs Ln (17406-8434)
PHONE..................717 764-8855
Daniel Baker,
Daniel Goulden,
EMP: 15
SALES (est): 924.6K **Privately Held**
SIC: 7699 3599 Hydraulic equipment repair; machine & other job shop work

(G-20750)
YORK STEEL RULE DIES INC
Also Called: Ditech Group
630 Loucks Mill Rd Ste 8 (17403-1019)
PHONE..................717 846-6002
Frederick Galiardo, *President*
James Osmolinski, *General Mgr*
EMP: 38
SQ FT: 52,000
SALES (est): 6.4MM **Privately Held**
SIC: 3544 Dies, steel rule

(G-20751)
YORK TEXTILE PRODUCTS INC
2110 Brougher Ln (17408-4522)
PHONE..................717 764-2528
Michael A Kristick, *President*
John J Kristick, *Vice Pres*
Clarence Kristick, *Treasurer*
Joseph R Kristick, *Admin Sec*
EMP: 6 **EST:** 1953
SQ FT: 1,600
SALES (est): 447K **Privately Held**
SIC: 2211 2259 5131 Tubing, seamless: cotton; meat bagging, knit; knit fabrics

(G-20752)
YORK TOOL & DIE INC
Also Called: Product Design and Development
2603 Keyway Dr (17402-4712)
PHONE..................717 741-4844
Larry Mifmitzel, *President*
Mike Brezler, *Treasurer*
EMP: 15
SQ FT: 2,200
SALES (est): 1.3MM **Privately Held**
SIC: 3599 Machine shop, jobbing & repair

(G-20753)
YORK TOWNE EMBROIDERY WORKS
220 W Philadelphia St (17401-2940)
PHONE..................717 854-0006
Lowell Davis, *Owner*
EMP: 4
SALES (est): 228.8K **Privately Held**
SIC: 2395 Embroidery products, except schiffli machine

(G-20754)
YORK WALLCOVERINGS INC (PA)
750 Linden Ave (17404-3373)
P.O. Box 5166 (17405-5166)
PHONE..................717 846-4456
Suzanne Jones, *General Mgr*
Stanley A Thomas, *Corp Secy*
Pierre J Delaye, *COO*
Ronald C Redding, *Vice Pres*
Gina Shaw, *Vice Pres*
◆ **EMP:** 225
SQ FT: 400,000
SALES (est): 54.4MM **Privately Held**
WEB: www.yorkwall.com
SIC: 2679 Wallpaper: made from purchased paper; wallpaper

(G-20755)
YORKAIRE INC
Also Called: Yorkaire Group, The
1877 Whiteford Rd (17402-2200)
PHONE..................717 755-2836
Lori Pearl-Guinan, *CEO*
Michael Hetrick, *CEO*
▼ **EMP:** 25
SQ FT: 4,800
SALES (est): 7.2MM **Privately Held**
WEB: www.yorkaire.com
SIC: 1711 3567 Mechanical contractor; industrial furnaces & ovens

---

York Haven
York County

(G-20756)
DAISY DATA DISPLAYS INC
2850 Lewisberry Rd (17370-9507)
PHONE..................717 932-9999
Henry Shefet, *CEO*
David Shefet, *President*
Michael Hadaway, *General Mgr*
Vered Shefet, *General Mgr*
Anna Poland, *Purchasing*
EMP: 50 **EST:** 1982
SQ FT: 28,000
SALES (est): 13.6MM **Privately Held**
WEB: www.daisydata.com
SIC: 3575 7373 3577 3571 Computer terminals, monitors & components; systems engineering, computer related; computer peripheral equipment; electronic computers

(G-20757)
DIE-TECH INC
295 Sipe Rd (17370-9218)
PHONE..................717 938-6771
Richard W Dennis, *President*
David W Hoover, *Vice Pres*
Cyndi Hiller, *CFO*
▼ **EMP:** 38
SQ FT: 32,000
SALES: 9MM **Privately Held**
WEB: www.die-tech.com
SIC: 3469 Metal stampings
PA: L-One, Inc.
295 Sipe Rd
York Haven PA 17370
717 938-6771

(G-20758)
EASTERN BAKERY EQUIPMENT CO
475 Stevens Rd (17370-9236)
PHONE..................717 938-8278
George Michels, *President*
EMP: 11
SQ FT: 12,000
SALES (est): 1.7MM **Privately Held**
WEB: www.comcastg.net
SIC: 3556 Bakery machinery

(G-20759)
JAMES CRAFT & SON INC (PA)
2780 York Haven Rd (17370)
P.O. Box 8 (17370-0008)
PHONE..................717 266-6629
James L Craft, *President*
Frederick A Craft, *Senior VP*
Thomas A Craft, *Senior VP*
William D Craft, *Senior VP*
Vicki E Kearns, *Treasurer*
EMP: 180 **EST:** 1900
SALES: 1.1MM **Privately Held**
WEB: www.jamescraftson.com
SIC: 1711 3444 Mechanical contractor; sheet metalwork; ducts, sheet metal; elbows, for air ducts, stovepipes, etc.: sheet metal

(G-20760)
L-ONE INC (PA)
295 Sipe Rd (17370-9218)
PHONE..................717 938-6771
Richard W Dennis, *President*
David W Hoover, *Vice Pres*
Cyndi Hiller, *Admin Sec*
▼ **EMP:** 41
SQ FT: 30,855
SALES (est): 9MM **Privately Held**
SIC: 3469 Metal stampings

(G-20761)
REESER BROS
Also Called: Reeser Bros Concrete
905 Pleasant Grove Rd (17370-9706)
PHONE..................717 266-6644
Verdell Reeser Jr, *Partner*
Lowell R Reeser, *Partner*
EMP: 8 **EST:** 1966
SQ FT: 10,000
SALES (est): 1MM **Privately Held**
SIC: 3273 1794 1711 Ready-mixed concrete; excavation & grading, building construction; septic system construction

(G-20762)
YORK HAVEN FABRICATORS INC
2850 Lewisberry Rd (17370-9507)
PHONE..................717 932-4000
Henry Shefet, *CEO*
Michael Shefet, *President*
Rich Washko, *General Mgr*
▲ **EMP:** 25
SQ FT: 25,000
SALES (est): 7.1MM **Privately Held**
WEB: www.yorkhavenfab.com
SIC: 3444 Sheet metal specialties, not stamped

York Springs
Adams County

(G-20763)
CONCRETE JUNGLE
7771 Carlisle Pike (17372-9524)
PHONE..................717 528-8851
Joseph Guarino, *Owner*
EMP: 5
SQ FT: 3,600
SALES (est): 290K **Privately Held**
WEB: www.theconcretejungle.com
SIC: 3999 Lawn ornaments

(G-20764)
CRYSTAL IMAGERY INC
680 S Ridge Rd (17372-8728)
PHONE..................888 440-6073
Eric Schuchart, *President*
EMP: 7
SALES: 1.1MM **Privately Held**
SIC: 5947 3231 Artcraft & carvings; decorated glassware: chipped, engraved, etched, etc.

(G-20765)
FLOWERS FOODS INC
101 High St (17372-9502)
PHONE..................717 528-4108
EMP: 43
SALES (corp-wide): 3.9B **Publicly Held**
SIC: 2051 Bakery: wholesale or wholesale/retail combined
PA: Flowers Foods, Inc.
1919 Flowers Cir
Thomasville GA 31757
229 226-9110

(G-20766)
GILBERT LOGGING AND SUPPLY
1440 Cranberry Rd (17372-8852)
PHONE..................717 528-4919
Viateur Gilbert, *Principal*
EMP: 3 **EST:** 2001
SALES (est): 301.2K **Privately Held**
SIC: 2411 Logging camps & contractors

(G-20767)
GUYON INDUSTRIES INC
100 Auction Dr (17372-9601)
PHONE..................717 528-0154
Eric Loftman, *President*
Katrina Loftman, *Vice Pres*
EMP: 9
SQ FT: 12,000
SALES: 800K **Privately Held**
SIC: 2421 Siding (dressed lumber)

(G-20768)
SUPRAWATER
20 Seneca Dr (17372-9730)
PHONE..................717 528-9949
William G Holland, *Principal*
EMP: 7
SALES: 950K **Privately Held**
SIC: 3999 Manufacturing industries

Youngsville
Warren County

(G-20769)
BROKEN STRAW OUTDOORS
488 E Main St (16371-1128)
PHONE..................814 563-2200
Kenneth Roberts, *Principal*
EMP: 4
SALES (est): 305.8K **Privately Held**
SIC: 3949 Sporting & athletic goods

(G-20770)
EDWARD OIL COMPANY
Brown HI (16371)
P.O. Box 202 (16371-0202)
PHONE..................814 726-9576
John E McCool, *Owner*
▲ **EMP:** 12 **EST:** 1978
SALES: 398K **Privately Held**
SIC: 1382 Oil & gas exploration services

▲ = Import ▼ =Export
◆ =Import/Export

(G-20771)
GAS & OIL MANAGEMENT ASSOC
80 Dillon Dr (16371-1602)
PHONE..................814 563-4601
Robert J Clark, *President*
EMP: 6
SQ FT: 800
SALES: 43K **Privately Held**
SIC: 1389 1381 Gas field services; oil field services; drilling oil & gas wells

(G-20772)
HYMA DEVORE LUMBER MILL INC
Also Called: Hyma Devore Lumber Co
Rt (16371)
PHONE..................814 563-4646
Wilbur Devore, *President*
Alan Downs, *Vice Pres*
Dora Devore, *Treasurer*
George Berlstein, *Admin Sec*
EMP: 32 EST: 1963
SQ FT: 48,000
SALES (est): 3.7MM **Privately Held**
WEB: www.hymadevore.com
SIC: 2421 5031 2426 Sawmills & planing mills, general; lumber, plywood & millwork; hardwood dimension & flooring mills

(G-20773)
LIGNETICS NEW ENGLAND INC
1055 Matthews Run Rd (16371-3127)
PHONE..................814 563-4358
EMP: 8
SALES (corp-wide): 27.9MM **Privately Held**
SIC: 2448 Wood pallets & skids
HQ: Lignetics Of New England, Inc.
1075 E S Boulder Rd
Louisville CO 80027
303 802-5400

(G-20774)
PETES BEVERAGE
29100 Route 6 (16371-2528)
PHONE..................814 563-7374
Brenda Savitz, *Owner*
Peter Savitz, *Co-Owner*
EMP: 5
SALES (est): 226.1K **Privately Held**
SIC: 2082 Beer (alcoholic beverage)

(G-20775)
ROBERT P WILLIAMS
Also Called: Robert Williams Truck Sales
29030 Route 6 (16371-2526)
PHONE..................814 563-7660
Robert P Williams, *Owner*
EMP: 3
SQ FT: 15,000
SALES: 700K **Privately Held**
WEB: www.robertpwilliams.com
SIC: 2789 5031 5012 5013 Deckling books, cards or paper; lumber: rough, dressed & finished; trucks, commercial; truck parts & accessories

Youngwood
Westmoreland County

(G-20776)
A & S FIREARM SUPPLIES INC
Also Called: A & S Indoor Pistol Range
617 Overhead Bridge Rd (15697-1551)
PHONE..................724 925-1212
Todd Edminston, *President*
Lynn Alcorn, *President*
Rich Snyder, *Vice Pres*
EMP: 4
SALES (est): 453.7K **Privately Held**
WEB: www.aandspistolrange.com
SIC: 5941 3949 7999 7699 Firearms; targets, archery & rifle shooting; shooting range operation; gun services

(G-20777)
ALL METAL FABRICATING CO INC
521 N 7th St (15697-1521)
P.O. Box J (15697-0344)
PHONE..................724 925-3537
Samuel Dragovich Jr, *President*
Kelli Miller, *Admin Sec*
EMP: 5 EST: 1957
SQ FT: 7,000
SALES: 500K **Privately Held**
SIC: 3443 3446 Fabricated plate work (boiler shop); architectural metalwork

(G-20778)
AMERICAN WATER TECHNOLOGIES (PA)
38 S 4th St (15697-1202)
PHONE..................724 850-9000
Gary E Restanio, *President*
EMP: 32
SQ FT: 2,000
SALES (est): 3.5MM **Privately Held**
SIC: 3589 Sewage & water treatment equipment

(G-20779)
APPALACHIAN TANK CAR SVCS INC
304 N 3rd St (15697-1614)
PHONE..................724 925-3919
EMP: 15
SALES (corp-wide): 46.3MM **Privately Held**
SIC: 3743 Mfg Railroad Equipment
HQ: Appalachian Tank Car Services, Inc.
3915 Hydro St
Lynchburg VA 24503
434 384-6200

(G-20780)
BUNCHER COMPANY
Also Called: Buncher Rail Car Svc Youngwood
304 N 3rd St (15697-1614)
P.O. Box 768, Pittsburgh (15230-0768)
PHONE..................724 925-3919
Fax: 724 925-2670
EMP: 4
SALES (corp-wide): 10.6MM **Privately Held**
SIC: 3743 4741 Mfg Railroad Equipment Railroad Car Rental
PA: The Buncher Company
1300 Penn Ave Ste 300
Pittsburgh PA 15222
412 422-9900

(G-20781)
POWEREX INC
200 E Hillis St (15697)
PHONE..................724 925-7272
Craig Morrow, *Owner*
EMP: 34
SQ FT: 82,116
SALES (corp-wide): 32.2MM **Privately Held**
SIC: 3674 5063 3634 3625 Semiconductor circuit networks; electrical supplies; electric housewares & fans; relays & industrial controls
PA: Powerex, Inc.
173 Pavilion Ln
Youngwood PA 15697
724 925-7272

(G-20782)
POWEREX INC (PA)
173 Pavilion Ln (15697-1814)
PHONE..................724 925-7272
John Hall, *President*
John Yurack, *General Mgr*
Ron Yurko, *Vice Pres*
Eric Motto, *Project Mgr*
Joe Wolfe, *CFO*
◆ EMP: 209
SQ FT: 98,000
SALES (est): 32.2MM **Privately Held**
WEB: www.pwrx.com
SIC: 3674 Semiconductor circuit networks

(G-20783)
R W SIDLEY INCORPORATED
88 E Hillis St (15697-4002)
PHONE..................724 755-0205

Clinton Boyd, *Branch Mgr*
EMP: 15
SALES (corp-wide): 132.6MM **Privately Held**
WEB: www.rwsidleyinc.com
SIC: 3273 Ready-mixed concrete
PA: R. W. Sidley Incorporated
436 Casement Ave
Painesville OH 44077
440 352-9343

Yukon
Westmoreland County

(G-20784)
ARC TECHNOLOGIES CORPORATION
226 Lumber St (15698)
P.O. Box 485 (15698-0485)
PHONE..................724 722-7066
Stanley Siegel, *President*
Pam Siegel, *Corp Secy*
EMP: 18 EST: 1978
SQ FT: 13,500
SALES (est): 341.1K **Privately Held**
WEB: www.yukonsoft.com
SIC: 3613 Control panels, electric

(G-20785)
TRICO WELDING COMPANY
100 Acorn Ln (15698)
P.O. Box 588 (15698-0588)
PHONE..................724 722-1300
Charles Trice, *President*
Ruth Trice, *Vice Pres*
Lisa Bialowas, *Admin Sec*
EMP: 10
SALES: 720K **Privately Held**
SIC: 1799 7692 3441 Welding on site; welding repair; fabricated structural metal

(G-20786)
VERTEX IMAGE PRODUCTS INC
173 Spring St (15698-1001)
PHONE..................724 722-3400
Charles E Bobich, *President*
Alan Benemelis, *Vice Pres*
▲ EMP: 4
SQ FT: 5,500
SALES (est): 542.1K **Privately Held**
WEB: www.imagetherm.com
SIC: 3861 Developers, photographic (not made in chemical plants)

Zelienople
Butler County

(G-20787)
AIR TURBINE PROPELLER COMPANY (PA)
22329 Perry Hwy (16063-8921)
P.O. Box 218 (16063-0218)
PHONE..................724 452-9540
Scott Pennel, *President*
Terri Tankersley, *Corp Secy*
Tim Lefebvre, *Purch Mgr*
Jonathan Mrockosky, *Engineer*
David Silvers, *Sales Mgr*
EMP: 21 EST: 1946
SQ FT: 35,000
SALES (est): 5.6MM **Privately Held**
WEB: www.airturbine.com
SIC: 3564 Filters, air: furnaces, air conditioning equipment, etc.

(G-20788)
ALLEGHENY TECHNOLOGIES INC
Also Called: ATI Flat Rolled Products
700 W New Castle St (16063-1028)
PHONE..................724 452-1726
EMP: 3 **Publicly Held**
SIC: 3312 Stainless steel
PA: Allegheny Technologies Incorporated
1000 Six Ppg Pl
Pittsburgh PA 15222

(G-20789)
AMERICAN CONTRACT SYSTEMS
4050 Jacksons Pointe Ct (16063-2838)
PHONE..................952 926-3515
Jeff Kruger, *Principal*
EMP: 5
SALES (est): 198.4K **Privately Held**
SIC: 3841 Surgical & medical instruments

(G-20790)
ATI PRECISION FINISHING LLC
W Newcastle St Rr 288 (16063)
PHONE..................724 452-1726
Carol Difrischia, *Branch Mgr*
EMP: 20 **Publicly Held**
WEB: www.romemetals.com
SIC: 3471 5051 Finishing, metals or formed products; metals service centers & offices
HQ: Ati Precision Finishing, Llc
499 Delaware Ave
Rochester PA 15074
724 775-1664

(G-20791)
BEER 4 LESS
114 S Main St Ste 1 (16063-1148)
PHONE..................724 452-7860
Harold Cooper, *Owner*
EMP: 3
SALES (est): 164.7K **Privately Held**
SIC: 2082 Beer (alcoholic beverage)

(G-20792)
BILLCO MANUFACTURING INC
100 Halstead Blvd (16063-9799)
PHONE..................724 452-7390
Phillip Plant, *President*
William Billinger, *Principal*
David Simko, *Vice Pres*
Daniel Allen, *Treasurer*
Martino Aron, *Admin Sec*
▼ EMP: 118 EST: 1948
SQ FT: 90,000
SALES (est): 36.9MM **Privately Held**
WEB: www.billco-mfg.com
SIC: 3559 Glass making machinery: blowing, molding, forming, etc.

(G-20793)
BNZ MATERIALS INC
191 Front St (16063-1088)
PHONE..................724 452-8650
Ben Holder, *Plant Engr*
Carrie Baker, *Human Res Mgr*
Bill P Pietisch, *Manager*
EMP: 75
SALES (corp-wide): 47MM **Privately Held**
WEB: www.bnzmaterials.com
SIC: 3255 Clay refractories
PA: Bnz Materials, Inc.
6901 S Pierce St Ste 180
Littleton CO 80128
303 978-1199

(G-20794)
CANNON U S A INC
300 W Grandview Ave (16063-1103)
PHONE..................724 452-5358
Butch Sloan, *Branch Mgr*
EMP: 6
SALES (corp-wide): 83.5K **Privately Held**
SIC: 3559 Plastics working machinery
HQ: Cannon U. S. A., Inc.
1235 Freedom Rd
Cranberry Township PA 16066
724 772-5600

(G-20795)
CON YEAGER COMPANY (PA)
Also Called: Con Yeager Spice
144 Magill Rd (16063-3424)
PHONE..................724 452-4120
William Y Kreuer, *President*
Glenn W Frederick, *Vice Pres*
Betty Burr, *Purch Mgr*
Chad Hollenbaugh, *Sales Staff*
Tabetha Fisher, *Director*
EMP: 25
SQ FT: 7,800
SALES (est): 2.6MM **Privately Held**
SIC: 2099 Seasonings & spices

G E O G R A P H I C

(G-20796)
EAGLE RUBBER PRODUCTS INC
306 Halstead Blvd (16063-1906)
P.O. Box 519 (16063-0519)
PHONE....................................724 452-3200
John R Chickos, *President*
Richard Green, *Principal*
Donald W Neff, *Principal*
Gary Westerman, *Principal*
EMP: 18
SQ FT: 17,000
SALES (est): 3.2MM **Privately Held**
WEB: www.eaglerubber.com
SIC: 3069 3061 Rubber rolls & roll coverings; roll coverings, rubber; mechanical rubber goods

(G-20797)
EASTERN ARCHITECTURAL PDTS LLC
213 Front St (16063-2029)
PHONE....................................724 513-1630
John R Beighey, *Principal*
▲ **EMP:** 3
SALES (est): 382.3K **Privately Held**
SIC: 3241 8712 Natural cement; architectural services

(G-20798)
ELM ENTERPRISES INC
Also Called: Sign Innovation
50 Halstead Blvd Ste 1 (16063-1914)
PHONE....................................724 452-8699
Raymond Roccon, *President*
Lana K Melberg, *Treasurer*
EMP: 30 **EST:** 1985
SALES: 3.5MM **Privately Held**
SIC: 3993 Electric signs

(G-20799)
EV PRODUCTS INC
Also Called: Kromek
143 Zehner School Rd (16063)
PHONE....................................724 352-5288
Arnab Basu, *President*
Richard J Smith, *Vice Pres*
Derek Bulmer, *CFO*
EMP: 45
SQ FT: 35,000
SALES (est): 11.3MM
SALES (corp-wide): 16.6MM **Privately Held**
SIC: 3829 Measuring & controlling devices
PA: Kromek Group Plc
Thomas Wright Way
Stockton-On-Tees TS21
174 062-6050

(G-20800)
FB LEOPOLD COMPANY INC
227 S Division St Ste 1 (16063-1397)
PHONE....................................724 452-6300
Sean Petraitis, *Project Mgr*
Pug Daugherty, *Purch Mgr*
Donna Eppinger, *Engineer*
John Geibel, *Engineer*
Thomas Morando, *Engineer*
▲ **EMP:** 19
SALES (est): 2.6MM **Privately Held**
SIC: 3589 Water treatment equipment, industrial

(G-20801)
FORNEY LP
2050 Jacksons Pointe Ct (16063-2840)
PHONE....................................724 346-7400
Jeff Dziki, *Principal*
Stacey Evans, *Accounts Exec*
Jennifer Grady, *Sales Staff*
EMP: 28 **EST:** 2011
SQ FT: 33,000
SALES (est): 6.1MM **Privately Held**
SIC: 3829 Measuring & controlling devices

(G-20802)
FRANKENSTEIN BUILDERS SUPPLY
Also Called: Frankenstein Builders Supplies
404 Walnut St (16063-1072)
PHONE....................................724 333-5260
Kenneth Altemus, *Partner*
John C Frankenstein, *Partner*
EMP: 5

SALES (est): 813.1K **Privately Held**
SIC: 5032 3273 Concrete & cinder building products; ready-mixed concrete

(G-20803)
HUCKSTEIN PRINTING
107 E New Castle St Ste A (16063-1373)
PHONE....................................724 452-5777
Gary Williams, *Owner*
EMP: 4 **EST:** 1980
SQ FT: 1,500
SALES (est): 517.7K **Privately Held**
SIC: 2752 Commercial printing, offset

(G-20804)
INDUSTRIAL MACHINE INC
1870 Route 588 Ste 1 (16063-3916)
PHONE....................................724 452-7730
Michael Sheridan, *President*
Beverly Sheridan, *Vice Pres*
EMP: 10
SQ FT: 20,000
SALES (est): 1.3MM
SALES (corp-wide): 1.5MM **Privately Held**
WEB: www.industrialmachine.net
SIC: 3599 Machine shop, jobbing & repair
PA: Cain Fabrication And Machine, Llc
1870 State Rte 588
Zelienople PA 16063
725 452-7730

(G-20805)
J B BOOTH AND CO (PA)
Also Called: Pittsburgh Welding & Forge Div
1761 Rt 588 (16063)
PHONE....................................724 452-8400
John W Mowry Jr, *President*
John N Mowry, *Vice Pres*
Lauren M Cesnales, *Admin Sec*
EMP: 15 **EST:** 1888
SQ FT: 40,000
SALES (est): 3.5MM **Privately Held**
WEB: www.jbbooth.com
SIC: 3452 3441 3462 5051 Bolts, metal; expansion joints (structural shapes), iron or steel; iron & steel forgings; iron & steel (ferrous) products

(G-20806)
J B BOOTH AND CO
Pittsburgh Welding & Forge Div
1761 Rte 588 W (16063)
P.O. Box 98 (16063-0098)
PHONE....................................724 452-1313
Nancy Valentine, *Manager*
EMP: 7
SALES (est): 795.2K
SALES (corp-wide): 3.5MM **Privately Held**
WEB: www.jbbooth.com
SIC: 3452 3462 Bolts, metal; iron & steel forgings
PA: J B Booth And Co
1761 Rt 588
Zelienople PA 16063
724 452-8400

(G-20807)
JEDCO PRODUCTS INC
155 Zehner School Rd (16063-2717)
PHONE....................................724 453-3490
Linda Hodak, *President*
EMP: 5
SQ FT: 10,000
SALES (est): 406.1K **Privately Held**
WEB: www.jedcopro.com
SIC: 3949 Swimming pools, plastic

(G-20808)
JET INDUSTRIES INC
416 Halstead Blvd (16063-1908)
PHONE....................................724 452-5780
EMP: 20
SQ FT: 32,000
SALES (est): 4.4MM **Privately Held**
SIC: 3441 Structural Metal Fabrication

(G-20809)
LABCHEM INC
1010 Jacksons Pointe Ct (16063-2826)
PHONE....................................412 826-5230
Leroy House, *President*
William Nichols, *Vice Pres*
Linda Thier, *CFO*
Janice Umbaugh, *Manager*

▲ **EMP:** 42
SQ FT: 27,000
SALES (est): 12.1MM
SALES (corp-wide): 6.9MM **Privately Held**
WEB: www.labchem.net
SIC: 2899 Chemical preparations
PA: Produits Chimiques Acp Chemicals Inc
4601 Boul Des Grandes-Prairies
Saint-Leonard QC H1R 1
514 327-0323

(G-20810)
MARKOVITZ ENTERPRISES INC (PA)
Also Called: Flowline Division
100 Badger Dr (16063-9726)
PHONE....................................724 452-4500
James S Markovitz, *President*
Brad Hood, *President*
Anthony W Bartley, *Treasurer*
Eric Maser, *Accounting Mgr*
David Bender, *Sales Mgr*
▲ **EMP:** 55 **EST:** 1930
SQ FT: 70,000
SALES (est): 12.8MM **Privately Held**
WEB: www.badgerind.com
SIC: 3498 3462 Pipe fittings, fabricated from purchased pipe; iron & steel forgings

(G-20811)
MOODY CORPORATION
1688 Route 288 (16063-3904)
PHONE....................................724 453-9470
Dalton N Moody, *President*
Mark S Calhoun, *Vice Pres*
John Rhoden, *Engineer*
EMP: 15
SQ FT: 4,000
SALES (est): 3.4MM **Privately Held**
WEB: www.moodycorp.com
SIC: 3599 Machine shop, jobbing & repair

(G-20812)
NELSONS COMPETITION ENGINES
121 Pebble Creek Ln (16063-3133)
PHONE....................................724 538-5282
Henry E Nelson, *Owner*
EMP: 4
SALES: 500K **Privately Held**
SIC: 3944 Engines, miniature

(G-20813)
OVERDRIVE HOLDINGS INC
22073 Perry Hwy (16063-8711)
PHONE....................................724 452-1500
Lou Dimaria, *Branch Mgr*
EMP: 10
SALES (corp-wide): 23.4MM **Privately Held**
SIC: 5013 3714 5531 Trailer parts & accessories; automotive brakes; truck parts & accessories; wheels, motor vehicle; transmissions, motor vehicle; differentials & parts, motor vehicle; truck equipment & parts
PA: Overdrive Holdings, Inc.
2501 Route 73
Cinnaminson NJ
856 665-4445

(G-20814)
PENN FAN INC
22329 Perry Hwy (16063-8921)
P.O. Box 52 (16063-0052)
PHONE....................................724 452-4570
Tony Perry, *President*
Nick Perry, *Marketing Staff*
Terry Tankersley, *Admin Sec*
EMP: 5
SQ FT: 35,000
SALES (est): 786.1K
SALES (corp-wide): 5.6MM **Privately Held**
WEB: www.pennfan.com
SIC: 3564 Air purification equipment
PA: Air Turbine Propeller Company
22329 Perry Hwy
Zelienople PA 16063
724 452-9540

(G-20815)
PENNA FLAME INDUSTRIES INC
1856 Route 588 (16063-3902)
PHONE....................................724 452-8750

James P Orr, *President*
▲ **EMP:** 30
SQ FT: 29,700
SALES (est): 7.7MM **Privately Held**
WEB: www.pennaflame.com
SIC: 3398 3321 3452 3316 Brazing (hardening) of metal; rolling mill rolls, cast iron; bolts, nuts, rivets & washers; cold finishing of steel shapes; blast furnaces & steel mills

(G-20816)
PITTSBURGH JET CENTER
1859 Route 588 (16063-3901)
PHONE....................................724 452-4719
Clayton Pegher, *Principal*
EMP: 14
SALES (est): 2.5MM **Privately Held**
SIC: 3721 Aircraft

(G-20817)
ROBINSON FANS INC (HQ)
400 Robinson Dr (16063)
P.O. Box 100 (16063-0100)
PHONE....................................863 646-5270
Carl E Staible, *President*
Carrie Casey, *Principal*
Alfred Grove, *Principal*
H Leslie Gutzwiller, *Principal*
Peter M Beringer, *Vice Pres*
◆ **EMP:** 275 **EST:** 2008
SQ FT: 85,000
SALES (est): 39.1MM **Privately Held**
WEB: www.robinsonfans.com
SIC: 3564 7699 Blowers & fans; industrial machinery & equipment repair

(G-20818)
ROBINSON FANS HOLDINGS INC (PA)
400 Robinson Dr (16063)
P.O. Box 100 (16063-0100)
PHONE....................................724 452-6121
Carl E Staible, *President*
Doug Bollinger, *Treasurer*
Ronald Marburger, *Treasurer*
Nancy H Staible, *Admin Sec*
EMP: 1
SALES: 57MM **Privately Held**
SIC: 3564 Blowers & fans

(G-20819)
ROCHESTER ALLOY CASTING CO
2 Brookview Ct (16063-9314)
P.O. Box 66 (16063-0066)
PHONE....................................724 452-5659
S Dale Benedum, *President*
EMP: 20
SQ FT: 10,000
SALES (est): 1.8MM **Privately Held**
SIC: 3325 Alloy steel castings, except investment

(G-20820)
SUN ENERGY SERVICES LLC
Deep Well Services
719 W New Castle St (16063-1027)
PHONE....................................724 473-0687
Tracy J Weekley, *Branch Mgr*
EMP: 105 **Privately Held**
SIC: 1382 Oil & gas exploration services
PA: Sun Energy Services Llc
307 W New Castle St
Zelienople PA 16063

(G-20821)
SUN ENERGY SERVICES LLC (PA)
307 W New Castle St (16063-1122)
PHONE....................................724 473-0687
Mark Marmo, *CEO*
EMP: 35
SALES: 28MM **Privately Held**
SIC: 1382 Oil & gas exploration services

(G-20822)
SUPERIOR AUTOGLASS LLC
22056 Perry Hwy (16063-8714)
PHONE....................................724 452-9870
Charles E Spangler III,
EMP: 8
SALES (est): 764.9K **Privately Held**
SIC: 3231 Products of purchased glass

(G-20823)
T SHIRT LOFT
420 S Main St (16063-2522)
PHONE...............................724 452-4380
Linda Cole, *Mng Member*
EMP: 4
SQ FT: 750
SALES (est): 310K Privately Held
SIC: 5699 2759 2396 T-shirts, custom
printed; screen printing; automotive & apparel trimmings

(G-20824)
TIN MAN SWEETS
205 S Main St (16063-1151)
PHONE...............................724 432-3930
EMP: 6 EST: 2012
SALES (est): 289.5K Privately Held
SIC: 3356 Tin

(G-20825)
UNION CHILL MAT CO (PA)
160 Dean Ln (16063-3918)
P.O. Box 250 (16063-0250)
PHONE...............................724 452-6400
Gladys M Gillespie, *President*
Stacie Lowery, *Treasurer*
EMP: 6 EST: 1945
SQ FT: 14,500
SALES (est): 5MM Privately Held
WEB: www.unionchill.com
SIC: 3585 5075 5149 Heating & air conditioning combination units; warm air heating equipment & supplies; coffee, green or roasted; water, distilled

(G-20826)
UNIVERSAL MANUFACTURING CORP
550 W New Castle St (16063-1047)
P.O. Box 220 (16063-0220)
PHONE...............................724 452-8300
Robert L Carbeau Jr, *President*
Terri Rusnock, *Managing Dir*
John Makar, *Purch Mgr*
Michael P O'Halloran, *Treasurer*
Jennifer Corrigan, *Credit Mgr*
◆ EMP: 50
SQ FT: 113,000
SALES (est): 10.7MM Privately Held
WEB: www.universalscaffold.com
SIC: 3446 Scaffolds, mobile or stationary: metal

(G-20827)
URSOFT INC
134 S Main St Ste A (16063-1184)
PHONE...............................724 452-2150
Joel Tipton, *President*
EMP: 15
SALES (est): 1.3MM Privately Held
WEB: www.ursofamily.com
SIC: 7371 7372 Computer software development; prepackaged software

(G-20828)
XYLEM WATER SOLUTIONS USA INC
227 S Division St (16063-1313)
PHONE...............................724 452-6300
Michael J Ulizio, *CEO*
Steven R Loranger, *President*
Robert M Clements, *Vice Pres*
Robert Laird, *Vice Pres*
Richard W Matz, *Vice Pres*
EMP: 17
SALES (est): 4MM Publicly Held
SIC: 3561 Pumps & pumping equipment
PA: Xylem Inc.
1 International Dr
Rye Brook NY 10573

(G-20829)
XYLEM WTR SLTONS ZLIENOPLE LLC
610 W Beaver St (16063-1824)
PHONE...............................724 452-6300
Michael Ulizio, *President*
EMP: 15 Publicly Held
WEB: www.fbleopold.com
SIC: 3599 3823 Machine shop, jobbing & repair; water quality monitoring & control systems

HQ: Xylem Water Solutions Zelienople Llc
227 S Division St Ste 1
Zelienople PA 16063
724 452-6300

(G-20830)
XYLEM WTR SLTONS ZLIENOPLE LLC (HQ)
Also Called: ITT Awt F B Leopold
227 S Division St Ste 1 (16063-1313)
PHONE...............................724 452-6300
Michael J Ulizio, *CEO*
Marvin A Brown, *President*
Steve Schieler, *President*
Rob Laird, *General Mgr*
Robert Clements, *Vice Pres*
◆ EMP: 142
SQ FT: 90,000
SALES (est): 36.1MM Publicly Held
WEB: www.fbleopold.com
SIC: 3589 Water treatment equipment, industrial; sewage treatment equipment

---

Zieglerville
Montgomery County

(G-20831)
AMERICAN CLASSIC MOTORS INC
315 Big Rd (19492-9712)
P.O. Box 298 (19492-0298)
PHONE...............................610 754-8500
David Vulakh, *President*
John Chinofski, *Vice Pres*
Brian Eshbach, *Manager*
Joseph Major, *Manager*
Trey Turner, *Asst Mgr*
EMP: 12
SALES (est): 4.5MM Privately Held
WEB: www.americanclassicmotors.net
SIC: 5571 3711 Motorcycles; motor vehicles & car bodies

(G-20832)
DETAYL MANUFACTURING CO INC
303a Big Rd (19492-9712)
PHONE...............................610 754-7123
Chris Taylor, *President*
Sherry Taylor, *Corp Secy*
Alice Taylor, *Vice Pres*
EMP: 12
SQ FT: 3,500
SALES (est): 1MM Privately Held
SIC: 3599 Machine shop, jobbing & repair

(G-20833)
MASTER REPLICAS GROUP INC
313 Big Rd (19492-9712)
PHONE...............................610 652-2265
Steve Dymzso, *Principal*
EMP: 3
SALES (est): 152.7K Privately Held
SIC: 3369 Aerospace castings, nonferrous: except aluminum

(G-20834)
QUAKER STATE TUBE MFG CORP
Also Called: Spring House Specialty
1303 Gravel Pike Rt 29 (19492)
PHONE...............................610 287-8841
▲ EMP: 20
SQ FT: 25,000
SALES (est): 2.9MM Privately Held
SIC: 3498 Mfg Fabricated Pipe/Fittings

Zionsville
Lehigh County

(G-20835)
HABERLE UPHOLSTERY
6024 Palm Rd (18092-2425)
PHONE...............................215 679-8195
Jessie Haberle, *Principal*
Michael Haberle, *Principal*
EMP: 3
SQ FT: 4,000

SALES (est): 249.1K Privately Held
SIC: 7641 8711 2512 Reupholstery; upholstery work; building construction consultant; upholstered household furniture

(G-20836)
S T M HEAVY DUTY ELECTRIC INC
Also Called: Stm Heavyduty Electric
7601 Chestnut St (18092-2309)
PHONE...............................610 967-3810
Thomas Laessig, *President*
EMP: 10
SQ FT: 6,500
SALES: 2MM Privately Held
SIC: 3694 3621 Alternators, automotive; starters, for motors

(G-20837)
UPPER MILFORD WESTERN DST FIRE
6341 Chestnut St (18092-2111)
P.O. Box 302, Old Zionsville (18068-0302)
PHONE...............................610 966-3541
Daniel J Mohr, *Chairman*
EMP: 3
SALES: 140.1K Privately Held
SIC: 3711 Fire department vehicles (motor vehicles), assembly of

---

Zullinger
Franklin County

(G-20838)
PRO TUBE INC
4872 Zane A Miller Dr (17272)
P.O. Box 146 (17272-0146)
PHONE...............................717 765-9400
William Bowers, *President*
Chris Dawson, *President*
EMP: 18
SQ FT: 18,200
SALES (est): 4.2MM Privately Held
WEB: www.protube.net
SIC: 3498 Tube fabricating (contract bending & shaping)

SIC INDEX

Standard Industrial Classification Alphabetical Index

SIC NO	PRODUCT

A

3291 Abrasive Prdts
2891 Adhesives & Sealants
3563 Air & Gas Compressors
3585 Air Conditioning & Heating Eqpt
3721 Aircraft
3724 Aircraft Engines & Engine Parts
3728 Aircraft Parts & Eqpt, NEC
2812 Alkalies & Chlorine
3363 Aluminum Die Castings
3354 Aluminum Extruded Prdts
3365 Aluminum Foundries
3355 Aluminum Rolling & Drawing, NEC
3353 Aluminum Sheet, Plate & Foil
3483 Ammunition, Large
3826 Analytical Instruments
2077 Animal, Marine Fats & Oils
1231 Anthracite Mining
2389 Apparel & Accessories, NEC
3446 Architectural & Ornamental Metal Work
7694 Armature Rewinding Shops
3292 Asbestos products
2952 Asphalt Felts & Coatings
3822 Automatic Temperature Controls
3581 Automatic Vending Machines
3465 Automotive Stampings
2396 Automotive Trimmings, Apparel Findings, Related Prdts

B

2673 Bags: Plastics, Laminated & Coated
2674 Bags: Uncoated Paper & Multiwall
3562 Ball & Roller Bearings
2836 Biological Prdts, Exc Diagnostic Substances
1221 Bituminous Coal & Lignite: Surface Mining
1222 Bituminous Coal: Underground Mining
2782 Blankbooks & Looseleaf Binders
3312 Blast Furnaces, Coke Ovens, Steel & Rolling Mills
3564 Blowers & Fans
3732 Boat Building & Repairing
3452 Bolts, Nuts, Screws, Rivets & Washers
2732 Book Printing, Not Publishing
2789 Bookbinding
2731 Books: Publishing & Printing
3131 Boot & Shoe Cut Stock & Findings
2342 Brassieres, Girdles & Garments
2051 Bread, Bakery Prdts Exc Cookies & Crackers
3251 Brick & Structural Clay Tile
3991 Brooms & Brushes
3995 Burial Caskets
2021 Butter

C

3578 Calculating & Accounting Eqpt
2064 Candy & Confectionery Prdts
2033 Canned Fruits, Vegetables & Preserves
2032 Canned Specialties
2394 Canvas Prdts
3624 Carbon & Graphite Prdts
2895 Carbon Black
3955 Carbon Paper & Inked Ribbons
3592 Carburetors, Pistons, Rings & Valves
2273 Carpets & Rugs
2823 Cellulosic Man-Made Fibers
3241 Cement, Hydraulic
3253 Ceramic Tile
2043 Cereal Breakfast Foods
2022 Cheese
1479 Chemical & Fertilizer Mining
2899 Chemical Preparations, NEC
2361 Children's & Infants' Dresses & Blouses
3261 China Plumbing Fixtures & Fittings
3262 China, Table & Kitchen Articles
2066 Chocolate & Cocoa Prdts
2111 Cigarettes
2121 Cigars
2257 Circular Knit Fabric Mills
3255 Clay Refractories
1459 Clay, Ceramic & Refractory Minerals, NEC
1241 Coal Mining Svcs
3479 Coating & Engraving, NEC
2095 Coffee
3316 Cold Rolled Steel Sheet, Strip & Bars
3582 Commercial Laundry, Dry Clean & Pressing Mchs
2759 Commercial Printing
2754 Commercial Printing: Gravure
2752 Commercial Printing: Lithographic

3646 Commercial, Indl & Institutional Lighting Fixtures
3669 Communications Eqpt, NEC
3577 Computer Peripheral Eqpt, NEC
3572 Computer Storage Devices
3575 Computer Terminals
3271 Concrete Block & Brick
3272 Concrete Prdts
3531 Construction Machinery & Eqpt
1442 Construction Sand & Gravel
2679 Converted Paper Prdts, NEC
3535 Conveyors & Eqpt
2052 Cookies & Crackers
3366 Copper Foundries
2298 Cordage & Twine
2653 Corrugated & Solid Fiber Boxes
3961 Costume Jewelry & Novelties
2261 Cotton Fabric Finishers
2211 Cotton, Woven Fabric
3466 Crowns & Closures
1311 Crude Petroleum & Natural Gas
1423 Crushed & Broken Granite
1422 Crushed & Broken Limestone
1429 Crushed & Broken Stone, NEC
3643 Current-Carrying Wiring Devices
2391 Curtains & Draperies
3087 Custom Compounding Of Purchased Plastic Resins
3281 Cut Stone Prdts
3421 Cutlery
2865 Cyclic-Crudes, Intermediates, Dyes & Org Pigments

D

3843 Dental Eqpt & Splys
2835 Diagnostic Substances
2675 Die-Cut Paper & Board
3544 Dies, Tools, Jigs, Fixtures & Indl Molds
1411 Dimension Stone
2047 Dog & Cat Food
3942 Dolls & Stuffed Toys
2591 Drapery Hardware, Window Blinds & Shades
2381 Dress & Work Gloves
2034 Dried Fruits, Vegetables & Soup
1381 Drilling Oil & Gas Wells

E

3263 Earthenware, Whiteware, Table & Kitchen Articles
3634 Electric Household Appliances
3641 Electric Lamps
3694 Electrical Eqpt For Internal Combustion Engines
3629 Electrical Indl Apparatus, NEC
3699 Electrical Machinery, Eqpt & Splys, NEC
3845 Electromedical & Electrotherapeutic Apparatus
3313 Electrometallurgical Prdts
3675 Electronic Capacitors
3677 Electronic Coils & Transformers
3679 Electronic Components, NEC
3571 Electronic Computers
3678 Electronic Connectors
3676 Electronic Resistors
3471 Electroplating, Plating, Polishing, Anodizing & Coloring
3534 Elevators & Moving Stairways
3431 Enameled Iron & Metal Sanitary Ware
2677 Envelopes
2892 Explosives

F

2241 Fabric Mills, Cotton, Wool, Silk & Man-Made
3499 Fabricated Metal Prdts, NEC
3498 Fabricated Pipe & Pipe Fittings
3443 Fabricated Plate Work
3069 Fabricated Rubber Prdts, NEC
3441 Fabricated Structural Steel
2399 Fabricated Textile Prdts, NEC
2295 Fabrics Coated Not Rubberized
2297 Fabrics, Nonwoven
3523 Farm Machinery & Eqpt
3965 Fasteners, Buttons, Needles & Pins
1061 Ferroalloy Ores, Except Vanadium
2875 Fertilizers, Mixing Only
2655 Fiber Cans, Tubes & Drums
2091 Fish & Seafoods, Canned & Cured
2092 Fish & Seafoods, Fresh & Frozen
3211 Flat Glass
2087 Flavoring Extracts & Syrups
2045 Flour, Blended & Prepared
2041 Flour, Grain Milling
3824 Fluid Meters & Counters

3593 Fluid Power Cylinders & Actuators
3594 Fluid Power Pumps & Motors
3492 Fluid Power Valves & Hose Fittings
2657 Folding Paperboard Boxes
3556 Food Prdts Machinery
2099 Food Preparations, NEC
3149 Footwear, NEC
2053 Frozen Bakery Prdts
2037 Frozen Fruits, Juices & Vegetables
2038 Frozen Specialties
2371 Fur Goods
2599 Furniture & Fixtures, NEC

G

3944 Games, Toys & Children's Vehicles
3524 Garden, Lawn Tractors & Eqpt
3053 Gaskets, Packing & Sealing Devices
2369 Girls' & Infants' Outerwear, NEC
3221 Glass Containers
3231 Glass Prdts Made Of Purchased Glass
3321 Gray Iron Foundries
2771 Greeting Card Publishing
3769 Guided Missile/Space Vehicle Parts & Eqpt, NEC
3764 Guided Missile/Space Vehicle Propulsion Units & parts
3761 Guided Missiles & Space Vehicles
2861 Gum & Wood Chemicals
3275 Gypsum Prdts

H

3423 Hand & Edge Tools
3425 Hand Saws & Saw Blades
3171 Handbags & Purses
3429 Hardware, NEC
2426 Hardwood Dimension & Flooring Mills
2435 Hardwood Veneer & Plywood
2353 Hats, Caps & Millinery
3433 Heating Eqpt
3536 Hoists, Cranes & Monorails
2252 Hosiery, Except Women's
2251 Hosiery, Women's Full & Knee Length
2392 House furnishings: Textile
3639 Household Appliances, NEC
3651 Household Audio & Video Eqpt
3631 Household Cooking Eqpt
2519 Household Furniture, NEC
3635 Household Vacuum Cleaners

I

2097 Ice
2024 Ice Cream
2819 Indl Inorganic Chemicals, NEC
3823 Indl Instruments For Meas, Display & Control
3569 Indl Machinery & Eqpt, NEC
3567 Indl Process Furnaces & Ovens
3537 Indl Trucks, Tractors, Trailers & Stackers
2813 Industrial Gases
2869 Industrial Organic Chemicals, NEC
3543 Industrial Patterns
1446 Industrial Sand
3491 Industrial Valves
2816 Inorganic Pigments
3825 Instrs For Measuring & Testing Electricity
3519 Internal Combustion Engines, NEC
3462 Iron & Steel Forgings
1011 Iron Ores

J

3915 Jewelers Findings & Lapidary Work
3911 Jewelry: Precious Metal

K

1455 Kaolin & Ball Clay
2253 Knit Outerwear Mills
2254 Knit Underwear Mills
2259 Knitting Mills, NEC

L

3821 Laboratory Apparatus & Furniture
2258 Lace & Warp Knit Fabric Mills
3952 Lead Pencils, Crayons & Artist's Mtrls
2386 Leather & Sheep Lined Clothing
3151 Leather Gloves & Mittens
3199 Leather Goods, NEC
3111 Leather Tanning & Finishing
3648 Lighting Eqpt, NEC
3274 Lime
3996 Linoleum & Hard Surface Floor Coverings, NEC

S I C

SIC NO	PRODUCT
2085	Liquors, Distilled, Rectified & Blended
2411	Logging
2992	Lubricating Oils & Greases
3161	Luggage

M

SIC NO	PRODUCT
2098	Macaroni, Spaghetti & Noodles
3545	Machine Tool Access
3541	Machine Tools: Cutting
3542	Machine Tools: Forming
3599	Machinery & Eqpt, Indl & Commercial, NEC
3322	Malleable Iron Foundries
2083	Malt
2082	Malt Beverages
2761	Manifold Business Forms
3999	Manufacturing Industries, NEC
3953	Marking Devices
2515	Mattresses & Bedsprings
3829	Measuring & Controlling Devices, NEC
3586	Measuring & Dispensing Pumps
2011	Meat Packing Plants
3568	Mechanical Power Transmission Eqpt, NEC
2833	Medicinal Chemicals & Botanical Prdts
2329	Men's & Boys' Clothing, NEC
2323	Men's & Boys' Neckwear
2325	Men's & Boys' Separate Trousers & Casual Slacks
2321	Men's & Boys' Shirts
2311	Men's & Boys' Suits, Coats & Overcoats
2322	Men's & Boys' Underwear & Nightwear
2326	Men's & Boys' Work Clothing
3143	Men's Footwear, Exc Athletic
3412	Metal Barrels, Drums, Kegs & Pails
3411	Metal Cans
3442	Metal Doors, Sash, Frames, Molding & Trim
3497	Metal Foil & Leaf
3398	Metal Heat Treating
2514	Metal Household Furniture
1081	Metal Mining Svcs
1099	Metal Ores, NEC
3469	Metal Stampings, NEC
3549	Metalworking Machinery, NEC
2026	Milk
2023	Milk, Condensed & Evaporated
2431	Millwork
3296	Mineral Wool
3295	Minerals & Earths: Ground Or Treated
3532	Mining Machinery & Eqpt
3496	Misc Fabricated Wire Prdts
2741	Misc Publishing
3449	Misc Structural Metal Work
1499	Miscellaneous Nonmetallic Mining
2451	Mobile Homes
3061	Molded, Extruded & Lathe-Cut Rubber Mechanical Goods
3716	Motor Homes
3714	Motor Vehicle Parts & Access
3711	Motor Vehicles & Car Bodies
3751	Motorcycles, Bicycles & Parts
3621	Motors & Generators
3931	Musical Instruments

N

SIC NO	PRODUCT
1321	Natural Gas Liquids
2711	Newspapers: Publishing & Printing
2873	Nitrogenous Fertilizers
3297	Nonclay Refractories
3644	Noncurrent-Carrying Wiring Devices
3364	Nonferrous Die Castings, Exc Aluminum
3463	Nonferrous Forgings
3369	Nonferrous Foundries: Castings, NEC
3357	Nonferrous Wire Drawing
3299	Nonmetallic Mineral Prdts, NEC
1481	Nonmetallic Minerals Svcs, Except Fuels

O

SIC NO	PRODUCT
2522	Office Furniture, Except Wood
3579	Office Machines, NEC
1382	Oil & Gas Field Exploration Svcs
1389	Oil & Gas Field Svcs, NEC
3533	Oil Field Machinery & Eqpt
3851	Ophthalmic Goods
3827	Optical Instruments
3489	Ordnance & Access, NEC
3842	Orthopedic, Prosthetic & Surgical Appliances/Splys

P

SIC NO	PRODUCT
3565	Packaging Machinery
2851	Paints, Varnishes, Lacquers, Enamels
2671	Paper Coating & Laminating for Packaging
2672	Paper Coating & Laminating, Exc for Packaging
3554	Paper Inds Machinery
2621	Paper Mills
2631	Paperboard Mills
2542	Partitions & Fixtures, Except Wood
2951	Paving Mixtures & Blocks
3951	Pens & Mechanical Pencils
2844	Perfumes, Cosmetics & Toilet Preparations
2721	Periodicals: Publishing & Printing
3172	Personal Leather Goods
2879	Pesticides & Agricultural Chemicals, NEC
2911	Petroleum Refining
2834	Pharmaceuticals
3652	Phonograph Records & Magnetic Tape
2874	Phosphatic Fertilizers
3861	Photographic Eqpt & Splys
2035	Pickled Fruits, Vegetables, Sauces & Dressings
3085	Plastic Bottles
3086	Plastic Foam Prdts
3083	Plastic Laminated Plate & Sheet
3084	Plastic Pipe
3088	Plastic Plumbing Fixtures
3089	Plastic Prdts
3082	Plastic Unsupported Profile Shapes
3081	Plastic Unsupported Sheet & Film
2821	Plastics, Mtrls & Nonvulcanizable Elastomers
2796	Platemaking & Related Svcs
2395	Pleating & Stitching For The Trade
3432	Plumbing Fixture Fittings & Trim, Brass
3264	Porcelain Electrical Splys
2096	Potato Chips & Similar Prdts
3269	Pottery Prdts, NEC
2015	Poultry Slaughtering, Dressing & Processing
3546	Power Hand Tools
3612	Power, Distribution & Specialty Transformers
3448	Prefabricated Metal Buildings & Cmpnts
2452	Prefabricated Wood Buildings & Cmpnts
7372	Prepackaged Software
2048	Prepared Feeds For Animals & Fowls
3229	Pressed & Blown Glassware, NEC
3692	Primary Batteries: Dry & Wet
3399	Primary Metal Prdts, NEC
3339	Primary Nonferrous Metals, NEC
3334	Primary Production Of Aluminum
3331	Primary Smelting & Refining Of Copper
3672	Printed Circuit Boards
2893	Printing Ink
3555	Printing Trades Machinery & Eqpt
2999	Products Of Petroleum & Coal, NEC
2531	Public Building & Related Furniture
2611	Pulp Mills
3561	Pumps & Pumping Eqpt

R

SIC NO	PRODUCT
3663	Radio & T V Communications, Systs & Eqpt, Broadcast/Studio
3671	Radio & T V Receiving Electron Tubes
3743	Railroad Eqpt
3273	Ready-Mixed Concrete
2493	Reconstituted Wood Prdts
3695	Recording Media
3625	Relays & Indl Controls
3645	Residential Lighting Fixtures
2384	Robes & Dressing Gowns
3547	Rolling Mill Machinery & Eqpt
3351	Rolling, Drawing & Extruding Of Copper
3356	Rolling, Drawing-Extruding Of Nonferrous Metals
3021	Rubber & Plastic Footwear
3052	Rubber & Plastic Hose & Belting

S

SIC NO	PRODUCT
2068	Salted & Roasted Nuts & Seeds
2656	Sanitary Food Containers
2676	Sanitary Paper Prdts
2013	Sausages & Meat Prdts
2421	Saw & Planing Mills
3596	Scales & Balances, Exc Laboratory
2397	Schiffli Machine Embroideries
3451	Screw Machine Prdts
3812	Search, Detection, Navigation & Guidance Systs & Instrs
3341	Secondary Smelting & Refining Of Nonferrous Metals
3674	Semiconductors
3589	Service Ind Machines, NEC
2652	Set-Up Paperboard Boxes
3444	Sheet Metal Work
3731	Shipbuilding & Repairing
2079	Shortening, Oils & Margarine
3993	Signs & Advertising Displays
2262	Silk & Man-Made Fabric Finishers
2221	Silk & Man-Made Fiber
1044	Silver Ores
3914	Silverware, Plated & Stainless Steel Ware
3484	Small Arms
3482	Small Arms Ammunition
2841	Soap & Detergents
2086	Soft Drinks
2436	Softwood Veneer & Plywood
2075	Soybean Oil Mills
2842	Spec Cleaning, Polishing & Sanitation Preparations
3559	Special Ind Machinery, NEC
2429	Special Prdt Sawmills, NEC
3566	Speed Changers, Drives & Gears
3949	Sporting & Athletic Goods, NEC
2678	Stationery Prdts
3511	Steam, Gas & Hydraulic Turbines & Engines
3325	Steel Foundries, NEC
3324	Steel Investment Foundries
3317	Steel Pipe & Tubes
3493	Steel Springs, Except Wire
3315	Steel Wire Drawing & Nails & Spikes
3691	Storage Batteries
3259	Structural Clay Prdts, NEC
2439	Structural Wood Members, NEC
2063	Sugar, Beet
2061	Sugar, Cane
2062	Sugar, Cane Refining
2843	Surface Active & Finishing Agents, Sulfonated Oils
3841	Surgical & Medical Instrs & Apparatus
3613	Switchgear & Switchboard Apparatus
2824	Synthetic Organic Fibers, Exc Cellulosic
2822	Synthetic Rubber (Vulcanizable Elastomers)

T

SIC NO	PRODUCT
3795	Tanks & Tank Components
3661	Telephone & Telegraph Apparatus
2393	Textile Bags
2269	Textile Finishers, NEC
2299	Textile Goods, NEC
3552	Textile Machinery
2284	Thread Mills
2296	Tire Cord & Fabric
3011	Tires & Inner Tubes
2141	Tobacco Stemming & Redrying
2131	Tobacco, Chewing & Snuff
3799	Transportation Eqpt, NEC
3792	Travel Trailers & Campers
3713	Truck & Bus Bodies
3715	Truck Trailers
2791	Typesetting

V

SIC NO	PRODUCT
3494	Valves & Pipe Fittings, NEC
2076	Vegetable Oil Mills
3647	Vehicular Lighting Eqpt

W

SIC NO	PRODUCT
3873	Watch & Clock Devices & Parts
2385	Waterproof Outerwear
3548	Welding Apparatus
7692	Welding Repair
2046	Wet Corn Milling
2084	Wine & Brandy
3495	Wire Springs
2331	Women's & Misses' Blouses
2335	Women's & Misses' Dresses
2339	Women's & Misses' Outerwear, NEC
2337	Women's & Misses' Suits, Coats & Skirts
3144	Women's Footwear, Exc Athletic
2341	Women's, Misses' & Children's Underwear & Nightwear
2441	Wood Boxes
2449	Wood Containers, NEC
2511	Wood Household Furniture
2512	Wood Household Furniture, Upholstered
2434	Wood Kitchen Cabinets
2521	Wood Office Furniture
2448	Wood Pallets & Skids
2499	Wood Prdts, NEC
2491	Wood Preserving
2517	Wood T V, Radio, Phono & Sewing Cabinets
2541	Wood, Office & Store Fixtures
3553	Woodworking Machinery
2231	Wool, Woven Fabric

X

SIC NO	PRODUCT
3844	X-ray Apparatus & Tubes

Y

SIC NO	PRODUCT
2281	Yarn Spinning Mills
2282	Yarn Texturizing, Throwing, Twisting & Winding Mills

SIC INDEX

Standard Industrial Classification Numerical Index

SIC NO	PRODUCT

10 metal mining
1011 Iron Ores
1044 Silver Ores
1061 Ferroalloy Ores, Except Vanadium
1081 Metal Mining Svcs
1099 Metal Ores, NEC

12 coal mining
1221 Bituminous Coal & Lignite: Surface Mining
1222 Bituminous Coal: Underground Mining
1231 Anthracite Mining
1241 Coal Mining Svcs

13 oil and gas extraction
1311 Crude Petroleum & Natural Gas
1321 Natural Gas Liquids
1381 Drilling Oil & Gas Wells
1382 Oil & Gas Field Exploration Svcs
1389 Oil & Gas Field Svcs, NEC

14 mining and quarrying of nonmetallic minerals, except fuels
1411 Dimension Stone
1422 Crushed & Broken Limestone
1423 Crushed & Broken Granite
1429 Crushed & Broken Stone, NEC
1442 Construction Sand & Gravel
1446 Industrial Sand
1455 Kaolin & Ball Clay
1459 Clay, Ceramic & Refractory Minerals, NEC
1479 Chemical & Fertilizer Mining
1481 Nonmetallic Minerals Svcs, Except Fuels
1499 Miscellaneous Nonmetallic Mining

20 food and kindred products
2011 Meat Packing Plants
2013 Sausages & Meat Prdts
2015 Poultry Slaughtering, Dressing & Processing
2021 Butter
2022 Cheese
2023 Milk, Condensed & Evaporated
2024 Ice Cream
2026 Milk
2032 Canned Specialties
2033 Canned Fruits, Vegetables & Preserves
2034 Dried Fruits, Vegetables & Soup
2035 Pickled Fruits, Vegetables, Sauces & Dressings
2037 Frozen Fruits, Juices & Vegetables
2038 Frozen Specialties
2041 Flour, Grain Milling
2043 Cereal Breakfast Foods
2045 Flour, Blended & Prepared
2046 Wet Corn Milling
2047 Dog & Cat Food
2048 Prepared Feeds For Animals & Fowls
2051 Bread, Bakery Prdts Exc Cookies & Crackers
2052 Cookies & Crackers
2053 Frozen Bakery Prdts
2061 Sugar, Cane
2062 Sugar, Cane Refining
2063 Sugar, Beet
2064 Candy & Confectionery Prdts
2066 Chocolate & Cocoa Prdts
2068 Salted & Roasted Nuts & Seeds
2075 Soybean Oil Mills
2076 Vegetable Oil Mills
2077 Animal, Marine Fats & Oils
2079 Shortening, Oils & Margarine
2082 Malt Beverages
2083 Malt
2084 Wine & Brandy
2085 Liquors, Distilled, Rectified & Blended
2086 Soft Drinks
2087 Flavoring Extracts & Syrups
2091 Fish & Seafoods, Canned & Cured
2092 Fish & Seafoods, Fresh & Frozen
2095 Coffee
2096 Potato Chips & Similar Prdts
2097 Ice
2098 Macaroni, Spaghetti & Noodles
2099 Food Preparations, NEC

21 tobacco products
2111 Cigarettes
2121 Cigars
2131 Tobacco, Chewing & Snuff
2141 Tobacco Stemming & Redrying

22 textile mill products
2211 Cotton, Woven Fabric
2221 Silk & Man-Made Fiber
2231 Wool, Woven Fabric
2241 Fabric Mills, Cotton, Wool, Silk & Man-Made
2251 Hosiery, Women's Full & Knee Length
2252 Hosiery, Except Women's
2253 Knit Outerwear Mills
2254 Knit Underwear Mills
2257 Circular Knit Fabric Mills
2258 Lace & Warp Knit Fabric Mills
2259 Knitting Mills, NEC
2261 Cotton Fabric Finishers
2262 Silk & Man-Made Fabric Finishers
2269 Textile Finishers, NEC
2273 Carpets & Rugs
2281 Yarn Spinning Mills
2282 Yarn Texturizing, Throwing, Twisting & Winding Mills
2284 Thread Mills
2295 Fabrics Coated Not Rubberized
2296 Tire Cord & Fabric
2297 Fabrics, Nonwoven
2298 Cordage & Twine
2299 Textile Goods, NEC

23 apparel and other finished products made from fabrics and similar material
2311 Men's & Boys' Suits, Coats & Overcoats
2321 Men's & Boys' Shirts
2322 Men's & Boys' Underwear & Nightwear
2323 Men's & Boys' Neckwear
2325 Men's & Boys' Separate Trousers & Casual Slacks
2326 Men's & Boys' Work Clothing
2329 Men's & Boys' Clothing, NEC
2331 Women's & Misses' Blouses
2335 Women's & Misses' Dresses
2337 Women's & Misses' Suits, Coats & Skirts
2339 Women's & Misses' Outerwear, NEC
2341 Women's, Misses' & Children's Underwear & Nightwear
2342 Brassieres, Girdles & Garments
2353 Hats, Caps & Millinery
2361 Children's & Infants' Dresses & Blouses
2369 Girls' & Infants' Outerwear, NEC
2371 Fur Goods
2381 Dress & Work Gloves
2384 Robes & Dressing Gowns
2385 Waterproof Outerwear
2386 Leather & Sheep Lined Clothing
2389 Apparel & Accessories, NEC
2391 Curtains & Draperies
2392 House furnishings: Textile
2393 Textile Bags
2394 Canvas Prdts
2395 Pleating & Stitching For The Trade
2396 Automotive Trimmings, Apparel Findings, Related Prdts
2397 Schiffli Machine Embroideries
2399 Fabricated Textile Prdts, NEC

24 lumber and wood products, except furniture
2411 Logging
2421 Saw & Planing Mills
2426 Hardwood Dimension & Flooring Mills
2429 Special Prdt Sawmills, NEC
2431 Millwork
2434 Wood Kitchen Cabinets
2435 Hardwood Veneer & Plywood
2436 Softwood Veneer & Plywood
2439 Structural Wood Members, NEC
2441 Wood Boxes
2448 Wood Pallets & Skids
2449 Wood Containers, NEC
2451 Mobile Homes
2452 Prefabricated Wood Buildings & Cmpnts
2491 Wood Preserving
2493 Reconstituted Wood Prdts
2499 Wood Prdts, NEC

25 furniture and fixtures
2511 Wood Household Furniture
2512 Wood Household Furniture, Upholstered
2514 Metal Household Furniture
2515 Mattresses & Bedsprings
2517 Wood T V, Radio, Phono & Sewing Cabinets
2519 Household Furniture, NEC
2521 Wood Office Furniture
2522 Office Furniture, Except Wood
2531 Public Building & Related Furniture
2541 Wood, Office & Store Fixtures
2542 Partitions & Fixtures, Except Wood
2591 Drapery Hardware, Window Blinds & Shades
2599 Furniture & Fixtures, NEC

26 paper and allied products
2611 Pulp Mills
2621 Paper Mills
2631 Paperboard Mills
2652 Set-Up Paperboard Boxes
2653 Corrugated & Solid Fiber Boxes
2655 Fiber Cans, Tubes & Drums
2656 Sanitary Food Containers
2657 Folding Paperboard Boxes
2671 Paper Coating & Laminating for Packaging
2672 Paper Coating & Laminating, Exc for Packaging
2673 Bags: Plastics, Laminated & Coated
2674 Bags: Uncoated Paper & Multiwall
2675 Die-Cut Paper & Board
2676 Sanitary Paper Prdts
2677 Envelopes
2678 Stationery Prdts
2679 Converted Paper Prdts, NEC

27 printing, publishing, and allied industries
2711 Newspapers: Publishing & Printing
2721 Periodicals: Publishing & Printing
2731 Books: Publishing & Printing
2732 Book Printing, Not Publishing
2741 Misc Publishing
2752 Commercial Printing: Lithographic
2754 Commercial Printing: Gravure
2759 Commercial Printing
2761 Manifold Business Forms
2771 Greeting Card Publishing
2782 Blankbooks & Looseleaf Binders
2789 Bookbinding
2791 Typesetting
2796 Platemaking & Related Svcs

28 chemicals and allied products
2812 Alkalies & Chlorine
2813 Industrial Gases
2816 Inorganic Pigments
2819 Indl Inorganic Chemicals, NEC
2821 Plastics, Mtrls & Nonvulcanizable Elastomers
2822 Synthetic Rubber (Vulcanizable Elastomers)
2823 Cellulosic Man-Made Fibers
2824 Synthetic Organic Fibers, Exc Cellulosic
2833 Medicinal Chemicals & Botanical Prdts
2834 Pharmaceuticals
2835 Diagnostic Substances
2836 Biological Prdts, Exc Diagnostic Substances
2841 Soap & Detergents
2842 Spec Cleaning, Polishing & Sanitation Preparations
2843 Surface Active & Finishing Agents, Sulfonated Oils
2844 Perfumes, Cosmetics & Toilet Preparations
2851 Paints, Varnishes, Lacquers, Enamels
2861 Gum & Wood Chemicals
2865 Cyclic-Crudes, Intermediates, Dyes & Org Pigments
2869 Industrial Organic Chemicals, NEC
2873 Nitrogenous Fertilizers
2874 Phosphatic Fertilizers
2875 Fertilizers, Mixing Only
2879 Pesticides & Agricultural Chemicals, NEC
2891 Adhesives & Sealants
2892 Explosives
2893 Printing Ink
2895 Carbon Black
2899 Chemical Preparations, NEC

29 petroleum refining and related industries
2911 Petroleum Refining

SIC NO	PRODUCT

2951 Paving Mixtures & Blocks
2952 Asphalt Felts & Coatings
2992 Lubricating Oils & Greases
2999 Products Of Petroleum & Coal, NEC

30 rubber and miscellaneous plastics products

3011 Tires & Inner Tubes
3021 Rubber & Plastic Footwear
3052 Rubber & Plastic Hose & Belting
3053 Gaskets, Packing & Sealing Devices
3061 Molded, Extruded & Lathe-Cut Rubber Mechanical Goods
3069 Fabricated Rubber Prdts, NEC
3081 Plastic Unsupported Sheet & Film
3082 Plastic Unsupported Profile Shapes
3083 Plastic Laminated Plate & Sheet
3084 Plastic Pipe
3085 Plastic Bottles
3086 Plastic Foam Prdts
3087 Custom Compounding Of Purchased Plastic Resins
3088 Plastic Plumbing Fixtures
3089 Plastic Prdts

31 leather and leather products

3111 Leather Tanning & Finishing
3131 Boot & Shoe Cut Stock & Findings
3143 Men's Footwear, Exc Athletic
3144 Women's Footwear, Exc Athletic
3149 Footwear, NEC
3151 Leather Gloves & Mittens
3161 Luggage
3171 Handbags & Purses
3172 Personal Leather Goods
3199 Leather Goods, NEC

32 stone, clay, glass, and concrete products

3211 Flat Glass
3221 Glass Containers
3229 Pressed & Blown Glassware, NEC
3231 Glass Prdts Made Of Purchased Glass
3241 Cement, Hydraulic
3251 Brick & Structural Clay Tile
3253 Ceramic Tile
3255 Clay Refractories
3259 Structural Clay Prdts, NEC
3261 China Plumbing Fixtures & Fittings
3262 China, Table & Kitchen Articles
3263 Earthenware, Whiteware, Table & Kitchen Articles
3264 Porcelain Electrical Splys
3269 Pottery Prdts, NEC
3271 Concrete Block & Brick
3272 Concrete Prdts
3273 Ready-Mixed Concrete
3274 Lime
3275 Gypsum Prdts
3281 Cut Stone Prdts
3291 Abrasive Prdts
3292 Asbestos products
3295 Minerals & Earths: Ground Or Treated
3296 Mineral Wool
3297 Nonclay Refractories
3299 Nonmetallic Mineral Prdts, NEC

33 primary metal industries

3312 Blast Furnaces, Coke Ovens, Steel & Rolling Mills
3313 Electrometallurgical Prdts
3315 Steel Wire Drawing & Nails & Spikes
3316 Cold Rolled Steel Sheet, Strip & Bars
3317 Steel Pipe & Tubes
3321 Gray Iron Foundries
3322 Malleable Iron Foundries
3324 Steel Investment Foundries
3325 Steel Foundries, NEC
3331 Primary Smelting & Refining Of Copper
3334 Primary Production Of Aluminum
3339 Primary Nonferrous Metals, NEC
3341 Secondary Smelting & Refining Of Nonferrous Metals
3351 Rolling, Drawing & Extruding Of Copper
3353 Aluminum Sheet, Plate & Foil
3354 Aluminum Extruded Prdts
3355 Aluminum Rolling & Drawing, NEC
3356 Rolling, Drawing-Extruding Of Nonferrous Metals
3357 Nonferrous Wire Drawing
3363 Aluminum Die Castings
3364 Nonferrous Die Castings, Exc Aluminum
3365 Aluminum Foundries
3366 Copper Foundries
3369 Nonferrous Foundries: Castings, NEC
3398 Metal Heat Treating
3399 Primary Metal Prdts, NEC

34 fabricated metal products, except machinery and transportation equipment

3411 Metal Cans
3412 Metal Barrels, Drums, Kegs & Pails
3421 Cutlery
3423 Hand & Edge Tools
3425 Hand Saws & Saw Blades
3429 Hardware, NEC
3431 Enameled Iron & Metal Sanitary Ware
3432 Plumbing Fixture Fittings & Trim, Brass
3433 Heating Eqpt
3441 Fabricated Structural Steel
3442 Metal Doors, Sash, Frames, Molding & Trim
3443 Fabricated Plate Work
3444 Sheet Metal Work
3446 Architectural & Ornamental Metal Work
3448 Prefabricated Metal Buildings & Cmpnts
3449 Misc Structural Metal Work
3451 Screw Machine Prdts
3452 Bolts, Nuts, Screws, Rivets & Washers
3462 Iron & Steel Forgings
3463 Nonferrous Forgings
3465 Automotive Stampings
3466 Crowns & Closures
3469 Metal Stampings, NEC
3471 Electroplating, Plating, Polishing, Anodizing & Coloring
3479 Coating & Engraving, NEC
3482 Small Arms Ammunition
3483 Ammunition, Large
3484 Small Arms
3489 Ordnance & Access, NEC
3491 Industrial Valves
3492 Fluid Power Valves & Hose Fittings
3493 Steel Springs, Except Wire
3494 Valves & Pipe Fittings, NEC
3495 Wire Springs
3496 Misc Fabricated Wire Prdts
3497 Metal Foil & Leaf
3498 Fabricated Pipe & Pipe Fittings
3499 Fabricated Metal Prdts, NEC

35 industrial and commercial machinery and computer equipment

3511 Steam, Gas & Hydraulic Turbines & Engines
3519 Internal Combustion Engines, NEC
3523 Farm Machinery & Eqpt
3524 Garden, Lawn Tractors & Eqpt
3531 Construction Machinery & Eqpt
3532 Mining Machinery & Eqpt
3533 Oil Field Machinery & Eqpt
3534 Elevators & Moving Stairways
3535 Conveyors & Eqpt
3536 Hoists, Cranes & Monorails
3537 Indl Trucks, Tractors, Trailers & Stackers
3541 Machine Tools: Cutting
3542 Machine Tools: Forming
3543 Industrial Patterns
3544 Dies, Tools, Jigs, Fixtures & Indl Molds
3545 Machine Tool Access
3546 Power Hand Tools
3547 Rolling Mill Machinery & Eqpt
3548 Welding Apparatus
3549 Metalworking Machinery, NEC
3552 Textile Machinery
3553 Woodworking Machinery
3554 Paper Inds Machinery
3555 Printing Trades Machinery & Eqpt
3556 Food Prdts Machinery
3559 Special Ind Machinery, NEC
3561 Pumps & Pumping Eqpt
3562 Ball & Roller Bearings
3563 Air & Gas Compressors
3564 Blowers & Fans
3565 Packaging Machinery
3566 Speed Changers, Drives & Gears
3567 Indl Process Furnaces & Ovens
3568 Mechanical Power Transmission Eqpt, NEC
3569 Indl Machinery & Eqpt, NEC
3571 Electronic Computers
3572 Computer Storage Devices
3575 Computer Terminals
3577 Computer Peripheral Eqpt, NEC
3578 Calculating & Accounting Eqpt
3579 Office Machines, NEC
3581 Automatic Vending Machines
3582 Commercial Laundry, Dry Clean & Pressing Mchs
3585 Air Conditioning & Heating Eqpt
3586 Measuring & Dispensing Pumps
3589 Service Ind Machines, NEC

3592 Carburetors, Pistons, Rings & Valves
3593 Fluid Power Cylinders & Actuators
3594 Fluid Power Pumps & Motors
3596 Scales & Balances, Exc Laboratory
3599 Machinery & Eqpt, Indl & Commercial, NEC

36 electronic and other electrical equipment and components, except computer

3612 Power, Distribution & Specialty Transformers
3613 Switchgear & Switchboard Apparatus
3621 Motors & Generators
3624 Carbon & Graphite Prdts
3625 Relays & Indl Controls
3629 Electrical Indl Apparatus, NEC
3631 Household Cooking Eqpt
3634 Electric Household Appliances
3635 Household Vacuum Cleaners
3639 Household Appliances, NEC
3641 Electric Lamps
3643 Current-Carrying Wiring Devices
3644 Noncurrent-Carrying Wiring Devices
3645 Residential Lighting Fixtures
3646 Commercial, Indl & Institutional Lighting Fixtures
3647 Vehicular Lighting Eqpt
3648 Lighting Eqpt, NEC
3651 Household Audio & Video Eqpt
3652 Phonograph Records & Magnetic Tape
3661 Telephone & Telegraph Apparatus
3663 Radio & T V Communications, Systs & Eqpt, Broadcast/Studio
3669 Communications Eqpt, NEC
3671 Radio & T V Receiving Electron Tubes
3672 Printed Circuit Boards
3674 Semiconductors
3675 Electronic Capacitors
3676 Electronic Resistors
3677 Electronic Coils & Transformers
3678 Electronic Connectors
3679 Electronic Components, NEC
3691 Storage Batteries
3692 Primary Batteries: Dry & Wet
3694 Electrical Eqpt For Internal Combustion Engines
3695 Recording Media
3699 Electrical Machinery, Eqpt & Splys, NEC

37 transportation equipment

3711 Motor Vehicles & Car Bodies
3713 Truck & Bus Bodies
3714 Motor Vehicle Parts & Access
3715 Truck Trailers
3716 Motor Homes
3721 Aircraft
3724 Aircraft Engines & Engine Parts
3728 Aircraft Parts & Eqpt, NEC
3731 Shipbuilding & Repairing
3732 Boat Building & Repairing
3743 Railroad Eqpt
3751 Motorcycles, Bicycles & Parts
3761 Guided Missiles & Space Vehicles
3764 Guided Missile/Space Vehicle Propulsion Units & parts
3769 Guided Missile/Space Vehicle Parts & Eqpt, NEC
3792 Travel Trailers & Campers
3795 Tanks & Tank Components
3799 Transportation Eqpt, NEC

38 measuring, analyzing and controlling instruments; photographic, medical an

3812 Search, Detection, Navigation & Guidance Systs & Instrs
3821 Laboratory Apparatus & Furniture
3822 Automatic Temperature Controls
3823 Indl Instruments For Meas, Display & Control
3824 Fluid Meters & Counters
3825 Instrs For Measuring & Testing Electricity
3826 Analytical Instruments
3827 Optical Instruments
3829 Measuring & Controlling Devices, NEC
3841 Surgical & Medical Instrs & Apparatus
3842 Orthopedic, Prosthetic & Surgical Appliances/Splys
3843 Dental Eqpt & Splys
3844 X-ray Apparatus & Tubes
3845 Electromedical & Electrotherapeutic Apparatus
3851 Ophthalmic Goods
3861 Photographic Eqpt & Splys
3873 Watch & Clock Devices & Parts

39 miscellaneous manufacturing industries

3911 Jewelry: Precious Metal
3914 Silverware, Plated & Stainless Steel Ware
3915 Jewelers Findings & Lapidary Work
3931 Musical Instruments

SIC

SIC SECTION

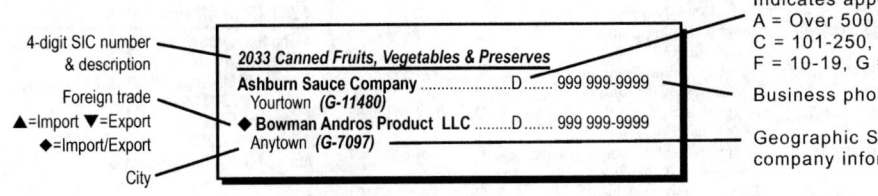

4-digit SIC number & description

Foreign trade
▲=Import ▼=Export
◆=Import/Export
City

2033 Canned Fruits, Vegetables & Preserves
Ashburn Sauce Company ....D 999 999-9999
Yourtown *(G-11480)*
◆ **Bowman Andros Product LLC** ....D 999 999-9999
Anytown *(G-7097)*

Indicates approximate employment figure
A = Over 500 employees, B = 251-500
C = 101-250, D = 51-100, E = 20-50
F = 10-19, G = 3-9

Business phone

Geographic Section entry number where full company information appears.

See footnotes for symbols and codes identification.

• The SIC codes in this section are from the latest Standard Industrial Classification manual published by the U.S. Government's Office of Management and Budget. For more information regarding SICs, see the Explanatory Notes.

• Companies may be listed under multiple classifications.

10 METAL MINING

1011 Iron Ores

Horlacher & Sherwood ....G... 570 836-6298
Tunkhannock *(G-18539)*
Mountaineer Mining Corporation ....G... 814 445-5806
Berlin *(G-1291)*
◆ **Norton Oglebay Company** ....F... 412 995-5500
Pittsburgh *(G-15347)*
Thyssnkrupp Indus Slutions USA ....D...... 412 257-8277
Bridgeville *(G-2095)*

1044 Silver Ores

Cleogeo Inc ....G... 610 868-7200
Bethlehem *(G-1485)*

1061 Ferroalloy Ores, Except Vanadium

◆ **Langeloth Metallurgical Co LLC**......C...... 724 947-2201
Langeloth *(G-9270)*

1081 Metal Mining Svcs

◆ **Alcoa World Alumina LLC**............E...... 412 315-2900
Pittsburgh *(G-14670)*
▲ **Cbmm North America Inc** ....G... 412 221-7008
Pittsburgh *(G-14829)*
Cru Group ....G... 724 940-7100
Wexford *(G-19797)*
Daleco Resources Corporation ....G... 570 795-4347
West Chester *(G-19531)*
▼ **Duquesne Mine Supply Company** ....G....... 412 821-2100
Pittsburgh *(G-14944)*
E D I Enviro-Drill Inc ....F... 412 788-1046
Pittsburgh *(G-14949)*
Joe Bento Construction Co Inc ....G... 215 969-1505
Philadelphia *(G-13901)*
Latona Mining LLC ....F... 570 654-3525
Pittston *(G-15761)*
Leber Mining Company Inc ....G... 717 367-1453
Elizabethtown *(G-4876)*
McKay & Gould Drilling Inc............E... 724 436-6823
Darlington *(G-4030)*
McKinney Drilling Company LLC ....E... 724 468-4139
Delmont *(G-4051)*
Metallurg Inc.......................G... 610 293-2501
Wayne *(G-19355)*
Metallurg Holdings Inc ....G... 610 293-2501
Wayne *(G-19356)*
Mine Vision Systems Inc ....G... 412 626-7461
Pittsburgh *(G-15292)*
Minichi Inc.........................D...... 570 654-8332
Dupont *(G-4491)*
Nexgen Industrial Services Inc............E... 724 592-5133
Rices Landing *(G-16670)*
▲ **Prco America Inc** ....F... 412 837-2798
Pittsburgh *(G-15431)*
Preferred Rocks LLC ....F... 484 684-1221
Wayne *(G-19363)*
Robindale Export LLC ....B... 724 879-4264
Latrobe *(G-9517)*
Sheridan Supply Company Inc ....G... 610 589-4361
Newmanstown *(G-12484)*
Surface Mining Reclamation Off.........G...... 717 782-4036
Harrisburg *(G-7224)*
Takraf Usa Inc.....................F... 215 822-4485
Lansdale *(G-9413)*
US Crossings Unlimited LLC ....G....... 888 359-1115
Cranberry Township *(G-3861)*

1099 Metal Ores, NEC

Alcoa USA Corp ....G... 212 518-5400
Pittsburgh *(G-14666)*
◆ **Alcoa World Alumina LLC** ....E... 412 315-2900
Pittsburgh *(G-14670)*
Boke Investment Company................A... 412 321-4252
Pittsburgh *(G-14780)*
Compagnie Des Bxites De Guinee ....A... 412 235-0279
Pittsburgh *(G-14870)*
Halco (mining) Inc ....A... 412 235-0265
Pittsburgh *(G-15074)*
Jigging Technologies LLC ....G... 814 254-4376
Johnstown *(G-8386)*
Westmoreland Iron and Met LLC.........G... 724 523-8151
Jeannette *(G-8267)*

12 COAL MINING

1221 Bituminous Coal & Lignite: Surface Mining

Alpha Coal Sales Co ....G... 304 256-1015
Clearfield *(G-3210)*
Amerikohl Mining Inc ....D... 724 282-2339
Butler *(G-2374)*
Amerikohl Mining Inc ....E... 724 282-2339
Stahlstown *(G-17935)*
Bentley Development Co Inc ....F... 724 459-5775
Blairsville *(G-1715)*
Beth Mining Co ....G... 814 845-7390
Glen Campbell *(G-6423)*
Black Hawk Mining Inc ....E... 724 783-6433
Rural Valley *(G-16876)*
▲ **Bognar and Company Inc** ....G... 412 344-9900
Pittsburgh *(G-14779)*
Buchanan Mining Company LLC........F... 724 485-4000
Canonsburg *(G-2553)*
Bullskin Tipple Company ....G... 724 628-7807
Perryopolis *(G-13303)*
C & M Aggregate Company Inc ....E... 724 796-3821
Bulger *(G-2342)*
Carlson Mining......................F... 724 924-2188
New Castle *(G-12069)*
Central Ohio Coal Company ....C...... 740 338-3100
Canonsburg *(G-2558)*
Charles L Swenglish Sons Coal ....G... 724 437-3541
Smithfield *(G-17646)*
Chemstream Holdings Inc...............F... 724 545-6222
Kittanning *(G-8761)*
Ckl Augering Inc ....G... 724 479-0213
Homer City *(G-7673)*
Coal Loaders Inc ....F... 724 238-6601
Ligonier *(G-9958)*
Coalview Recovery Group LLC ....G... 814 443-6454
Somerset *(G-17681)*
Consol Amonate Mining Co LLC ....G... 724 485-4000
Canonsburg *(G-2566)*
Consol Energy Inc ....C...... 724 785-6242
East Millsboro *(G-4583)*
Consol Energy Inc ....E... 412 854-6600
Canonsburg *(G-2569)*
Consol Energy Inc ....F... 724 485-3300
Canonsburg *(G-2568)*
Consol Mining Company LLC ....F... 724 485-4000
Canonsburg *(G-2570)*
▲ **Consolidation Coal Company** ....C...... 740 338-3100
Canonsburg *(G-2572)*
Cookport Coal Co Inc ....G... 814 938-4253
Kittanning *(G-8762)*

Corsa Coal Corp.....................G... 724 754-0028
Canonsburg *(G-2574)*
Durant Excavating ....G... 724 583-9800
Masontown *(G-10535)*
E E S Augering Company ....G... 724 397-8821
Home *(G-7668)*
E P Bender Coal Company.............E... 814 344-8063
Carrolltown *(G-2808)*
Enercorp Inc ....G... 814 345-6225
Morrisdale *(G-11548)*
Fairview Coal Co Inc.................G... 814 776-1158
Ridgway *(G-16708)*
Fieg Brothers Coal...................F... 814 893-5270
Stoystown *(G-18077)*
Finch Flagstone ....G... 570 965-0982
Springville *(G-17929)*
Freno Jr A J Mining ....G... 814 845-2286
Glen Campbell *(G-6424)*
G L R Mining Inc.....................G... 724 254-4043
Clymer *(G-3272)*
GM&s Coal Corp.....................D...... 814 629-5661
Stoystown *(G-18079)*
Godin Bros Inc ....F... 814 629-5117
Friedens *(G-6220)*
Gre Mining Company ....G... 814 226-6911
Clarion *(G-3178)*
Gre Ventures Inc ....G... 814 226-6911
Clarion *(G-3179)*
Greenley Engery Holdings of PA.........G... 724 238-8177
Central City *(G-2838)*
Greenwood Enterprises ....E... 412 429-6800
Carnegie *(G-2770)*
Hal Ben Mining Co ....G... 724 748-4528
Grove City *(G-6789)*
Hanson Aggregates Bmc Inc ....G... 724 626-0080
Connellsville *(G-3498)*
Hepburnia Coal Company ....G... 814 236-0473
Grampian *(G-6571)*
Homer City Coal Proc Corp............E... 724 348-4800
Finleyville *(G-5960)*
Junior Coal Contracting Inc ....E... 814 342-2012
Philipsburg *(G-14516)*
Kerry Coal Company Inc ....F... 724 535-1311
Wampum *(G-18801)*
Keystone Coal Mining Corp............B... 740 338-3100
Canonsburg *(G-2598)*
King Coal Sales Inc...................E... 814 342-6610
Philipsburg *(G-14517)*
L and J Equipment Co Inc ....G... 724 437-5405
Uniontown *(G-18633)*
Larry D Baumgardner Coal Co ....F... 814 345-6404
Lanse *(G-9446)*
Larson Enterprises Inc ....F... 814 345-5101
Kylertown *(G-8866)*
Lehigh Anthracite Coal LLC............G... 814 446-6700
Armagh *(G-724)*
Lost Creek Mining....................G... 724 335-8780
New Kensington *(G-12353)*
McElroy Coal Company ....F... 724 485-4000
Canonsburg *(G-2602)*
Mincorp Inc.........................F... 814 443-4668
Friedens *(G-6222)*
Montour Creek Mining Co ....G... 717 582-7526
Elliottsburg *(G-4921)*
New Enterprise Stone Lime Inc..........E... 570 823-0531
Plains *(G-15787)*
Original Fuels Inc....................E... 814 938-5171
Coolspring *(G-3622)*
P & N Coal Co Inc....................E... 814 938-7660
Punxsutawney *(G-16152)*

SIC

▼ Pbs Coals Inc ....E 814 443-4668
Canonsburg *(G-2617)*

Philip Reese Coal Co Inc ....G 814 263-4231
Karthaus *(G-8483)*

Piccolomini Contractors Inc ....G 724 437-7946
Waltersburg *(G-18795)*

Quality Aggregates Inc ....E 724 924-2198
Portersville *(G-15935)*

Quality Aggregates Inc ....F 412 777-6704
Pittsburgh *(G-15459)*

R S Carlin Inc ....F 814 387-4190
Snow Shoe *(G-17670)*

Rausch Creek Land LP ....E 570 682-4600
Valley View *(G-18717)*

Reclamation Inc ....F 814 265-2564
Brockway *(G-2233)*

River Hill Coal Co Inc ....D 814 345-5642
Kylertown *(G-8867)*

River Hill Coal Co Inc ....G 814 263-4506
Karthaus *(G-8484)*

River Hill Coal Co Inc ....F 814 263-4506
Karthaus *(G-8485)*

River Hill Coal Co Inc ....F 814 263-4341
Karthaus *(G-8486)*

Rjc Kohl Inc ....F 814 948-5903
Nicktown *(G-12621)*

Rosebud Mining Company ....E 724 354-4050
Shelocta *(G-17488)*

Rosebud Mining Company ....E 724 545-6222
Kittanning *(G-8790)*

Schuylkill Coal Processing ....G 570 875-3123
Ashland *(G-736)*

Senate Coal Mines ....G 724 537-2062
Latrobe *(G-9519)*

Seven Sisters Mining Company .....G 724 468-8232
Delmont *(G-4058)*

Sky Haven Coal Inc ....C 814 765-1665
Penfield *(G-13223)*

State Industries Inc ....G 724 548-8101
Kittanning *(G-8797)*

Strishock Coal Co ....E 814 375-1245
Du Bois *(G-4422)*

Twin Brook Coal Co ....G 724 254-4030
Clymer *(G-3274)*

Usnr LLC ....F 724 929-8405
Belle Vernon *(G-1089)*

Valier Coal Yard ....F 814 938-5171
Valier *(G-18706)*

Victor LLC ....G 814 765-5681
Clearfield *(G-3233)*

▲ Waroquier Coal Inc ....G 814 765-5681
Clearfield *(G-3235)*

Warren C Hartman Contracting .....G 814 765-8842
Clearfield *(G-3237)*

WJM Coal Co Inc ....F 724 354-2922
Shelocta *(G-17491)*

Xecol Corporation ....G 412 262-5222
Coraopolis *(G-3736)*

Zubek Inc ....G 814 443-4441
Berlin *(G-1294)*

1222 Bituminous Coal: Underground Mining

Black Hawk Mining Inc ....E 724 783-6433
Rural Valley *(G-16876)*

Chemstream Holdings Inc ....G 724 545-6222
Kittanning *(G-8761)*

Consol Coal Resources LP ....A 724 485-3300
Canonsburg *(G-2567)*

Consol Energy Inc ....F 724 485-3300
Canonsburg *(G-2568)*

Consol PA Coal Co LLC ....A 724 485-4000
Canonsburg *(G-2571)*

▼ Cumberland Coal Resources LP ....E 724 852-5845
Waynesburg *(G-19436)*

Cumberland Coal Resources LP .....A 724 627-7500
Waynesburg *(G-19437)*

Cumberland Contura LLC ....G 724 627-7500
Waynesburg *(G-19438)*

Eighty-Four Mining Company ....G 740 338-3100
Canonsburg *(G-2581)*

▲ Emerald Coal Resources LP ......A 724 627-7500
Waynesburg *(G-19440)*

F/K Industries Inc ....G 412 655-4982
Pittsburgh *(G-15001)*

GM&s Coal Corp ....D 814 629-5661
Stoystown *(G-18079)*

Hanson Aggregates Bmc Inc ....F 724 626-0080
Connellsville *(G-3498)*

Honey-Creek Stone Co ....F 724 654-5538
Edinburg *(G-4822)*

Laurel Run Mining Company LLC ......D 412 831-4000
Canonsburg *(G-2599)*

Marquise Mining Corp ....F 724 459-5775
Johnstown *(G-8406)*

Rosebud Mining Company ....E 724 354-4050
Shelocta *(G-17488)*

Rosebud Mining Company ....E 724 545-6222
Kittanning *(G-8790)*

Roxcoal Inc ....D 814 443-4668
Friedens *(G-6226)*

◆ Snyder Assod Companies Inc ......E 724 548-8101
Kittanning *(G-8793)*

Snyder Enterprises Inc ....G 724 548-8101
Kittanning *(G-8795)*

Southern Ohio Coal Company ....G 740 338-3100
Canonsburg *(G-2638)*

Swisher Contracting Inc ....F 814 765-6006
Clearfield *(G-3232)*

Waroquier Coal Inc ....E 814 765-5681
Clearfield *(G-3236)*

Wilson Creek Energy LLC ....E 724 754-0028
Canonsburg *(G-2660)*

Wilson Creek Energy LLC ....E 814 443-4668
Friedens *(G-6228)*

1231 Anthracite Mining

Anthracite Industries Inc ....E 570 286-2176
Sunbury *(G-18163)*

B D Mining Co Inc ....F 570 874-1602
Gilberton *(G-6365)*

Carol Fetterolf ....G 570 875-2026
Ashland *(G-728)*

Coal Contractors (1991) Inc ....D 570 450-5086
Hazle Township *(G-7449)*

Denis Bell Inc ....E 570 450-5086
Hazle Township *(G-7451)*

Dennis Snyder ....F 570 682-9698
Hegins *(G-7540)*

E O J Incorporated ....G 570 943-2860
New Ringgold *(G-12438)*

Filter Media Inc ....G 570 874-2537
Gilberton *(G-6366)*

Gilberton Coal Company ....E 570 874-1602
Gilberton *(G-6367)*

Hecla Machinery & Equipment Co ....F 570 385-4783
Schuylkill Haven *(G-17158)*

Hudson Anthracite Inc ....G 570 823-0531
Plains *(G-15785)*

Hudson Anthracite Inc ....F 570 655-4151
Avoca *(G-844)*

▼ Jeddo-Highland Coal Company ...G 570 825-8700
Wilkes Barre *(G-19933)*

Joe Kuperavage ....F 570 622-8080
Port Carbon *(G-15897)*

K & K Coal Company ....G 570 622-0220
Port Carbon *(G-15898)*

Keystone Anthracite Co Inc ....E 570 276-6480
Girardville *(G-6406)*

Kuperavage Enterprises Inc ....E 570 668-1633
Middleport *(G-11045)*

Mallard Contracting Co Inc ....E 570 339-2930
Mount Carmel *(G-11626)*

Mammoth Materials ....G 570 385-4232
Schuylkill Haven *(G-17162)*

Mountaintop Anthracite Inc ....F 570 474-1222
Mountain Top *(G-11766)*

Northeast Energy Co Inc ....G 570 823-1719
Wilkes Barre *(G-19951)*

Pagnotti Enterprises Inc ....E 570 825-8700
Wilkes Barre *(G-19954)*

Postupack Russell Culm Corp ....G 570 929-1699
McAdoo *(G-10657)*

R & R Energy Corp ....E 570 874-1602
Gilberton *(G-6369)*

▲ Reading Anthracite Company ....E 570 622-5150
Pottsville *(G-16093)*

RNS Services Inc ....G 570 638-3322
Blossburg *(G-1808)*

Rossi Excavating Company ....G 570 455-9607
Beaver Meadows *(G-1018)*

Sherman Coal Company Inc ....G 570 695-2690
Elysburg *(G-19482)*

Silverbrook Anthracite Inc ....F 570 654-3560
Wilkes Barre *(G-19963)*

Sky Top Coal Company Inc ....G 570 773-2000
Mahanoy City *(G-10174)*

South Tamaqua Coal Pockets ....F 570 386-5445
Tamaqua *(G-18226)*

Waste Management & Processors ....E 570 874-2003
Frackville *(G-6109)*

West Point Mining Corp ....E 570 339-5259
Stoystown *(G-18089)*

1241 Coal Mining Svcs

Alpha Safety USA ....G 814 236-3344
Clearfield *(G-3211)*

Amerihohl Mining ....G 724 455-4450
Mill Run *(G-11185)*

Amfire Mining Co ....G 724 254-9554
Clymer *(G-3269)*

Amfire Mining Company LLC ....F 724 532-4307
Latrobe *(G-9455)*

B & B Anthracite Coal ....G 570 695-3707
Tremont *(G-18478)*

B & B Coal Company ....G 570 695-3188
Tremont *(G-18479)*

Bellaire Corporation ....G 814 446-5631
Armagh *(G-723)*

Britt Resources Inc ....G 724 465-9333
Spring Church *(G-17855)*

Buckley Associates Inc ....G 412 963-7070
Pittsburgh *(G-14796)*

Burrell Mining Services Inc ....G 724 339-2220
New Kensington *(G-12330)*

▲ C & J Welding & Cnstr LLC ....C 724 564-7120
Mc Clellandtown *(G-10555)*

C & K Coal Company ....D 814 226-6911
Clarion *(G-3172)*

C L I Corporation ....G 724 348-4800
Finleyville *(G-5952)*

Christopher Resources Inc ....G 724 430-9610
Uniontown *(G-18620)*

Coal Innovations LLC ....G 814 893-5790
Friedens *(G-6219)*

D L Enterprise Inc ....G 814 948-6060
Barnesboro *(G-939)*

Donald Greathouse ....G 814 242-7624
Stoystown *(G-18076)*

Drill Management Inc ....G 717 227-8189
Glen Rock *(G-6456)*

▼ Duquesne Mine Supply Company ....G 412 821-2100
Pittsburgh *(G-14944)*

E P Bender Coal Company ....E 814 344-8063
Carrolltown *(G-2808)*

F & D Coal Sales Co Inc ....G 570 455-4745
Hazle Township *(G-7456)*

◆ Frank Calandra Inc ....E 412 963-9071
Pittsburgh *(G-15032)*

Freys Farm Dairy LLC ....G 717 860-8015
Chambersburg *(G-2934)*

Gale Mining Co ....G 570 622-2524
Pottsville *(G-16079)*

Gary Gioia Coal Co ....G 412 754-0994
Elizabeth *(G-4859)*

George Skebeck ....G 814 674-8169
Patton *(G-13188)*

Girard Estate Fee ....E 570 276-1404
Girardville *(G-6405)*

Joliett Coal Co ....G 717 647-9628
Tower City *(G-18438)*

Kentucky Berwind Land Company ....G 215 563-2800
Philadelphia *(G-13927)*

▼ Kimmels Coal and Packaging Inc ....E 717 453-7151
Wiconisco *(G-19895)*

Kovalchick Corporation ....E 724 349-3300
Indiana *(G-8110)*

Laurel Energy LP ....G 724 537-5731
Latrobe *(G-9496)*

Lincoln Contg & Eqp Co Inc ....D 814 629-6641
Stoystown *(G-18082)*

Longwall Mining Services Inc ....G 724 816-7871
Allison Park *(G-456)*

McKee Drilling ....G 814 427-2444
Rossiter *(G-16823)*

Mirada Energy Inc ....E 717 730-9412
Camp Hill *(G-2505)*

Mulligan Mining Inc ....G 412 831-1787
Bethel Park *(G-1427)*

Northern Son Inc ....E 724 548-1137
Du Bois *(G-4407)*

Orchard Coal Company ....G 570 695-2301
Tremont *(G-18482)*

PA Mining Professional ....G 717 761-4646
Camp Hill *(G-2509)*

Parkwood Resources Inc ....E 724 479-4090
Kittanning *(G-8787)*

Penn Crossing Limited ....G 724 744-7725
Harrison City *(G-7250)*

▲ R G Johnson Company Inc ....F 724 222-6810
Washington *(G-19220)*

R G Johnson Company Inc	D	724 225-4969	
Washington (G-19221)			
Reading Fracture Inc	G	570 628-2308	
Pottsville (G-16094)			
RES Coal LLC	E	814 765-7525	
Clearfield (G-3230)			
RES Coal LLC	D	814 765-0352	
West Decatur (G-19690)			
RNS Services Inc	E	814 472-5202	
Ebensburg (G-4794)			
Rosebud Coal Sales Inc	G	724 545-6222	
Kittanning (G-8789)			
Rosebud Mining Co	D	814 948-6390	
Heilwood (G-7548)			
Rosebud Mining Company	E	724 459-4970	
Clarksburg (G-3199)			
Rosini Coal Inc	E	570 874-2879	
Frackville (G-6107)			
Sebastian Management LLC	D	412 203-1273	
Pittsburgh (G-15519)			
Sherpa Mining Contractors Inc	E	814 754-5560	
Hooversville (G-7771)			
Snyder Exploration Co	G	724 548-8101	
Kittanning (G-8796)			
Solar Fuel Co Inc	G	814 443-2646	
Friedens (G-6227)			
South Penn Resources LLC	F	724 880-5882	
Mc Clellandtown (G-10556)			
Summit Packaging LLC	G	570 622-5150	
Pottsville (G-16098)			
Superior Coal Prep Coop LLC	F	570 682-3246	
Hegins (G-7545)			
Uae Coalcorp Associates	G	570 339-4090	
Mount Carmel (G-11630)			
Waste Management & Processors	E	570 874-2003	
Frackville (G-6109)			
Wilson Creek Energy LLC	G	814 619-4600	
Johnstown (G-8445)			
WJM Coal Co Inc	F	724 354-2922	
Shelocta (G-17491)			
Xylem Wtr Sltons Zlienople LLC	G	570 538-2260	
Watsontown (G-19281)			

13 OIL AND GAS EXTRACTION

1311 Crude Petroleum & Natural Gas

Afco Energy Production Co Inc	G	724 463-3350	
Barnesboro (G-937)			
Anadarko Petroleum Corp	F	570 323-4157	
Williamsport (G-19987)			
Anadarko Petroleum Corporation	G	570 323-4157	
Williamsport (G-19988)			
Apex Energy LLC	E	724 719-2611	
Wexford (G-19788)			
Ardent Resources Inc	G	412 854-1193	
Pittsburgh (G-14720)			
Arg Resources Inc	E	814 837-7477	
Kane (G-8459)			
Arg Resources Inc	E	610 940-4420	
West Conshohocken (G-19685)			
Atlas America Pub 11-2002 Ltd	G	412 262-2830	
Moon Township (G-11480)			
Atlas Resources LLC	F	800 251-0171	
Pittsburgh (G-14734)			
Atlas Rsrces Pub 18-2009 B LP	G	330 896-8510	
Coraopolis (G-3661)			
Atlas Rsrces Series 28-2010 LP	G	412 489-0006	
Pittsburgh (G-14735)			
B & B Oil & Gas Production Co	G	814 257-8760	
Dayton (G-4035)			
Baker Gas Inc	F	724 297-3456	
Worthington (G-20227)			
Bakwell LLC	G	570 724-7067	
Wellsboro (G-19462)			
Baron Development Company	G	814 676-8703	
Oil City (G-12940)			
BDH Oil Inc	G	814 362-5447	
Bradford (G-1957)			
Belden & Blake Corporation	F	814 589-7091	
Pleasantville (G-15797)			
Blx Inc	G	724 543-5743	
Kittanning (G-8758)			
Brymone Inc	G	724 746-4004	
Canonsburg (G-2552)			
Bucher Jj Producing Corp	G	814 697-6593	
Shinglehouse (G-17504)			
Campbell Oil LLC	G	814 749-0002	
Nanty Glo (G-11905)			
Carlson Technologies Inc	F	814 371-5500	
Du Bois (G-4386)			

Carpenter Co	D	610 366-5110	
Fogelsville (G-5993)			
Carpenter Co	C	814 944-8612	
Altoona (G-486)			
Carrizo (marcellus) LLC	G	570 278-7450	
Montrose (G-11460)			
Carrizo Oil & Gas Inc	G	570 278-7009	
Montrose (G-11461)			
CE Ready Mix	E	724 727-3331	
Apollo (G-667)			
Center Independent Oil Company	G	724 437-6607	
Lemont Furnace (G-9734)			
Chevron Ae Resources LLC	E	724 662-0300	
Jackson Center (G-8226)			
Cline Oil Inc	G	814 368-5395	
Bradford (G-1961)			
Cnx Gas Company LLC	G	724 485-4000	
Canonsburg (G-2559)			
Cnx Gas Corporation	D	724 485-4000	
Canonsburg (G-2560)			
Cnx Land LLC	G	724 485-4000	
Canonsburg (G-2561)			
Cnx Resources Corporation	B	724 485-4000	
Canonsburg (G-2562)			
Consol PA Coal Co LLC	A	724 485-4000	
Canonsburg (G-2571)			
Cumberland Farms Inc	G	412 331-4419	
Pittsburgh (G-14892)			
Dannic Energy Corporation	G	724 465-6663	
Indiana (G-8089)			
Davies & Sons LLC	G	814 723-7430	
Warren (G-19020)			
De Limited Family Partnership	F	814 938-0800	
Punxsutawney (G-16133)			
Devon Energy Corporation	F	412 366-7474	
Pittsburgh (G-14920)			
Devonian Resources Inc	E	814 589-7061	
Pleasantville (G-15800)			
Dominion Energy Transm Inc	G	724 354-3433	
Shelocta (G-17485)			
Dominion Exploration and Prod	G	724 349-4450	
Indiana (G-8091)			
Eagle Line Corporation	F	814 589-7724	
Pleasantville (G-15801)			
Eastern American Energy Corp	G	724 463-8400	
Indiana (G-8093)			
Eclipse Resources Holdings LP	C	814 308-9754	
State College (G-17959)			
Eclipse Resources I LP	F	814 308-9754	
State College (G-17960)			
Elkhorn Operating Company	G	814 723-4390	
Warren (G-19023)			
Em Energy Employer LLC	E	412 564-1300	
Canonsburg (G-2629)			
Em Energy Pennsylvania LLC	E	412 564-1300	
Canonsburg (G-2583)			
Eog Resources Inc	E	724 745-9063	
Canonsburg (G-2586)			
Eqt Corporation	C	412 553-5700	
Pittsburgh (G-14981)			
Eqt Re LLC	G	274 271-7200	
Canonsburg (G-2587)			
Exco Resources LLC	D	724 720-2500	
Kittanning (G-8768)			
Frederick Drilling Co & Sons	G	814 744-8581	
Tylersburg (G-18573)			
Grayco Controls LLC	G	724 545-2300	
Adrian (G-29)			
Imod Oil Production LLC	G	814 589-7539	
Pleasantville (G-15802)			
Inflection Energy	G	303 531-2343	
Williamsport (G-20025)			
J R Resources L P	G	814 365-5821	
Ringgold (G-16751)			
Jj Bucher Producing Corp	G	814 697-6593	
Shinglehouse (G-17508)			
John Wallace	G	814 374-4619	
Cooperstown (G-3637)			
KCS Energy Inc	G	814 723-4672	
Warren (G-19035)			
Kriebel Gas Inc	D	814 226-4160	
Clarion (G-3181)			
Kriebel Gas Inc	G	814 938-2010	
Punxsutawney (G-16146)			
Kriebel Minerals Inc	E	814 226-4160	
Clarion (G-3182)			
Laurel Mountain Production LLC	G	412 595-8700	
Pittsburgh (G-15221)			
▼ Lehigh Anthracite LP	G	570 668-9060	
Tamaqua (G-18215)			

▲ Lock 3 Company	F	724 258-7773	
Monongahela (G-11310)			
Maple Grove Enterprises Inc	G	814 473-6272	
Rimersburg (G-16750)			
Mds Energy Development LLC	E	724 548-2501	
Kittanning (G-8781)			
Mds Energy Partners Gp LLC	G	724 548-2501	
Kittanning (G-8782)			
Mds Well Holdings LLC	G	724 548-2501	
Kittanning (G-8784)			
Midnight Oil Express	G	215 933-9690	
Quakertown (G-16217)			
Minard Run Oil Company	G	814 368-4931	
Bradford (G-1983)			
Minichi Energy LLC	G	570 654-8332	
Dupont (G-4492)			
Mmscc-2 LLC	F	610 266-8990	
Allentown (G-317)			
Montauk Energy Holdings LLC	D	412 747-8700	
Pittsburgh (G-15301)			
Mountain Energy Inc	G	724 428-5200	
Aleppo (G-61)			
N A Petroleum Corp	G	610 438-5463	
Easton (G-4728)			
New Century Energy Inc	G	724 693-9266	
Oakdale (G-12908)			
Northwestern Energy Corp	G	814 277-9935	
Mahaffey (G-10172)			
Open Flow Gas Supply Corp	F	814 371-2228	
Du Bois (G-4409)			
Papco Inc	F	814 726-2130	
Warren (G-19042)			
Pennsylvania Gen Enrgy Corp	D	814 723-3230	
Warren (G-19043)			
Pennzoil-Quaker State Company	B	724 756-0110	
Karns City (G-8482)			
Petronorth Ltd	G	814 368-6992	
Smethport (G-17636)			
Phillips Exploration LLC	D	724 772-3500	
Warrendale (G-19092)			
Questa Petroleum Co	G	724 832-7297	
Greensburg (G-6708)			
Questa Petroleum Company	G	412 220-9210	
Pittsburgh (G-15462)			
R C Southwell	G	814 723-7182	
Warren (G-19045)			
Regency Energy Partners LP	G	610 687-8900	
Wayne (G-19369)			
Repsol Oil & Gas Usa LLC	G	724 814-5300	
Warrendale (G-19096)			
Rex Energy Corporation	D	814 278-7267	
State College (G-18014)			
Rice Olympus Midstream LLC	D	724 746-6720	
Canonsburg (G-2629)			
Rice Poseidon Midstream LLC	C	724 746-6720	
Canonsburg (G-2630)			
Royal Oil & Gas Corporation	E	724 463-0246	
Indiana (G-8124)			
Royal Production Company Inc	E	724 463-0246	
Indiana (G-8125)			
Rustys Oil and Propane Inc	G	814 497-4423	
Houtzdale (G-7884)			
Tall Oak Energy Inc	G	724 636-0621	
Boyers (G-1891)			
Targa Energy LP	F	412 489-0006	
Pittsburgh (G-15598)			
Targa Pipeline Oper Partnr LP	G	412 489-0006	
Philadelphia (G-14371)			
Targa Pipeline Partners GP LLC	D	215 546-5005	
Philadelphia (G-14372)			
Trans Energy Inc	F	304 684-7053	
Pittsburgh (G-15638)			
Triangle Petroleum Inc	G	908 380-2685	
Warren (G-19052)			
Van Hampton Gas & Oil Inc	F	814 589-7061	
Pleasantville (G-15805)			
Vineyard Oil & Gas Company	F	814 725-8742	
North East (G-12764)			
Williams Companies Inc	G	717 490-6857	
Lancaster (G-9241)			
Wilmoth Interests Inc	G	724 397-5558	
Marion Center (G-10478)			
Xto Energy Inc	D	540 772-3220	
Renfrew (G-16644)			
Xto Energy Inc	D	724 772-3500	
Warrendale (G-19103)			
Xto Energy Inc	G	570 368-8920	
Montoursville (G-11458)			
Zama Petroleum Inc	G	360 321-6160	
Pittsburgh (G-15732)			

Employee Codes: A=Over 500 employees, B=251-500
C=101-250, D=51-100, E=20-50, F=10-19, G=3-9

2019 Harris Pennsylvania
Manufacturers Directory

795

SIC

Zavillas Oil Co ....G....... 724 445-3702
Chicora *(G-3130)*

1321 Natural Gas Liquids

American Petroleum Partners ....G....... 844 835-5277
Canonsburg *(G-2539)*

Arsenal Resources Energy LLC ....F....... 724 940-1100
Wexford *(G-19790)*

De Limited Family Partnership ....F....... 814 938-0800
Punxsutawney *(G-16133)*

E F Laudenslager Inc ....F....... 610 395-1582
Orefield *(G-13011)*

Eqt Corporation..................................G....... 412 395-2080
Pittsburgh *(G-14982)*

Falcon Propane LLC ....G....... 570 207-1711
Blakely *(G-1747)*

Finnegan Gas Corp ....G....... 724 428-3688
Wind Ridge *(G-20176)*

Four Three Energy Services LLC ....G....... 814 797-0021
Knox *(G-8810)*

Kriebel Wells ....G....... 814 226-4160
Clarion *(G-3183)*

Lancaster Propane Gas Inc..................F....... 717 898-0800
Lancaster *(G-9104)*

M W Gary and Associates ....G....... 724 206-0071
Washington *(G-19197)*

M/D Gas Inc ....G....... 724 548-2501
Kittanning *(G-8778)*

Markwest Hydrocarbon Inc ....E....... 724 514-4398
Washington *(G-19198)*

Markwest Liberty Midstream..................D....... 724 514-4401
Washington *(G-19199)*

Mds Associated Companies Inc ....D....... 724 548-2501
Kittanning *(G-8780)*

Plains Lpg Services ....G....... 717 376-0830
Lebanon *(G-9622)*

Praxair Inc...G....... 215 721-9099
Souderton *(G-17760)*

Streamline Propane Llc ....G....... 215 919-4500
Green Lane *(G-6593)*

Trans Energy Inc ....F....... 304 684-7053
Pittsburgh *(G-15638)*

UGI Europe Inc ....G....... 610 337-1000
King of Prussia *(G-8692)*

Williams Companies Inc ....D....... 717 490-6857
Lancaster *(G-9241)*

1381 Drilling Oil & Gas Wells

A & S Production Inc ....G....... 814 463-9310
Endeavor *(G-5078)*

AEC Services Company LLC ....G....... 610 246-6470
Plymouth Meeting *(G-15828)*

AES Drilling Fluids LLC.........................E....... 724 743-2934
Canonsburg *(G-2533)*

Alternative Petroleum Svcs LLC ....G....... 570 807-1797
Milford *(G-11155)*

Andrew E Trautner & Sons Inc ....G....... 570 494-0191
Cogan Station *(G-3358)*

Appalachian Drillers LLC ....G....... 724 548-2501
Kittanning *(G-8754)*

Ardent Resources Inc...........................G....... 412 854-1193
Pittsburgh *(G-14720)*

Arsenal Resources LLC ....E....... 724 940-1100
Wexford *(G-19791)*

Atlas America Public 10 Ltd..................G....... 412 262-2830
Coraopolis *(G-3659)*

Atlas Energy Operating Co LLC ....B....... 412 262-2830
Coraopolis *(G-3660)*

Baron Crest Energy Company ....G....... 724 478-1121
Apollo *(G-663)*

Bittinger Drilling Co ....G....... 724 727-3822
Apollo *(G-664)*

Black Viper Energy Services ....D....... 432 561-8801
Cuddy *(G-3940)*

Brown Brothers Drilling Inc ....G....... 717 548-2500
Nottingham *(G-12881)*

Bucks Cnty Artesian Well Drlg ....F....... 215 493-1867
Washington Crossing *(G-19253)*

Calder Transport ....G....... 724 787-8390
Greensburg *(G-6654)*

Catalyst Energy Inc..............................E....... 412 325-4350
Pittsburgh *(G-14828)*

Chevron Ae Resources LLC ....E....... 724 662-0300
Jackson Center *(G-8226)*

Collins Drilling LLC.............................F....... 814 489-3297
Sugar Grove *(G-18144)*

Commonwealth Drilling Company ....G....... 610 940-4015
Plymouth Meeting *(G-15839)*

Curtis and Son Oil Inc ....G....... 814 489-7858
Sugargrove *(G-18150)*

D K Gas Inc ....G....... 814 365-5621
Hawthorn *(G-7443)*

Dallas - Morris Drilling Inc.....................D....... 814 362-6493
Bradford *(G-1964)*

Dallas - Morris Drilling Inc.....................E....... 814 362-6493
Bradford *(G-1965)*

Deepwell Energy Services LLC ....E....... 412 316-5243
Eighty Four *(G-4837)*

Donald W Deitz...................................G....... 814 745-2857
Clarion *(G-3177)*

Drillmasters LLC ....G....... 717 319-8657
Telford *(G-18285)*

Eagle Line Corporation ....F....... 814 589-7724
Pleasantville *(G-15801)*

Eastern Environmental Inds LLC ....E....... 814 371-2221
Brockway *(G-2224)*

Edgemarc Energy Holdings LLC ....E....... 724 749-8466
Canonsburg *(G-2580)*

Empire Energy E&P LLC ....E....... 724 483-2070
Canonsburg *(G-2584)*

Exco Resources LLC ....D....... 724 720-2500
Kittanning *(G-8768)*

First Class Energy LLC ....E....... 724 548-2501
Kittanning *(G-8771)*

First Class Energy LLC ....E....... 724 548-2501
Kittanning *(G-8770)*

Frederick Drilling Co & Sons ....G....... 814 744-8581
Tylersburg *(G-18573)*

Gas & Oil Management Assoc ....G....... 814 563-4601
Youngsville *(G-20771)*

▲ Gill Rock Drill Company Inc...............E....... 717 272-3861
Lebanon *(G-9573)*

Great Plains Oilfld Rentl LLC.................G....... 570 882-7700
Sayre *(G-17115)*

Greene County Gas & Oil Co ....G....... 724 627-3393
Waynesburg *(G-19444)*

Helmerich & Payne Intl Drlg Co ....C....... 814 353-3450
Howard *(G-7891)*

Hemlock Oil & Gas Co Inc ....G....... 814 368-6261
Bradford *(G-1972)*

Howard Drilling Inc ....G....... 814 778-5820
Mount Jewett *(G-11642)*

J H R Inc..G....... 412 221-1617
Bridgeville *(G-2072)*

JM Enterprise LLC ....G....... 814 758-5998
Tionesta *(G-18373)*

Keane Frac LP ....E....... 570 302-4050
Mansfield *(G-10417)*

Keane Frac Tx LLC ....G....... 570 302-4050
Mansfield *(G-10418)*

Key Energy Services Inc ....E....... 878 302-3333
New Kensington *(G-12351)*

Kriebel Gas Inc ....D....... 814 226-4160
Clarion *(G-3181)*

Kriebel Gas Inc ....G....... 814 938-2010
Punxsutawney *(G-16146)*

Michels Corporation ....G....... 724 249-2065
Washington *(G-19202)*

Minard Run Oil Company ....D....... 814 362-3531
Bradford *(G-1982)*

Mine Drilling Services LL ....F....... 814 765-1075
Clearfield *(G-3225)*

Nabors Drilling Tech USA ....G....... 814 768-4640
Clearfield *(G-3226)*

Northeast Energy MGT Inc....................C....... 724 465-7958
Indiana *(G-8115)*

Northstern Cnsld Enrgy Prtners..............G....... 412 491-6660
Wexford *(G-19816)*

Northwest Synergy Corp ....G....... 814 726-0543
Warren *(G-19040)*

Papco Inc ....F....... 814 726-2130
Warren *(G-19042)*

Patriot Exploration ....G....... 724 593-4427
Stahlstown *(G-17936)*

Patriot Exploration Corp ....G....... 724 282-2339
Butler *(G-2432)*

Penn Production Group LLC ....G....... 724 349-6690
Indiana *(G-8117)*

Penneco Oil Company...........................F....... 724 468-8232
Delmont *(G-4052)*

Phillips Drilling Company ....F....... 724 479-1135
Warrendale *(G-19091)*

Phillips Drilling Company ....G....... 724 479-1135
Indiana *(G-8120)*

Pioneer Drilling Services Ltd ....G....... 724 592-6707
Rices Landing *(G-16671)*

Precision Drilling Oilfld Svcs..................G....... 570 329-5100
Williamsport *(G-20062)*

Ristau Drilling Co ....G....... 814 723-4858
Warren *(G-19046)*

Rock Run Enterprises LLC ....G....... 814 938-8778
Punxsutawney *(G-16159)*

S & S Sbsrface Invstgtions Inc ....G....... 610 738-8762
West Chester *(G-19634)*

S & T Supply Co ....F....... 814 589-7025
Pleasantville *(G-15803)*

Sallack Well Services Inc ....G....... 814 938-8179
Punxsutawney *(G-16160)*

Silver Vly Drlg & Blastg Inc ....G....... 570 992-1125
Saylorsburg *(G-17107)*

Simon of Bolivar Enterprises.................G....... 814 697-7891
Shinglehouse *(G-17513)*

Sonic Energy Services USA Inc ....G....... 724 782-0560
Venetia *(G-18744)*

Southwell Oil Co ....G....... 814 723-5178
Warren *(G-19047)*

Target Drilling Inc................................E....... 724 633-3927
Smithton *(G-17663)*

Texas Keystone Inc..............................E....... 412 435-6555
Oakmont *(G-12926)*

Tophole Drilling LLC ....F....... 724 272-1932
Saxonburg *(G-17098)*

Universal Pressure Pumping Inc ....G....... 814 373-3226
Meadville *(G-10806)*

Universal Well Services Inc ....G....... 814 938-5327
Punxsutawney *(G-16165)*

US Crossings Unlimited LLC ....G....... 888 359-1115
Cranberry Township *(G-3861)*

US Energy Expl Corp ....G....... 724 783-7624
Rural Valley *(G-16878)*

Vertical Resources Inc..........................F....... 814 489-3931
Sugar Grove *(G-18148)*

Victory Energy Corporation ....E....... 724 349-6366
Indiana *(G-8133)*

Vista Resources Inc ....G....... 412 833-8884
Pittsburgh *(G-15699)*

Wgm Gas Company Inc ....E....... 724 397-9600
Creekside *(G-3878)*

Yost Drilling LLC ....D....... 724 324-2253
Mount Morris *(G-11684)*

1382 Oil & Gas Field Exploration Svcs

639 E Congress Realty Corp..................F....... 610 434-5195
Allentown *(G-110)*

Abarta Oil & Gas Co Inc ....E....... 412 963-6226
Pittsburgh *(G-14632)*

AEG Holdings Inc.................................E....... 412 262-2830
Coraopolis *(G-3654)*

Alpha Safety USA.................................G....... 814 236-3344
Clearfield *(G-3211)*

American Oil & Gas LLC ....G....... 724 852-2222
Mount Morris *(G-11677)*

American Petroleum Partners ....G....... 844 835-5277
Canonsburg *(G-2539)*

Anadarko Petroleum..............................G....... 570 326-1535
Williamsport *(G-19986)*

Anderson Family Farm Inc....................F....... 814 463-0202
Tionesta *(G-18369)*

Apex Energy LLC.................................F....... 724 719-2611
Wexford *(G-19787)*

Ard Operating LLC...............................D....... 570 979-1240
Williamsport *(G-19989)*

Atlas Energy Company LLC....................E....... 877 280-2857
Philadelphia *(G-13423)*

Atlas Growth Partners LP ....C....... 412 489-0006
Pittsburgh *(G-14733)*

Atls Production Company LLC................C....... 412 489-0006
Pittsburgh *(G-14736)*

Beckman Production Svcs Inc ....G....... 814 425-1066
Cochranton *(G-3336)*

Belden & Blake Corporation ....F....... 814 589-7091
Pleasantville *(G-15797)*

Blackhawk Specialty Tools LLC ....G....... 570 323-7100
Muncy *(G-11811)*

Bop Land Services LP ....F....... 724 747-1594
Pittsburgh *(G-14785)*

Brighton Resources Inc ....G....... 412 661-1025
Pittsburgh *(G-14792)*

◆ Cameron Technologies Us Inc ....D....... 724 695-3798
Coraopolis *(G-3671)*

Campbell Oil & Gas Inc ....G....... 724 465-9199
Indiana *(G-8085)*

Civic Mapper LLC.................................G....... 315 729-7869
Pittsburgh *(G-14856)*

Cody Well Service................................G....... 814 726-3542
Clarendon *(G-3168)*

Core Laboratories LP ....F....... 412 884-9250
Pittsburgh *(G-14876)*

Dale Property Services Penn LP ....G....... 724 705-0444
Canonsburg *(G-2576)*

Daleco Resources Corporation ....G...... 570 795-4347
West Chester (G-19531)
Dean Construction LLC...............G...... 814 887-8750
Smethport (G-17634)
Direct Energy Products Inc...........F...... 216 255-7777
Tionesta (G-18370)
Discovery Oil Gas LLC................G...... 724 746-4004
Canonsburg (G-2578)
Dominion Exploration and Prod.........G...... 724 349-4450
Indiana (G-8091)
Doran & Associates Inc...............G...... 412 344-5200
Pittsburgh (G-14933)
Dorso LLC.............................G...... 724 934-7710
Wexford (G-19798)
Duncan Land & Energy Inc.............G...... 412 922-0135
Pittsburgh (G-14943)
Eastern American Energy Corp.........F...... 814 938-9000
Punxsutawney (G-16136)
Eclipse Resources I LP...............F...... 814 308-9754
State College (G-17960)
Eclipse Resources Oper LLC...........G...... 814 308-9731
State College (G-17961)
Eclipse Resources-Pa LP..............F...... 814 409-7006
State College (G-17962)
▲ Edward Oil Company ....F...... 814 726-9576
Youngsville (G-20770)
Energy Corporation of America........G...... 724 966-9000
Carmichaels (G-2756)
Eog Resources Inc....................F...... 724 349-7620
Indiana (G-8095)
Esmark Inc...........................F...... 412 259-8868
Sewickley (G-17386)
Evolution Energy Services LLC........D...... 412 946-1371
Mc Murray (G-10644)
Exco Resources LLC...................D...... 724 720-2500
Kittanning (G-8768)
Explorations Inc.....................G...... 814 365-2105
Punxsutawney (G-16137)
Eye-Bot Aerial Solutions LLC.........G...... 724 904-7706
New Kensington (G-12340)
Fault Line Oil Corporation...........G...... 814 368-5901
Bradford (G-1968)
Fossil Rock LLC......................G...... 724 355-3747
Harmony (G-7067)
Fts International LLC.................G...... 724 873-1021
Canonsburg (G-2589)
Haddad and Brooks Inc................G...... 724 228-8811
Washington (G-19184)
Hep Pennsylvania Gathering LLC.......E...... 210 298-2229
Towanda (G-18430)
Hg Energy LLC........................G...... 724 935-8952
Sewickley (G-17391)
Huntley & Huntley Inc................F...... 412 380-2355
Monroeville (G-11341)
Keystone Wireline Inc................G...... 814 362-0230
Bradford (G-1977)
Little Pine Resources................E...... 814 765-6300
Clearfield (G-3223)
Natural Oil & Gas Corp...............G...... 814 362-6890
Bradford (G-1985)
Oil & Gas Management Inc.............G...... 724 925-1568
Hunker (G-7930)
Oleum Exploration LLC................F...... 855 912-6200
Brodheadsville (G-2237)
Pardee Resources Company.............F...... 215 405-1260
Philadelphia (G-14122)
Paul G Benedum Jr....................G...... 412 288-0280
Pittsburgh (G-15371)
Pennico Oil Co Inc...................E...... 724 468-8232
Delmont (G-4053)
Per Midstream LLC....................E...... 412 275-3200
Pittsburgh (G-15377)
Phoenix Energy Productions...........G...... 724 295-9220
Freeport (G-6213)
Plants and Goodwin Inc...............E...... 814 697-6330
Shinglehouse (G-17511)
Preferred Proppants LLC..............F...... 610 834-1969
Radnor (G-16297)
Range Resources......................G...... 570 858-1200
Bradford (G-1989)
Range Rsurces - Appalachia LLC.......F...... 724 887-5715
Scottdale (G-17198)
Range Rsurces - Appalachia LLC.......E...... 724 783-7144
Yatesboro (G-20348)
Range Rsurces - Appalachia LLC.......D...... 724 743-6700
Canonsburg (G-2624)
Range Rsurces - Appalachia LLC.......D...... 817 870-2601
Carlton (G-2753)
RE Gas Development LLC...............E...... 814 278-7267
State College (G-18013)

Rex Energy Corporation...............F...... 724 814-3230
Cranberry Township (G-3846)
Rex Energy IV LLC....................E...... 814 278-7267
State College (G-18015)
Rex Energy Operating Corp............E...... 814 278-7267
State College (G-18016)
Rice Drilling B LLC..................E...... 274 281-7200
Canonsburg (G-2627)
Rice Drilling D LLC..................D...... 274 281-7200
Canonsburg (G-2628)
Rjb Well Services Inc................F...... 814 368-9570
Bradford (G-1990)
Royal Oil & Gas Corporation..........E...... 724 463-0246
Indiana (G-8124)
Schlumberger Technology Corp.........C...... 814 220-1900
Brookville (G-2271)
Seneca Resources Company LLC.........D...... 412 548-2500
Pittsburgh (G-15523)
Snyder Brothers Inc..................E...... 724 548-8101
Kittanning (G-8794)
Star Energy Inc......................G...... 814 257-8485
Dayton (G-4040)
Straub Industries Inc................G...... 814 364-9789
Centre Hall (G-2844)
Sun Energy Services LLC..............C...... 724 473-0687
Zelienople (G-20820)
Sun Energy Services LLC..............E...... 724 473-0687
Zelienople (G-20821)
Superior Applchian Ppeline LLC.......G...... 724 746-6744
Canonsburg (G-2643)
Terraviz Geospatial Inc..............G...... 717 938-3591
Conshohocken (G-3612)
Terraviz Geospatial Inc..............G...... 717 512-9658
Etters (G-5554)
Trans Energy Inc.....................F...... 304 684-7053
Pittsburgh (G-15638)
Universal Well Services Inc..........F...... 570 321-5302
Williamsport (G-20086)
Universal Well Services Inc..........E...... 814 337-1983
Meadville (G-10807)
US Energy Expl Corp..................G...... 724 783-7624
Rural Valley (G-16878)
Vantage Energy LLC...................D...... 724 746-6720
Canonsburg (G-2653)
Vineyard Oil & Gas Company...........F...... 814 725-8742
North East (G-12764)
Weaver Glen A & Son LLC..............G...... 814 432-3013
Franklin (G-6168)
Welltech Products Inc................G...... 610 417-8928
Macungie (G-10161)
White Oak Farms Inc..................G...... 814 257-8485
Dayton (G-4041)

1389 Oil & Gas Field Svcs, NEC

A & P Support Inc....................D...... 570 265-9157
Pittsburgh (G-14627)
Alderdice Inc........................D...... 570 996-1609
Meshoppen (G-11005)
All Climate Servicing................G...... 570 686-4629
Milford (G-11153)
Alma Gas Inc.........................G...... 814 225-3480
Eldred (G-4852)
American Engineers Group LLC.........G...... 484 920-8010
Phoenixville (G-14527)
American Exploration Company.........D...... 610 940-4015
Plymouth Meeting (G-15830)
American Well Service LLC............D...... 724 206-9372
Washington (G-19149)
Appalachian Drilling Svcs Inc........F...... 570 907-0136
Beech Creek (G-1081)
AR Trucking.........................E...... 814 723-1245
Warren (G-19010)
Archrock Inc.........................E...... 724 464-2291
Indiana (G-8080)
Archrock Services LP.................G...... 724 935-7660
Wexford (G-19789)
Archrock Services LP.................G...... 570 567-7162
Canton (G-2662)
Arrowwood Construction...............G...... 610 799-6040
Coplay (G-3639)
Avc Solutions LLC....................G...... 412 737-8945
Pittsburgh (G-14743)
B & C Meter Inc......................G...... 814 257-8464
Dayton (G-4036)
B B Oilfield Equipment...............F...... 724 668-2509
New Alexandria (G-12017)
Baker Hghes Olfld Oprtions LLC.......G...... 724 695-2266
Imperial (G-8059)
Baker Hughes A GE Company LLC........D...... 724 696-3059
Mount Pleasant (G-11687)

Baron Crest Energy Company...........G...... 724 478-1121
Apollo (G-663)
Beckley Perforating Corp.............G...... 570 267-2092
Carbondale (G-2669)
Belden & Blake Corporation...........F...... 814 589-7091
Pleasantville (G-15797)
C&J Energy Services Inc..............D...... 724 354-5225
Shelocta (G-17484)
C&J Well Services Inc................E...... 724 746-2467
Canonsburg (G-2555)
Calfrac Well Services Corp...........E...... 724 564-5350
Smithfield (G-17643)
◆ Cameron Technologies Us Inc.......D...... 724 695-3798
Coraopolis (G-3671)
Canary LLC...........................F...... 724 483-2224
Charleroi (G-3007)
Capstone Energy Services LLC.........E...... 724 326-0190
Allenport (G-104)
CDK Perforating LLC..................G...... 724 222-8900
Washington (G-19155)
CDK Perforating LLC..................G...... 570 358-3250
Ulster (G-18598)
Cellar Tech LLC......................E...... 724 519-2139
Murrysville (G-11849)
Cimarron Energy.....................G...... 724 801-8517
Indiana (G-8086)
City of Pittsburgh...................E...... 412 255-2883
Pittsburgh (G-14854)
Clearfield Ohio Holdings Inc.........G...... 610 293-0410
Radnor (G-16291)
Cogan Wind LLC.......................G...... 570 998-9554
Trout Run (G-18513)
Complete Fluid Control Inc...........E...... 570 382-3376
S Abingtn Twp (G-16893)
Completion Snubbing Servi............G...... 940 668-5109
Smithton (G-17659)
Cory Reservior Testing Inc...........G...... 814 438-2006
Union City (G-18606)
Costys Energy Services...............G...... 570 662-2752
Mansfield (G-10413)
Crg Resources LLC....................G...... 814 571-7190
Curwensville (G-3950)
Cs Trucking LLC......................G...... 814 224-0395
East Freedom (G-4563)
Cudd Pressure Control Inc............E...... 570 250-9043
Lemont Furnace (G-9735)
Curtis Well Service Company..........F...... 814 489-7858
Sugargrove (G-18151)
Dan-Beck Well Services Inc...........E...... 724 538-1001
Evans City (G-5557)
Dean Construction LLC................G...... 814 887-8750
Smethport (G-17634)
Default Servicing Inc................D...... 502 968-1400
Pittsburgh (G-14915)
Developed Resources Inc..............G...... 724 274-6956
Cheswick (G-3106)
Dg Services LLC......................G...... 724 845-7300
Leechburg (G-9644)
Dmand Energy........................F...... 970 201-4976
Cabot (G-2455)
Donawald Enterprises LLC.............F...... 215 962-3635
Doylestown (G-4295)
Eden Green Energy Inc................G...... 267 255-9462
Philadelphia (G-13659)
Elements Direct LLC..................G...... 903 343-5441
New Brighton (G-12035)
Elite Oil Field Services Inc.........G...... 724 627-6060
Uniontown (G-18624)
Elk Lake Services LLC................F...... 724 463-7303
Indiana (G-8094)
Em1 Services LLC.....................F...... 570 560-2561
Unityville (G-18650)
Energy Field Services LLC............G...... 717 791-1018
Dillsburg (G-4128)
Energy Worx Inc......................G...... 321 610-4676
Mansfield (G-10414)
Evergreen Oilfld Solutions LLC.......F...... 570 485-9998
Wyalusing (G-20251)
Exterran Energy Solutions LP.........D...... 724 935-7660
Wexford (G-19799)
Fawnwood Energy Inc..................G...... 724 753-2416
Bruin (G-2314)
Franklin Brine Treatment Corp........G...... 814 437-3593
Franklin (G-6125)
Franks International LLC.............G...... 724 943-3243
Greensboro (G-6646)
G B Well Service.....................G...... 412 221-3102
Bridgeville (G-2065)
Gas & Oil Management Assoc............G...... 814 563-4601
Youngsville (G-20771)

S
I
C

Gas Analytical Services Inc ....G...... 724 349-8133
Indiana (G-8102)

Gas Field Specialists Inc...................D...... 814 698-2122
Shinglehouse (G-17507)

Gas Well Services 24-7 LLC..................G...... 570 398-7879
Jersey Shore (G-8313)

General Civil Company Inc ....F....... 484 571-1998
Aston (G-767)

Geyer & Son Inc ....F....... 412 431-5231
Pittsburgh (G-15049)

Glasgow Hauling Inc.....................D...... 215 884-8800
Glenside (G-6522)

Great Lakes Wellhead Inc ....G...... 570 723-8995
Wellsboro (G-19463)

Great Oak Energy Inc ....G...... 412 828-2900
Oakmont (G-12918)

Greene County Drilling Co Inc ....G...... 724 627-3393
Waynesburg (G-19443)

Halliburton Company....................C...... 570 547-5800
Montgomery (G-11370)

Henderson Resource Group LLC ......G...... 814 203-3226
Hazel Hurst (G-7445)

Homescapers ....G...... 814 353-0507
Bellefonte (G-1105)

▲ Homestead Inspection Service......G...... 717 691-1586
Mechanicsburg (G-10853)

Horizontal Wireline Svcs LLC ....E...... 724 382-5012
Irwin (G-8169)

Howard Drilling Inc ....G...... 814 778-5820
Mount Jewett (G-11642)

I L Geer and Sons ....G...... 814 723-7569
Clarendon (G-3169)

In A Week Guaranteed Inc ....G...... 610 965-7700
Emmaus (G-5028)

Infinity Oilfield Services LLC ....G...... 570 327-8114
Montoursville (G-11442)

J C K Services ....G...... 814 755-7772
Tionesta (G-18372)

J C& Well Services Inc ....E...... 724 475-4881
Fredonia (G-6184)

Jackie L Trout Septic ....G...... 717 244-6640
Felton (G-5940)

Jcs Oilfield Services LLC ....F...... 814 665-4008
Corry (G-3766)

Jklm Energy LLC........................G...... 561 826-3620
Sewickley (G-17398)

Joseph F Mariani Contrs Inc ....F....... 610 358-9746
Aston (G-770)

Kada Energy Resources LLC..........G...... 215 839-9159
Philadelphia (G-13919)

Kapanick Construction Inc ....F....... 814 763-3681
Meadville (G-10742)

Karp Excavating Ltd ....G...... 570 840-9026
Factoryville (G-5757)

Kenic Gas & Oil Company................G...... 724 445-7701
Fenelton (G-5946)

Key Energy Services Inc ....E...... 878 302-3333
New Kensington (G-12351)

Kimzey Casing Service LLC...............G...... 724 225-0529
Washington (G-19192)

Klapec Excavating Inc ....G...... 814 678-3478
Oil City (G-12949)

Klx Energy Services LLC ....G...... 570 835-0149
Tioga (G-18363)

Kozik Bros Inc ....E...... 724 443-2230
Cranberry Township (G-3829)

Linde Corporation ....G...... 570 299-5700
Pittston (G-15765)

Magee and Magee Inc ....F....... 814 966-3623
Rixford (G-16759)

Markwest Liberty Midstream..........D...... 724 514-4401
Washington (G-19199)

Marshall Flp LP ....G...... 570 465-3817
New Milford (G-12398)

Mds Securities LLC ....G...... 724 548-2501
Kittanning (G-8783)

MI Swaco.................................G...... 724 820-3306
Canonsburg (G-2603)

Michael R Skrip Excavating ....G...... 610 965-5331
Emmaus (G-5034)

Minard Run Oil Company ....D...... 814 362-3531
Bradford (G-1982)

Mountain Resources Inc ....G...... 814 734-1496
Edinboro (G-4817)

Msl Oil & Gas Corp ....E...... 814 362-6891
Lewis Run (G-9878)

Newpark Mats Intgrted Svcs LLC ....F...... 570 323-4970
Williamsport (G-20047)

Nortech Energy Solutions LLC............G...... 570 323-3060
Williamsport (G-20049)

Northern Hot Shot Services LLC ....G...... 724 664-5477
Kittanning (G-8786)

Northern Tier Inc ....G...... 814 465-2299
Rew (G-16654)

Oakes Gas Co Inc ....G...... 814 837-7972
Kane (G-8475)

Oil States Energy Services LLC ....D...... 570 538-1623
Watsontown (G-19278)

Oil States Energy Services LLC ....G...... 814 290-6755
Clearfield (G-3227)

Oxford Construction PA Inc ....D...... 215 809-2245
Philadelphia (G-14106)

Pacific Process Systems Inc ....C...... 724 993-4445
Washington (G-19214)

Penn Quaker Site Contrs Inc ....G...... 610 614-0401
Nazareth (G-11985)

Pennsylvania Production Svcs...........E...... 724 463-0729
Indiana (G-8118)

Petroleum Service Partners ....G...... 724 349-1536
Indiana (G-8119)

Petta Enterprises ....G...... 607 857-5915
Mansfield (G-10425)

Phillips & Dart Oil Field Svc ....G...... 814 465-2292
Gifford (G-6360)

Power Ign Cntrls Applachia LLC ....G...... 724 746-3700
Lawrence (G-9539)

Pruftechnik Inc ....E...... 844 242-6296
Philadelphia (G-14211)

◆ Pruftechnik Service Inc ....E...... 856 401-3095
Philadelphia (G-14212)

Puraglobe Florida LLC ....G...... 813 247-1754
Wayne (G-19366)

Quality Process Services ....G...... 724 455-1687
Normalville (G-12625)

R P Neese & Sons LLC ....G...... 724 465-5718
Marion Center (G-10476)

Randy Larkin ....G...... 814 358-2508
Callensburg (G-2465)

RB Farms Inc ....G...... 570 842-7246
Moscow (G-11602)

Reliance Well Services LLC ....E...... 814 454-1644
Erie (G-5461)

Rettew Field Services Inc...............E...... 717 697-3551
Lancaster (G-9187)

Rjb Well Services Inc....................F...... 814 368-9570
Bradford (G-1990)

Roach & Associates Inc ....G...... 412 344-9310
Pittsburgh (G-15491)

ROC Service Company Ltd ....G...... 724 745-3319
Canonsburg (G-2631)

Rpc Inc ....E...... 570 673-5965
Canton (G-2667)

Saybolt LP ....G...... 412 464-7380
West Mifflin (G-19744)

Schlumberger Technology Corp ....C...... 814 220-1900
Brookville (G-2271)

Scott Neilly ....G...... 814 362-4443
Bradford (G-1991)

Seahorse Oilfield Services LLC...........G...... 724 597-2039
Canonsburg (G-2633)

Select Dismantling Corp ....F...... 724 861-6004
Wendel (G-19482)

Select Energy Services LLC ....D...... 724 239-2056
Eighty Four (G-4848)

Sentry Wellhead Systems LLC ....E...... 724 422-8108
Canonsburg (G-2634)

Shallenberger Construction Inc ....D...... 724 628-8408
Connellsville (G-3508)

Shearer Elbie ....G...... 814 266-7548
Johnstown (G-8434)

Silver Creek Services Inc ....E...... 724 710-0440
Canonsburg (G-2637)

Sooner Pipe LLC ....G...... 570 368-4590
Montoursville (G-11450)

SPM Flow Control Inc ....C...... 570 546-1005
Muncy (G-11833)

Springhill Well Service Inc ....E...... 724 447-2449
New Freeport (G-12218)

Staar Distributing Llc...................D...... 814 612-2115
Reynoldsville (G-16666)

Stallion Littlefield Services ....G...... 724 966-2272
Carmichaels (G-2761)

Stallion Oilfield Services Ltd ....E...... 724 743-4801
Canonsburg (G-2639)

Stallion Oilfield Services Ltd ....G...... 570 494-0760
Cogan Station (G-3362)

Stallion Oilfield Services Ltd ....E...... 724 222-9059
Washington (G-19229)

Steven E Tachoir ....G...... 814 726-1572
Marienville (G-10459)

Streamline Energy Services LLC..........F....... 610 415-1220
Valley Forge (G-18715)

Subterranean Tech Inc ....G...... 610 517-0995
West Chester (G-19647)

Sunbelt Drilling Services Inc ....F....... 215 764-9544
Blue Bell (G-1853)

Superior Energy Resources LLC.........G...... 814 265-1080
Brockway (G-2235)

▲ Superior Energy Resources LLC.....E...... 814 265-1080
Brockway (G-2236)

Susquehanna Services LLC ....G...... 570 288-5269
Swoyersville (G-18200)

T C S Industries Inc ....G...... 717 657-7032
Harrisburg (G-7225)

Tarpon Energy Services LLC ....D...... 570 547-0442
Bridgeville (G-2093)

Team Oil Tools LP ....G...... 724 301-2659
Grove City (G-6806)

Tetra Technologies Inc ....E...... 570 659-5357
Mansfield (G-10426)

Texas Ces Inc ....B...... 412 490-9200
Pittsburgh (G-15606)

Thru Tubing Solutions Inc...............G...... 412 787-8060
Imperial (G-8078)

Thru Tubing Solutions Inc...............G...... 570 546-0323
Montoursville (G-11453)

Thyssnkrupp Indus Slutions USA.........D...... 412 257-8277
Bridgeville (G-2095)

Timothy A Musser & Co Inc ....G...... 610 433-6380
Allentown (G-410)

Timothy R Brennan Jr ....G...... 570 281-9504
Carbondale (G-2686)

Titan Wireline Service Inc ....F...... 724 354-2629
Shelocta (G-17489)

U S Weatherford L P ....E...... 724 745-7050
Canonsburg (G-2649)

Uav Aviation Services...................G...... 717 691-8882
Mechanicsburg (G-10901)

UGI Newco LLC ....C...... 610 337-7000
King of Prussia (G-8693)

Universal Well Services Inc ....C...... 724 430-6201
Lemont Furnace (G-9739)

Universal Well Services Inc ....E...... 814 337-1983
Meadville (G-10807)

Universal Well Services Inc ....E...... 814 333-2656
Meadville (G-10808)

Universal Well Services Inc ....E...... 814 938-2051
Punxsutawney (G-16166)

Universal Well Services Inc ....E...... 814 368-6175
Meadville (G-10809)

Ursa Mjor Drctnal Crssings LLC..........F...... 866 410-9719
Greentown (G-6735)

Vulcan Oilfield Services LLC ....G...... 724 698-1008
New Castle (G-12165)

Warrior Energy Services Corp ....F...... 814 637-5191
Penfield (G-13225)

Washita Valley Enterprises Inc ....F...... 724 437-1593
Hopwood (G-7777)

Weatherford International LLC ....F...... 724 745-7050
Canonsburg (G-2656)

Welltec Inc ....G...... 724 553-5922
Cranberry Township (G-3864)

West Penn Energy Services LLC..........C...... 724 354-4118
Shelocta (G-17490)

Wild Well Control Inc ....G...... 724 873-5083
Canonsburg (G-2659)

Williams Field Services ....G...... 570 965-7643
Tunkhannock (G-18552)

Willow Terrace ....G...... 215 951-8500
Philadelphia (G-14478)

Winn-Marion Barber LLC ....G...... 412 319-7392
Bridgeville (G-2099)

Wolverine Enterprise LLC ....E...... 570 463-4103
Mansfield (G-10427)

Wood Group Usa Inc ....G...... 724 514-1600
Canonsburg (G-2661)

Wyoming Casing Service Inc ....E...... 570 363-2883
New Albany (G-12016)

Youth Services Agency ....F...... 215 752-7050
Penndel (G-13242)

14 MINING AND QUARRYING OF NONMETALLIC MINERALS, EXCEPT FUELS

1411 Dimension Stone

Allegheny Mineral Corporation...............E 724 794-6911
Slippery Rock (G-17617)

Allegheny Urn Company .... G 814 437-3208
Franklin *(G-6115)*
API Americas Inc .... F 785 842-7674
Levittown *(G-9817)*
Balducci Stoneyard LLC .... G 410 627-0594
New Freedom *(G-12201)*
Bluegrass Materials Co LLC .... G 410 683-1250
Warfordsburg *(G-18811)*
Bluestone Inc .... F 215 364-1415
Southampton *(G-17799)*
Cava Intl MBL & Gran Inc .... E 215 732-7800
Philadelphia *(G-13516)*
Chilewski Flagstone .... F 570 756-3096
Susquehanna *(G-18179)*
CK Stone LLC .... G 570 903-5868
Tunkhannock *(G-18534)*
Compton Quarry .... G 570 222-9489
Greenfield Township *(G-6643)*
Coolspring Stone Supply Inc .... E 724 437-8663
Uniontown *(G-18621)*
Coolspring Stone Supply Inc .... G 724 437-5200
Uniontown *(G-18622)*
E&J Construction .... F 570 924-4455
Canton *(G-2664)*
Glasgow Inc .... E 610 279-6840
King of Prussia *(G-8620)*
Glenwood Stone Co Inc .... E 570 942-6420
Nicholson *(G-12614)*
Godino West Mtn Stone Quar .... G 570 342-4340
Scranton *(G-17240)*
Graymont Inc .... F 814 359-2313
Bellefonte *(G-1098)*
H&K Group Inc .... E 717 445-0961
Narvon *(G-11922)*
H&K Group Inc .... F 717 548-2147
Peach Bottom *(G-13198)*
H&K Group Inc .... C 610 705-0500
Pottstown *(G-15947)*
Hanson Aggregates PA LLC .... D 610 269-1710
Downingtown *(G-4232)*
Hepco Quarries Inc .... G 484 844-5024
West Chester *(G-19561)*
Highway Materials Inc .... E 610 828-4300
Plymouth Meeting *(G-15846)*
J & E Flagstone .... F 570 869-2718
Laceyville *(G-8871)*
Johnson & Son Stone Works .... G 570 278-9385
Montrose *(G-11467)*
Johnson Quarries Inc .... E 570 744-1284
Stevensville *(G-18059)*
M&M Stone Co .... D 215 723-1177
Telford *(G-18301)*
◆ **Marble Crafters Inc** .... D 610 497-6000
Marcus Hook *(G-10448)*
Media Quarry Co Inc .... E 610 566-6667
Media *(G-10938)*
Mid-Life Stone Works LLC .... G 570 928-8802
Dushore *(G-4509)*
Miller and Roebuck Inc .... G 724 398-3054
Vanderbilt *(G-18720)*
Newport Aggregate Inc .... G 570 736-6612
Nanticoke *(G-11900)*
North Star Leasing Inc .... G 814 629-6999
Friedens *(G-6224)*
P & P Stone LLC .... G 570 967-2279
Hallstead *(G-6835)*
Pottstown Trap Rock Quarries .... F 610 326-4843
Pottstown *(G-16034)*
▲ **Powers Stone Inc** .... E 570 553-4276
Montrose *(G-11475)*
◆ **Princeton Trade Consulting Gro** .... E 610 683-9348
Kutztown *(G-8856)*
Robert Johnson .... G 570 746-1287
Wyalusing *(G-20256)*
Rock Lake Inc .... F 570 465-2986
New Milford *(G-12399)*
South Bend Limestone Company .... G 724 468-8232
Delmont *(G-4059)*
Stoney Lonesome Quarry Inc .... G 570 434-2509
Kingsley *(G-8709)*
Valley Quarries Inc .... G 814 766-2211
Fayetteville *(G-5879)*

1422 Crushed & Broken Limestone

Allan Myers Inc .... E 717 442-4191
Paradise *(G-13152)*
Allan Myers Management Inc .... D 717 656-2411
Leola *(G-9768)*
Allan Myers Management Inc .... F 717 548-2191
Peach Bottom *(G-13195)*
Allan Myers Materials Inc .... C 610 560-7900
Worcester *(G-20222)*
Black Knight Quarries Inc .... G 570 265-8991
Towanda *(G-18421)*
Bradys Bend Corporation .... G 724 526-3353
East Brady *(G-4527)*
Bradys Bend Corporation .... E 724 526-3353
East Brady *(G-4528)*
C & M Aggregate Company Inc .... E 724 796-3821
Bulger *(G-2342)*
▲ **Carmeuse Lime Inc** .... D 412 995-5500
Pittsburgh *(G-14814)*
Carmeuse Lime Inc .... G 717 867-4441
Annville *(G-644)*
Carmeuse Lime & Stone Inc .... F 412 777-0724
Pittsburgh *(G-14815)*
◆ **Carmeuse Lime & Stone Inc** .... C 412 995-5500
Pittsburgh *(G-14816)*
Cemex Cnstr Mtls ATL LLC .... C 724 535-4311
Wampum *(G-18798)*
County Line Quarry Inc .... E 717 252-1584
Wrightsville *(G-20235)*
Eastern Industries Inc .... E 717 667-2015
Milroy *(G-11230)*
Edward M Arnold Jr .... F 610 689-5636
Douglassville *(G-4175)*
▲ **Erie Sand & Gravel Co Inc** .... E 412 995-5500
Pittsburgh *(G-14984)*
Eureka Stone Quarry Inc .... E 570 992-4210
Stroudsburg *(G-18116)*
Glasgow Inc .... E 610 251-0760
Malvern *(G-10240)*
Glenn O Hawbaker Inc .... D 814 237-1444
State College *(G-17970)*
Graymont Inc .... F 814 357-4500
Bellefonte *(G-1099)*
▼ **Graymont Inc** .... D 814 353-4613
Bellefonte *(G-1097)*
Greystone Materials BT .... G 814 748-7652
Colver *(G-3454)*
Greystone Materials BT .... G 570 244-2082
Herndon *(G-7598)*
Greystone Quarries Inc .... G 610 987-8055
Boyertown *(G-1915)*
H&K Group Inc .... C 570 646-3324
Pocono Lake *(G-15880)*
H&K Group Inc .... F 610 250-7700
Easton *(G-4693)*
▲ **H&K Group Inc** .... C 610 584-8500
Skippack *(G-17597)*
Hanson Aggregates Bmc Inc .... F 724 626-0080
Connellsville *(G-3498)*
Hanson Aggregates PA LLC .... E 610 366-4626
Allentown *(G-243)*
Hanson Aggregates PA LLC .... F 570 368-2481
Jersey Shore *(G-8314)*
Hanson Aggregates PA LLC .... F 570 584-2153
Muncy *(G-11818)*
Hanson Aggregates PA LLC .... E 814 355-4226
Bellefonte *(G-1103)*
Hanson Aggregates PA LLC .... F 814 466-5101
Boalsburg *(G-1867)*
Hepco Quarries Incorporated .... G 570 955-8545
New Milford *(G-12396)*
Honey-Creek Stone Co .... F 724 654-5538
Edinburg *(G-4822)*
Hoovers Stone Quarry LLC .... F 724 639-9813
Saltsburg *(G-17051)*
Iddings Quarry Inc .... G 570 966-1551
Mifflinburg *(G-11096)*
International Mill Service .... A 215 956-5500
Horsham *(G-7824)*
Keystone Lime Company .... E 814 662-2025
Springs *(G-17925)*
▼ **Kimmels Coal and Packaging Inc** .... E 717 453-7151
Wiconisco *(G-19895)*
Kowalewski Quarries .... G 570 465-7025
New Milford *(G-12397)*
Laurel Aggregates Inc .... E 724 564-5099
Uniontown *(G-18634)*
Legacy Vulcan LLC .... G 717 792-6996
York *(G-20564)*
Legacy Vulcan LLC .... D 717 637-7121
Hanover *(G-6913)*
◆ **Lwb Holding Company** .... G 717 792-3611
York *(G-20570)*
M & M Lime Co Inc .... E 724 297-3958
Worthington *(G-20231)*
◆ **Magnesita Refractories Company** .... B 717 792-3611
York *(G-20572)*
Magnesita Refractories Company .... B 717 792-4216
York *(G-20573)*
Martin Limestone Inc .... B 717 354-1370
East Earl *(G-4549)*
▼ **Martin Limestone Inc** .... E 717 335-4500
East Earl *(G-4548)*
Meckleys Limestone Pdts Inc .... D 570 758-3011
Herndon *(G-7601)*
Meckleys Limestone Pdts Inc .... G 570 837-5228
Beavertown *(G-1027)*
◆ **Mill Services Corp** .... F 412 678-6141
Glassport *(G-6413)*
Miller and Son Paving Inc .... F 215 598-7801
Rushland *(G-16879)*
National Limestone Quarry .... E 570 837-1635
Middleburg *(G-11033)*
New Enterprise Stone Lime Inc .... D 814 224-6883
New Enterprise *(G-12194)*
New Enterprise Stone Lime Inc .... G 717 349-2412
Dry Run *(G-4384)*
New Enterprise Stone Lime Inc .... D 814 652-5121
Everett *(G-5576)*
New Enterprise Stone Lime Inc .... G 610 683-3302
East Earl *(G-4551)*
New Enterprise Stone Lime Inc .... E 814 342-7096
West Decatur *(G-19689)*
New Enterprise Stone Lime Inc .... E 814 796-1413
Cambridge Springs *(G-2484)*
New Enterprise Stone Lime Inc .... E 814 754-4921
Cairnbrook *(G-2463)*
New Enterprise Stone Lime Inc .... E 814 684-4905
Tyrone *(G-18587)*
New Enterprise Stone Lime Inc .... E 814 443-6494
Somerset *(G-17698)*
New Hope Crushed Stone Lime Co .... E 215 862-5295
New Hope *(G-12310)*
◆ **Norton Oglebay Company** .... F 412 995-5500
Pittsburgh *(G-15347)*
Norton Oglebay Specialty Mnrl .... D 412 995-5500
Pittsburgh *(G-15348)*
▲ **O-N Minerals Chemstone Company** . C 412 995-5500
Pittsburgh *(G-15352)*
O-N Minerals Company (ohio) .... G 412 995-5500
Pittsburgh *(G-15353)*
O-N Minerals Luttrell Company .... F 412 995-5500
Pittsburgh *(G-15354)*
▲ **O-N Minerals Michigan Company** .... G 412 995-5500
Pittsburgh *(G-15355)*
O-N Minerals Portage Co LLC .... D 412 995-5500
Pittsburgh *(G-15356)*
P Stone Inc .... G 570 745-7166
Jersey Shore *(G-8319)*
Pennsy Supply Inc .... D 717 274-3661
Lebanon *(G-9619)*
Pennsy Supply Inc .... F 717 486-5414
Mount Holly Springs *(G-11638)*
Pickett Quarries Inc .... G 570 869-1817
Laceyville *(G-8873)*
Quarry Management LLC .... F 646 599-5893
Lackawaxen *(G-8876)*
Rock Star Quarries LLC .... G 570 721-1426
Wyalusing *(G-20257)*
Rohrers Quarry Inc .... D 717 626-9760
Lititz *(G-10043)*
Rohrers Quarry Inc .... G 717 626-9756
Lititz *(G-10044)*
Stabler Companies Inc .... G 610 799-2421
Coplay *(G-3650)*
Thomas E Siegel .... G 814 226-7421
Shippenville *(G-17564)*
Tms International LLC .... F 814 535-5081
Johnstown *(G-8439)*
Tms International LLC .... D 215 956-5500
Horsham *(G-7859)*
Union Quarries Inc .... E 717 249-5012
Carlisle *(G-2745)*
Valley Quarries Inc .... E 717 334-3281
Gettysburg *(G-6320)*
Valley Quarries Inc .... E 717 263-9186
Chambersburg *(G-2993)*
Valley Quarries Inc .... G 717 264-5811
Chambersburg *(G-2996)*
Valley Quarries Inc .... F 717 532-4456
Shippensburg *(G-17553)*
Valley Quarries Inc .... G 717 642-8535
Fairfield *(G-5770)*
Valley Quarries Inc .... F 717 267-2244
Chambersburg *(G-2994)*
Valley Quarries Inc .... E 717 264-4178
Chambersburg *(G-2995)*

Employee Codes: A=Over 500 employees, B=251-500
C=101-250, D=51-100, E=20-50, F=10-19, G=3-9
2019 Harris Pennsylvania
Manufacturers Directory
799

Winfield Lime & Stone Co Inc ....F 724 352-3596
Cabot (G-2461)

York Building Products Co Inc ....F 717 792-9922
Thomasville (G-18344)

▲ York Building Products Co Inc ....E 717 848-2831
York (G-20726)

1423 Crushed & Broken Granite

Grannas Bros Stone Asp Co Inc ....D 814 695-5021
Hollidaysburg (G-7649)

▲ Keystone Granite Tile Inc ....F 717 394-4972
Lancaster (G-9084)

Penn Run Quarry Spruce Mine ....F 724 465-0272
Penn Run (G-13231)

Pennsylvanin Flagstone Inc ....F 814 544-7575
Coudersport (G-3787)

▲ Signline LLC ....G 610 973-3600
Allentown (G-391)

1429 Crushed & Broken Stone, NEC

Allan Myers Inc ....E 717 442-4191
Paradise (G-13152)

Bear Gap Stone Inc ....G 570 337-9831
Elysburg (G-4971)

Blue Mountain Buildng Stone Co ....G 717 671-8711
Harrisburg (G-7096)

Capozzolo Brothers ....G 610 588-7702
Bangor (G-909)

Dyer Quarry Inc ....E 610 582-6010
Birdsboro (G-1693)

Edison Quarry Inc ....G 215 348-4382
Doylestown (G-4297)

H&K Group Inc ....G 570 347-1800
Dunmore (G-4474)

Hanson Aggregates PA LLC ....E 814 355-4226
Bellefonte (G-1103)

Hanson Aggregates PA LLC ....E 610 366-4626
Allentown (G-243)

Hanson Aggrgates Southeast Inc ....G 570 784-2888
Bloomsburg (G-1786)

Highway Materials Inc ....E 215 234-4522
Perkiomenville (G-13301)

Mammoth Materials ....G 570 385-4232
Schuylkill Haven (G-17162)

McClure Enterprises Inc ....G 570 562-1180
Old Forge (G-12970)

Pennsy Supply Inc ....F 570 754-7508
Schuylkill Haven (G-17163)

Slatedale Aggregate Mtls Inc ....G 610 767-4601
Slatington (G-17613)

1442 Construction Sand & Gravel

A C A Sand & Gravel ....G 814 665-6087
Corry (G-3741)

Afton Trucking Inc ....F 814 825-7449
Erie (G-5177)

Allegheny Mineral Corporation ....E 724 735-2088
Harrisville (G-7252)

Alliance Sand Co Inc ....F 610 826-2248
Palmerton (G-13099)

▼ American Asphalt Paving Co ....C 570 696-1181
Shavertown (G-17478)

Belvidere Sand Gravel ....G 267 880-2422
Doylestown (G-4274)

Bill Barry Excavating Inc ....G 570 595-2269
Cresco (G-3891)

Brokenstraw Gravel Co Inc ....G 814 563-7911
Pittsfield (G-15738)

C & M Aggregate Company Inc ....E 724 796-3821
Bulger (G-2342)

Chad Cross ....G 570 549-3234
Mansfield (G-10412)

Dalyrmple Gravel and Contracti ....G 570 297-0340
Troy (G-18521)

Dingmans Ferry Stone Inc ....G 570 828-2617
Dingmans Ferry (G-4142)

Earl F Dean Inc ....G 814 435-6581
Galeton (G-6239)

Eastern Industries Inc ....E 610 683-7400
Kutztown (G-8842)

Eastern Industries Inc ....E 570 265-9191
Towanda (G-18425)

▲ EJ Bognar Incorporated ....G 412 344-9900
Pittsburgh (G-14960)

▼ Erie Strayer Company ....C 814 456-7001
Erie (G-5275)

Fairmount Minerals ....G 724 873-9039
Eighty Four (G-4840)

Fiesler Sand & Gravel LLC ....G 814 899-6161
Erie (G-5289)

Georgetown Sand & Gravel Inc ....G 724 573-9518
Georgetown (G-6276)

Glacial Sand & Gravel Co ....G 724 548-8101
Kittanning (G-8773)

Glen Mills Sand & Gravel Inc ....E 610 459-4988
Media (G-10929)

Gravel ....G 215 675-3960
Hatboro (G-7286)

Gravel Bar Inc ....G 724 568-3518
Vandergrift (G-18729)

H & H Materials Inc ....E 724 376-2834
Stoneboro (G-18069)

Hanson Aggregates PA LLC ....D 610 269-1710
Downingtown (G-4232)

Hanson Aggregates PA LLC ....D 570 992-4951
Stroudsburg (G-18122)

Hanson Aggregates PA LLC ....F 570 368-2481
Jersey Shore (G-8314)

Hanson Aggregates PA LLC ....F 570 584-2153
Muncy (G-11818)

Hanson Aggregates PA LLC ....F 570 324-2514
Blossburg (G-1807)

Hanson Aggregates PA LLC ....F 570 437-4068
Milton (G-11240)

Hanson Aggregates PA LLC ....F 570 726-4511
Salona (G-17049)

Hanson Aggregates PA LLC ....F 570 784-1640
Bloomsburg (G-1784)

Hanson Aggregates PA LLC ....E 570 784-2888
Bloomsburg (G-1785)

Hanson Aggregates PA LLC ....F 814 466-5101
Boalsburg (G-1867)

Hanson Aggregates PA LLC ....E 610 366-4626
Allentown (G-243)

Hempt Bros Inc ....G 717 486-5111
Gardners (G-6260)

Hempt Bros Inc ....D 717 774-2911
Camp Hill (G-2500)

Hunlock Sand & Gravel Company ....F 570 256-3036
Bath (G-960)

J A & W A Hess Inc ....E 570 454-3731
Hazleton (G-7504)

Lakeland Sand & Gravel Inc ....E 724 588-7020
Conneaut Lake (G-3475)

Lane Construction Corporation ....D 412 838-0251
Pittsburgh (G-15218)

Legacy Vulcan LLC ....D 717 637-7121
Hanover (G-6913)

Linen Sand Supplies ....G 610 399-8305
West Chester (G-19594)

Martin Marietta Materials Inc ....F 724 573-9518
Georgetown (G-6277)

Mayer Brothers Construction Co ....F 814 452-3748
Erie (G-5383)

McDonald Sand & Gravel Inc ....G 814 774-8149
Girard (G-6397)

Middleport Materials Inc ....F 570 277-0335
Middleport (G-11046)

New Enterprise Stone Lime Inc ....C 814 224-2121
Roaring Spring (G-16766)

North Star Aggregates Inc ....G 814 637-5599
Penfield (G-13222)

Pennsy Supply Inc ....F 717 486-5414
Mount Holly Springs (G-11638)

Pennsy Supply Inc ....F 570 754-7508
Schuylkill Haven (G-17163)

Pennsy Supply Inc ....D 717 274-3661
Lebanon (G-9619)

Pocono Industries Inc ....G 570 421-3889
Stroudsburg (G-18134)

Preferred Sands LLC ....D 610 834-1969
Radnor (G-16298)

Shenango Valley Sand and Grav ....G 724 932-5600
Jamestown (G-8240)

Slippery Rock Materials Inc ....E 724 530-7472
Volant (G-18777)

◆ Snyder Assod Companies Inc ....E 724 548-8101
Kittanning (G-8793)

Summers Construction ....G 724 924-1700
New Castle (G-12157)

Svonavec Inc ....G 814 926-2815
Rockwood (G-17017)

T-M-T Gravel and Contg Inc ....F 570 537-2647
Millerton (G-11216)

▲ Tri-State River Products Inc ....F 724 775-2221
Beaver (G-993)

Valley Quarries Inc ....F 717 267-2244
Chambersburg (G-2994)

Valley Quarries Inc ....E 717 264-4178
Chambersburg (G-2995)

Waterford Sand & Gravel Co ....E 814 796-6250
Union City (G-18613)

Wendell H Stone Company Inc ....E 724 483-6571
Charleroi (G-3025)

Williams Garden Center Inc ....G 570 842-7277
Covington Township (G-3794)

Wysox S&G Inc ....F 570 265-6760
Wysox (G-20291)

▲ York Building Products Co Inc ....E 717 848-2831
York (G-20726)

1446 Industrial Sand

Allegheny Metals & Minerals ....G 412 344-9900
Pittsburgh (G-14681)

American Hard Chrome LLC ....G 412 951-9051
New Castle (G-12057)

Aztec Materials LLC ....G 215 675-8900
Hatboro (G-7271)

Aztec Materials LLC ....G 215 675-8900
Hatboro (G-7272)

Custom Entryways & Millwork ....G 814 798-2500
Stoystown (G-18074)

G&U Sand Svcs ....G 717 246-6724
Windsor (G-20196)

Hanson Aggregates PA LLC ....F 570 726-4511
Salona (G-17049)

◆ Norton Oglebay Company ....F 412 995-5500
Pittsburgh (G-15347)

U S Silica Company ....D 814 542-2561
Mapleton Depot (G-10432)

1455 Kaolin & Ball Clay

Resco Group Inc ....F 412 494-4491
Pittsburgh (G-15479)

Stephens Excavating Svc LLC ....G 484 888-1010
Kennett Square (G-8545)

1459 Clay, Ceramic & Refractory Minerals, NEC

American Colloid Company ....E 717 845-3077
York (G-20371)

E J Bognar Inc ....F 814 443-6000
Somerset (G-17686)

▲ EJ Bognar Incorporated ....G 412 344-9900
Pittsburgh (G-14960)

Fink & Stackhouse Inc ....G 570 323-3475
Williamsport (G-20013)

G & K Watterson Company ....G 724 827-2800
New Brighton (G-12037)

Harbisnwlker Intl Holdings Inc ....G 412 375-6600
Moon Township (G-11488)

◆ Harbisonwalker Intl Inc ....C 412 375-6600
Moon Township (G-11490)

▲ Refractory Machining Services ....F 724 285-7674
Butler (G-2438)

1479 Chemical & Fertilizer Mining

Corry Peat Products Co Inc ....G 814 665-7101
Corry (G-3756)

◆ Morton International LLC ....C 989 636-1000
Collegeville (G-3384)

1481 Nonmetallic Minerals Svcs, Except Fuels

C S Garber & Sons Inc ....E 610 367-2861
Boyertown (G-1902)

Covia Holdings Corporation ....G 412 431-4777
Pittsburgh (G-14883)

Envirnrnmntal Protection PA Dept ....F 570 621-3139
Pottsville (G-16078)

Hazleton Shaft Corporation ....E 570 450-0900
Hazleton (G-7503)

Nolt Services LLC ....G 717 738-1066
Lititz (G-10026)

▲ North American Drillers LLC ....C 304 291-0175
Mount Morris (G-11683)

▲ Preptech Inc ....G 724 727-3439
Apollo (G-684)

Rosebud Mining Co ....E 814 749-5208
Twin Rocks (G-18572)

Seneca Mineral Co Inc ....G 814 476-0076
Erie (G-5474)

Sheridan Construction Group ....G 717 948-0507
Middletown (G-11076)

Te Stone Products LLC ....G 570 335-4921
Mayfield (G-10543)

Test Boring Services Inc ....F 724 267-4649
Scenery Hill (G-17126)

1499 Miscellaneous Nonmetallic Mining

Allegheny Mineral Corporation ....E 724 735-2088
Harrisville *(G-7252)*

Black Diamond Mining Inc ....G 570 672-9917
Elysburg *(G-4972)*

Gma Garnet (usa) Corp ....E 215 736-1868
Fairless Hills *(G-5780)*

Grc Holding Inc ....G 610 667-6640
Bala Cynwyd *(G-879)*

Harleysville Materials LLC ....F 856 768-8493
Harleysville *(G-7037)*

Jigging Tech LLC DBA Atoll ....G 814 619-5187
Johnstown *(G-8385)*

Martin Limestone Inc ....B 717 354-1370
East Earl *(G-4549)*

New Enterprise Stone Lime Inc ....F 717 442-4148
Gap *(G-6254)*

◆ Norton Oglebay Company ....F 412 995-5500
Pittsburgh *(G-15347)*

Premier Chemicals LLC ....G 610 420-7500
Kennett Square *(G-8536)*

RC Cement Co Inc ....G 610 866-4400
Bethlehem *(G-1607)*

Specialty Vermiculite Corp ....D 610 660-8840
Bala Cynwyd *(G-893)*

Vermiculite Association Inc ....G 717 238-9902
Harrisburg *(G-7242)*

20 FOOD AND KINDRED PRODUCTS

2011 Meat Packing Plants

1732 Meats LLC ....G 267 879-7214
Yeadon *(G-20350)*

Al Marwa LLC ....G 215 536-6050
Quakertown *(G-16168)*

Alex Froehlich Packing Co ....F 814 535-7694
Johnstown *(G-8349)*

Alpine Wurst & Meathouse Inc ....E 570 253-5899
Honesdale *(G-7700)*

American Foods Inc ....F 724 223-0820
Washington *(G-19147)*

Astra Foods Inc ....D 610 352-4400
Upper Darby *(G-18681)*

Atlantic Veal and Lamb Inc ....E 570 489-4781
Olyphant *(G-12984)*

Bingman Packing Co ....G 814 267-3413
Berlin *(G-1283)*

Cargill Incorporated ....F 717 273-1133
Lebanon *(G-9552)*

Cargill Meat Solutions Corp ....A 570 384-8350
Hazleton *(G-7493)*

Cargill Meat Solutions Corp ....A 570 746-3000
Wyalusing *(G-20248)*

Cck Inc ....C 814 684-2270
Tyrone *(G-18578)*

▼ Clemens Family Corporation ....A 800 523-5291
Hatfield *(G-7324)*

◆ Clemens Food Group LLC ....A 215 368-2500
Hatfield *(G-7325)*

Clemens Food Group LLC ....D 215 368-2500
Emmaus *(G-5023)*

Country Butcher Shop ....F 717 249-4691
Carlisle *(G-2703)*

▼ CTI King of Prussia LLC ....G 610 879-2868
King of Prussia *(G-8603)*

Darlings Locker Plant ....G 570 945-5716
La Plume *(G-8869)*

Dave Fine Meat Packer Inc ....G 724 352-1537
Saxonburg *(G-17083)*

▲ Devault Packing Company Inc ....C 610 644-2536
Devault *(G-4111)*

▲ Dibruno Bros Inc ....G 215 665-9220
Philadelphia *(G-13630)*

▲ Dietz & Watson Inc ....A 800 333-1974
Philadelphia *(G-13631)*

Doug Pfers Deer Ctng Smoke Hse ....G 724 758-7965
Ellwood City *(G-4929)*

Drexel Foods Inc ....E 215 425-9900
Philadelphia *(G-13646)*

Emericks Meat & Packing Co ....E 814 842-6779
Hyndman *(G-8050)*

Farrs Meat Processing ....G 570 827-2241
Lawrenceville *(G-9542)*

Ferncliff Meat Processing ....G 724 592-6042
Rices Landing *(G-16669)*

George Farms ....F 570 275-0239
Danville *(G-4003)*

▲ Grammeco Inc ....C 610 352-4400
Upper Darby *(G-18686)*

▼ Hazle Park Packing Co ....E 570 455-7571
Hazle Township *(G-7461)*

Heinnickel Farms Inc ....G 724 837-9254
Greensburg *(G-6673)*

Herfurth Brothers Inc ....G 610 681-4515
Gilbert *(G-6361)*

Howard & Son Meatpacking ....G 724 662-3700
Mercer *(G-10963)*

J R Kline Butchery LLC ....G 570 220-4229
New Albany *(G-12012)*

J R Kline Butchery LLC ....G 570 220-4229
New Albany *(G-12013)*

Jbs Packerland Inc ....F 215 723-5559
Souderton *(G-17743)*

Jbs Souderton Inc ....A 215 723-5555
Souderton *(G-17744)*

Johnston Meat Processing ....G 814 225-3495
Eldred *(G-4853)*

K Heeps Inc ....G 610 434-4312
Allentown *(G-275)*

Korte & Co Inc ....F 610 253-9141
Easton *(G-4712)*

Kunzler & Company Inc ....B 717 299-6301
Lancaster *(G-9089)*

Laudermilch Meats Inc ....D 717 867-1251
Annville *(G-652)*

Leidys Inc ....D 215 723-4606
Souderton *(G-17749)*

Leona Meat Plant Inc ....F 570 297-3574
Troy *(G-18523)*

Locker Plant LLC ....G 814 652-2714
Everett *(G-5574)*

Lone Star Western Beef Inc ....E 484 509-2093
Reading *(G-16433)*

Louis G Sredy ....G 814 445-7229
Somerset *(G-17696)*

M Robzen Inc ....E 570 283-1226
Kingston *(G-8723)*

▼ Marcho Farms Inc ....C 215 721-7131
Harleysville *(G-7045)*

Mc Kruit Meat Packing ....G 724 352-2988
Cabot *(G-2459)*

Mikes Packing Company ....F 724 222-5476
Washington *(G-19203)*

Mountain Man Deer Processing ....G 717 532-7295
Orrstown *(G-13034)*

Mrg Food LLC ....F 412 482-7430
McKeesport *(G-10676)*

Murrys of Maryland Inc ....C 301 420-6400
Lebanon *(G-9612)*

National Beef Packing Co LLC ....C 570 743-4420
Hummels Wharf *(G-7900)*

Nema Usa Inc ....E 412 678-9541
Pittsburgh *(G-15325)*

Nicholas Meat LLC ....D 570 725-3511
Loganton *(G-10096)*

Nicholas Meat Packing Co ....C 570 725-3511
Loganton *(G-10097)*

October 6 2011 ....G 814 422-8810
Spring Mills *(G-17891)*

OJacks Inc ....E 814 225-4755
Eldred *(G-4854)*

P & N Packing Inc ....E 570 746-1974
Wyalusing *(G-20255)*

Painter Meat Processing ....G 814 258-7283
Elkland *(G-4917)*

Palmyra Bologna Company ....G 717 273-9581
Lebanon *(G-9614)*

Phillys Best Steak Company Inc ....F 610 259-6000
Lansdowne *(G-9441)*

Polarized Meat Co Inc ....B 570 347-3396
Dunmore *(G-4481)*

Pudliners Packing ....G 814 539-5422
Johnstown *(G-8425)*

R & R Provision Co ....D 610 258-5366
Easton *(G-4746)*

R C Silivis & Sons ....G 814 257-8401
Dayton *(G-4039)*

R L Sipes Locker Plant ....G 814 652-2714
Everett *(G-5578)*

▲ Rendulic Packing Company ....E 412 678-9541
McKeesport *(G-10679)*

Richard Baringer ....G 610 346-7661
Richlandtown *(G-16690)*

Rosss Custom Butchering ....F 570 634-3571
Trout Run *(G-18516)*

S Schiff Restaurant Svc Inc ....C 570 343-1294
Scranton *(G-17282)*

Sechrist Bros Inc ....F 717 244-2975
Dallastown *(G-3981)*

Sharon McGuigan Inc ....E 610 361-8100
Aston *(G-793)*

Silver Springs Farm Inc ....E 215 256-4321
Harleysville *(G-7058)*

Silver Star Meats Inc ....D 412 771-5539
Mc Kees Rocks *(G-10635)*

Smithfield Foods Inc ....A 215 752-1090
Middletown *(G-11077)*

Smithfield Packaged Meats Corp ....B 724 335-5800
New Kensington *(G-12378)*

Tags Processing ....G 724 345-8279
Washington *(G-19230)*

Thoma Meat Market Inc ....E 724 352-2020
Saxonburg *(G-17097)*

Tyson ....G 717 755-4782
Red Lion *(G-16618)*

Tyson Foods Inc ....E 717 653-8326
Mount Joy *(G-11673)*

Tyson Foods Inc ....B 412 257-3224
Pittsburgh *(G-15664)*

▼ USA Pork Packers Inc ....E 570 501-7675
Hazleton *(G-7533)*

Wright Meat Packing Co Inc ....G 724 368-8571
Fombell *(G-6039)*

Zrile Brothers Packing Inc ....G 724 528-9246
West Middlesex *(G-19733)*

2013 Sausages & Meat Prdts

Alderfer Inc ....D 215 256-8819
Harleysville *(G-7016)*

Alex Froehlich Packing Co ....F 814 535-7694
Johnstown *(G-8349)*

Alpine Wurst & Meathouse Inc ....E 570 253-5899
Honesdale *(G-7700)*

Ask Foods Inc ....E 717 838-6356
Palmyra *(G-13118)*

Bethlehem Sausage Works Inc ....G 800 478-2302
Easton *(G-4655)*

▲ Brother and Sister Fd Svc Inc ....G 717 558-0108
Camp Hill *(G-2493)*

Cargill Meat Solutions Corp ....A 570 746-3000
Wyalusing *(G-20248)*

Cck Inc ....C 814 684-2270
Tyrone *(G-18578)*

CFC Leola Properties Inc ....F 717 390-1978
Middletown *(G-11050)*

Charles Ritter Incorporated ....C 215 320-5000
Philadelphia *(G-13531)*

Clair D Thompson & Sons Inc ....E 570 398-1880
Jersey Shore *(G-8311)*

◆ Clemens Food Group LLC ....A 215 368-2500
Hatfield *(G-7325)*

CP Food Stores Inc ....F 412 831-7777
Pittsburgh *(G-14884)*

Daniel Weaver Company Inc ....E 717 274-6100
Lebanon *(G-9558)*

▲ Devault Packing Company Inc ....C 610 644-2536
Devault *(G-4111)*

▲ Dietz & Watson Inc ....A 800 333-1974
Philadelphia *(G-13631)*

Drexel Foods Inc ....E 215 425-9900
Philadelphia *(G-13646)*

Ernest Ricci ....G 412 490-9531
Mc Kees Rocks *(G-10607)*

◆ Euro Foods Inc ....C 570 636-3171
Freeland *(G-6194)*

European & American Sausage Co ....G 215 232-1716
Philadelphia *(G-13682)*

Family Food Products Inc ....D 215 633-1515
Bensalem *(G-1193)*

Gillo Brothers ....G 724 254-4845
Clymer *(G-3273)*

▼ Hazle Park Packing Co ....E 570 455-7571
Hazle Township *(G-7461)*

Hillshire Brands Company ....F 724 772-3440
Cranberry Township *(G-3822)*

Jbs Packerland Inc ....F 215 723-5559
Souderton *(G-17743)*

Jbs Souderton Inc ....A 215 723-5555
Souderton *(G-17744)*

John F Martin & Sons LLC ....C 717 336-2804
Stevens *(G-18054)*

Ken Weaver Meats Inc ....E 717 502-0118
Wellsville *(G-19479)*

Knauss Inc ....D 215 536-4220
Quakertown *(G-16206)*

Kunzler & Company Inc ....B 717 299-6301
Lancaster *(G-9089)*

Labriola Sausage Co ....G 412 281-5966
Pittsburgh *(G-15214)*

Laudermilch Meats Inc ....D 717 867-1251
Annville **(G-652)**

Leona Meat Plant Inc ....F 570 297-3574
Troy **(G-18523)**

Liberty Bell Steak Co ....E 215 537-4797
Philadelphia **(G-13968)**

Louis G Sredy ....G 814 445-7229
Somerset **(G-17696)**

M Robzen Inc ....E 570 283-1226
Kingston **(G-8723)**

Maglio Bros Inc ....D 215 465-3902
Philadelphia **(G-13987)**

Maid-Rite Specialty Foods LLC .....F 570 346-3572
Scranton **(G-17258)**

Mikes Packing Company ....F 724 222-5476
Washington **(G-19203)**

Moms Wholesale Foods Inc ....G 724 856-3049
New Castle **(G-12122)**

Mondelez Global LLC ....A 570 820-1200
Wilkes Barre **(G-19945)**

▲ Mrs Resslers Food Products Co ......D 215 744-4700
Philadelphia **(G-14043)**

Murazzi Provision Co ....F 570 344-2285
Scranton **(G-17262)**

Murrys of Maryland Inc ....C 301 420-6400
Lebanon **(G-9612)**

Nicholas Meat Packing Co ....C 570 725-3511
Loganton **(G-10097)**

OJacks Inc ....E 814 225-4755
Eldred **(G-4854)**

Olde Recipe Foods Inc ....G 724 654-5779
Portersville **(G-15934)**

Original Philly Holdings Inc ....C 215 423-3333
Southampton **(G-17829)**

Palmyra Bologna Company ....E 717 838-6336
Palmyra **(G-13128)**

Palumbos Meats Dubois Inc ....E 814 371-2150
Du Bois **(G-4412)**

Parma Sausage Products Inc ....F 412 261-2532
Pittsburgh **(G-15370)**

Perfection Foods Company Inc ....D 215 455-5400
Philadelphia **(G-14137)**

Philadelphia Provision Co ....C 215 423-1707
Philadelphia **(G-14151)**

Philadlphia Pr-Coked Steak Inc .....E 215 426-4949
Philadelphia **(G-14164)**

Pittsburgh Spice Seasoning Co ....G 412 288-5036
Pittsburgh **(G-15408)**

Polarized Meat Co Inc ....B 570 347-3396
Dunmore **(G-4481)**

Protos Foods Inc ....G 724 836-1802
Greensburg **(G-6705)**

▲ Quaker Maid Meats Inc ....C 610 376-1500
Reading **(G-16478)**

Quaker Maid Meats Inc ....E 610 376-1500
Reading **(G-16479)**

S M E Foods LLC ....G 717 852-8515
York **(G-20662)**

S Schiff Restaurant Svc Inc ....C 570 343-1294
Scranton **(G-17282)**

Sheinman Provision Co Inc ....E 305 592-0300
Philadelphia **(G-14300)**

Silver Springs Farm Inc ....E 215 256-4321
Harleysville **(G-7058)**

Silver Star Meats Inc ....D 412 771-5539
Mc Kees Rocks **(G-10635)**

Smith Provision Co Inc ....E 814 459-4974
Erie **(G-5482)**

Smith Provision Co Inc ....G 814 459-4974
Erie **(G-5483)**

Theodore Fazen ....E 215 672-1122
Horsham **(G-7858)**

Topsmal Dairy LLC ....G 814 880-3724
Bellefonte **(G-1123)**

Tri-Our Brands ....G 570 655-1512
Pittston **(G-15783)**

Uncle Charleys Sausage Co LLC .....E 724 845-3302
Vandergrift **(G-18736)**

Vantage Foods PA LP ....E 717 691-4728
Camp Hill **(G-2522)**

▲ Vincent Giordano Corp ....D 215 467-6629
Philadelphia **(G-14447)**

2015 Poultry Slaughtering, Dressing & Processing

A La Henri Inc ....G 724 856-1374
New Castle **(G-12052)**

Birdsboro Kosher Farms Corp ....C 610 404-0001
Birdsboro **(G-1690)**

Browns Mill Farm LLC ....G 570 345-3153
Schuylkill Haven **(G-17149)**

Cargill Incorporated ....F 717 273-1133
Lebanon **(G-9552)**

Crystal Frms Refrigerated Dist ....B 570 425-2910
Klingerstown **(G-8807)**

David Elliot Poultry Farm Inc ....C 570 344-6348
Scranton **(G-17228)**

Drexel Foods Inc ....E 215 425-9900
Philadelphia **(G-13646)**

▲ E G Emils and Son Inc ....E 215 763-3311
Philadelphia **(G-13653)**

E K Holdings Inc ....G 717 436-5921
Mifflintown **(G-11113)**

E S H Poultry ....F 717 517-9535
Lancaster **(G-9005)**

EG Emils and Son Inc ....G 800 228-3645
Philadelphia **(G-13663)**

Egglands Best Inc ....E 610 265-6500
Malvern **(G-10228)**

Empire Kosher Poultry Inc ....E 570 374-0501
Selinsgrove **(G-17324)**

◆ Empire Kosher Poultry Inc ....A 717 436-5921
Mifflintown **(G-11114)**

▲ Farmers Pride Inc ....A 717 865-6626
Fredericksburg **(G-6174)**

Fourth Street Barbecue Inc ....C 724 483-2000
Charleroi **(G-3013)**

Hain Pure Protein Corporation ....F 717 865-2136
Fredericksburg **(G-6175)**

Hain Pure Protein Corporation ....D 717 624-2191
New Oxford **(G-12411)**

Hillandale Farms of Pa Inc ....E 717 229-0601
Gettysburg **(G-6299)**

Hillandale-Gettysburg LP ....C 717 334-1973
Gettysburg **(G-6300)**

Jaindls Incorporated ....D 610 395-3333
Orefield **(G-13013)**

Jim Neidermyer Poultry ....E 717 738-1036
Denver **(G-4078)**

▲ Joe Jurgielewicz & Son Ltd ....E 610 562-3825
Hamburg **(G-6842)**

Lewistown Valley Entps Inc ....D 570 668-2089
Tamaqua **(G-18218)**

Mac Millan William Company ....F 215 627-3273
Philadelphia **(G-13985)**

Mitchel Loading Crew ....F 570 837-5907
Middleburg **(G-11032)**

▲ Mrs Resslers Food Products Co ......D 215 744-4700
Philadelphia **(G-14043)**

Murrys of Maryland Inc ....C 301 420-6400
Lebanon **(G-9612)**

Oaks Poultry Co Inc ....F 814 798-3631
Stoystown **(G-18083)**

Perdue Farms Inc ....B 717 426-1961
Marietta **(G-10466)**

Perdue Farms Inc ....C 610 388-1385
Chadds Ford **(G-2858)**

Philadelphia Poultry Inc ....E 215 574-0343
Philadelphia **(G-14150)**

Sechler Family Foods Inc ....F 717 865-6626
Fredericksburg **(G-6176)**

Sharon McGuigan Inc ....E 610 361-8100
Aston **(G-793)**

Tran Hoang ....G 215 833-0923
Philadelphia **(G-14402)**

Tri-Our Brands ....G 570 655-1512
Pittston **(G-15783)**

Tyson Foods Inc ....A 717 354-4211
New Holland **(G-12289)**

2021 Butter

Calkins Creamery LLC ....F 570 729-8103
Honesdale **(G-7704)**

Campus Creamery LLC ....G 570 351-1738
S Abingtn Twp **(G-16890)**

Cathys Creamery ....G 570 916-3386
Milton **(G-11235)**

Creamery On Main ....G 610 928-1500
Emmaus **(G-5024)**

Dairy Farmers America Inc ....E 724 946-8729
West Middlesex **(G-19722)**

Dietrichs Milk Products LLC ....D 570 376-2001
Middlebury Center **(G-11044)**

Fresh Made Inc ....G 215 725-9013
Philadelphia **(G-13724)**

Half Pint Creamery LLC ....G 717 634-5459
Hanover **(G-6890)**

Half Pint Creamery LLC ....G 717 420-2110
Gettysburg **(G-6297)**

High View Inc ....E 814 886-7171
Loretto **(G-10104)**

Honey Butter Products Co Inc ....G 717 665-9323
Manheim **(G-10389)**

Ironstone Creamery ....G 610 952-2748
Pottstown **(G-15949)**

Kellers Creamery LLC ....D 215 256-8871
Harleysville **(G-7043)**

L D Kallman Inc ....F 610 384-1200
Coatesville **(G-3312)**

Land OLakes Inc ....C 717 486-7000
Carlisle **(G-2719)**

Liberty View Creamery LLC ....G 717 359-8206
Littlestown **(G-10070)**

Paula Keswick ....G 574 298-2022
Reynoldsville **(G-16660)**

Pocono Mountain Creamery LLC ....G 570 443-9868
White Haven **(G-19850)**

Strasburg Creamery LLC ....G 717 456-7497
Delta **(G-4064)**

Turner Dairy Farms Inc ....D 412 372-7155
Pittsburgh **(G-15661)**

2022 Cheese

▼ AFP Advanced Food Products LLC..C 717 355-8667
New Holland **(G-12227)**

Calandra Cheese ....G 610 759-2299
Nazareth **(G-11958)**

Caputo Brothers Creamery LLC ......G 717 739-1087
Spring Grove **(G-17876)**

▲ Castle Cheese Inc ....E 724 368-3022
Pittsburgh **(G-14826)**

Cowz Leap Creamery LLC ....G 717 653-1532
Mount Joy **(G-11651)**

Dairiconcepts LP ....E 717 566-4500
Hummelstown **(G-7908)**

Dairy Farmers America Inc ....E 724 946-8729
West Middlesex **(G-19722)**

▲ Dibruno Bros Inc ....G 215 665-9220
Philadelphia **(G-13630)**

Euclid Technologies Inc ....G 610 515-1842
Easton **(G-4682)**

▲ Fleur De Lait East LLC ....G 717 355-8580
New Holland **(G-12249)**

Gods Country Creamery ....G 814 848-7262
Ulysses **(G-18602)**

HP Hood LLC ....C 215 637-2507
Philadelphia **(G-13837)**

▲ Ingretec Ltd ....F 717 273-0711
Lebanon **(G-9582)**

John F Kraft ....G 570 516-1092
Auburn **(G-817)**

▲ John Koller and Son Inc ....F 724 475-4154
Fredonia **(G-6185)**

Key Ingredient Market LLC ....G 484 281-3900
Bath **(G-961)**

Kraft and Jute Incorporated ....G 814 969-8121
Cambridge Springs **(G-2480)**

▼ Kraft Heinz Foods Company ....C 412 456-5700
Pittsburgh **(G-15197)**

Kraft Home Solutions LLC ....G 717 819-2690
York **(G-20559)**

KS Krafts ....G 717 764-7033
York **(G-20561)**

Leprino Foods Company ....C 570 888-9658
Sayre **(G-17118)**

Mondelez Global LLC ....A 570 820-1200
Wilkes Barre **(G-19945)**

Mrckl Closeco Inc ....E 412 828-6112
Verona **(G-18758)**

Ncc Wholesome Foods Inc ....F 724 652-3440
New Castle **(G-12124)**

Oak Shade Cheese LLC ....G 717 529-6049
Kirkwood **(G-8752)**

Penn Cheese Corporation ....F 570 524-7700
Winfield **(G-20202)**

Penn Dairy LLC ....G 570 524-7700
Winfield **(G-20203)**

◆ Savencia Cheese USA LLC ....D 717 355-8500
New Holland **(G-12281)**

Scents Krafts & Stitches ....G 610 770-0204
Allentown **(G-385)**

Schreiber Foods Inc ....C 717 530-5000
Shippensburg **(G-17546)**

Shenks Foods Inc ....G 717 393-4240
Lancaster **(G-9195)**

Sun-RE Cheese Corp ....E 570 286-1511
Sunbury **(G-18173)**

Three Belle Cheese ....G 570 713-8722
Mifflinburg **(G-11103)**

Turner Dairy Farms Inc ....D 412 372-7155
Pittsburgh (G-15661)
Vetch LLC ....F 570 524-7700
Winfield (G-20204)
Villanova Cheese Shop Inc ....F 610 495-8343
Pottstown (G-16069)
Wakefield Dairy LLC ....G 717 548-2179
Peach Bottom (G-13203)
Whitehall Specialties ....G 724 368-3959
Slippery Rock (G-17629)
Zausner Foods Corp ....B 717 355-8505
New Holland (G-12296)

2023 Milk, Condensed & Evaporated

Dairy Farmers America Inc ....E 724 946-8729
West Middlesex (G-19722)
Dietrichs Milk Products LLC ....D 610 929-5736
Reading (G-16361)
Dietrichs Milk Products LLC ....D 570 376-2001
Middlebury Center (G-11044)
Exclusive Supplements Inc ....F 412 787-2770
Oakdale (G-12898)
General Nutrition Centers Inc ......B 412 288-4600
Pittsburgh (G-15046)
GNC Corporation ....G 412 288-4600
Pittsburgh (G-15054)
GNC Parent LLC ....G 412 288-4600
Pittsburgh (G-15055)
▲ HB Trading LLC ....G 610 212-4565
Wayne (G-19336)
▲ Hi-Tech Nutraceuticals LLC .....E 717 667-2142
Reedsville (G-16623)
Hpf LLC ....G 215 321-8170
Yardley (G-20321)
Kellers Creamery LLC ....D 215 256-8871
Harleysville (G-7043)
Land OLakes Inc ....C 717 486-7000
Carlisle (G-2719)
Nestle Usa Inc ....C 610 391-7900
Breinigsville (G-2020)
Nestle Usa Inc ....C 818 549-6000
King of Prussia (G-8655)
Powder City LLC ....F 717 745-4795
York (G-20634)
Proper Nutrition Inc ....G 610 692-2060
West Chester (G-19621)
Trugen3 LLC ....G 412 668-3831
Pittsburgh (G-15657)
Vinomis Laboratories LLC ....G 877 484-6664
Aliquippa (G-101)

2024 Ice Cream

Allen McKinney Inc ....G 717 428-2321
Loganville (G-10101)
Arties Unlimited LLC ....G 267 516-2575
Philadelphia (G-13413)
Awesome Ice Inc ....F 717 519-2423
East Petersburg (G-4586)
Back Mountain Creamery ....G 570 855-3487
Shavertown (G-17479)
Berkey Creamery ....G 814 865-7535
University Park (G-18651)
Bill Macks Ice Cream ....E 717 292-1931
Dover (G-4188)
Blue Ribbon Farm Dairy ....G 570 763-5570
Swoyersville (G-18195)
Bobs Diner Enterprises Inc ....F 412 221-7474
Pittsburgh (G-14778)
Brook Meadow Dairy Company ....C 814 899-3191
Erie (G-5215)
Brusters Old Fashioned Ice Cre .....G 724 772-9999
Seven Fields (G-17374)
Buffs Ice Cream ....G 814 849-8335
Brookville (G-2257)
Chill Frozen Desserts ....G 724 695-8855
Imperial (G-8060)
Creperie Bechamel LLC ....G 610 964-9700
Radnor (G-16292)
Dairy Farmers America Inc ....E 724 946-8729
West Middlesex (G-19722)
Deer Creek Winery LLC ....D 814 354-7392
Shippenville (G-17560)
Donna Stanton ....G 412 561-2661
South Park (G-17781)
Dudley Enterprises Inc ....E 724 523-5522
Jeannette (G-8253)
Fikes Dairy Inc ....C 724 437-7931
Uniontown (G-18627)
Fox Meadows Creamery Inc ....E 717 721-6455
Ephrata (G-5104)

Fritz Tastee Creme ....G 570 925-2404
Benton (G-1279)
Frogurt LLC ....F 724 263-4299
Monroeville (G-11338)
Galliker Dairy Company ....C 814 266-8702
Johnstown (G-8374)
Gelateria ....G 484 466-4228
Primos (G-16108)
▲ Georgeos Water Ice Inc ....F 610 494-4975
Marcus Hook (G-10443)
Gibbys Ice Cream Inc ....F 215 547-7253
Levittown (G-9840)
Goodie Bar Ice-Cream Co Inc ....G 412 828-2840
Oakmont (G-12917)
Goose Bros Inc ....G 717 477-0010
Shippensburg (G-17530)
Halls Ice Cream Inc ....F 717 589-3290
Millerstown (G-11204)
Hayloft Candles ....G 717 656-9463
Leola (G-9786)
▲ Hershey Creamery Company ......C 717 238-8134
Harrisburg (G-7149)
High View Inc ....E 814 886-7171
Loretto (G-10104)
▲ J&J Snack Foods Corp/Mia ....E 570 457-7431
Moosic (G-11509)
Jackson Farms Dairy ....E 724 246-7010
New Salem (G-12445)
JAS Wholesale & Supply Co Inc .....E 610 967-0663
Emmaus (G-5031)
Joshi Bharkatkumar ....F 610 861-7733
Bethlehem (G-1547)
Justfroyo Inc ....G 215 355-7555
Feasterville Trevose (G-5914)
Kelley ....G 412 833-4559
Pittsburgh (G-15163)
Leibys Ichr LLC ....G 570 778-0108
Tamaqua (G-18217)
Manning Farm Dairy ....G 570 563-2016
Dalton (G-3987)
Marcies Homemade Ice Cream ......G 814 336-1749
Meadville (G-10756)
Mazzolis Ice Cream ....G 717 533-2252
Hershey (G-7620)
Mercurios Mulberry Creamery ....F 412 621-6220
Pittsburgh (G-15278)
▲ Mia Products Company ....E 570 457-7431
Avoca (G-846)
MJM Ices LLC ....G 412 401-4610
North Huntingdon (G-12770)
Mr Moo Cow LLC ....G 570 235-1061
Wilkes Barre (G-19947)
Nelsons Creamery LLC ....E 610 948-3000
Plymouth Meeting (G-15859)
Parkside Creamery LLC ....G 412 372-1110
Trafford (G-18460)
Paul Erivan ....G 215 887-2009
Oreland (G-13026)
Penn Gold Hughes ....G 724 735-2121
Harrisville (G-7254)
Premise Maid Candies Inc ....E 610 395-3221
Breinigsville (G-2024)
Purple Cow Creamery Ltd ....G 610 252-5544
Easton (G-4745)
Ritcheys Dairy Inc ....E 814 793-2157
Martinsburg (G-10529)
Robert Gerenser ....F 215 646-1853
New Hope (G-12314)
Shake and Twist Chartiers Ave ......G 412 331-9606
Mc Kees Rocks (G-10634)
Sinfully Sweet ....G 412 523-1887
Pittsburgh (G-15541)
Six Pack Creamery LLC ....G 267 261-2727
Hatboro (G-7305)
Snack Shack ....G 570 270-2929
Wilkes Barre (G-19964)
Specialty Ice ....G 724 283-7000
Butler (G-2443)
▲ SR Rosati Inc ....F 610 626-1818
Clifton Heights (G-3258)
Steffees ....F 814 827-4332
Titusville (G-18397)
Sterns Soft Serve LLC ....G 724 349-4118
Creekside (G-3877)
Sugar Magnolia Inc ....G 610 649-9462
Ardmore (G-719)
Sunset Ice Cream ....E 570 326-3902
Williamsport (G-20077)
Sweetdreams Brusters LLC ....G 717 261-1484
Chambersburg (G-2982)

Titusville Dairy Products Co ....E 814 827-1833
Titusville (G-18399)
Todd Curyto ....G 215 906-8097
Narberth (G-11913)
Topit Toppings LLC ....G 267 263-2590
Harleysville (G-7062)
Trickling Springs Creamery LLC .....E 717 709-0711
Chambersburg (G-2988)
Turkey Hill LP ....B 717 872-5461
Conestoga (G-3462)
Turner Dairy Farms Inc ....D 412 372-7155
Pittsburgh (G-15661)
Union Square Frog LLC ....G 717 561-0623
Harrisburg (G-7241)
Via Veneto Italian Ice Inc ....G 610 630-3355
Norristown (G-12722)

2026 Milk

▼ AFP Advanced Food Products LLC .C 717 355-8667
New Holland (G-12227)
Ayrshire Dairy ....F 814 781-1978
Saint Marys (G-16950)
Barchemy LLC ....E 724 379-4405
Donora (G-4147)
Brook Meadow Dairy Company ....C 814 899-3191
Erie (G-5215)
Clover Farms Dairy Company ....B 610 921-9111
Reading (G-16346)
Clover Farms Transportation Co .....G 610 921-9111
Reading (G-16347)
Country Food LLC ....G 717 506-0393
Mechanicsburg (G-10831)
Dairy Farmers America Inc ....E 717 691-4141
Mechanicsburg (G-10836)
Dairy Farmers America Inc ....D 724 946-8729
New Wilmington (G-12465)
Dairy Farmers America Inc ....E 724 946-8729
West Middlesex (G-19722)
▲ Dean Dairy Products Company .....B 724 962-7801
Sharpsville (G-17471)
Dean Foods Company ....G 717 522-5653
Mountville (G-11793)
Dean Foods Company ....G 215 855-8205
Lansdale (G-9358)
Dean Foods Company ....G 724 962-7801
Sharpsville (G-17472)
Dean Foods Company ....G 717 228-0445
Lebanon (G-9560)
Dean Transportation Inc ....G 570 385-1884
Schuylkill Haven (G-17153)
Dell Perry Farms ....E 717 741-3485
York (G-20447)
Dietrichs Milk Products LLC ....D 610 929-5736
Reading (G-16361)
Family Farm Creamery ....G 412 418-2596
Washington (G-19174)
Fikes Dairy Inc ....C 724 437-7931
Uniontown (G-18627)
Fresh Made Inc ....G 215 725-9013
Philadelphia (G-13724)
Galliker Dairy Company ....C 814 266-8702
Johnstown (G-8374)
Galliker Dairy Company ....F 814 944-8193
Altoona (G-508)
Galliker Dairy Company ....G 814 623-8597
Bedford (G-1051)
Galliker Dairy Company ....G 717 258-6199
Carlisle (G-2716)
Harrisburg Dairies Inc ....G 717 233-8701
Harrisburg (G-7142)
Herb & Lous LLC ....G 267 626-7913
Blue Bell (G-1833)
High View Inc ....E 814 886-7171
Loretto (G-10104)
HP Hood LLC ....B 215 855-9074
Allentown (G-248)
HP Hood LLC ....G 215 637-2507
Philadelphia (G-13837)
Hyproca Nutrition USA Inc ....F 416 565-4364
Pittsburgh (G-15108)
Jackson Farms Dairy ....E 724 246-7010
New Salem (G-12445)
Land OLakes Inc ....C 717 486-7000
Carlisle (G-2719)
Loco Yoco ....G 570 331-4529
Kingston (G-8722)
Longacres Modern Dairy Inc ....E 610 845-7551
Barto (G-945)
Montdale Farm Dairy ....G 570 254-6511
Scott Township (G-17186)

Paul Erivan ....G....... 215 887-2009
Oreland (G-13026)

Pittsburgh Special-T Dairy LLC ....E....... 412 881-1409
Pittsburgh (G-15407)

Polar Peach LLC ....G....... 717 517-9497
Lancaster (G-9172)

Razzy Fresh Frz Yogurt Forbes ....G....... 412 586-5270
Pittsburgh (G-15470)

Ready Food Products Inc ....C....... 215 824-2800
Philadelphia (G-14231)

Ritcheys Dairy Inc ....E....... 814 793-2157
Martinsburg (G-10529)

Rutter Bros Dairy Inc ....C....... 717 848-9827
York (G-20661)

Rutter Bros Dairy Inc ....F....... 717 388-1665
Middletown (G-11073)

Schneiders Dairy Inc ....C....... 412 881-3525
Pittsburgh (G-15516)

Schneiders Dairy Holdings Inc ....R....... 412 881-3525
Pittsburgh (G-15517)

Three Rivers Mothers Milk Bank ....F....... 412 281-4400
Pittsburgh (G-15619)

Topsmal Dairy LLC ....G....... 814 880-3724
Bellefonte (G-1123)

Trickling Springs Creamery LLC ....E....... 717 709-0711
Chambersburg (G-2988)

Turner Dairy Farms Inc ....D....... 412 372-7155
Pittsburgh (G-15661)

Tuscan/Lehigh Dairies Inc ....F....... 215 855-8205
Lansdale (G-9420)

Tuscan/Lehigh Dairies Inc ....F....... 610 434-9666
Allentown (G-415)

Upstate Niagara Coop Inc ....D....... 570 326-2021
Williamsport (G-20087)

Villanova Cheese Shop Inc ....F....... 610 495-8343
Pottstown (G-16069)

Whirled Peace Inc ....G....... 484 318-7735
Paoli (G-13151)

Wwf Operating Company ....C....... 814 590-8511
Du Bois (G-4429)

Yogo Factories ....G....... 215 230-9646
Doylestown (G-4347)

2032 Canned Specialties

AFP Advanced Food Products LLC ......E....... 717 354-6560
New Holland (G-12228)

▼ AFP Advanced Food Products LLC..C....... 717 355-8667
New Holland (G-12227)

Anitas Vegan Kitchen ....G....... 786 512-1428
Philadelphia (G-13393)

Ask Foods Inc ....E....... 717 838-6356
Palmyra (G-13118)

▲ Baby Matters LLC ....G....... 919 724-7087
Wayne (G-19304)

Barbato Foods Inc ....F....... 814 899-3721
Erie (G-5202)

Down Home Rice Pudding ....G....... 570 945-5744
Madison Township (G-10168)

Farmers From Italy Foods LLC ....G....... 484 480-3836
Upper Chichester (G-18661)

Fourth Street Barbecue Inc ....C....... 724 483-2000
Charleroi (G-3013)

◆ Hanover Foods Corporation ....A....... 717 632-6000
Hanover (G-6894)

Hazel and Ash Organics LLC ....G....... 717 521-9593
Coatesville (G-3307)

Kraft Heinz Company ....B....... 412 456-5700
Pittsburgh (G-15196)

Kraft Heinz Foods Company ....E....... 412 237-5868
Gibsonia (G-6341)

Kraft Heinz Foods Company ....E....... 412 237-5715
Carnegie (G-2774)

▼ Kraft Heinz Foods Company ....C....... 412 456-5700
Pittsburgh (G-15197)

Nestle Usa Inc ....C....... 818 549-6000
King of Prussia (G-8655)

Riverbend Foods LLC ....B....... 412 442-6989
Pittsburgh (G-15488)

Taif Inc ....F....... 610 534-0669
Ridley Park (G-16742)

Taif Inc ....E....... 610 522-0122
Folcroft (G-6017)

Taste of Puebla ....G....... 484 467-8597
Kennett Square (G-8548)

Valdez Foods Inc ....F....... 215 634-6106
Philadelphia (G-14436)

Winter Gardens Qulty Foods Inc ......C....... 717 624-4911
New Oxford (G-12427)

Zausner Foods Corp ....B....... 717 355-8505
New Holland (G-12296)

2033 Canned Fruits, Vegetables & Preserves

◆ American Beverage Corporation ......C....... 412 828-9020
Verona (G-18747)

American Beverage Corporation ....G....... 412 828-9020
Pittsburgh (G-14701)

Appeeling Fruit Inc ....F....... 610 926-6601
Dauberville (G-4032)

Bacon Jams ....G....... 484 681-5674
Norristown (G-12640)

Bauman Family ....F....... 610 754-7251
Sassamansville (G-17080)

Bel Aire Foods Inc ....E....... 412 364-7277
Pittsburgh (G-14760)

Brook Meadow Dairy Company ....C....... 814 899-3191
Erie (G-5215)

▲ California Mushroom Farm Inc ....B....... 805 642-3253
Toughkenamon (G-18417)

Charles & Alice Inc ....E....... 717 537-4700
Lancaster (G-8977)

Cliffstar LLC ....E....... 814 725-3801
North East (G-12735)

Clover Farms Dairy Company ....B....... 610 921-9111
Reading (G-16346)

Coca-Cola Company ....C....... 610 530-3900
Allentown (G-172)

Del Monte Foods Inc ....C....... 412 222-2200
Pittsburgh (G-14917)

▼ Delgrosso Foods Inc ....D....... 814 684-5880
Tipton (G-18374)

◆ Dell Sunny Foods LLC ....D....... 610 932-5164
Oxford (G-13078)

▲ Digiorgio Mushroom Corp ....B....... 610 926-2139
Reading (G-16362)

Eat This ....E....... 215 391-5807
Erwinna (G-5538)

Electric Pepper Company LLC ....G....... 812 340-4321
Russell (G-16880)

Florida Key West ....G....... 717 208-3084
Lancaster (G-9022)

◆ Furman Foods Inc ....C....... 570 473-3516
Northumberland (G-12867)

▲ Giorgio Foods Inc ....C....... 610 926-2139
Reading (G-16391)

Good Crop Inc ....F....... 585 944-7982
Malvern (G-10241)

Greenline Foods Inc ....G....... 717 630-9200
Hanover (G-6889)

Grouse Hunt Farms Inc ....F....... 570 573-2868
Tamaqua (G-18211)

Hanover Foods Corporation ....C....... 814 364-1482
Centre Hall (G-2841)

Hanover Foods Corporation ....F....... 717 843-0738
York (G-20522)

◆ Hanover Foods Corporation ....A....... 717 632-6000
Hanover (G-6894)

Hazel and Ash Organics LLC ....G....... 717 521-9593
Coatesville (G-3307)

High View Inc ....E....... 814 886-7171
Loretto (G-10104)

Hot Jams Dj Service ....G....... 814 246-8144
Punxsutawney (G-16144)

Hot Sauce Spot LLC ....G....... 717 341-7573
Lititz (G-10018)

House of Wings Foods LLC ....G....... 570 627-6116
Sayre (G-17116)

HP Hood LLC ....B....... 215 855-9074
Allentown (G-248)

J M Smucker Company ....F....... 724 228-6633
Washington (G-19187)

Kime Cider Mill ....F....... 717 677-7539
Bendersville (G-1139)

◆ Knouse Foods Cooperative Inc ....B....... 717 677-8181
Peach Glen (G-13205)

Knouse Foods Cooperative Inc ....B....... 717 263-9177
Chambersburg (G-2949)

Knouse Foods Cooperative Inc ....C....... 717 642-8291
Orrtanna (G-13036)

Knouse Foods Cooperative Inc ....G....... 717 328-3065
Mercersburg (G-10989)

Knouse Foods Cooperative Inc ....C....... 717 677-9115
Biglerville (G-1666)

Kraft Heinz Company ....B....... 412 456-5700
Pittsburgh (G-15196)

Kraft Heinz Foods Company ....B....... 724 778-5700
Warrendale (G-19085)

Kraft Heinz Foods Company ....B....... 412 456-2482
Moon Township (G-11496)

Kraft Heinz Foods Company ....E....... 412 237-5757
Pittsburgh (G-15198)

Kraft Heinz Foods Company ....F....... 412 456-5773
Pittsburgh (G-15199)

▼ Kraft Heinz Foods Company ....C....... 412 456-5700
Pittsburgh (G-15197)

Modern Mushroom Farms Inc ....B....... 610 268-3535
Toughkenamon (G-18420)

Motts LLP ....B....... 717 677-7121
Aspers (G-743)

▲ Myers Canning Co ....C....... 610 929-8644
Reading (G-16451)

Nestle Usa Inc ....C....... 818 549-6000
King of Prussia (G-8655)

Ocean Spray Cranberries Inc ....B....... 609 298-0905
Breinigsville (G-2022)

Ocean Spray Cranberries Inc ....E....... 508 946-1000
Breinigsville (G-2023)

▲ PCA Group Inc ....G....... 610 558-2802
Garnet Valley (G-6267)

▲ River Run Foods Inc ....E....... 570 701-1192
Northumberland (G-12875)

Roadside Products Inc ....F....... 412 220-9694
Bridgeville (G-2087)

Sam Beachy & Sons ....G....... 814 662-2220
Salisbury (G-17045)

Shenks Foods Inc ....G....... 717 393-4240
Lancaster (G-9195)

Snowtop LLC ....F....... 724 297-5491
Worthington (G-20233)

▲ Spring Glen Fresh Foods Inc ....D....... 717 733-2201
Ephrata (G-5145)

Sunsweet Growers Inc ....C....... 610 944-1005
Fleetwood (G-5980)

Welch Foods Inc A Cooperative ....B....... 814 725-4577
North East (G-12766)

◆ Zentis North America LLC ....D....... 215 676-3900
Philadelphia (G-14504)

2034 Dried Fruits, Vegetables & Soup

◆ A L Bazzini Co Inc........................E....... 610 366-1606
Allentown (G-111)

Ames Enterprises Inc ....G....... 814 474-2700
Fairview (G-5813)

Cooke Tavern Ltd.............................G....... 814 422-7687
Spring Mills (G-17887)

E S H Poultry ....F....... 717 517-9535
Lancaster (G-9005)

Hanover Foods Corporation ....B....... 800 888-4646
Hanover (G-6895)

▼ Keystone Potato Products LLC ....D....... 570 695-0909
Hegins (G-7542)

Monterey Mushrooms Inc ....F....... 610 929-1961
Temple (G-18333)

Moyer Specialty Foods LLC...............F....... 215 703-0100
Souderton (G-17754)

Ncc Wholesome Foods Inc ....F....... 724 652-3440
New Castle (G-12124)

Sunsweet Growers Inc ....C....... 610 944-1005
Fleetwood (G-5980)

2035 Pickled Fruits, Vegetables, Sauces & Dressings

▼ AFP Advanced Food Products LLC..C....... 717 355-8667
New Holland (G-12227)

Angelos Inc ....E....... 724 350-8715
Washington (G-19150)

Ask Foods Inc ....E....... 717 838-6356
Palmyra (G-13118)

▲ Bay Valley Foods LLC ....C....... 814 725-9617
North East (G-12731)

Belletieri Sauces Inc ....G....... 610 433-4334
Allentown (G-197)

Best Dressed Associates Inc ....F....... 717 938-2222
Lewisberry (G-9881)

Byler Relish House LLC ....G....... 814 763-6510
Saegertown (G-16908)

▼ Conroy Foods Inc ....F....... 412 781-0977
Pittsburgh (G-14872)

Dairiconcepts LP ....E....... 717 566-4500
Hummelstown (G-7908)

Epic Pickles LLC ....G....... 717 487-1323
Yoe (G-20360)

Fresh Foods Manufacturing ....E....... 724 683-3639
Freedom (G-6190)

Frito-Lay North America Inc ....E....... 570 323-6175
Williamsport (G-20014)

Golden Path LLC ....G....... 215 290-1582
Philadelphia (G-13776)

▲ Gourmet Specialty Imports ....F....... 610 345-1113
Kelton (G-8488)

Herlocher Foods Inc ....G...... 814 237-0134
State College (G-17975)

Lancaster Fine Foods Inc..................E...... 717 397-9578
Lancaster (G-9094)

Lionette Enterprises ....G...... 814 274-9401
Coudersport (G-3784)

Longs Horseradish ....G...... 717 872-9343
Lancaster (G-9114)

Mondelez Global LLC ....A...... 570 820-1200
Wilkes Barre (G-19945)

Reckitt Benckiser LLC ....C...... 717 506-0165
Mechanicsburg (G-10883)

Ronald J Stidmon ....G...... 724 336-0501
Enon Valley (G-5088)

▲ Spring Glen Fresh Foods Inc ....D...... 717 733-2201
Ephrata (G-5145)

▲ Stello Foods Inc ....E...... 814 938-8764
Punxsutawney (G-16164)

Sunrise Maple ....F...... 814 628-3110
Westfield (G-19781)

Treehouse Foods Inc ....G...... 814 725-5696
North East (G-12763)

Ventura Foods LLC ....G...... 215 223-8700
Philadelphia (G-14439)

Ventura Foods LLC ....C...... 717 263-6900
Chambersburg (G-2997)

William Kleinberger & Sons ....E...... 570 347-9331
Scranton (G-17314)

William Kleinberger & Sons ....E...... 570 347-9331
Scranton (G-17315)

Woods Wings ....G...... 610 417-5684
Kintnersville (G-8730)

Zukay Live Foods LLC ....G...... 610 286-3077
Palm (G-13097)

2037 Frozen Fruits, Juices & Vegetables

Bel Aire Foods Inc ....E...... 412 364-7277
Pittsburgh (G-14760)

Birds Eye Foods Inc ....C...... 814 267-4641
Berlin (G-1284)

Birds Eye Foods Inc ....F...... 814 942-6031
Altoona (G-478)

▲ Cambridge Farms Hanover LLC ......G...... 717 945-5178
Lancaster (G-8969)

Cliffstar LLC ....E...... 814 725-3801
North East (G-12735)

Coca-Cola Company ....C...... 610 530-3900
Allentown (G-172)

▲ Digiorgio Mushroom Corp ....B...... 610 926-2139
Reading (G-16362)

▲ Giorgio Foods Inc ....C...... 610 926-2139
Reading (G-16391)

H J Heinz Company Brands LLC ....G...... 412 456-5700
Pittsburgh (G-15072)

◆ Hanover Foods Corporation ....A...... 717 632-6000
Hanover (G-6894)

▼ Heinz Frozen Food Company ....A...... 412 237-5700
Pittsburgh (G-15088)

Icy Feet Inc ....G...... 610 462-3887
Whitehall (G-19876)

Inventure Foods Inc ....B...... 623 932-6200
Hanover (G-6903)

Juice Merchant ....G...... 215 483-8888
Philadelphia (G-13913)

Kreider Foods Inc ....F...... 717 898-3372
Lancaster (G-9088)

Mgk Produce Co...............................G...... 610 853-3678
Lansdowne (G-9438)

Mr Smoothie ....G...... 412 630-9065
Pittsburgh (G-15306)

Ocean Spray Cranberries Inc ....E...... 508 946-1000
Breinigsville (G-2023)

2038 Frozen Specialties

Almi Group Inc ....G...... 215 987-5768
Philadelphia (G-13371)

Ask Foods Inc ....C...... 717 838-6356
Palmyra (G-13117)

Ask Foods Inc ....E...... 717 838-6356
Palmyra (G-13118)

Ateeco Inc ....E...... 570 462-2745
Shenandoah (G-17492)

Atlantic Dev Corp of PA ....F...... 717 243-0212
Carlisle (G-2690)

B WS Pizza ....G...... 724 495-2898
Beaver (G-978)

Davenmark Inc ....F...... 484 461-8683
Upper Darby (G-18684)

Dawn Food Products Inc....................C...... 717 840-0044
York (G-20445)

Delicious Bite LLC ....F...... 610 701-4213
West Chester (G-19534)

▲ Ethnic Gourmet Foods Inc ....E...... 610 692-2209
West Chester (G-19552)

▲ Georgeos Water Ice Inc ....F...... 610 494-4975
Marcus Hook (G-10443)

▲ Giorgio Foods Inc ....C...... 610 926-2139
Reading (G-16391)

◆ H J Heinz Company LP ....C...... 412 237-5757
Pittsburgh (G-15071)

◆ Hanover Foods Corporation ....A...... 717 632-6000
Hanover (G-6894)

▼ Heinz Frozen Food Company ....A...... 412 237-5700
Pittsburgh (G-15088)

Icon Marketing LLC ....G...... 610 356-4050
Broomall (G-2289)

Kraft Heinz Company ....B...... 412 456-5700
Pittsburgh (G-15196)

Kraft Heinz Foods Company ....F...... 610 430-1536
West Chester (G-19584)

▼ Kraft Heinz Foods Company ....C...... 412 456-5700
Pittsburgh (G-15197)

▲ Lees Orntal Gourmet Foods Inc ......E...... 570 462-9505
Shenandoah (G-17494)

Leonetti Food Distributors Inc ....E...... 215 729-4200
Philadelphia (G-13966)

Luccis ....G...... 903 600-5848
Hatboro (G-7293)

Moms Wholesale Foods Inc ....G...... 724 856-3049
New Castle (G-12122)

Murrys of Maryland Inc ....C...... 301 420-6400
Lebanon (G-9612)

Mybiani LLC ....G...... 267 253-1866
Willow Grove (G-20130)

▲ Nardone Brothers Baking Co...........C...... 570 823-0141
Hanover Township (G-6999)

Ne Foods Inc ....A...... 814 725-4835
North East (G-12753)

Nestle Pizza Company Inc ....F...... 717 737-7268
Camp Hill (G-2506)

Petruzzi Pizza Mfg Inc ....E...... 570 454-5887
Hazleton (G-7517)

Poppi Als Inc ....G...... 717 652-6263
Harrisburg (G-7200)

Preferred Meal Systems Inc ....C...... 570 457-8311
Moosic (G-11512)

Rae Foods Inc ....G...... 716 326-7437
North East (G-12755)

Real English Foods Inc ....G...... 610 863-9091
Pen Argyl (G-13215)

▲ Roccas Italian Foods Inc ....F...... 724 654-3344
New Castle (G-12144)

Rome At Home ....G...... 412 361-3782
East Liberty (G-4579)

▼ Sb Global Foods Inc ....G...... 215 361-9500
Hatboro (G-7303)

Sfc Global Supply Chain Inc ....B...... 610 327-5074
Pottstown (G-16045)

Van Bennett Food Co Inc ....E...... 610 374-8348
Mohnton (G-11272)

Wakins Food Corporation ....G...... 215 785-3420
Bristol (G-2216)

2041 Flour, Grain Milling

ADM Milling Co..................................E...... 717 737-0529
Camp Hill (G-2485)

Archer-Daniels-Midland Company ....E...... 717 761-5200
Camp Hill (G-2491)

Archer-Daniels-Midland Company ....E...... 215 547-8424
Langhorne (G-9278)

Ardent Mills LLC ....E...... 717 846-7773
York (G-20385)

Ardent Mills LLC ....F...... 972 660-9980
Treichlers (G-18476)

Ardent Mills LLC ....G...... 717 244-4559
Red Lion (G-16588)

Ardent Mills LLC ....E...... 570 839-8322
Pocono Summit (G-15885)

Bedford Farm Bureau Coop Assn ......F...... 814 793-2721
Curryville (G-3945)

Bessie Grove ....G...... 570 524-2436
Lewisburg (G-9898)

Conagra Brands Inc ....F...... 717 846-7773
York (G-20431)

Cornell Bros Inc ....F...... 570 376-2471
Middlebury Center (G-11043)

Curry Flour Mills Inc ....F...... 717 838-2421
Palmyra (G-13119)

F M Browns Sons Incorporated ....E...... 610 944-7654
Fleetwood (G-5972)

◆ F M Browns Sons Incorporated ......D...... 800 334-8816
Reading (G-16384)

General Mills Inc ....E...... 717 838-7600
Palmyra (G-13124)

General Mills Inc ....D...... 215 784-5100
Dresher (G-4355)

Imperial Dough Company Inc ....G...... 724 695-3625
Oakdale (G-12904)

James F Sargent ....G...... 570 549-2168
Millerton (G-11215)

Jpmn Partners LLC ....G...... 484 888-8558
Parkesburg (G-13178)

Pillsbury Company LLC ....E...... 610 593-5133
Parkesburg (G-13182)

Roch Grande Gst Waffles LLC ....C...... 484 840-9179
Glen Mills (G-6442)

Rockfish Venture LLP ....F...... 215 968-5054
Newtown (G-12545)

Ross Feeds Inc ....F...... 570 289-4388
Kingsley (G-8707)

Snavelys Mill Inc ....G...... 717 626-6256
Lititz (G-10050)

Snavelys Mill Inc ....F...... 570 726-4747
Mill Hall (G-11182)

Tomanetti Food Products Inc ....E...... 412 828-3040
Oakmont (G-12928)

White Oak Mills Inc ....E...... 717 367-1525
Elizabethtown (G-4891)

Wpp Dough Company Inc ....F...... 814 539-7799
Johnstown (G-8446)

2043 Cereal Breakfast Foods

General Mills Inc ....E...... 717 838-7600
Palmyra (G-13124)

Gluten Free Food Group LLC ....G...... 570 689-9694
Moscow (G-11597)

Homestat Farm Ltd ....F...... 717 939-0407
Highspire (G-7633)

Kellogg Company ....A...... 717 898-0161
Lancaster (G-9079)

Kellogg Company ....B...... 570 546-0200
Muncy (G-11823)

Mondelez Global LLC ....A...... 570 820-1200
Wilkes Barre (G-19945)

▲ North American Packaging LLC ....D...... 570 296-4200
Milford (G-11165)

Treehouse Private Brands Inc ....G...... 610 589-4526
Womelsdorf (G-20209)

2045 Flour, Blended & Prepared

Better Bowls LLC ....G...... 717 298-1257
Hummelstown (G-7902)

Byrnes and Kiefer Company ....E...... 724 538-5200
Callery (G-2467)

Charlies Specialties Inc.....................D...... 724 346-2350
Hermitage (G-7577)

Country Fresh Batter Inc ....F...... 610 272-5751
King of Prussia (G-8600)

Moms Wholesale Foods Inc...............G...... 724 856-3049
New Castle (G-12122)

Plumpys Pierogies Inc......................G...... 570 489-5520
Jessup (G-8335)

Roch Grande Gst Waffles LLC.............C...... 484 840-9179
Glen Mills (G-6442)

2046 Wet Corn Milling

Cargill Incorporated..........................F...... 717 273-1133
Lebanon (G-9552)

Penford Carolina LLC ....E...... 570 218-4321
Berwick (G-1340)

Tate Lyle Ingrdnts Amricas LLC ....D...... 215 295-5011
Morrisville (G-11584)

2047 Dog & Cat Food

Ainsworth Pet Ntrtn Parent LLC ....G...... 814 724-7710
Meadville (G-10697)

Ainsworth Pet Nutrition LLC ....F...... 814 724-7710
Meadville (G-10698)

Ainsworth Pet Nutrition LLC ....C...... 814 724-7710
Meadville (G-10699)

▲ Annamaet Pet Foods Inc ....G...... 215 453-0381
Sellersville (G-17340)

Best Feeds & Farm Supplies Inc ....C...... 724 693-9417
Oakdale (G-12894)

Big Heart Pet Brands ....C...... 570 389-7650
Bloomsburg (G-1772)

Big Heart Pet Brands ....C...... 570 784-8200
Bloomsburg (G-1773)

S I C

Dpc Pet Specialties LLC ....E 814 724-7710
Meadville *(G-10719)*

Freshpet Inc ....F 610 997-7192
Bethlehem *(G-1520)*

Healthy Alternative Pet Diets ....G 210 745-1493
Tamiment *(G-18233)*

Meow Mix Company ....E 412 222-2200
Pittsburgh *(G-15276)*

Nestle Purina Petcare Company ....C 717 795-5454
Mechanicsburg *(G-10872)*

Nestle Purina Petcare Company ....D 610 398-4667
Allentown *(G-328)*

Nestle Purina Petcare Company ....C 610 395-3301
Allentown *(G-329)*

Nestle Usa Inc ....C 818 549-6000
King of Prussia *(G-8655)*

Oscar & Banks LLC ....G 701 922-1005
Ligonier *(G-9962)*

Pup E Luv LLC ....D 610 458-5280
Chester Springs *(G-3084)*

Valley Proteins Inc ....D 717 445-6890
East Earl *(G-4556)*

X F Enterprises Inc ....E 717 859-1166
Ephrata *(G-5157)*

2048 Prepared Feeds For Animals & Fowls

Albrights Mill LLC ....E 610 756-6022
Kempton *(G-8489)*

Bedford Farm Bureau Coop Assn ....F 814 793-2721
Curryville *(G-3945)*

Bedford Farm Bureau Coop Assn ....F 814 623-6194
Bedford *(G-1040)*

Benebone LLC ....G 610 366-3718
Macungie *(G-10142)*

Bessie Grove ....G 570 524-2436
Lewisburg *(G-9898)*

Cargill Incorporated ....E 717 530-7778
Shippensburg *(G-17521)*

Cargill Incorporated ....G 570 524-4777
Winfield *(G-20198)*

Cargill Incorporated ....E 814 793-3701
Martinsburg *(G-10520)*

Cargill Incorporated ....E 814 793-2137
Martinsburg *(G-10521)*

Cargill Incorporated ....F 717 273-1133
Lebanon *(G-9552)*

Chestnut Ridge LLC ....G 717 354-5741
New Holland *(G-12232)*

▲ Clarks Feed Mills Inc ....E 570 648-4351
Shamokin *(G-17423)*

Cochecton Mills Inc ....E 570 224-4144
Honesdale *(G-7707)*

Cornell Bros Inc ....F 570 376-2471
Middletown Center *(G-11043)*

Cumberland Valley Coop Assn ....E 717 532-2197
Shippensburg *(G-17525)*

Davis Feed of Bucks County ....G 215 257-2966
Perkasie *(G-13272)*

Diamond Milling Company Inc ....G 724 846-0920
New Brighton *(G-12034)*

Dietrich Bros Dream Catchr Fly ....G 717 267-0515
Chambersburg *(G-2925)*

Dyets Inc ....G 610 868-7701
Bethlehem *(G-1499)*

Equine Specialty Feed Co ....F 610 796-5670
Reading *(G-16378)*

Esbenshade Inc ....C 717 653-8061
Mount Joy *(G-11655)*

Extra Factors ....F 717 859-1166
Ephrata *(G-5102)*

F M Browns Sons Incorporated ....E 610 582-2741
Birdsboro *(G-1695)*

◆ F M Browns Sons Incorporated ....D 800 334-8816
Reading *(G-16384)*

Farmers Union Coop Assn ....F 717 597-3191
Greencastle *(G-6612)*

Hampsons Farm & Garden Inc ....G 570 724-3012
Wellsboro *(G-19464)*

▲ J Maze Corp ....G 717 329-8350
Hummelstown *(G-7915)*

Kaytee Products Incorporated ....E 570 385-1530
Cressona *(G-3905)*

Kreamer Feed Inc ....E 570 374-8148
Kreamer *(G-8818)*

Laneys Feed Mill Inc ....F 814 643-3211
Huntingdon *(G-7950)*

Lawn & Garden ....G 724 458-6141
Grove City *(G-6794)*

Leroy M Sensenig Inc ....E 717 354-4756
New Holland *(G-12257)*

◆ M Simon Zook Co ....C 610 273-3776
Honey Brook *(G-7753)*

Mark Hershey Farms Inc ....E 717 867-4624
Lebanon *(G-9608)*

Martins Feed Mill Inc ....F 814 349-8787
Coburn *(G-3333)*

Mc Crackens Feed Mill Inc ....F 717 665-2186
Manheim *(G-10395)*

Meiserville Milling Co ....G 570 539-8855
Mount Pleasant Mills *(G-11727)*

Mike Dupuy Hawk Food ....G 570 837-1551
Middleburg *(G-11031)*

Mw/Td Inspired LLC ....G 724 741-0473
Warrendale *(G-19090)*

Nestle Purina Petcare Company ....C 717 795-5454
Mechanicsburg *(G-10872)*

Nestle Purina Petcare Company ....D 610 398-4667
Allentown *(G-328)*

Nufeeds Inc ....G 570 278-3767
Montrose *(G-11473)*

Nufeeds Inc ....G 570 836-2866
Tunkhannock *(G-18545)*

Occidental Chemical Corp ....F 610 327-4145
Pottstown *(G-16022)*

Oesterlings Feed ....G 724 283-1819
Fenelton *(G-5947)*

▲ Organic Unlimited Inc ....G 610 593-2995
Atglen *(G-802)*

Purina Animal Nutrition LLC ....D 717 737-4581
Camp Hill *(G-2511)*

Purina Animal Nutrition LLC ....G 717 393-1361
Lancaster *(G-9178)*

Purina Mills LLC ....F 717 737-4581
Camp Hill *(G-2512)*

Purina Mills LLC ....G 717 393-1299
Lancaster *(G-9179)*

◆ Qlf Inc ....E 717 445-6225
New Holland *(G-12274)*

Renaissance Nutrition Inc ....E 814 793-2113
Roaring Spring *(G-16767)*

Renewal Processing Inc ....E 570 838-3838
Watsontown *(G-19280)*

Ridley USA Inc ....F 717 509-1078
Lancaster *(G-9188)*

Rockwells Feed Farm & Pet Sup ....G 877 797-4575
Wellsboro *(G-19472)*

Ross Feeds Inc ....F 570 289-4388
Kingsley *(G-8707)*

S Wenger Feed Mill Inc ....G 717 361-4223
Elizabethtown *(G-4886)*

Select Veal Feeds Inc ....F 215 721-7131
Souderton *(G-17762)*

Shade Gap Farm Supplies ....G 814 259-3258
Shade Gap *(G-17416)*

Shaffers Feed Service Inc ....F 570 265-3300
Monroeton *(G-11321)*

Songbird Sanctuary LLC ....G 412 780-1270
Pittsburgh *(G-15556)*

Sporting Valley Feeds LLC ....E 717 665-6122
Manheim *(G-10404)*

Valley Proteins Inc ....D 717 445-6890
East Earl *(G-4556)*

▲ Vita-Line Products Inc ....C 570 450-0192
Hazle Township *(G-7490)*

Waynesburg Milling Co ....G 724 627-6137
Waynesburg *(G-19452)*

Wenger Corporate Services LLC ....G 800 692-6008
Rheems *(G-16668)*

Wenger Feeds LLC ....G 717 367-1195
Muncy *(G-11841)*

Wenger Feeds LLC ....E 717 367-1195
Spring Glen *(G-17874)*

Wenger Feeds LLC ....B 717 367-1195
Lancaster *(G-9238)*

Wenger Feeds LLC ....F 717 367-1195
Mount Joy *(G-11676)*

Wenger Feeds LLC ....C 717 367-1195
Shippensburg *(G-17554)*

Wenger Feeds LLC ....E 570 682-8812
Hegins *(G-7546)*

Westway Feed Products LLC ....F 215 425-3707
Philadelphia *(G-14469)*

White Oak Mills Inc ....E 717 367-1525
Elizabethtown *(G-4891)*

Wild Birds Unlimited ....G 610 366-1725
Allentown *(G-434)*

X F Enterprises Inc ....E 717 859-1166
Ephrata *(G-5157)*

◆ Zeigler Bros Inc ....E 717 677-6181
Gardners *(G-6262)*

2051 Bread, Bakery Prdts Exc Cookies & Crackers

▼ 5 Generation Bakers LLC ....E 412 444-8200
Mc Kees Rocks *(G-10597)*

A Cupcake Wonderland LLC ....G 267 324-5579
Philadelphia *(G-13327)*

A T V Bakery Inc ....E 610 374-5577
Reading *(G-16307)*

Abes Bakery ....G 717 232-1330
Harrisburg *(G-7081)*

Achenbachs Pastry Inc ....E 717 656-6671
Leola *(G-9765)*

Acme Markets Inc ....C 215 725-9310
Philadelphia *(G-13341)*

Addison Baking Company ....E 215 464-8055
Philadelphia *(G-13344)*

Agostini Bakery Inc ....G 570 457-2021
Old Forge *(G-12962)*

Alfred and Sam Italian Bakery ....F 717 392-6311
Lancaster *(G-8927)*

Alfred Nickles Bakery Inc ....F 814 471-6913
Ebensburg *(G-4778)*

Amega Holdings LLC ....G 718 775-7188
Jamison *(G-8242)*

Anthony Mieczkowski ....G 610 489-2523
Collegeville *(G-3369)*

◆ Arnold Foods Company Inc ....A 215 672-8010
Horsham *(G-7788)*

ASA Baking Corp ....G 267 535-1618
Philadelphia *(G-13418)*

Au Fournil Inc ....G 610 664-0235
Narberth *(G-11908)*

Auntie Annes Inc ....D 717 435-1435
Lancaster *(G-8947)*

Backdoor Bakershop ....G 610 625-0987
Bethlehem *(G-1456)*

Bakerly Barn LLC ....E 610 829-1500
Easton *(G-4647)*

Bakkavor Foods Usa Inc ....F 570 383-9800
Jessup *(G-8327)*

Bb and CC Inc ....D 215 288-7440
Philadelphia *(G-13448)*

◆ Bbu Inc ....C 215 347-5500
Horsham *(G-7795)*

▲ Best Bakery Inc ....G 215 855-3831
Lansdale *(G-9345)*

Better Baked Foods LLC ....B 814 725-8778
North East *(G-12732)*

Better Baked Foods LLC ....E 814 899-6128
Erie *(G-5210)*

Bimbo Bakeries ....G 570 888-2289
Sayre *(G-17112)*

Bimbo Bakeries Usa Inc ....B 610 825-1140
Conshohocken *(G-3522)*

Bimbo Bakeries Usa Inc ....F 814 941-1102
Altoona *(G-477)*

Bimbo Bakeries Usa Inc ....E 800 222-7495
York *(G-20406)*

Bimbo Bakeries Usa Inc ....C 717 764-9999
York *(G-20407)*

Bimbo Bakeries Usa Inc ....G 610 478-9369
Reading *(G-16332)*

Bimbo Bakeries Usa Inc ....E 724 251-0971
Leetsdale *(G-9684)*

Bimbo Bakeries Usa Inc ....E 814 456-2596
Erie *(G-5211)*

Bimbo Bakeries Usa Inc ....F 412 443-3499
Leetsdale *(G-9685)*

Bimbo Bakeries Usa Inc ....F 570 455-7691
West Hazleton *(G-19707)*

Bimbo Bakeries Usa Inc ....E 610 921-2715
Reading *(G-16333)*

Bimbo Bakeries Usa Inc ....F 814 456-4575
Erie *(G-5212)*

Bimbo Bakeries Usa Inc ....D 610 391-7490
Breinigsville *(G-2010)*

Bimbo Bakeries Usa Inc ....D 610 865-7402
Bethlehem *(G-1466)*

▲ Bimbo Bakeries Usa Inc ....B 215 347-5500
Horsham *(G-7796)*

Bimbo Bakeries Usa Inc ....B 570 455-2066
West Hazleton *(G-19708)*

Bimbo Bakeries Usa Inc ....F 570 494-1191
Williamsport *(G-19993)*

Bimbo Bakeries Usa Inc ....F 724 733-2332
Pittsburgh *(G-14766)*

Bimbo Bakeries Usa Inc ....D 570 654-4668
Pittston *(G-15743)*

Bimbo Bakeries Usa Inc ....E 800 635-1685
Aston *(G-752)*

Bimbo Bakeries USA Inc ....B 610 258-7131
Easton (G-4656)

Bimbo Hungria Company ....F 866 506-6807
Horsham (G-7797)

Brinic Donuts Inc ....E 814 944-5242
Altoona (G-484)

Cakeworks LLC ....G 917 744-1375
Henryville (G-7565)

▲ Carlisle Foods Inc ....C 717 218-9880
Carlisle (G-2696)

Ccffg Inc ....D 570 270-3976
Wilkes Barre (G-19911)

Chau Fresh Donuts ....G 215 474-1533
Philadelphia (G-13535)

Community Services Group Inc .....E 570 286-0111
Sunbury (G-18167)

Conshohocken Italian Bakery ....E 610 825-9334
Conshohocken (G-3533)

Cora Lee Cupcakes ....G 724 681-5498
New Kensington (G-12336)

Cordova ....G 570 578-7413
Whitehall (G-19868)

Country Club Restaurant ....D 215 722-0500
Philadelphia (G-13575)

Country Cupboard Cookies Lt ......G 724 325-3045
Pittsburgh (G-14880)

Cramer Partnership ....G 215 378-6024
Yardley (G-20301)

Crave Cupcakes By Tamara LLC ..G 610 417-4909
Allentown (G-184)

Crofchick Inc ....G 570 287-3940
Swoyersville (G-18197)

Cupcake Momma ....G 724 516-5098
Jeannette (G-8251)

Dalos Bakery Inc ....E 570 752-4519
Berwick (G-1322)

D'Ambrosio Bakery LLC ....E 610 560-4700
King of Prussia (G-8604)

Dawn Food Products Inc ....C 717 840-0044
York (G-20445)

Daye-Licious Baking ....G 570 965-2491
Springville (G-17928)

Deangelis Bros Inc ....E 724 775-1641
Rochester (G-16784)

Demestia Baking Company LLC ....G 215 896-2289
Lansdale (G-9360)

Dharini LLC ....F 215 595-3915
Yardley (G-20306)

Dia Doce ....G 610 476-5684
Glenmoore (G-6465)

Dianas Heavenly Cupcakes ....G 412 628-0642
Jeannette (G-8252)

Don Saylors Markets Inc ....C 717 776-7551
Newville (G-12600)

Dons Lykens Food Market Inc ......D 717 453-7042
Lykens (G-10132)

Donut Connection ....F 724 282-6214
Butler (G-2395)

Donut Shack ....G 412 793-4222
Pittsburgh (G-14931)

Dough Nuts For Doughnuts LLC ....F 610 642-6186
Haverford (G-7409)

Dunkin Donuts ....G 610 992-0111
King of Prussia (G-8613)

Duritzas Enterprises Inc ....C 724 223-5494
Washington (G-19165)

Early Morning Donuts Corp ....G 570 961-5150
Scranton (G-17230)

Earthgrains Distribution LLC ....F 215 672-8010
Horsham (G-7813)

Egypt Star Inc ....E 610 434-8516
Allentown (G-204)

Enrico Biscotti Company ....G 412 281-2602
Pittsburgh (G-14977)

Federal Pretzel Baking Co ....E 215 467-0505
Philadelphia (G-13695)

Ferguson and Hassler Inc ....C 717 786-7301
Quarryville (G-16269)

◆ Flowers Baking Co Oxford Inc ....E 610 932-2147
Oxford (G-13079)

Flowers Foods Inc ....E 717 528-4108
York Springs (G-20765)

Ford City National Bakery ....G 724 763-7684
Ford City (G-6046)

Fred Fairburn ....E 570 282-3364
Carbondale (G-2675)

Fresh Donuts ....G 717 273-8886
Lebanon (G-9572)

Fresh Foods Manufacturing ....E 724 683-3639
Freedom (G-6190)

Frosted Fantasia Cupcakes LLC ....G 724 601-9440
Oakdale (G-12899)

G Weston Bakeries ....G 570 455-2066
West Hazleton (G-19710)

Ganesh Donuts Inc ....G 215 351-9370
Philadelphia (G-13743)

Gannons Gourmet ....F 610 439-8949
Allentown (G-223)

Gerritys Super Market Inc ....D 570 961-9030
Scranton (G-17239)

Giant Eagle ....C 724 772-1030
Cranberry Township (G-3821)

Gonnella Frozen Products LLC .....F 570 455-3194
Hazle Township (G-7459)

Grand Finale Desserts ....G 610 864-3824
Paoli (G-13141)

Half Plus Half Inc Enterprise ....D 800 252-4545
Philadelphia (G-13796)

Hallelujah Ink ....G 215 510-1152
Philadelphia (G-13798)

Harrys Famous Pudding ....F 484 494-6400
Glenolden (G-6475)

Hartings Bakery Inc ....E 717 445-5644
Bowmansville (G-1887)

Heathers Cupcakes N Things LLC ..G 717 329-2324
Harrisburg (G-7147)

Howard Donuts Inc ....E 215 634-7750
Philadelphia (G-13836)

Hoyt Inc ....F 570 326-9426
South Williamsport (G-17792)

Imperial Bakery ....G 570 343-4537
Scranton (G-17243)

International Bakery ....E 814 452-3435
Erie (G-5329)

Ising LLC ....G 610 216-2644
Allentown (G-266)

Its Only Cupcakes LLC ....G 717 421-6646
Wayne (G-19340)

J F M Philadelphia Donut Inc ....G 215 676-0700
Philadelphia (G-13883)

James J Tuzzi Jr ....E 570 752-2704
Berwick (G-1329)

Jo Suzy Donuts ....G 610 279-1350
Bridgeport (G-2038)

▲ Jtm Foods LLC ....D 814 899-0886
Erie (G-5340)

Kaplans New Model Baking Co ......E 215 627-5288
Philadelphia (G-13921)

Kellogg Company ....B 570 546-0200
Muncy (G-11823)

Kesser Baking Co ....F 215 878-8080
Philadelphia (G-13928)

Klosterman Baking Co ....G 412 564-1023
Bridgeville (G-2076)

Kretchmar Bakery Inc ....E 724 774-2324
Beaver (G-986)

Krispy Kreme Doughnuts ....G 724 228-1800
Washington (G-19194)

Kurts Making Whoopie ....G 570 888-9102
Sayre (G-17117)

Kyjs Bakery ....E 610 494-9400
Chester (G-3054)

La Gourmandine LLC ....G 412 682-2210
Pittsburgh (G-15210)

La Gourmandine LLC ....G 412 200-7969
Pittsburgh (G-15211)

La Gourmandine LLC ....G 412 291-8146
Hazelwood (G-7446)

Larry Darling ....G 215 677-1452
Philadelphia (G-13957)

Le Bus Bakery Inc ....E 610 337-1444
King of Prussia (G-8639)

Lee High Valley Bakers LLC ....F 610 868-2392
Bethlehem (G-1556)

Leibys Ichr LLC ....G 570 778-0108
Tamaqua (G-18217)

Lizzie BS Bakery ....G 717 817-1791
Glenville (G-6545)

Longos Bakery Inc ....F 570 233-0558
Hazleton (G-7508)

Luccis Bakery ....F 570 876-3830
Archbald (G-692)

M Cibrone & Sons Bakery Inc ....E 412 885-6200
Pittsburgh (G-15244)

Macs Donut Shop Inc ....E 724 375-6776
Aliquippa (G-82)

Mama DS Buns Inc ....G 724 752-1700
Ellwood City (G-4944)

Mama Nardone Baking Co Inc ......E 570 825-3421
Hazleton (G-7509)

Maple Donuts Inc ....C 717 757-7826
York (G-20578)

Maple Donuts Inc ....F 717 843-4276
York (G-20579)

Maple Donuts Inc ....D 814 774-3131
Lake City (G-8905)

◆ Martins Fmous Pstry Shoppe Inc ..C 717 263-9580
Chambersburg (G-2957)

Martins Fmous Pstry Shoppe Inc ...C 717 263-9580
Chambersburg (G-2958)

McClures Pie and Salad Inc ....F 717 442-4461
Gap (G-6253)

Megan Sweet Baking Company ......G 267 288-5080
Holland (G-7641)

Michels Bakery Inc ....C 215 742-3900
Philadelphia (G-14022)

Mighty Fine Inc ....D 814 455-6408
Erie (G-5391)

Moms Wholesale Foods Inc ....G 724 856-3049
New Castle (G-12122)

Morabito Baking Co Inc ....D 610 275-5419
Norristown (G-12688)

Mr ZS Food Mart ....G 570 421-7070
Stroudsburg (G-18132)

National Bakery Inc ....E 570 343-1609
Scranton (G-17264)

Native Foods LLC ....E 717 298-6157
Hershey (G-7622)

Nawalany-Franciotti LLC ....F 215 342-3005
Philadelphia (G-14059)

New Lycoming Bakery Inc ....E 570 326-9426
Williamsport (G-20046)

Northeast Foods Inc ....E 215 638-2400
Bensalem (G-1231)

Northwest Bagel Corporation ....G 610 237-0586
Downingtown (G-4245)

Odellick Baking LLC ....G 814 515-1337
Altoona (G-533)

OH Little Town Cupcakes LLC ....G 484 353-9709
Bethlehem (G-1586)

Paddycake Bakery ....E 412 621-4477
Pittsburgh (G-15367)

Petruzzis Manufacturing Inc ....G 570 459-5957
Hazleton (G-7518)

Philadelphia Soft Pretzels ....E 215 324-4315
Philadelphia (G-14155)

Philly Originals ....G 724 728-3011
Beaver (G-989)

Pittston Baking Co Inc ....G 570 343-2102
Scranton (G-17272)

Potomac Bakery Inc ....E 412 531-5066
Pittsburgh (G-15421)

Prantls of Shadyside LLC ....F 412 621-2092
Pittsburgh (G-15428)

Queen of Hearts Inc ....E 610 889-0477
Malvern (G-10305)

▼ Red Mill Farms LLC ....F 570 457-2400
Moosic (G-11513)

Redners Markets Inc ....C 610 678-2900
Reading (G-16494)

Redners Markets Inc ....D 610 776-2726
Allentown (G-372)

Robert Bath ....G 610 588-0423
Roseto (G-16822)

Rosciolis Bakery ....E 570 961-1151
Scranton (G-17279)

Royal Bake Shop ....G 570 654-2011
Exeter (G-5584)

S Don Food Market Inc ....E 717 453-7470
Lykens (G-10135)

Safran Brothers Inc ....E 724 266-9758
Ambridge (G-633)

Schiel Inc ....G 570 970-4460
Wilkes Barre (G-19962)

Schwebel Baking Co of PA Inc ....E 412 751-4080
McKeesport (G-10680)

Schwebel Baking Company ....G 814 333-2498
Meadville (G-10789)

Schwebel Baking Company ....E 412 257-6067
Bridgeville (G-2088)

Scratch Cupcakes ....G 717 271-2466
Ephrata (G-5139)

Senapes Bakery Inc ....E 570 454-0839
Hazleton (G-7526)

Shivkanta Corporation ....E 610 376-3515
Reading (G-16517)

Shree Swami Narayan Corp ....E 610 272-8404
Norristown (G-12713)

Simple Treat Bakery ....F 412 681-0303
Pittsburgh (G-15538)

S
I
C

Smucker Management Corporation ......G....... 717 768-1501
Bird In Hand ***(G-1681)***
Soft Pretzels Franchise System ....G....... 215 338-4606
Bensalem ***(G-1254)***
Sophisticakes Inc....................................G....... 610 626-9991
Drexel Hill ***(G-4371)***
Soumaya & Sons Bakery LLC...............G....... 610 432-0405
Whitehall ***(G-19889)***
Specialty Bakers LLC ....D....... 717 626-8002
Marysville ***(G-10533)***
Spin-A-Latte Tm ....G....... 215 285-1567
Lansdale ***(G-9412)***
Stagnos Bakery Inc.................................E....... 412 441-3485
East Liberty ***(G-4581)***
Stagnos Bakery Inc.................................G....... 412 361-2093
Pittsburgh ***(G-15574)***
Sunnyway Foods Inc ....D....... 717 264-6001
Chambersburg ***(G-2980)***
Sunnyway Foods Inc ....D....... 717 597-7121
Greencastle ***(G-6637)***
T & P Bagels Inc......................................G....... 610 867-8695
Bethlehem ***(G-1637)***
▲ **Tasty Baking Company** ....E....... 215 221-8500
Philadelphia ***(G-14374)***
Tasty Baking Company ....G....... 717 295-2530
Lancaster ***(G-9212)***
Tasty Baking Company ....G....... 717 651-0307
Harrisburg ***(G-7227)***
Tasty Baking Company ....G....... 570 961-8211
Dunmore ***(G-4485)***
Tasty Baking Company ....A....... 215 221-8500
Philadelphia ***(G-14375)***
Teris Deli & Bakery LLC ....G....... 570 785-7007
Forest City ***(G-6055)***
Termini Brothers Inc...............................E....... 215 334-1816
Philadelphia ***(G-14381)***
Terranettis Italian Bakery ....E....... 717 697-5434
Mechanicsburg ***(G-10896)***
Tops Markets LLC ....C....... 570 882-9188
Sayre ***(G-17123)***
Travaglini Enterprises Inc ....E....... 814 898-1212
Erie ***(G-5515)***
Travaglini Enterprises Inc ....E....... 724 342-3334
Hermitage ***(G-7596)***
Trofi Idoni Specialty Baking...................G....... 484 892-0876
Bethlehem ***(G-1643)***
Tsb Group LLC..G....... 412 224-2306
Pittsburgh ***(G-15659)***
Unique Desserts Inc ....G....... 610 372-7879
Reading ***(G-16552)***
Vallos Bakery LLC...................................E....... 610 866-1012
Bethlehem ***(G-1650)***
▲ **Village Farm Market**...........................G....... 717 733-5340
Ephrata ***(G-5154)***
Wakefern Food Corp...............................D....... 215 744-9500
Philadelphia ***(G-14457)***
Warrington Pastry Shop.........................F....... 215 343-1946
Warrington ***(G-19139)***
Weinrich Bakery......................................E....... 215 659-7062
Willow Grove ***(G-20148)***
Weis Markets Inc.....................................C....... 570 724-6364
Wellsboro ***(G-19474)***
William Aupperle......................................G....... 724 583-8310
Masontown ***(G-10538)***
Wixons Bakery Inc...................................F....... 610 777-6056
Reading ***(G-16568)***
Yum Yum Bake Shops Inc.......................G....... 215 675-9874
Warminster ***(G-19005)***
Yum-Yum Colmar Inc...............................E....... 215 822-9468
Colmar ***(G-3426)***
Zakes Cakes ....G....... 215 654-7600
Fort Washington ***(G-6097)***
Zynnie Bakes...G....... 610 905-6283
Philadelphia ***(G-14506)***

2052 Cookies & Crackers

A Taste of Philly ....G....... 215 639-3997
Feasterville Trevose ***(G-5882)***
Als Conezone ....G....... 412 405-9601
Clairton ***(G-3147)***
Amarriage Entertainment LLC.................F....... 267 973-5288
Upper Darby ***(G-18678)***
Amco Biscuit Distributors Inc ....F....... 215 467-8775
Philadelphia ***(G-13376)***
Auntie Annes Soft Pretzels.....................G....... 724 349-2825
Indiana ***(G-8084)***
Bainbridge Group Inc ....F....... 215 922-3274
Philadelphia ***(G-13442)***
Bakers Best Snack Foods Inc.................E....... 215 822-3511
Hatfield ***(G-7320)***
Better Batter Gluten Free Flur ....G....... 814 946-0958
Altoona ***(G-476)***
▲ **Bickels Snack Foods Inc**.....................E....... 800 233-1933
York ***(G-20403)***
Bucks Creamery LLC...............................E....... 732 387-3535
Feasterville Trevose ***(G-5895)***
Center City Pretzel Co ....F....... 215 463-5664
Philadelphia ***(G-13519)***
Charlies Specialties Inc..........................D....... 724 346-2350
Hermitage ***(G-7577)***
Claudes Creamery ....G....... 610 826-2663
Palmerton ***(G-13103)***
▲ **Condor Corporation**.............................C....... 717 560-1882
Lititz ***(G-10001)***
Cone Guys Ltd ....F....... 215 781-6996
Bristol ***(G-2128)***
Cookie Grams...G....... 814 942-4220
Altoona ***(G-494)***
Country Fresh Batter Inc.........................D....... 610 272-5751
King of Prussia ***(G-8600)***
Cramer Partnership ....G....... 215 378-6024
Yardley ***(G-20301)***
Cupoladua Oven LLC ....G....... 412 592-5378
Mars ***(G-10493)***
▲ **D F Stauffer Biscuit Co Inc**..................B....... 717 815-4600
York ***(G-20441)***
Dalos Bakery Inc......................................E....... 570 752-4519
Berwick ***(G-1322)***
Davis Cookie Company...........................D....... 814 473-3125
Rimersburg ***(G-16749)***
Dutch Cntry Soft Pretzels LLC................G....... 717 354-4493
New Holland ***(G-12244)***
Egypt Star Inc...E....... 610 434-8516
Allentown ***(G-204)***
Epex Soft Petals.......................................F....... 717 848-8488
York ***(G-20469)***
◆ **Flowers Baking Co Oxford Inc**..........E....... 610 932-2147
Oxford ***(G-13079)***
Gotcha Covered Pretzels LLC ....G....... 215 253-3176
Warrington ***(G-19118)***
Hammond Pretzel Bakery Inc ....E....... 717 392-7532
Lancaster ***(G-9038)***
Intercourse Pretzel Factory....................E....... 717 768-3432
Intercourse ***(G-8137)***
Jims Soft Pretzel Bakery LLC................G....... 215 431-1045
Ivyland ***(G-8213)***
◆ **Joy Cone Co** ....B....... 724 962-5747
Hermitage ***(G-7589)***
Keebler Company ....F....... 717 790-9886
Mechanicsburg ***(G-10862)***
Keebler Company ....E....... 215 752-4010
Horsham ***(G-7830)***
Kelloggs Snacks.......................................G....... 412 787-1183
Pittsburgh ***(G-15165)***
Kings Potato Chip Company ....E....... 717 445-4521
Mohnton ***(G-11268)***
Kretchmar Bakery Inc..............................E....... 724 774-2324
Beaver ***(G-986)***
▲ **Leclerc Foods Usa Inc**........................D....... 570 547-6295
Montgomery ***(G-11375)***
M Cibrone & Sons Bakery Inc................E....... 412 885-6200
Pittsburgh ***(G-15244)***
Martins Pretzel Bakery ....E....... 717 859-1272
Akron ***(G-36)***
Mondelez Global LLC ....E....... 215 673-4800
Philadelphia ***(G-14034)***
Nabisco Brands Inc ....G....... 570 820-1669
Wilkes Barre ***(G-19948)***
Nuts & Such Ltd.......................................G....... 215 708-8500
Philadelphia ***(G-14089)***
Paddycake Bakery ....E....... 412 621-4477
Pittsburgh ***(G-15367)***
Pati Petite Butter Cookies Inc................E....... 412 221-4033
Bridgeville ***(G-2085)***
Pepperidge Farm Incorporated..............G....... 610 356-0553
Broomall ***(G-2301)***
Pepperidge Farm Incorporated..............G....... 717 336-8500
Denver ***(G-4087)***
Philadelphia Soft Pretzels ....E....... 215 324-4315
Philadelphia ***(G-14155)***
Philly Pretzel Factory...............................E....... 215 962-5593
Philadelphia ***(G-14169)***
Pretzel Lady..G....... 717 632-7046
Hanover ***(G-6937)***
Pretzel Shop ....F....... 412 431-2574
Pittsburgh ***(G-15437)***
Pretzels Plus...G....... 724 228-9785
Washington ***(G-19218)***
Revonah Pretzel LLC ....E....... 717 632-4477
Hanover ***(G-6943)***
Rjj Mobile LLC..F....... 215 796-1935
Philadelphia ***(G-14253)***
Rjj Wayne LLC..G....... 215 796-1935
Lafayette Hill ***(G-8884)***
▼ **S-L Snacks Real Estate Inc** ....A....... 717 632-4477
Hanover ***(G-6948)***
Sansom Street Soft Pretzel Fac.............G....... 215 569-3988
Philadelphia ***(G-14279)***
▲ **Savor Street Foods Inc**.......................E....... 610 320-7800
Wyomissing ***(G-20288)***
Scooperman Water Ice Inc.....................G....... 267 623-8494
Philadelphia ***(G-14285)***
Shearers Fods Canonsburg Plant.........G....... 724 746-1162
Canonsburg ***(G-2635)***
Shirleys Cookie Company Inc ....D....... 814 239-2208
Claysburg ***(G-3208)***
Snyders Hanover Mfg Inc.......................G....... 800 233-7125
Hanover ***(G-6954)***
Snyders-Lance Inc...................................B....... 724 929-6270
Rostraver Township ***(G-16830)***
Snyders-Lance Inc...................................D....... 717 632-4477
Hanover ***(G-6955)***
Sophisticakes Inc.....................................G....... 610 626-9991
Drexel Hill ***(G-4371)***
Star Brands North America Inc..............G....... 610 775-4100
Mohnton ***(G-11270)***
Suzie BS Pretzeltown Inc ....G....... 814 868-8443
Erie ***(G-5498)***
Sweetzels Foods LLC ....G....... 610 278-8700
Blue Bell ***(G-1854)***
▲ **Tasty Baking Company** ....E....... 215 221-8500
Philadelphia ***(G-14374)***
Tasty Baking Company ....A....... 215 221-8500
Philadelphia ***(G-14375)***
Tasty Twisters Inc ....G....... 215 487-7828
Philadelphia ***(G-14376)***
▼ **Todds Snax Inc**....................................C....... 717 637-5931
Hanover ***(G-6961)***
▲ **Tom Sturgis Pretzels Inc** ....E....... 610 775-0335
Reading ***(G-16544)***
Troyer Inc..E....... 724 746-1162
Canonsburg ***(G-2648)***
Tshudy Snacks Inc...................................F....... 717 626-4354
Lititz ***(G-10055)***
Uncle Henrys Pretzel Bakery ....E....... 717 445-4698
Bowmansville ***(G-1888)***
Unique Desserts Inc ....G....... 610 372-7879
Reading ***(G-16552)***
Unique Pretzel Bakery Inc......................E....... 610 929-3172
Reading ***(G-16553)***
Utz Quality Foods Inc ....C....... 717 637-5666
Hanover ***(G-6966)***
◆ **Utz Quality Foods LLC**.......................A....... 800 367-7629
Hanover ***(G-6967)***
Village Pretzels...F....... 215 674-5070
Hatboro ***(G-7309)***
Wege Pretzel Co Inc................................D....... 717 843-0738
Hanover ***(G-6973)***

2053 Frozen Bakery Prdts

Dawn Food Products Inc.........................C....... 717 840-0044
York ***(G-20445)***
Dices Creative Cakes...............................G....... 610 367-0107
Boyertown ***(G-1906)***
Happy Baking Co ....G....... 412 621-4020
Pittsburgh ***(G-15081)***
Icy Bites Inc..G....... 570 558-5558
Scranton ***(G-17242)***
Luscious Layers..G....... 724 967-2357
Grove City ***(G-6796)***
Pepperidge Farm Incorporated..............G....... 610 356-0553
Broomall ***(G-2301)***
Pepperidge Farm Incorporated..............G....... 717 336-8500
Denver ***(G-4087)***
Pretzelworks Inc.......................................D....... 215 288-4002
Philadelphia ***(G-14199)***
Sunbeam Morrisville Inc..........................G....... 215 736-9991
Morrisville ***(G-11583)***

2061 Sugar, Cane

Good Food Inc..C....... 610 273-3776
Honey Brook ***(G-7745)***

2062 Sugar, Cane Refining

CSC Sugar LLC ....F....... 215 428-3670
Fairless Hills ***(G-5777)***
Sugar Shack..F....... 814 425-2220
Cochranton ***(G-3352)***
Sugaright LLC ....F....... 215 295-4709
Fairless Hills ***(G-5800)***

2063 Sugar, Beet

CSC Sugar LLC ......F 215 428-3670
Fairless Hills (G-5777)

2064 Candy & Confectionery Prdts

4sis LLC ......E 814 459-2451
Erie (G-5162)
Adrenalation Inc ......F 215 324-3412
Philadelphia (G-13346)
Andersons Candies Inc ......E 724 869-3018
Baden (G-869)
Anstines Candy Box ......G 717 854-9269
York (G-20379)
B & E Candy ......G 724 327-8898
Jeannette (G-8247)
Barchemy LLC ......E 724 379-4405
Donora (G-4147)
▲ Bazzini Holdings LLC ......C 610 366-1606
Allentown (G-147)
Bevans Candies Inc ......F 610 566-0581
Media (G-10915)
Blaine Boring Chocolates ......G 814 539-6244
Johnstown (G-8358)
Boyer Candy Company Inc ......D 814 944-9401
Altoona (G-483)
Byrnes and Kiefer Company ......E 724 538-5200
Callery (G-2467)
Callies Candy Kitchens Inc ......E 570 595-3257
Cresco (G-3892)
Callies Candy Kitchens Inc ......F 570 595-2280
Mountainhome (G-11786)
Catoris Candies Inc ......F 724 335-4371
New Kensington (G-12333)
Char-Val Candies ......G 814 275-1602
New Bethlehem (G-12025)
Chester A Asher Inc ......G 717 248-8613
Lewistown (G-9925)
▲ Chester A Asher Inc ......C 215 721-3000
Souderton (G-17729)
▲ Chris Candies Inc ......E 412 322-9400
Pittsburgh (G-14849)
Clark Candies Inc ......G 724 226-0866
Tarentum (G-18239)
Copper Kettle Fudge Factory ......F 412 824-1233
North Versailles (G-12773)
▲ Daffins Inc ......E 724 342-2892
Sharon (G-17432)
Daffins Inc ......E 724 983-8336
Farrell (G-5867)
Dan Smith Candies Inc ......F 814 849-8221
Brookville (G-2259)
Edwards Sherm Candies Inc ......E 412 372-4331
Trafford (G-18454)
Elite Sweets Inc ......F 610 391-1719
Trexlertown (G-18510)
Esthers Sweet Shop Inc ......G 412 884-4224
Pittsburgh (G-14986)
Evans Candy LLC ......G 717 295-7510
Lancaster (G-9012)
Fitzkees Candies Inc ......F 717 741-1031
York (G-20482)
▲ Fox Run Usa LLC ......D 215 675-7700
Ivyland (G-8211)
◆ Gertrude Hawk Chocolates Inc ......B 570 342-7556
Dunmore (G-4473)
Godiva Chocolatier Inc ......B 610 779-3797
Reading (G-16394)
Groffs Candies ......G 717 872-2845
Lancaster (G-9033)
Halls Candies LLC ......G 570 596-2267
Gillett (G-6381)
Hershey Company ......B 717 534-4100
Hershey (G-7614)
Hershey Company ......A 717 509-9795
Lancaster (G-9045)
Hershey Company ......B 717 534-4200
Hershey (G-7615)
Hershey Company ......B 570 384-3271
Hazle Township (G-7463)
◆ Hershey Company ......B 717 534-4200
Hershey (G-7613)
Hershey Foods Corporation - MA ......F 717 534-6799
Hershey (G-7616)
Hiddie Kitchen Inc ......F 717 566-2211
Hummelstown (G-7913)
James A Marquette ......G 570 523-3873
Lewisburg (G-9913)
Jamesons Candy Inc ......F 724 658-7441
New Castle (G-12107)
John L Stopay LLC ......G 570 562-6541
Taylor (G-18259)
Josh Early Candies Inc ......F 610 395-4321
Allentown (G-271)
◆ Just Born Inc ......B 610 867-7568
Bethlehem (G-1548)
Just Born Inc ......D 215 335-4500
Philadelphia (G-13915)
Lerro Candy Co ......F 610 461-8886
Darby (G-4021)
Lifestyle Evolution Inc ......F 412 828-4115
Oakmont (G-12920)
Lollipop HM Halthcare Svcs LLC ......G 570 286-9460
Sunbury (G-18171)
Lukas Confections Inc ......E 717 843-0921
Ebensburg (G-4787)
▼ Marc Edward Brands Inc ......D 412 380-0888
Pittsburgh (G-15250)
Mars Incorporated ......E 717 367-1500
Elizabethtown (G-4877)
Mars Chocolate North Amer LLC ......B 717 367-1500
Elizabethtown (G-4878)
Marshmallowmba ......G 703 340-7157
Red Lion (G-16607)
Matangos Candies Inc ......G 717 234-0882
Harrisburg (G-7174)
Michael Mootz Candies Inc ......F 570 823-8272
Hanover Township (G-6997)
Miesse Candies Corp ......G 717 299-5427
Lancaster (G-9135)
Mostollers Mfg & Distrg ......F 814 445-7281
Friedens (G-6223)
Moyer Specialty Foods LLC ......F 215 703-0100
Souderton (G-17754)
My Aunties Candies ......G 610 269-0919
Downingtown (G-4243)
Naylor Candies Inc ......F 717 266-2706
Mount Wolf (G-11748)
Nestle Usa Inc ......C 818 549-6000
King of Prussia (G-8655)
Nuts & Such Ltd ......G 215 708-8500
Philadelphia (G-14089)
Nuts About Granola LLC ......G 717 814-9648
York (G-20613)
Oak Spring Enterprises Inc ......F 570 622-2001
Pottsville (G-16090)
OH Ryans Irish Potatoes ......F 610 494-7123
Marcus Hook (G-10452)
OSheas Candies ......F 814 536-4800
Johnstown (G-8414)
OSheas Candies ......G 814 266-7041
Johnstown (G-8415)
▲ Pharmaloz Manufacturing Inc ......E 717 274-9800
Lebanon (G-9621)
Plantation Candies Inc ......F 215 723-6810
Telford (G-18309)
Popcorn Alley Inc ......F 877 292-5611
Dover (G-4199)
Popcorn Buddha Inc ......F 570 476-5676
East Stroudsburg (G-4629)
Purity Candy Co ......F 570 538-9502
Allenwood (G-442)
R M Palmer Company ......E 610 582-5551
Reading (G-16483)
R M Palmer Company ......C 610 374-5224
Wyomissing (G-20287)
Remarkable Designs Inc ......G 412 512-6564
Glenshaw (G-6499)
Repperts Candy ......F 610 689-9200
Oley (G-12980)
Resource Dynamics Incorporated ......G 412 369-7760
Pittsburgh (G-15480)
Robert W Gastel Jr ......E 412 678-2723
White Oak (G-19858)
Romolo Chocolates Inc ......E 814 452-1933
Erie (G-5466)
Rosalind Candy Castle Inc ......F 724 843-1144
New Brighton (G-12041)
Sarris Candies Inc ......B 724 745-4042
Canonsburg (G-2632)
Shane Candy Co ......F 215 922-1048
Philadelphia (G-14296)
Shannons Kandy Kitchen ......G 724 662-5211
Mercer (G-10975)
Specialty Snacks Inc ......G 215 721-0414
Telford (G-18317)
Stutz Candy Company ......E 215 675-2630
Hatboro (G-7307)
Suzannes Choclat & Confections ......G 570 753-8545
Avis (G-838)
Thomson Candies ......G 610 268-8337
Avondale (G-861)
Three Rivers Confections LLC ......D 412 402-0388
Pittsburgh (G-15618)
Toad-Ally Snax Inc ......E 215 788-7500
Bristol (G-2208)
Tootsie Roll Industries Inc ......G 570 455-2975
Hazle Township (G-7485)
Topps Company Inc ......D 570 346-5874
Scranton (G-17305)
Topps Company Inc ......G 570 471-7649
Old Forge (G-12975)
▲ Trufood Mfg Inc ......C 412 963-2330
Pittsburgh (G-15656)
Valos House of Candy ......G 724 339-2669
New Kensington (G-12385)
Victorias Candies Inc ......G 570 455-6341
Hazleton (G-7534)
Victorias Candies Inc ......G 570 455-6345
West Hazleton (G-19718)
WA Dehart Inc ......D 570 568-1551
New Columbia (G-12179)
Warners Candies ......G 215 639-1615
Bensalem (G-1269)
▲ Warrell Corporation ......B 717 761-5440
Camp Hill (G-2523)
Werther Partners LLC ......G 215 677-5200
Philadelphia (G-14465)
Wfc & C Inc ......F 215 627-3233
Philadelphia (G-14471)
Wilson Candy Co Inc ......F 724 523-3151
Jeannette (G-8268)
Wolfgang Operations LLC ......D 717 843-5536
York (G-20718)
Wolfgang Operations LLC ......E 717 843-5536
York (G-20719)
Zitner Candy Corp ......E 215 229-4990
Philadelphia (G-14505)

2066 Chocolate & Cocoa Prdts

4sis LLC ......E 814 459-2451
Erie (G-5162)
926 Partners Inc ......F 814 452-4026
Erie (G-5163)
Andersons Candies Inc ......E 724 869-3018
Baden (G-869)
▲ Artisan Confections Company ......G 717 534-4200
Hershey (G-7604)
Barry Callebaut USA LLC ......E 610 872-4528
Eddystone (G-4798)
Barry Callebaut USA LLC ......G 312 496-7305
Bethlehem (G-1457)
Barry Callebaut USA LLC ......B 570 342-7556
Dunmore (G-4470)
Basket Works Inc ......G 516 367-9200
Tannersville (G-18234)
Beckers Cafe ......G 412 331-1373
Mc Kees Rocks (G-10604)
Bevans Candies Inc ......F 610 566-0581
Media (G-10915)
Blaine Boring Chocolates ......G 814 539-6244
Johnstown (G-8358)
◆ Blommer Chocolate Company ......D 800 825-8181
East Greenville (G-4565)
Blommer Chocolate Company ......C 215 679-4472
East Greenville (G-4566)
Candy Cottage Co Inc ......G 215 322-6618
Huntingdon Valley (G-7967)
Cargill Cocoa & Chocolate Inc ......B 717 653-1471
Mount Joy (G-11647)
Cargill Cocoa & Chocolate Inc ......B 570 453-6825
Hazle Township (G-7448)
Casa Luker USA Inc ......G 412 854-9012
Pittsburgh (G-14824)
Cherrydale Fundraising LLC ......G 610 366-1606
Allentown (G-169)
▲ Chester A Asher Inc ......C 215 721-3000
Souderton (G-17729)
▲ Choccobutter Inc ......G 717 756-5590
New Cumberland (G-12184)
Chocodiem ......G 908 200-7044
Easton (G-4661)
Chocolate Creations ......G 570 383-9931
Peckville (G-13207)
Chocolate Creations ......G 724 774-7675
Monaca (G-11288)
Colebrook Chocolate Co LLC ......G 724 628-8383
Connellsville (G-3492)
▲ Confiseurs Inc ......E 610 932-2706
Oxford (G-13076)

S I C

Daffins Inc...E....... 724 983-8336
Farrell *(G-5867)*
Edwards Sherm Candies Inc...E....... 412 372-4331
Trafford *(G-18454)*
Event Horizon LLC...G....... 717 557-1427
Hershey *(G-7610)*
◆ **Frankford Candy LLC**...C....... 215 735-5200
Philadelphia *(G-13720)*
◆ **Gertrude Hawk Chocolates Inc**...B....... 570 342-7556
Dunmore *(G-4473)*
Godiva Chocolatier Inc...B....... 610 779-3797
Reading *(G-16394)*
◆ **Hershey Company**...B....... 717 534-4200
Hershey *(G-7613)*
Hershey Company...B....... 717 534-4100
Hershey *(G-7614)*
Hershey Company...B....... 570 384-3271
Hazle Township *(G-7463)*
Hershey Digital...G....... 717 431-9602
Willow Street *(G-20151)*
Lifestyle Evolution Inc...F....... 412 828-4115
Oakmont *(G-12920)*
Mars Chocolate North Amer LLC...B....... 717 367-1500
Elizabethtown *(G-4878)*
Matangos Candies Inc...G....... 717 234-0882
Harrisburg *(G-7174)*
My Aunties Candies...G....... 610 269-0919
Downingtown *(G-4243)*
OSheas Candies...F....... 814 536-4800
Johnstown *(G-8414)*
Painted Truffle...G....... 215 996-0606
North Wales *(G-12823)*
Pardoes Perky Peanuts Inc...E....... 570 524-9595
Montandon *(G-11366)*
Premise Maid Candies Inc...E....... 610 395-3221
Breinigsville *(G-2024)*
Purity Candy Co...F....... 570 538-9502
Allenwood *(G-442)*
R M Palmer Company...E....... 610 582-5551
Reading *(G-16483)*
R M Palmer Company...C....... 610 374-5224
Wyomissing *(G-20287)*
Robert W Gastel Jr...E....... 412 678-2723
White Oak *(G-19858)*
Romolo Chocolates Inc...E....... 814 452-1933
Erie *(G-5466)*
Sarris Candies Inc...B....... 724 745-4042
Canonsburg *(G-2632)*
Stutz Candy Company...E....... 215 675-2630
Hatboro *(G-7307)*
Suzannes Choclat & Confections...G....... 570 753-8545
Avis *(G-838)*
Sweet Jubilee Gourmet...G....... 717 691-9782
Mechanicsburg *(G-10893)*
Sweet Salvation Truffle...G....... 610 220-4157
Haverford *(G-7415)*
Trufood Mfg Inc...B....... 412 963-6600
Pittsburgh *(G-15655)*
▲ **Trufood Mfg Inc**...C....... 412 963-2330
Pittsburgh *(G-15656)*
Victorias Candies Inc...G....... 570 455-6341
Hazleton *(G-7534)*
▲ **Warrell Corporation**...B....... 717 761-5440
Camp Hill *(G-2523)*
Wfc & C Inc...F....... 215 627-3233
Philadelphia *(G-14471)*

2068 Salted & Roasted Nuts & Seeds

◆ **A L Bazzini Co Inc**...E....... 610 366-1606
Allentown *(G-111)*
Bal Nut Inc...G....... 570 675-2712
Dallas *(G-3958)*
▲ **Bazzini Holdings LLC**...C....... 610 366-1606
Allentown *(G-147)*
Moyer Specialty Foods LLC...F....... 215 703-0100
Souderton *(G-17754)*
Pardoes Perky Peanuts Inc...E....... 570 524-9595
Montandon *(G-11366)*
Stutz Candy Company...E....... 215 675-2630
Hatboro *(G-7307)*

2075 Soybean Oil Mills

Ardent Mills LLC...E....... 570 839-8322
Pocono Summit *(G-15885)*
Cargill Incorporated...F....... 717 273-1133
Lebanon *(G-9552)*
▲ **Nature Soy LLC**...F....... 215 765-3289
Philadelphia *(G-14058)*

2076 Vegetable Oil Mills

Boyd Station LLC...E....... 866 411-2693
Danville *(G-3998)*

2077 Animal, Marine Fats & Oils

A F Moyer Inc...G....... 215 723-5555
Souderton *(G-17719)*
Darling Ingredients Inc...F....... 724 695-1212
Imperial *(G-8063)*
Griffin Industries LLC...E....... 610 273-7014
Honey Brook *(G-7746)*
Jbs Souderton Inc...A....... 215 723-5555
Souderton *(G-17744)*
▲ **Marine Ingredients LLC**...E....... 570 260-6900
Mount Bethel *(G-11613)*
Mountain View Rendering Co...E....... 215 723-5555
Souderton *(G-17752)*
▼ **Neatsfoot Oil Refineries Corp**...E....... 215 739-1291
Philadelphia *(G-14061)*
Valley Proteins Inc...D....... 717 445-6890
East Earl *(G-4556)*
Valley Proteins Inc...D....... 717 436-0004
Mifflintown *(G-11140)*
▲ **Vigon International Inc**...D....... 877 844-6639
East Stroudsburg *(G-4638)*

2079 Shortening, Oils & Margarine

A & S Olive Oil Company Inc...G....... 267 483-8379
Chalfont *(G-2862)*
Cape May Olive Oil Company...G....... 610 256-3667
Morton *(G-11590)*
Cardenas Oil & Vinegar Taproom...G....... 570 401-4718
Philadelphia *(G-13501)*
Good Food Inc...C....... 610 273-3776
Honey Brook *(G-7745)*
▲ **Kalamata Farms Llc**...F....... 570 972-1021
Allentown *(G-279)*
Kapothanasis Group Inc...G....... 207 939-5680
Harrisburg *(G-7160)*
L D Kallman Inc...F....... 610 384-1200
Coatesville *(G-3312)*
▲ **Maeva Usa Inc**...G....... 215 461-2453
Philadelphia *(G-13986)*
◆ **Mallet and Company Inc**...G....... 412 276-9000
Carnegie *(G-2776)*
Olio Fresca Olive Oil Company...G....... 585 820-8400
Ridgway *(G-16722)*
Olive Kastania Oil...G....... 610 347-6736
Kennett Square *(G-8533)*
Olive Oakmont Oil Company...G....... 412 435-6912
Oakmont *(G-12921)*
Olive Olio Oils and Balsamics...G....... 717 627-0088
Lititz *(G-10027)*
▲ **PCA Group Inc**...G....... 610 558-2802
Garnet Valley *(G-6267)*
Two Rivers Olives Oil Company...G....... 724 775-2748
Beaver *(G-994)*
Ventura Foods LLC...C....... 717 263-6900
Chambersburg *(G-2997)*

2082 Malt Beverages

2124 Brewing Company LLC...G....... 724 260-8737
Pittsburgh *(G-14624)*
American Beer Beverage Ltd...G....... 610 352-2211
Upper Darby *(G-18679)*
American Craft Brewery LLC...B....... 610 391-4700
Breinigsville *(G-2007)*
Appalachian Brewing Co Inc...D....... 717 221-1080
Harrisburg *(G-7087)*
AR Tart LLC...G....... 267 408-6507
Philadelphia *(G-13404)*
B & B Beverage...G....... 570 742-7782
Milton *(G-11233)*
B & S Beverage L L C...G....... 814 674-2223
Patton *(G-13187)*
Battlefield Brew Works...G....... 717 398-2907
Gettysburg *(G-6284)*
Bayfront Brewing Co...G....... 814 333-8641
Meadville *(G-10705)*
Beer 4 Less...G....... 724 452-7860
Zelienople *(G-20791)*
Beer Brothers...G....... 610 438-3900
Easton *(G-4652)*
Beer To Go Inc...G....... 610 253-2954
Easton *(G-4653)*
Benny Brewing Company LLC...G....... 570 235-6995
Hanover Township *(G-6980)*
Bernies Beer & Beverage Inc...G....... 215 744-1946
Philadelphia *(G-13457)*
Berrys Beverage Inc...G....... 724 867-9480
Emlenton *(G-5006)*
Better World Spirits Inc...G....... 717 758-9346
York *(G-20402)*
Big Valley Beverage Inc...G....... 717 667-1414
Reedsville *(G-16622)*
Boneshire Brew Works...G....... 717 469-5007
Harrisburg *(G-7098)*
Bonn Place Brewing Inc...G....... 845 325-6748
Bethlehem *(G-1469)*
Boston Beer Company Inc...C....... 610 395-1885
Breinigsville *(G-2011)*
Brewers Outlet...G....... 717 848-5250
York *(G-20413)*
Brewskees of Shiloh...G....... 717 764-2994
York *(G-20414)*
Broker Brewing Company LLC...G....... 610 304-0822
Creamery *(G-3873)*
Bucks Cnty Brewing Distlg LLC...G....... 215 766-7711
Pipersville *(G-14612)*
Buddys Brews...G....... 724 970-2739
Lemont Furnace *(G-9733)*
Chesapeake Del Brewing Co LLC...C....... 610 627-9000
Media *(G-10918)*
City Brewing...F....... 724 532-5454
Latrobe *(G-9466)*
Clarion River Brewing Co...G....... 814 297-8399
Clarion *(G-3174)*
Cnc Malting Company...G....... 570 954-4500
Fenelton *(G-5944)*
Costar Brewing Inc...G....... 412 401-8433
Pittsburgh *(G-14877)*
Cranberry Beverage Corp...G....... 814 437-7998
Franklin *(G-6123)*
▲ **D G Yuengling and Son Inc**...E....... 570 622-4141
Pottsville *(G-16075)*
D G Yuengling and Son Inc...E....... 570 622-0153
Pottsville *(G-16076)*
Desi S Interstate Beer...G....... 814 528-5914
Erie *(G-5246)*
East End Brewing Company Inc...F....... 412 361-2848
Pittsburgh *(G-14955)*
East Falls Beverage LLC...G....... 215 844-5600
Philadelphia *(G-13656)*
Easton Beer...G....... 215 884-1252
Glenside *(G-6514)*
Firewlkers Small Btch Dist LLC...G....... 610 737-7900
Coplay *(G-3643)*
Frankensteins...G....... 814 938-2571
Punxsutawney *(G-16140)*
Guys Round Brewing Company...F....... 215 368-2640
Lansdale *(G-9374)*
Here and Now Brewing Co LLC...G....... 570 647-6085
Honesdale *(G-7713)*
Highway Manor Brewing...G....... 717 743-0613
Camp Hill *(G-2501)*
Icb Acquisitions LLC...F....... 412 682-7400
Pittsburgh *(G-15112)*
Jones Brewing Company Inc...G....... 724 872-2337
Smithton *(G-17661)*
Jskc LLC...G....... 724 933-5575
Wexford *(G-19809)*
Kennedy Beverage LLC...G....... 724 302-0123
Aliquippa *(G-78)*
Kreiders Mulch...G....... 717 871-9177
Washington Boro *(G-19250)*
Lackawanna Distributor Corp...G....... 570 342-8245
Dunmore *(G-4476)*
Lancaster Brewing Company...E....... 717 391-6258
Lancaster *(G-9090)*
Linda K Woodward Inc...G....... 610 791-3694
Allentown *(G-296)*
▲ **Lion Brewery Inc**...C....... 570 823-8801
Wilkes Barre *(G-19936)*
Lost Tavern Brewing LLC...F....... 484 851-3980
Hellertown *(G-7558)*
Mary Ann Pensiero Inc...G....... 717 545-8289
Harrisburg *(G-7173)*
Marzonies...D....... 814 695-2931
Duncansville *(G-4456)*
McLaughlin Distillery...G....... 315 486-1372
Sewickley *(G-17400)*
ME 5 Cents LLC...F....... 570 574-4701
Hanover Township *(G-6994)*
Mindful Brewing Company LLC...G....... 412 965-8428
Pittsburgh *(G-15290)*
Miscreation Brewing...G....... 717 698-3666
Hanover *(G-6922)*
Molly Pitcher Brewing Company...G....... 717 609-0969
Carlisle *(G-2727)*

Mudhook Brewing Company LLC ....F 717 747-3605
York *(G-20606)*

▲ Muller Inc ....C 215 676-7575
Philadelphia *(G-14044)*

New Liberty Distillery ....G..... 800 996-0595
Philadelphia *(G-14067)*

One Brew At A Time ....G..... 267 797-5437
Morrisville *(G-11575)*

▲ Pennsylvania Brewing Company .....E 412 237-9400
Pittsburgh *(G-15375)*

Petes Beverage ....G..... 814 563-7374
Youngsville *(G-20774)*

Philadelphia Beer Works Inc ....C 215 482-8220
Philadelphia *(G-14142)*

▲ Pittsburgh Brewing Company ....B 412 682-7400
Pittsburgh *(G-15388)*

Purblu Beverages Inc ....G..... 412 281-9808
Pittsburgh *(G-15456)*

Reclamation Brewing Company ....F 724 282-0831
Butler *(G-2437)*

Schnoch Corporation ....E 570 326-4700
Williamsport *(G-20070)*

SMK & Son Inc ....G..... 215 455-7867
Philadelphia *(G-14317)*

Sole Artisan Ales Llc ....F 570 977-0053
Easton *(G-4753)*

Something Wicked Brewing LLC..........G..... 717 316-5488
Hanover *(G-6956)*

South Hills Brewing Supply ....G..... 412 937-0773
Monroeville *(G-11356)*

Southside Brew-Thru LLC...................G..... 814 254-4828
Johnstown *(G-8437)*

St Benjamins Brewing Co ....F 215 232-4305
Philadelphia *(G-14338)*

Stickman Brews ....G..... 484 938-5900
Royersford *(G-16866)*

Stickman Brews ....G..... 856 912-4372
Wayne *(G-19373)*

▲ Stoudt Brewing Company ....E 717 484-4386
Adamstown *(G-24)*

Sunrise Naturals LLC ....G..... 717 350-6169
Millersburg *(G-11201)*

Symphony Brewing Systems LLC........G..... 215 493-0430
Yardley *(G-20342)*

Terry Baker ....G..... 717 263-5942
Chambersburg *(G-2985)*

Tk Beer Inc ....G..... 610 446-2337
Upper Darby *(G-18693)*

Tower Hill Berery ....G..... 267 308-8992
Chalfont *(G-2893)*

◆ Victory Brewing Company LLC........E 610 873-0881
Downingtown *(G-4261)*

Victory Parkesburg ....G..... 610 574-4000
Parkesburg *(G-13183)*

▲ Vink & Beri LLC ....F 215 654-5252
Montgomeryville *(G-11426)*

West End Beer Mart ....G..... 814 536-1846
Johnstown *(G-8443)*

▲ Weyerbacher Brewing Co ....G..... 610 559-5561
Easton *(G-4775)*

Wilbos Inc ....G..... 267 490-5168
Quakertown *(G-16259)*

Wissahickon Brewing Company ....G..... 267 239-6596
Philadelphia *(G-14480)*

▲ Ybc Holdings Inc ....F 215 634-2600
Philadelphia *(G-14499)*

2083 Malt

Deer Creek Malthouse LLC ....G..... 717 746-6258
Glen Mills *(G-6433)*

Deer Creek Malthouse LLC ....G..... 717 746-6258
Glen Mills *(G-6434)*

Philadelphia Beer Works Inc ....C 215 482-8220
Philadelphia *(G-14142)*

2084 Wine & Brandy

A & R Nissley Inc ....E 717 426-3514
Bainbridge *(G-871)*

A & R Nissley Inc ....G..... 717 541-1004
Harrisburg *(G-7078)*

Adams Vintner LLC ....G..... 717 685-1336
Annville *(G-641)*

ADello Vineyard & Winery LLC ....G..... 610 754-0006
Perkiomenville *(G-13299)*

Amore Vineyards and Winery ....G..... 610 837-1683
Nazareth *(G-11954)*

Antler Ridge Winery ....G..... 570 247-7222
Ulster *(G-18597)*

Arrowhead Wine Cellars Inc ....F 814 725-5509
North East *(G-12729)*

Arundel Cellars Inc ....F 814 725-1079
North East *(G-12730)*

Benignas Creek Vineyard & Wine ....G..... 570 546-0744
Muncy *(G-11809)*

Benignas Creek Vineyard Wine ....G..... 570 374-4750
Selinsgrove *(G-17321)*

Benignas Creek Vnyrd Wnery Inc ....G..... 570 523-4997
Klingerstown *(G-8805)*

Big Creek Vineyard ....G..... 570 325-8138
Jim Thorpe *(G-8337)*

Big Hill Winery ....G..... 717 226-8702
Gardners *(G-6259)*

Black Walnut Winery ....G..... 610 857-5566
Sadsburyville *(G-16904)*

Blair Vineyards ....G..... 610 682-0075
Mertztown *(G-11001)*

Blue Mtn Vineyards & Cellars ....G..... 610 298-3068
New Tripoli *(G-12453)*

Bostwick Enterprises Inc ....F 814 725-8015
North East *(G-12733)*

Broad Mountain Vineyard LLC ....G..... 717 362-8044
Elizabethville *(G-4892)*

Buckingham Valley Vineyards ....G..... 215 794-7188
Buckingham *(G-2338)*

Buddy Boy Winery ....G..... 814 772-3751
Ridgway *(G-16698)*

Buddy Boy Winery & Vineyard ....F 717 834-5606
Duncannon *(G-4444)*

Capra Collina Vineyard Inc ....G..... 570 489-0489
Blakely *(G-1746)*

Cassel Vineyards Hershey LLC ....G..... 717 533-2008
Hummelstown *(G-7905)*

Chaddsford Winery Ltd ....E 610 388-6221
Chadds Ford *(G-2849)*

▲ Charles Jacquin Et Cie Inc.............D..... 215 425-9300
Philadelphia *(G-13529)*

Christian W Klay Winery Inc ....F 724 439-3424
Chalk Hill *(G-2895)*

Clover Hill Enterprises Inc ....G..... 610 395-2468
Breinigsville *(G-2012)*

Country Creek Winery ....G..... 215 723-6516
Telford *(G-18278)*

Courtyard Wineries LLC ....G..... 814 725-0236
North East *(G-12736)*

Crossing Vineyards and Winery ....E 215 493-6500
Washington Crossing *(G-19255)*

Cullari Vineyards & Winery Inc ....F 717 571-2376
Hershey *(G-7607)*

Deer Creek Winery LLC ....D..... 814 354-7392
Shippenville *(G-17560)*

Direnzo Inc ....G..... 215 740-6166
Warrington *(G-19115)*

Eagle Rock Winery ....G..... 570 567-7715
Williamsport *(G-20009)*

El Serrano Inc ....G..... 717 397-6191
York *(G-20465)*

Fero Vineyards and Winery LLC ....F 570 568-0846
Lewisburg *(G-9907)*

Folino Estate LLC ....G..... 484 256-5300
Kutztown *(G-8843)*

Foxburg Wine Cellars Inc ....G..... 724 659-0021
Foxburg *(G-6101)*

Franklin Hill Vineyards Inc ....G..... 610 332-9463
Bethlehem *(G-1519)*

Franklin Hill Vineyards Inc ....G..... 610 588-8708
Bangor *(G-914)*

Franklin Hill Vineyards Inc ....G..... 610 559-8966
Easton *(G-4686)*

Galer Estates Vinyrd & Winery ....G..... 484 899-8013
Kennett Square *(G-8511)*

Germantown Winery LLC ....G..... 814 241-8458
Portage *(G-15917)*

Glades Pike Winery Inc ....F 814 445-3753
Somerset *(G-17689)*

Glendale Valley Winery ....G..... 814 687-3438
Flinton *(G-5983)*

Grace Winery LLC ....G..... 610 459-4711
Glen Mills *(G-6437)*

Greenhouse Winery ....G..... 412 892-9017
Pittsburgh *(G-15063)*

Grovedale Winery & Vinyard ....G..... 570 746-1400
Wyalusing *(G-20253)*

Happy Vly Vinyrd & Winery LLC ....G..... 814 308-8756
State College *(G-17973)*

Hauser Estate Inc ....D..... 717 334-4888
Biglerville *(G-1663)*

Hauser Estate Inc ....G..... 717 334-4888
Gettysburg *(G-6298)*

Hawstone Hollow Winery LLC ....G..... 717 953-9613
Lewistown *(G-9935)*

Heritage Wine Cellars ....G..... 724 748-5070
Grove City *(G-6790)*

Heritage Wine Cellars Inc ....F 814 725-8015
North East *(G-12748)*

Hiwassee Acres LLC ....G..... 717 334-1381
Gettysburg *(G-6301)*

Hunter Valley Winery ....G..... 717 444-7211
Liverpool *(G-10078)*

James Kirkpatrick ....D..... 610 869-4412
West Grove *(G-19701)*

Lacasa Narcisi Winery ....F 724 444-4744
Gibsonia *(G-6342)*

Lancaster County Winery Ltd ....G..... 717 464-3555
Willow Street *(G-20153)*

Liquor Control Board PA ....G..... 570 383-5248
Scranton *(G-17255)*

Long Trout Enterprises Inc ....G..... 570 366-6443
Auburn *(G-818)*

Maiolatesi Wine Cellar ....G..... 570 254-9977
Scott Township *(G-17185)*

Marilake Winery LLC ....G..... 570 536-6575
Childs *(G-3131)*

Mazza Chautauqua Cellars LLC..........G..... 814 725-8695
North East *(G-12751)*

Mazza Vineyards Inc ....E 717 665-7021
Manheim *(G-10394)*

Mobilia Fruit Farm Inc ....F 814 725-4077
North East *(G-12752)*

Moon Dancer Vineyards & Winery ....G..... 717 252-9463
Wrightsville *(G-20242)*

Mountain Lake Winery LLC ....G..... 267 664-6343
Towanda *(G-18433)*

Mountain Top Distillery ....G..... 570 745-2227
Williamsport *(G-20043)*

Newman Wine & Spirits Gp LLC ....G..... 610 476-3964
Bryn Mawr *(G-2331)*

Nordberg John ....G..... 814 371-2217
Falls Creek *(G-5856)*

Novosel LLC ....G..... 724 230-6686
New Wilmington *(G-12468)*

Oak Spring Winery Incorporated.........G..... 814 946-3799
Altoona *(G-532)*

Oliveros Vineyard LLC ....G..... 717 856-4566
Mc Alisterville *(G-10551)*

Paradocx Vineyard LLC......................G..... 610 255-5684
Landenberg *(G-9252)*

◆ Penn Sauna Corp ....E 610 932-5700
Oxford *(G-13087)*

Penn Sauna Corp ....E 610 932-5700
Paoli *(G-13146)*

Pickering Winery ....G..... 570 247-7269
Wysox *(G-20290)*

Pinnacle Ridge Winery ....G..... 610 756-4481
Kutztown *(G-8855)*

Pittsburgh Winery ....G..... 412 566-1000
Pittsburgh *(G-15412)*

Purple Cow Winery ....G..... 570 854-6969
Bloomsburg *(G-1797)*

Radical Wine Company ....G..... 610 365-7969
Lehighton *(G-9723)*

Renegade Winery LLC ....G..... 570 664-6626
Stroudsburg *(G-18139)*

Ridgewood Winery ....G..... 484 509-0100
Birdsboro *(G-1705)*

▲ Robert Mazza Inc ....F 814 725-8695
North East *(G-12759)*

Royal Welsh Winery ....G..... 724 396-7560
Ligonier *(G-9964)*

Rushland Rdge Vineyards Winery ....G..... 215 598-0251
Jamison *(G-8246)*

Sand Castle Winery ....G..... 484 924-9530
Phoenixville *(G-14578)*

Sand Castle Winery ....F 610 294-9181
Erwinna *(G-5539)*

Shade Mountain Winery Inc ....G..... 570 837-3644
Middleburg *(G-11040)*

Shawn Paul Zimmerman Kevin Joh .....G..... 814 594-1371
Weedville *(G-19459)*

Sorrenti Orchards Inc ....G..... 570 992-2255
Saylorsburg *(G-17108)*

Spitzenburg Cider House LLC ....G..... 484 357-2058
Kempton *(G-8494)*

Spring Gate Vineyard ....F 717 599-5574
Harrisburg *(G-7218)*

Starr Financial Group Inc ....G..... 814 236-0910
Curwensville *(G-3955)*

Thistlethwaite Vineyards ....G..... 724 883-3372
Jefferson *(G-8271)*

Thorn Hill Vineyards ....G..... 717 517-7839
Lancaster *(G-9218)*

S
I
C

Tolino Vineyards LLC ....G....610 588-9463
Bangor (G-931)
Totem Pole Ranch and Winery ....G....717 448-8370
Carlisle (G-2742)
Twisted Vine Winery ....G....814 512-4330
Kane (G-8479)
Unami Ridge Winery ....G....215 804-5445
Quakertown (G-16253)
Vineyard At Grandview LLC ....G....717 653-4825
Mount Joy (G-11675)
Vinoski Winery LLC ....G....724 872-3333
Rostraver Township (G-16832)
Vivino Selections Inc ....G....412 920-1336
Pittsburgh (G-15700)
Volant Enterprises Ltd ....G....724 533-2500
Volant (G-18778)
Vynecrest LLC ....F....610 398-7525
Breinigsville (G-2030)
Vynecrest LLC ....G....610 398-7525
Breinigsville (G-2031)
Weathered Vineyards LLC ....G....484 560-1528
New Tripoli (G-12462)
West Hanover Winery Inc ....G....717 652-3711
Harrisburg (G-7246)
Whispering Oaks Vineyard ....G....570 495-4054
Sunbury (G-18176)
Wilhelm Winery Inc ....G....724 253-3700
Hadley (G-6823)
Windgate Vineyards Inc ....E....814 257-8797
Smicksburg (G-17640)
Winery At Wilcox Inc ....G....412 490-9590
Pittsburgh (G-15720)
Winery At Wilcox Inc ....E....814 929-5598
Wilcox (G-19901)
Winery of Wilcox ....G....814 375-4501
Du Bois (G-4428)
Winfield Winery LLC ....G....724 352-9589
Cabot (G-2462)
Wooden Door Winery LLC ....G....724 889-7244
New Kensington (G-12390)

2085 Liquors, Distilled, Rectified & Blended

Allegheny Distilling LLC ....G....412 709-6480
Pittsburgh (G-14677)
Bald Hills Distillery ....G....717 858-2152
Dover (G-4184)
Blue Ridge Distillery LLC ....G....610 895-4205
Saylorsburg (G-17103)
Blue Steel Distillery ....G....610 820-7116
Allentown (G-155)
Bluebird Distilling LLC ....F....610 933-7827
Phoenixville (G-14535)
Brandywine Branch Distillers ....G....610 326-8151
Pottstown (G-15945)
Brandywine Branch Distlrs LLC ....G....610 901-3668
Elverson (G-4962)
Brave Spirits LLC ....G....610 453-3917
Narberth (G-11909)
Central Penn Distilling ....G....717 808-7695
Gettysburg (G-6285)
Chambord Et Cie Sarl ....E....215 425-9300
Philadelphia (G-13523)
▲ Charles Jacquin Et Cie Inc ....D....215 425-9300
Philadelphia (G-13529)
Custom Blends Inc ....G....215 934-7080
Philadelphia (G-13592)
Dead Lightning Distillery ....G....717 695-0927
New Cumberland (G-12185)
Dead Lightning Distillery LLC ....G....717 798-2021
Lemoyne (G-9743)
Eight Oaks Craft Distillery Co ....G....484 387-5287
New Tripoli (G-12455)
Five STS Dstlg Intl Sprits LLC ....G....610 279-5364
Norristown (G-12659)
Hazards Distillery Inc ....G....717 994-4860
Mifflintown (G-11121)
Hidden Still Inc ....G....717 270-1753
Lebanon (G-9581)
Kilimanjaro Distillery ....G....484 661-2488
Allentown (G-282)
Mac Beverage Inc ....G....215 474-2024
Philadelphia (G-13984)
Manatawny Still Works ....G....484 624-8271
Pottstown (G-16014)
Mason-Dixon Distillery ....G....717 314-2070
Gettysburg (G-6306)
Midnight Madness Distlg LLC ....G....215 268-6071
Trumbauersville (G-18532)
Mingo Creek Craft Distillers ....G....724 503-4014
Washington (G-19207)
Moonshine Mine Distillery Inc ....G....814 749-3038
Nanty Glo (G-11906)
▲ Olifant USA Inc ....G....916 996-6207
Camp Hill (G-2507)
Pennsylvnia Pure Dstllries LLC ....F....412 486-8666
Glenshaw (G-6496)
Pittsburgh Distilling Co LLC ....D....412 224-2827
Pittsburgh (G-15394)
Pollyodd ....G....215 271-1161
Philadelphia (G-14186)
Ponfeigh Distillery Inc ....G....919 606-0526
Meyersdale (G-11018)
Port Pittsburgh Distillery LLC ....G....412 294-8071
Pittsburgh (G-15420)
Social Still LLC ....E....610 625-4585
Bethlehem (G-1621)
Tall Pines Distillery LLC ....G....814 442-2245
Salisbury (G-17046)
This Life Forever Inc ....G....707 733-0383
Lansford (G-9450)
Vodka Brands Corp ....G....412 681-7777
Pittsburgh (G-15704)

2086 Soft Drinks

A&A Beverages Warehouse ....F....570 344-0024
Scranton (G-17204)
Abarta Inc ....G....610 807-5319
Bethlehem (G-1441)
Alfreds Village Beverage Inc ....G....215 676-2537
Philadelphia (G-13363)
Altoona Soft Water Company ....F....814 943-2768
Altoona (G-473)
American Bottling Company ....E....724 776-6111
Cranberry Township (G-3802)
B&B Sales Consulting Corp Inc ....G....215 225-3200
Philadelphia (G-13439)
Biagio Schiano Di Cola Debora ....E....724 224-9906
Natrona Heights (G-11935)
▲ Bottling Group LLC ....G....215 676-6400
Philadelphia (G-13474)
C S M Bottling Inc ....G....570 489-6071
Jessup (G-8328)
Cassidys Brew Zoo ....G....814 946-2739
Altoona (G-487)
Cbc Latrobe Acquisition LLC ....C....724 532-5444
Latrobe (G-9462)
City Btlg Co of New Kensington ....F....724 335-3350
New Kensington (G-12334)
Clover Farms Dairy Company ....B....610 921-9111
Reading (G-16346)
Coatesvlle Coca Cola Btlg Wrks ....E....610 384-4343
Downingtown (G-4221)
Coca Cola Refreshments US ....G....814 357-8628
Howard (G-7887)
Coca- Cola ....G....412 726-1482
Pittsburgh (G-14864)
Coca-Cola Btlg Co of NY Inc ....C....718 326-3334
Philadelphia (G-13556)
Coca-Cola Btlg Co Pottsville ....E....570 622-6991
Reading (G-16349)
Coca-Cola Btlg of Lehigh Vly ....C....610 866-8020
Bethlehem (G-1486)
Coca-Cola Company ....C....610 530-3900
Allentown (G-172)
Coca-Cola Refreshments USA Inc ....E....570 839-6706
Mount Pocono (G-11734)
Cola International LLC ....G....267 977-6700
Bensalem (G-1170)
▲ Cott Beverages Wyomissing Inc ....C....484 840-4800
Concordville (G-3456)
Creekside Springs LLC ....E....724 266-9000
Ambridge (G-613)
Creekside Springs LLC ....E....724 266-9000
Ambridge (G-614)
Crossroads Beverage Group LLC ....G....352 509-3127
Reading (G-16355)
Dahill Bottling Company Inc ....G....215 699-6432
Blue Bell (G-1825)
Days Beverage Inc ....D....215 990-0983
Newtown Square (G-12572)
Djquesne Bottling Company ....G....412 831-2779
Pittsburgh (G-14927)
Dr Pepper Snapple Group ....G....724 776-6111
Cranberry Township (G-3816)
Duquesne Distributing Co ....G....724 465-6141
Indiana (G-8092)
Everfresh Juice Co Pgh ....G....412 777-9660
Mc Kees Rocks (G-10608)
▲ Fentimans North America Inc ....F....877 326-3248
Wilkes Barre (G-19921)
Gablers Beverage Distributors ....G....717 532-2241
Shippensburg (G-17528)
Galliker Dairy Company ....C....814 266-8702
Johnstown (G-8374)
▼ GE Infrastructure Sensing ....F....617 926-1749
Feasterville Trevose (G-5912)
Glen Carbonic Gas Co ....F....570 779-1226
Plymouth (G-15819)
Hanks Beverage Company ....G....215 396-2809
Southampton (G-17815)
Happy Valley Com ....G....814 238-8066
State College (G-17972)
Ice River Springs Usa Inc ....F....828 391-6900
Allentown (G-249)
Jordan Draft Service ....G....412 382-4299
Clairton (G-3152)
Kamila Farm LLC ....G....570 427-8318
Weatherly (G-19454)
Keurig Dr Pepper Inc ....C....610 264-5151
Bethlehem (G-1549)
Keurig Dr Pepper Inc ....D....570 547-0777
Montgomery (G-11372)
Keurig Dr Pepper Inc ....D....717 677-7121
Aspers (G-741)
Kutztown Bottling Works Inc ....G....610 683-7377
Kutztown (G-8847)
Liberty Bell Beverages ....G....610 799-6600
Schnecksville (G-17141)
Liberty Coca-Cola Bevs LLC ....F....215 427-4500
Philadelphia (G-13969)
▲ Lion Brewery Inc ....C....570 823-8801
Wilkes Barre (G-19936)
Mr TS Sixpack ....G....814 226-8890
Clarion (G-3184)
Mvc Industries Inc ....D....610 650-0500
Norristown (G-12690)
Natrona Bottling Works Inc ....G....724 224-9224
Natrona Heights (G-11947)
Natures Way Prwter Systems Inc ....D....570 655-7755
Pittston (G-15769)
Natures Way Pure Water ....G....800 407-7873
Pittston (G-15770)
Nestle Waters ....E....484 221-0876
Breinigsville (G-2021)
New Bern Pbg Pepsi ....G....570 320-3324
Williamsport (G-20045)
Niagara Bottling LLC ....E....610 562-2176
Hamburg (G-6847)
▲ Northern Tier Beverage Inc ....G....570 662-2523
Mansfield (G-10423)
Pavlish Beverage Co Inc ....G....610 866-7722
Bethlehem (G-1592)
Pbg Johnstown ....G....814 262-1125
Johnstown (G-8420)
Pbg Philadelphia 2120 ....E....215 676-6401
Philadelphia (G-14127)
Pepsi Beverages Company ....E....412 778-4552
Mc Kees Rocks (G-10624)
Pepsi Co Inc ....G....717 792-2935
York (G-20623)
Pepsi-Cola Btlg Co of Scranton ....D....570 344-1159
Pittston (G-15774)
Pepsi-Cola Metro Btlg Co Inc ....C....814 266-9556
Johnstown (G-8422)
Pepsi-Cola Metro Btlg Co Inc ....F....215 937-6102
Philadelphia (G-14135)
Pepsi-Cola Metro Btlg Co Inc ....E....412 331-6775
Mc Kees Rocks (G-10625)
Pepsi-Cola Metro Btlg Co Inc ....D....570 326-9086
Williamsport (G-20056)
Pepsi-Cola Metro Btlg Co Inc ....D....570 344-1159
Pittston (G-15775)
Pepsi-Cola Metro Btlg Co Inc ....E....814 834-5700
Saint Marys (G-17005)
Pepsico Inc ....B....814 266-6005
Johnstown (G-8423)
Posties Beverages Inc ....G....570 929-2464
McAdoo (G-10656)
Potter Distributing Co ....G....724 495-3189
Monaca (G-11294)
Pure Flow Water Co ....G....215 723-0237
Souderton (G-17761)
Quaker Oats Company ....C....570 474-3800
Mountain Top (G-11774)
Reading Draft Birch Co ....G....610 372-2565
Reading (G-16487)
Reading Soda Works & Carbonic ....G....610 372-2565
Reading (G-16491)
Refresco Beverages US Inc ....F....484 840-4800
Glen Mills (G-6441)

Renewal Kombucha LLC ....G...... 484 525-3575
Lititz *(G-10040)*
Roaring Spring Blank Book Co ....E...... 717 334-8080
Gettysburg *(G-6313)*
Roaring Spring Water ....G...... 814 942-9844
Roaring Spring *(G-16770)*
Rochester Coca Cola Bottling ....G...... 570 655-2874
Pittston *(G-15782)*
Rochester Coca Cola Bottling ....D...... 717 730-2100
Lemoyne *(G-9752)*
Rochester Cola Cola Bottling ....D...... 717 209-4411
Lancaster *(G-9190)*
Rochester Coca Cola Bottling ....E...... 724 834-2700
Greensburg *(G-6712)*
Rochester Coca Cola Bottling ....D...... 814 472-6113
Ebensburg *(G-4795)*
Rochester Coca Cola Bottling ....D...... 610 916-3996
Reading *(G-16502)*
Rochester Coca Cola Bottling ....D...... 814 833-0101
Erie *(G-5465)*
Rochester Coca Cola Bottling ....D...... 412 787-3610
Houston *(G-7879)*
▲ Safe Pac Pasteurization LLC ....F...... 267 324-5631
Philadelphia *(G-14275)*
Schneiders Dairy Inc ....C...... 412 881-3525
Pittsburgh *(G-15516)*
Shangri-La Beverage LLC ....G...... 724 222-2222
Washington *(G-19225)*
Shared Financial Services ....E...... 412 968-1178
Pittsburgh *(G-15528)*
Shs Drinks Us LLC ....G...... 412 854-9012
Pittsburgh *(G-15535)*
Six Pak Shack ....G...... 724 593-2401
Jones Mills *(G-8448)*
◆ Suez Wts Systems Usa Inc ....B...... 781 359-7000
Trevose *(G-18505)*
Superior Value Beverage Co ....G...... 610 935-3111
Phoenixville *(G-14581)*
Take Six ....G...... 814 237-4350
State College *(G-18035)*
Terry Baker ....G...... 717 263-5942
Chambersburg *(G-2985)*
◆ Victory Brewing Company LLC ......E...... 610 873-0881
Downingtown *(G-4261)*
Wychocks Mountaintop Beverage ......G...... 570 474-5577
Mountain Top *(G-11782)*
▲ Zeiglers Beverages LLC ....E...... 215 855-5161
Lansdale *(G-9428)*

2087 Flavoring Extracts & Syrups

Byrnes and Kiefer Company ....E...... 724 538-5200
Callery *(G-2468)*
Byrnes and Kiefer Company ....E...... 724 538-5200
Callery *(G-2467)*
Cameron Supply Corporation ....F...... 610 866-9632
Bethlehem *(G-1478)*
Carbonator Rental Service Inc ....E...... 215 726-9100
Philadelphia *(G-13500)*
Coca-Cola Company ....C...... 610 530-3900
Allentown *(G-172)*
Creative Flavor Concepts Inc ....G...... 949 705-6584
Lancaster *(G-8988)*
David Michael & Co Inc ....F...... 909 887-3800
Philadelphia *(G-13608)*
▲ David Michael & Co Inc ....D...... 215 632-3100
Philadelphia *(G-13607)*
Emericks Maple Products ....G...... 814 324-4536
Hyndman *(G-8049)*
◆ Henry H Ottens Mfg Co Inc ....D...... 215 365-7800
Philadelphia *(G-13814)*
Imperial Beverage Systems Inc ....F...... 717 238-6870
Harrisburg *(G-7154)*
Interntnal Flvors Frgrnces Inc ....C...... 215 365-7800
Philadelphia *(G-13868)*
Kauffmantreatscom LLC ....G...... 717 715-6409
Ronks *(G-16809)*
Knouse Foods Cooperative Inc ....C...... 717 677-9115
Biglerville *(G-1666)*
Liberty Coca-Cola Bevs LLC ....F...... 215 427-4500
Philadelphia *(G-13969)*
Mondelez Global LLC ....A...... 570 820-1200
Wilkes Barre *(G-19945)*
Multi-Flow Industries LLC ....C...... 215 322-1800
Huntingdon Valley *(G-8015)*
Pardoes Perky Peanuts Inc ....E...... 570 524-9595
Montandon *(G-11366)*
Pitts Doggn It LLC ....G...... 412 687-1440
Pittsburgh *(G-15385)*
Quaker Oats Company ....C...... 570 474-3800
Mountain Top *(G-11774)*

Richards and Danielson LLC ....F...... 610 435-4300
Allentown *(G-375)*
Sensoryeffects Inc ....G...... 610 582-2170
Reading *(G-16512)*
Ungerer Industries Inc ....D...... 610 868-7266
Bethlehem *(G-1647)*
Upinya Beverages LLC ....G...... 717 398-7309
Fairfield *(G-5769)*
Welch Foods Inc A Cooperative ....B...... 814 725-4577
North East *(G-12766)*
◆ World Flavors Inc ....D...... 215 672-4400
Warminster *(G-19003)*

2091 Fish & Seafoods, Canned & Cured

Bar Bq Town Inc ....G...... 215 549-9666
Philadelphia *(G-13444)*
◆ Starkist Co ....D...... 412 323-7400
Pittsburgh *(G-15578)*

2092 Fish & Seafoods, Fresh & Frozen

A C Kissling Company ....F...... 215 423-4700
Philadelphia *(G-13325)*
Charles Ernsts Sons LLC ....G...... 267 237-1271
Springfield *(G-17910)*
H & G Diners Corp ....E...... 610 494-5107
Marcus Hook *(G-10445)*
Herkys Food Products Inc ....E...... 412 683-8511
Pittsburgh *(G-15092)*
Hills Qulty Seafood Mkts Inc ....F...... 610 359-1888
Newtown Square *(G-12576)*
Ocean King Enterprises Inc ....C...... 215 365-2500
Philadelphia *(G-14092)*
Rebecca Wilson Ltd Lblty Co ....G...... 973 670-7089
York *(G-20654)*
Seaco Foods International ....F...... 844 579-1133
Newtown *(G-12547)*
Seafood Enterprises LP ....C...... 215 672-2211
Warminster *(G-18964)*
Stone Silo Foods Inc ....G...... 570 676-0809
South Sterling *(G-17788)*

2095 Coffee

Coffee and Tea Exchange Corp ....G...... 570 445-8778
Olyphant *(G-12987)*
▲ East Indies Coffee & Tea ....F...... 717 228-2000
Lebanon *(G-9566)*
Flavorpros LLC ....F...... 610 435-4300
Allentown *(G-215)*
Fresh Roasted Coffee LLC ....F...... 570 743-9228
Sunbury *(G-18169)*
Fresh Start Vend & Cof Svc LLC ....G...... 215 322-8647
Southampton *(G-17813)*
Gamut Enterprises Inc ....G...... 717 627-5282
Lititz *(G-10011)*
Gerhart Coffee Co ....G...... 717 397-8788
Lancaster *(G-9028)*
La Prima Expresso Co ....G...... 412 565-7070
Pittsburgh *(G-15212)*
Melitta Usa Inc ....G...... 215 355-5581
Southampton *(G-17826)*
Mondelez Global LLC ....A...... 570 820-1200
Wilkes Barre *(G-19945)*
Noltpak LLC ....G...... 717 725-9862
Quarryville *(G-16274)*
◆ Thomas Miller & Co Inc ....F...... 215 822-3118
Colmar *(G-3420)*
▲ Valerio Coffee Roasters Inc ....G...... 610 676-0034
Audubon *(G-831)*
Van Maanen Albert ....G...... 610 373-7292
Reading *(G-16559)*
Wilbur Enterprises Inc ....G...... 724 625-8010
Gibsonia *(G-6358)*
Yum-Yum Colmar Inc ....E...... 215 822-9468
Colmar *(G-3426)*

2096 Potato Chips & Similar Prdts

▲ Bickels Snack Foods Inc ....E...... 800 233-1933
York *(G-20403)*
Bickels Snack Foods Inc ....D...... 717 843-0738
York *(G-20404)*
Birds Eye Foods Inc ....C...... 814 267-4641
Berlin *(G-1284)*
Birds Eye Foods Inc ....F...... 814 942-6031
Altoona *(G-478)*
Birds Eye Foods LLC ....B...... 814 267-4641
Berlin *(G-1285)*
Brothers Wood Company ....G...... 814 462-2422
Corry *(G-3746)*

Burkey Acquisition Inc ....D...... 717 292-5611
Dover *(G-4189)*
Condor Snack Company ....C...... 303 333-6075
Hanover *(G-6868)*
Cuthbert & Son Inc ....E...... 717 657-1050
Harrisburg *(G-7111)*
▼ Dieffenbachs Potato Chips Inc ....D...... 610 589-2385
Womelsdorf *(G-20206)*
Frito-Lay North America Inc ....E...... 570 323-6175
Williamsport *(G-20014)*
Frito-Lay North America Inc ....C...... 717 624-4206
New Oxford *(G-12409)*
Frito-Lay North America Inc ....B...... 717 792-2611
York *(G-20488)*
G & S Foods Inc ....E...... 717 259-5323
Abbottstown *(G-4)*
Good Health Natural Pdts Inc ....G...... 570 655-0823
Pittston *(G-15753)*
▲ Good Health Natural Pdts Inc ....F...... 336 285-0735
Hanover *(G-6888)*
Gruma Corporation ....B...... 570 474-6890
Mountain Top *(G-11763)*
Hanover Foods Corporation ....C...... 717 665-2002
York *(G-20521)*
Hartleys Potato Chip Mfg ....F...... 717 248-0526
Lewistown *(G-9934)*
◆ Herr Foods Incorporated ....A...... 610 932-9330
Nottingham *(G-12882)*
Herr Foods Incorporated ....E...... 610 395-6200
Allentown *(G-245)*
Herr Foods Incorporated ....E...... 215 934-7144
Philadelphia *(G-13819)*
Herr Foods Incorporated ....D...... 215 492-5990
Philadelphia *(G-13820)*
Herr Foods Incorporated ....A...... 610 932-9330
Nottingham *(G-12883)*
Innovative Advg Vend Svcs LLC ....G...... 814 528-7204
Erie *(G-5325)*
Inventure Foods Inc ....B...... 623 932-6200
Hanover *(G-6903)*
Ira Middleswarth and Son Inc ....G...... 717 248-3093
Lewistown *(G-9936)*
▲ Keystone Food Products Inc ....C...... 610 258-2706
Easton *(G-4711)*
Kings Potato Chip Company ....E...... 717 445-4521
Mohnton *(G-11268)*
▲ Martins Potato Chips Inc ....C...... 717 792-3065
Thomasville *(G-18341)*
Martins Potato Chips Inc ....G...... 610 777-3643
Reading *(G-16438)*
Middleswarth and Son Inc ....D...... 570 837-1431
Middleburg *(G-11030)*
Ralph Good Inc ....E...... 717 484-4884
Adamstown *(G-23)*
Ralph Good Inc ....F...... 610 367-2253
Boyertown *(G-1925)*
Reyna Foods Inc ....G...... 412 904-1242
Pittsburgh *(G-15481)*
▼ S-L Snacks Real Estate Inc ....A...... 717 632-4477
Hanover *(G-6948)*
▲ Savor Street Foods Inc ....E...... 610 320-7800
Wyomissing *(G-20288)*
Sensible Portions ....G...... 717 898-7131
Mountville *(G-11802)*
Svc Manufacturing Inc ....G...... 623 907-1822
Mountain Top *(G-11777)*
Tastysnack Quality Foods Inc ....E...... 717 259-6961
Abbottstown *(G-7)*
Utz Quality Foods Inc ....F...... 570 368-8050
Montoursville *(G-11455)*
Utz Quality Foods Inc ....D...... 717 637-6644
Hanover *(G-6965)*
Utz Quality Foods Inc ....C...... 717 637-5666
Hanover *(G-6966)*
◆ Utz Quality Foods LLC ....G...... 800 367-7629
Hanover *(G-6967)*
Utz Quality Foods LLC ....B...... 717 698-4032
Hanover *(G-6968)*
◆ Wise Foods Inc ....A...... 888 759-4401
Berwick *(G-1347)*
Wise Foods Employees Chrtble E.......G...... 570 759-4095
Berwick *(G-1348)*
▲ World Gourmet Acquisition LLC ......D...... 717 285-1884
Mountville *(G-11804)*

2097 Ice

A E Falgiani Ice Co Inc ....G...... 412 344-7538
Pittsburgh *(G-14629)*
Americold Logistics LLC ....C...... 215 721-0700
Hatfield *(G-7316)*

S
I
C

Arctic Glacier Texas Inc ..... G 610 494-8200
Upper Chichester *(G-18656)*
Carl R Harry ..... G 610 865-7104
Bethlehem *(G-1480)*
Conjelko Dairy & Ice Service ..... G 814 467-9997
Windber *(G-20179)*
Gaia Enterprises Inc ..... F 800 783-7841
Huntingdon Valley *(G-7988)*
Good Time Ice ..... G 717 234-1479
Harrisburg *(G-7135)*
Hanover Ice Co Inc ..... G 717 637-9137
Spring Grove *(G-17878)*
Ice Butler ..... G 610 644-3243
Malvern *(G-10249)*
Kelly Dry Ice ..... G 412 766-1555
Pittsburgh *(G-15167)*
Lansdale Packaged Ice Inc ..... F 215 256-8808
Harleysville *(G-7044)*
Lansdowne Ice & Coal Co Inc ..... E 610 353-6500
Broomall *(G-2293)*
Martin Associates Ephrata LLC ..... F 717 733-7968
Ephrata *(G-5122)*
Mastro Ice Inc ..... G 412 681-4423
Pittsburgh *(G-15261)*
Michalski Refrigeration Inc ..... G 724 352-1666
Butler *(G-2423)*
Nicholas Caputo ..... G 570 454-8280
Hazleton *(G-7513)*
Refrigeration Care Inc ..... F 724 746-1525
Canonsburg *(G-2625)*
Rosenbergers Cold Storage ..... B 215 721-0700
Hatfield *(G-7392)*
Sculpted Ice Works Inc ..... F 570 226-6246
Lakeville *(G-8913)*
Sugar Magnolia Inc ..... G 610 649-9462
Ardmore *(G-719)*
TLC Refreshments Inc ..... F 610 429-4124
West Chester *(G-19665)*
Vision Warehousing and Dist ..... G 717 762-5912
Waynesboro *(G-19429)*
Wheeland Inc ..... F 570 323-3237
Williamsport *(G-20091)*
White Oak Ice Company LLC ..... G 717 354-5322
New Holland *(G-12294)*
Winola Ice Co ..... F 570 378-2726
Dalton *(G-3988)*
York Ice Co Inc ..... E 717 848-2639
York *(G-20739)*
Zero Ice Corporation ..... G 717 264-7912
Chambersburg *(G-3002)*

2098 Macaroni, Spaghetti & Noodles

Cheu Noodle Bar ..... G 267 639-4136
Philadelphia *(G-13540)*
Dim Sum & Noodle ..... G 215 515-3992
Philadelphia *(G-13632)*
Innofoods Usa Inc ..... G 412 854-9012
Pittsburgh *(G-15126)*
Kraft Heinz Company ..... B 412 456-5700
Pittsburgh *(G-15196)*
▼ **Kraft Heinz Foods Company** ..... C 412 456-5700
Pittsburgh *(G-15197)*
Lees Mister Noodle Bar ..... G 610 829-2799
Easton *(G-4713)*
Nissin Foods USA Company Inc ..... C 717 291-5901
Lancaster *(G-9146)*
Noodle 88 ..... G 215 721-0888
Souderton *(G-17757)*
Noodle King ..... G 717 299-2799
Lancaster *(G-9147)*
P & S Ravioli Co ..... G 215 339-9929
Philadelphia *(G-14109)*
P & S Ravioli Co ..... F 215 465-8888
Philadelphia *(G-14108)*
Pasta Acquisition Corp ..... G 559 485-8110
Harrisburg *(G-7189)*
▲ **PCA Group Inc** ..... G 610 558-2802
Garnet Valley *(G-6267)*
Philadelphia Macaroni Company ..... E 215 441-5220
Warminster *(G-18940)*
Prince Company Inc ..... G 717 526-2200
Harrisburg *(G-7201)*
Ptb Rice Noodle ..... G 717 569-0330
Lancaster *(G-9177)*
Riviana Foods Inc ..... C 717 526-2200
Harrisburg *(G-7207)*
Saucy Noodle ..... G 412 440-0432
Pittsburgh *(G-15512)*
Superior Pasta Company Inc ..... G 215 627-3306
Philadelphia *(G-14358)*

Taif Inc ..... E 610 522-0122
Folcroft *(G-6017)*

2099 Food Preparations, NEC

▼ **AFP Advanced Food Products LLC** ..... C 717 355-8667
New Holland *(G-12227)*
Aldon Food Corporation ..... E 484 991-1000
Schwenksville *(G-17172)*
Andorra Salad Inc ..... G 215 482-5750
Philadelphia *(G-13390)*
Angle Foods LLC ..... G 724 900-0908
Pittsburgh *(G-14711)*
Arrow Supply Company Inc ..... G 773 863-8655
Willow Grove *(G-20108)*
Ask Foods Inc ..... C 717 838-6356
Palmyra *(G-13117)*
Ask Foods Inc ..... E 717 838-6356
Palmyra *(G-13118)*
Awesome Foods Inc ..... F 610 757-1048
Norristown *(G-12639)*
Bacon Jams LLC ..... G 856 720-0255
West Chester *(G-19507)*
Bee Positive Foundation ..... G 484 302-8234
Phoenixville *(G-14530)*
Bickels Snack Foods Inc ..... D 717 843-0738
York *(G-20404)*
Blue Mountain Farms LLC ..... G 717 599-5110
Harrisburg *(G-7097)*
▲ **Brads Raw Chips LLC** ..... F 215 766-3739
Doylestown *(G-4279)*
Brennemans Maple Syrup & Eqp ..... G 814 941-8974
Salisbury *(G-17044)*
▲ **Castle Cheese Inc** ..... E 724 368-3022
Pittsburgh *(G-14826)*
Charles Jacquin Et Cie Inc ..... F 215 425-9300
Philadelphia *(G-13530)*
Chestnut Acres Specialty ..... G 717 949-2875
Myerstown *(G-11879)*
Choo R Choo Snacks Inc ..... G 717 273-7499
Lebanon *(G-9554)*
Chucks Salsa ..... G 724 513-5708
Baden *(G-870)*
Citadelle ..... G 610 777-8844
Shillington *(G-17503)*
Compass Group Usa Inc ..... D 717 569-2671
Lancaster *(G-8982)*
Con Yeager Company ..... E 724 452-4120
Zelienople *(G-20795)*
Conagra Brands Inc ..... A 570 742-7621
Milton *(G-11236)*
Conagra Brands Inc ..... C 570 742-6607
Milton *(G-11237)*
Conagra Brands Inc ..... E 570 742-8910
Milton *(G-11238)*
Cooke Tavern Ltd ..... G 814 422-7687
Spring Mills *(G-17887)*
Country Acres Cider & Prod Inc ..... G 717 263-9349
Waynesboro *(G-19406)*
▲ **Country Fresh Pennsylvania LLC** ..... C 215 855-2408
Hatfield *(G-7327)*
▲ **Custom Particle Reduction Inc** ..... F 215 766-9791
Plumsteadville *(G-15808)*
Dalos Bakery Inc ..... E 570 752-4519
Berwick *(G-1322)*
Darling Blends LLC ..... G 215 630-2802
Langhorne *(G-9288)*
Davis & Davis Gourmet Foods ..... G 412 487-7770
Allison Park *(G-449)*
Delicious Bite LLC ..... F 610 701-4213
West Chester *(G-19534)*
Diabetic Pastry Chef Inc ..... G 412 260-6468
Pittsburgh *(G-14921)*
◆ **Dutch Gold Honey Inc** ..... D 717 393-1716
Lancaster *(G-9004)*
E S H Poultry ..... F 717 517-9535
Lancaster *(G-9005)*
E&M Wholesale Foods ..... F 610 367-2299
Boyertown *(G-1909)*
East Asia Noodle Inc ..... F 215 923-6838
Philadelphia *(G-13654)*
▲ **East Indies Coffee & Tea** ..... F 717 228-2000
Lebanon *(G-9566)*
Easton Salsa Company LLC ..... G 610 923-3692
Easton *(G-4674)*
El Milagro ..... G 412 668-2627
Pittsburgh *(G-14961)*
▲ **Ethnic Gourmet Foods Inc** ..... E 610 692-2209
West Chester *(G-19552)*
F Ferrato Foods Company ..... G 412 431-1479
Pittsburgh *(G-14998)*

Federal Pretzel Baking Co ..... E 215 467-0505
Philadelphia *(G-13695)*
▼ **Firth Maple Products Inc** ..... F 814 654-7265
Spartansburg *(G-17850)*
Fit Fuel Foods LLC ..... G 267 342-1559
Langhorne *(G-9297)*
Flavorpros LLC ..... F 610 435-4300
Allentown *(G-215)*
Fresh Express Mid-Atlantic LLC ..... C 717 561-2900
Harrisburg *(G-7131)*
Fresh Food Manufacturing Co ..... A 412 963-6200
Pittsburgh *(G-15037)*
Fresh Tofu Inc ..... E 610 433-4711
Allentown *(G-219)*
Frito-Lay North America Inc ..... E 570 323-6175
Williamsport *(G-20014)*
Gmp Nutraceuticals Inc ..... F 484 924-9042
King of Prussia *(G-8625)*
Goldfam Inc ..... G 215 379-6433
Cheltenham *(G-3028)*
▲ **Gourmail Inc** ..... G 610 522-2650
Berwyn *(G-1364)*
Gourmet Vinegars By Linda Lu ..... G 724 353-2026
Sarver *(G-17070)*
Grinders On Go ..... G 717 712-0977
Camp Hill *(G-2498)*
Gruma Corporation ..... B 570 474-6890
Mountain Top *(G-11763)*
Gtf Worldwide LLC ..... D 610 873-3663
Downingtown *(G-4231)*
Hall Foods Inc ..... G 412 257-9877
Bridgeville *(G-2067)*
◆ **Hanover Foods Corporation** ..... A 717 632-6000
Hanover *(G-6894)*
Hanover Potato Products Inc ..... G 717 632-0700
Hanover *(G-6898)*
Harrowgate Fine Foods Inc ..... G 717 823-6855
Lancaster *(G-9039)*
▲ **Herb Penn Co Ltd** ..... E 215 632-6100
Philadelphia *(G-13816)*
◆ **Hershey Company** ..... B 717 534-4200
Hershey *(G-7613)*
Honey Sandts Co ..... G 610 252-6511
Easton *(G-4700)*
Hurry Hill Maple Syrup ..... G 814 734-1358
Edinboro *(G-4814)*
Innofoods Usa Inc ..... G 412 854-9012
Pittsburgh *(G-15126)*
Intercourse Pretzel Factory ..... E 717 768-3432
Intercourse *(G-8137)*
International Bakery ..... E 814 452-3435
Erie *(G-5329)*
Isabelles Kitchen Inc ..... D 215 256-7987
Harleysville *(G-7040)*
It Takes A Village To Feed ..... G 888 702-9610
Ridley Park *(G-16739)*
J M Smucker PA Inc ..... E 814 275-1323
New Bethlehem *(G-12026)*
J S Zimmerman Co ..... G 717 232-6842
Harrisburg *(G-7157)*
Jackson Farms Dairy ..... E 724 246-7010
New Salem *(G-12445)*
Jacobsons Farm Syrup Co ..... G 814 367-2880
Westfield *(G-19778)*
▲ **Jadeite Foods LLC** ..... G 267 522-8193
Bensalem *(G-1211)*
Jamaica Way Limited ..... G 267 593-9724
Philadelphia *(G-13889)*
James J Tuzzi Jr ..... E 570 752-2704
Berwick *(G-1329)*
Jioios Italian Corner Inc ..... G 724 837-4576
Greensburg *(G-6680)*
Johnnie Lustigs Hotdogs LLC ..... G 484 661-8333
Bethlehem *(G-1546)*
Joo Young Inc ..... G 267 298-0054
Willow Grove *(G-20122)*
◆ **Joy Cone Co** ..... B 724 962-5747
Hermitage *(G-7589)*
Kestrel Growth Brands Inc ..... G 484 932-8447
Phoenixville *(G-14556)*
Kime Cider Mill ..... F 717 677-7539
Bendersville *(G-1139)*
Knouse Foods Cooperative Inc ..... C 717 677-9115
Biglerville *(G-1666)*
Leonetti Food Distributors Inc ..... E 215 729-4200
Philadelphia *(G-13966)*
Lettuce Turnip The Beet ..... G 412 334-8631
South Park *(G-17784)*
Lochs Maple Fiber Mill Inc ..... G 570 965-2679
Springville *(G-17931)*

Lung Hing Noodle Company Inc ....G..... 215 829-1988
   Philadelphia (G-13976)
◆ Mallet and Company Inc ....G..... 412 276-9000
   Carnegie (G-2776)
Mama Nardone Baking Co Inc ....E..... 570 825-3421
   Hazleton (G-7509)
▲ Martins Potato Chips Inc ....C..... 717 792-3065
   Thomasville (G-18341)
Masteros Homestyle Foods Inc ....G..... 215 551-2530
   Philadelphia (G-13994)
Melt Enterprises LLC ....G..... 570 244-2970
   Gouldsboro (G-6569)
Modern Mushroom Farms Inc ....B..... 610 268-3535
   Toughkenamon (G-18420)
Moshes Foods LLC ....G..... 215 291-8333
   Philadelphia (G-14041)
▲ Nardone Brothers Baking Co ....C..... 570 823-0141
   Hanover Township (G-6999)
▲ Neillys Food LLC ....F..... 717 428-6431
   York (G-20610)
Nestle Usa Inc ....C..... 818 549-6000
   King of Prussia (G-8655)
Newly Weds Foods Inc ....C..... 610 758-9100
   Bethlehem (G-1584)
Nissin Foods USA Company Inc ....C..... 717 291-5901
   Lancaster (G-9146)
Nutrition Inc ....E..... 724 978-2100
   Irwin (G-8185)
Nutrition Inc ....E..... 814 382-3656
   Irwin (G-8186)
O Land Lakes ....F..... 717 845-8076
   York (G-20614)
Oil & Vinegar ....G..... 724 840-9656
   Chicora (G-3128)
Ooh Lala Salad ....G..... 215 769-1006
   Philadelphia (G-14097)
Packer Avenue Foods Inc ....F..... 215 271-0300
   Philadelphia (G-14112)
Palace Foods Inc ....F..... 610 939-0631
   Wilkes Barre (G-19955)
Palace Foods Inc ....F..... 610 775-9947
   Reading (G-16464)
Paul Family Farms LLC ....G..... 570 772-2420
   Galeton (G-6242)
▲ PCA Group Inc ....G..... 610 558-2802
   Garnet Valley (G-6267)
Pepperidge Farm Incorporated ....G..... 610 356-0553
   Broomall (G-2301)
Pepperidge Farm Incorporated ....G..... 717 336-8500
   Denver (G-4087)
Petruzzi Pizza Mfg Inc ....E..... 570 454-5887
   Hazleton (G-7517)
Philadelphia Macaroni Company ....E..... 215 441-5220
   Warminster (G-18940)
Pizza Associates Incorporated ....C..... 570 822-6600
   Wilkes Barre (G-19957)
Positively Pasta ....G..... 484 945-1007
   Pottstown (G-16032)
▲ Protica Inc ....E..... 610 832-2000
   Whitehall (G-19887)
Purity Candy Co ....F..... 570 538-9502
   Allenwood (G-442)
Qtg Qu Trop Gat9084 ....G..... 570 474-9995
   Mountain Top (G-11773)
▼ Quality Pasta Company LLC ....G..... 855 878-9630
   Charleroi (G-3020)
Radiance ....G..... 717 290-1517
   Lancaster (G-9185)
Reist Popcorn Company ....G..... 717 653-8078
   Mount Joy (G-11669)
Revonah Pretzel LLC ....E..... 717 632-4477
   Hanover (G-6943)
Rtcsnacks LLC ....G..... 570 234-7266
   Effort (G-4828)
S & K Vending ....G..... 570 675-5180
   Hunlock Creek (G-7934)
Sadies Salads ....G..... 717 768-3774
   Gordonville (G-6563)
Saturnalian N Y A ....G..... 215 271-9181
   Philadelphia (G-14282)
▲ Savello USA Incorporated ....F..... 570 822-9743
   Hanover Township (G-7005)
▲ Savor Street Foods Inc ....E..... 610 320-7800
   Wyomissing (G-20288)
Seneca Foods Corporation ....E..... 717 675-2074
   Lebanon (G-9629)
Smuckers Salad ....G..... 267 757-0944
   Newtown (G-12550)
Snap Kitchen 3 LLC ....G..... 215 845-0001
   Philadelphia (G-14318)

Speedwell Garage ....G..... 607 434-2376
   Klingerstown (G-8808)
Spices Inc ....E..... 570 509-2340
   Elysburg (G-4982)
▲ Spring Glen Fresh Foods Inc ....D..... 717 733-2201
   Ephrata (G-5145)
Springfield Pasta ....G..... 610 543-5687
   Springfield (G-17923)
Stone County Specialties Inc ....G..... 570 467-2850
   Tamaqua (G-18228)
Subway ....F..... 814 368-2576
   Bradford (G-1993)
▲ Sun Kee Tofu Food Co ....G..... 215 625-3818
   Philadelphia (G-14355)
Sunrise Maple ....F..... 814 628-3110
   Westfield (G-19781)
Sunsweet Growers Inc ....C..... 610 944-1005
   Fleetwood (G-5980)
Superior Pasta Company Inc ....G..... 215 627-3306
   Philadelphia (G-14358)
T & L Pierogie Incorporated ....E..... 570 454-3198
   Hazleton (G-7528)
▼ Todds Snax Inc ....G..... 717 637-5931
   Hanover (G-6961)
Torchbearer Sauces LLC ....G..... 717 697-3568
   Mechanicsburg (G-10898)
Triple Creek ....G..... 814 756-4500
   Cranesville (G-3872)
Troyer Inc ....E..... 724 746-1162
   Canonsburg (G-2648)
Tshudy Snacks Inc ....F..... 717 626-4354
   Lititz (G-10055)
▲ U S Durum Products Limited ....F..... 717 293-8698
   Lancaster (G-9226)
Uncle Henrys Pretzel Bakery ....E..... 717 445-4698
   Bowmansville (G-1888)
Unique Pretzel Bakery Inc ....E..... 610 929-3172
   Reading (G-16553)
Utz Quality Foods Inc ....D..... 717 637-6644
   Hanover (G-6965)
Utz Quality Foods Inc ....G..... 717 637-5666
   Hanover (G-6966)
◆ Utz Quality Foods LLC ....A..... 800 367-7629
   Hanover (G-6967)
Van Bennett Food Co Inc ....E..... 610 374-8348
   Mohnton (G-11272)
Verls Salads Inc ....F..... 717 865-2771
   Fredericksburg (G-6177)
Vinegar Hill Picture Works ....G..... 724 596-0023
   Indiana (G-8134)
William Plange ....G..... 215 303-0069
   Philadelphia (G-14475)
Winter Gardens Qulty Foods Inc ....C..... 717 624-4911
   New Oxford (G-12427)
Wittmans Pure Maple Syrup LLC ....G..... 814 781-7523
   Saint Marys (G-17030)
◆ World Flavors Inc ....D..... 215 672-4400
   Warminster (G-19003)
Zappone Bros Foods ....G..... 724 539-1430
   Latrobe (G-9529)
Zukay Live Foods LLC ....G..... 610 286-3077
   Palm (G-13097)

21 TOBACCO PRODUCTS

2111 Cigarettes

Klafters Inc ....G..... 814 833-7444
   Erie (G-5346)
R J Reynolds Tobacco Company ....G..... 215 244-9071
   Bensalem (G-1247)
Rebel Indian Smoke Shop ....G..... 610 499-1711
   Brookhaven (G-2247)
Tabacos USA Inc ....G..... 610 438-2005
   Easton (G-4762)
Tobacco Plus Cash Checking ....G..... 267 585-3802
   Levittown (G-9868)

2121 Cigars

Altadis USA Inc ....D..... 570 929-2220
   McAdoo (G-10655)
F X Smiths Sons Co ....F..... 717 637-5232
   Mc Sherrystown (G-10650)
John Middleton Co ....F..... 804 274-2000
   King of Prussia (G-8636)
Parodi Holdings LLC ....E..... 570 344-8566
   Dunmore (G-4479)
Rebel Indian Smoke Shop ....G..... 610 499-1711
   Brookhaven (G-2247)

2131 Tobacco, Chewing & Snuff

Planet Ryo ....G..... 717 938-8860
   Etters (G-5552)

2141 Tobacco Stemming & Redrying

Lancaster Leaf Tob Co PA Inc ....E..... 717 291-1528
   Lancaster (G-9098)
◆ Lancaster Leaf Tob Co PA Inc ....E..... 717 394-2676
   Lancaster (G-9097)
Lancaster Leaf Tob Co PA Inc ....G..... 717 393-1526
   Lancaster (G-9099)

22 TEXTILE MILL PRODUCTS

2211 Cotton, Woven Fabric

▲ A Olek & Son Inc ....F..... 215 638-4550
   Bensalem (G-1141)
Akas Tex LLC ....F..... 215 244-2589
   Bensalem (G-1146)
American Silk Mills LLC ....G..... 215 561-4901
   Jenkintown (G-8281)
American Trench LLC ....G..... 215 360-3493
   Ardmore (G-700)
▲ Armstrong/Kover Kwick Inc ....E..... 412 771-2200
   Mc Kees Rocks (G-10603)
Aura Tiedye ....G..... 888 474-2872
   Equinunk (G-5159)
Bachman Drapery Studio Inc ....G..... 215 257-8810
   Tylersport (G-18574)
Bright Banners ....G..... 570 326-3524
   Williamsport (G-19994)
Casner Fabrics ....G..... 215 946-3334
   Levittown (G-9823)
Cloverleaf Alpacas ....G..... 717 492-0504
   Mount Joy (G-11650)
▲ Craftex Mills Inc Pennsylvania ....E..... 610 941-1212
   Blue Bell (G-1824)
Cressona Textile Waste Inc ....G..... 570 385-4556
   Cressona (G-3903)
Denim Inc Division ....F..... 215 627-1400
   Philadelphia (G-13619)
Dwell America LLC ....G..... 717 272-4666
   Lebanon (G-9562)
◆ East Cast Erosion Blankets LLC ......F..... 610 488-8496
   Bernville (G-1298)
Ed Cini Enterprises Inc ....E..... 215 432-3855
   Plumsteadville (G-15809)
Ems Surgical LP ....F..... 570 374-0569
   Selinsgrove (G-17325)
Factory Linens Inc ....E..... 610 825-2790
   Conshohocken (G-3545)
Globe Dye Works ....G..... 215 288-4554
   Philadelphia (G-13772)
Hanesbrands Inc ....G..... 336 519-8080
   Philadelphia (G-13800)
Johnnys Discount Furniture ....G..... 717 564-1898
   Harrisburg (G-7159)
Juniata Fabrics Inc ....F..... 814 944-9381
   Altoona (G-519)
Lachina Drapery Company Inc ....E..... 412 665-4900
   Pittsburgh (G-15215)
▲ Lmt Corp of Pennsylvania ....E..... 610 921-3926
   Reading (G-16432)
▲ Medico International Inc ....F..... 610 253-7009
   Allentown (G-314)
Microsilver Wear LLC ....G..... 215 917-7203
   Yardley (G-20325)
◆ Monarch Global Brands Inc ....D..... 215 482-6100
   Philadelphia (G-14033)
▲ Norfab Corporation ....E..... 610 275-7270
   Norristown (G-12694)
O S A Global LLC ....G..... 724 698-7042
   New Castle (G-12135)
▲ Oc Canvas Studio LLC ....G..... 717 510-4847
   Harrisburg (G-7187)
▲ Oscar Daniels & Company Inc ....F..... 610 678-8144
   Reading (G-16460)
Phoenix Trim Works Inc ....E..... 570 320-0322
   Williamsport (G-20057)
▲ Romar Textile Co Inc ....C..... 724 535-7787
   Wampum (G-18804)
Sears Carpet and Uphl Care Inc ....G..... 412 821-5200
   Sharpsburg (G-17468)
Shen Manufacturing Company Inc .....G..... 570 278-3707
   Montrose (G-11476)
Tmu Inc ....F..... 717 392-0578
   Lancaster (G-9220)
Weave Hub LLC ....G..... 215 809-2082
   Newtown (G-12562)

SIC

▲ Yes Towels Inc ....G...... 215 538-5230
Quakertown (G-16261)

York Textile Products Inc ......G...... 717 764-2528
York (G-20751)

2221 Silk & Man-Made Fiber

Advanced Tex Composites Inc ....E... 570 207-7000
Scranton (G-17206)

Akas Tex LLC ....F... 215 244-2589
Bensalem (G-1146)

▲ Amatex Corporation ....D... 610 277-6100
Norristown (G-12632)

American Silk Mills LLC ....G... 215 561-4901
Jenkintown (G-8281)

▲ Atlantex Manufacturing Corp .....F... 610 518-6601
Downingtown (G-4213)

Bachman Drapery Studio Inc ....G... 215 257-8810
Tylersport (G-18574)

Cambria County Asso ....B... 814 536-3531
Johnstown (G-8360)

▲ Chapel Hill Mfg Co ....F... 215 884-3614
Oreland (G-13020)

▲ Craftex Mills Inc Pennsylvania ....E... 610 941-1212
Blue Bell (G-1824)

Dwell America LLC ....G... 717 272-4666
Lebanon (G-9562)

▲ Dwell America Holdings Inc ....E... 717 272-4665
Lebanon (G-9563)

▲ Fabric Development Inc ....E... 215 536-1420
Quakertown (G-16192)

Fabtex Inc ....D... 910 739-0019
Danville (G-4001)

▲ Fabtex Inc ....C... 570 275-7500
Danville (G-4000)

Fisher S Hand Made Quilts ....G... 717 392-5440
Bird In Hand (G-1674)

Fortune Fabrics Inc...................E... 570 288-3666
Kingston (G-8717)

Greenbriar Indus Systems Inc ....D... 814 474-1400
Fairview (G-5824)

Honeywell International Inc ....B... 570 621-6000
Pottsville (G-16080)

▲ Huntingdon Fiberglass Pdts LLC .....E... 814 641-8129
Huntingdon (G-7945)

◆ Jetnet Corporation ....D... 412 741-0100
Sewickley (G-17396)

Juniata Fabrics Inc ....F... 814 944-9381
Altoona (G-519)

▲ Material Tech & Logistics Inc ....D... 570 487-6162
Jessup (G-8332)

▲ MBA Design & Display Pdts Corp ...G... 610 524-7590
Exton (G-5709)

▲ Mutual Industries North Inc ....E... 215 927-6000
Philadelphia (G-14046)

New York Wire Company ....C... 717 637-3795
Hanover (G-6926)

Ono Industries Inc ....E... 717 865-6619
Ono (G-13004)

Quilting Stone House ....G... 610 495-8762
Pottstown (G-15956)

▼ Sauquoit Industries LLC ....D... 570 348-2751
Scranton (G-17283)

Shaffer Desouza Brown Inc ....F... 610 449-6400
Havertown (G-7427)

▲ Thomaston Manufacturing LLC ....G... 215 576-6352
Wyncote (G-20266)

Todd Lengle & Co Inc ....E... 610 777-0731
Reading (G-16541)

2231 Wool, Woven Fabric

▲ Armstrong/Kover Kwick Inc ....E... 412 771-2200
Mc Kees Rocks (G-10603)

Bucks County Alpacas LLC ....G... 215 795-2453
Perkasie (G-13269)

C J Apparel Inc ....E... 610 432-8265
Allentown (G-159)

Chloe Textiles Incorporated ....D... 717 848-2800
York (G-20425)

▲ Craftex Mills Inc Pennsylvania ....E... 610 941-1212
Blue Bell (G-1824)

Dark Star Alpacas LLC ....G... 610 235-6638
Schwenksville (G-17175)

◆ Dualsun International Inc ....G... 412 421-7934
Pittsburgh (G-14939)

▲ Finishing Associates LLC ....F... 517 371-2460
Warminster (G-18880)

▲ G J Littlewood & Son Inc ....E... 215 483-3970
Philadelphia (G-13739)

▲ Immersion Research Inc ....F... 814 395-9191
Confluence (G-3466)

Little Bear Creek Alpacas...............G... 814 788-0971
Kane (G-8471)

Mamaux Supply Co ....F... 412 782-3456
Pittsburgh (G-15249)

Nobility Alpacas ....G... 484 332-1499
Wernersville (G-19486)

Rejniaks Alpaca ....G... 724 265-4062
Gibsonia (G-6349)

Rockafellow John ....G... 717 359-4276
Littlestown (G-10076)

▲ Woolrich Inc ....C... 570 769-6464
Woolrich (G-20220)

2241 Fabric Mills, Cotton, Wool, Silk & Man-Made

American Ribbon Manufacturers ....E... 570 421-7470
Stroudsburg (G-18102)

American Ribbon Manufacturers ....E... 570 421-7470
Stroudsburg (G-18103)

B & N Trophies & Awards LLC ....G... 814 723-8130
Warren (G-19012)

▲ Bally Ribbon Mills ....C... 610 845-2211
Bally (G-900)

Bally Ribbon Mills ....E... 610 845-2211
Bally (G-901)

Bally Ribbon Mills ....E... 610 845-2211
Bally (G-902)

◆ Barbett Industries Inc ....F... 610 372-2872
Reading (G-16327)

Chase Corporation ....E... 412 828-1500
Pittsburgh (G-14840)

◆ Eam-Mosca Corp ....C... 570 459-3426
Hazle Township (G-7452)

Fine Trim Line LLC......................G... 717 642-9032
Fairfield (G-5767)

Get It Right Tape Company Inc ....G... 570 383-6960
Olyphant (G-12991)

▲ Horn Textile Inc ....E... 814 827-3606
Titusville (G-18384)

Huepenbecker Enterprises Inc ....F... 717 393-3941
Lancaster (G-9052)

Juniata Fabrics Inc ....F... 814 944-9381
Altoona (G-519)

Lear Corporation ....G... 570 345-2611
Pine Grove (G-14598)

Liberty Throwing Company ....D... 570 287-1114
Kingston (G-8721)

Mutual Industries North Inc ....D... 215 679-7682
Red Hill (G-16583)

Otex Specialty Narrow Fabrics ....F... 570 538-5990
Watsontown (G-19279)

Plum Manufacturing Co Inc ....G... 215 520-2236
North Wales (G-12825)

Russell Ribbon & Trim Co ....G... 215 938-8550
Huntingdon Valley (G-8031)

Tapestration ....G... 215 536-0977
Quakertown (G-16248)

Textemp LLC ....F... 215 322-9670
Quakertown (G-16249)

▲ Trims ....F... 215 541-1946
East Greenville (G-4578)

▲ Wayne Mills Company Inc ....D... 215 842-2134
Philadelphia (G-14463)

Western PA Weather LLC ....G... 814 341-5086
Johnstown (G-8444)

◆ William J Dixon Company ....E... 610 524-1131
Exton (G-5750)

◆ Yarrington Mills Corporation ....E... 215 674-5125
Hatboro (G-7311)

▲ Zip-Net Inc ....E... 610 939-9762
Reading (G-16572)

2251 Hosiery, Women's Full & Knee Length

Highland Hosiery Mills Inc ....F... 215 249-3934
Dublin (G-4433)

Sculptz Inc ....E... 215 494-2900
Trevose (G-18503)

U S Textile Corp ....B... 828 733-9244
Feasterville Trevose (G-5934)

◆ U S Textile Corp ....E... 803 283-6800
Feasterville Trevose (G-5935)

2252 Hosiery, Except Women's

▲ CM Industries Inc ....C... 717 336-4545
Lancaster (G-8980)

Comfort Sportswear Inc ....G... 215 781-0300
Croydon (G-3914)

Eric L Socks ....G... 717 762-7488
Waynesboro (G-19409)

Frog Creek Socks ....G... 215 997-6104
Chalfont (G-2875)

Inspyr Apparel Co LLC ....G... 267 784-3036
Oreland (G-13022)

▲ Top Circle Hosiery Mills Co............E... 610 379-0470
Weissport (G-19461)

2253 Knit Outerwear Mills

▲ Alpha Mills Corporation................D... 570 385-1791
Schuylkill Haven (G-17145)

Alpha Mills Corporation ....D... 570 385-2400
Pottsville (G-16072)

Alpha Mills Corporation ....E... 570 385-1791
Schuylkill Haven (G-17146)

▲ Apex Apparel Inc ....D... 610 432-8007
Allentown (G-140)

C & L Enterprises LLC ....G... 215 589-4553
Doylestown (G-4284)

Calvin Taylor Corporation ....E... 570 983-2288
Scranton (G-17214)

Continental Apparel Corp ....G... 814 495-4625
South Fork (G-17773)

Effective Plan Inc ....G... 717 428-6190
Seven Valleys (G-17378)

El-Ana Collection Inc ....F... 215 953-8820
Huntingdon Valley (G-7977)

Ems Clothing & Novelty Inc ....G... 570 752-2896
Berwick (G-1324)

▲ Franklin Clothing Company Inc ....C... 717 264-5768
Chambersburg (G-2932)

Gemanias Jeans Collection Inc ....G... 610 776-1777
Allentown (G-225)

▲ Gloray If LLC ....F... 610 921-3300
Bernville (G-1299)

Hanesbrands Inc ....G... 610 970-5767
Pottstown (G-15996)

Lawrence R Gilman LLC................G... 215 432-2733
Philadelphia (G-13960)

Levis Only Stores Inc ....G... 717 337-1294
Gettysburg (G-6305)

Lifewear Inc ....E... 610 327-2884
Pottstown (G-16011)

Lifewear Inc ....G... 610 327-9938
Pottstown (G-15953)

Merry Maid Novelties ....F... 610 599-4104
Bangor (G-922)

Warrior Fashions Inc ....G... 215 925-7905
Philadelphia (G-14460)

Wet Paint T Shirts Inc ....G... 570 822-2221
Wilkes Barre (G-19973)

2254 Knit Underwear Mills

▲ Alpha Mills Corporation................D... 570 385-1791
Schuylkill Haven (G-17145)

Alpha Mills Corporation ....D... 570 385-2400
Pottsville (G-16072)

Alpha Mills Corporation ....E... 570 385-1791
Schuylkill Haven (G-17146)

American Sports Apparel Inc ....D... 570 357-8155
Avoca (G-839)

City Shirt Co ....G... 570 874-4251
Frackville (G-6104)

Lake Erie Regional Center For..............G... 814 725-4601
North East (G-12749)

2257 Circular Knit Fabric Mills

▲ Chapel Hill Mfg Co ....F... 215 884-3614
Oreland (G-13020)

Chloe Textiles Incorporated..............D... 717 848-2800
York (G-20425)

◆ Jetnet Corporation ....D... 412 741-0100
Sewickley (G-17396)

Robert W Turner ....G... 610 372-8863
Reading (G-16501)

2258 Lace & Warp Knit Fabric Mills

◆ Milco Industries Inc ....C... 570 784-0400
Bloomsburg (G-1790)

2259 Knitting Mills, NEC

Annville Shoulder Strap Co ....E... 717 867-4831
Annville (G-642)

Dbi Inc ....D... 814 653-7625
Fairmount City (G-5808)

◆ Jetnet Corporation ....D... 412 741-0100
Sewickley (G-17396)

◆ Yarrington Mills Corporation ....E... 215 674-5125
Hatboro (G-7311)

York Textile Products Inc ....G....... 717 764-2528
York (G-20751)

2261 Cotton Fabric Finishers

Academy Sports Center Inc ....G....... 570 339-3399
Mount Carmel (G-11622)

All ADS Up ....G....... 412 881-4114
Pittsburgh (G-14673)

C Jthomas Screening Inc ....F....... 412 384-4279
Monongahela (G-11305)

Chloe Textiles Incorporated ....D....... 717 848-2800
York (G-20425)

▲ Columbia Silk Dyeing Company ....E....... 215 739-2289
Philadelphia (G-13561)

Country Keepsakes ....G....... 570 744-2246
Rome (G-16796)

Craig Hollern ....E....... 814 539-2974
Johnstown (G-8366)

Dante Defranco Printing ....E....... 610 588-7300
Roseto (G-16819)

Edwin Ringer ....G....... 724 746-3374
Westland (G-19782)

▲ G J Littlewood & Son Inc ....E....... 215 483-3970
Philadelphia (G-13739)

Greater Pitts Speciality ....G....... 412 821-5976
Pittsburgh (G-15061)

Hlc Industries Inc ....F....... 610 668-9112
Bala Cynwyd (G-880)

J P Tees Inc ....G....... 215 634-2348
Philadelphia (G-13887)

Larry D Mays ....F....... 814 833-7988
Erie (G-5360)

Lawrence Schiff Silk Mills Inc ....F....... 215 536-5460
Quakertown (G-16209)

Lerko Products ....F....... 570 473-3501
Northumberland (G-12869)

▲ Maroco Ltd ....B....... 610 746-6800
Easton (G-4719)

Milford Sportswear Inc ....G....... 215 529-9316
Quakertown (G-16219)

Mindy Inc ....F....... 215 739-0432
Philadelphia (G-14024)

Mountainview Graphics ....G....... 610 939-1471
Reading (G-16449)

▲ Quality Crrctons Inspctons Inc ....D....... 814 696-3737
Duncansville (G-4462)

▲ Romar Textile Co Inc ....C....... 724 535-7787
Wampum (G-18804)

Royalty Promotions Inc ....G....... 215 794-2707
Furlong (G-6233)

Shenk Athletic Equipment Co ....F....... 717 766-6600
Mechanicsburg (G-10888)

Southern Alleghenies Advg Inc ....G....... 814 472-8593
Ebensburg (G-4797)

Trbz Ink LLC ....G....... 267 918-2242
Philadelphia (G-14403)

Village Idiot Designs ....G....... 724 545-7477
Kittanning (G-8802)

◆ William J Dixon Company ....E....... 610 524-1131
Exton (G-5750)

Youre Putting ME On Inc ....E....... 412 655-9666
Pittsburgh (G-15731)

2262 Silk & Man-Made Fabric Finishers

A & W Screen Printing Inc ....F....... 717 738-2726
Ephrata (G-5089)

Academy Sports Center Inc ....G....... 570 339-3399
Mount Carmel (G-11622)

Bell Graphics ....G....... 814 385-6222
Kennerdell (G-8497)

Blue Heron Sportswear Inc ....G....... 570 742-3228
Milton (G-11234)

▲ Columbia Silk Dyeing Company ....E....... 215 739-2289
Philadelphia (G-13561)

DOC Printing LLC ....G....... 267 702-6196
Philadelphia (G-13637)

Double M Productions LLC ....F....... 570 476-8000
Stroudsburg (G-18114)

Erie OEM Inc ....B....... 814 459-8024
Erie (G-5271)

Finish Line Screen Prtg Inc ....G....... 814 238-0122
State College (G-17964)

▲ G J Littlewood & Son Inc ....E....... 215 483-3970
Philadelphia (G-13739)

Go Tell It Inc ....G....... 212 769-3220
Robesonia (G-16774)

Lawrence Schiff Silk Mills Inc ....F....... 215 536-5460
Quakertown (G-16209)

◆ Milco Industries Inc ....C....... 570 784-0400
Bloomsburg (G-1790)

Mindy Inc ....F....... 215 739-0432
Philadelphia (G-14024)

Newtown Printing Corp ....G....... 215 968-6876
Newtown (G-12528)

Pennsylvania Promotions Inc ....F....... 800 360-2800
Exton (G-5724)

Prince Printing ....G....... 412 233-3555
Clairton (G-3156)

▲ Romar Textile Co Inc ....C....... 724 535-7787
Wampum (G-18804)

Tee Printing Inc ....F....... 717 394-2978
Lancaster (G-9215)

Valley Silk Screening Inc ....G....... 724 962-5255
Sharpsville (G-17477)

2269 Textile Finishers, NEC

Art Stitch Inc ....G....... 717 652-8992
Harrisburg (G-7091)

▲ Caledonian Dye Works ....E....... 215 739-2322
Philadelphia (G-13494)

Charles F May Co ....E....... 215 634-7257
Philadelphia (G-13527)

▲ Columbia Silk Dyeing Company ....E....... 215 739-2289
Philadelphia (G-13561)

▲ G J Littlewood & Son Inc ....E....... 215 483-3970
Philadelphia (G-13739)

Holly Label Company Inc ....E....... 570 222-9000
Nicholson (G-12615)

Lawrence Schiff Silk Mills Inc ....E....... 215 536-5460
Quakertown (G-16209)

Magiseal Services ....G....... 724 327-3068
Export (G-5617)

Sterling Finishing ....F....... 267 682-0844
Glenside (G-6541)

▲ Supreme Trading Ltd ....E....... 215 739-2237
Philadelphia (G-14361)

Sure Fold Co Inc ....F....... 215 634-7480
Philadelphia (G-14362)

Tom Russell ....G....... 724 746-5029
Houston (G-7882)

Wolfe Dye and Bleach Works Inc ....E....... 610 562-7639
Shoemakersville (G-17577)

2273 Carpets & Rugs

All Floor Supplies Inc ....F....... 412 793-6421
Monroeville (G-11323)

◆ Bloomsburg Carpet Inds Inc ....C....... 800 233-8773
Bloomsburg (G-1775)

Carpenter Co ....C....... 814 944-8612
Altoona (G-486)

Durex Coverings Inc ....E....... 717 626-8566
Brownstown (G-2307)

▲ Flextron Industries Inc ....F....... 610 459-4600
Aston (G-763)

Great Northern Foam ....E....... 610 791-3356
Allentown (G-237)

House of Price Inc ....G....... 724 625-3415
Mars (G-10499)

Hurlock Bros Co Inc ....F....... 610 659-8153
Drexel Hill (G-4366)

Jordans Bear Den ....G....... 814 938-4081
Northport (G-12864)

▲ Langhorne Carpet Company Inc ......E....... 215 757-5155
Penndel (G-13239)

Municipal Publications ....G....... 724 397-9812
Marion Center (G-10474)

Office Mats Inc ....G....... 717 359-9571
Littlestown (G-10073)

Oxford Market Place Inc ....G....... 610 998-9080
Oxford (G-13086)

Prosource of Lancaster ....G....... 717 299-5680
Lancaster (G-9176)

Shaw Industries Group Inc ....E....... 724 266-0315
Leetsdale (G-9705)

Steam Mad Carpet Cleaners Inc ....G....... 215 283-9833
Horsham (G-7853)

Stone Mill Rug Co ....G....... 215 744-2331
Philadelphia (G-14349)

2281 Yarn Spinning Mills

Chima Inc ....E....... 610 372-6508
Reading (G-16345)

Coren-Indik Inc ....F....... 267 288-1200
Levittown (G-9827)

Elkay Weaving Co Inc ....G....... 570 822-5371
Wilkes Barre (G-19917)

Family Heir-Loom Weavers Inc ....F....... 717 246-2431
Red Lion (G-16594)

Globe Dye Works ....G....... 215 288-4554
Philadelphia (G-13772)

▲ Kraemer Textiles Inc ....C....... 610 759-4030
Nazareth (G-11975)

Middleburg Yarn Processing Co ....D....... 570 374-1284
Selinsgrove (G-17331)

▲ Roselon Industries Inc ....D....... 215 536-3275
Quakertown (G-16242)

Warp Processing Inc ....C....... 570 655-1275
Exeter (G-5585)

2282 Yarn Texturizing, Throwing, Twisting & Winding Mills

Atwater Inc ....D....... 570 779-9568
Plymouth (G-15815)

BRB Technology Corporation ....G....... 215 364-4115
Feasterville Trevose (G-5893)

Globe Dye Works ....E....... 215 288-4554
Philadelphia (G-13772)

Huntingdon Offset Printing Co ....G....... 814 641-7310
Huntingdon (G-7946)

Middleburg Yarn Processing Co ....D....... 570 374-1284
Selinsgrove (G-17331)

▲ Roselon Industries Inc ....D....... 215 536-3275
Quakertown (G-16242)

Warp Processing Inc ....C....... 570 655-1275
Exeter (G-5585)

2284 Thread Mills

Eddington Thread Mfg Co Inc ....E....... 215 639-8900
Bensalem (G-1186)

Lets Get Personal ....G....... 412 829-0975
Monroeville (G-11343)

Liberty Throwing Company ....D....... 570 287-1114
Kingston (G-8721)

Middleburg Yarn Processing Co ....D....... 570 374-1284
Selinsgrove (G-17331)

Natural Textiles Solutions LLC ....G....... 484 660-4085
Macungie (G-10155)

▲ Roselon Industries Inc ....E....... 215 536-3275
Quakertown (G-16242)

▼ Sauquoit Industries LLC ....D....... 570 348-2751
Scranton (G-17283)

SYN Apparel LLC ....G....... 484 821-3664
Bethlehem (G-1636)

2295 Fabrics Coated Not Rubberized

◆ Aberdeen Road Company ....D....... 717 764-1192
Emigsville (G-4983)

Akas Tex LLC ....F....... 215 244-2589
Bensalem (G-1146)

Bruce Banning ....G....... 724 226-0818
Natrona Heights (G-11936)

Carlisle Construction Mtls Inc ....E....... 717 245-7142
Carlisle (G-2693)

▲ Chapel Hill Mfg Co ....F....... 215 884-3614
Oreland (G-13020)

◆ Clarion Boards LLC ....C....... 814 226-0851
Shippenville (G-17557)

▲ Clarion Laminates LLC ....D....... 814 226-8032
Shippenville (G-17559)

▲ Converters Inc ....E....... 215 355-5400
Huntingdon Valley (G-7971)

Curbell Inc ....G....... 724 772-6800
Cranberry Township (G-3813)

◆ D C Humphrys Co ....D....... 215 307-3363
Philadelphia (G-13599)

Fabricated Products ....G....... 570 588-1794
Bushkill (G-2365)

▲ Fielco LLC ....G....... 215 674-8700
Huntingdon Valley (G-7981)

Fortune Fabrics Inc ....E....... 570 288-3666
Kingston (G-8717)

Freckled Sage ....G....... 610 888-2037
Philadelphia (G-13722)

▲ Gentex Corporation ....E....... 570 282-3550
Simpson (G-17593)

Henderson Construction Fabrics ....G....... 724 368-1145
Harmony (G-7069)

Hill Crest Laminating LLC ....G....... 570 437-3357
Danville (G-4005)

Lite Fibers LLC ....G....... 724 758-0123
Ellwood City (G-4943)

▲ Ltl Color Compounders LLC ....D....... 215 736-1126
Morrisville (G-11570)

Nye Technical Sales ....G....... 610 639-9985
Downingtown (G-4246)

Penlin Fabricators LLC ....G....... 610 837-6667
Bath (G-968)

Performnce Ctngs Intl Labs LLC ....F....... 610 588-7900
Bangor (G-924)

SIC

Phb Inc ....C....... 814 474-1552
Fairview (G-5839)
▲ Poward Plastics Incorporated ....G....... 484 660-3690
Hamburg (G-6849)

2296 Tire Cord & Fabric

Dynacell Life Sciences LLC ....F....... 215 813-8775
Ambler (G-576)

2297 Fabrics, Nonwoven

▲ Armstrong/Kover Kwick Inc ....E....... 412 771-2200
Mc Kees Rocks (G-10603)
Chicopee Inc ....G....... 800 835-2442
Smithfield (G-17647)
First Quality Enterprises Inc ....C....... 570 384-1600
Hazleton (G-7498)
Horizon House Inc ....G....... 610 532-7423
Darby (G-4019)
Microsilver Wear LLC ....G....... 215 917-7203
Yardley (G-20325)
Monadnock Non-Wovens LLC ....E....... 570 839-9210
Mount Pocono (G-11735)
◆ Pfnonwovens LLC ....B....... 570 384-1600
Hazle Township (G-7472)
Sellars Nonwovens ....E....... 610 593-5145
Atglen (G-807)
United States Hardmetal ....G....... 724 834-8381
Greensburg (G-6725)

2298 Cordage & Twine

American Manufacturing & Engrg........F....... 215 362-9694
Montgomeryville (G-11385)
Eddington Thread Mfg Co Inc.............E....... 215 639-8900
Bensalem (G-1186)
▲ Gudebrod Inc ....C....... 610 327-4050
Pottstown (G-15993)
Hahn Universal ....G....... 724 941-6444
Canonsburg (G-2594)
◆ I & I Sling Inc ....E....... 800 874-3539
Aston (G-769)
▲ Lift-Tech Inc ....G....... 717 898-6615
Landisville (G-9263)
Muncy Industries LLC ....G....... 570 649-5188
Turbotville (G-18554)
Network Products & Services.............G....... 724 229-0332
Washington (G-19210)
◆ Phillystran Inc ....E....... 215 368-6611
Montgomeryville (G-11415)
Plum Manufacturing Co Inc ....G....... 215 520-2236
North Wales (G-12825)
Safety Sling Company Inc ....F....... 412 231-6684
Pittsburgh (G-15506)
Schermerhorn Bros Co ....G....... 610 284-7402
Lansdowne (G-9443)
Spencer Industries Inc ....G....... 570 969-9931
Scranton (G-17292)
Squid Wire LLC ....G....... 484 235-5155
Conshohocken (G-3606)
Thunder Basin Corporation ....F....... 610 962-3770
King of Prussia (G-8688)
▲ Troyer Rope Co ....G....... 814 587-3891
Conneautville (G-3488)
◆ TVC Communications LLC ....E....... 717 838-3790
Annville (G-661)
◆ Whitehill Mfg Corp ....E....... 610 494-2378
Chester (G-3068)
◆ Wirerope Works Inc ....B....... 570 327-4229
Williamsport (G-20096)
Wirerope Works Inc ....E....... 570 286-0115
Sunbury (G-18177)
▲ Zippercord Llc ....F....... 610 797-6564
Allentown (G-440)

2299 Textile Goods, NEC

▲ Aetna Felt Corp ....D....... 610 791-0900
Allentown (G-117)
▲ Alphasource Inc ....F....... 215 844-6470
Philadelphia (G-13372)
Arkwright LLC ....G....... 732 246-1506
Philadelphia (G-13411)
▲ Armstrong/Kover Kwick Inc ....E....... 412 771-2200
Mc Kees Rocks (G-10603)
◆ Atd-American Co ....E....... 215 576-1000
Wyncote (G-20261)
Bed Bath & Beyond Inc ....G....... 717 397-0206
Lancaster (G-8950)
Blue Mountain Farms LLC ....G....... 717 599-5110
Harrisburg (G-7097)

Bollman Industries Inc ....C....... 717 484-4361
Adamstown (G-20)
CF Textile Inc ....G....... 215 817-5867
Huntingdon Valley (G-7969)
Executive Distributors Intl ....G....... 610 608-1664
Bryn Mawr (G-2323)
Fiber Quest Composites LLC ....G....... 610 419-0387
Hellertown (G-7555)
Fiberland Inc..E....... 215 744-5446
Philadelphia (G-13699)
▲ FP Woll & Company ....E....... 215 934-5966
Philadelphia (G-13717)
Great American Weaving Corp ....F....... 610 845-9200
Bally (G-903)
Huntingdon Yarn Mills Inc ....E....... 215 425-5656
Philadelphia (G-13844)
▼ Jade Industries Inc ....G....... 610 828-4830
Conshohocken (G-3568)
Jmd Ersion Ctrl Instlltons Inc ....G....... 412 833-7100
Bethel Park (G-1420)
▲ Johnston-Morehouse-Dickey Co .....E....... 412 833-7100
Bethel Park (G-1421)
Johnston-Morehouse-Dickey Co..........G....... 814 684-0916
Tyrone (G-18584)
◆ Knoll Inc ....D....... 215 679-7991
East Greenville (G-4570)
Marionette Company Inc ....F....... 570 644-1936
Shamokin (G-17425)
▲ Milliken Nonwovens LLC ....G....... 610 544-7117
Broomall (G-2298)
Natural Textiles Solutions LLC ....G....... 484 660-4085
Macungie (G-10155)
▲ Noble Biomaterials Inc ....D....... 570 955-1800
Scranton (G-17265)
Oaks Industrial Supply Inc ....G....... 610 539-7008
Norristown (G-12696)
▲ Oscar Daniels & Company Inc ....F....... 610 678-8144
Reading (G-16460)
Penn Pro Manufacturing Inc ....F....... 724 222-6450
Washington (G-19215)
◆ Pinnacle Textile Inds LLC ....E....... 800 901-4784
King of Prussia (G-8663)
Rockwood Pigments Na Inc ....F....... 610 279-6450
King of Prussia (G-8670)
▲ Secant Group LLC ....C....... 877 774-2835
Telford (G-18314)
Secant Group LLC ....F....... 215 538-9601
Quakertown (G-16245)
▲ Tetratec Corp ....F....... 215 396-8349
Warminster (G-18978)
Thread International Pbc Inc ....G....... 814 876-9999
Pittsburgh (G-15617)
▲ Unitex Group Usa LLC ....E....... 864 846-8700
Warminster (G-18991)
Wholesale Linens Supply Inc ....G....... 814 886-7000
Cresson (G-3902)

23 APPAREL AND OTHER FINISHED PRODUCTS MADE FROM FABRICS AND SIMILAR MATERIAL

2311 Men's & Boys' Suits, Coats & Overcoats

◆ Aramark Unf Creer AP Group Inc......A....... 215 238-3000
Philadelphia (G-13406)
▲ Bodine Business Products ....G....... 610 827-0138
Malvern (G-10194)
Cintas Corporation No 2......................D....... 440 352-4003
Erie (G-5224)
D & S Clothing Inc.............................G....... 856 383-3794
Philadelphia (G-13598)
Donora Sportswear Company Inc ....G....... 724 929-2387
Donora (G-4151)
▲ Dream World International Inc ....G....... 215 320-0200
Philadelphia (G-13644)
Dynamic Team Sports Inc ....D....... 610 518-3300
Exton (G-5670)
◆ F&T Apparel LLC ....D....... 646 839-7000
Plymouth Meeting (G-15843)
F&T Apparel LLC................................D....... 610 828-8400
Plymouth Meeting (G-15844)
◆ Flagstaff Industries Corp ....C....... 215 638-9662
Bensalem (G-1195)
▲ Flynn & OHara Uniforms Inc ....D....... 800 441-4122
Philadelphia (G-13707)
Hope Uniform Co Inc ....E....... 908 496-4899
Bangor (G-916)
▲ Ideal Products America LP..............F....... 484 320-6194
Malvern (G-10250)

Ikor Industries Inc ....D....... 302 456-0280
Kennett Square (G-8514)
Jack OReilly Tuxedos ....G....... 610 929-9409
Reading (G-16412)
◆ Jacob Siegel LP ....G....... 610 828-8400
Conshohocken (G-3567)
▲ Majer Brand Company Inc ....F....... 717 632-1320
Hanover (G-6916)
Northside Manufacturing Inc ....E....... 814 342-4638
Philipsburg (G-14521)
Stonemak Enterprises Inc ....G....... 570 752-3209
Berwick (G-1345)
Tlr Redwood Inc ....G....... 215 322-1005
Southampton (G-17841)
Tom James Company ....E....... 570 875-3100
Ashland (G-737)
Tom James Company ....F....... 412 642-2797
Pittsburgh (G-15631)
Tom James Company ....D....... 717 264-5768
Chambersburg (G-2986)
◆ Union Apparel Inc ....A....... 724 423-4900
Norvelt (G-12879)
▲ Woolrich Inc ....C....... 570 769-6464
Woolrich (G-20220)

2321 Men's & Boys' Shirts

E-Nanomedsys LLC ....G....... 917 734-1462
State College (G-17958)
◆ Elbeco Incorporated ....D....... 610 921-0651
Reading (G-16370)
◆ F&T Apparel LLC ....D....... 646 839-7000
Plymouth Meeting (G-15843)
▲ Hancock Company ....G....... 570 875-3100
Ashland (G-731)
Kaylin Mfg Co ....F....... 610 820-6224
Allentown (G-280)
Lifewear Inc ....E....... 610 327-2884
Pottstown (G-16011)
Ocello Inc..C....... 717 866-5778
Richland (G-16688)
Taraco Sportswear Inc ....G....... 570 669-9004
Nesquehoning (G-12009)
Tom James Company ....D....... 717 264-5768
Chambersburg (G-2986)
Trademark Specialties ....G....... 412 353-3752
Cheswick (G-3119)
▲ Trau & Loevner Inc ....D....... 412 361-7700
Braddock (G-1949)
Vf Imagewear Inc.................................G....... 610 746-6800
Easton (G-4768)
Vf Outdoor LLC...................................G....... 610 265-2193
King of Prussia (G-8696)
Windjammer Corporation Inc...............E....... 610 588-0626
Bangor (G-935)
Windjammer Corporation Inc...............G....... 610 588-2137
Bangor (G-936)
▲ Woolrich Inc ....C....... 570 769-6464
Woolrich (G-20220)

2322 Men's & Boys' Underwear & Nightwear

Wundies ....G....... 570 322-7245
Williamsport (G-20102)

2323 Men's & Boys' Neckwear

Joyce Inc ....G....... 206 937-4633
Pittsburgh (G-15156)
Tom James Company ....D....... 717 264-5768
Chambersburg (G-2986)

2325 Men's & Boys' Separate Trousers & Casual Slacks

▲ Astro Apparel Inc ....E....... 570 346-1700
Scranton (G-17209)
D D J Manufacturing Inc......................D....... 814 378-7625
Madera (G-10162)
◆ F&T Apparel LLC ....D....... 646 839-7000
Plymouth Meeting (G-15843)
Freespiritjeanscom Inc ....G....... 302 319-9313
Philadelphia (G-13723)
L & G Manufacturing ....G....... 570 876-1550
Archbald (G-689)
Levi Strauss & Co ....F....... 610 337-0388
King of Prussia (G-8640)
▲ Majer Brand Company Inc ....F....... 717 632-1320
Hanover (G-6916)
Tan Clothing Co Inc ....E....... 215 625-2536
Philadelphia (G-14370)
Tom James Company ....D....... 717 264-5768
Chambersburg (G-2986)

Vf Outdoor LLC ....G..... 610 265-2193
King of Prussia (G-8696)
Windjammer Corporation Inc ....E..... 610 588-0626
Bangor (G-935)
Windjammer Corporation Inc ....G..... 610 588-2137
Bangor (G-936)

2326 Men's & Boys' Work Clothing

◆ AC Fashion LLC ....G..... 570 291-5982
Moosic (G-11501)
Amrit Works LLC ....G..... 267 475-7129
Morton (G-11589)
Bashlin Industries Inc ....D..... 724 458-8340
Grove City (G-6780)
Blind and Vision Rehab ....F..... 412 325-7504
Homestead (G-7683)
Blind and Vision Rehab ....D..... 412 368-4400
Pittsburgh (G-14771)
C K Sportwear Inc ....E..... 717 733-4786
Ephrata (G-5094)
Cintas Corporation No 2 ....D..... 724 696-5640
Mount Pleasant (G-11692)
▲ Combined Tactical Systems Inc ....C..... 724 932-2177
Jamestown (G-8236)
D & S Clothing Inc ....G..... 856 383-3794
Philadelphia (G-13598)
Davy Manufacturing Inc ....F..... 610 583-8240
Havertown (G-7420)
◆ Elbeco Incorporated ....D..... 610 921-0651
Reading (G-16370)
Enterprise Fashions ....G..... 570 489-1863
Olyphant (G-12989)
▲ Executive Apparel Inc ....F..... 215 464-5400
Philadelphia (G-13686)
G H Lainez Manufacturing Inc ....F..... 610 776-0778
Allentown (G-221)
Hatcrafters Inc ....G..... 610 623-2620
Clifton Heights (G-3253)
Hings Lai Fashion ....E..... 215 530-0348
Philadelphia (G-13827)
Hope Uniform Co Inc ....E..... 908 496-4899
Bangor (G-916)
Innovative Designs Inc ....G..... 412 799-0350
Pittsburgh (G-15127)
▲ Majestic Fire Apparel Inc ....E..... 610 377-6273
Lehighton (G-9719)
Mifflin Valley Inc ....E..... 610 775-0505
Reading (G-16443)
◆ Pinnacle Textile Inds LLC ....E..... 800 901-4784
King of Prussia (G-8663)
Roeberg Enterprises Inc ....E..... 800 523-8197
Reading (G-16503)
Suns Manufacturing Inc ....E..... 610 837-0798
Bath (G-971)
▲ Threshold Rhblitation Svcs Inc .....B..... 610 777-7691
Reading (G-16538)
Unek Designs EMB & Sew Sp LLC .....G..... 610 563-6676
Coatesville (G-3327)

2329 Men's & Boys' Clothing, NEC

Adidas North America Inc ....F..... 610 327-9565
Pottstown (G-15960)
▲ Alpha Mills Corporation ....D..... 570 385-1791
Schuylkill Haven (G-17145)
American Trench LLC ....G..... 215 360-3493
Ardmore (G-700)
Aramark Services Inc ....F..... 800 999-8989
Philadelphia (G-13405)
Bitars Sportswear ....G..... 610 435-4923
Allentown (G-153)
▲ Boathouse Row Sports Ltd ....C..... 215 425-4300
Philadelphia (G-13469)
C K Sportwear Inc ....E..... 717 733-4786
Ephrata (G-5094)
Camber Sportswear Inc ....E..... 610 239-9910
Norristown (G-12643)
▲ Coopersburg Products LLC ....G..... 610 282-1360
Center Valley (G-2826)
◆ Cycling Sports Group Inc ....D..... 203 749-7000
Bedford (G-1048)
D & S Clothing Inc ....G..... 856 383-3794
Philadelphia (G-13598)
Footers Inc ....G..... 610 437-2233
Allentown (G-217)
Gregg Shirtmakers Inc ....G..... 215 329-7700
Philadelphia (G-13787)
▲ HB Sportswear Inc ....G..... 717 354-2306
New Holland (G-12252)
▲ Henson Company Inc ....D..... 800 486-2788
Reading (G-16400)

Innovative Designs Inc ....G..... 412 799-0350
Pittsburgh (G-15127)
Iwom Outerwear LLC ....G..... 814 272-5400
State College (G-17979)
Kenum Distribution LLC ....G..... 814 383-2626
Mingoville (G-11256)
La Salle Products Inc ....F..... 412 488-1585
Pittsburgh (G-15213)
◆ Majestic Athletic Intl Ltd ....G..... 610 746-7494
Easton (G-4718)
▲ Maroco Ltd ....B..... 610 746-6800
Easton (G-4719)
▲ Meke Corp ....F..... 717 354-6353
East Earl (G-4550)
Nautica of Lancaster ....F..... 717 396-9414
Lancaster (G-9143)
▲ Outback Trading Company Ltd .....E..... 610 932-5314
Oxford (G-13084)
P & S Sportswear Inc ....E..... 215 455-7133
Philadelphia (G-14110)
▲ Performance Sports Apparel Inc ...E..... 508 384-8036
Reading (G-16468)
Prosco Inc ....E..... 814 375-0484
Du Bois (G-4414)
PS & QS Inc ....G..... 215 592-0888
Philadelphia (G-14213)
Roeberg Enterprises Inc ....E..... 800 523-8197
Reading (G-16503)
▼ Scottys Fashion of Lehighton ......G..... 610 377-3032
Pen Argyl (G-13216)
▲ Ski Haus LLC ....G..... 412 760-7547
Bradfordwoods (G-1999)
▲ Total Equestrian Inc ....G..... 215 721-1247
Souderton (G-17768)
Transfer Junction ....G..... 814 942-4434
Williamsport (G-19982)
Urban Outfitters Wholesale Inc ....G..... 215 454-5500
Philadelphia (G-14431)
Vf Outdoor LLC ....G..... 610 323-6575
Pottstown (G-16066)
Vf Outdoor LLC ....G..... 610 265-2193
King of Prussia (G-8696)
Windjammer Corporation Inc ....F..... 610 588-0626
Bangor (G-934)
Windjammer Corporation Inc ....E..... 610 588-0626
Bangor (G-935)
Windjammer Corporation Inc ....G..... 610 588-2137
Bangor (G-936)
▲ Woolrich Inc ....C..... 570 769-6464
Woolrich (G-20220)

2331 Women's & Misses' Blouses

Dallco Industries Inc ....E..... 717 854-7875
York (G-20443)
Designer Fashions Plus ....G..... 215 416-5062
Philadelphia (G-13621)
E-Nanomedsys LLC ....G..... 917 734-1462
State College (G-17958)
Gloninger Brothers Inc ....G..... 215 456-5100
Philadelphia (G-13774)
Jarmens Fashion ....G..... 215 441-5242
Warminster (G-18901)
Lifewear Inc ....E..... 610 327-2884
Pottstown (G-16011)
Meredith Banzhoff LLC ....G..... 717 919-5074
Mechanicsburg (G-10868)
Mona Lisa Fashions ....G..... 610 770-0806
Allentown (G-319)
▲ Notations Inc ....E..... 215 259-2000
Warminster (G-18930)
R & M Apparel Inc ....C..... 814 886-9272
Gallitzin (G-6247)
▲ Sarah Lynn Sportswear Inc ....E..... 610 770-1702
Allentown (G-384)
Taraco Sportswear Inc ....G..... 570 669-9004
Nesquehoning (G-12009)
▲ Trau & Loevner Inc ....D..... 412 361-7700
Braddock (G-1949)
▲ Woolrich Inc ....C..... 570 769-6464
Woolrich (G-20220)

2335 Women's & Misses' Dresses

Alfred Angelo - The Brdes Std ....F..... 813 872-1881
Fort Washington (G-6061)
Amc Inc ....G..... 412 531-3160
Pittsburgh (G-14698)
Center Fashions Inc ....D..... 570 655-2861
Dupont (G-4489)
CFM Designs Inc ....G..... 610 520-7777
Bryn Mawr (G-2318)

Davids Bridal Inc ....E..... 610 943-6210
Conshohocken (G-3536)
Donna Karan Company LLC ....C..... 610 625-4410
Bethlehem (G-1498)
Donna Karan Company LLC ....C..... 717 299-1706
Lancaster (G-9001)
Icbridal LLC ....G..... 570 409-6333
Milford (G-11161)
Joel Mfg Co Inc ....G..... 570 822-1182
Wilkes Barre (G-19934)
Johnny Appleseeds Inc ....G..... 800 546-4554
Warren (G-19034)
▲ Priscilla of Boston Inc ....D..... 610 943-5000
Conshohocken (G-3592)
R & M Apparel Inc ....C..... 814 886-9272
Gallitzin (G-6247)
Runway Liquidation LLC ....G..... 401 351-4994
Philadelphia (G-14264)
Sweethearts Bridal Formalwear ......G..... 610 750-5087
Reading (G-16532)
Tan Clothing Co Inc ....E..... 215 625-2536
Philadelphia (G-14370)

2337 Women's & Misses' Suits, Coats & Skirts

Amrit Works LLC ....G..... 267 475-7129
Morton (G-11589)
◆ Aramark Unf Creer AP Group Inc ....A..... 215 238-3000
Philadelphia (G-13406)
Cintas Corporation No 2 ....D..... 724 696-5640
Mount Pleasant (G-11692)
D D J Manufacturing Inc ....D..... 814 378-7625
Madera (G-10162)
Donora Sportswear Company Inc .....G..... 724 929-2387
Donora (G-4151)
▲ Executive Apparel Inc ....F..... 215 464-5400
Philadelphia (G-13686)
◆ Flagstaff Industries Corp ....E..... 215 638-9662
Bensalem (G-1195)
▲ Flynn & OHara Uniforms Inc ....D..... 800 441-4122
Philadelphia (G-13707)
▲ Greco International Inc ....F..... 215 628-2557
Ambler (G-580)
Mona Lisa Fashions ....G..... 610 770-0806
Allentown (G-319)
Premier Brnds Group Hldngs LLC .....G..... 215 785-4000
Bristol (G-2187)
Premier Brnds Group Hldngs LLC .....F..... 212 642-3860
Bristol (G-2188)
R & M Apparel Inc ....C..... 814 886-9272
Gallitzin (G-6247)
▲ Tama Mfg Co Inc ....B..... 610 231-3100
Allentown (G-407)
Tan Clothing Co Inc ....E..... 215 625-2536
Philadelphia (G-14370)
Theory LLC ....D..... 610 326-5040
Pottstown (G-16054)
◆ Union Apparel Inc ....A..... 724 423-4900
Norvelt (G-12879)
▲ Woolrich Inc ....C..... 570 769-6464
Woolrich (G-20220)

2339 Women's & Misses' Outerwear, NEC

A & H Sportswear Co Inc ....D..... 610 746-0922
Nazareth (G-11951)
◆ A & H Sportswear Co Inc ....D..... 484 373-3600
Easton (G-4643)
A & H Sportswear Co Inc ....C..... 610 759-9550
Stockertown (G-18063)
Aeo Management Co ....G..... 724 776-4857
Warrendale (G-19067)
▲ Aeo Management Co ....F..... 412 432-3300
Pittsburgh (G-14654)
▲ Alpha Mills Corporation ....D..... 570 385-1791
Schuylkill Haven (G-17145)
Alpha Mills Corporation ....D..... 570 385-2400
Pottsville (G-16072)
Anthony Hauze ....G..... 610 432-3533
Allentown (G-137)
Atkins Kareemah ....G..... 267 428-0019
Upper Darby (G-18682)
◆ Bendinger Inc ....G..... 484 342-3522
Plymouth Meeting (G-15833)
Bitars Sportswear ....G..... 610 435-4923
Allentown (G-153)
▲ Boathouse Row Sports Ltd ....C..... 215 425-4300
Philadelphia (G-13469)
Bryan Mfg Co ....E..... 724 245-8200
Eighty Four (G-4835)

C K Sportwear Inc ....E 717 733-4786
Ephrata (G-5094)

▲ Cheryl Nash Apparel LLC ....G 610 692-1919
Kennett Square (G-8504)

Cute Loops ....G 484 318-7175
Chesterbrook (G-3091)

D & S Clothing Inc 856 383-3794
Philadelphia (G-13598)

D D J Manufacturing Inc ....D 814 378-7625
Madera (G-10162)

Dallco Industries Inc ....E 717 854-7875
York (G-20443)

▲ Danskin ....F 717 747-3051
York (G-20444)

Eco Product Group LLC ....G 412 364-1792
Pittsburgh (G-14958)

Farnsworth Gowns and Fnrl Sups ......G 412 881-4696
Pittsburgh (G-15004)

▲ Flynn & OHara Uniforms Inc ....D 800 441-4122
Philadelphia (G-13707)

Footers Inc ....G 610 437-2233
Allentown (G-217)

Frox ....G 215 822-9011
Perkasie (G-13277)

G H Lainez Manufacturing Inc ....F 610 776-0778
Allentown (G-221)

▲ Gear Racewear Inc ....F 724 458-6336
Grove City (G-6786)

▲ HB Sportswear Inc ....G 717 354-2306
New Holland (G-12252)

▲ Henson Company Inc ....D 800 486-2788
Reading (G-16400)

Hey Girl Inc ....G 610 945-6138
Newtown Square (G-12575)

Idlewild Ski Shop Inc ....F 570 222-4200
Clifford Township (G-3248)

Jade Fashion Corporation ....G 215 922-3953
Philadelphia (G-13888)

▲ Kevin OBrien Studio Inc ....G 215 923-6378
Philadelphia (G-13929)

Lavender Badge LLC ....G 610 994-9476
King of Prussia (G-8638)

Lindas Stuff Inc ....F 215 956-9190
Hatboro (G-7292)

▲ Little Earth Productions Inc ....E 412 471-0909
Pittsburgh (G-15237)

Longevity Brands LLC ....E 484 373-3600
Easton (G-4715)

Mainstream Swimsuits Inc ....E 484 373-3600
Easton (G-4717)

◆ Majestic Athletic Intl Ltd ....G 610 746-7494
Easton (G-4718)

▲ Maroco LLC ....B 610 746-6800
Easton (G-4719)

Matthew Cole Inc ....G 215 425-6606
Philadelphia (G-13995)

▲ Meke Corp ....F 717 354-4550
East Earl (G-4550)

Merry Maid Inc ....E 800 360-3836
Bangor (G-921)

Mifflinburg Farmers Exchange ....G 570 966-4030
Mifflinburg (G-11098)

◆ Milco Industries Inc ....C 570 784-0400
Bloomsburg (G-1790)

Nightlife & Clothing Co ....G 718 415-6391
Philadelphia (G-14074)

▲ Notations Inc ....C 215 259-2000
Warminster (G-18930)

▲ Outback Trading Company Ltd ....E 610 932-5314
Oxford (G-13084)

P & L Sportswear Inc ....G 717 359-9000
Littlestown (G-10074)

P & S Sportswear Inc ....E 215 455-7133
Philadelphia (G-14110)

▲ Perform Group LLC ....B 717 852-6950
York (G-20624)

Perform Group LLC ....C 717 252-1578
York (G-20625)

Premier Brnds Group Hldngs LLC ......E 212 835-3672
Bristol (G-2186)

R & M Apparel Inc ....C 814 886-9272
Gallitzin (G-6247)

▲ Red Lion Manufacturing Inc ....C 717 767-6511
York (G-20656)

▲ Rich Reenie Inc ....F 610 439-7962
Allentown (G-374)

Roeberg Enterprises Inc ....E 800 523-8197
Reading (G-16503)

Roseys Creations Inc ....G 610 704-8591
Allentown (G-379)

▲ Sugartown Worldwide LLC ....C 610 878-5550
King of Prussia (G-8682)

T A E Ltd ....G 215 925-7860
Philadelphia (G-14364)

▲ Tama Mfg Co Inc ....B 610 231-3100
Allentown (G-407)

Tan Clothing Co Inc ....E 215 625-2536
Philadelphia (G-14370)

▲ Total Equestrian Inc ....G 215 721-1247
Souderton (G-17768)

Tukes Tearoff ....G 570 695-3171
Tremont (G-18483)

Vf Imagewear Inc ....G 610 746-6800
Easton (G-4768)

▲ Windridge Design Inc ....F 610 692-1919
West Chester (G-19678)

2341 Women's, Misses' & Children's Underwear & Nightwear

Alpha Mills Corporation ....D 570 385-2400
Pottsville (G-16072)

▲ Alpha Mills Corporation ....D 570 385-1791
Schuylkill Haven (G-17145)

Ariela and Associates Intl LLC ....G 570 385-8340
Schuylkill Haven (G-17147)

Artworks Silk Screen Printers ....G 717 238-5087
Harrisburg (G-7092)

Charles Komar & Sons Inc ....C 570 326-3741
Williamsport (G-19997)

Dallco Industries Inc ....E 717 854-7875
York (G-20443)

Delta Galil USA Inc ....B 570 326-2451
Williamsport (G-20004)

Flo Ann Garments ....G 717 445-5268
Ephrata (G-5103)

Glamorise Foundations Inc ....C 570 322-7806
Williamsport (G-20018)

◆ Milco Industries Inc ....C 570 784-0400
Bloomsburg (G-1790)

Ocello Inc ....C 717 866-5778
Richland (G-16688)

Sculptz Inc ....E 215 494-2900
Trevose (G-18503)

Wundies ....G 570 322-7245
Williamsport (G-20102)

2342 Brassieres, Girdles & Garments

Farel Corp ....E 814 495-4625
South Fork (G-17774)

Glamorise Foundations Inc ....C 570 322-7806
Williamsport (G-20018)

Hanesbrands Inc ....G 610 970-5767
Pottstown (G-15996)

▲ Lontex Corporation ....E 610 272-5040
Norristown (G-12678)

2353 Hats, Caps & Millinery

Birch Cutting Corporation ....E 570 343-7477
Scranton (G-17212)

▲ Bollman Hat Company ....B 717 484-4361
Adamstown (G-19)

Bollman Hat Company ....D 717 336-0545
Denver (G-4069)

Bollman Industries Inc ....C 717 484-4361
Adamstown (G-20)

▲ F & M Hat Company Inc ....E 717 336-5505
Denver (G-4073)

Hatcrafters Inc ....G 610 623-2620
Clifton Heights (G-3253)

◆ Jacobson Hat Co Inc ....D 570 342-7887
Scranton (G-17246)

Keystone Uniform Cap LP ....E 215 821-3434
Philadelphia (G-13933)

Lids Corporation ....G 814 868-1944
Erie (G-5364)

▲ Outback Trading Company Ltd ....E 610 932-5314
Oxford (G-13084)

P & L Sportswear Inc ....G 717 359-9000
Littlestown (G-10074)

Under Armour Inc ....E 717 393-7671
Lancaster (G-9228)

Weisman Novelty Co Inc ....F 215 635-0147
Elkins Park (G-4914)

2361 Children's & Infants' Dresses & Blouses

Baby Sparkles ....G 267 304-8787
Philadelphia (G-13440)

Emma One Sock Inc ....G 215 542-1082
Dresher (G-4354)

▲ HB Sportswear Inc ....G 717 354-2306
New Holland (G-12252)

◆ Kahn-Lucas-Lancaster Inc ....E 717 537-4140
Mountville (G-11797)

▲ Rosenau Beck Inc ....E 215 364-1714
Southampton (G-17835)

▲ Sugartown Worldwide LLC ....C 610 878-5550
King of Prussia (G-8682)

2369 Girls' & Infants' Outerwear, NEC

▲ Alpha Mills Corporation ....D 570 385-1791
Schuylkill Haven (G-17145)

Alpha Mills Corporation ....E 570 385-1791
Schuylkill Haven (G-17146)

Alpha Mills Corporation ....D 570 385-2400
Pottsville (G-16072)

C&H7 LLC ....G 215 887-7411
Exton (G-5658)

Coloratura Inc ....G 717 867-1144
Lebanon (G-9555)

Delta Galil USA Inc ....B 570 326-2451
Williamsport (G-20004)

Good Lad Co ....B 215 739-0200
Philadelphia (G-13777)

▲ HB Sportswear Inc ....G 717 354-2306
New Holland (G-12252)

◆ Kahn-Lucas-Lancaster Inc ....E 717 537-4140
Mountville (G-11797)

▲ Meke Corp ....F 717 354-6353
East Earl (G-4550)

R & M Apparel Inc ....C 814 886-9272
Gallitzin (G-6247)

2371 Fur Goods

Charles L Simpson Sr ....F 717 763-7023
New Cumberland (G-12182)

Hal-Jo Corp ....F 215 885-4747
Jenkintown (G-8289)

2381 Dress & Work Gloves

Brookville Glove Mfg Co Inc ....E 814 849-7324
Brookville (G-2253)

◆ G N F Produts Inc ....G 215 781-6222
Croydon (G-3917)

Ladyfingers Sewing Studio ....G 610 689-0068
Oley (G-12979)

▲ Red Lion Manufacturing Inc ....C 717 767-6511
York (G-20656)

Stone Breaker LLC ....G 312 203-5632
Ardmore (G-718)

2384 Robes & Dressing Gowns

Bentley Robe Factory Inc ....G 215 531-3862
Philadelphia (G-13455)

◆ Milco Industries Inc ....C 570 784-0400
Bloomsburg (G-1790)

2385 Waterproof Outerwear

▲ Harris Manufacturing Company ....G 609 393-3717
Southampton (G-17816)

▲ Keystone Niteware Co Inc ....E 717 336-7534
Reinholds (G-16634)

▲ Red Lion Manufacturing Inc ....C 717 767-6511
York (G-20656)

2386 Leather & Sheep Lined Clothing

Fusion Five USA LLC ....G 267 507-6127
Philadelphia (G-13735)

Hal-Jo Corp ....F 215 885-4747
Jenkintown (G-8289)

Pocono Mountain Leather Co ....G 570 814-6672
Hanover Township (G-7004)

Samuelson Leather LLC ....G 484 328-3273
Malvern (G-10314)

▲ Sickafus Sheepskins ....E 610 488-1782
Strausstown (G-18100)

Torgeman Gabi ....G 215 563-0882
Philadelphia (G-14397)

Vf Outdoor LLC ....G 610 265-2193
King of Prussia (G-8696)

2389 Apparel & Accessories, NEC

Aeo Management Co ....G 724 776-4857
Warrendale (G-19067)

▲ Aeo Management Co ....F 412 432-3300
Pittsburgh (G-14654)

Alex and Ani LLC ....G 412 367-1362
Pittsburgh (G-14672)

American Legion Post 548 ....D...... 724 443-0047
  Gibsonia (G-6324)
Angelie Original ....G...... 814 798-3312
  Hooversville (G-7770)
B & D Advertising Inc ....D...... 717 852-6950
  York (G-20394)
Breet Incorporated ....G...... 610 558-4006
  Glen Mills (G-6432)
C K Sportwear Inc ....E...... 717 733-4786
  Ephrata (G-5094)
Character Translation Inc ....G...... 610 279-3970
  Norristown (G-12644)
▲ Cicci Dance Supply Inc ....E...... 724 348-7359
  Finleyville (G-5953)
CSS Industries Inc ....C...... 610 729-3959
  Plymouth Meeting (G-15840)
David Moscinski ....G...... 215 271-6193
  Philadelphia (G-13609)
▲ Eros Hosiery Co Del Vly Inc ....G...... 215 342-2121
  Huntingdon Valley (G-7978)
Futernal Order Police Lodge...........G...... 610 655-6116
  Reading (G-16386)
Gardinier Associates Inc ....E...... 570 385-2721
  Schuylkill Haven (G-17157)
Gift Is In You Llc ....G...... 267 974-3376
  Philadelphia (G-13761)
Imagewear International Inc ....G...... 724 335-2425
  Murrysville (G-11853)
Imposters LLC ....G...... 412 781-3443
  Pittsburgh (G-15115)
James May Costume Co ....G...... 610 532-3430
  Folsom (G-6026)
Lakeland Industries Inc ....G...... 610 775-0505
  Reading (G-16426)
Meredith Banzhoff LLC....................G...... 717 919-5074
  Mechanicsburg (G-10868)
▲ Perform Group LLC ....B...... 717 852-6950
  York (G-20624)
Perform Group LLC ....C...... 717 252-1578
  York (G-20625)
Premier Brnds Group Hldngs LLC ....E...... 212 835-3672
  Bristol (G-2186)
Roeberg Enterprises Inc ....E...... 800 523-8197
  Reading (G-16503)
Steve Goldberg Company ....G...... 215 322-0615
  Southampton (G-17837)
Sugartown Worldwide LLC ....F...... 610 265-7607
  King of Prussia (G-8681)
▲ Supreme Trading Ltd ....E...... 215 739-2237
  Philadelphia (G-14361)
▲ T J Corporation ....E...... 724 929-7300
  Verona (G-18763)
◆ Valumax International Inc ....F...... 610 336-0101
  Allentown (G-421)
▲ Vivid Products LLC ....G...... 215 394-0235
  Warminster (G-18996)
Williamson Costume Company ....F...... 215 925-7121
  Philadelphia (G-14476)

2391 Curtains & Draperies

Bishops Inc ....G...... 412 821-3333
  Mars (G-10488)
Brookline Fabrics Co Inc..................E...... 412 665-4925
  Pittsburgh (G-14794)
Caldwells Windoware Inc ....E...... 412 922-1132
  Pittsburgh (G-14800)
De Lucas Draperys ....G...... 610 284-2464
  Clifton Heights (G-3251)
Decopro Inc ....G...... 215 939-7983
  Philadelphia (G-13613)
Fabtex Inc ....D...... 910 739-0019
  Danville (G-4001)
▲ Fabtex Inc ....C...... 570 275-7500
  Danville (G-4000)
Fay Studios.....................................G...... 215 672-2599
  Hatboro (G-7285)
Ferrante Uphlstrng & Crptng ....F...... 724 535-8866
  Wampum (G-18800)
Hamilton Awning Co ....F...... 724 774-7644
  Beaver (G-983)
▲ Kartri Sales Company Inc ....E...... 570 785-3365
  Forest City (G-6054)
L A Draperies Inc ....G...... 610 375-2224
  Reading (G-16425)
Lafayette Venetian Blind Inc ....E...... 717 652-3750
  Harrisburg (G-7167)
Lewrene Interiors ....G...... 717 263-8300
  Chambersburg (G-2953)
▲ Lincoln Textile Pdts Co Inc ....D...... 484 281-3999
  Bath (G-965)

Martins Draperies & Interiors...........G...... 717 239-0501
  Lancaster (G-9125)
Merrill Y Landis Ltd ....D...... 215 723-8177
  Telford (G-18302)
Morantz Inc ....G...... 215 969-0266
  Philadelphia (G-14038)
Plymouth Blind Co Inc ....E...... 412 771-8569
  Mc Kees Rocks (G-10626)
Plymouth Interiors LP ....F...... 412 771-8569
  Mc Kees Rocks (G-10627)
S Morantz Inc ....D...... 215 969-0266
  Philadelphia (G-14273)
Samuel Gerber Inc ....G...... 717 761-0250
  Harrisburg (G-7212)
Westerbrook Custom Made Drap ....G...... 717 737-8185
  Camp Hill (G-2525)

2392 House furnishings: Textile

◆ American Textile Company Inc ......C...... 412 948-1020
  Duquesne (G-4494)
▲ Armstrong/Kover Kwick Inc ....E...... 412 771-2200
  Mc Kees Rocks (G-10603)
▲ Belmont Fabrics LLC ....F...... 717 768-0077
  Paradise (G-13154)
▲ Bess Manufacturing Company ....G...... 215 447-1032
  Bensalem (G-1157)
▲ Bond Products Inc ....F...... 215 842-0200
  Philadelphia (G-13470)
Brookline Fabrics Co Inc..................E...... 412 665-4925
  Pittsburgh (G-14794)
Bryan Mfg Co ....E...... 724 245-8200
  Eighty Four (G-4835)
Carpenter Co ....C...... 814 944-8612
  Altoona (G-486)
▲ Chestnut Ridge Foam Inc ....C...... 724 537-9000
  Latrobe (G-9464)
CMI Systems ....F...... 215 596-0306
  Philadelphia (G-13553)
Dallco Industries Inc ....E...... 717 854-7875
  York (G-20443)
Dame Design LLC ....G...... 610 458-3290
  Phoenixville (G-14541)
Fabtex Inc ....D...... 910 739-0019
  Danville (G-4001)
▲ Fabtex Inc ....C...... 570 275-7500
  Danville (G-4000)
Factory Linens Inc ....E...... 610 825-2790
  Conshohocken (G-3545)
◆ Fibematics Inc ....E...... 215 226-2672
  Philadelphia (G-13698)
General Medical Mfg LLC ....G...... 610 599-0961
  Bangor (G-915)
▲ Harmonic Rays Mfg Group Inc .....G...... 267 761-9558
  Philadelphia (G-13803)
Hollander Sleep Products LLC ....E...... 570 874-2114
  Frackville (G-6105)
Home Grown Inc ....G...... 610 642-3601
  Haverford (G-7411)
Hotlineglass-Usa LLC ....G...... 800 634-9252
  Butler (G-2406)
▲ Kartri Sales Company Inc ....E...... 570 785-3365
  Forest City (G-6054)
▲ Lincoln Textile Pdts Co Inc ....D...... 484 281-3999
  Bath (G-965)
◆ Monarch Global Brands Inc ....D...... 215 482-6100
  Philadelphia (G-14033)
▲ National Furniture Assoc Inc ....G...... 814 342-2007
  Philipsburg (G-14520)
◆ Natures Pillows Inc ....G...... 215 633-9801
  Feasterville Trevose (G-5921)
Neuropedic LLC ....F...... 570 501-7713
  West Hazleton (G-19714)
▲ Norshel Industries Inc ....E...... 215 788-2200
  Croydon (G-3922)
Organic Climbing LLC ....G...... 651 245-1079
  Philipsburg (G-14523)
▲ Paradise Pillow Inc ....E...... 215 225-8700
  Philadelphia (G-14120)
Peter Sheims Cow Mattress ....G...... 717 786-2918
  Quarryville (G-16276)
Precision Rehab Manufacturing ....G...... 814 899-8731
  Erie (G-5432)
Salmon Pillowmakers Inc ....G...... 717 767-4978
  York (G-20663)
Samuel Gerber Inc ....G...... 717 761-0250
  Harrisburg (G-7212)
Shen Manufacturing Company Inc ....G...... 570 278-3707
  Montrose (G-11476)
Sonoco Products Company ....E...... 610 323-9221
  Pottstown (G-16049)

▲ Trillion Source Inc ....F...... 631 949-2304
  Emmaus (G-5045)
William H Kies Jr ....G...... 610 252-6261
  Easton (G-4776)

2393 Textile Bags

◆ A Rifkin Co ....D...... 570 825-9551
  Hanover Township (G-6978)
Cambria County Asso ....B...... 814 536-3531
  Johnstown (G-8360)
Covers All Canvas Products ....G...... 412 653-6010
  Pittsburgh (G-14881)
◆ D C Humphrys Co ....D...... 215 307-3363
  Philadelphia (G-13599)
Darling Blends LLC..........................G...... 215 630-2802
  Langhorne (G-9288)
▲ Equinox Ltd ....E...... 570 322-5900
  Williamsport (G-20011)
Hamilton Awning Co ....F...... 724 774-7644
  Beaver (G-983)
◆ Jetnet Corporation ....D...... 412 741-0100
  Sewickley (G-17396)
Nicole Lynn Inc ....G...... 717 292-6130
  Dover (G-4197)
Nyp Corp (frmr Ny-Pters Corp) ....G...... 717 656-0299
  Leola (G-9796)
▲ Redco Foods Inc ....G...... 800 556-6674
  Bethlehem (G-1609)
Wester Burlap Bag & Supply Co ....G...... 412 835-4314
  Bethel Park (G-1439)

2394 Canvas Prdts

549 Industrial Holdings Inc ....F...... 610 622-7211
  Philadelphia (G-13320)
A Mamaux & Son Inc ....F...... 412 771-8432
  Mc Kees Rocks (G-10599)
A Wbrown Awning ....G...... 610 372-2908
  Reading (G-16308)
Aerial Signs & Awnings Inc ....F...... 610 494-1415
  Chester (G-3037)
Als Awning Shop Inc ....G...... 814 456-6262
  Erie (G-5183)
American Cruising Sails Inc ....G...... 814 456-7245
  Erie (G-5186)
◆ Amish Country Gazebos Inc ....G...... 717 665-0365
  Manheim (G-10367)
Auto Seat Cover Company ....G...... 814 453-5897
  Erie (G-5196)
Canvas Awnings Inc ....G...... 215 423-1213
  Philadelphia (G-13498)
Canvas Specialties Inc ....G...... 570 825-9282
  Hanover Township (G-6983)
Covers All Canvas Products ....G...... 412 653-6010
  Pittsburgh (G-14881)
▲ Craft-Bilt Manufacturing Co ....D...... 215 721-7700
  Souderton (G-17731)
Creative Awnings Inc ....E...... 610 282-3305
  Coopersburg (G-3626)
Creative Logistics Ltd ....E...... 724 458-6560
  Grove City (G-6782)
◆ D C Humphrys Co ....D...... 215 307-3363
  Philadelphia (G-13599)
David A Bierig ....G...... 814 459-8001
  North East (G-12737)
E R Schantz Inc ....G...... 610 272-3603
  Norristown (G-12652)
▲ Ehmke Manufacturing Co Inc ....D...... 215 324-4200
  Philadelphia (G-13664)
F Creative Impressions Inc ....G...... 215 743-7577
  Philadelphia (G-13690)
Fehl Awning Company Inc ....G...... 717 776-3162
  Walnut Bottom (G-18789)
G T Watts Inc ....G...... 717 732-1111
  Enola (G-5080)
▲ Garrett Liners Inc ....E...... 215 295-0200
  Levittown (G-9838)
Grid Electric Inc ....E...... 610 466-7030
  Coatesville (G-3306)
Grimms Inc ....G...... 724 346-4952
  Sharon (G-17435)
HA Harper Sons Inc ....G...... 610 485-4776
  Upper Chichester (G-18663)
Hamilton Awning Co ....F...... 724 774-7644
  Beaver (G-983)
Hendersons Tarpaulin Covers ....G...... 717 944-5865
  Middletown (G-11056)
Hibbs Awning Company Inc ....G...... 724 437-1494
  Uniontown (G-18630)
Indutex Inc ....F...... 724 935-1482
  McKeesport (G-10673)

S
I
C

Jefco Manufacturing Inc..............F 215 334-3220
Wynnewood *(G-20270)*

Kreiders Canvas Service Inc..............G...... 717 656-7387
Leola *(G-9791)*

Laurel Industrial Fabric Entps ....E 724 567-5689
Apollo *(G-681)*

Leathersmith Inc ....G...... 717 933-8084
Myerstown *(G-11891)*

▲ Lightweight Manufacturing Inc........F 610 435-4720
Whitehall *(G-19883)*

Madhavan Inc ....G...... 610 534-2600
Folcroft *(G-6009)*

Mamaux Supply Co ....F 412 782-3456
Pittsburgh *(G-15249)*

McCloy Awning Company ....F 412 271-4044
Swissvale *(G-18192)*

McCullough Manufacturing Inc ....G...... 717 687-8784
Strasburg *(G-18092)*

▲ Merlot Trpulin Sidekit Mfg Inc ....E 412 828-7664
Verona *(G-18757)*

Mid-State Awning Inc ....G...... 814 355-8979
Bellefonte *(G-1108)*

◆ Monarch Global Brands Inc..............D...... 215 482-6100
Philadelphia *(G-14033)*

Mt Lebanon Awning & Tent Co ....F 412 221-2233
Presto *(G-16104)*

Nicewonger Awning Co ....G...... 724 837-5920
Greensburg *(G-6692)*

O K McCloyawnings Inc ....F 412 271-4044
Swissvale *(G-18193)*

Organic Climbing LLC ....G...... 651 245-1079
Philipsburg *(G-14523)*

Quality Canvas ....G...... 724 329-1571
Confluence *(G-3468)*

Quality Canvas ....G...... 814 695-8343
Duncansville *(G-4461)*

Reeves Awning Inc ....F 570 876-0350
Jermyn *(G-8309)*

Reinhardt Awning Co..............G...... 610 965-2544
Emmaus *(G-5041)*

Robertson Manufacturing Inc..............E 610 869-9600
West Grove *(G-19705)*

Rose A Rupp ....G...... 412 622-6827
Pittsburgh *(G-15496)*

Rothman Awning Co Inc ....F 412 589-9974
Pittsburgh *(G-15498)*

Sprung Instant Structures Inc ....G...... 610 391-9553
Allentown *(G-399)*

Tarp America Inc ....G...... 724 339-4771
Murrysville *(G-11869)*

Tmu Inc ....F 717 392-0578
Lancaster *(G-9220)*

Todd Lengle & Co Inc ....E 610 777-0731
Reading *(G-16541)*

Tumacs Corp ....E 412 653-1188
Pittsburgh *(G-15660)*

Undercoveralls Inc ....F 610 519-0858
Bryn Mawr *(G-2336)*

Wagner Tarps Inc ....G...... 814 849-3422
Brookville *(G-2275)*

Waugaman Awnings ....G...... 724 837-1239
Greensburg *(G-6728)*

Wondering Canvas Tattoos ....G...... 717 244-8260
Dallastown *(G-3983)*

Y T & A Inc ....F 717 854-3806
York *(G-20722)*

2395 Pleating & Stitching For The Trade

4 Life Promotions LLC ....G...... 215 919-4985
Philadelphia *(G-13319)*

A & D Fashions Inc ....G...... 610 967-1440
Emmaus *(G-5017)*

A R Groff Transport Inc ....G...... 717 859-4661
Leola *(G-9764)*

Air Conway Inc ....F 610 534-0500
Collingdale *(G-3402)*

All Pro Embroidery Inc ....F 412 942-0735
Pittsburgh *(G-14675)*

Anything Sews ....G...... 412 486-1055
Glenshaw *(G-6480)*

Art Stitch Inc ....G...... 717 652-8992
Harrisburg *(G-7091)*

Art Tech Designs ....G...... 412 754-0391
Elizabeth *(G-4855)*

Artistagraphics Inc ....F 412 271-3252
Pittsburgh *(G-14727)*

Arty Embroidery & Design Inc ....F....... 215 423-8114
Philadelphia *(G-13417)*

Atlantic Embroidery Company ....G...... 215 514-2154
Glenside *(G-6507)*

Awards & More ....G...... 724 444-1040
Gibsonia *(G-6325)*

Blue Mountain Sports AP Inc ....G...... 717 263-4124
Chambersburg *(G-2912)*

Bluestar Marketing Inc ....G...... 215 886-4002
Elkins Park *(G-4900)*

Bsg Custom Designs LLC ....G...... 610 867-7361
Bethlehem *(G-1475)*

Busy Bee Embroidery & More ....G...... 717 540-1955
Harrisburg *(G-7102)*

C & S Sports & Promotions ....G...... 724 775-1655
Monaca *(G-11287)*

Caffrey Michael & Sons ....G...... 610 252-1299
Easton *(G-4659)*

Callery Sr John ....G...... 412 344-9010
Pittsburgh *(G-14805)*

Charles F May Co ....G...... 215 634-7257
Philadelphia *(G-13527)*

Craig Hollern ....E 814 539-2974
Johnstown *(G-8366)*

Creative Embroidery Designs ....G...... 412 793-1923
Douglassville *(G-4173)*

Creative Stitches By Dina Inc ....G...... 724 863-4104
Irwin *(G-8152)*

Cross Works Embroidery Sp Inc ....G...... 610 261-1690
Coplay *(G-3642)*

Custom Corner Sportswear ....G...... 724 588-1667
Greenville *(G-6740)*

Cutting Edge Embroidery Inc ....G...... 412 732-9990
Pittsburgh *(G-14897)*

Danowski ....G...... 717 328-5057
Mercersburg *(G-10985)*

Designs Unlimited ....G...... 717 367-4405
Elizabethtown *(G-4872)*

Donora Sportswear Company Inc ....G...... 724 929-2387
Donora *(G-4151)*

Eberharts Cstm Embroidery Inc ....G...... 215 639-9530
Bensalem *(G-1185)*

Embroider Smith ....G...... 570 961-8781
Scranton *(G-17234)*

Embroidery Etc Inc ....G...... 412 381-6884
Pittsburgh *(G-14968)*

Embroidery Concepts ....G...... 724 225-3644
Washington *(G-19168)*

Embroidery Factory Inc ....G...... 570 654-7640
Pittston *(G-15749)*

Fawn Embroidery Punching Svcs ....G...... 717 382-4855
New Park *(G-12430)*

Fawn Industries Inc ....D...... 717 382-4855
New Park *(G-12431)*

Great Lakes Custom Graphics ....G...... 814 723-0110
Warren *(G-19029)*

Greater Pttsbrgh Spcialty Advg ....E 412 821-5976
Millvale *(G-11223)*

Griffith Pottery House Inc ....G...... 215 887-2222
Oreland *(G-13021)*

Heritage Gallery of Lace & Int ....G...... 717 359-4121
Littlestown *(G-10067)*

Hess Embroidery & Uniforms LLC ....G...... 610 816-5234
Reading *(G-16401)*

Hollys Embroidery ....G...... 717 599-5975
Harrisburg *(G-7151)*

Home Town Sports Inc ....G...... 412 672-2242
McKeesport *(G-10671)*

Hub LLC ....G...... 215 561-8090
Philadelphia *(G-13839)*

Ibis Tek Apparel LLC ....E 724 586-2179
Butler *(G-2408)*

Iehle Enterprises Inc ....E 717 859-1113
Lancaster *(G-9055)*

Imagewear Ltd ....G...... 704 999-9979
Easton *(G-4704)*

In Stitches Embroidery ....G...... 570 368-5525
Montoursville *(G-11441)*

Kampus Klothes Inc ....E 215 357-0892
Warminster *(G-18904)*

▲ Kartri Sales Company Inc ....E 570 785-3365
Forest City *(G-6054)*

▲ Kevins Wholesale LLC ....D...... 570 344-9055
Scranton *(G-17250)*

Keystone Uniform Cap LP ....E 215 821-3434
Philadelphia *(G-13933)*

La Perla LLC ....G...... 717 561-1257
Harrisburg *(G-7166)*

Larry D Mays ....F 814 833-7988
Erie *(G-5360)*

Lee Regional Health System Inc ....G...... 814 254-4716
Johnstown *(G-8403)*

Log Cabin Embroidery Inc ....G...... 724 327-5929
Murrysville *(G-11855)*

Marathon Embroidery ....G...... 215 627-8848
Philadelphia *(G-13990)*

Mark Im Com ....G...... 724 282-0997
Butler *(G-2421)*

Mayport Cottons & Quilt Shop ....G...... 814 365-2212
Mayport *(G-10546)*

▲ Milliken Nonwovens LLC ....G...... 610 544-7117
Broomall *(G-2298)*

Mister Bobbin Embroidery Inc ....F 717 838-5841
Annville *(G-654)*

▲ Moritz Embroidery Works Inc ....E 570 839-9600
Mount Pocono *(G-11736)*

N J K Lettering ....G...... 724 356-2583
Avella *(G-837)*

National Embroidery ....G...... 610 323-4400
Pottstown *(G-16020)*

New Look Uniform & Embroidery ....F 814 944-5515
Altoona *(G-530)*

Nice Threads International ....G...... 610 259-0788
Clifton Heights *(G-3257)*

Nicholas Wohlfarth ....F 412 373-6811
Pittsburgh *(G-15337)*

Nittany EMB & Digitizing ....F 814 359-0905
State College *(G-17998)*

▲ Penn Emblem Company ....D...... 215 632-7800
Feasterville Trevose *(G-5926)*

Perennial Pleasures LLC ....G...... 484 318-8376
Paoli *(G-13147)*

Physical Graffi-Tees ....G...... 610 439-3344
Allentown *(G-351)*

Preferred Sportswear Inc ....G...... 484 494-3067
Darby *(G-4024)*

Ras Sports Inc ....E 814 833-9111
Erie *(G-5457)*

Ravine Inc ....F 814 946-5006
Altoona *(G-541)*

Ray Derstine ....G...... 215 723-6573
Telford *(G-18311)*

Reid S Tannery ....G...... 610 929-4403
Reading *(G-16495)*

Rockland Embroidery Inc ....E 610 682-5042
Topton *(G-18415)*

▲ Rowe Screen Print Inc ....F 717 774-8920
New Cumberland *(G-12190)*

Royalty Promotions Inc ....G...... 215 794-2707
Furlong *(G-6233)*

S B I Inc ....G...... 610 595-3300
Prospect Park *(G-16119)*

Samfam Inc ....G...... 814 941-1915
Altoona *(G-546)*

Sansom Quilting & EMB Co ....F 215 627-6990
Philadelphia *(G-14278)*

Schuylkill Vly Spt Trappe Ctr ....F 877 711-8100
Pottstown *(G-16044)*

Sew Special ....G...... 724 438-1765
Uniontown *(G-18641)*

Sez Special Stitching Inc ....F 814 339-6734
Osceola Mills *(G-13057)*

Sharper Embroidery Inc ....G...... 570 714-3617
Swoyersville *(G-18199)*

Shenk Athletic Equipment Co ....F 717 766-6600
Mechanicsburg *(G-10888)*

Shields Embroidery By Design ....F 412 531-2321
Pittsburgh *(G-15533)*

Smith Prints Inc ....G...... 215 997-8077
Chalfont *(G-2888)*

Snowberger Embroidery ....G...... 814 696-6499
Duncansville *(G-4464)*

Stitch Art Custom Embroidery ....G...... 814 382-2702
Conneaut Lake *(G-3479)*

Stitch Crazy ....G...... 610 526-0154
Conshohocken *(G-3607)*

Stitch U S A Inc ....F 215 699-0123
North Wales *(G-12828)*

Stitch Wizards Inc ....G...... 412 264-9973
Coraopolis *(G-3726)*

Stitches Embroidery Inc ....E 412 781-7046
Pittsburgh *(G-15585)*

Summer Valley EMB ....F 570 386-3711
New Ringgold *(G-12443)*

T Shirt Printer ....G...... 717 367-1167
Elizabethtown *(G-4889)*

Thomas A Laskowski ....F 215 957-1544
Warminster *(G-18981)*

Tiadaghton Embroidery ....G...... 570 398-4477
Jersey Shore *(G-8323)*

Tom Russell ....G...... 724 746-5029
Houston *(G-7882)*

Trautman Associates Inc ....F 570 743-0430
Shamokin Dam *(G-17429)*

Tukes Tearoff ....G....... 570 695-3171
  Tremont (G-18483)
USA Embroidery & Silkscre ....G....... 570 837-7700
  Beavertown (G-1029)
Vitabru Embroidery ....G....... 610 296-0181
  Malvern (G-10345)
W S Lee & Sons LP ....G....... 814 317-5010
  Altoona (G-556)
Waterfront Embroidery ....G....... 412 337-9269
  Homestead (G-7697)
X-Deco LLC ....F....... 412 257-9755
  Pittsburgh (G-15725)
York Towne Embroidery Works ....G....... 717 854-0006
  York (G-20753)

2396 Automotive Trimmings, Apparel Findings, Related Prdts

4 Life Promotions LLC ....G....... 215 919-4985
  Philadelphia (G-13319)
A & W Screen Printing Inc ....F....... 717 738-2726
  Ephrata (G-5089)
Action Sportswear Inc ....F....... 610 623-1820
  Primos (G-16106)
Ad-Art Sign Co ....G....... 412 373-0960
  Pittsburgh (G-14649)
◆ Advantech US Inc ....E....... 412 706-5400
  Beaver (G-977)
Al Tedeschi ....G....... 724 746-3755
  Canonsburg (G-2535)
Allegheny Plastics Inc ....D....... 724 776-0100
  Cranberry Township (G-3800)
▲ American Process Lettering Inc .....C....... 610 623-9000
  Primos (G-16107)
American Ribbon Manufacturers ....E....... 570 421-7470
  Stroudsburg (G-18103)
Annville Shoulder Strap Co ....E....... 717 867-4831
  Annville (G-642)
▲ Auto Accessories America Inc ....C....... 717 667-3004
  Reedsville (G-16621)
▲ B L Tees Inc ....F....... 724 325-1882
  Export (G-5591)
◆ Berwick Offray LLC ....B....... 570 752-5934
  Berwick (G-1311)
Berwick Offray LLC ....A....... 570 752-5934
  Berwick (G-1312)
C & S Sports & Promotions ....G....... 724 775-1655
  Monaca (G-11287)
Coinco Inc ....E....... 814 425-7476
  Cochranton (G-3338)
Craig Hollern ....E....... 814 539-2974
  Johnstown (G-8366)
CSS Industries Inc ....C....... 610 729-3959
  Plymouth Meeting (G-15840)
Custom Corner Sportswear ....G....... 724 588-1667
  Greenville (G-6740)
Custom Printed Graphics Inc ....E....... 412 881-8208
  Pittsburgh (G-14895)
Daves Pro Shop Inc ....E....... 814 834-6116
  Saint Marys (G-16961)
Dispatch Printing Inc ....F....... 814 870-9600
  Erie (G-5248)
East Penn Container Dctg Inc ....E....... 610 944-3227
  Fleetwood (G-5971)
Epic Apparel LLC ....G....... 412 350-9543
  West Mifflin (G-19736)
Excl Inc ....E....... 412 856-7616
  Trafford (G-18456)
Grafika Commercial Prtg Inc ....B....... 610 678-8630
  Reading (G-16396)
Grip-Flex Corp ....E....... 215 743-7492
  Philadelphia (G-13789)
Heritage Screen Printing Inc ....G....... 215 672-2382
  Warminster (G-18894)
Hunts Promotions ....G....... 814 623-2751
  Bedford (G-1054)
Industrial Nameplate Inc ....E....... 215 322-1111
  Warminster (G-18898)
Joseph Lagrua ....G....... 814 274-7163
  Coudersport (G-3783)
Kampus Klothes Inc ....E....... 215 357-0892
  Warminster (G-18904)
Karl Dodson ....G....... 717 938-6132
  New Cumberland (G-12188)
Kinteco Inc ....G....... 610 921-1494
  Temple (G-18332)
Lawrence Schiff Silk Mills Inc ....D....... 717 776-4073
  Newville (G-12605)
Lesko Enterprises Inc ....C....... 814 756-4030
  Albion (G-46)

Log Cabin Embroidery Inc ....G....... 724 327-5929
  Murrysville (G-11855)
M & M Manufacturing Co ....E....... 724 274-0767
  Cheswick (G-3111)
Magnum Screening ....G....... 570 489-2902
  Olyphant (G-12993)
▲ Marco Manufacturing Co Inc ....E....... 215 463-2332
  Philadelphia (G-13992)
Mt Lebanon Awning & Tent Co ....E....... 412 221-2233
  Presto (G-16104)
Mystic Assembly & Dctg Co ....E....... 215 957-0280
  Warminster (G-18926)
Nittany EMB & Digitizing ....F....... 814 359-0905
  State College (G-17998)
Nittany Printing and Pubg Co ....D....... 814 238-5000
  State College (G-18000)
Nk Graphics Inc ....G....... 717 838-8324
  Palmyra (G-13127)
▲ Ohiopyle Prints Inc ....C....... 724 329-4652
  Ohiopyle (G-12939)
Peerless Printery ....G....... 610 258-5226
  Easton (G-4741)
Print Shop Inc ....G....... 570 784-4020
  Bloomsburg (G-1796)
Printdropper Inc ....F....... 412 657-6170
  Pittsburgh (G-15443)
Printex LLC ....G....... 412 371-6667
  Pittsburgh (G-15444)
▲ Priscilla of Boston Inc ....D....... 610 943-5000
  Conshohocken (G-3592)
Quick Print Center PA ....G....... 717 637-2838
  Hanover (G-6939)
Ras Sports Inc ....E....... 814 833-9111
  Erie (G-5457)
Ravine Inc ....F....... 814 946-5006
  Altoona (G-541)
Ron Lee Inc ....F....... 570 784-6020
  Bloomsburg (G-1799)
▲ Rowe Screen Print Inc ....F....... 717 774-8920
  New Cumberland (G-12190)
▲ Rowland Printing Inc ....E....... 610 933-7400
  Phoenixville (G-14575)
Schuylkill Vly Spt Trappe Ctr ....F....... 877 711-8100
  Pottstown (G-16044)
Scream Graphix Inc ....G....... 215 638-3900
  Philadelphia (G-14288)
Screening Room Inc ....G....... 610 363-5405
  Exton (G-5729)
Sez Sew Stitching Inc ....F....... 814 339-6734
  Osceola Mills (G-13057)
Shenk Athletic Equipment Co ....F....... 717 766-6600
  Mechanicsburg (G-10888)
Statement Walls LLC ....G....... 267 266-0869
  Philadelphia (G-14341)
Stineman Management Corp ....E....... 814 495-4686
  South Fork (G-17778)
Sunset Tees ....G....... 717 737-9919
  Camp Hill (G-2519)
T Shirt Loft ....G....... 724 452-4380
  Zelienople (G-20823)
T Shirt Printer ....G....... 717 367-1167
  Elizabethtown (G-4889)
Thomas A Laskowski ....F....... 215 957-1544
  Warminster (G-18981)
Three Soles Corp ....G....... 717 762-1945
  Waynesboro (G-19428)
Todd Lengle & Co Inc ....E....... 610 777-0731
  Reading (G-16541)
Todd Weikel ....G....... 610 779-5508
  Reading (G-16542)
Trbz Ink LLC ....G....... 267 918-2242
  Philadelphia (G-14403)
Triple D Screen Printing ....E....... 215 788-4877
  Bristol (G-2211)
Tukes Tearoff ....G....... 570 695-3171
  Tremont (G-18483)
Vocam Corp ....G....... 215 348-7115
  Doylestown (G-4344)
◆ Wallquest Inc ....D....... 610 293-1330
  Wayne (G-19389)
Warrior Wiper Wraps LLC ....G....... 720 577-9499
  Philadelphia (G-14461)
Xiii Touches Printing ....F....... 484 754-6504
  King of Prussia (G-8700)
◆ Yarrington Mills Corporation ....E....... 215 674-5125
  Hatboro (G-7311)

2397 Schiffli Machine Embroideries

▲ Moritz Embroidery Works Inc ....E....... 570 839-9600
  Mount Pocono (G-11736)

2399 Fabricated Textile Prdts, NEC

Ad Distinction ....G....... 215 736-0672
  Morrisville (G-11552)
◆ Agas Mfg Inc ....E....... 212 777-1178
  Philadelphia (G-13354)
All American Sweats Inc ....F....... 412 922-8999
  Pittsburgh (G-14674)
Ambassador Bags & Spats Mfg Co ......G....... 610 532-7840
  Folcroft (G-5998)
Ameri Print Flag Inc ....G....... 610 409-9603
  Collegeville (G-3367)
American Fence Inc ....F....... 610 437-1944
  Whitehall (G-19861)
▼ Baker Ballistics LLC ....F....... 717 625-2016
  Lititz (G-9994)
▲ Beilers Manufacturing & Supply .....G....... 717 768-0174
  Ronks (G-16804)
Beilers Manufacturing & Supply ....F....... 717 656-2179
  Leola (G-9772)
C&H7 LLC ....G....... 215 887-7411
  Exton (G-5658)
Del Val Flag Philadelphia Sp ....G....... 610 235-7179
  Aston (G-758)
Fenner Inc ....G....... 717 665-2421
  Manheim (G-10381)
▲ Fenner Inc ....F....... 717 665-2421
  Manheim (G-10382)
Fenner Dunlop Americas LLC ....C....... 412 249-0692
  Pittsburgh (G-15012)
Flags For All Seasons Inc ....G....... 610 688-4235
  Wayne (G-19331)
▲ Flagzone LLC ....C....... 610 367-9900
  Gilbertsville (G-6372)
Graphcom Inc ....C....... 800 699-1664
  Gettysburg (G-6295)
Hillside Horse Sew-It ....G....... 717 548-2293
  Peach Bottom (G-13199)
Humphrys Flag Company Inc ....E....... 215 922-0510
  Pottstown (G-15999)
Innovative Designs Inc ....G....... 412 799-0350
  Pittsburgh (G-15127)
J Carlton Jones & Associates ....G....... 267 538-5009
  Philadelphia (G-13881)
Jan Lew Textile Corp ....D....... 610 857-8050
  Parkesburg (G-13176)
◆ Jetnet Corporation ....D....... 412 741-0100
  Sewickley (G-17396)
John W Keplinger & Son ....G....... 610 666-6191
  Norristown (G-12674)
K & B Outfitters Inc ....E....... 724 266-1133
  Ambridge (G-623)
Kabar Tack and Feed ....G....... 717 416-0069
  New Oxford (G-12414)
▼ Life Support International ....E....... 215 785-2870
  Langhorne (G-9308)
Majestic Windsocks ....G....... 717 264-3113
  Chambersburg (G-2956)
▲ Msjc Inc ....G....... 717 930-0718
  Middletown (G-11065)
▲ N F C Industries Inc ....E....... 215 766-8890
  Plumsteadville (G-15812)
Otte Gear LLC ....F....... 917 923-6230
  New Hope (G-12311)
▲ Penn Emblem Company ....D....... 215 632-7800
  Feasterville Trevose (G-5926)
Port Richman Holdings LLC ....G....... 212 777-1178
  Philadelphia (G-14189)
▲ S & H Ltd ....G....... 215 426-2775
  West Chester (G-19633)
Sheep Thrills ....G....... 724 465-2617
  Indiana (G-8127)
Showtex Logistics LLC ....E....... 570 218-0054
  Berwick (G-1343)
Skydive Store Inc ....G....... 856 629-4600
  Bushkill (G-2369)
Skyline Technology Inc ....G....... 610 296-7501
  Malvern (G-10319)
Standard Pennant Company Inc ....E....... 814 427-2066
  Big Run (G-1657)
Stineman Management Corp ....E....... 814 495-4686
  South Fork (G-17778)
Swirling Silks Inc ....G....... 610 584-5595
  Harleysville (G-7061)
▲ Total Equestrian Inc ....G....... 215 721-1247
  Souderton (G-17768)
Willow Grove Auto Top Inc ....G....... 215 659-3276
  Willow Grove (G-20150)

S I C

24 LUMBER AND WOOD PRODUCTS, EXCEPT FURNITURE

2411 Logging

A M Logging LLC ....F 814 349-8089
  Spring Mills (G-17884)
Accurate Logging LLC ....G 724 354-3094
  Creekside (G-3874)
Albert Miller Logging Inc ....G 570 295-4040
  Lock Haven (G-10084)
▼ Appalachian Timber Products ....F 724 329-1990
  Markleysburg (G-10479)
Awf Logging ....G 814 577-5070
  Penfield (G-13221)
Basinger Logging ....G 724 455-1067
  Connellsville (G-3491)
Beavers Logging Inc ....G 570 842-4034
  Gouldsboro (G-6567)
▼ Bedford Forest Products Inc ....G 814 977-3712
  Bedford (G-1041)
Berdines Custom Hardwoods ....G 724 447-2535
  Holbrook (G-7637)
Black Logging ....G 717 263-6446
  Chambersburg (G-2911)
Blue Ox Timber Resources Inc ....F 814 437-2019
  Franklin (G-6116)
Brian Kingsley ....G 570 888-8668
  Athens (G-810)
Brown & Lounsberry Inc ....G 610 847-2242
  Ottsville (G-13060)
Byers Logging LLC ....G 717 530-5995
  Shippensburg (G-17520)
C Clark & Sons ....G 814 652-5370
  Everett (G-5568)
Cable Hardwoods Inc ....F 724 452-5927
  Portersville (G-15926)
Cameron Lumber LLP ....E 814 749-9635
  Homer City (G-7671)
Canfield Logging LLC ....G 570 224-4507
  Damascus (G-3990)
CB Excavating & Logging LLC ....G 570 756-2749
  Susquehanna (G-18178)
Charlies Tree Service ....G 814 943-1131
  Altoona (G-491)
CL Logging Inc ....G 814 842-3725
  Hyndman (G-8048)
CLB Logging ....G 814 784-3301
  Clearville (G-3240)
Coastal Treated Products Co ....E 610 932-5100
  Oxford (G-13075)
Colonial Logging ....F 814 583-5901
  Luthersburg (G-10122)
Coulter Logging ....G 814 236-2855
  Curwensville (G-3949)
Crown Hardwood West Inc ....G 717 436-9677
  Mifflintown (G-11112)
Curtis Leljedal Trading Loggn ....G 570 924-3938
  Forksville (G-6056)
D & K Logging Inc ....G 814 663-0210
  Spartansburg (G-17849)
D E Hyde Contracting ....G 814 228-3685
  Genesee (G-6271)
D Luther Trucking ....G 814 952-2136
  Punxsutawney (G-16132)
D&R Logging ....G 570 345-4632
  Pine Grove (G-14591)
Dean W Brouse & Sons ....G 570 374-7695
  Kreamer (G-8817)
Deems Logging ....G 724 657-7384
  Volant (G-18772)
Diiulio Logging ....G 814 965-3183
  Johnsonburg (G-8345)
Dimec Rail Service ....E 844 362-9221
  Pottstown (G-15983)
Diversified Logging ....G 724 228-4143
  Eighty Four (G-4838)
Donnelley Jr Joseph ....G 570 998-2541
  Cogan Station (G-3359)
Double A Logging LLC ....G 814 885-6844
  Kersey (G-8556)
Dunns Sawmill LLP ....G 570 253-5217
  Honesdale (G-7710)
E & E Logging & Sons ....G 814 886-4440
  Loretto (G-10102)
Edmund Burke Inc ....F 724 932-5200
  Adamsville (G-25)
Edsell & Edsell Logging ....G 570 746-3203
  Wyalusing (G-20250)

Elick Logging Inc ....G 814 743-5546
  Cherry Tree (G-3032)
Elite Timber Harvesting LLC ....G 570 836-2453
  Factoryville (G-5756)
Elk River Logging Inc ....G 814 787-4327
  Weedville (G-19458)
Emanuel K Fisher ....G 570 547-2599
  Allenwood (G-441)
Energex Inc ....G 717 436-2400
  Mifflintown (G-11115)
Eschrich and Son Logging ....G 814 362-1371
  Lewis Run (G-9875)
Eugene Flynn Logging ....G 814 772-1219
  Kersey (G-8558)
Fowlers Logging ....G 814 684-9883
  Tyrone (G-18583)
Fritz Logging ....G 814 623-6011
  Bedford (G-1050)
Full Strut Logging LLC ....G 814 323-5292
  Corry (G-3761)
Fulton Forest Products ....E 814 782-3448
  Shippenville (G-17561)
Gaberseck Bros ....G 814 274-0763
  Coudersport (G-3781)
Gary Fike Logging ....G 724 329-7175
  Farmington (G-5861)
Gary T Rossman ....G 814 837-7017
  Kane (G-8463)
Gates Logging LLC ....G 814 353-1238
  Howard (G-7890)
Gessner Logging & Sawmill Inc ....F 717 365-3883
  Lykens (G-10133)
Gilbert Logging and Supply ....G 717 528-4919
  York Springs (G-20766)
Gillens Logging Inc ....G 814 236-3999
  Curwensville (G-3951)
Gosnell Logging ....G 814 776-2038
  Ridgway (G-16710)
Guy Sexton Timber Mgmt ....G 717 548-3422
  Peach Bottom (G-13197)
Harold Graves Trucking ....G 814 654-7836
  Spartansburg (G-17851)
Heritage Fence & Deck LLC ....G 610 476-0003
  Skippack (G-17598)
Hopkins Logging ....G 814 827-1681
  Titusville (G-18383)
Horlacher & Sherwood ....G 570 836-6298
  Tunkhannock (G-18539)
Horsepower Logging ....G 814 274-2236
  Coudersport (G-3782)
J & L Logging ....G 717 687-8096
  Lancaster (G-9067)
J&B Tree Service ....G 570 282-1193
  Carbondale (G-2678)
James Confer ....G 814 945-7013
  Ludlow (G-10118)
James K Reisinger ....G 717 275-2124
  Loysville (G-10116)
James Sluga ....G 814 778-5100
  Mount Jewett (G-11643)
Je Logging ....G 724 455-5723
  Normalville (G-12623)
Jersey Shore Steel Company ....C 570 368-2601
  Montoursville (G-11443)
JOB Logging Inc ....G 814 772-0513
  Ridgway (G-16714)
John Carvell Logging ....G 717 354-8136
  New Holland (G-12254)
John F Biel ....G 814 945-6306
  Ludlow (G-10119)
John Hunt Logging ....G 814 967-4464
  Townville (G-18445)
John L Luchs Logging ....G 814 772-5767
  Ridgway (G-16715)
John R Holt ....G 814 837-8687
  Kane (G-8468)
John W Burdge ....G 814 259-3901
  Blairs Mills (G-1711)
Johnson Sawmill Logging ....G 717 532-7784
  Orrstown (G-13033)
Joni Britton Logging ....G 814 887-9920
  Smethport (G-17635)
Justick & Justick Inc ....G 570 840-0187
  Sprng Brk Twp (G-17933)
Justin L Zehr ....G 717 582-6436
  Ickesburg (G-8052)
K J Shaffer Milled Products ....F 570 698-8650
  Lake Ariel (G-8889)
Kio Logging LLC ....G 570 584-0283
  Hughesville (G-7895)

Klingler Family Sawmill ....G 717 677-4957
  Biglerville (G-1665)
Koppers Industries Inc ....E 412 227-2001
  Pittsburgh (G-15189)
Koppers Utility Indus Pdts Inc ....D 412 620-6238
  Pittsburgh (G-15193)
Kovalick Lumber Co ....F 814 263-4928
  Frenchville (G-6217)
Krause C W & Son Lumber ....G 814 378-8919
  Houtzdale (G-7883)
Kt Zimmerman Lumber & Logging ......G 570 345-2542
  Pine Grove (G-14595)
Lapps Logging ....G 814 642-7949
  Port Allegany (G-15894)
Lefever Logging ....G 717 587-7889
  Bethel (G-1396)
Lipinski Logging and Lbr Inc ....G 814 385-4101
  Kennerdell (G-8498)
Malsom Logging ....G 570 840-1044
  Moscow (G-11598)
Marietta Fence Experts LLC ....G 724 925-6100
  Hunker (G-7929)
Mark A Kulka ....G 814 726-7331
  Warren (G-19039)
Mark Case Logging ....G 570 729-8856
  Beach Lake (G-975)
Mark R Stairs ....G 814 634-0871
  Meyersdale (G-11016)
Mason Hill Logging ....G 814 546-2478
  Driftwood (G-4377)
Matteson Logging Inc ....G 814 848-9863
  Genesee (G-6273)
McVeys Logging & Lumbe ....G 814 542-2776
  Mount Union (G-11745)
Mitcheltree Bros ....G 814 665-4019
  Corry (G-3768)
Mitcheltree Bros Logging & Lbr ....G 724 598-7885
  Pulaski (G-16125)
New Growth Resources Inc ....G 814 837-2206
  Kane (G-8473)
Nicole M Reasner ....G 814 259-3827
  Neelyton (G-11997)
Noga Logging ....G 724 224-6369
  New Kensington (G-12363)
Northwest Logging LLC ....G 814 598-1350
  Kane (G-8474)
Oak Ridge Logging LLC ....G 717 687-8168
  Quarryville (G-16275)
Omega Logging Inc ....F 724 342-5430
  Wheatland (G-19839)
Out of Site Stump Removal LLC ....G 610 692-9907
  West Chester (G-19614)
Patrick Donovan ....G 724 238-9038
  Ligonier (G-9963)
Paul Danfelt ....G 814 448-2592
  Mapleton Depot (G-10431)
▲ Pendu Manufacturing Inc ....E 717 354-4348
  New Holland (G-12272)
Penn West Trading Co Inc ....G 814 664-7649
  Corry (G-3771)
Pequignot Logging ....G 570 659-5251
  Covington (G-3792)
Perry S Swanson Logging ....G 814 837-7020
  Kane (G-8477)
R & J Logging Inc ....G 717 933-5646
  Bethel (G-1398)
R & K Wettlaufer Logging Inc ....G 570 924-4752
  New Albany (G-12015)
R and C Logging ....G 814 590-4422
  Reynoldsville (G-16661)
R E B Bloxham Inc ....G 570 222-4693
  Clifford Township (G-3249)
R J & Sons Hoffman ....E 570 539-2428
  Mount Pleasant Mills (G-11730)
Rhoades Logging ....G 814 757-4711
  Sugar Grove (G-18145)
Ricky E Shaffer ....G 814 328-2318
  Brookville (G-2270)
Robbins Logging & Lumber ....F 814 236-3384
  Olanta (G-12961)
Robert A Crooks ....G 724 541-2746
  Marion Center (G-10477)
Rockwell Lumber Co Inc ....G 717 597-7428
  Greencastle (G-6631)
Roderick Duvall ....G 814 735-4969
  Crystal Spring (G-3938)
Ron Andrus Logging ....G 814 435-6484
  Gaines (G-6237)
Ronnas Ruff Bark Trucking Inc ....G 814 221-4410
  Shippenville (G-17563)

Ruffcutt Timber LLC ....G....... 724 626-7306
Connellsville (G-3507)

S & H Logging LLC ....G....... 570 966-8958
Mifflinburg (G-11102)

S & S Loggs Inc ....G....... 814 339-7375
West Decatur (G-19691)

Scalpy Hollow Timber Service ....G....... 717 284-2862
Drumore (G-4379)

Scott Zimmerman Logging Inc ....G....... 814 965-5070
Wilcox (G-19900)

Sewell Logging ....G....... 814 837-7136
Harrisburg (G-7214)

Shaffer Logging ....G....... 814 827-1729
Titusville (G-18395)

▼ Shetler Lumber Company Inc ....E....... 814 796-0303
Waterford (G-19269)

Shields Logging LLC ....G....... 814 778-6183
Kane (G-8478)

Smith Logging ....G....... 814 371-2698
Reynoldsville (G-16665)

Smith Lumber Co ....F....... 570 923-0188
Renovo (G-16650)

Smoker Logging Inc ....G....... 814 486-2570
Emporium (G-5075)

Snyder & Sons Tree Surgeons ....G....... 610 932-2966
Lincoln University (G-9975)

Spigelmyer Wood Products Inc ....F....... 717 248-6555
Lewistown (G-9948)

Stalnaker Lumber ....G....... 724 447-2248
New Freeport (G-12219)

Stella-Jones Corporation ....E....... 814 371-7331
Du Bois (G-4421)

Stout Lumber Company ....G....... 814 443-9920
Somerset (G-17712)

T & B Logging Inc ....G....... 570 561-4847
Tunkhannock (G-18549)

T&G Logging ....G....... 814 589-1731
Grand Valley (G-6573)

Taylor Logging ....G....... 814 642-2788
Port Allegany (G-15895)

Thoman Logging ....G....... 570 265-4993
Le Raysville (G-9543)

Thomas Timberland Enterprises ....G....... 814 359-2890
Bellefonte (G-1122)

Timinski Logging Co ....G....... 570 457-2641
Sprng Brk Twp (G-17934)

Todd A Forsythe ....G....... 814 512-1457
Weedville (G-19460)

Todd Smith Logging Inc ....G....... 814 887-2183
Smethport (G-17637)

Trumco Inc ....E....... 814 382-7767
Atlantic (G-814)

Twisted Tmber Deadwood Log Inc ....G....... 215 541-4140
Pennsburg (G-13258)

W D Zwicky & Son Inc ....E....... 484 248-5300
Fleetwood (G-5982)

◆ Wenturine Bros Lumber Inc ....D....... 814 948-6050
Nicktown (G-12622)

Wodrig Logging Corporation ....G....... 570 435-0783
Muncy (G-11842)

Ye Logging Veneer ....G....... 814 387-6503
Moshannon (G-11604)

2421 Saw & Planing Mills

A & L Wood Inc ....E....... 570 539-8922
Mount Pleasant Mills (G-11724)

A W Sawmill ....G....... 717 535-5081
Mifflintown (G-11107)

Aldenville Log and Lumberinc ....G....... 570 785-3141
Prompton (G-16109)

Allegheny Wood Pdts Intl Inc ....E....... 814 354-7304
Marble (G-10433)

Allegheny Wood Products Inc ....D....... 814 354-7304
Marble (G-10434)

Andreas Lumber Inc ....G....... 570 379-3644
Wapwallopen (G-18807)

Axion LLC ....G....... 484 243-6127
Blue Bell (G-1813)

Bailey Wood Products Inc ....G....... 610 756-6827
Kempton (G-8490)

Baillie Lumber Co LP ....D....... 814 827-1877
Titusville (G-18375)

Bakers Lumber Company Inc ....F....... 814 743-6671
Cherry Tree (G-3031)

Baumerts Wood Shavings ....G....... 570 758-1744
Herndon (G-7597)

Beegle Saw Mill ....G....... 814 784-5697
Clearville (G-3238)

Beiler Sawmill ....G....... 717 284-5271
Quarryville (G-16264)

Belden Brick Sales & Svc Inc ....F....... 215 639-6561
Trevose (G-18487)

Big Valley Hardwood ....F....... 717 483-6440
Allensville (G-107)

Bingaman & Son Lumber Inc ....E....... 814 723-2612
Clarendon (G-3167)

Bingaman & Son Lumber Inc ....E....... 570 726-7795
Mill Hall (G-11173)

▼ Blue Triangle Hardwoods LLC ....C....... 814 652-9111
Everett (G-5567)

Boswell Lumber Company ....E....... 814 629-5625
Boswell (G-1881)

Bowser Lumber Co Inc ....F....... 814 277-9956
Mahaffey (G-10170)

Bradford Forest Inc ....E....... 570 835-5000
Bradford (G-1958)

Brett W Shope ....G....... 814 643-2921
Huntingdon (G-7940)

Brian O Keffe ....G....... 570 477-3962
Sweet Valley (G-18187)

Brode Lumber Inc ....F....... 814 635-3436
Saxton (G-17100)

Brown Timber and Land Co Inc ....F....... 724 547-7777
Acme (G-15)

Brumbaugh Lumber LLC ....G....... 814 542-8880
Shirleysburg (G-17569)

Bucks Valley Sawmill LLC ....G....... 717 567-9663
Newport (G-12488)

Burke Parsons Bowlby Corp ....G....... 814 371-3042
Du Bois (G-4385)

Buterbaugh Bros Land & Timber ....G....... 814 948-9510
Barnesboro (G-938)

Buttonwood Lumber Company Inc ....G....... 570 324-3421
Liberty (G-9951)

Bwp Hardwoods Inc ....D....... 814 849-7331
Brookville (G-2258)

Bylers Saw Mill ....G....... 724 964-8528
New Wilmington (G-12464)

C & S Lumber Company Inc ....G....... 814 544-7544
Roulette (G-16833)

C C Allis & Sons Inc ....E....... 570 744-2631
Wyalusing (G-20247)

Cadosia Valley Lumber Company ....G....... 570 676-3400
Newfoundland (G-12476)

Cameron Lumber LLP ....E....... 814 749-9635
Homer City (G-7671)

Carol Zuzek ....G....... 814 837-7090
Kane (G-8460)

Center Hardwood LLC ....F....... 814 684-3600
Tyrone (G-18579)

Cessna Bros Lumber ....F....... 814 767-9518
Clearville (G-3239)

Champion Lumber Company Inc ....F....... 724 455-3401
Champion (G-3003)

Charles Shavings Inc ....G....... 570 458-4945
Benton (G-1278)

Clark F Burger Inc ....G....... 610 681-4762
Kresgeville (G-8820)

Clark H Ream Lumber ....G....... 814 445-8185
Somerset (G-17680)

▼ Clear Lake Lumber Inc ....E....... 800 237-1191
Spartansburg (G-17847)

Coastal Forest Resources Co ....G....... 814 654-7111
Spartansburg (G-17848)

Collins Pine Company ....D....... 814 837-6941
Kane (G-8461)

Collins Tool Corporation ....E....... 717 543-6070
Lewistown (G-9927)

Cover Lumber Co ....G....... 814 750-2006
Bedford (G-1047)

Curry Lumber Co ....G....... 724 438-1911
Hopwood (G-7776)

Curtis Baker Lumber Inc ....F....... 814 425-3020
Cochranton (G-3340)

Custeads Sawmill Inc ....G....... 814 425-3863
Guys Mills (G-6810)

D & D Wood Sales Inc ....E....... 814 948-8672
Nicktown (G-12620)

◆ Danzer Services Inc ....E....... 724 827-3700
Darlington (G-4025)

David Copeland ....G....... 814 756-3250
Albion (G-42)

David M Byler ....F....... 717 667-6157
Belleville (G-1130)

▼ Deer Park Lumber Inc ....D....... 570 836-1133
Tunkhannock (G-18538)

Diamond Road Resawing LLC ....G....... 717 738-3741
Ephrata (G-5100)

Donald Beiswenger Inc ....G....... 814 886-8341
Gallitzin (G-6245)

Donald EBY ....G....... 814 767-9406
Clearville (G-3241)

Dubel D H Mill & Lumber Co ....G....... 717 993-2566
Stewartstown (G-18060)

Dwight Lewis Lumber Co Inc ....E....... 570 924-3507
Hillsgrove (G-7635)

E H Beiler Sawmill LLC ....G....... 610 593-5989
Paradise (G-13156)

EBY Sawmill ....E....... 814 767-8060
Clearville (G-3242)

Ed Nicholson & Sons Lumber Co ....F....... 724 628-4440
Connellsville (G-3496)

EDM Co ....E....... 717 626-2186
Lititz (G-10005)

Edwin Johnson & Sons ....G....... 570 458-4488
Bloomsburg (G-1780)

Efflands Sawmill Repair S ....G....... 717 369-2391
Fort Loudon (G-6058)

Emily J High ....G....... 570 345-6268
Pine Grove (G-14593)

▲ Emporium Hardwoods Oper Co LLC C
814 486-3764
Emporium (G-5057)

Estemerwalt Lumber Pdts LLC ....F....... 570 729-8572
Honesdale (G-7711)

Eutsey Lumber Co Inc ....F....... 724 887-8404
Scottdale (G-17191)

Everlast Plastic Lumber Inc ....F....... 610 562-8336
Hamburg (G-6839)

Fairmans Wood Processing Inc ....G....... 724 349-6778
Creekside (G-3876)

Fedinetz Sawmill ....G....... 724 796-9461
Mc Donald (G-10573)

▼ Forcey Lumber Co Inc ....E....... 814 857-5002
Woodland (G-20211)

Foulk Equipment Leasing Inc ....G....... 610 838-2260
Bethlehem (G-1516)

Frank D Suppa Lumber Inc ....F....... 814 723-7360
Warren (G-19026)

Frey Lumber Company Inc ....E....... 724 564-1888
Smithfield (G-17648)

▲ Frontier Wood Products Inc ....E....... 215 538-2330
Quakertown (G-16195)

Frosty Hollow Hardwoods ....G....... 724 568-2406
Vandergrift (G-18728)

Fulton Forest Products ....E....... 814 782-3448
Shippenville (G-17561)

Gerald King Lumber Co Inc ....F....... 724 887-3688
Ruffs Dale (G-16872)

Gessner Logging & Sawmill Inc ....E....... 717 365-3883
Lykens (G-10133)

Gift Lumber Co Inc ....G....... 610 689-9483
Douglassville (G-4176)

Great Meadows Sawmill Frm Inc ....G....... 724 329-7771
Farmington (G-5862)

Greentree Lumber ....F....... 814 257-9878
Smicksburg (G-17638)

Greenwood Products ....G....... 717 337-2050
Gettysburg (G-6296)

Gutchess Lumber Co Inc ....D....... 724 537-6447
Latrobe (G-9479)

Guyon Industries Inc ....G....... 717 528-0154
York Springs (G-20767)

H & H General Excavating Co ....D....... 717 225-4669
Spring Grove (G-17877)

Harmony Hill Forestry ....E....... 570 247-2676
Rome (G-16799)

Herndon Reload Company ....E....... 570 758-2597
Herndon (G-7599)

Hickman Lumber Company ....G....... 724 867-9441
Emlenton (G-5010)

Hickman Lumber Company ....F....... 814 797-0555
Emlenton (G-5011)

Higgins Saw Mill ....G....... 717 235-4189
Glen Rock (G-6457)

Highland Forest Resources Inc ....E....... 814 927-2226
Marienville (G-10457)

▼ Highland Forest Resources Inc ....E....... 814 837-6760
Kane (G-8466)

Hitchcock E & R & Sons Lbr Inc ....G....... 814 229-9402
Strattanville (G-18097)

Hoffman Brothers Lumber Inc ....F....... 717 694-3340
Richfield (G-16679)

Holt and Bugbee Company ....E....... 724 277-8510
Mount Braddock (G-11619)

Horner Lumber Company ....G....... 814 629-5861
Boswell (G-1883)

Horsepower Wood Products ....G....... 814 447-5662
Orbisonia (G-13006)

Hyma Devore Lumber Mill Inc ....E....... 814 563-4646
Youngsville (G-20772)

S
I
C

Imperial Eagle Products Inc ....F 717 252-1573
Wrightsville (G-20238)

J C Moore Industries Inc ....F 724 475-3185
Fredonia (G-6181)

J F Rohrbaugh & Co ....D...... 800 800-4353
Hanover (G-6906)

J Mastrocola Hauling Inc ....G...... 610 631-1773
Norristown (G-12672)

John L Luchs Logging ....G...... 814 772-5767
Ridgway (G-16715)

John M Fink Lumber ....G...... 570 435-0362
Montoursville (G-11444)

Kerex Inc ....E 814 735-3838
Breezewood (G-2003)

Kern Brothers Lumber Inc ....E 814 893-5042
Stoystown (G-18081)

Keslar Lumber Co ....G...... 724 455-3210
White (G-19845)

King Logging and Sawmill ....G...... 717 365-3341
Spring Glen (G-17873)

Klingler Family Sawmill ....G...... 717 677-4957
Biglerville (G-1665)

Kochs Portable Sawmill & Lbr ....G...... 717 776-7961
Newville (G-12604)

◆ Koppers Industries Del Inc ....G...... 412 227-2001
Pittsburgh (G-15191)

Kovalick Lumber Co ....F 814 263-4928
Frenchville (G-6217)

▼ Kuhns Bros Lumber Co Inc ....E 570 568-1412
Lewisburg (G-9914)

L & R Lumber Inc ....G...... 717 463-3411
Mc Alisterville (G-10550)

Laceyville Lumber Inc ....G...... 570 869-1212
Laceyville (G-8872)

Lapp Lumber Co ....G...... 717 442-4116
Paradise (G-13162)

Larimer & Norton Inc ....F 814 757-4532
Russell (G-16881)

Leonard Forest Products ....F 724 329-4703
Markleysburg (G-10481)

Lewis Lumber & Supply Co Inc ....G...... 412 828-3810
Oakmont (G-12919)

Lindenmuth Saw Mill ....G...... 570 875-3546
Ashland (G-734)

Lindner Wood Technology Inc ....F 610 820-8310
Allentown (G-297)

Lipinski Logging and Lbr Inc ....G...... 814 385-4101
Kennerdell (G-8498)

Marsh Planing Inc ....G...... 814 827-9947
Titusville (G-18388)

Martin Fabricating Inc ....E 610 435-5700
Allentown (G-309)

Martindale Lumber Co Inc ....E 814 736-3032
Portage (G-15919)

Mastowski Lumber Company Inc ....E 724 455-7502
Normalville (G-12624)

Matson Industries Inc ....E 814 849-5334
Brookville (G-2263)

◆ Matson Lumber Company ....F 814 849-5334
Brookville (G-2264)

Mayberry Supply Company Inc ....G...... 724 652-6008
Volant (G-18775)

Mellott Wood Preserving Inc ....E 717 573-2519
Needmore (G-11996)

Mitchell Hardwood ....G...... 814 796-4925
Waterford (G-19266)

Mount Hope Lumber ....G...... 814 789-4953
Guys Mills (G-6811)

Moxham Lumber Co ....E 814 536-5186
Johnstown (G-8411)

Moyers Sawmill Company ....G...... 610 488-1462
Bernville (G-1302)

New Growth Resources Inc ....G...... 814 837-2206
Kane (G-8473)

Nicholas Shea Co Inc ....G...... 610 296-9036
Reading (G-16456)

Noah Shirk Sawmill ....G...... 717 354-0192
Ephrata (G-5132)

Noll Pallet Inc ....E 610 926-2500
Leesport (G-9671)

Oakes & McClelland Co ....F 724 588-6400
Greenville (G-6761)

OConnell Hardwood Inc ....E 814 796-2297
Waterford (G-19267)

Omega Logging Inc ....F 724 342-5430
Wheatland (G-19839)

▼ Ordie Price Sawmill Inc ....F 570 222-3986
South Gibson (G-17780)

PA Pellets LLC ....F 814 848-9970
Ulysses (G-18604)

Patiova LLC ....G...... 610 857-1359
Parkesburg (G-13181)

Patterson Lumber Co Inc ....E 814 435-2210
Galeton (G-6241)

Peacheys Sawmill Inc ....F 717 483-6336
Belleville (G-1134)

Pellheat Inc ....G...... 724 850-8169
Greensburg (G-6699)

Penn-Sylvan International Inc ....G...... 724 932-5200
Adamsville (G-26)

Penn-Sylvan International Inc ....F 814 654-7111
Spartansburg (G-17853)

Phillips Wood Products Inc ....F 570 726-3515
Mill Hall (G-11180)

Pinch Road Sawmill ....G...... 717 665-1096
Manheim (G-10403)

Pittman Bros Lumber ....G...... 814 652-6396
Everett (G-5577)

Pittston Lumber & Mfg Co ....E 570 654-3328
Pittston (G-15776)

Pleasant Valley Saw Mill ....G...... 814 767-9016
Clearville (G-3243)

Porosky Lumber Company Inc ....F 570 798-2326
Preston Park (G-16105)

Portzlines Pallets ....G...... 717 694-3951
Mount Pleasant Mills (G-11729)

Precision Pallets & Lumber Inc ....F 814 395-5351
Addison (G-28)

Price C L Lumber LLC ....F 814 349-5505
Aaronsburg (G-2)

Price Lumber Company ....G...... 814 231-0260
Port Matilda (G-15904)

▲ Quaker Hardwoods Company ....G...... 215 538-0401
Quakertown (G-16237)

R J & Sons Hoffman ....E 570 539-2428
Mount Pleasant Mills (G-11730)

R J Junk ....G...... 717 734-3838
Honey Grove (G-7768)

R J S Wood Products Inc ....G...... 570 689-7630
Lake Ariel (G-8890)

R L Kingsley Lumber Company ....F 570 596-3575
Milan (G-11148)

R Vbridendolph & Sons Inc ....G...... 717 328-3650
Mercersburg (G-10994)

Ralph Stuck Lumber Company ....G...... 570 539-8666
Mount Pleasant Mills (G-11731)

◆ Ram Forest Products Inc ....D...... 814 697-7185
Shinglehouse (G-17512)

◆ Red Square Corp ....G...... 412 422-8631
Pittsburgh (G-15473)

Rgm Hardwoods Inc ....E 570 842-4533
Moscow (G-11603)

Richard K Mohn ....G...... 717 762-7646
Waynesboro (G-19423)

Robbins Logging & Lumber ....F 814 236-3384
Olanta (G-12961)

Robert Pearce & Sons ....F 724 286-9757
Smicksburg (G-17639)

Robinson Sawmill Works ....G...... 570 559-7454
Shohola (G-17579)

Rock Creek Lumber ....F 570 756-2909
Thompson (G-18346)

Rockwell Lumber Co Inc ....G...... 717 597-7428
Greencastle (G-6631)

Roderick Duvall ....G...... 814 735-4969
Crystal Spring (G-3938)

Ronald Kauffman ....G...... 717 589-3789
Millerstown (G-11208)

Rorabaugh Lumber Co ....F 814 845-2277
Burnside (G-2363)

Rosenberry Bros Lumber Co ....F 717 349-7196
Fannettsburg (G-5858)

S & S Processing Inc ....E 724 535-3110
West Pittsburg (G-19752)

S&S Custom Sawing ....G...... 717 694-3248
Richfield (G-16682)

Sand Patch Mill LLC ....G...... 814 634-9772
Meyersdale (G-11019)

Scalpy Hollow Timber Service ....G...... 717 284-2862
Drumore (G-4379)

Schetler Lumber - Sawmill ....G...... 814 590-9592
Punxsutawney (G-16162)

Seneca Hardwood Lumber Co Inc ....E 814 498-2241
Cranberry (G-3797)

Sensenigs Wood Shavings ....G...... 717 336-2047
Denver (G-4093)

Sfk Ventures Inc ....D...... 610 825-5151
King of Prussia (G-8672)

Shady Elms Sawmill LLC ....G...... 724 356-2594
Hickory (G-7631)

Shady Hill Hardwood Inc ....G...... 717 463-9475
Mifflintown (G-11135)

Shaffer Brothers Lumber Co ....G...... 814 842-3996
Hyndman (G-8051)

Shaffer Products LLC ....F 717 597-2688
Greencastle (G-6633)

Shanks Portable Sawmills ....G...... 717 334-0352
Orrtanna (G-13037)

Shedio Logging & Lumber ....G...... 724 794-1321
Renfrew (G-16642)

▼ Shetler Lumber Company Inc ....E 814 796-0303
Waterford (G-19269)

Shirks Saw Mill ....G...... 717 776-7083
Shippensburg (G-17550)

Snooks Rhine & Arnold ....G...... 570 658-3410
Mc Clure (G-10561)

Solts Sawmill Inc ....E 610 682-6179
Mertztown (G-11004)

Somerset Door and Column Co ....E 814 445-9608
Somerset (G-17708)

Spigelmyer Wood Products Inc ....F 717 248-6555
Lewistown (G-9948)

Stella-Jones Corporation ....G...... 814 371-7331
Du Bois (G-4421)

Sterling Forest Products ....G...... 570 226-4233
Tafton (G-18205)

Straightline Saw Mill Inc ....G...... 724 639-3090
Saltsburg (G-17053)

Summit Forest Resources Inc ....E 724 329-3314
Markleysburg (G-10484)

Superior Lumber Inc ....F 814 684-3420
Tyrone (G-18594)

◆ T Baird McIlvain Company ....C 717 630-0025
Hanover (G-6960)

Thomas Timberland Enterprises ....G...... 814 359-2890
Bellefonte (G-1122)

Timberstrong LLC ....G...... 484 357-8730
Kempton (G-8496)

Tom Cesarino Lumber ....G...... 724 329-0467
Farmington (G-5863)

▼ Tony L Stec Lumber Company ....F 814 563-9002
Garland (G-6263)

True Cut Sawmills Inc ....G...... 814 694-2192
Centerville (G-2836)

Trumco Inc ....E 814 382-7767
Atlantic (G-814)

▼ Tuscarora Hardwoods Inc ....D...... 717 582-4122
Elliottsburg (G-4922)

Ufp Eastern Division Inc ....G...... 724 399-2992
Parker (G-13166)

Ufp Parker LLC ....G...... 724 399-2992
Parker (G-13167)

W J Reining & Sons Inc ....F 570 729-7325
Beach Lake (G-976)

Walker Lumber Co Inc ....E 814 857-7642
Woodland (G-20215)

Wattsburg Lumber Co LLC ....G...... 814 739-2770
Wattsburg (G-19284)

◆ Wenturine Bros Lumber Inc ....D...... 814 948-6050
Nicktown (G-12622)

◆ Werzalit of America Inc ....D...... 814 362-3881
Bradford (G-1995)

Weyerhaeuser Company ....C 814 827-4621
Titusville (G-18404)

◆ Wheeland Lumber Co Inc ....D...... 570 324-6042
Liberty (G-9952)

William Richter Lumber ....G...... 814 926-4608
Rockwood (G-16794)

Williams and Sons Lumber Co ....E 814 735-4295
Crystal Spring (G-3939)

Wilmer R EBY ....G...... 717 597-1090
Waynesboro (G-19430)

▼ Wilson Hardwoods Inc ....E 814 827-0277
Titusville (G-18405)

Winters Lumber Co ....G...... 570 435-2231
Cogan Station (G-3363)

Wlh Enterprise ....G...... 814 498-2040
Emlenton (G-5016)

Wood Mizer ....G...... 814 259-9976
Shade Gap (G-17418)

Wood-Mizer Holdings Inc ....G...... 814 259-9976
Shade Gap (G-17419)

Yardcraft Products LLC ....G...... 866 210-9273
New Holland (G-12295)

Yoder Lumber Co Inc ....G...... 717 463-9253
Mc Alisterville (G-10554)

Zooks Sawmill LLC ....G...... 610 593-1040
Christiana (G-3145)

2426 Hardwood Dimension & Flooring Mills

A W Everett Furniture Frames ....F 610 377-0170
  Lehighton (G-9708)
◆ Ahf Products LLC ....A 800 233-3823
  Lancaster (G-8923)
Allegheny Mtn Hardwood Flrg ....F 724 867-9441
  Emlenton (G-5004)
Allegheny Wood Products Inc ....D 814 354-7304
  Marble (G-10434)
◆ Appalachian Wood Products Inc .....B 814 765-2003
  Clearfield (G-3212)
Armstrong Flooring Inc ....A 717 672-9611
  Lancaster (G-8940)
▲ Armstrong Hardwood Flooring Co ..A 717 672-9611
  Lancaster (G-8941)
Babcock Lumber Company ....G 814 239-2281
  Pittsburgh (G-14746)
▲ Bareville Woodcraft Co ....F 717 656-6261
  Leola (G-9771)
Bennett Flooring LLC ....E 724 586-9350
  Butler (G-2378)
Bingaman & Son Lumber Inc ....E 570 726-7795
  Mill Hall (G-11173)
Boswell Lumber Company ....E 814 629-5625
  Boswell (G-1881)
Brian O Keffe ....G 570 477-3962
  Sweet Valley (G-18187)
Brodart Co ....E 570 326-2461
  Montgomery (G-11368)
Brown Timber and Land Co Inc ....F 724 547-7777
  Acme (G-15)
▼ Brownlee Lumber Inc ....E 814 328-2991
  Brookville (G-2255)
C A Elliot Lumber Co Inc ....F 814 544-7523
  Roulette (G-16834)
Carol Zuzek ....G 814 837-7090
  Kane (G-8460)
Center Hardwood LLC ....F 814 684-3600
  Tyrone (G-18579)
Centria Inc ....E 724 251-2208
  Coraopolis (G-3674)
Clymer Quality Hardwood ....G 724 463-1827
  Clymer (G-3271)
Collins Pine Company ....D 814 837-6941
  Kane (G-8461)
Colonial Hardwoods & Logging ....F 814 583-5901
  Luthersburg (G-10121)
Conestoga Wood Spc Corp ....C 570 658-9663
  Beavertown (G-1025)
Culver Hardwoods ....G 814 827-3202
  Titusville (G-18377)
Czar Imports Inc ....D 800 577-2927
  Huntingdon Valley (G-7973)
◆ Danzer Lumber North Amer Inc ......C 814 368-3701
  Bradford (G-1966)
▼ Deer Park Lumber Inc ....D 570 836-1133
  Tunkhannock (G-18538)
Dsc2 Inc ....F 980 223-2270
  York (G-20458)
Ed Nicholson & Sons Lumber Co........F 724 628-4440
  Connellsville (G-3496)
Facio Concepts LLC ....G 717 945-8609
  East Earl (G-4543)
Frank D Suppa Lumber Inc ....F 814 723-7360
  Warren (G-19026)
Fulton Forest Products ....E 814 782-3448
  Shippenville (G-17561)
Gutchess Lumber Co Inc ....D 724 537-6447
  Latrobe (G-9479)
Gwynn-E-Co Inc ....G 215 423-6400
  Philadelphia (G-13794)
Heritage Wood Products LLC ....G 814 629-9265
  Boswell (G-1882)
▼ Highland Forest Resources Inc ....E 814 837-6760
  Kane (G-8466)
▲ Homerwood Hardwood Flooring Co .D 814 827-3855
  Titusville (G-18382)
Hope Good Hardwoods Inc ....G 610 350-1556
  Landenberg (G-9250)
Horstcraft Millworks LLC ....G 717 694-9222
  Richfield (G-16680)
Hyma Devore Lumber Mill Inc ....E 814 563-4646
  Youngsville (G-20772)
Infinite Quest Cabinetry Corp ....G 301 222-3592
  Red Lion (G-16601)
Itl Corp ....D 814 463-7701
  Endeavor (G-5079)
J M Wood Products ....F 717 483-6700
  Allensville (G-108)

John L Luchs Logging ....G 814 772-5767
  Ridgway (G-16715)
John M Rohrbaugh Co Inc ....G 717 244-2895
  Red Lion (G-16602)
Keiths Cabinet Company ....E 814 793-2614
  Martinsburg (G-10525)
▲ Kgm Gaming LLC ....E 215 430-0388
  Philadelphia (G-13934)
Kovalick Lumber Co ....F 814 263-4928
  Frenchville (G-6217)
Lew-Hoc Wood Products Inc ....E 814 486-0359
  Emporium (G-5067)
▼ Lewis & Hockenberry Inc ....E 814 486-0359
  Emporium (G-5068)
Lewis Lumber Products Inc ....D 570 584-6167
  Picture Rocks (G-14585)
M & C Lumber Co Inc ....E 717 573-2200
  Warfordsburg (G-18813)
Mick Brothers Lumber Inc ....E 814 664-8700
  Corry (G-3767)
Mitcheltree Bros Logging & Lbr ....G 724 598-7885
  Pulaski (G-16125)
Modern Cabinet and Cnstr Co............F 814 942-1000
  Altoona (G-528)
Musselman Lumber - US Lbm LLC......D 717 354-4321
  New Holland (G-12264)
Nelson Bridge Inc ....G 908 996-6646
  New Hope (G-12309)
New Germany Wood Products Inc ....F 814 495-5923
  Summerhill (G-18154)
New Wave Custom Wdwkg Inc ....E 570 251-8218
  Honesdale (G-7718)
Noah Shirk Sawmill ....G 717 354-0192
  Ephrata (G-5132)
Oakes & McClelland Co ....D 724 588-6400
  Greenville (G-6761)
▼ Ordie Price Sawmill Inc ....F 570 222-3986
  South Gibson (G-17780)
Patterson Lumber Co Inc ....D 814 435-2210
  Galeton (G-6241)
▲ Pendu Manufacturing Inc ....E 717 354-4348
  New Holland (G-12272)
▲ Penn Wood Products Inc ....D 717 259-9551
  East Berlin (G-4524)
▲ RAD Mfg LLC ....D 570 752-4514
  Nescopeck (G-12001)
RAD Mfg LLC ....E 570 752-4514
  Nescopeck (G-12002)
◆ Ram Forest Products Inc ....D 814 697-7185
  Shinglehouse (G-17512)
Rgm Hardwoods Inc ....E 570 842-4533
  Moscow (G-11603)
Richard K Mohn ....G 717 762-7646
  Waynesboro (G-19423)
Robbins Logging & Lumber ....F 814 236-3384
  Olanta (G-12961)
Seneca Hardwood Lumber Co Inc ....E 814 498-2241
  Cranberry (G-3797)
▼ Shetler Lumber Company Inc ....E 814 796-0303
  Waterford (G-19269)
▲ Specialty Surfaces Intl Inc ....C 877 686-8873
  King of Prussia (G-8679)
▲ Strick Corporation ....F 215 949-3600
  Fairless Hills (G-5799)
Structural Glulam LLC ....E 717 355-9813
  New Holland (G-12286)
Tellus Three Sixty ....E 717 628-1866
  Palmyra (G-13133)
Thomas Gross Woodworking ....G 724 593-7044
  Ligonier (G-9967)
Thomas Timberland Enterprises ....G 814 359-2890
  Bellefonte (G-1122)
▼ Thompson Maple Products Inc ....E 814 664-7717
  Corry (G-3775)
Tindall Virgin Timbers Clnl WD...........G 717 548-2435
  Peach Bottom (G-13202)
Walker Lumber Co Inc ....E 814 857-7642
  Woodland (G-20215)
Walter and Jackson Inc ....E 610 593-5195
  Christiana (G-3144)
▼ Weaber Inc ....C 717 867-2212
  Lebanon (G-9638)
Weaber Inc ....E 814 827-4621
  Titusville (G-18403)
◆ Wenturine Bros Lumber Inc ....D 814 948-6050
  Nicktown (G-12622)
◆ Werzalit of America Inc ....D 814 362-3881
  Bradford (G-1995)
Weyerhaeuser Company ....E 814 827-4621
  Titusville (G-18404)

◆ Wheeland Lumber Co Inc ....D 570 324-6042
  Liberty (G-9952)
◆ Wilson Global Inc ....D 724 883-4952
  Jefferson (G-8272)
Wood Specialty Company Inc ....F 610 539-6384
  Norristown (G-12724)
◆ Woodcraft Products Co Inc ....D 215 329-2793
  Philadelphia (G-14485)
Woodcraft Products Co Inc ....E 215 426-6123
  Philadelphia (G-14486)
Woodside Glueing ....G 814 349-5646
  Rebersburg (G-16579)
Wt Hardwoods Group Inc ....F 717 867-2212
  Lebanon (G-9639)

2429 Special Prdt Sawmills, NEC

Scenic Road Manufacturing.................G 717 768-7300
  Gordonville (G-6565)
◆ Wilson Global Inc ....D 724 883-4952
  Jefferson (G-8272)

2431 Millwork

▲ 4 Daughters LLC ....D 570 283-5934
  Kingston (G-8711)
▼ 84 Lumber Company ....B 724 228-8820
  Eighty Four (G-4830)
A & V Woodwork Co ....F 215 727-8832
  Philadelphia (G-13322)
Abel Millwork LLC ....G 412 296-2254
  Finleyville (G-5951)
▲ Advanced Stair Systems - Penns .....F 215 256-7981
  Harleysville (G-7013)
Advanced Trim Specialties ....E 717 442-8098
  Kinzers (G-8731)
▲ Ajjp Corporation ....C 215 968-6677
  Newtown (G-12495)
▲ Al Lorenzi Lumber Co Inc ....D 724 222-6100
  Canonsburg (G-2534)
Alan Pepper Designs ....G 412 244-9299
  Pittsburgh (G-14659)
Allegheny Millwork Pbt ....C 724 873-8700
  Lawrence (G-9534)
Allegheny Wood Works Inc ....E 814 774-7338
  Lake City (G-8897)
Allensville Planing Mill Inc ....F 717 543-4954
  Huntingdon (G-7938)
Allensville Planing Mill Inc ....F 717 248-9688
  Lewistown (G-9924)
Allied Millwork of Pittsburgh ....G 412 471-9229
  Pittsburgh (G-14685)
Alvin Reiff Woodworking ....G 570 966-1149
  Mifflinburg (G-11092)
AMD Group Inc ....G 610 972-4491
  Riegelsville (G-16743)
American Mllwk & Cabinetry Inc ....E 610 965-0040
  Emmaus (G-5019)
American Stair & Cabinetry Inc ....C 717 709-1061
  Chambersburg (G-2904)
American Wood Design Inc ....F 302 792-2100
  Chester (G-3039)
Appalachian Millwork ....G 724 539-1944
  Latrobe (G-9456)
◆ Appalachian Wood Products Inc ......B 814 765-2003
  Clearfield (G-3212)
Apple Way Cstm Stairs Railing ....E 717 369-0502
  Saint Thomas (G-17036)
Architectural Millwork Assoc ....G 215 699-0346
  North Wales (G-12789)
Architectural Woodsmiths Inc ....D 717 532-7700
  Shippensburg (G-17515)
Asels Cabinet Company ....G 814 677-3063
  Rouseville (G-16835)
B & L Manufacturing Corp ....F 412 784-9400
  Pittsburgh (G-14745)
B & L Woodworking ....G 717 354-5430
  Kinzers (G-8732)
Barmah Co ....G 724 539-8477
  Latrobe (G-9459)
Beam S Custom Woodworking ....F 610 286-9040
  Morgantown (G-11518)
Beaver Dam Woodworks LLC ....G 610 273-7656
  Honey Brook (G-7737)
Bentley & Collins Company ....E 570 546-3250
  Muncy (G-11810)
Best Group Holdings Inc ....E 814 536-1422
  Johnstown (G-8357)
Biltwood Architectural Mllwk ....F 717 593-9400
  Greencastle (G-6600)
BMC East LLC ....E 717 866-2167
  Myerstown (G-11877)

Boswell Lumber Company ....E....... 814 629-5625
Boswell *(G-1881)*

Bounds Wood Products Ltd ....G....... 215 646-2122
North Wales *(G-12793)*

Brahma Building Products LLC ....F....... 717 567-2571
Newport *(G-12487)*

Brampton Entp & Design LLC ....G....... 484 678-4855
Thorndale *(G-18353)*

Brandywine Woodworks LLC ....G....... 610 793-7979
West Chester *(G-19514)*

Breezecraft LLC ....G....... 717 397-8584
Lancaster *(G-8958)*

Bristol Millwork Co Inc ....F....... 215 533-1921
Philadelphia *(G-13484)*

Brookside Woodworks ....G....... 717 768-0241
Narvon *(G-11917)*

Burke & Sons Inc ....E....... 814 938-7303
Punxsutawney *(G-16129)*

Campbells Custom Woodworks LLC ....G....... 484 300-4175
Pottstown *(G-15969)*

Cantwell Woodworking LLC ....E....... 215 710-3030
Fort Washington *(G-6064)*

Carpenter Shop Inc ....F....... 814 848-7448
Ulysses *(G-18601)*

Cedars Wdwkg & Renovations LLC ....G....... 717 392-1736
Lancaster *(G-8972)*

Center Hardwood LLC ....F....... 814 684-3600
Tyrone *(G-18579)*

Cider Press Woodworks LLC ....G....... 215 804-1100
Quakertown *(G-16178)*

Ciw Enterprises Inc ....E....... 800 233-8366
Mountain Top *(G-11755)*

◆ **Clarion Boards LLC** ....C....... 814 226-0851
Shippenville *(G-17557)*

▲ **Clarion Laminates LLC** ....D....... 814 226-8032
Shippenville *(G-17559)*

Clear Visions Inc ....G....... 717 236-4526
Harrisburg *(G-7106)*

Closet-Tier ....G....... 412 421-7838
Pittsburgh *(G-14862)*

◆ **Conestoga Wood Spc Corp** ....A....... 717 445-6701
East Earl *(G-4540)*

Conoco Woodworking ....G....... 717 536-3948
Blain *(G-1710)*

▼ **Contemprary Artisans Cabinetry** ....E....... 215 723-8803
Telford *(G-18276)*

Cornellcookson Inc ....C....... 570 474-6773
Mountain Top *(G-11757)*

Cornerstone Woodworks LLC ....G....... 717 866-0230
Myerstown *(G-11880)*

Craig A Scholedice Inc ....F....... 610 683-8910
Kutztown *(G-8838)*

Cumberland Woodcraft Co Inc ....E....... 717 243-0063
Carlisle *(G-2705)*

Custer Ave Woodworking LLC ....G....... 717 354-3999
New Holland *(G-12242)*

▲ **Custom Doorcraft LLC** ....F....... 717 768-7613
Bird In Hand *(G-1672)*

Custom Entryways & Millwork ....G....... 814 798-2500
Stoystown *(G-18074)*

Custom Stair Builders Inc ....G....... 717 261-0551
Chambersburg *(G-2922)*

D and S Artistic Wdwkg LLC ....G....... 973 495-7008
Henryville *(G-7566)*

D and S Artistic Wdwkg LLC ....G....... 973 495-7008
Stroudsburg *(G-18113)*

D G Woodworks LLC ....G....... 215 368-8001
Lansdale *(G-9356)*

David M Oley ....F....... 570 247-5599
Rome *(G-16797)*

Dennis Downing ....G....... 724 598-0043
New Castle *(G-12081)*

▲ **Detroit Switch Inc** ....E....... 412 322-9144
Pittsburgh *(G-14919)*

Dimpter Woodworking ....G....... 215 855-2335
Lansdale *(G-9361)*

Dmm Woodworking ....G....... 717 390-2828
Lancaster *(G-8999)*

Doellken- Woodtape Inc ....G....... 610 929-1910
Temple *(G-18328)*

Donald Beiswenger Inc ....G....... 814 886-8341
Gallitzin *(G-6245)*

Doyle Design ....G....... 215 456-9745
Philadelphia *(G-13642)*

Dp Millwork Inc ....G....... 215 996-1179
Hatfield *(G-7335)*

▲ **Durawood Products Inc** ....C....... 717 336-0220
Denver *(G-4071)*

E B Endres Inc ....E....... 814 643-1860
Huntingdon *(G-7942)*

Eagle Woodworking LLC ....G....... 484 764-7275
Northampton *(G-12849)*

Ed Nicholson & Sons Lumber Co ....F....... 724 628-4440
Connellsville *(G-3496)*

▲ **Eden Inc** ....E....... 814 797-1160
Knox *(G-8809)*

EDM Co ....E....... 717 626-2186
Lititz *(G-10005)*

Eidemiller Door Co ....G....... 724 668-8294
New Alexandria *(G-12018)*

Eisenhardt Mills Inc ....E....... 610 253-2791
Easton *(G-4677)*

Elc Manufacturing ....G....... 570 655-3060
West Pittston *(G-19755)*

Eli K Lapp Jr ....G....... 717 768-0258
Gordonville *(G-6553)*

Elite Vinyl Railings LLC ....G....... 717 354-0524
New Holland *(G-12248)*

Everite Door Company ....F....... 814 652-5143
Everett *(G-5571)*

Fine Line Homes ....F....... 717 561-2040
Harrisburg *(G-7129)*

Fiorella Woodworking Inc ....G....... 215 843-5870
Philadelphia *(G-13702)*

Fishers Woodworking ....G....... 570 725-2310
Loganton *(G-10095)*

Flagship City Hardwoods ....G....... 814 835-1178
Erie *(G-5292)*

Forest Hill Woodworking ....G....... 717 806-0193
Paradise *(G-13157)*

Forest Ridge Woodworking ....G....... 717 442-3191
Paradise *(G-13158)*

Foster-Kmetz Woodworking ....G....... 570 325-8222
Jim Thorpe *(G-8340)*

Frank Daddario Wdwrkng ....G....... 610 476-3414
Audubon *(G-825)*

Freedom Millwork Corp ....G....... 215 642-2213
Pipersville *(G-14616)*

Fremer Moulding Inc ....F....... 814 265-0671
Brockway *(G-2226)*

Frosty Hollow Hardwoods ....G....... 724 568-2406
Vandergrift *(G-18728)*

Frp Door Concepts Inc ....G....... 215 604-1545
Bensalem *(G-1200)*

Fulton Forest Products ....E....... 814 782-3448
Shippenville *(G-17561)*

Gene Forrey Millwork ....F....... 717 285-4046
Mountville *(G-11795)*

General Doors Corporation ....D....... 215 788-9277
Bristol *(G-2146)*

Giuntas Fine Woodworking ....G....... 610 287-1749
Schwenksville *(G-17176)*

Glenn A Hissim Woodworking LLC ....G....... 610 847-8961
Kintnersville *(G-8727)*

Glicks Woodworking ....G....... 717 768-8958
Gordonville *(G-6556)*

Global Custom ....G....... 844 782-2653
Folsom *(G-6023)*

▲ **Goebelwood Industries Inc** ....F....... 610 532-4644
Folsom *(G-6024)*

Goods From Woods ....G....... 215 699-6866
North Wales *(G-12804)*

Greenville Wood Products Inc ....G....... 724 646-1193
Greenville *(G-6743)*

Grothouse Lumber Company ....F....... 610 767-6515
Germansville *(G-6278)*

Haas Architectural Mllwk Inc ....E....... 717 840-4227
York *(G-20519)*

Halkett Woodworking Inc ....E....... 215 721-9331
Souderton *(G-17739)*

▲ **Hampton Cabinet Shop** ....G....... 717 898-7806
Manheim *(G-10387)*

Hand Crafted Furniture Co Inc ....G....... 717 630-0036
Hanover *(G-6891)*

Hardwoods Millworking ....G....... 814 395-5474
Confluence *(G-3465)*

Harmony Products Inc ....E....... 717 767-2779
Emigsville *(G-4987)*

Harris Woodworking ....G....... 610 932-2646
Oxford *(G-13080)*

Harvest Moon Woodworking ....G....... 717 521-4204
Mc Sherrystown *(G-10651)*

Heister House Millworks Inc ....D....... 570 539-2611
Mount Pleasant Mills *(G-11725)*

Highpoint Woodworks LLC ....G....... 610 346-7739
Coopersburg *(G-3629)*

Historic Doors LLC ....G....... 610 756-6187
Kempton *(G-8492)*

Hoff Enterprises Inc ....E....... 814 535-8371
Johnstown *(G-8381)*

Hoff Woodworking ....G....... 717 259-6040
East Berlin *(G-4522)*

HOP Millwork Inc ....G....... 724 934-3880
Wexford *(G-19806)*

Hordis Doors Inc ....G....... 215 957-9585
Warminster *(G-18895)*

Horstcraft Millworks LLC ....G....... 717 694-9222
Richfield *(G-16680)*

Howell Manufacturing Company ....F....... 814 652-5143
Everett *(G-5573)*

Industrial Shipping Pdts Isp ....G....... 724 423-6533
Latrobe *(G-9481)*

Innovative Displays ....G....... 570 386-8121
New Ringgold *(G-12439)*

Ivan C Dutterer Inc ....D....... 717 637-8977
Hanover *(G-6904)*

J C Snavely & Sons Inc ....E....... 717 291-8989
Lancaster *(G-9068)*

J D R Fixtures Inc ....E....... 610 323-6599
Pottstown *(G-16003)*

Jack Burnley Son Stair Contrs ....E....... 610 948-4166
Spring City *(G-17862)*

James Richard Woodworking ....F....... 717 397-4790
Lancaster *(G-9071)*

Jay Zimmerman ....G....... 717 445-7246
East Earl *(G-4546)*

JC Woodworking Inc ....G....... 215 651-2049
Quakertown *(G-16203)*

JC Woodworking Inc ....F....... 215 651-2049
Sellersville *(G-17351)*

Jeffrey R Knudsen ....G....... 717 529-4011
Kirkwood *(G-8749)*

Jeld-Wen Inc ....A....... 570 628-5317
Pottsville *(G-16084)*

Jeld-Wen Inc ....C....... 570 889-3173
Ringtown *(G-16754)*

Jerry G Martin ....G....... 814 395-5475
Confluence *(G-3467)*

JF Mill and Lumber Co ....G....... 724 654-9542
New Castle *(G-12109)*

John J Peachey ....F....... 717 667-9373
Reedsville *(G-16625)*

Johns Cstm Stairways Mllwk Co ....G....... 215 463-1211
Philadelphia *(G-13908)*

Jonathan Fallos Cabinetmaker ....G....... 610 253-4063
Easton *(G-4709)*

Joseph Mikstas ....G....... 215 271-2419
Philadelphia *(G-13911)*

Joyce Stair Corp ....G....... 570 345-8000
Pine Grove *(G-14594)*

Jwi Architectural Millwork Inc ....E....... 717 328-5880
Mercersburg *(G-10988)*

K & L Woodworking Inc ....E....... 610 372-0738
Reading *(G-16417)*

K & M Wood Products ....F....... 814 967-4613
Centerville *(G-2834)*

KB Woodcraft Inc ....G....... 502 533-2773
Phoenixville *(G-14555)*

Kellner Millwork Co Inc ....G....... 412 784-1414
Pittsburgh *(G-15164)*

▲ **Kestner Wood Products Inc** ....G....... 724 368-3605
Portersville *(G-15929)*

▼ **Kestrel Shutters & Doors Inc** ....F....... 610 326-6679
Stowe *(G-18072)*

▼ **Keystone Wood Specialties Inc** ....D....... 717 299-6288
Lancaster *(G-9085)*

Keystone Wood Turning ....G....... 717 354-2435
Ephrata *(G-5114)*

Kilbane Wood Creations ....G....... 814 664-0563
Union City *(G-18608)*

Knock On Woodwork ....G....... 717 579-8179
Mechanicsburg *(G-10865)*

Koch S Custom Woodworking ....G....... 610 261-2607
Northampton *(G-12854)*

Larkin C Company Inc ....G....... 610 696-9096
West Chester *(G-19586)*

Lb Woodworking LLC ....G....... 570 729-0000
Beach Lake *(G-974)*

Legacy Restoration LLC ....G....... 716 239-0695
Philadelphia *(G-13965)*

Leidys Custom Woodworking ....G....... 717 328-9323
Mercersburg *(G-10990)*

Lew-Hoc Wood Products Inc ....E....... 814 486-0359
Emporium *(G-5067)*

Lewis Lumber Products Inc ....D....... 570 584-6167
Picture Rocks *(G-14585)*

Lexyline Millwork ....E....... 267 895-1733
Doylestown *(G-4312)*

Lignitech Inc ....F....... 814 474-9590
Fairview *(G-5832)*

Locust Ridge Woodworks LLC ....G...... 610 350-6029
  Kirkwood (G-8750)
Longs Hardwoods Inc ....F...... 814 472-4740
  Ebensburg (G-4786)
M & M Cabinets LLC ....G...... 412 220-9663
  Cecil (G-2822)
M & R Woodworks Inc ....G...... 724 378-7677
  Aliquippa (G-81)
M4I Inc ....G...... 717 566-1610
  Hummelstown (G-7916)
Mario Dinardo Jr Custom WD Wkg ....E...... 610 495-7010
  Pottstown (G-16015)
Markraft Company ....G...... 724 733-3654
  Murrysville (G-11857)
Mars Lumber Inc ....G...... 724 625-2224
  Mars (G-10506)
Marsh Planing Inc ....G...... 814 827-9947
  Titusville (G-18388)
Marshall Woodworks Ltd ....F...... 412 321-1685
  Pittsburgh (G-15257)
Masco Cabinetry LLC ....B...... 570 882-8565
  Athens (G-812)
Masonite Corporation ....C...... 570 473-3557
  Northumberland (G-12870)
Master Woodcraft Corporation ....E...... 724 225-5530
  Washington (G-19201)
Merrigan Corporation ....F...... 610 317-6300
  Bethlehem (G-1568)
MI Windows and Doors Inc ....C...... 570 682-1206
  Hegins (G-7543)
Mil-Del Corporation ....G...... 215 788-9277
  Bristol (G-2168)
Millwork Solutions Inc ....E...... 814 446-4009
  Seward (G-17382)
Millwork Specialties ....G...... 610 261-2878
  Northampton (G-12855)
▲ Mohawk Flush Doors ....E...... 570 473-3557
  Northumberland (G-12872)
Moorhouse Stair ....G...... 610 367-9275
  Bechtelsville (G-1033)
Morris Millwork LLC ....G...... 215 667-1889
  Philadelphia (G-14039)
Morris Millwork LLC ....G...... 215 736-0708
  Yardley (G-20327)
▼ Mountain Mouldings ....F...... 814 535-8563
  Johnstown (G-8410)
Moxham Lumber Co ....E...... 814 536-5186
  Johnstown (G-8411)
Muldoon Window Door & Awning ....G...... 570 347-9453
  Scranton (G-17261)
National Woodworks LLC ....G...... 412 431-7071
  Pittsburgh (G-15322)
▲ Nature Flooring Industries Inc ....E...... 610 280-9800
  Malvern (G-10283)
Neshaminy Valley Millwork ....F...... 215 604-0251
  Bensalem (G-1230)
Newtown Mfg & Bldg Sup Corp ....D...... 570 825-3675
  Wilkes Barre (G-19950)
North Country Woodworking Inc ....G...... 570 549-8105
  Mansfield (G-10422)
Northeast Building Pdts Corp ....C...... 215 535-7110
  Philadelphia (G-14079)
Northern Millwork Inc ....F...... 215 393-7242
  Lansdale (G-9394)
Oakes & McClelland Co ....F...... 724 588-6400
  Greenville (G-6761)
Old Town Woodworking Inc ....G...... 570 562-2117
  Old Forge (G-12972)
Orwin Lathe & Dowel ....F...... 717 647-4397
  Tower City (G-18439)
Oskis Woodworks ....G...... 215 444-0523
  Warminster (G-18935)
Overhead Door Corporation ....C...... 570 326-7325
  Williamsport (G-20053)
Overhead Door Corporation ....B...... 717 248-0131
  Lewistown (G-9942)
Overhead Door Corporation ....D...... 215 368-8700
  Lansdale (G-9396)
P & H Lumber Millwork Co Inc ....E...... 215 699-9365
  North Wales (G-12822)
Pappajohn Woodworking Inc ....G...... 215 289-8625
  Philadelphia (G-14117)
Pella Corporation ....G...... 610 648-0922
  Berwyn (G-1370)
Pella Corporation ....B...... 610 648-0922
  Berwyn (G-1371)
Pella Corporation ....B...... 610 648-0922
  Berwyn (G-1372)
Pella Corporation ....D...... 717 334-0099
  Gettysburg (G-6310)

▲ Penn Wood Products Inc ....D...... 717 259-9551
  East Berlin (G-4524)
Peyty Construction ....G...... 570 764-5995
  Bloomsburg (G-1793)
Philadelphia Shutter Company ....G...... 610 685-2344
  Temple (G-18335)
Philadelphia Woodworks LLC ....G...... 267 331-5880
  Philadelphia (G-14160)
Phoenix Woodworking Inc ....F...... 610 209-9030
  East Earl (G-4553)
Pioneer Woodcrafts LLC ....F...... 717 656-0776
  Leola (G-9797)
Pittsburgh Shed Company Inc ....G...... 724 745-4422
  Canonsburg (G-2619)
Pittston Lumber & Mfg Co ....E...... 570 654-3328
  Pittston (G-15776)
Port Richmond Millwork ....G...... 215 423-4803
  Philadelphia (G-14190)
Precision Millwork & Cabinetry ....E...... 814 445-9669
  Somerset (G-17700)
Presta Contractor Supply Inc ....F...... 814 833-0655
  Erie (G-5436)
Progressive Door Corporation ....G...... 724 733-4636
  Murrysville (G-11862)
Quality Millwork Inc ....E...... 412 831-3500
  Finleyville (G-5964)
Quehanna Millwork ....G...... 814 263-4145
  Frenchville (G-6218)
R & C Foltz LLC ....F...... 717 927-9771
  Brogue (G-2239)
RAD Mfg LLC ....E...... 570 752-4514
  Nescopeck (G-12002)
Ralston Shop Inc ....F...... 610 268-3829
  Avondale (G-858)
Randy George Wdwkg Cstm Signs ....G...... 724 514-7201
  Canonsburg (G-2623)
Recon Enterprises ....G...... 570 836-1179
  Tunkhannock (G-18548)
Rehmeyer Precision Mllwk Inc ....F...... 717 235-0607
  Shrewsbury (G-17587)
Reinert & Sons Inc ....F...... 215 781-8311
  Bristol (G-2194)
Ridge Craft ....F...... 717 355-2254
  New Holland (G-12279)
Ridgeview Forest Products LLC ....E...... 717 423-6465
  Shippensburg (G-17544)
Ritescreen Company LLC ....C...... 717 362-7483
  Elizabethville (G-4897)
Roderick Duvall ....G...... 814 735-4969
  Crystal Spring (G-3938)
Rolands Special Millwork Inc ....G...... 215 885-5588
  Glenside (G-6534)
Rosenberry Bros Lumber Co ....F...... 717 349-7196
  Fannettsburg (G-5858)
Roth Woodworking LLC ....G...... 717 476-8609
  New Oxford (G-12423)
S F Spector Inc ....G...... 717 236-0805
  Harrisburg (G-7211)
▲ Sa-Fe Windows Inc ....F...... 717 464-9605
  Willow Street (G-20157)
Salem Millwork Inc ....F...... 724 468-5701
  Delmont (G-4056)
Saner Architecture Millwork ....G...... 717 786-2014
  Quarryville (G-16279)
Seaquay Archtctural Mllwk Corp ....F...... 610 279-1201
  Bridgeport (G-2045)
Seay Custom Woodworking ....G...... 814 422-8986
  Spring Mills (G-17892)
Selectrim Corporation ....E...... 570 326-3662
  Williamsport (G-20071)
Seneca Hardwood Lumber Co Inc ....E...... 814 498-2241
  Cranberry (G-3797)
▲ Seven D Industries LP ....C...... 814 317-4077
  Hollidaysburg (G-7654)
Seven Trees Woodworking LLC ....F...... 717 351-6300
  New Holland (G-12282)
Shady Grove Woodworking ....G...... 610 273-7038
  Narvon (G-11925)
Shane Hostetter ....G...... 717 949-6563
  Newmanstown (G-12483)
Shelly Enterprises -US Lbm LLC ....D...... 215 723-5108
  Telford (G-18315)
Shelly Enterprises -US Lbm LLC ....E...... 610 432-4511
  Bethlehem (G-1617)
Shelly Enterprises -US Lbm LLC ....F...... 610 933-1116
  Kimberton (G-8574)
Shirks Custom Wood Turning ....G...... 717 656-6295
  New Holland (G-12283)
Shuler Woodworking ....G...... 724 679-5222
  Fenelton (G-5948)

Signature Door Inc ....D...... 814 949-2770
  Altoona (G-549)
Slate Belt Woodworkers Inc ....G...... 610 588-1922
  Bangor (G-927)
Smith Lawton Millwork ....G...... 570 934-2544
  Montrose (G-11477)
Smokey Mountain Woodworking ....G...... 717 445-5120
  Ephrata (G-5143)
Solidays Millwork ....G...... 717 274-2841
  Lebanon (G-9633)
Somerset Door & Column Company ....F...... 814 444-9427
  Somerset (G-17707)
Somerset Door and Column Co ....E...... 814 445-9608
  Somerset (G-17708)
Souto Mould ....G...... 570 596-3128
  Milan (G-11150)
▲ Spectrim Building Products LLC ....F...... 267 223-1030
  Bensalem (G-1256)
Spring Hill Woodworks ....G...... 724 762-0111
  Cherry Tree (G-3036)
Spring Mill Woodworks ....G...... 267 408-9469
  Glenside (G-6540)
Spring Valley Millwork Inc ....E...... 610 927-0144
  Reading (G-16523)
▲ Stairworks Inc ....E...... 215 703-0823
  Telford (G-18320)
Stanley Access Tech LLC ....E...... 800 722-2377
  Pittsburgh (G-15577)
▲ Starke Millwork Inc ....F...... 610 759-1753
  Nazareth (G-11990)
Staurowsky Woodworking ....G...... 610 489-0770
  Collegeville (G-3394)
Steigrwalds Kitchens Baths Inc ....F...... 724 458-0280
  Grove City (G-6804)
Stevens Woodworks ....G...... 412 487-4408
  Allison Park (G-463)
▲ Stoltzfus Woodturning ....G...... 717 687-8237
  Ronks (G-16816)
Stoltzfus Woodworking ....G...... 717 656-4823
  Lancaster (G-9207)
Sweet Water Woodworks LLC ....G...... 610 273-1270
  Narvon (G-11929)
◆ TC Millwork Inc ....C...... 215 245-4210
  Bensalem (G-1259)
Thermal Industries Inc ....E...... 724 325-6100
  Murrysville (G-11870)
Thermal Windows & Doors LLC ....G...... 724 325-6100
  Murrysville (G-11871)
Thermo-Twin Industries Inc ....C...... 412 826-1000
  Oakmont (G-12927)
Thomas Gross Woodworking ....G...... 724 593-7044
  Ligonier (G-9967)
Tilo Industries ....G...... 570 524-9990
  Lewisburg (G-9921)
▼ Timberlane Inc ....E...... 215 616-0600
  Montgomeryville (G-11424)
Top Shop ....G...... 610 622-6101
  Philadelphia (G-14396)
Tri-Vet Design Fabrication LLC ....F...... 570 462-4941
  Shenandoah (G-17497)
Trimline Windows Inc ....G...... 215 672-5233
  Ivyland (G-8224)
Turner John ....G...... 610 524-2050
  Exton (G-5740)
Tyger Construction ....G...... 814 467-9342
  Windber (G-20193)
Ufp Stockertown LLC ....E...... 610 759-8536
  Stockertown (G-18067)
Vangura Kitchen Tops Inc ....D...... 412 824-0772
  Irwin (G-8204)
Vynex Window Systems Inc ....F...... 412 681-3800
  North Versailles (G-12783)
Wagner Masters Custom Wdwkg ....G...... 570 748-9424
  Lock Haven (G-10093)
Weather Shield Mfg Inc ....B...... 717 761-7131
  Camp Hill (G-2524)
Weyerhaeuser Company ....C...... 814 827-4621
  Titusville (G-18404)
Whispering Pine Woodworking ....G...... 570 922-4530
  Mifflinburg (G-11105)
White Deer Woodworking ....G...... 570 547-1664
  Allenwood (G-443)
William Bender Trimming ....G...... 570 922-4274
  Millmont (G-11221)
William H Hammonds & Bros ....G...... 610 489-7924
  Collegeville (G-3399)
Wilson & Mc Cracken Inc ....G...... 412 784-1772
  Pittsburgh (G-15718)
Wolf Lumber and Millwork Inc ....G...... 814 317-5111
  Duncansville (G-4466)

▲ Wood Moulding and Millwork ....F 215 324-8400
Philadelphia (G-14484)
Woodshop LLC ....G 610 647-4190
Malvern (G-10348)
Wyatt Incorporated ....E 724 684-7060
Monessen (G-11302)
Wyatt Woodworking ....G 717 246-8740
Felton (G-5943)
Zaveta Millwork Spc Inc ....G 215 489-4065
Doylestown (G-4348)
Zooks Woodworking ....G 570 758-3579
Dornsife (G-4165)

2434 Wood Kitchen Cabinets

75 Cabinets LLC ....G 215 343-7500
Warrington (G-19104)
A Kuhns Cabinets ....G 717 263-4306
Chambersburg (G-2896)
Adelphi Kitchens Inc ....C 610 693-3101
Robesonia (G-16772)
▲ Aiellos International Inc ....F 717 451-3910
New Oxford (G-12403)
Alan Pepper Designs ....G 412 244-9299
Pittsburgh (G-14659)
Alvin Reiff Woodworking ....G 570 966-1149
Mifflinburg (G-11092)
American Mllwk & Cabinetry Inc ....E 610 965-0040
Emmaus (G-5019)
Ames Construction Inc ....E 717 299-1395
Lancaster (G-8932)
Antones At The Mark Inc ....G 610 798-9218
Allentown (G-138)
Appalachian Mill Inc ....E 717 328-2805
Greencastle (G-6598)
Art Craft Cabinets Inc ....G 717 397-7817
Lancaster (G-8943)
Asels Cabinet Company ....G 814 677-3063
Rouseville (G-16835)
Beilers Woodworking ....G 717 656-8956
Talmage (G-18206)
Bentley & Collins Company ....F 570 546-3250
Muncy (G-11810)
Bhagyas Kitchen ....G 215 233-1587
Glenside (G-6508)
Birchcraft Kitchens Inc ....E 610 375-4391
Reading (G-16334)
Bittner Distributors Company ....G 412 261-8000
Pittsburgh (G-14770)
Blue Mountain Woodworking ....E 610 746-2588
Bath (G-952)
Braders Woodcraft Inc ....F 610 262-3452
Laurys Station (G-9532)
Brightbill Industries Inc ....E 717 233-4121
Harrisburg (G-7099)
Brubaker Kitchens Inc ....E 717 394-5622
Lancaster (G-8963)
Cabinet Connections ....G 215 429-9431
Feasterville Trevose (G-5899)
Cabinet Store ....G 814 677-5522
Seneca (G-17365)
Cameo Kitchens Inc ....E 717 436-9598
Mifflintown (G-11111)
Canaan Cabinetry Inc ....G 215 348-0551
Doylestown (G-4286)
Cbc Cabinetry & Home Services ....F 717 564-2521
Harrisburg (G-7103)
Centerville Cabinet Shop ....G 717 351-0708
Gordonville (G-6551)
Chadds Ford Cabinet Inc ....G 610 388-6005
Kennett Square (G-8503)
Churchtowne Cabinetry ....G 717 354-6682
Narvon (G-11918)
Closet City Ltd ....F 215 855-4400
Harleysville (G-7028)
Cold Spring Cabinetry Inc ....G 215 348-8001
Doylestown (G-4293)
Colonial Craft Kitchens Inc ....G 717 867-1145
Annville (G-645)
Conestoga Valley Cstm Kitchens ....E 717 445-5415
Narvon (G-11919)
◆ Conestoga Wood Spc Corp ....A 717 445-6701
East Earl (G-4540)
▼ Contemprary Artisans Cabinetry ......E 215 723-8803
Telford (G-18276)
▲ Craft-Maid Kitchen Inc ....E 610 376-8686
Reading (G-16352)
Crawford Dzignes Inc ....G 724 872-4644
West Newton (G-19750)
Creekhill Cabinetry ....G 717 656-7438
Paradise (G-13155)

Crownwood LLC ....G 717 463-2942
Mc Alisterville (G-10548)
Crystal Custom Kitchens Inc ....G 610 683-8187
Kutztown (G-8839)
Custom Cabinetry Unlimited LLC ....G 717 656-9170
Leola (G-9776)
Custom Designs & Mfg Co ....E 570 207-4432
Scranton (G-17226)
Custom Woodworking ....E 610 273-2907
Honey Brook (G-7743)
Daniel W Benedict ....G 717 709-0149
Waynesboro (G-19408)
David Jonathan Wdwkg & Mfg Co ....G 724 499-5225
Rogersville (G-16795)
Db & S Cabinets ....G 814 437-2529
Franklin (G-6124)
Deely Custom Cabinetry ....G 267 566-5704
North Wales (G-12798)
Del-Wood Kitchens Inc ....E 717 637-9320
Hanover (G-6876)
Dennis Downing ....G 724 598-0043
New Castle (G-12081)
Dinneen & Son Inc ....G 412 241-2727
Pittsburgh (G-14924)
Dodson Bros Inc ....G 412 793-0600
Verona (G-18755)
Donatucci Kitchens & Appls ....E 215 545-5755
Philadelphia (G-13639)
Dutch Wood LLC ....G 717 933-5133
Myerstown (G-11882)
E Beiler Cabinetry ....G 717 354-5515
New Holland (G-12245)
Eagle Displays LLC ....F 724 335-8900
North Apollo (G-12726)
EDM Co ....E 717 626-2186
Lititz (G-10005)
Effort Woodcraft Inc ....E 570 629-1160
Effort (G-4825)
Ehst Custom Kitchens Inc ....F 610 367-2074
Boyertown (G-1910)
Elegant Marble Products Inc ....F 717 939-0373
Middletown (G-11052)
Elite Cabinetry Inc ....G 717 993-5269
New Park (G-12429)
Elkay Wood Products Company ....B 570 966-1076
Mifflinburg (G-11094)
▲ Empire Building Products Inc ....F 610 926-0500
Leesport (G-9662)
Ethan Horwitz Cabinet Mak ....G 610 948-4889
Pottstown (G-15987)
F DEFrank& Son Custom Cabinets ....G 724 430-1812
Smock (G-17665)
Fedor Fabrication Inc ....F 610 431-7150
West Chester (G-19554)
Fine Line Cabinets Inc ....F 814 695-8133
Hollidaysburg (G-7647)
Fiorella Woodworking Inc ....G 215 843-5870
Philadelphia (G-13702)
Foxcraft Cabinets ....G 717 859-3261
Ephrata (G-5105)
Frank Griffith ....G 570 524-7175
Lewisburg (G-9909)
Freelands Fine Wood Finishings ....G 814 922-7101
West Springfield (G-19768)
Glicks Woodcraft LLC ....G 717 536-3670
Loysville (G-10115)
Goebel Cabinetry ....G 610 363-8970
Exton (G-5690)
▲ Goebelwood Industries Inc ....F 610 532-4644
Folsom (G-6024)
GP Cabinets LLC ....G 814 933-8902
Snow Shoe (G-17669)
▲ Hampton Cabinet Shop ....G 717 898-7806
Manheim (G-10387)
Harmony Plus Woodworks Inc ....G 717 432-0372
Dillsburg (G-4131)
Harrison Custom Cabinets ....G 215 548-2450
Philadelphia (G-13804)
Haugh Woodworking ....G 724 894-2205
West Sunbury (G-19770)
Heirloom Cabinetry PA Inc ....F 717 436-8091
Mifflintown (G-11122)
Hess C & Sons Cabinets Inc ....G 717 597-3295
Greencastle (G-6618)
Hilltop Woodshop Inc ....G 724 697-4506
Avonmore (G-865)
Hoff Enterprises Inc ....E 814 535-8371
Johnstown (G-8381)
Homestead Custom Cabinetry ....E 717 859-8788
Akron (G-35)

Honey Brook Cstm Cabinets Inc ....E 610 273-2436
Honey Brook (G-7749)
Infinite Quest Cabinetry Corp ....G 301 222-3592
Red Lion (G-16601)
Innovative Custom Cabinetry ....G 724 624-0164
Rochester (G-16786)
Irving K Doremus Jr ....G 215 679-6653
Pennsburg (G-13249)
Jay Zimmerman ....G 717 445-7246
East Earl (G-4546)
Jeffrey R Knudsen ....G 717 529-4011
Kirkwood (G-8749)
Jemson Cabinetry Inc ....G 717 733-0540
Ephrata (G-5112)
Jerry D Watson Jr ....G 814 355-7104
Milesburg (G-11152)
JI Cabinet Company ....G 412 931-8580
Pittsburgh (G-15154)
John Kegges Jr ....G 412 821-5535
Pittsburgh (G-15155)
Joseph Mikstas ....G 215 271-2419
Philadelphia (G-13911)
K & H Cabinet Company Inc ....F 717 949-6551
Newmanstown (G-12478)
Kabinet Koncepts Inc ....G 724 327-7737
Murrysville (G-11854)
Kahles Kitchens Inc ....D 814 744-9388
Leeper (G-9656)
Kares Krafted Kitchen Inc ....G 610 694-0180
Freemansburg (G-6197)
Kelly Custom Furn & Cabinetry ....G 412 781-3997
Pittsburgh (G-15166)
Kitchen Express Inc ....F 570 693-0285
Wyoming (G-20281)
Kitchen Express of Wyoming ....G 570 693-0285
Wyoming (G-20282)
Kitchen Gallery Inc ....G 724 838-0911
Greensburg (G-6682)
Kitchens By Meade Inc ....F 814 453-4888
Erie (G-5345)
Kitchenview Custom Cabinets ....G 717 687-6740
Paradise (G-13161)
Kountry Kraft Kitchens Inc ....C 610 589-4575
Newmanstown (G-12479)
Kountry Kustom Kitchens ....G 717 768-3091
Bird In Hand (G-1677)
Kross Cabinets ....G 724 375-7504
Aliquippa (G-79)
L & D Cabinetry ....G 717 484-1272
Denver (G-4080)
Lancaster Cabinet Company LLC ....G 717 556-8420
Bird In Hand (G-1678)
Lancaster Maid Cabinets Inc ....F 717 336-0111
Reinholds (G-16635)
Larkin C Company Inc ....G 610 696-9096
West Chester (G-19586)
▲ Leo Taur Technology Group Inc ....F 610 966-3484
Macungie (G-10153)
Lewistown Cabinet Center Inc ....D 717 667-2121
Milroy (G-11231)
Lyndan Cabinets Inc ....G 724 626-9630
Connellsville (G-3502)
Lyndan Designs Inc ....G 724 626-9630
Connellsville (G-3503)
Macson Company ....G 610 264-7733
Allentown (G-305)
Mar-Van Industries Inc ....G 215 249-3336
Dublin (G-4435)
Mario Dinardo Jr Custom WD Wkg ....E 610 495-7010
Pottstown (G-16015)
Martins Wood Products LLC ....E 717 933-5115
Myerstown (G-11893)
Master Woodcraft Corporation ....E 724 225-5530
Washington (G-19201)
Masterbrand Cabinets Inc ....A 717 359-4131
Carlisle (G-2725)
Mc Norton Cabinet Co ....G 724 538-5680
Cranberry Township (G-3834)
Melvin Stoltzfus ....F 717 656-3520
Talmage (G-18207)
▼ Meridian Products Inc ....D 717 355-7700
New Holland (G-12263)
Millwork Solutions Inc ....E 814 446-4009
Seward (G-17382)
Mountain City Cabinets Inc ....G 814 652-3977
Everett (G-865)
Mountainside Wood Products ....F 717 935-5753
Belleville (G-1133)
Myers Cabinet Co ....G 724 887-4070
Scottdale (G-17196)

Nailed It II LLC ....G........ 215 803-2060
  Langhorne (G-9312)
National Forest Products Ltd ....G........ 814 927-5622
  Marienville (G-10458)
Natures Blend Wood Pdts Inc ....D........ 724 763-7057
  Ford City (G-6050)
Noah F Boyle Cabinets ....G........ 717 944-1007
  Elizabethtown (G-4880)
North Country Woodworking Inc ....G........ 570 549-8105
  Mansfield (G-10422)
Northeast Cabinet Center Inc ....G........ 570 226-5005
  Hawley (G-7434)
Oak Park Cabinetry Inc ....F........ 717 561-4216
  Harrisburg (G-7186)
Olde Mill Cabinet Co ....G........ 717 866-6504
  Myerstown (G-11895)
Otto Design Casefixture Inc ....G........ 412 378-6460
  Irwin (G-8187)
Oxford Cabinetry LLC ....G........ 610 932-3793
  Nottingham (G-12884)
Pannebaker Holdings Inc ....D........ 717 463-3615
  Thompsontown (G-18350)
Patrick Aiello Cabinetry LLC ....G........ 610 681-7167
  Kunkletown (G-8834)
Paul H Nolt Woodworking ....G........ 717 445-4972
  East Earl (G-4552)
Paul Scalese ....G........ 814 743-5121
  Cherry Tree (G-3034)
Paulus & Son Cabinet Co ....G........ 717 896-3610
  Halifax (G-6828)
Penncraft Cabinet Co ....G........ 724 379-7040
  Monongahela (G-11313)
Philip J Stofanak Inc ....E........ 610 759-9311
  Bethlehem (G-1595)
Phoenix Cabinetry Inc ....G........ 484 831-5741
  Phoenixville (G-14568)
▲ Plain n Fancy Kitchens Inc ....C........ 717 949-6571
  Schaefferstown (G-17129)
Precision Cuntertops Mllwk Inc ....G........ 215 598-7161
  Hatboro (G-7298)
Precision Dimension Inc ....F........ 814 684-4150
  Tyrone (G-18590)
Precision Wood Works ....G........ 814 793-9900
  Martinsburg (G-10528)
Quaker Valley Specialties ....G........ 717 694-3999
  Richfield (G-16681)
Quality Custom Cabinetry Inc ....C........ 717 656-2721
  New Holland (G-12275)
Quality Custom Cabinetry Inc ....F........ 717 661-6565
  Leola (G-9798)
Ram-Wood Custom Cabinetry LLC ......G........ 717 242-6357
  Lewistown (G-9945)
Red Rose Cabinetry ....G........ 717 625-4456
  Lititz (G-10038)
Renningers Cabinetree Inc ....E........ 570 726-6494
  Mill Hall (G-11181)
Richard Hurst ....G........ 717 866-2343
  Myerstown (G-11897)
Richard Riberich ....G........ 412 271-8427
  Pittsburgh (G-15484)
Rissler Custom Kitchens ....G........ 717 656-6101
  Leola (G-9800)
Riverwoods Cabinetry ....G........ 724 991-0097
  Grove City (G-6803)
Rj Custom Products Llc ....F........ 717 246-2693
  Dallastown (G-3980)
Rocher Incorporated ....G........ 717 637-9320
  Hanover (G-6945)
Rosewood Kitchens Inc ....E........ 717 436-9878
  Mifflintown (G-11134)
Rossi Brothers Cabinet Makers ....F........ 215 426-9960
  Philadelphia (G-14260)
◆ Rynone Manufacturing Corp ....C........ 570 888-5272
  Sayre (G-17121)
Salix Cabinetry Inc ....G........ 814 266-4181
  Salix (G-17048)
Schubert Custom Cabinetry Inc ....G........ 610 372-5559
  Reading (G-16508)
Schutte Woodworking & Mfg Co ....G........ 814 453-5110
  Erie (G-5470)
Shady Grove Cabinet Shop Inc ....G........ 717 597-0825
  Greencastle (G-6632)
Shawn Harr ....G........ 215 258-5434
  Perkasie (G-13292)
Sherman & Gosweiler Inc ....G........ 610 270-0825
  Bridgeport (G-2046)
Signature Custom Cabinetry Inc ....C........ 717 738-4884
  Ephrata (G-5140)
Smith Lawton Millwork ....G........ 570 934-2544
  Montrose (G-11477)

▲ Snitz Creek Cabinet Shop LLC ....F........ 717 273-9861
  Lebanon (G-9632)
▲ Solid Wood Cabinet Company LLC..C........ 267 288-1200
  Levittown (G-9864)
▲ St Martin America Inc ....E........ 570 593-8596
  Cressona (G-3908)
Stansons Kitchens & Vanities ....G........ 570 648-4660
  Coal Township (G-3282)
Stasik Custom Cabinetry ....G........ 215 357-7277
  Feasterville Trevose (G-5931)
Stauffer Wood Products ....G........ 717 647-4372
  Tower City (G-18441)
Steigrwalds Kitchens Baths Inc ....F........ 724 458-0280
  Grove City (G-6804)
Superior Cabinet Co ....G........ 724 569-9581
  Smithfield (G-17655)
Superior Cabinet Company ....G........ 215 536-5228
  Quakertown (G-16247)
Superior Woodcraft Inc ....E........ 215 348-9942
  Doylestown (G-4340)
▲ Susquhnna Vly Woodcrafters Inc....E........ 717 898-7564
  Salunga (G-17057)
Sykes-Scholtz-Collins Lbr Inc ....E........ 610 494-2700
  Chester (G-3066)
Taylormaid Custom Cabinetry ....G........ 717 865-6598
  Annville (G-660)
Tedd Wood LLC ....D........ 717 463-3615
  Thompsontown (G-18352)
Trim Tech Inc ....F........ 215 321-0841
  Newtown (G-12556)
Trinity Sup & Installation LLC ....F........ 412 331-3044
  Pittsburgh (G-15650) .
Valley Custom Cabinetry ....G........ 717 957-2819
  Marysville (G-10534)
Viking Woodworking Llc ....G........ 412 381-5171
  Pittsburgh (G-15698)
Village Hndcrfted Cbinetry Inc............G........ 215 393-3040
  Lansdale (G-9424)
Wagner Masters Custom Wdwkg ....G........ 570 748-9424
  Lock Haven (G-10093)
Walnut Burl Woodmill ....G........ 717 259-8479
  Thomasville (G-18343)
Walter S Custom Cabinetry ....G........ 570 420-9800
  Stroudsburg (G-18142)
Waterloo Woodcraft ....G........ 724 221-0438
  Blairsville (G-1744)
Wayneco Inc ....D........ 717 225-4413
  York (G-20704)
Weir Kitchens ....F........ 717 292-6829
  Dover (G-4207)
Wellborn Holdings Inc ....C........ 717 351-1700
  New Holland (G-12293)
Whole House Cabinetry ....G........ 610 286-2901
  Elverson (G-4969)
Wood Creations LLC ....G........ 717 445-7007
  Terre Hill (G-18340)
Wood Ya Like Cabinets ....G........ 570 725-2523
  Loganton (G-10100)
▲ Wood-Mode Incorporated ....A........ 570 374-2711
  Kreamer (G-8819)
Wood-Mode Incorporated ....E........ 570 374-1176
  Selinsgrove (G-17338)
Woodcraft Industries ....G........ 570 323-4458
  Williamsport (G-20098)
Woodcraft Industries Inc ....E........ 724 638-4044
  Greenville (G-6777)
Woodmasters Cabinetry Inc ....E........ 717 949-3937
  Newmanstown (G-12485)
Woodshop LLC ....G........ 610 647-4190
  Malvern (G-10348)
▲ Y&Q Home Plus LLC ....G........ 412 642-6708
  Pittsburgh (G-15728)
Ye Olde Village Workshop ....G........ 570 595-2593
  Mountainhome (G-11788)

2435 Hardwood Veneer & Plywood

Collins Pine Company ....D........ 814 837-6941
  Kane (G-8461)
▲ Cummings Veneer Products Inc......G........ 570 995-1892
  Troy (G-18520)
Dally Slate Company Inc ....D........ 610 863-4172
  Pen Argyl (G-13213)
Danzer Veneer Americas Inc ....D........ 570 322-4400
  Williamsport (G-20002)
◆ Danzer Veneer Americas Inc ....D........ 724 827-8366
  Darlington (G-4026)
▲ Edgemate Inc ....C........ 814 224-5717
  Roaring Spring (G-16764)
Graham Paining Co ....G........ 215 447-8552
  Bensalem (G-1206)

Heirloom Engraving LLC ....G........ 717 336-8451
  Stevens (G-18052)
◆ Interforest Corp ....D........ 724 827-8366
  Darlington (G-4029)
▼ Interntional Timber Veneer LLC......C........ 724 662-0880
  Jackson Center (G-8228)
J C Snavely & Sons Inc ....C........ 717 898-2241
  Landisville (G-9262)
Mars Lumber Inc ....G........ 724 625-2224
  Mars (G-10506)
Mike Woodshop ....G........ 724 272-0259
  Mars (G-10507)
Northeast Products & Svcs Inc ....G........ 610 899-0286
  Topton (G-18414)
◆ Oak Hill Veneer Inc ....D........ 570 297-4137
  Troy (G-18524)
◆ Ram Forest Products Inc ....G........ 814 697-7185
  Shinglehouse (G-17512)
▲ Sieling and Jones Inc ....D........ 717 235-7931
  New Freedom (G-12215)
Signature Stone Inc ....G........ 717 397-2364
  Lancaster (G-9200)
Somerset Door and Column Co ....E........ 814 445-9608
  Somerset (G-17708)
United Panel Inc ....E........ 610 588-6871
  Mount Bethel (G-11615)
Wehrungs Specialty Woods ....D........ 610 847-6002
  Ottsville (G-13069)

2436 Softwood Veneer & Plywood

▲ Howe Wood Products Inc ....F........ 717 266-9855
  York (G-20529)
Ufp Gordon LLC ....E........ 570 875-2811
  Gordon (G-6547)
Ufp Stockertown LLC ....E........ 610 759-8536
  Stockertown (G-18067)
◆ Wilson Global Inc ....D........ 724 883-4952
  Jefferson (G-8272)

2439 Structural Wood Members, NEC

▼ 84 Lumber Company ....B........ 724 228-8820
  Eighty Four (G-4830)
Allensville Planing Mill Inc ....C........ 717 483-6386
  Allensville (G-106)
Bell Wall & Truss LLC ....F........ 717 768-8338
  Gordonville (G-6549)
▼ Brownlee Lumber Inc ....E........ 814 328-2991
  Brookville (G-2255)
Cussewago Truss LLC ....E........ 814 763-3229
  Cambridge Springs (G-2476)
DI Truss LLC ....G........ 717 355-9813
  New Holland (G-12243)
F DEFrank& Son Custom Cabinets ......G........ 724 430-1812
  Smock (G-17665)
Fairmans Roof Trusses Inc ....E........ 724 349-6778
  Creekside (G-3875)
J C Snavely & Sons Inc ....C........ 717 898-2241
  Landisville (G-9262)
Keystone Casework Inc ....E........ 814 941-7250
  Altoona (G-520)
Maronda Systems Inc Florida ....G........ 724 695-1200
  Imperial (G-8072)
Montgomery Truss & Panel Inc ....D........ 724 458-7500
  Grove City (G-6798)
Musselman Lumber - US Lbm LLC ......C........ 717 354-4321
  New Holland (G-12264)
New Enterprise Stone Lime Inc ....D........ 610 374-5131
  Kutztown (G-8851)
New Enterprise Stone Lime Inc ....B........ 610 374-5131
  Leesport (G-9668)
Oakes & McClelland Co ....F........ 724 588-6400
  Greenville (G-6761)
▲ Pocopson Industries Inc ....F........ 610 793-0344
  West Chester (G-19618)
Provance Truss LLC ....G........ 724 437-0585
  Lemont Furnace (G-9736)
R & R Components Inc ....C........ 717 792-4641
  York (G-20649)
Rigidply Rafters Inc ....E........ 717 866-6581
  Richland (G-16689)
S R Sloan Inc ....E........ 570 366-8934
  Orwigsburg (G-13051)
Salem Millwork Inc ....E........ 724 468-5701
  Delmont (G-4056)
Seals of Blossburg ....G........ 570 638-2161
  Blossburg (G-1809)
Seven D Truss LP ....E........ 814 317-4077
  Altoona (G-547)
Shelly Enterprises -US Lbm LLC ....D........ 215 723-5108
  Telford (G-18315)

S
I
C

Shelly Enterprises -US Lbm LLC..........E 610 432-4511
Bethlehem *(G-1617)*

Superior Trusses LLC ....E 717 721-2411
Ephrata *(G-5151)*

Triple D Truss LLC ....E 570 726-7092
Mill Hall *(G-11183)*

Truss-Tech Inc ....E 717 436-9778
Mifflintown *(G-11138)*

United Panel Inc ....E 610 588-6871
Mount Bethel *(G-11615)*

V Menghini & Sons Inc ....F 570 455-6315
Hazle Township *(G-7489)*

Whipple Bros Inc ....G 570 836-6262
Mountain Top *(G-11780)*

Wood Fabricators Inc ....F 717 284-4849
Quarryville *(G-16284)*

York P-B Truss Inc ....F 717 779-0327
York *(G-20748)*

Your Building Centers Inc ....E 570 962-2129
Beech Creek *(G-1084)*

2441 Wood Boxes

Achieva ....D 412 221-6609
Bridgeville *(G-2052)*

Achieva ....D 412 995-5000
Pittsburgh *(G-14640)*

Bomboy Inc ....F 610 266-1553
Allentown *(G-157)*

C & S Wood Products Inc ....E 570 489-8633
Olyphant *(G-12985)*

Carl Amore Greenhouses ....G 610 837-7038
Nazareth *(G-11959)*

Carson Street Commons ....G 412 431-1183
Pittsburgh *(G-14823)*

Export Boxing & Crating Inc ....F 412 675-1000
Glassport *(G-6412)*

Heritage Box Co ....G 724 728-0200
Aliquippa *(G-76)*

Honeybrook Woods ....G 610 380-7108
Coatesville *(G-3308)*

Industrial Shipping Pdts Isp ....G 724 423-6533
Latrobe *(G-9481)*

Integrated Metal Products Inc ....G 717 824-4052
Lancaster *(G-9058)*

Ishman Plastic & Wood Cutting ....G 814 849-9961
Brookville *(G-2262)*

James C Richards ....G 724 758-9032
Ellwood City *(G-4941)*

▼ JB Mill & Fabricating Inc ....E 724 202-6814
New Castle *(G-12108)*

Limpach Industries Inc ....F 724 646-4011
Sharpsville *(G-17473)*

Millennium Packaging Svc Inc ....E 570 282-2990
Carbondale *(G-2683)*

Molded Fiber Glass Companies ....C 814 683-4500
Linesville *(G-9984)*

Nelson Company Inc ....G 717 593-0600
Greencastle *(G-6624)*

OMalley Wood Products Inc ....E 717 677-6550
Gardners *(G-6261)*

Overend & Krill Lumber Inc ....G 724 348-7511
Finleyville *(G-5962)*

Reading Box Company Inc ....F 610 374-2080
Reading *(G-16485)*

Ron Anthony Wood Products Inc ....F 724 459-7620
Blairsville *(G-1740)*

Sheffield Container Corp...................E 814 968-3287
Sheffield *(G-17483)*

Ted Venesky Co Inc ....G 724 224-7992
Tarentum *(G-18248)*

Timber Pallet & Lumber Co Inc ....G 610 562-8442
Hamburg *(G-6853)*

Treen Box & Pallet Corp ....E 717 535-5800
Mifflintown *(G-11136)*

Wayne Lawson ....G 814 757-8424
Russell *(G-16882)*

Woodruff Corporation ....G 570 675-0890
Shavertown *(G-17481)*

2448 Wood Pallets & Skids

A & L Wood Inc................................E 570 539-8922
Mount Pleasant Mills *(G-11724)*

Absolute Pallet Inc ....G 215 331-4510
Bensalem *(G-1142)*

Achieva ....D 412 221-6609
Bridgeville *(G-2052)*

Achieva ....D 412 995-5000
Pittsburgh *(G-14640)*

Aj Pallet LLC ....E 717 597-3545
Waynesboro *(G-19395)*

Albert Gray ....F 717 436-8585
Mifflintown *(G-11109)*

All Pallet Inc....................................C 610 614-1905
Wind Gap *(G-20164)*

American Fibertech Corporation ....E 717 597-5708
Greencastle *(G-6595)*

Annalee Wood Products Inc ....F 610 436-0142
Coatesville *(G-3288)*

Annalee Wood Products Inc ....G 610 436-0142
West Chester *(G-19499)*

B V Pallets ....F 717 935-5740
Belleville *(G-1125)*

Barville Lumber ....G 717 667-9600
Belleville *(G-1126)*

Bass Pallets LLC ....E 717 731-1091
Shiremanstown *(G-17568)*

Bedford Pallets.................................F 814 623-1521
Bedford *(G-1043)*

Beenah Enterprises LLC ....G 570 546-9388
Muncy *(G-11808)*

Better Built Products ....G 724 423-5268
Mount Pleasant *(G-11688)*

Bio-Diversity LLC ....F 570 884-3057
Selinsgrove *(G-17322)*

Bishop Wood Products Inc ....F 215 723-6644
Souderton *(G-17726)*

Brian M Pallet ....G 484 720-8052
Landenberg *(G-9247)*

C & G Pallet Company Inc ....F 610 759-5625
Bath *(G-953)*

C & S Wood Products Inc ....E 570 489-8633
Olyphant *(G-12985)*

C Knaub & Sons ....G 717 292-3908
Dover *(G-4190)*

Carpenter Pallets ....G 570 465-2573
New Milford *(G-12395)*

Cedar Lane Pallets ....G 717 365-4014
Lykens *(G-10131)*

Centre Pallets LLC ....F 814 349-8693
Rebersburg *(G-16578)*

Chep (usa) Inc ....D 717 778-4279
Biglerville *(G-1661)*

Clark H Ream Lumber ....G 814 445-8185
Somerset *(G-17680)*

Clinton Pallet Company Inc ....F 570 753-3010
Jersey Shore *(G-8312)*

Colebrook Supply ....G 717 684-6287
Columbia *(G-3433)*

Columbia Wood Industries Inc ....F 570 458-4311
Millville *(G-11224)*

Cove Stake & Wood Products GP ......G 814 793-3257
Martinsburg *(G-10522)*

Crouses Pallet Service ....G 717 577-9012
Red Lion *(G-16592)*

Custom Bins Pallet Mfg ....G 570 539-4158
Port Trevorton *(G-15912)*

Custom Pallet Recycler ....G 724 658-6086
New Castle *(G-12080)*

D&J Pallet Services Inc ....G 717 275-1064
Landisburg *(G-9257)*

Dach Dime Manufacture ....G 814 336-2376
Meadville *(G-10717)*

Davco Pallet.....................................G 570 837-5910
Middleburg *(G-11024)*

Delco Pallets LLC ....G 267 438-1227
Morton *(G-11591)*

Diaz Stone and Pallet Inc ....E 570 289-8760
Kingsley *(G-8704)*

Dick Warner Sales & Contg ....G 814 683-4606
Linesville *(G-9980)*

Donald B Remmey Inc ....G 570 386-5379
Lehighton *(G-9711)*

Donald B Remmey Inc ....E 570 386-5379
Lehighton *(G-9712)*

Donovan Schoonover Lumber Co........G 814 697-7266
Shinglehouse *(G-17506)*

EMC Global Technologies Inc..........F 267 347-5100
Telford *(G-18287)*

▲ Erie Wood Products LLC..............F 814 452-4961
Erie *(G-5279)*

Esten Lumber Products Inc ....G 215 536-4976
Quakertown *(G-16190)*

Evergreen Pallet Company ....G 717 463-3217
Mc Alisterville *(G-10549)*

Frank Ferris Industries Inc................G 724 352-9477
Cabot *(G-2457)*

Frey Pallet Corporation ....F 724 564-1888
Smithfield *(G-17649)*

Gerald S Stillman ....G 610 377-7650
Allentown *(G-230)*

Gilliland Pallet Company Inc..............G 724 946-2222
New Wilmington *(G-12467)*

◆ Gupta Permold Corporation ....C 412 793-3511
Pittsburgh *(G-15067)*

H & M Lumber...................................G 717 535-5080
Mifflintown *(G-11120)*

Hannahoes Pallets & Skids ....F 610 926-4699
Reading *(G-16398)*

Harvey Leon ....G 570 337-2665
South Williamsport *(G-17791)*

Hess Wood Recycling Inc ....F 610 614-9070
Easton *(G-4698)*

Hornings Pallet Forks ....G 570 966-1025
Mifflinburg *(G-11095)*

House Wood Products Co ....G 570 662-3868
Mansfield *(G-10416)*

▲ Howe Wood Products Inc ....F 717 266-9855
York *(G-20529)*

J & J Pallet Co Inc ....E 570 489-7705
Throop *(G-18359)*

J & M Pallet LLC ....G 717 463-9205
Mifflintown *(G-11124)*

J F Rohrbaugh & Co ....D 800 800-4353
Hanover *(G-6906)*

Jacob E Leisenring Lumber ....G 570 672-9793
Elysburg *(G-4977)*

James C Richards ....G 724 758-9032
Ellwood City *(G-4941)*

▼ JB Mill & Fabricating Inc ....E 724 202-6814
New Castle *(G-12108)*

Jo Ml Pallet Co Inc ....G 570 875-3540
Ashland *(G-732)*

John Dibble Tree Service ....G 814 825-4543
Erie *(G-5338)*

▲ John Rock Inc ....D 610 857-8080
Coatesville *(G-3311)*

Jos Pallets ....G 570 278-8935
Montrose *(G-11468)*

Jrm Pallets Inc.................................G 717 926-6812
Myerstown *(G-11888)*

Keystone Pallet and Recycl LLC ....F 570 279-7236
Milton *(G-11245)*

Kiefer Pallet ....G 610 599-0971
Bangor *(G-920)*

Kopenitz Lumber Co ....G 570 544-2131
Pottsville *(G-16087)*

▼ Kuhns Bros Lumber Co Inc ....E 570 568-1412
Lewisburg *(G-9914)*

Lapps Pallet Repair LLC ....F 717 806-5348
Quarryville *(G-16273)*

Latrobe Pallet Inc ....G 724 537-9636
Latrobe *(G-9491)*

Laurel Run Pallet Company LLC ....F 717 436-5428
Mifflintown *(G-11128)*

Lignetics New England Inc ....G 814 563-4358
Youngsville *(G-20773)*

Limpach Industries Inc ....F 724 646-4011
Sharpsville *(G-17473)*

Little Johns Woodshop ....G 724 924-9029
New Castle *(G-12116)*

Locust Run Pallet LLC ....F 717 535-5883
Thompsontown *(G-18348)*

Lumber and Things Inc ....G 717 848-1622
York *(G-20568)*

M & M Salt & Pallet ....G 717 845-4039
Dallastown *(G-3979)*

M & M Wood Products Inc.................F 570 638-2234
Morris Run *(G-11546)*

M and M Pallet LLC ....F 717 845-4039
York *(G-20571)*

Mark Rioux Pallets ....G 610 562-7030
Hamburg *(G-6845)*

Mhp Industries Inc ....E 717 450-4753
Lebanon *(G-9609)*

Michael Meyer Pallets ....G 814 781-1107
Saint Marys *(G-16995)*

Middlecreek Pallet............................G 570 658-7667
Beaver Springs *(G-1019)*

Midlantic Pallet LLC..........................F 717 266-0300
York *(G-20597)*

▲ Nazareth Pallet Co Inc ....E 610 262-9799
Northampton *(G-12856)*

Nelson Company ....G 724 652-6681
New Castle *(G-12126)*

Nelson Company Inc ....G 717 593-0600
Greencastle *(G-6624)*

Noll Pallet & Lumber Co ....E 610 926-3502
Leesport *(G-9670)*

Noll Pallet Inc ....E 610 926-2500
Leesport *(G-9671)*

Northern Pallet Inc ....F 570 945-3920
Factoryville (G-5759)
Nova Global Inc ....F 619 822-2465
Philadelphia (G-14086)
OMalley Wood Products Inc ....E 717 677-6550
Gardners (G-6261)
Overend & Krill Lumber Inc ....G 724 348-7511
Finleyville (G-5962)
P & S Pallet Inc ....G 570 655-4628
Pittston (G-15772)
P G Recycling Incorporated ....F 814 696-6000
Tyrone (G-18588)
Palcon LLC ....F 570 546-9032
Muncy (G-11828)
Palcon LLC ....F 570 546-9032
Muncy (G-11829)
Pallet Connection ....G 570 963-1432
Scranton (G-17269)
Pallet Express Inc ....D 610 258-8846
Easton (G-4738)
Pallets Unlimited Inc ....G 717 755-3691
York (G-20617)
Paser Inc ....G 814 623-7221
Bedford (G-1070)
Peachey-Yoder LP ....F 570 658-8371
Beaver Springs (G-1020)
Penn Pallet Inc ....G 814 857-2988
Woodland (G-20213)
Penn Pallet Inc ....D 814 834-1700
Saint Marys (G-17002)
Perry Pallet Inc ....E 717 589-3345
Millerstown (G-11207)
Pieces By Pallets LLC ....G 717 872-7238
Quarryville (G-16277)
Precision Pallets & Lumber Inc ....F 814 395-5351
Addison (G-28)
Pro Pallet LLC ....C 717 292-5510
Dover (G-4201)
Pro Pallet Partners ....G 717 741-2418
York (G-20642)
Quality Penn Products Inc ....G 215 430-0117
Philadelphia (G-14220)
R & D Pallett Co ....G 610 944-9484
Blandon (G-1758)
R & R Wood Products Inc ....E 215 723-3470
Mainland (G-10175)
R&F Pallet Co ....G 717 463-3560
Mifflintown (G-11133)
Rebs Pallet Co Inc ....G 570 386-5516
Andreas (G-640)
Recycled Pallets ....G 717 754-3114
Schuylkill Haven (G-17165)
Recycled Pallets Inc ....G 724 657-6978
New Castle (G-12141)
Refined Pallet ....G 570 238-9455
Middleburg (G-11037)
Remington Pallets & Crates ....G 814 749-7557
Vintondale (G-18769)
Remmey Pallet Co ....E 570 658-7575
Beaver Springs (G-1021)
Rick Degeorge ....G 717 684-4555
Columbia (G-3449)
Robert Aguglia ....F 412 487-6511
Glenshaw (G-6500)
Robert D Rennick ....G 570 429-0784
Saint Clair (G-16940)
Rockwell Lumber Co Inc ....G 717 597-7428
Greencastle (G-6631)
Rosewood Company A Partnership ....G 717 349-2289
Fort Loudon (G-6060)
S Frey Pallets ....G 717 284-9937
Quarryville (G-16278)
S&K Pallet LLC ....G 717 667-0001
Reedsville (G-16627)
Shade Lumber Company Inc ....E 570 658-2425
Beaver Springs (G-1023)
Shank Pallet Recyclers Inc ....G 717 597-3545
Greencastle (G-6634)
Shank Pallet Recyclers Inc ....G 717 597-3545
Greencastle (G-6635)
Sheffield Container Corp ....E 814 968-3287
Sheffield (G-17483)
Sheltons Pallet Company ....E 610 932-3182
Oxford (G-13091)
Sovereign Services Inc ....E 412 331-6704
Pittsburgh (G-15565)
Strasburg Pallet Co Inc ....E 717 687-8131
Strasburg (G-18094)
Superior Pallet LLC ....G 717 789-9525
Ickesburg (G-8053)

Sutherland Lumber Co ....E 724 947-3388
Burgettstown (G-2355)
T/A Reborn Pallets ....G 484 841-3085
Bath (G-972)
Ted Venesky Co Inc ....G 724 224-7992
Tarentum (G-18248)
▲ Top Box Inc ....E 724 258-8966
Monongahela (G-11318)
Treen Box & Pallet Corp ....E 717 535-5800
Mifflintown (G-11136)
Troyer Pallet Company ....G 717 535-4499
Mifflintown (G-11137)
Ufp Gordon LLC ....G 570 875-2811
Gordon (G-6547)
Vepar LLC ....G 610 462-4545
Spring City (G-17871)
W W McFarland Inc ....G 724 946-9663
New Wilmington (G-12472)
W W Pallet Co ....F 717 362-9388
Elizabethville (G-4899)
Wayne Lawson ....G 814 757-8424
Russell (G-16882)
Weaver Pallet Company ....F 717 463-3037
Mifflintown (G-11142)
Weaver Pallet Company LLC ....G 717 463-2770
Mc Alisterville (G-10553)
Weaver Sawmill ....F 570 539-8420
Liverpool (G-10080)
Wengerd Pallet Company ....E 717 463-3274
Mifflintown (G-11144)
West Side Wood Products Inc ....F 610 562-8166
Hamburg (G-6856)
Woodruff Corporation ....G 570 675-0890
Shavertown (G-17481)
Wyoming Valley Pallets Inc ....G 570 655-3640
Exeter (G-5586)
Zooks Pallets Inc ....G 717 935-5030
Belleville (G-1135)
Zooks Pallets LLC ....F 717 667-9077
Belleville (G-1136)
Zooks Pallets LLC ....G 717 899-5212
Mc Veytown (G-10654)

2449 Wood Containers, NEC

A+ Packaging ....G 610 864-1758
Narvon (G-11916)
Bishop Wood Products Inc ....F 215 723-6644
Souderton (G-17726)
Bkts Inc ....G 814 724-1547
Meadville (G-10707)
Fulton Forest Products ....E 814 782-3448
Shippenville (G-17561)
Greenfield Basket Factory Inc ....E 814 725-3419
North East (G-12744)
Hall-Woolford Wood Tank Co Inc .....G 215 329-9022
Philadelphia (G-13797)
▲ Howe Wood Products Inc ....F 717 266-9855
York (G-20529)
▼ JB Mill & Fabricating Inc ....E 724 202-6814
New Castle (G-12108)
Little Johns Woodshop ....G 724 924-9029
New Castle (G-12116)
Newshams Woodshop Inc ....G 610 622-5800
Clifton Heights (G-3256)
PA Packing Products & Svcs Inc ......G 717 486-8100
Carlisle (G-2728)
Saylors Farm & Wood Products ....F 814 745-2306
Sligo (G-17616)
Strasburg Pallet Co Inc ....E 717 687-8131
Strasburg (G-18094)
Sutherland Baskets ....G 610 438-8233
Easton (G-4759)
Treen Box & Pallet Corp ....E 717 535-5800
Mifflintown (G-11136)
Ufp Gordon LLC ....G 570 875-2811
Gordon (G-6547)
Van Mar Manufacturing ....G 717 733-8948
Ephrata (G-5153)
Walker Wood Products Inc ....F 717 436-2105
Mifflintown (G-11141)
Zeiglers Packing and Crating ....G 814 238-4021
Port Matilda (G-15908)

2451 Mobile Homes

Commodore Corporation ....C 814 226-9210
Clarion (G-3175)
Garretts Fabricating ....G 724 528-8193
West Middlesex (G-19725)
Liberty Homes Inc ....C 717 656-2381
Leola (G-9793)

Mobile Concepts By Scotty Inc ....E 724 542-7640
Mount Pleasant (G-11706)
Pine Grove Mnfctured Homes Inc .....D 570 345-2011
Pine Grove (G-14602)
Pleasant Valley Homes Inc ....C 570 345-2011
Pine Grove (G-14603)
R S W Enterprises Inc ....G 570 888-2184
Milan (G-11149)
Simplex Industries Inc ....C 570 346-5113
Scranton (G-17291)
Skyline Champion Corporation ....E 717 656-2071
Leola (G-9803)
Stoltzfoos Layers ....G 717 826-0371
Kinzers (G-8743)
Taylored Building Solutions ....G 570 898-5361
Taylor (G-18263)
United States Hardware Mfg Inc ....C 724 222-5110
Washington (G-19235)
Village At Overlook LLC ....G 570 538-9167
New Columbia (G-12178)
Wireless Experience of PA Inc ....G 215 340-1382
Doylestown (G-4345)

2452 Prefabricated Wood Buildings & Cmpnts

All American Homes Colo LLC ....E 970 587-0544
Mechanicsburg (G-10818)
Apex Homes Inc ....C 570 837-2333
Middleburg (G-11021)
Apex Homes of Pa LLC ....C 570 837-2333
Middleburg (G-11022)
Appalachian Woodcrafts LLC ....G 570 726-7149
Mill Hall (G-11170)
B & B Structures ....G 717 656-0783
Bird In Hand (G-1669)
Barn Yard LLC ....G 717 314-9667
Paradise (G-13153)
Black Bear Structures Inc ....E 717 824-0983
Peach Bottom (G-13196)
Black Bear Structures Inc ....G 717 225-0377
York (G-20410)
Buchanan Trail Industries Inc ....G 717 597-7166
Greencastle (G-6601)
Cappelli Enterprises Inc ....C 845 856-9033
Mechanicsburg (G-10826)
Cedar Forest Products Company ....F 815 946-3994
Media (G-10917)
Cove Stake & Wood Products GP ......G 814 793-3257
Martinsburg (G-10522)
Cozy Cabins LLC ....G 717 354-3278
New Holland (G-12239)
Crockett Log Homes of PA Inc ....G 717 697-6198
Mechanicsburg (G-10834)
Cv Anglers Club ....G 814 203-3861
Westfield (G-19776)
Dalton Pavillions Inc ....G 215 721-1492
Telford (G-18279)
David S Stoltzsus ....G 717 556-0462
Bird In Hand (G-1673)
Eastern Exterior Wall ....D 610 868-5522
Allentown (G-200)
Elvin B Zimmerman ....G 717 656-9327
Leola (G-9780)
▲ Farmer Boy Ag Inc ....D 717 866-7565
Myerstown (G-11885)
Fisher Structures ....G 717 789-4569
Loysville (G-10114)
Foxs Country Sheds ....F 717 626-9560
Lititz (G-10010)
Gardner S Construction ....G 610 395-6614
Macungie (G-10146)
Greg Kline ....G 610 367-4060
Boyertown (G-1914)
Haven Homes Inc ....C 410 694-0091
King of Prussia (G-8628)
Icon Lgacy Cstm Mdlar Hmes LLC .....E 570 374-3280
Selinsgrove (G-17326)
Innovative Building Systems, L ....F 717 458-1400
Mechanicsburg (G-10859)
J C Snavely & Sons Inc ....C 717 898-2241
Landisville (G-9262)
Jacob B Kauffman ....G 717 529-6522
Christiana (G-3139)
K S M Enterprises Inc ....G 717 463-2383
Mifflintown (G-11126)
Lake Cy Manufactured Hsing Inc ......E 814 774-2033
Lake City (G-8903)
Lancaster Log Cabins LLC ....G 717 445-5522
Denver (G-4081)

Lanco Sheds Inc ....F 717 351-7100
New Holland (G-12256)

Lantz Structures LLC ....G 717 656-9418
Leola (G-9792)

Martins Buildings ....G 717 733-6689
Ephrata (G-5125)

Millcreek Structures ....F 717 656-2797
Leola (G-9794)

Milton Home Systems Inc ....D 800 533-4402
Milton (G-11249)

Modern Precast Concrete Inc ....E 484 548-6200
Easton (G-4726)

Morey General Contracting ....G 570 759-2021
Berwick (G-1336)

Morton Buildings Inc ....E 717 624-8000
Gettysburg (G-6308)

Mountainside Log Homes ....G 570 745-2388
Williamsport (G-20044)

Mr Luck Inc ....G 570 766-8734
Greentown (G-6734)

Muncy Homes ....B 570 546-2261
Muncy (G-11827)

Myerstown Sheds ....G 717 866-7644
Lebanon (G-9613)

Myerstown Sheds and Fencing ....G 717 866-7015
Myerstown (G-11894)

New Enterprise Stone Lime Inc ....D 610 374-5131
Kutztown (G-8851)

Noble Road Woodworks LLC ....G 610 593-5122
Christiana (G-3143)

North Mountain Structures LLC ....G 717 369-3400
Chambersburg (G-2964)

Peak Industries Inc ....E 717 306-4490
Lebanon (G-9617)

Peak Ventures Inc ....E 717 306-4490
Lebanon (G-9618)

Pear Tree Mfg ....G 610 273-9281
Honey Brook (G-7755)

◆ Penn Sauna Corp ....E 610 932-5700
Oxford (G-13087)

Penn Sauna Corp ....E 610 932-5700
Paoli (G-13146)

Pequea Storage Sheds LLC ....F 717 768-8980
Kinzers (G-8740)

Pittsburgh Shed Company Inc ....G 724 745-4422
Canonsburg (G-2619)

Pleasant Valley Homes Inc ....C 570 345-2011
Pine Grove (G-14603)

Professional Bldg Systems Inc ....C 570 837-1424
Middleburg (G-11036)

Reynolds Building Systems Inc ....G 724 646-0771
Greenville (G-6769)

Ridgeview Mdlar Hsing Group LP .....D 570 837-2333
Middleburg (G-11038)

Riehl Quality Stor Barns LLC ....F 717 442-8655
Kinzers (G-8741)

Sarik Corporation ....G 215 538-2269
Quakertown (G-16243)

Service Construction Co Inc ....F 610 377-2111
Lehighton (G-9727)

Shawnee Structures ....G 814 623-8212
Bedford (G-1076)

Sheds Unlimited Inc ....F 717 442-3281
Morgantown (G-11534)

Signature Building Systems Inc ....E 570 774-1000
Moosic (G-11515)

Signature Building Systems Inc ....D 570 774-1000
Moosic (G-11516)

Stoltzfus Ephram ....G 717 656-0513
Bird In Hand (G-1682)

Stoltzfus Structures ....F 610 593-7700
Atglen (G-808)

Strat-O-Span Buildings Inc ....G 717 334-4606
Gettysburg (G-6316)

Sunset Valley Structures ....G 570 758-2840
Dalmatia (G-3986)

T-Town Sheds & Supply ....G 570 836-5686
Tunkhannock (G-18550)

Tcc Pennwest LLC ....C 724 867-0047
Emlenton (G-5015)

▼ Timberhaven Log Homes LLC ....F 570 568-1422
Lewisburg (G-9922)

Tuscarora Structures Inc ....G 717 436-5591
Mifflin (G-11091)

Wargo Interior Systems Inc ....D 215 723-6200
Telford (G-18325)

Waterloo Structures ....G 610 857-2170
Parkesburg (G-13184)

Whipple Bros Inc ....G 570 836-6262
Mountain Top (G-11780)

Woodhouse Post & Beam ....E 570 549-6232
Mansfield (G-10428)

2491 Wood Preserving

Arrison H B West Virginia Inc ....G 724 324-2106
Mount Morris (G-11678)

Beecher & Myers Company Inc ....F 717 292-3031
York (G-20401)

Champion Lumber Company Inc ....F 724 455-3401
Champion (G-3003)

Effort Woodcraft Inc ....E 570 629-1160
Effort (G-4825)

Great Lakes Framing LLC ....G 724 399-0220
Parker (G-13165)

Gutchess Lumber Co Inc ....D 724 537-6447
Latrobe (G-9479)

Hoover Treated Wood Pdts Inc ....G 800 220-6046
Oxford (G-13081)

Koppers Holdings Inc ....C 412 227-2001
Pittsburgh (G-15187)

◆ Koppers Inc ....C 412 227-2001
Pittsburgh (G-15188)

Koppers Industries Inc ....E 412 227-2001
Pittsburgh (G-15189)

Koppers Industries Inc ....E 570 547-1651
Montgomery (G-11373)

Koppers Industries Inc ....E 412 826-3970
Pittsburgh (G-15190)

Koppers Industries Inc ....G 724 684-1000
Monessen (G-11299)

Koppers Performance Chem Inc ....G 412 227-2001
Pittsburgh (G-15192)

Lancaster Composite Inc ....F 717 872-8999
Columbia (G-3441)

Mellott Wood Preserving Inc ....E 717 573-2519
Needmore (G-11996)

Patrick Donovan ....G 724 238-9038
Ligonier (G-9963)

Perrotte Wood Finishing Co ....G 412 322-2592
Pittsburgh (G-15379)

Property Preservers ....G 267 975-3990
Philadelphia (G-14209)

Redstone International Inc ....D 724 439-1500
Scenery Hill (G-17125)

◆ Rockwell Venture Capital ....G 412 281-4620
Pittsburgh (G-15495)

Schroth Industries Inc ....G 724 465-5701
Indiana (G-8126)

Sewsations LLC ....G 484 842-1024
Garnet Valley (G-6268)

Somerset Enterprises Inc ....F 724 734-9497
Farrell (G-5874)

Stella-Jones Corporation ....G 717 721-3113
Ephrata (G-5148)

Stella-Jones Corporation ....E 814 371-7331
Du Bois (G-4421)

◆ Stella-Jones Corporation ....E 412 325-0202
Pittsburgh (G-15581)

▼ Stella-Jones US Holding Corp ....E 304 372-2211
Pittsburgh (G-15582)

Steve Eversoll ....G 717 768-3298
Gap (G-6256)

Sutherland Lumber Co ....E 724 947-3388
Burgettstown (G-2355)

▲ Tangent Rail Corporation ....G 412 325-0202
Pittsburgh (G-15596)

Tangent Rail Products Inc ....F 412 325-0202
Pittsburgh (G-15597)

TSO of Ohio Inc ....G 724 452-6161
Fombell (G-6035)

Ufp Stockertown LLC ....E 610 759-8536
Stockertown (G-18067)

▼ Woods Company Inc ....E 717 263-6524
Chambersburg (G-3000)

2493 Reconstituted Wood Prdts

Applegate Insul Systems Inc ....E 717 709-0533
Chambersburg (G-2905)

Aywon Chalkboard Corkboard Inc .....E 570 459-3490
Hazleton (G-7491)

▲ Clarion Industries LLC ....E 814 226-0851
Shippenville (G-17558)

Energex American Inc ....E 717 436-2400
Mifflintown (G-11116)

▼ Energex Corporation ....D 717 436-2400
Mifflintown (G-11117)

Engine Cycle Inc ....G 717 214-4177
Highspire (G-7632)

Erie Energy Products Inc ....F 814 454-2828
Erie (G-5266)

Georgia-Pacific LLC ....C 814 778-6000
Kane (G-8465)

Ipi Co Inc ....F 412 487-3995
Glenshaw (G-6491)

Jeld-Wen Inc ....C 570 265-9121
Towanda (G-18431)

New Heights LLC ....G 717 768-0070
Leola (G-9795)

◆ Rynone Manufacturing Corp ....C 570 888-5272
Sayre (G-17121)

▲ Saint-Gobain Corporation ....A 610 893-6000
Malvern (G-10313)

Soroka Sales Inc ....E 412 381-7700
Pittsburgh (G-15560)

Wirthmore Pdts & Svc Co Inc ....G 610 430-0300
West Chester (G-19680)

2499 Wood Prdts, NEC

A A A Engraving ....G 412 281-7756
Pittsburgh (G-14628)

A Word Concepts Inc ....G 215 924-2226
Philadelphia (G-13329)

A/S Custom Furniture Company ....E 215 491-3100
Warrington (G-19105)

Aaron E Beiler ....G 717 656-9596
New Holland (G-12224)

All Type Fence Co Inc ....G 610 718-1151
Douglassville (G-4166)

Applegate Insul Systems Inc ....E 717 709-0533
Chambersburg (G-2905)

Aunt Barbies ....G 717 445-6386
East Earl (G-4537)

B V Landscape Supplies Inc ....G 610 316-1099
Malvern (G-10191)

Bally Block Company ....D 610 845-7511
Bally (G-898)

Bally Holding Company PA ....G 610 845-7511
Bally (G-899)

Baut Studios Inc ....E 570 288-1431
Swoyersville (G-18194)

Beck & Ness Woodworking LLC ....G 717 764-3984
Emigsville (G-4984)

Beechdale Frames ....G 717 288-2723
Ronks (G-16803)

Bemenn Wood Products Inc ....G 717 738-3530
Ephrata (G-5093)

Black Lick Stake Plant ....G 724 459-7670
Blairsville (G-1716)

▲ Blue Mountain Processors Inc ....F 717 438-3296
Elliottsburg (G-4919)

Bon Air Products Inc ....G 412 793-8600
Verona (G-18749)

Byerstown Woodwork Shop ....G 717 442-8586
Kinzers (G-8734)

Calvert Lumber Company Inc ....F 724 346-5553
Sharon (G-17430)

Cedar Craft ....G 610 273-9224
Honey Brook (G-7741)

▲ Chef Specialties Inc ....E 814 887-5652
Smethport (G-17633)

Cheryl Hewitt ....G 814 943-7222
Altoona (G-492)

▲ Christopher Co Ltd ....G 215 331-8290
Philadelphia (G-13543)

Country Cupola Ltd ....G 717 866-8801
Myerstown (G-11881)

Country Lane Woodworking LLC ....E 717 351-9250
New Holland (G-12238)

▲ Countryside Woodcrafts Inc ....F 717 627-5641
Lititz (G-10004)

Cove Stake & Wood Products GP ......G 814 793-3257
Martinsburg (G-10522)

Creative Kink LLC ....G 610 506-9809
Royersford (G-16848)

D E Gemill Inc ....E 717 755-9794
Red Lion (G-16593)

David R Webb Company Inc ....C 570 322-7186
Williamsport (G-20003)

Door Stop Ltd ....G 610 353-8707
Wayne (G-19318)

E D Woodworks ....G 610 857-1465
Parkesburg (G-13174)

◆ Ecore International Inc ....C 717 295-3400
Lancaster (G-9007)

▲ Elmwood ....F 570 524-9663
Lewisburg (G-9905)

Erector Sets Inc ....G 215 289-1505
Philadelphia (G-13677)

Flexcut Tool Co Inc ....E 814 864-7855
Erie (G-5294)

Fogle Forest Products ....G..... 570 524-2580
Lewisburg (G-9908)
Frame Outlet Inc ....G..... 412 351-7283
Pittsburgh (G-15029)
Frey Group LLC ....F..... 717 786-2146
Quarryville (G-16270)
▼ Gish Logging Inc ....E..... 717 369-2783
Fort Loudon (G-6059)
Glenshaw Distributors Inc ....E..... 412 753-0231
Allison Park (G-451)
▲ Great Coasters Intl Inc ....F..... 570 286-9330
Sunbury (G-18170)
Groman Restoration Inc ....G..... 724 235-5000
New Florence (G-12197)
Heartland Kitchens & Bath ....G..... 814 744-8266
Leeper (G-9655)
Helm Fencing Inc ....E..... 215 822-5595
Hatfield (G-7348)
Honeybrook Woodworks ....F..... 610 593-6884
Christiana (G-3135)
Identification Systems Inc ....E..... 814 774-9656
Girard (G-6391)
Infinite Quest Cabinetry Corp ....G..... 301 222-3592
Red Lion (G-16601)
Ironstone Mills Inc ....G..... 717 656-4539
Leola (G-9787)
J & J Pallet Co Inc ....E..... 570 489-7705
Throop (G-18359)
J/M Fence & Deck Company ....G..... 610 488-7382
Mohrsville (G-11276)
Jay Weller ....G..... 215 257-4859
Sellersville (G-17350)
Jmg Inc ....G..... 215 659-4087
Willow Grove (G-20121)
John M Rohrbaugh Co Inc ....G..... 717 244-2895
Red Lion (G-16602)
Jones Crafts Inc ....G..... 610 346-6247
Kintnersville (G-8729)
Kaiser Mulch ....G..... 610 588-8111
Bangor (G-918)
▼ Kampel Enterprises Inc ....E..... 717 432-9688
Wellsville (G-19478)
Kennett Square Specialties LLC ....D..... 610 444-8122
Kennett Square (G-8520)
Kings Kountry Korner LLC ....G..... 717 768-3425
Gordonville (G-6560)
Kings Woodwork Shop ....G..... 717 768-7721
Kinzers (G-8739)
▼ Kuhns Bros Lumber Co Inc ....E..... 570 568-1412
Lewisburg (G-9914)
L W Green Frames ....G..... 610 432-3726
Westfield (G-19779)
Lanchester Woodworking ....G..... 717 355-2184
Narvon (G-11923)
Larson-Juhl US LLC ....G..... 215 638-5940
Bensalem (G-1219)
Leahmarlin Corp ....G..... 610 692-7378
West Chester (G-19589)
Limpach Industries Inc ....F..... 724 646-4011
Sharpsville (G-17473)
M & R Woodworks Inc ....G..... 724 378-7677
Aliquippa (G-81).
M K Crafts ....G..... 717 786-6080
Strasburg (G-18091)
Manley Fence Co ....G..... 610 842-8833
Coatesville (G-3316)
Martin Custom Cabinets LLC ....G..... 717 721-1859
East Earl (G-4547)
Mike Steck ....G..... 610 287-3518
Harleysville (G-7048)
Miller Country Craft ....G..... 717 336-1318
Denver (G-4084)
New Holland Fence LLC ....F..... 717 355-2204
New Holland (G-12265)
New Werner Holding Co Inc ....G..... 724 588-2000
Greenville (G-6758)
Newshams Woodshop Inc ....G..... 610 622-5800
Clifton Heights (G-3256)
Norse Paddle Co ....G..... 814 422-8844
Spring Mills (G-17890)
North Penn Art Inc ....F..... 215 362-2494
Lansdale (G-9393)
Northeast Products & Svcs Inc ....G..... 610 899-0286
Topton (G-18414)
▲ Patton Picture Company ....C..... 717 796-1508
Mechanicsburg (G-10877)
Pennypack Supply Company ....G..... 215 338-2200
Philadelphia (G-14133)
Perakis Frames Inc ....G..... 215 627-7700
Philadelphia (G-14136)

Precision Woodworking & C ....G..... 215 317-3533
Warminster (G-18943)
◆ Prestige Fence Co Inc ....D..... 215 362-8200
Hatfield (G-7385)
Ridge Woodworking ....G..... 814 839-0151
Schellsburg (G-17135)
Riley Tool Incorporated ....F..... 814 425-4140
Cochranton (G-3350)
Robert Wirth ....G..... 724 947-3615
Burgettstown (G-2354)
Round River Woodworking ....G..... 717 776-5876
Newville (G-12610)
Rusticraft Fence Co ....G..... 610 644-6770
Malvern (G-10311)
S & S Processing Inc ....E..... 724 535-3110
West Pittsburg (G-19752)
▲ Sauders Nursery ....F..... 717 354-9851
East Earl (G-4555)
Sensenigs Wood Shavings ....G..... 717 336-2047
Denver (G-4093)
South Penn Restoration Shop ......G..... 717 264-2602
Chambersburg (G-2977)
Spectra Inc ....E..... 814 238-6332
State College (G-18030)
Spoonwood Inc ....G..... 610 756-6464
Kempton (G-8495)
Spring Mill Woodworking ....G..... 610 286-7051
Morgantown (G-11536)
Stauffers Mini Barns ....G..... 724 479-0760
Indiana (G-8130)
Staurowsky Woodworking ....G..... 610 489-0770
Collegeville (G-3394)
Steve A Vitelli ....G..... 570 937-4546
Lake Ariel (G-8893)
Summitvile Woodworking ....G..... 717 355-5337
New Holland (G-12287)
▲ The Adirondack Group Inc ....E..... 610 431-4343
West Chester (G-19660)
Thomas Pennise Jr ....G..... 215 822-1832
Colmar (G-3421)
▼ Thompson Maple Products Inc ....E..... 814 664-7717
Corry (G-3775)
▲ Threshold Rhblitation Svcs Inc ...B..... 610 777-7691
Reading (G-16538)
Trotwood Manor ....G..... 724 635-3057
New Stanton (G-12452)
Turnings By Edric ....G..... 412 833-5127
Bethel Park (G-1436)
▼ Tuscarora Hardwoods Inc ....D..... 717 582-4122
Elliottsburg (G-4922)
Van Heyneker Fine Woodworking ...G..... 610 388-1772
West Chester (G-19671)
▲ Visconti Garment Hangers Inc ...G..... 570 366-7745
Orwigsburg (G-13054)
Walter E Lee Inc ....G..... 215 443-0271
Hatboro (G-7310)
Waltersdorf Manufacturing Co ......G..... 717 630-0036
Hanover (G-6971)
▲ Weaver Mulch LLC ....E..... 610 383-6818
Coatesville (G-3329)
◆ Werner Co ....C..... 724 588-2000
Greenville (G-6775)
Werner Holding Co Inc ....A..... 888 523-3371
Greenville (G-6776)
William Cottage ....G..... 724 266-2961
Ambridge (G-639)
Wilson & Mc Cracken Inc ....G..... 412 784-1772
Pittsburgh (G-15718)
Woodline Productions Inc ....G..... 814 362-5397
Bradford (G-1996)
Worthington Stowe Fine Woodwor ..F..... 215 504-5500
Newtown (G-12564)
Wyatt Incorporated ....E..... 724 684-7060
Monessen (G-11302)
Zell Manufacturing Co Inc ....G..... 724 327-4771
Export (G-5632)

25 FURNITURE AND FIXTURES

2511 Wood Household Furniture

2820 Associates Inc ....G..... 412 471-2525
Pittsburgh (G-14625)
▲ 4 Less Furniture and Rugs LLC ....F..... 610 650-4000
Oaks (G-12930)
Acorn Trail Woodcraft ....G..... 717 279-0261
Lebanon (G-9545)
Advantage Millwork Inc ....G..... 610 925-2785
Kennett Square (G-8502)
Alan Pepper Designs ....G..... 412 244-9299
Pittsburgh (G-14659)

Alvin Reiff Woodworking ....G..... 570 966-1149
Mifflinburg (G-11092)
Amanda Reiche ....G..... 570 424-0334
East Stroudsburg (G-4605)
▲ American Atelier Inc ....C..... 610 439-4040
Allentown (G-133)
Ames Construction Inc ....E..... 717 299-1395
Lancaster (G-8932)
Ashley Furniture Inds Inc ....A..... 610 926-0897
Leesport (G-9657)
B & S Woodcraft ....G..... 717 786-8154
Quarryville (G-16262)
▲ Bareville Woodcraft Co ....F..... 717 656-6261
Leola (G-9771)
◆ Benchsmith LLC ....G..... 215 491-1171
Warrington (G-19109)
Big Boyz Industries Inc ....G..... 215 942-9971
Warminster (G-18837)
◆ Bird-In-Hand Woodworks Inc .....D..... 717 397-5686
Lancaster (G-8954)
Bones and All LLC ....G..... 216 870-7177
Pittsburgh (G-14783)
Braders Woodcraft Inc ....F..... 610 262-3452
Laurys Station (G-9532)
Brodart Inc ....E..... 570 326-2461
Montgomery (G-11368)
Brodys Furniture Inc ....G..... 724 745-4630
Canonsburg (G-2551)
◆ Bush Industries of PA ....C..... 814 868-2874
Erie (G-5219)
Carpet and Furniture Depot Inc ....G..... 814 239-5865
Claysburg (G-3201)
Carter Handcrafted Furniture ....G..... 610 847-2101
Ottsville (G-13061)
Cedar Ridge Furniture ....G..... 610 286-6225
Morgantown (G-11519)
Charles Ginty Associates Inc ....G..... 610 347-1101
Unionville (G-18647)
Childcraft Education Corp ....C..... 717 653-7500
Mount Joy (G-11649)
Chris S Sensenig ....G..... 717 423-5311
Shippensburg (G-17522)
Classic Furniture ....G..... 717 738-0088
Lititz (G-9999)
Clifton Custom Furn & Design ....F..... 724 727-2045
Apollo (G-670)
▲ Closet Works Inc ....E..... 215 675-6430
Montgomeryville (G-11388)
▼ Collegiate Furnishings Inc ....E..... 814 234-1660
State College (G-17954)
Colonial Furniture Company ....D..... 570 374-6016
Freeburg (G-6188)
Colonial Road Woodworks LLC .....E..... 717 354-8998
New Holland (G-12237)
▲ Coopersburg Associates Inc .....E..... 610 282-1360
Center Valley (G-2825)
Country Additions Inc ....G..... 610 404-2062
Birdsboro (G-1692)
Country Barns of Pittsburgh ....G..... 412 221-1630
Pittsburgh (G-14879)
Country Heirlooms Inc ....G..... 610 869-9550
West Grove (G-19698)
Country Value Woodworks LLC .....E..... 717 786-7949
Quarryville (G-16267)
◆ Cramco Inc ....C..... 215 427-9500
Philadelphia (G-13577)
Creekside Structures LLC ....G..... 717 627-5267
Leola (G-9775)
Daniel G Berg ....G..... 610 856-7095
Mohnton (G-11261)
David Esh ....G..... 610 286-6225
Morgantown (G-11521)
David Karr ....G..... 814 669-4406
Alexandria (G-63)
David Lee Designs ....F..... 814 725-4289
North East (G-12738)
Delex Co ....G..... 724 938-2366
Brownsville (G-2311)
Destefanos Hardwood Lumber ......G..... 724 483-6196
Charleroi (G-3009)
◆ Diamond Trpcl Hardwoods Intl ...G..... 215 257-2556
Sellersville (G-17345)
Duckloe Frederick and Bros ....F..... 570 897-6172
Portland (G-15939)
E H Woodworking ....G..... 717 445-6595
East Earl (G-4542)
Edward Hennessy Co Inc ....G..... 215 426-4154
Philadelphia (G-13662)
▲ Elmwood ....F..... 570 524-9663
Lewisburg (G-9905)

S
I
C

Fab Dubrufaut Woodworking G 215 533-4853
Philadelphia *(G-13691)*

Federal Prison Industries B 570 524-0096
Lewisburg *(G-9906)*

Frame Up & Gallery G 724 627-0552
Waynesburg *(G-19441)*

Genesee River Trading Company G 724 533-5354
Volant *(G-18774)*

George Nkashima Woodworker S A F 215 862-2272
New Hope *(G-12302)*

Giffin Interior & Fixture Inc C 412 221-1166
Bridgeville *(G-2066)*

▲ **Gleepet Inc** F 347 607-7850
Trevose *(G-18497)*

Godshall Woodcraft G 610 530-9386
Breinigsville *(G-2017)*

Haltemans Hardwood Products G 814 745-2519
Sligo *(G-17615)*

▲ **Hampton Cabinet Shop** G 717 898-7806
Manheim *(G-10387)*

Harmony Plus Woodworks Inc G 717 432-0372
Dillsburg *(G-4131)*

Harrison Custom Cabinets G 215 548-2450
Philadelphia *(G-13804)*

Henderson Bernard Furn Ardison G 215 930-0400
Philadelphia *(G-13813)*

Hillside Enterprise G 724 479-3678
Homer City *(G-7675)*

Honey Brook Woodcrafts G 610 273-2928
Honey Brook *(G-7750)*

Ingrain Construction LLC G 717 205-1475
Columbia *(G-3439)*

Ingrain Construction LLC F 717 205-1475
Lancaster *(G-9057)*

Interior Motives Inc G 814 672-3100
Coalport *(G-3283)*

Interstate Self Storage G 724 662-1186
Mercer *(G-10965)*

J D Lohr Woodworking Inc G 610 287-7802
Schwenksville *(G-17177)*

Jacoby Transportation Inc E 717 677-7733
Gettysburg *(G-6302)*

Jonathans Woodcraft G 610 857-1359
Parkesburg *(G-13177)*

KB Woodcraft Inc G 502 533-2773
Phoenixville *(G-14555)*

Kinloch Woodworking Ltd G 610 347-2070
Unionville *(G-18648)*

Kitko Wood Products Inc C 814 672-3606
Glen Hope *(G-6426)*

Kosko Wood Products Inc G 814 427-2499
Stump Creek *(G-18143)*

Kountry Kraft Kitchens Inc C 610 589-4575
Newmanstown *(G-12479)*

Krehling Industries Inc D 717 232-7936
Harrisburg *(G-7165)*

Lamens Furniture G 814 733-4537
Schellsburg *(G-17134)*

Lapp John G 717 442-8583
Gap *(G-6252)*

Lehman Cabinetry G 717 432-5014
Dillsburg *(G-4133)*

Leisters Furniture Inc D 717 632-8177
Hanover *(G-6914)*

Lightning Group Inc G 717 834-3031
Duncannon *(G-4447)*

Lime Rock Gazebos LLC G 717 625-4066
Lititz *(G-10022)*

▲ **Little Partners Inc** G 318 220-7005
Reading *(G-16431)*

M & M Creative Laminates Inc G 412 781-4700
Aspinwall *(G-746)*

▲ **Maple Mountain Industries Inc** E 724 676-4703
New Florence *(G-12198)*

Martins Furniture LLC F 717 354-5657
Ephrata *(G-5126)*

Martins Wood Products LLC E 717 933-5115
Myerstown *(G-11893)*

Missing Piece G 610 759-4033
Nazareth *(G-11982)*

New Wave Custom Wdwkg Inc E 570 251-8218
Honesdale *(G-7718)*

Newburg Woodcrafts G 717 530-8823
Shippensburg *(G-17539)*

Newswanger Woods Specialties G 717 355-9274
New Holland *(G-12269)*

Patterson Furniture Co G 412 771-0600
Mc Kees Rocks *(G-10622)*

Paul Dorazio Custom Furniture G 215 836-1057
Flourtown *(G-5989)*

Pine Creek Construction LLC G 717 362-6974
Elizabethville *(G-4896)*

Pittsburgh Shed Company Inc G 724 745-4422
Canonsburg *(G-2619)*

PS Furniture Inc E 814 587-6313
Conneautville *(G-3486)*

▲ **RAD Mfg LLC** D 570 752-4514
Nescopeck *(G-12001)*

Renningers Cabinetree Inc E 570 726-6494
Mill Hall *(G-11181)*

Ricks Custom Wood Design Inc F 717 627-2701
Akron *(G-37)*

Robert Trate Hogg Cbinetmakers G 717 529-2522
Oxford *(G-13088)*

Ruby Custom Woodcraft Inc G 570 698-7741
Lake Ariel *(G-8891)*

◆ **Rynone Manufacturing Corp** C 570 888-5272
Sayre *(G-17121)*

S & R Woodworking G 717 354-8628
Gordonville *(G-6562)*

S D L Custom Cabinetry Inc G 215 355-8188
Langhorne *(G-9323)*

S F Spector Inc G 717 236-0805
Harrisburg *(G-7211)*

Sam Beiler G 717 442-8990
Kinzers *(G-8742)*

Saw Rocking Horse G 610 683-8075
Kutztown *(G-8860)*

◆ **Schultz Richard Design & Mfg** F 215 679-2222
East Greenville *(G-4574)*

Schutte Woodworking & Mfg Co G 814 453-5110
Erie *(G-5470)*

Selectrim Corporation E 570 326-3662
Williamsport *(G-20071)*

Sensenig Chair Shop G 717 463-3480
Thompsontown *(G-18351)*

Signature Gallery G 610 792-5399
Royersford *(G-16864)*

Smith Lawton Millwork G 570 934-2544
Montrose *(G-11477)*

Soltrace Inc E 215 765-5700
Philadelphia *(G-14324)*

Spectra Inc E 814 238-6332
State College *(G-18030)*

Stauffer Wood Products G 717 647-4372
Tower City *(G-18441)*

Stoltzfus John G 717 786-2481
Quarryville *(G-16281)*

Stony Hill Woodworks G 717 786-8358
Quarryville *(G-16283)*

▲ **Susquehanna Grdn Concepts LLC** G 717 826-5144
Fleetwood *(G-5981)*

T L King Cabinetmaker G 610 869-4220
Cochranville *(G-3356)*

Tiki Kevs G 267 718-4527
Chalfont *(G-2892)*

Top Shop G 610 622-6101
Philadelphia *(G-14396)*

Trim P A C LLC G 717 375-2366
Chambersburg *(G-2989)*

Unique Wood Creation LLC G 717 687-7900
Paradise *(G-13164)*

Van Etten James G 215 453-8228
Perkasie *(G-13297)*

Varchettis Furniture G 814 733-4318
Berlin *(G-1293)*

Village Craft Iron & Stone Inc E 814 353-1777
Julian *(G-8457)*

Wallace Moving & Storage G 724 568-2411
Vandergrift *(G-18737)*

Wanner Road Woodcraft G 717 768-0207
Narvon *(G-11931)*

Wayneco Inc D 717 225-4413
York *(G-20704)*

Weaver Wood Specialties G 610 589-5889
Womelsdorf *(G-20210)*

◆ **Werzalit of America Inc** D 814 362-3881
Bradford *(G-1995)*

White Oak Woodcraft G 717 665-4738
Manheim *(G-10406)*

William Cottage G 724 266-2961
Ambridge *(G-639)*

Winterhouse Furniture Inc G 215 249-3410
Dublin *(G-4437)*

Woodpeckers Woodcraft Inc G 814 397-2282
Erie *(G-5533)*

Woxall Woodcraft Inc G 215 234-8774
Green Lane *(G-6594)*

Wyomissing Structures LLC G 610 374-2370
New Providence *(G-12436)*

Zimmerman Chair Shop E 717 273-2706
Lebanon *(G-9640)*

2512 Wood Household Furniture, Upholstered

▲ **American Atelier Inc** C 610 439-4040
Allentown *(G-133)*

Anthony Cocco Inc G 215 629-4100
Philadelphia *(G-13394)*

Ashley Furniture Inds Inc A 610 926-0897
Leesport *(G-9657)*

B K Barrit Corp D 267 345-1200
Philadelphia *(G-13438)*

Chair Shoppe G 570 353-2735
Morris *(G-11544)*

Dronetti Upholstery Inc G 610 435-2957
Allentown *(G-196)*

Dsc2 Inc F 980 223-2270
York *(G-20458)*

Easton Upholstery Furn Mfg Co G 610 252-3169
Easton *(G-4675)*

Ed RE Invent G 814 590-0771
Luthersburg *(G-10123)*

Everclear Valley Inc G 724 676-4703
New Florence *(G-12196)*

▲ **Fabtex Inc** C 570 275-7500
Danville *(G-4000)*

Ferrante Uphlstrng & Crptng F 724 535-8866
Wampum *(G-18800)*

Flexsteel Industries Inc C 717 392-4161
Lancaster *(G-9019)*

Golden Brothers Inc E 570 714-5002
Kingston *(G-8718)*

◆ **Golden Brothers Inc** C 570 457-0867
Old Forge *(G-12965)*

Golden Technologies Inc G 570 451-7477
Old Forge *(G-12966)*

Guildcraft Inc F 717 854-3888
York *(G-20517)*

Haberle Upholstery G 215 679-8195
Zionsville *(G-20835)*

Jerry Lister Custom Upholsteri G 215 639-3880
Bensalem *(G-1213)*

Jerry Lister Custom Upholsteri F 215 639-3882
Huntingdon Valley *(G-8004)*

Kauffmans Upholstery Inc G 610 262-8298
Northampton *(G-12852)*

Keystone Quality Products LLC E 717 354-2762
Leola *(G-9790)*

Lusch Frames LLC G 215 739-6264
Philadelphia *(G-13977)*

Maple Mountain Industries Inc F 724 439-1234
Uniontown *(G-18637)*

Maple Mountain Industries Inc E 570 662-3200
Mansfield *(G-10421)*

▲ **Maple Mountain Industries Inc** E 724 676-4703
New Florence *(G-12198)*

Maple Mountain Industries Inc G 814 634-0674
Meyersdale *(G-11015)*

Mega Motion LLC E 800 800-8586
Exeter *(G-5583)*

Noor Furniture Inc G 215 533-0703
Philadelphia *(G-14077)*

Patterson Furniture Co G 412 771-0600
Mc Kees Rocks *(G-10622)*

Russell Upholstery Co Inc G 814 455-9021
Erie *(G-5467)*

S DRocco Upholstery G 215 745-2869
Philadelphia *(G-14270)*

Schuibbeo Holdings Inc G 610 268-2825
Avondale *(G-859)*

Tiffany Tiffany Designers Inc G 215 297-0550
Point Pleasant *(G-15888)*

2514 Metal Household Furniture

Casual Living Unlimited LLC G 717 351-7177
New Holland *(G-12231)*

Clear Creek Industries Inc F 814 834-9880
Saint Marys *(G-16954)*

◆ **Cramco Inc** C 215 427-9500
Philadelphia *(G-13577)*

Delweld Industries Corp F 814 535-2412
Stoystown *(G-18075)*

Earl West Industries G 717 656-6600
Leola *(G-9779)*

Federal Prison Industries B 570 524-0096
Lewisburg *(G-9906)*

Francis J Nowalk G 412 687-4017
Pittsburgh *(G-15030)*

George J Bush Kitchen Center ....G 724 694-9533
Derry *(G-4101)*

Gk Inc ....F 215 223-7207
Philadelphia *(G-13764)*

Harold M Horst Inc ....G 717 354-5815
New Holland *(G-12251)*

▲ Lee Sandusky Corporation ....E 717 359-4111
Littlestown *(G-10069)*

▲ Little Partners Inc ....G 318 220-7005
Reading *(G-16431)*

Maple Mountain Industries Inc ....G 814 634-0674
Meyersdale *(G-11015)*

Racechairs LLC ....G 267 632-5003
Perkasie *(G-13291)*

Rio Brands LLC ....D 610 629-6200
Conshohocken *(G-3601)*

▲ Robern Inc ....D 215 826-0280
Bristol *(G-2195)*

Sam Mannino Enterprises LLC ....E 814 692-4100
Pennsylvania Furnace *(G-13264)*

◆ Schultz Richard Design & Mfg .....F 215 679-2222
East Greenville *(G-4574)*

▲ Sett ....G 215 322-9301
Huntingdon Valley *(G-8037)*

Tri State Kitchens and Baths ....F ....
Pottstown *(G-16058)*

Village Craft Iron & Stone Inc ....E 814 353-1777
Julian *(G-8457)*

2515 Mattresses & Bedsprings

▼ Bergad Inc ....E 724 763-2883
Kittanning *(G-8757)*

▲ Chestnut Ridge Foam Inc ....C 724 537-9000
Latrobe *(G-9464)*

Classic Bedding Mfg Co Inc ....G 800 810-0930
Conneaut Lake *(G-3470)*

Custom Bedframe Products ....F 570 539-8770
Port Trevorton *(G-15911)*

Custom Carpet & Bedding Inc ....G 570 344-7533
Dunmore *(G-4472)*

Eastern Sleep Products Company .....E 610 582-7228
Reading *(G-16369)*

Elby Bedding Inc ....G 610 292-8700
Norristown *(G-12653)*

▲ ES Kluft & Co East LLC ....E 570 384-2800
Denver *(G-4072)*

ES Kluft & Company Inc ....D 570 384-2800
Hazle Township *(G-7455)*

Honey Brook Woodcrafts ....G 610 273-2928
Honey Brook *(G-7750)*

Jbs Woodwork Shop ....F 570 374-4883
Port Trevorton *(G-15914)*

Leggett & Platt Incorporated ....D 724 748-3057
Mercer *(G-10966)*

Leggett & Platt Incorporated ....D 570 824-6622
Hanover Township *(G-6992)*

Leggett & Platt Incorporated ....D 570 542-4171
Berwick *(G-1332)*

M B Bedding Co ....G 570 822-2491
Wilkes Barre *(G-19939)*

Magic Sleeper Inc ....F 610 327-2322
Pottstown *(G-16013)*

Manns Sickroom Service Inc ....E 412 672-5680
White Oak *(G-19856)*

McMullens Furniture Store ....G 814 942-1202
Altoona *(G-526)*

Neuropedic LLC ....F 570 501-7713
West Hazleton *(G-19714)*

Nuvanna LLC ....G 844 611-2324
Chadds Ford *(G-2857)*

Ohio Mat Lcnsing Cmpnnts Group ...D 570 715-7200
Mountain Top *(G-11768)*

Park Place Pa LLC ....D 717 336-2846
Denver *(G-4086)*

▲ Pennsylvania Bedding Inc ....E 570 457-0933
Old Forge *(G-12974)*

Stauffer Frames ....E 570 374-7100
Port Trevorton *(G-15915)*

Tempur Production Usa LLC ....F 570 715-7200
Mountain Top *(G-11778)*

▲ Z Wood Products Co Inc ....E 215 423-9891
Philadelphia *(G-14503)*

2517 Wood T V, Radio, Phono & Sewing Cabinets

Ames Construction Inc ....E 717 299-1395
Lancaster *(G-8932)*

Bostock Company Inc ....E 215 343-7040
Warrington *(G-19110)*

Conestoga Valley Cstm Kitchens ......E 717 445-5415
Narvon *(G-11919)*

Effort Woodcraft Inc ....E 570 629-1160
Effort *(G-4825)*

▲ Identity Group ....G 610 767-4700
Slatington *(G-17607)*

Richard Riberich ....G 412 271-8427
Pittsburgh *(G-15484)*

Sam King ....G 610 273-7979
Honey Brook *(G-7760)*

Schubert Custom Cabinetry Inc ....G 610 372-5559
Reading *(G-16508)*

◆ Touchstone Home Products Inc .....G 510 782-1282
Exton *(G-5738)*

2519 Household Furniture, NEC

Edward Hennessy Co Inc ....G 215 426-4154
Philadelphia *(G-13662)*

Gene Sanes & Associates ....E 412 471-8224
Pittsburgh *(G-15043)*

Gregg Lane LLC ....G 215 269-9900
Fairless Hills *(G-5781)*

Guildcraft Inc ....F 717 854-3888
York *(G-20517)*

K T & Co ....G 610 520-0221
Bryn Mawr *(G-2328)*

2521 Wood Office Furniture

A/S Custom Furniture Company ....E 215 491-3100
Warrington *(G-19105)*

▲ ABF USA Ltd ....G 570 788-0888
Drums *(G-4380)*

▲ Ajjp Corporation ....C 215 968-6677
Newtown *(G-12495)*

▲ American Atelier Inc ....C 610 439-4040
Allentown *(G-133)*

B K Barrit Corp ....D 267 345-1200
Philadelphia *(G-13438)*

Biltwood Architectural Mllwk ....F 717 593-9400
Greencastle *(G-6600)*

◆ Bush Industries of PA ....C 814 868-2874
Erie *(G-5219)*

Cedar Ridge Furniture ....G 610 286-6225
Morgantown *(G-11519)*

Ceraln Corp ....E 570 322-8400
South Williamsport *(G-17790)*

Conestoga Valley Cstm Kitchens ......E 717 445-5415
Narvon *(G-11919)*

Conestoga Wood Spc Corp ....C 570 658-9663
Beavertown *(G-1025)*

◆ Conestoga Wood Spc Corp ....A 717 445-6701
East Earl *(G-4540)*

▼ Contemprary Artisans Cabinetry .....E 215 723-8803
Telford *(G-18276)*

◆ Datum Filing Systems Inc ....C 717 764-6350
Emigsville *(G-4986)*

David Jonathan Wdwkg & Mfg Co .....G 724 499-5225
Rogersville *(G-16795)*

Dsc2 Inc ....F 980 223-2270
York *(G-20458)*

Duckloe Frederick and Bros ....F 570 897-6172
Portland *(G-15939)*

Epic Industries Inc ....G 570 586-0253
Clarks Summit *(G-3192)*

Eye Design LLC ....E 610 409-1900
Trappe *(G-18468)*

Federal Prison Industries ....E 570 544-7343
Minersville *(G-11254)*

French Creek Woodworking Inc ....G 610 286-9295
Elverson *(G-4963)*

Gerald Maier ....G 215 744-9999
Philadelphia *(G-13757)*

Home Woodwork ....G 570 295-2185
Port Trevorton *(G-15913)*

Infinite Quest Cabinetry Corp ....G 301 222-3592
Red Lion *(G-16601)*

Joseph Mikstas ....G 215 271-2419
Philadelphia *(G-13911)*

Knoll Inc ....E 215 988-1788
Philadelphia *(G-13940)*

Knoll Inc ....D 484 224-3760
Allentown *(G-285)*

◆ Knoll Inc ....D 215 679-7991
East Greenville *(G-4570)*

Knoll Inc ....E 215 679-1218
East Greenville *(G-4571)*

Krehling Industries Inc ....D 717 232-7936
Harrisburg *(G-7165)*

◆ Mahogany and More Inc ....F 610 666-6500
Oaks *(G-12934)*

Martins Furniture LLC ....F 717 354-5657
Ephrata *(G-5126)*

Milder Office Inc ....G 215 717-7027
Philadelphia *(G-14023)*

Millwork Solutions Inc ....E 814 446-4009
Seward *(G-17382)*

Missing Piece ....G 610 759-4033
Nazareth *(G-11982)*

Odhner and Odhner Fine Wdwkg ....G 610 258-9300
Easton *(G-4734)*

Paul Downs Cabinet Makers Inc ....F 610 239-0142
Bridgeport *(G-2043)*

Primrose Consulting Inc ....G 724 816-5769
Mars *(G-10510)*

Richard Riberich ....G 412 271-8427
Pittsburgh *(G-15484)*

Robert Trate Hogg Cbinetmakers ....G 717 529-2522
Oxford *(G-13088)*

Robisons Cabinet Studio ....G 717 677-9828
Aspers *(G-745)*

Selinsgrove Instnl Csework LLC ....E 570 374-1176
Selinsgrove *(G-17333)*

Spectra Inc ....E 814 238-6332
State College *(G-18030)*

Tha Inc ....G 215 804-0220
Quakertown *(G-16250)*

Vitra Inc ....E 610 391-9780
Allentown *(G-424)*

William Cottage ....G 724 266-2961
Ambridge *(G-639)*

Winterhouse Furniture Inc ....G 215 249-3410
Dublin *(G-4437)*

Wood-Mode Incorporated ....E 570 374-1176
Selinsgrove *(G-17338)*

2522 Office Furniture, Except Wood

A/S Custom Furniture Company ....E 215 491-3100
Warrington *(G-19105)*

AAA Business Solutions LLC ....G 412 787-3333
Pittsburgh *(G-14631)*

Adelphia Steel Eqp Co Inc ....E 800 865-8211
Philadelphia *(G-13345)*

▲ Ajjp Corporation ....C 215 968-6677
Newtown *(G-12495)*

Ceraln Corp ....E 570 322-8400
South Williamsport *(G-17790)*

▼ Charles Beseler Co Inc ....D 800 237-3537
Stroudsburg *(G-18109)*

◆ Datum Filing Systems Inc ....C 717 764-6350
Emigsville *(G-4986)*

Design Options Holdings LLC ....E 610 667-8180
Bala Cynwyd *(G-877)*

◆ Emeco Industries Inc ....E 717 637-5951
Hanover *(G-6883)*

Ergogenic Technology Inc ....E 215 766-8545
Quakertown *(G-16188)*

Flex-Y-Plan Industries Inc ....E 814 881-3436
Fairview *(G-5822)*

▲ Gichner Systems Group LLC ....B 717 244-7611
Dallastown *(G-3977)*

Gk Inc ....F 215 223-7207
Philadelphia *(G-13764)*

▲ Innovative Office Products LLC ......C 610 559-6369
Easton *(G-4707)*

Interior Creations Inc ....E 215 425-9390
Philadelphia *(G-13864)*

◆ Knoll Inc ....D 215 679-7991
East Greenville *(G-4570)*

Patterson Furniture Co ....E 412 771-0600
Mc Kees Rocks *(G-10622)*

Perpetual Enterprises Inc ....G 412 299-6356
Coraopolis *(G-3712)*

Perpetual Enterprises Inc ....G 412 299-6356
Coraopolis *(G-3713)*

Perpetual Enterprises Inc ....G 814 437-3705
Franklin *(G-6151)*

Pickell Enterprises Inc ....E 215 244-7800
Bensalem *(G-1243)*

Precise Graphix LLC ....E 610 965-9400
Allentown *(G-357)*

Primrose Consulting Inc ....G 724 816-5769
Mars *(G-10510)*

Racechairs LLC ....G 267 632-5003
Perkasie *(G-13291)*

Robert Trate Hogg Cbinetmakers ....G 717 529-2522
Oxford *(G-13088)*

Spectra Inc ....E 814 238-6332
State College *(G-18030)*

▲ Stanley Storage Systems Inc ....G 610 797-6600
Allentown *(G-401)*

Superior Cabinet Company....................G....... 215 536-5228
Quakertown *(G-16247)*

◆ TC Millwork Inc.................................C....... 215 245-4210
Bensalem *(G-1259)*

Transwall Office Systems Inc...............E....... 610 429-1400
West Chester *(G-19669)*

Vicjah Corporation...................................G....... 610 826-7475
Palmerton *(G-13114)*

Vitra Inc...E....... 610 391-9780
Allentown *(G-424)*

2531 Public Building & Related Furniture

▲ Ajjp Corporation.................................C....... 215 968-6677
Newtown *(G-12495)*

▲ American Atelier Inc.........................C....... 610 439-4040
Allentown *(G-133)*

B/E Aerospace Inc.................................G....... 570 595-7491
Mountainhome *(G-11785)*

Bahrets Church Interiors.........................G....... 717 540-1747
Harrisburg *(G-7094)*

◆ Bird-In-Hand Woodworks Inc...........D....... 717 397-5686
Lancaster *(G-8954)*

Brodart Co...C....... 570 769-7412
Mc Elhattan *(G-10585)*

◆ Brodart Co...D....... 570 326-2461
Williamsport *(G-19995)*

Carrier Class Green Infras.......................G....... 267 419-8496
Willow Grove *(G-20110)*

Cedar Ridge Furniture.............................G....... 610 286-6225
Morgantown *(G-11519)*

Ceraln Corp...E....... 570 322-8400
South Williamsport *(G-17790)*

Childcraft Education Corp......................C....... 717 653-7500
Mount Joy *(G-11649)*

Contour Seats Inc...................................G....... 610 395-5144
Allentown *(G-179)*

County of Montgomery...........................E....... 215 234-4528
Green Lane *(G-6586)*

Custom Seats Inc....................................D....... 570 602-7408
Wilkes Barre *(G-19915)*

Duckloe Frederick and Bros....................F....... 570 897-6172
Portland *(G-15939)*

◆ Enginred Arrsting Systems Corp......C....... 610 494-8000
Upper Chichester *(G-18660)*

Freedman Seating Company....................C....... 610 265-3610
Exton *(G-5681)*

Great Eastern Seating Co........................G....... 610 366-8132
Breinigsville *(G-2018)*

Johnson Controls Inc..............................D....... 717 765-2461
Waynesboro *(G-19414)*

Johnson Controls Inc..............................G....... 800 877-9675
Audubon *(G-828)*

Johnson Controls Inc..............................D....... 717 815-4200
York *(G-20544)*

Kettle Creek Corporation........................G....... 800 527-7848
Ottsville *(G-13064)*

Keystone Ridge Designs Inc....................E....... 724 284-1213
Butler *(G-2417)*

Legnini RC Architectural Mllwk..............F....... 610 640-1227
Malvern *(G-10266)*

Missing Piece...G....... 610 759-4033
Nazareth *(G-11982)*

◆ Oakworks Inc.....................................D....... 717 227-0516
New Freedom *(G-12213)*

PS Furniture Inc......................................E....... 814 587-6313
Conneautville *(G-3486)*

Racechairs LLC.......................................G....... 267 632-5003
Perkasie *(G-13291)*

Robert Trate Hogg Cbinetmakers............G....... 717 529-2522
Oxford *(G-13088)*

Schalow Visual Concepts Inc..................G....... 570 336-2714
Benton *(G-1282)*

Schutte Woodworking & Mfg Co............G....... 814 453-5110
Erie *(G-5470)*

Stadium Solutions Inc.............................F....... 724 287-5330
Butler *(G-2444)*

▲ Ussc Group Inc..................................D....... 610 265-3610
Exton *(G-5743)*

◆ Ussc LLC..D....... 610 265-3610
Exton *(G-5744)*

2541 Wood, Office & Store Fixtures

3-D Creative Services Inc.......................F....... 570 329-1111
Williamsport *(G-19983)*

A & V Woodwork Co...............................F....... 215 727-8832
Philadelphia *(G-13322)*

A/S Custom Furniture Company.............E....... 215 491-3100
Warrington *(G-19105)*

▲ Ajjp Corporation.................................C....... 215 968-6677
Newtown *(G-12495)*

Allegheny Solid Surfc Tech LLC............E....... 717 630-1251
Mc Sherrystown *(G-10649)*

▲ Allegheny Store Fixtures Inc..............E....... 814 362-6805
Bradford *(G-1954)*

Ames Construction Inc............................E....... 717 299-1395
Lancaster *(G-8932)*

API Americas Inc....................................F....... 785 842-7674
Levittown *(G-9817)*

Architectural Woodsmiths Inc.................D....... 717 532-7700
Shippensburg *(G-17515)*

Atlantic Shelving Systems LLC..............G....... 215 245-1310
Bensalem *(G-1151)*

Bendersville Wood Crafts........................G....... 717 677-6458
Bendersville *(G-1138)*

Berkman John A Display Sls Inc............G....... 412 421-0201
Pittsburgh *(G-14763)*

Big Valley Cabinets.................................G....... 717 935-2788
Belleville *(G-1127)*

▲ Boyce Products Ltd...........................F....... 570 224-6570
Damascus *(G-3989)*

▲ Bradford Clocks Limited....................F....... 570 427-4493
Weatherly *(G-19453)*

Brightbill Industries Inc...........................E....... 717 233-4121
Harrisburg *(G-7099)*

Broc Supply Co Inc.................................E....... 610 433-4646
Emmaus *(G-5022)*

Caseworks Inc..F....... 724 522-5068
Jeannette *(G-8249)*

Cedars Wdwkg & Renovations LLC......G....... 717 392-1736
Lancaster *(G-8972)*

Charles Steckman.....................................G....... 724 789-7066
Renfrew *(G-16638)*

CNT Fixture Company Inc......................E....... 412 443-6260
Glenshaw *(G-6484)*

Compass Ret Display Group Inc.............G....... 215 744-2787
Philadelphia *(G-13562)*

Countertek Inc..E....... 717 336-2371
Ephrata *(G-5097)*

Country Woodcrafts.................................G....... 814 793-4417
Roaring Spring *(G-16763)*

▲ Craft-Maid Kitchen Inc.......................E....... 610 376-8686
Reading *(G-16352)*

Custom Designs & Mfg Co.....................E....... 570 207-4432
Scranton *(G-17226)*

Custom Kitchens Inc................................G....... 814 833-5338
Erie *(G-5238)*

Custom Wood Crafters Inc......................G....... 215 357-6677
Warminster *(G-18853)*

Dally Slate Company Inc.........................D....... 610 863-4172
Pen Argyl *(G-13213)*

David Walters...G....... 610 435-5433
Allentown *(G-192)*

Dennis Downing.......................................G....... 724 598-0043
New Castle *(G-12081)*

Desavino & Sons Inc...............................E....... 570 383-3988
Olyphant *(G-12988)*

Desmond Wholesale Distrs Inc...............F....... 215 225-0300
Philadelphia *(G-13623)*

Donatucci Kitchens & Appls...................E....... 215 545-5755
Philadelphia *(G-13639)*

Dutka Inc..G....... 717 285-5880
Mountville *(G-11794)*

Earnest Industries Inc..............................G....... 412 323-1911
Pittsburgh *(G-14953)*

EDM Co...E....... 717 626-2186
Lititz *(G-10005)*

Eye Design LLC.......................................E....... 610 409-1900
Trappe *(G-18468)*

Frederick Wohlgemuth Inc......................E....... 215 638-9672
Bensalem *(G-1199)*

Gh Silver Asset Corp...............................G....... 404 432-3707
Philadelphia *(G-13760)*

Giffin Interior & Fixture Inc....................C....... 412 221-1166
Bridgeville *(G-2066)*

Gwiz Products...G....... 724 864-0200
Irwin *(G-8165)*

Harrison Custom Cabinets.......................G....... 215 548-2450
Philadelphia *(G-13804)*

Henry H Ross & Son Inc.........................E....... 717 626-6268
Lititz *(G-10014)*

Hilltop Woodshop Inc..............................G....... 724 697-4506
Avonmore *(G-865)*

Hoff Enterprises Inc.................................E....... 814 535-8371
Johnstown *(G-8381)*

Holly Woodcrafters Inc............................E....... 717 486-5862
Mount Holly Springs *(G-11634)*

Imperial Counter Top Company...............G....... 610 435-4803
Allentown *(G-255)*

Interactive Worldwide Corp....................D....... 906 370-7609
Philadelphia *(G-13863)*

Interior Creations Inc...............................E....... 215 425-9390
Philadelphia *(G-13864)*

◆ Intermetro Industries Corp................B....... 570 825-2741
Wilkes Barre *(G-19929)*

J D R Fixtures Inc....................................E....... 610 323-6599
Pottstown *(G-16003)*

K M B Inc...G....... 215 643-7999
Ambler *(G-585)*

▲ K S Manufacturing Co LP..................F....... 412 931-5365
Pittsburgh *(G-15160)*

Keystone Casework Inc...........................E....... 814 941-7250
Altoona *(G-520)*

Kitchens By Meade Inc............................F....... 814 453-4888
Erie *(G-5345)*

Kol Industries Inc.....................................F....... 717 630-0600
Hanover *(G-6911)*

Kountry Kraft Kitchens Inc.....................C....... 610 589-4575
Newmanstown *(G-12479)*

Krehling Industries Inc............................D....... 717 232-7936
Harrisburg *(G-7165)*

▲ Krg Enterprises Inc............................C....... 215 708-2811
Philadelphia *(G-13945)*

Lozier Corporation...................................C....... 570 658-8111
Mc Clure *(G-10560)*

M & M Creative Laminates Inc...............G....... 412 781-4700
Aspinwall *(G-746)*

M & M Manufacturing Co.......................E....... 724 274-0767
Cheswick *(G-3111)*

Macson Company.....................................G....... 610 264-7733
Allentown *(G-305)*

Markraft Company....................................G....... 724 733-3654
Murrysville *(G-11857)*

McGrory Inc...D....... 610 444-1512
Kennett Square *(G-8526)*

Melvin Stoltzfus.......................................F....... 717 656-3520
Talmage *(G-18207)*

Merchandising Solutions Inc...................G....... 717 898-1800
Lancaster *(G-9132)*

Merrigan Corporation...............................F....... 610 317-6300
Bethlehem *(G-1568)*

▲ Milford Enterprises Inc.......................D....... 215 538-2778
Quakertown *(G-16218)*

Millers Fabricating...................................G....... 717 733-9311
Ephrata *(G-5129)*

Millwork Solutions Inc............................E....... 814 446-4009
Seward *(G-17382)*

Misko Inc..F....... 610 524-1881
Exton *(G-5712)*

Mitre Wright Inc.......................................E....... 717 812-1000
York *(G-20600)*

Morrow Bros Countertop LP...................F....... 724 327-8980
Export *(G-5619)*

Northeast Fabricators Inc........................G....... 570 883-0936
Pittston *(G-15771)*

Northway Industries Inc...........................C....... 570 837-1564
Middleburg *(G-11034)*

Odhner and Odhner Fine Wdwkg............G....... 610 258-9300
Easton *(G-4734)*

Project Enterprise......................................G....... 717 933-9517
Womelsdorf *(G-20208)*

Quality Custom Cabinetry Inc.................C....... 717 656-2721
New Holland *(G-12275)*

Ralston Shop Inc......................................F....... 610 268-3829
Avondale *(G-858)*

REA Jobber Inc..G....... 814 226-9552
Clarion *(G-3186)*

Richard Riberich......................................G....... 412 271-8427
Pittsburgh *(G-15484)*

▲ RLB Ventures Inc...............................E....... 717 964-1111
Denver *(G-4091)*

Robertsons Inc..G....... 814 838-2313
Erie *(G-5464)*

Ruby Custom Woodcraft Inc....................G....... 570 698-7741
Lake Ariel *(G-8891)*

◆ Rynone Manufacturing Corp..............C....... 570 888-5272
Sayre *(G-17121)*

S F U LLC...G....... 610 473-0730
Gilbertsville *(G-6377)*

Schubert Custom Cabinetry Inc...............G....... 610 372-5559
Reading *(G-16508)*

Shade Mountain Countertops...................F....... 717 463-2729
Mc Alisterville *(G-10552)*

Staurowsky Woodworking.......................G....... 610 489-0770
Collegeville *(G-3394)*

Sunworks Etc LLC...................................G....... 717 473-3743
Annville *(G-659)*

Superior Cabinet Co................................G....... 724 569-9581
Smithfield *(G-17655)*

Superior Cabinet Company......................G....... 215 536-5228
Quakertown *(G-16247)*

Superior Flrcvgs Kitchens LLC ....G 717 264-9096
  Chambersburg *(G-2981)*
T L King Cabinetmaker ....G 610 869-4220
  Cochranville *(G-3356)*
Top Shop ....G 610 622-6101
  Philadelphia *(G-14396)*
Vangura Kitchen Tops Inc ....D 412 824-0772
  Irwin *(G-8204)*
Versatek Enterprises LLC ....D 717 626-6390
  Lititz *(G-10057)*
Visual Display Products LLC ....G 570 271-0815
  Danville *(G-4015)*
▲ Visual Merchandising LLC ....G 610 353-7550
  Newtown Square *(G-12597)*
William Cottage ....G 724 266-2961
  Ambridge *(G-639)*
Wood-Mode Incorporated ....E 570 374-1176
  Selinsgrove *(G-17338)*

2542 Partitions & Fixtures, Except Wood

A W Mercer Inc ....C 610 367-8460
  Boyertown *(G-1892)*
Adelphia Steel Eqp Co Inc ....E 800 865-8211
  Philadelphia *(G-13345)*
▲ Allegheny Store Fixtures Inc ....E 814 362-6805
  Bradford *(G-1954)*
Architectural Woodsmiths Inc ....D 717 532-7700
  Shippensburg *(G-17515)*
Bentech Inc ....E 215 223-9420
  Philadelphia *(G-13454)*
Bishop Metals Incorporated ....F 412 481-5501
  Pittsburgh *(G-14768)*
Bornmann Mfg Co Inc ....G 215 228-5826
  Philadelphia *(G-13473)*
▼ Charles Beseler Co Inc ....D 800 237-3537
  Stroudsburg *(G-18109)*
CNT Fixture Company Inc ....E 412 443-6260
  Glenshaw *(G-6484)*
Consolidated Stor Companies Inc ......C 610 253-2775
  Tatamy *(G-18256)*
Consolidated Stor Companies Inc ......C 610 253-2775
  Tatamy *(G-18257)*
Cpg International LLC ....F 570 348-0997
  Scranton *(G-17223)*
Crawford Dzignes Inc ....G 724 872-4644
  West Newton *(G-19750)*
Custom Craft Cabinets ....G 215 886-6105
  Abington *(G-10)*
Customfold Inc ....F 724 376-8565
  Stoneboro *(G-18068)*
Duckloe Frederick and Bros ....F 570 897-6172
  Portland *(G-15939)*
Federal Prison Industries ....B 570 524-0096
  Lewisburg *(G-9906)*
General Metal Company Inc ....E 215 638-3242
  Bensalem *(G-1203)*
▼ General Partitions Mfg Corp ....E 814 833-1154
  Erie *(G-5302)*
Getaways On Display Inc ....F 717 653-8070
  Manheim *(G-10386)*
Graphic Display Systems ....F 717 274-3954
  Lebanon *(G-9576)*
Interior Creations Inc ....E 215 425-9390
  Philadelphia *(G-13864)*
◆ Intermetro Industries Corp ....B 570 825-2741
  Wilkes Barre *(G-19929)*
▲ Jaboa Enterprises Inc ....F 610 703-5185
  Emmaus *(G-5030)*
▲ Kardex Systems Inc ....G 610 296-9730
  Paoli *(G-13142)*
L&D Millwork Inc ....G 570 285-3200
  Kingston *(G-8720)*
M & M Manufacturing Co ....E 724 274-0767
  Cheswick *(G-3111)*
Mastercraft Woodworking Co Inc ......E 610 926-1500
  Shoemakersville *(G-17571)*
Metro International Corp ....E 570 825-2741
  Wilkes Barre *(G-19943)*
▲ Moore Push Pin Company ....D 215 233-5700
  Glenside *(G-6531)*
Northway Industries Inc ....C 570 837-1564
  Middleburg *(G-11034)*
ODonnell Metal Fabricators ....F 610 279-8810
  Norristown *(G-12697)*
Otto Design Casefixture Inc ....G 412 824-3580
  Greenock *(G-6645)*
P A Office and Closet Systems ....F 610 944-1333
  Fleetwood *(G-5977)*
Promotion Centre Inc ....E 717 843-1582
  York *(G-20645)*

Resun Modspace Inc ....F 610 232-1200
  Berwyn *(G-1373)*
▼ Ridg-U-Rak Inc ....B 814 725-8751
  North East *(G-12756)*
Ridg-U-Rak Inc ....G 814 725-8751
  North East *(G-12757)*
Ridg-U-Rak Inc ....E 814 725-8751
  North East *(G-12758)*
School Gate Guardian Inc ....F 800 805-3808
  State College *(G-18020)*
▼ Scranton Products Inc ....C 570 558-8000
  Scranton *(G-17287)*
Southeastern PA Trnsp Auth ....B 215 580-7800
  Malvern *(G-10323)*
◆ Sparks Custom Retail LLC ....E 215 602-8100
  Philadelphia *(G-14328)*
Superior Cabinet Co ....G 724 569-9581
  Smithfield *(G-17455)*
Superior Cabinet Company ....G 215 536-5228
  Quakertown *(G-16247)*
T C B Displays Inc ....G 610 983-0500
  Phoenixville *(G-14582)*
Transwall Corp ....D 610 429-1400
  West Chester *(G-19668)*
▼ Vertirack Manufacturing Co ....G 484 971-7341
  Bernville *(G-1306)*
Vicjah Corporation ....G 610 826-7475
  Palmerton *(G-13114)*
Visual Display Products LLC ....G 570 271-0815
  Danville *(G-4015)*
Vitra Retail Inc ....G 610 366-1658
  Allentown *(G-425)*
Vmf Inc ....E 570 575-0997
  Scranton *(G-17310)*
Walco Fabricating Inc ....F 570 628-4523
  Pottsville *(G-16101)*
Wescho Company Inc ....E 610 436-5866
  West Chester *(G-19676)*

2591 Drapery Hardware, Window Blinds & Shades

Acacia Corp ....F 412 771-6144
  Mc Kees Rocks *(G-10600)*
Age-Craft Manufacturing Inc ....F 724 838-5580
  Greensburg *(G-6648)*
◆ Apple Fasteners Inc ....E 717 761-8962
  Camp Hill *(G-2490)*
Bishops Inc ....G 412 821-3333
  Mars *(G-10488)*
Blind Doctors ....G 412 822-8580
  Pittsburgh *(G-14772)*
Burton Springcrest Interiors ....G 724 468-3000
  Delmont *(G-4049)*
Caldwells Windoware Inc ....E 412 922-1132
  Pittsburgh *(G-14800)*
Carol Vinck Window Creation ....G 717 730-0303
  Camp Hill *(G-2494)*
Columbia Porch Shade Co ....G 570 639-1223
  Dallas *(G-3961)*
Hamilton Awning Co ....F 724 774-7644
  Beaver *(G-983)*
Indoor Sky LLC ....G 570 220-1903
  Williamsport *(G-20024)*
Jerry Lister Custom Upholsteri ....G 215 639-3880
  Bensalem *(G-1213)*
Jerry Lister Custom Upholsteri ....F 215 639-3882
  Huntingdon Valley *(G-8004)*
Lafayette Venetian Blind Inc ....E 717 652-3750
  Harrisburg *(G-7167)*
Morantz Inc ....G 215 969-0266
  Philadelphia *(G-14038)*
New Home Window Shade Co Inc ......E 570 346-2047
  Clarks Green *(G-3189)*
Nicholas Meyokovich ....G 724 439-0955
  Uniontown *(G-18638)*
▲ OEM Shades Inc ....E 724 763-3600
  Sarver *(G-17077)*
Penn Blind Manufacturing Inc ....F 610 770-1700
  Allentown *(G-347)*
Plymouth Blind Co Inc ....E 412 771-8569
  Mc Kees Rocks *(G-10626)*
Plymouth Interiors LP ....F 412 771-8569
  Mc Kees Rocks *(G-10627)*
S Morantz Inc ....D 215 969-0266
  Philadelphia *(G-14273)*
Shaffer Desouza Brown Inc ....F 610 449-6400
  Havertown *(G-7427)*
▲ Skotz Manufacturing Inc ....G 610 286-0710
  Elverson *(G-4966)*

Springs Window Fashions LLC ....E 570 547-6671
  Montgomery *(G-11378)*
TMW Associates Inc ....G 215 624-3940
  Philadelphia *(G-14393)*
Todd Lengle & Co Inc ....E 610 777-0731
  Reading *(G-16541)*
Vertical Access Solutions LLC ....G 412 787-9102
  Pittsburgh *(G-15693)*
Vertical Access Solutions LLC ....F 412 787-9102
  Lancaster *(G-9234)*
▲ Worldwide Fabricating Ltd ....D 215 455-2266
  Philadelphia *(G-14489)*

2599 Furniture & Fixtures, NEC

Acorn Manufacturing Inc ....E 717 964-1111
  Denver *(G-4065)*
▲ Ajjp Corporation ....C 215 968-6677
  Newtown *(G-12495)*
Apontes Latin Flavor Inc ....G 727 247-2001
  Glenshaw *(G-6481)*
▲ Blair Fixtures & Millwork Inc ....E 814 940-1913
  Altoona *(G-482)*
Brodart Co ....C 570 769-7412
  Mc Elhattan *(G-10585)*
Caseworks Inc ....G 724 522-5068
  Jeannette *(G-8249)*
Digital Designed Solutions LLC ....G 484 440-9665
  Media *(G-10921)*
Double DS Roadhouse LLc ....G 814 395-3535
  Confluence *(G-3464)*
◆ Econoco ....E 570 384-3000
  Hazle Township *(G-7453)*
G Case Inc ....G 717 737-5000
  Mechanicsburg *(G-10847)*
Gepharts Furniture ....G 814 276-3357
  Alum Bank *(G-561)*
Goodwest Industries LLC ....E 215 340-3100
  Douglassville *(G-4177)*
Hawk Industries Inc ....G 717 359-4138
  Littlestown *(G-10066)*
Hornings Woodcraft ....G 717 949-3524
  Newmanstown *(G-12477)*
Hurdles Inc ....G 814 467-8787
  Windber *(G-20182)*
Hurlock Bros Co Inc ....F 610 659-8153
  Drexel Hill *(G-4366)*
Jamies Courtside Spt & Spirits ....E 717 757-7689
  York *(G-20540)*
Kaufer Associates Inc ....G 814 756-4997
  Girard *(G-6394)*
Laurence Ronald Entps Inc ....F 215 677-3801
  Warminster *(G-18910)*
Markraft Company ....G 724 733-3654
  Murrysville *(G-11857)*
Mayberry Hospitality LLC ....G 570 275-9292
  Northumberland *(G-12871)*
Missing Piece ....G 610 759-4033
  Nazareth *(G-11982)*
Officelogic Inc ....G 215 752-3069
  Bensalem *(G-1235)*
ONeils Custom Cab & Design ....F 412 422-4723
  Pittsburgh *(G-15359)*
▲ Panel Solutions Inc ....E 570 459-3490
  Hazleton *(G-7515)*
Piscis ....G 412 464-5181
  Homestead *(G-7690)*
Quakermaid Cabinets Inc ....E 570 207-4432
  Scranton *(G-17277)*
Riverwoods Cabinetry LLC ....G 724 807-1045
  Harrisville *(G-7255)*
Siu King ....F 215 769-9863
  Philadelphia *(G-14313)*
▲ Sovana Bistro Inc ....D 610 444-5600
  Kennett Square *(G-8543)*
Spare Time Bowling ....G 570 668-3210
  Tamaqua *(G-18227)*
Top Shop ....G 610 622-6101
  Philadelphia *(G-14396)*

26 PAPER AND ALLIED PRODUCTS

2611 Pulp Mills

A J Blosenski Inc ....D 610 942-2707
  Honey Brook *(G-7734)*
Graybill Farms Inc ....G 717 361-8455
  Elizabethtown *(G-4874)*
K Diamond Incorporated ....E 570 346-4684
  Scranton *(G-17249)*
▼ Maslo Company Inc ....F 610 540-9000
  Malvern *(G-10276)*

S
I
C

Newstech PA LP ....G....... 315 955-6710
Northampton *(G-12857)*

Paper Recovery Systems Inc................G....... 215 423-6624
Philadelphia *(G-14115)*

▼ Rapid Recycling Inc ....D....... 610 650-0737
Oaks *(G-12936)*

Recycled Oil ....F....... 610 250-8747
Easton *(G-4748)*

Roderick Duvall ....G....... 814 735-4969
Crystal Spring *(G-3938)*

Staiman Recycling Corporation..........D....... 717 646-0951
Williamsport *(G-20074)*

Take Away Refuse................................G....... 717 490-9258
Lancaster *(G-9211)*

▼ Tin Technology and Ref LLC ....G....... 610 430-2225
West Chester *(G-19663)*

Unipaper Recycling Company ....F....... 412 429-8522
Carnegie *(G-2801)*

Westrock Rkt LLC ....D....... 570 476-0120
Delaware Water Gap *(G-4045)*

2621 Paper Mills

465 Devon Park Drive Inc ....G....... 610 293-1330
Wayne *(G-19292)*

Access Credential Systems LLC ....G....... 724 820-1160
Eighty Four *(G-4831)*

▲ Ahlstrom Mount Holly Sprng LLC ....E....... 717 486-3438
Mount Holly Springs *(G-11631)*

Ahlstrom Mount Holly Sprng LLC ....C....... 717 486-3438
Mount Holly Springs *(G-11632)*

American Crepe Corporation ....G....... 570 433-3319
Montoursville *(G-11430)*

Anderson Prints Inc............................F....... 610 293-1330
Wayne *(G-19298)*

Appvion Operations Inc ....B....... 814 224-2131
Roaring Spring *(G-16761)*

▲ Atlantic Enterprise Inc ....G....... 800 367-8547
Ivyland *(G-8206)*

Avery Dennison Corporation ....D....... 215 536-9000
Quakertown *(G-16170)*

◆ Beistle Company ....B....... 717 532-2131
Shippensburg *(G-17517)*

Burpee Willow Hill..............................G....... 717 349-0065
Fannettsburg *(G-5857)*

Cascades Tissue Group - PA Inc.........F....... 570 388-6161
Ransom *(G-16306)*

◆ Cascades Tissue Group - PA Inc......C....... 570 388-4307
Pittston *(G-15744)*

Case Paper Co Inc ....C....... 215 430-6400
Philadelphia *(G-13510)*

◆ Chiyoda America Inc ....D....... 610 286-3100
Morgantown *(G-11520)*

Crestwood Membranes Inc ....D....... 570 474-6741
Mountain Top *(G-11758)*

CSS Industries Inc ....C....... 610 729-3959
Plymouth Meeting *(G-15840)*

Devra Party Corp.................................G....... 718 522-7421
Philadelphia *(G-13626)*

Digital-Ink Inc ....D....... 717 731-8890
Dillsburg *(G-4126)*

Doellken- Woodtape Inc ....G....... 610 929-1910
Temple *(G-18328)*

Domtar Paper Company LLC................A....... 814 965-2521
Johnsonburg *(G-8346)*

Domtar Paper Company LLC................E....... 814 371-0630
Du Bois *(G-4387)*

Essity North America Inc ....G....... 610 499-3700
Eddystone *(G-4801)*

▲ Essity North America Inc..................C....... 610 499-3700
Philadelphia *(G-13680)*

Everything Postal Inc ....G....... 610 367-7444
Bechtelsville *(G-1032)*

Factor X Graffics ....G....... 717 590-7402
Mechanicsburg *(G-10842)*

First Quality Products Inc ....B....... 570 769-6900
Mc Elhattan *(G-10588)*

▲ First Quality Tissue LLC ....B....... 570 748-1200
Lock Haven *(G-10089)*

▲ Flextron Industries Inc ....F....... 610 459-4600
Aston *(G-763)*

Fortney Packages Inc ....G....... 717 243-1826
Carlisle *(G-2714)*

Georgia-Pacific LLC............................E....... 215 538-7549
Quakertown *(G-16196)*

Georgia-Pacific LLC............................E....... 610 250-7402
Easton *(G-4691)*

Glatfelter Holdings LLC......................G....... 717 225-2772
York *(G-20500)*

▲ Gty Inc ....D....... 717 764-8969
York *(G-20516)*

Hampden Papers Inc ....G....... 610 255-4166
Landenberg *(G-9249)*

▲ Harmony Paper Company LLC ....G 724 991-1110
Harmony *(G-7068)*

Hawk Mountain Editions Ltd...............G....... 484 220-0524
Leesport *(G-9666)*

Hibachi Grill Supreme Buffet ....F....... 215 728-7222
Philadelphia *(G-13822)*

Hispanic Media LLC............................E....... 215 424-1200
Philadelphia *(G-13829)*

Historical Documents Co ....G....... 215 533-4500
Philadelphia *(G-13830)*

Inservio3 LLC ....G....... 310 343-3486
Pittsburgh *(G-15129)*

International Paper Company ....C....... 570 384-3251
Hazle Township *(G-7464)*

International Paper Company ....F....... 724 745-2288
Eighty Four *(G-4843)*

International Paper Company ....C....... 717 391-3400
Lancaster *(G-9060)*

International Paper Company ....C....... 814 454-9001
Erie *(G-5330)*

Jerry James Trdng As Mnls BSC ....G....... 425 255-0199
Lafayette Hill *(G-8882)*

Kimberly-Clark Corporation.................D....... 610 874-4331
Chester *(G-3053)*

Kmn Packaging Inc.............................G....... 610 376-3606
Reading *(G-16422)*

▲ Kurtz Bros.......................................D....... 814 765-6561
Clearfield *(G-3222)*

▲ Lectromat Inc ....F....... 724 625-3502
Mars *(G-10505)*

Maiden Formats Inc ....G....... 412 884-4716
Pittsburgh *(G-15248)*

Metso Minerals Industries Inc............C....... 717 843-8671
York *(G-20591)*

Michael Z Gehman ....G....... 814 483-0488
Friedens *(G-6221)*

Minton Holdings LLC ....G....... 412 787-5912
Pittsburgh *(G-15293)*

Mri Flexible Packaging Company.........F 215 860-7676
Newtown *(G-12525)*

▼ Mt Holly Sprng Specialty Ppr...........F....... 717 486-8500
Mount Holly Springs *(G-11637)*

Ne Fibers LLC......................................E....... 570 445-2086
Wilkes Barre *(G-19949)*

New Ngc Inc ....D....... 570 538-2531
New Columbia *(G-12174)*

◆ Nittany Paper Mills Inc ....D....... 888 288-7907
Lewistown *(G-9940)*

P H Glatfelter Company ....A....... 717 225-4711
York *(G-20615)*

Penn Pro Manufacturing Inc ....F....... 724 222-6450
Washington *(G-19215)*

Pixelle Spcialty Solutions LLC ....G....... 717 225-4711
Spring Grove *(G-17880)*

Pratt Industries USA Inc ....D....... 610 967-6027
Emmaus *(G-5040)*

R & D Americas Best Packaging ....G 610 435-4300
Allentown *(G-364)*

R C Paper Company ....G....... 610 821-9610
Allentown *(G-366)*

Roddy Products ....G....... 610 623-7040
Aldan *(G-60)*

▲ S E Hagarman Designs LLC.............G....... 717 633-5336
Hanover *(G-6947)*

Sealed Air Corporation ....E....... 610 384-2650
Modena *(G-11259)*

Sealed Air Corporation ....E....... 610 375-4281
Reading *(G-16510)*

Select Tissue Pennsylvania LLC ....E....... 570 785-2000
Vandling *(G-18739)*

Statement Walls LLC ....G....... 267 266-0869
Philadelphia *(G-14341)*

Suplee Envelope Co Inc ....E....... 610 352-2900
Garnet Valley *(G-6269)*

Supra Office Solutions Inc ....G....... 267 275-8888
Philadelphia *(G-14360)*

◆ Team Ten LLC..................................B....... 814 684-1610
Tyrone *(G-18595)*

UPS Store Inc ....G....... 724 934-1088
Wexford *(G-19831)*

▲ Viking Importing Co ....G....... 610 690-2900
Springfield *(G-17924)*

Vornhold Wallpapers Inc ....G....... 215 757-6641
Langhorne *(G-9334)*

Warren Products Inc ....G....... 570 655-4596
West Pittston *(G-19757)*

Wausau Paper Corp ....D....... 866 722-8675
Philadelphia *(G-14462)*

Weyerhaeuser Company ....D....... 814 371-0630
Du Bois *(G-4427)*

2631 Paperboard Mills

American Paper Products of PHI ....E....... 508 879-1141
Lansdale *(G-9341)*

◆ Beistle Company ....B....... 717 532-2131
Shippensburg *(G-17517)*

Brandywine Industrial Paper ....G....... 610 212-9949
Coatesville *(G-3294)*

▼ Brazilian Paper Corporation ....G....... 215 369-7000
New Hope *(G-12299)*

Brown Jr Merritt ....G....... 610 253-0425
Easton *(G-4658)*

Caraustar Industries Inc.....................G....... 717 534-2206
Hershey *(G-7605)*

Case Paper Co Inc ....C....... 215 430-6400
Philadelphia *(G-13510)*

Century Packaging Co Inc ....E....... 610 262-8860
Whitehall *(G-19864)*

Danaken Designs Inc...........................F....... 570 445-9797
Scranton *(G-17227)*

General Partition Company Inc ....E....... 215 785-1000
Croydon *(G-3918)*

Georgia-Pacific LLC............................B....... 610 250-1400
Easton *(G-4690)*

Graphic Packaging Intl LLC ....B....... 610 725-9840
Phoenixville *(G-14552)*

Great Northern Corporation ....E....... 610 706-0910
Allentown *(G-236)*

Hurlock Bros Co Inc ....F....... 610 659-8153
Drexel Hill *(G-4366)*

Industrial Packaging Supplies ....G....... 724 459-8299
Blairsville *(G-1725)*

McLean Packaging Corporation ....E....... 610 759-3550
Nazareth *(G-11981)*

Neenah Northeast LLC ....C....... 215 536-4600
Quakertown *(G-16223)*

Neenah Northeast LLC ....E....... 610 926-1996
Reading *(G-16453)*

New Ngc Inc ....D....... 570 538-2531
New Columbia *(G-12174)*

◆ Newman & Company Inc ....C....... 215 333-8700
Philadelphia *(G-14070)*

▼ Northeastern PA Carton Co Inc ....E....... 570 457-7711
Moosic *(G-11510)*

Ox Paperboard LLC ....E....... 304 725-2076
Hanover *(G-6928)*

Pro Pak Containers Inc........................G....... 412 741-0549
Sewickley *(G-17404)*

Rixie Paper Products Inc......................F....... 610 323-9220
Pottstown *(G-16040)*

Sheffield Container Corp ....E....... 814 968-3287
Sheffield *(G-17483)*

◆ Sig Combibloc Inc ....E....... 610 546-4200
Chester *(G-3062)*

Signode Industrial Group LLC ....E....... 570 450-0123
Hazle Township *(G-7479)*

Somerset Enterprises Inc.....................F....... 724 734-9497
Farrell *(G-5874)*

Sonoco Prtective Solutions Inc ....E....... 215 643-3555
Montgomeryville *(G-11419)*

St Marys Box Company ....E....... 814 834-3819
Saint Marys *(G-17015)*

Sterling Paper Company ....D....... 215 744-5550
Philadelphia *(G-14347)*

Superior Packaging Inc ....F....... 570 824-3577
Plains *(G-15789)*

Turck Engineered Packaging................G....... 717 421-7371
Harrisburg *(G-7239)*

▲ United Corrstack LLC ....D....... 610 374-3000
Reading *(G-16554)*

Vogel Carton LLC ....E....... 215 957-0612
Warminster *(G-18997)*

Westrock Company ....G....... 215 826-2497
Croydon *(G-3932)*

Westrock Cp LLC.................................C....... 904 751-6400
York *(G-20709)*

Westrock Cp LLC.................................F....... 215 699-4444
North Wales *(G-12840)*

Westrock Cp LLC.................................C....... 215 984-7000
Philadelphia *(G-14468)*

Westrock Rkt LLC ....D....... 570 476-0120
Delaware Water Gap *(G-4045)*

Westrock Rkt LLC ....D....... 570 454-0433
Hazleton *(G-7538)*

Westrock Rkt LLC ....C....... 717 393-0436
Lancaster *(G-9239)*

2652 Set-Up Paperboard Boxes

Achieva ....F 412 391-4660
  Pittsburgh (G-14641)
Albright Paper & Box Corp ....G 484 524-8424
  Boyertown (G-1895)
Concept Products Corporation ....G 610 722-0830
  Mertztown (G-11002)
Duerr Packaging Company Inc...........E 724 695-2226
  Imperial (G-8064)
Friendly City Box Co Inc ....F 814 266-6287
  Johnstown (G-8373)
Gateway Packaging Corp ....E 724 327-7400
  Export (G-5607)
Hanover Paper Box Company Inc ....E 215 432-5033
  Allentown (G-242)
McLean Packaging Corporation ....C 610 759-3550
  Nazareth (G-11981)
Michael J Doyle ....G 215 587-1000
  Philadelphia (G-14021)
▼ Northeastern PA Carton Co Inc ......E 570 457-7711
  Moosic (G-11510)
Opi Holdings Inc ....E 610 857-2000
  Old Forge (G-12973)
PCA Corrugated and Display LLC ....G 610 489-8740
  Collegeville (G-3386)
Pittsburgh File & Box Co......................G 412 431-5465
  Pittsburgh (G-15396)
Raymond Sherman Co Inc ....G 610 272-4640
  Conshohocken (G-3597)
Reliance Paragon Paper Box ....G 215 743-1231
  Philadelphia (G-14239)
Simkins Corporation ....E 215 739-4033
  Jenkintown (G-8301)
Simplex Paper Box Corp ....E 717 757-3611
  Hellam (G-7552)
Superior Packaging Inc ....F 570 824-3577
  Plains (G-15789)
Unipak Inc ....E 610 436-6600
  West Chester (G-19670)
Westrock Rkt LLC ....C 717 393-0436
  Lancaster (G-9239)

2653 Corrugated & Solid Fiber Boxes

Acco Gbc ....G 267 880-6797
  Doylestown (G-4267)
Achieva ....F 412 391-4660
  Pittsburgh (G-14641)
Achieva ....D 412 995-5000
  Pittsburgh (G-14640)
▲ Acme Corrugated Box Co Inc ....C 215 444-8000
  Hatboro (G-7264)
Alden Industries Inc............................G 267 460-8904
  North Wales (G-12787)
Alpha Packaging Corporation ....F 610 926-5100
  Mohrsville (G-11273)
Beacon Container Corporation.............C 610 582-2222
  Birdsboro (G-1688)
Beacon Container Corporation.............E 570 433-3800
  Montoursville (G-11433)
Brown Jr Merritt ....G 610 253-0425
  Easton (G-4658)
Buckeye Corrugated Inc ....E 717 684-6921
  Columbia (G-3432)
◆ Carton Edge International Inc ....F 215 699-8755
  North Wales (G-12794)
▼ Cas Pack Corporation ....E 215 254-7225
  Bensalem (G-1165)
Century Packaging Co Inc ....E 610 262-8860
  Whitehall (G-19864)
Cor-Rite Inc...F 570 287-1718
  Swoyersville (G-18196)
Cor-Rite Corrugated Inc ....E 570 287-1718
  Kingston (G-8714)
Corrugated Specialties........................F 814 337-5705
  Meadville (G-10715)
Creative Management Svcs LLC ....G 610 863-1900
  Pen Argyl (G-13212)
Cummings Custom Saw Milling ....G 570 586-3277
  Clarks Summit (G-3190)
▲ David Weber Co Inc ....C 215 426-3500
  Philadelphia (G-13610)
▼ Dee Paper Company Inc ....D 610 876-9285
  Chester (G-3046)
Duerr Packaging Company Inc...........E 724 695-2226
  Imperial (G-8064)
▲ Edwin Bell Cooperage Company......E 412 221-1830
  Cuddy (G-3942)
Fca LLC ....E 309 792-3444
  Corry (G-3760)

Fitzpatrick Container Company............E 215 699-3515
  Allentown (G-214)
▲ Flextron Industries Inc ....F 610 459-4600
  Aston (G-763)
Freedom Corrugated LLC ....D 570 384-7500
  Hazle Township (G-7458)
Gateway Packaging Corp ....E 724 327-7400
  Export (G-5607)
General Partition Company Inc ....E 215 785-1000
  Croydon (G-3918)
Georgia-Pacific Bldg Pdts LLC............F 814 778-6000
  Kane (G-8464)
Georgia-Pacific LLC.............................B 610 250-1400
  Easton (G-4690)
Georgia-Pacific LLC.............................C 717 266-3621
  Mount Wolf (G-11747)
Georgia-Pacific LLC.............................C 814 368-8700
  Bradford (G-1969)
Global Packaging Solutions Inc ....G 717 653-2345
  Mount Joy (G-11658)
Graphex Inc ....G 610 524-9525
  Exton (G-5691)
▲ H P Cadwallader Inc ....E 215 256-6651
  Harleysville (G-7036)
Harford Stone Company ....F 570 434-9141
  Kingsley (G-8705)
International Paper Company ....D 717 677-8121
  Biglerville (G-1664)
International Paper Company ....C 570 339-1611
  Mount Carmel (G-11625)
International Paper Company ....E 610 268-5456
  Toughkenamon (G-18419)
▲ Interstate Cont Brunswick LLC........E 610 208-9300
  Reading (G-16408)
▲ Interstate Cont Reading LLC ....C 800 822-2002
  Reading (G-16409)
Jem Pallets ....G 717 532-5304
  Orrstown (G-13032)
Jmg Inc ....G 215 659-4087
  Willow Grove (G-20121)
Keystone Displays Corporation ....G 717 612-0340
  Lemoyne (G-9746)
Laurel Ridge Resawing ....G 814 629-5026
  Boswell (G-1884)
Lemac Packaging Inc ....G 814 453-7652
  Erie (G-5361)
M & G Packaging Corp ....F 610 363-7455
  Exton (G-5707)
Menasha Packaging Company LLC ......G 570 243-5512
  Tobyhanna (G-18407)
Menasha Packaging Company LLC ......C 630 236-4925
  Bethlehem (G-1567)
Menasha Packaging Company LLC ......E 717 776-2900
  Newville (G-12607)
Menasha Packaging Company LLC ......D 800 477-8746
  York (G-20587)
Menasha Packaging Company LLC ......E 800 477-8746
  York (G-20588)
Menasha Packaging Company LLC ......E 800 245-2486
  Ruffs Dale (G-16874)
Menasha Packaging Company LLC ......C 215 426-7110
  Philadelphia (G-14008)
Menasha Packaging Company LLC ......G 215 426-7110
  Philadelphia (G-14009)
Menasha Packaging Company LLC ......D 800 783-4563
  Latrobe (G-9504)
▲ Montco Packaging Co Inc ....G 610 935-9545
  Phoenixville (G-14562)
Montgomery Products Ltd ....E 610 933-2500
  Phoenixville (G-14563)
Multicell North Inc ....F 610 683-9000
  Kutztown (G-8850)
Npc Acquisition Inc ....E 215 946-2000
  Bristol (G-2176)
Packaging Corp O ....G 717 293-2877
  Lancaster (G-9158)
Packaging Corporation America ....E 301 497-9090
  Hanover (G-6929)
Packaging Corporation America ....G 610 366-6501
  Allentown (G-342)
Packaging Corporation America ....C 610 366-6500
  Allentown (G-343)
Packaging Corporation America ....E 610 916-3200
  Reading (G-16462)
Packaging Corporation America ....D 724 275-3700
  Cheswick (G-3114)
Packaging Corporation America ....G 717 624-2122
  New Oxford (G-12418)
Packaging Corporation America ....G 717 632-4800
  Hanover (G-6930)

Packaging Corporation America ....D 717 632-4727
  New Oxford (G-12419)
Packaging Corporation America ....C 717 397-3591
  Lancaster (G-9159)
Packaging Corporation America ....E 717 637-3758
  Hanover (G-6931)
Packaging Corporation America ....E 717 653-0420
  Manheim (G-10398)
◆ Paperworks Industries Inc ....C 215 984-7000
  Bala Cynwyd (G-888)
PCA Corrugated and Display LLC ....G 800 572-6061
  Hanover (G-6932)
PCA Corrugated and Display LLC ....G 717 624-3500
  New Oxford (G-12420)
PCA Corrugated and Display LLC ....G 800 572-6061
  Hanover (G-6933)
PCA Corrugated and Display LLC ....G 800 572-6061
  Hanover (G-6934)
PCA Corrugated and Display LLC ....D 717 624-2122
  New Oxford (G-12421)
PCA Corrugated and Display LLC ....G 610 489-8740
  Collegeville (G-3386)
Perkasie Container Corporation ....F 215 257-3683
  Perkasie (G-13287)
Pittsburgh File & Box Co......................G 412 431-5465
  Pittsburgh (G-15396)
Pratt Industries USA Inc ....D 610 967-6027
  Emmaus (G-5040)
Pratt Rock Solid Displays LLC ....E 610 929-4800
  Reading (G-16474)
Pro Pac Inc ....G 717 646-9555
  Hanover (G-6938)
PSI Container Inc ....E 570 929-1600
  McAdoo (G-10658)
PSI Packaging Services Inc ....D 724 626-0100
  Connellsville (G-3506)
Reliance Packaging & Supply Co ....G 724 468-8849
  Export (G-5624)
Righters Associat Ferry ....E 610 667-6767
  Bala Cynwyd (G-891)
Roaring Spring Blank Book Co ....E 814 224-2222
  Roaring Spring (G-16769)
◆ Roaring Spring Blank Book Co ....E 814 224-2306
  Roaring Spring (G-16768)
RTS Packaging LLC ....C 724 489-4495
  Charleroi (G-3021)
S & G Corrugated Packaging Inc ....F 570 287-1718
  Swoyersville (G-18198)
Schrage Box & Design Inc ....F 215 604-0800
  Bensalem (G-1252)
Service Die Cutng & Packg Corp..........F 215 739-8809
  Philadelphia (G-14294)
Sheffield Container Corp......................E 814 968-3287
  Sheffield (G-17483)
Shenango Operating Inc ....E 724 657-3650
  New Castle (G-12151)
Sonoco Display & Packaging LLC ....C 717 757-2683
  York (G-20672)
Sonoco Products Company ....E 610 323-9221
  Pottstown (G-16049)
Southern Container Corp ....E 717 393-0436
  Lancaster (G-9203)
◆ Sparks Exhibits Holding Corp..........G 215 676-1100
  Philadelphia (G-14330)
▲ Specialty Industries Inc..................C 717 246-1661
  Red Lion (G-16613)
St Marys Box Company ....E 814 834-3819
  Saint Marys (G-17015)
Strine Corrugated Products ....G 717 764-4800
  Emigsville (G-5000)
Supplyone Holdings Company Inc........D 484 582-5005
  Newtown Square (G-12593)
Tri-State Container Corp ....E 215 638-1311
  Bensalem (G-1263)
▲ Tyoga Container Company Inc ....E 570 835-5295
  Tioga (G-18366)
US Corrugated Inc ....E 724 345-2050
  Washington (G-19237)
Westrock Cp LLC ....C 610 485-8700
  Aston (G-798)
Westrock Rkt LLC ....C 717 393-0436
  Lancaster (G-9239)
Westrock Rkt Company ....G 717 520-7600
  Hershey (G-7626)
Westrock Rkt Company ....G 717 790-1596
  Mechanicsburg (G-10909)
Westrock Usc Inc ....G 724 938-3020
  Coal Center (G-3278)
◆ York Container Company ....C 717 757-7611
  York (G-20733)

2655 Fiber Cans, Tubes & Drums

American Paper Products of PHI..........G....... 215 739-5718
Philadelphia (G-13387)

American Paper Products of PHI..........E....... 215 855-3327
Lansdale (G-9340)

American Paper Products of PHI..........E....... 508 879-1141
Lansdale (G-9341)

Bushnell Alvah Company ....E....... 215 842-9520
Philadelphia (G-13488)

Caraustar Industrial and Con..........E....... 717 295-0047
Lancaster (G-8970)

Caraustar Industries Inc ....F....... 717 846-4559
York (G-20418)

Consolidated Container Co LLC..........C....... 570 759-0823
Berwick (G-1319)

Greif Inc ....D....... 610 485-8148
Upper Chichester (G-18662)

Greif Inc ....D....... 215 956-9049
Warminster (G-18892)

Jst Corporation ....G....... 717 920-7700
Middletown (G-11059)

Mauser Usa LLC ....E....... 610 258-2700
Easton (G-4720)

Micronic America LLC ....G....... 484 483-8075
Aston (G-777)

Nem-Pak Llc ....G....... 215 785-6430
Croydon (G-3921)

▼ Ox Paper Tube and Core Inc ....E....... 800 414-2476
Hanover (G-6927)

Plastic Options LLC ....G....... 724 730-5225
New Castle (G-12137)

Proline Composites Corp ....G....... 814 536-8491
South Fork (G-17776)

Pyrotek Incorporated..........D....... 717 249-2075
Carlisle (G-2733)

▲ Rose Plastic Usa Lllp ....D....... 724 938-8530
Coal Center (G-3277)

Self-Seal Cont Corp Del Vly ....G....... 610 275-2300
Boyertown (G-1929)

Sheen Kleen Inc ....G....... 610 337-3969
King of Prussia (G-8673)

Sonoco Products Company ....C....... 717 637-2103
Hanover (G-6957)

Sonoco Products Company ....E....... 610 693-5804
Robesonia (G-16779)

Stealth Composites Inc ....G....... 215 919-7584
Pottstown (G-16051)

Temtek Solutions Inc ....G....... 724 980-4270
Canonsburg (G-2647)

United Ammunition Container ....G....... 610 658-0888
Wynnewood (G-20273)

◆ Yazoo Mills Incorporated ....D....... 717 624-8993
New Oxford (G-12428)

2656 Sanitary Food Containers

Consolidated Container Co LLC..........C....... 570 759-0823
Berwick (G-1319)

▲ Ecopax LLC ....D....... 484 546-0700
Easton (G-4676)

Georgia-Pacific LLC..........B....... 610 250-1400
Easton (G-4690)

Letica Corporation ....C....... 570 883-0299
Pittston (G-15764)

Northstar Sales ....G....... 215 364-5540
Southampton (G-17828)

2657 Folding Paperboard Boxes

◆ Beistle Company ....B....... 717 532-2131
Shippensburg (G-17517)

Corrugated Specialties..........F....... 814 337-5705
Meadville (G-10715)

Corrugated Specialties..........F....... 814 337-5705
Meadville (G-10714)

Duerr Packaging Company Inc ....E....... 724 695-2226
Imperial (G-8064)

Graphic Packaging Intl LLC ....C....... 610 935-4000
Phoenixville (G-14551)

K & L Operating Co ....G....... 215 646-0760
Ambler (G-584)

Menasha Packaging Company LLC ....E....... 800 477-8746
York (G-20588)

Midvale Paper Box Company ....G....... 610 649-6992
Haverford (G-7413)

◆ Midvale Paper Box Company ....F....... 570 824-3577
Plains (G-15786)

▼ Northeastern PA Carton Co Inc ....E....... 570 457-7711
Moosic (G-11510)

Opi Holdings Inc ....E....... 610 857-2000
Old Forge (G-12973)

Prestige Gift Box Systems ....F....... 610 865-6768
Bethlehem (G-1605)

Service Die Cutng & Packg Corp ....F....... 215 739-8809
Philadelphia (G-14294)

Southern Container Corp ....C....... 717 393-0436
Lancaster (G-9203)

Sterling Paper Company ....D....... 215 744-5350
Philadelphia (G-14347)

Superior Packaging Inc ....F....... 570 824-3577
Plains (G-15789)

Tapestration ....G....... 215 536-0977
Quakertown (G-16248)

▲ Tavo Packaging Inc ....D....... 215 428-0900
Fairless Hills (G-5802)

▲ Union Packaging LLC ....D....... 610 572-7265
Yeadon (G-20356)

Unipak Inc ....E....... 610 436-6600
West Chester (G-19670)

Vogel Carton LLC ....E....... 215 957-0612
Warminster (G-18997)

Xomox Corporation ....G....... 570 824-3577
Wilkes Barre (G-19980)

2671 Paper Coating & Laminating for Packaging

Acro Labels Inc ....E....... 215 657-5366
Willow Grove (G-20105)

Amatech Inc..........E....... 814 452-0010
Erie (G-5185)

B W E Ltd ....E....... 724 246-0470
Republic (G-16652)

Bemis Company Inc..........C....... 570 501-1400
West Hazleton (G-19706)

Bemis Packaging Inc ....E....... 717 279-5000
Lebanon (G-9547)

Bestway Printing..........G....... 215 368-4140
Lansdale (G-9346)

▼ Cas Pack Corporation ....E....... 215 254-7225
Bensalem (G-1165)

Central Distribution Co Inc ....G....... 717 393-4851
Lancaster (G-8973)

Century Packaging Co Inc ....E....... 610 262-8860
Whitehall (G-19864)

▲ Cjc Contract Packaging Inc ....G....... 570 209-7836
Avoca (G-842)

▲ Coating & Converting Tech Corp..........E....... 215 271-0610
Philadelphia (G-13554)

▲ Constantia Colmar LLC ....D....... 215 997-6222
Colmar (G-3411)

Cw Thomas LLC ....E....... 215 335-0200
Philadelphia (G-13596)

Donald B Remmey Inc ....G....... 570 386-5379
Lehighton (G-9711)

Easter Unlimited Inc ....E....... 814 542-8661
Mount Union (G-11744)

▲ Emball Iso Inc ....G....... 267 687-8570
Montgomeryville (G-11395)

▲ FP Woll & Company ....E....... 215 934-5966
Philadelphia (G-13717)

Great Northern Corporation..........E....... 610 706-0910
Allentown (G-236)

▲ Greiner Packaging Corp ....F....... 570 602-3900
Pittsburgh (G-15754)

Guildcraft Inc ....F....... 717 854-3888
York (G-20517)

Harbor Bay Group Inc ....G....... 610 566-5290
Prospect Park (G-16115)

Harte Hanks Inc ....C....... 570 826-0414
Hanover Township (G-6989)

Holly Label Company Inc ....E....... 570 222-9000
Nicholson (G-12615)

▲ Ideal Sleeves Intl LLC ....F....... 570 823-8456
Wilkes Barre (G-19926)

Interstate Paper Supply Co Inc ....D....... 724 938-2218
Roscoe (G-16817)

Labelcom ....G....... 814 362-3252
Bradford (G-1978)

Lbp Manufacturing LLC..........E....... 570 291-5463
Jessup (G-8330)

▲ Mangar Industries Inc..........C....... 215 230-0300
New Britain (G-12047)

▲ Mangar Medical Inc..........C....... 215 230-0300
New Britain (G-12048)

McCourt Label Cabinet Company ....D....... 800 458-2390
Lewis Run (G-9877)

Nanopack Inc ....G....... 484 367-7015
Wayne (G-19359)

News Chronicle Co Inc ....E....... 717 532-4101
Shippensburg (G-17540)

▲ Okumus Enterprises Ltd ....E....... 215 295-3340
Fairless Hills (G-5790)

▲ Oliver-Tlas Hlthcare Packg Inc ....C....... 215 322-7900
Feasterville Trevose (G-5923)

◆ Opsec Security Inc ....D....... 717 293-4110
Lancaster (G-9155)

Presto Packaging Inc..........G....... 215 646-7514
Ambler (G-599)

Prime Packaging LLC ....D....... 215 499-0446
Yardley (G-20333)

Print Solutions Ltd ....G....... 484 538-3938
Coopersburg (G-3635)

R & G Gorr Enterprises Inc ....G....... 610 356-8500
Phoenixville (G-14573)

Reynolds Presto Products Inc ....B....... 866 254-3310
Pittsburgh (G-15483)

Sealed Air Corporation ....G....... 610 926-7517
Reading (G-16509)

Signode Industrial Group LLC ....E....... 570 450-0123
Hazle Township (G-7479)

Steele Print Inc ....G....... 724 758-6178
Ellwood City (G-4952)

Taba Labels Company ....G....... 215 455-9977
Philadelphia (G-14366)

Tredegar Corporation ....C....... 570 544-7600
Pottsville (G-16100)

◆ U S Textile Corp ....E....... 803 283-6800
Feasterville Trevose (G-5935)

◆ Universal Protective Packg Inc ....D....... 717 766-1578
Mechanicsburg (G-10903)

Vanguard Identification ....E....... 610 719-0700
West Chester (G-19672)

▲ Westrock Packaging Inc..........D....... 215 785-3350
Croydon (G-3933)

2672 Paper Coating & Laminating, Exc for Packaging

Acro Labels Inc ....E....... 215 657-5366
Willow Grove (G-20105)

Appvion Operations Inc ....B....... 814 224-2131
Roaring Spring (G-16761)

Avery Dennison Corporation ....D....... 570 888-6641
Sayre (G-17110)

Avery Dennison Corporation ....D....... 570 748-7701
Mill Hall (G-11172)

Avery Dennison Corporation ....D....... 215 536-9000
Quakertown (G-16170)

Bestway Printing..........G....... 215 368-4140
Lansdale (G-9346)

Boyertown Label Co ....G....... 800 260-4934
Boyertown (G-1901)

Butler Technologies Inc ....D....... 724 283-6656
Butler (G-2386)

▼ Cas Pack Corporation ....E....... 215 254-7225
Bensalem (G-1165)

◆ Chiyoda America Inc ....D....... 610 286-3100
Morgantown (G-11520)

▲ Converters Inc ....E....... 215 355-5400
Huntingdon Valley (G-7971)

▲ Cortape Ne Inc..........F....... 610 997-7900
Bethlehem (G-1488)

Fedex Office & Print Svcs Inc ....E....... 412 835-4005
Pittsburgh (G-15010)

Fedex Office & Print Svcs Inc ....F....... 412 788-0552
Pittsburgh (G-15009)

Grafika Commercial Prtg Inc..........B....... 610 678-8630
Reading (G-16396)

Great Northern Corporation..........E....... 610 706-0910
Allentown (G-236)

Guy Coder..........G....... 814 265-0519
Brockway (G-2227)

Holly Label Company Inc ....E....... 570 222-9000
Nicholson (G-12615)

J F Chobert Associates Inc ....G....... 610 431-2200
Wayne (G-19341)

Jon Swan Inc ....E....... 412 264-9000
Coraopolis (G-3700)

Kraemer Properties Inc ....G....... 717 246-0208
Red Lion (G-16603)

Label Converters Inc ....G....... 215 675-6900
Ivyland (G-8214)

Labels By Pulizzi Inc..........E....... 570 326-1244
Williamsport (G-20034)

Labelworx Inc ....G....... 215 945-5645
Levittown (G-9844)

Lemac Packaging Inc ....G....... 814 453-7652
Erie (G-5361)

▲ M & C Specialties Co ....B....... 215 322-7441
Southampton (G-17823)

M B Graphics ....G...... 717 246-9000
Red Lion (G-16606)

Mgi Seagull Inc ....E...... 610 380-6470
Downingtown (G-4241)

Mito Insulation Company ....E...... 724 335-8551
New Kensington (G-12359)

Mjs LLC ....G...... 215 732-3501
Philadelphia (G-14028)

Modern Reproductions Inc ....F...... 412 488-7700
Pittsburgh (G-15298)

▲ Moore Push Pin Company ....D...... 215 233-5700
Glenside (G-6531)

Mri Flexible Packaging Company ....F...... 215 860-7676
Newtown (G-12525)

Neenah Northeast LLC ....C...... 215 536-4600
Quakertown (G-16223)

Neenah Northeast LLC ....E...... 610 926-1996
Reading (G-16453)

▲ Penn Emblem Company ....D...... 215 632-7800
Feasterville Trevose (G-5926)

Reed & Witting Company ....E...... 412 682-1000
Pittsburgh (G-15476)

Rekord Printing Co ....G...... 570 648-3231
Elysburg (G-4980)

Shepherd Good Work Services .....C...... 610 776-8353
Allentown (G-388)

Spectra-Kote Corporation ....E...... 717 334-3177
Gettysburg (G-6314)

Status Label Corporation ....G...... 215 443-0124
Hatboro (G-7306)

▲ Tekni-Plex Inc ....E...... 484 690-1520
Wayne (G-19381)

▲ Tele-Media Sfp LLC ....E...... 570 271-0810
Danville (G-4014)

Tinicum Research Company ....G...... 610 294-9390
Erwinna (G-5540)

▲ Topflight Corporation ....C...... 717 227-5400
Glen Rock (G-6461)

Trident Tpi Holdings Inc ....A...... 484 690-1520
Wayne (G-19384)

Uniflex Holdings Inc ....E...... 516 932-2000
Philadelphia (G-14419)

▲ Westrock Packaging Inc ....D...... 215 785-3350
Croydon (G-3933)

Xode Inc ....E...... 610 683-8777
Kutztown (G-8864)

▼ Yerecic Label Co Inc ....D...... 724 334-3300
New Kensington (G-12393)

2673 Bags: Plastics, Laminated & Coated

Alpine Packaging Inc ....E...... 412 664-4000
North Versailles (G-12771)

Bemis Company Inc ....C...... 570 501-1400
West Hazleton (G-19706)

Bomboy Inc ....F...... 610 266-1553
Allentown (G-157)

Chalmur Bag LLC ....F...... 215 455-1360
Philadelphia (G-13522)

CJ Packaging Inc ....G...... 570 209-7836
Avoca (G-841)

▲ Cjc Contract Packaging Inc ......G...... 570 209-7836
Avoca (G-842)

Closet Space ....G...... 610 359-0583
Broomall (G-2283)

▲ Consolidated Packaging LLC .....G...... 215 968-6260
Langhorne (G-9286)

Gateway Packaging Corp ....E...... 724 327-7400
Export (G-5607)

Harmony LL Plastics Inc ....G...... 215 943-8888
Bristol (G-2151)

Hilex Poly Co LLC ....C...... 814 355-7410
Milesburg (G-11151)

Innovative Plastics of PA LLC ....G...... 717 529-2699
Christiana (G-3136)

◆ Knf Flexpak Corporation ....D...... 570 386-3550
Tamaqua (G-18214)

Lancaster Extrusion Inc ....G...... 717 392-9622
Lancaster (G-9093)

Mri Flexible Packaging Company ....F...... 215 860-7676
Newtown (G-12525)

North Coast Plastics Inc ....F...... 814 838-1343
Erie (G-5407)

▼ Peace Products Co Inc ....E...... 610 296-4222
Malvern (G-10294)

Retal Pa LLC ....F...... 724 705-3975
Donora (G-4160)

Reynolds Presto Products Inc ....B...... 866 254-3310
Pittsburgh (G-15483)

Royco Packaging Inc ....G...... 215 322-8082
Huntingdon Valley (G-8030)

Sealed Air Corporation ....C...... 717 637-5905
Hanover (G-6949)

Sealed Air Corporation ....G...... 610 926-7517
Reading (G-16509)

▲ Sheth International Inc ....G...... 610 584-8670
Norristown (G-12712)

Sunshine Plastics Inc ....F...... 215 943-8888
Bristol (G-2202)

Superior Packaging Inc ....F...... 570 824-3577
Plains (G-15789)

Transcontinental US LLC ....C...... 570 384-4674
Hazle Township (G-7486)

Trinity Plastics Inc ....B...... 717 242-2355
Lewistown (G-9950)

Uniflex Holdings Inc ....E...... 516 932-2000
Philadelphia (G-14419)

Viridor Global ....G...... 202 360-1617
Philadelphia (G-14450)

▲ West Pharmaceutical Svcs Inc ......B...... 610 594-2900
Exton (G-5748)

Wester Burlap Bag & Supply Co ....G...... 412 835-4314
Bethel Park (G-1439)

2674 Bags: Uncoated Paper & Multiwall

Dade Paper Co ....G...... 570 579-6780
Hazle Township (G-7450)

▲ Handelok Bag Company Inc ......E...... 215 362-3400
Lansdale (G-9375)

▲ Knight Corporation ....E...... 610 853-2161
Havertown (G-7423)

Superior Packaging Inc ....F...... 570 824-3577
Plains (G-15789)

Uniflex Holdings Inc ....E...... 516 932-2000
Philadelphia (G-14419)

2675 Die-Cut Paper & Board

Acme Specialties Inc ....G...... 215 822-5900
Hatfield (G-7314)

Alfred Envelope Company Inc ....F...... 215 739-1500
Philadelphia (G-13362)

American Products Inc ....D...... 717 767-6510
York (G-20375)

◆ Beistle Company ....B...... 717 532-2131
Shippensburg (G-17517)

CCT Manufacturing & Fulfillmen ......F...... 724 652-0818
New Castle (G-12072)

Club Coin Boards Inc ....G...... 570 473-0429
Northumberland (G-12866)

Complete Hand Assembly Finshg ......E...... 215 634-7490
Philadelphia (G-13563)

▲ Converters Inc ....E...... 215 355-5400
Huntingdon Valley (G-7971)

Delaware Valley Shipping & Pac ......E...... 215 638-8900
Bensalem (G-1182)

Folded Structures Company LLC ......G...... 908 237-1955
Newtown (G-12502)

Harrier Mfg Corp ....G...... 814 838-9957
Erie (G-5310)

Hot Off Press Inc ....F...... 610 473-5700
Boyertown (G-1916)

Kisel Printing Service Inc ....E...... 570 489-7666
Dickson City (G-4121)

Lemac Packaging Inc ....G...... 814 453-7652
Erie (G-5361)

◆ Nupak Printing LLC ....D...... 717 244-4041
Red Lion (G-16610)

Paper Magic Group Inc ....B...... 570 644-0842
Elysburg (G-4978)

Penn State Paper & Box Co Inc ......E...... 610 433-7468
Allentown (G-349)

Phillips Graphic Finishing LLC ....D...... 717 653-4565
Manheim (G-10402)

Raymond Sherman Co Inc ....G...... 610 272-4640
Conshohocken (G-3597)

Superior Packaging Inc ....F...... 570 824-3577
Plains (G-15789)

▲ Tele-Media Sfp LLC ....E...... 570 271-0810
Danville (G-4014)

2676 Sanitary Paper Prdts

▲ Bellemarque LLC ....E...... 855 262-7783
Hazle Township (G-7447)

◆ Berk International LLC ....D...... 610 369-0600
Boyertown (G-1898)

▲ Cellucap Manufacturing Co ....E...... 800 523-3814
Philadelphia (G-13518)

▲ Essity North America Inc ....C...... 610 499-3700
Philadelphia (G-13680)

F M P Healthcare Products ....G...... 800 611-7776
Bridgeville (G-2063)

◆ First Quality Baby Pdts LLC ....A...... 717 247-3516
Lewistown (G-9928)

First Quality Enterprises Inc ....C...... 570 384-1600
Hazleton (G-7498)

▲ First Quality Hygienic Inc ....G...... 570 769-6900
Mc Elhattan (G-10587)

First Quality Products Inc ....B...... 570 769-6900
Mc Elhattan (G-10588)

First Quality Products Inc ....B...... 610 265-5000
King of Prussia (G-8618)

Kimberly-Clark Corporation ....D...... 610 874-4331
Chester (G-3053)

Lake Paper Products Inc ....E...... 570 836-8815
Tunkhannock (G-18541)

▲ Nutek Disposables Inc ....D...... 570 769-6900
Mc Elhattan (G-10589)

Procter & Gamble Paper Pdts Co ......B...... 570 833-5141
Mehoopany (G-10957)

2677 Envelopes

Cenveo Worldwide Limited ....F...... 717 285-9095
Lancaster (G-8975)

Direct Line Productions Inc ....G...... 610 633-7082
Glen Mills (G-6435)

Great Northern Press of Wilkes ......F...... 570 822-3147
Wilkes Barre (G-19922)

National Imprint Corporation ....E...... 814 239-8141
Claysburg (G-3205)

National Imprint Corporation ....E...... 814 239-5116
Claysburg (G-3206)

National Mail Graphics Corp ....D...... 610 524-1600
Exton (G-5713)

North Amrcn Communications Inc ......A...... 814 696-3553
Duncansville (G-4458)

◆ Northeastern Envelope Company ......D...... 800 233-4285
Old Forge (G-12971)

Suplee Envelope Co Inc ....E...... 610 352-2900
Garnet Valley (G-6269)

Tension Envelope Corporation ....E...... 570 429-1444
Saint Clair (G-16942)

Tri-State Envelope Corporation ......B...... 570 875-0433
Ashland (G-738)

2678 Stationery Prdts

◆ Bay Sales LLC ....G...... 215 331-6466
Bristol (G-2117)

D-K Trading Corporation Inc ....G...... 570 586-9662
Clarks Summit (G-3191)

Digibuddha Design LLC ....F...... 267 387-8165
Hatboro (G-7280)

Foto-Wear Inc ....G...... 570 307-3600
Lake Ariel (G-8888)

Ligonier Outfitters Newsstands ....G...... 724 238-4900
Ligonier (G-9961)

▲ Mbm Industries Inc ....E...... 215 844-2490
Philadelphia (G-13998)

National Imprint Corporation ....E...... 814 239-8141
Claysburg (G-3205)

▲ Paper Magic Group Inc ....C...... 570 961-3863
Moosic (G-11511)

Progressive Converting Inc ....D...... 570 384-2979
Hazle Township (G-7475)

◆ Roaring Spring Blank Book Co ......B...... 814 224-2306
Roaring Spring (G-16768)

Roaring Spring Blank Book Co ....C...... 814 793-3744
Martinsburg (G-10530)

▲ Vanroden Inc ....E...... 717 509-2600
Lancaster (G-9230)

2679 Converted Paper Prdts, NEC

Aegis Technologies Inc ....F...... 610 676-0300
Oaks (G-12931)

Allflex Packaging Products Inc ....F...... 215 542-9200
Ambler (G-566)

Alumagraphics Inc ....E...... 412 787-7594
Pittsburgh (G-14694)

◆ Amercareroyal LLC ....E...... 610 384-3400
Exton (G-5642)

American Crepe Corporation ....G...... 570 433-3319
Montoursville (G-11430)

◆ Beistle Company ....B...... 717 532-2131
Shippensburg (G-17517)

▲ Bengal Converting Services Inc ......E...... 610 787-0900
Linfield (G-9987)

Bengal Direct LLC ....F...... 610 245-5901
Linfield (G-9988)

Beverage Coasters Inc ....G...... 610 916-4864
Centerport (G-2832)

Brodart Co ....C...... 570 769-3265
Mc Elhattan (G-10586)

Cariks Custom Decor ....G...... 412 882-1511
Pittsburgh *(G-14812)*

CSS Industries Inc ....C...... 610 729-3959
Plymouth Meeting *(G-15840)*

CSS Industries Inc ....G...... 570 275-5241
Danville *(G-3999)*

Devra Party Corp...................G...... 718 522-7421
Philadelphia *(G-13626)*

East-West Label Co Inc ....E...... 610 825-0410
Conshohocken *(G-3540)*

Erie Energy Products Inc ....F...... 814 454-2828
Erie *(G-5266)*

◆ Fibematics Inc ....E...... 215 226-2672
Philadelphia *(G-13698)*

Formica Corporation ....D...... 570 897-6319
Mount Bethel *(G-11610)*

Four Stars Pipe & Supply Inc ....G...... 724 746-2029
Eighty Four *(G-4841)*

Fox IV Technologies Inc ....E...... 724 387-3500
Export *(G-5603)*

Hampshire Paper Company ....G...... 570 759-7245
Berwick *(G-1328)*

Harmony Designs Inc ....G...... 610 869-4234
West Grove *(G-19700)*

◆ Hpi Plastics Incorporated ....F...... 610 273-7113
Honey Brook *(G-7751)*

Industrial Nameplate Inc ....E...... 215 322-1111
Warminster *(G-18898)*

Interstate Paper Supply Co Inc ....D...... 724 938-2218
Roscoe *(G-16817)*

Ivy Graphics Inc ....F...... 215 396-9446
Warminster *(G-18900)*

J F Chobert Associates Inc ....G...... 610 431-2200
Wayne *(G-19341)*

◆ Jacobson Hat Co Inc ....D...... 570 342-7887
Scranton *(G-17246)*

Keebar Enterprises Inc ....G...... 610 873-0150
West Chester *(G-19579)*

▲ Keystone Converting Inc ....F...... 215 661-9004
Montgomeryville *(G-11400)*

Labelcom ....G...... 814 362-3252
Bradford *(G-1978)*

◆ Lamtec Corporation ....C...... 570 897-8200
Mount Bethel *(G-11611)*

Lap Distributors Inc ....G...... 215 744-4000
Philadelphia *(G-13955)*

Lemac Packaging Inc ....G...... 814 453-7652
Erie *(G-5361)*

Leonards Auto Tag Service ....G...... 570 489-4777
Dickson Cty *(G-4124)*

Leonards Auto Tag Service ....G...... 570 693-0122
Scranton *(G-17254)*

Manchester Industries Inc VA ....E...... 570 822-9308
Hanover Township *(G-6993)*

◆ Max Intrntional Converters Inc ....E...... 717 898-0147
Lancaster *(G-9128)*

McCourt Label Cabinet Company ....D...... 800 458-2390
Lewis Run *(G-9877)*

Mri Flexible Packaging Company ....F...... 215 860-7676
Newtown *(G-12525)*

▲ N F String & Son Inc ....D...... 717 234-2441
Harrisburg *(G-7182)*

National Imprint Corporation ....E...... 814 239-8141
Claysburg *(G-3205)*

Neenah Northeast LLC ....C...... 215 536-4600
Quakertown *(G-16223)*

Northwoods Ppr Converting Inc ....D...... 570 424-8786
East Stroudsburg *(G-4625)*

Paper Exchange Inc ....F...... 412 325-7075
Allison Park *(G-457)*

▲ Paper Magic Group Inc ....C...... 570 961-3863
Moosic *(G-11511)*

▲ Party Time Manufacturing Co ....D...... 800 346-3847
Hughestown *(G-7894)*

Peerless Paper Specialty Inc ....G...... 215 657-3460
Willow Grove *(G-20133)*

Pocket Cross Inc ....G...... 724 745-1140
Houston *(G-7877)*

Progressive Converting Inc ....D...... 570 384-2979
Hazle Township *(G-7475)*

Reese Daryl C Wallpapering ....G...... 717 597-2532
Greencastle *(G-6629)*

Sappi North America Inc ....D...... 610 398-8400
Allentown *(G-383)*

Signode Industrial Group LLC ....E...... 570 450-0123
Hazle Township *(G-7479)*

Sonoco Prtective Solutions Inc ....E...... 412 415-3784
Pittsburgh *(G-15559)*

Southwind Studios Ltd ....G...... 610 664-4110
Lower Merion *(G-10109)*

▲ Specialty Industries Inc ....C...... 717 246-1661
Red Lion *(G-16613)*

Spring Mills Manufacturing Inc ....G...... 814 422-8892
Spring Mills *(G-17893)*

Taba Labels Company ....G...... 215 455-9977
Philadelphia *(G-14366)*

▼ Tagline Inc ....G...... 610 594-9300
Exton *(G-5735)*

▲ Tech Tag & Label Inc ....F...... 215 822-2400
Hatfield *(G-7398)*

▲ Tekni-Plex Inc ....E...... 484 690-1520
Wayne *(G-19381)*

▲ Tele-Media Sfp LLC ....E...... 570 271-0810
Danville *(G-4014)*

▲ Thomas Catanese & Co ....G...... 610 277-6230
Plymouth Meeting *(G-15876)*

Todd Weikel ....G...... 610 779-5508
Reading *(G-16542)*

Trautman Associates Inc ....F...... 570 743-0430
Shamokin Dam *(G-17429)*

Treco Incorporated ....F...... 215 226-0908
Philadelphia *(G-14405)*

Trident Tpi Holdings Inc ....A...... 484 690-1520
Wayne *(G-19384)*

Vetpack Enterprises LLC ....G...... 215 680-8637
Merion Station *(G-10999)*

◆ Wallquest Inc ....D...... 610 293-1330
Wayne *(G-19889)*

Weyerhaeuser Company ....D...... 814 371-0630
Du Bois *(G-4427)*

◆ York Wallcoverings Inc ....C...... 717 846-4456
York *(G-20754)*

27 PRINTING, PUBLISHING, AND ALLIED INDUSTRIES

2711 Newspapers: Publishing & Printing

21st Century Media Newsppr LLC ....D...... 610 692-3790
Exton *(G-5633)*

21st Century Media Newsppr LLC ....E...... 814 238-3071
State College *(G-17939)*

21st Century Newspapers Inc ....G...... 215 504-4200
Yardley *(G-20292)*

21st Cntury Mdia Newpapers LLC ....G...... 215 368-6973
Lansdale *(G-9338)*

21st Cntury Mdia Nwspapers LLC ....G...... 610 622-4186
Secane *(G-17316)*

A & T News Service ....G...... 610 454-7787
Collegeville *(G-3366)*

A T J Printing Inc ....F...... 814 641-9614
Huntingdon *(G-7936)*

Acme Newspapers Inc ....C...... 610 642-4300
Ardmore *(G-699)*

Advance Publications ....F...... 717 582-4305
New Bloomfield *(G-12029)*

Advance Publications ....F...... 717 436-8206
Mifflintown *(G-11108)*

Advertsing Otsourcing Svcs LLC ....E...... 570 793-2000
Wilkes Barre *(G-19903)*

Al Dia Newspaper Inc ....F...... 215 569-4666
Philadelphia *(G-13361)*

Alm Media LLC ....E...... 215 557-2300
Philadelphia *(G-13370)*

Altoona Mirror ....D...... 814 946-7506
Altoona *(G-471)*

Alvin Engle Associates Inc ....E...... 717 653-1833
Mount Joy *(G-11645)*

▲ Alvin Engle Associates Inc ....G...... 717 653-1833
Mount Joy *(G-11646)*

American Chief Company ....G...... 267 984-8852
Philadelphia *(G-13383)*

Anthony Ds Daily Numbers ....G...... 215 537-0618
Philadelphia *(G-13395)*

Area Shopper ....G...... 814 425-7272
Cochranton *(G-3335)*

Atlantic Publishing Group Inc ....F...... 800 832-3747
Flourtown *(G-5985)*

Balloon Flights Daily ....G...... 610 469-0782
Saint Peters *(G-17033)*

Barrys Lobby Shop ....F...... 215 925-1998
Philadelphia *(G-13446)*

Bcmi Ad Concepts Inc ....E...... 215 354-3000
Bensalem *(G-1154)*

Beaver Newspapers Inc ....B...... 724 775-3200
Beaver *(G-979)*

Bedford Gazette LLC ....E...... 814 623-1151
Bedford *(G-1042)*

Berks-Mont Newspapers Inc ....F...... 610 683-7343
Pottstown *(G-15966)*

Bill ONeill ....G...... 610 688-6135
Wayne *(G-19306)*

Bradford Journal Miner ....G...... 814 465-3468
Bradford *(G-1959)*

Bradford Publishing Company ....D...... 814 368-3173
Bradford *(G-1960)*

Broad St Cmnty Newspapers Inc ....G...... 215 354-3135
Berlin *(G-1286)*

Broadtop Bulletin ....G...... 814 635-2851
Saxton *(G-17099)*

▲ Brookshire Printing Inc ....E...... 717 392-1321
Lancaster *(G-8961)*

Bucks County Herald ....E...... 215 794-1096
Buckingham *(G-2339)*

Bucks County Herald Corp ....G...... 215 794-2601
Doylestown *(G-4282)*

Bucks County Midweek ....G...... 215 355-1234
Feasterville Trevose *(G-5894)*

Burrells Information Services ....E...... 717 671-3872
Harrisburg *(G-7101)*

Butler Circulation Calls ....G...... 724 282-1859
Butler *(G-2384)*

Calkins Media Incorporated ....C...... 215 949-4000
Levittown *(G-9822)*

Call Newspapers Inc ....F...... 570 385-3120
Schuylkill Haven *(G-17150)*

Cameron County Community Chest ....G...... 814 486-0612
Emporium *(G-5052)*

Cameron County Echo Inc ....G...... 814 486-3711
Emporium *(G-5053)*

Car Gazette Co ....G...... 412 951-5572
Pittsburgh *(G-14807)*

Carbondale News ....G...... 570 282-3300
Honesdale *(G-7705)*

Carbondale News ....G...... 570 282-3300
Honesdale *(G-7706)*

Career Lfstyle Enhncment Jurnl ....G...... 724 872-5344
West Newton *(G-19749)*

Carnegie Mellon University ....E...... 412 268-2111
Pittsburgh *(G-14818)*

Carreon Publishing LLC ....G...... 570 673-5151
Canton *(G-2663)*

Catholic Light Publishing Co ....G...... 570 207-2229
Scranton *(G-17215)*

Catholic Register ....G...... 814 695-7563
Hollidaysburg *(G-7643)*

Catholic Scl Svcs of Scranton ....D...... 570 207-2283
Scranton *(G-17216)*

Catholic Scl Svcs of Scranton ....G...... 570 454-6693
Hazleton *(G-7494)*

Central Pennsylvania ....G...... 814 946-7411
Altoona *(G-489)*

Centre County Womens Journal ....G...... 814 349-8202
Millheim *(G-11217)*

Chestnut Hill Local ....E...... 215 248-8800
Philadelphia *(G-13539)*

Citizen ....F...... 412 766-6679
Pittsburgh *(G-14853)*

Citizens Voice ....B...... 570 821-2000
Wilkes Barre *(G-19912)*

City Suburban News ....G...... 610 667-6623
Penn Valley *(G-13234)*

Citywide Exclusive Newsppr Inc ....G...... 215 467-8214
Phila *(G-13309)*

Civitas Media LLC ....G...... 570 829-7100
Wilkes Barre *(G-19913)*

Classified Advertising ....G...... 814 723-1400
Warren *(G-19016)*

Cnhi LLC ....E...... 814 781-1596
Saint Marys *(G-16955)*

Collegian Inc ....E...... 814 865-2531
State College *(G-17953)*

Community Newspaper ....G...... 814 683-4841
Linesville *(G-9979)*

Community Newspaper Group LLC ....G...... 570 275-3235
Sunbury *(G-18166)*

Commuters Express Inc ....G...... 570 476-0601
East Stroudsburg *(G-4610)*

Construction Equipment Guide ....E...... 215 885-2900
Fort Washington *(G-6066)*

Corporate Distribution Ltd ....E...... 717 697-6900
Harrisburg *(G-7109)*

Corry Journal Inc ....F...... 814 665-8291
Corry *(G-3750)*

Country Impressions Inc ....F...... 570 477-5000
Hunlock Creek *(G-7931)*

Courier Times Inc ....A...... 215 949-4011
Levittown *(G-9828)*

Daily ....G...... 610 384-0372
Coatesville *(G-3300)*

Daily American	E	814 444-5900	Somerset (G-17683)
Daily Dove Care LLC	G	215 316-5888	Philadelphia (G-13604)
Daily Informer LLC	G	717 634-9087	Hanover (G-6872)
Delaware County Legal Journal	G	717 337-9812	Gettysburg (G-6289)
Derrick Publishing Company	E	814 676-7444	Oil City (G-12944)
Derrick Publishing Company	E	412 364-8202	Pittsburgh (G-14918)
Derrick Publishing Company	E	814 226-7000	Clarion (G-3176)
Digital First Media Inc	G	215 504-4200	Yardley (G-20307)
Drdavesbestbodies Inc	G	610 926-5728	Fleetwood (G-5970)
Eagle Printing Company	D	724 282-8000	Butler (G-2398)
Eagle Printing Company	G	724 776-4270	Cranberry Township (G-3817)
Echo Pilot	G	717 597-2164	Greencastle (G-6609)
El Torero Spanish Newspaper	G	610 435-6608	Allentown (G-205)
Elizabethtown Advocate	G	717 361-0340	Elizabethtown (G-4873)
Elsol Latino Newspaper	G	215 424-1200	Philadelphia (G-13671)
Eric Nemeyer Corporation	G	215 887-8880	Glenside (G-6516)
Fairylogue Press	G	717 713-5788	Mechanicsburg (G-10843)
Family Business Publishing Co	G	215 567-3200	Philadelphia (G-13692)
Family-Life Media-Com Inc	F	724 543-6397	Kittanning (G-8769)
Fly Magazine	G	717 293-9772	Lancaster (G-9024)
Forest City News Inc	G	570 785-3800	Forest City (G-6053)
Franklin Penn Publishing Co	F	724 327-3471	Murrysville (G-11851)
Franklin Shopper	F	717 263-0359	Chambersburg (G-2933)
Frediani Printing Company	G	412 281-8533	Pittsburgh (G-15035)
Fresh Press LLC	G	717 504-9223	Hummelstown (G-7911)
Fulton County News	F	717 485-4513	Mc Connellsburg (G-10565)
Fulton County Reporter	G	717 325-0079	Mc Connellsburg (G-10566)
Gannett Co Inc	D	724 778-3388	Warrendale (G-19074)
Gannett Stllite Info Ntwrk Inc	G	215 679-9561	Red Hill (G-16581)
Gannett Stllite Info Ntwrk LLC	G	703 854-6185	Dillsburg (G-4130)
Gant Media Llc	G	814 765-5256	Clearfield (G-3219)
Gary Edward Soden	G	215 723-5964	Telford (G-18291)
Gatehouse Media LLC	E	570 253-3055	Honesdale (G-7712)
Gatehouse Media LLC	E	570 742-9671	Milton (G-11239)
Gateway Newspapers	G	412 856-7400	Pittsburgh (G-15041)
Gateway Publications	C	412 856-7400	Monroeville (G-11339)
Gateway Publications	G	412 856-7400	Mckees Rocks (G-10660)
Gazette Two DOT O	G	412 458-1526	Mc Kees Rocks (G-10611)
Gettysburg Times Pubg LLC	E	717 253-9403	Gettysburg (G-6292)
Gibson Journal	G	717 656-2582	Leola (G-9784)
▲ Goodson Holding Company	C	215 370-6069	Bristol (G-2149)
Great Valley Publishing Co	E	610 948-7639	Spring City (G-17858)
Green Tree Times	G	412 481-7830	Pittsburgh (G-15062)
Greenville Record Argus Inc	E	724 588-5000	Greenville (G-6742)
Hamburg Area Item	G	610 367-6041	Pottstown (G-15994)

Hammond Press Inc	E	412 821-4100	Pittsburgh (G-15078)
Hanover Publishing Co	C	717 637-3736	Hanover (G-6901)
Hari Jayanti News Inc	G	215 546-1350	Philadelphia (G-13802)
Hellenic News of America Inc	G	484 427-7446	Havertown (G-7422)
Herald Newspapers Company Inc	D	412 782-2121	Pittsburgh (G-15090)
Herald Standard	G	724 626-8345	Dunbar (G-4440)
Hocking Printing Co Inc	D	717 738-1151	Ephrata (G-5109)
Horsey Darden Enterprises LLC	G	215 309-3139	Philadelphia (G-13834)
Humble Elephant LLC	G	814 434-1743	Erie (G-5320)
Impressions Media	C	570 829-7140	Wilkes Barre (G-19927)
Independent-Observer	E	724 887-7400	Scottdale (G-17193)
Independent-Observer	G	724 238-2111	Ligonier (G-9959)
Independent-Observer	G	724 547-5722	Connellsville (G-3499)
Indiana Printing and Pubg Co	C	724 465-5555	Indiana (G-8105)
Inquirer & Daily News Fed CU	G	610 292-6762	Conshohocken (G-3564)
Irish Edition	G	215 836-4900	Oreland (G-13023)
Irish Network Philadelphia	G	215 690-1353	Upper Darby (G-18687)
Islamic Communication Network	G	215 227-0640	Philadelphia (G-13877)
J H Zerbey Newspapers Inc	F	570 622-3456	Pottsville (G-16082)
Jewish Chronicle	G	412 687-1000	Pittsburgh (G-15153)
Jewish Exponent Inc	E	215 832-0700	Philadelphia (G-13896)
Jimmi News	G	215 988-9095	Philadelphia (G-13899)
Johnson Communications Inc	G	215 474-7411	Philadelphia (G-13910)
Johnsonburg Press Inc	G	814 965-2503	Johnsonburg (G-8347)
Joseph F Biddle Publishing Co	G	814 684-4000	Tyrone (G-18585)
Journal Newspapers Inc	G	570 443-9131	White Haven (G-19849)
Journal Register Company	D	610 323-3000	Exton (G-5702)
Journal Register Company	D	610 280-2295	Exton (G-5703)
Journal Register Company	D	215 368-6976	Lansdale (G-9382)
Journal Register Company	C	610 696-1775	Exton (G-5704)
JS&d Graphics Inc	G	717 397-3440	Lancaster (G-9075)
Jyoti N Stand	G	215 843-5354	Philadelphia (G-13916)
Kane Republican	G	814 837-6000	Kane (G-8470)
Kapp Advertising Services Inc	D	717 270-2742	Lebanon (G-9587)
Kapp Advertising Services Inc	F	717 632-8303	Hanover (G-6909)
Knight Ridder Inc	G	570 829-7100	Wilkes Barre (G-19935)
Korea Daily News Inc	G	215 277-1112	Elkins Park (G-4908)
▲ Korean Phila Time Inc	F	215 663-2400	Rockledge (G-16791)
Krieg Dieter	G	717 656-8050	Brownstown (G-2308)
La Cronica Newspaper	G	484 357-2903	Allentown (G-290)
Lancaster County Weeklies	A	717 626-2191	Ephrata (G-5119)
Latrobe Printing and Pubg Co	E	724 537-3351	Latrobe (G-9493)
Lebanon Daily News	F	717 272-5615	Lebanon (G-9599)
Ledger Newspapers	G	610 444-6590	West Chester (G-19590)
Lee Enterprises Inc Sentinel	C	717 240-7135	Carlisle (G-2721)

Lee Publication Inc	G	717 240-7167	Carlisle (G-2722)
Lehigh Valley Chronicle	G	610 965-1636	Emmaus (G-5032)
Leon Spangler	F	570 837-7903	Middleburg (G-11028)
Lewistown Sentinel Inc	F	717 248-6741	Lewistown (G-9939)
Lititz Record Express Inc	G	717 626-2191	Lititz (G-10023)
Lnp Media Group Inc	D	717 733-6397	Ephrata (G-5121)
Local Media Group Inc	C	570 421-3000	Stroudsburg (G-18125)
Local Media Group Inc	F	724 458-5010	Grove City (G-6795)
Local Media Group Inc	G	570 524-2261	Lewisburg (G-9915)
Lock Haven Express	E	570 748-6791	Lock Haven (G-10090)
Mainline Newspapers	E	814 472-4110	Ebensburg (G-4789)
Margaret Mary Music Publishing	G	570 282-3503	Carbondale (G-2681)
Marie Chomicki	G	717 432-3456	Dillsburg (G-4136)
Masco Communications Inc	F	215 625-8501	Philadelphia (G-13993)
McLean Publishing Co	F	814 275-3131	New Bethlehem (G-12027)
McNear Charles & Associates	G	215 514-9431	Philadelphia (G-13999)
Medianews Group Inc	C	717 637-3736	Hanover (G-6919)
Mercersburg Journal	G	717 485-3162	Mc Connellsburg (G-10571)
Mercersburg Journal	G	717 328-3223	Mercersburg (G-10992)
Metal Bulletin Holdings LLC	F	412 765-2580	Pittsburgh (G-15279)
Metro News Gifts	G	610 734-2262	Upper Darby (G-18689)
Metroweek Corp	D	215 735-8444	Philadelphia (G-14017)
Mgtf Paper Company LLC	E	412 316-3342	Pittsburgh (G-15283)
Mid-Atlantic Tech Publications	F	610 783-6100	Valley Forge (G-18709)
Mifflinburg Telegraph Inc	G	570 966-2255	Mifflinburg (G-11099)
Miller Printing & Publishing	E	814 425-7272	Cochranton (G-3345)
Millersville University PA	E	717 871-4636	Millersville (G-11213)
Milton Daily Standard	E	570 742-9077	Montgomery (G-11376)
Molloy Associates Inc	G	610 293-1300	Bryn Mawr (G-2330)
Mon Valley Independent	G	724 314-0030	Charleroi (G-3016)
Morning Call LLC	F	610 379-3200	Lehighton (G-9720)
Morning Call LLC	A	610 820-6500	Allentown (G-322)
Morning Call Inc	E	610 861-3600	Bethlehem (G-1575)
Morrisons Cove Herald Inc	G	814 793-2144	Martinsburg (G-10527)
Mountaintop Eagle Inc	G	570 474-6397	Wilkes Barre (G-19946)
Moving Out	G	724 794-6831	Slippery Rock (G-17623)
Mpc Liquidation Inc	G	814 849-6737	Brookville (G-2266)
MSP Corporation	G	570 344-7670	Scranton (G-17260)
Mulligan Printing Corporation	E	570 278-3271	Tunkhannock (G-18544)
Muncy Luminary	G	570 584-0111	Hughesville (G-7897)
National Hot Rod Association	D	717 584-1200	Lancaster (G-9142)
Nazareth Key Youngs Press	G	610 759-5000	Nazareth (G-11984)
Neighborhood Publications Inc	G	412 481-0266	Pittsburgh (G-15324)
New Pittsburgh Courier Pubg Co	F	412 481-8302	Pittsburgh (G-15333)
New Republic	G	814 634-8321	Meyersdale (G-11017)

News Chronicle Co Inc ....E .... 717 532-4101 Shippensburg (G-17540)	Philadelphia Media Network Pbc ....D ..... 215 854-2000 Philadelphia (G-14147)	Sip Bulletin LLC ....G .... 267 235-3359 Philadelphia (G-14310)
News Eagle ....E ..... 570 226-4547 Honesdale (G-7719)	Philadelphia Newspapers Inc ....F ..... 610 292-6200 Conshohocken (G-3587)	Snyder County Times ....G ..... 570 837-6065 Middleburg (G-11041)
News Eagle ....G .... 570 296-4547 Milford (G-11164)	Philadelphia Public Record ....F ..... 215 755-2000 Philadelphia (G-14152)	Society of Good Shepherd ....G .... 717 349-7033 Amberson (G-565)
News Item Cin 5 ....F ..... 570 644-0891 Shamokin (G-17426)	Philadelphia Sun Group Inc ....G ..... 215 848-7864 Philadelphia (G-14157)	South Fork News Agency ....G ..... 814 495-9394 South Fork (G-17777)
News of Delaware County ....G .... 610 583-4432 Swarthmore (G-18185)	Philadelphia Tribune Company ....D ..... 215 893-5356 Philadelphia (G-14158)	Spirit Media Group Inc ....G ..... 610 447-8484 Chester (G-3064)
Newspaper Guild of Philadelphi ....G ..... 215 928-0118 Philadelphia (G-14071)	Philadlphia Media Holdings LLC ....F ..... 215 854-2000 Philadelphia (G-14162)	Spirit Publishing Company ....E ..... 814 938-8740 Punxsutawney (G-16163)
Newspaper Holding Inc ....D ..... 814 532-5102 Johnstown (G-8412)	▲ Philadelphia-Newspapers-Llc ....A ..... 215 854-2000 Philadelphia (G-14167)	Stott Publications Inc ....G ..... 814 632-6700 Tyrone (G-18593)
Newspaper Holding Inc ....D ..... 724 981-6100 Sharon (G-17440)	Phildelphia-Newspapers-Llc ....A ..... 610 292-6200 Conshohocken (G-3588)	Suburban Advertiser ....G ..... 610 363-2815 Exton (G-5734)
Newspaper Holding Inc ....D ..... 814 724-6370 Meadville (G-10769)	Philipsburg Journal ....G ..... 814 342-1320 Philipsburg (G-14524)	Suburban Newspaper of America ....G ..... 215 513-4145 Harleysville (G-7060)
Newspaper Holding Inc ....D ..... 724 654-6651 New Castle (G-12131)	Pike County Dispatch Inc ....F ..... 570 296-2611 Milford (G-11166)	Sullivan Review ....G ..... 570 928-8403 Dushore (G-4511)
Newspaper Networks Inc ....G ..... 610 853-2121 Upper Darby (G-18691)	Pittsburgh Business Times ....G ..... 412 481-6397 Pittsburgh (G-15389)	Sun-Gazette Company ....C ..... 570 326-1551 Williamsport (G-20076)
Newtown Gazette ....G ..... 215 702-3405 Langhorne (G-9314)	Pittsburgh Catholic Pubg Assoc ....F ..... 412 471-1252 Pittsburgh (G-15390)	Sunday Review ....G ..... 570 265-2151 Towanda (G-18434)
Nittany Printing and Pubg Co ....D ..... 814 238-5000 State College (G-18000)	Pittsburgh City Paper Inc ....E ..... 412 316-3342 Pittsburgh (G-15391)	▲ Sunday Topic Korean News ....G ..... 215 935-1111 Elkins Park (G-4912)
Northampton Herald ....G ..... 215 702-3405 Langhorne (G-9316)	Pittsburgh Jewish Publication ....F ..... 412 687-1000 Pittsburgh (G-15399)	Susquehanna Independent Wkndr ....G ..... 570 278-6397 Montrose (G-11479)
Observer Publishing Company ....B ..... 724 222-2200 Washington (G-19212)	Pittsburgh Post Gazette ....G ..... 724 266-2701 Leetsdale (G-9701)	Susquehanna Transcript Inc ....G ..... 570 853-3134 Susquehanna (G-18183)
Observer Publishing Company ....G ..... 724 852-2602 Waynesburg (G-19449)	Pittsburgh Postgazette ....G ..... 412 858-1850 Monroeville (G-11348)	Technically Media Inc ....G ..... 215 821-8745 Philadelphia (G-14379)
Observer Publishing Company ....E ..... 724 941-7725 Canonsburg (G-2614)	Pocono Times ....G ..... 570 421-4800 East Stroudsburg (G-4628)	Texas-New Mxico Newspapers LLC ....D ..... 717 767-3554 York (G-20686)
Ogden Newspapers Inc ....C ..... 814 946-7411 Altoona (G-535)	Pollock Advertising ....G ..... 724 794-6857 Slippery Rock (G-17624)	The M & A Journal Inc ....G ..... 215 238-0506 Philadelphia (G-14386)
Ogden Newspapers Inc ....F ..... 570 584-2134 Hughesville (G-7898)	Post Gazette ....G ..... 412 854-9722 Bethel Park (G-1428)	The Scranton Times L P ....D ..... 570 348-9146 Scranton (G-17297)
Ogden Newspapers of PA ....D ..... 717 248-6741 Lewistown (G-9941)	Post Gazette ....G ..... 412 965-6738 Mc Donald (G-10578)	The Scranton Times L P ....C ..... 570 348-9100 Scranton (G-17298)
Our Town ....F ..... 814 269-9704 Johnstown (G-8418)	▲ Pottsville Republican Inc ....E ..... 570 622-3456 Pottsville (G-16092)	The Scranton Times L P ....D ..... 570 644-6397 Shamokin (G-17427)
Oxford Daily LLC ....G ..... 215 533-5656 Philadelphia (G-14107)	Press and Journal ....E ..... 717 944-4628 Middletown (G-11071)	The Scranton Times L P ....C ..... 570 821-2095 Wilkes Barre (G-19965)
P & N Holdings Inc ....C ..... 570 455-3636 Hazleton (G-7514)	Press-Enterprise Inc ....G ..... 570 752-3645 Bloomsburg (G-1794)	The Scranton Times L P ....E ..... 410 523-2300 Scranton (G-17299)
Page 1 Publishers Inc ....G ..... 610 380-8264 Downingtown (G-4248)	Press-Enterprise Inc ....F ..... 610 807-9619 Bethlehem (G-1604)	The Scranton Times L P ....G ..... 570 682-9081 Valley View (G-18718)
Paradies Pleasant News LL ....G ..... 610 521-2936 Essington (G-5545)	Press-Enterprise Inc ....C ..... 570 784-2121 Bloomsburg (G-1795)	The Scranton Times L P ....G ..... 570 265-2151 Towanda (G-18435)
Patriot Kutztown Area ....G ..... 610 367-6041 Pottstown (G-16026)	Priceless Times ....G ..... 267 538-5723 Philadelphia (G-14200)	Thepaperframercom ....G ..... 570 239-1444 Ashley (G-740)
Patriot-News Co ....B ..... 717 255-8100 Mechanicsburg (G-10875)	Progress News ....G ..... 724 867-2435 Emlenton (G-5014)	Times Partner LLC ....G ..... 570 348-9100 Scranton (G-17302)
Patriot-News Co ....G ..... 717 255-8100 Mechanicsburg (G-10876)	Progressive Publishing Company ....D ..... 814 765-5051 Clearfield (G-3229)	Times Pubg Newspapers Inc ....F ..... 215 702-3405 Langhorne (G-9329)
Patriot-News Co ....G ..... 717 243-1758 Carlisle (G-2729)	Publicsource ....G ..... 412 315-0264 Pittsburgh (G-15455)	Times Publishing Company ....D ..... 814 453-4691 Erie (G-5509)
Paxton Herald ....F ..... 717 545-9868 Harrisburg (G-7190)	Quickel International Corp ....G ..... 215 862-1313 New Hope (G-12313)	Times Shamrock Newspaper Group ......G ..... 570 348-9100 Scranton (G-17303)
Payal News ....G ..... 215 625-3699 Philadelphia (G-14126)	Reading Eagle Company ....E ..... 610 371-5000 Reading (G-16488)	Times-Shamrock ....D ..... 570 501-0278 Hazleton (G-7531)
Peerless Publications Inc ....C ..... 610 323-3000 Pottstown (G-16027)	Reading Eagle Company ....E ..... 610 371-5180 Reading (G-16489)	Tioga Publishing Company ....A ..... 814 371-4200 Du Bois (G-4424)
Peerless Publications Inc ....F ..... 610 970-3210 Pottstown (G-16028)	Record Herald Publishing Co ....E ..... 717 762-2151 Waynesboro (G-19422)	Tioga Publishing Company ....F ..... 814 274-8044 Coudersport (G-3789)
Penco Products Inc ....G ..... 800 562-1000 Skippack (G-17603)	Review Publishing Ltd Partnr ....D ..... 215 563-7400 Philadelphia (G-14242)	Tioga Publishing Company ....G ..... 814 849-6737 Brookville (G-2273)
Pencor Services Inc ....G ..... 570 668-1250 Tamaqua (G-18223)	Ridgway Record ....G ..... 814 773-3161 Ridgway (G-16728)	Tioga Publishing Company ....E ..... 570 724-2287 Wellsboro (G-19473)
Pencor Services Inc ....E ..... 610 826-2115 Palmerton (G-13110)	Rocket-Courier Newspaper ....F ..... 570 746-1217 Wyalusing (G-20258)	Titusville Herald Inc ....E ..... 814 827-3634 Titusville (G-18400)
Pencor Services Inc ....C ..... 570 386-2660 Lehighton (G-9721)	Sample News Group LLC ....C ..... 814 665-8291 Corry (G-3773)	Towanda Printing Co Inc ....G ..... 570 297-4158 Troy (G-18528)
Pencor Services Inc ....E ..... 610 740-0944 Allentown (G-346)	Sample News Group LLC ....F ..... 814 774-7073 Girard (G-6401)	Towanda Printing Co Inc ....C ..... 570 265-2151 Towanda (G-18436)
Penn Jersey Advance Inc ....B ..... 610 258-7171 Easton (G-4742)	Sample News Group LLC ....E ..... 570 888-9643 Sayre (G-17122)	Town Talk Newspapers Inc ....E ..... 610 583-4432 Holmes (G-7666)
Penn Jersey Advance Inc ....G ..... 610 258-7171 Bethlehem (G-1593)	Saucon Source LLC ....G ..... 610 442-3370 Fountain Hill (G-6100)	Tri County Record ....G ..... 610 970-3218 Pottstown (G-16056)
Pennsylvnia Soc Newsppr Editor ....G ..... 717 703-3000 Harrisburg (G-7197)	Sb New York Inc ....E ..... 215 717-2600 Philadelphia (G-14284)	Trib Total Media Inc ....D ..... 724 684-5200 Greensburg (G-6719)
Penny Mansfield Saver Inc ....G ..... 570 662-3277 Mansfield (G-10424)	Scranton Times-Tribune ....F ..... 570 348-9100 Scranton (G-17289)	Trib Total Media LLC ....B ..... 412 321-6460 Greensburg (G-6720)
Penny Power Ltd ....F ..... 610 282-4808 Coopersburg (G-3633)	Sell-It ....G ..... 215 453-8937 Sellersville (G-17358)	Trib Total Media LLC ....E ..... 724 543-1303 Kittanning (G-8800)
▲ Pg Publishing Company ....A ..... 412 263-1100 Clinton (G-3265)	Sewickley Herald ....G ..... 412 324-1403 Sewickley (G-17409)	Trib Total Media LLC ....D ..... 412 871-2301 Tarentum (G-18250)
Philadelphia Media Network Pbc ....F ..... 610 292-6389 Conshohocken (G-3586)	Shoppers Guide ....G ..... 724 349-0336 Indiana (G-8128)	Trib Total Media LLC ....C ..... 724 834-1151 Greensburg (G-6721)

Triboro Banner ....G..... 570 348-9185
Scranton (G-17306)

Tribune-Review Publishing Co ....G..... 724 779-8742
Tarentum (G-18251)

Trustees of The Univ of PA ....G..... 215 898-5555
Philadelphia (G-14413)

Twanda Printing ....G..... 570 421-4800
Scranton (G-17307)

Union News ....G..... 570 343-4958
Dunmore (G-4486)

Uniontown Newspapers Inc ....C..... 724 439-7500
Uniontown (G-18644)

University City Review Inc ....G..... 215 222-2846
Philadelphia (G-14428)

University of Pittsburgh ....C..... 412 648-7980
Pittsburgh (G-15683)

Valley Mirror ....G..... 412 462-0626
Homestead (G-7696)

Valley Voice Inc ....G..... 610 838-2066
Hellertown (G-7564)

Vetmed Communications Inc ....G..... 610 361-0555
Glen Mills (G-6448)

Victorian Publishing Co Inc ....G..... 814 634-8321
Meyersdale (G-11020)

Warren Times Observer......................E..... 814 723-8200
Warren (G-19063)

Wced News Talk ....G..... 814 372-1420
Du Bois (G-4426)

Webb Communications Inc ....E..... 570 326-7634
Plymouth (G-15823)

Webb Communications Inc ....D..... 570 326-7634
Williamsport (G-20089)

Webb Weekly ....F..... 570 326-9322
Williamsport (G-20090)

Weekender ....F..... 570 831-7320
Wilkes Barre (G-19971)

Weekly Bargain Bulletin Inc ....G..... 724 654-5529
New Castle (G-12166)

Weekly Piper Ltd ....G..... 717 341-3726
Lititz (G-10058)

Weekly Shopper ....D..... 412 243-4215
Tarentum (G-18254)

Western PA Newsppr Co ....F..... 814 226-7000
Clarion (G-3187)

▲ Wilkes-Barre Publishing Co ....C..... 570 829-7100
Wilkes Barre (G-19976)

▲ Wilkes-Barre Publishing Co Inc......G..... 570 829-7100
Wilkes Barre (G-19977)

▲ Windsor-Press Inc ....E..... 610 562-3624
Hamburg (G-6857)

Wwb Holdings LLC ....E..... 267 519-4500
Philadelphia (G-14493)

Wyoming County Press Inc ....F..... 570 348-9185
Tunkhannock (G-18553)

Wyoming Valley Times Jurnl Inc ....G..... 570 288-8362
Kingston (G-8726)

Wysocki-Cole Enterprises Inc ....E..... 724 567-5656
Vandergrift (G-18738)

Xpress Energy ....F..... 610 935-9200
Phoenixville (G-14584)

Y H Newspaper Inc ....G..... 215 546-0372
Philadelphia (G-14497)

York County Womens Journal ....G..... 717 634-1658
York (G-20735)

York Daily Record Sunday News..........F....... 717 771-2000
York (G-20736)

York Newspaper Company.....................B..... 717 767-6397
York (G-20746)

2721 Periodicals: Publishing & Printing

310 Publishing LLC ....G..... 717 564-0161
Harrisburg (G-7077)

Act Inc ....G..... 484 562-0063
Bala Cynwyd (G-872)

Advertising Specialty Inst Inc..............B..... 800 546-1350
Feasterville Trevose (G-5883)

American Association For Cance..........D..... 215 440-9300
Philadelphia (G-13378)

American Baptst HM Mission Soc........D..... 610 768-2465
King of Prussia (G-8581)

American Cllege Physicians Inc...........B..... 215 351-2400
Philadelphia (G-13384)

American Economic Association ....F..... 412 432-2300
Pittsburgh (G-14702)

American Future Systems Inc ....E..... 610 375-8012
Reading (G-16319)

American Law Institute........................D..... 215 243-1600
Philadelphia (G-13385)

American Soc For Deaf Children..........G....... 717 909-5577
Camp Hill (G-2486)

American Waste Digest Corp ....G..... 610 326-9480
Pottstown (G-15942)

Association Test Publishers ....G..... 717 755-9747
York (G-20388)

B P S Communications Inc ....F..... 215 830-8467
Willow Grove (G-20109)

Bb Vintage Magazine ADS...................G..... 717 235-1109
New Freedom (G-12202)

Benchmark Group Media Inc ....G..... 610 691-8833
Bethlehem (G-1459)

Bible Lighthouse Inc..........................G..... 570 888-6615
Sayre (G-17111)

Blue Star Basketball ....G..... 215 638-7060
Bensalem (G-1158)

BNP Media Inc ....F..... 610 436-4220
West Chester (G-19512)

BNP Media Inc ....G..... 412 531-3370
Pittsburgh (G-19081)

Bradford County Sanitation Inc...........G..... 570 673-3128
Troy (G-18518)

Bradley Communications Corp ....E..... 484 477-4220
Broomall (G-2281)

Breakthrough Publications Inc.............G..... 610 928-4061
Emmaus (G-5021)

▲ Brookshire Printing Inc ....E..... 717 392-1321
Lancaster (G-8961)

Bryn Mawr Communications LLC ....F..... 610 687-0887
Wayne (G-19309)

Bwhip Magazine LLC ....G..... 412 607-3963
Pittsburgh (G-14798)

Campbell 3 ....G..... 724 322-1043
New Stanton (G-12447)

Career Communications Inc ....G..... 215 256-3130
Harleysville (G-7024)

Catholic Golden Age Inc ....F..... 570 586-1091
Scott Township (G-17183)

▲ Chitra Publications ....E..... 570 278-1984
Montrose (G-11462)

Cibo Media Group LLC ....G..... 215 732-6700
Philadelphia (G-13544)

Clipper Magazine LLC ....B..... 717 569-5100
Mountville (G-11791)

Computertalk Associates Inc...............G..... 610 825-7686
Blue Bell (G-1823)

Connections Magazine ....G..... 570 647-0085
Honesdale (G-7708)

Construction Equipment Guide............E..... 215 885-2900
Fort Washington (G-6066)

Critic Publications Inc ....G..... 215 536-8884
Quakertown (G-16181)

Current History Inc ....G..... 610 772-5709
Philadelphia (G-13591)

Current Therapeutics Inc ....G..... 610 644-5995
Berwyn (G-1359)

Cycle Source Magazine ....G..... 724 226-2867
Tarentum (G-18240)

D Dietrich Associates Inc ....G..... 215 258-1071
Sellersville (G-17342)

Daily American ....E..... 814 444-5900
Somerset (G-17683)

Daniel Parent ....G..... 914 850-5473
Milford (G-11158)

Days Communication Inc ....G..... 215 538-1240
Quakertown (G-16183)

Diamond Rock Productions..................G..... 215 564-3401
Philadelphia (G-13629)

Dirt Rag Magazine ....G..... 412 767-9910
Pittsburgh (G-14926)

Drexel University ....G..... 215 590-8863
Philadelphia (G-13647)

Easton Publishing Company ....G..... 610 258-7171
Easton (G-4673)

Edgell Communications ....E..... 570 296-8330
Milford (G-11159)

Engle Printing & Pubg Co Inc..............F..... 717 892-6800
Lancaster (G-9010)

Engle Printing & Pubg Co Inc..............F..... 717 653-1833
Mount Joy (G-11654)

Engle Printing & Pubg Co Inc..............C..... 717 653-1833
Lancaster (G-9009)

Ep World Inc ....G..... 814 361-3860
Indiana (G-8096)

Farm Journal Inc ....E..... 215 557-8900
Philadelphia (G-13694)

Feast Mag LLC ....F..... 484 343-5483
Wynnewood (G-20267)

Ferdic Inc ....G..... 717 731-1426
Camp Hill (G-2497)

Flagship Multimedia Inc ....G..... 814 314-9364
Erie (G-5293)

Foreign Policy Research Inst...............E..... 215 732-3774
Philadelphia (G-13714)

Friends Boarding Ho Buc Qua ME ......G..... 215 968-3346
Newtown (G-12503)

Fx Express Publications Inc ....G..... 267 364-5811
Yardley (G-20312)

Garden Pond Promotions Inc ....G..... 814 695-4325
Duncansville (G-4452)

Gene Szczurek S Quarterly P R ....G..... 215 887-7377
Wyncote (G-20263)

Great American Printer Inc ....G..... 570 752-7341
Berwick (G-1326)

Harrisburg Magazine Inc ....F..... 717 233-0109
Harrisburg (G-7143)

Health Care Council Western PA ....F..... 724 776-6400
Warrendale (G-19080)

Healthcare Information Corp ....F..... 724 776-9411
Warrendale (G-19081)

Highlights For Children Inc ....E..... 570 253-1080
Honesdale (G-7714)

Hmp Cmmunications Holdings LLC......G..... 610 560-0500
Malvern (G-10247)

Hmp Communications LLC..................E..... 610 560-0500
Malvern (G-10248)

Holistic Horse Inc ....G..... 215 249-1965
Perkasie (G-13279)

Horty Springer & Mattern ....E..... 412 687-7677
Pittsburgh (G-15100)

Hounds & Hunting Publishing ....G..... 812 820-1588
Bradford (G-1973)

▲ Idea Group Inc ....E..... 717 533-3673
Hershey (G-7617)

Industrial Data Exchange Inc ....B..... 717 653-1833
Mount Joy (G-11662)

Innovative Advertising & Mktg ....G..... 717 788-1385
Waynesboro (G-19413)

Innovative Designs & Pubg..................E..... 610 923-8000
Palmer (G-13098)

J A Mitch Printing & Copy Ctr ....G..... 724 847-2940
Beaver Falls (G-1002)

J G Press Inc ....G..... 610 967-4135
Emmaus (G-5029)

J P R Publications Inc ....F..... 570 587-3532
Clarks Summit (G-3196)

Jewish Exponent Inc ....E..... 215 832-0700
Philadelphia (G-13896)

Jobson Medical Information LLC ....E..... 610 492-1000
Newtown Square (G-12579)

Joseph Jenkins Inc ....G..... 814 786-9085
Grove City (G-6792)

JS Little Publication ....G..... 412 343-5288
Pittsburgh (G-15157)

Kane Communications Inc...................F..... 610 645-6940
Ardmore (G-711)

Kappa Books Publishers LLC...............G..... 215 643-6385
Blue Bell (G-1839)

▲ Kappa Graphics L P ....C..... 570 655-9681
Hughestown (G-7893)

Kappa Media Group Inc ....C..... 215 643-5800
Fort Washington (G-6080)

Kappa Publishing Group Inc ....G..... 215 643-6385
Blue Bell (G-1842)

Kappa Publishing Group Inc ....E..... 215 643-6385
Blue Bell (G-1843)

Kappa Publishing Group Inc ....G..... 215 643-6385
Ambler (G-586)

Kappa Publishing Group Inc ....E..... 215 643-6385
Ambler (G-587)

Kappa Publishing Group Inc ....D..... 215 643-6385
Ambler (G-588)

Koren Publications ....G..... 267 498-0071
Philadelphia (G-13941)

Koren Publications Inc ....G..... 267 498-0071
Hatfield (G-7360)

Lrp Magazine Group ....B..... 215 784-0860
Dresher (G-4356)

Lrp Publications Inc ....F..... 215 784-0941
Horsham (G-7832)

Lutz and Associates ....G..... 724 776-9800
Cranberry Township (G-3833)

M Shanken Communications Inc..........G..... 610 967-1083
Emmaus (G-5033)

Manor House Publishing Co Inc ....F..... 215 259-1700
Warminster (G-18916)

▼ Metro Corp ....D..... 215 564-7700
Philadelphia (G-14014)

Metro Corp ....G..... 215 564-7700
Philadelphia (G-14015)

Metro Corp Holdings Inc ....E..... 215 564-7700
Philadelphia (G-14016)

Mlr Holdings LLC ....F....215 567-3200
Philadelphia *(G-14029)*
Morgan Signs Inc ....E....814 238-5051
State College *(G-17994)*
Morning Call Inc ....E....610 861-3600
Bethlehem *(G-1575)*
Morningstar Credit Ratings LLC ....E....800 299-1665
Horsham *(G-7833)*
Motivos LLC ....G....267 283-1733
Philadelphia *(G-14042)*
Motorama Assoc ....G....717 359-4310
Hanover *(G-6924)*
Mount Lebanon Municipality ....G....412 343-3400
Pittsburgh *(G-15305)*
Mountaineer Publishing ....G....724 880-3753
Waynesburg *(G-19448)*
National Assn Cllges Employers ....E....610 868-1421
Bethlehem *(G-1577)*
Natural Marketing Inst Inc ....E....215 513-7300
Harleysville *(G-7049)*
▲ **New Visions Magazine** ....F....215 627-0102
Philadelphia *(G-14069)*
News Chronicle Co Inc ....E....717 532-4101
Shippensburg *(G-17540)*
Newsline Publishing Inc ....E....610 337-1050
King of Prussia *(G-8656)*
O & B Communications ....G....610 647-8585
Paoli *(G-13144)*
On Line Publishers Inc ....G....717 285-1350
Columbia *(G-3445)*
Pathfinders Travel Inc ....G....215 438-2140
Philadelphia *(G-14123)*
Paul Withers ....G....717 896-3173
Halifax *(G-6827)*
Penn Medical Education LLC ....G....215 524-2785
Newtown *(G-12534)*
Pennsylvania Institute of CPA ....E....215 496-9272
Philadelphia *(G-14132)*
Pennsylvania Motor Truck Assn ....G....717 761-7122
Camp Hill *(G-2510)*
Pentavision LLC ....E....215 628-6550
Ambler *(G-597)*
Philadelphia Style Mag LLC ....F....215 468-6670
Philadelphia *(G-14156)*
Pittsburgh Business Times ....G....412 481-6397
Pittsburgh *(G-15389)*
Pittsburgh Magazine ....F....412 622-1360
Pittsburgh *(G-15400)*
Pittsburgh Professional Magazi ....G....412 221-2992
Pittsburgh *(G-15405)*
Pittsburgh Technology Council ....E....412 687-2700
Pittsburgh *(G-15410)*
Pocono Land & Homes Magazine P ....G....570 424-1000
Stroudsburg *(G-18135)*
Postal History Society Inc ....F....717 624-5941
New Oxford *(G-12422)*
Printing Consulting Inc ....G....610 933-9311
Phoenixville *(G-14571)*
Printing Craftsmen Inc ....F....570 646-2121
Pocono Pines *(G-15883)*
Printing Inds Amer Foundation ....F....412 741-6860
Warrendale *(G-19094)*
Quad/Graphics Inc ....B....215 541-2729
Pennsburg *(G-13253)*
Red Flag Media Inc ....G....215 625-9850
Philadelphia *(G-14237)*
Religious Theological Abstract ....G....717 866-6734
Myerstown *(G-11896)*
Relx Inc ....E....610 964-4516
Radnor *(G-16300)*
Rjw Hired Hands Inc ....F....412 341-1477
Pittsburgh *(G-15490)*
Rodale Inc ....E....610 398-2255
Allentown *(G-377)*
Rodale Institute ....E....610 683-6009
Kutztown *(G-8859)*
Roland Lynagh Associates LLC ....G....570 467-2528
Barnesville *(G-940)*
Roman Press Inc ....G....215 997-9650
Chalfont *(G-2886)*
Ronald D Jones Financial Svc ....G....724 352-5020
Saxonburg *(G-17094)*
Roxanne Toser Non-Sport Entps ....G....717 238-1936
Harrisburg *(G-7209)*
RSC Worldwide (us) Inc ....G....215 966-6206
Philadelphia *(G-14261)*
Scripture Union ....F....610 935-2807
Valley Forge *(G-18714)*
Seak Inc ....G....215 288-7209
Philadelphia *(G-14291)*
Seapoint Enterprises Inc ....G....215 230-6933
Doylestown *(G-4337)*
Sharedxpertise Media LLC ....F....215 606-9520
Philadelphia *(G-14297)*
Shojoberry Magazine ....G....814 736-3210
Portage *(G-15921)*
Sing-Out Corporation ....G....610 865-5366
Bethlehem *(G-1619)*
Smith-Freeman & Associates ....F....610 929-5728
Temple *(G-18336)*
Snb Publishing Inc ....G....215 464-2500
Philadelphia *(G-14319)*
Society For Industrial & Appli ....D....215 382-9800
Philadelphia *(G-14320)*
Southside Holdings Inc ....E....412 431-8300
Pittsburgh *(G-15564)*
Sovereign Media Company Inc ....E....570 322-7848
Williamsport *(G-20073)*
Springer Adis Us LLC ....G....215 574-2201
Philadelphia *(G-14335)*
Stott Publications Inc ....G....814 632-6700
Tyrone *(G-18593)*
Strategic Reports Inc ....G....610 370-5640
Reading *(G-16526)*
Susquehanna Fishing Mag LLC ....G....570 441-4606
Bloomsburg *(G-1802)*
Susquehanna Life Magazine ....G....570 522-0149
Lewisburg *(G-9920)*
Susquehanna Times & Magazine ....G....717 898-9207
Salunga *(G-17056)*
▲ **Suza Inc** ....F....817 877-0067
East Petersburg *(G-4592)*
Synchrgnix Info Strategies Inc ....G....302 892-4800
Malvern *(G-10325)*
Technology Data Exchange Inc ....G....610 668-4717
Bala Cynwyd *(G-894)*
Three Bridges Media LLC ....G....717 695-2621
Harrisburg *(G-7231)*
Toastmasters International ....E....215 355-4838
Warminster *(G-18983)*
Transport For Christ Inc ....G....717 426-9977
Marietta *(G-10469)*
Tri State Golf Inc ....G....215 200-7000
Philadelphia *(G-14407)*
Tri-State Events Magazine Inc ....G....215 947-8600
Huntingdon Valley *(G-8044)*
Turner White Cmmunications Inc ....F....610 975-4541
Bryn Mawr *(G-2335)*
TV Guide Distribution Inc ....B....610 293-8500
Wayne *(G-19385)*
TV Guide Magazine LLC ....E....212 852-7500
Radnor *(G-16303)*
USA Media LLC ....F....215 571-9241
Folcroft *(G-6019)*
Ventasia Inc ....G....412 661-6600
Pittsburgh *(G-15691)*
Vert Markets Inc ....G....215 675-1800
Horsham *(G-7864)*
Victory Media Inc ....G....412 269-1663
Coraopolis *(G-3731)*
Washington Radio Reports Inc ....F....717 334-0668
Gettysburg *(G-6321)*
Washington Radio Reports Inc ....F....717 334-0668
Gettysburg *(G-6322)*
Whirl Publishing ....F....412 431-7888
Pittsburgh *(G-15716)*
Wilkes Barre Law & Lib Assn ....G....570 822-6712
Wilkes Barre *(G-19975)*
Williams Company Limited ....G....610 409-0520
Collegeville *(G-3401)*
Wmpm LLC ....E....303 662-5231
Pittsburgh *(G-15721)*
▲ **Wolters Kluwer Health Inc** ....C....215 521-8300
Philadelphia *(G-14482)*
World Poetry Inc ....G....215 309-3722
Philadelphia *(G-14488)*
Ygs Group Inc ....D....717 505-9701
York *(G-20723)*
York Graphic Services Co ....C....717 505-9701
York *(G-20738)*
Z Publication LLC ....G....484 574-5321
Coatesville *(G-3332)*

2731 Books: Publishing & Printing

American Baptst HM Mission Soc ....D....610 768-2465
King of Prussia *(G-8581)*
◆ **American Bible Society** ....C....212 408-1200
Philadelphia *(G-13379)*
American Law Institute ....D....215 243-1600
Philadelphia *(G-13385)*
Ascension Publishing LLC ....G....610 696-7795
West Chester *(G-19502)*
Assemblies of Yahweh ....F....717 933-4518
Bethel *(G-1392)*
Atlantic Alliance Pubg Co ....G....267 319-1659
Philadelphia *(G-13421)*
Atlantic Cmmncations Group Inc ....E....215 836-4683
Flourtown *(G-5984)*
Beard Group Inc ....E....240 629-3300
Fairless Hills *(G-5773)*
Beidel Printing House Inc ....E....717 532-5063
Shippensburg *(G-17516)*
Benetvison ....G....814 459-9224
Erie *(G-5208)*
Beverly Hall Co ....E....215 536-7048
Quakertown *(G-16172)*
Bible Visuals International ....G....717 859-1131
Akron *(G-34)*
▲ **Boyds Mills Press Inc** ....F....570 253-1164
Honesdale *(G-7703)*
Breakthrough Publications Inc ....G....610 928-4061
Emmaus *(G-5021)*
Brick Wall Ministries ....G....717 592-1798
Middletown *(G-11049)*
Brooks Group and Assoc Inc ....G....610 429-8990
West Chester *(G-19515)*
▲ **Brookshire Printing Inc** ....E....717 392-1321
Lancaster *(G-8961)*
Business 21 Publishing LLC ....D....484 479-2700
Springfield *(G-17908)*
Caribbean Elite Magazine Inc ....G....718 702-0161
Allentown *(G-162)*
Center Edctn & Empymnt Law ....E....800 365-4900
Malvern *(G-10202)*
Chandler-White Publishing Co ....G....312 907-3271
Philadelphia *(G-13524)*
Charlene Crawford ....G....215 432-7542
Elkins Park *(G-4901)*
Charlesworth Group (usa) Inc ....G....215 922-1611
Philadelphia *(G-13533)*
▲ **Church Publishing Incorporated** ....E....212 592-4229
Harrisburg *(G-7104)*
Clarence Larkin Estate ....G....215 576-5590
Glenside *(G-6512)*
▲ **Clement Communications Inc** ....D....610 497-6800
Upper Chichester *(G-18658)*
▲ **Clp Publications Inc** ....C....215 567-5080
Philadelphia *(G-13551)*
Cmmunications U Krienr-Ptthoff ....G....484 547-5261
Macungie *(G-10144)*
Concentrated Knowledge Corp ....E....610 388-5020
Kennett Square *(G-8507)*
Consumer Network Inc ....G....215 235-2400
Philadelphia *(G-13572)*
▼ **Continental Press Inc** ....C....717 367-1836
Elizabethtown *(G-4869)*
Coronet Books Inc ....G....215 925-2762
Philadelphia *(G-13574)*
Cottage Communications Inc ....G....610 678-7473
Reading *(G-16351)*
Creative Nonfiction Foundation ....G....412 688-0304
Pittsburgh *(G-14886)*
Dawn Evening Inc ....G....610 272-0518
Blue Bell *(G-1826)*
▼ **Destech Publications Inc** ....G....717 290-1660
Lancaster *(G-8996)*
▲ **Destiny Image Inc** ....E....717 532-3040
Shippensburg *(G-17526)*
Direct Marketing Publishers ....G....215 321-3068
Yardley *(G-20308)*
Dooner Ventures LLC ....G....610 420-1100
Bryn Mawr *(G-2320)*
Dorchester Publishing Co Inc ....E....212 725-8811
Wayne *(G-19319)*
Dorrance Publishing Co Inc ....E....800 788-7654
Pittsburgh *(G-14934)*
Dubose Printing & Bus Svcs ....G....215 877-9071
Philadelphia *(G-13649)*
Duquesne Univ of Holy Spirit ....G....412 396-6610
Pittsburgh *(G-14945)*
Elsevier Inc ....G....215 239-3900
Philadelphia *(G-13670)*
▲ **F A Davis Company** ....D....215 568-2270
Philadelphia *(G-13689)*
▲ **Fox Chapel Publishing Co Inc** ....E....800 457-9112
East Petersburg *(G-4587)*
From Heart ....G....570 278-6343
Montrose *(G-11464)*
Galeron Consulting LLC ....E....267 293-9230
Bensalem *(G-1202)*

George T Bisel Co Inc.................F 215 922-5760
  Philadelphia *(G-13755)*

Gutenberg Inc.................G 570 488-9820
  Waymart *(G-19287)*

Harpercollins Publishers LLC.................C 570 941-1500
  Moosic *(G-11507)*

◆ Harrison House Inc.................C 918 523-5700
  Shippensburg *(G-17531)*

◆ Himalayan International Instit.................E 570 253-5551
  Honesdale *(G-7715)*

▲ Idea Group Inc.................E 717 533-3673
  Hershey *(G-7617)*

In-Tec Inc.................G 570 342-8464
  Waverly *(G-19285)*

J S Paluch Co Inc.................E 724 772-8850
  Cranberry Township *(G-3825)*

▲ Jeremiah Junction Inc.................G 215 529-6430
  Quakertown *(G-16204)*

Jessica Kingsley Publishers.................G 215 922-1161
  Philadelphia *(G-13895)*

Jewish Publication Soc of Amer.................F 215 832-0600
  Philadelphia *(G-13897)*

Job Training Systems Inc.................G 610 444-0868
  Kennett Square *(G-8515)*

Kerygma Inc.................G 412 344-6062
  Bradford *(G-1976)*

Keyword Communications Inc.................G 717 481-2960
  Harrisburg *(G-7163)*

Knittle & Frey AG-Center Inc.................G 570 323-7554
  Williamsport *(G-20032)*

Knowledge In A Nut Shell Inc.................G 412 765-2020
  Pittsburgh *(G-15179)*

▲ Korea Week Inc.................G 215 782-8883
  Ambler *(G-589)*

Landes Bioscience Inc.................E 512 637-6050
  Philadelphia *(G-13951)*

Larry Arnold.................G 717 236-0080
  Harrisburg *(G-7168)*

Lippincott Williams & Wilkins.................G 215 521-8300
  Philadelphia *(G-13972)*

▲ Louis Neibauer Co Inc.................E 215 322-6200
  Warminster *(G-18913)*

Lunacor Inc.................G 610 328-6150
  Springfield *(G-17917)*

Markowski International Pubg.................G 717 566-0468
  Hummelstown *(G-7917)*

Mason Crest Publishers Inc.................G 610 543-6200
  Broomall *(G-2297)*

Meniscus Limited.................D 610 567-2725
  Conshohocken *(G-3575)*

▲ Michael Furman Photography.................G 215 925-4233
  Philadelphia *(G-14020)*

Mid Mon Valley Pub.................E 724 314-0030
  Monessen *(G-11300)*

Miroglyphics.................G 215 224-2486
  Philadelphia *(G-14027)*

Morning Call Inc.................E 610 861-3600
  Bethlehem *(G-1575)*

Mosaic Entertainment House.................D 215 353-1729
  Philadelphia *(G-14040)*

Moyer Music Test Inc.................G 717 566-8778
  Hummelstown *(G-7918)*

▲ National Publishing Company.................B 215 676-1863
  Philadelphia *(G-14055)*

Neil M Davis.................G 215 442-7430
  Warminster *(G-18928)*

Nine 2 Five Ceo.................G 919 729-2536
  Philadelphia *(G-14075)*

Nori Medical Group.................G 717 532-3040
  Shippensburg *(G-17542)*

Offset Paperback Mfrs Inc.................A 570 675-5261
  Dallas *(G-3964)*

Organization Design & Dev Inc.................E 610 279-2202
  West Chester *(G-19612)*

Oz World Media LLC.................E 202 470-6757
  Devon *(G-4115)*

Paul Withers.................G 717 896-3173
  Halifax *(G-6827)*

Pennsylvania Fireman Inc.................F 717 397-9174
  Lititz *(G-10031)*

Pennsylvania State University.................G 814 863-3764
  University Park *(G-18653)*

Pennsylvania State University.................E 814 865-1327
  University Park *(G-18654)*

Police Shield Corp.................E 215 788-3489
  Bristol *(G-2184)*

Printing Inds Amer Foundation.................F 412 741-6860
  Warrendale *(G-19094)*

Private Zone Productions Corp.................G 267 592-5447
  Philadelphia *(G-14204)*

Proofreaders LLC.................G 215 295-9400
  Penns Park *(G-13243)*

PSC Publishing.................E 570 443-9749
  White Haven *(G-19851)*

Puchalski Inc.................G 570 842-0361
  Covington Township *(G-3793)*

▲ Quirk Productions Inc.................F 215 627-3581
  Philadelphia *(G-14221)*

▲ Reading Reading Books LLC.................G 757 329-4224
  Morgantown *(G-11532)*

Renaissance Press Inc.................G 717 534-0708
  Hummelstown *(G-7924)*

Robar Industries Inc.................G 484 688-0300
  Plymouth Meeting *(G-15868)*

Rodale Inc.................E 610 398-2255
  Allentown *(G-377)*

Rodale Institute.................G 610 683-6009
  Kutztown *(G-8859)*

Rowman & Littlefield Publish.................B 717 794-3800
  Blue Ridge Summit *(G-1859)*

Rowman & Littlefield Publs Inc.................G 717 794-3800
  Blue Ridge Summit *(G-1860)*

S&P Global Inc.................C 215 430-6000
  Philadelphia *(G-14274)*

Scribe Inc.................G 215 336-5095
  Allentown *(G-387)*

Scribe Inc.................G 215 336-5094
  Philadelphia *(G-14289)*

Sea Group Graphics Inc.................G 215 805-0290
  Huntingdon Valley *(G-8036)*

Secrets of Big Dogs.................G 814 696-0469
  Hollidaysburg *(G-7653)*

Shepherd Press Inc.................G 570 379-2015
  Wapwallopen *(G-18809)*

Sing-Out Corporation.................G 610 865-5366
  Bethlehem *(G-1619)*

Society For Industrial & Appli.................D 215 382-9800
  Philadelphia *(G-14320)*

Southside Holdings Inc.................E 412 431-8300
  Pittsburgh *(G-15564)*

Springer Adis Us LLC.................G 215 574-2201
  Philadelphia *(G-14335)*

▲ Stackpole Inc.................E 717 796-0411
  Blue Ridge Summit *(G-1862)*

Stan Clark Military Books.................G 717 337-1728
  Gettysburg *(G-6315)*

Sunrise Publishing & Distrg.................G 724 946-9057
  Sharpsville *(G-17476)*

Swedenborg Foundation Inc.................G 610 430-3222
  West Chester *(G-19649)*

▼ Taylor & Francis Inc.................D 215 625-8900
  Philadelphia *(G-14378)*

Thespiderfriends Com LLC.................G 412 257-2346
  Bridgeville *(G-2094)*

Thomas.................G 717 642-6600
  Gettysburg *(G-6318)*

Three Brothers Publishing LLC.................G 412 656-3905
  Norristown *(G-12718)*

Tims Printing Inc.................G 215 208-0699
  Philadelphia *(G-14390)*

University of Pittsburgh.................F 412 383-2456
  Pittsburgh *(G-15682)*

▲ Vanroden Inc.................E 717 509-2600
  Lancaster *(G-9230)*

▲ Warner-Crivellaro Stained Glas.................F 610 264-1100
  Whitehall *(G-19893)*

Waza Inc.................G 610 827-7800
  Chester Springs *(G-3087)*

Whispering Leaf Inc.................E 267 437-2991
  Philadelphia *(G-14473)*

▼ Whitaker Corporation.................C 724 334-7000
  New Kensington *(G-12389)*

▲ Wolters Kluwer Health Inc.................C 215 521-8300
  Philadelphia *(G-14482)*

Zondervan Corporation LLC.................C 570 941-1366
  Dunmore *(G-4488)*

▲ Zur Ltd.................E 717 761-7044
  Camp Hill *(G-2528)*

2732 Book Printing, Not Publishing

Amrep Corporation.................F 609 487-0905
  Plymouth Meeting *(G-15831)*

Armstrong Supply Co.................G 215 643-0310
  Ambler *(G-567)*

Beidel Printing House Inc.................E 717 532-5063
  Shippensburg *(G-17516)*

Bela Printing & Packaging Corp.................G 215 664-7090
  Lansdale *(G-9344)*

Community Resource Svcs Inc.................G 717 338-9100
  Gettysburg *(G-6286)*

Corporate Print Solutions Inc.................G 215 774-1119
  Glenolden *(G-6472)*

Great American Printer Inc.................G 570 752-7341
  Berwick *(G-1326)*

Hf Group LLC.................E 215 855-2293
  Hatfield *(G-7350)*

Kappa Graphics L P.................F 215 542-2800
  Blue Bell *(G-1840)*

▲ Lisa Leleu Studios Inc.................G 215 345-1233
  Doylestown *(G-4313)*

▲ Maple Press Company.................C 717 764-5911
  York *(G-20580)*

Murrelle Printing Co Inc.................G 570 888-2244
  Sayre *(G-17119)*

▲ National Publishing Company.................B 215 676-1863
  Philadelphia *(G-14055)*

P A Hutchison Company.................C 570 876-4560
  Mayfield *(G-10542)*

Parker-Hannifin Corporation.................C 814 860-5700
  Erie *(G-5415)*

◆ Sheridan Group Inc.................D 717 632-3535
  Hanover *(G-6950)*

Squibb Alvah M Company Inc.................F 412 751-2301
  McKeesport *(G-10682)*

Triangle Press Inc.................E 717 541-9315
  Harrisburg *(G-7238)*

▼ Valley Business Services Inc.................F 610 366-1970
  Trexlertown *(G-18511)*

2741 Misc Publishing

3p Ltd.................G 717 566-5643
  Hummelstown *(G-7901)*

Acorn Press Inc.................G 717 569-3264
  Lititz *(G-9992)*

Ad Star Inc.................F 724 439-5519
  Uniontown *(G-18614)*

AMD Pennsylvania LLC.................F 610 485-4400
  King of Prussia *(G-8579)*

American Culture Publs LLC.................G 267 608-9734
  Chalfont *(G-2863)*

American Future Systems Inc.................D 610 695-8600
  Malvern *(G-10186)*

American Future Systems Inc.................G 610 375-8012
  Reading *(G-16319)*

Amigo Express.................G 484 461-3135
  Upper Darby *(G-18680)*

Amy Semler.................G 717 593-9243
  Greencastle *(G-6596)*

▲ Artistworks Wholesale Inc.................G 610 622-9940
  Lansdowne *(G-9430)*

Asphalt Press Industries.................G 610 489-7283
  Arcola *(G-697)*

Aspx LLC.................G 215 345-6782
  Doylestown *(G-4271)*

Associates In Medical Mktg Co.................E 215 860-9600
  Newtown *(G-12497)*

Avantext Inc.................E 610 796-2383
  Philadelphia *(G-13425)*

Awwsum Internet Services.................G 215 543-9078
  Philadelphia *(G-13430)*

Bacon Press.................G 484 328-3118
  Malvern *(G-10192)*

Baip Inc.................G 412 913-9826
  Export *(G-5592)*

Baldwin Publishing Inc.................F 215 369-1369
  Washington Crossing *(G-19252)*

Barkleigh Productions Inc.................F 717 691-3388
  Mechanicsburg *(G-10822)*

Beye LLC.................G 484 581-1840
  Wayne *(G-19305)*

Bill Straley Printing.................G 717 328-5404
  Lemasters *(G-9731)*

Blazing Passion Publ.................G 215 247-2024
  Philadelphia *(G-13468)*

BNP Media Inc.................E 412 531-3370
  Pittsburgh *(G-14776)*

Bookhaven Press LLC.................G 412 494-6926
  Coraopolis *(G-3663)*

Bpes Barr Publicatio Co.................G 215 765-0383
  Philadelphia *(G-13475)*

Bradley Communications Corp.................E 484 477-4220
  Broomall *(G-2281)*

Brown Brothers LLP.................G 570 689-9688
  Sterling *(G-18048)*

Bryn and Danes LLC.................G 844 328-2823
  Horsham *(G-7800)*

Business 21 Publishing LLC.................G 484 490-9205
  Wayne *(G-19310)*

Buy Photo Stock Lowes Digita.................G 814 954-0273
  Reynoldsville *(G-16655)*

Carnegie Learning Inc ....C 412 690-2442
Pittsburgh (G-14817)

Carson Publishing Inc ....G 412 548-3798
Pittsburgh (G-14822)

Cellco Partnership ....D 610 431-5800
West Chester (G-19520)

Centre Publications Inc ....G 814 364-2000
Centre Hall (G-2840)

Chandler-White Publishing Co ....G 312 907-3271
Philadelphia (G-13524)

Cider Press Woodworks LLC ....G 215 804-0880
Quakertown (G-16179)

Clarivate Analytics (us) LLC ....A 215 386-0100
Philadelphia (G-13548)

Coffee Cup Publishing ....G 215 887-7365
Jenkintown (G-8282)

▲ Collins Harper Publishers ....G 570 941-1557
Moosic (G-11504)

Commonwealth Press LLC ....G 412 431-4207
Pittsburgh (G-14869)

Community Resource Svcs Inc ....G 717 338-9100
Gettysburg (G-6286)

Contempory Pubg Group E LLC ....G 215 953-8210
Feasterville Trevose (G-5900)

Creative Nonfiction Foundation ....G 412 688-0304
Pittsburgh (G-14886)

Creative Printing Co ....G 570 875-1811
Ashland (G-729)

Critical Path Project Inc ....G 215 545-2212
Philadelphia (G-13583)

▲ Culturenik Publishing Inc ....G 570 424-9848
Stroudsburg (G-18112)

Cutts Group LLC ....F 610 366-9620
Allentown (G-190)

D & A Business Services Inc ....G 610 837-7748
Nazareth (G-11960)

David Jefferys LLC ....G 215 977-9900
Wallingford (G-18783)

Dex Media Inc ....E 412 858-4800
White Oak (G-19854)

Digital Grapes LLC ....E 866 458-4226
King of Prussia (G-8610)

Dorland Healthcare Information ....G 800 784-2332
Philadelphia (G-13640)

Dorrance Publishing Co Inc ....E 800 788-7654
Pittsburgh (G-14934)

Dream Publishing ....G 610 945-2017
King of Prussia (G-8612)

Dreamspring Institute ....G 570 829-1378
Wilkes Barre (G-19916)

Drexler Associates Inc ....G 724 888-2042
Mars (G-10495)

Dubose Printing & Bus Svcs ....G 215 877-9071
Philadelphia (G-13649)

Easy To Use Big Books ....D 814 946-7442
Altoona (G-500)

Eber & Wein Inc ....F 717 759-8065
New Freedom (G-12205)

Eber & Wein Inc ....F 717 759-8065
Shrewsbury (G-17582)

Elsevier Inc ....E 215 239-3441
Philadelphia (G-13669)

Energize Inc ....G 215 438-8342
Philadelphia (G-13674)

Engle Printing & Pubg Co Inc ....C 717 653-1833
Lancaster (G-9009)

Ernie Saxton ....G 215 752-7797
Langhorne (G-9294)

Express Money Services Inc ....G 717 235-5993
New Freedom (G-12208)

EZ To Use Directories Inc ....E 814 949-7100
Altoona (G-503)

Farm Journal Inc ....E 215 557-8900
Philadelphia (G-13694)

Ficore Incorporated ....E 717 735-9740
York (G-20480)

Franchise Bsness Opportunities ....G 412 831-2522
Bethel Park (G-1414)

Friends Publishing Corp ....F 215 563-8629
Philadelphia (G-13727)

Galeron Consulting LLC ....E 267 293-9230
Bensalem (G-1202)

Gentle Revolution Press ....G 215 233-2050
Glenside (G-6519)

Ggs Information Services Inc ....C 717 764-2222
York (G-20499)

Global Institute For Strgc Inv ....G 215 300-0907
Philadelphia (G-13769)

Glory Fibers ....G 610 444-5646
Kennett Square (G-8512)

Great Valley Publishing Co ....E 610 948-7639
Spring City (G-17858)

Grelin Press ....G 724 334-8240
New Kensington (G-12343)

Harpercollins Publishers LLC ....G 800 242-7737
Moosic (G-11508)

Harte Hanks Inc ....C 570 826-0414
Hanover Township (G-6989)

Head & The Hand Press LLC ....G 856 562-8545
Philadelphia (G-13807)

▲ Herman Geer Communications Inc ..G 724 652-0511
New Castle (G-12102)

Hocking Printing Co Inc ....D 717 738-1151
Ephrata (G-5109)

Hodgsons Quick Printing ....G 215 362-1356
Kulpsville (G-8830)

Hollinger Tchncal Pblctons Inc ....G 717 755-8800
York (G-20524)

Icon/Information Concepts Inc ....G 215 545-6700
Langhorne (G-9303)

Image Makers Art Inc ....G 610 722-5807
Berwyn (G-1365)

Infinity Publishing ....F 610 941-9999
Conshohocken (G-3562)

Infomat Associates Inc ....G 610 668-8306
Narberth (G-11911)

Informing Design Inc ....G 412 465-0047
Pittsburgh (G-15124)

Intelligent Direct Inc ....E 570 724-7355
Wellsboro (G-19466)

International Watch Magazine ....F 484 417-2122
Ardmore (G-709)

Iop Publishing Incorporated ....F 215 627-0880
Philadelphia (G-13872)

J L Communications Inc ....G 215 675-9133
Horsham (G-7826)

Jay Weiss Corporation ....G 610 834-8585
Lafayette Hill (G-8881)

Jayco Grafix Inc ....D 610 678-2640
Reinholds (G-16633)

Jcpds International Centre ....E 610 325-9814
Newtown Square (G-12578)

Just Kidstuff Inc ....D 610 336-9200
Allentown (G-274)

Kapp Advertising Services Inc ....E 610 670-2595
Reading (G-16418)

Kapp Advertising Services Inc ....F 717 632-8303
Hanover (G-6909)

Kappa Map Group LLC ....G 215 643-5800
Blue Bell (G-1841)

Kappa Media Group Inc ....C 215 643-5800
Fort Washington (G-6080)

Kappa Publishing Group Inc ....D 215 643-6385
Blue Bell (G-1842)

Ker Communications ....G 412 310-1973
Pittsburgh (G-15172)

Kgb Usa Inc ....D 610 997-1000
Bethlehem (G-1552)

King Publications ....G 610 395-4074
Allentown (G-284)

Kutztown Publishing Co Inc ....G 610 683-7341
Allentown (G-286)

Lancaster General Svcs Bus Tr ....F 717 544-5474
Lancaster (G-9095)

Leon Spangler ....F 570 837-7903
Middleburg (G-11028)

Library Video Company ....D 610 645-4000
Conshohocken (G-3572)

Lionshare Media Services ....G 724 837-9700
Greensburg (G-6685)

Local Pages Publishing LLC ....F 610 579-3809
Norristown (G-12677)

Localedge Media Inc ....E 716 875-9100
Erie (G-5369)

Louise Grace Publishing ....G 610 781-6874
Reading (G-16434)

Macnificent Pages ....G 610 323-6253
Pottstown (G-16012)

Marcan Advertising Inc ....G 717 270-6929
Cleona (G-3245)

Marcom Group Ltd ....F 610 859-8989
Upper Chichester (G-18667)

Marietta Closson ....G 724 337-4482
Apollo (G-683)

Media Management Services Inc ....E 800 523-5948
Newtown (G-12521)

Meniscus Limited ....D 610 567-2725
Conshohocken (G-3575)

Millenium Medical Educational ....E 215 230-1960
Doylestown (G-4316)

Miller Printing & Publishing ....E 814 425-7272
Cochranton (G-3345)

Mm USA Holdings LLC ....B 267 685-2300
Yardley (G-20326)

Monroe Press Inc ....G 215 778-7868
Philadelphia (G-14035)

Morgan Signs Inc ....E 814 238-5051
State College (G-17994)

Multiscope Incorporated ....E 724 743-1083
Canonsburg (G-2606)

My Biblical Perception LLC ....G 267 450-9655
Perkasie (G-13285)

National Assn Cllges Employers ....E 610 868-1421
Bethlehem (G-1577)

National Hot Rod Association ....D 717 584-1200
Lancaster (G-9142)

New Mainstream Press Inc ....G 610 617-8800
Bala Cynwyd (G-887)

Newsletters Ink Corp ....E 717 393-1000
Lancaster (G-9145)

Newsline Publishing Inc ....E 610 337-1050
King of Prussia (G-8656)

Newtown Business Forms Corp ....F 215 364-3898
Huntingdon Valley (G-8017)

Noel Interactive Group LLC ....G 732 991-1484
Easton (G-4732)

Ogden Directories PA Inc ....C 814 946-7404
Altoona (G-534)

Old City Publishing ....F 215 925-4390
Philadelphia (G-14093)

Omni Publlishing Eastern PA ....G 610 626-8819
Lansdowne (G-9440)

On Line Publishers Inc ....G 717 285-1350
Lancaster (G-9154)

Organ Historical Society ....G 804 353-9226
Villanova (G-18768)

P H A Finance Inc ....E 610 272-4700
Plymouth Meeting (G-15862)

P R X ....G 570 578-0136
Hanover Township (G-7002)

PA Outdoor Times ....G 814 946-7400
Altoona (G-536)

Paul Dry Books Inc ....G 215 231-9939
Philadelphia (G-14124)

Penns Valley Publishers ....G 215 855-4948
Lansdale (G-9397)

Pennsylvania Equestrian ....G 717 509-9800
Lancaster (G-9167)

Pennsylvania State University ....E 814 865-1327
University Park (G-18654)

Penny Mansfield Saver Inc ....G 570 662-3277
Mansfield (G-10424)

Philadelphia Photo Review ....G 215 364-9185
Langhorne (G-9318)

Pittsburgh Business Times ....G 412 481-6397
Pittsburgh (G-15389)

Pittsburgh Technology Council ....E 412 687-2700
Pittsburgh (G-15410)

Police Shield Corp ....E 215 788-3489
Bristol (G-2184)

Press and Journal ....E 717 944-4628
Middletown (G-11071)

Press Bistro ....G 814 254-4835
Johnstown (G-8424)

Press Start Games ....G 267 253-0595
East Berlin (G-4525)

PRI International Inc ....G 610 436-8292
West Chester (G-19619)

Prisma Inc ....E 412 503-4006
Pittsburgh (G-15448)

Publication Connexion LLC ....F 215 944-9400
Newtown (G-12539)

Publishing Office US Gvernment ....G 215 364-6465
Southampton (G-17832)

R M G Enterprises Inc ....G 814 866-2247
Erie (G-5448)

Real Estate Book South Cent ....G 814 943-8110
Altoona (G-542)

Recon Publications ....G 215 843-4256
Philadelphia (G-14233)

Regency Typographic Svcs Inc ....F 215 425-8810
Philadelphia (G-14238)

Riecks Publishing ....G 610 685-1222
Reading (G-16499)

Robar Industries Inc ....G 484 688-0300
Plymouth Meeting (G-15868)

Rwg Company ....G 215 552-9541
Malvern (G-10312)

Saj Publishing ....G 814 445-9695
Somerset (G-17703)

Saj Publishing ....G 610 544-5484
  Springfield (G-17922)
Sandvik Pubg Interactive Inc ....E 203 205-0188
  Yardley (G-20338)
Sapling Press ....G 412 681-1003
  Pittsburgh (G-15511)
Sb Distribution Center Inc ....G 215 717-2600
  Philadelphia (G-14283)
▲ Schiffer Publishing Ltd ....E 610 593-1777
  Atglen (G-806)
Schultz Mktg & Communications ....G 814 455-4772
  Erie (G-5469)
Scroll Publishing Co ....G 717 349-7033
  Doylesburg (G-4265)
Second Century Media LLC ....E 610 948-9500
  Spring City (G-17866)
Selah Publshng Co Inc ....G 412 886-1020
  Pittsburgh (G-15521)
Simplicity Creative Corp ....G 800 653-7301
  Plymouth Meeting (G-15871)
Sire Press LLC ....G 267 909-9233
  Philadelphia (G-14312)
Solo Soundz LLC ....G 610 931-8448
  Philadelphia (G-14323)
Source Halthcare Analytics LLC ....D 602 381-9500
  Conshohocken (G-3605)
Sports Images International ....G 412 851-1610
  Pittsburgh (G-15571)
Sports Management News Inc ....G 610 459-4040
  Glen Mills (G-6445)
Strassheim Grphic Dsign & Pres ....F 215 525-5134
  Philadelphia (G-14350)
Sunbury Press ....G 717 254-7274
  Mechanicsburg (G-10892)
Supermedia LLC ....D 814 833-2121
  Erie (G-5497)
Supermedia LLC ....B 610 317-5500
  Bethlehem (G-1635)
Supermedia LLC ....B 717 540-6500
  Harrisburg (G-7223)
Swanson Publishing Company Inc ....G 724 940-2444
  Wexford (G-19830)
Taylor & Francis Group LLC ....D 215 625-8900
  Philadelphia (G-14377)
▼ Taylor & Francis Inc ....D 215 625-8900
  Philadelphia (G-14378)
Textbook LLC ....G 717 779-7101
  York (G-20687)
Thats True Media LLC ....G 215 437-3292
  Philadelphia (G-14384)
The Scranton Times L P ....D 570 348-9146
  Scranton (G-17297)
▲ Theodore Presser Company ....E 610 592-1222
  King of Prussia (G-8687)
Towanda Printing Co Inc ....C 570 265-2151
  Towanda (G-18436)
Training Resource Corporation ....F 717 652-3100
  Harrisburg (G-7234)
Upper Perk Shoppers Guide Inc ....G 215 679-4133
  Pennsburg (G-13260)
Vaughens Price Pubg Co Inc ....G 412 367-5100
  Bradfordwoods (G-2000)
Veritas Press Inc ....F 717 519-1974
  Lancaster (G-9233)
Verizon Communications Inc ....C 570 387-3840
  Bloomsburg (G-1806)
Verizon Pennsylvania Inc ....D 215 879-7898
  Philadelphia (G-14441)
Vert Markets Inc ....D 814 897-9000
  Erie (G-5525)
Vivid Publishing Inc ....G 570 567-7808
  Williamsport (G-20088)
Washington Radio Reports Inc ....F 717 334-0668
  Gettysburg (G-6321)
Wharton School Univ of PA ....C 215 746-7846
  Philadelphia (G-14472)
White Mane Publishing Co Inc ....F 717 532-2237
  Shippensburg (G-17555)
Wild Cat Publishing LLC ....G 570 966-1120
  Mifflinburg (G-11106)
▲ Wolters Kluwer Health Inc ....C 215 521-8300
  Philadelphia (G-14482)
Womens Yellw Pages Gtr Phil ....G 610 446-4747
  Havertown (G-7433)
Yellow Pages Group LLC ....E 610 825-7720
  Blue Bell (G-1858)
Young Face ....G 412 928-2676
  Pittsburgh (G-15730)
▲ Zenescope Entertainment Inc ....F 215 442-9094
  Horsham (G-7866)

2752 Commercial Printing: Lithographic

21st Century Media Newsppr LLC ....E 814 238-3071
  State College (G-17939)
21st N College ....G 814 502-1542
  Martinsburg (G-10518)
3d Printing and Copy Ctr Inc ....F 215 968-7900
  Bensalem (G-1140)
3d Printing Service LLC ....G 215 426-1510
  Philadelphia (G-13317)
69th St Commercial Printers ....G 610 539-8412
  Norristown (G-12627)
A Archery and Printing Place ....G 717 274-1811
  Lebanon (G-9544)
A J Printing ....F 610 337-7468
  King of Prussia (G-8575)
A Link Prtg & Promotions LLC ....G 412 220-0290
  Bridgeville (G-2049)
A Stuart Morton Inc ....F 610 692-1190
  West Chester (G-19492)
A+ Printing Inc ....G 814 942-4257
  Altoona (G-468)
AAA Color Card Company ....G 814 793-2342
  Martinsburg (G-10519)
Abbi Print LLC ....G 215 471-8801
  Philadelphia (G-13335)
Abboud Samar ....G 412 343-6899
  Pittsburgh (G-14634)
▲ Acorn Company ....F 215 743-6100
  Philadelphia (G-13342)
Action Screen Printing Inc ....F 610 359-1777
  Broomall (G-2277)
◆ Acumark Inc ....G 570 883-1800
  West Pittston (G-19753)
Ad Forms LLC ....G 724 379-6022
  Charleroi (G-3004)
Ad Post Graphics Inc ....F 412 405-9163
  Library (G-9953)
Ad-Net Services Incorporated ....F 610 374-4200
  Reading (G-16310)
Adcomm Inc ....F 610 820-8565
  Allentown (G-115)
Advanced Color Graphics ....E 814 235-1200
  Huntingdon (G-7937)
Aeroprint Graphics Inc ....G 215 752-1089
  Langhorne (G-9274)
Air Conway Inc ....F 610 534-0500
  Collingdale (G-3402)
▲ Alcom Printing Group Inc ....C 215 513-1600
  Harleysville (G-7015)
Alfred Envelope Company Inc ....F 215 739-1500
  Philadelphia (G-13362)
Allegheny Plastics Inc ....D 724 776-0100
  Cranberry Township (G-3800)
Allegra Mktg Print Mail 408 ....G 717 839-6390
  Harrisburg (G-7085)
Allegra Print & Imaging ....G 412 922-0422
  Pittsburgh (G-14683)
Allegra Print & Imaging ....E 717 397-3440
  Lancaster (G-8929)
Allegra Print Imaging ....G 610 882-2229
  Allentown (G-125)
AlphaGraphics ....G 717 731-8444
  Mechanicsburg (G-10819)
AMD Graphics Inc ....G 215 728-8600
  Philadelphia (G-13377)
▲ American Bank Note Company ....E 215 396-8707
  Trevose (G-18486)
American Bank Note Holographic ....E 215 357-5300
  Huntingdon Valley (G-7963)
▲ American Bank Printers ....G 412 566-6737
  Pittsburgh (G-14700)
American Brchure Catalogue Inc ....E 215 259-1600
  Warminster (G-18827)
American Calendar Inc ....F 215 743-3834
  Philadelphia (G-13382)
American Printing Group Inc ....G 215 442-0500
  Horsham (G-7783)
Amherst Corporation ....F 610 589-1090
  Womelsdorf (G-20205)
Andrew H Lawson Co ....G 215 235-1609
  Philadelphia (G-13391)
Anstadt Printing Corporation ....E 717 767-6891
  York (G-20378)
Apparel Print Promotionals ....G 717 233-4277
  Harrisburg (G-7088)
Apple Press Ltd ....E 610 363-1776
  Exton (G-5644)
ARA Corporation ....G 724 843-5378
  Koppel (G-8813)

Arbil Enterprises Inc ....G 215 969-0500
  Philadelphia (G-13407)
Arch Parent Inc ....A 570 534-6026
  Stroudsburg (G-18104)
Archway Press Inc ....F 610 583-4004
  Sharon Hill (G-17452)
Arcs Design & Printing Inc ....G 215 238-1831
  Philadelphia (G-13408)
Art Communication Systems Inc ....E 717 232-0144
  Harrisburg (G-7090)
Art Printing Co of Lancaster ....G 717 397-6029
  Columbia (G-3430)
Artcraft Printers Inc ....G 724 537-5231
  Latrobe (G-9457)
ASAP Printing & Copying Inc ....F 215 357-5033
  Southampton (G-17798)
Astro Printing Services Inc ....F 215 441-4444
  Warminster (G-18831)
Athens Reproduction ....G 610 649-5761
  Ardmore (G-701)
Atlantic Prtg Grphic Cmmnctons ....G 610 584-2060
  Schwenksville (G-17173)
Atlas Printing Company ....G 814 445-2516
  Somerset (G-17675)
Atlas Rubber Stamp & Printing ....G 717 755-3882
  York (G-20390)
Auch Printing Inc ....G 215 886-9133
  Dresher (G-4353)
Auxiliary Business Services ....G 215 836-4833
  Fort Washington (G-6063)
Awesome Dudes Printingg LLC ....G 267 886-8492
  Philadelphia (G-13429)
B O H I C A Inc ....G 610 489-4540
  Trappe (G-18467)
B P S Communications Inc ....F 215 830-8467
  Willow Grove (G-20109)
Badzik Printing Service Inc ....G 724 379-4299
  Donora (G-4146)
Bai Printing ....G 412 400-5555
  Pittsburgh (G-14749)
Balfour Sales Company ....G 215 542-9745
  Ambler (G-569)
Banes and Mayer Inc ....G 215 641-1750
  Blue Bell (G-1814)
Becotte Design Inc ....G 215 641-1257
  Philadelphia (G-13451)
Bedford Gazette LLC ....E 814 623-1151
  Bedford (G-1042)
Bedwick and Jones Printing Inc ....F 570 829-1951
  Hanover Township (G-6979)
Bee Offset Printing ....G 610 253-0926
  Easton (G-4651)
Beggs Brothers Printing Co ....G 814 395-3241
  Confluence (G-3463)
Beidel Printing House Inc ....E 717 532-5063
  Shippensburg (G-17516)
Beiler Printing LLC ....G 717 336-1148
  Denver (G-4068)
Bela Printing & Packaging Corp ....G 215 664-7090
  Lansdale (G-9344)
Benkalu Group Lmtd Ta Jaguar ....G 215 646-5896
  Huntingdon Valley (G-7965)
Bentley Grphic Cmmncations Inc ....E 610 933-7400
  Phoenixville (G-14531)
Berks Digital Inc ....G 610 929-1200
  Reading (G-16329)
Bestway Printing ....G 215 368-4140
  Lansdale (G-9346)
Bill Straley Printing ....G 717 328-5404
  Lemasters (G-9731)
Birds Printing ....G 570 784-8136
  Bloomsburg (G-1774)
Birrbatt Printing Inc ....G 412 373-9047
  Trafford (G-18451)
Blasi Printing Inc ....F 570 824-3557
  Hanover Township (G-6981)
Blatts Printing Co ....G 610 926-2289
  Mohrsville (G-11274)
Blose Printing ....G 717 838-9129
  Campbelltown (G-2529)
Blue Bell Print Solutions ....G 215 591-3903
  Blue Bell (G-1817)
Blue Dog Printing & Design ....G 610 430-7992
  West Chester (G-19511)
Bodrie Inc ....G 724 836-3666
  Smithton (G-17658)
Boggs Printing Inc ....G 215 675-1203
  Hatboro (G-7274)
Boltz Printing Company LLC ....G 724 772-4941
  Cranberry Township (G-3809)

Bondi Printing Co Inc F 724 327-6022
Murrysville *(G-11848)*

Bonnie Kaiser G 215 331-6555
Philadelphia *(G-13471)*

Bradco Printers Inc G 570 297-3024
Troy *(G-18517)*

Bradley Graphic Solutions Inc E 215 638-8771
Bensalem *(G-1160)*

Brendan G Stover Printing G 610 459-2851
Boothwyn *(G-1876)*

Brenneman Printing Inc E 717 299-2847
Lancaster *(G-8959)*

Brilliant Inc G 215 271-5041
Philadelphia *(G-13482)*

▲ Brilliant Studio Inc G 610 458-7977
Exton *(G-5657)*

Brindle Printing Co Inc G 724 658-8549
New Castle *(G-12067)*

Brodak Printing Company G 724 966-5178
Carmichaels *(G-2755)*

◆ Brodart Co D 570 326-2461
Williamsport *(G-19995)*

▲ Brookshire Printing Inc E 717 392-1321
Lancaster *(G-8961)*

Buck County Print G 215 741-3250
Langhorne *(G-9283)*

Bucks County Off Svcs & Prtg G 215 295-7060
Bristol *(G-2121)*

Bucks Ship & Print G 215 493-8100
Yardley *(G-20299)*

Buhl Bros Printing Inc F 724 335-0970
Creighton *(G-3880)*

▲ Butler Color Press Inc C 724 283-9132
Butler *(G-2385)*

Butter Milk Falls Inc G 724 548-7388
Kittanning *(G-8759)*

Butts Ticket Company Inc F 610 869-7450
Cochranville *(G-3355)*

Byrne Enterprises Inc G 610 670-0767
Reading *(G-16338)*

C P Commercial Printing Inc G 215 675-7605
Warminster *(G-18843)*

C3 Media LLC E 610 832-8077
Philadelphia *(G-13492)*

Cab Technologies & Printing So G 724 457-8880
Coraopolis *(G-3667)*

Call Newspapers Inc F 570 385-3120
Schuylkill Haven *(G-17150)*

Cameron County Echo Inc G 814 486-3711
Emporium *(G-5053)*

Campbell Business Forms Inc G 610 356-0626
Newtown Square *(G-12568)*

Campus Copy Center F 215 386-6410
Philadelphia *(G-13496)*

Card Prsnlzation Solutions LLC D 610 231-1860
Allentown *(G-161)*

Carnegie Printing Company G 412 788-4399
Oakdale *(G-12895)*

Carol Fanelli G 717 945-7418
Lancaster *(G-8971)*

Caskey Printing Inc E 717 764-4500
York *(G-20420)*

Castor Printing Company Inc F 215 535-1471
Philadelphia *(G-13512)*

Catalogs By Design E 610 337-9133
King of Prussia *(G-8591)*

CDI Printing Services Inc F 724 444-6160
Gibsonia *(G-6330)*

Cerra Signs Inc G 570 282-6283
Carbondale *(G-2670)*

Chambersburg Screen Print EMB G 717 262-2111
Chambersburg *(G-2918)*

Champ Printing Company Inc E 412 269-0197
Coraopolis *(G-3675)*

Charles A Henderson Prtg Svc G 724 775-2623
Rochester *(G-16783)*

Chaucer Press Inc D 570 825-2005
Hanover Township *(G-6986)*

▲ Chernay Printing Inc D 610 282-3774
Coopersburg *(G-3625)*

Chester Multi Copy Inc G 610 876-1285
Brookhaven *(G-2243)*

Child Evngelism Fellowship Inc E 215 837-6324
Philadelphia *(G-13541)*

Child Evngelism Fellowship Inc E 724 463-1600
Somerset *(G-17679)*

Child Evngelism Fellowship Inc E 724 339-4825
Apollo *(G-669)*

Chrisber Corporation E 800 872-7436
West Chester *(G-19525)*

Christmas City Printing Co Inc E 610 868-5844
Bethlehem *(G-1483)*

Chroma Graphics G 724 693-9050
Oakdale *(G-12896)*

Citizen Publishing Company G 570 454-5911
Hazleton *(G-7495)*

Clarion Printing - Litho G 814 226-9453
Clarion *(G-3173)*

Clever Inc G 717 762-7508
Waynesboro *(G-19404)*

Clinton Press Inc G 814 455-9089
Erie *(G-5227)*

Clore Enterprise G 724 745-0673
Houston *(G-7871)*

College Town Inc G 717 532-7354
Shippensburg *(G-17523)*

College Town Inc G 717 532-3034
Shippensburg *(G-17524)*

Colonial Press LLC G 814 466-3380
Boalsburg *(G-1865)*

Color House Company Ltd F 215 322-4310
Warminster *(G-18845)*

Color Impressions Inc G 717 872-2666
Millersville *(G-11210)*

▲ Colortech Inc E 717 450-5416
Lebanon *(G-9556)*

Colorworks Graphic Svcs Inc E 610 367-7599
Gilbertsville *(G-6371)*

Commercial Job Printing Inc G 814 765-1925
Clearfield *(G-3216)*

Commercial Prtg & Off Suppy G 814 765-4731
Clearfield *(G-3217)*

Communication Graphics Inc F 215 646-2225
Blue Bell *(G-1821)*

Communication Svcs & Support G 215 540-5888
Blue Bell *(G-1822)*

Computer Print Inc G 717 397-9174
Lancaster *(G-8983)*

Con-Wald Corp E 215 879-1400
Philadelphia *(G-13568)*

Conant Corporation F 215 557-7466
Philadelphia *(G-13569)*

Conestoga Dpi LLC G 717 665-0298
Manheim *(G-10378)*

Conner Printing Inc G 610 494-2222
Aston *(G-756)*

Conrad Printing Co Inc G 717 637-5414
Hanover *(G-6870)*

Consolidated Printing Inc E 215 879-1400
Philadelphia *(G-13571)*

▼ Continental Press Inc C 717 367-1836
Elizabethtown *(G-4869)*

Cooper Printing Inc G 717 871-8856
Lancaster *(G-8986)*

Copy Center Plus G 724 547-5850
Mount Pleasant *(G-11694)*

Copy Management Inc G 610 993-8686
Malvern *(G-10217)*

Copy Management Inc F 215 269-5000
Huntingdon Valley *(G-7972)*

Copy Right Printing & Graphics G 814 838-6255
Erie *(G-5233)*

Corcoran Printing Inc F 570 822-1991
Wilkes Barre *(G-19914)*

Corles Printing G 814 276-3775
Imler *(G-8055)*

Corporate Arts Inc G 610 298-8374
New Tripoli *(G-12454)*

Corporate Graphics Inc G 570 424-0475
East Stroudsburg *(G-4612)*

Corporate Graphics Intl Inc F 800 247-2751
Waynesboro *(G-19405)*

Corporate Print Solutions Inc G 215 774-1119
Glenolden *(G-6472)*

Cortineo Creative LLC F 215 348-1100
Doylestown *(G-4294)*

Country Press Inc F 610 565-8808
Media *(G-10919)*

Courtside Document Svcs Inc G 570 969-2991
Scranton *(G-17220)*

Creative Characters G 215 923-2679
Philadelphia *(G-13578)*

Creative Printing & Graphics G 724 222-8304
Washington *(G-19158)*

Creative Printing Co G 570 875-1811
Ashland *(G-729)*

Creighton Printing Inc G 724 224-0444
Creighton *(G-3882)*

Creps United Publications Inc D 724 463-9722
Indiana *(G-8088)*

Cs-B2 Investments Inc E 412 261-1300
Pittsburgh *(G-14890)*

Curry Printing & Copy G 610 373-2890
Reading *(G-16358)*

D & A Associates G 610 534-4840
Darby *(G-4017)*

D & H Inc G 800 340-1001
Harrisburg *(G-7112)*

D & S Business Services Inc G 724 545-3143
Kittanning *(G-8765)*

▲ D & Sr Inc D 717 569-3264
Lancaster *(G-8989)*

D & Z Printers G 724 539-8922
Latrobe *(G-9470)*

D G A Inc G 717 249-8542
Carlisle *(G-2706)*

D L Dravis & Associates Inc G 814 943-6155
Altoona *(G-496)*

D L Dravis & Associates Inc G 814 944-5880
Altoona *(G-497)*

D R M Services Corporation G 610 789-2685
Havertown *(G-7419)*

Daedal Group Inc G 215 745-8718
Philadelphia *(G-13603)*

Damin Printing Co LLC G 814 472-9530
Ebensburg *(G-4784)*

Data Print G 484 329-7553
Malvern *(G-10221)*

Davco Advertising Inc E 717 442-4155
Kinzers *(G-8736)*

Dave Zerbe Studio G 610 376-0379
Reading *(G-16360)*

David A Smith Printing Inc E 717 564-3719
Harrisburg *(G-7114)*

David Bream G 717 334-1513
Gettysburg *(G-6288)*

Davinci Graphics Inc G 215 441-8180
Horsham *(G-7808)*

Degadan Corp G 610 940-1282
Conshohocken *(G-3537)*

Delco Trade Services Inc G 610 659-9978
Wayne *(G-19317)*

Democratic Print Shop E 717 787-3307
Harrisburg *(G-7118)*

Dennis Albertson LLC G 570 784-1677
Bloomsburg *(G-1778)*

Digital Color Graphics Inc E 215 942-7500
Southampton *(G-17808)*

Digital Impact LLC G 610 623-1269
Yeadon *(G-20353)*

Digital Print & Design Inc G 570 347-6001
Old Forge *(G-12963)*

Digital-Ink Inc D 717 731-8890
Dillsburg *(G-4126)*

Dilullo Graphics Inc E 610 775-4360
Mohnton *(G-11262)*

Direct Mail Service & Press F 610 432-4538
Allentown *(G-194)*

Direct Mail Service Inc D 412 471-6300
Pittsburgh *(G-14925)*

Dispatch Printing Inc F 814 870-9600
Erie *(G-5248)*

Dixon-Saunders Enterprises G 215 335-2150
Lafayette Hill *(G-8878)*

Djf Print Xpress G 215 964-1258
Levittown *(G-9833)*

Dla Document Services F 717 605-3777
Mechanicsburg *(G-10837)*

Dn Printer Solutions G 717 606-6233
Ephrata *(G-5101)*

Donald Blyler Offset Inc D 717 949-6831
Lebanon *(G-9561)*

Donnelley Financial LLC F 717 293-3725
Glen Mills *(G-6436)*

Doodad Printing LLC D 800 383-6973
Lancaster *(G-9002)*

Drexel Bindery Inc F 215 232-3808
Philadelphia *(G-13645)*

Drs Printing Services Inc G 717 502-1117
Dillsburg *(G-4127)*

Dubose Printing & Bus Svcs G 215 877-9071
Philadelphia *(G-13649)*

Dupli Craft Printing Inc G 570 344-8980
Scranton *(G-17229)*

Durham Press Inc G 610 346-6133
Durham *(G-4502)*

Dynamic Printing Inc G 215 793-9453
Ambler *(G-577)*

Dynamic Systems F 412 835-6100
Library *(G-9954)*

◆ Eagle Graphics Inc .... D 717 867-5576
Annville (G-647)

Eagle Printery Inc .... F 724 287-0754
Butler (G-2397)

Eagle Printing Company .... D 724 282-8000
Butler (G-2398)

East Associates Inc .... G 610 667-3980
Bala Cynwyd (G-878)

Eastern Die Cutting & Finshg .... F 610 917-9765
Phoenixville (G-14546)

Edwin Ringer .... G 724 746-3374
Westland (G-19782)

Elizabeth C Baker .... F 610 566-0691
Media (G-10923)

Engle Printing & Pubg Co Inc .... F 717 892-6800
Lancaster (G-9010)

Engle Printing & Pubg Co Inc .... F 717 653-1833
Mount Joy (G-11654)

Engle Printing & Pubg Co Inc .... C 717 653-1833
Lancaster (G-9009)

Ensinger Printing Service .... G 717 484-4451
Adamstown (G-21)

Epic Litho .... E 610 933-7400
Phoenixville (G-14548)

Evolution Printing Systems .... G 814 724-5831
Meadville (G-10723)

Executive Print Solutions LLC .... G 570 421-1437
Stroudsburg (G-18117)

Executive Printing Company Inc .... F 717 664-3636
Elm (G-4956)

Express Press Inc .... G 412 824-1000
Pittsburgh (G-14994)

Express Printing .... G 215 357-7033
Southampton (G-17810)

Express Prtg & Graphics Inc .... G 724 274-7700
Cheswick (G-3107)

Express Screenprinting .... G 215 579-8819
Langhorne (G-9296)

Expressway Printing Inc .... G 215 244-0233
Warminster (G-18876)

Fantasy Printing Supplies LLC .... G 215 569-3744
Philadelphia (G-13693)

FB Shoemaker LLC .... G 717 852-8029
York (G-20476)

Federal Business Products Inc .... D 570 454-2451
West Hazleton (G-19709)

Fedex Corporation .... G 412 441-2379
Pittsburgh (G-15008)

Fencor Graphics Inc .... E 215 745-2266
Bensalem (G-1194)

Filmet Color Lab Inc .... D 724 275-1700
Cheswick (G-3108)

Fine Print Commercial Printers .... G 814 337-7468
Meadville (G-10726)

First Shelburne Corporation .... G 610 544-8660
Springfield (G-17914)

Five Thousand Forms Inc .... F 610 395-0900
Fogelsville (G-5994)

Formex Business Printing .... G 717 737-3430
Lemoyne (G-9744)

Fort Dearborn Company .... G 814 686-7656
Tyrone (G-18582)

Fortney Printing .... F 717 939-6422
Harrisburg (G-7130)

Fotorecord Print Center Inc .... G 724 837-0530
Greensburg (G-6667)

Foundation Print Solutions .... G 717 330-0544
Lititz (G-10009)

French Creek Offset Inc .... G 610 582-3241
Birdsboro (G-1696)

▲ Fry Communications Inc .... A 717 766-0211
Mechanicsburg (G-10846)

G R Graphics .... G 814 774-9592
Girard (G-6389)

Gable Printing .... G 724 443-3444
Gibsonia (G-6335)

Gallagher Printing Inc .... G 717 838-1527
Palmyra (G-13123)

Gallop Printing .... G 215 542-0887
Fort Washington (G-6071)

Garlits Industries Inc .... F 215 736-2121
Morrisville (G-11559)

Gary Murelle .... G 570 888-7006
Sayre (G-17114)

▲ General Press Corporation .... E 724 224-3500
Natrona Heights (G-11943)

Gesualdi Printing .... G 215 785-3960
Bristol (G-2148)

Gibson Graphics Group Inc .... G 717 755-7192
Hellam (G-7550)

Gilbert Printing Services .... G 215 483-7772
Philadelphia (G-13763)

Gillespie Printing Inc .... F 610 264-1863
Allentown (G-232)

Globe Data Systems Inc .... D 215 443-7960
Warminster (G-18889)

Globe Print Shop .... G 570 454-8031
Hazleton (G-7499)

Gloroy Inc .... G 610 435-7800
Allentown (G-235)

Godfreys Custom Printing .... G 717 530-8818
Shippensburg (G-17529)

Goodway Graphics Inc .... B 215 887-5700
Jenkintown (G-8288)

Grace Press Inc .... F 717 354-0475
Ephrata (G-5107)

Grafika Commercial Prtg Inc .... B 610 678-8630
Reading (G-16396)

Gran Enterprises .... G 215 634-2883
Philadelphia (G-13780)

Graphcom Inc .... C 800 699-1664
Gettysburg (G-6295)

Graphic Arts Incorporated .... E 215 382-5500
Philadelphia (G-13782)

Graphic Impressions of America .... G 610 296-3939
Malvern (G-10243)

Graphic Print Solutions L .... G 610 845-0280
Barto (G-943)

Great American Printer Inc .... G 570 752-7341
Berwick (G-1326)

Great Atlantic Graphics Inc .... D 610 296-8711
Lansdale (G-9373)

Great Northern Press of Wilkes .... E 570 822-3147
Wilkes Barre (G-19922)

Greentree Printing Inc .... F 412 921-5570
Pittsburgh (G-15064)

Greenwood Business Printing .... G 610 337-8887
King of Prussia (G-8626)

Griffiths Printing Co .... F 610 623-3822
Lansdowne (G-9433)

Grit Commercial Printing Inc .... E 570 368-8021
Montoursville (G-11440)

Groffs Printing Company .... G 717 786-1511
Quarryville (G-16272)

Grove Printing Inc .... G 814 355-2197
Bellefonte (G-1101)

Guy Coder .... G 814 265-0519
Brockway (G-2227)

Guy Hrezik .... G 610 779-7609
Reading (G-16397)

Guyasuta Printing Co .... G 412 782-0112
Pittsburgh (G-15068)

H & H Graphics Inc .... E 717 393-3941
Lancaster (G-9035)

H & H Graphics Inc .... E 717 393-3941
Lancaster (G-9036)

H B South Printing .... F 412 751-1300
McKeesport (G-10669)

Haas Printing Co Inc .... E 717 761-0277
Lemoyne (G-9745)

Hammond Press Inc .... E 412 821-4100
Pittsburgh (G-15078)

Hapsco Design and Prtg Svcs .... G 717 564-2323
Harrisburg (G-7139)

Harman Beach Corporation .... F 717 652-0556
Harrisburg (G-7141)

Harmony Press Inc .... E 610 559-9800
Easton (G-4695)

Harper Printing Service .... G 412 884-2666
Pittsburgh (G-15082)

Hayden Printing Co .... F 610 642-2105
Ardmore (G-708)

Healthcare Information Corp .... F 724 776-9411
Warrendale (G-19081)

Heatha Henrys LLC .... G 215 968-2080
Newtown (G-12509)

Heeter Printing Company Inc .... D 724 746-8900
Canonsburg (G-2595)

Heirloom Engraving LLC .... G 717 336-8451
Stevens (G-18052)

Hendersons Printing Inc .... E 814 944-0855
Altoona (G-512)

Herrmann Printing & Litho Inc .... E 412 243-4100
Pittsburgh (G-15093)

Hesford Keystone Printing Co .... G 814 942-2911
Altoona (G-513)

Hess Commercial Printing Inc .... E 724 652-6802
New Castle (G-12103)

▲ Hessinger Group Inc .... G 814 480-8912
Erie (G-5316)

HI-Tech Color Inc .... F 724 463-8522
Indiana (G-8104)

Hocking Printing Co Inc .... D 717 738-1151
Ephrata (G-5109)

Hodgsons Quick Printing .... G 215 362-1356
Kulpsville (G-8830)

Hoffman Enterprises Inc .... G 610 944-8481
Fleetwood (G-5974)

Homer Reproductions Inc .... F 610 539-8400
Norristown (G-12667)

Horton Printing .... G 717 938-2777
Etters (G-5549)

Hot Frog Print Media LLC .... E 717 697-2204
Mechanicsburg (G-10855)

Houck Printing Company Inc .... F 717 233-5205
Harrisburg (G-7152)

House of Printing .... G 814 723-3701
Warren (G-19031)

Huckstein Printing .... G 724 452-5777
Zelienople (G-20803)

Huepenbecker Enterprises Inc .... F 717 393-3941
Lancaster (G-9052)

Hullihens Printery .... G 570 288-6804
Wilkes Barre (G-19925)

Huston National Printing Co .... G 412 431-5335
Pittsburgh (G-15106)

Ideal Prtg Co Lancaster Inc .... G 717 299-2643
Lancaster (G-9054)

Imaging Fx Inc .... G 484 223-3311
Allentown (G-252)

Imf Printing LLC .... G 844 463-2726
Allentown (G-253)

Impact Printing and Embroidery .... G 814 857-7246
Woodland (G-20212)

Independent Graphics Inc .... E 570 609-5267
Wyoming (G-20279)

Independent-Observer .... E 724 887-7400
Scottdale (G-17193)

Indian Valley Printing Co Inc .... E 215 723-7884
Souderton (G-17741)

Indiana Printing and Pubg Co .... C 724 465-5555
Indiana (G-8105)

Indiana Printing and Pubg Co .... G 724 349-3434
Indiana (G-8106)

Indus Graphics Inc .... G 215 443-7773
Warminster (G-18896)

Ink Spot Printing .... G 570 743-7979
Selinsgrove (G-17327)

Ink Spot Printing & Copy Ctr .... G 610 647-0776
Malvern (G-10255)

Instant Response Inc .... G 215 322-1271
Huntingdon Valley (G-7997)

Instant Web Inc .... G 952 474-0961
Warminster (G-18899)

Intercon Printer & Consultants .... G 724 837-5428
Greensburg (G-6678)

Interform Corporation .... C 412 221-7321
Bridgeville (G-2070)

Itp of Usa Inc .... D 717 367-3670
Elizabethtown (G-4875)

J & B Printing .... G 570 587-4427
Clarks Summit (G-3195)

J & R Beck Inc .... F 724 981-5220
Sharon (G-17437)

J A Mitch Printing & Copy Ctr .... G 724 847-2940
Beaver Falls (G-1002)

J D Enterprise-Mp LLC .... G 215 855-4003
Lansdale (G-9377)

J D Printing Inc .... G 724 327-0006
Pittsburgh (G-15141)

J R B Printing .... G 570 689-9114
Jefferson Township (G-8278)

J R Finio & Sons Inc .... F 610 623-5800
Lansdowne (G-9435)

Jaak Holdings LLC .... G 267 462-4092
Ambler (G-582)

Jack Pressman .... G 610 668-8847
Bala Cynwyd (G-882)

James Irwin .... G 724 867-6083
Emlenton (G-5012)

James Saks .... G 570 343-8150
Scranton (G-17247)

Jaren Enterprises Inc .... G 717 394-2671
Lancaster (G-9072)

Jayco Grafix Inc .... D 610 678-2640
Reinholds (G-16633)

▼ Jaz Forms .... G 610 272-0770
Norristown (G-12673)

JC Printing .... G 570 282-1187
Carbondale (G-2679)

Jem Graphics LLC ... G ... 412 220-0290
Bridgeville *(G-2074)*
Jerden Industries Inc ... F ... 814 375-7822
Du Bois *(G-4399)*
Jiffy Printing Inc ... G ... 814 452-2067
Erie *(G-5336)*
Jim Mannello ... G ... 610 681-6467
Gilbert *(G-6362)*
Jka Inc ... F ... 412 741-9288
Sewickley *(G-17397)*
Jma Group ... G ... 724 444-0004
Allison Park *(G-454)*
Jnb Screen Printing Inc ... G ... 610 845-7680
Alburtis *(G-52)*
Joan Vadyak Printing Inc ... G ... 570 645-5507
Lansford *(G-9448)*
Joseph H Tees & Son Inc ... G ... 215 638-3368
Bensalem *(G-1214)*
Joseph Lagrua ... G ... 814 274-7163
Coudersport *(G-3783)*
Jpa Printing ... G ... 610 270-8855
Blue Bell *(G-1838)*
JS Little Publication ... G ... 412 343-5288
Pittsburgh *(G-15157)*
K B Offset Printing Inc ... E ... 814 238-8445
State College *(G-17982)*
Kalil Printing Inc ... E ... 610 948-9330
Royersford *(G-16854)*
Kalnin Graphics Inc ... E ... 215 887-3203
Jenkintown *(G-8292)*
▲ **Kappa Graphics L P** ... C ... 570 655-9681
Hughestown *(G-7893)*
Kappa Media LLC ... C ... 215 643-5800
Fort Washington *(G-6079)*
Karen Holbrook ... G ... 724 628-3858
Connellsville *(G-3500)*
Keeney Printing Group Inc ... G ... 215 855-6116
Lansdale *(G-9383)*
Kelly Line Inc ... F ... 570 527-6822
Pottsville *(G-16085)*
Kendalls Kreations ... G ... 814 427-2517
Big Run *(G-1656)*
Kennedy Printing Co Inc ... F ... 215 474-5150
Philadelphia *(G-13926)*
Kestone Digital Press ... E ... 484 318-7017
Paoli *(G-13143)*
Keystone Printed Spc Co LLC ... C ... 570 457-8334
Old Forge *(G-12967)*
Keystone Printing Co ... F ... 570 622-4377
Pottsville *(G-16086)*
Keystone Printing Services ... G ... 215 675-6464
Hatboro *(G-7288)*
Keystone Prtg & Graphics Inc ... G ... 570 648-5785
Coal Township *(G-3280)*
Killeen Printing Co ... G ... 412 381-4090
Pittsburgh *(G-15177)*
King Printing and Pubg Inc ... G ... 814 238-2536
State College *(G-17985)*
Kingdom Exposure Ltd ... G ... 215 621-8291
Drexel Hill *(G-4368)*
Kirkland Printing Inc ... G ... 215 706-2399
Willow Grove *(G-20124)*
Kisel Printing Service Inc ... E ... 570 489-7666
Dickson City *(G-4121)*
Kistler & Dinapoli Inc ... G ... 215 428-4740
Morrisville *(G-11567)*
Kistler Printing Co Inc ... F ... 570 421-2050
East Stroudsburg *(G-4622)*
▲ **Knepper Press Corporation** ... C ... 724 899-4200
Clinton *(G-3263)*
Konhaus Farms Inc ... G ... 717 731-9456
Camp Hill *(G-2502)*
Kreider Digital Communications ... G ... 412 446-2784
Pittsburgh *(G-15200)*
Krohmalys Printing Co ... G ... 412 271-4234
Pittsburgh *(G-15201)*
▲ **Kurtz Bros** ... D ... 814 765-6561
Clearfield *(G-3222)*
Kutztown Publishing Company ... E ... 610 683-7341
Allentown *(G-287)*
Kwik Quality Press Inc ... G ... 717 273-0005
Lebanon *(G-9596)*
Kwikticketscom Inc ... F ... 724 438-7712
Uniontown *(G-18632)*
L D H Printing Ltd Inc ... F ... 609 924-4664
Morrisville *(G-11568)*
L G Graphics Inc ... F ... 412 421-6330
Pittsburgh *(G-15208)*
Labelcraft Press Inc ... G ... 215 257-6368
Perkasie *(G-13282)*
Labels By Pulizzi Inc ... E ... 570 326-1244
Williamsport *(G-20034)*
Labue Printing Inc ... G ... 814 371-5059
Du Bois *(G-4402)*
Lackawanna Printing Co ... G ... 570 342-0528
Scranton *(G-17253)*
Lancaster General Svcs Bus Tr ... F ... 800 341-2121
Lancaster *(G-9096)*
Lancaster General Svcs Bus Tr ... F ... 717 544-5474
Lancaster *(G-9095)*
Lapsley Printing Inc ... G ... 215 332-7451
Philadelphia *(G-13956)*
▲ **Larry Myers** ... G ... 717 564-8300
Harrisburg *(G-7169)*
Laurel Printing ... G ... 724 459-7554
Blairsville *(G-1731)*
Laurel Valley Graphics Inc ... F ... 724 539-4545
Latrobe *(G-9498)*
Lawrence Printing Service ... G ... 215 799-2332
Souderton *(G-17748)*
Lee Enterprises Inc Sentinel ... C ... 717 240-7135
Carlisle *(G-2721)*
Legacy Printing and Pubg Co ... G ... 724 567-5657
Vandergrift *(G-18732)*
Lehigh Print & Data LLC ... G ... 610 421-8891
Macungie *(G-10151)*
◆ **Lem Products Inc** ... E ... 800 220-2400
Montgomeryville *(G-11403)*
Leon Spangler ... F ... 570 837-7903
Middleburg *(G-11028)*
Lesko Enterprises Inc ... C ... 814 756-4030
Albion *(G-46)*
Levittown Printing Inc ... G ... 215 945-8156
Levittown *(G-9845)*
Liberty Craftsmen Inc ... G ... 717 871-0125
Millersville *(G-11211)*
Liberty Press LLC ... G ... 215 943-3788
Levittown *(G-9846)*
Liberty Products Group Inc ... G ... 215 631-1700
Hatfield *(G-7364)*
Little Mountain Printing ... F ... 717 933-8091
Myerstown *(G-11892)*
Little Printing Co Inc ... F ... 724 437-4831
Uniontown *(G-18635)*
Lls Graphics ... G ... 610 435-9055
Allentown *(G-299)*
Lock Haven Express ... E ... 570 748-6791
Lock Haven *(G-10090)*
Lsc Communications Us LLC ... A ... 717 392-4074
Lancaster *(G-9116)*
M3 Media LLC ... F ... 215 463-6348
Philadelphia *(G-13983)*
Magna Graphics Inc ... G ... 412 687-0500
Pittsburgh *(G-15247)*
Main Line Print Shop Inc ... G ... 610 688-7782
Wayne *(G-19349)*
Main St Prtg & Copy Ctr Inc ... G ... 570 424-0800
Stroudsburg *(G-18126)*
Mandelbroks ... G ... 814 813-5555
Meadville *(G-10755)*
▲ **Maple Press Company** ... C ... 717 764-5911
York *(G-20580)*
Marathon Printing Inc ... F ... 215 238-1100
Philadelphia *(G-13991)*
Marcan Advertising Inc ... G ... 717 270-6929
Cleona *(G-3245)*
Marlin A Inch ... G ... 570 374-1106
Selinsgrove *(G-17330)*
Marlo Enterprises Inc ... F ... 412 678-3800
Duquesne *(G-4498)*
Masters Ink Corporation ... G ... 724 745-1122
Canonsburg *(G-2601)*
Maximum Graphics Corporation ... F ... 215 639-6700
Bensalem *(G-1223)*
▲ **McCarty Printing Corp** ... D ... 814 454-4561
Erie *(G-5385)*
McCourt Label Cabinet Company ... D ... 800 458-2390
Lewis Run *(G-9877)*
McLean Publishing Co ... F ... 814 275-3131
New Bethlehem *(G-12027)*
Mdg Associates ... E ... 215 969-6623
Philadelphia *(G-14000)*
Medianews Group Inc ... C ... 717 637-3736
Hanover *(G-6919)*
Meinert Holdings Inc ... F ... 412 835-2727
Bethel Park *(G-1424)*
Mercersburg Printing Inc ... E ... 717 328-3902
Mercersburg *(G-10993)*
Mercersburg Printing Inc ... G ... 717 762-8204
Waynesboro *(G-19418)*
Metal Photo Service Inc ... G ... 412 829-2992
Wall *(G-18779)*
Michael Anthony Salvatori ... G ... 570 326-9222
Williamsport *(G-20041)*
Michael S Cwalina ... G ... 412 341-1606
Pittsburgh *(G-15284)*
Mifflin Press Inc ... G ... 717 684-2253
Columbia *(G-3443)*
Mifflinburg Telegraph Inc ... G ... 570 966-2255
Mifflinburg *(G-11099)*
Migu Press Inc ... E ... 215 957-9763
Warminster *(G-18923)*
Milan Printing ... G ... 570 325-2649
Jim Thorpe *(G-8342)*
Miller Printing Inc ... G ... 717 626-5800
Ephrata *(G-5128)*
Minit Rubber Stamps ... G ... 610 352-8600
Upper Darby *(G-18690)*
Minnich Limited ... G ... 717 697-2204
Mechanicsburg *(G-10871)*
Minuteman Press ... G ... 412 621-7456
Pittsburgh *(G-15294)*
Minuteman Press ... G ... 724 346-1105
Hermitage *(G-7592)*
Minuteman Press ... G ... 610 272-6220
Norristown *(G-12685)*
Minuteman Press ... G ... 724 236-0261
Leechburg *(G-9649)*
Minuteman Press ... G ... 724 846-9740
Beaver Falls *(G-1005)*
Minuteman Press ... G ... 215 538-2200
Quakertown *(G-16221)*
Minuteman Press Inc ... G ... 610 923-9266
Easton *(G-4724)*
Minuteman Press International ... G ... 610 539-6707
Norristown *(G-12686)*
Minuteman Press Intl Inc ... G ... 610 902-0203
Wayne *(G-19357)*
Minuteman Press of Glenside ... G ... 267 626-2706
Glenside *(G-6528)*
Minuteman Press of Hanover ... G ... 717 632-5400
Hanover *(G-6921)*
Minuteman Press South Hills ... G ... 412 531-0809
Pittsburgh *(G-15295)*
Mjjm Enterprises Inc ... E ... 717 392-1711
Lancaster *(G-9137)*
Modern Reproductions Inc ... F ... 412 488-7700
Pittsburgh *(G-15298)*
Mondlak Printery ... G ... 570 654-9871
Pittston *(G-15768)*
Morgan Printing Company ... G ... 215 784-0966
Willow Grove *(G-20129)*
Morlatton Post Card Club ... E ... 717 263-1638
Chambersburg *(G-2961)*
Morning Call LLC ... A ... 610 820-6500
Allentown *(G-322)*
Morris Printing Company ... G ... 412 881-8626
Pittsburgh *(G-15302)*
Motto Graphics Inc ... G ... 570 639-5555
Dallas *(G-3963)*
Movad LLC ... F ... 215 638-2679
Plymouth Meeting *(G-15858)*
Mr Printer Inc ... G ... 215 354-5533
Richboro *(G-16676)*
Mulligan Printing Corporation ... E ... 570 278-3271
Tunkhannock *(G-18544)*
Multi-Color Corporation ... D ... 717 266-9675
York *(G-20607)*
Multiscope Incorporated ... E ... 724 743-1083
Canonsburg *(G-2606)*
Munro Prtg Graphic Design LLC ... G ... 610 485-1966
Marcus Hook *(G-10451)*
Murphy Printing Free Press ... E ... 724 927-2222
Linesville *(G-9985)*
Murrelle Printing Co Inc ... F ... 570 888-2244
Sayre *(G-17119)*
My Instant Benefits ... G ... 724 465-6075
Indiana *(G-8114)*
N H Morgan Inc ... G ... 412 561-1046
Pittsburgh *(G-15314)*
Nacci Printing Inc ... E ... 610 434-1224
Allentown *(G-324)*
Nash Printing LLC ... F ... 215 855-4267
Lansdale *(G-9391)*
National Center For Def ... E ... 724 539-8811
Blairsville *(G-1735)*
▲ **National Dermalogy Image Corp** ... G ... 610 756-0065
Kempton *(G-8493)*
National Imprint Corporation ... E ... 814 239-5116
Claysburg *(G-3206)*

National Mail Graphics Corp .... D 610 524-1600
Exton (G-5713)

▼ National Ticket Company .... C 570 672-2900
Paxinos (G-13190)

Navitor Inc .... B 717 765-3121
Waynesboro (G-19419)

Nazareth Key Youngs Press .... G 610 759-5000
Nazareth (G-11984)

New Centuries LLC .... G 724 347-3030
Hermitage (G-7593)

News Chronicle Co Inc .... E 717 532-4101
Shippensburg (G-17540)

News Eagle .... E 570 226-4547
Honesdale (G-7719)

Newspaper Holding Inc .... D 814 724-6370
Meadville (G-10769)

Newspaper Holding Inc .... D 724 654-6651
New Castle (G-12131)

Newtown Business Forms Corp .... F 215 364-3898
Huntingdon Valley (G-8017)

Newville Print Shop .... G 717 776-7673
Newville (G-12608)

Nittany Printing and Pubg Co .... D 814 238-5000
State College (G-18000)

Norcorp Inc .... G 814 445-2523
Somerset (G-17699)

North Amrcn Communications Inc .... A 814 696-3553
Duncansville (G-4458)

◆ Northeastern Envelope Company .... D 800 233-4285
Old Forge (G-12971)

Northern Hardwoods Inc .... G 814 274-8060
Coudersport (G-3786)

Northern Liberty Press LLC .... G 215 634-3000
Philadelphia (G-14084)

Nosco Inc .... G 215 788-1105
Bristol (G-2175)

Npc Inc .... B 814 239-8787
Claysburg (G-3207)

Nuss Printing Inc .... F 610 853-3005
Havertown (G-7424)

▲ Oberthur Card Systems Inc .... B 610 280-2707
Exton (G-5717)

Offset Paperback Mfrs Inc .... A 570 675-5261
Dallas (G-3964)

Ogden Brothers Incorporated .... F 610 789-1258
Havertown (G-7425)

▲ Okumus Enterprises Ltd .... E 215 295-3340
Fairless Hills (G-5790)

Old York Road Printing LLC .... E 215 957-6200
Warminster (G-18931)

Olenicks Prtg & Photography Sp .... G 814 342-2853
Philipsburg (G-14522)

Outlook Printing Solutions Inc .... G 215 680-4014
Harleysville (G-7050)

P A Hutchison Company .... C 570 876-4560
Mayfield (G-10542)

P/S Printing & Copy Services .... G 814 623-7033
Bedford (G-1069)

Pace Resources Inc .... E 717 852-1300
York (G-20616)

Pacemaker Press PP&s Inc .... E 301 696-9629
Waynesboro (G-19421)

Paoli Print & Copy Inc .... G 610 644-7471
Paoli (G-13145)

Pap Technologies Inc .... E 717 399-3333
Lancaster (G-9160)

Paravano Company Inc .... G 215 659-4600
Willow Grove (G-20132)

Parc Productions .... G 724 283-3300
Butler (G-2431)

Park Press Inc .... G 724 465-5812
Indiana (G-8116)

Parkland Bindery Inc .... G 610 433-6153
Allentown (G-344)

Parks Design & Ink .... G 814 643-1120
Huntingdon (G-7955)

Parkside Graphics Inc .... G 215 453-1123
Sellersville (G-17356)

Parkway Printing .... G 610 928-3433
Emmaus (G-5039)

Partners Press Inc .... F 610 666-7960
Oaks (G-12935)

Partridge Wirth Company Inc .... F 570 344-8514
Scranton (G-17270)

Patrick Mc Cool .... F 814 359-2447
Bellefonte (G-1110)

Payne Printery Inc .... D 570 675-1147
Dallas (G-3965)

Peacock Printing .... D 814 336-5009
Erie (G-5418)

Pecks Graphics LLC .... G 717 963-7588
Harrisburg (G-7191)

Pegasus Print & Copy Centers .... G 610 356-8787
Broomall (G-2300)

Pemcor Printing Company LLC .... D 717 898-1555
Lancaster (G-9162)

Pencor Services Inc .... C 570 386-2660
Lehighton (G-9721)

Penn Print & Graphics .... G 724 239-5849
Bentleyville (G-1273)

Penn Valley Printing Company .... G 215 295-5755
Morrisville (G-11576)

Penny Mansfield Saver Inc .... G 570 662-3277
Mansfield (G-10424)

Penny Press of York Inc .... G 717 843-4078
York (G-20622)

Perfect Impression .... G 610 444-9493
Kennett Square (G-8535)

Perry Printing .... G 215 256-8074
Harleysville (G-7052)

Perry Printing Company .... G 717 582-2838
New Bloomfield (G-12030)

Philadelphia Photo Arts Center .... G 215 232-5678
Philadelphia (G-14148)

Philly Banner Express LLC .... G 267 385-5451
Philadelphia (G-14168)

Phoenix Data Inc .... D 570 547-1665
Montgomery (G-11377)

Phoenix Design & Print Inc .... F 412 264-4895
Coraopolis (G-3715)

Phoenix Lithographing Corp .... D 215 969-4600
Philadelphia (G-14170)

Phoenix Lithographing Corp .... C 215 698-9000
Philadelphia (G-14171)

Phresh Prints Ink LLC .... G 267 687-7483
Philadelphia (G-14173)

Pic Mobile Advertising LLC .... G 570 208-1459
Wilkes Barre (G-19956)

Pik-A-Boo Photos LLC .... G 267 334-6379
Philadelphia (G-14177)

Pikewood Inc .... F 610 974-8000
Bethlehem (G-1597)

Pjr Printing Inc .... G 724 283-2666
Butler (G-2434)

Placemat Printers Inc .... F 610 285-2255
Fogelsville (G-5996)

Pleasant Luck Corp .... G 215 968-2080
Newtown (G-12537)

Pomco Graphics Inc .... F 215 455-9500
Philadelphia (G-14188)

Portico Group LLC .... G 610 566-8499
Media (G-10943)

Portico Printing LLC .... G 215 717-5151
Philadelphia (G-14192)

Precise Graphic Products Inc .... G 412 481-0952
Coraopolis (G-3717)

Premier Printing Solutions LLC .... G 570 426-1570
East Stroudsburg (G-4630)

Press and Journal .... E 717 944-4628
Middletown (G-11071)

Press Box Printing .... G 814 944-3057
Altoona (G-538)

Press Craft Printers Inc .... G 412 761-8200
Pittsburgh (G-15434)

Prince Printing .... G 412 233-3555
Clairton (G-3156)

Print & Copy Center Inc .... F 412 828-2205
Verona (G-18760)

Print and Graphics Scholrship .... G 412 741-6860
Warrendale (G-19093)

Print Box Inc .... G 212 741-1381
Downingtown (G-4251)

Print Charming Design .... G 412 519-5226
Clairton (G-3157)

Print Escape LLC .... G 888 524-8690
Pittsburgh (G-15439)

Print Shop .... G 215 788-1883
Croydon (G-3925)

Print Shop .... G 570 327-9005
Williamsport (G-20064)

Print Shop Inc .... G 610 692-1810
West Chester (G-19620)

Print Tech Western PA .... E 412 963-1500
Pittsburgh (G-15440)

Print Works On Demand Inc .... G 717 545-5215
Harrisburg (G-7202)

Print-O-Stat Inc .... F 724 742-9811
Cranberry Township (G-3845)

Print-O-Stat Inc .... E 717 812-9476
York (G-20640)

Print-O-Stat Inc .... G 610 265-5470
King of Prussia (G-8664)

Print-O-Stat Inc .... F 717 795-9255
Mechanicsburg (G-10882)

◆ Print2finish LLC .... G 215 369-5494
Yardley (G-20334)

Printaway Inc .... G 717 263-1839
Chambersburg (G-2971)

Printbiz LLC .... G 412 881-3318
Pittsburgh (G-15442)

Printcompass LLC .... G 610 541-6763
Springfield (G-17921)

Printers Edge .... G 570 454-4803
Hazleton (G-7520)

Printers Parts Store Inc .... F 610 279-6660
Bridgeport (G-2044)

Printforce Inc .... G 610 797-6455
Allentown (G-360)

Printing 4u .... G 610 377-0111
Lehighton (G-9722)

Printing Concepts Inc .... E 814 833-8080
Erie (G-5437)

Printing Craftsmen Inc .... F 570 646-2121
Pocono Pines (G-15883)

Printing Express Inc .... G 717 600-1111
York (G-20641)

Printing Mas .... G 570 326-9222
Williamsport (G-20065)

Printing Plus+ Inc .... F 814 834-1000
Saint Marys (G-17009)

Printing Post LLC .... G 412 367-7468
Pittsburgh (G-15445)

Printing Press .... G 412 264-3355
Coraopolis (G-3718)

Printing Works .... G 215 357-5609
Southampton (G-17831)

Printwearonline .... G 267 987-6118
Yardley (G-20335)

Printworks & Company Inc .... E 215 721-8500
Lansdale (G-9400)

Process Reproductions Inc .... E 412 321-3120
Pittsburgh (G-15452)

Procopy Inc .... F 814 231-1256
State College (G-18010)

Professional Duplicating Inc .... E 610 891-7979
Media (G-10944)

Professional Graphic Co .... E 724 318-8530
Sewickley (G-17405)

Proforma Graphic Impressions .... G 610 759-2430
Nazareth (G-11986)

Promark Industries Inc .... G 724 356-4060
Mc Donald (G-10579)

Promotional Printing Assoc .... G 215 639-1662
Bensalem (G-1245)

Prova Inc .... G 412 278-3010
Carnegie (G-2783)

Public Image Printing Inc .... G 215 677-4088
Philadelphia (G-14216)

Q D F Inc .... G 610 670-2090
Reading (G-16477)

Qg LLC .... C 414 208-2700
Atglen (G-803)

Qg Printing II Corp .... A 610 593-1445
Atglen (G-804)

Qg Printing II Corp .... B 717 642-5871
Fairfield (G-5768)

Quad/Graphics Inc .... B 215 541-2729
Pennsburg (G-13253)

Quad/Graphics Inc .... B 570 459-5700
Hazleton (G-7522)

Quality Print Shop Inc .... G 570 473-1122
Northumberland (G-12874)

Quick Print Center PA .... G 717 637-2838
Hanover (G-6939)

Quiet Valley Printing LLC .... G 908 400-3689
Mount Bethel (G-11614)

R Graphics Inc .... G 610 918-0373
West Chester (G-19625)

R M S Graphics Inc .... G 215 322-6000
Huntingdon Valley (G-8028)

R R Donnelley & Sons Company .... C 570 524-2224
Lewisburg (G-9918)

R R Donnelley & Sons Company .... C 215 671-9500
Philadelphia (G-14225)

R R Donnelley & Sons Company .... C 717 209-7700
Lancaster (G-9184)

Raff Printing Inc .... D 412 431-4044
Pittsburgh (G-15466)

Rainbow Graphics Inc .... G 724 228-3007
Bentleyville (G-1275)

S I C

Rancatore & Lavender Inc ....G....... 412 829-7456
North Versailles *(G-12782)*

Reading Eagle Company ....E....... 610 371-5000
Reading *(G-16488)*

Ream Printing Co Inc ....E....... 717 764-5663
York *(G-20653)*

Record Herald Publishing Co ....E....... 717 762-2151
Waynesboro *(G-19422)*

Red Gravel Partners LLC ....G....... 570 445-3553
Scranton *(G-17278)*

Reed & Witting Company ....E....... 412 682-1000
Pittsburgh *(G-15476)*

Reidler Decal Corporation ....E....... 800 628-7770
Saint Clair *(G-16939)*

Rekord Printing Co ....G....... 570 648-3231
Elysburg *(G-4980)*

Rhodes & Hammers Printing ....G....... 724 852-1457
Waynesburg *(G-19451)*

Ricks Quick Printing Inc ....E....... 412 571-0333
Pittsburgh *(G-15485)*

Ridgways Inc ....E....... 215 735-8055
Philadelphia *(G-14250)*

Riecks Letter Service Inc ....F....... 610 375-8581
Reading *(G-16498)*

Rittenhouse Instant Press ....G....... 215 854-0505
Philadelphia *(G-14251)*

Rocket-Courier Newspaper ....F....... 570 746-1217
Wyalusing *(G-20258)*

Rogers & Deturck Printing Inc ....G....... 412 828-8868
Verona *(G-18762)*

Roller Printing Company Inc ....G....... 717 632-1433
Hanover *(G-6946)*

Rowe Printing Shop ....F....... 717 249-5485
Carlisle *(G-2737)*

▲ Rowland Printing Inc ....E....... 610 933-7400
Phoenixville *(G-14575)*

Royalton Press Inc ....G....... 610 929-4040
Camp Hill *(G-2516)*

Rozema Printing LLC ....G....... 717 564-4143
Harrisburg *(G-7210)*

RR Donnelley & Sons Company ....D....... 412 281-7401
Pittsburgh *(G-15501)*

S G Business Services Inc ....G....... 215 567-7107
Philadelphia *(G-14271)*

S P Printing ....G....... 610 562-8551
Shoemakersville *(G-17574)*

Safeguard Business Systems Inc ....C....... 215 631-7500
Lansdale *(G-9408)*

Salem Printing Inc ....F....... 724 468-8604
Delmont *(G-4057)*

Samuel C Rizzo Jr ....G....... 814 725-3047
North East *(G-12760)*

Sandt Printing Co Inc ....G....... 610 258-7445
Easton *(G-4751)*

Scantron Corporation ....C....... 717 684-4600
Columbia *(G-3450)*

Schank Printing Inc ....F....... 610 828-1623
Conshohocken *(G-3603)*

Seiders Printing Co Inc ....G....... 570 622-0570
Pottsville *(G-16097)*

Semler Enterprises Inc ....G....... 717 242-0322
Burnham *(G-2361)*

Seneca Enterprises Inc ....G....... 814 432-7890
Franklin *(G-6156)*

Seneca Printing & Label Inc ....D....... 814 437-5364
Franklin *(G-6157)*

Seneca Printing Express Inc ....G....... 814 437-5364
Franklin *(G-6158)*

Serve Inc ....G....... 570 265-3119
Monroeton *(G-11320)*

Services Unlimited Mstr Prtg ....G....... 610 891-7877
Media *(G-10949)*

Shemco Corp ....F....... 412 831-6022
Pittsburgh *(G-15529)*

◆ Sheridan Group Inc ....D....... 717 632-3535
Hanover *(G-6950)*

▲ Sheridan Press Inc ....G....... 717 632-3535
Hanover *(G-6951)*

Silverline Screen Printing ....G....... 570 275-8866
Danville *(G-4011)*

Simply Business LLC ....G....... 814 241-7113
Summerhill *(G-18155)*

Sir James Prtg & Bus Forms Inc ....G....... 724 339-2122
New Kensington *(G-12377)*

Sir Speedy Inc ....F....... 215 877-8888
Philadelphia *(G-14311)*

Sir Speedy 7108 Inc ....F....... 412 787-9898
Pittsburgh *(G-15542)*

Sir Speedy Printing Center ....G....... 412 687-0500
Pittsburgh *(G-15543)*

Slate Belt Printers Inc ....G....... 610 863-6752
Pen Argyl *(G-13217)*

Slate Lick Printing Inc ....G....... 724 295-2053
Freeport *(G-6214)*

Slates Enterprises Inc ....G....... 814 695-2851
Duncansville *(G-4463)*

Slavia Printing Co Inc ....G....... 412 343-4444
Pittsburgh *(G-15545)*

Smales Printery Inc ....G....... 610 323-7775
Pottstown *(G-16047)*

Smart Print Technologies Inc ....G....... 412 771-8307
Mc Kees Rocks *(G-10636)*

Snellbaker Printing Inc ....G....... 215 885-0674
Glenside *(G-6536)*

South Greensburg Printing Co ....F....... 724 834-0295
Greensburg *(G-6715)*

Spahr-Evans Printers ....G....... 215 886-4057
Glenside *(G-6539)*

Specialty Group Printing Inc ....F....... 814 425-3061
Cochranton *(G-3351)*

Spencer Graphics Inc ....G....... 610 793-2348
West Chester *(G-19643)*

Spencer Printing Inc ....G....... 570 253-2001
Honesdale *(G-7725)*

Sprint Print Inc ....G....... 570 586-5947
Chinchilla *(G-3132)*

St Clair Graphics Inc ....F....... 570 253-6692
Honesdale *(G-7726)*

Standard Offset Prtg Co Inc ....D....... 610 375-6174
Reading *(G-16524)*

Star Printing Company ....G....... 717 456-5692
Delta *(G-4063)*

◆ Starprint Publications Inc ....E....... 814 736-9666
Portage *(G-15922)*

State Street Copy and Press ....G....... 717 232-6684
Harrisburg *(G-7220)*

Stauffer Acquisition Corp ....E....... 717 569-3200
East Petersburg *(G-4591)*

Steckel Printing Inc ....D....... 717 898-1555
Lancaster *(G-9205)*

Steel City Graphics Inc ....G....... 724 942-5699
Canonsburg *(G-2640)*

Steele Print Inc ....G....... 724 758-6178
Ellwood City *(G-4952)*

Stefanos Printing Inc ....G....... 724 277-8374
Dunbar *(G-4443)*

Steffy Printing Inc ....G....... 717 859-5040
Brownstown *(G-2309)*

Strassheim Printing Co Inc ....G....... 610 446-3637
Havertown *(G-7428)*

Sullivan Review ....G....... 570 928-8403
Dushore *(G-4511)*

Sun Litho Print Inc ....F....... 570 421-3250
East Stroudsburg *(G-4636)*

Sunshine Screen Print ....G....... 610 678-9034
Reading *(G-16529)*

Sycamore Partners MGT LP ....G....... 724 748-0052
Grove City *(G-6805)*

Synergy Business Forms Inc ....G....... 814 833-3344
Erie *(G-5502)*

T & T Prtg T & Symbol T Printi ....G....... 724 938-9495
Allenport *(G-105)*

Taggart Printing Corporation ....F....... 610 431-2500
West Chester *(G-19655)*

Tammy M Tibbens ....G....... 717 979-3063
Harrisburg *(G-7226)*

Tcg Document Solutions LLC ....F....... 215 957-0600
Huntingdon Valley *(G-8043)*

Tcg Document Solutions LLC ....E....... 610 356-4700
Paoli *(G-13150)*

▲ Tech Support Screen P ....E....... 412 697-0171
Pittsburgh *(G-15601)*

▲ Telepole Manufacturing Inc ....G....... 570 546-3699
Muncy *(G-11835)*

Theprinterscom Inc ....G....... 814 238-8445
State College *(G-18038)*

Third Dimension Spc LLC ....G....... 570 969-0623
Scranton *(G-17301)*

Thorndale Press Inc ....G....... 610 384-3363
Downingtown *(G-4258)*

Tiger Printing Group LLC ....E....... 215 799-0500
Telford *(G-18323)*

Times Publishing Company ....D....... 814 453-4691
Erie *(G-5509)*

Tioga Publishing Company ....A....... 814 371-4200
Du Bois *(G-4424)*

Tioga Publishing Company ....E....... 570 724-2287
Wellsboro *(G-19473)*

Todays Graphics Inc ....D....... 215 634-6200
Philadelphia *(G-14394)*

▲ Toppan Interamerica Inc ....E....... 610 286-3100
Morgantown *(G-11541)*

Tor Industries Inc ....G....... 570 622-7370
Pottsville *(G-16099)*

Total Document Resource Inc ....G....... 717 648-6234
Lancaster *(G-9221)*

Towanda Printing Co Inc ....C....... 570 265-2151
Towanda *(G-18436)*

TP (old) LLC ....E....... 412 488-1600
Pittsburgh *(G-15634)*

Tre Graphics Etc Inc ....G....... 610 821-8508
Allentown *(G-411)*

Tri-Ad Litho Inc ....F....... 412 795-3110
Pittsburgh *(G-15645)*

Triangle Printing Company Inc ....E....... 717 854-1521
York *(G-20692)*

Tricounty Printers Ltd ....G....... 215 886-3737
Oreland *(G-13031)*

Tristate Blue Printing Inc ....E....... 412 281-3538
Pittsburgh *(G-15653)*

Triune Color Corporation ....D....... 856 829-5600
Huntingdon Valley *(G-8045)*

Trust Franklin Press Co ....F....... 412 481-6442
Pittsburgh *(G-15658)*

▲ Tsi Associates Inc ....F....... 610 375-4371
Reading *(G-16551)*

Type & Print Inc ....E....... 412 241-6070
Clinton *(G-3267)*

Type Set Print ....G....... 570 542-5910
Hunlock Creek *(G-7935)*

Typecraft Press Inc ....E....... 412 488-1600
Pittsburgh *(G-15663)*

TYT LLC ....E....... 800 511-2009
Bethlehem *(G-1645)*

Unigraphics Communications ....G....... 717 697-8132
Mechanicsburg *(G-10902)*

Unipak Inc ....E....... 610 436-6600
West Chester *(G-19670)*

United Offset ....G....... 215 721-2251
Franconia *(G-6111)*

United Partners Ltd ....F....... 570 288-7603
Taylor *(G-18264)*

United Partners Ltd ....G....... 570 283-0995
Taylor *(G-18265)*

▲ Unity Printing Company Inc ....E....... 724 537-5800
Latrobe *(G-9527)*

Universal Network Technologies ....G....... 412 490-0990
Monroeville *(G-11362)*

Universal Printing Company LLC ....D....... 570 342-1243
Dunmore *(G-4487)*

Universal Transfers Inc ....E....... 215 744-6227
Philadelphia *(G-14427)*

University Copy Service Inc ....G....... 215 898-5574
Philadelphia *(G-14429)*

▲ Uticom Systems Inc ....E....... 610 857-2655
Coatesville *(G-3328)*

▼ Valley Business Services Inc ....F....... 610 366-1970
Trexlertown *(G-18511)*

Valley Instant Printing ....G....... 610 439-4122
Orefield *(G-13016)*

Valley Litho Inc ....G....... 610 437-5122
Whitehall *(G-19892)*

Valley Press Inc ....E....... 610 664-7770
Bala Cynwyd *(G-895)*

Velocity Color Inc ....G....... 717 431-2591
Lancaster *(G-9232)*

Vernon Printing Inc ....F....... 724 283-9242
Butler *(G-2447)*

▲ Victor Printing Inc ....D....... 724 342-2106
Sharon *(G-17444)*

Village Publishing Operations ....G....... 215 794-0202
Furlong *(G-6235)*

VIP Advertising & Printing ....G....... 570 251-7897
Honesdale *(G-7731)*

Virgo Investment LLC ....F....... 215 339-1596
Philadelphia *(G-14449)*

Vocam Corp ....G....... 215 348-7115
Doylestown *(G-4344)*

W B Mason Co Inc ....D....... 888 926-2766
Allentown *(G-427)*

W B Mason Co Inc ....E....... 888 926-2766
Altoona *(G-555)*

W L Fegley & Son Inc ....G....... 610 779-0277
Reading *(G-16561)*

W M Abene Co ....G....... 570 457-8334
Old Forge *(G-12977)*

Wakefoose Office Supply & Prtg ....G....... 814 623-5742
Bedford *(G-1079)*

Waveline Direct Llc ....E....... 717 795-8830
Mechanicsburg *(G-10905)*

Webb Communications Inc ....E 570 326-7634
Plymouth (G-15824)

Webb Communications Inc ....F 570 779-9543
Plymouth (G-15825)

Webb Communications Inc ....E 570 326-7634
Plymouth (G-15823)

Webb Communications Inc ....D 570 326-7634
Williamsport (G-20089)

Webb-Mason Inc ....E 724 935-1770
Wexford (G-19833)

West Penn Printing ....G 724 546-2020
New Castle (G-12168)

West Shore Prtg & Dist Corp ....E 717 691-8282
Mechanicsburg (G-10908)

Wheeler Enterprises Inc ....G 610 975-9230
Wayne (G-19392)

White Castle Services LLC ....G 484 560-5961
New Tripoli (G-12463)

White Oak Group Inc ....E 717 291-2222
Lancaster (G-9240)

Whitehead Eagle Corporation ....G 724 346-4280
Sharon (G-17447)

William A Fraser Inc ....G 570 622-7347
Pottsville (G-16102)

William Penn Printing Company ....G 412 322-3660
Pittsburgh (G-15717)

Wise Printing Co Inc ....G 717 741-2751
York (G-20715)

WM Enterprises Inc ....E 717 238-5751
Harrisburg (G-7248)

Wolf Printing ....G 717 755-1560
York (G-20716)

Ygs West LLC ....E 425 251-5005
York (G-20725)

York Newspaper Company ....B 717 767-6397
York (G-20746)

York Newspapers Inc ....D 717 767-6397
York (G-20747)

Yurchak Printing Inc ....G 717 399-9551
Lancaster (G-9244)

Yurchak Printing Inc ....E 717 399-0209
Landisville (G-9269)

Zodiac Printing Corporation ....E 570 474-9220
Mountain Top (G-11784)

2754 Commercial Printing: Gravure

Allimage Graphics LLC ....G 814 728-8650
Warren (G-19009)

Alm Media LLC ....E 215 557-2300
Philadelphia (G-13370)

Alpine Packaging Inc ....E 412 664-4000
North Versailles (G-12771)

Chelsea Partners Inc ....E 215 603-7300
Philadelphia (G-13537)

Chroma Graphics ....G 724 693-9050
Oakdale (G-12896)

Clipper Magazine LLC ....B 717 569-5100
Mountville (G-11791)

Colorworks Graphic Svcs Inc ....E 610 367-7599
Gilbertsville (G-6371)

Dupli Graphics Corporation ....E 610 644-4188
Malvern (G-10225)

Dynamic Business Systems ....G 800 782-2946
South Park (G-17782)

Griffith Pottery House Inc ....G 215 887-2222
Oreland (G-13021)

Innovtive Print Mdia Group Inc ....D 610 489-4800
Phoenixville (G-14553)

Jon Swan Inc ....E 412 264-9000
Coraopolis (G-3700)

▲ Keystone Converting Inc ....F 215 661-9004
Montgomeryville (G-11400)

Kim Kraft Inc ....F 814 870-9600
Fairview (G-5830)

Kustom Cards International ....G 215 233-1678
Glenside (G-6525)

Magagna Associates Inc ....F 610 213-2335
Souderton (G-17751)

Nocopi Technologies Inc ....G 610 834-9600
King of Prussia (G-8657)

Paravano Company Inc ....G 215 659-4600
Willow Grove (G-20132)

Qg LLC ....C 414 208-2700
Atglen (G-803)

Quad/Graphics Inc ....B 215 541-2729
Pennsburg (G-13253)

R R Donnelley & Sons Company ....D 610 391-3900
Breinigsville (G-2025)

Samson Paper Co Inc ....E 610 630-9090
Norristown (G-12708)

▲ Westrock Packaging Inc ....D 215 785-3350
Croydon (G-3933)

Ygs Group Inc ....D 717 505-9701
York (G-20723)

Ygs Group Inc ....G 425 251-5005
York (G-20724)

2759 Commercial Printing

69th St Commercial Printers ....G 610 539-8412
Norristown (G-12627)

A A A Engraving ....G 412 281-7756
Pittsburgh (G-14628)

A Funky Little Sign Shop ....G 215 489-2880
Doylestown (G-4266)

A J Printing ....F 610 337-7468
King of Prussia (G-8575)

Abardia Media ....G 215 893-5100
Philadelphia (G-13333)

Accu-Decal Inc ....G 215 535-0320
Philadelphia (G-13338)

Acro Labels Inc ....E 215 657-5366
Willow Grove (G-20105)

Action Printing and Bus Forms ....F 814 453-5977
Erie (G-5173)

Ad-Art Sign Co ....G 412 373-0960
Pittsburgh (G-14649)

▲ Ad-Rax Productions LLC ....G 610 264-8405
Catasauqua (G-2812)

ADM Publications Inc ....G 610 565-8895
Media (G-10914)

Advance Central Services PA ....G 717 255-8400
Mechanicsburg (G-10816)

Al Tedeschi ....G 724 746-3755
Canonsburg (G-2535)

Alpha Advertising & Mktg LLC ....G 717 445-4200
Bowmansville (G-1886)

Alpha Printing ....G 814 536-8721
Johnstown (G-8352)

Alpha Screen Graphics Inc ....G 412 431-9000
Pittsburgh (G-14687)

Altris Incorporated ....G 724 259-8338
Greensburg (G-6649)

Altus Group Inc ....F 215 977-9900
Philadelphia (G-13374)

American Additive Mfg LLC ....F 215 559-1200
Horsham (G-7782)

▲ American Bank Note Company ....E 215 396-8707
Trevose (G-18486)

American Brchure Catalogue Inc ....E 215 259-1600
Warminster (G-18827)

American Calendar Inc ....F 215 743-3834
Philadelphia (G-13382)

American Future Systems Inc ....E 814 724-2035
Meadville (G-10702)

American Printing Co & Pdts ....G 412 422-3488
Pittsburgh (G-14704)

Anstadt Printing Corporation ....E 717 767-6891
York (G-20378)

Ap-O-Gee Industries Inc ....F 610 719-8010
West Chester (G-19500)

Apex Screen Printing & EMB ....G 814 634-5992
Meyersdale (G-11008)

Apple Press Ltd ....E 610 363-1776
Exton (G-5644)

Argus Printing ....G 610 687-0411
Wayne (G-19301)

Argus Printing & Copy ....G 610 687-0411
Wayne (G-19302)

Arkwood Products Inc ....G 412 835-8730
Bethel Park (G-1404)

Art & Ink ....G 814 486-0606
Emporium (G-5049)

Art Printing Co of Lancaster ....G 717 397-6029
Columbia (G-3430)

Artistagraphics Inc ....F 412 271-3252
Pittsburgh (G-14727)

Artistic Image ....G 717 567-7070
Newport (G-12486)

Ask IV Screen Printing ....G 412 200-5610
Imperial (G-8058)

Associated Prtg Graphics Svcs ....G 215 322-6762
Feasterville Trevose (G-5887)

Atiyeh Printing Inc ....G 610 439-8978
Allentown (G-145)

Auskin Inc ....G 610 696-0234
West Chester (G-19503)

Aviation Technologies Inc ....G 570 457-4147
Avoca (G-840)

Awards & More ....G 724 444-1040
Gibsonia (G-6325)

Axelrad LLC ....G 570 714-3278
Wilkes Barre (G-19907)

B & E Sportswear LP ....F 610 328-9266
Broomall (G-2280)

▲ B L Tees Inc ....F 724 325-1882
Export (G-5591)

▼ Baltimore Corp ....E 215 957-6200
Warminster (G-18835)

Bangtees LLC ....G 484 767-2382
Easton (G-4649)

Berks-Mont Newspapers Inc ....F 610 683-7343
Pottstown (G-15966)

Birds Printing ....G 570 784-8136
Bloomsburg (G-1774)

Blue Mountain Sports AP Inc ....G 717 263-4124
Chambersburg (G-2912)

Bluegill Graphix ....G 814 827-7003
Titusville (G-18376)

Bonnie Kaiser ....G 215 331-6555
Philadelphia (G-13471)

Boulevard Sports ....G 724 378-9191
Aliquippa (G-69)

Bourne Graphics Inc ....G 610 584-6120
Worcester (G-20224)

Bradco Printers Inc ....G 570 297-3024
Troy (G-18517)

Brandywine Envelope Corp ....G 800 887-9399
Cochranville (G-3354)

Brindle Printing Co Inc ....G 724 658-8549
New Castle (G-12067)

Bsg Custom Designs LLC ....G 610 867-7361
Bethlehem (G-1475)

Bubco Enterprise Inc ....G 724 274-4930
Cheswick (G-3102)

Buhl Bros Printing Inc ....F 724 335-0970
Creighton (G-3880)

Butts Ticket Company Inc ....F 610 869-7450
Cochranville (G-3355)

▲ C P Converters Inc ....D 717 764-1193
York (G-20415)

Caffrey Michael & Sons ....G 610 252-1299
Easton (G-4659)

Call Newspapers Inc ....G 570 385-3120
Schuylkill Haven (G-17150)

Cannon Graphics Inc ....G 215 676-5114
Philadelphia (G-13497)

Carrollsisters ....E 215 969-4688
Philadelphia (G-13509)

Castor Printing Company Inc ....F 215 535-1471
Philadelphia (G-13512)

Cenveo Worldwide Limited ....C 724 887-5400
Mount Pleasant (G-11691)

Champ Printing Company Inc ....E 412 269-0197
Coraopolis (G-3675)

Champion Choice Sports ....G 814 236-2930
Curwensville (G-3948)

Charles A Henderson Prtg Svc ....G 724 775-2623
Rochester (G-16783)

Charles R Eckert Signs Inc ....G 717 733-4601
Ephrata (G-5096)

Chocolatecovers Ltd Inc ....G 717 534-1992
Hershey (G-7606)

Choice Marketing Inc ....E 610 494-1270
Aston (G-755)

Chrisber Corporation ....E 800 872-7436
West Chester (G-19525)

Christmas City Printing Co Inc ....E 610 868-5844
Bethlehem (G-1483)

Chroma Graphics ....G 724 693-9050
Oakdale (G-12896)

Citizen Publishing Company ....G 570 454-5911
Hazleton (G-7495)

City Engraving & Awards LLC ....G 215 731-0200
Philadelphia (G-13547)

Clarion Safety Systems LLC ....E 570 296-5686
Milford (G-11157)

Classic Ink USA LLC ....G 724 482-1727
Butler (G-2389)

▲ Clayton Kendall Inc ....C 412 798-7120
Monroeville (G-11327)

Clockwise Tees ....G 412 727-1602
Pittsburg (G-14861)

CMI Printgraphix Inc ....G 717 697-4567
Mechanicsburg (G-10827)

Cobb & Dabaldo Printing Co ....G 724 942-0544
Canonsburg (G-2563)

Commercial Color Inc ....G 610 391-7444
Allentown (G-173)

Comporto LLC ....G 215 595-6224
Philadelphia (G-13564)

Composing Room Inc .... G 215 310-5559
Philadelphia ***(G-13565)***

Concepts .... G 717 600-2964
York ***(G-20432)***

Conrad Printing Co Inc .... G 717 637-5414
Hanover ***(G-6870)***

▲ Constantia Colmar LLC .... D 215 997-6222
Colmar ***(G-3411)***

Copy Corner Inc .... G 570 992-4769
Saylorsburg ***(G-17104)***

Copy Shop .... G 724 654-6515
New Castle ***(G-12078)***

Copy Stop Inc .... G 412 271-4444
Swissvale ***(G-18191)***

Cornerstone Printing Services .... G 717 626-7895
Lititz ***(G-10003)***

Corporate Distribution Ltd .... E 717 697-6900
Harrisburg ***(G-7109)***

Corporate Images Company .... G 610 439-7961
Allentown ***(G-182)***

Corporate Print Solutions Inc .... G 215 774-1119
Glenolden ***(G-6472)***

Cotton Bureau .... F 412 573-9041
Pittsburgh ***(G-14878)***

Country Tees & Grafx LLC .... G 570 568-0973
Lewisburg ***(G-9901)***

County Line Screenprinting .... G 570 758-5397
Dalmatia ***(G-3984)***

Courier Times Inc .... C 215 949-4219
Fairless Hills ***(G-5776)***

▲ Creative Impressions Advg LLC .... G 215 357-1228
Langhorne ***(G-9287)***

Creative Printing Co .... G 570 875-1811
Ashland ***(G-729)***

Creighton Printing Inc .... G 724 224-0444
Creighton ***(G-3882)***

Crogan Inc .... G 814 944-3057
Altoona ***(G-495)***

Cross Works Embroidery Sp Inc .... G 610 261-1690
Coplay ***(G-3642)***

Custom Design .... G 570 462-0041
Shenandoah ***(G-17493)***

Custom Printing Unlimited .... F 724 339-3000
New Kensington ***(G-12338)***

Cyberink LLC .... G 814 870-1600
Erie ***(G-5242)***

▲ D & Sr Inc .... D 717 569-3264
Lancaster ***(G-8989)***

Daisy Mae Prtg & Design LLC .... G 610 467-1989
Oxford ***(G-13077)***

Danowski .... G 717 328-5057
Mercersburg ***(G-10985)***

Darra Group Inc .... G 724 684-6040
Monessen ***(G-11298)***

David Bream .... G 717 334-1513
Gettysburg ***(G-6288)***

Decalcraft Corp .... G 215 822-0517
Hatfield ***(G-7332)***

Del Martin Screen Prtg & EMB .... F 717 597-5751
Greencastle ***(G-6606)***

Design Dynamics Inc .... F 724 266-4826
Ambridge ***(G-615)***

Diamond Graphics Inc .... E 610 269-7335
Downingtown ***(G-4223)***

Digital Color Graphics Inc .... E 215 942-7500
Southampton ***(G-17808)***

Digital Direct Tm Inc .... G 215 491-1725
Warrington ***(G-19114)***

Dilullo Graphics Inc .... E 610 775-4360
Mohnton ***(G-11262)***

Direct Mail Service Inc .... D 412 471-6300
Pittsburgh ***(G-14925)***

Dispatch Printing Inc .... F 814 870-9600
Erie ***(G-5248)***

Duff Al Bag Screenprinting Co .... G 717 249-8686
Carlisle ***(G-2708)***

Dupli Graphics Corporation .... E 610 644-4188
Malvern ***(G-10225)***

Dynamic Creations Screen Prtg .... G 724 229-1157
Washington ***(G-19166)***

Dynamic Graphic Finishing Inc .... E 215 441-8880
Horsham ***(G-7811)***

Dynamic Systems .... F 412 835-6100
Library ***(G-9954)***

▼ E P M Corporation .... F 814 825-6650
Erie ***(G-5252)***

Eagle Printery Inc .... F 724 287-0754
Butler ***(G-2397)***

▲ Easton Photoworks Inc .... G 610 559-1998
Easton ***(G-4671)***

Ed Cini Enterprises Inc .... G 215 432-3855
Plumsteadville ***(G-15809)***

Electronic Imaging Svcs Inc .... G 215 785-2284
Bristol ***(G-2139)***

Elliott Printing Services LLC .... F 610 614-1500
Bethlehem ***(G-1503)***

Embroidery Concepts .... G 724 225-3644
Washington ***(G-19168)***

Emerald Printing & Imaging .... G 814 899-6959
Erie ***(G-5258)***

Emp Sales Associates Inc .... G 412 731-9899
Pittsburgh ***(G-14972)***

Eps Printing Services Inc .... G 610 701-6403
West Chester ***(G-19551)***

Eric and Christopher LLC .... F 215 257-2400
Perkasie ***(G-13276)***

Etched In Time .... G 717 334-3600
Gettysburg ***(G-6290)***

Excel Sportswear Inc .... D 412 856-7616
Trafford ***(G-18455)***

Express Business Center Inc .... G 610 366-1970
Allentown ***(G-209)***

Expression Tees .... G 631 523-5673
Exton ***(G-5674)***

EZ Garment Printing Inc .... G 570 703-0961
Scranton ***(G-17236)***

Fast Ink Apparel .... G 717 328-5057
Mercersburg ***(G-10986)***

Fast Time Screen Printing .... F 724 463-9007
Indiana ***(G-8099)***

Fedex Office & Print Svcs Inc .... G 215 576-1687
Jenkintown ***(G-8287)***

Fedex Office & Print Svcs Inc .... F 412 788-0552
Pittsburgh ***(G-15009)***

Fedex Office & Print Svcs Inc .... F 412 366-9750
Pittsburgh ***(G-15011)***

Filmet Color Lab Inc .... D 724 275-1700
Cheswick ***(G-3108)***

First Class Specialties .... F 724 446-1000
Herminie ***(G-7570)***

Fleet Decal & Graphics Inc .... F 570 779-4343
Plymouth ***(G-15818)***

Focus One Promotions Inc .... G 610 459-7781
Aston ***(G-764)***

Forms Graphics LLC .... F 215 639-3504
Bensalem ***(G-1197)***

Forsythe Marketing .... G 717 764-9863
York ***(G-20486)***

Frontline Graphics Inc .... G 610 941-2750
Conshohocken ***(G-3550)***

G&R Designs LLC .... G 717 697-4538
Mechanicsburg ***(G-10848)***

Galaxy Products .... G 215 426-8640
Philadelphia ***(G-13740)***

Gambal Printing & Design .... G 570 265-8968
Towanda ***(G-18427)***

Gary James Designs .... G 814 623-2477
Bedford ***(G-1052)***

Gary Murelle .... G 570 888-7006
Sayre ***(G-17114)***

Gate 7 LLC .... F 717 593-0204
Greencastle ***(G-6614)***

General Graphics .... G 724 337-1470
New Kensington ***(G-12342)***

▲ General Press Corporation .... E 724 224-3500
Natrona Heights ***(G-11943)***

Gillespie Printing Inc .... F 610 264-1863
Allentown ***(G-232)***

Giving Tree Inc .... G 215 968-2487
New Hope ***(G-12303)***

Globe Print Shop .... G 570 454-8031
Hazleton ***(G-7499)***

Good .... G 717 271-2917
Stevens ***(G-18051)***

Grafika Commercial Prtg Inc .... B 610 678-8630
Reading ***(G-16396)***

Gran Enterprises .... G 215 634-2883
Philadelphia ***(G-13780)***

Grandshare LLC .... G 919 308-5115
Philadelphia ***(G-13781)***

Graphic Communications Inc .... F 215 441-5335
Warminster ***(G-18891)***

Graphic Connections .... G 814 948-5810
Cresson ***(G-3898)***

Graphic Garage .... G 724 274-4930
Cheswick ***(G-3110)***

Graphic Products Inc .... G 724 935-6600
Warrendale ***(G-19079)***

Graphic Search Associates .... G 610 344-0644
Glen Mills ***(G-6438)***

Great Northern Press of Wilkes .... E 570 822-3147
Wilkes Barre ***(G-19922)***

Greg Speece .... G 717 838-8365
Palmyra ***(G-13125)***

Gregory Troyer .... G 717 393-0233
Bird In Hand ***(G-1676)***

Griffith Pottery House Inc .... G 215 887-2222
Oreland ***(G-13021)***

Griffiths Printing Co .... F 610 623-3822
Lansdowne ***(G-9433)***

Guyasuta Printing Co .... G 412 782-0112
Pittsburgh ***(G-15068)***

H B Fowler Co Inc .... G 610 688-0567
Wayne ***(G-19334)***

Haines Printing Co .... G 814 725-1955
North East ***(G-12746)***

Harmony Labels Inc .... G 570 664-6700
East Stroudsburg ***(G-4616)***

Harte Hanks Inc .... C 570 826-0414
Hanover Township ***(G-6989)***

▲ HB Trading LLC .... G 610 212-4565
Wayne ***(G-19336)***

▲ Hds Marketing Inc .... E 412 279-1600
Pittsburgh ***(G-15084)***

Head To Toe Sportswear .... G 814 371-5119
Du Bois ***(G-4395)***

Heatha Henrys LLC .... G 215 968-2080
Newtown ***(G-12509)***

Heraclitean Corporation .... F 215 862-5518
New Hope ***(G-12305)***

Heritage Screen Printing Inc .... G 215 672-2382
Warrington ***(G-19120)***

Heritage Screen Printing Inc .... G 215 672-2382
Warminster ***(G-18894)***

Hesford Keystone Printing Co .... G 814 942-2911
Altoona ***(G-513)***

High Printing & Graphics Inc .... G 610 693-5399
Robesonia ***(G-16776)***

Hilden Enterprises Inc .... E 412 257-8459
Pittsburgh ***(G-15094)***

Hilsher Graphics Flp .... F 570 326-9159
Williamsport ***(G-20023)***

Himalayan Intl Ins of Yoga Ins .... G 570 634-5168
Honesdale ***(G-7716)***

Holly Label Company Inc .... E 570 222-9000
Nicholson ***(G-12615)***

Homer Reproductions Inc .... F 610 539-8400
Norristown ***(G-12667)***

▲ Hope Paige Designs LLC .... E 610 234-0093
Conshohocken ***(G-3558)***

Hot Off Press Inc .... F 610 473-5700
Boyertown ***(G-1916)***

Houck Printing Company Inc .... F 717 233-5205
Harrisburg ***(G-7152)***

House of Printing .... G 814 723-3701
Warren ***(G-19031)***

Howetts Custom Screen Printing .... G 610 932-3697
Oxford ***(G-13082)***

Hullihens Printery .... G 570 288-6804
Wilkes Barre ***(G-19925)***

Huntingdon Offset Printing Co .... G 814 641-7310
Huntingdon ***(G-7946)***

Icon Screenprinting Inc .... G 814 454-0086
Erie ***(G-5321)***

ID Technology LLC .... E 717 848-3875
York ***(G-20533)***

Impressions Printing & Pubg .... G 717 436-2034
Mifflintown ***(G-11123)***

Imprinted Promotions .... G 215 342-7226
Philadelphia ***(G-13852)***

Imprints Unlimited .... G 215 879-9484
Philadelphia ***(G-13853)***

In Stitches Embroidery .... G 570 368-5525
Montoursville ***(G-11441)***

Indiana Printing and Pubg Co .... C 724 349-3434
Indiana ***(G-8106)***

Industrial Nameplate Inc .... E 215 322-1111
Warminster ***(G-18898)***

Ink Spot Printing .... G 570 743-7979
Selinsgrove ***(G-17327)***

Inkster Prints .... G 267 886-0021
Philadelphia ***(G-13857)***

Instant Print .... G 724 261-5153
Greensburg ***(G-6677)***

Integra Graphix Inc .... G 717 626-7895
Lititz ***(G-10019)***

Interform Corporation .... F 610 566-1515
Media ***(G-10934)***

Interform Corporation .... C 412 221-7321
Bridgeville ***(G-2070)***

Interstate Cont New Castle LLC	E	724 657-3650	
New Castle (G-12106)			
Invitations Plus	G	412 421-7778	
Pittsburgh (G-15135)			
Ivy Graphics Inc	F	215 396-9446	
Warminster (G-18900)			
Izzo Embroidery & Screen Prtg	F	724 843-2334	
Beaver Falls (G-1001)			
J B Kreider Co Inc	F	412 246-0343	
Pittsburgh (G-15140)			
J Carlton Jones & Associates	G	267 538-5009	
Philadelphia (G-13881)			
J D Printing Inc	G	724 327-0006	
Pittsburgh (G-15141)			
J Davis Printing LLC	G	215 483-1006	
Philadelphia (G-13882)			
J L Screen Printing	G	724 696-5630	
Ruffs Dale (G-16873)			
Jankensteph Inc	G	412 446-2777	
Bridgeville (G-2073)			
Jaren Enterprises Inc	G	717 394-2671	
Lancaster (G-9072)			
Jayco Grafix Inc	D	610 678-2640	
Reinholds (G-16633)			
Jbr Associates Inc	G	215 362-1318	
Lansdale (G-9380)			
Jerome W Sinclair	G	215 477-3996	
Philadelphia (G-13894)			
Jerry James Trdng As Mnls BSC	G	425 255-0199	
Lafayette Hill (G-8882)			
John Schmidt Printing Co	G	215 624-2945	
Philadelphia (G-13905)			
Joseph H Tees & Son Inc	G	215 638-3368	
Bensalem (G-1214)			
Joseph Lagrua	G	814 274-7163	
Coudersport (G-3783)			
Kalil Printing Inc	E	610 948-9330	
Royersford (G-16854)			
▲ Kappa Graphics L P	C	570 655-9681	
Hughestown (G-7893)			
Kappa Publishing Group Inc	D	215 643-6385	
Blue Bell (G-1842)			
Karen Holbrook	G	724 628-3858	
Connellsville (G-3500)			
Kelly Line Inc	F	570 527-6822	
Pottsville (G-16085)			
Kemko Industries Inc	G	267 613-8651	
Upper Gwynedd (G-18695)			
Keystone Expressions Ltd	E	570 648-5785	
Coal Township (G-3279)			
Keystone Printed Spc Co LLC	C	570 457-8334	
Old Forge (G-12967)			
Keystone Prtg & Graphics Inc	G	570 648-5785	
Coal Township (G-3280)			
Killeen Printing Co	G	412 381-4090	
Pittsburgh (G-15177)			
Kim Kraft Inc	F	814 870-9600	
Fairview (G-5830)			
Kimkopy Printing Inc	G	814 454-6635	
Erie (G-5343)			
Kisel Printing Service Inc	E	570 489-7666	
Dickson City (G-4121)			
Kistler Printing Co Inc	F	570 421-2050	
East Stroudsburg (G-4622)			
Kunz Business Products Inc	C	814 643-4320	
Huntingdon (G-7949)			
Labelcraft Press Inc	G	215 257-6368	
Perkasie (G-13282)			
Labels By Pulizzi Inc	E	570 326-1244	
Williamsport (G-20034)			
Laser Imaging Systems Inc	E	717 266-1700	
Lancaster (G-9108)			
▲ Lebanon Valley Engraving Inc	F	717 273-7913	
Lebanon (G-9605)			
Lee Engraving Services Inc	G	412 788-4224	
Oakdale (G-12905)			
Lehigh Valley Printing LLC	G	610 905-5686	
Bethlehem (G-1559)			
Leisure Graphics Inc	G	610 692-9872	
West Chester (G-19591)			
◆ Lem Products Inc	E	800 220-2400	
Montgomeryville (G-11403)			
Lemac Packaging Inc	F	814 866-7469	
Erie (G-5362)			
Lemar Mast	G	610 286-0258	
Morgantown (G-11524)			
Letterpress Shop	G	412 231-2282	
Pittsburgh (G-15225)			
Levittown Printing Inc	G	215 945-8156	
Levittown (G-9845)			

Liberty Craftsmen Inc	G	717 871-0125	
Millersville (G-11211)			
Lighthouse Studios Inc	G	717 394-1300	
Lancaster (G-9111)			
Lime Sportswear	F	484 461-7000	
Secane (G-17318)			
Logo Depot Inc	G	610 543-3890	
Broomall (G-2294)			
Lowlander Corporation	G	412 221-1240	
Monaca (G-11291)			
Lsc Communications Us LLC	A	717 392-4074	
Lancaster (G-9116)			
Luminite Products Corporation	D	814 817-1420	
Bradford (G-1980)			
Luposello Enterprises	F	570 994-2500	
Milford (G-11162)			
Lycoming Screen Printing Co	G	570 326-3301	
Williamsport (G-20038)			
Lykens Corporation	F	814 375-9961	
Du Bois (G-4403)			
Major League Screen Prtg & EMB	F	717 270-9511	
Lebanon (G-9607)			
Marcus Uppe Inc	G	412 391-1218	
Pittsburgh (G-15254)			
▲ Marine Information Tech LLC	G	610 429-5180	
West Chester (G-19595)			
Marlin A Inch	G	570 374-1106	
Selinsgrove (G-17330)			
Marquee Graphx LLC	G	215 538-2992	
Quakertown (G-16212)			
Martin Design Group LLC	G	717 633-9214	
Hanover (G-6917)			
Mary J Backaroo	E	570 819-4809	
Wilkes Barre (G-19941)			
Mbr2 Graphic Services LLC	G	610 490-8996	
Norristown (G-12680)			
▲ McCarty Printing Corp	D	814 454-4561	
Erie (G-5385)			
McCourt Label Cabinet Company	D	800 458-2390	
Lewis Run (G-9877)			
Medianews Group Inc	C	717 637-3736	
Hanover (G-6919)			
▲ Memory Makers Ltd	E	215 679-3636	
Pennsburg (G-13250)			
Menu World Inc	G	267 784-8515	
Willow Grove (G-20127)			
Mercersburg Printing Inc	E	717 328-3902	
Mercersburg (G-10993)			
Mercersburg Printing Inc	G	717 762-8204	
Waynesboro (G-19418)			
Merrill Corporation	F	215 405-8443	
Philadelphia (G-14010)			
Michael Dahma Associates	G	412 607-1151	
Irwin (G-8183)			
Mifflin Press Inc	G	717 684-2253	
Columbia (G-3443)			
Mifflinburg Telegraph Inc	G	570 966-2255	
Mifflinburg (G-11099)			
Milan Printing	G	570 325-2649	
Jim Thorpe (G-8342)			
Miller Printing Inc	G	717 626-5800	
Ephrata (G-5128)			
Miller Printing & Publishing	E	814 425-7272	
Cochranton (G-3345)			
Miller Process Coatingmiller	G	724 274-5880	
Pittsburgh (G-15289)			
Mirage Advertising Inc	G	412 372-4181	
Monroeville (G-11345)			
Modern Reproductions Inc	F	412 488-7700	
Pittsburgh (G-15298)			
Montco Advertising Spc Inc	E	610 270-9800	
Norristown (G-12687)			
Montco Scientific Inc	G	215 699-8057	
Lansdale (G-9389)			
Moonlight Graphics Studio	G	570 322-6570	
Williamsport (G-20042)			
Morris Print Management	G	610 408-8922	
Berwyn (G-1369)			
Motson Graphics Inc	F	215 233-0500	
Flourtown (G-5988)			
Motto Graphics Inc	G	570 639-5555	
Dallas (G-3963)			
Mountain Side Scrn Prnt/Desgn	G	570 539-2400	
Mount Pleasant Mills (G-11728)			
Movad LLC	F	215 638-2679	
Plymouth Meeting (G-15858)			
Mri Flexible Packaging Company	E	800 448-8183	
Bristol (G-2170)			
▲ Mri Flexible Packaging Company	E	215 860-7676	
Bristol (G-2171)			

Multiscope Dcment Slutions Inc	E	724 743-1083	
Bridgeville (G-2080)			
Munro Prtg Graphic Design LLC	G	610 485-1966	
Marcus Hook (G-10451)			
Mystic Assembly & Dctg Co	E	215 957-0280	
Warminster (G-18926)			
Mystic Screen Printing and EMB	F	570 628-3520	
Pottsville (G-16089)			
N H Morgan Inc	G	412 561-1046	
Pittsburgh (G-15314)			
Nash Printing LLC	G	215 855-4267	
Lansdale (G-9391)			
National Cthlic Bthics Ctr Inc	F	215 877-2660	
Philadelphia (G-14054)			
National Decal Craft Corp	G	215 822-0517	
Hatfield (G-7371)			
National Film Converting Inc	F	800 422-6651	
Berwick (G-1338)			
National Imprint Corporation	E	814 239-5116	
Claysburg (G-3206)			
▼ National Ticket Company	G	570 672-2900	
Paxinos (G-13190)			
Navitor Inc	B	717 765-3121	
Waynesboro (G-19419)			
Nefra Communication Center	E	717 509-1430	
Lancaster (G-9144)			
Newell Brands Inc	G	814 278-6771	
State College (G-17997)			
Newtown Printing Corp	G	215 968-6876	
Newtown (G-12528)			
Nicholas Wohlfarth	F	412 373-6811	
Pittsburgh (G-15337)			
Nittany EMB & Digitizing	F	814 359-0905	
State College (G-17998)			
Nittany Printing and Pubg Co	G	814 238-5000	
State College (G-18000)			
Nk Graphics Inc	G	717 838-8324	
Palmyra (G-13127)			
NMB Signs Inc	F	412 344-5700	
Pittsburgh (G-15342)			
Northeast Discount Printing	G	215 742-3111	
Philadelphia (G-14081)			
Novelli Inc	F	215 739-3538	
Philadelphia (G-14088)			
Npc Inc	B	814 239-8787	
Claysburg (G-3207)			
Nu-Art Graphics Inc	F	610 436-4336	
West Chester (G-19608)			
▲ Okumus Enterprises Ltd	E	215 295-3340	
Fairless Hills (G-5790)			
Oldskool Produxins Inc	G	215 638-4804	
Bensalem (G-1236)			
Olenicks Prtg & Photography Sp	G	814 342-2853	
Philipsburg (G-14522)			
Omnipress Inc	G	610 631-2171	
Norristown (G-12698)			
On Demand Printing	G	610 696-2258	
West Chester (G-19610)			
Paper Magic Group Inc	B	570 644-0842	
Elysburg (G-4978)			
Paperia	G	215 247-8521	
Philadelphia (G-14116)			
Papyrus Inc	F	610 354-9480	
King of Prussia (G-8659)			
Parabo Press LLC	G	484 843-1230	
Philadelphia (G-14118)			
Paramount Games Inc	D	800 282-5766	
Wheatland (G-19840)			
Paravano Company Inc	G	215 659-4600	
Willow Grove (G-20132)			
Parc Productions	G	724 283-3300	
Butler (G-2431)			
Park Press Inc	G	724 465-5812	
Indiana (G-8116)			
Parkland Bindery Inc	G	610 433-6153	
Allentown (G-344)			
Parrot Graphics	G	570 746-1745	
New Albany (G-12014)			
Pathfnder Eqine Pblcations LLC	G	610 488-1282	
Mohrsville (G-11278)			
Patrick Mc Cool	F	814 359-2447	
Bellefonte (G-1110)			
Payne Printery Inc	D	570 675-1147	
Dallas (G-3965)			
PDQ Print Center	G	570 283-0995	
Kingston (G-8724)			
PDQ Printing Services	G	717 691-4777	
Mechanicsburg (G-10878)			
Pedco-Hill Inc	F	215 942-5193	
Warminster (G-18938)			

Pemcor Printing Company LLC ....D 717 898-1555
Lancaster (G-9162)

▲ Penn Graphics Equipment Inc ......E 610 488-7414
Hamburg (G-6848)

Penn Jersey Advance Inc ....B 610 258-7171
Easton (G-4742)

Penn Print & Graphics ....G 724 239-5849
Bentleyville (G-1273)

Penn Valley Printing Company ....G 215 295-5755
Morrisville (G-11576)

Pennsylvania Legislative Svcs ....G 717 236-6984
Harrisburg (G-7194)

Perkiomen Valley Printing Inc..............G 215 679-4000
East Greenville (G-4573)

Perry Printing Company ....G 717 582-2838
New Bloomfield (G-12030)

Phila Legnds of Jazz Orchestra ....F 215 763-2819
Philadelphia (G-14140)

Phoenix Printers Inc ....G 610 427-3069
Phoenixville (G-14569)

Photo Process Screen Mfg Co..............F 215 426-5473
Philadelphia (G-14172)

Pittsburgh Prtg Solutions LLC ....G 412 977-2026
Pittsburgh (G-15406)

Plymouth Graphics Inc ....G 570 779-9645
Plymouth (G-15820)

Preferred Sportswear Inc ....G 484 494-3067
Darby (G-4024)

Premier Graphics LLC ....F 814 894-2467
Sykesville (G-18202)

Premier Printing Services Inc ....G 724 588-5577
Greenville (G-6767)

Premier Screen Printing Inc ....G 717 560-9088
Lititz (G-10036)

Press Box Printing ....G 814 944-3057
Altoona (G-538)

Press Craft Printers Inc ....G 412 761-8200
Pittsburgh (G-15434)

Prime Packaging LLC ....D 215 499-0446
Yardley (G-20333)

Prince Printing ....G 412 233-3555
Clairton (G-3156)

Print and Sew Inc ....G 215 281-3909
Philadelphia (G-14201)

Print City Graphics Inc ....G 610 495-5524
Phoenixville (G-14570)

Print Factory ....G 570 961-2111
Scranton (G-17275)

Print Shop Inc ....G 570 784-4020
Bloomsburg (G-1796)

Print Tech Western PA ....F 412 963-1500
Pittsburgh (G-15441)

Print Works On Demand Inc ....G 717 545-5215
Harrisburg (G-7202)

Printers Printer Inc ....F 610 454-0102
Collegeville (G-3389)

Printfly Corporation ....E 800 620-1233
Philadelphia (G-14202)

Printmark Industries Inc ....E 570 501-0547
Hazleton (G-7521)

Prints & More By Holly ....G 814 453-5548
Erie (G-5438)

Printworx Inc ....G 412 939-6004
Pittsburgh (G-15446)

Prism Graphics Inc ....G 215 782-1600
Elkins Park (G-4910)

Pro Active Sports Inc ....G 814 943-4651
Altoona (G-539)

Pro Printing & Office LLC ....G 814 834-3006
Saint Marys (G-17010)

Professional Graphic Co ....E 724 318-8530
Sewickley (G-17405)

Promo Gear ....G 570 775-4078
Hawley (G-7436)

Promote ME Printing ....G 412 486-2504
Pittsburgh (G-15454)

Prosit LLC..G 610 430-1470
West Chester (G-19622)

Pure Screenprinting Inc ....G 412 246-2048
Pittsburgh (G-15457)

Quality Brand Printing Inc....................G 724 864-1731
Irwin (G-8194)

Quality Laser Alternatives....................G 610 373-0788
Reading (G-16480)

Quality Print Shop Inc ....G 570 473-1122
Northumberland (G-12874)

Quick Print Center PA............................G 717 637-2838
Hanover (G-6939)

R A Palmer Products Company ....F 412 823-5971
Monroeville (G-11351)

R C Print Specialist..............................G 814 942-1204
Altoona (G-540)

R Graphics Inc ....G 610 918-0373
West Chester (G-19625)

R R Donnelley & Sons Company ....G 610 688-9090
Wayne (G-19367)

R R Donnelley & Sons Company ....A 717 295-4002
Lancaster (G-9183)

R R Donnelley & Sons Company ....G 814 266-6031
Johnstown (G-8428)

R R Donnelley & Sons Company ....E 215 564-3220
Philadelphia (G-14226)

R R Donnelley & Sons Company ....C 610 391-0203
Breinigsville (G-2026)

R R Donnelley & Sons Company ....C 215 671-9500
Philadelphia (G-14225)

R&S Ventures LLC ....G 610 532-2950
Prospect Park (G-16118)

Rainbow Graphics Inc ....G 724 228-3007
Bentleyville (G-1275)

Randall A Reese ....G 570 748-6528
Lock Haven (G-10091)

Ras Sports Inc ....E 814 833-9111
Erie (G-5457)

Ravine Inc ....F 814 946-5006
Altoona (G-541)

RB Concepts LLC ....G 484 351-8211
Conshohocken (G-3598)

Ream Printing Co Inc ....E 717 764-5663
York (G-20653)

▲ Red Rose Screen Prtg Awrds Inc ......G 717 625-1581
Lititz (G-10039)

Reed & Witting Company ....E 412 682-1000
Pittsburgh (G-15476)

▲ Reed Drabick Inc ....G 215 794-2068
Doylestown (G-4334)

Richman Industries Inc ....G 717 561-1766
Harrisburg (G-7206)

Ricks Quick Printing Inc ....E 412 571-0333
Pittsburgh (G-15485)

Ridgways Inc ....E 215 735-8055
Philadelphia (G-14250)

Riecks Letter Service Inc ....F 610 375-8581
Reading (G-16498)

Riggans Advg Specialty Co ....F 724 654-5741
New Castle (G-12143)

Rite Envelope and Graphics Inc ....F 610 518-1601
Downingtown (G-4255)

Rmb Specialtees LLC ....G 570 578-8258
Beaver Meadows (G-1017)

RMH Image Group LLC..........................G 610 731-0050
Conshohocken (G-3602)

Robanco ....G 412 795-7444
Pittsburgh (G-15493)

Rock It Printwear ....G 717 697-3983
Mechanicsburg (G-10885)

Rockpetz Ventures LLC ....G 610 608-2788
Philadelphia (G-14256)

Roo Tees Inc ....G 412 279-9889
Carnegie (G-2788)

Rowe Printing Shop ....F 717 249-5485
Carlisle (G-2737)

Royalton Press Inc................................G 610 929-4040
Camp Hill (G-2516)

RR Donnelley & Sons Company ....C 412 241-8200
Pittsburgh (G-15500)

Rush Order Tees ....G 215 677-9200
Philadelphia (G-14266)

Sandt Printing Co Inc ....G 610 258-7445
Easton (G-4751)

Santees Love ....G 215 821-9679
Philadelphia (G-14280)

Schank Printing Inc ....F 610 828-1623
Conshohocken (G-3603)

School Colors Inc ....G 570 561-2632
Scranton (G-17284)

Schuylkill Valley Sports Inc ....D 717 627-0417
Lititz (G-10046)

Scream Graphix Inc ....G 215 638-3900
Philadelphia (G-14288)

Screen Images Inc ....G 610 926-3061
Shoemakersville (G-17575)

Screening Room Inc ....G 610 363-5405
Exton (G-5729)

Screenprinted Grafix Inc ....G 717 564-7464
Halifax (G-6830)

Scullin Group Inc ....G 215 640-3330
Philadelphia (G-14290)

Sea Group Graphics Inc ....G 215 805-0290
Huntingdon Valley (G-8036)

Seiders Printing Co Inc ....G 570 622-0570
Pottsville (G-16097)

Serigraph Factory ....G 570 647-0644
Honesdale (G-7723)

Serve Inc ....G 570 265-3119
Monroeton (G-11320)

Services Unlimited Mstr Prtg ....G 610 891-7877
Media (G-10949)

Shirt Gallery Inc ....G 215 364-1212
Feasterville Trevose (G-5929)

Sign Creators Inc ....G 412 461-3567
West Homestead (G-19720)

Silk Screen Printers ....G 717 761-1121
Camp Hill (G-2518)

Skylon Inc ....F 814 489-3622
Sugar Grove (G-18147)

Slavia Printing Co Inc ....G 412 343-4444
Pittsburgh (G-15545)

Slavic Group Inc....................................G 724 437-6756
Lemont Furnace (G-9737)

Smales Printery Inc...............................G 610 323-7775
Pottstown (G-16047)

Smith Prints Inc ....G 215 997-8077
Chalfont (G-2888)

Snyder Printing & Promotional ....G 215 358-3178
Ambler (G-602)

Specialty Group Printing Inc ....F 814 425-3061
Cochranton (G-3351)

Spencer Industries Inc ....F 215 634-2700
Philadelphia (G-14334)

Sportin My Stuff ....G 724 457-7005
Crescent (G-3889)

Sports Factory Promotions Inc ....G 724 847-2684
New Brighton (G-12042)

Spring Hill Laser Services....................E 570 689-0970
Lake Ariel (G-8892)

Standard Pennant Company Inc..........E 814 427-2066
Big Run (G-1657)

Star Printing Company ....G 717 456-5692
Delta (G-4063)

Stationary Engravers Inc ....F 215 739-3538
Philadelphia (G-14342)

Steele Print Inc ....G 724 758-6178
Ellwood City (G-4952)

Straz ....G 570 344-1513
Scranton (G-17294)

Sun Litho Print Inc ....F 570 421-3250
East Stroudsburg (G-4636)

Sunflower Graphics ....G 412 369-7769
Pittsburgh (G-15587)

Sunsational Signs Win Tinting ....G 610 277-4344
Norristown (G-12715)

Superior Printing & Engraving ....G 610 352-1966
Upper Darby (G-18692)

▲ Superpac Inc ....C 215 322-1010
Southampton (G-17838)

Susan Becker ....G 610 378-7844
Reading (G-16531)

SYN Apparel LLC ....G 484 821-3664
Bethlehem (G-1636)

Synergy Print Design LLC......................G 610 532-2950
Prospect Park (G-16121)

T N T Manufacturing ....G 724 745-6242
Canonsburg (G-2644)

T Shirt Loft ....G 724 452-4380
Zelienople (G-20823)

Taylor Communications Inc ....G 412 594-2800
Pittsburgh (G-15599)

Taylor Communications Inc ....D 717 755-1051
York (G-20684)

Teamwork Graphic Inc..........................G 570 368-2360
Montoursville (G-11452)

Technosystems Service Corp................F 412 288-2525
Pittsburgh (G-15602)

Teeship LLC ....G 717 497-2970
Hummelstown (G-7926)

Tex Styles LLC ....G 610 562-4939
Shoemakersville (G-17576)

◆ Tex Visions LLC ....D 717 240-0213
Carlisle (G-2741)

Third Dimension Spc LLC ....G 570 969-0623
Scranton (G-17301)

Thomas A Laskowski ....F 215 957-1544
Warminster (G-18981)

Thorn Hill Printing Inc ....E 724 774-4700
Freedom (G-6192)

Timber Skate Shop ....G 570 492-6063
Sunbury (G-18175)

TN TS..G 717 248-2278
Lewistown (G-9949)

Tokarick Printing Services ....F 570 385-4639
Schuylkill Haven (G-17168)
Tom Russell ....G 724 746-5029
Houston (G-7882)
Tookan Screening & Design Inc ....G 724 846-2264
Beaver Falls (G-1015)
Tor Industries Inc ....G 570 622-7370
Pottsville (G-16099)
Trans Atlantic Publications ....G 215 925-2762
Schwenksville (G-17180)
Trautman Associates Inc ....F 570 743-0430
Shamokin Dam (G-17429)
Tri-State Reprographics Inc ....F 412 281-3538
Pittsburgh (G-15647)
Triangle Poster and Prtg Co ....F 412 371-0774
Pittsburgh (G-15648)
Triple Play Sports ....F 215 923-5466
Philadelphia (G-14412)
Two Letters Ink ....E 717 393-8989
Lancaster (G-9225)
Two Paperdolls LLC ....F 610 293-4933
Wayne (G-19386)
Typecraft Press Inc ....E 412 488-1600
Pittsburgh (G-15663)
United Envelope LLC ....B 570 839-1600
Mount Pocono (G-11738)
Upper Perk Sportswear Inc ....G 215 541-3211
Pennsburg (G-13261)
Upper Room Inc ....F 724 437-5815
Uniontown (G-18646)
UPS Store 6410 ....G 484 816-0252
Aston (G-795)
Urban Enterprises T & M LLC ....G 215 485-5209
Feasterville Trevose (G-5936)
Urban Tees Inc DBA Soho G ....G 646 295-8923
Philadelphia (G-14432)
▲ Uticom Systems Inc ....E 610 857-2655
Coatesville (G-3328)
▼ Valley Business Services Inc ....F 610 366-1970
Trexlertown (G-18511)
Valley Forge Tape Label Co Inc ....D 610 524-8900
Exton (G-5745)
Valley Litho Inc ....G 610 437-5122
Whitehall (G-19892)
Valley Printing and Design Co ....G 814 536-5990
Johnstown (G-8442)
Vernon Printing Inc ....F 724 283-9242
Butler (G-2447)
Vertees ....G 570 630-0678
Hawley (G-7441)
Victory Athletics ....G 814 886-4866
Cresson (G-3900)
Vintage Color Graphics Inc ....G 215 646-6589
Ambler (G-604)
▲ Visual Resources LLC ....G 484 351-8100
Conshohocken (G-3616)
Vocam Corp ....G 215 348-7115
Doylestown (G-4344)
W L Fegley & Son Inc ....G 610 779-0277
Reading (G-16561)
Wakefoose Office Supply & Prtg ....G 814 623-5742
Bedford (G-1079)
Weaver Screen Printing Inc ....G 717 632-9158
Hanover (G-6972)
◆ Werzalit of America Inc ....D 814 362-3881
Bradford (G-1995)
Wick Copy Center ....G 814 942-8040
Altoona (G-558)
Williams Business Forms Ltd ....F 724 444-6771
Gibsonia (G-6359)
Williamsigns ....G 610 530-0300
Allentown (G-435)
Wise Business Forms Inc ....D 724 789-0010
Butler (G-2449)
Wise Printing Co Inc ....F 717 741-2751
York (G-20715)
World Chronicle Inc ....G 724 745-3808
Mc Donald (G-10584)
Wright Appellate Services LLC ....G 215 733-9870
Philadelphia (G-14490)
X-Deco LLC ....F 412 257-9755
Pittsburgh (G-15725)
York Graphic Services Co ....C 717 505-9701
York (G-20738)
Yurchak Printing Inc ....E 717 399-0209
Landisville (G-9269)

2761 Manifold Business Forms

Borough of Slippery Rock ....G 724 794-3823
Slippery Rock (G-17618)

Campbell Business Forms Inc ....G 610 356-0626
Newtown Square (G-12568)
Federal Business Products Inc ....D 570 454-2451
West Hazleton (G-19709)
Graphcom Inc ....C 800 699-1664
Gettysburg (G-6295)
Interform Corporation ....C 412 221-7321
Bridgeville (G-2070)
Phoenix Data Inc ....D 570 547-1665
Montgomery (G-11377)
RPM Nittany Printing ....G 814 941-7775
Altoona (G-545)
RR Donnelley & Sons Company ....E 610 391-8825
Allentown (G-380)
Safeguard Business Systems Inc .....C 215 631-7500
Lansdale (G-9408)
Star Continuous Card Systems ....G 800 458-1413
Glenmoore (G-6470)
Steele Print Inc ....G 724 758-6178
Ellwood City (G-4952)
Steve Schwartz Associates Inc ....E 412 765-3400
Pittsburgh (G-15583)
Taylor Communications Inc ....G 610 688-9090
Wayne (G-19378)
Techni-Forms Inc ....E 215 345-0333
Doylestown (G-4341)
The Reynolds and Reynolds Co ....E 717 767-5264
Emigsville (G-5001)
Tor Industries Inc ....G 570 622-7370
Pottsville (G-16099)
▲ Victor Printing Inc ....D 724 342-2106
Sharon (G-17444)
Wise Business Forms Inc ....D 724 789-0010
Butler (G-2449)

2771 Greeting Card Publishing

CSS Industries Inc ....C 610 729-3959
Plymouth Meeting (G-15840)
CSS Industries Inc ....G 570 275-5241
Danville (G-3999)
Jennifers Cards & Gifts ....G 412 462-8505
Homestead (G-7689)
▲ Paper Magic Group Inc ....C 570 961-3863
Moosic (G-11511)
Paper Magic Group Inc ....B 570 644-0842
Elysburg (G-4978)
Rekord Printing Co ....G 570 648-3231
Elysburg (G-4980)
▲ S E Hagarman Designs LLC ....G 717 633-5336
Hanover (G-6947)

2782 Blankbooks & Looseleaf Binders

Anthony J Mascherino PC ....G 610 269-6833
Downingtown (G-4210)
◆ Brodart Co ....D 570 326-2461
Williamsport (G-19995)
Crg Holding Inc ....G 215 569-9900
Philadelphia (G-13581)
Deluxe Corporation ....C 215 631-7500
Lansdale (G-9359)
Dialogue Institute ....G 215 204-7520
Philadelphia (G-13628)
Get Hip Inc ....G 412 231-4766
Pittsburgh (G-15048)
HW Marston & Co. ....G 610 328-6669
West Chester (G-19565)
Kunz Business Products Inc ....C 814 643-4320
Huntingdon (G-7949)
M & M Manufacturing Co ....E 724 274-0767
Cheswick (G-3111)
Scrapbook Station ....G 724 287-4311
Butler (G-2440)
Sperry Graphic Inc ....E 610 534-8585
Folcroft (G-6016)
Tamarack Packaging Ltd ....E 814 724-2860
Meadville (G-10798)
Wise Business Forms Inc ....D 724 789-0010
Butler (G-2449)

2789 Bookbinding

69th St Commercial Printers ....G 610 539-8412
Norristown (G-12627)
A J Printing ....F 610 337-7468
King of Prussia (G-8575)
Ace Bindery Corporation ....E 412 784-3669
Pittsburgh (G-14639)
▲ Acuity Finishing LLC ....D 724 935-9190
Cranberry Township (G-3798)
Afterprint Services Inc ....G 215 674-3082
Warminster (G-18823)

▲ Alcom Printing Group Inc ....C 215 513-1600
Harleysville (G-7015)
Allen L Geiser & Son Inc ....F 215 426-0211
Philadelphia (G-13367)
Apple Press Ltd ....E 610 363-1776
Exton (G-5644)
Benkalu Group Lmtd Ta Jaguar ....G 215 646-5896
Huntingdon Valley (G-7965)
Bestway Printing ....G 215 368-4140
Lansdale (G-9346)
Bindery Associates Inc ....E 717 295-7443
Lancaster (G-8953)
Bonnie Kaiser ....G 215 331-6555
Philadelphia (G-13471)
Book Bindery Co Inc ....G 717 244-4343
Dallastown (G-3972)
Bridget Morris ....G 215 828-9261
Philadelphia (G-13480)
◆ Brodart Co ....D 570 326-2461
Williamsport (G-19995)
▲ Brookshire Printing Inc ....E 717 392-1321
Lancaster (G-8961)
C3 Media LLC ....E 610 832-8077
Philadelphia (G-13492)
Castor Printing Company Inc ....F 215 535-1471
Philadelphia (G-13512)
Champ Printing Company Inc ....E 412 269-0197
Coraopolis (G-3675)
▲ Chernay Printing Inc ....D 610 282-3774
Coopersburg (G-3625)
Chrisber Corporation ....G 800 872-7436
West Chester (G-19525)
Christmas City Printing Co Inc ....E 610 868-5844
Bethlehem (G-1483)
Clinton Press Inc ....G 814 455-9089
Erie (G-5227)
Complete Hand Assembly Finshg .....E 215 634-7490
Philadelphia (G-13563)
Copy Management Inc ....G 610 993-8686
Malvern (G-10217)
Copy Management Inc ....F 215 269-5000
Huntingdon Valley (G-7972)
▲ D & Sr Inc ....D 717 569-3264
Lancaster (G-8989)
Davco Advertising Inc ....E 717 442-4155
Kinzers (G-8736)
Degadan Corp ....G 610 940-1282
Conshohocken (G-3537)
Digital-Ink Inc ....D 717 731-8890
Dillsburg (G-4126)
Dilullo Graphics Inc ....E 610 775-4360
Mohnton (G-11262)
Direct Mail Service Inc ....D 412 471-6300
Pittsburgh (G-14925)
Donald Blyler Offset Inc ....D 717 949-6831
Lebanon (G-9561)
Drexel Bindery Inc ....F 215 232-3808
Philadelphia (G-13645)
Fedex Office & Print Svcs Inc ....E 412 856-8016
Monroeville (G-11337)
Fedex Office & Print Svcs Inc ....G 215 386-5679
Philadelphia (G-13696)
Fedex Office & Print Svcs Inc ....F 412 788-0552
Pittsburgh (G-15009)
Fedex Office & Print Svcs Inc ....F 412 366-9750
Pittsburgh (G-15011)
Fox Bindery Inc ....C 215 538-5380
Lansdale (G-9369)
Fox Group Inc ....E 215 538-5380
Lansdale (G-9370)
Fox Specialties Inc ....G 215 822-5775
Lansdale (G-9371)
Grafika Commercial Prtg Inc ....B 610 678-8630
Reading (G-16396)
Griffiths Printing Co ....F 610 623-3822
Lansdowne (G-9433)
Guy Coder ....G 814 265-0519
Brockway (G-2227)
Guy Hrezik ....G 610 779-7609
Reading (G-16397)
Hapsco Design and Prtg Svcs ....G 717 564-2323
Harrisburg (G-7139)
Harmony Press Inc ....G 610 559-9800
Easton (G-4695)
Harper Printing Service ....G 412 884-2666
Pittsburgh (G-15082)
Hf Group LLC ....E 215 368-7308
Hatfield (G-7349)
Indiana Printing and Pubg Co ....C 724 349-3434
Indiana (G-8106)

S I C

Indus Graphics Inc .... G 215 443-7773
Warminster *(G-18896)*
Jim Mannello .... G 610 681-6467
Gilbert *(G-6362)*
John Galt Bndery Publ Svcs Inc .... E 724 733-1439
Export *(G-5611)*
Joseph Lagrua .... G 814 274-7163
Coudersport *(G-3783)*
K B Offset Printing Inc .... E 814 238-8445
State College *(G-17982)*
▲ **Kappa Graphics L P** .... C 570 655-9681
Hughestown *(G-7893)*
Killeen Printing Co .... G 412 381-4090
Pittsburgh *(G-15177)*
Kisel Printing Service Inc .... E 570 489-7666
Dickson City *(G-4121)*
Labels By Pulizzi Inc .... E 570 326-1244
Williamsport *(G-20034)*
Lancaster General Svcs Bus Tr .... F 717 544-5474
Lancaster *(G-9095)*
Leon Spangler .... F 570 837-7903
Middleburg *(G-11028)*
Lesko Enterprises Inc .... C 814 756-4030
Albion *(G-46)*
Library Bindery Co of PA Inc .... E 215 855-2293
Hatfield *(G-7365)*
Lsc Communications Us LLC .... A 717 392-4074
Lancaster *(G-9116)*
M & M Manufacturing Co .... E 724 274-0767
Cheswick *(G-3111)*
▲ **Maple Press Company** .... C 717 764-5911
York *(G-20580)*
▲ **McCarty Printing Corp** .... D 814 454-4561
Erie *(G-5385)*
McGivern Bindery Inc .... F 610 770-9611
Allentown *(G-312)*
Mdg Associates .... E 215 969-6623
Philadelphia *(G-14000)*
Mechling Associates Inc .... F 724 287-2120
Butler *(G-2422)*
Mifflinburg Telegraph Inc .... G 570 966-2255
Mifflinburg *(G-11099)*
Minuteman Press .... G 412 621-7456
Pittsburgh *(G-15294)*
Minuteman Press .... G 724 846-9740
Beaver Falls *(G-1005)*
Movad LLC .... F 215 638-2679
Plymouth Meeting *(G-15858)*
▲ **National Publishing Company** .... B 215 676-1863
Philadelphia *(G-14055)*
▼ **National Ticket Company** .... C 570 672-2900
Paxinos *(G-13190)*
Npc Inc .... B 814 239-8787
Claysburg *(G-3207)*
Oakwood Bindery .... E 717 396-9559
Lancaster *(G-9149)*
Pace Resources Inc .... E 717 852-1300
York *(G-20616)*
Parkland Bindery Inc .... G 610 433-6153
Allentown *(G-344)*
Partners Press Inc .... F 610 666-7960
Oaks *(G-12935)*
Payne Printery Inc .... D 570 675-1147
Dallas *(G-3965)*
Pikewood Inc .... F 610 974-8000
Bethlehem *(G-1597)*
Pittsburgh Binding .... E 412 481-8108
Pittsburgh *(G-15387)*
Pleasant Luck Corp .... G 215 968-2080
Newtown *(G-12537)*
Print Works On Demand Inc .... G 717 545-5215
Harrisburg *(G-7202)*
Print-O-Stat Inc .... E 717 812-9476
York *(G-20640)*
R R Donnelley & Sons Company .... C 215 671-9500
Philadelphia *(G-14225)*
Raff Printing Inc .... D 412 431-4044
Pittsburgh *(G-15466)*
Reed & Witting Company .... E 412 682-1000
Pittsburgh *(G-15476)*
Ricks Quick Printing Inc .... E 412 571-0333
Pittsburgh *(G-15485)*
Ridgways Inc .... E 215 735-8055
Philadelphia *(G-14250)*
Robert P Williams .... G 814 563-7660
Youngsville *(G-20775)*
▲ **Rowland Printing Inc** .... E 610 933-7400
Phoenixville *(G-14575)*
S G Business Services Inc .... G 215 567-7107
Philadelphia *(G-14271)*
Sir James Prtg & Bus Forms Inc .... G 724 339-2122
New Kensington *(G-12377)*
Slavia Printing Co Inc .... G 412 343-4444
Pittsburgh *(G-15545)*
Specialty Group Printing Inc .... F 814 425-3061
Cochranton *(G-3351)*
St Clair Graphics Inc .... F 570 253-6692
Honesdale *(G-7726)*
Stauffer Acquisition Corp .... E 717 569-3200
East Petersburg *(G-4591)*
Sun Litho Print Inc .... F 570 421-3250
East Stroudsburg *(G-4636)*
Third Dimension Spc LLC .... G 570 969-0623
Scranton *(G-17301)*
Tinicum Research Company .... F 215 766-7277
Plumsteadville *(G-15814)*
Typecraft Press Inc .... E 412 488-1600
Pittsburgh *(G-15663)*
▲ **Unity Printing Company Inc** .... E 724 537-5800
Latrobe *(G-9527)*
University Copy Service Inc .... G 215 898-5574
Philadelphia *(G-14429)*
Venango Training & Dev Ctr Inc .... D 814 676-5755
Seneca *(G-17371)*
Vocam Corp .... G 215 348-7115
Doylestown *(G-4344)*
Webb Communications Inc .... E 570 326-7634
Plymouth *(G-15824)*
▲ **Wert Bookbinding Inc** .... E 717 469-0626
Grantville *(G-6576)*

2791 Typesetting

A Stuart Morton Inc .... F 610 692-1190
West Chester *(G-19492)*
Adams Graphics Inc .... G 215 751-1114
Philadelphia *(G-13343)*
Adcomm Inc .... F 610 820-8565
Allentown *(G-115)*
▲ **Alcom Printing Group Inc** .... C 215 513-1600
Harleysville *(G-7015)*
AlphaGraphics .... G 717 731-8444
Mechanicsburg *(G-10819)*
American Brchure Catalogue Inc .... E 215 259-1600
Warminster *(G-18827)*
American Directory Systems Co .... F 610 640-1774
Malvern *(G-10185)*
Athens Reproduction .... G 610 649-5761
Ardmore *(G-701)*
Benkalu Group Lmtd Ta Jaguar .... G 215 646-5896
Huntingdon Valley *(G-7965)*
Bentley Grphic Cmmncations Inc .... E 610 933-7400
Phoenixville *(G-14531)*
Borris Information Group Inc .... G 717 285-9141
Mountville *(G-11790)*
Brindle Printing Co Inc .... G 724 658-8549
New Castle *(G-12067)*
▲ **Brookshire Printing Inc** .... E 717 392-1321
Lancaster *(G-8961)*
Bucks County Type & Design Inc .... F 215 579-4200
Newtown *(G-12499)*
Castor Printing Company Inc .... F 215 535-1471
Philadelphia *(G-13512)*
Champ Printing Company Inc .... E 412 269-0197
Coraopolis *(G-3675)*
Chandler-White Publishing Co .... G 312 907-3271
Philadelphia *(G-13524)*
▲ **Chernay Printing Inc** .... D 610 282-3774
Coopersburg *(G-3625)*
Chrisber Corporation .... E 800 872-7436
West Chester *(G-19525)*
Christmas City Printing Co Inc .... E 610 868-5844
Bethlehem *(G-1483)*
Clinton Press Inc .... G 814 455-9089
Erie *(G-5227)*
▲ **Clp Publications Inc** .... C 215 567-5080
Philadelphia *(G-13551)*
Colorworks Graphic Svcs Inc .... E 610 367-7599
Gilbertsville *(G-6371)*
Copy Corner Inc .... G 570 992-4769
Saylorsburg *(G-17104)*
Copy Management Inc .... G 610 993-8686
Malvern *(G-10217)*
Copy Management Inc .... F 215 269-5000
Huntingdon Valley *(G-7972)*
Copy Right Printing & Graphics .... G 814 838-6255
Erie *(G-5233)*
Copy Systems Group Inc .... G 215 355-2223
Southampton *(G-17806)*
Creative Graphics Inc .... E 610 973-8300
Allentown *(G-185)*
Davco Advertising Inc .... E 717 442-4155
Kinzers *(G-8736)*
David Bream .... G 717 334-1513
Gettysburg *(G-6288)*
Digital-Ink Inc .... D 717 731-8890
Dillsburg *(G-4126)*
Dilullo Graphics Inc .... E 610 775-4360
Mohnton *(G-11262)*
Dispatch Printing Inc .... F 814 870-9600
Erie *(G-5248)*
Donald Blyler Offset Inc .... D 717 949-6831
Lebanon *(G-9561)*
Engle Printing & Pubg Co Inc .... C 717 653-1833
Lancaster *(G-9009)*
Fedex Office & Print Svcs Inc .... E 412 856-8016
Monroeville *(G-11337)*
Fedex Office & Print Svcs Inc .... G 215 386-5679
Philadelphia *(G-13696)*
Fedex Office & Print Svcs Inc .... F 412 788-0552
Pittsburgh *(G-15009)*
Fedex Office & Print Svcs Inc .... E 412 835-4005
Pittsburgh *(G-15010)*
Fedex Office & Print Svcs Inc .... F 412 366-9750
Pittsburgh *(G-15011)*
Fidelity Graphics .... F 610 586-9300
Holmes *(G-7662)*
Gary Murelle .... G 570 888-7006
Sayre *(G-17114)*
Ggs Information Services Inc .... C 717 764-2222
York *(G-20499)*
Gillespie Printing Inc .... F 610 264-1863
Allentown *(G-232)*
Graphic Arts Camera Service .... G 610 647-6395
Malvern *(G-10242)*
Griffiths Printing Co .... F 610 623-3822
Lansdowne *(G-9433)*
Guy Coder .... G 814 265-0519
Brockway *(G-2227)*
Guy Hrezik .... G 610 779-7609
Reading *(G-16397)*
Harmony Press Inc .... E 610 559-9800
Easton *(G-4695)*
Harper Printing Service .... G 412 884-2666
Pittsburgh *(G-15082)*
Herrmann Printing & Litho Inc .... E 412 243-4100
Pittsburgh *(G-15093)*
I P Graphics Inc .... E 215 673-2600
Philadelphia *(G-13845)*
Indiana Printing and Pubg Co .... C 724 349-3434
Indiana *(G-8106)*
Indus Graphics Inc .... G 215 443-7773
Warminster *(G-18896)*
Infotechnologies Inc .... G 717 285-7105
Mountville *(G-11796)*
Interform Corporation .... C 412 221-7321
Bridgeville *(G-2070)*
James Saks .... G 570 343-8150
Scranton *(G-17247)*
Jim Mannello .... G 610 681-6467
Gilbert *(G-6362)*
Joseph Lagrua .... G 814 274-7163
Coudersport *(G-3783)*
K B Offset Printing Inc .... E 814 238-8445
State College *(G-17982)*
Keeney Printing Group Inc .... G 215 855-6116
Lansdale *(G-9383)*
Keystone Printed Spc Co LLC .... C 570 457-8334
Old Forge *(G-12967)*
Killeen Printing Co .... G 412 381-4090
Pittsburgh *(G-15177)*
Kisel Printing Service Inc .... E 570 489-7666
Dickson City *(G-4121)*
L D H Printing Ltd Inc .... F 609 924-4664
Morrisville *(G-11568)*
L G Graphics Inc .... F 412 421-6330
Pittsburgh *(G-15208)*
Labels By Pulizzi Inc .... E 570 326-1244
Williamsport *(G-20034)*
Magnus Group Inc .... E 717 764-5908
York *(G-20575)*
Malone & Blunt Inc .... G 215 563-1368
Philadelphia *(G-13988)*
▲ **Maple Press Company** .... C 717 764-5911
York *(G-20580)*
Matrix Publishing Services Inc .... F 717 764-9673
York *(G-20583)*
▲ **McCarty Printing Corp** .... D 814 454-4561
Erie *(G-5385)*
Me Ken + Jen Crative Svcs LLC .... G 215 997-2355
Chalfont *(G-2883)*

Medianews Group Inc ....C 717 637-3736
Hanover (G-6919)

Mifflinburg Telegraph Inc ....G 570 966-2255
Mifflinburg (G-11099)

Minuteman Press ....G 724 846-9740
Beaver Falls (G-1005)

Movad LLC ....F 215 638-2679
Plymouth Meeting (G-15858)

Multilingual Communications ....G 412 621-7450
Pittsburgh (G-15307)

Murrelle Printing Co Inc ....F 570 888-2244
Sayre (G-17119)

Nartak Media Group ....F 412 276-4000
Pittsburgh (G-15319)

▼ National Ticket Company ....C 570 672-2900
Paxinos (G-13190)

P A Hutchison Company ....C 570 876-4560
Mayfield (G-10542)

Partners Press Inc ....F 610 666-7960
Oaks (G-12935)

Payne Printery Inc ....D 570 675-1147
Dallas (G-3965)

Pikewood Inc ....F 610 974-8000
Bethlehem (G-1597)

Pindar Set Inc ....C 610 731-2921
King of Prussia (G-8662)

Pleasant Luck Corp ....G 215 968-2080
Newtown (G-12537)

Print Tech Western PA ....E 412 963-1500
Pittsburgh (G-15440)

Printworks & Company Inc ....E 215 721-8500
Lansdale (G-9400)

Professional Graphic Co ....E 724 318-8530
Sewickley (G-17405)

Public Image Printing Inc ....G 215 677-4088
Philadelphia (G-14216)

R Graphics Inc ....G 610 918-0373
West Chester (G-19625)

R R Donnelley & Sons Company ....C 215 671-9500
Philadelphia (G-14225)

Raff Printing Inc ....D 412 431-4044
Pittsburgh (G-15466)

Rainbow Graphics Inc ....G 724 228-3007
Bentleyville (G-1275)

Reed Tech & Info Svcs Inc ....B 215 441-6400
Horsham (G-7844)

Regency Typographic Svcs Inc ....F 215 425-8810
Philadelphia (G-14238)

Ricks Quick Printing Inc ....E 412 571-0333
Pittsburgh (G-15485)

Ridgways Inc ....E 215 735-8055
Philadelphia (G-14250)

▲ Rowland Printing Inc ....E 610 933-7400
Phoenixville (G-14575)

RR Donnelley & Sons Company ....D 412 281-7401
Pittsburgh (G-15501)

S G Business Services Inc ....G 215 567-7107
Philadelphia (G-14271)

Serve Inc ....G 570 265-3119
Monroeton (G-11320)

Specialty Group Printing Inc ....F 814 425-3061
Cochranton (G-3351)

Stauffer Acquisition Corp ....E 717 569-3200
East Petersburg (G-4591)

Third Dimension Spc LLC ....G 570 969-0623
Scranton (G-17301)

Towanda Printing Co Inc ....C 570 265-2151
Towanda (G-18436)

Type & Print Inc ....E 412 241-6070
Clinton (G-3267)

Typecraft Press Inc ....E 412 488-1600
Pittsburgh (G-15663)

United Partners Ltd ....F 570 288-7603
Taylor (G-18264)

▲ Unity Printing Company Inc ....E 724 537-5800
Latrobe (G-9527)

University Copy Service Inc ....G 215 898-5574
Philadelphia (G-14429)

Victorian Publishing Co Inc ....G 814 634-8321
Meyersdale (G-11020)

Vocam Corp ....G 215 348-7115
Doylestown (G-4344)

Wakefoose Office Supply & Prtg ....G 814 623-5742
Bedford (G-1079)

Webb Communications Inc ....E 570 326-7634
Plymouth (G-15824)

2796 Platemaking & Related Svcs

Aeco Service Inc ....G 610 372-0561
Pottstown (G-15941)

American Bank Note Holographic ....E 215 357-5300
Huntingdon Valley (G-7963)

Color House Company Ltd ....F 215 322-4310
Warminster (G-18845)

Color Scan LLC ....G 814 949-2032
Altoona (G-493)

▲ Colortech Inc ....E 717 450-5416
Lebanon (G-9556)

Dynamic Dies Inc ....E 724 325-1514
Pittsburgh (G-14947)

▼ E P M Corporation ....F 814 825-6650
Erie (G-5252)

Ggs Information Services Inc ....C 717 764-2222
York (G-20499)

Holly Label Company Inc ....E 570 222-9000
Nicholson (G-12615)

I P Graphics Inc ....E 215 673-2600
Philadelphia (G-13845)

Jbr Associates Inc ....G 215 362-1318
Lansdale (G-9380)

◆ Matthews International Corp ....E 412 442-8200
Pittsburgh (G-15264)

▲ McCarty Printing Corp ....D 814 454-4561
Erie (G-5385)

Movad LLC ....F 215 638-2679
Plymouth Meeting (G-15858)

Navitor Inc ....B 717 765-3121
Waynesboro (G-19419)

Payne Printery Inc ....D 570 675-1147
Dallas (G-3965)

▲ Photonis Defense Inc ....F 717 295-6000
Lancaster (G-9170)

Professional Graphic Co ....E 724 318-8530
Sewickley (G-17405)

R R Donnelley & Sons Company ....C 215 671-9500
Philadelphia (G-14225)

▼ Select Industries Inc ....G 724 654-7747
New Castle (G-12147)

Trophy Works ....G 412 279-0111
Carnegie (G-2799)

Van Eerden Coatings Company ....G 484 368-3073
Plymouth Meeting (G-15877)

W Graphics Digital Services ....G 610 252-3565
Easton (G-4773)

28 CHEMICALS AND ALLIED PRODUCTS

2812 Alkalies & Chlorine

◆ Arkema Delaware Inc ....A 610 205-7000
King of Prussia (G-8582)

Arkema Inc ....C 215 826-2600
Bristol (G-2109)

Arkema Inc ....B 610 878-6500
King of Prussia (G-8583)

FMC Asia-Pacific Inc ....E 215 299-6000
Philadelphia (G-13708)

◆ FMC Corporation ....B 215 299-6000
Philadelphia (G-13709)

FMC Corporation ....G 215 717-7500
Philadelphia (G-13710)

FMC Corporation ....B 800 526-3649
Philadelphia (G-13711)

Genesis Alkali Wyoming LP ....E 215 299-6904
Philadelphia (G-13751)

Genesis Alkali Wyoming LP ....D 215 845-4500
Philadelphia (G-13752)

Genesis Specialty Alkali LLC ....D 215 845-4550
Philadelphia (G-13753)

Occidental Chemical Corp ....F 610 327-4145
Pottstown (G-16022)

PPG Industries Inc ....A 412 434-3131
Pittsburgh (G-15425)

Univar USA Inc ....D 717 944-7471
Middletown (G-11084)

2813 Industrial Gases

Air Liquide America LP ....E 610 383-5500
Coatesville (G-3286)

Air Liquide Electronics US LP ....F 215 428-4600
Morrisville (G-11553)

Air Liquide Electronics US LP ....G 570 897-2000
Mount Bethel (G-11606)

Air Liquide Electronics US LP ....E 215 736-2796
Morrisville (G-11554)

Air Products and Chemicals Inc ....E 610 317-8706
Bethlehem (G-1445)

Air Products and Chemicals Inc ....D 724 226-4434
Creighton (G-3879)

Air Products and Chemicals Inc ....D 717 291-1617
Lancaster (G-8925)

Air Products and Chemicals Inc ....E 610 317-8715
Bethlehem (G-1446)

Air Products and Chemicals Inc ....B 570 467-2981
Tamaqua (G-18208)

Air Products and Chemicals Inc ....E 610 395-2101
Allentown (G-120)

Air Products and Chemicals Inc ....G 610 481-2057
Allentown (G-121)

Air Products and Chemicals Inc ....D 610 481-3706
Allentown (G-122)

◆ Air Products and Chemicals Inc ....A 610 481-4911
Allentown (G-119)

Air Products and Chemicals Inc ....E 724 266-1563
Leetsdale (G-9677)

Air Products LLC ....G 610 481-4911
Allentown (G-123)

Airgas Usa LLC ....G 814 437-2431
Franklin (G-6113)

Airgas Usa LLC ....G 215 766-8860
Plumsteadville (G-15806)

Alig LLC ....G 570 544-2540
Minersville (G-11253)

American Welding & Gas Inc ....F 570 323-8400
Williamsport (G-19985)

Bethlehem Hydrogen Inc ....G 610 762-1706
Northampton (G-12845)

Carbon Capture Scientific LLC ....G 412 854-6713
Bethel Park (G-1409)

Debbie Dengler ....G 717 755-5226
York (G-20446)

Glen Carbonic Gas Co ....F 570 779-1226
Plymouth (G-15819)

Hyrdogen Corp ....G 412 405-1000
McKeesport (G-10672)

Keiper Tech LLC ....G 717 938-1674
Etters (G-5551)

Linde Gas North America LLC ....F 610 539-6510
Norristown (G-12675)

Linde Gas North America LLC ....F 412 741-6613
Sewickley (G-17399)

Marcellus Shale Coalition ....F 412 706-5160
Pittsburgh (G-15251)

Matheson Tri-Gas Inc ....F 724 379-4104
Donora (G-4156)

Matheson Tri-Gas Inc ....F 814 781-6990
Saint Marys (G-16987)

Messer Gt & S ....F 717 232-3173
Harrisburg (G-7177)

Messer LLC ....G 610 317-8500
Bethlehem (G-1569)

Messer LLC ....F 412 351-4580
Braddock (G-1947)

Neon Moon ....G 814 332-0302
Meadville (G-10767)

Nitrogen ....G 440 208-7474
Yardley (G-20329)

Nitrogen (was Dorland ....G 215 928-2727
Philadelphia (G-14076)

Praxair Inc ....C 610 691-2474
Bethlehem (G-1603)

Praxair Inc ....D 610 759-3923
Stockertown (G-18066)

Praxair Inc ....E 610 530-3885
Allentown (G-354)

Praxair Distribution Inc ....G 570 655-3721
Pittston (G-15778)

Praxair Distribution Inc ....G 717 393-3681
Lancaster (G-9174)

Praxair Distribution Inc ....F 215 736-8005
Morrisville (G-11579)

Praxair Distribution Inc ....E 610 921-9230
Reading (G-16475)

Praxair Distribution Inc ....F 412 781-6273
Pittsburgh (G-15429)

R K Neon Company ....G 724 539-9605
Latrobe (G-9515)

▼ Specgas Inc ....G 215 355-2405
Warminster (G-18971)

◆ Spray Products Corporation ....D 610 277-1010
Plymouth Meeting (G-15872)

Ucg Georgia LLC ....G 610 515-8589
Bethlehem (G-1646)

United Hydrogen Group Inc ....F 866 942-7763
Canonsburg (G-2651)

Wilson Pdts Compressed Gas Co ....E 610 253-9608
Easton (G-4777)

2816 Inorganic Pigments

Amdex Metallizing Inc ....G...... 724 887-4977
Scottdale (G-17189)

Bailey Oxides LLC ....G...... 724 745-9500
Canonsburg (G-2548)

▼ Ceramic Color and Chem Mfg Co ...E...... 724 846-4000
New Brighton (G-12032)

Edgmont Metallic Pigment Inc ....F...... 610 429-1345
West Chester (G-19546)

Ferro Corporation ....E...... 412 331-3550
Pittsburgh (G-15015)

Ferro Corporation ....C...... 724 207-2152
Washington (G-19176)

Hammond Group Inc ....E...... 610 327-1400
Pottstown (G-15995)

▲ Impact Colors Inc ....E...... 302 224-8310
Conshohocken (G-3561)

◆ Lanxess Corporation ....A...... 800 526-9377
Pittsburgh (G-15219)

Lanxess Corporation ....E...... 412 809-4735
Burgettstown (G-2348)

Lord Corporation ....A...... 877 275-5673
Erie (G-5373)

◆ McAdoo & Allen Inc ....E...... 215 536-3520
Quakertown (G-16214)

◆ Penn Color Inc ....E...... 215 345-6550
Doylestown (G-4322)

Penn Color Inc ....C...... 215 997-2221
Hatfield (G-7380)

PVS Steel Services Inc ....C...... 412 929-0177
Pittsburgh (G-15458)

▲ Rebus Inc ....E...... 610 459-1597
West Chester (G-19628)

Rockwood Pigments Na Inc ....F...... 610 279-6450
King of Prussia (G-8670)

◆ Silberline Holding Co ....F...... 570 668-6050
Tamaqua (G-18224)

◆ Silberline Mfg Co Inc ....C...... 570 668-6050
Tamaqua (G-18225)

Silberline Mfg Co Inc ....D...... 570 668-6050
Lansford (G-9449)

▲ Sussex Wire Inc ....D...... 610 250-7750
Easton (G-4758)

Venator Americas LLC ....C...... 610 279-6450
King of Prussia (G-8695)

◆ Whitford Corporation ....D...... 610 286-3500
Elverson (G-4967)

2819 Indl Inorganic Chemicals, NEC

4 Elements of Life LLC ....G...... 215 668-1643
Philadelphia (G-13318)

Active Chemical Corporation ....F...... 215 322-0377
Langhorne (G-9272)

▲ Advanced Carbide Grinding Inc ....E...... 724 537-3393
Derry (G-4099)

▲ Afab Industrial Services Inc ....E...... 215 245-1280
Bensalem (G-1145)

Agsalt Processing ....G...... 717 632-9144
Gettysburg (G-6283)

Akzo Nobel Chemicals Inc ....D...... 724 258-6200
Monongahela (G-11303)

Albemarle Corporation ....C...... 814 684-4310
Tyrone (G-18575)

Alcoa Corporation ....G...... 412 553-4001
Pittsburgh (G-14661)

Alcoa Corporation ....E...... 412 315-2900
Pittsburgh (G-14662)

▲ Allegheny Alloys ....G...... 412 833-9733
Pittsburgh (G-14676)

◆ Almatis Inc ....D...... 412 630-2800
Leetsdale (G-9681)

Alpont II Inc ....E...... 814 456-7561
Erie (G-5182)

Altuglas International ....G...... 610 878-6423
King of Prussia (G-8578)

▲ Angstrom Sciences Inc ....E...... 412 469-8466
Duquesne (G-4495)

◆ Arkema Delaware Inc ....A...... 610 205-7000
King of Prussia (G-8582)

Arkema Inc ....C...... 610 582-1551
Birdsboro (G-1686)

Arkema Inc ....C...... 610 363-4100
Exton (G-5646)

Arkema Inc ....C...... 215 826-2600
Bristol (G-2109)

Avantor Inc ....F...... 610 386-1700
Radnor (G-16286)

◆ Avantor Performance Mtls LLC ....C...... 610 573-2600
Radnor (G-16287)

Avantor Prfmce Mtls Hldngs LLC ....G...... 610 573-2600
Radnor (G-16288)

Barbers Chemicals Inc ....F...... 724 962-7886
Sharpsville (G-17469)

Basic Carbide Corporation ....D...... 412 751-3774
Buena Vista (G-2340)

◆ Bayer Corporation ....A...... 412 777-2000
Pittsburgh (G-14750)

◆ Bethlehem Apparatus Co Inc ....F...... 610 838-7034
Hellertown (G-7554)

Bethlehem Apparatus Co Inc ....G...... 610 882-2611
Bethlehem (G-1460)

Bethlehem Apparatus Co Inc ....E...... 610 838-7034
Bethlehem (G-1461)

▲ Bimax Inc ....E...... 717 235-3136
Glen Rock (G-6453)

Blind and Vision Rehab ....F...... 412 325-7504
Homestead (G-7683)

▲ Bulk Chemicals Inc ....E...... 610 926-4128
Reading (G-16337)

Bulk Chemicals Inc ....F...... 610 926-4128
Mohrsville (G-11275)

◆ Calgon Carbon Corporation ....C...... 412 787-6700
Moon Township (G-11482)

Calgon Carbon Corporation ....F...... 724 218-7001
Coraopolis (G-3668)

Calgon Carbon Corporation ....D...... 412 771-4050
Pittsburgh (G-14801)

Calgon Carbon Corporation ....G...... 610 873-3071
Downingtown (G-4218)

Calgon Carbon Corporation ....F...... 412 269-4188
Pittsburgh (G-14802)

Calgon Carbon Corporation ....B...... 412 787-6700
Pittsburgh (G-14803)

Calgon Carbon Investments Inc ....E...... 412 787-6700
Coraopolis (G-3669)

Cantol USA Inc ....F...... 905 475-6141
Sharon Hill (G-17455)

Carbon Sales Inc ....E...... 570 823-7664
Wilkes Barre (G-19909)

▼ Ceramic Color and Chem Mfg Co .....E...... 724 846-4000
New Brighton (G-12032)

Chem Service Inc ....E...... 610 692-3026
West Chester (G-19523)

▲ Chemalloy Company LLC ....E...... 610 527-3700
Conshohocken (G-3527)

Chemtrade Chemicals Corp ....G...... 814 965-4118
Johnsonburg (G-8344)

Compound Technology Inc ....G...... 717 845-8646
York (G-20430)

Craft Products Co Inc ....G...... 412 821-8102
Pittsburgh (G-14885)

◆ Curtiss Laboratories Inc ....G...... 215 245-8833
Bensalem (G-1177)

Cyanide Vs Xaneria ....G...... 570 968-4522
Orwigsburg (G-13041)

D K P -Hardy Inc ....G...... 215 441-0383
Warminster (G-18854)

Deangelis Carbide Tooling Inc ....G...... 724 224-7280
Brackenridge (G-1938)

Dischem ....G...... 814 772-6603
Ridgway (G-16704)

Doctor Bart Ayurveda ....G...... 717 524-4208
Hanover (G-6878)

Dow Chemical Co ....G...... 610 244-7101
Lansdale (G-9363)

Dow Chemical Company ....D...... 215 641-7000
Collegeville (G-3375)

Dow Chemical Company ....C...... 610 775-6640
Reading (G-16365)

Dow Chemical Company ....G...... 215 592-3000
Philadelphia (G-13641)

Dow Chemical Company ....D...... 215 785-7000
Bristol (G-2133)

Dupont Specialty Pdts USA LLC ....E...... 570 265-6141
Towanda (G-18424)

Dyno Nobel Inc ....E...... 724 379-8100
Donora (G-4152)

E I Du Pont De Nemours & Co ....G...... 302 996-7165
Avondale (G-850)

Eco Services Operations Corp ....D...... 610 251-9118
Malvern (G-10227)

Edt ....G...... 724 217-4008
Greensburg (G-6663)

Element 1 LLC ....G...... 570 593-8177
Schuylkill Haven (G-17156)

Element Granite & Quartz ....G...... 215 437-9368
Philadelphia (G-13666)

Element Roofing LLC ....G...... 610 737-0641
Bethlehem (G-1502)

▲ Elements For Motion LLC ....G...... 215 768-1641
Kulpsville (G-8826)

Elements Home Accents LLC ....G...... 412 521-0724
Pittsburgh (G-14963)

Elements of Love ....G...... 267 262-9796
Philadelphia (G-13668)

Elements Skin Care LLC ....G...... 814 254-4227
Johnstown (G-8371)

◆ Elkem Materials Inc ....G...... 412 299-7200
Moon Township (G-11486)

▲ EMD Performance Materials Corp ....G...... 888 367-3275
Philadelphia (G-13672)

▲ Envirotrol Inc ....E...... 412 741-2030
Rochester (G-16785)

Esm Group Inc ....E...... 724 538-8974
Mars (G-10496)

Evonik Corporation ....G...... 610 990-8100
Chester (G-3050)

Evoqua Water Technologies LLC ....E...... 724 827-8181
Darlington (G-4028)

Fedchem LLC ....F...... 610 837-1808
Bethlehem (G-1507)

◆ Fedchem LLC ....G...... 610 837-1808
Bethlehem (G-1508)

Filmtronics Inc ....G...... 724 352-3790
Butler (G-2401)

▲ Fine Grinding Corporation ....E...... 610 828-7250
Conshohocken (G-3547)

▲ Fisher Scientific Company LLC ....B...... 724 517-1500
Pittsburgh (G-15019)

FMC Asia-Pacific Inc ....G...... 215 299-6000
Philadelphia (G-13708)

Gb Biosciences Corporation ....G...... 713 453-7281
Willow Grove (G-20118)

◆ Gelest Inc ....E...... 215 547-1015
Morrisville (G-11561)

Gelest Realty Inc ....G...... 215 547-1015
Morrisville (G-11562)

Gelest Technologies Inc ....G...... 215 547-1015
Morrisville (G-11563)

▲ General Carbide Corporation ....C...... 724 836-3000
Greensburg (G-6668)

Geo Specialty Chemicals Inc ....E...... 215 773-9280
Horsham (G-7821)

Geo Specialty Chemicals Inc ....D...... 610 433-6331
Allentown (G-229)

▲ Gharda Chemicals Limited ....G...... 215 968-9474
Newtown (G-12505)

Gilberton Energy Corporation ....G...... 570 874-1602
Gilberton (G-6368)

GKN Sinter Metals LLC ....C...... 814 781-6500
Kersey (G-8561)

Grotto ....G...... 610 570-9060
Allentown (G-238)

▲ Haycarb Usa Inc ....G...... 281 292-8678
Oakdale (G-12900)

Helena Agri-Enterprises LLC ....G...... 814 632-5177
Warriors Mark (G-19142)

Helena Chemical Company ....G...... 724 538-3304
Evans City (G-5559)

▲ Hydro Carbide Inc ....C...... 724 539-9701
Latrobe (G-9480)

Indocarb AC LLC ....G...... 412 928-4970
Pittsburgh (G-15117)

Indspec Chemical Corporation ....E...... 412 826-3666
Pittsburgh (G-15118)

◆ Indspec Chemical Corporation ....B...... 724 756-2370
Petrolia (G-13305)

◆ International Raw Mtls Ltd ....E...... 215 928-1010
Philadelphia (G-13867)

▲ Interstate Chemical Co Inc ....C...... 724 981-3771
Hermitage (G-7588)

Interstate Chemical Co Inc ....E...... 724 813-2576
Erie (G-5331)

Interstate Chemical Co Inc ....G...... 724 774-1669
Beaver (G-985)

J & B Blending & Technologies ....G...... 412 331-2850
Mc Kees Rocks (G-10615)

Kimre Inc ....G...... 305 233-4249
Bensalem (G-1215)

L R M Inc ....G...... 215 721-4840
Souderton (G-17747)

Lamberti Usa Incorporated ....G...... 610 862-1400
Conshohocken (G-3571)

◆ Lanxess Corporation ....A...... 800 526-9377
Pittsburgh (G-15219)

▲ Laurel Products LLC ....C...... 610 286-2534
Elverson (G-4964)

Livent Corporation ....A...... 215 299-6000
Philadelphia (G-13973)

◆ Lockhart Chemical Company ....E 724 444-1900
Gibsonia (G-6344)

Lockhart Company ....E 724 444-1900
Gibsonia (G-6345)

Lockhart Holdings Inc ....E 724 444-1900
Gibsonia (G-6346)

Lonza Inc ....C 570 321-3900
Williamsport (G-20035)

Luxfer Magtech Inc ....E 570 668-0001
Tamaqua (G-18219)

▲ Macherey-Nagel Inc ....F 484 821-0984
Bethlehem (G-1564)

Magnesium Elektron ....F 570 668-0001
Tamaqua (G-18220)

Metal Exchange Corporation ....G 724 373-8471
Greenville (G-6755)

◆ Metallurgical Products Company ......E 610 696-6770
West Chester (G-19601)

Milazzo Industries Inc ....E 570 722-0522
Pittston (G-15767)

Monomer-Polymer and Dajac Labs ......G 215 364-1155
Ambler (G-592)

Multisorb Tech Intl LLC ....G 412 521-3685
Pittsburgh (G-15309)

◆ Murlin Chemical Inc ....F 610 825-1165
Conshohocken (G-3579)

National Magnetics Group Inc ....G 610 867-7600
Bethlehem (G-1579)

Neo-Solutions Inc ....E 724 728-7360
Beaver (G-988)

Niagara Holdings Inc ....A 610 651-4200
Malvern (G-10286)

Occidental Chemical Corp ....F 610 327-4145
Pottstown (G-16022)

Omya PCC USA Inc ....E 814 965-3400
Johnsonburg (G-8348)

Oxbow Activated Carbon LLC ....F 724 791-2411
Emlenton (G-5013)

▼ Penn United Technologies Inc ....A 724 352-1507
Cabot (G-2460)

◆ Peroxychem LLC ....E 267 422-2400
Philadelphia (G-14138)

Phoenix Cfb Inc ....G 215 957-0500
Warminster (G-18941)

Powsus Inc ....F 610 296-2237
Chesterbrook (G-3095)

PPG Architectural Finishes Inc ....D 610 380-6200
Downingtown (G-4250)

PQ Corporation ....E 610 447-3900
Chester (G-3059)

PQ Corporation ....D 610 651-4600
Conshohocken (G-3591)

◆ PQ Corporation ....C 610 651-4200
Malvern (G-10299)

PQ Export Company ....G 610 651-4200
Malvern (G-10300)

PQ Group Holdings Inc ....F 610 651-4400
Malvern (G-10301)

PQ Holding Inc ....F 610 651-4400
Malvern (G-10302)

▲ Pressure Chemical Co ....E 412 682-5882
Pittsburgh (G-15435)

R H Carbide & Epoxy Inc ....G 724 356-2277
Hickory (G-7630)

◆ Reaxis Inc ....E 412 517-6070
Mc Donald (G-10580)

Ridgway Industries Inc ....F 610 259-5534
Lansdowne (G-9442)

◆ Rohm and Haas Company ....A 989 636-1000
Collegeville (G-3392)

Royal Chemical Company Ltd ....F 570 421-7850
East Stroudsburg (G-4634)

Russell Standard Corporation ....G 724 748-3700
Mercer (G-10973)

▲ Saint-Gobain Ceramics Plas Inc ......A 508 795-5000
Valley Forge (G-18711)

Siem Tool Company Inc ....E 724 520-1904
Latrobe (G-9520)

◆ Silberline Mfg Co Inc ....C 570 668-6050
Tamaqua (G-18225)

Silberline Mfg Co Inc ....D 570 668-6050
Lansford (G-9449)

Solvay USA Inc ....C 609 860-4000
Pittsburgh (G-15555)

Solvay USA Inc ....E 570 748-4450
Castanea (G-2811)

Solvay USA Inc ....D 215 781-6001
Bristol (G-2199)

▲ Specialty Chemical Systems Inc ......F 610 323-2716
Pottstown (G-16050)

Specialty Minerals Inc ....B 860 824-5435
Bethlehem (G-1624)

Specialty Minerals Inc ....B 610 861-3400
Bethlehem (G-1625)

Specialty Minerals Inc ....C 212 878-1800
Bethlehem (G-1626)

▲ Ssw International Inc ....E 412 922-9100
Pittsburgh (G-15572)

Synergy Core Elements ....G 267 885-5832
New Hope (G-12316)

Tetra Technologies Inc ....E 717 545-3580
Harrisburg (G-7230)

Tetra Technologies Inc ....E 610 853-1679
Havertown (G-7430)

Tetra Technologies Inc ....E 570 659-5357
Mansfield (G-10426)

▲ Thermo Shandon Inc ....G 412 788-1133
Pittsburgh (G-15615)

Uct Inc ....E 215 781-9255
Bristol (G-2213)

Ultra Chem LLC ....G 215 778-5967
Warminster (G-18990)

Univar USA Inc ....D 717 944-7471
Middletown (G-11084)

▲ Valtech Corporation ....E 610 705-5900
Pottstown (G-16064)

◆ Van Air Inc ....E 814 774-2631
Lake City (G-8909)

◆ Vexcon Chemicals Inc ....E 215 332-7709
Philadelphia (G-14443)

▼ Vision Technology UHS LLC ....G 717 465-0694
Hanover (G-6969)

VWR Corporation ....C 610 386-1700
Radnor (G-16304)

◆ Westinghouse Electric Co LLC ....A 412 374-2020
Cranberry Township (G-3865)

Westinghouse Electric Co LLC ....D 412 256-1085
Pittsburgh (G-15710)

Zeolyst International ....E 610 651-4200
Malvern (G-10352)

2821 Plastics, Mtrls & Nonvulcanizable Elastomers

3M Company ....F 610 497-7032
Aston (G-748)

7106 Dow Chemical ....F 610 244-6000
Collegeville (G-3365)

A Schulman Inc ....G 610 398-5900
Allentown (G-112)

Advanced Solutions Network LLC ....F 814 464-0791
Erie (G-5175)

Advansix Inc ....C 215 533-3000
Philadelphia (G-13349)

▲ Afab Industrial Services Inc ....E 215 245-1280
Bensalem (G-1145)

AGC Chemicals Americas Inc ....E 610 380-6200
Downingtown (G-4209)

Air Products and Chemicals Inc ....E 724 266-1563
Leetsdale (G-9677)

Akzo Nobel Coatings Inc ....E 610 372-3600
Reading (G-16314)

▲ Anholt Technologies Inc ....F 610 268-2758
Avondale (G-848)

▲ Apexco-Ppsi LLC ....G 937 935-0164
Horsham (G-7787)

▲ APT Advanced Polymer Tech Corp ..D 724 452-1330
Harmony (G-7066)

Arlanxeo USA Holdings Corp ....G 412 809-1000
Pittsburgh (G-14723)

Arlanxeo USA LLC ....B 412 809-1000
Pittsburgh (G-14724)

Ashland LLC ....E 215 446-7900
Philadelphia (G-13420)

Asm Industries Inc ....E 717 656-2166
Leola (G-9769)

Atochem Intl Inc/Polymers Div ....G 610 582-1551
Birdsboro (G-1687)

Atrp Solutions Inc ....G 412 735-4799
Pittsburgh (G-14737)

Audia International Inc ....F 724 228-1260
Washington (G-19151)

◆ Bayer Corporation ....A 412 777-2000
Pittsburgh (G-14750)

Bayer Cropscience Holding Inc ....G 412 777-2000
Pittsburgh (G-14752)

Bayer Intl Trade Svcs Corp ....G 412 777-2000
Pittsburgh (G-14755)

Bellisimo LLC ....B 215 781-1700
Croydon (G-3912)

Berry Global Films LLC ....C 570 474-9700
Mountain Top (G-11752)

◆ Biocoat Incorporated ....E 215 734-0888
Horsham (G-7799)

Blair Tool and Plastics Co LLC ....G 814 695-2726
East Freedom (G-4561)

Braskem America Inc ....E 412 208-8100
Pittsburgh (G-14790)

Braskem America Inc ....E 610 497-8378
Marcus Hook (G-10438)

▲ Braskem America Inc ....C 215 841-3100
Philadelphia (G-13478)

▲ C E N Inc ....E 412 749-0442
Leetsdale (G-9686)

▲ C P Converters Inc ....D 717 764-1193
York (G-20415)

C Purolite Corporation ....A 610 668-9090
Bala Cynwyd (G-874)

Cambria Plastics LLC ....G 814 472-6189
Ebensburg (G-4783)

▼ Cashel LLC ....G 610 853-8227
Havertown (G-7417)

Cellomics Inc ....E 412 770-2500
Pittsburgh (G-14833)

Chase Corporation ....E 412 828-1500
Pittsburgh (G-14840)

▲ Chestnut Ridge Foam Inc ....C 724 537-9000
Latrobe (G-9464)

Cott Manufacturing Company ....E 724 625-3730
Glassport (G-6411)

◆ Covestro LLC ....A 412 413-2000
Pittsburgh (G-14882)

Cpg International I Inc ....G 570 346-8797
Scranton (G-17222)

◆ Creative Pultrusions Inc ....E 814 839-4186
Alum Bank (G-560)

Custom Kitchens Inc ....G 814 833-5338
Erie (G-5238)

Ddp Specialty Electronic MA ....E 610 244-6000
Collegeville (G-3374)

Desavino & Sons Inc ....E 570 383-3988
Olyphant (G-12988)

Dow Chemical Company ....E 610 775-6640
Reading (G-16365)

Dow Chemical Company ....G 215 592-3000
Philadelphia (G-13641)

Dow Chemical Company ....G 215 785-7000
Bristol (G-2133)

Eagle Spinco Inc ....G 412 434-3131
Pittsburgh (G-14952)

Eastman Chemical Company ....E 412 384-2520
Jefferson Hills (G-8274)

Eastman Chemical Company ....A 423 229-2000
Jefferson Hills (G-8275)

Eastman Chemical Resins Inc ....E 412 384-2520
Jefferson Hills (G-8276)

▲ Edlon Inc ....D 610 268-3101
Avondale (G-852)

Efs Plastics US Inc ....G 570 455-0925
Hazle Township (G-7454)

Em-Bed-It & Co Inc ....F 412 781-8585
Pittsburgh (G-14966)

▲ Esschem Inc ....D 610 497-9000
Linwood (G-9989)

Evolution Mlding Solutions Inc ....E 814 807-1982
Meadville (G-10722)

Execumold Inc ....E 814 864-2535
Waterford (G-19262)

Extruded Plastic Solutions ....G 610 756-6602
Kempton (G-8491)

▲ Fenner Precision Inc ....C 800 327-2288
Manheim (G-10383)

Foam Fabricators Inc ....F 814 838-4538
Erie (G-5298)

◆ Forta Corporation ....E 724 458-5221
Grove City (G-6785)

▲ FP Woll & Company ....E 215 934-5966
Philadelphia (G-13717)

▲ G Scudese Consultants Inc ....F 610 250-7800
Nazareth (G-11968)

Gampe Machine & Tool Co Inc ....E 814 696-6206
Hollidaysburg (G-7648)

▲ Gellner Industrial LLC ....G 570 668-8800
Tamaqua (G-18210)

▲ General Polymeric Corporation ....D 610 374-5171
Reading (G-16390)

Geo Specialty Chemicals Inc ....E 215 773-9280
Ambler (G-579)

Graham Recycling Company LP ....D 717 852-7744
York (G-20512)

S I C

◆ Haysite Reinforced Plas LLC ....D...... 814 868-3691
Erie *(G-5313)*

▲ Highline Polycarbonate LLC ....G...... 267 847-0056
Philadelphia *(G-13824)*

Honeywell International Inc ....A...... 215 533-3000
Philadelphia *(G-13832)*

▲ Hydra-Matic Packing Co Inc ....E...... 215 676-2992
Huntingdon Valley *(G-7995)*

ICO Polymers North America Inc ....C...... 610 398-5900
Allentown *(G-250)*

Idemia America Corp ....C...... 610 524-2410
Exton *(G-5694)*

Illinois Tool Works Inc ....D...... 215 855-8450
Montgomeryville *(G-11399)*

▲ Impact Guard LLC ....E...... 724 318-8800
Leetsdale *(G-9695)*

Imperial Tool Co ....G...... 215 947-7650
Huntingdon Valley *(G-7996)*

▲ Inolex Group Inc ....D...... 215 271-0800
Philadelphia *(G-13859)*

Insta-Mold Products Inc ....F...... 610 935-7270
Oaks *(G-12933)*

J-M Manufacturing Company Inc ....C...... 814 432-2166
Franklin *(G-6141)*

J-M Manufacturing Company Inc ....G...... 814 337-7675
Cochranton *(G-3343)*

Jsp International Group Ltd ....G...... 610 651-8600
Wayne *(G-19342)*

▲ Jsp International LLC ....F...... 610 651-8600
Wayne *(G-19343)*

Jsp International LLC ....C...... 724 477-5100
Butler *(G-2415)*

Jsp Resins LLC ....F...... 610 651-8600
Wayne *(G-19344)*

▲ Knf Corporation ....E...... 570 386-3550
Tamaqua *(G-18213)*

Kozmer Technologies Ltd ....G...... 610 358-4099
Newtown Square *(G-12580)*

▲ Laminations Inc ....C...... 570 876-8199
Archbald *(G-690)*

◆ Lanxess Corporation ....A...... 800 526-9377
Pittsburgh *(G-15219)*

Lanxess Corporation ....E...... 412 809-4735
Burgettstown *(G-2348)*

Lehigh Valley Plastics Inc ....D...... 484 893-5500
Bethlehem *(G-1558)*

Lord Corporation ....B...... 814 868-0924
Erie *(G-5371)*

Mitsubishi Chemical Advncd Mtr ....G...... 610 320-6600
Reading *(G-16446)*

◆ Multi-Plastics Extrusions Inc ....C...... 570 455-2021
Hazleton *(G-7512)*

National Plas Acquisition LLC ....G...... 610 250-7800
Easton *(G-4731)*

National Plastics ....G...... 610 252-6172
Bethlehem *(G-1583)*

North Amrcn Specialty Pdts LLC ....D...... 484 253-4545
Wayne *(G-19360)*

Northern Lehigh Erectors Corp ....E...... 610 791-4200
Allentown *(G-335)*

▼ Nova Chemicals Inc ....C...... 412 490-4000
Moon Township *(G-11497)*

Nova Chemicals Inc ....B...... 724 770-5542
Monaca *(G-11293)*

Occidental Chemical Corp ....F...... 610 327-4145
Pottstown *(G-16022)*

▲ Ocp Inc ....E...... 814 827-3661
Titusville *(G-18389)*

Old Glory Corp ....F...... 724 423-3580
Mount Pleasant *(G-11709)*

Ono Industries Inc ....E...... 717 865-6619
Ono *(G-13004)*

▲ Opco Inc ....E...... 724 537-9300
Latrobe *(G-9507)*

Otoole Plastic Surgery Dr ....E...... 412 345-1615
Pittsburgh *(G-15365)*

Pak Innovations Inc ....G...... 215 723-0498
Souderton *(G-17759)*

▲ Palram 2000 Inc ....E...... 610 285-9918
Kutztown *(G-8852)*

◆ Palram Americas Inc ....D...... 610 285-9918
Kutztown *(G-8853)*

▲ Penn Foam Corporation ....D...... 610 797-7500
Allentown *(G-348)*

Pepperell Braiding Company Inc ....D...... 814 368-4454
Bradford *(G-1986)*

▲ Performance Additives LLC ....F...... 215 321-4388
Yardley *(G-20332)*

Piccolo Group Inc ....G...... 610 738-7733
West Chester *(G-19617)*

▲ Plasti-Coat Corp ....E...... 475 235-2761
Sellersville *(G-17357)*

▲ Plastic Dip Moldings Inc ....E...... 215 766-2020
Quakertown *(G-16229)*

Plastic Profiles LLC ....G...... 717 593-9200
Greencastle *(G-6626)*

◆ Pleiger Plastics Company ....D...... 724 228-2244
Washington *(G-19216)*

Poly Lite Windshield Repr Sups ....G...... 717 845-1596
York *(G-20631)*

Poly Sat Inc ....E...... 215 332-7700
Philadelphia *(G-14187)*

▲ Polymer Instrumentation & C ....E...... 814 357-5860
State College *(G-18007)*

◆ Polymeric Systems Inc ....D...... 610 286-2500
Elverson *(G-4965)*

Polyone Corporation ....F...... 570 474-7770
Mountain Top *(G-11770)*

Polyone Corporation ....F...... 610 317-3300
Bethlehem *(G-1602)*

▼ Polytek Development Corp ....E...... 610 559-8620
Easton *(G-4743)*

Polyvisions Holdings Inc ....F...... 717 266-3031
Manchester *(G-10361)*

PPG Architectural Finishes Inc ....D...... 610 380-6200
Downingtown *(G-4250)*

PPG Industries Inc ....A...... 412 434-3131
Pittsburgh *(G-15425)*

Prestige Institute For Plastic ....G...... 215 275-1011
Doylestown *(G-4328)*

◆ Purolite Corporation ....C...... 610 668-9090
Bala Cynwyd *(G-889)*

Purolite Corporation ....C...... 610 668-9090
Philadelphia *(G-14218)*

Quadrant Holding Inc ....C...... 724 468-7062
Delmont *(G-4054)*

◆ Ranbar Electrical Mtls LLC ....E...... 724 864-8200
Harrison City *(G-7251)*

Ravago Americas LLC ....G...... 215 591-9641
Ambler *(G-601)*

Rebtech Corporation ....F...... 570 421-6616
Stroudsburg *(G-18138)*

Riverdale Global LLC ....G...... 610 358-2900
Aston *(G-792)*

Sabic Innovative Plas US LLC ....C...... 610 383-8900
Exton *(G-5728)*

◆ Sartomer Company Divison Total ....E...... 610 692-8401
West Chester *(G-19637)*

Sealguard Inc ....F...... 724 625-4550
Gibsonia *(G-6351)*

◆ Sekisui Polymr Innovations LLC ....B...... 570 387-6997
Bloomsburg *(G-1801)*

◆ Simtech Industrial Pdts Inc ....F...... 215 547-0444
Levittown *(G-9863)*

◆ Smooth-On Inc ....C...... 610 252-5800
Macungie *(G-10159)*

Soroka Sales Inc ....E...... 412 381-7700
Pittsburgh *(G-15560)*

Steinmetz Inc ....E...... 570 842-6161
Roaring Brook Twp *(G-16760)*

Sunnyside Supply Inc ....G...... 724 947-9966
Slovan *(G-17630)*

▲ T P Schwartz Inc ....G...... 724 266-7045
Pittsburgh *(G-15594)*

Taylor Chemical Inc ....F...... 570 562-7771
Taylor *(G-18262)*

Technetics ....G...... 215 855-9916
Hatfield *(G-7399)*

Teflex Inc ....F...... 570 945-9185
Factoryville *(G-5762)*

▲ TMI International LLC ....D...... 412 787-9750
Pittsburgh *(G-15628)*

Total Systems Technology Inc ....F...... 412 653-7690
Pittsburgh *(G-15633)*

◆ Trinseo LLC ....C...... 610 240-3200
Berwyn *(G-1378)*

Trinseo Materials Finance Inc ....C...... 610 240-3200
Berwyn *(G-1379)*

Trinseo S A ....E...... 610 240-3200
Berwyn *(G-1380)*

True Form Plastics LLC ....G...... 717 875-4521
Strasburg *(G-18096)*

▲ Ultra-Poly Corporation ....E...... 570 897-7500
Portland *(G-15940)*

Ultra-Poly Corporation ....G...... 570 784-1586
Bloomsburg *(G-1805)*

Usnr LLC ....G...... 724 929-8405
Belle Vernon *(G-1090)*

W L Gore & Associates Inc ....A...... 610 268-1864
Landenberg *(G-9255)*

Washington Penn Plastic Co Inc ....E...... 724 206-2120
Washington *(G-19242)*

2822 Synthetic Rubber (Vulcanizable Elastomers)

▲ APT Advanced Polymer Tech Corp ..D...... 724 452-1330
Harmony *(G-7066)*

Covestro LLC ....F...... 215 428-4400
Morrisville *(G-11556)*

◆ Lanxess Corporation ....A...... 800 526-9377
Pittsburgh *(G-15219)*

Lanxess Corporation ....E...... 412 809-4735
Burgettstown *(G-2348)*

▲ Lebanon Gasket and Seal Inc ....G...... 717 274-3684
Lebanon *(G-9600)*

◆ Morton International LLC ....C...... 989 636-1000
Collegeville *(G-3384)*

◆ Palmer International Inc ....E...... 610 584-4241
Skippack *(G-17602)*

Palmer International Inc ....E...... 610 584-3204
Worcester *(G-20225)*

▲ Pelmor Laboratories Inc ....E...... 215 968-3334
Newtown *(G-12533)*

▼ Polytek Development Corp ....E...... 610 559-8620
Easton *(G-4743)*

◆ Sartomer Company Divison Total ....E...... 610 692-8401
West Chester *(G-19637)*

◆ Smooth-On Inc ....C...... 610 252-5800
Macungie *(G-10159)*

◆ SRC Elastomerics Inc ....D...... 215 335-2049
Philadelphia *(G-14336)*

2823 Cellulosic Man-Made Fibers

Atwater Inc ....D...... 570 779-9568
Plymouth *(G-15815)*

▲ C P Converters Inc ....D...... 717 764-1193
York *(G-20415)*

Carpenter Co ....C...... 814 944-8612
Altoona *(G-486)*

◆ Forta Corporation ....E...... 724 458-5221
Grove City *(G-6785)*

▲ FP Woll & Company ....E...... 215 934-5966
Philadelphia *(G-13717)*

Ne Fibers LLC ....E...... 610 366-8600
Allentown *(G-326)*

Quik Piks & Paks Inc ....G...... 570 459-3099
Hazle Township *(G-7477)*

2824 Synthetic Organic Fibers, Exc Cellulosic

Abtrex Industries Inc ....E...... 724 266-5425
Leetsdale *(G-9676)*

Arlanxeo USA Holdings Corp ....G...... 412 809-1000
Pittsburgh *(G-14723)*

Arlanxeo USA LLC ....B...... 412 809-1000
Pittsburgh *(G-14724)*

▲ Gudebrod Inc ....C...... 610 327-4050
Pottstown *(G-15993)*

Honeywell International Inc ....A...... 215 533-3000
Philadelphia *(G-13832)*

James R Hanlon Inc ....E...... 610 631-9999
Eagleville *(G-4514)*

Quadrant Holding Inc ....C...... 724 468-7062
Delmont *(G-4054)*

Solutia Inc ....C...... 724 258-6200
Monongahela *(G-11316)*

◆ SRC Elastomerics Inc ....D...... 215 335-2049
Philadelphia *(G-14336)*

2833 Medicinal Chemicals & Botanical Prdts

▲ Boiron Inc ....E...... 610 325-7464
Newtown Square *(G-12567)*

Croda Inc ....E...... 570 893-7650
Mill Hall *(G-11175)*

Di Chem Concentrate Inc ....E...... 717 938-8391
Lewisberry *(G-9883)*

Douglas Laboratories ....E...... 412 494-0122
Pittsburgh *(G-14935)*

Frontida Biopharm Inc ....E...... 215 288-6500
Philadelphia *(G-13728)*

Frontida Biopharm Inc ....G...... 610 232-0112
Philadelphia *(G-13729)*

Gilmore & Assoc Inc ....F...... 215 345-4330
Doylestown *(G-4301)*

▲ Goodstate Inc ....G...... 215 366-2030
Glenside *(G-6523)*

▲ Herb Penn Co Ltd ....E...... 215 632-6100
Philadelphia *(G-13816)*

Ilera Healthcare LLC ....G...... 610 440-8443
Plymouth Meeting (G-15850)

▲ Kauffmans Animal Health Inc ....G... 717 274-3676
Lebanon (G-9588)

Lampire Biological Labs Inc ....E... 215 795-2838
Ottsville (G-13065)

Longevity Prmier Ntraceuticals ....E... 877 529-1118
Philadelphia (G-13975)

▲ Muscle Gauge Nutrition LLC ....F... 484 840-8006
West Chester (G-19602)

Nabi Genmed LLC ....G... 610 258-5627
Easton (G-4729)

Nabriva Therapeutics Us Inc ....F... 610 816-6640
King of Prussia (G-8653)

Natures Bounty Co ....F... 570 384-2270
Hazle Township (G-7470)

Niramaya Inc ....G... 267 799-2120
Wallingford (G-18785)

Prwt Services Inc ....D... 570 275-2220
Riverside (G-16758)

▲ Reaction Nutrition LLC ....F... 412 276-7800
Carnegie (G-2784)

Sani-Brands Inc ....G... 610 841-1599
Allentown (G-382)

SDC Nutrition Inc ....F... 412 276-7800
Carnegie (G-2791)

Specialty Measurements Inc ....F... 908 534-1500
Bethlehem (G-1623)

Stemmetry ....G... 678 770-6781
Sewickley (G-17413)

◆ Teva Pharmaceuticals Usa Inc ....B... 215 591-3000
North Wales (G-12834)

Thg/Paradigm Health Intl Inc ....G... 610 998-1080
Oxford (G-13093)

▲ V L H Inc ....B... 800 245-4440
Pittsburgh (G-15688)

Venatorx Pharmaceuticals Inc ....G... 610 644-8935
Malvern (G-10339)

2834 Pharmaceuticals

▲ A & C Pharmtech Inc ....G... 215 968-5605
Newtown (G-12493)

Abbott Laboratories ....E... 610 265-9100
King of Prussia (G-8576)

Abbott Laboratories ....G... 570 347-0319
Scranton (G-17205)

Abbott Laboratories ....D... 717 545-8159
Harrisburg (G-7080)

Abbott Laboratories ....G... 610 444-9818
Kennett Square (G-8500)

▲ Accucorp Packaging Inc ....C... 215 673-3375
Philadelphia (G-13339)

Aclaris Therapeutics Inc ....D... 484 324-7933
Wayne (G-19293)

Actavis Pharma Inc ....F... 847 377-5508
North Wales (G-12785)

Actavis Pharma Inc ....C... 847 855-0812
North Wales (G-12786)

Adapt Pharma Inc ....F... 844 232-7811
Radnor (G-16285)

Aevi Genomic Medicine Inc ....F... 610 254-4201
Wayne (G-19294)

Akamara Therapeutics Inc ....G... 617 888-9191
Philadelphia (G-13360)

▲ Alacer Corp ....C... 717 258-2000
Carlisle (G-2688)

Alcobra Inc ....G... 610 940-1630
Conshohocken (G-3517)

Allergan Inc ....G... 610 262-4844
Northampton (G-12842)

Allergan Inc ....F... 610 352-4992
Upper Darby (G-18677)

Allergan Inc ....D... 610 691-2880
Center Valley (G-2824)

Alliance Contract Pharma LLC ....F... 215 256-5920
Harleysville (G-7017)

Alliqua Biomedical Inc ....D... 215 702-8550
Langhorne (G-9275)

Allpure Technologies Inc ....G... 717 624-3241
New Oxford (G-12404)

Almac Central Management LLC ....C... 215 660-8500
Souderton (G-17721)

Almac Clinical Services LLC ....F... 610 666-9500
Souderton (G-17722)

Almac Group Incorporated ....A... 215 660-8500
Souderton (G-17723)

▲ Almac Pharma Services LLC ....C... 610 666-9500
Audubon (G-823)

Almirall LLC ....D... 610 644-7000
Exton (G-5641)

Amchemteq Inc ....G... 814 234-0123
State College (G-17940)

Amedra Pharmaceuticals LLC ....F... 215 259-3601
Fort Washington (G-6062)

American Medical Systems Inc ....F... 512 808-4974
Malvern (G-10187)

American Pharmaceutical ....G... 610 366-9000
Allentown (G-136)

American Regent Inc ....E... 610 650-4200
Norristown (G-12634)

Angiotech Pharmaceuticals Inc ....G... 610 404-1000
Reading (G-16322)

Applied Clinical Concepts Inc ....G... 215 660-8500
Souderton (G-17725)

Aquacap Pharmaceutical Inc ....G... 610 361-2800
Chadds Ford (G-2847)

Aquamed Technologies Inc ....G... 215 970-7194
Yardley (G-20296)

AR Scientific Inc ....G... 215 288-6500
Philadelphia (G-13402)

AR Scientific Inc ....G... 215 807-1312
Philadelphia (G-13403)

Aralez Pharmaceuticals MGT Inc ....G... 609 917-9330
Royersford (G-16843)

Aralez Pharmaceuticals R&D Inc ....G... 609 917-9330
Royersford (G-16844)

Aralez Pharmaceuticals US Inc ....F... 609 917-9330
Royersford (G-16845)

Arbutus Biopharma Corporation ....F... 267 469-0914
Warminster (G-18828)

Arbutus Biopharma Inc ....G... 215 675-5921
Warminster (G-18829)

Arx LLC ....E... 717 253-7979
Glen Rock (G-6451)

Astrazeneca Pharmaceuticals LP.........G... 215 501-1739
Bensalem (G-1150)

Aumapharma LLC ....G... 215 345-4150
Doylestown (G-4272)

Auxilium Pharmaceuticals LLC ....C... 484 321-5900
Malvern (G-10189)

▲ Axcentria Pharmaceutical LLC ....F... 215 453-5055
Telford (G-18268)

Azur Pharma Inc ....G... 215 832-3750
Philadelphia (G-13434)

◆ Barr Laboratories Inc ....C... 215 591-3000
North Wales (G-12790)

Barr Laboratories Inc ....C... 845 362-1100
North Wales (G-12791)

Bayer Corporation ....A... 717 866-2141
Myerstown (G-11875)

◆ Bayer Corporation ....A... 412 777-2000
Pittsburgh (G-14750)

Bayer Data Center Pittsburgh ....G... 412 920-2950
Pittsburgh (G-14753)

Bayer Healthcare LLC ....B... 717 866-2141
Myerstown (G-11876)

Bayer Healthcare LLC ....C... 412 777-2000
Pittsburgh (G-14754)

Bayer Hlthcare Phrmcticals Inc ....C... 717 713-7173
Mechanicsburg (G-10823)

Becton Dickinson and Company ....G... 610 948-3492
Royersford (G-16846)

Best Medical International Inc ....D... 412 312-6700
Pittsburgh (G-14764)

Bilcare Inc ....C... 610 935-4300
Phoenixville (G-14532)

Bioleap Inc ....G... 609 575-8645
Doylestown (G-4276)

Biomed Healthcare Inc ....G... 888 244-2340
Sharon Hill (G-17453)

Biotest Pharmaceuticals Corp ....G... 570 383-5341
Dickson City (G-4119)

▲ Boiron Inc ....E... 610 325-7464
Newtown Square (G-12567)

Braeburn Pharmaceuticals Inc ....D... 609 751-5375
Plymouth Meeting (G-15835)

Brandywine Pharmaceuticals Inc ....F... 800 647-0172
West Chester (G-19513)

Bristol-Myers Squibb Company ....D... 609 818-5513
Southampton (G-17800)

Btg International Inc ....D... 610 943-6000
West Conshohocken (G-19686)

Bvi C/O Genco ....G... 712 228-3338
Lebanon (G-9550)

Caliber Therapeutics Inc ....F... 215 862-5797
New Hope (G-12300)

Canticle Pharmaceuticals Inc ....G... 404 380-9263
Conshohocken (G-3526)

Capnostics LLC ....G... 610 442-1363
Doylestown (G-4288)

Catalent Cts Inc ....C... 816 767-6013
Philadelphia (G-13513)

Catalent Micron Tech Inc ....D... 610 251-7400
Malvern (G-10200)

Catalent Pharma Solutions Inc ....E... 215 637-3565
Philadelphia (G-13514)

Catalent Pharma Solutions Inc ....E... 215 613-3001
Philadelphia (G-13515)

Ccn America LP ....G... 412 349-6300
Pittsburgh (G-14831)

Centocor Inc ....G... 215 325-2297
Horsham (G-7802)

Central Admxture Phrm Svcs Inc ....E... 215 706-4001
Horsham (G-7803)

Cephalon Inc ....B... 610 738-6410
West Chester (G-19521)

▲ Cephalon Inc ....A... 610 344-0200
Malvern (G-10203)

Cephalon Clinical Partners LP...........G... 610 883-5260
West Chester (G-19522)

Ch James G Thornton ....G... 412 207-2153
Pittsburgh (G-14836)

Chemgenex Pharmaceuticals Inc........F... 650 804-7660
Malvern (G-10207)

◆ Cherokee Pharmaceuticals LLC ....B... 570 271-4195
Riverside (G-16757)

Chiltern International Inc................E... 484 679-2400
King of Prussia (G-8592)

Choice Therapeutics Inc ....G... 508 384-0425
Langhorne (G-9284)

Chromatan Corporation ....F... 617 529-0784
Ambler (G-573)

Cima Labs Inc ....E... 763 315-4178
North Wales (G-12796)

Cima Labs Inc ....D... 763 488-4700
North Wales (G-12795)

Clinical Supplies MGT LLC ....F... 215 596-4356
Malvern (G-10212)

Coeptis Pharmaceuticals Inc ....G... 724 290-1183
Wexford (G-19795)

Cognition Therapeutics Inc ....G... 412 481-2210
Pittsburgh (G-14865)

Colorcon Inc ....E... 215 256-7700
Harleysville (G-7029)

◆ Colorcon Inc ....B... 215 699-7733
West Point (G-19758)

Colorcon Inc ....F... 267 695-7700
Chalfont (G-2867)

Complete Intrvnous Access Svcs ....F... 724 226-2618
Creighton (G-3881)

Complexa Inc ....G... 412 727-8727
Berwyn (G-1356)

Connie Fogarty ....G... 610 647-3172
Malvern (G-10216)

Cool Bio Inc ....G... 973 452-8309
Wayne (G-19314)

▼ Copperhead Chemical Co Inc ....E... 570 386-6123
Tamaqua (G-18209)

Correvio LLC ....F... 610 833-6050
Chadds Ford (G-2850)

Corry Opothecary ....G... 814 452-4220
Corry (G-3755)

Cortendo AB Inc ....G... 610 254-9200
Trevose (G-18490)

Cslb Holdings Inc ....C... 610 878-4000
King of Prussia (G-8602)

Curtis Pharmaceutical Service ....F... 724 223-1114
Washington (G-19160)

Cutanea Life Sciences Inc..............E... 484 568-0100
Chesterbrook (G-3090)

Cutix Inc ....G... 610 246-7518
Wayne (G-19316)

Daniel Baum Company ....F... 717 509-5724
Lancaster (G-8991)

Danmir Therapeutics LLC ....G... 610 896-8826
Haverford (G-7407)

Dbex Tek LLC ....G... 267 566-0354
Bensalem (G-1180)

▲ Delavau LLC ....G... 215 671-1400
Philadelphia (G-13617)

Dercher Enterprises Inc ....E... 610 734-2011
Upper Darby (G-18685)

Dermavance Pharmaceuticals Inc ....F... 610 727-3935
Berwyn (G-1360)

Design Space Inpharmatics LLC ....G... 215 272-4275
Green Lane (G-6587)

▼ Digestive Care Inc ....E... 610 882-5950
Bethlehem (G-1496)

Dolphin Group ....G... 610 640-7513
Paoli (G-13139)

Double DS Roadhouse LLc G 814 395-3535
Confluence *(G-3464)*
Douglas Pharma Us Inc F 267 317-2010
Warminster *(G-18862)*
Drugdev Inc F 888 650-1860
Wayne *(G-19320)*
Duchesnay Usa Inc G 484 380-2641
Bryn Mawr *(G-2321)*
Edward A Shelly Vmd G 610 826-2793
Palmerton *(G-13104)*
Egalet Corporation E 610 833-4200
Wayne *(G-19322)*
Egalet Ltd F 484 875-3095
Wayne *(G-19323)*
Egalet US Inc F 610 833-4200
Wayne *(G-19324)*
Endo Finance Co G 484 216-0000
Malvern *(G-10231)*
Endo Health Solutions Inc B 484 216-0000
Malvern *(G-10232)*
Endo Pharmaceutical Inc G 484 216-2759
Horsham *(G-7815)*
▲ **Endo Pharmaceuticals Inc** F 484 216-0000
Malvern *(G-10233)*
Endo Phrmcticals Solutions Inc E 484 216-0000
Malvern *(G-10234)*
Epharmasolutions G 610 832-2100
Conshohocken *(G-3543)*
Escalon Medical Corp E 610 688-6830
Wayne *(G-19325)*
Eurand Pharmaceuticals Inc E 937 898-9669
Yardley *(G-20309)*
▲ **Eusa Pharma (usa) Inc** E 215 867-4900
Langhorne *(G-9295)*
▲ **Fallien Cosmeceuticals Ltd** F 610 630-6800
Norristown *(G-12655)*
Femmephrma Cnsmr Halthcare LLC G 610 995-0801
Wayne *(G-19328)*
Fiberopticscom G 215 499-8959
Quakertown *(G-16193)*
Fibrocell Science Inc D 484 713-6000
Exton *(G-5678)*
Formula Pharmaceuticals Inc G 610 727-4172
Berwyn *(G-1363)*
Fresenius Kabi Usa Inc G 724 772-6900
Warrendale *(G-19073)*
Frontage Laboratories Inc C 610 232-0100
Exton *(G-5682)*
Frontage Laboratories Inc E 610 232-0100
Exton *(G-5683)*
Frontida Biopharm Inc E 215 288-6500
Philadelphia *(G-13728)*
G&W PA Laboratories LLC C 215 799-5333
Sellersville *(G-17348)*
Gendx Products Inc G 443 543-5254
Downingtown *(G-4230)*
Genentech G 717 572-8001
Lititz *(G-10012)*
▲ **Generics International US Inc** G 256 859-2575
Malvern *(G-10239)*
Genoa Healthcare LLC G 215 426-1007
Philadelphia *(G-13754)*
Genomind LLC E 877 895-8658
Chalfont *(G-2876)*
▲ **Gentell Inc** D 215 788-2700
Bristol *(G-2147)*
Genus Lifesciences Inc C 610 782-9780
Allentown *(G-227)*
Genzyme Corporation F 610 594-8590
Exton *(G-5688)*
Gjv Pharma LLC G 267 880-6375
Doylestown *(G-4302)*
Glaxosmithkline E 717 426-6644
Marietta *(G-10462)*
Glaxosmithkline Consumer D 717 268-0110
York *(G-20501)*
◆ **Glaxosmithkline LLC** G 215 751-4000
Philadelphia *(G-13766)*
Glaxosmithkline LLC E 610 223-9089
Blandon *(G-1754)*
Glaxosmithkline LLC E 717 898-6853
Lancaster *(G-9029)*
Glaxosmithkline LLC E 610 917-4085
Royersford *(G-16850)*
Glaxosmithkline LLC E 610 270-5836
Harleysville *(G-7034)*
Glaxosmithkline LLC E 610 962-7548
Willow Grove *(G-20119)*
Glaxosmithkline LLC E 814 243-0366
Johnstown *(G-8378)*
Glaxosmithkline LLC E 412 860-5475
Export *(G-5608)*
Glaxosmithkline LLC E 412 726-6041
Imperial *(G-8066)*
Glaxosmithkline LLC G 717 268-0319
York *(G-20502)*
Glaxosmithkline LLC E 412 398-2600
Pittsburgh *(G-15050)*
Glaxosmithkline LLC D 610 270-7125
King of Prussia *(G-8621)*
Glaxosmithkline LLC E 610 270-4692
King of Prussia *(G-8622)*
Glaxosmithkline LLC E 610 917-4941
Collegeville *(G-3379)*
Glaxosmithkline LLC F 610 768-3150
King of Prussia *(G-8623)*
Glaxosmithkline LLC E 610 779-4774
Reading *(G-16392)*
Glaxosmithkline LLC E 610 270-4800
King of Prussia *(G-8624)*
Glaxosmithkline LLC E 610 270-4800
Conshohocken *(G-3551)*
Glaxosmithkline LLC E 814 935-5693
Newville *(G-12603)*
Glaxosmithkline LLC F 610 917-3493
Collegeville *(G-3380)*
Glaxosmithkline PLC E 215 336-0824
Philadelphia *(G-13767)*
▲ **Gnosis USA Inc** G 215 340-7960
Doylestown *(G-4303)*
Harmony Biosciences LLC E 847 715-0500
Plymouth Meeting *(G-15845)*
◆ **Heraeus Precious Metals Nor** C 610 825-6050
Conshohocken *(G-3556)*
Hercon Laboratories Inc D 717 764-1191
Emigsville *(G-4990)*
▲ **Hercon Pharmaceuticals LLC** E 717 764-1191
Emigsville *(G-4991)*
HLS Therapeutics (usa) Inc F 844 457-8900
Bryn Mawr *(G-2324)*
Horse Systems Inc G 724 544-9686
Fombell *(G-6032)*
▼ **Hr Pharmaceuticals Inc** E 877 302-1110
York *(G-20530)*
Iceutica Inc G 267 546-1400
King of Prussia *(G-8632)*
Ictv Holdings Inc F 484 598-2300
Wayne *(G-19337)*
Idera Pharmaceuticals Inc D 484 348-1600
Exton *(G-5695)*
Immunocore G 484 534-5261
Conshohocken *(G-3560)*
Immunome Inc G 610 716-3599
Exton *(G-5696)*
Impax Laboratories Inc D 215 289-2220
Fort Washington *(G-6075)*
Impax Laboratories LLC D 215 558-4300
Fort Washington *(G-6076)*
Incyte Corporation D 302 498-6700
Broomall *(G-2290)*
Infacare Pharmaceutical Corp G 267 515-5850
Trevose *(G-18499)*
◆ **Innochem Inc** G 610 323-0730
Pottstown *(G-16002)*
Innocoll Inc F 484 406-5200
Newtown Square *(G-12577)*
Iroko Intermediate Holdings G 267 546-3003
Philadelphia *(G-13874)*
Iroko Pharmaceuticals Inc G 267 546-3003
Philadelphia *(G-13875)*
▲ **Iroko Pharmaceuticals LLC** C 267 546-3003
Philadelphia *(G-13876)*
Itf Pharma Inc G 484 328-4964
Berwyn *(G-1366)*
Ivax Pharmaceuticals LLC G 215 591-3000
North Wales *(G-12807)*
Ivd LLC G 949 664-5500
Philadelphia *(G-13879)*
Janssen Biotech Inc G 610 407-0194
Malvern *(G-10259)*
Janssen Biotech Inc D 610 651-6000
Malvern *(G-10260)*
Janssen Biotech Inc D 610 651-7200
Royersford *(G-16853)*
▲ **Janssen Biotech Inc** B 610 651-6000
Horsham *(G-7827)*
Janssen Biotech Inc G 215 325-4250
Malvern *(G-10261)*
Janssen Biotech Inc G 610 651-6000
Malvern *(G-10262)*
Janssen Research & Dev LLC C 610 458-2192
Exton *(G-5701)*
Janssen Research & Dev LLC C 215 628-5000
Spring House *(G-17882)*
Jazz Pharmaceuticals F 215 832-3750
Philadelphia *(G-13892)*
Jazz Pharmaceuticals E 215 867-4900
Langhorne *(G-9304)*
Jdp Therapeutics Inc G 215 661-8557
Lansdale *(G-9381)*
Johnson & Johnson Consumer Inc C 717 207-3500
Lancaster *(G-9074)*
Johnsons Pharmaceuticals F 412 655-2151
West Mifflin *(G-19741)*
K & H Pharma LLC G 267 893-6578
Doylestown *(G-4310)*
▲ **Kadmon Pharmaceuticals LLC** D 724 778-6100
Warrendale *(G-19084)*
Kdl Pharmaceutical Co Ltd G 215 259-3024
Hatfield *(G-7357)*
Kremers Urban Pharmaceuticals G 609 936-5940
Philadelphia *(G-13942)*
Kremers Urban Phrmcuticals Inc F 609 936-5940
Philadelphia *(G-13943)*
Krystal Biotech Inc E 412 586-5830
Pittsburgh *(G-15202)*
Kvk-Tech Inc E 215 579-1842
Newtown *(G-12515)*
▲ **Kvk-Tech Inc** B 215 579-1842
Newtown *(G-12516)*
Lannett Company Inc B 215 333-9000
Philadelphia *(G-13952)*
Lannett Company Inc D 215 333-9000
Philadelphia *(G-13953)*
Laron Pharma Inc F 267 575-1470
Fort Washington *(G-6082)*
Life Tree Pharmacy Svcs LLC G 610 522-2010
Sharon Hill *(G-17458)*
Lipella Pharmaceuticals Inc F 412 901-0315
Pittsburgh *(G-15234)*
Locus Pharmaceuticals Inc D 215 358-2000
Blue Bell *(G-1845)*
Lomed Inc G 800 477-0239
Ottsville *(G-13066)*
Louston International Inc G 610 859-9860
Marcus Hook *(G-10447)*
Lucky Vitamin LLC C 412 741-2598
Leetsdale *(G-9698)*
M D Pharma Connection LLC G 814 371-7726
Du Bois *(G-4404)*
Madrigal Pharmaceuticals Inc G 484 380-9263
Conshohocken *(G-3573)*
Main Line Center For Skin Surg G 610 664-1414
Bala Cynwyd *(G-884)*
Mainline Biosciences LLC G 610 643-4881
Malvern *(G-10273)*
Mallinckrodt LLC F 570 824-8980
Wilkes Barre *(G-19940)*
Marinus Pharmaceuticals Inc F 267 440-4200
Radnor *(G-16295)*
◆ **Matthey Johnson Holdings Inc** E 610 971-3000
Wayne *(G-19350)*
◆ **Matthey Johnson Inc** E 610 971-3000
Wayne *(G-19351)*
Matthey Johnson Inc C 610 341-8300
Wayne *(G-19353)*
McCahans Pharmacy Inc G 814 635-2911
Saxton *(G-17102)*
McNeil Consmr Pharmaceuticals C 215 273-7700
Fort Washington *(G-6083)*
Med-Fast Pharmacy LP G 866 979-7378
Aliquippa *(G-83)*
Medarbor LLC G 732 887-6111
Bristol *(G-2165)*
▲ **Medical Products Labs Inc** C 215 677-2700
Philadelphia *(G-14005)*
Medicine Shoppe G 717 208-3415
Lancaster *(G-9131)*
Medimmune G 240 751-5625
Royersford *(G-16858)*
Medunik Usa Inc F 484 380-2641
Bryn Mawr *(G-2329)*
Merck & Co Inc D 215 652-5000
North Wales *(G-12814)*
Merck and Company Inc F 215 993-1616
North Wales *(G-12815)*
Merck Sharp & Dohme Corp F 215 652-6777
West Point *(G-19760)*
Merck Sharp & Dohme Corp C 215 652-5000
North Wales *(G-12816)*

Merck Sharp & Dohme Corp ....E 215 652-8368
West Point *(G-19761)*
Merck Sharp & Dohme Corp ....B 484 344-2493
Blue Bell *(G-1847)*
Merck Sharp & Dohme Corp ....C 267 305-5000
North Wales *(G-12817)*
Merck Sharp & Dohme Corp ....G 215 397-2541
Hatfield *(G-7368)*
Merck Sharp & Dohme Corp ....B 215 652-5000
West Point *(G-19763)*
Merck Sharp & Dohme Corp ....C 215 631-5000
West Point *(G-19762)*
Merck Sharp Dhme Argentina Inc ....F 215 996-3806
Lansdale *(G-9386)*
Metcure Inc ....G 813 601-3533
Newtown Square *(G-12585)*
Microgenics ....G 412 490-8365
Pittsburgh *(G-15285)*
Mirador Global LP ....G 302 983-3430
Kennett Square *(G-8529)*
Mito Biopharm ....G 215 767-9700
Radnor *(G-16296)*
Mlre LLC ....G 724 514-1800
Canonsburg *(G-2604)*
Montgomery Laboratories Inc ....F 570 752-7712
Berwick *(G-1335)*
Mrlrx LLC ....F 610 485-7750
Marcus Hook *(G-10450)*
MSP Distribution Svcs C LLC ....C 215 652-6160
North Wales *(G-12819)*
▲ Mutual Pharmaceutical Co Inc ....C 215 288-6500
Philadelphia *(G-14047)*
Mutual Pharmaceutical Co Inc ....G 215 807-1312
Philadelphia *(G-14048)*
Myers Drugstore Inc ....F 610 233-3300
Norristown *(G-12691)*
▲ Mylan Inc ....G 724 514-1800
Canonsburg *(G-2607)*
Mylan Pharmaceuticals Inc ....E 724 514-1800
Canonsburg *(G-2608)*
Nanoscan Imaging LLC ....G 215 699-1703
Lansdale *(G-9390)*
National Generic Distributors ....G 215 788-3113
Levittown *(G-9852)*
Neurokine Therapeutics LLC ....G 609 937-0409
Philadelphia *(G-14065)*
Norcom Systems Inc ....F 610 592-0167
Norristown *(G-12693)*
◆ Norquay Technology Inc ....E 610 874-4330
Chester *(G-3058)*
Nova Aurora Corp ....G 817 467-7567
Pittsburgh *(G-15349)*
Novartis Corporation ....D 215 255-4200
Philadelphia *(G-14087)*
Novartis Pharmaceuticals Corp ....G 717 901-1916
Mechanicsburg *(G-10874)*
Nupathe Inc ....F 610 232-0800
Malvern *(G-10289)*
Oncoceutics Inc ....G 678 897-0563
Philadelphia *(G-14095)*
Onconova Therapeutics Inc ....F 267 759-3680
Newtown *(G-12532)*
Oncore Biopharma Inc ....F 215 589-6378
Doylestown *(G-4320)*
Opertech Bio Inc ....G 215 456-8765
Philadelphia *(G-14098)*
Optinose Inc ....G 267 364-3500
Yardley *(G-20330)*
Optofluidics Inc ....F 215 253-5777
Philadelphia *(G-14100)*
Othera Pharmaceuticals Inc ....G 484 879-2800
Conshohocken *(G-3584)*
Packaging Coordinators Inc ....F 215 613-3600
Philadelphia *(G-14111)*
Par Pharmaceutical 2 Inc ....D 484 216-7741
Malvern *(G-10293)*
Paratek Pharmaceuticals Inc ....G 484 751-4920
King of Prussia *(G-8660)*
Particle Sciences Inc ....E 610 861-4701
Bethlehem *(G-1591)*
Patriot Pharmaceuticals LLC ....G 215 325-7676
Horsham *(G-7839)*
Patwell Phrm Solutions LLC ....G 610 380-7101
Coatesville *(G-3321)*
Pentec Health Inc ....C 800 223-4376
Upper Chichester *(G-18670)*
Pentec Health Inc ....C 610 494-8700
Glen Mills *(G-6440)*
Pentec Health Inc ....E 610 494-8700
Upper Chichester *(G-18671)*
Pfizer Inc ....G 484 865-5000
Collegeville *(G-3387)*
Pfizer Inc ....A 717 627-2211
Lititz *(G-10032)*
Pfizer Inc ....G 484 865-0288
Collegeville *(G-3388)*
Pfizer Inc ....F 717 932-3701
Lewisberry *(G-9891)*
Pfizer Inc ....B 717 932-3701
Lewisberry *(G-9890)*
Pharma Acumen LLC ....G 215 885-1029
Rydal *(G-16886)*
Pharma Innvtion Srcing Ctr LLC ....G 203 314-8095
Newtown *(G-12535)*
Pharma Rep Training ....G 215 369-1719
Washington Crossing *(G-19258)*
Pharma Tech Pro LLC ....G 570 412-4008
Danville *(G-4009)*
Pharmaceutical Procurement ....F 610 680-7708
Coatesville *(G-3324)*
▲ Pharmceutical Mfg RES Svcs Inc ....E 267 960-3300
Horsham *(G-7841)*
Pharmctcal Stffing Sltons Inc ....G 215 322-5392
Richboro *(G-16677)*
Phasebio Pharmaceuticals Inc ....F 610 981-6500
Malvern *(G-10295)*
Phibro Animal Health Corp ....F 201 329-7300
State College *(G-18005)*
Philadelphia Animal Health LLC ....G 215 573-4503
Philadelphia *(G-14141)*
Philarx Pharmacy Inc ....G 267 324-5231
Philadelphia *(G-14166)*
Photomedex Inc ....G 215 619-3286
Willow Grove *(G-20134)*
Photomedex Inc ....F 215 619-3235
Willow Grove *(G-20135)*
Physician Transformations LLC ....G 484 420-4407
Newtown Square *(G-12590)*
▲ Piramal Critical Care Inc ....E 800 414-1901
Bethlehem *(G-1598)*
Piramal Healthcare Inc ....G 610 974-9760
Bethlehem *(G-1600)*
Plurogen Therapeutics LLC ....G 610 539-3670
Norristown *(G-12703)*
Pompa Trssler Chiropractic LLC ....G 724 327-5665
Monroeville *(G-11349)*
Prophase Labs Inc ....E 215 345-0919
Doylestown *(G-4329)*
Protarga Inc ....G 610 260-4000
King of Prussia *(G-8666)*
Protherics Inc ....C 615 327-1027
Conshohocken *(G-3593)*
Provell Pharmaceuticals LLC ....G 610 942-8970
Honey Brook *(G-7757)*
PSI Pharma Support America Inc ....C 267 464-2500
King of Prussia *(G-8667)*
Qilu Pharma Inc ....D 484 443-2935
Malvern *(G-10304)*
Qol Meds ....G 724 602-0532
Butler *(G-2436)*
Qualitox Laboratories LLC ....G 412 458-5431
Mc Kees Rocks *(G-10629)*
Quality Health and Life Inc ....G 866 547-8447
Philadelphia *(G-14219)*
Quigley Nutraceuticals LLC ....F 646 499-5100
Exton *(G-5725)*
Quinnova Pharmaceuticals Inc ....G 215 860-6263
Jamison *(G-8245)*
Quotient Sciences - Phila ....C 610 485-4270
Boothwyn *(G-1880)*
Recro Pharma Inc ....D 484 395-2470
Malvern *(G-10309)*
◆ Reliable Products Inc ....G 215 860-2011
Newtown *(G-12543)*
Renaissance Ssa LLC ....F 267 685-0340
Newtown *(G-12544)*
Renee Awad ND ....G 717 875-3056
Columbia *(G-3448)*
Rhotau Pharma Services LLC ....G 484 437-2654
West Chester *(G-19629)*
Ribonova Inc ....G 610 801-2541
Wynnewood *(G-20272)*
Rochester Pharmaceuticals ....G 215 345-4880
Doylestown *(G-4335)*
Sfa Therapeutics LLC ....G 267 584-1080
Jenkintown *(G-8300)*
Shire Holdings US AG ....F 484 595-8800
Chesterbrook *(G-3096)*
Shire Pharmaceuticals LLC ....C 484 595-8800
Chesterbrook *(G-3097)*
▲ Shire US Manufacturing Inc ....E 484 595-8800
Chesterbrook *(G-3098)*
Shire Viropharma Incorporated ....E 610 644-9929
Exton *(G-5731)*
▲ Sigmapharm Laboratories LLC ....C 215 352-6655
Bensalem *(G-1253)*
Silarx Pharmaceuticals Inc ....G 845 225-1500
Philadelphia *(G-14305)*
Sirtris Pharmaceuticals Inc ....D 585 275-5774
Collegeville *(G-3393)*
Slate Pharmaceuticals Inc ....D 484 321-5900
Malvern *(G-10320)*
Smithkline Beecham Corporation ....G 215 751-4000
Philadelphia *(G-14316)*
Soleo Health Holdings Inc ....G 888 244-2340
Sharon Hill *(G-17460)*
Soleo Health Inc ....D 888 244-2340
Sharon Hill *(G-17461)*
Specialty Phrm Pdts LLC ....F 215 321-5836
Yardley *(G-20340)*
STI Pharma LLC ....G 215 710-3270
Newtown *(G-12553)*
Storeflex LLC ....G 856 498-0079
New Hope *(G-12315)*
Strategic Medicine Inc ....G 814 659-5450
Kennett Square *(G-8546)*
Strongbridge Biopharma PLC ....E 610 254-9200
Trevose *(G-18504)*
Summers Laboratories Inc ....F 610 454-1471
Collegeville *(G-3395)*
Sunshine Biologics Inc ....E 484 494-0818
Sharon Hill *(G-17463)*
Svm2 Pharma Inc ....G 717 369-4636
Saint Thomas *(G-17042)*
Synchrony Medical LLC ....E 484 947-5003
Kennett Square *(G-8547)*
Synergy Health Systems Inc ....E 570 473-7506
Northumberland *(G-12877)*
Tarsa Therapeutics Inc ....F 267 273-7940
Philadelphia *(G-14373)*
Tasman Pharma Inc ....G 267 317-2010
Warminster *(G-18975)*
▲ Techniserv Inc ....D 570 759-2315
Berwick *(G-1346)*
Telesis Therapeutics LLC ....G 215 848-4773
Philadelphia *(G-14380)*
Tetralgic Pharmaceuticals Corp ....F 610 889-9900
Malvern *(G-10328)*
Teva Bopharmaceuticals USA Inc ....D 240 821-9000
West Chester *(G-19658)*
Teva Branded Phrm Pdts R&D Inc ....D 215 591-3000
West Chester *(G-19659)*
Teva Branded Phrm Pdts R&D Inc ....G 215 591-3000
Malvern *(G-10329)*
Teva Neuroscience ....G 215 591-6309
Horsham *(G-7856)*
Teva Pharmaceutical Fin Co LLC ....G 215 591-3000
North Wales *(G-12832)*
Teva Pharmaceutical Fin IV LLC ....F 215 591-3000
North Wales *(G-12833)*
Teva Pharmaceuticals Usa Inc ....D 215 591-3000
North Wales *(G-12835)*
Teva Pharmaceuticals Usa Inc ....G 240 821-9000
North Wales *(G-12836)*
Teva Pharmaceuticals Usa Inc ....C 215 591-3000
Sellersville *(G-17359)*
Teva Pharmaceuticals Usa Inc ....D 215 591-3000
Horsham *(G-7857)*
Teva Pharmaceuticals Usa Inc ....D 215 591-3000
Chalfont *(G-2891)*
◆ Teva Pharmaceuticals Usa Inc ....B 215 591-3000
North Wales *(G-12834)*
Teva Respiratory LLC ....D 610 344-0200
Malvern *(G-10330)*
Thar Pharmaceuticals Inc ....E 412 963-6800
Pittsburgh *(G-15609)*
Thresher Pharmaceuticals ....G 215 826-0227
Bristol *(G-2206)*
Tmw Products LLC ....G 215 997-9687
Perkasie *(G-13296)*
Tomayko Group LLC ....F 412 481-0600
Pittsburgh *(G-15632)*
Torrent Pharma Inc ....D 215 949-3711
Levittown *(G-9869)*
Torresdale Pharmacy ....G 215 612-5400
Philadelphia *(G-14398)*
Transcelerate Biopharma ....G 484 539-1236
Conshohocken *(G-3613)*
Trevena Inc ....D 610 354-8840
Chesterbrook *(G-3099)*

Tri- Med Laboratories Inc......E...... 732 249-6363
York *(G-20691)*
Triad Isotopes Inc......G...... 717 558-8640
Harrisburg *(G-7237)*
Trinity Partners LLC......F...... 610 233-1210
East Norriton *(G-4585)*
Troy Healthcare LLC......G...... 570 453-5252
Hazle Township *(G-7487)*
▲ **Troy Manufacturing Co Inc**......E...... 570 453-5252
Hazle Township *(G-7488)*
▲ **Unipack Inc**......G...... 724 733-7381
Pittsburgh *(G-15673)*
United Research Labs Inc......E...... 215 535-7460
Philadelphia *(G-14422)*
University Pittsburgh Med Ctr......F...... 412 647-8762
Pittsburgh *(G-15684)*
Upreach Inc......G...... 215 536-8758
Easton *(G-4766)*
Url Pharma Inc......E...... 215 288-6500
Philadelphia *(G-14433)*
US Specialty Formulations LLC......F...... 610 849-5030
Bethlehem *(G-1648)*
▲ **V L H Inc**......B...... 800 245-4440
Pittsburgh *(G-15688)*
Varinel Inc......G...... 610 256-3119
West Chester *(G-19673)*
Velicept Therapeutics Inc......G...... 484 318-2988
Wayne *(G-19387)*
Verrica Pharmaceuticals Inc......F...... 484 453-3300
West Chester *(G-19674)*
Vgx Pharmaceuticals LLC......E...... 215 542-5912
Plymouth Meeting *(G-15878)*
Vintage Pharmaceuticals LLC......D...... 256 859-2222
Malvern *(G-10340)*
Viral Genomix Inc......F...... 267 440-4200
Blue Bell *(G-1856)*
Virtus Pharmaceuticals LLC......E...... 267 938-4850
Bristol *(G-2215)*
▲ **Virtus Pharmaceuticals LLC**......E...... 267 938-4850
Langhorne *(G-9331)*
Virtus Pharmaceuticals LLC......G...... 813 283-1344
Newtown *(G-12561)*
Virtus Phrmctcals Holdings LLC......G...... 267 938-4850
Langhorne *(G-9332)*
Virtus Phrmcticals Opco II LLC......G...... 267 938-4850
Langhorne *(G-9333)*
Wakeem Inc......F...... 610 258-2311
Easton *(G-4774)*
Wallace Pharmaceuticals Inc......C...... 732 564-2700
Canonsburg *(G-2654)*
Watson Laboratories Inc......G...... 951 493-5300
North Wales *(G-12839)*
West Pharmaceutical Svcs Inc......C...... 570 398-5411
Jersey Shore *(G-8325)*
West Pharmaceutical Svcs Inc......E...... 717 560-8460
Lititz *(G-10059)*
West Pharmaceutical Svcs Inc......F...... 610 853-3200
Upper Darby *(G-18694)*
Williams Richard H Pharmacist......G...... 717 393-6708
Lancaster *(G-9242)*
Windtree Therapeutics Inc......D...... 215 488-9300
Warrington *(G-19140)*
Workcenter......E...... 570 320-7444
Williamsport *(G-20100)*
Wuxi Apptec Inc......G...... 215 334-1380
Philadelphia *(G-14491)*
Wyeth LLC......G...... 610 696-3100
West Chester *(G-19682)*
Zavante Therapeutics Inc......G...... 610 816-6640
King of Prussia *(G-8701)*
Zeomedix Inc......G...... 610 517-7818
Malvern *(G-10353)*
Zoetis Inc......F...... 908 901-1116
Exton *(G-5752)*
Zoetis LLC......G...... 717 932-3702
Lewisberry *(G-9895)*
Zynerba Pharmaceuticals Inc......F...... 484 581-7505
Devon *(G-4117)*

2835 Diagnostic Substances

Abbott Laboratories......G...... 610 444-9818
Kennett Square *(G-8500)*
◆ **Aquaphoenix Scientific Inc**......D...... 717 632-1291
Hanover *(G-6861)*
Avid Radiopharmaceuticals Inc......F...... 215 298-0700
Philadelphia *(G-13427)*
Avidtox Inc......G...... 610 738-7938
West Chester *(G-19504)*
Bio-Nucleonics Inc......F...... 305 576-0996
Philadelphia *(G-13461)*
Bio/Data Corporation......E...... 215 441-4000
Horsham *(G-7798)*
Biodetego LLC......G...... 856 701-2453
Philadelphia *(G-13464)*
Biomagnetic Solutions LLC......G...... 814 689-1801
State College *(G-17945)*
Biorealize Inc......G...... 610 216-5554
Philadelphia *(G-13466)*
Bramante Bioscience LLC......G...... 860 634-0015
Philadelphia *(G-13476)*
Celsense Inc......G...... 412 263-2870
Pittsburgh *(G-14834)*
Cernostics Inc......G...... 412 315-7359
Pittsburgh *(G-14835)*
East York Diagnostic Center......G...... 717 851-1850
York *(G-20460)*
Esoterix Genetic Labs LLC......E...... 215 351-2331
Philadelphia *(G-13679)*
Excela Health Holding Co Inc......G...... 724 832-4450
Greensburg *(G-6665)*
Interntnal Soc of Nurovirology......G...... 215 707-9788
Philadelphia *(G-13870)*
Janssen Biotech Inc......G...... 610 407-0194
Malvern *(G-10259)*
▲ **Janssen Biotech Inc**......B...... 610 651-6000
Horsham *(G-7827)*
Janssen Biotech Inc......G...... 610 651-6000
Malvern *(G-10262)*
Jt-Mesh Diagnostics LLC......G...... 610 299-7482
Kennett Square *(G-8517)*
Lia Diagnostics Inc......G...... 267 362-9670
Philadelphia *(G-13967)*
▲ **Lifescan Inc**......A...... 800 227-8862
Chesterbrook *(G-3093)*
Limitless Longevity LLC......F...... 215 279-8376
Philadelphia *(G-13971)*
Microbiology Lab Co......G...... 570 800-5795
Scranton *(G-17259)*
N-Zyme Scientifics LLC......G...... 267 218-1098
Doylestown *(G-4317)*
Orasure Technologies Inc......B...... 610 882-1820
Bethlehem *(G-1588)*
Orasure Technologies Inc......E...... 610 882-1820
Bethlehem *(G-1589)*
Orasure Technologies Inc......E...... 610 882-1820
Bethlehem *(G-1590)*
Petnet Solutions Inc......G...... 865 218-2000
North Wales *(G-12824)*
Rapid Pathogen Screening Inc......E...... 718 288-4318
Montoursville *(G-11449)*
Saint Lukes Hosp Bethlehem PA......G...... 610 954-3531
Bethlehem *(G-1614)*
Saladax Biomedical Inc......E...... 610 419-6731
Bethlehem *(G-1615)*
Salimetrics LLC......E...... 814 234-7748
State College *(G-18019)*
SMC Direct LLC......E...... 800 521-1635
Evans City *(G-5563)*

2836 Biological Prdts, Exc Diagnostic Substances

AA Plasma LLC......G...... 312 371-7947
Warminster *(G-18817)*
Advanced Plasma Solutions Inc......F...... 484 568-4942
Richboro *(G-16672)*
Avax Technologies Inc......E...... 215 241-9760
Philadelphia *(G-13426)*
▼ **Bioscience Management Inc**......F...... 484 245-5232
Allentown *(G-152)*
Biospectra Inc......E...... 610 599-3400
Bangor *(G-908)*
▲ **Biospectra Inc**......D...... 610 599-3400
Stroudsburg *(G-18108)*
Cocalico Biologicals Inc......E...... 717 336-1990
Reamstown *(G-16575)*
▲ **Csl Behring LLC**......B...... 610 878-4000
King of Prussia *(G-8601)*
Csl Plasma Inc......G...... 717 767-2348
York *(G-20439)*
▲ **Eusa Pharma (usa) Inc**......E...... 215 867-4900
Langhorne *(G-9295)*
Fibrocell Science Inc......D...... 484 713-6000
Exton *(G-5678)*
Fibrocell Technologies Inc......F...... 484 713-6000
Exton *(G-5679)*
Genomind LLC......E...... 877 895-8658
Chalfont *(G-2876)*
Herbal Extracts Plus......G...... 215 245-5055
Bensalem *(G-1209)*
Hersehy Veterinary Hospital......F...... 717 534-2244
Hershey *(G-7612)*
Idera Pharmaceuticals Inc......D...... 484 348-1600
Exton *(G-5695)*
Immunotek Bio Centers LLC......E...... 570 300-7940
Pittston *(G-15756)*
Immunotek Bio Centers LLC......E...... 484 408-6376
Allentown *(G-254)*
Immunotek Bio Centers LLC......E...... 814 283-6421
Altoona *(G-516)*
Immunotope Inc......G...... 215 489-4945
Doylestown *(G-4307)*
Integrated Tech Svcs Intl LLC......F...... 814 262-7332
Johnstown *(G-8382)*
Janus Biogenics LLC......G...... 814 215-3013
Clarion *(G-3180)*
Krystal Biotech Inc......E...... 412 586-5830
Pittsburgh *(G-15202)*
Lehigh Valley Venom Basbal CLB......G...... 610 262-1750
Whitehall *(G-19882)*
McM Vaccine Co......G...... 570 957-7187
Swiftwater *(G-18188)*
Medimmune LLC......B...... 215 501-1300
Bensalem *(G-1225)*
Merck Sharp & Dohme Corp......C...... 215 631-5000
West Point *(G-19762)*
Novavax Execoffice......G...... 484 913-1200
Malvern *(G-10288)*
Plasma Source......G...... 215 942-6370
Southampton *(G-17830)*
Quotient Biodiagnostics Inc......F...... 215 497-8820
Newtown *(G-12541)*
Rapid Pathogen Screening Inc......E...... 718 288-4318
Montoursville *(G-11449)*
Renaptys Vaccines LLC......G...... 917 620-2256
Philadelphia *(G-14240)*
Renmatix Inc......D...... 484 681-9246
King of Prussia *(G-8669)*
Richard J McMenamin Inc......G...... 215 673-1200
Philadelphia *(G-14246)*
River City Venom......G...... 724 316-5886
Butler *(G-2439)*
Rockland Immunochemicals Inc......D...... 484 791-3823
Pottstown *(G-16041)*
Safc Biosciences Inc......G...... 610 750-8801
Reading *(G-16507)*
▲ **Sanofi Pasteur Inc**......A...... 570 839-7187
Swiftwater *(G-18190)*
Sanofi Pasteur Inc......F...... 570 957-7187
Taylor *(G-18261)*
Sigma Biologics Inc......G...... 215 741-1523
Yardley *(G-20339)*
Spark Therapeutics Inc......C...... 888 772-7560
Philadelphia *(G-14327)*
Spectragenetics Inc......G...... 412 488-9350
Pittsburgh *(G-15570)*
Spider Venom Racing Pdts LLC......G...... 484 547-1400
East Texas *(G-4639)*
▲ **Sylvan Bio Inc**......G...... 724 543-3900
Kittanning *(G-8798)*
Tulip Biolabs Inc......G...... 610 584-2706
Lansdale *(G-9419)*
Venom Power Sports......G...... 717 467-5190
Dover *(G-4206)*
Windtree Therapeutics Inc......D...... 215 488-9300
Warrington *(G-19140)*
Wuxi Apptec Inc......D...... 215 218-5500
Philadelphia *(G-14492)*

2841 Soap & Detergents

Advanced Skin Technologies Inc......G...... 610 488-7643
Bernville *(G-1295)*
◆ **Alex C Fergusson LLC**......D...... 717 264-9147
Chambersburg *(G-2899)*
Big 3 Packaging LLC......F...... 215 743-4201
Philadelphia *(G-13459)*
Blendco Systems LLC......E...... 215 785-3147
Bristol *(G-2119)*
Bulk Chemicals Inc......F...... 610 926-4128
Mohrsville *(G-11275)*
▲ **Cei-Douglassville Inc**......D...... 610 385-9500
Douglassville *(G-4172)*
Clean Concepts Group LLC......G...... 908 229-8812
Washington Crossing *(G-19254)*
Diversey Inc......D...... 570 421-7850
East Stroudsburg *(G-4613)*
▲ **Dreumex USA Inc**......E...... 717 767-6881
York *(G-20457)*
Eco Solution Distributing LLC......F...... 724 941-4140
Pittsburgh *(G-14959)*

Ecolab Inc ....E 610 521-1072
  Philadelphia *(G-13314)*
Essence of Old Woods ....G...... 215 258-0852
  Green Lane *(G-6588)*
▲ Evergreen Synergies LLC ....E 610 239-9425
  King of Prussia *(G-8617)*
Friendly Organic LLC ....G...... 609 709-2924
  Philadelphia *(G-13726)*
Good Health Natural Pdts Inc ....G...... 570 655-0823
  Pittston *(G-15753)*
Gretchen Maser ....G...... 717 295-9426
  Lancaster *(G-9032)*
Hand In Hand Soap LLC ....G...... 267 714-4168
  Philadelphia *(G-13799)*
Henkel US Operations Corp ....C...... 570 455-9980
  West Hazleton *(G-19712)*
James Austin Company ....C...... 724 625-1535
  Mars *(G-10504)*
Jay Design Inc ....G...... 412 683-1184
  Pittsburgh *(G-15146)*
Lincoln Industrial Chemical Co ....F 610 375-4596
  Reading *(G-16430)*
Misco Products Corporation ....D...... 610 926-4106
  Reading *(G-16445)*
◆ National Chemical Labs PA Inc .....C...... 215 922-1200
  Philadelphia *(G-14053)*
Oneill Industries Inc ....G...... 215 533-2101
  Philadelphia *(G-14096)*
Pagoda Products Inc ....G...... 610 678-8096
  Reading *(G-16463)*
▼ Precision Finishing Inc ....E 215 257-6862
  Quakertown *(G-16232)*
Royal Chemical Company Ltd ....F 570 421-7850
  East Stroudsburg *(G-4634)*
▲ Select Medical Systems Inc ....F 215 207-9003
  Philadelphia *(G-14293)*
Sensible Organics Inc ....E 724 891-4560
  Beaver Falls *(G-1011)*
Soap Plant Inc ....G...... 724 656-3601
  New Castle *(G-12154)*
Soaphies ....G...... 814 861-7627
  State College *(G-18027)*
Straight Arrow Products Inc ....G...... 610 882-9606
  Bethlehem *(G-1633)*
T&T Buttas LLC ....G...... 833 251-1357
  Philadelphia *(G-14365)*
Tip Top Resources LLC ....G...... 407 818-6937
  Reedsville *(G-16628)*
United Refining Company ....G...... 724 274-0885
  Springdale *(G-17904)*
Windglo Manufacturing Co ....G...... 717 859-2932
  Akron *(G-39)*
Wound Care Concepts Inc ....E 215 788-2700
  Bristol *(G-2218)*
Zep Inc ....C...... 610 295-1360
  Breinigsville *(G-2033)*

2842 Spec Cleaning, Polishing & Sanitation Preparations

A Better Power LLC ....G...... 412 498-6537
  Ligonier *(G-9956)*
Afco C&S LLC ....G...... 717 264-9147
  Chambersburg *(G-2898)*
◆ Air Products and Chemicals Inc .....A 610 481-4911
  Allentown *(G-119)*
Air Products and Chemicals Inc ....E 724 266-1563
  Leetsdale *(G-9677)*
▼ Air-Scent International ....D...... 412 252-2000
  Pittsburgh *(G-14658)*
◆ Alex C Fergusson LLC ....D...... 717 264-9147
  Chambersburg *(G-2899)*
Alkali Beaver Products ....G...... 724 709-7857
  Rochester *(G-16781)*
Apter Industries Inc ....F 412 672-9628
  White Oak *(G-19853)*
Aquachempacs LLC ....E 215 396-7200
  Feasterville Trevose *(G-5885)*
Arete Qis LLC ....D...... 814 781-1194
  Ridgway *(G-16696)*
Associated Products LLC ....E 412 486-2255
  Glenshaw *(G-6482)*
Berkley Products Company ....F 717 859-1104
  Akron *(G-33)*
Better Air Management LLC ....G...... 215 362-5677
  Lansdale *(G-9347)*
Big 3 Packaging LLC ....F 215 743-4201
  Philadelphia *(G-13459)*
Big Oaks Ltd Partnership II ....F 724 444-0055
  Gibsonia *(G-6326)*

Bio Sun Systems Inc ....G...... 570 537-2200
  Millerton *(G-11214)*
Car Cleen Systems Inc ....F 717 795-8995
  Bethel Park *(G-1408)*
Carbon Clean Industries Inc ....E 570 288-1155
  Kingston *(G-8713)*
▲ Cei-Douglassville Inc ....D...... 610 385-9500
  Douglassville *(G-4172)*
Church & Dwight Co Inc ....D...... 717 781-8800
  York *(G-20426)*
Clarkson Chemical Company Inc ....G...... 570 323-3631
  Williamsport *(G-20000)*
CPA Operations LLC ....G...... 215 743-6860
  Philadelphia *(G-13576)*
◆ CRC Industries Inc ....C...... 215 674-4300
  Horsham *(G-7806)*
▲ Crystal Inc - PMC ....D...... 215 368-1661
  Lansdale *(G-9355)*
Curtis Glenchem Corp ....G...... 610 876-9906
  Eddystone *(G-4800)*
D&B Tailors Inc ....E 610 356-9279
  Newtown Square *(G-12571)*
Ddp Specialty Electronic MA ....G...... 610 244-6000
  Collegeville *(G-3374)*
Decon Laboratories Inc ....E 610 755-0800
  King of Prussia *(G-8606)*
Diversey Inc ....D...... 570 421-7850
  East Stroudsburg *(G-4613)*
Dixie S Young Cleaning ....G...... 814 623-3015
  Bedford *(G-1049)*
▲ Dreumex USA Inc ....E 717 767-6881
  York *(G-20457)*
DW Services LLC ....G...... 484 241-8915
  Allentown *(G-198)*
Dyvex Industries Inc ....F 570 281-7141
  Carbondale *(G-2674)*
E E Zimmerman Company ....F 412 963-0949
  Pittsburgh *(G-14950)*
◆ Emsco Inc ....C...... 814 774-3137
  Girard *(G-6386)*
Environmental Chem & Lubr Co ....G...... 610 923-6492
  Easton *(G-4680)*
Evoqua Water Technologies LLC ....E 724 827-8181
  Darlington *(G-4028)*
Houghton Chemical Corporation ....G...... 800 777-2466
  Scranton *(G-17241)*
Industrial Floor Corporation ....F 215 886-1800
  Jenkintown *(G-8291)*
▼ International Chemical Company .....F 215 739-2313
  Philadelphia *(G-13865)*
Island Fragrances Inc ....E 570 793-1680
  Pittston *(G-15759)*
James Austin Company ....C...... 724 625-1535
  Mars *(G-10504)*
Lincoln Industrial Chemical Co ....F 610 375-4596
  Reading *(G-16430)*
Milazzo Industries Inc ....E 570 722-0522
  Pittston *(G-15767)*
Misco Products Corporation ....D...... 610 926-4106
  Reading *(G-16445)*
Mspi Enterprises LLC ....G...... 814 258-7500
  Knoxville *(G-8812)*
N B Garber Inc ....G...... 267 387-6225
  Warminster *(G-18927)*
◆ National Chemical Labs PA Inc ....C...... 215 922-1200
  Philadelphia *(G-14053)*
Nu-Chem Corp ....F 610 770-2000
  Allentown *(G-336)*
Ogi Inc ....G...... 610 623-6747
  Drexel Hill *(G-4370)*
On Track Enterprises Inc ....F 610 277-4995
  Norristown *(G-12699)*
▲ Oscar Daniels & Company Inc ....F 610 678-8144
  Reading *(G-16460)*
Penn Kleen Ex-Its Inc ....G...... 717 792-3608
  York *(G-20620)*
Perfectdata Corporation ....G...... 800 973-7332
  Plymouth Meeting *(G-15863)*
▲ Quantum Global Tech LLC ....C...... 215 892-9300
  Quakertown *(G-16239)*
Randall Inds Ltd Liability Co ....F 814 743-6630
  Cherry Tree *(G-3035)*
Recirculation Technologies LLC ....F 215 682-7099
  Fort Washington *(G-6090)*
Reckitt Benckiser LLC ....C...... 717 506-0165
  Mechanicsburg *(G-10883)*
◆ Richardsapex Inc ....E 215 487-1100
  Philadelphia *(G-14247)*
Rugani & Rugani LLC ....G...... 412 223-6472
  Mc Kees Rocks *(G-10632)*

◆ Schaffner Manufacturing Co ....D...... 412 761-9902
  Pittsburgh *(G-15515)*
▲ Senoret Chemical Company ....E 717 626-2125
  Lititz *(G-10047)*
Shore Corporation ....F 412 471-3330
  Pittsburgh *(G-15534)*
Singerman Laboratories ....E 412 798-0447
  Murrysville *(G-11868)*
Spilltech Environmental Inc ....G...... 814 247-8566
  Hastings *(G-7263)*
◆ Stoner Incorporated ....F 717 786-7355
  Quarryville *(G-16282)*
Svt Inc ....F 215 245-5055
  Bensalem *(G-1258)*
Sweeper City Inc ....G...... 724 283-0859
  Butler *(G-2445)*
Titusville Laundry Center ....G...... 814 827-9127
  Titusville *(G-18401)*
Total Systems Technology Inc ....F 412 653-7690
  Pittsburgh *(G-15633)*
Ultronix Inc ....E 215 822-8206
  Hatfield *(G-7404)*
Univar USA Inc ....D...... 717 944-7471
  Middletown *(G-11084)*
Valley Wholesale & Supply ....F 724 783-6531
  Kittanning *(G-8801)*
◆ Veltek Associates Inc ....E 610 644-8335
  Malvern *(G-10338)*
Versum Materials Us LLC ....F 610 481-3946
  Allentown *(G-423)*
Versum Materials Us LLC ....G...... 570 467-2981
  Tamaqua *(G-18231)*
Viking LLC ....F 570 645-3633
  Nesquehoning *(G-12010)*
▼ Vision Technology UHS LLC ....G...... 717 465-0694
  Hanover *(G-6969)*
Zep Inc ....C...... 610 295-1360
  Breinigsville *(G-2033)*

2843 Surface Active & Finishing Agents, Sulfonated Oils

▲ Acton Technologies Inc ....D...... 570 654-0612
  Pittston *(G-15741)*
Independent Concepts Inc ....G...... 412 741-7903
  Sewickley *(G-17394)*
Leatex Chemical Co ....E 215 739-2000
  Philadelphia *(G-13964)*
Lonza Inc ....C...... 570 321-3900
  Williamsport *(G-20035)*
Neo-Solutions Inc ....E 724 728-7360
  Beaver *(G-988)*

2844 Perfumes, Cosmetics & Toilet Preparations

AAA Nail ....G...... 814 362-2863
  Bradford *(G-1953)*
Advanced Skin Technologies Inc ....G...... 610 488-7643
  Bernville *(G-1295)*
◆ Alpha Aromatics Inc ....D...... 412 252-1012
  Pittsburgh *(G-14686)*
Art of Shaving - Fl LLC ....G...... 610 962-1000
  King of Prussia *(G-8585)*
Aucourant LLC ....F 800 682-1623
  East Stroudsburg *(G-4606)*
Beautifulbody Skincare LLC ....G...... 610 255-2255
  King of Prussia *(G-8587)*
Bed Bath & Beyond Inc ....G...... 717 397-0206
  Lancaster *(G-8950)*
Bismoline Manufacturing Co ....G...... 717 394-8795
  Lancaster *(G-8955)*
Bodybuilders Bodywash LLC ....G...... 954 682-8191
  Quakertown *(G-16174)*
▲ Conrex Pharmaceutical Corp ....F 610 355-2454
  West Chester *(G-19529)*
▼ Copperhead Chemical Co Inc ....E 570 386-6123
  Tamaqua *(G-18209)*
Davidson Supply Co Inc ....C...... 412 635-2671
  Pittsburgh *(G-14908)*
Decon Laboratories Inc ....E 610 755-0800
  King of Prussia *(G-8606)*
Designer Michael Todd LLC ....F 215 376-0145
  Jenkintown *(G-8283)*
Donald Trammell ....G...... 484 238-5467
  Coatesville *(G-3301)*
Estee Lauder Companies Inc ....A 215 826-4247
  Bristol *(G-2142)*
Function Inc ....G...... 570 317-0737
  Catawissa *(G-2818)*

▲ Gentell Inc ....D 215 788-2700
Bristol (G-2147)

Hawkeye-Jensen Inc ....E 610 488-8500
Bernville (G-1300)

▲ Hayward Laboratories Inc ....C 570 424-9512
East Stroudsburg (G-4619)

Honest Industries LLC ....E 724 588-1540
Greenville (G-6747)

▲ Jean Alexander Cosmetics Inc ....G 412 331-6069
Mc Kees Rocks (G-10617)

▲ Jpms Manufacturing LLC ....E 610 373-1007
Reading (G-16416)

Makes Scents LLC ....G 717 824-3094
Lancaster (G-9124)

Marula Oil Holdings LLC ....G 310 559-8600
Ardmore (G-712)

Melinessence LLC ....G 717 668-3730
York (G-20586)

Nail Central ....G 717 664-5051
Manheim (G-10396)

▲ National Dermalogy Image Corp ......G 610 756-0065
Kempton (G-8493)

▲ National Towelette Company ....E 215 245-7300
Bensalem (G-1229)

▲ New Stars LLC ....E 215 962-4239
Philadelphia (G-14068)

Northtec LLC ....F 215 781-2731
Bristol (G-2173)

Northtec LLC ....E 215 781-1600
Bristol (G-2174)

▲ Padc 1 ....C 215 781-1600
Bristol (G-2179)

Padc 1 ....E 215 322-3300
Feasterville Trevose (G-5925)

▲ Paper Magic Group Inc ....C 570 961-3863
Moosic (G-11511)

Phytogenx Inc ....E 610 286-0111
Morgantown (G-11530)

▲ Power Line Packaging Inc ....E 610 239-7088
Conshohocken (G-3590)

▲ Process Tech & Packg LLC ....C 570 587-8326
Scott Township (G-17188)

Procter & Gamble Company ....C 570 833-5141
Tunkhannock (G-18547)

Profresh International Corp ....F 800 610-5110
Philadelphia (G-14206)

▲ Renu Labs Inc ....G 215 675-5227
Warminster (G-18952)

Retrohair Inc ....G 412 278-2383
Carnegie (G-2787)

▲ Revelations Perfume Cosmt Inc ......G 215 396-7286
Hatboro (G-7300)

Revoltnary Elctrnic Design LLC ....G 814 977-9546
Bedford (G-1073)

▲ Rgl Distributors LLC ....G 610 207-9000
Ardmore (G-715)

Rice Aesthetics LLC ....G 814 503-8540
Du Bois (G-4416)

Sandys Nail ....G 215 848-0299
Philadelphia (G-14276)

Sensible Organics Inc ....E 724 891-4560
Beaver Falls (G-1011)

Sharp & Wily LLC ....G 717 893-2970
York (G-20667)

▼ Straight Arrow Products Inc ....D 610 882-9606
Bethlehem (G-1632)

Strong Body Care Products Inc ....G 717 786-8947
New Providence (G-12435)

Sun Laboratories Inc ....E 215 659-1111
Willow Grove (G-20144)

▼ Surco Products Inc ....F 412 252-7000
Pittsburgh (G-15590)

T&T Buttas LLC ....G 833 251-1357
Philadelphia (G-14365)

Teeter Enterprises Inc ....G 717 732-5994
Enola (G-5086)

Una Biologicals LLC ....G 412 889-9746
Pittsburgh (G-15668)

Ungerer Industries Inc ....D 610 868-7266
Bethlehem (G-1647)

Unilever ....F 717 776-2180
Newville (G-12611)

▲ Unipack Inc ....G 724 733-7381
Pittsburgh (G-15673)

Venus Nail & Spa ....G 610 660-6180
Narberth (G-11914)

Westlab Distribution Inc ....G 800 699-0301
Montoursville (G-11456)

Williams Fresh Scents LLC ....G 484 838-0147
Nazareth (G-11995)

2851 Paints, Varnishes, Lacquers, Enamels

A & L Paint Co Llc ....G 814 349-8064
Rebersburg (G-16577)

A I Floor Products ....G 215 355-2798
Feasterville Trevose (G-5881)

▼ Acrysystems Laboratories Inc ....G 610 273-1355
Reading (G-16309)

Advanced Finishing Usa Inc ....E 814 474-5200
Fairview (G-5810)

Akzo Nobel Coatings Inc ....E 610 372-3600
Reading (G-16314)

Amdex Metallizing Inc ....G 724 887-4977
Scottdale (G-17189)

American Inks & Coatings Corp ....D 610 933-5848
Phoenixville (G-14528)

▲ APT Advanced Polymer Tech Corp ..D 724 452-1330
Harmony (G-7066)

Aurora International Coat ....F 412 782-2984
Pittsburgh (G-14740)

Axalta Coating Systems LLC ....C 215 255-4347
Philadelphia (G-13431)

Axalta Coating Systems LLC ....E 610 358-2228
Glen Mills (G-6430)

Axalta Coating Systems Ip LLC ....G 855 547-1461
Philadelphia (G-13432)

Axalta Coating Systems Ltd ....B 855 547-1461
Philadelphia (G-13433)

B & T Contractors Inc ....C 814 368-7199
Bradford (G-1956)

Baxter Group Inc ....F 717 263-7341
Chambersburg (G-2909)

Behr Process Corporation ....C 610 391-1085
Allentown (G-148)

Belden Inc ....C 724 222-7060
Washington (G-19153)

Berkley Products Company ....F 717 859-1104
Akron (G-33)

◆ Biocoat Incorporated ....E 215 734-0888
Horsham (G-7799)

▲ Bonnit Brush LLC ....G 215 355-4115
Bensalem (G-1159)

Bradley Coatings Group Inc ....F 724 444-4400
Gibsonia (G-6329)

▲ Brunner Industrial Group Inc ....F 717 233-8781
Harrisburg (G-7100)

Bulk Chemicals Inc ....F 610 926-4128
Mohrsville (G-11275)

Capital Coating Inc ....F 717 442-0979
Kinzers (G-8735)

Carboline Company ....G 724 838-5750
Greensburg (G-6655)

Cardinal Industrial Finishes ....G 814 723-0721
Warren (G-19015)

Chase Corporation ....E 412 828-1500
Pittsburgh (G-14840)

▲ Chem-Clay Corporation ....E 412 276-6333
Carnegie (G-2765)

Chemcoat Inc ....E 570 368-8631
Montoursville (G-11436)

▲ Chroma Acrylics Inc ....E 717 626-8866
Lititz (G-2667)

▼ Clearkin Chemical Corp ....G 215 426-7230
Philadelphia (G-13549)

Coating Development Group Inc ....F 215 426-6216
Philadelphia (G-13555)

Coating Innovations LLC ....F 412 269-0100
Coraopolis (G-3679)

Consolidated Coatings Inc ....G 215 949-1474
Levittown (G-9826)

▲ Coopers Creek Chemical Corp ....E 610 828-0375
Conshohocken (G-3534)

Corban Corporation ....D 610 837-9700
Bath (G-956)

▼ Cork Industries Inc ....E 610 522-9550
Folcroft (G-6001)

Craig R Wickett ....G 610 599-6882
Bangor (G-910)

▲ Custom Mil & Consulting Inc ....E 610 926-0984
Fleetwood (G-5969)

Dajr Enterprises Inc ....F 215 949-0800
Levittown (G-9830)

Donaldson Company Inc ....G 215 396-8349
Warminster (G-18859)

Dow Chemical Company ....C 215 785-8000
Bristol (G-2132)

▼ Dumond Chemicals Inc ....G 609 655-7700
West Chester (G-19544)

Dura-Bond Coating Inc ....E 412 436-2411
Duquesne (G-4496)

Dura-Bond Coating Inc ....E 724 327-0782
Export (G-5598)

E E Zimmerman Company ....F 412 963-0949
Pittsburgh (G-14950)

Evaporated Coatings Inc ....E 215 659-3080
Willow Grove (G-20116)

Evonik Corporation ....G 800 345-3148
Allentown (G-208)

Fuchs Lubricants Co ....E 724 867-5000
Emlenton (G-5008)

Gateway Paint & Chemical Co ....E 412 261-6642
Pittsburgh (G-15042)

Gryphin Elements LLC ....G 215 694-7727
Philadelphia (G-13790)

▼ Haley Paint Company ....D 717 299-6771
Lancaster (G-9037)

Harsco Corporation ....C 570 421-7500
East Stroudsburg (G-4617)

Henry Company LLC ....B 610 933-8888
Kimberton (G-8573)

▲ IC&s Distributing Co ....E 717 391-6250
Lancaster (G-9053)

Innovative Finishers Inc ....G 215 536-2222
Quakertown (G-16201)

◆ International Marketing Inc ....F 717 264-5819
Chambersburg (G-2942)

J & M Industrial Coatings Inc ....G 570 547-1825
Montgomery (G-11371)

James G Bohn ....G 717 597-1901
Greencastle (G-6619)

◆ Kop-Coat Inc ....F 412 227-2426
Pittsburgh (G-15183)

Kop-Coat Inc ....F 412 826-3387
Pittsburgh (G-15184)

Lafarge Rd Marking Inc ....G 570 547-1621
Montgomery (G-11374)

Lockhart Company ....E 724 444-1900
Gibsonia (G-6345)

Lord Corporation ....C 814 763-2345
Saegertown (G-16923)

Lord Corporation ....A 877 275-5673
Erie (G-5373)

M-B Companies Inc ....E 570 547-1621
Muncy (G-11825)

Mark Gingerella ....G 570 213-5603
Susquehanna (G-18181)

◆ McAdoo & Allen Inc ....E 215 536-3520
Quakertown (G-16214)

Mg Industries Erie Inc ....G 814 806-6826
Erie (G-5388)

Minusnine Technologies Inc ....G 215 704-9396
Philadelphia (G-14025)

◆ Morton International LLC ....C 989 636-1000
Collegeville (G-3384)

▲ Mxl Industries Inc ....D 717 569-8711
Lancaster (G-9141)

▲ Norstone Incorporated ....G 484 684-6986
Bridgeport (G-2041)

One Day Baths Inc ....E 570 402-2337
Effort (G-4827)

Pandalai Coatings Company Inc ....G 724 224-5600
Brackenridge (G-1940)

Parrish R Varnish ....G 814 242-1786
Johnstown (G-8419)

▲ Pelmor Laboratories Inc ....E 215 968-3334
Newtown (G-12533)

▲ Performance Coatings Corp ....F 610 525-1190
Levittown (G-9854)

Pittsburgh Glass Works LLC ....B 419 683-2400
Creighton (G-3884)

Pittsburgh Glass Works LLC ....B 814 336-4411
Cochranton (G-3347)

Pittsburgh Powder Coat L ....G 724 348-8434
Bridgeville (G-2086)

◆ Polymeric Systems Inc ....D 610 286-2500
Elverson (G-4965)

PPG Industries Inc ....A 412 434-3131
Pittsburgh (G-15425)

PPG Industries Inc ....E 724 274-7900
Springdale (G-17899)

PPG Industries Inc ....G 215 873-8940
Philadelphia (G-14193)

PPG Industries Inc ....G 717 218-5400
Carlisle (G-2730)

PPG Industries Inc ....E 724 224-6500
Creighton (G-3885)

PPG Industries Inc ....G 717 763-1030
Lemoyne (G-9748)

PPG Industries Inc ....G 610 544-1925
  Springfield (G-17920)
PPG Industries Inc ....G 888 774-1010
  Reading (G-16473)
PPG Industries Inc ....F 412 820-8116
  Carlisle (G-2731)
PPG Industries Inc ....C 412 820-8500
  Cheswick (G-3116)
PPG Industries Inc ....G 412 276-1922
  Carnegie (G-2781)
PPG Industries Inc ....F 412 434-4463
  Pittsburgh (G-15426)
PPG Industries Inc ....G 724 772-0005
  Cranberry Township (G-3843)
PPG Industries Inc ....G 724 863-4473
  Irwin (G-8192)
PPG Industries Inc ....E 412 487-4500
  Allison Park (G-459)
PPG Industries Inc ....E 724 327-3000
  Monroeville (G-11350)
PPG Industries Foundation ....G 412 434-3131
  Pittsburgh (G-15427)
Premier Ink Systems Inc ....G 570 459-2300
  West Hazleton (G-19715)
Pro Guard Coatings Inc ....F 717 336-7900
  Denver (G-4089)
◆ Protech Powder Coatings ....G 814 456-1243
  Erie (G-5440)
Protech Powder Coatings Inc ....E 717 767-6996
  York (G-20646)
Protech Powder Coatings Inc ....F 814 899-7628
  York (G-20647)
Qovalent ....G 610 269-3075
  Downingtown (G-4253)
▲ R & D Coatings Inc ....F 412 771-8110
  Mc Kees Rocks (G-10630)
◆ Ranbar Electrical Mtls LLC ....E 724 864-8200
  Harrison City (G-7251)
Randall Publications ....G 610 871-1427
  Allentown (G-371)
Richardson Paint Co Inc ....F 215 535-4500
  Philadelphia (G-14248)
▲ Richter Precision Inc ....D 717 560-9990
  East Petersburg (G-4589)
◆ Rohm and Haas Company ....A 989 636-1000
  Collegeville (G-3392)
◆ Sargent Realty Inc ....D 570 454-3596
  Hazleton (G-7525)
Sarver Hardware Co Inc ....G 724 295-5131
  Sarver (G-17079)
◆ Sauereisen Inc ....E 412 963-0303
  Pittsburgh (G-15514)
Schaefer Paint Company ....F 717 687-7017
  Ronks (G-16813)
Sealmark Manufacturing Corp ....G 724 379-4442
  Donora (G-4161)
Sherwin-Williams Company ....G 610 975-0126
  Wayne (G-19371)
Specialty Paints Coatings Inc ....G 717 249-5523
  Carlisle (G-2739)
Spectra-Kote Corporation ....E 717 334-3177
  Gettysburg (G-6314)
◆ Spray Products Corporation ....D 610 277-1010
  Plymouth Meeting (G-15872)
Steves Ventures ....G 717 808-2501
  Ephrata (G-5149)
◆ Thermoclad Company ....F 814 456-1243
  Erie (G-5507)
Thermoclad Company ....E 814 899-7628
  Erie (G-5508)
Total Systems Technology Inc ....F 412 653-7690
  Pittsburgh (G-15633)
▲ United Gilsonite Laboratories ....D 570 344-1202
  Scranton (G-17308)
◆ Vexcon Chemicals Inc ....E 215 332-7709
  Philadelphia (G-14443)
Walton Paint Company Inc ....G 724 932-3101
  Jamestown (G-8241)
Walton Paint Company Inc ....F 814 774-3042
  Girard (G-6403)
Watson Industries Inc ....E 724 275-1000
  Harwick (G-7257)
◆ Watson Standard Adhesives Co ......G 724 274-5014
  Harwick (G-7258)
◆ Watson Standard Company ....D 724 275-1000
  Harwick (G-7259)
Wendells Prfmce Trck Sp LLC ....G 717 458-8404
  Mechanicsburg (G-10906)

2861 Gum & Wood Chemicals

▲ Coopers Creek Chemical Corp ....E 610 828-0375
  Conshohocken (G-3534)
Milazzo Industries Inc ....E 570 722-0522
  Pittston (G-15767)

2865 Cyclic-Crudes, Intermediates, Dyes & Org Pigments

◆ Abbey Color Incorporated ....E 215 739-9960
  Philadelphia (G-13334)
Alex Color Company Inc ....G 570 875-3300
  Ashland (G-725)
Blue Mountain Pigment ....G 610 261-4963
  Northampton (G-12846)
Braskem America Inc ....E 412 208-8100
  Pittsburgh (G-14790)
Braskem America Inc ....C 610 497-8378
  Marcus Hook (G-10438)
▲ Braskem America Inc ....C 215 841-3100
  Philadelphia (G-13478)
Byrnes and Kiefer Company ....R 724 538-5200
  Callery (G-2467)
Chem Service Inc ....E 610 692-3026
  West Chester (G-19523)
▲ Coopers Creek Chemical Corp ....E 610 828-0375
  Conshohocken (G-3534)
Coppers Inc ....E 412 233-2137
  Pittsburgh (G-14875)
CSS Industries Inc ....C 610 729-3959
  Plymouth Meeting (G-15840)
▲ Custom Mil & Consulting Inc ....E 610 926-0984
  Fleetwood (G-5969)
Dura-Bond Coating Inc ....E 412 436-2411
  Duquesne (G-4496)
▲ Hamburger Color Company Inc ......F 610 279-6450
  King of Prussia (G-8627)
◆ Heucotech Ltd A NJ Ltd Partnr ......D 215 736-0712
  Fairless Hills (G-5785)
Honeywell Resins & Chem LLC ....C 215 533-3000
  Philadelphia (G-13833)
◆ Indspec Chemical Corporation ....B 724 756-2370
  Petrolia (G-13305)
▲ Itc Supplies LLC ....G 610 430-1300
  West Chester (G-19574)
Koppers Asia LLC ....G 412 227-2001
  Pittsburgh (G-15185)
Koppers Concrete Products Inc ....G 412 227-2001
  Pittsburgh (G-15186)
Koppers Holdings Inc ....C 412 227-2001
  Pittsburgh (G-15187)
◆ Koppers Inc ....C 412 227-2001
  Pittsburgh (G-15188)
◆ Lockhart Chemical Company ....E 724 444-1900
  Gibsonia (G-6344)
Lyondell Chemical Company ....D 610 359-2360
  Newtown Square (G-12583)
◆ Palmer International Inc ....E 610 584-4241
  Skippack (G-17602)
▲ Paper Magic Group Inc ....C 570 961-3863
  Moosic (G-11511)
◆ Penn Color Inc ....E 215 345-6550
  Doylestown (G-4322)
Penn Color Inc ....G 215 997-9206
  Hatfield (G-7379)
Penn Color Inc ....C 215 997-2221
  Hatfield (G-7380)
Presto Dyechem Co Inc ....G 215 627-1863
  Philadelphia (G-14198)
▲ Sanyo Chemical & Resins LLC ....G 412 384-5700
  West Elizabeth (G-19697)
Sealmaster Pennsylvania Inc ....F 724 667-0444
  Hillsville (G-7636)
▲ Sunoco Inc ....D 215 977-3000
  Newtown Square (G-12591)
▲ Tangent Rail Corporation ....G 412 325-0202
  Pittsburgh (G-15596)
Tangent Rail Products Inc ....F 412 325-0202
  Pittsburgh (G-15597)
◆ Toner Holdings LLC ....E 570 675-1131
  Dallas (G-3969)
▲ United Color Manufacturing Inc ......F 215 860-2165
  Newtown (G-12557)
United Color Manufacturing Inc ....F 215 423-2527
  Philadelphia (G-14420)
▼ Verichem Inc ....E 412 331-2616
  Pittsburgh (G-15692)
Youghiogheny Opalescent GL Inc ......E 724 628-3000
  Connellsville (G-3512)

2869 Industrial Organic Chemicals, NEC

3 Prime LLC ....G 610 459-3468
  Aston (G-747)
Affordable Home Fuel LLC ....G 610 847-0972
  Ottsville (G-13058)
Agrofresh Solutions Inc ....G 267 317-9139
  Philadelphia (G-13356)
Air Products and Chemicals Inc ....E 724 266-1563
  Leetsdale (G-9677)
Air Products and Chemicals Inc ....E 610 317-8715
  Bethlehem (G-1446)
Ajay Fuel Inc ....G 570 223-1580
  East Stroudsburg (G-4604)
Akzo Nobel Inc ....G 312 544-7000
  Reading (G-16315)
Albemarle Corporation ....C 814 684-4310
  Tyrone (G-18575)
Alco Fuel Inc ....G 215 638-4800
  Bensalem (G-1147)
Alex Color Company Inc ....G 570 875-3300
  Ashland (G-725)
Alex Color Company Inc ....G 570 875-3300
  Ashland (G-726)
Alien Fuel Inc ....G 609 306-8592
  Yardley (G-20294)
Ambition - The Fuel For Sccess ....G 215 668-9561
  Philadelphia (G-13375)
American Fuels LLC ....G 610 222-3569
  Skippack (G-17594)
◆ Arkema Delaware Inc ....A 610 205-7000
  King of Prussia (G-8582)
Arkema Inc ....C 215 826-2600
  Bristol (G-2109)
◆ Astatech Inc ....E 215 785-3197
  Bristol (G-2110)
B Asf Corp ....G 814 453-7186
  Erie (G-5201)
Baker Outlaw Fuel Systems ....G 717 795-9383
  Liverpool (G-10077)
Bam Fuel LLC ....G 814 255-1689
  Johnstown (G-8355)
Barbary ....G 215 634-7400
  Philadelphia (G-13445)
BASF Catalysts LLC ....C 814 870-3900
  Erie (G-5204)
BASF Corporation ....C 724 728-6900
  Monaca (G-11281)
Biofuel Boiler Tech LLC ....G 717 436-9300
  Mifflintown (G-11110)
Bionol Clearfield LLC ....F 814 913-3100
  Clearfield (G-3213)
Borchers Americas Inc ....E 814 432-2125
  Franklin (G-6117)
Brandywine Fuel Inc ....G 610 455-0123
  Chester (G-3041)
Brandywine Fuel Inc ....G 484 357-7683
  Glen Mills (G-6431)
Brandywine Fuel Inc ....G 484 574-8274
  Aston (G-753)
Braskem America Inc ....E 412 208-8100
  Pittsburgh (G-14790)
Braskem America Inc ....C 610 497-8378
  Marcus Hook (G-10438)
▲ Braskem America Inc ....C 215 841-3100
  Philadelphia (G-13478)
Bucks County Fuel LLC ....G 215 245-0807
  Bensalem (G-1162)
C Ruffs Mini Mart Fuel ....G 484 619-6832
  Coplay (G-3641)
Car Fuel 1 Inc ....G 215 545-2002
  Philadelphia (G-13499)
Carpenter Co ....D 610 366-5110
  Fogelsville (G-5993)
Carpenter Co ....C 814 944-8612
  Altoona (G-486)
Chem Service Inc ....E 610 692-3026
  West Chester (G-19523)
Citi Fuel Convenience Inc ....F 215 724-2395
  Philadelphia (G-13546)
CMA Refinishing Solutions Inc ....G 215 427-1141
  Philadelphia (G-13552)
CNG Mtor Fuels Clarion Cnty LP ....G 814 590-4498
  Coolspring (G-3621)
Connective Tssue Gene Tsts LLC ....F 484 244-2900
  Allentown (G-176)
Craft Products Co Inc ....G 412 821-8102
  Pittsburgh (G-14885)
Creative Chemical Co ....G 724 443-5010
  Allison Park (G-448)

▲ David Michael & Co Inc ....D 215 632-3100
Philadelphia *(G-13607)*

David Michael & Co Inc ....F 909 887-3800
Philadelphia *(G-13608)*

Ddp Specialty Electronic MA ....G 610 244-6000
Collegeville *(G-3374)*

Dl1 Processing LLC ....G 215 582-3263
Chester *(G-3048)*

Dow Chemical Company ....F 215 785-8000
Croydon *(G-3916)*

Dr G H Michel Restor-Skin Co ....G 724 526-5551
East Brady *(G-4529)*

Duco Holdings LLC......................G 215 942-6274
Ivyland *(G-8209)*

Edmil Fuels Inc...........................G 717 249-4901
Carlisle *(G-2709)*

Elf Atochem ....G 215 826-2600
Bristol *(G-2140)*

Emil Rarick Fuel Delivery ....G 570 345-8584
Pine Grove *(G-14592)*

Esstech Inc ....F 610 521-3800
Essington *(G-5543)*

◆ Evonik Oil Additives Usa Inc ....D 215 706-5800
Horsham *(G-7817)*

Evoqua Water Technologies LLC .....E 724 827-8181
Darlington *(G-4028)*

▲ Fenner Precision Inc ....C 800 327-2288
Manheim *(G-10383)*

Filmtronics Inc ....E 724 352-3790
Butler *(G-2401)*

▲ Fine Grinding Corporation ....E 610 828-7250
Conshohocken *(G-3547)*

▲ Fisher Scientific Company LLC .....B 724 517-1500
Pittsburgh *(G-15019)*

Five Star Group Inc ....G 814 237-0241
State College *(G-17965)*

Fluorous Technologies Inc ....F 267 225-5384
Pittsburgh *(G-15022)*

◆ FMC Corporation ....B 215 299-6000
Philadelphia *(G-13709)*

FMC Overseas Ltd ....G 215 299-6000
Philadelphia *(G-13712)*

▲ Fragrance Manufacturing Inc ....E 610 266-7580
Allentown *(G-218)*

Friendly Fuel.............................G 717 254-1932
Newburg *(G-12475)*

Fuel ....G 215 468-3835
Philadelphia *(G-13730)*

Fuel ....G 215 922-3835
Philadelphia *(G-13731)*

Fuel & Save Inc ....G 814 857-5356
Bigler *(G-1659)*

Fuel Cell Inc ....E 610 759-0143
Nazareth *(G-11967)*

Fuel Doctor Inc ....G 904 521-9889
Ronks *(G-16807)*

Fuel ME Green LLC ....G 267 825-7193
Philadelphia *(G-13732)*

Fuel On Whitehaven LLC ....G 570 443-8830
White Haven *(G-19847)*

Fuel One Gas Cnvnience Str LLC .....G 551 208-3490
Mountain Top *(G-11761)*

Fuel Recharge Yourself Inc 3 ....G 215 468-3835
Philadelphia *(G-13733)*

Fuel Treatment Solutions LLC ....G 215 914-1006
Huntingdon Valley *(G-7986)*

Fuel7 Inc ....G 267 980-7888
Langhorne *(G-9299)*

Fuelone Gas Cnvenience Str LLC .....G 570 443-8830
White Haven *(G-19848)*

Fuels & Lubes Technologies LLC .....G 724 282-8264
Fenelton *(G-5945)*

Gas N Go Washington ....G 724 228-2850
Washington *(G-19178)*

Gelest Inc ....G 215 547-1015
Morrisville *(G-11560)*

Geo Fuels LLC...........................G 570 331-0800
Mountain Top *(G-11762)*

Geo Specialty Chemicals Inc ....E 215 773-9280
Ambler *(G-579)*

Gh Holdings Inc ....G 610 666-4000
Valley Forge *(G-18707)*

Glycol Technologies Inc................G 724 776-3554
Warrendale *(G-19077)*

Greenerways LLC ....F 215 280-7658
Yardley *(G-20313)*

Gs Fuel Inc...............................G 484 751-5414
Blue Bell *(G-1831)*

Gurpreet Fuel Company Llc............G 215 493-6322
Philadelphia *(G-13792)*

Haller Energy Services LLC ....F 717 721-9560
Adamstown *(G-22)*

Henkel Corp ....G 267 424-5645
Sellersville *(G-17349)*

Hercon Laboratories Corp ....E 717 764-1191
Emigsville *(G-4989)*

Hii Holding Corporation ....G 610 666-0219
Norristown *(G-12666)*

◆ Houghton International Inc...........C 888 459-9844
Norristown *(G-12668)*

Hydac Technology Corp ....G 610 266-3143
Bethlehem *(G-1535)*

Hydrol Chemical Company Inc ....F 610 622-3603
Yeadon *(G-20354)*

I Fuel.......................................G 570 524-6851
Lewisburg *(G-9912)*

Innaventure LLC ....G 570 371-9390
Wilkes Barre *(G-19928)*

▲ Inolex Group Inc ....D 215 271-0800
Philadelphia *(G-13859)*

Interntnal Flvors Frgrnces Inc ....G 215 365-7800
Philadelphia *(G-13869)*

Interphase Materials Inc ....G 814 282-8119
Pittsburgh *(G-15133)*

J & B Blending & Technologies ....G 412 331-2850
Mc Kees Rocks *(G-10615)*

Kelly Fuel Co Inc ....G 610 444-5055
Kennett Square *(G-8518)*

Keystone Fuels LLC ....G 724 357-1710
Blairsville *(G-1730)*

Kreiser Fuel Service Inc ....G 570 455-0418
Hazleton *(G-7506)*

Lake Erie Biofuels LLC ....E 814 528-9200
Erie *(G-5353)*

Lamberti Usa Incorporated ....G 610 862-1400
Conshohocken *(G-3571)*

Lancaster Fuels ....G 717 687-5390
Strasburg *(G-18090)*

Lanxess Corporation ....E 412 809-4735
Burgettstown *(G-2348)*

◆ Lanxess Corporation ....A 800 526-9377
Pittsburgh *(G-15219)*

Liquid Ion Solutions LLC ....G 412 275-0919
Pittsburgh *(G-15235)*

Louis Nardello Company................G 215 467-1420
Newtown Square *(G-12582)*

Lyco I LLC.................................G 570 784-0903
Bloomsburg *(G-1788)*

Lyondell Chemical Company ....D 610 359-2360
Newtown Square *(G-12583)*

Martino Fuel ....G 484 802-2183
Broomall *(G-2296)*

Maya Devi Inc ....G 717 420-7060
Gettysburg *(G-6307)*

Merisol Antioxidants LLC...............E 814 677-2028
Oil City *(G-12952)*

Mobinol Fuel Company ....G 484 432-9007
Collegeville *(G-3382)*

Mtr Fuel LLC ....G 609 610-0783
Morrisville *(G-11573)*

N3 Oceanic Inc ....E 215 541-1073
Pennsburg *(G-13251)*

National Fuel Gas Dist Corp ....G 814 837-9585
Kane *(G-8472)*

Naughton Energy Corporation ....F 570 646-0422
Pocono Pines *(G-15882)*

Neo-Solutions Inc ....E 724 728-7360
Beaver *(G-988)*

◆ Nonlethal Technologies Inc ....E 724 479-5100
Homer City *(G-7679)*

◆ Norquay Technology Inc..............E 610 874-4330
Chester *(G-3058)*

Nu-Chem Corp ....F 610 770-2000
Allentown *(G-336)*

Nurture Inc ....G 610 989-0945
Devon *(G-4114)*

Occidental Chemical Corp ....F 610 327-4145
Pottstown *(G-16022)*

On Fuel....................................G 570 288-5805
Luzerne *(G-10128)*

On Fuel....................................G 570 784-5320
Bloomsburg *(G-1792)*

On Fuel....................................G 814 837-1017
Kane *(G-8476)*

On Fuel....................................G 570 275-0170
Danville *(G-4008)*

Penn Fuel Gas Incorporated ....G 814 353-0404
Bellefonte *(G-1111)*

Pennsylvania Agri-Fuel Inc ....G 717 733-1050
Ephrata *(G-5137)*

Pennsylvania Grains Proc LLC.........E 877 871-0774
Clearfield *(G-3228)*

▼ Polonier Corporation ....G 267 994-1698
Fairless Hills *(G-5792)*

◆ Polymeric Systems Inc ....D 610 286-2500
Elverson *(G-4965)*

Pottsville Fuel Stop Inc ....G 570 429-2970
Pottsville *(G-16091)*

PST Fuel Inc ....G 215 676-3545
Phila *(G-13312)*

Quaker Chemical Corporation ....A 610 832-4000
Conshohocken *(G-3595)*

Quanta Technologies Inc ....G 610 644-7101
Lancaster *(G-9180)*

Rawlee Fuels LLC ....G 724 349-3320
Indiana *(G-8123)*

REO & Sons Fuels LLC ....G 267 374-6400
Quakertown *(G-16241)*

Ritters Fuel Delivery LLC ....G 717 957-4477
Shermans Dale *(G-17501)*

Road Runner Race Fuels LLC ....G 717 587-1693
Mohnton *(G-16241)*

Royal Chemical Company Ltd ....F 570 421-7850
East Stroudsburg *(G-4634)*

Sanda Corporation......................G 502 510-8782
Media *(G-10947)*

Sasol Chemicals (usa) LLC ....C 814 677-2028
Oil City *(G-12957)*

Sbn Holding LLC.........................G 724 756-2210
Petrolia *(G-13307)*

Sewickley Village Fuel and Svc ....G 412 741-9972
Sewickley *(G-17410)*

Shereen Fuel Inc ....G 215 632-2160
Philadelphia *(G-14302)*

Sign Fuel..................................G 989 245-6284
Coplay *(G-3648)*

Sky Fuel Inc ....G 215 343-3825
Warrington *(G-19134)*

Sky Fuel Inc ....G 215 257-5392
Perkasie *(G-13294)*

Smart Fuels LLC ....G 717 645-8983
Mechanicsburg *(G-10890)*

Smarterfuel Inc ....E 570 972-4727
Wind Gap *(G-20173)*

Sonneborn LLC ....C 724 756-9337
Petrolia *(G-13308)*

Spring Vly Altrntive Fuels LLC ....G 814 587-3002
Conneautville *(G-3487)*

▲ Sunoco Inc ....D 215 977-3000
Newtown Square *(G-12591)*

▲ Sunoco (R&m) LLC ....D 215 977-3000
Newtown Square *(G-12592)*

Synthex Organics LLC ....G 814 941-8375
Altoona *(G-550)*

▲ Thermo Shandon Inc ....G 412 788-1133
Pittsburgh *(G-15615)*

Total Ptrchemicals Ref USA Inc ....B 877 871-2729
Exton *(G-5737)*

Total Ptrchemicals Ref USA Inc ....D 610 692-8401
West Chester *(G-19667)*

Town & Country Fuel LLC ....F 717 252-2152
Conestoga *(G-3461)*

Uct Inc ....E 215 781-9255
Bristol *(G-2213)*

Uct LLC....................................E 215 781-9255
Bristol *(G-2214)*

Ungerer Industries Inc..................D 610 868-7266
Bethlehem *(G-1647)*

United Enrgy Plus Trminals LLC ....E 610 774-5151
Allentown *(G-418)*

Vertellus DWG LLC ....B 800 344-3426
Delaware Water Gap *(G-4044)*

▲ Vigon International Inc ....D 877 844-6639
East Stroudsburg *(G-4638)*

▼ Vision Technology UHS LLC..........G 717 465-0694
Hanover *(G-6969)*

Vista Fuels LLC ....G 570 385-7274
Schuylkill Haven *(G-17170)*

VWR Corporation ....C 610 386-1700
Radnor *(G-16304)*

Wacker Chemical Corporation.........D 610 336-2700
Allentown *(G-428)*

Watt Fuel Cell Corp ....E 724 547-9170
Mount Pleasant *(G-11722)*

Wayne Fueling Systems ....G 215 257-1046
Perkasie *(G-13298)*

Westlake Chemical Partners LP ....G 484 253-4545
Wayne *(G-19391)*

2873 Nitrogenous Fertilizers

Agrium Advanced Tech US Inc ....G 724 865-9180
Butler *(G-2372)*

Chemgro Fertilizer Co Inc ....F 717 935-2185
Belleville *(G-1129)*

Cumberland Valley Coop Assn ....E 717 532-2197
Shippensburg *(G-17525)*

Dyno Nobel Inc ....E 724 379-8100
Donora *(G-4152)*

Growmark Fs LLC ....G 814 359-2725
Bellefonte *(G-1102)*

Growmark Fs LLC ....E 724 543-1101
Adrian *(G-30)*

Hillendale Peat Moss Inc ....G 610 444-5591
Avondale *(G-853)*

Hyponex Corporation ....D 610 932-4200
Oxford *(G-13083)*

◆ International Raw Mtls Ltd ....E 215 928-1010
Philadelphia *(G-13867)*

J J C L Inc ....G 570 619-7347
Reeders *(G-16619)*

▲ Laurel Valley Farms Inc ....E 610 268-2074
Landenberg *(G-9251)*

Peach Bottom Transport LLC ....G 717 278-8055
Peach Bottom *(G-13200)*

Scotts Company LLC ....G 215 538-0191
Quakertown *(G-16244)*

Smart Fertilizer LLC ....G 814 880-8873
State College *(G-18026)*

▲ Timac Agro Usa Inc ....E 610 375-7272
Reading *(G-16539)*

2874 Phosphatic Fertilizers

Agricultural Commodities Inc ....D 717 624-6858
Gettysburg *(G-6282)*

Growmark Fs LLC ....E 724 543-1101
Adrian *(G-30)*

Growmark Fs LLC ....E 610 926-6339
Leesport *(G-9664)*

Growmark Fs LLC ....F 717 854-3818
York *(G-20515)*

Growmark Fs LLC ....G 814 359-2725
Bellefonte *(G-1102)*

◆ International Raw Mtls Ltd ....E 215 928-1010
Philadelphia *(G-13867)*

Occidental Chemical Corp ....F 610 327-4145
Pottstown *(G-16022)*

Willard Agri-Service Inc ....F 717 375-2229
Marion *(G-10471)*

2875 Fertilizers, Mixing Only

A & M Compost ....F 215 256-1900
Norristown *(G-12629)*

Barnside Mulch and Compost ....G 610 287-8880
Schwenksville *(G-17174)*

Bedford Farm Bureau Coop Assn ....F 814 623-6194
Bedford *(G-1040)*

Bedford Farm Bureau Coop Assn ....F 814 793-2721
Curryville *(G-3945)*

Bennett Compost ....G 215 520-2406
Philadelphia *(G-13453)*

Compost Films Inc ....G 215 668-3001
Wallingford *(G-18782)*

Cornell Bros Inc ....F 570 376-2471
Middlebury Center *(G-11043)*

Dyno Nobel Inc ....E 724 379-8100
Donora *(G-4152)*

Earth Friendly Compost Inc ....G 570 760-4510
Harveys Lake *(G-7256)*

First Regional Compost Auth ....G 610 262-1000
Northampton *(G-12850)*

Green n Grow Compost LLC ....G 717 284-5710
Holtwood *(G-7667)*

Growmark Fs LLC ....G 814 359-2725
Bellefonte *(G-1102)*

Growmark Fs LLC ....E 724 543-1101
Adrian *(G-30)*

◆ International Raw Mtls Ltd ....E 215 928-1010
Philadelphia *(G-13867)*

◆ J R Peters Inc ....E 610 395-7104
Allentown *(G-267)*

Joe Grow Inc ....F 814 355-2878
Bellefonte *(G-1106)*

Kirby Agri Inc ....E 717 299-2541
Lancaster *(G-9087)*

Klingler Incorporated ....F 717 535-5151
Thompsontown *(G-18347)*

▲ Laurel Valley Farms Inc ....E 610 268-2074
Landenberg *(G-9251)*

▲ Laurel Valley Soils ....G 610 268-5555
Avondale *(G-854)*

Magnesita Refractories Company ....C 717 792-3611
York *(G-20574)*

Mainville AG Services Inc ....G 570 784-6922
Bloomsburg *(G-1789)*

Mastermix Inc ....G 610 346-8723
Quakertown *(G-16213)*

▼ Moyer & Son Inc ....C 215 799-2000
Souderton *(G-17753)*

Mulch Works Recycling Inc ....F 888 214-4628
Aston *(G-779)*

Natural Soil Products Company ....D 570 695-2211
Tremont *(G-18481)*

▲ Ontelaunee Farms Inc ....E 610 929-5753
Temple *(G-18334)*

Organic Mechanics Soil Co LLC...........G 484 557-2961
Modena *(G-11258)*

Penn Jersey Farms Inc ....G 610 488-7003
Bethel *(G-1397)*

Pine Valley Supply Corporation ....G 215 676-8100
Philadelphia *(G-14178)*

Scotts Company LLC ....E 610 268-3006
Avondale *(G-860)*

Spring Valley Mulch Brian ....G 717 292-7945
Dover *(G-4205)*

Synatek LP ....D 888 408-5433
Souderton *(G-17767)*

Webbs Super-Gro Products Inc............E 570 726-4525
Mill Hall *(G-11184)*

2879 Pesticides & Agricultural Chemicals, NEC

All Star Pest Servcies LLC ....G 215 828-9099
Philadelphia *(G-13365)*

◆ Bayer Corporation ....A 412 777-2000
Pittsburgh *(G-14750)*

Bayer Cropscience LP ....D 412 777-2000
Pittsburgh *(G-14752)*

Boos Bug Stoppers LLC ....G 724 601-3223
Fombell *(G-6030)*

Chem Service Inc ....E 610 692-3026
West Chester *(G-19523)*

Chemgro Fertilizer Co Inc ....F 717 935-2185
Belleville *(G-1129)*

FMC Asia-Pacific Inc ....G 215 299-6000
Philadelphia *(G-13708)*

◆ FMC Corporation ....B 215 299-6000
Philadelphia *(G-13709)*

FMC Corporation ....B 800 526-3649
Philadelphia *(G-13711)*

Gallimed Sciences Inc ....G 814 777-2973
State College *(G-17967)*

Koch Industries Inc ....G 717 949-3469
Schaefferstown *(G-17128)*

Koch Industries Inc ....F 814 453-5444
Erie *(G-5349)*

▲ Liquid Fence Co Inc ....E 570 722-8165
Blakeslee *(G-1748)*

Miller Chemical & Fert Corp ....G 717 632-8921
Hanover *(G-6920)*

Nutra-Soils Inc ....E 610 869-7645
West Grove *(G-19703)*

▲ Nutrient Control Systems Inc ....G 717 261-5711
Chambersburg *(G-2965)*

▲ Senoret Chemical Company ....E 717 626-2125
Lititz *(G-10047)*

Specilized Svcs Promotions Inc...........G 814 864-4984
Erie *(G-5487)*

▲ Upl NA Inc ....E 610 491-2800
King of Prussia *(G-8694)*

Weiser Group LLC ....F 724 452-6535
Evans City *(G-5565)*

Zep Inc ....C 610 295-1360
Breinigsville *(G-2033)*

2891 Adhesives & Sealants

Accu Bond Corporation ....F 610 269-8433
Downingtown *(G-4208)*

ACE Company ....G 215 234-4615
Harleysville *(G-7012)*

Acrymax Technologies Inc ....F 610 566-7470
Media *(G-10913)*

◆ Adhesives Research Inc ....B 717 235-7979
Glen Rock *(G-6449)*

▲ Adhesives Specialists Inc ....E 610 266-8910
Allentown *(G-116)*

▲ Adlamco Inc ....G 717 292-1577
York *(G-20367)*

◆ Air Products and Chemicals Inc ....A 610 481-4911
Allentown *(G-119)*

Air Products and Chemicals Inc...........E 724 266-1563
Leetsdale *(G-9677)*

▲ American Cnsld Mfg Co Inc ....E 610 825-2630
Conshohocken *(G-3519)*

▲ Arkema Delaware Inc ....A 610 205-7000
King of Prussia *(G-8582)*

Arkema Inc ....C 215 826-2600
Bristol *(G-2109)*

◆ Atlas Minerals & Chemicals Inc ....E 800 523-8269
Mertztown *(G-11000)*

Bemis Packaging Inc ....E 717 279-5000
Lebanon *(G-9481)*

◆ Berwind Consumer Products LLC......A 215 563-2800
Philadelphia *(G-13458)*

▲ C P Converters Inc ....D 717 764-1193
York *(G-20415)*

◆ Cardolite Corporation ....E 609 436-0902
Bristol *(G-2123)*

◆ Carlisle Construction Mtls LLC ....B 717 245-7000
Carlisle *(G-2695)*

Chrysler Encpsulated Seals Inc ....E 570 319-1694
S Abingtn Twp *(G-16891)*

Clarance J Venne Inc ....G 215 547-7110
Levittown *(G-9825)*

Concrete Service Materials Co ....G 610 825-1554
Conshohocken *(G-3532)*

Concure Inc ....G 610 497-0198
Chester *(G-3044)*

◆ Covestro LLC ....A 412 413-2000
Pittsburgh *(G-14882)*

Ddp Specialty Electronic MA ....G 610 244-6000
Collegeville *(G-3374)*

DSM Biomedical Inc ....G 610 321-2720
Exton *(G-5669)*

▲ Eastern Adhesives Inc ....F 215 348-0119
Doylestown *(G-4296)*

Fielco Adhesives ....G 267 282-5311
Huntingdon Valley *(G-7982)*

Fielco Industries Inc ....E 215 674-8700
Huntingdon Valley *(G-7983)*

◆ Fres-Co Systems Usa Inc ....B 215 721-4600
Telford *(G-18290)*

Fuchs Lubricants Co ....E 724 867-5000
Emlenton *(G-5008)*

Hahn Universal ....G 724 941-6444
Canonsburg *(G-2594)*

Haraeuc Inc Cermalloy Div ....G 610 825-8387
Conshohocken *(G-3553)*

Harsco Corporation ....G 215 295-8675
Fairless Hills *(G-5783)*

HB Fuller Company ....E 610 688-1234
Wayne *(G-19335)*

Heraeus Incorporated Hic ....C 610 825-6050
Conshohocken *(G-3555)*

Laticrete International Inc ....E 610 326-9970
Pottstown *(G-16009)*

▲ LD Davis Industries Inc ....E 800 883-6199
Jenkintown *(G-8293)*

Lord Corporation ....C 724 260-5541
Eighty Four *(G-4844)*

Lord Corporation ....B 814 868-0924
Erie *(G-5371)*

Lord Corporation ....C 814 763-2345
Saegertown *(G-16923)*

Lord Corporation ....A 877 275-5673
Erie *(G-5373)*

Lutech Inc ....G 717 898-9150
Salunga *(G-17054)*

Lynx Specialty Tapes Inc ....G 215 348-1382
Doylestown *(G-4314)*

Marsh Laboratories Inc ....F 412 271-3060
Pittsburgh *(G-15256)*

Modern Blending Tech Inc ....F 267 580-1000
Levittown *(G-9850)*

◆ Morton International LLC ....C 989 636-1000
Collegeville *(G-3384)*

Nanogriptech Inc ....G 412 224-2136
Pittsburgh *(G-15318)*

Oneida Instant Log ....E 814 336-2125
Meadville *(G-10770)*

◆ Pecora Corporation ....G 215 723-6051
Harleysville *(G-7051)*

▲ Pelmor Laboratories Inc ....E 215 968-3334
Newtown *(G-12533)*

Pelseal Technologies LLC ....F 215 245-0581
Bensalem *(G-1239)*

▲ Performance Coatings Corp ....F 610 525-1190
Levittown *(G-9854)*

S I C

Permabond LLC ....G....... 732 868-1372
Pottstown **(G-16029)**
◆ Polymeric Systems Inc ....D....... 610 286-2500
Elverson **(G-4965)**
▼ Polytek Development Corp ....E....... 610 559-8620
Easton **(G-4743)**
PPG Industries Inc ....E....... 412 487-4500
Allison Park **(G-459)**
PRC - Desoto International Inc ....G....... 412 434-3131
Pittsburgh **(G-15430)**
Quaker Chemical Corporation ....A....... 610 832-4000
Conshohocken **(G-3595)**
R H Carbide & Epoxy Inc ....G....... 724 356-2277
Hickory **(G-7630)**
◆ Rohm and Haas Company ....A....... 989 636-1000
Collegeville **(G-3392)**
S-Bond Technologies LLC ....G....... 215 631-7114
Hatfield **(G-7393)**
▲ Saint-Gobain Corporation ....A....... 610 893-6000
Malvern **(G-10313)**
◆ Saint-Gobain Delaware Corp ....G....... 610 341-7000
Valley Forge **(G-18712)**
◆ Sauereisen Inc ....E....... 412 963-0303
Pittsburgh **(G-15514)**
Sensible Components LLC ....F....... 855 548-7587
Oakdale **(G-12911)**
Sensus USA Inc ....C....... 800 375-8875
Du Bois **(G-4419)**
Sensus USA Inc ....C....... 724 430-3956
Pittsburgh **(G-15524)**
◆ Smooth-On Inc ....C....... 610 252-5800
Macungie **(G-10159)**
Specialty Adhesives Inc ....G....... 484 524-5324
Coatesville **(G-3326)**
Tremco Incorporated ....D....... 717 944-9702
Middletown **(G-11083)**
Union Sealants LLC ....G....... 610 473-2892
Gilbertsville **(G-6379)**
▲ United Gilsonite Laboratories ....D....... 570 344-1202
Scranton **(G-17308)**
Versum Materials Us LLC ....F....... 610 481-3946
Allentown **(G-423)**
Versum Materials Us LLC ....G....... 570 467-2981
Tamaqua **(G-18231)**
Vilimia Inc ....F....... 570 654-6735
Yatesville **(G-20349)**
▼ Wall Firma Inc ....F....... 724 258-6873
Monongahela **(G-11319)**
◆ Whitford Corporation ....D....... 610 286-3500
Elverson **(G-4967)**
◆ Whitford Worldwide Company LLC ..D....... 610 286-3500
Elverson **(G-4968)**
Whitmore Manufacturing Company ......F....... 724 225-8008
Washington **(G-19246)**
▲ WW Henry Company LP ....E....... 704 203-5000
Aliquippa **(G-103)**

2892 Explosives

▼ Action Manufacturing Company ....B....... 267 540-4041
Bristol **(G-2103)**
Action Manufacturing Company ....E....... 610 593-1800
Atglen **(G-799)**
Ametek Inc ....D....... 215 256-6601
Harleysville **(G-7020)**
Blasting Products Inc ....E....... 412 221-5722
Cuddy **(G-3941)**
Cheri-Lee Inc ....G....... 570 339-4195
Kulpmont **(G-8822)**
▼ Copperhead Chemical Co Inc ....E....... 570 386-6123
Tamaqua **(G-18209)**
Douglas Explosives Inc ....E....... 814 342-0782
Philipsburg **(G-14511)**
Dyno Nobel Inc ....E....... 814 938-2035
Punxsutawney **(G-16135)**
◆ Nonlethal Technologies Inc ....E....... 724 479-5100
Homer City **(G-7679)**
Tripwire Operations Group LLC ....F....... 717 648-2792
Gettysburg **(G-6319)**
Wampum Hardware Co ....G....... 724 336-4501
New Galilee **(G-12223)**

2893 Printing Ink

American Inks & Coatings Corp ....D....... 610 933-5848
Phoenixville **(G-14528)**
Bell-Mark Sales Co Inc ....E....... 717 292-5641
Dover **(G-4186)**
Bell-Mark Technologies Corp ....E....... 717 292-5641
Dover **(G-4187)**
Cabrun Ink Products Corp ....E....... 215 533-2990
Philadelphia **(G-13493)**

Constaflow Pump Company LLC ....G....... 610 515-1753
Easton **(G-4662)**
Dynamic Printing Inc ....G....... 215 793-9453
Ambler **(G-577)**
Flint Group US LLC ....G....... 717 392-1953
Lancaster **(G-9021)**
Ink Division LLC ....G....... 412 381-1104
Braddock **(G-1945)**
Ink RE Phill ....G....... 717 840-0835
York **(G-20537)**
Keystone Printing Ink Co ....F....... 215 228-8100
Philadelphia **(G-13932)**
Liquid X Printed Metals Inc ....F....... 412 426-3521
Pittsburgh **(G-15236)**
N H Laboratories Inc ....F....... 717 545-3221
Harrisburg **(G-7183)**
Penn Color Inc ....C....... 215 997-2221
Hatfield **(G-7380)**
Print Happy LLC ....G....... 717 699-4465
York **(G-20639)**
Printed Ink LLC ....G....... 215 355-1683
Huntingdon Valley **(G-8027)**
▲ Quality Dispersions Inc ....F....... 814 781-7927
Kersey **(G-8567)**
◆ Raven Industries Inc ....D....... 724 539-8230
Latrobe **(G-9516)**
▲ Sanyo Chemical & Resins LLC ....G....... 412 384-5700
West Elizabeth **(G-19697)**
Siegwerk USA Inc ....G....... 570 708-0267
Drums **(G-4383)**
Standard Ink & Color Corp ....G....... 570 424-5214
East Stroudsburg **(G-4635)**
Sun Chemical Corporation ....D....... 215 223-8220
Philadelphia **(G-14353)**
Sun Chemical Corporation ....D....... 215 223-8220
Philadelphia **(G-14354)**
Tek Products & Services Inc ....F....... 610 376-0690
Reading **(G-16534)**
Two Cousins Holdings LLC ....G....... 717 637-1311
Hanover **(G-6963)**
Wampum Hardware Co ....F....... 814 893-5470
Stoystown **(G-18088)**
Wikoff Color Corporation ....G....... 484 681-4065
King of Prussia **(G-8699)**

2895 Carbon Black

Koppers Holdings Inc ....C....... 412 227-2001
Pittsburgh **(G-15187)**
Rockwood Pigments Na Inc ....F....... 610 279-6450
King of Prussia **(G-8670)**

2899 Chemical Preparations, NEC

Acrymax Technologies Inc ....F....... 610 566-7470
Media **(G-10913)**
◆ Advanced Lubrication Spc Inc ....E....... 215 244-2114
Bensalem **(G-1144)**
Advanced Powder Products Inc ....F....... 814 342-5898
Philipsburg **(G-14507)**
Advanced Skin Technologies Inc ....G....... 610 488-7643
Bernville **(G-1295)**
African Cultural Art Forum LLC ....G....... 215 476-0680
Philadelphia **(G-13353)**
Air Products and Chemicals Inc ....B....... 570 467-2981
Tamaqua **(G-18208)**
Allied Foam Tech Corp ....G....... 215 540-2666
Montgomeryville **(G-11384)**
◆ Allsorce Scrning Solutions LLC ....E....... 724 515-2637
Irwin **(G-8143)**
American Colloid Company ....E....... 717 845-3077
York **(G-20371)**
American Inks & Coatings Corp ....D....... 610 933-5848
Phoenixville **(G-14528)**
American Solder & Flux Co Inc ....F....... 610 647-2375
Paoli **(G-13134)**
American Solder & Flux Co Inc ....G....... 610 647-3575
Paoli **(G-13135)**
◆ Arkema Delaware Inc ....A....... 610 205-7000
King of Prussia **(G-8582)**
Arkema Inc ....C....... 215 826-2600
Bristol **(G-2109)**
Armstrongs ....G....... 717 543-5488
Mc Clure **(G-10557)**
◆ Astatech Inc ....E....... 215 785-3197
Bristol **(G-2110)**
Atotech Usa LLC ....E....... 814 238-0514
State College **(G-17943)**
◆ Axiall LLC ....A....... 412 515-8149
Pittsburgh **(G-14744)**
Baker Petrolite LLC ....F....... 610 876-2200
Crum Lynne **(G-3935)**

BASF Construction Chem LLC ....G....... 215 945-3900
Levittown **(G-9818)**
BASF Construction Chem LLC ....G....... 610 391-0633
Allentown **(G-146)**
Blue Boy Products Inc ....G....... 610 284-1055
Downingtown **(G-4215)**
Bms Inc ....G....... 609 883-5155
Yardley **(G-20297)**
▲ Bpi Inc ....F....... 412 371-8554
Pittsburgh **(G-14788)**
Bpi Inc ....F....... 412 771-8176
Mc Kees Rocks **(G-10605)**
Bulk Chemicals Inc ....G....... 610 926-4128
Mohrsville **(G-11275)**
Callery LLC ....G....... 724 538-1200
Evans City **(G-5556)**
◆ Carlisle Construction Mtls LLC ....B....... 717 245-7000
Carlisle **(G-2695)**
Castrol Industrial N Amer Inc ....D....... 877 641-1600
Levittown **(G-9824)**
Charkit Chemical Company LLC ....G....... 267 573-4062
Yardley **(G-20300)**
Chase Corporation ....E....... 412 828-1500
Pittsburgh **(G-14840)**
▲ Chemalloy Company LLC ....E....... 610 527-3700
Conshohocken **(G-3527)**
▲ Chemical Equipment Labs VA Inc ....E....... 610 497-9390
Newtown Square **(G-12570)**
▲ Cheminova Inc ....G....... 919 474-6600
Philadelphia **(G-13538)**
Chemstream Inc ....F....... 814 629-7118
Homer City **(G-7672)**
Clean World Industries Inc ....G....... 724 962-0720
Hermitage **(G-7578)**
▲ Coates Electrographics Inc ....E....... 570 675-1131
Dallas **(G-3960)**
Concrete Service Materials Co ....G....... 610 825-1554
Conshohocken **(G-3532)**
▲ Coopers Creek Chemical Corp ....E....... 610 828-0375
Conshohocken **(G-3534)**
CRC Industries Inc ....G....... 800 556-5074
Warminster **(G-18850)**
◆ CRC Industries Inc ....C....... 215 674-4300
Horsham **(G-7806)**
Creative Chemical Co ....G....... 724 443-5010
Allison Park **(G-448)**
Croda Inc ....E....... 570 893-7650
Mill Hall **(G-11175)**
▲ Crystal Inc - PMC ....D....... 215 368-1661
Lansdale **(G-9355)**
Custom Blends Inc ....G....... 215 934-7080
Philadelphia **(G-13592)**
▲ Custom Mil & Consulting Inc ....E....... 610 926-0984
Fleetwood **(G-5969)**
Dacar Industries ....G....... 412 921-3620
Pittsburgh **(G-14902)**
▼ Dimesol Usa LLC ....F....... 717 938-0796
Lewisberry **(G-9884)**
Dynalene Inc ....F....... 610 262-9686
Whitehall **(G-19871)**
Dyneon LLC ....D....... 610 497-8899
Aston **(G-759)**
E E Zimmerman Company ....F....... 412 963-0949
Pittsburgh **(G-14950)**
East Loop Sand Company Inc ....F....... 814 695-3082
Hollidaysburg **(G-7646)**
Eastern Technologies Inc ....F....... 610 286-2010
Morgantown **(G-11522)**
Elizabeth Milling Company LLC ....F....... 724 872-9404
Smithton **(G-17660)**
◆ Elkem Materials Inc ....G....... 412 299-7200
Moon Township **(G-11486)**
Enchlor Inc ....G....... 215 453-2533
Silverdale **(G-17591)**
Engineered Pressed Materials ....G....... 814 772-6127
Ridgway **(G-16707)**
Esf Enterprise LLC ....G....... 610 334-2615
Reading **(G-16380)**
Euclid Chemical Company ....G....... 610 438-2409
Easton **(G-4681)**
F P Engbert Discount Guns ....G....... 724 465-9756
Indiana **(G-8098)**
Flint Group US LLC ....G....... 717 285-5454
Lancaster **(G-9020)**
Foam Fabricators Inc ....E....... 570 752-7110
Bloomsburg **(G-1782)**
▼ Force Industries Inc ....F....... 610 647-3575
Paoli **(G-13140)**
▲ Fragrance Manufacturing Inc ....E....... 610 266-7580
Allentown **(G-218)**

Fuchs Lubricants Co ... E ... 724 867-5000
Emlenton *(G-5008)*
GE Betz International Inc ... E ... 215 957-2200
Langhorne *(G-9300)*
▼ **GE Infrastructure Sensing** ... F ... 617 926-1749
Feasterville Trevose *(G-5912)*
Gerson Associates PC ... E ... 215 637-6800
Philadelphia *(G-13759)*
Haas Chem Managment of Mexico ... F ... 610 656-7454
West Chester *(G-19558)*
Harsco Corporation ... C ... 570 421-7500
East Stroudsburg *(G-4617)*
Hollyfrontier Corporation ... G ... 800 395-2786
Plymouth Meeting *(G-15848)*
Honeywell Resins & Chem LLC ... C ... 215 533-3000
Philadelphia *(G-13833)*
Houghton Chemical Corporation ... G ... 800 777-2466
Scranton *(G-17241)*
Hydrol Chemical Company Inc ... F ... 610 622-3603
Yeadon *(G-20354)*
◆ **Ifs Industries Inc** ... C ... 610 378-1381
Reading *(G-16406)*
Industrial Terminal Systems ... E ... 724 335-9837
New Kensington *(G-12346)*
Inksewn USA ... F ... 570 534-5199
Philadelphia *(G-13856)*
◆ **International Raw Mtls Ltd** ... E ... 215 928-1010
Philadelphia *(G-13867)*
Interstate Foundry Products ... F ... 814 456-4202
Erie *(G-5332)*
▼ **IPA Systems Inc** ... F ... 215 425-6607
Philadelphia *(G-13873)*
Justi Group Inc ... E ... 484 318-7158
Berwyn *(G-1367)*
K2 Concepts Inc ... F ... 717 207-0820
Lancaster *(G-9077)*
▲ **Keystone Frewrks Specialty Sls** ... G ... 724 277-4294
Dunbar *(G-4442)*
Klenzoid Inc ... F ... 610 825-9494
Conshohocken *(G-3570)*
Koppers Holdings Inc ... C ... 412 227-2001
Pittsburgh *(G-15187)*
◆ **Koppers Inc** ... C ... 412 227-2001
Pittsburgh *(G-15188)*
▲ **Labchem Inc** ... E ... 412 826-5230
Zelienople *(G-20809)*
Lamberti Usa Incorporated ... G ... 610 862-1400
Conshohocken *(G-3571)*
◆ **Langeloth Metallurgical Co LLC** ... C ... 724 947-2201
Langeloth *(G-9270)*
◆ **Lockhart Chemical Company** ... E ... 724 444-1900
Gibsonia *(G-6344)*
Lonza Inc ... C ... 570 321-3900
Williamsport *(G-20035)*
Lord Corporation ... C ... 814 763-2345
Saegertown *(G-16923)*
Lyondell Chemical Company ... D ... 610 359-2360
Newtown Square *(G-12583)*
Mark Gingerella ... G ... 570 213-5603
Susquehanna *(G-18181)*
▲ **McGee Industries Inc** ... E ... 610 459-1890
Aston *(G-775)*
Mg Industrial Products Inc ... G ... 814 255-2471
Johnstown *(G-8408)*
Milazzo Industries Inc ... E ... 570 722-0522
Pittston *(G-15767)*
Mimco Products LLC ... G ... 724 258-8208
Monongahela *(G-11311)*
◆ **Montgomery Chemicals LLC** ... E ... 610 567-0877
Conshohocken *(G-3577)*
Morgan Advanced Ceramics Inc ... D ... 724 537-7791
Latrobe *(G-9505)*
◆ **Morton International LLC** ... C ... 989 636-1000
Collegeville *(G-3384)*
Morton Salt Inc ... F ... 215 428-2012
Fairless Hills *(G-5789)*
Nanohorizons Inc ... E ... 814 355-4700
Bellefonte *(G-1109)*
◆ **National Chemical Labs PA Inc** ... C ... 215 922-1200
Philadelphia *(G-14053)*
National Foam Inc ... G ... 610 363-1400
West Chester *(G-19607)*
▼ **National Foam Inc** ... D ... 610 363-1400
West Chester *(G-19606)*
◆ **Norquay Technology Inc** ... E ... 610 874-4330
Chester *(G-3058)*
▼ **Paper and Ink of Pa LLC** ... E ... 717 709-0533
Chambersburg *(G-2967)*
Paradigm Labs Inc ... F ... 570 345-2600
Pine Grove *(G-14601)*
Parkin Chemical Corporation ... G ... 412 828-7355
Oakmont *(G-12922)*
Pepper Italian Bistro ... G ... 717 392-3000
Lancaster *(G-9168)*
▲ **Performance Coatings Corp** ... F ... 610 525-1190
Levittown *(G-9854)*
Phoenix Laboratories Inc ... F ... 215 295-5222
Levittown *(G-9855)*
▲ **Pike Creek Salt Company** ... F ... 570 585-8818
Clarks Summit *(G-3198)*
Pitt Penn Oil Co LLC ... D ... 813 968-9635
Creighton *(G-3883)*
◆ **Plastic Lumber Yard LLC** ... G ... 610 277-3900
Plymouth Meeting *(G-15864)*
Poly Sat Inc ... E ... 215 332-7700
Philadelphia *(G-14187)*
▲ **Polysciences Inc** ... C ... 215 343-6484
Warrington *(G-19128)*
Polysciences Inc ... G ... 215 520-9358
Warrington *(G-19129)*
Premier Ink Systems Inc ... G ... 570 459-2300
West Hazleton *(G-19715)*
Preservation Technologies LP ... D ... 724 779-2111
Cranberry Township *(G-3844)*
▲ **Pressure Chemical Co** ... E ... 412 682-5882
Pittsburgh *(G-15435)*
Prochemtech International Inc ... E ... 814 265-0959
Brockway *(G-2231)*
Prwt Services Inc ... D ... 570 275-2220
Riverside *(G-16758)*
Quaker Chemical Corporation ... A ... 610 832-4000
Conshohocken *(G-3595)*
◆ **Raven Industries Inc** ... D ... 724 539-8230
Latrobe *(G-9516)*
Recovery Environment Inc ... G ... 717 625-0040
Lititz *(G-10037)*
Revoltnary Elctrnic Design LLC ... G ... 814 977-9546
Bedford *(G-1073)*
Rohm and Haas Chemicals LLC ... G ... 215 592-3696
Philadelphia *(G-14257)*
◆ **Rohm and Haas Chemicals LLC** ... C ... 989 636-1000
Collegeville *(G-3391)*
◆ **Rohm and Haas Company** ... A ... 989 636-1000
Collegeville *(G-3392)*
▲ **Rowa Corporation** ... G ... 609 567-8600
Croydon *(G-3927)*
▲ **Rusmar Incorporated** ... F ... 610 436-4314
West Chester *(G-19632)*
Sabrosa Salt Company LLC ... G ... 610 250-9002
Easton *(G-4750)*
Salt Fctry By Snow Ice MGT Inc ... G ... 412 321-7669
Pittsburgh *(G-15508)*
◆ **Sauereisen Inc** ... E ... 412 963-0303
Pittsburgh *(G-15514)*
▲ **Schaefer Pyrotechnics Inc** ... G ... 717 687-0647
Ronks *(G-16814)*
Sealmaster Pennsylvania Inc ... F ... 724 667-0444
Hillsville *(G-7636)*
Seneca Mineral Company ... G ... 814 476-0076
Erie *(G-5475)*
Service Rite ... G ... 814 774-8716
Cranesville *(G-3871)*
▲ **Skm Industries Inc** ... F ... 570 383-3062
Olyphant *(G-12999)*
▲ **SOS Products Company Inc** ... E ... 215 679-6262
East Greenville *(G-4576)*
Spectacular Fire Works USA ... G ... 570 465-2100
New Milford *(G-12400)*
◆ **Spray Products Corporation** ... D ... 610 277-1010
Plymouth Meeting *(G-15872)*
Staar Distributing Llc ... E ... 814 371-3500
Du Bois *(G-4420)*
Standard Fusee Corporation ... G ... 215 788-3001
Croydon *(G-3929)*
▲ **Starfire Corporation** ... G ... 814 948-5164
Carrolltown *(G-2810)*
Starfire Corporation ... G ... 814 948-5164
Northern Cambria *(G-12863)*
◆ **Suez Wts Systems Usa Inc** ... B ... 781 359-7000
Trevose *(G-18505)*
◆ **Suez Wts Usa Inc** ... A ... 215 355-3300
Trevose *(G-18506)*
Thomas E Ferro ... G ... 610 485-1356
Upper Chichester *(G-18673)*
Total Ptrchemicals Ref USA Inc ... B ... 877 871-2729
Exton *(G-5737)*
Total Ptrchemicals Ref USA Inc ... D ... 610 692-8401
West Chester *(G-19667)*
Total Systems Technology Inc ... F ... 412 653-7690
Pittsburgh *(G-15633)*
Toxicity Assssors Globl PA LLC ... G ... 215 921-6972
Philadelphia *(G-14401)*
Tricorn Inc ... G ... 610 777-6823
Reading *(G-16550)*
Ungerer Industries Inc ... D ... 610 868-7266
Bethlehem *(G-1647)*
◆ **Vtg Tanktainer North Amer Inc** ... F ... 610 429-5440
West Chester *(G-19675)*
W R Meadows Inc ... E ... 717 792-2627
York *(G-20701)*
▼ **Wall Firma Inc** ... F ... 724 258-6873
Monongahela *(G-11319)*
Water Treatment Services Inc ... F ... 800 817-5116
Monroeville *(G-11363)*
Watson Industries Inc ... E ... 724 275-1000
Harwick *(G-7257)*
▲ **White Engrg Surfaces Corp** ... C ... 215 968-5021
Newtown *(G-12563)*
◆ **Whitford Corporation** ... D ... 610 286-3500
Elverson *(G-4967)*
Wicktek Inc ... G ... 513 474-4518
Farmington *(G-5864)*
Wilkinsburg Penn Joint Wtr ... D ... 412 243-6254
Verona *(G-18764)*
Wilson Pdts Compressed Gas Co ... E ... 610 253-9608
Easton *(G-4777)*
Youghiogheny Opalescent GL Inc ... E ... 724 628-3000
Connellsville *(G-3512)*
Zambelli Fireworks Mfg Co ... G ... 724 652-1156
New Castle *(G-12172)*

29 PETROLEUM REFINING AND RELATED INDUSTRIES

2911 Petroleum Refining

Airgas Usa LLC ... G ... 215 766-8860
Plumsteadville *(G-15806)*
American Natural Retail PA LLC ... G ... 212 359-4483
Wexford *(G-19786)*
American Ref & Biochem Inc ... G ... 610 940-4420
Conshohocken *(G-3520)*
American Refining Group Inc ... B ... 814 368-1378
Bradford *(G-1955)*
American Refining Group Inc ... F ... 412 826-3014
Pittsburgh *(G-14705)*
Atlantic Refining & Marketing ... C ... 215 977-3000
Philadelphia *(G-13422)*
Atls Production Company LLC ... C ... 412 489-0006
Pittsburgh *(G-14736)*
Aviation Technologies Inc ... G ... 570 457-4147
Avoca *(G-840)*
B&B Gas & Oil Shop ... G ... 814 257-8032
Dayton *(G-4037)*
Bognar and Company Inc ... E ... 724 336-5000
New Galilee *(G-12220)*
BP Oil Co Svc Stns Diesl Fuel ... G ... 412 264-6140
Coraopolis *(G-3664)*
BP Stop N Go ... G ... 412 823-4500
Turtle Creek *(G-18559)*
C R Augenstein Inc ... G ... 724 206-0679
Eighty Four *(G-4836)*
Calumet Karns City Ref LLC ... G ... 724 756-9212
Karns City *(G-8480)*
Chevron USA Inc ... E ... 412 262-2830
Coraopolis *(G-3677)*
▲ **Coopers Creek Chemical Corp** ... E ... 610 828-0375
Conshohocken *(G-3534)*
Coppers Inc ... E ... 412 233-2137
Pittsburgh *(G-14875)*
Eagle Bio Diesel Inc ... E ... 814 773-3133
Ridgway *(G-16706)*
Elroy Turpentine Company ... G ... 412 963-0949
Pittsburgh *(G-14964)*
▼ **Equipment & Contrls Africa Inc** ... C ... 412 489-3000
Pittsburgh *(G-14983)*
Ergon Asphalt & Emulsions Inc ... G ... 610 921-0271
Reading *(G-16379)*
Fisher-Klosterman Inc ... F ... 717 274-7280
Lebanon *(G-9568)*
Haller Energy Services LLC ... F ... 717 721-9560
Adamstown *(G-22)*
Hollyfrontier Corporation ... G ... 800 456-4786
Plymouth Meeting *(G-15847)*
Industrial Systems & Process C ... G ... 412 279-4750
Pittsburgh *(G-15122)*
Innovalgae LLC ... G ... 412 996-2556
Wexford *(G-19807)*
◆ **International Group Inc** ... E ... 814 827-4900
Titusville *(G-18385)*

SIC

Jadden Inc ....G....... 724 212-3715
New Kensington *(G-12349)*

Lakeside Stop-N-Go LLC ....G....... 814 213-0202
Conneaut Lake *(G-3476)*

Lanxess Solutions US Inc ....C....... 724 756-2210
Petrolia *(G-13306)*

Lyondell Chemical Company ....D....... 610 359-2360
Newtown Square *(G-12583)*

Main St Stop N Go ....G....... 570 424-5505
Stroudsburg *(G-18127)*

Matreya LLC ....F....... 814 355-1030
State College *(G-17988)*

Maxwell Canby Fuel Oil Co ....G....... 610 269-0288
Upper Darby *(G-18688)*

Mipc LLC ....B....... 610 364-8660
Marcus Hook *(G-10449)*

▲ Monroe Energy LLC ....B....... 610 364-8000
Trainer *(G-18464)*

Pennzoil-Quaker State Company ......B....... 724 756-0110
Karns City *(G-8482)*

Petroleum Products Corp ....G....... 412 264-8242
Coraopolis *(G-3714)*

Philadelphia Energy Solutions ....C....... 267 238-4300
Philadelphia *(G-14144)*

Philadelphia Energy Solutions ....A....... 215 339-1200
Philadelphia *(G-14145)*

▲ Philadlphia Enrgy Slutions LLC .....G....... 267 238-4300
Philadelphia *(G-14161)*

Pricetown Ephrata Gas &F ....G....... 610 939-1701
Fleetwood *(G-5978)*

Rohmax Additives GMBH LLC ....E....... 215 706-5800
Philadelphia *(G-14258)*

Sunoco Inc ....E....... 717 564-1440
Harrisburg *(G-7222)*

▲ Sunoco Inc ....D....... 215 977-3000
Newtown Square *(G-12591)*

Sunoco Inc (R&m) ....A....... 610 859-1000
Marcus Hook *(G-10455)*

▲ Sunoco (R&m) LLC ....D....... 215 977-3000
Newtown Square *(G-12592)*

▲ Tangent Rail Corporation ....G....... 412 325-0202
Pittsburgh *(G-15596)*

Total Ptrchemicals Ref USA Inc ....B....... 877 871-2729
Exton *(G-5737)*

Total Ptrchemicals Ref USA Inc ....D....... 610 692-8401
West Chester *(G-19667)*

Tresco Paving Corporation ....G....... 412 793-0651
Pittsburgh *(G-15643)*

Tri-State Petroleum Corp ....D....... 724 226-0135
Tarentum *(G-18249)*

Turtle Moon Gardens ....G....... 814 639-0287
Port Matilda *(G-15907)*

▲ United Refining Inc ....D....... 814 723-1500
Warren *(G-19054)*

United Refining Company ....G....... 814 723-6511
Warren *(G-19056)*

United Refining Company ....C....... 814 723-1500
Warren *(G-19055)*

Van Tongeren America LLC ....G....... 717 450-3835
Lebanon *(G-9637)*

World Energy Harrisburg LLC ....F....... 717 412-0374
Camp Hill *(G-2526)*

2951 Paving Mixtures & Blocks

A-One Asphalt Paving ....G....... 215 658-1616
Philadelphia *(G-13331)*

Advanced Asphalt LLC ....G....... 717 965-2406
New Oxford *(G-12402)*

Allan Myers Materials Inc ....G....... 610 442-4191
Devault *(G-4110)*

Allegheny Asphalt Services LLC ....G....... 724 732-6637
Ambridge *(G-607)*

▼ American Asphalt Paving Co ....C....... 570 696-1181
Shavertown *(G-17478)*

◆ Atlas Minerals & Chemicals Inc ......E....... 800 523-8269
Mertztown *(G-11000)*

Beaver Valley Slag Inc ....G....... 724 375-8173
Monaca *(G-11285)*

Becks Paving ....G....... 814 692-7797
Port Matilda *(G-15901)*

Bituminous Pav Mtls York Inc ....G....... 717 843-4573
York *(G-20408)*

Bituminous Pav Mtls York Inc ....G....... 717 632-8919
Hanover *(G-6863)*

Clairton Slag Inc ....F....... 412 384-8420
West Elizabeth *(G-19693)*

Cole Construction Inc ....G....... 570 888-5501
Milan *(G-11146)*

▲ Coopers Creek Chemical Corp ....E....... 610 828-0375
Conshohocken *(G-3534)*

Crafco Inc ....G....... 610 264-7541
Allentown *(G-183)*

Derry Construction Co Inc ....F....... 724 539-7600
Latrobe *(G-9471)*

Dunbar Asphalt Products Inc ....G....... 724 346-3594
Wheatland *(G-19837)*

Dunbar Asphalt Products Inc ....G....... 724 528-9310
West Middlesex *(G-19723)*

Eastern Industries Inc ....E....... 570 265-9191
Towanda *(G-18425)*

Eastern Industries Inc ....E....... 570 524-2251
Winfield *(G-20199)*

Eastern Industries Inc ....E....... 717 362-3388
Elizabethville *(G-4893)*

Ergon Asphalt & Emulsions Inc ....G....... 484 471-3999
Springfield *(G-17912)*

Erie Asphalt Paving Co ....D....... 814 898-4151
Erie *(G-5262)*

Eureka Stone Quarry Inc ....E....... 215 822-0593
Chalfont *(G-2874)*

Getz Paving ....G....... 570 629-3007
Kunkletown *(G-8833)*

Glasgow Inc ....D....... 215 884-8800
Glenside *(G-6521)*

Glen Blooming Contractors Inc ....C....... 717 566-3711
Hummelstown *(G-7912)*

Glenn O Hawbaker Inc ....D....... 814 237-1444
State College *(G-17970)*

Glenn O Hawbaker Inc ....C....... 724 458-0991
Grove City *(G-6788)*

Glenn O Hawbaker Inc ....E....... 814 359-3411
Pleasant Gap *(G-15792)*

Golden Eagle Construction Co ....E....... 724 437-6495
Uniontown *(G-18628)*

Grannas Bros Stone Asp Co Inc ....D....... 814 695-5021
Hollidaysburg *(G-7649)*

H&K Group Inc ....C....... 610 705-0500
Pottstown *(G-15947)*

H&K Group Inc ....G....... 717 867-0701
Annville *(G-650)*

▲ H&K Group Inc ....C....... 610 584-8500
Skippack *(G-17597)*

Hammaker East ....G....... 717 263-0434
Chambersburg *(G-2937)*

Hammaker East ....E....... 412 221-7300
Pittsburgh *(G-15076)*

Hammaker East Emulsions LLC ....E....... 412 449-0700
Pittsburgh *(G-15077)*

◆ Hanover Prest-Paving Company ......E....... 717 637-0500
Hanover *(G-6900)*

Hanson Aggregates PA LLC ....F....... 570 322-6737
Williamsport *(G-20020)*

Hanson Aggregates PA LLC ....D....... 570 992-4951
Stroudsburg *(G-18122)*

Hanson Aggregates PA LLC ....E....... 610 366-4626
Allentown *(G-243)*

HEI-Way LLC ....F....... 724 353-2700
Sarver *(G-17072)*

Heilman Pavement Specialties ....G....... 724 353-2700
Sarver *(G-17073)*

Hempt Bros Inc ....D....... 717 774-2911
Camp Hill *(G-2500)*

Henry Company LLC ....B....... 610 933-8888
Kimberton *(G-8573)*

▲ Highway Materials Inc ....F....... 610 832-8000
Flourtown *(G-5987)*

Highway Materials Inc ....G....... 610 647-5902
Malvern *(G-10245)*

Highway Materials Inc ....F....... 717 626-8571
Lititz *(G-10017)*

Highway Materials Inc ....G....... 215 225-7020
Blue Bell *(G-1834)*

Highway Materials Inc ....G....... 610 828-9525
Conshohocken *(G-3557)*

Highway Materials Inc ....G....... 717 252-3636
Wrightsville *(G-20237)*

Highway Materials Inc ....E....... 215 234-4522
Perkiomenville *(G-13301)*

Hri Inc ....G....... 570 437-4315
Milton *(G-11242)*

Hri Inc ....D....... 570 322-6737
Muncy *(G-11821)*

IA Construction Corporation ....E....... 724 368-2140
Franklin *(G-6137)*

IA Construction Corporation ....G....... 724 479-9690
Homer City *(G-7676)*

IA Construction Corporation ....E....... 814 432-3184
Franklin *(G-6136)*

Integrated Cnstr Systems Inc ....F....... 724 528-9310
West Middlesex *(G-19726)*

Jason A Kreinbrook ....G....... 724 493-6202
Natrona Heights *(G-11944)*

Jem Industries LLC ....G....... 412 818-2606
Pittsburgh *(G-15148)*

Joseph McCormick Cnstr Co Inc ....E....... 814 899-3111
Erie *(G-5339)*

K-R-K Paving LLC ....G....... 267 602-7715
Philadelphia *(G-13918)*

Landfried Paving Inc ....F....... 724 646-2505
Greenville *(G-6753)*

Lehigh Asphalt Pav & Cnstr Co ....F....... 570 668-2040
Tamaqua *(G-18216)*

M&M Stone Co ....D....... 215 723-1177
Telford *(G-18301)*

Martin Limestone Inc ....D....... 717 354-1340
Ephrata *(G-5123)*

Mayer Brothers Construction Co ....F....... 814 452-3748
Erie *(G-5383)*

Mukies/Mccarty Seal Coating C ....G....... 717 684-2799
Columbia *(G-3444)*

New Enterprise Stone Lime Inc ....E....... 814 443-6494
Somerset *(G-17698)*

New Enterprise Stone Lime Inc ....C....... 814 224-2121
Roaring Spring *(G-16766)*

New Enterprise Stone Lime Inc ....E....... 610 678-1913
Reading *(G-16454)*

New Enterprise Stone Lime Inc ....D....... 814 652-5121
Everett *(G-5576)*

New Enterprise Stone Lime Inc ....G....... 610 678-1913
Leesport *(G-9669)*

Pcm Contracting Inc ....G....... 215 675-8846
Hatboro *(G-7296)*

Pennsy Supply Inc ....F....... 717 867-5925
Annville *(G-656)*

Pennsy Supply Inc ....D....... 717 274-3661
Lebanon *(G-9619)*

Petrunak & Company Inc ....E....... 814 467-7860
Windber *(G-20191)*

Pignuts Inc ....G....... 610 530-8788
Allentown *(G-352)*

Pottstown Trap Rock Quarries ....F....... 610 326-4843
Pottstown *(G-16034)*

Quaker Sales Corporation ....G....... 814 539-1376
Johnstown *(G-8427)*

Quaker Sales Corporation ....F....... 814 536-7541
Johnstown *(G-8426)*

Redland Brick Inc ....E....... 412 828-8046
Cheswick *(G-3117)*

Riverside Materials Inc ....F....... 215 426-7299
Philadelphia *(G-14252)*

Rs Asphalt Maintenance Inc ....G....... 717 367-4914
Elizabethtown *(G-4884)*

Russell Standard Corporation ....G....... 724 748-3700
Mercer *(G-10973)*

Russell Standard Corporation ....F....... 412 449-0700
Pittsburgh *(G-15504)*

Russell Standard Corporation ....E....... 724 625-1505
Valencia *(G-18701)*

Sealmaster Pennsylvania Inc ....F....... 724 667-0444
Hillsville *(G-7636)*

Specialty Emulsions Inc ....G....... 717 849-5020
York *(G-20676)*

St Thomas Development Inc ....G....... 717 369-3030
Saint Thomas *(G-17041)*

Stopper Construction Co Inc ....E....... 570 322-5947
Williamsport *(G-20075)*

Stouffers Asphalt Construction ....G....... 724 527-0917
Mount Pleasant *(G-11719)*

Suit-Kote Corporation ....D....... 814 337-1171
Meadville *(G-10796)*

Sunoco (R&m) LLC ....E....... 215 339-2000
Philadelphia *(G-14356)*

▲ Tangent Rail Corporation ....G....... 412 325-0202
Pittsburgh *(G-15596)*

Treyco Manufacturing Inc ....E....... 717 273-6504
Lebanon *(G-9636)*

Valley Quarries Inc ....E....... 717 264-4178
Chambersburg *(G-2995)*

Valley Quarries Inc ....F....... 717 267-2244
Chambersburg *(G-2994)*

Walter R Erle - Mrrisville LLC ....G....... 215 736-1708
Morrisville *(G-11588)*

Wiest Asphalt Products and Pav ....F....... 724 282-6913
Butler *(G-2448)*

Wilkes-Barre Materials LLC ....E....... 570 829-1181
Plains *(G-15790)*

Wilson Paving Inc ....E....... 717 249-3227
Carlisle *(G-2751)*

Windsor Service Trucking Corp ....C....... 610 929-0716
Reading *(G-16567)*

▲ York Building Products Co Inc ....E 717 848-2831
York *(G-20726)*

2952 Asphalt Felts & Coatings

◆ Atlas Minerals & Chemicals Inc ....E 800 523-8269
Mertztown *(G-11000)*

Atlas Roofing Corporation ....E 717 760-5460
Camp Hill *(G-2492)*

Carlisle Construction Mtls Inc ....E 717 245-7142
Carlisle *(G-2693)*

Carlisle Construction Mtls LLC ....G 717 245-7000
Carlisle *(G-2694)*

◆ Carlisle Construction Mtls LLC ....B 717 245-7000
Carlisle *(G-2695)*

Chase Corporation ....G 412 828-5470
Pittsburgh *(G-14838)*

Choose Blackstone LLC ....G 570 754-7800
Schuylkill Haven *(G-17152)*

Dally Slate Company Inc ....D 610 863-4172
Pen Argyl *(G-13213)*

Dectile Harkus Construction ....E 724 789-7125
Butler *(G-2393)*

Designer Cabinets and Hdwr Co ....E 610 622-4455
Clifton Heights *(G-3252)*

Domar Group Inc ....G 714 674-0391
Finleyville *(G-5955)*

Elk Premium Building Products ....G 717 866-8300
Myerstown *(G-11884)*

Fairmans Roof Trusses Inc ....E 724 349-6778
Creekside *(G-3875)*

▼ FBC Chemical Corporation ....G 724 625-3116
Mars *(G-10497)*

Gateway Paint & Chemical Co ....E 412 261-6642
Pittsburgh *(G-15042)*

Henry Company LLC ....B 610 933-8888
Kimberton *(G-8573)*

Kunsman Aggregates ....G 610 882-1455
Bethlehem *(G-1554)*

Maintain-It ....E 484 684-6766
Eagleville *(G-4515)*

Mountain Brook Industrial Coat ....G 717 369-4040
Saint Thomas *(G-17040)*

Omnova Solutions Inc ....B 724 523-5441
Jeannette *(G-8263)*

Penn Big Bed Slate Co Inc ....D 610 767-4601
Slatington *(G-17611)*

▲ Performance Coatings Corp ....F 610 525-1190
Levittown *(G-9854)*

Polyglass USA Inc ....E 570 384-1230
Hazle Township *(G-7474)*

R F Fager Company ....F 717 564-1166
Harrisburg *(G-7203)*

Russell Standard Corporation ....E 724 625-1505
Valencia *(G-18701)*

▲ Slate and Copper Sales Co ....F 814 455-7430
Erie *(G-5481)*

▲ Tangent Rail Corporation ....G 412 325-0202
Pittsburgh *(G-15596)*

Tarco Inc ....E 717 597-1876
Greencastle *(G-6638)*

Versico Incorporated ....E 717 960-4024
Carlisle *(G-2747)*

Warrior Roofing Mfg Inc ....E 717 709-0323
Chambersburg *(G-2998)*

2992 Lubricating Oils & Greases

◆ Advanced Lubrication Spc Inc ....E 215 244-2114
Bensalem *(G-1144)*

Afco C&S LLC ....G 717 264-9147
Chambersburg *(G-2898)*

Akj Industries Inc ....G 412 233-7222
Clairton *(G-3146)*

◆ Alex C Fergusson LLC ....D 717 264-9147
Chambersburg *(G-2899)*

Allegheny Petroleum Pdts Co ....G 724 266-3247
Ambridge *(G-608)*

◆ Allegheny Petroleum Pdts Co ....D 412 829-1990
Wilmerding *(G-20158)*

Applied Creativity Inc ....G 724 327-0054
Export *(G-5589)*

◆ Arkema Delaware Inc ....A 610 205-7000
King of Prussia *(G-8582)*

Arkema Inc ....C 215 826-2600
Bristol *(G-2109)*

BP Lubricants USA Inc ....D 215 443-5220
Warminster *(G-18840)*

BP Lubricants USA Inc ....E 215 674-5301
Warminster *(G-18841)*

Byrne Energy Corp ....G 570 895-4333
Mount Pocono *(G-11733)*

Castrol Industrial N Amer Inc ....D 877 641-1600
Levittown *(G-9824)*

CRC Industries Inc ....G 800 556-5074
Warminster *(G-18850)*

◆ CRC Industries Inc ....C 215 674-4300
Horsham *(G-7806)*

CRC Industries Inc ....G 215 441-4380
Warminster *(G-18851)*

Eni USA R & M Co Inc ....E 724 352-4451
Cabot *(G-2456)*

Fuchs Lubricants Co ....E 724 867-5000
Emlenton *(G-5008)*

▲ General Polymeric Corporation ....D 610 374-5171
Reading *(G-16390)*

Gh Holdings Inc ....G 610 666-4000
Valley Forge *(G-18707)*

Gordon Terminal Service Co PA ....C 412 331-9410
Mckees Rocks *(G-10661)*

Graham Packaging Company LP ....E 717 849-8500
York *(G-20511)*

◆ GTS Enterprises Inc ....G 610 798-9922
Allentown *(G-239)*

◆ Houghton International Inc ....C 888 459-9844
Norristown *(G-12668)*

Kenum Distribution LLC ....G 814 383-2626
Mingoville *(G-11256)*

Levroil LLC ....G 412 722-9849
Pittsburgh *(G-15227)*

Lube Center ....G 717 848-4885
York *(G-20567)*

Lubedealercom ....G 814 521-9625
Berlin *(G-1290)*

McMillan Music Co LLC ....G 215 441-0212
New Britain *(G-12049)*

▲ Muscle Products Corporation ....F 814 786-0166
Jackson Center *(G-8229)*

Noco Distribution LLC ....G 866 946-3927
Ridgway *(G-16719)*

Pennstar LLC ....F 484 275-7990
Northampton *(G-12859)*

Pennzoil-Quaker State Company ....B 724 756-0110
Karns City *(G-8482)*

Pitt Oil Service Inc ....G 412 771-6950
Pittsburgh *(G-15384)*

PPG Architectural Finishes Inc ....D 610 380-6200
Downingtown *(G-4250)*

Quaker Chemical Corporation ....A 610 832-4000
Conshohocken *(G-3595)*

Recoil Inc ....G 814 623-3921
Bedford *(G-1072)*

◆ Richardsapex Inc ....E 215 487-1100
Philadelphia *(G-14247)*

Sean Naughton ....G 570 646-0422
Pocono Pines *(G-15884)*

Sensible Components LLC ....F 855 548-7587
Oakdale *(G-12911)*

▼ Stevenson-Cooper Inc ....G 215 223-2600
Philadelphia *(G-14348)*

Stoner Incorporated ....F 800 227-5538
Lancaster *(G-9208)*

Twin Specialties Corporation ....G 610 834-7900
Conshohocken *(G-3614)*

United Oil Company Corp ....F 412 231-1269
Pittsburgh *(G-15674)*

Whitmore Manufacturing Company ....G 724 225-4151
Washington *(G-19245)*

Whitmore Manufacturing Company ....F 724 225-8008
Washington *(G-19246)*

2999 Products Of Petroleum & Coal, NEC

International Waxes Inc ....E 814 827-3609
Titusville *(G-18386)*

▼ Stevenson-Cooper Inc ....G 215 223-2600
Philadelphia *(G-14348)*

▼ Wall Firma Inc ....F 724 258-6873
Monongahela *(G-11319)*

30 RUBBER AND MISCELLANEOUS PLASTICS PRODUCTS

3011 Tires & Inner Tubes

American Industrial Parts ....G 800 421-1180
Monroeville *(G-11324)*

Barnes P S P Inc ....G 724 287-6711
Butler *(G-2376)*

Bastian Tire Sales Inc ....E 570 323-8651
Williamsport *(G-19992)*

BF Hiestand House ....G 717 426-8415
Marietta *(G-10461)*

Cooper Tire & Rubber Company ....E 610 967-0860
Alburtis *(G-51)*

◆ International Marketing Inc ....F 717 264-5819
Chambersburg *(G-2942)*

Jack Williams Tire Co Inc ....F 610 437-4651
Whitehall *(G-19878)*

Johnstown Tube Laser LLC ....E 814 532-4121
Johnstown *(G-8392)*

Michelin North America Inc ....B 301 641-0121
Seven Fields *(G-17376)*

Micronic Manufacturingusa LLC ....F 484 483-8075
Aston *(G-778)*

◆ Polymer Enterprises Inc ....G 724 838-2340
Greensburg *(G-6703)*

◆ Polymer Tennessee Holdings ....G 724 838-2340
Indiana *(G-8121)*

Pomps Tire Service Inc ....G 814 623-6764
Bedford *(G-1071)*

Steve Shannon Tire Company Inc ....G 570 675-8473
Dallas *(G-3968)*

◆ Superior Tire & Rubber Corp ....E 814 723-2370
Warren *(G-19049)*

Superior Tire & Rubber Corp ....D 814 723-2370
Warren *(G-19050)*

Valley Retreading Inc ....F 724 489-4483
Charleroi *(G-3023)*

3021 Rubber & Plastic Footwear

HH Brown Shoe Company Inc ....D 814 793-3786
Martinsburg *(G-10524)*

▲ Joneric Products Inc ....F 215 441-9669
Horsham *(G-7829)*

Nike Inc ....G 412 922-3660
Coraopolis *(G-3707)*

Paragon Development Corp ....F 724 254-1551
Penn Run *(G-13230)*

Vans Inc ....F 215 632-2481
Philadelphia *(G-14437)*

Vans Inc ....G 717 291-8936
Lancaster *(G-9231)*

3052 Rubber & Plastic Hose & Belting

▲ All-American Holdings LLc ....C 814 438-7616
Union City *(G-18605)*

All-American Hose LLC ....E 814 438-7616
Erie *(G-5180)*

All-American Hose LLC ....E 814 838-3381
Erie *(G-5181)*

Allied Rubber & Rigging Sup Co ....G 724 535-7380
Wampum *(G-18796)*

▲ American Metal & Rubber Inc ....F 215 225-3700
Philadelphia *(G-13386)*

Corry Rubber Corporation ....E 814 664-2313
Corry *(G-3757)*

Fenner Inc ....C 717 665-2421
Manheim *(G-10380)*

Fenner Inc ....D 717 665-2421
Manheim *(G-10381)*

▲ Fenner Inc ....G 717 665-2421
Manheim *(G-10382)*

Gates Corporation ....C 717 267-7000
Chambersburg *(G-2935)*

Iron Hose Company LLC ....G 877 277-9035
Corry *(G-3765)*

Jnb Industrial Supply Inc ....G 412 455-5170
Blawnox *(G-1764)*

Mason East Inc ....G 631 254-2240
Feasterville Trevose *(G-5917)*

▼ National Foam Inc ....D 610 363-1400
West Chester *(G-19606)*

▲ Newage Industries Inc ....C 215 526-2151
Southampton *(G-17827)*

Paragon America LLC ....F 412 408-3447
Sharpsburg *(G-17467)*

Parker-Hannifin Corporation ....A 814 866-4100
Erie *(G-5414)*

Polymeric Extruded Products ....G 215 943-1288
Levittown *(G-9858)*

Powell Electro Systems LLC ....F 610 869-8393
West Grove *(G-19704)*

▲ Powertrack International LLC ....E 412 787-4444
Pittsburgh *(G-15423)*

Quadrant Holding Inc ....C 724 468-7062
Delmont *(G-4054)*

▲ R/W Connection Inc ....E 717 898-5257
Landisville *(G-9266)*

R/W Connection Inc ....G 717 767-3660
Emigsville *(G-4998)*

Raymond Dunn ....G 412 734-2135
Pittsburgh *(G-15469)*

◆ Shingle Belting Inc ....E 610 825-5500
King of Prussia (G-8674)

▲ Tekni-Plex Inc ....E 484 690-1520
Wayne (G-19381)

Trident Tpi Holdings Inc ....A 484 690-1520
Wayne (G-19384)

▲ Zena Associates Llc ....E 215 730-9000
Folcroft (G-6021)

3053 Gaskets, Packing & Sealing Devices

◆ Accutrex Products Inc ....C 724 746-4300
Canonsburg (G-2532)

Al Xander Co Inc ....E 814 665-8268
Corry (G-3743)

▲ Allegheny-York Co ....E 717 266-6617
Manchester (G-10354)

▲ American High Prfmce Seals Inc ......F 412 788-8815
Oakdale (G-12889)

AP Services LLC ....D 724 295-6200
Freeport (G-6199)

Argosy Capital Group LLC ....F 610 971-9685
Wayne (G-19299)

Argosy Inv Partners IV LP ....F 610 971-9685
Wayne (G-19300)

Aviva Technology Inc ....G 610 228-4689
Broomall (G-2279)

C E Conover & Co Inc ....E 215 639-6666
Bensalem (G-1164)

Canfields Outdoor Pwr Eqp Inc ....G 814 697-6233
Shinglehouse (G-17505)

Compressed Air Specialists Co ....G 814 835-2420
Erie (G-5230)

Corona Corporation ....G 215 679-9538
Red Hill (G-16580)

▲ D A R Industrial Pdts Inc ....G 610 825-4900
Conshohocken (G-3535)

D E Errick Corporation ....F 814 642-2589
Port Allegany (G-15893)

▲ Dooley Gasket and Seal Inc ....E 610 328-2720
Broomall (G-2286)

▲ Dudlik Industries Inc ....E 215 674-4383
Hatboro (G-7282)

Dynamic Sealing Systems LLC ....G 724 537-6315
Latrobe (G-9473)

Effective Shielding Company ....F 610 429-9449
West Chester (G-19547)

Enpro Industries Inc ....E 800 618-4701
Hatfield (G-7340)

Enpro Industries Inc ....G 215 946-0845
Bristol (G-2141)

Ensinger Penn Fibre Inc ....D 215 702-9551
Bensalem (G-1190)

Eraseal Technologies LLC ....G 215 350-3633
Hatfield (G-7342)

Fabritech Inc ....G 610 430-0027
Chester Springs (G-3078)

Federal-Mogul Powertrain LLC ....D 610 363-2600
Exton (G-5677)

▼ Fibreflex Packing & Mfg Co ....E 215 482-1490
Philadelphia (G-13700)

▲ Flextron Industries Inc ....F 610 459-4600
Aston (G-763)

G F C Inc ....E 570 587-4588
Clarks Summit (G-3193)

Garlock Sealing Tech LLC ....D 570 323-9409
Williamsport (G-20016)

◆ Gasket Resources Inc ....E 610 363-5800
Downingtown (G-4229)

◆ Greene Tweed & Co Inc ....A 215 256-9521
Kulpsville (G-8827)

Has-Mor Industries Inc ....F 570 383-0185
Olyphant (G-12992)

Hunter Sales Corporation ....F 412 341-2444
Bethel Park (G-1416)

Hussey Performance LLC ....G 724 318-8292
Ambridge (G-619)

▲ Igs Industries Inc ....C 724 222-5800
Meadow Lands (G-10690)

▲ Inter Tech Supplies Inc ....G 610 435-1333
Allentown (G-265)

Interface Solutions Inc ....G 717 824-8009
Lancaster (G-9059)

Irp Group Inc ....D 412 276-6400
Pittsburgh (G-15138)

Laird Technologies Inc ....G 570 424-8510
Delaware Water Gap (G-4043)

▲ Lehigh Gasket Inc ....F 610 837-1818
Bath (G-964)

Lydall Performance Mtls US Inc ....C 717 207-6000
Lancaster (G-9119)

Lydall Performance Mtls US Inc ....C 717 207-6025
Lancaster (G-9120)

◆ Lydall Performance Mtls US Inc ....E 717 390-1886
Lancaster (G-9121)

Manufactured Rubber Pdts Co ....F 215 533-3600
Philadelphia (G-13989)

Melrath Gasket Inc ....D 215 223-6000
Philadelphia (G-14007)

▲ Morgan Advanced Mtls Tech Inc ......C 814 781-1573
Saint Marys (G-16998)

Nrf US Inc ....G 814 947-1378
Plymouth Meeting (G-15861)

Oliver Products Company ....G 215 230-0300
New Britain (G-12050)

Plum Manufacturing Co Inc ....G 215 520-2236
North Wales (G-12825)

Poly-TEC Products Inc ....F 215 547-3366
Bristol (G-2185)

Prime Contract Pkg Svcs Corp ....E 570 876-2300
Olyphant (G-12996)

Process Technologies Inc ....G 412 771-8555
Mc Kees Rocks (G-10628)

R Way Gasket & Supply Company ......F 215 743-1650
Philadelphia (G-14229)

▲ R/W Connection Inc ....E 717 898-5257
Landisville (G-9266)

R/W Connection Inc ....G 717 767-3660
Emigsville (G-4998)

Scott H Payne ....G 215 723-0510
Telford (G-18313)

Seal Science Inc ....F 610 868-2800
Bethlehem (G-1616)

SKF USA Inc ....F 610 954-7000
Allentown (G-395)

▲ St Marys Carbon Co Inc ....C 814 781-7333
Saint Marys (G-17016)

Staver Hydraulics Co Inc ....G 610 837-1818
Bath (G-970)

◆ Stein Seal Company ....C 215 256-0201
Kulpsville (G-8831)

Susquehanna Capitl Acquisition ....A 800 942-7538
Lancaster (G-9210)

Target Industrial Products ....G 412 486-2627
Glenshaw (G-6501)

▲ Tegrant Corporation ....F 215 643-3555
Montgomeryville (G-11422)

Toss Machine Components Inc ....E 610 759-8883
Nazareth (G-11992)

3061 Molded, Extruded & Lathe-Cut Rubber Mechanical Goods

C E Conover & Co Inc ....E 215 639-6666
Bensalem (G-1164)

Corry Rubber Corporation ....E 814 664-2313
Corry (G-3757)

Eagle Rubber Products Inc ....F 724 452-3200
Zelienople (G-20796)

▲ Fenner Precision Inc ....C 800 327-2288
Manheim (G-10383)

Greenbriar Indus Systems Inc ....D 814 474-1400
Fairview (G-5824)

▲ Pelmor Laboratories Inc ....E 215 968-3334
Newtown (G-12533)

Phb Inc ....D 814 474-2683
Fairview (G-5838)

Ross Enterprises Inc ....D 215 968-3334
Newtown (G-12546)

Rubber Rolls Inc ....E 724 225-9240
Meadow Lands (G-10692)

Spadone Machine Inc ....F 215 396-8005
Willow Grove (G-20143)

Valmet Inc ....D 570 587-5111
S Abingtn Twp (G-16900)

3069 Fabricated Rubber Prdts, NEC

Abacus Surfaces Inc ....F 717 560-8050
Lancaster (G-8920)

Ace Panels Company ....G 814 583-5015
Luthersburg (G-10120)

▲ Advanced Scientifics Inc ....B 717 692-2104
Millersburg (G-11186)

Arkmedica LLC ....F 724 349-0856
Indiana (G-8083)

Aspol LLC ....G 412 628-0078
New Kensington (G-12325)

Associated Rubber Inc ....E 215 536-2800
Quakertown (G-16169)

▲ Business Applications Ltd ....G 814 677-7056
Reno (G-16645)

▲ California Med Innovations LLC ......E 909 621-5871
Easton (G-4660)

▲ Capri Cork LLC ....F 717 627-5701
Lititz (G-9995)

Carlisle Construction Mtls Inc ....E 717 245-7142
Carlisle (G-2693)

Carlisle Construction Mtls LLC ....G 717 245-7000
Carlisle (G-2694)

◆ Carlisle Construction Mtls LLC ....B 717 245-7000
Carlisle (G-2695)

Certified Carpet Service Inc ....D 717 393-3012
Lancaster (G-8976)

▲ Chestnut Ridge Foam Inc ....C 724 537-9000
Latrobe (G-9464)

◆ Crazy Aaron Enterprises Inc ....F 866 578-2845
Nornstown (G-12649)

Devcom Manufacturing LLC ....G 484 462-4907
Easton (G-4669)

Dykema Rubber Band ....G 412 771-1955
Pittsburgh (G-14946)

Eagle Rubber Products Inc ....F 724 452-3200
Zelienople (G-20796)

◆ Ecore International Inc ....C 717 295-3400
Lancaster (G-9007)

Edge Rubber Recycling LLC ....E 717 660-2353
Chambersburg (G-2928)

Fast Shelter Inc ....G 610 415-0225
Phoenixville (G-14549)

▲ Ferotec Friction Inc ....F 717 492-9600
Manheim (G-10384)

Flexsys America LP ....D 724 258-6200
Monongahela (G-11308)

Fred Foust ....G 724 845-7028
Vandergrift (G-18727)

Fxi Building Products Corp ....C 610 744-2230
Media (G-10927)

General Rubber Corporation ....F 412 424-0270
Coraopolis (G-3693)

Global Rubber LLC ....G 610 878-9200
Wayne (G-19333)

Glw Global Inc ....G 412 664-7946
McKeesport (G-10668)

Gordon Seaver ....G 724 356-2313
Hickory (G-7628)

Gothic Inc ....G 610 923-9180
Easton (G-4692)

Grant Belcher ....F 814 853-9640
Greenville (G-6741)

▲ Harris Manufacturing Company ....G 609 393-3717
Southampton (G-17816)

Healing Environments Intl Inc ....G 215 758-2107
Philadelphia (G-13808)

Herbert Cooper Company Inc ....E 814 228-3417
Genesee (G-6272)

Hilmarr Rubber Co Inc ....G 215 426-3628
Philadelphia (G-13826)

Innocor Foam Tech - Acp Inc ....G 570 876-4544
Archbald (G-687)

Interntional Track Systems Inc ....G 724 658-5970
New Castle (G-12105)

JM Industries Inc ....G 724 452-6060
Harmony (G-7071)

Lake Erie Rubber & Mfg LLC ....F 814 835-0170
Erie (G-5354)

Lake Erie Rubber Works Inc ....F 814 835-0170
Erie (G-5355)

Lambert-Jones Rubber Co ....G 412 781-8100
Pittsburgh (G-15217)

▲ Lebanon Gasket and Seal Inc ....G 717 274-3684
Lebanon (G-9600)

▼ Life Support International ....E 215 785-2870
Langhorne (G-9308)

Lord Corporation ....D 814 398-4641
Cambridge Springs (G-2481)

Lord Corporation ....A 877 275-5673
Erie (G-5373)

M B Bedding Co ....G 570 822-2491
Wilkes Barre (G-19939)

Martech Medical Products Inc ....E 215 256-8833
Harleysville (G-7046)

Mary Hail Rubber Co Inc ....F 215 343-1955
Warrington (G-19124)

Mason East Inc ....G 631 254-2240
Feasterville Trevose (G-5917)

▲ Mason Rubber Co Inc ....F 215 355-3440
Feasterville Trevose (G-5918)

Mat Penn Company Inc ....G 724 837-7060
Greensburg (G-6687)

Matamatic Inc ....G 724 696-5678
Mount Pleasant (G-11705)

▲ Mondo Usa Inc ....G...... 610 834-3835
  Conshohocken *(G-3576)*
▲ Montrose Machine Works Inc ....F...... 570 278-7655
  Montrose *(G-11471)*
▲ Nation Ruskin Holdings Inc ....F...... 267 654-4000
  Montgomeryville *(G-11409)*
◆ National Polymers Inc ....E...... 724 483-9300
  Charleroi *(G-3017)*
◆ National Rubber Corporation ....F...... 412 831-6100
  Canonsburg *(G-2612)*
▲ Norstone Incorporated ....G...... 484 684-6986
  Bridgeport *(G-2041)*
  Overtime Tool Inc ....F...... 814 734-0848
  Edinboro *(G-4818)*
▲ Penn Foam Corporation ....D...... 610 797-7500
  Allentown *(G-348)*
◆ Polymer Enterprises Inc ....G...... 724 838-2340
  Greensburg *(G-6703)*
  Polymeric Extruded Products ....G...... 215 943-1288
  Levittown *(G-9858)*
  Port Richman Holdings LLC ....G...... 212 777-1178
  Philadelphia *(G-14189)*
  Presti Group Inc ....F...... 215 340-2870
  Doylestown *(G-4327)*
  Q-Cast Inc ....E...... 724 728-7440
  Rochester *(G-16789)*
▲ Recycling Tech Intl LLC ....E...... 717 633-9008
  York *(G-20655)*
◆ Regupol America LLC ....E...... 717 675-2198
  Lebanon *(G-9626)*
◆ Reilly Foam Corp ....D...... 610 834-1900
  King of Prussia *(G-8668)*
  Rubber Rolls Inc ....E...... 412 276-6400
  Pittsburgh *(G-15502)*
  Rubber Rolls Inc ....E...... 724 225-9240
  Meadow Lands *(G-10692)*
▲ Rubber Technology Inc ....G...... 724 838-2340
  Greensburg *(G-6713)*
▲ Scrub Daddy Inc ....E...... 610 583-4883
  Folcroft *(G-6015)*
▲ Scully Enterprises Inc ....G...... 814 835-0173
  Erie *(G-5471)*
  Specialty Roller and Mch Inc ....F...... 570 759-1278
  Berwick *(G-1344)*
◆ SRC Elastomerics Inc ....D...... 215 335-2049
  Philadelphia *(G-14336)*
  Starrhock Silicones Inc ....F...... 610 837-4883
  Bath *(G-969)*
  Stingfree Technologies Company ....G...... 610 444-2806
  West Chester *(G-19644)*
  Surco Inc ....F...... 215 855-9551
  Hatfield *(G-7397)*
  Svt Inc ....F...... 215 245-5055
  Bensalem *(G-1258)*
  Tech-Seal Products Inc ....G...... 847 805-6400
  Wayne *(G-19379)*
▼ Techline Technologies Inc ....E...... 215 657-1909
  Willow Grove *(G-20146)*
  Thermo Fisher Scientific Inc ....B...... 717 692-2104
  Millersburg *(G-11203)*
  Unicast Inc ....E...... 610 559-9998
  Easton *(G-4765)*
  Valmet Inc ....D...... 570 587-5111
  S Abingtn Twp *(G-16900)*
  Valmet Inc ....E...... 570 587-5111
  S Abingtn Twp *(G-16901)*
  Washington Greene County Blind ....F...... 724 228-0770
  Washington *(G-19238)*
▲ West Pharmaceutical Svcs Inc ....B...... 610 594-2900
  Exton *(G-5748)*
  West Phrm Svcs Del Inc ....F...... 610 594-2900
  Exton *(G-5749)*
◆ William F Kempf & Son Inc ....G...... 610 532-2000
  Folcroft *(G-6020)*

3081 Plastic Unsupported Sheet & Film

  Abtrex Industries Inc ....E...... 724 266-5425
  Leetsdale *(G-9676)*
▲ Acton Technologies Inc ....D...... 570 654-0612
  Pittston *(G-15741)*
▼ Azek Building Products Inc ....E...... 877 275-2935
  Scranton *(G-17210)*
  Berry Global Inc ....B...... 570 759-6240
  Berwick *(G-1309)*
  Berry Global Inc ....E...... 814 849-4234
  Brookville *(G-2248)*
  Berry Global Films LLC ....C...... 570 474-9700
  Mountain Top *(G-11752)*
◆ Berwick Offray LLC ....B...... 570 752-5934
  Berwick *(G-1311)*

  Berwick Offray LLC ....A...... 570 752-5934
  Berwick *(G-1312)*
◆ Centric Plastics LLC ....G...... 215 309-1999
  Hatfield *(G-7323)*
  CJ Packaging Inc ....G...... 570 209-7836
  Avoca *(G-841)*
▲ Cjc Contract Packaging Inc ....G...... 570 209-7836
  Avoca *(G-842)*
  Compression Polymers ....G...... 570 558-8000
  Scranton *(G-17217)*
  Computer Designs Inc ....D...... 610 261-2100
  Whitehall *(G-19867)*
  Coupler Enterprises Inc ....G...... 267 487-8982
  Warrington *(G-19113)*
  Cpg International Holdings LP ....A...... 570 558-8000
  Scranton *(G-17221)*
  Cpg International I Inc ....G...... 570 346-8797
  Scranton *(G-17222)*
  Cpg International LLC ....F...... 570 348-0997
  Scranton *(G-17223)*
  CPI Scranton Inc ....B...... 570 558-8000
  Scranton *(G-17225)*
  Crestwood Membranes Inc ....D...... 570 474-6741
  Mountain Top *(G-11758)*
  Crosstex International Inc ....E...... 724 347-0400
  Sharon *(G-17431)*
  Delstar Technologies Inc ....G...... 717 866-7472
  Richland *(G-16685)*
◆ Dunmore Corporation ....D...... 215 781-8895
  Bristol *(G-2134)*
  Dunmore International Corp ....G...... 215 781-8895
  Bristol *(G-2135)*
  Easter Unlimited Inc ....E...... 814 542-8661
  Mount Union *(G-11744)*
  Ensinger Penn Fibre Inc ....D...... 215 702-9551
  Bensalem *(G-1190)*
▲ Filmtech Corp ....D...... 610 709-9999
  Allentown *(G-213)*
▲ FP Woll & Company ....E...... 215 934-5966
  Philadelphia *(G-13717)*
  Gateway Packaging Corp ....E...... 724 327-7400
  Export *(G-5607)*
  General Plastics Inc ....G...... 215 423-8200
  Philadelphia *(G-13750)*
  Honeywell International Inc ....B...... 570 621-6000
  Pottsville *(G-16080)*
  International Vectors Ltd ....E...... 717 767-4008
  Emigsville *(G-4993)*
  J Benson Corp ....G...... 610 678-2692
  Reading *(G-16411)*
  Kw Plastics ....E...... 334 566-1563
  Allentown *(G-288)*
▲ Laminations Inc ....C...... 570 876-8199
  Archbald *(G-288)*
  Lion Ribbon Company LLC ....G...... 570 752-5934
  Berwick *(G-1333)*
  Meadville New Products Inc ....F...... 814 336-2174
  Meadville *(G-10759)*
  Nova Chemicals Inc ....B...... 724 770-5542
  Monaca *(G-11293)*
  Omnova Solutions Inc ....B...... 724 523-5441
  Jeannette *(G-8263)*
  Omnova Solutions Inc ....B...... 570 366-1051
  Auburn *(G-820)*
  Packaging Science Inc ....F...... 610 992-9991
  King of Prussia *(G-8658)*
◆ Palram Panels Inc ....G...... 610 285-9918
  Kutztown *(G-8854)*
  Penn Fibre & Specialty Co ....G...... 215 702-9551
  Bensalem *(G-1242)*
  PPG Architectural Finishes Inc ....D...... 610 380-6200
  Downingtown *(G-4250)*
  Precision Polymer Processors ....F...... 570 344-9916
  Scranton *(G-17274)*
  Proplastix International Inc ....C...... 717 692-4733
  Millersburg *(G-11198)*
  Protostar Technologies ....G...... 484 988-0964
  Lincoln University *(G-9974)*
◆ Robert Mrvel Plastic Mulch LLC ......F...... 717 838-0976
  Annville *(G-658)*
▲ Rose Plastic Usa Lllp ....D...... 724 938-8530
  Coal Center *(G-3277)*
  S & S Packaging Products Inc ....E...... 800 633-0272
  Cranesville *(G-3870)*
▲ Simona America Inc ....D...... 570 579-1300
  Archbald *(G-694)*
  Specialty Extrusion Inc ....G...... 610 792-3800
  Royersford *(G-16865)*
  Tarp America Inc ....G...... 724 339-4771
  Murrysville *(G-11869)*

  Tech Packaging Inc ....E...... 570 759-7717
  Hazle Township *(G-7483)*
  Transparent Protection Syst ....E...... 215 638-0800
  Bensalem *(G-1262)*
  Tredegar Corporation ....C...... 570 544-7600
  Pottsville *(G-16100)*
  United Laminations Inc ....F...... 570 876-1360
  Mayfield *(G-10544)*
  Vinyl Window Wells LLC ....F...... 717 768-0618
  Gordonville *(G-6566)*
▲ Westlake Plastics Company ....C...... 610 459-1000
  Lenni *(G-9763)*
  Westlake United Corporation ....F...... 570 876-0222
  Mayfield *(G-10545)*
  Wexco Incorporated ....G...... 717 764-8585
  York *(G-20710)*

3082 Plastic Unsupported Profile Shapes

  Cambria Plastics LLC ....G...... 814 535-5467
  Johnstown *(G-8361)*
  Ensinger Penn Fibre Inc ....D...... 215 702-9551
  Bensalem *(G-1190)*
  Essentra Porous Tech Corp ....E...... 814 898-3238
  Erie *(G-5283)*
  Formtech Enterprises Inc ....E...... 814 474-1940
  Fairview *(G-5823)*
  Gateway Packaging Corp ....E...... 724 327-7400
  Export *(G-5607)*
  H R Edgar Machining & Fabg Inc ....D...... 724 339-6694
  New Kensington *(G-12344)*
▲ Iridium Industries Inc ....C...... 570 476-8800
  East Stroudsburg *(G-4621)*
  J Benson Corp ....G...... 610 678-2692
  Reading *(G-16411)*
  Lehigh Valley Plastics Inc ....D...... 484 893-5500
  Bethlehem *(G-1558)*
▲ Markel Corp ....C...... 610 272-8960
  Plymouth Meeting *(G-15855)*
  Meadville New Products Inc ....F...... 814 336-2174
  Meadville *(G-10759)*
  Oilfield LLC ....G...... 814 623-8125
  Bedford *(G-1067)*
  Ono Industries Inc ....E...... 717 865-6619
  Ono *(G-13004)*
  Quadrant Holding Inc ....C...... 570 558-6000
  Scranton *(G-17276)*
  Quadrant Holding Inc ....C...... 724 468-7062
  Delmont *(G-4054)*
  Resdel Corporation ....C...... 215 343-2400
  Warrington *(G-19131)*
▲ Westlake Plastics Company ....C...... 610 459-1000
  Lenni *(G-9763)*
▲ Westrock Packaging Inc ....D...... 215 785-3350
  Croydon *(G-3933)*

3083 Plastic Laminated Plate & Sheet

  AAR Plastic & Glass Llc ....G...... 410 200-6369
  Gettysburg *(G-6281)*
  Acrylics Unlimited ....G...... 215 443-2365
  Horsham *(G-7778)*
  Adams Manufacturing Corp ....G...... 724 758-2125
  Ellwood City *(G-4923)*
▲ Adept Corporation ....D...... 800 451-2254
  York *(G-20366)*
  Advanced Coil Industries ....F...... 724 225-1885
  Washington *(G-19145)*
  Adventek Corporation ....E...... 215 736-0961
  Levittown *(G-9813)*
◆ American Made LLC ....C...... 724 776-4044
  Cranberry Township *(G-3803)*
▲ Anholt Technologies Inc ....F...... 610 268-2758
  Avondale *(G-848)*
▲ Apexco-Ppsi LLC ....G...... 937 935-0164
  Horsham *(G-7787)*
  Baw Plastics Inc ....C...... 412 384-3100
  Jefferson Hills *(G-8273)*
  C-Thru Products Inc ....E...... 610 586-1130
  Ridley Park *(G-16738)*
  CCL Tube Inc ....C...... 570 824-8485
  Hanover Township *(G-6984)*
  Dilworth Manufacturing Co ....G...... 717 354-8956
  Narvon *(G-11920)*
  Duco Holdings LLC ....G...... 215 942-6274
  Ivyland *(G-8209)*
  Ensinger Penn Fibre Inc ....D...... 215 702-9551
  Bensalem *(G-1190)*
  Finish Tech Corp ....F...... 215 396-8800
  Warminster *(G-18878)*
▲ Finish Tech Corp ....E...... 215 396-8800
  Warminster *(G-18879)*

S
I
C

Fluortek Inc....................................D....... 610 438-1800
Easton (G-4683)

Gateway Packaging Corp ....E....... 724 327-7400
Export (G-5607)

▲ Global Epp Inc ....G....... 412 580-4780
Pittsburgh (G-15052)

Grims Plastics ....G....... 717 526-7980
Harrisburg (G-7136)

Gt Services LLC ....E....... 215 256-9521
Kulpsville (G-8829)

Gtr Industries Incorporated ....E....... 610 705-5900
Pottstown (G-15992)

Hoff Enterprises Inc........................E....... 814 535-8371
Johnstown (G-8381)

Isola Services Inc ....G....... 724 547-5142
Mount Pleasant (G-11702)

J Benson Corp ....G....... 610 678-2692
Reading (G-16411)

Joseph Piazza ....G....... 610 593-3053
Atglen (G-801)

Krehling Industries Inc ....D....... 717 232-7936
Harrisburg (G-7165)

Lambert-Jones Rubber Co ....G....... 412 781-8100
Pittsburgh (G-15217)

▲ Laminations Inc ....C....... 570 876-8199
Archbald (G-690)

Lawrie Technology Inc ....G....... 814 402-1208
Girard (G-6396)

Lehigh Valley Plastics Inc ....D....... 484 893-5500
Bethlehem (G-1558)

M-B Companies Inc ....E....... 570 547-1621
Muncy (G-11825)

Magee Plastics Company ....D....... 724 776-2220
Warrendale (G-19087)

▲ Markel Corp ....C....... 610 272-8960
Plymouth Meeting (G-15855)

Martech Medical Products Inc ....E....... 215 256-8833
Harleysville (G-7046)

◆ McClarin Plastics Llc ....C....... 717 637-2241
Hanover (G-6918)

Meadville New Products Inc.............F....... 814 336-2174
Meadville (G-10759)

Metplas Inc ....D....... 724 295-5200
Natrona Heights (G-11946)

Milner Enterprises Inc ....F....... 610 252-0700
Easton (G-4722)

Mohawk Inc......................................G....... 717 243-9231
Carlisle (G-2726)

Northway Industries Inc ....C....... 570 837-1564
Middleburg (G-11034)

Old Epp Inc ....G....... 570 430-9089
Tunkhannock (G-18546)

Panel Technologies Inc ....G....... 215 538-7055
Quakertown (G-16226)

Patrick Industries Inc.....................E....... 717 653-2086
Mount Joy (G-11668)

Perkasie Industries Corp.................D....... 215 257-6581
Perkasie (G-13288)

Precise Plastics Inc ....D....... 814 474-5504
Fairview (G-5840)

Rapid Tpc LLC ....F....... 412 450-0482
Pittsburgh (G-15468)

▲ Rochling Machined Plastics ....E....... 724 696-5200
Mount Pleasant (G-11717)

Romax Hose Inc ....F....... 570 869-0860
Laceyville (G-8874)

Superior Dual Laminates Inc ....G....... 610 965-9061
Emmaus (G-5043)

Tomark-Worthen LLC ....G....... 610 978-1889
Chadds Ford (G-2861)

Total Plastics Inc ....G....... 877 677-8872
Philadelphia (G-14399)

Total Plastics Resources LLC..........E....... 215 637-2221
Bensalem (G-1261)

◆ U E C Inc ....D....... 724 772-5225
Cranberry Township (G-3860)

United Laminations Inc ....F....... 570 876-1360
Mayfield (G-10544)

Washington Penn Mexico Holding ....G....... 724 228-1260
Washington (G-19239)

◆ Washington Penn Plastic Co Inc......C....... 724 228-1260
Washington (G-19240)

Washington Penn Plastic Co Inc ....E....... 724 228-3709
Eighty Four (G-4851)

William Deleeuw Co ....G....... 570 296-2694
Milford (G-11168)

3084 Plastic Pipe

Advanced Drainage Systems Inc ....E....... 570 546-7686
Muncy (G-11805)

◆ Certainteed Corporation ....B....... 610 893-5000
Malvern (G-10204)

Certainteed Corporation ....G....... 610 651-8706
Malvern (G-10205)

Charlotte Pipe and Foundry Co ....E....... 570 546-7666
Muncy (G-11812)

▼ Chemex Inc ....G....... 610 398-6200
Allentown (G-168)

Cresline Plastic Pipe Co Inc ....D....... 717 766-9262
Mechanicsburg (G-10833)

D A R A Inc ....F....... 717 274-1800
Lebanon (G-9557)

▲ Georg Fischer Harvel LLC..............C....... 610 252-7355
Easton (G-4688)

Georg Fischer Harvel LLC.................E....... 610 252-7355
Easton (G-4689)

Harvel Plastics Inc ....G....... 610 252-7355
Easton (G-4696)

J-M Manufacturing Company Inc ....C....... 814 432-2166
Franklin (G-6141)

J-M Manufacturing Company Inc ....D....... 814 337-7675
Cochranton (G-3343)

Miller Plastic Products Inc ....F....... 724 947-5000
Burgettstown (G-2350)

▲ Ocp Inc ....E....... 814 827-3661
Titusville (G-18389)

Ono Industries Inc ....E....... 717 865-6619
Ono (G-13004)

Premier Conduit Inc ....G....... 814 451-0898
Erie (G-5433)

Premier Conduit Inc ....G....... 814 451-0898
Erie (G-5434)

◆ Saint-Gobain Delaware Corp ....G....... 610 341-7000
Valley Forge (G-18712)

Spears Manufacturing Co ....E....... 717 938-8844
Lewisberry (G-9893)

3085 Plastic Bottles

Alpha Packaging North East Inc...........D....... 610 974-9001
Bethlehem (G-1448)

Alpla Inc ....E....... 770 914-1407
Bethlehem (G-1449)

Consolidated Container Co LLC...........D....... 724 658-4578
New Castle (G-12075)

Consolidated Container Co LLC...........D....... 412 828-1111
Verona (G-18754)

Consolidated Container Co LLC...........C....... 570 759-0823
Berwick (G-1319)

Diamond Drinks Inc ....D....... 570 326-2003
Williamsport (G-20005)

Drug Plastics and Glass Co Inc ....D....... 724 548-5654
Kittanning (G-8767)

Drug Plastics and Glass Co Inc ....D....... 570 672-3215
Elysburg (G-4975)

Graham Packaging Company LP ....E....... 717 849-8700
York (G-20509)

Graham Packaging Company LP ....E....... 717 849-8500
York (G-20511)

Mohawk Inc......................................G....... 717 243-9231
Carlisle (G-2726)

Novapak Corporation ....F....... 717 266-6687
Manchester (G-10359)

Pvc Container Corporation ....E....... 570 384-3930
Hazle Township (G-7476)

Pvc Container Corporation ....D....... 717 266-9100
Manchester (G-10363)

Sean S Zuniga ....G....... 215 757-2676
Langhorne (G-9324)

Silgan Plastics LLC..........................D....... 215 727-2676
Langhorne (G-9325)

Springdale Specialty Plas Inc ....E....... 724 274-4144
Springdale (G-17901)

Staychilled Usa LLC ....G....... 215 284-6018
Plymouth Meeting (G-15874)

Suscon Inc ....D....... 570 326-2003
Williamsport (G-20078)

▲ West Pharmaceutical Svcs Inc ....B....... 610 594-2900
Exton (G-5748)

3086 Plastic Foam Prdts

A C F Ltd ....G....... 610 459-5397
Glen Mills (G-6429)

Alberts Spray Solutions LLC.............G....... 570 368-6653
Montoursville (G-11429)

Amatech Inc ....E....... 814 452-0010
Erie (G-5185)

Arctic Blast Covers..........................E....... 724 213-8460
Indiana (G-8081)

Atlas Roofing Corporation ....E....... 717 760-5460
Camp Hill (G-2492)

▼ Azek Building Products Inc.............E....... 877 275-2935
Scranton (G-17210)

B H B Industries ....G....... 814 398-8011
Cambridge Springs (G-2474)

▼ Bergad Inc ....E....... 724 763-2883
Kittanning (G-8757)

Brd Noise & Vibration Ctrl Inc ....G....... 610 863-6300
Wind Gap (G-20167)

Bryn Hill Industries Inc ....E....... 610 623-4005
Yeadon (G-20351)

Cardinal Health 407 Inc ....A....... 215 501-1210
Philadelphia (G-13502)

Carlisle Construction Mtls LLC ....C....... 724 564-5440
Smithfield (G-17644)

Carlisle Construction Mtls LLC ....E....... 724 564-5440
Smithfield (G-17645)

Carpenter Co ....F....... 717 627-1878
Lititz (G-9996)

▲ Carpenter Co ....G....... 610 366-5110
Allentown (G-163)

Carpenter Co ....E....... 610 366-8349
Allentown (G-164)

Carpenter Co ....D....... 610 366-5110
Fogelsville (G-5993)

Carpenter Co ....C....... 814 944-8612
Altoona (G-486)

Clarke Container Inc ....F....... 814 452-4848
Erie (G-5226)

Corrugated Specialties ....F....... 814 337-5705
Meadville (G-10715)

Corrugated Specialties ....F....... 814 337-5705
Meadville (G-10714)

Cpg International I Inc ....G....... 570 346-8797
Scranton (G-17222)

Cryovac Inc.....................................C....... 610 926-7500
Reading (G-16356)

Cryovac Inc.....................................F....... 610 929-9190
Reading (G-16357)

Custom Pack Inc ....F....... 610 363-1900
Exton (G-5663)

◆ Dart Container Corp PA ....G....... 717 656-2236
Leola (G-9777)

Dart Container Corp PA ....A....... 717 397-1032
Lancaster (G-8992)

Ddp Specialty Electronic MA ....G....... 610 244-6000
Collegeville (G-3374)

◆ Downing Enterprises Inc ....E....... 610 873-0070
Downingtown (G-4224)

Duerr Packaging Company Inc...........D....... 724 947-1234
Burgettstown (G-2346)

Duerr Packaging Company Inc...........E....... 724 695-2226
Imperial (G-8064)

Ekopak Inc ....F....... 412 264-9800
Coraopolis (G-3686)

Energy Innovation Ctr Inst Inc...........G....... 412 894-9800
Pittsburgh (G-14976)

Epe Industries Usa Inc ....G....... 800 315-0336
Carlisle (G-2710)

▲ Essity North America Inc................C....... 610 499-3700
Philadelphia (G-13680)

▲ Flextron Industries Inc ....F....... 610 459-4600
Aston (G-763)

Foam Fabricators Inc.......................F....... 814 838-4538
Erie (G-5298)

Foam Fabricators Inc.......................E....... 570 752-7110
Bloomsburg (G-1782)

▲ Foam Fair Industries Inc ....E....... 610 622-4665
Aldan (G-59)

◆ Foamex International Inc ....C....... 610 744-2300
Media (G-10924)

▲ Foamex LP ....D....... 610 565-2374
Media (G-10925)

▲ FP Woll & Company ....E....... 215 934-5966
Philadelphia (G-13717)

Future Foam Inc ....D....... 215 736-8611
Fairless Hills (G-5779)

Fxi Inc..C....... 610 245-2800
Aston (G-766)

Fxi Inc..C....... 814 664-7771
Corry (G-3762)

◆ Fxi Inc ....C....... 610 744-2300
Media (G-10926)

▼ Fxi Holdings Inc ....C....... 610 744-2300
Media (G-10928)

G I S Inc...F....... 412 771-8860
Mc Kees Rocks (G-10610)

Great Northern Foam ....E....... 610 791-3356
Allentown (G-237)

▲ Greiner Packaging Corp ....F....... 570 602-3900
Pittston (G-15754)

Highwood Usa LLC ....E 570 668-6113
Tamaqua *(G-18212)*

Ica Inc ....F 610 377-6100
Lehighton *(G-9716)*

Innocor Foam Tech - Acp Inc ....G 570 876-4544
Archbald *(G-688)*

▲ Insul-Board Inc ....E 814 833-7400
Erie *(G-5327)*

▲ Insulation Corporation America ....E 610 791-4200
Allentown *(G-262)*

Interstate Paper Supply Co Inc ....D 724 938-2218
Roscoe *(G-16817)*

Johns Manville Corporation ....D 570 455-5340
Hazle Township *(G-7467)*

Laurel Parcel Services Inc ....G 724 850-6245
Greensburg *(G-6683)*

Northeastern Foam and Fiber ....G 570 488-6859
Waymart *(G-19288)*

Novipax LLC ....E 570 644-0314
Paxinos *(G-13191)*

Polar Tech Industries Inc ....E 800 423-2749
Elysburg *(G-4979)*

Presto Packaging Inc ....G 215 822-9598
Hatfield *(G-7386)*

Presto Packaging Inc ....G 215 646-7514
Ambler *(G-599)*

Protective Packaging Corp ....G 610 398-2229
Allentown *(G-362)*

R W Pefferle Inc ....G 724 265-2764
Oakmont *(G-12925)*

Rogers Foam Corporation ....D 215 295-8720
Morrisville *(G-11580)*

Rpw Group Inc ....E 215 493-7456
Yardley *(G-20337)*

Sealed Air Corporation ....E 610 384-2650
Modena *(G-11259)*

Sealed Air Corporation ....E 610 375-4281
Reading *(G-16510)*

Sealed Air Corporation ....G 610 926-7517
Reading *(G-16509)*

Sonoco Prtective Solutions Inc ....D 800 377-2692
Pittsburgh *(G-15557)*

Sonoco Prtective Solutions Inc ....E 412 415-1462
Pittsburgh *(G-15558)*

Sonoco Prtective Solutions Inc ....E 412 415-3784
Pittsburgh *(G-15559)*

Stephen Gould Corporation ....G 724 933-1400
Wexford *(G-19829)*

Sterling Paper Company ....D 215 744-5350
Philadelphia *(G-14347)*

Temperatsure LLC ....E 775 358-1999
Hatfield *(G-7401)*

▲ Ty-Pak Inc ....E 570 835-5269
Tioga *(G-18365)*

3087 Custom Compounding Of Purchased Plastic Resins

Dyneon LLC ....D 610 497-8899
Aston *(G-759)*

Fielco Industries Inc ....E 215 674-8700
Huntingdon Valley *(G-7983)*

Hayes-Ivy Mfg Inc ....E 610 767-3865
New Tripoli *(G-12457)*

J Meyer & Sons Inc ....C 215 699-7003
West Point *(G-19759)*

▲ Ltl Color Compounders LLC ....D 215 736-1126
Morrisville *(G-11570)*

▼ Polytek Development Corp ....E 610 559-8620
Easton *(G-4743)*

◆ Ranbar Electrical Mtls LLC ....E 724 864-8200
Harrison City *(G-7251)*

Sabic Innovative Plas US LLC ....D 610 363-4500
Exton *(G-5727)*

Sealed Air Corporation ....G 610 926-7517
Reading *(G-16509)*

▲ Ultra-Poly Corporation ....E 570 897-7500
Portland *(G-15940)*

Washington Penn Plastic Co Inc ....G 724 228-1260
Washington *(G-19241)*

Washington Penn Plastic Co Inc ....E 724 228-3709
Eighty Four *(G-4851)*

◆ Washington Penn Plastic Co Inc ......C 724 228-1260
Washington *(G-19240)*

3088 Plastic Plumbing Fixtures

Abtrex Industries Inc ....E 724 266-5425
Leetsdale *(G-9676)*

Aquatic Co ....C 717 367-1100
Elizabethtown *(G-4865)*

Clarion Bathware Inc ....C 814 782-3016
Marble *(G-10435)*

Clarion Bathware Inc ....D 814 782-3016
Marble *(G-10436)*

▲ Clarion Bathware Inc ....C 814 226-5374
Shippenville *(G-17556)*

Containment Solutions Inc ....C 814 542-8621
Mount Union *(G-11741)*

Elegant Marble Products Inc ....F 717 939-0373
Middletown *(G-11052)*

Frameless Shower Doors ....G 215 534-0021
Jamison *(G-8243)*

Grape Fiberglass Inc ....F 814 938-8118
Punxsutawney *(G-16142)*

Hunter Kitchen & Bath LLC ....G 570 926-0777
Exton *(G-5693)*

Legacy Polymer Products Inc ....G 570 344-5019
Dunmore *(G-4477)*

▲ Leo Taur Technology Group Inc ....F 610 966-3484
Macungie *(G-10153)*

Macson Company ....E 610 264-7733
Allentown *(G-305)*

▼ Plastic Development Company PA ....E 800 451-1420
Williamsport *(G-20058)*

Robert J Fleig Inc ....E 215 702-7676
Langhorne *(G-9322)*

Space Age Plastics Inc ....F 570 630-6060
Jefferson Township *(G-8279)*

Top Notch Products Inc ....G 724 475-2341
Fredonia *(G-6187)*

Yarmouth Construction ....G 267 592-1432
Philadelphia *(G-14498)*

3089 Plastic Prdts

100 Thompson Street LLC ....G 866 654-2676
Pittston *(G-15740)*

AAR Plastic & Glass Llc ....G 410 200-6369
Gettysburg *(G-6281)*

Abtec Incorporated ....D 215 788-0950
Bristol *(G-2102)*

▼ Accu-Mold & Tool Company Inc ....E 717 896-3937
Halifax *(G-6824)*

▲ Accudyn Products Inc ....D 814 833-7615
Erie *(G-5167)*

Accurate Marking Products Inc ....F 724 337-8390
New Kensington *(G-12321)*

▼ Adams Mfg Corp ....E 800 237-8287
Portersville *(G-15923)*

Advanced Alloy Dvsion/Nmc Corp ....F 724 266-8770
Ambridge *(G-605)*

Advanced Composite Pdts Inc ....E 717 232-8237
Harrisburg *(G-7083)*

Advanced Mold Technologies ....F 814 899-1233
Erie *(G-5174)*

◆ Advanced Pultrusions LLC ....D 412 466-8611
West Mifflin *(G-19735)*

Advanced Solutions Network LLC ....F 814 464-0791
Erie *(G-5175)*

Advantage Precision Plastics ....E 814 337-8535
Meadville *(G-10696)*

Adventek Corporation ....E 215 736-0961
Levittown *(G-9813)*

Afca Company Inc ....E 215 425-2300
Philadelphia *(G-13351)*

◆ Agd Products Inc ....G 215 682-9643
Warminster *(G-18824)*

AIN Plastics ....G 717 291-9300
Lancaster *(G-8924)*

Airlite Plastics Co ....D 610 759-0280
Nazareth *(G-11952)*

Aline Components Inc ....E 215 368-0300
Kulpsville *(G-8823)*

Allegheny Performance Plas LLC ....E 412 741-4416
Leetsdale *(G-9678)*

Allegheny Plastics Inc ....E 412 741-4416
Leetsdale *(G-9680)*

▲ Allegheny Plastics Inc ....C 412 741-4416
Leetsdale *(G-9679)*

Allentown Plastics Inc ....E 610 391-8383
Breinigsville *(G-2006)*

▼ Alltrista Plastics Corporation ....E 717 667-2131
Reedsville *(G-16620)*

Almega Plastics Inc ....E 724 652-6411
New Castle *(G-12056)*

Amcor Group GMBH ....G 570 474-9739
Mountain Top *(G-11750)*

▲ Amcor Rigid Plastics Usa Inc ....E 610 871-9000
Allentown *(G-130)*

Amcor Rigid Plastics Usa LLC ....C 610 871-9035
Allentown *(G-131)*

American Molding and Tech Inc ....E 814 836-0202
Fairview *(G-5811)*

American Molding Incorporated ....G 215 822-5544
Hatfield *(G-7315)*

▲ Ames Industries Inc ....E 877 296-9977
Hershey *(G-7603)*

▲ Ammeraal Beltech Modular Inc ....E 610 372-1800
Reading *(G-16321)*

Analytic Plastic Inc ....E 215 638-7505
Philadelphia *(G-13389)*

◆ Anderson Plastics Inc ....F 814 774-0076
Girard *(G-6384)*

▲ Anholt Technologies Inc ....F 610 268-2758
Avondale *(G-848)*

▼ Apex Urethane Millworks LLC ....E 717 246-1948
Red Lion *(G-16587)*

▲ Apexco-Ppsi LLC ....G 937 935-0164
Horsham *(G-7787)*

Aspire Technologies ....G 610 491-8162
King of Prussia *(G-8586)*

▲ Associated Packaging Entps Inc .....B 484 785-1120
Chadds Ford *(G-2848)*

Atalanti Polymer Inc ....G 412 321-7411
Pittsburgh *(G-14730)*

◆ Atlas Minerals & Chemicals Inc ......D 800 523-8269
Mertztown *(G-11000)*

▲ Atlas Molding LLC ....F 717 556-8193
Leola *(G-9770)*

Atlas Neon Sign Corp ....G 724 935-2171
Warrendale *(G-19068)*

▲ Augustine Plastics Inc ....E 814 443-7428
Somerset *(G-17677)*

Automating Molding Tech LLC ....G 610 497-7162
Marcus Hook *(G-10437)*

B-TEC Solutions Inc ....E 215 785-2400
Croydon *(G-3911)*

Back 2 Earth Recycling LLC ....G 717 389-6591
Myerstown *(G-11874)*

▲ Bardot Plastics Inc ....C 610 252-5900
Easton *(G-4650)*

Baw Plastics Inc ....D 215 333-6508
Philadelphia *(G-13447)*

Beaumont Advanced Proc LLC ....F 814 899-6390
Erie *(G-5206)*

Beaumont Development LLC ....F 814 899-6390
Erie *(G-5207)*

◆ Bedford Reinforced Plas Inc ....D 814 623-8125
Bedford *(G-1044)*

Belco Tool & Mfg Inc ....F 814 337-3403
Meadville *(G-10706)*

▲ Berger Building Products Inc ....G 215 355-1200
Feasterville Trevose *(G-5889)*

Berry Global Inc ....G 814 455-9051
Erie *(G-5209)*

Berry Global Inc ....B 570 889-3131
Ringtown *(G-16752)*

Berry Global Inc ....G 717 393-3498
Lancaster *(G-8951)*

Berry Global Inc ....B 570 759-6240
Berwick *(G-1309)*

Berry Global Inc ....E 814 849-4234
Brookville *(G-2248)*

Berry Global Inc ....G 717 299-6511
Lancaster *(G-8952)*

◆ Berwick Offray LLC ....B 570 752-5934
Berwick *(G-1311)*

Berwick Offray LLC ....A 570 752-5934
Berwick *(G-1312)*

Berwick Offray LLC ....G 570 752-5934
Berwick *(G-1313)*

Best Group Holdings Inc ....E 814 536-1422
Johnstown *(G-8357)*

Bidwell Machining Inc ....G 570 222-5575
Clifford Township *(G-3247)*

Blair Tool & Plastic Co Inc ....E 814 695-2726
East Freedom *(G-4560)*

Blanchard Mfg & Engrg ....G 814 454-8995
Erie *(G-5213)*

Boyer Machine ....G 570 473-1212
Northumberland *(G-12865)*

Bprex Plastic Packaging Inc ....C 814 849-4240
Brookville *(G-2251)*

◆ Brentwood Industries Inc ....C 610 374-5109
Reading *(G-16336)*

Brentwood Industries Inc ....D 717 274-1827
Lebanon *(G-9548)*

C & E Plastic East ....F 724 457-0594
Coraopolis *(G-3666)*

C & E Plastics Inc ....E 724 947-4949
Georgetown *(G-6274)*

▲ C & J Industries Inc .... B 814 724-4950
  Meadville (G-10709)

C & M Mold & Tool Inc .... G 215 741-2081
  Feasterville Trevose (G-5897)

C Sharkey Keyboard Covers Inc .... F ... 215 969-8783
  Philadelphia (G-13491)

▲ C-K Composites Co LLC .... D 724 547-4581
  Mount Pleasant (G-11690)

Cardinal Health 407 Inc .... A 215 501-1210
  Philadelphia (G-13502)

Carlisle Tpo Inc .... G 717 245-7000
  Carlisle (G-2698)

CCL Tube Inc .... D 570 824-8485
  Hanover Township (G-6984)

Cellcon Plastics Inc .... F 814 763-2195
  Saegertown (G-16909)

◆ Certainteed Corporation .... B 610 893-5000
  Malvern (G-10204)

Certainteed Corporation .... G 610 651-8706
  Malvern (G-10205)

Chautauqua Mfg Corp .... G 513 423-8840
  Sharpsville (G-17470)

▲ Chelsea Building Products .... C 412 826-8077
  Oakmont (G-12914)

Chem-Tainer Industries Inc .... F 717 469-7316
  Hummelstown (G-7906)

Ci Medical Technologies Inc .... E 724 537-9600
  Latrobe (G-9465)

▲ Cjc Contract Packaging Inc .... G 570 209-7836
  Avoca (G-842)

Comor Inc .... G 814 425-3943
  Cochranton (G-3339)

Composite Pnels Innvations LLC .... G 814 317-5023
  Hollidaysburg (G-7644)

Consolidated Cont Holdings LLC .... D 717 854-3454
  York (G-20437)

Consolidated Container Co LLC .... G 724 658-4570
  New Castle (G-12074)

Consolidated Container Co LLC .... D 724 658-4578
  New Castle (G-12075)

Consolidated Container Co LLC .... D 412 828-1111
  Verona (G-18754)

Consolidated Container Co LLC .... G 724 658-0549
  New Castle (G-12076)

Consolidated Container Co LLC .... F 717 267-3533
  Chambersburg (G-2920)

Consolidated Container Co LLC .... E 610 869-4021
  York (G-20438)

Consolidated Container Co LP .... E 814 676-5671
  Oil City (G-12943)

Controlled Molding Inc .... E 724 253-3550
  Hadley (G-6817)

▲ Cook & Frey Inc .... E 717 336-1200
  Lititz (G-10002)

Coreco Fiberglass Inc .... F 724 463-3726
  Indiana (G-8087)

Coretec Plastics Inc .... F 717 866-7472
  Richland (G-16684)

Covington Plastic Molding .... G 717 624-1111
  New Oxford (G-12408)

Cpg International LLC .... G 570 558-8000
  Scranton (G-17224)

Cpk Manufacturing LLC .... G 814 839-4186
  Alum Bank (G-559)

▲ Crescent Industries Inc .... C 717 235-3844
  New Freedom (G-12203)

Crescent Industries Inc .... D 717 235-3844
  New Freedom (G-12204)

Crighton Plastics Inc .... E 724 457-0594
  Coraopolis (G-3681)

Crncte LLC .... F 610 648-0419
  Malvern (G-10219)

Crown Molding .... G 412 779-9209
  Pittsburgh (G-14888)

CSP Technologies Inc .... G 610 635-1202
  Audubon (G-824)

Ctp Carrera Inc .... D 724 733-2994
  Export (G-5596)

▲ Ctp Carrera Inc .... C 724 539-6995
  Latrobe (G-9468)

Custom Extruders Inc .... G 570 345-6600
  Pine Grove (G-14590)

Custom Molds Plastic .... G 717 417-5639
  Yoe (G-20359)

Custom Pack Inc .... F 610 363-1900
  Exton (G-5663)

Cw Thomas LLC .... E 215 335-0200
  Philadelphia (G-13596)

D A R A Inc .... F 717 274-1800
  Lebanon (G-9557)

D&W Fine Pack LLC .... B 215 362-1501
  Hatfield (G-7331)

Delstar Technologies Inc .... E 717 866-7472
  Richland (G-16686)

▲ Diamond Manufacturing Company .. C 570 693-0300
  Wyoming (G-20275)

Diamond Manufacturing Company ..... F 570 693-0300
  Wyoming (G-20276)

Diamond Tech Group Inc .... F 814 445-8953
  Somerset (G-17685)

Dove Plastics Inc .... E 610 562-2600
  Hamburg (G-6837)

▲ Drinkworks Corporation .... E 800 825-5575
  Warren (G-19021)

Drug Plastics and Glass Co .... G 610 367-5000
  Boyertown (G-1907)

Drug Plastics and Glass Co Inc .... D 570 672-3215
  Elysburg (G-4974)

▼ Drug Plastics Closures Inc .... D 610 367-5000
  Boyertown (G-1908)

◆ Dual Core LLC .... D 800 233-0298
  Manheim (G-10379)

Dyneon LLC .... D 610 497-8899
  Aston (G-759)

E-Slinger LLC .... G 412 848-1742
  Meadville (G-10720)

Easygo Drinkware LLC .... E 814 723-7600
  Warren (G-19022)

Edon Corporation .... E 215 672-8050
  Horsham (G-7814)

Eks Vinyl Structures .... G 570 725-3439
  Loganton (G-10094)

Electroline Corp .... E 215 766-2229
  Pipersville (G-14614)

Eljobo Inc .... D 215 822-5544
  Hatfield (G-7338)

Em-Bed-It & Co Inc .... F 412 781-8585
  Pittsburgh (G-14966)

Emperor Aquatics Inc .... F 610 970-0440
  Pottstown (G-15986)

Emporeum Plastics Corporation .... G 610 698-6347
  Birdsboro (G-1694)

◆ Emsco Inc .... C 814 774-3137
  Girard (G-6386)

Engineered Plastics LLC .... D 814 452-6632
  Erie (G-5259)

▲ Engineered Plastics LLC .... D 814 774-2970
  Lake City (G-8899)

Enpro Industries Inc .... G 215 946-0845
  Bristol (G-2141)

Ensinger Inc .... E 724 746-6050
  Washington (G-19170)

▲ Ensinger Industries Inc .... D 724 746-6050
  Washington (G-19171)

Entech Plastics Inc .... E 814 664-7205
  Corry (G-3759)

Entrance Inc .... F 610 926-0126
  Leesport (G-9663)

Epc Inc .... E 215 464-1440
  Philadelphia (G-13675)

Erie OEM Inc .... B 814 459-8024
  Erie (G-5271)

▲ Essentra Plastics LLC .... C 814 899-7671
  Erie (G-5282)

Essentra Porous Tech Corp .... E 814 898-3238
  Erie (G-5283)

Evolution Mlding Solutions Inc .... G 814 807-1982
  Meadville (G-10722)

▲ Executool Prcision Tooling Inc ...... E 814 836-1141
  Erie (G-5285)

Eznergy LLC .... G 215 361-7332
  Lansdale (G-9366)

F R P Fabricators Inc .... G 814 643-2525
  Huntingdon (G-7943)

Fabri-Kal Corporation .... B 570 501-2018
  Hazle Township (G-7457)

Fabri-Kal Corporation .... C 570 454-6672
  Mountain Top (G-11759)

Faivre Mch & Fabrication Inc .... G 814 724-7160
  Meadville (G-10725)

Falcon Plastics Inc .... D 724 222-2620
  Washington (G-19172)

▲ Fenner Precision Inc .... C 800 327-2288
  Manheim (G-10383)

Fiberglass Technologies Inc .... E 215 943-4567
  Levittown (G-9836)

▲ Flontech USA LLC .... E 866 654-2676
  Pittston (G-15751)

▲ Fluoro-Plastics Inc .... F 215 425-5500
  Philadelphia (G-13705)

Fluortek Inc .... D 610 438-1800
  Easton (G-4683)

Focus Noise Ltd Liability Co .... G 484 886-7242
  Exton (G-5680)

Formtech Enterprises Inc .... E 814 474-1940
  Fairview (G-5823)

Franconia Plastics Corp .... G 215 723-8926
  Souderton (G-17735)

Galomb Inc .... G 610 434-3283
  Allentown (G-222)

▲ Gemini Plastics Inc .... E 215 736-1313
  Levittown (G-9839)

General Technical Plastics .... E 610 363-5480
  Exton (G-5687)

▼ George-Ko Industries Inc .... E 814 838-6992
  Erie (G-5303)

Georgia-Pacific LLC .... B 610 250-1400
  Easton (G-4690)

Glass Molders Pottry Plstc .... D 814 756-4042
  Albion (G-44)

Good Neighbors Inc .... F 610 444-1860
  Kennett Square (G-8513)

Gpc Capital Corp II .... A 717 849-8500
  York (G-20505)

Graham Packaging Co Europe LLC .... E 209 572-5187
  York (G-20508)

Graham Packaging Company LP .... D 814 362-3861
  Bradford (G-1970)

Graham Packaging Company LP .... E 717 849-8700
  York (G-20509)

Graham Packaging Company LP .... E 717 849-1800
  York (G-20510)

Graham Packaging Company LP .... E 717 849-8500
  York (G-20511)

Graham Packaging Company LP .... E 570 454-8261
  Hazle Township (G-7460)

▲ Graham Packaging Company Inc .... C 717 849-8500
  Lancaster (G-9031)

Grand Openings Inc .... G 724 325-2029
  Murrysville (G-11852)

Grate Clip Company Inc .... G 215 230-8015
  Doylestown (G-4304)

Greenbriar Indus Systems Inc .... D 814 474-1400
  Fairview (G-5824)

Greif Inc .... E 570 459-9075
  West Hazleton (G-19711)

▲ Greiner Packaging Corp .... F 570 602-3900
  Pittston (G-15754)

Grimm Industries Inc .... C 814 474-2648
  Fairview (G-5825)

Guenther & Sons Enterprises .... G 570 676-0585
  Gouldsboro (G-6568)

◆ H & F Manufacturing Corp .... F 215 355-0250
  Ivyland (G-8212)

Haemer/Wright Tool & Die Inc .... E 814 763-6076
  Saegertown (G-16916)

Halsey Inc .... F 570 278-3610
  Montrose (G-11466)

▲ Hanes Erie Inc .... C 814 474-1999
  Fairview (G-5826)

Harry Rhoades .... F 814 474-1099
  Fairview (G-5827)

Havis Inc .... G 215 354-3280
  Warminster (G-18893)

Havpack .... G 814 452-4989
  Erie (G-5312)

Helix Scientific Inc .... G 215 953-2072
  Southampton (G-17817)

Heritage Fence & Deck LLC .... G 610 476-0003
  Skippack (G-17598)

Hidensee Inc .... G 614 465-3375
  Wallingford (G-18784)

Holbrook Tool & Molding Inc .... E 814 336-4113
  Meadville (G-10736)

Honeywell International Inc .... B 570 621-6000
  Pottsville (G-16080)

Hunsinger Plastics .... G 610 845-9111
  Bally (G-904)

Independent Tool & Mfg .... G 814 336-5168
  Meadville (G-10738)

Industrial Floor Corporation .... F 215 886-1800
  Jenkintown (G-8291)

Industrial Plas Fabrication .... G 610 524-7090
  Exton (G-5697)

Infinity Marketing Inc .... G 610 296-0653
  Malvern (G-10253)

Insert Molding Tech Inc .... E 814 406-7033
  Warren (G-19032)

Interstate Building Mtls Inc .... D 570 655-8496
  Pittston (G-15757)

▼ **Interstate Building Mtls Inc** ....E 570 655-2811
Pittston *(G-15758)*

Ipeg Inc ....F 814 437-6861
Franklin *(G-6139)*

Ishman Plastic & Wood Cutting ....G 814 849-9961
Brookville *(G-2262)*

▲ **J & L Building Materials Inc** ....C 610 644-6311
Malvern *(G-10257)*

J Meyer & Sons Inc ....F 215 324-4440
Philadelphia *(G-13885)*

Jan-Stix LLC ....G 267 918-9561
Huntingdon Valley *(G-8002)*

Jarden Corporation ....C 717 667-2131
Reedsville *(G-16624)*

Jbr Associates Inc ....G 215 362-1318
Lansdale *(G-9380)*

JC Vinyl Fence Rail & Deck ....G 570 282-2222
Carbondale *(G-2680)*

Jenard Corporation ....G 610 622-3600
Lansdowne *(G-9436)*

Jet Plastica Industries Inc ....B 800 220-5381
Hatfield *(G-7356)*

◆ **Jetnet Corporation** ....D 412 741-0100
Sewickley *(G-17396)*

Jmc Engraving Inc ....G 610 759-0140
Nazareth *(G-11974)*

▲ **Jml Industries Inc** ....F 570 453-1201
Hazle Township *(G-7466)*

▲ **John Wall Inc** ....F 724 966-9255
Carmichaels *(G-2759)*

▲ **Johnston-Morehouse-Dickey Co** ....E 412 833-7100
Bethel Park *(G-1421)*

Johnston-Morehouse-Dickey Co ....G 814 684-0916
Tyrone *(G-18584)*

K & H Die and Mold Inc ....G 814 445-9584
Somerset *(G-17694)*

K D Home & Garden Inc ....F 610 929-5794
Temple *(G-18331)*

Keltrol Enterprises Inc ....G 717 764-5940
York *(G-20550)*

Kena Corporation ....F 717 292-7097
Dover *(G-4193)*

Kenson Plastics Inc ....E 724 776-6820
Beaver Falls *(G-1003)*

Ker Custom Molders Inc ....E 610 582-0967
Birdsboro *(G-1701)*

▲ **Kerotest Industries Inc** ....E 412 521-4200
Pittsburgh *(G-15173)*

▲ **Kerotest Manufacturing Corp** ....E 412 521-4200
Pittsburgh *(G-15174)*

◆ **Kerr Group LLC** ....E 812 424-2904
Lancaster *(G-9082)*

Kerr Group LLC ....C 812 424-2904
Lancaster *(G-9083)*

Keystone Containers Inc ....D 603 888-1315
Reading *(G-16420)*

Kindle Creations Inc ....E 215 997-6878
Chalfont *(G-2882)*

King Precision Solutions LLC ....F 877 312-3858
Erie *(G-5344)*

Klimek Molding Corp ....G 814 774-4051
Girard *(G-6395)*

▲ **Knf Corporation** ....E 570 386-3550
Tamaqua *(G-18213)*

Kw Plastics ....E 334 566-1563
Allentown *(G-288)*

L & L Industrial Chemical Inc ....G 215 368-7813
North Wales *(G-12811)*

L P Aero Plastics Inc ....E 724 744-4448
Jeannette *(G-8260)*

◆ **La France Corp** ....C 610 361-4300
Concordville *(G-3457)*

▲ **Laminated Materials Corp** ....E 215 425-4100
Bensalem *(G-1218)*

▲ **Laminations Inc** ....C 570 876-8199
Archbald *(G-690)*

▲ **Lancer Systems LP** ....E 610 973-2600
Quakertown *(G-16208)*

Latrobe Associates Inc ....E 724 539-1612
Latrobe *(G-9488)*

Lawrie Technology Inc ....G 814 402-1208
Girard *(G-6396)*

Lesko Enterprises Inc ....C 814 756-4030
Albion *(G-46)*

Letica Corporation ....D 570 654-2451
Pittston *(G-15763)*

▲ **LLC Snyder Gates** ....F 877 621-0195
Millerstown *(G-11205)*

▲ **M & Q Plastic Products Co** ....F 484 369-8906
Limerick *(G-9969)*

M&Q Holdings LLC ....F 570 385-4991
Schuylkill Haven *(G-17161)*

Maloney Plastics Inc ....E 814 337-8417
Meadville *(G-10753)*

Marietta Fence Experts LLC ....G 724 925-6100
Hunker *(G-7929)*

Mason Jars Company ....F 877 490-5565
Erie *(G-5381)*

Matamatic Inc ....G 724 696-5678
Mount Pleasant *(G-11705)*

Maxima Tech & Systems Inc ....B 717 569-5713
Lancaster *(G-9129)*

Meadville New Products Inc ....F 814 336-2174
Meadville *(G-10759)*

▲ **Medart Inc** ....E 724 752-3555
Ellwood City *(G-4946)*

Medical Precision Plastics Inc ....F 215 441-4800
Warminster *(G-18920)*

Meridian Precision Inc ....E 570 345-6600
Pine Grove *(G-14599)*

Metamora Products Corp Elkland ....C 814 258-7122
Elkland *(G-4916)*

▼ **MI Windows and Doors Inc** ....G 717 365-3300
Gratz *(G-6578)*

Micor Inc ....E 412 487-1113
Bethlehem *(G-1571)*

▲ **Micro Dimensional Products** ....D 610 239-7940
Norristown *(G-12683)*

Micro Mold Co Inc ....E 814 838-3404
Erie *(G-5389)*

Micro Plastics Inc ....G 814 337-0781
Meadville *(G-10763)*

▲ **Microsonic Inc** ....E 724 266-2031
Ambridge *(G-627)*

▲ **Midgard Inc** ....D 215 536-3174
Green Lane *(G-6590)*

Miller Plastic Products Inc ....F 724 947-5000
Burgettstown *(G-2350)*

▲ **Millet Plastics Inc** ....E 717 277-7404
Lebanon *(G-9611)*

Misterplexi ....G 724 759-7500
Wexford *(G-19812)*

Modern Plastics Corp ....E 570 822-1124
Wilkes Barre *(G-19944)*

Moldamatic LLC ....G 215 785-2356
Levittown *(G-9851)*

Molded Fiber Glass Companies ....C 814 438-3841
Union City *(G-18610)*

Molded Fiber Glass Companies ....C 814 683-4500
Linesville *(G-9984)*

Moog Inc ....C 610 328-4000
Springfield *(G-17919)*

Mr Spouting ....G 814 692-4880
Port Matilda *(G-15903)*

▼ **Mtl Holdings Inc** ....C 570 343-7921
Archbald *(G-693)*

Multicolor Corp ....G 610 262-8420
Coplay *(G-3646)*

Munot Plastics Inc ....E 814 838-7721
Erie *(G-5398)*

Munot Plastics Inc ....E 814 838-7721
Erie *(G-5399)*

▲ **Mxl Industries Inc** ....D 717 569-8711
Lancaster *(G-9141)*

▲ **Namsco Plastics Inds Inc** ....D 724 339-3591
New Kensington *(G-12360)*

Namsco Plastics Industries ....E 724 339-3100
New Kensington *(G-12361)*

▲ **Nation Ruskin Holdings Inc** ....F 267 654-4000
Montgomeryville *(G-11409)*

National Molding LLC ....E 724 266-8770
Ambridge *(G-630)*

Nazareth Industrial Corp ....F 610 759-9776
Nazareth *(G-11983)*

Nds Holdings LP ....A 610 408-0500
Newtown Square *(G-12586)*

Nethercraft Incorporated ....G 248 224-1963
Bridgeville *(G-2081)*

New Concept Manufacturing LLC ....C 717 741-0840
Emigsville *(G-4994)*

▲ **New Concept Technology Inc** ....E 717 741-0840
Emigsville *(G-4995)*

New Thermo-Serv Ltd ....D 215 646-7667
Ambler *(G-594)*

New Werner Holding Co Inc ....G 724 588-2000
Greenville *(G-6758)*

▲ **Newmetro Design LLC** ....G 814 696-2550
Duncansville *(G-4457)*

Newtown Mfg & Bldg Sup Corp ....D 570 825-3675
Wilkes Barre *(G-19950)*

Newtown-Slocomb Mfg Inc ....E 570 825-3675
Hanover Township *(G-7000)*

Newtown-Slocomb Mfg Inc ....G 570 825-3675
Hanover Township *(G-7001)*

Niagara Plastics ....G 814 464-8169
Erie *(G-5404)*

Normandy Industries Inc ....G 412 826-1825
Pittsburgh *(G-15344)*

Normandy Products Company ....G 412 826-1825
Pittsburgh *(G-15345)*

Northern Engrg Plas Corp PR ....G 724 658-9019
New Castle *(G-12133)*

Novares US LLC ....D 717 244-0151
Felton *(G-5941)*

Novares US LLC ....B 717 244-4581
Felton *(G-5942)*

▲ **Novelty Concepts Inc** ....E 215 245-5570
Bensalem *(G-1233)*

▼ **Nushield Inc** ....G 215 500-6426
Newtown *(G-12530)*

▲ **Nylacast LLC** ....E 717 270-5600
Harrisburg *(G-7185)*

▲ **Nytef Plastics Ltd** ....E 215 244-6950
Bensalem *(G-1234)*

▲ **Nzk Plastics LLC** ....E 412 823-8630
Turtle Creek *(G-18566)*

Obh Enterprises LLC ....G 610 436-0796
West Chester *(G-19609)*

▼ **Old Ladder Co** ....A 888 523-3371
Greenville *(G-6762)*

Olde Slate Mtn Color Co Inc ....G 570 421-8910
East Stroudsburg *(G-4626)*

▲ **Omega Plastics LLC** ....F 814 452-4989
Erie *(G-5409)*

Omnova Solutions Inc ....B 570 366-1051
Auburn *(G-820)*

Ono Industries Inc ....E 717 865-6619
Ono *(G-13004)*

Opi Holdings Inc ....E 610 857-2000
Old Forge *(G-12973)*

◆ **Orange Products Inc** ....D 610 791-9711
Allentown *(G-341)*

P & C Tool Co ....F 814 425-7050
Meadville *(G-10773)*

P E H Inc ....E 610 845-9111
Bally *(G-905)*

◆ **Pac Strapping Products Inc** ....E 610 363-8805
Exton *(G-5721)*

Pactiv LLC ....C 610 269-1776
Downingtown *(G-4247)*

Palmer Plastics Inc ....F 610 330-9900
Easton *(G-4739)*

Panel Technologies Inc ....E 215 538-7055
Quakertown *(G-16226)*

Panthera Products Inc ....G 724 532-3362
Latrobe *(G-9509)*

▲ **Parker Industries Inc** ....E 412 561-6902
Pittsburgh *(G-15369)*

Parker Precision Molding Inc ....E 724 930-8099
Rostraver Township *(G-16829)*

Penn Fibre Inc ....E 800 662-7366
Bensalem *(G-1241)*

Pennsylvania Insert Corp ....F 610 474-0112
Royersford *(G-16860)*

Pexco LLC ....E 215 736-2553
Morrisville *(G-11577)*

Pickar Brothers Inc ....E 610 582-0967
Birdsboro *(G-1703)*

Pittsburgh Technologies Inc ....E 724 339-0900
New Kensington *(G-12367)*

◆ **Plastek Industries Inc** ....D 814 878-4400
Erie *(G-5420)*

Plastek Industries Inc ....G 814 878-4741
Erie *(G-5421)*

Plastek Industries Inc ....E 814 878-4719
Erie *(G-5422)*

Plastek Industries Inc ....E 814 878-4601
Erie *(G-5423)*

Plastek Industries Inc ....B 814 878-4466
Erie *(G-5424)*

Plastek Industries Inc ....A 814 878-4515
Erie *(G-5425)*

Plastic Components Inc ....F 215 235-5550
Philadelphia *(G-14182)*

▲ **Plastic Dip Moldings Inc** ....E 215 766-2020
Quakertown *(G-16229)*

Plastic Fabricators Inc ....F 717 843-4222
York *(G-20628)*

Plastic Solutions Inc ....G 215 968-3242
Newtown *(G-12536)*

Plastic System Packaging Mille..........F 717 277-7404
Lebanon (G-9623)

Plasticoncentrates Inc ....G...... 215 243-4143
Philadelphia (G-14183)

Plastics Services Network ....G...... 814 898-6317
Erie (G-5426)

Plastikos Inc ....E 814 868-1656
Erie (G-5427)

◆ Pleiger Plastics Company ....D...... 724 228-2244
Washington (G-19216)

PMI Inc ....G...... 814 455-8085
Erie (G-5428)

Polar Tech Industries Inc ....E 800 423-2749
Elysburg (G-4979)

Polycube Company LLC...................F 215 946-2823
Levittown (G-9857)

▼ Polycycle Industrial Pdts Inc ....E 412 747-1101
Pittsburgh (G-15419)

Polyfab Corporation ....E 610 926-3245
Reading (G-16472)

▲ Polyflo Inc ....E 570 429-2340
Saint Clair (G-16938)

Polymer Div of Wyomissing Spc ....G...... 610 488-0981
Bernville (G-1303)

▲ Polymer Instrumentation & C ....E 814 357-5860
State College (G-18007)

◆ Polymer Molding Inc ....E 800 344-7584
Erie (G-5429)

Popit Inc ....G...... 215 752-8410
Langhorne (G-9320)

▲ Port Erie Plastics Inc ....E 814 899-7602
Harborcreek (G-7008)

Port Erie Plastics Inc ....G...... 814 899-7602
Harborcreek (G-7009)

Poux Plastics Inc ....G...... 814 425-2100
Cochranton (G-3348)

Precise Plastics Inc ....D...... 814 474-5504
Fairview (G-5840)

◆ Precision Polymer Products Inc ....C 610 326-0921
Pottstown (G-16035)

Precision Polymers Inc ....F 814 838-9288
Erie (G-5431)

Premier Spouting Design LLC ....G...... 717 336-1205
Reinholds (G-16636)

Premium Molding Inc......................G...... 724 424-7000
Derry (G-4106)

Premium Plastics Solutions LLC ....D...... 724 424-7000
Latrobe (G-9511)

Pretium Packaging LLC....................C 717 266-6687
Manchester (G-10362)

Prime Plastics Inc ....E 724 250-7172
Washington (G-19219)

Prism Plastics Inc ....C 814 724-8222
Meadville (G-10781)

Proplastix International Inc ....C 717 692-4733
Millersburg (G-11198)

Protective Industries Inc ....C 814 868-3671
Erie (G-5441)

Proto-Cast LLC ....E 610 326-1723
Douglassville (G-4180)

▲ Ptr Tool & Plastics LLC................E 814 724-6979
Meadville (G-10783)

Q-Cast Inc ....E 724 728-7440
Rochester (G-16789)

Qtd Plastics Inc ....E 814 724-1641
Meadville (G-10784)

Quadrant Holding Inc ....C 570 558-6000
Scranton (G-17276)

Quality Fencing & Supply ....E 717 355-7112
New Holland (G-12276)

Quality Mold Inc ....G...... 814 459-1084
Erie (G-5444)

◆ Quality Perforating Inc................D...... 570 267-2092
Carbondale (G-2685)

R & G Products Inc ....F 717 633-0011
Hanover (G-6940)

▲ R J Evercrest Polymers Inc............G...... 610 647-1555
West Chester (G-19626)

R-G-T Plastics Company ....G...... 814 683-2161
Linesville (G-9986)

Ram Precision Inc ....G...... 215 674-0663
Horsham (G-7843)

▲ Rapid Mold Solutions Inc ....G...... 814 833-2721
Erie (G-5456)

Reading Plastic Products Inc ....G...... 610 779-3128
Reading Station (G-16573)

Regency Plus Inc ....E 570 339-1390
Mount Carmel (G-11629)

Regenex Corporation ....D...... 724 528-5900
West Middlesex (G-19728)

Rehrig Pacific Company...................D...... 814 455-8023
Erie (G-5460)

Relianology International Ltd ....G...... 412 607-1503
Export (G-5625)

Reliant Molding Inc.......................E 814 756-5522
Cranesville (G-3869)

◆ Remcon Plastics Inc ....D...... 610 376-2666
Reading (G-16496)

▲ Reubes Plastics Co Inc ....E 215 368-3010
Hatfield (G-7390)

Rhkg Holdings Inc ....E 814 337-8407
Meadville (G-10787)

Richman Industries Inc ....E 717 561-1766
Harrisburg (G-7206)

Rick Leasure ....G...... 814 739-9521
Wattsburg (G-19282)

Rj Evercrests Inc ....G...... 610 431-4200
West Chester (G-19630)

▲ Rocal Corporation ....E 215 343-2400
Warrington (G-19132)

Rodon Group ....D...... 215 822-5544
Hatfield (G-7391)

▲ RPC Bramlage-Wiko-Usa Inc ....D...... 610 286-0805
Morgantown (G-11533)

Rubbermaid Commercial Pdts LLC.......F 570 622-7715
Pottsville (G-16096)

▲ Rwb Special Services Corp ....F 215 766-4800
Pipersville (G-14619)

▲ S E Moulding Inc ....G...... 717 385-4119
Carlisle (G-2738)

▲ Saint-Gobain Vetrotex Amer Inc .....F 610 893-6000
Valley Forge (G-18713)

▲ Say Plastics Inc ....E 717 633-6333
Mc Sherrystown (G-10652)

Say Plastics Inc ....G...... 717 624-3222
New Oxford (G-12424)

Scaffs Enterprises Inc ....G...... 570 725-3497
Logantown (G-10098)

Schlotter Precision Pdts Inc ....E 215 354-3280
Warminster (G-18963)

Schubert Plastics Inc.....................F 610 358-4920
Lenni (G-9762)

▲ Scully Enterprises Inc ....G...... 814 835-0173
Erie (G-5471)

Sealed Air Corporation ....G...... 610 926-7517
Reading (G-16509)

Seaway Manufacturing Corp..............D...... 814 898-2255
Erie (G-5472)

Sein Organizing Solutions ....G...... 215 932-8837
East Greenville (G-4575)

Selmax Corp ....E 570 374-2833
Selinsgrove (G-17334)

▲ Seven D Industries LP ....C 814 317-4077
Hollidaysburg (G-7654)

Seybert Castings Inc ....F 215 364-7115
Huntingdon Valley (G-8038)

Shades of Country ....G...... 570 297-3327
Troy (G-18526)

▲ Shape TEC Ltd ....G...... 610 689-8940
Limekiln (G-9968)

Sharp Coatings ....F 215 324-8500
Philadelphia (G-14298)

▲ Sharpsville Container Corp............E 724 962-1100
Sharpsville (G-17475)

Shop Vac Corporation ....B 570 673-5145
Williamsport (G-20072)

Shorts Tool & Mfg Inc ....E 814 763-2401
Saegertown (G-16933)

Shutter Tech Inc ....G...... 610 696-9322
West Chester (G-19639)

Silgan Ipec Corporation ....D...... 724 658-3004
New Castle (G-12152)

Silgan Ipec Corporation ....D...... 724 658-3004
New Castle (G-12153)

Silgan Plastics LLC ....D...... 215 727-2676
Langhorne (G-9325)

SLC Sales and Service Inc ....G...... 724 238-7692
Ligonier (G-9965)

Smart Systems Inc........................G...... 412 323-2128
Pittsburgh (G-15546)

▲ Smartshake.............................F 724 396-7947
Pittsburgh (G-15549)

Smooth Line Inc ....G...... 412 828-3599
Cheswick (G-3118)

Sonoco Prtective Solutions Inc ....E 412 415-1462
Pittsburgh (G-15558)

Southwest Vinyl Windows Inc ....F 610 626-8826
Lansdowne (G-9444)

Space Age Plastics Inc...................F 570 630-6060
Jefferson Township (G-8279)

Spears Manufacturing Co ....G...... 570 384-4832
Hazle Township (G-7482)

Stabler Companies Inc ....F 717 236-9307
Harrisburg (G-7219)

Staggert Disposal ....G...... 570 547-6150
Montgomery (G-11379)

Standard Industries Inc ....F 570 568-7230
New Columbia (G-12176)

Steinmetz Inc ....E 570 842-6161
Roaring Brook Twp (G-16760)

▲ Sterling Technologies Inc ....C 814 774-2500
Lake City (G-8908)

Strauss Engineering Company...........D...... 215 947-1083
Huntingdon Valley (G-8041)

Structural Fiberglass Inc ....F 814 623-0458
Bedford (G-1077)

Sun Star Inc ....G...... 724 537-5990
Latrobe (G-9523)

Suntuf 2000 Inc ....G...... 610 285-6968
Kutztown (G-8862)

Superior Plastic Products Inc ....E 717 355-7100
New Holland (G-12288)

Superior Plastic Products LLC ....G...... 717 556-3240
Leola (G-12594)

Superior Transparent Noise ....G...... 610 715-1969
Ardmore (G-720)

Superior Window Mfg Inc..................F 412 793-3500
Pittsburgh (G-15589)

Supreme Corq LLC........................G...... 610 408-0500
Newtown Square (G-12594)

T K Plastics Inc ....F 724 443-6760
Gibsonia (G-6355)

T M Fitzgerald & Assoc Inc ....G...... 610 853-2008
Havertown (G-7429)

Tamarack Packaging Ltd ....E 814 724-2860
Meadville (G-10798)

Target Precision ....F 814 382-3000
Harmonsburg (G-7065)

Tech Group North America Inc ....C 570 326-7673
Williamsport (G-20080)

Tech Group North America Inc ....G...... 480 281-4500
Exton (G-5736)

Techna-Plastic Services Inc ....E 570 386-2732
Lehighton (G-9729)

Tef - Cap Industries Inc ....G...... 610 692-2576
West Chester (G-19657)

Tetra Tool Company ....F 814 833-6127
Erie (G-5506)

Theodore W Styborski....................G...... 814 337-8535
Meadville (G-10800)

Tmf Corporation ....G...... 610 853-3080
Havertown (G-7431)

TNT Disposal ....G...... 570 297-0101
Troy (G-18527)

Todd Weikel ....G...... 610 779-5508
Reading (G-16542)

Tool-Rite Inc ....G...... 814 587-3151
Springboro (G-17896)

Top Gun Tool Inc ....G...... 814 454-4849
Erie (G-5513)

Torytown Sculpture ....G...... 215 458-8092
Bristol (G-2209)

Tpl Plastic Engraving ....G...... 412 771-3773
Coraopolis (G-3728)

▲ Trans Western Polymers Inc ....E 570 668-5690
Tamaqua (G-18230)

▲ Tray-Pak Corporation ....C 888 926-1777
Reading (G-16546)

Tray-Pak Corporation ....C 484 509-0046
Reading (G-16547)

Tri-State Plastics Inc......................F 724 457-2847
Coraopolis (G-3729)

Tri-Tech Injection Molding Inc ....E 814 476-7748
Mc Kean (G-10595)

Triangle Tool Company Inc ....C 814 878-4400
Erie (G-5517)

Trident Plastics Inc ....G...... 215 946-3999
Bristol (G-2210)

Trio Plastics Inc ....F 814 724-1640
Meadville (G-10803)

Trojan Inc ....E 814 336-4468
Meadville (G-10804)

▲ True Precision Plastics LLC............E 717 358-9251
Lancaster (G-9223)

▲ Tubro Company Inc ....E 800 673-7887
Warminster (G-18987)

Two Togethers Inc ....G...... 814 838-1234
Erie (G-5521)

▲ U S Plastic Coatings Corp.............E 215 257-5300
Sellersville (G-17361)

Ultra-Mold Corporation..................G.... 215 493-9840
Yardley (G-20344)

▲ Unipar Inc....................................E.... 717 667-3354
Reedsville (G-16629)

United Fence Supply Company..........G.... 570 307-0782
Olyphant (G-13002)

◆ Universal Protective Packg Inc.....D.... 717 766-1578
Mechanicsburg (G-10903)

Urban Outfitters Wholesale Inc.........G.... 215 454-5500
Philadelphia (G-14431)

Valley Extrusions LLC.....................E.... 610 266-8550
Allentown (G-420)

Valley Plastics Inc........................G.... 570 287-7964
Forty Fort (G-6099)

▲ Valtech Corporation.....................E.... 610 705-5900
Pottstown (G-16064)

▲ Vanguard Manufacturing Inc.........F.... 610 481-0655
Allentown (G-422)

Veka Holdings Inc.........................E.... 724 452-1000
Fombell (G-6036)

◆ Veka Inc...................................B.... 800 654-5589
Fombell (G-6037)

Veka West Inc..............................G.... 724 452-1000
Fombell (G-6038)

◆ Velocity Eqp Solutions LLC...........F.... 800 521-1368
New Castle (G-12162)

◆ Ventana USA.............................D.... 724 325-3400
Export (G-5630)

Venture Precision Tool Inc...............F.... 717 566-6496
Hummelstown (G-7927)

Veritiv Operating Company..............E.... 724 776-3122
Cranberry Township (G-3863)

▲ Versatex Building Products LLC.....D.... 724 857-1111
Aliquippa (G-100)

Viant Westfield LLC........................D.... 215 675-4653
Warminster (G-18994)

Vision Custom Tooling Inc...............F.... 610 582-1640
Birdsboro (G-1708)

Viwinco Inc.................................C.... 610 286-8884
Morgantown (G-11543)

VPI Acquisition LLC.......................C.... 814 664-8671
Corry (G-3779)

Walters Mlding Fabrication LLC.........G.... 724 662-4836
Mercer (G-10978)

Warren Plastics Mfg.......................G.... 814 726-9511
Warren (G-19060)

Wentzel Fabrication Inc...................F.... 610 987-6909
Oley (G-12981)

◆ Werner Co.................................C.... 724 588-2000
Greenville (G-6775)

Werner Holding Co Inc....................A.... 888 523-3371
Greenville (G-6776)

▲ West Pharmaceutical Svcs Inc.......B.... 610 594-2900
Exton (G-5748)

Westlake United Corporation............F.... 570 876-0222
Mayfield (G-10545)

Wexco Incorporated.......................G.... 717 764-8585
York (G-20710)

▼ WFC Company Inc......................D.... 215 953-1260
Southampton (G-17846)

▲ Whirley Industries Inc..................C.... 814 723-7600
Warren (G-19064)

Whirley Industries Inc.....................G.... 814 723-7600
Warren (G-19065)

Wise Plastics................................G.... 847 697-2840
Harrisburg (G-7247)

Wolverine Plastics Inc.....................E.... 724 856-5610
Ellwood City (G-4955)

X-Act Technology Incorporated.........G.... 814 824-6811
Erie (G-5534)

X-Cell Molding Inc.........................G.... 814 836-0202
Erie (G-5535)

Yonish Disposal Company................G.... 814 839-4797
Alum Bank (G-563)

▲ York Imperial Plastics Inc.............E.... 717 428-3939
York (G-20740)

Zehrco-Giancola Composites Inc........G.... 814 406-7033
Warren (G-19066)

Zemco Tool & Die Inc.....................D.... 717 647-7151
Williamstown (G-20104)

Zircon Corp.................................G.... 215 757-7156
Langhorne (G-9337)

31 LEATHER AND LEATHER PRODUCTS

3111 Leather Tanning & Finishing

Clemintines................................G.... 717 626-1378
Lititz (G-10000)

Columbia Organ Works Inc...............G.... 717 684-3573
Columbia (G-3436)

Daniel D Esh...............................G.... 814 383-4579
Howard (G-7889)

Empire Glove Inc...........................G.... 570 824-4400
Wilkes Barre (G-19918)

G & F Products Inc........................F.... 215 781-6222
Philadelphia (G-13737)

Interntnal Lthers of Phldlphia............G.... 610 793-1140
West Chester (G-19572)

Keystone Fur Dressing Inc...............G.... 717 677-4553
Aspers (G-742)

◆ McAdoo & Allen Inc....................E.... 215 536-3520
Quakertown (G-16214)

▲ New Gear Brands LLC.................G.... 407 674-6850
Milford (G-11163)

Sugar Valley Collar Shop Inc............G.... 570 725-3499
Loganton (G-10099)

▲ Thermo Electric Company Inc........D.... 610 692-7990
West Chester (G-19661)

Titan Group Ltd............................E.... 610 631-0831
Norristown (G-12719)

▲ Wickett & Craig America Inc..........D.... 814 236-2220
Curwensville (G-3956)

3131 Boot & Shoe Cut Stock & Findings

Country Flair Quarter Horses............G.... 724 822-8413
Worthington (G-20229)

Dotted Quarter Music......................G.... 724 541-4211
Mechanicsburg (G-10838)

Fighters Quarters..........................G.... 334 657-4128
Allentown (G-212)

French Quaters.............................G.... 724 845-7387
Leechburg (G-9645)

Hbg-Upper Saucon Inc....................G.... 215 491-7736
Jamison (G-8244)

Ingersoll Rand Co..........................G.... 215 345-4470
Furlong (G-6231)

Ingersoll-Rand Co..........................G.... 717 530-1160
Shippensburg (G-17533)

Ingersoll-Rand Co..........................G.... 610 882-8800
Bethlehem (G-1539)

▲ Keystone Leather Distrs LLC.........F.... 570 329-3780
Williamsport (G-20031)

L Rand Incorporated.......................G.... 215 490-8090
Philadelphia (G-13949)

Lucks Upper Bucks Gym LLC............G.... 610 847-2392
Upper Black Eddy (G-18655)

North Pittsburgh Upper Cervica.........G.... 724 553-8526
Cranberry Township (G-3842)

▲ Quality Crrctons Inspctons Inc......D.... 814 696-3737
Duncansville (G-4462)

Rand 2339 Haverford LP..................G.... 215 620-6993
Ardmore (G-714)

Richard Zerbe Ltd..........................G.... 717 564-2024
Harrisburg (G-7205)

Rob Rand Enterprises Inc.................G.... 724 927-6844
Jamestown (G-8239)

Stevens Clogging Supplies Inc...........G.... 724 662-0808
Mercer (G-10976)

Three Dimensions Systems Inc..........G.... 724 779-3890
Cranberry Township (G-3852)

Ticket Counter.............................G.... 717 536-3092
Mechanicsburg (G-10897)

Unequal Technologies Company.........E.... 610 444-5900
Glen Mills (G-6446)

Upper Case Living.........................G.... 724 229-8190
Washington (G-19236)

Upper Delaware Valley ID.................G.... 570 251-8040
Bethany (G-1391)

Upper Moreland............................G.... 215 773-9880
Horsham (G-7862)

Upper Perk Robotics.......................G.... 215 541-1654
Pennsburg (G-13259)

Upper Providence Township..............F.... 610 933-8179
Oaks (G-12937)

3143 Men's Footwear, Exc Athletic

▲ Abilene Boot Co Inc....................E.... 814 445-6545
Somerset (G-17672)

▲ Best-Made Shoes........................G.... 412 621-9363
Pittsburgh (G-14765)

C & J Clark America Inc...................D.... 717 632-2444
Hanover (G-6864)

HH Brown Shoe Company Inc...........E.... 814 793-3786
Martinsburg (G-10523)

HH Brown Shoe Company Inc...........G.... 814 793-3786
Martinsburg (G-10524)

Perry Ercolino Inc.........................G.... 215 348-5885
Doylestown (G-4324)

Primitive Country Tole.....................G.... 570 247-2719
Rome (G-16801)

▲ Quality Crrctons Inspctons Inc......D.... 814 696-3737
Duncansville (G-4462)

Relay Shoe Company LLC................G.... 610 970-6450
Pottstown (G-16039)

Vf Outdoor LLC............................G.... 610 327-1734
Pottstown (G-16065)

Vf Outdoor LLC............................G.... 610 265-2193
King of Prussia (G-8696)

3144 Women's Footwear, Exc Athletic

▲ Abilene Boot Co Inc....................E.... 814 445-6545
Somerset (G-17672)

Gleen.......................................G.... 570 457-3858
Moosic (G-11506)

HH Brown Shoe Company Inc...........D.... 814 793-3786
Martinsburg (G-10524)

Modzori LLC................................G.... 215 833-3618
Newtown (G-12522)

▲ Quality Crrctons Inspctons Inc......D.... 814 696-3737
Duncansville (G-4462)

Vf Outdoor LLC............................G.... 610 265-2193
King of Prussia (G-8696)

3149 Footwear, NEC

Greenkeepers Inc..........................G.... 215 464-7540
Philadelphia (G-13786)

▲ Kepner-Scott Shoe Co..................E.... 570 366-0229
Orwigsburg (G-13047)

Sunnys Fashions...........................G.... 724 527-1800
Jeannette (G-8266)

▲ Up-Front Footwear Inc.................G.... 717 492-1875
Mount Joy (G-11674)

3151 Leather Gloves & Mittens

▲ Red Lion Manufacturing Inc...........C.... 717 767-6511
York (G-20656)

Stingfree Technologies Company........G.... 610 444-2806
West Chester (G-19644)

3161 Luggage

American Accessories Inc.................E.... 215 639-8000
Bensalem (G-1148)

▲ Case Design Corporation..............D.... 215 703-0130
Telford (G-18270)

▲ Case Design Corporation..............G.... 800 847-4176
Telford (G-18271)

Ceramic Art Company Inc................A.... 952 944-5600
Bristol (G-2124)

▲ Codi Inc...................................F.... 717 540-1337
Harrisburg (G-7108)

David Trunk................................G.... 570 247-2012
Rome (G-16798)

Discovery Direct Inc.......................G.... 610 252-3809
Easton (G-4670)

▲ Lenox Corporation......................F.... 267 525-7800
Bristol (G-2159)

M & M Manufacturing Co..................E.... 724 274-0767
Cheswick (G-3111)

▲ Shine Moon L P.........................F.... 570 539-8602
Mount Pleasant Mills (G-11732)

Silver Charm Clothing Company.........G.... 484 274-6796
Allentown (G-393)

Susan Reabuck.............................G.... 610 797-7014
Allentown (G-405)

Tom James Company......................D.... 717 264-5768
Chambersburg (G-2986)

Tre-Ray Cases Inc.........................F.... 215 551-6811
Philadelphia (G-14404)

3171 Handbags & Purses

A Tru Diva LLC............................G.... 888 400-1034
Brookhaven (G-2241)

Coach Inc...................................F.... 215 659-6158
Willow Grove (G-20112)

Eternity Fashion Inc.......................G.... 215 567-5571
Philadelphia (G-13681)

Fleuri LLC..................................G.... 724 539-7566
Latrobe (G-9476)

▲ Marcus J Wholesalers Inc.............F.... 412 261-3315
Pittsburgh (G-15252)

Softkog Inc.................................G.... 717 490-1091
Harleysville (G-7059)

3172 Personal Leather Goods

American Accessories Inc.................E.... 215 639-8000
Bensalem (G-1148)

S I C

Bashlin Industries Inc..................D...... 724 458-8340
Grove City (G-6780)
Buffalo Billfold..........................G...... 814 422-8955
Spring Mills (G-17885)
Dmi Locksmith Inc......................G...... 412 232-3000
Pittsburgh (G-14928)
Dr Davies Products Inc................G...... 570 321-5423
Williamsport (G-20007)
Korsak Glass & Aluminum Inc.........G...... 610 987-9888
Boyertown (G-1923)
Leathersmith Inc........................G...... 717 933-8084
Myerstown (G-11891)

3199 Leather Goods, NEC

Ambassador Bags & Spats Mfg Co......G...... 610 532-7840
Folcroft (G-5998)
Bashlin Industries Inc.................D...... 724 458-8340
Grove City (G-6780)
C&G Arms LLC...........................G...... 724 858-2856
Natrona Heights (G-11937)
Dull Knife Terminator Inc..............G...... 717 512-8596
Mechanicsburg (G-10839)
E Z Sensenig & Son....................G...... 717 445-5580
New Holland (G-12246)
▲ Frenchcreek Production Inc.........E...... 814 437-1808
Franklin (G-6131)
▲ Graham International Inc............F...... 203 838-3355
Philadelphia (G-13779)
Helene Batoff Interiors................G...... 215 879-7727
Philadelphia (G-13812)
Kimberly A Spickler....................G...... 814 627-2316
Hesston (G-7627)
L M Robbins Co.........................F...... 610 760-8301
Slatington (G-17608)
Lb Full Circle Canine Fitness..........G...... 267 825-7375
Philadelphia (G-13961)
Mac Inc.................................G...... 717 560-0612
East Petersburg (G-4588)
McCabes Custom Leather...............G...... 814 414-1442
Altoona (G-525)
▲ Polar Manufacturing Co Inc.........F...... 215 535-6940
Philadelphia (G-14184)
Roberta Weissburg Leathers...........G...... 412 681-8188
Pittsburgh (G-15494)
Samuelson Leather LLC................G...... 610 719-7391
West Chester (G-19636)
Samuelson Leather LLC................G...... 484 328-3273
Malvern (G-10314)
Shady Acres Saddlery Inc..............G...... 412 963-9454
Pittsburgh (G-15526)
▲ Smuckers Harness Shop Inc.........F...... 717 445-5956
Narvon (G-11927)
▲ Sperian Fall Protection Inc.........C...... 814 432-2118
Franklin (G-6163)
Spiders Den Inc.........................G...... 724 445-7450
Chicora (G-3129)
Todd Weikel............................G...... 610 779-5508
Reading (G-16542)

32 STONE, CLAY, GLASS, AND CONCRETE PRODUCTS

3211 Flat Glass

AGC Flat Glass North Amer Inc.........E...... 215 538-9424
Quakertown (G-16167)
Associated Windows....................G...... 814 445-9744
Somerset (G-17674)
Baut Studios Inc.......................E...... 570 288-1431
Swoyersville (G-18194)
Bryn Mawr Shower Door Inc...........G...... 610 647-0357
Berwyn (G-1354)
Cascade Architectural Products........G...... 412 824-9313
Turtle Creek (G-18561)
Chango Inc.............................G...... 215 634-0400
Philadelphia (G-13525)
Consolidated GL Holdings Inc..........G...... 866 412-6977
East Butler (G-4531)
Emerald Art Glass Inc..................F...... 412 381-2274
Pittsburgh (G-14970)
Glass Machinery Works LLC...........G...... 724 473-0666
Ellwood City (G-4933)
▼ Global Custom Decorating Inc......E...... 814 236-2110
Curwensville (G-3952)
Greenheat LP...........................F...... 724 545-6540
Cowansville (G-3796)
Guardian Industries LLC...............D...... 717 242-2571
Lewistown (G-9933)
Hutts Glass Co Inc....................G...... 610 369-1028
Gilbertsville (G-6373)

▲ Kane Innovations Inc................D...... 814 838-7731
Erie (G-5342)
Lot Made Gallery LLC...................G...... 717 458-8716
Mechanicsburg (G-10866)
Mesko Glass and Mirror Co Inc.........D...... 570 457-1700
Avoca (G-845)
Northeast Laminated Glass Corp.......G...... 570 489-6421
Jessup (G-8334)
Pennsylvania Insulating Glass.........F...... 717 247-0560
Lewistown (G-9944)
Pittsburgh Aluminum Co LLC...........F...... 724 452-5900
Pittsburgh (G-15386)
◆ Pittsburgh Glass Works LLC.........D...... 412 995-6500
Pittsburgh (G-15398)
Poma GL Specialty Windows Inc........D...... 215 538-9424
Quakertown (G-16230)
PPG Industries Inc.....................A...... 412 434-3131
Pittsburgh (G-15425)
PPG Industries Inc.....................C...... 412 820-8500
Cheswick (G-3116)
R and R Glass Inc......................G...... 215 443-7010
Warminster (G-18950)
Schott North America Inc..............G...... 570 457-7485
Duryea (G-4507)
Spectrocell Inc.........................F...... 215 572-7605
Oreland (G-13030)
◆ Standard Bent Glass LLC...........D...... 724 287-3747
East Butler (G-4536)
Thermo-Twin Industries Inc...........C...... 412 826-1000
Oakmont (G-12927)
Thermolite Inc.........................E...... 570 969-1957
Scranton (G-17300)
Three Rivers Optical Company..........D...... 412 928-2020
Pittsburgh (G-15620)
▼ Traco Delaware Inc.................F...... 724 776-7000
Cranberry Township (G-3856)
Trulite GL Alum Solutions LLC.........D...... 570 282-6711
Carbondale (G-2687)
Universal Glass Cnstr Inc..............G...... 570 390-4900
Lake Ariel (G-8895)
Vitro Flat Glass LLC...................C...... 412 820-8500
Cheswick (G-3122)
Vitro Flat Glass LLC...................B...... 717 486-3366
Carlisle (G-2748)
Youghiogheny Opalescent GL Inc........E...... 724 628-3000
Connellsville (G-3512)

3221 Glass Containers

◆ Certainteed Corporation............B...... 610 893-5000
Malvern (G-10204)
Certainteed Corporation...............G...... 610 651-8706
Malvern (G-10205)
Homeopathic Natural Healing..........G...... 412 646-4151
Monroeville (G-11340)
Kelman Holdings Llc...................G...... 412 486-9100
Glenshaw (G-6493)
Mason Jars Company...................F...... 877 490-5565
Erie (G-5381)
▲ Ompi of America Inc...............F...... 267 757-8747
Newtown (G-12531)
Owens-Brockway Glass Cont Inc........C...... 814 226-0500
Clarion (G-3185)
Owens-Brockway Glass Cont Inc........C...... 814 461-5100
Erie (G-5412)
Owens-Brockway Glass Cont Inc........G...... 814 849-4265
Brookville (G-2267)
Owens-Brockway Glass Cont Inc........C...... 814 261-6284
Brockway (G-2229)
Owens-Illinois Inc.....................B...... 814 261-5200
Brockport (G-2222)
◆ Saint-Gobain Delaware Corp........G...... 610 341-7000
Valley Forge (G-18712)
Schott North America Inc..............C...... 717 228-4200
Lebanon (G-9628)
Sonoco Products Company.............E...... 610 323-9221
Pottstown (G-16049)
Verallia................................G...... 814 642-2521
Port Allegany (G-15896)

3229 Pressed & Blown Glassware, NEC

A A A Engraving.......................G...... 412 281-7756
Pittsburgh (G-14628)
▲ Bent Glass Design Inc.............E...... 215 441-9101
Hatboro (G-7273)
◆ Bethlehem Apparatus Co Inc........F...... 610 838-7034
Hellertown (G-7554)
▲ Blair Composites LLC..............E...... 423 638-5847
Altoona (G-481)
Brian Giniewski LLC...................G...... 610 858-2821
Philadelphia (G-13479)

Cellmylight Inc........................G...... 800 575-5913
Thorndale (G-18354)
Ceramic Art Company Inc..............A...... 952 944-5600
Bristol (G-2124)
▲ Chromaglass Inc...................F...... 724 325-1437
Export (G-5594)
Corning Incorporated..................D...... 570 883-9005
Pittston (G-15746)
Cpd Lighting LLC......................G...... 215 361-6100
Colmar (G-3412)
▲ Ctp Carrera Inc...................C...... 724 539-6995
Latrobe (G-9468)
Dally Slate Company Inc...............D...... 610 863-4172
Pen Argyl (G-13213)
Dielectric Sales LLC...................C...... 724 543-2333
Kittanning (G-8766)
▲ Dielectric Solutions LLC...........E...... 724 543-2333
Pittsburgh (G-14923)
▼ Dlubak Glass Company.............F...... 724 226-1991
Natrona Heights (G-11939)
Dlubak Glass Company.................F...... 724 224-5887
Natrona Heights (G-11940)
Dqe Communications LLC..............G...... 412 393-1033
Pittsburgh (G-14936)
▲ Drummond Scientific Company......D...... 610 353-0200
Broomall (G-2287)
E Victor Pesce..........................G...... 610 444-5903
Kennett Square (G-8508)
Electro-Glass Products Inc.............E...... 724 423-5000
Norvelt (G-12878)
Etched In Glass........................G...... 724 444-0808
Gibsonia (G-6333)
Eyeland Optical Corp..................D...... 215 368-1600
Philadelphia (G-13688)
Fibertel Inc............................F...... 570 714-7189
Plymouth (G-15817)
Ghp II LLC.............................A...... 724 775-0010
Monaca (G-11290)
Greenstar Allentown LLC...............E...... 610 262-6988
Northampton (G-12851)
▲ Ii-VI Incorporated.................B...... 724 352-4455
Saxonburg (G-17088)
JB Services of Indiana LLC.............G...... 215 862-2515
New Hope (G-12307)
▲ Jeannette Shade and Novelty Co.....D...... 724 523-5567
Jeannette (G-8257)
K & N Enterprises Inc..................G...... 724 334-0698
New Kensington (G-12350)
Kelman Bottles LLC....................F...... 412 486-9100
Glenshaw (G-6492)
Lenox Corporation.....................G...... 610 954-7590
Bethlehem (G-1560)
▲ Lenox Corporation.................F...... 267 525-7800
Bristol (G-2159)
Martra LLC.............................G...... 610 444-9469
Kennett Square (G-8525)
Novotny Micheal.......................F...... 724 785-2160
Brownsville (G-2313)
▲ Optical Filters USA LLC............E...... 814 333-2222
Meadville (G-10771)
Osram Sylvania Inc....................B...... 570 724-8200
Wellsboro (G-19471)
◆ Pittsburgh Corning LLC............B...... 724 327-6100
Pittsburgh (G-15392)
Port Augustus Glass Co LLC...........F...... 412 486-9100
Glenshaw (G-6498)
PPG Industries Inc.....................A...... 412 434-3131
Pittsburgh (G-15425)
Puchalski Inc...........................G...... 570 842-0361
Covington Township (G-3793)
Punxsutawney Tile & Glass Inc.........F...... 814 938-4200
Punxsutawney (G-16156)
Qualastat Electronics Inc..............E...... 717 253-9301
Gettysburg (G-6311)
▲ Rfsj Inc...........................G...... 724 547-4457
Mount Pleasant (G-11716)
Rob Kei Inc............................G...... 717 293-8991
Lancaster (G-9189)
▲ Sentinel Process Systems Inc.......F...... 215 675-5700
Hatboro (G-7304)
Specialty Seal Group Inc...............E...... 724 539-1626
Latrobe (G-9522)
Taylor-Backes Inc......................E...... 610 367-4600
Boyertown (G-1931)
Three Rivers Optical Company..........D...... 412 928-2020
Pittsburgh (G-15620)
USA Optical Inc........................F...... 717 757-5632
York (G-20695)
West Penn Optical Inc..................E...... 814 833-1194
Erie (G-5528)

3231 Glass Prdts Made Of Purchased Glass

A J Blosenski Inc ....D 610 942-2707
  Honey Brook **(G-7734)**

AGC Flat Glass North Amer Inc ....E 215 538-9424
  Quakertown **(G-16167)**

Amera Glass Inc ....G 814 696-0944
  Duncansville **(G-4449)**

Americana Art China Co Inc ....F 330 938-6133
  Mercer **(G-10959)**

Archetype Frameless Glass Co ....G 717 244-5240
  Yoe **(G-20358)**

Ardagh Glass Inc ....E 814 642-2521
  Port Allegany **(G-15891)**

Art Glass Sgo Inc ....G 215 884-8543
  Spring House **(G-17881)**

Atlantic Glass Etching Inc ....G 717 244-7045
  Red Lion **(G-16589)**

Bahrets Church Interiors ....G 717 540-1747
  Harrisburg **(G-7094)**

Bakers Lawn Ornaments ....F 814 445-7028
  Somerset **(G-17678)**

Baut Studios Inc ....E 570 288-1431
  Swoyersville **(G-18194)**

▲ Behrenberg Glass Company Inc ......F 724 468-4181
  Delmont **(G-4048)**

Cardinal Ig Company ....G 570 474-9204
  Mountain Top **(G-11753)**

Cardinal Lg Company ....F 570 489-6421
  Jessup **(G-8329)**

Cathedral Stained GL Studios ....G 215 379-5360
  Cheltenham **(G-3027)**

City Sign Service Inc ....E 800 523-4452
  Horsham **(G-7804)**

Clearview Mirror and Glass ....G 412 672-4122
  McKeesport **(G-10663)**

▲ Consolidated Glass Corporation ....E 724 658-4541
  New Castle **(G-12077)**

Crystal Imagery Inc ....G 888 440-6073
  York Springs **(G-20764)**

▼ Culver Industries Inc ....F 724 857-5770
  Aliquippa **(G-72)**

Davis Trophies & Sports Wear ....G 610 455-0640
  West Chester **(G-19533)**

▲ Dorman Products Inc ....C 215 997-1800
  Colmar **(G-3416)**

▲ Drummond Scientific Company ....D 610 353-0200
  Broomall **(G-2287)**

Electro-Glass Products Inc ....E 724 423-5000
  Norvelt **(G-12878)**

Emerald Art Glass Inc ....F 412 381-2274
  Pittsburgh **(G-14970)**

Etched In Glass ....G 724 444-0808
  Gibsonia **(G-6333)**

◆ Ferro Color & Glass Corp ....B 724 223-5900
  Washington **(G-19175)**

▲ Flabeg Automotive US Corp ....E 724 224-1800
  Brackenridge **(G-1939)**

Francis L Freas Glass Works ....E 610 828-0430
  Conshohocken **(G-3549)**

Fredericks Company Inc ....E 215 947-2500
  Huntingdon Valley **(G-7985)**

◆ Glassautomatic Inc ....E 724 547-7500
  Mount Pleasant **(G-11700)**

Greenstar Allentown LLC ....E 610 262-6988
  Northampton **(G-12851)**

Hausser Scientific Company ....G 215 675-7769
  Horsham **(G-7822)**

Hunt Stained Glass Studios ....G 412 391-1796
  Pittsburgh **(G-15105)**

Illadelph Glass Inc ....G 215 483-1801
  Philadelphia **(G-13849)**

▲ Jeannette Shade and Novelty Co ....D 724 523-5567
  Jeannette **(G-8257)**

John Beirs Studio ....G 215 627-1410
  Philadelphia **(G-13902)**

Kasmark & Marshall Inc ....G 570 287-3663
  Hunlock Creek **(G-7932)**

Kmz Enterprises LLC ....E 215 659-8400
  Willow Grove **(G-20126)**

Latrobe Glass & Mirror Inc ....G 724 539-2431
  Latrobe **(G-9490)**

Lifetime Bathtub Enclosures ....F 215 228-2500
  Philadelphia **(G-13970)**

Mark-A-Hydrant LLC ....G 888 399-5532
  Allentown **(G-308)**

▲ Martell Sales & Service Inc ....G 814 765-6557
  Hyde **(G-8047)**

Mesko Glass and Mirror Co Inc ....D 570 457-1700
  Avoca **(G-845)**

Micfralip Inc ....F 215 338-3293
  Philadelphia **(G-14019)**

▲ Mitchco Inc ....E 717 843-3345
  York **(G-20599)**

◆ Moderne Glass Company Inc ....C 724 857-5700
  Aliquippa **(G-86)**

National Scientific Company ....G 215 536-2577
  Quakertown **(G-16222)**

Neidighs Inc ....F 814 237-3985
  State College **(G-17996)**

Niagara Holdings Inc ....A 610 651-4200
  Malvern **(G-10286)**

Northeast Glass Co ....G 267 991-0054
  Philadelphia **(G-14083)**

Park & Park Norristown Inc ....G 267 346-0932
  Norristown **(G-12700)**

Pediatrix Medical Group PA PC ....F 717 782-3127
  Harrisburg **(G-7192)**

Pittsburgh Glass Works LLC ....B 814 684-2300
  Tyrone **(G-18589)**

Pittsburgh Stained GL Studio ....F 412 921-2500
  Pittsburgh **(G-15409)**

Potters Holdings II LP ....G 610 651-4200
  Malvern **(G-10297)**

◆ Potters Industries LLC ....E 610 651-4700
  Malvern **(G-10298)**

Potters Industries LLC ....G 610 651-4600
  Conshohocken **(G-3589)**

PPG Industries Inc ....A 412 434-3131
  Pittsburgh **(G-15425)**

◆ PQ Corporation ....C 610 651-4200
  Malvern **(G-10299)**

Precision Glass Products Co ....F 215 885-0145
  Oreland **(G-13028)**

Rainbow Vision Stained GL Ctr ....G 717 657-9737
  Harrisburg **(G-7204)**

▲ RB Distribution Inc ....B 215 997-1800
  Colmar **(G-3419)**

Renaissance Glassworks Inc ....G 724 969-9009
  Canonsburg **(G-2626)**

Roma Aluminum Co Inc ....F 215 545-5700
  Philadelphia **(G-14259)**

Santelli Tempered Glass Inc ....E 724 684-4144
  Monessen **(G-11301)**

Sarik Corporation ....G 215 538-2269
  Quakertown **(G-16243)**

Signature Door Inc ....D 814 949-2770
  Altoona **(G-549)**

Stained Glass Creations ....G 570 629-5070
  Tannersville **(G-18237)**

◆ Standard Bent Glass LLC ....D 724 287-3747
  East Butler **(G-4536)**

Stellar Images Imges Dcrtv GLS ....G 717 367-6500
  Elizabethtown **(G-4888)**

Studio 8 ....G 610 372-7065
  Reading **(G-16527)**

Superior Autoglass LLC ....G 724 452-9870
  Zelienople **(G-20822)**

▲ Susquehanna Glass Co ....E 717 684-2155
  Columbia **(G-3451)**

TFC LLC ....G 412 979-1670
  Brackenridge **(G-1941)**

Thermo-Twin Industries Inc ....C 412 826-1000
  Oakmont **(G-12927)**

▲ Tohickon Corp ....G 267 450-5020
  Sellersville **(G-17360)**

World Wide Plastics Inc ....E 215 357-0893
  Langhorne **(G-9336)**

▲ Yorkshire Lead Glass Company ......F 215 694-2727
  Bristol **(G-2219)**

Youghiogheny Opalescent GL Inc ....E 724 628-3000
  Connellsville **(G-3512)**

▲ Young Windows Inc ....D 610 828-5036
  Conshohocken **(G-3618)**

3241 Cement, Hydraulic

Antonio Colella Cement Work ....G 215 745-2951
  Philadelphia **(G-13396)**

◆ Ardex L P ....C 724 203-5000
  Aliquippa **(G-66)**

Armstrong Cement & Supply Corp ......D 724 352-9401
  Cabot **(G-2452)**

Buzzi Unicem USA Inc ....F 610 746-6222
  Stockertown **(G-18064)**

▲ Buzzi Unicem USA Inc ....E 610 882-5000
  Bethlehem **(G-1476)**

Cemex Cnstr Mtls ATL LLC ....C 724 535-4311
  Wampum **(G-18798)**

▲ Eastern Architectural Pdts LLC ......G 724 513-1630
  Zelienople **(G-20797)**

▼ Erie Strayer Company ....C 814 456-7001
  Erie **(G-5275)**

Essroc Cement ....C 610 882-2498
  Bethlehem **(G-1504)**

Essroc Corp ....F 610 759-4211
  Nazareth **(G-11963)**

◆ Essroc Corp ....G 610 837-6725
  Nazareth **(G-11964)**

Federal White Cement ....G 814 946-8950
  Altoona **(G-506)**

G M C Inc ....E 215 638-4400
  Bensalem **(G-1201)**

Happy Valley Blended Pdts LLC ....F 814 548-7090
  Pleasant Gap **(G-15793)**

Harsco Corporation ....C 570 421-7500
  East Stroudsburg **(G-4617)**

Hercules Cement Company LP ....C 610 759-6300
  Stockertown **(G-18065)**

Holcim (us) Inc ....G 724 226-1449
  Tarentum **(G-18245)**

◆ Keystone Cement Co ....E 610 837-1881
  Exton **(G-5705)**

▲ Keystone Cement Company ....C 610 837-1881
  Bath **(G-962)**

Lafarge North America Inc ....D 610 262-7831
  Whitehall **(G-19880)**

Lafarge North America Inc ....E 412 461-1163
  Pittsburgh **(G-15216)**

Lehigh Cement Company LLC ....C 610 926-1024
  Fleetwood **(G-5976)**

Lehigh Cement Company LLC ....C 610 562-3000
  Hamburg **(G-6844)**

Lehigh Cement Company LLC ....D 717 843-0811
  York **(G-20565)**

Midwest Material Inds Inc ....G 610 882-5000
  Bethlehem **(G-1573)**

Quikrete Companies LLC ....E 724 539-6600
  Latrobe **(G-9513)**

R & D Packaging PA Inc ....G 570 235-2310
  Wilkes Barre **(G-19960)**

▲ RC Lonestar Inc ....D 610 882-5000
  Bethlehem **(G-1608)**

▲ SAI Hydraulics Inc ....E 610 497-0190
  Linwood **(G-9991)**

3251 Brick & Structural Clay Tile

Cpg International LLC ....F 570 348-0997
  Scranton **(G-17223)**

Dectile Harkus Construction ....E 724 789-7125
  Butler **(G-2393)**

▲ Glen-Gery Corporation ....E 610 374-4011
  Reading **(G-16393)**

Glen-Gery Corporation ....D 610 374-4011
  Shoemakersville **(G-17570)**

Glen-Gery Corporation ....D 814 856-2171
  Summerville **(G-18158)**

Glen-Gery Corporation ....D 717 854-8802
  York **(G-20503)**

Glen-Gery Corporation ....G 484 240-4000
  Allentown **(G-233)**

Glen-Gery Corporation ....D 717 848-2589
  York **(G-20504)**

Glen-Gery Corporation ....G 570 742-4721
  Watsontown **(G-19274)**

Glen-Gery Corporation ....G 814 857-7688
  Bigler **(G-1660)**

Glen-Gery Corporation ....G 717 939-6061
  Middletown **(G-11054)**

Gruber Con Specialists Inc ....F 610 760-0925
  New Tripoli **(G-12456)**

McAvoy Brick Company ....G 610 933-2932
  Phoenixville **(G-14560)**

Midwest Material Inds Inc ....G 610 882-5000
  Bethlehem **(G-1573)**

Morgan Advanced Ceramics Inc ....E 610 366-7100
  Allentown **(G-321)**

Mulch Barn ....G 215 703-0300
  Souderton **(G-17755)**

Sil-Base Company Inc ....E 412 751-2314
  McKeesport **(G-10681)**

3253 Ceramic Tile

Alumina Ceramic Components Inc ....F 724 532-1900
  Latrobe **(G-9454)**

Dal-Tile Corporation ....F 484 530-9066
  Plymouth Meeting **(G-15841)**

Dal-Tile Corporation ....C 717 334-1181
  Gettysburg **(G-6287)**

Eric Snow ....G 267 602-3522
  Chester **(G-3049)**

Glenn O Hawbaker Inc ....E 814 359-3411
Pleasant Gap (G-15792)

Harvey Bell ....G 215 634-4900
Philadelphia (G-13806)

Hydro Lazer Inc ....G 724 295-9100
Freeport (G-6205)

Mohawk Industries Inc ....G 215 977-2871
Philadelphia (G-14031)

◆ Princeton Trade Consulting Gro ......E 610 683-9348
Kutztown (G-8856)

3255 Clay Refractories

◆ Altus Refractories LLC ....G 412 430-0138
Pittsburgh (G-14693)

▲ Bloom Engineering Company Inc ....F 412 653-3500
Pittsburgh (G-14773)

▲ Bloom Refractory Products LLC ......G 412 653-3500
Pittsburgh (G-14774)

▲ Bmi Refractory Services Inc ....G 412 429-1800
Pittsburgh (G-14775)

Bnz Materials Inc ....D 724 452-8650
Zelienople (G-20793)

◆ Carpenter Technology Corp ....B 610 208-2000
Philadelphia (G-13508)

Certech Inc ....C 570 823-7400
Hanover Township (G-6985)

Glen-Gery Corporation ....D 610 374-4011
Shoemakersville (G-17570)

Glen-Gery Corporation ....D 814 856-2171
Summerville (G-18158)

Glen-Gery Corporation ....D 717 848-2589
York (G-20504)

Glen-Gery Corporation ....D 814 857-7688
Bigler (G-1660)

Grc Holding Inc ....G 610 667-6640
Bala Cynwyd (G-879)

Harbison Walker ....G 215 364-5555
Trevose (G-18498)

Harbisonwalker Intl Foundation ....C 412 375-6600
Moon Township (G-11489)

Harbisonwalker Intl Inc ....E 412 469-3880
West Mifflin (G-19740)

Harbisonwalker Intl Inc ....D 814 239-2111
Claysburg (G-3204)

HWI Intermediate 1 Inc ....G 412 375-6800
Moon Township (G-11491)

Lionheart Holdings LLC ....D 215 283-8400
Newtown (G-12519)

Lwb Holding Company ....C 717 792-3611
York (G-20569)

M S S I Inc ....E 412 771-5533
Canonsburg (G-2600)

Magnesita Refractories Company ....C 717 792-3611
York (G-20574)

Minteq International Inc ....E 724 794-3000
Slippery Rock (G-17622)

Mssi Refractory LLC ....E 412 771-5533
Mc Kees Rocks (G-10621)

Ncri Inc ....E 724 654-7711
New Castle (G-12125)

New Castle Refactories Co In ....D 724 654-7711
New Castle (G-12130)

Ona Corporation ....C 610 378-1381
Reading (G-16458)

Psnergy LLC ....G 724 581-3845
Erie (G-5443)

Redland Brick Inc ....E 412 828-8046
Cheswick (G-3117)

Resco Group Inc ....F 412 494-4491
Pittsburgh (G-15479)

Selas Heat Technology Co LLC ....G 215 646-6600
Newtown (G-12549)

▲ Shenango Advanced Ceramics LLC E 724 652-6668
New Castle (G-12149)

Snow Shoe Refractories LLC ....E 814 387-6811
Clarence (G-3165)

T Helbling LLC ....G 724 601-9819
Beaver (G-992)

▲ Tyk America Inc ....E 412 384-4259
Clairton (G-3158)

Union Min Co of Allegheny Cnty ....E 412 344-9900
Pittsburgh (G-15669)

▲ Universal Refractories Inc ....G 724 535-4374
Wampum (G-18806)

Universal Refractories Inc ....E 412 787-7220
Coraopolis (G-3730)

▲ Worldwide Refractories Inc ....D 724 224-8800
Tarentum (G-18255)

Zampell Refractories Inc ....E 215 788-3000
Croydon (G-3934)

3259 Structural Clay Prdts, NEC

Brinkmann Bros Inc ....G 215 739-4769
Philadelphia (G-13483)

◆ Certainteed Corporation ....B 610 893-5000
Malvern (G-10204)

Certainteed Corporation ....G 610 651-8706
Malvern (G-10205)

JM Daugherty Industries LLC ....G 412 835-2135
Bethel Park (G-1419)

Mill Hall Clay Products Inc ....E 570 726-6752
Mill Hall (G-11179)

Polyglass USA Inc ....E 570 384-1230
Hazle Township (G-7474)

Septic Surgeons LLC ....G 570 224-4822
Equinunk (G-5160)

3261 China Plumbing Fixtures & Fittings

▲ Jdl Equipment Co ....G 215 489-0134
Doylestown (G-4309)

Soap Alchemy LLC ....E 412 671-4278
New Galilee (G-12222)

3262 China, Table & Kitchen Articles

Ceramic Art Company Inc ....A 952 944-5600
Bristol (G-2124)

3263 Earthenware, Whiteware, Table & Kitchen Articles

▲ Bryan China Company ....D 724 658-3098
New Castle (G-12068)

China Lenox Incorporated ....A 267 525-7800
Bristol (G-2125)

3264 Porcelain Electrical Splys

Alumina Ceramic Components Inc ......F 724 532-1900
Latrobe (G-9454)

▲ Associated Ceramics & Tech ....D 724 353-1585
Sarver (G-17065)

◆ Carson Industries Inc ....E 724 295-5147
Freeport (G-6201)

Du-Co Ceramics Company ....C 724 352-1511
Saxonburg (G-17085)

▼ Dynamic Ceramics Inc ....E 724 353-9527
Sarver (G-17068)

Electro-Glass Products Inc ....E 724 423-5000
Norvelt (G-12878)

Eneflux Armtek Magnetics Inc ....G 215 443-5303
Warminster (G-18872)

Insaco Incorporated ....D 215 536-3500
Quakertown (G-16202)

Kadco Ceramics LLC ....F 610 252-5424
Easton (G-4710)

Leco Corporation ....E 814 355-7903
Bellefonte (G-1107)

Mersen USA St Marys-PA Corp ....C 814 781-1234
Saint Marys (G-16990)

▲ Morgan Advanced Mtls Tech Inc ......C 814 781-1573
Saint Marys (G-16998)

▲ National Magnetics Group Inc ....E 610 867-7600
Bethlehem (G-1578)

National Magnetics Group Inc ....F 610 867-7600
Bethlehem (G-1580)

National Magnetics Group Inc ....E 610 867-7600
Bethlehem (G-1581)

Spectrum Control Inc ....C 814 835-4000
Fairview (G-5844)

◆ SPS Technologies LLC ....A 215 572-3000
Jenkintown (G-8302)

Vesuvius U S A Corporation ....F 412 429-1800
Pittsburgh (G-15697)

3269 Pottery Prdts, NEC

Americana Art China Co Inc ....F 330 938-6133
Mercer (G-10959)

Aud-A-Bud Ceramics ....G 717 898-7537
Landisville (G-9258)

Bakers Lawn Ornaments ....F 814 445-7028
Somerset (G-17678)

▲ Bryan China Company ....D 724 658-3098
New Castle (G-12068)

Campania International Inc ....D 215 541-4627
Pennsburg (G-13246)

Campbell Studios Inc ....E 814 398-2148
Cambridge Springs (G-2475)

▲ Chem-Clay Corporation ....E 412 276-6333
Carnegie (G-2765)

Creative Ceramics ....G 724 504-4318
Butler (G-2391)

Crow Valley Pottery ....G 360 376-4260
Jim Thorpe (G-8339)

Fired Up ....G 724 941-0302
Canonsburg (G-2588)

Grandville Hollow Pottery Inc ....G 814 355-7928
Julian (G-8455)

Horn Linda Collectibles & Co ....G 570 998-8401
Trout Run (G-18514)

Jens Flowers & More ....G 570 898-3176
Shamokin (G-17424)

Metalzed Ceramics For Elec Inc ....F 724 287-5752
East Butler (G-4535)

Pennsylvania Dry Mix ....G 717 509-3520
Lancaster (G-9166)

▲ Pfaltzgraff Factory Stores Inc ....B 717 848-5500
York (G-20626)

Pots By Deperrot ....G 717 627-6789
Lititz (G-10034)

▲ R A S Industries Inc ....E 215 541-4627
Pennsburg (G-13254)

Robin Morris ....G 814 395-9555
Confluence (G-3469)

▲ Saint-Gobain Corporation ....A 610 893-6000
Malvern (G-10313)

◆ Saint-Gobain Delaware Corp ....G 610 341-7000
Valley Forge (G-18712)

Sdi Custom Decow ....G 570 685-7278
Hawley (G-7438)

Steve Day ....E 610 916-1317
Blandon (G-1760)

Westerwald Corp of America ....G 724 945-6000
Scenery Hill (G-17127)

3271 Concrete Block & Brick

A A Robbins Inc ....F 814 398-4607
Cambridge Springs (G-2473)

A Duchini Inc ....E 814 456-7027
Erie (G-5165)

A Messinger Arch ....G 610 896-7227
Penn Valley (G-13232)

B V Landscape Supplies Inc ....G 610 316-1099
Malvern (G-10191)

Bauer Company Inc ....G 724 548-8101
Kittanning (G-8756)

Beaver Concrete & Supply Inc ....F 724 774-5100
Monaca (G-11282)

Beavertown Block Co Inc ....E 814 359-2771
Bellefonte (G-1093)

Beavertown Block Co Inc ....F 814 695-4448
East Freedom (G-4559)

Burrell Group Inc ....F 724 337-3557
New Kensington (G-12328)

Burrell Mining Products Inc ....F 724 339-2511
New Kensington (G-12329)

Burrell Mining Products Inc ....F 724 966-5183
Waynesburg (G-19435)

C Strunk Inc ....G 610 678-1960
Reading (G-16339)

Calcium Chloride Sales Inc ....G 724 458-5778
Grove City (G-6781)

Castle Builders Supply Inc ....E 724 981-4212
Hermitage (G-7573)

Castle Builders Supply Inc ....E 724 658-5656
New Castle (G-12070)

Cenprepavandcon ....G 215 778-6103
Willow Grove (G-20111)

Colussy Enterprises Inc ....G 412 221-4750
Bridgeville (G-2057)

Craigjill Inc ....E 570 803-0234
Ashley (G-739)

Crete NYCE Co Inc ....E 215 855-4628
Lansdale (G-9354)

CTS Bulk Terminals ....G 610 759-8330
Bethlehem (G-1491)

Distinctive Outdoor Spaces LLC ....F 484 718-5050
Parkesburg (G-13173)

Eastern Industries Inc ....E 570 265-9191
Towanda (G-18425)

EP Henry Corporation ....E 610 495-8533
Parker Ford (G-13168)

Fizzano Bros Concrete Pdts Inc ....E 610 363-6290
Malvern (G-10235)

Fizzano Bros Concrete Pdts Inc ....G 215 355-6160
Langhorne (G-9298)

Fizzano Bros Inc ....D 610 833-1100
Crum Lynne (G-3937)

Fizzano Bros Inc ....E 215 355-6160
Feasterville Trevose (G-5910)

Fleetwood Building Block Inc ....F 610 944-8385
Fleetwood (G-5973)

Green Scenes Landscape Inc ....G...... 610 566-3154
Media *(G-10930)*

H&K Group Inc ....E...... 610 494-5364
Media *(G-10933)*

H&K Group Inc ....E...... 610 250-7703
Easton *(G-4694)*

Hanover Brick and Block Co..............F...... 717 637-0500
Hanover *(G-6892)*

◆ Hanover Prest-Paving Company..............E...... 717 637-0500
Hanover *(G-6900)*

Hawk Construction Products..............G...... 610 873-8658
Downingtown *(G-4233)*

Hopper Lawn & Ldscp MGT LLC..............G...... 610 692-3879
West Chester *(G-19563)*

J A Kohlhepp Sons Inc..............D...... 814 371-5200
Du Bois *(G-4398)*

▼ Jdn Block Inc..............E...... 215 723-5506
Souderton *(G-17745)*

Jokers Coal & Building Sups..............G...... 570 724-4912
Wellsboro *(G-19468)*

Juniata Concrete Co..............G...... 717 567-3183
Newport *(G-12491)*

Keystone Con Block Sup Co Inc..............E...... 570 346-7701
Scranton *(G-17251)*

Klondike Block Masnry Sups Inc..............G...... 724 439-3888
Smithfield *(G-17652)*

Lane Holdings LLC..............E...... 412 279-1234
Carnegie *(G-2775)*

Leonard Block Company Inc..............G...... 570 398-3376
Jersey Shore *(G-8317)*

Lucisano Bros Inc..............E...... 215 945-2700
Bristol *(G-2162)*

▼ Martin Limestone Inc..............E...... 717 335-4500
East Earl *(G-4548)*

Martin Limestone Inc..............D...... 717 354-1200
New Holland *(G-12258)*

MBR Inc..............G...... 570 386-8820
Reading *(G-16440)*

Montgomery Block Works Inc..............F...... 724 735-2931
Harrisville *(G-7253)*

Mountain-Valley Services LLC..............G...... 814 594-3167
Ridgway *(G-16718)*

New Enterprise Stone Lime Inc..............E...... 814 443-6494
Somerset *(G-17698)*

▲ Nitterhouse Masonry Pdts LLC..............D...... 717 268-4137
Chambersburg *(G-2963)*

Nortons Building Supply Inc..............G...... 814 697-6351
Shinglehouse *(G-17510)*

Oesterlings Concrete Co Inc..............G...... 724 282-8556
Butler *(G-2428)*

Oldcastle Apg Northeast Inc..............F...... 484 240-2176
Allentown *(G-338)*

▲ R I Lampus Company..............C...... 412 362-3800
Springdale *(G-17900)*

R W Sidley Inc..............E...... 724 794-4451
Slippery Rock *(G-17625)*

Ray-Guard International Ltd..............G...... 215 543-3849
Pottstown *(G-16038)*

Refined Outoor Lvng Envirnmnts..............G...... 412 635-8440
Pittsburgh *(G-15477)*

Riverview Block Inc..............G...... 570 752-7191
Berwick *(G-1342)*

Santarelli Vibrated Block LLC..............F...... 570 693-2200
Wyoming *(G-20284)*

Seymore Bros Inc..............E...... 814 944-2074
Altoona *(G-548)*

Shaffer Block and Con Pdts Inc..............E...... 814 445-4414
Somerset *(G-17705)*

Standard Concrete Products Co..............E...... 717 843-8074
York *(G-20679)*

Sweetwater Natural Pdts LLC..............G...... 610 321-1900
Chester Springs *(G-3086)*

Swisher Concrete Products Inc..............G...... 814 765-9502
Clearfield *(G-3231)*

▲ Techo-Bloc Corp..............C...... 610 863-2300
Pen Argyl *(G-13220)*

▼ Trenwyth Industries Inc..............D...... 717 767-6868
Emigsville *(G-5002)*

Troemel Landscaping..............G...... 215 783-3150
Lansdale *(G-9418)*

Vcw Enterprises Inc..............G...... 610 847-5112
Ottsville *(G-13068)*

Wendell H Stone Company Inc..............E...... 724 483-6571
Charleroi *(G-3025)*

Wool Concrete Block..............G...... 570 322-1943
Williamsport *(G-20099)*

▲ York Building Products Co Inc..............E...... 717 848-2831
York *(G-20726)*

York Building Products Co Inc..............F...... 717 944-1488
Middletown *(G-11086)*

York Building Products Co Inc..............E...... 717 845-5333
York *(G-20727)*

York Building Products Co Inc..............E...... 717 324-2379
York *(G-20728)*

York Building Products Co Inc..............F...... 717 792-4700
Thomasville *(G-18345)*

York Building Products Co Inc..............F...... 717 792-1200
York *(G-20730)*

Young and Brothers Constuction..............G...... 215 852-5398
Philadelphia *(G-14502)*

3272 Concrete Prdts

A & A Concrete Products Inc..............F...... 724 538-1114
Evans City *(G-5555)*

▲ A C Miller Concrete Pdts Inc..............C...... 610 948-4600
Spring City *(G-17856)*

A C Miller Concrete Pdts Inc..............D...... 724 459-5950
Blairsville *(G-1712)*

Advanced Cast Stone Inc Inc..............F...... 817 572-0018
Girard *(G-6383)*

Advanced Drainage Systems Inc..............E...... 570 546-7686
Muncy *(G-11805)*

All Aspects..............G...... 610 292-1955
Norristown *(G-12631)*

Alternative Burial Corporation..............G...... 814 533-5832
Johnstown *(G-8353)*

Altomare Precast Inc..............F...... 215 225-8800
Philadelphia *(G-13373)*

American Tank & Concrete Svc..............F...... 724 837-4410
Greensburg *(G-6650)*

Annuity Vault..............G...... 215 830-8666
Willow Grove *(G-20107)*

Appleridge Stone Intl Inc..............E...... 724 459-9511
Blairsville *(G-1713)*

Architctral Prcast Innovations..............D...... 570 837-1774
Middleburg *(G-11023)*

Architectural Polymers Inc..............E...... 610 824-3322
Palmerton *(G-13102)*

▲ Atlantic Concrete Products Inc..............D...... 215 945-5600
Bristol *(G-2111)*

Atlantic Precast Concrete..............D...... 215 945-5600
Bristol *(G-2112)*

Atlantic Precast Industries..............C...... 215 945-5600
Bristol *(G-2113)*

Bauer Company Inc..............E...... 724 297-3200
Worthington *(G-20228)*

Bauer Company Inc..............E...... 724 548-8101
Kittanning *(G-8756)*

Beavertown Block Co Inc..............E...... 814 359-2771
Bellefonte *(G-1093)*

Bethlehem Pre-Cast Inc..............G...... 610 967-5531
Macungie *(G-10143)*

Bethlehem Pre-Cast Inc..............G...... 610 691-1336
Bethlehem *(G-1462)*

Big Bear Concrete Works..............G...... 570 584-0107
Lairdsville *(G-8886)*

Blairsville Wilbert Burial Vlt..............E...... 724 459-9677
Blairsville *(G-1717)*

Blairsville Wilbert Burial Vlt..............G...... 724 324-2010
Mount Morris *(G-11679)*

Blairsville Wilbert Burial Vlt..............G...... 724 547-2865
Mount Pleasant *(G-11689)*

Blairsville Wilbert Burial Vlt..............F...... 814 495-5921
South Fork *(G-17772)*

Bodon Industries Inc..............F...... 610 323-0700
Douglassville *(G-4170)*

Bonsal American Inc..............E...... 724 475-2511
Fredonia *(G-6179)*

Bonsal American Inc..............F...... 215 785-1290
Bristol *(G-2120)*

Bradley E Miller..............G...... 717 566-6243
Hummelstown *(G-7904)*

Brentano Concrete Connection..............G...... 412 731-8485
Pittsburgh *(G-14791)*

Building Specialties..............G...... 814 454-4345
Erie *(G-5217)*

Callahan David E Pool Plst Inc..............E...... 610 429-4496
West Chester *(G-19517)*

Carlisle Vault LLC..............G...... 717 382-8588
Carlisle *(G-2699)*

Castek Inc..............F...... 570 759-3540
Berwick *(G-1316)*

Cellular Concrete LLC..............F...... 610 398-7833
Allentown *(G-166)*

Centermoreland Concrete Pdts..............F...... 570 333-4944
Tunkhannock *(G-18533)*

Central PA Wilbert Vault..............G...... 717 248-3777
Burnham *(G-2359)*

Cfb LLC..............G...... 717 769-0857
Elizabethtown *(G-4868)*

◆ Cgm Incorporated..............E...... 215 638-4400
Bensalem *(G-1167)*

CMS East Inc..............D...... 724 527-6700
Jeannette *(G-8250)*

Coalisland Cast Stone Inc..............F...... 610 476-1683
Collegeville *(G-3372)*

Colonial Concrete Industries..............G...... 610 279-2102
King of Prussia *(G-8593)*

Colonial Concrete Industries..............G...... 610 279-2102
King of Prussia *(G-8594)*

Commercial Precast..............G...... 724 873-0708
Canonsburg *(G-2564)*

Commonwealth Precast Inc..............F...... 215 721-6005
Souderton *(G-17730)*

Concrete Concepts Inc..............F...... 412 331-1500
Mc Kees Rocks *(G-10606)*

Concrete Pipe & Precast LLC..............E...... 717 597-5000
Greencastle *(G-6603)*

Concrete Safety Systems LLC..............E...... 717 933-4107
Bethel *(G-1394)*

Concrete Simplicity Cons..............G...... 814 857-7500
Dover *(G-4191)*

Concrete Step Units Inc..............E...... 570 343-2458
Scranton *(G-17218)*

Concrete Texturing LLC..............E...... 570 489-6025
Throop *(G-18357)*

Continental Concrete Pdts Inc..............E...... 610 327-3700
Pottstown *(G-15974)*

Cooper Wilbert Vault Co Inc..............G...... 610 842-7782
Berwyn *(G-1357)*

Coudersport Precast Inc..............F...... 814 274-9634
Coudersport *(G-3780)*

Cpg International LLC..............G...... 570 558-8000
Scranton *(G-17224)*

Craig Walters..............G...... 570 645-3415
Summit Hill *(G-18159)*

Custom Pool Coping Inc..............G...... 215 822-9098
Hatfield *(G-7330)*

Dayton Superior Corporation..............G...... 570 695-3163
Tremont *(G-18480)*

Dectile Harkus Construction..............E...... 724 789-7125
Butler *(G-2393)*

Deihl Vault & Precast Inc..............F...... 570 458-6466
Orangeville *(G-13005)*

Dennis Lumber and Concrete..............E...... 724 329-5542
Markleysburg *(G-10480)*

Dogs In Cast Stone..............G...... 717 291-9696
Lancaster *(G-9000)*

▲ Doren Inc..............F...... 724 535-4397
Wampum *(G-18799)*

Doren Inc Parkway..............G...... 724 375-6637
Aliquippa *(G-74)*

Dutchland Inc..............C...... 717 442-8282
Gap *(G-6249)*

Dymonds Concrete Products..............G...... 717 352-2321
Fayetteville *(G-5876)*

Edge Building Products Inc..............E...... 717 567-2311
Newport *(G-12489)*

Edward T Christiansen & Sons..............G...... 215 368-1001
Montgomeryville *(G-11393)*

EP Henry Corporation..............E...... 610 495-8533
Parker Ford *(G-13168)*

Essroc Corp..............F...... 610 759-4211
Nazareth *(G-11963)*

Esterly Concrete Co Inc..............E...... 610 376-2791
West Reading *(G-19764)*

Evans Eagle Burial Vaults Inc..............F...... 717 656-2213
Leola *(G-9781)*

Evergreen Tank Solutions Inc..............G...... 484 268-5168
Philadelphia *(G-13684)*

F & G Monument Lettering LLC..............G...... 814 247-5032
Hastings *(G-7260)*

▲ F&M Surfaces Inc..............G...... 717 267-3799
Chambersburg *(G-2931)*

▲ Fabcon East LLC..............D...... 610 530-4470
Mahanoy City *(G-10173)*

Fi-Hoff Concrete Products Inc..............F...... 814 266-5834
Johnstown *(G-8372)*

Fizzano Bros Concrete Pdts Inc..............E...... 215 355-6160
Langhorne *(G-9298)*

Forsht Concrete Pdts Co Inc..............G...... 814 944-1617
Altoona *(G-507)*

Furnley H Frisch..............F...... 717 957-3261
Duncannon *(G-4445)*

Gamers Vault..............G...... 609 781-0938
Montgomeryville *(G-11398)*

Gcl Inc..............G...... 724 933-7260
Wexford *(G-19805)*

Glasgow Inc..............E...... 610 251-0760
Malvern *(G-10240)*

**S
I
C**

Great Lakes Cast Stone Inc F 814 402-1055 Girard *(G-6390)*
Guyers Superior Walls C 814 725-8575 North East *(G-12745)*
H Troxel Cemetery Service Inc G 610 489-4426 Norristown *(G-12663)*
H Y K Construction Co Inc D 610 489-2646 Collegeville *(G-3381)*
H&K Group Inc E 610 250-7703 Easton *(G-4694)*
Hampton Concrete Products Inc F 724 443-7205 Valencia *(G-18698)*
◆ Hanover Prest Paving Company E 717 637-0500 Hanover *(G-6899)*
◆ Hanover Prest-Paving Company E 717 637-0500 Hanover *(G-6900)*
Harbisnwlker Intl Holdings Inc G 412 375-6600 Moon Township *(G-11488)*
◆ Harbisonwalker Intl Inc C 412 375-6600 Moon Township *(G-11490)*
Harvil Inc E 412 682-1500 Pittsburgh *(G-15083)*
Henry S Esh G 717 627-2585 Lititz *(G-10015)*
Hessian Co Ltd G 610 683-5464 Kutztown *(G-8844)*
Hessian Co Ltd G 610 683-0067 Kutztown *(G-8845)*
Hessian Co Ltd E 610 269-4685 Honey Brook *(G-7747)*
Hessian Co Ltd G 610 683-0067 Kutztown *(G-8846)*
Hessian Co Ltd E 724 658-6638 New Castle *(G-12104)*
Hg Smith Wilbert Vault Company G 570 420-9599 Stroudsburg *(G-18123)*
▲ High Concrete Group LLC B 717 336-9300 Denver *(G-4075)*
High Industries Inc B 717 293-4444 Lancaster *(G-9046)*
High Steel Structures LLC G 717 299-5211 Lancaster *(G-9049)*
Hilltop Tank & Supply G 814 658-3915 James Creek *(G-8234)*
Hpkd Inc E 412 922-7600 Pittsburgh *(G-15104)*
▲ Hygrade Components D 610 866-2441 Bethlehem *(G-1537)*
Igneous Rock Gallery G 717 774-4074 Mechanicsburg *(G-10857)*
Ink Vault G 724 355-8616 Butler *(G-2410)*
Interstate Safety Service Inc E 570 563-1161 Clarks Summit *(G-3194)*
J & R Slaw Inc D 610 852-2020 Lehighton *(G-9717)*
James F Geibel G 724 287-1964 Butler *(G-2412)*
Jamison Bsmnt Wterproofing Inc G 215 885-2424 Oreland *(G-13025)*
Jefferson Memorial Park Inc E 412 655-4500 Pittsburgh *(G-15147)*
Jna Materials LLC G 215 233-0121 Ambler *(G-583)*
Joseph Riepole Construction G 412 833-6611 Library *(G-9955)*
Juniata Concrete Co E 717 436-2176 Mifflintown *(G-11125)*
Kemosabe Inc G 412 961-0190 Glenshaw *(G-6494)*
Kennedy Concrete Inc F 570 875-2780 Ashland *(G-733)*
Keystone Precast Inc G 570 837-1864 Middleburg *(G-11026)*
Kimenski Burial Vaults G 724 223-0364 Washington *(G-19191)*
Klocek Burial Vault Co G 724 547-2865 Mount Pleasant *(G-11704)*
◆ Koppers Industries Del Inc G 412 227-2001 Pittsburgh *(G-15191)*
Kuss Enterprises LLC G 412 583-0206 Pittsburgh *(G-15203)*
L B Foster Company D 412 928-3400 Pittsburgh *(G-15207)*
L B Foster Company E 814 623-6101 Bedford *(G-1060)*
Lebanon Valley Enterprises G 717 866-2030 Newmanstown *(G-12480)*
Lee Concrete Products G 814 467-4470 Windber *(G-20188)*
Lehigh Fabrication LLC E 908 791-4800 Whitehall *(G-19881)*
Lockcrete Bauer G 800 419-9255 Worthington *(G-20230)*
Lycoming Burial Vault Co Inc F 570 368-8642 Montoursville *(G-11446)*
Macinnis Group LLC D 814 695-2016 Roaring Spring *(G-16765)*
Marion Center Supply Inc F 724 397-5505 Marion Center *(G-10473)*
Martin Limestone Inc D 717 354-1200 New Holland *(G-12258)*
Masons Mark Stone Veneer Corp G 724 635-0082 New Stanton *(G-12449)*
Merchants Metals LLC D 570 384-3063 Hazle Township *(G-7469)*
Michael P Hoover Company Inc G 717 757-7842 York *(G-20593)*
Middleburg Pre Cast LLC F 570 837-1463 Middleburg *(G-11029)*
Miller Burial Vault Co G 570 386-5479 New Ringgold *(G-12441)*
Milroy Enterprises Inc E 610 678-4537 Reading *(G-16444)*
Modern Precast Concrete Inc E 484 548-6200 Easton *(G-4726)*
Monarch Precast Concrete Corp E 610 435-6746 Allentown *(G-320)*
Monumental Express G 570 501-1009 Hazleton *(G-7511)*
Monumental Touch G 484 226-7277 Walnutport *(G-18792)*
Mountain Side Supply LLC G 814 201-2525 Altoona *(G-529)*
New Bethlehem Burial Service F 814 275-3333 New Bethlehem *(G-12028)*
New Enterprise Stone Lime Inc C 814 224-2121 Roaring Spring *(G-16766)*
▲ Nitterhouse Concrete Pdts Inc C 717 207-7837 Chambersburg *(G-2962)*
▲ Northeast Prestressed Pdts LLC C 570 385-2352 Cressona *(G-3906)*
Northwest PA Burial Service G 814 425-2436 Cochranton *(G-3346)*
Oldcastle Precast Inc D 484 548-6200 Easton *(G-4735)*
Oldcastle Precast Inc D 888 965-3227 Croydon *(G-3923)*
Oldcastle Precast Inc C 215 257-8081 Telford *(G-18306)*
Oldcastle Precast Inc E 215 257-2255 Telford *(G-18307)*
Oldcastle Precast Inc D 215 736-9576 Morrisville *(G-11574)*
Omega Transworld Ltd F 724 966-5183 Waynesburg *(G-19450)*
Omni Precast Products Inc G 724 316-1582 Wampum *(G-18803)*
Parnell Enterprises Inc G 724 258-3320 Monongahela *(G-11312)*
Paxton Precast LLC G 717 692-5686 Dalmatia *(G-3985)*
Perma-Column East G 610 562-7161 Lenhartsville *(G-9760)*
Peter Mamienski G 215 822-3293 Hatfield *(G-7381)*
Piles Concrete Products Co Inc F 814 445-6619 Friedens *(G-6225)*
Pioneer Burial Vault Co Inc F 215 766-2943 Doylestown *(G-4325)*
Pipe & Precast Cnstr Pdts Inc F 610 644-7338 Devault *(G-4112)*
Pittsburgh Mobile Concrete Inc F 412 486-0186 Pittsburgh *(G-15402)*
Pre Cast Systems LLC F 717 369-3773 Greencastle *(G-6627)*
▲ Pre-Blend Products Inc E 215 295-6004 Fairless Hills *(G-5793)*
Precast Services Inc D 330 425-2880 Morgantown *(G-11531)*
Precast Systems LLC E 717 267-4500 Chambersburg *(G-2969)*
Quality Concrete Inc G 412 922-0200 Pittsburgh *(G-15460)*
Quikrete Companies Inc E 570 672-1063 Paxinos *(G-13192)*
Quikrete Companies LLC E 724 539-6600 Latrobe *(G-9513)*
▲ R A S Industries Inc E 215 541-4627 Pennsburg *(G-13254)*
▲ R I Lampus Company C 412 362-3800 Springdale *(G-17900)*
R W Sidley Inc E 724 794-4451 Slippery Rock *(G-17625)*
Rahns Construction Material Co G 610 584-8500 Collegeville *(G-3390)*
Ray Burial Vault Company Inc F 814 684-0104 Tyrone *(G-18591)*
Reading Precast Inc E 610 926-5000 Leesport *(G-9673)*
▲ Reecon North America LLC G 412 850-8001 Pittsburgh *(G-15475)*
Richard Rhodes F 814 535-3633 Johnstown *(G-8430)*
Ringtown Wilbert Vault Works F 570 889-3153 Ringtown *(G-16756)*
Ron Mulkerrin G 724 693-8920 Oakdale *(G-12910)*
Rosenberry Septic Tank Service G 717 532-4026 Shippensburg *(G-17545)*
Rotondo Weirich Entps Inc D 215 256-7940 Lansdale *(G-9407)*
Sakala Stone Products G 724 339-2224 New Kensington *(G-12374)*
▲ Say-Core Inc D 814 736-8018 Portage *(G-15920)*
Scranton Craftsmen Excvtg Inc D 800 775-1479 Throop *(G-18360)*
Scranton Wilbert Vault Inc F 570 489-5065 Jessup *(G-8336)*
Shetler Memorials Inc G 814 288-1087 Johnstown *(G-8435)*
Silbaugh Vault and Burial Svc G 724 437-3002 Uniontown *(G-18642)*
Silvi Concrete Products Inc C 215 295-0777 Fairless Hills *(G-5797)*
Slate Road Supply LLC G 717 445-5222 Ephrata *(G-5141)*
Smith Concrete Products G 724 349-5858 Homer City *(G-7682)*
Smiths Wilbert Vault Company E 610 588-5259 Bangor *(G-928)*
Solution People Inc G 215 750-2694 Newtown *(G-12551)*
St Clair Precast Concrete Inc G 412 221-2577 Bridgeville *(G-2091)*
Stacy Lloyd G 724 265-3445 Tarentum *(G-18247)*
Standard Concrete Products Co E 717 843-8074 York *(G-20679)*
Stauffer Con Pdts & Excvtg Inc G 570 629-1977 Kunkletown *(G-8835)*
Steel Stone Manufacturing Co F 610 837-9966 Lehigh Valley *(G-9707)*
Sun Precast Company E 570 658-8000 Beaver Springs *(G-1024)*
Superior Walls of Colorado F 412 664-7788 Glassport *(G-6417)*
▲ Taktl LLC C 412 486-1600 Turtle Creek *(G-18569)*
Techo-Bloc (ne) Corp G 610 863-2300 Pen Argyl *(G-13219)*
Techo-Bloc Corp E 610 326-3677 Douglassville *(G-4181)*
Terre Hill Concrete F 717 738-9164 Ephrata *(G-5152)*
Terre Hill Silo Company Inc E 717 445-3100 Terre Hill *(G-18339)*
Tervo Masonry Llc E 724 944-6179 New Wilmington *(G-12471)*
Toma Inc F 717 597-7194 Harrisburg *(G-7232)*
Unistress Corp G 610 395-5930 Macungie *(G-10160)*
Universal Concrete Pdts Corp F 610 323-0700 Stowe *(G-18073)*
Utility Service Group Inc E 717 737-6092 Camp Hill *(G-2521)*
Valmont Newmark Inc C 570 454-8730 West Hazleton *(G-19717)*
Vault Clothing Store G 570 871-4135 Scranton *(G-17309)*
Vault Clothing Store Inc G 570 780-8240 S Abingtn Twp *(G-16902)*
Vault My Keys LLC G 267 575-0506 Glenside *(G-6542)*
Vault Services G 814 282-8143 Saegertown *(G-16935)*
Vcw Enterprises Inc D 610 847-5112 Ottsville *(G-13068)*

W R Meadows Inc ....E 717 792-2627
York (G-20701)
Waterford Precast & Sales Inc ....G 814 864-4956
Erie (G-5527)
Wendell H Stone Company Inc ....E 724 836-1400
Greensburg (G-6729)
▲ Wenzco Supplies ....F 610 434-6157
Allentown (G-432)
Wilbert Vault Co ....G 724 459-8400
Blairsville (G-1745)
Wilkes Barre Burial Vault ....F 570 824-8268
Hanover Township (G-7007)
Willard Burial Service Inc ....G 724 528-9965
West Middlesex (G-19732)
William Elston Incorporated ....F 570 689-2203
Jefferson Township (G-8280)
Windy Hill Concrete Inc ....G 717 464-3889
Lancaster (G-9243)
Wine Concrete Products Inc ....E 724 266-9500
Sewickley (G-17415)
Wissahickon Stone Quarry LLC ....G 215 887-3330
Glenside (G-6544)
Wm S Long Inc ....G 724 538-3775
Callery (G-2471)
York Building Products Co Inc ....E 717 764-5996
York (G-20729)

3273 Ready-Mixed Concrete

43rd St Inc ....E 412 682-4090
Pittsburgh (G-14626)
A Anthony & Sons Inc ....E 814 454-2883
Erie (G-5164)
A D Swartzlander & Sons ....G 724 282-2706
Butler (G-2370)
Advance Transit Mix Inc ....F 610 461-2182
Glenolden (G-6471)
Allied Concrete & Supply Corp ....E 215 646-8484
Dresher (G-4352)
Baycrete Inc ....F 814 454-5001
Erie (G-5205)
Beaver Concrete & Supply Inc ....F 724 774-5100
Monaca (G-11282)
Big Valley Concrete ....G 717 483-6538
Belleville (G-1128)
Blank Concrete and Supply ....F 724 758-7596
Ellwood City (G-4928)
Castle Builders Supply Inc ....E 724 658-5656
New Castle (G-12070)
Castle Builders Supply Inc ....E 724 981-4212
Hermitage (G-7573)
CE Ready Mix ....E 724 727-3331
Apollo (G-667)
Central Builders Supply Co ....G 570 524-9147
Lewisburg (G-9899)
Central Concrete Co Inc ....E 215 953-9736
Southampton (G-17801)
Central Concrete Supply Coinc ....G 215 927-4686
Philadelphia (G-13520)
Centre Concrete Company ....F 570 748-7747
Lock Haven (G-10085)
Centre Concrete Company ....E 570 433-3186
Montoursville (G-11435)
Concrete Services Corporation ....E 814 774-8807
Fairview (G-5817)
Conewago Ready Mix ....G 717 633-5022
Hanover (G-6869)
Construction Dynamics Inc ....D 215 295-0777
Fairless Hills (G-5775)
Coon Industries Inc ....G 570 735-6852
Nanticoke (G-11899)
Coon Industries Inc ....E 570 341-8033
Dunmore (G-4471)
County Line Quarry Inc ....E 717 252-1584
Wrightsville (G-20235)
Crete NYCE Co Inc ....E 215 855-4628
Lansdale (G-9354)
De Paul Concrete ....G 610 832-8000
Flourtown (G-5986)
Delaware Valley Con Co Inc ....D 215 675-8900
Hatboro (G-7278)
Delco Mini Mix LLC ....G 610 809-0316
Chester (G-3047)
Dinardo Brothers Material Inc ....G 215 535-4645
Philadelphia (G-13633)
Donaldson Supply & Eqp Co ....F 724 745-5250
Canonsburg (G-2579)
Drd Inc ....G 215 879-1055
Philadelphia (G-13643)
Dubrook Inc ....G 814 371-3113
Du Bois (G-4389)

Dubrook Inc ....G 724 538-3111
Evans City (G-5558)
Dubrook Inc ....E 724 283-3111
Butler (G-2396)
Dubrook Inc ....E 814 371-3111
Du Bois (G-4390)
Dubrook Inc ....E 814 834-3111
Saint Marys (G-16964)
E M Brown Incorporated ....E 814 765-7519
Clearfield (G-3218)
East Side Concrete Supply Co ....F 814 944-8175
Altoona (G-499)
Eastern Industries Inc ....B 610 866-0932
Whitehall (G-19873)
Eastern Industries Inc ....F 717 362-3388
Elizabethville (G-4893)
Eastern Industries Inc ....E 570 265-9191
Towanda (G-18425)
Edwards Concrete ....F 570 842-8438
Elmhurst Township (G-4957)
Eles Bros Inc ....G 412 824-6161
Monroeville (G-11335)
Emporium Contractors Inc ....E 814 562-0631
Emporium (G-5056)
◆ Essroc Corp ....G 610 837-6725
Nazareth (G-11964)
Eureka Stone Quarry Inc ....F 570 842-7694
Moscow (G-11596)
Eureka Stone Quarry Inc ....G 215 723-9801
Telford (G-18288)
Family Ready Labor Inc ....G 717 615-4900
Lancaster (G-9014)
Fi-Hoff Concrete Products Inc ....F 814 266-5834
Johnstown (G-8372)
Fly Mix Entertainment ....G 215 722-6287
Philadelphia (G-13706)
Four Winds Concrete Inc ....E 610 865-1788
Bethlehem (G-1517)
Four Winds Concrete Inc ....E 610 865-1788
Center Valley (G-2827)
Frank Bryan Inc ....G 412 331-1630
Mc Kees Rocks (G-10609)
Frank Bryan Inc ....F 412 431-2700
Pittsburgh (G-15031)
Frank Casilio and Sons Inc ....G 610 253-3558
Easton (G-4685)
Frank Casilio and Sons Inc ....F 610 867-5886
Bethlehem (G-1518)
Frankenstein Builders Supply ....G 724 333-5260
Zelienople (G-20802)
G F Edwards Inc ....G 570 842-8438
Elmhurst Township (G-4958)
Gettysburg Concrete Co Inc ....G 717 334-1494
Gettysburg (G-6291)
GF Edwards Inc ....G 570 842-8438
Elmhurst Township (G-4959)
GF Edwards Inc ....E 570 676-3200
South Sterling (G-17787)
Giovanni Demarco ....G 724 898-7239
Valencia (G-18697)
Glenside Ready Mix Concrete Co ......G 215 659-1500
Erie (G-5304)
Glossners Concrete Inc ....G 570 962-2564
Beech Creek (G-1082)
H & L Concrete ....F 610 562-8273
Virginville (G-18770)
H Y K Construction Co Inc ....D 610 489-2646
Collegeville (G-3381)
H Y K Construction Co Inc ....E 610 282-2300
Coopersburg (G-3628)
Hanover Concrete Co ....E 717 637-2288
Hanover (G-6893)
Hanson Aggregates Bmc Inc ....G 610 847-5211
Ottsville (G-13062)
Hanson Aggregates Bmc Inc ....F 724 229-5840
Eighty Four (G-4842)
Hanson Lehigh Inc ....G 610 366-4600
Allentown (G-244)
Hanson Ready Mix Inc ....F 814 238-1781
State College (G-17971)
Hanson Ready Mix Inc ....F 814 269-9600
Johnstown (G-8379)
Hanson Ready Mix Inc ....E 412 431-6001
Pittsburgh (G-15080)
Hanson Ready Mix Inc ....G 610 837-6725
Nazareth (G-11971)
Hempt Bros Inc ....D 717 774-2911
Camp Hill (G-2500)
Hess Ready Mix Inc ....F 570 385-0300
Schuylkill Haven (G-17159)

Hopper T and J Building Sups ....F 724 443-2222
Gibsonia (G-6340)
Hosmer Supply Company Inc ....F 412 892-2525
Pittsburgh (G-15101)
Hoys Construction Company Inc ......F 724 852-1112
Waynesburg (G-19445)
Hunlock Sand & Gravel Company ......F 570 256-3036
Bath (G-960)
Irwin Concrete Co ....F 724 863-1848
Apollo (G-677)
J & H Concrete Co ....E 570 824-3565
Wilkes Barre (G-19931)
J A & W A Hess Inc ....E 570 454-3731
Hazleton (G-7504)
J A & W A Hess Inc ....F 570 271-0227
Danville (G-4007)
J A & W A Hess Inc ....F 570 385-0300
Schuylkill Haven (G-17160)
James D Morrissey Inc ....G 267 554-7946
Bristol (G-2156)
James W Quandel & Sons Inc ....F 570 544-2261
Minersville (G-11255)
JDM Materials ....E 215 357-5505
Huntingdon Valley (G-8003)
Jfi Redi-Mix LLC ....F 215 428-3560
Morrisville (G-11564)
Jj Kennedy Inc ....G 724 452-6260
Fombell (G-6033)
Jj Kennedy Inc ....G 724 783-6081
Kittanning (G-8776)
Jj Kennedy Inc ....G 814 226-6320
Shippenville (G-17562)
Jj Kennedy Inc ....G 724 357-9696
Penn Run (G-13228)
Jj Kennedy Inc ....G 724 368-8660
Portersville (G-15928)
John Stephen Golob ....G 717 469-7931
Harrisburg (G-7158)
John W Thrower Inc ....G 724 352-9421
Saxonburg (G-17090)
Juniata Concrete Co ....E 717 436-2176
Mifflintown (G-11125)
Juniata Concrete Co ....G 717 567-3183
Newport (G-12491)
Juniata Concrete Co ....G 717 248-9677
Lewistown (G-9937)
Kibbes Concrete ....G 814 334-5537
Mills (G-11222)
Kiefer Coal and Supply Co ....G 412 835-7900
Bethel Park (G-1422)
Kinsley Construction Inc ....E 717 846-6711
York (G-20554)
Koller Concrete Inc ....G 610 865-5034
Bethlehem (G-1553)
Kraft Concrete Products Inc ....E 814 677-3019
Oil City (G-12950)
Lane Holdings LLC ....G 412 279-1234
Carnegie (G-2775)
Lehigh Cement Company LLC ....G 610 366-4600
Allentown (G-292)
Lehigh Cement Company LLC ....G 610 837-6725
Nazareth (G-11976)
Lehigh Cement Company LLC ....G 610 759-2222
Nazareth (G-11977)
Lehigh Cement Company LLC ....G 724 378-2232
Aliquippa (G-80)
Lehigh Cement Company LLC ....G 610 366-0500
Macungie (G-10149)
Lehigh Cement Company LLC ....C 610 926-1024
Fleetwood (G-5976)
▲ Lehigh Hanson Ecc Inc ....D 610 837-6725
Nazareth (G-11978)
Lehigh Hanson Ecc Inc ....D 610 837-3312
Nazareth (G-11979)
Lehigh Hanson Ecc Inc ....D 610 759-2222
Nazareth (G-11980)
Ligonier Stone & Lime Company ......E 724 537-6023
Latrobe (G-9500)
Limestone Mobile Concrete ....G 570 437-2640
Milton (G-11247)
Limestone Products & Supply Co ......G 412 221-5120
Bridgeville (G-2077)
Lisa Little Inc ....G 814 697-7500
Shinglehouse (G-17509)
Main Line Concrete & Sup Inc ....F 610 269-5556
Downingtown (G-4238)
Marion Center Supply Inc ....F 724 397-5505
Marion Center (G-10473)
Marion Center Supply Inc ....G 724 354-2143
Shelocta (G-17487)

S
I
C

Marstellar Concrete Inc ....G...... 717 834-6200
Duncannon *(G-4448)*

▼ Martin Limestone Inc ....E...... 717 335-4500
East Earl *(G-4548)*

Martin Limestone Inc ....D...... 717 354-1200
New Holland *(G-12258)*

Martin Limestone Inc ....E...... 717 335-4523
Denver *(G-4082)*

Martin Limestone Inc ....G...... 814 224-6837
West Chester *(G-19597)*

Martin Limestone Inc ....D...... 717 354-1298
New Holland *(G-12259)*

Masters Concrete ....E...... 570 798-2680
Lakewood *(G-8915)*

Meadville Redi-Mix Concrete ....G...... 814 734-1644
Edinboro *(G-4816)*

Middleburg Pre Cast LLC ....F...... 570 837-1463
Middleburg *(G-11029)*

Midwest Material Inds Inc ....G...... 610 882-5000
Bethlehem *(G-1573)*

Mix Earl ....G...... 610 444-3245
Kennett Square *(G-8530)*

Mon River Supply LLC.....................G...... 412 382-7178
West Elizabeth *(G-19695)*

Montgomery Block Works Inc ....F...... 724 735-2931
Harrisville *(G-7253)*

Naceville Materials JV ....F...... 215 453-8933
Sellersville *(G-17354)*

New Enterprise Stone Lime Inc ....E...... 814 472-4717
Ebensburg *(G-4790)*

New Enterprise Stone Lime Inc ....E...... 610 374-5131
Allentown *(G-330)*

New Enterprise Stone Lime Inc ....G...... 717 349-2412
Dry Run *(G-4384)*

New Enterprise Stone Lime Inc ....D...... 814 652-5121
Everett *(G-5576)*

New Enterprise Stone Lime Inc ....E...... 814 443-6494
Somerset *(G-17698)*

New Enterprise Stone Lime Inc ....B...... 610 374-5131
Leesport *(G-9668)*

New Enterprise Stone Lime Inc ....C...... 814 224-2121
Roaring Spring *(G-16766)*

Oldcastle Materials Inc ....G...... 717 898-2278
Annville *(G-655)*

Parmer Metered Concrete Inc ....G...... 717 533-3344
Hershey *(G-7624)*

Pennsy Supply Inc ....G...... 570 833-4497
Montrose *(G-11474)*

Pennsy Supply Inc ....G...... 717 569-2623
Manheim *(G-10400)*

Pennsy Supply Inc ....G...... 717 397-0391
Lancaster *(G-9165)*

Pennsy Supply Inc ....G...... 570 471-7358
Avoca *(G-847)*

Pennsy Supply Inc ....D...... 717 792-2631
Thomasville *(G-18342)*

Pennsy Supply Inc ....E...... 570 868-6936
Wapwallopen *(G-18808)*

Pennsy Supply Inc ....F...... 570 654-3462
Pittston *(G-15773)*

Pennsy Supply Inc ....E...... 717 566-0222
Hummelstown *(G-7921)*

Pennsy Supply Inc ....E...... 717 766-7676
Mechanicsburg *(G-10879)*

Pennsy Supply Inc ....D...... 717 274-3661
Lebanon *(G-9619)*

Pennsylvania Supply Inc ....G...... 717 567-3197
Harrisburg *(G-7196)*

Pike County Concrete Inc ....F...... 570 775-7880
Hawley *(G-7435)*

Pocono Transcrete Incorporated .....E...... 570 646-2662
Blakeslee *(G-1749)*

Pocono Transcrete Incorporated......G...... 570 655-9166
Pittston *(G-15777)*

Prospect Concrete Inc ....F...... 717 898-2277
Landisville *(G-9265)*

Quality Concrete Inc ....G...... 412 922-0200
Pittsburgh *(G-15460)*

R W Sidley Inc ....E...... 724 794-4451
Slippery Rock *(G-17625)*

R W Sidley Incorporated ....F...... 724 755-0205
Youngwood *(G-20783)*

R W Sidley Incorporated ....E...... 724 794-4451
Slippery Rock *(G-17626)*

Rahns Construction Material Co ......G...... 610 584-8500
Collegeville *(G-3390)*

RC Concrete Inc ....G...... 724 947-9005
Burgettstown *(G-2353)*

Ready Set Live Inc ....G...... 215 953-1509
Feasterville Trevose *(G-5928)*

Ready Training Inc ....G...... 717 366-4253
Elizabethtown *(G-4883)*

Redmonds Ready Mix Inc ....G...... 814 776-1437
Ridgway *(G-16726)*

Reeser Bros ....G...... 717 266-6644
York Haven *(G-20761)*

Riverside Builders Supply ....E...... 412 264-8835
Coraopolis *(G-3721)*

Robert J Quinn Jr ....G...... 570 622-4420
Pottsville *(G-16095)*

Rock Hill Materials Company ....E...... 610 264-5586
Catasauqua *(G-2817)*

Rock Hill Materials Company ....G...... 610 852-2314
Parryville *(G-13186)*

Rohrers Quarry Inc ....D...... 717 626-9760
Lititz *(G-10043)*

Rohrers Quarry Inc ....G...... 717 626-9756
Lititz *(G-10044)*

Rose Wild Inc ....G...... 570 835-4329
Tioga *(G-18364)*

S J A Construction Inc ....E...... 856 985-3400
Philadelphia *(G-14272)*

Santarelli Vibrated Block LLC............F...... 570 693-2200
Wyoming *(G-20284)*

Scott R Mix ....G...... 570 220-5887
Bellefonte *(G-1117)*

Scranton Craftsmen Excvtg Inc........D...... 800 775-1479
Throop *(G-18360)*

Scranton Craftsmen Inc ....D...... 570 347-5125
Throop *(G-18361)*

Sebastian Brothers ....F...... 717 930-8797
Middletown *(G-11075)*

Shaffer Block and Con Pdts Inc ....E...... 814 445-4414
Somerset *(G-17705)*

Shamrock Metered Concrete Inc ....G...... 570 672-3223
Paxinos *(G-13193)*

Shawnee Ready Mix Con & Asp Co .....E...... 570 779-9586
Plymouth *(G-15821)*

Sikorsky Concrete Product LLC ....G...... 610 826-3676
Palmerton *(G-13111)*

Sil Kemp Concrete Inc ....G...... 215 295-0777
Fairless Hills *(G-5796)*

Silhol Builders Supply Co Inc ....E...... 412 221-7400
Bridgeville *(G-2089)*

Skrapits Concrete Company ....G...... 610 262-8830
Northampton *(G-12861)*

Skrapits Concrete Company ....F...... 610 442-5355
Coplay *(G-3649)*

Stacy Lloyd ....G...... 724 265-3445
Tarentum *(G-18247)*

T C Redi Mix Youngstown Inc............G...... 724 652-7878
New Castle *(G-12158)*

Tafisco Inc ....G...... 215 493-3167
Philadelphia *(G-14368)*

Tarrs Concrete & Supplies ....G...... 724 438-4114
Washington *(G-19231)*

Toma Inc ....G...... 717 597-7194
Greencastle *(G-6641)*

Trenton Group Inc ....E...... 717 637-2288
Hanover *(G-6962)*

Trenton Group Inc ....G...... 717 235-3807
Shrewsbury *(G-17589)*

Tresco Concrete Products Inc ....F...... 724 468-4640
Export *(G-5629)*

Tri-Boro Construction Sups Inc..........E...... 717 249-6448
Carlisle *(G-2743)*

Union Quarries Inc ....E...... 717 249-5012
Carlisle *(G-2745)*

Universal Ready Mix & Supply ....F...... 724 529-2950
Dawson *(G-4033)*

US Concrete Inc ....E...... 610 532-6290
Sharon Hill *(G-17465)*

Valley Quarries Inc ....F...... 717 267-2244
Chambersburg *(G-2994)*

Valley Quarries Inc ....F...... 717 532-4161
Shippensburg *(G-17552)*

Valley Quarries Inc ....E...... 717 264-4178
Chambersburg *(G-2995)*

Vincent Lohuvey ....G...... 724 527-2994
Greensburg *(G-6727)*

Wayne Concrete Inc ....F...... 814 697-7500
Shinglehouse *(G-17514)*

Wayne County Ready Mix Inc ....F...... 570 253-4341
Honesdale *(G-7733)*

Wendell H Stone and Company ....G...... 412 331-1944
Mc Kees Rocks *(G-10641)*

Wendell H Stone Company Inc ....F...... 724 836-1400
Connellsville *(G-3510)*

Wendell H Stone Company Inc ....E...... 724 224-7688
Connellsville *(G-3511)*

Wendell H Stone Company Inc ....E...... 724 836-1400
Greensburg *(G-6729)*

Wendell H Stone Company Inc ....F...... 412 373-6235
Monroeville *(G-11364)*

Wendell H Stone Company Inc ....E...... 724 483-6571
Charleroi *(G-3025)*

▲ Westmoreland Advanced Mtls Inc ....G...... 724 684-5902
Charleroi *(G-3026)*

Wine Concrete Products Inc ....E...... 724 266-9500
Sewickley *(G-17415)*

Wolyniec Construction Inc ....E...... 570 322-8634
Williamsport *(G-20097)*

Wysox S&G Inc ....F...... 570 265-6760
Wysox *(G-20291)*

York Concrete Company ....F...... 717 843-8746
York *(G-20732)*

3274 Lime

Allegheny Mineral Corporation............E...... 724 735-2088
Harrisville *(G-7252)*

Allegheny Mineral Corporation............G...... 724 548-8101
Kittanning *(G-8753)*

Bullskin Stone & Lime LLC ....F...... 724 537-7505
Laughlintown *(G-9531)*

▲ Carmeuse Lime Inc ....D...... 412 995-5500
Pittsburgh *(G-14814)*

Carmeuse Lime Inc ....G...... 717 867-4441
Annville *(G-644)*

Glasgow Inc ....E...... 610 251-0760
Malvern *(G-10240)*

▼ Graymont Inc ....D...... 814 353-4613
Bellefonte *(G-1097)*

Highway Materials Inc ....E...... 610 828-4300
Plymouth Meeting *(G-15846)*

Keystone Lime Company ....E...... 814 662-2025
Springs *(G-17925)*

Lancaster Lime Works.........................F...... 717 207-7014
Lancaster *(G-9100)*

Luxfer Magtech Inc ....E...... 570 668-0001
Tamaqua *(G-18219)*

◆ Magnesia Refractories Company ....B...... 717 792-3611
York *(G-20572)*

Magnesita Refractories Company ....B...... 717 792-4216
York *(G-20573)*

Magnesita Refractories Company ....C...... 717 792-3611
York *(G-20574)*

Martin Limestone Inc ....B...... 717 354-1370
East Earl *(G-4549)*

Mercer Lime Company ....G...... 412 220-0316
Bridgeville *(G-2078)*

Rohrers Quarry Inc ....D...... 717 626-9760
Lititz *(G-10043)*

3275 Gypsum Prdts

▼ Agri Marketing Inc ....G...... 717 335-0379
Denver *(G-4066)*

◆ Certainteed Gypsum Inc ....D...... 610 893-6000
Malvern *(G-10206)*

Certainteed Gypsum Mfg Inc ....E...... 813 286-3900
Wayne *(G-19312)*

Dentsply Holding Company ....E...... 717 845-7511
York *(G-20448)*

New Ngc Inc...D...... 724 643-3440
Shippingport *(G-17567)*

New Ngc Inc...D...... 570 538-2531
New Columbia *(G-12174)*

Patrick Industries Inc ....E...... 717 653-2086
Mount Joy *(G-11668)*

▲ Saint-Gobain Corporation ....A...... 610 893-6000
Malvern *(G-10313)*

Tate Access Floors Inc ....C...... 717 244-4071
Red Lion *(G-16617)*

United States Gypsum Company ....D...... 724 857-4300
Aliquippa *(G-98)*

3281 Cut Stone Prdts

▲ AAA Hellenic Marble Inc ....E...... 610 344-7700
West Chester *(G-19493)*

Allegheny Cut Stone Co ....G...... 814 943-4157
Altoona *(G-469)*

Allegheny Mineral Corporation............G...... 724 548-8101
Kittanning *(G-8753)*

Armina Stone Inc ....G...... 412 406-8442
Cheswick *(G-3101)*

Aywon Chalkboard Corkboard Inc........E...... 570 459-3490
Hazleton *(G-7491)*

Bakers Quarry ....G...... 570 942-6005
Nicholson *(G-12612)*

Berkheimer Realty Company Inc..........G...... 610 588-0965
Pen Argyl *(G-13211)*

Bob Johnson Flagstone Inc....G.... 570 746-0907
Wyalusing (G-20246)
Brandywine Quarry Inc....G.... 610 857-4200
Parkesburg (G-13172)
Britt Energies Inc....G.... 724 465-9333
Spring Church (G-17854)
BS Quarries Inc....C.... 570 278-4901
Montrose (G-11459)
Butler Stonecraft Inc....G.... 724 352-3520
Cabot (G-2453)
Carl J Kaetzel....G.... 570 434-2391
Kingsley (G-8702)
Carlini Brothers Co....G.... 412 421-9301
Pittsburgh (G-14813)
Cava Intl MBL & Gran Inc....E.... 215 732-7800
Philadelphia (G-13516)
Charles Steckman....G.... 724 789-7066
Renfrew (G-16638)
▲ Choice Granite and Marble LLC....G.... 412 821-3900
Pittsburgh (G-14848)
Compton Flagstone Quarry....G.... 570 942-6359
Hop Bottom (G-7773)
Concure Inc....G.... 610 497-0198
Chester (G-3044)
Craig Walters....G.... 570 645-3415
Summit Hill (G-18159)
Custom Stone Interiors Inc....G.... 814 548-0120
Bellefonte (G-1096)
Czar Imports Inc....D.... 800 577-2927
Huntingdon Valley (G-7973)
Dally Slate Company Inc....D.... 610 863-4172
Pen Argyl (G-13213)
David R Kipar....E.... 570 833-4068
Meshoppen (G-11006)
Dente Pittsburgh Inc....G.... 412 828-1772
Oakmont (G-12916)
Derry Stone & Lime Co Inc....F.... 724 459-3971
Latrobe (G-9472)
Designs In Stone Inc....G.... 800 878-6631
Hatboro (G-7279)
Devido Ranier Stone Co....E.... 724 658-8518
New Castle (G-12082)
Diaz Stone and Pallet Inc....F.... 570 289-8760
Kingsley (G-8703)
Diaz Stone and Pallet Inc....E.... 570 289-8760
Kingsley (G-8704)
Dingmans Ferry Stone Inc....G.... 570 828-2617
Dingmans Ferry (G-4142)
Dyer Quarry Inc....E.... 610 582-6010
Birdsboro (G-1693)
Earl Wenz Inc....F.... 610 395-2331
Breinigsville (G-2014)
▲ Eastern Surfaces Inc....D.... 610 266-3121
Allentown (G-201)
Elegant Marble Products Inc....F.... 717 939-0373
Middletown (G-11052)
Environmental Materials LLC....C.... 570 366-6460
Orwigsburg (G-13042)
Environmental Stoneworks LLC....E.... 570 366-6460
Orwigsburg (G-13043)
EP Henry Corporation....E.... 610 495-8533
Parker Ford (G-13168)
Eureka Stone Quarry Inc....G.... 570 689-2901
Sterling (G-18049)
Eureka Stone Quarry Inc....G.... 570 296-6632
Milford (G-11160)
Eureka Stone Quarry Inc....G.... 570 992-4444
Stroudsburg (G-18115)
▲ Excel Glass and Granite....E.... 724 523-6190
Jeannette (G-8255)
Flagstone Small Bus Vltons LLC....G.... 484 515-2621
Bethlehem (G-1509)
▲ Franks Marble & Granite LLC....G.... 717 244-2685
Red Lion (G-16595)
G and H Contracting Inc....G.... 610 826-7542
Palmerton (G-13106)
▲ G Wb European Treasures....G.... 610 275-4395
Bridgeport (G-2037)
Gary Foster....G.... 717 248-5322
Lewistown (G-9932)
Gill Quarries Incorporated....G.... 610 584-6061
East Norriton (G-4584)
Gingrich Memorials Inc....F.... 717 272-0901
Lebanon (G-9574)
GK Flagstone Inc....G.... 570 942-4393
Nicholson (G-12613)
Glenn O Hawbaker Inc....D.... 814 237-1444
State College (G-17970)
▲ Granite Gllria Fabrication Inc....G.... 215 283-0341
Fort Washington (G-6073)

H B Mellott Estate Inc....F.... 301 678-2050
Warfordsburg (G-18812)
Hanson Aggregates LLC....E.... 724 459-6031
Blairsville (G-1722)
Hanson Aggregates PA LLC....F.... 570 324-2514
Blossburg (G-1807)
Harford Stone Company....F.... 570 434-9141
Kingsley (G-8705)
Harmony Flagstone LLC....G.... 570 727-2077
Susquehanna (G-18180)
Herb Kilmer & Sons Flagstone....E.... 570 434-2060
Kingsley (G-8706)
Heritage Stone & Marble Inc....G.... 610 222-0856
Lansdale (G-9376)
Howell Craft Inc....G.... 412 751-6861
Elizabeth (G-4860)
Indoor City Granite & MBL Inc....F.... 717 393-3931
Lancaster (G-9056)
J A Kohlepp and Sons Stone....F.... 814 371-5200
Du Bois (G-4397)
Jet Stream Manufacturing Inc....G.... 610 532-6632
Darby (G-4020)
Jones Stone & Marble Inc....G.... 724 838-7625
Greensburg (G-6681)
Kenneth E Decker....G.... 570 677-3710
Hop Bottom (G-7774)
Kerrico Corporation....E.... 570 374-9831
Selinsgrove (G-17329)
Kwik Kerb of Valley....G.... 610 419-8854
Bethlehem (G-1555)
L & D Stoneworks Inc....E.... 570 553-1670
Montrose (G-11469)
L and J Equipment Co Inc....G.... 724 437-5405
Uniontown (G-18633)
L&S Stone LLC....F.... 717 264-3559
Chambersburg (G-2950)
Lesher Inc....F.... 717 944-4431
Middletown (G-11062)
Lexmarusa Inc....G.... 412 896-9266
McKeesport (G-10675)
Luicana Industries Inc....G.... 570 325-9699
Jim Thorpe (G-8341)
Macson Company....G.... 610 264-7733
Allentown (G-305)
Magnesita Refractories Company....C.... 717 792-3611
York (G-20574)
▲ Majesty Marble and Granite Inc....E.... 610 859-8181
Aston (G-774)
Marble Source Inc....G.... 610 847-5694
Ottsville (G-13067)
Matt Kilmer Flagstone LLC....G.... 570 756-2591
South Gibson (G-17779)
Matthews International Corp....B.... 412 571-5500
Pittsburgh (G-15266)
McAvoy Brick Company....G.... 610 933-2932
Phoenixville (G-14560)
Media Quarry Co Inc....E.... 610 566-6667
Media (G-10938)
Meshoppen Stone Incorporated....C.... 570 833-2767
Meshoppen (G-11007)
Mid-Life Stone Works LLC....G.... 570 928-8802
Dushore (G-4509)
▲ Monticello Granite Ltd....F.... 215 677-1000
Collegeville (G-3383)
Natstone LLC....E.... 570 278-1611
Montrose (G-11472)
New Way Homes....G.... 570 967-2187
Hallstead (G-6834)
Oliver T Korb & Sons Inc....G.... 814 371-4545
Du Bois (G-4408)
Owens Monumental Company....G.... 610 588-3370
Bangor (G-923)
Patrick G Stinely....G.... 814 528-3832
Erie (G-5417)
Penn Big Bed Slate Co Inc....D.... 610 767-4601
Slatington (G-17611)
Pennsylvania Monument Co....F.... 570 454-2621
Hazleton (G-7516)
Porto Exim Usa LLC....G.... 412 406-8442
Cheswick (G-3115)
Pottstown Trap Rock Quarries....F.... 610 326-4843
Pottstown (G-16034)
Pottstown Trap Rock Quarries....F.... 610 326-5921
Douglassville (G-4179)
▲ Powers Stone Inc....E.... 570 553-4276
Montrose (G-11475)
Prada Company Inc....F.... 412 751-4900
McKeesport (G-10678)
Premier Bluestone Inc....E.... 570 465-7200
Susquehanna (G-18182)

◆ Princeton Trade Consulting Gro....E.... 610 683-9348
Kutztown (G-8856)
Richard Freeman....G.... 717 597-4580
Greencastle (G-6630)
▲ Rolling Rock Bldg Stone Inc....D.... 610 987-6226
Boyertown (G-1926)
▲ Russell Stone Products Inc....G.... 814 236-2449
Grampian (G-6572)
◆ Rynone Manufacturing Corp....C.... 570 888-5272
Sayre (G-17121)
Scranton Materials LLC....F.... 570 961-8586
Scranton (G-17286)
◆ Snyder Assod Companies Inc....E.... 724 548-8101
Kittanning (G-8793)
Suburban Marble LLC....G.... 215 734-9100
Warminster (G-18974)
Tony Bennett Flagstone....G.... 570 746-6015
Wyalusing (G-20259)
Tri City Marble Inc....E.... 610 481-0177
Allentown (G-412)
Tri-City Marble LLC....F.... 610 481-0177
Allentown (G-413)
Unity Marble and Granite Inc....G.... 412 793-4220
Pittsburgh (G-15681)
Wenz Co Inc....G.... 610 434-6157
Allentown (G-431)
▲ Wenzco Supplies....F.... 610 434-6157
Allentown (G-432)
Whitley East LLC....D.... 717 656-2081
Leola (G-9808)
▲ Wilder Diamond Blades Inc....G.... 570 222-9590
Kingsley (G-8710)
William J Judge....F.... 610 348-8070
Collegeville (G-3400)
▲ Williams & Sons Slate & Tile....E.... 610 863-4161
Wind Gap (G-20175)
Wirthmore Pdts & Svc Co Inc....G.... 610 430-0300
West Chester (G-19680)
▲ York Building Products Co Inc....E.... 717 848-2831
York (G-20726)

3291 Abrasive Prdts

▲ Associated Ceramics & Tech....D.... 724 353-1585
Sarver (G-17065)
▲ Basic Carbide Corporation....E.... 724 446-1630
Irwin (G-8146)
Basic Carbide Corporation....D.... 412 754-0060
Elizabeth (G-4856)
Basic Carbide Corporation....D.... 412 751-3774
Buena Vista (G-2340)
Cady Enterprises....G.... 814 848-7408
Ulysses (G-18600)
Calder Industries Inc....F.... 814 422-8026
Spring Mills (G-17886)
Carbide Metals Inc....F.... 724 459-6355
Blairsville (G-1718)
Ceratizit Usa Inc....F.... 724 694-8100
Latrobe (G-9463)
Confluense LLC....G.... 215 530-6461
Allentown (G-175)
Dynacut Inc....G.... 610 346-7386
Springtown (G-17926)
▲ Edmar Abrasive Company....F.... 610 544-4900
Broomall (G-2288)
Elge Precision Machining Inc....F.... 610 376-5458
Reading (G-16372)
Ervin Industries Inc....D.... 724 282-1060
Butler (G-2399)
Extramet Products LLC....F.... 724 532-3041
Latrobe (G-9475)
◆ Global Tungsten & Powders Corp....B.... 570 268-5000
Towanda (G-18429)
Hewlett Manufacturing Co....G.... 814 683-4762
Linesville (G-9981)
▲ Innovative Carbide Inc....D.... 412 751-6900
Irwin (G-8171)
▲ Jowitt & Rodgers Company....E.... 215 824-0401
Philadelphia (G-13912)
Keystone Abrasives Co....F.... 610 939-1060
Reading (G-16419)
▲ Laminators Incorporated....D.... 215 723-5285
Hatfield (G-7362)
Laurel Carbide Inc....G.... 724 537-4810
Latrobe (G-9495)
▲ Morgan Advanced Mtls Tech Inc....C.... 814 781-1573
Saint Marys (G-16998)
▲ Norstone Incorporated....G.... 484 684-6986
Bridgeport (G-2041)
Pacer Industries Inc....F.... 610 383-4200
Coatesville (G-3320)

SIC

Penn Scientific Products Co..................F 888 238-6710
   Abington *(G-13)*

Phoenixx Intl Resources Inc..............G 412 782-7060
   Pittsburgh *(G-15380)*

▲ Power & Industrial Svcs Corp........E 800 676-7116
   Donora *(G-4158)*

▲ Ppt Research Inc...........................G 610 434-0103
   Allentown *(G-353)*

▼ Precision Finishing Inc..................E 215 257-6862
   Quakertown *(G-16232)*

▲ Production Abrasives Inc...............E 814 938-5490
   Hamilton *(G-6858)*

◆ Red Hill Grinding Wheel Corp........E 215 679-7964
   Pennsburg *(G-13255)*

Saint-Gobain Abrasives Inc.............E 215 855-4300
   Montgomeryville *(G-11416)*

Saint-Gobain Abrasives Inc.............E 267 218-7100
   Montgomeryville *(G-11417)*

◆ Saint-Gobain Delaware Corp...........G 610 341-7000
   Valley Forge *(G-18712)*

◆ Schaffner Manufacturing Co............D 412 761-9902
   Pittsburgh *(G-15515)*

Sponge-Jet Inc..............................G 570 278-4563
   Montrose *(G-11478)*

T B W Industries Inc.......................F 215 794-8070
   Furlong *(G-6234)*

United States Products Co................G 412 621-2130
   Pittsburgh *(G-15675)*

◆ Weiler Corporation ....B 570 595-7495
   Cresco *(G-3896)*

▲ Wilder Diamond Blades Inc............G 570 222-9590
   Kingsley *(G-8710)*

▲ Winterthur Wendt Usa Inc.............C 610 495-2850
   Royersford *(G-16869)*

3292 Asbestos products

Abmech Acquisitions LLC ....E 412 462-7440
   West Homestead *(G-19719)*

Cdr Contracting ....G 814 536-7675
   Johnstown *(G-8363)*

◆ Certainteed Corporation ....B 610 893-5000
   Malvern *(G-10204)*

Certainteed Corporation ....G 610 651-8706
   Malvern *(G-10205)*

Control Temp Insulation LLC............G 610 393-0943
   Northampton *(G-12848)*

3295 Minerals & Earths: Ground Or Treated

Allegheny Mineral Corporation..........G 724 548-8101
   Kittanning *(G-8753)*

Anthracite Industries Inc..................E 570 286-2176
   Sunbury *(G-18163)*

Asbury Graphite Mills Inc.................D 724 543-1343
   Kittanning *(G-8755)*

▲ Beaver Valley Slag Inc...................F 724 378-8888
   Aliquippa *(G-68)*

Beaver Valley Slag Inc.....................F 724 773-0444
   Monaca *(G-11284)*

Bpi Inc..F 412 771-8176
   Mc Kees Rocks *(G-10605)*

C-E Minerals Inc ....G 610 768-8800
   King of Prussia *(G-8589)*

▲ Chemalloy Company LLC ....E 610 527-3700
   Conshohocken *(G-3527)*

▼ Chemrock Corporation ....F 610 667-6640
   Bala Cynwyd *(G-875)*

Du Penn Inc...................................F 814 371-6280
   Du Bois *(G-4388)*

East Loop Sand Company Inc...........F 814 695-3082
   Hollidaysburg *(G-7646)*

▲ Fluid Energy Proc & Eqp Co ....G 215 721-8990
   Telford *(G-18289)*

Fluid Energy Proc & Eqp Co ....D 215 368-2510
   Hatfield *(G-7343)*

Harsco Corporation ....E 724 287-4791
   Butler *(G-2405)*

Harsco Minerals PA LLC..................G 717 506-7157
   Fairless Hills *(G-5784)*

International Mill Service..................A 215 956-5500
   Horsham *(G-7824)*

Jobomax Global Ltd ....G 215 253-3691
   Philadelphia *(G-13900)*

◆ Keystone Filler & Mfg Co ....E 570 546-3148
   Muncy *(G-11824)*

Latrobe Foundry Mch & Sup Co ....F 724 423-4210
   Whitney *(G-19894)*

▲ Metal Services LLC ....E 610 347-0444
   Kennett Square *(G-8527)*

◆ Mill Services Corp ....F 412 678-6141
   Glassport *(G-6413)*

Nittany Extraction Tech LLC ....G 814 571-4776
   State College *(G-17999)*

▼ Penn Mag Incorporated ....F 724 545-2300
   Adrian *(G-31)*

Pennsylvania Carbon Pdts LLC.........G 724 564-9211
   Smithfield *(G-17654)*

Pennsylvania Perlite Corp York ....G 610 868-0992
   Bethlehem *(G-1594)*

◆ Premier Magnesia LLC ....E 610 828-6929
   Wayne *(G-19364)*

Premier Magnesia LLC ....F 717 677-7313
   Aspers *(G-744)*

▲ Reed Minerals...............................G 215 295-8675
   Fairless Hills *(G-5794)*

Rwe Holding Company......................F 724 752-9082
   New Castle *(G-12146)*

▲ Shamokin Filler Co Inc ....E 570 644-0437
   Coal Township *(G-3281)*

Specialty Granules Inc ....C 717 794-2184
   Blue Ridge Summit *(G-1861)*

Specialty Minerals Inc ....F 610 250-3000
   Easton *(G-4755)*

▲ Therm-O-Rock East Inc ....D 724 258-3670
   New Eagle *(G-12193)*

Therm-O-Rock East Inc.....................E 724 379-8604
   Donora *(G-4163)*

Tms International LLC......................G 724 746-5377
   Houston *(G-7881)*

Tms International LLC......................D 215 956-5500
   Horsham *(G-7859)*

Tms International LLC......................F 724 929-4515
   Belle Vernon *(G-1088)*

Tms International Corp.....................E 215 956-5500
   Horsham *(G-7860)*

Worldwide EDM Graphite Inc............G 814 781-6939
   Kersey *(G-8572)*

3296 Mineral Wool

Alpha Assembly Solutions Inc ....C 814 946-1611
   Altoona *(G-470)*

Armstrong World Industries Inc ....A 717 397-0611
   Lancaster *(G-8942)*

▲ Bloom Engineering Company Inc ....F 412 653-3500
   Pittsburgh *(G-14773)*

Brd Noise & Vibration Ctrl Inc ....G 610 863-6300
   Wind Gap *(G-20167)*

Certainteed Corporation....................B 570 474-6731
   Mountain Top *(G-11754)*

▼ Chemrock Corporation ....F 610 667-6640
   Bala Cynwyd *(G-875)*

◆ Epic Metals Corporation ....D 412 351-3913
   Rankin *(G-16305)*

Ica Inc..F 610 377-6100
   Lehighton *(G-9716)*

Keith Bush Associates Inc................G 215 968-5255
   Langhorne *(G-9306)*

Mito Insulation Company..................E 724 335-8551
   New Kensington *(G-12359)*

Molded Acstcal Pdts Easton Inc.........F 610 250-6738
   Easton *(G-4727)*

Ohio Valley Indus Svcs Inc ....G 412 269-0020
   Moon Township *(G-11498)*

Ohio Valley Indus Svcs Inc ....F 412 335-5237
   Coraopolis *(G-3708)*

Owens Corning Sales LLC.................E 570 339-3374
   Mount Carmel *(G-11628)*

▲ Panel Solutions Inc ....E 570 459-3490
   Hazleton *(G-7515)*

▼ Quanta Technologies Inc ....G 610 644-7101
   Lancaster *(G-9181)*

Quiet Core Inc ....F 610 694-9190
   Bethlehem *(G-1606)*

◆ Ranbar Electrical Mtls LLC.............E 724 864-8200
   Harrison City *(G-7251)*

◆ Saint-Gobain Delaware Corp...........G 610 341-7000
   Valley Forge *(G-18712)*

Shearer Elbie ....G 814 266-7548
   Johnstown *(G-8434)*

SMC Industries Inc.........................G 610 647-5687
   Malvern *(G-10321)*

▲ Therm-O-Rock East Inc ....D 724 258-3670
   New Eagle *(G-12193)*

Trinity Fibrgls Composites LLC...........G 412 855-3398
   Carnegie *(G-2798)*

3297 Nonclay Refractories

A P Green Services Inc.....................F 412 375-6600
   Coraopolis *(G-3652)*

Alcoa Corporation............................G 412 553-4001
   Pittsburgh *(G-14661)*

Alcoa Corporation............................E 412 315-2900
   Pittsburgh *(G-14662)*

Envirosafe Services of Ohio ....F 717 354-1025
   Narvon *(G-11921)*

Fuzion Technologies Inc ....F 724 545-2223
   Kittanning *(G-8772)*

Harbisnwlker Intl Holdings Inc...........G 412 375-6600
   Moon Township *(G-11488)*

◆ Harbisonwalker Intl Inc ....C 412 375-6600
   Moon Township *(G-11490)*

▲ Intersource Inc ....F 724 940-2220
   Mars *(G-10501)*

J M S Fabricated Systems Inc ....E 724 832-3640
   Latrobe *(G-9482)*

Krosaki Mgnsita Rfrctories LLC ....E 717 793-5536
   York *(G-20560)*

Lehigh Cement Company LLC.............D 717 843-0811
   York *(G-20565)*

Lwb Holding Company......................C 717 792-3611
   York *(G-20569)*

◆ Lwb Holding Company ....G 717 792-3611
   York *(G-20570)*

M J Stranko Inc ....G 610 929-8080
   Reading *(G-16436)*

M S S I Inc ....E 412 771-5533
   Canonsburg *(G-2600)*

◆ Magnesita Refractories Company ....B 717 792-3611
   York *(G-20572)*

Magnesita Refractories Company ....B 717 792-4216
   York *(G-20573)*

Magnesita Refractories Company ....C 717 792-3611
   York *(G-20574)*

Minteq International Inc.....................E 610 250-3000
   Easton *(G-4723)*

Minteq International Inc.....................E 724 794-3000
   Slippery Rock *(G-17622)*

▲ Minteq International Inc..................A 724 794-3000
   Bethlehem *(G-1574)*

Mount Svage Spclty Rfractories ....F 814 236-8370
   Curwensville *(G-3954)*

Mssi Refractory LLC ....E 412 771-5533
   Mc Kees Rocks *(G-10621)*

Ncri Inc...E 724 654-7711
   New Castle *(G-12125)*

Ona Corporation.............................C 610 378-1381
   Reading *(G-16458)*

Osram Sylvania Inc.........................B 570 724-8200
   Wellsboro *(G-19471)*

Osram Sylvania Inc.........................D 412 856-2111
   Monroeville *(G-11347)*

Penn-MO Fire Brick Co Inc................G 717 234-4504
   Harrisburg *(G-7193)*

Pennsylvania Perlite Corp York ....G 610 868-0992
   Bethlehem *(G-1594)*

Pennsylvania Perlite Corp York ....G 717 755-6206
   York *(G-20621)*

Pyrotek Incorporated ....D 717 249-2075
   Carlisle *(G-2733)*

Reading Refractories Company ....F 610 375-4422
   Bala Cynwyd *(G-890)*

Resco Group Inc ....E 412 494-4491
   Pittsburgh *(G-15479)*

Saint-Gobain Ceramics Plas Inc ....E 570 383-3261
   Olyphant *(G-12998)*

Saint-Gobain Ceramics Plas Inc ....D 724 539-6000
   Latrobe *(G-9518)*

▲ Saint-Gobain Ceramics Plas Inc .....A 508 795-5000
   Valley Forge *(G-18711)*

◆ Sauereisen Inc ....E 412 963-0303
   Pittsburgh *(G-15514)*

Sil-Base Company Inc ....E 412 751-2314
   McKeesport *(G-10681)*

Snow Shoe Refractories LLC..............E 814 387-6811
   Clarence *(G-3165)*

▲ Tyk America Inc ....E 412 384-4259
   Clairton *(G-3158)*

▼ UNI-Ref United Refractories Co........G 724 941-9390
   Canonsburg *(G-2650)*

Universal Refractories Inc.................E 412 787-7220
   Coraopolis *(G-3730)*

▲ Universal Refractories Inc..............E 724 535-4374
   Wampum *(G-18806)*

◆ Varsal LLC ....C 215 957-5880
   Warminster *(G-18993)*

Vesuvius U S A Corporation ....G 215 708-7404
   Philadelphia *(G-14442)*

Vesuvius U S A Corporation ....C 412 276-1750
   Pittsburgh *(G-15694)*

Vesuvius U S A Corporation ....E 419 986-5126
   Pittsburgh *(G-15695)*

Vesuvius U S A Corporation ....D...... 412 788-4441
  Pittsburgh (G-15696)
Vesuvius U S A Corporation ....D...... 814 387-6811
  Snow Shoe (G-17671)
▲ Worldwide Refractories Inc ....D...... 724 224-8800
  Tarentum (G-18255)

3299 Nonmetallic Mineral Prdts, NEC

Arlington Industries Inc ....G...... 267 580-2620
  Taylor (G-18258)
Complete Imaging Corp ....G...... 610 827-1561
  Chester Springs (G-3074)
Custom Sintered Specialties ....G...... 814 834-5154
  Saint Marys (G-16959)
Franks Ice Service LLC ....G...... 215 741-2026
  Bensalem (G-1198)
G R G Technologies LLC ....F...... 610 325-6701
  Newtown Square (G-12573)
▲ McDanel Advnced Crmic Tech LLC..C...... 724 843-8300
  Beaver Falls (G-1004)
Nikal Imaging Products In ....G...... 215 887-1319
  Wyncote (G-20265)
Outcast Studios LLC ....G...... 267 242-1332
  Philadelphia (G-14105)
Sam Andrew ....G...... 724 224-5445
  Tarentum (G-18246)
Sculpted Ice Works Inc ....F...... 570 226-6246
  Lakeville (G-8913)
Stucco Code Inc ....G...... 610 348-3905
  Drexel Hill (G-4372)

33 PRIMARY METAL INDUSTRIES

3312 Blast Furnaces, Coke Ovens, Steel & Rolling Mills

A & R Iron Works Inc ....F...... 610 497-8770
  Trainer (G-18462)
▲ Accu Machining Center Inc ....E...... 610 252-6855
  Easton (G-4644)
Acrelormittal Us LLC ....D...... 724 222-7769
  Washington (G-19144)
Action Materials Inc ....G...... 610 377-3037
  Lehighton (G-9709)
◆ Affival Inc ....G...... 412 826-9430
  Verona (G-18745)
Affival Inc ....E...... 412 826-9430
  Verona (G-18746)
Aii Acquisition LLC ....G...... 412 394-2800
  Pittsburgh (G-14657)
Aii Acquisition LLC ....G...... 724 226-5947
  Brackenridge (G-1936)
AK Steel Corporation ....A...... 724 284-2854
  Butler (G-2373)
Allegheny Iron & Metal Co ....E...... 215 743-7759
  Philadelphia (G-13366)
Allegheny Ludlum LLC..........................D...... 724 226-5000
  Brackenridge (G-1937)
▼ Allegheny Ludlum LLC ....B...... 412 394-2800
  Pittsburgh (G-14679)
Allegheny Ludlum LLC..........................D...... 724 773-2700
  Pittsburgh (G-14680)
Allegheny Ludlum LLC..........................F...... 724 537-5551
  Latrobe (G-9453)
Allegheny Technologies Inc ....G...... 724 224-1000
  Oakdale (G-12888)
Allegheny Technologies Inc ....G...... 724 452-1726
  Zelienople (G-20788)
Allegheny Technologies Inc ....D...... 412 394-2800
  Pittsburgh (G-14682)
◆ Allomet Corporation ....F...... 724 864-4787
  Irwin (G-8142)
Alpha Assembly Solutions Inc ....C...... 814 946-1611
  Altoona (G-470)
◆ AMG Resources Corporation ....E...... 412 777-7300
  Pittsburgh (G-14710)
▲ Ampco-Pittsburgh Corporation ....D...... 412 456-4400
  Carnegie (G-2763)
Anthracite Industries Inc ....E...... 570 286-2176
  Sunbury (G-18163)
Arcelormittal Holdings LLC ....C...... 724 684-1000
  Monessen (G-11297)
◆ Arcelormittal Plate LLC ....A...... 610 383-2000
  Coatesville (G-3289)
▲ Arcelormittal Steelton LLC ....A...... 717 986-2000
  Steelton (G-18044)
Arcelormittal USA LLC ....A...... 610 383-2000
  Coatesville (G-3290)
Arcelormittal USA LLC ....A...... 717 986-2887
  Steelton (G-18045)

Arcelormittal USA LLC ....B...... 610 825-6020
  Conshohocken (G-3521)
Ashby Mfg Co Inc ....F...... 724 776-5566
  Cranberry Township (G-3805)
Ashland Foundry & Mch Work LLC.......C...... 570 875-6100
  Ashland (G-727)
ATI Flat Rlled Pdts Hldngs LLC...........G...... 800 323-1240
  Natrona Heights (G-11933)
ATI Powder Metals ....F...... 412 923-2670
  Oakdale (G-12891)
ATI Powder Metals LLC ....D...... 412 923-2670
  Oakdale (G-12892)
ATI Powder Metals LLC ....D...... 412 394-2800
  Pittsburgh (G-14732)
ATI Precision Finishing LLC ....F...... 724 775-2618
  Monaca (G-11280)
Atlantic Track & Turnout Co ....E...... 570 429-1462
  Pottsville (G-16073)
Baileys Steel & Supply LLC ....G...... 724 267-4648
  Waynesburg (G-19433)
Bangor Steel Erectors Inc ....E...... 215 338-1200
  Philadelphia (G-13443)
◆ Bedford Reinforced Plas Inc ....D...... 814 623-8125
  Bedford (G-1044)
▲ Blair Strip Steel Company ....D...... 724 658-2611
  New Castle (G-12064)
Bosio Metal Specialties Inc ....F...... 215 699-4100
  North Wales (G-12792)
Bpi Inc ....F...... 412 771-8176
  Mc Kees Rocks (G-10605)
Brown Tool & Die Inc ....G...... 724 547-3366
  Acme (G-16)
Camden Iron & Metal Llc ....C...... 610 532-1080
  Sharon Hill (G-17454)
Capo and Kifer Pultrusions ....G...... 412 751-3489
  Greenock (G-6644)
◆ Carpenter Technology Corp ....B...... 610 208-2000
  Philadelphia (G-13508)
Carpenter Technology Corp ....G...... 610 208-2000
  Reading (G-16343)
Carpenter Technology Corp ....E...... 610 208-2000
  Reading (G-16344)
Classic Tool Inc ....E...... 814 763-4805
  Saegertown (G-16911)
Composidie Inc ....E...... 724 845-8602
  Leechburg (G-9643)
◆ Cronimet Corporation ....D...... 724 375-5004
  Aliquippa (G-71)
▲ D I Furnace LLC ....G...... 412 231-1200
  Pittsburgh (G-14901)
Ds Machine LLC ....H...... 717 768-3853
  Gordonville (G-6552)
Dyer Industries Inc ....F...... 724 258-3400
  Bunola (G-2343)
Dyer Quarry Inc ....E...... 610 582-6010
  Birdsboro (G-1693)
East Coast Metals Inc ....E...... 215 256-9550
  Harleysville (G-7031)
Eastern Manufacturing LLC ....G...... 215 702-3600
  Langhorne (G-9292)
Eastern Tool Steel Service Inc ....G...... 814 834-7224
  Saint Marys (G-16967)
Economy Tooling Corp PA ....G...... 724 266-4546
  Ambridge (G-617)
Eden Tool Company ....G...... 717 235-7009
  New Freedom (G-12206)
Electrospray Incorporated ....F...... 215 322-5255
  Feasterville Trevose (G-5904)
Electrospray Incorporated ....G...... 215 322-5255
  Feasterville Trevose (G-5905)
▲ Elliott Bros Steel Company ....E...... 724 658-5561
  Volant (G-18773)
Ellis Machine ....G...... 724 657-4519
  Pulaski (G-16123)
Ellwood Group Inc ....E...... 724 658-3685
  New Castle (G-12084)
Ellwood Mill Products Company ....E...... 724 752-0055
  New Castle (G-12085)
▲ Ellwood Mill Products Company ....E...... 724 658-9632
  New Castle (G-12086)
◆ Ellwood National Forge Company ....C...... 814 563-7522
  Irvine (G-8140)
▲ Ellwood Quality Steels Company .....C...... 724 658-6502
  New Castle (G-12087)
▲ Ellwood Specialty Steel Co ....D...... 724 657-1160
  New Castle (G-12088)
Erie Coke Corp ....F...... 814 454-0177
  Erie (G-5264)
Erie Coke Corporation ....C...... 814 454-0177
  Erie (G-5265)

▲ Erie Forge and Steel Inc ....D...... 814 452-2300
  Erie (G-5267)
Evraz Inc NA ....A...... 610 743-5970
  Reading (G-16381)
◆ Exim Steel & Shipbroking Inc ....G...... 215 369-9746
  Yardley (G-20310)
Flowline ....F...... 724 658-3711
  New Castle (G-12094)
Franklin Industries Co ....B...... 814 437-3726
  Franklin (G-6128)
▼ Franklin Industries Inc. ....B...... 814 437-3726
  Franklin (G-6129)
▼ Franklin Investment Corp. ....C...... 814 437-3726
  Franklin (G-6130)
G O Carlson Inc ....B...... 610 384-2800
  Downingtown (G-4228)
Gautier Steel Ltd ....D...... 814 535-9200
  Johnstown (G-8376)
▲ Geemacher LLC ....G...... 484 524-8251
  Pottstown (G-15990)
▲ General Carbide Corporation ....C...... 724 836-3000
  Greensburg (G-6668)
Gerdau Ameristeel US Inc ....C...... 717 751-6898
  York (G-20497)
▲ Gill Rock Drill Company Inc ....E...... 717 272-3861
  Lebanon (G-9573)
GKN Sinter Metals LLC ....A...... 814 486-3314
  Emporium (G-5060)
Goc Property Holdings LLC ....F...... 814 678-4127
  Oil City (G-12946)
Goldsborough & Vansant Inc ....G...... 724 287-5590
  East Butler (G-4532)
▲ Halferty Metals Company Inc ....G...... 724 694-5280
  Derry (G-4102)
Harsco Corporation ....G...... 724 287-4791
  Butler (G-2405)
Harter Precision ....G...... 724 459-5060
  Blairsville (G-1723)
Himes Machine Inc ....F...... 724 927-6850
  Linesville (G-9982)
Hoodco Inc ....F...... 215 236-0951
  Drexel Hill (G-4365)
Industrial Composites Inc ....G...... 412 221-2662
  Bridgeville (G-2069)
◆ Inweld Corporation ....F...... 610 261-1900
  Coplay (G-3644)
▲ Ipsco Koppel Tubulars LLC..............B...... 724 847-6389
  Koppel (G-8814)
Ipsco Koppel Tubulars Llc ....B...... 724 266-8830
  Ambridge (G-620)
Istil (usa) Milton Inc ....C...... 570 742-7420
  Milton (G-11243)
◆ J W T Holding Corp ....B...... 814 532-5600
  Johnstown (G-8383)
▲ Jadco Manufacturing Inc. ....G...... 724 452-5252
  Harmony (G-7070)
James A & Paulette M Berry ....G...... 814 486-2323
  Emporium (G-5064)
◆ Jersey Shore Steel Company ....B...... 570 753-3000
  Jersey Shore (G-8315)
Jersey Shore Steel Company ....C...... 570 368-2601
  Montoursville (G-11443)
Jessop Steel LLC ....G...... 724 222-4000
  Washington (G-19188)
JM Welding Company Inc ....G...... 610 872-2049
  Chester (G-3052)
John W Czech ....E...... 814 763-4470
  Saegertown (G-16920)
Johnstown Specialty Castings ....B...... 814 535-9002
  Johnstown (G-8391)
▲ Johnstown Wire Tech Inc ....B...... 814 532-5600
  Johnstown (G-8393)
Kasunick Welding & Fabg Co Inc ....F...... 412 321-2722
  Pittsburgh (G-15161)
Kca Enterprises ....G...... 724 880-2534
  Connellsville (G-3501)
Keystone Spike ....G...... 717 270-2700
  Lebanon (G-9594)
Klk Welding Inc ....F...... 717 637-0080
  Hanover (G-6910)
Kloeckner Metals Corporation ....A...... 215 245-3300
  Bensalem (G-1216)
Koppers Holdings Inc ....C...... 412 227-2001
  Pittsburgh (G-15187)
◆ Koppers Inc. ....C...... 412 227-2001
  Pittsburgh (G-15188)
L B Foster Company ....D...... 412 928-3400
  Pittsburgh (G-15207)

S
I
C

Larimer & Norton Inc ....G...... 814 435-2202
Galeton (G-6240)

◆ Latrobe Specialty Mtls Co LLC ....A 724 537-7711
Latrobe (G-9494)

Latrobe Specialty Mtls Co LLC ....D...... 814 432-8575
Franklin (G-6147)

Laurel Valley Metals LLC ....G...... 724 990-8189
Blairsville (G-1732)

◆ Lehigh Heavy Forge Corporation ....C...... 610 332-8100
Bethlehem (G-1557)

Lehigh Specialty Melting Inc ....D...... 724 537-7731
Latrobe (G-9499)

▲ Lloyd Industries Inc ....E...... 215 367-5863
Montgomeryville (G-11404)

▼ Lukens Inc ....D...... 610 383-2000
Coatesville (G-3315)

Luzerne Ironworks Inc ....G...... 570 288-1950
Luzerne (G-10127)

Magnetic Lifting Tech US LLC ....F...... 724 202-7987
New Castle (G-12118)

Manufctring Technical Svcs Inc ....G...... 610 857-3500
Sadsburyville (G-16905)

◆ Marcegaglia Usa Inc ....C...... 412 462-2185
Munhall (G-11844)

Markovitz Enterprises Inc ....C...... 412 381-2305
Pittsburgh (G-15255)

Markovitz Enterprises Inc ....E...... 724 658-6575
New Castle (G-12119)

Materion Brush Inc ....C...... 610 562-2211
Shoemakersville (G-17572)

Mercer Co ....G...... 724 347-4534
Sharon (G-17438)

Metal Service Company Inc ....F...... 724 567-6500
Vandergrift (G-18733)

Millcraft Corporation ....G...... 724 743-3400
Washington (G-19204)

Millcraft Industries Inc ....F...... 724 229-8800
Washington (G-19205)

▲ Millcraft SMS Services LLC ....C...... 724 222-5000
Washington (G-19206)

Molek Brothers ....G...... 717 248-8032
Yeagertown (G-20357)

▲ Molyneux Industries Inc ....F...... 724 695-3406
Coraopolis (G-3705)

▲ Morgardshammar Inc ....G...... 724 778-5400
Cranberry Township (G-3837)

N M A ....F...... 814 453-6787
Erie (G-5401)

New York Wire Company ....G...... 717 266-5626
Mount Wolf (G-11749)

Nexarc Inc ....G...... 570 458-6990
Bloomsburg (G-1791)

▲ Nlmk Pennsylvania LLC ....B...... 724 983-6464
Farrell (G-5869)

North Jckson Specialty Stl LLC ....E...... 412 257-7600
Bridgeville (G-2082)

▲ Olympia Chimney Supply Inc ....D...... 570 496-8890
Scranton (G-17268)

Olympic Steel Inc ....E...... 717 709-1515
Chambersburg (G-2966)

▲ Penna Flame Industries Inc ....E...... 724 452-8750
Zelienople (G-20815)

Perryman Company ....F...... 724 746-9390
Coal Center (G-3276)

Philadelphia Pipe Bending Co ....E...... 215 225-8955
Philadelphia (G-14149)

Pickar Brothers Inc ....E...... 610 582-0967
Birdsboro (G-1703)

Pittsburgh Flatroll Company ....G...... 412 237-2260
Pittsburgh (G-15397)

▼ PM Kalco Inc ....E...... 724 347-2208
Wheatland (G-19841)

Poormans Wldg Fabrication Inc ....F...... 814 349-5893
Aaronsburg (G-1)

▲ Precision Kidd Steel Co Inc ....E...... 724 695-2216
Aliquippa (G-89)

Precision Kidd Steel Co Inc ....E...... 724 695-2216
Clinton (G-3266)

Premier Fence & Iron Works Inc ....G...... 267 567-2078
Philadelphia (G-14197)

Primetals Technologies USA LLC ....C...... 724 514-8500
Canonsburg (G-2620)

Progress Rail Services Corp ....E...... 610 779-2039
Reading (G-16476)

Quality Steel Fabricators ....F...... 724 646-0500
Greenville (G-6768)

Rolled Steel Products Corp PA ....G...... 610 647-6264
Berwyn (G-1374)

Rose Corporation ....D...... 610 376-5004
Reading (G-16504)

Rossi Precision Inc ....G...... 724 667-9334
New Castle (G-12145)

Samuel Grossi & Sons Inc ....D...... 215 638-4470
Bensalem (G-1249)

Sandvik Inc ....B...... 570 585-7500
S Abingtn Twp (G-16899)

Sb Specialty Metals LLC ....G...... 814 337-8804
Meadville (G-10788)

▲ Sharon Coating LLC ....C...... 724 983-6464
Sharon (G-17442)

Sharp Tool and Die Inc ....G...... 814 763-1133
Guys Mills (G-6812)

Shenango Group Inc ....C...... 412 771-4400
Pittsburgh (G-15530)

Shenango Incorporated ....C...... 412 771-4400
Pittsburgh (G-15531)

SMS Demag Inc ....C...... 412 231-1200
Pittsburgh (G-15551)

◆ Spang & Company ....C...... 412 963-9363
Pittsburgh (G-15566)

Spomin Metals Inc ....F...... 724 924-9718
New Castle (G-12155)

Sssi Inc ....B...... 724 743-5815
Washington (G-19228)

Standard Forged Products LLC ....D...... 412 778-2020
Mc Kees Rocks (G-10637)

Standard Iron Works ....E...... 570 347-2058
Scranton (G-17293)

▲ Standard Steel LLC ....B...... 717 242-4615
Burnham (G-2362)

Sterling-Fleischman Inc ....F...... 610 647-1717
Media (G-10951)

Summerill Tube Corporation ....G...... 724 887-9700
Koppel (G-8816)

Superior Forge & Steel Corp ....D...... 412 431-8250
Pittsburgh (G-15588)

Superior Tooling Tech Inc ....F...... 814 486-9498
Emporium (G-5076)

▲ Susini Specialty Steels Inc ....F...... 724 295-6511
Natrona Heights (G-11949)

Tatano Wire and Steel Inc ....G...... 724 746-3118
Houston (G-7880)

◆ Tdy Industries LLC ....D...... 412 394-2896
Pittsburgh (G-15600)

Te Connectivity Corporation ....C...... 717 762-9186
Waynesboro (G-19426)

TI Oregon Inc ....C...... 412 394-2800
Pittsburgh (G-15624)

Titusville Enterprises Inc ....G...... 412 826-8140
Pittsburgh (G-15627)

Titusville Fabricators Inc ....E...... 814 432-2551
Franklin (G-6165)

◆ Tms International LLC ....D...... 412 678-6141
Glassport (G-6419)

Tms International LLC ....G...... 724 658-2004
New Castle (G-12159)

Tms International LLC ....G...... 814 535-1911
Johnstown (G-8438)

Tms International LLC ....G...... 412 271-4430
Braddock (G-1948)

Tms International LLC ....G...... 610 208-3293
Reading (G-16540)

Tms International Corp ....C...... 412 678-6141
Glassport (G-6420)

◆ Tms International Corporation ....E...... 412 675-8251
Glassport (G-6421)

Tonda Inc ....G...... 570 454-3323
Hazle Township (G-7484)

Union Electric Company ....G...... 814 452-0587
Erie (G-5523)

Union Electric Steel Corp ....D...... 724 947-9595
Burgettstown (G-2358)

◆ Union Electric Steel Corp ....D...... 412 429-7655
Carnegie (G-2800)

United States Steel Corp ....C...... 412 675-7459
West Mifflin (G-19746)

◆ United States Steel Corp ....B...... 412 433-1121
Pittsburgh (G-15677)

United States Steel Corp ....D...... 412 273-7000
Braddock (G-1950)

United States Steel Corp ....C...... 412 433-1121
Pittsburgh (G-15678)

United States Steel Corp ....D...... 215 736-4000
Fairless Hills (G-5805)

United States Steel Corp ....E...... 412 810-0286
Homestead (G-7694)

United States Steel Corp ....E...... 724 439-1116
Uniontown (G-18645)

United States Steel Corp ....C...... 412 433-1419
Pittsburgh (G-15679)

United States Steel Corp ....C...... 215 736-4600
Fairless Hills (G-5806)

United States Steel Corp ....C...... 412 433-7215
Homestead (G-7695)

Unitrac Railroad Materials Inc ....G...... 570 923-1514
Renovo (G-16651)

▲ Universal Stainless & Alloy ....B...... 412 257-7600
Bridgeville (G-2097)

Universal STAinless& Alloy ....D...... 814 827-9723
Titusville (G-18402)

US Steel Holdings Inc ....G...... 412 433-1121
Pittsburgh (G-15687)

Vai Pomini Inc ....F...... 610 921-9101
Reading (G-16558)

Vb Fabricators Inc ....F...... 412 486-6385
Glenshaw (G-6502)

Victaulic Company of America ....C...... 610 966-3966
Alburtis (G-58)

Weichert Machining Inc ....G...... 717 235-6761
Glen Rock (G-6462)

Wescott Steel Inc ....E...... 215 364-3636
Langhorne (G-9335)

Wheatland Steel Processing Co ....E...... 724 981-4242
Wheatland (G-19843)

▼ Whemco Inc ....E...... 412 390-2700
Pittsburgh (G-15715)

Woodward Inc ....E...... 724 538-3110
Mars (G-10516)

X-Cell Tool and Mold Inc ....E...... 814 474-9100
Fairview (G-5850)

3313 Electrometallurgical Prdts

Aviva Technology Inc ....G...... 610 228-4689
Broomall (G-2279)

BMC Liquidation Company ....E...... 724 431-2800
Butler (G-2382)

◆ Elkem Holding Inc ....B...... 412 299-7200
Coraopolis (G-3687)

◆ Elkem Materials Inc ....C...... 412 299-7200
Coraopolis (G-3688)

Evergreen Metallurgical LLC ....G...... 724 431-2800
Butler (G-2400)

G O Carlson Inc ....E...... 814 678-4100
Oil City (G-12945)

General Electric Company ....G...... 646 682-5601
Imperial (G-8065)

◆ Global Tungsten & Powders Corp ....B...... 570 268-5000
Towanda (G-18429)

◆ Greenville Metals Inc ....D...... 724 509-1861
Transfer (G-18445)

Ironmaster LLC ....G...... 412 554-6705
Export (G-5609)

▲ Kennametal Inc ....A...... 412 248-8000
Pittsburgh (G-15169)

Metallurg Inc ....G...... 610 293-2501
Wayne (G-19355)

Metallurg Holdings Inc ....F...... 610 293-2501
Wayne (G-19356)

◆ Neh Inc ....B...... 412 299-7200
Coraopolis (G-3706)

◆ Reading Alloys Inc ....C...... 610 693-5822
Robesonia (G-16777)

3315 Steel Wire Drawing & Nails & Spikes

A & B Steelworks LLC ....F...... 717 823-8599
Myerstown (G-11872)

◆ Ace Wire Spring & Form Co Inc ....E...... 412 331-3353
Mc Kees Rocks (G-10601)

All Steel Supply Inc ....E...... 215 672-0883
Horsham (G-7781)

▲ American Wire Research Inc ....E...... 412 349-8431
Wilmerding (G-20159)

Aristo-TEC Metal Forms Inc ....E...... 724 626-5900
Connellsville (G-3489)

Avant-Garde Technology Inc ....G...... 215 345-8228
Doylestown (G-4273)

Belden Inc ....C...... 724 222-7060
Washington (G-19153)

◆ Bombardier Transportation ....A...... 412 655-5700
Pittsburgh (G-14782)

Business Wire Inc ....G...... 610 617-9560
Plymouth Meeting (G-15836)

◆ Carpenter Technology Corp ....B...... 610 208-2000
Philadelphia (G-13508)

▲ Cedar Ridge Manufacturing LLC ....G...... 717 656-0404
Ronks (G-16805)

County Line Fence Co ....F...... 215 343-5085
Warrington (G-19112)

Dellovade Fabricators Inc ....F...... 615 370-7000
Avella (G-835)

Drs Laurel Technologies ....B 814 534-8900
Johnstown (G-8370)
▲ DSI-Lang Geotech LLC ....G 610 268-2221
Toughkenamon (G-18418)
Erisco Industries Inc ....D 814 459-2720
North East (G-12741)
ESAB Group Inc ....B 717 637-8911
Hanover (G-6884)
ESAB Group Inc ....C 843 673-7700
Hanover (G-6885)
Esmark Excalibur LLC ....E 814 382-5696
Meadville (G-10721)
Forest Hill Manufacturing LLC ....G 717 556-0363
Leola (G-9782)
Glenfield Supply Company Inc ....G 412 781-8188
Pittsburgh (G-15051)
Grassroots Unwired Inc ....G 215 788-1210
Bristol (G-2150)
HIG Capital LLC ....C 610 495-7011
Royersford (G-16851)
▲ Ism Enterprises Inc ....G 800 378-3430
Butler (G-2411)
Ivy Steel & Wire Inc ....D 570 450-2090
Hazle Township (G-7465)
Iwm International LLC ....G 800 323-5585
York (G-20538)
Keystone Spike ....G 717 270-2700
Lebanon (G-9594)
▲ Legrand Home Systems Inc ....D 717 702-2532
Middletown (G-11060)
▲ Lift-Tech Inc ....G 717 898-6615
Landisville (G-9263)
Marietta Fence Experts LLC ....G 724 925-6100
Hunker (G-7929)
▲ Markel Corp ....C 610 272-8960
Plymouth Meeting (G-15855)
Mlp Steel LLC ....E 724 887-7720
Everson (G-5580)
Mlp Steel LLC ....E 724 887-8100
Scottdale (G-17195)
▲ Moore Push Pin Company ....D 215 233-5700
Glenside (G-6531)
▲ Mount Joy Wire Corporation ....C 717 653-1461
Mount Joy (G-11666)
Muncy Machine & Tool Co Inc ....E 570 649-5188
Turbotville (G-18555)
▲ Nelson Steel Products Inc ....E 215 721-9449
Hatfield (G-7372)
Nexans USA Inc ....B 717 354-6200
New Holland (G-12271)
North Jckson Specialty Stl LLC ....C 412 257-7600
Bridgeville (G-2083)
Northeast Fence & Ir Works Inc ....E 215 335-1681
Philadelphia (G-14082)
Omega Fence Co ....G 215 729-7474
Philadelphia (G-14094)
Pennheat LLC ....E 814 282-6774
Meadville (G-10777)
Perryman Company ....F 724 746-9390
Coal Center (G-3276)
▲ Precision Kidd Steel Co Inc ....E 724 695-2216
Aliquippa (G-89)
Precision Kidd Steel Co Inc ....E 724 695-2216
Clinton (G-3266)
▲ Quality Wire Forming ....G 717 656-4478
Leola (G-9799)
Rapid Tag & Wire Co ....G 724 452-7760
Fombell (G-6034)
Rocky Ridge Steel LLC ....G 717 626-0153
Lititz (G-10042)
Shirk Manufacturing ....G 717 445-9353
Narvon (G-11926)
Sonco Worldwide Inc ....F 215 337-9651
Bristol (G-2200)
Susquhnna Wire Rope Rgging Inc ....G 814 772-4766
Ridgway (G-16731)
Tatano Wire and Steel Inc ....E 724 746-3118
Canonsburg (G-2645)
◆ Three M Tool and Die Corp ....F 717 854-6379
York (G-20688)
▲ Wire and Cable Specialties Inc ....D 610 466-6200
Coatesville (G-3330)
◆ Wirerope Works Inc ....B 570 327-4229
Williamsport (G-20096)
Z & F USA ....G 412 257-8575
Bridgeville (G-2100)

3316 Cold Rolled Steel Sheet, Strip & Bars

▲ All-Clad Metalcrafters LLC ....D 724 745-8300
Canonsburg (G-2537)

Allegheny Ludlum LLC ....C 724 567-2001
Vandergrift (G-18721)
ATI Powder Metals LLC ....D 412 394-2800
Pittsburgh (G-14732)
▲ Blair Strip Steel Company ....D 724 658-2611
New Castle (G-12064)
◆ Carpenter Technology Corp ....B 610 208-2000
Philadelphia (G-13508)
Colonial Metal Products Inc ....E 724 346-5550
Hermitage (G-7579)
▲ Elliott Bros Steel Company ....E 724 658-5561
Volant (G-18773)
Hygrade Acquisition Corp ....D 610 866-2441
Bethlehem (G-1536)
▲ Hygrade Mtal Moulding Mfg Corp ...E 610 866-2441
Bethlehem (G-1538)
Jabtek LLC ....G 724 796-5656
New Kensington (G-12348)
Joseph T Ryerson & Son Inc ....F 215 736-8970
Morrisville (G-11565)
Kloeckner Metals Corporation ....A 215 245-3300
Bensalem (G-1216)
Kloeckner Metals Corporation ....D 717 755-1923
York (G-20557)
Laneko Roll Form Inc ....E 215 822-1930
Hatfield (G-7363)
Markovitz Enterprises Inc ....E 724 658-6575
New Castle (G-12119)
▲ Nlmk Pennsylvania LLC ....B 724 983-6464
Farrell (G-5869)
▲ Penna Flame Industries Inc ....E 724 452-8750
Zelienople (G-20815)
Perryman Company ....F 724 746-9390
Coal Center (G-3276)
Pilot-Run Stamping Company ....E 440 255-8821
Corry (G-3772)
▲ Precision Industries Inc ....D 724 222-2100
Washington (G-19217)
▲ Precision Kidd Steel Co Inc ....E 724 695-2216
Aliquippa (G-89)
Precision Kidd Steel Co Inc ....E 724 695-2216
Clinton (G-3266)
Rose Corporation ....F 610 921-9647
Reading (G-16505)
Saegertown Manufacturing Corp ......C 814 763-2655
Saegertown (G-16932)
Shalmet Corporation ....C 570 366-1414
Orwigsburg (G-13052)
Superior Forge & Steel Corp ....D 412 431-8250
Pittsburgh (G-15588)
◆ Tdy Industries LLC ....D 412 394-2896
Pittsburgh (G-15600)

3317 Steel Pipe & Tubes

A & L Tubular Specialties ....G 724 667-6101
New Castle (G-12051)
A F Necastro Inc ....G 724 981-3239
Farrell (G-5865)
▲ ABT LLC ....E 412 826-8002
Pittsburgh (G-14636)
Abtrex Industries Inc ....E 724 266-5425
Leetsdale (G-9676)
▼ Accumetrics Limited ....E 610 948-0181
Royersford (G-16840)
Allied Tube & Conduit Corp ....B 215 676-6464
Philadelphia (G-13369)
American Tube Company Inc ....D 610 759-8700
Nazareth (G-11953)
▼ Arcelrmttal Tblar Pdts USA LLC ....E 419 342-1200
Pittsburgh (G-14716)
Avidon Welding Inc ....G 570 421-2307
East Stroudsburg (G-4607)
Baileys Steel & Supply LLC ....G 724 267-4648
Waynesburg (G-19433)
◆ Bradford Allegheny Corporation ....C 814 362-2590
Lewis Run (G-9871)
Bradford Allegheny Corporation ......D 814 362-2593
Lewis Run (G-9874)
Crp Inc ....G 610 970-7663
Pottstown (G-15977)
Custom Fab Inc ....G 717 721-5008
Ephrata (G-5098)
Dura-Bond Coating Inc ....E 724 327-0782
Export (G-5598)
Dura-Bond Pipe LLC ....D 717 986-1100
Steelton (G-18047)
Dura-Bond Steel Corp ....C 724 327-0280
Export (G-5599)
◆ Handy & Harman Tube Co Inc ......B 610 539-3900
Norristown (G-12664)

▲ Hofmann Industries Inc ....B 610 678-8051
Reading (G-16403)
Ipsco Koppel Tubulars Llc ....B 724 266-8830
Ambridge (G-620)
Kloeckner Metals Corporation ....A 215 245-3300
Bensalem (G-1216)
L B Foster Company ....D 412 928-3400
Pittsburgh (G-15207)
◆ Marcegaglia Usa Inc ....C 412 462-2185
Munhall (G-11844)
▲ Parade Strapping & Baling LLC ....G 215 537-9473
Philadelphia (G-14119)
▲ Penn State Special Metals LLC .....E 724 847-4623
Koppel (G-8815)
Pennsylvania Steel Company ....E 610 432-4541
Whitehall (G-19886)
▲ Phoenix Tube Co Inc ....B 610 865-5337
Bethlehem (G-1596)
◆ Ptc Alliance Corp ....D 412 299-7900
Wexford (G-19823)
Ptc Alliance Corp ....C 724 847-7137
Beaver Falls (G-1008)
Ptc Group Holdings Corp ....D 724 847-7137
Beaver Falls (G-1009)
◆ Ptc Group Holdings Corp ....E 412 299-7900
Wexford (G-19824)
Ptc Holdings I Corp ....E 412 299-7900
Wexford (G-19825)
◆ Salem Tube Inc ....C 724 646-4301
Greenville (G-6772)
Sinnott Industries Inc ....G 215 677-7793
Philadelphia (G-14309)
State Line Supply Company ....F 814 362-7433
Bradford (G-1992)
Steel Consulting Services LLC ....C 412 727-6645
Pittsburgh (G-15580)
▲ Summerill Tube Corporation ....D 724 887-9700
Scottdale (G-17202)
◆ Summit Steel & Mfg Inc ....D 610 921-1119
Reading (G-16528)
▲ Superior Group Inc ....E 610 397-2040
Conshohocken (G-3610)
T Helbling LLC ....G 724 601-9819
Beaver (G-992)
Tapco Tube Company ....G 814 336-2201
Meadville (G-10799)
Tech Tube Inc ....D 610 491-8000
King of Prussia (G-8684)
▲ Tube Methods Inc ....D 610 279-7700
Bridgeport (G-2047)
United States Steel Corp ....C 215 736-4600
Fairless Hills (G-5806)
United States Steel Corp ....C 412 433-7215
Homestead (G-7695)
◆ United States Steel Corp ....B 412 433-1121
Pittsburgh (G-15677)
US Steel Holdings Inc ....B 412 433-1121
Pittsburgh (G-15687)
Valmont Newmark Inc ....C 570 454-8730
West Hazleton (G-19717)
Victaulic Company of America ....C 610 966-3966
Alburtis (G-58)
Webco Industries Inc ....C 814 678-1325
Oil City (G-12959)
Wheatland Tube LLC ....D 724 981-5200
Sharon (G-17445)
Wheatland Tube LLC ....D 724 342-6851
Sharon (G-17446)
Zekelman Industries Inc ....D 610 889-3337
Newtown Square (G-12599)
Zekelman Industries Inc ....C 724 342-6851
Sharon (G-17450)
Zekelman Industries Inc ....D 724 342-6851
Sharon (G-17451)

3321 Gray Iron Foundries

Advanced Metals Group LLC ....F 610 408-8006
Malvern (G-10180)
B & B Foundry Inc ....E 215 333-7100
Philadelphia (G-13435)
Benton Foundry Inc ....C 570 925-6711
Benton (G-1277)
▲ Betts Industries Inc ....C 814 723-1250
Warren (G-19013)
Buck Company Inc ....G 717 284-4114
Quarryville (G-16266)
Charter Dura-Bar Inc ....F 717 779-0807
York (G-20424)
Clearfield Machine Company ....F 814 765-6544
Clearfield (G-3214)

Craigg Manufacturing Corp ....G...... 610 678-8200
Reading (G-16353)

Donsco Inc...C....... 717 653-1851
Mount Joy (G-11653)

Donsco Inc...C....... 717 252-1561
Belleville (G-1131)

▲ Donsco Inc.......................................B....... 717 252-1561
Wrightsville (G-20236)

Ej Usa Inc ....F....... 412 795-6000
Monroeville (G-11334)

Fry & 146 Cast Division ....G....... 570 546-2109
Muncy (G-11817)

General Foundry LLC ....G....... 610 997-8660
Bethlehem (G-1525)

H and H Foundry Machine Co...............G....... 724 863-3251
Manor (G-10411)

Hamburg Manufacturing Inc ....E....... 610 562-2203
Hamburg (G-6840)

▲ Hodge Foundry Inc ....C....... 724 588-4100
Greenville (G-6746)

Jdh Pacific Inc ....E....... 562 926-8088
Reading (G-16413)

Kulp Foundry Inc ....D...... 610 881-8093
Wind Gap (G-20170)

Louis P Canuso Inc.............................F....... 610 366-7914
Allentown (G-301)

Man Pan LLC ....G....... 724 942-9500
Mc Murray (G-10645)

◆ McLanahan Corporation ....B....... 814 695-9807
Hollidaysburg (G-7651)

Metso Minerals Industries Inc..............B....... 717 843-8671
York (G-20590)

Metso Minerals Industries Inc..............C....... 210 491-9521
Greenville (G-6757)

Penn Mar Castings Inc ....D....... 717 632-4165
Hanover (G-6935)

▲ Penna Flame Industries Inc ....E....... 724 452-8750
Zelienople (G-20815)

Perfomance Castings LLC ....G....... 814 454-1243
Fairview (G-5836)

◆ R H Sheppard Co Inc.......................A....... 717 637-3751
Hanover (G-6941)

◆ Rolls Technology Inc.......................B....... 724 697-4533
Avonmore (G-868)

▲ Ross Sand Casting ....G....... 724 222-7006
Washington (G-19223)

S & B Foundry Co ....E....... 570 784-2047
Bloomsburg (G-1800)

Somerset Consolidated Inds Inc ....E....... 814 445-7927
Somerset (G-17706)

▼ Tyco Fire Products LP ....C....... 215 362-0700
Lansdale (G-9421)

▲ Unicast Company.............................D....... 610 366-8836
Boyertown (G-1934)

Unicast Company................................G....... 610 366-8836
Allentown (G-417)

◆ Victaulic Company...........................A....... 610 559-3300
Easton (G-4770)

▲ Ward Manufacturing LLC ....C....... 570 638-2131
Blossburg (G-1810)

Waupaca Foundry Inc.........................C....... 570 724-5191
Tioga (G-18367)

Waupaca Foundry Inc.........................B....... 570 827-3245
Tioga (G-18368)

▼ Weatherly Casting and Mch Co ....D....... 570 427-8611
Weatherly (G-19455)

Wellsville Foundry Inc ....E....... 330 532-2995
Meadville (G-10812)

West Salisbury Fndry Mch Inc..............E....... 814 662-2809
West Salisbury (G-19765)

Williamsport Foundry Co Inc ....E....... 570 323-6216
Williamsport (G-20093)

Workmaster Inc ....G....... 866 476-9217
Malvern (G-10349)

3322 Malleable Iron Foundries

Beaver Valley Alloy Foundry Co............E....... 724 775-1987
Monaca (G-11283)

Buck Company Inc..............................G....... 717 284-4114
Quarryville (G-16266)

Kulp Foundry Inc ....D...... 610 881-8093
Wind Gap (G-20170)

Metso Minerals Industries Inc..............C....... 210 491-9521
Greenville (G-6757)

Prime Metals Acquisition LLC ....D....... 724 479-4155
Homer City (G-7680)

Ridge Tool Company ....D....... 814 454-2461
Erie (G-5463)

▲ Sinacom North America Inc ....E....... 610 337-2250
King of Prussia (G-8677)

▲ Ward Manufacturing LLC ....C...... 570 638-2131
Blossburg (G-1810)

3324 Steel Investment Foundries

▲ Bowser Manufacturing Co ....F....... 570 368-5045
Montoursville (G-11434)

Esmark Inc..F....... 412 259-8868
Sewickley (G-17386)

Howmet Aluminum Casting Inc ....C....... 610 266-0270
Bethlehem (G-1532)

◆ Lee Industries Inc............................C....... 814 342-0460
Philipsburg (G-14519)

▲ Nova Precision Casting Corp ....E....... 570 366-2679
Auburn (G-819)

Pennsylvannia Precision Cast P ....C....... 717 273-3338
Lebanon (G-9620)

▲ Post Precision Castings Inc..............C....... 610 488-1011
Strausstown (G-18099)

Precision Castparts Corp ....B....... 570 474-6371
Mountain Top (G-11771)

Wolf Technologies LLC ....E....... 610 385-6091
Douglassville (G-4182)

3325 Steel Foundries, NEC

◆ Akers National Roll Company ....C....... 724 697-4533
Avonmore (G-862)

Amsi US LLC ....G....... 814 479-3380
Hollsopple (G-7656)

Beaver Valley Alloy Foundry Co............E....... 724 775-1987
Monaca (G-11283)

Brighton Electric ....G....... 412 269-7000
Coraopolis (G-3665)

Brighton Steel Inc...............................E....... 724 846-7377
Beaver Falls (G-997)

Ccx Inc ....E....... 724 224-6900
Lower Burrell (G-10105)

Dickson Investment Hdwr Inc...............E....... 610 272-0764
King of Prussia (G-8609)

Duraloy Technologies Inc ....C....... 724 887-5100
Scottdale (G-17190)

Effort Foundry Inc ....D....... 610 837-1837
Bath (G-958)

Eureka Foundry Co..............................G....... 412 963-7881
Pittsburgh (G-14988)

Export USA LLC ....G....... 215 949-3380
Levittown (G-9835)

Falvey Steel Castings ....G....... 484 678-2174
Mohnton (G-11263)

▼ Frog Switch and Mfg Co ....C....... 717 243-2454
Carlisle (G-2715)

Gautier Steel Ltd ....D....... 814 535-9200
Johnstown (G-8376)

Grid Company LLC ....E....... 610 341-7307
Valley Forge (G-18708)

Hazleton Casting Company ....E....... 570 453-0199
Hazleton (G-7500)

Lisa Thomas ....G....... 724 748-3600
Mercer (G-10967)

Lzk Manufacturing Inc ....G....... 717 891-5792
Shrewsbury (G-17585)

◆ McConway & Torley LLC ....E....... 412 622-0494
Pittsburgh (G-15269)

McConway & Torley LLC ....F....... 610 683-7351
Kutztown (G-8849)

▲ Montrose Machine Works Inc ....F....... 570 278-7655
Montrose (G-11471)

Raser Industries Inc............................F....... 610 320-5130
Reading (G-16484)

Regal Cast Inc ....F....... 717 270-1888
Lebanon (G-9625)

Rochester Alloy Casting Co..................E....... 724 452-5659
Zelienople (G-20819)

Tiger Brand Jack Post Co ....E....... 814 333-4302
Meadville (G-10801)

Trinity Industries ....G....... 724 588-7000
Greenville (G-6774)

◆ Union Electric Steel Corp ....D....... 412 429-7655
Carnegie (G-2800)

Union Electric Steel Corp ....D....... 724 947-9595
Burgettstown (G-2358)

United States Steel Corp ....A....... 412 433-1121
Pittsburgh (G-15676)

Universal STAinless& Alloy ....D....... 814 827-9723
Titusville (G-18402)

Victaulic Company of America ....G....... 610 614-1261
Nazareth (G-11993)

Wescott Steel Inc ....E....... 215 364-3636
Langhorne (G-9335)

Whemco - Steel Castings Inc................F....... 724 643-7001
Midland (G-11089)

▼ Whemco - Steel Castings Inc............D....... 412 390-2700
Pittsburgh (G-15714)

▼ Whemco Inc....................................E....... 412 390-2700
Pittsburgh (G-15715)

Whemco-Steel Castings Inc.................G....... 724 643-7001
Homestead (G-7698)

3331 Primary Smelting & Refining Of Copper

▲ All-Clad Metalcrafters LLC ....D....... 724 745-8300
Canonsburg (G-2537)

▲ Birdsboro Extrusions LLC ....G....... 610 582-0400
Birdsboro (G-1689)

▲ Edward C Rinck Associates Inc..........G....... 610 397-1727
Lafayette Hill (G-8879)

▲ Electric Materials Company ....C....... 814 725-9621
North East (G-12739)

Eric Herr ....G....... 717 464-1829
Lancaster (G-9011)

▲ Heyco Metals Inc.............................D....... 610 926-4131
Reading (G-16402)

WMS Metals - Welding Alloys ....G....... 412 231-3811
Pittsburgh (G-15722)

3334 Primary Production Of Aluminum

Alcoa USA Corp ....G....... 212 518-5400
Pittsburgh (G-14666)

Alcoa USA Corp ....G....... 412 553-4545
Pittsburgh (G-14667)

Alumax LLC ....C....... 412 553-4545
Pittsburgh (G-14695)

Alumisource Corporation ....F....... 412 250-0360
Monessen (G-11296)

Arconic Mexico Holdings LLC ....A....... 412 553-4545
Pittsburgh (G-14719)

Custom Manufacturing Corp ....E....... 215 638-3888
Bensalem (G-1178)

Hollowell Aluminum ....G....... 717 597-0826
Waynesboro (G-19411)

▼ Old Ladder Co ....A....... 888 523-3371
Greenville (G-6762)

3339 Primary Nonferrous Metals, NEC

A Plus Precious Metals ....G....... 215 821-3751
Philadelphia (G-13328)

Ae Polysilicon Corporation ....E....... 215 337-8183
Fairless Hills (G-5771)

Allegheny Technologies Inc..................D....... 412 394-2800
Pittsburgh (G-14682)

Alpha Assembly Solutions Inc ....C....... 814 946-1611
Altoona (G-470)

◆ American Zinc Recycling Corp ....E....... 724 774-1020
Pittsburgh (G-14708)

American Zinc Recycling LLC ....E....... 724 773-2203
Pittsburgh (G-14709)

◆ AMG Aluminum North America LLC .F....... 610 293-2501
Wayne (G-19297)

ATI Powder Metals LLC ....D....... 412 394-2800
Pittsburgh (G-14732)

Crown Precious Metals ....G....... 267 923-5263
Pennsburg (G-13247)

Dallice Precious Metals ....G....... 570 501-0850
Hazleton (G-7496)

Geneva Roth International LLC ....G....... 724 887-8771
Scottdale (G-17192)

Global Advanced Metals USA Inc ....D....... 610 367-2181
Boyertown (G-1912)

Gold Bug Exchange...............................G....... 724 770-9008
Beaver (G-982)

Hammond Group Inc ....E....... 610 327-1400
Pottstown (G-15995)

◆ Heraeus Incorporated ....G....... 215 944-9981
Yardley (G-20314)

Heraeus Incorporated ....B....... 480 961-9200
Yardley (G-20315)

Heraeus Kulzer LLC ....G....... 215 944-9968
Langhorne (G-9302)

Hipps Sons Coins Precious Mtls............G....... 215 550-6854
Newtown (G-12511)

Horsehead Corporation ....E....... 610 826-2111
Palmerton (G-13107)

◆ KB Alloys Holdings LLC ....F....... 484 582-3520
Wayne (G-19345)

Luxfer Magtech Inc ....E....... 570 668-0001
Tamaqua (G-18219)

Materion Brush Inc ....C....... 610 562-2211
Shoemakersville (G-17572)

◆ Matthey Johnson Holdings Inc ....E....... 610 971-3000
Wayne (G-19350)

◆ Matthey Johnson Inc........................E....... 610 971-3000
Wayne (G-19351)

Matthey Johnson Inc ....C 484 320-2223
Audubon (G-830)

Matthey Johnson Inc ....C 610 341-8300
Wayne (G-19353)

Matthey Johnson Inc ....C 610 648-8000
West Chester (G-19598)

▼ New Way Machine Components Inc .E 610 494-6700
Aston (G-781)

▲ Oregon Metallurgical LLC ....F 541 967-9000
Pittsburgh (G-15363)

Patriot Metal Products Inc ....E 570 759-3634
Berwick (G-1339)

▲ Pyropure Inc ....E 610 497-1743
Aston (G-789)

▲ R I Lampus Company ....C 412 362-3800
Springdale (G-17900)

◆ Reichdrill LLC ....D 814 342-5500
Philipsburg (G-14525)

RSI Silicon Products LLC ....E 610 258-3100
Easton (G-4749)

T M P Refining Corporation ....G 484 318-8285
Malvern (G-10326)

◆ Tdy Industries LLC ....D 412 394-2896
Pittsburgh (G-15600)

◆ Thermoclad Company ....F 814 456-1243
Erie (G-5507)

TI Oregon Inc ....G 412 394-2800
Pittsburgh (G-15624)

▼ Tin Technology and Ref LLC ....G 610 430-2225
West Chester (G-19663)

Titanium Metals Corporation ....E 702 564-2544
Morgantown (G-11539)

3341 Secondary Smelting & Refining Of Non-ferrous Metals

A Allan Industries Inc ....E 570 826-0123
Wilkes Barre (G-19902)

A J Blosenski Inc ....D 610 942-2707
Honey Brook (G-7734)

Allegheny Iron & Metal Co ....E 215 743-7759
Philadelphia (G-13366)

Alpha Assembly Solutions Inc ....C 814 946-1611
Altoona (G-470)

◆ AMG Resources Corporation ....E 412 777-7300
Pittsburgh (G-14710)

Bolton Metal Products Co Inc ....G 814 355-6217
Bellefonte (G-1094)

Brandywine Valley Fabricators ....F 610 384-7440
Coatesville (G-3295)

Charles Casturo ....G 412 672-1407
McKeesport (G-10662)

Coatesville Scrap Ir Met Inc ....E 610 384-9230
Coatesville (G-3299)

◆ Colonial Metals Co ....E 717 684-2311
Columbia (G-3434)

Consoldted Scrap Resources Inc ....F 717 843-0931
York (G-20434)

Consoldted Scrap Resources Inc ....G 717 843-0931
York (G-20436)

Culpepper Corporation ....E 215 425-6532
Philadelphia (G-13590)

DMC Global Inc ....E 724 277-9710
Mount Braddock (G-11616)

E Schneider & Sons Inc ....E 610 435-3527
Allentown (G-199)

▲ Electric Materials Company ....C 814 725-9621
North East (G-12739)

Grant Mfg & Alloying Inc ....G 610 404-1380
Birdsboro (G-1697)

Greenstar Allentown LLC ....E 610 262-6988
Northampton (G-12851)

Harsco Minerals PA LLC ....G 724 352-0066
Sarver (G-17071)

Heraeus Incorporated ....B 480 961-9200
Yardley (G-20315)

▲ Heyco Metals Inc ....D 610 926-4131
Reading (G-16402)

International Mill Service ....A 215 956-5500
Horsham (G-7824)

▲ Interntnal Mtal Rclaiming Corp ....C 724 758-5515
Ellwood City (G-4939)

J W Zaprazny Inc ....D 570 943-2860
New Ringgold (G-12440)

◆ Kalumetals Inc ....F 724 694-2800
Derry (G-4104)

Keywell Metals LLC ....F 412 462-5555
West Mifflin (G-19742)

Kovalchick Corporation ....E 724 349-3300
Indiana (G-8110)

▲ Lee Metals Inc ....G 412 331-8630
Coraopolis (G-3701)

◆ Matthey Johnson Holdings Inc ....E 610 971-3000
Wayne (G-19350)

◆ Matthey Johnson Inc ....E 610 971-3000
Wayne (G-19351)

Matthey Johnson Inc ....C 610 648-8000
West Chester (G-19598)

Matthey Johnson Inc ....C 484 320-2223
Audubon (G-830)

Matthey Johnson Inc ....F 610 292-4300
Conshohocken (G-3574)

Matthey Johnson Inc ....E 610 873-3200
Downingtown (G-4240)

Matthey Johnson Inc ....C 610 341-8300
Wayne (G-19353)

◆ Metallurgical Products Company ....E 610 696-6770
West Chester (G-19601)

◆ Mill Services Corp ....F 412 678-6141
Glassport (G-6413)

Nak International Corp ....E 724 774-9200
Monaca (G-11292)

New Frontier Industries Inc ....G 814 337-4234
Meadville (G-10768)

Penn Recycling Inc ....E 570 326-9041
Williamsport (G-20054)

Phoenix Metals of Pa Inc ....F 724 282-0679
Butler (G-2433)

Pittsburgh Flatroll Company ....G 412 237-2260
Pittsburgh (G-15397)

Profiners Inc ....G 215 997-1060
Hatfield (G-7387)

◆ Reading Alloys Inc ....C 610 693-5822
Robesonia (G-16777)

Slates Salvage ....G 814 448-3218
Three Springs (G-18356)

▲ Specilty Mtallurgical Pdts Inc ....F 717 246-0385
Red Lion (G-16614)

◆ SPS Technologies LLC ....A 215 572-3000
Jenkintown (G-8302)

Staiman Recycling Corporation ....D 717 646-0951
Williamsport (G-20074)

▲ Telex Metals LLC ....E 215 781-6335
Croydon (G-3931)

Titanium Metals Corporation ....E 702 564-2544
Morgantown (G-11539)

Tms International LLC ....E 412 885-3600
Pittsburgh (G-15629)

Tms International LLC ....D 215 956-5500
Horsham (G-7859)

Tms International Corp ....E 215 956-5500
Horsham (G-7860)

United Metal Traders Inc ....E 215 288-6555
Philadelphia (G-14421)

US Bronze Foundry & Mch Inc ....D 814 337-4234
Meadville (G-10810)

3351 Rolling, Drawing & Extruding Of Copper

American Alloy Fabricators ....G 610 635-0205
Norristown (G-12633)

▲ Ampco-Pittsburgh Corporation ....D 412 456-4400
Carnegie (G-2763)

C F Moores Co Inc ....F 215 248-1250
Philadelphia (G-13490)

Cambridge-Lee Holdings Inc ....F 610 926-4141
Reading (G-16340)

◆ Cambridge-Lee Industries LLC ....C 610 926-4141
Reading (G-16341)

Cerro Fabricated Products LLC ....G 724 451-8202
Brave (G-2002)

▲ Eagle Metals Inc ....E 610 926-4111
Leesport (G-9661)

▲ Electric Materials Company ....C 814 725-9621
North East (G-12739)

Garretts Fabricating ....G 724 528-8193
West Middlesex (G-19725)

General Cable Corporation ....C 570 321-7750
Williamsport (G-20017)

Gesco Inc ....F 724 846-8700
Beaver Falls (G-999)

▲ Hcl Liquidation Ltd ....A 724 251-4200
Leetsdale (G-9693)

▲ Heyco Metals Inc ....D 610 926-4131
Reading (G-16402)

Iusa Wire Inc ....G 610 926-4141
Reading (G-16410)

▲ Libertas Copper LLC ....A 724 251-4200
Leetsdale (G-9697)

Philadelphia Pipe Bending Co ....E 215 225-8955
Philadelphia (G-14149)

▼ Precision Tube Company Inc ....C 215 699-5801
North Wales (G-12826)

Ptubes Inc ....F 201 560-7127
Honesdale (G-7721)

Southwire Company LLC ....F 717 266-2004
York (G-20674)

3353 Aluminum Sheet, Plate & Foil

Alcoa N Amercn Rolled Proudcts ....G 717 393-9641
Lancaster (G-8926)

Alcoa USA Corp ....G 212 518-5400
Pittsburgh (G-14666)

Alumax LLC ....E 570 784-7481
Bloomsburg (G-1768)

Alumax LLC ....C 412 553-4545
Pittsburgh (G-14695)

◆ Alumax Mill Products Inc ....E 717 393-9641
Lancaster (G-8930)

▲ Ampco-Pittsburgh Corporation ....D 412 456-4400
Carnegie (G-2763)

Arconic Inc ....C 717 393-9641
Lancaster (G-8938)

Arconic Inc ....C 412 553-4545
Pittsburgh (G-14718)

Arconic Inc ....E 724 337-5300
New Kensington (G-12324)

Evapco Alcoil Inc ....E 717 347-7500
York (G-20472)

JW Aluminum Company ....C 570 323-4430
Williamsport (G-20030)

Modern Specialties Inc ....G 814 643-0410
Huntingdon (G-7952)

Mueller Industries Inc ....D 215 699-5801
North Wales (G-12820)

▼ Precision Tube Company Inc ....C 215 699-5801
North Wales (G-12826)

Swampy Hollow Mfg LLC ....F 610 273-0157
Honey Brook (G-7765)

3354 Aluminum Extruded Prdts

▲ Accuride Erie LP ....B 814 480-6400
Erie (G-5170)

▲ All-Clad Metalcrafters LLC ....D 724 745-8300
Canonsburg (G-2537)

▲ Alloy America LLC ....F 412 828-8270
Cheswick (G-3100)

Alumax LLC ....C 412 553-4545
Pittsburgh (G-14695)

Aluminum & Carbon Plus Inc ....G 724 368-9200
Portersville (G-15924)

◆ AMG Aluminum North America LLC .F 610 293-2501
Wayne (G-19297)

▲ Associated Ceramics & Tech ....D 724 353-1585
Sarver (G-17065)

Ballews Aluminum Products Inc ....F 717 492-8956
Manheim (G-10369)

Bristol Aluminum Co ....E 215 946-1566
Levittown (G-9820)

Construction Specialties Inc ....B 570 546-2255
Muncy (G-11813)

▲ Craft-Bilt Manufacturing Co ....D 215 721-7700
Souderton (G-17731)

Hopewell Manufacturing Inc ....G 717 593-9400
Waynesboro (G-19412)

Hydro Extruder LLC ....C 570 474-5935
Mountain Top (G-11764)

▲ Hydro Extruder LLC ....C 412 299-7600
Moon Township (G-11492)

Hydro Extruder LLC ....C 570 474-5935
Mountain Top (G-11765)

Hydro Extrusion Usa LLC ....C 877 966-7272
Moon Township (G-11493)

Hydro Extrusion Usa LLC ....G 318 878-9703
Cressona (G-3904)

Hygrade Acquisition Corp ....D 610 866-2441
Bethlehem (G-1536)

▲ Hygrade Mtal Moulding Mfg Corp ......E 610 866-2441
Bethlehem (G-1538)

Ilsco Extrusions Inc ....E 724 589-5888
Greenville (G-6748)

◆ KB Alloys Holdings LLC ....F 484 582-3520
Wayne (G-19345)

Matthews International Corp ....B 412 571-5500
Pittsburgh (G-15266)

MI Metals Inc ....F 717 692-4851
Millersburg (G-11196)

Mountain Ridge Metals LLC ....C 717 692-4851
Millersburg (G-11197)

▲ Paletti Usa LLC ....E 267 289-0020
Montgomeryville (G-11410)

S I C

Railway Specialties Corp ....E 215 788-9242
Croydon (G-3926)

Ralph McClure ....G... 610 738-1440
Reynoldsville (G-16662)

▼ Reitnouer Inc ....E 610 929-4856
Birdsboro (G-1704)

▲ Rockwood Manufacturing Company C 814 926-2026
Rockwood (G-16792)

Sapa Extrusions Inc ....G... 870 235-2609
Bensalem (G-1251)

▲ Sapa North America Inc ....B 877 922-7272
Cressona (G-3907)

Sapa Precision Tubing LLC ....F 412 893-1300
Moon Township (G-11499)

▲ Specilty Mtallurgical Pdts Inc ....F 717 246-0385
Red Lion (G-16614)

▼ Traco Delaware Inc ....F 724 776-7000
Cranberry Township (G-3856)

Tredegar Corporation ....C 570 544-7600
Pottsville (G-16100)

▲ Tri City Aluminum Company ....A 724 799-8917
Cranberry Township (G-3857)

▲ Tyk America Inc ....E 412 384-4259
Clairton (G-3158)

Victor Sun Ctrl of Phladelphia ....E 215 743-0800
Philadelphia (G-14446)

3355 Aluminum Rolling & Drawing, NEC

Alcoa Business Park LLC ....G... 412 553-4545
Pittsburgh (G-14660)

Alcoa Corporation ....G... 412 553-4001
Pittsburgh (G-14661)

Alcoa Corporation ....E 412 315-2900
Pittsburgh (G-14662)

Alcoa Remediation MGT LLC ....G... 412 553-4545
Pittsburgh (G-14663)

Alcoa South Carolina Inc ....G... 412 553-4545
Pittsburgh (G-14664)

Alcoa Technical Center LLC ....G... 724 337-5300
New Kensington (G-12322)

Alcoa Technical Center LLC ....G... 412 553-4545
Pittsburgh (G-14665)

Alcoa Warrick LLC ....F 412 553-4545
Pittsburgh (G-14668)

▲ Alcoa Wenatchee LLC ....G... 412 553-4545
Pittsburgh (G-14669)

Aluminum Company of America ....G... 412 553-4545
Pittsburgh (G-14696)

◆ AMG Aluminum North America LLC .F 610 293-2501
Wayne (G-19297)

Badin Business Park LLC ....G... 412 553-4545
Pittsburgh (G-14748)

C F Moores Co Inc ....F 215 248-1250
Philadelphia (G-13490)

General Cable Corporation ....C 570 321-7750
Williamsport (G-20017)

H & M Diversified Entps Inc ....E 717 277-0680
Lebanon (G-9577)

H & M Diversified Entps Inc ....G... 717 531-3490
Hershey (G-7611)

Hampton Concrete Products Inc ....F 724 443-7205
Valencia (G-18698)

◆ Inweld Corporation ....F 610 261-1900
Coplay (G-3644)

Kane Innovations Inc ....D 814 838-7731
Kane (G-8469)

◆ KB Alloys Holdings LLC ....F 484 582-3520
Wayne (G-19345)

New Werner Holding Co Inc ....G... 724 588-2000
Greenville (G-6758)

Panel Technologies Inc ....G... 215 538-7055
Quakertown (G-16226)

Prime Metals Acquisition LLC ....D 724 479-4155
Homer City (G-7680)

Southwire Company LLC ....F 717 266-2004
York (G-20674)

St Croix Alumina LLC ....G... 412 553-4545
Pittsburgh (G-15573)

Torpedo Specialty Wire Inc ....E 814 563-7505
Pittsfield (G-15739)

Trulite GL Alum Solutions LLC ....F 724 274-9050
Cheswick (G-3120)

Valley Precision TI & Tech Inc ....E 717 647-7550
Tower City (G-18443)

◆ Werner Co ....C 724 588-2000
Greenville (G-6775)

Werner Holding Co Inc ....A 888 523-3371
Greenville (G-6776)

3356 Rolling, Drawing-Extruding Of Nonferrous Metals

Alpha Assembly Solutions Inc ....C 814 946-1611
Altoona (G-470)

ATI Powder Metals LLC ....D 412 394-2800
Pittsburgh (G-14732)

Atomic Industries Inc ....F 610 754-6400
Frederick (G-6171)

Basically Nickel ....G... 717 292-7232
East Berlin (G-4519)

Double Nickel Delivery LLC ....G... 412 721-0550
Irwin (G-8157)

▲ Eagle Metals Inc ....E 610 926-4111
Leesport (G-9661)

ESAB Group Inc ....C 843 673-7700
Hanover (G-6885)

G O Carlson Inc ....E 814 678-4100
Oil City (G-12945)

G O Carlson Inc ....D 610 384-2800
Downingtown (G-4228)

G O Carlson Inc ....E 814 678-4168
Titusville (G-18378)

Hammond Group Inc ....E 610 327-1400
Pottstown (G-15995)

Hygrade Acquisition Corp ....D 610 866-2441
Bethlehem (G-1536)

▲ Hygrade Mtal Moulding Mfg Corp .....E 610 866-2441
Bethlehem (G-1538)

◆ Inweld Corporation ....F 610 261-1900
Coplay (G-3644)

Kapp Alloy & Wire Inc ....F 814 676-0613
Oil City (G-12948)

▲ Leech Inc ....D 814 724-5454
Meadville (G-10749)

◆ Matthey Johnson Holdings Inc ....E 610 971-3000
Wayne (G-19350)

◆ Matthey Johnson Inc ....E 610 971-3000
Wayne (G-19351)

Matthey Johnson Inc ....C 610 341-8300
Wayne (G-19353)

Milner Enterprises Inc ....F 610 252-0700
Easton (G-4722)

Nak International Corp ....E 724 774-9200
Monaca (G-11292)

Nexarc Inc ....G... 570 458-6990
Bloomsburg (G-1791)

Nichols4nickels ....G... 215 317-6717
Philadelphia (G-14073)

▲ Nlmk Pennsylvania LLC ....B 724 983-6464
Farrell (G-5869)

▲ Oregon Metallurgical LLC ....F 541 967-9000
Pittsburgh (G-15363)

▲ Perryman Company ....C 724 743-4239
Houston (G-7876)

Perryman Company ....F 724 746-9390
Coal Center (G-3276)

Rin Tin Tim Inc ....G... 412 403-5378
Pittsburgh (G-15486)

▲ Robinson Technical Pdts Corp ....E 610 261-1900
Coplay (G-3647)

◆ Salem Tube Inc ....C 724 646-4301
Greenville (G-6772)

Selectrode Industries Inc ....E 724 378-6351
Aliquippa (G-93)

▲ Sintermet LLC ....D 724 548-7631
Kittanning (G-8792)

▲ Susini Specialty Steels Inc ....F 724 295-6511
Natrona Heights (G-11949)

◆ Tdy Industries LLC ....D 412 394-2896
Pittsburgh (G-15600)

Techspec Inc ....E 724 694-2716
Derry (G-4108)

Tel Tin ....G... 717 259-9004
Abbottstown (G-8)

Tin Cup Inc ....G... 570 322-1115
Williamsport (G-20083)

Tin Lizzy Inc ....G... 724 836-0281
Greensburg (G-6718)

Tin Man Sweets ....G... 724 432-3930
Zelienople (G-20824)

Tin Roof Enterprises LLC ....G... 610 659-3989
Media (G-10954)

Tin Tinker ....G... 215 230-9619
Doylestown (G-4342)

Titanium 40 LLC ....G... 610 338-0446
Swarthmore (G-18186)

Titanium Brkg Solutions LLC ....G... 267 506-6642
Philadelphia (G-14391)

Titanium Foundation ....G... 717 668-8423
New Freedom (G-12217)

Titanium Wealth Advisors LLC ....G... 610 429-1700
West Chester (G-19664)

Torpedo Specialty Wire Inc ....E 814 563-7505
Pittsfield (G-15739)

United States Steel Corp ....C 215 736-4600
Fairless Hills (G-5806)

United States Steel Corp ....C 412 433-7215
Homestead (G-7695)

◆ United States Steel Corp ....B 412 433-1121
Pittsburgh (G-15677)

◆ Uniti Titanium LLC ....E 412 424-0440
Pittsburgh (G-15680)

US Steel Holdings Inc ....G... 412 433-1121
Pittsburgh (G-15687)

▲ Vargo Outdoors Incorporated ....G... 570 437-0990
Lewisburg (G-9923)

Vsmpo-Tirus US LLC ....G... 724 251-9400
Leetsdale (G-9706)

Watson Metal Products Corp ....D 908 276-2202
Lancaster (G-9236)

Wooden Nickels LLC ....G... 484 408-4901
Pottstown (G-15958)

3357 Nonferrous Wire Drawing

Alpha Assembly Solutions Inc ....C 814 946-1611
Altoona (G-470)

▲ American Data Link Inc ....G... 724 503-4290
Washington (G-19146)

Belden Inc ....D 724 228-7373
Washington (G-19152)

Belden Inc ....C 724 222-7060
Washington (G-19153)

▼ Berk-Tek LLC ....G... 717 354-6200
New Holland (G-12230)

Bower Wire Cloth TI & Die Inc ....G... 570 398-4488
Jersey Shore (G-8310)

Brop Tech LLC ....F 323 229-7390
Upper Darby (G-18683)

Cable Associates Inc ....E 570 876-4565
Archbald (G-686)

Coleman Cable LLC ....E 717 845-5100
York (G-20428)

▲ Direct Wire & Cable Inc ....D 717 336-2842
Denver (G-4070)

▲ Diversified Traffic Pdts Inc ....C 717 428-0222
Seven Valleys (G-17377)

Fiber Optic Marketplace LLC ....F 610 973-6000
Breinigsville (G-2015)

▲ Fiberopticscom Inc ....E 610 973-6000
Breinigsville (G-2016)

Fortmex Corporation ....G... 215 990-9688
Merion Station (G-10997)

General Cable Corporation ....C 570 321-7750
Williamsport (G-20017)

General Cable Industries Inc ....C 814 944-5002
Altoona (G-510)

Genergy Power LLC ....G... 717 584-0375
Lancaster (G-9027)

▲ Industrial Enterprises Inc ....D 215 355-7080
Southampton (G-17819)

Industrial Harness Company Inc ....D 717 477-0100
Shippensburg (G-17532)

▲ Kalas Mfg Inc ....D 717 336-5575
Lancaster (G-9078)

Kalas Mfg Inc ....D 717 335-0193
Denver (G-4079)

▲ Lancer Systems LP ....E 610 973-2600
Quakertown (G-16208)

Marine Tech Wire and Cable Inc ....E 717 854-1992
York (G-20581)

▲ Markel Corp ....C 610 272-8960
Plymouth Meeting (G-15855)

Micro-Coax Inc ....C 610 495-4438
Pottstown (G-16019)

Mueller Industries Inc ....D 215 699-5801
North Wales (G-12820)

Naval Company Inc ....G... 215 348-8982
Doylestown (G-4318)

▲ Nexans Aerospace USA LLC ....C 252 236-4311
New Holland (G-12270)

Nexans USA Inc ....B 717 354-6200
New Holland (G-12271)

▲ Optium Corporation ....D 215 675-3105
Horsham (G-7838)

Ospcom LLC ....G... 267 356-7124
Doylestown (G-4321)

Point 2 Point Wireless Inc ....G... 347 543-5227
Macungie (G-10156)

Professional Electronic Compon ....G... 215 245-1550
Philadelphia (G-14205)

Prysmian Cbles Systems USA LLC......D 570 385-4381
Schuylkill Haven *(G-17164)*

Ruckus Wireless Inc ....E 814 231-3710
State College *(G-18018)*

▲ Superior Group Inc ....E 610 397-2040
Conshohocken *(G-3610)*

Torpedo Specialty Wire Inc ....F 814 563-7505
Pittsfield *(G-15739)*

Trojan Inc ....E 814 336-4468
Meadville *(G-10804)*

Tru Temp Sensors Inc ....G 215 396-1550
Southampton *(G-17844)*

US Custom Wiring LLC ....G 856 905-0250
Philadelphia *(G-14435)*

W L Gore & Associates Inc ....A 610 268-1864
Landenberg *(G-9255)*

3363 Aluminum Die Castings

▲ Accuride Erie LP ....B 814 480-6400
Erie *(G-5170)*

Alcast Metals Inc ....E 215 368-5865
Montgomeryville *(G-11382)*

Alcoa Corporation............................G 412 553-4001
Pittsburgh *(G-14661)*

Alcoa Corporation............................E 412 315-2900
Pittsburgh *(G-14662)*

▲ Bardane Mfg Co ....D 570 876-4844
Jermyn *(G-8305)*

C Palmer Manufacturing Inc ....F 724 872-8200
West Newton *(G-19748)*

E A Quirin Machine Shop Inc ....E 570 429-0590
Saint Clair *(G-16937)*

Howmet Castings & Services Inc ....F 973 361-2310
Pittsburgh *(G-15102)*

J Clem Kline & Son Inc ....G 610 258-6071
Easton *(G-4708)*

K Castings Inc ....G 724 539-9753
Latrobe *(G-9485)*

Pace Industries LLC ....B 724 539-4527
Loyalhanna *(G-10112)*

▲ Parker White Metal Company ....A 814 474-5511
Fairview *(G-5835)*

Phb Inc ....A 814 474-5511
Fairview *(G-5837)*

Phb Inc ....D 814 474-2683
Fairview *(G-5838)*

▲ Scicast International Inc ....E 610 369-3060
Bechtelsville *(G-1036)*

Sensus USA Inc ....C 800 375-8875
Du Bois *(G-4419)*

Sensus USA Inc ....C 724 430-3956
Pittsburgh *(G-15524)*

T Helbling LLC.................................G 724 601-9819
Beaver *(G-992)*

Tilden Manufacturing Inc ....G 610 562-4682
Hamburg *(G-6852)*

West Phila Bronze Co Inc ....E 610 874-1454
Chester *(G-3067)*

3364 Nonferrous Die Castings, Exc Aluminum

▲ Bardane Mfg Co ....D 570 876-4844
Jermyn *(G-8305)*

▲ Franklin Bronze Precision Comp .....D 814 437-6891
Franklin *(G-6127)*

J Clem Kline & Son Inc...................G 610 258-6071
Easton *(G-4708)*

K Castings Inc ....G 724 539-9753
Latrobe *(G-9485)*

◆ La France Corp ....C 610 361-4300
Concordville *(G-3457)*

◆ Metallurgical Products Company .....E 610 696-6770
West Chester *(G-19601)*

▲ Parker White Metal Company ....A 814 474-5511
Fairview *(G-5835)*

Phb Inc ....A 814 474-5511
Fairview *(G-5837)*

▲ Scicast International Inc ....E 610 369-3060
Bechtelsville *(G-1036)*

West Phila Bronze Co Inc................E 610 874-1454
Chester *(G-3067)*

3365 Aluminum Foundries

Active Brass Foundry Inc.................F 215 257-6519
Telford *(G-18266)*

Advanced Metals Group LLC............F 610 408-8006
Malvern *(G-10180)*

Ajax Xray Inc ....E 570 888-6605
Sayre *(G-17109)*

Altman Manufacturing Inc..............F 814 756-5254
Albion *(G-40)*

◆ AMG Aluminum North America LLC .F 610 293-2501
Wayne *(G-19297)*

Aqua Enterprises ....F 215 257-2231
Perkasie *(G-13266)*

Ashland Foundry & Mch Work LLC......C 570 875-6100
Ashland *(G-727)*

▲ Boose Aluminum Foundry Co Inc ......C 717 336-5581
Reamstown *(G-16574)*

Bridesburg Foundry Company ....D 610 266-0900
Whitehall *(G-19863)*

Buck Company Inc..........................G 717 284-4114
Quarryville *(G-16266)*

Buckeye Aluminum Foundry Inc ....E 814 683-4011
Linesville *(G-9978)*

▲ Carroll Manufacturing Co LLC.........G 724 266-0400
Leetsdale *(G-9688)*

Carson Industries Inc ....G 724 295-5147
Kittanning *(G-8760)*

◆ Carson Industries Inc....................E 724 295-5147
Freeport *(G-6201)*

Cast-Rite Metal Company ....E 610 582-1300
Birdsboro *(G-1691)*

▲ Cera-Met LLC ....C 610 266-0270
Bethlehem *(G-1481)*

◆ Erie Bronze & Aluminum Company ..E 814 838-8602
Erie *(G-5263)*

◆ Gupta Permold Corporation ....C 412 793-3511
Pittsburgh *(G-15067)*

H & H Castings Inc ....D 717 751-0064
York *(G-20518)*

Hopewell Non-Ferrous Foundry ....G 610 385-6747
Douglassville *(G-4178)*

Jacob Pattern Works Inc ....E 610 326-1100
Pottstown *(G-16004)*

K & S Castings Inc ....E 717 272-9775
Lebanon *(G-9585)*

◆ KB Alloys Holdings LLC ....F 484 582-3520
Wayne *(G-19345)*

Kebeico Inc ....E 610 241-8163
Chadds Ford *(G-2852)*

▲ Laminators Incorporated................D 215 723-5285
Hatfield *(G-7362)*

Latrobe Foundry Mch & Sup Co ....F 724 537-3341
Latrobe *(G-9489)*

Lenape Tooling Inc ....E 215 257-0431
Perkasie *(G-13283)*

Lincoln Foundry Inc ....E 814 833-1514
Erie *(G-5366)*

New Hegedus Aluminum Co Inc ....E 814 676-5635
Oil City *(G-12953)*

New Jersey Shell Casting Corp ....E 717 426-1835
Marietta *(G-10465)*

Paul W Zimmerman Foundries Co ......F 717 285-5253
Columbia *(G-3446)*

Pennex Aluminum Company LLC ......E 724 373-8471
Greenville *(G-6764)*

Perfect Stride Ltd............................G 412 221-1722
Pittsburgh *(G-15378)*

▲ Performance Metals Inc................D 610 369-3060
Bechtelsville *(G-1034)*

Poormans Wldg Fabrication Inc ....F 814 349-5893
Aaronsburg *(G-1)*

Q Aluminum LLC..............................F 570 966-2800
New Berlin *(G-12021)*

Quality Aluminum Casting Co ....F 717 484-4545
Denver *(G-4090)*

Royer Quality Castings Inc ....G 610 367-1390
Boyertown *(G-1927)*

Schmitt Aluminum Foundry Inc..........F 717 299-5651
Smoketown *(G-17668)*

Smoyer L M Brass Products Inc ....G 610 867-5011
Bethlehem *(G-1620)*

▲ Trega Corporation.........................F 610 562-5558
Hamburg *(G-6854)*

United Bronze of Pittsburgh ....G 724 226-8500
Tarentum *(G-18252)*

▼ Viking Tool & Gage Inc..................G 814 382-8691
Conneaut Lake *(G-3482)*

WER Corporation ....C 610 678-8023
Reading *(G-16564)*

Williamsport Foundry Co Inc ....E 570 323-6216
Williamsport *(G-20093)*

3366 Copper Foundries

▲ A Cubed Corporation.....................C 724 538-4000
Mars *(G-10485)*

Active Brass Foundry Inc..................F 215 257-6519
Telford *(G-18266)*

Arrow Castings Co...........................F 814 838-3561
Erie *(G-5194)*

ART Research Enterprises ....E 717 290-1303
Lancaster *(G-8944)*

▲ Bowser Manufacturing Co ....F 570 368-5045
Montoursville *(G-11434)*

Bridesburg Foundry Company ....D 610 266-0900
Whitehall *(G-19863)*

Buck Company Inc...........................G 717 284-4114
Quarryville *(G-16266)*

Carbide Metals Inc ....F 724 459-6355
Blairsville *(G-1718)*

Century Propeller Corporation ....F 814 677-7100
Franklin *(G-6119)*

Clearfield Energy Inc ....G 610 293-0410
Conshohocken *(G-3529)*

▲ Concast Metal Products Company ....C 724 538-4000
Mars *(G-10492)*

Considine Studios Inc......................G 215 362-8922
Lansdale *(G-9353)*

◆ Erie Bronze & Aluminum Company ..E 814 838-8602
Erie *(G-5263)*

Eureka Electrical Products ....E 814 725-9638
North East *(G-12742)*

Fenner Inc ....C 717 665-2421
Manheim *(G-10380)*

Flury Foundry Company ....F 717 397-9080
Lancaster *(G-9023)*

Franklin Bronze & Alloy Co Inc ....F 814 437-6891
Franklin *(G-6126)*

▲ Franklin Bronze Precision Comp .....D 814 437-6891
Franklin *(G-6127)*

◆ GKN Sinter Metals - Dubois Inc ......D 814 375-0938
Du Bois *(G-4393)*

Goldsborough & Vansant Inc............G 724 782-0393
Finleyville *(G-5959)*

▲ Heyco Metals Inc.........................D 610 926-4131
Reading *(G-16402)*

Hines Flask Div Bckeye Alnimum ....E 814 683-4420
Linesville *(G-9983)*

Laran Bronze Inc.............................G 610 874-4414
Chester *(G-3055)*

▲ Libertas Copper LLC ....A 724 251-4200
Leetsdale *(G-9697)*

Lincoln Foundry Inc ....E 814 833-1514
Erie *(G-5366)*

◆ Matthews International Corp ....E 412 442-8200
Pittsburgh *(G-15264)*

Matthews International Corp.............B 412 571-5500
Pittsburgh *(G-15266)*

Matthews International Corp.............G 717 854-9566
York *(G-20584)*

Metaltech Inc ....E 814 375-9399
Du Bois *(G-4406)*

Miller J Walter Company Inc ....E 717 392-7428
Lancaster *(G-9136)*

New Jersey Shell Casting Corp ....E 717 426-1835
Marietta *(G-10465)*

Paul W Zimmerman Foundries Co ......F 717 285-5253
Columbia *(G-3446)*

▲ Perma Cast LLC ....E 724 325-1662
Export *(G-5620)*

Phoenix Bronze Resources LLC ....G 724 857-2225
Aliquippa *(G-88)*

▲ Piad Precision Casting Corp...........C 724 838-5500
Greensburg *(G-6700)*

Precision Bushing Inc ....F 717 264-6461
Chambersburg *(G-2970)*

Proform Powdered Metals Inc ....E 814 938-7411
Punxsutawney *(G-16154)*

Roser Technologies Inc....................D 814 589-7031
Titusville *(G-18394)*

Sensenich Propeller Company ....E 717 560-3711
Lititz *(G-10048)*

Smoyer L M Brass Products Inc........G 610 867-5011
Bethlehem *(G-1620)*

▲ St Marys Carbon Co Inc ....C 814 781-7333
Saint Marys *(G-17016)*

Superior Bronze Corporation ....F 814 452-3474
Erie *(G-5496)*

Temple Aluminum Foundry Inc..........E 610 926-2125
Blandon *(G-1761)*

United Brass Works Inc....................E 814 456-4296
Erie *(G-5524)*

United Bronze of Pittsburgh ....G 724 226-8500
Tarentum *(G-18252)*

United Foundry Company Inc ....E 814 539-8840
Johnstown *(G-8440)*

United States Dept of Navy ....C 215 897-3537
Philadelphia *(G-14423)*

S
I
C

Vallorbs Jewel Company ....C...... 717 392-3978
Bird In Hand *(G-1684)*

Williamsport Foundry Co Inc ....E...... 570 323-6216
Williamsport *(G-20093)*

3369 Nonferrous Foundries: Castings, NEC

A M Industries Inc ....G...... 215 362-2525
Lansdale *(G-9339)*

ATI Powder Metals LLC ....D...... 412 394-2800
Pittsburgh *(G-14732)*

B & B Foundry Inc ....E...... 215 333-7100
Philadelphia *(G-13435)*

Beaver Valley Alloy Foundry Co ....E...... 724 775-1987
Monaca *(G-11283)*

Complexx Gases Inc ....G...... 610 969-6661
East Stroudsburg *(G-4611)*

D & M Precision Mfg Inc ....G...... 724 727-3039
Apollo *(G-674)*

De Technologies Inc ....E...... 610 337-2800
King of Prussia *(G-8605)*

Donsco Inc ....C...... 717 653-1851
Mount Joy *(G-11653)*

Duraloy Technologies Inc ....C...... 724 887-5100
Scottdale *(G-17190)*

Elecast Inc ....F...... 570 587-5105
S Abingtn Twp *(G-16895)*

Eureka Electrical Products ....E...... 814 725-9638
North East *(G-12742)*

G O Carlson Inc ....D...... 610 384-2800
Downingtown *(G-4228)*

George J Anderton ....G...... 814 382-9201
Conneaut Lake *(G-3473)*

◆ Gupta Permold Corporation ....C...... 412 793-3511
Pittsburgh *(G-15067)*

Haas Group ....A...... 484 564-4500
West Chester *(G-19559)*

Hopewell Non-Ferrous Foundry ....G...... 610 385-6747
Douglassville *(G-4178)*

Hussey Marine Alloys Ltd ....E...... 724 251-4200
Leetsdale *(G-9694)*

K & S Castings Inc ....E...... 717 272-9775
Lebanon *(G-9585)*

◆ Latrobe Specialty Mtls Co LLC ......A...... 724 537-7711
Latrobe *(G-9494)*

▼ M & M Industries Inc ....E...... 610 447-0663
Chester *(G-3056)*

Master Replicas Group Inc ....G...... 610 652-2265
Zieglerville *(G-20833)*

◆ McC Holdings Company LLC ....D...... 724 745-0300
Mc Donald *(G-10576)*

Miller J Walter Company Inc ....E...... 717 392-7428
Lancaster *(G-9136)*

▲ Nova Precision Casting Corp ....E...... 570 366-2679
Auburn *(G-819)*

O-Z/Gedney Co Inc ....G...... 610 926-3645
Shoemakersville *(G-17573)*

▲ Oregon Metallurgical LLC ....F...... 541 967-9000
Pittsburgh *(G-15363)*

Phb Inc ....C...... 814 474-1552
Fairview *(G-5839)*

▲ Piad Precision Casting Corp ....C...... 724 838-5500
Greensburg *(G-6700)*

Precision Castparts Corp ....B...... 570 474-6371
Mountain Top *(G-11771)*

Prl Industries Inc ....E...... 717 273-6787
Cornwall *(G-3740)*

Regal Cast Inc ....F...... 717 270-1888
Lebanon *(G-9625)*

Royer Quality Castings Inc ....G...... 610 367-1390
Boyertown *(G-1927)*

Schmitt Aluminum Foundry Inc ....F...... 717 299-5651
Smoketown *(G-17668)*

Seybert Castings Inc ....F...... 215 364-7115
Huntingdon Valley *(G-8038)*

◆ Tdy Industries LLC ....D...... 412 394-2896
Pittsburgh *(G-15600)*

◆ Union City Non-Ferrous Inc ....E...... 937 968-5460
Washington *(G-19233)*

US Bronze Foundry & Mch Inc ....D...... 814 337-4234
Meadville *(G-10810)*

▼ Weatherly Casting and Mch Co ....D...... 570 427-8611
Weatherly *(G-19455)*

WER Corporation ....C...... 610 678-8023
Reading *(G-16564)*

▼ Whemco Inc ....E...... 412 390-2700
Pittsburgh *(G-15715)*

3398 Metal Heat Treating

Acme Heat Treating Co....................F...... 215 743-8500
Philadelphia *(G-13340)*

Aht Inc ....D...... 724 445-2155
Chicora *(G-3125)*

Bennett Heat Trting Brzing Inc ....F...... 215 674-8120
Warminster *(G-18836)*

Bluewater Thermal Services ....G...... 814 772-8474
Ridgway *(G-16697)*

Bodycote Thermal Proc Inc ....E...... 717 767-6757
Emigsville *(G-4985)*

▼ Bvht Inc ....G...... 724 728-4328
Monaca *(G-11286)*

Cooperheat Mqs Proj ....G...... 412 787-8690
Pittsburgh *(G-14874)*

DMC Global Inc ....E...... 724 277-9710
Mount Braddock *(G-11616)*

▲ Donsco Inc ....B...... 717 252-1561
Wrightsville *(G-20236)*

Elk County Heat Treaters Inc ....F...... 814 834-0056
Saint Marys *(G-16968)*

Evans Heat Treating Company ....F...... 215 938-8791
Huntingdon Valley *(G-7979)*

F Tinker and Sons Company ....E...... 412 781-3553
Pittsburgh *(G-15000)*

Fenton Heat Treating Inc ....G...... 412 466-3960
West Mifflin *(G-19738)*

Goc Property Holdings LLC ....G...... 814 678-4193
Rouseville *(G-16836)*

Irwin Automation Inc ....E...... 724 834-7160
Greensburg *(G-6679)*

Irwin Car & Equipment Inc ....F...... 724 864-5170
Irwin *(G-8173)*

▲ Irwin Car & Equipment Inc ....E...... 724 864-8900
Irwin *(G-8174)*

Jarex Enterprises ....G...... 215 855-2149
Lansdale *(G-9378)*

Kinton Carbide Inc ....F...... 724 327-3141
Export *(G-5613)*

▲ L B Toney Co ....F...... 814 375-9974
Du Bois *(G-4401)*

Machinery & Industrial Eqp Co ....F...... 412 781-8053
Pittsburgh *(G-15245)*

Madison Inds Holdings LLC................C...... 717 762-3151
Waynesboro *(G-19416)*

Mannings USA Inc ....D...... 412 816-1264
North Versailles *(G-12779)*

▲ Mannings USA...............................G...... 863 619-8099
North Versailles *(G-12780)*

Metal Menders LLC ....G...... 412 580-8625
Trafford *(G-18458)*

Mexico Heat Treating ....G...... 717 535-5034
Mifflintown *(G-11130)*

Modern Industries Inc.....................F...... 814 885-8514
Kersey *(G-8564)*

▲ Modern Industries Inc..................C...... 814 455-8061
Erie *(G-5394)*

▲ Orbel Corporation ....E...... 610 829-5000
Easton *(G-4736)*

▲ Penna Flame Industries Inc ....E...... 724 452-8750
Zelienople *(G-20815)*

Peters Heat Treating Inc ....E...... 814 333-1782
Meadville *(G-10779)*

Piht LLC ....D...... 814 781-6262
Saint Marys *(G-17007)*

Pittsburgh Metal Processing Co............F...... 412 781-8053
Pittsburgh *(G-15401)*

▲ Podcon Inc ....E...... 215 233-2600
Glenside *(G-6533)*

▼ Precision Finishing Inc.................E...... 215 257-6862
Quakertown *(G-16232)*

Pressure Technology Inc ....F...... 215 674-8844
Warminster *(G-18946)*

R & R Heat Treating Inc ....G...... 570 424-8750
East Stroudsburg *(G-4633)*

R H Carbide & Epoxy Inc ....G...... 724 356-2277
Hickory *(G-7630)*

Reading Coml Heat Treating Co ....G...... 610 376-3994
Reading *(G-16486)*

Rex Heat Treat -Lansdale Inc ....D...... 215 855-1131
Lansdale *(G-9405)*

Rex Heat Treat -Lansdale Inc............E...... 814 623-1701
Bedford *(G-1074)*

▲ Richter Precision Inc ....D...... 717 560-9990
East Petersburg *(G-4589)*

Robert Wooler Company ....E...... 215 542-7600
Dresher *(G-4357)*

Ronal Tool Company Inc ....F...... 717 741-0880
York *(G-20660)*

Solar Atmospheres Inc ....D...... 215 721-1502
Souderton *(G-17765)*

Solar Atmospheres Wstn PA Inc ....D...... 742 982-0660
Hermitage *(G-7595)*

Specialty Alloy Proc Co Inc ....G...... 724 339-0464
New Kensington *(G-12379)*

▲ Specialty Bar Products Company ....C...... 724 459-0544
Blairsville *(G-1742)*

Ultramet Heat Treating Inc ....G...... 814 781-7215
Saint Marys *(G-17025)*

◆ Union Electric Steel Corp ....D...... 412 429-7655
Carnegie *(G-2800)*

Vacu-Braze Inc ....F...... 215 453-0414
Quakertown *(G-16254)*

3399 Primary Metal Prdts, NEC

Accu-Grind Inc ....D...... 814 965-5475
Johnsonburg *(G-8343)*

Advanced Research Systems Inc............E...... 610 967-2120
Macungie *(G-10138)*

Advantage Metal Powders Inc ....F...... 814 772-5363
Ridgway *(G-16691)*

▲ Allegheny Blending Tech Inc ....G...... 814 772-9279
Ridgway *(G-16692)*

Alpha Precision Group LLC ....G...... 814 773-3191
Ridgway *(G-16693)*

Alpha Sintered Metals LLC ....C...... 814 773-3191
Ridgway *(G-16694)*

▲ American Metal & Rubber Inc ....F...... 215 225-3700
Philadelphia *(G-13386)*

◆ Ampal Inc ....G...... 610 826-7020
Palmerton *(G-13100)*

Ampal Inc ....E...... 610 826-7020
Palmerton *(G-13101)*

APS Advance Products & Svcs ....G...... 610 863-0570
Wind Gap *(G-20165)*

◆ ARC Metals Corporation ....G...... 814 776-2116
Ridgway *(G-16695)*

B & B Tool and Die Inc....................F...... 814 486-5355
Emporium *(G-5050)*

B B Express ....G...... 717 573-2686
Warfordsburg *(G-18810)*

Back Bay Industries Inc ....G...... 724 941-5825
Venetia *(G-18741)*

Biltwood Powder Coating LLC ....F...... 717 655-5664
Waynesboro *(G-19400)*

Brockway Sintered Technology............G...... 814 265-8090
Brockway *(G-2223)*

Cameron Diversified Pdts Inc ....E...... 814 929-5834
Wilcox *(G-19897)*

Carbon City Products Inc ....D...... 814 834-2886
Saint Marys *(G-16952)*

Catalus Corporation ....F...... 814 781-7004
Saint Marys *(G-16953)*

Catalus Corporation ....D...... 814 435-6541
Galeton *(G-6238)*

▲ Chemalloy Company LLC ....E...... 610 527-3700
Conshohocken *(G-3527)*

▼ Clarion Sintered Metals Inc ....B...... 814 773-3124
Ridgway *(G-16699)*

▲ Cmg Process Inc ....E...... 724 962-8717
Clark *(G-3188)*

Continuous Metal Tech Inc ....E...... 814 772-9274
Ridgway *(G-16701)*

▲ Cordray Corporation ....F...... 610 644-6200
King of Prussia *(G-8598)*

Cryo Tempering Tech of Ne PA............G...... 570 287-7443
Kingston *(G-8715)*

▲ Custom Laminating Corporation............F...... 570 897-8300
Mount Bethel *(G-11609)*

Djk Properties LLC ....G...... 717 597-5965
Greencastle *(G-6607)*

Dominion Powdered Metals ....G...... 814 598-4684
Saint Marys *(G-16963)*

Eastern Sintered Alloys Inc ....B...... 814 834-1216
Saint Marys *(G-16966)*

Edgmont Metallic Pigment Inc............F...... 610 429-1345
West Chester *(G-19546)*

Elcam Tool & Die Inc.......................E...... 814 929-5831
Wilcox *(G-19898)*

Elco Sintered Alloys Co Inc ....E...... 814 885-8031
Kersey *(G-8557)*

Elk Metals Inc ....F...... 814 834-4959
Saint Marys *(G-16971)*

Embassy Powdered Metals Inc............E...... 814 486-1011
Emporium *(G-5055)*

Emporium Powdered Metal Inc............F...... 814 486-0136
Emporium *(G-5058)*

Emporium Secondaries Inc................F...... 814 486-1881
Emporium *(G-5059)*

Engineered Pressed Materials............G...... 814 834-3189
Saint Marys *(G-16972)*

Engineered Pressed Materials............G...... 814 772-6127
Ridgway *(G-16707)*

▲ **EPC Powder Manufacturing Inc**........G....... 814 725-2012
North East *(G-12740)*

Falls Creek Powdered Metals................F....... 814 265-8771
Brockway *(G-2225)*

Formfast Powder Mtl Tech LLC.............G....... 814 201-5292
Ridgway *(G-16709)*

GKN Sinter Metals LLC..........................A....... 814 486-9234
Emporium *(G-5061)*

GKN Sinter Metals LLC..........................D....... 814 885-8053
Kersey *(G-8559)*

GKN Sinter Metals LLC..........................C....... 814 781-6500
Kersey *(G-8560)*

◆ **GKN Sinter Metals - Dubois Inc**........D....... 814 375-0938
Du Bois *(G-4393)*

◆ **Global Metal Powders LLC**...............G....... 724 654-9171
New Castle *(G-12097)*

▲ **Global Metal Products Inc**.................G....... 814 834-2214
Saint Marys *(G-16978)*

Griffin Sealing LLC...............................G....... 267 328-6600
Kulpsville *(G-8828)*

Hawk Precision Components...............G....... 814 371-0184
Falls Creek *(G-5854)*

◆ **Heraeus Incorporated**........................G....... 215 944-9981
Yardley *(G-20314)*

Heraeus Incorporated Hic....................C....... 610 825-6050
Conshohocken *(G-3555)*

◆ **Heraeus Precious Metals Nor**............C....... 610 825-6050
Conshohocken *(G-3556)*

Hoeganaes Corporation.........................E....... 570 538-3587
Watsontown *(G-19275)*

HRP Metals Inc.......................................G....... 412 741-6781
Sewickley *(G-17393)*

▲ **Industrial Services**.............................F....... 610 437-1453
Whitehall *(G-19877)*

Intech P/M Stainless Inc.........................E....... 814 776-6150
Ridgway *(G-16711)*

J S H Enterprises Inc.............................E....... 814 486-3939
Emporium *(G-5063)*

▲ **Jet Metals Inc**.....................................F....... 814 781-7399
Saint Marys *(G-16982)*

▲ **Kennametal Inc**...................................A....... 412 248-8000
Pittsburgh *(G-15169)*

Keystone Powdered Metal Co................D....... 814 368-5320
Lewis Run *(G-9876)*

Liberty Pressed Metals LLC....................F....... 814 885-6277
Kersey *(G-8563)*

◆ **Matthey Johnson Holdings Inc**.........E....... 610 971-3000
Wayne *(G-19350)*

◆ **Matthey Johnson Inc**..........................E....... 610 971-3000
Wayne *(G-19351)*

Mersen USA St Marys-PA Corp..............C....... 814 781-1234
Saint Marys *(G-16990)*

Metal Group..G....... 215 438-6156
Philadelphia *(G-14012)*

Metal Powder Products LLC.................D....... 814 834-2886
Saint Marys *(G-16991)*

Metal Powder Products LLC.................C....... 814 834-7261
Saint Marys *(G-16992)*

Metal Powder Products LLC.................C....... 814 776-2141
Ridgway *(G-16716)*

◆ **Metaldyne Sintered Ridgway LLC**.....D....... 814 776-1141
Ridgway *(G-16717)*

Metaltech Inc...E....... 814 375-9399
Du Bois *(G-4406)*

▲ **Metco Industries Inc**..........................D....... 814 781-3630
Saint Marys *(G-16994)*

Metkote Laminated Products Inc...........F....... 570 562-0107
Taylor *(G-18260)*

Netshape Technologies LLC..................C....... 814 371-0184
Falls Creek *(G-5855)*

◆ **North Amer Hoganas High Alloys**.....D....... 814 361-6800
Johnstown *(G-8413)*

◆ **North American Hoganas Company**.B....... 814 479-3500
Hollsopple *(G-7658)*

Northeastern Hydro-Seeding Inc..........G....... 570 668-1108
Tamaqua *(G-18222)*

Northern Powdered Metals Inc..............G....... 814 772-0882
Ridgway *(G-16720)*

O Alpine Pressed Metals Inc.................D....... 814 776-2141
Ridgway *(G-16721)*

P D Q Tooling Inc....................................G....... 412 751-2214
Mckeesport *(G-10677)*

P R L Inc..E....... 717 273-2470
Cornwall *(G-3739)*

P/M National Inc.....................................E....... 814 781-1960
Saint Marys *(G-17001)*

▲ **Particle Size Technology Inc**..............E....... 215 529-9771
Quakertown *(G-16227)*

Pennsylvania Powdered Mtls Inc..........E....... 814 834-9565
Saint Marys *(G-17004)*

Pennsylvania Sintered Mtls Inc.............E....... 814 486-1768
Emporium *(G-5071)*

Phoenix Sintered Metals LLC...............E....... 814 268-3455
Brockway *(G-2230)*

Powder Metal Products Inc....................C....... 814 834-7261
Saint Marys *(G-17008)*

▲ **Precision Cmpcted Cmpnents LLC**..D....... 814 929-5805
Wilcox *(G-19899)*

Quality Compacted Metals Inc..............F....... 814 486-1500
Emporium *(G-5072)*

Quality Metal Coatings Inc.....................G....... 814 781-6161
Saint Marys *(G-17012)*

Rebco Inc..C....... 814 885-8035
Kersey *(G-8568)*

Rideltin Powder Metal Inc......................G....... 412 788-0956
Mc Kees Rocks *(G-10631)*

Ridgway Powdered Metals Inc..............E....... 814 772-5551
Ridgway *(G-16727)*

Robvon Backing Ring Co Inc.................F....... 570 945-3800
Factoryville *(G-5761)*

Rolling Ridge Metals LLC.......................G....... 724 588-2375
Greenville *(G-6771)*

Silcotek Corp..E....... 814 353-1778
Bellefonte *(G-1118)*

▲ **Sinacom North America Inc**..............E....... 610 337-2250
King of Prussia *(G-8677)*

Sinterfire Inc..F....... 814 885-6672
Kersey *(G-8570)*

▲ **Specilty Mtallurgical Pdts Inc**...........F....... 717 246-0385
Red Lion *(G-16614)*

Spinworks LLC...G....... 814 725-1188
North East *(G-12761)*

▲ **Ssw International Inc**........................E....... 412 922-9100
Pittsburgh *(G-15572)*

St Marys Carbon Co Inc..........................D....... 814 781-7333
Saint Marys *(G-17017)*

St Marys Carbon Co Inc..........................D....... 814 781-7333
Saint Marys *(G-17018)*

St Marys Pressed Metals Inc.................E....... 814 772-7455
Ridgway *(G-16730)*

Summit Materials LLC.............................G....... 412 260-8048
Mc Donald *(G-10582)*

Superior Powder Coating Inc.................G....... 412 221-8250
Mc Donald *(G-10583)*

Symmco Inc...C....... 814 894-2461
Sykesville *(G-18203)*

Symmco Group Inc..................................D....... 814 894-2461
Sykesville *(G-18204)*

Technitrol Inc..G....... 215 355-2900
Feasterville Trevose *(G-5932)*

◆ **Tms International LLC**........................D....... 412 678-6141
Glassport *(G-6419)*

Tms International Corp...........................E....... 215 956-5500
Horsham *(G-7860)*

Tms International Corp...........................C....... 412 678-6141
Glassport *(G-6420)*

◆ **Tms International Corporation**..........E....... 412 675-8251
Glassport *(G-6421)*

▲ **United Sttes Metal Powders Inc**........F....... 908 782-5454
Palmerton *(G-13113)*

Vision Quality Components Inc..............F....... 814 765-1903
Clearfield *(G-3234)*

World Resources Company....................E....... 570 622-4747
Pottsville *(G-16103)*

34 FABRICATED METAL PRODUCTS, EXCEPT MACHINERY AND TRANSPORTATION EQUIPMENT

3411 Metal Cans

American Keg Company LLC...............E....... 484 524-8251
Pottstown *(G-15963)*

Ardagh Metal Packaging USA Inc.........C....... 570 389-5563
Bloomsburg *(G-1770)*

Ball Arosol Specialty Cont Inc................C....... 215 442-5462
Horsham *(G-7794)*

▲ **Can Corporation America Inc**..............C....... 610 926-3044
Blandon *(G-1752)*

Can Corporation America Inc................E....... 610 921-3460
Reading *(G-16342)*

CCL Container (hermitage) Inc..............G....... 724 981-4420
Hermitage *(G-7574)*

◆ **CCL Container Corporation**................C....... 724 981-4420
Hermitage *(G-7575)*

Crown Americas LLC...............................E....... 215 698-5100
Philadelphia *(G-13584)*

◆ **Crown Beverage Packaging LLC**.....B....... 215 698-5100
Philadelphia *(G-13585)*

Crown Cork & Seal Company Inc..........A....... 215 698-5100
Yardley *(G-20302)*

Crown Cork & Seal Usa Inc....................C....... 215 322-5507
Feasterville Trevose *(G-5901)*

Crown Cork & Seal Usa Inc....................G....... 215 698-5100
Philadelphia *(G-13587)*

Crown Cork & Seal Usa Inc....................C....... 724 626-0121
Connellsville *(G-3493)*

Crown Cork & Seal Usa Inc....................D....... 717 633-1163
Hanover *(G-6871)*

◆ **Crown Cork & Seal Usa Inc**.................B....... 215 698-5100
Yardley *(G-20303)*

Crown Cork Seal.......................................G....... 610 687-2616
Wayne *(G-19315)*

◆ **Crown Holdings Inc**..............................C....... 215 698-5100
Yardley *(G-20304)*

Crown Holdings Inc.................................E....... 215 322-3533
Feasterville Trevose *(G-5902)*

Crown Intl Holdings Inc..........................B....... 215 698-5100
Yardley *(G-20305)*

Deist Industries Inc..................................E....... 800 233-0867
Hadley *(G-6819)*

JL Clark LLC..C....... 717 392-4125
Lancaster *(G-9073)*

Lanco Industries.......................................G....... 717 949-3435
Lebanon *(G-9597)*

Lilys LLC..G....... 814 938-9419
Punxsutawney *(G-16147)*

Michelman Steel Entps LLC....................F....... 610 395-3472
Allentown *(G-315)*

Nationwide Recyclers Inc........................G....... 215 698-5100
Philadelphia *(G-14057)*

Nestle Purina Petcare Company.............D....... 610 398-4667
Allentown *(G-328)*

Reynolds Metals Company LLC.............F....... 412 343-5020
Pittsburgh *(G-15482)*

Silgan Containers Corporation..............G....... 484 223-3189
Breinigsville *(G-2027)*

Silgan Containers Mfg Corp...................D....... 610 337-2203
King of Prussia *(G-8676)*

Silgan White Cap Corporation...............C....... 570 455-7781
Hazle Township *(G-7480)*

◆ **Universal Protective Packg Inc**..........D....... 717 766-1578
Mechanicsburg *(G-10903)*

3412 Metal Barrels, Drums, Kegs & Pails

Altrax..G....... 814 379-3706
Summerville *(G-18156)*

Berenfield Cntrs Northeast Inc..............C....... 610 258-2700
Easton *(G-4654)*

Cleveland Steel Container Corp............E....... 215 536-4477
Quakertown *(G-16180)*

▲ **Container Research Corporation**.......C....... 610 459-2160
Aston *(G-757)*

Georgia-Pacific LLC.................................C....... 814 368-8700
Bradford *(G-1969)*

Italian Mutual Benefit Society................G....... 412 221-0751
Bridgeville *(G-2071)*

Lancaster Container Inc..........................E....... 717 285-3312
Columbia *(G-3442)*

Northeast Industrial Mfg Inc..................E....... 724 588-7711
Greenville *(G-6760)*

Sonoco Display & Packaging LLC.........C....... 717 757-2683
York *(G-20672)*

Talk Express...G....... 412 977-1786
Natrona Heights *(G-11950)*

▼ **Williamsport Steel Cont Corp**.............E....... 570 323-9473
Williamsport *(G-20095)*

3421 Cutlery

Art of Shaving - Fl LLC............................G....... 610 962-1000
King of Prussia *(G-8585)*

Backus Company.......................................E....... 814 887-5705
Smethport *(G-17632)*

Brysi Inc..G....... 215 573-7918
Philadelphia *(G-13487)*

Columbian Cutlery Company Inc...........G....... 610 374-5762
Reading *(G-16350)*

Deffibaugh Butcher Supply....................G....... 814 944-1297
Altoona *(G-498)*

Easy Use Air Tools Inc.............................G....... 412 486-2270
Allison Park *(G-450)*

Guardian Tactical Inc...............................G....... 814 558-6761
Emporium *(G-5062)*

Jet Plastica Industries Inc.......................B....... 800 220-5381
Hatfield *(G-7356)*

Renees Cold Cut Hut.................................G....... 570 215-0057
White Haven *(G-19852)*

Sweet Sanctions.......................................G....... 717 222-1859
Lebanon *(G-9635)*

Employee Codes: A=Over 500 employees, B=251-500
C=101-250, D=51-100, E=20-50, F=10-19, G=3-9

2019 Harris Pennsylvania
Manufacturers Directory

905

3423 Hand & Edge Tools

Ames Companies Inc.....................C 717 258-3001
  Carlisle *(G-2689)*

Ames Companies Inc.....................D...... 717 737-1500
  Camp Hill *(G-2487)*

◆ Ames Companies Inc ....B 717 737-1500
  Camp Hill *(G-2488)*

Ames True Temper Inc.....................D...... 717 231-7856
  Harrisburg *(G-7086)*

Antares Instruments Inc...................F 215 441-5250
  Horsham *(G-7786)*

Aquador...G 724 942-1525
  Canonsburg *(G-2542)*

▲ Auger Fabrication Inc ....E 610 524-3350
  Exton *(G-5648)*

Auger Mfg Specialists Co..................E 610 647-4677
  Malvern *(G-10188)*

Augers Unlimited Inc.......................E 610 380-1660
  Coatesville *(G-3292)*

B N S Woodcrafts............................G 717 284-1035
  Quarryville *(G-16263)*

◆ Barco Industries Inc....................E 610 374-3117
  Reading *(G-16328)*

▲ Bolttech Mannings Inc..................D...... 724 872-4873
  North Versailles *(G-12772)*

◆ Bon Tool Company ....D...... 724 443-7080
  Gibsonia *(G-6328)*

Bostock Inc.....................................G...... 610 650-9650
  Norristown *(G-12641)*

▲ Channellock Inc ....B 814 337-9200
  Meadville *(G-10711)*

Cornwell Quality Tools Company.........G 814 756-5484
  Albion *(G-41)*

CP Precision Inc..............................G 267 364-0870
  Warminster *(G-18849)*

▼ Craig Colabaugh Gunsmith Inc........G 570 992-4499
  Stroudsburg *(G-18111)*

Cutting Edge Knives Inc....................E 412 279-9350
  Pittsburgh *(G-14898)*

▲ Diatome U S Joint Venture ....G 215 646-1478
  Hatfield *(G-7334)*

Electro-Glass Products Inc ....E 724 423-5000
  Norvelt *(G-12878)*

Electroline Corp..............................E 215 766-2229
  Pipersville *(G-14614)*

Elge Precision Machining Inc ....F 610 376-5458
  Reading *(G-16372)*

Emporium Specialties Company.........E 814 647-8661
  Austin *(G-833)*

◆ Emsco Inc ....C 814 774-3137
  Girard *(G-6386)*

F Tinker and Sons Company ....E 412 781-3553
  Pittsburgh *(G-15000)*

Flexcut Tool Co Inc..........................E 814 864-7855
  Erie *(G-5294)*

▲ General Wire Spring Company.........C 412 771-6300
  Mc Kees Rocks *(G-10612)*

Halex Corporation...........................E 909 622-3537
  Fairless Hills *(G-5782)*

Hewlett Manufacturing Co.................E 814 683-4762
  Linesville *(G-9981)*

Ingrain Construction LLC..................F 717 205-1475
  Lancaster *(G-9057)*

▲ Jiba LLC.....................................F 215 739-9644
  Philadelphia *(G-13898)*

◆ John Stortz and Son Inc................G 215 627-3855
  Philadelphia *(G-13906)*

Kal-Cameron Manufacturing..............F 814 486-3394
  Emporium *(G-5065)*

Lion Industrial Knife Co Inc...............G 717 244-8195
  Red Lion *(G-16605)*

Nu-TEC Tooling Co ....F 570 538-2571
  Watsontown *(G-19277)*

Paramount Die Corporation ....F 814 734-6999
  Edinboro *(G-4819)*

Pro Tool Industries Inc ....F 484 945-5001
  Pottstown *(G-16037)*

Quality Tool & Die Enterprises...........G...... 814 834-2384
  Saint Marys *(G-17013)*

◆ Reed Manufacturing Company.........D....... 814 452-3691
  Erie *(G-5459)*

Reliable Equipment Mfg Co................E 215 357-7015
  Warminster *(G-18951)*

Ronal Tool Company Inc ....F 717 741-0880
  York *(G-20660)*

Ruch Carbide Burs Inc ....E 215 657-3660
  Willow Grove *(G-20139)*

▲ Sanders Saws & Blades Inc ....E 610 273-3733
  Honey Brook *(G-7761)*

◆ SPS Technologies LLC ....A 215 572-3000
  Jenkintown *(G-8302)*

◆ Tamco Inc...................................E 724 258-6622
  Monongahela *(G-11317)*

◆ Three M Tool and Die Corp ....F 717 854-6379
  York *(G-20688)*

Transportation Eqp Sup Co ....E 814 866-1952
  Erie *(G-5514)*

Vollman Pershing H Inc.....................G....... 215 956-1971
  Warminster *(G-18998)*

W Rose Inc......................................E 610 583-4125
  Sharon Hill *(G-17466)*

◆ Woodings Industrial Corp...............C 724 625-3131
  Mars *(G-10515)*

▲ York Saw & Knife Company Inc ....E 717 767-6402
  Emigsville *(G-5003)*

3425 Hand Saws & Saw Blades

▲ A Lindemann Inc ....G 412 487-7282
  Glenshaw *(G-6477)*

American Carbide Saw Co ....F 215 672-1466
  Hatboro *(G-7267)*

Dinosaw Inc....................................F 570 374-5531
  Selinsgrove *(G-17323)*

Hoffman Diamond Products Inc ....E 814 938-7600
  Punxsutawney *(G-16143)*

MOr Saw Service Center Inc...............G 215 333-0441
  Philadelphia *(G-14037)*

Penn Scientific Products Co ....F 888 238-6710
  Abington *(G-13)*

▲ Sanders Saws & Blades Inc ....E 610 273-3733
  Honey Brook *(G-7761)*

Suffolk McHy & Pwr TI Corp..............G 631 289-7153
  Brockway *(G-2234)*

Victor Metals..................................G 570 925-2618
  Stillwater *(G-18062)*

▲ Wilder Diamond Blades Inc............G 570 222-9590
  Kingsley *(G-8710)*

▲ York Saw & Knife Company Inc ....E 717 767-6402
  Emigsville *(G-5003)*

3429 Hardware, NEC

A G Mauro Company ....E 717 938-4671
  Lewisberry *(G-9879)*

Austin Hardware.............................E 610 921-2723
  Reading *(G-16326)*

Aviva Technology Inc........................G 610 228-4689
  Broomall *(G-2279)*

B G M Fastener Co Inc......................E 570 253-5046
  Honesdale *(G-7701)*

Backus Company..............................E 814 887-5705
  Smethport *(G-17632)*

Baileys Steel & Supply LLC................G 724 267-4648
  Waynesburg *(G-19433)*

Baldt Inc...E 610 447-5200
  Bryn Mawr *(G-2315)*

Baldwin Hardware Corporation ....B 610 777-7811
  Leesport *(G-9659)*

▲ Ball & Ball LLP ....E 610 363-7330
  Exton *(G-5651)*

◆ Barco Industries Inc....................E 610 374-3117
  Reading *(G-16328)*

Bergen Pipe Supports Inc ....D...... 724 379-5212
  Donora *(G-4148)*

Calgon Carbon Uv Tech LLC ....G 724 218-7001
  Coraopolis *(G-3670)*

▼ Campbell Manufacturing Inc...........D...... 610 367-2107
  Bechtelsville *(G-1030)*

▲ Chick Wrkholding Solutions Inc.......D...... 724 772-1644
  Warrendale *(G-19070)*

Chief Fire ....G 484 356-5316
  West Chester *(G-19524)*

Cir-Cut Corporation.........................G 215 324-1000
  Philadelphia *(G-13545)*

Clark Deco Moldings Inc ....G 412 363-9602
  Pittsburgh *(G-14857)*

▲ Cobra Anchors Corp.....................D...... 610 929-5764
  Temple *(G-18326)*

Ctc Pressure Products LLC................G 814 315-6427
  Erie *(G-5235)*

Dayton Superior Corporation ....F 610 366-3890
  Allentown *(G-193)*

Delmar Enterprises Inc.....................F 215 674-4534
  Warminster *(G-18856)*

◆ Dormakaba USA Inc ....C 717 336-3881
  Reamstown *(G-16576)*

Draper Dbs Inc.................................E 215 257-3833
  Perkasie *(G-13275)*

Eastern Millwork Ltd ....G 570 344-7128
  Scranton *(G-17231)*

Elite Cabinetry Inc...........................G 717 993-5269
  New Park *(G-12429)*

▲ Emka-Incorporated ....E 717 986-1111
  Middletown *(G-11053)*

Foambeak LLC.................................G 814 452-3626
  Erie *(G-5299)*

▼ G G Greene Enterprises Inc ....E 814 723-5700
  Warren *(G-19027)*

▲ G G Schmitt & Sons Inc.................F 717 394-3701
  Lancaster *(G-9026)*

Gibson Stainless Specialty Inc...........F 724 838-8320
  Greensburg *(G-6669)*

Globe Metal Manufacturing Co ....F 215 763-1024
  Philadelphia *(G-13773)*

Grate Clip Company Inc ....G 215 230-8015
  Doylestown *(G-4304)*

Gregg Lane LLC................................G 215 269-9900
  Fairless Hills *(G-5781)*

H & B Enterprises Inc ....G 814 345-6416
  Kylertown *(G-8865)*

Hearth & Home Technologies LLC ....Quarry...... 717 362-9080
  Halifax *(G-6826)*

▲ Hiatt Thompson Corporation ....G 708 496-8585
  Greenville *(G-6745)*

HIG Capital LLC...............................C 610 495-7011
  Royersford *(G-16851)*

Idn Global Inc..................................G 215 698-8155
  Philadelphia *(G-13846)*

Ingersoll-Rand Company ....E 410 238-0542
  Shrewsbury *(G-17584)*

▲ Jacob Holtz Company LLC ....D...... 215 423-2800
  Philadelphia *(G-13316)*

JP Betz Inc......................................G 610 458-8787
  Glenmoore *(G-6468)*

Keys Wholesale Distributors ....G 610 626-4787
  Broomall *(G-2291)*

Larry Paige ....G 570 374-5650
  Middleburg *(G-11027)*

Loranger International Corp ....D...... 814 723-2250
  Warren *(G-19038)*

Martin Sprocket & Gear Inc...............D...... 610 837-1841
  Danielsville *(G-3994)*

Michael N Sullenberger ....G 724 725-5285
  Point Marion *(G-15886)*

Millheim Small Engine Inc.................G 814 349-5007
  Spring Mills *(G-17889)*

N3zn Keys LLC.................................G 412 389-7797
  Pittsburgh *(G-15315)*

New Home Window Shade Co Inc ....E 570 346-2047
  Clarks Green *(G-3189)*

▲ Norma Pennsylvania Inc ....B 724 639-3571
  Saltsburg *(G-17052)*

Omega Flex Inc ....C 610 524-7272
  Exton *(G-5719)*

▼ Onexia Brass Inc..........................G 610 431-3271
  West Chester *(G-19611)*

▲ Peerless Hardware Mfg Co.............F 717 684-2889
  Columbia *(G-3447)*

Penn Big Bed Slate Co Inc..................D...... 610 767-4601
  Slatington *(G-17611)*

▲ Penn Engineering & Mfg Corp.........B 215 766-8853
  Danboro *(G-3991)*

Penn Engineering & Mfg Corp ....F 215 766-8853
  Danboro *(G-3992)*

▲ Penn Lock Corp............................E 570 288-5547
  Kingston *(G-8725)*

▲ Philadelphia Security Pdts Inc........G....... 610 521-4400
  Essington *(G-5546)*

Pitcal Inc..G 412 433-1121
  Pittsburgh *(G-15382)*

▲ Powertrack International LLC ....E 412 787-4444
  Pittsburgh *(G-15423)*

R & H Manufacturing Inc ....E 570 288-6648
  Edwardsville *(G-4824)*

Rfcircuits Inc ....F 215 364-2450
  Huntingdon Valley *(G-8029)*

Roberts Manufacturing LLC...............F 855 763-7450
  Allentown *(G-376)*

▲ Rockwood Manufacturing Company.C 814 926-2026
  Rockwood *(G-16792)*

Roger S Wright Furniture Ltd ....G 215 257-5700
  Blooming Glen *(G-1765)*

Rollock Company.............................E 814 893-6421
  Stoystown *(G-18086)*

San-Fab Co Inc................................G 570 385-2551
  Schuylkill Haven *(G-17166)*

▲ Schmitt Mar Stering Wheels Inc .....G 717 431-2316
  Lancaster *(G-9191)*

Simpson Manufacturing Inc...............G 724 694-2708
  Derry *(G-4107)*

Southco Inc ....E 267 957-9260
  Warminster (G-18968)

Southco Cunterbalance Div - PA ....E 267 957-9260
  Warminster (G-18970)

▲ Standard Steel Specialty Co ....D 724 846-7600
  Beaver Falls (G-1014)

Stanley Black & Decker Inc ....C 215 710-9300
  Langhorne (G-9326)

Stanley Security Solutions Inc ....F 877 476-4968
  Monroeville (G-11357)

Stanley Security Solutions Inc ....F 888 265-0412
  Monroeville (G-11358)

Staver Hydraulics Co Inc ....G 610 837-1818
  Bath (G-970)

Summers Acquisition Corp ....G 724 652-4673
  New Castle (G-12156)

◆ Tell Manufacturing Inc ....E 717 625-2990
  Lititz (G-10054)

▲ The Keystone Friction Hinge Co ...C 570 321-0693
  Williamsport (G-20082)

Top Notch Distributors Inc ....F 800 233-4210
  Honesdale (G-7729)

United Commercial Supply LLC ......G 412 835-2690
  South Park (G-17786)

Upson-Walton Company ....G 570 649-5188
  Turbotville (G-18557)

V2r2 LLC ....G 215 277-2181
  Harleysville (G-7063)

Vanguard Identification ....E 610 719-0700
  West Chester (G-19672)

▲ W W Patterson Company ....E 412 322-2012
  Pittsburgh (G-15706)

▲ Winner International Inc ....D 724 981-1152
  Sharon (G-17448)

Yardley Products LLC ....E 215 493-2700
  Yardley (G-20346)

3431 Enameled Iron & Metal Sanitary Ware

▲ Clarion Bathware Inc ....C 814 226-5374
  Shippenville (G-17556)

Crystal Shower Doors ....G 717 642-9689
  Fairfield (G-5766)

▲ Jeannette Shade and Novelty Co ...D 724 523-5567
  Jeannette (G-8257)

Kebeico Inc ....E 610 241-8163
  Chadds Ford (G-2852)

▲ Speakman Company ....G 302 764-7100
  Glen Mills (G-6444)

◆ Zurn Industries LLC ....G 814 455-0921
  Erie (G-5537)

Zurn Industries LLC ....G 215 946-0216
  Levittown (G-9870)

3432 Plumbing Fixture Fittings & Trim, Brass

Apr Supply Co ....G 215 592-1935
  Philadelphia (G-13401)

◆ Certainteed Corporation ....B 610 893-5000
  Malvern (G-10204)

Certainteed Corporation ....G 610 651-8706
  Malvern (G-10205)

▲ Cimberio Valve Co Inc ....G 610 560-0802
  Malvern (G-10208)

Corry Rubber Corporation ....E 814 664-2313
  Corry (G-3757)

E S Specialty Manufacturing ....G 215 635-0973
  Wyncote (G-20262)

Four Guys Stnless Tank Eqp Inc ....D 814 634-8373
  Meyersdale (G-11010)

Green Garden Inc ....E 814 623-2735
  Bedford (G-1053)

▲ Greenfield Mfg Co Inc ....F 215 535-4141
  Philadelphia (G-13785)

Hajoca Corporation ....G 215 657-0700
  Willow Grove (G-20120)

Innovative Pressure Tech LLC ......D 814 833-5200
  Erie (G-5326)

Moen Incorporated ....F 570 345-8021
  Pine Grove (G-14600)

Pipe Dreams Plumbing Sup Inc .....G 215 741-0889
  Langhorne (G-9319)

Rayco Process Services Inc ....G 717 464-2572
  Willow Street (G-20155)

Rowe Sprinkler Systems Inc ....E 570 837-7647
  Middleburg (G-11039)

Space Age Plastics Inc ....F 570 630-6060
  Jefferson Township (G-8279)

▲ Speakman Company ....C 302 764-7100
  Glen Mills (G-6444)

Triumph Sales Inc ....G 412 781-0950
  Pittsburgh (G-15654)

3433 Heating Eqpt

A W Mercer Inc ....C 610 367-8460
  Boyertown (G-1892)

ABB Installation Products Inc ....B 724 662-4400
  Mercer (G-10958)

Advanced Cooling Tech Inc ....D 717 208-2612
  Lancaster (G-8921)

Alaska Company Inc ....F 570 387-0260
  Bloomsburg (G-1766)

Alfa Laval Inc ....D 717 453-7143
  Lykens (G-10129)

American Slar Envmtl Technolog .....G 570 279-0338
  Lewisburg (G-9897)

◆ Applied Test Systems LLC ....E 724 283-1212
  Butler (G-2375)

Arthur L Baker Enterprises ....G 717 432-9788
  Lewisberry (G-9880)

Axeman-Anderson Company ....E 570 326-9114
  Williamsport (G-19991)

Black Rock Manufacturing Co ....G 570 752-1811
  Berwick (G-1314)

▲ Bloom Engineering Company Inc ...F 412 653-3500
  Pittsburgh (G-14773)

▲ Boyertown Foundry Company ......C 610 473-1000
  Boyertown (G-1899)

Boyertown Furnace Company ....E 610 369-1450
  Boyertown (G-1900)

◆ Bradford White Corporation ....D 215 641-9400
  Ambler (G-571)

▲ Burnham Holdings Inc ....C 717 390-7800
  Lancaster (G-8964)

Columbia Boiler Company ....E 610 323-9200
  Pottstown (G-15972)

Combustion Service & Eqp Co ....D 412 821-8900
  Pittsburgh (G-14867)

▲ Crown Boiler Co ....E 215 535-8900
  Philadelphia (G-13586)

Division of Thermo Dynamics ....G 570 385-0731
  Schuylkill Haven (G-17154)

Ds Machine LLC ....E 717 768-3853
  Gordonville (G-6552)

Emporium Specialties Company .....E 814 647-8661
  Austin (G-833)

Faber Burner Company ....E 570 748-4009
  Lock Haven (G-10088)

Fives N Amercn Combustn Inc ....E 717 228-0714
  Lebanon (G-9570)

Fives N Amercn Combustn Inc ....E 610 996-8005
  West Chester (G-19555)

▲ Flabeg Solar US Corporation ......E 724 899-4622
  Clinton (G-3262)

General Fabricating Svcs LLC ....F 412 262-1131
  Coraopolis (G-3692)

General Machine & Mfg Co ....G 570 383-0990
  Peckville (G-13209)

▼ Hauck Manufacturing Company ...D 717 272-3051
  Cleona (G-3244)

Havaco Technologies Inc ....G 814 878-5509
  Erie (G-5311)

Hoover Pump Works ....G 717 733-0630
  Ephrata (G-5110)

Industrial Systems & Controls ....G 412 638-4977
  Pittsburgh (G-15121)

Kottcamp Sheet Metal ....E 717 845-7616
  York (G-20558)

▲ Kt-Grant Inc ....D 724 468-4700
  Export (G-5614)

Lccm Solar LLC ....G 717 514-0751
  Harrisburg (G-7170)

Lionheart Holdings LLC ....D 215 283-8400
  Newtown (G-12519)

Log Hard Premium Pellets Inc ....G 814 654-2100
  Spartansburg (G-17852)

Mahoning Outdoor Furnace Inc ......E 814 277-6675
  Mahaffey (G-10171)

McCleary Heating & Cooling LLC ...F 717 263-3833
  Chambersburg (G-2959)

Nacah Tech LLC ....G 412 833-0687
  Pittsburgh (G-15316)

New Berry Inc ....F 724 452-8040
  Harmony (G-7074)

Oerlikon Management USA Inc ....F 412 967-7016
  Pittsburgh (G-15357)

Penn Manufacturing ....G 717 626-8879
  Lititz (G-10030)

▲ Ritter Group Usa Inc ....G 570 517-5380
  Stroudsburg (G-18140)

▼ S P Kinney Engineers Inc ....E 412 276-4600
  Carnegie (G-2789)

Sil-Base Company Inc ....E 412 751-2314
  McKeesport (G-10681)

Solar Technology Solutions ....G 610 916-0864
  Leesport (G-9674)

Spinworks International Corp ....E 814 725-1188
  North East (G-12762)

Tdc Manufacturing Inc ....F 570 385-0731
  Schuylkill Haven (G-17167)

USA Coil & Air Inc ....E 610 296-9668
  Malvern (G-10336)

◆ Van Air Inc ....E 814 774-2631
  Lake City (G-8909)

Vari Corporation ....G 570 385-0731
  Schuylkill Haven (G-17169)

Yeagers Field ....G 610 434-1516
  Allentown (G-439)

3441 Fabricated Structural Steel

A & R Iron Works Inc ....F 610 497-8770
  Trainer (G-18462)

A D M Welding & Fabrication ....G 814 723-7227
  Warren (G-19007)

A M Sheet Metal Inc ....F 570 322-5417
  South Williamsport (G-17789)

Aaron S Myers ....G 717 339-9304
  New Oxford (G-12401)

Abex Industries ....G 717 246-2611
  Red Lion (G-16586)

◆ Accutrex Products Inc ....C 724 746-4300
  Canonsburg (G-2532)

◆ Ace Metal Inc ....E 610 623-2204
  Clifton Heights (G-3250)

Acf Group LLC ....E 724 364-7027
  Allison (G-444)

Acme Metals Co ....G 412 331-4301
  Pittsburgh (G-14642)

▲ Advanced Fabrication Svcs Inc ...E 717 763-0286
  Lemoyne (G-9741)

▲ Advanced Industrial Svcs Inc ......C 717 764-9811
  York (G-20368)

Afco C&S LLC ....G 717 264-9147
  Chambersburg (G-2898)

Agar Welding Service & Stl Sup .....E 717 532-1000
  Walnut Bottom (G-18788)

Al Kaczmarczyk ....G 724 775-1366
  Beaver Falls (G-996)

◆ Alex C Fergusson LLC ....D 717 264-9147
  Chambersburg (G-2899)

All Weld Steel Co Inc ....F 215 884-6985
  Glenside (G-6504)

Allegheny Strl Components Inc ....G 724 867-1100
  Emlenton (G-5005)

Allfab Manufacturing Inc ....G 724 924-2725
  New Castle (G-12055)

Alloy Design Inc ....G 610 369-9265
  Boyertown (G-1896)

Altrax ....G 814 379-3706
  Summerville (G-18156)

American Bridge Mfg Co ....E 412 631-3000
  Coraopolis (G-3655)

American Bridge Mfg Co ....G 541 271-1100
  Coraopolis (G-3656)

American Roll Suppliers Inc ....G 610 857-2988
  Parkesburg (G-13171)

Amthor Steel Inc ....G 814 452-4700
  Erie (G-5193)

Anvil Craft Corp ....E 610 250-9600
  Easton (G-4645)

Anvil Iron Works Inc ....G 215 468-8300
  Philadelphia (G-13397)

Apex Fabrication & Design Inc ....E 610 689-5880
  Boyertown (G-1897)

Apex Manufacturing Co Inc ....G 215 343-4850
  Warrington (G-19108)

Architectural Stl & Assod Pdts ....F 215 368-8113
  Lansdale (G-9343)

Armin Ironworks Inc ....G 412 322-1622
  Pittsburgh (G-14725)

ASP Services Inc ....E 570 374-5333
  Selinsgrove (G-17320)

Atlantic Metal Industries LLC ....G 908 445-4299
  Stroudsburg (G-18106)

Australtek LLC ....G 412 257-2377
  Bridgeville (G-2054)

Auto Weld Chassis & Components ...G 570 275-1411
  Danville (G-3997)

▼ Azek Building Products Inc ....E 877 275-2935
  Scranton (G-17210)

B & T Fabrication ....G 814 634-0638
  Meyersdale (G-11009)

▲ B D & D Spclty Fabrication Mch ....E....... 814 236-3810
Curwensville (G-3946)
Baileys Steel & Supply LLC ....G....... 724 267-4648
Waynesburg (G-19433)
Baillie Fabricating & Wldg Inc ....G....... 610 701-5808
West Chester (G-19508)
◆ Ballymore Holdings Inc ....E....... 610 593-5062
Coatesville (G-3293)
Baut Studios Inc.....................................E....... 570 288-1431
Swoyersville (G-18194)
Ben Swaney...G....... 412 372-8109
Monroeville (G-11325)
Berlin Steel Construction Co ....F....... 610 240-8953
West Chester (G-19510)
Bethlehem Aluminum Inc ....F....... 610 432-4541
Allentown (G-150)
Big B Manufacturing Inc........................E....... 570 648-2084
Klingerstown (G-8806)
Biofab Products Inc...............................E....... 724 283-4801
Butler (G-2379)
Black Rock Fabrication LLC ....G....... 610 212-3528
Phoenixville (G-14533)
Black Rock Repair LLC ....G....... 717 529-6553
Kirkwood (G-8744)
▼ Blue Valley Industries Inc ....G....... 717 436-8266
Port Royal (G-15909)
Bortnick Construction Inc.....................G....... 814 587-6023
Springboro (G-17894)
Brad Foote Gear Works Inc...................E....... 412 264-1428
Pittsburgh (G-14789)
Brandywine Valley Fabricators.............F....... 610 384-7440
Coatesville (G-3295)
Bridges & Towers Inc ....F....... 724 654-6672
New Castle (G-12066)
Bryce Saylor & Sons Inc ....F....... 814 942-2288
Altoona (G-485)
▲ Byrne Chiarlone LP.........................E....... 610 874-8436
Chester (G-3042)
C M C Steel Fabricators Inc ....C....... 570 568-6761
New Columbia (G-12173)
Carl E Reichert Corp..............................G....... 215 723-9525
Telford (G-18269)
Carrara Steel Inc ....E....... 814 452-4600
Erie (G-5222)
Carriage Machine Shop LLC ....F....... 717 397-4079
Bird In Hand (G-1671)
▲ Carroll Manufacturing Co LLC..........G....... 724 266-0400
Leetsdale (G-9688)
Cast Pac Inc..E....... 610 264-8131
Allentown (G-165)
Cava Intl MBL & Gran Inc......................E....... 215 732-7800
Philadelphia (G-13516)
▲ Challenger Fabrication ....G....... 570 788-7911
Drums (G-4381)
Charters Fabg Pwdr Coating LLC ....E....... 412 203-5421
Coraopolis (G-3676)
Chase Industries Inc..............................F....... 412 449-0160
Pittsburgh (G-14841)
Cherry Steel Corp ....F....... 215 340-2239
Doylestown (G-4291)
Chowns Fabrication Rigging Inc...........D....... 610 584-0240
Skippack (G-17595)
▲ Cid Associates Inc ....E....... 724 353-0300
Sarver (G-17066)
Clipper Pipe & Service Inc ....G....... 610 872-9067
Eddystone (G-4799)
Compu-Craft Fabricators Inc ....E....... 215 646-2381
Montgomeryville (G-11390)
Conrad Enterprises Inc ....E....... 717 274-5151
Cornwall (G-3738)
Conshohocken Steel Pdts Inc ....E....... 215 283-9222
Ambler (G-574)
Consolidated Steel Svcs Inc ....E....... 814 944-5890
Fallentimber (G-5851)
▲ Container Research Corporation .....C....... 610 459-2160
Aston (G-757)
▲ Converters Inc..................................E....... 215 355-5400
Huntingdon Valley (G-7971)
Cooks Machine Work..............................G....... 814 589-5141
Pleasantville (G-15799)
Craftweld Fabrication Co Inc ....E....... 267 492-1100
Montgomeryville (G-11391)
Craig Sidleck ....F....... 610 261-9580
Whitehall (G-19869)
Crowell Metal Fabrication ....G....... 814 486-2664
Emporium (G-5054)
Custom Mfg & Indus Svcs LLC.............G....... 412 621-2982
Pittsburgh (G-14894)
Custom Steel Products Inc ....G....... 412 215-9923
Bridgeville (G-2058)
Cutting Edge Countertops ....G....... 724 397-8605
Marion Center (G-10472)
D & S Fabricating & Welding ....G....... 412 653-9185
Clairton (G-3148)
D A D Fabrication and Welding.............G....... 814 781-1886
Saint Marys (G-16960)
D L George & Sons Mfg Inc...................D....... 717 765-4700
Waynesboro (G-19407)
D L Machine LLC....................................F....... 724 627-7870
Jefferson (G-8269)
Daniel C Tanney Inc...............................D....... 215 639-3131
Bensalem (G-1179)
Dasco Inc..G....... 412 771-4140
Pittsburgh (G-14906)
David J Hohenshilt Welding LLC...........G....... 610 349-2937
Neffs (G-11998)
David Seidel..F....... 610 921-8310
Temple (G-18327)
Delvania Indus Fabrication Inc..............G....... 732 417-0333
Pine Forge (G-14587)
Demarchi John..G....... 724 547-6440
Mount Pleasant (G-11696)
DH Steel Products LLC...........................E....... 814 459-2715
Erie (G-5247)
Diamond Fabrications Inc......................G....... 724 228-8422
Washington (G-19163)
Dinsmore Wldg Fabrication Inc.............G....... 814 885-6407
Kersey (G-8555)
Dolans Wldg Stl Fbrication Inc..............E....... 814 749-8639
Johnstown (G-8369)
Dunbar Machine Co Inc ....G....... 724 277-8711
Dunbar (G-4439)
Dura-Bond Coating Inc...........................E....... 724 327-0782
Export (G-5598)
Dura-Bond Steel Corp ....C....... 724 327-0280
Export (G-5599)
Duraloy Technologies Inc ....C....... 724 887-5100
Scottdale (G-17190)
◆ Dynamic Surfc Applications Ltd ....E....... 570 546-6041
Pennsdale (G-13262)
E & E Metal Fabrications Inc.................E....... 717 228-3727
Lebanon (G-9565)
◆ Eagle Far East Inc ....E....... 215 957-9333
Warminster (G-18866)
Earlys Body Machine & Welding...........G....... 717 838-1663
Palmyra (G-13122)
Eastern Alloy Inc.....................................G....... 724 379-5776
Donora (G-4153)
Economy Metal Inc ....G....... 724 869-2887
Freedom (G-6189)
▲ Edlon Inc...D....... 610 268-3101
Avondale (G-852)
Edro Engineering Inc..............................F....... 610 940-1993
Conshohocken (G-3541)
Enclosures Direct Corporation..............G....... 724 837-7600
Greensburg (G-6664)
Energy Control Systems Inc ....E....... 412 781-8500
Pittsburgh (G-14974)
▼ Erie Weld Products Inc......................F....... 814 899-6320
Erie (G-5278)
Esmark Excalibur LLC............................E....... 724 371-3059
Beaver (G-981)
Esmark Excalibur LLC............................E....... 814 382-5696
Conneaut Lake (G-3472)
Esmark Industrial Group LLC ....F....... 412 259-8868
Sewickley (G-17387)
Evco Embouchure Visualizer Co...........G....... 724 224-4817
Tarentum (G-18243)
F F Frickanisce Iron Works ....G....... 724 568-2001
Vandergrift (G-18726)
Fab Tech Industries ....G....... 717 597-4919
Greencastle (G-6610)
Fab Tech V Industries Inc.......................E....... 717 597-4919
Greencastle (G-6611)
Fab-Rick Industries Inc ....E....... 717 859-5633
Lancaster (G-9013)
▲ Fab-TEC Industries Inc......................E....... 412 262-1144
Coraopolis (G-3690)
Fabbco Steel Inc ....E....... 717 792-4904
York (G-20474)
Fabco Inc ....F....... 814 944-1631
Altoona (G-505)
Fabricon Inc...E....... 610 921-0203
Temple (G-18329)
Fisher & Ludlow Inc................................D....... 217 324-6106
Wexford (G-19802)
Flint Road Welding ....G....... 717 535-5282
Mifflintown (G-11118)
Flintwood Metals Inc...............................E....... 717 274-9481
Lebanon (G-9571)
Formit Metal Fabricators LLC ....G....... 717 650-2895
York (G-20485)
Forrest Steel Corporation ....F....... 412 884-5533
Pittsburgh (G-15027)
Frazier-Simplex Machine Co ....E....... 724 222-5700
Washington (G-19177)
Freedom Components Inc.......................G....... 717 242-0101
Lewistown (G-9930)
Frey Lutz Corp..C....... 717 394-4635
Lancaster (G-9025)
Fronti Fabrications Inc ....G....... 610 900-6160
Palmerton (G-13105)
Gambone Steel Company Inc ....E....... 610 539-6505
Norristown (G-12660)
Gateco Inc...F....... 610 433-2100
Allentown (G-224)
Gcl Inc...G....... 724 933-7260
Wexford (G-19805)
General Weldments Inc ....F....... 724 744-2105
Irwin (G-8164)
George I Reitz & Sons Inc ....E....... 814 849-2308
Brookville (G-2261)
George I Reitz & Sons Inc ....G....... 412 824-9976
East Pittsburgh (G-4595)
▲ Gfs LLC ....D....... 412 262-1131
Coraopolis (G-3694)
▼ Global Fabrication Inc ....D....... 814 372-1500
Du Bois (G-4394)
Global Utility Structures LLC..................G....... 570 788-0826
Sugarloaf (G-18153)
Goldsborough & Vansant Inc..................G....... 724 782-0393
Finleyville (G-5959)
Goodhart Sons Inc....................................C....... 717 656-2404
Lancaster (G-9030)
▲ Grand Valley Manufacturing Co........D....... 814 728-8760
Titusville (G-18379)
Gray Wldg Fabrication Svcs Inc..............E....... 412 271-6900
Braddock (G-1944)
▼ Greiner Industries Inc ....B....... 717 653-8111
Mount Joy (G-11660)
▲ Groffdale Machine Co Inc...................G....... 717 656-3249
Leola (G-9785)
H & P Manufacturing................................G....... 610 565-7344
Media (G-10932)
H R Edgar Machining & Fabg Inc ....D....... 724 339-6694
New Kensington (G-12344)
H W Nicholson Wldg & Mfg Inc...............E....... 724 727-3461
Apollo (G-676)
◆ Haberle Steel Inc ....D....... 215 723-8848
Souderton (G-17738)
▲ Harris Rebar Atlantic Inc ....D....... 610 882-1401
Bethlehem (G-1529)
Hayes Metal Fabrication LLC...................G....... 724 694-5280
Derry (G-4103)
Hazleton Custom Metal Pdts Inc ....G....... 570 455-0450
Hazle Township (G-7462)
Hazleton Custom Metal Products...........F....... 570 455-0450
Hazleton (G-7501)
Hazleton Iron Works Inc ....G....... 570 455-0445
Hazleton (G-7502)
Helcrist LLC...F....... 215 727-2050
Philadelphia (G-13811)
Heslin-Steel Fab Inc..................................G....... 724 745-8282
Canonsburg (G-2596)
Hetran-B Inc...G....... 570 366-1411
Orwigsburg (G-13044)
High Industries Inc.....................................B....... 717 293-4444
Lancaster (G-9046)
High Steel Structures LLC ....F....... 717 390-4227
Lancaster (G-9047)
High Steel Structures LLC ....F....... 570 326-9051
Williamsport (G-20022)
▲ High Steel Structures LLC ....B....... 717 299-5211
Lancaster (G-9048)
High Steel Structures LLC ....G....... 717 299-5211
Lancaster (G-9049)
Hipps Tool & Design..................................G....... 814 236-3600
Curwensville (G-3953)
HMS Industries Inc.....................................E....... 724 459-5090
Blairsville (G-1724)
Hwp Fabrications.......................................G....... 814 487-5507
Windber (G-20183)
Industrial Welding and Fabg.....................G....... 724 266-2887
Leetsdale (G-9696)
Interlocking Deck Systems Inte................D....... 412 682-3041
Sewickley (G-17395)
Interstate Equipment Corp........................G....... 412 563-5556
Pittsburgh (G-15134)
Ira G Steffy and Son Inc ....D....... 717 626-6500
Ephrata (G-5111)

J & R Emerick Inc..................G...... 724 752-1251
Ellwood City **(G-4940)**

J B Booth and Co......................F...... 724 452-8400
Zelienople **(G-20805)**

J B Cooper and Cooper Co Inc...F...... 724 573-9860
Hookstown **(G-7769)**

J M S Fabricated Systems Inc.....E...... 724 832-3640
Latrobe **(G-9482)**

J Thomas Ltd...........................E...... 717 397-3483
Lancaster **(G-9069)**

▲ **J W Steel Fabricating Co**..........E...... 724 625-1355
Mars **(G-10503)**

James E Roth Inc.....................D...... 724 776-1910
Cranberry Township **(G-3826)**

Jasper Steel Fabrication Inc.......G...... 570 329-3330
Williamsport **(G-20027)**

Jeff Hills..............................G...... 570 322-4536
Williamsport **(G-20029)**

Jet Industries LLC..................D...... 724 758-5601
Ellwood City **(G-4942)**

Jet Industries Inc...................E...... 724 452-5780
Zelienople **(G-20808)**

JGM Fabricators & Constrs LLC....D...... 484 698-6201
Coatesville **(G-3309)**

JGM Welding & Fabg Svcs Inc......G...... 610 873-0081
Coatesville **(G-3310)**

JM Fabrications LLC..................G...... 267 354-1741
Sellersville **(G-17352)**

Job-Fab Inc...........................G...... 724 225-8225
Washington **(G-19190)**

Joes Welding Repairs................G...... 570 546-5223
Muncy **(G-11822)**

John H Bricker Welding..............F...... 717 263-5588
Chambersburg **(G-2946)**

John Jost Jr Inc.....................G...... 610 395-5461
Allentown **(G-269)**

▲ **Johnstown Wldg Fabrication Inc**...C...... 800 225-9353
Johnstown **(G-8394)**

Kbm Industries Inc...................G...... 717 938-2870
Etters **(G-5550)**

Keiths Truck Service.................G...... 814 696-6008
Duncansville **(G-4454)**

Kelly Iron Works Inc................G...... 610 872-5436
Hazleton **(G-7505)**

Ken F Smith Custom Shtmtl LLC.....G...... 717 624-4214
New Oxford **(G-12415)**

Ken-Fab & Weld Inc...................G...... 724 283-8815
East Butler **(G-4533)**

Ken-Fab & Weld Inc...................G...... 724 283-8815
East Butler **(G-4534)**

Kiczan Manufacturing Inc..........E...... 412 678-0980
North Versailles **(G-12777)**

Kincaid Manufacturing Inc..........G...... 412 795-9811
Verona **(G-18756)**

Kloeckner Metals Corporation.......D...... 717 755-1923
York **(G-20557)**

Kreitz Wldg & Fabrication Inc......F...... 610 678-6010
Reading **(G-16423)**

Krimes Industrial and Mech Inc.....G...... 717 628-1301
Ephrata **(G-5115)**

▲ **Kt-Grant Inc**........................D...... 724 468-4700
Export **(G-5614)**

Kutz Fabricating Inc................F...... 412 771-4161
Pittsburgh **(G-15204)**

L & M Fabrication and Mch Inc.....D...... 610 837-1848
Bath **(G-963)**

L B Foster Company...................E...... 814 623-6101
Bedford **(G-1060)**

Lafayette Welding Inc..............G...... 610 489-3529
Royersford **(G-16857)**

Lebanon Machine & Mfg Co LLC......G...... 717 274-3636
Lebanon **(G-9601)**

Lee Antenna & Line Service Inc.....F...... 610 346-7999
Springtown **(G-17927)**

▲ **Leiss Tool & Die**....................C...... 814 444-1444
Somerset **(G-17695)**

Leman Machine Company...............E...... 814 736-9696
Portage **(G-15918)**

Lincoln Contg & Eqp Co Inc.........D...... 814 629-6641
Stoystown **(G-18082)**

Lincoln Fabricating Co Inc.........E...... 412 361-2400
Pittsburgh **(G-15232)**

Lisa Mikolajczak.....................G...... 814 898-4700
Erie **(G-5367)**

Longwood Manufacturing Corp.......F...... 610 444-4200
Kennett Square **(G-8523)**

Lyons Industries Inc.................E...... 814 472-9770
Ebensburg **(G-4788)**

M & D Industries Inc................F...... 814 723-2381
Clarendon **(G-3170)**

M E Enterprise Services Inc........E...... 570 457-5221
Old Forge **(G-12968)**

Mancinci Metal Specialty Inc.......G...... 215 529-5800
Quakertown **(G-16211)**

Mariani Metal Fabricators Usa......G...... 717 432-9241
Dillsburg **(G-4135)**

Marlowes Metal Fabricating.........G...... 717 292-7360
Dover **(G-4195)**

Marstrand Industries Inc...........D...... 412 921-1511
Pittsburgh **(G-15258)**

Martin Rollison Inc..................E...... 570 253-4141
Honesdale **(G-7717)**

Mas-Fab Inc..........................E...... 717 244-4561
Red Lion **(G-16608)**

Mass Machine & Fabricating Co......F...... 724 225-1125
Washington **(G-19200)**

Master Machine Co Inc................F...... 814 495-4900
South Fork **(G-17777)**

Maverick Steel Company LLC.........D...... 412 271-1620
Braddock **(G-1946)**

▲ **Maxwell Welding and Mch Inc**.......E...... 724 729-3160
Burgettstown **(G-2349)**

Mc Grew Welding and Fabg Inc......F...... 724 379-9303
Donora **(G-4157)**

Mc Iron Works Inc....................D...... 610 837-9444
Bath **(G-966)**

McKinley Blacksmith Limited........G...... 610 459-2730
Boothwyn **(G-1879)**

McMillen Welding Inc................G...... 724 745-4507
Houston **(G-7874)**

McShane Welding Company Inc.......E...... 814 459-3797
Erie **(G-5387)**

Mechancal Fbrication Group Inc.....F...... 717 351-0437
New Holland **(G-12262)**

Metal USA Plates and Shapes........D...... 724 266-1283
Ambridge **(G-626)**

◆ **Metaldyne Sintered Ridgway LLC**....D...... 814 776-1141
Ridgway **(G-16717)**

Metals Usa Inc.......................F...... 215 540-8004
Fort Washington **(G-6084)**

Metals Usa Inc.......................F...... 215 540-8004
Fort Washington **(G-6085)**

Micale Fabricators Inc...............G...... 814 368-7133
Bradford **(G-1981)**

Michelmn-Cncllere Irnworks Inc.....C...... 610 837-9914
Bath **(G-967)**

Mid Atlntic Stl Fbrication LLC......G...... 717 687-0292
Ronks **(G-16811)**

Miller Fabrication Inc..............G...... 717 359-4433
Greencastle **(G-6622)**

Miller Metalcraft Inc...............E...... 717 399-8100
Millersville **(G-11212)**

Minnotte Manufacturing Corp........D...... 412 373-5270
Trafford **(G-18459)**

Mkt Metal Manufacturing.............E...... 717 764-9090
York **(G-20602)**

Mohney Fabricating & Mfg LLC.......G...... 724 349-6136
Penn Run **(G-13229)**

Mong Fabrication & Machine.........G...... 724 745-8370
Canonsburg **(G-2605)**

Monocacy Fabs Inc....................E...... 610 866-7311
Pen Argyl **(G-13214)**

Moore & Morford Inc.................E...... 724 834-1100
Greensburg **(G-6689)**

Moore Design Inc......................G...... 215 627-3379
Philadelphia **(G-14036)**

MRS and Son LLC......................G...... 215 750-7828
Morrisville **(G-11572)**

Multifab & Machine Inc...............F...... 724 947-7700
Burgettstown **(G-2351)**

Myers Steel Works Inc...............E...... 717 502-0266
Dillsburg **(G-4138)**

N C Stauffer & Sons Inc............D...... 570 945-3401
Factoryville **(G-5758)**

Nabco Inc.............................G...... 724 746-9617
Canonsburg **(G-2609)**

Nadine Corporation...................E...... 412 795-5100
Verona **(G-18759)**

Nestors Welding Co...................G...... 570 668-3401
Tamaqua **(G-18221)**

Northeast Industrial Mfg Inc........E...... 724 588-7711
Greenville **(G-6760)**

Northwestern Welding & Mch Co......G...... 814 774-2866
Lake City **(G-8907)**

Nuweld Inc............................C...... 570 505-1500
Williamsport **(G-20051)**

Oldcastle Precast Inc................C...... 215 257-8081
Telford **(G-18306)**

Outlaw Performance Inc...............E...... 724 697-4876
Avonmore **(G-866)**

Pabcor Inc............................G...... 724 652-1930
New Castle **(G-12136)**

Palladino Mtal Fabrication Inc......G...... 610 323-9439
Pottstown **(G-16025)**

Pelets Welding Inc..................E...... 610 384-5048
Coatesville **(G-3323)**

Penn Steel Fabrication Inc.........E...... 267 878-0705
Bristol **(G-2180)**

Penn Weld Inc.........................E...... 814 332-3682
Meadville **(G-10775)**

Penn-American Inc...................E...... 570 649-5173
Muncy **(G-11830)**

Pennheat LLC.........................E...... 814 282-6774
Meadville **(G-10777)**

Performance Proc Ventures LLC......G...... 724 704-8827
Farrell **(G-5870)**

Philadelphia Pipe Bending Co........E...... 215 225-8955
Philadelphia **(G-14149)**

Pittsburgh Fabrication Mch Inc......E...... 412 771-1400
Pittsburgh **(G-15395)**

Pleasant Mount Welding Inc.........G...... 570 282-6164
Carbondale **(G-2684)**

Poormans Wldg Fabrication Inc......F...... 814 349-5893
Aaronsburg **(G-1)**

▲ **Power Pipe Supports Inc**...........G...... 724 379-5212
Donora **(G-4159)**

Precision Cut Industries Inc.......D...... 717 632-2550
Hanover **(G-6936)**

Precision Fabg Group LLC............G...... 610 438-3156
Easton **(G-4744)**

Precision Steel Services Inc.......F...... 724 347-2770
Farrell **(G-5871)**

Preferred Sheet Metal Inc..........E...... 717 732-7100
Enola **(G-5084)**

Prodex Inc............................F...... 215 679-2405
Red Hill **(G-16584)**

▲ **Psb Industries Inc**.................D...... 814 453-3651
Erie **(G-5442)**

Pti Machine Inc.......................G...... 410 452-8855
Delta **(G-4062)**

Quality Metal Works Inc............F...... 717 367-2120
Elizabethtown **(G-4882)**

R & M Ship Tech USA Inc.............E...... 352 403-8365
Philadelphia **(G-14223)**

R G Steel Corp.......................E...... 724 656-1722
Pulaski **(G-16126)**

R H Benedix Contracting.............G...... 610 889-7472
Malvern **(G-10306)**

R PS Machinery Sales Inc.............E...... 570 398-7456
Jersey Shore **(G-8322)**

▲ **R&M American Marine Pdts Inc**......F...... 352 345-4866
Philadelphia **(G-14230)**

R&N Manufacturing LLC...............E...... 412 778-4103
Pittsburgh **(G-15464)**

Rackem Mfg LLC.......................G...... 570 226-6093
Hawley **(G-7442)**

Railway Specialties Corp............E...... 215 788-9242
Croydon **(G-3926)**

Ray-Guard International Ltd..........G...... 215 543-3849
Pottstown **(G-16038)**

Replicant Metals.....................G...... 717 626-1618
Lititz **(G-10041)**

Reuss Industries Inc................E...... 724 722-3300
Madison **(G-10166)**

Reynolds Iron Works Inc..............G...... 570 323-4663
Williamsport **(G-20068)**

▲ **Reynolds Manufacturing Co Inc**.....F...... 724 697-4522
Avonmore **(G-867)**

Reynolds Sales Co Inc................G...... 412 461-7877
Homestead **(G-7692)**

Riggs Industries Inc................E...... 814 629-5621
Stoystown **(G-18085)**

Rissler E Manufacturing LLC.........E...... 814 766-2246
New Enterprise **(G-12195)**

Ritner Steel Inc.....................E...... 717 249-1449
Carlisle **(G-2736)**

Ritter Industries Inc...............F...... 724 225-6563
Eighty Four **(G-4847)**

Robo Construction LLC...............E...... 570 494-1028
Williamsport **(G-20069)**

Rochester Machine Corporation.......E...... 724 843-7820
New Brighton **(G-12040)**

Rose Corporation.....................D...... 610 376-5004
Reading **(G-16504)**

Russell Rolls Inc.....................G...... 412 321-6623
Pittsburgh **(G-15503)**

Sabre Tblar Strctures - PA LLC......D...... 724 201-9968
Ellwood City **(G-4948)**

Sac Industries Inc..................F...... 412 787-7500
Pittsburgh **(G-15505)**

S I C

Safety Guard Steel Fabg Co ....F....... 412 821-1177
McKnight (G-10688)
Samuel Grossi & Sons Inc ....D....... 215 638-4470
Bensalem (G-1249)
Saylorsburg Stl Fbricators Inc ....G....... 610 381-4444
Saylorsburg (G-17106)
Scenic Ridge Company ....D....... 717 768-7522
Gordonville (G-6564)
Scranton Craftsmen Excvtg Inc ....D....... 800 775-1479
Throop (G-18360)
Sender Ornamental Iron Works ....E....... 814 536-5139
Johnstown (G-8433)
Shoemaker Mfg Solutions Inc ....E....... 215 723-5567
Souderton (G-17764)
Shrock Fabrication ....G....... 717 397-9500
Bird In Hand (G-1680)
Shumars Welding & Mch Svc Inc ....D....... 724 246-8095
Grindstone (G-6779)
Signal Machine Co ....G....... 717 354-9994
New Holland (G-12284)
Sippel Co Inc ....E....... 724 266-9800
Ambridge (G-635)
Siu King ....F....... 215 769-9863
Philadelphia (G-14313)
Skias Chuck Wldg & Fabricators ....G....... 610 375-0912
Reading (G-16519)
Smg Fab Inc ....F....... 717 556-8263
Leola (G-9804)
Solarian US ....G....... 610 550-6350
Ardmore (G-717)
Solid Steel Buildings Inc ....F....... 800 377-6543
Pittsburgh (G-15553)
Somerset Welding & Steel Inc ....E....... 814 444-7000
Somerset (G-17709)
Soul Customs Metal Works ....G....... 610 881-4300
Pen Argyl (G-13218)
Southern Stretch Forming & ....G....... 724 256-8474
Butler (G-2442)
▲ Specialty Fabrication and Powd ....D....... 814 432-6406
Franklin (G-6161)
Specialty Retail Fabricators ....F....... 215 477-5977
Philadelphia (G-14332)
Specialty Steel Supply Co Inc ....F....... 215 949-8800
Fairless Hills (G-5798)
Specialty Support Systems Inc ....F....... 215 945-1033
Levittown (G-9865)
Staar Distributing Llc ....D....... 814 612-2115
Reynoldsville (G-16666)
Stambaugh Metal Inc ....E....... 717 632-5957
Hanover (G-6958)
Standard Iron Works ....E....... 570 347-2058
Scranton (G-17293)
Standard Tool & Machine Co ....E....... 724 758-5522
Ellwood City (G-4951)
State of ARC Wldg & Fabg LLC ....G....... 610 216-6862
Bangor (G-930)
Steel Fab Enterprises LLC ....E....... 717 464-0330
Lancaster (G-9206)
Steel Fabricators LLC ....G....... 610 775-3532
Reading (G-16525)
Steel Plus Inc ....E....... 717 274-9481
Lebanon (G-9634)
Steffan Industries Inc ....G....... 412 751-4484
McKeesport (G-10683)
Stewart Welding & Fabg Inc ....D....... 717 252-3948
Wrightsville (G-20244)
Stewart-Amos Steel Inc ....E....... 717 564-3931
Harrisburg (G-7221)
Stoltzfus Enterprises Ltd ....G....... 610 273-9266
Honey Brook (G-7763)
Strait Steel Inc ....D....... 717 597-3125
Greencastle (G-6636)
Structural Fiberglass Inc ....F....... 814 623-0458
Bedford (G-1077)
Structure Manufacturing Work ....G....... 570 271-2880
Danville (G-4012)
Subcon Tl/Cctool Mch Group Inc ....E....... 814 456-7797
Erie (G-5494)
Summit Contracting Svcs Inc ....G....... 570 943-2232
Orwigsburg (G-13053)
Sunset Creations ....G....... 717 768-7663
Narvon (G-11928)
Supreme Manufacturing Inc ....E....... 724 376-4110
Stoneboro (G-18071)
Szoke Iron Works Inc ....F....... 610 760-9565
Walnutport (G-18794)
T Bruce Campbell Cnstr Co Inc ....C....... 724 528-9944
West Middlesex (G-19730)
▲ T Bruce Sales Inc ....D....... 724 528-9961
West Middlesex (G-19731)
◆ Tbj Incorporated ....F....... 717 261-9700
Chambersburg (G-2984)
Temtek Solutions Inc ....G....... 724 980-4270
Canonsburg (G-2647)
Thompson Machine Company Inc ....E....... 814 941-4982
Altoona (G-552)
Tna Doors ....G....... 570 484-5858
Effort (G-4829)
Tool City Welding LLC ....G....... 814 333-9353
Meadville (G-10802)
Tri-Form Inc ....F....... 724 334-0237
New Kensington (G-12384)
Tri-State Rebar Company ....F....... 412 824-4000
Mount Pleasant (G-11720)
Tri-Vet Design Fabrication LLC ....F....... 570 462-4941
Shenandoah (G-17497)
Tri-Way Metalworkers Inc ....E....... 570 462-4941
Shenandoah (G-17498)
Trico Welding Company ....F....... 724 722-1300
Yukon (G-20785)
UNI-Pro Inc ....F....... 610 668-9191
Philadelphia (G-14418)
Unique Fabrication LLC ....G....... 814 227-2627
Shippenville (G-17565)
United Fabricating Inc ....F....... 724 663-5891
Claysville (G-3209)
United Industrial Electro ....D....... 814 539-6115
Johnstown (G-8441)
United Wldg & Fabrication Inc ....G....... 814 266-3598
Windber (G-20194)
Valero Service Inc ....E....... 724 468-1010
Delmont (G-4061)
Vangura Iron Inc ....F....... 412 461-7825
Clairton (G-3159)
▲ Vautid North America Inc ....G....... 412 429-3288
Carnegie (G-2803)
Venango Steel Inc ....E....... 814 437-9353
Franklin (G-6167)
Vmf Inc ....E....... 570 575-0997
Scranton (G-17310)
VSI Sales LLC ....F....... 724 625-4060
Hazleton (G-7536)
Vulcan Industries Inc ....F....... 412 269-7655
Coraopolis (G-3732)
W & K Steel LLC ....E....... 412 271-0540
Braddock (G-1951)
Waggoner Fbrction Mllwrght LLC ....E....... 717 486-7533
Mount Holly Springs (G-11641)
Walker Fabricating ....G....... 724 847-5111
Beaver Falls (G-1016)
Waltco Inc ....E....... 724 625-3110
Mars (G-10512)
Walter Long Mfg Co Inc ....E....... 724 348-6631
Finleyville (G-5965)
Warren Sheet Metal Inc ....G....... 814 726-5777
Warren (G-19062)
Waste Gas Fabricating Co Inc ....E....... 215 736-9240
Fairless Hills (G-5807)
▲ Wearforce North America LLC ....F....... 215 996-1770
Chalfont (G-2894)
Weaver Metal Fab LLC ....F....... 717 466-6601
Ephrata (G-5155)
Wegco Welding Inc ....G....... 412 833-7020
Bethel Park (G-1438)
Weir Welding Company Inc ....D....... 610 974-8140
Bethlehem (G-1654)
Westmrland Stl Fabrication Inc ....E....... 724 446-0555
Madison (G-10167)
Wesworld Fabrications Inc ....G....... 215 455-5015
Philadelphia (G-14470)
Wheaton & Sons Inc ....F....... 412 351-0405
McKeesport (G-10687)
▼ Whemco Inc ....E....... 412 390-2700
Pittsburgh (G-15715)
William Henry Orna Ir Works ....G....... 215 659-1887
Willow Grove (G-20149)
Wing Dynamics ....G....... 570 275-5502
Danville (G-4016)
◆ Woodings Industrial Corp ....C....... 724 625-3131
Mars (G-10515)
Woolf Steel Inc ....E....... 717 944-1423
Middletown (G-11085)
Youngstown Alloy & Chain Corp ....G....... 724 347-1920
Mercer (G-10980)
Zottola Fab A PA Bus Tr ....G....... 412 221-4488
Cuddy (G-3944)
Zottola Steel Corporation ....G....... 412 362-5577
Pittsburgh (G-15737)
Zurenko Welding & Fabricating ....G....... 724 254-1131
Commodore (G-3455)

3442 Metal Doors, Sash, Frames, Molding & Trim

A C Miller Concrete Pdts Inc ....D....... 724 459-5950
Blairsville (G-1712)
Action Materials Inc ....G....... 610 377-3037
Lehighton (G-9709)
▲ Advanced Door Technologies Inc ....E....... 570 421-5929
East Stroudsburg (G-4603)
Alto Garage Door Manufacturing ....G....... 717 546-0056
Middletown (G-11047)
Alumax LLC ....C....... 412 553-4545
Pittsburgh (G-14695)
▲ Aluminum 2000 Inc ....E....... 717 569-2300
Lititz (G-9993)
▼ Apex Urethane Millworks LLC ....E....... 717 246-1948
Red Lion (G-16587)
Armaclad Inc ....E....... 717 749-3141
Waynesboro (G-19398)
B & L Manufacturing Corp ....F....... 412 784-9400
Pittsburgh (G-14745)
Baut Studios Inc ....E....... 570 288-1431
Swoyersville (G-18194)
Bbk Industries LLC ....G....... 215 676-1500
Langhorne (G-9280)
Best Group Holdings Inc ....E....... 814 536-1422
Johnstown (G-8357)
Bristol Rolling Door Inc ....G....... 215 949-9090
Levittown (G-9821)
Bucks County Shutters LLC ....F....... 215 957-3333
Warminster (G-18842)
Bugstuff ....G....... 724 785-7000
Brownsville (G-2310)
▲ Burns Manufacturing Inc ....F....... 814 833-7428
Erie (G-5218)
Caff Co ....G....... 412 787-1761
Pittsburgh (G-14799)
Ciw Enterprises Inc ....E....... 800 233-8366
Mountain Top (G-11755)
Clearview Mirror and Glass ....G....... 412 672-4122
McKeesport (G-10663)
Colfab Industries LLC ....E....... 215 768-2135
Bensalem (G-1171)
◆ Cornellcookson LLC ....B....... 800 294-4358
Mountain Top (G-11756)
Cornellcookson Inc ....C....... 570 474-6773
Mountain Top (G-11757)
▲ Craft-Bilt Manufacturing Co ....D....... 215 721-7700
Souderton (G-17731)
Custom Entryways & Millwork ....G....... 814 798-2500
Stoystown (G-18074)
Cutting Edge Doors Inc ....G....... 215 425-5921
Phila (G-13310)
Dailey Manufacturing Co ....F....... 215 659-0477
Willow Grove (G-20113)
Dun Rite Window and Door ....G....... 412 781-8200
Pittsburgh (G-14942)
EDM Co ....E....... 717 626-2186
Lititz (G-10005)
▲ Emerald Windows Inc ....F....... 215 236-6767
Philadelphia (G-13673)
▲ Extech/Exterior Tech Inc ....E....... 412 781-0991
Pittsburgh (G-14995)
Ezy Products Co Inc ....G....... 570 822-9600
Wilkes Barre (G-19919)
Fleming Steel Co ....F....... 724 658-1511
New Castle (G-12093)
G & S Metal Products Inc ....G....... 412 462-7000
Pittsburgh (G-15039)
Glenn Shutter ....G....... 717 867-2589
Annville (G-649)
▲ Graham Architectural Pdts Corp ......B....... 717 849-8100
York (G-20506)
▲ Graham Thermal Products LLC ....E....... 724 658-0500
New Castle (G-12098)
Guida Inc ....E....... 215 727-2222
Marcus Hook (G-10444)
Hagerty Precision Tool ....G....... 814 734-8668
Edinboro (G-4813)
Hc Hoodco Inc ....F....... 814 355-4003
Bellefonte (G-1104)
Hc Quality Doors LLC ....F....... 717 768-7038
Gordonville (G-6557)
Hinkel-Hofmann Supply Co Inc ....E....... 412 231-3131
Pittsburgh (G-15095)
▲ Hormann Flexon LLC ....E....... 724 385-9150
Burgettstown (G-2347)
▲ Household Metals Inc ....D....... 215 634-2800
Philadelphia (G-13835)
Howell Manufacturing Company ....F....... 814 652-5143
Everett (G-5573)

Joe Gigliotti & Sons Ornament.............F 610 775-3532
Reading *(G-16415)*

▲ **Kane Innovations Inc**.......................D....... 814 838-7731
Erie *(G-5342)*

Kane Innovations Inc...........................D....... 814 838-7731
Kane *(G-8469)*

Kawneer Commercial Windows LLC.....D....... 724 776-7000
Cranberry Township *(G-3827)*

Kawneer Company Inc.........................B....... 570 784-8000
Bloomsburg *(G-1787)*

Kenbern Storm Doors............................G....... 412 678-7210
McKeesport *(G-10674)*

Kensington Hpp Inc..............................E....... 866 318-6628
Vandergrift *(G-18731)*

▼ **Kestrel Shutters & Doors Inc**...........F....... 610 326-6679
Stowe *(G-18072)*

McBrothers Inc.......................................F....... 215 675-3003
Warminster *(G-18918)*

MI Windows and Doors Inc..................B....... 717 362-8196
Elizabethville *(G-4895)*

MI Windows and Doors Inc..................C....... 717 365-3300
Gratz *(G-6579)*

MI Windows and Doors Inc..................C....... 570 682-1206
Hegins *(G-7543)*

▼ **MI Windows and Doors Inc**.............G....... 717 365-3300
Gratz *(G-6578)*

MI Windows and Doors LLC.................G....... 717 365-3300
Gratz *(G-6580)*

Mid Atlantic Retractable.......................G....... 610 496-8062
Malvern *(G-10279)*

Millcreek Metals Inc...............................G....... 814 764-3708
Strattanville *(G-18098)*

Muldoon Window Door & Awning.........G....... 570 347-9453
Scranton *(G-17261)*

Nortek Global Hvac LLC.........................B....... 814 938-1408
Punxsutawney *(G-16151)*

Northeast Building Pdts Corp...............C....... 215 535-7110
Philadelphia *(G-14079)*

Northeast Building Pdts Corp...............F....... 215 331-2400
Philadelphia *(G-14080)*

Northeast Glass Co................................G....... 267 991-0054
Philadelphia *(G-14083)*

Nova Molding...G....... 610 767-7858
Slatington *(G-17610)*

Overhead Door Corporation..................D....... 215 368-8700
Lansdale *(G-9396)*

Overhead Door Corporation..................C....... 570 326-7325
Williamsport *(G-20053)*

Overly Door Company............................D....... 724 834-7300
Greensburg *(G-6696)*

Pella Corporation....................................G....... 610 648-0922
Berwyn *(G-1370)*

Peters James & Son Inc.........................G....... 215 739-9500
Philadelphia *(G-14139)*

Philadelphia Safety Devices..................G....... 215 245-7554
Bristol *(G-2181)*

Pittsburgh Aluminum Co LLC................F....... 724 452-5900
Pittsburgh *(G-15386)*

Pompanette LLC......................................E....... 717 569-2300
Lititz *(G-10033)*

Q C M Corporation..................................F....... 610 586-4770
Folcroft *(G-6013)*

Railway Specialties Corp.......................E....... 215 788-9242
Croydon *(G-3926)*

Ray-Guard International Ltd.................G....... 215 543-3849
Pottstown *(G-16038)*

Regenex Corporation.............................D....... 724 528-5900
West Middlesex *(G-19728)*

Ritescreen Company LLC.......................C....... 717 362-7483
Elizabethville *(G-4897)*

Roma Aluminum Co Inc..........................F....... 215 545-5700
Philadelphia *(G-14259)*

Saha Industries Inc.................................G....... 610 383-5070
Coatesville *(G-3325)*

Scatton Bros Mfg Co...............................E....... 215 362-6830
Lansdale *(G-9409)*

Seaway Manufacturing Corp..................D....... 814 898-2255
Erie *(G-5472)*

Seneca Hardwood Lumber Co Inc.........E....... 814 498-2241
Cranberry *(G-3797)*

◆ **Solar Innovations Inc**..........................C....... 570 915-1500
Pine Grove *(G-14605)*

Southwest Vinyl Windows Inc...............F....... 610 626-8826
Lansdowne *(G-9444)*

▲ **Steelway Cellar Doors LLC**...............F....... 610 277-9988
King of Prussia *(G-8680)*

Tell Doors & Windows LLC....................G....... 717 625-2990
Lititz *(G-10053)*

Termac Corp..G....... 610 863-5356
Wind Gap *(G-20174)*

Thermal Industries Inc...........................G....... 814 944-4534
Altoona *(G-551)*

Thermo-Twin Industries Inc..................C....... 412 826-1000
Oakmont *(G-12927)*

Thermolite Inc..E....... 570 969-1957
Scranton *(G-17300)*

Three Rivers Aluminum Company........G....... 800 837-7002
Cranberry Township *(G-3853)*

Thruways Door Systems Inc...................F....... 412 781-4030
Pittsburgh *(G-15622)*

▼ **Traco Delaware Inc**.............................F....... 724 776-7000
Cranberry Township *(G-3856)*

▲ **Tri City Aluminum Company**..............A....... 724 799-8917
Cranberry Township *(G-3857)*

Tri-State Door and Hardware.................G....... 215 455-2100
Philadelphia *(G-14408)*

Trimline Windows Inc............................D....... 215 672-5233
Ivyland *(G-8224)*

Trinity Glass Intl Inc...............................D....... 610 395-2030
Breinigsville *(G-2028)*

Victor Sun Ctrl of Philadelphia.............E....... 215 743-0800
Philadelphia *(G-14446)*

Vista Custom Millwork Inc.....................F....... 724 376-4093
Sandy Lake *(G-17063)*

Voegele Company Inc.............................E....... 412 781-0940
Pittsburgh *(G-15705)*

Vynex Window Systems Inc...................F....... 412 681-3800
North Versailles *(G-12783)*

Weather Shield Mfg Inc..........................B....... 717 761-7131
Camp Hill *(G-2524)*

▲ **Young Windows Inc**.............................D....... 610 828-5036
Conshohocken *(G-3618)*

Zurn Aluminum Products Co..................G....... 814 774-2681
Girard *(G-6404)*

3443 Fabricated Plate Work

A & R Iron Works Inc..............................F....... 610 497-8770
Trainer *(G-18462)*

Aaron King..G....... 610 273-1365
Honey Brook *(G-7735)*

▲ **ABT LLC**..E....... 412 826-8002
Pittsburgh *(G-14636)*

Abtrex Industries Inc..............................E....... 724 266-5425
Leetsdale *(G-9676)*

Advanced Thermal Hydronics................F....... 610 473-1036
Boyertown *(G-1894)*

Advanced Welding Tech Inc...................E....... 814 899-3584
Erie *(G-5176)*

Alchemet Inc..G....... 610 566-5964
Wallingford *(G-18780)*

Alfa Laval Inc...D....... 717 453-7143
Lykens *(G-10129)*

All Metal Fabricating Co Inc...................G....... 724 925-3537
Youngwood *(G-20777)*

All-Steel Fabricators Co Inc...................G....... 610 687-2267
Wayne *(G-19296)*

▲ **Allegheny Plastics Inc**.........................C....... 412 741-4416
Leetsdale *(G-9679)*

Allentown Steel Fabg Co Inc..................F....... 610 264-2815
Catasauqua *(G-2813)*

Alloy Fabrication Inc...............................G....... 610 921-9212
Reading *(G-16318)*

Alternate Heating Systems LLC............E....... 717 261-0922
Chambersburg *(G-2901)*

Altrax...G....... 814 379-3706
Summerville *(G-18156)*

American Hollow Boring Company.......E....... 800 673-2458
Erie *(G-5187)*

American Made Systems Inc.................G....... 412 771-3300
Pittsburgh *(G-14703)*

Amity Industries Inc...............................D....... 610 385-6075
Douglassville *(G-4169)*

▼ **Anderson Tube Company Inc**............G....... 215 855-0118
Hatfield *(G-7317)*

Applied Equipment Co............................G....... 610 258-7941
Easton *(G-4646)*

▲ **Armstrong Engrg Assoc Inc**...............D....... 610 436-6080
Coatesville *(G-3291)*

Armstrong Engrg Assoc Inc...................G....... 610 436-6080
West Chester *(G-19501)*

Ax Heat Transfer Inc...............................F....... 724 654-7747
New Castle *(G-12060)*

Axeman-Anderson Company.................E....... 570 326-9114
Williamsport *(G-19991)*

Babcock Wlcox Ebnsburg Pwr Inc........G....... 814 472-1140
Ebensburg *(G-4780)*

Bigbee Steel and Tank Company..........C....... 814 893-5701
Manheim *(G-10370)*

Bigbee Steel and Tank Company..........D....... 717 664-0600
Manheim *(G-10371)*

Biofab Products Inc.................................E....... 724 283-4801
Butler *(G-2379)*

Blank River Services Inc........................E....... 412 384-2489
Elizabeth *(G-4857)*

Boilerroom Equipment Inc.....................G....... 724 327-0077
Export *(G-5593)*

Bradford Allegheny Corporation............F....... 814 362-2591
Lewis Run *(G-9872)*

Bradford Allegheny Corporation............D....... 814 362-2593
Lewis Run *(G-9874)*

Brandywine Machine Co Inc...................F....... 610 269-1221
Downingtown *(G-4216)*

Brandywine Valley Fabricators..............F....... 610 384-7440
Coatesville *(G-3295)*

Brentwood Industries Inc.......................D....... 717 274-1827
Lebanon *(G-9548)*

Bristol Tank & Welding Co Inc...............F....... 215 752-8727
Langhorne *(G-9282)*

Brumbaugh Body Co Inc.........................G....... 814 696-9552
Duncansville *(G-4450)*

Burnham LLC..D....... 717 293-5839
Lancaster *(G-8965)*

▲ **Byrne Chiarlone LP**.............................E....... 610 874-8436
Chester *(G-3042)*

▲ **Cannon Boiler Works Inc**....................D....... 724 335-8541
New Kensington *(G-12332)*

Careys Dumpster Services.....................G....... 717 258-1400
Carlisle *(G-2692)*

◆ **Carpenter Technology Corp**...............B....... 610 208-2000
Philadelphia *(G-13508)*

Cemline Corporation...............................D....... 724 274-5430
Cheswick *(G-3104)*

Charles R Kelley.......................................G....... 717 840-0181
York *(G-20423)*

◆ **Charleston Marine Cntrs Inc**...............D....... 843 745-0022
Dallastown *(G-3973)*

Clipper Pipe & Service Inc......................G....... 610 872-9067
Eddystone *(G-4799)*

Combustion Service & Eqp Co...............D....... 412 821-8900
Pittsburgh *(G-14867)*

Containment Solutions Inc.....................C....... 814 542-8621
Mount Union *(G-11741)*

Contech Engnered Solutions LLC..........E....... 717 597-2148
Greencastle *(G-6604)*

Conway-Phillips Holding LLC................E....... 412 315-7963
Braddock *(G-1943)*

Cooney Manufacturing Co LLC..............G....... 610 272-2100
Pottstown *(G-15976)*

▲ **Counterflow Inc**....................................G....... 814 734-9440
Edinboro *(G-4810)*

◆ **CP Industries Holdings Inc**................D....... 412 664-6604
McKeesport *(G-10665)*

Creekside Welding LLC...........................G....... 717 355-2008
New Holland *(G-12241)*

▲ **Crown Boiler Co**...................................E....... 215 535-8900
Philadelphia *(G-13586)*

Cryognic Inds Svc Cmpanies LLC.........G....... 724 695-1910
Imperial *(G-8062)*

Custom Container Vly Can LLC..............F....... 724 253-2038
Lewisburg *(G-9903)*

▲ **Custom Engineering Co**.......................C....... 814 898-1390
Erie *(G-5237)*

D L George & Sons Mfg Inc....................D....... 717 765-4700
Waynesboro *(G-19407)*

▲ **Davis Lattemann Inc**...........................G....... 877 576-5885
Tunkhannock *(G-18537)*

De Marco Waste Dumpster Svc..............G....... 412 904-4260
Pittsburgh *(G-14912)*

Dedicated Customs Inc...........................G....... 724 678-6609
Burgettstown *(G-2345)*

Deist Industries Inc.................................E....... 800 233-0867
Hadley *(G-6819)*

Delta Mechanical Inc...............................F....... 570 752-5511
Berwick *(G-1323)*

DHL Machine Co Inc................................E....... 215 536-3591
Quakertown *(G-16186)*

DMC Global Inc...E....... 724 277-9710
Mount Braddock *(G-11616)*

Dolans Wldg Stl Fbrication Inc..............E....... 814 749-8639
Johnstown *(G-8369)*

▼ **Doucette Industries Inc**.......................E....... 717 845-8746
York *(G-20456)*

Doyle & Roth Mfg Co Inc.........................E....... 570 282-5010
Simpson *(G-17592)*

Drv Metal Fab LLC....................................F....... 717 968-9028
East Waterford *(G-4640)*

Dunes Point Capital..................................G....... 610 666-1225
Oaks *(G-12932)*

Dura-Bond Steel Corp..............................C....... 724 327-0280
Export *(G-5599)*

SIC

▲ Edlon Inc.............................D...... 610 268-3101
Avondale (G-852)

Electronics Instrs & Optics..................E...... 215 245-6300
Bensalem (G-1188)

Energy Conversion Technology..........G...... 412 835-0191
Pittsburgh (G-14975)

F F Frickanisce Iron Works ....G...... 724 568-2001
Vandergrift (G-18726)

F R Industries Inc.............................F...... 412 242-5903
Pittsburgh (G-14999)

▲ Fab-TEC Industries Inc ....E...... 412 262-1144
Coraopolis (G-3690)

Faull Fabricating Inc.......................G...... 724 458-7662
Grove City (G-6784)

Fisher Tank Company..........................E...... 610 494-7200
Chester (G-3051)

Four Guys Stnless Tank Eqp Inc......D...... 814 634-8373
Meyersdale (G-11010)

▼ G G Greene Enterprises Inc ....E...... 814 723-5700
Warren (G-19027)

▼ Gardner Cryogenics Inc ....C...... 610 264-4523
Bethlehem (G-1523)

General Fabricating Svcs LLC............F...... 412 262-1131
Coraopolis (G-3692)

General Weldments Inc.....................F...... 724 744-2105
Irwin (G-8164)

George I Reitz & Sons Inc ....E...... 814 849-2308
Brookville (G-2261)

George I Reitz & Sons Inc ....G...... 412 824-9976
East Pittsburgh (G-4595)

▲ Gerome Manufacturing Co Inc.......D...... 724 438-8544
Smithfield (G-17650)

Glens Dumpster Service LLC............G...... 202 521-1493
Pottstown (G-15991)

▲ Gooch Thermal Mfg Inc ....F...... 610 285-2496
Whitehall (G-19874)

Goodhart Sons Inc..............................C...... 717 656-2404
Lancaster (G-9030)

Gouldey Welding & Fabrications..........E...... 215 721-9522
Souderton (G-17737)

Grape Fiberglass Inc ....F...... 814 938-8118
Punxsutawney (G-16142)

Grattons Fabricating & Mfg.............G...... 724 527-5681
Adamsburg (G-18)

▲ Greenetech Mfg Co Inc ....E...... 724 228-2400
Washington (G-19181)

Gyrotron Technology Inc ....G...... 215 244-4740
Bensalem (G-1207)

H & C Giamo Inc.................................G...... 610 941-0909
Conshohocken (G-3552)

Hanover Iron Works Inc...................E...... 717 632-5624
Hanover (G-6896)

Harbor Steel Inc ....F...... 724 658-7748
New Castle (G-12100)

Harliss Specialties Corp...................E...... 724 863-0321
Irwin (G-8166)

Harsco Corporation............................C...... 570 421-7500
East Stroudsburg (G-4617)

Harsco Corporation............................F...... 717 506-2071
Mechanicsburg (G-10851)

▼ Highland Tank and Mfg Co...........C...... 814 893-5701
Stoystown (G-18080)

Hpi Processes Inc ....G...... 215 799-0450
Telford (G-18294)

▲ Hydac Corp.......................................E...... 610 266-0100
Bethlehem (G-1533)

Hydroflex Systems Inc ....F...... 717 480-4200
Lewisberry (G-9887)

▲ Ice Qube Inc....................................D...... 724 837-7600
Greensburg (G-6676)

Ik Stotzfus Service Corp...................E...... 717 397-3503
Manheim (G-10390)

▲ Indeck Keystone Energy LLC ....E...... 814 452-6421
Erie (G-5322)

Industrial Eqp Fabricators Inc ....F...... 724 752-8819
Ellwood City (G-4938)

Integrated Fabrication Mch Inc.........E...... 724 962-3526
Greenville (G-6749)

J Thomas Ltd......................................E...... 717 397-3483
Lancaster (G-9069)

▲ J W Steel Fabricating Co ....E...... 724 625-1355
Mars (G-10503)

James F Kemp Inc..............................G...... 412 233-8166
Clairton (G-3151)

L & M Fabrication and Mch Inc ....D...... 610 837-1848
Bath (G-963)

Lancaster Composite ....G...... 717 872-8999
Lancaster (G-9091)

Lancaster Metal Mfg Inc ....D...... 717 293-4480
Lancaster (G-9101)

Larry J Epps.......................................G...... 724 712-1156
Butler (G-2419)

◆ Lee Industries Inc.........................C...... 814 342-0460
Philipsburg (G-14519)

Liberty Welding Co ....G...... 412 661-1776
Pittsburgh (G-15228)

Liquid Tech Tank Systems Inc...........F...... 717 796-7056
Dillsburg (G-4134)

Longwood Manufacturing Corp..........F...... 610 444-4200
Kennett Square (G-8523)

M & D Industries Inc ....F...... 814 723-2381
Clarendon (G-3170)

M & M Welding & Fabricating ....G...... 724 794-2045
Slippery Rock (G-17620)

M and P Custom Design Inc...............F...... 610 444-0244
Kennett Square (G-8524)

M Glosser & Sons Inc ....E...... 412 751-4700
Mc Keesport (G-10642)

◆ Maguire Products Inc.....................E...... 610 459-4300
Aston (G-773)

◆ Marg Inc...F...... 724 703-3020
Oakdale (G-12906)

McShane Welding Company Inc........E...... 814 459-3797
Erie (G-5387)

Messer LLC...F...... 484 281-3261
Bethlehem (G-1570)

Metplas Inc ....D...... 724 295-5200
Natrona Heights (G-11946)

Mgk Technologies Inc.......................E...... 814 849-3061
Homer City (G-7678)

▲ Mgs Inc...C...... 717 336-7528
Denver (G-4083)

Minnotte Manufacturing Corp..........D...... 412 373-5270
Trafford (G-18459)

Modern Precast Concrete Inc ....E...... 484 548-6200
Easton (G-4726)

Mounts Equipment Co Inc.................G...... 724 225-0460
Washington (G-19208)

Moyers Service Co............................G...... 267 205-1105
Feasterville Trevose (G-5920)

MSA Safety Incorporated..................A...... 724 733-9100
Murrysville (G-11859)

▲ Msf Management LLC ....E...... 724 371-3059
Beaver (G-987)

Multitherm Heat Transfer..................G...... 610 408-8361
Malvern (G-10281)

▲ Munroe Incorporated ....D...... 412 231-0600
Pittsburgh (G-15311)

Munroe Incorporated.........................G...... 412 231-0600
Ambridge (G-628)

Nabco Systems LLC..........................E...... 724 746-9617
Canonsburg (G-2610)

National Dumpster Service LLC ....G...... 484 949-1060
Coatesville (G-3319)

New Castle Industries Inc ....G...... 724 656-5600
New Castle (G-12129)

▲ Norstone Incorporated ....G...... 484 684-6986
Bridgeport (G-2041)

Northeast Industrial Mfg...................G...... 724 253-3110
Hadley (G-6820)

Nrf US Inc..G...... 814 947-1378
Plymouth Meeting (G-15861)

Olmsted Inc ....F...... 412 384-2161
West Elizabeth (G-19696)

◆ ORourke & Sons Inc ....F...... 610 436-0932
West Chester (G-19613)

▲ Panel Solutions Inc ....E...... 570 459-3490
Hazleton (G-7515)

Park Corporation...............................G...... 412 472-0500
Coraopolis (G-3711)

▲ Pb Heat LLC....................................E...... 610 845-6100
Bally (G-906)

Penguin Logistics Holdings LLC..........G...... 724 772-9800
Wexford (G-19819)

◆ Penn Iron Works Inc......................E...... 610 777-7656
Reading (G-16467)

Penn Manufacturing LLC...................F...... 724 845-4682
New Kensington (G-12365)

▼ Penn Separator Corp......................E...... 814 849-7328
Brookville (G-2269)

▲ Pennmark Technologies Corp.........C...... 570 255-5000
Dallas (G-3966)

◆ Petrex Inc..F...... 814 723-2050
Warren (G-19044)

Philadlphia Mtal Rsrce Rcovery ....E...... 215 423-4800
Philadelphia (G-14163)

Pittsburgh Tank Corporation.............E...... 724 258-0200
Monongahela (G-11314)

Precision Components Group LLC.......C...... 717 848-1126
York (G-20637)

▲ Precision Cstm Components LLC....B...... 717 848-1126
York (G-20638)

Precision Tool & Mfg Corp ....G...... 717 767-6454
Emigsville (G-4997)

Pressure-Tech Inc.............................F...... 717 597-1868
Greencastle (G-6628)

▲ Pro Dyne Corporation ....G...... 610 789-0606
Phoenixville (G-14572)

Pro Thermal Inc.................................G...... 412 203-1588
Pittsburgh (G-15450)

Prodex Inc..G...... 215 536-4078
Quakertown (G-16234)

Proweld...G...... 724 836-0207
Greensburg (G-6706)

Pts Industries Corp...........................F...... 814 345-5200
Drifting (G-4375)

▲ R-V Industries Inc ....C...... 610 273-2457
Honey Brook (G-7758)

Ray-Guard International Ltd ....G...... 215 543-3849
Pottstown (G-16038)

▲ Reynolds Manufacturing Co Inc.....F...... 724 697-4522
Avonmore (G-867)

Reynolds Sales Co Inc......................G...... 412 461-7877
Homestead (G-7692)

◆ Reynolds Services Inc ....D...... 724 646-2600
Greenville (G-6770)

RG Industries Inc...............................E...... 717 849-0345
York (G-20658)

Richard J Summons Sculpture............G...... 610 223-9013
Reading (G-16497)

◆ Richardson Coolg Packages LLC.....E...... 724 698-2302
New Castle (G-12142)

River Supply Inc.................................E...... 717 927-1555
Brogue (G-2240)

◆ Schutte Koerting Acquisition ....E...... 215 639-0900
Trevose (G-18502)

Scott Metals Inc.................................E...... 412 279-7021
Carnegie (G-2790)

Scranton Craftsmen Excvtg Inc.........D...... 800 775-1479
Throop (G-18360)

▼ Select Industries Inc ....G...... 724 654-7747
New Castle (G-12147)

▲ Sharpsville Container Corp.............E...... 724 962-1100
Sharpsville (G-17475)

Sheet Metal Specialists LLC.............E...... 717 910-7000
Harrisburg (G-7215)

Shoemaker Mfg Solutions Inc............E...... 215 723-5567
Souderton (G-17764)

▲ Sidehill Copper Works Inc ....G...... 814 451-0400
Erie (G-5477)

Solar Cool Coatings...........................G...... 267 664-3667
Glenside (G-6537)

Somerset Door and Column Co...........E...... 814 445-9608
Somerset (G-17708)

Specialty Tank & Wldg Co Inc............E...... 215 949-2939
Bristol (G-2201)

Spomin Metals Inc..............................F...... 724 924-9718
New Castle (G-12155)

SPX Cooling Technologies Inc............E...... 717 845-4830
York (G-20677)

SPX Corporation................................C...... 724 746-4240
Washington (G-19227)

▲ SPX Flow Us LLC ....G...... 814 476-5800
Mc Kean (G-10594)

SPX Heat Transfer LLC.......................E...... 610 250-1146
Bethlehem (G-1628)

Staar Distributing Llc.........................D...... 814 612-2115
Reynoldsville (G-16666)

Standard Tool & Machine Co ....E...... 724 758-5522
Ellwood City (G-4951)

Stoltzfus Steel Manufacturing............G...... 570 524-7835
Lewisburg (G-9919)

Stone Valley Welding LLC....................E...... 814 667-2046
Huntingdon (G-7956)

Stoystown Tank & Steel Co................E...... 814 893-5133
Stoystown (G-18087)

Superior Metalworks Inc ....F...... 717 245-2446
Carlisle (G-2740)

Therma-Fab Inc ....G...... 814 664-9429
Corry (G-3774)

▲ Therma-Fab Inc ....G...... 814 827-9455
Titusville (G-18398)

Thermacore International Inc..............B...... 717 569-6551
Lancaster (G-9216)

Thermal Engrg Intl USA Inc ....E...... 610 948-5400
Royersford (G-16868)

▲ Thermal Solutions Products LLC.....E...... 717 239-7642
Lancaster (G-9217)

◆ Thermal Transfer Corporation..........D...... 412 460-4004
Duquesne (G-4500)

Thomas Sales Inc................................G.... 717 597-9366
Greencastle (G-6639)

Thrifty Dumpster Inc..........................G.... 215 688-1774
Eagleville (G-4518)

Titan Co2 Inc.....................................G.... 814 669-4544
Alexandria (G-64)

▲ Tm Industrial Supply Inc ....E.... 814 453-5014
Erie (G-5510)

Trashcans Unlimited LLC....................G.... 800 279-3615
Honesdale (G-7730)

◆ TW Metals LLC...............................D.... 610 458-1300
Exton (G-5741)

US Boiler Company Inc.......................C.... 717 397-4701
Lancaster (G-9229)

Valley Can Inc....................................F.... 724 253-2038
Hadley (G-6822)

Valley Enterprise Cont Inc ....F.... 570 962-2194
Blanchard (G-1750)

Valley Enterprise Cont LLC ....F.... 570 962-2194
Blanchard (G-1751)

Van Industries Inc.............................E.... 610 582-1118
Birdsboro (G-1707)

Vari Corporation................................G.... 570 385-0731
Schuylkill Haven (G-17169)

Vcw Enterprises Inc...........................D.... 610 847-5112
Ottsville (G-13068)

Walter Long Mfg Co Inc......................E.... 724 348-6631
Finleyville (G-5965)

▼ Warren Industries Inc ....E.... 814 723-2050
Warren (G-19059)

Waste Gas Fabricating Co Inc ....E.... 215 736-9240
Fairless Hills (G-5807)

Wcr Inc..G.... 215 447-8152
Bensalem (G-1270)

Wedj/Three CS Inc.............................D.... 717 845-8685
York (G-20705)

Western PA Stl Fabg Inc.....................E.... 724 658-8575
New Castle (G-12169)

Wheaton & Sons Inc..........................F.... 412 351-0405
McKeesport (G-10687)

Witherup Fbrction Erection Inc ....E.... 814 385-6601
Kennerdell (G-8499)

Wolfe Metal Fab Inc...........................G.... 724 339-7790
Lower Burrell (G-10108)

◆ Woodings Industrial Corp...............C.... 724 625-3131
Mars (G-10515)

▼ X-Mark/Cdt Inc...............................G.... 724 228-7373
Washington (G-19248)

Zeyon Inc...E.... 814 899-3311
Erie (G-5536)

3444 Sheet Metal Work

486 Associates Inc.............................E.... 717 691-7077
Mechanicsburg (G-10815)

A & E Manufacturing Co Inc................C.... 215 943-9460
Levittown (G-9810)

A C Gentry Inc....................................F.... 215 927-9948
Philadelphia (G-13324)

A M E R Inc..E.... 724 229-8020
Washington (G-19143)

A W Mercer Inc...................................C.... 610 367-8460
Boyertown (G-1892)

Aaron S Myers.....................................G.... 717 339-9304
New Oxford (G-12401)

▲ ABT LLC...E.... 412 826-8002
Pittsburgh (G-14636)

Acacia Corp..F.... 412 771-6144
Mc Kees Rocks (G-10600)

Accrotool Inc......................................C.... 724 339-3560
New Kensington (G-12320)

▲ Accu Machining Center Inc.............E.... 610 252-6855
Easton (G-4644)

◆ Ace Metal Inc..................................E.... 610 623-2204
Clifton Heights (G-3250)

Acf Group LLC....................................E.... 724 364-7027
Allison (G-444)

Acme Roofing and Heating Inc...........G...... 412 921-8218
Pittsburgh (G-14643)

▼ Acurlite Strl Skylights Inc...............E.... 570 759-6882
Berwick (G-1307)

ADG Fabrication LLC...........................G.... 724 658-3000
New Castle (G-12053)

Advanced Drainage Systems Inc ....E.... 570 546-7686
Muncy (G-11805)

Aella Industries Corporation ....G.... 610 399-9086
Aston (G-749)

Aeroparts Fabg & Machining Inc.........E.... 814 948-6015
Nicktown (G-12618)

Afca Company Inc...............................E.... 215 425-2300
Philadelphia (G-13351)

Agape Precision Mfg LLC ....E.... 484 704-2601
Pottstown (G-15961)

Age-Craft Manufacturing Inc..............F.... 724 838-5580
Greensburg (G-6648)

Airsources Inc....................................G.... 610 983-0102
Malvern (G-10181)

Alaska Stoker Stove Inc......................G.... 570 387-0260
Bloomsburg (G-1767)

Albert C Phy & Sons Inc......................F.... 215 659-2125
Willow Grove (G-20106)

Alberts Custom Shtmtl & Wldg...........G.... 814 454-4461
Erie (G-5179)

Albright Precision Inc.........................E.... 570 457-5744
Moosic (G-11502)

◆ Allentech Inc...................................D.... 484 664-7887
Allentown (G-126)

Alumax LLC...E.... 570 784-7481
Bloomsburg (G-1768)

American Air Duct Inc.........................G.... 724 483-8057
Charleroi (G-3006)

American Alloy Fabricators ....G.... 610 635-0205
Norristown (G-12633)

American Architectural Metal M..........F.... 610 432-9787
Allentown (G-132)

American Metals & Mfg Co...................G.... 724 934-8866
Sarver (G-17064)

American Metals Company...................G.... 724 625-8666
Mars (G-10486)

American Roll Suppliers Inc ....G.... 610 857-2988
Parkesburg (G-13171)

Amity Industries Inc...........................D.... 610 385-6075
Douglassville (G-4169)

▲ Apx Enclosures Inc.........................E.... 717 328-9399
Mercersburg (G-10981)

Apx York Sheet Metal Inc...................E.... 717 767-2704
York (G-20382)

Arconic Inc...C.... 717 393-9641
Lancaster (G-8938)

ARS Metal Fabricators LLC.................G.... 215 855-6000
Hatfield (G-7318)

Arvite Technologies Inc......................F.... 814 838-9444
Erie (G-5195)

ATI Corporation..................................E.... 717 354-8721
New Holland (G-12229)

Atkinson Industries Inc......................G.... 570 366-2114
Orwigsburg (G-13039)

▲ Auger Fabrication Inc......................E.... 610 524-3350
Exton (G-5648)

Bcl Manufacturing Inc........................E.... 814 467-8225
Windber (G-20178)

Bellwether Corp.................................F.... 610 534-5382
Folcroft (G-5999)

Bensalem Metal Inc............................G.... 215 526-3355
Bensalem (G-1156)

▲ Berger Building Products Inc..........G.... 215 355-1200
Feasterville Trevose (G-5889)

▲ Berger Building Products Corp........D.... 215 355-1200
Feasterville Trevose (G-5890)

Bevilacqua Sheet Metal Inc.................G.... 570 558-0397
Scranton (G-17211)

Biofab Products Inc............................E.... 724 283-4801
Butler (G-2379)

Blank River Services Inc.....................E.... 412 384-2489
Elizabeth (G-4857)

Blanski Energy Management Inc.........E.... 610 373-5273
Reading (G-16335)

Bork Inc..G.... 215 324-1155
Philadelphia (G-13472)

Bornmann Mfg Co Inc.........................G.... 215 228-5826
Philadelphia (G-13473)

Boyertown Shtmtl Fbrcators Inc..........G.... 610 689-0991
Douglassville (G-4171)

Bradford Allegheny Corporation..........D.... 814 362-2593
Lewis Run (G-9874)

Brandywine Machine Co Inc................F.... 610 269-1221
Downingtown (G-4216)

Brandywine Valley Fabricators............F.... 610 384-7440
Coatesville (G-3295)

Brd Noise & Vibration Ctrl Inc ....G.... 610 863-6300
Wind Gap (G-20167)

Brown Machine Co Inc........................G.... 610 932-3359
Oxford (G-13073)

▲ Byrne Chiarlone LP.........................E.... 610 874-8436
Chester (G-3042)

C A Spalding Company ....E.... 267 550-9000
Bensalem (G-1163)

▲ Cardinal Systems Inc......................E.... 570 385-4733
Schuylkill Haven (G-17151)

Carlisle Systems LLC.........................G.... 610 821-4222
Fogelsville (G-5992)

◆ Centria Inc.......................................C.... 412 299-8000
Moon Township (G-11483)

CFC Manufacturing Co Inc..................G.... 570 281-9605
Carbondale (G-2671)

Charles Cracciolo Stl Met Yard...........E.... 814 944-4051
Altoona (G-490)

Charles F Woodill...............................G.... 215 457-5858
Philadelphia (G-13528)

▲ Charles Machine Inc........................E.... 814 379-3706
Summerville (G-18157)

Chefs Design Inc................................G.... 215 763-5252
Philadelphia (G-13536)

▲ Cid Associates Inc..........................E.... 724 353-0300
Sarver (G-17066)

Clarion Bathware Inc..........................D.... 814 782-3016
Marble (G-10436)

Clark Metal Products Co ....C.... 724 459-7550
Blairsville (G-1719)

Coilplus Inc..D.... 215 331-5200
Philadelphia (G-13559)

Colmetal Incorporated........................G.... 215 225-1060
Philadelphia (G-13560)

Commercial Stainless Inc....................E.... 570 387-8980
Bloomsburg (G-1776)

Compu-Craft Fabricators Inc ....E.... 215 646-2381
Montgomeryville (G-11390)

Computer Components Corp................D.... 215 676-7600
Philadelphia (G-13567)

Concrete Form Consultants Inc ....F.... 570 281-9605
Carbondale (G-2672)

Coopers...G.... 610 369-8992
Boyertown (G-1905)

Coraopolis Light Metal Inc..................G.... 412 264-2252
Coraopolis (G-3680)

Coren Metal Inc..................................E.... 215 244-4260
Bensalem (G-1173)

Coren Metalcrafts Company................F.... 215 244-0532
Bensalem (G-1174)

▲ Corry Contract Inc..........................E.... 814 665-8221
Corry (G-3748)

Craft Metal Products Inc.....................G.... 570 829-2441
Sugar Notch (G-18149)

▲ Craft-Bilt Manufacturing Co.............D.... 215 721-7700
Souderton (G-17731)

Craftweld Fabrication Co Inc ....E.... 267 492-1100
Montgomeryville (G-11391)

Creston E Lockbaum Inc.....................F.... 717 414-6885
Chambersburg (G-2921)

Cronan Sheet Metal Inc......................G.... 610 375-9230
Reading (G-16354)

Crusader Precision Shtmtl Co ....G.... 610 485-4321
Marcus Hook (G-10440)

▼ Csi Industries Inc............................E.... 814 474-9353
Fairview (G-5819)

Culverts Inc..G.... 412 262-3111
Coraopolis (G-3682)

Curbs Plus Inc....................................E.... 888 639-2872
Mount Union (G-11742)

Curbs Plus Inc....................................E.... 888 639-2872
Mount Union (G-11743)

Custom Manufacturing Corp ....E.... 215 638-3888
Bensalem (G-1178)

Custom Products................................G.... 814 453-6803
Erie (G-5240)

D L George & Sons Mfg Inc.................D.... 717 765-4700
Waynesboro (G-19407)

Daniel C Tanney Inc............................D.... 215 639-3131
Bensalem (G-1179)

▲ Daria Metal Fabricators Inc.............E.... 215 453-2110
Perkasie (G-13271)

David Seidel.......................................F.... 610 921-8310
Temple (G-18327)

Davidsons Fabricating Inc..................E.... 610 544-9750
Broomall (G-2285)

Dedicated Customs Inc.......................G.... 724 678-6609
Burgettstown (G-2345)

Dennis Filges Co Inc...........................E.... 724 287-3735
Chicora (G-3126)

Designer Cabinets and Hdwr Co..........E.... 610 622-4455
Clifton Heights (G-3252)

Diamond Awning Mfg Co.....................G.... 610 656-1924
Folcroft (G-6002)

Diversified Metal Products Co ....E.... 215 423-8877
Philadelphia (G-13636)

Division Seven Inc..............................G.... 724 449-8400
Gibsonia (G-6332)

DMC Global Inc...................................E.... 724 277-9710
Mount Braddock (G-11616)

Donald B Smith Incorporated ....E.... 717 632-2100
Hanover (G-6879)

SIC

Donald Campbell.................................G....... 412 793-6068
Pittsburgh *(G-14930)*

Double D Sheet Metal Inc.................G....... 610 987-3733
Oley *(G-12978)*

Dreamline...G....... 215 957-1411
Warminster *(G-18863)*

Duct Shop USA Inc.............................G....... 412 231-2330
Pittsburgh *(G-14940)*

Ductmate Industries Inc....................G....... 724 258-0500
Monongahela *(G-11307)*

▲ Ductmate Industries Inc................E....... 800 990-8459
Charleroi *(G-3011)*

Ductworks Inc....................................G....... 412 231-2330
Pittsburgh *(G-14941)*

▲ Dudlik Industries Inc......................E....... 215 674-4383
Hatboro *(G-7282)*

Dukane Radiator Inc..........................G....... 412 233-3300
Bethel Park *(G-1413)*

Dunbar Machine Co Inc......................G....... 724 277-8711
Dunbar *(G-4439)*

Dura-Bilt Products Inc........................D....... 570 596-2000
Gillett *(G-6380)*

E R Schantz Inc..................................G....... 610 272-3603
Norristown *(G-12652)*

▲ Edward J Deseta Co Inc.................C....... 302 691-2040
Harleysville *(G-7032)*

▲ Ehc Industries Inc..........................E....... 724 696-1212
Mount Pleasant *(G-11699)*

Electro-Space Fabricators Inc...........D....... 610 682-7181
Topton *(G-18412)*

Electronics Instrs & Optics...............E....... 215 245-6300
Bensalem *(G-1188)*

Emp Industries Inc.............................G....... 215 357-5333
Warminster *(G-18871)*

Enclosure Direct Corp.......................E....... 724 697-5191
Avonmore *(G-864)*

Environmental Air Inc........................E....... 412 922-8988
Pittsburgh *(G-14979)*

◆ Epic Metals Corporation.................D....... 412 351-3913
Rankin *(G-16305)*

Erie Metal Basket Inc.........................F....... 814 833-1745
Erie *(G-5270)*

Expert Process Systems LLC.............G....... 570 424-0581
Stroudsburg *(G-18118)*

▲ Extech/Exterior Tech Inc................E....... 412 781-0991
Pittsburgh *(G-14995)*

F & M Designs Inc..............................G....... 717 564-8120
Harrisburg *(G-7128)*

F Creative Impressions Inc................G....... 215 743-7577
Lansdowne *(G-9432)*

F F Frickanisce Iron Works................G....... 724 568-2001
Vandergrift *(G-18726)*

F W Lang Co..G....... 267 401-8293
Havertown *(G-7421)*

▲ Fabricated Components Inc...........D....... 570 421-4110
Stroudsburg *(G-18119)*

Fabricated Products...........................G....... 570 588-1794
Bushkill *(G-2365)*

Fabricon Inc..E....... 610 921-0203
Temple *(G-18329)*

Fairmans Roof Trusses Inc................G....... 724 349-6778
Creekside *(G-3875)*

FEC Technologies Inc.........................E....... 717 764-5959
York *(G-20477)*

Fedco Manufacturing Inc...................F....... 724 863-2252
Larimer *(G-9451)*

Fetchen Sheet Metal Inc....................E....... 570 457-3560
Old Forge *(G-12964)*

▼ First Rate Met Fabrication LLC.......F....... 724 515-7005
Manor *(G-10410)*

First State Sheet Metal Inc................G....... 215 766-9510
Bedminster *(G-1080)*

First State Sheet Metal Inc................G....... 302 521-0166
Pipersville *(G-14615)*

Fisher Iron Works...............................G....... 717 687-7595
Gordonville *(G-6554)*

Flexospan Steel Buildings Inc............D....... 724 376-7221
Sandy Lake *(G-17060)*

Form Tech Concrete Forms Inc..........F....... 412 331-4500
Gibsonia *(G-6334)*

Fountain Fabricating Co.....................G....... 570 682-9018
Hegins *(G-7541)*

Francis J Nowalk................................G....... 412 687-4017
Pittsburgh *(G-15030)*

Freedom Components Inc...................G....... 717 242-0101
Lewistown *(G-9930)*

Freedom Metals Mfg Inc.....................G....... 814 224-4438
Duncansville *(G-4451)*

Frey Lutz Corp....................................C....... 717 394-4635
Lancaster *(G-9025)*

G & S Metal Products Inc...................G....... 412 462-7000
Pittsburgh *(G-15039)*

G T Watts Inc......................................G....... 717 732-1111
Enola *(G-5080)*

Gamlet Inc..D....... 717 852-9200
York *(G-20489)*

General Metal Company Inc...............E....... 215 638-3242
Bensalem *(G-1203)*

General Weldments Inc......................F....... 724 744-2105
Irwin *(G-8164)*

George I Reitz & Sons Inc..................E....... 814 849-2308
Brookville *(G-2261)*

George I Reitz & Sons Inc..................G....... 412 824-9976
East Pittsburgh *(G-4595)*

George L Wilson & Co Inc A...............G....... 412 321-3217
Apollo *(G-675)*

Georgia Web Inc..................................F....... 215 887-6600
Glenside *(G-6520)*

▲ Gerome Manufacturing Co Inc.......D....... 724 438-8544
Smithfield *(G-17650)*

▲ Graham Thermal Products LLC......G....... 724 658-0500
New Castle *(G-12098)*

Great Lakes Manufacturing Inc.........C....... 814 734-2436
Corry *(G-3764)*

Greg Kiser...G....... 814 425-1678
Utica *(G-18696)*

Grid Electric Inc.................................E....... 610 466-7030
Coatesville *(G-3306)*

Grimms Inc...G....... 724 346-4952
Sharon *(G-17435)*

▲ GSM Industrial Inc.........................C....... 717 207-8985
Lancaster *(G-9034)*

▲ Hamill Manufacturing Company.....D....... 724 744-2131
Trafford *(G-18457)*

Harbor Steel Inc.................................F....... 724 658-7748
New Castle *(G-12100)*

Havaco Technologies Inc....................G....... 814 878-5509
Erie *(G-5311)*

Hawkins Metal...................................G....... 215 538-9668
Quakertown *(G-16199)*

▲ Hendrick Manufacturing Company..G....... 570 282-1010
Carbondale *(G-2677)*

Hennemuth Metal Fabricators...........G....... 724 693-9605
Oakdale *(G-12901)*

Hennemuth Metal Fabricators...........G....... 724 693-9605
Oakdale *(G-12902)*

Herb Sheet Metal Inc.........................F....... 717 273-8001
Lebanon *(G-9579)*

▲ Herwin Inc......................................G....... 724 446-2000
Rillton *(G-16746)*

Hibbs Awning Company Inc................G....... 724 437-1494
Uniontown *(G-18630)*

Hillside Custom Mac Wel & Fab.........F....... 610 942-3093
Honey Brook *(G-7748)*

Histand Brothers Inc..........................F....... 215 348-4121
Ambler *(G-581)*

Hoffman Manufacturing Inc...............F....... 610 821-4222
Fogelsville *(G-5995)*

Holly Metals Inc.................................F....... 610 692-4989
West Chester *(G-19562)*

Hoover Cnvyor Fabrication Corp........E....... 814 634-5431
Meyersdale *(G-11011)*

Hranec Sheet Metal Inc......................C....... 724 437-2211
Uniontown *(G-18631)*

Hutchinson & Gunter Inc....................F....... 724 837-3200
Greensburg *(G-6675)*

Interlock Industries Inc......................D....... 570 366-2020
Orwigsburg *(G-13045)*

Ira G Steffy and Son Inc.....................D....... 717 626-6500
Ephrata *(G-5111)*

Ironridge Inc......................................G....... 800 227-9523
Fort Washington *(G-6077)*

▲ J & S Fabrication Inc......................F....... 717 469-1409
Grantville *(G-6574)*

J A Smith Inc......................................G....... 724 295-1133
Freeport *(G-6206)*

J M S Fabricated Systems Inc...........E....... 724 832-3640
Latrobe *(G-9482)*

▲ J W Steel Fabricating Co................E....... 724 625-1355
Mars *(G-10503)*

J-Mar Metal Fabricating Co................G....... 215 785-6521
Croydon *(G-3920)*

James Craft & Son Inc........................C....... 717 266-6629
York Haven *(G-20759)*

James McAtee....................................G....... 724 789-9078
Renfrew *(G-16640)*

Jefco Manufacturing Inc.....................F....... 215 334-3220
Wynnewood *(G-20270)*

JL Clark LLC.......................................C....... 717 392-4125
Lancaster *(G-9073)*

John R Novak & Son Inc.....................G....... 724 285-6802
Butler *(G-2414)*

K & I Sheet Metal Inc.........................E....... 412 781-8111
Pittsburgh *(G-15159)*

▼ Kampel Enterprises Inc..................E....... 717 432-9688
Wellsville *(G-19478)*

Kendred F Hunt...................................G....... 610 327-4131
Pottstown *(G-16007)*

Keystone Cstm Fabricators Inc.........E....... 412 384-9131
Elizabeth *(G-4861)*

Keystone Fabricating Inc...................E....... 610 868-0900
Bethlehem *(G-1551)*

Keystone Flashing Co.........................G....... 215 329-8500
Philadelphia *(G-13930)*

Keystone Truck & Trailer LLC.............G....... 570 903-1902
Madison Township *(G-10169)*

Kline Bros...F....... 717 469-0699
Grantville *(G-6575)*

Kloeckner Metals Corporation...........D....... 717 755-1923
York *(G-20557)*

▲ Kms Fab LLC...................................E....... 570 338-0200
Luzerne *(G-10125)*

Kottcamp Sheet Metal.......................E....... 717 845-7616
York *(G-20558)*

Kutzner Manufacturing Inds Inc.........E....... 215 721-1712
Telford *(G-18300)*

L & M Fabrication and Mch Inc...........D....... 610 837-1848
Bath *(G-963)*

L B Foster Company............................G....... 814 623-6101
Bedford *(G-1060)*

Lane Enterprises Inc..........................E....... 724 652-7747
Pulaski *(G-16124)*

Lane Enterprises Inc..........................E....... 814 623-1191
Bedford *(G-1061)*

Lane Enterprises Inc..........................E....... 717 532-5959
Shippensburg *(G-17537)*

▼ Lane Enterprises Inc......................F....... 717 761-8175
Camp Hill *(G-2503)*

Leedom Welding & Fabricating..........G....... 215 757-8787
Newtown *(G-12518)*

Legacy Service USA LLC....................D....... 215 675-7770
Southampton *(G-17822)*

Lehigh Gap Seamless Gutter LLC.......G....... 610 824-4888
Palmerton *(G-13108)*

Lehigh Services Inc............................G....... 610 966-2525
Macungie *(G-10152)*

▲ Leiss Tool & Die.............................C....... 814 444-1444
Somerset *(G-17695)*

Leman Machine Company...................E....... 814 736-9696
Portage *(G-15918)*

Lighthouse Electric Contrls Co..........F....... 814 835-2348
Erie *(G-5365)*

▲ Lingenfelter Awning.......................G....... 814 696-4353
Duncansville *(G-4455)*

Little Round Industries LLC...............G....... 215 361-1456
Hatfield *(G-7366)*

Little Sheet Metal Inc........................F....... 215 946-9970
Bristol *(G-2161)*

Lockheed Martin Aeroparts...............C....... 814 262-3000
Johnstown *(G-8404)*

Logue Industries Inc..........................E....... 570 368-2639
Montoursville *(G-11445)*

Lukjan Supply & Manufacturing.........F....... 814 838-1328
Erie *(G-5374)*

M & M Sheet Metal Inc.......................F....... 570 326-4655
Williamsport *(G-20039)*

Marc-Service Inc................................E....... 814 467-8611
Windber *(G-20189)*

Marine Sheet Metal Works..................G....... 814 455-9700
Erie *(G-5380)*

Martin Metal Works Inc......................F....... 717 292-5691
East Berlin *(G-4523)*

Martys Muffler & Weld Shop...............G....... 412 673-4141
North Versailles *(G-12781)*

Matthey Johnson Inc..........................C....... 610 648-8000
West Chester *(G-19598)*

Mc Mahon Welding Inc.......................G....... 215 794-0260
Mechanicsville *(G-10912)*

McShane Welding Company Inc.........E....... 814 459-3797
Erie *(G-5387)*

Mdl Manufacturing Inds Inc...............E....... 814 623-0888
Bedford *(G-1064)*

Mellinger Manufacturing Co Inc.........F....... 717 464-3318
Willow Street *(G-20154)*

Mestek Inc..C....... 570 746-1888
Wyalusing *(G-20254)*

Metal Finishing Systems Inc..............E....... 610 524-9336
Exton *(G-5710)*

Metal Integrity LLC.............................F....... 570 281-2303
Carbondale *(G-2682)*

Metal Sales Manufacturing Corp .... E 570 366-2020
Orwigsburg *(G-13049)*
Metalwerks Inc .... E 724 378-9020
Aliquippa *(G-84)*
Mi-Kee-Tro Metal Mfg Inc .... D 717 764-9090
York *(G-20592)*
▲ **Miller Welding and Machine Co** .... C 814 849-3061
Brookville *(G-2265)*
Moltec Heating and AC .... F 215 755-2169
Philadelphia *(G-14032)*
▲ **Munroe Incorporated** .... D 412 231-0600
Pittsburgh *(G-15311)*
N C Stauffer & Sons Inc .... D 570 945-3047
Factoryville *(G-5758)*
Narvon Construction LLC .... F 717 989-2026
Narvon *(G-11924)*
National Material LP .... E 724 337-6551
New Kensington *(G-12362)*
Neosystemsusa Inc .... G 717 586-5040
Shrewsbury *(G-17586)*
Newport Fabricators Inc .... F 215 234-4400
Green Lane *(G-6591)*
Noftz Sheet Metal Inc .... E 412 471-1983
Pittsburgh *(G-15343)*
▲ **North American Mfg Co** .... E 570 348-1163
Scranton *(G-17266)*
Northstern Precision Pdts Corp .... E 215 245-6300
Bensalem *(G-1232)*
ODonnell Metal Fabricators .... F 610 279-8810
Norristown *(G-12697)*
▼ **Old Ladder Co** .... A 888 523-3371
Greenville *(G-6762)*
Omni Fab Inc .... F 724 334-8851
New Kensington *(G-12364)*
Omnimax International Inc .... C 215 355-1200
Feasterville Trevose *(G-5924)*
Omnimax International Inc .... E 717 299-3711
Lancaster *(G-9152)*
Omnimax International Inc .... B 717 397-2741
Lancaster *(G-9153)*
Palermo Metal Products Inc .... E 610 253-6230
Easton *(G-4737)*
Palladino Mtal Fabrication Inc .... G 610 323-9439
Pottstown *(G-16025)*
Panagraphics Inc .... E 717 292-5606
Dover *(G-4198)*
Panel Technologies Inc .... G 215 538-7055
Quakertown *(G-16226)*
Paul Groth & Sons Inc .... F 724 843-8086
New Brighton *(G-12039)*
Pbz LLC .... E 800 578-1121
Lititz *(G-10029)*
▲ **Pennmark Technologies Corp** .... C 570 255-5000
Dallas *(G-3966)*
Pennsylvania Aluminum .... G 570 752-2666
Berwick *(G-1341)*
◆ **Petrex Inc** .... E 814 723-2050
Warren *(G-19044)*
Pfa Inc .... G 717 664-4216
Manheim *(G-10401)*
Philadelphia Pipe Bending Co .... E 215 225-8955
Philadelphia *(G-14149)*
Pinnacle Systems .... G 412 262-3950
Coraopolis *(G-3716)*
Pioneer Electric Supply Co Inc .... G 814 437-1342
Franklin *(G-6152)*
Pioneer Energy Products LLC .... F 814 676-5688
Oil City *(G-12954)*
▲ **Pittsburgh Design Services Inc** .... F 412 276-3000
Carnegie *(G-2779)*
Pittsburgh Fence Co Inc .... E 724 775-6550
Carnegie *(G-2780)*
Plum Corporation .... F 724 836-7261
Greensburg *(G-6702)*
▲ **PMF Industries Inc** .... D 570 323-9944
Williamsport *(G-20059)*
Poff Sheet Metal Inc .... G 717 845-9622
York *(G-20629)*
Power Mechanical Corp .... E 570 823-8824
Wilkes Barre *(G-19958)*
Precision Sheet Metal LLC .... G 570 254-6670
Scott Township *(G-17187)*
Preferred Sheet Metal Inc .... E 717 732-7100
Enola *(G-5084)*
Presco Sheet Metal Fabricators .... G 215 672-7200
Warminster *(G-18944)*
Pressure-Tech Inc .... F 717 597-1868
Greencastle *(G-6628)*
▲ **Prizer-Painter Stove Works Inc** .... E 610 376-7479
Blandon *(G-1757)*
Prl Industries Inc .... E 717 273-6787
Cornwall *(G-3740)*
Production Components Corp .... E 215 368-7416
Lansdale *(G-9402)*
Proshort Stamping Services Inc .... G 814 371-9633
Brockway *(G-2232)*
PSMLV Inc .... F 610 395-8214
Allentown *(G-363)*
▲ **R A Egan Sign & Awng Co Inc** .... F 610 777-3795
Reading *(G-16482)*
R E Wildes Sheet Metal Inc .... G 570 501-3828
Hazle Township *(G-7478)*
R M Metals Inc .... G 717 656-8737
Lancaster *(G-9182)*
Rabe Environmental Systems Inc .... D 814 456-5374
Erie *(G-5451)*
Radiant Steel Products Company .... F 570 322-7828
Williamsport *(G-20067)*
Rado Enterprises Inc .... E 570 759-0303
Benton *(G-1281)*
Rainbow Awnings Inc .... F 610 534-5380
Folcroft *(G-6014)*
Randy Brensinger .... G 610 562-2184
Hamburg *(G-6851)*
Raytec LLC .... E 717 445-0510
Ephrata *(G-5138)*
Raytec Fabricating LLC .... E 717 355-5333
New Holland *(G-12278)*
Rdy Gutters Plus LLC .... G 610 488-5666
Bernville *(G-1304)*
Reh Holdings Inc .... G 717 843-0021
York *(G-20657)*
Robert G Dent Heating & AC .... F 570 784-6721
Bloomsburg *(G-1798)*
▼ **Roll Former Corporation** .... E 215 997-2511
Chalfont *(G-2885)*
Russo Heating & Cooling Inc .... F 814 454-6263
Erie *(G-5468)*
S & N Industries LLC .... G 724 406-0322
Slippery Rock *(G-17627)*
Saeger Machine Inc .... F 215 256-8754
Harleysville *(G-7056)*
Sanitary Process Systems Inc .... E 717 627-6630
Lititz *(G-10045)*
Scatton Bros Mfg Co .... E 215 362-6830
Lansdale *(G-9409)*
Schatzie Ltd .... G 610 834-1240
Conshohocken *(G-3604)*
Schiller Grounds Care Inc .... D 215 322-4970
Huntingdon Valley *(G-8035)*
Scranton Sheet Metal Inc .... E 570 342-2904
Scranton *(G-17288)*
Sensenigs Spouting .... F 717 627-6886
Lititz *(G-10049)*
Sheet Metal Wkrs Local Un 19 .... G 215 952-1999
Philadelphia *(G-14299)*
Shoemaker Mfg Solutions Inc .... E 215 723-5567
Souderton *(G-17764)*
Sk Sales Company Inc .... F 570 474-5600
Mountain Top *(G-11775)*
Somerset Welding & Steel Inc .... E 814 444-7000
Somerset *(G-17709)*
Somerset Welding & Steel Inc .... E 814 444-7000
Somerset *(G-17711)*
▲ **Sonic Systems Inc** .... E 267 803-1964
Warminster *(G-18967)*
Southwest Vinyl Windows Inc .... F 610 626-8826
Lansdowne *(G-9444)*
Ssm Industries Inc .... D 215 288-7777
Philadelphia *(G-14337)*
Stambaugh Metal Inc .... E 717 632-5957
Hanover *(G-6958)*
Standard Awnings & Aluminum .... G 570 824-3535
Hanover Township *(G-7006)*
Standard Tool & Machine Co .... E 724 758-5522
Ellwood City *(G-4951)*
Stewart Welding & Fabg Inc .... D 717 252-3948
Wrightsville *(G-20244)*
Stewarts Fabrication Inc .... G 610 921-1600
Temple *(G-18338)*
Subcon Tl/Cctool Mch Group Inc .... E 814 456-7797
Erie *(G-5494)*
Suez Wts Systems Usa Inc .... C 724 743-0270
Canonsburg *(G-2642)*
Summers & Zims Inc .... E 610 593-2420
Atglen *(G-809)*
Superior Metal Products Co .... E 610 326-0607
Pottstown *(G-16052)*
Superior Metalworks Inc .... F 717 245-2446
Carlisle *(G-2740)*
Supply Technologies LLC .... E 724 745-8877
Carnegie *(G-2797)*
T D Landis Air Flow Design .... G 215 679-4395
Pennsburg *(G-13257)*
Tate Access Floors Inc .... C 717 244-4071
Red Lion *(G-16617)*
Tech Manufacturing Corporation .... E 610 586-0620
Sharon Hill *(G-17464)*
Tech Sheet Metal Company Inc .... F 724 539-3763
Bradenville *(G-1952)*
Titan Metal & Machine Co Inc .... G 724 747-9528
Washington *(G-19232)*
▼ **Traco Delaware Inc** .... F 724 776-7000
Cranberry Township *(G-3856)*
Trexler Industries Inc .... E 610 974-9800
Bethlehem *(G-1641)*
Tuckey Metal Fabricators Inc .... E 717 249-8111
Carlisle *(G-2744)*
◆ **TW Metals LLC** .... D 610 458-1300
Exton *(G-5741)*
Union Roofing and Shtmtl Co .... E 814 946-0824
Altoona *(G-553)*
United Metal Products Corp .... G 570 226-3084
Hawley *(G-7440)*
United States Steel Corp .... C 412 675-7459
West Mifflin *(G-19746)*
Vari Corporation .... G 570 385-0731
Schuylkill Haven *(G-17169)*
Versa-Fab Inc .... E 724 889-0137
New Kensington *(G-12387)*
▲ **Vertech International Inc** .... E 215 529-0300
Quakertown *(G-16257)*
Vh Service LLC .... G 267 808-9745
Feasterville Trevose *(G-5938)*
Victor Group Inc .... D 814 899-1079
Erie *(G-5526)*
Voegele Company Inc .... E 412 781-0940
Pittsburgh *(G-15705)*
Walsh Sheet Metal Inc .... G 570 344-3495
Scranton *(G-17311)*
Walter B Staller Inc .... G 570 385-5386
Schuylkill Haven *(G-17171)*
Walter Long Mfg Co Inc .... E 724 348-6631
Finleyville *(G-5965)*
Waste Gas Fabricating Co Inc .... E 215 736-9240
Fairless Hills *(G-5807)*
Watson Metal Products Corp .... D 908 276-2202
Lancaster *(G-9236)*
Watt Enterprises Inc .... G 570 698-8081
Lake Ariel *(G-8896)*
WD Services Inc .... G 610 970-7946
Pottstown *(G-16071)*
Weaver Metal Fab LLC .... F 717 466-6601
Ephrata *(G-5155)*
▲ **Weaver Sheet Metal LLC** .... F 717 733-4763
Ephrata *(G-5156)*
Welded Shtmtl Specialty Co .... G 412 331-3534
Pittsburgh *(G-15708)*
Wierman Diller Inc .... G 717 637-3871
Hanover *(G-6975)*
William J Koshinskie .... G 570 742-4969
Milton *(G-11251)*
Wintercorp LLC .... G 717 848-3425
York *(G-20712)*
▼ **X-Mark/Cdt Inc** .... G 724 228-7373
Washington *(G-19248)*
Yeager Wire Works Inc .... G 570 752-2769
Berwick *(G-1349)*
▲ **York Haven Fabricators Inc** .... E 717 932-4000
York Haven *(G-20762)*
Zambotti Collision & Wldg Ctr .... G 724 545-2305
Kittanning *(G-8804)*

3446 Architectural & Ornamental Metal Work

A & R Iron Works Inc .... F 610 497-8770
Trainer *(G-18462)*
A B N A Inc .... E 724 527-2866
Penn *(G-13226)*
▼ **Above Rim International LLC** .... G 215 789-7893
Philadelphia *(G-13336)*
Advanced Cnstr Estimating LLC .... F 724 747-7032
Mc Murray *(G-10643)*
AJ Kane Incorporated .... G 215 953-5152
Warminster *(G-18825)*
All Metal Fabricating Co Inc .... G 724 925-3537
Youngwood *(G-20777)*
Alumax LLC .... C 412 553-4545
Pittsburgh *(G-14695)*
American Fence Inc .... F 610 437-1944
Whitehall *(G-19861)*

S I C

American Ornamental Iron Corp .... F 724 639-8684
Saltsburg *(G-17050)*
▼ **American Railing Systems Inc** .... E 814 899-7677
Erie *(G-5188)*
▲ **American Safety Technologies** .... G 215 855-8450
Montgomeryville *(G-11386)*
Anvil Forge & Hammer Ir Works .... G 610 837-9951
Allentown *(G-139)*
Anvil Iron Works Inc .... G 215 468-8300
Philadelphia *(G-13397)*
Architectural Woodsmiths Inc .... D 717 532-7700
Shippensburg *(G-17515)*
Armin Ironworks Inc .... G 412 322-1622
Pittsburgh *(G-14725)*
Artisans of The Anvil Inc .... G 570 476-7950
Stroudsburg *(G-18105)*
Artline Ornamental Iron Works .... G 215 727-2923
Philadelphia *(G-13416)*
Barretts Custom Wrought Iron .... G 814 676-4575
Oil City *(G-12941)*
Baut Studios Inc .... E 570 288-1431
Swoyersville *(G-18194)*
◆ **Bedford Reinforced Plas Inc** .... D 814 623-8125
Bedford *(G-1044)*
Benfab Inc .... F 610 626-9100
Folcroft *(G-6000)*
Bethlehem Aluminum Inc .... F 610 432-4541
Allentown *(G-150)*
◆ **Biros John** .... F 570 384-3473
Sheppton *(G-17499)*
◆ **Bon Tool Company** .... D 724 443-7080
Gibsonia *(G-6328)*
C & B Iron Inc .... G 215 536-7162
Quakertown *(G-16176)*
C & C Manufacturing & Fabg .... G 570 454-0819
Hazleton *(G-7492)*
Carl E Reichert Corp .... G 215 723-9525
Telford *(G-18269)*
▲ **Cid Associates Inc** .... E 724 353-0300
Sarver *(G-17066)*
Ciw Enterprises Inc .... E 800 233-8366
Mountain Top *(G-11755)*
Concrete Step Units Inc .... E 570 343-2458
Scranton *(G-17218)*
Cornellcookson Inc .... C 570 474-6773
Mountain Top *(G-11757)*
Country Accents .... G 570 478-4127
Williamsport *(G-20001)*
Creative Architectural Metals .... E 215 638-1650
Bensalem *(G-1175)*
Del Ren Assoc Inc .... G 215 467-7000
Philadelphia *(G-13616)*
Dura-Bilt Products Inc .... D 570 596-2000
Gillett *(G-6380)*
Ebinger Iron Works Inc .... E 570 385-3460
Schuylkill Haven *(G-17155)*
EPI of Cleveland Inc .... D 330 468-2872
Pittsburgh *(G-14980)*
Exeter Architectural Products .... F 570 693-4220
Wyoming *(G-20277)*
F F Frickanisce Iron Works .... G 724 568-2001
Vandergrift *(G-18726)*
Facchiano Ironworks Inc .... G 610 865-1503
Bethlehem *(G-1506)*
Fairway Building Products LLC .... D 717 653-6777
Mount Joy *(G-11657)*
Fairwinds Manufacturing Inc .... G 724 662-5210
Jackson Center *(G-8227)*
Filippi Bros Inc .... G 215 247-5973
Philadelphia *(G-13701)*
Fisher & Ludlow Inc .... F 859 282-7767
Wexford *(G-19801)*
Fisher & Ludlow Inc .... G 814 763-5914
Saegertown *(G-16914)*
Fisher & Ludlow Inc .... D 724 934-5320
Wexford *(G-19803)*
Fisher & Ludlow Inc .... D 217 324-6106
Wexford *(G-19802)*
◆ **Forms and Surfaces Inc** .... A 412 781-9003
Pittsburgh *(G-15026)*
Frank Bellace Welding .... G 856 488-8099
Danville *(G-4002)*
Frey Lutz Corp .... C 717 394-4635
Lancaster *(G-9025)*
Genie Electronics Co Inc .... D 717 244-1099
Red Lion *(G-16598)*
Genie Electronics Co Inc .... C 717 244-1099
Red Lion *(G-16599)*
Goldsborough & Vansant Inc .... G 724 782-0393
Finleyville *(G-5959)*
▲ **Gratz Industries LLC** .... E 215 739-7373
Philadelphia *(G-13783)*
Groll Ornamental Ir Works LLC .... G 412 431-4444
Pittsburgh *(G-15065)*
Guida Inc .... E 215 727-2222
Marcus Hook *(G-10444)*
Hampton Concrete Products Inc .... F 724 443-7205
Valencia *(G-18698)*
▲ **Handrail Design Inc** .... D 717 285-4088
Columbia *(G-3438)*
Hanover Iron Works Inc .... E 717 632-5624
Hanover *(G-6896)*
Hendricks Welding Service Inc .... G 215 757-5369
Langhorne *(G-9301)*
Heritage Fence & Deck LLC .... G 610 476-0003
Skippack *(G-17598)*
Heritage Fence Company .... F 610 584-6710
Skippack *(G-17599)*
Heritage Industries Inc .... G 412 435-0091
Pittsburgh *(G-15091)*
Heritage Metalworks Ltd .... G 610 518-3999
Downingtown *(G-4234)*
Herman Iron Works Inc .... G 215 727-1127
Philadelphia *(G-13817)*
Hess S Ornamental Iron .... F 717 927-9160
Red Lion *(G-16600)*
▲ **International Gate Devices** .... G 610 461-0811
Folsom *(G-6025)*
Janzer Corporation .... G 215 757-1168
Bensalem *(G-1212)*
Jays Railing & Fabrication Co .... G 717 933-9244
Bethel *(G-1395)*
▼ **Jerith Manufacturing LLC** .... D 215 676-4068
Philadelphia *(G-13893)*
John Jost Jr Inc .... G 610 395-5461
Allentown *(G-269)*
Joseph Lee & Son Inc .... G 610 825-1944
Lafayette Hill *(G-8883)*
▲ **Kane Innovations Inc** .... D 814 838-7731
Erie *(G-5342)*
Kauffmans Welding Iron Wo .... G 717 361-9844
Manheim *(G-10392)*
Kawneer Company Inc .... B 570 784-8000
Bloomsburg *(G-1787)*
Kawneer Company Inc .... D 570 784-8000
Pittsburgh *(G-15162)*
Kebb Inc .... G 610 859-0907
Upper Chichester *(G-18666)*
L B Foster Company .... E 814 623-6101
Bedford *(G-1060)*
▲ **Laminators Incorporated** .... D 215 723-5285
Hatfield *(G-7362)*
Lehigh Services Inc .... G 610 966-2525
Macungie *(G-10152)*
Louis Emmel Co .... G 412 859-6781
Boyers *(G-1889)*
Lux Ornamental Iron Works Inc .... G 412 481-5677
Pittsburgh *(G-15243)*
Manley Fence Co .... G 610 842-8833
Coatesville *(G-3316)*
▲ **McGregor Industries Inc** .... E 570 343-2436
Dunmore *(G-4478)*
McM Architectural Products LLC .... G 240 416-2809
Indiana *(G-8112)*
McShane Welding Company Inc .... E 814 459-3797
Erie *(G-5387)*
Mendel Steel & Orna Ir Co .... F 412 341-7778
Bethel Park *(G-1425)*
Mountain Metal Studio Inc .... G 724 329-0238
Markleysburg *(G-10482)*
Multi-Metals Co Inc .... D 724 836-2720
Greensburg *(G-6691)*
N C Stauffer & Sons Inc .... D 570 945-3047
Factoryville *(G-5758)*
Neville Grating LLC .... G 412 771-6973
Pittsburgh *(G-15332)*
New Werner Holding Co Inc .... G 724 588-2000
Greenville *(G-6758)*
North East Louvers Inc .... F 717 436-5300
Mifflintown *(G-11131)*
Northern Iron Works Inc .... F 215 947-1867
Huntingdon Valley *(G-8018)*
Nucor Grating .... G 724 934-5320
Wexford *(G-19817)*
▼ **Old Ladder Co** .... A 888 523-3371
Greenville *(G-6762)*
Oldcastle Precast Inc .... D 484 548-6200
Easton *(G-4735)*
Omni Fab Inc .... F 724 334-8851
New Kensington *(G-12364)*
Overly Manufacturing Company .... E 724 834-7300
Greensburg *(G-6697)*
Peifer Welding Inc .... G 717 687-7581
Ronks *(G-16812)*
Pencoyd Iron Works Inc .... E 610 522-5000
Folcroft *(G-6012)*
Pennsylvania Stair Lifts Inc .... G 215 914-0800
Huntingdon Valley *(G-8023)*
Peter Mamienski .... G 215 822-3293
Hatfield *(G-7381)*
Pleasant Mount Welding Inc .... D 570 282-6164
Carbondale *(G-2684)*
Randy Brensinger .... G 610 562-2184
Hamburg *(G-6851)*
Redstar Ironworks LLC .... G 412 821-3630
Pittsburgh *(G-15474)*
Reynolds Iron Works Inc .... F 570 323-4663
Williamsport *(G-20068)*
▲ **Robern Inc** .... D 215 826-0280
Bristol *(G-2195)*
Robert L Baker .... F 443 617-0164
Chambersburg *(G-2973)*
Safety Rail Source LLC .... G 610 539-9535
Norristown *(G-12707)*
Samuel Yellin Metalworkers Co .... G 610 527-2334
Bryn Mawr *(G-2333)*
Scranton Craftsmen Excvtg Inc .... D 800 775-1479
Throop *(G-18360)*
Scranton Craftsmen Inc .... D 570 347-5125
Throop *(G-18361)*
Shedaker Metal Arts Inc .... E 215 788-3383
Croydon *(G-3928)*
Shetron Wldg & Fabrication Inc .... E 717 776-4344
Shippensburg *(G-17548)*
Skitco Manufacturing Inc .... G 570 929-2100
Hazle Township *(G-7481)*
Snaptex International LLC .... G 215 283-0152
Montgomeryville *(G-11418)*
Specialty Building Systems .... G 610 954-0595
Easton *(G-4754)*
▼ **Spiral Stairs of America LLC** .... E 800 422-3700
Erie *(G-5489)*
Spring Lock Scaffolding Eqp Co .... G 215 426-5727
Plymouth Meeting *(G-15873)*
Standard & Custom LLC .... G 412 345-7901
Pittsburgh *(G-15575)*
Standard Iron Works .... E 570 347-2058
Scranton *(G-17293)*
▲ **Standard Steel Specialty Co** .... D 724 846-7600
Beaver Falls *(G-1014)*
Standard Tool & Machine Co .... E 724 758-5522
Ellwood City *(G-4951)*
▲ **Sterling Dula Architectural** .... C 814 838-7731
Erie *(G-5493)*
Structural Fiberglass Inc .... F 814 623-0458
Bedford *(G-1077)*
Swick Ornamental Iron .... G 412 487-5755
Gibsonia *(G-6354)*
Technique Architectural Pdts .... G 412 241-1644
Wilkinsburg *(G-19981)*
Termaco USA Inc .... E 610 916-2600
Reading *(G-16535)*
Trailgate Tailgate Systems .... G 724 321-6558
Rostraver Township *(G-16831)*
Tri-Vet Design Fabrication LLC .... F 570 462-4941
Shenandoah *(G-17497)*
▼ **Unisource Associates Inc** .... E 610 489-5799
Collegeville *(G-3398)*
◆ **Universal Manufacturing Corp** .... E 724 452-8300
Zelienople *(G-20826)*
Vangura Iron Inc .... F 412 461-7825
Clairton *(G-3159)*
Vanquish Fencing Incorporated .... F 215 295-2863
Morrisville *(G-11586)*
◆ **Werner Co** .... C 724 588-2000
Greenville *(G-6775)*
Werner Holding Co Inc .... A 888 523-3371
Greenville *(G-6776)*
William Henry Orna Ir Works .... G 215 659-1887
Willow Grove *(G-20149)*
Wilmington Metalcraft .... G 717 442-9834
Gap *(G-6258)*
Worthington Armstrong Intl LLC .... G 610 722-1200
Malvern *(G-10350)*
▲ **Worthington Armstrong Venture** ...... C 610 722-1200
Malvern *(G-10351)*
Zottola Fab A PA Bus Tr .... G 412 221-4488
Cuddy *(G-3944)*

3448 Prefabricated Metal Buildings & Cmpnts

1998 Equipment Leasing Corp ....G...... 412 771-2944
Mc Kees Rocks (G-10596)

▲ Advanced Building Products ....G...... 717 661-7520
Leola (G-9766)

American Conservatory Co Inc ....F...... 724 465-1800
Indiana (G-8079)

American Manufactured Struc ....G...... 703 403-4656
Hellertown (G-7553)

American Steel Carports Inc ....F...... 570 825-8260
Wilkes Barre (G-19905)

Bluescope Buildings N Amer Inc ....D...... 717 867-4651
Annville (G-643)

◆ Bracalente Global Ltd ....C...... 215 536-3077
Trumbauersville (G-18530)

Brock Associates LLC ....F...... 412 919-0690
Pittsburgh (G-14793)

Central States Mfg Inc ....E...... 814 239-2764
Claysburg (G-3202)

Century Buildings ....G...... 814 336-1446
Saegertown (G-16910)

▲ Cid Associates Inc ....E...... 724 353-0300
Sarver (G-17066)

Corle Building Systems Inc ....B...... 814 276-9611
Imler (G-8054)

Custom Container Solutions LLC ....F...... 570 524-7835
Lewisburg (G-9902)

Dura-Bilt Products Inc ....D...... 570 596-2000
Gillett (G-6380)

Eagle Industrial Solutions ....G...... 610 509-8275
Nazareth (G-11962)

◆ Epic Metals Corporation ....D...... 412 351-3913
Rankin (G-16305)

▲ Farmer Boy Ag Inc ....D...... 717 866-7565
Myerstown (G-11885)

Flexospan Steel Buildings Inc ....D...... 724 376-7221
Sandy Lake (G-17060)

Fork Creek Cabins LLC ....F...... 717 442-1902
Paradise (G-13159)

G & D Erectors Inc ....E...... 724 587-0590
Avella (G-836)

▲ Gichner Systems Group LLC ....B...... 717 244-7611
Dallastown (G-3977)

Gichner Systems Intl Inc ....G...... 717 244-7611
Dallastown (G-3978)

Great Additions Inc ....F...... 570 675-0852
Luzerne (G-10124)

Great Day Improvements LLC ....E...... 412 304-0089
Pittsburgh (G-15060)

Heintz Storage Center ....G...... 412 931-3444
Pittsburgh (G-15087)

Integrated Metal Products Inc ....G...... 717 824-4052
Lancaster (G-9058)

▲ Jadco Manufacturing Inc ....E...... 724 452-5252
Harmony (G-7070)

JE Lyons Construction Inc ....G...... 724 686-3967
Latrobe (G-9483)

Johnathan Stoltzfus ....G...... 717 768-7922
Ronks (G-16808)

Keystone Metal Structures LLC ....G...... 717 816-3631
Chambersburg (G-2947)

Keystone Structures Inc ....E...... 610 444-9525
Kennett Square (G-8521)

Marcon & Boyer Inc ....D...... 610 866-5959
Allentown (G-307)

Metal Sales Manufacturing Corp ....E...... 570 366-2020
Orwigsburg (G-13049)

Mobile Mini Inc ....E...... 484 540-9072
Allentown (G-318)

Mobile Mini Inc ....E...... 412 220-4477
Bridgeville (G-2079)

Mobile Mini Inc ....F...... 484 540-9073
Essington (G-5544)

Modern Precast Concrete Inc ....E...... 484 548-6200
Easton (G-4726)

Morton Buildings Inc ....E...... 717 624-8000
Gettysburg (G-6308)

Morton Buildings Inc ....F...... 814 364-9500
Centre Hall (G-2843)

Morton Buildings Inc ....G...... 724 542-7930
Mount Pleasant (G-11707)

Nucor Corporation ....G...... 717 735-7766
Lancaster (G-9148)

Oldcastle Precast Inc ....C...... 215 257-8081
Telford (G-18306)

Penn State Cnstr J&D LLC ....G...... 717 953-9200
Lewistown (G-9943)

Pennsylvania Aluminum ....G...... 570 752-2666
Berwick (G-1341)

Poly-Growers Inc ....F...... 570 546-3216
Muncy (G-11831)

Scatton Bros Mfg Co ....E...... 215 362-6830
Lansdale (G-9409)

Scenic Ridge Company ....D...... 717 768-7522
Gordonville (G-6564)

Sewickley Creek Greenhouse ....G...... 724 935-8500
Sewickley (G-17408)

Shelter Structures Inc ....G...... 267 239-5906
Philadelphia (G-14301)

Signature Structures LLC ....G...... 610 882-9030
Bethlehem (G-1618)

◆ Solar Innovations Inc ....C...... 570 915-1500
Pine Grove (G-14605)

Sollenberger Silos LLC ....G...... 717 264-9588
Chambersburg (G-2976)

Speed Partz LLC ....G...... 513 874-2034
Fayetteville (G-5878)

Starflite Systems Inc ....E...... 724 789-9200
Connoquenessing (G-3513)

▲ Steel Factory Corp ....F...... 412 771-2944
Mc Kees Rocks (G-10638)

Sukup Steel Structures LLC ....C...... 724 266-6484
Ambridge (G-636)

Timber Mill Woodcraft LLC ....G...... 717 597-7433
Greencastle (G-6640)

▼ Traco Delaware Inc ....F...... 724 776-7000
Cranberry Township (G-3856)

▼ Uh Structures Inc ....F...... 724 628-6100
Connellsville (G-3509)

United Fence Supply Company ....G...... 570 307-0782
Olyphant (G-13002)

3449 Misc Structural Metal Work

A & L Iron Works LLC ....G...... 717 768-0705
Narvon (G-11915)

▲ Acco Mtl Hdlg Solutions Inc ....D...... 800 967-7333
York (G-20365)

Alumax LLC ....C...... 412 553-4545
Pittsburgh (G-14695)

Baileys Steel & Supply LLC ....G...... 724 267-4648
Waynesburg (G-19433)

Brandywine Valley Fabricators ....F...... 610 384-7440
Coatesville (G-3295)

C & C Welding and Fabg Inc ....G...... 814 387-6556
Clarence (G-3161)

◆ Centria Inc ....C...... 412 299-8000
Moon Township (G-11483)

Cmw Technologies Inc ....F...... 215 721-5824
Telford (G-18274)

Contrast Metalworks LLC ....E...... 484 624-5542
Pottstown (G-15975)

▲ Craft-Bilt Manufacturing Co ....D...... 215 721-7700
Souderton (G-17731)

Custom Mfg & Indus Svcs LLC ....C...... 412 621-2982
Pittsburgh (G-14894)

Dek Machine Co Inc ....G...... 215 794-5791
Mechanicsville (G-10911)

Diversified Fabrications Inc ....G...... 814 344-8434
Carrolltown (G-2807)

DMS Shredding Inc ....F...... 570 819-3339
Hanover Township (G-6988)

Doerschner Machine ....G...... 724 625-1350
Mars (G-10494)

Dura-Bilt Products Inc ....D...... 570 596-2000
Gillett (G-6380)

Enhanced Sintered Products Inc ....G...... 814 834-2470
Saint Marys (G-16973)

Extreme Manufacturing Inc ....F...... 717 369-0044
Saint Thomas (G-17039)

▲ Florig R & J Industrial Co Inc ......E...... 610 825-6655
Conshohocken (G-3548)

Gerdau Ameristeel US Inc ....D...... 717 846-7865
York (G-20498)

Guida Inc ....E...... 215 727-2222
Marcus Hook (G-10444)

▲ Harris Rebar Atlantic Inc ....D...... 610 882-1401
Bethlehem (G-1529)

Hunter Highway Inc ....F...... 570 454-8161
Lattimer Mines (G-9530)

Industrial Polsg & Grinding ....D...... 717 854-9001
York (G-20536)

Ivy Steel & Wire Inc ....D...... 570 450-2090
Hazle Township (G-7465)

Jasper Steel Fabrication Inc ....G...... 570 329-3330
Williamsport (G-20027)

Keamco Industries Inc ....E...... 215 938-6050
Feasterville Trevose (G-5916)

Kreico LLC ....G...... 717 228-7312
Lebanon (G-9595)

Laneko Roll Form Inc ....E...... 215 822-1930
Hatfield (G-7363)

Lee Michael Industries Inc ....G...... 724 656-0890
New Castle (G-12115)

Lineman & Sons ....G...... 814 677-7215
Oil City (G-12951)

Little Wash Fabricators Inc ....F...... 717 768-7356
Christiana (G-3141)

M & S Conversion Company Inc ....F...... 570 368-1991
Montoursville (G-11447)

Martellis Mtal Fabrication Inc ....E...... 215 957-9700
Ivyland (G-8217)

Men of Steel Enterprises LLC ....E...... 609 871-2000
Bensalem (G-1226)

Morgan Brothers Company ....F...... 724 843-7485
Beaver Falls (G-1006)

▲ Mpc Industries LLC ....E...... 717 393-4100
Lancaster (G-9138)

Neville Grating LLC ....G...... 412 771-6973
Pittsburgh (G-15332)

New Hudson Facades LLC ....C...... 610 494-8100
Upper Chichester (G-18668)

Omni Fab Inc ....F...... 724 334-8851
New Kensington (G-12364)

P G A Machine Co Inc ....E...... 610 874-1335
Eddystone (G-4806)

Penn Fabrication LLC ....F...... 610 292-1980
Norristown (G-12702)

Pennsylvania Insert Corp ....E...... 610 474-0112
Royersford (G-16860)

▲ Precision Roll Grinders Inc ....D...... 610 395-6966
Allentown (G-358)

Rapid Reaction Inc ....F...... 814 432-9832
Franklin (G-6155)

Roll Forming Corp - Sharon ....G...... 724 982-0400
Farrell (G-5873)

Simpson Reinforcing Inc ....F...... 412 362-6200
New Kensington (G-12376)

Sippel Co Inc ....G...... 724 266-9800
Ambridge (G-634)

▲ Standard Metal Industries LLC ....G...... 610 377-5400
Lehighton (G-9728)

Standard Tool & Machine Co ....G...... 724 758-5522
Ellwood City (G-4951)

Structural Services Inc ....G...... 610 282-5810
Coopersburg (G-3636)

Tye Bar LLC ....F...... 412 896-1376
Glassport (G-6422)

Van Varick Inc ....G...... 610 588-9997
Bangor (G-932)

Walter Long Mfg Co Inc ....E...... 724 348-6631
Finleyville (G-5965)

Ward Fabricating Inc ....G...... 814 345-6707
Morrisdale (G-11549)

Welding Technologies Inc ....F...... 814 432-0954
Franklin (G-6169)

Zenzel III Michael ....G...... 570 752-2666
Berwick (G-1350)

3451 Screw Machine Prdts

American Turned Products Inc ....C...... 814 824-7600
Erie (G-5191)

▲ American Turned Products Inc ....D...... 814 474-4200
Fairview (G-5812)

Automatic Machining Mfg Co Inc ....E...... 717 767-4448
York (G-20393)

◆ Bonney Forge Corporation ....B...... 814 542-2545
Mount Union (G-11739)

▲ Bracalentes Mfg Co Inc ....C...... 215 536-3077
Trumbauersville (G-18531)

C E Holden Inc ....F...... 412 767-5050
Cheswick (G-3103)

▲ Cbh of Lancaster Company ....D...... 717 569-0485
Manheim (G-10375)

Chestnut Group Inc ....G...... 610 688-3300
Wayne (G-19313)

Clifton Tube Cutting Inc ....E...... 724 588-3241
Greenville (G-6739)

Compu-Craft Fabricators Inc ....E...... 215 646-2381
Montgomeryville (G-11390)

Corry Metal Products Inc ....G...... 814 664-7087
Corry (G-3753)

CP Precision Inc ....G...... 267 364-0870
Warminster (G-18848)

Diane A Walters ....G...... 215 453-0890
Perkasie (G-13273)

Elge Precision Machining Inc ....F...... 610 376-5458
Reading (G-16372)

Erie Specialty Products Inc ....E...... 814 453-5611
Erie (G-5274)

S I C

Ernst Timing Screw Company ....E 215 639-1438
Bensalem (G-1191)

Fostermation Inc ....G 814 336-6211
Meadville (G-10727)

Fostermation Inc ....F 814 336-6211
Meadville (G-10728)

Freedom Components Inc ....G 717 242-0101
Lewistown (G-9930)

G H Forbes Screw Machine Pdts ....G 215 884-4343
Glenside (G-6518)

Giordano Incorporated ....F 215 632-3470
Bensalem (G-1205)

◆ Hall Industries Incorporated ....E 724 752-2000
Ellwood City (G-4934)

Hall Industries Incorporated ....F 724 758-5522
Ellwood City (G-4935)

Hall Technical Services LLC ....G 724 752-2000
Ellwood City (G-4936)

Helix Inc ....F 215 679-7924
Red Hill (G-16582)

Imperial Specialty Inc ....F 610 323-4531
Pottstown (G-16001)

In Speck Corporation ....E 610 272-9500
Norristown (G-12669)

J & J Precision Tech LLC ....F 717 625-0130
Lititz (G-10020)

Jensen Machine Co Inc ....G 724 568-3787
Vandergrift (G-18730)

▲ John R Bromiley Company Inc ....E 215 822-7723
Chalfont (G-2878)

Kdl Industries ....G 814 398-1555
Cambridge Springs (G-2479)

Kevro Precision Components Inc ....G 814 834-5387
Saint Marys (G-16983)

▲ Keystone Machine Inc ....E 717 359-9256
Littlestown (G-10068)

Lakeview Forge Co ....F 814 454-4518
Erie (G-5358)

▲ Lsc Acquistion Company Inc ....E 412 795-6400
Pittsburgh (G-15239)

Mac-It Corporation ....E 717 397-3535
Lancaster (G-9122)

Orr Screw Machine Products ....E 724 668-2256
Greensburg (G-6695)

P & M Precision Machining Inc ....G 215 357-3313
Huntingdon Valley (G-8020)

Parker Snap-Tite Qdv Assembly ....D 814 438-3821
Union City (G-18611)

Perry Screw Machine Co Inc ....E 814 452-3095
Erie (G-5419)

▼ Pittsburgh Precision ....E 412 712-1111
Pittsburgh (G-15404)

▲ Precision Feedscrews Inc ....E 724 654-9676
New Castle (G-12139)

Precisionform Incorporated ....D 717 560-7610
Lititz (G-10035)

Q-E Manufacturing Company ....E 570 966-1017
New Berlin (G-12023)

Richlyn Manufacturing Inc ....E 814 833-8925
Erie (G-5462)

Shoemaker Mfg Solutions Inc ....E 215 723-5567
Souderton (G-17764)

South Erie Production Co Inc ....E 814 864-0311
Erie (G-5485)

Spectrum Automated Inc ....G 610 433-7755
Allentown (G-398)

Thomas W Springer Inc ....E 610 274-8400
Landenberg (G-9254)

Turning Solutions Inc ....F 814 723-1134
Warren (G-19053)

Turnmatic ....G 717 898-3200
Lancaster (G-9224)

Ultimate Screw Machine Pdts ....G 610 565-1565
Media (G-10955)

V R Machine Co Inc ....F 717 846-9203
York (G-20696)

Vallorbs Jewel Company ....C 717 392-3978
Bird In Hand (G-1684)

Wagman Manufacturing Inc ....F 717 266-5616
Manchester (G-10365)

▲ White Engrg Surfaces Corp ....C 215 968-5021
Newtown (G-12563)

3452 Bolts, Nuts, Screws, Rivets & Washers

Accurate Tool Co Inc ....E 610 436-4500
West Chester (G-19494)

◆ Accutrex Products Inc ....C 724 746-4300
Canonsburg (G-2532)

All America Threaded Pdts Inc ....D 317 921-3000
Lancaster (G-8928)

Alvord-Polk Inc ....G 800 925-2126
Millersburg (G-11187)

American Fastener Tech Corp ....F 724 444-6940
Gibsonia (G-6323)

American Patch and Pin ....G 814 935-4289
Altoona (G-474)

Amsteel Inc ....F 724 758-5566
Ellwood City (G-4926)

Angel Pins and More ....G 717 692-5086
Millersburg (G-11190)

Associated Fasteners Inc ....F 610 837-9200
Bath (G-951)

Automatic Machining Mfg Co Inc ....E 717 767-4448
York (G-20393)

▲ B&G Manufacturing Co Inc ....C 215 822-1925
Hatfield (G-7319)

Baden Steelbar & Bolt Corp ....F 724 266-3003
Sewickley (G-17383)

Belleville International LLC ....E 724 431-0444
Butler (G-2377)

C & L Rivet Co Inc ....E 215 672-1113
Hatboro (G-7275)

Cambria County Asso ....C 814 472-5077
Ebensburg (G-4782)

Chicago Rivet & Machine Co ....D 814 684-2430
Tyrone (G-18580)

Clothes-Pin ....G 215 888-5784
Philadelphia (G-13550)

▲ Cobra Anchors Corp ....D 610 929-5764
Temple (G-18326)

▲ Connex Inc ....F 814 474-4550
Fairview (G-5818)

Duco Holdings LLC ....G 215 942-6274
Ivyland (G-8209)

East Coast Metals Inc ....E 215 256-9550
Harleysville (G-7031)

East Coast Threading Company ....G 610 970-9933
Pine Forge (G-14588)

Emerson Company ....G 310 940-1755
Harrisburg (G-7126)

Ensinger Penn Fibre Inc ....D 215 702-9551
Bensalem (G-1190)

Erie Bolt Corporation ....D 814 456-4287
Blairsville (G-1720)

Fhritp Holdings LLC ....F 215 675-4590
Warminster (G-18877)

Harter Precision ....G 724 459-5060
Blairsville (G-1723)

Hastings Machine Company Inc ....E 814 247-6562
Hastings (G-7261)

History Washer Inc ....G 717 275-3101
Elliottsburg (G-4920)

J B Booth and Co ....F 724 452-8400
Zelienople (G-20805)

J B Booth and Co ....G 724 452-1313
Zelienople (G-20806)

J F Burns Machine Co Inc ....E 724 327-2870
Export (G-5610)

Jennmar Corp of West Virginia ....E 412 963-9071
Pittsburgh (G-15149)

Jennmar Corporation ....D 814 886-4121
Cresson (G-3899)

Jim Airgood Pressure Washer ....G 814 837-7626
Kane (G-8467)

Keystone Automatic Tech Inc ....E 814 486-0513
Emporium (G-5066)

◆ Keystone Scrw Corp ....D 215 657-7100
Willow Grove (G-20123)

Kingpin Production Vans Inc ....G 305 772-0687
Germansville (G-6279)

Mac-It Corporation ....E 717 397-3535
Lancaster (G-9122)

▲ Military and Coml Fas Corp ....D 717 767-6856
York (G-20598)

Mitchell Apx Machine Shop Inc ....G 717 597-2157
Greencastle (G-6623)

Needle and Pin ....G 412 207-9724
Pittsburgh (G-15323)

Nick Charles Kravitch ....G 412 882-6262
Pittsburgh (G-15340)

Outlaw Performance Inc ....E 724 697-4876
Avonmore (G-866)

P G A Machine Co Inc ....G 610 874-1335
Eddystone (G-4806)

▲ Peerless Hardware Mfg Co ....F 717 684-2889
Columbia (G-3447)

Penn Engineering & Mfg Corp ....E 215 766-8853
Danboro (G-3993)

Penn Fasteners Inc ....E 215 674-2772
Hatboro (G-7297)

▲ Penna Flame Industries Inc ....E 724 452-8750
Zelienople (G-20815)

Philadelphia Window Washers ....G 215 742-3875
Philadelphia (G-14159)

Pin Hsun Kuo ....G 717 795-7297
Mechanicsburg (G-10880)

Pittsburgh Bolt Company LLC ....G 724 935-6844
Wexford (G-19820)

Pressure Water Systems of PA ....G 412 668-0878
Pittsburgh (G-15436)

Q-E Manufacturing Company ....E 570 966-1017
New Berlin (G-12023)

Rocwel Industries Inc ....G 610 459-5490
Concordville (G-3458)

S & S Fasteners Inc ....G 724 251-9288
Ambridge (G-632)

Saegertown Manufacturing Corp ....C 814 763-2655
Saegertown (G-16932)

Secure Components LLC ....F 610 551-3475
Norristown (G-12711)

Sfs Group Usa Inc ....D 610 376-5751
Reading (G-16513)

Shoemaker Mfg Solutions Inc ....E 215 723-5567
Souderton (G-17764)

▲ Specialty Bar Products Company ....C 724 459-0544
Blairsville (G-1742)

▲ Speedbear Fasteners ....G 724 695-3696
Imperial (G-8076)

SPS Technologies LLC ....A 215 572-3000
Jenkintown (G-8303)

◆ SPS Technologies LLC ....A 215 572-3000
Jenkintown (G-8302)

St Marys Pressed Metals Inc ....E 814 772-7455
Ridgway (G-16730)

▲ Standard Horse Nail Corp ....F 724 846-4660
New Brighton (G-12043)

Subcon Tl/Cctool Mch Group Inc ....E 814 456-7797
Erie (G-5494)

▲ Superbolt Inc ....D 412 279-1149
Carnegie (G-2795)

Touchpoint Inc ....A 610 459-4000
Concordville (G-3460)

Tri-State Tubular Rivet Co ....F 610 644-6060
Malvern (G-10335)

Turning Solutions Inc ....F 814 723-1134
Warren (G-19053)

Watson Metal Products Corp ....D 908 276-2202
Lancaster (G-9236)

Westbrook Window Washers LLC ....G 610 873-0245
Downingtown (G-4263)

3462 Iron & Steel Forgings

A & A Gear Inc ....G 215 364-3952
Huntingdon Valley (G-7959)

Accuride Akw LP ....G 814 459-7589
Erie (G-5168)

Adomis Industrial Mch Maint ....G 717 244-0716
Windsor (G-20195)

Allegheny Ludlum LLC ....F 724 567-2670
Vandergrift (G-18722)

American Hollow Boring Company ....E 800 673-2458
Erie (G-5187)

Architectural Iron Company ....E 570 296-7722
Milford (G-11156)

Arro Forge Inc ....F 814 724-4223
Meadville (G-10704)

ATI Operating Holdings LLC ....G 412 394-2800
Pittsburgh (G-14731)

B C Fabrications Inc ....G 610 369-2882
New Berlinville (G-12024)

Baldt Inc ....E 610 447-5200
Bryn Mawr (G-2315)

◆ Bonney Forge Corporation ....B 814 542-2545
Mount Union (G-11739)

Brad Foote Gear Works Inc ....E 412 264-1428
Pittsburgh (G-14789)

Cleveland Brothers Eqp Co Inc ....F 717 564-2121
Harrisburg (G-7107)

▲ Cobra Anchors Corp ....D 610 929-5764
Temple (G-18326)

Corry Forge Company ....E 814 664-9664
Corry (G-3749)

Corry Forge Company ....E 814 459-4495
Erie (G-5234)

Damian Hntz Locomotive Svc Inc ....G 814 748-7222
Colver (G-3453)

E-Tech Industrial ....G 570 297-1300
Troy (G-18522)

Eaton Electric Holdings LLC ....D 717 755-2933
York (G-20462)

Ecm ....C.... 724 347-0250
Hermitage (G-7580)

Ellwood City Forge Company ....G.. 724 202-5008
New Castle (G-12083)

Ellwood Group Inc ....E.. 724 658-3685
New Castle (G-12084)

Ellwood Group Inc ....B.. 724 752-0055
Ellwood City (G-4931)

Ellwood Group Inc ....C.. 724 981-1012
Hermitage (G-7582)

◆ Ellwood National Crankshaft Co.......C.. 814 563-7522
Irvine (G-8139)

◆ Enginred Arrsting Systems Corp.......C.. 610 494-8000
Upper Chichester (G-18660)

Environmental Inc ....G.. 412 394-2800
Pittsburgh (G-14978)

Erie Bolt Corporation ....D.. 814 456-4287
Blairsville (G-1720)

▲ Erie Forge and Steel Inc ....D.. 814 452-2300
Erie (G-5267)

Erie Tool and Forge Inc ....E.. 814 587-2841
Springboro (G-17895)

Federal-Mogul Motorparts LLC..........G.. 717 430-5021
York (G-20478)

Fessler Machine Company ....E.. 724 346-0878
Sharon (G-17433)

▲ Fluid Gear Products LLC ....G.. 484 480-3923
Marcus Hook (G-10441)

◆ G & B Specialties Inc ....C.. 570 752-5901
Berwick (G-1325)

General Dynamics Ots PA Inc...........C.. 570 342-7801
Scranton (G-17238)

General Electric Company ....D.. 412 469-6080
West Mifflin (G-19739)

Goldsborough & Vansant Inc ....G.. 724 782-0393
Finleyville (G-5959)

Homewood Products Corporation ......E.. 412 665-2700
Pittsburgh (G-15099)

J B Booth and Co ....G.. 724 452-1313
Zelienople (G-20806)

J B Booth and Co ....F.. 724 452-8400
Zelienople (G-20805)

Kal-Cameron Manufacturing..............F.. 814 486-3394
Emporium (G-5065)

Kepco Plant Service & Engrg Co ......C.. 412 374-3410
Cranberry Township (G-3828)

▲ Keystone Forging Company ....C.. 570 473-3524
Northumberland (G-12868)

▲ Klaric Forge & Machine Inc ....F.. 814 382-6290
Farrell (G-5868)

Lenape Forged Products Corp ....D.. 610 793-5090
West Chester (G-19592)

▲ Markovitz Enterprises Inc ....D.. 724 452-4500
Zelienople (G-20810)

Markovitz Enterprises Inc ....E.. 724 658-6575
New Castle (G-12119)

Martin Sprocket & Gear Inc ....D.. 610 837-1841
Danielsville (G-3994)

McKees Rocks Forgings Inc ....D.. 412 778-2020
Mc Kees Rocks (G-10620)

▲ Meadville Forging Company LP ....B.. 814 332-8200
Meadville (G-10758)

Meadville Forging Company LP ....D.. 814 398-2203
Cambridge Springs (G-2483)

◆ Medico Industries Inc ....C.. 570 825-7711
Wilkes Barre (G-19942)

Medico Industries Inc ....E.. 570 825-7711
Hanover Township (G-6996)

▲ Mercer Forge Corporation..............C.. 724 662-2750
Mercer (G-10968)

◆ Metaldyne Sintered Ridgway LLC....D.. 814 776-1141
Ridgway (G-16717)

Metaltech Inc ....E.. 814 375-9399
Du Bois (G-4406)

Mg Industries Inc ....G.. 724 694-8290
Derry (G-4105)

North American Forgemasters Co ......E.. 724 656-6440
New Castle (G-12132)

◆ North Amrcn Hgnas Holdings Inc....C.. 814 479-2551
Hollsopple (G-7659)

Peerless Chain Company ....F.. 800 395-2445
Mount Pleasant (G-11710)

▲ Penn Machine Company ....D.. 814 288-1547
Johnstown (G-8421)

◆ Pennsylvania Machine Works Inc....C.. 610 497-3300
Upper Chichester (G-18669)

Phoenix Forge Group LLC ....F.. 800 234-8665
Reading (G-16470)

Phoenix Forging Company Inc..........G.. 610 530-8249
Allentown (G-350)

▲ Phoenix Forging Company Inc ....G.. 610 264-2861
Catasauqua (G-2816)

Prl Industries Inc ....E.. 717 273-6787
Cornwall (G-3740)

Process Science & Innovation ....G.. 717 428-3511
Glen Rock (G-6460)

Qdp Inc ....F.. 610 828-2324
Plymouth Meeting (G-15866)

S & S Slides Inc ....G.. 724 545-2001
Kittanning (G-8791)

Sac Industries Inc ....F.. 412 787-7500
Pittsburgh (G-15505)

Safari Tools Inc ....D.. 717 350-9869
Mercer (G-10974)

Soundhorse Technologies LLC ....G.. 610 347-0453
Unionville (G-18649)

St Marys Pressed Metals Inc ....E.. 814 772-7455
Ridgway (G-16720)

Stainless Distributors Inc.................G.. 215 369-9746
Yardley (G-20341)

▲ Standard Steel LLC ....B.. 717 242-4615
Burnham (G-2362)

T S K Partners Inc ....D.. 814 459-4495
Erie (G-5503)

▲ Tekni-Plex Inc ....E.. 484 690-1520
Wayne (G-19381)

Thompson Gear & Machine Co..........G.. 724 468-5625
Delmont (G-4060)

▲ Timken Gears & Services Inc ....G.. 610 265-3000
King of Prussia (G-8689)

Trident Tpi Holdings Inc ....A.. 484 690-1520
Wayne (G-19384)

Union Electric Steel Corp.................D.. 724 947-9595
Burgettstown (G-2358)

Unisteel LLC ....G.. 724 657-1160
New Castle (G-12161)

▼ Whemco Inc ....E.. 412 390-2700
Pittsburgh (G-15715)

Winston & Duke Inc ....E.. 814 456-0582
Erie (G-5530)

▲ Wyman-Gordon Pennsylvania LLC .E.. 570 474-6371
Mountain Top (G-11783)

3463 Nonferrous Forgings

▲ Electric Materials Company ....C.. 814 725-9621
North East (G-12739)

Eureka Electrical Products ....E.. 814 725-9638
North East (G-12742)

General Dynamics Ots PA Inc...........C.. 570 342-7801
Scranton (G-17238)

Hussey Marine Alloys Ltd ....E.. 724 251-4200
Leetsdale (G-9694)

▲ Keystone Forging Company ....C.. 570 473-3524
Northumberland (G-12868)

Symmco Inc ....C.. 814 894-2461
Sykesville (G-18203)

▲ Wendell August Forge Inc ....D.. 724 748-9500
Mercer (G-10979)

Winston & Duke Inc ....E.. 814 456-0582
Erie (G-5530)

3465 Automotive Stampings

Addev Walco Inc ....E.. 412 486-4400
Glenshaw (G-6479)

Angel Colon ....G.. 215 455-4000
Philadelphia (G-13392)

◆ Cardone Industries Inc ....B.. 215 912-3000
Philadelphia (G-13504)

Century Motors Inc ....G.. 215 724-8845
Philadelphia (G-13521)

Colours Inc ....G.. 814 542-4215
Mount Union (G-11740)

Cosma USA LLC ....G.. 412 551-0708
Wexford (G-19796)

▲ Designs By Lawrence Inc..............E.. 215 698-4555
Philadelphia (G-13622)

Eugene Zapsky ....G.. 814 378-6157
Madera (G-10163)

Finish Technology Inc ....E.. 570 421-4110
Stroudsburg (G-18120)

G Adasavage LLC ....E.. 215 355-3105
Huntingdon Valley (G-7987)

Henshell Corp ....E.. 215 225-7755
Philadelphia (G-13815)

HMS Industries Inc ....E.. 724 459-5090
Blairsville (G-1724)

Metro Manufacturing & Supply ....G.. 610 891-1899
Media (G-10939)

Mikey Gs ....G.. 717 820-4053
Jonestown (G-8450)

▲ New Standard Corporation ....D.. 717 757-9450
York (G-20611)

Norplas Industries Inc ....G.. 724 705-7483
Washington (G-19211)

▲ Osterwalder Inc ....G.. 570 325-2500
Northampton (G-12858)

Quality Stamping ....G.. 724 459-5060
Blairsville (G-1739)

Sikkens Inc ....G.. 610 337-8710
King of Prussia (G-8675)

Sjm Manufacturing Inc ....G.. 724 478-5580
Apollo (G-685)

Waupaca Foundry Inc.....................C.. 570 724-5191
Tioga (G-18367)

Waupaca Foundry Inc.....................B.. 570 827-3245
Tioga (G-18368)

York Corrugating Company ....D.. 717 845-3512
York (G-20734)

3466 Crowns & Closures

◆ Crown Beverage Packaging LLC .....B.. 215 698-5100
Philadelphia (G-13585)

◆ Crown Cork & Seal Usa Inc ....B.. 215 698-5100
Yardley (G-20303)

Crown Holdings Inc ....E.. 215 322-3533
Feasterville Trevose (G-5902)

◆ Crown Holdings Inc ....C.. 215 698-5100
Yardley (G-20304)

Dayton Superior Corporation ....G.. 570 695-3163
Tremont (G-18480)

Guida Inc ....E.. 215 727-2222
Marcus Hook (G-10444)

Keystone Cap Co Inc ....G.. 717 684-3716
Columbia (G-3440)

◆ Maugus Manufacturing Inc ....F.. 717 299-5681
Lancaster (G-9126)

▲ West Pharmaceutical Svcs Inc ......B.. 610 594-2900
Exton (G-5748)

3469 Metal Stampings, NEC

A & S Manufacturing Co ....F.. 888 651-6149
Philadelphia (G-13321)

A V Weber Co Inc ....G.. 215 699-3527
North Wales (G-12784)

A W Mercer Inc ....C.. 610 367-8460
Boyertown (G-1892)

Abbottstown Stamping Co Inc ....F.. 717 632-0588
Hanover (G-6859)

Accrotool Inc ....C.. 724 339-3560
New Kensington (G-12320)

◆ Accutrex Products Inc ....C.. 724 746-4300
Canonsburg (G-2532)

Acme Stamping Wire Forming Co ......E.. 412 771-5720
Pittsburgh (G-14644)

Action Materials Inc ....G.. 610 377-3037
Lehighton (G-9709)

▲ Adept Corporation ....D.. 800 451-2254
York (G-20366)

Advanced Feedscrews Inc ....E.. 724 924-9877
New Castle (G-12054)

Aeroparts Fabg & Machining Inc........E.. 814 948-6015
Nicktown (G-12618)

Aetna Machine Company ....F.. 814 425-3881
Cochranton (G-3334)

▲ All-Clad Holdings Inc ....G.. 724 745-8300
Canonsburg (G-2536)

All-Clad Metalcrafters LLC ....G.. 724 745-8300
Canonsburg (G-2538)

▲ All-Clad Metalcrafters LLC ....D.. 724 745-8300
Canonsburg (G-2537)

American Machine Co ....G.. 717 533-5678
Palmyra (G-13115)

American Metal Finishers Inc ....F.. 610 323-1394
Pottstown (G-15964)

American Trim LLC ....C.. 814 833-7758
Erie (G-5190)

▲ Arai Helmet Americas Inc ....G.. 610 366-7220
Allentown (G-142)

▲ Archetype Design Studio LLC ....G.. 412 369-2900
West View (G-19773)

Ardsley Auto Tags ....G.. 215 572-1409
Glenside (G-6506)

Axiom Inc ....F.. 570 385-1944
Schuylkill Haven (G-17148)

B-TEC Solutions Inc ....D.. 215 785-2400
Croydon (G-3911)

Backus Company ....E.. 814 887-5705
Smethport (G-17632)

◆ Barco Industries Inc ....E.. 610 374-3117
Reading (G-16328)

S I C

Barnes Group Inc...........................C.......814 663-6082
Corry (G-3745)

Bhm Metal Products & Inds LLC.........G.......570 785-2032
Crescent (G-3886)

Blind and Vision Rehab........................F.......412 325-7504
Homestead (G-7683)

Bra-Vor Tool & Die Co Inc ....E.......814 724-1557
Meadville (G-10708)

Brd Noise & Vibration Ctrl Inc ....G.......610 863-6300
Wind Gap (G-20167)

Bridge Auto Tags.................................G.......215 946-8026
Levittown (G-9819)

C & J Metals.......................................F.......562 634-3101
Avella (G-834)

C G S Enterprises Inc ....F.......610 758-9263
Bethlehem (G-1477)

▲ C T E Inc.......................................E.......717 767-6636
York (G-20416)

Camco Manufacturing Inc ....E.......570 731-4109
Sayre (G-17113)

Century Propeller Corporation ....F.......814 677-7100
Franklin (G-6119)

▲ Charles Schillinger Co Inc ....E.......215 638-7200
Bensalem (G-1168)

Chase Manufacturing ....E.......814 664-9069
Corry (G-3747)

Chestnut Group Inc ....G.......610 688-3300
Wayne (G-19313)

Clark Metal Products Co ....C.......724 459-7550
Blairsville (G-1719)

▲ Coinco Inc.....................................E.......814 425-7407
Cochranton (G-3337)

▲ Composidie Inc..............................C.......724 845-8602
Apollo (G-673)

Composidie Inc...................................E.......724 845-8602
Leechburg (G-9643)

Corona Corporation.............................F.......215 679-9538
Red Hill (G-16580)

Cumberland Tool & Die Inc ....E.......717 691-1125
Mechanicsburg (G-10835)

Dallas Machine Inc.............................E.......610 799-2800
Schnecksville (G-17138)

Danco Precision Inc...........................F.......610 933-8981
Phoenixville (G-14542)

Danco Precision Inc...........................E.......610 933-1090
Phoenixville (G-14543)

▲ Diamond Manufacturing Company ...C.......570 693-0300
Wyoming (G-20275)

Diamond Manufacturing Company ....F.......570 693-0300
Wyoming (G-20276)

▼ Die-Tech Inc...................................E.......717 938-6771
York Haven (G-20757)

▲ Dudlik Industries Inc......................E.......215 674-4383
Hatboro (G-7282)

Dyna East Corporation........................E.......610 270-9900
King of Prussia (G-8614)

E F E Laboratories Inc ....E.......215 672-2400
Horsham (G-7812)

E H Schwab Company ....E.......412 823-5003
Turtle Creek (G-18564)

Eagle Displays LLC.............................F.......724 335-8900
North Apollo (G-12726)

Electronic Tool & Die Works ....G.......215 639-0730
Bensalem (G-1187)

Emporium Specialties Company ....E.......814 647-8661
Austin (G-833)

Evans Machining Service Inc...............G.......412 233-3556
Clairton (G-3150)

F B F Inc..E.......215 322-7110
Southampton (G-17811)

F B F Industries Inc............................D.......215 322-7110
Southampton (G-17812)

▲ Falls Mfg Co..................................D.......215 736-2557
Fairless Hills (G-5778)

Federal Metal Products Inc ....G.......610 847-2077
Ferndale (G-5950)

Ferguson Perforating Company ....E.......724 657-8703
New Castle (G-12092)

Fox Welding Shop Inc ....G.......215 225-3069
Philadelphia (G-13716)

Frank Custom Stainless Inc................G.......412 784-0300
Pittsburgh (G-15033)

Freedom Components Inc....................G.......717 242-0101
Lewistown (G-9930)

G & M Co Inc.....................................F.......610 779-7812
Reading (G-16387)

G Adasavage LLC ....E.......215 355-3105
Huntingdon Valley (G-7987)

▼ G G Greene Enterprises Inc ....E.......814 723-5700
Warren (G-19027)

▲ Gap Stamping LLC..........................G.......610 759-7820
Bethlehem (G-1522)

Gcl Inc..F.......724 282-2221
Butler (G-2403)

Gemel Precision Tool Inc ....E.......215 355-2174
Warminster (G-18886)

▲ Gerome Manufacturing Co Inc..........D.......724 438-8544
Smithfield (G-17650)

Get-A-Grip Chafing Pans.....................G.......724 443-6037
Gibsonia (G-6338)

Glenfield Supply Company Inc ....G.......412 781-8188
Pittsburgh (G-15051)

Globe Metal Manufacturing Co ....F.......215 763-1024
Philadelphia (G-13773)

Gma Tooling Company ....E.......215 355-3107
Huntingdon Valley (G-7991)

Harter Precision.................................G.......724 459-5060
Blairsville (G-1723)

▲ Hendrick Manufacturing Company ..G.......570 282-1010
Carbondale (G-2677)

Heraeus Incorporated.........................B.......480 961-9200
Yardley (G-20315)

◆ Heraeus Incorporated ....G.......215 944-9981
Yardley (G-20314)

Heritage Maintenance Pdts LLC ....G.......610 277-5070
Harleysville (G-7038)

Hillcrest Tool & Die Inc ....F.......814 827-1296
Titusville (G-18381)

HMS Industries Inc.............................G.......724 459-5090
Blairsville (G-1724)

Hpt Pharma LLC.................................F.......215 792-0020
Warrington (G-19121)

Hunter Kitchen & Bath LLC.................G.......570 926-0777
Exton (G-5693)

▲ Ice Qube Inc...................................D.......724 837-7600
Greensburg (G-6676)

Igb Tool & Machine Inc.......................G.......215 338-1420
Philadelphia (G-13847)

▲ Igs Industries Inc...........................C.......724 222-5800
Meadow Lands (G-10690)

▲ IKEA Indirect Mtl & Svcs LLC...........G.......610 834-0150
Conshohocken (G-3559)

Independent Tool & Mfg......................G.......814 336-5168
Meadville (G-10738)

J & R Metal Products LLC...................G.......717 656-6241
Leola (G-9788)

Jackson & Sons Machine Co ....G.......724 744-2116
Harrison City (G-7249)

▲ Jacob Holtz Company LLC ....D.......215 423-2800
Philadelphia (G-13316)

▲ Jade Equipment Corporation...........C.......215 947-3333
Huntingdon Valley (G-7999)

▼ Jade Holdings Inc...........................C.......215 947-3333
Huntingdon Valley (G-8000)

Kajevi Services LLC............................G.......215 722-0711
Philadelphia (G-13920)

Keystone North Inc.............................E.......570 662-3882
Mansfield (G-10420)

Kimjohn Industries Inc ....F.......610 436-8600
West Chester (G-19582)

Kreckel Enterprises Inc.......................F.......814 834-1874
Saint Marys (G-16986)

▲ Kyles Auto Tags & Insurance...........G.......610 429-1447
West Chester (G-19585)

▼ L-One Inc.......................................E.......717 938-6771
York Haven (G-20760)

Laminar Flow Inc................................D.......215 672-0232
Warminster (G-18903)

Langhorne Metal Spinning Inc.............G.......215 497-8876
Langhorne (G-9307)

▲ Leefson Tool & Die Company ....E.......610 461-7772
Folcroft (G-6008)

▲ Leiss Tool & Die..............................C.......814 444-1444
Somerset (G-17695)

Lewistown Manufacturing Inc.............F.......717 242-1468
Lewistown (G-9938)

▲ Marco Manufacturing Co Inc............E.......215 463-2332
Philadelphia (G-13992)

Metal Fabricating Co...........................G.......717 442-4729
Parkesburg (G-13180)

Metal Peddler Inc................................G.......724 476-1061
West Sunbury (G-19772)

Metal Powder Products LLC.................D.......814 834-2886
Saint Marys (G-16991)

Metalkraft Industries Inc.....................E.......570 724-6800
Wellsboro (G-19469)

▲ Moore Push Pin Company.................D.......215 233-5700
Glenside (G-6531)

N C B Technologies Inc........................G.......724 658-5544
New Castle (G-12123)

▲ New Standard Corporation ....D.......717 757-9450
York (G-20611)

New Standard Corporation ....G.......717 757-9450
Mount Joy (G-11667)

New Standard Corporation ....B.......717 764-2409
Emigsville (G-4996)

Northeast Industrial Mfg Inc ....E.......724 588-7711
Greenville (G-6760)

Norwood Manufacture Co LLC ....G.......724 652-0698
New Castle (G-12134)

◆ Oberg Industries Inc.......................A.......724 295-2121
Freeport (G-6209)

Oberg Industries Inc...........................C.......724 353-9700
Sarver (G-17074)

Oberg Industries Inc...........................C.......724 353-9700
Sarver (G-17075)

▲ Orbel Corporation ....E.......610 829-5000
Easton (G-4736)

Orlotronics Corporation.......................E.......610 239-8200
Bridgeport (G-2042)

Osram Sylvania Inc.............................B.......717 854-3499
Saint Marys (G-17000)

P G A Machine Co Inc ....G.......610 874-1335
Eddystone (G-4806)

Paulsonbilt Ltd ....F.......610 384-6112
Coatesville (G-3322)

Pb Holdings Inc..................................G.......215 947-3333
Huntingdon Valley (G-8021)

Penn Metal Stamping Inc ....E.......814 834-7171
Kersey (G-8565)

Penn-Elkco Inc...................................F.......814 834-4304
Saint Marys (G-17003)

Perry C Ritter....................................G.......215 699-7079
Lansdale (G-9398)

Pilot-Run Stamping Company ....E.......440 255-8821
Corry (G-3772)

PMI Stainless.....................................E.......412 461-1463
Homestead (G-7691)

◆ Premier Pan Company Inc................D.......724 457-4220
Crescent (G-3887)

▲ Prizer-Painter Stove Works Inc.........E.......610 376-7479
Blandon (G-1757)

Qdp Inc...F.......610 828-2324
Plymouth Meeting (G-15866)

◆ Quality Perforating Inc....................D.......570 267-2092
Carbondale (G-2685)

◆ Reading Truck Body LLC..................C.......610 775-3301
Reading (G-16493)

Robert L Baker...................................F.......443 617-0164
Chambersburg (G-2973)

◆ Schaffner Manufacturing Co ....D.......412 761-9902
Pittsburgh (G-15515)

Schiller Grounds Care Inc...................D.......215 322-4970
Huntingdon Valley (G-8035)

Smoyer L M Brass Products Inc...........G.......610 867-5011
Bethlehem (G-1620)

Specialty Products Inc ....G.......814 455-6978
Erie (G-5486)

Stellar Machine Incorporated..............F.......570 718-1733
Nanticoke (G-11903)

▲ Steril-Sil Co LLC.............................G.......617 739-2970
Denver (G-4094)

▲ Superior Group Inc.........................E.......610 397-2040
Conshohocken (G-3610)

Tate Access Floors Inc.......................C.......717 244-4071
Red Lion (G-16616)

Tecklane Manufacturing Inc................F.......724 274-9464
Springdale (G-17903)

▲ The Keystone Friction Hinge Co ......C.......570 321-0693
Williamsport (G-20082)

Tonnard Manufacturing Corp...............D.......814 664-7794
Corry (G-3776)

◆ Tooling Dynamics LLC.....................C.......717 764-8873
York (G-20690)

▲ Tottser Tool and Die Shop Inc.........D.......215 357-7600
Southampton (G-17842)

Tottser Tool and Die Shop Inc ....D.......215 357-7600
Southampton (G-17843)

Transportation PA Dept ....E.......717 787-2304
Harrisburg (G-7236)

Tucker Industries Incorporated ....D.......215 638-1900
Bensalem (G-1265)

United Fabricating Inc.........................F.......724 663-5891
Claysville (G-3209)

United Panel Inc.................................E.......610 588-6871
Mount Bethel (G-11615)

Venango County Notary.......................G.......814 677-2216
Seneca (G-17370)

▲ Vertech International Inc ....E.......215 529-0300
Quakertown (G-16257)

▲ Veterinary Tag Supply Co Inc ....G..... 610 649-1550
  Bridgeport *(G-2048)*
Vic Auto Tech Place ....G..... 215 969-2083
  Philadelphia *(G-14445)*
Waverly Partners Inc ....C..... 610 687-7867
  Wayne *(G-19390)*
Westwood Precision LLC ....G..... 610 264-7020
  Allentown *(G-433)*
Windle Mech Solutions Inc ....G..... 215 624-8600
  Philadelphia *(G-14479)*
Winston & Duke Inc ....E..... 814 456-0582
  Erie *(G-5530)*
▲ Winston Industries Inc ....F..... 215 394-8178
  Warminster *(G-19001)*
Witmer Public Safety Group Inc ....D..... 800 852-6088
  Coatesville *(G-3331)*
Wm C Haldeman ....G..... 215 324-2400
  Philadelphia *(G-14481)*
▲ Wrapmaster Usa LLC ....G..... 215 782-2285
  Elkins Park *(G-4915)*
York Corrugating Company ....D..... 717 845-3512
  York *(G-20734)*

3471 Electroplating, Plating, Polishing, Anodizing & Coloring

24k Gold Plating ....G..... 610 255-4676
  Landenberg *(G-9246)*
A L Finishing Co Inc ....F..... 215 855-9422
  Hatfield *(G-7313)*
Accent Metals Inc ....F..... 717 699-5676
  York *(G-20363)*
Accent Metals Inc ....F..... 717 699-5676
  York *(G-20364)*
Accu-Grind Inc ....D..... 814 965-5475
  Johnsonburg *(G-8343)*
Advanced Finishing Usa Inc ....E..... 814 474-5200
  Fairview *(G-5810)*
▲ Advanced Metal Coatings Inc ....E..... 570 538-1249
  Watsontown *(G-19273)*
Aeco Inc ....G..... 215 335-2974
  Philadelphia *(G-13350)*
All-Clad Metalcrafters LLC ....G..... 724 745-8300
  Canonsburg *(G-2538)*
Allegheny Ludlum LLC ....C..... 724 567-2001
  Vandergrift *(G-18721)*
Allegheny Metal Finishing ....G..... 724 695-3233
  Imperial *(G-8057)*
Allegheny Technologies Inc ....F..... 724 775-1554
  Monaca *(G-11279)*
American Hard Chrome LLC ....G..... 412 951-9051
  New Castle *(G-12057)*
American Metal Finishers Inc ....F..... 610 323-1394
  Pottstown *(G-15964)*
American Nickeloid Company ....G..... 610 767-3842
  Walnutport *(G-18790)*
American Tinning Galvanizing ....D..... 814 456-7053
  Erie *(G-5189)*
Amz Manufacturing Corporation ....E..... 717 751-2714
  York *(G-20376)*
Amz Manufacturing Corporation ....F..... 717 848-2565
  York *(G-20377)*
Anodizing Plus Inc ....G..... 717 246-0584
  Dallastown *(G-3971)*
▲ Apollo Metals Ltd ....E..... 610 867-5826
  Bethlehem *(G-1450)*
▲ ATI Precision Finishing LLC ....E..... 724 775-1664
  Rochester *(G-16782)*
ATI Precision Finishing LLC ....E..... 724 452-1726
  Zelienople *(G-20790)*
B & G Finishing LLC ....G..... 267 229-2569
  Philadelphia *(G-13436)*
B&B Metal Finishing Inc ....G..... 717 764-8941
  Manchester *(G-10355)*
Benco Technology LLC ....F..... 610 273-3364
  Honey Brook *(G-7738)*
Benders Buffing & Polishing ....G..... 717 226-1850
  Elizabethtown *(G-4866)*
Bfg Manufacturing Services Inc ....D..... 814 938-9164
  Punxsutawney *(G-16128)*
Blastco ....G..... 215 529-7100
  Quakertown *(G-16173)*
Blue Mountain Metal Finishing ....G..... 717 933-1643
  Bethel *(G-1393)*
Bradford Allegheny Corporation ....F..... 814 368-4465
  Lewis Run *(G-9873)*
Canalley Painting ....G..... 215 443-9505
  Hatboro *(G-7276)*
Centria Inc ....F..... 724 251-2300
  Ambridge *(G-612)*

Clark Metal Products Co ....C..... 724 459-7550
  Blairsville *(G-1719)*
Classic Metal ....G..... 724 991-2659
  Prospect *(G-16111)*
Cnc Specialties Mfg Inc ....E..... 724 727-5680
  Apollo *(G-671)*
Commercial Metal Polishing ....F..... 610 837-0267
  Bath *(G-954)*
▲ Composidie Inc ....C..... 724 845-8602
  Apollo *(G-673)*
◆ CRC Industries Inc ....C..... 215 674-4300
  Horsham *(G-7806)*
Crile Consolidated Inds Inc ....F..... 724 228-0880
  Washington *(G-19159)*
Custom Industrial Processing ....F..... 814 834-1883
  Saint Marys *(G-16958)*
Custom Polishing and Finishing ....G..... 215 331-0960
  Philadelphia *(G-13595)*
Dgm Custom Plsg Finsg C ....G..... 215 331-0960
  Philadelphia *(G-13627)*
▲ Diamond Manufacturing Company ..C..... 570 693-0300
  Wyoming *(G-20275)*
Diamond Manufacturing Company ....F..... 570 693-0300
  Wyoming *(G-20276)*
East Liberty Elcpltg Inc ....E..... 412 487-4080
  Glenshaw *(G-6487)*
Easton Pltg & Met Finshg Inc ....E..... 610 252-9007
  Easton *(G-4672)*
Electro-Platers of York Inc ....F..... 717 751-2712
  York *(G-20466)*
Elsie A Mundkowsky ....G..... 814 922-3072
  West Springfield *(G-19767)*
Epy Industries Inc ....F..... 717 751-2712
  York *(G-20470)*
Erie Hard Chrome Inc ....E..... 814 459-5114
  Erie *(G-5268)*
Erie Plating Company ....D..... 814 453-7531
  Erie *(G-5272)*
Erie Protective Coatings Inc ....G..... 814 833-0095
  Erie *(G-5273)*
▲ Evergreen Synergies LLC ....E..... 610 239-9425
  King of Prussia *(G-8617)*
Francis J Nowalk ....G..... 412 687-4017
  Pittsburgh *(G-15030)*
Frank Mance Plating Service ....G..... 412 281-5748
  Pittsburgh *(G-15034)*
Frankford Plating Inc ....G..... 215 288-4518
  Philadelphia *(G-13721)*
G Beswick Enterprises Inc ....G..... 412 829-3068
  North Versailles *(G-12775)*
G O Carlson Inc ....D..... 610 384-2800
  Downingtown *(G-4228)*
Great Lakes Metal Finishing ....E..... 814 452-1886
  Erie *(G-5306)*
◆ Hall Industries Incorporated ....E..... 724 752-2000
  Ellwood City *(G-4934)*
Harvey M Stern & Co ....G..... 610 649-1728
  Wynnewood *(G-20268)*
HI Tech Plating Co Inc ....F..... 814 455-4231
  Erie *(G-5317)*
Hillock Anodizing Inc ....E..... 215 535-8090
  Philadelphia *(G-13825)*
Hkp Metals Inc ....G..... 412 751-0500
  McKeesport *(G-10670)*
▲ Hofmann Industries Inc ....B..... 610 678-8051
  Reading *(G-16403)*
Imp Inc ....G..... 610 458-1533
  West Chester *(G-19568)*
Industrial Machine Works Inc ....E..... 412 782-5055
  Pittsburgh *(G-15119)*
Industrial Metal Plating Inc ....D..... 610 374-5107
  Reading *(G-16407)*
Industrial Polsg & Grinding ....D..... 717 854-9001
  York *(G-20536)*
Insaco Incorporated ....D..... 215 536-3500
  Quakertown *(G-16202)*
Ion Technologies Inc ....F..... 814 772-0440
  Ridgway *(G-16712)*
J M Caldwell Co Inc ....G..... 610 436-9997
  West Chester *(G-19576)*
J P Cerini Technologies Inc ....G..... 215 457-7337
  Philadelphia *(G-13886)*
Jamarco ....G..... 814 833-3159
  Erie *(G-5333)*
▲ James Abbott ....F..... 215 426-8070
  Philadelphia *(G-13890)*
James K Wallick ....G..... 717 471-8152
  Lancaster *(G-9070)*
Jaws Inc ....G..... 215 423-2234
  Philadelphia *(G-13891)*

Jersey Chrome Plating Co ....F..... 412 681-7044
  Pittsburgh *(G-15152)*
JMJ Finishing ....G..... 814 838-4050
  Erie *(G-5337)*
John R Armstrong ....G..... 717 464-3239
  Willow Street *(G-20152)*
K&L Plating Company Inc ....F..... 717 397-9819
  Lancaster *(G-9076)*
Keystone Automotive Inds Inc ....E..... 814 467-5531
  Windber *(G-20184)*
Keystone Coating LLC ....G..... 717 440-5922
  Boiling Springs *(G-1874)*
Keystone Rustproofing Inc ....E..... 724 339-7588
  New Kensington *(G-12352)*
▲ Klein Plating Works Inc ....D..... 814 452-3793
  Erie *(G-5347)*
Lasermation Inc ....E..... 215 228-7900
  Philadelphia *(G-13959)*
▲ Leading Technologies Inc ....E..... 724 842-3400
  Leechburg *(G-9647)*
Leonhardt Manufacturing Co Inc ....D..... 717 632-4150
  Hanover *(G-6915)*
Lepko J D Finishing ....G..... 215 538-9717
  Quakertown *(G-16210)*
Librandi Machine Shop Inc ....F..... 717 944-9442
  Middletown *(G-11063)*
M & A Coatings LLC ....F..... 724 267-2868
  Washington *(G-19196)*
M & P Refinishing Co ....G..... 724 527-6360
  Jeannette *(G-8262)*
M J M Industries ....G..... 724 368-8400
  Portersville *(G-15931)*
Main Steel LLC ....G..... 724 453-3000
  Harmony *(G-7073)*
Mance Plating Co ....G..... 724 695-0550
  Imperial *(G-8071)*
Meadville Plating Company Inc ....F..... 814 724-1084
  Meadville *(G-10760)*
Met-Fin Co Inc ....G..... 215 699-3505
  North Wales *(G-12818)*
Metal Finishing Industries ....G..... 724 836-1003
  Greensburg *(G-6688)*
Metalife Industries Inc ....G..... 814 676-5661
  Reno *(G-16647)*
Micro Plating Inc ....G..... 814 866-0073
  Erie *(G-5390)*
Millcreek Metal Finishing Inc ....G..... 814 833-9045
  Erie *(G-5393)*
Molecular Finishing Systems ....G..... 724 695-0554
  Imperial *(G-8073)*
Multiflex Plating Company Inc ....E..... 610 461-7700
  Collingdale *(G-3408)*
Multiple Metal Processing Inc ....G..... 570 620-7254
  Effort *(G-4826)*
Nak International Corp ....E..... 724 774-9200
  Monaca *(G-11292)*
New Castle Industries Inc ....E..... 724 656-5600
  New Castle *(G-12129)*
North Penn Polishing and Pltg ....E..... 215 257-4945
  Sellersville *(G-17355)*
Oesterlings Sndblst & Pntg Inc ....E..... 724 282-1391
  Butler *(G-2429)*
▲ Orbel Corporation ....E..... 610 829-5000
  Easton *(G-4736)*
▲ Ore Enterprises Inc ....G..... 814 898-3933
  Erie *(G-5410)*
P R Finishing Inc ....G..... 610 565-0378
  Folcroft *(G-6011)*
Pauls Chrome Plating Inc ....E..... 724 538-3367
  Evans City *(G-5560)*
Philadelphia Chrome ....G..... 267 988-5834
  Philadelphia *(G-14143)*
Philadelphia Rust Proof Co ....F..... 215 425-3000
  Philadelphia *(G-14153)*
Pittsburgh Anodizing Co ....E..... 724 265-5110
  Russellton *(G-16884)*
Plating Unlimited LLC ....G..... 814 952-3135
  Punxsutawney *(G-16153)*
Polish This Inc ....G..... 484 269-9450
  Royersford *(G-16861)*
Pottsgrove Metal Finishers ....F..... 610 323-7004
  Pottstown *(G-16033)*
Precious Metal Plating Co Inc ....G..... 610 586-1500
  Glenolden *(G-6476)*
▼ Precision Finishing Inc ....E..... 215 257-6862
  Quakertown *(G-16232)*
Precision Plating Co Inc ....G..... 724 652-2393
  New Castle *(G-12140)*
▲ Precision Roll Grinders Inc ....D..... 610 395-6966
  Allentown *(G-358)*

Prism Powder Coating Services ....G 724 457-2836
Crescent (G-3888)

Products Finishing Inc ....F 814 452-4887
Erie (G-5439)

Progress For Industry Inc ....F 814 763-3707
Saegertown (G-16928)

Punxsutawney Finshg Works Inc ....C 814 938-9164
Punxsutawney (G-16155)

▲ Quality Dispersions Inc ....F 814 781-7927
Kersey (G-8567)

Quality Metal Coatings Inc ....G 814 781-6161
Saint Marys (G-17012)

Quantum Plating Inc ....G 814 835-9213
Erie (G-5446)

Reilly Plating Company Inc ....D 570 735-7777
Nanticoke (G-11902)

Reisingers Precision Polsg LLC ....G 814 763-2226
Saegertown (G-16931)

Revel Capewell Inc ....G 610 272-8075
Norristown (G-12705)

Rick Radvansky & Sons ....G 724 335-7411
New Kensington (G-12371)

▲ Schake Industries Inc ....E 814 677-9333
Seneca (G-17369)

Scoopermarket Inc ....G 215 925-1132
Philadelphia (G-14286)

Select-Tron Industries Inc ....F 814 459-0847
Erie (G-5473)

Shalmet Corporation ....C 570 366-1414
Orwigsburg (G-13052)

Shammy Solutions ....G 412 871-0939
Pittsburgh (G-15527)

▲ Sharretts Plating Co Inc ....D 717 767-6702
Emigsville (G-4999)

Simms Abrasives ....G 610 327-1877
Pottstown (G-16046)

St Marys Metal Finishing Inc................G 814 834-6500
Saint Marys (G-17019)

▲ Stainless Steel Services Inc ....F 215 831-1471
Philadelphia (G-14340)

Stambaugh Metal Inc ....E 717 632-5957
Hanover (G-6958)

Steel City Chromium Plating Co ....G 610 838-8441
Hellertown (G-7563)

Sunshine Polishing Systems ....G 610 828-6197
Conshohocken (G-3609)

Surtech Industries Inc ....E 717 767-6808
York (G-20682)

Tiger Enterprises Inc ....G 717 786-5441
Strasburg (G-18095)

Titanium Finishing Co ....F 215 679-4181
East Greenville (G-4577)

Torpedo Specialty Wire Inc ....E 814 563-7505
Pittsfield (G-15739)

Tri State Metal Cleaning Inc ....G 814 898-3933
Erie (G-5516)

Tumbling With Jojo ....G 267 574-5074
King of Prussia (G-8691)

Vallorbs Jewel Company ....C 717 392-3978
Bird In Hand (G-1684)

▼ Vibroplating Inc ....G 215 638-4413
Bensalem (G-1267)

Wade Technology Incorporated.............G 215 765-2478
Philadelphia (G-14456)

Williams Metalfinishing Inc ....D 610 670-1077
Reading (G-16566)

3479 Coating & Engraving, NEC

A A A Engraving ....G 412 281-7756
Pittsburgh (G-14628)

Absolute Powder Coating LLC ....G 814 781-1160
Saint Marys (G-16944)

Addies Inc ....G 570 748-2966
Lock Haven (G-10081)

Advanced Finishing Usa Inc ....E 814 474-5200
Fairview (G-5810)

▲ Advanced Metal Coatings Inc ....E 570 538-1249
Watsontown (G-19273)

Advanced Polymer Coatings Inc ....G 215 943-1466
Levittown (G-9812)

Amanita Technologies LLC ....G 215 353-1984
Dublin (G-4430)

Amdex Metallizing Inc ....G 724 887-4977
Scottdale (G-17189)

American Metal Finishers Inc ....F 610 323-1394
Pottstown (G-65)

▲ American Precision Powder..............G 724 788-1691
Aliquippa (G-65)

▲ American Safety Technologies ....G 215 855-8450
Montgomeryville (G-11386)

American Tinning Galvanizing ....D 814 456-7053
Erie (G-5189)

Andrew W Nissly Inc ....G 717 393-3841
Lancaster (G-8934)

Antietam Iron Works LLC ....G 717 485-5557
Mc Connellsburg (G-10562)

Apply Powder & Coating ....G 610 361-1889
Middletown (G-11048)

Apx Industrial Coatings Inc ....E 717 369-0037
Saint Thomas (G-17037)

Armoloy Co of Philadelphia ....G 215 788-0841
Croydon (G-3910)

Armoloy Western Pennsylvania ....F 412 823-1030
Turtle Creek (G-18558)

Atkinson Industries Inc ....G 570 366-2114
Orwigsburg (G-13039)

Axalta Coating Systems LLC ....E 610 358-2228
Glen Mills (G-6430)

Bbm Technologies Inc ....G 412 269-4546
Coraopolis (G-3662)

Blastmaster Surface Restoratio ....G 724 282-7669
Butler (G-2381)

Bonehead Performance Inc ....F 215 674-8206
Warminster (G-18839)

Bridge Deck Solutions LLC..................E 724 424-1001
Latrobe (G-9461)

◆ Cardolite Corporation ....E 609 436-0902
Bristol (G-2123)

◆ Carma Industrial Coatings Inc ....G 717 624-6239
New Oxford (G-12405)

Cedar Hollow Sales Inc ....G 610 644-2660
Malvern (G-10201)

Celf Services LLC ....G 717 643-0039
Greencastle (G-6602)

Centria Inc ....F 724 251-2300
Ambridge (G-612)

Chase Corporation...............................F 412 963-6285
Pittsburgh (G-14837)

City Engraving & Awards LLC ....G 215 731-0200
Philadelphia (G-13547)

Coating Concepts LLC ....G 717 240-0010
Carlisle (G-2701)

Coating Technology Inc ....G 610 296-7722
Malvern (G-10213)

Commercial Metal Polishing ....F 610 837-0267
Bath (G-954)

▲ Composidie Inc ....C 724 845-8602
Apollo (G-673)

Cronimet Spcialty Mtls USA Inc ....E 724 347-2208
Wheatland (G-19835)

Cummings Group Ltd ....F 814 774-8238
Girard (G-6385)

Custom Etch Inc ....E 724 652-7117
New Castle (G-12079)

Custom Polishing and Finishing ....G 215 331-0960
Philadelphia (G-13595)

Deane Carbide Products Inc ....F 215 639-3333
Trevose (G-18492)

Delp Family Powder Coatings ....G 724 287-3200
Butler (G-2394)

▲ Diamond Manufacturing Company ..C 570 693-0300
Wyoming (G-20275)

Diamond Manufacturing Company ....F 570 693-0300
Wyoming (G-20276)

Diversified Coatings Inc ....C 814 772-3850
Ridgway (G-16705)

Dm Coatings Inc...................................E 717 561-1175
Harrisburg (G-7121)

Dura-Bond Coating Inc ....E 412 436-2411
Duquesne (G-4496)

Dura-Bond Coating Inc ....C 717 939-1079
Steelton (G-18046)

Dura-Bond Pipe LLC ....G 412 672-0764
McKeesport (G-10666)

▲ East Coast Atv Inc ....F 267 733-7364
Coopersburg (G-3627)

▲ Eclat Industries Inc ....G 215 547-2684
Levittown (G-9834)

Ems Engnred Mtls Solutions LLC ....D 610 562-3841
Hamburg (G-6838)

Evaporated Coatings Inc ....E 215 659-3080
Willow Grove (G-20116)

◆ F3 Metalworx Inc ....E 814 725-8637
North East (G-12743)

FAD Corporation ....G 610 872-3844
Eddystone (G-4802)

First Line Coatings Inc ....G 814 452-0046
Erie (G-5291)

FMR Industries Inc ....G 215 536-2222
Quakertown (G-16194)

Freys Research Inc ....G 724 586-5659
Renfrew (G-16639)

Fusion Coatings Inc ....E 610 693-5886
Robesonia (G-16773)

G V D Inc ....G 724 537-5586
Latrobe (G-9477)

Ganoe Paving Inc ....E 717 597-2567
Greencastle (G-6613)

Gill Powder Coating Inc ....E 215 639-5486
Bensalem (G-1204)

Great Lakes Finishes LLC ....G 814 438-2518
Union City (G-18607)

H & H Wholesale LLC ....G 724 733-8338
Pittsburgh (G-15069)

H & W Global Industries Inc.................E 724 459-5316
Blairsville (G-1721)

▲ Hadco Aluminum & Metal Corp PA ..D 215 695-2705
Philadelphia (G-13795)

Hd Laser Engrv & Etching LLC ....G 724 924-9241
New Castle (G-12101)

Healy Glass Artistry LLC ....E 484 241-0989
Bethlehem (G-1530)

Helfran Glass ....G 570 287-8105
Kingston (G-8719)

Hoffman Powder Coating ....G 610 845-1422
Macungie (G-10147)

▲ Hofmann Industries Inc ....B 610 678-8051
Reading (G-16403)

ICP Industries LLC ....E 888 672-2123
Birdsboro (G-1700)

Industrial Nameplate Inc ....E 215 322-1111
Warminster (G-18898)

Inghams Regrooving Service Inc ....E 717 336-8473
Denver (G-4076)

Inghams Regrooving Service Inc ....E 717 336-8473
Stevens (G-18053)

Innovative Finishers Inc ....G 215 536-2222
Telford (G-18296)

Ivy Graphics Inc ....F 215 396-9446
Warminster (G-18900)

J & M Custom Powdr Coating LLC.......G 717 445-4869
Denver (G-4077)

Jerico Bolt Co......................................G 215 721-9567
Souderton (G-17746)

John Pasquarello ....G 610 825-3069
Conshohocken (G-3569)

▲ Johnstown Wldg Fabrication Inc......C 800 225-9353
Johnstown (G-8394)

K Matkem of Morrisville LP ....G 215 428-3664
Allentown (G-276)

K Matkem of Morrisville LP ....G 215 295-4158
Morrisville (G-11566)

Keener Coatings Inc ....E 717 764-9412
York (G-20549)

Keystone Koating LLC ....E 717 738-2148
Lititz (G-10021)

Keystone Koating LLC ....D 717 436-2056
Mifflintown (G-11127)

King Coatings LLC...............................G 610 435-1212
Allentown (G-283)

Korns Galvanizing Company Inc ....E 814 535-3293
Johnstown (G-8401)

▼ Lane Enterprises Inc ....F 717 761-8175
Camp Hill (G-2503)

Lane Enterprises Inc............................E 610 272-4531
King of Prussia (G-8637)

Lane Enterprises Inc............................D 717 249-8342
Carlisle (G-2720)

Laurel Highlands Finishing ....G 724 537-9850
Latrobe (G-9497)

Lee Engraving Services Inc ....G 412 788-4224
Oakdale (G-12905)

Longevity Coatings..............................G 610 871-1427
Saylorsburg (G-17105)

Luna Collison Ltd.................................F 412 466-8866
Duquesne (G-4497)

M J M Industries ....G 724 368-8400
Portersville (G-15931)

Metal Litho and Laminating LLC ....E 724 646-1222
Greenville (G-6756)

Metaltech ....D 412 464-5000
Pittsburgh (G-15280)

Mshar Power Train Specialists ....G 717 231-3900
Harrisburg (G-7181)

▲ Mxl Industries Inc ....D 717 569-8711
Lancaster (G-9141)

Mystic Assembly & Dctg Co ....E 215 957-0280
Warminster (G-18926)

NC Industries Inc ....F 248 528-5200
Reynoldsville (G-16658)

Neville Galvanizing Inc ....E 412 771-9799
  Pittsburgh (G-15331)
Nittany Coatings Inc ....G 724 588-1898
  Greenville (G-6759)
North American Compounding ....E 814 899-0621
  Erie (G-5406)
Patriot Armory & Coatings LLC ......G 215 723-7228
  Telford (G-18308)
Patriot Metal Products Inc ....E 570 759-3634
  Berwick (G-1339)
Pbz LLC ....E 800 578-1121
  Lititz (G-10029)
Penn Protective Coatings Corp ....F 215 355-0708
  Huntingdon Valley (G-8022)
▲ Performance Coatings Corp ....F 610 525-1190
  Levittown (G-9854)
Pittsburgh Powder Coat ....G 412 419-8434
  Finleyville (G-5963)
▲ Plastic Dip Moldings Inc ....E 215 766-2020
  Quakertown (G-16229)
Polymer Surface Systems LLC ....G 724 222-6544
  Eighty Four (G-4845)
Powder Coating ....G 570 837-3325
  Middleburg (G-11035)
Powder Coating Co ....G 610 273-9007
  Honey Brook (G-7756)
Precision Coating Tech Mfg Inc ....E 717 336-5030
  Denver (G-4088)
Precision Grit Etching & Engrv ....G 412 828-5790
  Oakmont (G-12924)
Precision Metal Crafters Ltd ....E 724 837-2511
  Greensburg (G-6704)
Premier Applied Coatings Inc ....F 610 367-2635
  Boyertown (G-1924)
Punxsutawney Finshg Works Inc .....C 814 938-9164
  Punxsutawney (G-16155)
Purtech Inc ....F 570 424-1669
  East Stroudsburg (G-4632)
Quality Metal Coatings Inc ....G 814 781-6161
  Saint Marys (G-17012)
R & H Jewelers ....G 215 928-1240
  Philadelphia (G-14222)
Reh Holdings Inc ....G 717 843-0021
  York (G-20657)
▲ Richter Precision Inc ....D 717 560-9990
  East Petersburg (G-4589)
Robert H Berenson ....G 610 642-9380
  Haverford (G-7414)
▲ Schake Industries Inc ....E 814 677-9333
  Seneca (G-17369)
▲ Sharon Coating LLC ....C 724 983-6464
  Sharon (G-17442)
Shawcor Pipe Protection LLC ....E 215 736-1111
  Morrisville (G-11581)
Spec Industries Inc ....G 610 497-4220
  Chester (G-3063)
Surtech Industries Inc ....E 717 767-6808
  York (G-20682)
Surtreat Holding LLC ....G 412 281-1202
  Pittsburgh (G-15592)
Tech Met Inc ....E 412 678-8277
  Glassport (G-6418)
Techs Industries Inc ....F 412 464-5000
  Turtle Creek (G-18570)
Techs Industries Inc ....E 412 464-5000
  Pittsburgh (G-15603)
▲ Techs Industries Inc ....C 412 464-5000
  Pittsburgh (G-15604)
◆ Thermoclad Company ....F 814 456-1243
  Erie (G-5507)
Tms International LLC ....G 412 257-1083
  Bridgeville (G-2096)
Total Systems Technology Inc ....F 412 653-7690
  Pittsburgh (G-15633)
◆ Triumph Group Operations Inc .....F 610 251-1000
  Berwyn (G-1386)
Tucker Indus Lquid Catings Inc ......E 717 259-8339
  East Berlin (G-4526)
Turri Associates Incorporated ....F 717 795-9936
  Mechanicsburg (G-10900)
▲ U S Plastic Coatings Corp ....E 215 257-5300
  Sellersville (G-17361)
V and S Lbanon Galvanizing LLC .....E 717 861-7777
  Jonestown (G-8453)
Vci Coatings LLC ....G 412 281-1202
  Pittsburgh (G-15689)
Velocity Powder Coating LLC ....G 704 287-1024
  New Castle (G-12164)
Voigt & Schweitzer LLC ....E 717 861-7777
  Jonestown (G-8454)

Vorteq Coil Finishers LLC ....D 610 797-5200
  Allentown (G-426)
Vorteq Coil Finishers LLC ....F 724 898-1511
  Valencia (G-18704)
▲ White Engrg Surfaces Corp ....E 215 968-5021
  Newtown (G-12563)
Wismarq Valencia LLC ....F 724 898-1511
  Valencia (G-18705)
Xser Coatings Llc ....G 732 754-9887
  Philadelphia (G-14495)

3482 Small Arms Ammunition

Ballistic Scientific Usa LLC ....G 267 282-6666
  Corry (G-3744)
Classic Shotshell Co Inc ....G 570 553-1651
  Friendsville (G-6229)
▲ Combined Tactical Systems Inc ....C 724 932-2177
  Jamestown (G-8236)
Ford City Gun Workd ....G 724 994-9501
  Ford City (G-6045)
▼ G G Greene Enterprises Inc ....E 814 723-5700
  Warren (G-19027)
◆ International Cartridge Corp ....E 814 938-6820
  Reynoldsville (G-16657)
Joint Ammunition and Tech Inc ....F 703 926-5509
  Johnstown (G-8395)
◆ Nonlethal Technologies Inc ....E 724 479-5100
  Homer City (G-7679)
Pocono Pistol Club LLC ....G 570 424-2940
  Stroudsburg (G-18136)
▲ Precision Custom Ammunition ....G 717 274-8762
  Lebanon (G-9624)
Steel Valley Casting LLC ....G 724 777-4025
  New Brighton (G-12044)
Velocity Munitions Inc ....G 724 966-2140
  Carmichaels (G-2762)

3483 Ammunition, Large

3si Security Systems Holdg Inc ....G 610 280-2000
  Malvern (G-10177)
▼ Action Manufacturing Company .....B 267 540-4041
  Bristol (G-2103)
Action Manufacturing Company ....D 610 593-1800
  Atglen (G-799)
▼ Combined Systems Inc ....C 724 932-2177
  Jamestown (G-8235)
General Dynamics Ots PA Inc ....C 717 244-4551
  Red Lion (G-16596)
▲ General Dynamics Ots PA Inc ....G 717 246-8208
  Red Lion (G-16597)
General Dynamics Ots PA Inc ....C 570 342-7801
  Scranton (G-17238)
Lockheed Martin Corporation ....B 570 876-2132
  Archbald (G-691)
◆ Medico Industries Inc ....C 570 825-7711
  Wilkes Barre (G-19942)
Medico Industries Inc ....E 570 825-7711
  Hanover Township (G-6996)
▲ Nammo Pocal Inc ....E 570 961-1999
  Scranton (G-17263)
Nammo Pocal Inc ....F 570 842-2288
  Moscow (G-11599)
◆ Nonlethal Technologies Inc ....E 724 479-5100
  Homer City (G-7679)
Steel Valley Casting LLC ....G 724 777-4025
  New Brighton (G-12044)

3484 Small Arms

American Built Arms Company ....G 443 807-3022
  Glen Rock (G-6450)
Anthony Burney ....G 412 606-7336
  Monongahela (G-11304)
Combat Arms LLC ....G 412 245-0824
  Carlisle (G-2702)
E R Shaw Inc ....E 412 212-4343
  Bridgeville (G-2059)
Ford City Gun Workd ....G 724 994-9501
  Ford City (G-6045)
Garrett & Co Inc ....G 800 748-4608
  New Kensington (G-12341)
Geissele Automatics LLC ....F 610 272-2060
  North Wales (G-12803)
▲ Gog Paintball USA ....G 724 520-8690
  Loyalhanna (G-10111)
Gunsmiths Stainless Clg Rods ....G 215 256-9208
  Harleysville (G-7035)
Gwynedd Manufacturing Inc ....E 610 272-2060
  North Wales (G-12805)
Iwi Us Inc ....E 717 695-2081
  Middletown (G-11058)

▲ Keystone Sporting Arms Llc ....D 570 742-2066
  Milton (G-11246)
▲ Lancer Systems LP ....E 610 973-2600
  Quakertown (G-16208)
Lesleh Precision Inc ....E 724 823-0901
  Rostraver Township (G-16827)
Micro Facture LLC ....E 717 285-9700
  Mountville (G-11799)
◆ Nonlethal Technologies Inc ....E 724 479-5100
  Homer City (G-7679)
▲ North American Arms Inc ....G 610 940-1668
  Plymouth Meeting (G-15860)
Penn Arms Inc ....E 814 938-5279
  Jamestown (G-8238)
▼ Pneu-Dart Inc ....D 570 323-2710
  Williamsport (G-20061)
S & K Scope Mounts ....G 814 489-3091
  Sugar Grove (G-18146)
Saeilo Inc ....F 845 735-4500
  Greeley (G-6583)
▲ Tar Hunt Custom Rifles Inc ....G 570 784-6368
  Bloomsburg (G-1803)
Wyss-Gallifent Corporation ....G 215 343-3974
  Warrington (G-19141)

3489 Ordnance & Access, NEC

▼ Action Manufacturing Company .....B 267 540-4041
  Bristol (G-2103)
Action Manufacturing Company ....G 610 593-1800
  Atglen (G-799)
▼ Alloy Surfaces Company Inc ....C 610 497-7979
  Chester (G-3038)
Alloy Surfaces Company Inc ....E 610 558-7100
  Boothwyn (G-1875)
Avant-Garde Technology Inc ....E 215 345-8228
  Doylestown (G-4273)
E W Yost Co ....F 215 699-4868
  Blue Bell (G-1828)
Evolution Gun Works Inc ....E 215 538-1012
  Quakertown (G-16191)
▼ G G Greene Enterprises Inc ....E 814 723-5700
  Warren (G-19027)
General Dynamics Corporation ....F 570 340-1136
  Scranton (G-17237)
Jim Borden ....G 570 965-2505
  Springville (G-17930)
▲ Kongsberg Protech Systems ....D 814 269-5700
  Johnstown (G-8400)
Lockheed Martin Corporation ....B 570 876-2132
  Archbald (G-691)
◆ Medico Industries Inc ....E 570 825-7711
  Wilkes Barre (G-19942)
Medico Industries Inc ....G 570 208-3140
  Hanover Township (G-6995)
Medico Industries Inc ....E 570 825-7711
  Hanover Township (G-6996)
Naval Company Inc ....E 215 348-8982
  Doylestown (G-4318)
Orlotronics Corporation ....E 610 239-8200
  Bridgeport (G-2042)

3491 Industrial Valves

A/C Service and Repair Inc ....E 717 792-3492
  York (G-20361)
Actaire Inc ....G 412 851-1040
  Pittsburgh (G-14645)
▲ Advanced Valve Design Inc ....F 610 435-8820
  Whitehall (G-19860)
▲ Air-Con Inc ....F 814 838-6373
  Erie (G-5178)
Al Xander Co Inc ....E 814 665-8268
  Corry (G-3743)
◆ American Cap Company LLC ....D 724 981-4461
  Wheatland (G-19834)
American Cone Valve Inc ....F 717 792-3492
  York (G-20372)
Co-Ax Valves Inc ....F 215 757-3725
  Bristol (G-2127)
▲ Crispin Valve LLC ....G 570 752-4524
  Berwick (G-1321)
Curtiss-Wright Corporation ....A 724 275-5277
  New Kensington (G-12337)
Curtiss-Wright Corporation ....F 215 721-1100
  Hatfield (G-7328)
Curtiss-Wright Flow Control ....G 724 295-6200
  Freeport (G-6202)
▲ DFT Inc ....E 610 363-8903
  Exton (G-5664)
Ecco/Gregory Inc ....E 610 840-0390
  West Chester (G-19545)

Elite Midstream Services Inc ....E 412 220-3082
Cuddy (G-3943)

Eriks Na LLC ....E 412 787-2400
Pittsburgh (G-14985)

◆ Fetterolf Corporation ....D 610 584-1500
Skippack (G-17596)

Gas Breaker Inc ....E 610 407-7200
Malvern (G-10238)

▼ Global Trade Links LLC ....E 888 777-1577
Chester Springs (G-3079)

Graco High Pressure Eqp Inc ....G 800 289-7447
Erie (G-5305)

Industrial Controls & Eqp Inc ....E 724 746-3705
Lawrence (G-9537)

Innovative Pressure Tech LLC ....D 814 833-5200
Erie (G-5326)

ITT Engineered Valves LLC ....F 717 509-2200
Lancaster (G-9066)

▲ K- Flo Butterfly ....G 570 752-4524
Berwick (G-1330)

Keims Machine & Tool Co Inc ....G 570 758-2605
Herndon (G-7600)

Mawa Inc ....G 610 539-5007
Norristown (G-12679)

▲ Multiplex Manufacturing Co ....G 570 752-4524
Berwick (G-1337)

Nutech LLC ....F 215 361-0373
Hatfield (G-7375)

Ogontz Corporation ....F 215 657-4770
Willow Grove (G-20131)

▲ Olson Technologies Inc ....E 610 770-1100
Allentown (G-339)

◆ Penn Troy Manufacturing Inc ....E 570 297-2125
Troy (G-18525)

▲ Quadax Valves Inc ....F 713 429-5458
Bristol (G-2191)

▲ R Conrader Company ....G 814 898-2727
Erie (G-5447)

▲ Red Valve Company Inc ....D 412 279-0044
Carnegie (G-2785)

Red Valve Company Inc ....E 412 279-0044
Carnegie (G-2786)

▼ S P Kinney Engineers Inc ....E 412 276-4600
Carnegie (G-2789)

◆ Schutte Koerting Acquisition ....E 215 639-0900
Trevose (G-18502)

Sensus USA Inc ....C 800 375-8875
Du Bois (G-4419)

Sensus USA Inc ....C 724 430-3956
Pittsburgh (G-15524)

◆ Sherwood Valve LLC ....C 724 225-8000
Pittsburgh (G-15532)

Sigelock Systems LLC ....G 814 673-2791
Franklin (G-6160)

▲ Solenoid Solutions Inc ....E 814 838-3190
Erie (G-5484)

Sooner Pipe LLC ....G 570 368-4590
Montoursville (G-11450)

Spirax Sarco Inc ....G 610 807-3500
Center Valley (G-2831)

SPX Corporation ....F 814 476-5800
Mc Kean (G-10592)

Strahman Industries Inc ....C 484 893-5080
Bethlehem (G-1630)

Sunbury Controls Inc ....G 570 274-7847
Sunbury (G-18174)

▲ Superior Group Inc ....E 610 397-2040
Conshohocken (G-3610)

Taylor-Wharton Intl LLC ....D 717 763-5060
Mechanicsburg (G-10894)

▲ Therm-Omega-Tech Inc ....D 877 379-8258
Warminster (G-18980)

▲ Tru-Tech Industries Inc ....D 724 776-1020
Cranberry Township (G-3858)

Turning Solutions Inc ....F 814 723-1134
Warren (G-19053)

◆ Victaulic Company ....A 610 559-3300
Easton (G-4770)

Vmd Machine Co Inc ....G 215 723-7782
Telford (G-18324)

▲ Warren Controls Inc ....D 610 317-0800
Bethlehem (G-1653)

Watson McDaniel Company ....G 610 367-7191
Boyertown (G-1935)

◆ Watson McDaniel Company ....E 610 495-5131
Pottstown (G-16070)

World Wide Plastics Inc ....E 215 357-0893
Langhorne (G-9336)

Wyman-Gordon Pennsylvania LLC ......F 570 474-3059
Wilkes Barre (G-19978)

Zeyon Inc ....E 814 899-3311
Erie (G-5536)

3492 Fluid Power Valves & Hose Fittings

Admiral Valve LLC ....E 215 386-6508
Kennett Square (G-8501)

Al Xander Co Inc ....E 814 665-8268
Corry (G-3743)

Appalachian Tank Car Svcs Inc ....D 412 741-1500
Leetsdale (G-9682)

Applied Indus Tech — PA LLC ....G 724 696-3099
Mount Pleasant (G-11686)

▼ Autoclave Engineers ....G 814 860-5700
Erie (G-5197)

Crane Co ....D 610 631-7700
Norristown (G-12647)

Custom Hydraulics Inc ....F 724 729-3170
Burgettstown (G-2344)

▲ Cypher Company Inc ....F 412 661-4913
Monroeville (G-11331)

Delri Industrial Supplies Inc ....G 610 833-2070
Crum Lynne (G-3936)

Dispersion Tech Systems LLC ....G 610 832-2040
Conshohocken (G-3539)

Fessler Machine Company ....E 724 346-0878
Sharon (G-17433)

Flotran Exton Inc ....G 610 640-4141
Malvern (G-10236)

Fluid Intelligence LLC ....G 610 405-2698
Berwyn (G-1362)

Genuine Parts Company ....G 215 968-4266
Newtown (G-12504)

Ghx Industrial LLC ....G 410 687-7900
Greencastle (G-6615)

▲ Global Passive Safety Systems ....G 267 297-2340
Springfield (G-17916)

▲ Hydac Technology Corp ....C 205 520-1220
Bethlehem (G-1534)

I D Technologies Inc ....G 610 652-2418
Gilbertsville (G-6374)

Independent Hose Co ....G 570 544-9528
Pottsville (G-16081)

Innovative Pressure Tech LLC ....D 814 833-5200
Erie (G-5326)

J & K Industrial Sales ....G 724 458-7670
Grove City (G-6791)

▲ Kobold Instruments Inc ....E 412 490-4806
Pittsburgh (G-15180)

Maxpro Technologies Inc ....F 814 474-9191
Fairview (G-5833)

National Hydraulic Systems LLC ....G 724 628-4010
Connellsville (G-3505)

National Hydraulic Systems LLC ....D 724 547-9222
Mount Pleasant (G-11708)

Nick Charles Kravitch ....G 412 882-6262
Pittsburgh (G-15340)

Parker-Hannifin Corporation ....A 814 866-4100
Erie (G-5414)

▲ PBM Inc ....D 724 863-0550
Irwin (G-8189)

Penndel Hydraulic Sls & Svc Co ....G 215 757-2000
Langhorne (G-9317)

▲ Powertrack International LLC ....E 412 787-4444
Pittsburgh (G-15423)

Powertrack International LLC ....G 412 787-4444
Pittsburgh (G-15424)

Q-E Manufacturing Company ....E 570 966-1017
New Berlin (G-12023)

R/W Connection Inc ....G 717 767-3660
Emigsville (G-4998)

▲ R/W Connection Inc ....E 717 898-5257
Landisville (G-9266)

▲ Rle Systems LLC ....G 610 518-3751
West Chester (G-19631)

Seventy-Three Mfg Co Inc ....E 610 845-7823
Bechtelsville (G-1037)

Superior Energy Resources LLC ....G 814 265-1080
Brockway (G-2235)

▲ Superior Energy Resources LLC .....G 814 265-1080
Brockway (G-2236)

Universal Fluids Inc ....G 267 639-2238
Philadelphia (G-14426)

▲ York Industries Inc ....E 717 764-8855
York (G-20742)

3493 Steel Springs, Except Wire

◆ Ace Wire Spring & Form Co Inc ....E 412 331-3353
Mc Kees Rocks (G-10601)

Ametek Inc ....G 215 355-6900
Horsham (G-7785)

Cambria Springs Service Inc ....G 814 539-1629
Johnstown (G-8362)

Fulmer Company Inc ....G 724 325-7140
Export (G-5606)

▲ General Wire Spring Company ....C 412 771-6300
Mc Kees Rocks (G-10612)

Glenfield Supply Company Inc ....G 412 781-8188
Pittsburgh (G-15051)

Keystone Spring Service Inc ....E 412 621-4800
Pittsburgh (G-15176)

◆ Lesjofors Springs America Inc ....C 800 551-0298
Pittston (G-15762)

Standard Car Truck Company ....D 412 782-7300
Pittsburgh (G-15576)

▲ Standard Steel Specialty Co ....D 724 846-7600
Beaver Falls (G-1014)

▲ Triangle Sspension Systems Inc ....D 814 375-7211
Du Bois (G-4425)

Tricor Industries Inc ....F 610 265-1111
Norristown (G-12721)

Union Spring & Mfg Corp ....C 412 843-5900
Monroeville (G-11361)

Union Spring & Mfg Corp ....E 814 967-2545
Townville (G-18449)

3494 Valves & Pipe Fittings, NEC

▲ Acme Cryogenics Inc ....D 610 966-4488
Allentown (G-114)

Advanced Welding Tech Inc ....E 814 899-3584
Erie (G-5176)

Allegheny Valve & Coupling Inc ....E 814 723-8150
Warren (G-19008)

American Pipe and Supply LLC ....D 724 228-6360
Washington (G-19148)

Anthracite Industries Inc ....E 570 286-2176
Sunbury (G-18163)

Anvil International LLC ....C 717 684-4400
Columbia (G-3428)

Atsco Holdings Corp ....D 440 701-1021
Cranberry Township (G-3807)

▲ Betts Industries Inc ....C 814 723-1250
Warren (G-19013)

Bitrekpasub Inc ....D 717 762-9141
Waynesboro (G-19401)

◆ Bonney Forge Corporation ....B 814 542-2545
Mount Union (G-11739)

◆ Bradford Allegheny Corporation ......C 814 362-2590
Lewis Run (G-9871)

Bradford Allegheny Corporation ....D 814 362-2593
Lewis Run (G-9874)

▲ Campbell Fittings Inc ....E 610 367-6916
Boyertown (G-1903)

▼ Campbell Manufacturing Inc ....D 610 367-2107
Bechtelsville (G-1030)

Carpenter & Paterson Inc ....F 724 379-8461
Donora (G-4150)

Ctc Pressure Products LLC ....G 814 315-6427
Erie (G-5235)

Danzi Energy ....G 814 723-8640
Warren (G-19019)

Derbyshire Marine Products LLC ....G 267 222-8900
Harleysville (G-7030)

Dresser LLC ....C 814 362-9200
Bradford (G-1967)

Exigo Manufacturing Inc ....F 484 285-0200
Nazareth (G-11966)

Expansion Seal Technologies ....G 215 513-4300
Harleysville (G-7033)

▲ Ezeflow Usa Inc ....C 724 658-3711
New Castle (G-12090)

Fessler Machine Company ....E 724 346-0878
Sharon (G-17433)

Flexible Compensators Inc ....F 610 837-3812
Bath (G-959)

▼ Global Trade Links LLC ....E 888 777-1577
Chester Springs (G-3079)

▲ Hailiang America Corporation ....F 877 515-4522
Leesport (G-9665)

Hajoca Corporation ....G 610 432-0551
Allentown (G-240)

◆ Hall Industries Incorporated ....E 724 752-2000
Ellwood City (G-4934)

▲ Hy-Tech Machine Inc ....D 724 776-6800
Cranberry Township (G-3823)

Hy-Tech Machine Inc ....D 724 776-2400
Cranberry Township (G-3824)

Ideal Aerosmith Inc ....E 412 963-1495
Pittsburgh (G-15113)

Jet Tool Company Inc ....G 814 756-3169
Albion (G-45)

▲ Kerotest Industries Inc ....E 412 521-4200
Pittsburgh (G-15173)

▲ Kerotest Manufacturing Corp ....E 412 521-4200
Pittsburgh (G-15174)

Lasco Fittings Inc ....F 570 301-1170
Pittston (G-15760)

◆ Lee Industries Inc ....C 814 342-0460
Philipsburg (G-14519)

Merit Manufacturing Corp ....D 610 327-4000
Pottstown (G-16018)

▲ Multiplex Manufacturing Co ....E 570 752-4524
Berwick (G-1337)

Nick Charles Kravitch ....G 412 882-6262
Pittsburgh (G-15340)

Norwin Mfg Inc ....G 724 515-7092
Irwin (G-8184)

Ogontz Corporation ....F 215 657-4770
Willow Grove (G-20131)

Parker-Hannifin Corporation ....A 814 866-4100
Erie (G-5414)

Parker-Hannifin Corporation ....C 215 723-4000
Hatfield (G-7377)

▲ PBM Inc ....D 724 863-0550
Irwin (G-8189)

▲ Phoenix Forging Company Inc ....G 610 264-2861
Catasauqua (G-2816)

Pittsburgh Plug and Pdts Corp ....E 724 538-4022
Evans City (G-5561)

Pittsburgh Plug and Pdts Corp ....E 724 538-4022
Evans City (G-5562)

Plastinetics Inc ....G 570 384-4832
Hazle Township (G-7473)

Popit Inc ....G 215 945-5201
Levittown (G-9859)

Process Development & Ctrl LLC ....E 724 695-3440
Coraopolis (G-3719)

Process Technology of PA ....F 215 628-2222
Ambler (G-600)

Q-E Manufacturing Company ....E 570 966-1017
New Berlin (G-12023)

▼ S P Kinney Engineers Inc ....E 412 276-4600
Carnegie (G-2789)

Sfc Valve Corporation ....D 814 445-9671
Somerset (G-17704)

Spears Manufacturing Co ....G 570 384-4832
Hazle Township (G-7482)

Spirax Sarco Inc ....G 610 807-3500
Center Valley (G-2831)

SPX Flow Us LLC ....G 814 476-5842
Mc Kean (G-10593)

▲ SPX Flow Us LLC ....G 814 476-5800
Mc Kean (G-10594)

Staver Hydraulics Co Inc ....G 610 837-1818
Bath (G-970)

▲ Strahman Valves Inc ....D 877 787-2462
Bethlehem (G-1631)

Swagelok Company ....G 610 799-9001
Schnecksville (G-17144)

▲ Therm-Omega-Tech Inc ....D 877 379-8258
Warminster (G-18980)

Titan Metal & Machine Co Inc ....G 724 747-9528
Washington (G-19232)

Turning Solutions Inc ....F 814 723-1134
Warren (G-19053)

▼ Tyco Fire Products LP ....C 215 362-0700
Lansdale (G-9421)

Vag USA LLC ....G 978 544-2511
Cranberry Township (G-3862)

Valves Inc ....F 724 378-0600
Aliquippa (G-99)

Victaulic LLC ....G 610 559-3300
Easton (G-4769)

◆ Victaulic Company ....A 610 559-3300
Easton (G-4770)

Victaulic Holding Company LLC ....G 610 559-3300
Easton (G-4771)

◆ Watson McDaniel Company ....E 610 495-5131
Pottstown (G-16070)

World Wide Plastics Inc ....E 215 357-0893
Langhorne (G-9336)

▲ Wtk Holdings Inc ....E 724 695-3440
Coraopolis (G-3735)

3495 Wire Springs

A V Weber Co Inc ....G 215 699-3527
North Wales (G-12784)

◆ Ace Wire Spring & Form Co Inc ....E 412 331-3353
Mc Kees Rocks (G-10601)

Barnes Group Inc ....C 814 663-6082
Corry (G-3745)

Barnes Group Inc ....G 215 785-4466
Bristol (G-2116)

Chestnut Group Inc ....G 610 688-3300
Wayne (G-19313)

Diamond Wire Spring Company ....E 412 821-2703
Pittsburgh (G-14922)

▲ Evans John Sons Incorporated ....D 215 368-7700
Lansdale (G-9365)

▲ General Wire Spring Company ....C 412 771-6300
Mc Kees Rocks (G-10612)

◆ Lesjofors Springs America Inc ....G 800 551-0298
Pittston (G-15762)

Liberty Spring Company Inc ....F 484 652-1100
Collingdale (G-3406)

Liberty Spring Usa LLC ....F 484 652-1100
Darby (G-4022)

Mercer Spring & Wire LLC ....E 814 967-2545
Townville (G-18446)

Navarro Spring Company ....G 610 259-3177
Lansdowne (G-9439)

Nelmark Electric Inc ....G 724 290-0314
Renfrew (G-16641)

Northeast Spring Inc ....E 610 374-8508
Reading (G-16457)

Oak Hill Controls LLC ....G 610 967-3985
Emmaus (G-5035)

Oak Hill Controls LLC ....F 610 758-9500
Bethlehem (G-1585)

Penn Central Spring Corp ....E 717 564-6792
Middletown (G-11067)

Penn-Elkco Inc ....F 814 834-4304
Saint Marys (G-17003)

▲ Royersford Spring Co ....F 610 948-4440
Royersford (G-16863)

St Marys Spring Co ....G 814 834-2460
Saint Marys (G-17020)

Union Spring & Mfg Corp ....E 814 967-2545
Townville (G-18449)

Vodvarka Springs ....G 724 695-3268
Clinton (G-3268)

W C Wolff Company ....F 610 359-9600
Newtown Square (G-12598)

▲ Wilder Diamond Blades Inc ....Fc 570 222-9590
Kingsley (G-8710)

3496 Misc Fabricated Wire Prdts

A V Weber Co Inc ....G 215 699-3527
North Wales (G-12784)

◆ Ace Wire Spring & Form Co Inc ....E 412 331-3353
Mc Kees Rocks (G-10601)

Acme Stamping Wire Forming Co ....E 412 771-5720
Pittsburgh (G-14644)

Aeroparts Fabg & Machining Inc ....E 814 948-6015
Nicktown (G-12618)

▼ American Lifting Products Inc ....G 610 384-1300
Coatesville (G-3287)

Amsteel Inc ....F 724 758-5566
Ellwood City (G-4926)

Apple Belting Company ....G 717 293-8903
Lancaster (G-8936)

Apx-Seetech Systems Inc ....G 717 751-6445
York (G-20383)

Aristo-TEC Metal Forms Inc ....E 724 626-5900
Connellsville (G-3489)

◆ Bedford Reinforced Plas Inc ....E 814 623-8125
Bedford (G-1044)

▲ Blair Fixtures & Millwork Inc ....E 814 940-1913
Altoona (G-482)

Blue Ridge Mtn Cookery Inc ....E 717 762-1211
Waynesboro (G-19402)

Bridon-American Corporation ....C 570 822-3349
Exeter (G-5581)

C C B B Inc ....F 215 364-5377
Feasterville Trevose (G-5898)

Cambria County Asso ....B 814 536-3531
Johnstown (G-8360)

Cambria County Asso ....C 814 472-5077
Ebensburg (G-4782)

◆ Cobra Wire & Cable Inc ....E 215 674-8773
Huntingdon Valley (G-7970)

◆ Daniel Gerard Worldwide Inc ....D 800 232-3332
Hanover (G-6873)

Daniel Gerard Worldwide Inc ....F 717 630-3787
Hanover (G-6874)

Daniel Gerard Worldwide Inc ....C 717 637-3250
Hanover (G-6875)

Display Source Alliance LLC ....G 717 534-0884
Hershey (G-7608)

Eis Inc ....E 215 674-8773
Huntingdon Valley (G-7976)

Erisco Industries Inc ....D 814 459-2720
North East (G-12741)

ESAB Group Inc ....B 717 637-8911
Hanover (G-6884)

ESAB Group Inc ....C 843 673-7700
Hanover (G-6885)

Eysters Machine Shop Inc ....E 717 227-8400
Shrewsbury (G-17583)

Federal-Mogul Powertrain LLC ....D 610 363-2600
Exton (G-5677)

◆ Fenner Dunlop Americas LLC ....C 412 249-0700
Pittsburgh (G-15013)

Ferguson Perforating Company ....E 724 657-8703
New Castle (G-12092)

Frames & More ....G 724 933-5557
Wexford (G-19804)

Gehret Wire Works Inc ....G 215 236-3322
Philadelphia (G-13745)

Gemel Precision Tool Inc ....E 215 355-2174
Warminster (G-18886)

Gems Services Inc ....G 215 399-8932
Philadelphia (G-13748)

General Cable Corporation ....C 570 321-7750
Williamsport (G-20017)

Hanover Wire Cloth ....E 717 637-3795
Hanover (G-6902)

▲ Hendrick Manufacturing Company ...G 570 282-1010
Carbondale (G-2677)

Heritage Fence Company ....F 610 584-6710
Skippack (G-17599)

Hohmann & Barnard Inc ....E 610 873-0070
Chester Springs (G-3080)

◆ I & I Sling Inc ....E 800 874-3539
Aston (G-769)

International Conveyor Rbr LLC ....G 724 343-4225
Blairsville (G-1726)

Ivy Steel & Wire Inc ....G 570 450-2090
Hazle Township (G-7465)

▲ Iwm International LLC ....G 717 637-3795
Hanover (G-6905)

▲ J & R Wire Inc ....F 570 342-3193
Scranton (G-17245)

Jackburn Corporation ....G 814 774-3573
Girard (G-6392)

▲ Jackburn Mfg Inc ....F 814 774-3573
Girard (G-6393)

▼ Jerith Manufacturing LLC ....D 215 676-4068
Philadelphia (G-13893)

▲ Kane Innovations Inc ....D 814 838-7731
Erie (G-5342)

Keystone Automatic Tech Inc ....E 814 486-0513
Emporium (G-5066)

Leahmarlin Corp ....F 610 692-7378
West Chester (G-19589)

Leonard Leibensperger ....G 610 926-7491
Mohrsville (G-11277)

▲ Lumsden Corporation ....E 717 394-6871
Lancaster (G-9117)

M Dobron & Sons Inc ....G 215 297-5331
Point Pleasant (G-15887)

Manley Fence Co ....G 610 842-8833
Coatesville (G-3316)

▲ Markel Corp ....C 610 272-8960
Plymouth Meeting (G-15855)

Melrath Gasket Inc ....G 215 223-6000
Philadelphia (G-14007)

Metro International Corp ....E 570 825-2741
Wilkes Barre (G-19943)

▲ Miller Edge Inc ....D 610 869-4422
West Grove (G-19702)

Myerstown Sheds ....G 717 866-7644
Lebanon (G-9613)

N C Stauffer & Sons Inc ....D 570 945-3047
Factoryville (G-5758)

Nelson Wire Rope Corporation ....F 215 721-9449
Hatfield (G-7373)

Nick-Of-Time Textiles Ltd ....G 610 395-4641
Allentown (G-332)

North American Fencing Corp ....E 412 362-3900
Cheswick (G-3113)

North American Stl & Wire Inc ....E 724 431-0626
Butler (G-2426)

North American Wire LLC ....G 724 431-0626
Butler (G-2427)

Northeast Fence & Ir Works Inc ....E 215 335-1681
Philadelphia (G-14082)

Northeimer Manufacturing ....G 610 926-1136
Leesport (G-9672)

Peerless Chain Company ....F 800 395-2445
Mount Pleasant (G-11710)

S
I
C

▲ Pendu Manufacturing Inc ....E 717 354-4348
New Holland (G-12272)

Penn Wire Products Corporation ....G 717 664-4411
Manheim (G-10399)

▲ Penn Wire Products Corporation .....G 717 393-2352
Lancaster (G-9164)

Penn-Elkco Inc ....F 814 834-4304
Saint Marys (G-17003)

▲ Pennsylvania Sling Co ....G 717 657-7700
Harrisburg (G-7195)

Pittsburgh Fence Co Inc ....E 724 775-6550
Carnegie (G-2780)

Pointer Hill Pets Inc ....G 610 754-7830
Bechtelsville (G-1035)

Precision Wire Products Inc ....E 724 459-5601
Blairsville (G-1737)

Quality Fencing & Supply ....E 717 355-7112
New Holland (G-12276)

◆ Quality Perforating Inc ....D 570 267-2092
Carbondale (G-2685)

Rfcircuits Inc ....F 215 364-2450
Huntingdon Valley (G-8029)

▲ Safeguard Products Inc ....E 717 354-4586
New Holland (G-12280)

Safety Sling Company Inc ....F 412 231-6684
Pittsburgh (G-15506)

Selectrode Industries Inc ....E 724 378-6351
Aliquippa (G-93)

Sheffield Container Corp ....E 814 968-3287
Sheffield (G-17483)

▲ South Fork Hardware Company ....G 814 248-3375
Johnstown (G-8436)

▲ Stanton Dynamics Inc ....F 814 849-6255
Brookville (G-2272)

Tatano Wire and Steel Inc ....G 724 746-3118
Canonsburg (G-2645)

Tatano Wire and Steel Inc ....G 724 746-3118
Houston (G-7880)

TG Marcis Wire Designs LLC ....G 412 391-5532
Pittsburgh (G-15607)

Torpedo Specialty Wire Inc ....E 814 563-7505
Pittsfield (G-15739)

Tri-Boro Construction Sups Inc ....D 717 246-3095
Dallastown (G-3982)

▲ Tri-Com Inc ....E 610 259-7400
Clifton Heights (G-3259)

Tricor Industries Inc ....F 610 265-1111
Norristown (G-12721)

▲ Victor-Balata Belting Company ....E 610 258-2010
Easton (G-4772)

Vogan Mfg Inc ....G 717 354-9954
New Holland (G-12292)

◆ Voith Paper Fabric and Roll Sy ....C 717 792-7000
York (G-20700)

▲ Wire and Cable Specialties Inc ....D 610 466-6200
Coatesville (G-3330)

Wire and Cable Specialties Inc ....E 610 692-7551
West Chester (G-19679)

Wire Company Holdings Inc ....B 717 637-3795
Hanover (G-6977)

Wire Crafters ....D 610 296-2538
Malvern (G-10347)

◆ Wire Mesh Products Inc ....E 717 848-3620
York (G-20714)

Wire Mesh Sales LLC ....E 724 245-9577
New Salem (G-12446)

Wireco Worldgroup Inc ....F 412 373-6122
Trafford (G-18461)

◆ Wirerope Works Inc ....B 570 327-4229
Williamsport (G-20096)

◆ Woodstream Corporation ....E 717 626-2125
Lititz (G-10060)

Yeager Wire Works Inc ....G 570 752-2769
Berwick (G-1349)

3497 Metal Foil & Leaf

Custom Processing Services Inc ....E 610 779-7001
Reading (G-16359)

JW Aluminum Company ....C 570 323-4430
Williamsport (G-20030)

Kurz-Hastings Inc ....E 215 632-2300
Philadelphia (G-13946)

Original Little Pepis Inc ....F 215 822-9650
Hatfield (G-7376)

▲ Performance Coatings Corp ....F 610 525-1190
Levittown (G-9854)

South Pole Magnetics ....G 412 537-5625
Pittsburgh (G-15563)

3498 Fabricated Pipe & Pipe Fittings

A M Sheet Metal Inc ....F 570 322-5417
South Williamsport (G-17789)

▲ ABT LLC ....E 412 826-8002
Pittsburgh (G-14636)

Abtrex Industries Inc ....E 724 266-5425
Leetsdale (G-9676)

▲ Accu-Fire Fabrication Inc ....E 800 641-0005
Morrisville (G-11550)

▼ Accumetrics Limited ....E 610 948-0181
Royersford (G-16840)

Acme Cryogenics Inc ....E 610 966-4488
Alburtis (G-49)

▲ Acme Cryogenics Inc ....D 610 966-4488
Allentown (G-114)

Admiral Valve LLC ....E 215 386-6508
Kennett Square (G-8501)

Al Xander Co Inc ....E 814 665-8268
Corry (G-3743)

American Air Duct Inc ....E 724 483-8057
Charleroi (G-3006)

Anvil International LLC ....G 717 684-4400
Columbia (G-3427)

Anvil International LLC ....C 256 238-0579
Columbia (G-3429)

Anvil International LLC ....G 717 762-9141
Waynesboro (G-19396)

Appellation Cnstr Svcs LLC ....D 570 601-4765
Montoursville (G-11431)

Beck Manufacturing Company ....F 717 593-0197
Greencastle (G-6599)

▲ Beck Manufacturing Company ....E 717 762-9141
Waynesboro (G-19399)

Bentech Inc ....E 215 223-9420
Philadelphia (G-13454)

Bergen Pipe Supports Inc ....D 724 379-5212
Donora (G-4148)

Bitrekpasub Inc ....D 717 762-9141
Waynesboro (G-19401)

BJ REO Inc ....E 412 384-2161
West Elizabeth (G-19692)

Boiler Erection and Repair Co ....E 215 721-7900
Souderton (G-17727)

◆ Bonney Forge Corporation ....B 814 542-2545
Mount Union (G-11739)

Brandywine Valley Fabricators ....F 610 384-7440
Coatesville (G-3295)

Browns Welding Inc ....G 717 762-6467
Waynesboro (G-19403)

▼ Campbell Manufacturing Inc ....D 610 367-2107
Bechtelsville (G-1030)

Clipper Pipe & Service Inc ....G 610 872-9067
Eddystone (G-4799)

▼ Coil Company LLC ....E 610 408-8361
Malvern (G-10214)

Colonial Machine Company Inc ....E 814 589-7033
Pleasantville (G-15798)

Cooney Manufacturing Co LLC ....G 610 272-2100
Pottstown (G-15976)

Crees Wldg & Fabrication Inc ....G 717 795-8711
Mechanicsburg (G-10832)

▲ Cvip Inc ....D 610 967-1525
Emmaus (G-5025)

D & R Steel Construction Inc ....F 570 265-6216
Milan (G-11147)

D L George & Sons Mfg Inc ....D 717 765-4700
Waynesboro (G-19407)

Dedicated Customs Inc ....G 724 678-6609
Burgettstown (G-2345)

Dlubak Fabrication Inc ....F 724 224-5887
Natrona Heights (G-11938)

▲ Dormont Manufacturing Company ...C 724 327-7909
Export (G-5597)

Dresser LLC ....C 814 362-9200
Bradford (G-1967)

East Coast Constructors Inc ....F 610 532-3650
Holmes (G-7661)

◆ Eastern Manufacturing LLC ....D 215 702-3600
Langhorne (G-9293)

Flexsteel Pipeline Tech Inc ....G 570 505-3491
Montoursville (G-11439)

General Fabricating Svcs LLC ....F 412 262-1131
Coraopolis (G-3692)

Greenbank Group Inc ....G 724 229-1180
Washington (G-19180)

Hastings Machine Company Inc ....E 814 247-6562
Hastings (G-7261)

High Pressure Equipment Co Inc ....D 800 289-7447
Erie (G-5318)

▲ Hofmann Industries Inc ....B 610 678-8051
Reading (G-16403)

Industrial Eqp Fabricators Inc ....F 724 752-8819
Ellwood City (G-4938)

Ipsco Tubulars Inc ....G 724 251-2539
Ambridge (G-621)

J Rybnick Mech Contr Inc ....E 570 222-2544
Nicholson (G-12616)

JI Hartman Stainless LLC ....G 724 646-1150
Greenville (G-6751)

▲ Judson A Smith Company ....C 610 367-2021
Boyertown (G-1920)

Kennedy Tubular Products Inc ....F 724 658-5508
New Castle (G-12113)

L S Martin LLC ....G 717 859-3073
Ephrata (G-5118)

Leonhardt Manufacturing Co Inc ....D 717 632-4150
Hanover (G-6915)

▼ Maclean Saegertown LLC ....G 814 763-2655
Saegertown (G-16924)

Madison Inds Holdings LLC ....C 717 762-3151
Waynesboro (G-19416)

▲ Markovitz Enterprises Inc ....D 724 452-4500
Zelienople (G-20810)

McCarls Inc ....F 724 581-5409
Muncy (G-11826)

MCS Inc ....E 412 429-8991
Carnegie (G-2777)

Michels Corporation ....G 724 249-2065
Washington (G-19202)

◆ Morris Coupling Company ....D 814 459-1741
Erie (G-5396)

Mueller Industries Inc ....D 215 699-5801
North Wales (G-12820)

P & R United Welding and Fabg ....F 610 375-9928
Reading (G-16461)

◆ Pennsylvania Machine Works Inc .....C 610 497-3300
Upper Chichester (G-18669)

Philadelphia Pipe Bending Co ....E 215 225-8955
Philadelphia (G-14149)

▼ Pittsbrgh Tubular Shafting Inc ....E 724 774-7212
Rochester (G-16787)

Pittsbrgh Tubular Shafting Inc ....G 724 774-7212
Rochester (G-16788)

Pro Tube Inc ....F 717 765-9400
Zullinger (G-20838)

Propipe ....G 610 518-6320
Downingtown (G-4252)

▲ Quaker State Tube Mfg Corp ....E 610 287-8841
Zieglerville (G-20834)

RG Industries Inc ....E 717 849-0345
York (G-20658)

Saegertown Manufacturing Corp ....C 814 763-2655
Saegertown (G-16932)

Scott Metals Inc ....E 412 279-7021
Carnegie (G-2790)

Sentry Fire Protection Inc ....F 717 843-4973
York (G-20666)

Trojan Tube Sls & Fabrications ....F 570 546-8860
Muncy (G-11836)

▼ TW Metals LLC ....D 610 458-1300
Exton (G-5741)

▲ Ward Manufacturing LLC ....C 570 638-2131
Blossburg (G-1810)

◆ Watson McDaniel Company ....E 610 495-5131
Pottstown (G-16070)

Wm T Spaeder Co Inc ....D 814 456-7014
Erie (G-5532)

3499 Fabricated Metal Prdts, NEC

Adams County Laser LLC ....G 717 359-4030
Littlestown (G-10062)

All - American Trophy Company ....G 570 342-2613
Scranton (G-17207)

▲ Ames Reese Inc ....E 717 393-1591
Bird In Hand (G-1668)

Ametek Inc ....G 215 355-6900
Horsham (G-7785)

Ashcombe Products Company Inc ....G 717 848-1271
York (G-20387)

B & N Trophies & Awards LLC ....G 814 723-8130
Warren (G-19012)

B Wise Trailers ....F 717 261-0922
Chambersburg (G-2908)

◆ Ballymore Holdings Inc ....E 610 593-5062
Coatesville (G-3293)

Banc Technic Inc ....F 610 756-4440
Kutztown (G-8836)

▲ Bassett Industries Inc ....E 610 327-1200
Pottstown (G-15965)

Becky Kens Duck & Geese Creat ....G....... 717 684-0252
  Columbia *(G-3431)*

Bolsan Company Inc ....F....... 724 225-0446
  Eighty Four *(G-4834)*

Bond Caster and Wheel Corp ....F....... 717 665-2275
  Manheim *(G-10372)*

C L Ward Family ....F....... 724 743-5903
  Canonsburg *(G-2554)*

◆ Cardolite Corporation ....E....... 609 436-0902
  Bristol *(G-2123)*

CDM Holdings Inc ....E....... 215 724-8640
  Philadelphia *(G-13517)*

Celf Services LLC ....G....... 717 643-0039
  Greencastle *(G-6602)*

Chelate Incorporated ....G....... 717 203-0415
  Lititz *(G-9997)*

Coinco Inc ....E....... 814 425-7476
  Cochranton *(G-3338)*

▲ Compression Components Svc LLCF 267 387-2000
  Warrington *(G-19111)*

Comtec Mfg Inc ....D....... 814 834-9300
  Saint Marys *(G-16956)*

Crouse Run Ventures Inc ....G....... 412 491-5738
  Sewickley *(G-17385)*

◆ Crown Holdings Inc ....C....... 215 698-5100
  Yardley *(G-20304)*

Crumbs ....F....... 717 609-1120
  Mount Holly Springs *(G-11633)*

Custom Built Products Inc ....F....... 215 946-9555
  Bristol *(G-2130)*

Custom Corner Sportswear ....G....... 724 588-1667
  Greenville *(G-6740)*

D & M Welding Co Inc ....E....... 717 767-9353
  York *(G-20440)*

Daniel C Tanney Inc ....D....... 215 639-3131
  Bensalem *(G-1179)*

▲ David B Lytle Products Inc ....G....... 724 352-3322
  Cabot *(G-2454)*

▲ Edward Hecht Importers Inc ....G....... 215 925-5520
  Philadelphia *(G-13661)*

Edwards Co ....G....... 215 343-2133
  Warrington *(G-19116)*

▲ Electron Energy Corporation ....E....... 717 898-2294
  Landisville *(G-9259)*

Emporium Specialties Company ....E....... 814 647-8661
  Austin *(G-833)*

F R Industries Inc ....F....... 412 242-5903
  Pittsburgh *(G-14999)*

Fabco Inc ....G....... 814 944-1631
  Altoona *(G-504)*

Fisher & Ludlow Inc ....F....... 859 282-7767
  Wexford *(G-19801)*

◆ Fox Run Holdings Inc ....G....... 215 675-7700
  Warminster *(G-18882)*

Gaven Industries Inc ....E....... 724 352-8100
  Saxonburg *(G-17087)*

Germantown Tool Machine Sp Inc ....E....... 215 322-4970
  Huntingdon Valley *(G-7989)*

GP Metal Fabrication ....G....... 570 494-1002
  Williamsport *(G-20019)*

Great Lakes Case & Cab Co Inc ....G....... 814 663-6015
  Corry *(G-3763)*

◆ Great Lakes Case & Cab Co Inc ....G....... 814 734-7303
  Edinboro *(G-4812)*

Hart McHncl-Lctrcal Contrs Inc ....E....... 215 257-1666
  Perkasie *(G-13278)*

Hi-TEC Magnetics Inc ....G....... 484 681-4265
  King of Prussia *(G-8631)*

Horizon Technology Inc ....E....... 814 834-4004
  Saint Marys *(G-16980)*

Hutton Metalcrafts Inc ....G....... 570 646-7778
  Pocono Pines *(G-15881)*

▲ Ideal Products America LP ....F....... 484 320-6194
  Malvern *(G-10250)*

▲ Igs Industries Inc ....C....... 724 222-5800
  Meadow Lands *(G-10690)*

Innovative Sintered Metals Inc ....E....... 814 781-1033
  Saint Marys *(G-16981)*

▲ Irvins Corp ....D....... 570 539-8200
  Mount Pleasant Mills *(G-11726)*

James Derr ....G....... 724 475-2094
  Greenville *(G-6750)*

▲ K & J Magnetics Inc ....E....... 215 766-8055
  Pipersville *(G-14617)*

▲ Keystone Powdered Metal Co ....B....... 814 781-1591
  Saint Marys *(G-16984)*

Linett Co Inc ....C....... 412 826-8531
  Pittsburgh *(G-15233)*

Louisville Ladder Inc ....G....... 215 638-8904
  Bensalem *(G-1222)*

Lpw Technology Inc ....F....... 844 480-7663
  Imperial *(G-8070)*

M D Cline Metal Fabg Inc ....G....... 724 459-8968
  Blairsville *(G-1733)*

▲ Moore Push Pin Company ....D....... 215 233-5700
  Glenside *(G-6531)*

Musumeci Santo ....G....... 215 467-2158
  Philadelphia *(G-14045)*

◆ New View Gifts & ACC Ltd ....E....... 610 627-0190
  Media *(G-10940)*

New Werner Holding Co Inc ....G....... 724 588-2000
  Greenville *(G-6758)*

▼ Old Ladder Co ....A....... 888 523-3371
  Greenville *(G-6762)*

Phoenix Corporation ....E....... 215 295-9510
  Morrisville *(G-11578)*

▲ Primitives By Kathy Inc ....D....... 717 394-4220
  Lancaster *(G-9175)*

Pro Barrier Engineering LLC ....G....... 717 944-6056
  Hummelstown *(G-7922)*

Proform Powdered Metals Inc ....E....... 814 938-7411
  Punxsutawney *(G-16154)*

Reiff Metal Fabrications ....G....... 717 445-7050
  East Earl *(G-4554)*

Roadsafe Traffic Systems Inc ....D....... 412 559-1396
  Gibsonia *(G-6350)*

Sandlex Corporation ....G....... 570 820-8568
  Wilkes Barre *(G-19961)*

Significant Developments LLC ....G....... 724 348-5277
  Moon Township *(G-11500)*

Smiths Wilbert Vault Company ....F....... 610 588-5259
  Bangor *(G-929)*

Sosko Manufacturing Inc ....G....... 724 879-4117
  Latrobe *(G-9521)*

▲ Specialty Bar Products Company ....C....... 724 459-0544
  Blairsville *(G-1742)*

◆ SPS Technologies LLC ....A....... 215 572-3000
  Jenkintown *(G-8302)*

Stellar Machine Incorporated ....F....... 570 718-1733
  Nanticoke *(G-11903)*

Stineman Management Corp ....E....... 814 495-4686
  South Fork *(G-17778)*

Talaris Inc ....G....... 215 674-2882
  Horsham *(G-7855)*

Tamis Corporation ....F....... 412 241-7161
  Pittsburgh *(G-15595)*

◆ TJ Cope Inc ....D....... 215 961-2570
  Philadelphia *(G-14392)*

Todd Weikel ....G....... 610 779-5508
  Reading *(G-16542)*

Trinity Highway Rentals Inc ....G....... 570 380-2856
  Bloomsburg *(G-1804)*

▲ Trinity Mining Services Inc ....G....... 412 605-0612
  Pittsburgh *(G-15649)*

Tritech Applied Sciences Inc ....G....... 215 362-6890
  Lansdale *(G-9417)*

Veyko Design Inc ....G....... 215 928-1349
  Philadelphia *(G-14444)*

Vicjah Corporation ....G....... 610 826-7475
  Palmerton *(G-13114)*

▲ Wendell August Forge Inc ....D....... 724 748-9500
  Mercer *(G-10979)*

◆ Werner Co ....C....... 724 588-2000
  Greenville *(G-6775)*

Werner Holding Co Inc ....A....... 888 523-3371
  Greenville *(G-6776)*

Win-Holt Equipment Corp ....C....... 516 222-0335
  Allentown *(G-436)*

Yarde Metals Inc ....G....... 610 495-7545
  Limerick *(G-9972)*

Zachary R Marella ....G....... 724 557-1671
  Smithfield *(G-17656)*

35 INDUSTRIAL AND COMMERCIAL MACHINERY AND COMPUTER EQUIPMENT

3511 Steam, Gas & Hydraulic Turbines & Engines

ABB Inc ....F....... 412 963-7530
  Pittsburgh *(G-14633)*

Adaconn ....E....... 215 643-1900
  Blue Bell *(G-1812)*

Agripower Mfg & Svcs Inc ....G....... 814 781-1009
  Saint Marys *(G-16946)*

▲ Alessi Manufacturing Corp ....E....... 610 586-4200
  Collingdale *(G-3403)*

▲ American Hydro Corporation ....C....... 717 755-5300
  York *(G-20374)*

Apache Turbines ....G....... 814 880-0053
  Bellefonte *(G-1092)*

Babcock & Wilcox Company ....G....... 724 479-3585
  Homer City *(G-7670)*

▲ Curtiss-Wright Electro- ....A....... 724 275-5000
  Cheswick *(G-3105)*

Dynamic Manufacturing LLC ....D....... 724 295-4200
  Freeport *(G-6203)*

▲ E C T Inc ....G....... 610 239-5120
  Bridgeport *(G-2035)*

E-Finity Dstrbted Gnration LLC ....G....... 610 688-6212
  Wayne *(G-19321)*

E-Harvest Systems ....G....... 908 832-0400
  Mechanicsburg *(G-10840)*

Eaton Aerospace LLC ....D....... 610 522-4000
  Glenolden *(G-6473)*

◆ Elliott Company ....A....... 724 527-2811
  Jeannette *(G-8254)*

▲ Erie Forge and Steel Inc ....D....... 814 452-2300
  Erie *(G-5267)*

Everpower Wind Holdings Inc ....E....... 412 253-9400
  Pittsburgh *(G-14989)*

Eznergy LLC ....G....... 215 361-7332
  Lansdale *(G-9366)*

Genx Sustainable Solutions Inc ....G....... 484 244-7016
  Allentown *(G-228)*

▼ Hydrocoil Power Inc ....G....... 610 745-1990
  Bryn Mawr *(G-2325)*

ITT Water & Wastewater USA Inc......E....... 610 647-6620
  Malvern *(G-10256)*

◆ Matric Group LLC ....B....... 814 677-0716
  Seneca *(G-17366)*

Nickles Industries ....G....... 724 422-7211
  Marion Center *(G-10475)*

Penn Wind Energy LLC ....G....... 814 288-8064
  Ebensburg *(G-4792)*

Precision Castparts Corp ....B....... 570 474-6371
  Mountain Top *(G-11771)*

Solar Turbines Incorporated ....D....... 724 759-7800
  Sewickley *(G-17411)*

Trireme Energy Development LLC .....D....... 412 253-9400
  Pittsburgh *(G-15652)*

▲ Voith Hydro Inc ....B....... 717 792-7000
  York *(G-20699)*

▲ Windkits LLC ....E....... 610 530-5704
  Allentown *(G-437)*

Windstax Inc ....G....... 412 235-7907
  Pittsburgh *(G-15719)*

▲ Windurance LLC ....B....... 412 424-8900
  Coraopolis *(G-3733)*

▲ Worldwide Turbine LLC ....G....... 610 821-9500
  Allentown *(G-438)*

3519 Internal Combustion Engines, NEC

◆ Ash/Tec Inc ....E....... 570 682-0933
  Hegins *(G-7539)*

◆ Aztec Products Inc ....F....... 215 393-4700
  Montgomeryville *(G-11387)*

Boyesen Inc ....E....... 610 756-6818
  Lenhartsville *(G-9756)*

Cummins - Allison Corp ....F....... 610 355-1400
  Broomall *(G-2284)*

Cummins - Allison Corp ....G....... 215 245-8436
  Bensalem *(G-1176)*

Cummins Inc ....G....... 724 798-4511
  Belle Vernon *(G-1085)*

Cummins Inc ....G....... 412 820-0330
  Pittsburgh *(G-14893)*

Cummins Inc ....D....... 717 564-1344
  Harrisburg *(G-7110)*

Cummins Inc ....G....... 570 333-0360
  Tunkhannock *(G-18535)*

Cummins Inc ....G....... 215 785-6005
  Bristol *(G-2129)*

Cummins-Wagner Company Inc ....E....... 717 367-8294
  Elizabethtown *(G-4870)*

Ecobee Advanced Tech LLC ....G....... 609 474-0010
  Warminster *(G-18869)*

Efi Connection LLC ....G....... 814 566-0946
  Erie *(G-5257)*

Enpro Industries Inc ....G....... 215 946-0845
  Bristol *(G-2141)*

Fyda Frghtliner Pittsburgh Inc ....D....... 724 514-2055
  Canonsburg *(G-2590)*

G2 Diesel Products Inc ....F....... 717 525-8709
  Harrisburg *(G-7132)*

General Electric Company ....B....... 724 450-1887
  Grove City *(G-6787)*

Employee Codes: A=Over 500 employees, B=251-500
C=101-250, D=51-100, E=20-50, F=10-19, G=3-9   2019 Harris Pennsylvania
Manufacturers Directory   927

S I C

Hassinger Diesel Service LLC .... G 570 837-3412
Middleburg (G-11025)

HIG Capital LLC .... C 610 495-7011
Royersford (G-16851)

Industrial Diesel Power Inc .... F 215 781-2378
Croydon (G-3919)

James E Krack .... G 724 864-4150
Irwin (G-8176)

L & M Engines Inc .... G 215 675-8485
Hatboro (G-7291)

Mack Trucks Inc .... C 717 939-1338
Middletown (G-11064)

Navistar Inc .... B 610 375-4230
Reading (G-16452)

Optimus Technologies Inc .... F 412 727-8228
Pittsburgh (G-15362)

Penn Power Group LLC .... E 570 208-1192
Hanover Township (G-7003)

Precision Castparts Corp .... B 570 474-6371
Mountain Top (G-11771)

Ransome Idealease LLC .... G 215 639-4300
Bensalem (G-1248)

Ritter Precision Machining .... G 610 377-2011
Lehighton (G-9725)

Rutts Machine Inc .... F 717 367-3011
Elizabethtown (G-4885)

▲ Sardello Inc .... G 724 827-8835
Darlington (G-4031)

W W Engine and Supply Inc .... E 814 345-5693
Kylertown (G-8868)

3523 Farm Machinery & Eqpt

5 Star Plus Inc .... G 610 470-9187
Oxford (G-13070)

Aaron Wenger .... G 717 656-9876
New Holland (G-12225)

Allegheny-Wagner Inds Inc .... E 724 468-4300
Delmont (G-4047)

American Baling Products Inc .... G 724 758-5566
Ellwood City (G-4925)

Andritz Inc .... B 570 546-1253
Muncy (G-11806)

Angell Industries Inc .... G 412 269-2956
Coraopolis (G-3658)

ATI Corporation .... E 717 354-8721
New Holland (G-12229)

▲ AZS Brusher Equipment LLC .... G 717 733-2584
Ephrata (G-5092)

Barebo Inc .... E 610 965-6018
Emmaus (G-5020)

Bhs Energy LLC .... G 570 696-3754
Wyoming (G-20274)

Bishop Equipment Manufacturing .... G 215 368-5307
Hatfield (G-7321)

C E Sauder & Sons LLC .... G 717 445-4822
East Earl (G-4539)

Case Modern Work .... G 717 785-1232
Fairfield (G-5765)

▲ CK Manufacturing LLC .... E 717 442-8912
Lancaster (G-8978)

Closet Cases .... G 570 262-9092
Jim Thorpe (G-8338)

▼ Cnh Inc .... G 717 355-1121
New Holland (G-12233)

Cnh Industrial America LLC .... B 262 636-6011
Lancaster (G-8981)

Cnh Industrial America LLC .... E 800 501-5711
New Holland (G-12234)

Cnh Industrial America LLC .... C 717 355-1121
New Holland (G-12235)

Cnh Industrial America LLC .... C 717 355-1902
New Holland (G-12236)

Cold Case Beverage LLC .... G 570 388-2297
Harding (G-7010)

Conestoga Mfg LLC .... G 717 529-0199
Kirkwood (G-8745)

Custom Linings Spray On Bed .... G 570 779-4609
Plymouth (G-15816)

Demuth Steel Products Inc .... F 717 653-2239
Mount Joy (G-11652)

◆ Earth & Turf Products LLC .... G 717 355-2276
New Holland (G-12247)

Els Manufacturing LLC .... F 717 442-8569
Kinzers (G-8737)

Ez-Flo Injection Systems Inc .... G 412 996-2161
Moon Township (G-11487)

◆ Farm-Bilt Machine LLC .... F 717 442-5020
Gap (G-6251)

Farmco Manufacturing LP .... G 717 768-7769
Ronks (G-16806)

▲ Farmer Boy Ag Inc .... D 717 866-7565
Myerstown (G-11885)

Feedmobile Inc .... F 717 626-8318
Lititz (G-10007)

▲ Groffdale Machine Co Inc .... G 717 656-3249
Leola (G-9785)

▲ Gvm Inc .... D 717 677-6197
Biglerville (G-1662)

Harvestmore Inc .... F 814 725-5258
North East (G-12747)

Horning Manufacturing LLC .... F 717 354-5040
East Earl (G-4545)

▲ I & J Manufacturing LLC .... G 717 442-9451
Gordonville (G-6558)

I H Rissler Mfg LLC .... G 717 484-0551
Mohnton (G-11265)

John H Bricker Welding .... F 717 263-5588
Chambersburg (G-2946)

Kennedys Powder Coating .... F 717 866-6747
Myerstown (G-11889)

Keystone Dehorner .... G 610 857-9728
Pomeroy (G-15890)

Kneppco Equipment LLC .... G 814 483-0108
Berlin (G-1289)

◆ Lancaster Parts & Eqp Inc .... F 717 299-3721
Lancaster (G-9103)

◆ Mc Dowell Implement Company .... G 814 786-7955
Grove City (G-6797)

◆ McLanahan Corporation .... B 814 695-9807
Hollidaysburg (G-7651)

MDC Romani Inc .... F 724 349-5533
Indiana (G-8113)

Middlecreek Welding & Mfg .... G 315 853-3936
Newmanstown (G-12481)

Mill Run Carriage .... G 717 438-3149
Millerstown (G-11206)

Morris Twnship Spervisors Barn .... G 724 627-3096
Sycamore (G-18201)

New Holland North America .... B 717 354-4514
New Holland (G-12266)

◆ New Holland North America .... A 717 355-1121
New Holland (G-12267)

New Holland North America .... B 717 355-1121
New Holland (G-12268)

▼ Pannell Mfg Corp .... G 610 268-2012
Avondale (G-856)

Pbz LLC .... E 800 578-1121
Lititz (G-10029)

Pequea Planter LLC .... F 717 442-4406
Gap (G-6255)

Quality Fencing & Supply .... E 717 355-7112
New Holland (G-12276)

Raytec LLC .... E 717 445-0510
Ephrata (G-5138)

Richard Shilling Jr .... G 814 319-4326
Seminole (G-17363)

Scenic Road Manufacturing .... G 717 768-7300
Gordonville (G-6565)

Smouse Trucks & Vans Inc .... G 724 887-7777
Mount Pleasant (G-11718)

Stengels Welding Shop Inc .... G 610 444-4110
Kennett Square (G-8544)

▼ Stoltz Mfg LLC .... E 610 286-5146
Morgantown (G-11537)

Stoltzfus Manufacturing Inc .... G 610 273-3603
Honey Brook (G-7764)

▲ Sturdy Built Manufacturing LLC .... E 717 484-2233
Denver (G-4095)

▼ Superior Tech Inc .... G 717 569-3359
Ephrata (G-5150)

Synatek LP .... D 888 408-5433
Souderton (G-17767)

Taty Bug Inc .... G 814 856-3323
Mayport (G-10547)

Tj Manufacturing LLC .... G 717 575-0675
Narvon (G-11930)

Tree Equipment Design Inc .... G 570 386-3515
New Ringgold (G-12444)

Tuscarora Electric Mfg Co .... G 570 836-2101
Tunkhannock (G-18551)

Val Products Inc .... F 717 354-4586
New Holland (G-12291)

◆ Val Products Inc .... D 717 392-3978
Bird In Hand (G-1683)

▲ Weaverline LLC .... F 717 445-6724
Narvon (G-11932)

Weeds Inc .... E 610 358-9430
Aston (G-797)

White Horse Machine LLC .... F 717 768-8313
Gap (G-6257)

Wolfe Metal Fab Inc .... G 724 339-7790
Lower Burrell (G-10108)

3524 Garden, Lawn Tractors & Eqpt

A Cut Above Lawn Care & Landsp .... G 484 239-6825
Northampton (G-12841)

Ames Companies Inc .... C 717 258-3001
Carlisle (G-2689)

◆ Ames Companies Inc .... B 717 737-1500
Camp Hill (G-2488)

Antonio Centeno Lawnkeeping .... G 267 580-0443
Levittown (G-9816)

Betts Equipment Inc .... G 215 598-7501
New Hope (G-12298)

Brickhouse Services .... G 570 869-1871
Laceyville (G-8870)

Buchanan Hauling .... G 412 373-6760
Trafford (G-18452)

Bullgater Limited .... G 717 606-5414
Bird In Hand (G-1670)

Calgon Carbon Corporation .... F 412 269-4000
Pittsburgh (G-14804)

Custom Turf Inc .... G 412 384-4111
Finleyville (G-5954)

Edward T Regina .... G 570 223-8358
East Stroudsburg (G-4614)

Ephraim L King .... G 570 837-9470
Winfield (G-20200)

▲ Good Ideas Inc .... E 814 774-8231
Lake City (G-8900)

Hirt Powersports LLC .... G 717 834-9126
Duncannon (G-4446)

Iceblox Inc .... G 717 697-1900
Mechanicsburg (G-10856)

Lane Cherry Manufacturing .... G 717 687-9059
Ronks (G-16810)

▼ Mackissic Inc .... E 610 495-7181
Parker Ford (G-13169)

◆ Pride Group Inc .... E 484 540-8059
Ridley Park (G-16740)

▲ Pride Group Inc .... G 484 540-8059
Ridley Park (G-16741)

Robert J Brown .... E 814 486-1768
Emporium (G-5074)

Saylor Industries Inc .... G 814 479-4964
Johnstown (G-8432)

Schiller Grounds Care Inc .... G 215 355-9700
Southampton (G-17836)

Schiller Grounds Care Inc .... D 215 322-4970
Huntingdon Valley (G-8035)

Stines Equipment & Maintenance .... G 717 432-4374
Dillsburg (G-4140)

Sunnys Sweeping Service Inc .... G 570 785-5564
Prompton (G-16110)

▲ Terrain Merchandising LLC .... F 310 709-8784
Philadelphia (G-14382)

Thomas Nay LLC .... F 215 613-8367
Philadelphia (G-14388)

◆ Walnut Industries Inc .... E 215 638-7847
Bensalem (G-1268)

3531 Construction Machinery & Eqpt

A Crane Rental LLC .... E 412 469-1776
Dravosburg (G-4350)

Abbottstown Stamping Co Inc .... F 717 632-0588
Hanover (G-6859)

Aces Inc .... G 215 458-7143
Morrisville (G-11551)

Acumix Inc .... G 717 540-9738
Harrisburg (G-7082)

Admixtures Inc .... F 610 775-0371
Wernersville (G-19483)

Advanced Cnstr Robotics Inc .... G 412 756-3360
Allison Park (G-445)

Altec Industries Inc .... C 570 822-3104
Wilkes Barre (G-19904)

Altrax .... G 814 379-3706
Summerville (G-18156)

Artman Equipment Company Inc .... F 724 337-3700
Apollo (G-662)

Atlantic Track & Turnout Co .... G 610 916-2840
Leesport (G-9658)

August Transport Inc .... E 724 462-1445
Leetsdale (G-9683)

Beaver Concrete & Supply Inc .... F 724 774-5100
Monaca (G-11282)

Blazing Technologies Inc .... G 484 722-4800
Mohnton (G-11260)

◆ Bon Tool Company .... D 724 443-7080
Gibsonia (G-6328)

Bramley Machinery Corporation F 610 326-2500
Pottstown *(G-15968)*

Brookville Locomotive Inc C 814 849-2000
Brookville *(G-2254)*

Buffalo Limestone Inc G 724 545-7478
Ford City *(G-6044)*

C&C Backhoe Service LLC G 724 438-5283
Uniontown *(G-18619)*

Caterpillar Inc B 724 743-0566
Houston *(G-7870)*

Caterpillar Inc B 717 751-5123
York *(G-20421)*

Caterpillar URS Storeroom F 610 293-5576
Radnor *(G-16290)*

Caulfield Associates Inc E 215 480-1940
Doylestown *(G-4290)*

Cellular Concrete LLC F 610 398-7833
Allentown *(G-166)*

City of Washington G 724 225-4883
Washington *(G-19156)*

Cnh Industrial America LLC C 717 355-1902
New Holland *(G-12236)*

Concept Engineering Group G 412 826-8800
Verona *(G-18753)*

Conrad Enterprises Inc E 717 274-5151
Cornwall *(G-3738)*

Craneco LLC G 610 948-1400
Royersford *(G-16847)*

Cwi Inc E 610 652-2211
Barto *(G-941)*

Dant Enterprises G 570 379-3121
Nescopeck *(G-12000)*

Darkar Railway Equipment Inc G 610 296-5712
Malvern *(G-10220)*

Dayton Superior Corporation D 570 695-3163
Tremont *(G-18480)*

Dieci United States LLC G 724 215-7081
Wyalusing *(G-20249)*

Disston Precision Inc G 215 338-1200
Philadelphia *(G-13635)*

Doyle Equipment Company G 724 837-4500
Delmont *(G-4050)*

▼ **Erie Strayer Company** C 814 456-7001
Erie *(G-5275)*

Force Inc E 724 465-9399
Indiana *(G-8100)*

▼ **Frog Switch and Mfg Co** C 717 243-2454
Carlisle *(G-2715)*

▲ **Future-All Inc** E 412 279-2670
Carnegie *(G-2768)*

G W Becker Inc D 724 983-1000
Hermitage *(G-7586)*

Gantrex Crane Rail I Installat G 412 655-1400
Canonsburg *(G-2592)*

General Electric Company G 814 875-2234
Erie *(G-5301)*

◆ **General Machine Pdts Kt LLC** D 215 357-5500
Trevose *(G-18496)*

Glenn O Hawbaker Inc F 814 642-7869
Turtlepoint *(G-18571)*

Global Polishing Solutions LLC F 619 295-0893
Folcroft *(G-6003)*

Greenwood Township G 570 458-0212
Millville *(G-11225)*

Groff Tractor & Equipment LLC F 814 353-8400
Bellefonte *(G-1100)*

Grove Investors Inc A 717 597-8121
Greencastle *(G-6616)*

◆ **Grove US LLc** D 717 597-8121
Shady Grove *(G-17420)*

Helping Hnds For Wnded Vterans G 724 600-4965
White Oak *(G-19855)*

Highway Materials Inc E 215 234-4522
Perkiomenville *(G-13301)*

Hobart Corporation E 717 397-5100
Lancaster *(G-9050)*

Ironshore Marine LLC G 484 941-3914
Spring City *(G-17861)*

J R Young G 717 935-2919
Belleville *(G-1132)*

James P Wolfley G 570 541-0414
Mc Clure *(G-10559)*

Jlg Industries Inc C 717 530-9000
Shippensburg *(G-17534)*

▼ **Jlg Industries Inc** A 717 485-5161
Mc Connellsburg *(G-10568)*

Jlg Industries Inc C 814 623-0045
Bedford *(G-1056)*

Jlg Industries Inc C 717 485-5161
Mc Connellsburg *(G-10569)*

Jlg Industries Inc E 717 485-6464
Mc Connellsburg *(G-10570)*

Jlg Industries Inc F 814 623-2156
Bedford *(G-1055)*

K & B Aqua Express Co LLC G 215 343-2247
Chalfont *(G-2879)*

Keenan Cnstr & Excvtg Inc G 610 724-4157
West Chester *(G-19580)*

Kenco Construction Pdts Inc F 724 238-3387
Ligonier *(G-9960)*

▲ **Kennametal Inc** A 412 248-8000
Pittsburgh *(G-15169)*

Kennametal Inc C 276 646-0080
Bedford *(G-1059)*

▲ **Keystone Technologies LLC** G 215 283-2600
North Wales *(G-12810)*

L & M Construction G 610 326-9970
Pottstown *(G-15951)*

L A Welte Inc G 412 341-9400
Pittsburgh *(G-15206)*

Lanco Manufacturing Company G 717 556-4143
Bird In Hand *(G-1679)*

◆ **Lee Industries Inc** C 814 342-0460
Philipsburg *(G-14519)*

▲ **Lemco Tool Corporation** E 570 494-0620
Cogan Station *(G-3361)*

Ls Steel Inc G 717 669-4581
Coatesville *(G-3314)*

M C E Development Inc G 412 952-0918
Irwin *(G-8181)*

M-B Companies Inc E 570 547-1621
Muncy *(G-11825)*

◆ **Maguire Products Inc** E 610 459-4300
Aston *(G-773)*

▲ **Marine Acquisition US Inc** E 610 495-7011
Limerick *(G-9970)*

Masters RMC Inc E 570 278-3258
Montrose *(G-11470)*

Mayer Brothers Construction Co F 814 452-3748
Erie *(G-5383)*

McNeilus Truck and Mfg Inc E 610 286-0400
Morgantown *(G-11527)*

MIC Industries Inc D 814 266-8226
Elton *(G-4960)*

▼ **Mongoose Products Inc** G 215 887-6600
Glenside *(G-6529)*

▲ **Mzp Kiln Services Inc** G 412 825-5100
Pittsburgh *(G-15313)*

◆ **National Crane Corporation** G 717 597-8121
Shady Grove *(G-17422)*

Pohl Railroad Mtls Corp LLC G 610 916-7645
Reading *(G-16471)*

Promachining and Technology F 814 796-3254
Waterford *(G-19268)*

Pulva Corporation E 724 898-3000
Valencia *(G-18700)*

▲ **Ratchet Rake LLC** G 717 249-1228
Carlisle *(G-2734)*

Richard E Krall Inc E 717 432-4179
Rossville *(G-16824)*

Roadsafe Traffic Systems Inc F 904 350-0080
Lemoyne *(G-9751)*

◆ **Rockland Inc** B 814 623-1115
Bedford *(G-1075)*

Rooftop Equipment Inc G 724 946-9999
New Wilmington *(G-12470)*

Russ Industrial Solutions LLC G 724 736-2580
Perryopolis *(G-13304)*

Saba Holding Company Inc G 717 737-3431
Camp Hill *(G-2517)*

Screen Service Tech Inc G 610 497-3555
Marcus Hook *(G-10454)*

Speciality Precast Company G 724 865-9255
Prospect *(G-16113)*

Stabler Companies Inc F 717 236-9307
Harrisburg *(G-7219)*

Star Surplus One G 215 654-9237
Ambler *(G-603)*

Sunnyburn Welding G 717 862-3878
Airville *(G-32)*

T & N Excavating LLC G 717 801-5525
Etters *(G-5553)*

▲ **Tamco Inc** E 724 258-6622
Monongahela *(G-11317)*

Top of Line Auto Svc II LLC G 215 727-6958
Philadelphia *(G-14395)*

Trench Shoring Services G 412 331-8118
Pittsburgh *(G-15642)*

Try Tek Machine Works Inc E 717 428-1477
Jacobus *(G-8232)*

Tybot LLC G 412 756-3360
Allison Park *(G-465)*

Umoja Erectors LLC G 215 235-7662
Philadelphia *(G-14417)*

United Theatrical Services G 215 242-2134
Philadelphia *(G-14424)*

Valk Manufacturing Company D 717 766-0711
New Kingstown *(G-12394)*

Valley Broom Inc G 717 349-2614
East Waterford *(G-4642)*

Vollmer Tar & Chip Inc G 814 834-1332
Saint Marys *(G-17027)*

▲ **Wagman Metal Products Inc** E 717 854-2120
York *(G-20702)*

Waldrich GMBH Inc G 724 763-3889
Ford City *(G-6052)*

◆ **Weir Hazleton Inc** D 570 455-7711
Hazleton *(G-7537)*

William Sport Crane & Rigging G 570 433-3300
Montoursville *(G-11457)*

Woodings Doweling Tech Inc G 724 625-3131
Mars *(G-10514)*

◆ **Zimmerman Industries Inc** E 717 733-6166
Ephrata *(G-5158)*

3532 Mining Machinery & Eqpt

◆ **Acker Drill Co Inc** E 570 586-2061
S Abingtn Twp *(G-16888)*

▼ **Advanced Processes Inc** F 724 266-7274
Ambridge *(G-606)*

American Bit & Drill Steel G 570 474-6788
Mountain Top *(G-11751)*

▼ **Angelo Nieto Inc** F 570 489-6761
Jessup *(G-8326)*

Atlas Copco Secoroc LLC E 717 369-3177
Fort Loudon *(G-6057)*

▲ **Balco Inc** F 724 459-6814
Blairsville *(G-1714)*

▲ **Barefoot Pellet Company** G 570 297-4771
York *(G-20400)*

▲ **Becker/Wholesale Mine Sup LLC** E 724 515-4993
Greensburg *(G-6653)*

Blue Mountain Lawn Service G 610 759-6979
Wind Gap *(G-20166)*

◆ **Bradley Pulverizer Company** F 610 432-2101
Allentown *(G-158)*

▲ **Bridon-American Corporation** B 570 822-3349
Hanover Township *(G-6982)*

Brookville Locomotive Inc C 814 849-2000
Brookville *(G-2254)*

Bucyrus America Inc E 724 743-1200
Houston *(G-7867)*

Burch Supplies Company Inc G 610 640-4877
Malvern *(G-10197)*

◆ **Caterpillar Globl Min Amer LLC** C 724 743-1200
Houston *(G-7869)*

▲ **Center Rock Inc** G 814 267-7100
Berlin *(G-1287)*

Daves Airport Shuttle LLC G 215 288-1000
Philadelphia *(G-13606)*

DSI Underground Systems Inc D 740 432-7302
Pittsburgh *(G-14938)*

◆ **Eastern Machine & Convyrs Inc** F 724 379-4701
Donora *(G-4154)*

▲ **Eickhoff Corporation** F 724 218-1856
Georgetown *(G-6275)*

Epiroc USA LLC G 717 552-9694
Chambersburg *(G-2930)*

Epiroc USA LLC G 724 324-2391
Mount Morris *(G-11680)*

◆ **FLS US Holdings Inc** F 610 264-6011
Bethlehem *(G-1512)*

Gcl Inc G 724 933-7260
Wexford *(G-19805)*

▲ **Gill Rock Drill Company Inc** E 717 272-3861
Lebanon *(G-9573)*

Hoffman Diamond Products Inc E 814 938-7600
Punxsutawney *(G-16143)*

Irwin Car & Equipment Inc F 724 864-5170
Irwin *(G-8173)*

▲ **Irwin Car & Equipment Inc** E 724 864-8900
Irwin *(G-8174)*

J & L Professional Sales Inc G 412 788-4927
Mc Kees Rocks *(G-10616)*

Jennmar Corporation D 814 886-4121
Cresson *(G-3899)*

▲ **Jennmar of Kentucky Inc** E 412 963-9071
Pittsburgh *(G-15150)*

◆ **Jennmar of Pennsylvania LLC** E 412 963-9071
Pittsburgh *(G-15151)*

▲ Joy Global Inc ....C 814 432-1202
Franklin *(G-6142)*

Joy Global Underground Min LLC ....D 814 676-8531
Franklin *(G-6143)*

Joy Global Underground Min LLC ....D 814 432-1647
Franklin *(G-6144)*

Joy Global Underground Min LLC ....C 814 437-5731
Franklin *(G-6145)*

◆ Joy Global Underground Min LLC ....C 724 779-4500
Warrendale *(G-19083)*

K & K Mine Products Inc ....E 724 463-5000
Indiana *(G-8109)*

▲ Kennametal Inc ....A 412 248-8000
Pittsburgh *(G-15169)*

Kennametal Inc ....C 276 646-0080
Bedford *(G-1059)*

Klinger Machinery Co Inc ....G 717 362-8656
Elizabethville *(G-4894)*

Leman Machine Company ....E 814 736-9696
Portage *(G-15918)*

▲ Longwall Services Inc ....G 724 228-9898
Meadow Lands *(G-10691)*

▼ Maclean Saegertown LLC ....G 814 763-2655
Saegertown *(G-16924)*

Master Machine Co Inc ....F 814 495-4900
South Fork *(G-17775)*

◆ McLanahan Corporation ....B 814 695-9807
Hollidaysburg *(G-7651)*

▲ Metadyne Inc ....E 570 265-6963
Towanda *(G-18432)*

Mineral Processing Spc Inc ....G 724 339-8630
New Kensington *(G-12358)*

Mining Clamps Fasteners & More ....G 724 324-2430
Mount Morris *(G-11681)*

Mpi Supply Incorporated ....G 412 664-9320
Glassport *(G-6414)*

▼ Northeast Geotechnical Sup LLC ....G 570 307-1283
Olyphant *(G-12995)*

Ottinger Machine Co Inc ....G 610 933-2101
Phoenixville *(G-14565)*

▲ Penn Machine Company ....D 814 288-1547
Johnstown *(G-8421)*

Pennsylvania Drilling Company ....E 412 771-2110
Mc Kees Rocks *(G-10623)*

▲ Pennsylvania Drilling Company ......E 412 771-2110
Imperial *(G-8074)*

▼ R Q I Inc ....G 724 209-4100
Venetia *(G-18743)*

◆ Reichdrill LLC ....D 814 342-5500
Philipsburg *(G-14525)*

Saegertown Manufacturing Corp ....C 814 763-2655
Saegertown *(G-16932)*

Sandvik Inc ....E 724 246-2901
Brier Hill *(G-2101)*

▲ Sandvik Mining and Cnstr ....G 215 245-0280
Bensalem *(G-1250)*

Scheirer Machine Company Inc ....E 412 833-6500
Bethel Park *(G-1433)*

▼ Steel Systems Installation Inc ....E 717 786-1264
Quarryville *(G-16280)*

Strata Products Worldwide LLC ....G 724 745-5030
Canonsburg *(G-2641)*

Tallman Supply Company ....G 717 647-2123
Tower City *(G-18442)*

Terrasource Global Corporation ....E 610 544-7200
Media *(G-10953)*

Testa Machine Company Inc ....E 724 947-9397
Slovan *(G-17631)*

Titan Metal & Machine Co Inc ....G 724 747-9528
Washington *(G-19232)*

Watts Brothers Tool Works Inc ....F 412 823-7877
Wilmerding *(G-20162)*

3533 Oil Field Machinery & Eqpt

Baker Hghes Olfld Oprtions Inc..........G 724 266-4725
Ambridge *(G-610)*

Blowout Tools Inc ....F 724 627-0208
Waynesburg *(G-19434)*

▲ Bridon-American Corporation ....B 570 822-3349
Hanover Township *(G-6982)*

Cactus Wellhead LLC ....G 814 308-0344
Reynoldsville *(G-16656)*

Central Penn Rig Service ....G 814 342-4800
Morrisdale *(G-11547)*

Electrichp USA Corp ....E 724 678-5084
Venetia *(G-18742)*

FMC Technologies Inc ....E 570 546-2441
Muncy *(G-11816)*

FMC Technologies Inc ....F 215 822-4485
Lansdale *(G-9368)*

Funks Drilling Incorporated ....F 717 423-6688
Newville *(G-12601)*

General Electric Company ....G 610 876-2200
Eddystone *(G-4803)*

▲ Gill Rock Drill Company Inc ....E 717 272-3861
Lebanon *(G-9573)*

Gt Services LLC ....E 215 256-9521
Kulpsville *(G-8829)*

Heisey Machine Co Inc ....G 717 293-1373
Lancaster *(G-9042)*

Matheson Tri-Gas Inc....................D 215 641-2700
Montgomeryville *(G-11406)*

National Oilwell Varco Inc ....F 724 745-6005
Canonsburg *(G-2611)*

National Oilwell Varco Inc ....F 724 947-4581
Burgettstown *(G-2352)*

National Oilwell Varco Inc ....E 318 243-5910
Washington *(G-19209)*

National Oilwell Varco Inc ....D 814 427-2555
Punxsutawney *(G-16150)*

National Oilwell Varco LP ....E 570 862-2548
Leetsdale *(G-9700)*

Oil Process Systems Inc ....E 610 437-4618
Allentown *(G-337)*

Oil States Energy Services LLC ....G 724 746-1168
Canonsburg *(G-2615)*

Pcs Ferguson Inc ....G 412 264-6000
Brookville *(G-2268)*

◆ Reichdrill LLC ....D 814 342-5500
Philipsburg *(G-14525)*

▲ Robroy Industries Inc ....F 412 828-2100
Verona *(G-18761)*

◆ Schramm Inc ....C 610 696-2500
West Chester *(G-19638)*

Specialized Desanders USA Inc ....E 412 535-3396
Pittsburgh *(G-15569)*

Stream-Flo USA LLC ....G 724 349-6090
Indiana *(G-8131)*

▲ Superior Energy Resources LLC....E 814 265-1080
Brockway *(G-2236)*

Superior Energy Resources LLC........G 814 265-1080
Brockway *(G-2235)*

Technipfmc US Holdings Inc ....G 303 217-2030
Erie *(G-5504)*

Technipfmc US Holdings Inc ....F 724 459-7350
Blairsville *(G-17743)*

Technipfmc US Holdings Inc ....E 570 546-2380
Muncy *(G-11834)*

Technipfmc US Holdings Inc ....E 724 820-5023
Canonsburg *(G-2646)*

Torquato Drilling ACC Inc ....G 570 457-8565
Old Forge *(G-12976)*

Tru-Gas Inc ....G 814 723-9260
Clarendon *(G-3171)*

Vetco Gray Inc ....G 570 435-8027
Muncy *(G-11837)*

Wc Welding Services ....G 570 798-2300
Lakewood *(G-8916)*

Weatherford International LLC ....E 570 326-2754
Muncy *(G-11839)*

Weatherford International LLC ....D 570 546-0745
Muncy *(G-11840)*

Wise Intervention Svcs USA Inc ....D 724 405-6660
Smithton *(G-17664)*

3534 Elevators & Moving Stairways

A Plus Stair Lift Pittsburgh ....G 412 260-7469
Monroeville *(G-11322)*

Ashland Industrial Svcs LLC ....G 717 347-5616
Shrewsbury *(G-17581)*

Benton Elevator ....G 215 795-0650
Ottsville *(G-13059)*

◆ Buddy Butlers Inc ....G 570 759-0550
Berwick *(G-1315)*

▲ Custom Elevator Mfg Co Inc ....E 215 766-3380
Plumsteadville *(G-15807)*

Door Guard Inc ....G 724 695-8936
Pittsburgh *(G-14932)*

International Union-Elevator..............G 570 842-5430
Sprng Brk Twp *(G-17932)*

Otis Elevator Company ....G 814 452-2703
Erie *(G-5411)*

Stiltz Inc ....G 610 443-2282
Bethlehem *(G-1629)*

Thyssenkrupp Elevator Corp ....E 610 366-0161
Allentown *(G-409)*

◆ Unlimited Mobility ....G 484 620-9587
Reading *(G-16557)*

Zipf Associates Inc ....G 610 667-1717
Bala Cynwyd *(G-897)*

3535 Conveyors & Eqpt

Advanced Bulk & Conveying Inc.........F 724 588-9327
Greenville *(G-6736)*

Advanced Bulk & Conveying Inc.........G 724 588-9327
Greenville *(G-6737)*

Advantage Puck Technologies ....G 814 664-4810
Corry *(G-3742)*

▲ Aggregates Equipment Inc...........E 717 656-2131
Leola *(G-9767)*

▲ Asgco ....G 610 821-0216
Allentown *(G-144)*

Augers Unlimited Inc ....E 610 380-1660
Coatesville *(G-3292)*

Automted Conveying Systems Inc.......G 215 368-0500
Harleysville *(G-7022)*

B & C Material Handling Inc ....G 724 814-7910
Cranberry Township *(G-3808)*

C C B B Inc ....F 215 364-5377
Feasterville Trevose *(G-5898)*

▲ Capway Systems Inc ....E 717 843-0003
York *(G-20417)*

Cbf Systems ....F 717 793-2941
York *(G-20422)*

Dairy Conveyor Corp ....G 717 431-3121
Lancaster *(G-8990)*

Daniel B Proffitt Jr ....F 717 529-2194
Kirkwood *(G-8747)*

Delta/Ducon Conveying Techlgy ....E 610 695-9700
Malvern *(G-10222)*

Demco Enterprises Inc ....F 888 419-3343
Quakertown *(G-16184)*

◆ Dyco Inc ....D 800 545-3926
Bloomsburg *(G-1779)*

Erie Technical Systems Inc ....G 814 899-2103
Erie *(G-5276)*

Esco Windber ....G 814 509-8927
Windber *(G-20181)*

Eta Industries Inc ....G 724 453-1722
New Brighton *(G-12036)*

Fenner Inc ....C 717 665-2421
Manheim *(G-10380)*

Ferag Inc ....D 215 788-0892
Bristol *(G-2144)*

Fessler Machine Company...............E 724 346-0878
Sharon *(G-17433)*

▲ Flexicon Corporation ....C 610 814-2400
Bethlehem *(G-1510)*

▲ Flexlink Systems Inc ....D 610 973-8200
Allentown *(G-216)*

▲ Flexmove Americas LLC ....G 267 203-8351
Souderton *(G-17734)*

◆ FLS US Holdings Inc ....F 610 264-6011
Bethlehem *(G-1512)*

Flsmidth Inc ....C 717 665-2224
Manheim *(G-10385)*

▲ Fluidtechnik USA ....G 610 321-2407
Glenmoore *(G-6466)*

Hamilton High Heat Inc ....G 814 635-4131
Saxton *(G-17101)*

Hammertek Corporation ....E 717 898-7665
Bethlehem *(G-1528)*

Handling Products Inc....................G 724 443-1100
Gibsonia *(G-6339)*

▲ Homer City Automation Inc ....G 724 479-4503
New Alexandria *(G-12019)*

Hoover Cnvyor Fabrication Corp ....E 814 634-5431
Meyersdale *(G-11011)*

▲ Hosch Company LP ....E 724 695-3002
Oakdale *(G-12903)*

Industrial Composites Inc.................G 412 221-2662
Bridgeville *(G-2069)*

Industrial Svc Instllation Inc ....D 717 767-1129
Emigsville *(G-4992)*

Ipeg Inc ....C 814 437-6861
Franklin *(G-6138)*

Irwin Car & Equipment Inc ....F 724 864-5170
Irwin *(G-8173)*

▲ Irwin Car & Equipment Inc ....E 724 864-8900
Irwin *(G-8174)*

▲ ITOH Denki USA Inc ....E 570 820-8811
Wilkes Barre *(G-19930)*

J & L Professional Sales Inc ....G 412 788-4927
Mc Kees Rocks *(G-10616)*

J A Emilius Sons Inc ....F 215 379-6162
Cheltenham *(G-3030)*

▲ J W Steel Fabricating Co ....E 724 625-1355
Mars *(G-10503)*

Jam Works LLC..........................G 570 972-1562
Mayfield *(G-10541)*

James Eagen Sons Company................E....... 570 693-2100
Wyoming *(G-20280)*
Jlg Industries Inc................................C....... 717 485-5161
Mc Connellsburg *(G-10569)*
Jmg Inc..G....... 215 659-4087
Willow Grove *(G-20121)*
Joy Global Underground Min LLC.........C....... 724 873-4200
Houston *(G-7872)*
Joy Global Underground Min LLC.........D....... 724 915-2200
Homer City *(G-7677)*
Joy Global Underground Min LLC.........G....... 724 873-4200
Houston *(G-7873)*
◆ **Joy Global Underground Min LLC**....C....... 724 779-4500
Warrendale *(G-19083)*
K & K Mine Products Inc......................E....... 724 463-5000
Indiana *(G-8109)*
▲ **Lumsden Corporation**.......................C....... 717 394-6871
Lancaster *(G-9117)*
◆ **Master Solutions Inc**........................E....... 717 243-6849
Carlisle *(G-2724)*
▲ **Muller Martini Mailroom**...................C....... 610 266-7000
Allentown *(G-323)*
N C Stauffer & Sons Inc........................D....... 570 945-3047
Factoryville *(G-5758)*
▲ **Ncc Automated Systems Inc**............E....... 215 721-1900
Souderton *(G-17756)*
New Castle Company Inc.......................G....... 724 658-4516
New Castle *(G-12128)*
Paragon Technologies Inc....................E....... 610 252-7321
Easton *(G-4740)*
▼ **Pennram Diversified Mfg Corp**.........E....... 570 327-2802
Williamsport *(G-20055)*
Platypus LLC..G....... 412 979-4629
Pittsburgh *(G-15416)*
▲ **Precision Feedscrews Inc**.................E....... 724 654-9676
New Castle *(G-12139)*
Proconveyor LLC...................................G....... 717 887-5897
York *(G-20643)*
Production Systems Automtn LLC........F....... 610 358-0500
Aston *(G-788)*
Production Systems Automtn LLC........E....... 570 602-4200
Duryea *(G-4506)*
Rage Bulk Systems Ltd..........................E....... 215 489-5373
Doylestown *(G-4333)*
Rissler Conveyors.................................G....... 717 336-2244
Stevens *(G-18055)*
Rissler E Manufacturing LLC................G....... 814 766-2246
New Enterprise *(G-12195)*
◆ **Ropro Design Inc**................................G....... 724 630-1976
Beaver *(G-991)*
▲ **Rtj Inc A Close Corporation**..............F....... 215 943-9220
Levittown *(G-9862)*
▲ **Sapient Automation LLC**...................E....... 877 451-4044
Hatfield *(G-7394)*
▲ **Schake Industries Inc**.......................E....... 814 677-9333
Seneca *(G-17369)*
Sensible Components LLC....................F....... 855 548-7587
Oakdale *(G-12911)*
◆ **Shingle Belting Inc**............................E....... 610 825-5500
King of Prussia *(G-8674)*
Shumars Welding & Mch Svc Inc..........D....... 724 246-8095
Grindstone *(G-6779)*
SKF USA Inc..F....... 610 954-7000
Allentown *(G-395)*
Sparks Belting Company Inc.................G....... 717 767-1490
York *(G-20675)*
▼ **Steel Systems Installation Inc**...........E....... 717 786-1264
Quarryville *(G-16280)*
Thomas & Muller Systems Ltd...............G....... 215 541-1961
Red Hill *(G-16585)*
Unimove LLC..G....... 610 826-7855
Palmerton *(G-13112)*
Vibro Industries Inc...............................G....... 717 527-2094
Fogelsville *(G-5997)*
Walsh Tool Company Inc........................G....... 570 823-1375
Wilkes Barre *(G-19969)*
Weldon Machine Tool Inc.......................E....... 717 846-4000
York *(G-20706)*
▲ **Westfalia Technologies Inc**...............D....... 717 764-1115
York *(G-20708)*

3536 Hoists, Cranes & Monorails

▲ **Acco Mtl Hdlg Solutions Inc**..............D....... 800 967-7333
York *(G-20365)*
Altec Industries Inc...............................C....... 570 822-3104
Wilkes Barre *(G-19904)*
American Crane & Eqp Corp..................F....... 484 945-0420
Douglassville *(G-4167)*
American Crane & Eqp Corp..................F....... 610 521-9000
Essington *(G-5541)*
▲ **American Crane & Eqp Corp**.............C....... 610 385-6061
Douglassville *(G-4168)*
Atlantic Crane Inc..................................F....... 610 366-1540
Fogelsville *(G-5991)*
▼ **B E Wallace Products Corp**...............F....... 610 647-1400
Malvern *(G-10190)*
Bashlin Industries Inc...........................D....... 724 458-8340
Grove City *(G-6780)*
Brad Foote Gear Works Inc...................E....... 412 264-1428
Pittsburgh *(G-14789)*
Crane Man Inc..G....... 215 996-1033
Chalfont *(G-2870)*
D & S Industrial Contg Inc.....................E....... 412 490-3215
Coraopolis *(G-3683)*
◆ **D L Carmody Holdings LLC**..............C....... 717 741-4863
York *(G-20442)*
▲ **DMW Marine Group LLC**...................G....... 610 827-2032
Chester Springs *(G-3075)*
▲ **East Coast Hoist Inc**..........................D....... 215 646-2336
Telford *(G-18286)*
▼ **Erie Strayer Company**........................C....... 814 456-7001
Erie *(G-5275)*
Funks Drilling Incorporated...................F....... 717 423-6688
Newville *(G-12601)*
Gantrex Inc...F....... 412 347-0300
Canonsburg *(G-2591)*
◆ **Grove Worldwide LLC**.........................D....... 717 597-8121
Shady Grove *(G-17421)*
◆ **Harrington Hoists Inc**.........................C....... 717 665-2000
Manheim *(G-10388)*
Interstate Equipment Corp....................G....... 412 563-5556
Pittsburgh *(G-15134)*
J W Hoist and Crane LLC.......................G....... 814 696-0350
Duncansville *(G-4453)*
Jlg Industries Inc...................................F....... 814 623-2156
Bedford *(G-1055)*
Jlg Industries Inc...................................C....... 814 623-0045
Bedford *(G-1056)*
Johnson Memorial Co.............................G....... 814 634-0622
Meyersdale *(G-11014)*
KKR & Co LP..C....... 717 741-4863
York *(G-20555)*
Kone Cranes Inc......................................F....... 814 878-8070
Erie *(G-5351)*
Konecranes Inc.......................................F....... 814 237-2663
Philipsburg *(G-14518)*
Konecranes Inc.......................................E....... 610 321-2900
Pottstown *(G-16008)*
Konecranes Inc.......................................F....... 814 878-8070
Erie *(G-5352)*
▲ **Liftex Corporation**..............................D....... 800 478-4651
Ivyland *(G-8215)*
▲ **Lug-All Co Inc**.....................................E....... 610 286-9884
Morgantown *(G-11526)*
McDal Corporation..................................F....... 800 626-2325
King of Prussia *(G-8649)*
◆ **National Crane Corporation**...............G....... 717 597-8121
Shady Grove *(G-17422)*
Overhead Crane Sales Svc LLC............G....... 724 335-1415
Lower Burrell *(G-10107)*
▲ **Pittsburgh Design Services Inc**........F....... 412 276-3000
Carnegie *(G-2779)*
▲ **T Bruce Sales Inc**..............................D....... 724 528-9961
West Middlesex *(G-19731)*
Transol Corporation................................G....... 610 527-0234
Morgantown *(G-11542)*
▲ **Universal Electric Corporation**..........B....... 724 597-7800
Canonsburg *(G-2652)*

3537 Indl Trucks, Tractors, Trailers & Stackers

▲ **Acco Mtl Hdlg Solutions Inc**..............D....... 800 967-7333
York *(G-20365)*
Altec Industries Inc...............................C....... 570 822-3104
Wilkes Barre *(G-19904)*
◆ **Ballymore Holdings Inc**......................E....... 610 593-5062
Coatesville *(G-3293)*
Beco Truck Cap Outlet............................F....... 717 336-3141
Denver *(G-4067)*
Bornmann Mfg Co Inc..............................G....... 215 228-5826
Philadelphia *(G-13473)*
Brookville Locomotive Inc......................C....... 814 849-2000
Brookville *(G-2254)*
Cascade Corporation...............................C....... 570 995-5099
Trout Run *(G-18512)*
Central Road LLC....................................G....... 888 319-7778
Bethel Park *(G-1410)*
▲ **Cheetah Chassis Corporation**.............C....... 570 752-2708
Berwick *(G-1317)*
Commonwealth Utility Eqp Inc................E....... 724 283-8400
Butler *(G-2390)*
Conrad Enterprises Inc............................E....... 717 274-5151
Cornwall *(G-3738)*
Craneco LLC..G....... 610 948-1400
Royersford *(G-16847)*
Crown Equipment Corporation................E....... 724 696-3533
Mount Pleasant *(G-11695)*
Crown Food Carts Incorporated..............G....... 610 628-9612
Allentown *(G-187)*
▲ **D L Martin Co**..C....... 717 328-2141
Mercersburg *(G-10984)*
David J Klein Inc......................................F....... 610 385-4888
Douglassville *(G-4174)*
Daynight Transport LLC..........................G....... 800 288-4996
Carlisle *(G-2707)*
Deval Life Cycle Support LLC..................E....... 865 786-8675
Philadelphia *(G-13624)*
Devaltronix Inc...F....... 215 331-9600
Philadelphia *(G-13625)*
F & R Cargo Express LLC........................G....... 610 351-9200
Allentown *(G-211)*
Ferag Inc...D....... 215 788-0892
Bristol *(G-2144)*
◆ **General Transervice Inc**........................E....... 610 857-1900
Coatesville *(G-3304)*
George Taylor Forklift Repair..................G....... 412 221-7206
Morgan *(G-11517)*
Global Capital Corp..................................G....... 610 857-1900
Coatesville *(G-3305)*
Gold Rush Inc..E....... 717 484-2424
Denver *(G-4074)*
◆ **Grove US LLc**...D....... 717 597-8121
Shady Grove *(G-17420)*
High Country Motors LLC.........................E....... 814 886-9375
Loretto *(G-10103)*
Hoover Cnvyor Fabrication Corp.............E....... 814 634-5431
Meyersdale *(G-11011)*
▲ **Hosch Company LP**..............................E....... 724 695-3002
Oakdale *(G-12903)*
J & Ak Inc...D....... 412 787-9750
Pittsburgh *(G-15139)*
J&J Carriers Inc..G....... 814 285-0217
Schellsburg *(G-17132)*
Jkr Prolift...G....... 724 547-5955
Mount Pleasant *(G-11703)*
Jlg Industries Inc......................................F....... 814 623-2156
Bedford *(G-1055)*
K & K Mine Products Inc...........................E....... 724 463-5000
Indiana *(G-8109)*
Mack Trucks Inc...A....... 610 966-8800
Macungie *(G-10154)*
Martin Sprocket & Gear Inc......................D....... 610 837-1841
Danielsville *(G-3994)*
Metro International Corp..........................E....... 570 825-2741
Wilkes Barre *(G-19943)*
Molded Fiber Glass Companies...............C....... 814 683-4500
Linesville *(G-9984)*
Oppenheimer Precision Pdts Inc..............D....... 215 674-9100
Horsham *(G-7837)*
Oram Transport Co Inc...............................F....... 702 559-4067
Allentown *(G-340)*
Overhead Door Corporation......................D....... 215 368-8700
Lansdale *(G-9396)*
Penn Manufacturing...................................G....... 717 626-8879
Lititz *(G-10030)*
▼ **Reitnouer Inc**..E....... 610 929-4856
Birdsboro *(G-1704)*
Robinson Vacuum Tanks Inc.....................G....... 814 355-4474
Bellefonte *(G-1116)*
Rock-Built Inc..E....... 878 302-3978
New Kensington *(G-12372)*
Sha Co Welding & Fabrication..................G....... 724 588-0993
Greenville *(G-6773)*
Smeal Ltc LLC..E....... 717 918-1806
Ephrata *(G-5142)*
Stanko Products Inc....................................F....... 724 834-8080
Greensburg *(G-6717)*
▼ **Steel Systems Installation Inc**..............E....... 717 786-1264
Quarryville *(G-16280)*
Sterling-Fleischman Inc..............................F....... 610 647-1717
Media *(G-10951)*
▲ **Strick Corporation**...................................F....... 215 949-3600
Fairless Hills *(G-5799)*
Superior Custom Designs Inc.....................G....... 412 744-0110
Glassport *(G-6416)*
▲ **T Bruce Sales Inc**.....................................D....... 724 528-9961
West Middlesex *(G-19731)*
T S Beh Trucking Services..........................G....... 267 918-0493
Bristol *(G-2203)*

Team Biondi LLC ....E 570 503-7087
Lake Ariel (G-8894)

Terex Corporation ....E 717 840-0226
Mountville (G-11803)

Thompson Logging and Trckg Inc ....E 570 923-2590
North Bend (G-12727)

Top-Notch Trucking Inc ....G 267 456-1744
Elkins Park (G-4913)

◆ Weldship Industries Inc ....F 610 861-7330
Bethlehem (G-1655)

Wilsons Outdoor Services LLC ....E 724 503-4261
Washington (G-19247)

Win-Holt Equipment Corp ....C 516 222-0335
Allentown (G-436)

Wolenski Enterprises Inc ....E 205 307-9862
White Oak (G-19859)

3541 Machine Tools: Cutting

Aaron Enterprises Inc ....D 717 854-2641
York (G-20362)

Abe Custom Metal Products ....G 412 298-0200
Bethel Park (G-1399)

Adams County Laser LLC ....G 717 359-4030
Littlestown (G-10062)

Andritz Herr-Voss Stamco Inc ....E 724 251-8745
Ambridge (G-609)

▼ Arthur R Warner Company ....F 724 539-9229
Latrobe (G-9458)

Asm Products Inc ....G 724 861-8026
North Huntingdon (G-12768)

Branson Ultrasonics Corp ....E 610 251-9776
Paoli (G-13136)

Brighton Machine Company Inc ....F 724 378-0960
Aliquippa (G-70)

Brubaker Tool Corporation ....B 717 692-2113
Millersburg (G-11191)

◆ CAM Industries Inc ....E 717 637-5988
Hanover (G-6866)

◆ Carton Edge International Inc ....F 215 699-8755
North Wales (G-12794)

Center Machine Company ....G 724 379-4066
Webster (G-19456)

Cherryhill Manufacturing Corp ....F 724 254-2185
Clymer (G-3270)

Clln Directional Drilling Inc ....G 814 460-0248
Centerville (G-2833)

CNT Motion Systems Inc ....E 412 244-5770
Glenshaw (G-6485)

Commercial Metal Polishing ....F 610 837-0267
Bath (G-954)

▲ Composidie Inc ....C 724 845-8602
Apollo (G-673)

Conicity Technologies LLC ....G 412 601-1874
Turtle Creek (G-18563)

Coretech International Inc ....F 908 454-7999
Allentown (G-181)

▲ Custom Engineering Co ....C 814 898-1390
Erie (G-5237)

▲ Custom Mil & Consulting Inc ....E 610 926-0984
Fleetwood (G-5969)

D & D Machine ....G 412 821-3725
Pittsburgh (G-14900)

◆ Ellwood Crankshaft and Mch Co ....C 724 347-0250
Hermitage (G-7581)

Ellwood Group Inc ....C 724 981-1012
Hermitage (G-7582)

Emporium Specialties Company ....E 814 647-8661
Austin (G-833)

Ettco Tool & Machine Co Inc ....F 717 792-1417
York (G-20471)

Exact Machine Service Inc ....G 717 848-2121
York (G-20473)

▲ Extrude Hone LLC ....D 724 863-5900
Irwin (G-8162)

F Tinker and Sons Company ....E 412 781-3553
Pittsburgh (G-15000)

Fabworks Inc ....F 570 814-1515
Dallas (G-3962)

Faivre Mch & Fabrication Inc ....G 814 724-7160
Meadville (G-10725)

Forest Scientific Corporation ....G 814 463-5006
Tionesta (G-18371)

Frazier Machine Company Inc ....G 717 632-1101
Hanover (G-6887)

Freedom Components Inc ....G 717 242-0101
Lewistown (G-9930)

◆ G F Goodman & Son Inc ....F 215 672-8810
Warminster (G-18884)

Gardner Associate Enterprises ....G 717 624-2003
New Oxford (G-12410)

◆ Genesis Worldwide II Inc ....B 724 538-3180
Callery (G-2469)

Golis Machine Inc ....F 570 278-1963
Montrose (G-11465)

▲ Greenleaf Corporation ....B 814 763-2915
Saegertown (G-16915)

Heisey Machine Co Inc ....G 717 293-1373
Lancaster (G-9042)

▲ Herkules USA Corporation ....C 724 763-2066
Ford City (G-6047)

Herkules USA Corporation ....D 724 763-2066
Ford City (G-6048)

Hetrick Mfg Inc ....F 724 335-0455
Lower Burrell (G-10106)

Highland Carbide Tool Co ....F 724 863-7151
Irwin (G-8167)

HMS Industries Inc ....E 724 459-5090
Blairsville (G-1724)

Hone Alone Inc ....G 610 495-5832
Spring City (G-17859)

I T C Industrial Tube Cleaning ....F 724 752-3100
Ellwood City (G-4937)

Imperial Newbould Inc ....F 814 337-8155
Meadville (G-10737)

Innovative Design Inc ....E 717 202-1306
Lebanon (G-9583)

▲ John R Bromiley Company Inc ....E 215 822-7723
Chalfont (G-2878)

K Tool Inc ....G 717 624-3866
New Oxford (G-12413)

◆ Kaast Machine Tools Inc ....G 224 216-8886
Ardmore (G-710)

Kaleidas Machining Inc ....G 814 398-4337
Cambridge Springs (G-2478)

Kauffman Elec Contrls & Contg ....E 717 252-3667
Wrightsville (G-20240)

Keane Group Holdings LLC ....E 570 302-4050
Mansfield (G-10419)

Kinetigear LLC ....G 412 810-0049
Pittsburgh (G-15178)

▲ Lehigh Machine Tools Inc ....G 215 493-6446
Morrisville (G-11569)

M & S Centerless Grinding Inc ....F 215 675-4144
Hatboro (G-7294)

Machine TI Rebuild Specialists ....G 717 423-6073
Shippensburg (G-17538)

Madison Inds Holdings LLC ....C 717 762-3151
Waynesboro (G-19416)

Mazak Corporation ....G 610 481-0850
Allentown (G-311)

Medco Process Inc ....G 717 453-7298
Wiconisco (G-19896)

Mk Precision ....G 215 675-4590
Warminster (G-18924)

Mpe Machine Tool Inc ....E 814 664-4822
Corry (G-3769)

Orr Screw Machine Products ....E 724 668-2256
Greensburg (G-6695)

Penn United Technologies Inc ....E 724 431-2482
Sarver (G-17078)

Plasma Automation Incorporated ....F 814 333-2181
Meadville (G-10780)

▲ PR Hoffman Machine Pdts Inc ....E 717 243-9900
Carlisle (G-2732)

Price Machine Tool Repair ....G 215 631-9440
Lansdale (G-9399)

Quality Metal Products Inc ....E 570 333-4248
Dallas (G-3967)

◆ Reed Manufacturing Company ....D 814 452-3691
Erie (G-5459)

▲ Ressler Enterprises Inc ....E 717 933-5611
Mount Aetna (G-11605)

Risco Industries Inc ....G 412 767-0349
Pittsburgh (G-15487)

Ruch Carbide Burs Inc ....E 215 657-3660
Willow Grove (G-20139)

S Morantz Inc ....D 215 969-0266
Philadelphia (G-14273)

Scientific Tool Inc ....E 724 446-9311
New Stanton (G-12450)

South Morgan Technologies LLC ....G 814 774-2000
Girard (G-6402)

▼ Srd Design Corp ....G 717 699-0005
York (G-20678)

Stone & Wood Inc ....G 814 857-7621
Woodland (G-20214)

Talbot Holdings LLC ....C 717 692-2113
Millersburg (G-11202)

Td & Company ....G 610 637-6100
Morgantown (G-11538)

Time Machine Inc ....D 814 432-5281
Polk (G-15889)

Tms Precision Machining Inc ....G 215 547-6070
Bristol (G-2207)

Top Notch Cnc Machining Inc ....F 570 658-3725
Beavertown (G-1028)

Trident Plastics Inc ....E 215 443-7147
Warminster (G-18986)

Universal Pioneers LLC ....G 570 239-3950
Plymouth (G-15822)

US Energy ....G 724 783-7532
Rural Valley (G-16877)

USA Spares Inc ....E 717 241-9222
Carlisle (G-2746)

Vallorbs Jewel Company ....C 717 392-3978
Bird In Hand (G-1684)

Vanalstine Manufacturing Co ....G 610 489-7670
Trappe (G-18475)

▲ Vollmer of America Corp ....F 412 278-0655
Carnegie (G-2804)

Waldrich GMBH Inc ....C 724 763-3889
Ford City (G-6052)

Weldon Machine Tool Inc ....E 717 846-4000
York (G-20706)

◆ Woodings Industrial Corp ....C 724 625-3131
Mars (G-10515)

Yardley Products LLC ....E 215 493-2700
Yardley (G-20346)

3542 Machine Tools: Forming

Anvil Forge & Hammer Ir Works ....G 610 837-9951
Allentown (G-139)

Auto Care ....G 814 943-8155
Altoona (G-475)

Automated Indus Systems Inc ....E 814 838-2270
Erie (G-5198)

Baltec Corporation ....E 724 873-5757
Canonsburg (G-2549)

Bell-Mark Sales Co Inc ....E 717 292-5641
Dover (G-4186)

▲ C I Hayes Inc ....E 814 834-2200
Saint Marys (G-16951)

Chant Engineering Co Inc ....E 215 230-4260
New Britain (G-12046)

Chicago Rivet & Machine Co ....D 814 684-2430
Tyrone (G-18580)

Clearfield Metal Tech Inc ....F 814 765-7860
Clearfield (G-3215)

▲ Composidie Inc ....C 724 845-8602
Apollo (G-673)

▲ CPM Wolverine Proctor LLC ....D 215 443-5200
Horsham (G-7805)

▲ Custom Engineering Co ....C 814 898-1390
Erie (G-5237)

Daugherty Tool and Die Inc ....D 412 754-0200
Buena Vista (G-2341)

Die-Quip Corporation ....F 412 833-1662
Bethel Park (G-1411)

▲ Dreistern Inc ....G 215 799-0220
Telford (G-18284)

◆ Efco Inc ....E 814 455-3941
Erie (G-5256)

◆ Elizabeth Carbide Die Co Inc ....C 412 751-3000
McKeesport (G-10667)

Elizabeth Carbide Die Co Inc ....E 412 829-7700
Irwin (G-8160)

Engineered Devices Corporation ....F 570 455-4897
Hazleton (G-7497)

▲ Erie M & P Company Inc ....E 814 454-1581
Erie (G-5269)

Gasbarre Products Inc ....E 814 236-3108
Olanta (G-12960)

◆ Gasbarre Products Inc ....D 814 371-3015
Du Bois (G-4392)

Gasbarre Products Inc ....E 814 834-2200
Saint Marys (G-16975)

◆ Kaast Machine Tools Inc ....G 224 216-8886
Ardmore (G-710)

▲ Loomis Products Company ....F 215 547-2121
Levittown (G-9847)

Machine Rebuilders ....G 724 694-3190
New Derry (G-12191)

Machine TI Rebuild Specialists ....G 717 423-6073
Shippensburg (G-17538)

Max Levy Autograph Inc ....G 215 842-3675
Philadelphia (G-13996)

▲ Morlin Inc ....G 814 454-5559
Erie (G-5395)

Oakwood Bindery ....E 717 396-9559
Lancaster (G-9149)

▲ Pannier Corporation ....F 412 323-4900
Pittsburgh (G-15368)

▲ PR Hoffman Machine Pdts Inc ....E 717 243-9900
Carlisle (G-2732)

Pro Tech Machining Inc ....E 814 587-3200
Conneautville (G-3484)

▲ PTX - Pentronix Inc ....G 734 667-2897
Du Bois (G-4415)

Samuel Stamping Tech LLC ....E 724 981-5042
Hermitage (G-7594)

Schmidt Technology Corporation ....F 724 772-4600
Cranberry Township (G-3848)

Schwenk Custom Machining Inc ....G 610 367-1777
Boyertown (G-1928)

Showmark LLC ....G 610 458-0304
Exton (G-5732)

SMS Group Inc ....C 412 231-1200
Pittsburgh (G-15552)

Talbot Holdings LLC ....C 717 692-2113
Millersburg (G-11202)

Wemco Inc ....F 570 869-9660
Laceyville (G-8875)

Wesel Manufacturing Company ....E 570 586-8978
S Abingtn Twp (G-16903)

3543 Industrial Patterns

A B Patterns Models ....G 215 322-8226
Huntingdon Valley (G-7960)

Able Pattern Company ....F 724 327-1401
Export (G-5587)

Armstrong Patterns & Mfg ....G 724 845-1452
Ford City (G-6042)

Bassler Wllmsport Pttern Works ....G 570 368-2471
Montoursville (G-11432)

Baum & Hersh Inc ....G 717 229-2255
Codorus (G-3357)

Blatts Pattern Shop ....F 717 933-5633
Fredericksburg (G-6172)

Castek Innovations Inc ....E 717 267-2748
Chambersburg (G-2915)

Effort Enterprises Inc ....E 610 837-7003
Bath (G-957)

Frederick Wohlgemuth Inc ....E 215 638-9672
Bensalem (G-1199)

Hains Pattern Shop Inc ....F 717 273-6351
Lebanon (G-9578)

Independent Pattern Shop ....G 814 459-2591
Erie (G-5323)

J Clem Kline & Son Inc ....G 610 258-6071
Easton (G-4708)

Jacob Pattern Works Inc ....F 610 326-1100
Pottstown (G-16004)

Johnson Pattern & Machine Shop ....G 724 697-4079
Salina (G-17043)

Kore Mart Ltd ....E 610 562-5900
Hamburg (G-6843)

Latrobe Pattern Co ....E 724 539-9753
Latrobe (G-9492)

Lebanon Pattern Shop Inc ....G 717 273-8159
Lebanon (G-9603)

Patterson Plastics & Mfg ....G 215 736-3020
Levittown (G-9853)

Pennsylvania Patterns ....G 717 533-4188
Hershey (G-7625)

Precision Pattern & Wdwkg ....G 724 588-2224
Greenville (G-6766)

Spring Ford Castings Inc ....G 610 489-2600
Trappe (G-18473)

Standard Pattern Works Inc ....G 814 455-5145
Erie (G-5490)

Steffys Pattern Shop ....G 717 656-6032
Leola (G-9805)

Swope & Bartholomew Inc ....F 610 264-2672
Whitehall (G-19890)

Tammy Williams ....G 814 654-7127
Conneaut Lake (G-3481)

Threeway Pattern Enterprises ....G 610 929-2889
Reading (G-16537)

▼ Weatherly Casting and Mch Co ....D 570 427-8611
Weatherly (G-19455)

3544 Dies, Tools, Jigs, Fixtures & Indl Molds

A & H Industries Inc ....E 717 866-7591
Myerstown (G-11873)

Abbottstown Industries Inc ....E 717 259-8715
Abbottstown (G-3)

Accudie Inc ....G 724 222-8447
Meadow Lands (G-10689)

Accudyn Products Inc ....G 814 835-5088
Fairview (G-5809)

Accurate Marking Products Inc ....F 724 337-8390
New Kensington (G-12321)

▲ Accuride Erie LP ....B 814 480-6400
Erie (G-5170)

Actco Tool & Mfg Co ....E 814 336-4235
Meadville (G-10694)

Advanced Plastix Injection Mol ....F 215 453-7808
Perkasie (G-13265)

Allegheny Tool & Mfg Co ....F 814 337-2795
Meadville (G-10700)

Allegheny Tool Mold & Mfg Inc ....F 814 726-0200
Clarendon (G-3166)

▲ Alpha Carb Enterprises Inc ....E 724 845-2500
Leechburg (G-9641)

Alston Machine Company Inc ....E 412 795-1000
Pittsburgh (G-14690)

Alvord-Polk Inc ....F 717 692-2128
Millersburg (G-11189)

American Additive Mfg LLC ....F 215 559-1200
Horsham (G-7782)

▲ Ames Industries Inc ....F 877 296-9977
Hershey (G-7603)

Anchor Machine Inc ....G 610 261-4924
Northampton (G-12843)

Angermeier Tool & Die Inc ....G 814 445-2285
Somerset (G-17673)

Area Tool & Manufacturing Inc ....F 814 724-3166
Meadville (G-10703)

Arkay Tool & Die Inc ....F 215 322-2039
Langhorne (G-9279)

Arrow Tool Die & Machine Co ....F 215 676-1300
Hatboro (G-7270)

▼ Arthur R Warner Company ....F 724 539-9229
Latrobe (G-9458)

Associated Tool & Machine ....G 814 783-0083
Saegertown (G-16907)

Augustine Die & Mold Inc ....G 814 443-2390
Somerset (G-17676)

B-TEC Solutions Inc ....D 215 785-2400
Croydon (G-3911)

Backus Company ....E 814 887-5705
Smethport (G-17632)

Basic Carbide Corporation ....D 412 754-0060
Elizabeth (G-4856)

Beck Tool Inc ....E 814 734-8513
Edinboro (G-4809)

Belco Tool & Mfg Inc ....F 814 337-3403
Meadville (G-10706)

Biggs Tool and Die Inc ....F 215 674-9911
Warminster (G-18838)

Billet Industries Inc ....E 717 840-0280
York (G-20405)

Blair Tool and Plastics Co LLC ....G 814 695-2726
East Freedom (G-4561)

Blatts Pattern Shop ....F 717 933-5633
Fredericksburg (G-6172)

Bloom Machine Works Inc ....G 814 789-4234
Guys Mills (G-6808)

Bower Wire Cloth Tl & Die Inc ....G 570 398-4488
Jersey Shore (G-8310)

Boyle Incorporated ....G 724 295-2420
Freeport (G-6200)

Bra-Vor Tool & Die Co Inc ....E 814 724-1557
Meadville (G-10708)

Brandt Tool & Die Co Inc ....F 717 359-5995
Littlestown (G-10064)

Brian L Dewey ....G 814 967-3246
Townville (G-18444)

C & C Tooling Inc ....F 724 845-0939
Leechburg (G-9642)

C A Spalding Company ....E 267 550-9000
Bensalem (G-1163)

C Palmer Manufacturing Inc ....F 724 872-8200
West Newton (G-19748)

▲ C T E Inc ....E 717 767-6636
York (G-20416)

Cannon Tool Company ....F 724 745-1070
Canonsburg (G-2556)

Canto Tool Corporation ....F 814 724-2865
Meadville (G-10710)

Carbide Metals Inc ....F 724 459-6355
Blairsville (G-1718)

Carbigrind Inc ....G 724 722-3536
Ruffs Dale (G-16871)

Castek Innovations Inc ....E 717 267-2748
Chambersburg (G-2915)

Castle Mold & Tool Co Inc ....G 724 652-4737
New Castle (G-12071)

Central Penna Tool & Mfg Inc ....G 717 932-1294
New Cumberland (G-12181)

Char-Mark Inc ....G 570 754-7310
Auburn (G-815)

Choice Tool ....G 814 474-4656
Fairview (G-5815)

Christiansbrunn Die Fmlies Der ....G 570 425-2548
Pitman (G-14621)

Cir-Cut Corporation ....G 215 324-1000
Philadelphia (G-13545)

CK Tool & Die Inc ....G 814 836-9600
Erie (G-5225)

▲ Coinco Inc ....E 814 425-7407
Cochranton (G-3337)

Coinco Inc ....E 814 425-7476
Cochranton (G-3338)

Compacting Tooling Inc ....E 412 751-3535
McKeesport (G-10664)

Composidie Inc ....D 717 764-2233
York (G-20429)

▲ Composidie Inc ....C 724 845-8602
Apollo (G-673)

Composidie Inc ....E 724 845-8602
Vandergrift (G-18723)

Composidie Inc ....E 724 845-8602
Leechburg (G-9643)

Cooks Machine Work ....G 814 589-5141
Pleasantville (G-15799)

Crescent Industries Inc ....F 717 235-3844
New Freedom (G-12204)

Culver Tool & Die Inc ....G 717 932-2000
Lewisberry (G-9882)

Cumberland Tool & Die Inc ....E 717 691-1125
Mechanicsburg (G-10835)

Custom Die Services Inc ....F 717 867-5400
Annville (G-646)

Custom Tool & Design Inc ....E 814 838-9777
Erie (G-5241)

Custom Tool and Die Inc ....F 717 522-1440
Mountville (G-11792)

D & F Tool Inc ....G 814 899-6364
Erie (G-5244)

D W Machine Co Inc ....G 215 672-3340
Hatboro (G-7277)

D&M Tool Inc ....F 814 724-6743
Meadville (G-10716)

Danco Precision Inc ....E 610 933-1090
Phoenixville (G-14543)

Danco Precision Inc ....F 610 933-8981
Phoenixville (G-14544)

Danco Precision Inc ....F 610 933-8981
Phoenixville (G-14542)

Daugherty Tool and Die Inc ....D 412 754-0200
Buena Vista (G-2341)

Davis Tool Company ....G 215 368-0300
Kulpsville (G-8825)

De Vore Tool Co Inc ....G 814 425-2566
Cochranton (G-3341)

Deasey Machine Tl & Die Works ....G 814 847-2728
Everett (G-5570)

Dennis Sanders ....G 814 833-5497
Erie (G-5245)

Detwiler Tool Co ....G 215 257-5770
Sellersville (G-17344)

Die Botschaft ....G 717 433-4417
Millersburg (G-11193)

Die Urglaawisch Sippschaft ....G 215 499-1323
Bristol (G-2131)

Dietech Tool & Die Inc ....F 814 834-2779
Saint Marys (G-16962)

Dixon Tool & Die Inc ....F 814 684-0266
Tyrone (G-18581)

Do-Co Inc ....F 814 382-8339
Conneaut Lake (G-3471)

Dock Tool & Machine Inc ....G 215 338-8989
Philadelphia (G-13638)

Donlee Tool Corp ....F 814 398-8215
Cambridge Springs (G-2477)

Double H Manufacturing Corp ....D 215 674-4100
Warminster (G-18860)

Double H Manufacturing Corp ....G 215 674-4100
Warminster (G-18861)

Doutt Tool Inc ....E 814 398-2989
Venango (G-18740)

Drumm & Oharah Tl & Design Inc ....G 814 476-1349
Erie (G-5251)

Dunay Tool & Die Co ....G 724 335-7972
Tarentum (G-18241)

Dyer Industries Inc ....F 724 258-3400
Bunola (G-2343)

Dynamic Dies Inc ....E 724 325-1514
Pittsburgh (G-14947)

Employee Codes: A=Over 500 employees, B=251-500
C=101-250, D=51-100, E=20-50, F=10-19, G=3-9   2019 Harris Pennsylvania
Manufacturers Directory   933

S
I
C

E L W Manufacturing Inc ....F 717 246-6600
Dallastown (G-3974)
Eagle Precision Tooling Inc ....F 814 838-3515
Erie (G-5253)
Eagle Tool & Die Co Inc ....G 610 264-6011
Malvern (G-10226)
Effort Enterprises Inc ....G 610 837-7003
Bath (G-957)
Elbach & Johnson Inc ....G 724 457-6180
Glenwillard (G-6546)
Elcam Tool & Die Inc ....E 814 929-5831
Wilcox (G-19898)
Electronic Tool & Die Works ....G 215 639-0730
Bensalem (G-1187)
Elizabeth Carbide Die Co ....E 412 829-7700
Irwin (G-8159)
◆ Elizabeth Carbide Die Co Inc ....C 412 751-3000
McKeesport (G-10667)
Elizabeth Carbide Die Co Inc ....E 412 829-7700
Irwin (G-8160)
▲ Elk County Tool & Die Inc ....E 814 834-1434
Saint Marys (G-16970)
EMC Global Technologies Inc ....F 267 347-5100
Telford (G-18287)
Emp Industries Inc ....G 215 357-5333
Warminster (G-18871)
Engdahl Manufacturing Inc ....G 717 854-7114
York (G-20468)
Ernest Hill Machine Co Inc ....F 215 467-7750
Philadelphia (G-13678)
Evansburg Tool Corporation ....G 610 489-7580
Collegeville (G-3376)
Excellent Tool Inc ....G 814 337-7705
Meadville (G-10724)
Executool ....G 814 836-1141
Erie (G-5284)
F & S Tool Inc ....E 814 838-7991
Erie (G-5286)
F B F Inc ....E 215 322-7110
Southampton (G-17811)
Fiber Productions II Inc ....G 267 546-7025
Bristol (G-2145)
Florio Tooling Inc ....G 814 781-3973
Saint Marys (G-16974)
Franconia Plastics Corp ....G 215 723-8926
Souderton (G-17735)
Frew Mill Die Crafts Inc ....F 724 658-9026
New Castle (G-12095)
G & M Co Inc ....F 610 779-7812
Reading (G-16387)
G Adasavage LLC ....E 215 355-3105
Huntingdon Valley (G-7987)
Gasbarre Products Inc ....E 814 236-3108
Olanta (G-12960)
◆ Gasbarre Products Inc ....D 814 371-3015
Du Bois (G-4392)
▲ General Carbide Corporation ....C 724 836-3000
Greensburg (G-6668)
General Machine & Mfg Co ....G 570 383-0990
Peckville (G-13209)
General Welding & Machine Co ....G 570 889-3776
Ringtown (G-16753)
George J Anderton ....G 814 382-9201
Conneaut Lake (G-3473)
Gil Prebelli ....F 215 281-0300
Philadelphia (G-13762)
Glen Carbide Inc ....E 412 279-7500
Carnegie (G-2769)
Gma Manufacturing Inc ....F 215 355-3105
Huntingdon Valley (G-7990)
Gma Tooling Company ....E 215 355-3107
Huntingdon Valley (G-7991)
Graham Tech Inc ....G 814 807-1778
Meadville (G-10729)
Greenbriar Indus Systems Inc ....D 814 474-1400
Fairview (G-5824)
H and H Tool ....G 814 333-4677
Meadville (G-10732)
H and K Tool and Mch Co Inc ....E 215 322-0380
Huntingdon Valley (G-7993)
Haemer/Wright Tool & Die Inc ....E 814 763-6076
Saegertown (G-16916)
Hagerty Precision Tool ....G 814 734-8668
Edinboro (G-4813)
Hill Precision Manufacturing ....G 814 827-4333
Titusville (G-18380)
HMS Industries Inc ....E 724 459-5090
Blairsville (G-1724)
▲ Hodge Tool Co Inc ....E 717 393-5543
Lancaster (G-9051)
Holbrook Tool & Molding Inc ....E 814 336-4113
Meadville (G-10736)
Holt Precision Tool Co ....G 814 342-3595
West Decatur (G-19688)
Howmet Aluminum Casting Inc ....C 610 266-0270
Bethlehem (G-1532)
Hyde Special Tools ....G 814 763-4140
Saegertown (G-16918)
Hytech Tool & Design Co ....F 814 734-6000
Edinboro (G-4815)
Imperial Newbould Inc ....F 814 337-8155
Meadville (G-10737)
Imperial Tool Co ....G 215 947-7650
Huntingdon Valley (G-7996)
▼ Indiana Tool & Die LLC ....G 724 463-0386
Indiana (G-8107)
Inlet Tools Inc ....G 814 382-3511
Conneautville (G-3483)
Innotech Industries Inc ....E 215 533-6400
Philadelphia (G-13858)
▲ Innovative Carbide Inc ....D 412 751-6900
Irwin (G-8171)
J I T Tool & Die Inc ....E 814 265-0257
Brockport (G-2221)
J K J Tool Co ....F 570 322-1411
Williamsport (G-20026)
J K Tool Inc ....E 724 727-2490
Apollo (G-678)
J K Tool Die Co ....G 724 339-1858
New Kensington (G-12347)
J L W Ventures Incorporated ....F 814 765-9648
Clearfield (G-3221)
▲ Jade Equipment Corporation ....C 215 947-3333
Huntingdon Valley (G-7999)
Jatco Machine & Tool Co Inc ....E 412 761-4344
Pittsburgh (G-15145)
Jay-Ell Industries Inc ....F 610 326-0921
Pottstown (G-16005)
◆ Jennison Corporation ....E 412 429-0500
Carnegie (G-2771)
Jepson Precision Tool Inc ....F 814 756-4806
Cranesville (G-3867)
Jit Global Enterprises LLC ....E 724 478-1135
Apollo (G-679)
John W Czech ....E 814 763-4470
Saegertown (G-16920)
Johnson Pattern & Machine Shop ....G 724 697-4079
Salina (G-17043)
Johnstown Foundry Castings Inc ....G 814 539-8840
Johnstown (G-8389)
▲ JV Manufacturing Co Inc ....D 724 224-1704
Natrona Heights (G-11945)
K & A Tool Co ....G 814 835-1405
Erie (G-5341)
K & S Tool & Die Inc ....G 814 336-6932
Meadville (G-10741)
K S Tooling Inc ....E 717 764-5817
York (G-20546)
K V Inc ....F 215 322-4044
Huntingdon Valley (G-8006)
▲ K-Fab Inc ....D 570 759-8411
Berwick (G-1331)
Karadon Corporation ....F 724 676-5790
Blairsville (G-1729)
Kdc Engineering ....G 267 203-8487
Telford (G-18298)
Ken-Tex Corp ....E 570 374-4476
Selinsgrove (G-17328)
Kersey Tool and Die Co Inc ....G 814 885-8045
Kersey (G-8562)
Key Dies Inc ....E 717 838-5200
Annville (G-651)
Keystone Precision Inc ....G 814 336-2187
Meadville (G-10743)
Krauss S E Tool & Die Co ....G 215 957-1517
Warminster (G-18906)
Kroesen Tool Co Inc ....F 717 653-1392
Mount Joy (G-11665)
Kuhn Tool & Die Co ....E 814 336-2123
Meadville (G-10747)
Kw Inc ....E 610 582-8735
Birdsboro (G-1702)
▲ L L Brown Inc ....E 717 766-1885
Enola (G-5081)
Lake Tool Inc ....G 814 374-4401
Franklin (G-6146)
Lakeland Precision Inc ....G 814 382-6811
Conneaut Lake (G-3474)
▲ Lamms Machine Inc ....E 610 797-2023
Allentown (G-291)
Laneko Roll Form Inc ....E 215 822-1930
Hatfield (G-7363)
Lanum Metal Products LLC ....G 215 329-5010
Philadelphia (G-13954)
Laser Tool Inc ....E 814 763-2032
Saegertown (G-16921)
Laureldale Tool Co Inc ....G 610 929-5406
Reading (G-16427)
Layke Tool & Manufacturing Co ....E 814 333-1169
Meadville (G-10748)
Lebanon Pattern Shop Inc ....G 717 273-8159
Lebanon (G-9603)
▲ Leefson Tool & Die Company ....E 610 461-7772
Folcroft (G-6008)
Lehr Design & Manufacturing ....G 717 428-1828
Jacobus (G-8230)
▲ Leiss Tool & Die ....C 814 444-1444
Somerset (G-17695)
▲ Lemm Liquidating Company LLC ....D 724 325-7140
Export (G-5615)
Librandi Machine Shop Inc ....D 717 944-9442
Middletown (G-11063)
Lionheart Industrial Group LLC ....G 215 283-8400
Newtown (G-12520)
M & M Tool & Die Inc ....G 717 359-7178
Littlestown (G-10071)
M & M Tool & Die Inc ....G 717 359-7178
Littlestown (G-10072)
M C Tool & Die Inc ....G 814 944-8654
Altoona (G-523)
M S & M Manufacturing Co Inc ....G 215 743-3930
Philadelphia (G-13982)
Mac Tool & Die Inc ....G 814 337-9105
Meadville (G-10752)
Magdic Precision Tooling Inc ....E 412 824-6661
North Versailles (G-12778)
Mal-Ber Manufacturing Company ....E 215 672-6440
Huntingdon Valley (G-8010)
Maloney Tool & Mold Inc ....E 814 337-8407
Meadville (G-10754)
Marlan Tool Inc ....E 814 382-2744
Meadville (G-10757)
Master Tool and Mold Inc ....F 717 757-3671
York (G-20582)
McNulty Tool Die ....G 215 957-9900
Warminster (G-18919)
Mears Tool & Die Inc ....F 814 425-8304
Cochranton (G-3344)
Medl Tool & Die Inc ....G 215 443-5457
Warminster (G-18921)
Merlin Machine & Tool Co Inc ....G 215 493-6322
Collingdale (G-3407)
Mervine Corp ....F 215 257-0431
Perkasie (G-13284)
Metco Manufacturing Co Inc ....E 215 518-7400
Huntingdon Valley (G-8013)
Minco Tool & Mold Inc ....G 814 724-1376
Meadville (G-10764)
Mitchell Apx Machine Shop Inc ....G 717 597-2157
Greencastle (G-6623)
Mold 911 LLC ....G 267 312-1432
Blue Bell (G-1849)
Mold-Base Industries Inc ....D 717 564-7960
Harrisburg (G-7180)
▲ Moldex Tool & Design Corp ....D 814 337-3190
Meadville (G-10766)
Mountain Vly Mold Solution LLC ....G 570 460-6592
Stroudsburg (G-18131)
▲ Mxl Industries Inc ....D 717 569-8711
Lancaster (G-9141)
Nemco ....E 215 355-2100
Feasterville Trevose (G-5922)
▲ Neu Dynamics Corp ....F 215 355-2460
Warminster (G-18929)
New Castle Company Inc ....G 724 658-4516
New Castle (G-12128)
Nordic Tool & Die Co ....G 570 889-5650
Ringtown (G-16755)
North American Tooling Inc ....G 814 486-3700
Emporium (G-5070)
▲ North Coast Tool Inc ....F 814 836-7685
Lake City (G-8906)
Northwest Tool & Die Inc ....F 814 763-5087
Saegertown (G-16926)
Oberg Carbide Punch & Die ....G 724 295-2118
Freeport (G-6208)
Oberg Industries Inc ....E 724 295-5151
Freeport (G-6210)
Oberg Industries Inc ....C 724 353-9700
Sarver (G-17075)

Ofcg Inc.....G....... 570 655-0804
Dupont *(G-4493)*

Omca Cast Metals Inc.....G....... 724 222-7006
Washington *(G-19213)*

P D Q Tooling Inc.....G....... 412 751-2214
Mckeesport *(G-10677)*

Pace Precisions Products Inc.....E....... 814 371-6201
Du Bois *(G-4411)*

Paramount Die Corporation.....F....... 814 734-6999
Edinboro *(G-4819)*

▲ **Parker Industries Inc**.....E....... 412 561-6902
Pittsburgh *(G-15369)*

Paul E Seymour Tool & Die LLC.....F....... 814 725-5170
North East *(G-12754)*

Penn United Technologies Inc.....E....... 724 431-2482
Sarver *(G-17078)*

Penn United Technologies Inc.....C....... 724 352-5151
Saxonburg *(G-17092)*

▼ **Penn United Technologies Inc**.....A....... 724 352-1507
Cabot *(G-2460)*

Pennco Tool & Die Inc.....E....... 814 336-5035
Meadville *(G-10776)*

Phaztech Inc.....E....... 814 834-3262
Saint Marys *(G-17006)*

Philadelphia Carbide Co Inc.....G....... 215 885-0770
Oreland *(G-13027)*

Phoenix Mold and Machine LLC.....G....... 215 355-1985
Warminster *(G-18942)*

Pickar Brothers Inc.....E....... 610 582-0967
Birdsboro *(G-1703)*

Pittsburgh Carbide Die Co LLC.....F....... 412 384-5785
Elizabeth *(G-4862)*

Port Richmond Tool & Die Inc.....F....... 215 426-2287
Philadelphia *(G-14191)*

Prebola Enterprises Inc.....E....... 570 693-3036
Wyoming *(G-20283)*

Precise Plastics Inc.....D....... 814 474-5504
Fairview *(G-5840)*

Precise Polish.....F....... 814 453-4220
Erie *(G-5430)*

Precise Tool & Die Inc.....E....... 724 845-1285
Leechburg *(G-9650)*

Precision Carbide Inc.....G....... 215 355-4220
Feasterville Trevose *(G-5927)*

Precision Tool & Mfg Corp.....G....... 717 767-6454
Emigsville *(G-4997)*

Presto Packaging Inc.....G....... 215 646-7514
Ambler *(G-599)*

Prism Technologies Inc.....G....... 412 751-3090
Elizabeth *(G-4863)*

Pro Cel Inc.....G....... 215 322-9883
Warminster *(G-18948)*

Products Finishing Inc.....F....... 814 452-4887
Erie *(G-5439)*

Progressive Tool & Die Inc.....F....... 814 333-2992
Meadville *(G-10782)*

Proto Fab Technologies.....G....... 570 682-2000
Valley View *(G-18716)*

Proto-Cast LLC.....E....... 610 326-1723
Douglassville *(G-4180)*

Ptc-In-Liquidation Inc.....E....... 814 763-2000
Saegertown *(G-16930)*

Quality Die Makers Inc.....E....... 724 325-1264
Turtle Creek *(G-18568)*

Quality Metal Products Inc.....E....... 570 333-4248
Dallas *(G-3967)*

Quality Mold Inc.....E....... 814 866-2255
Erie *(G-5445)*

Quality Mould Inc.....E....... 724 532-3678
Latrobe *(G-9512)*

Quality Tool & Die Enterprises.....G....... 814 834-2384
Saint Marys *(G-17013)*

Ram Precision Inc.....G....... 215 674-0663
Horsham *(G-7843)*

Ram Tool Co Inc.....F....... 814 382-1842
Conneaut Lake *(G-3478)*

▲ **Rapid Mold Solutions Inc**.....G....... 814 833-2721
Erie *(G-5456)*

Rbs Fab Inc.....F....... 717 566-9513
Hummelstown *(G-7923)*

Realco Diversified Inc.....E....... 814 638-0800
Cochranton *(G-3349)*

▲ **Reddog Industries Inc**.....D....... 814 898-4321
Erie *(G-5458)*

Reed Tool & Die Inc.....E....... 724 547-3500
Mount Pleasant *(G-11713)*

Reiner Associates Inc.....G....... 717 647-7454
Tower City *(G-18440)*

Reliable Equipment Mfg Co.....E....... 215 357-7015
Warminster *(G-18951)*

Reubes Machine & Tool Co Inc.....G....... 215 368-0200
Lansdale *(G-9404)*

Rhkg Holdings Inc.....E....... 814 337-8407
Meadville *(G-10787)*

▲ **Richter Precision Inc**.....D....... 717 560-9990
East Petersburg *(G-4589)*

Robert I Oldfield.....G....... 215 533-5860
Philadelphia *(G-14254)*

Ronal Tool Company Inc.....F....... 717 741-0880
York *(G-20660)*

▲ **Roser Technologies Inc**.....D....... 814 827-7717
Titusville *(G-18393)*

◆ **Ross Mould LLC**.....C....... 724 222-7006
Washington *(G-19222)*

▲ **Saint-Gobain Ceramics Plas Inc**.....A....... 508 795-5000
Valley Forge *(G-18711)*

Samuel Stamping Tech LLC.....E....... 724 981-5042
Hermitage *(G-7594)*

Sansom Tool & Die Inc.....G....... 814 967-4985
Centerville *(G-2835)*

Schiller Grounds Care Inc.....D....... 215 322-4970
Huntingdon Valley *(G-8035)*

Schultz Precision Tooling.....G....... 724 334-4491
Leechburg *(G-9653)*

Scientific Tool Inc.....E....... 724 446-9311
New Stanton *(G-12450)*

Sedco Manufacturing.....G....... 570 323-1232
Hughesville *(G-7899)*

Shaw Industries Inc.....E....... 814 432-0954
Franklin *(G-6159)*

Sidelinger Bros Tool & Die.....G....... 814 885-8001
Kersey *(G-8569)*

Sigbet Manufacturing.....G....... 724 459-7920
Blairsville *(G-1741)*

Signal Machine Co.....G....... 717 354-9994
New Holland *(G-12284)*

Skylon Inc.....F....... 814 489-3622
Sugar Grove *(G-18147)*

Spark Technologies Inc.....F....... 724 295-3860
Schenley *(G-17136)*

Specialty Design & Mfg Co Inc.....E....... 610 779-1357
Reading *(G-16520)*

Spring Tool & Die Co Inc.....G....... 814 224-5173
Roaring Spring *(G-16771)*

Square Tool and Die Corp Inc.....F....... 570 489-8657
Throop *(G-18362)*

St Marys Tool & Die Co Inc.....E....... 814 834-7420
Saint Marys *(G-17021)*

Standard Precision Mfg Inc.....E....... 814 724-1202
Meadville *(G-10792)*

Stanko Products Inc.....F....... 724 834-8080
Greensburg *(G-6717)*

▲ **Starn Tool & Manufacturing Co**.....D....... 814 724-1057
Meadville *(G-10794)*

Steadman Tool & Die Inc.....G....... 814 967-4333
Townville *(G-18447)*

Steer Machine Tool & Die Corp.....F....... 570 253-5152
Honesdale *(G-7727)*

Steinmetz Inc.....E....... 570 842-6161
Roaring Brook Twp *(G-16760)*

Subcon Tl/Cctool Mch Group Inc.....E....... 814 456-7797
Erie *(G-5494)*

Suburban Precison Mold Company.....F....... 814 337-3413
Meadville *(G-10795)*

Suburban Tool & Die Co Inc.....E....... 814 833-4882
Erie *(G-5495)*

Superior Tool and Die Co.....F....... 215 638-1904
Bensalem *(G-1257)*

Sutley Tool Co.....G....... 814 789-4332
Guys Mills *(G-6813)*

Talbar Inc.....E....... 814 337-8400
Meadville *(G-10797)*

Target Tool Inc.....G....... 717 949-2407
Schaefferstown *(G-17131)*

Taylor Tool Inc.....G....... 814 967-4642
Townville *(G-18448)*

Technical Precision Inc.....E....... 724 253-2800
Hadley *(G-6821)*

Tetra Tool Company.....F....... 814 833-6127
Erie *(G-5506)*

Theodore W Styborski.....G....... 814 337-8535
Meadville *(G-10800)*

Tohickon Tool & Die Co.....G....... 215 766-8285
Doylestown *(G-4343)*

Tool & Die Productions.....G....... 814 838-3304
Erie *(G-5511)*

Tool-All Inc.....D....... 814 898-3917
Erie *(G-5512)*

◆ **Tooling Dynamics LLC**.....C....... 717 764-8873
York *(G-20690)*

Tory Tool Inc.....E....... 814 772-5439
Saint Marys *(G-17023)*

Tory Tool Inc.....E....... 814 772-5439
Ridgway *(G-16732)*

▲ **Tottser Tool and Die Shop Inc**.....D....... 215 357-7600
Southampton *(G-17842)*

Tottser Tool and Die Shop Inc.....D....... 215 357-7600
Southampton *(G-17843)*

Triangle Tool Company Inc.....E....... 814 878-4400
Erie *(G-5518)*

Triangle Tool Company Inc.....E....... 814 878-4603
Erie *(G-5519)*

Trimetric Enterprises Inc.....G....... 610 670-2099
Wernersville *(G-19487)*

Turner Tool & Die Inc.....F....... 570 378-3233
Lake Winola *(G-8912)*

Ultimate Tool Inc.....F....... 814 835-2291
Erie *(G-5522)*

Ultra Precision Incorporated.....E....... 724 295-5161
Freeport *(G-6216)*

Unique Machine & Tool.....F....... 412 331-2717
Mc Kees Rocks *(G-10640)*

Unique Machine Co.....E....... 215 368-8550
Montgomeryville *(G-11425)*

United Tool & Die Inc.....F....... 814 763-1133
Meadville *(G-10805)*

Universal Pen & Pencil Co Inc.....G....... 610 670-4720
Reading *(G-16555)*

Vangura Tool Inc.....E....... 412 233-6401
Clairton *(G-3160)*

Vanicek Precision Machining Co.....G....... 814 774-9012
Lake City *(G-8910)*

Viant Westfield LLC.....D....... 215 675-4653
Warminster *(G-18994)*

▼ **Viking Tool & Gage Inc**.....C....... 814 382-8691
Conneaut Lake *(G-3482)*

Vision Tool & Manufacturing.....E....... 814 724-6363
Meadville *(G-10811)*

Walsh Tool Company Inc.....G....... 570 823-1375
Wilkes Barre *(G-19969)*

West End Precision.....G....... 570 695-3911
Tremont *(G-18484)*

Whitehead Tool & Design Inc.....F....... 814 967-3064
Guys Mills *(G-6814)*

Willamsport Dies & Cuts Inc.....G....... 570 323-8351
Williamsport *(G-20092)*

Wilmington Die Inc.....G....... 724 946-8020
New Wilmington *(G-12473)*

Wolfe Tool & Machine Company.....F....... 717 848-6375
York *(G-20717)*

Wycon Mold & Tool Inc.....G....... 215 675-2945
Warminster *(G-19004)*

Xaloy Superior Holdings Inc.....G....... 724 656-5600
New Castle *(G-12170)*

York Steel Rule Dies Inc.....E....... 717 846-6002
York *(G-20750)*

Zemco Tool & Die Inc.....D....... 717 647-7151
Williamstown *(G-20104)*

3545 Machine Tool Access

A & H Industries Inc.....E....... 717 866-7591
Myerstown *(G-11873)*

A and M Tool LLC.....G....... 215 513-0968
Harleysville *(G-7011)*

A Landau Diamond Co.....G....... 215 675-2700
Warminster *(G-18815)*

Accurate Tool Co Inc.....E....... 610 436-4500
West Chester *(G-19494)*

◆ **Acker Drill Co Inc**.....E....... 570 586-2061
S Abingtn Twp *(G-16888)*

Advanced Carbide Tool Company.....F....... 267 960-1222
Southampton *(G-17797)*

Al Xander Co Inc.....E....... 814 665-8268
Corry *(G-3743)*

Allegheny Technologies Inc.....D....... 412 394-2800
Pittsburgh *(G-14682)*

Allegheny Tool & Supply Inc.....F....... 814 437-7062
Franklin *(G-6114)*

Allen Gauge & Tool Company.....E....... 412 241-6410
Pittsburgh *(G-14684)*

▲ **Alvord-Polk Inc**.....D....... 605 847-4823
Millersburg *(G-11188)*

Amat Inc.....G....... 717 235-8003
New Freedom *(G-12200)*

American Hollow Boring Company.....E....... 800 673-2458
Erie *(G-5187)*

ARC Diamond Tooling.....G....... 724 593-5814
Ligonier *(G-9957)*

Ashcombe Products Company Inc.....G....... 717 848-1271
York *(G-20387)*

S I C

▲ Bock Workholding Inc ....G...... 724 763-1776
Ford City *(G-6043)*

▲ Bolttech Mannings Inc ....D...... 724 872-4873
North Versailles *(G-12772)*

◆ Bon Tool Company ....D...... 724 443-7080
Gibsonia *(G-6328)*

Brubaker Tool Corporation ....B...... 717 692-2113
Millersburg *(G-11191)*

Calder Industries Inc ....F...... 814 422-8026
Spring Mills *(G-17886)*

Carbide Metals Inc ....F...... 724 459-6355
Blairsville *(G-1718)*

Cenco Grinding Corporation ....G...... 610 434-5740
Allentown *(G-167)*

▼ Chemcut Corporation ....B...... 814 272-2800
State College *(G-17950)*

▲ Chick Wrkholding Solutions Inc ......D...... 724 772-1644
Warrendale *(G-19070)*

Cianflone Scientific LLC ....G...... 412 787-3600
Pittsburgh *(G-14851)*

Clarks Expert Sales & Service ....G...... 570 321-8206
Williamsport *(G-19999)*

Clifford Cnc Tling Surgeon LLC ....G...... 717 528-4264
New Oxford *(G-12406)*

Construction Tool Service Inc ....G...... 814 231-3090
State College *(G-17955)*

Custom Tool & Grinding Inc ....F...... 724 223-1555
Washington *(G-19161)*

Dacval LLC ....F...... 215 331-9600
Philadelphia *(G-13601)*

▲ Dauphin Precision Tool LLC ....C...... 800 522-8665
Millersburg *(G-11192)*

Deane Carbide Products Inc ....F...... 215 639-3333
Trevose *(G-18492)*

Decherts Machine Shop Inc ....E...... 717 838-1326
Palmyra *(G-13121)*

Deetag USA Inc ....G...... 828 465-2644
Chambersburg *(G-2924)*

Dj Machining LLC ....G...... 724 938-0812
Greensburg *(G-6659)*

Dock Tool & Machine Inc ....G...... 215 338-8989
Philadelphia *(G-13638)*

Drebo America Inc ....D...... 724 938-0690
Coal Center *(G-3275)*

Dynacut Inc ....G...... 610 346-7386
Springtown *(G-17926)*

Dynamic Balancing Co Inc ....G...... 610 337-2757
King of Prussia *(G-8615)*

Eastcoast Cutter Inc ....G...... 717 933-5566
Myerstown *(G-11883)*

Elbach & Johnson Inc ....G...... 724 457-6180
Glenwillard *(G-6546)*

Electroline Corp ....E...... 215 766-2229
Pipersville *(G-14614)*

Elizabeth Carbide Components ....E...... 724 539-3574
Latrobe *(G-9474)*

▲ Ernst Hoffmann Inc ....G...... 610 593-2280
Atglen *(G-800)*

◆ Exim Steel & Shipbroking Inc ....G...... 215 369-9746
Yardley *(G-20310)*

Eysters Machine Shop Inc ....E...... 717 227-8400
Shrewsbury *(G-17583)*

F Tinker and Sons Company ....E...... 412 781-3553
Pittsburgh *(G-15000)*

Fabricating Technology Inc ....E...... 814 774-4403
Girard *(G-6388)*

Form Tool Technology Inc ....E...... 717 792-3626
York *(G-20484)*

Foust Machine & Tool ....G...... 717 766-7841
Mechanicsburg *(G-10845)*

Frazier-Simplex Machine Co ....E...... 724 222-5700
Washington *(G-19177)*

Frew Mill Die Crafts Inc ....F...... 724 658-9026
New Castle *(G-12095)*

Gasbarre Products Inc ....E...... 814 236-3108
Olanta *(G-12960)*

Gemel Precision Tool Inc ....E...... 215 355-2174
Warminster *(G-18886)*

▲ General Carbide Corporation ....C...... 724 836-3000
Greensburg *(G-6668)*

General Dynamics Ots PA Inc ....C...... 570 342-7801
Scranton *(G-17238)*

Gesco Inc ....F...... 724 846-8700
Beaver Falls *(G-999)*

▲ Greenleaf Corporation ....B...... 814 763-2915
Saegertown *(G-6915)*

Hamilton Tool Co Inc ....G...... 814 382-3419
Meadville *(G-10734)*

Harpoint Holdings Inc ....G...... 717 692-2113
Millersburg *(G-11194)*

Hewlett Manufacturing Co...............G...... 814 683-4762
Linesville *(G-9981)*

▲ Hosch Company LP ....E...... 724 695-3002
Oakdale *(G-12903)*

▲ Hy-Tech Machine Inc ....D...... 724 776-6800
Cranberry Township *(G-3823)*

Ideal Aerosmith Inc ....E...... 412 963-1495
Pittsburgh *(G-15113)*

Imex Pa LLC ....G...... 607 343-3160
Hallstead *(G-6833)*

Intra Corporation ....G...... 215 672-7003
Horsham *(G-7825)*

J & J Carbide Tool Co Inc ....G...... 570 538-9283
Watsontown *(G-19276)*

J K J Tool Co ....F...... 570 322-1411
Williamsport *(G-20026)*

▲ Jade Equipment Corporation ....C...... 215 947-3333
Huntingdon Valley *(G-7999)*

▼ Jade Holdings Inc ....C...... 215 947-3333
Huntingdon Valley *(G-8000)*

JB Anderson & Son Inc ....G...... 724 523-9610
Irwin *(G-8177)*

Jepson Precision Tool Inc ....F...... 814 756-4806
Cranesville *(G-3867)*

▲ John R Bromiley Company Inc ....E...... 215 822-7723
Chalfont *(G-2878)*

▲ JV Manufacturing Co Inc ....D...... 724 224-1704
Natrona Heights *(G-11945)*

K-Tool Inc ....F...... 717 632-3015
Gettysburg *(G-6303)*

Kdc Engineering ....G...... 267 203-8487
Telford *(G-18298)*

Kennametal Inc ....C...... 814 623-2711
Bedford *(G-1057)*

Kennametal Inc ....A...... 412 539-5000
Latrobe *(G-9486)*

Kennametal Inc ....C...... 814 624-2406
Bedford *(G-1058)*

Kennametal Inc ....C...... 276 646-0080
Bedford *(G-1059)*

Kennametal Inc ....C...... 724 864-5900
Irwin *(G-8178)*

Kennametal Inc ....F...... 724 657-1967
New Castle *(G-12112)*

▲ Kennametal Inc ....A...... 412 248-8000
Pittsburgh *(G-15169)*

Kermitool Liquidation Company ....F...... 717 846-8665
York *(G-20551)*

Kurtzs Machining LLC ....G...... 717 899-6125
Mc Veytown *(G-10653)*

Layke Tool & Manufacturing Co ....E...... 814 333-1169
Meadville *(G-10748)*

Leverwood Machine Works Inc ....F...... 717 246-4105
Red Lion *(G-16604)*

Loudon Industries Inc ....E...... 717 328-9808
Mercersburg *(G-10991)*

Madison Inds Holdings LLC ....C...... 717 762-3151
Waynesboro *(G-19416)*

▲ Magnum Carbide LLC ....G...... 717 762-7181
Waynesboro *(G-19417)*

Molinaro Tool & Die Inc ....F...... 724 654-5141
New Castle *(G-12121)*

NC Industries Inc ....F...... 248 528-5200
Reynoldsville *(G-16658)*

Niagara Cutter PA Inc ....E...... 814 653-8211
Reynoldsville *(G-16659)*

Oberg Carbide Punch & Die ....G...... 724 295-2118
Freeport *(G-6208)*

Oberg Industries Inc ....C...... 724 353-9700
Sarver *(G-17076)*

◆ Oberg Industries Inc ....A...... 724 295-2121
Freeport *(G-6209)*

Ofcg Inc ....G...... 570 655-0804
Dupont *(G-4493)*

Oppenheimer Precision Pdts Inc........D...... 215 674-9100
Horsham *(G-7837)*

Paco Winders Mfg LLC ....E...... 215 673-6265
Philadelphia *(G-14113)*

Parker Machine and Fabrication.........G...... 570 673-4160
Canton *(G-2666)*

Parker-Hannifin Corporation.............C...... 724 861-8200
Irwin *(G-8188)*

Pb Holdings Inc ....G...... 215 947-3333
Huntingdon Valley *(G-8021)*

▲ PDC Machines Inc ....D...... 215 443-9442
Warminster *(G-18937)*

Penn Scientific Products Co ....F...... 888 238-6710
Abington *(G-13)*

Penn United Technologies Inc...........E...... 724 431-2482
Sarver *(G-17078)*

Phb Inc ....A...... 814 474-5511
Fairview *(G-5837)*

▲ Pioneer Tool & Forge Inc.............F...... 724 337-4700
New Kensington *(G-12366)*

Precision Carbide Tooling Inc ....G...... 717 244-4771
Red Lion *(G-16611)*

Preform Specialties Inc ....E...... 724 459-0808
Blairsville *(G-1738)*

Pressure Innovators LLC ....G...... 215 431-6520
Warminster *(G-18945)*

Price Tool Inc ....F...... 814 763-4410
Saegertown *(G-16927)*

Product Design and Development ....E...... 717 741-4844
York *(G-20644)*

Q Company LLC ....E...... 570 966-1017
New Berlin *(G-12022)*

Quality Machine Tools LLC ....G...... 412 787-2876
Coraopolis *(G-3720)*

Quality Tool & Die Inc ....F...... 814 336-6364
Meadville *(G-10785)*

Reed Tool & Die Inc ....E...... 724 547-3500
Mount Pleasant *(G-11713)*

▲ Reiff & Nestor Company ....D...... 717 453-7113
Lykens *(G-10134)*

▲ Richter Precision Inc ....D...... 717 560-9990
East Petersburg *(G-4589)*

Rjc Manufacturing Services LLC.........G...... 724 836-3636
Irwin *(G-8197)*

Robert Boone Company ....G...... 215 362-2577
Lansdale *(G-9406)*

Ronal Tool Company Inc ....F...... 717 741-0880
York *(G-20660)*

Ruch Carbide Burs Inc ....E...... 215 657-3660
Willow Grove *(G-20139)*

Saegertown Manufacturing Corp ....C...... 814 763-2655
Saegertown *(G-16932)*

Siemens Industry Inc.....................D...... 215 646-7400
Spring House *(G-17883)*

Southco Inc ....E...... 215 957-9260
Warminster *(G-18969)*

Starlite Industries Inc ....E...... 610 527-1300
Bryn Mawr *(G-2334)*

▲ Starn Tool & Manufacturing Co ......D...... 814 724-1057
Meadville *(G-10794)*

Steven Laucks...............................G...... 717 244-6310
Red Lion *(G-16615)*

▲ Stone Supply Inc ....G...... 570 434-2076
Kingsley *(G-8708)*

▲ Sureflow Corporation ....F...... 412 828-5900
Pittsburgh *(G-15591)*

Swissaero Inc ....F...... 814 796-4166
Waterford *(G-19271)*

T-Bird McHning Fabrication LLC ....F...... 717 384-8362
York *(G-20683)*

Talbot Holdings LLC ....C...... 717 692-2113
Millersburg *(G-11202)*

TI Oregon Inc ....C...... 412 394-2800
Pittsburgh *(G-15624)*

▼ Titan Tool Company ....F...... 814 474-1583
Fairview *(G-5848)*

Trilion Quality Systems LLC ....E...... 215 710-3000
King of Prussia *(G-8690)*

▼ Uhl Technologies LLC ....G...... 814 437-6346
Franklin *(G-6166)*

Unison Engine Components Inc...........C...... 570 825-4544
Wilkes Barre *(G-19967)*

◆ Velocity Eqp Solutions LLC............F...... 800 521-1368
New Castle *(G-12162)*

Venus Machines & Tool ....G...... 570 421-4564
Stroudsburg *(G-18141)*

▲ Vista Metals Inc ....C...... 412 751-4600
McKeesport *(G-10685)*

Vista Metals Inc ....G...... 724 545-7750
Kittanning *(G-8803)*

Washington Rotating Control ....F...... 724 228-8889
Washington *(G-19243)*

Wheeler Tool Co ....G...... 570 888-2275
Athens *(G-813)*

William Lammers ....G...... 610 894-9502
Kutztown *(G-8863)*

▲ Winterthur Wendt Usa Inc ....C...... 610 495-2850
Royersford *(G-16869)*

3546 Power Hand Tools

Atsco Holdings Corp ....D...... 440 701-1021
Cranberry Township *(G-3807)*

Black & Decker (us) Inc ....F...... 215 271-0402
Philadelphia *(G-13467)*

Black & Decker (us) Inc ....G...... 717 755-3441
York *(G-20409)*

▲ Bolttech Mannings Inc ....D 724 872-4873
North Versailles *(G-12772)*

◆ Bon Tool Company ....D 724 443-7080
Gibsonia *(G-6328)*

CDI Lawn Equipment & Grdn Sup ....E 610 489-3474
Collegeville *(G-3371)*

Eaton Electric Holdings LLC ....D 717 755-2933
York *(G-20462)*

▼ Fsm Tools ....G 717 867-5359
Annville *(G-648)*

JD Delta Company Inc ....G 484 320-7600
Malvern *(G-10263)*

Kdc Engineering ....G 267 203-8487
Telford *(G-18298)*

▲ Keystone Machine Inc ....E 717 359-9256
Littlestown *(G-10068)*

▲ Lemco Tool Corporation...............E 570 494-0620
Cogan Station *(G-3361)*

Marilyn Strawser Beauty Salon ....E 717 463-2804
Thompsontown *(G-18349)*

Modern Manufacturing Co Inc ....F 215 659-4820
Willow Grove *(G-20128)*

▲ Novative Designs Inc ....G 215 794-3380
Blue Bell *(G-1850)*

R E Dupill & Associates Ltd ....G 724 845-7300
Leechburg *(G-9651)*

▲ Sanders Saws & Blades Inc ....E 610 273-3733
Honey Brook *(G-7761)*

▲ Tamco Inc ....E 724 258-6622
Monongahela *(G-11317)*

▲ Torcup Inc ....F 610 250-5800
Easton *(G-4763)*

Transportation Eqp Sup Co ....E 814 866-1952
Erie *(G-5514)*

Velocity Robotics ....G 412 254-3011
Pittsburgh *(G-15690)*

Wheeler Tool Co ....G 570 888-2275
Athens *(G-813)*

◆ Woodings Industrial Corp.............C 724 625-3131
Mars *(G-10515)*

3547 Rolling Mill Machinery & Eqpt

▲ Alpine Metal Tech N Amer Inc ....E 412 787-2832
Pittsburgh *(G-14688)*

Bailey Engineers Inc ....E 724 745-6200
Canonsburg *(G-2547)*

Custom Mfg & Indus Svcs LLC............G 412 621-2982
Pittsburgh *(G-14894)*

◆ Danieli Corporation ....D 724 778-5400
Cranberry Township *(G-3814)*

▲ Ewald A Stellrecht Inc ....F 610 363-1141
Coatesville *(G-3302)*

Fessler Machine Company ....E 724 346-0878
Sharon *(G-17433)*

Karadon Corporation ....F 724 676-5790
Blairsville *(G-1729)*

▲ Kocks Pittsburgh Corporation........G 412 367-4174
Pittsburgh *(G-15181)*

Laneko Roll Form Inc ....E 215 822-1930
Hatfield *(G-7363)*

Leman Machine Company...................E 814 736-9696
Portage *(G-15918)*

▲ Medart Inc ....E 724 752-3555
Ellwood City *(G-4946)*

Park Corporation ....G 412 472-0500
Coraopolis *(G-3711)*

Presto Packaging Inc.......................G 215 822-9598
Hatfield *(G-7386)*

Presto Packaging Inc.......................G 215 646-7514
Ambler *(G-599)*

Rotation Dynamics Corporation...........E 717 656-4252
Leola *(G-9802)*

▼ S P Kinney Engineers Inc ....E 412 276-4600
Carnegie *(G-2789)*

S S Salvage Recycling Inc ....F 717 444-0008
Liverpool *(G-10079)*

▲ Sme Sales and Service Inc...........C 724 384-1159
Beaver Falls *(G-1012)*

SMS Group Inc ....C 412 231-1200
Pittsburgh *(G-15552)*

▲ T Bruce Sales Inc ....D 724 528-9961
West Middlesex *(G-19731)*

Testa Machine Company Inc ....E 724 947-9397
Slovan *(G-17631)*

Titan Metal & Machine Co Inc ....G 724 747-9528
Washington *(G-19232)*

3548 Welding Apparatus

▲ Arcos Industries LLC...................D 570 339-5200
Mount Carmel *(G-11623)*

▲ Bestweld Inc ....E 610 718-9700
Pottstown *(G-15967)*

Branson Ultrasonics Corp ....E 610 251-9776
Paoli *(G-13136)*

▲ Direct Wire & Cable Inc ....D 717 336-2842
Denver *(G-4070)*

Electro-Glass Products Inc ....G 724 423-5000
Norvelt *(G-12878)*

ESAB Group Inc ....B 717 637-8911
Hanover *(G-6884)*

ESAB Group Inc ....E 717 637-8911
Hanover *(G-6886)*

ESAB Group Inc ....C 843 673-7700
Hanover *(G-6885)*

Garretts Fabricating ....G 724 528-8193
West Middlesex *(G-19725)*

◆ Goss Inc ....D 412 486-6100
Glenshaw *(G-6489)*

Joseph Nedorezov ....G 215 661-0600
North Wales *(G-12808)*

Joseph Nedorezov ....G 610 278-9325
Blue Bell *(G-1837)*

Matheson Tri-Gas Inc ....G 814 453-5637
Erie *(G-5382)*

New Berry Inc ....F 724 452-8040
Harmony *(G-7074)*

Nexarc Inc ....G 570 458-6990
Bloomsburg *(G-1791)*

Oaks Welding LLC ....G 570 527-7328
Ashland *(G-735)*

Omnitech Automation Inc ....E 610 965-3279
Emmaus *(G-5036)*

▲ Praxair Dist Mid-Atlantic LLC ....A 610 398-2211
Allentown *(G-355)*

Praxair Distribution Inc ....F 814 238-5092
State College *(G-18009)*

Praxair Distribution Inc ....A 610 398-2211
Allentown *(G-356)*

Stored Energy Concepts Inc.............F 610 469-6543
Saint Peters *(G-17035)*

▲ Systematics ....D 610 696-9040
West Chester *(G-19654)*

Weld Tooling Corporation ....E 412 331-1776
Canonsburg *(G-2658)*

Welding Alloys USA.........................G 724 202-7497
New Castle *(G-12167)*

▲ Weldsale Company LLC ....G 215 739-7474
Philadelphia *(G-14464)*

▲ Xcell Automation Inc....................D 717 755-6800
York *(G-20721)*

3549 Metalworking Machinery, NEC

◆ All-Fill Corporation ....D 866 255-3455
Exton *(G-5639)*

Astro Automation Inc ....G 724 864-2500
Irwin *(G-8145)*

Automated Concepts Tooling Inc........F 814 796-6302
Waterford *(G-19259)*

Automation Products Inc ....F 814 453-5841
Erie *(G-5199)*

Ay Machine Co ....F 717 733-0335
Ephrata *(G-5091)*

Bella Machine Inc ....G 570 826-9127
Wilkes Barre *(G-19908)*

▲ C I Hayes Inc ....G 814 834-2200
Saint Marys *(G-16951)*

◆ CAM Industries Inc ....E 717 637-5988
Hanover *(G-6866)*

Charles Smith ....G 724 727-3455
Apollo *(G-668)*

Cnc Technology Inc ....G 610 444-4437
Coatesville *(G-3298)*

▲ Coinco Inc ....E 814 425-7407
Cochranton *(G-3337)*

Daltech Inc ....E 570 823-9911
Hanover Township *(G-6987)*

Emp Industries Inc..........................G 215 357-5333
Warminster *(G-18871)*

◆ Exim Steel & Shipbroking Inc ....G 215 369-9746
Yardley *(G-20310)*

◆ FLS US Holdings Inc ....F 610 264-6011
Bethlehem *(G-1512)*

Frazier-Simplex Machine Co ....E 724 222-5700
Washington *(G-19177)*

Gasbarre Products Inc ....E 814 834-2200
Saint Marys *(G-16975)*

Geissele Automatics LLC..................F 610 272-2060
North Wales *(G-12803)*

Grattons Fabricating & Mfg ....G 724 527-5681
Adamsburg *(G-18)*

Holdrens Precision Machining ....F 570 358-3377
Ulster *(G-18599)*

Industrial Machine Designs Inc ....G 724 981-2707
Wheatland *(G-19838)*

J & S Machining Corp ....F 717 653-6358
Manheim *(G-10391)*

John A Manning Jr ....G 215 233-0976
Glenside *(G-6524)*

▲ Joseph Machine Company Inc ....E 717 432-3442
Dillsburg *(G-4132)*

K & N Machine Shop LLC ....G 717 624-3403
New Oxford *(G-12412)*

Keystone Diamond Blades Inc ....G 570 942-4526
Nicholson *(G-12617)*

LAY Machine and Tool Inc ....G 610 469-0928
Pottstown *(G-15952)*

▲ Leefson Tool & Die Company ....E 610 461-7772
Folcroft *(G-6008)*

◆ Mae-Eitel Inc ....D 570 366-0585
Orwigsburg *(G-13048)*

Matthews International Corp...............D 412 665-2500
Pittsburgh *(G-15265)*

▲ McC International Inc....................D 724 745-0300
Mc Donald *(G-10577)*

Mecco Partners LLC ....F 724 779-9555
Cranberry Township *(G-3835)*

MIC Industries Inc ....D 814 266-8226
Elton *(G-4960)*

Micro Miniature Manufacturing............G 724 481-1033
Butler *(G-2424)*

Omnitech Automation Inc ....E 610 965-3279
Emmaus *(G-5036)*

▲ Pannier Corporation ....E 412 323-4900
Pittsburgh *(G-15368)*

▲ Penn Engineering & Mfg Corp ....B 215 766-8853
Danboro *(G-3991)*

Precision Tool & Mfg Corp ....G 717 767-6454
Emigsville *(G-4997)*

Precision Tool and Machine Co ....F 570 868-3920
Mountain Top *(G-11772)*

▲ Readco Kurimoto LLC ....E 717 848-2801
York *(G-20652)*

Ribarchik John ....G 215 547-8901
Levittown *(G-9861)*

▲ Schake Industries Inc ....E 814 677-9333
Seneca *(G-17369)*

Scheirer Machine Company Inc..........E 412 833-6500
Bethel Park *(G-1433)*

▲ Seegrid Corporation ....D 412 379-4500
Pittsburgh *(G-15520)*

Shaffers Fabricating Inc ....G 724 583-2833
Masontown *(G-10536)*

Specialty Design & Mfg Co Inc ....E 610 779-1357
Reading *(G-16520)*

Specialty Holdings Corp ....E 610 779-1357
Reading *(G-16521)*

Steimer and Co Inc ....F 610 933-7450
Phoenixville *(G-14579)*

▲ Tool Tec Inc................................F 610 688-9086
Wayne *(G-19383)*

Universal Mch Co Pottstown Inc ....D 610 323-1810
Pottstown *(G-16062)*

▲ Weld Tooling Corporation ....D 412 331-1776
Canonsburg *(G-2657)*

Wesel Manufacturing Company ....E 570 586-8978
S Abingtn Twp *(G-16903)*

▲ Westerly Incorporated ....G 610 693-8866
Robesonia *(G-16780)*

X Material Processing Company ....G 717 968-8765
State College *(G-18042)*

Xact Metal Inc ....G 814 777-7727
State College *(G-18043)*

3552 Textile Machinery

Andrew W Nissly Inc ....G 717 393-3841
Lancaster *(G-8934)*

▲ Automated Components Intl ....E 570 344-4000
Dunmore *(G-4469)*

Aztec Machinery Company ....E 215 672-2600
Warminster *(G-18833)*

Bearing Products Company................E 215 659-4768
Philadelphia *(G-13449)*

Bell-Mark Technologies Corp ....E 717 292-5641
Dover *(G-4187)*

Caldwells of Bucks County ....E 215 345-1348
Doylestown *(G-4285)*

Elk County Machining ....G 814 781-3502
Saint Marys *(G-16969)*

▲ Finetex Rotary Engraving Inc ....G 717 273-6841
Lebanon *(G-9567)*

S I C

Frontier LLC ....F 570 265-2500
Towanda (G-18426)

Ken-Tex Corp ....E 570 374-4476
Selinsgrove (G-17328)

Miller Screen & Design Inc ....F 724 625-1870
Mars (G-10508)

No Fear Inc ....F 484 527-8000
Malvern (G-10287)

OP Schuman & Sons Inc ....D 215 343-1530
Warminster (G-18932)

Pennsylvania Sewing Res Co ....F 570 344-4000
Dunmore (G-4480)

S Morantz Inc ....D 215 969-0266
Philadelphia (G-14273)

▲ Sheerlund Products LLC ....F 484 248-2650
Reading (G-16516)

▲ Stahls Special Projects Inc ....G 724 583-1176
Masontown (G-10537)

◆ Stretch Devices Inc ....E 215 739-3000
Philadelphia (G-14352)

Strutz Fabricators Inc ....E 724 625-1501
Valencia (G-18702)

T Shirt Printer ....G 717 367-1167
Elizabethtown (G-4889)

Textured Yarn Co Inc ....G 610 444-5400
Kennett Square (G-8549)

Tsg Finishing ....F 828 850-4381
North Wales (G-12838)

▲ Westerly Incorporated ....G 610 693-8866
Robesonia (G-16780)

3553 Woodworking Machinery

Casework Cabinetry Cnstr ....G 814 236-7601
Curwensville (G-3947)

CNE Machinery Ltd ....G 814 723-1685
Warren (G-19017)

Dan Dulls Specialty Wdwkg ....G 724 843-6223
New Brighton (G-12033)

E & E Building Group LP ....F 215 453-5124
Ambler (G-578)

Econotool Inc ....G 215 947-2404
Huntingdon Valley (G-7975)

G&M Bandsaw Inc ....F 570 547-2386
Montgomery (G-11369)

▲ Hermance Machine Company ......E 570 326-9156
Williamsport (G-20021)

▲ John M Sensenig ....G 717 445-4669
New Holland (G-12255)

KB Woodcraft Inc ....G 502 533-2773
Phoenixville (G-14555)

▲ Pendu Manufacturing Inc ....E 717 354-4348
New Holland (G-12272)

Steves Refacing ....G 724 274-4740
Springdale (G-17902)

Unique Wood Creation LLC ....G 717 687-8843
Paradise (G-13163)

Unique Wood Creation LLC ....G 717 687-7900
Paradise (G-13164)

Wood Machinery Mfrs Amer ....G 215 564-3484
Philadelphia (G-14483)

3554 Paper Inds Machinery

A & F Holdings LLC ....E 215 289-8300
Feasterville Trevose (G-5880)

Accurate Die Wrks of Phldlphia .....F 610 667-9200
Penn Valley (G-13233)

▲ Andritz Inc ....C 724 597-7801
Canonsburg (G-2540)

Andritz Inc ....B 570 546-1253
Muncy (G-11806)

Andritz Inc ....B 570 546-8211
Muncy (G-11807)

▲ Elsner Engineering Works Inc ....D 717 637-5991
Hanover (G-6882)

Ferag Inc ....D 215 788-0892
Bristol (G-2144)

◆ FLS US Holdings Inc ....F 610 264-6011
Bethlehem (G-1512)

H M Spencer Wire ....G 570 726-7495
Mill Hall (G-11177)

Hobart Corporation ....E 717 397-5100
Lancaster (G-9050)

John Eppler Machine Works ....E 215 624-3400
Orwigsburg (G-13046)

Marquip Ward United ....G 570 742-7859
Milton (G-11248)

Norton Pulpstones Incorporated .....F 610 964-0544
Villanova (G-18767)

Paco Winders Mfg LLC ....E 215 673-6265
Philadelphia (G-14113)

Paper Converting Machine Co ....C 814 695-5521
Duncansville (G-4459)

Pcmc ....G 814 934-3262
Duncansville (G-4460)

◆ Sig Combibloc Inc ....E 610 546-4200
Chester (G-3062)

3555 Printing Trades Machinery & Eqpt

Advance Graphics Eqp of York .....E 717 292-9183
Dover (G-4183)

◆ Apex North America LLC ....E 866 273-9872
Donora (G-4145)

Aradiant Corporation ....G 717 838-7220
Palmyra (G-13116)

Baldwin Technology Company Inc ..G 610 829-4240
Easton (G-4648)

Bell-Mark Sales Co Inc ....E 717 292-5641
Dover (G-4186)

Chant Engineering Co Inc ....E 215 230-4260
New Britain (G-12046)

Consolidated Printing Inc ....E 215 879-1400
Philadelphia (G-13571)

Copy Rite ....G 814 644-0360
Huntingdon (G-7941)

Custom Platecrafters Inc ....F 215 997-1990
Colmar (G-3414)

David K Hart Co ....G 610 527-0388
Bryn Mawr (G-2319)

▲ Exone Company ....E 724 863-9663
North Huntingdon (G-12769)

Expert Pr-Press Consulting Ltd ......G 484 401-9821
Downingtown (G-4227)

Ferag Inc ....D 215 788-0892
Bristol (G-2144)

Global Inserting Systems LLC ....E 610 217-3019
Emmaus (G-5027)

◆ Glunz & Jensen K&F Inc ....C 267 227-3493
Quakertown (G-16198)

H D Sampey Inc ....G 215 723-3471
Telford (G-18293)

J & J Specialties of PA ....F 717 838-7220
Palmyra (G-13126)

Jls Automation LLC ....E 717 505-3800
York (G-20541)

Kba North America Inc ....C 717 505-1150
York (G-20548)

Kennett Advance Printing House .....G 610 444-5840
Kennett Square (G-8519)

Keystone Printing Services ....G 215 675-6464
Hatboro (G-7289)

Lycoming Screen Printing Co ....G 570 326-3301
Williamsport (G-20038)

▲ Manugraph Americas Inc ....E 717 362-3243
Millersville (G-11195)

Marcus Uppe Inc ....E 412 261-4233
Pittsburgh (G-15253)

Matthews International Corp ....D 412 665-2500
Pittsburgh (G-15265)

▲ Muller Martini Mailroom ....C 610 266-7000
Allentown (G-323)

R W Hartnett Company ....E 215 969-9190
Philadelphia (G-14228)

Recognition Engraving ....G 717 242-1166
Lewistown (G-9946)

Rotation Dynamics Corporation ......F 717 464-2724
Willow Street (G-20156)

S Morantz Inc ....D 215 969-0266
Philadelphia (G-14273)

Sh Quints Sons Company ....F 215 533-1988
Philadelphia (G-14295)

Southern Graphic Systems LLC .....C 215 843-2243
Philadelphia (G-14325)

▲ Susquehanna Glass Co ....E 717 684-2155
Columbia (G-3451)

▲ W O Hickok Manufacturing Co .....E 717 234-8041
Harrisburg (G-7243)

Wood Specialty Company Inc ....F 610 539-6384
Norristown (G-12724)

3556 Food Prdts Machinery

◆ Abec Inc ....C 610 882-1541
Bethlehem (G-1442)

Allen Gauge & Tool Company ....E 412 241-6410
Pittsburgh (G-14684)

▲ American Waffle Company LLC .....E 717 632-6000
Hanover (G-6860)

▲ Arcobaleno LLC ....F 717 394-1402
Lancaster (G-8937)

B & J Sheet Metal Inc ....F 215 538-9543
Trumbauersville (G-18529)

Beverage-Air Corporation ....C 814 849-7336
Brookville (G-2250)

▲ Boardroom Spirits LLC ....G 215 815-5351
Lansdale (G-9348)

Bog Turtle Brewery LLC ....G 484 758-0416
Oxford (G-13072)

◆ Boy Machines Inc ....E 610 363-9121
Exton (G-5656)

◆ Bradford Allegheny Corporation ...C 814 362-2590
Lewis Run (G-9871)

Bradford Allegheny Corporation ......D 814 362-2593
Lewis Run (G-9874)

Captain Chuckys Crab Cake Co I ..G 610 355-7525
Newtown Square (G-12569)

Chop - Rite Two Inc ....F 215 256-4620
Harleysville (G-7027)

Christmas City Spirits LLC ....G 484 893-0590
Bethlehem (G-1484)

Conair Corporation ....D 717 485-4871
Mc Connellsburg (G-10563)

Craft Manufacturing Inc ....F 724 532-2702
Latrobe (G-9467)

D Cooper Works LLC ....G 717 733-4220
Ephrata (G-5099)

Eastern Bakery Equipment Co ....F 717 938-8278
York Haven (G-20758)

Fairfield Confectionery ....G 724 654-3888
New Castle (G-12091)

◆ Gemini Bakery Equipment Co ....D 215 673-3520
Philadelphia (G-13747)

Gold Medal Products Co ....G 412 787-1030
Pittsburgh (G-15056)

Graybill Machines Inc ....E 717 626-5221
Lititz (G-10013)

Idreco USA Ltd ....F 610 701-9944
West Chester (G-19566)

▲ Insinger Machine Company ....D 215 624-4800
Philadelphia (G-13860)

JD Product Solutions LLC ....G 570 234-9421
Bartonsville (G-947)

John Bean Technologies Corp ....C 215 822-4600
Chalfont (G-2877)

▲ KB Systems Inc ....D 610 588-7788
Bangor (G-919)

▲ Krishna Protects Cows Inc ....G 717 527-4101
Port Royal (G-15910)

▲ Le Jo Enterprises Incorporated ....E 484 921-9000
Phoenixville (G-14559)

◆ Lee Industries Inc ....C 814 342-0460
Philipsburg (G-14519)

◆ Mallet and Company Inc ....G 412 276-9000
Carnegie (G-2776)

▲ Mgs Inc ....C 717 336-7528
Denver (G-4083)

N C Stauffer & Sons Inc ....D 570 945-3047
Factoryville (G-5758)

New York Bagelry ....G 610 678-6420
Reading (G-16455)

ODonnell Metal Fabricators ....F 610 279-8810
Norristown (G-12697)

▲ Oshikiri Corporation America ....F 215 637-6005
Philadelphia (G-14103)

Packaging Progressions Inc ....E 610 489-9096
Souderton (G-17758)

Pittsburgh Bakery Equipment Co .....G 724 533-2158
Volant (G-18776)

Purcell Company ....E 717 838-5611
Palmyra (G-13130)

◆ Reading Bakery Systems Inc ....D 610 693-5816
Robesonia (G-16778)

Santucci Process Development ....G 412 787-0747
Mc Kees Rocks (G-10633)

Schnupps Grain Roasting LLC ....F 717 865-6611
Lebanon (G-9627)

Smokers Outlet ....G 814 827-1104
Titusville (G-18396)

▼ Top Line Process Equipment ....D 814 362-4626
Bradford (G-1994)

Victoria Orchard LLC ....G 610 873-2848
Downingtown (G-4260)

Win-Holt Equipment Corp ....C 516 222-0335
Allentown (G-436)

▲ Woody Associates Inc ....F 717 843-3975
York (G-20720)

3559 Special Ind Machinery, NEC

▲ Abps, Inc. ....E 800 552-9980
Exton (G-5635)

Acme Cryogenics Inc ....E 610 966-4488
Alburtis (G-49)

▲ Acme Cryogenics Inc..................D...... 610 966-4488
   Allentown *(G-114)*

▲ Alexanderwerk Inc.....................G...... 215 442-0270
   Montgomeryville *(G-11383)*

Allegheny Fabg & Sups Inc..............G...... 412 828-3320
   Pittsburgh *(G-14678)*

▲ Allegheny Plastics Inc.................C...... 412 741-4416
   Leetsdale *(G-9679)*

Allegheny-Wagner Inds Inc..............E...... 724 468-4300
   Delmont *(G-4047)*

Allied Foam Tech Corp.................G...... 215 540-2666
   Montgomeryville *(G-11384)*

▲ Andritz Herr-Voss Stamco Inc.......C...... 724 538-3180
   Callery *(G-2466)*

▲ Angstrom Sciences Inc................E...... 412 469-8466
   Duquesne *(G-4495)*

Approved Info Destruction Inc...........G...... 412 722-8124
   Bethel Park *(G-1403)*

Astro Automation Inc..................G...... 724 864-2500
   Irwin *(G-8145)*

Berner Industries Inc.................F...... 724 924-9240
   New Castle *(G-12062)*

Bethlehem Apparatus Co Inc............G...... 610 882-2611
   Bethlehem *(G-1460)*

Bethlehem Apparatus Co Inc............E...... 610 838-7034
   Bethlehem *(G-1461)*

Bethlehem Hydrogen Inc................G...... 610 762-1706
   Northampton *(G-12845)*

▼ Billco Manufacturing Inc.............C...... 724 452-7390
   Zelienople *(G-20792)*

Biokinetics Inc......................G...... 570 538-3089
   Dewart *(G-4118)*

▼ Blue Valley Industries Inc............G...... 717 436-8266
   Port Royal *(G-15909)*

◆ Bradford Allegheny Corporation......C...... 814 362-2590
   Lewis Run *(G-9871)*

Brockport Glass Components LLC........G...... 814 265-1479
   Brockport *(G-2220)*

Camden Iron & Metal Inc...............G...... 215 952-1500
   Philadelphia *(G-13495)*

◆ Cannon U S A Inc....................E...... 724 772-5600
   Cranberry Township *(G-3810)*

Cannon U S A Inc.....................G...... 724 452-5358
   Zelienople *(G-20794)*

Carl Strutz & Company Inc.............E...... 724 625-1501
   Mars *(G-10489)*

Carl Strutz & Company Inc.............D...... 724 625-1501
   Mars *(G-10490)*

Carlson Erie Corporation...............F...... 814 455-2768
   Erie *(G-5220)*

Castec Inc...........................G...... 724 258-8700
   Monongahela *(G-11306)*

Ccr Electronics......................G...... 317 469-4855
   Pittsburgh *(G-14832)*

Chant Engineering Co Inc..............E...... 215 230-4260
   New Britain *(G-12046)*

▼ Chemcut Corporation................B...... 814 272-2800
   State College *(G-17950)*

◆ Chemcut Holdings LLC...............D...... 814 272-2800
   State College *(G-17951)*

Chestnut Rd Lumber & Dry Kiln.........G...... 717 423-5941
   Newburg *(G-12474)*

Churchville Mech Assoc LLC............G...... 267 231-5968
   Southampton *(G-17803)*

City of Pittsburgh....................E...... 412 255-2330
   Pittsburgh *(G-14855)*

Clearfield Machine Company.............F...... 814 765-6544
   Clearfield *(G-3214)*

Collegecart Innovations Inc............G...... 215 813-3900
   Holland *(G-7640)*

▲ Conair Group Inc....................E...... 724 584-5500
   Cranberry Township *(G-3811)*

Cryocal.............................G...... 714 568-0201
   Imperial *(G-8061)*

▲ Cryogenic Gas Technologies Inc......E...... 610 530-7288
   Allentown *(G-188)*

Crystalplex Corporation................G...... 412 787-1525
   Pittsburgh *(G-14889)*

Dartonya Manufacturing Inc............G...... 814 849-3240
   Brookville *(G-2260)*

▲ Ddm Novastar Inc...................E...... 610 337-3050
   Warminster *(G-18855)*

▼ Economy Industrial Corporation......G...... 724 266-5720
   Ambridge *(G-616)*

◆ Efco Inc...........................E...... 814 455-3941
   Erie *(G-5256)*

Electro-Optical Systems Inc............F...... 610 935-5838
   Phoenixville *(G-14547)*

Emp Industries Inc...................G...... 215 357-5333
   Warminster *(G-18871)*

◆ Eriez Manufacturing Co..............B...... 814 835-6000
   Erie *(G-5280)*

Eriez Manufacturing Co................G...... 814 520-8540
   Erie *(G-5281)*

Federal-Mogul Motorparts LLC..........G...... 717 430-5021
   York *(G-20479)*

◆ FLS US Holdings Inc.................F...... 610 264-6011
   Bethlehem *(G-1512)*

▲ Fluid Energy Proc & Eqp Co..........G...... 215 721-8990
   Telford *(G-18289)*

Fluid Energy Proc & Eqp Co............D...... 215 368-2510
   Hatfield *(G-7343)*

Frontier LLC.........................F...... 570 265-2500
   Towanda *(G-18426)*

Garl Machine & Fabrication Inc.........G...... 610 929-7886
   Temple *(G-18330)*

▼ GE Infrastructure Sensing............F...... 617 926-1749
   Feasterville Trevose *(G-5912)*

Gil Prebelli.........................F...... 215 281-0300
   Philadelphia *(G-13762)*

▼ Global Chem Feed Solutions LLC.....E...... 215 675-2777
   Warminster *(G-18888)*

Global Machine and Maint LLC..........G...... 215 356-3077
   Rydal *(G-16885)*

◆ Graham Engineering Corporation.....C...... 717 848-3755
   York *(G-20507)*

Handygas Corporation.................G...... 717 428-2506
   Seven Valleys *(G-17379)*

◆ Hanover Prest-Paving Company.......E...... 717 637-0500
   Hanover *(G-6900)*

▼ Herr Industrial Inc..................E...... 717 569-6619
   Lititz *(G-10016)*

◆ Hn Automotive Inc...................D...... 570 724-5191
   Wellsboro *(G-19465)*

Hub Parking Technology USA Inc........E...... 724 772-2400
   Warrendale *(G-19082)*

Hunter Engineering Company............D...... 610 330-9024
   Easton *(G-4702)*

Iheadbones Inc.......................G...... 888 866-0807
   Newtown *(G-12512)*

▲ Ilsemann Corp......................G...... 610 323-4143
   Pottstown *(G-16000)*

◆ International Marketing Inc...........F...... 717 264-5819
   Chambersburg *(G-2942)*

Ipeg Inc............................E...... 814 437-6861
   Franklin *(G-6140)*

Isaac Stephens & Assoc Inc............G...... 215 576-5414
   Oreland *(G-13024)*

J-Mar Metal Fabricating Co.............G...... 215 785-6521
   Croydon *(G-3920)*

Jay-Ell Industries Inc.................F...... 610 326-0921
   Pottstown *(G-16005)*

Jet Plate Inc........................F...... 610 373-6600
   Reading *(G-16414)*

▲ Kercher Industries Inc...............E...... 717 273-2111
   Lebanon *(G-9592)*

Kleen Line Service Co Inc..............G...... 412 466-6277
   Dravosburg *(G-4351)*

Kras Corporation.....................E...... 610 566-0271
   Media *(G-10935)*

Kuper Technologies LLC................G...... 610 358-5120
   Garnet Valley *(G-6266)*

▲ Kurt J Lesker Company...............C...... 412 387-9200
   Jefferson Hills *(G-8277)*

Ladisch Corporation Inc...............C...... 267 313-4189
   Alburtis *(G-55)*

▲ LB Bohle LLC.......................F...... 215 957-1240
   Warminster *(G-18911)*

◆ Lee Industries Inc...................C...... 814 342-0460
   Philipsburg *(G-14519)*

Lime Kiln AG LLC.....................G...... 610 589-4302
   Womelsdorf *(G-20207)*

M A Hanna Color......................F...... 610 317-3300
   Bethlehem *(G-1563)*

▲ McC International Inc................D...... 724 745-0300
   Mc Donald *(G-10577)*

Mega Enterprises Inc..................G...... 610 380-0255
   Parkesburg *(G-13179)*

Microprocess Technolgies LLC...........G...... 570 778-0925
   Palm *(G-13095)*

Mivatek Global LLC...................F...... 610 358-5120
   Chadds Ford *(G-2856)*

Molded Fiber Glass Companies..........C...... 814 683-4500
   Linesville *(G-9984)*

Montgmrys Atomtn Parts Sls Svc.......G...... 724 368-3001
   Portersville *(G-15933)*

Mzp Kiln Services Inc.................G...... 724 318-8653
   Ambridge *(G-629)*

Naura Akrion Inc.....................D...... 610 391-9200
   Allentown *(G-325)*

Nestor Systems International............G...... 610 767-5000
   Treichlers *(G-18477)*

New Precision Technology Inc...........G...... 412 596-5948
   Pittsburgh *(G-15334)*

Ntec Inc............................G...... 215 768-0261
   Newtown *(G-12529)*

Orchem Pumps Inc....................G...... 215 743-6352
   Philadelphia *(G-14101)*

Pds Paint Inc........................F...... 717 393-5838
   Lancaster *(G-9161)*

Plastrac Inc.........................G...... 610 356-3000
   Edgemont *(G-4807)*

Powder Coating Specialists LLC.........G...... 717 968-1479
   York *(G-20635)*

Primaxx Inc.........................E...... 610 336-0314
   Allentown *(G-359)*

Production Systems Automtn LLC........E...... 570 602-4200
   Duryea *(G-4506)*

▲ Quantum Engineered Pdts Inc........E...... 724 352-5100
   Saxonburg *(G-17093)*

R-V Industries Inc....................G...... 800 552-9980
   Exton *(G-5726)*

▲ Rapid Granulator Inc.................G...... 724 584-5220
   Leetsdale *(G-9702)*

Rapid Granulator Inc..................F...... 814 437-6861
   Franklin *(G-6154)*

◆ Rbna Fluid Exchange Inc.............E...... 717 840-0678
   York *(G-20651)*

Riethmiller Lumber Mfg Corp............G...... 724 946-8608
   New Wilmington *(G-12469)*

Rocksolid Installation Inc..............G...... 717 548-8700
   Peach Bottom *(G-13201)*

▲ Rusmar Incorporated................F...... 610 436-4314
   West Chester *(G-19632)*

S K P Company.......................G...... 570 344-0561
   Scranton *(G-17281)*

◆ Schutte Koerting Acquisition.........E...... 215 639-0900
   Trevose *(G-18502)*

◆ Sergood Corp.......................G...... 724 772-5600
   Cranberry Township *(G-3849)*

Shenango Auto Mall LLC...............C...... 724 698-7304
   New Castle *(G-12150)*

Shredstation Express of Montgo.........G...... 215 723-1694
   Franconia *(G-6110)*

Simkins Corporation..................E...... 215 739-4033
   Jenkintown *(G-8301)*

Specialty Automation Inc...............G...... 215 453-0817
   Perkasie *(G-13295)*

Specialty Measurements Inc.............F...... 908 534-1500
   Bethlehem *(G-1623)*

Stanko Products Inc...................F...... 724 834-8080
   Greensburg *(G-6717)*

Steq America LLC.....................G...... 267 644-5477
   Doylestown *(G-4339)*

◆ Suez Wts Systems Usa Inc............B...... 781 359-7000
   Trevose *(G-18505)*

▲ Sumitomo Shi Crygnics Amer Inc.....D...... 610 791-6700
   Allentown *(G-404)*

Sunoco (R&m) LLC....................E...... 215 339-2000
   Philadelphia *(G-14356)*

Technical Process & Engrg Inc..........G...... 570 386-4777
   Lehighton *(G-9730)*

Thyssnkrupp Indus Slutions USA.........D...... 412 257-8277
   Bridgeville *(G-2095)*

▲ Tm Industrial Supply Inc.............E...... 814 453-5014
   Erie *(G-5510)*

Tsb Nclear Enrgy USA Group Inc........G...... 412 374-4111
   Cranberry Township *(G-3859)*

United Plastics Machinery Inc...........E...... 610 363-0990
   Exton *(G-5742)*

▼ Veeco Precision Surfc Proc LLC.......D...... 215 328-0700
   Horsham *(G-7863)*

Victaulic Company of America............C...... 610 966-3966
   Alburtis *(G-58)*

Vmf Inc.............................E...... 570 575-0997
   Scranton *(G-17310)*

Waupaca Foundry Inc..................D...... 570 724-5191
   Tioga *(G-18367)*

Waupaca Foundry Inc..................B...... 570 827-3245
   Tioga *(G-18368)*

Wepco Inc...........................G...... 570 368-8184
   Pittston *(G-15784)*

West Pharmaceutical Services D.........E...... 610 594-2900
   Exton *(G-5747)*

Wiggins Shredding Inc.................G...... 610 692-8327
   West Chester *(G-19677)*

▲ Wise Machine Co Inc.................E...... 724 287-2705
   Butler *(G-2450)*

SIC

3561 Pumps & Pumping Eqpt

▲ Airgas Safety Inc ....C....... 215 826-9000
Levittown (G-9814)

American Pipe and Supply LLC ...G....... 724 228-6360
Washington (G-19148)

▲ Ampco-Pittsburgh Corporation ....D....... 412 456-4400
Carnegie (G-2763)

▲ Amt Pump Company ....E....... 610 948-3800
Royersford (G-16842)

◆ Asm Industries Inc ....G....... 717 656-2161
Lancaster (G-8945)

Asm Industries Inc ....E....... 717 656-2166
Leola (G-9769)

Asm Industries Inc ....E....... 717 656-2161
Lancaster (G-8946)

Barebo Inc ....E....... 610 965-6018
Emmaus (G-5020)

C W S Inc ....G....... 800 800-7867
North East (G-12734)

▲ C-B Tool Co ....E....... 717 397-3521
Lancaster (G-8967)

C-B Tool Co ....E....... 717 393-3953
Lancaster (G-8968)

▼ Campbell Manufacturing Inc ....D....... 610 367-2107
Bechtelsville (G-1030)

◆ Campbell Manufacturing LLC ....E....... 610 367-2107
Bechtelsville (G-1031)

Chant Engineering Co Inc ....E....... 215 230-4260
New Britain (G-12046)

◆ Chesterfield Special Cylinders ....E....... 832 252-1082
Pittsburgh (G-14847)

Coleman Water Services ....G....... 814 382-8004
Meadville (G-10713)

Compressed Air Specialists Co ....G....... 814 835-2420
Erie (G-5230)

▲ Curtiss-Wright Electro- ....A....... 724 275-5000
Cheswick (G-3105)

Curtiss-Wright Electro- ....D....... 610 997-6400
Bethlehem (G-1493)

Derbyshire Marine Products LLC ....G....... 267 222-8900
Harleysville (G-7030)

Ds Fabrication ....G....... 717 529-2282
Kirkwood (G-8748)

Dynaflo Inc ....G....... 610 200-8017
Reading (G-16367)

▲ Eastern Industrial Pdts Inc ....E....... 610 459-1212
Aston (G-760)

Ecotech Inc ....D....... 610 954-8480
Allentown (G-202)

▲ Ecotech Marine LLC ....F....... 610 954-8480
Allentown (G-203)

Fessler Machine Company ....G....... 412 367-3663
Sharon (G-17434)

▲ Finish Thompson Inc ....E....... 814 455-4478
Erie (G-5290)

Flowserve Corporation ....D....... 570 451-2200
S Abingtn Twp (G-16896)

Flowserve Corporation ....F....... 908 859-7408
Bethlehem (G-1511)

Flowserve Corporation ....D....... 570 451-2325
Moosic (G-11505)

Flowserve Corporation ....D....... 412 257-4600
Bridgeville (G-2064)

Four Guys Stnless Tank Eqp Inc ....D....... 814 634-8373
Meyersdale (G-11010)

▲ Fresh Link Industrial Ltd ....G....... 724 779-6880
Cranberry Township (G-3819)

Gardner Denver Nash LLC ....E....... 724 239-1522
Charleroi (G-3014)

Gardner Denver Nash LLC ....G....... 203 459-3923
Charleroi (G-3015)

Goulds Pumps LLC ....C....... 570 875-2660
Ashland (G-730)

Greentree Machine Works ....E....... 717 786-4047
Quarryville (G-16271)

Hannmann Machinery Systems Inc ....E....... 610 583-6900
Folcroft (G-6005)

Hoover Pump Works ....G....... 717 733-0630
Ephrata (G-5110)

◆ Hydra-Tech Pumps Inc ....F....... 570 645-3779
Nesquehoning (G-12005)

◆ Hydro-Pac Inc ....E....... 814 474-1511
Fairview (G-5829)

Idac Corporation ....G....... 570 534-4400
Sciota (G-17181)

Industrial Service Co Ltd ....F....... 484 373-0410
Easton (G-4705)

Ingersoll-Rand Company ....D....... 717 532-9181
Chambersburg (G-2941)

Ingersoll-Rand Company ....E....... 410 238-0542
Shrewsbury (G-17584)

Instech Laboratories Inc ....E....... 610 941-0132
Plymouth Meeting (G-15852)

Integrated Envmtl Tech Inc ....G....... 412 298-5845
Washington (G-19185)

ITT Water & Wastewater USA Inc ....E....... 610 647-6620
Malvern (G-10256)

▼ Jaeco Fluid Solutions Inc ....G....... 610 407-7207
Malvern (G-10258)

▼ Johnson March Systems Inc ....E....... 215 364-2500
Warminster (G-18903)

Keystone Containment Contrs LP ....F....... 412 921-2070
Pittsburgh (G-15175)

Kitco Tool Inc ....G....... 570 726-6190
Mill Hall (G-11178)

Lionheart Holdings LLC ....D....... 215 283-8400
Newtown (G-12519)

Lonergan Pump Systems Inc ....G....... 610 770-2050
Allentown (G-300)

◆ Maguire Products Inc ....E....... 610 459-4300
Aston (G-773)

Manchester Township ....G....... 717 779-0297
York (G-20577)

Masterflo Pump Inc ....G....... 724 443-1122
Gibsonia (G-6347)

▲ Megator Corporation ....G....... 412 963-9200
Pittsburgh (G-15275)

Met-Pro Technologies LLC ....D....... 215 723-4700
Telford (G-18304)

▲ Milton Roy LLC ....C....... 215 441-0800
Ivyland (G-8218)

Milton Roy LLC ....G....... 215 293-0401
Ivyland (G-8219)

Monarch Precast Concrete Corp ....E....... 610 435-6746
Allentown (G-320)

Neac Compressor Svcs USA Inc ....G....... 814 437-3711
Franklin (G-6150)

Neco Equipment Company ....E....... 215 721-2200
Malvern (G-10284)

Neptune Pump Manufacturing Co ....G....... 484 901-4100
Pottstown (G-15955)

▲ Netzsch Pumps North Amer LLC ....E....... 610 363-8010
Exton (G-5714)

Orchem Pumps Inc ....G....... 215 743-6352
Philadelphia (G-14101)

Orr Screw Machine Products ....E....... 724 668-2256
Greensburg (G-6695)

▲ PDC Machines Inc ....D....... 215 443-9442
Warminster (G-18937)

Pump Shop Inc ....G....... 610 431-6570
West Chester (G-19623)

Pump Station Ridgway ....G....... 814 772-3251
Ridgway (G-16725)

Service Filtration Corp ....E....... 717 656-2161
Lancaster (G-9194)

Shippensburg Pump Co Inc ....E....... 717 532-7321
Shippensburg (G-17549)

Skc Inc ....D....... 724 260-0741
Eighty Four (G-4849)

Spirax Sarco Inc ....G....... 610 807-3500
Center Valley (G-2831)

Springer Pumps LLC ....F....... 484 949-2900
Telford (G-18319)

▲ Travaini Pumps USA Inc ....E....... 757 988-3930
Norristown (G-12720)

Vacuum Works LLC ....G....... 570 202-8407
East Stroudsburg (G-4637)

Watson McDaniel Company ....G....... 610 367-7191
Boyertown (G-1935)

Weatherford Artificia ....E....... 570 308-3400
Muncy (G-11838)

◆ Weir Hazleton Inc ....D....... 570 455-7711
Hazleton (G-7537)

◆ Whittco Inc ....F....... 570 645-3779
Nesquehoning (G-12011)

Xylem Water Solutions USA Inc ....F....... 724 452-6300
Zelienople (G-20828)

3562 Ball & Roller Bearings

Barkby Group Inc ....G....... 717 292-4148
Dover (G-4185)

▲ Bearing Service Company PA ....D....... 412 963-7710
Pittsburgh (G-14758)

▲ Cbh of Lancaster Company ....D....... 717 569-0485
Manheim (G-10375)

Hollow Ball Group LLC ....G....... 215 822-3380
Hatfield (G-7351)

Keystone North Inc ....E....... 570 662-3882
Mansfield (G-10420)

Kingsbury Inc ....E....... 215 824-4000
Philadelphia (G-13939)

Metalkraft Industries Inc ....E....... 570 724-6800
Wellsboro (G-19469)

Penn A Caster Loft Offices ....G....... 412 471-3285
Pittsburgh (G-15373)

Precision Metal Pdts Co Inc ....F....... 724 758-5555
Ellwood City (G-4947)

Proform Powdered Metals Inc ....E....... 814 938-7411
Punxsutawney (G-16154)

Royersford Fndry & Mch Co Inc ....E....... 610 935-7200
Phoenixville (G-14576)

◆ Scheerer Bearing Corporation ....E....... 215 443-5252
Willow Grove (G-20140)

Scheerer Bearing Corporation ....E....... 215 443-5252
Horsham (G-7848)

SKF Motion Technologies LLC ....E....... 267 436-6000
Lansdale (G-9411)

Timken Company ....G....... 215 654-7606
Malvern (G-10331)

Tribology Systems ....G....... 610 466-7547
Warminster (G-18985)

3563 Air & Gas Compressors

◆ Aerzen USA Corp ....D....... 610 380-0244
Coatesville (G-3285)

▲ Air Products Corporation ....D....... 800 345-8207
Exton (G-5637)

Applied Equipment Co ....G....... 610 258-7941
Easton (G-4646)

Atlas Copco Compressors LLC ....E....... 610 916-4002
Reading (G-16325)

Barts Pneumatics Corp ....G....... 717 392-1568
Lancaster (G-8949)

Blue Mtn A Comprsr Svcs LLC ....G....... 717 423-5262
Shippensburg (G-17519)

C H Reed Inc ....E....... 717 632-4261
Hanover (G-6865)

C H Reed Inc ....G....... 412 380-1334
Monroeville (G-11326)

Cameron Compression Systems ....G....... 610 265-2410
King of Prussia (G-8590)

▲ Cersell Company LLC ....G....... 484 753-2655
Exton (G-5661)

▲ CFM Air Inc ....G....... 814 539-6922
Johnstown (G-8365)

Chant Engineering Co Inc ....E....... 215 230-4260
New Britain (G-12046)

Cmpressed A Zeks Solutions LLC ....C....... 610 692-9100
West Chester (G-19526)

Columbia Industries Inc ....E....... 570 520-4048
Berwick (G-1318)

Compressed Air Systems Inc ....G....... 215 340-1307
Pipersville (G-14613)

Diversified Air Systems Inc ....G....... 724 873-0884
Washington (G-19164)

Dresser-Rand Company ....E....... 215 441-0400
Horsham (G-7810)

Dynaflo Inc ....G....... 610 200-8017
Reading (G-16367)

Earl E Knox Company ....F....... 814 459-2754
Erie (G-5254)

Earl E Knox Company ....E....... 814 459-2754
Erie (G-5255)

◆ Elliott Company ....A....... 724 527-2811
Jeannette (G-8254)

Elliott Company ....D....... 724 379-5440
Donora (G-4155)

Flsmidth Inc ....C....... 717 665-2224
Manheim (G-10385)

◆ Fs-Elliott Co LLC ....B....... 724 387-3200
Export (G-5604)

Fs-North America Inc ....G....... 724 387-3200
Export (G-5605)

Gap Pollution & Envmtl Ctrl ....E....... 814 266-9469
Johnstown (G-8375)

Gardner Denver Nash LLC ....G....... 203 459-3923
Charleroi (G-3015)

▲ Gas & Air Systems Inc ....F....... 610 838-9625
Hellertown (G-7556)

▲ General Air Products Inc ....E....... 610 524-8950
Exton (G-5685)

▲ Howden Compressors Inc ....F....... 610 313-9800
Plymouth Meeting (G-15849)

◆ Hydro-Pac Inc ....E....... 814 474-1511
Fairview (G-5829)

Ingersoll-Rand Company ....E....... 410 238-0542
Shrewsbury (G-17584)

▲ Jenny Products Inc ....E....... 814 445-3400
Somerset (G-17693)

Kingsly Compression Inc......................E 724 524-1840
Saxonburg (G-17091)

▲ Knox-Western Inc ....G 814 459-2754
Erie (G-5348)

▲ Leybold USA Inc ....D 724 327-5700
Export (G-5616)

Maxpro Technologies Inc ....F 814 474-9191
Fairview (G-5833)

Myers Vacuum Repair Svcs Inc ....F 724 545-8331
Kittanning (G-8785)

Neac Compressor Svcs USA Inc ....G 814 437-3711
Franklin (G-6150)

Nordson Corporation ....B 610 829-4240
Easton (G-4733)

▲ PDC Machines Inc ....D 215 443-9442
Warminster (G-18937)

Polvac Corp ....G 610 625-1505
Bethlehem (G-1601)

Smuckers Sales & Services LLC ....G 717 354-4158
New Holland (G-12285)

Spray-Tek Inc ....E 610 814-2922
Bethlehem (G-1627)

Stauffer Compressor N Machine ....G 717 733-4128
Ephrata (G-5146)

▲ Travaini Pumps USA Inc ....E 757 988-3930
Norristown (G-12720)

Vacuum Works LLC ....G 570 202-8407
East Stroudsburg (G-4637)

◆ Van Air Inc ....E 814 774-2631
Lake City (G-8909)

Ventwell Inc ....G 717 683-1477
York (G-20697)

3564 Blowers & Fans

Advanced Design and Ctrl Corp............F 215 723-7200
Souderton (G-17720)

Advanced Industrial Tech Corp ....F 201 483-7235
Langhorne (G-9273)

▲ Air Dynmics Indus Systems Corp .....F 717 854-4050
York (G-20370)

Air Turbine Propeller Company ....E 724 452-9540
Zelienople (G-20787)

▲ Air/Tak Inc ....F 724 297-3416
Worthington (G-20226)

▲ Aircon Filter Sales & Svc Co ....E 215 922-7727
Philadelphia (G-13359)

Beach Filter Products Inc ....G 717 235-1136
Hanover (G-6862)

Berner International LLC ....E 724 658-3551
New Castle (G-12063)

Bradford Allegheny Corporation ....D 814 362-2593
Lewis Run (G-9874)

Brentwood Industries Inc ....D 717 274-1827
Lebanon (G-9548)

◆ Calgon Carbon Corporation ....C 412 787-6700
Moon Township (G-11482)

Calgon Carbon Corporation..................B 412 787-6700
Pittsburgh (G-14803)

▲ Ceco Filters Inc ....F 215 723-8155
Telford (G-18272)

◆ Centria Inc ....C 412 299-8000
Moon Township (G-11483)

Clarcor Air Filtration Pdts ....D 570 602-6274
Pittston (G-15745)

▼ Clark Filter Inc ....G 717 285-5941
Lancaster (G-8979)

Coil Specialty Co Inc ....E 814 234-7044
State College (G-17952)

Diamond Power Intl Inc ....D 484 875-1600
Exton (G-5667)

Eastern Manufacturing LLC ....G 215 702-3600
Langhorne (G-9292)

▲ Excelsior Blower Systems Inc ....F 610 921-9558
Blandon (G-1753)

Exhaust Track Inc ....G 215 675-1021
Warminster (G-18875)

Filter Service & Installation..................G 724 274-5220
Cheswick (G-3109)

Filter Technology Inc ....G 866 992-9490
Gladwyne (G-6407)

Flsmidth Inc ....A 610 264-6101
Bethlehem (G-1513)

▼ Full-On Filters ....G 610 970-4701
Pottstown (G-15989)

G-O-Metric Incorporated ....G 814 376-6940
Philipsburg (G-14514)

Galaxy Global Products LLC ....G 610 692-7400
West Chester (G-19557)

Gardner Denver Holdings Inc ....F 814 742-9600
Altoona (G-509)

◆ General Air Products Inc ....E 610 524-8950
Exton (G-5685)

▼ Hauck Manufacturing Company ....D 717 272-3051
Cleona (G-3244)

Historic York Inc ....G 717 843-0320
York (G-20523)

▲ Hydra-Matic Packing Co Inc ....E 215 676-2992
Huntingdon Valley (G-7995)

Imperial Systems Inc ....E 724 662-2801
Mercer (G-10964)

▲ Jadco Manufacturing Inc ....E 724 452-5252
Harmony (G-7070)

Jaybird Manufacturing Inc ....G 814 364-1800
Centre Hall (G-2842)

▼ Johnson March Systems Inc ....E 215 364-2500
Warminster (G-18903)

Kottcamp Sheet Metal ....E 717 845-7616
York (G-20558)

Laminar Flow Inc ....D 215 672-0232
Warminster (G-18909)

◆ Lasko Products LLC ....G 610 692-7400
West Chester (G-19588)

Lifeaire Systems LLC ....G 484 224-3042
Allentown (G-295)

Loranger International Corp ....D 814 723-2250
Warren (G-19038)

Luftrol Inc ....G 215 355-0532
Warminster (G-18914)

M & M Sheet Metal Inc ....F 570 326-4655
Williamsport (G-20039)

◆ Marg Inc ....F 724 703-3020
Oakdale (G-12906)

Mas Engineering LLC ....F 724 652-1367
New Castle (G-12120)

Matthey Johnson Inc ....B 610 341-8300
Wayne (G-19352)

McCleary Heating & Cooling LLC ....F 717 263-3833
Chambersburg (G-2959)

Met-Pro Technologies LLC...................D 215 723-8155
Telford (G-18305)

Met-Pro Technologies LLC...................E 215 822-1963
Telford (G-18303)

Micro-Coax Inc ....C 610 495-4438
Pottstown (G-16019)

New Busch Co Inc ....G 724 940-2326
Wexford (G-19815)

ODonnell Metal Fabricators ....F 610 279-8810
Norristown (G-12697)

Penn Fan Inc ....G 724 452-4570
Zelienople (G-20814)

Precision Filtration Pdts Inc ....E 215 679-6645
Pennsburg (G-13252)

RAF Industries Inc ....F 215 572-0738
Jenkintown (G-8299)

Respironics Inc ....B 724 387-4270
Monroeville (G-11354)

Respironics Inc ....C 724 334-3100
New Kensington (G-12370)

◆ Respironics Inc ....D 724 387-5200
Murrysville (G-11865)

RM Benney Technical Sls Inc ....G 724 935-0150
Wexford (G-19828)

◆ Robinson Fans Inc ....B 863 646-5270
Zelienople (G-20817)

Robinson Fans Holdings Inc ....G 724 452-6121
Zelienople (G-20818)

◆ Schutte Koerting Acquisition ....E 215 639-0900
Trevose (G-18502)

Skc Inc ....D 724 260-0741
Eighty Four (G-4849)

▲ Sp Environmental Inc ....E 724 935-1300
Sewickley (G-17412)

Spectrum Control Inc ....C 814 835-4000
Fairview (G-5844)

◆ Strobic Air Corporation ....F 215 723-4700
Telford (G-18321)

▲ Tm Industrial Supply Inc ....E 814 453-5014
Erie (G-5510)

▲ Tps LLC ....C 570 538-7200
New Columbia (G-12177)

▲ Tri Bms LLC ....E 610 495-9700
Spring City (G-17870)

Tri State Filter Mfg Co ....D 412 621-8491
Pittsburgh (G-15644)

Tuscarora Electric Mfg Co ....G 570 836-2101
Tunkhannock (G-18551)

USA Coil & Air Inc ....E 610 296-9668
Malvern (G-10336)

▲ Wayne Products Inc ....F 800 255-5665
Broomall (G-2305)

3565 Packaging Machinery

▼ Advanced Machine Systems Inc......F 610 837-8677
Bath (G-949)

◆ All-Fill Corporation ....D 866 255-3455
Exton (G-5639)

All-Fill Inc ....G 610 524-7350
Exton (G-5640)

Ameripak ....E 215 343-1530
Warrington (G-19107)

AMS Liquidating Co Inc ....G 610 942-4200
Honey Brook (G-7736)

◆ Ardagh Metal Packaging USA Inc ...E 412 923-1080
Carnegie (G-2764)

Beta Industries Inc ....G 610 363-6555
Exton (G-5655)

Carleton Inc ....E 215 230-8900
Doylestown (G-4289)

▼ Charles Beseler Co Inc ....D 800 237-3537
Stroudsburg (G-18109)

CSS International Corporation ....F 215 533-6110
Philadelphia (G-13589)

◆ Dyco Inc ....D 800 545-3926
Bloomsburg (G-1779)

▲ E S S Packaging Machinery ....E 610 588-8579
Roseto (G-16820)

Emp Industries Inc ....E 215 357-5333
Warminster (G-18871)

Enchanted Acres Farm Group LLC ....G 877 707-3833
Reading (G-16373)

▼ Ergonomic Mfg Group Inc ....G 800 223-6430
Quakertown (G-16189)

Erie Technical Systems Inc ....G 814 899-2103
Erie (G-5276)

Farason Corporation ....E 610 383-6224
Coatesville (G-3303)

Fox IV Technologies Inc ....E 724 387-3500
Export (G-5603)

◆ Fres-Co Systems Usa Inc ....B 215 721-4600
Telford (G-18290)

Gideon B Stoltzfus ....G 717 656-4903
Bird In Hand (G-1675)

Gottscho Printing Systems Inc..............G 267 387-3005
Warminster (G-18890)

▲ Harro Hofliger Packg Systems ....E 215 345-4256
Doylestown (G-4305)

◆ Horix Manufacturing Company ....E 412 771-1111
Mc Kees Rocks (G-10614)

Hostvedt Pavoni Inc ....F 215 489-7300
Doylestown (G-4306)

I D Tek Inc ....E 215 699-8888
North Wales (G-12806)

ID Technology LLC ....G 717 235-8345
New Freedom (G-12209)

ID Technology LLC ....E 717 848-3875
York (G-20533)

Jls Automation LLC ....E 717 505-3800
York (G-20541)

Kinsley Incorporated ....G 215 348-7723
Doylestown (G-4311)

Labelpack Automation Inc ....E 814 362-1528
Bradford (G-1979)

Libra Three Inc ....G 610 217-9992
Palmerton (G-13109)

▼ Loveshaw Corporation ....C 570 937-4921
South Canaan (G-17769)

McNeilus Truck and Mfg Inc.................E 610 286-0400
Morgantown (G-11527)

Millwood Inc ....C 610 421-6230
Alburtis (G-57)

Millwood Inc ....F 724 266-7030
Leetsdale (G-9699)

Millwood Inc ....F 717 790-9118
Mechanicsburg (G-10869)

Millwood Inc ....F 570 836-9280
Tunkhannock (G-18543)

Nelson Wrap Dispenser Inc ....G 814 623-1317
Bedford (G-1066)

New Way Packaging Machinery ....G 717 637-2133
Hanover (G-6925)

◆ Omega Design Corporation ....D 610 363-6555
Exton (G-5718)

OP Schuman & Sons Inc ....D 215 343-1530
Warminster (G-18932)

Pack Pro Technologies LLC.................G 717 517-9065
Lititz (G-10028)

▲ Packaging Enterprises Inc ....G 215 379-1234
Jenkintown (G-8298)

Packaging Progressions Inc ....E 610 489-9096
Souderton (G-17758)

Pak-Rapid Inc ....G 610 828-3511
Conshohocken (G-3585)

▲ Palace Packaging Machines Inc ......E 610 873-7252
Downingtown (G-4249)

Paragon Print Systems Inc ....F 814 456-8331
Erie (G-5413)

Peters Equipment Corp ....G 215 364-9147
Huntingdon Valley (G-8024)

R R Pankratz Inc.............................G 610 696-1043
West Chester (G-19627)

▲ RE Pack Inc ....G 215 699-9252
Lansdale (G-9403)

Signode Industrial Group LLC ....C 570 937-4921
South Canaan (G-17770)

Signode Industrial Group LLC ....C 570 937-4921
South Canaan (G-17771)

▲ Smit Corporation ....E 215 396-2200
Warminster (G-18965)

Tek ID ....F 215 699-8888
North Wales (G-12831)

▲ Telstar North America Inc................A 215 826-0770
Bristol (G-2205)

Urania Engineering Co Inc ....E 570 455-0776
Hazleton (G-7532)

▼ Veeco Precision Surfc Proc LLC .....D 215 328-0700
Horsham (G-7863)

◆ Velocity Eqp Solutions LLC ....F 800 521-1368
New Castle (G-12162)

Wayne Automation Corporation ....D 610 630-8900
Norristown (G-12723)

3566 Speed Changers, Drives & Gears

Alcast Metals Inc ....E 215 368-5865
Montgomeryville (G-11382)

Altec Industries Inc........................C 570 822-3104
Wilkes Barre (G-19904)

Ametek Inc ....D 215 256-6601
Harleysville (G-7020)

Atch-Mont Gear Co Inc ....F 215 355-5146
Ivyland (G-8205)

B & F Tool & Gear Inc ....G 717 632-8977
Spring Grove (G-17875)

Brad Foote Gear Works Inc ....E 412 264-1428
Pittsburgh (G-14789)

Charles Bond Company ....F 610 593-5171
Christiana (G-3134)

Gearmakers Inc ....F 215 703-0390
Souderton (G-17736)

Harold Beck & Sons Inc ....C 215 968-4600
Newtown (G-12506)

Heclyn Precision Gear Company ....F 215 739-7094
Philadelphia (G-13810)

Martin Sprocket & Gear Inc ....D 610 837-1841
Danielsville (G-3994)

Motor Actuator Specialties Inc ....G 215 919-1437
Coatesville (G-3317)

▲ PDC Machines Inc.....................D 215 443-9442
Warminster (G-18937)

Penngear LLC................................G 215 968-2403
Yardley (G-20331)

▼ Quigley Motor Company Inc ....D 717 266-5631
Manchester (G-10364)

Rockwell Automation Inc ....G 412 375-4700
Coraopolis (G-3723)

Strube Inc ....F 717 426-1906
Marietta (G-10468)

Thunder Basin Corporation ....F 610 962-3770
King of Prussia (G-8688)

Voith Digital Solutions Inc................F 717 792-7000
York (G-20698)

Zia-Tech Gear Mfg Inc.....................G 412 321-0770
Pittsburgh (G-15733)

3567 Indl Process Furnaces & Ovens

A Stucki Company ....E 724 746-4240
Canonsburg (G-2531)

Abbott Furnace Company ....D 814 781-6355
Saint Marys (G-16943)

▲ Air/Tak Inc ....F 724 297-3416
Worthington (G-20226)

Ajax Electric Company ....E 215 947-8500
Huntingdon Valley (G-7962)

◆ Applied Test Systems LLC ....E 724 283-1212
Butler (G-2375)

Armstrong Engrg Assoc Inc ....G 610 436-6080
West Chester (G-19501)

▲ Armstrong Engrg Assoc Inc.........D 610 436-6080
Coatesville (G-3291)

Aztec Machinery Company ....E 215 672-2600
Warminster (G-18833)

Boyertown Furnace Company ....E 610 369-1450
Boyertown (G-1900)

▲ C I Hayes Inc............................E 814 834-2200
Saint Marys (G-16951)

Ceramic Services Inc......................G 215 245-4040
Bensalem (G-1166)

◆ Chromalox Inc...........................D 412 967-3800
Pittsburgh (G-14850)

Clean Energy Htg Systems LLC ....F 888 519-2347
Honey Brook (G-7742)

CMI America Inc ....F 814 897-7000
Erie (G-5228)

Concept Products Corporation ....G 610 722-0830
Mertztown (G-11002)

Creative Energy Distributors ....G 717 354-6090
New Holland (G-12240)

Dayco Inc ....G 610 326-4500
Pottstown (G-15981)

◆ Eastern Manufacturing LLC ....D 215 702-3600
Langhorne (G-9293)

Ecco/Gregory Inc ....E 610 840-0390
West Chester (G-19545)

Fce LLC..G 215 947-7333
Huntingdon Valley (G-7980)

Frazier-Simplex Machine Co ....E 724 222-5700
Washington (G-19177)

Frontier LLC..................................F 570 265-2500
Towanda (G-18426)

Gasbarre Products Inc ....E 814 834-2200
Saint Marys (G-16975)

◆ Gasbarre Products Inc ....D 814 371-3015
Du Bois (G-4392)

▲ Graftech Usa LLC.....................C 814 781-2478
Saint Marys (G-16979)

Gyrotron Technology Inc ....G 215 244-4740
Bensalem (G-1207)

Ipsen Inc ....G 215 723-8125
Souderton (G-17742)

J&R Cad Enterprise LLC ....G 724 695-4279
Imperial (G-8069)

Jmg Inc ....G 215 659-4087
Willow Grove (G-20121)

Jpw Design & Manufacturing Inc ....E 570 995-5025
Trout Run (G-18515)

▲ L & L Special Furnace Co Inc..........F 610 459-9216
Aston (G-772)

Linde Engineering N Amer Inc...........E 610 834-0300
Blue Bell (G-1844)

Lucifer Furnaces Inc........................F 215 343-0411
Warrington (G-19123)

Metvac Inc ....G 215 541-4495
Hereford (G-7568)

Nass Inc ....G 717 846-3685
York (G-20609)

▼ Pennram Diversified Mfg Corp ....E 570 327-2802
Williamsport (G-20055)

Pinnacle Climate Tech Inc ....G 215 891-8460
Bristol (G-2182)

Quartz Tubing Inc...........................F 215 638-0909
Bensalem (G-1246)

Riise Inc ....G 724 528-3305
West Middlesex (G-19729)

Seco/Vacuum Technologies LLC........G 814 332-8520
Meadville (G-10790)

◆ Seco/Warwick Corporation ....D 814 332-8400
Meadville (G-10791)

Signature Vacuum Systems Inc..........G 814 333-1110
Harmonsburg (G-7064)

Solar Atmospheres Mfg Inc ....E 267 384-5040
Souderton (G-17766)

▲ SPX Flow Us LLC ....G 814 476-5800
Mc Kean (G-10594)

▲ T Bruce Sales Inc ....D 724 528-9961
West Middlesex (G-19731)

Tate Jones Inc ....G 412 771-4200
Portersville (G-15937)

Thermtrend Inc ....G 215 752-0711
Bensalem (G-1260)

▲ Tps LLC....................................C 570 538-7200
New Columbia (G-12177)

Trent Inc ....F 215 482-5000
Philadelphia (G-14406)

V P L Inc ....G 814 652-6767
Everett (G-5579)

◆ World Marketing of America ....E 814 643-6500
Mill Creek (G-11169)

▼ Yorkaire Inc..............................E 717 755-2836
York (G-20755)

3568 Mechanical Power Transmission Eqpt, NEC

Altra Industrial Motion......................G 781 917-0600
Chambersburg (G-2902)

Altra Industrial Motion Corp ....G 717 261-2550
Chambersburg (G-2903)

American Hollow Boring Company ......E 800 673-2458
Erie (G-5187)

▲ Ameridrives International LLC........D 814 480-5000
Erie (G-5192)

▲ Cbh of Lancaster Company ....D 717 569-0485
Manheim (G-10375)

Certainteed Gypsum Mfg Inc ....E 813 286-3900
Wayne (G-19312)

Converter Accessory Corp ....F 610 863-6008
Wind Gap (G-20168)

Dana Driveshaft Products LLC ....B 610 323-4200
Pottstown (G-15979)

▲ Edlon Inc ....D 610 268-3101
Avondale (G-852)

Elliott Company.............................D 724 379-5440
Donora (G-4155)

Fenner Inc ....E 717 665-2421
Lancaster (G-9015)

Fenner Inc ....D 717 665-2421
Manheim (G-10381)

▲ Fenner Inc ....G 717 665-2421
Manheim (G-10382)

Fenner Inc ....C 717 665-2421
Manheim (G-10380)

Force America Inc ....E 610 495-4590
Pottstown (G-15988)

▲ General Carbide Corporation ....C 724 836-3000
Greensburg (G-6668)

General Dynamics Ots PA Inc............E 570 342-7801
Scranton (G-17238)

◆ GKN Sinter Metals - Dubois Inc .....D 814 375-0938
Du Bois (G-4393)

Keystone Powdered Metal Co............D 814 368-5320
Lewis Run (G-9876)

◆ Kingsbury Inc...........................C 215 824-4000
Philadelphia (G-13938)

Kingsbury Inc ....E 215 824-4000
Philadelphia (G-13939)

Kingsbury Inc ....F 215 824-4000
Hatboro (G-7290)

Lord Corporation ....B 814 868-3180
Erie (G-5372)

Lord Corporation ....D 814 398-4641
Cambridge Springs (G-2481)

Lord Corporation ....B 814 868-0924
Erie (G-5371)

Lubrite LLC...................................E 814 337-4234
Meadville (G-10750)

Martin Sprocket & Gear Inc ....D 610 837-1841
Danielsville (G-3994)

▲ Medart Inc ....E 724 752-3555
Ellwood City (G-4946)

Metal Powder Products LLC ....C 814 834-7261
Saint Marys (G-16992)

Metalkraft Industries Inc...................E 570 724-6800
Wellsboro (G-19469)

Metaltech Inc ....E 814 375-9399
Du Bois (G-4406)

▲ Morgan Advanced Mtls Tech Inc .....C 814 781-1573
Saint Marys (G-16998)

◆ Morris Coupling Company ....D 814 459-1741
Erie (G-5396)

N C B Technologies Inc ....G 724 658-5544
New Castle (G-12123)

▲ Neapco Components LLC ....E 610 323-6000
Pottstown (G-16021)

Nearhoof Machine Inc......................G 814 339-6621
Osceola Mills (G-13056)

Nick Charles Kravitch......................G 412 882-6262
Pittsburgh (G-15340)

Orville Bronze and Alum LLC ....G 330 948-1231
Meadville (G-10772)

Oswald & Associates Inc ....G 814 627-0300
Huntingdon (G-7954)

▼ Pittsbrgh Tubular Shafting Inc........E 724 774-7212
Rochester (G-16787)

Proform Powdered Metals Inc ....E 814 938-7411
Punxsutawney (G-16154)

Royersford Fndry & Mch Co Inc..........E 610 935-7200
Phoenixville (G-14576)

◆ Scheerer Bearing Corporation ....E 215 443-5252
Willow Grove (G-20140)

Scheerer Bearing Corporation............E 215 443-5252
Horsham (G-7848)

Schneider Electric It Corp .... G 215 230-7270
  Doylestown *(G-4336)*

SKF USA Inc .... C 717 637-8981
  Hanover *(G-6953)*

St Marys Pressed Metals Inc .... E 814 772-7455
  Ridgway *(G-16730)*

Stapf Energy Services .... G 610 831-1500
  Trappe *(G-18474)*

◆ Tb Woods Incorporated .... C 717 264-7161
  Chambersburg *(G-2983)*

Triple W Enterprises Inc .... G 610 865-0071
  Bethlehem *(G-1642)*

Vallorbs Jewel Company .... C 717 392-3978
  Bird In Hand *(G-1684)*

▲ Wise Machine Co Inc .... E 724 287-2705
  Butler *(G-2450)*

3569 Indl Machinery & Eqpt, NEC

▲ A G F Manufacturing Co Inc .... E 610 240-4900
  Malvern *(G-10178)*

▲ A Stucki Company .... E 412 424-0560
  Coraopolis *(G-3653)*

A-1 Babbitt Co Inc .... F 724 379-6588
  Donora *(G-4144)*

Advanced Machine Technologies ..... G 717 871-9724
  Millersville *(G-11209)*

▲ Advent Design Corporation .... C 215 781-0500
  Bristol *(G-2104)*

▲ Air Liquid Systems Inc .... G 724 834-8090
  Forbes Road *(G-6040)*

Air Liquide America LP .... E 610 383-5500
  Coatesville *(G-3286)*

◆ Air Products and Chemicals Inc ..... A 610 481-4911
  Allentown *(G-119)*

Air Products and Chemicals Inc ...... E 724 266-1563
  Leetsdale *(G-9677)*

▲ Air Products Corporation .... D 800 345-8207
  Exton *(G-5637)*

Airtek Inc .... E 412 351-3837
  Irwin *(G-8141)*

◆ Ameri-Surce Specialty Pdts Inc ..... E 412 831-9400
  Bethel Park *(G-1402)*

American Robot Corporation .... G 724 695-9000
  Oakdale *(G-12890)*

▲ American Tool Mfg LLC .... G 610 837-8573
  Bath *(G-950)*

Aml Industries Inc .... D 215 674-2424
  Hatboro *(G-7269)*

Apex Hydraulic & Machine Inc .... F 814 342-1010
  Philipsburg *(G-14508)*

Apss Inc .... F 724 368-3001
  Portersville *(G-15925)*

Automation Devices Inc .... E 814 474-5561
  Fairview *(G-5814)*

Barebo Inc .... E 610 965-6018
  Emmaus *(G-5020)*

Bnb Fire Protection Inc .... G 610 944-0594
  Fleetwood *(G-5968)*

▲ C and M Sales Co .... F 814 437-3095
  Franklin *(G-6118)*

Chant Engineering Co Inc .... E 215 230-4260
  New Britain *(G-12046)*

Chief Technologies LLC .... F 484 693-0750
  Downingtown *(G-4220)*

Coal Centrifuge Service .... G 724 478-4205
  Apollo *(G-672)*

Consoldted Scrap Resources Inc ..... E 717 843-0660
  York *(G-20435)*

D & A Emergency Equipment Inc ..... G 610 691-6847
  Bethlehem *(G-1495)*

▲ D L Martin Co .... C 717 328-2141
  Mercersburg *(G-10984)*

Ddp Specialty Electronic MA .... G 610 244-6000
  Collegeville *(G-3374)*

Demco Enterprises Inc .... F 888 419-3343
  Quakertown *(G-16184)*

Diversatech Industrial LLC .... G 724 887-4199
  Connellsville *(G-3495)*

▲ Drake Refrigeration Inc .... F 215 638-5515
  Bensalem *(G-1183)*

▲ Drucker Company Intl Inc .... E 814 342-6210
  Philipsburg *(G-14512)*

Duncan Associates Inc .... G 717 299-6940
  Lancaster *(G-9003)*

Dynamic Manufacturing LLC .... D 724 295-4200
  Freeport *(G-6203)*

Ecco/Gregory Inc .... E 610 840-0390
  West Chester *(G-19545)*

Eisenhower Tool Inc .... F 215 538-9381
  Quakertown *(G-16187)*

Empire Energy E&P LLC .... F 814 365-5621
  Hawthorn *(G-7444)*

Enhanced Systems & Products .... G 215 794-6942
  Doylestown *(G-4299)*

Equipment Technology Inc .... G 570 489-8651
  Peckville *(G-13208)*

Erie Metal Basket Inc .... F 814 833-1745
  Erie *(G-5270)*

▲ Filpro Corporation .... F 215 699-4510
  North Wales *(G-12801)*

Filter Shine Inc .... G 866 977-4463
  Reinholds *(G-16631)*

Filter Technology Inc .... G 866 992-9490
  Gladwyne *(G-6407)*

▲ Filterfab Manufacturing Corp .... G 724 643-4000
  Industry *(G-8136)*

Filtrtion of Wstn Pnnsylvania .... G 412 855-7372
  Cranberry Township *(G-3818)*

Fluid Conditioning Pdts Inc .... E 717 627-1550
  Lititz *(G-10008)*

▼ Full-On Filters .... G 610 970-4701
  Pottstown *(G-15989)*

Gaydos Equipment LLC .... E 724 272-6951
  Gibsonia *(G-6336)*

Gecco Inc .... G 570 945-3568
  Fleetville *(G-5966)*

Grace Filter Company Inc .... G 610 664-5790
  Philadelphia *(G-13778)*

▲ Green Filter Usa Inc .... E 724 430-2050
  Mount Braddock *(G-11617)*

▲ Hennecke Inc .... D 724 271-3686
  Bridgeville *(G-2068)*

Homeland Mfg Svcs Inc .... F 814 862-9103
  State College *(G-17976)*

Hydrogen Electrics LLC .... G 267 334-3155
  Jenkintown *(G-8290)*

Iam Robotics LLC .... G 412 636-7425
  Pittsburgh *(G-15110)*

JM Automation Services .... G 215 675-0125
  Warminster *(G-18902)*

Jnb Industrial Supply Inc .... G 412 455-5170
  Blawnox *(G-1764)*

Jomarr Safety Systems Inc .... D 570 346-5330
  Dunmore *(G-4475)*

Keystone Fire Apparatus Inc .... G 412 771-7722
  Mc Kees Rocks *(G-10618)*

▲ Knight Corporation .... E 610 853-2161
  Havertown *(G-7423)*

Laessig Associates .... G 610 353-3543
  Newtown Square *(G-12581)*

Lawrence R McGuigan .... G 724 493-9175
  Warren *(G-19037)*

Lube Systems Company .... G 724 335-4050
  Apollo *(G-682)*

▲ Mar Cor Purification Inc .... C 800 633-3080
  Skippack *(G-17600)*

Marando Industries Inc .... G 610 621-2536
  Reading *(G-16437)*

Matheson Tri-Gas Inc .... D 215 641-2700
  Montgomeryville *(G-11406)*

◆ Matric Group LLC .... B 814 677-0716
  Seneca *(G-17366)*

Matthew McKeon .... G 215 234-8505
  Green Lane *(G-6589)*

◆ Matthews International Corp .... E 412 442-8200
  Pittsburgh *(G-15264)*

Matthey Johnson Inc .... E 610 232-1900
  West Chester *(G-19599)*

McFadden Machine & Mfg Co .... E 724 459-9278
  Blairsville *(G-1734)*

Met-Pro Technologies LLC .... E 215 822-1963
  Telford *(G-18303)*

Metalworking Machinery Co Inc .... F 724 625-3181
  New Kensington *(G-12355)*

Modern Industries Inc .... F 814 885-8514
  Kersey *(G-8564)*

▲ Modern Industries Inc .... C 814 455-8061
  Erie *(G-5394)*

Municipal Fire Equipment Inc .... G 412 366-8180
  Pittsburgh *(G-15310)*

National Foam Inc .... G 610 363-1400
  West Chester *(G-19607)*

▼ National Foam Inc .... D 610 363-1400
  West Chester *(G-19606)*

Newco Industries .... F 717 566-9560
  Hummelstown *(G-7919)*

Next Generation Filtration .... G 412 548-1659
  Pittsburgh *(G-15335)*

Oil Process Systems Inc .... E 610 437-4618
  Allentown *(G-337)*

▲ Paletti Usa LLC .... E 267 289-0020
  Montgomeryville *(G-11410)*

Pall Corporation .... D 610 458-9500
  Exton *(G-5722)*

Penn-Central Industries Inc .... G 814 371-3211
  Du Bois *(G-4413)*

▼ Philadlphia Tramrail Entps Inc ...... E 215 743-4359
  Philadelphia *(G-14165)*

Pkt Technologies .... E 412 494-5600
  Pittsburgh *(G-15414)*

Precision Assembly Inc .... E 215 784-0861
  Willow Grove *(G-20136)*

▲ Projectile Tube Cleaning Inc .... E 724 763-7633
  Ford City *(G-6051)*

▲ Psb Industries Inc .... D 814 453-3651
  Erie *(G-5442)*

◆ Ptr Baler and Compactor Co .... E 215 533-5100
  Philadelphia *(G-14215)*

Raceresq Inc .... G 724 891-3473
  Beaver Falls *(G-1010)*

Rhino Inc .... F 215 442-1504
  Hatboro *(G-7301)*

Rowe Sprinkler Systems Inc .... E 570 837-7647
  Middleburg *(G-11039)*

S G Frantz Co Inc .... G 215 943-2930
  Bristol *(G-2196)*

▼ S P Kinney Engineers Inc .... E 412 276-4600
  Carnegie *(G-2789)*

Salmen Tech Co Inc .... G 412 854-1822
  Bethel Park *(G-1432)*

▲ Schroeder Industries LLC .... D 724 318-1100
  Leetsdale *(G-9194)*

Separation Technologies Inc .... E 724 325-4546
  Export *(G-5626)*

Service Filtration Corp .... E 717 656-2161
  Lancaster *(G-9194)*

Skc Gulf Coast Inc .... G 724 677-0340
  Smock *(G-17667)*

Smeal Ltc LLC .... G 717 918-1806
  Ephrata *(G-5142)*

SMS Group Inc .... C 412 231-1200
  Pittsburgh *(G-15552)*

Spectrum Microwave Inc .... E 814 272-2700
  State College *(G-18033)*

Swanson Systems Inc .... D 814 453-5841
  Erie *(G-5499)*

Swanson-Erie Corporation .... D 814 453-5841
  Erie *(G-5500)*

Synergy Applications Inc .... F 814 454-8803
  Erie *(G-5501)*

▼ Titan Abrasive Systems LLC .... G 215 310-5055
  Ivyland *(G-8223)*

◆ Titus Company .... E 610 913-9100
  Morgantown *(G-11540)*

Tool O Matic Inc .... G 724 776-3232
  Cranberry Township *(G-3855)*

Tri-Dim Filter Corporation .... F 610 481-9926
  Allentown *(G-414)*

▲ Trident Emergency Products LLC ... G 215 293-0700
  Hatboro *(G-7308)*

▼ Tyco Fire Products LP .... C 215 362-0700
  Lansdale *(G-9421)*

Tyco Fire Products LP .... E 256 238-0579
  Columbia *(G-3452)*

Versum Materials Us LLC .... F 610 481-3946
  Allentown *(G-423)*

Versum Materials Us LLC .... G 570 467-2981
  Tamaqua *(G-18231)*

▲ W O Hickok Manufacturing Co ..... E 717 234-8041
  Harrisburg *(G-7243)*

▲ Wayne Products Inc .... F 800 255-5665
  Broomall *(G-2305)*

▲ Xcell Automation Inc .... D 717 755-6800
  York *(G-20721)*

▼ Ziamatic Corp .... E 215 493-2777
  Yardley *(G-20347)*

3571 Electronic Computers

ABS and Apples .... G 646 847-8262
  Tobyhanna *(G-18406)*

Apple Alley Associates-Ii LP .... G 215 817-2828
  Langhorne *(G-9276)*

Apple Fox .... G 484 388-0011
  Bernville *(G-1296)*

Audio Video Automation SEC Inc ..... G 814 313-1108
  Warren *(G-19011)*

Aurora Computer Systems Inc .... G 814 535-8371
  Johnstown *(G-8354)*

Blue Toro Technologies LLC .... G 610 428-0891
  Bethlehem *(G-1468)*

Cobalt Computers Inc....F.... 610 395-3771
Schnecksville *(G-17137)*
Consyst Inc....G.... 610 398-0752
Orefield *(G-13010)*
Daisy Data Displays Inc....E.... 717 932-9999
York Haven *(G-20756)*
▲ **Devon International Group Inc**....D.... 866 312-3373
King of Prussia *(G-8607)*
▲ **Devon It Inc**....E.... 610 757-4220
King of Prussia *(G-8608)*
Dynamic Manufacturing LLC....D.... 724 295-4200
Freeport *(G-6203)*
Eagle Mfg & Design Corp....E.... 717 848-9767
York *(G-20459)*
Effective Software Products....G.... 717 267-2054
Chambersburg *(G-2929)*
Egg To Apples LLC....G.... 610 822-3670
Haverford *(G-7410)*
Electrovue LLC....G.... 855 226-4430
Aston *(G-762)*
Element 27 Inc....G.... 610 502-2727
Schnecksville *(G-17139)*
Elk Systems Inc....G.... 717 884-9355
Lewisberry *(G-9885)*
Evergreen Group Inc....G.... 610 799-2263
Schnecksville *(G-17140)*
▲ **Flight Systems Inc**....E.... 717 590-7330
Mechanicsburg *(G-10844)*
General Dynamics Mission....E.... 412 488-8605
Pittsburgh *(G-15045)*
H M W Enterprises Inc....F.... 717 765-4690
Waynesboro *(G-19410)*
Horeb Inc....G.... 610 285-1917
West Chester *(G-19564)*
HP Inc....F.... 412 928-4978
Pittsburgh *(G-15103)*
International Bus Mchs Corp....A.... 610 578-2017
Wayne *(G-19339)*
J J Cacchio Enterprises....G.... 610 399-9750
West Chester *(G-19575)*
▲ **Jli Electronics Inc**....G.... 215 256-3200
Harleysville *(G-7042)*
Lexicon International Corp....E.... 215 639-8220
Bensalem *(G-1220)*
Library Video Company....D.... 610 645-4000
Conshohocken *(G-3572)*
◆ **Matric Group LLC**....B.... 814 677-0716
Seneca *(G-17366)*
Medcomp Technologies Inc....G.... 814 504-3328
East Springfield *(G-4600)*
National Hybrid Inc....D.... 814 467-9060
Windber *(G-20190)*
Not For Radio LLC....G.... 484 437-9962
Manheim *(G-10397)*
Progeny Systems Corporation....F.... 724 239-3939
Charleroi *(G-3019)*
Real Automotive Pc Inc....G.... 609 876-7450
Paoli *(G-13148)*
Reclamere Inc....E.... 814 684-5505
Tyrone *(G-18592)*
Right Reason Technologies LLC....F.... 570 234-0324
Tobyhanna *(G-18408)*
RMS Systems Inc....G.... 724 458-7580
Mercer *(G-10972)*
Sparton Aydin LLC....D.... 610 404-7400
Birdsboro *(G-1706)*
Sterling Computer Sales LLC....G.... 610 255-0198
Landenberg *(G-9253)*
T-R Associates Inc....E.... 570 876-4067
Archbald *(G-696)*
Time Man Jr Corporation....D.... 856 244-1485
Philadelphia *(G-14389)*
▲ **Two Technologies Inc**....E.... 215 441-5305
Horsham *(G-7861)*
▲ **Venture 3 Systems LLC**....F.... 267 954-0100
Hatfield *(G-7405)*
VIP Tech LLC....G.... 267 582-1554
Philadelphia *(G-14448)*
Viper Network Systems LLC....G.... 855 758-4737
West View *(G-19774)*
Voci Technologies Incorporated....F.... 412 621-9310
Pittsburgh *(G-15701)*
Vocollect Inc....C.... 412 829-8145
Pittsburgh *(G-15702)*
White Box Systems LLC....G.... 717 612-9911
Lemoyne *(G-9755)*

3572 Computer Storage Devices

Ecm Energy Services Inc....E.... 888 659-2413
Williamsport *(G-20010)*
EMC Corporation....C.... 484 322-1000
Norristown *(G-12654)*
EMC Corporation....B.... 610 834-0471
Conshohocken *(G-3542)*
EMC Fintech....G.... 814 230-9157
Warren *(G-19024)*
EMC Metals Inc....G.... 412 299-7200
Coraopolis *(G-3689)*
Griffith Inc....C.... 215 322-8100
Huntingdon Valley *(G-7992)*
High Avlblity Stor Systems Inc....E.... 610 254-5090
Audubon *(G-827)*
Integration Tech Systems Inc....E.... 724 696-3000
Mount Pleasant *(G-11701)*
International Bus Mchs Corp....A.... 610 578-2017
Wayne *(G-19339)*
Mtekka LLC....G.... 610 619-3555
Kennett Square *(G-8532)*
North Central Sight Svcs Inc....D.... 570 323-9401
Williamsport *(G-20050)*
▲ **Progressive Computer Svcs Inc**....E.... 215 226-2220
Philadelphia *(G-14207)*
Quantum Connection....G.... 814 333-9398
Meadville *(G-10786)*
Quantum One....F.... 412 432-5234
Pittsburgh *(G-15461)*
Quantum Qube Inc....G.... 412 767-0506
Sewickley *(G-17406)*
Quantum Restoration LLC....G.... 215 259-3402
Conshohocken *(G-3596)*
Quantum Vortex Inc....G.... 814 325-0148
State College *(G-18011)*
Seagate Technology LLC....C.... 412 918-7000
Pittsburgh *(G-15518)*
Seiberts Computers....G.... 717 349-7859
Fannettsburg *(G-5859)*

3575 Computer Terminals

Accustar Inc....G.... 610 459-0123
Garnet Valley *(G-6264)*
Capsen Robotics Inc....G.... 203 218-0204
Pittsburgh *(G-14806)*
Daisy Data Displays Inc....E.... 717 932-9999
York Haven *(G-20756)*
Datacap Systems Inc....E.... 215 997-8989
Chalfont *(G-2871)*
Gc Enterprises LLC....G.... 570 655-5543
Pittston *(G-15752)*
Global Data Consultants LLC....E.... 717 697-7500
Mechanicsburg *(G-10849)*
Go Main Domains LLC....G.... 480 624-2500
Darby *(G-4018)*
H M W Enterprises Inc....F.... 717 765-4690
Waynesboro *(G-19410)*
Internet Probation and....G.... 610 701-8921
West Chester *(G-19571)*
▲ **Marco Manufacturing Co Inc**....E.... 215 463-2332
Philadelphia *(G-13992)*
Northern Winding Inc....G.... 724 776-4983
Mars *(G-10509)*
▲ **Two Technologies Inc**....E.... 215 441-5305
Horsham *(G-7861)*

3577 Computer Peripheral Eqpt, NEC

ACS Investors LLC....G.... 724 746-5500
Lawrence *(G-9533)*
Advanced Mobile Group LLC....F.... 215 489-2538
Doylestown *(G-4268)*
Advanced Network Products Inc....E.... 215 572-0111
Glenside *(G-6503)*
Alfred Troilo....G.... 610 544-0115
Springfield *(G-17906)*
Application Consultants Inc....F.... 610 521-1529
Ridley Park *(G-16733)*
Aurora Electrical & Data Svcs....G.... 412 255-4060
Pittsburgh *(G-14739)*
▲ **Birdbrain Technologies LLC**....G.... 412 216-5833
Pittsburgh *(G-14767)*
◆ **Black Box Corporation**....G.... 724 746-5500
Lawrence *(G-9535)*
Black Box Corporation....G.... 215 274-1044
Blue Bell *(G-1816)*
Black Box Services Company....G.... 724 746-5500
Lawrence *(G-9536)*
Brocade Cmmnctions Systems Inc....G.... 610 648-3915
Malvern *(G-10195)*
Butler Technologies Inc....D.... 724 283-6656
Butler *(G-2386)*
Bxvideo Solutions LLC....G.... 724 940-4190
Wexford *(G-19793)*
Capsen Robotics Inc....G.... 203 218-0204
Pittsburgh *(G-14806)*
◆ **Carpenter Connection Inc**....E.... 412 881-3900
Pittsburgh *(G-14821)*
Cisco Systems Inc....A.... 814 789-2990
Guys Mills *(G-6809)*
Cisco Systems Inc....D.... 610 695-6000
Malvern *(G-10210)*
Cisco Systems Inc....A.... 610 336-8500
Allentown *(G-170)*
Claypoole Hex Signs....G.... 610 562-8911
Lenhartsville *(G-9757)*
Comdoc Inc....D.... 800 321-1009
Pittsburgh *(G-14868)*
▲ **Commerce Drive Enterprises LLC**....D.... 215 362-2766
Montgomeryville *(G-11389)*
Copiers Inc....G.... 610 837-7400
Bath *(G-955)*
Craddock & Lerro Associates....G.... 610 543-0200
Drexel Hill *(G-4363)*
Cybertech Inc....F.... 215 957-6220
Horsham *(G-7807)*
Daisy Data Displays Inc....E.... 717 932-9999
York Haven *(G-20756)*
Datalogic Usa Inc....B.... 215 723-0981
Telford *(G-18280)*
▲ **Datapath North America Inc**....G.... 484 679-1553
Norristown *(G-12650)*
▲ **Dawar Technologies Inc**....E.... 412 322-9900
Pittsburgh *(G-14909)*
▲ **Decal Specialties Inc**....G.... 610 644-9200
Paoli *(G-13137)*
▲ **Decora Industries Inc**....D.... 215 698-2600
Philadelphia *(G-13614)*
◆ **Deltronic Labs Inc**....E.... 215 997-8616
Chalfont *(G-2872)*
Digital Media Solutions LLC....G.... 610 234-3834
Conshohocken *(G-3538)*
Effective CD Llc....G.... 607 351-5949
Lawrenceville *(G-9541)*
Fox IV Technologies Inc....E.... 724 387-3500
Export *(G-5603)*
G&R Designs LLC....G.... 717 697-4538
Mechanicsburg *(G-10848)*
Gda Corp....F.... 814 237-4060
State College *(G-17968)*
General Metal Company Inc....E.... 215 638-3242
Bensalem *(G-1203)*
Goodway Graphics Inc....B.... 215 887-5700
Jenkintown *(G-8288)*
Griffith Inc....C.... 215 322-8100
Huntingdon Valley *(G-7992)*
H M W Enterprises Inc....F.... 717 765-4690
Waynesboro *(G-19410)*
Integrted Productivity Systems....G.... 215 646-1374
Blue Bell *(G-1836)*
Intel Corporation....G.... 908 894-6035
Allentown *(G-263)*
Intel Network Systems Inc....F.... 610 973-5566
Allentown *(G-264)*
Intermec Technologies Corp....F.... 724 218-1444
Imperial *(G-8068)*
J Penner Corporation....E.... 215 340-9700
Doylestown *(G-4308)*
Lee Rj Group Inc....C.... 800 860-1775
Monroeville *(G-11342)*
Legrand Home Systems Inc....E.... 717 702-2532
Middletown *(G-11061)*
▲ **Legrand Home Systems Inc**....D.... 717 702-2532
Middletown *(G-11060)*
Lexicon International Corp....E.... 215 639-8220
Bensalem *(G-1220)*
Lexmark International Inc....F.... 610 966-8283
Coopersburg *(G-3630)*
Library Video Company....D.... 610 645-4000
Conshohocken *(G-3572)*
Light My Fiber LLC....G.... 888 428-4454
West Chester *(G-19593)*
Loranger International Corp....D.... 814 723-2250
Warren *(G-19038)*
▼ **Loveshaw Corporation**....C.... 570 937-4921
South Canaan *(G-17769)*
Matthews International Corp....D.... 412 665-2500
Pittsburgh *(G-15265)*
Mecco....G.... 412 548-3549
Pittsburgh *(G-15271)*
Menu For Less....G.... 215 240-1582
Feasterville Trevose *(G-5919)*
Mergtech Inc....G.... 570 584-3388
Hughesville *(G-7896)*

Monroeville Ink Refills Inc...................G...... 412 374-1700
  Monroeville (G-11346)

Moog Inc...C...... 610 328-4000
  Springfield (G-17919)

Next Rev Distribution Inc.................G...... 717 576-9050
  Hershey (G-7623)

Oberon Inc.......................................F...... 814 867-2312
  State College (G-18003)

▲ Omega Piezo Technologies Inc....F...... 814 861-4160
  State College (G-18004)

Online Data Systems Inc.................E...... 610 967-5821
  Emmaus (G-5037)

▲ Pannier Corporation.....................F...... 412 323-4900
  Pittsburgh (G-15368)

Phxco LLC..D...... 608 203-1500
  Middletown (G-11069)

Pixel Innovations Inc.......................G...... 724 935-8366
  Wexford (G-19821)

R T R Business Products Inc...........E...... 724 733-7373
  Export (G-5622)

Riverbed Technology Inc..................G...... 610 648-3819
  Malvern (G-10310)

RMS Omega Tech Grouping..............G...... 610 917-0472
  Phoenixville (G-14574)

RTD Embedded Technologies Inc.....G...... 814 234-8087
  State College (G-18017)

Saxon Office Technology Inc............F...... 215 736-2620
  Fairless Hills (G-5795)

Solvay...D...... 412 423-2030
  Pittsburgh (G-15554)

Support McRcomputers Assoc Inc......F...... 215 496-0303
  Philadelphia (G-14359)

Symbol Technologies LLC..................F...... 610 834-8900
  Plymouth Meeting (G-15875)

Tsitouch Inc.....................................E...... 802 874-0123
  Uniontown (G-18643)

Vanguard Identification....................E...... 610 719-0700
  West Chester (G-19672)

▲ Videotek Inc.................................C...... 610 327-2292
  Pottstown (G-16068)

Vocollect Inc....................................C...... 412 829-8145
  Pittsburgh (G-15702)

Vocollect Healthcare Systems..........E...... 412 829-8145
  Pittsburgh (G-15703)

W Graphics Digital Services.............G...... 610 252-3565
  Easton (G-4773)

Watch My Net Inc.............................G...... 267 625-6000
  Glenside (G-6543)

Whiskey Dicks..................................G...... 570 342-9824
  Scranton (G-17312)

▼ Whiteman Tower Inc......................G...... 800 748-3891
  Wilkes Barre (G-19974)

World Video Sales Co Inc..................G...... 610 754-6800
  Bechtelsville (G-1038)

Xerox Corporation...........................C...... 412 506-4000
  Pittsburgh (G-15726)

Zemco Tool & Die Inc.......................D...... 717 647-7151
  Williamstown (G-20104)

3578 Calculating & Accounting Eqpt

Atm Bancorp Inc..............................G...... 610 279-9550
  Norristown (G-12636)

Beaver Valley Cash Register Co..........G...... 724 728-0800
  New Brighton (G-12031)

Blessed Dough LLC..........................F...... 717 368-4109
  Easton (G-4657)

◆ Crane Payment Innovations Inc.....B...... 610 430-2700
  Malvern (G-10218)

Data Tech Pos Inc............................G...... 215 925-8888
  Philadelphia (G-13605)

Datacap Systems Inc........................E...... 215 997-8989
  Chalfont (G-2871)

Garda CL Technical Svcs Inc.............D...... 610 926-7400
  Reading (G-16389)

Matrix Atm......................................G...... 215 661-2916
  North Wales (G-12813)

Menasha Packaging Company LLC.....G...... 717 520-5990
  Hershey (G-7621)

▲ Remcal Products Corporation........F...... 215 343-5500
  Warrington (G-19130)

◆ Sicom Systems Inc.......................D...... 215 489-2500
  Lansdale (G-9410)

Talaris Inc.......................................G...... 215 674-2882
  Horsham (G-7855)

Ukani Brothers Enterprise................G...... 412 269-0499
  Pittsburgh (G-15667)

3579 Office Machines, NEC

▼ Advanced Pstioning Systems Inc.....G...... 717 582-3915
  Elliottsburg (G-4918)

Allegheny-Wagner Inds Inc...............E...... 724 468-4300
  Delmont (G-4047)

Bowe Bell + Howell Postal Syst.........F...... 610 317-4300
  Bethlehem (G-1472)

Contrado BBH Holdings LLC.............F...... 215 609-3400
  Philadelphia (G-13573)

Dein-Verbit Associates Inc...............F...... 610 649-9674
  Ardmore (G-707)

Keystone Typewriter Company..........G...... 814 539-6077
  Johnstown (G-8397)

Mg Financial Services Inc.................E...... 215 364-7555
  Fort Washington (G-6086)

Neopost USA Inc..............................E...... 717 939-2700
  Middletown (G-11066)

Neopost USA Inc..............................G...... 717 939-2700
  King of Prussia (G-8654)

Packaging Progressions Inc.............E...... 610 489-9096
  Souderton (G-17758)

Paper Converting Machine Co...........C...... 814 695-5521
  Duncansville (G-4459)

Pitney Bowes Inc..............................E...... 717 884-1882
  Harrisburg (G-7199)

Pitney Bowes Inc..............................E...... 412 689-6639
  Pittsburgh (G-15383)

Pitney Bowes Inc..............................C...... 215 751-9800
  Philadelphia (G-14180)

Pitney Bowes Inc..............................E...... 215 946-2863
  Levittown (G-9856)

Roovers Inc.....................................G...... 570 455-7548
  Hazleton (G-7523)

▲ Sapling Inc..................................E...... 215 322-6063
  Warminster (G-18961)

William A Fraser Inc.........................F...... 717 766-1126
  Mechanicsburg (G-10910)

3581 Automatic Vending Machines

Compass Group USA Investments.......F...... 717 939-1200
  Middletown (G-11051)

▲ Evive Station LLC.........................G...... 724 972-6421
  Rostraver Township (G-16825)

Jennison Ice LLC..............................G...... 412 596-5914
  Carnegie (G-2772)

Mk Solutions Inc..............................G...... 860 760-0438
  York (G-20601)

Sapor Food Group LLC......................F...... 267 714-4382
  Philadelphia (G-14281)

Tasty Fries Inc.................................G...... 610 941-2109
  Blue Bell (G-1855)

Teutech LLC.....................................E...... 814 486-1896
  Emporium (G-5077)

Vend Natural of Western PA...............G...... 724 518-6594
  Donora (G-4164)

Vendors 1st Choice Inc.....................G...... 215 804-1011
  Quakertown (G-16256)

West Dairy Inc.................................E...... 610 495-0100
  Parker Ford (G-13170)

3582 Commercial Laundry, Dry Clean & Pressing Mchs

◆ Apparel Machinery & Supply Co......E...... 215 634-2626
  Philadelphia (G-13400)

Hang Xing Fa Inc..............................G...... 646 250-7175
  Allentown (G-241)

Schreiber & Goldberg Ltd.................E...... 570 344-4000
  Dunmore (G-4483)

Shamaseen Hamzah...........................G...... 484 557-5051
  Center Valley (G-2830)

3585 Air Conditioning & Heating Eqpt

A M Parts Inc...................................G...... 412 367-8040
  Pittsburgh (G-14630)

Advanced Thermal Solutions LLC.......G...... 610 966-2500
  Emmaus (G-5018)

▲ Air/Tak Inc...................................F...... 724 297-3416
  Worthington (G-20226)

Airgreen LLC....................................G...... 610 209-8067
  West Chester (G-19495)

▲ American Cooling Tech Inc............F...... 717 767-2775
  York (G-20373)

Apex Fountain Sales Inc...................G...... 215 627-4526
  Philadelphia (G-13398)

Beneficial Enrgy Solutions LLC.........G...... 844 237-7697
  Jonestown (G-8449)

◆ Beverage Air.................................F...... 814 849-2022
  Brookville (G-2249)

Beverage-Air Corporation.................C...... 814 849-7336
  Brookville (G-2250)

Bti-Coopermatics Inc........................G...... 610 262-7700
  Northampton (G-12847)

Building Inspectors Contrs Inc...........G...... 215 481-0606
  Glenside (G-6509)

Capital Coil & Air LLC.......................G...... 484 498-6880
  West Chester (G-19518)

Carel Usa Inc...................................G...... 410 497-5128
  Manheim (G-10374)

Carrier Corporation...........................E...... 610 834-1717
  Plymouth Meeting (G-15838)

▲ Chipblaster Inc.............................D...... 814 724-6278
  Meadville (G-10712)

▲ Cni Inc..E...... 215 244-9650
  Bensalem (G-1169)

▼ Coil Company LLC..........................E...... 610 408-8361
  Malvern (G-10214)

▲ Crown Boiler Co.............................E...... 215 535-8900
  Philadelphia (G-13586)

Crystaline Bus & Rail Inc...................F...... 570 645-3145
  Nesquehoning (G-12004)

Custom Chill Inc..............................G...... 215 676-7600
  Philadelphia (G-13593)

▲ Drake Refrigeration Inc.................G...... 215 638-5515
  Bensalem (G-1183)

E-Finity Dstrbted Gnration LLC.........G...... 610 688-6212
  Wayne (G-19321)

◆ Eic Solutions Inc..........................E...... 215 443-5190
  Warminster (G-18870)

EMC Technology LLC.........................G...... 814 728-8857
  Warren (G-19025)

Enerflex Energy Systems Inc.............E...... 724 627-0751
  Canonsburg (G-2585)

Enerflex Energy Systems Inc.............D...... 570 726-0500
  Muncy (G-11815)

Energy Products & Technologies.........G...... 717 485-3137
  Mc Connellsburg (G-10564)

Evapco Alcoil Inc.............................E...... 717 347-7500
  York (G-20472)

▲ Everything Ice Inc.........................E...... 814 244-5477
  Salix (G-17047)

F W Lang Co.....................................G...... 267 401-8293
  Havertown (G-7421)

◆ Follett LLC...................................B...... 610 252-7301
  Easton (G-4684)

Follett LLC.......................................G...... 800 523-9361
  Bethlehem (G-1515)

Galaxy Global Products LLC..............G...... 610 692-7400
  West Chester (G-19557)

Gap Ridge Contractors LLC...............F...... 717 442-4386
  Kinzers (G-8738)

Gea Systems North America Llc.........C...... 717 767-6411
  York (G-20493)

Gem Refrigerator Co.........................F...... 877 436-7374
  Philadelphia (G-13746)

Goodwest Industries LLC..................E...... 215 340-3100
  Douglassville (G-4177)

Grokas Inc.......................................F...... 610 565-1498
  Media (G-10931)

Harsco Corporation...........................E...... 570 421-7500
  East Stroudsburg (G-4618)

Havaco Technologies Inc..................G...... 814 878-5509
  Erie (G-5311)

Hermetics Inc...................................G...... 215 848-9522
  Philadelphia (G-13818)

▲ HMC Enterprises LLC.....................E...... 215 464-6800
  Philadelphia (G-13831)

Honeywell International Inc...............A...... 215 533-3000
  Philadelphia (G-13832)

▲ Imprintables Warehouse LLC.........G...... 724 966-8599
  Carmichaels (G-2758)

Industrial Systems & Controls...........G...... 412 638-4977
  Pittsburgh (G-15121)

J&M Fluidics Inc...............................G...... 888 539-1731
  Telford (G-18297)

John Bachman Hvac...........................G...... 610 266-3877
  Catasauqua (G-2815)

Johnson Controls Inc........................D...... 717 771-7890
  York (G-20543)

Johnstone Supply Inc........................E...... 484 765-1160
  Breinigsville (G-2019)

K C Stoves & Fireplaces Inc..............G...... 610 966-3556
  Alburtis (G-54)

Keller Enterprises Inc.......................G...... 866 359-6828
  Northampton (G-12853)

◆ Klinge Corporation........................D...... 717 840-4500
  York (G-20556)

Koch Filter Corporation.....................F...... 215 679-3135
  East Greenville (G-4572)

◆ Kold Draft International LLC...........E...... 814 453-6761
  Erie (G-5350)

Kottcamp Sheet Metal.......................E...... 717 845-7616
  York (G-20558)

◆ **Lasko Products LLC** C 610 692-7400
West Chester *(G-19588)*

Liberty Bell Bottling Co Inc G 610 820-6020
Allentown *(G-294)*

Memrs Inc G 724 589-5567
Greenville *(G-6754)*

Micro Matic Usa Inc F 610 625-4464
Center Valley *(G-2828)*

▼ **Multi-Flow Dispensers LP** D 215 322-1800
Huntingdon Valley *(G-8014)*

Narsa F 724 799-8415
Wexford *(G-19814)*

National Rfrgn & AC Pdts Inc F 215 638-8909
Langhorne *(G-9313)*

▲ **National Rfrgn & AC Pdts Inc** E 215 244-1400
Bensalem *(G-1228)*

Nevco Service Co LLC G 717 626-1479
Lititz *(G-10025)*

Nortek Global Hvac LLC B 814 938-1408
Punxsutawney *(G-16151)*

Ocean Thermal Energy Corp F 717 299-1344
Lancaster *(G-9150)*

Oxicool Inc G 215 462-2665
Malvern *(G-10292)*

Parts To Your Door LP G 610 916-5380
Reading *(G-16466)*

Pennergy Solutions LLC G 484 393-1539
Royersford *(G-16859)*

▲ **Pinnacle Products Intl Inc** F 215 302-1417
Bristol *(G-2183)*

Poolpak Inc D 717 757-2648
York *(G-20632)*

Poolpak LLC G 717 757-2648
York *(G-20633)*

Precision Technology Assoc Inc G 412 881-8006
Pittsburgh *(G-15433)*

▲ **Reliable Products Intl LLC** G 717 261-1291
Mercersburg *(G-10995)*

▲ **Reznor LLC** A 724 662-4400
Mercer *(G-10971)*

RG Industries Inc E 717 849-0345
York *(G-20658)*

Rich Industrial Services Inc F 610 534-0195
Holmes *(G-7664)*

▲ **S P Industries Inc** D 215 672-7800
Warminster *(G-18959)*

Tek-Temp Instruments Inc E 215 788-5528
Croydon *(G-3930)*

Tekgard Inc D 717 854-0005
York *(G-20685)*

Texan Corporation E 215 441-8967
Warminster *(G-18979)*

Thd Contracting Service LLC G 215 626-1548
Philadelphia *(G-14385)*

Thermal Care Inc G 724 584-5500
Franklin *(G-6164)*

Time Tech Industries Inc G 412 670-5498
Mc Kees Rocks *(G-10639)*

Trane US Inc D 412 747-3000
Pittsburgh *(G-15635)*

Trane US Inc F 412 394-9021
Pittsburgh *(G-15636)*

Trane US Inc G 412 963-9021
Pittsburgh *(G-15637)*

Trane US Inc E 717 561-5400
Harrisburg *(G-7235)*

Trilli Holdings Inc G 724 736-8000
Star Junction *(G-17938)*

TS McCorry Heating and Cooling G 215 379-2800
Rydal *(G-16887)*

Tuna Enterprises G 724 205-6535
Greensburg *(G-6722)*

U R I Compressors Inc G 484 223-3265
Allentown *(G-416)*

Union Chill Mat Co G 724 452-6400
Zelienople *(G-20825)*

United Coolair Corporation C 717 845-8685
York *(G-20694)*

▼ **United States Thermoamp Inc** E 724 537-3500
Latrobe *(G-9526)*

United Technologies Corp B 800 227-7437
Scottdale *(G-17203)*

US Boiler G 215 535-8900
Philadelphia *(G-14434)*

USA Coil & Air Inc E 610 296-9668
Malvern *(G-10336)*

Waste Recovery Designed Pdts G 724 926-5713
Bethel Park *(G-1437)*

▲ **Wayne Products Inc** F 800 255-5665
Broomall *(G-2305)*

Wedj/Three CS Inc D 717 845-8685
York *(G-20705)*

York International Corporation E 414 524-1200
Audubon *(G-832)*

York International Corporation F 814 479-4005
Johnstown *(G-8447)*

York International Corporation C 717 815-4200
York *(G-20744)*

York International Corporation B 717 762-1440
Waynesboro *(G-19431)*

◆ **York International Corporation** A 717 771-7890
York *(G-20745)*

York International Corporation B 717 762-2121
Waynesboro *(G-19432)*

3586 Measuring & Dispensing Pumps

Atlantis Technologies LLC G 724 695-2900
Oakdale *(G-12893)*

▲ **Drummond Scientific Company** D 610 353-0200
Broomall *(G-2287)*

Fluid Dynamics Inc E 215 699-8700
North Wales *(G-12802)*

▼ **Jaeco Fluid Solutions Inc** G 610 407-7207
Malvern *(G-10258)*

◆ **Maguire Products Inc** E 610 459-4300
Aston *(G-773)*

▲ **Mechanical Service Co Inc** F 610 351-1655
Allentown *(G-313)*

▲ **Milton Roy LLC** C 215 441-0800
Ivyland *(G-8218)*

Milton Roy LLC G 215 293-0401
Ivyland *(G-8219)*

Seventy-Three Mfg Co Inc E 610 845-7823
Bechtelsville *(G-1037)*

3589 Service Ind Machines, NEC

A I Floor Products G 215 355-2798
Feasterville Trevose *(G-5881)*

A3-Usa Inc G 724 871-7170
Westmoreland City *(G-19783)*

▼ **Agape Water Solutions Inc** G 215 631-7035
Harleysville *(G-7014)*

Alfa Laval Inc G 610 594-1830
Exton *(G-5638)*

Allegheny Paper Shredders Corp E 800 245-2497
Delmont *(G-4046)*

Allegheny-Wagner Inds Inc E 724 468-4300
Delmont *(G-4047)*

Altair Equipment Company Inc E 215 672-9000
Warminster *(G-18826)*

American Auto Wash Inc F 610 265-3222
King of Prussia *(G-8580)*

American Water Technologies E 724 850-9000
Youngwood *(G-20778)*

▲ **Aqua Treatment Services Inc** E 717 697-4998
Mechanicsburg *(G-10820)*

◆ **Aquatech International LLC** C 724 746-5300
Canonsburg *(G-2543)*

Aquatech Intl Sls Corp G 724 746-5300
Canonsburg *(G-2544)*

◆ **Aztec Products Inc** F 215 393-4700
Montgomeryville *(G-11387)*

Biss Nuss Inc G 412 221-1200
Pittsburgh *(G-14769)*

Blue Boy Products Inc G 610 284-1055
Downingtown *(G-4215)*

Borough of Tyrone G 814 684-5396
Tyrone *(G-18577)*

BSC Technologies Inc G 570 825-9196
Dallas *(G-3959)*

Bti-Coopermatics Inc G 610 262-7700
Northampton *(G-12847)*

▲ **C-B Tool Co** E 717 397-3521
Lancaster *(G-8967)*

◆ **Calgon Carbon Corporation** C 412 787-6700
Moon Township *(G-11482)*

Calgon Carbon Corporation B 412 787-6700
Pittsburgh *(G-14803)*

▼ **Campbell Manufacturing Inc** D 610 367-2107
Bechtelsville *(G-1030)*

▼ **Cardinal Resources Inc** G 412 374-0989
Pittsburgh *(G-14809)*

Cardinal Resources LLC G 412 374-0989
Pittsburgh *(G-14810)*

▲ **Cardinal Systems Inc** E 570 385-4733
Schuylkill Haven *(G-17151)*

Cawley Environmental Svcs Inc F 610 594-0101
Downingtown *(G-4219)*

CCL Restoration LLC G 412 926-6156
Pittsburgh *(G-14830)*

▲ **Chemical Equipment Labs VA Inc** E 610 497-9390
Newtown Square *(G-12570)*

Chippewa Twp Sewage Plant G 724 846-3820
Beaver Falls *(G-998)*

City of New Castle G 724 654-1627
New Castle *(G-12073)*

▼ **CK Construction & Indus Inc** G 570 286-4128
Pitman *(G-14622)*

Clapper Leon Plbg Htg Wtr Cond F 570 629-2833
Stroudsburg *(G-18110)*

Collins Deck Sealing G 717 789-3322
Landisburg *(G-9256)*

Comtech Industries Inc E 724 884-0101
Canonsburg *(G-2565)*

Concept Products Corporation G 610 722-0830
Mertztown *(G-11002)*

Corrosion Technology Inc G 610 429-1450
West Chester *(G-19530)*

County of Somerset G 814 629-9460
Hollsopple *(G-7657)*

Craft Products Co Inc G 412 821-8102
Pittsburgh *(G-14885)*

◆ **Cromaflow Inc** F 570 546-3557
Montoursville *(G-11437)*

Crown Food Carts Incorporated G 610 628-9612
Allentown *(G-187)*

Ctc Pressure Products LLC G 814 315-6427
Erie *(G-5235)*

Custom Blends Inc G 215 934-7080
Philadelphia *(G-13592)*

Custom Fab Co Inc F 570 784-0874
Bloomsburg *(G-1777)*

De Nora Water Technologies Inc G 412 494-4077
Pittsburgh *(G-14913)*

De Nora Water Technologies Inc E 412 788-8300
Pittsburgh *(G-14914)*

Double D Service Center LLC F 717 201-2800
Columbia *(G-3437)*

Ds Services of America Inc F 717 901-4620
Harrisburg *(G-7122)*

DW Services LLC G 484 241-8915
Allentown *(G-198)*

▲ **East West Component Inc** G 215 616-4414
North Wales *(G-12799)*

▲ **Easy Liner LLC** G 717 825-7962
York *(G-20461)*

Electrocell Systems Inc G 610 438-2969
Easton *(G-4678)*

Elm Ave Car Wash G 717 637-7392
Hanover *(G-6881)*

EMC Global Technologies Inc G 215 340-0650
Doylestown *(G-4298)*

EMC Global Technologies Inc F 267 347-5100
Telford *(G-18287)*

Emsco Inc E 814 774-3137
Girard *(G-6387)*

Encotech Inc E 724 222-3334
Eighty Four *(G-4839)*

Enquip Co G 610 363-8275
Exton *(G-5672)*

◆ **Envirodyne Systems Inc** E 717 763-0500
Camp Hill *(G-2496)*

Equisol LLC F 866 629-7646
Conshohocken *(G-3544)*

Espresso Analysts G 724 541-2151
Indiana *(G-8097)*

Espresso Solutions G 412 326-0170
West Mifflin *(G-19737)*

Essential Water Technologies F 570 317-2583
Bloomsburg *(G-1781)*

Evoqua Water Technologies Corp D 724 772-0044
Pittsburgh *(G-14990)*

Ewt Holdings III Corp G 724 772-0044
Pittsburgh *(G-14991)*

▲ **FB Leopold Company Inc** F 724 452-6300
Zelienople *(G-20800)*

Fermentec Inc G 203 809-8078
Philadelphia *(G-13697)*

Filson Water Treatment Inc F 717 240-0763
Carlisle *(G-2712)*

Filter & Water Technologies G 267 450-4900
Montgomeryville *(G-11397)*

Filter Technology Inc G 866 992-9490
Gladwyne *(G-6407)*

Foxcroft Equipment & Svcs Co F 610 942-2888
Glenmoore *(G-6467)*

Fresh Roasted Coffee LLC F 570 743-9228
Sunbury *(G-18169)*

▼ **Full-On Filters** G 610 970-4701
Pottstown *(G-15989)*

▲ Gamajet Cleaning Systems Inc......F 610 408-9940
Exton *(G-5684)*

▼ GE Infrastructure Sensing ....F 617 926-1749
Feasterville Trevose *(G-5912)*

▲ General Ecology Inc ....E 610 363-7900
Exton *(G-5686)*

▲ General Wire Spring Company ....C 412 771-6300
Mc Kees Rocks *(G-10612)*

Global Environmental Tech ....G 610 821-4901
Allentown *(G-234)*

GSM Hold Co ....G 412 487-7140
Allison Park *(G-452)*

Guardian CSC Corporation ....F 717 848-2540
Hellam *(G-7551)*

Guardian Filtration Pdts LLC ....G 724 646-0450
Greenville *(G-6744)*

▼ Hess Machine International ....G 717 733-0005
Ephrata *(G-5108)*

High Tech Aquatics Inc ....G 570 546-3557
Muncy *(G-11819)*

Hobart Corporation ....E 717 397-5100
Lancaster *(G-9050)*

Hobart Sales and Service Inc ....G 301 733-6560
Harrisburg *(G-7150)*

Hotwash ....F 610 351-2119
Allentown *(G-247)*

▲ Hsm of America LLC ....E 610 918-4894
Downingtown *(G-4235)*

Hydroflow Pennsylvania LLC ....G 814 643-7135
Pennsylvania Furnace *(G-13263)*

Ial Assoc LLC ....E 215 887-5114
Elkins Park *(G-4906)*

Idreco USA Ltd ....F 610 701-9944
West Chester *(G-19566)*

Inframark LLC ....D 215 822-2258
Colmar *(G-3417)*

▲ Inframark LLC ....E 215 646-9201
Horsham *(G-7823)*

Infrastructure H Environmental ....F 866 629-7646
Conshohocken *(G-3563)*

Innovative Control Systems Inc ....E 610 881-8061
Easton *(G-4706)*

▲ Innovative Control Systems Inc ....C 610 881-8000
Wind Gap *(G-20169)*

▲ Insinger Machine Company ....D 215 624-4800
Philadelphia *(G-13860)*

▲ Jenny Products Inc ....E 814 445-3400
Somerset *(G-17693)*

Kneppers Kleen Water ....G 717 264-9715
Chambersburg *(G-2948)*

Lancaster Pump ....E 717 397-3521
Lancaster *(G-9105)*

Landons Car Wash and Laundry ....G 570 673-4188
Canton *(G-2665)*

Lang Filter Media LP ....F 570 459-7005
Hazleton *(G-7507)*

Lebanon Water Treatment Plant ....F 717 865-2191
Lebanon *(G-9606)*

Lester Water Inc ....F 610 444-4660
Kennett Square *(G-8522)*

Longs Water Technol ....G 610 398-3737
Orefield *(G-13014)*

Mannis Wash Systems ....G 724 337-8255
New Kensington *(G-12354)*

◆ Marg Inc ....F 724 703-3020
Oakdale *(G-12906)*

Master Water Conditioning Corp ....F 610 323-8358
Pottstown *(G-16017)*

Mendit Chemical Inc ....F 610 239-5120
Bridgeport *(G-2039)*

Metro Building Services ....G 412 221-1284
Pittsburgh *(G-15281)*

Mfg Water Treat Prod ....G 814 438-3959
Union City *(G-18609)*

Mid-Atlntic Bldg Solutions LLC ....G 484 532-7269
Blue Bell *(G-1848)*

Mobile Wash Power Wash Inc ....G 814 327-3820
Bedford *(G-1065)*

Morantz Inc ....G 215 969-0266
Philadelphia *(G-14038)*

Mount Plsnt Twnshp-Wshngtn CNT .....F 724 356-7974
Hickory *(G-7629)*

MPW Industrial Services Inc ....G 412 233-4060
Clairton *(G-3154)*

N/S Corporation ....G 610 436-5552
West Chester *(G-19605)*

Nalco Company LLC ....E 412 278-8600
Pittsburgh *(G-15317)*

Nalco Wtr Prtrtment Sltons LLC ....E 610 358-0717
Aston *(G-780)*

Neptune-Benson Inc ....G 724 772-0044
Pittsburgh *(G-15327)*

Newterra Inc ....G 610 631-7700
Norristown *(G-12692)*

Orbisonia Rockhill Joint ....G 814 447-5414
Orbisonia *(G-13007)*

Otterbine Barebo Inc ....G 610 965-6018
Emmaus *(G-5038)*

Overhead Door Corporation ....D 215 368-8700
Lansdale *(G-9266)*

Oxford Area Sewer Authority ....G 610 932-3493
Oxford *(G-13085)*

Pennsylvania American Water - ....D 412 884-5113
Pittsburgh *(G-15374)*

◆ Philadlphia Mxing Slutions Ltd ....D 717 832-2800
Palmyra *(G-13129)*

▼ Philadlphia Tramrail Entps Inc ....C 215 743-4359
Philadelphia *(G-14165)*

◆ PNC Equity Partners LP ....F 412 914-0175
Pittsburgh *(G-15417)*

Pocono Water Centers Inc ....G 570 839-8012
Moscow *(G-11600)*

Process Masters Corporation ....G 610 683-5674
Kutztown *(G-8857)*

Protechs LLC ....G 717 768-0800
New Holland *(G-12273)*

◆ Ptr Baler and Compactor Co ....C 215 533-5100
Philadelphia *(G-14215)*

Pump-Warehouse Inc ....E 215 536-0500
Quakertown *(G-16236)*

Pure Flow Water Co ....G 215 723-0237
Souderton *(G-17761)*

Pure Power ....G 412 673-5285
White Oak *(G-19857)*

R & R Briggs Inc ....G 215 357-3413
Southampton *(G-17833)*

R M Frantz Inc ....G 570 421-3020
Stroudsburg *(G-18137)*

▲ Rdp Technologies Inc ....F 610 650-9900
Conshohocken *(G-3599)*

Realm Therapeutics Inc ....D 484 321-2700
Malvern *(G-10308)*

Roberts Filter Holding Company ....G 610 583-3131
Media *(G-10946)*

Ronald Hines ....G 570 256-3355
Shickshinny *(G-17502)*

S & G Water Conditioning Inc ....G 215 672-2030
Warminster *(G-18957)*

S H Sharpless & Son Inc ....G 570 454-6685
Hazleton *(G-7524)*

S Morantz Inc ....D 215 969-0266
Philadelphia *(G-14273)*

Safety House Inc ....F 610 344-0637
Glen Mills *(G-6443)*

Sanatoga Water Cond Inc ....G 610 326-9803
Pottstown *(G-16042)*

Sawcom Tech Inc ....G 610 433-7900
Whitehall *(G-19888)*

▲ Scale Watcher North Amer Inc ....G 610 932-6888
Oxford *(G-13089)*

Shenandoah Water Trtmnt Plant ....G 570 462-4918
Shenandoah *(G-17496)*

Siemens Industry Inc ....E 724 772-0044
Warrendale *(G-19097)*

Solar Laundry & Dry Cleaning ....G 610 323-2121
Pottstown *(G-16048)*

Somat Company ....E 717 397-5100
Lancaster *(G-9202)*

Spec Sciences Inc ....G 607 972-3159
Sharon *(G-17443)*

Sponge-Jet Inc ....G 570 278-4563
Montrose *(G-11478)*

◆ Suez Wts Systems Usa Inc ....B 781 359-7000
Trevose *(G-18505)*

Suez Wts Systems Usa Inc ....C 724 743-0270
Canonsburg *(G-2642)*

Taylor Run ....G 610 436-1369
West Chester *(G-19656)*

Terra Group Corp ....E 610 821-7003
Allentown *(G-408)*

▲ Trijay Systems Inc ....F 215 997-5833
Line Lexington *(G-9977)*

Trilli Holdings Inc ....G 724 736-8000
Star Junction *(G-17938)*

TSS Industries Inc ....G 717 821-6570
Pine Grove *(G-14606)*

▲ Turf Teq LLC ....E 484 798-6300
Honey Brook *(G-7767)*

Ultra Pure Products Inc ....E 717 589-7001
Mifflintown *(G-11139)*

USA All Pro Auto Salon Inc ....G 267 230-7442
Warminster *(G-18992)*

Water Gem Inc ....F 717 561-4440
Harrisburg *(G-7244)*

Water Master Inc ....G 717 561-4440
Harrisburg *(G-7245)*

Water Treatment By Design LLC ....G 717 938-0670
Lewisberry *(G-9894)*

Watermark Usa LLC ....F 610 983-0500
Gladwyne *(G-6409)*

▲ Wsg & Solutions Inc ....E 267 638-3000
Montgomeryville *(G-11427)*

◆ Xylem Wtr Sltons Zlienople LLC ....C 724 452-6300
Zelienople *(G-20830)*

▲ Zero Technologies LLC ....F 215 244-0823
Trevose *(G-18509)*

3592 Carburetors, Pistons, Rings & Valves

Mercer Valve Co Inc ....G 412 859-0300
Pittsburgh *(G-15277)*

Mikron Valve & Mfr Inc ....G 814 453-2337
Erie *(G-5392)*

▲ Morgan Advanced Mtls Tech Inc ....C 814 781-1573
Saint Marys *(G-16998)*

Niagara Piston Ring Works Inc ....F 716 782-2307
Corry *(G-3770)*

Philadelphia Valve Company Inc ....E 570 669-9461
Nesquehoning *(G-12008)*

Philapack LLC ....G 215 322-2122
Huntingdon Valley *(G-8025)*

Precision Controls LLC ....E 267 337-9812
Levittown *(G-9860)*

Sloan Valve Company ....G 717 387-3959
Mechanicsburg *(G-10889)*

▲ Tru Tech Valve LLC ....G 724 916-4805
New Castle *(G-12160)*

3593 Fluid Power Cylinders & Actuators

▲ Alliance Remanufacturing Inc ....C 215 291-4640
Philadelphia *(G-13368)*

American Hydraulic Mfg ....G 610 264-8542
Allentown *(G-135)*

◆ Auma Actuators Inc ....C 724 743-2862
Canonsburg *(G-2545)*

Auma Actuators Inc ....G 714 247-1250
Canonsburg *(G-2546)*

Basic - Psa Inc ....E 814 266-8646
Johnstown *(G-8356)*

Burnside America Inc ....G 717 414-1509
Chambersburg *(G-2914)*

Ecobee Advanced Tech LLC ....G 609 474-0010
Warminster *(G-18869)*

Fessler Machine Company ....E 724 346-0878
Sharon *(G-17433)*

▲ Fluidtechnik USA ....G 610 321-2407
Glenmoore *(G-6466)*

▲ Hydac Corp ....G 610 266-0100
Bethlehem *(G-1533)*

Hydac Technology Corp ....G 610 266-3143
Bethlehem *(G-1535)*

Kerry Company Inc ....F 412 486-3388
Allison Park *(G-455)*

Manchester Hydraulics Inc ....G 717 764-5226
Manchester *(G-10357)*

Moog Inc ....C 610 328-4000
Springfield *(G-17919)*

Morgantown Technical Services ....D 724 324-5433
Mount Morris *(G-11682)*

National Hydraulics Inc ....D 724 547-9222
Mount Pleasant *(G-11708)*

Parker-Hannifin Corporation ....E 814 866-4100
Erie *(G-5416)*

▲ PBM Inc ....D 724 863-0550
Irwin *(G-8189)*

◆ Ralph A Hiller Company ....E 724 325-1200
Export *(G-5623)*

RG Industries Inc ....E 717 849-0345
York *(G-20658)*

Tri-State Hydraulics Inc ....E 724 483-1790
Charleroi *(G-3022)*

Wellm Dyna Mach and Asse Inc ....E 717 764-8855
York *(G-20707)*

Wipro Enterprises Inc ....G 717 496-8877
Chambersburg *(G-2999)*

▲ York Industries Inc ....E 717 764-8855
York *(G-20742)*

3594 Fluid Power Pumps & Motors

American Hydraulic Mfg ....G 610 264-8542
Allentown *(G-135)*

S
I
C

Bosch Rexroth Corporation................A...... 610 694-8300
Bethlehem *(G-1471)*

Bosch Rexroth Corporation................A...... 610 694-8300
Bethlehem *(G-1470)*

Conestoga USA Inc.............................G...... 610 327-2882
Pottstown *(G-15973)*

▲ Eastern Industrial Pdts Inc.............E...... 610 459-1212
Aston *(G-760)*

Eaton Aerospace LLC.........................D...... 610 522-4000
Glenolden *(G-6473)*

Eaton Corporation...............................E...... 412 893-3300
Moon Township *(G-11484)*

◆ Eaton Electrical Inc.........................E...... 412 893-3300
Moon Township *(G-11485)*

▼ Global Trade Links LLC...................E...... 888 777-1577
Chester Springs *(G-3079)*

▲ Hydac Corp......................................G...... 610 266-0100
Bethlehem *(G-1533)*

▲ Hydromotion Inc..............................D...... 610 948-4150
Spring City *(G-17860)*

ITT Corporation...................................G...... 717 262-2945
Chambersburg *(G-2944)*

Lionheart Holdings LLC.......................D...... 215 283-8400
Newtown *(G-12519)*

Manchester Hydraulics Inc.................G...... 717 764-5226
Manchester *(G-10357)*

N-Jay Machines...................................G...... 724 232-0110
Karns City *(G-8481)*

National Hydraulics Inc.......................D...... 724 547-9222
Mount Pleasant *(G-11708)*

Nick Charles Kravitch.........................G...... 412 882-6262
Pittsburgh *(G-15340)*

Parker-Hannifin Corporation...............D...... 814 438-3821
Union City *(G-18612)*

Parker-Hannifin Corporation...............C...... 717 263-5099
Chambersburg *(G-2968)*

Penndel Hydraulic Sls & Svc Co.........G...... 215 757-2000
Langhorne *(G-9317)*

◆ R H Sheppard Co Inc......................A...... 717 637-3751
Hanover *(G-6941)*

◆ Ralph A Hiller Company..................E...... 724 325-1200
Export *(G-5623)*

▲ Seko Dosing Systems Corp.............G...... 215 945-0125
Bristol *(G-2197)*

Sencillo Systems Inc.........................G...... 610 340-2848
Warrington *(G-19133)*

Siemens Industry Inc.........................C...... 724 339-9500
New Kensington *(G-12375)*

◆ Weir Hazleton Inc...........................D...... 570 455-7711
Hazleton *(G-7537)*

▼ Wojanis Supply Company................E...... 724 695-1415
Coraopolis *(G-3734)*

▲ York Industries Inc.........................E...... 717 764-8855
York *(G-20742)*

3596 Scales & Balances, Exc Laboratory

A H Emery Company............................F....... 717 295-6935
Lancaster *(G-8918)*

◆ All-Fill Corporation.........................D...... 866 255-3455
Exton *(G-5639)*

▲ Cambridge Scale Works Inc............F....... 610 273-7040
Honey Brook *(G-7740)*

Drafto Corporation..............................D...... 814 425-7445
Cochranton *(G-3342)*

▲ Jiba LLC..F....... 215 739-9644
Philadelphia *(G-13898)*

Kanawha Scales & Systems Inc..........F....... 724 258-6650
Monongahela *(G-11309)*

Libra Scale...G...... 412 782-0611
Pittsburgh *(G-15229)*

Malvern Scale Data Systems..............G...... 610 296-9642
Malvern *(G-10274)*

Measurement Specialties Inc..............G...... 610 971-9893
Wayne *(G-19354)*

Monroe Scale Company Inc.................G...... 412 793-8134
Pittsburgh *(G-15300)*

Raytec LLC...E...... 717 445-0510
Ephrata *(G-5138)*

Scaletron Industries Ltd......................F....... 215 766-2670
Plumsteadville *(G-15813)*

Tri State Scales LLC...........................G...... 610 779-5361
Reading *(G-16548)*

Zurex Corporation...............................E...... 814 425-7445
Cochranton *(G-3353)*

3599 Machinery & Eqpt, Indl & Commercial, NEC

A & M McHining Fabrication Inc...........G...... 724 842-0314
Ford City *(G-6041)*

A & R Jadczak Company......................G...... 215 752-3438
Langhorne *(G-9271)*

A C Grinding & Supply Co Inc..............G...... 215 946-3760
Levittown *(G-9811)*

A F Paul Company...............................F....... 412 264-2111
Coraopolis *(G-3651)*

A G Source Inc....................................F....... 484 459-9292
Pottstown *(G-15959)*

A J Drgon Associates Inc....................G...... 412 771-5160
Mc Kees Rocks *(G-10598)*

A K U Wire Inc.....................................G...... 215 672-8071
Warminster *(G-18814)*

A&A Machine Co Inc............................E...... 215 355-8330
Southampton *(G-17795)*

A-1 Babbitt Co Inc...............................F....... 724 379-6588
Donora *(G-4144)*

A-One Machine LLC.............................G...... 570 289-4347
Hop Bottom *(G-7772)*

Able Tool Co Inc..................................E...... 724 863-2508
Trafford *(G-18450)*

Abrill Industries.................................G...... 814 437-5354
Franklin *(G-6112)*

Accra Machine Shop Inc......................G...... 814 623-8009
Bedford *(G-4204)*

▲ Accu Machining Center Inc.............E...... 610 252-6855
Easton *(G-4644)*

Accu-Chek Machining Inc....................F....... 814 834-2342
Saint Marys *(G-16945)*

Accu-Cut Industries Inc.......................G...... 814 456-6616
Erie *(G-5166)*

▲ Accu-Turn Tool Company Inc..........F....... 412 492-7270
Glenshaw *(G-6478)*

Accurate Machine Tech Inc.................G...... 267 885-7344
Warminster *(G-18820)*

Accurate Tool Co Inc..........................E...... 610 436-4500
West Chester *(G-19494)*

Acme Cryogenics Inc..........................E...... 610 966-4488
Alburtis *(G-49)*

▲ Acme Cryogenics Inc......................D...... 610 966-4488
Allentown *(G-114)*

▲ Acme Machine & Welding Co LLC....D...... 814 938-6702
Punxsutawney *(G-16127)*

▲ Adept Corporation...........................G...... 800 451-2254
York *(G-20366)*

Advance Graphics Eqp of York............E...... 717 292-9183
Dover *(G-4183)*

▼ Advanced Carbon Tech Inc.............F....... 610 682-1086
Topton *(G-18409)*

Advanced Machining Tech....................G...... 215 672-4899
Hatboro *(G-7265)*

Advanced Precision Pdts LLC..............E...... 570 487-2830
Olyphant *(G-12983)*

Advanced VSR Technology...................G...... 215 366-3315
Philadelphia *(G-13348)*

Advanced Welding Tech Inc.................E...... 814 899-3584
Erie *(G-5176)*

Agape Precision Mfg LLC.....................E...... 484 704-2601
Pottstown *(G-15961)*

Al Kaczmarczyk..................................G...... 724 775-1366
Beaver Falls *(G-996)*

Alan Mazzaferro..................................F....... 814 885-6744
Kersey *(G-8553)*

Alberts Jennings.................................G...... 215 766-2852
Pipersville *(G-14610)*

ALe Hydraulic McHy Co LLC................G...... 215 547-3351
Levittown *(G-9815)*

▲ Alessi Manufacturing Corp.............E...... 610 586-4200
Collingdale *(G-3403)*

Alibert Industries Inc..........................G...... 610 872-3900
Woodlyn *(G-20217)*

▼ Alkab Contract Mfg Inc...................E...... 724 335-7050
New Kensington *(G-12323)*

Allcams Machine Co............................F....... 610 534-9004
Folsom *(G-6022)*

Allen P Sutton...................................G...... 717 957-2047
Marysville *(G-10531)*

Allen Zimmmerman..............................G...... 570 966-6924
Lewisburg *(G-9896)*

Almac Machine Co...............................G...... 814 539-5539
Johnstown *(G-8351)*

Alpha Laser-US....................................G...... 814 724-3666
Meadville *(G-10701)*

Alpha Omega Machine Shop.................G...... 570 573-4610
Pine Grove *(G-14589)*

Alston Machine Company Inc...............E...... 412 795-1000
Pittsburgh *(G-14690)*

Amacoil Inc...E...... 610 485-8300
Aston *(G-750)*

◆ American Cap Company LLC............D...... 724 981-4461
Wheatland *(G-19834)*

American Leak Detection.....................G...... 412 859-6000
Coraopolis *(G-3657)*

▲ American Machine LLC....................G...... 215 674-4886
Orwigsburg *(G-13038)*

American Machining Inc.......................G...... 724 938-2120
Daisytown *(G-3957)*

American Manufacturing & Engrg.........F....... 215 362-9694
Montgomeryville *(G-11385)*

American Metal Finishers Inc...............F....... 610 323-1394
Pottstown *(G-15964)*

American Prcsion Machining LLC.........G...... 484 632-9449
Portland *(G-15938)*

American Tool & Machine Co................G...... 724 654-0971
New Castle *(G-12058)*

▲ Ames Industries Inc.......................E...... 877 296-9977
Hershey *(G-7603)*

▲ Amity Machine Corporation.............E...... 610 966-3115
Alburtis *(G-50)*

Anchor Machine Inc.............................E...... 610 261-4924
Northampton *(G-12843)*

Anderson Machine Co..........................G...... 724 834-5135
Greensburg *(G-6651)*

Andritz Herr-Voss Stamco Inc.............D...... 724 538-3180
Conway *(G-3619)*

Antrim Machine Company.....................E...... 717 369-3184
Greencastle *(G-6597)*

ARC Manufacturing Co Inc...................E...... 215 355-8500
Feasterville Trevose *(G-5886)*

Arco Sales Co......................................F....... 215 743-9425
Glenside *(G-6505)*

Arkay Tool & Die Inc............................F....... 215 322-2039
Langhorne *(G-9279)*

Armor Manufacturing Inc.....................F....... 724 658-1848
New Castle *(G-12059)*

Arrow Tool Die & Machine Co...............F....... 215 676-1300
Hatboro *(G-7270)*

Artisan Specialist Tech........................G...... 215 849-0509
Philadelphia *(G-13415)*

Artman and Artman Inc........................E...... 610 821-3970
Allentown *(G-143)*

◆ Ash/Tec Inc......................................E...... 570 682-0933
Hegins *(G-7539)*

Ashby Mfg Co Inc................................F....... 724 776-5566
Cranberry Township *(G-3805)*

Ashland Foundry & Mch Work LLC.......C...... 570 875-6100
Ashland *(G-727)*

▼ Ashley Machine & Tool Co...............E...... 570 287-0966
West Wyoming *(G-19775)*

Asmac Inc..E...... 814 781-3358
Saint Marys *(G-16949)*

Assured Toll & Gauge Inc.....................G...... 724 722-3410
Ruffs Dale *(G-16870)*

Astley Precision Mch Co Inc.................F....... 724 861-5000
Irwin *(G-8144)*

Astro Automation Inc...........................G...... 724 864-2500
Irwin *(G-8145)*

▲ Astro Machine Works Inc.................D...... 717 738-4281
Ephrata *(G-5090)*

▲ Atlas Machining & Welding Inc........E...... 610 262-1374
Northampton *(G-12844)*

Atlas Material Handling Inc..................G...... 610 262-0644
Whitehall *(G-19862)*

Atomatic Manufacturing Co Inc............F....... 412 824-6400
East Pittsburgh *(G-4594)*

▲ Auman Machine Company Inc..........E...... 717 273-4604
Lebanon *(G-9546)*

Automated Concepts Tooling Inc..........F....... 814 796-6302
Waterford *(G-19259)*

Avanti Engineering and Mfg Inc...........F....... 724 834-0752
Greensburg *(G-6652)*

Aviva Technology Inc...........................G...... 610 228-4689
Broomall *(G-2279)*

Avondale Machine Products Inc...........G...... 610 268-2121
Avondale *(G-849)*

Axiom Inc...F....... 570 385-1944
Schuylkill Haven *(G-17148)*

Ay Machine Co....................................F....... 717 733-0335
Ephrata *(G-5091)*

B & B Machine Inc...............................G...... 717 898-3081
Manheim *(G-10368)*

B & B Tool and Die Inc.........................F....... 814 486-5355
Emporium *(G-5050)*

B & D Machine Shop.............................G...... 717 843-0312
York *(G-20395)*

B & F General Machine Inc...................F....... 610 767-2448
Slatington *(G-17604)*

B & J Machine Inc...............................G...... 215 639-8800
Bensalem *(G-1153)*

B & J Sheet Metal Inc..........................F....... 215 538-9543
Trumbauersville *(G-18529)*

B & R Speed Shop ....G... 412 795-7022
Verona (G-18748)

B & W Machine Works Inc ....G... 215 529-2990
Quakertown (G-16171)

B-TEC Solutions Inc ....D... 215 785-2400
Croydon (G-3911)

Bailey Machine Company ....E... 724 628-4730
Connellsville (G-3490)

Bar Machining ....G... 724 226-1050
Natrona Heights (G-11934)

Baum Precision Machining Inc ....E... 215 766-3066
Pipersville (G-14611)

Beach Machine Inc ....G... 570 752-7786
Berwick (G-1308)

Bear Ridge Mch & Fabrication ....G... 570 874-4083
Frackville (G-6103)

Bear Springs Manufacturing ....G... 717 667-3200
Milroy (G-11228)

Beaver Tool and Machine Co Inc ....F... 215 322-0660
Feasterville Trevose (G-5888)

▲ BEC Systems Inc ....E... 215 256-3100
Harleysville (G-7023)

Begonia Tool Co ....G... 724 446-1102
Herminie (G-7569)

Beljan Manufacturing Corp ....G... 717 432-2891
Wellsville (G-19477)

Bell Manufacturing ....G... 717 529-2600
Christiana (G-3133)

Berks Engineering Company ....E... 610 926-4146
Reading (G-16330)

Berks Precision Machine Corp ....G... 610 603-0948
Reading (G-16331)

Bertram Tool and Mch Co Inc ....F... 724 983-2222
Farrell (G-5866)

Berwick Machine LLC ....G... 570 759-1888
Berwick (G-1310)

▲ Bestweld Inc ....E... 610 718-9700
Pottstown (G-15967)

Bethel Machine & Manufacturing ....F... 412 833-5522
Bethel Park (G-1406)

Big B Manufacturing Inc ....G... 570 648-2084
Klingerstown (G-8806)

Biggs Tool and Die Inc ....F... 215 674-9911
Warminster (G-18838)

Bill Hards ....F... 814 677-2460
Seneca (G-17364)

Billet Industries Inc ....E... 717 840-0280
York (G-20405)

Bissinger and Stein Inc ....E... 215 256-1122
Kulpsville (G-8824)

Bless Precision Tool Inc ....E... 215 536-7836
Pennsburg (G-13245)

Blue Mountain Machine Inc ....D... 610 377-4690
Lehighton (G-9710)

Boeh Tool & Die Co Inc ....G... 412 833-8707
Bethel Park (G-1407)

Boekeloo Inc ....F... 814 723-5950
Warren (G-19014)

Bolt Works Inc ....G... 724 776-7273
Warrendale (G-19069)

▲ Bolttech Mannings Inc ....D... 724 872-4873
North Versailles (G-12772)

Bond Machine & Fabrication LLC ....E... 717 665-9030
Manheim (G-10373)

Boquet Tool & Die ....G... 724 539-8250
Latrobe (G-9460)

Bowman Tool ....G... 717 432-1403
East Berlin (G-4520)

Boyd Machine Co Inc ....F... 215 723-8941
Souderton (G-17728)

▲ Bracalentes Mfg Co Inc ....C... 215 536-3077
Trumbauersville (G-18531)

Brackett Machine Co Inc ....G... 724 287-5804
Butler (G-2383)

Brandywine Machine Co Inc ....F... 610 269-1221
Downingtown (G-4216)

Brenner Machine Co ....C... 717 274-3411
Cornwall (G-3737)

Brent A Lindberg ....G... 814 796-9068
Waterford (G-19260)

Brent D Beistel ....G... 724 823-0099
Donora (G-4149)

Breons Inc A Close Corporation ....G... 814 359-3182
Pleasant Gap (G-15791)

Brighton Machine Company Inc ....F... 724 378-0960
Aliquippa (G-70)

Brown Machine Co Inc ....G... 610 932-3359
Oxford (G-13073)

Brush Industries Inc ....D... 570 286-5611
Sunbury (G-18165)

Buck-A-Lew Tooling Machining ....E... 570 321-0640
Williamsport (G-19996)

Budd Lake Machine and Tool Inc ....F... 570 897-5899
Mount Bethel (G-11607)

Bushkill Tool Company Inc ....G... 570 588-7000
Bushkill (G-2364)

Butler Machine Inc ....G... 814 355-5605
Bellefonte (G-1095)

C & M Custom Machining Inc ....G... 610 458-0897
Glenmoore (G-6464)

C & T Machining Inc ....E... 717 328-9572
Mercersburg (G-10982)

C Crouthamel & Co Inc ....G... 215 822-1911
Chalfont (G-2865)

C Everwine Machine LLC ....G... 717 656-5451
Leola (G-9774)

▲ C-B Tool Co ....E... 717 397-3521
Lancaster (G-8967)

Calfab and Machine Inc ....G... 570 654-4004
Exeter (G-5582)

◆ CAM Industries Inc ....E... 717 637-5988
Hanover (G-6866)

◆ CAM Innovation Inc ....E... 717 637-5988
Hanover (G-6867)

Cambria Machining Co LLC ....G... 814 948-8128
Nicktown (G-12619)

Cannon Tool Company ....F... 724 745-1070
Canonsburg (G-2556)

Capitol Tool & Mfg Co Inc ....F... 717 938-6165
New Cumberland (G-12180)

Cardinal Precision Company ....G... 215 885-2050
Oreland (G-13018)

Carlisle Machine Shop Inc ....G... 717 243-0289
Carlisle (G-2697)

Carlsons Industrial Grinding ....G... 814 864-8640
Erie (G-5221)

Caro Brothers Inc ....F... 724 265-1538
Russellton (G-16883)

CCS Machining Inc ....G... 724 668-7706
Greensburg (G-6657)

Central Blair Electric Co ....F... 814 949-8280
Altoona (G-488)

Central Hydraulics Inc ....E... 814 224-0375
East Freedom (G-4562)

Central Machine Co Inc ....F... 215 536-5071
Quakertown (G-16177)

Cewa Technologies Inc ....G... 484 695-5489
Bethlehem (G-1482)

Chambersburg Machine Co Inc ....F... 717 264-7111
Chambersburg (G-2916)

Chantelau Inc ....F... 215 723-1383
Telford (G-18273)

▲ Charles Machine Inc ....E... 814 379-3706
Summerville (G-18157)

Charlotte Industries Inc ....G... 717 653-6721
Mount Joy (G-11648)

Chick Machine Company LLC ....E... 724 352-3330
Butler (G-2388)

Choice Precision Machine Inc ....G... 610 502-1111
Whitehall (G-19865)

Chris Machine Co Inc ....F... 215 348-1229
Doylestown (G-4292)

Cigas Machine Shop Inc ....E... 610 384-5239
Coatesville (G-3296)

Cingle Brothers Machine Shop ....G... 814 387-4994
Clarence (G-3163)

Cipco Industries LLC ....G... 215 785-2976
Croydon (G-3913)

Clark Industrial Supply Inc ....F... 610 705-3333
Pottstown (G-15970)

Clifton Tube Cutting Inc ....E... 724 588-3241
Greenville (G-6739)

Cnc Manufacturing Inc ....E... 610 444-4437
Coatesville (G-3297)

Cnc Specialties Mfg Inc ....E... 724 727-5680
Apollo (G-671)

CNG One Source Inc ....F... 814 673-4980
Franklin (G-6120)

Colonial Auto Supply Co ....C... 215 643-3699
Fort Washington (G-6065)

Columbia Motor Parts Inc ....G... 717 684-2501
Columbia (G-3435)

Concentric Machining Grinding ....G... 610 692-9450
West Chester (G-19528)

Conn & Company LLC ....G... 814 723-7980
Warren (G-19018)

Contine Corporation ....E... 814 899-0006
Erie (G-5231)

Cooper Machine LLC ....G... 717 529-6155
Kirkwood (G-8746)

Corestar International Corp ....G... 724 744-4094
Irwin (G-8150)

Cox Machining Inc ....G... 814 642-5009
Port Allegany (G-15892)

Coxs Machine Shop ....G... 724 796-7815
Midway (G-11090)

Craftweld Fabrication Co Inc ....E... 267 492-1100
Montgomeryville (G-11391)

CRC Manufacturing Inc ....G... 703 408-0645
Everett (G-5569)

Creative Design & Machining ....E... 570 587-3077
S Abingtn Twp (G-16894)

Creotech Industries LLC ....G... 724 267-3100
Marianna (G-10456)

Crismor Machine Inc ....G... 717 292-9646
East Berlin (G-4521)

▲ Cromie Machine Tool Co Inc ....F... 724 385-0729
Pittsburgh (G-14887)

Crystal Metal Products Co Inc ....E... 215 423-2500
Philadelphia (G-13588)

Curtis Sure-Grip Inc ....F... 724 545-8333
Kittanning (G-8763)

Cusick Tool Inc ....F... 724 253-4455
Hadley (G-6818)

Custom Carbioe Grinding ....G... 724 539-8826
Latrobe (G-9469)

Custom Heliarc Welding & Mch ....E... 570 897-0400
Mount Bethel (G-11608)

Custom Hydraulics Inc ....F... 724 729-3170
Burgettstown (G-2344)

Custom Machine & Design Inc ....F... 610 932-4717
West Grove (G-19699)

Custom Machined Spc Inc ....G... 814 938-1031
Punxsutawney (G-16130)

Custom McHining Great Bend Inc ....F... 570 879-2559
Great Bend (G-6581)

Custom Mfg & Indus Svcs LLC ....G... 412 621-2982
Pittsburgh (G-14894)

▲ Cutting Edge Machining ....G... 814 345-6690
Drifting (G-4374)

Cyb Machining Inc ....G... 814 938-8133
Punxsutawney (G-16131)

▲ Cygnus Manufacturing Co LLC ....C... 724 352-8000
Saxonburg (G-17082)

▲ D & B Services Inc ....F... 610 381-2848
Kunkletown (G-8832)

D & G Machine ....G... 724 864-0043
Irwin (G-8154)

D & K Machine Company Inc ....G... 814 328-2382
Ridgway (G-16702)

D & R Machine Co ....E... 215 526-2080
Southampton (G-17807)

D A Tool and Machine Company ....G... 215 887-1673
Glenside (G-6513)

D Gillette Indus Svcs Inc ....F... 610 588-4939
Bangor (G-911)

D J Precision Instrument Corp ....F... 570 836-2229
Tunkhannock (G-18536)

D L George & Sons Mfg Inc ....D... 717 765-4700
Waynesboro (G-19407)

D L Machine LLC ....F... 724 627-7870
Jefferson (G-8269)

D&E Machining Ltd ....E... 814 664-3531
Corry (G-3758)

D/R Machine & Weld Co Inc ....G... 412 655-4452
Clairton (G-3149)

Dagus Machining Inc ....G... 814 834-3491
Ridgway (G-16703)

Daily Grind Quarryville ....G... 717 786-0615
Quarryville (G-16268)

Daltech Inc ....E... 570 823-9911
Hanover Township (G-6987)

Data Machine LLC ....E... 724 864-4370
Irwin (G-8155)

Davan Manufacturing Inc ....F... 724 228-0115
Washington (G-19162)

Daven Sharpe Machine Products ....G... 610 821-4022
Allentown (G-191)

David Kovalcik ....G... 724 539-3181
Loyalhanna (G-10110)

Davies Precision Machining Inc ....F... 717 273-5495
Lebanon (G-9559)

Davis Machine Inc ....G... 724 265-2266
Saxonburg (G-17084)

Davis Ne Company Inc ....G... 412 751-5122
Irwin (G-8156)

▼ Dawson Performance Inc ....F... 717 261-1414
Chambersburg (G-2923)

Dean Barrett ....G... 814 427-2586
Punxsutawney (G-16134)

S
I
C

Deasey Machine Tl & Die Works............G...... 814 847-2728
Everett (G-5570)

Dechert Dynamics Corporation............E...... 717 838-1326
Palmyra (G-13120)

Decherts Machine Shop Inc................E...... 717 838-1326
Palmyra (G-13121)

Deck Machine Co.................G...... 570 879-2833
Hallstead (G-6832)

Dedicated Customs Inc...............G...... 724 678-6609
Burgettstown (G-2345)

Delaware Tool & Machine Co..............E...... 610 259-1810
Yeadon (G-20352)

Demarchi John.................G...... 724 547-6440
Mount Pleasant (G-11696)

Demco Enterprises Inc................F...... 888 419-3343
Quakertown (G-16184)

Deshlers Machine Inc................G...... 610 588-5622
Bangor (G-912)

Detayl Manufacturing Co Inc.............F...... 610 754-7123
Zieglerville (G-20832)

DHL Machine Co Inc................G...... 215 536-3591
Quakertown (G-16186)

Dick Rughs Auto Parts Inc..............G...... 724 438-3425
Uniontown (G-18623)

Digital Machine Company Inc.............E...... 215 672-6454
Warminster (G-18858)

Digital Press Inc.................G...... 610 758-9680
Bethlehem (G-1497)

Diken Machine Inc................G...... 610 495-9995
Pottstown (G-15982)

Dimension Carbide.................G...... 814 789-2102
Saegertown (G-16912)

▲ Diversified Design & Mfg Inc...........G...... 610 337-1969
King of Prussia (G-8611)

Diversified Machine Inc...............E...... 717 397-5347
Lancaster (G-8998)

Diversified Mfg Systems...............F...... 814 455-2400
Erie (G-5249)

DMC Global Inc.................E...... 724 277-9710
Mount Braddock (G-11616)

Donald Campbell.................G...... 412 793-6068
Pittsburgh (G-14930)

Dons Machine Shop Inc................E...... 570 655-1950
West Pittston (G-19754)

Dor-Mae Industries Inc...............E...... 610 929-5003
Reading (G-16364)

Downing Machines Inc................G...... 412 461-0580
Homestead (G-7684)

Dpi Inc.................F...... 215 953-9800
Hatboro (G-7281)

Dri Machine Shop Inc................F...... 717 633-9306
Hanover (G-6880)

Drifton Precision Machining.............G...... 570 636-1408
Drifton (G-4376)

Dunbar Machine Co Inc................G...... 724 277-8711
Dunbar (G-4439)

Dunhuntin Machine Shop Inc.............G...... 724 794-5404
Slippery Rock (G-17619)

Dupont Tool & Machine Co..............E...... 570 655-1728
Dupont (G-4490)

Dutchie Manufacturing LLC..............G...... 717 656-2186
Leola (G-9778)

Duvinage LLC.................F...... 717 283-6111
Greencastle (G-6608)

Dw Machine & Fabricating..............G...... 570 788-8144
Drums (G-4382)

Dyer Industries Inc................F...... 724 258-3400
Bunola (G-2343)

Dynamic Concepts Mfg LLC..............G...... 215 675-9006
Warminster (G-18865)

E K L Machine Inc................E...... 215 639-0150
Bensalem (G-1184)

Eagle Microsystems.................G...... 610 323-2250
Pottstown (G-15984)

Eamco Inc.................F...... 610 262-5731
Whitehall (G-19872)

Earl E Knox Company................E...... 814 459-2754
Erie (G-5255)

East Bank Machine Inc................G...... 412 384-4721
Finleyville (G-5956)

◆ East West Drilling Inc...............E...... 570 966-7312
Mifflinburg (G-11093)

Ebersole Engineering.................G...... 215 675-0106
Hatboro (G-7283)

Ed Fish Maching Co.................G...... 724 224-0992
Tarentum (G-18242)

Edward Thompson.................G...... 717 442-4550
Gap (G-6250)

EF Precision Inc.................D...... 215 784-0861
Willow Grove (G-20115)

Ei Machine Inc.................G...... 724 348-0296
Finleyville (G-5957)

Elite Tool Company Inc................F...... 724 379-5800
Webster (G-19457)

Elizabeth Carbide Die Co Inc.............E...... 412 829-7700
Irwin (G-8160)

Elk County Machining.................G...... 814 781-3502
Saint Marys (G-16969)

Ellco Products Inc................G...... 724 758-3526
Ellwood City (G-6045)

Elliott Machine Company...............G...... 610 485-5345
Upper Chichester (G-18659)

◆ Ellwood Crankshaft and Mch Co......C...... 724 347-0250
Hermitage (G-7581)

▲ Ellwood Nat Crankshaft Svcs...........G...... 724 342-4965
Hermitage (G-7583)

◆ Ellwood National Forge Company....C...... 814 563-7522
Irvine (G-8140)

EMC Global Technologies Inc.............F...... 267 347-5100
Telford (G-18287)

Enjet Aero Erie Inc................G...... 814 860-3104
Erie (G-5260)

Enrico J Fiore.................G...... 570 489-8430
Throop (G-17358)

Enterprise Machine.................G...... 215 679-7490
East Greenville (G-4567)

Enterprise Machine and Tool Co..........G...... 570 969-2587
Scranton (G-17235)

Enterprise Machine Co................G...... 215 855-0868
Hatfield (G-7341)

Equipment Technology Inc...............G...... 570 489-8651
Peckville (G-13208)

Erickson Corporation.................E...... 814 371-4350
Du Bois (G-4391)

Essay Precision Machining..............G...... 724 446-2422
Madison (G-10165)

Excel Machine Co.................G...... 215 624-8600
Philadelphia (G-13685)

Excellent Tool Inc................G...... 814 337-7705
Meadville (G-10724)

Exedyne Manufacturing Services..........G...... 724 651-5100
Pittsburgh (G-14993)

▲ Extreme Machine and Fabg Inc..........D...... 724 342-4340
West Middlesex (G-19724)

F W Lang Co.................G...... 267 401-8293
Havertown (G-7421)

F&F Machine Works.................G...... 717 335-3008
Stevens (G-18050)

Fabricon Inc.................E...... 610 921-0203
Temple (G-18329)

Fairfax Precision Mfg................G...... 814 348-1184
Everett (G-5572)

▼ Fairfield Manufacturing Co Inc..........F...... 570 368-8624
Montoursville (G-11438)

Fairview Manufacturing Corp.............F...... 814 474-5581
Fairview (G-5821)

Falcon Manufacturing Company..........G...... 215 249-0212
Dublin (G-4432)

Falosk Contract Machine Inc.............G...... 724 228-0567
Washington (G-19173)

Farzati Manufacturing Corp..............E...... 724 836-3508
Greensburg (G-6666)

Fassett Mfg Co.................G...... 724 446-7870
Wendel (G-19480)

Femco Holdings LLC................E...... 906 576-0418
Punxsutawney (G-16138)

◆ Femco Machine Company LLC..........C...... 814 938-9763
Punxsutawney (G-16139)

Filter Technology Inc................G...... 866 992-9490
Gladwyne (G-6407)

Finch Manufacturing & Tech LLC.........E...... 570 655-2277
West Pittston (G-19756)

First Article Inc................E...... 267 382-0761
Souderton (G-17733)

Flex-Cell Precision.................G...... 717 393-3335
Lancaster (G-9017)

Flex-Cell Precision Inc................G...... 717 824-4086
Lancaster (G-9018)

Flinchbaugh Company Inc...............E...... 717 266-2202
Manchester (G-10356)

◆ Flinchbaugh Engineering Inc............C...... 717 755-1900
York (G-20483)

▲ Florig R & J Industrial Co Inc............E...... 610 825-6655
Conshohocken (G-3548)

Florio Tooling Inc................G...... 814 781-3973
Saint Marys (G-16974)

▲ Fluid Energy Proc & Eqp Co............G...... 215 721-8990
Telford (G-18289)

Fluid Energy Proc & Eqp Co.............D...... 215 368-2510
Hatfield (G-7343)

Flurer Machine and Tool...............G...... 610 759-6114
Bethlehem (G-1514)

Folsom Tool & Mold Corp..............E...... 610 358-5030
Aston (G-765)

Foradora Welding & Machine............E...... 814 375-2176
Falls Creek (G-5853)

Foranne Manufacturing Inc..............E...... 215 357-4650
Warminster (G-18881)

Ford City Gun Workd.................G...... 724 994-9501
Ford City (G-6045)

Forging Parts & Machining Co............E...... 717 530-8810
Shippensburg (G-17527)

Fraccaro Industries Inc................E...... 610 367-2777
Boyertown (G-1911)

Francis Latovich.................G...... 570 339-1059
Mount Carmel (G-11624)

Frank Bellace Welding.................G...... 856 488-8099
Danville (G-4002)

Frank J Butch Co Inc................F...... 215 322-7399
Philadelphia (G-13718)

Frazier-Simplex Machine Co.............G...... 724 222-5700
Washington (G-19177)

Frb Machine Inc.................G...... 724 867-0111
Emlenton (G-5007)

Freedom Components Inc...............G...... 717 242-0101
Lewistown (G-9930)

Freedom Technologies Inc...............G...... 717 242-0101
Lewistown (G-9931)

Fruehauf Manufacturing.................G...... 412 771-4200
Portersville (G-15927)

▲ Fulton Precision Inds Inc...............E...... 717 485-5158
Mc Connellsburg (G-10567)

◆ G & B Specialties Inc................C...... 570 752-5901
Berwick (G-1325)

G & M Co Inc.................F...... 610 779-7812
Reading (G-16387)

G C Carl Klemmer Inc................G...... 215 329-4100
Philadelphia (G-13738)

Gar-Ren Tool & Machine Co Inc..........F...... 610 534-1897
Prospect Park (G-16114)

Gardan Manufacturing Company..........G...... 724 652-8171
New Wilmington (G-12466)

Gaumer Tool Machine Co Inc............E...... 717 266-0273
York (G-20492)

Geitz Machine Inc................G...... 215 257-6752
Telford (G-18292)

Gemini Machining Company Inc..........F...... 610 746-5000
Easton (G-4687)

General Machine Works Inc.............F...... 717 848-2713
York (G-20494)

General Manufacturing Co...............F...... 412 833-4300
Bethel Park (G-1415)

General Nuclear Corp.................D...... 724 925-3565
Hunker (G-7928)

General Regulator Corp................E...... 717 848-5960
York (G-20495)

General Weldments Inc................F...... 724 744-2105
Irwin (G-8164)

Gerg Tool & Die Inc................E...... 814 834-3888
Saint Marys (G-16977)

Germantown Welding Co................G...... 215 843-2643
Philadelphia (G-13758)

Giesler Engineering Inc................G...... 800 428-8616
Aston (G-768)

Giordano Incorporated.................F...... 215 632-3470
Bensalem (G-1205)

Gittens Corp.................G...... 215 945-0944
Levittown (G-9841)

Glenn Machine Co.................F...... 724 457-7750
Coraopolis (G-3695)

Global Incorporated.................E...... 814 445-9671
Somerset (G-17690)

Goldsborough & Vansant Inc.............G...... 724 782-0393
Finleyville (G-5959)

Golis Machine Inc................F...... 570 278-1963
Montrose (G-11465)

Goodhart Sons Inc................C...... 717 656-2404
Lancaster (G-9030)

Goshorn Industries LLC................G...... 717 369-3654
Chambersburg (G-2936)

Gosiger Inc.................F...... 724 778-3220
Warrendale (G-19078)

Graham Machine Inc................E...... 814 437-7190
Franklin (G-6133)

▲ Grand Valley Manufacturing Co..........D...... 814 728-8760
Titusville (G-18379)

Grand Valley Manufacturing Co...........G...... 814 728-8760
Warren (G-19028)

Grandview Manufacturing Co.............G...... 724 887-0631
Alverton (G-564)

Graphite Machining Inc ....G..... 610 682-0080	Hill John M Machine Co Inc ....E..... 610 562-8690	J Baur Machining Inc ....F...... 724 625-2680
Robesonia *(G-16775)*	Hamburg *(G-6841)*	Mars *(G-10502)*
Grauch Enterprises Inc ....F..... 814 342-7320	Hills Machine Shop ....G..... 570 645-8787	J Brown Machine LLC ....G..... 724 543-4044
Philipsburg *(G-14515)*	Lansford *(G-9447)*	Kittanning *(G-8775)*
Great Lakes Automtn Svcs Inc ......E..... 814 476-7710	Hillside Custom Mac Wel & Fab ....F..... 610 942-3093	J C Moore Industries Inc ....F...... 724 475-3185
Mc Kean *(G-10591)*	Honey Brook *(G-7748)*	Fredonia *(G-6181)*
Great Lakes Automtn Svcs Inc ......F..... 814 774-3144	▲ Hoffman-Kane Distributors Inc ....F...... 412 653-6886	▼ J D Kauffman Machine Sp Inc ....F...... 610 593-2033
Lake City *(G-8901)*	Pittsburgh *(G-15097)*	Christiana *(G-3137)*
▲ Greenetech Mfg Co Inc ....E..... 724 228-2400	Hoffmans Machine Shop Inc ....G..... 570 437-2788	J D Kauffman Machine Sp Inc ....F...... 610 593-2033
Washington *(G-19181)*	Milton *(G-11241)*	Christiana *(G-3138)*
Greentree Machine Works ....G..... 717 786-4047	Holan Inc ....F...... 724 744-1660	J F Burns Machine Co Inc ....G..... 724 327-2870
Quarryville *(G-16271)*	Irwin *(G-8168)*	Export *(G-5610)*
Gretz Machine Products ....G..... 215 247-2495	Holden Precision Machine ....G..... 814 968-3833	J G Mundy Machine LLC ....G..... 610 583-1200
Philadelphia *(G-13788)*	Sheffield *(G-17482)*	Collingdale *(G-3405)*
Grimm Machine & Model ....G..... 724 228-2133	Holt Le Grinding Service ....F...... 724 864-6865	J I T Tool & Die Inc ....E..... 814 265-0257
Washington *(G-19182)*	Rillton *(G-16747)*	Brockport *(G-2221)*
▲ Groffdale Machine Co Inc ....G..... 717 656-3249	Homestead Automotive Supply ....G..... 412 462-4467	J M Schmidt Precision Tool Co ....F...... 610 436-5010
Leola *(G-9785)*	Homestead *(G-7686)*	Chester Springs *(G-3081)*
Gross Machine Inc ....G..... 215 491-7077	Hondels Machine Shop ....G..... 814 677-7768	J M T Machine Company ....E..... 215 934-7600
Warrington *(G-19119)*	Oil City *(G-12947)*	Huntingdon Valley *(G-7998)*
Gsg Manufacturing Inc ....G..... 814 336-4287	Hood & Son Inc ....G..... 215 822-5750	J P Tine Tool Co ....G..... 724 863-0332
Meadville *(G-10731)*	Line Lexington *(G-9976)*	Irwin *(G-8175)*
Gtf Corporation ....E..... 717 752-3631	Hoover Design & Manufacturing ....G..... 717 767-9555	J R M Machinery Inc ....G..... 570 544-9505
Berwick *(G-1327)*	York *(G-20528)*	Pottsville *(G-16083)*
Guardian Tactical Inc ....G..... 814 558-6761	Hoover Precision Machine Works ......G..... 717 445-9190	J Russel Tooling Co ....G..... 724 423-2766
Emporium *(G-5062)*	East Earl *(G-4544)*	Calumet *(G-2472)*
Gutierrez Machine Corporation ......F..... 570 888-6088	Horoschuck Inc ....F...... 814 860-3104	Jack Garner & Sons Inc ....G..... 717 367-8866
Athens *(G-811)*	Erie *(G-5319)*	Mount Joy *(G-11663)*
H & H Manufacturing Co Inc ....D..... 610 532-1250	Hotronix LLC ....G..... 800 727-8520	Jacob Schmidt & Son Inc ....F...... 215 234-4641
Folcroft *(G-6004)*	Carmichaels *(G-2757)*	Harleysville *(G-7041)*
H & H Precision Wire LLC ....F..... 717 567-9600	Houseknechts Mch & TI Co Inc ....G..... 570 584-3010	Jacobs Tool & Mfg Inc ....G..... 717 630-0083
Newport *(G-12490)*	Muncy *(G-11820)*	Hanover *(G-6907)*
H & K Equipment Inc ....D..... 412 490-5300	Hsk Manufacturing Inc ....G..... 610 404-1940	▲ Jade Equipment Corporation ....C..... 215 947-3333
Coraopolis *(G-3696)*	Birdsboro *(G-1699)*	Huntingdon Valley *(G-7999)*
H and K Tool and Mch Co Inc ....E..... 215 322-0380	▲ Hy-Tech Machine Inc ....D..... 724 776-6800	▼ Jade Holdings Inc ....E..... 215 947-3333
Huntingdon Valley *(G-7993)*	Cranberry Township *(G-3823)*	Huntingdon Valley *(G-8000)*
H D Sampey Inc ....G..... 215 723-3471	Hydra Service Inc ....G..... 724 852-2423	Jag Fabrication LLC ....G..... 724 457-2347
Telford *(G-18293)*	Waynesburg *(G-19446)*	Moon Township *(G-11495)*
▲ H H Fluorescent Parts Inc ....D..... 215 379-2750	Hydrojet Services Inc ....E..... 610 375-7500	James G Beaver ....G..... 570 799-0388
Cheltenham *(G-3029)*	Reading *(G-16405)*	Catawissa *(G-2819)*
H P Gazzam Machine Company ......G..... 412 471-6647	▲ Hydromotion Inc ....D..... 610 948-4150	James McAtee ....G..... 724 789-9078
Pittsburgh *(G-15073)*	Spring City *(G-17860)*	Renfrew *(G-16640)*
H R Edgar Machining & Fabg Inc ......D..... 724 339-6694	Ideal-Pmt Machine Inc ....F...... 570 879-2165	Jarrett Machine Co ....E..... 814 362-2755
New Kensington *(G-12344)*	Great Bend *(G-6582)*	Bradford *(G-1974)*
H W Nicholson Wldg & Mfg Inc ......E..... 724 727-3461	Image Components Inc ....G..... 215 739-3599	Jarrett Machine Co ....F...... 814 362-2755
Apollo *(G-676)*	Philadelphia *(G-13850)*	Bradford *(G-1975)*
▲ Hamill Manufacturing Company ......D..... 724 744-2131	Indian Head TI Cutter Grinding ....G..... 814 796-4954	JB Machine Inc ....G..... 570 824-2003
Trafford *(G-18457)*	Waterford *(G-19263)*	Wilkes Barre *(G-19932)*
Hampton Machining Inc ....G..... 717 734-2497	Industrial Consortium Inc ....G..... 610 775-5760	Jbm Metalcraft Corp ....G..... 814 241-0448
East Waterford *(G-4641)*	Mohnton *(G-11266)*	Johnstown *(G-8384)*
▲ Hanel Storage Systems ....E..... 412 788-0509	Industrial Consortium Inc ....F...... 610 777-1653	Jeglinski Group Inc ....E..... 814 807-0681
Pittsburgh *(G-15079)*	Mohnton *(G-11267)*	Meadville *(G-10739)*
Hardy Machine Inc ....E..... 215 822-9359	Industrial Machine Inc ....F...... 724 452-7730	Jeneral Machine Company ....G..... 610 837-5206
Hatfield *(G-7345)*	Zelienople *(G-20804)*	Stroudsburg *(G-18124)*
Harnish Production Machine ....G..... 717 866-4562	Industrial Machine Works Inc ....E..... 412 782-5055	Jenkins Machine Inc ....E..... 610 837-6723
Myerstown *(G-11886)*	Pittsburgh *(G-15119)*	Bethlehem *(G-1545)*
Harrington Machine and Tool Co ......E..... 814 432-7339	▲ Industrial Sales & Mfg Inc ....D..... 814 833-9876	◆ Jennison Corporation ....F...... 412 429-0500
Franklin *(G-6134)*	Erie *(G-5324)*	Carnegie *(G-2771)*
▲ Hartzell Machine Works Inc ....E..... 610 485-3502	Innovative Machining Tech Inc ....G..... 610 473-5600	Jennison Precision Machine Inc ....E..... 412 279-3007
Upper Chichester *(G-18664)*	Boyertown *(G-1917)*	Carnegie *(G-2773)*
Hastings Machine Company Inc ......E..... 814 247-6562	Innovative Machining Tech Inc ....E..... 610 473-5600	Jess Miller Machine Shop Inc ....G..... 610 692-2193
Hastings *(G-7261)*	Boyertown *(G-1918)*	West Chester *(G-19577)*
Hastings Machine Company Inc ......G..... 814 533-5777	Inserta Products Inc ....E..... 215 643-0192	Jet Tool Company Inc ....G..... 814 756-3169
Johnstown *(G-8380)*	Blue Bell *(G-1835)*	Albion *(G-45)*
Haverstick Bros Inc ....F..... 717 392-5722	Integrated Power Services LLC ....F...... 724 225-2900	Jex Manufacturing Inc ....G..... 412 292-5516
Lancaster *(G-9040)*	Washington *(G-19186)*	Bridgeville *(G-2075)*
Hawkins Metal ....G..... 215 538-9668	Intricate Edm LLC ....G..... 717 392-8244	Jim Conrath ....F...... 724 423-6363
Quakertown *(G-16199)*	Lancaster *(G-9062)*	Pleasant Unity *(G-15796)*
Hayes Enterprises Inc ....G..... 610 252-2530	Intricate Precision Mfg LLC ....G..... 717 392-8244	Jle Industries LLC ....E..... 724 603-2228
Easton *(G-4697)*	Lancaster *(G-9063)*	Dunbar *(G-4441)*
▼ Hayes Industries Inc ....G..... 484 624-5314	Irwin Automation Inc ....E..... 724 834-7160	Joel Freidhoff ....G..... 814 536-6458
Pottstown *(G-15998)*	Greensburg *(G-6679)*	Johnstown *(G-8387)*
Hefner Machine & Tool Inc ....E..... 215 721-5900	Isimac Machine Company Inc ....E..... 610 926-6400	John O Machine Co ....G..... 215 228-1155
Hatfield *(G-7347)*	Blandon *(G-1755)*	Philadelphia *(G-13904)*
Helix Inc ....F...... 215 679-7924	Isimac Machine Company Inc ....E..... 610 926-6400	John Prosock Machine Inc ....G..... 215 804-0321
Red Hill *(G-16582)*	Blandon *(G-1756)*	Quakertown *(G-16205)*
▲ Herkules USA Corporation ....C..... 724 763-2066	J & E Industries ....E..... 570 876-1361	▲ John R Bromiley Company Inc ....E..... 215 822-7723
Ford City *(G-6047)*	Jermyn *(G-8307)*	Chalfont *(G-2878)*
Hertz Machine & Fabrication ....G..... 610 874-7848	J & L Precision Machine Co Inc ....E..... 610 691-8411	▲ John R Wald Company Inc ....E..... 814 643-3908
Brookhaven *(G-2245)*	Bethlehem *(G-1543)*	Huntingdon *(G-7947)*
Heslin-Steel Fab Inc ....G..... 724 745-8282	J & S Grinding Co Inc ....F...... 814 776-1113	John V Potero Enterprises Inc ....G..... 215 537-3320
Canonsburg *(G-2596)*	Ridgway *(G-16713)*	Philadelphia *(G-13907)*
Hetran-B Inc ....G..... 570 366-1411	J & S Machining Corp ....F...... 717 653-6358	Johnson Bros Machine ....G..... 610 749-2313
Orwigsburg *(G-13044)*	Manheim *(G-10391)*	Riegelsville *(G-16745)*
Hetrick Mfg Inc ....F...... 724 335-0455	J A Emilius Sons Inc ....F...... 215 379-6162	Johnson Machine & Prod Inc ....G..... 570 724-2042
Lower Burrell *(G-10106)*	Cheltenham *(G-3030)*	Wellsboro *(G-19467)*
Highland Tool & Die Company ....G..... 215 426-4116	J A K Machine Co ....G..... 610 346-6906	Johnstown McHning Fbrction Inc ......E..... 814 539-2209
Philadelphia *(G-13823)*	Kintnersville *(G-8728)*	Johnstown *(G-8390)*
Highpoint Tool & Machine Inc ....E..... 814 763-5453	J and B Precision Machine Co ....G..... 215 822-1400	Jonny T Fletcher ....G..... 814 724-6687
Saegertown *(G-16917)*	Hatfield *(G-7355)*	Meadville *(G-10740)*

Employee Codes: A=Over 500 employees, B=251-500   2019 Harris Pennsylvania
C=101-250, D=51-100, E=20-50, F=10-19, G=3-9   Manufacturers Directory

951

S I C

Jr Machine & Tool Inc ..... G 610 873-4100
Downingtown (G-4236)
Judy Raymond Corporation ..... G 814 677-4058
Rouseville (G-16837)
▲ Jwf Defense Systems LLC ..... D 814 539-6922
Johnstown (G-8396)
K & C Machine ..... G 724 266-1737
Ambridge (G-624)
K & C Machining Company Inc ..... F 610 588-6749
Bangor (G-917)
K & K Precision Enterprises ..... F 215 364-4120
Perkasie (G-13280)
K & K Precision Grinding Co ..... G 215 333-1276
Philadelphia (G-13917)
K & L Machining Inc ..... E 717 656-0948
Leola (G-9789)
K & S Tool & Die Inc ..... G 814 336-6932
Meadville (G-10741)
K D Machine Inc ..... F 724 652-8833
New Castle (G-12110)
K Machine & Tool Inc ..... G 717 272-2241
Lebanon (G-9586)
K Wagner Machine Inc ..... G 610 485-3831
Marcus Hook (G-10446)
K&C Machine Inc ..... G 724 375-3633
Aliquippa (G-77)
K&J Machine Shop ..... G 814 364-1101
Spring Mills (G-17888)
▲ K-Fab Inc ..... D 570 759-8411
Berwick (G-1331)
Kaf-Tech Industries Inc ..... G 724 523-2343
Jeannette (G-8259)
Kelley-Tron Machine Company ..... G 717 545-8814
Harrisburg (G-7161)
Kelly Machine Works ..... G 717 273-0303
Lebanon (G-9590)
Kelly Precision Machining Co ..... G 717 396-8622
Lancaster (G-9080)
Ken Hall Machine Shop Inc ..... G 724 637-3273
West Sunbury (G-19771)
Ken Imler ..... G 814 695-1310
East Freedom (G-4564)
Kena Corporation ..... F 717 292-7097
Dover (G-4193)
Kercher Enterprises Inc ..... E 717 273-2111
Lebanon (G-9591)
Kercher Machine Works Inc ..... E 717 273-2111
Lebanon (G-9593)
Keystone Honing Corporation ..... D 814 827-9641
Titusville (G-18387)
Keystone Machinery Corporation ..... G 717 859-4977
Ephrata (G-5113)
Keystone Pine Machine Inc Co ..... G 215 425-0605
Philadelphia (G-13931)
Keystone Precision Machining ..... F 215 699-5553
North Wales (G-12809)
Kfw Automation Inc ..... G 610 266-5731
Allentown (G-281)
Khs Corp ..... E 215 947-4010
Huntingdon Valley (G-8007)
Kiczan Manufacturing Inc ..... E 412 678-0980
North Versailles (G-12777)
Kin-Tech Manufacturing Inc ..... F 724 446-0777
Irwin (G-8179)
Kincaid Manufacturing Inc ..... G 412 795-9811
Verona (G-18756)
Kinsley Incorporated ..... G 215 348-7723
Doylestown (G-4311)
Kiski Precision Industries LLC ..... E 724 845-2799
Leechburg (G-9646)
Kittatinny Manufacturing Svcs ..... F 717 530-1242
Shippensburg (G-17536)
Klt Group Inc ..... G 215 525-0902
Pottstown (G-15950)
Knm Machine and Tool Inc ..... G 215 443-9660
Warminster (G-18905)
Kono Co ..... G 724 462-3333
Meadville (G-10744)
Kovacs Manufacturing Inc ..... F 215 355-1985
Southampton (G-17821)
Kress Manufacturing Inc ..... G 724 864-5056
Irwin (G-8180)
Krimes Machine Shop Inc ..... G 717 733-1271
Ephrata (G-5116)
Kutzner Manufacturing Inds Inc ..... E 215 721-1712
Telford (G-18300)
L & M Machine Inc ..... G 724 733-2283
Pittsburgh (G-15205)
L & P Machine Shop Inc ..... G 610 262-7356
Coplay (G-3645)

L B G Machine Inc ..... F 610 770-2550
Allentown (G-289)
▲ L L Brown Inc ..... E 717 766-1885
Enola (G-5081)
L M Stevenson Company Inc ..... G 724 458-7510
Hermitage (G-7590)
L S Wimmer Machine Co Inc ..... F 215 257-3006
Perkasie (G-13281)
Laboratory Testing Inc ..... C 215 997-9080
Hatfield (G-7361)
Lagonda Machine LLC ..... E 724 222-2710
Washington (G-19195)
Lamjen Inc ..... E 814 459-5277
Erie (G-5359)
▲ Lamms Machine Inc ..... E 610 797-2023
Allentown (G-291)
Lancaster Metals Science Corp ..... E 717 299-9709
Lancaster (G-9102)
Lanum Metal Products LLC ..... G 215 329-5010
Philadelphia (G-13954)
Laurel Holdings Inc ..... G 814 533-5777
Johnstown (G-8402)
Laurel Machine Inc ..... D 724 438-8661
Mount Braddock (G-11620)
Lawruk Machine & Tool Co Inc ..... E 814 943-6136
Altoona (G-521)
Leading Edge Composites Inc ..... E 610 932-9055
Coatesville (G-3313)
Leading Edge Tooling Inc ..... G 215 953-9717
Huntingdon Valley (G-8008)
Lebanon Parts Service Inc ..... G 717 272-0181
Lebanon (G-9602)
Lebanon Tool Co Inc ..... C 717 273-3711
Lebanon (G-9604)
Leese & Co Inc ..... E 724 834-5810
Greensburg (G-6684)
Leico Manufacturing Corp ..... G 610 376-8288
Reading (G-16428)
▲ Leiss Tool & Die ..... C 814 444-1444
Somerset (G-17695)
Leister Machine ..... G 814 623-5992
Bedford (G-1062)
Leman Machine Company ..... E 814 736-9696
Portage (G-15918)
Len Sabatine Automotive ..... G 610 258-8020
Easton (G-4714)
Lennys Machine Company ..... G 814 490-4407
Lake City (G-8904)
Lennys Machine Company ..... G 814 474-5510
Fairview (G-5831)
Lenox Machine Inc ..... G 717 394-8760
Lancaster (G-9110)
Leonhardt Manufacturing Co Inc ..... D 717 632-4150
Hanover (G-6915)
Lesher Machine Shop Inc ..... G 717 263-0673
Chambersburg (G-2952)
Lewis Welding & Xcavating ..... G 570 353-7301
Morris (G-11545)
Liberty Welding Co ..... G 412 661-1776
Pittsburgh (G-15228)
Librandi Machine Shop Inc ..... D 717 944-9442
Middletown (G-11063)
Light Tool and Machine Inc ..... F 814 684-2755
Tyrone (G-18586)
Lindstrom Machine Shop ..... G 717 848-2983
York (G-20566)
Logue Industries Inc ..... E 570 368-2639
Montoursville (G-11445)
Lon Hyde ..... G 814 763-4140
Saegertown (G-16922)
Longwood Manufacturing Corp ..... F 610 444-4200
Kennett Square (G-8523)
Lorenzo Fst Flw Cylinder Heads ..... G 215 750-8324
Langhorne (G-9310)
Loudon Industries Inc ..... E 717 328-9808
Mercersburg (G-10991)
Louis Mattes Jr ..... G 412 653-1266
Clairton (G-3153)
Lovell Strouble Inc ..... G 570 326-5561
Williamsport (G-20036)
LRG Corporation ..... E 724 523-3131
Jeannette (G-8261)
Lu-Mac Inc ..... F 724 763-3750
Ford City (G-6049)
Luxcelis Technologies LLC ..... G 724 424-1800
Latrobe (G-9501)
Lwe Inc ..... G 814 336-3553
Meadville (G-10751)
Lynar Corporation ..... F 610 395-3155
Allentown (G-303)

M & B Machine Inc ..... G 717 766-7879
Mechanicsburg (G-10867)
M & S Centerless Grinding Inc ..... F 215 675-4144
Hatboro (G-7294)
M and P Custom Design Inc ..... F 610 444-0244
Kennett Square (G-8524)
M C M Machine & Tool Inc ..... G 570 897-5472
Mount Bethel (G-11612)
M D Cline Metal Fabg Inc ..... G 724 459-8968
Blairsville (G-1733)
M E Inc ..... E 610 820-5250
Whitehall (G-19884)
M E Kmachine ..... G 570 636-0710
Freeland (G-6195)
M I P Inc ..... G 724 643-5114
Midland (G-11087)
M L Scott & Sons ..... G 610 847-5671
Revere (G-16653)
Mac Machine LLC ..... F 610 583-3055
Brookhaven (G-2246)
Machine Fabg & Weight Eqp Sp ..... G 724 439-1222
Uniontown (G-18636)
Machine Specialties ..... G 717 264-0061
Chambersburg (G-2955)
Machined Products Company ..... E 717 299-3757
Lancaster (G-9123)
Machining America Inc ..... F 717 249-8635
Carlisle (G-2723)
Machining Center ..... G 724 530-7212
Slippery Rock (G-17621)
Machining Concepts Inc ..... F 814 838-8896
Erie (G-5378)
Machining Solutions ..... G 412 798-6590
Murrysville (G-11856)
Machining Technology Inc ..... G 570 459-3440
Hazle Township (G-7468)
Magdic Precision Tooling Inc ..... E 412 824-6661
North Versailles (G-12778)
Magnetic Lifting Tech US LLC ..... G 412 490-5300
Coraopolis (G-3703)
Main Engines & Service Center ..... G 570 457-7081
Old Forge (G-12969)
Manheim Specialty Machine ..... F 717 665-5400
Manheim (G-10393)
Marando Industries Inc ..... G 610 621-2536
Reading (G-16437)
Mardinly Enterprises LLC ..... E 610 544-9490
Broomall (G-2295)
Martin Truck Bodies Inc ..... E 814 793-3353
Martinsburg (G-10526)
Martinos Delicatessen Inc ..... F 814 432-2525
Franklin (G-6149)
Martins Steel LLC ..... G 570 966-3775
Mifflinburg (G-11097)
Marwood Machine Company Inc ..... G 724 352-2646
Cabot (G-2458)
Master Machine and Mfg ..... G 412 262-1550
Coraopolis (G-3704)
Master Machine Co Inc ..... F 814 495-4900
South Fork (G-17775)
Mastrorocco Machine ..... G 724 539-4511
Latrobe (G-9503)
Matt Machine & Mfg Inc ..... E 412 793-6020
Pittsburgh (G-15263)
▲ Matt Nabeja ..... G 412 787-2876
Mc Donald (G-10575)
Max Machine LLC ..... G 717 361-8744
Elizabethtown (G-4879)
▲ Maxwell Welding and Mch Inc ..... E 724 729-3160
Burgettstown (G-2349)
Mc Cullough Machine Inc ..... F 724 694-8485
New Derry (G-12192)
Mc Gear Co Inc ..... G 412 767-5502
Pittsburgh (G-15268)
McAdoo Machine Company ..... F 570 929-3717
Kelayres (G-8487)
McFadden Machine & Mfg Co ..... E 724 459-9278
Blairsville (G-1734)
◆ McLanahan Corporation ..... B 814 695-9807
Hollidaysburg (G-7651)
McMillen Welding Inc ..... G 724 745-4507
Houston (G-7874)
McNulty Tool Die ..... G 215 957-9900
Warminster (G-18919)
Mdc Machine Incorporated ..... F 814 372-2345
Du Bois (G-4405)
Mdl Manufacturing Inds Inc ..... E 814 623-0888
Bedford (G-1064)
Meadville Tool & Manufacturing ..... G 814 337-7555
Meadville (G-10761)

▲ **Mechanical Service Co Inc** .... F 610 351-1655
Allentown *(G-313)*
Meck Manufacturing .... G 610 756-6284
Lenhartsville *(G-9759)*
Medl Tool & Die Inc .... G 215 443-5457
Warminster *(G-18921)*
Melvin Leid .... G 717 776-4940
Newville *(G-12606)*
▲ **Mensco Inc** .... G 610 863-9233
Wind Gap *(G-20171)*
Metal Finishing Corporation .... G 215 788-9246
Bristol *(G-2166)*
Metal Integrity Inc .... E 814 234-7399
State College *(G-17989)*
Metal Tech Machine Company .... G 412 833-3239
Bethel Park *(G-1426)*
Meyer Machine Company Inc .... G 724 368-3711
Portersville *(G-15932)*
Mg Welding & Fabrication .... G 717 292-5206
Dover *(G-4196)*
Michael Bryan .... G 610 273-2535
Honey Brook *(G-7754)*
Michael J Zellers .... G 610 562-2825
Hamburg *(G-6846)*
Mickelson Mfg Inds Inc .... G 215 529-5442
Quakertown *(G-16216)*
Micro Facture LLC .... E 717 285-9700
Mountville *(G-11799)*
Micro Machine Design Inc .... F 717 274-3500
Lebanon *(G-9610)*
Micro Precision Corporation .... D 717 393-4100
Lancaster *(G-9133)*
Micro Tool Company .... D 610 882-3740
Bethlehem *(G-1572)*
Microcut Inc .... G 717 848-4150
York *(G-20594)*
Midway Automotive & Indus Mch .... G 570 339-2411
Mount Carmel *(G-11627)*
Mikron Valve & Mfr Inc .... G 814 453-2337
Erie *(G-5392)*
Millennium Machining Spc .... G 570 501-2002
Hazleton *(G-7510)*
Millennium Manufacturing Inc .... F 215 536-3006
Quakertown *(G-16220)*
Miller Machine Shop Inc .... G 814 834-2114
Saint Marys *(G-16996)*
▲ **Miller Welding and Machine Co** .... C 814 849-3061
Brookville *(G-2265)*
Million Dollar Machining Inc .... G 814 834-9224
Saint Marys *(G-16997)*
Mines and Meadows LLC .... G 724 535-6026
Wampum *(G-18802)*
Minnotte Manufacturing Corp .... D 412 373-5270
Trafford *(G-18459)*
Modern Industries Inc .... E 814 724-6242
Meadville *(G-10765)*
Moldcraft Co .... F 610 399-1404
Kennett Square *(G-8531)*
Mong Fabrication & Machine .... G 724 745-8370
Canonsburg *(G-2605)*
Montco Manufacturing Co Inc .... G 215 822-1291
Hatfield *(G-7370)*
Moody Corporation .... F 724 453-9470
Zelienople *(G-20811)*
Moritz Machine & Repairs LLC .... G 717 677-6838
Biglerville *(G-1667)*
Morocco Welding LLC .... F 814 444-9353
Somerset *(G-17697)*
Morton Tool Company .... G 717 824-1723
Ephrata *(G-5131)*
Moss Machine & Design LLC .... G 570 724-9119
Wellsboro *(G-19470)*
Mosse Blocks Inc .... G 717 624-2597
New Oxford *(G-12416)*
Mountain Top Welding & Repair .... G 570 888-7174
Gillett *(G-6382)*
Muncy Machine & Tool Co Inc .... E 570 649-5188
Turbotville *(G-18555)*
Murdick Auto Parts & Racg Sups .... G 724 482-2177
Butler *(G-2425)*
N T M Inc .... E 717 567-9374
Newport *(G-12492)*
National Hydraulics Inc .... G 724 887-3850
Scottdale *(G-17197)*
Nemco .... E 215 355-2100
Feasterville Trevose *(G-5922)*
New Oxford Tool & Die Inc .... G 717 624-8441
New Oxford *(G-12417)*
▼ **Niagara Machine Inc** .... G 814 455-8838
Erie *(G-5402)*
Niagara Manufacturing Co .... F 814 838-4511
Erie *(G-5403)*
Nick Charles Kravitch .... G 412 882-6262
Pittsburgh *(G-15340)*
Nick Charles Kravitch .... G 412 341-7265
Pittsburgh *(G-15339)*
Nolt Bros Inc .... G 717 733-8761
Ephrata *(G-5133)*
Non Mtallic Machining Assembly .... F 814 453-6787
Erie *(G-5405)*
North American Tooling Inc .... G 814 486-3700
Emporium *(G-5070)*
North Penn Industries Corp .... G 215 453-9775
Perkasie *(G-13286)*
Northwestern Welding & Mch Co .... G 814 774-2866
Lake City *(G-8907)*
Novosel Instrument Shop Inc .... F 814 359-2249
Pleasant Gap *(G-15795)*
NP Precision Inc .... E 610 586-5100
Folcroft *(G-6010)*
Null Machine Shop Inc .... G 717 597-3330
Greencastle *(G-6625)*
Nyes Machine and Design .... G 717 533-9514
Elizabethtown *(G-4881)*
Nyes Machine and Design .... F 717 533-9514
Hummelstown *(G-7920)*
O & S Machine Co Inc .... G 724 539-9431
Latrobe *(G-9506)*
Ofcg Inc .... G 570 655-0804
Dupont *(G-4493)*
Olympic Tool & Machine Corp .... D 610 494-1600
Aston *(G-784)*
Omega Flex Inc .... C 610 524-7272
Exton *(G-5719)*
Onexia Inc .... E 610 431-7271
Exton *(G-5720)*
Ordnance Research Inc .... F 717 738-6941
Ephrata *(G-5135)*
Orr Screw Machine Products .... E 724 668-2256
Greensburg *(G-6695)*
Otw Tool Co .... F 724 539-8952
Latrobe *(G-9508)*
P & M Precision Machining Inc .... G 215 357-3313
Huntingdon Valley *(G-8020)*
P & R Engine Rebuilders .... G 724 837-7590
Greensburg *(G-6698)*
▲ **P M Supply Co Inc** .... E 814 472-4430
Ebensburg *(G-4791)*
P R L Inc .... E 717 273-2470
Cornwall *(G-3739)*
Paar Precision Industries .... G 610 807-9230
Freemansburg *(G-6198)*
Pabcor Inc .... G 724 652-1930
New Castle *(G-12136)*
Paradigm Corporation .... F 215 675-9488
Hatboro *(G-7295)*
Paragon America LLC .... F 412 408-3447
Sharpsburg *(G-17467)*
Parker Machine Company .... G 814 772-0135
Ridgway *(G-16723)*
Parker-Hannifin Corporation .... F 610 926-1115
Reading *(G-16465)*
Patricia Morris .... G 717 272-5594
Lebanon *(G-9615)*
Pb Holdings Inc .... G 215 947-3333
Huntingdon Valley *(G-8021)*
Peak Precision Inc .... G 215 799-1929
Hatfield *(G-7378)*
Pen Dor Manufacturing Inc .... G 724 863-7180
Westmoreland City *(G-19784)*
▲ **Penflex Corporation** .... D 610 367-2260
Gilbertsville *(G-6375)*
▼ **Penn Cigar Machines Inc** .... E 570 740-1112
Nanticoke *(G-11901)*
Penn Equipment Corporation .... E 570 622-9933
Port Carbon *(G-15899)*
Penn Machine Company .... F 724 459-0302
Blairsville *(G-1736)*
◆ **Penn Manufacturing Inds Inc** .... D 215 362-1217
Montgomeryville *(G-11411)*
Penn Public Truck & Equipment .... F 814 944-5314
Altoona *(G-537)*
Pennside Machining LLC .... G 814 774-2075
Girard *(G-6399)*
Pennsylvania State University .... G 814 865-4963
University Park *(G-18652)*
Pennsylvania Tool & Gages Inc .... E 814 336-3136
Meadville *(G-10778)*
Pennsylvnia Precision Pdts Inc .... G 724 568-4397
Vandergrift *(G-18735)*
Performance Machining Inc .... F 724 864-2499
Irwin *(G-8190)*
Petersen Machine Shop Inc .... F 412 233-8077
Clairton *(G-3155)*
Phb Inc .... C 814 474-1552
Fairview *(G-5839)*
Phil Skrzat .... G 215 257-8583
Perkasie *(G-13289)*
Philadelphia Toboggan Coaster .... F 215 799-2155
Hatfield *(G-7382)*
Phoenix Forging Company Inc .... G 610 530-8249
Allentown *(G-350)*
Pinnacle Precision Co .... F 412 678-6816
Glassport *(G-6415)*
Pioneer Machine & Tooling LLC .... F 610 623-3908
Secane *(G-17319)*
Plouse Machine Shop Inc .... D 717 558-8530
Highspire *(G-7634)*
Pmt Machining Inc .... G 570 329-0349
Williamsport *(G-20060)*
Porter Ao Co .... G 570 366-1387
Auburn *(G-821)*
Powderco Inc .... G 814 437-3705
Franklin *(G-6153)*
▲ **Practical Machine Solutions** .... G 717 949-3345
Schaefferstown *(G-17130)*
Pre-Mach Inc .... E 717 757-5685
York *(G-20636)*
Precision Automatic Machine Co .... F 724 339-2360
New Kensington *(G-12368)*
Precision Defense Services Inc .... C 724 863-1100
Irwin *(G-8193)*
Precision Metal Crafters Ltd .... E 724 837-2511
Greensburg *(G-6704)*
Precision Parts & Machine Co .... G 412 824-9367
Turtle Creek *(G-18567)*
Precision Production Turning .... G 610 872-8557
Chester *(G-3060)*
Precision Products Ltd .... E 215 538-1795
Quakertown *(G-16233)*
Precision Profiles LLC .... G 814 827-9887
Titusville *(G-18390)*
Precision Secondary Machining .... G 814 885-6572
Kersey *(G-8566)*
Precision Tl & Die Mfg Co Inc .... F 814 676-1864
Oil City *(G-12955)*
▼ **Precision Tool & Die Co Inc** .... E 814 676-1864
Oil City *(G-12956)*
Precision Tool & Mfg Corp .... G 717 767-6454
Emigsville *(G-4997)*
Precision Tool and Machine Co .... F 570 868-3920
Mountain Top *(G-11772)*
Precisioneering Inc .... G 724 423-2472
Latrobe *(G-9510)*
Premax Tool Machine Inc .... G 610 326-3860
Pottstown *(G-16036)*
▲ **Premier Hydraulics LLC** .... D 724 342-6506
Farrell *(G-5872)*
Premium Tool Co Inc .... F 570 753-5070
Jersey Shore *(G-8320)*
Prieto Machine Co Inc .... F 215 675-6061
Warminster *(G-18947)*
▼ **Prion Manufacturing Co Inc** .... E 724 693-0200
Oakdale *(G-12909)*
Pro-Machine LLC .... F 724 342-9895
Wheatland *(G-19842)*
Progressive Machine Works Inc .... F 610 562-2281
Hamburg *(G-6850)*
Progressive Machining .... G 610 469-6204
Spring City *(G-17864)*
▲ **Projectile Tube Cleaning Inc** .... E 724 763-7633
Ford City *(G-6051)*
Prompton Tool Inc .... D 570 253-4141
Honesdale *(G-7720)*
Protect Machining Inc .... F 814 587-3200
Conneautville *(G-3485)*
Pt Industries Inc .... F 717 755-1679
York *(G-20648)*
Purcell Company .... E 717 838-5611
Palmyra *(G-13130)*
Pyle Machine Manufacturing Inc .... G 814 443-3171
Somerset *(G-17701)*
Q-E Manufacturing Company .... E 570 966-1017
New Berlin *(G-12023)*
Qmac-Quality Machining Inc .... D 814 548-2000
Bellefonte *(G-1113)*
Quala-Die Inc .... D 814 781-6280
Saint Marys *(G-17011)*
Quality Die Makers Inc .... E 724 325-1264
Turtle Creek *(G-18568)*

Quality Gear & Machine Inc .... F 814 938-5552
Punxsutawney *(G-16157)*

Quality Machine Inc .... G 610 942-2488
Glenmoore *(G-6469)*

Quality Machined Pdts Mfg Inc .... E 724 339-2360
New Kensington *(G-12369)*

Quality Mould Inc .... E 724 532-3678
Latrobe *(G-9512)*

Quality Tooling & Repair Inc .... F 724 522-1555
Irwin *(G-8195)*

Quantum Mfg Services Inc .... G 570 785-9716
Waymart *(G-19289)*

R & R Automotive Machine Shop .... G 717 732-5521
Enola *(G-5085)*

R & S Machine Inc .... F 814 938-7540
Punxsutawney *(G-16158)*

R and M Machining Company Inc .... F 724 532-0890
Latrobe *(G-9514)*

R C Kletzing Inc .... G 215 357-1788
Southampton *(G-17834)*

R G S Machine Inc .... G 610 532-1850
Folsom *(G-6027)*

▲ R H Fink Inc .... F 717 266-1054
York *(G-20650)*

R Illig Machining .... G 814 344-6202
Carrolltown *(G-2809)*

R J Machine Co Inc .... G 610 494-8107
Upper Chichester *(G-18672)*

R L Sgath McHining Fabrication .... G 724 327-3895
Murrysville *(G-11863)*

R M Kerner Co .... B 814 898-2000
Erie *(G-5449)*

R M Kerner Co .... C 814 898-2000
Erie *(G-5450)*

R S Machine & Tool Inc .... G 610 857-1644
Sadsburyville *(G-16906)*

R T Callahan Machine Pdts Inc .... G 215 256-8765
Harleysville *(G-7054)*

R&R Machine Inc .... G 724 286-9507
Rochester Mills *(G-16790)*

Racoh Products Inc .... E 814 486-3288
Emporium *(G-5073)*

Ramac Industries Inc .... F 814 456-6159
Erie *(G-5455)*

Ramsay Machine Development .... F 610 395-4764
Allentown *(G-370)*

Randall Lesso .... G 724 746-2100
Houston *(G-7878)*

Randolph Manufacturing Corp .... E 610 253-9626
Easton *(G-4747)*

Rasley Enterprise .... G 610 588-9520
Bangor *(G-925)*

Raytec LLC .... E 717 445-0510
Ephrata *(G-5138)*

Rbs Fab Inc .... F 717 566-9513
Hummelstown *(G-7923)*

Rebco Machining Inc .... G 215 957-5133
Hatboro *(G-7299)*

▲ Refractory Machining Services .... F 724 285-7674
Butler *(G-2438)*

Rego Precision Machine LLC .... G 610 434-1582
Allentown *(G-373)*

Reilly Plating Company Inc .... D 570 735-7777
Nanticoke *(G-11902)*

Reist Precision Machine Inc .... G 717 606-3166
Mountville *(G-11801)*

▲ Ressler Enterprises Inc .... E 717 933-5611
Mount Aetna *(G-11605)*

Reuss Industries Inc .... E 724 722-3300
Madison *(G-10166)*

Reynolds Machine Co Inc .... G 724 925-1982
Ruffs Dale *(G-16875)*

Reynolds Sales Co Inc .... G 412 461-7877
Homestead *(G-7692)*

Rhoads Industries Inc .... D 267 728-6300
Philadelphia *(G-14244)*

Richard Meyers .... F 814 359-4340
Bellefonte *(G-1114)*

Ridge Machine Shop Inc .... G 717 896-8348
Halifax *(G-6829)*

Rightnour Machining .... F 814 383-4176
Bellefonte *(G-1115)*

▲ Rightnour Manufacturing Co Inc .... E 800 326-9113
Mingoville *(G-11257)*

Rochester Machine Corporation .... E 724 843-7820
New Brighton *(G-12040)*

Rod Quellette .... G 814 274-8812
Coudersport *(G-3788)*

Rokat Machine .... G 610 432-1830
Allentown *(G-378)*

Romans Precision Machining .... G 724 774-6444
Beaver *(G-990)*

Ronald Copeland .... G 814 827-3968
Titusville *(G-18392)*

Rose Corporation .... D 610 376-5004
Reading *(G-16504)*

Royalton Tool and Die Inc .... G 717 944-5838
Middletown *(G-11072)*

Royersford Fndry & Mch Co Inc .... E 610 935-7200
Phoenixville *(G-14576)*

Rsj Technologies LLC .... E 570 673-4173
Canton *(G-2668)*

Ruch Carbide Burs Inc .... E 215 657-3660
Willow Grove *(G-20139)*

Ruck Engineering .... G 412 835-2408
Bethel Park *(G-1431)*

▲ Rudys Fabricating & Mch Inc .... G 724 377-1425
Fredericktown *(G-6178)*

Ruscomb Tool & Machine Co Inc .... G 215 455-1301
Philadelphia *(G-14265)*

Russo Machine Works .... G 215 634-1630
Philadelphia *(G-14267)*

S & L Motors Inc .... G 570 342-9718
Scranton *(G-17280)*

S & M Machine Company .... G 724 339-2035
New Kensington *(G-12373)*

S & S Machine & Tool Company .... G 610 265-1582
King of Prussia *(G-8671)*

S & S Precision Tool Inc .... G 717 244-1600
Red Lion *(G-16612)*

◆ S & W Metal Products Inc .... E 610 473-2400
Gilbertsville *(G-6376)*

S W Machine .... G 717 336-2699
Stevens *(G-18056)*

S W U Automotive Machinery LLC .... G 570 457-4299
Moosic *(G-11514)*

Saeger Machine Inc .... F 215 256-8754
Harleysville *(G-7056)*

Saeilo Inc .... F 845 735-4500
Greeley *(G-6583)*

Saeilo Enterprises Inc .... E 845 735-6500
Greeley *(G-6584)*

Santucci Process Development .... G 412 787-0747
Mc Kees Rocks *(G-10633)*

▲ Sbi Survivor Corporation .... C 215 997-8900
Center Valley *(G-2829)*

Schaefer Machine Inc .... G 724 796-7755
Mc Donald *(G-10581)*

Scientific Tool Inc .... E 724 446-9311
New Stanton *(G-12450)*

Sciullo Machine Shop & Tool Co .... G 412 466-9571
Homestead *(G-7693)*

Sciullo Machine Shop & Tool Co .... G 412 462-1604
West Mifflin *(G-19745)*

Scranton Grinder & Hardware .... E 570 344-2520
Scranton *(G-17285)*

Secondary Development & Res .... E 814 772-3882
Ridgway *(G-16729)*

Sedco Manufacturing .... G 570 323-1232
Hughesville *(G-7899)*

Seel Tool & Die Inc .... G 814 834-4561
Saint Marys *(G-17014)*

Sepco Erie .... F 814 864-0311
Erie *(G-5476)*

Seths Auto Machine Shop .... G 570 658-2886
Beaver Springs *(G-1022)*

Shasta Inc .... E 724 378-8280
Aliquippa *(G-94)*

Shasta Holdings Company .... C 724 378-8280
Aliquippa *(G-95)*

Shaw Industries Inc .... E 814 432-0954
Franklin *(G-6159)*

Shed-Shop Incorporated .... G 215 723-4209
Souderton *(G-17763)*

Shook Specialty Welding Inc .... F 724 368-8419
Portersville *(G-15936)*

Sidelinger Bros Tool & Die .... G 814 885-8001
Kersey *(G-8569)*

Sigbet Manufacturing .... G 724 459-7920
Blairsville *(G-1741)*

Simpson Technical Sales Inc .... G 724 375-7133
Aliquippa *(G-96)*

▲ Sinacom North America Inc .... E 610 337-2250
King of Prussia *(G-8677)*

Sintergy Inc .... F 814 653-9640
Reynoldsville *(G-16664)*

Skovira Fabrication Mch Sp Inc .... G 717 323-0056
Mount Holly Springs *(G-11639)*

Skovira Machine Company .... F 724 887-4896
Scottdale *(G-17201)*

Skylon Inc .... F 814 489-3622
Sugar Grove *(G-18147)*

Skytop Machine & Tool Inc .... G 814 234-3430
Port Matilda *(G-15906)*

Slothower Machine Shop LLC .... F 717 846-3409
York *(G-20669)*

Small Parts Machine Inc .... G 724 452-6116
Harmony *(G-7076)*

SMI IL Inc .... E 847 228-0090
Greeley *(G-6585)*

Snyder County Automotive Inc .... G 570 374-2072
Selinsgrove *(G-17335)*

South Erie Production Co Inc .... E 814 864-0311
Erie *(G-5485)*

Specialized Welding Inc .... G 724 733-7801
Export *(G-5627)*

Specialty Design & Mfg Co Inc .... E 610 779-1357
Reading *(G-16520)*

Specialty Holdings Corp .... E 610 779-1357
Reading *(G-16521)*

Specialty Machine & Hydraulic .... G 814 589-7381
Pleasantville *(G-15804)*

Specialty Products Inc .... G 814 455-6978
Erie *(G-5486)*

Spektra Manufacturing Inc .... G 814 454-6879
Erie *(G-5488)*

Speranza Specialty Machining .... G 724 733-8045
Export *(G-5628)*

Spiral Tool Corporation .... G 570 409-1331
Shohola *(G-17580)*

Spreng Machine Co Inc .... F 724 352-9467
Saxonburg *(G-17095)*

Spring Tool & Die Co Inc .... G 814 224-5173
Roaring Spring *(G-16771)*

Square Tool and Die Corp Inc .... F 570 489-8657
Throop *(G-18362)*

Squibb Custom Machine Inc .... G 610 258-0923
Easton *(G-4756)*

◆ Stahls Hotronix .... G 724 966-5996
Carmichaels *(G-2760)*

Standard Tool & Machine Co .... D 724 758-5522
Ellwood City *(G-4950)*

Standard Tool & Machine Co .... E 724 758-5522
Ellwood City *(G-4951)*

Stanko Products Inc .... F 724 834-8080
Greensburg *(G-6717)*

Starlite Group Inc .... G 814 333-1377
Meadville *(G-10793)*

State of ARC Wldg & Fabg LLC .... G 610 216-6862
Bangor *(G-930)*

Statlers Repair Shop .... G 717 263-5074
Chambersburg *(G-2979)*

Staudt Machine Company .... F 215 598-7225
Newtown *(G-12552)*

Stauffer Compressor N Machine .... G 717 733-4128
Ephrata *(G-5146)*

Stellar Machine Incorporated .... F 570 718-1733
Nanticoke *(G-11903)*

Stellar Prcsion Components Ltd .... D 724 523-5559
Jeannette *(G-8265)*

Stephen R Lechman .... G 570 636-3159
Freeland *(G-6196)*

Sterling Machine Tech Inc .... E 717 838-1234
Palmyra *(G-13131)*

Steve Jones .... G 717 845-7700
York *(G-20680)*

Strobel Machine Inc .... F 724 297-3441
Worthington *(G-20234)*

Subcon Tl/Cctool Mch Group Inc .... E 814 456-7797
Erie *(G-5494)*

Suburban Pump and Mch Co Inc .... G 412 221-2823
Bridgeville *(G-2092)*

Superior Machining Inc .... F 814 372-2270
Du Bois *(G-4423)*

Swissaero Inc .... F 814 796-4166
Waterford *(G-19271)*

Syncom Specialty Inc .... G 215 322-9708
Southampton *(G-17839)*

Syncom Specialty Inc .... E 215 322-9708
Huntingdon Valley *(G-8042)*

Synergy Metal Solutions Inc .... G 215 699-7060
North Wales *(G-12830)*

T H E M Services Inc .... G 610 559-9341
Easton *(G-4761)*

Tancredi Machining Inc .... G 215 679-8985
Bally *(G-907)*

Tecklane Manufacturing Inc .... F 724 274-9464
Springdale *(G-17903)*

Tennett Manufacturing Inc .... F 215 721-3803
Telford *(G-18322)*

Terry D Miles.................................G...... 814 686-1997
Tyrone (G-18596)

Testa Machine Company Inc........E...... 724 947-9397
Slovan (G-17631)

Thompson Gear & Machine Co......G...... 724 468-5625
Delmont (G-4060)

Thompson Machine Company Inc....E...... 814 941-4982
Altoona (G-552)

Thornton Industries Inc................F...... 814 756-3578
Albion (G-47)

Thorsens Precision Grinding.........G...... 717 765-9090
Waynesboro (G-19427)

Tiberi Gun Shop............................G...... 724 245-6151
Fairbank (G-5764)

Tigereye Enterprise Inc.................G...... 724 443-7810
Warrendale (G-19099)

Time Machine Inc..........................D...... 814 432-5281
Polk (G-15889)

Timothy Emig................................G...... 215 443-7810
Warminster (G-18982)

Tiros Machine & Tool Company......G...... 215 322-9965
Feasterville Trevose (G-5933)

Tita Machine & Tool Inc................G...... 724 535-4988
Wampum (G-18805)

Toolco Inc....................................E...... 724 337-9119
New Kensington (G-12382)

Tooling Specialists Inc.................D...... 724 539-2534
Latrobe (G-9524)

Tooling Specialists Inc.................G...... 724 837-0433
Latrobe (G-9525)

Torcomp Usa LLC.........................G...... 717 261-1530
Chambersburg (G-2987)

Tory Tool Inc................................E...... 814 772-5439
Saint Marys (G-17023)

Tory Tool Inc................................E...... 814 772-5439
Ridgway (G-16732)

Trans American Tool Company......G...... 610 948-4411
Spring City (G-17869)

Tri Max Manufacturing Co Inc.......G...... 724 898-1400
Valencia (G-18703)

Tri Star Precision Mfg...................G...... 215 443-8610
Warminster (G-18984)

Tri-Kris Co Inc.............................G...... 215 855-5183
Lansdale (G-9415)

Tri-Kris Company..........................F...... 215 855-5183
Lansdale (G-9416)

Trimach LLC.................................G...... 610 252-8983
Easton (G-4764)

Trout Run Secondary....................G...... 814 834-0075
Saint Marys (G-17024)

True Position Inc..........................F...... 724 444-0300
Gibsonia (G-6357)

Turning Solutions, Inc..................F...... 814 723-1134
Warren (G-19053)

Twenty First Century Tool Co........G...... 724 423-5357
Acme (G-17)

Twin Pines Manuifacturing Corp....G...... 724 459-3850
Clarksburg (G-3200)

UGm Precision Machining Inc........G...... 215 957-6175
Warminster (G-18989)

Under Pressure Connections LLC...G...... 570 326-1117
South Williamsport (G-17793)

Unimach Manufacturing.................G...... 724 285-5505
Fenelton (G-5949)

Unique Machine & Tool.................F...... 412 331-2717
Mc Kees Rocks (G-10640)

Unique Machine Co.......................E...... 215 368-8550
Montgomeryville (G-11425)

United Fabricating Inc...................F...... 724 663-5891
Claysville (G-3209)

United Foundry Company Inc.........E...... 814 539-8840
Johnstown (G-8440)

United Precision Mfg Co Inc..........G...... 215 938-5890
Huntingdon Valley (G-8046)

United Theatrical Services.............G...... 215 242-2134
Philadelphia (G-14424)

Universal Mch Co Pottstown Inc.....D...... 610 323-1810
Pottstown (G-16062)

Urania Engineering Co Inc.............E...... 570 455-0776
Hazleton (G-7532)

▼ US Axle Inc...............................D...... 610 323-3800
Pottstown (G-16063)

USA Precision..............................G...... 724 924-2838
Ellwood City (G-4954)

V I P Machining Inc......................F...... 814 665-1840
Corry (G-3777)

V I P Machining Inc......................G...... 814 665-1840
Corry (G-3778)

V2r2 LLC.....................................G...... 215 277-2181
Harleysville (G-7063)

Valco Investment Corporation........E...... 610 770-1881
Allentown (G-419)

Valley Machine and Tool Co..........G...... 814 637-5621
Penfield (G-13224)

Valley Machine Ltd.......................G...... 814 259-3624
Shade Gap (G-17417)

Valley Precision LLC.....................F...... 215 536-0676
Quakertown (G-16255)

Vanderslice Machine Company.......G...... 215 659-0429
Willow Grove (G-20147)

Vangura Tool Inc..........................E...... 412 233-6401
Clairton (G-3160)

▲ Vanzel Inc................................G...... 215 223-1000
Philadelphia (G-14438)

Velocity Powder Coating LLC........G...... 704 287-1024
New Castle (G-12164)

Venango Machine Company Inc......F...... 814 739-2211
Wattsburg (G-19283)

Venango Machine Products Inc.......F...... 814 676-5741
Reno (G-16648)

Versa-Fab Inc..............................F...... 724 889-0137
New Kensington (G-12387)

Versatech Incorporated.................D...... 724 327-8324
Export (G-5631)

Victoria Precision Inc....................F...... 215 355-7576
Feasterville Trevose (G-5939)

Vision Grinding & Tool Co.............G...... 215 744-5069
Philadelphia (G-14451)

Vista Manufacturing Inc................G...... 724 495-6860
Aliquippa (G-102)

Vista Manufacturing Inc................G...... 724 495-6860
Midland (G-11088)

Vitols Tool & Machine Corp............G...... 215 464-8240
Philadelphia (G-14454)

Vollmer Patterns Inc.....................G...... 610 562-7920
Hamburg (G-6855)

Von Machine Co............................G...... 412 276-4505
Carnegie (G-2805)

Vortx United Inc...........................G...... 570 742-7859
Milton (G-11250)

W & H Machine Shop Co LLC........F...... 814 834-6258
Saint Marys (G-17028)

W & H Machine Shop Inc...............F...... 814 834-6258
Saint Marys (G-17029)

W E Keller Machining Welding........G...... 724 337-8327
Leechburg (G-9654)

Wagman Manufacturing Inc............F...... 717 266-5616
Manchester (G-10365)

Wagner & Sons Machine Shop........G...... 610 434-6640
Allentown (G-429)

Wagner Industries Inc...................G...... 570 874-4400
Frackville (G-6108)

Walsh Tool Company Inc...............G...... 570 823-1375
Wilkes Barre (G-19969)

Warren Industrial Solutions...........F...... 814 728-8500
Warren (G-19058)

Warren Machine Technology Inc.....G...... 215 491-5500
Warrington (G-19137)

▲ Warwick Machine & Tool Company..E...... 717 892-6814
Landisville (G-9268)

Wash n Grind LLC........................G...... 814 383-4707
Bellefonte (G-1124)

Watermark Usa LLC......................F...... 610 983-0500
Gladwyne (G-6409)

Waverly Partners Inc....................C...... 610 687-7867
Wayne (G-19390)

Weaver Machine & Hardware LLC....G...... 717 445-9927
East Earl (G-4558)

Webco Inc....................................F...... 215 942-9366
Richboro (G-16678)

Wel-Mac Inc.................................G...... 717 637-6921
Hanover (G-6974)

WER Corporation..........................C...... 610 678-8023
Reading (G-16564)

Weskem Technologies Inc.............G...... 717 697-8228
Mechanicsburg (G-10907)

West Moreland Precision Tool........G...... 724 537-6558
Latrobe (G-9528)

West Side Tool and Die Company....G...... 570 331-7016
Wilkes Barre (G-19972)

▲ Westrock Packaging Inc.............D...... 215 785-3350
Croydon (G-3933)

White Horse Machine LLC..............F...... 717 768-8313
Gap (G-6257)

White-Brook Inc...........................E...... 814 849-8441
Brookville (G-2276)

Whites Machine Inc.......................G...... 570 345-1142
Pine Grove (G-14607)

Wilke Enginuity Inc......................E...... 717 632-5937
Hanover (G-6976)

William A Moddrel........................G...... 610 327-8296
Pottstown (G-15957)

William J Labb Sons Inc................E...... 215 289-3450
Philadelphia (G-14474)

Williams Machining Co..................G...... 814 734-3121
Edinboro (G-4821)

Wilsey Tool Company Inc..............D...... 215 538-0800
Quakertown (G-16260)

Windsor Beach Technologies Inc....E...... 814 474-4900
Fairview (G-5849)

Winston & Duke Inc......................F...... 814 456-0582
Erie (G-5529)

Winston & Duke Inc......................F...... 814 456-0582
Erie (G-5530)

Wintercorp LLC............................G...... 717 848-3425
York (G-20712)

Wire Tech & Tool Inc....................G...... 814 333-3175
Meadville (G-10813)

Wismer Machine Company Inc........G...... 215 257-5081
Sellersville (G-17362)

Wolfe Tool & Machine Company.....F...... 717 848-6375
York (G-20717)

Woodstock Mfg Services Inc..........G...... 814 336-4426
Meadville (G-10814)

Wpmw Inc....................................F...... 610 286-5071
Elverson (G-4970)

XI Precision Technologies.............F...... 610 696-6800
West Chester (G-19683)

Xpert Machining Inc......................G...... 724 694-0123
Derry (G-4109)

Xylem Wtr Sltons Zlienople LLC.....F...... 724 452-6300
Zelienople (G-20829)

Xynatech Mfg Co..........................F...... 215 423-0804
Philadelphia (G-14496)

Yarger Precision Machining...........F...... 814 364-1961
Centre Hall (G-2846)

Yoder Industries LLC....................G...... 717 656-6770
Leola (G-9809)

Yoh Industrial LLC........................E...... 215 656-2650
Philadelphia (G-14501)

York Electro-Mechanical Corp........G...... 717 764-5262
York (G-20737)

York Industrial Tool Inc................G...... 717 200-1149
York (G-20741)

York Precision............................F...... 717 764-8855
York (G-20749)

York Tool & Die Inc.....................F...... 717 741-4844
York (G-20752)

York-Seaway Indus Pdts Inc..........D...... 814 774-7080
Lake City (G-8911)

▲ YS Manufacturing Inc...............D...... 610 444-4832
Kennett Square (G-8552)

Z & Z Machine Inc.........................G...... 717 428-0354
Jacobus (G-8233)

Z-Axis Connector Company............F...... 267 803-9000
Warminster (G-19006)

Zeb Machine Co Inc......................G...... 610 926-4766
Leesport (G-9675)

Zeiglers Machine Shop..................G...... 570 374-5535
Middleburg (G-11042)

Zemco Tool & Die Inc...................D...... 717 647-7151
Williamstown (G-20104)

Zenco Machine & Tool Co Inc.........G...... 215 345-6262
Doylestown (G-4349)

Zero Error Racing Inc....................G...... 724 588-5898
Greenville (G-6778)

Zimm-O-Matic LLC........................G...... 717 445-6432
Denver (G-4098)

Zrm Enterprises LLC.....................F...... 724 437-3116
Smithfield (G-17657)

Zurenko Welding & Fabricating.......G...... 724 254-1131
Commodore (G-3455)

36 ELECTRONIC AND OTHER ELECTRICAL EQUIPMENT AND COMPONENTS, EXCEPT COMPUTER

3612 Power, Distribution & Specialty Transformers

ABB Inc.......................................D...... 724 838-8622
Greensburg (G-6647)

ABB Inc.......................................C...... 215 674-6000
Warminster (G-18818)

ABB Inc.......................................D...... 724 696-1300
Mount Pleasant (G-11685)

Acutran LP...................................E...... 724 452-4130
Fombell (G-6029)

SIC

Agileswitch LLC .... F 484 483-3256
Philadelphia *(G-13355)*
Alstom Grid LLC .... D 412 967-0765
Pittsburgh *(G-14689)*
◆ **Alstom Power Conversion Inc** .... C 412 967-0765
Cranberry Township *(G-3801)*
American Powernet MGT LP .... G 610 372-8500
Wyomissing *(G-20286)*
Associated Specialty Co .... F 610 395-9172
Orefield *(G-13008)*
◆ **C&D Technologies Inc** .... C 215 619-2700
Blue Bell *(G-1820)*
Central Penn Wire and Cable .... G 717 945-5540
Lancaster *(G-8974)*
Coil Specialty Co Inc .... E 814 234-7044
State College *(G-17952)*
Cooper Power Systems LLC .... G 636 394-2877
Canonsburg *(G-2573)*
Eaton Corporation .... B 724 773-1231
Beaver *(G-980)*
Evans Commercial Services LLC .... F 412 573-9442
Bridgeville *(G-2061)*
▲ **Fortune Electric Co Ltd** .... F 724 346-2722
Hermitage *(G-7585)*
Gentherm Incorporated .... G 215 362-9191
Lansdale *(G-9372)*
Gettysburg Transformer Corp .... E 717 334-2191
Gettysburg *(G-6293)*
High Voltage Solutions Sls Inc .... G 412 523-0238
Sharon *(G-17436)*
Hindle Power Inc .... D 610 330-9000
Easton *(G-4699)*
Hydro Partners LLC .... G 717 825-1332
York *(G-20532)*
Ifco Enterprises Inc .... C 610 651-0999
Malvern *(G-10251)*
▲ **Innovative Control Systems Inc** .... C 610 881-8000
Wind Gap *(G-20169)*
▲ **Invensys Energy Metering Corp** .... B 814 371-3011
Du Bois *(G-4396)*
Kongsberg Integrated Tactical .... E 814 269-5700
Johnstown *(G-8399)*
Magnetic Windings Company Inc .... E 610 253-2751
Easton *(G-4716)*
Micro-Coax Inc .... C 610 495-4438
Pottstown *(G-16019)*
Mimco Equipment Inc .... F 610 494-7400
Linwood *(G-9990)*
Myers Power Products Inc .... D 610 868-3500
Bethlehem *(G-1576)*
Orlotronics Corporation .... E 610 239-8200
Bridgeport *(G-2042)*
Parker-Hannifin Corporation .... C 215 723-4000
Hatfield *(G-7377)*
▲ **Pennsylvania Trans Tech Inc** .... B 724 873-2100
Canonsburg *(G-2618)*
▼ **Philadelphia Electrical Eqp Co** .... F 484 840-0860
Aston *(G-786)*
Power Systems Specialists Inc .... F 570 296-4573
Milford *(G-11167)*
▲ **Progressive Power Tech LLC** .... F 724 452-6064
Harmony *(G-7075)*
▲ **RE Uptegraff Mfg Co LLC** .... D 724 887-7700
Scottdale *(G-17199)*
Schneider Electric It Corp .... B 717 948-1200
Middletown *(G-11074)*
Siemens Industry Inc .... D 724 743-5913
Canonsburg *(G-2636)*
Silicon Power Corporation .... D 610 407-4700
Malvern *(G-10317)*
◆ **Spang & Company** .... C 412 963-9363
Pittsburgh *(G-15566)*
Spang & Company .... E 724 376-7515
Sandy Lake *(G-17062)*
SPD Electrical Systems Inc .... B 215 698-6426
Philadelphia *(G-14331)*
▲ **Spectrum Control Inc** .... B 814 474-2207
Fairview *(G-5842)*
Spectrum Control Inc .... G 814 474-4315
Fairview *(G-5845)*
Tamini Transformers USA LLC .... G 412 534-4275
Sewickley *(G-17414)*
Thomas Magnetix Inc .... E 570 879-4363
Hallstead *(G-6836)*
Transicoil LLC .... C 484 902-1100
Collegeville *(G-3397)*
Vishay Intertechnology Inc .... B 610 644-1300
Malvern *(G-10341)*
VSI Meter Services Inc .... G 484 482-2480
Aston *(G-796)*
Yesco Pittsburgh Inc .... G 330 747-8593
Pittsburgh *(G-15729)*

3613 Switchgear & Switchboard Apparatus

Accurate Control & Design Co .... G 412 884-3723
Pittsburgh *(G-14638)*
Action Manufacturing Company .... D 610 593-1800
Atglen *(G-799)*
Ai Control Systems Inc .... F 610 921-9670
Reading *(G-16313)*
Ajax Electric Company .... E 215 947-8500
Huntingdon Valley *(G-7962)*
Alstom Grid LLC .... D 724 483-7308
Charleroi *(G-3005)*
American Mfg & Integration LLC .... F 724 861-2080
North Huntingdon *(G-12767)*
ARc Technologies Corporation .... F 724 722-7066
Yukon *(G-20784)*
B & C Controls Inc .... F 610 738-9204
West Chester *(G-19506)*
Basic Power Inc .... G 570 872-9666
East Stroudsburg *(G-4608)*
Butler Technologies Inc .... D 724 283-6656
Butler *(G-2386)*
◆ **C&D Technologies Inc** .... C 215 619-2700
Blue Bell *(G-1820)*
Carpenter Engineering Inc .... G 717 274-8808
Lebanon *(G-9553)*
Caruso Inc .... G 717 738-0248
Ephrata *(G-5095)*
Central Panel Inc .... G 215 947-8500
Huntingdon Valley *(G-7968)*
Clark Metal Products Co .... C 724 459-7550
Blairsville *(G-1719)*
Clinton Controls Inc .... G 570 748-4042
Lock Haven *(G-10086)*
Coflex Inc .... G 570 296-2100
Shohola *(G-17578)*
▼ **Control Design Inc** .... E 412 788-2280
Pittsburgh *(G-14873)*
Control Design Inc .... F 814 833-4663
Erie *(G-5232)*
Cooper Bussmann LLC .... B 724 553-5449
Cranberry Township *(G-3812)*
Crisp Control Inc .... D 724 864-6777
Irwin *(G-8153)*
Del Electronic Co .... G 412 787-1177
Pittsburgh *(G-14916)*
◆ **Deltronic Labs Inc** .... E 215 997-8616
Chalfont *(G-2872)*
▲ **Detroit Switch Inc** .... E 412 322-9144
Pittsburgh *(G-14919)*
Dr Controls Inc .... G 570 622-7109
Pottsville *(G-16077)*
▼ **Duquesne Mine Supply Company** .... G 412 821-2100
Pittsburgh *(G-14944)*
E F E Laboratories Inc .... E 215 672-2400
Horsham *(G-7812)*
Eaton Corporation .... B 724 773-1231
Beaver *(G-980)*
Eaton Corporation .... E 610 497-6100
Boothwyn *(G-1877)*
Eaton Corporation .... E 412 893-3300
Moon Township *(G-11484)*
◆ **Eaton Electrical Inc** .... E 412 893-3300
Moon Township *(G-11485)*
Edwin L Heim Co .... E 717 233-8711
Harrisburg *(G-7125)*
▲ **Electric Materials Company** .... C 814 725-9621
North East *(G-12739)*
Electro Soft Inc .... E 215 654-0701
Montgomeryville *(G-11394)*
Ellison Industrial Contrls LLC .... G 724 483-0251
Belle Vernon *(G-1086)*
Erickson Corporation .... E 814 371-4350
Du Bois *(G-4391)*
Essex Engineering Corp .... G 215 322-5880
Warminster *(G-18874)*
FEC Technologies Inc .... E 717 764-5959
York *(G-20477)*
Fenner Inc .... C 717 665-2421
Manheim *(G-10380)*
Genesys Controls Corporation .... G 717 291-1116
Landisville *(G-9260)*
Genesys Controls Corporation .... F 717 291-1116
Landisville *(G-9261)*
▲ **Gerome Manufacturing Co Inc** .... D 724 438-8544
Smithfield *(G-17650)*
Ges Automation Technology .... E 717 236-8733
Harrisburg *(G-7133)*
Homewood Products Corporation .... E 412 665-2700
Pittsburgh *(G-15099)*
Industrial Ctrl Concepts Inc .... G 412 464-1905
Homestead *(G-7687)*
Industrial Ctrl Concepts Inc .... G 412 464-1905
Homestead *(G-7688)*
Industrial Systems & Controls .... G 412 638-4977
Pittsburgh *(G-15121)*
▲ **Invensys Energy Metering Corp** .... B 814 371-3011
Du Bois *(G-4396)*
Io Solutions & Controls .... F 215 635-4480
Elkins Park *(G-4907)*
J C H Associates Inc .... G 610 367-5000
Boyertown *(G-1919)*
Kauffman Elec Contrls & Contg .... E 717 252-3667
Wrightsville *(G-20240)*
Kennametal Inc .... C 276 646-0080
Bedford *(G-1059)*
Lighthouse Electric Contrls Co .... F 814 835-2348
Erie *(G-5365)*
Marvin Dale Slaymaker .... G 717 684-5050
Washington Boro *(G-19251)*
Mauell Corporation .... E 717 432-8686
Dillsburg *(G-4137)*
▲ **Maxima Tech & Systems LLC** .... C 717 581-1000
Lancaster *(G-9130)*
▲ **Miller Edge Inc** .... D 610 869-4422
West Grove *(G-19702)*
Mitsubishi Elc Pwr Pdts Inc .... C 724 772-2555
Freedom *(G-6191)*
◆ **Mitsubishi Elc Pwr Pdts Inc** .... C 724 772-2555
Warrendale *(G-19088)*
Mitsubishi Elc Pwr Pdts Inc .... G 724 778-5112
Warrendale *(G-19089)*
Oak Hill Controls LLC .... F 610 758-9500
Bethlehem *(G-1585)*
Penn Panel & Box Company .... E 610 586-2700
Collingdale *(G-3409)*
Premier Automotive .... G 570 966-0363
Mifflinburg *(G-11100)*
▲ **Prominent Fluid Controls Inc** .... E 412 787-2484
Pittsburgh *(G-15453)*
R & D Machine Controls Inc .... G 267 205-5976
Bristol *(G-2192)*
▲ **Rtb Products Inc** .... F 724 861-2080
Irwin *(G-8198)*
RTD Embedded Technologies Inc .... E 814 234-8087
State College *(G-18017)*
Schrantz Indus Electricians .... G 610 435-8255
Allentown *(G-386)*
Scott Metals Inc .... E 412 279-7021
Carnegie *(G-2790)*
Siemens Industry Inc .... F 610 921-3135
Reading *(G-16518)*
Siemens Industry Inc .... D 724 743-5913
Canonsburg *(G-2636)*
◆ **Spang & Company** .... C 412 963-9363
Pittsburgh *(G-15566)*
SPD Electrical Systems Inc .... B 215 698-6426
Philadelphia *(G-14331)*
Spectrum Microwave Inc .... D 215 464-0586
Philadelphia *(G-14333)*
Staneco Corporation .... E 215 672-6500
Horsham *(G-7852)*
Te Connectivity Corporation .... B 717 986-3743
Middletown *(G-11081)*
U B R LLC .... G 717 432-3490
Dillsburg *(G-4141)*
▲ **Videotek Inc** .... C 610 327-2292
Pottstown *(G-16068)*
Vishay Intertechnology Inc .... B 610 644-1300
Malvern *(G-10341)*
W T Storey Inc .... F 570 923-2400
North Bend *(G-12728)*

3621 Motors & Generators

A B M Motors Inc .... G 215 781-9400
Croydon *(G-3909)*
Advanced Mobile Power Systems .... G 610 440-0195
Coplay *(G-3638)*
Agustawestland Tilt-Rotor LLC .... F 215 281-1400
Philadelphia *(G-13357)*
Allegheny Mfg & Elec Svc Inc .... E 814 288-1597
Johnstown *(G-8350)*
Alstom Signaling Operation LLC .... A 814 486-0235
Emporium *(G-5048)*
American Eagle Windmills LLC .... G 814 922-3180
West Springfield *(G-19766)*
Ametek Inc .... D 215 355-6900
Horsham *(G-7784)*

Ametek Inc .... D 570 645-2191
Nesquehoning *(G-12003)*
Ametek Inc .... D 215 256-6601
Harleysville *(G-7020)*
Ametek Inc .... D 717 569-7061
Lancaster *(G-8933)*
◆ **Ametek Inc** .... D 610 647-2121
Berwyn *(G-1351)*
Ametek Emg Holdings Inc .... G 610 647-2121
Berwyn *(G-1352)*
Ametek Inc .... D 724 225-8400
Eighty Four *(G-4833)*
Berrena Jseph T McHanicals Inc .... E 814 643-2645
Huntingdon *(G-7939)*
▼ **Bohlinger Inc** .... G 610 825-0440
Conshohocken *(G-3524)*
Brodrick Hughes Energy LLC .... G 570 662-2464
Covington *(G-3791)*
Brush Aftermarket N Amer Inc .... F 412 829-7500
Turtle Creek *(G-18560)*
California Linear Devices Inc .... F 610 328-4000
Springfield *(G-17909)*
Capital Coil & Air LLC .... G 484 498-6880
West Chester *(G-19518)*
Coil Specialty Co Inc .... E 814 234-7044
State College *(G-17952)*
Colonial EP LLC .... E 844 376-9374
King of Prussia *(G-8595)*
Computer Pwr Solutions PA Inc .... F 724 898-2223
Mars *(G-10491)*
Converter Accessory Corp .... F 610 863-6008
Wind Gap *(G-20168)*
Critical Systems LLC .... G 570 643-6903
Tannersville *(G-18235)*
Crystal Engineering Corp .... G 610 647-2121
Berwyn *(G-1358)*
▲ **Curtiss-Wright Electro-** .... A 724 275-5000
Cheswick *(G-3105)*
Danaher Corporation .... D 610 692-2700
West Chester *(G-19532)*
Danco Precision Inc .... F 610 933-8981
Phoenixville *(G-14542)*
▼ **Duryea Technologies Inc** .... G 610 939-0480
Reading *(G-16366)*
Dyna-Tech Industries Ltd .... F 717 274-3099
Lebanon *(G-9564)*
Ecolution Energy LLC .... G 908 707-1400
Lehighton *(G-9713)*
Evans Commercial Services LLC .... F 412 573-9442
Bridgeville *(G-2061)*
◆ **Everson Tesla Inc** .... D 610 746-1520
Nazareth *(G-11965)*
▲ **Fiberblade LLC** .... C 814 361-8730
Feasterville Trevose *(G-5908)*
Gamesa Energy Usa Inc .... F 215 665-9810
Trevose *(G-18495)*
▼ **Gamesa Wind Pa LLC** .... F 215 665-9810
Philadelphia *(G-13742)*
◆ **Generator and Mtr Svcs PA LLC** .... D 412 829-7500
Turtle Creek *(G-18565)*
Gettysburg Transformer Corp .... E 717 334-2191
Gettysburg *(G-6293)*
Go2power LLC .... E 215 244-4202
Feasterville Trevose *(G-5913)*
Grays Automotive Speed Eqp .... G 717 436-8777
Mifflintown *(G-11119)*
◆ **Gupta Permold Corporation** .... C 412 793-3511
Pittsburgh *(G-15067)*
Hannon Company .... G 724 266-2712
Ambridge *(G-618)*
Holtrys LLC .... G 717 532-7261
Roxbury *(G-16838)*
Homewood Products Corporation .... E 412 665-2700
Pittsburgh *(G-15099)*
▲ **Hydromotion Inc** .... D 610 948-4150
Spring City *(G-17860)*
Iberdrola Renewable .... F 610 254-9800
Radnor *(G-16294)*
Integrated Power Services LLC .... F 724 225-2900
Washington *(G-19186)*
◆ **Klinge Corporation** .... D 717 840-4500
York *(G-20556)*
Lake City Power Systems LLC .... G 814 774-2034
Lake City *(G-8902)*
▲ **Lemm Liquidating Company LLC** .... D 724 325-7140
Export *(G-5615)*
Lesleh Precision Inc .... E 724 823-0901
Rostraver Township *(G-16827)*
LLC Armstrong Power .... F 724 354-5300
Shelocta *(G-17486)*

◆ **Marino Indus Systems Svcs Inc** .... E 610 872-3630
Chester *(G-3057)*
Martin Associates Ephrata LLC .... F 717 733-7968
Ephrata *(G-5122)*
Marvin Dale Slaymaker .... G 717 684-5050
Washington Boro *(G-19251)*
Mechanical Service Company .... F 570 654-2445
Pittston *(G-15766)*
▲ **Mgs Inc** .... C 717 336-7528
Denver *(G-4083)*
Milan Energy LLC .... G 724 933-0140
Pittsburgh *(G-15287)*
Nearhoof Machine Inc .... G 814 339-6621
Osceola Mills *(G-13056)*
NRG Texas Power LLC .... G 412 655-4134
West Mifflin *(G-19743)*
Patriot Sensors & Contrls Corp .... C 336 449-3400
Horsham *(G-7840)*
Powerhouse Generator Inc .... G 717 759-8535
New Freedom *(G-12214)*
Rockwell Automation Inc .... G 412 375-4700
Coraopolis *(G-3723)*
▲ **RR Enterprises Inc** .... G 610 266-9600
Allentown *(G-381)*
S & L Motors Inc .... G 570 342-9718
Scranton *(G-17280)*
S T M Heavy Duty Electric Inc .... F 610 967-3810
Zionsville *(G-20836)*
Servo Repair International .... F 412 492-8116
Allison Park *(G-462)*
Siemens Gamesa Renewable .... G 215 665-9810
Philadelphia *(G-14303)*
◆ **Siemens Gamesa Renewable** .... G 215 710-3100
Feasterville Trevose *(G-5930)*
Siemens Industry Inc .... D 724 743-5913
Canonsburg *(G-2636)*
Solaris Select .... G 267 987-2082
Morrisville *(G-11582)*
Stimple and Ward Company .... G 724 772-0049
Cranberry Township *(G-3851)*
Toshiba International Corp .... G 215 830-3340
Dresher *(G-4359)*
Ultra Lite Brakes An C .... G 724 696-3743
Mount Pleasant *(G-11721)*
▲ **Videotek Inc** .... C 610 327-2292
Pottstown *(G-16068)*
W M S Phase Converters .... G 717 336-6566
Stevens *(G-18057)*
Wg Products Pittsburgh LLC .... G 412 795-7177
Pittsburgh *(G-15713)*
Windurance .... G 814 678-1318
Seneca *(G-17372)*
World of Wheels Inc .... F 814 676-5721
Seneca *(G-17373)*

3624 Carbon & Graphite Prdts

Aluminum & Carbon Plus Inc .... G 724 368-9200
Portersville *(G-15924)*
◆ **Ameri-Surce Specialty Pdts Inc** .... E 412 831-9400
Bethel Park *(G-1402)*
Anthracite Industries Inc .... E 570 286-2176
Sunbury *(G-18163)*
Asbury Carbons Inc .... G 570 286-9721
Sunbury *(G-18164)*
Asbury Graphite Mills Inc .... D 724 543-1343
Kittanning *(G-8755)*
Caldwell Corporation .... E 814 486-3493
Emporium *(G-5051)*
E-Carbon America LLC .... F 814 834-7777
Saint Marys *(G-16965)*
▲ **Galaxy Mfg Company Inc** .... F 570 457-5199
Avoca *(G-843)*
Ges Graphite .... G 205 838-0820
Emlenton *(G-5009)*
▲ **Graftech Usa LLC** .... C 814 781-2478
Saint Marys *(G-16979)*
▲ **Graphite Machining Inc** .... E 610 682-0080
Topton *(G-18413)*
Graphtek LLC .... F 724 564-9211
Smithfield *(G-17651)*
▲ **Lancer Systems LP** .... E 610 973-2600
Quakertown *(G-16208)*
Mersen USA Bn Corp .... C 814 781-1234
Saint Marys *(G-16988)*
◆ **Mersen USA St Marys-PA Corp** .... D 814 781-1234
Saint Marys *(G-16989)*
Mersen USA St Marys-PA Corp .... C 814 781-1234
Saint Marys *(G-16990)*
Micron Research Corporation .... E 814 486-2444
Emporium *(G-5069)*

Morgan Advanced Mtls Tech Inc .... D 814 274-6132
Coudersport *(G-3785)*
Morgan Advanced Mtls Tech Inc .... G 570 421-9921
East Stroudsburg *(G-4623)*
▲ **Morgan Advanced Mtls Tech Inc** .... C 814 781-1573
Saint Marys *(G-16998)*
Nac Carbon Products Inc .... E 814 938-7450
Punxsutawney *(G-16148)*
Nac Joint Venture Pipline .... D 814 938-7450
Punxsutawney *(G-16149)*
National Elec Carbn Pdts Inc .... D 570 476-9004
East Stroudsburg *(G-4624)*
Samuel Son & Co (usa) Inc .... E 412 865-4444
Pittsburgh *(G-15510)*
▲ **Sgl LLC** .... E 610 670-4040
Reading *(G-16514)*
▲ **Shamokin Filler Co Inc** .... E 570 644-0437
Coal Township *(G-3281)*
Smith Group Inc .... E 215 957-7800
Warminster *(G-18966)*
St Marys Carbon Co Inc .... D 814 781-7333
Saint Marys *(G-17018)*
▲ **St Marys Carbon Co Inc** .... C 814 781-7333
Saint Marys *(G-17016)*
◆ **Stein Seal Company** .... C 215 256-0201
Kulpsville *(G-8831)*
▲ **Tyk America Inc** .... E 412 384-4259
Clairton *(G-3158)*
◆ **Weaver Industries Inc** .... D 717 336-7507
Denver *(G-4097)*

3625 Relays & Indl Controls

3si Security Systems Holdg Inc .... G 610 280-2000
Malvern *(G-10177)*
Aaim Controls Inc .... F 717 765-9100
Waynesboro *(G-19393)*
Abbott Furnace Company .... D 814 781-6355
Saint Marys *(G-16943)*
Accelight Networks Inc .... D 412 220-2102
Bridgeville *(G-2050)*
Advanced Controls Inc .... G 724 776-0224
Cranberry Township *(G-3799)*
Advanced Systems Technologies .... G 610 682-0610
Topton *(G-18410)*
American Sensors Corporation .... F 412 242-5903
Pittsburgh *(G-14706)*
Ametek Inc .... D 215 256-6601
Harleysville *(G-7020)*
Amtek Inc .... F 814 734-3327
Edinboro *(G-4808)*
Arbutus Electronics Inc .... F 717 764-3565
York *(G-20384)*
Auma Actuators Inc .... G 714 247-1250
Canonsburg *(G-2546)*
◆ **Auma Actuators Inc** .... C 724 743-2862
Canonsburg *(G-2545)*
Automatic Control Elec Co .... F 210 661-4111
Harleysville *(G-7021)*
Automation Devices Inc .... E 814 474-5561
Fairview *(G-5814)*
Automted Lgic Corp Kennesaw GA .... G 717 909-7000
Harrisburg *(G-7093)*
Belden Inc .... E 717 263-7655
Chambersburg *(G-2910)*
◆ **Bender Electronics Inc** .... D 610 383-9200
Exton *(G-5652)*
◆ **Benshaw Inc** .... D 412 968-0100
Pittsburgh *(G-14762)*
Benshaw Inc .... G 412 487-8235
Glenshaw *(G-6483)*
Brd Noise & Vibration Ctrl Inc .... G 610 863-6300
Wind Gap *(G-20167)*
Brentek International Inc .... G 814 259-3333
York *(G-20412)*
▲ **Bwi Eagle Inc** .... F 724 283-4681
Butler *(G-2387)*
Canterbery Industries LLC .... G 724 697-4231
Avonmore *(G-863)*
Carnegie Robotics LLC .... D 412 251-0321
Pittsburgh *(G-14819)*
▲ **Centroid Corporation** .... E 814 353-9290
Howard *(G-7886)*
Chestnut Vly Ctrl Systems LLC .... G 717 330-2356
Manheim *(G-10376)*
Cieco Inc .... G 412 262-5581
Clinton *(G-3261)*
Cmu Robotics .... G 412 681-6900
Pittsburgh *(G-14863)*
◆ **Columbia Research Labs Inc** .... E 610 872-3900
Woodlyn *(G-20218)*

SIC

Control Chief Corporation ....E 814 362-6811
   Bradford *(G-1962)*

Control Chief Holdings Inc ....D 814 362-6811
   Bradford *(G-1963)*

▼ Control Design Inc ....E 412 788-2280
   Pittsburgh *(G-14873)*

Control Dynamics Corporation ....G 215 956-0700
   Warminster *(G-18846)*

Corby Industries Inc ....G 610 433-1412
   Allentown *(G-180)*

Crisp Control Inc ....D 724 864-6777
   Irwin *(G-8153)*

Cse Corporation ....E 724 733-2247
   Pittsburgh *(G-14891)*

◆ Deltronic Labs Inc ....E 215 997-8616
   Chalfont *(G-2872)*

Dew Electric Inc ....G 724 628-9711
   Connellsville *(G-3494)*

Domenic Stangherlin ....G 610 434-5624
   Allentown *(G-195)*

East Coast Control Systems ....G 814 857-5420
   Bigler *(G-1658)*

Eaton Corporation ....B 412 893-3300
   Coraopolis *(G-3685)*

Eaton Corporation ....B 724 773-1231
   Beaver *(G-980)*

Eaton Corporation ....E 412 893-3300
   Moon Township *(G-11484)*

◆ Eaton Electrical Inc ....E 412 893-3300
   Moon Township *(G-11485)*

Egr Ventures Inc ....E 610 358-0500
   Aston *(G-761)*

Electronic Instrument Res Ltd ....G 724 744-7028
   Irwin *(G-8158)*

Ellison Industrial Contrls LLC ....G 724 483-0251
   Belle Vernon *(G-1086)*

Ernst Timing Screw Company ....E 215 639-1438
   Bensalem *(G-1191)*

Ges Automation Technology ....G 717 236-8733
   Harrisburg *(G-7133)*

Hampton Controls Inc ....F 724 861-0150
   Wendel *(G-19481)*

Harold Beck & Sons Inc ....C 215 968-4600
   Newtown *(G-12506)*

Hartronics ....G 717 597-3931
   Greencastle *(G-6617)*

HIG Capital LLC ....C 610 495-1011
   Royersford *(G-16851)*

Hillside Equity Inc ....G 484 707-9012
   Bethlehem *(G-1531)*

Homewood Products Corporation ....E 412 665-2700
   Pittsburgh *(G-15099)*

Honeywell International Inc ....C 717 771-8100
   York *(G-20526)*

▲ Hullvac Pump Corp ....G 215 355-3995
   Southampton *(G-17818)*

Icreate Automation Inc ....E 610 443-1758
   Allentown *(G-251)*

Industrial Controls Inc ....G 717 697-7555
   Mechanicsburg *(G-10858)*

Industrial Systems & Controls ....E 412 638-4977
   Pittsburgh *(G-15121)*

Infinite Control Systems Inc ....G 610 696-8600
   West Chester *(G-19570)*

Intellidrives Inc ....F 215 728-6804
   Philadelphia *(G-13862)*

Intervala LLC ....C 412 829-4800
   East Pittsburgh *(G-4596)*

ITT Corporation ....B 717 509-2200
   Lancaster *(G-9065)*

ITT LLC ....D 215 218-7400
   Philadelphia *(G-13878)*

J & Ak Inc ....D 412 787-9750
   Pittsburgh *(G-15139)*

J A Brown Company ....G 610 832-0400
   Conshohocken *(G-3566)*

Jls Automation LLC ....E 717 505-3800
   York *(G-20541)*

Jordan Acquisition Group LLC ....D 724 733-2000
   Export *(G-5612)*

Karma Industrial Services LLC ....G 717 814-7101
   York *(G-20547)*

Limpet Inc ....F 610 273-7155
   Honey Brook *(G-7752)*

Lutron Electronics Co Inc ....D 610 282-6617
   Alburtis *(G-56)*

Lutron Electronics Co Inc ....D 610 282-6268
   Allentown *(G-302)*

◆ M Squared Electronics Inc ....F 215 945-6658
   Levittown *(G-9848)*

Malvern Scale Data Systems ....G 610 296-9642
   Malvern *(G-10274)*

◆ Marino Indus Systems Svcs Inc ....E 610 872-3630
   Chester *(G-3057)*

Mason East Inc ....G 631 254-2240
   Feasterville Trevose *(G-5917)*

Mass Industrial Control ....G 610 678-8228
   Reading *(G-16439)*

Metso Automation USA Inc ....G 215 393-3900
   Lansdale *(G-9387)*

▲ Metso Automation USA Inc ....E 215 393-3947
   Lansdale *(G-9388)*

◆ Morningstar Corporation ....F 267 685-0500
   Newtown *(G-12523)*

Nickel Cobalt Battery LLC ....G 412 567-6828
   Pittsburgh *(G-15341)*

Noise Solutions (usa) Inc ....E 724 308-6901
   Sharon *(G-17441)*

Novasentis Inc ....F 814 238-7400
   State College *(G-18001)*

Novatech LLC ....C 484 812-6000
   Quakertown *(G-16224)*

Oakwood Controls Corporation ....F 717 801-1515
   Glen Rock *(G-6458)*

Onexia Inc ....E 610 431-7271
   Exton *(G-5720)*

Optimum Controls Corporation ....D 610 375-0990
   Reading *(G-16459)*

▲ Oven Industries Inc ....E 717 766-0721
   Camp Hill *(G-2508)*

Parker-Hannifin Corporation ....C 215 723-4000
   Hatfield *(G-7377)*

Parker-Hannifin Corporation ....C 724 861-8200
   Irwin *(G-8188)*

◆ Pine Instrument Company ....D 724 458-6391
   Grove City *(G-6801)*

Powerex Inc ....E 724 925-7272
   Youngwood *(G-20781)*

Process Instruments Inc ....E 412 431-4600
   Pittsburgh *(G-15451)*

R L Snelbecker Inc ....G 717 292-4971
   Dover *(G-4202)*

◆ Ralph A Hiller Company ....E 724 325-1200
   Export *(G-5623)*

▲ Rdp Technologies Inc ....F 610 650-9900
   Conshohocken *(G-3599)*

Rockwell Automation Inc ....F 717 747-8240
   York *(G-20659)*

Rockwell Automation Inc ....E 610 650-6840
   Norristown *(G-12706)*

Rockwell Automation Inc ....D 724 741-4000
   Coraopolis *(G-3722)*

Rockwell Automation Inc ....G 412 375-4700
   Coraopolis *(G-3723)*

RPM Industries LLC ....E 724 228-5130
   Washington *(G-19224)*

▲ RSR Industries Inc ....G 215 543-3350
   Warminster *(G-18956)*

Sauer Industries Inc ....G 412 687-4100
   Pittsburgh *(G-15513)*

Seastar Solutions ....G 610 495-1011
   Limerick *(G-9971)*

Sensor Corporation ....G 724 887-4080
   Scottdale *(G-17200)*

Servedio A Elc Mtr Svc Inc ....F 724 658-8041
   New Castle *(G-12148)*

Seventy-Three Mfg Co Inc ....E 610 845-7823
   Bechtelsville *(G-1037)*

Siemens Industry Inc ....C 724 339-9500
   New Kensington *(G-12375)*

Siemens Industry Inc ....C 724 733-2569
   Murrysville *(G-11866)*

Siemens Industry Inc ....D 724 743-5913
   Canonsburg *(G-2636)*

Sigma Controls Inc ....F 215 257-3412
   Perkasie *(G-13293)*

▲ Solcon USA LLC ....F 724 728-2100
   Monroeville *(G-11355)*

Spang & Company ....E 724 376-7515
   Sandy Lake *(G-17062)*

Spectrum Microwave Inc ....D 215 464-0586
   Philadelphia *(G-14333)*

Steel City Controls Inc ....G 412 851-8566
   Bethel Park *(G-1434)*

Synergistic Systems Inc ....G 814 796-4217
   Waterford *(G-19272)*

Te Connectivity Corporation ....C 717 762-9186
   Waynesboro *(G-19425)*

Technical Applications Inc ....G 610 353-0722
   Broomall *(G-2303)*

Techsource Engineering Inc ....G 814 459-2150
   Erie *(G-5505)*

Teleflex Incorporated ....C 610 495-7011
   Royersford *(G-16867)*

Thackray Inc ....G 800 245-4387
   Philadelphia *(G-14383)*

Trio Motion Technology LLC ....G 724 472-4100
   Freeport *(G-6215)*

Urania Engineering Co Inc ....E 570 455-0776
   Hazleton *(G-7532)*

▲ Vacon LLC ....C 717 261-5000
   Chambersburg *(G-2992)*

Valley Forge Instrument Co ....G 610 933-1806
   Phoenixville *(G-14583)*

▲ Vektron Corporation ....G 215 354-0300
   Southampton *(G-17845)*

WAsnyder An Son LLC ....G 724 260-0695
   Canonsburg *(G-2655)*

Wells Technology Inc ....G 215 672-7000
   Warminster *(G-18999)*

Westinghouse Industry Products ....C 412 374-2020
   Cranberry Township *(G-3866)*

3629 Electrical Indl Apparatus, NEC

Advanced Electronics Systems ....G 717 263-5681
   Chambersburg *(G-2897)*

Afterglo Lighting Co Inc ....G 215 355-7942
   Warminster *(G-18822)*

▲ Alencon Acquisition Co LLC ....G 484 436-0035
   Hatboro *(G-7266)*

Alencon Systems Inc ....G 610 825-7094
   Plymouth Meeting *(G-15829)*

◆ American Zinc Recycling Corp ....E 724 774-1020
   Pittsburgh *(G-14708)*

C&D Intrntnal Inv Holdings Inc ....G 215 619-2700
   Blue Bell *(G-1819)*

CM Technologies Corporation ....F 412 262-0734
   Coraopolis *(G-3678)*

Cmsjlp LLC ....F 814 834-2817
   Ridgway *(G-16700)*

▼ E I T Corporation Phoenix ....F 570 286-7744
   Sunbury *(G-18168)*

Electrostatics Inc ....F 215 513-0850
   Hatfield *(G-7337)*

Exide Technologies ....C 717 464-2721
   Lampeter *(G-8917)*

Exide Technologies ....G 610 269-0429
   Downingtown *(G-4226)*

Exide Technologies ....G 724 239-2006
   Charleroi *(G-3012)*

Exide Technologies ....E 610 921-4055
   Reading *(G-16383)*

Exide Technologies ....G 304 345-5616
   Rostraver Township *(G-16826)*

▲ GE Enrgy Pwr Cnversion USA Inc ....C 412 967-0765
   Cranberry Township *(G-3820)*

◆ High Energy Corp ....E 610 593-2800
   Parkesburg *(G-13175)*

Illinois Tool Works Inc ....D 215 822-2171
   Hatfield *(G-7352)*

▲ K H Controls Inc ....D 724 459-7474
   Blairsville *(G-1728)*

K&L Services ....G 610 349-1358
   Allentown *(G-277)*

Mayer Electric Supply Co Inc ....G 814 765-7531
   Clearfield *(G-3224)*

Myers Power Products Inc ....D 610 868-3500
   Bethlehem *(G-1576)*

Northeast Indus Batteries Inc ....E 215 788-8000
   Bristol *(G-2172)*

Power One Inc ....G 267 429-0374
   Perkasie *(G-13290)*

▲ Power Products Inc ....G 610 532-3880
   Sharon Hill *(G-17459)*

Schneider Electric It Corp ....B 717 948-1200
   Middletown *(G-11074)*

Strainsense Enterprises Inc ....G 412 751-3055
   McKeesport *(G-10684)*

Wirecard North America Inc ....D 610 234-4410
   Conshohocken *(G-3617)*

3631 Household Cooking Eqpt

Alaska Company Inc ....F 570 387-0260
   Bloomsburg *(G-1766)*

Appalachain Grills ....G 717 762-3321
   Waynesboro *(G-19397)*

Breeo LLC ....F 800 413-9848
   Kinzers *(G-8733)*

Ellco Products Inc ....G 724 758-3526
   Ellwood City *(G-4930)*

3634 Electric Household Appliances

Conair Corporation.....D..... 717 485-4871
Mc Connellsburg *(G-10563)*
▲ Edgecraft Corporation.....C..... 610 268-0500
Avondale *(G-851)*
Harsco Corporation.....C..... 570 421-7500
East Stroudsburg *(G-4617)*
Heatron Inc.....E..... 814 868-8554
Erie *(G-5314)*
Heatron Inc.....E..... 814 868-8554
Erie *(G-5315)*
Hvl LLC.....E..... 412 494-9600
Pittsburgh *(G-15107)*
Lasko Group Inc.....D..... 610 692-7400
West Chester *(G-19587)*
▲ Mosebach Manufacturing Company D..... 412 220-0200
Pittsburgh *(G-15303)*
▲ Munroe Incorporated.....D..... 412 231-0600
Pittsburgh *(G-15311)*
▲ Pelonis Technologies Inc.....F..... 888 546-0524
Exton *(G-5723)*
Powerex Inc.....E..... 724 925-7272
Youngwood *(G-20781)*
Rebel Indian Smoke Shop.....G..... 610 499-1711
Brookhaven *(G-2247)*
Schmitt Walter H and Assoc.....E..... 724 872-5007
West Newton *(G-19751)*
Steel Fitness Premier LLC.....E..... 610 973-1500
Allentown *(G-403)*

3635 Household Vacuum Cleaners

▲ Nilfisk Inc.....D..... 800 645-3475
Morgantown *(G-11529)*
▲ Supercleanscom Inc.....G..... 412 429-1640
Carnegie *(G-2796)*

3639 Household Appliances, NEC

Cemline Corporation.....D..... 724 274-5430
Cheswick *(G-3104)*
Clearnav Instruments.....G..... 610 925-0198
Kennett Square *(G-8506)*
▲ Fretz Corporation.....E..... 215 671-8300
Philadelphia *(G-13725)*
Harsco Corporation.....C..... 570 421-7500
East Stroudsburg *(G-4617)*
▲ Leslie S Geissel.....G..... 215 884-1050
Jenkintown *(G-8294)*
Merkin Body and Hoist Company.....G..... 610 258-6179
Easton *(G-4721)*
Molek Brothers.....G..... 717 248-8032
Yeagertown *(G-20357)*
Petrillos Appliance.....G..... 215 491-9400
Warrington *(G-19127)*
Rent-A-Center Inc.....G..... 724 845-1070
Leechburg *(G-9652)*
Sewing Equipment Co Inc.....G..... 610 825-2581
Plymouth Meeting *(G-15869)*
Therma-Tek Range Corp.....E..... 570 455-3000
West Hazleton *(G-19716)*
Versalot Enterprises LLC.....G..... 610 213-1017
New Tripoli *(G-12461)*
Vistappliances.....G..... 215 600-1232
Morrisville *(G-11587)*

3641 Electric Lamps

Adapt Technologies LLC.....G..... 610 896-7274
Conshohocken *(G-3516)*
Arcman Corporation.....G..... 570 489-6402
Dunmore *(G-4467)*
Davis Lamp & Shade Inc.....E..... 215 426-2777
Philadelphia *(G-13611)*
Ecotech Inc.....D..... 610 954-8480
Allentown *(G-202)*
Fangio Enterprises Inc.....G..... 570 383-1030
Dickson City *(G-4120)*
▲ Fangio Enterprises Inc.....E..... 570 383-1030
Olyphant *(G-12990)*
▲ H H Fluorescent Parts Inc.....D..... 215 379-2750
Cheltenham *(G-3029)*
▲ Interlectric Corporation.....C..... 814 723-6061
Warren *(G-19033)*
K-B Lighting Manufacturing Co.....E..... 215 953-6663
Feasterville Trevose *(G-5915)*
◆ Koehler-Bright Star LLC.....E..... 570 825-1900
Hanover Township *(G-6991)*
Led Tube USA.....G..... 724 650-0691
Ambridge *(G-625)*
◆ Lightbox Inc.....E..... 610 954-8480
Bethlehem *(G-1561)*
Luxtech LLC.....F..... 888 340-4266
Philadelphia *(G-13978)*
▲ Minleon Intl USA Ltd LLC.....G..... 717 991-1432
Mechanicsburg *(G-10870)*
Osram Sylvania Inc.....C..... 814 834-1800
Saint Marys *(G-16999)*
Osram Sylvania Inc.....C..... 814 726-6600
Warren *(G-19041)*
Osram Sylvania Inc.....B..... 717 854-3499
Saint Marys *(G-17000)*
Osram Sylvania Inc.....B..... 814 269-1418
Johnstown *(G-8416)*
Osram Sylvania Inc.....B..... 570 724-8200
Wellsboro *(G-19471)*
Osram Sylvania Inc.....D..... 412 856-2111
Monroeville *(G-11347)*
Pureland Supply LLC.....F..... 610 444-0590
Kennett Square *(G-8537)*
Respironics Inc.....G..... 724 771-7837
Mount Pleasant *(G-11715)*
◆ Respironics Inc.....D..... 724 387-5200
Murrysville *(G-11865)*
▲ Retrolite Corporation America.....G..... 215 443-9370
Warminster *(G-18954)*
Strategic Medicine Inc.....G..... 814 659-5450
Kennett Square *(G-8546)*
▲ Superior Quartz Products Inc.....D..... 610 317-3450
Bethlehem *(G-1634)*
Trojan Inc.....E..... 814 336-4468
Meadville *(G-10804)*
▲ Westinghouse Lighting Corp.....D..... 215 671-2000
Philadelphia *(G-14466)*

3643 Current-Carrying Wiring Devices

3si Security Systems Holdg Inc.....G..... 610 280-2000
Malvern *(G-10177)*
A E Pakos Inc.....G..... 724 539-1790
Latrobe *(G-9452)*
Achieva.....D..... 412 995-5000
Pittsburgh *(G-14640)*
Ava Electronics Corp.....E..... 610 284-2500
Drexel Hill *(G-4360)*
Burndy LLC.....G..... 717 938-7258
Etters *(G-5547)*
Checon Powder Met Contacts LLC.....G..... 814 753-4466
Kersey *(G-8554)*
▲ Cjc Contract Packaging Inc.....G..... 570 209-7836
Avoca *(G-842)*
▲ Contact Technologies Inc.....C..... 814 834-9000
Saint Marys *(G-16957)*
Cooper Interconnect Inc.....E..... 630 248-4007
King of Prussia *(G-8597)*
Corey Associates Inc.....E..... 570 676-4800
Greentown *(G-6733)*
Custom Systems Technology Inc.....G..... 215 822-2525
Colmar *(G-3415)*
Datacap Systems Inc.....E..... 215 997-8989
Chalfont *(G-2871)*
Dean Technology Inc.....E..... 724 479-3533
Lucernemines *(G-10117)*
E F E Laboratories Inc.....E..... 215 672-2400
Horsham *(G-7812)*
Eaton Corporation.....B..... 724 773-1231
Beaver *(G-980)*
Eaton Corporation.....E..... 412 893-3300
Moon Township *(G-11484)*
◆ Eaton Electrical Inc.....E..... 412 893-3300
Moon Township *(G-11485)*
EBY Group LLC.....E..... 215 537-4700
Philadelphia *(G-13657)*
Elec Const Jt.....G..... 610 777-3150
Reading *(G-16371)*
Electro Soft Inc.....E..... 215 654-0701
Montgomeryville *(G-11394)*
F Tinker and Sons Company.....E..... 412 781-3553
Pittsburgh *(G-15000)*
◆ Fci USA LLC.....B..... 717 938-7200
Etters *(G-5548)*
G&W Solutions Inc.....G..... 610 704-6959
Emmaus *(G-5026)*
Gettysburg Village Factory Str.....F..... 717 334-2332
Gettysburg *(G-6294)*
Greenbriar Indus Systems Inc.....D..... 814 474-1400
Fairview *(G-5824)*
▲ H H Fluorescent Parts Inc.....D..... 215 379-2750
Cheltenham *(G-3029)*
Halsit Holdings LLC.....E..... 814 724-6440
Meadville *(G-10733)*
Hartstrings LLC.....G..... 610 326-8221
Pottstown *(G-15997)*
Ilsco Extrusions Inc.....G..... 724 589-5888
Greenville *(G-6748)*
▲ Industrial Enterprises Inc.....D..... 215 355-7080
Southampton *(G-17819)*
▲ King Associates Ltd.....D..... 717 556-5673
Lancaster *(G-9086)*
Leggs Hanes Bali Factory Otlt.....G..... 717 392-2511
Lancaster *(G-9109)*
▲ Lynn Electronics Corp.....D..... 215 355-8200
Ivyland *(G-8216)*
Lynn Electronics Corp.....E..... 215 826-9600
Bristol *(G-2163)*
Lynn Electronics Corp.....G..... 954 977-3800
Warminster *(G-18915)*
▲ Marco Manufacturing Co Inc.....E..... 215 463-2332
Philadelphia *(G-13992)*
◆ Metallurgical Products Company.....E..... 610 696-6770
West Chester *(G-19601)*
▲ Metalor Electronics USA Corp.....C..... 724 733-8332
Export *(G-5618)*
Micro Facture LLC.....E..... 717 285-9700
Mountville *(G-11799)*
Milli-Switch Manufacturing Co.....G..... 610 270-9222
Bridgeport *(G-2040)*
N T M Inc.....E..... 717 567-9374
Newport *(G-12492)*
Nexans USA Inc.....B..... 717 354-6200
New Holland *(G-12271)*
Orion Systems Inc.....E..... 215 346-8200
Huntingdon Valley *(G-8019)*
Osram Sylvania Inc.....B..... 570 724-8200
Wellsboro *(G-19471)*
Osram Sylvania Inc.....D..... 412 856-2111
Monroeville *(G-11347)*
Paxson Lightning Rods Inc.....G..... 610 696-8290
West Chester *(G-19615)*
▲ PC Systems Inc.....E..... 814 772-6359
Ridgway *(G-16724)*
▲ Penn-Union Corp.....D..... 814 734-1631
Edinboro *(G-4820)*
Phoenix Contact Dev & Mfg Inc.....B..... 717 944-1300
Middletown *(G-11068)*
Powersafe Inc.....G..... 717 436-5380
Mifflintown *(G-11132)*
Precise Plastics Inc.....D..... 814 474-5504
Fairview *(G-5840)*
Precision Assembly Inc.....E..... 215 784-0861
Willow Grove *(G-20136)*
Precision Fbrction Contrls Inc.....E..... 814 368-7320
Bradford *(G-1987)*
Prysmian Cbles Systems USA LLC.....D..... 570 385-4381
Schuylkill Haven *(G-17164)*
Qualastat Electronics Inc.....E..... 717 253-9301
Gettysburg *(G-6311)*
Reiner Associates Inc.....G..... 717 647-7454
Tower City *(G-18440)*
Rubbermaid Commercial Pdts LLC.....F..... 570 622-7715
Pottsville *(G-16096)*
Sensor Corporation.....G..... 724 887-4080
Scottdale *(G-17200)*
Silicon Power Corporation.....D..... 610 407-4700
Malvern *(G-10317)*
Souriau Usa Inc.....F..... 717 718-8810
York *(G-20673)*
Spectrum Control Inc.....C..... 814 835-4000
Fairview *(G-5844)*
Spectrum Microwave Inc.....D..... 215 464-0586
Philadelphia *(G-14333)*
▲ St Marys Carbon Co Inc.....C..... 814 781-7333
Saint Marys *(G-17016)*
Te Connectivity Corporation.....C..... 717 986-3028
Middletown *(G-11079)*
Te Connectivity Corporation.....B..... 717 227-4400
Shrewsbury *(G-17588)*
▲ Te Connectivity Corporation.....C..... 610 893-9800
Berwyn *(G-1376)*
Te Connectivity Corporation.....C..... 717 564-0100
Middletown *(G-11078)*
Te Connectivity Corporation.....B..... 717 861-5000
Jonestown *(G-8452)*
Te Connectivity Corporation.....B..... 717 653-8151
Mount Joy *(G-11672)*
Tilsit Corporation.....F..... 610 681-5951
Gilbert *(G-6364)*
Torpedo Specialty Wire Inc.....E..... 814 563-7505
Pittsfield *(G-15739)*
Tyco Elec Latin Amer Holdg LLC.....G..... 610 893-9800
Berwyn *(G-1389)*
▲ Universal Electric Corporation.....B..... 724 597-7800
Canonsburg *(G-2652)*

SIC

▲ Warners Innvtive Solutions Inc ....F 814 201-2429
Altoona (G-557)

Woolrich Inc ....G 570 769-7401
Woolrich (G-20221)

Z-Axis Connector Company ....F 267 803-9000
Warminster (G-19006)

3644 Noncurrent-Carrying Wiring Devices

A W Mercer Inc ....C 610 367-8460
Boyertown (G-1892)

Allegheny Mountain Raceway ....G 814 598-9077
Kane (G-8458)

▲ Bedford Materials Co Inc ....D 800 773-4276
Manns Choice (G-10408)

▲ Carroll Manufacturing Co LLC ....G 724 266-0400
Leetsdale (G-9688)

Chase Corporation ....F 800 245-3209
Blawnox (G-1763)

Chase Corporation ....F 412 828-1500
Pittsburgh (G-14839)

Conestoga USA Inc ....G 610 327-2882
Pottstown (G-15973)

Cott Manufacturing Company ....F 412 675-0101
Glassport (G-6410)

Cott Manufacturing Company ....G 724 625-3730
Glassport (G-6411)

Dcm Slot Car Raceway ....G 215 805-6887
Newtown (G-12501)

▲ Electrical Design Developm ....G 412 747-4970
Pittsburgh (G-14962)

Gibson Stainless Specialty Inc ....F 724 838-8320
Greensburg (G-6669)

▲ Marco Manufacturing Co Inc ....E 215 463-2332
Philadelphia (G-13992)

Penn Panel & Box Company ....E 610 586-2700
Collingdale (G-3409)

Penns Creek Raceway Park ....G 570 473-9599
Northumberland (G-12873)

Pikes Creek Raceway Park Inc ....G 570 477-2226
Hunlock Creek (G-7933)

R & D Raceway Inc ....G 724 258-8754
Bentleyville (G-1274)

Raceway Beverage Center ....G 724 695-3130
Imperial (G-8075)

▲ Robroy Industries Inc ....F 412 828-2100
Verona (G-18761)

▲ Rochling Machined Plastics ....E 724 696-5200
Mount Pleasant (G-11717)

▲ Silvine Inc ....E 215 657-2345
Willow Grove (G-20142)

Smithton Raceway LLC ....G 724 797-1822
Smithton (G-17662)

Specialty Conduit & Mfg LLC ....F 724 439-9371
Mount Braddock (G-11621)

Specialty Products & Insul Co ....G 717 569-3900
East Petersburg (G-4590)

▲ Speed Raceway ....F 215 672-6128
Horsham (G-7851)

◆ Spring City Electrical Mfg Co ....C 610 948-4000
Spring City (G-17867)

Spring City Electrical Mfg Co ....G 610 948-4000
Spring City (G-17868)

Stuart Kranzel ....G 717 737-7223
Lemoyne (G-9754)

Tom Hester Hiesters Ho Raceway ....G 610 796-0490
Reading (G-16543)

Wheatland Tube LLC ....D 724 981-5200
Sharon (G-17445)

Winola Industrial Inc ....F 570 378-3808
Factoryville (G-5763)

3645 Residential Lighting Fixtures

American Period Lighting Inc ....G 717 392-5649
Lancaster (G-8931)

Andromeda Led Lighting LLC ....G 610 336-7474
Macungie (G-10140)

▲ Appalachian Ltg Systems Inc ....E 724 752-0326
Ellwood City (G-4927)

Bahdeebahdu ....G 215 627-5002
Philadelphia (G-13441)

▲ Brightline LP ....F 412 206-0106
Bridgeville (G-2056)

Brontech Industries Inc ....G 717 672-0240
Lancaster (G-8960)

Candela Corporation ....G 610 861-8772
Bethlehem (G-1479)

Craft Lite Inc ....G 717 359-7131
Littlestown (G-10065)

Davis Lamp & Shade Inc ....E 215 426-2777
Philadelphia (G-13611)

▲ Decora Industries Inc ....D 215 698-2600
Philadelphia (G-13614)

Dine-Glow Dblo Fd Svc Fels LLC ....E 800 526-7583
Phoenixville (G-14545)

▲ Elk Group International LLC ....G 800 613-3261
Easton (G-4679)

Elk Lighting Inc ....G 610 767-0511
Walnutport (G-18791)

Elk Lighting Inc ....F 800 613-3261
Summit Hill (G-18160)

Francis J Nowalk ....G 412 687-4017
Pittsburgh (G-15030)

Gexpro ....G 570 265-2420
Towanda (G-18428)

Glasslight Inc ....G 610 469-9066
Saint Peters (G-17034)

Hartman Design Inc ....G 610 670-2517
Wernersville (G-19484)

Hopper Lawn & Ldscp MGT LLC ....G 610 692-3879
West Chester (G-19563)

Horizon Lamps Inc ....F 610 829-4220
Easton (G-4701)

Hutton Metalcrafts Inc ....G 570 646-7778
Pocono Pines (G-15881)

K-B Lighting Manufacturing Co ....E 215 953-6663
Feasterville Trevose (G-5915)

Led Living Technologies Inc ....E 215 633-1558
Bristol (G-2158)

▲ Lighting Accents Inc ....E 412 761-5000
Pittsburgh (G-15230)

Makefield Collection Inc ....F 610 496-4649
Coopersburg (G-3631)

Oaklawn Metal Craft Shop Inc ....G 215 794-7387
Lahaska (G-8885)

▲ Penn Shadecrafters Inc ....E 570 342-3193
Scranton (G-17271)

Philips-Hadco ....F 717 359-7131
Littlestown (G-10075)

◆ Pieri Creations LLC ....E 215 634-4000
Philadelphia (G-14176)

RC & Design Company ....G 484 626-1216
Lehighton (G-9724)

▲ Remilux LLC ....G 717 737-7120
Camp Hill (G-2515)

▲ Retrolite Corporation America ....G 215 443-9370
Warminster (G-18954)

Richard Scofield Hstorc Lghtng ....F 860 767-7032
Downingtown (G-4254)

Rjf Enterprises Inc ....F 570 383-1030
Olyphant (G-12997)

Salem Antiquities ....G 724 309-1781
Delmont (G-4055)

▲ Silvine Inc ....E 215 657-2345
Willow Grove (G-20142)

Sitka Enterprises Inc ....G 610 393-6708
Macungie (G-10158)

Soltech Solutions LLC ....G 484 821-1001
Bethlehem (G-1622)

Stellar Industries Inc ....G 724 335-5525
New Kensington (G-12380)

United Electric Supply Co Inc ....G 717 632-7640
Hanover (G-6964)

◆ Varsal LLC ....C 215 957-5880
Warminster (G-18993)

Victorian Lighting Works Inc ....G 814 364-9577
Centre Hall (G-2845)

▲ Westinghouse Lighting Corp ....D 215 671-2000
Philadelphia (G-14466)

3646 Commercial, Indl & Institutional Lighting Fixtures

8 12 Illumination LLC ....G 717 285-9700
Mountville (G-11789)

American Period Lighting Inc ....G 717 392-5649
Lancaster (G-8931)

Andromeda Led Lighting LLC ....G 610 336-7474
Macungie (G-10140)

▲ Appalachian Ltg Systems Inc ....E 724 752-0326
Ellwood City (G-4927)

Armstrong World Industries Inc ....A 717 397-0611
Lancaster (G-8942)

Bluestem Industries Pa LLC ....G 412 585-6220
Moon Township (G-11481)

Camman Industries Inc ....E 724 539-7670
Derry (G-4100)

Carey Schuster LLC ....G 610 431-2512
West Chester (G-19519)

CNT Fixture Company Inc ....E 412 443-6260
Glenshaw (G-6484)

Custom Manufactured Products ....E 215 228-3830
Philadelphia (G-13594)

Donohoe Corporation ....F 724 850-2433
Greensburg (G-6660)

Eaton Electric Holdings LLC ....G 724 228-7333
Washington (G-19167)

Ecotech Inc ....D 610 954-8480
Allentown (G-202)

◆ Elegant Furniture & Lighting ....G 888 388-3390
Philadelphia (G-13665)

▲ Elk Group International LLC ....G 800 613-3261
Easton (G-4679)

Elk Lighting Inc ....F 800 613-3261
Summit Hill (G-18160)

Emw Inc ....F 717 626-0248
Lititz (G-10006)

Envoy Lighting Inc ....G 215 512-7000
Trevose (G-18493)

Exit Store LLC ....G 310 305-4646
Wayne (G-19326)

Forum Inc ....D 412 781-5970
Pittsburgh (G-15028)

Global Indus Ltg Solutions LLC ....E 215 671-2029
Philadelphia (G-13768)

Innogreen USA LLC ....G 814 880-4493
State College (G-17977)

▲ Le Jo Enterprises Incorporated ....E 484 921-9000
Phoenixville (G-14559)

Led Saving Solutions LLC ....E 484 588-5401
Wayne (G-19347)

Led Tube USA ....G 724 650-0691
Ambridge (G-625)

▲ Lighting Accents Inc ....E 412 761-5000
Pittsburgh (G-15230)

Lumenoptix LLC ....E 215 671-2029
Montgomeryville (G-11405)

Metal Light Manufacturing ....F 215 430-7200
Philadelphia (G-14013)

▲ Modular International Inc ....E 412 734-9000
Pittsburgh (G-15299)

Neo Lights Holdings Inc ....G 215 831-7700
Philadelphia (G-14062)

▲ Nu Tech Inc ....E 215 297-8889
Doylestown (G-4319)

Olde Mill Lighting Limited ....G 717 299-7240
Lancaster (G-9151)

Osram Sylvania Inc ....B 570 724-8200
Wellsboro (G-19471)

Osram Sylvania Inc ....D 412 856-2111
Monroeville (G-11347)

▲ Pendants Systems Mfg Co ....F 215 638-8552
Bensalem (G-1240)

Perkasie Industries Corp ....D 215 257-6581
Perkasie (G-13288)

◆ Pieri Creations LLC ....E 215 634-4000
Philadelphia (G-14176)

▲ Plant Growers Workshop Inc ....G 724 473-1079
Callery (G-2470)

Practicom ....G 267 979-5446
Philadelphia (G-14194)

Pureoptix Led LLC ....G 610 301-9767
Macungie (G-10157)

RC & Design Company ....G 484 626-1216
Lehighton (G-9724)

Reece Lighting & Prod LLC ....G 215 460-8560
Bristol (G-2193)

▲ Retrolite Corporation America ....G 215 443-9370
Warminster (G-18954)

Rogerson & Associates ....G 724 943-3934
Dilliner (G-4125)

Self-Powered Lighting Inc ....G 484 595-9130
Berwyn (G-1375)

◆ Simkar LLC ....C 215 831-7700
Philadelphia (G-14307)

Stellar Industries Inc ....G 724 335-5525
New Kensington (G-12380)

Terra-Glo Lighting Corporation ....G 267 430-1259
Ivyland (G-8222)

Trans-Tech Technologies Inc ....G 724 327-6600
Pittsburgh (G-15639)

Tristar Lighting Company ....E 215 245-3400
Bensalem (G-1264)

3647 Vehicular Lighting Eqpt

B/E Aerospace Inc ....G 570 595-7491
Mountainhome (G-11785)

▲ Betts Industries Inc ....C 814 723-1250
Warren (G-19013)

Liberty Vhcl Ltg & Safety Sup ....G 610 356-5320
Prospect Park (G-16116)

Osram Sylvania Inc....B....570 724-8200
Wellsboro *(G-19471)*
Osram Sylvania Inc....D....412 856-2111
Monroeville *(G-11347)*
Railpower LLC....C....814 835-2212
Erie *(G-5453)*
TRM Emergency Vehicles LLC....G....610 689-0702
Boyertown *(G-1932)*
Truck Lite Co Inc....G....716 664-3519
Beech Creek *(G-1083)*
Truck-Lite Co LLC....D....570 769-7231
Mc Elhattan *(G-10590)*
Truck-Lite Co LLC....D....814 274-5400
Coudersport *(G-3790)*
▼ Ziamatic Corp....E....215 493-2777
Yardley *(G-20347)*

3648 Lighting Eqpt, NEC

◆ American Gas Lamp Works LLC....G....724 274-7131
Springdale *(G-17897)*
American Gas Lamp Works LLC....F....724 274-7131
Springdale *(G-17898)*
▲ American Tack & Hdwr Co Inc....E....610 336-1330
Breinigsville *(G-2008)*
Anaconda Enterprises LLC....G....908 910-7150
Nazareth *(G-11955)*
Black Bear Associates LLC....G....610 470-6477
Lancaster *(G-8956)*
Bluestem Industries Pa LLC....G....412 585-6220
Moon Township *(G-11481)*
Challenger Manufacturing Ltd....C....215 968-6004
Southampton *(G-17802)*
Comcast Spotlight....G....610 784-2560
Conshohocken *(G-3530)*
Craze For Rayz Tanning Center....G....484 231-1164
Norristown *(G-12648)*
Doner Design Inc....G....717 786-4172
New Providence *(G-12433)*
▲ Evenlite Inc....E....215 244-4201
Feasterville Trevose *(G-5906)*
Feng Shui Lighting Inc....G....215 393-5500
Lansdale *(G-9367)*
▲ H B Instrument Co....E....610 489-5500
Trappe *(G-18469)*
Jcr Sales & Mfg LLC....G....814 897-8870
Erie *(G-5335)*
▲ Just Normlicht Inc....G....267 852-2200
Langhorne *(G-9305)*
◆ Koehler-Bright Star LLC....E....570 825-1900
Hanover Township *(G-6991)*
Lehigh Electric Products Co....E....610 395-3386
Allentown *(G-293)*
▲ Lighting Accents Inc....E....412 761-5000
Pittsburgh *(G-15230)*
▲ Lighting By Led LLC....F....412 600-3132
Pittsburgh *(G-15231)*
Litescaping LLC....G....814 833-6200
Erie *(G-5368)*
Lloyd Jones....E....610 395-3386
Allentown *(G-298)*
Lumi Trak Inc....F....717 235-2863
New Freedom *(G-12212)*
Mdl Lighting LLC....E....267 968-3611
Philadelphia *(G-14001)*
▲ Mine Safety Appliances Co LLC....B....724 776-8600
Cranberry Township *(G-3836)*
MSA Safety Incorporated....B....724 733-9100
Murrysville *(G-11858)*
MSA Safety Incorporated....B....724 776-8600
Cranberry Township *(G-3839)*
MSA Safety Sales LLC....G....724 776-8600
Cranberry Township *(G-3841)*
Nitebrite Ltd....G....215 493-9361
Washington Crossing *(G-19257)*
Orlotronics Corporation....E....610 239-8200
Bridgeport *(G-2042)*
Peak Beam Systems Inc....E....610 353-8505
Newtown Square *(G-12588)*
RC & Design Company....G....484 626-1216
Lehighton *(G-9724)*
Solar Light Company Inc....D....215 517-8700
Glenside *(G-6538)*
▲ Special-Lite Products LLC....F....724 537-4711
Loyalhanna *(G-10113)*
◆ Spring City Electrical Mfg Co....C....610 948-4000
Spring City *(G-17867)*
Spring City Electrical Mfg Co....D....610 948-4000
Spring City *(G-17868)*
Stabler Companies Inc....F....717 236-9307
Harrisburg *(G-7219)*
◆ Streamlight Inc....B....610 631-0600
Eagleville *(G-4517)*
Sylvan Corporation....G....724 864-9350
Irwin *(G-8203)*
▲ Tait Towers Inc....D....717 626-9571
Lititz *(G-10051)*
Theotek Corporation....F....610 336-9191
Orefield *(G-13015)*
▲ We-Ef Lighting USA LLC....G....724 742-0027
Warrendale *(G-19100)*

3651 Household Audio & Video Eqpt

All American Installs....G....215 888-0046
Penndel *(G-13238)*
Altec Lansing Inc....F....570 296-4434
Milford *(G-11154)*
▲ Aviom Inc....D....610 738-9005
West Chester *(G-19505)*
Better Living Center LLC....G....724 266-3750
Ambridge *(G-611)*
Burnt Circuit Inc....G....215 913-6594
Ambler *(G-572)*
Castgrabber LLC....F....412 362-6802
Pittsburgh *(G-14825)*
Cinemaplex Technologies Corp....G....610 935-8366
Spring City *(G-17857)*
▲ Clair Bros Audio Entps Inc....D....717 626-4000
Manheim *(G-10377)*
▲ Community Light & Sound Inc....D....610 876-3400
Chester *(G-3043)*
▲ Dnh Speakers Inc....G....484 494-5790
Sharon Hill *(G-17457)*
East Hill Video Prod Co LLC....F....215 855-4457
Lansdale *(G-9364)*
Electronic Concepts Inc....G....717 235-9450
New Freedom *(G-12207)*
Global Home Automation LLC....G....484 686-7374
Fort Washington *(G-6072)*
Jcm Audio Inc....G....570 323-9014
Williamsport *(G-20028)*
Legrand Home Systems Inc....E....717 702-2532
Middletown *(G-11061)*
▲ Legrand Home Systems Inc....D....717 702-2532
Middletown *(G-11060)*
Lord Corporation....D....814 398-4641
Cambridge Springs *(G-2481)*
Lord Corporation....A....877 275-5673
Erie *(G-5373)*
▲ Luzerne Trading Company Inc....F....866 954-4440
Wilkes Barre *(G-19938)*
Media Rooms Inc....G....610 719-8500
West Chester *(G-19600)*
Mobile Video Devices Inc....G....610 921-5720
Reading *(G-16447)*
Optima Plus International LLC....G....717 207-9037
Lancaster *(G-9156)*
Oswaldsmill Inc....G....610 298-3271
New Tripoli *(G-12459)*
Phoenix Avs LLC....G....610 910-6251
Broomall *(G-2302)*
Rogue Audio Inc....G....570 992-9901
Brodheadsville *(G-2238)*
Shangri La Productions....G....610 838-5188
Hellertown *(G-7562)*
Siemens Industry Inc....C....724 339-9500
New Kensington *(G-12375)*
Sigma Technology Systems LLC....F....717 569-2926
Lancaster *(G-9197)*
Simply Automated Llc....G....412 343-0348
Pittsburgh *(G-15539)*
Spectrum Microwave Inc....D....215 464-0586
Philadelphia *(G-14333)*
Technicolor Usa Inc....C....717 295-6100
Lancaster *(G-9214)*
Teledyne Defense Elec LLC....D....814 238-3450
State College *(G-18036)*
Videon Central Inc....D....814 235-1111
State College *(G-18041)*
▲ Videotek Inc....C....610 327-2292
Pottstown *(G-16068)*
World Video Sales Co Inc....G....610 754-6800
Bechtelsville *(G-1038)*
▲ Zylux America Inc....G....412 221-5530
Bethel Park *(G-1440)*

3652 Phonograph Records & Magnetic Tape

Atr Magnetics LLC....G....717 718-8008
York *(G-20391)*
Brooke Production Inc....G....610 296-9394
Malvern *(G-10196)*
▲ Cinram Manufacturing Inc....A....570 383-3291
Olyphant *(G-12986)*
Digital Dynamics Audio Inc....G....412 434-1630
Bethel Park *(G-1412)*
Disc Hounds LLC....G....610 696-8668
West Chester *(G-19542)*
Gilead Enterprises Inc....G....717 733-2003
Ephrata *(G-5106)*
His Light Kingdom LLC....G....267 777-3866
Philadelphia *(G-13828)*
Najafi Companies LLC....G....570 383-3291
Olyphant *(G-12994)*
Private Zone Productions Corp....G....267 592-5447
Philadelphia *(G-14204)*
Sony Music Holdings Inc....E....724 794-8500
Boyers *(G-1890)*
Sour Junkie LLC....G....412 612-6860
Pittsburgh *(G-15562)*
Technicolor HM Entrmt Svcs Inc....F....570 383-3291
Olyphant *(G-13001)*
Tuscarora Usa Inc....G....717 491-2861
Chambersburg *(G-2991)*
Warner Music Inc....D....570 383-3291
Olyphant *(G-13003)*
▼ Whitaker Corporation....C....724 334-7000
New Kensington *(G-12389)*

3661 Telephone & Telegraph Apparatus

Accelbeam Photonics LLC....G....215 715-4345
Huntingdon Valley *(G-7961)*
Advanced Laser Printer S....G....717 764-3272
York *(G-20369)*
Alcatel-Lucent Tech Inc....G....215 752-1847
Feasterville Trevose *(G-5884)*
All Tech-D Out LLC....F....610 814-0888
Allentown *(G-124)*
Amtel Systems Corporation....G....610 458-3320
Chester Springs *(G-3071)*
Arris Global Services Inc....G....215 323-1000
Horsham *(G-7789)*
Aurora Optics Inc....G....215 646-0690
Ambler *(G-568)*
B N I Solutions LLC....G....814 237-4073
State College *(G-17944)*
◆ Black Box Corporation....G....724 746-5500
Lawrence *(G-9535)*
Bluephone....G....412 337-1965
Bridgeville *(G-2055)*
Broadband Networks Inc....D....814 237-4073
State College *(G-17947)*
C Dcap Modem Line....G....814 966-3954
Duke Center *(G-4438)*
▲ Cardo Systems Inc....E....412 788-4533
Pittsburgh *(G-14811)*
Compunetix Inc....B....412 373-8110
Monroeville *(G-11330)*
Copitech Associates....G....570 963-1391
Scranton *(G-17219)*
Cott Manufacturing Company....F....412 675-0101
Glassport *(G-6410)*
Cott Manufacturing Company....E....724 625-3730
Glassport *(G-6411)*
D&E Communications LLC....E....814 238-0000
State College *(G-17956)*
D&E Communications LLC....G....570 524-2200
Lewisburg *(G-9904)*
Delktech Systems Inc....G....267 341-8391
Philadelphia *(G-13618)*
Fetterolf Group Inc....G....814 443-4688
Somerset *(G-17688)*
Finisar Corporation....C....267 803-3800
Horsham *(G-7818)*
◆ Gai-Tronics Corporation....C....610 777-1374
Reading *(G-16388)*
Greg Norton....E....724 625-3426
Mars *(G-10498)*
ITI Inmate Telephone Inc....D....814 944-0405
Altoona *(G-518)*
▲ Legrand Home Systems Inc....D....717 702-2532
Middletown *(G-11060)*
Lexicon International Corp....E....215 639-8220
Bensalem *(G-1220)*
Library Video Company....D....610 645-4000
Conshohocken *(G-3572)*
▲ Mobile Outfitters LLC....F....215 325-0747
Philadelphia *(G-14030)*
Netgear Inc....G....724 941-5748
Canonsburg *(G-2613)*
Omnispread Communications Inc....G....215 654-9900
North Wales *(G-12821)*

S I C

Ospcom LLC ....G 267 356-7124
Doylestown (G-4321)

Pittsburgh Photon Studio LLC ....G 724 263-6502
Pittsburgh (G-15403)

Quintech Elec Cmmnications Inc ....D 724 349-1412
Indiana (G-8122)

Rajant Corporation ....D 484 595-0233
Malvern (G-10307)

Ruckus Wireless Inc ....E 215 323-1000
Horsham (G-7847)

Ruckus Wireless Inc ....G 215 209-6160
Philadelphia (G-14263)

Ruckus Wireless Inc ....E 814 231-3710
State College (G-18018)

Siemens Industry Inc ....F 412 829-7511
East Pittsburgh (G-4597)

Tech Modem CB Comcast ....G 267 288-5661
Warminster (G-18976)

Telamon Corporation ....E 800 945-8800
Levittown (G-9867)

▲ Thales Transport & SEC Inc ......E 412 366-8814
Pittsburgh (G-15608)

▲ Tollgrade Communications Inc ....E 724 720-1400
Cranberry Township (G-3854)

Voicestar Inc ....F 267 514-0000
Philadelphia (G-14455)

Woodbine Properties ....C 814 443-4688
Somerset (G-17718)

3663 Radio & T V Communications, Systs & Eqpt, Broadcast/Studio

Activeblu Corporation ....G 412 490-1929
Pittsburgh (G-14646)

▲ Alstom Signaling Operation LLC ......B 800 825-3178
Erie (G-5184)

Ameritech Network Corp ....E 215 441-8310
Hatboro (G-7268)

▲ Amplifier Research Corp ....C 215 723-8181
Souderton (G-17724)

Amplifier Solutions Corp ....F 215 799-2561
Telford (G-18267)

App-Techs Corporation ....F 717 735-0848
Lancaster (G-8935)

Arris Technology Inc ....F 215 323-2590
Horsham (G-7790)

Ats-Needham LLC ....F 617 375-7500
Philadelphia (G-13424)

Belar Electronics Lab Inc ....E 610 687-5550
West Chester (G-19509)

Broadband Networks Inc ....D 814 237-4073
State College (G-17947)

Cheetah Technologies LP ....G 412 928-7707
Pittsburgh (G-14842)

▲ Comtrol International ....E 724 864-3800
Irwin (G-8149)

Contrail Systems Inc ....F 724 353-1127
Sarver (G-17067)

Control Dynamics Corporation ....G 215 956-0700
Warminster (G-18846)

CPI Locus Microwave Inc ....E 814 466-6275
Boalsburg (G-1866)

Cricket Communications LLC ....G 267 687-5949
Philadelphia (G-13582)

Delta Information Systems Inc ....E 215 657-5270
Horsham (G-7809)

Digital Card Inc ....F 215 275-7100
Langhorne (G-9290)

Dynamic Manufacturing LLC ....D 724 295-4200
Freeport (G-6203)

E-Nanomedsys LLC ....G 917 734-1462
State College (G-17958)

▲ Fidelity Technologies Corp ....C 610 929-3330
Reading (G-16385)

◆ Gai-Tronics Corporation ....C 610 777-1374
Reading (G-16388)

Gaintenna ....G 724 654-9900
New Castle (G-12096)

General Dynmics Stcom Tech Inc ....C 814 238-2700
State College (G-17969)

Global Monitoring LLC ....G 610 604-0760
Springfield (G-17915)

H & S Electronics ....G 717 354-2200
New Holland (G-12250)

Hilltop Tower Leasing Inc ....E 814 942-1888
Altoona (G-514)

Hirschmann Electronics Inc ....F 717 217-2200
Chambersburg (G-2940)

Hughes Network Systems LLC ......E 610 363-1427
Exton (G-5692)

Hughes Network Systems LLC ......E 717 792-2987
York (G-20531)

Idsi LLC ....G 717 227-9055
New Freedom (G-12210)

Idsi LLC ....E 717 235-5474
New Freedom (G-12211)

Katz Media Group Inc ....E 215 567-5166
Philadelphia (G-13924)

Kreco Antennas ....G 570 595-2212
Cresco (G-3894)

Kykayke Inc ....G 610 522-0106
Holmes (G-7663)

L3 Electron Devices Inc ....C 570 326-3561
Williamsport (G-20033)

L3 Technologies Inc ....C 267 545-7000
Bristol (G-2157)

Liberty Uplink Inc ....G 215 964-5222
Malvern (G-10267)

Library Video Company ....D 610 645-4000
Conshohocken (G-3572)

Linear Acoustic Inc ....G 717 735-6142
Lancaster (G-9112)

◆ Matric Group LLC ....B 814 677-0716
Seneca (G-17366)

Mechantech Inc ....F 570 389-1039
Catawissa (G-2820)

Metroplitan Communications Inc ....F 610 874-7100
Eddystone (G-4805)

Micro-Coax Inc ....C 610 495-4438
Pottstown (G-16019)

Motorola Mobility LLC ....D 215 674-4800
Horsham (G-7834)

Motorola Mobility LLC ....G 610 238-0109
Plymouth Meeting (G-15857)

Motorola Solutions Inc ....C 724 837-3030
Greensburg (G-6690)

Ospcom LLC ....G 267 356-7124
Doylestown (G-4321)

Payloadz Inc ....G 609 510-3074
Newtown Square (G-12587)

Phasetek Inc ....G 215 536-6648
Quakertown (G-16228)

Prime Image Delaware Inc ....G 215 822-1561
Chalfont (G-2884)

Professional Electronic Compon ....G 215 245-1550
Philadelphia (G-14205)

R F Specialties Pennsylvania ....G 814 472-2000
Ebensburg (G-4793)

Raytheon Company ....B 814 278-2256
State College (G-18012)

Rockwell Automation Inc ....G 412 375-4700
Coraopolis (G-3723)

Ruckus Wireless Inc ....E 215 323-1000
Horsham (G-7847)

Ruckus Wireless Inc ....E 814 231-3710
State College (G-18018)

Satcom Digital Networks LLC ....G 724 824-1699
Cranberry Township (G-3847)

Sierra Media Services Inc ....G 412 722-1701
Pittsburgh (G-15537)

▲ Spectrum Control Inc ....B 814 474-2207
Fairview (G-5842)

Spectrum Control Inc ....G 814 474-4315
Fairview (G-5845)

Spyware ....F 215 444-0405
Warminster (G-18973)

Star-H Corporation ....G 717 826-7587
Lancaster (G-9204)

Structured Mining Systems Inc ......E 724 741-9000
Warrendale (G-19098)

Symbol Technologies LLC ....F 610 834-8900
Plymouth Meeting (G-15875)

Teledyne Defense Elec LLC ....D 814 238-3450
State College (G-18036)

▲ Tm Systems Inc ....F 814 272-2700
State College (G-18039)

◆ TVC Communications LLC ....E 717 838-3790
Annville (G-661)

Validity LLC ....G 610 768-8042
Malvern (G-10337)

Video Visions Inc ....F 215 942-6642
Trevose (G-18508)

▲ Videotek Inc ....C 610 327-2292
Pottstown (G-16068)

Warren Installations Inc ....F 717 517-9321
Lancaster (G-9235)

Wave Central LLC ....F 717 503-7157
Carlisle (G-2750)

Westcom Wireless Inc ....G 412 228-5507
McKeesport (G-10686)

Wireless Acquisition LLC ....G 602 315-9979
Mountain Top (G-11781)

World Video Sales Co Inc ....G 610 754-6800
Bechtelsville (G-1038)

3669 Communications Eqpt, NEC

▲ Acra Control Inc ....G 714 382-1863
Newtown (G-12494)

Ademco Inc ....G 215 244-6377
Bensalem (G-1143)

▲ Alertone Services Inc ....F 570 321-5433
Williamsport (G-19984)

Alpha Space Control Co Inc ....G 717 263-0182
Chambersburg (G-2900)

▲ Alstom Signaling Operation LLC ......B 800 825-3178
Erie (G-5184)

Atlas Flasher & Supply Co Inc ....E 610 469-2602
Pottstown (G-15944)

Ballistic Applications ....F 724 282-0416
East Butler (G-4530)

▲ Big Brother Hd Ltd Lblty Co ....G 201 355-8166
Tamiment (G-18232)

Business Cmmunications Systems ....G 610 827-7061
Chester Springs (G-3073)

Clark Traffic Control Inc ....F 724 388-4023
Homer City (G-7674)

▲ Comtrol International ....E 724 864-3800
Irwin (G-8149)

Digital Care Sysytems Inc ....F 215 946-7700
Levittown (G-9831)

Ecomm Life Safety Systems LLC ....G 215 953-5858
Ivyland (G-8210)

Gaadt Perspectives LLC ....G 610 388-7641
Chadds Ford (G-2851)

Harrison Electronic Systems ....F 570 639-5695
Wilkes Barre (G-19924)

Hirschmann Electronics Inc ....F 717 217-2200
Chambersburg (G-2940)

◆ Hitachi Rail STS Usa Inc ....B 412 688-2400
Pittsburgh (G-15096)

Hri Networks Inc ....F 267 515-5880
Philadelphia (G-13838)

Hubbell Incorporated Delaware ......B 574 234-7151
Mohnton (G-11264)

Infinera Corporation ....G 408 572-5200
Allentown (G-259)

Intuidex Inc ....E 484 851-3423
Hellertown (G-7557)

Johnson Controls ....D 717 610-8100
New Cumberland (G-12187)

Johnson Controls ....D 610 398-7260
Allentown (G-270)

Keystone Fire Co Apparatus ....F 610 587-3859
Boyertown (G-1921)

◆ Kidde Fire Protection Inc ....E 610 363-1400
West Chester (G-19581)

Kongsberg Integrated Tactical ....E 814 269-5700
Johnstown (G-8399)

Kykayke Inc ....G 610 522-0106
Holmes (G-7663)

L3 Technologies Inc ....C 267 545-7000
Bristol (G-2157)

Mainstream Industries ....G 610 488-1148
Bernville (G-1301)

Mashan Inc ....G 724 397-4008
Home (G-7669)

▲ Medical Alarm Concepts LLC ....G 877 639-2929
King of Prussia (G-8650)

Mercury Systems Inc ....G 215 245-0546
Bensalem (G-1227)

Metabloc Inc ....G 717 764-4937
York (G-20589)

Micro-Trap Corporation ....G 215 295-8208
Morrisville (G-11571)

Ncn Data Networks LLC ....G 570 213-8300
Stroudsburg (G-18133)

Orion Systems Inc ....E 215 346-8200
Huntingdon Valley (G-8019)

Orlotronics Corporation ....E 610 239-8200
Bridgeport (G-2042)

Ospcom LLC ....G 267 356-7124
Doylestown (G-4321)

Otx Logistics Inc ....G 412 567-8821
Clinton (G-3264)

Pls Signs LLC ....G 215 269-1400
Fairless Hills (G-5791)

Probee Safety LLC ....G 302 893-0258
Telford (G-18310)

▼ Solar Technology Inc ....D 610 391-8600
Allentown (G-396)

Traffic Control Eqp & Sups Co ....G...... 412 882-2012
 Bentleyville (G-1276)

Two Toys Inc ....G...... 717 840-6400
 York (G-20693)

Unique Systems Inc ....G...... 610 499-1463
 Wallingford (G-18787)

◆ Van Air Inc ....E...... 814 774-2631
 Lake City (G-8909)

Wearable Health Solutions Inc ....F...... 877 639-2929
 King of Prussia (G-8698)

3671 Radio & T V Receiving Electron Tubes

▲ Eag Electronics Corp ....C...... 814 836-8080
 Fairview (G-5820)

Hamamatsu Corporation ....G...... 724 935-3600
 Sewickley (G-17390)

Lockheed Martin Corporation ....B...... 570 876-2132
 Archbald (G-691)

▲ Optilumen Inc ....G...... 717 547-5417
 Pillow (G-14586)

▲ Photonis Defense Inc ....D...... 717 295-6000
 Lancaster (G-9170)

Triton Services Inc ....G...... 484 851-3883
 Breinigsville (G-2029)

Vectron International Inc ....E...... 603 598-0070
 Mount Holly Springs (G-11640)

3672 Printed Circuit Boards

▲ 4front Solutions LLC ....C...... 814 464-2000
 Erie (G-5161)

Aci Technologies Inc ....E...... 610 362-1200
 Philadelphia (G-13313)

Advanced Electrocircuits Corp ....E...... 412 278-5200
 Pittsburgh (G-14652)

Advanced Mfg Tech Inc ....D...... 724 327-3001
 Export (G-5588)

Advanced Technology Labs Inc ....B...... 215 355-8111
 Richboro (G-16673)

Allen Integrated Assemblies ....G...... 610 966-2200
 Macungie (G-10139)

◆ Alstom Power Conversion Inc ....C...... 412 967-0765
 Cranberry Township (G-3801)

▲ Alstom Signaling Operation LLC .....B...... 800 825-3178
 Erie (G-5184)

Amptech Inc ....E...... 724 843-7605
 Wampum (G-18797)

Ansen Corporation ....G...... 315 393-3573
 Pittsburgh (G-14712)

AOC Acquisition Inc ....B...... 610 966-2200
 Macungie (G-10141)

Bayter Technologies Inc ....G...... 610 948-7447
 Phoenixville (G-14529)

▲ Circuit Foil Trading Inc ....G...... 215 887-7255
 Glenside (G-6511)

Communication Automation Corp ....E...... 610 692-9526
 West Chester (G-19527)

Compunetics Inc ....E...... 724 519-4773
 Murrysville (G-11850)

Compunetics Inc ....D...... 412 373-8110
 Monroeville (G-11328)

Compunetix Inc ....D...... 412 373-8110
 Monroeville (G-11329)

Currency Inc ....E...... 814 509-6157
 Windber (G-20180)

▲ Ddm Novastar Inc ....E...... 610 337-3050
 Warminster (G-18855)

▲ Diamond Mt Inc ....E...... 814 535-3505
 Johnstown (G-8368)

Drs Laurel Technologies ....B...... 814 534-8900
 Johnstown (G-8370)

Dynamic Manufacturing LLC ....D...... 724 295-4200
 Freeport (G-6203)

Electro Soft Inc ....E...... 215 654-0701
 Montgomeryville (G-11394)

▲ Electronic Integration Inc ....F...... 215 364-3390
 Feasterville Trevose (G-5903)

Electronic Mfg Svcs Group Inc ....D...... 717 764-0002
 York (G-20467)

Electronic Prototype Dev Inc ....E...... 412 767-4111
 Natrona Heights (G-11941)

Electronic Service & Design ....G...... 717 243-7743
 Hummelstown (G-7909)

▲ Electronic Test Eqp Mfg Co ....E...... 717 393-9653
 Lancaster (G-9008)

Fineline Circuits Inc ....E...... 215 364-3311
 Feasterville Trevose (G-5909)

Flex Rig Inc ....F...... 215 638-5743
 Bensalem (G-1196)

Ford City Gun Workd ....G...... 724 994-9501
 Ford City (G-6045)

Genie Electronics Co Inc ....E...... 717 840-6999
 York (G-20496)

Genie Electronics Co Inc ....D...... 717 244-1099
 Red Lion (G-16598)

Genie Electronics Co Inc ....C...... 717 244-1099
 Red Lion (G-16599)

In Speck Corporation ....E...... 610 272-9500
 Norristown (G-12669)

Keystone Electronics Inc ....E...... 717 747-5900
 York (G-20553)

Kitron Technologies Inc ....C...... 814 474-4300
 Windber (G-20187)

Loranger International Corp ....D...... 814 723-2250
 Warren (G-19038)

▲ Manncorp Inc ....F...... 215 830-1200
 Huntingdon Valley (G-8011)

◆ Matric Group LLC ....B...... 814 677-0716
 Seneca (G-17366)

▲ Mid-Atlantic Circuit Inc ....F...... 215 672-8480
 Warminster (G-18922)

Millennium Circuits Limited ....F...... 717 558-5975
 Harrisburg (G-7178)

▲ Monach Associates Inc ....G...... 888 849-0149
 Bristol (G-2169)

National Hybrid Inc ....D...... 814 467-9060
 Windber (G-20190)

Niche Electronics Tech Inc ....E...... 717 532-6620
 Shippensburg (G-17541)

◆ Nupak Printing LLC ....D...... 717 244-4041
 Red Lion (G-16610)

Pennatronics Corporation ....D...... 724 938-1800
 California (G-2464)

▲ Pergamon Corp ....F...... 610 239-0721
 King of Prussia (G-8661)

Pine Electronics Inc ....D...... 724 458-6391
 Grove City (G-6800)

◆ Pine Instrument Company ....D...... 724 458-6391
 Grove City (G-6801)

▲ Positran Manufacturing Inc ....D...... 610 277-0500
 Norristown (G-12704)

▲ Primus Technologies Corp ....B...... 570 326-6591
 Williamsport (G-20063)

R&D Sockets Inc ....G...... 610 443-2299
 Allentown (G-369)

Reed Micro Automation Inc ....G...... 814 941-0225
 Altoona (G-543)

Rfcircuits Inc ....F...... 215 364-2450
 Huntingdon Valley (G-8029)

Secure Components LLC ....F...... 610 551-3475
 Norristown (G-12711)

Sen Dec Corp ....F...... 585 425-3390
 Fairview (G-5841)

▲ Smg-Global Circuits Inc ....E...... 724 229-3200
 Washington (G-19226)

◆ Spang & Company ....C...... 412 963-9363
 Pittsburgh (G-15566)

Strategic Mfg Tech LLC ....E...... 610 269-0054
 Downingtown (G-4257)

Technical Fabrication Inc ....E...... 717 227-0909
 New Freedom (G-12216)

Ted J Tedesco ....G...... 215 316-8303
 Media (G-10952)

Telan Corporation ....E...... 215 822-1234
 Hatfield (G-7400)

Tudor Design ....G...... 215 638-3366
 Bensalem (G-1266)

▲ Wintronics Inc ....E...... 724 981-5770
 Sharon (G-17449)

Woodward McCoach Inc ....F...... 610 692-9526
 West Chester (G-19681)

▲ World Elec Sls & Svc Inc ....C...... 610 939-9800
 Reading (G-16569)

Youngtron Inc ....E...... 215 822-7866
 Hatfield (G-7406)

Ziel Technologies LLC ....G...... 717 951-7485
 Lancaster (G-9245)

3674 Semiconductors

Advanced Plasma Solutions ....G...... 267 679-4077
 Reading (G-16312)

▲ Agere Systems Inc ....A...... 610 712-1000
 Allentown (G-118)

American Innovations Inc ....G...... 215 249-1840
 Dublin (G-4431)

Applied Materials Inc ....G...... 610 409-9187
 Collegeville (G-3370)

Applied Micro Circuits Corp ....E...... 267 757-8722
 Newtown (G-12496)

Aron Lighting LLC ....G...... 484 681-5687
 King of Prussia (G-8584)

Aural Harmonics ....F...... 610 488-0232
 Bernville (G-1297)

Bfhj Enrgy Solutions Ltd Lblty ....G...... 717 458-0927
 Mechanicsburg (G-10824)

◆ C&D Technologies Inc ....C...... 215 619-2700
 Blue Bell (G-1820)

Conductive Technologies Inc ....D...... 717 764-6931
 York (G-20433)

Cymatics Laboratories Corp ....G...... 412 578-0280
 Pittsburgh (G-14899)

Dean Technology Inc ....E...... 724 479-3533
 Lucernemines (G-10117)

Dean Technology Inc ....E...... 724 349-9440
 Indiana (G-8090)

Electromagnetic Liberation ....G...... 724 568-2869
 Vandergrift (G-18725)

Esilicon Corporation ....G...... 610 439-6800
 Allentown (G-207)

◆ Everson Tesla Inc ....D...... 610 746-1520
 Nazareth (G-11965)

F S Convergent ....F...... 484 581-7065
 Wayne (G-19327)

Fairchild Semiconductor Corp ....C...... 570 474-6761
 Mountain Top (G-11760)

Filmtronics Inc ....E...... 724 352-3790
 Butler (G-2401)

First Level Inc ....F...... 717 266-2450
 York (G-20481)

▲ Griff and Associates LP ....D...... 215 428-1075
 Levittown (G-9842)

H & M Net Works ....F...... 484 344-2161
 Blue Bell (G-1832)

◆ Heraeus Precious Metals Nor ....C...... 610 825-6050
 Conshohocken (G-3556)

Hoffman Materials LLC ....G...... 717 243-2011
 Carlisle (G-2717)

▲ Ii-VI Incorporated ....B...... 724 352-4455
 Saxonburg (G-17088)

Ii-VI Laser Enterprise Inc ....E...... 724 352-4455
 Saxonburg (G-17089)

Infineon Tech Americas Corp ....E...... 408 503-2655
 Allentown (G-257)

Infineon Tech Americas Corp ....G...... 610 712-7100
 Allentown (G-258)

Infinera Corporation ....G...... 484 866-4600
 Allentown (G-260)

Intel Homes Ltd Liability Co ....G...... 570 872-9559
 East Stroudsburg (G-4620)

Intervideo Inc ....G...... 717 435-9433
 Lancaster (G-9061)

▲ Invensys Energy Metering Corp ....B...... 814 371-3011
 Du Bois (G-4396)

▲ Iqe Inc ....G...... 610 861-6930
 Bethlehem (G-1540)

Keytronics Inc ....D...... 814 272-2700
 State College (G-17984)

Kontron America Incorporated ....F...... 412 921-3322
 Pittsburgh (G-15182)

▲ Laurell Technologies Corp ....G...... 215 699-7278
 North Wales (G-12812)

Linear Technology LLC ....F...... 215 638-9667
 Bensalem (G-1221)

Mesta Electronics Inc ....F...... 412 754-3000
 Irwin (G-8182)

Microchip Technology Inc ....F...... 610 630-0556
 Norristown (G-12684)

Microsemi Corp ....E...... 610 929-7142
 Reading (G-16442)

Microsemi Corp - High ....D...... 717 486-3411
 Mount Holly Springs (G-11636)

Microsemi Corp - Mntgmeryville ....E...... 215 631-9840
 Montgomeryville (G-11407)

Microsemi Stor Solutions Inc ....E...... 610 289-5200
 Allentown (G-316)

Micross Components Inc ....G...... 215 997-3200
 Hatfield (G-7369)

Moglabs Usa LLC ....G...... 814 251-4363
 Huntingdon (G-7953)

▲ Montco Enterprises Ltd ....E...... 610 948-5316
 Spring City (G-17863)

Moog Inc ....C...... 610 328-4000
 Springfield (G-17919)

National Hybrid Inc ....D...... 814 467-9060
 Windber (G-20190)

NORTH PENN TECHNOLOGY INC ....E...... 215 997-3200
 Hatfield (G-7374)

Novatech Industries Inc ....G...... 610 584-8996
 Skippack (G-17601)

▲ OEM Group East Inc ....D... 610 282-0105
Coopersburg *(G-3632)*

On Semiconductor ....G....... 570 475-6030
Mountain Top *(G-11769)*

On Semiconductor Corp ....E... 602 244-6600
Amber *(G-595)*

On Semiconductor Corporation ....E... 215 654-9700
Amber *(G-596)*

Phase Guard Co Inc..........................G...... 412 276-3415
Carnegie *(G-2778)*

Power & Energy Inc ....F... 215 942-4600
Ivyland *(G-8221)*

Powerex Inc ....E... 724 925-7272
Youngwood *(G-20781)*

◆ Powerex Inc ....C... 724 925-7272
Youngwood *(G-20782)*

▲ Premier Semiconductor Svcs LLC ...D... 267 954-0130
Hatfield *(G-7384)*

Process Sltions Consulting Inc ....G....... 610 248-2002
New Tripoli *(G-12460)*

Quad Tron Inc....................................G... 215 441-9303
Warminster *(G-18949)*

▲ Quick Assembly Inc ....F... 215 361-4100
Hatfield *(G-7388)*

R & D Assembly Inc ....G... 610 770-0700
Allentown *(G-365)*

R & E International Inc.......................F... 610 664-5637
Merion Station *(G-10998)*

R&D Circuits Inc.................................G... 610 443-2299
Allentown *(G-368)*

Raytheon Company ....B... 814 278-2256
State College *(G-18012)*

Rose Network Solutions......................G... 610 563-1958
Honey Brook *(G-7759)*

RTD Embedded Technologies Inc ....E... 814 234-8087
State College *(G-18017)*

Scitech Assoc Holdings Inc ....G... 201 218-3777
State College *(G-18021)*

Secure Components LLC ....F... 610 551-3475
Norristown *(G-12711)*

Semicndctor Ozone Slutions LLC ....G... 541 936-0844
Fleetwood *(G-5979)*

Semilab USA LLC...............................F... 610 377-5990
Lehighton *(G-9726)*

Sensortex Inc ....G... 302 444-2383
Kennett Square *(G-8542)*

▼ Sentinel Power Inc ....G... 724 925-8181
New Stanton *(G-12451)*

SES Inc..G... 484 767-3280
Nazareth *(G-11987)*

Silicon Power Corporation..................D...... 610 407-4700
Malvern *(G-10317)*

▲ Solar Power Solutions LLC ....G... 724 379-2002
Belle Vernon *(G-1087)*

Spectrum Control Tech Inc ....F... 814 474-2207
Fairview *(G-5846)*

▼ Spectrum Devices Corporation ....G... 215 997-7870
Telford *(G-18318)*

Sun Prime Energy LLC ....G... 215 962-4196
Chalfont *(G-2890)*

Texas Instrs Lehigh Vly Inc ....G... 610 849-5100
Bethlehem *(G-1638)*

Texas Instruments Incorporated ....E... 610 849-5100
Bethlehem *(G-1639)*

Thermigate LLC..................................G... 610 931-1023
Lansdowne *(G-9445)*

Universal Display Corporation ....G... 609 671-0980
Newtown *(G-12558)*

Victor Associates Inc..........................G... 215 393-5437
Lansdale *(G-9423)*

Vishay Intertechnology Inc ....B... 610 644-1300
Malvern *(G-10341)*

Vishay Siliconix LLC...........................A... 408 567-8177
Malvern *(G-10344)*

Xensor Corporation............................E... 610 284-2508
Drexel Hill *(G-4373)*

▲ Yingli Green Enrgy Amricas Inc........F 212 609-4909
Philadelphia *(G-14500)*

3675 *Electronic Capacitors*

Dean Technology Inc ....E... 724 479-3533
Lucernemines *(G-10117)*

Evaporated Coatings Inc ....E... 215 659-3080
Willow Grove *(G-20116)*

◆ High Energy Corp ....E... 610 593-2800
Parkesburg *(G-13175)*

Kemet Investment Ltd Partnr................G....... 215 822-1550
Chalfont *(G-2880)*

Kemet Investments Inc ....F... 215 822-1550
Chalfont *(G-2881)*

Optixtal Inc ....G....... 215 254-5225
Philadelphia *(G-14099)*

Spectrum Control Inc ....C....... 814 474-1571
Fairview *(G-5843)*

Spectrum Control Inc ....C....... 814 835-4000
Fairview *(G-5844)*

Vishay Intertechnology Inc ....B....... 610 644-1300
Malvern *(G-10341)*

3676 *Electronic Resistors*

Dean Technology Inc ....E... 724 479-3533
Lucernemines *(G-10117)*

Grued Corporation..............................C... 610 644-1300
Malvern *(G-10244)*

In Speck Corporation..........................E... 610 272-9500
Norristown *(G-12669)*

▲ Spectrum Control Inc ....B... 814 474-2207
Fairview *(G-5842)*

▲ State of Art Inc..............................C... 814 355-2714
State College *(G-18034)*

Thermistors Unlimited Inc....................G... 814 781-5920
Saint Marys *(G-17022)*

Triaxial Structures Inc ....G... 215 248-0380
Philadelphia *(G-14409)*

▲ US Resistor Inc.............................G... 814 834-9369
Saint Marys *(G-17026)*

Vishay Intertechnology Inc ....B... 610 644-1300
Malvern *(G-10341)*

Vishay Precision Foil Inc......................A... 484 321-5300
Malvern *(G-10342)*

Vishay Precision Group Inc ....D... 484 321-5300
Malvern *(G-10343)*

3677 *Electronic Coils & Transformers*

API Technologies Corp.........................G... 215 464-4000
Philadelphia *(G-13399)*

▼ Chemrock Corporation ....F... 610 667-6640
Bala Cynwyd *(G-875)*

Coil Specialty Co Inc ....E... 814 234-7044
State College *(G-17952)*

Customized Envmtl Systems ....G... 412 380-2311
Pittsburgh *(G-14896)*

Danco Precision Inc............................F... 610 933-8981
Phoenixville *(G-14542)*

Digital Plaza LLC................................F... 267 515-8000
Ambler *(G-575)*

Gettysburg Transformer Corp ....E... 717 334-2191
Gettysburg *(G-6293)*

Gkld Corp...G... 215 643-6950
Blue Bell *(G-1830)*

Halsit Holdings LLC............................E... 814 724-6440
Meadville *(G-10733)*

Ikor Industries Inc...............................D... 302 456-0280
Kennett Square *(G-8514)*

Lrt Sensors Inc ....G... 877 299-8595
Huntingdon Valley *(G-8009)*

▲ Mar Cor Purification Inc ....C... 800 633-3080
Skippack *(G-17600)*

Micro-Coax Inc ....C... 610 495-4438
Pottstown *(G-16019)*

Northern Winding Inc ....G... 724 776-4983
Mars *(G-10509)*

Pei/Genesis Inc ....G... 215 638-1645
Bensalem *(G-1238)*

▲ Pei/Genesis Inc ....C... 215 464-1410
Philadelphia *(G-14129)*

▲ Pennsylvania Trans Tech Inc ....B... 724 873-2100
Canonsburg *(G-2618)*

Precisian Inc.......................................G... 610 861-0844
Tannersville *(G-18236)*

Raycom Electronics Inc ....D... 717 292-3641
Dover *(G-4203)*

Schneider Electric It Corp ....B... 717 948-1200
Middletown *(G-11074)*

Solid State Ceramics Inc ....G... 570 322-2700
State College *(G-18028)*

Spang & Company ....E... 724 376-7515
Sandy Lake *(G-17062)*

▲ Spectrum Control Inc ....B... 814 474-2207
Fairview *(G-5842)*

Spectrum Control Inc ....C... 814 272-2700
State College *(G-18031)*

Spectrum Control Inc ....C... 814 474-1571
Fairview *(G-5843)*

Spectrum Control Inc ....C... 814 835-4000
Fairview *(G-5844)*

Spectrum Control Inc ....E... 814 272-2700
State College *(G-18032)*

Spectrum Control Inc ....G... 814 474-4315
Fairview *(G-5845)*

▲ Stimple and Ward Company ....E... 412 364-5200
Pittsburgh *(G-15584)*

Tinicum Magnetics Inc ....F 717 530-2424
Shippensburg *(G-17551)*

▼ Unifilt Corporation ....G... 717 823-0313
Wilkes Barre *(G-19966)*

Vishay Intertechnology Inc ....B....... 610 644-1300
Malvern *(G-10341)*

Wist Enterprises Inc ....F 724 283-7230
Butler *(G-2451)*

3678 *Electronic Connectors*

Avant-Garde Technology Inc ....G... 215 345-8228
Doylestown *(G-4273)*

▲ Bel Connector Inc..........................D... 717 235-7512
Glen Rock *(G-6452)*

Belden Inc...E... 717 263-7655
Chambersburg *(G-2910)*

Component Enterprises Co Inc ....E... 610 272-7900
Norristown *(G-12646)*

Continental-Wirt Elec Corp ....C... 215 355-7080
Southampton *(G-17805)*

Cooper Interconnect Inc......................E... 630 248-4007
King of Prussia *(G-8597)*

▲ Eagle Design Group........................E... 610 321-2488
Chester Springs *(G-3076)*

Eagle Design Innovation LLC ....F... 610 321-2488
Chester Springs *(G-3077)*

EBY Group LLC...................................E... 215 537-4700
Philadelphia *(G-13657)*

Electroline Corp ....E... 215 766-2229
Pipersville *(G-14614)*

◆ Fci USA LLC ....B... 717 938-7200
Etters *(G-5548)*

Halsit Holdings LLC............................E... 814 724-6440
Meadville *(G-10733)*

Hirschmann Electronics Inc..................F... 717 217-2200
Chambersburg *(G-2940)*

▲ Industrial Enterprises Inc...............D... 215 355-7080
Southampton *(G-17819)*

Keystone Controls Company ....G... 215 355-7080
Southampton *(G-17820)*

Koaxis Inc ....E... 610 222-0154
Schwenksville *(G-17178)*

Loranger International Corp ....D... 814 723-2250
Warren *(G-19038)*

Megaphase LLC ....E... 570 424-8400
Stroudsburg *(G-18130)*

▲ Optima Technology Assoc Inc ....D... 717 932-5877
Lewisberry *(G-9889)*

Ospcom LLC.......................................G... 267 356-7124
Doylestown *(G-4321)*

Osram Sylvania Inc.............................C... 814 726-6600
Warren *(G-19041)*

Pei/Genesis Inc ....G... 215 638-1645
Bensalem *(G-1238)*

▲ Pei/Genesis Inc ....C... 215 464-1410
Philadelphia *(G-14129)*

Pennatronics Corporation.....................D... 724 938-1800
California *(G-2464)*

Phoenix Contact Dev & Mfg Inc...........B... 717 944-1300
Middletown *(G-11068)*

Precise Plastics Inc ....D... 814 474-5504
Fairview *(G-5840)*

▲ Rocal Corporation ....E... 215 343-2400
Warrington *(G-19132)*

▲ Rosenberger N Amer Akron LLC ......C....... 717 859-8900
Akron *(G-38)*

▲ Sentinel Connector Systems Inc ......E... 717 843-4240
York *(G-20664)*

▲ Sentinel Holding Inc ....E... 717 843-4240
York *(G-20665)*

▲ Te Connectivity Corporation ....C... 610 893-9800
Berwyn *(G-1376)*

Te Connectivity Corporation.................C... 717 564-0100
Middletown *(G-11078)*

Te Connectivity Corporation.................D... 717 564-0100
Harrisburg *(G-7228)*

Te Connectivity Corporation.................B... 717 861-5000
Jonestown *(G-8452)*

Te Connectivity Corporation.................F... 717 492-1000
Mount Joy *(G-11671)*

Te Connectivity Corporation.................A... 866 743-6440
Middletown *(G-11080)*

Te Connectivity Corporation.................B... 717 986-3743
Middletown *(G-11081)*

Te Connectivity Corporation.................B... 717 653-8151
Mount Joy *(G-11672)*

Te Connectivity Corporation.................B... 717 564-0100
Middletown *(G-11082)*

Te Connectivity Corporation................B......717 564-0100
Harrisburg (G-7229)
Te Connectivity Corporation................C......717 762-9186
Waynesboro (G-19426)
Valley Precision TI & Tech Inc............E......717 647-7550
Tower City (G-18443)
Video Display Corporation.................F......770 938-2080
Howard (G-7892)

3679 Electronic Components, NEC

Ability Systems Corporation...............G......215 657-4338
Abington (G-9)
▲ Acousticsheep LLC.........................F......814 380-9296
Erie (G-5172)
Advanced Electronics Systems............G......717 263-5681
Chambersburg (G-2897)
Ambit Switch.................................G......610 705-9695
Pottstown (G-15962)
▲ American Cable Company.................D......215 456-0700
Philadelphia (G-13380)
American Mfg & Integration LLC..........F......724 861-2080
North Huntingdon (G-12767)
American Military Technologies...........G......215 550-7970
Huntingdon Valley (G-7964)
American Precision Inds Inc...............C......610 235-5499
West Chester (G-19498)
American Products Inc.....................D......717 767-6510
York (G-20375)
Ametek Europe LLC.........................G......610 647-2121
Berwyn (G-1353)
Anderson Electronics LLC.................E......814 695-4428
Hollidaysburg (G-7642)
▲ APC International Ltd......................E......570 726-6961
Mackeyville (G-10137)
Apogee Labs Inc............................E......215 699-2060
North Wales (G-12788)
▲ Avex Electronics Corp....................E......215 245-4848
Bensalem (G-1152)
B and N Electronics........................G......724 484-0164
West Alexander (G-19490)
◆ Black Box Corporation....................G......724 746-5500
Lawrence (G-9535)
Blatek Industries Inc.......................D......814 231-2085
State College (G-17946)
Bliley Technologies Inc....................C......814 838-3571
Erie (G-5214)
Brush Industries Inc........................D......570 286-5611
Sunbury (G-18165)
C M R Usa LLC..............................F......724 452-2200
Leetsdale (G-9687)
Caron Enterprises Inc......................B......814 774-5658
Lake City (G-8898)
Clear Microwave Inc........................F......610 844-6421
Malvern (G-10211)
▲ CMR USA Inc...............................F......724 452-2200
Leetsdale (G-9689)
Coax Incorporated..........................F......717 227-0045
Glen Rock (G-6454)
Com Pros Inc................................G......717 264-2769
Chambersburg (G-2919)
▲ Component Intrtechnologies Inc........E......724 253-3161
Hadley (G-6816)
Conductive Technologies Inc.............D......717 764-6931
York (G-20433)
Continental-Wirt Elec Corp...............C......215 355-7080
Southampton (G-17805)
Controls Service & Repair.................G......412 487-7310
Glenshaw (G-6486)
Corey Associates Inc.......................E......570 676-4800
Greentown (G-6733)
▲ Corry Micronics Inc.......................F......814 664-7728
Corry (G-3754)
Cougar Metals Inc...........................G......724 251-9030
Leetsdale (G-9690)
Cryostar USA.................................G......484 281-3261
Bethlehem (G-1490)
Currency Inc..................................E......814 509-6157
Windber (G-20180)
Current Circuits Inc.........................G......215 444-9295
Warminster (G-18852)
Custom Systems Technology Inc.........G......215 822-2525
Colmar (G-3415)
D L Electronics Inc..........................F......215 742-2666
Philadelphia (G-13600)
Danco Precision Inc.........................E......610 933-1090
Phoenixville (G-14543)
Danco Precision Inc.........................F......610 933-8981
Phoenixville (G-14542)
Dbwave Technologies LLC.................G......412 345-8081
Cranberry Township (G-3815)

◆ Deltronic Labs Inc..........................E......215 997-8616
Chalfont (G-2872)
Diverse Tchnical Solutions LLC...........G......717 630-8522
Hanover (G-6877)
▲ Diversified Traffic Pdts Inc...............C......717 428-0222
Seven Valleys (G-17377)
Dynamic Manufacturing LLC...............D......724 295-4200
Freeport (G-6203)
E-Nanomedsys LLC.........................G......917 734-1462
State College (G-17958)
▲ Eaglerise E&E Inc..........................E......215 675-5953
Warminster (G-18867)
EBY Group LLC..............................E......215 537-4700
Philadelphia (G-13657)
Effective Shielding Company..............F......610 429-9449
West Chester (G-19547)
Electro Soft Inc..............................E......215 654-0701
Montgomeryville (G-11394)
Electronic Assembly Co Inc................E......215 799-0600
Souderton (G-17732)
Electronic Prototype Dev Inc...............E......412 767-4111
Natrona Heights (G-11941)
Element Id Inc................................F......610 419-8822
Bethlehem (G-1501)
Energy Products & Technologies..........G......717 485-3137
Mc Connellsburg (G-10564)
Epoxtal LLC..................................G......908 376-9825
Philadelphia (G-13676)
Equate Space-Time Tech LLC.............G......814 838-3571
Erie (G-5261)
Erie Specialty Products Inc.................E......814 453-5611
Erie (G-5274)
◆ Everson Tesla Inc...........................D......610 746-1520
Nazareth (G-11965)
Excel-Pro.....................................G......610 845-9752
Barto (G-942)
Fargo Assemblies...........................G......610 272-5726
Norristown (G-12656)
Fargo Assembly of Pa Inc..................C......717 866-5800
Richland (G-16687)
▲ Fargo Assembly of Pa Inc................C......610 272-6850
Norristown (G-12657)
▲ FCG Inc......................................C......215 343-4617
Warrington (G-19117)
Ford City Gun Workd........................G......724 994-9501
Ford City (G-6045)
Galaxy Wire and Cable Inc.................F......215 957-8714
Horsham (G-7820)
Gby Corporation.............................D......724 539-1626
Latrobe (G-9478)
Genesys Controls Corporation............F......717 291-1116
Landisville (G-9261)
Genie Electronics Co Inc...................E......717 840-6999
York (G-20496)
Gorden Inc...................................G......610 644-4476
Reading (G-16395)
Greenray Industries Inc....................E......717 766-0223
Mechanicsburg (G-10850)
Halsit Holdings LLC.........................E......814 724-6440
Meadville (G-10733)
▲ Heraeus Quartz America LLC............D......512 703-9000
Yardley (G-20317)
Heraeus Quartz America LLC..............G......512 251-2027
Yardley (G-20318)
Herley Industries Inc........................E......717 397-2779
Lancaster (G-9044)
Herley Industries Inc........................B......717 397-2777
Lancaster (G-9043)
Hoffman Materials Inc.......................E......717 243-2011
Carlisle (G-2718)
Homeland Mfg Svcs Inc....................F......814 862-9103
State College (G-17976)
Hound Dog Corp.............................G......215 355-6424
Huntingdon Valley (G-7994)
Ifm Efector Inc...............................D......610 524-2000
Auburn (G-816)
▲ Ifm Efector Inc..............................C......800 441-8246
Malvern (G-10252)
▲ Industrial Enterprises Inc.................D......215 355-7080
Southampton (G-17819)
Industrial Enterprises Inc...................G......215 355-7080
Warminster (G-18897)
Infineon Tech Americas Corp..............D......610 712-7100
Allentown (G-258)
▲ Integrated Power Designs Inc............D......570 824-4666
Hanover Township (G-6990)
Integrted Assembly Systems Inc..........E......724 746-6532
Canonsburg (G-2597)
◆ Iqe Rf LLC...................................D......732 271-5990
Bethlehem (G-1541)

Iqe Usa Inc...................................D......610 861-6930
Bethlehem (G-1542)
J K Miller Corp...............................E......412 922-5070
Pittsburgh (G-15143)
Juergensen Defense Corporation.........G......814 395-9509
Addison (G-27)
Keystone Controls Company...............G......215 355-7080
Southampton (G-17820)
Keystone Crystal Corporation.............G......724 282-1506
Butler (G-2416)
Keystone Electronics Inc...................E......717 747-5900
York (G-20553)
Keystone Test Solutions Inc...............G......814 733-4490
Schellsburg (G-17133)
Kinetic Ceramics LLC.......................G......510 264-2140
Philadelphia (G-13937)
Kitron Holding USA Inc.....................G......814 467-9060
Windber (G-20186)
L3 Electron Devices Inc....................C......570 326-3561
Williamsport (G-20033)
L3 Technologies Inc........................C......267 545-7000
Bristol (G-2157)
Laboratory Control Systems Inc...........G......570 487-2490
Scott Township (G-17184)
Liberty Electronics.........................B......814 676-0600
Reno (G-16646)
▲ Liberty Electronics Inc....................B......814 432-7505
Franklin (G-6148)
▲ Lynn Electronics Corp.....................D......215 355-8200
Ivyland (G-8216)
Lynn Electronics Corp.......................E......215 826-9600
Bristol (G-2163)
Lynn Electronics Corp......................G......954 977-3800
Warminster (G-18915)
▲ Majr Products Corporation................E......814 763-3211
Saegertown (G-16925)
Malvern Scale Data Systems...............G......610 296-9642
Malvern (G-10274)
Maro Electronics Inc........................E......215 788-7919
Bristol (G-2164)
Martek Power Laser Drive LLC.............D......805 383-5548
Pittsburgh (G-15259)
◆ Matric Group LLC...........................B......814 677-0716
Seneca (G-17366)
Mbpj Corporation............................G......814 461-9120
Erie (G-5384)
Mdbel Inc.....................................G......215 738-3383
Southampton (G-17825)
Micro Oscillator Inc.........................G......610 617-8682
Bala Cynwyd (G-886)
Micro-Coax Inc..............................C......610 495-4438
Pottstown (G-16019)
Micromechatronics Inc.....................G......814 861-5688
State College (G-17990)
Microsphere Inc.............................G......610 444-3450
Kennett Square (G-8528)
National Magnetics Group Inc.............G......610 867-6003
Bethlehem (G-1582)
National Scientific Company...............G......215 536-2577
Quakertown (G-16222)
Nichols Electronics Inc.....................G......724 668-2526
Greensburg (G-6693)
◆ Nicomatic LP................................E......215 444-9580
Horsham (G-7836)
Nolatron Inc..................................G......717 564-3398
Harrisburg (G-7184)
Northeimer Manufacturing..................E......610 926-1136
Leesport (G-9672)
Nth Solutions LLC...........................G......610 594-2191
Exton (G-5715)
Olympus Advanced Tech LLC.............G......814 838-3571
Erie (G-5408)
Oneida Instant Log.........................E......814 336-2125
Meadville (G-10770)
▲ Performance Controls Inc.................E......215 619-4920
Montgomeryville (G-11412)
Phlexglobal Inc..............................D......484 324-7921
Malvern (G-10296)
▲ Piezo Kinetics Inc..........................E......814 355-1593
Bellefonte (G-1112)
Powell Electro Systems LLC...............F......610 869-8393
West Grove (G-19704)
▲ Power Products Inc.........................G......610 532-3880
Sharon Hill (G-17459)
Powercast Corporation.....................G......412 455-5800
Pittsburgh (G-15422)
Precision Glass Products Co...............F......215 885-0145
Oreland (G-13028)
◆ Pulser LLC...................................E......215 781-6400
Bristol (G-2189)

**S
I
C**

Pulser LLC ....E 215 781-6400
Bristol (G-2190)

Qualastat Electronics Inc ....E 717 253-9301
Gettysburg (G-6311)

R F Circuits & Cad Services ......G 215 368-6483
Harleysville (G-7053)

Rcd Technology Inc ....F 215 529-9440
Newtown (G-12542)

Retrolinear Inc ....G 215 699-8000
North Wales (G-12827)

Richard J Clickett Inc ....E 814 827-7548
Titusville (G-18391)

▲ Saint-Gobain Ceramics Plas Inc ......A 508 795-5000
Valley Forge (G-18711)

Sanford Miller Inc ....G 724 479-5090
Homer City (G-7681)

▲ Sendec Corp ....C 585 425-3390
Windber (G-20192)

Sense Technology Inc ....G 724 733-2277
Halifax (G-6831)

Sensor Corporation ....G 724 887-4080
Scottdale (G-17200)

Servedio A Elc Mtr Svc Inc ....F 724 658-8041
New Castle (G-12148)

Silicon Power Corporation ....D 610 407-4700
Malvern (G-10317)

Simco Industrial Static Cntrl ......D 215 822-2171
Hatfield (G-7396)

◆ Smiths Group North America Inc ......F 772 286-9300
Malvern (G-10322)

Smt Manufacturing Group LLC ....E 717 767-4900
York (G-20670)

Snakable Inc ....G 347 449-3378
Prospect Park (G-16120)

Solar Transformers Inc ....F 267 384-5231
Telford (G-18316)

Souders Industries Inc ....E 717 271-4975
Waynesboro (G-19424)

▲ Souders Industries Inc ....D 717 749-3900
Mont Alto (G-11365)

▲ Sound Technology Inc ....C 814 234-4377
State College (G-18029)

Spang & Company ....C 412 963-9363
Pittsburgh (G-15567)

◆ Spectrum Microwave Inc ....D 814 474-4300
Fairview (G-5847)

Spectrum Microwave Inc ....D 215 464-0586
Philadelphia (G-14333)

Spectrum Microwave Inc ....E 814 272-2700
State College (G-18033)

◆ SPS Technologies LLC ....A 215 572-3000
Jenkintown (G-8302)

Te Connectivity Corporation ....C 717 492-2000
Manheim (G-10405)

Te Connectivity Corporation ....C 717 898-4302
Landisville (G-9267)

Te Connectivity Corporation ....D 717 691-5842
Mechanicsburg (G-10895)

Te Connectivity Foundation ....E 717 810-2987
Berwyn (G-1377)

Telan Corporation ....E 215 822-1234
Hatfield (G-7400)

Thin Film Industries Inc ....G 267 316-9999
Morrisville (G-11585)

Thin Labs Inc ....G 215 269-3322
Fairless Hills (G-5804)

▲ Tobii Dynavox LLC ....C 412 381-4883
Pittsburgh (G-15630)

Tq Electronics Inc ....G 570 320-1760
Williamsport (G-20084)

Traffic Maintenance Attenuator ....G 215 997-1272
Hatfield (G-7403)

Trak Ceramics Inc ....E 610 867-7600
Bethlehem (G-1640)

Trs Technologies Inc ....E 814 238-7485
State College (G-18040)

▲ Tsrubnus Liquidation Inc ....D 814 461-9120
Erie (G-5520)

Ultravoice Ltd ....G 610 356-6443
Newtown Square (G-12595)

Union Switch and Signal ....G 412 688-2400
Pittsburgh (G-15672)

Vizinex LLC ....G 215 529-9440
Bethlehem (G-1652)

Weld Tooling Corporation ....E 412 331-1776
Canonsburg (G-2658)

Wire Works Enterprises Inc ....F 610 485-1981
Chester (G-3069)

▲ Wmi Group Inc ....F 215 822-2525
Colmar (G-3425)

Wunsch Technologies Corp ....E 610 207-0628
Birdsboro (G-1709)

Z-Band Technologies LLC ....G 717 249-2606
Carlisle (G-2752)

3691 Storage Batteries

◆ Aquion Energy Inc ....C 412 904-6400
Pittsburgh (G-14715)

▲ Avex Electronics Corp ....E 215 245-4848
Bensalem (G-1152)

Battery Tech LLC ....G 570 253-6908
Honesdale (G-7702)

▲ Battery Zone ....F 800 371-5033
Bethlehem (G-1458)

◆ C&D Technologies Inc ....C 215 619-2700
Blue Bell (G-1820)

CD Technologies Inc ....E 215 619-2700
Horsham (G-7801)

▲ Cell-Con Inc ....D 800 771-7139
Exton (G-5660)

Cell-Con Inc ....E 814 623-7057
Bedford (G-1046)

East Penn Manufacturing Co ....F 412 793-0283
Pittsburgh (G-14956)

East Penn Manufacturing Co ....F 610 682-6361
Topton (G-18411)

East Penn Manufacturing Co ....E 610 682-6361
Kutztown (G-8840)

Enersys ....D 724 223-4255
Washington (G-19169)

Enersys ....F 215 420-1000
Warminster (G-18873)

◆ Enersys ....C 610 208-1991
Reading (G-16375)

Enersys Capital Inc ....F 610 208-1991
Reading (G-16376)

▲ Enersys Delaware Inc ....B 214 324-8990
Reading (G-16377)

Enersys Delaware Inc ....G 484 244-4150
Allentown (G-206)

Exide Corporation Smelter ....F 610 921-4003
Reading (G-16382)

Exide Technologies ....C 717 464-2721
Lampeter (G-8917)

Exide Technologies ....G 610 269-0429
Downingtown (G-4226)

Exide Technologies ....G 304 345-5616
Rostraver Township (G-16826)

Juline-Titans LLC ....F 412 352-4744
Pittsburgh (G-15158)

Lithium Technology Corporation ....G 888 776-0942
Plymouth Meeting (G-15854)

Maxpower Inc ....F 215 256-4575
Harleysville (G-7047)

New Castle Battery Mfg Co ....C 724 658-5501
New Castle (G-12127)

Northeast Indus Batteries Inc ....E 215 788-8000
Bristol (G-2172)

▲ Philadelphia Scientific LLC ....E 215 616-0390
Montgomeryville (G-11414)

Rm Battery Doctors LLC ....G 570 441-9184
Millville (G-11227)

3692 Primary Batteries: Dry & Wet

▲ Axion Power Battery Mfg Inc .....E 724 654-9300
New Castle (G-12061)

▲ Battery Builders Inc ....G 717 751-2705
Red Lion (G-16590)

▲ Battery Zone ....F 800 371-5033
Bethlehem (G-1458)

◆ C&D Technologies Inc ....C 215 619-2700
Blue Bell (G-1820)

CD Technologies Inc ....E 215 619-2700
Horsham (G-7801)

▼ E I T Corporation Phoenix ....F 570 286-7744
Sunbury (G-18168)

Energizer Battery Co ....G 215 572-0200
Jenkintown (G-8286)

▲ Enersys Advanced Systems Inc ......D 215 674-3800
Horsham (G-7816)

◆ Yuasa Battery Inc ....B 610 929-5781
Reading (G-16571)

3694 Electrical Eqpt For Internal Combustion Engines

Alcolock PA Inc ....G 800 452-1759
Mechanicsburg (G-10817)

Allied Tube & Conduit Corp ....B 215 676-6464
Philadelphia (G-13369)

◆ Atc Technology Corporation ......E 412 820-3700
Cranberry Township (G-3806)

Auto Diesel Electric Inc ....G 570 874-2100
Frackville (G-6102)

▲ Chargeitspot LLC ....C 215 220-6600
Philadelphia (G-13526)

Creative Engnred Solutions Inc .....G 570 655-3399
Pittston (G-15747)

East Penn Manufacturing Co ....G 610 929-4920
Reading (G-16368)

East Penn Manufacturing Co ....E 610 682-6361
Kutztown (G-8840)

Ecobee Advanced Tech LLC ....G 609 474-0010
Warminster (G-18869)

◆ Fci USA LLC ....B 717 938-7200
Etters (G-5548)

▲ Flight Systems Auto Group LLC ......C 717 932-7000
Lewisberry (G-9886)

Industrial Harness Company Inc .....D 717 477-0100
Shippensburg (G-17532)

▲ Kalas Mfg Inc ....G 717 336-5575
Lancaster (G-9078)

Keystone Automatic Tech Inc ....E 814 486-0513
Emporium (G-5066)

Kuhn Auto Electric ....G 717 632-4197
Hanover (G-6912)

Martins Starter Service ....G 814 398-2496
Cambridge Springs (G-2482)

Moore Performance Pwr Pdts LLC ......G 610 507-2344
Reading (G-16448)

Northeimer Manufacturing ....E 610 926-1136
Leesport (G-9672)

Penntex Industries Inc ....G 717 266-8762
Manchester (G-10360)

Pittsburgh Electric Engs Inc ....F 724 547-9170
Mount Pleasant (G-11711)

Plan B Consultants LLC ....G 215 638-0767
Huntington Valley (G-8026)

R T Grim Co ....E 717 761-4113
Camp Hill (G-2513)

▲ Reading Electric Motor Svc Inc ......D 610 929-5777
Reading (G-16490)

Remote Remotes ....G 215 420-7934
Horsham (G-7846)

S T M Heavy Duty Electric Inc ......F 610 967-3810
Zionsville (G-20836)

Steins Pasco Battery Starter ....G 215 969-6900
Philadelphia (G-14343)

3695 Recording Media

Agent Dynamics Inc ....G 412 441-4604
Pittsburgh (G-14656)

Binary Research Inc ....E 215 233-3200
Ambler (G-570)

Blue Golf Com ....G 909 592-6411
Wayne (G-19308)

Caliburn Inc ....G 610 429-9500
West Chester (G-19516)

E Instruments Group LLC ....G 215 750-1212
Langhorne (G-9291)

Integrted Productivity Systems ......G 215 646-1374
Blue Bell (G-1836)

▲ James Jesse & Co Inc ....E 610 419-9880
Bethlehem (G-1544)

▼ Magnetizer Industrial Tech ....G 215 766-9150
Hatfield (G-7367)

▲ Optium Corporation ....D 215 675-3105
Horsham (G-7838)

Poonam International Inc ....G 215 968-1555
Newtown (G-12538)

Spang & Company ....E 724 376-7515
Sandy Lake (G-17062)

3699 Electrical Machinery, Eqpt & Splys, NEC

3 T Secuirty LLC ....G 717 653-0019
Manheim (G-10366)

3si Security Systems Inc ....D 800 523-1430
Malvern (G-10176)

3si Security Systems Holdg Inc .....G 610 280-2000
Malvern (G-10177)

Abe Alarm Service ....G 484 664-7304
Allentown (G-113)

Advanced Integration Group Inc .....E 412 722-0065
Mc Kees Rocks (G-10602)

Advanced PDT Design & Mfg Inc ......E 610 380-9140
Coatesville (G-3284)

◆ Aerotech Inc ....B 412 963-7470
Pittsburgh (G-14655)

▼ Air-Scent International ....D 412 252-2000
Pittsburgh (G-14658)

Ajm Electric Inc ..... G 610 494-5735
Chester Township (G-3088)
Alert Enterprises Ltd Lblty Co ..... G 570 373-2821
Kulpmont (G-8821)
Allentown Auto Electric LLC ..... G 610 432-2888
Allentown (G-127)
Alpine Electric ..... G 412 257-4827
Bridgeville (G-2053)
API Cryptek Inc ..... F 908 546-3900
State College (G-17941)
Arm Camco LLC ..... E 814 472-7980
Ebensburg (G-4779)
Asr Enterprises Inc ..... G 610 873-7484
Downingtown (G-4211)
▲ Battery Zone ..... F 800 371-5033
Bethlehem (G-1458)
Black & Decker (us) Inc ..... A 610 797-6600
Allentown (G-154)
Bosch Security Systems Inc ..... B 717 735-6300
Lancaster (G-8957)
Branson Ultrasonics Corp ..... E 610 251-9776
Paoli (G-13136)
Bsg Corporation ..... G 267 230-0514
Huntingdon Valley (G-7966)
Colonial Electric Supply Inc ..... G 610 935-2493
Phoenixville (G-14540)
Corey Associates Inc ..... E 570 676-4800
Greentown (G-6733)
Covenant Group of China Inc ..... D 610 660-7828
Bala Cynwyd (G-876)
Custom Ultrasonics Inc ..... D 215 364-1477
Ivyland (G-8208)
D L George & Sons Mfg Inc ..... D 717 765-4700
Waynesboro (G-19407)
D&D Security Solutions LLC ..... G 484 614-7024
Landenberg (G-9248)
Delta Information Systems Inc ..... E 215 657-5270
Horsham (G-7809)
Demco Enterprises Inc ..... F 888 419-3343
Quakertown (G-16184)
▲ Design Decorators ..... E 215 634-8300
Philadelphia (G-13620)
Digital Designs Inc ..... F 215 781-2525
Levittown (G-9832)
▲ Direct Wire & Cable Inc ..... D 717 336-2842
Denver (G-4070)
◆ Dual Core LLC ..... D 800 233-0298
Manheim (G-10379)
▼ Duryea Technologies Inc ..... G 610 939-0480
Reading (G-16366)
Dvm Manufacturing LLC ..... F 215 839-3425
Warminster (G-18864)
E F E Laboratories Inc ..... E 215 672-2400
Horsham (G-7812)
Eagle Energy Systems Ltd ..... E 610 444-3388
Kennett Square (G-8509)
Eko Solutions Plus Inc ..... G 215 856-9517
Elkins Park (G-4902)
▲ Electri-Cord Manufacturing Co ..... C 814 367-2265
Westfield (G-19777)
Electric City Baseball & Soft ..... G 570 955-0471
Scranton (G-17232)
Electric City Yoga ..... G 570 558-9642
Scranton (G-17233)
Emergensee Inc ..... E 610 804-9007
Malvern (G-10230)
◆ Enersys ..... C 610 208-1991
Reading (G-16375)
Evaporated Coatings Inc ..... E 215 659-3080
Willow Grove (G-20116)
◆ Everson Tesla Inc ..... D 610 746-1520
Nazareth (G-11965)
Extorr Inc ..... F 724 337-3000
New Kensington (G-12339)
Fargo Assembly of Pa Inc ..... C 717 866-5800
Richland (G-16687)
Faro Laser Division LLC ..... G 610 444-2300
Kennett Square (G-8510)
Faro Technologies Inc ..... G 412 559-7737
Pittsburgh (G-15005)
Fclz Holdings Inc ..... F 412 788-4991
Pittsburgh (G-15007)
FEC Technologies Inc ..... E 717 764-5959
York (G-20477)
Fiber Optic Designs Inc ..... G 215 321-9750
Yardley (G-20311)
Fidelity Flight Simulation Inc ..... F 412 321-3280
Pittsburgh (G-15016)
Fitz Security Co Inc ..... G 717 272-5020
Lebanon (G-9569)
Five Star Associates Inc ..... F 610 588-7426
Bangor (G-913)
Fluid Intelligence LLC ..... G 610 405-2698
Berwyn (G-1362)
Fromm Elc Sup Corp Rding Penna ..... G 570 387-9711
Bloomsburg (G-1783)
Gamlet Inc ..... D 717 852-9200
York (G-20489)
▲ Gerome Manufacturing Co Inc ..... D 724 438-8544
Smithfield (G-17650)
Gexpro ..... G 570 265-2420
Towanda (G-18428)
Glen L Myers Inc ..... G 717 352-0035
Fayetteville (G-5877)
Grid Elc & Solar Solutions LLC ..... G 717 885-5249
York (G-20514)
Gsi ..... G 610 667-4271
Penn Valley (G-13236)
◆ Gupta Permold Corporation ..... C 412 793-3511
Pittsburgh (G-15067)
Harlan Electric ..... G 717 243-4600
Harrisburg (G-7140)
Homewood Energy Services Corp ..... G 256 882-2796
Pittsburgh (G-15098)
Horizon Electric Lighting LLC ..... G 267 288-5353
Richboro (G-16675)
Ictv Holdings Inc ..... F 484 598-2300
Wayne (G-19337)
Ifco Enterprises Inc ..... C 610 651-0999
Malvern (G-10251)
▲ Ii-VI Incorporated ..... B 724 352-4455
Saxonburg (G-17088)
Integrated Securty & Communctn ..... E 610 397-0988
Plymouth Meeting (G-15853)
Jeffers & Leek Electric Inc ..... G 724 384-0315
New Brighton (G-12038)
Jod Contracting Inc ..... G 724 323-2124
Fayette City (G-5875)
John A Romeo & Associates Inc ..... F 724 586-6961
Butler (G-2413)
Kirkwood Electric ..... G 814 467-7171
Windber (G-20185)
Kykayke Inc ..... G 610 522-0106
Holmes (G-7663)
Laserfab Inc ..... F 717 272-0060
Lebanon (G-9598)
Lengyel Electric ..... G 724 475-2045
Fredonia (G-6186)
Lighthouse Enrgy Solutions LLC ..... G 610 269-0113
Morgantown (G-11525)
Maro Electronics Inc ..... E 215 788-7919
Bristol (G-2164)
Martin Communications Inc ..... F 412 498-0157
Mc Kees Rocks (G-10619)
▲ Miller Edge Inc ..... D 610 869-4422
West Grove (G-19702)
Millstat LLC ..... F 610 783-0181
Phoenixville (G-14561)
Mititech LLC ..... G 410 309-9447
Chambersburg (G-2960)
▲ Navitek Group Inc ..... G 814 474-2312
Fairview (G-5834)
Northeimer Manufacturing ..... E 610 926-1136
Leesport (G-9672)
Novasentis Inc ..... F 814 238-7400
State College (G-18002)
Nuwave Technologies Inc ..... G 610 584-8428
Norristown (G-12695)
Oakwood Controls Corporation ..... F 717 801-1515
Glen Rock (G-6458)
Overhead Door Corporation ..... D 215 368-8700
Lansdale (G-9396)
▲ Precision Cstm Components LLC ..... B 717 848-1126
York (G-20638)
Precision Technical Sales LLC ..... G 610 282-4541
Coopersburg (G-3634)
Profi Vision Inc ..... G 610 530-2025
Allentown (G-361)
Qortek Inc ..... G 570 322-2700
Williamsport (G-20066)
Raco International LP ..... F 412 835-5744
Bethel Park (G-1430)
▲ Reecon North America LLC ..... G 412 850-8001
Pittsburgh (G-15475)
Reliant Systems LLC ..... G 412 496-2580
Irwin (G-8196)
Response Electric Inc ..... G 215 799-2400
Green Lane (G-6592)
Reynolds & Reynolds Elec Inc ..... F 484 221-6381
Bethlehem (G-1610)
Rfcircuits Inc ..... F 215 364-2450
Huntingdon Valley (G-8029)
Right Reason Technologies LLC ..... G 484 898-1967
Bethlehem (G-1611)
Rockwell Collins Inc ..... F 610 925-5844
Kennett Square (G-8540)
▼ Ross Security Systems LLC ..... E 717 656-2200
Leola (G-9801)
Royal Karina Air Service Inc ..... G 215 321-3981
Yardley (G-20336)
Sales Marketing Group Inc ..... G 412 928-0422
Pittsburgh (G-15507)
Salus Security Devices LLC ..... G 610 388-6387
West Chester (G-19635)
Schneder Elc Bldngs Amrcas Inc ..... E 215 441-4389
Horsham (G-7849)
Semilab USA LLC ..... F 610 377-5990
Lehighton (G-9726)
Sensor Networks Inc ..... E 814 466-7207
Boalsburg (G-1869)
Shepherd Good Work Services ..... C 610 776-8353
Allentown (G-388)
Simulation Live Fire Training ..... G 412 787-2832
Pittsburgh (G-15540)
▲ Sinacom North America Inc ..... E 610 337-2250
King of Prussia (G-8677)
Slater Electric & Sons ..... G 724 306-1060
Prospect (G-16112)
Solid State Eqp Holdings LLC ..... G 215 328-0700
Horsham (G-7850)
▲ Sonic Systems Inc ..... E 267 803-1964
Warminster (G-18967)
Sonobond Ultrasonics Inc ..... F 610 696-4710
West Chester (G-19642)
Spang & Company ..... E 724 376-7515
Sandy Lake (G-17062)
SPD Electrical Systems Inc ..... B 215 698-6426
Philadelphia (G-14331)
Spec Sciences Inc ..... G 607 972-3159
Sharon (G-17443)
Stanley Access Tech LLC ..... G 570 368-1435
Montgomery (G-11380)
Stanley Industrial & Auto LLC ..... C 800 523-9462
Allentown (G-400)
▲ Stanley Vidmar ..... E 610 797-6600
Allentown (G-402)
Steimer and Co Inc ..... F 610 933-7450
Phoenixville (G-14579)
Synergy Contracting Svcs LLC ..... E 724 349-0855
Indiana (G-8132)
Synergy Electrical Sales Inc ..... F 215 428-1130
Fairless Hills (G-5801)
T T M Contacts Corporation ..... G 215 497-1078
Newtown (G-12554)
Tactical Technologies Inc ..... E 610 522-0106
Holmes (G-7665)
Tecnomasium Inc ..... F 412 264-7364
Coraopolis (G-3727)
Tgb I LLC ..... C 724 431-3090
Saxonburg (G-17096)
Titan Security Group LLC ..... F 914 474-2221
Lancaster (G-9219)
Titanium Metals Corporation ..... E 702 564-2544
Morgantown (G-11539)
Trexler Industries Inc ..... E 610 974-9800
Bethlehem (G-1641)
Tri-Rivers Electric Inc ..... G 412 290-6525
Pittsburgh (G-15646)
Tridex Technology Ltd ..... F 484 388-5000
Philadelphia (G-14410)
Tru-Lite International Inc ..... G 724 443-6821
Gibsonia (G-6356)
Two M Electric Inc ..... F 215 530-9964
Warminster (G-18988)
▲ Universal Electric Corporation ..... B 724 597-7800
Canonsburg (G-2652)
Videoray LLC ..... E 610 458-3000
Pottstown (G-16067)
Wesco Distribution Inc ..... F 724 772-5000
Warrendale (G-19101)
▲ Windurance LLC ..... B 412 424-8900
Coraopolis (G-3733)
Wistex II LLC ..... G 215 328-9100
Warminster (G-19002)
Wm Industries Inc ..... G 215 822-2525
Colmar (G-3423)
Wm Robots, LLC ..... F 215 822-2525
Colmar (G-3424)
▼ Zareba Systems Inc ..... D 763 551-1125
Lititz (G-10061)

37 TRANSPORTATION EQUIPMENT

3711 Motor Vehicles & Car Bodies

Aircooled Racing and Parts ....G 717 432-4116
Wellsville *(G-19476)*

American Classic Motors Inc ....F 610 754-8500
Zieglerville *(G-20831)*

B & C Auto Wreckers Inc ....G 570 547-1040
Montgomery *(G-11367)*

Ben Cook Racing Ltd ....G 570 788-4223
Sugarloaf *(G-18152)*

Blockcom ....G 215 794-9575
Doylestown *(G-4277)*

Bowser Pontiac Inc ....C 412 469-2100
Pittsburgh *(G-14787)*

Bugstuff ....G 724 785-7000
Brownsville *(G-2310)*

Carriers Wreckers By Kimes ....G 724 342-2930
Mercer *(G-10960)*

▲ Cheetah Chassis Corporation ....C 570 752-2708
Berwick *(G-1317)*

Dan Donahue ....G 814 336-3262
Meadville *(G-10718)*

Dangelos Custom Built Mfg LLC ....F 814 837-6053
Kane *(G-8462)*

Diamond Hvy Vhcl Solutions LLC ....G 717 695-9378
Harrisburg *(G-7119)*

East Coast Partners LLC ....D 215 207-9360
Philadelphia *(G-13655)*

Edward H Quay Welding Spc ....G 610 326-8050
Pottstown *(G-15985)*

Filly Fabricating Inc ....G 412 896-6452
North Versailles *(G-12774)*

Garnon Truck Equipment Inc ....F 814 833-6000
Erie *(G-5300)*

Gregory Racing Fabrications ....G 610 759-8217
Nazareth *(G-11970)*

Harners Auto Body Inc ....G 610 385-3825
Birdsboro *(G-1698)*

Hot Rod Fabrications LLP ....G 717 774-6302
New Cumberland *(G-12186)*

▲ Ibis Tek Inc ....D 724 431-3000
Butler *(G-2407)*

Ibis Tek Holdings Inc ....G 724 431-3000
Butler *(G-2409)*

Industrial Food Truck LLC ....F 215 596-0010
Philadelphia *(G-13854)*

Interntnal Def Systems USA LLC ....G 610 973-2228
Orefield *(G-13012)*

▲ Kovatch Corp ....D 570 669-5130
Nesquehoning *(G-12006)*

◆ Kovatch Mobile Equipment Corp ......A 570 669-9461
Nesquehoning *(G-12007)*

▲ Lge Coachworks Inc ....G 814 434-0856
North East *(G-12750)*

◆ Louis Berkman Company ....E 740 283-3722
Pittsburgh *(G-15238)*

◆ Mack Defense LLC ....E 484 387-5911
Allentown *(G-304)*

Mack Trucks Inc ....C 717 939-1338
Middletown *(G-11064)*

Mack Trucks Inc ....A 610 966-8800
Macungie *(G-10154)*

Martz Chassis Inc ....G 814 623-9501
Bedford *(G-1063)*

Murrysville Auto LLC ....F 724 387-1607
Murrysville *(G-11860)*

Navistar Inc ....D 717 767-3800
Manchester *(G-10358)*

Outlaw Performance Inc ....E 724 697-4876
Avonmore *(G-866)*

Paccar Inc ....E 717 397-4111
Lancaster *(G-9157)*

◆ Philip Cooke ....G 717 854-4081
York *(G-20627)*

Riggeals Performance Fibrgls ....G 717 677-4167
Gettysburg *(G-6312)*

Rizworks ....G 570 226-7611
Hawley *(G-7437)*

Roadside PA LLC ....G 412 464-1452
Pittsburgh *(G-15492)*

Rockland Coach Works LLC ....G 610 682-2830
Mertztown *(G-11003)*

S & W Race Cars Components Inc ....E 610 948-7303
Spring City *(G-17865)*

Skyline Auto Supply LLC ....G 484 365-4040
Easton *(G-4752)*

Smeal Ltc LLC ....E 717 918-1806
Ephrata *(G-5142)*

Spartan Motors Usa Inc ....F 605 582-4000
Ephrata *(G-5144)*

◆ Specialty Vhcl Solutions LLC ....E 609 882-1900
Warminster *(G-18972)*

▲ Steelway Cellar Doors LLC ....F 610 277-9988
King of Prussia *(G-8680)*

Superior Custom Designs Inc ....G 412 744-0110
Glassport *(G-6416)*

Tesla Inc ....F 484 235-5858
King of Prussia *(G-8686)*

Upper Milford Western Dst Fire ....G 610 966-3541
Zionsville *(G-20837)*

Versalift East LLC ....C 610 866-1400
Bethlehem *(G-1651)*

Wayne Abel Repairs ....G 610 857-1708
Parkesburg *(G-13185)*

William T Jenkins ....G 610 644-7052
Malvern *(G-10346)*

◆ Wolfington Body Company Inc ....C 610 458-8501
Exton *(G-5751)*

Wood Racing Products LLC ....G 717 454-7003
Pine Grove *(G-14608)*

3713 Truck & Bus Bodies

Altec Industries Inc ....C 570 822-3104
Wilkes Barre *(G-19904)*

Andrew Billets & Son Inc ....G 570 207-7253
Scranton *(G-17208)*

Asco Enterprises Inc ....G 724 945-5525
Scenery Hill *(G-17124)*

Asone Technologies Inc ....E 570 443-5700
White Haven *(G-19846)*

▲ Champion Carrier Corporation ....E 724 981-3328
Hermitage *(G-7576)*

Columbia Industries Inc ....E 570 520-4048
Berwick *(G-1318)*

Commonwealth Utility Eqp Inc ....E 724 283-8400
Butler *(G-2390)*

Conrad Enterprises Inc ....E 717 274-5151
Cornwall *(G-3738)*

D K Hostetler Inc ....F 717 667-3921
Milroy *(G-11229)*

Darco Inc ....E 717 597-7139
Greencastle *(G-6605)*

Dayton Parts LLC ....F 717 255-8548
Harrisburg *(G-7115)*

Driban Body Works Inc ....G 215 468-6900
Philadelphia *(G-13648)*

East Penn Truck Eqp W Inc ....G 724 342-1800
Mercer *(G-10961)*

East Penn Truck Equipment Inc ....G 610 694-9234
Bethlehem *(G-1500)*

Envirnmntal Enrgy Slutions LLC ....G 814 446-5625
Seward *(G-17381)*

Gra-Ter Industries Inc ....G 570 658-7652
Beavertown *(G-1026)*

Gsp Marketing Inc ....E 814 445-5866
Somerset *(G-17692)*

Harners Auto Body Inc ....G 610 385-3825
Birdsboro *(G-1698)*

Heritage Truck Equipment LLC ....G 215 256-0951
Harleysville *(G-7039)*

Hewey Welding ....G 717 867-5222
Lebanon *(G-9580)*

Hill John M Machine Co Inc ....E 610 562-8690
Hamburg *(G-6841)*

Imperial Truck Body & Eqp ....F 724 695-3165
Imperial *(G-8067)*

J C Moore Industries Inc ....F 724 475-3185
Fredonia *(G-6181)*

J C Moore Industries Sales ....G 724 475-3185
Fredonia *(G-6182)*

J C Moore Sales Corp ....G 724 475-4605
Fredonia *(G-6183)*

J Thomas Ltd ....E 717 397-3483
Lancaster *(G-9069)*

Jerrdan Corporation ....D 717 597-7111
Greencastle *(G-6620)*

▲ Jones Performance Products Inc ......D 724 528-3569
West Middlesex *(G-19727)*

Ken-Co Company Inc ....E 724 887-7070
Scottdale *(G-17194)*

◆ M H EBY Inc ....C 800 292-4752
Blue Ball *(G-1811)*

Maxwell Truck & Equipment LLC ....G 814 359-2672
Pleasant Gap *(G-15794)*

McNeilus Truck and Mfg Inc ....E 610 286-0400
Morgantown *(G-11527)*

▲ Merlot Trpulin Sidekit Mfg Inc ....E 412 828-7664
Verona *(G-18757)*

Metalsa SA De CV ....C 610 371-7000
Reading *(G-16441)*

Mid Atlantic Municipal LLC ....E 717 394-2647
Lancaster *(G-9134)*

Morgan Truck Body LLC ....C 717 733-8644
Ephrata *(G-5130)*

New Harrisburg Truck Body Co ....E 717 766-7651
Mechanicsburg *(G-10873)*

Penn Fabrication LLC ....F 610 292-1980
Norristown *(G-12702)*

R E B Inc ....G 215 538-7875
Quakertown *(G-16240)*

Reading Equipment & Dist LLC ....E 717 445-6746
Abington *(G-14)*

◆ Reading Truck Body LLC ....C 610 775-3301
Reading *(G-16493)*

Riggs Industries Inc ....F 814 629-5621
Stoystown *(G-18085)*

Rizworks ....G 570 226-7611
Hawley *(G-7437)*

Sabre Equipment Inc ....E 412 262-3080
Coraopolis *(G-3725)*

Samco Inc ....G 814 495-4632
Saint Michael *(G-17032)*

Sixth Wheel Inc ....G 610 647-0880
Malvern *(G-10318)*

Somerset Welding & Steel Inc ....C 814 443-2671
Somerset *(G-17710)*

Standard Iron Works ....E 570 347-2058
Scranton *(G-17293)*

Statler Body Works Inc ....G 717 261-5936
Chambersburg *(G-2978)*

▲ Strick Corporation ....F 215 949-3600
Fairless Hills *(G-5799)*

Superior Custom Designs Inc ....G 412 744-0110
Glassport *(G-6416)*

▲ Supreme Mid-Atlantic Corp ....D 717 865-0031
Jonestown *(G-8451)*

Swab Wagon Company ....E 717 362-8151
Elizabethville *(G-4898)*

Tamaqua Truck & Trailer Inc ....G 570 386-5994
Tamaqua *(G-18229)*

Triad Truck Equipment ....G 484 614-7349
Pottstown *(G-16059)*

Truckcraft Corporation ....E 717 375-2900
Chambersburg *(G-2990)*

VT Hackney Inc ....D 570 547-1681
Montgomery *(G-11381)*

Wade Holdings LLC ....G 717 375-2251
Marion *(G-10470)*

Warrington Equipment Mfg Co ....E 215 343-1714
Warrington *(G-19138)*

◆ Wolfington Body Company Inc ....C 610 458-8501
Exton *(G-5751)*

3714 Motor Vehicle Parts & Access

A-1 Racing Products Inc ....G 215 675-8442
Warminster *(G-18816)*

Accuride Corporation ....B 814 480-6400
Erie *(G-5169)*

Advance Stores Company Inc ....E 610 939-0120
Reading *(G-16311)*

▲ Alliance Remanufacturing Inc ....C 215 291-4640
Philadelphia *(G-13368)*

American Cable Systems LLC ....G 215 456-0700
Philadelphia *(G-13381)*

◆ American Cycle Fabrication ....G 570 752-8715
Bloomsburg *(G-1769)*

Angel Colon ....G 215 455-4000
Philadelphia *(G-13392)*

Ansa Electric Vehicles LLC ....G 610 955-5686
Narberth *(G-11907)*

▲ Auto Accessories America Inc ....C 717 667-3004
Reedsville *(G-16621)*

Auto Tops Inc ....F 215 785-3310
Bristol *(G-2115)*

Autocare Service Center Inc ....G 717 854-0242
York *(G-20392)*

Automated Unmanned Vehicle Sys ......G 570 748-3844
Mill Hall *(G-11171)*

Autoneum North America Inc ....A 570 784-4100
Bloomsburg *(G-1771)*

Bigbee Steel and Tank Company ....C 814 893-5701
Manheim *(G-10370)*

Bluhms Gas Sales Inc ....F 570 746-2440
Wyalusing *(G-20245)*

Boninfante Friction Inc ....E 610 626-2194
Lansdowne *(G-9431)*

Boyesen Inc ....E 610 756-6818
Lenhartsville *(G-9756)*

Bugstuff....G....724 785-7000
Brownsville (G-2310)

Cardone Industries Inc....C....215 912-3000
Philadelphia (G-13503)

Cardone Industries Inc....B....215 912-3000
Philadelphia (G-13505)

Cardone Industries Inc....C....215 912-3000
Philadelphia (G-13506)

Cardone Industries Inc....C....215 912-3000
Philadelphia (G-13507)

◆ Cardone Industries Inc....B....215 912-3000
Philadelphia (G-13504)

Centech Inc....G....610 754-0720
Perkiomenville (G-13300)

▼ Clark Filter Inc....G....717 285-5941
Lancaster (G-8979)

Conrad Enterprises Inc....E....717 274-5151
Cornwall (G-3738)

Continental Auto Systems Inc....E....610 289-1390
Allentown (G-177)

Continental Corporation....G....610 289-0488
Allentown (G-178)

Corry Manufacturing Company....C....814 664-9611
Corry (G-3752)

Dana Auto Systems Group LLC....B....610 323-4200
Pottstown (G-15978)

Dana Driveshaft Products LLC....B....610 323-4200
Pottstown (G-15979)

▲ Darby Industries Inc....G....570 388-6173
Falls (G-5852)

◆ Dayton Parts LLC....C....717 255-8500
Harrisburg (G-7116)

▲ Diamondback Automotive ACC Inc..E....800 935-4002
Philipsburg (G-14510)

Diesel Pro Inc....G....717 235-4996
Glen Rock (G-6455)

Diverse Sales Company Inc....G....215 317-1815
Perkasie (G-13274)

▲ Dorman Products Inc....C....215 997-1800
Colmar (G-3416)

Dukane Radiator Inc....G....412 233-3300
Bethel Park (G-1413)

EBY Group LLC....E....215 537-4700
Philadelphia (G-13657)

Efi Connection LLC....G....814 566-0946
Erie (G-5257)

Emporium Specialties Company....E....814 647-8661
Austin (G-833)

Exotic Car Gear Inc....G....215 371-2855
North Wales (G-12800)

Fenner Inc....C....717 665-2421
Manheim (G-10380)

FJ Performance Inc....G....724 681-7430
Export (G-5602)

▲ Flextron Industries Inc....F....610 459-4600
Aston (G-763)

G Adasavage LLC....E....215 355-3105
Huntingdon Valley (G-7987)

General Electric Company....B....724 450-1887
Grove City (G-6787)

George I Reitz & Sons Inc....E....814 849-2308
Brookville (G-2261)

George I Reitz & Sons Inc....G....412 824-9976
East Pittsburgh (G-4595)

Graco Inc....A....412 771-5774
Mc Kees Rocks (G-10613)

Great Lakes Power Products Inc....G....724 266-4000
Leetsdale (G-9691)

Great Valley Automotive....G....412 829-8904
North Versailles (G-12776)

Greensburg Mch & Driveline LLC....G....724 837-8233
Greensburg (G-6670)

Gregory Racing Fabrications....G....610 759-8217
Nazareth (G-11970)

▲ Ground Force Marketing Co....E....724 430-2068
Mount Braddock (G-11618)

H R Sales Inc....G....215 639-7150
Bensalem (G-1208)

Haldex Brake Products Corp....F....717 939-5928
Middletown (G-11055)

HIG Capital LLC....C....610 495-7011
Royersford (G-16851)

Hoffman Bros Speed....G....610 760-6274
New Tripoli (G-12458)

Industrial Brake Company Inc....G....724 625-0010
Mars (G-10500)

Industrial Harness Company Inc....D....717 477-0100
Shippensburg (G-17532)

Innotech Industries Inc....E....215 533-6400
Philadelphia (G-13858)

▲ J S H Industries LLC....G....717 267-3566
Chambersburg (G-2945)

Jack Williams Tire Co Inc....F....610 437-4651
Whitehall (G-19878)

Johnson Controls Inc....G....717 771-7890
York (G-20542)

Jones Machine Racing Products....G....610 847-2028
Ottsville (G-13063)

▲ Jones Performance Products Inc....D....724 528-3569
West Middlesex (G-19727)

Keystone Automotive Inds Inc....D....610 866-0313
Bethlehem (G-1550)

Keystone Automotive Inds Inc....F....717 843-8927
York (G-20552)

Krem Speed Equipment Inc....G....814 724-4806
Meadville (G-10746)

L & P Machine Shop Inc....G....610 262-7356
Coplay (G-3645)

Ladmac Services....G....724 679-8047
Butler (G-2418)

Lear Corporation....B....570 345-6725
Pine Grove (G-14597)

Lord Corporation....B....814 868-0924
Erie (G-5371)

Lpw Racing Products Inc....G....717 394-7432
Lancaster (G-9115)

▲ Lynn Parker Associates LLC....G....561 406-6472
Rose Valley (G-16818)

▲ M P N Inc....C....215 289-9480
Philadelphia (G-13981)

Mack Trucks Inc....C....717 939-1338
Middletown (G-11064)

▼ Maclean Saegertown LLC....G....814 763-2655
Saegertown (G-16924)

◆ Mancor-Pa Inc....D....610 398-2300
Allentown (G-306)

▲ Markel Corp....C....610 272-8960
Plymouth Meeting (G-15855)

Marko Radiator Inc....F....570 462-2281
Shenandoah (G-17495)

Matthewas Auto Supplies....G....610 797-3729
Allentown (G-310)

◆ Matthey Johnson Holdings Inc....E....610 971-3000
Wayne (G-19350)

Matthey Johnson Inc....F....724 564-7200
Smithfield (G-17653)

Matthey Johnson Inc....B....610 341-8300
Wayne (G-19352)

◆ Matthey Johnson Inc....E....610 971-3000
Wayne (G-19351)

Metal Powder Products LLC....C....814 834-7261
Saint Marys (G-16992)

▲ Metaldyne Snterforged Pdts LLC....A....814 834-1222
Saint Marys (G-16993)

▲ Modern Industries Inc....C....814 455-8061
Erie (G-5394)

Modern Industries Inc....F....814 885-8514
Kersey (G-8564)

Motorsport Green Engineer....G....570 386-8600
New Ringgold (G-12442)

Mr Rebuildables Inc....G....610 767-2100
Walnutport (G-18793)

N C B Technologies Inc....G....724 658-5544
New Castle (G-12123)

▲ N F C Industries Inc....E....215 766-8890
Plumsteadville (G-15812)

NC Industries Antiq Auto Parts....G....570 888-6216
Sayre (G-17120)

▲ Neapco Components LLC....E....610 323-6000
Pottstown (G-16021)

Nrf US Inc....G....814 947-1378
Plymouth Meeting (G-15861)

O & N Arcft Modification Inc....E....570 945-3769
Factoryville (G-5760)

Osram Sylvania Inc....C....814 726-6600
Warren (G-19041)

Overdrive Holdings Inc....F....724 452-1500
Zelienople (G-20813)

Park Place Transmission Inc....G....717 859-2998
Ephrata (G-5136)

▲ Penn Machine Company....D....814 288-1547
Johnstown (G-8421)

▲ Penntecq Inc....C....724 646-4250
Greenville (G-6765)

Pillings FRP....F....570 538-9202
New Columbia (G-12175)

Point Spring Company....F....724 658-9076
New Castle (G-12138)

▲ Precision Transmission Inc....G....215 822-8300
Colmar (G-3418)

Quality Trailer Products LP....F....717 354-7070
New Holland (G-12277)

Quick Clamp 2....G....724 336-5719
Enon Valley (G-5087)

▼ Quigley Motor Company Inc....D....717 266-5631
Manchester (G-10364)

R E M Automotive Parts Inc....F....717 838-4242
Annville (G-657)

◆ R H Sheppard Co Inc....A....717 637-3751
Hanover (G-6941)

R H Sheppard Co Inc....F....717 633-4106
Hanover (G-6942)

▲ Raineater LLC....G....814 806-3100
Erie (G-5454)

▲ RB Distribution Inc....B....215 997-1800
Colmar (G-3419)

▲ Red Devil Brakes Inc....F....724 696-3744
Mount Pleasant (G-11712)

RG Industries Inc....E....717 849-0345
York (G-20658)

Robert Bosch LLC....B....610 694-8200
Bethlehem (G-1612)

RPM Industries LLC....E....724 228-5130
Washington (G-19224)

Rtr Manufacturing Co....F....412 665-1500
East Liberty (G-4580)

S & W Race Cars Components Inc....E....610 948-7303
Spring City (G-17865)

Saegertown Manufacturing Corp....C....814 763-2655
Saegertown (G-16932)

Slawko Racing Heads Inc....G....610 286-1822
Morgantown (G-11535)

Smith Auto Service....G....215 788-2401
Bristol (G-2198)

▲ Spalding Automotive Inc....E....215 638-3334
Bensalem (G-1255)

▲ Spohn Performance Inc....G....717 866-6033
Myerstown (G-11898)

Steel Shield Technologies Inc....G....412 479-0024
Bethel Park (G-1435)

▼ Stk LLC....F....724 430-2477
Lemont Furnace (G-9738)

◆ Strobic Air Corporation....F....215 723-4700
Telford (G-18321)

Technology Fabricators Inc....E....215 699-0731
Montgomeryville (G-11421)

Thermalblade LLC....G....570 995-1425
Muncy Valley (G-11843)

Torcomp Usa LLC....G....717 261-1530
Chambersburg (G-2987)

Ultra Lite Brakes An C....G....724 696-3743
Mount Pleasant (G-11721)

Universal Carnegie Mfg....G....800 867-9554
Carnegie (G-2802)

▼ US Axle Inc....D....610 323-3800
Pottstown (G-16063)

W W Engine and Supply Inc....E....814 345-5693
Kylertown (G-8868)

Westmoreland Machine & Elc Co....G....412 784-1991
Pittsburgh (G-15712)

▲ Westport Axle....B....610 366-2900
Breinigsville (G-2032)

Wheeler Bros Inc....G....814 443-3269
Somerset (G-17716)

◆ Wheeler Bros Inc....D....814 443-7000
Somerset (G-17717)

▲ Winters Performance Pdts Inc....E....717 764-9844
York (G-20713)

World Motorsports Inc....G....610 929-1982
Reading (G-16570)

▲ Young Windows Inc....D....610 828-5036
Conshohocken (G-3618)

3715 Truck Trailers

3nt-3 Nieces Trucking Inc....G....360 815-0938
Grassflat (G-6577)

Belmont Machine Co....G....717 556-0040
Leola (G-9773)

▼ Borco Equipment Inc....E....814 535-1400
Johnstown (G-8359)

Bri-Mar Manufacturing LLC....E....717 263-6116
Chambersburg (G-2913)

Comanche Manufacturing Inc....G....724 530-7278
Volant (G-18771)

Custom Fab Trailers Inc....G....724 548-5529
Kittanning (G-8764)

Daniel Leo Olesnevich....G....724 352-3160
Butler (G-2392)

Delaware Valley Shippers Inc....F....215 633-1535
Bensalem (G-1181)

Dively Manufacture Co Inc ....F 814 239-5441
Claysburg *(G-3203)*

Ehb Logisitics Inc ....F 717 764-5800
York *(G-20464)*

Great Dane LLC ....B 570 437-3141
Danville *(G-4004)*

Great Dane LLC ....B 717 492-0057
Mount Joy *(G-11659)*

Great Dane Trailers Inc ....G 570 221-6920
Elysburg *(G-4976)*

Gregory Racing Fabrications ....G 610 759-8217
Nazareth *(G-11970)*

International Trailers Inc ....D 814 634-1922
Meyersdale *(G-11012)*

ITI Trailers & Trck Bodies Inc ....E 814 634-0080
Meyersdale *(G-11013)*

Lang Speciality Trailers LLC ....G 724 972-6590
Latrobe *(G-9487)*

Manac Trailers Inc ....G 724 294-0007
Freeport *(G-6207)*

◆ Master Solutions Inc ....F 717 243-6849
Carlisle *(G-2724)*

Phoenix Coach Works Inc ....G 610 495-2266
Pottstown *(G-16030)*

Pine Hill Manufacturing LLC ....F 717 288-2443
Gordonville *(G-6561)*

▼ Reitnouer Inc ....E 610 929-4856
Birdsboro *(G-1704)*

▲ Rt 66 Tractor Supply ....G 724 668-2000
New Alexandria *(G-12020)*

▲ Schnure Manufacturing Co Inc ....F 610 273-3352
Honey Brook *(G-7762)*

Shetron Manufacturing LLC ....G 717 532-4400
Shippensburg *(G-17547)*

Somerset Welding & Steel Inc ....C 814 443-2671
Somerset *(G-17710)*

◆ Spector Manufacturing Inc ....E 570 429-2510
Saint Clair *(G-16941)*

▲ Stanton Dynamics Inc ....F 814 849-6255
Brookville *(G-2272)*

▲ Strick Corporation ....F 215 949-3600
Fairless Hills *(G-5799)*

▼ Summit Trailer Sales Inc ....E 570 754-3511
Summit Station *(G-18161)*

Transport Custom Designs LLC ....G 570 368-1403
Montoursville *(G-11454)*

Universal Trlr Crgo Group Inc ....F 570 929-3761
McAdoo *(G-10659)*

Viking Vee Inc ....G 724 789-9194
Renfrew *(G-16643)*

Wherleys Trailer Inc ....G 717 624-2268
New Oxford *(G-12426)*

Windview Truck & Trlr Repr LLC ....G 570 374-8077
Port Trevorton *(G-15916)*

Worthington Trailers LP ....F 570 567-7921
Williamsport *(G-20101)*

3716 Motor Homes

GM Home Inc ....G 888 352-3442
Southampton *(G-17814)*

3721 Aircraft

◆ Agustwstland Philadelphia Corp ......D 215 281-1400
Philadelphia *(G-13358)*

Air Ventures Balloon Rides ....G 610 827-2138
Chester Springs *(G-3070)*

Boeing Company ....D 610 828-7764
Lafayette Hill *(G-8877)*

Boeing Company ....G 610 591-1978
Ridley Park *(G-16734)*

Boeing Company ....G 610 591-2121
Ridley Park *(G-16735)*

Boeing Company ....B 610 591-2121
Ridley Park *(G-16736)*

Boeing Company ....A 610 591-2121
Ridley Park *(G-16737)*

Bombardier Transportation ....F 412 655-0325
Pittsburgh *(G-14781)*

Dragonfly Pictures Inc ....G 610 521-6115
Essington *(G-5542)*

General Electric Company ....G 610 770-1881
Allentown *(G-226)*

Learjet Inc ....A 215 246-3454
Philadelphia *(G-13963)*

Lockheed Martin Corporation ....G 610 337-9560
Malvern *(G-10270)*

Lockheed Martin Corporation ....B 610 531-5640
Malvern *(G-10271)*

Pittsburgh Jet Center ....F 724 452-4719
Zelienople *(G-20816)*

Textron Inc ....D 570 323-6181
Williamsport *(G-20081)*

Usm Aerostructures Corp ....E 570 613-1234
Wyoming *(G-20285)*

3724 Aircraft Engines & Engine Parts

▲ Acutec Precision Aerospace Inc ......B 814 336-2214
Meadville *(G-10695)*

Ametek Inc ....D 267 933-2121
Harleysville *(G-7018)*

Ametek Inc ....E 267 933-2121
Harleysville *(G-7019)*

Avco Corporation ....C 570 323-6181
Williamsport *(G-19990)*

Cnc Metalworks Inc ....G 717 624-8436
New Oxford *(G-12407)*

Corry Manufacturing Company ....C 814 664-9611
Corry *(G-3752)*

Eaton Aerospace LLC ....D 610 522-4000
Glenolden *(G-6473)*

▲ Holtec International ....G 215 646-5842
Maple Glen *(G-10430)*

Honeywell International Inc ....A 215 533-3000
Philadelphia *(G-13832)*

Honeywell International Inc ....D 724 452-1300
Fombell *(G-6031)*

Honeywell International Inc ....A 717 741-3799
York *(G-20527)*

Honeywell International Inc ....C 814 432-2118
Franklin *(G-6135)*

Innodyn LLC ....G 814 339-7328
Osceola Mills *(G-13055)*

Lionheart Holdings LLC ....G 215 283-8400
Newtown *(G-12519)*

Lockheed Martin Aeroparts ....C 814 262-3000
Johnstown *(G-8404)*

Lord Corporation ....B 814 868-0924
Erie *(G-5371)*

Mecaer Aviation Group Inc ....E 301 790-3645
Philadelphia *(G-14002)*

Netmercatus LLC ....G 646 822-7900
Sutersville *(G-18184)*

◆ Pratt & Whitney Americon Inc ....C 717 546-0220
Middletown *(G-11070)*

Precision Castparts Corp ....C 570 825-4544
Wilkes Barre *(G-19959)*

Precision Castparts Corp ....B 570 474-6371
Mountain Top *(G-11771)*

Prime Turbines LLC ....G 724 586-0124
Butler *(G-2435)*

◆ Stein Seal Company ....C 215 256-0201
Kulpsville *(G-8831)*

Summit Aerospace USA Inc ....F 570 839-8615
Mount Pocono *(G-11737)*

Teledyne Scientific Imaging LLC ....F 215 368-6900
Montgomeryville *(G-11423)*

◆ Triumph Group Inc ....C 610 251-1000
Berwyn *(G-1383)*

◆ Triumph Group Operations Inc ....F 610 251-1000
Berwyn *(G-1386)*

Unison Engine Components Inc ....C 570 825-4544
Wilkes Barre *(G-19967)*

Vector Aerospace Usa Inc ....G 610 559-2191
Easton *(G-4767)*

3728 Aircraft Parts & Eqpt, NEC

▲ Acutec Precision Aerospace Inc ......B 814 336-2214
Meadville *(G-10695)*

Air Parts of Lock Haven ....F 570 748-0823
Lock Haven *(G-10683)*

Alvord-Polk Inc ....G 800 925-2126
Millersburg *(G-11187)*

American Sun Inc ....F 610 497-2210
Aston *(G-751)*

Ametek Inc ....D 267 933-2121
Harleysville *(G-7018)*

Ametek Inc ....E 267 933-2121
Harleysville *(G-7019)*

Amies Airparts LLC ....G 570 871-7991
Clifton Twp *(G-3260)*

▲ Anholt Technologies Inc ....F 610 268-2758
Avondale *(G-848)*

B/E Aerospace Inc ....G 570 595-7491
Mountainhome *(G-11785)*

Blue Avionics Inc ....F 310 433-9431
Chester Springs *(G-3072)*

Brenner Aerostructures LLC ....E 215 638-3884
Bensalem *(G-1161)*

Bridge Acpuncture Natural Hlth ....G 215 348-8058
Doylestown *(G-4281)*

Bsm Enterprises Company Inc ....F 215 257-2231
Perkasie *(G-13268)*

Carson Helicopters Inc ....D 215 249-3535
Perkasie *(G-13270)*

Eaton Aerospace LLC ....D 610 522-4000
Glenolden *(G-6473)*

Eaton Corporation ....C 610 522-4059
Glenolden *(G-6474)*

▲ Enersys Advanced Systems Inc ....D 215 674-3800
Horsham *(G-7816)*

◆ Enginred Arrsting Systems Corp .....C 610 494-8000
Upper Chichester *(G-18660)*

▲ Environmental Tectonics Corp ....C 215 355-9100
Southampton *(G-17809)*

Foranne Manufacturing Inc ....E 215 357-4650
Warminster *(G-18881)*

Gogreenapu LLC ....G 814 943-9948
Altoona *(G-511)*

H-D Advanced Manufacturing Co ....G 724 759-2850
Sewickley *(G-17389)*

Helicopter Tech Inc ....F 610 272-8090
King of Prussia *(G-8630)*

▲ J A Reinhardt & Co Inc ....C 570 595-7491
Mountainhome *(G-11787)*

L P Aero Plastics Inc ....E 724 744-4448
Jeannette *(G-8260)*

Lockheed Martin Aeroparts ....C 814 262-3000
Johnstown *(G-8404)*

Lockheed Martin Corporation ....B 814 262-3000
Johnstown *(G-8405)*

Magee Plastics Company ....D 724 776-2220
Warrendale *(G-19087)*

▲ Martin-Baker America Inc ....C 814 262-9325
Johnstown *(G-8407)*

▼ Mike Barta and Sons Inc ....G 215 757-1162
Langhorne *(G-9311)*

Mitchell Aviation Ltd ....G 717 232-7575
Harrisburg *(G-7179)*

Moritz Aerospace Inc ....B 215 249-1300
Dublin *(G-4436)*

O & N Arcft Modification Inc ....E 570 945-3769
Factoryville *(G-5760)*

Olympic Tool & Machine Corp ....D 610 494-1600
Aston *(G-784)*

◆ Pratt & Whitney Americon Inc ....C 717 546-0220
Middletown *(G-11070)*

Redstone Corporation ....G 321 213-2135
Johnstown *(G-8429)*

Sgrignoli Brothers ....G 717 766-2812
Mechanicsburg *(G-10887)*

Smiths Aerospace Components I ....G 570 474-3011
Mountain Top *(G-11776)*

Strube Inc ....F 717 426-1906
Marietta *(G-10468)*

Titan Robotics Inc ....G 724 986-6737
Pittsburgh *(G-15625)*

Transicoil LLC ....E 484 902-1100
Collegeville *(G-3397)*

Trigon Holding Inc ....E 724 941-5540
Mc Murray *(G-10647)*

▲ Trigon Incorporated ....D 724 941-5540
Mc Murray *(G-10648)*

Triumph Aerospace Systems Grp ....E 610 251-1000
Berwyn *(G-1381)*

Triumph Aviations Inc ....G 610 251-1000
Berwyn *(G-1382)*

◆ Triumph Group Inc ....C 610 251-1000
Berwyn *(G-1383)*

Triumph Group Acquisition Corp ....G 610 251-1000
Berwyn *(G-1384)*

Triumph Group Holdings - Mexic ....D 610 251-1000
Berwyn *(G-1385)*

Triumph Insulation Systems LLC ....G 610 251-1000
Berwyn *(G-1387)*

Triumph Structures - E Texas ....A 610 251-1000
Berwyn *(G-1388)*

Usm Aerostructures Corp ....E 570 613-1234
Wyoming *(G-20285)*

▲ Victor-Balata Belting Company ....E 610 258-2010
Easton *(G-4772)*

3731 Shipbuilding & Repairing

C & C Marine Maintenance Co ....C 724 746-9550
Houston *(G-7868)*

Donjon Shipbuilding & Repr LLC ....F 814 455-6442
Erie *(G-5250)*

▲ Erie Forge and Steel Inc ....D 814 452-2300
Erie *(G-5267)*

General Dynamics Corporation ....E 412 432-2200
Pittsburgh *(G-15044)*

Heartland Fabrication LLC ....C 724 785-2575
Brownsville (G-2312)

HIG Capital LLC ....C 610 495-7011
Royersford (G-16851)

Hli Rail & Rigging LLC ....F 215 277-5558
Elkins Park (G-4905)

Interntonal Mar Outfitting LLC ....G 215 875-9911
Philadelphia (G-13871)

Kennedy Fuels Inc ....G 412 721-7404
Pittsburgh (G-15171)

Kvaerner Philadelphia Shi ....G 215 875-2725
Philadelphia (G-13947)

Lion Energy Co LLC ....G 724 444-7501
Gibsonia (G-6343)

Loeffler Corporation ....F 215 757-2404
Langhorne (G-9309)

NCM Barge Maintence ....F 724 469-0083
Rostraver Township (G-16828)

Philadelphia Ship Repair LLC ....F 215 339-1026
Philadelphia (G-14154)

Rhoads Industries Inc ....E 267 728-6544
Philadelphia (G-14243)

Rhoads Industries Inc ....D 267 728-6300
Philadelphia (G-14244)

Supreme - DSC Dredge LLC ....G 724 376-4368
Stoneboro (G-18070)

▼ Whemco Inc ....E 412 390-2700
Pittsburgh (G-15715)

3732 Boat Building & Repairing

24-7 Innovations LLC ....G 570 676-8888
Greentown (G-6732)

Altra Marine ....G 814 786-8346
Jackson Center (G-8225)

▼ Blackbird Industries Inc ....F 724 283-2537
West Sunbury (G-19769)

C & C Marine Maintenance Co ....C 724 746-9550
Houston (G-7868)

Coletech ....G 814 474-3370
Fairview (G-5816)

Daves Boat Repair LLC ....G 215 453-6904
Sellersville (G-17343)

George Kranich ....G 610 295-2039
Marcus Hook (G-10442)

Hydrosource ....F 570 676-8500
Canadensis (G-2530)

Indian Lake Marina Inc ....G 814 754-4774
Central City (G-2839)

Mellinger Manufacturing Co Inc ....F 717 464-3318
Willow Street (G-20154)

P S Composites Inc ....G 724 329-4413
Markleysburg (G-10483)

Rock Proof Boats ....G 717 957-3282
Marysville (G-10532)

◆ Stoltzfus Trailer Sales Inc ....D 610 399-0628
West Chester (G-19645)

3743 Railroad Eqpt

▲ A Stucki Company ....E 412 424-0560
Coraopolis (G-3653)

Acf Industries LLC ....D 570 742-7601
Milton (G-11232)

▼ Amsted Rail Company Inc ....D 717 761-3690
Camp Hill (G-2489)

Appalachian Tank Car Svcs Inc ....F 724 925-3919
Youngwood (G-20779)

Appalachian Tank Car Svcs Inc ....D 412 741-1500
Leetsdale (G-9682)

◆ Bombardier Transportation ....A 412 655-5700
Pittsburgh (G-14782)

▲ Brookville Equipment Corp ....C 814 849-2000
Brookville (G-2252)

Brookville Locomotive Inc ....C 814 849-2000
Brookville (G-2254)

Buncher Company ....G 724 925-3919
Youngwood (G-20780)

Carly Railcar Components LLC ....G 724 864-8170
Irwin (G-8147)

Curry Rail Services Inc ....G 814 793-7245
Hollidaysburg (G-7645)

Damian Hntz Locomotive Svc Inc ....G 814 748-7222
Colver (G-3453)

Donohue Railroad Equipment Inc ....E 724 827-8104
Darlington (G-4027)

Edens Ticketing ....D 215 625-0314
Philadelphia (G-13660)

▲ G G Schmitt & Sons Inc ....F 717 394-3701
Lancaster (G-9026)

General Electric Company ....G 814 875-2234
Erie (G-5301)

◆ Gupta Permold Corporation ....C 412 793-3511
Pittsburgh (G-15067)

▲ Hyundai Rotem USA Corporation ....F 215 227-6836
Fort Washington (G-6074)

Ionx LLC ....G 484 653-2600
West Chester (G-19573)

◆ Johnstown America Corporation ....D 877 739-2006
Johnstown (G-8388)

◆ Kasgro Rail Corp ....D 724 658-9061
New Castle (G-12111)

Keystone Rail Recovery LLC ....G 865 567-2166
Jersey Shore (G-8316)

Keystone Spike ....G 717 270-2700
Lebanon (G-9594)

Kinkisharyo USA Inc ....G 724 778-0100
Seven Fields (G-17375)

Magee Plastics Company ....D 724 776-2220
Warrendale (G-19087)

▼ McHugh Railroad Maint Eqp ....F 215 949-0430
Fairless Hills (G-5788)

Nascent Energy Systems LLC ....G 203 722-1101
Pittsburgh (G-15320)

Neville Island RR Holdings Inc ....F 724 981-4100
Sharon (G-17439)

Norfolk Southern Corporation ....E 814 949-1551
Altoona (G-531)

Powerrail Distribution Inc ....D 570 883-7005
Duryea (G-4504)

▲ Powerrail Holdings Inc ....E 570 883-7005
Duryea (G-4505)

Precision Runners LLC ....E 330 240-5988
Sharpsville (G-17474)

Priest Enterprises ....G 724 658-7692
Grove City (G-6802)

Rail Car Service Co ....G 724 662-3660
Mercer (G-10970)

Rail Transit Products Inc ....G 724 527-2386
Penn (G-13227)

Renovo Rail Industries LLC ....G 570 923-2093
Renovo (G-16649)

▲ Sardello Inc ....D 724 375-4101
Aliquippa (G-91)

Standard Car Truck Company ....D 412 782-7300
Pittsburgh (G-15576)

Synergy Industries LLC ....F 215 699-4045
North Wales (G-12829)

▲ Toyo Denki Usa Inc ....E 724 774-1760
Freedom (G-6193)

Trac Products Inc ....G 610 789-7853
Havertown (G-7432)

Transco Railway Products Inc ....E 570 322-3411
Williamsport (G-20085)

Union Tank Car Company ....D 814 944-4523
Altoona (G-554)

▲ Utcras Inc ....D 610 328-1100
Morton (G-11594)

Utcras LLC ....D 610 328-1100
Morton (G-11595)

Verail Technologies Inc ....G 513 454-8192
Lansdale (G-9422)

▲ Vossloh Track Material Inc ....D 610 926-5400
Reading (G-16560)

◆ Wabtec Corporation ....B 412 825-1000
Wilmerding (G-20160)

Wabtec Investments Limited LLC ....B 412 825-1000
Wilmerding (G-20161)

Warren Railcar Service Inc ....F 814 723-2500
Warren (G-19061)

Webtrans Limited LLC ....E 215 260-3313
Lansdale (G-9427)

Westinghouse A Brake Tech Corp ....E 724 838-1317
Greensburg (G-6730)

▲ Westinghouse A Brake Tech Corp ....B 412 825-1000
Wilmerding (G-20163)

3751 Motorcycles, Bicycles & Parts

Advanced Sports Inc ....D 215 824-3854
Philadelphia (G-13347)

Arthur K Miller ....G 724 588-1118
Greenville (G-6738)

Barnharts Honda Suzuki ....F 724 627-5819
Prosperity (G-16122)

Bikes & Trikes For ....D 267 304-1534
Philadelphia (G-13460)

Boyesen Inc ....E 610 756-6818
Lenhartsville (G-9756)

▲ Christini Technologies Inc ....G 215 351-9895
Philadelphia (G-13542)

◆ Cycling Sports Group Inc ....D 203 749-7000
Bedford (G-1048)

David Tuttle ....G 570 280-8441
Waymart (G-19286)

▲ Fast By Ferracci Inc ....F 215 657-1276
Abington (G-12)

Freeze Thaw Cycles ....G 814 272-0178
State College (G-17966)

Gatto Moto LLC ....E 412 487-3377
Glenshaw (G-6488)

Integrated Machine Company ....G 814 835-4949
Erie (G-5328)

▲ Mxl Industries Inc ....D 717 569-8711
Lancaster (G-9141)

P K Choppers Mobile ....G 570 458-6983
Millville (G-11226)

Price Chopper Oper Co of PA ....G 570 223-2410
East Stroudsburg (G-4631)

Pro Action Inc ....F 724 846-9055
Beaver Falls (G-1007)

Road Ready LLC ....G 717 647-7902
Williamstown (G-20103)

Tech Cycle Performance Pdts ....G 215 702-8324
Langhorne (G-9328)

Torcomp Usa LLC ....G 717 261-1530
Chambersburg (G-2987)

Vicious Cycle Works Llc ....G 724 662-0581
Mercer (G-10977)

3761 Guided Missiles & Space Vehicles

Astrobotic Technology Inc ....F 412 682-3282
Pittsburgh (G-14729)

Converging Sciences Tech Inc ....G 215 626-5705
Warminster (G-18847)

Kyron Naval Architecture ....G 516 304-1769
Bensalem (G-1217)

Lockheed Martin Corporation ....B 610 531-5640
Malvern (G-10271)

Lockheed Martin Corporation ....A 610 382-3200
King of Prussia (G-8641)

Lockheed Martin Corporation ....A 610 531-7400
King of Prussia (G-8643)

Lockheed Martin Corporation ....B 570 876-2132
Archbald (G-691)

3764 Guided Missile/Space Vehicle Propulsion Units & parts

Kyron Naval Architecture ....G 516 304-1769
Bensalem (G-1217)

Reaction Chemicals ....G 610 838-5496
Hellertown (G-7561)

3769 Guided Missile/Space Vehicle Parts & Eqpt, NEC

Delaware Tool & Machine Co ....E 610 259-1810
Yeadon (G-20352)

G Adasavage LLC ....E 215 355-3105
Huntingdon Valley (G-7987)

General Dynamics Ots PA Inc ....C 570 342-7801
Scranton (G-17238)

L3 Technologies Inc ....C 267 545-7000
Bristol (G-2157)

Stellar Prcsion Components Ltd ....D 724 523-5559
Jeannette (G-8265)

▲ York Industries Inc ....E 717 764-8855
York (G-20742)

3792 Travel Trailers & Campers

Bailey Leasing Inc ....D 717 718-0490
York (G-20398)

◆ Columbia Northwest Inc ....F 724 423-7440
Mount Pleasant (G-11693)

Conrad Enterprises Inc ....E 717 274-5151
Cornwall (G-3738)

Fame Manufacturing Inc ....F 814 763-5645
Saegertown (G-16913)

Jeraco Enterprises Inc ....D 570 742-9688
Milton (G-11244)

Keystone Truck Caps LLC ....G 570 836-4322
Tunkhannock (G-18540)

Mobile Concepts By Scotty Inc ....E 724 542-7640
Mount Pleasant (G-11706)

Quantum Leap Engnered Pdts LLC ....G 814 289-1476
Somerset (G-17702)

◆ Reading Truck Body LLC ....C 610 775-3301
Reading (G-16493)

Transport Custom Designs LLC ....G 570 368-1403
Montoursville (G-11454)

Warrington Equipment Mfg Co ....E 215 343-1714
Warrington (G-19138)

3795 Tanks & Tank Components

Bae Systems Land Armaments LP ....D 717 225-8000
  York *(G-20397)*

Bosch Rexroth Corporation ....A 610 694-8300
  Bethlehem *(G-1470)*

Gichner Systems Group Inc ....B 877 520-1773
  Dallastown *(G-3976)*

Hiltz Propane Systems Inc ....E 717 799-4322
  Marietta *(G-10464)*

Humanistic Robotics Inc ....G 215 922-7803
  Philadelphia *(G-13840)*

Humanistic Robotics Inc ....G 267 515-5880
  Philadelphia *(G-13841)*

◆ Medico Industries Inc ....C 570 825-7711
  Wilkes Barre *(G-19942)*

Medico Industries Inc ....E 570 825-7711
  Hanover Township *(G-6996)*

Shale Tank Solutions LLC ....F 724 823-0953
  Donora *(G-4162)*

3799 Transportation Eqpt, NEC

101 Cameo Appearances LLC ....G 412 787-7981
  Pittsburgh *(G-14623)*

Allan A Myers ....G 610 584-6020
  Worcester *(G-20223)*

◆ Ames Companies Inc ....B 717 737-1500
  Camp Hill *(G-2488)*

Anderson Inc ....F 412 486-2211
  Allison Park *(G-447)*

Arthur L Baker Enterprises ....G 717 432-9788
  Lewisberry *(G-9880)*

Bri-Mar Manufacturing LLC ....E 717 263-6116
  Chambersburg *(G-2913)*

C & C Manufacturing & Fabg ....G 570 454-0819
  Hazleton *(G-7492)*

Carriage Machine Shop LLC ....F 717 397-4079
  Bird In Hand *(G-1671)*

Dutchie Manufacturing LLC ....G 717 656-2186
  Leola *(G-9778)*

Fiba Technologies Inc ....F 215 679-7823
  East Greenville *(G-4568)*

Four Wheeling For Less LLC ....G 724 287-7852
  Butler *(G-2402)*

Gold Rush Inc ....E 717 484-2424
  Denver *(G-4074)*

Hilltown Services ....G 215 249-3694
  Dublin *(G-4434)*

J&B Outdoor Center ....G 814 848-3838
  Ulysses *(G-18603)*

▲ JB Racing Inc ....G 814 922-3523
  East Springfield *(G-4599)*

John L Mary D Shaffer ....G 814 427-2894
  Punxsutawney *(G-16145)*

▲ Kutz Farm Equipment Inc ....G 570 345-4882
  Pine Grove *(G-14596)*

Lblock Transportation Inc ....G 347 533-0943
  York *(G-20563)*

▲ Mgs Inc ....C 717 336-7528
  Denver *(G-4083)*

Miller Inds Towing Eqp Inc ....G 724 981-3328
  Hermitage *(G-7591)*

◆ Mission Critical Solutions LLC ....E 814 839-2078
  Alum Bank *(G-562)*

Mustang Trailer Mfg ....F 724 628-1000
  Connellsville *(G-3504)*

Polar Blox Inc ....G 814 629-7397
  Hollsopple *(G-7660)*

Pushcart USA Inc ....G 570 622-2479
  Port Carbon *(G-15900)*

Rail Ryder LLC ....G 814 873-1623
  Erie *(G-5452)*

Rock Run Recreation Area ....G 814 674-6026
  Patton *(G-13189)*

Smouse Trucks & Vans Inc ....G 724 887-7777
  Mount Pleasant *(G-11718)*

▲ Stanton Dynamics Inc ....F 814 849-6255
  Brookville *(G-2272)*

Stauffer Manufacturing LLC ....G 717 445-6122
  Ephrata *(G-5147)*

Superior Custom Designs Inc ....G 412 744-0110
  Glassport *(G-6416)*

T E Fletcher Snowmobiles ....G 724 253-3225
  Conneaut Lake *(G-3480)*

Transport Custom Designs LLC ....G 570 368-1403
  Montoursville *(G-11454)*

Vicksburg Buggy Shop ....G 570 966-3658
  Mifflinburg *(G-11104)*

Weaver Carriage Shop ....G 717 445-7191
  East Earl *(G-4557)*

Weavertown Coach Shop ....G 717 768-3299
  Bird In Hand *(G-1685)*

World of Wheels Inc ....F 814 676-5721
  Seneca *(G-17373)*

Worthington Trailers LP ....F 570 567-7921
  Williamsport *(G-20101)*

38 MEASURING, ANALYZING AND CONTROLLING INSTRUMENTS; PHOTOGRAPHIC, MEDICAL AN

3812 Search, Detection, Navigation & Guidance Systs & Instrs

Acutronic Company ....G 412 926-1200
  Pittsburgh *(G-14647)*

Acutronic USA Inc ....G 412 926-1200
  Pittsburgh *(G-14648)*

Advanced Acoustic Concepts LLC ....D 724 434-5100
  Lemont Furnace *(G-9732)*

▼ Aircraft Instruments Company ....G 215 348-5274
  Doylestown *(G-4269)*

Ametek Inc ....D 267 933-2121
  Harleysville *(G-7018)*

Ametek Inc ....E 267 933-2121
  Harleysville *(G-7019)*

▲ Applied Magnetics Lab Inc ....G 717 430-2774
  York *(G-20381)*

Argon St Inc ....E 724 564-4100
  Smithfield *(G-17641)*

Arin Technologies Inc ....G 412 877-2877
  Pittsburgh *(G-14722)*

Bae Systems Land Armaments LP ....D 717 225-8000
  York *(G-20397)*

Bayhill Defense LLC ....G 412 877-9372
  Pittsburgh *(G-14757)*

Blue Avionics Inc ....F 310 433-9431
  Chester Springs *(G-3072)*

Clear Align LLC ....D 484 956-0510
  Eagleville *(G-4512)*

Coastal Defense ....G 570 858-1139
  Lock Haven *(G-10087)*

Cobham Adv Elec Sol Inc ....B 215 996-2000
  Lansdale *(G-9351)*

Conspec Controls Inc ....F 724 489-8450
  Charleroi *(G-3008)*

Damsel In Defense ....G 215 262-3643
  Morrisville *(G-11557)*

Defense Training Solutions LLC ....G 484 240-1188
  Nazareth *(G-11961)*

Dep Technologies LLC ....G 800 578-7929
  Lancaster *(G-8995)*

Discovery Machine Inc ....F 570 601-1966
  Williamsport *(G-20006)*

Eaton Corporation ....E 412 893-3300
  Moon Township *(G-11484)*

◆ Eaton Electrical Inc ....E 412 893-3300
  Moon Township *(G-11485)*

Endless Mountains Specialties ....G 570 432-4018
  Montrose *(G-11463)*

◆ Enginred Arrsting Systems Corp ......C 610 494-8000
  Upper Chichester *(G-18660)*

Enjet Aero Erie Inc ....C 814 860-3104
  Erie *(G-5260)*

Environmental Solut World Inc ....E 215 699-0730
  Montgomeryville *(G-11396)*

Geissele Automatics LLC ....F 610 272-2060
  North Wales *(G-12803)*

▲ Gerome Manufacturing Co Inc ....D 724 438-8544
  Smithfield *(G-17650)*

Gray Space Defense ....G 814 475-2749
  Berlin *(G-1288)*

Heilig Defense LLC ....G 717 490-6833
  Lancaster *(G-9041)*

Herley Industries Inc ....B 717 397-2777
  Lancaster *(G-9043)*

Honeywell International Inc ....A 215 533-3000
  Philadelphia *(G-13832)*

I2r Electronics Inc ....E 610 928-1045
  Macungie *(G-10148)*

Innovtive Slutions Support Inc ....D 610 646-9800
  Exton *(G-5699)*

Kitron Inc ....E 814 619-0523
  Johnstown *(G-8398)*

L3 Technologies Inc ....C 412 967-7700
  Pittsburgh *(G-15209)*

L3 Technologies Inc ....C 267 545-7000
  Bristol *(G-2157)*

◆ Laser-View Technologies Inc ....F 610 497-8910
  Chester Springs *(G-3082)*

Lighthouse Electric Contrls Co ....F 814 835-2348
  Erie *(G-5365)*

Lockheed Martin Corporation ....B 570 307-1590
  Jessup *(G-8331)*

Lockheed Martin Corporation 717 267-5796
  Chambersburg *(G-2954)*

Lockheed Martin Corporation ....A 610 382-3200
  King of Prussia *(G-8641)*

Lockheed Martin Corporation 610 354-7782
  Audubon *(G-829)*

Lockheed Martin Corporation ....A 610 354-3083
  King of Prussia *(G-8642)*

Lockheed Martin Corporation ....A 610 531-7400
  King of Prussia *(G-8643)*

Lockheed Martin Corporation ....B 610 962-4954
  King of Prussia *(G-8644)*

Lockheed Martin Corporation ....C 610 531-7400
  King of Prussia *(G-8645)*

Lockheed Martin Corporation ....C 610 962-2264
  King of Prussia *(G-8646)*

Matthey Johnson Inc ....C 610 341-8300
  Wayne *(G-19353)*

▲ Maxima Tech & Systems LLC ....C 717 581-1000
  Lancaster *(G-9130)*

▲ Miller Edge Inc ....D 610 869-4422
  West Grove *(G-19702)*

Moog Inc ....E 610 328-4000
  Springfield *(G-17919)*

MSI Acquisition Corp ....G 717 397-2777
  Lancaster *(G-9139)*

Nexgen Ats ....G 717 779-9580
  Mountville *(G-11800)*

Night Vision Devices Inc ....F 610 395-9743
  Allentown *(G-333)*

Oppenheimer Precision Pdts Inc ....D 215 674-9100
  Horsham *(G-7837)*

Oto Melara North America Inc ....G 314 707-4223
  Johnstown *(G-8417)*

Pennsylvania State University ....E 215 682-4000
  Warminster *(G-18939)*

▲ Photonis Defense Inc ....D 717 295-6000
  Lancaster *(G-9170)*

Point Blank Defense LLC ....G 717 801-2632
  York *(G-20630)*

R G B Business Tech Solutions ....G 215 745-3646
  Philadelphia *(G-14224)*

Raytheon Company ....G 717 267-4200
  Chambersburg *(G-2972)*

Raytheon Company ....B 814 278-2256
  State College *(G-18012)*

Re2 Inc ....E 412 681-6382
  Pittsburgh *(G-15472)*

▲ Remcal Products Corporation ....F 215 343-5500
  Warrington *(G-19130)*

Sensing Devices Inc ....E 717 295-4735
  Lancaster *(G-9193)*

Shock Solutions Inc ....G 610 767-7090
  Danielsville *(G-3995)*

Smart Avionics Inc ....G 717 928-4360
  Marietta *(G-10467)*

◆ Smiths Group North America Inc ......F 772 286-9300
  Malvern *(G-10322)*

Strategic Defense Unit LLC ....G 267 591-0725
  Philadelphia *(G-14351)*

Strube Inc ....F 717 426-1906
  Marietta *(G-10468)*

Suburban Deer Defense Llc ....G 717 632-8844
  Hanover *(G-6959)*

Tcw Technologies LLC ....G 610 928-3420
  Emmaus *(G-5044)*

Teletronics Technology Corp ....C 267 352-2020
  Newtown *(G-12555)*

Then Defense Group ....G 717 465-0584
  Gettysburg *(G-6317)*

Tiger PC Defense ....G 888 531-1530
  Whitehall *(G-19891)*

Tortel Products ....G 267 477-1805
  Hatfield *(G-7402)*

Track Trail Search Rescue Inc ....G 814 715-5608
  Brookville *(G-2274)*

Triumph Controls LLC ....C 215 699-4861
  North Wales *(G-12837)*

◆ Triumph Group Inc ....C 610 251-1000
  Berwyn *(G-1383)*

Tru Temp Sensors Inc ....G 215 396-1550
  Southampton *(G-17844)*

Ufc Aerospace ....G 610 485-4704
  Upper Chichester *(G-18675)*

Unison Engine Components Inc..........C..... 570 825-4544
  Wilkes Barre (G-19967)
Validus Inc..................................G..... 215 822-2525
  Colmar (G-3422)
▲ Velocity Magnetics Inc.................G..... 724 657-8290
  New Castle (G-12163)
Warren Machine Co Inc....................F..... 215 491-5500
  Warrington (G-19136)
Wm Robots, LLC.............................F..... 215 822-2525
  Colmar (G-3424)
Xensor Corporation.........................E..... 610 284-2508
  Drexel Hill (G-4373)

3821 Laboratory Apparatus & Furniture

Ajikabe Inc....................................G..... 484 424-9415
  Holland (G-7639)
▼ American Lyophilizer Inc...............F..... 610 999-4151
  Yardley (G-20295)
Applied Equipment Co......................G..... 610 258-7941
  Easton (G-4646)
▲ Applied Magnetics Lab Inc............G..... 717 430-2774
  York (G-20381)
▲ Applied Separations Inc...............E..... 610 770-0900
  Allentown (G-141)
◆ Applied Test Systems LLC.............E..... 724 283-1212
  Butler (G-2375)
▲ Aqua Treatment Services Inc.........E..... 717 697-4998
  Mechanicsburg (G-10820)
Archer Instruments LLC...................G..... 215 589-0356
  Catasauqua (G-2814)
Base Lab Tools Inc.........................G..... 570 371-5710
  Stroudsburg (G-18107)
Biorealize Inc................................G..... 610 216-5554
  Philadelphia (G-13466)
Blue Spin LLC................................G..... 814 863-4630
  Boalsburg (G-1864)
▲ Boekel Industries Inc..................E..... 215 396-8200
  Feasterville Trevose (G-5892)
▲ Brady Instruments.......................G..... 717 453-7171
  Lykens (G-10130)
▼ Burrell Scientific LLC..................F..... 412 747-2111
  Pittsburgh (G-14797)
Chatillon Scales Tester Co...............G..... 215 745-3304
  Philadelphia (G-13534)
David R Englehart..........................G..... 814 238-6734
  State College (G-17957)
Diversified Modular Casework...........G..... 484 442-8007
  Media (G-10922)
▲ Drucker Company LLC...................D..... 814 692-7661
  Philipsburg (G-14513)
▲ Drummond Scientific Company......D..... 610 353-0200
  Broomall (G-2287)
▲ Euthanex Corporation..................F..... 610 559-0159
  Bethlehem (G-1505)
Eye Design LLC..............................E..... 610 409-1900
  Trappe (G-18468)
Fedegari Technologies Inc...............F..... 215 453-0400
  Sellersville (G-17346)
▲ Fedegari Technologies Inc............F..... 215 453-2180
  Sellersville (G-17347)
▲ Finish Thompson Inc....................E..... 814 455-4478
  Erie (G-5290)
▲ Fisher Scientific Company LLC.......B..... 724 517-1500
  Pittsburgh (G-15019)
Hamilton L Fisher L C......................G..... 412 490-8300
  Pittsburgh (G-15075)
HB Instrment Div Bel-Art Produ..........G..... 610 489-5500
  Trappe (G-18470)
▲ Hvac Products Inc.......................F..... 484 901-4100
  Pottstown (G-15948)
J H C Fabrications Inc.....................G..... 570 277-6150
  New Philadelphia (G-12432)
Jrt Calibration Services Inc.............G..... 610 327-9610
  Pottstown (G-16006)
Leco Corporation...........................E..... 814 355-7903
  Bellefonte (G-1107)
▲ Leybold USA Inc..........................D..... 724 327-5700
  Export (G-5616)
Market Service Corp........................G..... 610 644-6211
  Malvern (G-10275)
Matachana USA Corp.......................G..... 484 873-2763
  Exton (G-5708)
Mdi Membrane Technologies Inc........G..... 717 412-0943
  Harrisburg (G-7175)
▼ Morehouse Instrument Company.....F..... 717 843-0081
  York (G-20603)
Oakwood Controls Corporation.........F..... 717 801-1515
  Glen Rock (G-6458)
▲ Omnia LLC...................................G..... 717 259-1633
  Abbottstown (G-5)

◆ Powdersize LLC...........................E..... 215 536-5605
  Quakertown (G-16231)
Prosoft Software Inc......................F..... 484 580-8162
  Wayne (G-19365)
Reed Associates Inc.......................F..... 215 256-9572
  Hatfield (G-7389)
S P Industries Inc..........................E..... 215 396-2200
  Warminster (G-18958)
▲ S P Industries Inc.......................D..... 215 672-7800
  Warminster (G-18959)
Skc Inc..D..... 724 260-0741
  Eighty Four (G-4849)
Spectra Hardware Inc......................G..... 724 863-7527
  Westmoreland City (G-19785)
T B W Industries Inc.......................F..... 215 794-8070
  Furlong (G-6234)
◆ Tbj Incorporated..........................F..... 717 261-9700
  Chambersburg (G-2984)
Tech Equipment Sales Inc................E..... 610 279-0370
  Norristown (G-12716)
▲ Thermo Hypersil-Keystone LLC......E..... 814 353-2300
  Bellefonte (G-1121)
▲ Thermo Shandon Inc....................G..... 412 788-1133
  Pittsburgh (G-15615)
▲ Thoren Caging Systems Inc...........G..... 570 454-3517
  Hazleton (G-7529)
Thoren Industries Inc......................F..... 570 454-3514
  Hazleton (G-7530)
Towerview Health Inc......................G..... 715 771-9831
  Philadelphia (G-14400)
▲ Tps LLC......................................C..... 570 538-7200
  New Columbia (G-12177)
▲ Verder Scientific Inc....................F..... 267 757-0351
  Newtown (G-12559)
Vere Inc.......................................F..... 724 335-5530
  New Kensington (G-12386)
VWR Corporation............................C..... 610 386-1700
  Radnor (G-16304)
VWR Scientific Inc.........................G..... 412 487-1983
  Allison Park (G-466)

3822 Automatic Temperature Controls

Absolute Acstic Noise Ctrl LLC.........F..... 304 670-0095
  Oakdale (G-12887)
Advanced Enviromation Inc..............G..... 610 422-3770
  Fleetwood (G-5967)
Advanced Technical Peddler Inc........G..... 610 689-4017
  Boyertown (G-1893)
▲ Advanced Valve Design Inc............F..... 610 435-8820
  Whitehall (G-19860)
Arbutus Electronics Inc..................F..... 717 764-3565
  York (G-20384)
Astrometrics Inc............................G..... 610 280-0869
  Downingtown (G-4212)
Automatic Control Elec Co...............F..... 210 661-4111
  Harleysville (G-7021)
Boss Controls LLC..........................G..... 724 396-8131
  Pittsburgh (G-14786)
C S Fuller Inc................................G..... 610 941-9225
  Plymouth Meeting (G-15837)
Clean Power Resources Inc..............G..... 724 863-3768
  Irwin (G-8148)
Control Tech USA Ltd......................D..... 570 529-6011
  Troy (G-18519)
Controlsoft Inc..............................E..... 724 733-2000
  Export (G-5595)
Eccotrol LLC.................................G..... 877 322-6876
  Huntingdon Valley (G-7974)
Evolve Guest Controls LLC..............F..... 855 750-9090
  West Chester (G-19553)
▲ First Quality Retail Svcs LLC.........C..... 610 265-5000
  King of Prussia (G-8619)
Healthy Home Resources.................F..... 412 431-4449
  Pittsburgh (G-15086)
Hri Networks Inc............................F..... 267 515-5880
  Philadelphia (G-13838)
Hvl LLC..E..... 412 494-9600
  Pittsburgh (G-15107)
Institute Prof Envmtl Practice..........G..... 412 396-1703
  Pittsburgh (G-15130)
Integritas Inc...............................G..... 814 941-7006
  Altoona (G-517)
Janatics USA Inc...........................G..... 610 443-2400
  Whitehall (G-19879)
Johnson Controls Inc......................D..... 610 276-3700
  Horsham (G-7828)
Johnson Controls Inc......................E..... 717 531-5371
  Hershey (G-7619)
Jordan Acquisition Group LLC...........D..... 724 733-2000
  Export (G-5612)

◆ Julabo Usa Inc............................E..... 610 231-0250
  Allentown (G-272)
Kanawha Scales & Systems Inc........F..... 724 258-6650
  Monongahela (G-11309)
Keenan and Meier LLC.....................G..... 215 766-3010
  Plumsteadville (G-15810)
Kustom Komponents.......................G..... 484 671-3076
  Leesport (G-9667)
Laminar Flow Inc............................D..... 215 672-0232
  Warminster (G-18909)
▲ Lloyd Industries Inc.....................E..... 215 367-5863
  Montgomeryville (G-11404)
Lundy Warehousing Inc....................G..... 570 327-4541
  Williamsport (G-20037)
Mainline Environmental LLC.............G..... 215 651-6635
  Trevose (G-18501)
MSA Advanced Detection LLC (..........G..... 724 776-8600
  Cranberry Township (G-3838)
Myexposome Inc............................G..... 610 668-0145
  Philadelphia (G-14049)
◆ National Refrigerants Inc.............E..... 215 698-6620
  Philadelphia (G-14056)
Novatech LLC................................C..... 484 812-6000
  Quakertown (G-16224)
Optimum Controls Corporation.........G..... 610 375-0990
  Reading (G-16459)
▲ Oven Industries Inc.....................E..... 717 766-0721
  Camp Hill (G-2508)
P D Q Pest Control Inc....................G..... 814 774-8882
  Girard (G-6398)
Philadelphia Instrs & Contrls...........F..... 215 329-8828
  Philadelphia (G-14146)
Phonetics Inc...............................E..... 610 558-2700
  Aston (G-787)
Precision Technology Assoc Inc.........G..... 412 881-8006
  Pittsburgh (G-15433)
◆ Probes Unlimited Inc....................E..... 267 263-0400
  Lansdale (G-9401)
Process Instruments Inc..................E..... 412 431-4600
  Pittsburgh (G-15451)
◆ Psg Controls Inc.........................D..... 215 257-3621
  Philadelphia (G-14214)
Radius Systems LLC........................E..... 610 388-9940
  Chadds Ford (G-2859)
Resolve Trnchless Slutions Inc..........G..... 215 441-5544
  Warminster (G-18953)
Siemens Industry Inc......................G..... 215 654-8040
  Blue Bell (G-1852)
◆ Strobic Air Corporation................F..... 215 723-4700
  Telford (G-18321)
Strubles Fire and Safety.................G..... 814 594-0840
  Kersey (G-8571)
▲ Therm-Omega-Tech Inc................G..... 877 379-8258
  Warminster (G-18980)
▲ Thermo Electric Company Inc........D..... 610 692-7990
  West Chester (G-19661)
▲ Warren Controls Inc....................G..... 610 317-0800
  Bethlehem (G-1653)
White Refrigeration Inc...................G..... 570 265-7335
  Towanda (G-18437)

3823 Indl Instruments For Meas, Display & Control

2000 F Process Htg & Contrls...........G..... 724 224-2800
  Tarentum (G-18238)
ABB Inc..D..... 724 295-6000
  Oakmont (G-12913)
Ace Controls & Instrumentation........G..... 610 876-2000
  Brookhaven (G-2242)
Action Manufacturing Company.........G..... 610 593-1800
  Atglen (G-799)
ADS LLC.......................................G..... 717 554-7552
  Lemoyne (G-9740)
Advanced Automated Controls Co......F..... 570 842-5842
  Lake Ariel (G-8887)
Ajax Electric Company....................E..... 215 947-8500
  Huntingdon Valley (G-7962)
Allen Gauge & Tool Company............E..... 412 241-6410
  Pittsburgh (G-14684)
◆ Alstom Power Conversion Inc.........C..... 412 967-0765
  Cranberry Township (G-3801)
▲ Ametek Inc.................................D..... 610 647-2121
  Berwyn (G-1351)
Ametek Inc....................................D..... 215 355-6900
  Horsham (G-7784)
▲ Amphenol Thermometrics Inc........C..... 814 834-9140
  Saint Marys (G-16948)
Analytical Technology Inc................F..... 610 917-0991
  Collegeville (G-3368)

S I C

▲ Apantec LLC ....F 267 436-3991
Lansdale (G-9342)

Arcadia Controls ....G 724 538-8931
Cranberry Township (G-3804)

Astra Corporation ....G 215 674-3539
Warminster (G-18830)

▲ Athena Controls Inc ....D 610 828-2490
Plymouth Meeting (G-15832)

Automatic Control Elec Co ....F 210 661-4111
Harleysville (G-7021)

Avure Autoclave Systems Inc ......G 814 833-4331
Erie (G-5200)

▲ Bacharach Inc ....C 724 334-5000
New Kensington (G-12326)

Backe Digital Brand Marketing ....F 610 947-6922
Radnor (G-16289)

▲ Bafco Inc ....E 215 674-1700
Warminster (G-18834)

Bethlehem Waste Water ....E 610 865-7169
Bethlehem (G-1463)

◆ Bombardier Transportation ....A 412 655-5700
Pittsburgh (G-14782)

Bronkhorst USA Inc ....G 610 866-6750
Bethlehem (G-1474)

Brooks Instrument LLC ....C 215 362-3500
Hatfield (G-7322)

Burlington Instr Sls Assoc ....G 215 322-8750
Trevose (G-18488)

Cameron Technologies Us Inc ......D 724 273-9300
Coraopolis (G-3672)

Cameron Technologies Us Inc ......F 724 273-9300
Coraopolis (G-3673)

▼ Campbell Manufacturing Inc .....D 610 367-2107
Bechtelsville (G-1030)

Cannon Instrument Company ....D 814 353-8000
State College (G-17948)

◆ Columbia Research Labs Inc .....E 610 872-3900
Woodlyn (G-20218)

▲ Conflow Inc ....F 724 746-0200
Washington (G-19157)

Conspec Controls Inc ....F 724 489-8450
Charleroi (G-3008)

▼ Control Design Inc ....E 412 788-2280
Pittsburgh (G-14873)

Control Electronics Inc ....G 610 942-3190
Brandamore (G-2001)

Cryoguard Corporation ....G 215 712-9018
Colmar (G-3413)

Cyberscan Technologies Inc ....G 215 321-0447
Washington Crossing (G-19256)

Dansway Incorporated ....G 570 672-1550
Elysburg (G-4973)

Delaware County Pennsylvania .....G 610 891-4865
Media (G-10920)

Delta Information Systems Inc ......E 215 657-5270
Horsham (G-7809)

Delta Usa Inc ....G 412 429-3574
Carnegie (G-2766)

Direct Digital Master Inc ....G 215 634-2235
Philadelphia (G-13634)

E F E Laboratories Inc ....E 215 672-2400
Horsham (G-7812)

Eaton Aerospace LLC ....D 610 522-4000
Glenolden (G-6473)

Eaton Corporation ....B 724 773-1231
Beaver (G-980)

Eaton Corporation ....C 610 522-4059
Glenolden (G-6474)

Edwin L Heim Co ....E 717 233-8711
Harrisburg (G-7125)

Electronic Tech Systems Inc ....D 724 295-6000
Natrona Heights (G-11942)

Ellison Industrial Contrls LLC ......G 724 483-0251
Belle Vernon (G-1086)

Emerson Electric Co ....E 610 569-4023
Royersford (G-16849)

Emerson Electric Co ....G 215 638-8904
Bensalem (G-1189)

◆ Emerson Process Management ...A 412 963-4000
Pittsburgh (G-14971)

Endress + Hauser Inc ....G 317 535-7138
Chalfont (G-2873)

▲ Environmental Tectonics Corp ...C 215 355-9100
Southampton (G-17809)

▼ Erie Strayer Company ....C 814 456-7001
Erie (G-5275)

Erie Technical Systems Inc ....G 814 899-2103
Erie (G-5277)

ESAB Group Inc ....B 717 637-8911
Hanover (G-6884)

Evoqua Water Technologies LLC ...E 215 638-7700
Bensalem (G-1192)

Fairmount Automation Inc ....F 610 356-9840
Conshohocken (G-3546)

FEC Technologies Inc ....E 717 764-5959
York (G-20477)

Fives N Amercn Combustn Inc ......G 412 655-0101
Pittsburgh (G-15020)

Flow Measurement Technologies ....G 610 377-6050
Lehighton (G-9714)

Flw of Pa Inc ....G 610 251-9700
Malvern (G-10237)

◆ FMC Technologies Measurement S ..C 281 591-4000
Erie (G-5297)

Francis L Freas Glass Works ....E 610 828-0430
Conshohocken (G-3549)

▲ Freas Glass Works Inc ....F 610 825-0430
Bridgeport (G-2036)

Fredericks Company Inc ....E 215 947-2500
Huntingdon Valley (G-7985)

Freshtemp LLC ....G 844 370-1782
Pittsburgh (G-15038)

▲ G & W Instruments Inc ....G 570 282-7352
Carbondale (G-2676)

Garrett Precision LLC ....G 717 779-1384
York (G-20490)

▼ GE Infrastructure Sensing ....F 617 926-1749
Feasterville Trevose (G-5912)

GE Infrastructure Sensing Inc ....B 814 834-5506
Saint Marys (G-16976)

General Nuclear Corp ....D 724 925-3565
Hunker (G-7928)

General Regulator Corp ....E 717 848-5960
York (G-20495)

George J Anderton ....G 814 382-9201
Conneaut Lake (G-3473)

Ges Automation Technology ....E 717 236-8733
Harrisburg (G-7133)

◆ Global Trade Links LLC ....E 888 777-1577
Chester Springs (G-3079)

Gow-Mac Instrument Co ....E 610 954-9000
Bethlehem (G-1526)

▲ Graftech Usa LLC ....C 814 781-2478
Saint Marys (G-16979)

▲ H B Instrument Co ....E 610 489-5500
Trappe (G-18469)

H M W Enterprises Inc ....F 717 765-4690
Waynesboro (G-19410)

◆ Heraeus Incorporated ....G 215 944-9981
Yardley (G-20314)

▲ Heraeus Sensor Tech USA LLC ...G 732 940-4400
Yardley (G-20319)

Homewood Products Corporation ...E 412 665-2700
Pittsburgh (G-15099)

Horiba Instruments Inc ....D 724 457-2424
Coraopolis (G-3698)

▲ Hydro Instruments Inc ....E 215 799-0980
Telford (G-18295)

I F H Industries Inc ....G 215 699-9344
Royersford (G-16852)

Industrial Control & Elec Inc ....G 610 859-9272
Upper Chichester (G-18665)

Industrial Instrs & Sups Inc ....F 215 396-0822
Wycombe (G-20260)

Industrial Learning Systems ....G 412 512-8257
Allison Park (G-453)

Instrument & Valve Services Co .....E 724 205-3348
Irwin (G-8172)

Jeffery Faust ....G 610 759-1951
Nazareth (G-11973)

Johnson Controls Inc ....D 610 276-3700
Horsham (G-7828)

▼ Johnson March Systems Inc ....E 215 364-2500
Warminster (G-18903)

◆ Julabo Usa Inc ....E 610 231-0250
Allentown (G-272)

Kenai Associates Inc ....G 412 655-2079
Pittsburgh (G-15168)

Keystone Powdered Metal Co ....C 814 834-9140
Saint Marys (G-16985)

◆ Kidde Fire Protection Inc ....E 610 363-1400
West Chester (G-19581)

Kontrol Automation Inc ....G 610 284-4106
Secane (G-17317)

Lawco Inc ....G 717 691-6965
Enola (G-5082)

Lawson Labs Inc ....G 610 725-8800
Malvern (G-10265)

Leco Corporation ....E 814 355-7903
Bellefonte (G-1107)

Lee Rj Group Inc ....C 800 860-1775
Monroeville (G-11342)

Lin Kay Associates Inc ....G 610 469-6833
Pottstown (G-15954)

Lionheart Holdings LLC ....D 215 283-8400
Newtown (G-12519)

Liquid Meter Company Inc ....G 814 756-5602
Cranesville (G-3868)

Lord Corporation ....A 877 275-5673
Erie (G-5373)

LSI Controls Inc ....E 717 762-2191
Waynesboro (G-19415)

◆ Maguire Products Inc ....E 610 459-4300
Aston (G-773)

▲ Mansco Products Inc ....G 215 674-4395
Warminster (G-18917)

◆ Marg Inc ....F 724 703-3020
Oakdale (G-12906)

Master-Lee Engineered Products ...G 724 537-6002
Latrobe (G-9502)

Matthey Johnson Inc ....E 610 232-1900
West Chester (G-19599)

▲ Maxima Tech & Systems LLC ......G 717 581-1000
Lancaster (G-9130)

Meeco Inc ....E 215 343-6600
Warrington (G-19125)

Mikron Valve & Mfr Inc ....G 814 453-2337
Erie (G-5392)

▲ Mine Safety Appliances Co LLC ...B 724 776-8600
Cranberry Township (G-3836)

MSA Safety Incorporated ....B 724 776-8600
Cranberry Township (G-3839)

MSA Safety Incorporated ....B 724 733-9100
Murrysville (G-11858)

MSA Safety Sales LLC ....G 724 776-8600
Cranberry Township (G-3841)

Nac Carbon Products Inc ....E 814 938-7450
Punxsutawney (G-16148)

▼ Nao Inc ....E 215 743-5300
Philadelphia (G-14051)

National Airoil Burner Co Inc ....G 215 743-5300
Philadelphia (G-14052)

Nu-Chem Corp ....F 610 770-2000
Allentown (G-336)

Parker-Hannifin Corporation ....C 215 723-4000
Hatfield (G-7377)

Parker-Hannifin Corporation ....C 724 861-8200
Irwin (G-8188)

Pdir Inc ....F 215 794-5011
Norristown (G-12701)

Philadelphia Instrs & Contrls ....F 215 329-8828
Philadelphia (G-14146)

Phoenix Combustion Inc ....F 610 495-5800
Pottstown (G-16031)

Pro-Mic Corp ....G 610 783-7901
King of Prussia (G-8665)

Process Control Spc Inc ....G 570 753-5799
Jersey Shore (G-8321)

Process Instruments Inc ....E 412 431-4600
Pittsburgh (G-15451)

◆ Psg Controls Inc ....D 215 257-3621
Philadelphia (G-14214)

Pyco LLC ....G 215 757-3704
Penndel (G-13241)

Responselogix Inc ....E 215 256-1700
Harleysville (G-7055)

Ridge Tool Company ....D 814 454-2461
Erie (G-5463)

Rieker Electronics Inc ....E 610 500-2000
Aston (G-790)

Rosemount Inc ....F 412 788-1160
Pittsburgh (G-15497)

Rosemount Inc ....F 724 746-3400
Lawrence (G-9540)

RTD Embedded Technologies Inc ...E 814 234-8087
State College (G-18017)

S & G Water Conditioning Inc ....G 215 672-2030
Warminster (G-18957)

Scritchfield Controls LLC ....G 717 887-5992
Wrightsville (G-20243)

Sensing Devices LLC ....F 717 295-4735
Lancaster (G-9192)

Sensing Devices Inc ....E 717 295-4735
Lancaster (G-9193)

Sensitron Associates Inc ....G 610 779-0939
Reading (G-16511)

Sensor Corporation ....G 724 887-4080
Scottdale (G-17200)

Serv-I-Quip Inc ....E 610 873-7010
Downingtown (G-4256)

Seventy-Three Mfg Co Inc ... E ... 610 845-7823
Bechtelsville (G-1037)

Siemens Industry Inc ... E ... 215 712-0280
Chalfont (G-2887)

Siemens Industry Inc ... D ... 215 646-7400
Spring House (G-17883)

Spectrodyne Inc ... F ... 215 804-1044
Quakertown (G-16246)

Staneco Corporation ... E ... 215 672-6500
Horsham (G-7852)

Stel Life Inc ... G ... 610 724-3688
Philadelphia (G-14344)

Suburban Water Technology Inc ... F ... 610 696-1495
West Chester (G-19648)

◆ Suez Wts Systems Usa Inc ... B ... 781 359-7000
Trevose (G-18505)

◆ Suez Wts Usa Inc ... A ... 215 355-3300
Trevose (G-18506)

Te Connectivity Corporation ... C ... 717 762-9186
Waynesboro (G-19425)

Texan Corporation ... E ... 215 441-8967
Warminster (G-18979)

▲ Thar Process Inc ... G ... 412 968-9180
Pittsburgh (G-15610)

Thermal Instrument Co Inc ... F ... 215 355-8400
Trevose (G-18507)

Thermocouple Technologies Inc ... G ... 215 529-9394
Quakertown (G-16251)

Thermocouple Technology LLC ... E ... 215 529-9394
Quakertown (G-16252)

Tru Temp Sensors Inc ... G ... 215 396-1550
Southampton (G-17844)

Tsb Nclear Enrgy USA Group Inc ... G ... 412 374-4111
Cranberry Township (G-3859)

United Partners Ltd ... G ... 570 283-0995
Taylor (G-18265)

Valley Instrument Co Inc ... F ... 610 363-2650
Exton (G-5746)

Veeder-Root Company ... E ... 814 695-4476
Duncansville (G-4465)

Vishay Precision Group Inc ... D ... 484 321-5300
Malvern (G-10343)

▲ W H Cooke & Co Inc ... G ... 717 630-2222
Hanover (G-6970)

◆ Westinghouse Electric Co LLC ... A ... 412 374-2020
Cranberry Township (G-3865)

Westinghouse Electric Co LLC ... D ... 412 256-1085
Pittsburgh (G-15710)

▼ Westinghouse Plasma Corp ... F ... 724 722-7053
Mount Pleasant (G-11723)

▲ Wgs Equipment & Controls ... F ... 610 459-8800
Garnet Valley (G-6270)

Wise Electronic Systems Inc ... G ... 717 244-0111
Windsor (G-20197)

Wistex II LLC ... G ... 215 328-9100
Warminster (G-19002)

World Video Sales Co Inc ... G ... 610 754-6800
Bechtelsville (G-1038)

World Wide Plastics Inc ... E ... 215 357-0893
Langhorne (G-9336)

Wortman Controls Inc ... G ... 814 834-1299
Saint Marys (G-17031)

Wyman-Gordon Pennsylvania LLC ... F ... 570 474-3059
Wilkes Barre (G-19978)

Xylem Wtr Sltons Zlienople LLC ... F ... 724 452-6300
Zelienople (G-20829)

3824 Fluid Meters & Counters

◆ Ametek Inc ... D ... 610 647-2121
Berwyn (G-1351)

Elster American Meter Co LLC ... G ... 412 833-2550
Pittsburgh (G-14965)

Emw Inc ... F ... 717 626-0248
Lititz (G-10006)

FMC Technologies Inc ... F ... 814 898-5000
Erie (G-5296)

◆ FMC Technologies Measurement S ... C ... 281 591-4000
Erie (G-5297)

Integrated Myers Systems LLC ... G ... 814 937-3958
Gallitzin (G-6246)

▲ Invensys Energy Metering Corp ... B ... 814 371-3011
Du Bois (G-4396)

◆ Maguire Products Inc ... E ... 610 459-4300
Aston (G-773)

Maguire Products Inc ... G ... 610 494-6566
Media (G-10937)

Matheson Tri-Gas Inc ... D ... 215 641-2700
Montgomeryville (G-11406)

▲ Maxima Tech & Systems LLC ... C ... 717 581-1000
Lancaster (G-9130)

Mol Communications & Elec ... G ... 570 383-3658
Dickson City (G-4122)

Monitor Data Corp ... F ... 215 887-8343
Glenside (G-6530)

Parker-Hannifin Corporation ... C ... 215 723-4000
Hatfield (G-7377)

▲ Prominent Fluid Controls Inc ... E ... 412 787-2484
Pittsburgh (G-15453)

Schlumberger Technology Corp ... C ... 814 220-1900
Brookville (G-2271)

▲ Sensus Metering Systems-North ... A ... 724 439-7700
Uniontown (G-18639)

Sensus USA Inc ... C ... 814 375-8354
Du Bois (G-4418)

Sensus USA Inc ... B ... 724 439-7700
Uniontown (G-18640)

Sensus USA Inc ... C ... 800 375-8875
Du Bois (G-4419)

Sensus USA Inc ... C ... 724 430-3956
Pittsburgh (G-15524)

Seventy-Three Mfg Co Inc ... E ... 610 845-7823
Bechtelsville (G-1037)

Strube Inc ... F ... 717 426-1906
Marietta (G-10468)

Techsource Engineering Inc ... G ... 814 459-2150
Erie (G-5505)

Utilities & Industries Inc ... D ... 814 653-8269
Reynoldsville (G-16667)

Veeder-Root Company ... E ... 814 695-4476
Duncansville (G-4465)

Wellspring Wireless Inc ... F ... 215 788-8485
Bensalem (G-1271)

World Wide Plastics Inc ... E ... 215 357-0893
Langhorne (G-9336)

3825 Instrs For Measuring & Testing Electricity

Abl Engineering ... G ... 814 364-1333
Boalsburg (G-1863)

Advance Stores Company Inc ... E ... 610 939-0120
Reading (G-16311)

Advanced Avionics Inc ... F ... 215 441-0449
Warminster (G-18821)

Advanced McRo Cmpt Specialists ... G ... 215 773-9700
Plymouth Meeting (G-15827)

▲ Advent Design Corporation ... C ... 215 781-0500
Bristol (G-2104)

◆ Aerotech Inc ... B ... 412 963-7470
Pittsburgh (G-14655)

Ametek Inc ... D ... 267 933-2121
Harleysville (G-7018)

Ametek Inc ... E ... 267 933-2121
Harleysville (G-7019)

◆ Ametek Inc ... D ... 610 647-2121
Berwyn (G-1351)

◆ Applied Test Systems LLC ... E ... 724 283-1212
Butler (G-2375)

Asr Instruments Inc ... F ... 412 833-7577
Bethel Park (G-1405)

▲ Avex Electronics Corp ... E ... 215 245-4848
Bensalem (G-1152)

Avo International Inc ... G ... 610 676-8500
Norristown (G-12637)

Avo Multi-AMP Corporation ... C ... 610 676-8501
Norristown (G-12638)

Avox Inc ... G ... 267 404-2676
Perkasie (G-13267)

Basic Power Inc ... G ... 570 872-9666
East Stroudsburg (G-4608)

Bionix Safety Technologies ... G ... 610 408-0555
Wayne (G-19307)

Bitronics LLC ... E ... 610 997-5100
Bethlehem (G-1467)

Brynavon Group Inc ... G ... 610 525-2102
Villanova (G-18765)

◆ Columbia Research Labs Inc ... E ... 610 872-3900
Woodlyn (G-20218)

Core Technology Group Inc ... G ... 215 822-0120
Chalfont (G-2869)

Cygnus Technology Inc ... G ... 570 424-5701
Delaware Water Gap (G-4042)

Donart Electronics Inc ... G ... 724 796-3011
Mc Donald (G-10572)

E F E Laboratories Inc ... E ... 215 672-2400
Horsham (G-7812)

Eastern Gauge & Regulator ... F ... 215 443-5192
Warminster (G-18868)

Eko Solutions Plus Inc ... G ... 215 856-9517
Elkins Park (G-4902)

▲ Electric Metering Corp USA ... D ... 215 949-1900
Bristol (G-2138)

Electro-Tech Systems Inc ... E ... 215 887-2196
Glenside (G-6515)

◆ FMC Technologies Measurement S ... C ... 281 591-4000
Erie (G-5297)

▲ Foerster Instruments Inc ... E ... 412 788-8976
Pittsburgh (G-15023)

Francis L Freas Glass Works ... E ... 610 828-0430
Conshohocken (G-3549)

Geosonics Inc ... F ... 724 934-2900
Warrendale (G-19076)

Hannon Company ... G ... 724 266-2712
Ambridge (G-618)

Hapeman Electronics Inc ... G ... 724 475-2033
Mercer (G-10962)

Hirschmann Electronics Inc ... F ... 717 217-2200
Chambersburg (G-2940)

Ic Mechanics Inc ... F ... 412 682-5560
Pittsburgh (G-15111)

Industrial Instrs & Sups Inc ... F ... 215 396-0822
Wycombe (G-20260)

Inteligistics Inc ... G ... 412 826-0379
Pittsburgh (G-15132)

Islip Transformer and Metal Co ... F ... 814 272-2700
State College (G-17978)

K&S Interconnect Inc ... D ... 267 256-1725
Fort Washington (G-6078)

Keystone Nap LLC ... G ... 215 280-6614
Fairless Hills (G-5786)

Leco Corporation ... E ... 814 355-7903
Bellefonte (G-1107)

Lee Rj Group Inc ... C ... 800 860-1775
Monroeville (G-11342)

Lehighton Electronics Inc ... F ... 610 377-5990
Lehighton (G-9718)

Lehman Scientific LLC ... G ... 717 244-7540
Wrightsville (G-20241)

Link Group Inc ... E ... 215 957-6061
Warminster (G-18912)

Loranger International Corp ... D ... 814 723-2250
Warren (G-19038)

Mack Information Systems Inc ... F ... 215 884-8123
Wyncote (G-20264)

▲ Maxima Tech & Systems LLC ... C ... 717 581-1000
Lancaster (G-9130)

MMS Technologies LLC ... G ... 814 238-2323
State College (G-17993)

▼ Morehouse Instrument Company ... F ... 717 843-0081
York (G-20603)

Oakwood Controls Corporation ... F ... 717 801-1515
Glen Rock (G-6458)

OHM- Labs Inc ... F ... 412 431-0640
Pittsburgh (G-15358)

Optimum Controls Corporation ... D ... 610 375-0990
Reading (G-16459)

▲ Orbit Advanced Tech Inc ... E ... 215 674-5100
Warminster (G-18933)

▲ Orbit/Fr Inc ... E ... 215 674-5100
Warminster (G-18934)

Pasadena Scientific Inc ... G ... 717 227-1220
Glen Rock (G-6459)

Process Instruments Inc ... E ... 412 431-4600
Pittsburgh (G-15451)

▲ Prominent Fluid Controls Inc ... E ... 412 787-2484
Pittsburgh (G-15453)

Rfcircuits Inc ... F ... 215 364-2450
Huntingdon Valley (G-8029)

▲ RLC Electronic Systems Inc ... E ... 610 898-4902
Reading (G-16500)

Schlumberger Technology Corp ... C ... 814 220-1900
Brookville (G-2271)

Semilab USA LLC ... F ... 610 377-5990
Lehighton (G-9726)

Sensor Corporation ... G ... 724 887-4080
Scottdale (G-17200)

Sentech Inc ... F ... 215 887-8665
Glenside (G-6535)

Spectrum Microwave Inc ... D ... 215 464-0586
Philadelphia (G-14333)

Square Wheel Inc ... G ... 610 921-8561
Temple (G-18337)

Strainsert Company ... E ... 610 825-3310
Conshohocken (G-3608)

Testlink Corp ... G ... 267 743-2956
New Hope (G-12317)

▲ Thermo Shandon Inc ... G ... 412 788-1133
Pittsburgh (G-15615)

Vizinex LLC ... G ... 215 529-9440
Bethlehem (G-1652)

S I C

World Wide Plastics Inc ....E 215 357-0893
Langhorne *(G-9336)*

3826 Analytical Instruments

Abbott Laboratories ....G 610 444-9818
Kennett Square *(G-8500)*

▲ Advent Design Corporation ....C 215 781-0500
Bristol *(G-2104)*

Altamira Instruments Inc ....F 412 963-6385
Pittsburgh *(G-14691)*

Applied RES & Photonics Inc ....G 717 220-1003
Harrisburg *(G-7089)*

▲ Applied Separations Inc ....E 610 770-0900
Allentown *(G-141)*

◆ Applied Test Systems LLC ....E 724 283-1212
Butler *(G-2375)*

Ardara Technologies LP ....F 724 863-0418
Ardara *(G-698)*

Avo Multi-AMP Corporation ....C 610 676-8501
Norristown *(G-12638)*

Bio-RAD Laboratories Inc ....B 267 322-6931
Philadelphia *(G-13462)*

Bio-RAD Laboratories Inc ....E 267 322-6945
Philadelphia *(G-13463)*

Bio/Data Corporation ....E 215 441-4000
Horsham *(G-7798)*

Biomeme Inc ....F 267 519-9066
Philadelphia *(G-13465)*

Bionix Safety Technologies ....G 610 408-0555
Wayne *(G-19307)*

▼ Bioscience Management Inc ....F 484 245-5232
Allentown *(G-152)*

▲ Boekel Industries Inc ....E 215 396-8200
Feasterville Trevose *(G-5892)*

Busch Company ....F 724 940-2326
Wexford *(G-19792)*

Cdprintexpress LLC ....G 610 450-6176
Phoenixville *(G-14539)*

Cds Analytical LLC ....G 610 932-3636
Oxford *(G-13074)*

Chem Image Bio Threat LLC ....E 412 241-7335
Pittsburgh *(G-14843)*

Chemimage Corporation ....E 412 241-7335
Pittsburgh *(G-14845)*

Chemimage Filter Tech LLC ....E 412 241-7335
Pittsburgh *(G-14846)*

Cianflone Scientific LLC ....G 412 787-3600
Pittsburgh *(G-14851)*

◆ Climatic Testing Systems Inc ....E 215 773-9322
Hatfield *(G-7326)*

Conair Group Inc ....E 814 437-6861
Franklin *(G-6122)*

Conspec Controls Inc ....F 724 489-8450
Charleroi *(G-3008)*

Delta Analytical Instruments ....G 412 372-0739
Trafford *(G-18453)*

EA Fischione Instruments ....E 724 325-5444
Export *(G-5600)*

EMD Millipore Corporation ....B 484 652-5600
Philadelphia *(G-13315)*

▲ Ems Acquisition Corp ....E 215 412-8400
Hatfield *(G-7339)*

▲ Environmental Tectonics Corp ....C 215 355-9100
Southampton *(G-17809)*

Extrel Cms LLC ....E 412 963-7530
Pittsburgh *(G-14996)*

Extremity Imaging Partners ....G 610 432-1055
Allentown *(G-210)*

First Choice Radon Testing Co ....G 215 947-1995
Huntingdon Valley *(G-7984)*

▲ Fisher Scientific Company LLC ....B 724 517-1500
Pittsburgh *(G-15019)*

Flir Systems Inc ....C 412 423-2100
Pittsburgh *(G-15021)*

▲ Foerster Instruments Inc ....E 412 788-8976
Pittsburgh *(G-15023)*

Gatan Inc ....D 724 779-2572
Warrendale *(G-19075)*

Gow-Mac Instrument Co ....E 610 954-9000
Bethlehem *(G-1526)*

Greendesign LLC ....G 215 242-0700
Philadelphia *(G-13784)*

Hamot Imaging Facility ....F 814 877-5381
Erie *(G-5309)*

Hazardous Materials Mgt Team ....G 215 968-4044
Newtown *(G-12507)*

▲ Holo Image Technology Inc ....G 215 946-2190
Bristol *(G-2153)*

Humanistic Robotics Inc ....G 267 515-5880
Philadelphia *(G-13842)*

Ideal Aerosmith Inc ....E 412 963-1495
Pittsburgh *(G-15113)*

Industrial Instrs & Sups Inc ....F 215 396-0822
Wycombe *(G-20260)*

Instech Laboratories Inc ....E 610 941-0132
Plymouth Meeting *(G-15852)*

Inteprod LLC ....F 610 650-9002
Norristown *(G-12670)*

Leco Corporation ....E 814 355-7903
Bellefonte *(G-1107)*

Lee Rj Group Inc ....C 800 860-1775
Monroeville *(G-11342)*

Lemos Labs LLC ....G 724 519-2936
Butler *(G-2420)*

Magritek Inc ....G 855 667-6835
Malvern *(G-10272)*

Microtrac Inc ....E 215 619-9920
Montgomeryville *(G-11408)*

Microtrac Inc ....F 717 843-4433
York *(G-20595)*

Microtrac Inc ....F 717 843-4433
York *(G-20596)*

▲ Milton Roy LLC ....C 215 441-0800
Ivyland *(G-8218)*

Milton Roy LLC ....G 215 293-0401
Ivyland *(G-8219)*

▲ Mine Safety Appliances Co LLC ....B 724 776-8600
Cranberry Township *(G-3836)*

Mitigator Inc ....G 717 576-9589
New Cumberland *(G-12189)*

Moa Instrumentation Inc ....F 609 352-9329
Levittown *(G-9849)*

Molecular Devices LLC ....E 610 873-5610
Downingtown *(G-4242)*

MSA Safety Incorporated ....B 724 776-8600
Cranberry Township *(G-3839)*

MSA Safety Sales LLC ....G 724 776-8600
Cranberry Township *(G-3841)*

N Pgh Imaging Specialists ....F 724 935-6200
Wexford *(G-19813)*

Nanomagnetics Instrs USA LLC ....G 610 417-3857
Easton *(G-4730)*

Nikon Precision Inc ....G 610 439-6203
Allentown *(G-334)*

Perkinelmer Inc ....D 215 368-6900
Montgomeryville *(G-11413)*

Phenomenex ....G 484 680-0678
Avondale *(G-857)*

Princeton Security Tech LLC ....G 609 915-9700
Croydon *(G-3924)*

Reading Thermal Systems Inc ....G 610 678-5890
Reading *(G-16492)*

▲ S P Industries Inc ....D 215 672-7800
Warminster *(G-18959)*

Sanda Corporation ....G 502 510-8782
Media *(G-10947)*

Sanguis LLC ....G 267 228-7502
Philadelphia *(G-14277)*

Scs Inc ....G 866 727-4436
Harleysville *(G-7057)*

Sloan Equipment Sales Co Inc ....G 215 784-0771
Dresher *(G-4358)*

Solar Light Company Inc ....D 215 517-8700
Glenside *(G-6538)*

Specac Inc ....G 215 793-4044
Fort Washington *(G-6092)*

Specialty Tstg & Dev Co Inc ....G 717 428-0186
Seven Valleys *(G-17380)*

▲ Structure Probe Inc ....E 610 436-5400
West Chester *(G-19646)*

◆ Suez Wts Usa Inc ....A 215 355-3300
Trevose *(G-18506)*

Teledyne Instruments Inc ....D 814 234-7311
State College *(G-18037)*

◆ Tescor Inc ....E 215 957-6061
Warminster *(G-18977)*

Thermo Fisher Scientific Inc ....F 610 837-5091
Nazareth *(G-11991)*

Thermo Fisher Scientific Inc ....B 561 688-8725
Stahlstown *(G-17937)*

Thermo Fisher Scientific Inc ....G 412 490-8000
Pittsburgh *(G-15611)*

Thermo Fisher Scientific Inc ....E 814 353-2300
Bellefonte *(G-1120)*

Thermo Fisher Scientific Inc ....C 215 964-6020
Philadelphia *(G-14387)*

Thermo Fisher Scientific Inc ....B 412 770-2326
Pittsburgh *(G-15612)*

Thermo Fisher Scientific Inc ....A 412 490-8300
Pittsburgh *(G-15613)*

Thermo Fisher Scientific Inc ....D 412 490-8000
Pittsburgh *(G-15614)*

▲ Thermo Hypersil-Keystone LLC ....E 814 353-2300
Bellefonte *(G-1121)*

▲ Thermo Shandon Inc ....G 412 788-1133
Pittsburgh *(G-15615)*

▲ Thermo-Electric Co ....G 724 695-2774
Imperial *(G-8077)*

Tiger Optics LLC ....F 215 343-6600
Warrington *(G-19135)*

Uct Inc ....G 215 781-9255
Bristol *(G-2212)*

US Web Converting McHy Corp ....F 570 644-1401
Paxinos *(G-13194)*

Vere Inc ....F 724 335-5530
New Kensington *(G-12386)*

Waters Corporation ....F 412 967-5665
Pittsburgh *(G-15707)*

Waters Corporation ....G 484 344-5404
Plymouth Meeting *(G-15879)*

Wel Instrument Co ....G 724 625-9041
Mars *(G-10513)*

Welltech Products Inc ....G 610 417-8928
Macungie *(G-10161)*

3827 Optical Instruments

A&J Optical Inc ....G 215 338-7645
Philadelphia *(G-13330)*

▲ Accutome Inc ....E 800 979-2020
Malvern *(G-10179)*

▲ Allentown Optical Corp ....E 610 433-5269
Allentown *(G-129)*

American Polarizers Inc ....E 610 373-5177
Reading *(G-16320)*

American Precision Glass Corp ....G 570 457-9664
Duryea *(G-4503)*

Atlas Instrument Co Inc ....G 717 267-1250
Chambersburg *(G-2907)*

Avo Photonics Inc ....F 215 441-0107
Horsham *(G-7793)*

Bioptechs Inc ....F 724 282-7145
Butler *(G-2380)*

Broadband Networks Inc ....D 814 237-4073
State College *(G-17947)*

Captek Inc ....G 610 296-2111
Berwyn *(G-1355)*

CJ Optical Holdings LLC ....F 610 264-8537
Whitehall *(G-19866)*

Co Optics Inc ....G 610 478-1884
Reading *(G-16348)*

▲ Ctp Carrera Inc ....C 724 539-6995
Latrobe *(G-9468)*

Cybel LLC ....G 610 691-7012
Bethlehem *(G-1494)*

▼ Cyoptics Inc ....B 484 397-2000
Breinigsville *(G-2013)*

Davro Optical Systems Inc ....G 215 362-3870
Lansdale *(G-9357)*

E O S Group Inc ....G 412 781-6023
Pittsburgh *(G-14951)*

Evaporated Coatings Inc ....E 215 659-3080
Willow Grove *(G-20116)*

Eyeland Optical ....G 888 603-3937
Mount Joy *(G-11656)*

◆ Flir Government Systems Pittsb ....D 724 295-2880
Freeport *(G-6204)*

Fraser Optics LLC ....E 215 443-5240
Trevose *(G-18494)*

Fraser-Volpe LLC ....E 215 443-5240
Feasterville Trevose *(G-5911)*

Gatan Inc ....D 724 779-2572
Warrendale *(G-19075)*

Hampton Controls Inc ....F 724 861-0150
Wendel *(G-19481)*

I Optical City ....G 412 881-3090
Pittsburgh *(G-15109)*

▲ Ii-VI Incorporated ....B 724 352-4455
Saxonburg *(G-17088)*

Ii-VI Optical Systems Inc ....E 215 842-3675
Philadelphia *(G-13848)*

Infinera Corporation ....G 408 572-5200
Allentown *(G-259)*

Insaco Incorporated ....D 215 536-3500
Quakertown *(G-16202)*

James B Carty Jr MD ....G 610 527-0897
Bryn Mawr *(G-2327)*

JAS Precision Inc ....G 215 239-7299
Yardley *(G-20322)*

John E Stiles Jr ....G 215 947-5571
Huntingdon Valley *(G-8005)*

L3 Technologies Inc..............................C......412 967-7700
Pittsburgh *(G-15209)*

Leica Microsystems Inc.....................G......610 321-0434
Exton *(G-5706)*

◆ Lenox Instrument Co Inc................E......215 322-9990
Trevose *(G-18500)*

Leonard Anderson...............................G......724 463-3615
Indiana *(G-8111)*

Lost Creek Shoe Shop Inc.................G......717 463-3117
Mifflintown *(G-11129)*

▲ Luzerne Optical Laboratories........C......570 822-3183
Wilkes Barre *(G-19937)*

Martin Rawdin Od...............................G......610 323-8007
Pottstown *(G-16016)*

Metaphase Technologies Inc.............E......215 639-8699
Bristol *(G-2167)*

▲ N Vision Group Inc..........................G......610 278-1900
Morton *(G-11592)*

Ncrx Optical Solutions Inc.................G......724 745-1011
Lawrence *(G-9538)*

Nexans USA Inc...................................B......717 354-6200
New Holland *(G-12271)*

Omnitech Partners Inc........................G......724 295-2880
Freeport *(G-6211)*

Onyx Optical...G......570 951-7750
Wilkes Barre *(G-19953)*

Ophthalmic Associates PC.................E......215 368-1646
Lansdale *(G-9395)*

Optical Crosslinks Inc.........................G......610 444-9469
Kennett Square *(G-8534)*

▲ Optical Systems Technology..........E......724 295-2880
Freeport *(G-6212)*

Opticscampcom....................................G......888 978-5330
Williamsport *(G-20052)*

P D Plastics...G......724 941-3930
Canonsburg *(G-2616)*

Parker-Hannifin Corporation..............C......724 861-8200
Irwin *(G-8188)*

Precision Glass Technologies.............G......610 323-2825
Sanatoga *(G-17058)*

Proteus Optics LLC.............................G......215 204-5241
Media *(G-10945)*

Questar Corporation............................E......215 862-5277
New Hope *(G-12312)*

Republic Lens Co Inc..........................F......610 588-7867
Bangor *(G-926)*

Sarclad (north America) LP................F......412 466-2000
Duquesne *(G-4499)*

▲ Shadowfax Inc..................................E......610 373-5177
Reading *(G-16515)*

Solar Light Company Inc.....................D......215 517-8700
Glenside *(G-6538)*

▲ Spitz Inc...D......610 459-5200
Chadds Ford *(G-2860)*

Te Connectivity Corporation...............B......717 986-3743
Middletown *(G-11081)*

Telefactor Robotics LLC......................G......610 940-6040
Conshohocken *(G-3611)*

Three Rivers Optical Company...........D......412 928-2020
Pittsburgh *(G-15620)*

View Thru Technologies Inc................F......215 703-0950
Quakertown *(G-16258)*

Vision Optics.......................................G......267 639-5773
Philadelphia *(G-14452)*

Vista Optical..G......724 458-0333
Grove City *(G-6807)*

3829 Measuring & Controlling Devices, NEC

Aaron J Michael..................................G......724 745-0656
Cecil *(G-2821)*

Advanced Controls Inc........................F......412 322-0991
Pittsburgh *(G-14651)*

AGR International Inc..........................E......724 482-2164
Butler *(G-2371)*

American Leak Detection....................G......412 859-6000
Coraopolis *(G-3657)*

American Stress Tech Inc...................F......412 784-8400
Pittsburgh *(G-14707)*

Ametek Inc...D......215 355-6900
Horsham *(G-7784)*

Amphenol Corporation........................G......814 834-9140
Saint Marys *(G-16947)*

Analytical Technology Inc...................F......610 917-0991
Collegeville *(G-3368)*

▲ Apantec LLC......................................F......267 436-3991
Lansdale *(G-9342)*

Applied Controls Inc............................E......717 854-2889
York *(G-20380)*

▲ Applied Separations Inc...................E......610 770-0900
Allentown *(G-141)*

◆ Applied Test Systems LLC..............E......724 283-1212
Butler *(G-2375)*

▲ Associated Ceramics & Tech...........D......724 353-1585
Sarver *(G-17065)*

Assured Polygraph Services Inc.........G......412 492-9980
Pittsburgh *(G-14728)*

▲ Audiology & Hearing Aid Center.....G......570 822-6122
Wilkes Barre *(G-19906)*

Audiology & Hearing Aid Center.........G......570 383-0500
Peckville *(G-13206)*

Avo Multi-AMP Corporation................C......610 676-8501
Norristown *(G-12638)*

B & Q Technical Service Inc..............G......610 872-8428
Wallingford *(G-18781)*

Batterytest Equipment Co...................G......610 746-9449
Nazareth *(G-11956)*

◆ Biocoat Incorporated.......................E......215 734-0888
Horsham *(G-7790)*

Bionix Safety Technologies................G......610 408-0555
Wayne *(G-19307)*

Blatek Industries Inc...........................B......814 231-2085
State College *(G-17946)*

◆ Bon Tool Company...........................D......724 443-7080
Gibsonia *(G-6328)*

Bondata Inc...G......717 566-5550
Hummelstown *(G-7903)*

▲ Boschung America LLC.....................F......724 658-3300
New Castle *(G-12065)*

Bvs Inc...G......610 273-2842
Honey Brook *(G-7739)*

Cdl Nuclear Technologies Inc............G......724 933-5570
Wexford *(G-19794)*

▼ Chant Engineering Co Inc...............E......215 230-4260
New Britain *(G-12045)*

Chemdaq Inc..F......412 787-0202
Pittsburgh *(G-14844)*

Cianflone Scientific LLC......................G......412 787-3600
Pittsburgh *(G-14851)*

Circa Healthcare LLC.........................G......610 954-2340
Malvern *(G-10209)*

Clickcadence LLC................................G......412 434-4911
Pittsburgh *(G-14860)*

Coinco Inc...E......814 425-7476
Cochranton *(G-3338)*

◆ Columbia Research Labs Inc...........E......610 872-3900
Woodlyn *(G-20218)*

Cornerstone Automation LLC..............G......215 513-4111
Telford *(G-18277)*

Custom Scientific Instruments............G......610 923-6500
Easton *(G-4667)*

Delta Information Systems Inc.............E......215 657-5270
Horsham *(G-7809)*

Dynamic Control Systems Inc............G......484 674-1408
King of Prussia *(G-8616)*

Eaton Aerospace LLC.........................D......610 522-4000
Glenolden *(G-6473)*

Embedded Energy Technology LLC....G......412 254-3381
Pittsburgh *(G-14967)*

Encompass Health Corporation..........F......610 478-8797
Reading *(G-16374)*

◆ Enginred Arrsting Systems Corp.....C......610 494-8000
Upper Chichester *(G-18660)*

Ev Products Inc....................................E......724 352-5288
Zelienople *(G-20799)*

▲ Evans John Sons Incorporated.......D......215 368-7700
Lansdale *(G-9365)*

Everight Position Tech Corp...............G......856 727-9500
Narberth *(G-11910)*

Faro Technologies Inc........................G......407 333-9911
Exton *(G-5675)*

◆ FMC Technologies Measurement S..C......281 591-4000
Erie *(G-5297)*

▲ Foerster Instruments Inc.................E......412 788-8976
Pittsburgh *(G-15023)*

◆ Forney Holdings Inc.........................E......724 346-7400
Hermitage *(G-7584)*

Forney LP...E......724 346-7400
Zelienople *(G-20801)*

Francis L Freas Glass Works..............E......610 828-0430
Conshohocken *(G-3549)*

Gamry Instruments Inc.......................E......215 682-9330
Warminster *(G-18885)*

Garment Dimensions Inc.....................G......610 838-0484
Bethlehem *(G-1524)*

General Nuclear Corp.........................D......724 925-3565
Hunker *(G-7928)*

Genisphere LLC...................................G......215 996-3002
Hatfield *(G-7344)*

Geosonics Inc......................................F......724 934-2900
Warrendale *(G-19076)*

Gerhart Systems & Contrls Corp........F......610 264-2800
Allentown *(G-231)*

Grace Industries Inc...........................E......724 962-9231
Fredonia *(G-6180)*

Greenbank Energy Solutions Inc........G......724 229-4454
Washington *(G-19179)*

Greenbank Group Inc..........................G......724 229-1180
Washington *(G-19180)*

Guth Laboratories Inc.........................F......717 564-5470
Harrisburg *(G-7137)*

Hawk Grips..G......484 351-8050
Conshohocken *(G-3554)*

Heart Masters Diagnsostics LLC........G......267 503-3803
Philadelphia *(G-13809)*

Hy-Tech Machine Inc..........................D......724 776-2400
Cranberry Township *(G-3824)*

Ideal Aerosmith Inc............................E......412 963-1495
Pittsburgh *(G-15113)*

▲ Imac Systems Inc............................E......215 946-2200
Bristol *(G-2155)*

Industrial Instrs & Sups Inc..............F......215 396-0822
Wycombe *(G-20260)*

▲ Industrial Scientific Corp...............B......412 788-4353
Pittsburgh *(G-15120)*

▲ Invensys Energy Metering Corp.....B......814 371-3011
Du Bois *(G-4396)*

Johnson Controls Inc..........................E......717 531-5371
Hershey *(G-7619)*

Jomarr Safety Systems Inc.................G......570 346-5330
Dunmore *(G-4475)*

Julabo West Inc...................................F......610 231-0250
Allentown *(G-273)*

Kinetics Hydro Inc...............................G......717 532-6016
Shippensburg *(G-17535)*

King Tester Corporation.......................F......610 279-6010
Phoenixville *(G-14557)*

King Tester Corporation.......................F......610 279-6010
Phoenixville *(G-14558)*

Lakeshore Isotopes LLC......................F......814 836-0207
Erie *(G-5357)*

Lasersense Inc.....................................G......856 207-5701
Media *(G-10936)*

◆ Lenox Instrument Co Inc.................E......215 322-9990
Trevose *(G-18500)*

Long Island Pllution Strippers............G......215 752-2709
Yardley *(G-20323)*

Lord Corporation.................................D......814 398-4641
Cambridge Springs *(G-2481)*

Lpg Industries Inc...............................E......610 622-2900
Clifton Heights *(G-3254)*

◆ M Squared Electronics Inc.............F......215 945-6658
Levittown *(G-9848)*

Marvel Manufacturing Company.........G......570 421-6221
Stroudsburg *(G-18128)*

Marvel Manufacturing Company.........G......570 421-6221
Stroudsburg *(G-18129)*

Matt Machine & Mfg Inc.....................E......412 793-6020
Pittsburgh *(G-15263)*

Measurement Specialties Inc..............G......610 971-9893
Wayne *(G-19354)*

▲ Mine Safety Appliances Co LLC......B......724 776-8600
Cranberry Township *(G-3836)*

Mistras Group Inc................................E......610 497-0400
Trainer *(G-18463)*

Mp Machinery and Testing LLC...........E......814 234-8860
Port Matilda *(G-15902)*

MSA Safety Incorporated....................B......724 776-8600
Cranberry Township *(G-3839)*

MSA Safety Sales LLC........................G......724 776-8600
Cranberry Township *(G-3841)*

National Basic Sensor Corp...............F......215 322-4700
Huntingdon Valley *(G-8016)*

▲ Newage Testing Instruments..........E......215 355-6900
Horsham *(G-7835)*

OP Schuman & Sons Inc....................D......215 343-1530
Warminster *(G-18932)*

▲ Optotech Optical Machinery Inc.....F......215 679-2091
Palm *(G-13096)*

Optotherm Inc......................................G......724 940-7600
Sewickley *(G-17401)*

P J Electronics Inc..............................G......412 793-3912
Pittsburgh *(G-15366)*

Pace Environmental.............................G......610 262-3818
Whitehall *(G-19885)*

PH Tool LLC...E......267 203-1600
Pipersville *(G-14618)*

Photonis Digital Imaging LLC.............G......972 987-1460
Lancaster *(G-9171)*

Precision Laser and Instr Inc..............E......724 266-1600
Ambridge *(G-631)*

Employee Codes: A=Over 500 employees, B=251-500
C=101-250, D=51-100, E=20-50, F=10-19, G=3-9

▲ Precision Medical Inc ....C...... 610 262-6090
   Northampton (G-12860)
◆ Probes Unlimited Inc ....E...... 267 263-0400
   Lansdale (G-9401)
Proceq USA Inc ....G...... 724 512-0330
   Aliquippa (G-90)
Process Instruments Inc ....E...... 412 431-4600
   Pittsburgh (G-15451)
Pruftechnik Inc ....E...... 844 242-6296
   Philadelphia (G-14211)
◆ Pruftechnik Service Inc ....E...... 856 401-3095
   Philadelphia (G-14212)
R L Holliday Company Inc ....E...... 412 561-7620
   Pittsburgh (G-15463)
Rel-Tek Corporation ....F...... 412 373-4417
   Monroeville (G-11353)
Reliefband Technologies LLC ....F...... 877 735-2263
   Horsham (G-7845)
▲ Rieker Instrument Company Inc ......E...... 610 500-2000
   Aston (G-791)
Sanavita Medical LLC ....E...... 267 517-3220
   Telford (G-18312)
Scanmaster ....G...... 215 208-4732
   Warminster (G-18962)
Sensing Devices Inc ....E...... 717 295-4735
   Lancaster (G-9193)
Sensor Networks Inc ....E...... 814 466-7207
   Boalsburg (G-1869)
Sensor Networks Inc ....G...... 814 441-2476
   Boalsburg (G-1870)
Sensor Networks Corporation ....G...... 717 466-7207
   Boalsburg (G-1871)
Skantra Diagnostics Inc ....G...... 215 990-0381
   Radnor (G-16302)
Skc Inc ....D...... 724 260-0741
   Eighty Four (G-4849)
Solar Light Company Inc ....D...... 215 517-8700
   Glenside (G-6538)
Special T Electronic LLC ....G...... 412 635-4997
   Pittsburgh (G-15568)
Strainsert Company ....E...... 610 825-3310
   Conshohocken (G-3608)
◆ Stretch Devices Inc ....E...... 215 739-3000
   Philadelphia (G-14352)
Summit Control Panels ....G...... 814 431-4402
   Waterford (G-19270)
◆ Tasseron Sensors Inc ....D...... 570 601-1971
   Montoursville (G-11451)
Technology Development Corp ....F...... 610 631-5043
   Norristown (G-12717)
Teeco Associates Inc ....E...... 610 539-4708
   Schwenksville (G-17179)
Teletrix Corp ....G...... 412 798-3636
   Pittsburgh (G-15605)
▲ Thermo Electric Company Inc ....D...... 610 692-7990
   West Chester (G-19661)
Thermo Electric Pa Inc ....D...... 610 692-7990
   West Chester (G-19662)
Thermocouple Technology LLC ....E...... 215 529-9394
   Quakertown (G-16252)
Tri County Transit Service Inc ....D...... 610 495-5640
   Pottstown (G-16057)
Valco ....E...... 610 691-3205
   Bethlehem (G-1649)
▲ Videotek Inc ....C...... 610 327-2292
   Pottstown (G-16068)
Warren Industries Incorporated ....E...... 215 464-9300
   Philadelphia (G-14458)
Warren Industries Incorporated ....F...... 215 969-5011
   Philadelphia (G-14459)
Watermark Usa LLC ....F...... 610 983-0500
   Gladwyne (G-6409)
◆ Westinghouse Electric Co LLC ....A...... 412 374-2020
   Cranberry Township (G-3865)
Westinghouse Electric Co LLC ....A...... 412 374-4252
   Warrendale (G-19102)
Westinghouse Electric Co LLC ....D...... 412 256-1085
   Pittsburgh (G-15710)
Westinghouse Electric Company ....E...... 866 442-7873
   Pittsburgh (G-15711)
World Video Sales Co Inc ....G...... 610 754-6800
   Bechtelsville (G-1038)
X-Bar Diagnostics Systems Inc ....G...... 610 388-2071
   Kennett Square (G-8551)
Xensor Corporation ....E...... 610 284-2508
   Drexel Hill (G-4373)

3841 Surgical & Medical Instrs & Apparatus

Abbott Laboratories ....G...... 610 444-9818
   Kennett Square (G-8500)

Accellent ....F...... 610 489-0300
   Trappe (G-18466)
◆ Accutome Inc ....E...... 800 979-2020
   Malvern (G-10179)
Actuated Medical Inc ....F...... 814 355-0003
   Bellefonte (G-1091)
Aesculap Biologics LLC ....E...... 610 984-9000
   Breinigsville (G-2004)
Aesculap Implant Systems LLC ....G...... 610 984-9404
   Breinigsville (G-2005)
Aesculap Implant Systems LLC ....G...... 610 984-9000
   Center Valley (G-2823)
Airgas Safety Inc ....C...... 215 826-9000
   Levittown (G-9814)
Airos Medical Inc ....G...... 866 991-6956
   Audubon (G-822)
Alcon Manufacturing Ltd ....A...... 610 670-3500
   Reading (G-16316)
Alcon Research Ltd ....B...... 610 670-3500
   Reading (G-16317)
Alliqua Biomedical Inc ....D...... 215 702-8550
   Langhorne (G-9275)
Altus Partners LLC ....E...... 610 355-4156
   West Chester (G-19497)
Amax Solutions Inc ....G...... 717 798-8070
   Lemoyne (G-8742)
American Contract Systems ....G...... 952 926-3515
   Zelienople (G-20789)
American Proven Products LLC ....G...... 215 876-5274
   Philadelphia (G-13388)
Ardiem Medical Inc ....F...... 724 349-0855
   Indiana (G-8082)
▲ Arrow International Inc ....A...... 610 225-6800
   Wayne (G-19303)
Arrow International Inc ....C...... 610 655-8522
   Reading (G-16323)
Arrow International Inc ....C...... 610 378-0131
   Reading (G-16324)
Aspire Bariatrics Inc ....E...... 610 590-1577
   Exton (G-5647)
◆ B Braun Medical Inc ....A...... 610 691-5400
   Bethlehem (G-1454)
B Braun Medical Inc ....A...... 610 336-9595
   Breinigsville (G-2009)
B Braun of America Inc ....G...... 610 691-5400
   Bethlehem (G-1455)
Bacharach Instruments Ltd ....F...... 724 334-5000
   Pittsburgh (G-14747)
Barc Developmental Services .....E...... 215 794-0800
   Holicong (G-7638)
Baxano Surgical Inc ....E...... 919 800-0020
   Blue Bell (G-1815)
Baxter Healthcare Corporation ....B...... 717 232-1901
   Harrisburg (G-7095)
◆ Bayer Corporation ....A...... 412 777-2000
   Pittsburgh (G-14750)
▼ Bayer Medical Care Inc ....A...... 724 940-6800
   Indianola (G-8135)
Bayer Medical Care Inc ....D...... 724 337-8176
   New Kensington (G-12327)
Bayer Medical Care Inc ....D...... 724 360-7600
   Saxonburg (G-17081)
Bayer Medical Care Inc ....D...... 412 767-2400
   Pittsburgh (G-14756)
Bayter Technologies Inc ....G...... 610 948-7447
   Phoenixville (G-14529)
Berkley Medical Resources Inc ....D...... 724 438-3000
   Uniontown (G-18617)
◆ Berkley Medical Resources Inc ....C...... 724 564-5002
   Smithfield (G-17642)
▲ Berkley Surgical Corporation ....C...... 724 438-3000
   Uniontown (G-18618)
Best Medical International Inc ....D...... 412 312-6700
   Pittsburgh (G-14764)
Bio Med Sciences Inc ....F...... 610 530-3193
   Allentown (G-151)
▲ Biochem Technology Inc ....G...... 484 674-7003
   King of Prussia (G-8588)
Biomeme Inc. ....F...... 267 519-9066
   Philadelphia (G-13465)
Bioplast Manufacturing LLC ......E...... 609 807-3070
   Bristol (G-2118)
Boehringer Laboratories Inc ......E...... 610 278-0900
   Phoenixville (G-14536)
Boehringer Laboratories LLC ......E...... 610 278-0900
   Phoenixville (G-14537)
Boehringer Wound Systems LLC ....E...... 610 278-0900
   Phoenixville (G-14538)
Branch Medical Group LLC ....D...... 877 992-7262
   Norristown (G-12642)

C L Sturkey Inc ....G...... 717 274-9441
   Lebanon (G-9551)
Cardiac Telecom Corporation .....F...... 800 355-2594
   Greensburg (G-6656)
Cardiacassist Inc ....E...... 412 963-8883
   Pittsburgh (G-14808)
Chrono-Log Corp ....E...... 610 853-1130
   Havertown (G-7418)
◆ Clinton Industries Inc ....E...... 717 848-2391
   York (G-20427)
Cook Vandergrift Inc ....C...... 724 845-8621
   Vandergrift (G-18724)
Coordinated Health Systems ....C...... 610 861-8080
   Bethlehem (G-1487)
Cybersonics Inc ....G...... 814 898-4734
   Erie (G-5243)
Depuy Synthes Inc ....B...... 610 647-9700
   Paoli (G-13138)
Depuy Synthes Products Inc ......G...... 610 719-5000
   West Chester (G-19539)
Depuy Synthes Sales Inc ....G...... 610 719-5000
   West Chester (G-19540)
Depuy Synthes Sales Inc ....F...... 610 738-4600
   West Chester (G-19541)
Dermamed Usa Inc ....F...... 610 358-4447
   Lenni (G-9761)
Dgh Koi Inc ....G...... 717 582-7749
   Shermans Dale (G-17500)
▲ Dgh Technology Inc ....F...... 610 594-9100
   Exton (G-5665)
Dghkoi Inc ....G...... 610 594-9100
   Exton (G-5666)
▲ Doctor In The House Inc ....G...... 610 277-1998
   Blue Bell (G-1827)
Draeger Inc ....F...... 215 721-5400
   Telford (G-18281)
Draeger Inc ....F...... 215 660-2252
   Telford (G-18282)
▲ Draeger Medical Systems Inc ....C...... 800 437-2437
   Telford (G-18283)
Drt Medical LLC ....E...... 215 997-2900
   Hatfield (G-7336)
DSM Biomedical Inc. ....G...... 484 713-2100
   Exton (G-5668)
Duane Grant ....G...... 412 856-1357
   Monroeville (G-11333)
Eastern Rail Systems Inc ....G...... 215 826-9980
   Bristol (G-2137)
Easy Walking Inc ....G...... 215 654-1626
   Maple Glen (G-10429)
Endologix Inc ....G...... 412 661-5877
   Pittsburgh (G-14973)
▲ Environmental Tectonics Corp ....C...... 215 355-9100
   Southampton (G-17809)
Escalon Medical Corp ....E...... 610 688-6830
   Wayne (G-19325)
Essential Medical Inc ....G...... 610 557-1009
   Exton (G-5673)
▲ Eyenavision Inc ....F...... 412 456-2736
   Pittsburgh (G-14997)
Fluortek Inc ....D...... 610 438-1800
   Easton (G-4683)
Foranne Manufacturing Inc ....E...... 215 357-4650
   Warminster (G-18881)
Foundation Surgery Center ....E...... 215 628-4300
   Fort Washington (G-6070)
General Anesthetic Services ......F...... 412 851-4390
   South Park (G-17783)
Globus Medical Inc ....G...... 610 930-1800
   Norristown (G-12661)
Globus Medical Inc ....B...... 610 930-1800
   Audubon (G-826)
Glutalor Medical Inc ....F...... 610 492-5710
   Exton (G-5689)
▲ Gulden Ophthalmics Inc ....F...... 215 884-8105
   Elkins Park (G-4904)
Haemonetics Corporation ....C...... 412 741-7399
   Leetsdale (G-9692)
▲ Health-Chem Corporation ....D...... 717 764-1191
   Emigsville (G-4988)
▲ Hill Laboratories Co ....E...... 610 644-2867
   Malvern (G-10246)
Hunter Russell Group ....G...... 724 445-7228
   Chicora (G-3127)
Hyq Research Solutions LLC ......G...... 717 439-9320
   Hummelstown (G-7914)
Icu Medical Sales Inc ....G...... 610 265-9100
   King of Prussia (G-8633)
Implant Research Center ....G...... 215 571-4345
   Philadelphia (G-13851)

Infrascan Inc ....G...... 215 387-6784
  Philadelphia (G-13855)
Ingmar Medical Ltd ....G...... 412 441-8228
  Pittsburgh (G-15125)
▼ Instrumentation Industries Inc .....E...... 412 854-1133
  Bethel Park (G-1418)
Intact Vascular Inc ....E...... 484 253-1048
  Wayne (G-19338)
Intelomed Inc ....F...... 412 536-7661
  Wexford (G-19808)
Invibio Inc ....E...... 484 342-6004
  Conshohocken (G-3565)
Jade Prcsion Med Cmponents LLC .....G...... 215 947-5762
  Huntingdon Valley (G-8001)
Kc-13 LLC ....G...... 484 887-8900
  West Chester (G-19578)
Keeler Instruments Inc ....E...... 610 353-4359
  Malvern (G-10264)
Keyscripts LLC ....G...... 866 446-2848
  Mechanicsburg (G-10863)
Kmi Surgical Ltd ....G...... 610 518-7110
  Downingtown (G-4237)
Lake Region Medical Inc ....C...... 610 489-0300
  Trappe (G-18471)
Lampire Biological Labs Inc ....E...... 215 795-2838
  Ottsville (G-13065)
Legend Spine LLC ....G...... 267 566-3273
  Pottstown (G-16010)
▲ Lifescan Inc ....A...... 800 227-8862
  Chesterbrook (G-3093)
Lifescan Global Corporation ....F...... 800 227-8862
  Chesterbrook (G-3094)
Lifesensors Inc ....F...... 610 644-8845
  Malvern (G-10268)
▼ Loh Enterprises LLC ....E...... 570 737-4143
  Clarks Summit (G-3197)
Maculogix Inc ....F...... 717 982-6751
  Harrisburg (G-7172)
▲ Mangar Medical Inc ....C...... 215 230-0300
  New Britain (G-12048)
Matt Machine & Mfg Inc ....E...... 412 793-6020
  Pittsburgh (G-15263)
Medcontrol Technologies LLC ....G...... 508 479-8109
  Pittsburgh (G-15272)
Medical Creative Technologies ....G...... 267 347-4436
  Quakertown (G-16215)
Medicapture Inc ....F...... 610 238-0700
  Plymouth Meeting (G-15856)
Medisurg Ltd ....G...... 610 277-3937
  Norristown (G-12682)
Medplast Engineered Pdts Inc ....D...... 814 367-2246
  Westfield (G-19780)
Medrad Incorporated Ohara ....G...... 412 967-9700
  Pittsburgh (G-15273)
Medtronic Usa Inc ....G...... 724 933-8100
  Wexford (G-19811)
Medtronic Usa Inc ....G...... 717 657-6140
  Harrisburg (G-7176)
Merit Medical ....G...... 610 651-5000
  Malvern (G-10277)
Micro Facture LLC ....E...... 717 285-9700
  Mountville (G-11799)
Micromed LLC ....G...... 480 236-4705
  Ambler (G-590)
▲ Micronic ....G...... 484 480-3372
  Aston (G-776)
Molecular Devices LLC ....E...... 610 873-5610
  Downingtown (G-4242)
Mytamed Inc ....G...... 877 444-6982
  Malvern (G-10282)
N E D LLC ....G...... 610 442-1017
  Slatington (G-17609)
N T M Inc ....E...... 717 567-9374
  Newport (G-12492)
Neuro Kinetics Inc ....F...... 412 963-6649
  Pittsburgh (G-15329)
Neurodx Development LLC ....G...... 609 865-4426
  Yardley (G-20328)
Neurologix Technologies Inc ....F...... 512 914-7941
  Cherry Tree (G-3033)
Neuronetics Inc ....C...... 610 640-4202
  Malvern (G-10285)
Neurontrvntnal Thrapeutics Inc .....G...... 412 726-3111
  Pittsburgh (G-15330)
◆ Oakworks Inc ....D...... 717 227-0516
  New Freedom (G-12213)
Onsite Sterilization LLC ....G...... 484 624-8566
  Pottstown (G-16023)
Operating Room Safety LLC ....G...... 866 498-6882
  Conshohocken (G-3580)

Orasure Technologies Inc ....B...... 610 882-1820
  Bethlehem (G-1588)
▲ Orthovita Inc ....B...... 610 640-1775
  Malvern (G-10291)
Ot Medical LLC ....G...... 484 588-2063
  Collegeville (G-3385)
Parker-Hannifin Corporation ....C...... 215 723-4000
  Hatfield (G-7377)
Peca Labs Inc ....G...... 412 589-9847
  Pittsburgh (G-15372)
Penn-Century Inc ....G...... 215 843-6540
  Philadelphia (G-14131)
Peregrine Surgical Ltd ....E...... 215 348-0456
  Doylestown (G-4323)
Permegear Inc ....G...... 484 851-3688
  Hellertown (G-7560)
Perryman Company ....D...... 724 745-7272
  Houston (G-7875)
Pilling Company ....F...... 215 643-2600
  Fort Washington (G-6088)
Piramal Critical Care Inc ....D...... 610 974-9760
  Bethlehem (G-1599)
▲ Piramal Critical Care Inc ....E...... 800 414-1901
  Bethlehem (G-1598)
▼ Pneu-Dart Inc ....D...... 570 323-2710
  Williamsport (G-20061)
Porter Instrument ....F...... 215 723-4000
  Hatfield (G-7383)
Ppk Animal Healthcare LLC ....G...... 718 288-4318
  Montoursville (G-11448)
Precise Medical ....E...... 215 345-6729
  Furlong (G-6232)
Precision Medical Devices Inc ....F...... 717 795-9480
  Mechanicsburg (G-10881)
▲ Premier Dental Products Co ....E...... 610 239-6000
  Plymouth Meeting (G-15865)
Premier Dental Products Co Inc ......E...... 215 676-9090
  Philadelphia (G-14196)
▲ Pulse Technologies Inc ....C...... 267 733-0200
  Quakertown (G-16235)
▲ Qbc Diagnostics LLC ....C...... 814 342-6210
  Port Matilda (G-15905)
Qualtek Molecular Laboratories ......G...... 215 504-7402
  Newtown (G-12540)
▼ Recathco LLC ....F...... 412 487-1482
  Allison Park (G-461)
Renerva LLC ....G...... 412 841-7966
  Pittsburgh (G-15478)
Respironics Inc ....B...... 724 387-4270
  Monroeville (G-11354)
Respironics Inc ....C...... 724 334-3100
  New Kensington (G-12370)
◆ Respironics Inc ....D...... 724 387-5200
  Murrysville (G-11865)
Rex Medical Inc ....E...... 610 940-0665
  Conshohocken (G-3600)
▲ Roechling Med Lancaster LLC ......C...... 717 335-3700
  Denver (G-4092)
Safe-TEC Clinical Products LLC ....G...... 215 364-5582
  Warminster (G-18960)
Safeguard Scientifics Inc ....E...... 610 293-0600
  Radnor (G-16301)
Seitz Tech LLC ....G...... 610 268-2228
  Oxford (G-13090)
Sekisui Diagnostics LLC ....G...... 610 594-8590
  Exton (G-5730)
Siemens Med Solutions USA Inc ......E...... 610 834-1220
  Plymouth Meeting (G-15870)
Sigma Instruments Inc ....F...... 724 776-9500
  Cranberry Township (G-3850)
Sleep Specialists LLC ....G...... 610 304-6408
  Bala Cynwyd (G-892)
◆ Smiths Group North America Inc ...F...... 772 286-9300
  Malvern (G-10322)
Snake Creek Lasers LLC ....E...... 570 553-1120
  Friendsville (G-6230)
Somni Scientific LLC ....F...... 412 851-4390
  South Park (G-17785)
▲ Sonic Systems Inc ....E...... 267 803-1964
  Warminster (G-18967)
Spectrasonics Inc ....G...... 610 964-9637
  Wayne (G-19372)
Spinal Acoustics LLC ....G...... 724 846-3600
  Beaver Falls (G-1013)
Sterilzer Rfurbishing Svcs Inc ....G...... 814 882-4116
  Erie (G-5491)
Strata Skin Sciences Inc ....D...... 215 619-3200
  Horsham (G-7854)
Stryker Orthobiologics ....G...... 610 407-5259
  Malvern (G-10324)

◆ Superior Surgical Ltd Lblty Co ....G...... 877 669-7646
  Pottstown (G-16053)
Surgeoneering LLC ....G...... 412 292-2816
  Gibsonia (G-6353)
Surgical Specialties Corp ....F...... 610 404-1000
  Wyomissing (G-20289)
▲ Synthes Inc ....G...... 610 647-9700
  West Chester (G-19650)
Synthes Spine Inc ....E...... 610 695-2424
  West Chester (G-19651)
Synthes USA Products LLC ....G...... 610 719-5000
  West Chester (G-19653)
Talexmedical LLC ....G...... 888 327-2221
  Malvern (G-10327)
▲ Tar Hunt Custom Rifles Inc ....G...... 570 784-6368
  Bloomsburg (G-1803)
Tecomet Inc ....F...... 215 826-8250
  Bristol (G-2204)
▲ Teleflex Incorporated ....B...... 610 225-6800
  Wayne (G-19382)
▲ Thermo-Electric Co ....G...... 724 695-2774
  Imperial (G-8077)
Timm Medical Technologies Inc ......E...... 484 321-5900
  Fort Washington (G-6093)
Titan Manufacturing Inc ....G...... 610 935-8203
  Malvern (G-10332)
Titan Manufacturing Inc ....G...... 781 767-1963
  Malvern (G-10333)
Tyber Medical LLC ....F...... 303 717-5060
  Bethlehem (G-1644)
▼ Ue Lifesciences Inc ....G...... 631 980-8340
  Philadelphia (G-14416)
Ultraoptics Inc ....G...... 724 838-7155
  Greensburg (G-6723)
Unique Technologies Inc ....F...... 610 775-9191
  Mohnton (G-11271)
Varitronics Inc ....F...... 610 356-3995
  Broomall (G-2304)
Vcp Mobility Inc ....B...... 814 443-4881
  Somerset (G-17715)
Viant Westfield LLC ....D...... 215 675-4653
  Warminster (G-18994)
Vicor Technologies Inc ....F...... 570 897-5797
  Bangor (G-933)
Wilmand Labglass ....G...... 215 672-7800
  Warminster (G-19000)
World Video Sales Co Inc ....G...... 610 754-6800
  Bechtelsville (G-1038)
Wright Linear Pump Inc ....G...... 724 695-0800
  Oakdale (G-12912)
Xodus Medical Inc ....G...... 724 337-5500
  New Kensington (G-12391)
▲ Xodus Medical Inc ....E...... 724 337-5500
  New Kensington (G-12392)
York Integra PA Inc ....G...... 717 840-3438
  York (G-20743)
Zynitech Medical Inc ....G...... 610 592-0755
  Exton (G-5753)

3842 Orthopedic, Prosthetic & Surgical Appliances/Splys

911 Safety Equipment LLC ....F...... 610 279-6808
  Norristown (G-12628)
Ability Prsthtics Orthtics Inc ....G...... 717 337-2277
  Exton (G-5634)
Activaided Orthotics LLC ....G...... 412 901-2658
  West Mifflin (G-19734)
Allentown Limb & Brace Inc ....G...... 610 437-2254
  Allentown (G-128)
Alpha Scientific Instrument ....G...... 610 647-7000
  Malvern (G-10182)
Altamira Ltd ....G...... 800 343-1066
  Pittsburgh (G-14692)
Altus Partners LLC ....E...... 610 355-4156
  West Chester (G-19497)
America Hears Inc ....F...... 215 785-5437
  Bristol (G-2105)
American Artisan Orthotics ....G...... 724 776-6030
  Hermitage (G-7571)
American Innovations Inc ....G...... 215 249-1840
  Dublin (G-4431)
American Safety Clothing Inc ....E...... 215 257-7667
  Sellersville (G-17339)
Anatomical Designs Inc ....F...... 724 430-1470
  Uniontown (G-18615)
▲ Animas LLC ....B...... 610 644-8990
  Chesterbrook (G-3089)
Applied Technology Intl Ltd ....F...... 610 363-1077
  Exton (G-5645)

S I C

Aquamed Technologies Inc ....F 215 702-8550
Langhorne (G-9277)

ARC Rmediation Specialists Inc...........F 386 405-6760
Bristol (G-2108)

Arma Co LLC ....E 717 295-6805
Lancaster (G-8939)

Authorized Earmold Labs ....D 215 788-0330
Bristol (G-2114)

Avanta Orthopaedics Inc....................G 215 428-1792
Morrisville (G-11555)

Axial Medical ....F 267 961-2600
Ivyland (G-8207)

Baker Hydro Incorporated..................D 717 764-8581
York (G-20399)

▲ Bar-Ray Products Inc ....D 717 359-9100
Littlestown (G-10063)

Bashlin Industries Inc.......................D 724 458-8340
Grove City (G-6780)

Beltone Corporation ....G 717 300-7163
Shippensburg (G-17518)

Beltone Corporation ....G 717 386-5640
Carlisle (G-2691)

Beltone Corporation ....G 412 490-4902
Pittsburgh (G-14761)

Benchmark Orthot & Prosth Inc.........G 724 825-4200
Washington (G-19154)

Biowerk USA Inc ....G 717 697-3310
Mechanicsburg (G-10825)

Boas Surgical Inc.............................E 484 895-3451
Allentown (G-156)

Boehringer Laboratories Inc ....E 610 278-0900
Phoenixville (G-14536)

C-Fab-1 Inc ....G 215 331-2797
Trevose (G-18489)

Cape Prosthetics-Orthotics ....G 610 644-7824
Exton (G-5659)

Center For Orthtic and Prsthtc ....F 570 382-8208
Dickson Cty (G-4123)

Central Orthotic Prosthetic Co ....F 814 535-8221
Johnstown (G-8364)

Choice Cleangear LLC.......................G 610 497-9756
Aston (G-754)

Church Communities PA Inc...............G 724 329-8573
Farmington (G-5860)

Circadiance LLC ....F 724 858-2837
Turtle Creek (G-18562)

Clearcount Med Solutions Inc ....F 412 931-7233
Pittsburgh (G-14859)

CMS Orthotic Lab LLC.......................G 717 329-9301
Carlisle (G-2700)

Cocco Bros ....E 215 334-3816
Philadelphia (G-13557)

Colburn Orthopedics Inc...................G 814 432-5252
Franklin (G-6121)

▲ Comfort Stump Sock Mfg Co ....F 215 781-0300
Croydon (G-3915)

Core Essence Orthopedics Inc...........F 215 660-5014
King of Prussia (G-8599)

Crew Systems Corporation................G 570 281-9221
Carbondale (G-2673)

Curvebeam LLC ....E 267 483-8081
Hatfield (G-7329)

Decon Laboratories Inc ....E 610 755-0800
King of Prussia (G-8606)

Def Medical Technologies LLC ....G 802 299-8457
Philadelphia (G-13615)

Depuy Synthes Inc ....B 610 647-9700
Paoli (G-13138)

Depuy Synthes Inc ....B 610 701-7078
West Chester (G-19536)

Depuy Synthes Inc ....B 610 738-4600
West Chester (G-19537)

Depuy Synthes Inc ....B 610 719-5000
West Chester (G-19538)

▲ DT Davis Enterprises Ltd ....D 610 694-9600
Allentown (G-197)

Duralife Inc ....E 570 323-9743
Philadelphia (G-13651)

Ellwood Safety Appliance Co ....F 724 758-7538
Ellwood City (G-4932)

▲ Environmental Tectonics Corp ....C 215 355-9100
Southampton (G-17809)

Envision Products Inc ....E 215 428-1791
Morrisville (G-11558)

Factor Medical LLC ....G 215 862-5345
New Hope (G-12301)

Fort Washington Pharma LLC ....G 800 279-7434
Fort Washington (G-6069)

Freedom Management Svcs LLC ....G 215 328-9111
Horsham (G-7819)

Garnes Park E Jr ....G 757 502-3381
Newville (G-12602)

Genesis Hearing Systems ....G 610 759-0459
Nazareth (G-11969)

▲ Gentex Corporation ....B 570 282-3550
Simpson (G-17593)

Gerber Chair Mates Inc.....................G 814 266-6588
Johnstown (G-8377)

Global Medical Solutions Inc ....G 215 440-7701
Philadelphia (G-13770)

◆ Golden Brothers Inc ....C 570 457-0867
Old Forge (G-12965)

Green Prosthetics & Orthotics ....F 814 833-2311
Erie (G-5307)

Green Prosthetics & Orthotics ....G 814 833-2311
Erie (G-5308)

Green Prosthetics & Orthotics ....G 814 337-1159
Meadville (G-10730)

Groman Restoration Inc.....................G 724 235-5000
New Florence (G-12197)

Hanger Inc ....F 877 442-6437
Wilkes Barre (G-19923)

Hanger Inc ....E 724 836-4949
Greensburg (G-6671)

Hanger Prsthetcs & Ortho Inc............G 215 365-1532
Philadelphia (G-13801)

Hanger Prsthetcs & Ortho Inc............E 714 774-0637
West Bridgewater (G-19491)

Hanger Prsthetcs & Ortho Inc............G 814 368-3702
Bradford (G-1971)

Hanger Prsthetcs & Ortho Inc............G 717 731-8181
Camp Hill (G-2499)

Hanger Prsthetcs & Ortho Inc............G 724 836-4949
Greensburg (G-6672)

Hanger Prsthetcs & Ortho Inc............G 724 285-1284
Butler (G-2404)

Hanger Prsthetcs & Ortho Inc............G 570 421-8221
East Stroudsburg (G-4615)

Hanger Prsthetcs & Ortho Inc............G 717 264-7117
Chambersburg (G-2938)

Hanger Prsthetcs & Ortho Inc............G 717 564-4521
Harrisburg (G-7138)

Hanger Prsthetcs & Ortho Inc............G 724 981-5775
Hermitage (G-7587)

Hanger Prsthetcs & Ortho Inc............G 717 767-6667
York (G-20520)

Hanger Prsthetcs & Ortho Inc............G 724 438-4582
Uniontown (G-18629)

Harry J Lawall & Son Inc...................C 215 338-6611
Philadelphia (G-13805)

Haveco Div of Ace Mobility ....F 717 558-4301
Harrisburg (G-7145)

Health Solutions Inc ....G 610 379-0300
Lehighton (G-9715)

Hearing Lab Technology LLC ....A 215 785-5437
Bristol (G-2152)

Howmedica Osteonics Corp ....F 610 760-7007
Neffs (G-11999)

▼ Hydroworx International Inc ....E 717 902-1923
Middletown (G-11057)

Implant Research Center....................G 215 571-4345
Philadelphia (G-13851)

▼ Instrumentation Industries Inc ....E 412 854-1133
Bethel Park (G-1418)

Iron Lung LLC ....G 412 291-8928
Pittsburgh (G-15136)

J G McGinness Prosthetics ....F 610 278-1866
Norristown (G-12671)

J Walker & Associates LLC................G 717 755-7142
York (G-20539)

Jeffrey L Roberts ....G 724 627-4600
Waynesburg (G-19447)

Johnson & Johnson ....A 215 273-7000
Philadelphia (G-13909)

Jumpers Shoe Service ....G 717 766-3422
Mechanicsburg (G-10860)

Keystone Surgical Systems Inc...........G 717 412-4383
Harrisburg (G-7162)

Kinetic ....G 814 603-1131
Du Bois (G-4400)

Kinetic Concepts Inc ....G 717 558-0985
Harrisburg (G-7164)

Lakeland Industries Inc ....G 610 775-0505
Reading (G-16426)

Laveings Mobility ....G 724 368-9417
Portersville (G-15930)

▼ Life Support International ....E 215 785-2870
Langhorne (G-9308)

Limb Technologies Inc ....F 215 781-8454
Bristol (G-2160)

▲ Lite Tech Inc ....F 610 650-8690
Norristown (G-12676)

M-B Companies Inc...........................E 570 547-1621
Muncy (G-11825)

Martech Medical Products Inc ....E 215 256-8833
Harleysville (G-7046)

McGinness Group LLC ....G 610 278-1866
Norristown (G-12681)

McKesson Ptent Care Sltons Inc.........D 814 860-8160
Erie (G-5386)

▲ Mechanical Safety Equipment ....E 215 676-7828
Philadelphia (G-14003)

▲ Mechanical Service Co Inc ....F 610 351-1655
Allentown (G-313)

Medeast Post-Op & Surgical Inc.........G 888 629-2030
Bethlehem (G-1566)

Medical Device Bus Svcs Inc ....G 724 933-0288
Wexford (G-19810)

Mgs04 Corporation ....G 267 249-2372
Philadelphia (G-14018)

Michels Hearing Aid Center ....G 570 622-9151
Pottsville (G-16088)

Micro-Fusion LLC ....G 717 244-4648
Red Lion (G-16609)

Mifflin Valley Inc ....E 610 775-0505
Reading (G-16443)

▲ Mine Safety Appliances Co LLC ......B 724 776-8600
Cranberry Township (G-3836)

▲ Mio Mechanical Corporation ....F 215 613-8189
Philadelphia (G-14026)

Moberg Research Inc........................F 215 283-0860
Ambler (G-591)

Ms Wheelchair PA Program ....G 814 331-1722
Bradford (G-1984)

▲ MSA Pittsburgh Dist Ctr ....G 724 742-8090
New Galilee (G-12221)

MSA Safety Incorporated ....B 724 733-9100
Murrysville (G-11858)

MSA Safety Incorporated ....D 724 776-7700
Cranberry Township (G-3840)

MSA Safety Incorporated ....A 724 733-9100
Murrysville (G-11859)

MSA Safety Incorporated ....B 724 776-8600
Cranberry Township (G-3839)

MSA Safety Sales LLC ....G 724 776-8600
Cranberry Township (G-3841)

▲ Mutual Industries North Inc ....E 215 927-6000
Philadelphia (G-14046)

National Artificial Limb Co ....G 412 608-9910
Pittsburgh (G-15321)

O & P Benchmark Holdings Inc ....G 610 644-7824
Exton (G-5716)

O and P Svetz Inc ....F 724 834-1448
Greensburg (G-6694)

O2s LLC ....E 215 299-8500
Philadelphia (G-14091)

◆ Oakworks Inc ....D 717 227-0516
New Freedom (G-12213)

Occuped Orthotics............................G 717 949-2377
Newmanstown (G-12482)

Olde Town Grove City ....G 724 458-0301
Grove City (G-6799)

▲ Ortho Depot LLC ....G 800 992-9999
Salunga (G-17055)

Ototech Inc ....D 215 781-7987
Bristol (G-2177)

Out On A Limb Creations ....G 570 287-3778
Forty Fort (G-6098)

PA & Implant Surgery LLC................G 814 375-0500
Du Bois (G-4410)

PA Artificial Limb & Brace Co ....G 724 588-6860
Greenville (G-6763)

Phufar...G 215 483-0487
Philadelphia (G-14174)

Plum Enterprises Inc ....E 610 783-7377
Valley Forge (G-18710)

Precision Castparts Corp ....B 570 474-6371
Mountain Top (G-11771)

Presque Isle Orthpd Lab Inc ....F 814 838-0002
Erie (G-5435)

Pride Mobility Products Corp ....E 570 655-5574
Pittston (G-15779)

Professional Hearing Aid Svc ....G 724 548-4801
Kittanning (G-8788)

Profile Shop Inc................................F 215 633-3461
Bensalem (G-1244)

Prosthetic Artworks LLC ....G 570 828-6177
Dingmans Ferry (G-4143)

Prosthetic Cad-CAM Tech Inc.............G 814 763-1151
Saegertown (G-16929)

Quaker Safety Products Corp .... E 215 536-2991
  Quakertown (G-16238)
Reaction Orthotics .... G 717 609-2361
  Carlisle (G-2735)
Respironics Inc .... C 724 387-5200
  Mount Pleasant (G-11714)
Respironics Inc .... B 724 733-0200
  Murrysville (G-11864)
Respironics Inc .... C 724 733-5803
  Sewickley (G-17407)
Respironics Inc .... B 724 387-4270
  Monroeville (G-11354)
Respironics Inc .... C 724 334-3100
  New Kensington (G-12370)
Restorative Care America Inc .... G 215 592-8880
  Philadelphia (G-14241)
Reynolds Presto Products Inc .... B 866 254-3310
  Pittsburgh (G-15483)
Ricochet Manufacturing Corp .... E 888 462-1999
  Philadelphia (G-14249)
River Street Pedorthics Inc .... G 570 299-5472
  Gouldsboro (G-6570)
Riverview Orthotics .... G 570 270-6231
  Plains (G-15788)
Riverview Orthtics Prosthetics .... G 570 743-1414
  Selinsgrove (G-17332)
Riverview Orthtics Prosthetics .... F 570 284-4291
  Danville (G-4010)
Robert John Enterprises Inc .... F 814 944-0187
  Altoona (G-544)
Safeware Inc .... G 215 354-1401
  Huntingdon Valley (G-8034)
Scott Gordon .... G 717 652-2828
  Harrisburg (G-7213)
Seal Glove Mfg Inc .... F 717 692-4837
  Millersburg (G-11200)
◆ Siemens Med Solutions USA Inc ...... B 888 826-9702
  Malvern (G-10315)
Smith & Nephew Inc .... E 412 914-1190
  Bridgeville (G-2090)
▲ Snapper Cane LLC .... G 516 770-3569
  West Chester (G-19641)
Specialty Millworks Inc .... G 610 682-6334
  Topton (G-18416)
Sr Jan Fisher .... G 724 841-0508
  Lyndora (G-10136)
State of Art Prosthetics .... G 215 914-1222
  Huntingdon Valley (G-8040)
Stelkast Inc .... E 888 273-1583
  Mc Murray (G-10646)
Sterilzer Rfurbishing Svcs Inc .... F 814 456-2616
  Erie (G-5492)
Steris Barrier Pdts Solutions .... D 215 763-8200
  Sharon Hill (G-17462)
Steris Corporation .... G 215 763-8200
  Philadelphia (G-14346)
Suburban Audiology Balance Ctr .... G 610 647-3710
  Paoli (G-13149)
Super Can Industries Inc .... G 215 945-1075
  Levittown (G-9866)
Surgical Institute Reading LP .... G 610 378-8800
  Reading (G-16530)
Surgical Specialties Corp .... F 610 404-1000
  Wyomissing (G-20289)
Susquehanna Valley Prosthetics .... F 570 743-1414
  Selinsgrove (G-17337)
Svpo Inc .... F 570 743-1414
  Shamokin Dam (G-17428)
▲ Synthes Inc .... G 610 647-9700
  West Chester (G-19650)
Synthes Usa LLC .... G 610 719-5000
  West Chester (G-19652)
T G Faust Inc .... F 610 375-8549
  Reading (G-16533)
▲ Teleflex Incorporated .... B 610 225-6800
  Wayne (G-19382)
▲ Thomas Fetterman Inc .... G 215 355-8849
  Southampton (G-17840)
Three Rivers Orthotics Prsthti .... G 412 371-2318
  Pittsburgh (G-15621)
Tornier Inc .... G 610 585-2111
  West Chester (G-19666)
▲ Tps LLC .... C 570 538-7200
  New Columbia (G-12177)
Trac Fabrication Inc .... G 717 862-8722
  Slippery Rock (G-17628)
Trigon Holding Inc .... E 724 941-5540
  Mc Murray (G-10647)
▲ Trigon Incorporated .... D 724 941-5540
  Mc Murray (G-10648)

Troutman Machine Shop Inc .... G 610 363-5480
  Exton (G-5739)
Uds Home Medical Equipment LLC ...... G 717 665-1490
  Lancaster (G-9227)
Ultraflex Systems Inc .... E 610 906-1410
  Pottstown (G-16061)
Union Orthotics Prosthetics Co .... G 724 836-6656
  Greensburg (G-6724)
Union Orthotics Prosthetics Co .... G 412 943-1950
  Pittsburgh (G-15670)
Union Orthotics Prosthetics Co .... E 412 621-2698
  Pittsburgh (G-15671)
Vcp Mobility Inc .... B 814 443-4881
  Somerset (G-17715)
Visco .... G 215 420-7437
  Warminster (G-18995)
West Penn Ear Nose and Throat .... G 412 621-2656
  Pittsburgh (G-15709)
West Penn Optical Inc .... E 814 833-1194
  Erie (G-5528)
Williamsport Orthopedic .... G 570 322-5277
  Williamsport (G-20094)
Wyoming Vly Prsthtic Orthotics .... G 570 283-3835
  Wilkes Barre (G-19979)
Xerothera Inc .... G 610 525-9916
  Bryn Mawr (G-2337)

3843 Dental Eqpt & Splys

▲ 5p Corporation .... G 215 997-5666
  Hatfield (G-7312)
▲ American Cnsld Mfg Co Inc .... E 610 825-2630
  Conshohocken (G-3519)
▲ American Dental Supply Inc .... F 484 223-3940
  Allentown (G-134)
B E V O L .... G 570 962-3644
  Howard (G-7885)
Benjamin Industries and Mfg .... G 724 523-9615
  Jeannette (G-8248)
▲ Bti of America LLC .... G 215 646-4067
  Blue Bell (G-1818)
Burmans Medical Supplies Inc .... F 610 876-6068
  Upper Chichester (G-18657)
Conicella-Fessler Dental Lab .... G 610 622-3298
  Drexel Hill (G-4362)
David C Weigle .... G 610 327-1616
  Pottstown (G-15980)
Dent-Chew Brush LLC .... G 610 520-9941
  Haverford (G-7408)
Dental Corp of America .... F 610 344-7488
  West Chester (G-19535)
▲ Dental Imaging Tech Corp .... D 215 997-5666
  Hatfield (G-7333)
▲ Dentalez Inc .... E 610 725-8004
  Malvern (G-10223)
Dentalez Inc .... C 717 291-1161
  Lancaster (G-8993)
Dentsply Holding Company .... E 717 845-7511
  York (G-20448)
Dentsply International Inc .... D 717 767-8500
  York (G-20449)
Dentsply International Inc .... D 717 487-0100
  York (G-20450)
Dentsply LLC .... D 800 323-0970
  York (G-20451)
Dentsply North America LLC .... G 717 849-4229
  York (G-20452)
Dentsply Sirona Inc .... C 717 849-7747
  Lancaster (G-8994)
Dentsply Sirona Inc .... E 717 699-4100
  York (G-20453)
◆ Dentsply Sirona Inc .... A 717 845-7511
  York (G-20454)
Dentsply Sirona Inc .... F 717 845-7511
  York (G-20455)
Everest Dental LLC .... G 215 671-0188
  Philadelphia (G-13683)
Flenniken & Flenniken PC .... G 717 249-7777
  Carlisle (G-2713)
Frank J May Co Inc .... G 215 923-3165
  Philadelphia (G-13719)
▲ Gudebrod Inc .... C 610 327-4050
  Pottstown (G-15993)
Harbor Orthodontic Services .... G 724 654-3599
  New Castle (G-12099)
Holmes Dental Company .... G 215 675-2877
  Hatboro (G-7287)
J R Ramos Dental Lab Inc .... G 717 272-5821
  Lebanon (G-9584)
Jasinski Dental Lab Inc .... E 215 699-8861
  Lansdale (G-9379)

Margraf Dental Mfg Inc .... G 215 884-0369
  Jenkintown (G-8296)
Mobility and Access Inc .... G 724 695-1590
  Oakdale (G-12907)
MTI Precision Products LLC .... F 610 679-5280
  Coatesville (G-3318)
Northeast Dental Laboratories .... G 215 725-0950
  Elkins Park (G-4909)
Orahealth International .... G 610 971-9600
  Wayne (G-19361)
Orthopli Corp .... E 215 671-1000
  Philadelphia (G-14102)
Osspray Inc .... G 866 238-9902
  Abbottstown (G-6)
▲ Premier Dental Products Co .... E 610 239-6000
  Plymouth Meeting (G-15865)
Premier Dental Products Co Inc .... E 215 676-9090
  Philadelphia (G-14196)
Print A Tooth Inc .... G 610 647-6990
  Malvern (G-10303)
Prosthetic Arts Inc .... G 570 842-2929
  Moscow (G-11601)
Quanotech Inc .... G 610 658-0116
  Wynnewood (G-20271)
◆ Radius Corporation .... E 484 646-9122
  Kutztown (G-8858)
RED Orthodontic Lab .... G 610 237-1100
  Kennett Square (G-8539)
Sentage Corporation .... D 412 431-3353
  Pittsburgh (G-15525)
◆ Siemens Med Solutions USA Inc ...... B 888 826-9702
  Malvern (G-10315)
Sodium Systems LLC .... F 800 821-8962
  York (G-20671)
Spring Health Products Inc .... F 610 630-8024
  Norristown (G-12714)
Stan Bender .... G 610 759-4021
  Nazareth (G-11989)
Taylor Made Smiles .... G 724 212-3167
  New Kensington (G-12381)
Urgent Denture Repair LLC .... G 412 714-8157
  Pittsburgh (G-15685)
West Hills Specialty Supply Co .... G 412 279-6766
  Carnegie (G-2806)

3844 X-ray Apparatus & Tubes

American Access Care Holdings .... G 717 235-0181
  Malvern (G-10183)
American Access Care Intermedi .... G 717 235-0181
  Malvern (G-10184)
▲ Anholt Technologies Inc .... F 610 268-2758
  Avondale (G-848)
▲ Arrow International Inc .... A 610 225-6800
  Wayne (G-19303)
Best Solutions Med Systems LLC .... G 814 577-4184
  Philipsburg (G-14509)
Dentsply Holding Company .... E 717 845-7511
  York (G-20448)
Dentsply LLC .... D 800 323-0970
  York (G-20451)
Endicott Interconnect Tech .... G 724 352-6315
  Saxonburg (G-17086)
Gamma Irradiator Service LLC .... G 570 925-5681
  Benton (G-1280)
▲ Imaging Sciences Intl LLC .... G 215 997-5666
  Hatfield (G-7353)
▲ Lustra-Line Inc .... E 412 766-5757
  Pittsburgh (G-15242)
Novus X-Ray LLC .... F 215 962-3171
  Blue Bell (G-1851)

3845 Electromedical & Electrotherapeutic Apparatus

Acryl8 LLC .... G 484 695-6209
  Coopersburg (G-3623)
Alung Technologies Inc .... E 412 697-3370
  Pittsburgh (G-14697)
Applied RES & Photonics Inc .... G 717 220-1003
  Harrisburg (G-7089)
Atoptix LLC .... G 814 808-7056
  State College (G-17942)
Biotelemetry Inc .... D 610 729-7000
  Malvern (G-10193)
Boehringer Laboratories Inc .... E 610 278-0900
  Phoenixville (G-14536)
Bond With Me LLC .... G 267 334-1233
  Doylestown (G-4278)
C W E Inc .... G 610 642-7719
  Ardmore (G-704)

Cardionet Inc...........................G.......888 312-2328
Malvern *(G-10199)*

▲ Composiflex Inc...................D.......814 866-8616
Erie *(G-5229)*

Cpo 2 Inc................................G.......570 759-1233
Berwick *(G-1320)*

▲ Cygnus Manufacturing Co LLC.......C...724 352-8000
Saxonburg *(G-17082)*

Dbmtion Inc...........................G.......412 605-1952
Pittsburgh *(G-14911)*

◆ Devilbiss Healthcare LLC.........B.......814 443-4881
Somerset *(G-17684)*

▲ Dymax Corporation................E.......800 296-4146
Warrendale *(G-19072)*

Endoscopic Laser Technologies..........G....443 205-9340
Stewartstown *(G-18061)*

Eveos Corporation..................G.......412 366-0159
Sewickley *(G-17388)*

▲ Extremity Imaging Partners.......F.......724 493-7452
Wexford *(G-19800)*

Forest Devices Inc.................G.......724 612-1504
Pittsburgh *(G-15025)*

Gianna Skin & Laser Ltd..........G.......610 356-7870
Newtown Square *(G-12574)*

Gregory W Moyer Defibrillato.....G.......570 421-9993
Stroudsburg *(G-18121)*

◆ Heartsine Technologies LLC.......E...215 860-8100
Newtown *(G-12508)*

Helius Medical Tech Inc............F.......215 944-6100
Newtown *(G-12510)*

Ictv Holdings Inc....................F.......484 598-2300
Wayne *(G-19337)*

Instrumental Associates...........G.......610 992-3300
Phoenixville *(G-14554)*

Laser Center of Central PA........G.......814 867-1852
State College *(G-17986)*

Laser Hair Enhancemen...........G.......724 591-5670
Harmony *(G-7072)*

Laser Vginal Rejuvenation Inst...G.......610 584-0584
Lansdale *(G-9384)*

Lifewatch Services Inc.............B.......847 720-2100
Malvern *(G-10269)*

Market Service Corp................G.......610 696-1884
West Chester *(G-19596)*

▲ Medihill Inc..........................G.......215 464-7016
Bensalem *(G-1224)*

Medtronic Monitoring Inc..........G.......610 257-3640
Bala Cynwyd *(G-885)*

Mg Development America Inc.....G....412 288-9959
Pittsburgh *(G-15282)*

Moberg Research Inc...............F.......215 283-0860
Ambler *(G-591)*

Mobile Medical Innovations........G....724 646-2200
Mercer *(G-10969)*

Neurohabilitation Corporation.....G.......215 809-2018
Newtown *(G-12527)*

Nian-Crae Inc..........................G.......732 545-5881
Philadelphia *(G-14072)*

Nu-U Laser Center...................G.......717 718-7880
York *(G-20612)*

Perfusion Management Group.....F.......717 392-4112
Lancaster *(G-9169)*

Perseon Corporation................G.......201 486-5924
Newtown Square *(G-12589)*

Philips Ultrasound Inc..............E.......717 667-5000
Reedsville *(G-16626)*

Photosonix Medical Inc............G.......215 641-4909
Ambler *(G-598)*

Pittsburgh Medical Device.........F.......724 325-1869
Murrysville *(G-11861)*

Pro-Sltons For Chiropractic Inc...G....724 942-4284
Canonsburg *(G-2621)*

Pyxidis..................................G.......267 614-8348
Doylestown *(G-4330)*

▲ Radiancy Inc.........................F.......845 398-1647
Willow Grove *(G-20138)*

Reccare Incorporated...............E.......215 886-0880
Philadelphia *(G-14232)*

Reha Technology Usa Inc.........G.......267 419-8690
Plymouth Meeting *(G-15867)*

Renal Solutions Inc.................E.......724 772-6900
Warrendale *(G-19095)*

Respironics Inc......................B.......724 387-4270
Monroeville *(G-11354)*

Respironics Inc......................C.......724 334-3100
New Kensington *(G-12370)*

Respironics Inc......................C.......724 387-5200
Mount Pleasant *(G-11714)*

◆ Respironics Inc....................D.......724 387-5200
Murrysville *(G-11865)*

Rijuven Corp..........................G.......412 404-6292
Wexford *(G-19827)*

Rtm Vital Signs LLC................G.......215 643-1286
Fort Washington *(G-6091)*

Samir Corp............................G.......412 647-6000
Pittsburgh *(G-15509)*

Sense Technology Inc..............G.......724 733-2277
Halifax *(G-6831)*

◆ Siemens Med Solutions USA Inc......B...888 826-9702
Malvern *(G-10315)*

Snake Creek Lasers LLC..........F.......570 553-1120
Friendsville *(G-6230)*

Spec Sciences Inc..................G.......607 972-3159
Sharon *(G-17443)*

Spectrum Healthcare Inc..........E.......888 210-5576
Eagleville *(G-4516)*

Surgical Laser Tech Inc...........G.......215 619-3600
Montgomeryville *(G-11420)*

Technical Vision Inc.................F.......215 205-6084
Pipersville *(G-14620)*

Total Scope Inc......................E.......484 490-2100
Upper Chichester *(G-18674)*

Triomi Inc..............................G.......215 756-2771
Philadelphia *(G-14411)*

Ursus Medical LLC..................G.......412 779-4016
Pittsburgh *(G-15686)*

Valira LLC..............................G.......973 216-5803
Conshohocken *(G-3615)*

▲ Xgen LLC............................F.......877 450-9436
Horsham *(G-7865)*

Zoll.......................................G.......717 761-1842
Camp Hill *(G-2527)*

Zoll Manufacturing Corporation.......D...412 968-3333
Pittsburgh *(G-15734)*

Zoll Manufacturing Corporation.......D...412 968-3333
Cheswick *(G-3123)*

Zoll Medical Corporation...........F.......800 543-3267
Pittsburgh *(G-15735)*

Zoll Medical Corporation...........G.......412 968-3333
Cheswick *(G-3124)*

Zoll Services LLC....................A.......412 968-3333
Pittsburgh *(G-15736)*

3851 Ophthalmic Goods

A-Boss Opticians....................G.......412 271-4424
Braddock *(G-1942)*

▲ Allentown Optical Corp...........E.......610 433-5269
Allentown *(G-129)*

B & G Optics Inc.....................E.......215 289-2480
Philadelphia *(G-13437)*

Bartolotta Vision Care LLC.......G.......814 472-8010
Ebensburg *(G-4781)*

Beitler-Mckee Optical Company.......G...412 381-7953
Pittsburgh *(G-14759)*

Bruce N Pelsh Inc...................G.......724 346-2020
Hermitage *(G-7572)*

Chadwick Optical Inc...............G.......267 203-8665
Harleysville *(G-7026)*

Chambersburg Optical Service.....G...717 263-4898
Chambersburg *(G-2917)*

Chromagen Vision LLC.............G.......610 628-2941
Kennett Square *(G-8505)*

▲ Cima Technology Inc............F.......724 733-2627
Pittsburgh *(G-14852)*

Curry Spectacle Shop Inc........G.......814 899-6833
Erie *(G-5236)*

Dalmo Optical Corporation........G.......412 521-2100
Pittsburgh *(G-14903)*

Dalmo Optical Corporation........G.......412 937-1112
Pittsburgh *(G-14904)*

Fashion Optical Inc.................G.......724 339-4595
Sarver *(G-17069)*

Gary N Snyder........................G.......215 735-5656
Philadelphia *(G-13744)*

Geryville Eye Associates PC......F.......215 679-3500
Pennsburg *(G-13248)*

Homer Optical Company Inc......F.......717 843-1822
York *(G-20525)*

John J Kelley Associates Ltd......G.......215 545-0939
Philadelphia *(G-13903)*

Karen Wrigley Dr....................G.......215 563-8440
Philadelphia *(G-13922)*

Kutztown Optical Corp.............G.......610 683-5544
Kutztown *(G-8848)*

Lancaster Contact Lens Inc........G.......717 569-7386
Lancaster *(G-9092)*

Le Grand Assoc of Pittsburgh.....G...215 496-1307
Philadelphia *(G-13962)*

Leechburg Contact Lens Lab.......G....724 845-7777
Leechburg *(G-9648)*

Lens Contact Center.................G.......724 543-2702
Kittanning *(G-8777)*

Luxottica of America Inc...........E.......412 373-2200
Monroeville *(G-11344)*

Luxottica of America Inc...........E.......610 543-8622
Springfield *(G-17918)*

Luxottica of America Inc...........E.......610 962-5945
King of Prussia *(G-8647)*

Luxottica of America Inc...........E.......814 868-7502
Erie *(G-5375)*

Luxottica of America Inc...........E.......717 295-3001
Lancaster *(G-9118)*

Morgantown Eye Care Center.....G...610 286-0206
Morgantown *(G-11528)*

▲ Mxl Industries Inc.................D.......717 569-8711
Lancaster *(G-9141)*

New Vision Lens Lab LLC.........G.......610 351-7376
Allentown *(G-331)*

Nix Optical Co Inc....................G.......724 483-6527
Charleroi *(G-3018)*

Novotny Micheal.....................F.......724 785-2160
Brownsville *(G-2313)*

◆ Peppers Performance Eyeware.......E...412 688-8555
Pittsburgh *(G-15376)*

◆ PNC Equity Partners LP..........F.......412 914-0175
Pittsburgh *(G-15417)*

Point of View LLC...................G.......215 340-1725
Doylestown *(G-4326)*

Prairie Products Inc.................G.......717 292-0421
Dover *(G-4200)*

▲ R & R Eyewear Imports Inc......E.......215 393-5895
Willow Grove *(G-20137)*

Ross Mc Donnell Optical..........G.......570 348-0464
Dunmore *(G-4482)*

Rss Optometry LLC.................G.......610 933-2177
Phoenixville *(G-14577)*

Schneck Art Optical Co.............F.......610 965-4066
Emmaus *(G-5042)*

Scott Smith G.........................G.......724 378-2880
Aliquippa *(G-92)*

Sosniak Opticians...................G.......412 281-9199
Pittsburgh *(G-15561)*

Three Rivers Optical Company.....D...412 928-2020
Pittsburgh *(G-15620)*

▲ Tohickon Corp......................G.......267 450-5020
Sellersville *(G-17360)*

Usv Optical Inc.......................G.......412 655-8311
West Mifflin *(G-19747)*

Walman Optical Company..........E.......717 767-5193
York *(G-20703)*

West Penn Optical Inc..............E.......814 833-1194
Erie *(G-5528)*

Xray Eyewear.........................G.......215 545-3361
Philadelphia *(G-14494)*

3861 Photographic Eqpt & Splys

Allison Park Group Inc..............G.......412 487-8211
Allison Park *(G-446)*

Aserdiv Inc............................E.......800 966-7770
Springfield *(G-17907)*

Bms Inc.................................G.......609 883-5155
Yardley *(G-20297)*

▼ Charles Beseler Co Inc..........D.......800 237-3537
Stroudsburg *(G-18109)*

Clover Technologies Group LLC.......F...818 407-7500
Exton *(G-5662)*

▲ Coates Electrographics Inc......E.......570 675-1131
Dallas *(G-3960)*

Copitech Associates................G.......570 963-1391
Scranton *(G-17219)*

Corporate Arts Inc...................G.......610 298-8374
New Tripoli *(G-12454)*

Creative Systems Usa LLC........G.......610 450-6580
Collegeville *(G-3373)*

Creative Thought Media LLC......G.......267 270-5147
Philadelphia *(G-13579)*

Debenham Media Group...........F.......412 264-2526
Coraopolis *(G-3684)*

◆ Dual Core LLC......................D.......800 233-0298
Manheim *(G-10379)*

Evaporated Coatings Inc...........E.......215 659-3080
Willow Grove *(G-20116)*

▲ FCG Inc...............................C.......215 343-4617
Warrington *(G-19117)*

George T Faraghan Studios........G.......215 928-0499
Philadelphia *(G-13756)*

◆ Glunz & Jensen Inc...............E.......574 272-9950
Quakertown *(G-16197)*

Griffith Inc.............................C.......215 322-8100
Huntingdon Valley *(G-7992)*

▲ Itc Supplies LLC ....G...... 610 430-1300
  West Chester (G-19574)
Lasertek Tner Crtrdge Rchrging..........G...... 412 244-9505
  Pittsburgh (G-15220)
Lions World Media LLC ....F...... 917 645-7590
  Bushkill (G-2366)
Lunacor Inc ....G...... 610 328-6150
  Springfield (G-17917)
Mobile Video Corporation ....F...... 215 863-1072
  Broomall (G-2299)
Mosaic Engineering Inc ....G...... 406 544-7902
  State College (G-17995)
Mvp Prnting Prmtional Pdts LLC..........G...... 814 520-8392
  Erie (G-5400)
Nick Mulone & Son ....G...... 724 274-3221
  Cheswick (G-3112)
Photo Process Screen Mfg Co...........F...... 215 426-5473
  Philadelphia (G-14172)
Pixcontroller Inc ....G...... 724 733-0970
  Export (G-5621)
▲ Pocono Screen Supply LLC ....G...... 570 253-6375
  Scranton (G-17273)
◆ Raven Industries Inc ....D...... 724 539-8230
  Latrobe (G-9516)
Red Associates ....G...... 215 722-4895
  Philadelphia (G-14235)
Rockwell Collins Inc ....F...... 610 925-5844
  Kennett Square (G-8540)
▲ Spitz Inc ....D...... 610 459-5200
  Chadds Ford (G-2860)
Stanhope Microworks..................G...... 717 796-9000
  Mechanicsburg (G-10891)
Steel City Optronics LLC ....G...... 412 501-3849
  Gibsonia (G-6352)
Sun Valley Film Wash Inc ....G...... 610 497-1743
  Aston (G-794)
UTC Fire SEC Americas Corp Inc.........C...... 717 569-5797
  Lititz (G-10056)
▲ Vertex Image Products Inc ....G...... 724 722-3400
  Yukon (G-20786)
Xerox Corporation ....C...... 412 506-4000
  Pittsburgh (G-15726)

3873 Watch & Clock Devices & Parts

3si Security Systems Holdg Inc..........G...... 610 280-2000
  Malvern (G-10177)
▲ Calconix Inc ....F...... 610 642-5921
  Ardmore (G-705)
◆ Dernier Cree Inc ....G...... 917 287-7452
  Shavertown (G-17480)
Elderhorst Bells Inc ....G...... 215 679-3264
  Palm (G-13094)
◆ Franklin Instrument Co Inc ....F...... 215 355-7942
  Warminster (G-18883)
Rgm Watch Company ....F...... 717 653-9799
  Mount Joy (G-11670)
Watch U Want Inc ....G...... 954 961-1445
  Bala Cynwyd (G-896)

39 MISCELLANEOUS MANUFACTURING INDUSTRIES

3911 Jewelry: Precious Metal

A Jacoby & Company ....G...... 610 828-0500
  Conshohocken (G-3515)
Al May Manufacturing Jewelers ....G...... 412 391-8736
  Bethel Park (G-1401)
Alex and Ani LLC ....G...... 412 742-4968
  Pittsburgh (G-14671)
Alex and Ani LLC ....G...... 412 367-1362
  Pittsburgh (G-14672)
Armadani Inc ....G...... 215 627-2601
  Philadelphia (G-13412)
Bella Turka Inc ....G...... 215 560-8733
  Philadelphia (G-13452)
Body Gems ....G...... 215 357-9552
  Feasterville Trevose (G-5891)
Brown Industries Inc ....E...... 610 544-8888
  Media (G-10916)
Byard F Brogan Inc ....F...... 215 885-3550
  Glenside (G-6510)
C Leslie Smith Inc ....E...... 610 439-8833
  Allentown (G-160)
Casting Headquarters Inc ....G...... 215 922-2278
  Philadelphia (G-13511)
Colucci and Co...........................G...... 717 243-5562
  Boiling Springs (G-1873)
Courtney Metal Design ....G...... 610 932-6065
  Lincoln University (G-9973)

David Craig Jewelers Ltd ....G...... 215 968-8900
  Langhorne (G-9289)
Dexter Rosettes Inc ....G...... 215 542-0118
  Gwynedd Valley (G-6815)
Dutcher Brothers Inc ....G...... 215 922-4555
  Philadelphia (G-13652)
E R Kinley & Sons ....G...... 570 323-6740
  Williamsport (G-20008)
Fenstemaker John ....G...... 215 572-1444
  Glenside (G-6517)
G C Wyant Ltd ....G...... 724 357-8000
  Indiana (G-8101)
G D C Manufacturing Inc ....G...... 724 864-5000
  Irwin (G-8163)
Goldcrafters Corner ....G...... 717 412-4616
  Harrisburg (G-7134)
Golden Specialties Ltd ....G...... 717 273-9731
  Lebanon (G-9575)
Helm & Hahn Co Inc ....G...... 412 854-4367
  Pittsburgh (G-15089)
Herff Jones LLC ....G...... 717 526-4373
  Harrisburg (G-7148)
Herff Jones LLC ....F...... 215 638-2490
  Bensalem (G-1210)
Herff Jones LLC ....G...... 717 697-0649
  Mechanicsburg (G-10852)
Hersh Imports Inc ....G...... 215 627-1128
  Philadelphia (G-13821)
International Mfg Corp ....F...... 215 925-7558
  Philadelphia (G-13866)
J & D Jewelers Inc ....F...... 215 592-8956
  Philadelphia (G-13880)
Jan & Dans Jewelry ....G...... 814 452-3336
  Erie (G-5334)
Janette Jewelers ....G...... 717 632-9478
  Hanover (G-6908)
Jo-An Inc ....G...... 610 664-8777
  Bala Cynwyd (G-883)
Jostens Inc ....B...... 814 237-5771
  State College (G-17981)
Katz Imports Inc ....G...... 215 238-0197
  Philadelphia (G-13923)
▲ Lagos Inc ....D...... 215 925-1693
  Philadelphia (G-13950)
Larry Paul Casting Co Inc ....G...... 215 928-1644
  Philadelphia (G-13958)
Leon Miller & Company Ltd ....F...... 412 281-8498
  Pittsburgh (G-15224)
Levine Design Incorporated ....G...... 412 288-0220
  Pittsburgh (G-15226)
M B Mumma Inc.........................G...... 610 372-6962
  Reading (G-16435)
Majestic Creations Inc ....G...... 215 968-5411
  Southampton (G-17824)
Marc Williams Goldsmith Inc ....G...... 570 322-4248
  Williamsport (G-20040)
Marilyn Cohen Designs ....G...... 610 664-6219
  Penn Valley (G-13237)
Maximal Art Inc ....G...... 484 840-0600
  Philadelphia (G-13997)
Meighen Jinjou ....G...... 717 846-5600
  York (G-20585)
My Jewel Shop Inc ....G...... 215 887-3881
  Jenkintown (G-8297)
N Barsky & Sons ....F...... 215 925-8639
  Philadelphia (G-14050)
Nexus Inc ....G...... 412 391-2444
  Pittsburgh (G-15336)
Norman Kivitz Co Inc ....E...... 215 922-3038
  Philadelphia (G-14078)
O C Tanner Company ....G...... 610 458-1245
  Chester Springs (G-3083)
Paul F Rothstein Inc ....F...... 215 884-4720
  Glenside (G-6532)
▲ Paul Morelli Design Inc ....F...... 215 922-7392
  Philadelphia (G-14125)
RBS Impex Inc ....G...... 412 566-2488
  Pittsburgh (G-15471)
Roll Your Own ....G...... 215 420-7441
  Hatboro (G-7302)
Rubertones Casting Division ....G...... 215 922-1314
  Philadelphia (G-14262)
Ruud Kahle Master Goldsmith..........F...... 215 947-5050
  Huntingdon Valley (G-8032)
Semi-Mounts Inc ....G...... 412 422-7988
  Pittsburgh (G-15522)
Simons Bros Company ....F...... 215 426-9901
  Philadelphia (G-14308)
Stonebraker John ....G...... 724 238-6466
  Ligonier (G-9966)

▲ Superfit Inc ....F...... 215 391-4380
  Philadelphia (G-14357)
T Foster & Co Inc ....G...... 215 493-1044
  Yardley (G-20343)
Uniquely Diamonds ....G...... 610 356-5025
  Newtown Square (G-12596)

3914 Silverware, Plated & Stainless Steel Ware

Award Products Inc ....E...... 215 324-0414
  Philadelphia (G-13428)
Bob Allen & Sons Inc ....G...... 610 874-4391
  Chester (G-3040)
Bry Mar Trophy Inc ....G...... 215 295-4053
  Yardley (G-20298)
◆ Carson Industries Inc ....E...... 724 295-5147
  Freeport (G-6201)
Coventry Pewter Inc ....G...... 610 328-1557
  Springfield (G-17911)
Creative Embedments ....G...... 717 299-0385
  Lancaster (G-8987)
Daniel C Tanney Inc ....D...... 215 639-3131
  Bensalem (G-1179)
Kellys Trophies ....F...... 610 626-3300
  Drexel Hill (G-4367)
▲ L & L K Incorporated................E...... 215 732-2614
  Philadelphia (G-13948)
Martina Guerra Goldsmith ....G...... 570 398-1833
  Jersey Shore (G-8318)
Meighen Jinjou ....G...... 717 846-5600
  York (G-20585)
Micheners Engraving Inc ....G...... 717 738-9630
  Ephrata (G-5127)
Old Glory Corp ....F...... 724 423-3580
  Mount Pleasant (G-11709)
Pittsburgh Trophy Company Inc ....G...... 412 261-4376
  Pittsburgh (G-15411)
R & J Trophy ....G...... 570 345-2277
  Pine Grove (G-14604)
Richland Plastics & Engraving ....G...... 814 266-3002
  Johnstown (G-8431)
Rothrocks Silversmiths Inc............G...... 570 253-1990
  Honesdale (G-7722)
Superior Trophy & Engraving Co ....G...... 570 343-4087
  Scranton (G-17295)
Trophy Works ....G...... 412 279-0111
  Carnegie (G-2799)
▲ Wendell August Forge Inc ....D...... 724 748-9500
  Mercer (G-10979)
White Trophy Co Inc ....G...... 215 638-9134
  Bensalem (G-1272)

3915 Jewelers Findings & Lapidary Work

Aurele M Gatti Inc ....G...... 215 428-4500
  Fairless Hills (G-5772)
David I Helfer Inc ....G...... 412 281-6734
  Pittsburgh (G-14907)
E R Kinley & Sons ....G...... 570 323-6740
  Williamsport (G-20008)
Keystone Findings Inc..................D...... 215 723-4600
  Telford (G-18299)
Meighen Jinjou ....G...... 717 846-5600
  York (G-20585)
Metal Crafters Inc ....G...... 215 491-9925
  Warrington (G-19126)
White Light Productions ....F...... 610 518-0644
  Downingtown (G-4264)

3931 Musical Instruments

B X S Bass Inc ....G...... 724 378-8697
  Aliquippa (G-67)
Bedside Harp LLC ....F...... 215 752-7599
  Bensalem (G-1155)
Blocki Flute Method LLC ....G...... 866 463-5883
  Gibsonia (G-6327)
Breezy Ridge Instruments Ltd ....G...... 610 691-3302
  Bethlehem (G-1473)
Bucks Musical Instrument Pdts..........G...... 215 345-9442
  Doylestown (G-4283)
C F Martin & Co Inc ....A...... 610 759-2837
  Nazareth (G-11957)
◆ Carson Industries Inc ....E...... 724 295-5147
  Freeport (G-6201)
Catania Folk Instruments Inc ....G...... 570 922-4487
  Millmont (G-11219)
Chimneys Violin Shop ....G...... 717 258-3203
  Boiling Springs (G-1872)
Columbia Organ Works Inc.............G...... 717 684-3573
  Columbia (G-3436)

SIC

DAddario & Company Inc ....D 856 217-4954
Philadelphia *(G-13602)*

David R Houser ....G 610 505-5924
Norristown *(G-12651)*

Elderhorst Bells Inc ....G 215 679-3264
Palm *(G-13094)*

Fritzsche Organ Co Inc ....G 610 797-2510
Allentown *(G-220)*

Hunter Mudler Inc ....F 215 229-5470
Philadelphia *(G-13843)*

Lawless Assoc Pipe Organ Inc ....G 717 593-0398
Greencastle *(G-6621)*

Luson Drums LLC ....G 412 867-9404
Pittsburgh *(G-15241)*

Lyrrus Inc ....E 215 922-0880
Philadelphia *(G-13979)*

Malmark Incorporated ....E 215 766-7200
Plumsteadville *(G-15811)*

▲ Qrs Music Inc ....G 239 597-5888
Seneca *(G-17367)*

▲ Qrs Music Technologies Inc ....G 814 676-6683
Seneca *(G-17368)*

R J Brunner & Company ....G 717 285-3534
Silver Spring *(G-17590)*

Schulmerich Bells LLC ....F 215 257-2771
Hatfield *(G-7395)*

▲ Smuckers Harness Shop Inc ....F 717 445-5956
Narvon *(G-11927)*

Summer Music Festival ....G 570 343-7271
Dunmore *(G-4484)*

3942 Dolls & Stuffed Toys

Aimee & Darias Doll Outlet ....G 717 687-8118
Ronks *(G-16802)*

▲ B J Toy Company Inc ....F 610 863-9191
Pen Argyl *(G-13210)*

Country Traditions ....G 570 386-3621
New Ringgold *(G-12437)*

▲ Curto Toy Manufacturing Co ....F 610 438-5241
Easton *(G-4666)*

Ladie & Friends Inc ....G 215 453-8200
Sellersville *(G-17353)*

Lily Kay Doll Clothes LLC ....G 724 814-2210
Cranberry Township *(G-3832)*

Little Souls Inc ....E 610 278-0500
Devon *(G-4113)*

▲ Madame Alexander Doll Co LLC ....E 717 537-4140
Mountville *(G-11798)*

Teddy Wears ....G 610 273-3234
Honey Brook *(G-7766)*

3944 Games, Toys & Children's Vehicles

Accent Shop ....G 724 695-7580
Imperial *(G-8056)*

Ack Displays Inc ....G 215 236-3000
Merion Station *(G-10996)*

Action Centered Training Inc ....G 610 630-3325
Norristown *(G-12630)*

Apex Manufacturing Co ....G 610 272-0659
Norristown *(G-12635)*

▲ Artskills Inc ....E 610 253-6663
Bethlehem *(G-1453)*

▲ Bleacher Creatures LLC ....G 484 534-2398
Plymouth Meeting *(G-15834)*

▲ Bowser Manufacturing Co ....F 570 368-5045
Montoursville *(G-11434)*

▲ Brodak Manufacturing & Distrg ....G 724 966-2726
Carmichaels *(G-2754)*

Christopher Gans ....G 610 353-8585
Broomall *(G-2282)*

Church Communities PA Inc ....G 724 329-8573
Farmington *(G-5860)*

Compleat Strategist Inc ....G 610 265-8562
King of Prussia *(G-8596)*

Conestoga Co Inc ....G 610 866-0777
Allentown *(G-174)*

Cook Forest Saw Mill Center ....F 814 927-6655
Cooksburg *(G-3620)*

Country Accents ....G 570 478-4127
Williamsport *(G-20001)*

▲ Creative Designs Intl Ltd ....D 215 953-2800
Trevose *(G-18491)*

▲ Dimensions ....G 610 939-9900
Reading *(G-16363)*

Dodie Sable ....G 610 756-3836
Lenhartsville *(G-9758)*

Engineered Plastics LLC ....D 814 452-6632
Erie *(G-5259)*

Fisher Woodcraft ....G 610 273-2076
Honey Brook *(G-7744)*

Gemini Precision Products Ltd ....G 724 452-8700
Gibsonia *(G-6337)*

Goliath Development LLC ....G 310 748-6288
Jermyn *(G-8306)*

Higley Enterprises ....G 610 693-4039
Levittown *(G-9843)*

Holly Woodcrafters Inc ....E 717 486-5862
Mount Holly Springs *(G-11634)*

Jake Stoltzfus ....F 717 529-4082
Christiana *(G-3140)*

Jay Weller ....G 215 257-4859
Sellersville *(G-17350)*

Jensen Manufacturing Co Inc ....G 800 525-5245
Jeannette *(G-8258)*

Jumpbutton Studio LLC ....E 267 407-7535
Philadelphia *(G-13914)*

Just Play ....E 215 953-1208
Newtown *(G-12513)*

Kelly Line Inc ....F 570 527-6822
Pottsville *(G-16085)*

◆ KNex Industries Inc ....C 215 997-7722
Hatfield *(G-7358)*

KNex Ltd Partnership Group ....D 215 997-7722
Hatfield *(G-7359)*

▲ Lisa Leleu Studios Inc ....G 215 345-1233
Doylestown *(G-4313)*

Loyal Gaming Rewards LLC ....G 814 822-2008
Altoona *(G-522)*

Martin Weaver R ....G 717 354-8970
New Holland *(G-12260)*

Nelsons Competition Engines ....G 724 538-5282
Zelienople *(G-20812)*

Nocopi Technologies Inc ....G 610 834-9600
King of Prussia *(G-8657)*

Old Bedford Village Inc ....G 814 623-1156
Bedford *(G-1068)*

Old Time Games Inc ....G 215 538-5422
Quakertown *(G-16225)*

◆ Orange Products Inc ....D 610 791-9711
Allentown *(G-341)*

▲ Paper Magic Group Inc ....C 570 961-3863
Moosic *(G-11511)*

▲ Second Play LLC ....G 267 229-8033
Newtown *(G-12548)*

Seder Gaming Inc ....G 814 736-3611
Ebensburg *(G-4796)*

Senior Craftsmens Shop ....G 570 344-7089
Scranton *(G-17290)*

Smart Potato LLC ....G 215 380-5050
Oreland *(G-13029)*

Sonic Tronics Inc ....G 215 635-6520
Elkins Park *(G-4911)*

◆ Spang & Company ....C 412 963-9363
Pittsburgh *(G-15566)*

Specialty Products Company ....G 570 729-7192
Honesdale *(G-7724)*

Srm Entertainment Group LLC ....F 610 825-1039
Doylestown *(G-4338)*

Susquehanna Games & Bingo Sups ....G 570 322-9941
Williamsport *(G-20079)*

Trivagory Enterprises ....F 570 474-6520
Mountain Top *(G-11779)*

▲ Verus Sports Inc ....F 215 283-0153
Fort Washington *(G-6096)*

◆ Wicked Cool Toys Holdings LLC ....E 267 536-9186
Bristol *(G-2217)*

Wood Hollow Crafts LLC ....G 215 428-0870
Yardley *(G-20345)*

3949 Sporting & Athletic Goods, NEC

2 Sports Inc ....G 484 679-1225
Norristown *(G-12626)*

25 Fathoms International Inc ....G 610 558-1101
Glen Mills *(G-6428)*

▲ 60x Custom Strings ....G 724 525-0507
Cowansville *(G-3795)*

A & B Homes Inc ....G 570 253-3888
Honesdale *(G-7699)*

A & S Firearm Supplies Inc ....G 724 925-1212
Youngwood *(G-20776)*

▲ Abcore Fitness Inc ....G 570 424-1006
East Stroudsburg *(G-4602)*

Accubar Engineering & Rorco ....G 814 669-9005
Alexandria *(G-62)*

Ace Sports Inc ....D 610 833-5513
Woodlyn *(G-20216)*

Adventure Systems Inc ....G 717 351-7177
New Holland *(G-12226)*

▼ Aluminum Athletic Equipment Co ......E 610 825-6565
Royersford *(G-16841)*

Aluminum Athletic Equipment Co ....E 610 825-6565
West Conshohocken *(G-19684)*

American Adventure Sports ....G 724 205-6450
Pittsburgh *(G-14699)*

American Built Arms Company ....G 443 807-3022
Glen Rock *(G-6450)*

▲ APT Advanced Polymer Tech Corp ......D 724 452-1330
Harmony *(G-7066)*

Archer Double Ds Product ....G 610 838-1121
Bethlehem *(G-1452)*

Arctic Star Sleds ....G 814 684-3594
Tyrone *(G-18576)*

Aul Company Jack ....G 412 882-1836
Pittsburgh *(G-14738)*

Bailey & Izett Inc ....G 610 642-1887
Ardmore *(G-702)*

Baseball Info Solutions Inc ....F 610 261-4316
Coplay *(G-3640)*

Be The Tree Llc ....G 717 887-0780
Hellam *(G-7549)*

Bellview Lawn Furniture ....G 717 786-1286
Quarryville *(G-16265)*

▲ Bigshot Archery LLC ....G 610 873-0147
Elverson *(G-4961)*

▲ Bike USA Inc ....G 610 868-7652
Bethlehem *(G-1465)*

▲ Black Knight Industries Inc ....G 814 676-3474
Oil City *(G-12942)*

Blue Sky International Inc ....G 610 306-1234
Phoenixville *(G-14534)*

Bradley Walter Myers ....G 717 413-0197
East Earl *(G-4538)*

▲ Brain-Pad Incorporated ....G 610 397-0893
Conshohocken *(G-3525)*

Broken Straw Outdoors ....G 814 563-2200
Youngsville *(G-20769)*

▲ Brutis Enterprises Inc ....G 412 431-5440
Pittsburgh *(G-14795)*

Buck Koola Inc ....G 814 849-9695
Brookville *(G-2256)*

▲ Cardinal Systems Inc ....E 570 385-4733
Schuylkill Haven *(G-17151)*

Carson Boxing LLC ....G 814 839-2768
Bedford *(G-1045)*

Casual Living Unlimited LLC ....G 717 351-7177
New Holland *(G-12231)*

▲ Charles Hardy ....G 610 366-9752
Orefield *(G-13009)*

Chester County Sports Products ....G 610 327-4843
Pottstown *(G-15946)*

Clelan Industries Inc ....G 717 248-5061
Lewistown *(G-9926)*

▲ Combined Tactical Systems Inc ....C 724 932-2177
Jamestown *(G-8236)*

Deadsolid Simulations Inc ....F 570 655-6500
Pittston *(G-15748)*

▲ Designed For Fun Inc ....G 215 675-4718
Warminster *(G-18857)*

Diamond Wear ....G 610 433-2680
Whitehall *(G-19870)*

Donald Plants ....G 412 384-5911
West Elizabeth *(G-19694)*

Dorothy M Nelson ....G 724 837-6210
Greensburg *(G-6662)*

Duracart Usa LLC ....G 888 743-9957
Philadelphia *(G-13650)*

Emsco Distributor Company ....G 412 754-1236
Irwin *(G-8161)*

Es & Son of Union I ....G 724 439-5589
Uniontown *(G-18625)*

Family First Sports Park ....E 814 866-5425
Erie *(G-5288)*

Fergies Bait & Tackle ....G 724 253-3655
Sandy Lake *(G-17059)*

◆ Ferrari Importing Company ....E 412 323-0335
Pittsburgh *(G-15014)*

Fit Engineering ....G 717 432-2626
Dillsburg *(G-4129)*

Fox Pool Lancaster Inc ....D 717 718-1977
York *(G-20487)*

▲ Foxpro Inc ....E 717 248-2507
Lewistown *(G-9929)*

Foxs Country Sheds ....F 717 626-9560
Lititz *(G-10010)*

Gaines Company ....G 814 435-2332
Gaines *(G-6236)*

▲ Garrett Liners Inc ....E 215 295-0200
Levittown *(G-9838)*

Gerald Laub ....G 570 658-2609
Mc Clure *(G-10558)*

Gilson Boards LLC ....F 570 798-9102
Winfield (G-20201)

▲ Gratz Industries LLC ....E 215 739-7373
Philadelphia (G-13783)

Hanford & Hockenbrock ....G 610 275-5373
Norristown (G-12665)

Heated Hunts ....G 570 575-5080
S Abingtn Twp (G-16897)

Henry Jack Water On Wheels ....G 724 925-1727
New Stanton (G-12448)

Hi-TEC Custom Painting Inc ....F 724 932-2631
Jamestown (G-8237)

Highlands of Donegal LLC ....G 717 653-2048
Mount Joy (G-11661)

Hoyes Outdoor Products ....G 570 275-2953
Danville (G-4006)

Huna Designs Ltd ....G 570 522-9800
Lewisburg (G-9911)

Impact Innovative Products LLC ....F 724 864-8440
Irwin (G-8170)

Inferno Sports & Athletics LLC ....G 610 633-0919
Exton (G-5698)

Innovative Designs Inc ....G 412 799-0350
Pittsburgh (G-15128)

International Vectors Ltd ....E 717 767-4008
Emigsville (G-4993)

J and D Custom Strings ....F 717 252-4078
Wrightsville (G-20239)

Jedco Products Inc ....G 724 453-3490
Zelienople (G-20807)

Jo Jan Sportsequip Co Inc ....G 724 225-5582
Washington (G-19189)

Johns Custom Leather ....G 724 459-6802
Blairsville (G-1727)

▲ Kinseys Archery Products Inc ....D 717 653-9074
Mount Joy (G-11664)

Kodabow Inc ....G 484 947-5471
West Chester (G-19583)

◆ Kwik Goal Ltd ....D 800 531-4252
Quakertown (G-16207)

Larimer & Norton Inc ....F 814 757-4532
Russell (G-16881)

Larimer & Norton Inc ....F 814 723-1778
Warren (G-19036)

Larimer & Norton Inc ....G 814 435-2202
Galeton (G-6240)

▼ Lilliput Play Homes Inc ....G 724 348-7071
Finleyville (G-5961)

Lomma Investments ....E 570 346-5555
Scranton (G-17256)

Louis Fliszar ....G 610 865-6494
Bethlehem (G-1562)

Macris Sports Inc ....G 724 654-6065
New Castle (G-12117)

▲ Mancino Manufacturing Co Inc ....F 800 338-6287
Lansdale (G-9385)

McKenzie Sports Products LLC ....C 717 731-9920
Camp Hill (G-2504)

Mgs04 Corporation ....G 267 249-2372
Philadelphia (G-14018)

Mini-Golf Inc ....E 570 489-8623
Jessup (G-8333)

Mvp Sports & Games Co ....G 302 250-4836
Lancaster (G-9140)

Mystic Lanes LLC ....G 724 898-2960
Valencia (G-18699)

Neff Specialties LLC ....F 814 247-8887
Hastings (G-7262)

Nest ....G 215 545-6378
Philadelphia (G-14063)

Oldco Ep Inc ....G 484 768-1000
Aston (G-782)

▼ Oldco Ep Inc ....G 888 314-9356
Aston (G-783)

Olympian Athletics ....G 717 765-8615
Waynesboro (G-19420)

Patternmaster Chokes LLC ....G 877 388-2259
Hollidaysburg (G-7652)

Penn Big Bed Slate Co Inc ....D 610 767-4601
Slatington (G-17611)

▲ Penn Fishing Tackle Mfg Co ....C 215 227-1087
Philadelphia (G-14130)

▲ Pennsbury Enterprises Inc ....F 215 741-5960
Penndel (G-13240)

Pennsylvania Avenue Sports ....G 610 533-4133
Roseto (G-16821)

Pete Rickard Company ....G 518 234-3758
Galeton (G-6243)

Philadelphia Skating Club A ....F 610 642-8700
Ardmore (G-713)

Pioneer Enterprises Inc ....G 717 938-9388
Lewisberry (G-9892)

Pipes Skate Park ....G 724 327-4247
Pittsburgh (G-15381)

▼ Plastic Development Company PA ......E 800 451-1420
Williamsport (G-20058)

Playpower Inc ....B 570 522-9800
Lewisburg (G-9916)

◆ Playworld Systems Incorporated ....E 570 522-5435
Lewisburg (G-9917)

Pocono Pool Products Inc ....E 570 839-9291
Swiftwater (G-18189)

Pond Hockey Brewing Co LLC ....G 814 429-9846
State College (G-18008)

Prosco Inc ....E 814 375-0484
Du Bois (G-4414)

Protektor Model ....G 814 435-2442
Galeton (G-6244)

▲ Pure Fishing America Inc ....G 215 229-9415
Philadelphia (G-14217)

Pure Hospitality LLC ....G 724 935-1515
Wexford (G-19826)

Quaker Boy Inc ....F 814 362-7073
Bradford (G-1988)

R & M Targets Inc ....G 814 774-0160
Girard (G-6400)

Real Scent ....G 717 692-0527
Millersburg (G-11199)

Recreation Resource Usa LLC ....G 610 444-4402
Kennett Square (G-8538)

▲ Rightnour Manufacturing Co Inc ....E 800 326-9113
Mingoville (G-11257)

Roller Derby Skate Corp ....E 610 593-6931
Atglen (G-805)

Ryan Kanaskie ....G 717 248-9822
Lewistown (G-9947)

▲ Sea Mar Tackle Co Inc ....G 610 769-0755
Schnecksville (G-17143)

Serendib Imports Inc ....G 610 203-3070
Media (G-10948)

Shubandit LLC ....G 610 916-8313
Blandon (G-1759)

Shydas Services Inc ....G 717 274-8676
Lebanon (G-9630)

Skunkwirkz LLC ....G 814 602-8936
Erie (G-5480)

Smokers Sports Store ....G 717 687-9445
Ronks (G-16815)

Space 1026 ....G 215 574-7630
Philadelphia (G-14326)

Specialty Fitness Systems LLC ....G 814 432-6406
Franklin (G-6162)

▲ Sport Manufacturing Group Inc ....G 718 575-1801
Huntingdon Valley (G-8039)

Sportsmansliquidationcom LLC ....G 717 263-6000
Harrisburg (G-7217)

State Line Fencing ....G 610 932-9352
Nottingham (G-12885)

Stateasy ....G 412 437-8287
Pittsburgh (G-15579)

Stingfree Technologies Company ....G 610 444-2806
West Chester (G-19644)

Stoltzfus Sylvan Lee ....G 570 682-9755
Hegins (G-7544)

Stonybrook Shooting Supplies ....G 717 757-1088
York (G-20681)

Strasburg Lawn Structures LLC ....G 717 687-8210
Strasburg (G-18093)

Sue N Doug Inc ....G 717 838-6341
Palmyra (G-13132)

Swimtech Distributing Inc ....G 570 595-7680
Cresco (G-3895)

Swing Kingdom LLC ....F 717 656-4449
Leola (G-9807)

T & J Bowling Products Corp ....F 717 428-0100
Jacobus (G-8231)

Talkin Stick Game Calls Inc ....G 724 758-3869
Ellwood City (G-4953)

Tee-To-Green ....G 570 275-8335
Danville (G-4013)

Thomas Spinning Lures Inc ....G 570 226-4011
Hawley (G-7439)

Titan Boards Inc ....G 814 516-1899
Oil City (G-12958)

Top Hats Drum and Baton Co ....G 724 339-7861
New Kensington (G-12383)

Tri County Sports Inc ....G 717 394-9169
Lancaster (G-9222)

Triple Trophy Products Inc ....G 412 781-8801
Pittsburgh (G-15651)

Unequal Technologies Company ....G 610 444-5900
Glen Mills (G-6447)

University Rifle Club Inc ....G 610 927-1810
Reading (G-16556)

Upper Perk Sportswear Inc ....G 215 541-3211
Pennsburg (G-13261)

Vergona Outdoors LLC ....G 814 967-4844
Centerville (G-2837)

Versitex of America Ltd ....F 610 948-4442
Spring City (G-17872)

▲ Verus Sports Inc ....F 215 283-0153
Fort Washington (G-6096)

Virtic Industries LLC ....G 610 246-9428
Wayne (G-19388)

Vision Quest Inc ....G 570 448-2845
Honesdale (G-7732)

Wexco Incorporated ....G 717 764-8585
York (G-20710)

Wild Asaph Outfitters ....G 570 724-5155
Wellsboro (G-19475)

Wilkes Pool Corp ....E 570 759-0317
Mifflinville (G-11145)

XA Fishing Inc ....G 610 356-0340
Broomall (G-2306)

Xpogo LLC ....G 717 650-5232
Pittsburgh (G-15727)

Xtreme Hunting Products ....G 610 967-4588
Emmaus (G-5047)

3951 Pens & Mechanical Pencils

Cartridge World York ....G 717 699-4465
York (G-20419)

▲ Clarence J Venne LLC ....D 215 547-7110
Bristol (G-2126)

▲ Hanover Pen Corp ....E 717 637-3729
Hanover (G-6897)

Pen Pal LLC ....G 917 882-1441
Allentown (G-345)

▲ Skm Industries Inc ....F 570 383-3062
Olyphant (G-12999)

Universal Pen & Pencil Co Inc ....G 610 670-4720
Reading (G-16555)

3952 Lead Pencils, Crayons & Artist's Mtrls

▲ Colorfin LLC ....G 484 646-9900
Kutztown (G-8837)

◆ Crayola LLC ....A 610 253-6272
Easton (G-4663)

Crayola LLC ....B 610 253-6271
Fredericksburg (G-6173)

Crayola LLC ....B 610 814-7681
Bethlehem (G-1489)

Crayola LLC ....F 610 253-6272
Easton (G-4664)

Crayola LLC ....B 610 515-8000
Easton (G-4665)

Graphic Display Systems ....F 717 274-3954
Lebanon (G-9576)

Kent Studios ....E 610 534-7777
Woodlyn (G-20219)

Nocopi Technologies Inc ....G 610 834-9600
King of Prussia (G-8657)

Odhner Corporation ....G 610 364-3200
Media (G-10941)

Pidilite Usa Inc ....G 800 424-3596
Hazleton (G-7519)

◆ Sargent Realty Inc ....D 570 454-3596
Hazleton (G-7525)

Statement Walls LLC ....G 267 266-0869
Philadelphia (G-14341)

3953 Marking Devices

Accurate Marking Products Inc ....F 724 337-8390
New Kensington (G-12321)

Ad-Art Sign Co ....G 412 373-0960
Pittsburgh (G-14649)

Advance Sign Company LLC ....E 412 481-6990
Pittsburgh (G-14650)

Allegheny Rubber Stamp Inc ....G 412 826-8662
Blawnox (G-1762)

Atlas Rubber Stamp & Printing ....G 717 755-3882
York (G-20390)

Automated Indus Systems Inc ....E 814 838-2270
Erie (G-5198)

Bosha Design Inc ....G 610 622-4422
Drexel Hill (G-4361)

Bunting Inc ....C 412 820-2200
Verona (G-18750)

Bunting Stamp Company ....C 412 820-2200
Verona (G-18752)

Causco ....G 814 452-2004
Erie *(G-5223)*

▲ Gvm Inc ....D 717 677-6197
Biglerville *(G-1662)*

Harrisburg Stamp & Stencil Co ....G 717 236-9000
Harrisburg *(G-7144)*

ID Technology LLC ....E 717 848-3875
York *(G-20533)*

Krengel Quaker City Corp ....E 215 969-9800
Philadelphia *(G-13944)*

Lasermation Inc ....E 215 228-7900
Philadelphia *(G-13959)*

Liberty Craftsmen Inc ....G 717 871-0125
Millersville *(G-11211)*

Marking Device Mfg Co Inc ....G 215 632-9583
Fairless Hills *(G-5787)*

Marvel Marking Products ....F 412 381-0700
Pittsburgh *(G-15260)*

Matthews International Corp ....D 412 665-2500
Pittsburgh *(G-15265)*

Matthews International Corp ....D 412 665-2500
Pittsburgh *(G-15267)*

Matthews International Corp ....B 412 571-5500
Pittsburgh *(G-15266)*

◆ Matthews International Corp ....E 412 442-8200
Pittsburgh *(G-15264)*

Mecco Partners LLC ....F 724 779-9555
Cranberry Township *(G-3835)*

Minton Holdings LLC ....G 412 787-5912
Pittsburgh *(G-15293)*

Notaries Equipment Co ....F 215 563-8190
Philadelphia *(G-14085)*

◆ Opsec Security Inc ....D 717 293-4110
Lancaster *(G-9155)*

Pannier Corporation ....E 724 265-4900
Gibsonia *(G-6348)*

Pannier Corporation ....E 412 492-1400
Glenshaw *(G-6495)*

▲ Pannier Corporation ....F 412 323-4900
Pittsburgh *(G-15368)*

Richland Plastics & Engraving ....G 814 266-3002
Johnstown *(G-8431)*

Sh Quints Sons Company ....F 215 533-1988
Philadelphia *(G-14295)*

Sic Marking Usa Inc ....G 412 487-1165
Pittsburgh *(G-15536)*

Srm-Avant Inc ....G 724 537-0300
Greensburg *(G-6716)*

Steele Print Inc ....G 724 758-6178
Ellwood City *(G-4952)*

▲ Unity Printing Company Inc ....E 724 537-5800
Latrobe *(G-9527)*

▲ Viking Electronic Services ....E 610 992-0400
King of Prussia *(G-8697)*

Wakefoose Office Supply & Prtg ....G 814 623-5742
Bedford *(G-1079)*

3955 Carbon Paper & Inked Ribbons

Aserdiv Inc ....E 800 966-7770
Springfield *(G-17907)*

Cartridge Specialist ....G 412 741-4442
Sewickley *(G-17384)*

▲ D B Products Inc ....E 215 628-0416
Montgomeryville *(G-11392)*

Dnp Imagingcomm America Corp ....D 724 696-7500
Mount Pleasant *(G-11697)*

Impression Technology Inc ....G 412 318-4437
Pittsburgh *(G-15116)*

▲ Itc Supplies LLC ....G 610 430-1300
West Chester *(G-19574)*

Laser Lab Inc ....F 717 738-3333
Ephrata *(G-5120)*

Mark Grim ....G 724 758-2270
Ellwood City *(G-4945)*

N H Laboratories Inc ....F 717 545-3221
Harrisburg *(G-7183)*

Prime Ribbon Inc ....G 412 761-4470
Pittsburgh *(G-15438)*

◆ West Point Acquisition LLC ....C 724 222-2354
Washington *(G-19244)*

3961 Costume Jewelry & Novelties

Becker Fashion Tech LLC ....G 215 776-2589
Philadelphia *(G-13450)*

Bg Jewelry ....G 610 691-0687
Bethlehem *(G-1464)*

Laura J Designs ....G 610 213-1082
Lansdowne *(G-9437)*

Lema Novelty Co Inc ....G 610 754-7242
Glenside *(G-6526)*

Pardees Jewelry & Accessories ....G 814 282-1172
Meadville *(G-10774)*

Sandys Fashion Jewelry LLC ....G 814 938-4356
Punxsutawney *(G-16161)*

▲ Sorrelli Inc ....F 610 894-9857
Kutztown *(G-8861)*

Swarovski North America Ltd ....G 412 833-3708
Pittsburgh *(G-15593)*

Swarovski North America Ltd ....G 215 752-3198
Langhorne *(G-9327)*

Swarovski Retail Ventures Ltd ....G 215 659-3649
Willow Grove *(G-20145)*

Swarovski US Holding Limited ....G 610 992-9661
King of Prussia *(G-8683)*

Treasures Inc ....G 412 920-5421
Pittsburgh *(G-15641)*

Wallace Brothers Mfg Co ....F 570 822-3808
Wilkes Barre *(G-19968)*

3965 Fasteners, Buttons, Needles & Pins

American Fastener Tech Corp ....F 724 444-6940
Gibsonia *(G-6323)*

Bolt Works Inc ....F 724 776-7273
Warrendale *(G-19069)*

Chima Inc ....E 610 372-6508
Reading *(G-16345)*

▲ Dorman Products Inc ....C 215 997-1800
Colmar *(G-3416)*

▲ Ideal Building Fasteners Inc ....F 412 299-6199
Coraopolis *(G-3699)*

▲ Innovation Plus Llc ....G 610 272-2600
King of Prussia *(G-8634)*

Inofast Manufacturing Inc ....G 215 996-9963
Hatfield *(G-7354)*

Lehigh Consumer Products LLC ....G 484 232-7100
Macungie *(G-10150)*

▼ Maclean Saegertown LLC ....G 814 763-2655
Saegertown *(G-16924)*

▲ Moore Push Pin Company ....D 215 233-5700
Glenside *(G-6531)*

▲ Southco Inc ....A 610 459-4000
Concordville *(G-3459)*

3991 Brooms & Brushes

▲ Alvord-Polk Inc ....D 605 847-4823
Millersburg *(G-11188)*

Anderson Products Incorporated ....D 570 595-7495
Cresco *(G-3890)*

Blind and Vision Rehab ....D 412 368-4400
Pittsburgh *(G-14771)*

Blind and Vision Rehab ....F 412 325-7504
Homestead *(G-7683)*

Cocker-Weber Brush Co ....F 215 723-3880
Telford *(G-18275)*

J Penner Corporation ....E 215 340-9700
Doylestown *(G-4308)*

◆ Maugus Manufacturing Inc ....F 717 299-5681
Lancaster *(G-9126)*

Maugus Manufacturing Inc ....D 717 481-4823
Lancaster *(G-9127)*

▲ Nation Ruskin Holdings Inc ....F 267 654-4000
Montgomeryville *(G-11409)*

◆ R S Quality Products Inc ....G 610 266-1916
Allentown *(G-367)*

◆ Radius Corporation ....E 484 646-9122
Kutztown *(G-8858)*

Silber Brush Manufacturing Co ....G 215 634-4063
Philadelphia *(G-14306)*

Valley Broom Inc ....G 717 349-2614
East Waterford *(G-4642)*

◆ Weiler Corporation ....B 570 595-7495
Cresco *(G-3896)*

3993 Signs & Advertising Displays

13 Big Bears Inc ....G 610 437-6123
Allentown *(G-109)*

39 Design Company Inc ....G 215 563-1320
Wayne *(G-19291)*

▲ A C Signs Inc ....G 215 465-0274
Philadelphia *(G-13326)*

Abby Signs of PA ....G 570 494-0600
Montoursville *(G-11428)*

Accel Sign Group Inc ....F 412 781-7735
Pittsburgh *(G-14637)*

Acorn Manufacturing Inc ....E 717 964-1111
Denver *(G-4065)*

Ad-Art Sign Co ....G 412 373-0960
Pittsburgh *(G-14649)*

Adams Outdoor Advg Ltd Partnr ....E 610 266-9461
Bethlehem *(G-1444)*

Addaren Holdings LLC ....G 267 387-6029
Horsham *(G-7779)*

Addies Awards & Printing LLC ....G 570 484-9060
Lock Haven *(G-10082)*

Adelphia Graphic Systems Inc ....D 610 363-8150
Exton *(G-5636)*

Advance Sign Company LLC ....E 412 481-6990
Pittsburgh *(G-14650)*

Advision Signs Inc ....F 412 788-8440
Pittsburgh *(G-14653)*

Aerial Signs & Awnings Inc ....E 610 494-1415
Chester *(G-3037)*

▲ Affordable Signs Co Inc ....F 215 671-0646
Philadelphia *(G-13352)*

Al Tedeschi ....G 724 746-3755
Canonsburg *(G-2535)*

All-Sign Graphics & Design ....E 814 467-9995
Windber *(G-20177)*

Allimage Graphics LLC ....G 814 728-8650
Warren *(G-19009)*

Alphabet Signs Inc ....G 800 582-6366
Gap *(G-6248)*

Alpine Sign and Lighting Inc ....F 717 246-2376
Dallastown *(G-3970)*

▲ Altoona Neon Sign Service ....G 814 942-7488
Altoona *(G-472)*

Ameraquick Inc ....G 724 733-5906
Murrysville *(G-11846)*

Ameraquick Sign Systems ....G 724 733-5906
Murrysville *(G-11847)*

American Brchure Catalogue Inc ....E 215 259-1600
Warminster *(G-18827)*

Americana Art China Co Inc ....F 330 938-6133
Mercer *(G-10959)*

Andrew W Nissly Inc ....G 717 393-3841
Lancaster *(G-8934)*

Architectural Sign Associates ....F 412 563-5657
Pittsburgh *(G-14717)*

Art Sign Company ....G 717 264-4211
Chambersburg *(G-2906)*

Athletic Lettering Inc ....F 717 840-6373
York *(G-20389)*

Atlas Neon Sign Corp ....G 724 935-2171
Warrendale *(G-19068)*

Atlas Sign Group LLC ....G 724 935-2160
Mars *(G-10487)*

Autograph Signs Inc ....G 412 371-2877
Pittsburgh *(G-14741)*

B and B Signs and Graphics ....G 717 737-4467
Mechanicsburg *(G-10821)*

Bartlett Signs ....G 814 392-7082
Erie *(G-5203)*

Bartush Signs Inc ....E 570 366-2311
Orwigsburg *(G-13040)*

◆ Bedford Reinforced Plas Inc ....D 814 623-8125
Bedford *(G-1044)*

◆ Beistle Company ....B 717 532-2131
Shippensburg *(G-17517)*

Berm Studios Incorporated ....D 610 622-2100
Garnet Valley *(G-6265)*

Bernard Sign Corporation ....E 215 425-1700
Philadelphia *(G-13456)*

Blair Companies ....D 814 949-8280
Altoona *(G-479)*

◆ Blair Companies ....C 814 949-8287
Altoona *(G-480)*

Blind and Vision Rehab ....F 412 325-7504
Homestead *(G-7683)*

Blind and Vision Rehab ....D 412 368-4400
Pittsburgh *(G-14771)*

Bonura Jr Cabinets By Bill ....G 412 793-6790
Pittsburgh *(G-14784)*

Boyd Geyer Sign Corporation ....G 215 860-3008
Newtown *(G-12498)*

Brands Imaging LLC ....G 215 279-7218
Philadelphia *(G-13477)*

Brenneman Printing Inc ....E 717 299-2847
Lancaster *(G-8959)*

Bright Sign and Maint Co Inc ....E 610 916-5100
Leesport *(G-9660)*

Bright Sign Co Inc ....G 215 563-9480
Philadelphia *(G-13481)*

Brown Signs Inc ....G 717 866-2669
Richland *(G-16683)*

Browns Graphic Solutions ....G 717 721-6160
Lancaster *(G-8962)*

Bruners Sign Service Inc ....G 717 896-7699
Halifax *(G-6825)*

Bunting Inc ....C 412 820-2200
Verona *(G-18750)*

▲ Bunting Graphics Inc ....C 412 481-0445
  Verona (G-18751)
Bunting Stamp Company ....C 412 820-2200
  Verona (G-18752)
Burkhart & Quinn Sign Co Inc ....F 717 367-1375
  Elizabethtown (G-4867)
Butz Sign Co ....G 717 397-8565
  Lancaster (G-8966)
Bux Mont Awards ....G 215 855-5052
  Lansdale (G-9349)
Bux Mont Awards ....G 215 257-5432
  Sellersville (G-17341)
C & G Wilcox Engrv & Images ....G 570 265-3621
  Towanda (G-18422)
Capitol Sign Company Inc ....D 215 822-0166
  Lansdale (G-9350)
Cariks Custom Decor ....G 412 882-1511
  Pittsburgh (G-14812)
Cerra Signs Inc ....G 570 282-6283
  Carbondale (G-2670)
Character Translation Inc ....G 610 279-3970
  Norristown (G-12644)
Charles R Eckert Signs Inc ....G 717 733-4601
  Ephrata (G-5096)
Charles Steckman ....G 724 789-7066
  Renfrew (G-16638)
CHI Signs & Designs Inc ....G 412 517-8691
  Oakmont (G-12915)
Cima Network Inc ....D 267 308-0575
  Chalfont (G-2866)
City Engraving & Awards LLC ....G 215 731-0200
  Philadelphia (G-13547)
City Sign Service Inc ....E 800 523-4452
  Horsham (G-7804)
Clapper Enterprises Inc ....E 570 368-3327
  Williamsport (G-19998)
Clarke System ....E 610 434-9889
  Allentown (G-171)
Coinco Inc ....E 814 425-7476
  Cochranton (G-3338)
▲ Coinco Inc ....E 814 425-7407
  Cochranton (G-3337)
Compass Sign Co LLC ....E 215 639-6777
  Bensalem (G-1172)
Connor Sign Group Ltd ....G 215 741-1299
  Langhorne (G-9285)
Cott Manufacturing Company ....E 724 625-3730
  Glassport (G-6411)
Crawford Dzignes Inc ....G 724 872-4644
  West Newton (G-19750)
Creation Cabinetry & Sign Co ....G 717 246-3386
  Red Lion (G-16591)
Creative Management Svcs LLC ....E 610 863-1900
  Pen Argyl (G-13212)
Crest Advertising Co ....F 724 774-4413
  Monaca (G-11289)
Crichton Diversfd Ventures LLC ....G 814 288-1561
  Johnstown (G-8367)
Custom Finishing Inc ....F 215 269-7500
  Levittown (G-9829)
Custom Plastic Specialties LLC ....C 814 838-6471
  Erie (G-5239)
Custom Signs Inc ....F 814 786-7232
  Grove City (G-6783)
D & N Enterprise Inc ....G 215 238-9050
  Philadelphia (G-13597)
Dan Orner Signs ....G 610 876-6042
  Chester (G-3045)
▲ David Weber Co Inc ....C 215 426-3500
  Philadelphia (G-13610)
Davis Sign Service LLC ....G 412 856-5535
  Monroeville (G-11332)
Davis Trophies & Sports Wear ....G 610 455-0640
  West Chester (G-19533)
▼ Dawson Performance Inc ....F 717 261-1414
  Chambersburg (G-2923)
Dayton Computer & Sign Inc ....G 814 257-8670
  Dayton (G-4038)
De Signs By Ben Pogue ....G 724 592-5013
  Jefferson (G-8270)
▲ Decora Industries Inc ....D 215 698-2600
  Philadelphia (G-13614)
Deforest Signs & Lighting Inc ....F 717 564-6102
  Harrisburg (G-7117)
◆ Deltronic Labs Inc ....E 215 997-8616
  Chalfont (G-2872)
Denron Sign Co Inc ....G 610 269-6622
  Downingtown (G-4222)
Derse Inc ....D 724 772-4853
  Warrendale (G-19071)

Devaltronix Inc ....F 215 331-9600
  Philadelphia (G-13625)
Deversign ....G 610 583-2312
  Sharon Hill (G-17456)
Digital Dsgns Grphics Sgns LLC ....G 724 568-1626
  Gibsonia (G-6331)
Digital Sign Id Corporation ....G 800 407-9188
  Richboro (G-16674)
Direct Results Bsp Inc ....F 724 627-2040
  Waynesburg (G-19439)
Displays and Graphics Inc ....G 717 540-1481
  Harrisburg (G-7120)
Dobish Signs & Display Inc ....G 724 375-3943
  Aliquippa (G-73)
DS Services Group Corp ....F 724 350-6429
  Charleroi (G-3010)
East Coast Sign Advg Co Inc ....C 888 724-0380
  Bristol (G-2136)
Edmiston Signs ....G 814 742-8930
  Bellwood (G-1137)
Elevated Sign Solutions LLC ....E 267 374-4758
  Abington (G-11)
ELM Enterprises Inc ....E 724 452-8699
  Zelienople (G-20798)
Elmark Sign & Graphics Inc ....F 610 692-0525
  West Chester (G-19550)
Elmark Sign & Graphics Inc ....F 610 692-0525
  West Chester (G-19549)
Endagraph Inc ....G 724 327-9384
  Export (G-5601)
Excel Signworks ....G 412 337-2966
  Pittsburgh (G-14992)
Excl Inc ....E 412 856-7616
  Trafford (G-18456)
Exhibit G LLC ....G 215 302-2260
  Philadelphia (G-13687)
Express Sign Outlet Inc ....G 610 336-9636
  Wescosville (G-19489)
Eye Catcher Graphics Inc ....G 814 946-4080
  Altoona (G-502)
Eye Design LLC ....E 610 409-1900
  Trappe (G-18468)
EZ Signs LLC ....G 866 349-5444
  Phila (G-13311)
F and T LP ....G 215 355-2060
  Feasterville Trevose (G-5907)
F Creative Impressions Inc ....G 215 743-7577
  Philadelphia (G-13690)
F Creative Impressions Inc ....G 215 743-7577
  Lansdowne (G-9432)
Factor X Graffics LLC ....F 717 458-8336
  Carlisle (G-2711)
Fassinger Products & Engraving ....G 412 563-6226
  Pittsburgh (G-15006)
Fast Signs of Willow Grove ....G 215 830-9960
  Willow Grove (G-20117)
Fast Signs of Wynnewood ....G 484 278-4839
  Penn Valley (G-13235)
Fastsigns ....G 570 824-7446
  Wilkes Barre (G-19920)
Fastsigns ....G 610 280-6100
  Exton (G-5676)
Fastsigns ....G 610 296-0400
  Phoenixville (G-14550)
Fastsigns International Inc ....G 717 840-6400
  York (G-20475)
Fastsigns of Uniontown ....G 724 430-7446
  Uniontown (G-18626)
Fejes Signs ....G 724 527-7446
  Jeannette (G-8256)
Ferri Design ....G 412 276-3700
  Carnegie (G-2767)
Fieseler Neon Sign Co ....G 570 655-2976
  Pittston (G-15750)
Fine Sign Designs Inc ....G 610 277-9860
  Norristown (G-12658)
Fleet Decal & Graphics Inc ....F 570 779-4343
  Plymouth (G-15818)
Fm2 Inc ....G 814 874-0090
  Erie (G-5295)
Forman Sign Co ....E 215 827-6500
  Philadelphia (G-13715)
Freds Signs ....G 412 741-3153
  Pittsburgh (G-15036)
Futura Identities Inc ....G 215 333-3337
  Philadelphia (G-13736)
G & L Designs ....G 610 868-1381
  Bethlehem (G-1521)
G S P Signs & Banners Inc ....G 610 430-7000
  West Chester (G-19556)

Gallo Design Group ....G 724 628-0198
  Connellsville (G-3497)
GEC Enterprises Inc ....G 570 662-8898
  Mansfield (G-10415)
Gerding Corp ....G 215 441-0900
  Warminster (G-18887)
Gesualdi Printing ....G 215 785-3960
  Bristol (G-2148)
Glass U LLC ....F 855 687-7423
  Philadelphia (G-13765)
Graber Letterin Inc ....G 610 369-1112
  Boyertown (G-1913)
Graham Sign Company ....G 814 765-7199
  Clearfield (G-3220)
Graphics 22 Signs Inc ....F 412 422-1125
  Pittsburgh (G-15058)
Gray Sign Advertising ....G 724 224-5008
  Tarentum (G-18244)
Grid Electric Inc ....E 610 466-7030
  Coatesville (G-3306)
H & R Neon Service Inc ....G 724 222-6115
  Washington (G-19183)
H H Seiferth Associates Inc ....G 412 281-4983
  Pittsburgh (G-15070)
▲ Hanover Pen Corp ....E 717 637-3729
  Hanover (G-6897)
Harris Graphics & Detailing ....G 610 532-0209
  Norwood (G-12880)
Heimer Enterprises Inc ....G 814 234-7446
  State College (G-17974)
Hicks Signs ....G 717 328-3300
  Mercersburg (G-10987)
Horizon Signs LLC ....F 215 538-2600
  Quakertown (G-16200)
Horst Signs ....G 717 866-8899
  Myerstown (G-11887)
Horsts Handpainting ....G 717 336-7098
  Reinholds (G-16632)
Howard Industries Inc ....E 814 833-7000
  Fairview (G-5828)
Identification Systems Inc ....E 814 774-9656
  Girard (G-6391)
Image 360 ....G 717 317-9147
  Harrisburg (G-7153)
Image Signs Inc ....G 814 946-4663
  Altoona (G-515)
Imagineered Signs & Display ....G 717 846-6114
  York (G-20534)
Impressive Signs Inc ....G 717 848-9305
  York (G-20535)
Interstate Self Storage ....G 724 662-1186
  Mercer (G-10965)
Ivy Graphics Inc ....F 215 396-9446
  Warminster (G-18900)
J & P Incorporated ....G 610 759-2378
  Nazareth (G-11972)
J & S Signco Inc ....G 717 657-3800
  Harrisburg (G-7156)
J L Screen Printing ....G 724 696-5630
  Ruffs Dale (G-16873)
J Margulis Inc ....G 215 739-9100
  Bala Cynwyd (G-881)
Jack Murray Design ....G 610 845-9154
  Barto (G-944)
▲ Jalite Inc ....G 570 491-2205
  Matamoras (G-10539)
Jeff Enterprises Inc ....F 610 434-7353
  Allentown (G-268)
JMB Signs LLC ....G 814 933-9725
  State College (G-17980)
Ken Leaman Signs ....G 717 295-4531
  Lancaster (G-9081)
Keystone Sign Systems Inc ....G 717 319-2265
  Mechanicsburg (G-10864)
Keystone Signs ....G 717 486-5381
  Mount Holly Springs (G-11635)
Kgc Enterprises Inc ....E 610 497-0111
  Aston (G-771)
Klein Electric Advertising Inc ....F 215 657-6984
  Willow Grove (G-20125)
Kochmer Graphics ....G 570 222-5713
  Clifford (G-3246)
Koroteo Investments Inc ....G 570 342-4422
  Scranton (G-17252)
Krohmalys Printing Co ....G 412 271-4234
  Pittsburgh (G-15201)
Kruppko Inc ....F 610 489-2334
  Royersford (G-16856)
Kurt Lebo ....G 610 682-4071
  Fleetwood (G-5975)

L & H Signs Inc................................E 610 374-2748
Reading (G-16424)

◆ La France Corp............................C...... 610 361-4300
Concordville (G-3457)

Lake Shore Industries Inc ....F 814 456-4277
Erie (G-5356)

▲ Laminators Incorporated..............D...... 215 723-5285
Hatfield (G-7362)

Lancaster Sign Co Inc.......................F 717 284-3500
New Providence (G-12434)

Lancaster Sign Source Inc..................G...... 717 569-7606
Lancaster (G-9106)

Landis Neon Sign Co Inc....................G...... 717 397-0588
Lancaster (G-9107)

Lane Display Inc................................G...... 610 361-1110
Chadds Ford (G-2854)

Laret Sign Co....................................G...... 814 695-4455
Hollidaysburg (G-7650)

Lark Enterprises Inc..........................E 724 657-2001
New Castle (G-12114)

Laucks and Spaulding Inc...................F 717 845-3312
York (G-20562)

Laurelind Corp...................................G...... 215 368-5800
Montgomeryville (G-11401)

Laurelind Corp...................................G...... 215 230-4737
Montgomeryville (G-11402)

Lehigh Valley Sign & Service ....G...... 610 760-8590
Germansville (G-6280)

Leiphart Enterprises LLC....................G...... 717 938-4100
Lewisberry (G-9888)

◆ Leon L Berkowitz Co......................F 215 654-0800
Glenside (G-6527)

Leonard Dick.....................................G...... 717 334-8992
Gettysburg (G-6304)

Letterco Inc.......................................G...... 215 721-9010
Souderton (G-17750)

Linbob LLC...G...... 610 375-7446
Reading (G-16429)

Lionette Enterprises ....G...... 814 274-9401
Coudersport (G-3784)

Lititz Sign Company ....G...... 717 626-7715
Lititz (G-10024)

Lucky Sign Shop Inc..........................G...... 610 459-5825
Glen Mills (G-6439)

M & M Displays Inc ....F 800 874-7171
Philadelphia (G-13980)

Mac Sign Systems Inc.......................F 570 347-7446
Scranton (G-17257)

Madera Cabinets ....F 412 793-5850
Pittsburgh (G-15246)

Marsh Creek Signs Inc.......................G...... 610 458-5503
Downingtown (G-4239)

Martino Signs Inc...............................F 610 622-7446
Yeadon (G-20355)

Martino Signs Inc...............................G...... 610 355-9269
Newtown Square (G-12584)

Matthews International Corp...............B...... 412 571-5500
Pittsburgh (G-15266)

Media Advantage Inc ....G...... 800 985-5596
Huntingdon Valley (G-8012)

Merchandising Methods Inc................E 215 262-4842
Doylestown (G-4315)

Minahan Corporation..........................G...... 814 288-1561
Johnstown (G-8409)

▲ Mobile Technology Graphics LLC ....G....... 610 838-8075
Hellertown (G-7559)

Montgomery Signs Inc ....G...... 610 834-5400
Conshohocken (G-3578)

Monument Sign Mfg LLC....................G...... 570 366-9505
Orwigsburg (G-13050)

Morgan Signs Inc ....E 814 238-5051
State College (G-17994)

MRC Electric......................................G...... 267 988-4370
Warminster (G-18925)

Mt Displays LLC.................................F 201 636-4144
Hanover Township (G-6998)

Mundorf Sign Co................................G...... 717 854-3071
York (G-20608)

MWM Graphics...................................F 610 692-0525
West Chester (G-19603)

Naamans Creek Co Inc.......................G...... 610 268-3833
Avondale (G-855)

▲ Nation-Wide Sign Service Inc ....G...... 888 234-5300
Drexel Hill (G-4369)

National Signs Inc..............................G...... 724 375-3083
Aliquippa (G-87)

Neon Doctor LLC................................G...... 412 885-7075
Pittsburgh (G-15326)

Neon Trading ....G...... 610 530-2988
Allentown (G-327)

Nite Lite Sign Co ....G...... 570 649-5825
Turbotville (G-18556)

NMB Signs Inc...................................F 412 344-5700
Pittsburgh (G-15342)

North American Display ....G...... 412 209-9988
Pittsburgh (G-15346)

One Sign Inc......................................G...... 412 478-6809
Natrona Heights (G-11948)

▲ Pak-It Displays Inc ....E 215 638-7510
Bensalem (G-1237)

Pannier Corporation ....E 724 265-4900
Gibsonia (G-6348)

Pannier Corporation ....E 412 492-1400
Glenshaw (G-6495)

▲ Pannier Corporation ....F 412 323-4900
Pittsburgh (G-15368)

Peachtree City Foamcraft Inc ....G...... 610 769-0661
Schnecksville (G-17142)

Penn Sign Company ....G...... 717 732-8900
Enola (G-5083)

Permanent Sign & Display ....G...... 610 736-3222
Reading (G-16469)

Pike Graphics Inc...............................F 215 836-9120
Flowertown (G-5990)

Pioneer Supply Company Inc..............G...... 856 314-8299
Greensburg (G-6701)

Pls Signs LLC.....................................G...... 215 269-1400
Fairless Hills (G-5791)

Pmdi Signs Inc...................................G...... 215 526-0898
Ivyland (G-8220)

Precision Sign & Awning.....................G...... 412 281-0330
Pittsburgh (G-15432)

Precisions Signs and Awning...............G...... 412 278-0400
Carnegie (G-2782)

Prism Fiber Optics Inc........................G...... 412 802-0750
Pittsburgh (G-15447)

Promark Industries Inc.......................G...... 724 356-4060
Mc Donald (G-10579)

Promotion Centre Inc ....E 717 843-1582
York (G-20645)

Purpose 1 LLC....................................G...... 717 232-9077
Lemoyne (G-9749)

R & K Neon Inc..................................G...... 724 834-8570
Greensburg (G-6709)

▲ R A Egan Sign & Awng Co Inc ....F 610 777-3795
Reading (G-16482)

Ras Sports Inc....................................E 814 833-9111
Erie (G-5457)

Raucmin Seven LLC............................G...... 412 374-1420
Monroeville (G-11352)

Reed Sign Company ....F 215 679-5066
Pennsburg (G-13256)

Rehoboth Signs ....G...... 717 458-8520
Mechanicsburg (G-10884)

Reidler Decal Corporation...................E 800 628-7770
Saint Clair (G-16939)

Reliable Sign & Striping Inc ....G...... 610 767-8090
Slatington (G-17612)

Rhoads Sign Systems ....G...... 717 776-7309
Newville (G-12609)

Rich-Art Sign Co Inc...........................G...... 215 922-1539
Philadelphia (G-14245)

Richland Plastics & Engraving ....G...... 814 266-3002
Johnstown (G-8431)

Richman Industries Inc ....G...... 717 561-1766
Harrisburg (G-7206)

Rick Weyand Signs ....G...... 814 893-5524
Stoystown (G-18084)

RMS Kunkle Inc..................................G...... 717 564-8829
Harrisburg (G-7208)

▲ Roe Fabricators Inc ....F 610 485-4990
Chester (G-3061)

Rosuco Inc...G...... 724 297-5610
Worthington (G-20232)

Ruck Engineering Inc..........................G...... 412 835-2408
Bethel Park (G-1431)

Ryder Graphics..................................G...... 717 697-0187
Mechanicsburg (G-10886)

S & H Hardware & Supply Co...............F 215 745-9375
Philadelphia (G-14269)

S & H Hardware & Supply Co...............G...... 267 288-5950
Huntingdon Valley (G-8033)

Sarro Signs Inc..................................G...... 610 444-2020
Kennett Square (G-8541)

Saupp Signs Co LLC ....G...... 814 342-2100
Philipsburg (G-14526)

Savemypixcom Inc.............................G...... 800 535-6299
Thornton (G-18355)

Scepter Signs Inc...............................G...... 610 326-7446
Pottstown (G-16043)

Sekula Sign Corporation.....................E 814 371-4650
Du Bois (G-4417)

Shamrock Building Services Inc ....E 412 279-2800
Carnegie (G-2792)

Sign Concepts Inc..............................G...... 610 586-7070
Folsom (G-6028)

Sign Design Associates Inc ....G...... 610 791-9301
Allentown (G-390)

Sign Guy ....G...... 724 483-2200
Monongahela (G-11315)

Sign Here Inc.....................................F 814 453-6711
Erie (G-5478)

Sign Here Sign Co Inc ....G...... 845 858-6366
Matamoras (G-10540)

Sign Maker Inc...................................G...... 215 676-6711
Philadelphia (G-14304)

Sign ME Up LLC..................................G...... 814 931-0933
Hollidaysburg (G-7655)

Sign Medix Inc....................................F 717 396-9749
Lancaster (G-9198)

Sign O Rama Inc.................................G...... 215 784-9494
Willow Grove (G-20141)

Sign Services Inc...............................G...... 412 996-0824
East Pittsburgh (G-4598)

Sign Shop of The Poconos Inc ....G...... 347 972-1775
Wind Gap (G-20172)

Sign Spot...G...... 570 455-7775
Hazleton (G-7527)

Sign Stop...G...... 814 238-3338
State College (G-18024)

Signage Unlimited Inc.........................F 610 647-6962
Malvern (G-10316)

Signarama..F 717 397-3173
Lancaster (G-9199)

Signs By Design ....G...... 717 626-6212
Lancaster (G-9201)

Signs By Renee ....G...... 814 763-4206
Saegertown (G-16934)

Signs By Rick Inc................................G...... 724 287-3887
Butler (G-2441)

Signs By Sam ....G...... 724 752-3711
Ellwood City (G-4949)

Signs By Tomorrow ....G...... 717 757-4909
York (G-20668)

Signs By Tomorrow ....G...... 724 838-9060
Greensburg (G-6714)

Signs By Tomorrow ....G...... 484 356-0707
West Chester (G-19640)

Signs By Tomorrow Inc ....G...... 717 975-2456
Lemoyne (G-9753)

Signs By Tomorrow USA Inc...............G...... 484 592-0404
Ardmore (G-716)

Signs Now ....G...... 717 633-5864
Hanover (G-6952)

Signs Now ....G...... 814 453-6564
Erie (G-5479)

Signs of Excellence Inc ....G...... 724 325-7446
Murrysville (G-11867)

Signs Service & Crane Inc ....G...... 724 515-5272
Irwin (G-8200)

Signstat..F 724 527-7475
Jeannette (G-8264)

Simco Sign Studios Inc.......................F 610 534-5550
Collingdale (G-3410)

Simone Associates Inc ....G...... 717 274-3621
Lebanon (G-9631)

Sir Speedy 7108 Inc ....F 412 787-9898
Pittsburgh (G-15542)

Skuta Signs of All Kinds ....G...... 724 863-6159
Irwin (G-8201)

Slavic Group Inc.................................G...... 724 437-6756
Lemont Furnace (G-9737)

Smart Systems Inc.............................G...... 412 323-2128
Pittsburgh (G-15546)

▼ Solar Technology Inc ....D...... 610 391-8600
Allentown (G-396)

▲ Southern Glazer s Wine and Sp........C...... 610 265-6800
King of Prussia (G-8678)

Spencer Industries Inc ....F 215 634-2700
Philadelphia (G-14334)

Sperry Graphic Inc.............................E 610 534-8585
Folcroft (G-6016)

Sskj Enterprises Inc...........................G...... 412 494-3308
Carnegie (G-2794)

Star Organization Inc ....G...... 412 374-1420
Monroeville (G-11359)

Steel City Graphics Inc ....G...... 724 942-5699
Canonsburg (G-2640)

Steele Print Inc..................................G...... 724 758-6178
Ellwood City (G-4952)

Stephanie McClain G 267 820-9273
Philadelphia *(G-14345)*
Steve Schwartz Associates Inc E 412 765-3400
Pittsburgh *(G-15583)*
Stoner Graphix Inc G 717 469-7716
Hummelstown *(G-7925)*
Stop N Go Signs G 570 374-3939
Selinsgrove *(G-17336)*
Sturdevant Signs G 814 723-3361
Warren *(G-19048)*
Sun and Shade Inc G 610 409-0366
Boyertown *(G-1930)*
Sunsational Signs Win Tinting G 610 277-4344
Norristown *(G-12715)*
Superior Respiratory Home Care G 717 560-7806
Lancaster *(G-9209)*
Surf & Turf Enterprises G 610 338-0274
Morton *(G-11593)*
T C B Displays Inc E 610 983-0500
Phoenixville *(G-14582)*
TApp Technology LLC G 800 288-3184
Ardmore *(G-721)*
Terre Trophy Co G 610 777-2050
Reading *(G-16536)*
Thomas Henry Potoeski G 570 922-3361
Millmont *(G-11220)*
Tjaws LLC G 570 344-2117
Scranton *(G-17304)*
Tomdel Inc G 724 519-2697
Monroeville *(G-11360)*
▲ **Trafcon Industries Inc** E 717 691-8007
Mechanicsburg *(G-10899)*
Traffic & Safety Signs Inc G 610 925-1990
Kennett Square *(G-8550)*
Triton Signs Incorporated G 610 495-4747
Pottstown *(G-16060)*
Two Toys Inc G 717 840-6400
York *(G-20693)*
Universal Awnings & Signs Inc G 215 634-7150
Philadelphia *(G-14425)*
Universal Services Assoc Inc E 610 461-0300
Folcroft *(G-6018)*
▼ **Upper Darby Sign Company** D 610 518-5881
Downingtown *(G-4259)*
Upper Room Inc F 724 437-5815
Uniontown *(G-18646)*
US Municipal Supply Inc E 610 292-9450
Huntingdon *(G-7958)*
Verners Paint Center Inc F 724 224-7445
Tarentum *(G-18253)*
Vh Service LLC G 267 808-9745
Feasterville Trevose *(G-5938)*
Viking Signs Inc G 570 455-4369
Hazleton *(G-7535)*
Vinyl Dizzign G 267 246-7725
Lansdale *(G-9425)*
Vinyl Graphics Unlimited G 814 226-7887
Shippenville *(G-17566)*
Vision Products Inc D 724 274-0767
Cheswick *(G-3121)*
Visual Information Services G 800 777-3565
Denver *(G-4096)*
Visualize Digitized LLC G 610 494-9504
Upper Chichester *(G-18676)*
Vpak Technology G 610 458-8600
Downingtown *(G-4262)*
W J Strickler Signs Inc E 717 624-8450
New Oxford *(G-12425)*
Web Paint Inc F 570 208-2528
Wilkes Barre *(G-19970)*
Weekend Directional Services D 800 494-4954
Beaver *(G-995)*
Wenning Entertainment LLC F 412 292-8776
East Mc Keesport *(G-4582)*
Wertner Signs G 717 597-4502
Greencastle *(G-6642)*
West Signs Inc G 724 443-5588
Allison Park *(G-467)*
White Trophy Co Inc G 215 638-9134
Bensalem *(G-1272)*
Widmer Sign Company Inc G 570 343-0319
Scranton *(G-17313)*
Wiley Electric Sign Service G 610 759-8167
Nazareth *(G-11994)*
William F and Kathy A Yeager G 717 665-6964
Manheim *(G-10407)*
William Klein Signs Inc G 610 374-5371
Reading *(G-16565)*
▲ **Wlek Inc** C 800 772-8247
Erie *(G-5531)*

Yesco Handyman Services G 724 206-9541
Washington *(G-19249)*
Yesco New Castle Elec Sup G 724 656-0911
New Castle *(G-12171)*

3995 Burial Caskets

Casket Shells Incorporated G 570 876-2642
Eynon *(G-5754)*
◆ **Matthews International Corp** E 412 442-8200
Pittsburgh *(G-15264)*
McKennas Woodworking G 570 836-3652
Tunkhannock *(G-18542)*
Miller Casket Company Inc D 570 876-3872
Jermyn *(G-8308)*
Reynoldsville Casket Company G 814 653-9666
Reynoldsville *(G-16663)*
Smiths Wilbert Vault Company E 610 588-5259
Bangor *(G-928)*
◆ **Werzalit of America Inc** D 814 362-3881
Bradford *(G-1995)*
▼ **York Casket Company** B 717 854-9566
York *(G-20731)*

3996 Linoleum & Hard Surface Floor Coverings, NEC

Ahf Holding Inc G 800 233-3823
Lancaster *(G-8922)*
Armstrong Flooring Inc A 717 672-9611
Lancaster *(G-8940)*
Armstrong World Industries Inc F 717 426-4171
Marietta *(G-10460)*
Commercial Flrg Professionals G 717 576-7847
Mechanicsburg *(G-10829)*
Congoleum Corporation B 609 584-3000
Marcus Hook *(G-10439)*

3999 Manufacturing Industries, NEC

201 Distributing Inc G 724 529-2320
Vanderbilt *(G-18719)*
7th Soul LLC G 917 880-8423
Stroudsburg *(G-18101)*
8 12 Innovations Inc G 717 413-7656
Mount Joy *(G-11644)*
A & D Manufacturing G 717 768-7330
Gordonville *(G-6548)*
A Class Corp G 717 695-0597
Harrisburg *(G-7079)*
▲ **Aavid Thermacore Inc** C 717 569-6551
Lancaster *(G-8919)*
Aaxis Distributors G 717 762-2947
Waynesboro *(G-19394)*
Abililife Inc G 443 326-6395
Pittsburgh *(G-14635)*
Accurate Components G 215 442-1023
Warminster *(G-18819)*
Acutronic Company G 412 926-1200
Pittsburgh *(G-14647)*
Acutronic USA Inc G 412 926-1200
Pittsburgh *(G-14648)*
Adams Mfg Corp G 724 758-2125
Ellwood City *(G-4924)*
Agri-Dynamics Inc G 610 250-9280
Martins Creek *(G-10517)*
Albrighten Industries Inc F 724 222-2959
Eighty Four *(G-4832)*
Allegheny Rubber Stamp Inc G 412 826-8662
Blawnox *(G-1762)*
Alpha Advertising & Mktg LLC G 717 445-4200
Bowmansville *(G-1886)*
◆ **Amekor Industries Inc** D 610 825-6747
Conshohocken *(G-3518)*
American Lady US Male Hair Sln G 570 286-7759
Sunbury *(G-18162)*
American Mfg & Integration LLC F 724 861-2080
North Huntingdon *(G-12767)*
▲ **American Plume Fancy Feather** F 570 586-8400
S Abingtn Twp *(G-16889)*
Ameripak E 215 343-1530
Warrington *(G-19107)*
▲ **AMI Entertainment Network Inc** E 215 826-1400
Bristol *(G-2106)*
Antonios Manufacturing Inc F 814 886-8171
Cresson *(G-3897)*
Apex Manufacturing Company G 215 345-4400
Doylestown *(G-4270)*
Arbco Industries LLC E 724 327-6300
Export *(G-5590)*
Arch Mfg LLC G 724 438-5170
Uniontown *(G-18616)*

Armark Authentication Tech LLC G 717 767-4651
York *(G-20386)*
Armstrong Precision Mfg LLC G 412 449-0160
Pittsburgh *(G-14726)*
Azar International Inc G 570 288-0786
Kingston *(G-8712)*
B & N Trophies & Awards LLC G 814 723-8130
Warren *(G-19012)*
Baar Products Company G 610 873-4591
Downingtown *(G-4214)*
▲ **Barhill Manufacturing Corp** E 570 655-2005
Pittston *(G-15742)*
Barkby Group Inc G 717 292-4148
Dover *(G-4185)*
Barrick Design Inc G 717 295-4800
Lancaster *(G-8948)*
Beaver Creek Aviary G 717 369-9983
Saint Thomas *(G-17038)*
Bedford Manufacturing LP G 717 419-2680
Everett *(G-5566)*
Bee Positive Foundation G 484 302-8234
Phoenixville *(G-14530)*
Bg Industries LLC G 267 374-8565
Pennsburg *(G-13244)*
◆ **Binder Industries-Candlewic** F 215 230-3601
Doylestown *(G-4275)*
Blue Flame Heater Mfg G 717 768-0301
Gordonville *(G-6550)*
Bonland Industries Inc D 215 949-3720
Fairless Hills *(G-5774)*
Boxwood Manufacturing Corp G 717 751-2712
York *(G-20411)*
Breeze Dryer G 215 794-2421
Doylestown *(G-4280)*
Bri-Mar Manufacturing LLC E 717 263-6116
Chambersburg *(G-2913)*
Bristol Industries Pennsylv G 215 493-7230
Langhorne *(G-9281)*
Broderick Industries LLC G 215 409-5771
Philadelphia *(G-13485)*
Browning-Ferris Industries Inc G 814 453-6608
Erie *(G-5216)*
Bry Mar Trophy Inc G 215 295-4053
Yardley *(G-20298)*
Bucks County Fur Products Inc G 215 536-6614
Quakertown *(G-16175)*
▲ **Buzzy Inc** F 570 621-2883
Pottsville *(G-16074)*
▲ **Byers Choice Ltd** C 215 822-6700
Chalfont *(G-2864)*
Byrne Candle Co Inc E 570 346-4070
Scranton *(G-17213)*
Caltech Manufacturing F 215 322-2025
Warminster *(G-18844)*
Candlerock G 724 503-2231
New Kensington *(G-12331)*
Candles In Cove G 518 368-3381
Roaring Spring *(G-16762)*
◆ **Candlewic Company** G 215 230-3601
Doylestown *(G-4287)*
▼ **Candlsetcetera Candles ACC LLC** G 610 507-7830
Reinholds *(G-16630)*
Cappelli Industries Inc G 724 745-6766
Canonsburg *(G-2557)*
Carla Bella Ent LLC G 570 704-0077
Wilkes Barre *(G-19910)*
Cbd Incorporated G 215 579-6337
Newtown *(G-12500)*
Cessna Industries G 610 636-9282
Harleysville *(G-7025)*
▼ **Chemcut Corporation** B 814 272-2800
State College *(G-17950)*
Chestnut Group Inc G 610 688-3300
Wayne *(G-19313)*
Childcraft Education Corp C 717 653-7500
Mount Joy *(G-11649)*
Cigar N More G 717 541-1341
Harrisburg *(G-7105)*
Cincinnatus Group G 724 600-0221
Greensburg *(G-6658)*
Circle Manufacturing Company G 570 585-2139
S Abingtn Twp *(G-16892)*
City Engraving & Awards LLC G 215 731-0200
Philadelphia *(G-13547)*
Cla Industries Inc G 724 858-7112
Oakdale *(G-12897)*
Cloud Chemistry LLC F 570 851-1680
East Stroudsburg *(G-4609)*
▲ **Coinco Inc** E 814 425-7407
Cochranton *(G-3337)*

S I C

Coinco Inc................................E...... 814 425-7476
Cochranton (G-3338)

Colonial Candlecrafters.................G...... 570 524-4556
Lewisburg (G-9900)

Concrete Jungle.........................G...... 717 528-8851
York Springs (G-20763)

Construction Specialties Inc...........D...... 570 546-5941
Muncy (G-11814)

Core House..............................G...... 717 566-3810
Hummelstown (G-7907)

Costa Industries LLC....................F...... 412 384-8170
Elizabeth (G-4858)

Creative Labworks Inc...................G...... 724 667-4093
Bessemer (G-1390)

Creative Touch Inc......................E...... 215 856-9177
Philadelphia (G-13580)

Creek View Manufacturing LLC...........G...... 717 445-4922
East Earl (G-4541)

Crespo & Diaz Industries LLC ....G...... 484 895-7139
Allentown (G-186)

CSS International Corporation...........F...... 215 533-6110
Philadelphia (G-13589)

Cummings Group Inc.....................G...... 714 237-1140
Bethlehem (G-1492)

Custom Metal Innovations Inc...........G...... 724 965-3929
Wheatland (G-19836)

Custom Nuclear Fabrication LLC.........G...... 724 271-3006
Canonsburg (G-2575)

D&D Cigar & Cigarette Emporium.........G...... 570 722-4665
Albrightsville (G-48)

Danchcks Extinguishers Svc Inc.........G...... 570 589-1610
Edwardsville (G-4823)

Danita Container Inc...................G...... 570 448-3606
Honesdale (G-7709)

Dig Family Business LLC................F...... 717 299-5703
Lancaster (G-8997)

Dine-Glow Dblo Fd Svc Fels LLC ....E...... 800 526-7583
Phoenixville (G-14545)

Doppelhauer Manufacturing ....G...... 724 691-0763
Greensburg (G-6661)

Drindustries............................G...... 412 704-5840
Pittsburgh (G-14937)

Eagle Displays LLC......................F...... 724 335-8900
North Apollo (G-12726)

Early American Pittsburgh Inc..........D...... 412 486-6757
Mount Pleasant (G-11698)

East West Manufacturing A..............F...... 412 207-7385
Pittsburgh (G-14957)

Eastern Oil Corporation................G...... 412 221-2911
Bridgeville (G-2060)

Ecco Industries Inc....................G...... 570 288-1226
Kingston (G-8716)

Echo Delta Charlie Inc.................G...... 267 278-7598
Mechanicsburg (G-10841)

Edge Rubber LLC.........................E...... 717 660-2353
Chambersburg (G-2927)

Edinboro Creations.....................G...... 412 462-0370
Homestead (G-7685)

Elyse Aion..............................G...... 215 663-8787
Jenkintown (G-8285)

Endeavour Sky LLC.......................G...... 610 872-5694
Brookhaven (G-2244)

Entech Industries.......................G...... 724 244-9805
New Castle (G-12089)

Eti Closeco.............................G...... 412 822-8250
Pittsburgh (G-14987)

Everclear Valley Inc...................G...... 724 676-4703
New Florence (G-12196)

F & H Wax Works Ltd....................E...... 610 336-0308
Macungie (G-10145)

◆ F C Young & Co Inc...................C...... 215 788-9226
Bristol (G-2143)

Factory Unlocked LLC...................G...... 724 882-9940
Pittsburgh (G-15003)

Felchar Manufacturing Corp.............G...... 607 723-4076
Williamsport (G-20012)

Fig Industries LLC.....................G...... 803 414-3950
Lancaster (G-9016)

Fire 1st Defense Inc...................G...... 610 296-7576
Berwyn (G-1361)

First Rspnse Ltg Solutions LLC ....G...... 412 585-6220
Pittsburgh (G-15018)

Five Points Pet Supply LLC ....G...... 724 857-6000
Aliquippa (G-75)

Frames & More...........................G...... 724 933-5557
Wexford (G-6648)

Free Energy Systems Inc ....E...... 610 583-2640
Collingdale (G-3404)

FSI Industries Inc.....................G...... 215 295-0552
Levittown (G-9837)

Ft Pitt Acquisition Corp...............E...... 412 269-2950
Coraopolis (G-3691)

Full Throttle Industries LLC...........G...... 724 926-2140
Mc Donald (G-10574)

◆ Fun-Time International Inc...........C...... 215 925-1450
Philadelphia (G-13734)

Future Generation Ag LLC...............G...... 844 993-3311
Leola (G-9783)

Gail Dagowitz..........................G...... 610 642-7634
Gladwyne (G-6408)

Galomb Inc..............................G...... 610 434-3283
Allentown (G-222)

Gardencraft Mfg.........................G...... 717 354-3430
Gordonville (G-6555)

Gerding Corp............................G...... 215 441-0900
Warminster (G-18887)

▲ Global Ceramic Services Inc.........F...... 724 545-7224
Kittanning (G-8774)

Glow Mfg................................G...... 814 798-2215
Stoystown (G-18078)

Gohn Mfg................................G...... 717 426-3875
Marietta (G-10463)

Golden Bone Pet Resort Inc.............E...... 412 661-7001
Pittsburgh (G-15057)

▲ Good Scents Candle Co Inc...........G...... 814 349-5848
Millheim (G-11218)

Gordon Industries......................G...... 516 354-8888
Indiana (G-8103)

Grundy Industries LLC..................G...... 570 609-5487
Wyoming (G-20278)

Hatfield Manufacturing Inc.............G...... 215 368-9574
Hatfield (G-7346)

Haveco Inc..............................G...... 717 558-4301
Harrisburg (G-7146)

Hawke Aerospace Holdings LLC...........F...... 610 372-5141
Reading (G-16399)

Hawke Aerospace Holdings LLC...........G...... 610 372-5191
Morgantown (G-11523)

Haylolt Candles........................G...... 717 656-9463
Leola (G-9786)

▼ Healthy Pet Foods Inc...............G...... 610 918-4702
West Chester (G-19560)

Heathen Mfg.............................G...... 724 887-0337
White (G-19844)

▲ Henry Margu Inc.....................F...... 610 622-0515
Lansdowne (G-9434)

Hoehl Assoc.............................G...... 412 741-4170
Sewickley (G-17392)

Hoff Industries LLC....................G...... 215 516-9849
Souderton (G-17740)

Homestead Valve Mfg Co.................G...... 610 770-1100
Allentown (G-246)

Hooke Mfg LLC...........................G...... 570 876-6787
Eynon (G-5755)

Hope Good Animal Clinic................G...... 717 766-5535
Mechanicsburg (G-10854)

Horning Manufacturing LLC..............F...... 717 354-5040
New Holland (G-12253)

House of Candles.......................F...... 570 629-1953
Henryville (G-7567)

▼ Howanitz Associates Inc............E...... 570 629-3388
Bartonsville (G-946)

Hv2 Enterprises Inc ....F...... 610 330-9300
Easton (G-4703)

Ideal Manufacturing LLC................G...... 717 629-3751
Gordonville (G-6559)

Idlewood Industries Inc ....G...... 724 624-1499
Beaver (G-984)

Ikan Industries Inc....................G...... 412 670-6026
Pittsburgh (G-15114)

Industrial Vision Systems Inc ....G...... 215 393-5300
Bryn Mawr (G-2326)

◆ Inert Products LLC..................F...... 570 341-3751
Scranton (G-17244)

Innovative Exhibit Productions ....G...... 610 770-9833
Allentown (G-261)

▲ Innovative Manufacturing Svcs......G...... 610 583-4883
Folcroft (G-6006)

Intents Mfg.............................G...... 215 527-6441
East Greenville (G-4569)

Ivy Graphics Inc........................F...... 215 396-9446
Warminster (G-18900)

▼ J Harris & Sons Co.................E...... 412 391-5532
Pittsburgh (G-15142)

▲ J Kinderman & Sons Inc.............E...... 215 271-7600
Philadelphia (G-13884)

Jacob Gerger & Sons Inc................G...... 215 491-4659
Warrington (G-19122)

▲ James Jesse & Co Inc...............E...... 610 419-9880
Bethlehem (G-1544)

Jarcandlestorecom......................G...... 412 758-8855
Pittsburgh (G-15144)

Johnson Machine & Prod Inc.............G...... 570 724-2042
Wellsboro (G-19467)

Joyce Langelier........................F...... 610 659-8859
Kennett Square (G-8516)

JRKN Industries LLC....................G...... 717 324-3996
York (G-20545)

Ke Custom PC Mfg.......................G...... 215 228-6437
Philadelphia (G-13925)

Kern Industries Inc....................G...... 814 691-4211
Dover (G-4194)

Kerr Light Manufacturing LLC...........G...... 724 309-6598
Apollo (G-680)

Kessler Industries LLC.................G...... 570 590-2333
Frackville (G-6106)

▲ Keystone Industries.................F...... 717 866-7571
Myerstown (G-11890)

◆ Kidde Fire Protection Inc..........E...... 610 363-1400
West Chester (G-19581)

King Coils Manufacturing Inc...........G...... 484 645-4054
Boyertown (G-1922)

Krem Cars/Racing Inc...................G...... 814 336-6619
Meadville (G-10745)

Kykayke Inc.............................G...... 610 522-0106
Holmes (G-7663)

L E Holt Grinding Service Inc..........G...... 724 446-0977
Rillton (G-16748)

Lasting Expressions....................G...... 724 776-3953
Cranberry Township (G-3831)

Lightning Gaming Inc...................F...... 610 494-5534
Boothwyn (G-1878)

Lock and Mane..........................G...... 215 221-2131
New Hope (G-12308)

Lombardo Industries....................G...... 412 264-4588
Coraopolis (G-3703)

London Wreath Co Inc...................G...... 215 739-6440
Philadelphia (G-13974)

M & T Industries LLC...................G...... 724 216-5256
Greensburg (G-6686)

M G Industries.........................F...... 814 238-5092
State College (G-17987)

Magnum Model Concepts Inc ....G...... 717 529-0912
Kirkwood (G-8751)

Malatesta Enterprises..................F...... 570 752-2516
Berwick (G-1334)

Malek Ham..............................G...... 610 691-7600
Bethlehem (G-1565)

Manchester Industries Inc..............F...... 717 764-1161
York (G-20576)

▼ Marc Edward Brands Inc.............D...... 412 380-0888
Pittsburgh (G-15250)

Marios Tree Service Inc................G...... 610 637-1405
King of Prussia (G-8648)

Martin Amr LLC.........................G...... 908 313-2459
Altoona (G-524)

Matthey Johnson Inc....................B...... 610 341-8300
Wayne (G-19352)

McKnight Surgical Inc..................G...... 412 821-9000
Pittsburgh (G-15270)

Meadville Tool Grinding Inc............F...... 814 382-1201
Conneaut Lake (G-3477)

Meeco Manufacturing Targe..............G...... 412 653-1323
Pittsburgh (G-15274)

Michael Cain...........................F...... 814 333-1852
Meadville (G-10762)

Millcraft Industries Inc...............C...... 412 281-7675
Pittsburgh (G-15288)

Mineral Manufacturing Corp.............E...... 814 643-0410
Huntingdon (G-7951)

Mognet Industries LLC..................G...... 814 418-0864
Mineral Point (G-11252)

Montco Industries......................G...... 610 233-1081
King of Prussia (G-8652)

Msh Industries.........................G...... 814 866-0777
Erie (G-5397)

Msk Industries LLC.....................G...... 570 485-4908
Rome (G-16800)

Mt Chemical Company LLC ....G...... 570 474-2200
Mountain Top (G-11767)

Musser Manufacturing...................G...... 717 271-2321
Denver (G-4085)

Natawill Industries LLC................G...... 610 574-8226
Phoenixville (G-14564)

Natures Best Cbd PA LLC................G...... 724 568-4657
Vandergrift (G-18734)

Nestle Purina Petcare Company..........D...... 610 398-4667
Allentown (G-328)

New Hope Industries LLC................G...... 570 994-6391
Bushkill (G-2367)

Nippon Panel Inc....G....570 326-4258
Williamsport (G-20048)
Nutricia Mfg USA Inc....G....412 288-4600
Pittsburgh (G-15351)
Oak Crest Industries Inc....G....610 246-9177
Wallingford (G-18786)
▲ Old Candle Barn Inc....E....717 768-3231
Intercourse (G-8138)
On The Edge Mfg Inc....F....724 285-6802
Butler (G-2430)
OSI Industries....G....412 741-3630
Sewickley (G-17402)
Paeonia Arts & Literature LLC....G....267 520-4572
Philadelphia (G-14114)
Palace Industries....G....215 442-5508
Warminster (G-18936)
Panache Plus....G....717 812-8999
York (G-20618)
Paul William Boyle....G....412 828-0883
Oakmont (G-12923)
Penn Fibre Inc....G....800 662-7366
Bensalem (G-1241)
Penn Pro Manufacturing Inc....F....724 222-6450
Washington (G-19215)
▲ Penn Shadecrafters Inc....E....570 342-3193
Scranton (G-17271)
Penn Veterinary Supply Inc....D....717 656-4121
Lancaster (G-9163)
Perfect Precision....G....610 461-3625
Darby (G-4023)
▲ Petnovations Inc....E....610 994-2103
Phoenixville (G-14566)
▼ Pets United LLC....G....570 384-5555
Hazle Township (G-7471)
Philadelphia Regalia Co....G....610 237-9757
Prospect Park (G-16117)
Philly Fades Inc....G....678 672-9727
Phoenixville (G-14567)
▲ Pinter Industries Inc....G....717 898-9517
Landisville (G-9264)
▲ Pittsburgh Stage Inc....E....412 534-4500
Sewickley (G-17403)
Pittsburgh Wool Co Inc....G....412 642-0606
Pittsburgh (G-15413)
Plantarium Living Envirom....G....215 338-2008
Philadelphia (G-14181)
Plantscape Inc....D....412 281-6352
Pittsburgh (G-15415)
▼ Plastic Development Company PA....E....800 451-1420
Williamsport (G-20058)
Pocono Candle Works Inc....F....570 421-1832
East Stroudsburg (G-4627)
Pocono Hydrponic Solutions LLC....G....570 730-4544
Bartonsville (G-948)
Pointer Hill Pets Inc....G....610 754-7830
Bechtelsville (G-1035)
Polkabla Industries LLC....G....724 322-7740
Smock (G-17666)
Prb Mfg Representatives....G....814 466-2161
Boalsburg (G-1868)
Premier Brnds Group Hldngs LLC....E....212 835-3672
Bristol (G-2186)
Premium Pet Division....G....215 364-0211
Langhorne (G-9321)
Quietflex Manufacturing....F....570 883-9019
Pittston (G-15780)
Quinlan Scenic Studio Inc....F....610 859-9130
Marcus Hook (G-10453)
R J Reynolds Tobacco Company....G....570 654-0770
Pittston (G-15781)
▲ Radio Parts Company....E....412 963-6202
Pittsburgh (G-15465)
Rakoczy Industries Inc....G....412 389-3123
Canonsburg (G-2622)
Randall Industries LLC....G....412 281-6901
Pittsburgh (G-15467)
Raster Manufacturing LLC....G....724 837-7354
Greensburg (G-6710)
Rearden Steel Fabrication Inc....F....717 503-1989
Lemoyne (G-9750)
Red Bandana Co....F....215 744-3144
Philadelphia (G-14236)
Rob Kei Inc....G....717 293-8991
Lancaster (G-9189)
Ronco Machine Inc....F....570 319-1832
S Abingtn Twp (G-16898)
Roppa Industries LLC....G....412 749-9250
Leetsdale (G-9703)
Ryan Foster Inc....G....215 769-0118
Philadelphia (G-14268)

Sabold Design Inc....G....610 401-4086
Bernville (G-1305)
Sageking Inc....G....717 540-0525
Irwin (G-8199)
Seasons Specialties Inc....F....570 928-9522
Dushore (G-4510)
Shaffer Block and Con Pdts Inc....E....814 445-4414
Somerset (G-17705)
Shiloh Industries....G....717 779-7654
Dover (G-4204)
Silberine Manufacturing....G....570 668-8361
Allentown (G-392)
Simplex Industries Inc....G....570 495-4333
Sunbury (G-18172)
Sinking Ship Premium Juice LLC....G....570 855-2316
Glen Lyon (G-6427)
Sky Point Crane LLC....G....724 471-5710
Indiana (G-8129)
Smart Systems Enterprises Inc....G....412 323-2128
Pittsburgh (G-15547)
Smoke Town LLC....G....570 383-7833
Olyphant (G-13000)
Smokers Stop....G....717 232-5206
Harrisburg (G-7216)
Sovereign Steel Mfg LLC....G....610 797-2800
Allentown (G-397)
Spadre Investments Inc....E....724 452-8440
Evans City (G-5564)
▲ Sparks Exhbits Envrnments Corp....D....215 676-1100
Philadelphia (G-14329)
▲ Stagestep Inc....F....267 672-2900
Philadelphia (G-14339)
Stampede Industries LLC....G....724 239-2104
Eighty Four (G-4850)
◆ Strong Industries Inc....C....570 275-2700
Northumberland (G-12876)
Stx Industries....G....412 513-6689
Pittsburgh (G-15586)
Sugar Creek Candles LLC....G....724 261-1927
Irwin (G-8202)
Suprawater....G....717 528-9949
York Springs (G-20768)
▲ Supreme Zipper Industries....G....570 226-9501
Lakeville (G-8914)
▲ Sure-Lok Inc....E....610 814-0300
Easton (G-4757)
Sylray Manufacturing LLC....G....570 640-0689
Allentown (G-406)
▲ Tait Towers Inc....D....717 626-9571
Lititz (G-10051)
Tait Towers Manufacturing LLC....G....717 626-9571
Lititz (G-10052)
Tangled Manes....G....717 581-0600
East Petersburg (G-4593)
Targeted Pet Treats LLC....C....814 406-7351
Warren (G-19051)
Temco Industries Inc....G....412 831-5620
Burgettstown (G-2356)
Terra Essential Scents Sy....G....412 213-3600
Allison Park (G-464)
Thompsons Candle Co....E....814 641-7490
Huntingdon (G-7957)
Thyssenkrupp Elevator Corp....E....412 364-2624
Pittsburgh (G-15623)
▲ Tkd Mfg Inc....F....717 266-3156
York (G-20689)
Tlb Industries Inc....G....570 729-7192
Honesdale (G-7728)
TMC Candies LLC....G....814 623-1545
Bedford (G-1078)
Tompkins Manufacturing Co....G....724 287-4927
Butler (G-2446)
Total Mobility Services Inc....G....814 629-9935
Boswell (G-1885)
▲ Towerstar Pets LLC....G....610 296-4970
Malvern (G-10334)
Transtar Industries Inc....G....412 441-7353
Pittsburgh (G-15640)
Trotter Industries....F....610 369-9473
Boyertown (G-1933)
Uhuru Mfg LLC....G....717 345-3366
New Holland (G-12290)
▼ Veeco Precision Surfc Proc LLC....D....215 328-0700
Horsham (G-7863)
View Works Inc....G....724 226-9773
Springdale (G-17905)
W S Display....G....717 460-3485
Carlisle (G-2749)
Wave Swimmer Inc....G....215 367-3778
Ardmore (G-722)

Weahterford Manufacturing....G....724 239-1404
Charleroi (G-3024)
West Collection....G....570 762-8844
Oaks (G-12938)
West Penn Mfg Tech LLC....F....814 886-4100
Cresson (G-3901)
Westmoreland Contract Fur....G....724 838-7748
Greensburg (G-6731)
Weston Commercial Group Inc....G....215 717-9675
Philadelphia (G-14467)
Wexco Incorporated....G....717 764-8585
York (G-20710)
Whistle Pig Pumpkin Patch....G....570 298-0962
Noxen (G-12886)
▲ Wilder Diamond Blades Inc....G....570 222-9590
Kingsley (G-8710)
Wkw Associates LLC....F....215 348-1257
Doylestown (G-4346)
World Manufacturing Inc....E....215 426-0500
Philadelphia (G-14487)
Zerbe Manufacturing....G....570 640-1528
Pine Grove (G-14609)
Zipcorp Inc....B....814 368-2700
Bradford (G-1997)

73 BUSINESS SERVICES

7372 Prepackaged Software

21st Century Software Tech Inc....E....610 341-9017
Wayne (G-19290)
2w Technologies LLC....G....814 333-3117
Meadville (G-10693)
9dots Management Corp LLC....E....610 825-2027
Conshohocken (G-3514)
Aapryl LLC....G....215 567-1100
Philadelphia (G-13332)
Aaxios Technologies LLC....G....267 545-7400
Warrington (G-19106)
ACC Accounting Solutions Inc....G....215 253-4738
Philadelphia (G-13337)
Accion Labs Us Inc....E....724 260-5139
Bridgeville (G-2051)
Accountable Software Inc....E....610 983-3100
Royersford (G-16839)
Accustar Inc....G....610 459-0123
Garnet Valley (G-6264)
Action Wireless Network....G....412 292-1712
Bethel Park (G-1400)
Active Data Inc....E....610 997-8100
Bethlehem (G-1443)
Activestrategy Inc....E....484 690-0700
Plymouth Meeting (G-15826)
Acutedge Inc....G....484 846-6275
King of Prussia (G-8577)
Adenine Solutions Inc....G....267 684-6013
Southampton (G-17796)
Advanced Education Service....G....717 545-8633
Harrisburg (G-7084)
Advanced Software Inc....F....215 369-7800
Yardley (G-20293)
Advantage Learning Technology....G....610 217-8022
Coopersburg (G-3624)
Advertising Specialty Inst Inc....B....800 546-1350
Feasterville Trevose (G-5883)
Aegis Industrial Software Corp....E....215 773-3571
Horsham (G-7780)
Aegis Software Corporation....G....724 325-5595
Murrysville (G-11845)
Airclic Inc....D....215 504-0560
Trevose (G-18485)
Algorhythm Diagnostics LLC....G....312 813-2959
Philadelphia (G-13364)
Ally Home Care Ltd Lblty Co....G....800 930-0587
West Chester (G-19496)
Alumties Inc....G....720 570-6259
Havertown (G-7416)
Amcs Group Inc....E....610 932-4006
Oxford (G-13071)
Analytical Graphics Inc....C....610 981-8000
Exton (G-5643)
Andrew Torba....G....570 209-1622
Moosic (G-11503)
Anju Sylogent LLC....F....215 504-7000
Bristol (G-2107)
Ansoft LLC....G....412 261-3200
Pittsburgh (G-14713)
Ansys Inc....C....884 462-6797
Canonsburg (G-2541)
Appitur Co....G....215 720-1420
Newtown Square (G-12565)

S I C

Applied Software Inc ....G....... 215 297-9441
New Hope *(G-12297)*

Appligent Inc ....E....... 610 284-4006
Lansdowne *(G-9429)*

Apprise Software Inc ....E....... 610 991-3600
Bethlehem *(G-1451)*

Aptech Computer Systems Inc ....E....... 412 963-7440
Pittsburgh *(G-14714)*

Arcweb Technologies LLC ....G....... 800 846-7980
Philadelphia *(G-13409)*

Ariba Inc ....F....... 215 246-3493
Philadelphia *(G-13410)*

Ariba Inc ....D....... 412 644-0160
Pittsburgh *(G-14721)*

Ariba Inc ....F....... 610 661-8413
Newtown Square *(G-12566)*

Ark Ideaz Inc ....G....... 610 246-9106
Pottstown *(G-15943)*

Artisan Mobile Inc ....F....... 610 209-1959
Philadelphia *(G-13414)*

Ascentive LLC ....D....... 215 395-8559
Philadelphia *(G-13419)*

Astea International Inc ....D....... 215 682-2500
Horsham *(G-7791)*

Ats Fleet Trcking MGT Slutions ....F....... 570 445-8805
Dunmore *(G-4468)*

Augmentir Inc ....G....... 949 432-6450
Horsham *(G-7792)*

Automated Enterprise Intl ....G....... 610 458-5810
Glenmoore *(G-6463)*

Automated Fincl Systems Inc ....B....... 484 875-1250
Exton *(G-5649)*

Automated Fincl Systems Inc ....B....... 610 594-1037
Exton *(G-5650)*

Automatic Forecasting Systems ....F....... 215 675-0652
Warminster *(G-18832)*

Autosoft Inc ....D....... 800 473-4630
West Middlesex *(G-19721)*

Avatar Data Pubg Solutions ....G....... 412 921-7747
Pittsburgh *(G-14742)*

B6 Systems Inc ....G....... 724 861-8080
Manor *(G-10409)*

Bagatrix Solutions Ltd ....G....... 610 574-9607
Gilbertsville *(G-6370)*

Bentley Systems Incorporated ....C....... 610 458-5000
Exton *(G-5653)*

Bentley Systems Incorporated ....B....... 610 458-5000
Exton *(G-5654)*

Best Medical International Inc ....D....... 412 312-6700
Pittsburgh *(G-14764)*

Bisil North America Inc ....G....... 610 747-0340
Bala Cynwyd *(G-873)*

Bloksberg Inc ....F....... 724 727-9925
Apollo *(G-665)*

Blupanda LLC ....G....... 724 494-2077
Apollo *(G-666)*

BMC Software Inc ....E....... 610 941-2750
Conshohocken *(G-3523)*

Bodyx LLC ....G....... 610 519-9999
Bryn Mawr *(G-2316)*

Bpl Global LLC ....F....... 724 933-7700
Canonsburg *(G-2550)*

Bryn Mawr Equipment Fin Inc ....F....... 610 581-4996
Bryn Mawr *(G-2317)*

Business & Decision North Amer ....C....... 610 230-2500
Malvern *(G-10198)*

Business Intelligence Intl Inc ....E....... 484 688-8300
Wayne *(G-19311)*

Business Planning Inc ....G....... 610 649-0550
Ardmore *(G-703)*

Businessone Technologies Inc ....G....... 215 953-6660
Feasterville Trevose *(G-5896)*

Byrd Alley LLC ....F....... 215 669-0068
Philadelphia *(G-13489)*

Carnegie Learning Inc ....C....... 412 690-2442
Pittsburgh *(G-14817)*

Carnegie Speech LLC ....F....... 412 471-1234
Pittsburgh *(G-14820)*

Catalyst Crossroads LLC ....G....... 412 969-2733
Pittsburgh *(G-14827)*

Centify LLC ....F....... 215 421-8375
Oreland *(G-13019)*

Centre of Web Inc ....G....... 814 235-9592
State College *(G-17949)*

Cherokee Software Systems ....G....... 717 932-5008
New Cumberland *(G-12183)*

Ciright Automation LLC ....G....... 855 247-4448
Conshohocken *(G-3528)*

Clarivate Analytics (us) LLC ....A....... 215 386-0100
Philadelphia *(G-13548)*

Classroom Salon LLC ....G....... 412 621-6287
Pittsburgh *(G-14858)*

Cleararmor Solutions Corp ....G....... 610 816-0101
Riegelsville *(G-16744)*

Cody Computer Services Inc ....E....... 610 326-7476
Pottstown *(G-15971)*

Cognitive Oprtonal Systems LLC ....G....... 908 672-4711
Philadelphia *(G-13558)*

Cognos Corporation ....G....... 412 490-9804
Pittsburgh *(G-14866)*

Collective Intelligence Inc ....G....... 717 545-9234
Mechanicsburg *(G-10828)*

Communimetrics Group LLC ....G....... 215 260-5382
Malvern *(G-10215)*

Componentone Enterprises LLC ....D....... 412 681-4343
Pittsburgh *(G-14871)*

Compudata Inc ....E....... 215 969-1000
Philadelphia *(G-13566)*

Computer Boss ....G....... 215 444-9393
Southampton *(G-17804)*

Computer Designs Inc ....D....... 610 261-2100
Whitehall *(G-19867)*

Computer Dev Systems LLC ....G....... 717 591-0995
Mechanicsburg *(G-10830)*

Computer Software Inc ....E....... 215 822-9100
Chalfont *(G-2868)*

Compututor Inc ....G....... 610 260-0300
Conshohocken *(G-3531)*

Conestoga Data Services Inc ....F....... 717 569-7728
Lancaster *(G-8984)*

Connectedsign LLC ....G....... 717 490-6431
Lancaster *(G-8985)*

▲ Connectify Inc ....F....... 215 854-8432
Philadelphia *(G-13570)*

Connectwo LLC ....G....... 215 421-4225
Lansdale *(G-9352)*

▼ Continental Press Inc ....C....... 717 367-1836
Elizabethtown *(G-4869)*

Corestar International Corp ....E....... 724 744-4094
Irwin *(G-8151)*

Corrugated Services Corp ....D....... 215 639-9540
Fort Washington *(G-6067)*

Creative Mountain Software LLC ....G....... 814 383-2685
Howard *(G-7888)*

Cyrus-Xp Inc ....E....... 610 986-8408
Ardmore *(G-706)*

Datatech Software Inc ....F....... 717 652-4344
Harrisburg *(G-7113)*

Datumrite Corporation ....F....... 215 407-4447
North Wales *(G-12797)*

Dbaza Inc ....F....... 412 681-1180
Philadelphia *(G-13612)*

Dbmotion Inc ....F....... 412 605-1952
Pittsburgh *(G-14910)*

Decilog Inc ....G....... 215 657-0817
Willow Grove *(G-20114)*

Digital Concepts Inc ....F....... 724 745-4000
Canonsburg *(G-2577)*

Dimension Data North Amer Inc ....E....... 484 362-2563
Malvern *(G-10224)*

Dita Exchange Inc ....E....... 267 327-4889
Radnor *(G-16293)*

DMS Computer Services Inc ....G....... 412 835-3570
Pittsburgh *(G-14929)*

Dorado Solutions Inc ....G....... 480 216-1056
West Chester *(G-19543)*

Dqe Communications LLC ....G....... 412 393-1033
Pittsburgh *(G-14936)*

Dreamlike Entertainment ....G....... 610 392-5614
Slatington *(G-17606)*

Dynavox Inc ....B....... 412 381-4883
Pittsburgh *(G-14948)*

E Z Net Solutions Inc ....G....... 215 887-7200
Jenkintown *(G-8284)*

E-Lynxx Corporation ....E....... 717 709-0990
Chambersburg *(G-2926)*

Earthware Corporation ....G....... 412 563-1920
Pittsburgh *(G-14954)*

Eastern Systems Management ....G....... 717 391-9700
Lancaster *(G-9006)*

Ebroker Software LLC ....G....... 717 540-3720
Harrisburg *(G-7124)*

Ed Jupiter Inc ....F....... 888 367-6175
Philadelphia *(G-13658)*

Edaptive Systems LLC ....G....... 717 718-1230
York *(G-20463)*

Education MGT Solutions LLC ....D....... 610 701-7002
Exton *(G-5671)*

Efficient Ip Inc ....F....... 888 228-4655
West Chester *(G-19548)*

Electronics Boutique Amer Inc ....G....... 610 518-5300
Downingtown *(G-4225)*

Elemental 3 LLC ....G....... 267 217-3592
Philadelphia *(G-13667)*

Ellucian Support Inc ....C....... 610 647-5930
Malvern *(G-10229)*

Embroidery Systems Inc ....G....... 412 967-9271
Pittsburgh *(G-14969)*

Emerging Computer Technologies ....G....... 717 761-4027
Camp Hill *(G-2495)*

Energycap Inc ....E....... 814 237-3744
State College *(G-17963)*

Enlightening Lrng Minds LLC ....F....... 412 880-9601
Monroeville *(G-11336)*

Enterprise Cloudworks Corp ....E....... 215 395-6311
Bryn Mawr *(G-2322)*

Environmental Systems Research ....E....... 909 793-2853
Chesterbrook *(G-3092)*

Epilogue Systems LLC ....G....... 281 249-5405
Villanova *(G-18766)*

Eplans Inc ....G....... 717 534-1183
Hershey *(G-7609)*

Eq Technologic Inc ....F....... 215 891-9010
Fort Washington *(G-6068)*

Estari Inc ....F....... 717 233-1518
Harrisburg *(G-7127)*

Everest Software LP ....E....... 412 206-0005
Bridgeville *(G-2062)*

Expensewatch Inc ....F....... 610 397-0532
Plymouth Meeting *(G-15842)*

Ez-Plant Software Inc ....G....... 814 421-6744
Ebensburg *(G-4785)*

Fab Universal Corp ....F....... 412 621-0902
Pittsburgh *(G-15002)*

Fiberlink Communications Corp ....C....... 215 664-1600
Blue Bell *(G-1829)*

Fiftyone K LLC ....G....... 908 222-8780
Pittsburgh *(G-15017)*

First Supply Chain LLC ....G....... 215 527-2264
Hummelstown *(G-7910)*

Fis Avantgard LLC ....E....... 800 468-7483
Wayne *(G-19329)*

Fis Avantgard LLC ....E....... 215 413-4700
Philadelphia *(G-13703)*

Fis Data Systems Inc ....E....... 484 582-2000
Collegeville *(G-3377)*

Fis Sg LLC ....C....... 484 582-5400
Wayne *(G-19330)*

Fis Sg LLC ....G....... 215 627-3800
Philadelphia *(G-13704)*

Fis Systems International LLC ....D....... 484 582-2000
Collegeville *(G-3378)*

Flexible Informatics LLC ....G....... 215 253-8765
Lafayette Hill *(G-8880)*

For Lenfest Institute ....G....... 215 854-5600
Philadelphia *(G-13713)*

Forallsecure Inc ....F....... 412 256-8809
Pittsburgh *(G-15024)*

Franklin Potter Associates ....G....... 215 345-0844
Doylestown *(G-4300)*

Freedom Cyber Marketing LLC ....G....... 717 654-2392
Dallastown *(G-3975)*

Fry International LLC ....G....... 215 847-6359
Elkins Park *(G-4903)*

Gamefreaks101 Inc ....G....... 215 587-9787
Philadelphia *(G-13741)*

Ganesco Incorporated ....G....... 931 284-9033
Pittsburgh *(G-15040)*

Garth Groft ....G....... 717 819-9479
York *(G-20491)*

Genilogix LLC ....E....... 412 444-0554
Pittsburgh *(G-15047)*

GL Trade Capitl Mkts Solutions ....D....... 484 530-4400
Wayne *(G-19332)*

Globalsubmit Inc ....F....... 215 253-7471
Philadelphia *(G-13771)*

Goji Systems Inc ....G....... 267 309-2000
Norristown *(G-12662)*

Gokaaf International Inc ....G....... 267 343-3075
Philadelphia *(G-13775)*

Grammaton Research LLC ....G....... 410 703-9237
York *(G-20513)*

Gray Bridge Software Inc ....G....... 412 401-1045
Pittsburgh *(G-15059)*

Green Hills Software LLC ....G....... 215 862-9474
New Hope *(G-12304)*

Ground 34 LLC ....G....... 914 299-7212
Pittsburgh *(G-15066)*

Guiding Technologies Corp ....G....... 609 605-9273
Philadelphia *(G-13791)*

Guru Technologies Inc	F	610 572-2086
Philadelphia (G-13793)		
H&R Block Inc	F	814 723-3001
Warren (G-19030)		
Hamiltonian Systems Inc	F	412 327-7204
Coraopolis (G-3697)		
Health Market Science Inc	C	610 940-4002
King of Prussia (G-8629)		
Healthstratica LLC	G	412 956-1000
Pittsburgh (G-15085)		
Help Every Addict Live	G	484 598-3285
Drexel Hill (G-4364)		
Heraeus Prcous Mtls N Amer LLC	G	562 921-7464
Yardley (G-20316)		
Hootboard LLC	G	610 844-2423
Yardley (G-20320)		
Horizon Software Solutions	G	610 225-0989
Reading (G-16404)		
Horsey Darden Enterprises LLC	G	215 309-3139
Philadelphia (G-13834)		
Ima North America Inc	G	215 826-8500
Bristol (G-2154)		
Image Net Ventures LLC	E	610 240-0800
West Chester (G-19567)		
Impac Technology Inc	E	610 430-1400
West Chester (G-19569)		
Impilo LLC	G	610 662-2867
Wynnewood (G-20269)		
Industry Weapon Inc	E	877 344-8450
Pittsburgh (G-15123)		
Industrybuilt Software Ltd	E	866 788-1086
Allentown (G-256)		
Infor (us) Inc	E	678 319-8000
Malvern (G-10254)		
Information Builders Inc	F	610 940-0790
Plymouth Meeting (G-15851)		
Information Mktg Group Inc	F	508 626-8682
Bethel Park (G-1417)		
Ingenuware Ltd	G	724 843-3140
Beaver Falls (G-1000)		
Innovate Software Inc	G	724 935-1790
Bradfordwoods (G-1998)		
Inspire Closing Services LLC	G	412 348-8367
Moon Township (G-11494)		
Inspro Technologies Corp	F	484 654-2200
Eddystone (G-4804)		
Integrated Software Services	G	717 534-1480
Hershey (G-7618)		
Integritas Inc	G	800 411-6281
Pittsburgh (G-15131)		
Intelipc	G	610 534-8268
Folcroft (G-6007)		
Intelligent Micro Systems Ltd	G	610 664-1207
Haverford (G-7412)		
Inter Media Outdoors	G	717 695-8171
Harrisburg (G-7155)		
International Bus Mchs Corp	A	610 578-2017
Wayne (G-19339)		
International Road Dynamics	G	717 264-2077
Chambersburg (G-2943)		
▲ Internet Pipeline Inc	D	484 348-6555
Exton (G-5700)		
Iota Communications Inc	G	855 743-6478
New Hope (G-12306)		
Ip Lasso LLC	G	484 352-2029
King of Prussia (G-8635)		
Iron Compass Map Company	G	717 295-1194
Lancaster (G-9064)		
Ironwood Learning LLC	G	412 784-1384
Pittsburgh (G-15137)		
Ividix Software Inc	G	484 580-9601
Eagleville (G-4513)		
J & J Consulting Corp	G	610 678-6611
Wernersville (G-19485)		
Jujama Inc	E	570 209-7670
Scranton (G-17248)		
Jumpbutton Studio LLC	E	267 407-7535
Philadelphia (G-13914)		
K-Systems Inc	F	717 795-7711
Mechanicsburg (G-10861)		
K12systems Inc	F	610 366-9540
Allentown (G-278)		
Kcf Technologies Inc	F	814 867-4097
State College (G-17983)		
Keffer Development Svcs LLC	G	724 458-5289
Grove City (G-6793)		
Kenexa Learning Inc	E	610 971-9171
Wayne (G-19346)		
Kennebec Inc	G	412 278-2040
Pittsburgh (G-15170)		

Keystone Sftwr Solutions Inc	G	610 685-2111
Reading (G-16421)		
Kickup LLC	G	610 256-1004
Philadelphia (G-13935)		
Kinesis Software LLC	G	610 353-4150
Broomall (G-2292)		
Kinetic Buildings LLC	G	203 858-0813
Philadelphia (G-13936)		
Knowledge MGT & Tech Corp	G	412 503-3657
Washington (G-19193)		
Koryak Consulting Inc	E	412 364-6600
Pittsburgh (G-15194)		
Kos & Associates Inc	F	412 367-7444
Pittsburgh (G-15195)		
Kronos Incorporated	E	724 772-2400
Warrendale (G-19086)		
Kronos Incorporated	G	724 742-3142
Cranberry Township (G-3830)		
Kronos Incorporated	G	610 567-2127
Royersford (G-16855)		
Kynectiv Inc	F	484 899-0746
Chadds Ford (G-2853)		
Lantica Software LLC	G	215 598-8419
Newtown (G-12517)		
Ldp Inc	D	570 455-8511
West Hazleton (G-19713)		
Ldp Inc	G	717 657-8500
Harrisburg (G-7171)		
Leanfm Technologies Inc	E	412 818-5167
Pittsburgh (G-15222)		
Lease More	G	814 796-4047
Waterford (G-19264)		
Lee Rj Group Inc	C	800 860-1775
Monroeville (G-11342)		
Legacy Mark LLC	G	800 444-9260
Chambersburg (G-2951)		
Legal Sifter Inc	G	724 221-7438
Pittsburgh (G-15223)		
Lifeguard Health Networks Inc	F	484 584-4071
Wayne (G-19348)		
Link Software Corp	G	717 399-3023
Lancaster (G-9113)		
Liquent Inc	C	215 957-6401
Horsham (G-7831)		
Long Drop Games LLC	G	814 460-7961
Erie (G-5370)		
Lunchera LLC	E	787 607-8914
Pittsburgh (G-15240)		
Luxury Electronics LLC	G	215 847-0937
Yardley (G-20324)		
Makteam Software Ltd Co	G	814 504-1283
Erie (G-5379)		
Mam Software Inc	D	610 336-9045
Blue Bell (G-1846)		
Managing Editor Inc	E	215 517-5116
Jenkintown (G-8295)		
Matrix Solutions LLC	E	412 697-3000
Pittsburgh (G-15262)		
McNs Technologies LLC	G	610 269-2891
Chadds Ford (G-2855)		
Medchive LLC	G	215 688-7475
Philadelphia (G-14004)		
Media Highway	F	610 647-2255
Berwyn (G-1368)		
Medshifts Inc	G	856 834-0074
Philadelphia (G-14006)		
Meshnet Inc	G	215 237-7712
Philadelphia (G-14011)		
Metavis Technologies Inc	E	484 288-2990
Exton (G-5711)		
Method Automation Services Inc	G	724 337-9064
New Kensington (G-12356)		
Microlite Corporation	G	724 375-6711
Aliquippa (G-85)		
Microsoft Corporation	G	484 754-7600
King of Prussia (G-8651)		
Microsoft Corporation	E	412 323-6700
Pittsburgh (G-15286)		
Microsoft Corporation	C	610 240-7000
Malvern (G-10278)		
Mindmatrix Inc	F	412 381-0230
Pittsburgh (G-15291)		
▼ Minitab LLC	B	814 238-3280
State College (G-17992)		
Moai Technologies Inc	E	412 454-5550
Pittsburgh (G-15296)		
Mobius Acquisition LLC	G	412 281-7000
Pittsburgh (G-15297)		
Modevity LLC	E	610 251-0700
Malvern (G-10280)		

Morrison Consulting Inc	E	717 268-8201
York (G-20604)		
Mother Nature Corporation	G	412 798-3911
Pittsburgh (G-15304)		
Mousley Consulting Inc	G	610 539-0150
Norristown (G-12689)		
Mpm Holdings Inc	E	610 678-8131
Reading (G-16450)		
Mpower Software Services LLC	D	215 497-9730
Newtown (G-12524)		
MSI Technologies LLC	G	215 968-5068
Newtown (G-12526)		
Multimedia Training Systems	G	412 341-2185
Pittsburgh (G-15308)		
Mumps Audiofax Inc	E	610 293-2160
Wayne (G-19358)		
Mxstrategies LLC	G	610 241-2099
West Chester (G-19604)		
Neat Company Inc	C	215 382-4283
Philadelphia (G-14060)		
Net Reach Technologies LLC	F	215 283-2300
Ambler (G-593)		
Netbeez Inc	G	412 465-0638
Pittsburgh (G-15328)		
Neuroflow Inc	G	347 881-6306
Philadelphia (G-14064)		
Neuxpower Inc	G	267 238-3833
Philadelphia (G-14066)		
Next Generation Software	G	215 361-2754
Lansdale (G-9392)		
Noblemedical LLC	G	917 750-9605
Bryn Mawr (G-2332)		
Noblesoft Solutions Inc	G	713 480-7510
Langhorne (G-9315)		
Novatech LLC	C	484 812-6000
Quakertown (G-16224)		
Nurelm Inc	F	724 430-0490
Pittsburgh (G-15350)		
Nzinganet Inc	G	877 709-6459
Fort Washington (G-6087)		
O S I Software	G	215 606-0612
Philadelphia (G-14090)		
Oa Systems Llc	G	888 347-7950
Wexford (G-19818)		
Offset Paperback	G	570 602-1316
Wilkes Barre (G-19952)		
Ois LLC	G	717 447-0265
Mount Union (G-11746)		
Onlyboth Inc	G	412 303-8798
Pittsburgh (G-15360)		
Open Solution	G	646 696-8686
Bushkill (G-2368)		
Opinionmeter International Ltd	E	888 676-3837
Bethlehem (G-1587)		
Optimized Markets Inc	G	412 654-5994
Pittsburgh (G-15361)		
Oracle America Inc	E	412 859-6051
Coraopolis (G-3709)		
Oracle America Inc	G	610 647-8530
Malvern (G-10290)		
Oracle America Inc	G	717 730-5501
Lemoyne (G-9747)		
Oracle Corporation	D	610 667-8600
Conshohocken (G-3581)		
Oracle Corporation	C	717 234-5858
Harrisburg (G-7188)		
Oracle Systems Corporation	G	412 262-5200
Coraopolis (G-3710)		
Oracle Systems Corporation	C	610 729-3600
Conshohocken (G-3582)		
Oracle Systems Corporation	G	610 260-9000
Conshohocken (G-3583)		
Orbit Software Inc	F	484 941-0820
Pottstown (G-16024)		
Orkist LLC	G	412 346-8316
Pittsburgh (G-15364)		
Osisoft LLC	F	215 606-0700
Philadelphia (G-14104)		
Pat Landgraf	G	412 221-0347
Bridgeville (G-2084)		
Paulhus and Associates Inc	F	717 274-5621
Lebanon (G-9616)		
Payserv Inc	G	610 524-3251
Media (G-10942)		
PC Network Inc	D	267 236-0015
Philadelphia (G-14128)		
Pcxpert Company Inc	G	717 792-0005
York (G-20619)		
Penn Assurance Software LLC	F	610 996-6124
Aston (G-785)		

Pensionpro Software LLC ....G...... 717 545-6060
  Harrisburg *(G-7198)*
Peoplejoy Inc ....G...... 267 603-7726
  Philadelphia *(G-14134)*
Personlytics LLC..............................G...... 484 929-0853
  West Chester *(G-19616)*
Phl Collective LLC ....G...... 610 496-7758
  Havertown *(G-7426)*
Physiic LLC ....G...... 424 653-6410
  Irwin *(G-8191)*
Picwell Inc.......................................F 215 563-0976
  Philadelphia *(G-14175)*
Pima LLC ....G...... 412 770-8130
  Glenshaw *(G-6497)*
Pita Pita LLC ....G...... 267 440-7482
  Philadelphia *(G-14179)*
Pittsburgh Digital ....G...... 412 431-6008
  Pittsburgh *(G-15393)*
Plan Management Corporation.............F 610 359-5870
  Wayne *(G-19362)*
Plumriver LLC ....F 781 577-9575
  State College *(G-18006)*
Poiesis Informatics Inc ....G...... 412 327-8766
  Pittsburgh *(G-15418)*
Policymap Inc ....G...... 866 923-6277
  Philadelphia *(G-14185)*
Popultion Hlth Innovations LLC ....G...... 717 735-8105
  Lancaster *(G-9173)*
Prairie Dog Tech LLC ....G...... 215 558-4975
  Philadelphia *(G-14195)*
Printfresh Studio LLC ....E 215 426-1661
  Philadelphia *(G-14203)*
◆ Prism Engineering LLC..................E 215 784-0800
  Horsham *(G-7842)*
Prismatic Consulting LLC ....G...... 412 915-9072
  Pittsburgh *(G-15449)*
Profit Engine LLC ....G...... 412 848-8187
  Wexford *(G-19822)*
Project One Inc ....G...... 267 901-7906
  Philadelphia *(G-14208)*
Proportal LLC ....G...... 215 923-7100
  Philadelphia *(G-14210)*
Prosoft Technologies Inc ....F 412 835-6217
  Bethel Park *(G-1429)*
Ptc Inc ....F 724 219-2600
  Greensburg *(G-6707)*
Pulsemetrics LLC ....G...... 412 656-5776
  Allison Park *(G-460)*
Purple Deck Media Inc ....G...... 717 884-9529
  Scotland *(G-17182)*
Q-Linx Inc ....G...... 610 941-2756
  Conshohocken *(G-3594)*
Quality Systems Associates ....G...... 215 345-5575
  Doylestown *(G-4331)*
Quality Systems Integrators ....G...... 610 458-0539
  Chester Springs *(G-3085)*
Quantam Software Solutions ....G...... 610 373-4770
  Reading *(G-16481)*
Qube Global Software Americas ....G...... 610 431-9080
  West Chester *(G-19624)*
Quintiq Inc ....D...... 610 964-8111
  Radnor *(G-16299)*
Quire LLC..G...... 267 935-9777
  Doylestown *(G-4332)*
R Fritz Enterprises Inc....................G...... 814 267-4204
  Berlin *(G-1292)*
Rackware Inc ....G...... 408 430-5821
  Trappe *(G-18472)*
Ragnasoft Inc ....F 866 471-2001
  Lancaster *(G-9186)*
Ram Technologies Inc ....E 215 654-8810
  Fort Washington *(G-6089)*
Rapid Learning Institute ....F 877 792-2172
  Wayne *(G-19368)*
Recovery Networks Inc ....G...... 215 809-1300
  Philadelphia *(G-14234)*
Relyence Corporation.......................F 724 433-1909
  Greensburg *(G-6711)*
Robotic Services Inc........................G...... 215 550-1823
  Philadelphia *(G-14255)*
Rocket Cloud Inc ....G...... 484 948-0327
  Bethlehem *(G-1613)*
Rough Stone Software LLC ....G...... 412 444-5295
  Pittsburgh *(G-15499)*
Rovi Corporation..............................G...... 610 293-8561
  Wayne *(G-19370)*
RTD Embedded Technologies Inc .....E 814 234-8087
  State College *(G-18017)*
Runwell Solutions Inc......................F 610 376-7773
  Reading *(G-16506)*

Safeguard Scientifics Inc ....E 610 293-0600
  Radnor *(G-16301)*
Schneider Electric It Corp ....B 717 948-1200
  Middletown *(G-11074)*
Scorecast Medical LLC ....G...... 877 475-1001
  Philadelphia *(G-14287)*
Search Live Today LLC ....G...... 610 805-7734
  Norristown *(G-12710)*
Searer Solutions Inc ....G...... 302 475-6944
  Philadelphia *(G-14292)*
Servant PC Resources Inc ....F 570 748-2800
  Lock Haven *(G-10092)*
Shift4 Payments LLC ....D...... 800 201-0461
  Allentown *(G-389)*
Sid Global Solutions LLC ....G...... 484 218-0021
  Exton *(G-5733)*
Siemens Product Life Mgmt Sftw.......G...... 717 299-1846
  Lancaster *(G-9196)*
Siemens Product Life Mgmt Sftw.......E 814 237-4999
  State College *(G-18022)*
Siemens Product Life Mgmt Sftw.......G...... 814 861-1651
  State College *(G-18023)*
Simplr Technologies LLC ....G...... 814 883-6463
  State College *(G-18025)*
Sinclair Technologies LLC ....G...... 610 296-8259
  Media *(G-10950)*
SIS Software LLC.............................G...... 888 844-6599
  Pittsburgh *(G-15544)*
Skaffl LLC ....G...... 484 809-9351
  Allentown *(G-394)*
Skyroc LLC ....G...... 215 840-5466
  Philadelphia *(G-14315)*
Smartops Corporation......................E 412 231-0115
  Pittsburgh *(G-15548)*
Smith Micro Software Inc ....C...... 412 837-5300
  Pittsburgh *(G-15550)*
Society of Clinical ....F 215 822-8644
  Chalfont *(G-2889)*
Softboss Corp ....G...... 215 563-7488
  Philadelphia *(G-14321)*
Softstuf Inc ....G...... 215 627-8850
  Philadelphia *(G-14322)*
Software Consulting Svcs LLC............E 610 746-7700
  Nazareth *(G-11988)*
Software Engineering Assoc ....F 570 803-0535
  Archbald *(G-695)*
Solution Systems Inc.......................F 610 668-4620
  Narberth *(G-11912)*
Southside Holdings LLC ....E 412 431-8300
  Pittsburgh *(G-15564)*
Spectrum Software Innovations ....G...... 610 779-6974
  Reading *(G-16522)*
Spm Global Services Inc ....D...... 610 340-2828
  Chester *(G-3065)*
Stone Edge Technologies Inc ....G...... 484 927-4804
  Phoenixville *(G-14580)*
Sungard AR Financing LLC ....G...... 484 582-2000
  Wayne *(G-19374)*
Sungard Asset MGT Systems Inc.........C...... 610 251-6500
  Collegeville *(G-3396)*
Sungard Capital Corp II ....F 484 582-2000
  Wayne *(G-19375)*
Sungard Holdco LLC ....A...... 484 582-2000
  Wayne *(G-19376)*
Sungard Holding Corp ....G...... 888 332-2564
  Wayne *(G-19377)*
Sustrana LLC ....G...... 610 651-2870
  Devon *(G-4116)*
Sweet Roll Studio Llc ....G...... 209 559-8219
  Philadelphia *(G-14363)*
Sy-Con Systems Inc ....G...... 610 253-0900
  Easton *(G-4760)*
Tactile Design Group LLC ....F 215 732-2311
  Philadelphia *(G-14367)*
Tal Technologies Inc ....E 215 496-0222
  Philadelphia *(G-14369)*
Tata America Intl Corp......................D...... 717 737-4737
  Camp Hill *(G-2520)*
Team Approach Inc ....G...... 847 259-0005
  Lancaster *(G-9213)*
Technology Dynamics Inc ....G...... 888 988-3243
  Wayne *(G-19380)*
Telefactor Robotics LLC...................G...... 610 940-6040
  Conshohocken *(G-3611)*
Tenex Systems Inc ....F 610 239-9988
  King of Prussia *(G-8685)*
Thebathoutlet LLC ....F 877 256-1645
  Lansdale *(G-9414)*
Thoroughcare Inc.............................G...... 412 737-7332
  Pittsburgh *(G-15616)*

Titan Technologies Inc ....G...... 888 671-6649
  Pittsburgh *(G-15626)*
Touchtown Inc ....E 412 826-0460
  Oakmont *(G-12929)*
Town Square Software LLC ....G...... 610 374-7900
  Reading *(G-16545)*
Traction Software Inc ....G...... 401 528-1145
  Harrisburg *(G-7233)*
Transporeon Group Americas Inc ....E 267 281-1555
  Fort Washington *(G-6094)*
Tunefly LLC ....G...... 570 392-9239
  Nanticoke *(G-11904)*
Turbo Software LLC..........................G...... 215 490-6806
  Philadelphia *(G-14414)*
Turnitin LLC ....G...... 724 272-7250
  Pittsburgh *(G-15662)*
Tutorgen Inc ....G...... 704 710-8445
  Mars *(G-10511)*
Twenty61 LLC ....G...... 215 370-7076
  Philadelphia *(G-14415)*
U Squared Interactive LLC ....G...... 214 770-7437
  Pittsburgh *(G-15665)*
Uber Atc ....G...... 412 587-2986
  Pittsburgh *(G-15666)*
Undernet Gaming Incorporated...........G...... 484 544-8943
  Harrisburg *(G-7240)*
Unlocked Entertainment Tech ....G...... 267 507-6028
  Philadelphia *(G-14430)*
Ursoft Inc ....F 724 452-2150
  Zelienople *(G-20827)*
Validity LLC ....G...... 610 768-8042
  Malvern *(G-10337)*
Vanadium Enterprises Corp ....E 412 206-2990
  Bridgeville *(G-2098)*
Vantage Learning Usa LLC ....D...... 800 230-2213
  New Hope *(G-12318)*
Vantage Learning Usa LLC ....E 800 230-2213
  Langhorne *(G-9330)*
Vantage Online Store LLC ....C...... 267 756-1155
  New Hope *(G-12319)*
Veeva Systems Inc ....G...... 215 422-3356
  Fort Washington *(G-6095)*
Vega Applications Development ....G...... 610 892-1812
  Media *(G-10956)*
Venus Video ....G...... 215 937-1545
  Philadelphia *(G-14440)*
Versatile Credit Inc..........................E 800 851-1281
  Mechanicsburg *(G-10904)*
Vetstreet Incorporated ....E 267 685-2400
  Feasterville Trevose *(G-5937)*
Via Design & Technologies ....G...... 215 579-5730
  Newtown *(G-12560)*
Viper Network Systems LLC ....G...... 855 758-4737
  West View *(G-19774)*
Virtix Consulting LLC ....G...... 412 440-4835
  Wexford *(G-19832)*
Vitaltrax LLC ....G...... 610 864-0211
  Philadelphia *(G-14453)*
Vocollect Inc ....C...... 412 829-8145
  Pittsburgh *(G-15702)*
Voicestars Inc ....G...... 305 902-9666
  Emmaus *(G-5046)*
Volian Enterprises Inc ....F 724 335-3744
  New Kensington *(G-12388)*
Watchword Worldwide.......................G...... 814 366-2770
  Ambridge *(G-638)*
Web Age Solutions Inc ....E 215 517-6540
  Jenkintown *(G-8304)*
Weidenhammer Systems Corp ....E 610 317-4000
  Allentown *(G-430)*
Weidenhammer Systems Corp ....D...... 610 378-1149
  Reading *(G-16562)*
Weidenhammer Systems Corp ....E 610 378-1149
  Lancaster *(G-9237)*
Weidenhammer Systems Corp ....E 610 687-0037
  Blue Bell *(G-1857)*
Winfosoft Inc ....E 717 226-1299
  York *(G-20711)*
▲ Wolters Kluwer Health Inc.............C...... 215 521-8300
  Philadelphia *(G-14482)*
Wombat Security Tech Inc ....E 412 621-1484
  Pittsburgh *(G-15723)*
Worktask Media Inc ....G...... 610 762-9014
  Bath *(G-973)*
Workzone LLC ....F 610 275-9861
  Norristown *(G-12725)*
Wov Inc ....D...... 412 261-3791
  Pittsburgh *(G-15724)*

76 MISCELLANEOUS REPAIR SERVICES

7692 Welding Repair

A A A Welding Service Inc ....E 215 426-2240
Philadelphia *(G-13323)*

A D M Welding & Fabrication ....G 814 723-7227
Warren *(G-19007)*

Aaron Wenger ....G 717 656-9876
New Holland *(G-12225)*

Abbottstown Industries Inc ....E 717 259-8715
Abbottstown *(G-3)*

▲ Accu Machining Center Inc ....E 610 252-6855
Easton *(G-4644)*

Affil Distributors ....G 610 977-3100
Wayne *(G-19295)*

Agri Welding Service Inc ....F 570 437-3330
Danville *(G-3996)*

Altrax ....G 814 379-3706
Summerville *(G-18156)*

American Machine Co ....G 717 533-5678
Palmyra *(G-13115)*

Anderson Welding & Sons LLC ....G 215 886-1726
Oreland *(G-13017)*

Andrew E Reken ....G 724 783-7878
Dayton *(G-4034)*

Artman Equipment Company Inc ....F 724 337-3700
Apollo *(G-662)*

▲ Auman Machine Company Inc ....E 717 273-4604
Lebanon *(G-9546)*

Auto Weld Chassis & Components ....G 570 275-1411
Danville *(G-3997)*

B & W Metal Works Inc ....G 717 848-1077
York *(G-20396)*

Bailey Machine Company ....E 724 628-4730
Connellsville *(G-3490)*

Barretts Custom Wrought Iron ....G 814 676-4575
Oil City *(G-12941)*

Bell-Mark Sales Co Inc ....E 717 292-5641
Dover *(G-4186)*

Bissinger and Stein Inc ....E 215 256-1122
Kulpsville *(G-8824)*

Blank River Services Inc ....E 412 384-2489
Elizabeth *(G-4857)*

Brighton Machine Company Inc ....F 724 378-0960
Aliquippa *(G-70)*

Brodys Welding and Mech Contrs ....G 215 941-7914
Philadelphia *(G-13486)*

Browns Welding Inc ....G 717 762-6467
Waynesboro *(G-19403)*

Budget Portable Welding Mch ....E 717 865-0473
Lebanon *(G-9549)*

Burnells Welding Corporation ....G 215 757-2896
Bristol *(G-2122)*

Butler Machine Inc ....G 814 355-5605
Bellefonte *(G-1095)*

C & C Welding and Fabg Inc ....G 814 387-6556
Clarence *(G-3161)*

C & T Machining Inc ....E 717 328-9572
Mercersburg *(G-10982)*

C A Spalding Company ....E 267 550-9000
Bensalem *(G-1163)*

C/C Welding/Fabrict Inc ....G 814 364-9460
Clarence *(G-3162)*

Caldwell Corporation ....E 814 486-3493
Emporium *(G-5051)*

Cambria Welding & Fabg Inc ....G 814 948-5072
Saint Benedict *(G-16936)*

Cannon Tool Company ....F 724 745-1070
Canonsburg *(G-2556)*

Claylick Enterprises LLC ....F 717 328-9876
Mercersburg *(G-10983)*

Comfab Inc ....G 724 339-1750
New Kensington *(G-12335)*

Compass Welding LLC ....G 570 928-7472
Dushore *(G-4508)*

Condos Incorporated ....E 570 748-9265
Mill Hall *(G-11174)*

Conshohocken Steel Pdts Inc ....E 215 283-9222
Ambler *(G-574)*

Construction On Site Welding ....G 610 367-1895
Boyertown *(G-1904)*

Corry Laser Technology Inc ....F 814 664-7212
Corry *(G-3751)*

Creative Design & Machining ....G 570 587-3077
S Abingtn Twp *(G-16894)*

Cumberland Valley Wldg & Repr ....G 717 249-1129
Carlisle *(G-2704)*

Custom Iron Works Welding ....F 814 444-1315
Somerset *(G-17682)*

D & M Welding Co Inc ....E 717 767-9353
York *(G-20440)*

D & S Fabricating & Welding ....G 412 653-9185
Clairton *(G-3148)*

D R Gaumer Metal Fabricating ....G 610 395-5101
Wescosville *(G-19488)*

Dallas Machine Inc ....E 610 799-2800
Schnecksville *(G-17138)*

Daves Welding Shop ....E 814 796-6520
Waterford *(G-19261)*

DC Welding ....G 717 361-9400
Elizabethtown *(G-4871)*

Decherts Machine Shop Inc ....E 717 838-1326
Palmyra *(G-13121)*

Dennys Welding ....G 570 265-8015
Towanda *(G-18423)*

Dewitt Fab Welding Co ....G 215 538-9477
Quakertown *(G-16185)*

DHL Machine Co Inc ....E 215 536-3591
Quakertown *(G-16186)*

Diversified Mech Svcs Inc ....G 215 368-3084
Lansdale *(G-9362)*

Donald Campbell ....G 412 793-6068
Pittsburgh *(G-14930)*

Doug Herhold ....G 814 756-5141
Albion *(G-43)*

Dressel Welding Supply Inc ....G 570 505-1994
Cogan Station *(G-3360)*

Dunbar Machine Co Inc ....G 724 277-8711
Dunbar *(G-4439)*

Dyeco Inc ....G 717 545-1882
Harrisburg *(G-7123)*

E K L Machine Inc ....G 215 639-0150
Bensalem *(G-1184)*

E M United Wldg & Fabrication ....G 570 595-0695
Cresco *(G-3893)*

East End Welding ....G 570 726-7925
Mill Hall *(G-11176)*

East Penn Welding Inc ....G 610 682-2290
Kutztown *(G-8841)*

Edgewood Welding & Fabrication ....F 814 445-7746
Somerset *(G-17687)*

Edinboro Industries ....G 814 734-1100
Edinboro *(G-4811)*

Edward H Quay Welding Spc ....G 610 326-8050
Pottstown *(G-15985)*

Elliott Machine Company ....G 610 485-5345
Upper Chichester *(G-18659)*

Enrico J Fiore ....G 570 489-8430
Throop *(G-18358)*

F F Frickanisce Iron Works ....G 724 568-2001
Vandergrift *(G-18726)*

F W B & Sons Welding Inc ....G 610 543-0348
Springfield *(G-17913)*

Fab Tech Industries ....G 717 597-4919
Greencastle *(G-6610)*

Fab Tech V Industries Inc ....E 717 597-4919
Greencastle *(G-6611)*

Fabri-Weld LLC ....G 814 490-7324
Erie *(G-5287)*

Facchiano Ironworks Inc ....G 610 865-1503
Bethlehem *(G-1506)*

Faull Fabricating Inc ....G 724 458-7662
Grove City *(G-6784)*

Fenton Welding LLC ....E 570 746-9018
Wyalusing *(G-20252)*

Ferguson Welding Inc ....F 717 292-4179
Dover *(G-4192)*

Flinchbaugh Company Inc ....E 717 266-2202
Manchester *(G-10356)*

Flint Road Welding ....G 717 535-5282
Mifflintown *(G-11118)*

Flurer Machine and Tool ....G 610 759-6114
Bethlehem *(G-1514)*

Fountain Fabricating Co ....G 570 682-9018
Hegins *(G-7541)*

Fox Welding Shop Inc ....G 215 225-3069
Philadelphia *(G-13716)*

Frank Bellace Welding ....G 856 488-8099
Danville *(G-4002)*

Frazier-Simplex Machine Co ....G 724 222-5700
Washington *(G-19177)*

Freedom Welding ....G 717 437-0943
Burnham *(G-2360)*

Friesens Welding ....G 570 523-3580
Lewisburg *(G-9910)*

G-S Hydraulics Inc ....F 814 938-2862
Punxsutawney *(G-16141)*

General Welding & Machine Co ....G 570 889-3776
Ringtown *(G-16753)*

General Weldments Inc ....F 724 744-2105
Irwin *(G-8164)*

George I Reitz & Sons Inc ....E 814 849-2308
Brookville *(G-2261)*

George I Reitz & Sons Inc ....G 412 824-9976
East Pittsburgh *(G-4595)*

Germantown Welding Co ....G 215 843-2643
Philadelphia *(G-13758)*

Gouldey Welding & Fabrications ....E 215 721-9522
Souderton *(G-17737)*

Grahams Welding ....G 724 627-6082
Waynesburg *(G-19442)*

Gregory Racing Fabrications ....G 610 759-8217
Nazareth *(G-11970)*

Grimm Machine & Model ....G 724 228-2133
Washington *(G-19182)*

Gross Bros Wldg Fbrication Inc ....G 814 443-1130
Somerset *(G-17691)*

H & H Manufacturing Co Inc ....D 610 532-1250
Folcroft *(G-6004)*

H and H Tool ....G 814 333-4677
Meadville *(G-10732)*

▲ Hamill Manufacturing Company ....D 724 744-2131
Trafford *(G-18457)*

Haverstick Bros Inc ....F 717 392-5722
Lancaster *(G-9040)*

Hawk Industrial Services LLC ....F 717 658-4332
Chambersburg *(G-2939)*

Hazleton Custom Metal Products ....F 570 455-0450
Hazleton *(G-7501)*

Healey Welding Co Inc ....G 570 655-9437
Pittston *(G-15755)*

Hendricks Welding Service Inc ....E 215 757-5369
Langhorne *(G-9301)*

Henrys Welding Inc ....G 717 548-2460
Drumore *(G-4378)*

▲ Herkules USA Corporation ....C 724 763-2066
Ford City *(G-6047)*

Hetrick Mfg Inc ....F 724 335-0455
Lower Burrell *(G-10106)*

Hill John M Machine Co Inc ....G 610 562-8690
Hamburg *(G-6841)*

Hills Machine Shop ....G 570 645-8787
Lansford *(G-9447)*

Hills Micro Weld Inc ....G 814 336-4511
Meadville *(G-10735)*

Hillside Custom Mac Wel & Fab ....F 610 942-3093
Honey Brook *(G-7748)*

Hines Industries Inc ....G 610 264-1656
Whitehall *(G-19875)*

▲ Hy-Tech Machine Inc ....D 724 776-6800
Cranberry Township *(G-3823)*

Innovative Machining Tech Inc ....E 610 473-5600
Boyertown *(G-1918)*

Integrated Power Services LLC ....F 724 225-2900
Washington *(G-19186)*

Ira G Steffy and Son Inc ....D 717 626-6500
Ephrata *(G-5111)*

J & S Machining Corp ....F 717 653-6358
Manheim *(G-10391)*

J and B Precision Machine Co ....G 215 822-1400
Hatfield *(G-7355)*

J C Moore Sales Corp ....G 724 475-4605
Fredonia *(G-6183)*

J M T Machine Company ....E 215 934-7600
Huntingdon Valley *(G-7998)*

J R Young ....G 717 935-2919
Belleville *(G-1132)*

J Russel Tooling Co ....G 724 423-2766
Calumet *(G-2472)*

Jack Garner & Sons Inc ....G 717 367-8866
Mount Joy *(G-11663)*

James A Schultz ....F 814 763-5561
Saegertown *(G-16919)*

Jeffery Faust ....G 610 759-1951
Nazareth *(G-11973)*

Jfs Welding ....G 717 687-6554
Paradise *(G-13160)*

Jobco Mfg & Stl Fabrication ....G 724 266-3210
Ambridge *(G-622)*

Joel Freidhoff ....G 814 536-6458
Johnstown *(G-8387)*

Joes Welding Repairs ....G 570 546-5223
Muncy *(G-11822)*

John H Bricker Welding ....F 717 263-5588
Chambersburg *(G-2946)*

John Jost Jr Inc ....G 610 395-5461
Allentown *(G-269)*

Johns Welding Shop ....G..... 814 643-4564	Napotnik Welding Inc ....G..... 814 446-4500	▲ Schnure Manufacturing Co Inc ....F 610 273-3352
Huntingdon (G-7948)	New Florence (G-12199)	Honey Brook (G-7762)
Johnsons Frog & Rail Wldg Inc ....G..... 724 475-2305	Nelson Stud Welding Inc ....G..... 610 873-0012	Scranton Sheet Metal Inc ....E 570 342-2904
Greenville (G-6752)	Downingtown (G-4244)	Scranton (G-17288)
▲ Johnstown Wldg Fabrication Inc ....C..... 800 225-9353	Nestors Welding Co ....G..... 570 668-3401	Servedio A Elc Mtr Svc Inc ....F 724 658-8041
Johnstown (G-8394)	Tamaqua (G-18221)	New Castle (G-12148)
Keystone Foundation Service ....G..... 215 968-2955	Niagara Manufacturing Co ....F..... 814 838-4511	Sha Co Welding & Fabrication ....G..... 724 588-0993
Newtown (G-12514)	Erie (G-5403)	Greenville (G-6773)
Kiski Precision Industries LLC ....E..... 724 845-2799	Nichols Welding Service Inc ....G..... 412 362-8855	Shearers Welding Inc ....G..... 717 361-9196
Leechburg (G-9646)	Pittsburgh (G-15338)	Elizabethtown (G-4887)
Kittatinny Manufacturing Svcs ....F..... 717 530-1242	Norman Hoover Welding LLC ....G..... 717 445-5333	Skias Chuck Wldg & Fabricators ....G..... 610 375-0912
Shippensburg (G-17536)	Ephrata (G-5134)	Reading (G-16519)
Kottcamp Sheet Metal ....E..... 717 845-7616	Novinger Welding Repair Inc ....G..... 570 758-6592	Sky Oxygen Inc ....E..... 412 278-3001
York (G-20558)	Herndon (G-7602)	Carnegie (G-2793)
Kovacs Manufacturing Inc ....F..... 215 355-1985	Nuweld Inc ....C..... 570 505-1500	Smoker Manufacturing ....G..... 717 529-6915
Southampton (G-17821)	Williamsport (G-20051)	Oxford (G-13092)
Kutzner Manufacturing Inds Inc ....E..... 215 721-1712	P & R United Welding and Fabg ....F..... 610 375-9928	Snyder Welding LLC ....G..... 610 657-4916
Telford (G-18300)	Reading (G-16461)	Slatington (G-17614)
L Richard Sensenig Co ....D..... 717 733-0364	P K B Inc ....G..... 215 826-1988	Soul Customs Metal Works ....G..... 610 881-4300
Ephrata (G-5117)	Bristol (G-2178)	Pen Argyl (G-13218)
▲ Leiss Tool & Die ....C..... 814 444-1444	▼ Pannell Mfg Corp ....G..... 610 268-2012	Specialized Welding Inc ....G..... 724 733-7801
Somerset (G-17695)	Avondale (G-856)	Export (G-5627)
Leonhardt Manufacturing Co Inc ....D..... 717 632-4150	Paragon Welding Company Inc ....G..... 215 634-7300	Speranza Specialty Machining ....G..... 724 733-8045
Hanover (G-6915)	Philadelphia (G-14121)	Export (G-5628)
Lesko Enterprises Inc ....C..... 814 756-4030	Pelets Welding Inc ....E..... 610 384-5048	Spicer Wldg & Fabrication Inc ....G..... 814 355-7046
Albion (G-46)	Coatesville (G-3323)	Bellefonte (G-1119)
Lewis Welding Services Inc ....G..... 814 838-1074	Penn Fabrication LLC ....F..... 610 292-1980	Spicer Wldg & Fabrication Inc ....G..... 814 355-7046
Erie (G-5363)	Norristown (G-12702)	Julian (G-8456)
Liberty Welding Co ....G..... 412 661-1776	Penn Weld Inc ....G..... 814 332-3682	State of ARC Wldg & Fabg LLC ....G..... 610 216-6862
Pittsburgh (G-15228)	Meadville (G-10775)	Bangor (G-930)
Lights Welding Inc ....F..... 717 838-3931	Phil Skrzat ....G..... 215 257-8583	Stengels Welding Shop Inc ....G..... 610 444-4110
Annville (G-653)	Perkasie (G-13289)	Kennett Square (G-8544)
Logue Industries Inc ....E..... 570 368-2639	Philadelphia Pipe Bending Co ....E..... 215 225-8955	Stephen R Lechman ....G..... 570 636-3159
Montoursville (G-11445)	Philadelphia (G-14149)	Freeland (G-6196)
Longwood Manufacturing Corp ....F..... 610 444-4200	Pocono Protech ....G..... 610 681-3550	Stoltzfus Custom Welding ....G..... 717 477-8200
Kennett Square (G-8523)	Gilbert (G-6363)	Orrstown (G-13035)
M and P Custom Design Inc ....F..... 610 444-0244	Precision Metal Crafters Ltd ....E..... 724 837-2511	Subcon Tl/Cctool Mch Group Inc ....E 814 456-7797
Kennett Square (G-8524)	Greensburg (G-6704)	Erie (G-5494)
M&B Enterprises Inc ....G..... 814 454-4461	Production Plus Steel Inc ....G..... 724 376-3634	Sullis Wldg & Pipe Fitting LLC ....G..... 814 445-9147
Erie (G-5377)	Sandy Lake (G-17061)	Somerset (G-17713)
Machine Specialties ....G..... 717 264-0061	Prompton Tool Inc ....D..... 570 253-4141	Sunnyburn Welding ....G..... 717 862-3878
Chambersburg (G-2955)	Honesdale (G-7720)	Airville (G-32)
Machining Center ....G..... 724 530-7212	Quality Metal Works Inc ....F..... 717 367-2120	Superior Welding Co ....G..... 570 344-4212
Slippery Rock (G-17621)	Elizabethtown (G-4882)	Scranton (G-17296)
Mariano Welding Corp ....G..... 610 626-0975	R G S Machine Inc ....G..... 610 532-1850	Swartfager Welding Inc ....D..... 814 797-0394
Clifton Heights (G-3255)	Folsom (G-6027)	Knox (G-8811)
Mark Tk Welding Inc ....F..... 724 545-2001	R H Benedix Contracting ....G..... 610 889-7472	T & L Welding ....F..... 724 354-3538
Kittanning (G-8779)	Malvern (G-10306)	Kittanning (G-8799)
Martindale Welding LLC ....G..... 717 445-4666	R S Myers Welding ....G..... 717 532-4714	T & T Machine & Welding Co ....G..... 814 845-9054
Ephrata (G-5124)	Shippensburg (G-17543)	Glen Campbell (G-6425)
Martins Steel LLC ....G..... 570 966-3775	Randy Brensinger ....G..... 610 562-2184	Temperature Ctrl Professionals ....G..... 215 295-1616
Mifflinburg (G-11097)	Hamburg (G-6851)	Fairless Hills (G-5803)
Martys Muffler & Weld Shop ....G..... 412 673-4141	Raphael A Ingaglio ....G..... 570 289-5000	Terry L Handwerk ....G..... 610 262-0986
North Versailles (G-12781)	Hop Bottom (G-7775)	Northampton (G-12862)
▲ Maxwell Welding and Mch Inc ....E 724 729-3160	Raser Industries Inc ....F..... 610 320-5130	Three Rivers Gamma Service ....G..... 724 947-9020
Burgettstown (G-2349)	Reading (G-16484)	Burgettstown (G-2357)
McKinley Blacksmith Limited ....G..... 610 459-2730	Reading Equipment & Dist LLC ....E..... 717 445-6746	Titan Metal & Machine Co Inc ....G..... 724 747-9528
Boothwyn (G-1879)	Abington (G-14)	Washington (G-19232)
McShane Welding Company Inc ....E..... 814 459-3797	Red Bank Welding ....G..... 570 966-0695	Tooling Specialists Inc ....D..... 724 539-2534
Erie (G-5387)	Mifflinburg (G-11101)	Latrobe (G-9524)
Meadowcreek Welding LLC ....G..... 717 354-7533	Revtur Welding Company LLC ....G..... 215 672-8233	Tri-State Welding Corp ....G..... 610 374-0321
New Holland (G-12261)	Warminster (G-18955)	Reading (G-16549)
Mill Professional Services ....F..... 724 335-4625	Riley Welding and Fabg Inc ....F..... 717 637-6014	Trico Welding Company ....F..... 724 722-1300
New Kensington (G-12357)	Hanover (G-6944)	Yukon (G-20785)
▲ Miller Welding and Machine Co ......C 814 849-3061	Rizzo & Sons Industrial Svc Co ....E..... 814 948-5381	Trs Welding & Fabrication Inc ....F..... 610 369-0897
Brookville (G-2265)	Pittsburgh (G-15489)	Gilbertsville (G-6378)
Miller Welding Service ....G..... 814 238-2950	Robbie Holland ....G..... 610 495-5441	True Position Inc ....F..... 724 444-0300
State College (G-17991)	Royersford (G-16862)	Gibsonia (G-6357)
Millers Welding & Repair ....G..... 610 593-6112	Robert Urda Jr ....G..... 724 775-9333	Unity Fabrication Tech Inc ....F..... 724 423-7500
Christiana (G-3142)	Monaca (G-11295)	Greensburg (G-6726)
Mobile Welding & Boiler Repair ....F 610 253-9688	Rochester Machine Corporation ....E..... 724 843-7820	Universal Mch Co Pottstown Inc ....D 610 323-1810
Easton (G-4725)	New Brighton (G-12040)	Pottstown (G-16062)
Mohney Fabricating & Mfg LLC ....G..... 724 349-6136	Rod Quellette ....G..... 814 274-8812	Vegely Welding Inc ....F..... 412 469-9808
Penn Run (G-13229)	Coudersport (G-3788)	Duquesne (G-4501)
Moore Welding ....G..... 814 328-2399	Ronald E Koller Welding ....G..... 412 859-6781	Versatech Incorporated ....D..... 724 327-8324
Brockway (G-2228)	Coraopolis (G-3724)	Export (G-5631)
Moreno Welding Service ....G..... 717 646-0000	Rose Corporation ....D..... 610 376-5004	Vr Enterprises Llc ....G..... 215 932-1113
Hanover (G-6923)	Reading (G-16504)	Lansdale (G-9426)
Moritz Machine & Repairs LLC ....G..... 717 677-6838	Royal Hydraulic Svc & Mfg Inc ....E..... 724 945-6800	W & W Welding Inc ....G..... 717 336-4314
Biglerville (G-1667)	Cokeburg (G-3364)	Reinholds (G-16637)
Mountain Top Welding & Repair ....G..... 570 888-7174	Ryders Welding LLC ....G..... 717 369-5198	W C H Inc ....G..... 814 725-8431
Gillett (G-6382)	Chambersburg (G-2974)	North East (G-12765)
Mountaintop Welding ....G..... 814 387-9353	S & D Welding Inc ....G..... 570 546-8772	W V Fabricating & Welding Inc ....G..... 724 266-3000
Clarence (G-3164)	Muncy (G-11832)	Ambridge (G-637)
Murslack Welding Inc ....G..... 412 364-5554	Sac Industries Inc ....F..... 412 787-7500	Wakefield Steel & Welding LLC ....E..... 717 548-2172
Pittsburgh (G-15312)	Pittsburgh (G-15505)	Peach Bottom (G-13204)
Mwi Service ....G..... 717 578-2324	Saeger Machine Inc ....F..... 215 256-8754	Walsh Tool Company Inc ....G..... 570 823-1375
Spring Grove (G-17879)	Harleysville (G-7056)	Wilkes Barre (G-19969)
Myers Wldg & Fabrication Inc ....G..... 717 502-7473	Sanfelice Wldg Fabrication LLC ....G..... 610 337-4125	Walter McClelland Jr LLC ....G..... 814 378-7434
Dillsburg (G-4139)	Norristown (G-12709)	Madera (G-10164)

Waste Gas Fabricating Co Inc ....E 215 736-9240
Fairless Hills (G-5807)

Watts Welding Shop LLC ....G 570 398-1184
Jersey Shore (G-8324)

Wegco Welding Inc ....G 412 833-7020
Bethel Park (G-1438)

Wel-Mac Inc ....G 717 637-6921
Hanover (G-6974)

Weld Tek Ltd ....G 717 367-0666
Elizabethtown (G-4890)

Welding & Thermal Technologies ....G 610 678-4847
Reading (G-16563)

Welding Alloys USA ....G 724 202-7497
New Castle (G-1167)

Werner Welding LLC ....G 724 379-4240
Elizabeth (G-4864)

Westmrland Stl Fabrication Inc ....E 724 446-0555
Madison (G-10167)

Wolbert Welding Inc ....G 814 437-2870
Franklin (G-6170)

▼ X-Mark/Cdt Inc ....G 724 228-7373
Washington (G-19248)

Y B Welding Inc ....G 717 267-0104
Chambersburg (G-3001)

Yarmouth Construction ....G 267 592-1432
Philadelphia (G-14498)

Youngs Truck Repair LLC ....F 570 329-3571
South Williamsport (G-17794)

Z Weldco ....G 610 689-8773
Oley (G-12982)

Zambotti Collision & Wldg Ctr ....G 724 545-2305
Kittanning (G-8804)

Zimm-O-Matic LLC ....G 717 445-6432
Denver (G-4098)

7694 Armature Rewinding Shops

A J Smith Electric Motor Svc ....G 570 424-8743
East Stroudsburg (G-4601)

Ace Viking Electric Mtr Co Inc ....G 814 897-9445
Erie (G-5171)

Action Cycle & Atv LLC ....G 814 765-2578
West Decatur (G-19687)

Albarell Electric Inc ....G 610 691-7030
Bethlehem (G-1447)

Allegheny Mfg & Elec Svc Inc ....E 814 288-1597
Johnstown (G-8350)

Ampere Electric Co ....G 215 426-5356
Broomall (G-2278)

Associated Machine Service ....G 215 335-1940
Bensalem (G-1149)

Breons Inc A Close Corporation ....G 814 359-3182
Pleasant Gap (G-15791)

Burkholder s Motor Repair ....G 717 866-9724
Myerstown (G-11878)

C & S Repair Center Inc ....G 610 524-9724
Downingtown (G-4217)

Charles W Romano Co ....G 215 535-3800
Philadelphia (G-13532)

Coleman & Schmidt Inc ....G 610 275-0796
Norristown (G-12645)

Curio Electrical Motor Repr Sp ....G 610 432-9923
Allentown (G-189)

D-Electric Inc ....F 215 529-6020
Quakertown (G-16182)

Daniels Electric Service ....G 412 821-2594
Pittsburgh (G-14905)

Deckman Electric Inc ....G 610 272-6944
Bridgeport (G-2034)

Delaware Electric Inc ....G 610 252-7803
Easton (G-4668)

Dorwards Electric Corp ....G 610 767-8148
Slatington (G-17605)

Edwin L Heim Co ....E 717 233-8711
Harrisburg (G-7125)

Electric Motor & Supply Inc ....E 814 946-0401
Altoona (G-501)

Electric Motor Service Inc ....G 724 348-6858
Finleyville (G-5958)

Electric Rewind Co Inc ....G 215 675-6912
Hatboro (G-7284)

G I Electric Company ....G 570 323-6147
Williamsport (G-20015)

General Electric Company ....D 412 469-6080
West Mifflin (G-19739)

General Electric Company ....D 215 289-0400
Philadelphia (G-13749)

Gerald Boughner ....G 814 432-3519
Franklin (G-6132)

▲ Globe Electric Company Inc ....E 412 781-2671
Pittsburgh (G-15053)

H & Z Auto LLC ....G 610 419-8012
Bethlehem (G-1527)

Habsco Inc ....G 724 337-9498
New Kensington (G-12345)

Hodge Electric Motors Inc ....G 724 834-8420
Greensburg (G-6674)

Huntingdon Elc Mtr Svc Inc ....E 814 643-3921
Huntingdon (G-7944)

Industrial Pump & Mtr Repr Inc ....F 412 369-5060
Glenshaw (G-6490)

Integrated Power Services LLC ....E 724 479-9066
Indiana (G-8108)

Integrated Power Services LLC ....E 215 365-1500
Philadelphia (G-13861)

Irvin G Tyson & Son Inc ....G 610 754-0930
Perkiomenville (G-13302)

Jeffrey Shepler ....G 724 537-7411
Latrobe (G-9484)

Johnstone Supply ....G 610 967-9900
Alburtis (G-53)

Keener Electric Motors Inc ....G 717 272-7686
Lebanon (G-9589)

Kufen Electric Motors Inc ....G 215 672-5250
Warminster (G-18907)

Kufen Motor and Pump Tech ....G 215 672-5250
Warminster (G-18908)

Leboeuf Industries Inc ....F 814 796-9000
Waterford (G-19265)

Ligus Electric Mtr & Pump Svc ....G 570 287-1272
Luzerne (G-10126)

▲ Lyons Electric Motor Service ....G 814 456-7127
Erie (G-5376)

M & R Electric Inc ....E 412 831-6101
Bethel Park (G-1423)

Mikron Valve & Mfr Inc ....G 814 453-2337
Erie (G-5392)

Miller Electric Service & Sup ....F 814 942-9943
Altoona (G-527)

Motor Technology Inc ....D 717 266-4045
York (G-20605)

Myers Electrical Repairs ....G 717 334-8105
Gettysburg (G-6309)

Nearhoof Machine Inc ....G 814 339-6621
Osceola Mills (G-13056)

▲ North End Electric Service Inc ....E 570 342-6740
Scranton (G-17267)

Pittsburgh Elc Mtr Repr Inc ....G 724 443-2333
Allison Park (G-458)

R Scheinert & Son Inc ....E 215 673-9800
Philadelphia (G-14227)

Ram Industrial Services LLC ....E 717 232-4414
Camp Hill (G-2514)

Rice Electric Company ....E 724 225-4180
Eighty Four (G-4846)

Royal Hydraulic Svc & Mfg Inc ....E 724 945-6800
Cokeburg (G-3364)

S & S Electric Motors Inc ....G 717 263-1919
Chambersburg (G-2975)

Servedio A Elc Mtr Svc Inc ....F 724 658-8041
New Castle (G-12148)

Special Electric Motor Company ....G 724 378-4200
Aliquippa (G-97)

Tims Electric Motor Repair Co ....G 814 445-5078
Somerset (G-17714)

◆ Topos Mondial Corp ....E 610 970-2270
Pottstown (G-16055)

United Industrial Group Inc ....F 724 746-4700
Washington (G-19234)

Warren Electric Motor Service ....G 814 723-2045
Warren (G-19057)

Weber Electmotor Service ....G 717 436-8120
Mifflintown (G-11143)

West End Electric Inc ....F 570 682-9292
Hegins (G-7547)

Willier Elc Mtr Repr Co Inc ....G 215 426-9920
Philadelphia (G-14477)

Witmer Motor Service ....G 717 336-2949
Stevens (G-18058)

S I C

ALPHABETIC SECTION

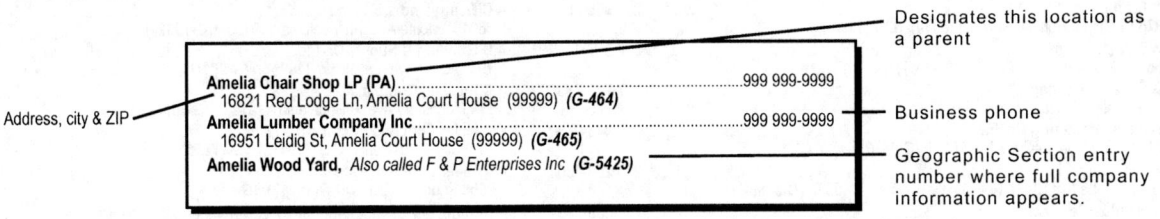

Designates this location as a parent

Amelia Chair Shop LP (PA)............999 999-9999
16821 Red Lodge Ln, Amelia Court House (99999) *(G-464)*

Business phone

Amelia Lumber Company Inc............999 999-9999
16951 Leidig St, Amelia Court House (99999) *(G-465)*

Geographic Section entry number where full company information appears.

Amelia Wood Yard, *Also called F & P Enterprises Inc (G-5425)*

Address, city & ZIP

See footnotes for symbols and codes identification.

* Companies listed alphabetically.

* Complete physical or mailing address.

---

100 Thompson Street LLC............866 654-2676
100 Thompson St Pittston (18640) *(G-15740)*

101 Cameo Appearances LLC............412 787-7981
770 Vista Park Dr Pittsburgh (15205) *(G-14623)*

101 Mobility of Pittsburgh, Pittsburgh *Also called 101 Cameo Appearances LLC (G-14623)*

13 Big Bears Inc............610 437-6123
5925 Tilghman St Ste 400 Allentown (18104) *(G-109)*

142-Tactical, Monongahela *Also called Anthony Burney (G-11304)*

1732 Meats LLC............267 879-7214
6250 Baltimore Ave Yeadon (19050) *(G-20350)*

1998 Equipment Leasing Corp............412 771-2944
400 Island Ave Mc Kees Rocks (15136) *(G-10596)*

1fh Industries, Royersford *Also called I F H Industries Inc (G-16852)*

1st Choice Athlete, Broomall *Also called Kinesis Software LLC (G-2292)*

2 Sports Inc............484 679-1225
1055 W Germantown Pike # 1 Norristown (19403) *(G-12626)*

2000 F Process Htg & Contrls............724 224-2800
221 James E Wolfe St Tarentum (15084) *(G-18238)*

201 Distributing Inc............724 529-2320
206 Round Barn Rd Vanderbilt (15486) *(G-18719)*

2124 Brewing Company LLC............724 260-8737
8321 Ohio River Blvd Pittsburgh (15202) *(G-14624)*

21st Century Media Newsppr LLC............610 692-3790
390 Eagleview Blvd Exton (19341) *(G-5633)*

21st Century Media Newsppr LLC............814 238-3071
1015 Benner Pike State College (16801) *(G-17939)*

21st Century Newspapers Inc............215 504-4200
Lower Makefield Corporate Yardley (19067) *(G-20292)*

21st Century Signs, Williamsport *Also called Clapper Enterprises Inc (G-19998)*

21st Century Software Tech Inc............610 341-9017
940 W Valley Rd Wayne (19087) *(G-19290)*

21st Cntury Mdia Newpapers LLC............215 368-6973
307 Derstine Ave Lansdale (19446) *(G-9338)*

21st Cntury Mdia Nwspapers LLC............610 622-4186
500 Mildred Ave Secane (19018) *(G-17316)*

21st N College............814 502-1542
1863 Piney Creek Rd Martinsburg (16662) *(G-10518)*

24-7 Innovations LLC............570 676-8888
176 Old Schoolhouse Rd Greentown (18426) *(G-6732)*

24k Gold Plating............610 255-4676
124 Woodhaven Dr Landenberg (19350) *(G-9246)*

25 Fathoms International Inc............610 558-1101
364 W Chesterpike Ste B7 Glen Mills (19342) *(G-6428)*

2508 Easton Ave, Bethlehem *Also called Dyets Inc (G-1499)*

2820 Associates Inc............412 471-2525
2820 Smallman St Ste 2 Pittsburgh (15222) *(G-14625)*

2w Technologies LLC (PA)............814 333-3117
1009 Water St Ste 2 Meadville (16335) *(G-10693)*

2z Medical, Bala Cynwyd *Also called Sleep Specialists LLC (G-892)*

3 D Printing & Digital Imaging, Bensalem *Also called 3d Printing and Copy Ctr Inc (G-1140)*

3 Prime LLC............610 459-3468
2 New Rd Ste 300 Aston (19014) *(G-747)*

3 T Secuirty LLC............717 653-0019
3045 Back Run Rd Manheim (17545) *(G-10366)*

3-D Creative Services Inc............570 329-1111
3500 W 4th St Williamsport (17701) *(G-19983)*

310 Publishing LLC............717 564-0161
4711 Queen St Ste 202 Harrisburg (17109) *(G-7077)*

39 Design Company Inc............215 563-1320
207b Highland Ave Wayne (19087) *(G-19291)*

3d Printing and Copy Ctr Inc............215 968-7900
1296 Adams Rd 150 Bensalem (19020) *(G-1140)*

3d Printing Service LLC............215 426-1510
833 E Allegheny Ave Philadelphia (19134) *(G-13317)*

3M Company............610 497-7032
50 Milton Dr Aston (19014) *(G-748)*

3nt-3 Nieces Trucking Inc............360 815-0938
108 Mini St Grassflat (16839) *(G-6577)*

3p Ltd............717 566-5643
286 E Main St Hummelstown (17036) *(G-7901)*

3si Security Systems Inc (HQ)............800 523-1430
101 Lindenwood Dr Ste 200 Malvern (19355) *(G-10176)*

3si Security Systems Holdg Inc............610 280-2000
101 Lindenwood Dr Ste 200 Malvern (19355) *(G-10177)*

4 Daughters LLC............570 283-5934
1 Korn St Kingston (18704) *(G-8711)*

4 Elements of Life LLC............215 668-1643
2131 Fitzwater St Philadelphia (19146) *(G-13318)*

4 GUY'S FIRETRUCKS, Meyersdale *Also called Four Guys Stnless Tank Eqp Inc (G-11010)*

4 Less Furniture and Rugs LLC............610 650-4000
122 Mill Rd Oaks (19456) *(G-12930)*

4 Life Promotions LLC............215 919-4985
1210 E Palmer St Philadelphia (19125) *(G-13319)*

43rd St Inc............412 682-4090
1 43rd St Pittsburgh (15201) *(G-14626)*

43rd St Concrete, Pittsburgh *Also called 43rd St Inc (G-14626)*

465 Devon Park Drive Inc............610 293-1330
465 Devon Park Dr Wayne (19087) *(G-19292)*

486 Associates Inc............717 691-7077
486 Covinton St Mechanicsburg (17055) *(G-10815)*

4front Solutions LLC............814 464-2000
8140 Hawthorne Dr Erie (16509) *(G-5161)*

4sis LLC (PA)............814 459-2451
2054 W 8th St Erie (16505) *(G-5162)*

5 Generation Bakers LLC............412 444-8200
1100 Chartiers Ave Mc Kees Rocks (15136) *(G-10597)*

5 Star Plus Inc............610 470-9187
716 Little Elk Creek Rd Oxford (19363) *(G-13070)*

549 Industrial Holdings Inc............610 622-7211
5000 Paschall Ave Philadelphia (19143) *(G-13320)*

5p Corporation............215 997-5666
2800 Crystal Dr Hatfield (19440) *(G-7312)*

5th Street Live Poultry, Philadelphia *Also called Tran Hoang (G-14402)*

60x Custom Strings............724 525-0507
1047 State Route 268 Cowansville (16218) *(G-3795)*

639 E Congress Realty Corp............610 434-5195
639 E Congress St Allentown (18109) *(G-110)*

69th St Commercial Printers............610 539-8412
4030 Redwing Ln Norristown (19403) *(G-12627)*

7106 Dow Chemical............610 244-6000
400 Arcola Rd Collegeville (19426) *(G-3365)*

75 Cabinets LLC............215 343-7500
646 Easton Rd Warrington (18976) *(G-19104)*

7th Soul LLC............917 880-8423
602 Thomas St Stroudsburg (18360) *(G-18101)*

8 12 Illumination LLC............717 285-9700
200 N Donnerville Rd Mountville (17554) *(G-11789)*

8 12 Innovations Inc............717 413-7656
11 Mount Joy St Mount Joy (17552) *(G-11644)*

84 Lumber Company (PA)............724 228-8820
1019 Route 519 Eighty Four (15330) *(G-4830)*

911 Safety Equipment LLC............610 279-6808
9 S Forrest Ave Ste 200 Norristown (19403) *(G-12628)*

926 Partners Inc (PA)............814 452-4026
2530 Parade St Erie (16503) *(G-5163)*

9dots Management Corp LLC............610 825-2027
1010 Spring Mill Ave # 200 Conshohocken (19428) *(G-3514)*

9th Street Management Company, Philadelphia *Also called Superior Pasta Company Inc (G-14358)*

A & A Concrete Products Inc............724 538-1114
1559 Mars Evans City Rd Evans City (16033) *(G-5555)*

A & A Gear Inc............215 364-3952
1840 County Line Rd # 204 Huntingdon Valley (19006) *(G-7959)*

A & B Homes Inc............570 253-3888
Rr 6 Honesdale (18431) *(G-7699)*

A
L
P
H
A
B
E
T
I
C

A & B Steelworks LLC 717 823-8599
464 E Main Ave Myerstown (17067) *(G-11872)*

A & C Pharmtech Inc 215 968-5605
375 Pheasant Run Newtown (18940) *(G-12493)*

A & D Fashions Inc 610 967-1440
55 S 7th St Emmaus (18049) *(G-5017)*

A & D Manufacturing 717 768-7330
345 Centerville Rd Gordonville (17529) *(G-6548)*

A & E Manufacturing Co Inc 215 943-9460
2110 Hartel Ave Levittown (19057) *(G-9810)*

A & F Holdings LLC 215 289-8300
1641 Loretta Ave Ste B Feasterville Trevose (19053) *(G-5880)*

A & H Industries Inc 717 866-7591
837 S Railroad St Myerstown (17067) *(G-11873)*

A & H Sportswear Co Inc 610 746-0922
50 Sycamore St Nazareth (18064) *(G-11951)*

A & H Sportswear Co Inc (PA) 484 373-3600
610 Uhler Rd Easton (18040) *(G-4643)*

A & H Sportswear Co Inc 610 759-9550
110 Commerce Way Stockertown (18083) *(G-18063)*

A & K Enterprises, Glenshaw Also called Robert Aguglia *(G-6500)*

A & L Iron Works LLC 717 768-0705
624 Buchland Rd Narvon (17555) *(G-11915)*

A & L Paint Co Llc 814 349-8064
112 4 Wheel Dr Ste 2 Rebersburg (16872) *(G-16577)*

A & L Tubular Specialties 724 667-6101
5124 Erie St New Castle (16102) *(G-12051)*

A & L Wood Inc 570 539-8922
2220 Paradise Church Rd Mount Pleasant Mills (17853) *(G-11724)*

A & M Compost 215 256-1900
2650 Audubon Rd Norristown (19403) *(G-12629)*

A & M McHining Fabrication Inc 724 842-0314
296 Robbs Fording Rd Ford City (16226) *(G-6041)*

A & P Support Inc 570 265-9157
525 William Penn Pl Pittsburgh (15219) *(G-14627)*

A & R Iron Works Inc 610 497-8770
21 Nealy Blvd Ste 2101 Trainer (19061) *(G-18462)*

A & R Jadczak Company 215 752-3438
135 Green St Langhorne (19047) *(G-9271)*

A & R Nissley Inc (PA) 717 426-3514
140 Vintage Dr Bainbridge (17502) *(G-871)*

A & R Nissley Inc 717 541-1004
22 Colonial Park Mall Harrisburg (17109) *(G-7078)*

A & S Firearm Supplies Inc 724 925-1212
617 Overhead Bridge Rd Youngwood (15697) *(G-20776)*

A & S Indoor Pistol Range, Youngwood Also called A & S Firearm Supplies Inc *(G-20776)*

A & S Manufacturing Co. 888 651-6149
3246 Collins St Philadelphia (19134) *(G-13321)*

A & S Olive Oil Company Inc 267 483-8379
1240 Lower State Rd Chalfont (18914) *(G-2862)*

A & S Production Inc 814 463-9310
666 Yellow Hammer Rd Endeavor (16322) *(G-5078)*

A & T News Service 610 454-7787
1005 Brassington Dr Collegeville (19426) *(G-3366)*

A & V Woodwork Co 215 727-8832
6525 Upland St Philadelphia (19142) *(G-13322)*

A & W Screen Printing Inc 717 738-2726
503 Alexander Dr Ephrata (17522) *(G-5089)*

A A A Awning Company, Philadelphia Also called Afca Company Inc *(G-13351)*

A A A Engraving 412 281-7756
1042 5th Ave Pittsburgh (15219) *(G-14628)*

A A A Welding Service Inc 215 426-2240
811 E Cayuga St Philadelphia (19124) *(G-13323)*

A A E, Royersford Also called Aluminum Athletic Equipment Co *(G-16841)*

A A I, Allentown Also called American Atelier Inc *(G-133)*

A A Robbins Inc 814 398-4607
260 Railroad St Cambridge Springs (16403) *(G-2473)*

A Allan Industries Inc 570 826-0123
Allan Rd Wilkes Barre (18703) *(G-19902)*

A and M Tool LLC 215 513-0968
106 Fairway Dr Harleysville (19438) *(G-7011)*

A Anthony & Sons Inc 814 454-2883
1450 W 21st St Erie (16502) *(G-5164)*

A Archery and Printing Place 717 274-1811
1705 E Cumberland St # 2 Lebanon (17042) *(G-9544)*

A B C Insert Co, Ambler Also called K & L Operating Co *(G-584)*

A B M Motors Inc 215 781-9400
300 Linton Ave Croydon (19021) *(G-3909)*

A B N A Inc 724 527-2866
100 Penn Ave Penn (15675) *(G-13226)*

A B Patterns Models 215 322-8226
390 Pike Rd Unit 7 Huntingdon Valley (19006) *(G-7960)*

A B T, Pittsburgh Also called ABT LLC *(G-14636)*

A Better Power LLC 412 498-6537
116 Timberlane Dr Ligonier (15658) *(G-9956)*

A C, Doylestown Also called Tohickon Tool & Die Co *(G-4343)*

A C A Sand & Gravel 814 665-6087
19144 Route 89 Corry (16407) *(G-3741)*

A C F Ltd 610 459-5397
124 Willits Way Glen Mills (19342) *(G-6429)*

A C Gentry Inc 215 927-9948
6631 Wyncote Ave Philadelphia (19138) *(G-13324)*

A C Grinding & Supply Co Inc 215 946-3760
1917 Hartel Ave Levittown (19057) *(G-9811)*

A C Kissling Company 215 423-4700
574 Monastery Ave Philadelphia (19128) *(G-13325)*

A C Miller Concrete Pdts Inc (PA) 610 948-4600
31 E Bridge St Spring City (19475) *(G-17856)*

A C Miller Concrete Pdts Inc. 724 459-5950
9558 Route 22 Blairsville (15717) *(G-1712)*

A C Rebuilders, Philadelphia Also called Angel Colon *(G-13392)*

A C Signs Inc 215 465-0274
1522 Alter St Ste 26 Philadelphia (19146) *(G-13326)*

A Class Corp 717 695-0597
1303 Market St 1 Harrisburg (17103) *(G-7079)*

A Crane Rental LLC (PA) 412 469-1776
200 Washington Ave Dravosburg (15034) *(G-4350)*

A Cubed Corporation (PA) 724 538-4000
131 Myoma Rd Mars (16046) *(G-10485)*

A Cupcake Wonderland LLC 267 324-5579
1620 Montrose St Philadelphia (19146) *(G-13327)*

A Cut Above Lawn Care & Landsp 484 239-6825
4884 Circle Dr Northampton (18067) *(G-12841)*

A D M Welding & Fabrication 814 723-7227
37 Broadhead St Warren (16365) *(G-19007)*

A D Swartzlander & Sons 724 282-2706
399 Keck Rd Butler (16002) *(G-2370)*

A Dema Company, Nesquehoning Also called Viking LLC *(G-12010)*

A Duchini Inc (PA) 814 456-7027
2550 Mckinley Ave Erie (16503) *(G-5165)*

A E Falgiani Ice Co Inc 412 344-7538
3639 Poplar Ave Pittsburgh (15234) *(G-14629)*

A E I, Leola Also called Aggregates Equipment Inc *(G-9767)*

A E Pakos Inc 724 539-1790
1106 Burns St Latrobe (15650) *(G-9452)*

A E Reken Welding & Fabg, Dayton Also called Andrew E Reken *(G-4034)*

A F Moyer Inc 215 723-5555
249 Allentown Rd Souderton (18964) *(G-17719)*

A F Necastro & Associates, Farrell Also called A F Necastro Inc *(G-5865)*

A F Necastro Inc 724 981-3239
713 Martin Luther King Jr Farrell (16121) *(G-5865)*

A F Paul Company 412 264-2111
859 2nd Ave Coraopolis (15108) *(G-3651)*

A F S, Exton Also called Automated Fincl Systems Inc *(G-5649)*

A Funky Little Sign Shop 215 489-2880
3605 Old Easton Rd Doylestown (18902) *(G-4266)*

A G F Manufacturing Co Inc 610 240-4900
100 Quaker Ln Malvern (19355) *(G-10178)*

A G Mauro Company 717 938-4671
580 Industrial Dr Lewisberry (17339) *(G-9879)*

A G Source Inc 484 459-9292
2029 Orlando Rd Pottstown (19464) *(G-15959)*

A H Emery Company 717 295-6935
665 N Reservoir St Lancaster (17602) *(G-8918)*

A I Floor Products 215 355-2798
4888 Hazel Ave Feasterville Trevose (19053) *(G-5881)*

A J Blosenski Inc (PA) 610 942-2707
1600 Chestnut Tree Rd Honey Brook (19344) *(G-7734)*

A J Drgon Associates Inc 412 771-5160
201 Chamber St Mc Kees Rocks (15136) *(G-10598)*

A J Printing 610 337-7468
150 Allendale Rd Ste 11 King of Prussia (19406) *(G-8575)*

A J Smith Electric Motor Svc 570 424-8743
210 Independence Rd East Stroudsburg (18301) *(G-4601)*

A Jacoby & Company 610 828-0500
300 Conshohocken State Rd # 180 Conshohocken (19428) *(G-3515)*

A K U Wire Inc 215 672-8071
1800 Mearns Rd Ste D Warminster (18974) *(G-18814)*

A Killeen Union Printing, Pittsburgh Also called Killeen Printing Co *(G-15177)*

A Kuhns Cabinets 717 263-4306
2979 Newcomer Rd Chambersburg (17202) *(G-2896)*

A L Bazzini Co Inc (PA) 610 366-1606
1035 Mill Rd Allentown (18106) *(G-111)*

A L Finishing Co Inc 215 855-9422
925 Schwab Rd Ste C Hatfield (19440) *(G-7313)*

A La Henri Inc 724 856-1374
3213 Lexington Dr New Castle (16105) *(G-12052)*

A Landau Diamond Co 215 675-2700
1811 Stout Dr Warminster (18974) *(G-18815)*

A Lindemann Inc 412 487-7282
1005 8th Ave Glenshaw (15116) *(G-6477)*

A Link Prtg & Promotions LLC 412 220-0290
3189 Washington Pike Bridgeville (15017) *(G-2049)*

A M E R Inc 724 229-8020
5 Commercial Dr Washington (15301) *(G-19143)*

A M Industries Inc 215 362-2525
151 Green St Lansdale (19446) *(G-9339)*

A M L, York *Also called Applied Magnetics Lab Inc* ***(G-20381)***
A M Logging LLC 814 349-8089
4873 Penns Valley Rd Spring Mills (16875) ***(G-17884)***
A M Metal Specialties, South Williamsport *Also called A M Sheet Metal Inc* ***(G-17789)***
A M Parts Inc 412 367-8040
3470 Babcock Blvd Pittsburgh (15237) ***(G-14630)***
A M Sheet Metal Inc 570 322-5417
410 W 2nd Ave South Williamsport (17702) ***(G-17789)***
A M T, Royersford *Also called Amt Pump Company* ***(G-16842)***
A M T, Export *Also called Advanced Mfg Tech Inc* ***(G-5588)***
A Mamaux & Son Inc 412 771-8432
102 Ella St Mc Kees Rocks (15136) ***(G-10599)***
A Messinger Arch 610 896-7227
1640 Oakwood Dr Apt W319 Penn Valley (19072) ***(G-13232)***
A Olek & Son Inc 215 638-4550
443 Mill Rd Bensalem (19020) ***(G-1141)***
A P Green Services Inc 412 375-6600
1305 Cherrington Pkwy # 100 Coraopolis (15108) ***(G-3652)***
A P P, Philipsburg *Also called Advanced Powder Products Inc* ***(G-14507)***
A P S, Elliottsburg *Also called Advanced Pstioning Systems Inc* ***(G-4918)***
A Plus Precious Metals 215 821-3751
6907 Torresdale Ave Philadelphia (19135) ***(G-13328)***
A Plus Printing, Altoona *Also called A+ Printing Inc* ***(G-468)***
A Plus Stair Lift Pittsburgh 412 260-7469
2828 Broadway Blvd Monroeville (15146) ***(G-11322)***
A R Groff Transport Inc 717 859-4661
20 Trinity Dr Leola (17540) ***(G-9764)***
A Ra, Koppel *Also called ARA Corporation* ***(G-8813)***
A Rifkin Co 570 825-9551
1400 Sans Souci Pkwy Hanover Township (18706) ***(G-6978)***
A S C, Telford *Also called Amplifier Solutions Corp* ***(G-18267)***
A S I, Feasterville Trevose *Also called Advertising Specialty Inst Inc* ***(G-5883)***
A S I, Malvern *Also called Alpha Scientific Instrument* ***(G-10182)***
A S I, Millersburg *Also called Advanced Scientifics Inc* ***(G-11186)***
A S T, Bernville *Also called Advanced Skin Technologies Inc* ***(G-1295)***
A Schulman Inc 610 398-5900
6355 Farm Bureau Rd Allentown (18106) ***(G-112)***
A Stuart Morton Inc 610 692-1190
315 Westtown Rd Ste 11 West Chester (19382) ***(G-19492)***
A Stuckeye, Pottstown *Also called Dimec Rail Service* ***(G-15983)***
A Stucki Company (PA) 412 424-0560
360 Wright Brothers Dr Coraopolis (15108) ***(G-3653)***
A Stucki Company 724 746-4240
1000 Philadelphia St Canonsburg (15317) ***(G-2531)***
A T I Systems A Garda Company, Reading *Also called Garda CL Technical Svcs Inc* ***(G-16389)***
A T J Printing Inc (PA) 814 641-9614
325 Penn St Ste 1 Huntingdon (16652) ***(G-7936)***
A T L, Richboro *Also called Advanced Technology Labs Inc* ***(G-16673)***
A T S, Mechanicsburg *Also called Aqua Treatment Services Inc* ***(G-10820)***
A T V Bakery Inc 610 374-5577
36 S 3rd St Reading (19602) ***(G-16307)***
A Taste of Philly 215 639-3997
1801 Bridgetown Pike # 2 Feasterville Trevose (19053) ***(G-5882)***
A Tru Diva LLC 888 400-1034
224 E Avon Rd Brookhaven (19015) ***(G-2241)***
A V Weber Co Inc 215 699-3527
101 Elm Ave Ste A North Wales (19454) ***(G-12784)***
A W Everett Furniture Frames 610 377-0170
95 Reber St Lehighton (18235) ***(G-9708)***
A W Mercer Inc 610 367-8460
104 Industrial Dr Boyertown (19512) ***(G-1892)***
A W Sawmill 717 535-5081
2144 Locust Run Rd Mifflintown (17059) ***(G-11107)***
A Wbrown Awning 610 372-2908
443 Buttonwood St Reading (19601) ***(G-16308)***
A Word Concepts Inc 215 924-2226
500 W Cheltenham Ave Philadelphia (19126) ***(G-13329)***
A Z S Brusher Equipment, Ephrata *Also called AZS Brusher Equipment LLC* ***(G-5092)***
A&A Beverages Warehouse 570 344-0024
949 Adams Ave Scranton (18510) ***(G-17204)***
A&A Machine Co Inc 215 355-8330
1085 Industrial Blvd Southampton (18966) ***(G-17795)***
A&D Dyestuffs, Philadelphia *Also called Presto Dyechem Co Inc* ***(G-14198)***
A&E, Levittown *Also called A & E Manufacturing Co Inc* ***(G-9810)***
A&J Optical Inc 215 338-7645
8002 Frankford Ave Philadelphia (19136) ***(G-13330)***
A&L Wood Products, Mount Pleasant Mills *Also called A & L Wood Inc* ***(G-11724)***
A+ Packaging 610 864-1758
2262 Laurel Ridge Rd Narvon (17555) ***(G-11916)***
A+ Printing Inc 814 942-4257
2415 13th Ave Altoona (16601) ***(G-468)***
A-1 Babbitt and Machine, Donora *Also called A-1 Babbitt Co Inc* ***(G-4144)***
A-1 Babbitt Co Inc 724 379-6588
1122 Scott Street Ext Donora (15033) ***(G-4144)***
A-1 Racing Products Inc 215 675-8442
1927 Stout Dr Ste 2 Warminster (18974) ***(G-18816)***
A-Boss Opticians (PA) 412 271-4424
634 Braddock Ave Braddock (15104) ***(G-1942)***
A-Link Printing & Promotions, Bridgeville *Also called Jem Graphics LLC* ***(G-2074)***
A-Lok Products, Bristol *Also called Poly-TEC Products Inc* ***(G-2185)***
A-One Asphalt Paving 215 658-1616
3716 Richmond St Philadelphia (19137) ***(G-13331)***
A-One Machine LLC 570 289-4347
3109 State Route 2096 Hop Bottom (18824) ***(G-7772)***
A.B.E. Materials, Easton *Also called H&K Group Inc* ***(G-4693)***
A.G.A.S. Flags, Philadelphia *Also called Agas Mfg Inc* ***(G-13354)***
A.M. Gatti, Inc, Fairless Hills *Also called Aurele M Gatti Inc* ***(G-5772)***
A.S.S.T., Mc Sherrystown *Also called Allegheny Solid Surfc Tech LLC* ***(G-10649)***
A.W.I., Shippensburg *Also called Architectural Woodsmiths Inc* ***(G-17515)***
A/C Service and Repair Inc 717 792-3492
5166 Commerce Dr York (17408) ***(G-20361)***
A/S Custom Furniture Company 215 491-3100
364 Valley Rd Ste C Warrington (18976) ***(G-19105)***
A3-Usa Inc 724 871-7170
1350 Biddle Ave Westmoreland City (15692) ***(G-19783)***
AA Plasma LLC 312 371-7947
32 Richard Rd Warminster (18974) ***(G-18817)***
AAA Business Solutions LLC 412 787-3333
500 Glass Rd Pittsburgh (15205) ***(G-14631)***
AAA Color Card Company 814 793-2342
115 S Wall St Martinsburg (16662) ***(G-10519)***
AAA Hellenic Marble Inc 610 344-7700
301 E Market St West Chester (19382) ***(G-19493)***
AAA Nail 814 362-2863
115 Main St Bradford (16701) ***(G-1953)***
AAC, Lemont Furnace *Also called Advanced Acoustic Concepts LLC* ***(G-9732)***
Aacr, Philadelphia *Also called American Association For Cance* ***(G-13378)***
Aaim Controls Inc 717 765-9100
11885 Mutual Dr Waynesboro (17268) ***(G-19393)***
Aapryl LLC 215 567-1100
1845 Walnut St Ste 800 Philadelphia (19103) ***(G-13332)***
AAR Plastic & Glass Llc 410 200-6369
43 E Middle St Gettysburg (17325) ***(G-6281)***
Aaron E Beiler 717 656-9596
905 W Main St New Holland (17557) ***(G-12224)***
Aaron Enterprises Inc 717 854-2641
300 Cloverleaf Rd York (17406) ***(G-20362)***
Aaron J Michael 724 745-0656
119 Valleycrest Dr Cecil (15321) ***(G-2821)***
Aaron King 610 273-1365
665 Pleasant View Rd Honey Brook (19344) ***(G-7735)***
Aaron Products, Wyoming *Also called Kitchen Express Inc* ***(G-20281)***
Aaron S Myers 717 339-9304
630 Cashman Rd New Oxford (17350) ***(G-12401)***
Aaron Wenger 717 656-9876
264 Voganville Rd New Holland (17557) ***(G-12225)***
Aavid Thermacore Inc (HQ) 717 569-6551
780 Eden Rd Ofc Lancaster (17601) ***(G-8919)***
Aaxios Technologies LLC 267 545-7400
272 Titus Ave Ste 217 Warrington (18976) ***(G-19106)***
Aaxis Distributors 717 762-2947
8605 Anthony Hwy Waynesboro (17268) ***(G-19394)***
Aba Thermal Windows & Doors, Murrysville *Also called Thermal Industries Inc* ***(G-11870)***
Abacus Surfaces Inc 717 560-8050
2330 Dairy Rd Lancaster (17601) ***(G-8920)***
Abardia Media 215 893-5100
301 S 19th St Ste 1s Philadelphia (19103) ***(G-13333)***
Abarta Energy, Pittsburgh *Also called Abarta Oil & Gas Co Inc* ***(G-14632)***
Abarta Inc 610 807-5319
2150 Industrial Dr Bethlehem (18017) ***(G-1441)***
Abarta Oil & Gas Co Inc (HQ) 412 963-6226
200 Alpha Dr Pittsburgh (15238) ***(G-14632)***
ABB High Voltage Technology, Mount Pleasant *Also called ABB Inc* ***(G-11685)***
ABB Inc 724 295-6000
201 Ann St B Oakmont (15139) ***(G-12913)***
ABB Inc 724 838-8622
125 Theobold Ave Ste 10 Greensburg (15601) ***(G-6647)***
ABB Inc 215 674-6000
125 County Line Rd Warminster (18974) ***(G-18818)***
ABB Inc 724 696-1300
100 Distribution Cir Mount Pleasant (15666) ***(G-11685)***
ABB Inc 412 963-7530
575 Epsilon Dr Ste 1 Pittsburgh (15238) ***(G-14633)***
ABB Installation Products Inc 724 662-4400
150 Mckinley Ave Mercer (16137) ***(G-10958)***
Abbatron, Meadville *Also called Halsit Holdings LLC* ***(G-10733)***
Abbey Color Incorporated 215 739-9960
400 E Tioga St Philadelphia (19134) ***(G-13334)***
Abbey Products, Philadelphia *Also called Abbey Color Incorporated* ***(G-13334)***
Abbi Print LLC 215 471-8801
321 S 60th St Philadelphia (19143) ***(G-13335)***

Abbott Furnace Company.................................814 781-6355
1068 Trout Run Rd Saint Marys (15857) *(G-16943)*

Abbott Laboratories.......................................610 265-9100
920 E 8th Ave King of Prussia (19406) *(G-8576)*

Abbott Laboratories.......................................570 347-0319
3271 Greenwood Ave Scranton (18505) *(G-17205)*

Abbott Laboratories.......................................610 444-9818
148 W State St Ste 103 Kennett Square (19348) *(G-8500)*

Abbott Laboratories.......................................717 545-8159
2405 Melbourne Dr Harrisburg (17112) *(G-7080)*

Abbott's Plating, Philadelphia *Also called James Abbott (G-13890)*

Abbottstown Industries Inc...........................717 259-8715
420 W Fleet St Abbottstown (17301) *(G-3)*

Abbottstown Stamping Co Inc........................717 632-0588
13 Barnhart Dr Hanover (17331) *(G-6859)*

Abboud Samar...412 343-6899
704 Brookline Blvd Pittsburg (15226) *(G-14634)*

Abby Signs of PA..570 494-0600
1128 Broad St Montoursville (17754) *(G-11428)*

ABC, Reading *Also called Reading Truck Body LLC (G-16493)*

ABC, Verona *Also called American Beverage Corporation (G-18747)*

ABC, Olyphant *Also called Saint-Gobain Ceramics Plas Inc (G-12998)*

ABC School Supply, Mount Joy *Also called Childcraft Education Corp (G-11649)*

Abcore Fitness Inc..570 424-1006
158 Progress St East Stroudsburg (18301) *(G-4602)*

Abe Alarm Service..484 664-7304
1014 N Quebec St Allentown (18109) *(G-113)*

Abe Custom Metal Products..........................412 298-0200
3500 Maplevue Dr Bethel Park (15102) *(G-1399)*

Abec Inc (PA)...610 882-1541
3998 Schelden Cir Bethlehem (18017) *(G-1442)*

Abel Millwork LLC...412 296-2254
550 Mcclelland Rd Finleyville (15332) *(G-5951)*

Aberdeen Road Company..............................717 764-1192
105 Sinking Springs Ln Emigsville (17318) *(G-4983)*

Abes Bakery...717 232-1330
1330 Marion St Harrisburg (17102) *(G-7081)*

Abex Industries..717 246-2611
1 Vulcan Ln Red Lion (17356) *(G-16586)*

ABF USA Ltd..570 788-0888
72 Hillside Dr Drums (18222) *(G-4380)*

Abilene Boot Co Inc......................................814 445-6545
841 S Center Ave Somerset (15501) *(G-17672)*

Abililife Inc...443 326-6395
100 S Commons Ste 102 Pittsburg (15212) *(G-14635)*

Ability Prosthetics Orthotics, Exton *Also called Ability Prsthtics Orthtics Inc (G-5634)*

Ability Prsthtics Orthtics Inc (PA).................717 337-2277
660 W Lincoln Hwy Exton (19341) *(G-5634)*

Ability Systems Corporation.........................215 657-4338
1422 Arnold Ave Abington (19001) *(G-9)*

Abl Engineering..814 364-1333
227 W Main St Boalsburg (16827) *(G-1863)*

Able Pattern Company...................................724 327-1401
5597 Fox Chase Dr Export (15632) *(G-5587)*

Able Tool Co Inc (PA)....................................724 863-2508
13160 Route 993 Trafford (15085) *(G-18450)*

Abmech Acquisitions LLC..............................412 462-7440
976 Forest Ave West Homestead (15120) *(G-19719)*

Above Rim International LLC..........................215 789-7893
1158 S 18th St Philadelphia (19146) *(G-13336)*

Abps, Inc....800 552-9980
435 Creamery Way Ste 100 Exton (19341) *(G-5635)*

Abrill Industries..814 437-5354
773 Meadville Pike Franklin (16323) *(G-6112)*

ABS, Philadelphia *Also called American Bible Society (G-13379)*

ABS and Apples..646 847-8262
5111 Juliet Rd Tobyhanna (18466) *(G-18406)*

ABS Print Management, Wayne *Also called Wheeler Enterprises Inc (G-19392)*

Absolute Acstic Noise Ctrl LLC......................304 670-0095
800 Imperial Indus Pkwy Oakdale (15071) *(G-12887)*

Absolute Pallet Inc.......................................215 331-4510
550 State Rd Ste B Bensalem (19020) *(G-1142)*

Absolute Powder Coating LLC........................814 781-1160
202 Grotzinger Rd Saint Marys (15857) *(G-16944)*

Abss, Feasterville Trevose *Also called Associated Prtg Graphics Svcs (G-5887)*

ABT LLC..412 826-8002
500 Fountain St Pittsburg (15238) *(G-14636)*

Abtec Incorporated.......................................215 788-0950
2570 Pearl Buck Rd Bristol (19007) *(G-2102)*

Abtrex Industries Inc.....................................724 266-5425
112 Ross Way Leetsdale (15056) *(G-9676)*

AC Fashion LLC...570 291-5982
330 Montage Mountain Rd Moosic (18507) *(G-11501)*

Acacia Corp...412 771-6144
7 Crawford St Mc Kees Rocks (15136) *(G-10600)*

Academy Sports Center Inc...........................570 339-3399
18 S Oak St 20 Mount Carmel (17851) *(G-11622)*

ACC Accounting Solutions Inc.......................215 253-4738
1800 Jfk Blvd Unit 300 Philadelphia (19103) *(G-13337)*

Accel Sign Group Inc.....................................412 781-7735
5600 Harrison St Pittsburg (15201) *(G-14637)*

Accelbeam Photonics LLC.............................215 715-4345
111 Buck Rd Unit 5001 Huntingdon Valley (19006) *(G-7961)*

Accelight Networks Inc..................................412 220-2102
70 Abele Rd Bridgeville (15017) *(G-2050)*

Accellent..610 489-0300
200 W 7th Ave Trappe (19426) *(G-18466)*

Accent Metals Inc..717 699-5676
3675 Sandhurst Dr York (17406) *(G-20363)*

Accent Metals Inc..717 699-5676
3675 Sandhurst Dr York (17406) *(G-20364)*

Accent Shop..724 695-7580
161 Main St Imperial (15126) *(G-8056)*

Access Credential Systems LLC.....................724 820-1160
104 Highcroft Cir Eighty Four (15330) *(G-4831)*

Access Floor Division, Red Lion *Also called Tate Access Floors Inc (G-16616)*

Access411, York *Also called Morrison Consulting Inc (G-20604)*

Accion Labs Us Inc (PA)................................724 260-5139
1225 Wash Pike Ste 401 Bridgeville (15017) *(G-2051)*

Acco Gbc...267 880-6797
1411 Whitehall Dr Doylestown (18901) *(G-4267)*

Acco Material Hdlg Solutions, York *Also called D L Carmody Holdings LLC (G-20442)*

Acco Mtl Hdlg Solutions Inc (HQ)...................800 967-7333
76 Acco Dr York (17402) *(G-20365)*

Accountable Software Inc..............................610 983-3100
70 Buckwalter Rd Ste 226 Royersford (19468) *(G-16839)*

Accounting Department, Indiana *Also called Royal Production Company Inc (G-8125)*

Accra Machine Shop Inc................................814 623-8009
554 N Thomas St Bedford (15522) *(G-1039)*

Accrotool Inc...724 339-3560
401 Hunt Valley Rd New Kensington (15068) *(G-12320)*

Accu Bond Corporation..................................610 269-8433
460 Acorn Ln Downingtown (19335) *(G-4208)*

Accu Machining Center Inc............................610 252-6855
3750 Nicholas St Easton (18045) *(G-4644)*

Accu Mold Plastics, Halifax *Also called Accu-Mold & Tool Company Inc (G-6824)*

Accu-Chek Machining Inc..............................814 834-2342
37 Accu Chek Dr Saint Marys (15857) *(G-16945)*

Accu-Cut Industries Inc.................................814 456-6616
141 E 26th St Erie (16504) *(G-5166)*

Accu-Decal Inc....215 535-0320
5301 Tacony St Ste 201 Philadelphia (19137) *(G-13338)*

Accu-Fire Fabrication Inc...............................800 641-0005
8 Progress Dr Morrisville (19067) *(G-11550)*

Accu-Grind Inc....814 965-5475
451 Center St Johnsonburg (15845) *(G-8343)*

Accu-Mold & Tool Company Inc......................717 896-3937
18 Powells Valley Rd Halifax (17032) *(G-6824)*

Accu-Turn Tool Company Inc..........................412 492-7270
1049 William Flynn Hwy # 400 Glenshaw (15116) *(G-6478)*

Accubar Engineering & Rorco........................814 669-9005
Woolverton Way Alexandria (16611) *(G-62)*

Accubond, Downingtown *Also called Accu Bond Corporation (G-4208)*

Accucorp Packaging Inc.................................215 673-3375
10101 Roosevelt Blvd Philadelphia (19154) *(G-13339)*

Accudie Inc...724 222-8447
175 S Country Club Rd Meadow Lands (15347) *(G-10689)*

Accudriv, York *Also called General Regulator Corp (G-20495)*

Accudyn Products Inc (PA)............................814 833-7615
2400 Yoder Dr Erie (16506) *(G-5167)*

Accudyn Products Inc....................................814 835-5088
6543 Sterrettania Rd Fairview (16415) *(G-5809)*

Accumetrics Limited......................................610 948-0181
134 Adams St Royersford (19468) *(G-16840)*

Accurate Components....................................215 442-1023
48 Vincent Cir Ste B Warminster (18974) *(G-18819)*

Accurate Control & Design Co.......................412 884-3723
2948 Meadowvue Dr Pittsburg (15227) *(G-14638)*

Accurate Die Wrks of Phldlphia.....................610 667-9200
954 Mcgomnery Ave Ste 3 Penn Valley (19072) *(G-13233)*

Accurate Logging LLC....................................724 354-3094
153 Aikens Rd Creekside (15732) *(G-3874)*

Accurate Machine Tech Inc............................267 885-7344
1800 Mearns Rd Ste L Warminster (18974) *(G-18820)*

Accurate Machine Technology, Warminster *Also called Accurate Machine Tech Inc (G-18820)*

Accurate Marking & Mfg, New Kensington *Also called Accurate Marking Products Inc (G-12321)*

Accurate Marking Products Inc......................724 337-8390
225 Prominence Dr New Kensington (15068) *(G-12321)*

Accurate Tool Co Inc.....................................610 436-4500
891 Fernhill Rd West Chester (19380) *(G-19494)*

Accuride Akw LP..814 459-7589
1015 E 12th St Erie (16503) *(G-5168)*

Accuride Corporation.....................................814 480-6400
1015 E 12th St Erie (16503) *(G-5169)*

Accuride Erie LP..814 480-6400
1015 E 12th St Ste 200 Erie (16503) *(G-5170)*

Accuspec Electronics, Erie *Also called 4front Solutions LLC (G-5161)*

Accustar Inc 610 459-0123
3060 Plaza Dr Ste 101 Garnet Valley (19060) *(G-6264)*

Accutome Inc (HQ) 800 979-2020
3222 Phoenixville Pike # 100 Malvern (19355) *(G-10179)*

Accutrex Products Inc (PA) 724 746-4300
112 Southpointe Blvd Canonsburg (15317) *(G-2532)*

Ace Bindery Corporation 412 784-3669
2323 Main St Pittsburgh (15215) *(G-14639)*

ACE Company 215 234-4615
19 Kratz Rd Harleysville (19438) *(G-7012)*

Ace Controls & Instrumentation 610 876-2000
601 Upland Ave Ste 219 Brookhaven (19015) *(G-2242)*

Ace Hardware, Erie Also called A Duchini Inc *(G-5165)*

Ace Metal Inc 610 623-2204
227 E Madison Ave Clifton Heights (19018) *(G-3250)*

Ace Overhead Door Co., Langhorne Also called Bbk Industries LLC *(G-9280)*

Ace Panels Company 814 583-5015
436 Evergreen Rd Luthersburg (15848) *(G-10120)*

Ace Sports Inc 610 833-5513
90 Randall Ave Ste F Woodlyn (19094) *(G-20216)*

Ace Trophy Co, Scranton Also called All - American Trophy Company *(G-17207)*

Ace Viking Electric Mtr Co Inc 814 897-9445
2222 E 30th St Erie (16510) *(G-5171)*

Ace Wire Spring & Form Co Inc 412 331-3353
1105 Thompson Ave Mc Kees Rocks (15136) *(G-10601)*

Ace-Co, Harleysville Also called Automatic Control Elec Co *(G-7021)*

Aceco, Douglassville Also called American Crane & Eqp Corp *(G-4168)*

Aces Inc 215 458-7143
1300 Steel Rd E Ste 3 Morrisville (19067) *(G-11551)*

Acf Group LLC 724 364-7027
120 Mine St Allison (15413) *(G-444)*

Acf Industries LLC 570 742-7601
417 N Arch St Milton (17847) *(G-11232)*

Achenbachs Pastry Inc 717 656-6671
375 E Main St Leola (17540) *(G-9765)*

Achieva (HQ) 412 995-5000
711 Bingham St Pittsburgh (15203) *(G-14640)*

Achieva 412 391-4660
711 Bingham St 1 Pittsburgh (15203) *(G-14641)*

Achieva 412 221-6609
360 Commercial St Bridgeville (15017) *(G-2052)*

ACHIEVA SUPPORT, Pittsburgh Also called Achieva *(G-14640)*

Aci, State College Also called Amchemteq Inc *(G-17940)*

Aci Technologies Inc 610 362-1200
1 International Plz # 600 Philadelphia (19113) *(G-13313)*

Ack Displays Inc 215 236-3000
232 Standish Rd Merion Station (19066) *(G-10996)*

Acker Drill Co Inc 570 586-2061
710 Shady Lane Rd S Abingtn Twp (18411) *(G-16888)*

Aclaris Therapeutics Inc (PA) 484 324-7933
640 Lee Rd Ste 200 Wayne (19087) *(G-19293)*

Acme Corrugated Box Co Inc 215 444-8000
2700 Turnpike Dr Hatboro (19040) *(G-7264)*

Acme Cryogenics Inc 610 966-4488
7662 Church St Alburtis (18011) *(G-49)*

Acme Cryogenics Inc (PA) 610 966-4488
2801 Mitchell Ave Allentown (18103) *(G-114)*

Acme Heat Treating Co 215 743-8500
4626 Hedge St Philadelphia (19124) *(G-13340)*

Acme Machine & Welding Co LLC 814 938-6702
46 Anchor Inn Rd Punxsutawney (15767) *(G-16127)*

Acme Markets Inc 215 725-9310
6640 Oxford Ave Philadelphia (19111) *(G-13341)*

Acme Metals Co 412 331-4301
3000 Grand Ave Ste 2 Pittsburgh (15225) *(G-14642)*

Acme Newspapers Inc (HQ) 610 642-4300
311 W Lancaster Ave Ardmore (19003) *(G-699)*

Acme Roofing and Heating Inc 412 921-8218
1610 Noblestown Rd Pittsburgh (15205) *(G-14643)*

Acme Specialties Inc 215 822-5900
2880 Bergey Rd Ste 100 Hatfield (19440) *(G-7314)*

Acme Stamping Wire Forming Co 412 771-5720
201 Corliss St Pittsburgh (15220) *(G-14644)*

Acorn Company (PA) 215 743-6100
4555 Tacony St Philadelphia (19124) *(G-13342)*

Acorn Design and Manufacturing, Denver Also called RLB Ventures Inc *(G-4091)*

Acorn Manufacturing Inc 717 964-1111
10 Industrial Way Denver (17517) *(G-4065)*

Acorn Press Inc 717 569-3264
500 E Oregon Rd Lititz (17543) *(G-9992)*

Acorn Trail Woodcraft 717 279-0261
1010 E Maple St Lebanon (17046) *(G-9545)*

Acousticsheep LLC 814 380-9296
2001 Peninsula Dr Erie (16506) *(G-5172)*

Acra Control Inc 714 382-1863
15 Terry Dr Newtown (18940) *(G-12494)*

Acrelormittal Us LLC 724 222-7769
Woodland & Griffith Ave Washington (15301) *(G-19144)*

Acro Labels Inc 215 657-5366
2530 Wyandotte Rd Willow Grove (19090) *(G-20105)*

Acryl8 LLC 484 695-6209
6517 Sugar Maple Cir Coopersburg (18036) *(G-3623)*

Acrylabs, Reading Also called Acrysystems Laboratories Inc *(G-16309)*

Acrylics Unlimited 215 443-2365
4 School Rd Horsham (19044) *(G-7778)*

Acrymax Technologies Inc 610 566-7470
221 Brooke St Media (19063) *(G-10913)*

Acrysystems Laboratories 610 273-1355
101 N Prospect St Reading (19606) *(G-16309)*

ACS, Harrisburg Also called Art Communication Systems Inc *(G-7090)*

ACS Investors LLC (HQ) 724 746-5500
1000 Park Dr Lawrence (15055) *(G-9533)*

Act, Lancaster Also called Advanced Cooling Tech Inc *(G-8921)*

Act Government Support Svcs, Norristown Also called Action Centered Training Inc *(G-12630)*

Act Inc 484 562-0063
29 Bala Ave Ste 114 Bala Cynwyd (19004) *(G-872)*

Actaire Inc 412 851-1040
1227 Prospect Rd Pittsburgh (15227) *(G-14645)*

Actavis Pharma Inc 847 377-5508
1090 Horsham Rd North Wales (19454) *(G-12785)*

Actavis Pharma Inc 847 855-0812
1090 Horsham Rd North Wales (19454) *(G-12786)*

Actco Tool & Mfg Co 814 336-4235
14421 Baldwin Street Ext Meadville (16335) *(G-10694)*

Action Centered Training Inc 610 630-3325
935 E Main St Norristown (19401) *(G-12630)*

Action Cycle & Atv LLC 814 765-2578
8081 Old Erie Pike West Decatur (16878) *(G-19687)*

Action Graphics, Clearfield Also called Commercial Job Printing Inc *(G-3216)*

Action Manufacturing Company 610 593-1800
500 Bailey Crossroads Rd Atglen (19310) *(G-799)*

Action Manufacturing Company (PA) 267 540-4041
190 Rittenhouse Cir Bristol (19007) *(G-2103)*

Action Materials Inc 610 377-3037
155157 Interchange Rd Lehighton (18235) *(G-9709)*

Action Printing and Bus Forms 814 453-5977
824 E 9th St Erie (16503) *(G-5173)*

Action Screen Printing Inc 610 359-1777
650 Park Way Frnt Frnt Broomall (19008) *(G-2277)*

Action Sportswear Inc 610 623-1820
30 Bunting Ln Primos (19018) *(G-16106)*

Action Supply, Sharon Hill Also called US Concrete Inc *(G-17465)*

Action Wireless Network 412 292-1712
3540 Maplevue Dr Bethel Park (15102) *(G-1400)*

Activaided Orthotics LLC 412 901-2658
5012 Ball Ave West Mifflin (15122) *(G-19734)*

Active Brass Foundry Inc 215 257-6519
330 Progress Dr Telford (18969) *(G-18266)*

Active Chemical Corporation (PA) 215 322-0377
4511 Old Lincoln Hwy Langhorne (19053) *(G-9272)*

Active Data Inc 610 997-8100
190 Brodhead Rd Ste 300 Bethlehem (18017) *(G-1443)*

Active Data Exchange, Bethlehem Also called Active Data Inc *(G-1443)*

Active Edge, Philadelphia Also called T A E Ltd *(G-14364)*

Active Heavy-Duty Cooling Pdts, Philadelphia Also called M P N Inc *(G-13981)*

Activeblu Corporation 412 490-1929
4638 Centre Ave Pittsburgh (15213) *(G-14646)*

Activestrategy Inc 484 690-0700
620 W Germantown Pike Plymouth Meeting (19462) *(G-15826)*

Acton Technologies Inc 570 654-0612
100 Thompson St Pittston (18640) *(G-15741)*

Actuated Medical Inc 814 355-0003
310 Rolling Ridge Dr Bellefonte (16823) *(G-1091)*

Acuity Finishing LLC 724 935-9190
230 W Kensinger Dr Ste B Cranberry Township (16066) *(G-3798)*

Acumark Inc 570 883-1800
702 Exeter Ave West Pittston (18643) *(G-19753)*

Acumix Inc (PA) 717 540-9738
805 Harrogate Dr Harrisburg (17111) *(G-7082)*

Acura-Cut, Bellefonte Also called Richard Meyers *(G-1114)*

Acurlite Strl Skylights Inc 570 759-6882
1017 N Vine St Berwick (18603) *(G-1307)*

Acutec Precision Aerospace Inc 814 336-2214
13555 Broadway Meadville (16335) *(G-10695)*

Acutedge Inc 484 846-6275
660 American Ave Ste 204 King of Prussia (19406) *(G-8577)*

Acutran LP 724 452-4130
1711 Route 588 Fombell (16123) *(G-6029)*

Acutronic Company (PA) 412 926-1200
700 Waterfront Dr Pittsburgh (15222) *(G-14647)*

Acutronic USA Inc 412 926-1200
700 Waterfront Dr Pittsburgh (15222) *(G-14648)*

Ad Distinction 215 736-0672
211 Winding Way Morrisville (19067) *(G-11552)*

Ad Forms LLC 724 379-6022
821 Jane Ave Charleroi (15022) *(G-3004)*

A
L
P
H
A
B
E
T
I
C

Ad Performance Polymers USA, Mill Hall *Also called Avery Dennison Corporation* ***(G-11172)***

Ad Post Graphics Inc 412 405-9163
6321 Library Rd Bldg 2 Library (15129) ***(G-9953)***

Ad Star Inc 724 439-5519
15 W Church St Uniontown (15401) ***(G-18614)***

Ad-Art Sign Co 412 373-0960
1380 Frey Rd Pittsburgh (15235) ***(G-14649)***

Ad-Net Services Incorporated 610 374-4200
1301 Allegheny Ave Reading (19601) ***(G-16310)***

Ad-Rax Productions LLC 610 264-8405
1225 7th St Catasauqua (18032) ***(G-2812)***

Adaconn 215 643-1900
538 Township Line Rd Blue Bell (19422) ***(G-1812)***

Adams Construction, Port Matilda *Also called Mr Spouting* ***(G-15903)***

Adams County Laser LLC 717 359-4030
1789 Frederick Pike Littlestown (17340) ***(G-10062)***

Adams Graphics Inc 215 751-1114
211 N 13th St Fl 9 Philadelphia (19107) ***(G-13343)***

Adams Manufacturing Corp 724 758-2125
1 Early St Ellwood City (16117) ***(G-4923)***

Adams Mfg Corp 724 758-2125
1 Early St Ellwood City (16117) ***(G-4924)***

Adams Mfg Corp (HQ) 800 237-8287
109 W Park Rd Portersville (16051) ***(G-15923)***

Adams Outdoor Advg Ltd Partnr 610 266-9461
2176 Avenue C Bethlehem (18017) ***(G-1444)***

Adams Vintner LLC 717 685-1336
30 E Main St Annville (17003) ***(G-641)***

Adapt Pharma Inc 844 232-7811
100 W Matsonford Rd # 4 Radnor (19087) ***(G-16285)***

Adapt Technologies LLC 610 896-7274
24 Portland Rd Ste 200 Conshohocken (19428) ***(G-3516)***

Adcomm Inc 610 820-8565
2626 W Washington St Allentown (18104) ***(G-115)***

Addaren Holdings LLC 267 387-6029
418 Caredean Dr Ste 6 Horsham (19044) ***(G-7779)***

Addev Walco Inc (PA) 412 486-4400
1651 E Sutter Rd Glenshaw (15116) ***(G-6479)***

Addie's Jewels, Lock Haven *Also called Addies Inc* ***(G-10081)***

Addies Inc 570 748-2966
202 E Main St Lock Haven (17745) ***(G-10081)***

Addies Awards & Printing LLC 570 484-9060
125 E Main St Lock Haven (17745) ***(G-10082)***

Addison Baking Company (PA) 215 464-8055
10865 Bustleton Ave Philadelphia (19116) ***(G-13344)***

ADello Vineyard & Winery LLC (PA) 610 754-0006
21 Simmons Rd Perkiomenville (18074) ***(G-13299)***

Adelphi Kitchens Inc 610 693-3101
E Penn Ave Freeman St Robesonia (19551) ***(G-16772)***

Adelphia Graphic Systems Inc 610 363-8150
302 Commerce Dr Exton (19341) ***(G-5636)***

Adelphia Steel Eqp Co Inc 800 865-8211
6218 Gillespie St Philadelphia (19135) ***(G-13345)***

Ademco Inc 215 244-6377
358 Dunksferry Rd Bensalem (19020) ***(G-1143)***

Adenine Solutions Inc 267 684-6013
285 Wisteria Dr Southampton (18966) ***(G-17796)***

Adept Corporation 800 451-2254
4601 N Susquehanna Trl York (17406) ***(G-20366)***

ADG Fabrication LLC 724 658-3000
540 Sampson St New Castle (16101) ***(G-12053)***

Adhesives & Chemicals, Yatesville *Also called Vilimia Inc* ***(G-20349)***

Adhesives Research Inc (PA) 717 235-7979
400 Seaks Run Rd Glen Rock (17327) ***(G-6449)***

Adhesives Specialists Inc 610 266-8910
739 Roble Rd Allentown (18109) ***(G-116)***

ADI Global Distribution, Bensalem *Also called Ademco Inc* ***(G-1143)***

Adidas North America Inc 610 327-9565
18 W Lightcap Rd Ste 789 Pottstown (19464) ***(G-15960)***

Adidas Outlet Store Pottstown, Pottstown *Also called Adidas North America Inc* ***(G-15960)***

Adlamco Inc 717 292-1577
1189 Smallbrook Ln York (17403) ***(G-20367)***

ADM, Camp Hill *Also called Archer-Daniels-Midland Company* ***(G-2491)***

ADM, Langhorne *Also called Archer-Daniels-Midland Company* ***(G-9278)***

ADM Milling Co 717 737-0529
811 Spangler Rd Camp Hill (17011) ***(G-2485)***

ADM Publications Inc 610 565-8895
326 W State St Media (19063) ***(G-10914)***

Admiral Valve LLC 215 386-6508
503 School House Rd Kennett Square (19348) ***(G-8501)***

Admixtures Inc (PA) 610 775-0371
200 Furnace Rd Wernersville (19565) ***(G-19483)***

Adomis Industrial Mch Maint 717 244-0716
1812 Snyder Corner Rd Windsor (17366) ***(G-20195)***

Adrenalation Inc 215 324-3412
4900 N 20th St Philadelphia (19144) ***(G-13346)***

ADS, Allentown *Also called American Dental Supply Inc* ***(G-134)***

ADS By Phone, Canonsburg *Also called Observer Publishing Company* ***(G-2614)***

ADS Environmental Services, Lemoyne *Also called ADS LLC* ***(G-9740)***

ADS LLC 717 554-7552
319 S 3rd St Lowr 3 Lemoyne (17043) ***(G-9740)***

Ads/Transicoil, Collegeville *Also called Transicoil LLC* ***(G-3397)***

Advance Auto Parts, Reading *Also called Advance Stores Company Inc* ***(G-16311)***

Advance Central Services PA 717 255-8400
1900 Patriot Dr Mechanicsburg (17050) ***(G-10816)***

Advance Graphics Eqp of York 717 292-9183
4700 Raycom Rd Dover (17315) ***(G-4183)***

Advance Publications (HQ) 717 582-4305
51 Church St New Bloomfield (17068) ***(G-12029)***

Advance Publications 717 436-8206
Old Rte 22 W Mifflintown (17059) ***(G-11108)***

Advance Sign Company LLC 412 481-6990
1010 Saw Mill Run Blvd Pittsburgh (15226) ***(G-14650)***

Advance Signs & Awnings, Pittsburgh *Also called Advance Sign Company LLC* ***(G-14650)***

Advance Stores Company Inc 610 939-0120
3409 N 5th Street Hwy Reading (19605) ***(G-16311)***

Advance Transit Mix Inc 610 461-2182
613 W Oak Ln Glenolden (19036) ***(G-6471)***

Advanced Acoustic Concepts LLC 724 434-5100
1080 Eberly Way Lemont Furnace (15456) ***(G-9732)***

Advanced Alloy Dvsion/Nmc Corp 724 266-8770
2305 Duss Ave Ambridge (15003) ***(G-605)***

Advanced Asphalt LLC 717 965-2406
59 Kelly Rd New Oxford (17350) ***(G-12402)***

Advanced Automated Contrls Inc, Lake Ariel *Also called Advanced Automated Controls Co* ***(G-8887)***

Advanced Automated Controls Co 570 842-5842
473 Easton Tpke Lake Ariel (18436) ***(G-8887)***

Advanced Avionics Inc 215 441-0449
607 Louis Dr Ste G Warminster (18974) ***(G-18821)***

Advanced Building Products (PA) 717 661-7520
132 Ashmore Dr Leola (17540) ***(G-9766)***

Advanced Bulk & Conveying Inc (PA) 724 588-9327
59 W Main St Greenville (16125) ***(G-6736)***

Advanced Bulk & Conveying Inc 724 588-9327
15 S Water St Greenville (16125) ***(G-6737)***

Advanced Carbide Grinding Inc 724 537-3393
5369 Route 982 Derry (15627) ***(G-4099)***

Advanced Carbide Tool Company (PA) 267 960-1222
1385 Industrial Blvd Southampton (18966) ***(G-17797)***

Advanced Carbon Tech Inc 610 682-1086
220 N Main St Ste 4 Topton (19562) ***(G-18409)***

Advanced Cast Stone Inc Inc 817 572-0018
711 Beaver Rd Girard (16417) ***(G-6383)***

Advanced Cnstr Estimating LLC 724 747-7032
240 Center Church Rd Mc Murray (15317) ***(G-10643)***

Advanced Cnstr Robotics Inc (PA) 412 756-3360
3812 William Flynn Hwy Allison Park (15101) ***(G-445)***

Advanced Coating Technology, Mechanicsburg *Also called Turri Associates Incorporated* ***(G-10900)***

Advanced Coil Industries 724 225-1885
175 Plumpton Ave Washington (15301) ***(G-19145)***

Advanced Color Graphics 814 235-1200
14660 Happy Hills Rd Huntingdon (16652) ***(G-7937)***

Advanced Composite Pdts Inc 717 232-8237
1740 Mulberry St Harrisburg (17104) ***(G-7083)***

Advanced Controls Inc 724 776-0224
243 Peace St Cranberry Township (16066) ***(G-3799)***

Advanced Controls Inc 412 322-0991
700 River Ave Ste 520 Pittsburgh (15212) ***(G-14651)***

Advanced Cooling Tech Inc 717 208-2612
1046 New Holland Ave Lancaster (17601) ***(G-8921)***

Advanced Design and Ctrl Corp 215 723-7200
535 Hagey Rd Souderton (18964) ***(G-17720)***

Advanced Door Service, Lansdale *Also called Overhead Door Corporation* ***(G-9396)***

Advanced Door Technologies Inc 570 421-5929
34 N Crystal St East Stroudsburg (18301) ***(G-4603)***

Advanced Drainage Systems Inc 570 546-7686
173 Industrial Pkwy Muncy (17756) ***(G-11805)***

Advanced Education Service 717 545-8633
3820 Walnut St Harrisburg (17109) ***(G-7084)***

Advanced Electrocircuits Corp 412 278-5200
750 Trumbull Dr Pittsburgh (15205) ***(G-14652)***

Advanced Electronics Systems (PA) 717 263-5681
2005 Lincoln Way E Chambersburg (17202) ***(G-2897)***

Advanced Enviromation Inc 610 422-3770
18 W Poplar St Fleetwood (19522) ***(G-5967)***

Advanced Equipment Sales, Souderton *Also called Advanced Design and Ctrl Corp* ***(G-17720)***

Advanced Fabrication Svcs Inc 717 763-0286
420 Oak St Lemoyne (17043) ***(G-9741)***

Advanced Feedscrews Inc 724 924-9877
3307 Us 422 New Castle (16101) ***(G-12054)***

Advanced Finishing Usa Inc 814 474-5200
7401 Klier Dr Fairview (16415) ***(G-5810)***

Advanced Fluid Connectors, Emigsville *Also called R/W Connection Inc* ***(G-4998)***

Advanced Graphic Services, Dover *Also called Advance Graphics Eqp of York* ***(G-4183)***

Advanced Industrial Svcs Inc 717 764-9811
3250 N Susquehanna Trl York (17406) *(G-20368)*

Advanced Industrial Tech Corp 201 483-7235
30 Goldfields Ave Langhorne (19047) *(G-9273)*

Advanced Integration Group Inc 412 722-0065
1 Mccormick Rd Ste A Mc Kees Rocks (15136) *(G-10602)*

Advanced Laser Printer S 717 764-3272
40 Aberdeen Rd York (17406) *(G-20369)*

Advanced Lubrication Spc, Bensalem *Also called Advanced Lubrication Spc Inc (G-1144)*

Advanced Lubrication Spc Inc (PA) 215 244-2114
420 Imperial Ct Bensalem (19020) *(G-1144)*

Advanced Machine Systems Inc 610 837-8677
7286 Penn Dr Bath (18014) *(G-949)*

Advanced Machine Technologies 717 871-9724
19 Russet Ln Millersville (17551) *(G-11209)*

Advanced Machining Tech 215 672-4899
220 Jacksonville Rd Hatboro (19040) *(G-7265)*

Advanced McRo Cmpt Specialists 215 773-9700
5100 Campus Dr Ste 140 Plymouth Meeting (19462) *(G-15827)*

Advanced Metal Coatings Inc 570 538-1249
1200a Matthew St Watsontown (17777) *(G-19273)*

Advanced Metals Group LLC (PA) 610 408-8006
18 Mystic Ln Malvern (19355) *(G-10180)*

Advanced Metals Machining, Olyphant *Also called Advanced Precision Pdts LLC (G-12983)*

Advanced Mfg Tech Inc 724 327-3001
9001 Corporate Cir Export (15632) *(G-5588)*

Advanced Mobile Group LLC 215 489-2538
301 S Main St Ste 1n Doylestown (18901) *(G-4268)*

Advanced Mobile Power Systems 610 440-0195
876 Barbara Dr Coplay (18037) *(G-3638)*

Advanced Mold Technologies 814 899-1233
2011 E 30th St Erie (16510) *(G-5174)*

Advanced Network Products Inc 215 572-0111
33 E Glenside Ave Glenside (19038) *(G-6503)*

Advanced PDT Design & Mfg Inc 610 380-9140
735 Fox Chase Ste 107 Coatesville (19320) *(G-3284)*

Advanced Photonic Sciences, Friendsville *Also called Snake Creek Lasers LLC (G-6230)*

Advanced Plasma Solutions 267 679-4077
200 Sherwood Dr Reading (19606) *(G-16312)*

Advanced Plasma Solutions Inc 484 568-4942
24 Purdue Dr Richboro (18954) *(G-16672)*

Advanced Plastix Injection Mol 215 453-7808
2819 Creek Rd Perkasie (18944) *(G-13265)*

Advanced Polymer Coatings Inc (PA) 215 943-1466
6000 Hibbs Ln Levittown (19057) *(G-9812)*

Advanced Powder Products Inc 814 342-5898
301 Enterprise Dr Philipsburg (16866) *(G-14507)*

Advanced Precision Pdts LLC 570 487-2830
1159 Mid Valley Dr Olyphant (18447) *(G-12983)*

Advanced Processes Inc 724 266-7274
2097 Duss Ave Ambridge (15003) *(G-606)*

Advanced Pstioning Systems Inc 717 582-3915
184 Butcher Shop Ln Elliottsburg (17024) *(G-4918)*

Advanced Pultrusions LLC 412 466-8611
1575 Lebanon School Rd West Mifflin (15122) *(G-19735)*

Advanced Research Systems Inc 610 967-2120
7476 Industrial Park Way Macungie (18062) *(G-10138)*

Advanced Scientifics Inc 717 692-2104
163 Research Ln Millersburg (17061) *(G-11186)*

Advanced Skin Technologies Inc (PA) 610 488-7643
7143 Bernville Rd Bernville (19506) *(G-1295)*

Advanced Software Inc 215 369-7800
301 Oxford Valley Rd Yardley (19067) *(G-20293)*

Advanced Solutions Network LLC 814 464-0791
5368 Kuhl Rd Erie (16510) *(G-5175)*

Advanced Sports Inc (HQ) 215 824-3854
10940 Dutton Rd Philadelphia (19154) *(G-13347)*

Advanced Sports International, Philadelphia *Also called Advanced Sports Inc (G-13347)*

Advanced Stair Systems - Penns 215 256-7981
1547 Gehman Rd Harleysville (19438) *(G-7013)*

Advanced Systems Technologies 610 682-0610
3 N Main St Fl 1 Topton (19562) *(G-18410)*

Advanced Technical Peddler Inc 610 689-4017
112 Edgewood Rd Boyertown (19512) *(G-1893)*

Advanced Technology Labs Inc (PA) 215 355-8111
12 E Georgianna Dr Richboro (18954) *(G-16673)*

Advanced Tex Composites Inc 570 207-7000
700 E Parker St Scranton (18509) *(G-17206)*

Advanced Thermal Hydronics 610 473-1036
203 W Spring St Boyertown (19512) *(G-1894)*

Advanced Thermal Solutions LLC 610 966-2500
154 E Minor St Emmaus (18049) *(G-5018)*

Advanced Trim and Kitchens, Kinzers *Also called Advanced Trim Specialties (G-8731)*

Advanced Trim Specialties 717 442-8098
4966 Lincoln Hwy Kinzers (17535) *(G-8731)*

Advanced Valve Design Inc 610 435-8820
480 Mickley Rd Whitehall (18052) *(G-19860)*

Advanced VSR Technology 215 366-3315
3615 Emerald St Philadelphia (19134) *(G-13348)*

Advanced Welding Tech Inc 814 899-3584
3110 Pearl Ave Erie (16510) *(G-5176)*

Advancing Alternative, Lancaster *Also called Integrated Metal Products Inc (G-9058)*

Advansix Frankford Plant, Philadelphia *Also called Advansix Inc (G-13349)*

Advansix Inc 215 533-3000
2501 Margaret St Philadelphia (19137) *(G-13349)*

Advantage Learning Technology 610 217-8022
6255 Robin Ln Coopersburg (18036) *(G-3624)*

Advantage Metal Powders Inc 814 772-5363
44 Spleen Rd Ridgway (15853) *(G-16691)*

Advantage Millwork Inc 610 925-2785
529 Rosedale Rd Ste 103 Kennett Square (19348) *(G-8502)*

Advantage Mold & Design, Meadville *Also called Theodore W Styborski (G-10800)*

Advantage Precision Plastics 814 337-8535
10246 Mercer Pike Meadville (16335) *(G-10696)*

Advantage Puck Technologies 814 664-4810
1 Plastics Rd Ste 6 Corry (16407) *(G-3742)*

Advantage Tool & Die-Div, Bethel Park *Also called Instrumentation Industries Inc (G-1418)*

Advantapure Division, Southampton *Also called Newage Industries Inc (G-17827)*

Advantech US Inc 412 706-5400
333 4th St Beaver (15009) *(G-977)*

Advent Design Corporation 215 781-0500
925 Canal St Ste 1301 Bristol (19007) *(G-2104)*

Adventek Corporation 215 736-0961
10 Headley Pl Levittown (19054) *(G-9813)*

Adventure Systems Inc 717 351-7177
172 Orlan Rd New Holland (17557) *(G-12226)*

Advertising Specialty Inst Inc (PA) 800 546-1350
4800 E Street Rd Ste 100a Feasterville Trevose (19053) *(G-5883)*

Advertsing Otsourcing Svcs LLC 570 793-2000
106 S Main St Fl 1 Wilkes Barre (18701) *(G-19903)*

Advision Signs Inc 412 788-8440
4735 Campbells Run Rd Pittsburgh (15205) *(G-14653)*

Ae Polysilicon Corporation (PA) 215 337-8183
150 Roebling Rd Fairless Hills (19030) *(G-5771)*

AEC Services Company LLC 610 246-6470
525 Plymouth Rd Ste 320 Plymouth Meeting (19462) *(G-15828)*

Aeco Inc 215 335-2974
4923 Arendell Ave 25 Philadelphia (19114) *(G-13350)*

Aeco Service Inc 610 372-0561
1214 Grandview Cir Pottstown (19465) *(G-15941)*

AEG Holdings Inc 412 262-2830
311 Rouser Rd Coraopolis (15108) *(G-3654)*

Aegis Industrial Software Corp (PA) 215 773-3571
5 Walnut Grove Dr Ste 320 Horsham (19044) *(G-7780)*

Aegis Software, Horsham *Also called Aegis Industrial Software Corp (G-7780)*

Aegis Software Corporation 724 325-5595
3840 Beatty Ct Murrysville (15668) *(G-11845)*

Aegis Technologies Inc 610 676-0300
98 Highland Ave Oaks (19456) *(G-12931)*

Aella Industries Corporation 610 399-9086
45 Milton Dr Aston (19014) *(G-749)*

Aeo Management Co 724 776-4857
150 Thorn Hill Rd Warrendale (15086) *(G-19067)*

Aeo Management Co (HQ) 412 432-3300
77 Hot Metal St Pittsburgh (15203) *(G-14654)*

Aerial Applications, Philadelphia *Also called Robotic Services Inc (G-14255)*

Aerial Signs & Awnings Inc 610 494-1415
2333 Concord Rd Chester (19013) *(G-3037)*

Aerix Industries, Allentown *Also called Cellular Concrete LLC (G-166)*

Aero Tool & Supply Division, Canonsburg *Also called Cannon Tool Company (G-2556)*

Aerofab, Nicktown *Also called Aeroparts Fabg & Machining Inc (G-12618)*

Aeroparts Fabg & Machining Inc 814 948-6015
722 Ridge Rd Nicktown (15762) *(G-12618)*

Aeroprint Graphics Inc 215 752-1089
134 W Lincoln Hwy Rear Langhorne (19047) *(G-9274)*

Aerospace Division, Jenkintown *Also called SPS Technologies LLC (G-8303)*

Aerospace Division, Erie *Also called Lord Corporation (G-5372)*

Aerotech Inc (PA) 412 963-7470
101 Zeta Dr Pittsburgh (15238) *(G-14655)*

Aerowings, Fayetteville *Also called Speed Partz LLC (G-5878)*

Aerzen USA Corp (HQ) 610 380-0244
108 Independence Way Coatesville (19320) *(G-3285)*

Aerzener Maschinenfabrik, Coatesville *Also called Aerzen USA Corp (G-3285)*

AES Drilling Fluids LLC 724 743-2934
4 Grandview Cir Canonsburg (15317) *(G-2533)*

Aesculap Biologics LLC 610 984-9000
9999 Hamilton Blvd Breinigsville (18031) *(G-2004)*

Aesculap Implant Systems LLC 610 984-9404
9999 Hamilton Blvd # 120 Breinigsville (18031) *(G-2005)*

Aesculap Implant Systems LLC (HQ) 610 984-9000
3773 Corp Pkwy Ste 200 Center Valley (18034) *(G-2823)*

Aeson Flooring, Philadelphia *Also called Stagestep Inc (G-14339)*

Aetna Felt Corp 610 791-0900
2401 W Emaus Ave Allentown (18103) *(G-117)*

Aetna Machine Company 814 425-3881
203 N Franklin St Cochranton (16314) *(G-3334)*

Aevi Genomic Medicine Inc (PA).............................610 254-4201
　435 Devon Park Dr Ste 715 Wayne (19087) *(G-19294)*

Afab Industrial Services Inc...................................215 245-1280
　350 Camer Dr Bensalem (19020) *(G-1145)*

Afca Company Inc..215 425-2300
　2901 Hedley St Philadelphia (19137) *(G-13351)*

Afco, Chambersburg *Also called Alex C Fergusson LLC (G-2899)*

Afco C&S LLC..717 264-9147
　5121 Coffey Ave Chambersburg (17201) *(G-2898)*

Afco Energy Production Co Inc................................724 463-3350
　857 Cameron Bottom Rd Barnesboro (15714) *(G-937)*

Affil Distributors..610 977-3100
　440 E Swedesford Rd # 1000 Wayne (19087) *(G-19295)*

Affimex Code Wire, Verona *Also called Affival Inc (G-18745)*

Affival Inc (HQ)...412 826-9430
　1967 Eastern Ave Verona (15147) *(G-18745)*

Affival Inc..412 826-9430
　1967 Eastern Ave Verona (15147) *(G-18746)*

Affordable Home Fuel LLC.....................................610 847-0972
　89 Oak Grove Rd Ottsville (18942) *(G-13058)*

Affordable Signs Co Inc...215 671-0646
　9986 Gantry Rd Ste 2 Philadelphia (19115) *(G-13352)*

AFI, Lancaster *Also called Armstrong Flooring Inc (G-8940)*

AFP Advanced Food Products LLC (HQ).................717 355-8667
　402 S Custer Ave New Holland (17557) *(G-12227)*

AFP Advanced Food Products LLC..........................717 354-6560
　158 W Jackson St New Holland (17557) *(G-12228)*

African Cultural Art Forum LLC..............................215 476-0680
　221 S 52nd St Philadelphia (19139) *(G-13353)*

Africvan American Publications, Chalfont *Also called American Culture Publs LLC (G-2863)*

Afs Energy Systems, Lemoyne *Also called Advanced Fabrication Svcs Inc (G-9741)*

Afterglo Lighting Co Inc..215 355-7942
　1825 Stout Dr Warminster (18974) *(G-18822)*

Afterprint Services Inc..215 674-3082
　1800 Mearns Rd Ste G Warminster (18974) *(G-18823)*

Afton Landscape Supply, Erie *Also called Afton Trucking Inc (G-5177)*

Afton Trucking Inc...814 825-7449
　8955 Wattsburg Rd Erie (16509) *(G-5177)*

AG Information Systems, Mountville *Also called Infotechnologies Inc (G-11796)*

Agape Precision Mfg LLC.......................................484 704-2601
　320 Circle Of Progress Dr # 108 Pottstown (19464) *(G-15961)*

Agape Water Solutions Inc.....................................215 631-7035
　1567 Gehman Rd Harleysville (19438) *(G-7014)*

Agar Welding Service & Stl Sup..............................717 532-1000
　93 Firehouse Rd Walnut Bottom (17266) *(G-18788)*

Agas Mfg Inc..212 777-1178
　2701 E Tioga St Philadelphia (19134) *(G-13354)*

AGC Chemicals Americas Inc.................................610 380-6200
　255 S Bailey Rd Downingtown (19335) *(G-4209)*

AGC Flat Glass North Amer Inc..............................215 538-9424
　480 California Rd Quakertown (18951) *(G-16167)*

Agd Products Inc..215 682-9643
　952 Thomas Dr Warminster (18974) *(G-18824)*

Age-Craft Manufacturing Inc (PA)..........................724 838-5580
　45 Madison Ave Greensburg (15601) *(G-6648)*

Agent Dynamics Inc..412 441-4604
　300 S Dallas Ave Pittsburgh (15208) *(G-14656)*

Agere Systems Inc..610 712-1000
　1110 American Pkwy Ne Allentown (18109) *(G-118)*

Aggregates Equipment Inc.....................................717 656-2131
　9 Horseshoe Rd Leola (17540) *(G-9767)*

Agi, Exton *Also called Analytical Graphics Inc (G-5643)*

Agile Displays, Allentown *Also called Solar Technology Inc (G-396)*

Agileswitch LLC..484 483-3256
　2002 Ludlow St Fl 2 Philadelphia (19103) *(G-13355)*

Ago Design Group, Jermyn *Also called Goliath Development LLC (G-8306)*

Agostini Bakery Inc...570 457-2021
　1216 S Main St Old Forge (18518) *(G-12962)*

AGR International Inc..724 482-2164
　603 Evans City Rd Butler (16001) *(G-2371)*

Agri Marketing Inc..717 335-0379
　1368 W Route 897 Denver (17517) *(G-4066)*

Agri Welding Service Inc..570 437-3330
　2468 Continental Blvd Danville (17821) *(G-3996)*

Agri-Dynamics Inc..610 250-9280
　6574 S Delaware Dr Martins Creek (18063) *(G-10517)*

Agricultural Commodities Inc.................................717 624-6858
　1585 Granite Station Rd Gettysburg (17325) *(G-6282)*

Agripower Mfg & Svcs Inc.....................................814 781-1009
　230 State St Saint Marys (15857) *(G-16946)*

Agrium Advanced Tech US Inc...............................724 865-9180
　121 Pflugh Rd Butler (16001) *(G-2372)*

Agrofresh Solutions Inc (PA).................................267 317-9139
　510-530 Wlnut St Ste 1350 Philadelphia (19106) *(G-13356)*

Agronomy Center, The, Thompsontown *Also called Klingler Incorporated (G-18347)*

Agsalt Processing...717 632-9144
　530 Storms Store Rd Gettysburg (17325) *(G-6283)*

Agusta Westland, Philadelphia *Also called Agustawestland Tilt-Rotor LLC (G-13357)*

Agustawestland Tilt-Rotor LLC...............................215 281-1400
　3076 Red Lion Rd Philadelphia (19114) *(G-13357)*

Agustwstland Philadelphia Corp (HQ).....................215 281-1400
　3050 Red Lion Rd Philadelphia (19114) *(G-13358)*

Agway, Wellsboro *Also called Hampsons Farm & Garden Inc (G-19464)*

Ahf Holding Inc (PA)...800 233-3823
　2500 Columbia Ave Lancaster (17603) *(G-8922)*

Ahf Products LLC...800 233-3823
　2500 Columbia Ave Lancaster (17603) *(G-8923)*

Ahlstrom Mount Holly Sprng LLC (HQ)...................717 486-3438
　122 W Butler St Mount Holly Springs (17065) *(G-11631)*

Ahlstrom Mount Holly Sprng LLC...........................717 486-3438
　Junction 34 94 Yates St 34 Junction Mount Holly Springs (17065) *(G-11632)*

Ahs Acquisition, Chambersburg *Also called Alternate Heating Systems LLC (G-2901)*

Aht Inc (HQ)...724 445-2155
　1024 Kittanning Pike Chicora (16025) *(G-3125)*

Ai Control Systems Inc..610 921-9670
　90 Water St Reading (19605) *(G-16313)*

Aiellos International Inc...717 451-3910
　60 Shamrock Ln New Oxford (17350) *(G-12403)*

Aii Acquisition LLC (HQ)..412 394-2800
　1000 Six Ppg Pl Pittsburgh (15222) *(G-14657)*

Aii Acquisition LLC...724 226-5947
　100 River Rd Brackenridge (15014) *(G-1936)*

Aimee & Darias Doll Outlet.....................................717 687-8118
　2682 Lincoln Hwy E Ste A Ronks (17572) *(G-16802)*

Aimm, Windsor *Also called Adomis Industrial Mch Maint (G-20195)*

AIN Plastics...717 291-9300
　499 Running Pump Rd # 116 Lancaster (17601) *(G-8924)*

Ainsworth Pet Ntrtn Parent LLC (HQ)......................814 724-7710
　18746 Mill St Meadville (16335) *(G-10697)*

Ainsworth Pet Nutrition, Meadville *Also called Dpc Pet Specialties LLC (G-10719)*

Ainsworth Pet Nutrition LLC (HQ)...........................814 724-7710
　18746 Mill St Meadville (16335) *(G-10698)*

Ainsworth Pet Nutrition LLC...................................814 724-7710
　18746 Mill St Meadville (16335) *(G-10699)*

Air Conway Inc...610 534-0500
　1116 Macdade Blvd Ste 6 Collingdale (19023) *(G-3402)*

Air Dynmics Indus Systems Corp............................717 854-4050
　180 Roosevelt Ave York (17401) *(G-20370)*

Air Liquid Systems Inc..724 834-8090
　315 Fire Station Rd Forbes Road (15633) *(G-6040)*

Air Liquide America LP...610 383-5500
　Modena Rd Coatesville (19320) *(G-3286)*

Air Liquide Electronics US LP.................................215 428-4600
　19 Steel Rd W Morrisville (19067) *(G-11553)*

Air Liquide Electronics US LP.................................570 897-2000
　103 Demi Rd Mount Bethel (18343) *(G-11606)*

Air Liquide Electronics US LP.................................215 736-2796
　19 Steel Rd W Morrisville (19067) *(G-11554)*

Air Parts of Lock Haven...570 748-0823
　1084 E Water St Lock Haven (17745) *(G-10083)*

Air Products and Chemicals Inc (PA).......................610 481-4911
　7201 Hamilton Blvd Allentown (18195) *(G-119)*

Air Products and Chemicals Inc..............................610 317-8706
　1025 E Market St Bethlehem (18017) *(G-1445)*

Air Products and Chemicals Inc..............................724 226-4434
　500 Freeport Rd Creighton (15030) *(G-3879)*

Air Products and Chemicals Inc..............................717 291-1617
　3250 Hempland Rd Lancaster (17601) *(G-8925)*

Air Products and Chemicals Inc..............................610 317-8715
　1011 E Market St Bethlehem (18017) *(G-1446)*

Air Products and Chemicals Inc..............................570 467-2981
　357 Marian Ave Tamaqua (18252) *(G-18208)*

Air Products and Chemicals Inc..............................610 395-2101
　7331 William Ave Allentown (18106) *(G-120)*

Air Products and Chemicals Inc..............................610 481-2057
　645 Hamilton St Allentown (18101) *(G-121)*

Air Products and Chemicals Inc..............................610 481-3706
　1919 Vultee St Allentown (18103) *(G-122)*

Air Products and Chemicals Inc..............................724 266-1563
　360 Leetsdale Indus Dr Leetsdale (15056) *(G-9677)*

Air Products Corporation (PA).................................800 345-8207
　118 Summit Dr Exton (19341) *(G-5637)*

Air Products LLC..610 481-4911
　7201 Hamilton Blvd Allentown (18195) *(G-123)*

Air Turbine Propeller Company (PA).........................724 452-9540
　22329 Perry Hwy Zelienople (16063) *(G-20787)*

Air Ventures Balloon Rides.....................................610 827-2138
　2145 Conestoga Rd Chester Springs (19425) *(G-3070)*

Air-Con Inc..814 838-6373
　4835 W 23rd St Erie (16506) *(G-5178)*

Air-Scent International..412 252-2000
　290a Alpha Dr Pittsburgh (15238) *(G-14658)*

Air/Tak Inc..724 297-3416
　107 W Main St Worthington (16262) *(G-20226)*

Airclic Inc (HQ)..215 504-0560
　900 Northbrook Dr Ste 100 Trevose (19053) *(G-18485)*

Aircon Filter Manufacturing Co, Philadelphia *Also called Aircon Filter Sales & Svc Co (G-13359)*

Aircon Filter Sales & Svc Co 215 922-7727
  441 Green St Philadelphia (19123) *(G-13359)*

Aircooled Racing and Parts 717 432-4116
  1560 Old Mountain Rd Wellsville (17365) *(G-19476)*

Aircraft Instruments Company 215 348-5274
  4039 Skyron Dr Doylestown (18902) *(G-4269)*

Airgas Safety Inc (HQ) 215 826-9000
  2501 Green Ln Levittown (19057) *(G-9814)*

Airgas Usa LLC 814 437-2431
  984 Mercer Rd Franklin (16323) *(G-6113)*

Airgas Usa LLC 215 766-8860
  6141 Easton Rd Plumsteadville (18949) *(G-15806)*

Airgreen LLC 610 209-8067
  515 Highland Rd West Chester (19380) *(G-19495)*

Airlite Plastics Co 610 759-0280
  2860 Bath Pike Nazareth (18064) *(G-11952)*

Airopek, Manchester Also called Pvc Container Corporation *(G-10363)*

Airos Medical Inc 866 991-6956
  2501 Monroe Blvd Ste 1200 Audubon (19403) *(G-822)*

Airscent International, Pittsburgh Also called Alpha Aromatics Inc *(G-14686)*

Airsources Inc 610 983-0102
  17 Country Ln Malvern (19355) *(G-10181)*

Airtek Inc (PA) 412 351-3837
  76 Clair St Irwin (15642) *(G-8141)*

Ais, Shrewsbury Also called Ashland Industrial Svcs LLC *(G-17581)*

AJ Kane Incorporated 215 953-5152
  92 Railroad Dr Warminster (18974) *(G-18825)*

Aj Pallet LLC 717 597-3545
  300 Walnut St Waynesboro (17268) *(G-19395)*

Ajax Comb Company, Cresson Also called Antonios Manufacturing Inc *(G-3897)*

Ajax Electric Company (PA) 215 947-8500
  60 Tomlinson Rd Huntingdon Valley (19006) *(G-7962)*

Ajax Xray Inc 570 888-6605
  150 Bradford St Sayre (18840) *(G-17109)*

Ajay Fuel Inc 570 223-1580
  2579 Milford Rd East Stroudsburg (18301) *(G-4604)*

Ajb Productions, Pittsburgh Also called Minuteman Press South Hills *(G-15295)*

Ajikabe Inc 484 424-9415
  207 Buck Rd Ste 1c Holland (18966) *(G-7639)*

Ajjp Corporation 215 968-6677
  305 Pheasant Run Newtown (18940) *(G-12495)*

Ajm Electric Inc 610 494-5735
  2333 Concord Rd Chester Township (19013) *(G-3088)*

AJW Jamaican and American Food, Philadelphia Also called William Plange *(G-14475)*

AK Steel Corporation 724 284-2854
  210 Pittsburgh Rd Butler (16001) *(G-2373)*

Akamara Therapeutics Inc 617 888-9191
  3411 Chestnut St Apt 602 Philadelphia (19104) *(G-13360)*

Akas Tex LLC 215 244-2589
  1360 Adams Rd Bensalem (19020) *(G-1146)*

Akas Textiles & Lamination, Bensalem Also called Akas Tex LLC *(G-1146)*

Akers National Roll Company (HQ) 724 697-4533
  400 Railroad Ave Avonmore (15618) *(G-862)*

Akj Industries Inc 412 233-7222
  1500 N State St Clairton (15025) *(G-3146)*

Akzo Nobel Chemicals Inc 724 258-6200
  829 Route 481 Monongahela (15063) *(G-11303)*

Akzo Nobel Coatings Inc 610 372-3600
  150 Columbia Ave Reading (19601) *(G-16314)*

Akzo Nobel Inc 312 544-7000
  150 Columbia Ave Reading (19601) *(G-16315)*

Al Dia Newspaper Inc 215 569-4666
  1835 Market St Ste 450 Philadelphia (19103) *(G-13361)*

Al Kaczmarczyk 724 775-1366
  3185 Bennetts Run Rd Beaver Falls (15010) *(G-996)*

Al Lorenzi Lumber Co Inc (PA) 724 222-6100
  3928 Washington Rd Canonsburg (15317) *(G-2534)*

Al Marwa LLC 215 536-6050
  670 E Cherry Rd Quakertown (18951) *(G-16168)*

Al May Manufacturing Jewelers 412 391-8736
  2309 Casswell Dr Bethel Park (15102) *(G-1401)*

Al Tedeschi 724 746-3755
  805 S Central Ave Canonsburg (15317) *(G-2535)*

Al Xander Co Inc (PA) 814 665-8268
  36 E South St Corry (16407) *(G-3743)*

Al's Awning Shop & Canvas Pdts, Erie Also called Als Awning Shop Inc *(G-5183)*

Al's Machining, Kersey Also called Alan Mazzaferro *(G-8553)*

Alacer Corp 717 258-2000
  219 Allen Rd Ste 300 Carlisle (17013) *(G-2688)*

Alan Mazzaferro 814 885-6744
  375 Main St Kersey (15846) *(G-8553)*

Alan Pepper Designs 412 244-9299
  827 S Trenton Ave Pittsburgh (15221) *(G-14659)*

Alaska Company Inc 570 387-0260
  3162 Columbia Blvd Bloomsburg (17815) *(G-1766)*

Alaska Stoker Stove Inc 570 387-0260
  3162 Columbia Blvd Bloomsburg (17815) *(G-1767)*

Alaska Stove, Bloomsburg Also called Alaska Company Inc *(G-1766)*

Albarell Electric Inc 610 691-7030
  1005c W Lehigh St Bethlehem (18018) *(G-1447)*

Albarell Electric Mtr Repr Sp, Bethlehem Also called Albarell Electric Inc *(G-1447)*

Albemarle Corporation 814 684-4310
  2858 Back Vail Rd Tyrone (16686) *(G-18575)*

Albert C Phy & Sons Inc 215 659-2125
  2290 Wyandotte Rd Willow Grove (19090) *(G-20106)*

Albert Gray 717 436-8585
  Off Rte 32222 Mifflintown (17059) *(G-11109)*

Albert Miller Logging Inc 570 295-4040
  143 Davis Ln Lock Haven (17745) *(G-10084)*

Alberts Custom Shtmtl & Wldg 814 454-4461
  209 E 21st St Erie (16503) *(G-5179)*

Alberts Jennings 215 766-2852
  6184 Easton Rd Pipersville (18947) *(G-14610)*

Alberts Spray Solutions LLC 570 368-6653
  60 Choate Cir Montoursville (17754) *(G-11429)*

Albright Paper & Box Corp 484 524-8424
  198 Popodickon Dr Boyertown (19512) *(G-1895)*

Albright Precision Inc 570 457-5744
  4 Rocky Glen Rd Moosic (18507) *(G-11502)*

Albrighten Industries Inc 724 222-2959
  45 Saint Cloud Rd Eighty Four (15330) *(G-4832)*

Albrights Mill LLC 610 756-6022
  9927 Kistler Valley Rd Kempton (19529) *(G-8489)*

Alcast Metals Inc 215 368-5865
  440 Stump Rd Montgomeryville (18936) *(G-11382)*

Alcatel-Lucent Tech Inc 215 752-1847
  34 Polder Dr Feasterville Trevose (19053) *(G-5884)*

Alchemet Inc 610 566-5964
  202 Highland Ave Wallingford (19086) *(G-18780)*

Alco Fuel Inc 215 638-4800
  2803 Bristol Pike Bensalem (19020) *(G-1147)*

Alcoa, Lancaster Also called Arconic Inc *(G-8938)*

Alcoa, Pittsburgh Also called Reynolds Metals Company LLC *(G-15482)*

Alcoa Business Park LLC (HQ) 412 553-4545
  201 Isabella St Ste 500 Pittsburgh (15212) *(G-14660)*

Alcoa Corporation 412 553-4001
  1590 Omega Dr Pittsburgh (15205) *(G-14661)*

Alcoa Corporation (PA) 412 315-2900
  201 Isabella St Ste 500 Pittsburgh (15212) *(G-14662)*

Alcoa N Amercn Rolled Proudcts 717 393-9641
  1480 Manheim Pike Lancaster (17601) *(G-8926)*

Alcoa Remediation MGT LLC 412 553-4545
  201 Isabella St Ste 500 Pittsburgh (15212) *(G-14663)*

Alcoa South Carolina Inc 412 553-4545
  201 Isabella St Ste 500 Pittsburgh (15212) *(G-14664)*

Alcoa Technical Center LLC 724 337-5300
  859 White Cloud Rd New Kensington (15068) *(G-12322)*

Alcoa Technical Center LLC (HQ) 412 553-4545
  201 Isabella St Ste 500 Pittsburgh (15212) *(G-14665)*

Alcoa USA Corp (HQ) 212 518-5400
  201 Isabella St Ste 500 Pittsburgh (15212) *(G-14666)*

Alcoa USA Corp 412 553-4545
  201 Isabella St Ste 500 Pittsburgh (15212) *(G-14667)*

Alcoa Warrick LLC (HQ) 412 553-4545
  201 Isabella St Ste 500 Pittsburgh (15212) *(G-14668)*

Alcoa Wenatchee LLC (HQ) 412 553-4545
  201 Isabella St Ste 500 Pittsburgh (15212) *(G-14669)*

Alcoa World Alumina LLC (HQ) 412 315-2900
  201 Isabella St Ste 500 Pittsburgh (15212) *(G-14670)*

Alcobra Inc 610 940-1630
  101 W Elm St Ste 350 Conshohocken (19428) *(G-3517)*

Alcolock PA Inc 800 452-1759
  273 Mulberry Dr Ste 2 Mechanicsburg (17050) *(G-10817)*

Alcom Printing Group Inc 215 513-1600
  140 Christopher Ln Harleysville (19438) *(G-7015)*

Alcon Manufacturing Ltd 610 670-3500
  714 Columbia Ave Reading (19608) *(G-16316)*

Alcon Precision Device, Reading Also called Alcon Manufacturing Ltd *(G-16316)*

Alcon Research Ltd 610 670-3500
  714 Columbia Ave Reading (19608) *(G-16317)*

Alden Industries Inc 267 460-8904
  1400 Welsh Rd North Wales (19454) *(G-12787)*

Aldenville Log and Lumberinc 570 785-3141
  936 Creek Dr Prompton (18456) *(G-16109)*

Alderdice Inc 570 996-1609
  524 Sr 4015 Meshoppen (18630) *(G-11005)*

Alderfer Inc (HQ) 215 256-8819
  382 Main St Harleysville (19438) *(G-7016)*

Aldon Food Corporation 484 991-1000
  4461 Township Line Rd Schwenksville (19473) *(G-17172)*

ALe Hydraulic McHy Co LLC 215 547-3351
  6215 Airport Rd Levittown (19057) *(G-9815)*

Aleghaney Mineral, Kittanning Also called Snyder Enterprises Inc *(G-8795)*

Alencon Acquisition Co LLC 484 436-0035
  330 S Warminster Rd # 380 Hatboro (19040) *(G-7266)*

Alencon Systems Inc 610 825-7094
  5150 Campus Dr Plymouth Meeting (19462) *(G-15829)*

A L P H A B E T I C

Alert Enterprises Ltd Lblty Co.................570 373-2821
  1109 Maple St Kulpmont (17834) *(G-8821)*

Alert Security Service, Kulpmont *Also called Alert Enterprises Ltd Lblty Co* *(G-8821)*

Alertone Services Inc.................570 321-5433
  24 W 4th St Williamsport (17701) *(G-19984)*

Alessandro Working Dog, Huntingdon Valley *Also called Hound Dog Corp* *(G-7994)*

Alessi Manufacturing Corp.................610 586-4200
  19 Jackson Ave Collingdale (19023) *(G-3403)*

Alex and Ani LLC.................412 742-4968
  5505 Walnut St Pittsburgh (15232) *(G-14671)*

Alex and Ani LLC.................412 367-1362
  1000 Ross Park Mall Dr Pittsburgh (15237) *(G-14672)*

Alex C Fergusson LLC (PA).................717 264-9147
  5121 Coffey Ave Ste D Chambersburg (17201) *(G-2899)*

Alex Color Company Inc (PA).................570 875-3300
  17th & Market St Ashland (17921) *(G-725)*

Alex Color Company Inc.................570 875-3300
  1638 Market St Ashland (17921) *(G-726)*

Alex Froehlich Packing Co.................814 535-7694
  77 D Street Ext Johnstown (15906) *(G-8349)*

Alexanderwerk Inc.................215 442-0270
  102 Commerce Dr Montgomeryville (18936) *(G-11383)*

Alfa Laval Inc.................717 453-7143
  300 Chestnut St Lykens (17048) *(G-10129)*

Alfa Laval Inc.................610 594-1830
  604 Jeffers Cir Exton (19341) *(G-5638)*

Alfery Sausage, Mc Kees Rocks *Also called Silver Star Meats Inc* *(G-10635)*

Alfred and Sam Italian Bakery.................717 392-6311
  17 Fairview Ave Lancaster (17603) *(G-8927)*

Alfred Angelo - The Brdes Std.................813 872-1881
  1301 Virginia Dr Fort Washington (19034) *(G-6061)*

Alfred Envelope Company Inc.................215 739-1500
  3536 N Mascher St Philadelphia (19140) *(G-13362)*

Alfred Nickles Bakery Inc.................814 471-6913
  131 Mini Mall Rd Ebensburg (15931) *(G-4778)*

Alfred Troilo.................610 544-0115
  434 Kennerly Rd Springfield (19064) *(G-17906)*

Alfred's Beverage, Philadelphia *Also called Alfreds Village Beverage Inc* *(G-13363)*

Alfreds Village Beverage Inc.................215 676-2537
  9218 Ashton Rd Philadelphia (19114) *(G-13363)*

Algorhythm Diagnostics LLC.................312 813-2959
  1125 E Columbia Ave # 201 Philadelphia (19125) *(G-13364)*

ALI-CLE, Philadelphia *Also called American Law Institute* *(G-13385)*

Alibert Industries Inc.................610 872-3900
  1925 Macdade Blvd Fl 1 Woodlyn (19094) *(G-20217)*

Alien Fuel Inc.................609 306-8592
  1220 Linden Ave Yardley (19067) *(G-20294)*

Alig LLC.................570 544-2540
  125 S Delaware Ave Minersville (17954) *(G-11253)*

Aline Components Inc.................215 368-0300
  1830 Tomlinson Rd Kulpsville (19443) *(G-8823)*

Alkab Contract Mfg Inc.................724 335-7050
  843 Industrial Blvd New Kensington (15068) *(G-12323)*

Alkali Beaver Products (PA).................724 709-7857
  25 New York Ave Rochester (15074) *(G-16781)*

All - American Trophy Company.................570 342-2613
  1415 Capouse Ave Scranton (18509) *(G-17207)*

All Aboard Railroad, Lancaster *Also called Barts Pneumatics Corp* *(G-8949)*

All About Eyes, Phoenixville *Also called Rss Optometry LLC* *(G-14577)*

All ADS Up.................412 881-4114
  2606 Brownsville Rd Pittsburgh (15227) *(G-14673)*

All America Threaded Pdts Inc.................317 921-3000
  731 Martha Ave Lancaster (17601) *(G-8928)*

All American Embroidery, Pittsburgh *Also called All American Sweats Inc* *(G-14674)*

All American Homes Colo LLC.................970 587-0544
  4900 Ritter Rd Ste 130 Mechanicsburg (17055) *(G-10818)*

All American Installs.................215 888-0046
  422 Madison Ave Penndel (19047) *(G-13238)*

All American Sweats Inc (PA).................412 922-8999
  15 Robinhood Rd Pittsburgh (15220) *(G-14674)*

All Aspects.................610 292-1955
  800 Stanbridge St Norristown (19401) *(G-12631)*

All Climate Servicing.................570 686-4629
  103 Dove Ct Milford (18337) *(G-11153)*

All Floor Supplies Inc.................412 793-6421
  168 Dexter Dr Monroeville (15146) *(G-11323)*

All Metal Fabricating Co Inc.................724 925-3537
  521 N 7th St Youngwood (15697) *(G-20777)*

All Pallet Inc.................610 614-1905
  198 W Mountain Rd Wind Gap (18091) *(G-20164)*

All Pro Embroidery Inc.................412 942-0735
  4854 Streets Run Rd Pittsburgh (15236) *(G-14675)*

All So Sites & Bites, Narberth *Also called Infomat Associates Inc* *(G-11911)*

All Star Pest Servcies LLC.................215 828-9099
  4351 N Marshall St Philadelphia (19140) *(G-13365)*

All State Signs, Philadelphia *Also called Affordable Signs Co Inc* *(G-13352)*

All Steel Supply Inc.................215 672-0883
  412 Caredean Dr Horsham (19044) *(G-7781)*

All Tech-D Out LLC.................610 814-0888
  1155 Union Blvd Allentown (18109) *(G-124)*

All Type Fence Co Inc (PA).................610 718-1151
  1600 W Schuylkill Rd Douglassville (19518) *(G-4166)*

All Weld Steel Co Inc.................215 884-6985
  3041 Chestnut Ave Glenside (19038) *(G-6504)*

All-American Holdings LLc (PA).................814 438-7616
  217 Titusville Rd Union City (16438) *(G-18605)*

All-American Hose LLC.................814 438-7616
  6424 W Ridge Rd Erie (16506) *(G-5180)*

All-American Hose LLC.................814 838-3381
  6420 W Ridge Rd Erie (16506) *(G-5181)*

All-Brite Metal Finishing, Philadelphia *Also called Jaws Inc* *(G-13891)*

All-Clad Holdings Inc.................724 745-8300
  424 Morganza Rd Canonsburg (15317) *(G-2536)*

All-Clad Metalcrafters LLC (HQ).................724 745-8300
  424 Morganza Rd Canonsburg (15317) *(G-2537)*

All-Clad Metalcrafters LLC.................724 745-8300
  424 Morganza Rd Canonsburg (15317) *(G-2538)*

All-Fill Corporation.................866 255-3455
  418 Creamery Way Exton (19341) *(G-5639)*

All-Fill Inc.................610 524-7350
  418 Creamery Way Exton (19341) *(G-5640)*

All-Pro, Horsham *Also called Steam Mad Carpet Cleaners Inc* *(G-7853)*

All-Sign Graphics & Design.................814 467-9995
  148 Minnow Creek Ln 1 Windber (15963) *(G-20177)*

All-Size Corrugated, Columbia *Also called Buckeye Corrugated Inc* *(G-3432)*

All-Steel Fabricators Co Inc..................610 687-2267
  292 Sunset Rd Wayne (19087) *(G-19296)*

Allan A Myers.................610 584-6020
  1805 Berks Rd Worcester (19490) *(G-20223)*

Allan Myers Inc.................717 442-4191
  47 Mcilvaine Rd Paradise (17562) *(G-13152)*

Allan Myers Management Inc (PA).................717 656-2411
  330 Quarry Rd Leola (17540) *(G-9768)*

Allan Myers Management Inc.................717 548-2191
  219 Quarry Rd Peach Bottom (17563) *(G-13195)*

Allan Myers Materials Inc (HQ).................610 560-7900
  1805 Berks Rd Worcester (19355) *(G-20222)*

Allan Myers Materials Inc..................610 442-4191
  4045 State Rd Devault (19432) *(G-4110)*

Allcams Machine Co.................610 534-9004
  116 Sycamore Ave Folsom (19033) *(G-6022)*

ALLE-KISKI INDUSTRIES, Leechburg *Also called Kiski Precision Industries LLC* *(G-9646)*

Allied, Ellwood City *Also called Appalachian Ltg Systems Inc* *(G-4927)*

Allegeny Mountain Hardwood, Emlenton *Also called Hickman Lumber Company* *(G-5011)*

Allegheny Alloys.................412 833-9733
  1700 N Highland Rd # 208 Pittsburgh (15241) *(G-14676)*

Allegheny Asphalt Services LLC.................724 732-6637
  921 Pine St Ambridge (15003) *(G-607)*

Allegheny Blending Tech Inc.................814 772-9279
  143 Maine Ln Ridgway (15853) *(G-16692)*

Allegheny Coatings, Ridgway *Also called Diversified Coatings Inc* *(G-16705)*

Allegheny Coupling Company, Warren *Also called Allegheny Valve & Coupling Inc* *(G-19008)*

Allegheny Cut Stone Co.................814 943-4157
  911 9th Ave Altoona (16602) *(G-469)*

Allegheny Distilling LLC.................412 709-6480
  3212 Smallman St Pittsburgh (15201) *(G-14677)*

Allegheny Fabg & Sups Inc.................412 828-3320
  208 Woodland Rd Pittsburgh (15238) *(G-14678)*

Allegheny Glass Technologies, Kittanning *Also called Dielectric Sales LLC* *(G-8766)*

Allegheny Group, The, Pittsburgh *Also called Allegheny Fabg & Sups Inc* *(G-14678)*

Allegheny Iron & Metal Co.................215 743-7759
  2200 Adams Ave Rear Philadelphia (19124) *(G-13366)*

Allegheny Ludlum LLC.................724 226-5000
  100 River Rd Brackenridge (15014) *(G-1937)*

Allegheny Ludlum LLC.................724 567-2001
  130 Lincoln Ave Vandergrift (15690) *(G-18721)*

Allegheny Ludlum LLC (HQ).................412 394-2800
  1000 Six Ppg Pl Pittsburgh (15222) *(G-14679)*

Allegheny Ludlum LLC.................724 773-2700
  6 Ppg Pl Ste 1000 Pittsburgh (15222) *(G-14680)*

Allegheny Ludlum LLC.................724 537-5551
  Rr 981 Box N Latrobe (15650) *(G-9453)*

Allegheny Ludlum LLC.................724 567-2670
  132 Lincoln Ave Vandergrift (15690) *(G-18722)*

Allegheny Marking Products, Blawnox *Also called Allegheny Rubber Stamp Inc* *(G-1762)*

Allegheny Metal Finishing.................724 695-3233
  8150 Steubenville Pike Imperial (15126) *(G-8057)*

Allegheny Metals & Minerals (PA).................412 344-9900
  733 Washington Rd Ste 2 Pittsburgh (15228) *(G-14681)*

Allegheny Mfg & Elec Svc Inc.................814 288-1597
  107 Station St Johnstown (15905) *(G-8350)*

Allegheny Millwork Pbt (PA).................724 873-8700
  104 Commerce Blvd Lawrence (15055) *(G-9534)*

Allegheny Mineral Corporation (HQ).................724 548-8101
  1 Glade Dr Kittanning (16201) *(G-8753)*

Allegheny Mineral Corporation.................724 735-2088
  133 Camp Ground Rd Harrisville (16038) *(G-7252)*

Allegheny Mineral Corporation 724 794-6911
140 Arner Ln Slippery Rock (16057) *(G-17617)*

Allegheny Mountain Raceway 814 598-9077
505 Gunsmoke Rd Kane (16735) *(G-8458)*

Allegheny Mtn Hardwood Flrg, Emlenton Also called Allegheny Mtn Hardwood Flrg *(G-5004)*

Allegheny Mtn Hardwood Flrg 724 867-9441
501 Main St Emlenton (16373) *(G-5004)*

Allegheny Orthtics Prosthetics, Altoona Also called Robert John Enterprises Inc *(G-544)*

Allegheny Paper Shredders Corp 800 245-2497
Old William Penn Hwy E Delmont (15626) *(G-4046)*

Allegheny Performance Plas LLC 412 741-4416
3 Avenue A Leetsdale (15056) *(G-9678)*

Allegheny Performance Plastics, Leetsdale Also called Allegheny Plastics Inc *(G-9679)*

Allegheny Petroleum Pdts Co 724 266-3247
2911 Duss Ave Ste 3 Ambridge (15003) *(G-608)*

Allegheny Petroleum Pdts Co (PA) 412 829-1990
999 Airbrake Ave Wilmerding (15148) *(G-20158)*

Allegheny Plastics Inc (PA) 412 741-4416
Ave A Bldg 3 Leetsdale (15056) *(G-9679)*

Allegheny Plastics Inc. 412 741-4416
3 Avenue A Leetsdale (15056) *(G-9680)*

Allegheny Plastics Inc. 724 776-0100
1224 Freedom Rd Cranberry Township (16066) *(G-3800)*

Allegheny Recycled Products, Pittsburgh Also called Sovereign Services Inc *(G-15565)*

Allegheny Rubber Stamp Inc 412 826-8662
122 4th St Blawnox (15238) *(G-1762)*

Allegheny Solid Surfc Tech LLC 717 630-1251
350 South St Mc Sherrystown (17344) *(G-10649)*

Allegheny Store Fixtures Inc 814 362-6805
57 Holley Ave Bradford (16701) *(G-1954)*

Allegheny Strl Components Inc 724 867-1100
3778 Oneida Valley Rd Emlenton (16373) *(G-5005)*

Allegheny Surface Technology, Lewis Run Also called Bradford Allegheny
Corporation *(G-9873)*

Allegheny Technologies ..., Oakdale Also called Allegheny Technologies Inc *(G-12888)*

Allegheny Technologies Inc 724 775-1554
2070 Pennsylvania Ave Monaca (15061) *(G-11279)*

Allegheny Technologies Inc 724 224-1000
1001 Robb Hill Rd Oakdale (15071) *(G-12888)*

Allegheny Technologies Inc 724 452-1726
700 W New Castle St Zelienople (16063) *(G-20788)*

Allegheny Technologies Inc (PA) 412 394-2800
1000 Six Ppg Pl Pittsburgh (15222) *(G-14682)*

Allegheny Tool & Mfg Co 814 337-2795
19320 Cochranton Rd Meadville (16335) *(G-10700)*

Allegheny Tool & Supply Inc 814 437-7062
725 Grant St Franklin (16323) *(G-6114)*

Allegheny Tool Mold & Mfg Inc 814 726-0200
15300 Route 6 Clarendon (16313) *(G-3166)*

Allegheny Trico, Bradford Also called Allegheny Store Fixtures Inc *(G-1954)*

Allegheny Urn Company 814 437-3208
4871 Us 322 Franklin (16323) *(G-6115)*

Allegheny Valve & Coupling Inc 814 723-8150
419 W 3rd Ave Warren (16365) *(G-19008)*

Allegheny Wood Pdts Intl Inc 814 354-7304
17761 Route 208 Marble (16334) *(G-10433)*

Allegheny Wood Products Inc 814 354-7304
17761 Route 208 Marble (16334) *(G-10434)*

Allegheny Wood Works Inc 814 774-7338
10003 Railroad St Lake City (16423) *(G-8897)*

Allegheny-Wagner Inds Inc (PA) 724 468-4300
Old William Penn Hwy E Delmont (15626) *(G-4047)*

Allegheny-York Co 717 266-6617
3995 N George Street Ext Manchester (17345) *(G-10354)*

Allegra Mktg Print Mail 408 ....717 839-6390
6951 Allentown Blvd Ste D Harrisburg (17112) *(G-7085)*

Allegra Print, Harrisburg Also called Allegra Mktg Print Mail 408 *(G-7085)*

Allegra Print & Imaging, Philadelphia Also called Arbil Enterprises Inc *(G-13407)*

Allegra Print & Imaging 412 922-0422
18 W Steuben St Pittsburgh (15205) *(G-14683)*

Allegra Print & Imaging 717 397-3440
1770 Hempstead Rd Lancaster (17601) *(G-8929)*

Allegra Print & Imaging No.233, Lancaster Also called Allegra Print & Imaging *(G-8929)*

Allegra Print Imaging 610 882-2229
435 Allentown Dr Allentown (18109) *(G-125)*

Allen Gauge & Tool Company 412 241-6410
421 N Braddock Ave Pittsburgh (15208) *(G-14684)*

Allen Integrated Assemblies 610 966-2200
150 Locust St Macungie (18062) *(G-10139)*

Allen L Geiser & Son Inc 215 426-0211
3237 Amber St Ste 2 Philadelphia (19134) *(G-13367)*

Allen McKinney Inc 717 428-2321
24 N Main St Loganville (17342) *(G-10101)*

Allen P Sutton 717 957-2047
222 Verbeke St Marysville (17053) *(G-10531)*

Allen Zimmmerman 570 966-6924
360 Young Rd Lewisburg (17837) *(G-9896)*

Allensville Planing Mill Inc (PA) 717 483-6386
108 E Main St Allensville (17002) *(G-106)*

Allensville Planing Mill Inc 717 248-9688
101 Kish Pike Lewistown (17044) *(G-9924)*

Allensville Planing Mill Inc 717 543-4954
10381 Fairgrounds Rd Huntingdon (16652) *(G-7938)*

Allentech Inc 484 664-7887
6350 Hedgewood Dr # 100 Allentown (18106) *(G-126)*

Allentown Auto Electric LLC 610 432-2888
527 N Madison St Allentown (18102) *(G-127)*

Allentown Limb & Brace Inc 610 437-2254
1808 W Allen St Allentown (18104) *(G-128)*

Allentown Optical Corp 610 433-5269
525 Business Park Ln Allentown (18109) *(G-129)*

Allentown Plastics Inc. 610 391-8383
405 Nestle Way Breinigsville (18031) *(G-2006)*

Allentown Scientific Assoc, Allentown Also called Oil Process Systems Inc *(G-337)*

Allentown Steel Fabg Co Inc 610 264-2815
260 Race St Catasauqua (18032) *(G-2813)*

Allergan Inc 610 262-4844
589 Coventry Ct Northampton (18067) *(G-12842)*

Allergan Inc 610 352-4992
423 Beverly Blvd Upper Darby (19082) *(G-18677)*

Allergan Inc 610 691-2880
4647 Saucon Creek Rd # 101 Center Valley (18034) *(G-2824)*

Allfab Manufacturing Inc 724 924-2725
1602 Old Princeton Rd New Castle (16101) *(G-12055)*

Allflex Packaging Products Inc (PA) 215 542-9200
100 Race St Ambler (19002) *(G-566)*

Alliance Contract Pharma LLC 215 256-5920
1510 Delp Dr Harleysville (19438) *(G-7017)*

Alliance Display, Mechanicsburg Also called Westrock Rkt Company *(G-10909)*

Alliance Display & Packaging, Hershey Also called Westrock Rkt Company *(G-7626)*

Alliance Plastics Shipg Dept, Erie Also called Essentra Porous Tech Corp *(G-5283)*

Alliance Remanufacturing Inc 215 291-4640
620 E Erie Ave Philadelphia (19134) *(G-13368)*

Alliance Sand Co Inc 610 826-2248
415 Golf Rd Palmerton (18071) *(G-13099)*

Alliance Sand Company Office, Palmerton Also called Alliance Sand Co Inc *(G-13099)*

Alliance Surface Technologies, Philadelphia Also called Alliance Remanufacturing
Inc *(G-13368)*

Allied Concrete & Supply Corp (PA) 215 646-8484
1752 Limekiln Pike Ste 1 Dresher (19025) *(G-4352)*

Allied Foam Tech Corp. 215 540-2666
146 Keystone Dr Montgomeryville (18936) *(G-11384)*

Allied Millwork of P G H, Pittsburgh Also called Allied Millwork of Pittsburgh *(G-14685)*

Allied Millwork of Pittsburgh 412 471-9229
3206 Penn Ave Pittsburgh (15201) *(G-14685)*

Allied News, Grove City Also called Local Media Group Inc *(G-6795)*

Allied Rubber & Rigging Sup Co 724 535-7380
Rr 18 Wampum (16157) *(G-18796)*

Allied Tube & Conduit Corp 215 676-6464
11350 Norcom Rd Philadelphia (19154) *(G-13369)*

Allied-Hrizontal Wireline Svcs, Irwin Also called Horizontal Wireline Svcs LLC *(G-8169)*

Allimage Graphics LLC 814 728-8650
900 4th Ave Warren (16365) *(G-19009)*

Alliqua Biomedical Inc (PA) 215 702-8550
2150 Cabot Blvd W Ste B Langhorne (19047) *(G-9275)*

Allison Custom Fabrication, Allison Also called Acf Group LLC *(G-444)*

Allison Park Group Inc 412 487-8211
4055 Alpha Dr Allison Park (15101) *(G-446)*

Allomet Corporation 724 864-4787
509 Hahntown Wendel Rd Irwin (15642) *(G-8142)*

Alloy America LLC 412 828-8270
820 Route 910 Cheswick (15024) *(G-3100)*

Alloy Design Inc 610 369-9265
320 Old State Rd Boyertown (19512) *(G-1896)*

Alloy Fabrication Inc 610 921-9212
1700 N 10th St Reading (19604) *(G-16318)*

Alloy Surfaces Company Inc (HQ) 610 497-7979
121 N Commerce Dr Chester (19014) *(G-3038)*

Alloy Surfaces Company Inc 610 558-7100
151 Garnet Mine Rd Boothwyn (19060) *(G-1875)*

Allpure Technologies Inc 717 624-3241
80 Progress Ave New Oxford (17350) *(G-12404)*

Allsorce Scrning Solutions LLC 724 515-2637
4 W Hempfield Dr Irwin (15642) *(G-8143)*

Alltrista Plastics Corporation 717 667-2131
20 Setar Way Reedsville (17084) *(G-16620)*

Ally Home Care Ltd Lblty Co 800 930-0587
1554 Paoli Pike Ste 251 West Chester (19380) *(G-19496)*

Allyms, West Chester Also called Ally Home Care Ltd Lblty Co *(G-19496)*

Alm Media LLC 215 557-2300
1617 Jf Kennedy Blvd # 1750 Philadelphia (19103) *(G-13370)*

Alma Gas Inc 814 225-3480
379 Loop Rd Eldred (16731) *(G-4852)*

Almac Central Management LLC 215 660-8500
25 Fretz Rd Souderton (18964) *(G-17721)*

Almac Clinical Services LLC 610 666-9500
25 Fretz Rd Souderton (18964) *(G-17722)*

A
L
P
H
A
B
E
T
I
C

Almac Clinical Svcs, Souderton *Also called Almac Clinical Services LLC* ***(G-17722)***
Almac Group Incorporated (HQ).....215 660-8500
25 Fretz Rd Souderton (18964) ***(G-17723)***
Almac Machine Co.....814 539-5539
205 Morgan Pl Johnstown (15901) ***(G-8351)***
Almac Pharma Services LLC.....610 666-9500
2661 Audubon Rd Audubon (19403) ***(G-823)***
Almatis Inc (HQ).....412 630-2800
501 W Park Rd Leetsdale (15056) ***(G-9681)***
Almega Plastics Inc.....724 652-6411
503 Commerce Ave New Castle (16101) ***(G-12056)***
Almi Group Inc.....215 987-5768
5419 N Mascher St Philadelphia (19120) ***(G-13371)***
Almirall LLC.....610 644-7000
707 Eagleview Blvd # 200 Exton (19341) ***(G-5641)***
Alpha Advanced Materials, Altoona *Also called Alpha Assembly Solutions Inc* ***(G-470)***
Alpha Advertising & Mktg LLC.....717 445-4200
1268 Reading Rd Bowmansville (17507) ***(G-1886)***
Alpha Aromatics Inc.....412 252-1012
294 Alpha Dr Pittsburgh (15238) ***(G-14686)***
Alpha Assembly Solutions Inc.....814 946-1611
4100 6th Ave Altoona (16602) ***(G-470)***
Alpha Carb Enterprises Inc.....724 845-2500
691 Hyde Park Rd Leechburg (15656) ***(G-9641)***
Alpha Coal Sales Co.....304 256-1015
51 Airport Rd Clearfield (16830) ***(G-3210)***
Alpha Label Tank Equipment, Exton *Also called Gamajet Cleaning Systems Inc* ***(G-5684)***
Alpha Laser-US.....814 724-3666
7799 Mchenry St Meadville (16335) ***(G-10701)***
Alpha Mills Corporation (PA).....570 385-1791
122 S Margaretta St Schuylkill Haven (17972) ***(G-17145)***
Alpha Mills Corporation.....570 385-2400
70 Argo Rd Pottsville (17901) ***(G-16072)***
Alpha Mills Corporation.....570 385-1791
301 S Margaretta St Schuylkill Haven (17972) ***(G-17146)***
Alpha Omega Machine Shop.....570 573-4610
992 Mountain Rd Pine Grove (17963) ***(G-14589)***
Alpha Packaging Corporation.....610 926-5100
589 Centerport Rd Mohrsville (19541) ***(G-11273)***
Alpha Packaging North East Inc.....610 974-9001
2115 Spillman Dr Bethlehem (18015) ***(G-1448)***
Alpha Precision Group LLC (PA).....814 773-3191
95 Mason Run Rd Ridgway (15853) ***(G-16693)***
Alpha Printing.....814 536-8721
215 Franklin St Johnstown (15901) ***(G-8352)***
Alpha Safety USA.....814 236-3344
9118 Clearfield Curwensvi Clearfield (16830) ***(G-3211)***
Alpha Scientific Instrument.....610 647-7000
287 Great Valley Pkwy Malvern (19355) ***(G-10182)***
Alpha Screen Graphics Inc.....412 431-9000
1200 Muriel St Pittsburgh (15203) ***(G-14687)***
Alpha Sintered Metals LLC (HQ).....814 773-3191
95 Mason Run Rd Ridgway (15853) ***(G-16694)***
Alpha Space Control Co Inc.....717 263-0182
1580 Gabler Rd Chambersburg (17201) ***(G-2900)***
Alpha Systems, Huntingdon Valley *Also called Griffith Inc* ***(G-7992)***
Alphabet Signs Inc.....800 582-6366
91 Newport Rd Ste 102 Gap (17527) ***(G-6248)***
AlphaGraphics, Conshohocken *Also called Degadan Corp* ***(G-3537)***
AlphaGraphics.....717 731-8444
4609 Gettysburg Rd Mechanicsburg (17055) ***(G-10819)***
AlphaGraphics 514, Pittsburgh *Also called Cs-B2 Investments Inc* ***(G-14890)***
Alphasource Inc.....215 844-6470
4837-49 N Stenton Ave Philadelphia (19144) ***(G-13372)***
Alphasrce Phldelphia Wiper Sup, Philadelphia *Also called Alphasource Inc* ***(G-13372)***
Alpine Electric.....412 257-4827
1273 Washington Pike Bridgeville (15017) ***(G-2053)***
Alpine Metal Tech N Amer Inc.....412 787-2832
4853 Campbells Run Rd Pittsburgh (15205) ***(G-14688)***
Alpine Packaging Inc.....412 664-4000
4000 Crooked Run Rd North Versailles (15137) ***(G-12771)***
Alpine Sales and Distribution, Bethlehem *Also called Louis Fliszar* ***(G-1562)***
Alpine Sign and Lighting Inc.....717 246-2376
280 N Park St Dallastown (17313) ***(G-3970)***
Alpine Wurst & Meathouse Inc.....570 253-5899
1106 Texas Palmyra Hwy Honesdale (18431) ***(G-7700)***
Alpla Inc.....770 914-1407
2120 Spillman Dr Bethlehem (18015) ***(G-1449)***
Alpont II Inc.....814 456-7561
1432 Chestnut St Erie (16502) ***(G-5182)***
Alps, York *Also called Advanced Laser Printer S* ***(G-20369)***
Als Awning Shop Inc.....814 456-6262
1721 W 26th St Erie (16508) ***(G-5183)***
Als Conezone.....412 405-9601
1211 State Route 885 Clairton (15025) ***(G-3147)***
Alstom Grid LLC.....412 967-0765
610 Epsilon Dr Pittsburgh (15238) ***(G-14689)***
Alstom Grid LLC.....724 483-7308
1 Power Ln Charleroi (15022) ***(G-3005)***
Alstom Power Conversion Inc (HQ).....412 967-0765
100 E Kensinger Dr # 500 Cranberry Township (16066) ***(G-3801)***
Alstom Signaling Operation LLC (PA).....800 825-3178
2901 E Lake Rd Bldg 122 Erie (16531) ***(G-5184)***
Alstom Signaling Operation LLC.....814 486-0235
55 S Pine St Emporium (15834) ***(G-5048)***
Alston Machine Company Inc.....412 795-1000
2 Commerce Dr Pittsburgh (15239) ***(G-14690)***
Altadis USA Inc.....570 929-2220
1000 Tresckow Rd McAdoo (18237) ***(G-10655)***
Altair Equipment Company Inc.....215 672-9000
335 Constance Dr Warminster (18974) ***(G-18826)***
Altamira Instruments Inc.....412 963-6385
149 Delta Dr Ste 200 Pittsburgh (15238) ***(G-14691)***
Altamira Ltd.....800 343-1066
517 Mcneilly Rd Pittsburgh (15226) ***(G-14692)***
Altec Industries Inc.....570 822-3104
250 Laird St Wilkes Barre (18705) ***(G-19904)***
Altec Lansing Inc.....570 296-4434
535 Route 6 And 209 Milford (18337) ***(G-11154)***
Alternate Heating Systems LLC.....717 261-0922
1086 Wayne Ave Chambersburg (17201) ***(G-2901)***
Alternative Burial Corporation.....814 533-5832
146 Chandler Ave Johnstown (15906) ***(G-8353)***
Alternative Petroleum Svcs LLC.....570 807-1797
301 W Ann St Milford (18337) ***(G-11155)***
Altier Archery Mfg Div, Honesdale *Also called A & B Homes Inc* ***(G-7699)***
Altivity Packaging, Phoenixville *Also called Graphic Packaging Intl LLC* ***(G-14551)***
Altman Manufacturing Inc.....814 756-5254
54 Umburn Dr Albion (16401) ***(G-40)***
Alto Garage Door Manufacturing.....717 546-0056
1451 Stoneridge Dr Middletown (17057) ***(G-11047)***
Altomare Construction, Philadelphia *Also called Altomare Precast Inc* ***(G-13373)***
Altomare Precast Inc.....215 225-8800
4300 Wissahickon Ave Philadelphia (19129) ***(G-13373)***
Altoona Division, Altoona *Also called Galliker Dairy Company* ***(G-508)***
Altoona Hoist & Crane, Duncansville *Also called J W Hoist and Crane LLC* ***(G-4453)***
Altoona Mirror, Altoona *Also called Ogden Newspapers Inc* ***(G-535)***
Altoona Mirror.....814 946-7506
301 Cayuga Ave Altoona (16602) ***(G-471)***
Altoona Neon Sign Service.....814 942-7488
809 S 10th St Altoona (16602) ***(G-472)***
Altoona Pipe & Steel, Altoona *Also called Fabco Inc* ***(G-505)***
Altoona Soft Water Company.....814 943-2768
445 Logan Blvd Lakemont Altoona (16602) ***(G-473)***
Altra Industrial Motion.....781 917-0600
440 5th Ave Chambersburg (17201) ***(G-2902)***
Altra Industrial Motion Corp.....717 261-2550
86 Monroe Dr Chambersburg (17201) ***(G-2903)***
Altra Marine.....814 786-8346
782 S Hazzard Rd Jackson Center (16133) ***(G-8225)***
Altrax.....814 379-3706
1557 Limestone Rd Summerville (15864) ***(G-18156)***
Altris Incorporated.....724 259-8338
119 Apple Ln Greensburg (15601) ***(G-6649)***
Altuglas International.....610 878-6423
900 1st Ave King of Prussia (19406) ***(G-8578)***
Altus Agency, Wallingford *Also called David Jefferys LLC* ***(G-18783)***
Altus Group Inc.....215 977-9900
211 N 13th St Ste 802 Philadelphia (19107) ***(G-13374)***
Altus Partners LLC.....610 355-4156
1340 Enterprise Dr West Chester (19380) ***(G-19497)***
Altus Refractories LLC.....412 430-0138
303 Murrays Ln Pittsburgh (15234) ***(G-14693)***
Altus Spine, West Chester *Also called Altus Partners LLC* ***(G-19497)***
Alumagraphics Inc.....412 787-7594
214 Parkway View Dr Pittsburgh (15205) ***(G-14694)***
Alumax LLC.....570 784-7481
851 Railroad St Bloomsburg (17815) ***(G-1768)***
Alumax LLC (HQ).....412 553-4545
201 Isabella St Pittsburgh (15212) ***(G-14695)***
Alumax Mill Products Inc.....717 393-9641
1480 Manheim Pike Lancaster (17601) ***(G-8930)***
Alumina Ceramic Components Inc.....724 532-1900
4532 State Route 982 Latrobe (15650) ***(G-9454)***
Aluminum & Carbon Plus Inc.....724 368-9200
2207 Erie Hwy Portersville (16051) ***(G-15924)***
Aluminum 2000 Inc.....717 569-2300
595 E Oregon Rd Lititz (17543) ***(G-9993)***
Aluminum Alloys, Reading *Also called WER Corporation* ***(G-16564)***
Aluminum Athletic Equipment Co.....610 825-6565
1000 Enterprise Dr Royersford (19468) ***(G-16841)***
Aluminum Athletic Equipment Co.....610 825-6565
1000 Enterprises St West Conshohocken (19428) ***(G-19684)***
Aluminum Company of America.....412 553-4545
201 Isabella St Pittsburgh (15212) ***(G-14696)***
Alumisource Corporation (PA).....412 250-0360
1145 Donner Ave Monessen (15062) ***(G-11296)***

Alumties Inc 720 570-6259
  638 Country Club Ln Havertown (19083) *(G-7416)*

Alung Technologies Inc (PA) 412 697-3370
  2500 Jane St Ste 1 Pittsburgh (15203) *(G-14697)*

Alvin Engle Associates Inc 717 653-1833
  1425 W Main St Mount Joy (17552) *(G-11645)*

Alvin Engle Associates Inc (PA) 717 653-1833
  1425 W Main St Mount Joy (17552) *(G-11646)*

Alvin Reiff Woodworking 570 966-1149
  1190 Green Ridge Rd Mifflinburg (17844) *(G-11092)*

Alvord-Polk Inc 800 925-2126
  125 Gehrhart St Millersburg (17061) *(G-11187)*

Alvord-Polk Inc (PA) 605 847-4823
  125 Gehrhart St Millersburg (17061) *(G-11188)*

Alvord-Polk Inc 717 692-2128
  135 Gehrhart St Millersburg (17061) *(G-11189)*

Alvord-Polk Tool Company, Millersburg *Also called Alvord-Polk Inc (G-11188)*

Alyan Pump Company, Folcroft *Also called Hannmann Machinery Systems Inc (G-6005)*

Amacoil Inc 610 485-8300
  2100 Bridgewater Rd Aston (19014) *(G-750)*

Amanda Reiche 570 424-0334
  127 Chariton Dr East Stroudsburg (18301) *(G-4605)*

Amanita Technologies LLC 215 353-1984
  123 N Main St Dublin (18917) *(G-4430)*

Amarriage Entertainment LLC 267 973-5288
  444 Glendale Rd Upper Darby (19082) *(G-18678)*

Amat Inc 717 235-8003
  10 E Franklin St New Freedom (17349) *(G-12200)*

Amatech Inc (PA) 814 452-0010
  1460 Grimm Dr Erie (16501) *(G-5185)*

Amatex Corporation (PA) 610 277-6100
  1032 Stanbridge St Norristown (19401) *(G-12632)*

Amax Solutions Inc 717 798-8070
  717 Market St Ste 221 Lemoyne (17043) *(G-9742)*

Ambassador Bags & Spats Mfg Co 610 532-7840
  900 Ashland Ave Folcroft (19032) *(G-5998)*

Ambassador Spat Co, Folcroft *Also called Ambassador Bags & Spats Mfg Co (G-5998)*

Ambit Switch 610 705-9695
  504 Walnut St Pottstown (19464) *(G-15962)*

Ambition - The Fuel For Sccess 215 668-9561
  1429 N 5th St Philadelphia (19122) *(G-13375)*

Ambridge Mobile Welding & Fabg, Monaca *Also called Robert Urda Jr (G-11295)*

Ambridge Shop N Save, Ambridge *Also called Safran Brothers Inc (G-633)*

Amc Inc 412 531-3160
  2975 W Liberty Ave Pittsburgh (15216) *(G-14698)*

Amchemteq Inc (PA) 814 234-0123
  2514 Shawn Cir State College (16801) *(G-17940)*

Amco Biscuit Distributors Inc (PA) 215 467-8775
  1717 S 26th St Ste 29 Philadelphia (19145) *(G-13376)*

Amco International, Conshohocken *Also called American Cnsld Mfg Co Inc (G-3519)*

Amcor Group GMBH 570 474-9739
  750 Oak Hill Rd Mountain Top (18707) *(G-11750)*

Amcor Rigid Plas - Allentown, Allentown *Also called Amcor Rigid Plastics Usa Inc (G-130)*

Amcor Rigid Plastics Usa Inc 610 871-9000
  6974 Schantz Rd Allentown (18106) *(G-130)*

Amcor Rigid Plastics Usa LLC 610 871-9035
  6974 Schantz Rd Ste C Allentown (18106) *(G-131)*

Amcs Group Inc 610 932-4006
  119 S 5th St Oxford (19363) *(G-13071)*

AMD Graphics Inc 215 728-8600
  10300 Drummond Rd Fl 2 Philadelphia (19154) *(G-13377)*

AMD Group Inc 610 972-4491
  2502 Slifer Valley Rd Riegelsville (18077) *(G-16743)*

AMD Pennsylvania LLC 610 485-4400
  3400 Horizon Dr Ste 400 King of Prussia (19406) *(G-8579)*

Amdex Metallizing Inc 724 887-4977
  2 Church St Scottdale (15683) *(G-17189)*

Amedra Pharmaceuticals LLC 215 259-3601
  602 W Office Center Dr # 200 Fort Washington (19034) *(G-6062)*

Amedra Specialty Generics, Fort Washington *Also called Amedra Pharmaceuticals LLC (G-6062)*

Amega Holdings LLC 718 775-7188
  2604 Heron Pt Jamison (18929) *(G-8242)*

Amekor Industries Inc 610 825-6747
  500 Brook Rd Ste 100 Conshohocken (19428) *(G-3518)*

Amera Glass Inc 814 696-0944
  2283 Plank Rd Duncansville (16635) *(G-4449)*

Ameraquick Inc 724 733-5906
  3821 Harwick Ct Murrysville (15668) *(G-11846)*

Ameraquick Sign Systems 724 733-5906
  3821 Harwick Ct Murrysville (15668) *(G-11847)*

Amercareroyal LLC (PA) 610 384-3400
  420 Clover Mill Rd Exton (19341) *(G-5642)*

Ameri Print Flag Inc 610 409-9603
  202 Jordan Ct Collegeville (19426) *(G-3367)*

Ameri-Surce Specialty Pdts Inc 412 831-9400
  5372 Enterprise Blvd Bethel Park (15102) *(G-1402)*

America Hears Inc (PA) 215 785-5437
  806 Beaver St Bristol (19007) *(G-2105)*

America In Wwii, Harrisburg *Also called 310 Publishing LLC (G-7077)*

American Access Care Holdings (HQ) 717 235-0181
  40 Valley Stream Pkwy Malvern (19355) *(G-10183)*

American Access Care Intermedi (HQ) 717 235-0181
  40 Valley Stream Pkwy Malvern (19355) *(G-10184)*

American Accessories Inc 215 639-8000
  1355 Adams Rd Bensalem (19020) *(G-1148)*

American Additive Mfg LLC 215 559-1200
  201 Witmer Rd Horsham (19044) *(G-7782)*

American Adventure Sports 724 205-6450
  1217 S Braddock Ave Pittsburgh (15218) *(G-14699)*

American Air Duct Inc 724 483-8057
  300 Arentzen Blvd Charleroi (15022) *(G-3006)*

American Alloy Fabricators 610 635-0205
  2559 Industry Ln Norristown (19403) *(G-12633)*

American Architectural Metal M 610 432-9787
  575 Business Park Ln Allentown (18109) *(G-132)*

American Artisan Orthotics 724 776-6030
  2532 S Neshannock Rd Hermitage (16148) *(G-7571)*

American Asphalt Paving Co (PA) 570 696-1181
  500 Chase Rd Shavertown (18708) *(G-17478)*

American Association For Cance 215 440-9300
  615 Chestnut St Fl 17 Philadelphia (19106) *(G-13378)*

American Atelier Inc 610 439-4040
  2132 Downyflake Ln Allentown (18103) *(G-133)*

American Auto Wash Inc 610 265-3222
  508 S Henderson Rd King of Prussia (19406) *(G-8580)*

American Auto-Matrix, Export *Also called Jordan Acquisition Group LLC (G-5612)*

American Baling Products Inc 724 758-5566
  103 Park Ave Ellwood City (16117) *(G-4925)*

American Bank Note Company (HQ) 215 396-8707
  2520 Metropolitan Dr Trevose (19053) *(G-18486)*

American Bank Note Holographic 215 357-5300
  1448 County Line Rd Huntingdon Valley (19006) *(G-7963)*

American Bank Printers 412 566-6737
  600 Chatham Park Dr Pittsburgh (15220) *(G-14700)*

American Baptst HM Mission Soc 610 768-2465
  588 N Gulph Rd Ste C King of Prussia (19406) *(G-8581)*

American Beauty Panels, Williamsport *Also called Nippon Panel Inc (G-20048)*

American Beer Beverage Ltd 610 352-2211
  770 Garrett Rd Upper Darby (19082) *(G-18679)*

American Beverage Corporation (HQ) 412 828-9020
  1 Daily Way Verona (15147) *(G-18747)*

American Beverage Corporation 412 828-9020
  100 Papercraft Park Pittsburgh (15238) *(G-14701)*

American Bible Society (PA) 212 408-1200
  101 N Indpdnc Mall E 8f Philadelphia (19106) *(G-13379)*

American Bit & Drill Steel 570 474-6788
  29 Independence Rd Mountain Top (18707) *(G-11751)*

American Bottling Company 724 776-6111
  125 E Kensinger Dr Cranberry Township (16066) *(G-3802)*

American Brchure Catalogue Inc 215 259-1600
  882 Louis Dr Warminster (18974) *(G-18827)*

American Bridge Mfg Co (HQ) 412 631-3000
  1000 American Bridge Way Coraopolis (15108) *(G-3655)*

American Bridge Mfg Co 541 271-1100
  1000 American Bridge Way Coraopolis (15108) *(G-3656)*

American Built Arms Company 443 807-3022
  322 Industrial Rd Glen Rock (17327) *(G-6450)*

American Cable Company 215 456-0700
  1200 E Erie Ave Philadelphia (19124) *(G-13380)*

American Cable Systems LLC 215 456-0700
  1200 E Erie Ave Philadelphia (19124) *(G-13381)*

American Calendar Inc 215 743-3834
  2080 Wheatsheaf Ln 1a Philadelphia (19124) *(G-13382)*

American Candle, Bartonsville *Also called Howanitz Associates Inc (G-946)*

American Cap Company LLC 724 981-4461
  15 Church St Wheatland (16161) *(G-19834)*

American Carbide Saw Co 215 672-1466
  320 Springdale Ave Hatboro (19040) *(G-7267)*

American Carbide Tooling Div, Cabot *Also called Penn United Technologies Inc (G-2460)*

American Chief Company 267 984-8852
  104 Tomlinson Rd Philadelphia (19116) *(G-13383)*

American Classic Motors Inc 610 754-8500
  315 Big Rd Zieglerville (19492) *(G-20831)*

American Cllege Physicians Inc (PA) 215 351-2400
  190 N Independence Mall W Philadelphia (19106) *(G-13384)*

American Cnsld Mfg Co Inc 610 825-2630
  2 Union Hill Rd Bldg 2 # 2 Conshohocken (19428) *(G-3519)*

American Colloid Company 717 845-3077
  600 Lincoln St York (17401) *(G-20371)*

American Cone Valve Inc 717 792-3492
  5166 Commerce Dr York (17408) *(G-20372)*

American Conservatory Co Inc 724 465-1800
  1380 Wayne Ave Indiana (15701) *(G-8079)*

American Contract Systems 952 926-3515
  4050 Jacksons Pointe Ct Zelienople (16063) *(G-20789)*

American Contracting Fabg, Glen Mills *Also called A C F Ltd (G-6429)*

American Conveyor Systems, Levittown *Also called Rtj Inc A Close Corporation (G-9862)*

American Cooling Tech Inc 717 767-2775
715 Willow Springs Ln York (17406) *(G-20373)*
American Craft Brewery LLC 610 391-4700
7880 Penn Dr Breinigsville (18031) *(G-2007)*
American Crane & Eqp Corp 484 945-0420
1440 Ben Franklin Hwy E Douglassville (19518) *(G-4167)*
American Crane & Eqp Corp 610 521-9000
10 Industrial Hwy Hwys Essington (19029) *(G-5541)*
American Crane & Eqp Corp (PA) 610 385-6061
531 Old Swede Rd Douglassville (19518) *(G-4168)*
American Crepe Corporation 570 433-3319
496 Fairfield Rd Montoursville (17754) *(G-11430)*
American Cruising Sails Inc 814 456-7245
2705 W 17th St Erie (16505) *(G-5186)*
American Ctr For Stdy of Dstnc, University Park *Also called Pennsylvania State
University (G-18653)*
American Culture Publs LLC 267 608-9734
127 Statesman Rd Chalfont (18914) *(G-2863)*
American Cycle Fabrication 570 752-8715
7175 Columbia Blvd Apt 1 Bloomsburg (17815) *(G-1769)*
American Data Link Inc 724 503-4290
124 W Maiden St Washington (15301) *(G-19146)*
American Dental Supply Inc 484 223-3940
1075 N Gilmore St Allentown (18109) *(G-134)*
American Directory Systems Co 610 640-1774
255 Great Valley Pkwy # 120 Malvern (19355) *(G-10185)*
American Eagle Outfitters, Pittsburgh *Also called Aeo Management Co (G-14654)*
American Eagle Paper Mills, Tyrone *Also called Team Ten LLC (G-18595)*
American Eagle Windmills LLC 814 922-3180
13053 Ridge Rd West Springfield (16443) *(G-19766)*
American Economic Association 412 432-2300
2403 Sidney St Ste 260 Pittsburgh (15203) *(G-14702)*
American Egle Screen Print EMB, Johnstown *Also called Craig Hollern (G-8366)*
American Engineers Group LLC 484 920-8010
1220 Valley Forge Rd # 4 Phoenixville (19460) *(G-14527)*
American Exploration Company (PA) 610 940-4015
525 Plymouth Rd Ste 320 Plymouth Meeting (19462) *(G-15830)*
American Fastener Tech Corp 724 444-6940
9 Frontier Dr Gibsonia (15044) *(G-6323)*
American Fence Inc 610 437-1944
2738 Eberhart Rd Whitehall (18052) *(G-19861)*
American Fibertech Corporation 717 597-5708
255 N Carlisle St Greencastle (17225) *(G-6595)*
American Fishing Wire Div, Coatesville *Also called Wire and Cable Specialties Inc (G-3330)*
American Foods Inc 724 223-0820
230 Oak Hill Dr Washington (15301) *(G-19147)*
American Fuels LLC 610 222-3569
2052 Lucon Rd Skippack (19474) *(G-17594)*
American Future Systems Inc (PA) 610 695-8600
370 Technology Dr Malvern (19355) *(G-10186)*
American Future Systems Inc 814 724-2035
660 Terrace St Meadville (16335) *(G-10702)*
American Future Systems Inc 610 375-8012
220 N Park Rd Bldg 5-2 Reading (19610) *(G-16319)*
American Gas Lamp Works LLC (PA) 724 274-7131
101 Hoeveler St Springdale (15144) *(G-17897)*
American Gas Lamp Works LLC 724 274-7131
101 Hoeveler St Springdale (15144) *(G-17898)*
American Glass Research, Butler *Also called AGR International Inc (G-2371)*
American Hard Chrome LLC 412 951-9051
925 Industrial St New Castle (16102) *(G-12057)*
American High Prfmce Seals, Oakdale *Also called American High Prfmce Seals
Inc (G-12889)*
American High Prfmce Seals Inc 412 788-8815
408 High Tech Dr Oakdale (15071) *(G-12889)*
American Hollow Boring Company 800 673-2458
1901 Raspberry St Erie (16502) *(G-5187)*
American Hydraulic Mfg 610 264-8542
109 Roble Rd Allentown (18103) *(G-135)*
American Hydro Corporation 717 755-5300
135 Stonewood Rd York (17402) *(G-20374)*
American Industrial Parts 800 421-1180
1610 Mcclure Rd Monroeville (15146) *(G-11324)*
American Inks & Coatings Corp 610 933-5848
330 Pawlings Rd Phoenixville (19460) *(G-14528)*
American Innovations Inc 215 249-1840
123 N Main St Dublin (18917) *(G-4431)*
American Keg Company LLC 484 524-8251
31 Robinson St Pottstown (19464) *(G-15963)*
American Lady Hair Care Center, Sunbury *Also called American Lady US Male Hair
Sln (G-18162)*
American Lady US Male Hair Sln 570 286-7759
12 N 5th St Sunbury (17801) *(G-18162)*
American Law Institute (PA) 215 243-1600
4025 Chestnut St Fl 5 Philadelphia (19104) *(G-13385)*
American Leak Detection 412 859-6000
113 Nanton Way Coraopolis (15108) *(G-3657)*
American Legion Post 548 ....724 443-0047
3724 Legion Dr Gibsonia (15044) *(G-6324)*

American Lifting Products Inc (HQ) 610 384-1300
1227 W Lincoln Hwy Coatesville (19320) *(G-3287)*
American Log Homes, Berwick *Also called Morey General Contracting (G-1336)*
American Lyophilizer Inc 610 999-4151
668 Stony Hill Rd Yardley (19067) *(G-20295)*
American Machine LLC 215 674-4886
206 N Washington St Orwigsburg (17961) *(G-13038)*
American Machine Co 717 533-5678
435 N Lingle Ave Palmyra (17078) *(G-13115)*
American Machining Fabrication, Beaver Falls *Also called Al Kaczmarczyk (G-996)*
American Machining Inc 724 938-2120
715 Scenic Dr Daisytown (15427) *(G-3957)*
American Made LLC 724 776-4044
19 Leonberg Rd Ste 1 Cranberry Township (16066) *(G-3803)*
American Made Liner Systems, Pittsburgh *Also called American Made Systems
Inc (G-14703)*
American Made Systems Inc 412 771-3300
2600 Neville Rd Pittsburgh (15225) *(G-14703)*
American Manufactured Struc 703 403-4656
1509 Jakes Pl Hellertown (18055) *(G-7553)*
American Manufacturing & Engrg 215 362-9694
506 Stump Rd Montgomeryville (18936) *(G-11385)*
American Medical Systems Inc 512 808-4974
1400 Atwater Dr Malvern (19355) *(G-10187)*
American Metal & Rubber Inc 215 225-3700
2545 N Broad St Philadelphia (19132) *(G-13386)*
American Metal Finishers Inc 610 323-1394
1346 Farmington Ave Pottstown (19464) *(G-15964)*
American Metals & Mfg Co 724 934-8866
200 Obringer Ln Sarver (16055) *(G-17064)*
American Metals Company 724 625-8666
311 Clark St Mars (16046) *(G-10486)*
American Mfg & Integration LLC 724 861-2080
1061 Main St North Huntingdon (15642) *(G-12767)*
American Military Technologies 215 550-7970
2516 Kirk Dr Huntingdon Valley (19006) *(G-7964)*
American Mllwk & Cabinetry Inc 610 965-0040
840 Broad St Emmaus (18049) *(G-5019)*
American Molding, Lake Ariel *Also called Steve A Vitelli (G-8893)*
American Molding and Tech Inc 814 836-0202
7700 Birkmire Dr Fairview (16415) *(G-5811)*
American Molding Incorporated 215 822-5544
2800 Sterling Dr Hatfield (19440) *(G-7315)*
American Natural Retail PA LLC 212 359-4483
115 Vip Dr Ste 205 Wexford (15090) *(G-19786)*
American Nickeloid Company 610 767-3842
200 Spruce St Walnutport (18088) *(G-18790)*
American Oil & Gas LLC 724 852-2222
130 Madow Ridge Rd Ste 26 Mount Morris (15349) *(G-11677)*
American Ornamental Iron Corp 724 639-8684
2484 Elders Ridge Rd Saltsburg (15681) *(G-17050)*
American Pan Company, Crescent *Also called Premier Pan Company Inc (G-3887)*
American Paper Products of PHI (PA) 215 739-5718
2113 E Rush St 25 Philadelphia (19134) *(G-13387)*
American Paper Products of PHI 215 855-3327
1802 Beth Ln Lansdale (19446) *(G-9340)*
American Paper Products of PHI 508 879-1141
1802 Beth Ln Lansdale (19446) *(G-9341)*
American Paper Tube Encore, Philadelphia *Also called American Paper Products of
PHI (G-13387)*
American Patch and Pin 814 935-4289
1503 Bell Ave Altoona (16602) *(G-474)*
American Period Lighting Inc 717 392-5649
118 Weaver Rd Lancaster (17603) *(G-8931)*
American Petroleum Partners 844 835-5277
380 Sthpinte Blvd Ste 120 Canonsburg (15317) *(G-2539)*
American Pharmaceutical 610 366-9000
4825 W Tilghman St Allentown (18104) *(G-136)*
American Piezo Ceramics, Mackeyville *Also called APC International Ltd (G-10137)*
American Pipe and Supply LLC 724 228-6360
124 W Maiden St Washington (15301) *(G-19148)*
American Plume Fancy Feather (PA) 570 586-8400
11 Skyline Dr E Ste 2 S Abingtn Twp (18411) *(G-16889)*
AMERICAN POETRY REVIEW, THE, Philadelphia *Also called World Poetry Inc (G-14488)*
American Polarizers Inc 610 373-5177
141 S 7th St Ste 1 Reading (19602) *(G-16320)*
American Power Company, Middletown *Also called Schneider Electric It Corp (G-11074)*
American Powernet MGT LP 610 372-8500
45 Commerce Dr Wyomissing (19610) *(G-20286)*
American Prcsion Machining LLC 484 632-9449
106 State St Portland (18351) *(G-15938)*
American Precision Glass Corp 570 457-9664
602 Main St Duryea (18642) *(G-4503)*
American Precision Inds Inc 610 235-5499
110 Westtown Rd Ste 101 West Chester (19382) *(G-19498)*
American Precision Powder 724 788-1691
1296 Airport Rd Aliquippa (15001) *(G-65)*
American Printing Co & Pdts 412 422-3488
5406 Guarino Rd Pittsburgh (15217) *(G-14704)*

American Printing Company, Pittsburgh *Also called American Printing Co & Pdts* ***(G-14704)***
American Printing Group Inc..........215 442-0500
935 Horsham Rd Ste P Horsham (19044) ***(G-7783)***
American Process Lettering Inc..........610 623-9000
30 Bunting Ln Primos (19018) ***(G-16107)***
American Products Inc (PA)..........717 767-6510
45 Leigh Dr York (17406) ***(G-20375)***
American Proven Products LLC..........215 876-5274
2000 S College Ave Ste 2 Philadelphia (19121) ***(G-13388)***
American Railing Systems Inc..........814 899-7677
1813 Mcclelland Ave Erie (16510) ***(G-5188)***
American Ref & Biochem Inc..........610 940-4420
100 4 Falls Corporate Ctr Conshohocken (19428) ***(G-3520)***
American Refining Group Inc..........814 368-1378
77 N Kendall Ave Bradford (16701) ***(G-1955)***
American Refining Group Inc..........412 826-3014
55 Alpha Dr W Ste 3 Pittsburgh (15238) ***(G-14705)***
American Regent Inc..........610 650-4200
800 Adams Ave Ste 200 Norristown (19403) ***(G-12634)***
American Ribbon Manufacturers..........570 421-7470
925 Ann St Stroudsburg (18360) ***(G-18102)***
American Ribbon Manufacturers (PA)..........570 421-7470
925 Ann St Stroudsburg (18360) ***(G-18103)***
American Robot Corporation..........724 695-9000
305 High Tech Dr Oakdale (15071) ***(G-12890)***
American Roll Suppliers Inc..........610 857-2988
186 Compass Rd Parkesburg (19365) ***(G-13171)***
American Safety Clothing Inc..........215 257-7667
30 E Park Ave Sellersville (18960) ***(G-17339)***
American Safety Technologies (PA)..........215 855-8450
130 Commerce Dr Montgomeryville (18936) ***(G-11386)***
American Sensors Corporation..........412 242-5903
557 Long Rd Pittsburgh (15235) ***(G-14706)***
American Silk Mills LLC..........215 561-4901
100 West Ave Ste 910 Jenkintown (19046) ***(G-8281)***
American Slar Envmtl Technolog..........570 279-0338
220 S 3rd St Lewisburg (17837) ***(G-9897)***
American Soc For Deaf Children..........717 909-5577
3820 Hartzdale Dr Camp Hill (17011) ***(G-2486)***
American Solder & Flux Co Inc..........610 647-2375
28 Industrial Blvd Paoli (19301) ***(G-13134)***
American Solder & Flux Co Inc..........610 647-3575
28 Industrial Blvd Paoli (19301) ***(G-13135)***
American Solder and Flux, Paoli *Also called Force Industries Inc* ***(G-13140)***
American Sports Apparel Inc..........570 357-8155
914 Hope St Avoca (18641) ***(G-839)***
American Stair & Cabinetry Inc..........717 709-1061
5171 Innovation Way Chambersburg (17201) ***(G-2904)***
American Steel Carports Inc..........570 825-8260
22 Ruddle St Wilkes Barre (18702) ***(G-19905)***
American Steel Co, Ellwood City *Also called Amsteel Inc* ***(G-4926)***
American Steel Span, Mc Kees Rocks *Also called Steel Factory Corp* ***(G-10638)***
American Stress Tech Inc..........412 784-8400
540 Alpha Dr Pittsburgh (15238) ***(G-14707)***
American Sun Inc..........610 497-2210
50 Mcdonald Blvd Aston (19014) ***(G-751)***
American Tack & Hdwr Co Inc (HQ)..........610 336-1330
250 Boulder Dr Breinigsville (18031) ***(G-2008)***
American Tank & Concrete Svc..........724 837-4410
813 Georges Station Rd Greensburg (15601) ***(G-6650)***
American Textile Company Inc (PA)..........412 948-1020
10 N Linden St Duquesne (15110) ***(G-4494)***
American Tinning Galvanizing (PA)..........814 456-7053
552 W 12th St Erie (16501) ***(G-5189)***
American Tool & Machine Co..........724 654-0971
1119 Butler Ave New Castle (16101) ***(G-12058)***
American Tool Mfg LLC..........610 837-8573
280 Smith Rd Bath (18014) ***(G-950)***
American Trench LLC..........215 360-3493
7 E Lancaster Ave Ste 220 Ardmore (19003) ***(G-700)***
American Trim LLC..........814 833-7758
3120 W 22nd St Erie (16506) ***(G-5190)***
American Tube & Paper Co Div, Lansdale *Also called American Paper Products of PHI* ***(G-9340)***
American Tube Company Inc..........610 759-8700
603 Gremar Rd Nazareth (18064) ***(G-11953)***
American Turned Products Inc..........814 824-7600
1944 Wager Rd Erie (16509) ***(G-5191)***
American Turned Products Inc (PA)..........814 474-4200
7626 Klier Dr S Fairview (16415) ***(G-5812)***
American Waffle Company LLC..........717 632-6000
1125 Wilson Ave Hanover (17331) ***(G-6860)***
American Waste Digest Corp (PA)..........610 326-9480
1345 Thomas Oakes Dr Pottstown (19465) ***(G-15942)***
American Water Technologies (PA)..........724 850-9000
38 S 4th St Youngwood (15697) ***(G-20778)***
American Welding & Gas Inc..........570 323-8400
100 Reading Ave Williamsport (17701) ***(G-19985)***
American Well Service LLC..........724 206-9372
1478 Jefferson Ave Washington (15301) ***(G-19149)***
American Whl Thermographers, Pittsburgh *Also called Hilden Enterprises Inc* ***(G-15094)***
American Wire Research Inc..........412 349-8431
1005 Airbrake Ave Wilmerding (15148) ***(G-20159)***
American Wood Design Inc..........302 792-2100
201 Fulton St Chester (19013) ***(G-3039)***
American Zinc Recycling Corp (HQ)..........724 774-1020
4955 Steubenville Pike # 405 Pittsburgh (15205) ***(G-14708)***
American Zinc Recycling LLC (PA)..........724 773-2203
4955 Steubenville Pike Pittsburgh (15205) ***(G-14709)***
Americana Art China Co Inc (PA)..........330 938-6133
316 Manito Trl Mercer (16137) ***(G-10959)***
Americold Logistics LLC..........215 721-0700
2525 Bergey Rd Hatfield (19440) ***(G-7316)***
Americor Press, Warminster *Also called American Brchure Catalogue Inc* ***(G-18827)***
Ameridrives Couplings, Erie *Also called Ameridrives International LLC* ***(G-5192)***
Ameridrives International LLC (HQ)..........814 480-5000
1802 Pittsburgh Ave Erie (16502) ***(G-5192)***
Amerihohl Mining..........724 455-4450
940 Jim Mountain Rd Mill Run (15464) ***(G-11185)***
Amerikohl Mining Inc (PA)..........724 282-2339
202 Sunset Dr Butler (16001) ***(G-2374)***
Amerikohl Mining Inc..........724 282-2339
1384 State Route 711 Stahlstown (15687) ***(G-17935)***
Amerimax Building Products, Bloomsburg *Also called Alumax LLC* ***(G-1768)***
Ameripak..........215 343-1530
2001 County Line Rd Warrington (18976) ***(G-19107)***
Ameritech Network Corp..........215 441-8310
2940 Turnpike Dr Ste 6 Hatboro (19040) ***(G-7268)***
Amertac, Breinigsville *Also called American Tack & Hdwr Co Inc* ***(G-2008)***
Ames Companies Inc..........717 258-3001
1 True Temper Dr Carlisle (17015) ***(G-2689)***
Ames Companies Inc..........717 737-1500
465 Railroad Ave Camp Hill (17011) ***(G-2487)***
Ames Companies Inc (HQ)..........717 737-1500
465 Railroad Ave Camp Hill (17011) ***(G-2488)***
Ames Construction Inc..........717 299-1395
351 Sprecher Rd Lancaster (17603) ***(G-8932)***
Ames Enterprises Inc..........814 474-2700
7359 W Ridge Rd Fairview (16415) ***(G-5813)***
Ames Industries Inc..........877 296-9977
2999 Elizabethtown Rd Hershey (17033) ***(G-7603)***
Ames Reese Inc..........717 393-1591
2575 Old Phladelphia Pike Bird In Hand (17505) ***(G-1668)***
Ames True Temper Inc..........717 231-7856
1500 S Cameron St Harrisburg (17104) ***(G-7086)***
Ametek Inc (PA)..........610 647-2121
1100 Cassatt Rd Berwyn (19312) ***(G-1351)***
Ametek Inc..........215 355-6900
205 Keith Valley Rd Horsham (19044) ***(G-7784)***
Ametek Inc..........570 645-2191
42 Mountain Ave Nesquehoning (18240) ***(G-12003)***
Ametek Inc..........215 355-6900
205 Keith Valley Rd Horsham (19044) ***(G-7785)***
Ametek Inc..........267 933-2121
343 Godshall Dr Harleysville (19438) ***(G-7018)***
Ametek Inc..........267 933-2121
343 Godshall Dr Harleysville (19438) ***(G-7019)***
Ametek Inc..........215 256-6601
343 Godshall Dr Harleysville (19438) ***(G-7020)***
Ametek Inc..........717 569-7061
1780 Rohrerstown Rd Lancaster (17601) ***(G-8933)***
Ametek Company, Horsham *Also called Newage Testing Instruments* ***(G-7835)***
Ametek Drexelbrook, Horsham *Also called Patriot Sensors & Contrls Corp* ***(G-7840)***
Ametek Emg Holdings Inc..........610 647-2121
1100 Cassatt Rd Berwyn (19312) ***(G-1352)***
Ametek Europe LLC..........610 647-2121
1100 Cassatt Rd Berwyn (19312) ***(G-1353)***
Ametek Inc..........724 225-8400
1085 Route 519 Eighty Four (15330) ***(G-4833)***
Ametek- Arspc Div Pwr Data Sys, Harleysville *Also called Ametek Inc* ***(G-7019)***
Amfire Mining Co..........724 254-9554
Plant Off Hwy 403 Clymer (15728) ***(G-3269)***
Amfire Mining Company LLC (HQ)..........724 532-4307
1 Energy Pl Ste 3000 Latrobe (15650) ***(G-9455)***
AMG Advnced Mtllrgcal Group NV, Wayne *Also called Metallurg Inc* ***(G-19355)***
AMG Aluminum North America LLC (HQ)..........610 293-2501
435 Devon Park Dr Ste 200 Wayne (19087) ***(G-19297)***
AMG Resources Corporation (HQ)..........412 777-7300
2 Robinson Plz Ste 350 Pittsburgh (15205) ***(G-14710)***
Amherst Corporation..........610 589-1090
80 Begonia Ct Womelsdorf (19567) ***(G-20205)***
AMI Entertainment Network Inc (HQ)..........215 826-1400
925 Canal St Bristol (19007) ***(G-2106)***
Amies Airparts LLC..........570 871-7991
11 Sunnyside Rd Clifton Twp (18424) ***(G-3260)***
Amigo Express..........484 461-3135
7209 W Chester Pike Upper Darby (19082) ***(G-18680)***
Amish Country Gazebos Inc..........717 665-0365
340 Hostetter Rd Manheim (17545) ***(G-10367)***

Amishtastes, Ronks *Also called Kauffmantreatscom LLC (G-16809)*

Amitec, Huntingdon Valley *Also called American Military Technologies (G-7964)*

Amity Carts, Shenandoah *Also called Tri-Way Metalworkers Inc (G-17498)*

Amity Industries Inc (PA) 610 385-6075
491 Old Swede Rd Douglassville (19518) *(G-4169)*

Amity Machine Corporation 610 966-3115
3750 Chestnut Rd Alburtis (18011) *(G-50)*

Aml Industries Inc 215 674-2424
3500 Davisville Rd Hatboro (19040) *(G-7269)*

Ammac, York *Also called Automatic Machining Mfg Co Inc (G-20393)*

Ammeraal Beltech Modular Inc 610 372-1800
500 Brentwood Dr Reading (19611) *(G-16321)*

Amore Vineyards and Winery 610 837-1683
6821 Steuben Rd Nazareth (18064) *(G-11954)*

AMP, Middletown *Also called Te Connectivity Corporation (G-11079)*

Ampal Inc (HQ) 610 826-7020
2115 Little Gap Rd Palmerton (18071) *(G-13100)*

Ampal Inc 610 826-7020
2125 Little Gap Rd Palmerton (18071) *(G-13101)*

Ampco-Pittsburgh Corporation (PA) 412 456-4400
726 Bell Ave Ste 301 Carnegie (15106) *(G-2763)*

Ampere Electric Co 215 426-5356
210 1st Ave Broomall (19008) *(G-2278)*

Amphenol Corporation 814 834-9140
967 Windfall Rd Saint Marys (15857) *(G-16947)*

Amphenol Thermometrics Inc (HQ) 814 834-9140
967 Windfall Rd Saint Marys (15857) *(G-16948)*

Amplifier Research Corp (PA) 215 723-8181
160 Schoolhouse Rd Souderton (18964) *(G-17724)*

Amplifier Solutions Corp 215 799-2561
3009 Old State Rd Telford (18969) *(G-18267)*

Ampm, Millersburg *Also called Alvord-Polk Inc (G-11187)*

Ampro Sportswear, Primos *Also called American Process Lettering Inc (G-16107)*

Ampros Trophies, Philadelphia *Also called Award Products Inc (G-13428)*

Amptech Inc 724 843-7605
1605 Old Route 18 9-26 Wampum (16157) *(G-18797)*

Amrep Corporation (PA) 609 487-0905
620 W Germantown Pike # 175 Plymouth Meeting (19462) *(G-15831)*

Amrit Works LLC 267 475-7129
108 Harding Ave Morton (19070) *(G-11589)*

AMS Filling Systems, Honey Brook *Also called AMS Liquidating Co Inc (G-7736)*

AMS Filling Systems, Honey Brook *Also called Hillside Custom Mac Wel & Fab (G-7748)*

AMS Liquidating Co Inc 610 942-4200
2500 Chestnut Tree Rd Honey Brook (19344) *(G-7736)*

AMS Services & Designs, Greencastle *Also called Amy Semler (G-6596)*

Amsi US LLC 814 479-3380
111 Hoganas Way Hollsopple (15935) *(G-7656)*

Amsted Rail Company Inc 717 761-3690
3420 Simpson Ferry Rd Camp Hill (17011) *(G-2489)*

Amsteel Inc 724 758-5566
103 Park Ave Ellwood City (16117) *(G-4926)*

Amt, Hatboro *Also called Advanced Machining Tech (G-7265)*

Amt Pump Company 610 948-3800
400 Spring St Royersford (19468) *(G-16842)*

Amtech, Fort Washington *Also called Corrugated Services Corp (G-6067)*

Amtek Inc (PA) 814 734-3327
10961 Route 98 Edinboro (16412) *(G-4808)*

Amtel Systems Corporation 610 458-3320
1955 Ticonderoga Blvd # 800 Chester Springs (19425) *(G-3071)*

Amthor Steel Inc (PA) 814 452-4700
1717 Gaskell Ave Erie (16503) *(G-5193)*

Amy Semler 717 593-9243
175 Hykes Rd E Greencastle (17225) *(G-6596)*

Amz Manufacturing Corporation 717 751-2714
100 Boxwood Ln York (17402) *(G-20376)*

Amz Manufacturing Corporation (PA) 717 848-2565
2206 Pennsylvania Ave York (17404) *(G-20377)*

An Emagen Company, Export *Also called Endagraph Inc (G-5601)*

Anaconda Enterprises LLC 908 910-7150
2104 Fieldview Dr Nazareth (18064) *(G-11955)*

Anadarko Petroleum 570 326-1535
2011 Lycoming Creek Rd Williamsport (17701) *(G-19986)*

Anadarko Petroleum Corp 570 323-4157
33 W 3rd St Ste 200 Williamsport (17701) *(G-19987)*

Anadarko Petroleum Corporation 570 323-4157
33 W 3rd St Ste 400 Williamsport (17701) *(G-19988)*

Analytic Plastic Inc 215 638-7505
8000 State Rd Philadelphia (19136) *(G-13389)*

Analytical Graphics Inc (PA) 610 981-8000
220 Valley Creek Blvd Exton (19341) *(G-5643)*

Analytical Technology Inc (PA) 610 917-0991
6 Iron Bridge Dr Collegeville (19426) *(G-3368)*

Anatomical Designs Inc 724 430-1470
383 Dixon Blvd Uniontown (15401) *(G-18615)*

Anchor Distributors, New Kensington *Also called Whitaker Corporation (G-12389)*

Anchor Hocking Packaging, Connellsville *Also called Crown Cork & Seal Usa Inc (G-3493)*

Anchor Machine Inc 610 261-4924
5432 Green Meadow Rd Northampton (18067) *(G-12843)*

Anderson Electronics LLC (PA) 814 695-4428
721 Scotch Valley Rd # 200 Hollidaysburg (16648) *(G-7642)*

Anderson Family Farm Inc 814 463-0202
15255 Route 66 Tionesta (16353) *(G-18369)*

Anderson Inc 412 486-2211
4715 William Flynn Hwy Allison Park (15101) *(G-447)*

Anderson Machine Co 724 834-5135
1131 Beaver Run Rd Greensburg (15601) *(G-6651)*

Anderson Plastics Inc 814 774-0076
227 Hathaway St E Girard (16417) *(G-6384)*

Anderson Prints LLC 610 293-1330
465 Devon Park Dr Wayne (19087) *(G-19298)*

Anderson Products Incorporated 570 595-7495
1 Weiler Dr Cresco (18326) *(G-3890)*

Anderson Tube Company Inc 215 855-0118
1400 Fairgrounds Rd Hatfield (19440) *(G-7317)*

Anderson Welding & Sons LLC 215 886-1726
100 Ehrenpfort Ave Oreland (19075) *(G-13017)*

Andersons Candies Inc 724 869-3018
1010 W State St Baden (15005) *(G-869)*

Andorra Salad Inc 215 482-5750
8500 Henry Ave Philadelphia (19128) *(G-13390)*

Andreas Lumber Inc 570 379-3644
16 Sawmill Ln Wapwallopen (18660) *(G-18807)*

Andrew Billets & Son Inc 570 207-7253
1105 Capouse Ave Scranton (18509) *(G-17208)*

Andrew E Reken 724 783-7878
134 Minich Rd Dayton (16222) *(G-4034)*

Andrew E Trautner & Sons Inc 570 494-0191
115 Elizabeth St Cogan Station (17728) *(G-3358)*

Andrew H Lawson Co 215 235-1609
2927 W Thompson St Philadelphia (19121) *(G-13391)*

Andrew Torba 570 209-1622
905 Marion Ln Moosic (18507) *(G-11503)*

Andrew W Nissly Inc 717 393-3841
544 W Mill Ave Lancaster (17603) *(G-8934)*

Andritz Herr-Voss Stamco Inc 724 538-3180
1500 1st Ave Conway (15027) *(G-3619)*

Andritz Herr-Voss Stamco Inc (HQ) 724 538-3180
130 Main St Callery (16024) *(G-2466)*

Andritz Herr-Voss Stamco Inc 724 251-8745
2970 Duss Ave Ambridge (15003) *(G-609)*

Andritz Inc (HQ) 724 597-7801
500 Technology Dr Canonsburg (15317) *(G-2540)*

Andritz Inc 570 546-1253
336 W Penn St Muncy (17756) *(G-11806)*

Andritz Inc 570 546-8211
35 Sherman St Muncy (17756) *(G-11807)*

Andromeda Led Lighting LLC 610 336-7474
2188 Greenmeadow Dr Macungie (18062) *(G-10140)*

Angel Colon 215 455-4000
4309 Rising Sun Ave Philadelphia (19140) *(G-13392)*

Angel Pins and More 717 692-5086
2141 State Route 209 Millersburg (17061) *(G-11190)*

Angelie Original 814 798-3312
1285 Whistler Rd Hooversville (15936) *(G-7770)*

Angell Industries Inc 412 269-2956
400 Chess St Coraopolis (15108) *(G-3658)*

Angelo Brothers Co, Philadelphia *Also called Westinghouse Lighting Corp (G-14466)*

Angelo Nieto Inc 570 489-6761
200 Clarkson Ave Jessup (18434) *(G-8326)*

Angelos Inc 724 350-8715
2109 N Franklin Dr Washington (15301) *(G-19150)*

Angermeier Tool & Die Inc 814 445-2285
2414 Glades Pike Somerset (15501) *(G-17673)*

Angiotech Pharmaceuticals Inc 610 404-1000
1100 Berkshire Blvd # 308 Reading (19610) *(G-16322)*

Angle Foods LLC 724 900-0908
3100 Penn Ave Pittsburgh (15201) *(G-14711)*

Angstrom Sciences Inc 412 469-8466
40 S Linden St Duquesne (15110) *(G-4495)*

Anh Refractories, Moon Township *Also called Harbisonwalker Intl Foundation (G-11489)*

Anholt Technologies Inc (PA) 610 268-2758
440 Church Rd Avondale (19311) *(G-848)*

Animas LLC (HQ) 610 644-8990
965 Chesterbrook Blvd Chesterbrook (19087) *(G-3089)*

Anitas Vegan Kitchen 786 512-1428
4500 Worth St Ste B101 Philadelphia (19124) *(G-13393)*

Anju Sylogent LLC 215 504-7000
1414 Radcliffe St Ste 115 Bristol (19007) *(G-2107)*

Ann Gregory For The Bride, Pittsburgh *Also called Amc Inc (G-14698)*

Annalee Wood Products Inc (PA) 610 436-0142
789 Cedar Knoll Rd Coatesville (19320) *(G-3288)*

Annalee Wood Products Inc 610 436-0142
701 S Franklin St West Chester (19382) *(G-19499)*

Annamaet Pet Foods Inc 215 453-0381
41 Daniels Rd Sellersville (18960) *(G-17340)*

Annuity Vault 215 830-8666
616 Easton Rd Willow Grove (19090) *(G-20107)*

Annville Shoulder Strap Co 717 867-4831
400 W Sheridan Ave Annville (17003) ***(G-642)***
Anodizing Plus Inc 717 246-0584
165 E Broad St Dallastown (17313) ***(G-3971)***
Ansa Electric Vehicles LLC 610 955-5686
209 Avon Rd Narberth (19072) ***(G-11907)***
Ansaldo STS Usa, Inc., Pittsburgh *Also called Hitachi Rail STS Usa Inc* ***(G-15096)***
Ansen Corporation 315 393-3573
720 Trumbull Dr Pittsburgh (15205) ***(G-14712)***
Ansoft LLC (HQ) 412 261-3200
225 W Station Square Dr # 200 Pittsburgh (15219) ***(G-14713)***
Anson Mold & Manufacturing, Erie *Also called Reddog Industries Inc* ***(G-5458)***
Anstadt Communications, York *Also called Anstadt Printing Corporation* ***(G-20378)***
Anstadt Printing Corporation 717 767-6891
3300 Farmtrail Rd York (17406) ***(G-20378)***
Anstines Candy Box 717 854-9269
1901 S Queen St York (17403) ***(G-20379)***
Anstines Home Made Candy, York *Also called Anstines Candy Box* ***(G-20379)***
Ansys Inc (PA) 884 462-6797
2600 Ansys Dr Canonsburg (15317) ***(G-2541)***
Antares Instruments Inc 215 441-5250
418 Caredean Dr Ste 4 Horsham (19044) ***(G-7786)***
Anthony Burney 412 606-7336
455 4th St Monongahela (15063) ***(G-11304)***
Anthony Cocco Inc 215 629-4100
529 Spring Garden St Philadelphia (19123) ***(G-13394)***
Anthony Ds Daily Numbers 215 537-0618
2617 Lefevre St Philadelphia (19137) ***(G-13395)***
Anthony Hauze 610 432-3533
391 Auburn St Ste A Allentown (18103) ***(G-137)***
Anthony J Mascherino PC 610 269-6833
341 E Lancaster Ave Ste 1 Downingtown (19335) ***(G-4210)***
Anthony Mieczkowski 610 489-2523
928 Dogwood Ln Collegeville (19426) ***(G-3369)***
Anthracite, Kittanning *Also called Asbury Graphite Mills Inc* ***(G-8755)***
Anthracite Industries Inc 570 286-2176
610 Anthracite Rd Sunbury (17801) ***(G-18163)***
Anthrafilt, Wilkes Barre *Also called Carbon Sales Inc* ***(G-19909)***
Anthrcite Non-Coal Mine Safety, Pottsville *Also called Envimmntal Protection PA Dept* ***(G-16078)***
Antietam Iron Works LLC 717 485-5557
201 Lincoln Way W Ste 100 Mc Connellsburg (17233) ***(G-10562)***
Antique Lighting, Wynnewood *Also called Harvey M Stern & Co* ***(G-20268)***
Antler Ridge Winery (PA) 570 247-7222
37 Antler Ridge Ln Ulster (18850) ***(G-18597)***
Antones At The Mark Inc 610 798-9218
1801 S 12th St Ste 5 Allentown (18103) ***(G-138)***
Antonio Centeno Lawnkeeping 267 580-0443
73 Kingwood Ln Levittown (19055) ***(G-9816)***
Antonio Colella Cement Work 215 745-2951
1414 Disston St Philadelphia (19111) ***(G-13396)***
Antonios Manufacturing Inc 814 886-8171
800 2nd St Cresson (16630) ***(G-3897)***
Antrim Machine Company 717 369-3184
5865 Bullitt Rd Greencastle (17225) ***(G-6597)***
Anvil Craft Corp 610 250-9600
1005 Aspen St Easton (18042) ***(G-4645)***
Anvil Forge & Hammer Ir Works 610 837-9951
6337 Airport Rd Allentown (18109) ***(G-139)***
Anvil International LLC 717 684-4400
800 Malleable Rd Columbia (17512) ***(G-3427)***
Anvil International LLC 717 684-4400
1411 Lancaster Ave Columbia (17512) ***(G-3428)***
Anvil International LLC 256 238-0579
1411 Lancaster Ave Columbia (17512) ***(G-3429)***
Anvil International LLC 717 762-9141
330 E 9th St Waynesboro (17268) ***(G-19396)***
Anvil Iron Works Inc (PA) 215 468-8300
1022 Washington Ave 26 Philadelphia (19147) ***(G-13397)***
Anything Sews 412 486-1055
2208 Mount Royal Blvd Glenshaw (15116) ***(G-6480)***
AOC Acquisition Inc (PA) 610 966-2200
150 Locust St Macungie (18062) ***(G-10141)***
AP Services LLC 724 295-6200
203 Armstrong Dr Freeport (16229) ***(G-6199)***
Ap-O-Gee Industries Inc 610 719-8010
827 Lincoln Ave Unit 4-6 West Chester (19380) ***(G-19500)***
Apache Turbines 814 880-0053
531 Saint Paul Cir Bellefonte (16823) ***(G-1092)***
Apantec LLC (PA) 267 436-3991
805 W 5th St Ste 13 Lansdale (19446) ***(G-9342)***
APC International Ltd 570 726-6961
213 Duck Run Rd Mackeyville (17750) ***(G-10137)***
Apelsteim, James, Huntingdon Valley *Also called State of Art Prosthetics* ***(G-8040)***
Apex Apparel Inc 610 432-8007
1801 S 12th St Ste 4 Allentown (18103) ***(G-140)***
Apex Energy LLC (PA) 724 719-2611
6041 Wallace Road Ext # 100 Wexford (15090) ***(G-19787)***
Apex Energy LLC 724 719-2611
6041 Wallace Road Ext # 100 Wexford (15090) ***(G-19788)***
Apex Engineered Products, Clark *Also called Cmg Process Inc* ***(G-3188)***
Apex Fabrication & Design Inc 610 689-5880
7938 Boyertown Pike Boyertown (19512) ***(G-1897)***
Apex Fountain Sales Inc 215 627-4526
1140 N American St Philadelphia (19123) ***(G-13398)***
Apex Homes Inc 570 837-2333
7172 Route 522 Middleburg (17842) ***(G-11021)***
Apex Homes of Pa LLC 570 837-2333
7172 Route 522 Middleburg (17842) ***(G-11022)***
Apex Hydraulic & Machine Inc 814 342-1010
2859 Phlpsburg Bigler Hwy Philipsburg (16866) ***(G-14508)***
Apex Manufacturing Co 610 272-0659
2706 Hillcrest Ave Norristown (19401) ***(G-12635)***
Apex Manufacturing Co Inc 215 343-4850
1750 Costner Dr Ste B Warrington (18976) ***(G-19108)***
Apex Manufacturing Company 215 345-4400
4800 Burnt House Hill Rd Doylestown (18902) ***(G-4270)***
Apex North America LLC 866 273-9872
65 Washington St Donora (15033) ***(G-4145)***
Apex Screen Printing & EMB 814 634-5992
102 Meyers Ave Meyersdale (15552) ***(G-11008)***
Apex Urethane Millworks LLC 717 246-1948
105 Church Ln Red Lion (17356) ***(G-16587)***
Apexco-Ppsi LLC 937 935-0164
430 Caredean Dr Horsham (19044) ***(G-7787)***
Apg, Allison Park *Also called Allison Park Group Inc* ***(G-446)***
API, Reading *Also called American Polarizers Inc* ***(G-16320)***
API, York *Also called American Products Inc* ***(G-20375)***
API, Bristol *Also called Advent Design Corporation* ***(G-2104)***
API Americas Inc 785 842-7674
47 Runway Dr Ste G Levittown (19057) ***(G-9817)***
API Cryptek Inc (HQ) 908 546-3900
1900 W College Ave State College (16801) ***(G-17941)***
API Technologies, Fairview *Also called Spectrum Control Inc* ***(G-5842)***
API Technologies, State College *Also called Tm Systems Inc* ***(G-18039)***
API Technologies, Windber *Also called Sendec Corp* ***(G-20192)***
API Technologies Corp, State College *Also called Islip Transformer and Metal Co* ***(G-17978)***
API Technologies Corp, Philadelphia *Also called Spectrum Microwave Inc* ***(G-14333)***
API Technologies Corp, State College *Also called Spectrum Microwave Inc* ***(G-18033)***
API Technologies Corp 215 464-4000
2707 Black Lake Pl Philadelphia (19154) ***(G-13399)***
APM Home Center, Lewistown *Also called Allensville Planing Mill Inc* ***(G-9924)***
Apogee Industries, West Chester *Also called Ap-O-Gee Industries Inc* ***(G-19500)***
Apogee Labs Inc 215 699-2060
210 S 3rd St North Wales (19454) ***(G-12788)***
Apollo Metals Ltd 610 867-5826
1001 14th Ave Bethlehem (18018) ***(G-1450)***
Apollo Metals, Ltd., Bethlehem *Also called Apollo Metals Ltd* ***(G-1450)***
Apontes Foodtrucks, Glenshaw *Also called Apontes Latin Flavor Inc* ***(G-6481)***
Apontes Latin Flavor Inc (PA) 727 247-2001
1606 Butler Plank Rd Glenshaw (15116) ***(G-6481)***
App, Canonsburg *Also called American Petroleum Partners* ***(G-2539)***
App-Techs Corporation 717 735-0848
505 Willow Ln Lancaster (17601) ***(G-8935)***
Appalachain Grills 717 762-3321
146 Briar Ridge Dr Waynesboro (17268) ***(G-19397)***
Appalachian Brewing Co Inc 717 221-1080
50 N Cameron St Harrisburg (17101) ***(G-7087)***
Appalachian Drillers LLC 724 548-2501
409 Butler Rd Ste A Kittanning (16201) ***(G-8754)***
Appalachian Drilling Svcs Inc 570 907-0136
105 Industrial Park Rd Beech Creek (16822) ***(G-1081)***
Appalachian Ltg Systems Inc 724 752-0326
101 Randolph St Ellwood City (16117) ***(G-4927)***
Appalachian Mill Inc 717 328-2805
2375 Buchanan Trl W Greencastle (17225) ***(G-6598)***
Appalachian Millwork 724 539-1944
166 Menasha Ln Latrobe (15650) ***(G-9456)***
Appalachian Tank Car Svcs Inc 412 741-1500
Ferry St & Ave C Leetsdale (15056) ***(G-9682)***
Appalachian Tank Car Svcs Inc 724 925-3919
304 N 3rd St Youngwood (15697) ***(G-20779)***
Appalachian Timber Products 724 329-1990
5441 National Pike Markleysburg (15459) ***(G-10479)***
Appalachian Wood Products Inc 814 765-2003
171 Appalachian Dr Clearfield (16830) ***(G-3212)***
Appalachian Woodcrafts LLC 570 726-7149
88 Airstrip Dr Mill Hall (17751) ***(G-11170)***
Apparel Machinery & Supply Co 215 634-2626
1836 E Ontario St Philadelphia (19134) ***(G-13400)***
Apparel Print Promotionals 717 233-4277
5010 Linglestown Rd Harrisburg (17112) ***(G-7088)***
Appcon, Ridley Park *Also called Application Consultants Inc* ***(G-16733)***
Appeeling Fruit Inc 610 926-6601
1149 Railroad Rd Dauberville (19533) ***(G-4032)***

Appellation Cnstr Svcs LLC (PA).....570 601-4765
999 N Loyalsock Ave Ste C Montoursville (17754) ***(G-11431)***
Appitur Co.....215 720-1420
3553 West Chester Pike Newtown Square (19073) ***(G-12565)***
Apple Alley Associates-Ii LP.....215 817-2828
413 Executive Dr Langhorne (19047) ***(G-9276)***
Apple Belting Company.....717 293-8903
3501 Hempland Rd Lancaster (17601) ***(G-8936)***
Apple Fasteners Inc.....717 761-8962
2850 Appleton St Ste A Camp Hill (17011) ***(G-2490)***
Apple Fox.....484 388-0011
5715 Mount Pleasant Rd Bernville (19506) ***(G-1296)***
Apple Press Ltd.....610 363-1776
307 Commerce Dr Exton (19341) ***(G-5644)***
Apple Printing Co, Carnegie *Also called Prova Inc* ***(G-2783)***
Apple Way Cstm Stairs Railing.....717 369-0502
9523 Lincoln Way W Saint Thomas (17252) ***(G-17036)***
Applegate Insul Systems Inc.....717 709-0533
1050 Superior Ave Bldg 53 Chambersburg (17201) ***(G-2905)***
Applegate Manufacturing, Chambersburg *Also called Applegate Insul Systems Inc* ***(G-2905)***
Applegate Mfg, Chambersburg *Also called Paper and Ink of Pa LLC* ***(G-2967)***
Appleridge Stone Intl Inc.....724 459-9511
1094 Old William Penn Hwy Blairsville (15717) ***(G-1713)***
Application Consultants Inc.....610 521-1529
119 W Chester Pike Ridley Park (19078) ***(G-16733)***
Applied Clinical Concepts Inc.....215 660-8500
25 Fretz Rd Souderton (18964) ***(G-17725)***
Applied Controls Inc.....717 854-2889
144 Roosevelt Ave Ste 400 York (17401) ***(G-20380)***
Applied Creativity Inc.....724 327-0054
101 Technology Ln Export (15632) ***(G-5589)***
Applied Electronics, York *Also called Metabloc Inc* ***(G-20589)***
Applied Equipment Co.....610 258-7941
8 Devon Dr Easton (18045) ***(G-4646)***
Applied Indus Tech — PA LLC.....724 696-3099
301 Westec Dr Mount Pleasant (15666) ***(G-11686)***
Applied Industrial Tech 0118, Mount Pleasant *Also called Applied Indus Tech — PA LLC* ***(G-11686)***
Applied Magnetics Lab Inc.....717 430-2774
401 Manor St York (17401) ***(G-20381)***
Applied Materials Inc.....610 409-9187
71 Longacre Dr Collegeville (19426) ***(G-3370)***
Applied Micro Circuits Corp.....267 757-8722
41 University Dr Ste 400 Newtown (18940) ***(G-12496)***
Applied RES & Photonics Inc.....717 220-1003
470 Friendship Rd Ste 10 Harrisburg (17111) ***(G-7089)***
Applied Research Lab, Warminster *Also called Pennsylvania State University* ***(G-18939)***
Applied Separations Inc.....610 770-0900
930 Hamilton St Ste 4 Allentown (18101) ***(G-141)***
Applied Software Inc (PA).....215 297-9441
6720 Paxson Rd New Hope (18938) ***(G-12297)***
Applied Technology Intl Ltd.....610 363-1077
900 Springdale Dr Exton (19341) ***(G-5645)***
Applied Test Systems LLC.....724 283-1212
154 Eastbrook Ln Butler (16002) ***(G-2375)***
Appligent Inc.....610 284-4006
22 E Baltimore Ave Lansdowne (19050) ***(G-9429)***
Apply Powder & Coating.....610 361-1889
394 Parkmount Rd Middletown (17057) ***(G-11048)***
Apprise Software Inc (PA).....610 991-3600
3101 Emrick Blvd Ste 301 Bethlehem (18020) ***(G-1451)***
Approved Info Destruction Inc.....412 722-8124
3946 Mimosa Dr Bethel Park (15102) ***(G-1403)***
Appvion Operations Inc.....814 224-2131
100 Paper Mill Rd Roaring Spring (16673) ***(G-16761)***
Apr Supply Co.....215 592-1935
462 N 4th St Philadelphia (19123) ***(G-13401)***
APS Advance Products & Svcs.....610 863-0570
316 N Broadway Wind Gap (18091) ***(G-20165)***
Apss Inc.....724 368-3001
120 Fisher Rd Portersville (16051) ***(G-15925)***
APT Advanced Polymer Tech Corp (PA).....724 452-1330
109 Conica Ln Harmony (16037) ***(G-7066)***
Aptech Computer Systems Inc.....412 963-7440
135 Delta Dr Pittsburgh (15238) ***(G-14714)***
Apter Industries Inc.....412 672-9628
1224 Long Run Rd Ste 1 White Oak (15131) ***(G-19853)***
Apx Enclosures Inc (PA).....717 328-9399
200 Oregon St Mercersburg (17236) ***(G-10981)***
Apx Industrial Coatings Inc.....717 369-0037
9473 Lincoln Way W Saint Thomas (17252) ***(G-17037)***
Apx York Sheet Metal Inc.....717 767-2704
255 Church Rd York (17406) ***(G-20382)***
Apx-Seetech Systems Inc.....717 751-6445
95 Willow Springs Cir York (17406) ***(G-20383)***
Aqua Enterprises.....215 257-2231
311 Wyckford Dr Perkasie (18944) ***(G-13266)***
Aqua Group, Canonsburg *Also called Aquatech International LLC* ***(G-2543)***
Aqua Treatment Services Inc.....717 697-4998
194 Hempt Rd Mechanicsburg (17050) ***(G-10820)***
Aquacap Pharmaceutical Inc.....610 361-2800
4 Hillman Dr Ste 190 Chadds Ford (19317) ***(G-2847)***
Aquachempacs LLC.....215 396-7200
515 Andrews Rd Feasterville Trevose (19053) ***(G-5885)***
Aquador.....724 942-1525
3855 Washington Rd Canonsburg (15317) ***(G-2542)***
Aquamed Technologies Inc.....215 702-8550
2150 Cabot Blvd W Ste B Langhorne (19047) ***(G-9277)***
Aquamed Technologies Inc.....215 970-7194
1010 Stony Hill Rd # 200 Yardley (19067) ***(G-20296)***
Aquaphoenix Scientific Inc.....717 632-1291
860 Gitts Run Rd Hanover (17331) ***(G-6861)***
Aquatech International LLC (PA).....724 746-5300
1 Four Coins Dr Canonsburg (15317) ***(G-2543)***
Aquatech Intl Sls Corp.....724 746-5300
1 Four Coins Dr Canonsburg (15317) ***(G-2544)***
Aquatic Co.....717 367-1100
40 Industrial Rd Elizabethtown (17022) ***(G-4865)***
Aquion Energy Inc.....412 904-6400
32 39th St Pittsburgh (15201) ***(G-14715)***
AR Rf/Mcrowave Instrumentation, Souderton *Also called Amplifier Research Corp* ***(G-17724)***
AR Scientific Inc (HQ).....215 288-6500
1100 Orthodox St Philadelphia (19124) ***(G-13402)***
AR Scientific Inc.....215 807-1312
7722 Dungan Rd Philadelphia (19111) ***(G-13403)***
AR Tart LLC.....267 408-6507
8229 Germantown Ave Ste D Philadelphia (19118) ***(G-13404)***
AR Trucking.....814 723-1245
2072 Pennsylvania Ave W Warren (16365) ***(G-19010)***
ARA Corporation.....724 843-5378
5227 Fifth Ave Koppel (16136) ***(G-8813)***
Aradiant Corporation.....717 838-7220
101 N Harrison St Palmyra (17078) ***(G-13116)***
Arai Helmet Americas Inc.....610 366-7220
7020 Snowdrift Rd Allentown (18106) ***(G-142)***
Arai Technical Services, Allentown *Also called Arai Helmet Americas Inc* ***(G-142)***
Aralez Management, Royersford *Also called Aralez Pharmaceuticals MGT Inc* ***(G-16843)***
Aralez Pharmaceuticals MGT Inc.....609 917-9330
70 Bayhill Cir Royersford (19468) ***(G-16843)***
Aralez Pharmaceuticals R&D Inc.....609 917-9330
70 Bayhill Cir Royersford (19468) ***(G-16844)***
Aralez Pharmaceuticals US Inc.....609 917-9330
70 Bayhill Cir Royersford (19468) ***(G-16845)***
Aralez R&D, Royersford *Also called Aralez Pharmaceuticals R&D Inc* ***(G-16844)***
Araloc, Malvern *Also called Modevity LLC* ***(G-10280)***
Aramark Services Inc.....800 999-8989
1101 Market St Ste 45 Philadelphia (19107) ***(G-13405)***
Aramark Unf Creer AP Group Inc (HQ).....215 238-3000
1101 Market St Ste 45 Philadelphia (19107) ***(G-13406)***
Arbco Industries LLC.....724 327-6300
2040 Borland Farm Rd Export (15632) ***(G-5590)***
Arbil Enterprises Inc.....215 969-0500
12285 Mcnulty Rd Ste 101 Philadelphia (19154) ***(G-13407)***
Arbutus Biopharma Corporation.....267 469-0914
701 Veterans Cir Warminster (18974) ***(G-18828)***
Arbutus Biopharma Inc.....215 675-5921
701 Veterans Cir Warminster (18974) ***(G-18829)***
Arbutus Electronics Inc.....717 764-3565
600 Farmbrook Ln York (17406) ***(G-20384)***
ARC Diamond Tooling.....724 593-5814
494 Bethel Church Rd Ligonier (15658) ***(G-9957)***
ARC Manufacturing Co Inc.....215 355-8500
1651 Loretta Ave Feasterville Trevose (19053) ***(G-5886)***
ARC Metals Corporation (HQ).....814 776-2116
224 River Rd Ste 9 Ridgway (15853) ***(G-16695)***
ARC Rmediation Specialists Inc.....386 405-6760
258 Main St Bristol (19007) ***(G-2108)***
ARc Technologies Corporation.....724 722-7066
226 Lumber St Yukon (15698) ***(G-20784)***
Arcadia Controls.....724 538-8931
392 Plains Church Rd Cranberry Township (16066) ***(G-3804)***
Arcelormittal Holdings LLC.....724 684-1000
345 Donner Ave Monessen (15062) ***(G-11297)***
Arcelormittal Plate, Coatesville *Also called Arcelormittal USA LLC* ***(G-3290)***
Arcelormittal Plate LLC.....610 383-2000
201 Stoyer Rd Coatesville (19320) ***(G-3289)***
Arcelormittal Steelton LLC.....717 986-2000
215 S Front St Steelton (17113) ***(G-18044)***
Arcelormittal USA LLC.....610 383-2000
139 Modena Rd Coatesville (19320) ***(G-3290)***
Arcelormittal USA LLC.....717 986-2887
215 S Front St Steelton (17113) ***(G-18045)***
Arcelormittal USA LLC.....610 825-6020
900 Conshohocken Rd Conshohocken (19428) ***(G-3521)***
Arcelrmttal Tblar Pdts USA LLC (HQ).....419 342-1200
4 Gateway Ctr Pittsburgh (15222) ***(G-14716)***
Arch Mfg LLC.....724 438-5170
336 E Main St Uniontown (15401) ***(G-18616)***

Arch Parent Inc 570 534-6026
205 Applegate Rd Stroudsburg (18360) *(G-18104)*

Archer Double Ds Product 610 838-1121
3215 Bingen Rd Bethlehem (18015) *(G-1452)*

Archer Instruments LLC 215 589-0356
411 Race St Catasauqua (18032) *(G-2814)*

Archer-Daniels-Midland Company 717 761-5200
2000 Hummel Ave Camp Hill (17011) *(G-2491)*

Archer-Daniels-Midland Company 215 547-8424
100 Cabot Blvd E Langhorne (19047) *(G-9278)*

Archetype Design Studio LLC 412 369-2900
176 Rochester Rd West View (15229) *(G-19773)*

Archetype Frameless Glass Co 717 244-5240
180 S Orchard St Yoe (17313) *(G-20358)*

Archi-Texture, Fairview Also called Advanced Finishing Usa Inc *(G-5810)*

Architctral Prcast Innovations 570 837-1774
3369 Paxtonville Rd Middleburg (17842) *(G-11023)*

Architectural Iron Company 570 296-7722
104 Ironwood Ct Milford (18337) *(G-11156)*

Architectural Millwork Assoc 215 699-0346
327 S 5th St North Wales (19454) *(G-12789)*

Architectural Polymers Inc 610 824-3322
1220 Little Gap Rd Palmerton (18071) *(G-13102)*

Architectural Sign Associates 412 563-5657
300 Mount Lebanon Blvd 201a Pittsburgh (15234) *(G-14717)*

Architectural Stl & Assod Pdts 215 368-8113
864 W 5th St Lansdale (19446) *(G-9343)*

Architectural Woodsmiths Inc (PA) 717 532-7700
40 Lurgan Ave Shippensburg (17257) *(G-17515)*

Archrock Inc 724 464-2291
488 Geesey Rd Indiana (15701) *(G-8080)*

Archrock Services LP 724 935-7660
3000 Stonewood Dr Wexford (15090) *(G-19789)*

Archrock Services LP 570 567-7162
9070 Route 414 Canton (17724) *(G-2662)*

Archway Press Inc 610 583-4004
825 Chester Pike Sharon Hill (19079) *(G-17452)*

Arcman Corporation 570 489-6402
1200 Meade St Dunmore (18512) *(G-4467)*

Arco Sales Co 215 743-9425
1230 E Mermaid Ln Ste 7 Glenside (19038) *(G-6505)*

Arcobaleno LLC 717 394-1402
160 Greenfield Rd Lancaster (17601) *(G-8937)*

Arconic Inc 717 393-9641
1480 Manheim Pike Lancaster (17601) *(G-8938)*

Arconic Inc 412 553-4545
201 Isabella St Ste 200 Pittsburgh (15212) *(G-14718)*

Arconic Inc 724 337-5300
100 Technical Dr New Kensington (15068) *(G-12324)*

Arconic Mexico Holdings LLC 412 553-4545
201 Isabella St Pittsburgh (15212) *(G-14719)*

Arcos Industries LLC 570 339-5200
394 Arcos Dr Mount Carmel (17851) *(G-11623)*

Arcs Design & Printing Inc 215 238-1831
211 N 9th St Philadelphia (19107) *(G-13408)*

Arctic Blast Covers 724 213-8460
1434 Florence Ave Indiana (15701) *(G-8081)*

Arctic Glacier Texas Inc 610 494-8200
410 Bethel Ave Upper Chichester (19014) *(G-18656)*

Arctic Star Sleds 814 684-3594
2842 Butternut Rd Tyrone (16686) *(G-18576)*

Arcweb Technologies LLC 800 846-7980
234 Market St Fl 5 Philadelphia (19106) *(G-13409)*

Ard Operating LLC 570 979-1240
33 W 3rd St Williamsport (17701) *(G-19989)*

Ardagh Glass Inc 814 642-2521
1 Glass Pl Port Allegany (16743) *(G-15891)*

Ardagh Metal Packaging USA Inc 570 389-5563
6670 Lowe St Bloomsburg (17815) *(G-1770)*

Ardagh Metal Packaging USA Inc (HQ) 412 923-1080
600 N Bell Ave Carnegie (15106) *(G-2764)*

Ardara Technologies LP 724 863-0418
12941 State Route 993 Ardara (15615) *(G-698)*

Ardent Mills LLC 717 846-7773
2800 Black Bridge Rd York (17406) *(G-20385)*

Ardent Mills LLC 972 660-9980
321 E Breadfruit Dr Treichlers (18086) *(G-18476)*

Ardent Mills LLC 717 244-4559
321 Taylor Ave Red Lion (17356) *(G-16588)*

Ardent Mills LLC 570 839-8322
258 Harvest Ln Pocono Summit (18346) *(G-15885)*

Ardent Resources Inc 412 854-1193
61 Mcmurray Rd Ste 204 Pittsburgh (15241) *(G-14720)*

Ardex L P (HQ) 724 203-5000
400 Ardex Park Dr Ste 1 Aliquippa (15001) *(G-66)*

Ardex Engineered Cements, Aliquippa Also called Ardex L P *(G-66)*

Ardiem Medical Inc 724 349-0855
1380 Route 286 Hwy E Indiana (15701) *(G-8082)*

ARDMORE ICE SKATING RINK, Ardmore Also called Philadelphia Skating Club A *(G-713)*

Ardsley Auto Tags (PA) 215 572-1409
2745 Jenkintown Rd Glenside (19038) *(G-6506)*

Area Shopper 814 425-7272
4095 Us Highway 19 Cochranton (16314) *(G-3335)*

Area Tool & Manufacturing Inc 814 724-3166
181 Baldwin Street Ext Meadville (16335) *(G-10703)*

Arete Qis LLC 814 781-1194
103 Bridge St Ridgway (15853) *(G-16696)*

Arg Resources Inc 814 837-7477
285 Custom Lumber Ln Kane (16735) *(G-8459)*

Arg Resources Inc (PA) 610 940-4420
100 Four Fls Ste 215 West Conshohocken (19428) *(G-19685)*

Argon St Inc 724 564-4100
90 Laurel View Dr Smithfield (15478) *(G-17641)*

Argosy Capital Group LLC 610 971-9685
950 W Valley Rd Ste 2902 Wayne (19087) *(G-19299)*

Argosy Inv Partners IV LP (PA) 610 971-9685
950 W Valley Rd Ste 2900 Wayne (19087) *(G-19300)*

Argosy Private Equity, Wayne Also called Argosy Capital Group LLC *(G-19299)*

Argus Printing 610 687-0411
168 E Lancaster Ave Wayne (19087) *(G-19301)*

Argus Printing & Copy 610 687-0411
168 E Lancaster Ave Wayne (19087) *(G-19302)*

Ariba Inc 215 246-3493
1500 Market St Fl 12 Philadelphia (19102) *(G-13410)*

Ariba Inc 412 644-0160
210 6th Ave Fl 25 Pittsburgh (15222) *(G-14721)*

Ariba Inc 610 661-8413
3999 West Chester Pike Newtown Square (19073) *(G-12566)*

Ariela and Associates Intl LLC 570 385-8340
301 S Margaretta St Schuylkill Haven (17972) *(G-17147)*

Arin Technologies Inc 412 877-2877
24 Terminal Way Ste 324 Pittsburgh (15219) *(G-14722)*

Aristo-TEC Metal Forms Inc 724 626-5900
401 Ridge Blvd Connellsville (15425) *(G-3489)*

Ark Ideaz Inc 610 246-9106
1198 Chestershire Pl Pottstown (19465) *(G-15943)*

Ark Safety, Millersburg Also called Seal Glove Mfg Inc *(G-11200)*

Arkay Tool & Die Inc 215 322-2039
41 Terry Dr Langhorne (19053) *(G-9279)*

Arkema Delaware Inc (HQ) 610 205-7000
900 First Ave King of Prussia (19406) *(G-8582)*

Arkema Inc 215 826-2600
100 Route 413 Bristol (19007) *(G-2109)*

Arkema Inc 610 582-1551
1112 Lincoln Rd Birdsboro (19508) *(G-1686)*

Arkema Inc 610 878-6500
900 1st Ave King of Prussia (19406) *(G-8583)*

Arkema Inc 610 363-4100
502 Thomas Jones Way Exton (19341) *(G-5646)*

Arkmedica LLC 724 349-0856
1125 Wayne Ave Indiana (15701) *(G-8083)*

Arkwood Products Inc 412 835-8730
5309 Enterprise Blvd Bethel Park (15102) *(G-1404)*

Arkwright LLC 732 246-1506
11350 Norcom Rd Philadelphia (19154) *(G-13411)*

Arlanxeo USA Holdings Corp (HQ) 412 809-1000
111 Ridc Park West Dr Pittsburgh (15275) *(G-14723)*

Arlanxeo USA LLC (HQ) 412 809-1000
111 Ridc Park West Dr Pittsburgh (15275) *(G-14724)*

Arlington Industries Inc 267 580-2620
1 Stauffer Industrial Par Taylor (18517) *(G-18258)*

Arm Camco LLC 814 472-7980
667 Industrial Park Rd Ebensburg (15931) *(G-4779)*

Arma Co LLC 717 295-6805
1048 New Holland Ave Lancaster (17601) *(G-8939)*

Armaclad Inc 717 749-3141
6806 Anthony Hwy Waynesboro (17268) *(G-19398)*

Armadani Inc 215 627-2601
740 Sansom St Ste 204 Philadelphia (19106) *(G-13412)*

Armark Authentication Tech LLC 717 767-4651
3400 Farmtrail Rd York (17406) *(G-20386)*

Armin Ironworks Inc 412 322-1622
1800 Preble Ave Pittsburgh (15233) *(G-14725)*

Armina Stone, Cheswick Also called Porto Exim Usa LLC *(G-3115)*

Armina Stone Inc 412 406-8442
780 Route 910 Ste 100 Cheswick (15024) *(G-3101)*

Armoloy Co of Philadelphia 215 788-0841
1105 Miller Ave Croydon (19021) *(G-3910)*

Armoloy Western Pennsylvania, Turtle Creek Also called Armoloy Western Pennsylvania *(G-18558)*

Armoloy Western Pennsylvania 412 823-1030
1231 Rodi Rd Turtle Creek (15145) *(G-18558)*

Armor Manufacturing Inc 724 658-1848
5220 State Route 18 New Castle (16102) *(G-12059)*

Armstrong Cement & Supply Corp 724 352-9401
100 Clearfield Rd Cabot (16023) *(G-2452)*

Armstrong Engrg Assoc Inc (PA) 610 436-6080
1845 W Strasburg Rd Coatesville (19320) *(G-3291)*

Armstrong Engrg Assoc Inc........................610 436-6080
1101 W Strasburg Rd West Chester (19382) *(G-19501)*

Armstrong Flooring, Lancaster *Also called Armstrong Hardwood Flooring Co* *(G-8941)*

Armstrong Flooring, Lancaster *Also called Ahf Products LLC* *(G-8923)*

Armstrong Flooring, Titusville *Also called Homerwood Hardwood Flooring Co* *(G-18382)*

Armstrong Flooring Inc (PA).....................717 672-9611
2500 Columbia Ave Lancaster (17603) *(G-8940)*

Armstrong Hardwood Flooring Co................717 672-9611
2500 Columbia Ave Lancaster (17603) *(G-8941)*

Armstrong Patterns & Mfg.........................724 845-1452
1509 Rearick Rd Ford City (16226) *(G-6042)*

Armstrong Precision Mfg LLC......................412 449-0160
1370 Old Frport Rd Ste 3b Pittsburgh (15238) *(G-14726)*

Armstrong Supply Co................................215 643-0310
22 Schiavone Dr Ambler (19002) *(G-567)*

Armstrong World Industries Inc (PA)..............717 397-0611
2500 Columbia Ave Lancaster (17603) *(G-8942)*

Armstrong World Industries Inc...................717 426-4171
1507 River Rd Marietta (17547) *(G-10460)*

Armstrong/Kover Kwick Inc........................412 771-2200
401 Sproul St Mc Kees Rocks (15136) *(G-10603)*

Armstrongs..717 543-5488
130 Armstrong Ln Mc Clure (17841) *(G-10557)*

Arnold Foods Company Inc.........................215 672-8010
255 Business Center Dr # 200 Horsham (19044) *(G-7788)*

Arnold Printed Communications, Sewickley *Also called Jka Inc* *(G-17397)*

Arnold's Meats, Bensalem *Also called Family Food Products Inc* *(G-1193)*

Aron Lighting LLC................................484 681-5687
307 E Church Rd Ste 3 King of Prussia (19406) *(G-8584)*

Arp, Harrisburg *Also called Applied RES & Photonics Inc* *(G-7089)*

Arris, Horsham *Also called Ruckus Wireless Inc* *(G-7847)*

Arris Global Services Inc.........................215 323-1000
101 Tournament Dr Horsham (19044) *(G-7789)*

Arris Technology Inc..............................215 323-2590
101 Tournament Dr Horsham (19044) *(G-7790)*

Arrison H B West Virginia Inc.....................724 324-2106
Rr 19 Mount Morris (15349) *(G-11678)*

Arro Forge Inc....................................814 724-4223
Kebert Industrial Park Meadville (16335) *(G-10704)*

Arrow Castings Co................................814 838-3561
2645 W 14th St Erie (16505) *(G-5194)*

Arrow International Inc (HQ).......................610 225-6800
550 E Swedesford Rd # 400 Wayne (19087) *(G-19303)*

Arrow International Inc............................610 655-8522
1001 Hill Ave Reading (19610) *(G-16323)*

Arrow International Inc............................610 378-0131
2400 Bernville Rd Reading (19605) *(G-16324)*

Arrow Supply Company Inc........................773 863-8655
2517 Wyandotte Rd Willow Grove (19090) *(G-20108)*

Arrow Tool Die & Machine Co (PA).................215 676-1300
56 Home Rd Hatboro (19040) *(G-7270)*

Arrowhead Wine Cellars Inc.......................814 725-5509
12073 E Main Rd North East (16428) *(G-12729)*

Arrowwood Construction..........................610 799-6040
4245 Hill St Coplay (18037) *(G-3639)*

ARS Metal Fabricators LLC........................215 855-6000
3430 Unionville Pike Hatfield (19440) *(G-7318)*

Arsenal Resources Energy LLC.....................724 940-1100
6031 Wallace Road Ext Wexford (15090) *(G-19790)*

Arsenal Resources LLC............................724 940-1100
6031 Wallace Road Ext # 300 Wexford (15090) *(G-19791)*

Art & Ink...814 486-0606
6 W 6th St Emporium (15834) *(G-5049)*

Art Communication Systems Inc....................717 232-0144
1340 N 17th St Harrisburg (17103) *(G-7090)*

Art Craft Cabinets Inc............................717 397-7817
720 Lafayette St Lancaster (17603) *(G-8943)*

Art Engraving, Pottstown *Also called Aeco Service Inc* *(G-15941)*

Art Glass Sgo Inc.................................215 884-8543
909 Bethlehem Pike Spring House (19477) *(G-17881)*

Art Kraft, Bristol *Also called Npc Acquisition Inc* *(G-2176)*

Art of Shaving - Fl LLC...........................610 962-1000
160 N Gulph Rd Ste 2184 King of Prussia (19406) *(G-8585)*

Art Printing Co of Lancaster.......................717 397-6029
131 Locust St Columbia (17512) *(G-3430)*

ART Research Enterprises.........................717 290-1303
3050 Industry Dr Lancaster (17603) *(G-8944)*

Art Sign Company.................................717 264-4211
470 Nelson St Chambersburg (17201) *(G-2906)*

Art Stitch Inc....................................717 652-8992
1308 N Mountain Rd Harrisburg (17112) *(G-7091)*

Art Tech Designs.................................412 754-0391
411 Spring Ln Elizabeth (15037) *(G-4855)*

Art Works, Canonsburg *Also called Al Tedeschi* *(G-2535)*

Artcraft Printers Inc.............................724 537-5231
400 Weldon St Latrobe (15650) *(G-9457)*

Arthur K Miller...................................724 588-1118
182 Sharon Rd Greenville (16125) *(G-6738)*

Arthur L Baker Enterprises........................717 432-9788
711 E Mount Airy Rd Lewisberry (17339) *(G-9880)*

Arthur R Warner Company (PA).....................724 539-9229
701 Depot St Latrobe (15650) *(G-9458)*

Artie's Waterice, Philadelphia *Also called Arties Unlimited LLC* *(G-13413)*

Arties Unlimited LLC..............................267 516-2575
6730 N Broad St Philadelphia (19126) *(G-13413)*

Artisan Confections Company (HQ).................717 534-4200
100 Crystal A Dr Hershey (17033) *(G-7604)*

Artisan Mobile Inc...............................610 209-1959
234 Market St Fl 4 Philadelphia (19106) *(G-13414)*

Artisan Specialist Tech...........................215 849-0509
439 E High St Philadelphia (19144) *(G-13415)*

Artisans of The Anvil Inc.........................570 476-7950
40 N 2nd St Stroudsburg (18360) *(G-18105)*

Artistagraphics Inc...............................412 271-3252
2148 Ardmore Blvd Pittsburgh (15221) *(G-14727)*

Artistic Image...................................717 567-7070
211 N 4th St Newport (17074) *(G-12486)*

Artistworks Wholesale Inc.........................610 622-9940
456 Penn St Lansdowne (19050) *(G-9430)*

Artline Ornamental Iron Works.....................215 727-2923
4820 Yocum St Philadelphia (19143) *(G-13416)*

Artman and Artman Inc...........................610 821-3970
1137 N Godfrey St Unit 2 Allentown (18109) *(G-143)*

Artman Equipment Company Inc....................724 337-3700
854 State Route 380 Apollo (15613) *(G-662)*

Artskills Inc.....................................610 253-6663
3935 Rabold Cir S Bethlehem (18020) *(G-1453)*

Artube, East Stroudsburg *Also called Iridium Industries Inc* *(G-4621)*

Artwear, Leola *Also called A R Groff Transport Inc* *(G-9764)*

Artworks Silk Screen Printers......................717 238-5087
4379 N 6th St Harrisburg (17110) *(G-7092)*

Arty Embroidery & Design Inc......................215 423-8114
3301 Frankford Ave Philadelphia (19134) *(G-13417)*

Arundel Cellars Inc...............................814 725-1079
11727 E Main Rd North East (16428) *(G-12730)*

Arundel Cellars & Brewing Co, North East *Also called Arundel Cellars Inc* *(G-12730)*

Arvite Technologies Inc...........................814 838-9444
2731 W 11th St Erie (16505) *(G-5195)*

Arx LLC..717 253-7979
400 Seaks Run Rd Glen Rock (17327) *(G-6451)*

As, Allentown *Also called Adhesives Specialists Inc* *(G-116)*

ASA Baking Corp.................................267 535-1618
2023 S Redfield St Philadelphia (19143) *(G-13418)*

ASAP Printing & Copying Inc......................215 357-5033
1300 Industrial Blvd # 100 Southampton (18966) *(G-17798)*

Asbury Carbons, Sunbury *Also called Anthracite Industries Inc* *(G-18163)*

Asbury Carbons Inc..............................570 286-9721
216 E Haas Manor Rd Sunbury (17801) *(G-18164)*

Asbury Graphite Mills Inc.........................724 543-1343
280 Linde Rd Kittanning (16201) *(G-8755)*

Ascension Publishing LLC.........................610 696-7795
20 Hagerty Blvd Ste 3 West Chester (19382) *(G-19502)*

Ascentive LLC....................................215 395-8559
50 S 16th St Ste 3575 Philadelphia (19102) *(G-13419)*

Asco Enterprises Inc.............................724 945-5525
1684 E National Pike Scenery Hill (15360) *(G-17124)*

Asels Cabinet Company...........................814 677-3063
Rouseville Rd Rr 8 Rouseville (16344) *(G-16835)*

Aserdiv Inc (HQ).................................800 966-7770
940 W Sproul Rd Springfield (19064) *(G-17907)*

Aset, Lewisburg *Also called American Slar Envmtl Technolog* *(G-9897)*

Asgco (PA).......................................610 821-0216
302 W Gordon St Allentown (18102) *(G-144)*

Ash/Tec Inc......................................570 682-0933
218 Dell Rd Hegins (17938) *(G-7539)*

Ashby Mfg Co Inc................................724 776-5566
12 Leonberg Rd Cranberry Township (16066) *(G-3805)*

Ashcombe Products Company Inc...................717 848-1271
1065 Box Hill Ln York (17403) *(G-20387)*

Asher Chocolates, Souderton *Also called Chester A Asher Inc* *(G-17729)*

Ashland Foundry & Mch Work LLC..................570 875-6100
500 E Centre St Ashland (17921) *(G-727)*

Ashland Industrial Svcs LLC (PA)..................717 347-5616
1 N Main St Shrewsbury (17361) *(G-17581)*

Ashland LLC.....................................215 446-7900
2801 Christopher Columbus Philadelphia (19148) *(G-13420)*

Ashland Technologies, Hegins *Also called Ash/Tec Inc* *(G-7539)*

Ashley Ant-Skid Aggregates Div, Old Forge *Also called McClure Enterprises Inc* *(G-12970)*

Ashley Furniture Inds Inc.........................610 926-0897
45 Ashley Way Leesport (19533) *(G-9657)*

Ashley Machine & Tool Co.........................570 287-0966
1450 1460 Shoemaker Ave West Wyoming (18644) *(G-19775)*

Ashlow, Reading *Also called Vai Pomini Inc* *(G-16558)*

Asi Holding, Allentown *Also called Applied Separations Inc* *(G-141)*

Ask Foods Inc (PA)...............................717 838-6356
77 N Hetrick Ave Palmyra (17078) *(G-13117)*

Ask Foods Inc 717 838-6356
  140 N Locust St Palmyra (17078) *(G-13118)*

Ask IV Screen Printing 412 200-5610
  7900 Steubenville Pike Imperial (15126) *(G-8058)*

Asm, Ridgway *Also called Alpha Sintered Metals LLC (G-16694)*

Asm Industries Inc (HQ) 717 656-2161
  41 Industrial Cir Lancaster (17601) *(G-8945)*

Asm Industries Inc 717 656-2166
  1 Lark Ave Leola (17540) *(G-9769)*

Asm Industries Inc 717 656-2161
  41 Industrial Cir Lancaster (17601) *(G-8946)*

Asm Products Inc 724 861-8026
  10830 Glass St North Huntingdon (15642) *(G-12768)*

Asmac Inc 814 781-3358
  338 West Creek Rd Saint Marys (15857) *(G-16949)*

Asone Technologies Inc 570 443-5700
  13 Berwick St White Haven (18661) *(G-19846)*

ASP Services Inc (PA) 570 374-5333
  10 Lisalyn Rd Selinsgrove (17870) *(G-17320)*

Asphalt Press Industries 610 489-7283
  3513 Arcola Rd Arcola (19420) *(G-697)*

Aspire Bariatrics Inc 610 590-1577
  319 N Pottstown Pike # 202 Exton (19341) *(G-5647)*

Aspire Technologies 610 491-8162
  970 Pulaski Dr King of Prussia (19406) *(G-8586)*

Aspol LLC 412 628-0078
  1504 Constitution Blvd New Kensington (15068) *(G-12325)*

Aspx LLC 215 345-6782
  1730 Lower State Rd Doylestown (18901) *(G-4271)*

Asr Enterprises Inc 610 873-7484
  801 E Lancaster Ave Downingtown (19335) *(G-4211)*

Asr Instruments Inc 412 833-7577
  5547 Saddlebrook Dr Bethel Park (15102) *(G-1405)*

Assemblies of Yahweh 717 933-4518
  190 Frantz Rd Bethel (19507) *(G-1392)*

Associated Box, New Castle *Also called Nelson Company (G-12126)*

Associated Ceramics & Tech (PA) 724 353-1585
  400 N Pike Rd Sarver (16055) *(G-17065)*

Associated Fasteners Inc 610 837-9200
  6854 Chrisphalt Dr Bath (18014) *(G-951)*

Associated Machine Service (PA) 215 335-1940
  6560 Senator Ln Bensalem (19020) *(G-1149)*

Associated Packaging Entps Inc 484 785-1120
  1 Dickinson Dr Ste 100 Chadds Ford (19317) *(G-2848)*

Associated Packaging Tech, Chadds Ford *Also called Associated Packaging Entps Inc (G-2848)*

Associated Products LLC 412 486-2255
  1901 William Flynn Hwy Glenshaw (15116) *(G-6482)*

Associated Prtg Graphics Svcs 215 322-6762
  4570 E Bristol Rd Ste A Feasterville Trevose (19053) *(G-5887)*

Associated Rubber Inc 215 536-2800
  115 S 6th St Quakertown (18951) *(G-16169)*

Associated Specialties, Orefield *Also called Associated Specialty Co (G-13008)*

Associated Specialty Co 610 395-9172
  3551 Route 309 Orefield (18069) *(G-13008)*

Associated Tool & Machine 814 783-0083
  19817 Bertram Dr Saegertown (16433) *(G-16907)*

Associated Windows 814 445-9744
  334 Emert Rd Somerset (15501) *(G-17674)*

Associates In Medical Mktg Co 215 860-9600
  6 Penns Trl Newtown (18940) *(G-12497)*

Association Test Publishers 717 755-9747
  2995 Round Hill Rd York (17402) *(G-20388)*

Assocted Grphic Communications, Wayne *Also called Main Line Print Shop Inc (G-19349)*

Assured Polygraph Services Inc 412 492-9980
  3242 Babcock Blvd Pittsburgh (15237) *(G-14728)*

Assured Toll & Gauge Inc 724 722-3410
  184 Gressly Rd Ruffs Dale (15679) *(G-16870)*

Astatech Inc (PA) 215 785-3197
  2525 Pearl Buck Rd Bristol (19007) *(G-2110)*

Astea International Inc (PA) 215 682-2500
  240 Gibraltar Rd Ste 300 Horsham (19044) *(G-7791)*

Astley Precision Mch Co Inc (PA) 724 861-5000
  160 S Thompson Ln Irwin (15642) *(G-8144)*

Astra Corporation 215 674-3539
  21 Industrial Dr Ste B Warminster (18974) *(G-18830)*

Astra Distributors, Upper Darby *Also called Grammeco Inc (G-18686)*

Astra Foods Inc 610 352-4400
  6430 Market St Upper Darby (19082) *(G-18681)*

Astrazeneca Pharmaceuticals LP 215 501-1739
  3600 Marshall Ln Bensalem (19020) *(G-1150)*

Astro Apparel Inc (PA) 570 346-1700
  300 Brook St Ste 2 Scranton (18505) *(G-17209)*

Astro Automation Inc 724 864-2500
  100 Productivity Pl Irwin (15642) *(G-8145)*

Astro Dynmc Print Graphic Svcs, Warminster *Also called Astro Printing Services Inc (G-18831)*

Astro Machine Works Inc 717 738-4281
  470 Wenger Dr Ephrata (17522) *(G-5090)*

Astro Printing Services Inc 215 441-4444
  882 Louis Dr Warminster (18974) *(G-18831)*

Astrobotic Technology Inc 412 682-3282
  2515 Liberty Ave Pittsburgh (15222) *(G-14729)*

Astrocomix, Milford *Also called Daniel Parent (G-11158)*

Astrometrics Inc 610 280-0869
  108 Ashland Dr Downingtown (19335) *(G-4212)*

At-Mar Glass, Kennett Square *Also called E Victor Pesce (G-8508)*

Atalanti Polymer Inc 412 321-7411
  1016 Constance St Pittsburgh (15212) *(G-14730)*

Atc Technology Corporation (HQ) 412 820-3700
  700 Cranberry Woods Dr Cranberry Township (16066) *(G-3806)*

Atch-Mont Gear Co Inc 215 355-5146
  65 Industrial Dr Ivyland (18974) *(G-8205)*

Atd-American Co 215 576-1000
  135 Greenwood Ave Wyncote (19095) *(G-20261)*

Ateeco Inc (PA) 570 462-2745
  600 E Centre St Shenandoah (17976) *(G-17492)*

Athena Controls Inc 610 828-2490
  5145 Campus Dr Ste 1 Plymouth Meeting (19462) *(G-15832)*

Athens Reproduction 610 649-5761
  19 W Athens Ave Ardmore (19003) *(G-701)*

Athletic Lettering Inc 717 840-6373
  2860 Eastern Blvd York (17402) *(G-20389)*

Athletic Trainer System, Grove City *Also called Keffer Development Svcs LLC (G-6793)*

ATI, Collegeville *Also called Analytical Technology Inc (G-3368)*

ATI, Pittsburgh *Also called Allegheny Technologies Inc (G-14682)*

ATI Albany Operations, Pittsburgh *Also called Oregon Metallurgical LLC (G-15363)*

ATI Allegheny Ludlum, Brackenridge *Also called Allegheny Ludlum LLC (G-1937)*

ATI Allegheny Ludlum, Vandergrift *Also called Allegheny Ludlum LLC (G-18721)*

ATI Allegheny Ludlum, Pittsburgh *Also called Allegheny Ludlum LLC (G-14679)*

ATI Allegheny Ludlum, Pittsburgh *Also called Allegheny Ludlum LLC (G-14680)*

ATI Allegheny Ludlum, Latrobe *Also called Allegheny Ludlum LLC (G-9453)*

ATI Allegheny Ludlum, Vandergrift *Also called Allegheny Ludlum LLC (G-18722)*

ATI Corporation 717 354-8721
  250 Earland Dr New Holland (17557) *(G-12229)*

ATI Flat Rlled Pdts Hldngs LLC 800 323-1240
  1300 Pacific Ave Natrona Heights (15065) *(G-11933)*

ATI Flat Rolled Products, Monaca *Also called ATI Precision Finishing LLC (G-11280)*

ATI Flat Rolled Products, Zelienople *Also called Allegheny Technologies Inc (G-20788)*

ATI Landis Threading Systems, Waynesboro *Also called Madison Inds Holdings LLC (G-19416)*

ATI Operating Holdings LLC (HQ) 412 394-2800
  1000 Six Ppg Pl Pittsburgh (15222) *(G-14731)*

ATI Powder Metals 412 923-2670
  1001 Robb Hill Rd Oakdale (15071) *(G-12891)*

ATI Powder Metals LLC 412 923-2670
  1001 Robb Hill Rd Oakdale (15071) *(G-12892)*

ATI Powder Metals LLC (HQ) 412 394-2800
  1000 Six Ppg Pl Pittsburgh (15222) *(G-14732)*

ATI Precision Finishing LLC (HQ) 724 775-1664
  499 Delaware Ave Rochester (15074) *(G-16782)*

ATI Precision Finishing LLC 724 775-2618
  2070 Pennsylvania Ave Monaca (15061) *(G-11280)*

ATI Precision Finishing LLC 724 452-1726
  W Newcastle St Rr 288 Zelienople (16063) *(G-20790)*

ATI Rome Metals, Rochester *Also called ATI Precision Finishing LLC (G-16782)*

ATI Specialty Materials, Pittsburgh *Also called Tdy Industries LLC (G-15600)*

Atiyeh Printing Inc 610 439-8978
  1002 W Tilghman St Allentown (18102) *(G-145)*

Atkins Kareemah 267 428-0019
  6 S Cedar Ln Upper Darby (19082) *(G-18682)*

Atkinson Industries Inc 570 366-2114
  Lincoln Ave Orwigsburg (17961) *(G-13039)*

Atkore International, Philadelphia *Also called TJ Cope Inc (G-14392)*

Atlantex Manufacturing Corp 610 518-6601
  600 Brandywine Ave # 500 Downingtown (19335) *(G-4213)*

Atlantic Alliance Pubg Co 267 319-1659
  318 Fitzwater St Philadelphia (19147) *(G-13421)*

Atlantic Cmmncations Group Inc 215 836-4683
  18 E Mill Rd Flourtown (19031) *(G-5984)*

Atlantic Concrete Products Inc (PA) 215 945-5600
  8900 Old Route 13 Bristol (19007) *(G-2111)*

Atlantic Crane Inc 610 366-1540
  7562 Penn Dr Ste 110 Fogelsville (18051) *(G-5991)*

Atlantic Dev Corp of PA 717 243-0212
  819 E High St Carlisle (17013) *(G-2690)*

Atlantic Embroidery Company 215 514-2154
  6 S Easton Rd Frnt Frnt Glenside (19038) *(G-6507)*

Atlantic Enterprise Inc 800 367-8547
  1800 Mearns Rd Ste P Ivyland (18974) *(G-8206)*

Atlantic Glass Etching Inc 717 244-7045
  450 Sterling Dr Red Lion (17356) *(G-16589)*

Atlantic Metal Industries LLC 908 445-4299
  2213 Shafer Rd Stroudsburg (18360) *(G-18106)*

Atlantic Novelties, Robesonia *Also called Go Tell It Inc (G-16774)*

Atlantic Papers, Ivyland *Also called Atlantic Enterprise Inc (G-8206)*

Atlantic Precast Concrete, Bristol *Also called Atlantic Precast Industries* ***(G-2113)***
Atlantic Precast Concrete......215 945-5600
8900 Old Route 13 Bristol (19007) ***(G-2112)***
Atlantic Precast Industries (PA)......215 945-5600
8900 Old Rte 13 Bristol (19007) ***(G-2113)***
Atlantic Prtg Grphic Cmmnctons......610 584-2060
2019 Lucon Rd Schwenksville (19473) ***(G-17173)***
Atlantic Publishing Group Inc......800 832-3747
18 E Mill Rd Flourtown (19031) ***(G-5985)***
Atlantic Refining & Marketing (HQ)......215 977-3000
1801 Market St Philadelphia (19103) ***(G-13422)***
Atlantic Shelving Systems LLC......215 245-1310
480 State Rd Ste D Bensalem (19020) ***(G-1151)***
Atlantic Spring & Mfg Co Div, Wayne *Also called Chestnut Group Inc* ***(G-19313)***
Atlantic Track & Turnout Co......570 429-1462
St Clair Business Park Pottsville (17901) ***(G-16073)***
Atlantic Track & Turnout Co......610 916-2840
5 S Cntre Ave Ste 200 Leesport (19533) ***(G-9658)***
Atlantic Veal & Lamb, Olyphant *Also called Atlantic Veal and Lamb Inc* ***(G-12984)***
Atlantic Veal and Lamb Inc......570 489-4781
218 Hull Ave Olyphant (18447) ***(G-12984)***
Atlantis Technologies LLC......724 695-2900
308 High Tech Dr Oakdale (15071) ***(G-12893)***
Atlas America, Coraopolis *Also called AEG Holdings Inc* ***(G-3654)***
Atlas America Pub 11-2002 Ltd......412 262-2830
311 Rouser Rd Moon Township (15108) ***(G-11480)***
Atlas America Public 10 Ltd......412 262-2830
311 Rouser Rd Coraopolis (15108) ***(G-3659)***
Atlas Copco Compressors LLC......610 916-4002
260 Corporate Dr Reading (19605) ***(G-16325)***
Atlas Copco Secoroc LLC......717 369-3177
13278 Lincoln Way W Fort Loudon (17224) ***(G-6057)***
Atlas Energy, Coraopolis *Also called Atlas Rsrces Pub 18-2009 B LP* ***(G-3661)***
Atlas Energy Company LLC (HQ)......877 280-2857
1845 Walnut St Ste 1000 Philadelphia (19103) ***(G-13423)***
Atlas Energy Operating Co LLC......412 262-2830
311 Rouser Rd Coraopolis (15108) ***(G-3660)***
Atlas Energy Resources, Pittsburgh *Also called Atlas Resources LLC* ***(G-14734)***
Atlas Energy, L.P., Pittsburgh *Also called Targa Energy LP* ***(G-15598)***
Atlas Flasher & Supply Co Inc......610 469-2602
2046 Pottstown Pike Pottstown (19465) ***(G-15944)***
Atlas Group The, Bensalem *Also called Brenner Aerostructures LLC* ***(G-1161)***
Atlas Growth Partners LP......412 489-0006
1000 Commerce Dr Ste 400 Pittsburgh (15275) ***(G-14733)***
Atlas Instrument Co Inc......717 267-1250
144 Oyler Dr Chambersburg (17201) ***(G-2907)***
Atlas Machining & Welding Inc......610 262-1374
777 Smith Ln Northampton (18067) ***(G-12844)***
Atlas Material Handling Inc......610 262-0644
4167 S Church St Whitehall (18052) ***(G-19862)***
Atlas Minerals & Chemicals Inc......800 523-8269
1227 Valley Rd Mertztown (19539) ***(G-11000)***
Atlas Molding LLC......717 556-8193
36 Glenbrook Rd Leola (17540) ***(G-9770)***
Atlas Neon Sign Corp (PA)......724 935-2171
230 Northgate Dr Warrendale (15086) ***(G-19068)***
Atlas Pipeline Oper Partnr LP, Philadelphia *Also called Targa Pipeline Oper Partnr LP* ***(G-14371)***
Atlas Pipeline Partners GP LLC, Philadelphia *Also called Targa Pipeline Partners GP LLC* ***(G-14372)***
Atlas Printing Company......814 445-2516
421 W Patriot St Somerset (15501) ***(G-17675)***
Atlas Resources LLC (HQ)......800 251-0171
1000 Commerce Dr Ste 510 Pittsburgh (15275) ***(G-14734)***
Atlas Roofing Corporation......717 760-5460
817 Spangler Rd Camp Hill (17011) ***(G-2492)***
Atlas Rsrces Pub 18-2009 B LP......330 896-8510
Westpointe Corp Ctr One Coraopolis (15108) ***(G-3661)***
Atlas Rsrces Series 28-2010 LP......412 489-0006
Park Pl Corp Ctr One 1000 Corporate Center Pittsburgh (15275) ***(G-14735)***
Atlas Rubber Stamp & Printing......717 755-3882
3755 E Market St Ste 5 York (17402) ***(G-20390)***
Atlas Sign Group LLC......724 935-2160
508 Pittsburgh St Ste 104 Mars (16046) ***(G-10487)***
Atls Production Company LLC......412 489-0006
1000 Commerce Dr Ste 400 Pittsburgh (15275) ***(G-14736)***
Atm Bancorp Inc......610 279-9550
2938 Dekalb Pike Norristown (19401) ***(G-12636)***
Atm's, Easton *Also called Blessed Dough LLC* ***(G-4657)***
Atochem Intl Inc/Polymers Div......610 582-1551
1112 Lincoln Rd Birdsboro (19508) ***(G-1687)***
Atoll, Johnstown *Also called Jigging Technologies LLC* ***(G-8386)***
Atomatic Manufacturing Co Inc......412 824-6400
300 Shadeland Ave East Pittsburgh (15112) ***(G-4594)***
Atomic Industries Inc......610 754-6400
2079 Big Rd Frederick (19435) ***(G-6171)***
Atoptix LLC......814 808-7056
200 Innovation Blvd State College (16803) ***(G-17942)***
Atotech Usa LLC......814 238-0514
270 Walker Dr State College (16801) ***(G-17943)***
Atp Associates, Boyertown *Also called Advanced Technical Peddler Inc* ***(G-1893)***
Atr Int'l, Philadelphia *Also called Above Rim International LLC* ***(G-13336)***
Atr Magnetics LLC......717 718-8008
385 Emig Rd Ste A York (17406) ***(G-20391)***
Atrp Solutions Inc......412 735-4799
855 William Pitt Way Pittsburgh (15238) ***(G-14737)***
Ats Equipment, Carlisle *Also called Master Solutions Inc* ***(G-2724)***
Ats Fleet Trcking MGT Slutions......570 445-8805
138 Willow St Dunmore (18512) ***(G-4468)***
Ats-Needham LLC......617 375-7500
Po Box 7501 Philadelphia (19101) ***(G-13424)***
Atsco Holdings Corp......440 701-1021
25 Leonberg Rd Cranberry Township (16066) ***(G-3807)***
Atwater Inc......570 779-9568
627 W Main St Plymouth (18651) ***(G-15815)***
Atwater Self Storage, Plymouth *Also called Atwater Inc* ***(G-15815)***
Au Fournil Inc......610 664-0235
234 Woodbine Ave Narberth (19072) ***(G-11908)***
Auch Printing Inc......215 886-9133
1351 Harris Rd Dresher (19025) ***(G-4353)***
Aucourant LLC......800 682-1623
140 Deer Path East Stroudsburg (18302) ***(G-4606)***
Aud-A-Bud Ceramics......717 898-7537
3090 Harrisburg Pike Landisville (17538) ***(G-9258)***
Audia International Inc (HQ)......724 228-1260
450 Racetrack Rd Washington (15301) ***(G-19151)***
Audio Critic, The, Quakertown *Also called Critic Publications Inc* ***(G-16181)***
Audio Video Automation SEC Inc......814 313-1108
920 Pennsylvania Ave W Warren (16365) ***(G-19011)***
Audiocare Systems, Wayne *Also called Mumps Audiofax Inc* ***(G-19358)***
Audiology & Hearing Aid Center (PA)......570 822-6122
34 S Main St Ste 19 Wilkes Barre (18701) ***(G-19906)***
Audiology & Hearing Aid Center......570 383-0500
1339 Main St Apt 4 Peckville (18452) ***(G-13206)***
Audubon Sales & Service, Feasterville Trevose *Also called C C B B Inc* ***(G-5898)***
Auger Fabrication Inc......610 524-3350
418 Creamery Way Exton (19341) ***(G-5648)***
Auger Mfg Specialists Co......610 647-4677
22a N Bacton Hill Rd Malvern (19355) ***(G-10188)***
Augers Unlimited Inc......610 380-1660
735 Fox Chase Ste 114 Coatesville (19320) ***(G-3292)***
Augmentir Inc......949 432-6450
425 Caredean Dr Horsham (19044) ***(G-7792)***
Augostinos, Bryn Mawr *Also called CFM Designs Inc* ***(G-2318)***
August Transport Inc......724 462-1445
17 Ferry St Leetsdale (15056) ***(G-9683)***
Augustine Die & Mold Inc......814 443-2390
492 Drum Ave Somerset (15501) ***(G-17676)***
Augustine Plastics Inc......814 443-7428
492 Drum Ave Somerset (15501) ***(G-17677)***
Aul Company Jack......412 882-1836
4687 Cook Ave Pittsburgh (15236) ***(G-14738)***
Auma Actuators Inc (HQ)......724 743-2862
100 Southpointe Blvd Canonsburg (15317) ***(G-2545)***
Auma Actuators Inc......714 247-1250
100 Southpointe Blvd Canonsburg (15317) ***(G-2546)***
Auman Machine Company Inc (PA)......717 273-4604
1525 Joel Dr Lebanon (17046) ***(G-9546)***
Aumapharma LLC......215 345-4150
215 Decatur St Doylestown (18901) ***(G-4272)***
Aunt Barbies......717 445-6386
234 Pleasant Valley Rd East Earl (17519) ***(G-4537)***
Auntie Annes Inc (HQ)......717 435-1435
48-50 W Chestnut St # 200 Lancaster (17603) ***(G-8947)***
Auntie Annes Soft Pretzels......724 349-2825
2334 Oakland Ave Ste 51 Indiana (15701) ***(G-8084)***
Aura Tiedye......888 474-2872
3095 Hancock Hwy Equinunk (18417) ***(G-5159)***
Aural Harmonics......610 488-0232
91 Miller Rd Bernville (19506) ***(G-1297)***
Aurele M Gatti Inc......215 428-4500
1 Canal Rd Fairless Hills (19030) ***(G-5772)***
Aurochs Brewing Company, Pittsburgh *Also called 2124 Brewing Company LLC* ***(G-14624)***
Aurora Computer Systems Inc......814 535-8371
151 Freidhoff Ln Johnstown (15902) ***(G-8354)***
Aurora Electrical & Data Svcs......412 255-4060
2740 Smallman St Ste 600 Pittsburgh (15222) ***(G-14739)***
Aurora International Coat......412 782-2984
20 Grant Ave Pittsburgh (15223) ***(G-14740)***
Aurora Optics Inc......215 646-0690
7 E Skippack Pike Ste 202 Ambler (19002) ***(G-568)***
Auskin Inc......610 696-0234
200 S Franklin St Ste 7 West Chester (19382) ***(G-19503)***
Austin Hardware......610 921-2723
1001 Rockland St Reading (19604) ***(G-16326)***
Australtek LLC......412 257-2377
800 Old Pond Rd Ste 706k Bridgeville (15017) ***(G-2054)***

Authorized Earmold Labs 215 788-0330
806 Beaver St Bristol (19007) *(G-2114)*

Auto Accessories America Inc 717 667-3004
100 Classic Car Dr Reedsville (17084) *(G-16621)*

Auto Addictions, Whitehall *Also called Jack Williams Tire Co Inc (G-19878)*

Auto B J, Warminster *Also called Automatic Forecasting Systems (G-18832)*

Auto Care 814 943-8155
1022 Old Mill Run Rd Altoona (16601) *(G-475)*

Auto Diesel Electric Inc 570 874-2100
9 Starter Dr Frackville (17931) *(G-6102)*

Auto Graphics Company, Manheim *Also called William F and Kathy A Yeager (G-10407)*

Auto Graphix, Wilkes Barre *Also called Web Paint Inc (G-19970)*

Auto Locater, Mount Joy *Also called Industrial Data Exchange Inc (G-11662)*

Auto Locator, Mount Joy *Also called Engle Printing & Pubg Co Inc (G-11654)*

Auto Seat Cover Company (PA) 814 453-5897
2125 Filmore Ave Erie (16506) *(G-5196)*

Auto Tops Inc (PA) 215 785-3310
320 Howell St Bristol (19007) *(G-2115)*

Auto Weld Chassis & Components 570 275-1411
21 Cherokee Rd Danville (17821) *(G-3997)*

Autocare Service Center Inc 717 854-0242
450 Loucks Rd York (17404) *(G-20392)*

Autoclave Engineers 814 860-5700
8325 Hessinger Dr Erie (16509) *(G-5197)*

Autograph Signs Inc 412 371-2877
508 Rodi Rd Pittsburgh (15235) *(G-14741)*

Automated Components Intl (PA) 570 344-4000
1321 E Drinker St Dunmore (18512) *(G-4469)*

Automated Concepts Tooling Inc 814 796-6302
14500 Willy Rd Waterford (16441) *(G-19259)*

Automated Enterprise Intl 610 458-5810
632 Greenridge Rd Glenmoore (19343) *(G-6463)*

Automated Fincl Systems Inc (PA) 484 875-1250
123 Summit Dr Ste 2 Exton (19341) *(G-5649)*

Automated Fincl Systems Inc 610 594-1037
770 Springdale Dr Exton (19341) *(G-5650)*

Automated Indus Systems Inc 814 838-2270
4238 W 12th St Erie (16505) *(G-5198)*

Automated Unmanned Vehicle Sys 570 748-3844
155 Orchard Hill Ln Mill Hall (17751) *(G-11171)*

Automatic Control Elec Co 210 661-4111
220 Stahl Rd Harleysville (19438) *(G-7021)*

Automatic Forecasting Systems 215 675-0652
759 Ivyland Rd Warminster (18974) *(G-18832)*

Automatic Machining Mfg Co Inc (PA) 717 767-4448
3405 Board Rd York (17406) *(G-20393)*

Automating Molding Tech LLC 610 497-7162
203 E 10th St Ste 16 Marcus Hook (19061) *(G-10437)*

Automation Aides, Warminster *Also called Vollman Pershing H Inc (G-18998)*

Automation Devices Inc 814 474-5561
7050 W Ridge Rd Fairview (16415) *(G-5814)*

Automation Parts Sales & Svc, Portersville *Also called Apss Inc (G-15925)*

Automation Products Inc (HQ) 814 453-5841
814 E 8th St Erie (16503) *(G-5199)*

Automted Conveying Systems Inc 215 368-0500
1551 Gehman Rd Harleysville (19438) *(G-7022)*

Automted Lgic Corp Kennesaw GA 717 909-7000
6345 Flank Dr Ste 100 Harrisburg (17112) *(G-7093)*

Automtion Tech Analytical Pdts, Pittsburgh *Also called ABB Inc (G-14633)*

Autoneum North America Inc 570 784-4100
480 W 5th St Bloomsburg (17815) *(G-1771)*

Autosoft Inc 800 473-4630
61 Executive Ct Ste 1 West Middlesex (16159) *(G-19721)*

Autosoft International, West Middlesex *Also called Autosoft Inc (G-19721)*

Auxiliary Business Services 215 836-4833
7157 Camp Hill Rd Fort Washington (19034) *(G-6063)*

Auxilium Pharmaceuticals LLC (HQ) 484 321-5900
1400 Atwater Dr Malvern (19355) *(G-10189)*

Ava Electronics Corp 610 284-2500
4000 Bridge St Drexel Hill (19026) *(G-4360)*

Avalon Natural Health Center, Columbia *Also called Renee Awad ND (G-3448)*

Avant-Garde Technology Inc 215 345-8228
631 Spring Valley Rd Doylestown (18901) *(G-4273)*

Avanta Orthopaedics Inc 215 428-1792
1711 S Pennsylvania Ave Morrisville (19067) *(G-11555)*

Avantext Inc 610 796-2383
30 S Bank St Philadelphia (19106) *(G-13425)*

Avanti Cigar Company, Dunmore *Also called Parodi Holdings LLC (G-4479)*

Avanti Engineering and Mfg Inc 724 834-0752
1666 Business Route 66 Greensburg (15601) *(G-6652)*

Avantor Inc (HQ) 610 386-1700
100 W Matsonford Rd # 1 Radnor (19087) *(G-16286)*

Avantor Performance Mtls LLC (HQ) 610 573-2600
100 W Matsonford Rd Radnor (19087) *(G-16287)*

Avantor Prfmce Mtls Hldngs LLC (HQ) 610 573-2600
100 W Matsonford Rd # 1 Radnor (19087) *(G-16288)*

Avas, Warren *Also called Audio Video Automation SEC Inc (G-19011)*

Avatar Data Pubg Solutions 412 921-7747
1815 Crafton Blvd Pittsburgh (15205) *(G-14742)*

Avax Technologies Inc 215 241-9760
2000 Hamilton St Ste 204 Philadelphia (19130) *(G-13426)*

Avc Solutions LLC 412 737-8945
2511 Sarah St Pittsburgh (15203) *(G-14743)*

Avco Corporation 570 323-6181
652 Oliver St Williamsport (17701) *(G-19990)*

Avery Dennison Corporation 570 888-6641
1 Wilcox St Sayre (18840) *(G-17110)*

Avery Dennison Corporation 570 748-7701
171 Draketown Rd Mill Hall (17751) *(G-11172)*

Avery Dennison Corporation 215 536-9000
35 Penn Am Dr Quakertown (18951) *(G-16170)*

Avex Electronics Corp 215 245-4848
1683 Winchester Rd Bensalem (19020) *(G-1152)*

Aviation Technologies Inc 570 457-4147
201 Hanger Rd Ste 2 Avoca (18641) *(G-840)*

Avid Radiopharmaceuticals Inc (HQ) 215 298-0700
3711 Market St Fl 7 Philadelphia (19104) *(G-13427)*

Avidon Welding Inc 570 421-2307
205 W 4th St East Stroudsburg (18301) *(G-4607)*

Avidtox Inc 610 738-7938
833 Lincoln Ave Unit 9 West Chester (19380) *(G-19504)*

Aviom Inc 610 738-9005
1157 Phoenixville Pike # 201 West Chester (19380) *(G-19505)*

Aviva Technology Inc 610 228-4689
511 Abbott Dr Fl 2 Broomall (19008) *(G-2279)*

Avm Services, Norristown *Also called Mvc Industries Inc (G-12690)*

Avo International Inc 610 676-8500
2621 Van Buren Ave Ste 40 Norristown (19403) *(G-12637)*

Avo Multi-AMP Corporation 610 676-8501
2621 Van Buren Ave # 400 Norristown (19403) *(G-12638)*

Avo Photonics Inc 215 441-0107
120 Welsh Rd Horsham (19044) *(G-7793)*

Avondale Machine Products Inc 610 268-2121
1304 Glen Willow Rd Avondale (19311) *(G-849)*

Avox Inc 267 404-2676
118 S 2nd St Perkasie (18944) *(G-13267)*

Avox Technologies, Perkasie *Also called Avox Inc (G-13267)*

Avure Autoclave Systems Inc 814 833-4331
2820 W 23rd St Ste 6 Erie (16506) *(G-5200)*

Award Products Inc 215 324-0414
4830 N Front St Philadelphia (19120) *(G-13428)*

Awards & More 724 444-1040
5418 William Flynn Hwy Gibsonia (15044) *(G-6325)*

AWC Mr Spouting, Somerset *Also called Associated Windows (G-17674)*

Awesome Dudes Printingg LLC 267 886-8492
1338 S 6th St Philadelphia (19147) *(G-13429)*

Awesome Foods Inc 610 757-1048
329 E Penn St Norristown (19401) *(G-12639)*

Awesome Ice Inc 717 519-2423
2235 Olde Meadow Ct East Petersburg (17520) *(G-4586)*

Awf Logging 814 577-5070
1905 Hoovertown Rd Penfield (15849) *(G-13221)*

Awp Mill 7, Marble *Also called Allegheny Wood Products Inc (G-10434)*

Awwsum Internet Services 215 543-9078
4227 Rhawn St Philadelphia (19136) *(G-13430)*

Ax Heat Transfer Inc 724 654-7747
420 S Cascade St New Castle (16101) *(G-12060)*

Axalta Coating Systems LLC (HQ) 215 255-4347
2001 Market St Ste 3600 Philadelphia (19103) *(G-13431)*

Axalta Coating Systems LLC 610 358-2228
50 Applied Bank Blvd # 300 Glen Mills (19342) *(G-6430)*

Axalta Coating Systems Ip LLC 855 547-1461
2001 Market St Ste 3600 Philadelphia (19103) *(G-13432)*

Axalta Coating Systems Ltd (PA) 855 547-1461
2001 Market St Ste 3600 Philadelphia (19103) *(G-13433)*

Axcentria Pharmaceutical LLC 215 453-5055
306 Keystone Dr Telford (18969) *(G-18268)*

Axco Valve, Corry *Also called Al Xander Co Inc (G-3743)*

Axelrad LLC (PA) 570 714-3278
152 N Pennsylvania Ave Wilkes Barre (18701) *(G-19907)*

Axeman-Anderson Company 570 326-9114
300 E Mountain Ave Williamsport (17702) *(G-19991)*

Axial Medical 267 961-2600
65 Richard Rd Ivyland (18974) *(G-8207)*

Axiall LLC 412 515-8149
11 Stanwix St Ste 1900 Pittsburgh (15222) *(G-14744)*

Axiom Inc 570 385-1944
200 Willow St Schuylkill Haven (17972) *(G-17148)*

Axiom Hydraulics, Schuylkill Haven *Also called Axiom Inc (G-17148)*

Axion LLC 484 243-6127
610 Sentry Pkwy Ste 220 Blue Bell (19422) *(G-1813)*

Axion Power Battery Mfg Inc 724 654-9300
3601 Clover Ln New Castle (16105) *(G-12061)*

Axion Power International, New Castle *Also called Axion Power Battery Mfg Inc (G-12061)*

Axon Magazine Group, Dresher *Also called Lrp Magazine Group (G-4356)*

AXR HOLDINGS, Plymouth Meeting *Also called Amrep Corporation (G-15831)*

Ay Machine Co 717 733-0335
    E King St Ephrata (17522) *(G-5091)*

Aydin Displays, Birdsboro *Also called Sparton Aydin LLC (G-1706)*

Ayrshire Dairy 814 781-1978
    347 Old Kersey Rd Saint Marys (15857) *(G-16950)*

Aywon Chalkboard Corkboard Inc 570 459-3490
    100 E Diamond Ave Hazleton (18201) *(G-7491)*

Azar International Inc 570 288-0786
    232 Division St Kingston (18704) *(G-8712)*

Azek Building Products Inc (HQ) 877 275-2935
    888 N Keyser Ave Scranton (18504) *(G-17210)*

AZS Brusher Equipment LLC 717 733-2584
    821 Crooked Ln Ephrata (17522) *(G-5092)*

Aztec Machinery Company 215 672-2600
    960 Jacksonville Rd Warminster (18974) *(G-18833)*

Aztec Materials LLC 215 675-8900
    248 E County Line Rd Hatboro (19040) *(G-7271)*

Aztec Materials LLC 215 675-8900
    348 E County Line Rd Hatboro (19040) *(G-7272)*

Aztec Products Inc 215 393-4700
    201 Commerce Dr Montgomeryville (18936) *(G-11387)*

Azur Pharma Inc 215 832-3750
    1818 Market St Philadelphia (19103) *(G-13434)*

B & B Anthracite Coal 570 695-3707
    225 W Main St Tremont (17981) *(G-18478)*

B & B Beverage 570 742-7782
    1220 N Front St Frnt Milton (17847) *(G-11233)*

B & B Coal Company 570 695-3188
    320 Main St Tremont (17981) *(G-18479)*

B & B Foundry Inc 215 333-7100
    6101 Keystone St Philadelphia (19135) *(G-13435)*

B & B Machine Inc 717 898-3081
    8820 S Chiques Rd Manheim (17545) *(G-10368)*

B & B Oil & Gas Production Co 814 257-8760
    370 Pipeline Rd Dayton (16222) *(G-4035)*

B & B Pole Buildings, Hummelstown *Also called Bradley E Miller (G-7904)*

B & B Structures 717 656-0783
    568 Gibbons Rd Bird In Hand (17505) *(G-1669)*

B & B Tool & Die, Subsidiary, Saint Marys *Also called Gerg Tool & Die Inc (G-16977)*

B & B Tool and Die Inc 814 486-5355
    5878 Beechwood Rd Emporium (15834) *(G-5050)*

B & C Auto Wreckers Inc 570 547-1040
    4867 Us Highway 15 Montgomery (17752) *(G-11367)*

B & C Controls Inc 610 738-9204
    1155 Phoenixville Pike # 107 West Chester (19380) *(G-19506)*

B & C Material Handling Inc 724 814-7910
    9276 Marshall Rd Cranberry Township (16066) *(G-3808)*

B & C Meter Inc 814 257-8464
    119 E Church Ave Dayton (16222) *(G-4036)*

B & D Advertising Inc 717 852-6950
    333 E 7th Ave Ste 1 York (17404) *(G-20394)*

B & D Machine Shop 717 843-0312
    808 W Mason Ave York (17401) *(G-20395)*

B & E Candy 724 327-8898
    1286 Hrrison Cy Export Rd Jeannette (15644) *(G-8247)*

B & E Sportswear LP 610 328-9266
    1005 Sussex Blvd Ste 9 Broomall (19008) *(G-2280)*

B & F General Machine Inc 610 767-2448
    4875 Park Ave Slatington (18080) *(G-17604)*

B & F Tool & Gear Inc 717 632-8977
    2551 Pine Tree Rd Spring Grove (17362) *(G-17875)*

B & G Finishing LLC 267 229-2569
    12417 Dunks Ferry Rd Philadelphia (19154) *(G-13436)*

B & G Optics Inc 215 289-2480
    1320 Unity St Philadelphia (19124) *(G-13437)*

B & J Machine Inc 215 639-8800
    309 Camer Dr Unit 3 Bensalem (19020) *(G-1153)*

B & J Sheet Metal Inc 215 538-9543
    1535 Allentown Rd Trumbauersville (18970) *(G-18529)*

B & K Sheet Metal Products, Milton *Also called William J Koshinskie (G-11251)*

B & L Manufacturing Corp 412 784-9400
    5629 Harrison St Pittsburgh (15201) *(G-14745)*

B & L Woodworking 717 354-5430
    250 Snake Ln Kinzers (17535) *(G-8732)*

B & N Trophies & Awards LLC 814 723-8130
    318 Pennsylvania Ave E Warren (16365) *(G-19012)*

B & Q Technical Service Inc 610 872-8428
    417 Karen Ln Wallingford (19086) *(G-18781)*

B & R Automotive, Verona *Also called B & R Speed Shop (G-18748)*

B & R Speed Shop 412 795-7022
    4859 Allegheny River Blvd Verona (15147) *(G-18748)*

B & R Welding & Fabricating, Penn Run *Also called Mohney Fabricating & Mfg LLC (G-13229)*

B & S Beverage L L C 814 674-2223
    614 5th Ave Patton (16668) *(G-13187)*

B & S Logging, Huntingdon *Also called Brett W Shope (G-7940)*

B & S Woodcraft 717 786-8154
    501 Furnace Rd Quarryville (17566) *(G-16262)*

B & T Contractors Inc 814 368-7199
    612 S Kendall Ave Bradford (16701) *(G-1956)*

B & T Fabrication 814 634-0638
    187 Maple Valley Rd Meyersdale (15552) *(G-11009)*

B & W Machine Works Inc 215 529-2990
    550 California Rd Ste 8 Quakertown (18951) *(G-16171)*

B & W Metal Works Inc 717 848-1077
    635 Hay St York (17403) *(G-20396)*

B and B Signs and Graphics 717 737-4467
    4713 Carlisle Pike Mechanicsburg (17050) *(G-10821)*

B and K Manufacturing, Callery *Also called Byrnes and Kiefer Company (G-2467)*

B and N Electronics 724 484-0164
    240 Chambers Ridge Rd West Alexander (15376) *(G-19490)*

B Asf Corp 814 453-7186
    1729 East Ave Erie (16503) *(G-5201)*

B B Express 717 573-2686
    3771 Pleasant Grove Rd Warfordsburg (17267) *(G-18810)*

B B Oilfield Equipment 724 668-2509
    8791 State Route 22 New Alexandria (15670) *(G-12017)*

B Braun Medical Inc (HQ) 610 691-5400
    824 12th Ave Bethlehem (18018) *(G-1454)*

B Braun Medical Inc 610 336-9595
    200 Boulder Dr Ste 1 Breinigsville (18031) *(G-2009)*

B Braun of America Inc (HQ) 610 691-5400
    824 12th Ave Bethlehem (18018) *(G-1455)*

B C Fabrications Inc 610 369-2882
    821 N Reading Ave New Berlinville (19545) *(G-12024)*

B C I Engineering, Leetsdale *Also called Carroll Manufacturing Co LLC (G-9688)*

B D & D Spclty Fabrication Mch 814 236-3810
    1181 Bailor Rd Curwensville (16833) *(G-3946)*

B D Medical Systems-Injection, Royersford *Also called Becton Dickinson and Company (G-16846)*

B D Mining Co Inc 570 874-1602
    10 Gilberton Rd Gilberton (17934) *(G-6365)*

B E V O L 570 962-3644
    118 Country Ln Howard (16841) *(G-7885)*

B E Wallace Products Corp 610 647-1400
    71 N Bacton Hill Rd Malvern (19355) *(G-10190)*

B G M Fastener Co Inc 570 253-5046
    759 Old Willow Ave Honesdale (18431) *(G-7701)*

B H B Industries 814 398-8011
    116 Railroad St Cambridge Springs (16403) *(G-2474)*

B I International, Wayne *Also called Business Intelligence Intl Inc (G-19311)*

B J Sales Co Div, Berwick *Also called Gtf Corporation (G-1327)*

B J Toy Company Inc 610 863-9191
    504 W Applegate Ave Pen Argyl (18072) *(G-13210)*

B J Toy Manufacturing Company, Pen Argyl *Also called B J Toy Company Inc (G-13210)*

B K Barrit Corp 267 345-1200
    4011 G St Philadelphia (19124) *(G-13438)*

B L Tees Inc 724 325-1882
    3005 Venture Ct Export (15632) *(G-5591)*

B N I Solutions LLC 814 237-4073
    2820 E College Ave Ste B State College (16801) *(G-17944)*

B N S Woodcrafts 717 284-1035
    722 Tress Rd Quarryville (17566) *(G-16263)*

B O H I C A Inc 610 489-4540
    521 W Main St Trappe (19426) *(G-18467)*

B P I, Pittsburgh *Also called Bpi Inc (G-14788)*

B P S Communications Inc 215 830-8467
    801 Easton Rd Ste 2 Willow Grove (19090) *(G-20109)*

B V Landscape Supplies Inc 610 316-1099
    154 Lancaster Ave Malvern (19355) *(G-10191)*

B V Pallets 717 935-5740
    2451 W Back Mountain Rd Belleville (17004) *(G-1125)*

B W E Ltd 724 246-0470
    Legion St Republic (15475) *(G-16652)*

B Wise Trailers 717 261-0922
    1086 Wayne Ave Chambersburg (17201) *(G-2908)*

B WS Pizza 724 495-2898
    4790 Tuscarawas Rd Beaver (15009) *(G-978)*

B X S Bass Inc 724 378-8697
    2256 Brodhead Rd Aliquippa (15001) *(G-67)*

B&B Gas & Oil Shop 814 257-8032
    370 Pipeline Rd Dayton (16222) *(G-4037)*

B&B Metal Finishing Inc 717 764-8941
    401 N Main St Manchester (17345) *(G-10355)*

B&B Sales Consulting Corp Inc 215 225-3200
    2015 W Allegheny Ave Philadelphia (19132) *(G-13439)*

B&G Manufacturing Co Inc (PA) 215 822-1925
    3067 Unionville Pike Hatfield (19440) *(G-7319)*

B-TEC Solutions Inc 215 785-2400
    913 Cedar Ave Croydon (19021) *(G-3911)*

B.R.p, Bedford *Also called Bedford Reinforced Plas Inc (G-1044)*

B/E Aerospace Inc 570 595-7491
    Spruce Cabin Rd Mountainhome (18342) *(G-11785)*

B2b Magazine, Harrisburg *Also called Keyword Communications Inc (G-7163)*

B6 Systems Inc 724 861-8080
    B 7 Manor Vly Plz Rte 993 Manor (15665) *(G-10409)*

Baar Products Company..610 873-4591
241 Boot Rd Downingtown (19335) *(G-4214)*

Babcock & Wilcox Company.....................................724 479-3585
81 Grover St Homer City (15748) *(G-7670)*

Babcock & Wilcox Pwr Gen, Ebensburg *Also called Babcock Wlcox Ebnsburg Pwr Inc (G-4780)*

Babcock Lumber Company...814 239-2281
905 Old Hickory Rd Pittsburgh (15243) *(G-14746)*

Babcock Wlcox Ebnsburg Pwr Inc...............................814 472-1140
2840 New Germany Rd Ebensburg (15931) *(G-4780)*

Babunyas Gourmets Spice, Gouldsboro *Also called Melt Enterprises LLC (G-6569)*

Baby Matters LLC...919 724-7087
153 Finn Ln Wayne (19087) *(G-19304)*

Baby Sparkles...267 304-8787
4821 Unruh Ave Philadelphia (19135) *(G-13440)*

Bacharach Inc (PA)..724 334-5000
621 Hunt Valley Cir New Kensington (15068) *(G-12326)*

Bacharach Instruments Ltd.......................................724 334-5000
625 Alpha Dr Pittsburgh (15238) *(G-14747)*

Bachman Drapery Studio Inc......................................215 257-8810
20 Ridge Rd Tylersport (18971) *(G-18574)*

Back 2 Earth Recycling LLC......................................717 389-6591
213 N Locust St Myerstown (17067) *(G-11874)*

Back Bay Industries Inc..724 941-5825
116 Sugar Camp Rd Venetia (15367) *(G-18741)*

Back Mountain Creamery...570 855-3487
24 Carverton Rd Shavertown (18708) *(G-17479)*

Backdoor Bakershop...610 625-0987
92 E Broad St Bethlehem (18018) *(G-1456)*

Backe Digital Brand Marketing..................................610 947-6922
100 W Matsonford Rd Radnor (19087) *(G-16289)*

Backus Company (PA)...814 887-5705
411 W Water St Smethport (16749) *(G-17632)*

Baco Plastics, Meadville *Also called Meadville New Products Inc (G-10759)*

Bacon Jams...484 681-5674
125 Noble St Norristown (19401) *(G-12640)*

Bacon Jams LLC...856 720-0255
1554 Paoli Pike Ste 254 West Chester (19380) *(G-19507)*

Bacon Press..484 328-3118
215 Lancaster Ave Malvern (19355) *(G-10192)*

Baden Steelbar & Bolt Corp.......................................724 266-3003
852 Big Sewickley Crk R Sewickley (15143) *(G-17383)*

Badin Business Park LLC (HQ)....................................412 553-4545
201 Isabella St Pittsburgh (15212) *(G-14748)*

Badzik Printing Service Inc.......................................724 379-4299
799 Meldon Ave Donora (15033) *(G-4146)*

Bae Systems Land Armaments LP................................717 225-8000
1100 Bairs Rd York (17408) *(G-20397)*

Bafco Inc..215 674-1700
717 Mearns Rd Warminster (18974) *(G-18834)*

Bagatrix Solutions Ltd...610 574-9607
462 Windy Hill Rd Gilbertsville (19525) *(G-6370)*

Bahdeebahdu..215 627-5002
1522 N American St Philadelphia (19122) *(G-13441)*

Bahrets Church Interiors..717 540-1747
135 N Fairville Ave Harrisburg (17112) *(G-7094)*

Bai Document Services, Export *Also called Baip Inc (G-5592)*

Bai Printing..412 400-5555
615 Plum Industrial Park Pittsburgh (15239) *(G-14749)*

Bailey & Izett Inc..610 642-1887
2538 Haverford Rd Ardmore (19003) *(G-702)*

Bailey Coach, York *Also called Bailey Leasing Inc (G-20398)*

Bailey Engineers Inc (PA)...724 745-6200
125 Technology Dr Ste 205 Canonsburg (15317) *(G-2547)*

Bailey Leasing Inc..717 718-0490
55 S Fayette St Ste 1 York (17404) *(G-20398)*

Bailey Machine Company...724 628-4730
1516 Morrell Ave Connellsville (15425) *(G-3490)*

Bailey Oxides LLC (PA)..724 745-9500
125 Technology Dr Canonsburg (15317) *(G-2548)*

Bailey Wood Products Inc...610 756-6827
441 Mountain Rd Kempton (19529) *(G-8490)*

Baileys Steel & Supply LLC..724 267-4648
60 Moscow Rd Waynesburg (15370) *(G-19433)*

Baillie Fabricating & Wldg Inc...................................610 701-5808
1109 Saunders Ct Ste 110 West Chester (19380) *(G-19508)*

Baillie Lumber Co LP..814 827-1877
45529 State Highway 27 The Titusville (16354) *(G-18375)*

Bainbridge Group Inc...215 922-3274
4177 Ridge Ave Philadelphia (19129) *(G-13442)*

Baip Inc..412 913-9826
3 Wesco Dr Ste 3 # 3 Export (15632) *(G-5592)*

Bake Rite Rolls, Bensalem *Also called Northeast Foods Inc (G-1231)*

Baker Ballistics LLC..717 625-2016
112 Koser Rd Lititz (17543) *(G-9994)*

Baker Beverage, Chambersburg *Also called Terry Baker (G-2985)*

Baker Curtis Lumber Sawmill, Cochranton *Also called Curtis Baker Lumber Inc (G-3340)*

Baker Gas Inc..724 297-3456
136 Baker Gas Dr Worthington (16262) *(G-20227)*

Baker Hghes Olfld Oprtions Inc..................................724 266-4725
100 Industry Dr Ambridge (15003) *(G-610)*

Baker Hghes Olfld Oprtions LLC.................................724 695-2266
400 Bakeman Imperial (15126) *(G-8059)*

Baker Hughes A GE Company LLC...............................724 696-3059
370 Westec Dr Mount Pleasant (15666) *(G-11687)*

Baker Hydro Incorporated...717 764-8581
3490 Board Rd York (17406) *(G-20399)*

Baker Outlaw Fuel Systems.......................................717 795-9383
130 Peach Rd Apt A Liverpool (17045) *(G-10077)*

Baker Petrolite LLC..610 876-2200
4 Saville Ave Crum Lynne (19022) *(G-3935)*

Baker Print Design, Media *Also called Elizabeth C Baker (G-10923)*

Baker Refractories, York *Also called Magnesita Refractories Company (G-20574)*

Baker The Sign Man, Wayne *Also called 39 Design Company Inc (G-19291)*

Baker WD & Coal Burning Stoves, Lewisberry *Also called Arthur L Baker Enterprises (G-9880)*

Baker's Maple, Klingerstown *Also called Speedwell Garage (G-8808)*

Bakerly Barn LLC..610 829-1500
4300 Braden Blvd E Easton (18040) *(G-4647)*

Bakers Best Snack Foods Inc.....................................215 822-3511
1880 N Penn Rd Hatfield (19440) *(G-7320)*

Bakers Lawn Ornaments..814 445-7028
570 Berlin Plank Rd Somerset (15501) *(G-17678)*

Bakers Lumber Company Inc......................................814 743-6671
1481 Shawna Rd Cherry Tree (15724) *(G-3031)*

Bakers Quarry...570 942-6005
18712 Dmock To Nchlson Rd Nicholson (18446) *(G-12612)*

Bakery Feeds, Honey Brook *Also called Griffin Industries LLC (G-7746)*

Bakkavor Foods Usa Inc...570 383-9800
46 Alberigi Dr Jessup (18434) *(G-8327)*

Bakwell LLC..570 724-7067
61 Bodine St Wellsboro (16901) *(G-19462)*

Bal Nut Inc (PA)..570 675-2712
191 E Center Hill Rd Dallas (18612) *(G-3958)*

Balco Inc...724 459-6814
400 Serell Dr Blairsville (15717) *(G-1714)*

Bald Eagle Precision, Tyrone *Also called Terry D Miles (G-18596)*

Bald Hills Distillery..717 858-2152
5061 Carlisle Rd Dover (17315) *(G-4184)*

Baldt Inc..610 447-5200
400 S Roberts Rd Bryn Mawr (19010) *(G-2315)*

Balducci Stoneyard LLC..410 627-0594
18159 Susquehanna Trl S New Freedom (17349) *(G-12201)*

Baldwin Hardware Corporation...................................610 777-7811
225 Peach St Leesport (19533) *(G-9659)*

Baldwin Publishing Inc..215 369-1369
1107 Tylrsvlle Rd Ste 101 Washington Crossing (18977) *(G-19252)*

Baldwin Technology Company Inc...............................610 829-4240
2 Danforth Dr Easton (18045) *(G-4648)*

Balfour Sales Company...215 542-9745
2 Balfour Cir Ambler (19002) *(G-569)*

Ball & Ball LLP..610 363-7330
463 W Lincoln Hwy Exton (19341) *(G-5651)*

Ball Arosol Specialty Cont Inc...................................215 442-5462
431 Privet Rd Horsham (19044) *(G-7794)*

Ballews Aluminum Products Inc..................................717 492-8956
166 Arrowhead Dr Manheim (17545) *(G-10369)*

Ballistic Applications...724 282-0416
1317 Grant Ave East Butler (16029) *(G-4530)*

Ballistic Scientific Usa LLC......................................267 282-6666
1 Plastics Rd Ste 1a Corry (16407) *(G-3744)*

Balloon Flights Daily..610 469-0782
490 Hopewell Rd Saint Peters (19470) *(G-17033)*

Bally Block Co, Bally *Also called Bally Holding Company PA (G-899)*

Bally Block Company (HQ)...610 845-7511
30 S 7th St Bally (19503) *(G-898)*

Bally Holding Company PA (PA)..................................610 845-7511
30 S 7th St Bally (19503) *(G-899)*

Bally Ribbon Mills (PA)...610 845-2211
23 N 7th St Bally (19503) *(G-900)*

Bally Ribbon Mills..610 845-2211
23 N 7th St Bally (19503) *(G-901)*

Bally Ribbon Mills..610 845-2211
24 N 7th St Bally (19503) *(G-902)*

Ballymore Company, Coatesville *Also called Ballymore Holdings Inc (G-3293)*

Ballymore Holdings Inc (PA).....................................610 593-5062
501 Gunnard Carlson Dr Coatesville (19320) *(G-3293)*

Baltec Corporation...724 873-5757
121 Hillpointe Dr Ste 900 Canonsburg (15317) *(G-2549)*

Baltic Leisure, Oxford *Also called Penn Sauna Corp (G-13087)*

Baltic Leisure, Paoli *Also called Penn Sauna Corp (G-13146)*

Baltimore Corp (PA)...215 957-6200
905 Louis Dr Warminster (18974) *(G-18835)*

Bam Fuel LLC...814 255-1689
1023 Willett Dr Johnstown (15905) *(G-8355)*

Bam International, East Butler *Also called Ballistic Applications (G-4530)*

ALPHABETIC

Banc Technic Inc 610 756-4440
  7 Tedway Ave Kutztown (19530) *(G-8836)*

Banes and Mayer Inc 215 641-1750
  6198 Butler Pike Ste 225 Blue Bell (19422) *(G-1814)*

Bangor Concrete, Bangor *Also called Smiths Wilbert Vault Company (G-928)*

Bangor Steel Erectors Inc 215 338-1200
  6795 State Rd Philadelphia (19135) *(G-13443)*

Bangtees LLC 484 767-2382
  217 E Madison St Easton (18042) *(G-4649)*

Banksville Express, Pittsburgh *Also called Ricks Quick Printing Inc (G-15485)*

Banning Specialty Co, Natrona Heights *Also called Bruce Banning (G-11936)*

Bar & Cap System, Venetia *Also called R Q I Inc (G-18743)*

Bar Bq Town Inc 215 549-9666
  7711 Ogontz Ave Philadelphia (19150) *(G-13444)*

Bar Machining 724 226-1050
  9 Kuhnert St Natrona Heights (15065) *(G-11934)*

Bar-Ray Products Inc 717 359-9100
  90 E Lakeview Dr Littlestown (17340) *(G-10063)*

Barash Group, The, State College *Also called Morgan Signs Inc (G-17994)*

Barbary 215 634-7400
  951 Frankford Ave Philadelphia (19125) *(G-13445)*

Barbato Foods Inc 814 899-3721
  1707 State St Erie (16501) *(G-5202)*

Barbers Chemicals Inc 724 962-7886
  950 W Main St Sharpsville (16150) *(G-17469)*

Barbett Industries Inc 610 372-2872
  226 Cedar St Reading (19601) *(G-16327)*

Barc Developmental Services (PA) 215 794-0800
  4950 York Rd Holicong (18928) *(G-7638)*

Barchemy LLC 724 379-4405
  65 E 1st St Donora (15033) *(G-4147)*

Barco Industries Inc 610 374-3117
  1020 Macarthur Rd Reading (19605) *(G-16328)*

BARD MFG CO, Phoenixville *Also called Royersford Fndry & Mch Co Inc (G-14576)*

Bardane Mfg Co 570 876-4844
  317 Delaware St Jermyn (18433) *(G-8305)*

Bardot Plastics Inc (PA) 610 252-5900
  10 Mcfadden Rd Easton (18045) *(G-4650)*

Barebo Inc 610 965-6018
  3840 Main Rd E Emmaus (18049) *(G-5020)*

Barefoot Pellet Company 570 297-4771
  Rr 14 Box North York (17315) *(G-20400)*

Bareville Furniture, Leola *Also called Quality Custom Cabinetry Inc (G-9798)*

Bareville Woodcraft Co 717 656-6261
  70 Farmland Rd Leola (17540) *(G-9771)*

Barfly Monthly, Lancaster *Also called Fly Magazine (G-9024)*

Bargain Beer & Soda, Harrisburg *Also called Mary Ann Pensiero Inc (G-7173)*

Bargain Sheet, The, Dillsburg *Also called Marie Chomicki (G-4136)*

Barhill Manufacturing Corp 570 655-2005
  396 S Township Blvd Pittston (18640) *(G-15742)*

Barkby Group Inc 717 292-4148
  127 Cranbrook Dr Dover (17315) *(G-4185)*

Barkleigh Productions Inc 717 691-3388
  970 W Trindle Rd Mechanicsburg (17055) *(G-10822)*

Barkleigh Publications, Mechanicsburg *Also called Barkleigh Productions Inc (G-10822)*

Barmah Co 724 539-8477
  Center Dr Bldg 1 Latrobe (15650) *(G-9459)*

Barn Yard LLC 717 314-9667
  3351 Lincoln Hwy E Paradise (17562) *(G-13153)*

Barnes Group Inc 814 663-6082
  226 S Center St Corry (16407) *(G-3745)*

Barnes Group Inc 215 785-4466
  1900 Frost Rd Ste 101 Bristol (19007) *(G-2116)*

Barnes P S P Inc 724 287-6711
  355 Unionville Rd Butler (16001) *(G-2376)*

Barnett Canvas Co, Folcroft *Also called Madhavan Inc (G-6009)*

Barnharts Honda Suzuki 724 627-5819
  883 Washington Rd Prosperity (15329) *(G-16122)*

Barnside Mulch and Compost 610 287-8880
  991 Haldeman Rd Schwenksville (19473) *(G-17174)*

Baron Crest Energy Company 724 478-1121
  601 1st Street Ext Apollo (15613) *(G-663)*

Baron Development Company 814 676-8703
  207 Maple Ave Oil City (16301) *(G-12940)*

Barr Laboratories Inc (HQ) 215 591-3000
  1090 Horsham Rd North Wales (19454) *(G-12790)*

Barr Laboratories Inc 845 362-1100
  1090 Horsham Rd North Wales (19454) *(G-12791)*

Barre Engraving Co, Hanover Township *Also called Blasi Printing Inc (G-6981)*

Barrett's Machine, Punxsutawney *Also called Dean Barrett (G-16134)*

Barretts Custom Wrought Iron 814 676-4575
  2237 Horsecreek Rd Oil City (16301) *(G-12941)*

Barrick Design Inc 717 295-4800
  541 N Mulberry St Lancaster (17603) *(G-8948)*

Barrville Lumber 717 667-9600
  52 Cherry Tree Ln Belleville (17004) *(G-1126)*

Barry Callebaut USA LLC 610 872-4528
  903 Industrial Hwy Eddystone (19022) *(G-4798)*

Barry Callebaut USA LLC 312 496-7305
  4863 Hanoverville Rd Bethlehem (18020) *(G-1457)*

Barry Callebaut USA LLC 570 342-7556
  9 Keystone Industrial Par Dunmore (18512) *(G-4470)*

Barrys Lobby Shop 215 925-1998
  399 Market St Ste 1 Philadelphia (19106) *(G-13446)*

Barsky Diamonds, Philadelphia *Also called N Barsky & Sons (G-14050)*

Barta, Pittsburgh *Also called Shared Financial Services (G-15528)*

Bartlett Signs 814 392-7082
  5148 Peach St Ste 328 Erie (16509) *(G-5203)*

Bartolotta Vision Care Inc 814 472-8010
  3133 New Germany Rd Ebensburg (15931) *(G-4781)*

Barts Pneumatics Corp 717 392-1568
  1952 Landis Valley Rd Lancaster (17601) *(G-8949)*

Bartush Signs Inc 570 366-2311
  302 N Washington St Apt A Orwigsburg (17961) *(G-13040)*

Base Lab Tools Inc 570 371-5710
  140 N 2nd St Unit 3 Stroudsburg (18360) *(G-18107)*

Baseball Info Solutions Inc 610 261-4316
  41 S 2nd St Coplay (18037) *(G-3640)*

BASF Catalysts LLC 814 870-3900
  1729 East Ave Erie (16503) *(G-5204)*

BASF Construction Chem LLC 215 945-3900
  6450 Bristol Pike Levittown (19057) *(G-9818)*

BASF Construction Chem LLC 610 391-0633
  7234 Penn Dr Allentown (18106) *(G-146)*

BASF Corporation 724 728-6900
  370 Frankfort Rd Monaca (15061) *(G-11281)*

Bashlin Industries Inc 724 458-8340
  119 W Pine St Grove City (16127) *(G-6780)*

Basic - Psa Inc 814 266-8646
  269 Jari Dr Johnstown (15904) *(G-8356)*

Basic Carbide Corporation (PA) 724 446-1630
  900 Main St Irwin (15642) *(G-8146)*

Basic Carbide Corporation 412 754-0060
  900 Blythedale Rd Elizabeth (15037) *(G-4856)*

Basic Carbide Corporation 412 751-3774
  900 Blythedale Rd Buena Vista (15018) *(G-2340)*

Basic Power Inc 570 872-9666
  530 Seven Bridge Rd East Stroudsburg (18301) *(G-4608)*

Basically Nickel 717 292-7232
  2042 Baltimore Pike East Berlin (17316) *(G-4519)*

Basinger Logging 724 455-1067
  3051 Springfield Pike Connellsville (15425) *(G-3491)*

Basket Works Inc 516 367-9200
  2951 Route 611 Ste 102 Tannersville (18372) *(G-18234)*

Bass Pallets LLC 717 731-1091
  311 Railroad Ave Shiremanstown (17011) *(G-17568)*

Bassett Industries Inc 610 327-1200
  2119 Sanatoga Station Rd Pottstown (19464) *(G-15965)*

Bassler Wllmsport Pttern Works 570 368-2471
  430 S Alley Montoursville (17754) *(G-11432)*

Bastian Tire and Auto, Williamsport *Also called Bastian Tire Sales Inc (G-19992)*

Bastian Tire Sales Inc 570 323-8651
  2940 Reach Rd Williamsport (17701) *(G-19992)*

Battery Builders Inc 717 751-2705
  237 N Church Ln Red Lion (17356) *(G-16590)*

Battery Tech LLC 570 253-6908
  203 Dunn Rd Honesdale (18431) *(G-7702)*

Battery Zone (PA) 800 371-5033
  902 4th Ave Ste 200 Bethlehem (18018) *(G-1458)*

Batterytest Equipment Co 610 746-9449
  539 S Main St Nazareth (18064) *(G-11956)*

Battlefield Brew Works 717 398-2907
  248 Hunterstown Rd Gettysburg (17325) *(G-6284)*

Bauer Company Inc 724 548-8101
  1 Glade Dr Kittanning (16201) *(G-8756)*

Bauer Company Inc 724 297-3200
  119 Ruth Hill Rd Worthington (16262) *(G-20228)*

Baum & Hersh Inc 717 229-2255
  11 Hanover St Codorus (17311) *(G-3357)*

Baum Precision Machining Inc 215 766-3066
  5136 Applebutter Rd Pipersville (18947) *(G-14611)*

Baum Printing Company, Philadelphia *Also called R R Donnelley & Sons Company (G-14225)*

Bauman Family 610 754-7251
  116 Hoffmansville Rd Sassamansville (19472) *(G-17080)*

Baumerts Wood Shavings 570 758-1744
  745 Mountain Top Rd Herndon (17830) *(G-7597)*

Baut Studios Inc 570 288-1431
  1095 Main St Swoyersville (18704) *(G-18194)*

Baw Plastics Inc (PA) 412 384-3100
  2148 Century Dr Jefferson Hills (15025) *(G-8273)*

Baw Plastics Inc 215 333-6508
  7236 Charles St Philadelphia (19135) *(G-13447)*

Baxano Surgical Inc (PA) 919 800-0020
  1301 Skippack Pike Ste 7a Blue Bell (19422) *(G-1815)*

Baxter Group Inc 717 263-7341
  941 Progress Rd Chambersburg (17201) *(G-2909)*

(G-0000) Company's Geographic Section entry number

Baxter Healthcare Corporation 717 232-1901
931 N 7th St Harrisburg (17102) *(G-7095)*

Bay Rat Lures, Erie *Also called Rapid Mold Solutions Inc (G-5456)*

Bay Sales LLC 215 331-6466
113 Fillmore St Bristol (19007) *(G-2117)*

Bay Valley Foods LLC 814 725-9617
11160 Parkway Dr North East (16428) *(G-12731)*

Bayard, Plymouth *Also called Webb Communications Inc (G-15824)*

Bayard Printing, Plymouth *Also called Webb Communications Inc (G-15825)*

Bayard Printing Group, Plymouth *Also called Webb Communications Inc (G-15823)*

Bayard Printing Group, Williamsport *Also called Webb Communications Inc (G-20089)*

Baycrete Inc 814 454-5001
1816 Greengarden Rd Erie (16502) *(G-5205)*

Bayer Corporation (HQ) 412 777-2000
100 Bayer Rd Bldg 14 Pittsburgh (15205) *(G-14750)*

Bayer Corporation 717 866-2141
400 W Stoever Ave Myerstown (17067) *(G-11875)*

Bayer Cropscience Holding Inc 412 777-2000
100 Bayer Rd Pittsburgh (15205) *(G-14751)*

Bayer Cropscience LP 412 777-2000
100 Bayer Rd Pittsburgh (15205) *(G-14752)*

Bayer Data Center Pittsburgh 412 920-2950
810 Parish St Pittsburgh (15220) *(G-14753)*

Bayer Healthcare, Indianola *Also called Bayer Medical Care Inc (G-8135)*

Bayer Healthcare, Pittsburgh *Also called Bayer Medical Care Inc (G-14756)*

Bayer Healthcare LLC 717 866-2141
400 W Stoever Ave Myerstown (17067) *(G-11876)*

Bayer Healthcare LLC 412 777-2000
100 Bayer Rd Pittsburgh (15205) *(G-14754)*

Bayer Hlthcare Phrmcticals Inc 717 713-7173
260 Salem Church Rd Mechanicsburg (17050) *(G-10823)*

Bayer Intl Trade Svcs Corp 412 777-2000
100 Bayer Rd Bldg 4 Pittsburgh (15205) *(G-14755)*

Bayer Medical Care Inc (HQ) 724 940-6800
1 Bayer Dr Indianola (15051) *(G-8135)*

Bayer Medical Care Inc 724 337-8176
2555 7th St New Kensington (15068) *(G-12327)*

Bayer Medical Care Inc 724 360-7600
150 Victory Rd Saxonburg (16056) *(G-17081)*

Bayer Medical Care Inc 412 767-2400
625 Alpha Dr Pittsburgh (15238) *(G-14756)*

Bayfront Brewing Co 814 333-8641
13388 Leslie Rd Meadville (16335) *(G-10705)*

Bayhill Defense LLC 412 877-9372
221 Paulson Ave Pittsburgh (15206) *(G-14757)*

Bayter Technologies Inc 610 948-7447
30 Thayer Way Phoenixville (19460) *(G-14529)*

Bazzini Holdings LLC 610 366-1606
1035 Mill Rd Allentown (18106) *(G-147)*

Bb and CC Inc (PA) 215 288-7440
1821 E Sedgley Ave Philadelphia (19124) *(G-13448)*

Bb Express Welding, Warfordsburg *Also called B B Express (G-18810)*

Bb Vintage Magazine ADS 717 235-1109
118 Windy Hill Rd New Freedom (17349) *(G-12202)*

Bbk Industries LLC 215 676-1500
585 Heatons Mill Dr Langhorne (19047) *(G-9280)*

Bbm Technologies Inc 412 269-4546
845 4th Ave Coraopolis (15108) *(G-3662)*

Bbu Inc (HQ) 215 347-5500
255 Business Center Dr # 200 Horsham (19044) *(G-7795)*

Bc USA, New Holland *Also called Zausner Foods Corp (G-12296)*

Bcbg, Philadelphia *Also called Runway Liquidation LLC (G-14264)*

Bcl Manufacturing Inc 814 467-8225
161 Bello Dr Windber (15963) *(G-20178)*

Bcmi Ad Concepts Inc 215 354-3000
3412 Progress Dr Ste C Bensalem (19020) *(G-1154)*

BCT, Bethel Park *Also called Meinert Holdings Inc (G-1424)*

BDH Oil Inc 814 362-5447
580 Interstate Pkwy Bradford (16701) *(G-1957)*

Be The Tree Llc 717 887-0780
1241 Chimney Rock Rd Hellam (17406) *(G-7549)*

Beach Filter Products Inc 717 235-1136
555 Centennial Ave # 120 Hanover (17331) *(G-6862)*

Beach Machine Inc 570 752-7786
61 Hosicks Rd Berwick (18603) *(G-1308)*

Beacon & Lively, Philadelphia *Also called Becker Fashion Tech LLC (G-13450)*

Beacon Container Corp PA, Birdsboro *Also called Beacon Container Corporation (G-1688)*

Beacon Container Corp Pennsylv, Montoursville *Also called Beacon Container Corporation (G-11433)*

Beacon Container Corporation (PA) 610 582-2222
700 W 1st St Birdsboro (19508) *(G-1688)*

Beacon Container Corporation 570 433-3800
326 S Maple St Montoursville (17754) *(G-11433)*

Beadazzle, Penn Valley *Also called Marilyn Cohen Designs (G-13237)*

Beam S Custom Woodworking 610 286-9040
95 Oak Tree Ln Morgantown (19543) *(G-11518)*

Bear Gap Stone Inc 570 337-9831
432 Quarry Rd Elysburg (17824) *(G-4971)*

Bear Metallurgical, Butler *Also called BMC Liquidation Company (G-2382)*

Bear Metallurgical, Butler *Also called Evergreen Metallurgical LLC (G-2400)*

Bear Paw Hand Cleaner, Knoxville *Also called Mspi Enterprises LLC (G-8812)*

Bear Ridge Mch & Fabrication 570 874-4083
10 S Eleanor Ave Frackville (17931) *(G-6103)*

Bear Springs Manufacturing 717 667-3200
107 S Main St Milroy (17063) *(G-11228)*

Beard Group Inc 240 629-3300
572 Fernwood Ln Fairless Hills (19030) *(G-5773)*

Bearing Products Company 215 659-4768
4567 Wayne Ave Philadelphia (19144) *(G-13449)*

Bearing Service Company PA (PA) 412 963-7710
630 Alpha Dr Pittsburgh (15238) *(G-14758)*

Beaumont Advanced Proc LLC 814 899-6390
1524 E 10th St Erie (16511) *(G-5206)*

Beaumont Development LLC 814 899-6390
6100 W Ridge Rd Erie (16506) *(G-5207)*

Beautifulbody Skincare LLC 610 255-2255
444 Dorothy Dr King of Prussia (19406) *(G-8587)*

Beaver Concrete & Supply Inc 724 774-5100
10 Industrial Park Rd Monaca (15061) *(G-11282)*

Beaver Creek Aviary 717 369-9983
942 Loudon Rd Saint Thomas (17252) *(G-17038)*

Beaver Dam Woodworks LLC 610 273-7656
2060 Beaver Dam Rd Honey Brook (19344) *(G-7737)*

Beaver Falls Tubular Products, Beaver Falls *Also called Ptc Alliance Corp (G-1008)*

Beaver Newspapers Inc 724 775-3200
400 Fair Ave Beaver (15009) *(G-979)*

Beaver Paint Company, Jamestown *Also called Walton Paint Company Inc (G-8241)*

Beaver Tool and Machine Co Inc 215 322-0660
1641 Loretta Ave Ste A Feasterville Trevose (19053) *(G-5888)*

Beaver Valley Alloy Foundry Co 724 775-1987
4165 Brodhead Rd Monaca (15061) *(G-11283)*

Beaver Valley Bowl, Rochester *Also called Alkali Beaver Products (G-16781)*

Beaver Valley Cash Register Co 724 728-0800
1408 Lexington Dr New Brighton (15066) *(G-12031)*

Beaver Valley Slag Inc 724 378-8888
6010 Woodlawn Rd Aliquippa (15001) *(G-68)*

Beaver Valley Slag Inc 724 773-0444
300 Constitution Blvd Monaca (15061) *(G-11284)*

Beaver Valley Slag Inc (PA) 724 375-8173
3468 Brodhead Rd Ste 3 Monaca (15061) *(G-11285)*

Beavers Logging Inc 570 842-4034
Rr 435 Gouldsboro (18424) *(G-6567)*

Beavertown Block Co Inc 814 359-2771
121 N Harrison Rd Bellefonte (16823) *(G-1093)*

Beavertown Block Co Inc 814 695-4448
16637 Dvecchis Spruce Sts East Freedom (16637) *(G-4559)*

BEC Machine Products, Harleysville *Also called BEC Systems Inc (G-7023)*

BEC Systems Inc 215 256-3100
100 Christopher Ln Harleysville (19438) *(G-7023)*

Beck & Ness Woodworking LLC 717 764-3984
3337 N George St Emigsville (17318) *(G-4984)*

Beck Electric Actuator, Newtown *Also called Harold Beck & Sons Inc (G-12506)*

Beck Manufacturing Company 717 593-0197
9170 Molly Pitcher Hwy Greencastle (17225) *(G-6599)*

Beck Manufacturing Company (HQ) 717 762-9141
330 E 9th St Waynesboro (17268) *(G-19399)*

Beck Tool Inc 814 734-8513
25741 Fry Rd Edinboro (16412) *(G-4809)*

Becker Fashion Tech LLC 215 776-2589
123 Monroe St Philadelphia (19147) *(G-13450)*

Becker's Printing, Sellersville *Also called Parkside Graphics Inc (G-17356)*

Becker/Wholesale Mine Sup LLC 724 515-4993
114 Equity Dr Ste E Greensburg (15601) *(G-6653)*

Beckers Cafe 412 331-1373
315 Olivia St Mc Kees Rocks (15136) *(G-10604)*

Beckley Perforating Corp 570 267-2092
166 Dundaff St Carbondale (18407) *(G-2669)*

Beckman Production Svcs Inc 814 425-1066
3052 St Rt 173 Cochranton (16314) *(G-3336)*

Becks Paving 814 692-7797
50 Peggy Cir Port Matilda (16870) *(G-15901)*

Becky Kens Duck & Geese Creat 717 684-0252
725 Poplar St Columbia (17512) *(G-3431)*

Beco Truck Cap Outlet 717 336-3141
143 Denver Rd Denver (17517) *(G-4067)*

Beco Truck Caps, Denver *Also called Beco Truck Cap Outlet (G-4067)*

Becotte Design Inc 215 641-1257
9999 Global Rd Philadelphia (19115) *(G-13451)*

Becton Dickinson and Company 610 948-3492
10 Galie Way Royersford (19468) *(G-16846)*

Bed Bath & Beyond Inc 717 397-0206
2350 Lincoln Hwy E # 100 Lancaster (17602) *(G-8950)*

Bedford Candies, Bedford *Also called TMC Candies LLC (G-1078)*

Bedford Depot, Bedford *Also called Galliker Dairy Company (G-1051)*

Bedford Farm Bureau Coop Assn (PA) 814 623-6194
102 Industrial Ave Bedford (15522) *(G-1040)*

Bedford Farm Bureau Coop Assn..............................814 793-2721
  Rr 866 Curryville (16631) (G-3945)

Bedford Forest Products Inc..................................814 977-3712
  205 Barclay St Bedford (15522) (G-1041)

Bedford Gazette LLC..814 623-1151
  424 W Penn St Bedford (15522) (G-1042)

Bedford Manufacturing LP.....................................717 419-2680
  227 Industrial Blvd Everett (15537) (G-5566)

Bedford Materials Co Inc.......................................800 773-4276
  7676 Allegheny Rd Manns Choice (15550) (G-10408)

Bedford Pallets..814 623-1521
  5425 Business 220 Bedford (15522) (G-1043)

Bedford Reinforced Plas Inc (PA)............................814 623-8125
  1 Corporate Dr Ste 106 Bedford (15522) (G-1044)

Bedside Harp LLC..215 752-7599
  4802 Neshaminy Blvd Ste 9 Bensalem (19020) (G-1155)

Bedwick and Jones Printing Inc..............................570 829-1951
  425 New Commerce Blvd Hanover Township (18706) (G-6979)

Bee Hempy, Homestead Also called Edinboro Creations (G-7685)

Bee Offset Printing...610 253-0926
  1130 Church St Easton (18042) (G-4651)

Bee Positive Foundation..484 302-8234
  497 Schuylkill Rd Phoenixville (19460) (G-14530)

Bee Positive Honey, Phoenixville Also called Bee Positive Foundation (G-14530)

Beechdale Frames...717 288-2723
  2856 Lincoln Hwy E Ronks (17572) (G-16803)

Beecher & Myers Company Inc...............................717 292-3031
  5176 Commerce Dr York (17408) (G-20401)

Beegle Saw Mill...814 784-5697
  1656 Rock Hill Church Rd Clearville (15535) (G-3238)

Beegles Logs and Lumber, Clearville Also called Beegle Saw Mill (G-3238)

Beenah Enterprises LLC..570 546-9388
  995 Gardner Rd Muncy (17756) (G-11808)

Beer 4 Less...724 452-7860
  114 S Main St Ste 1 Zelienople (16063) (G-20791)

Beer Brothers..610 438-3900
  1125 Northampton St Easton (18042) (G-4652)

Beer Stop, Philadelphia Also called SMK & Son Inc (G-14317)

Beer To Go Inc...610 253-2954
  250 Line St Easton (18042) (G-4653)

Beggs Brothers Printing Co....................................814 395-3241
  472 Latrobe Ave Confluence (15424) (G-3463)

Begonia Tool Co...724 446-1102
  573 Herminie Rd Herminie (15637) (G-7569)

Behr Process Corporation......................................610 391-1085
  7529 Morris Ct Ste 500 Allentown (18106) (G-148)

Behrenberg Glass Company Inc...............................724 468-4181
  57 Mark Dr Delmont (15626) (G-4048)

Beidel Printing House Inc.......................................717 532-5063
  63 W Burd St Shippensburg (17257) (G-17516)

Beiler Elam Sawmill, Quarryville Also called Beiler Sawmill (G-16264)

Beiler Printing LLC..717 336-1148
  115 N King St Denver (17517) (G-4068)

Beiler Sawmill..717 284-5271
  921 Lancaster Pike Quarryville (17566) (G-16264)

Beilers Manufacturing & Supply (PA).......................717 768-0174
  3025 Harvest Dr Ronks (17572) (G-16804)

Beilers Manufacturing & Supply.............................717 656-2179
  290 S Groffdale Rd Leola (17540) (G-9772)

Beilers Woodworking...717 656-8956
  81 Locust St Talmage (17580) (G-18206)

Beistel Machining, Donora Also called Brent D Beistel (G-4149)

Beistle Company (PA)...717 532-2131
  1 Beistle Plz Shippensburg (17257) (G-17517)

Beitler-Mckee Optical Company..............................412 381-7953
  160 S 22nd St Pittsburgh (15203) (G-14759)

Bel Aire Foods Inc...412 364-7277
  530 Camp Horne Rd Pittsburgh (15237) (G-14760)

Bel Connector Inc (HQ)...717 235-7512
  11118 Susquehanna Trl S Glen Rock (17327) (G-6452)

Bela Printing & Packaging Corp...............................215 664-7090
  650 N Cannon Ave Lansdale (19446) (G-9344)

Belar Electronics Lab Inc.......................................610 687-5550
  1140 Mcdermott Dr Ste 105 West Chester (19380) (G-19509)

Belco Tool & Mfg Inc..814 337-3403
  225 Terrace Street Ext Meadville (16335) (G-10706)

Belden & Blake Corporation...................................814 589-7091
  22811 Titusville Rd Pleasantville (16341) (G-15797)

Belden Brick Sales & Svc Inc..................................215 639-6561
  7 Neshaminy Interplex Dr # 117 Trevose (19053) (G-18487)

Belden Inc..724 228-7373
  2001 N Main St Washington (15301) (G-19152)

Belden Inc..724 222-7060
  2833 W Chestnut St Washington (15301) (G-19153)

Belden Inc..717 263-7655
  518 Cleveland Ave Ste 2a Chambersburg (17201) (G-2910)

Belden Tri-State Building Mtls, Trevose Also called Belden Brick Sales & Svc Inc (G-18487)

Beljan Manufacturing Corp....................................717 432-2891
  7675 Carlisle Rd Wellsville (17365) (G-19477)

Bell & Evans, Fredericksburg Also called Farmers Pride Inc (G-6174)

Bell Apothecary, Easton Also called Wakeem Inc (G-4774)

Bell Atlantic, Bloomsburg Also called Verizon Communications Inc (G-1806)

Bell Floor Covering, Philadelphia Also called Harvey Bell (G-13806)

Bell Fuel, Upper Darby Also called Maxwell Canby Fuel Oil Co (G-18688)

Bell Graphics...814 385-6222
  338 Donaldson Rd Kennerdell (16374) (G-8497)

Bell Manufacturing..717 529-2600
  195 Bell Rd Christiana (17509) (G-3133)

Bell Wall & Truss LLC...717 768-8338
  229 Osceola Mill Rd Gordonville (17529) (G-6549)

Bell, Edwin Containers, Cuddy Also called Edwin Bell Cooperage Company (G-3942)

Bell-Mark Sales Co Inc...717 292-5641
  4500 W Canal Rd Dover (17315) (G-4186)

Bell-Mark Technologies Corp..................................717 292-5641
  4500 W Canal Rd Dover (17315) (G-4187)

Bella Frte Bkbnding Ltterpress, Philadelphia Also called Bridget Morris (G-13480)

Bella Machine Inc..570 826-9127
  421 N Penna Ave Ste 1 Wilkes Barre (18702) (G-19908)

Bella Turka Inc (PA)...215 560-8733
  113 S 13th St Philadelphia (19107) (G-13452)

Bella Turka Jewelry, Philadelphia Also called Bella Turka Inc (G-13452)

Bellaire Corporation...814 446-5631
  196 Grange Hall Rd Armagh (15920) (G-723)

Bellefonte Gazette, Tyrone Also called Stott Publications Inc (G-18593)

Bellefonte Lime Co Quarry, Bellefonte Also called Graymont Inc (G-1098)

Bellemarque LLC..855 262-7783
  135 Lions Dr Hazle Township (18202) (G-7447)

Belletieri Sauces Inc (PA)......................................610 433-4334
  1207 Chew St Allentown (18102) (G-149)

Belleville International LLC.....................................724 431-0444
  330 E Cunningham St Butler (16001) (G-2377)

Bellisimo LLC..215 781-1700
  2925 State Rd Croydon (19021) (G-3912)

Bellview Lawn Furniture..717 786-1286
  87a Quarry Rd Quarryville (17566) (G-16265)

Bellville Foundry, Belleville Also called Donsco Inc (G-1131)

Bellwether Corp...610 534-5382
  622 Grant Rd Folcroft (19032) (G-5999)

Belmont Fabrics LLC...717 768-0077
  14 S Belmont Rd Paradise (17562) (G-13154)

Belmont Machine Co...717 556-0040
  40 Hess Rd Leola (17540) (G-9773)

Beltone Corporation..717 300-7163
  341 Baltimore Rd Shippensburg (17257) (G-17518)

Beltone Corporation..717 386-5640
  850 Walnut Bottom Rd Carlisle (17013) (G-2691)

Beltone Corporation..412 490-4902
  1000 Robinson Center Dr Pittsburgh (15205) (G-14761)

Beltone Hearing Center, Kittanning Also called Professional Hearing Aid Svc (G-8788)

Belvidere Sand Gravel...267 880-2422
  350 S Main St Ste 207 Doylestown (18901) (G-4274)

Bemenn Wood Products Inc...................................717 738-3530
  37 N Church St Ephrata (17522) (G-5093)

Bemis Company Inc...570 501-1400
  20 Jaycee Dr West Hazleton (18202) (G-19706)

Bemis North America, West Hazleton Also called Bemis Company Inc (G-19706)

Bemis Packaging Inc..717 279-5000
  5 Keystone Dr Lebanon (17042) (G-9547)

Ben Cook Racing Ltd...570 788-4223
  362 State Route 93 Hwy Sugarloaf (18249) (G-18152)

Ben Swaney...412 372-8109
  3704 Northern Pike Monroeville (15146) (G-11325)

Benchmark Group Media, Harrisburg Also called Harrisburg Magazine Inc (G-7143)

Benchmark Group Media Inc..................................610 691-8833
  65 E Elizabeth Ave # 307 Bethlehem (18018) (G-1459)

Benchmark Mtrials/ Cornerstone, Muncy Also called Hri Inc (G-11821)

Benchmark Orthot & Prosth Inc (HQ).......................724 825-4200
  351 W Beau St Ste A Washington (15301) (G-19154)

Benchsmith LLC...215 491-1711
  429 Easton Rd Ste B Warrington (18976) (G-19109)

Benco Technology LLC (PA)...................................610 273-3364
  625 Todd Rd Honey Brook (19344) (G-7738)

Bender Electronics Inc..610 383-9200
  420 Eagleview Blvd Exton (19341) (G-5652)

Benders Buffing & Polishing...................................717 226-1850
  19 Hess Ave Elizabethtown (17022) (G-4866)

Bendersville Wood Crafts......................................717 677-6458
  182 Park St Bendersville (17306) (G-1138)

Bendinger Inc..484 342-3522
  4110 Butler Pike Ste A101 Plymouth Meeting (19462) (G-15833)

Benebone LLC...610 366-3718
  7089 Queenscourt Ln Macungie (18062) (G-10142)

Benedict Cabinetry, Waynesboro Also called Daniel W Benedict (G-19408)

Benedum Interests, Pittsburgh Also called Paul G Benedum Jr (G-15371)

Beneficial Enrgy Solutions LLC (HQ)........................844 237-7697
  2632 State Route 72 Jonestown (17038) (G-8449)

Benetvison 814 459-9224
355 E 9th St Erie (16503) *(G-5208)*

Benfab Inc 610 626-9100
801 Carpenters Xing Ste 8 Folcroft (19032) *(G-6000)*

Bengal Converting Services Inc 610 787-0900
1155 Main St Linfield (19468) *(G-9987)*

Bengal Direct LLC 610 245-5901
1155 Main St Linfield (19468) *(G-9988)*

Benignas Creek Vineyard & Wine 570 546-0744
300 Lycoming Mall Cir Muncy (17756) *(G-11809)*

Benignas Creek Vineyard Wine 570 374-4750
1 Susquehanna Vly Mall Dr Selinsgrove (17870) *(G-17321)*

Benignas Creek Vnyrd Wnery Inc 570 523-4997
1585 Ridge Rd Klingerstown (17941) *(G-8805)*

Benjamin Company, Jeannette *Also called Benjamin Industries and Mfg (G-8248)*

Benjamin Industries and Mfg 724 523-9615
500 S 4th St Jeannette (15644) *(G-8248)*

Benkalu Group Lmtd Ta Jaguar 215 646-5896
1908 County Line Rd Huntingdon Valley (19006) *(G-7965)*

Bennett Compost 215 520-2406
2901 W Hunting Park Ave Philadelphia (19129) *(G-13453)*

Bennett Flooring LLC 724 586-9350
465 Pittsburgh Rd Butler (16002) *(G-2378)*

Bennett Heat Trting Brzing Inc 215 674-8120
82 Richard Rd Warminster (18974) *(G-18836)*

Benny Brewing Company LLC 570 235-6995
1429 Sans Souci Pkwy Hanover Township (18706) *(G-6980)*

Bensalem Metal Inc 215 526-3355
2424 State Rd Ste 3 Bensalem (19020) *(G-1156)*

Benshaw Inc 412 487-8235
1659 E Sutter Rd Glenshaw (15116) *(G-6483)*

Benshaw Inc (HQ) 412 968-0100
615 Alpha Dr Pittsburgh (15238) *(G-14762)*

Bensol Trousers, Scranton *Also called Astro Apparel Inc (G-17209)*

Bent Glass Design Inc 215 441-9101
3535 Davisville Rd Hatboro (19040) *(G-7273)*

Bentech, Philadelphia *Also called Philadelphia Pipe Bending Co (G-14149)*

Bentech Inc 215 223-9420
4135 N 5th St Philadelphia (19140) *(G-13454)*

Bentley & Collins Company 570 546-3250
195 Parkway Dr Muncy (17756) *(G-11810)*

Bentley Development Co Inc (PA) 724 459-5775
101 Serrell Dr Blairsville (15717) *(G-1715)*

Bentley Grphic Cmmncations Inc (PA) 610 933-7400
751 Pike Springs Rd Phoenixville (19460) *(G-14531)*

Bentley Robe Factory Inc 215 531-3862
2246 N 52nd St Philadelphia (19131) *(G-13455)*

Bentley Systems Incorporated 610 458-5000
690 Pennsylvania Dr Exton (19341) *(G-5653)*

Bentley Systems Incorporated (PA) 610 458-5000
685 Stockton Dr Exton (19341) *(G-5654)*

Benton Elevator 215 795-0650
3567 Spruce Hill Rd # 18942 Ottsville (18942) *(G-13059)*

Benton Foundry Inc 570 925-6711
5297 State Route 487 Benton (17814) *(G-1277)*

Berben Insignia Company, Jenkintown *Also called Elyse Aion (G-8285)*

Berdines Custom Hardwoods 724 447-2535
1276 Golden Oaks Rd Holbrook (15341) *(G-7637)*

Berenfield Cntrs Northeast Inc 610 258-2700
7 Mcfadden Rd Easton (18045) *(G-4654)*

Bergad Inc 724 763-2883
11858 State Route 85 Kittanning (16201) *(G-8757)*

Bergad Spclty Foams Composites, Kittanning *Also called Bergad Inc (G-8757)*

Bergen Pipe Supports Inc 724 379-5212
484 Galiffa Dr Donora (15033) *(G-4148)*

Bergen Power Pipe Supports, Donora *Also called Power Pipe Supports Inc (G-4159)*

Berger Building Products Inc 215 355-1200
805 Pennsylvania Blvd Feasterville Trevose (19053) *(G-5889)*

Berger Building Products Corp (HQ) 215 355-1200
805 Pennsylvania Blvd Feasterville Trevose (19053) *(G-5890)*

Bergs Custom Furniture, Mohnton *Also called Daniel G Berg (G-11261)*

Berk International LLC 610 369-0600
400 E 2nd St Boyertown (19512) *(G-1898)*

Berk Wiper Converting & Packg, Boyertown *Also called Berk International LLC (G-1898)*

Berk-Tek LLC 717 354-6200
132 White Oak Rd New Holland (17557) *(G-12230)*

Berkeley Surgicals, Uniontown *Also called Berkley Medical Resources Inc (G-18617)*

Berkey Creamery 814 865-7535
119 Food Science Bldg University Park (16802) *(G-18651)*

Berkheimer Realty Company Inc 610 588-0965
1883 Jury Rd Pen Argyl (18072) *(G-13211)*

Berkley Medical Resources Inc 724 438-3000
49 Virginia Ave Uniontown (15401) *(G-18617)*

Berkley Medical Resources Inc (PA) 724 564-5002
700 Mountain View Dr Smithfield (15478) *(G-17642)*

Berkley Products Company 717 859-1104
405 S 7th St A Akron (17501) *(G-33)*

Berkley Surgical Corporation 724 438-3000
49 Virginia Ave Uniontown (15401) *(G-18618)*

Berkman John A Display Sls Inc 412 421-0201
5715 Beacon St Apt 318 Pittsburgh (15217) *(G-14763)*

Berks Digital Inc 610 929-1200
2620 Hampden Blvd Reading (19604) *(G-16329)*

Berks Engineering Company 610 926-4146
1078 Stinson Dr Reading (19605) *(G-16330)*

BERKS PERSONNEL NETWORK, Reading *Also called Threshold Rhblitation Svcs Inc (G-16538)*

Berks Precision Machine Corp 610 603-0948
31 Catherine St Ste 1 Reading (19607) *(G-16331)*

Berks Products, Allentown *Also called New Enterprise Stone Lime Inc (G-330)*

Berks-Mont Newspapers Inc 610 683-7343
24 N Hanover St Pottstown (19464) *(G-15966)*

Berlin Steel Construction Co 610 240-8953
501 Garfield Ave West Chester (19380) *(G-19510)*

Berlin Steel Mid-Atlantic, West Chester *Also called Berlin Steel Construction Co (G-19510)*

Berm Studios Incorporated 610 622-2100
3070 Mccann Farm Dr # 104 Garnet Valley (19060) *(G-6265)*

Bernard Sign Corporation 215 425-1700
3325 Rorer St Philadelphia (19134) *(G-13456)*

Berner Industries Inc 724 924-9240
Rr 422 Box E New Castle (16101) *(G-12062)*

Berner International LLC (PA) 724 658-3551
111 Progress Ave New Castle (16101) *(G-12063)*

Bernies Beer & Beverage Inc 215 744-1946
4291 Paul St Philadelphia (19124) *(G-13457)*

Berrena Jeseph T McHanicals Inc 814 643-2645
279 Standing Stone Ave Huntingdon (16652) *(G-7939)*

Berry Enterprises Tool and Die, Emporium *Also called James A & Paulette M Berry (G-5064)*

Berry Global Inc 814 455-9051
316 W 16th St Erie (16502) *(G-5209)*

Berry Global Inc 570 889-3131
75 W Main St Ringtown (17967) *(G-16752)*

Berry Global Inc 717 393-3498
1846 Charter Ln Lancaster (17601) *(G-8951)*

Berry Global Inc 570 759-6240
910 E 7th St Berwick (18603) *(G-1309)*

Berry Global Inc 814 849-4234
2890 Maplevale Rd Brookville (15825) *(G-2248)*

Berry Global Inc 717 299-6511
1706 Hempstead Rd Lancaster (17601) *(G-8952)*

Berry Global Films LLC 570 474-9700
20 Elmwood Ave Mountain Top (18707) *(G-11752)*

Berry Metal Co, Harmony *Also called New Berry Inc (G-7074)*

Berrys Beverage Inc 724 867-9480
613 Main St Emlenton (16373) *(G-5006)*

Bertram Tool and Mch Co Inc 724 983-2222
1201 Mtn Ltr Kng Jr Blvd Farrell (16121) *(G-5866)*

Berwick Concrete & Aggergate, Berwick *Also called Riverview Block Inc (G-1342)*

Berwick Industries, Berwick *Also called Berwick Offray LLC (G-1311)*

Berwick Machine LLC 570 759-1888
705 Maple St Unit 1 Berwick (18603) *(G-1310)*

Berwick Offray LLC (HQ) 570 752-5934
2015 W Front St Berwick (18603) *(G-1311)*

Berwick Offray LLC 570 752-5934
Ninth St & Bombay Ln Berwick (18603) *(G-1312)*

Berwick Offray LLC 570 752-5934
1414 Susquehanna Ave Berwick (18603) *(G-1313)*

Berwind Consumer Products LLC 215 563-2800
1500 Market St Ste 3000w Philadelphia (19102) *(G-13458)*

Bes, Jonestown *Also called Beneficial Enrgy Solutions LLC (G-8449)*

Bess Manufacturing Company 215 447-1032
156 Dunksferry Rd Bensalem (19020) *(G-1157)*

Bessie Grove 570 524-2436
268 Wolfland Rd Lewisburg (17837) *(G-9898)*

Best Access Systems, Monroeville *Also called Stanley Security Solutions Inc (G-11357)*

Best Access Systems, Monroeville *Also called Stanley Security Solutions Inc (G-11358)*

Best Bakery Inc 215 855-3831
804 W 2nd St Lansdale (19446) *(G-9345)*

Best Dressed Associates Inc 717 938-2222
641 Lowther Rd Lewisberry (17339) *(G-9881)*

Best Feeds & Farm Supplies Inc (PA) 724 693-9417
106 Seminary Ave Oakdale (15071) *(G-12894)*

Best Group Holdings Inc (PA) 814 536-1422
501 Broad St Johnstown (15906) *(G-8357)*

Best Medical International Inc 412 312-6700
1 Best Dr Pittsburgh (15202) *(G-14764)*

Best Solutions Med Systems LLC 814 577-4184
516 Henrietta St Philipsburg (16866) *(G-14509)*

Best Window & Door Company, Johnstown *Also called Best Group Holdings Inc (G-8357)*

Best-Made Shoes 412 621-9363
5143 Liberty Ave Pittsburgh (15224) *(G-14765)*

Bestway Printing 215 368-4140
300 S Broad St Lansdale (19446) *(G-9346)*

Bestway Printing Service, Lansdale *Also called Bestway Printing (G-9346)*

Bestweld Inc 610 718-9700
40 Robinson St Pottstown (19464) *(G-15967)*

A
L
P
H
A
B
E
T
I
C

Beta Industries Inc 610 363-6555
211 Philips Rd Exton (19341) *(G-5655)*

Beth Mining Co 814 845-7390
815 Rock Run Rd Glen Campbell (15742) *(G-6423)*

Bethel Machine & Manufacturing 412 833-5522
3050 Industrial Blvd Bethel Park (15102) *(G-1406)*

Bethlehem Aluminum Inc. 610 432-4541
270 E Hamilton St Allentown (18109) *(G-150)*

Bethlehem Apparatus Co Inc (PA) 610 838-7034
890 Front St Hellertown (18055) *(G-7554)*

Bethlehem Apparatus Co Inc 610 882-2611
935 Bethlehem Dr Bethlehem (18017) *(G-1460)*

Bethlehem Apparatus Co Inc 610 838-7034
890 Front St Bethlehem (18017) *(G-1461)*

Bethlehem Hydrogen Inc 610 762-1706
600 Held Dr Northampton (18067) *(G-12845)*

Bethlehem Ice Service, Bethlehem *Also called Carl R Harry (G-1480)*

Bethlehem Pre-Cast Inc (PA) 610 967-5531
4702 Indian Creek Rd Macungie (18062) *(G-10143)*

Bethlehem Pre-Cast Inc 610 691-1336
835 E North St Bethlehem (18017) *(G-1462)*

Bethlehem Precast, Macungie *Also called Bethlehem Pre-Cast Inc (G-10143)*

Bethlehem Sausage Works Inc 800 478-2302
110 Mort Dr Easton (18040) *(G-4655)*

Bethlehem Waste Water 610 865-7169
144 Shimersville Rd Bethlehem (18015) *(G-1463)*

Bethlhem Resource Recovery Div, Hellertown *Also called Bethlehem Apparatus Co Inc (G-7554)*

Betmar, Adamstown *Also called Bollman Hat Company (G-19)*

Betmar, Denver *Also called Bollman Hat Company (G-4069)*

Better Air Management LLC 215 362-5677
810 E Hancock St Lansdale (19446) *(G-9347)*

Better Baked Foods LLC (HQ) 814 725-8778
56 Smedley St North East (16428) *(G-12732)*

Better Baked Foods LLC 814 899-6128
2200 E 38th St Erie (16510) *(G-5210)*

Better Batter Gluten Free Flur 814 946-0958
1885 E Pleasant Vly Blvd Altoona (16602) *(G-476)*

Better Bowls LLC 717 298-1257
1152 Mae St Ste 101 Hummelstown (17036) *(G-7902)*

Better Built Products 724 423-5268
320 Moccasin Hollow Rd Mount Pleasant (15666) *(G-11688)*

Better Living Center LLC 724 266-3750
607 Merchant St Ambridge (15003) *(G-611)*

Better World Spirits Inc 717 758-9346
131 E Philadelphia St York (17401) *(G-20402)*

Betts Equipment Inc 215 598-7501
3139 Windy Bush Rd New Hope (18938) *(G-12298)*

Betts Food Products, Pottstown *Also called Villanova Cheese Shop Inc (G-16069)*

Betts Industries Inc (PA) 814 723-1250
1800 Pennsylvania Ave W Warren (16365) *(G-19013)*

Betts Machine Shop, Rouseville *Also called Judy Raymond Corporation (G-16837)*

Betty's Salads, Mohnton *Also called Van Bennett Food Co Inc (G-11272)*

Beuerle, J Co, Willow Grove *Also called Jmg Inc (G-20121)*

Bevan's Own Make Candies, Media *Also called Bevans Candies Inc (G-10915)*

Bevans Candies Inc 610 566-0581
141 E Baltimore Ave # 143 Media (19063) *(G-10915)*

Beverage Air 814 849-2022
1082 Route 28 Brookville (15825) *(G-2249)*

Beverage Coasters Inc 610 916-4864
589 Centerport Rd Centerport (19516) *(G-2832)*

Beverage-Air Corporation 814 849-7336
Progress St Brookville (15825) *(G-2250)*

Beverly Hall Co 215 536-7048
5966 Clymer Rd Quakertown (18951) *(G-16172)*

Bevilacqua Sheet Metal Inc 570 558-0397
916 Capouse Ave Scranton (18509) *(G-17211)*

Beye LLC 484 581-1840
1008 Upper Gulph Rd Wayne (19087) *(G-19305)*

Beye.com, Wayne *Also called Beye LLC (G-19305)*

BF Hiestand House 717 426-8415
722 E Market St Marietta (17547) *(G-10461)*

Bfg Manufacturing Services Inc (PA) 814 938-9164
701 Martha St Punxsutawney (15767) *(G-16128)*

Bfhj Enrgy Solutions Ltd Lblty 717 458-0927
6427 Carlisle Pike Mechanicsburg (17050) *(G-10824)*

Bfr Hydraulics, Conshohocken *Also called Dispersion Tech Systems LLC (G-3539)*

Bg Industries LLC 267 374-8565
1510 View Rd Pennsburg (18073) *(G-13244)*

Bg Jewelry 610 691-0687
2189 Rovaldi Ave Bethlehem (18015) *(G-1464)*

Bhagyas Kitchen 215 233-1587
1010 E Willow Grove Ave Glenside (19038) *(G-6508)*

Bhm Metal Products & Inds LLC (PA) 570 785-2032
33 Mcgovern Blvd Crescent (15046) *(G-3886)*

Bhs Energy LLC 570 696-3754
56 Deer Path Ln Wyoming (18644) *(G-20274)*

Biagio Schiano Di Cola Debora 724 224-9906
1828 Union Ave Natrona Heights (15065) *(G-11935)*

Bible Channel, The, Ambridge *Also called Watchword Worldwide (G-638)*

Bible Lighthouse Book Store, Sayre *Also called Bible Lighthouse Inc (G-17111)*

Bible Lighthouse Inc 570 888-6615
518 N Keystone Ave Sayre (18840) *(G-17111)*

Bible Visuals International 717 859-1131
650 Main St Akron (17501) *(G-34)*

Bickels Potato Chips, York *Also called Hanover Foods Corporation (G-20521)*

Bickels Snack Foods Inc (HQ) 800 233-1933
1120 Zinns Quarry Rd York (17404) *(G-20403)*

Bickels Snack Foods Inc 717 843-0738
1000 W College Ave York (17404) *(G-20404)*

Bickle Snack Foods, York *Also called Hanover Foods Corporation (G-20522)*

Bico Machine and Tool, Marianna *Also called Creotech Industries LLC (G-10456)*

Bidwell Machining Inc 570 222-5575
1431 Oswald Johnson Rd Clifford Township (18441) *(G-3247)*

Biehn Printing, West Chester *Also called Auskin Inc (G-19503)*

Bierig Sailmakers, North East *Also called David A Bierig (G-12737)*

Big 3 Packaging LLC (PA) 215 743-4201
5039 Tomley St Ste B Philadelphia (19137) *(G-13459)*

Big B Manufacturing Inc (PA) 570 648-2084
17 Municipal Rd Klingerstown (17941) *(G-8806)*

Big Bear Concrete Works 570 584-0107
213 Mill Ln Lairdsville (17742) *(G-8886)*

Big Boyz Industries Inc 215 942-9971
128 Railroad Dr Warminster (18974) *(G-18837)*

Big Brother Hd Ltd Lblty Co 201 355-8166
107 Oakenshield Dr Tamiment (18371) *(G-18232)*

Big Creek Vineyard 570 325-8138
27 Race St Jim Thorpe (18229) *(G-8337)*

Big Daddy D Trucking, Waymart *Also called David Tuttle (G-19286)*

Big Heart Pet Brands 570 389-7650
6650 Lowe St Bloomsburg (17815) *(G-1772)*

Big Heart Pet Brands 570 784-8200
6670 Lowe St Bloomsburg (17815) *(G-1773)*

Big Hill Winery 717 226-8702
1365 Gablers Rd Gardners (17324) *(G-6259)*

Big John's Beef Jerky, York *Also called S M E Foods LLC (G-20662)*

Big Oaks Ltd Partnership II 724 444-0055
5360 William Flynn Hwy Gibsonia (15044) *(G-6326)*

Big Trucking Co, Media *Also called Glen Mills Sand & Gravel Inc (G-10929)*

Big Valley Beverage Inc 717 667-1414
8 Apple Ln Reedsville (17084) *(G-16622)*

Big Valley Cabinets 717 935-2788
80 Rockville Rd Belleville (17004) *(G-1127)*

Big Valley Concrete 717 483-6538
2649 Front Mountain Rd Belleville (17004) *(G-1128)*

Big Valley Hardwood 717 483-6440
12794 Fawn Ln Allensville (17002) *(G-107)*

Bigbee Steel and Tank Company (PA) 814 893-5701
4535 Elizabethtown Rd Manheim (17545) *(G-10370)*

Bigbee Steel and Tank Company 717 664-0600
4535 Elizabethtown Rd Manheim (17545) *(G-10371)*

Biggs Tool and Die Inc 215 674-9911
365 Patricia Dr Warminster (18974) *(G-18838)*

Bigshot Archery LLC 610 873-0147
2836 Creek Rd Elverson (19520) *(G-4961)*

Bike USA Inc 610 868-7652
2811 Brodhead Rd Ste 1 Bethlehem (18020) *(G-1465)*

Bikes & Trikes For 267 304-1534
2512 E Oakdale St Philadelphia (19125) *(G-13460)*

Bilcare Inc 610 935-4300
300 Kimberton Rd Ste 110 Phoenixville (19460) *(G-14532)*

Bill Barry Excavating Inc 570 595-2269
174 Quarry Ln Cresco (18326) *(G-3891)*

Bill Hards 814 677-2460
231 Gilmore Dr Seneca (16346) *(G-17364)*

Bill Macks Ice Cream 717 292-1931
3890 Carlisle Rd Dover (17315) *(G-4188)*

Bill ONeill 610 688-6135
46 Meadowbrook Rd Wayne (19087) *(G-19306)*

Bill Straley Printing 717 328-5404
4879 Steele Ave Lemasters (17231) *(G-9731)*

Bill's Woodworking & Rmdlg, Ambridge *Also called William Cottage (G-639)*

Billco Manufacturing Inc 724 452-7390
100 Halstead Blvd Zelienople (16063) *(G-20792)*

Billet Industries Inc 717 840-0280
247 Campbell Rd York (17402) *(G-20405)*

Bilt-Rite Mastex, Philadelphia *Also called Mutual Industries North Inc (G-14046)*

Biltwood Architectural Mllwk 717 593-9400
544 Buchanan Trl W Greencastle (17225) *(G-6600)*

Biltwood Interiors, Greencastle *Also called Biltwood Architectural Mllwk (G-6600)*

Biltwood Powder Coating LLC 717 655-5664
217 N Franklin St Waynesboro (17268) *(G-19400)*

Bimax Inc (PA) 717 235-3136
281 Industrial Rd Glen Rock (17327) *(G-6453)*

Bimbo Bakeries 570 888-2289
  901 N Elmer Ave Sayre (18840) *(G-17112)*

Bimbo Bakeries Usa Inc 610 825-1140
  1113 W Ridge Pike Conshohocken (19428) *(G-3522)*

Bimbo Bakeries Usa Inc 814 941-1102
  116 Stroehman Dr Altoona (16601) *(G-477)*

Bimbo Bakeries Usa Inc 800 222-7495
  1851 Loucks Rd York (17408) *(G-20406)*

Bimbo Bakeries Usa Inc 717 764-9999
  3670 Sandhurst Dr Ste A York (17406) *(G-20407)*

Bimbo Bakeries Usa Inc 610 478-9369
  640 Park Ave Reading (19611) *(G-16332)*

Bimbo Bakeries Usa Inc 724 251-0971
  140 Ferry St Leetsdale (15056) *(G-9684)*

Bimbo Bakeries Usa Inc 814 456-2596
  1220 W 20th St Erie (16502) *(G-5211)*

Bimbo Bakeries Usa Inc 412 443-3499
  140 Ferry St Bldg 24c Leetsdale (15056) *(G-9685)*

Bimbo Bakeries Usa Inc 570 455-7691
  350 Kiwanis Blvd West Hazleton (18202) *(G-19707)*

Bimbo Bakeries Usa Inc 610 921-2715
  4432 Pottsville Pike Reading (19605) *(G-16333)*

Bimbo Bakeries Usa Inc 814 456-4575
  1860 W 26th St Erie (16508) *(G-5212)*

Bimbo Bakeries Usa Inc 610 391-7490
  150 Boulder Dr Breinigsville (18031) *(G-2010)*

Bimbo Bakeries Usa Inc 610 865-7402
  2415 Brodhead Rd Bethlehem (18020) *(G-1466)*

Bimbo Bakeries Usa Inc (HQ) 215 347-5500
  255 Business Center Dr # 200 Horsham (19044) *(G-7796)*

Bimbo Bakeries Usa Inc 570 455-2066
  325 Kiwanis Blvd West Hazleton (18202) *(G-19708)*

Bimbo Bakeries Usa Inc 570 494-1191
  3375 Lycoming Creek Rd Williamsport (17701) *(G-19993)*

Bimbo Bakeries Usa Inc 724 733-2332
  780 Pine Valley Dr Ste D Pittsburgh (15239) *(G-14766)*

Bimbo Bakeries Usa Inc 570 654-4668
  1186 Sathers Dr Pittston (18640) *(G-15743)*

Bimbo Bakeries Usa Inc 800 635-1685
  75 Mcdonald Blvd Aston (19014) *(G-752)*

Bimbo Bakeries USA Inc 610 258-7131
  2400 Northampton St Easton (18045) *(G-4656)*

Bimbo Hungria Company (HQ) 866 506-6807
  255 Business Center Dr Horsham (19044) *(G-7797)*

Binary Research Inc 215 233-3200
  809 N Bethlehem Pike B Ambler (19002) *(G-570)*

Binder Industries-Candlewic 215 230-3601
  3765 Old Easton Rd Doylestown (18902) *(G-4275)*

Bindery Associates Inc 717 295-7443
  2025 Horseshoe Rd Lancaster (17602) *(G-8953)*

Bingaman & Son Lumber Inc 570 726-7795
  60 Lizardville Rd Mill Hall (17751) *(G-11173)*

Bingaman & Son Lumber Inc 814 723-2612
  22 Brown Ave Clarendon (16313) *(G-3167)*

Bingman Packing Co 814 267-3413
  165 5th Ave Berlin (15530) *(G-1283)*

Bio Med Sciences Inc 610 530-3193
  7584 Morris Ct Ste 218 Allentown (18106) *(G-151)*

Bio Sun Systems Inc 570 537-2200
  7088 Route 549 Ste 2 Millerton (16936) *(G-11214)*

Bio-Diversity LLC 570 884-3057
  2585 Route 522 Selinsgrove (17870) *(G-17322)*

Bio-Nucleonics Inc (PA) 305 576-0996
  1600 Market St Ste 13200 Philadelphia (19103) *(G-13461)*

Bio-RAD Laboratories Inc 267 322-6931
  1500 John F Kennedy Blvd # 800 Philadelphia (19102) *(G-13462)*

Bio-RAD Laboratories Inc 267 322-6945
  2000 Market St Ste 1460 Philadelphia (19103) *(G-13463)*

Bio/Data Corporation 215 441-4000
  155 Gibraltar Rd Horsham (19044) *(G-7798)*

Biochem Technology Inc 484 674-7003
  601 S Henderson Rd # 153 King of Prussia (19406) *(G-8588)*

Biocoat Incorporated 215 734-0888
  123 Rock Rd Horsham (19044) *(G-7799)*

Biodetego LLC 856 701-2453
  3711 Market St Ste 800 Philadelphia (19104) *(G-13464)*

Biofab Products Inc 724 283-4801
  140 Eastbrook Ln Butler (16002) *(G-2379)*

Bioflect Medical Group, Easton *Also called Discovery Direct Inc* *(G-4670)*

Biofuel Boiler Tech LLC 717 436-9300
  600 Airport Dr Mifflintown (17059) *(G-11110)*

Biokinetics Inc 570 538-3089
  Turbot Ave Dewart (17730) *(G-4118)*

Bioleap Inc 609 575-8645
  3805 Old Easton Rd Doylestown (18902) *(G-4276)*

Biomagnetic Solutions LLC 814 689-1801
  420 Amblewood Way State College (16803) *(G-17945)*

Biomed Healthcare (HQ) 888 244-2340
  950 Calcon Hook Rd Ste 19 Sharon Hill (19079) *(G-17453)*

Biomeme Inc 267 519-9066
  1015 Chestnut St Ste 1401 Philadelphia (19107) *(G-13465)*

Bionix Safety Technologies 610 408-0555
  996 Old Eagle School Rd # 1118 Wayne (19087) *(G-19307)*

Bionol Clearfield LLC 814 913-3100
  250 Technology Dr Clearfield (16830) *(G-3213)*

Bioplast Manufacturing LLC 609 807-3070
  128 Wharton Rd Bristol (19007) *(G-2118)*

Bioptechs Inc 724 282-7145
  3560 Beck Rd Butler (16002) *(G-2380)*

Biorealize Inc 610 216-5554
  3401 Grays Ferry Ave Philadelphia (19146) *(G-13466)*

Biorhythm, Oakdale *Also called Exclusive Supplements Inc* *(G-12898)*

Bioscience Management Inc 484 245-5232
  2201 Hangar Pl Ste 200 Allentown (18109) *(G-152)*

Biospectra Inc 610 599-3400
  100 Majestic Way Bangor (18013) *(G-908)*

Biospectra Inc (PA) 610 599-3400
  1474 Rockdale Ln Stroudsburg (18360) *(G-18108)*

Biotelemetry Inc (PA) 610 729-7000
  1000 Cedar Hollow Rd Malvern (19355) *(G-10193)*

Biotest Pharmaceuticals Corp 570 383-5341
  1027 Commerce Blvd Dickson City (18519) *(G-4119)*

Biowerk Inc 717 697-3310
  1115 S York St Mechanicsburg (17055) *(G-10825)*

Birch Cutting Corporation 570 343-7477
  Birch Street & Crown Ave Scranton (18510) *(G-17212)*

Birchcraft Kitchens Inc (PA) 610 375-4391
  425 Richmond St Reading (19605) *(G-16334)*

Bird In Hand Bakery, Bird In Hand *Also called Smucker Management Corporation* *(G-1681)*

Bird-In-Hand Woodworks Inc 717 397-5686
  3031 Industry Dr Lancaster (17603) *(G-8954)*

Birdbrain Technologies LLC 412 216-5833
  544 Miltenberger St Pittsburgh (15219) *(G-14767)*

Birds Eye Foods Inc 814 267-4641
  1313 Stadium St Berlin (15530) *(G-1284)*

Birds Eye Foods Inc 814 942-6031
  307 4th Ave Ste 1 Altoona (16602) *(G-478)*

Birds Eye Foods LLC 814 267-4641
  1313 Stadium St Berlin (15530) *(G-1285)*

Birds Printing 570 784-8136
  622 East St Bloomsburg (17815) *(G-1774)*

Birds' Paradise, The, Conneautville *Also called Troyer Rope Co* *(G-3488)*

Birdsboro Extrusions LLC 610 582-0400
  1 Industrial Dr Birdsboro (19508) *(G-1689)*

Birdsboro Kosher Farms Corp 610 404-0001
  1100 Lincoln Rd Birdsboro (19508) *(G-1690)*

Birdsboro Plant, Birdsboro *Also called Arkema Inc* *(G-1686)*

Biros John 570 384-3473
  14 Schoolhouse Rd Shepton (18248) *(G-17499)*

Biros Utilities, Shepton *Also called Biros John* *(G-17499)*

Birrbatt Printing Inc 412 373-9047
  421 Cavitt Ave Trafford (15085) *(G-18451)*

Bishop Equipment Manufacturing 215 368-5307
  63 E Broad St Ste 1 Hatfield (19440) *(G-7321)*

Bishop Metals Incorporated 412 481-5501
  422 Hays Ave Pittsburgh (15210) *(G-14768)*

Bishop Wood Products Inc 215 723-6644
  75 Schoolhouse Rd Souderton (18964) *(G-17726)*

Bishops Inc 412 821-3333
  1022 Sophia Ln Mars (16046) *(G-10488)*

Bishops Fencing & Outdoor Pdts, Souderton *Also called Bishop Wood Products Inc* *(G-17726)*

Bisil North America Inc 610 747-0340
  111 Presidential Blvd # 246 Bala Cynwyd (19004) *(G-873)*

Bismoline Manufacturing Co 717 394-8795
  411 S Queen St Lancaster (17603) *(G-8955)*

Biss Nuss Inc 412 221-1200
  2600 Boyce Plaza Rd # 141 Pittsburgh (15241) *(G-14769)*

Bissinger and Stein Inc 215 256-1122
  1500 Industrial Blvd Kulpsville (19443) *(G-8824)*

Bitars Sportswear 610 435-4923
  207 W Tilghman St Allentown (18102) *(G-153)*

Bitrekpasub Inc (HQ) 717 762-9141
  330 E 9th St Waynesboro (17268) *(G-19401)*

Bitronics LLC 610 997-5100
  261 Brodhead Rd Ste 100 Bethlehem (18017) *(G-1467)*

Bittinger Drilling Co 724 727-3822
  104 Spring Dr Apollo (15613) *(G-664)*

Bittner Distributors Company 412 261-8000
  26th & Smallman Sts Pittsburgh (15222) *(G-14770)*

Bituminous Pav Mtls York Inc (PA) 717 843-4573
  1300 Zinns Quarry Rd York (17404) *(G-20408)*

Bituminous Pav Mtls York Inc 717 632-8919
  100 Green Springs Rd Hanover (17331) *(G-6863)*

BJ REO Inc 412 384-2161
  Madison Ave West Elizabeth (15088) *(G-19692)*

Bk Barrit, Philadelphia *Also called B K Barrit Corp* *(G-13438)*

Bkts Inc 814 724-1547
  1347 S Main St Meadville (16335) *(G-10707)*

A L P H A B E T I C

Black & Decker (us) Inc...610 797-6600
    11 Grammes Rd Allentown (18103) *(G-154)*
Black & Decker (us) Inc...215 271-0402
    2715 S Front St Ste 5 Philadelphia (19148) *(G-13467)*
Black & Decker (us) Inc...717 755-3441
    2201 Industrial Hwy York (17402) *(G-20409)*
Black Bear Associates LLC.......................................610 470-6477
    923 E Orange St Unit 1 Lancaster (17602) *(G-8956)*
Black Bear Deli Meats, Philadelphia Also called Dietz & Watson Inc *(G-13631)*
Black Bear Structures Inc (PA)...............................717 824-0983
    1865 Lancaster Pike Peach Bottom (17563) *(G-13196)*
Black Bear Structures Inc.......................................717 225-0377
    1213 Hanover Rd York (17408) *(G-20410)*
Black Box Corporation (HQ).....................................724 746-5500
    1000 Park Dr Lawrence (15055) *(G-9535)*
Black Box Corporation...215 274-1044
    540 Township Line Rd Blue Bell (19422) *(G-1816)*
Black Box Services Company.....................................724 746-5500
    1000 Park Dr Lawrence (15055) *(G-9536)*
Black Diamond Mining Inc.......................................570 672-9917
    27 S Hickory St Elysburg (17824) *(G-4972)*
Black Hawk Mining Inc...724 783-6433
    221 Creek Rd Rural Valley (16249) *(G-16876)*
Black Knight Industries Inc.....................................814 676-3474
    382 State Route 227 Oil City (16301) *(G-12942)*
Black Knight Quarries Inc...570 265-8991
    293 Beacon Light Rd Towanda (18848) *(G-18421)*
Black Lick Stake Plant...724 459-7670
    1610 Cornell Rd Blairsville (15717) *(G-1716)*
Black Logging..717 263-6446
    3880 Crottlestown Rd Chambersburg (17202) *(G-2911)*
Black Rock Fabrication LLC.......................................610 212-3528
    485 Freemont St Phoenixville (19460) *(G-14533)*
Black Rock Manufacturing Co...................................570 752-1811
    R620 Broad St Berwick (18603) *(G-1314)*
Black Rock Repair LLC...717 529-6553
    858 Pumping Station Rd Kirkwood (17536) *(G-8744)*
Black Viper Energy Services.....................................432 561-8801
    3 Nicholson Dr Cuddy (15031) *(G-3940)*
Black Walnut Winery (PA)...610 857-5566
    3000 E Lincoln Hwy Sadsburyville (19369) *(G-16904)*
Blackbird Industries Inc..724 283-2537
    569 Mahood Rd West Sunbury (16061) *(G-19769)*
Blackhawk Specialty Tools LLC.................................570 323-7100
    285 Marcellus Dr Muncy (17756) *(G-11811)*
Blaine Boring Chocolates..814 539-6244
    123 Market St Johnstown (15901) *(G-8358)*
Blair Companies...814 949-8280
    259 Lakemont Park Blvd Altoona (16602) *(G-479)*
Blair Companies (PA)...814 949-8287
    5107 Kissell Ave Altoona (16601) *(G-480)*
Blair Composites LLC..423 638-5847
    259 Lakemont Park Blvd Altoona (16602) *(G-481)*
Blair Fixtures & Millwork Inc.....................................814 940-1913
    4100 Industrial Park Dr Altoona (16602) *(G-482)*
Blair Sign Company, Altoona Also called Blair Companies *(G-480)*
Blair Strip Steel Company...724 658-2611
    1209 Butler Ave New Castle (16101) *(G-12064)*
Blair Tool & Plastic Co Inc..814 695-2726
    Everette Rd East Freedom (16637) *(G-4560)*
Blair Tool and Plastics Co LLC..................................814 695-2726
    2846 Everett Rd East Freedom (16637) *(G-4561)*
Blair Vineyards...610 682-0075
    62 Five Points Rd Mertztown (19539) *(G-11001)*
Blairsville Wilbert Burial Vlt (PA).............................724 459-9677
    6 Decker St Blairsville (15717) *(G-1717)*
Blairsville Wilbert Burial Vlt.....................................724 324-2010
    Mechanic St Mount Morris (15349) *(G-11679)*
Blairsville Wilbert Burial Vlt.....................................724 547-2865
    153 S Quarry St Mount Pleasant (15666) *(G-11689)*
Blairsville Wilbert Burial Vlt.....................................814 495-5921
    530 Railroad St South Fork (15956) *(G-17772)*
Blanchard Mfg & Engrg...814 454-8995
    1322 E 12th St Erie (16503) *(G-5213)*
Blank Concrete and Supply.......................................724 758-7596
    804 Factory Ave Ellwood City (16117) *(G-4928)*
Blank River Services Inc (PA)...................................412 384-2489
    1 Chicago Ave Bldg 12 Elizabeth (15037) *(G-4857)*
Blanski Energy Management Inc................................610 373-5273
    1835 Pear St Reading (19601) *(G-16335)*
Blasi Printing Inc...570 824-3557
    1490 Sans Souci Pkwy Hanover Township (18706) *(G-6981)*
Blastco...215 529-7100
    1505 N West End Blvd Quakertown (18951) *(G-16173)*
Blasting Products Inc...412 221-5722
    710 Millers Run Rd Cuddy (15031) *(G-3941)*
Blastmaster Surface Restoratio.................................724 282-7669
    314 Broad St Butler (16001) *(G-2381)*
Blatek Industries Inc..814 231-2085
    2820 E College Ave Ste F State College (16801) *(G-17946)*

Blatts Pattern Shop...717 933-5633
    760 Meckville Rd Fredericksburg (17026) *(G-6172)*
Blatts Printing Co..610 926-2289
    637 Main St Mohrsville (19541) *(G-11274)*
Blazing Passion Publ...215 247-2024
    8600 Provident St Philadelphia (19150) *(G-13468)*
Blazing Technologies Inc...484 722-4800
    4631 Morgantown Rd Mohnton (19540) *(G-11260)*
Bleacher Creatures LLC..484 534-2398
    527 Plymouth Rd Ste 407 Plymouth Meeting (19462) *(G-15834)*
Blendco Systems LLC (HQ).....................................215 785-3147
    1 Pearl Buck Ct Bristol (19007) *(G-2119)*
Bless Precision Tool Inc...215 536-7836
    601 Montgomery Ave Pennsburg (18073) *(G-13245)*
Blessed Dough LLC..717 368-4109
    3722 Nazareth Rd Easton (18045) *(G-4657)*
Bliley Technologies Inc...814 838-3571
    2545 W Grandview Blvd Erie (16506) *(G-5214)*
Blind & Vision, Homestead Also called Blind and Vision Rehab *(G-7683)*
Blind and Vision Rehab (PA).....................................412 368-4400
    1816 Locust St Pittsburgh (15219) *(G-14771)*
Blind and Vision Rehab..412 325-7504
    1800 West St Side Homestead (15120) *(G-7683)*
Blind Doctors...412 822-8580
    506 Seavey Rd Pittsburgh (15209) *(G-14772)*
Blockcom, Doylestown Also called Blockcom *(G-4277)*
Blockcom...215 794-9575
    3667 Old Easton Rd Doylestown (18902) *(G-4277)*
Blocki Flute Method LLC..866 463-5883
    5368 Hardt Rd Gibsonia (15044) *(G-6327)*
Bloksberg Inc...724 727-9925
    4203 State Route 66 # 101 Apollo (15613) *(G-665)*
Blommer Chocolate Company (HQ)............................800 825-8181
    1101 Blommer Dr East Greenville (18041) *(G-4565)*
Blommer Chocolate Company.....................................215 679-4472
    1101 Blommer Dr East Greenville (18041) *(G-4566)*
Blommer Chocolate Company, The, East Greenville Also called Blommer Chocolate
Company *(G-4566)*
Bloom Engineering Company Inc (HQ)........................412 653-3500
    5460 Horning Rd Pittsburgh (15236) *(G-14773)*
Bloom Machine Works Inc...814 789-4234
    11860 State Highway 198 Guys Mills (16327) *(G-6808)*
Bloom Refractory Products LLC..................................412 653-3500
    5460 Curry Rd Pittsburgh (15236) *(G-14774)*
Bloomsburg Carpet Inds Inc (PA)..............................800 233-8773
    4999 Columbia Blvd Bloomsburg (17815) *(G-1775)*
Blose Printing...717 838-9129
    2709 Horseshoe Pike Campbelltown (17010) *(G-2529)*
Blowout Tools Inc...724 627-0208
    114 Baker Dr Waynesburg (15370) *(G-19434)*
Blue Avionics Inc...310 433-9431
    542 Black Horse Rd Chester Springs (19425) *(G-3072)*
Blue Bell Print Solutions..215 591-3903
    1018 Hickory Dr Blue Bell (19422) *(G-1817)*
Blue Boy Products Inc (PA).......................................610 284-1055
    104 Woodcrest Dr Downingtown (19335) *(G-4215)*
Blue Diamond Vodka, Pittsburgh Also called Vodka Brands Corp *(G-15704)*
Blue Dog Printing & Design.......................................610 430-7992
    1039 Andrew Dr West Chester (19380) *(G-19511)*
Blue Flame Heater Mfg...717 768-0301
    321 Osceola Mill Rd Gordonville (17529) *(G-6550)*
Blue Golf Com...909 592-6411
    724 W Lancaster Ave # 220 Wayne (19087) *(G-19308)*
Blue Heron Sporstwear, Milton Also called Blue Heron Sportswear Inc *(G-11234)*
Blue Heron Sportswear Inc..570 742-3228
    Rr 405 Box S Milton (17847) *(G-11234)*
Blue Horizons Dive Center, Glen Mills Also called 25 Fathoms International Inc *(G-6428)*
Blue Mountain Buildng Stone Co................................717 671-8711
    80 S Hershey Rd Harrisburg (17112) *(G-7096)*
Blue Mountain Farms LLC...717 599-5110
    605 Lesentier Ln Harrisburg (17112) *(G-7097)*
Blue Mountain Lawn Service......................................610 759-6979
    1433 Church Rd Wind Gap (18091) *(G-20166)*
Blue Mountain Machine Inc.......................................610 377-4690
    725 State Rd Lehighton (18235) *(G-9710)*
Blue Mountain Metal Finishing..................................717 933-1643
    137 Kline Rd Bethel (19507) *(G-1393)*
Blue Mountain Pigment...610 261-4963
    75 W 21st St Ste 3 Northampton (18067) *(G-12846)*
Blue Mountain Processors Inc....................................717 438-3296
    34 Blue Mountain Ln Fl 35 Elliottsburg (17024) *(G-4919)*
Blue Mountain Rock Drilling, Wind Gap Also called Blue Mountain Lawn Service *(G-20166)*
Blue Mountain Sports AP Inc.....................................717 263-4124
    763 S 2nd St Chambersburg (17201) *(G-2912)*
Blue Mountain Woodworking......................................610 746-2588
    2413 Community Dr Bath (18014) *(G-952)*
Blue Mtn A Comprsr Svcs LLC....................................717 423-5262
    26 Jumper Rd Shippensburg (17257) *(G-17519)*

Blue Mtn Vineyards & Cellars (PA)................610 298-3068
7627 Grape Vine Dr New Tripoli (18066) (G-12453)

Blue Ox Timber Resources Inc................814 437-2019
6708 Us 322 Franklin (16323) (G-6116)

Blue Ribbon Farm Dairy................570 763-5570
1209 Main St Swoyersville (18704) (G-18195)

Blue Ridge Distillery LLC................610 895-4205
239 Blue Ridge Rd Saylorsburg (18353) (G-17103)

Blue Ridge Mtn Cookery Inc................717 762-1211
6806 Anthony Hwy Waynesboro (17268) (G-19402)

Blue Sky International Inc................610 306-1234
534 Brighton Way Phoenixville (19460) (G-14534)

Blue Spin LLC................814 863-4630
1120 Kay St Boalsburg (16827) (G-1864)

Blue Star Basketball................215 638-7060
1950 Street Rd Ste 104 Bensalem (19020) (G-1158)

Blue Star Cooking, Blandon Also called Prizer-Painter Stove Works Inc (G-1757)

Blue Steel Distillery................610 820-7116
321 S Carlisle St Allentown (18109) (G-155)

Blue Toro Technologies LLC................610 428-0891
4431 Wagner Dr Bethlehem (18020) (G-1468)

Blue Triangle Hardwoods LLC................814 652-9111
156 Industrial Blvd Everett (15537) (G-5567)

Blue Valley Industries Inc................717 436-8266
304 N Third St Port Royal (17082) (G-15909)

Bluebird Distilling LLC................610 933-7827
100 Bridge St Phoenixville (19460) (G-14535)

Bluegill Graphix................814 827-7003
318 N Franklin St Titusville (16354) (G-18376)

Bluegolf, Wayne Also called Blue Golf Com (G-19308)

Bluegrass Materials Co LLC................410 683-1250
424 Pigeon Cove Rd Warfordsburg (17267) (G-18811)

Bluephone................412 337-1965
625 Elm St Bridgeville (15017) (G-2055)

Blueridge Furniture, East Earl Also called E H Woodworking (G-4542)

Bluescope Buildings N Amer Inc................717 867-4651
400 N Weaber St Annville (17003) (G-643)

Bluestar Marketing Inc................215 886-4002
915 Jenkintown Rd Elkins Park (19027) (G-4900)

Bluestem Industries Pa LLC................412 585-6220
944 Beaver Grade Rd Moon Township (15108) (G-11481)

Bluestone Inc................215 364-1415
170 Cherry Blossom Dr Southampton (18966) (G-17799)

Bluewater Thermal Services................814 772-8474
337 N Broad St Ridgway (15853) (G-16697)

Bluewater Thermal Solutions, Saint Marys Also called Piht LLC (G-17007)

Bluhms Gas Sales Inc................570 746-2440
44340 Route 6 Wyalusing (18853) (G-20245)

Blupanda LLC................724 494-2077
1719 Coulter Rd Apollo (15613) (G-666)

Blx Inc................724 543-5743
233 North Park Dr Kittanning (16201) (G-8758)

BMC East LLC................717 866-2167
50 W Stoever Ave Myerstown (17067) (G-11877)

BMC Liquidation Company................724 431-2800
679 E Butler Rd Butler (16002) (G-2382)

BMC Software Inc................610 941-2750
200 Barr Harbor Dr # 400 Conshohocken (19428) (G-3523)

Bmi Refractory Services Inc (HQ)................412 429-1800
250 Parkwest Dr Pittsburgh (15275) (G-14775)

Bms Inc (PA)................609 883-5155
679 Deerpath Rd Yardley (19067) (G-20297)

Bnb Fire Protection Inc................610 944-0594
16 Breezy Park Dr Fleetwood (19522) (G-5968)

BNP Media Inc................610 436-4220
600 Willowbrook Ln # 610 West Chester (19382) (G-19512)

BNP Media Inc................412 531-3370
1910 Cochran Rd Ste 450 Pittsburgh (15220) (G-14776)

BNP Media Inc................412 531-3370
1910 Cochran Rd Ste 450 Pittsburgh (15220) (G-14777)

Bnz Materials Inc................724 452-8650
191 Front St Zelienople (16063) (G-20793)

Boardmaker, Pittsburgh Also called Dynavox Inc (G-14948)

Boardroom Spirits................215 815-5351
575 W 3rd St Lansdale (19446) (G-9348)

Boardroom Spirits Distillery, Lansdale Also called Boardroom Spirits LLC (G-9348)

Boas Surgical Inc (PA)................484 895-3451
3050 Hamilton Blvd # 220 Allentown (18103) (G-156)

Boathouse Row Sports Ltd................215 425-4300
425 E Hunting Park Ave Philadelphia (19124) (G-13469)

Boathouse Sports, Philadelphia Also called Boathouse Row Sports Ltd (G-13469)

Bob Allen & Sons Inc................610 874-4391
1 W 9th St Chester (19013) (G-3040)

Bob Johnson Flagstone Inc................570 746-0907
3658 Old Stagecoach Rd Wyalusing (18853) (G-20246)

Bobs Diner Enterprises Inc................412 221-7474
1870 Painters Run Rd Pittsburgh (15241) (G-14778)

Bock Workholding Inc................724 763-1776
418 3rd Ave Ste 4 Ford City (16226) (G-6043)

Bodine Business Products................610 827-0138
2099 Bodine Rd Ste 100 Malvern (19355) (G-10194)

Bodon Industries Inc (PA)................610 323-0700
1513 Ben Franklin Hwy E Douglassville (19518) (G-4170)

Bodrie Inc................724 836-3666
138 Flora St B Smithton (15479) (G-17658)

Body Gems................215 357-9552
875 Pnnsylvania Blvd Ste 2 Feasterville Trevose (19053) (G-5891)

Bodybuilders Bodywash LLC................954 682-8191
128 Woodview Dr Quakertown (18951) (G-16174)

Bodycote Thermal Proc Inc................717 767-6757
270 Emig Rd Emigsville (17318) (G-4985)

Bodyx LLC................610 519-9999
22 N Bryn Mawr Ave Bryn Mawr (19010) (G-2316)

Boeh Tool & Die Co Inc................412 833-8707
1098 Highfield Rd Bethel Park (15102) (G-1407)

Boehringer Laboratories Inc................610 278-0900
300 Thoms Dr Ste 14 Phoenixville (19460) (G-14536)

Boehringer Laboratories LLC................610 278-0900
300 Thoms Dr Phoenixville (19460) (G-14537)

Boehringer Wound Systems LLC................610 278-0900
300 Thoms Dr Ste 14 Phoenixville (19460) (G-14538)

Boeing Company................610 828-7764
853 Hamilton Dr Lafayette Hill (19444) (G-8877)

Boeing Company................610 591-1978
300 Industrial Hwy Ridley Park (19078) (G-16734)

Boeing Company................610 591-2121
Stewart Ave Rr 291 Ridley Park (19078) (G-16735)

Boeing Company................610 591-2121
1 S Stewart Ave Ridley Park (19078) (G-16736)

Boeing Company................610 591-2121
Stewart Ave Rr 291 Ridley Park (19078) (G-16737)

Boekel Industries Inc (PA)................215 396-8200
855 Pennsylvania Blvd Feasterville Trevose (19053) (G-5892)

Boekel Scientific, Feasterville Trevose Also called Boekel Industries Inc (G-5892)

Boekeloo Inc................814 723-5950
1501 Pennsylvania Ave W Warren (16365) (G-19014)

Bog Turtle Brewery LLC................484 758-0416
145 Schoolview Ln Oxford (19363) (G-13072)

Boggs Printing Inc................215 675-1203
216 N York Rd Hatboro (19040) (G-7274)

Bognar and Company Inc (PA)................412 344-9900
733 Washington Rd Ste 500 Pittsburgh (15228) (G-14779)

Bognar and Company Inc................724 336-5000
Hc 168 New Galilee (16141) (G-12220)

Bohlinger Inc................610 825-0440
600 E Elm St Conshohocken (19428) (G-3524)

Bohn Painting & Decorating, Greencastle Also called James G Bohn (G-6619)

Boiler Erection and Repair Co................215 721-7900
142 Schoolhouse Rd Souderton (18964) (G-17727)

Boilerroom Equipment Inc................724 327-0077
2081 Borland Farm Rd B Export (15632) (G-5593)

Boiron Inc (HQ)................610 325-7464
6 Campus Blvd Newtown Square (19073) (G-12567)

Boke Investment Company (HQ)................412 321-4252
12 Federal St Ste 320 Pittsburgh (15212) (G-14780)

Bollman Hat Company (PA)................717 484-4361
110 E Main St Adamstown (19501) (G-19)

Bollman Hat Company................717 336-0545
50 Denver Rd Denver (17517) (G-4069)

Bollman Industries Inc (HQ)................717 484-4361
110 E Main St Adamstown (19501) (G-20)

Bollman Industries-San Angelo, Adamstown Also called Bollman Industries Inc (G-20)

Bolsan Company Inc................724 225-0446
163 Linnwood Rd Eighty Four (15330) (G-4834)

Bolt Works Inc................724 776-7273
2150 Woodland Rd Warrendale (15086) (G-19069)

Bolton Metal Products Co Inc................814 355-6217
2042 Axemann Rd 300 Bellefonte (16823) (G-1094)

Bolttech Mannings Inc (HQ)................724 872-4873
501 Mosside Blvd North Versailles (15137) (G-12772)

Boltz Printing Company LLC................724 772-4911
20325 Route 19 Cranberry Township (16066) (G-3809)

Bombardier Transportation................412 655-0325
1400 Lebanon Church Rd Pittsburgh (15236) (G-14781)

Bombardier Transportation (HQ)................412 655-5700
1501 Lebanon Church Rd Pittsburgh (15236) (G-14782)

Bombardier Trnsp Systems, Pittsburgh Also called Bombardier Transportation (G-14782)

Bomboy Inc................610 266-1553
1621 E Race St Allentown (18109) (G-157)

Bompadre Division, Newtown Also called Ajjp Corporation (G-12495)

Bon Air Products Inc................412 793-8600
147 Sandy Creek Rd Verona (15147) (G-18749)

Bon Tool Company (PA)................724 443-7080
4430 Gibsonia Rd Gibsonia (15044) (G-6328)

Bond Caster and Wheel Corp (PA)................717 665-2275
230 S Penn St Manheim (17545) (G-10372)

Bond Machine & Fabrication LLC................717 665-9030
230 S Penn St Manheim (17545) (G-10373)

A
L
P
H
A
B
E
T
I
C

Bond Machine and Fabrication, Manheim *Also called Bond Caster and Wheel Corp* ***(G-10372)***
Bond Products Inc....215 842-0200
4511 Wayne Ave Philadelphia (19144) ***(G-13470)***
Bond With Me LLC....267 334-1233
30 E Swamp Rd Doylestown (18901) ***(G-4278)***
Bondata Inc....717 566-5550
245 W High St Hummelstown (17036) ***(G-7903)***
Bondi Printing Co Inc....724 327-6022
3975 William Penn Hwy Murrysville (15668) ***(G-11848)***
Bonehead Performance Inc....215 674-8206
1836 Stout Dr Ste 18 Warminster (18974) ***(G-18839)***
Bones and All LLC....216 870-7177
6888 Hamilton Ave Rear Pittsburgh (15208) ***(G-14783)***
Boneshire Brew Works....717 469-5007
7462 Derry St Harrisburg (17111) ***(G-7098)***
Boninfante Enterprises, Lansdowne *Also called Boninfante Friction Inc* ***(G-9431)***
Boninfante Friction Inc....610 626-2194
555 Industrial Park Dr Lansdowne (19050) ***(G-9431)***
Bonland Fairless Hills, Fairless Hills *Also called Bonland Industries Inc* ***(G-5774)***
Bonland Industries Inc....215 949-3720
515 S Olds Blvd Ste 202 Fairless Hills (19030) ***(G-5774)***
Bonn Place Brewing Inc....845 325-6748
310 Taylor St Bethlehem (18015) ***(G-1469)***
Bonney Forge Corporation (PA)....814 542-2545
14496 Croghan Pike Mount Union (17066) ***(G-11739)***
Bonnie Kaiser....215 331-6555
8799 Frankford Ave Philadelphia (19136) ***(G-13471)***
Bonnit Brush LLC....215 355-4115
3161 State Rd Bensalem (19020) ***(G-1159)***
Bonsal American Inc....724 475-2511
97 Main St Fredonia (16124) ***(G-6179)***
Bonsal American Inc....215 785-1290
1214 Hayes Blvd Bristol (19007) ***(G-2120)***
Bonura Jr Cabinets By Bill....412 793-6790
7940 Saltsburg Rd Pittsburgh (15239) ***(G-14784)***
Book Bindery Co Inc....717 244-4343
401 E Locust St Ste 9 Dallastown (17313) ***(G-3972)***
Bookhaven Press LLC....412 494-6926
302 Scenic Ct Coraopolis (15108) ***(G-3663)***
Boos Bug Stoppers LLC....724 601-3223
207 Thomas Hill Rd Fombell (16123) ***(G-6030)***
Boose Aluminum Foundry Co Inc....717 336-5581
77 N Reamstown Rd Reamstown (17567) ***(G-16574)***
Bop Land Services LP....724 747-1594
2547 Washington Rd # 720 Pittsburgh (15241) ***(G-14785)***
Boquet Tool & Die....724 539-8250
143 Shawley Ln Latrobe (15650) ***(G-9460)***
Borchers Americas Inc....814 432-2125
240 Two Mile Run Rd Franklin (16323) ***(G-6117)***
Borco Equipment Inc....814 535-1400
50 Johns St Johnstown (15901) ***(G-8359)***
Borco Equipment Company, Johnstown *Also called Borco Equipment Inc* ***(G-8359)***
Borden Accuracy, Springville *Also called Jim Borden* ***(G-17930)***
Bork Inc....215 324-1155
5301 N 2nd St Ste 3 Philadelphia (19120) ***(G-13472)***
Bornmann Mfg Co Inc....215 228-5826
3731 Old York Rd Philadelphia (19140) ***(G-13473)***
Borough of Slippery Rock....724 794-3823
155 Branchton Rd Slippery Rock (16057) ***(G-17618)***
Borough of Tyrone....814 684-5396
1100 Logan Ave Tyrone (16686) ***(G-18577)***
Borris Information Group Inc....717 285-9141
306 Primrose Ln Mountville (17554) ***(G-11790)***
Bortnick Construction Inc (PA)....814 587-6023
146 Beaver St Springboro (16435) ***(G-17894)***
Bosch Rexroth Corporation....610 694-8300
2315 City Line Rd Bethlehem (18017) ***(G-1470)***
Bosch Rexroth Corporation....610 694-8300
2655 Brodhead Rd Ste 150 Bethlehem (18020) ***(G-1471)***
Bosch Security Systems Inc....717 735-6300
1706 Hempstead Rd Lancaster (17601) ***(G-8957)***
Boschung America LLC....724 658-3300
930 Cass St Ste 2 New Castle (16101) ***(G-12065)***
Bosha Design Inc....610 622-4422
707 Burmont Rd Drexel Hill (19026) ***(G-4361)***
Bosio Metal Specialties Inc....215 699-4100
409 Industrial Dr North Wales (19454) ***(G-12792)***
Boss Controls LLC....724 396-8131
4117 Liberty Ave Pittsburgh (15224) ***(G-14786)***
Bostock Company Inc (PA)....215 343-7040
175 Titus Ave Ste 200 Warrington (18976) ***(G-19110)***
Bostock Inc....610 650-9650
16 W Indian Ln Norristown (19403) ***(G-12641)***
Boston Beer Company Inc....610 395-1885
7880 Penn Dr Breinigsville (18031) ***(G-2011)***
Bostwick Enterprises Inc....814 725-8015
12162 E Main Rd North East (16428) ***(G-12733)***
Boswell Lumber Company....814 629-5625
4904 Penn Ave Boswell (15531) ***(G-1881)***
Bottling Group LLC....215 676-6400
11701 Roosevelt Blvd Philadelphia (19154) ***(G-13474)***
Boulevard Sports....724 378-9191
1503 Kennedy Blvd Aliquippa (15001) ***(G-69)***
Bounds Wood Products Ltd....215 646-2122
1076 Bethlehem Pike North Wales (19454) ***(G-12793)***
Bourne Graphics Inc....610 584-6120
2901 Skippack Park Worcester (19490) ***(G-20224)***
Bowe Bell + Howell Postal Syst....610 317-4300
2625 Brodhead Rd Bethlehem (18020) ***(G-1472)***
Bower Wire Cloth Tl & Die Inc....570 398-4488
328 Railroad St Jersey Shore (17740) ***(G-8310)***
Bowlder Metal, New Oxford *Also called Aaron S Myers* ***(G-12401)***
Bowman Tool....717 432-1403
1515 Braggtown Rd East Berlin (17316) ***(G-4520)***
Bowser Lumber Co Inc....814 277-9956
8530 Colonel Drake Hwy Mahaffey (15757) ***(G-10170)***
Bowser Manufacturing Co....570 368-5045
201 Streibeigh Ln Montoursville (17754) ***(G-11434)***
Bowser Pntc-Sbr-Suzu Oldsmbile, Pittsburgh *Also called Bowser Pontiac Inc* ***(G-14787)***
Bowser Pontiac Inc....412 469-2100
Lewis Run Rd & Rr 51 Pittsburgh (15236) ***(G-14787)***
Box King Products, Phoenixville *Also called Montgomery Products Ltd* ***(G-14563)***
Boxwood Manufacturing Corp....717 751-2712
100 Boxwood Ln York (17402) ***(G-20411)***
Boy Machines Inc (PA)....610 363-9121
199 Philips Rd Exton (19341) ***(G-5656)***
Boyce Products Ltd (PA)....570 224-6570
205 Conklin Hill Rd Damascus (18415) ***(G-3989)***
Boyd Geyer Sign Corporation....215 860-3008
444 S State St Ste C3 Newtown (18940) ***(G-12498)***
Boyd Machine Co Inc....215 723-8941
36 E Cherry Ln Souderton (18964) ***(G-17728)***
Boyd Station LLC....866 411-2693
557 Elysburg Rd Danville (17821) ***(G-3998)***
Boyds Mills Press Inc....570 253-1164
815 Church St Honesdale (18431) ***(G-7703)***
Boyer Candy Company Inc....814 944-9401
821 17th St Altoona (16601) ***(G-483)***
Boyer Machine....570 473-1212
465 Duke St Northumberland (17857) ***(G-12865)***
Boyertown Foundry Company....610 473-1000
9th St & Rothermel Dr Boyertown (19512) ***(G-1899)***
Boyertown Furnace Company....610 369-1450
156 Holly Rd Boyertown (19512) ***(G-1900)***
Boyertown Label Co....800 260-4934
1252 Montgomery Ave Boyertown (19512) ***(G-1901)***
Boyertown Plant, Boyertown *Also called Global Advanced Metals USA Inc* ***(G-1912)***
Boyertown Shtmtl Fbrcators Inc....610 689-0991
1 Shore Ave Douglassville (19518) ***(G-4171)***
Boyesen Inc (PA)....610 756-6818
8 Rhoades Rd Lenhartsville (19534) ***(G-9756)***
Boyle Incorporated....724 295-2420
102 Cherokee Ct Freeport (16229) ***(G-6200)***
BP Lubricants USA Inc....215 443-5220
775 Louis Dr Warminster (18974) ***(G-18840)***
BP Lubricants USA Inc....215 674-5301
1020 Louis Dr Warminster (18974) ***(G-18841)***
BP Oil Co Svc Stns Diesl Fuel....412 264-6140
921 Brodhead Rd Coraopolis (15108) ***(G-3664)***
BP Stop N Go....412 823-4500
638 Brown Ave Turtle Creek (15145) ***(G-18559)***
Bpes Barr Publicatio Co....215 765-0383
824 N Stillman St Philadelphia (19130) ***(G-13475)***
Bpi Inc (PA)....412 371-8554
612 S Trenton Ave Pittsburgh (15221) ***(G-14788)***
Bpi Inc....412 771-8176
149 Nichol Ave Ste 2 Mc Kees Rocks (15136) ***(G-10605)***
Bpl Global LLC....724 933-7700
2400 Ansys Dr Ste 102 Canonsburg (15317) ***(G-2550)***
Bprex Plastic Packaging Inc....814 849-4240
Maplevale Rd Brookville (15825) ***(G-2251)***
Bra-Vor Tool & Die Co Inc....814 724-1557
11189 Murray Rd Meadville (16335) ***(G-10708)***
Bracalente Global Ltd....215 536-3077
20 W Creamery Rd Trumbauersville (18970) ***(G-18530)***
Bracalente Manufacturing Group, Trumbauersville *Also called Bracalentes Mfg Co Inc* ***(G-18531)***
Bracalentes Mfg Co Inc (PA)....215 536-3077
20 W Creamery Rd Trumbauersville (18970) ***(G-18531)***
Brackett Machine Co Inc....724 287-5804
152 North Rd Butler (16001) ***(G-2383)***
Brad Foote Gear Works Inc....412 264-1428
5100 Neville Rd Pittsburgh (15225) ***(G-14789)***
Brad's Raw Foods, Doylestown *Also called Brads Raw Chips LLC* ***(G-4279)***
Bradco Printers Inc....570 297-3024
11 Canton St Troy (16947) ***(G-18517)***
Braders Woodcraft Inc....610 262-3452
5440 Route 145 Laurys Station (18059) ***(G-9532)***

Bradford Allegheny Corporation (PA)....814 362-2590
1522 South Ave Lewis Run (16738) ***(G-9871)***
Bradford Allegheny Corporation....814 362-2591
1522 South Ave Lewis Run (16738) ***(G-9872)***
Bradford Allegheny Corporation....814 368-4465
14 Egbert Ln Lewis Run (16738) ***(G-9873)***
Bradford Allegheny Corporation....814 362-2593
16 Valley Hunt Dr Lewis Run (16738) ***(G-9874)***
Bradford Clocks Limited....570 427-4493
1080 Hudson Dr Weatherly (18255) ***(G-19453)***
Bradford County Law Jurnl The, Sayre *Also called Murrelle Printing Co Inc* ***(G-17119)***
Bradford County Sanitation Inc....570 673-3128
9 Canton St Troy (16947) ***(G-18518)***
Bradford County Sanitation Svc, Troy *Also called Bradford County Sanitation Inc* ***(G-18518)***
Bradford Forest Inc....570 835-5000
444 High St Bradford (16701) ***(G-1958)***
Bradford Journal Miner....814 465-3468
69 Garlock Holw Bradford (16701) ***(G-1959)***
Bradford Publications Inc, Bradford *Also called Bradford Publishing Company* ***(G-1960)***
Bradford Publishing Company (HQ)....814 368-3173
43 Main St Bradford (16701) ***(G-1960)***
Bradford White Corporation (PA)....215 641-9400
725 Talamore Dr Ambler (19002) ***(G-571)***
Bradley Business Forms, Bensalem *Also called Bradley Graphic Solutions Inc* ***(G-1160)***
Bradley Coatings Group Inc (HQ)....724 444-4400
2873 W Hardies Rd Ste 1 Gibsonia (15044) ***(G-6329)***
Bradley Communications Corp....484 477-4220
390 Reed Rd Fl 1 Broomall (19008) ***(G-2281)***
Bradley E Miller....717 566-6243
602 W High St Hummelstown (17036) ***(G-7904)***
Bradley Graphic Solutions Inc....215 638-8771
941 Mill Rd Bensalem (19020) ***(G-1160)***
Bradley Pulverizer Company (PA)....610 432-2101
123 S 3rd St Allentown (18102) ***(G-158)***
Bradley Walter Myers....717 413-0197
653 Wentzel Rd East Earl (17519) ***(G-4538)***
Brads Raw Chips LLC (PA)....215 766-3739
4049 Landisville Rd Doylestown (18902) ***(G-4279)***
Brady Instruments....717 453-7171
1315 Pottsville St Lykens (17048) ***(G-10130)***
Bradys Bend Corporation (PA)....724 526-3353
209 Cove Run Rd East Brady (16028) ***(G-4527)***
Bradys Bend Corporation....724 526-3353
Cove Run Rd East Brady (16028) ***(G-4528)***
Braeburn Alloy Steel, Lower Burrell *Also called Ccx Inc* ***(G-10105)***
Braeburn Pharmaceuticals Inc....609 751-5375
450 Plymouth Rd Ste 400 Plymouth Meeting (19462) ***(G-15835)***
Brahma Building Products LLC....717 567-2571
224 Red Hill Rd Newport (17074) ***(G-12487)***
Brain-Pad Incorporated....610 397-0893
322 Fayette St Conshohocken (19428) ***(G-3525)***
Brainy Valley Sales, Honey Brook *Also called Bvs Inc* ***(G-7739)***
Bramante Bioscience LLC....860 634-0015
2100 Christian St Apt A Philadelphia (19146) ***(G-13476)***
Bramco Stainless, Downingtown *Also called Brandywine Machine Co Inc* ***(G-4216)***
Bramley Machinery Corporation....610 326-2500
824 Spruce St Pottstown (19464) ***(G-15968)***
Brampton Entp & Design LLC....484 678-4855
332 Garden View Dr Thorndale (19372) ***(G-18353)***
Branch Medical Group LLC....877 992-7262
1111 Adams Ave Norristown (19403) ***(G-12642)***
Branch Medical Group, Inc., Norristown *Also called Branch Medical Group LLC* ***(G-12642)***
Brand Graphic Solutions, Plymouth *Also called Fleet Decal & Graphics Inc* ***(G-15818)***
Brands Imaging LLC....215 279-7218
521 Cecil B Moore Ave Philadelphia (19122) ***(G-13477)***
Brandt Tool & Die Co Inc....717 359-5995
1908 Frederick Pike Littlestown (17340) ***(G-10064)***
Brandywine Branch Distillers....610 326-8151
247 Bishop Rd Pottstown (19465) ***(G-15945)***
Brandywine Branch Distlrs LLC....610 901-3668
350 Warwick Rd Elverson (19520) ***(G-4962)***
Brandywine Envelope Corp....800 887-9399
151 Hood Rd Cochranville (19330) ***(G-3354)***
Brandywine Fuel Inc....610 455-0123
913 Macadam St Chester (19013) ***(G-3041)***
Brandywine Fuel Inc....484 357-7683
83 Smithbridge Rd Glen Mills (19342) ***(G-6431)***
Brandywine Fuel Inc....484 574-8274
16 Crozerville Rd Aston (19014) ***(G-753)***
Brandywine Industrial Paper....610 212-9949
104 Sycamore Ln Coatesville (19320) ***(G-3294)***
Brandywine Machine Co Inc....610 269-1221
State Highway 282 Downingtown (19335) ***(G-4216)***
Brandywine Pharmaceuticals Inc....800 647-0172
600 W Strasburg Rd West Chester (19382) ***(G-19513)***
Brandywine Precision, Honey Brook *Also called Michael Bryan* ***(G-7754)***
Brandywine Quarry Inc....610 857-4200
151 N Church St Parkesburg (19365) ***(G-13172)***
Brandywine Valley Fabricators....610 384-7440
1102 Foundry St Coatesville (19320) ***(G-3295)***
Brandywine Woodworks LLC....610 793-7979
186 Bragg Hill Rd West Chester (19382) ***(G-19514)***
Branson Ultrasonics Corp....610 251-9776
136 W Lancaster Ave Paoli (19301) ***(G-13136)***
Braskem America Inc....412 208-8100
550 Technology Dr Pittsburgh (15219) ***(G-14790)***
Braskem America Inc....610 497-8378
750 W 10th St Marcus Hook (19061) ***(G-10438)***
Braskem America Inc (HQ)....215 841-3100
1735 Market St Fl 28 Philadelphia (19103) ***(G-13478)***
Braskem Pp Americas, Philadelphia *Also called Braskem America Inc* ***(G-13478)***
Brave Spirits LLC....610 453-3917
229 Forrest Ave Narberth (19072) ***(G-11909)***
Brazilian Paper Corporation (PA)....215 369-7000
6 Middle Rd New Hope (18938) ***(G-12299)***
BRB Technology Corporation....215 364-4115
1641 Loretta Ave Ste B Feasterville Trevose (19053) ***(G-5893)***
Brd Noise & Vibration Ctrl Inc (PA)....610 863-6300
112 Fairview Ave Wind Gap (18091) ***(G-20167)***
Breakthrough Publications Inc....610 928-4061
3 Iroquois St Emmaus (18049) ***(G-5021)***
Bream's Print Shop, Gettysburg *Also called David Bream* ***(G-6288)***
Brebling Plastics, Warrington *Also called Resdel Corporation* ***(G-19131)***
Breeo LLC....800 413-9848
5002 Lincoln Hwy Kinzers (17535) ***(G-8733)***
Breet Incorporated....610 558-4006
507 Glen Eagle Sq Glen Mills (19342) ***(G-6432)***
Breeze Dryer....215 794-2421
2567 Mill Rd Doylestown (18902) ***(G-4280)***
Breeze Industrial Products, Saltsburg *Also called Norma Pennsylvania Inc* ***(G-17052)***
Breezecraft LLC....717 397-8584
946 Gypsy Hill Rd Lancaster (17602) ***(G-8958)***
Breezy Ridge Instruments Ltd....610 691-3302
3644 Route 378 Unit B Bethlehem (18015) ***(G-1473)***
Brendan G Stover Printing....610 459-2851
1460 Garnet Mine Rd Boothwyn (19060) ***(G-1876)***
Brenneman Printing Inc....717 299-2847
1909 Olde Homestead Ln Lancaster (17601) ***(G-8959)***
Brennemans Maple Syrup & Eqp....814 941-8974
572 Oak Dale Rd Salisbury (15558) ***(G-17044)***
Brenner Aerostructures LLC....215 638-3884
450 Winks Ln 3 Bensalem (19020) ***(G-1161)***
Brenner Machine Co....717 274-3411
64 Rexmont Rd Cornwall (17016) ***(G-3737)***
Brent A Lindberg....814 796-9068
2930 Old Meadville Rd Waterford (16441) ***(G-19260)***
Brent D Beistel....724 823-0099
23 Mckean Ave Donora (15033) ***(G-4149)***
Brentano Concrete Connection....412 731-8485
518 Rodi Rd Ste 520 Pittsburgh (15235) ***(G-14791)***
Brentano's Concrete Connection, Pittsburgh *Also called Brentano Concrete Connection* ***(G-14791)***
Brentek International Inc....814 259-3333
1249 Ridgewood Rd York (17406) ***(G-20412)***
Brentwood Industries Inc (PA)....610 374-5109
500 Spring Ridge Dr Reading (19610) ***(G-16336)***
Brentwood Industries Inc....717 274-1827
2101 Lehman St Lebanon (17046) ***(G-9548)***
Brentwood Plastics Inc, Reading *Also called Brentwood Industries Inc* ***(G-16336)***
Breons Inc A Close Corporation....814 359-3182
330 S Main St Pleasant Gap (16823) ***(G-15791)***
Brett W Shope....814 643-2921
5272 Cold Springs Rd Huntingdon (16652) ***(G-7940)***
Brewers Outlet....717 848-5250
409 E Philadelphia St York (17403) ***(G-20413)***
Brewskees of Shiloh....717 764-2994
2010 Carlisle Rd York (17408) ***(G-20414)***
Bri-Mar Manufacturing LLC....717 263-6116
1086 Wayne Ave Ste 2 Chambersburg (17201) ***(G-2913)***
Brian Giniewski LLC....610 858-2821
4500 Worth St Philadelphia (19124) ***(G-13479)***
Brian Kingsley....570 888-8668
514 Round Top Rd Athens (18810) ***(G-810)***
Brian L Dewey....814 967-3246
33328 N Main St Townville (16360) ***(G-18444)***
Brian M Pallet....484 720-8052
860 Penn Green Rd Landenberg (19350) ***(G-9247)***
Brian O Keffe....570 477-3962
27 Scavone Ln Sweet Valley (18656) ***(G-18187)***
Brick Wall Ministries....717 592-1798
1371 Spring House Rd Middletown (17057) ***(G-11049)***
Brickhouse Services....570 869-1871
2 Main St Laceyville (18623) ***(G-8870)***
Bridesburg Foundry Company....610 266-0900
901 Front St Whitehall (18052) ***(G-19863)***
Bridge Acpuncture Natural Hlth....215 348-8058
30 Garden Aly Doylestown (18901) ***(G-4281)***

ALPHABETIC

Bridge Auto Tags 215 946-8026
   34 Indian Park Rd Levittown (19057) *(G-9819)*

Bridge Deck Solutions LLC 724 424-1001
   298 Cherry Hills Dr Latrobe (15650) *(G-9461)*

Bridges & Towers Inc 724 654-6672
   923 Industrial St New Castle (16102) *(G-12066)*

Bridget Morris 215 828-9261
   2202 Alter St Philadelphia (19146) *(G-13480)*

Bridgeville Italian Club, Bridgeville *Also called Italian Mutual Benefit Society* *(G-2071)*

Bridon-American Corporation (HQ) 570 822-3349
   280 New Commerce Blvd Hanover Township (18706) *(G-6982)*

Bridon-American Corporation 570 822-3349
   100 Stevens Ln Exeter (18643) *(G-5581)*

Brier Hill Press, Pittston *Also called Mondlak Printery* *(G-15768)*

Bright Banners 570 326-3524
   216 S Market St Williamsport (17702) *(G-19994)*

Bright Sign and Maint Co Inc 610 916-5100
   1025 James Dr Leesport (19533) *(G-9660)*

Bright Sign Co Inc 215 563-9480
   1215 Race St Philadelphia (19107) *(G-13481)*

Brightbill Industries Inc 717 233-4121
   1901 N Cameron St Harrisburg (17103) *(G-7099)*

Brightline LP 412 206-0106
   580 Mayer St Ste 7 Bridgeville (15017) *(G-2056)*

Brighton Electric 412 269-7000
   107 Patton Dr Coraopolis (15108) *(G-3665)*

Brighton Electric Stl Cast Co, Beaver Falls *Also called Brighton Steel Inc* *(G-997)*

Brighton Machine Company Inc 724 378-0960
   1306 Airport Rd Aliquippa (15001) *(G-70)*

Brighton Resources Inc 412 661-1025
   5851 Ellsworth Ave Ste 1 Pittsburgh (15232) *(G-14792)*

Brighton Steel Inc 724 846-7377
   2900 7th Avenue Ext Beaver Falls (15010) *(G-997)*

Brilliant Inc 215 271-5041
   1531 S 7th St Philadelphia (19147) *(G-13482)*

Brilliant Graphics, Exton *Also called Brilliant Studio Inc* *(G-5657)*

Brilliant Studio Inc (PA) 610 458-7977
   400 Eagleview Blvd # 104 Exton (19341) *(G-5657)*

Brindle Printing Co Inc 724 658-8549
   401 Sampson St New Castle (16101) *(G-12067)*

Brinic Donuts Inc 814 944-5242
   3132 Pleasant Valley Blvd Altoona (16602) *(G-484)*

Brinkmann Bros Inc 215 739-4769
   2617 Frankford Ave Philadelphia (19125) *(G-13483)*

Bristol Aluminum Co 215 946-1566
   5514 Bristol Emilie Rd Levittown (19057) *(G-9820)*

Bristol Industries Pennsylv 215 493-7230
   131 Old Oxford Valley Rd Langhorne (19047) *(G-9281)*

Bristol Millwork Co Inc 215 533-1921
   4560 Tacony St Philadelphia (19124) *(G-13484)*

Bristol Plant, Bristol *Also called Arkema Inc* *(G-2109)*

Bristol Rolling Door Inc 215 949-9090
   1990 Hartel Ave Levittown (19057) *(G-9821)*

Bristol Tank & Welding Co Inc 215 752-8727
   2400 Big Oak Rd Langhorne (19047) *(G-9282)*

Bristol-Myers Squibb Company 609 818-5513
   139 Lark Dr Southampton (18966) *(G-17800)*

Brite Star Manufacturing, Philadelphia *Also called J Kinderman & Sons Inc* *(G-13884)*

Britt Energies Inc 724 465-9333
   2960 State Route 156 Spring Church (15686) *(G-17854)*

Britt Resources Inc 724 465-9333
   2960 State Route 156 Spring Church (15686) *(G-17855)*

Briun Stone Plant, Shippenville *Also called Thomas E Siegel* *(G-17564)*

Brmc Fabrications, Waynesboro *Also called Blue Ridge Mtn Cookery Inc* *(G-19402)*

Broad Mountain Vineyard LLC 717 362-8044
   45 W Broad St Elizabethville (17023) *(G-4892)*

Broad St Cmnty Newspapers Inc 215 354-3135
   16 Haines Ave Berlin (15530) *(G-1286)*

Broadband Networks Inc (HQ) 814 237-4073
   2820 E College Ave Ste B State College (16801) *(G-17947)*

Broadcom Limited, Breinigsville *Also called Cyoptics Inc* *(G-2013)*

Broadtop Bulletin 814 635-2851
   900 6th St Saxton (16678) *(G-17099)*

Broc Supply Co Inc 610 433-4646
   30 S Keystone Ave Emmaus (18049) *(G-5022)*

Brocade Cmmnctions Systems Inc 610 648-3915
   5 Great Valley Pkwy # 325 Malvern (19355) *(G-10195)*

Brock Associates LLC 412 919-0690
   180 Bilmar Dr Ste 2 Pittsburgh (15205) *(G-14793)*

Brockport Glass Components LLC 814 265-1479
   6185 Route 219 Brockport (15823) *(G-2220)*

Brockway Sintered Technology (HQ) 814 265-8090
   1228 Main St Brockway (15824) *(G-2223)*

Brodak Manufacturing & Distrg 724 966-2726
   100 Park Ave Carmichaels (15320) *(G-2754)*

Brodak Printing Company 724 966-5178
   100 Park Ave Carmichaels (15320) *(G-2755)*

Brodart Co (PA) 570 326-2461
   500 Arch St Williamsport (17701) *(G-19995)*

Brodart Co 570 769-7412
   280 North Rd Mc Elhattan (17748) *(G-10585)*

Brodart Co 570 769-3265
   100 North Rd Mc Elhattan (17748) *(G-10586)*

Brodart Co 570 326-2461
   E S Thomas St Montgomery (17752) *(G-11368)*

Brode Lumber Inc 814 635-3436
   20188 Little Valley Rd Saxton (16678) *(G-17100)*

Broderick Industries LLC 215 409-5771
   6101 Keystone St Philadelphia (19135) *(G-13485)*

Brodrick Hughes Energy LLC 570 662-2464
   2050 N Williamson Rd Covington (16917) *(G-3791)*

Brodys Furniture Inc 724 745-4630
   111 W Pike St Canonsburg (15317) *(G-2551)*

Brodys Welding & Mech Contrs, Philadelphia *Also called Brodys Welding and Mech Contrs* *(G-13486)*

Brodys Welding and Mech Contrs 215 941-7914
   2020 Orthodox St Philadelphia (19124) *(G-13486)*

Broken Straw Outdoors 814 563-2200
   488 E Main St Youngsville (16371) *(G-20769)*

Brokenstraw Gravel Co Inc 814 563-7911
   Rr 6 Pittsfield (16340) *(G-15738)*

Broker Brewing Company LLC 610 304-0822
   1045 Bridge Rd Creamery (19430) *(G-3873)*

Bronkhorst USA Inc 610 866-6750
   57 S Commerce Way Bethlehem (18017) *(G-1474)*

Brontech Industries Inc 717 672-0240
   1115 Marietta Ave Apt 16 Lancaster (17603) *(G-8960)*

Brook Meadow Dairy Company (HQ) 814 899-3191
   2365 Buffalo Rd Erie (16510) *(G-5215)*

Brooke Production Inc 610 296-9394
   730 Monument Rd Malvern (19355) *(G-10196)*

Brookline Fabrics Co Inc 412 665-4925
   5750 Baum Blvd Pittsburgh (15206) *(G-14794)*

Brooks Group and Assoc Inc 610 429-8990
   16 E Market St West Chester (19382) *(G-19515)*

Brooks Instrument LLC (HQ) 215 362-3500
   407 W Vine St Hatfield (19440) *(G-7322)*

Brookshire Printing Inc (PA) 717 392-1321
   200 Hazel St Lancaster (17603) *(G-8961)*

Brookside Woodworks 717 768-0241
   615 Red Hill Rd Narvon (17555) *(G-11917)*

Brookville Equipment Corp 814 849-2000
   175 Evans St Brookville (15825) *(G-2252)*

Brookville Glove Mfg Co Inc (PA) 814 849-7324
   98 Service Center Rd B Brookville (15825) *(G-2253)*

Brookville Locomotive Inc 814 849-2000
   175 Evans St Brookville (15825) *(G-2254)*

Brookville Mining Equipment, Brookville *Also called Brookville Equipment Corp* *(G-2252)*

Brookville Tanks, Brookville *Also called George I Reitz & Sons Inc* *(G-2261)*

Brop Tech LLC 323 229-7390
   121 Normandy Rd Upper Darby (19082) *(G-18683)*

Brother and Sister Fd Svc Inc 717 558-0108
   811 Spangler Rd Camp Hill (17011) *(G-2493)*

Brothers Wood Company 814 462-2422
   Enterprise Rd Corry (16407) *(G-3746)*

Brown & Lounsberry Inc 610 847-2242
   8490 Easton Rd Ottsville (18942) *(G-13060)*

Brown Bro Stock Photography, Sterling *Also called Brown Brothers LLP* *(G-18048)*

Brown Brothers Drilling Inc 717 548-2500
   497 Kirks Mill Rd Nottingham (19362) *(G-12881)*

Brown Brothers LLP 570 689-9688
   100 Bortree Rd Sterling (18463) *(G-18048)*

Brown Industries Inc 610 544-8888
   344 W Front St Ste 100 Media (19063) *(G-10916)*

Brown Jr Merritt (PA) 610 253-0425
   2906 William Penn Hwy # 308 Easton (18045) *(G-4658)*

Brown Machine Co Inc 610 932-3359
   125 Limestone Rd Oxford (19363) *(G-13073)*

Brown Signs Inc 717 866-2669
   190 Millardsville Rd Richland (17087) *(G-16683)*

Brown Timber and Land Co Inc 724 547-7777
   2573 Rte 31 Acme (15610) *(G-15)*

Brown Tool & Die Inc 724 547-3366
   130 Redwood Rd Acme (15610) *(G-16)*

Browning-Ferris Industries Inc 814 453-6608
   1863 E 12th St Erie (16511) *(G-5216)*

Brownlee Lumber Inc 814 328-2991
   2652 Hzen Rchardsville Rd Brookville (15825) *(G-2255)*

Browns Graphic Solutions 717 721-6160
   1397 Arcadia Rd Ste 100 Lancaster (17601) *(G-8962)*

Browns Mill Farm LLC 570 345-3153
   21 Grist Mill Rd Schuylkill Haven (17972) *(G-17149)*

Browns Tree Farm, Spring Mills *Also called Norse Paddle Co* *(G-17890)*

Browns Welding Inc 717 762-6467
   2110a Market Square Blvd Waynesboro (17268) *(G-19403)*

Brubaker Kitchens Inc 717 394-5622
   1121 Manheim Pike Lancaster (17601) *(G-8963)*

Brubaker Tool Corporation (PA) 717 692-2113
   200 Front St Millersburg (17061) *(G-11191)*

Bruce Banning....724 226-0818
1546 Saxonburg Rd Natrona Heights (15065) ***(G-11936)***
Bruce N Pelsh Inc....724 346-2020
2926 E State St Hermitage (16148) ***(G-7572)***
Brumbaugh Body Co Inc....814 696-9552
71 Jennifer Rd Duncansville (16635) ***(G-4450)***
Brumbaugh Lumber LLC....814 542-8880
16460 Croghan Pike Shirleysburg (17260) ***(G-17569)***
Bruners Sign Service Inc....717 896-7699
97 Lehman Rd Halifax (17032) ***(G-6825)***
Brunner Industrial Group Inc....717 233-8781
2200 Paxton St Harrisburg (17111) ***(G-7100)***
Brush Aftermarket N Amer Inc....412 829-7500
601 Braddock Ave Turtle Creek (15145) ***(G-18560)***
Brush Aftermarket US, Turtle Creek *Also called Brush Aftermarket N Amer Inc* ***(G-18560)***
Brush G M S, Turtle Creek *Also called Generator and Mtr Svcs PA LLC* ***(G-18565)***
Brush Industries Inc....570 286-5611
301 Reagan St Sunbury (17801) ***(G-18165)***
Brusters Old Fashioned Ice Cre....724 772-9999
510 Northpointe Cir Seven Fields (16046) ***(G-17374)***
Brute Group, Reading *Also called Henson Company Inc* ***(G-16400)***
Brutis Enterprises Inc....412 431-5440
105 S 12th St Pittsburgh (15203) ***(G-14795)***
Bry Mar Trophy Inc....215 295-4053
85 Makefield Rd Ste 13 Yardley (19067) ***(G-20298)***
Bryan China Company....724 658-3098
657 Northgate Cir New Castle (16105) ***(G-12068)***
Bryan Management, Canonsburg *Also called Brymone Inc* ***(G-2552)***
Bryan Material Group, Mc Kees Rocks *Also called Concrete Concepts Inc* ***(G-10606)***
Bryan Mfg Co....724 245-8200
279 Valley Rd Eighty Four (15330) ***(G-4835)***
Bryce Saylor & Sons Inc....814 942-2288
4235 6th Ave Altoona (16602) ***(G-485)***
Brymone Inc....724 746-4004
125 Technology Dr Ste 105 Canonsburg (15317) ***(G-2552)***
Bryn and Danes LLC....844 328-2823
400 Privet Rd Horsham (19044) ***(G-7800)***
Bryn Hill Industries Inc....610 623-4005
407 Industrial Park Dr Yeadon (19050) ***(G-20351)***
Bryn Mawr Communications LLC....610 687-0887
1008 Upper Gulph Rd # 200 Wayne (19087) ***(G-19309)***
Bryn Mawr Equipment Fin Inc....610 581-4996
801 W Lancaster Ave Bryn Mawr (19010) ***(G-2317)***
Bryn Mawr Shower Door Inc....610 647-0357
579 Lancaster Ave Berwyn (19312) ***(G-1354)***
Brynavon Group Inc (PA)....610 525-2102
2000 Montgomery Ave Villanova (19085) ***(G-18765)***
Brysi Inc....215 573-7918
233 S 33rd St Philadelphia (19104) ***(G-13487)***
Bs Group, Huntingdon Valley *Also called Bsg Corporation* ***(G-7966)***
BS Quarries Inc....570 278-4901
859 John C Mcnamara Dr Montrose (18801) ***(G-11459)***
BSC Technologies Inc....570 825-9196
61 Sterling Ave Dallas (18612) ***(G-3959)***
Bsg Corporation....267 230-0514
3401 Sorrel Ln Huntingdon Valley (19006) ***(G-7966)***
Bsg Custom Designs LLC....610 867-7361
826 Monocacy St Bethlehem (18018) ***(G-1475)***
BSI Exhibits, Garnet Valley *Also called Berm Studios Incorporated* ***(G-6265)***
Bsm Enterprises Company Inc....215 257-2231
311 Wyckford Dr Perkasie (18944) ***(G-13268)***
Btg International Inc (HQ)....610 943-6000
300 Four Falls Corporate West Conshohocken (19428) ***(G-19686)***
Bti of America LLC....215 646-4067
1730 Walton Rd Ste 110 Blue Bell (19422) ***(G-1818)***
Bti of North America, Blue Bell *Also called Bti of America LLC* ***(G-1818)***
Bti-Coopermatics Inc....610 262-7700
600 Held Dr Northampton (18067) ***(G-12847)***
Bubco Enterprise Inc....724 274-4930
1415 Pittsburgh St Cheswick (15024) ***(G-3102)***
Buchanan Hauling....412 373-6760
1200 Commerce Cir Trafford (15085) ***(G-18452)***
Buchanan Mining Company LLC....724 485-4000
1000 Consol Energy Dr Canonsburg (15317) ***(G-2553)***
Buchanan Trail Industries Inc....717 597-7166
2375 Buchanan Trl W Greencastle (17225) ***(G-6601)***
Bucher Jj Producing Corp....814 697-6593
2568 Bells Run Rd Shinglehouse (16748) ***(G-17504)***
Buck Company Inc....717 284-4114
897 Lancaster Pike Quarryville (17566) ***(G-16266)***
Buck County Print....215 741-3250
17 Lady Slipper Ln Langhorne (19047) ***(G-9283)***
Buck Koola Inc....814 849-9695
494 Service Center Rd Brookville (15825) ***(G-2256)***
Buck's Fabricating Division, Hadley *Also called Deist Industries Inc* ***(G-6819)***
Buck-A-Lew Tooling Machining....570 321-0640
2401 Reach Rd Williamsport (17701) ***(G-19996)***
Buckeye Aluminum Foundry Inc....814 683-4011
5906 W Center Rd Linesville (16424) ***(G-9978)***
Buckeye Corrugated Inc....717 684-6921
3950 Continental Dr Columbia (17512) ***(G-3432)***
Buckingham Valley Vineyards....215 794-7188
1521 Rte 413 Buckingham (18912) ***(G-2338)***
Buckley Associates Inc....412 963-7070
636 Alpha Dr Pittsburgh (15238) ***(G-14796)***
Bucks Cnty Artesian Well Drlg....215 493-1867
1075 General Sullivan Rd Washington Crossing (18977) ***(G-19253)***
Bucks Cnty Brewing Distlg LLC....215 766-7711
31 Appletree Ln Pipersville (18947) ***(G-14612)***
Bucks County Alpacas LLC....215 795-2453
2736 Bedminster Rd Perkasie (18944) ***(G-13269)***
Bucks County Courier Times, Levittown *Also called Courier Times Inc* ***(G-9828)***
Bucks County Courier Times, Fairless Hills *Also called Courier Times Inc* ***(G-5776)***
Bucks County Digital Imaging, Newtown *Also called Bucks County Type & Design Inc* ***(G-12499)***
Bucks County Equipment, Levittown *Also called Ribarchik John* ***(G-9861)***
Bucks County Fuel LLC....215 245-0807
890 Jordan Dr Bensalem (19020) ***(G-1162)***
Bucks County Fur Products Inc....215 536-6614
220 N Ambler St Quakertown (18951) ***(G-16175)***
Bucks County Herald....215 794-1096
5667 York Rd Buckingham (18912) ***(G-2339)***
Bucks County Herald Corp....215 794-2601
3828 Lucy Dr Doylestown (18902) ***(G-4282)***
Bucks County Midweek....215 355-1234
2512 Metropolitan Dr Feasterville Trevose (19053) ***(G-5894)***
Bucks County Off Svcs & Prtg....215 295-7060
2297 Seabird Dr Bristol (19007) ***(G-2121)***
Bucks County Shutters LLC....215 957-3333
940 Thomas Dr Warminster (18974) ***(G-18842)***
Bucks County Type & Design Inc....215 579-4200
90 Walker Ln Newtown (18940) ***(G-12499)***
Bucks Creamery LLC....732 387-3535
140 E Street Rd Feasterville Trevose (19053) ***(G-5895)***
Bucks Musical Instrument Pdts....215 345-9442
40 S Sand Rd Doylestown (18901) ***(G-4283)***
Bucks Ship & Print....215 493-8100
25 S Main St Ste 6 Yardley (19067) ***(G-20299)***
Bucks Valley Sawmill LLC....717 567-9663
913 Bucks Valley Rd Newport (17074) ***(G-12488)***
Bucyrus America Inc....724 743-1200
2045 W Pike St Houston (15342) ***(G-7867)***
Budd Lake Machine and Tool Inc....570 897-5899
800 Jacoby Creek Rd Mount Bethel (18343) ***(G-11607)***
Buddy Boy Winery....814 772-3751
29 N Broad St Ridgway (15853) ***(G-16698)***
Buddy Boy Winery & Vineyard....717 834-5606
111 Barnett Dr Duncannon (17020) ***(G-4444)***
Buddy Butlers Inc....570 759-0550
1665 Spring Garden Ave Berwick (18603) ***(G-1315)***
Buddys Brews....724 970-2739
60 Nickman Plz Lemont Furnace (15456) ***(G-9733)***
Budget Portable Welding Mch....717 865-0473
2197 State Route 72 N Lebanon (17046) ***(G-9549)***
Budget Print Center, Reading *Also called Byrne Enterprises Inc* ***(G-16338)***
Budget Printing Center, Southampton *Also called Copy Systems Group Inc* ***(G-17806)***
Buffalo Billfold....814 422-8955
711 Upper Georges Vly Rd Spring Mills (16875) ***(G-17885)***
Buffalo Bills, Lebanon *Also called Choo R Choo Snacks Inc* ***(G-9554)***
Buffalo Crushed Stone, New Enterprise *Also called New Enterprise Stone Lime Inc* ***(G-12194)***
Buffalo Limestone Inc....724 545-7478
805 Garretts Run Rd Ford City (16226) ***(G-6044)***
Buffs Ice Cream....814 849-8335
1 Mabon St Brookville (15825) ***(G-2257)***
Bug-O Systems International, Canonsburg *Also called Weld Tooling Corporation* ***(G-2657)***
Bug-O Systems International, Canonsburg *Also called Weld Tooling Corporation* ***(G-2658)***
Bugstuff....724 785-7000
709 Jefferson Ave Brownsville (15417) ***(G-2310)***
Buhl Bros Printing Inc....724 335-0970
316 Crawford Run Rd Creighton (15030) ***(G-3880)***
Building G, New Kensington *Also called Alcoa Technical Center LLC* ***(G-12322)***
Building Inspectors Contrs Inc....215 481-0606
3003 Mount Carmel Ave Glenside (19038) ***(G-6509)***
Building Specialties....814 454-4345
2011 W 12th St Erie (16505) ***(G-5217)***
Bulk Chemicals Inc (PA)....610 926-4128
1074 Stinson Dr Reading (19605) ***(G-16337)***
Bulk Chemicals Inc....610 926-4128
809 Old Mohrsville Rd Mohrsville (19541) ***(G-11275)***
Bulk Material Handling, York *Also called Metso Minerals Industries Inc* ***(G-20591)***
Bullfrog Brewery, Williamsport *Also called Schnoch Corporation* ***(G-20070)***
Bullgater Limited....717 606-5414
159 Glenbrook Rd Bird In Hand (17505) ***(G-1670)***
Bullskin Stone & Lime LLC....724 537-7505
1350 Route 30 Laughlintown (15655) ***(G-9531)***

ALPHABETIC

Bullskin Tipple Company 724 628-7807
　2927 Pittsburgh Rd　Perryopolis (15473) *(G-13303)*

Buncher Company 724 925-3919
　304 N 3rd St　Youngwood (15697) *(G-20780)*

Buncher Rail Car Svc Youngwood, Youngwood *Also called Buncher Company (G-20780)*

Bunting Inc (PA) 412 820-2200
　20 River Rd　Verona (15147) *(G-18750)*

Bunting Graphics Inc 412 481-0445
　20 River Rd　Verona (15147) *(G-18751)*

Bunting Stamp Company 412 820-2200
　20 River Rd　Verona (15147) *(G-18752)*

Burch Materials & Supplies, Malvern *Also called Burch Supplies Company Inc (G-10197)*

Burch Supplies Company Inc 610 640-4877
　380 Lapp Rd　Malvern (19355) *(G-10197)*

Bureau of Motor Vehicles, Harrisburg *Also called Transportation PA Dept (G-7236)*

Burke & Sons Inc (PA) 814 938-7303
　110 Gaskill Ave　Punxsutawney (15767) *(G-16129)*

Burke Parsons Bowlby Corp 814 371-3042
　392 Larkeytown Rd　Du Bois (15801) *(G-4385)*

Burkey Acquisition Inc 717 292-5611
　1 Popcorn Ln　Dover (17315) *(G-4189)*

Burkhart & Quinn Sign Co Inc 717 367-1375
　105 Maytown Rd　Elizabethtown (17022) *(G-4867)*

Burkholder s Motor Repair 717 866-9724
　115 Martin Rd　Myerstown (17067) *(G-11878)*

Burlington Instr Sls Assoc 215 322-8750
　4921 Carver Ave　Trevose (19053) *(G-18488)*

Burman's Apothecary, Upper Chichester *Also called Burmans Medical Supplies Inc (G-18657)*

Burmans Medical Supplies Inc 610 876-6068
　7 Creek Pkwy Ste 700　Upper Chichester (19061) *(G-18657)*

Burndy LLC 717 938-7258
　825 Old Trail Rd　Etters (17319) *(G-5547)*

Burnells Welding Corporation 215 757-2896
　1231 Hayes Blvd　Bristol (19007) *(G-2122)*

Burnham Commercial, Lancaster *Also called Burnham LLC (G-8965)*

Burnham Holdings Inc (PA) 717 390-7800
　1241 Harrisburg Ave　Lancaster (17603) *(G-8964)*

Burnham LLC 717 293-5839
　1237 Harrisburg Ave　Lancaster (17603) *(G-8965)*

Burns & Wohlgemuth, Bensalem *Also called Frederick Wohlgemuth Inc (G-1199)*

Burns Manufacturing Inc 814 833-7428
　2001 Lowell Ave　Erie (16506) *(G-5218)*

Burnside America Inc 717 414-1509
　5900 Coffey Ave　Chambersburg (17201) *(G-2914)*

Burnt Circuit Inc 215 913-6594
　321 Norristown Rd Ste 210　Ambler (19002) *(G-572)*

Burpee Willow Hill 717 349-0065
　12844 Creek Rd　Fannettsburg (17221) *(G-5857)*

Burrell Group Inc (PA) 724 337-3557
　2400 Leechburg Rd Ste 216　New Kensington (15068) *(G-12328)*

Burrell Mining Products Inc (HQ) 724 339-2511
　2400 Leechburg Rd Ste 216　New Kensington (15068) *(G-12329)*

Burrell Mining Products Inc 724 966-5183
　I 79 S Ext Kirby George　Waynesburg (15370) *(G-19435)*

Burrell Mining Services Inc 724 339-2220
　2400 Leechburg Rd Ste 216　New Kensington (15068) *(G-12330)*

Burrell Scientific LLC 412 747-2111
　300 Parkway View Dr　Pittsburgh (15205) *(G-14797)*

Burrells Information Services 717 671-3872
　297 Care St Fl 1　Harrisburg (17109) *(G-7101)*

Burton Springcrest Interiors 724 468-3000
　135 Barrington Rdg　Delmont (15626) *(G-4049)*

Busch Company 724 940-2326
　10431 Perry Hwy Ste 210　Wexford (15090) *(G-19792)*

Busch International Division, Wexford *Also called New Busch Co Inc (G-19815)*

Bush Industries of PA 814 868-2874
　2455 Robison Rd W　Erie (16509) *(G-5219)*

Bushkill Tool Company Inc 570 588-7000
　5063 Milford Rd　Bushkill (18324) *(G-2364)*

Bushnell Alvah Company 215 842-9520
　519 E Chelten Ave　Philadelphia (19144) *(G-13488)*

Business & Decision North Amer (HQ) 610 230-2500
　5 Great Valley Pkwy # 210　Malvern (19355) *(G-10198)*

Business 21 Publishing LLC 484 490-9205
　435 Devon Park Dr Ste 510　Wayne (19087) *(G-19310)*

Business 21 Publishing LLC 484 479-2700
　477 Baltimore Pike　Springfield (19064) *(G-17908)*

Business Applications Ltd 814 677-7056
　805 Walnut St　Reno (16343) *(G-16645)*

Business Cmmunications Systems 610 827-7061
　1856 Art School Rd　Chester Springs (19425) *(G-3073)*

Business Intelligence Intl Inc 484 688-8300
　993 Old Eagle School Rd # 405　Wayne (19087) *(G-19311)*

Business Planning Inc 610 649-0550
　63 W Lancaster Ave Ste 1　Ardmore (19003) *(G-703)*

Business Wire Inc 610 617-9560
　2250 Hickory Rd Ste 410　Plymouth Meeting (19462) *(G-15836)*

Businessone Technologies Inc 215 953-6660
　1210 Northbrook Dr # 310　Feasterville Trevose (19053) *(G-5896)*

Busy Bee Embroidery & More 717 540-1955
　7044 Linglestown Rd　Harrisburg (17112) *(G-7102)*

Buterbaugh Bros Land & Timber 814 948-9510
　835 Shawna Rd Ste 2　Barnesboro (15714) *(G-938)*

Butler Circulation Calls 724 282-1859
　114 W Diamond St　Butler (16001) *(G-2384)*

Butler Color Press Inc 724 283-9132
　119 Bonnie Dr　Butler (16002) *(G-2385)*

Butler Eagle, Butler *Also called Eagle Printing Company (G-2398)*

Butler Fence Builders, Carnegie *Also called Pittsburgh Fence Co Inc (G-2780)*

Butler Forge & Metal Works, East Butler *Also called Goldsborough & Vansant Inc (G-4532)*

Butler Forge & Metal Works Div, Finleyville *Also called Goldsborough & Vansant Inc (G-5959)*

Butler Machine Inc 814 355-5605
　236 S Potter St　Bellefonte (16823) *(G-1095)*

Butler Steel Supply, East Butler *Also called Ken-Fab & Weld Inc (G-4533)*

Butler Stonecraft Inc 724 352-3520
　772 N Pike Rd　Cabot (16023) *(G-2453)*

Butler Technologies Inc 724 283-6656
　231 W Wayne St　Butler (16001) *(G-2386)*

Butler Winding, Butler *Also called Wist Enterprises Inc (G-2451)*

Butter Milk Falls Inc 724 548-7388
　341 N Grant Ave Ste C　Kittanning (16201) *(G-8759)*

Buttonwood Lumber Company Inc 570 324-3421
　1418 Beuterstown Rd　Liberty (16930) *(G-9951)*

Butts Ticket Company Inc 610 869-7450
　151 Hood Rd　Cochranville (19330) *(G-3355)*

Butz Sign Co 717 397-8565
　915 N Ann St　Lancaster (17602) *(G-8966)*

Bux Mont Awards 215 855-5052
　122 S Broad St　Lansdale (19446) *(G-9349)*

Bux Mont Awards (PA) 215 257-5432
　225 N Main St　Sellersville (18960) *(G-17341)*

Bux-Mont Awards and Engrv Svcs, Sellersville *Also called Bux Mont Awards (G-17341)*

Buy Photo Stock Lowes Digita 814 954-0273
　57 Yellow Brick Rd　Reynoldsville (15851) *(G-16655)*

Buzzi Unicem USA, Bethlehem *Also called RC Lonestar Inc (G-1608)*

Buzzi Unicem USA Inc 610 746-6222
　501 Hercules Dr　Stockertown (18083) *(G-18064)*

Buzzi Unicem USA Inc (HQ) 610 882-5000
　100 Brodhead Rd Ste 230　Bethlehem (18017) *(G-1476)*

Buzzy Inc (PA) 570 621-2883
　121 Progress Ave Ste 300　Pottsville (17901) *(G-16074)*

Bvht Inc 724 728-4328
　1585 Beaver Ave　Monaca (15061) *(G-11286)*

Bvi C/O Genco 712 228-3338
　1629 Willow St　Lebanon (17042) *(G-9550)*

Bvs Inc 610 273-2842
　949 Poplar Rd　Honey Brook (19344) *(G-7739)*

Bwhip Magazine LLC 412 607-3963
　2439 Lyzell St　Pittsburgh (15214) *(G-14798)*

Bwi Eagle Inc 724 283-4681
　105 Bonnie Dr　Butler (16002) *(G-2387)*

Bwp Hardwoods Inc 814 849-7331
　12942 Route 322　Brookville (15825) *(G-2258)*

Bxvideo Solutions LLC 724 940-4190
　12330 Perry Hwy Ste 101　Wexford (15090) *(G-19793)*

By-Products Industries, Mc Kees Rocks *Also called Bpi Inc (G-10605)*

Byard F Brogan Inc 215 885-3550
　124 S Keswick Ave　Glenside (19038) *(G-6510)*

Byers Choice Ltd 215 822-6700
　4355 County Line Rd　Chalfont (18914) *(G-2864)*

Byers Logging LLC 717 530-5995
　1275 Baltimore Rd　Shippensburg (17257) *(G-17520)*

Byerstown Woodwork Shop 717 442-8586
　5031 Newport Rd　Kinzers (17535) *(G-8734)*

Byler Relish House LLC 814 763-6510
　18258 Leimbach Rd　Saegertown (16433) *(G-16908)*

Bylers Saw Mill 724 964-8528
　23 Angel Rd　New Wilmington (16142) *(G-12464)*

Byrd Alley LLC 215 669-0068
　807 S Hancock St　Philadelphia (19147) *(G-13489)*

Byrne Candle Co Inc 570 346-4070
　1200 Remington Ave　Scranton (18505) *(G-17213)*

Byrne Chiarlone LP 610 874-8436
　418 W Front St　Chester (19013) *(G-3042)*

Byrne Energy Corp 570 895-4333
　187 Sterling Rd　Mount Pocono (18344) *(G-11733)*

Byrne Enterprises Inc (PA) 610 670-0767
　916 Bedford Ave　Reading (19607) *(G-16338)*

Byrnes and Kiefer Company (PA) 724 538-5200
　131 Kline Ave　Callery (16024) *(G-2467)*

Byrnes and Kiefer Company 724 538-5200
　131 Kline Ave　Callery (16024) *(G-2468)*

C & B Iron Inc 215 536-7162
　100 Richlandtown Pike　Quakertown (18951) *(G-16176)*

C & C Manufacturing & Fabg 570 454-0819
300 S Church St Hazleton (18201) *(G-7492)*

C & C Marine Maintenance Co (HQ) 724 746-9550
201 S Johnson Rd Ste 303 Houston (15342) *(G-7868)*

C & C Tooling Inc 724 845-0939
120 Siberian Ave Leechburg (15656) *(G-9642)*

C & C Welding and Fabg Inc 814 387-6556
803 Clarence Rd Clarence (16829) *(G-3161)*

C & D Fence Company, West Chester Also called Leahmarlin Corp *(G-19589)*

C & D Powercom, Horsham Also called CD Technologies Inc *(G-7801)*

C & E Plastic East 724 457-0594
392 Flaugherty Run Rd Coraopolis (15108) *(G-3666)*

C & E Plastics Inc 724 947-4949
2500 Route 168 Georgetown (15043) *(G-6274)*

C & G Pallet Company Inc 610 759-5625
1000 Deemer Rd Bath (18014) *(G-953)*

C & G Wilcox Engrv & Images 570 265-3621
502 Main St Towanda (18848) *(G-18422)*

C & J Clark America Inc 717 632-2444
455 Madison St Hanover (17331) *(G-6864)*

C & J Clarks, Hanover Also called C & J Clark America Inc *(G-6864)*

C & J Industries Inc 814 724-4950
760 Water St Meadville (16335) *(G-10709)*

C & J Metals 562 634-3101
25 Penny Ln Avella (15312) *(G-834)*

C & J Welding & Cnstr LLC 724 564-7120
116 Moonlite Dr Mc Clellandtown (15458) *(G-10555)*

C & K Coal Company 814 226-6911
1062 E Main St Clarion (16214) *(G-3172)*

C & L Enterprises LLC 215 589-4553
287 Fox Hound Dr Doylestown (18901) *(G-4284)*

C & L Rivet Co Inc 215 672-1113
220 Jacksonville Rd Hatboro (19040) *(G-7275)*

C & M Aggregate Company Inc 724 796-3821
76 Station St Bulger (15019) *(G-2342)*

C & M Custom Machining Inc 610 458-0897
237 Sweet Spring Rd Glenmoore (19343) *(G-6464)*

C & M Mold & Tool Inc 215 741-2081
2600 W Maple Ave Rear Feasterville Trevose (19053) *(G-5897)*

C & S Lumber Company Inc 814 544-7544
398 Main St Roulette (16746) *(G-16833)*

C & S Repair Center Inc 610 524-9724
507 W Uwchlan Ave Downingtown (19335) *(G-4217)*

C & S Sports & Promotions 724 775-1655
3433 Brodhead Rd Ste 2 Monaca (15061) *(G-11287)*

C & S Wood Products Inc 570 489-8633
944 Underwood Rd Olyphant (18447) *(G-12985)*

C & T Industrial Supply Co, Mercersburg Also called C & T Machining Inc *(G-10982)*

C & T Machining Inc 717 328-9572
12991 Buchanan Trl W Mercersburg (17236) *(G-10982)*

C A C, West Chester Also called Communication Automation Corp *(G-19527)*

C A Elliot Lumber Co Inc 814 544-7523
200 Main St Roulette (16746) *(G-16834)*

C A P S, Horsham Also called Central Admxture Phrm Svcs Inc *(G-7803)*

C A Spalding Company 267 550-9000
4529 Adams Cir Bensalem (19020) *(G-1163)*

C and M Sales Co 814 437-3095
1587 Pittsburgh Rd Franklin (16323) *(G-6118)*

C B W, New Kensington Also called Cannon Boiler Works Inc *(G-12332)*

C C, Blandon Also called Can Corporation America Inc *(G-1752)*

C C Allis & Sons Inc 570 744-2631
2 Miles E Of Rte 467 Wyalusing (18853) *(G-20247)*

C C B B Inc 215 364-5377
850 Pennsylvania Blvd Feasterville Trevose (19053) *(G-5898)*

C C L, Hermitage Also called CCL Container Corporation *(G-7575)*

C C P, Saint Marys Also called Carbon City Products Inc *(G-16952)*

C C Printing, North East Also called Samuel C Rizzo Jr *(G-12760)*

C Clark & Sons 814 652-5370
322 W Mattie Rd Everett (15537) *(G-5568)*

C Crouthamel & Co Inc 215 822-1911
186 New Galena Rd Chalfont (18914) *(G-2865)*

C D M I, S Abingtn Twp Also called Creative Design & Machining *(G-16894)*

C Dcap Modem Line 814 966-3954
691 Main St Duke Center (16729) *(G-4438)*

C E Conover & Co Inc 215 639-6666
4106 Blanche Rd Bensalem (19020) *(G-1164)*

C E Holden Inc 412 767-5050
938 Route 910 Cheswick (15024) *(G-3103)*

C E N Inc 412 749-0442
Buncher Commerce Pk Ave A Leetsdale (15056) *(G-9686)*

C E S, In, Pittsburgh Also called Customized Envmtl Systems *(G-14896)*

C E Sauder & Sons LLC 717 445-4822
359 Weaverland Valley Rd East Earl (17519) *(G-4539)*

C Everwine Machine LLC 717 656-5451
2 Site Rd Leola (17540) *(G-9774)*

C F Martin & Co Inc 610 759-2837
Green St Nazareth (18064) *(G-11957)*

C F Moores Co Inc 215 248-1250
1123 Ivy Hill Rd Philadelphia (19150) *(G-13490)*

C G S Enterprises Inc 610 758-9263
3864 Courtney St Ste 220 Bethlehem (18017) *(G-1477)*

C H Reed, Monroeville Also called C H Reed Inc *(G-11326)*

C H Reed Inc (PA) 717 632-4261
301 Poplar St Hanover (17331) *(G-6865)*

C H Reed Inc 412 380-1334
205 Seco Rd Monroeville (15146) *(G-11326)*

C I Hayes Inc 814 834-2200
310 State St Saint Marys (15857) *(G-16951)*

C J Apparel Inc 610 432-8265
747 Pittston St Ste 3 Allentown (18103) *(G-159)*

C Jthomas Screening Inc 412 384-4279
1213 Prospect St Monongahela (15063) *(G-11305)*

C K E, Indiana Also called Dean Technology Inc *(G-8090)*

C K Sportwear Inc 717 733-4786
178 Ridge Ave Ephrata (17522) *(G-5094)*

C Knaub & Sons 717 292-3908
1595 Jug Rd Dover (17315) *(G-4190)*

C L I Corporation (PA) 724 348-4800
6108 Brownsville Road Ext # 201 Finleyville (15332) *(G-5952)*

C L Sturkey Inc (PA) 717 274-9441
824 Cumberland St Ste 3 Lebanon (17042) *(G-9551)*

C L Ward Family 724 743-5903
1100 Ashwood Dr Ste 1101 Canonsburg (15317) *(G-2554)*

C Leslie Smith Inc 610 439-8833
3100 W Tilghman St Allentown (18104) *(G-160)*

C M C, Fleetwood Also called Custom Mil & Consulting Inc *(G-5969)*

C M C Steel Fabricators Inc 570 568-6761
2093 Old Hwy Ste 15 New Columbia (17856) *(G-12173)*

C M R Usa LLC 724 452-2200
940 Riverside Pl Leetsdale (15056) *(G-9687)*

C N C, Coatesville Also called Cnc Manufacturing Inc *(G-3297)*

C N C Auto Motion, Warren Also called CNE Machinery Ltd *(G-19017)*

C N W, Mount Pleasant Also called Columbia Northwest Inc *(G-11693)*

C P C Baking Group, Pittsburgh Also called Bimbo Bakeries Usa Inc *(G-14766)*

C P Commercial Printing Inc (PA) 215 675-7605
2031 Stout Dr Ste 2 Warminster (18974) *(G-18843)*

C P Commerical Printing, Warminster Also called C P Commercial Printing Inc *(G-18843)*

C P Converters Inc (HQ) 717 764-1193
15 Grumbacher Rd York (17406) *(G-20415)*

C P S, Allentown Also called Card Prsnlzation Solutions LLC *(G-161)*

C P S, Erie Also called Wlek Inc *(G-5531)*

C Palmer Manufacturing Inc 724 872-8200
5 Palmers Rd West Newton (15089) *(G-19748)*

C Purolite Corporation 610 668-9090
150 Monument Rd Ste 202 Bala Cynwyd (19004) *(G-874)*

C R Augenstein Inc 724 206-0679
2344 Route 136 Eighty Four (15330) *(G-4836)*

C R I, Berlin Also called Center Rock Inc *(G-1287)*

C Ruffs Mini Mart Fuel 484 619-6832
4563 Court St Coplay (18037) *(G-3641)*

C S Fuller Inc 610 941-9225
400 Stenton Ave Ste 104 Plymouth Meeting (19462) *(G-15837)*

C S Garber & Sons Inc 610 367-2861
7928 Boyertown Pike Boyertown (19512) *(G-1902)*

C S I, Eynon Also called Casket Shells Incorporated *(G-5754)*

C S I, Chalfont Also called Computer Software Inc *(G-2868)*

C S M, Ridgway Also called Clarion Sintered Metals Inc *(G-16699)*

C S M Bottling Inc 570 489-6071
214 Flynn St Jessup (18434) *(G-8328)*

C S R, York Also called Consoldted Scrap Resources Inc *(G-20434)*

C S S, Bethel Also called Concrete Safety Systems LLC *(G-1394)*

C Sharkey Keyboard Covers Inc (PA) 215 969-8783
9764 Redd Rambler Ter Philadelphia (19115) *(G-13491)*

C Strunk Inc 610 678-1960
128 Green Valley Rd Reading (19608) *(G-16339)*

C T E Inc 717 767-6636
30 Willow Springs Cir York (17406) *(G-20416)*

C T S, Hatfield Also called Climatic Testing Systems Inc *(G-7326)*

C W E Inc 610 642-7719
315 E County Line Rd Ardmore (19003) *(G-704)*

C W Graphics Co, Du Bois Also called Jerden Industries Inc *(G-4399)*

C W I, Barto Also called Cwi Inc *(G-941)*

C W S Inc 800 800-7867
11828 Old Lake Rd North East (16428) *(G-12734)*

C W Thomas, Philadelphia Also called Cw Thomas LLC *(G-13596)*

C&C Backhoe Service LLC 724 438-5283
1345 W Penn Blvd Uniontown (15401) *(G-18619)*

C&D Intrntnal Inv Holdings Inc (HQ) 215 619-2700
1400 Union Meeting Rd Blue Bell (19422) *(G-1819)*

C&D Technologies Inc (PA) 215 619-2700
1400 Union Meeting Rd # 110 Blue Bell (19422) *(G-1820)*

C&G Arms LLC 724 858-2856
160 York Dr Natrona Heights (15065) *(G-11937)*

C&G Holsters, Natrona Heights Also called C&G Arms LLC *(G-11937)*

A
L
P
H
A
B
E
T
I
C

C&H7 LLC (PA)..215 887-7411
  717 Constitution Dr # 112 Exton (19341) *(G-5658)*

C&J Energy Services Inc.......................................724 354-5225
  228 Lawton Rd Shelocta (15774) *(G-17484)*

C&J Well Services Inc..724 746-2467
  380 Southpointe Blvd # 210 Canonsburg (15317) *(G-2555)*

C-B Tool Co (PA)..717 397-3521
  640 Bean Hill Rd Lancaster (17603) *(G-8967)*

C-B Tool Co...717 393-3953
  640 Bean Hill Rd Lancaster (17603) *(G-8968)*

C-E Minerals Inc..610 768-8800
  901 E 8th Ave Ste 200 King of Prussia (19406) *(G-8589)*

C-Fab-1 Inc...215 331-2797
  2820 Old Lincoln Hwy # 1 Trevose (19053) *(G-18489)*

C-K Composites Co LLC.....................................724 547-4581
  361 Bridgeport St Mount Pleasant (15666) *(G-11690)*

C-P Flexible Packaging, York *Also called C P Converters Inc (G-20415)*

C-Thru Products Inc...610 586-1130
  400 W Chester Pike Ridley Park (19078) *(G-16738)*

C-W Industries, Southampton *Also called Industrial Enterprises Inc (G-17819)*

C. N. I., Bensalem *Also called Cni Inc (G-1169)*

C.C. Korns, Johnstown *Also called Korns Galvanizing Company Inc (G-8401)*

C.K.E., Lucernemines *Also called Dean Technology Inc (G-10117)*

C/C Welding/Fabric Inc......................................814 364-9460
  803 Main St Clarence (16829) *(G-3162)*

C3 Media LLC..610 832-8077
  442 Brown St Philadelphia (19123) *(G-13492)*

Cab Technologies & Printing So...........................724 457-8880
  438 Skylark Dr Coraopolis (15108) *(G-3667)*

Cabinet Connections...215 429-9431
  81 Bertha St Feasterville Trevose (19053) *(G-5899)*

Cabinet Fashions, Milesburg *Also called Jerry D Watson Jr (G-11152)*

Cabinet Store..814 677-5522
  3272 State Route 257 Seneca (16346) *(G-17365)*

Cable Associates Inc...570 876-4565
  1 Export Ln Archbald (18403) *(G-686)*

Cable Hardwoods Inc..724 452-5927
  4401 State Route 488 Portersville (16051) *(G-15926)*

Cabrun Ink Products Corp...................................215 533-2990
  2020 Valetta St Philadelphia (19124) *(G-13493)*

Cac, Wind Gap *Also called Converter Accessory Corp (G-20168)*

Cactus Wellhead LLC..814 308-0344
  194 Aviation Way Reynoldsville (15851) *(G-16656)*

Cadosia Valley Lumber Company.........................570 676-3400
  Rr 191 Newfoundland (18445) *(G-12476)*

Cady Enterprises...814 848-7408
  1336 Fox Hill Rd Ulysses (16948) *(G-18600)*

Caff Co..412 787-1761
  370 Vista Park Dr Pittsburgh (15205) *(G-14799)*

Caffrey Michael & Sons.......................................610 252-1299
  820 Newlins Rd E Easton (18040) *(G-4659)*

Caffrey's, Easton *Also called Caffrey Michael & Sons (G-4659)*

Cai, Greentown *Also called Corey Associates Inc (G-6733)*

Cakeworks LLC..917 744-1375
  2110 Post Hill Ct Henryville (18332) *(G-7565)*

Cal Fab Machine & Tool, Exeter *Also called Calfab and Machine Inc (G-5582)*

Calandra Cheese (PA)...610 759-2299
  350 E Lawn Rd Nazareth (18064) *(G-11958)*

Calandra Salvatore, Nazareth *Also called Calandra Cheese (G-11958)*

Calcium Chloride Sales Inc..................................724 458-5778
  713 W Main St Grove City (16127) *(G-6781)*

Calconix Inc...610 642-5921
  821 Aubrey Ave Ste B Ardmore (19003) *(G-705)*

Calder Enterprises, Greensburg *Also called Calder Transport (G-6654)*

Calder Industries Inc...814 422-8026
  187 Edgewood Ln Spring Mills (16875) *(G-17886)*

Calder Transport...724 787-8390
  314 Persian Ln Greensburg (15601) *(G-6654)*

Caldon Ultrasonics Div, Coraopolis *Also called Cameron Technologies Us Inc (G-3671)*

Caldwell Corporation...814 486-3493
  116 W 2nd St Emporium (15834) *(G-5051)*

Caldwell's Quality Embroidery, Doylestown *Also called Caldwells of Bucks County (G-4285)*

Caldwells of Bucks County..................................215 345-1348
  248 W State St Doylestown (18901) *(G-4285)*

Caldwells Windoware Inc.....................................412 922-1132
  166 Wabash St Pittsburgh (15220) *(G-14800)*

Caledonian Dye Works..215 739-2322
  3300 Emerald St Philadelphia (19134) *(G-13494)*

Calfab and Machine Inc.......................................570 654-4004
  201 Schooley Ave Exeter (18643) *(G-5582)*

Calfrac Well Services Corp..................................724 564-5350
  2001 Summit View Dr Smithfield (15478) *(G-17643)*

Calgon Carbon Corporation (HQ)........................412 787-6700
  3000 Gsk Dr Moon Township (15108) *(G-11482)*

Calgon Carbon Corporation.................................724 218-7001
  2000 Mcclaren Woods Dr Coraopolis (15108) *(G-3668)*

Calgon Carbon Corporation.................................412 771-4050
  200 Neville Rd Unit 1 Pittsburgh (15225) *(G-14801)*

Calgon Carbon Corporation.................................610 873-3071
  1061 Boot Rd Downingtown (19335) *(G-4218)*

Calgon Carbon Corporation.................................412 269-4188
  4301 Neville Rd Pittsburgh (15225) *(G-14802)*

Calgon Carbon Corporation.................................412 787-6700
  500 Calgon Carbon Dr Pittsburgh (15205) *(G-14803)*

Calgon Carbon Corporation.................................412 269-4000
  4301 Grand Ave Pittsburgh (15225) *(G-14804)*

Calgon Carbon Investments Inc (HQ)..................412 787-6700
  3000 Gsk Dr Coraopolis (15108) *(G-3669)*

Calgon Carbon Uv Tech LLC................................724 218-7001
  2000 Mcclaren Woods Dr Coraopolis (15108) *(G-3670)*

Caliber Therapeutics Inc......................................215 862-5797
  150 Union Square Dr New Hope (18938) *(G-12300)*

Caliburn Inc...610 429-9500
  7 N 5 Points Rd Ste 4 West Chester (19380) *(G-19516)*

California Linear Devices Inc................................610 328-4000
  750 W Sproul Rd Springfield (19064) *(G-17909)*

California Med Innovations LLC............................909 621-5871
  55 Hilton St Easton (18042) *(G-4660)*

California Mushroom Farm Inc.............................805 642-3253
  1320 Newark Rd Toughkenamon (19374) *(G-18417)*

California Pallet Mello, Horsham *Also called CPM Wolverine Proctor LLC (G-7805)*

California Scents, Glenshaw *Also called Associated Products LLC (G-6482)*

Calkins Creamery LLC...570 729-8103
  288 Calkins Rd Honesdale (18431) *(G-7704)*

Calkins Media Incorporated (PA).........................215 949-4000
  8400 Bristol Pike Levittown (19057) *(G-9822)*

Call Newspapers Inc (PA)....................................570 385-3120
  960 E Main St Schuylkill Haven (17972) *(G-17150)*

Callahan David E Pool Plst Inc............................610 429-4496
  1198 Phoenixville Pike West Chester (19380) *(G-19517)*

Callery LLC..724 538-1200
  1424 Mars Evans City Rd Evans City (16033) *(G-5556)*

Callery Sr John..412 344-9010
  1515 Potomac Ave Pittsburgh (15216) *(G-14805)*

Callie's Pretzel Factory, Mountainhome *Also called Callies Candy Kitchens Inc (G-11786)*

Callie's Pretzel Factory, Cresco *Also called Callies Candy Kitchens Inc (G-3892)*

Callies Candy Kitchens Inc (PA)...........................570 595-2280
  1111 Rte 390 Mountainhome (18342) *(G-11786)*

Callies Candy Kitchens Inc...................................570 595-3257
  Rr 390 Cresco (18326) *(G-3892)*

Calloway House, Lancaster *Also called Dig Family Business LLC (G-8997)*

Calloway Network, Reading *Also called Standard Offset Prtg Co Inc (G-16524)*

Caltech Manufacturing...215 322-2025
  109 Industrial Dr Warminster (18974) *(G-18844)*

Calumet Karns City Ref LLC................................724 756-9212
  138 Petrolia St Karns City (16041) *(G-8480)*

Calvert Lumber Company Inc...............................724 346-5553
  139 W Budd St Sharon (16146) *(G-17430)*

Calvin Taylor Corporation....................................570 983-2288
  101 Pittston Ave Ste 2 Scranton (18505) *(G-17214)*

CAM Industries Inc..717 637-5988
  215 Philadelphia St Hanover (17331) *(G-6866)*

CAM Innovation Inc...717 637-5988
  215 Philadelphia St Hanover (17331) *(G-6867)*

Camber Sportswear Inc.......................................610 239-9910
  2 Dekalb St Norristown (19401) *(G-12643)*

Cambria County Asso (PA)..................................814 536-3531
  211 Central Ave Johnstown (15902) *(G-8360)*

Cambria County Asso..814 472-5077
  175 Industrial Park Rd Ebensburg (15931) *(G-4782)*

Cambria Machining Co LLC.................................814 948-8128
  108 Kinter Rd Nicktown (15762) *(G-12619)*

Cambria Plastics LLC..814 472-6189
  502 E Crawford St Ebensburg (15931) *(G-4783)*

Cambria Plastics LLC..814 535-5467
  840 Horner St Johnstown (15902) *(G-8361)*

Cambria Springs Service Inc................................814 539-1629
  151 Horner St Johnstown (15902) *(G-8362)*

Cambria Welding & Fabg Inc...............................814 948-5072
  196 Shop Rd Saint Benedict (15773) *(G-16936)*

Cambridge Farms Hanover LLC..........................717 945-5178
  201 Granite Run Dr # 250 Lancaster (17601) *(G-8969)*

Cambridge Scale Works Inc (PA).........................610 273-7040
  5011 Horseshoe Pike Honey Brook (19344) *(G-7740)*

Cambridge-Lee Holdings Inc (HQ)........................610 926-4141
  86 Tube Dr Reading (19605) *(G-16340)*

Cambridge-Lee Industries LLC (HQ)......................610 926-4141
  86 Tube Dr Plant 4 4 Plant Reading (19605) *(G-16341)*

Camco Manufacturing Inc....................................570 731-4109
  317 S Thomas Ave Sayre (18840) *(G-17113)*

Camden Iron & Metal Inc.....................................215 952-1500
  2600 Penrose Ave Philadelphia (19145) *(G-13495)*

Camden Iron & Metal Llc.....................................610 532-1080
  3 Industrial Dr Sharon Hill (19079) *(G-17454)*

Cameo Kitchens Inc..717 436-9598
  Old Rt 22 Mifflintown (17059) *(G-11111)*

Cameron Compression Systems...........................610 265-2410
  156 Anderson Rd King of Prussia (19406) *(G-8590)*

(G-0000) Company's Geographic Section entry number

Cameron County Community Chest...................814 486-0612
33 E 4th St Emporium (15834) (G-5052)

Cameron County Echo Inc..........................814 486-3711
300 S Broad St Ste 1 Emporium (15834) (G-5053)

Cameron Diversified Pdts Inc......................814 929-5834
479 Buena Vista Hwy Wilcox (15870) (G-19897)

Cameron Lumber LLP................................814 749-9635
1386 Ridge Rd Homer City (15748) (G-7671)

Cameron Measurements Systems, Coraopolis Also called Cameron Technologies Us
Inc (G-3673)

Cameron Supply Corporation.......................610 866-9632
1850 W Market St Bethlehem (18018) (G-1478)

Cameron Technologies Us Inc (HQ)................724 695-3798
1000 Mcclaren Woods Dr Coraopolis (15108) (G-3671)

Cameron Technologies Us Inc.....................724 273-9300
1000 Mcclaren Woods Dr Coraopolis (15108) (G-3672)

Cameron Technologies Us Inc.....................724 273-9300
1000 Mcclaren Woods Dr Coraopolis (15108) (G-3673)

Camman Industries Inc............................724 539-7670
111 Strawcutter Rd Derry (15627) (G-4100)

Campania Imports, Pennsburg Also called Campania International Inc (G-13246)

Campania International Inc........................215 541-4627
2452 Quakertown Rd # 100 Pennsburg (18073) (G-13246)

Campbell 3...724 322-1043
418 Crossbow Dr New Stanton (15672) (G-12447)

Campbell Business Forms Inc......................610 356-0626
3558 Winding Way Newtown Square (19073) (G-12568)

Campbell Companies, Reading Also called J Benson Corp (G-16411)

Campbell Fittings Inc (PA).......................610 367-6916
301 S Washington St Boyertown (19512) (G-1903)

Campbell House Publishing, New Stanton Also called Campbell 3 (G-12447)

Campbell Machine & Fabricating, Pittsburgh Also called Donald Campbell (G-14930)

Campbell Manufacturing Inc (HQ).................610 367-2107
127 E Spring St Bechtelsville (19505) (G-1030)

Campbell Manufacturing LLC (HQ)................610 367-2107
127 E Spring St Bechtelsville (19505) (G-1031)

Campbell Oil & Gas Inc...........................724 465-9199
280 Indian Springs Rd 222a Indiana (15701) (G-8085)

Campbell Oil LLC..................................814 749-0002
1021 Wagner St Nanty Glo (15943) (G-11905)

Campbell Soup Co, Denver Also called Pepperidge Farm Incorporated (G-4087)

Campbell Studios Inc (PA).......................814 398-2148
146 Railroad St Cambridge Springs (16403) (G-2475)

Campbells Custom Woodworks LLC...................484 300-4175
62 Lemon St Pottstown (19464) (G-15969)

Campus Copy Center (PA)...........................215 386-6410
3907 Walnut St Philadelphia (19104) (G-13496)

Campus Creamery LLC..............................570 351-1738
1150 Northern Blvd S Abingtn Twp (18411) (G-16890)

Campus Shipping Center, Philadelphia Also called Campus Copy Center (G-13496)

Camrpc Electronics, Pittsburgh Also called Radio Parts Company (G-15465)

Can Corporation America Inc (PA).................610 926-3044
326 June Ave Blandon (19510) (G-1752)

Can Corporation America Inc.......................610 921-3460
3723 Pottsville Pike Reading (19605) (G-16342)

Canaan Cabinetry Inc..............................215 348-0551
415 E Butler Ave Ste A Doylestown (18901) (G-4286)

Canalley Painting.................................215 443-9505
400 Lincoln Ave Ste A Hatboro (19040) (G-7276)

Canary LLC.......................................724 483-2224
2975 Marginal W Charleroi (15022) (G-3007)

Candela Corporation...............................610 861-8772
2550 Brodhead Rd Ste 300 Bethlehem (18020) (G-1479)

Candlerock...724 503-2231
925 4th Ave New Kensington (15068) (G-12331)

Candles In Cove...................................518 368-3381
624 Locust St Roaring Spring (16673) (G-16762)

Candlesetcetera.com, Reinholds Also called Candlsetcetera Candles ACC LLC (G-16630)

Candlewic Company.................................215 230-3601
3765 Old Easton Rd Doylestown (18902) (G-4287)

Candlsetcetera Candles ACC LLC...................610 507-7830
550 Golf Rd Reinholds (17569) (G-16630)

Candy Cottage Co Inc..............................215 322-6618
465 Pike Rd Ste 103 Huntingdon Valley (19006) (G-7967)

Canfield Logging LLC..............................570 224-4507
120 Maverick Draw Damascus (18415) (G-3990)

Canfields Outdoor Pwr Eqp Inc....................814 697-6233
2932 Kings Run Rd Shinglehouse (16748) (G-17505)

Canis Major International, Hollidaysburg Also called Secrets of Big Dogs (G-7653)

Cannon Boiler Works Inc..........................724 335-8541
510 Constitution Blvd New Kensington (15068) (G-12332)

Cannon Graphics Inc...............................215 676-5114
12301 Mcnulty Rd Unit L Philadelphia (19154) (G-13497)

Cannon Instrument Company.........................814 353-8000
2139 High Tech Rd State College (16803) (G-17948)

Cannon Tool Company...............................724 745-1070
165 Valley Rd Canonsburg (15317) (G-2556)

Cannon U S A Inc (HQ).............................724 772-5600
1235 Freedom Rd Cranberry Township (16066) (G-3810)

Cannon U S A Inc.................................724 452-5358
300 W Grandview Ave Zelienople (16063) (G-20794)

Cannondale Sports Group, Bedford Also called Cycling Sports Group Inc (G-1048)

Canopy Foods, Downingtown Also called Gtf Worldwide LLC (G-4231)

Canteen, Lancaster Also called Compass Group Usa Inc (G-8982)

Canterbery Industries LLC.........................724 697-4231
435 Allshouse Rd Avonmore (15618) (G-863)

Canticle Pharmaceuticals Inc....................404 380-9263
200 Barr Harbor Dr # 400 Conshohocken (19428) (G-3526)

Canto Tool Corporation............................814 724-2865
11494 Airport Rd Meadville (16335) (G-10710)

Cantol USA Inc....................................905 475-6141
Sharon Ct 105 Hnderson Dr Sharon Hill (19079) (G-17455)

Canton Independent Sentinel, Canton Also called Carreon Publishing LLC (G-2663)

Cantwell Woodworking LLC.........................215 710-3030
175 Commerce Dr Ste 500 Fort Washington (19034) (G-6064)

Canvas Awnings Inc................................215 423-1213
3029 Ruth St Philadelphia (19134) (G-13498)

Canvas Specialties Inc............................570 825-9282
785 Hazle St Hanover Township (18706) (G-6983)

Cape May Olive Oil Company........................610 256-3667
618 N Morton Ave Morton (19070) (G-11590)

Cape Prosthetics-Orthotics (HQ)..................610 644-7824
855 Springdale Dr Ste 200 Exton (19341) (G-5659)

Capital Coating Inc..............................717 442-0979
7 S Kinzer Rd Kinzers (17535) (G-8735)

Capital Coil & Air LLC............................484 498-6880
1544 Mcdaniel Dr West Chester (19380) (G-19518)

Capital Crestings, Milford Also called Architectural Iron Company (G-11156)

Capital Manufacturing, Lansdale Also called Capitol Sign Company Inc (G-9350)

Capital Press, Duncansville Also called Slates Enterprises Inc (G-4463)

Capitol Manufacturing Division, Reading Also called Phoenix Forge Group LLC (G-16470)

Capitol Sign Company Inc.........................215 822-0166
Broad St & Rte 309 Lansdale (19446) (G-9350)

Capitol Tool & Mfg Co Inc.........................717 938-6165
429 Old York Rd New Cumberland (17070) (G-12180)

Caplugs Niagara, Erie Also called Protective Industries Inc (G-5441)

Capnostics LLC....................................610 442-1363
4639 Old Oak Rd Doylestown (18902) (G-4288)

Capo and Kifer Pultrusions........................412 751-3489
1 Locust Grv Greenock (15047) (G-6644)

Capozzolo Brothers................................610 588-7702
1342 Ridge Rd Bangor (18013) (G-909)

Cappelli Enterprises Inc.........................845 856-9033
4900 Ritter Rd Ste 130 Mechanicsburg (17055) (G-10826)

Cappelli Industries Inc..........................724 745-6766
218 Mcclelland Rd Canonsburg (15317) (G-2557)

Capra Collina Vineyard Inc........................570 489-0489
1971 Scranton Carbondale Blakely (18447) (G-1746)

Capri Cork LLC...................................717 627-5701
215 Bucky Dr Lititz (17543) (G-9995)

Capsen Robotics Inc..............................203 218-0204
4638 Centre Ave Pittsburgh (15213) (G-14806)

Capstone Energy Services LLC (PA)...............724 326-0190
1 Wheeling Pittsburgh Dr Allenport (15412) (G-104)

Captain Chuckys Crab Cake Co I....................610 355-7525
5149 West Chester Pike Newtown Square (19073) (G-12569)

Captek Inc..610 296-2111
1043 Lancaster Ave Berwyn (19312) (G-1355)

Caputo Brothers Creamery LLC....................717 739-1087
6403 Pahagaco Rd Spring Grove (17362) (G-17876)

Caputo Ice Plant, Hazleton Also called Nicholas Caputo (G-7513)

Capway Systems Inc................................717 843-0003
725 Vogelsong Rd York (17404) (G-20417)

Car Cleen Systems Inc............................717 795-8995
1000 Transit Blvd Bethel Park (15102) (G-1408)

Car Fuel 1 Inc....................................215 545-2002
914 Clinton St Philadelphia (19107) (G-13499)

Car Gazette Co....................................412 951-5572
450 Dawson Ave Pittsburgh (15202) (G-14807)

Caraustar Industrial and Con......................717 295-0047
1820 Olde Homestead Ln Lancaster (17601) (G-8970)

Caraustar Industries Inc.........................717 846-4559
2510 N George St York (17406) (G-20418)

Caraustar Industries Inc.........................717 534-2206
515 W Chocolate Ave Rear Hershey (17033) (G-7605)

Carb-Rite, Pittsburgh Also called EJ Bognar Incorporated (G-14960)

Carbide Metals Inc................................724 459-6355
176 Cherry St Blairsville (15717) (G-1718)

Carbigrind Inc....................................724 722-3536
186 Waltz Mill Rd Ruffs Dale (15679) (G-16871)

Carbinite Metal Coatings, Renfrew Also called Freys Research Inc (G-16639)

Carboline Company.................................724 838-5750
741 S Main St Greensburg (15601) (G-6655)

Carbon Capture Scientific LLC.....................412 854-6713
2940 Industrial Blvd Bethel Park (15102) (G-1409)

Carbon City Products Inc..........................814 834-2886
150 Ford Rd Saint Marys (15857) (G-16952)

A
L
P
H
A
B
E
T
I
C

Carbon Clean Industries Inc 570 288-1155
216 Courtdale Ave Kingston (18704) *(G-8713)*

Carbon Sales Inc 570 823-7664
375 Johnson St Wilkes Barre (18702) *(G-19909)*

Carbonator Rental Service Inc 215 726-9100
6500 Eastwick Ave Philadelphia (19142) *(G-13500)*

Carbondale News (PA) 570 282-3300
220 8th St Honesdale (18431) *(G-7705)*

Carbondale News 570 282-3300
220 8th St Honesdale (18431) *(G-7706)*

Carclo Technical Plastics, Latrobe *Also called Ctp Carrera Inc (G-9468)*

Card Prsnlzation Solutions LLC (PA) 610 231-1860
7520 Morris Ct Ste 100 Allentown (18106) *(G-161)*

Cardenas Oil & Vinegar Taproom 570 401-4718
942 S 9th St Philadelphia (19147) *(G-13501)*

Cardiac Telecom Corporation 800 355-2594
212 Outlet Way Ste 1 Greensburg (15601) *(G-6656)*

Cardiacassist Inc 412 963-8883
620 Alpha Dr Pittsburgh (15238) *(G-14808)*

Cardinal Health 407 Inc 215 501-1210
3001 Red Lion Rd Ste Ag Philadelphia (19114) *(G-13502)*

Cardinal Ig Company 570 474-9204
50 Elmwood Ave Mountain Top (18707) *(G-11753)*

Cardinal Industrial Finishes 814 723-0721
4 Harmar St Warren (16365) *(G-19015)*

Cardinal Lg Company 570 489-6421
42 Archbald Heights Rd Jessup (18434) *(G-8329)*

Cardinal Precision Company 215 885-2050
222 Roesch Ave Unit 24 Oreland (19075) *(G-13018)*

Cardinal Resources Inc 412 374-0989
201 Penn Center Blvd # 400 Pittsburgh (15235) *(G-14809)*

Cardinal Resources LLC 412 374-0989
201 Penn Center Blvd # 400 Pittsburgh (15235) *(G-14810)*

Cardinal Systems Inc 570 385-4733
250 Route 61 S Schuylkill Haven (17972) *(G-17151)*

Cardionet Inc 888 312-2328
1000 Cedar Hollow Rd Malvern (19355) *(G-10199)*

Cardo Systems Inc 412 788-4533
1204 Parkway View Dr Pittsburgh (15205) *(G-14811)*

Cardolite Corporation (PA) 609 436-0902
140 Wharton Rd Bristol (19007) *(G-2123)*

Cardone Industries Inc 215 912-3000
5670 Rising Sun Ave Philadelphia (19120) *(G-13503)*

Cardone Industries Inc (PA) 215 912-3000
5501 Whitaker Ave Philadelphia (19124) *(G-13504)*

Cardone Industries Inc 215 912-3000
550 E Erie Ave Philadelphia (19134) *(G-13505)*

Cardone Industries Inc 215 912-3000
5660 Rising Sun Ave Philadelphia (19120) *(G-13506)*

Cardone Industries Inc 215 912-3000
5501 Whitaker Ave Philadelphia (19124) *(G-13507)*

Career Communications Inc 215 256-3130
303 Maple Ave Ste 4 Harleysville (19438) *(G-7024)*

Career Lfstyle Enhncment Jurnl 724 872-5344
244 N 5th St West Newton (15089) *(G-19749)*

Carel Usa Inc 410 497-5128
385 S Oak St Manheim (17545) *(G-10374)*

Carey Schuster LLC 610 431-2512
120 S Church St West Chester (19382) *(G-19519)*

Careys Dumpster Services 717 258-1400
61 Heisers Ln Carlisle (17015) *(G-2692)*

Cargill Incorporated 717 530-7778
580 N Morris St Shippensburg (17257) *(G-17521)*

Cargill Incorporated 570 524-4777
70 Agway Ln Winfield (17889) *(G-20198)*

Cargill Incorporated 814 793-3701
965 Frederick Rd Martinsburg (16662) *(G-10520)*

Cargill Incorporated 814 793-2137
106 S Railroad St Martinsburg (16662) *(G-10521)*

Cargill Incorporated 717 273-1133
320 N 16th St Lebanon (17046) *(G-9552)*

Cargill Cocoa & Chocolate Inc 717 653-1471
200 Chocolate Ave Mount Joy (17552) *(G-11647)*

Cargill Cocoa & Chocolate Inc 570 453-6825
400 Stoney Creek Rd Hazle Township (18202) *(G-7448)*

Cargill Meat Solutions Corp 570 384-8350
65 Green Mountain Rd Hazleton (18202) *(G-7493)*

Cargill Meat Solutions Corp 570 746-3000
1252 Route 706 Wyalusing (18853) *(G-20248)*

Caribbean Elite Magazine Inc 718 702-0161
448 N 17th St Allentown (18104) *(G-162)*

Carik's Signs, Pittsburgh *Also called Cariks Custom Decor (G-14812)*

Cariks Custom Decor 412 882-1511
2523 Brownsville Rd Pittsburgh (15210) *(G-14812)*

Carl Amore Greenhouses 610 837-7038
6761 Steuben Rd Nazareth (18064) *(G-11959)*

Carl E Reichert Corp 215 723-9525
4120 Bethlehem Pike Telford (18969) *(G-18269)*

Carl J Kaetzel 570 434-2391
203 Reynolds Rd Kingsley (18826) *(G-8702)*

Carl J Kaetzel Flagstone, Kingsley *Also called Carl J Kaetzel (G-8702)*

Carl R Harry 610 865-7104
1521 Linden St Bethlehem (18017) *(G-1480)*

Carl Strutz & Company Inc (PA) 724 625-1501
440 Mars Valencia Rd Mars (16046) *(G-10489)*

Carl Strutz & Company Inc 724 625-1501
440 Mars Valencia Rd Mars (16046) *(G-10490)*

Carla Bella Ent LLC 570 704-0077
1 George Ave Wilkes Barre (18705) *(G-19910)*

Carleton Inc 215 230-8900
30 S Sand Rd Doylestown (18901) *(G-4289)*

Carleton Package Engineering, Doylestown *Also called Carleton Inc (G-4289)*

Carlin Coal Co, Snow Shoe *Also called R S Carlin Inc (G-17670)*

Carlini Brothers Co (PA) 412 421-9301
701 Hazelwood Ave Pittsburgh (15217) *(G-14813)*

Carlisle Construction Mtls Inc 717 245-7142
1555 Ritner Hwy Carlisle (17013) *(G-2693)*

Carlisle Construction Mtls LLC 724 564-5440
2000 Summit View Dr Smithfield (15478) *(G-17644)*

Carlisle Construction Mtls LLC 717 245-7000
1603 Industrial Dr Carlisle (17013) *(G-2694)*

Carlisle Construction Mtls LLC 724 564-5440
2000 Summit View Dr Smithfield (15478) *(G-17645)*

Carlisle Construction Mtls LLC (HQ) 717 245-7000
1285 Ritner Hwy Carlisle (17013) *(G-2695)*

Carlisle Depot, Carlisle *Also called Galliker Dairy Company (G-2716)*

Carlisle Distribution Center, Carlisle *Also called Ames Companies Inc (G-2689)*

Carlisle Foods Inc 717 218-9880
1605 Shearer Dr Carlisle (17013) *(G-2696)*

Carlisle Machine Shop Inc 717 243-0289
17 Donegal Dr Carlisle (17013) *(G-2697)*

Carlisle Syntec Systems, Carlisle *Also called Carlisle Construction Mtls LLC (G-2695)*

Carlisle Systems LLC 610 821-4222
210 Sunset Dr Fogelsville (18051) *(G-5992)*

Carlisle Tpo Inc 717 245-7000
1285 Ritner Hwy Carlisle (17013) *(G-2698)*

Carlisle Vault LLC 717 382-8588
31 S Hanover St Ste 4 Carlisle (17013) *(G-2699)*

Carlson Erie Corporation 814 455-2768
1115 Cherry St Erie (16501) *(G-5220)*

Carlson Mining 724 924-2188
166 Mount Herman Ch Rd New Castle (16101) *(G-12069)*

Carlson Technologies Inc 814 371-5500
213 Hahne Ct Du Bois (15801) *(G-4386)*

Carlsons Industrial Grinding 814 864-8640
8959 Perry Hwy Erie (16509) *(G-5221)*

Carly Railcar Components LLC 724 864-8170
1090 Sandy Hill Rd Irwin (15642) *(G-8147)*

Carlyd Fishers Products, East Earl *Also called Bradley Walter Myers (G-4538)*

Carma Industrial Coatings Inc 717 624-6239
45 Enterprise Dr New Oxford (17350) *(G-12405)*

Carman Ice Cream, Loganville *Also called Allen McKinney Inc (G-10101)*

Carmeuse Lime Inc (HQ) 412 995-5500
11 Stanwix St Fl 21 Pittsburgh (15222) *(G-14814)*

Carmeuse Lime Inc 717 867-4441
3 Clear Spring Rd Annville (17003) *(G-644)*

Carmeuse Lime & Stone, Pittsburgh *Also called Norton Oglebay Company (G-15347)*

Carmeuse Lime & Stone, Pittsburgh *Also called Erie Sand & Gravel Co Inc (G-14984)*

Carmeuse Lime & Stone, Pittsburgh *Also called O-N Minerals Company (ohio) (G-15353)*

Carmeuse Lime & Stone, Pittsburgh *Also called O-N Minerals Michigan Company (G-15355)*

Carmeuse Lime & Stone, Pittsburgh *Also called Norton Oglebay Specialty Mnrl (G-15348)*

Carmeuse Lime & Stone, Pittsburgh *Also called O-N Minerals Chemstone Company (G-15352)*

Carmeuse Lime & Stone, Pittsburgh *Also called O-N Minerals Luttrell Company (G-15354)*

Carmeuse Lime & Stone, Pittsburgh *Also called O-N Minerals Portage Co LLC (G-15356)*

Carmeuse Lime & Stone Inc 412 777-0724
3600 Neville Rd Pittsburgh (15225) *(G-14815)*

Carmeuse Lime & Stone Inc (HQ) 412 995-5500
11 Stanwix St Fl 21 Pittsburgh (15222) *(G-14816)*

Carmeuse Lime-Anville, Annville *Also called Carmeuse Lime Inc (G-644)*

Carmeuse Natural Chemicals, Pittsburgh *Also called Carmeuse Lime Inc (G-14814)*

Carnegie Learning Inc 412 690-2442
501 Grant St Ste 1075 Pittsburgh (15219) *(G-14817)*

Carnegie Mellon University 412 268-2111
5000 4th Ave Ste 314 Pittsburgh (15213) *(G-14818)*

Carnegie Printing Company 412 788-4399
7425 Steubenville Pike Oakdale (15071) *(G-12895)*

Carnegie Robotics LLC 412 251-0321
4501 Hatfield St Pittsburgh (15201) *(G-14819)*

Carnegie Speech LLC 412 471-1234
2425 Sidney St Pittsburgh (15203) *(G-14820)*

Caro Brothers Inc 724 265-1538
1 Main St Russellton (15076) *(G-16883)*

Carol Fanelli 717 945-7418
118 Parklawn Ct Lancaster (17601) *(G-8971)*

Carol Fetterolf 570 875-2026
26 Rolling Meadows Rd Ashland (17921) *(G-728)*

Carol Vinck Window Creation 717 730-0303
　4401 Carlisle Pike Ste J Camp Hill (17011) *(G-2494)*
Carol Zuzek 814 837-7090
　Off Rte 66 Rr 2 Kane (16735) *(G-8460)*
Caron Enterprises Inc 814 774-5658
　2700 Mechanic St Lake City (16423) *(G-8898)*
CARPENTER, Orwigsburg *Also called Kepner-Scott Shoe Co* *(G-13047)*
Carpenter & Paterson Inc 724 379-8461
　484 Galiffa Dr Donora (15033) *(G-4150)*
Carpenter Co 717 627-1878
　400 Arrowhead Dr Lititz (17543) *(G-9996)*
Carpenter Co 610 366-5110
　57 Olin Way Allentown (18106) *(G-163)*
Carpenter Co 610 366-8349
　1100 Mill Rd Allentown (18106) *(G-164)*
Carpenter Co 610 366-5110
　57 A Olin Way Fogelsville (18051) *(G-5993)*
Carpenter Co 814 944-8612
　2337 E Pleasant Vly Blvd Altoona (16601) *(G-486)*
Carpenter Connection Inc 412 881-3900
　901 Killarney Dr Pittsburgh (15234) *(G-14821)*
Carpenter Engineering Inc 717 274-8808
　808 Patmar Dr Lebanon (17046) *(G-9553)*
Carpenter Insulation Co, Fogelsville *Also called Carpenter Co* *(G-5993)*
Carpenter Pallets 570 465-2573
　301 Hall Rd New Milford (18834) *(G-12395)*
Carpenter Shop Inc 814 848-7448
　2228 Sr 49 W Ulysses (16948) *(G-18601)*
Carpenter Technology, Latrobe *Also called Latrobe Specialty Mtls Co LLC* *(G-9494)*
Carpenter Technology Corp (PA) 610 208-2000
　1735 Market St Fl 15 Philadelphia (19103) *(G-13508)*
Carpenter Technology Corp 610 208-2000
　2120 Centre Ave Reading (19605) *(G-16343)*
Carpenter Technology Corp 610 208-2000
　101 Bern St Reading (19601) *(G-16344)*
Carpet and Furniture Depot Inc 814 239-5865
　12756 Dunnings Hwy Ste 3 Claysburg (16625) *(G-3201)*
Carpet Depot Home Center, Claysburg *Also called Carpet and Furniture Depot Inc* *(G-3201)*
Carpet Steam Rentals, Lancaster *Also called Certified Carpet Service Inc* *(G-8976)*
Carrara Steel Erectors, Erie *Also called Carrara Steel Inc* *(G-5222)*
Carrara Steel Inc 814 452-4600
　1717 Gaskell Ave Erie (16503) *(G-5222)*
Carreon Publishing LLC 570 673-5151
　10 W Main St Canton (17724) *(G-2663)*
Carriage Machine Shop LLC 717 397-4079
　250 Maple Ave Bird In Hand (17505) *(G-1671)*
Carrier Class Green Infras 267 419-8496
　601 Davisville Rd Ste 210 Willow Grove (19090) *(G-20110)*
Carrier Corporation 610 834-1717
　4110 Butler Pike Ste A104 Plymouth Meeting (19462) *(G-15838)*
Carriers Wreckers By Kimes 724 342-2930
　7294 W Market St Mercer (16137) *(G-10960)*
Carrizo (marcellus) LLC 570 278-7450
　12231 State Route 706 Montrose (18801) *(G-11460)*
Carrizo Oil & Gas Inc 570 278-7009
　12231 State Route 706 Montrose (18801) *(G-11461)*
Carroll Manufacturing Co LLC 724 266-0400
　80 Leetsdale Indstrl 30 Leetsdale (15056) *(G-9688)*
Carrollsisters 215 969-4688
　13421 Kelvin Ave Philadelphia (19116) *(G-13509)*
Carson Boxing LLC 814 839-2768
　797 Sloans Hollow Rd Bedford (15522) *(G-1045)*
Carson Helicopters Inc 215 249-3535
　952 Blooming Glen Rd Perkasie (18944) *(G-13270)*
Carson Home Accents, Freeport *Also called Carson Industries Inc* *(G-6201)*
Carson Industries Inc 724 295-5147
　15 Glade Dr Kittanning (16201) *(G-8760)*
Carson Industries Inc (PA) 724 295-5147
　189 Foreman Rd Freeport (16229) *(G-6201)*
Carson Publishing Inc. 412 548-3798
　506 Mcknight Park Dr 506a Pittsburgh (15237) *(G-14822)*
Carson Street Commons 412 431-1183
　2529 E Carson St Pittsburgh (15203) *(G-14823)*
Carter Handcrafted Furniture 610 847-2101
　7541 Easton Rd Ottsville (18942) *(G-13061)*
Carton Edge International Inc (PA) 215 699-8755
　337 W Walnut St North Wales (19454) *(G-12794)*
Cartridge Specialist 412 741-4442
　111 Linda Vista Rd Sewickley (15143) *(G-17384)*
Cartridge World York 717 699-4465
　1805 Loucks Rd Ste 100 York (17408) *(G-20419)*
Caruso Inc 717 738-0248
　820 N Reading Rd Ephrata (17522) *(G-5095)*
Cas Pack Corporation 215 254-7225
　1750b Woodhaven Dr Bensalem (19020) *(G-1165)*
Casa Luker USA Inc 412 854-9012
　71 Mcmurray Rd Ste 104 Pittsburgh (15241) *(G-14824)*
Cascade Architectural Products 412 824-9313
　132 George St Turtle Creek (15145) *(G-18561)*

Cascade Corporation 570 995-5099
　1456 Kelly Rd Trout Run (17771) *(G-18512)*
Cascades Tissue Group - PA Inc 570 388-6161
　1 Main St Ransom (18653) *(G-16306)*
Cascades Tissue Group - PA Inc (HQ) 570 388-4307
　901 Sathers Dr Pittston (18640) *(G-15744)*
Casco USA, Erie *Also called Compressed Air Specialists Co* *(G-5230)*
Case Design Corporation 215 703-0130
　333 School Ln Telford (18969) *(G-18270)*
Case Design Corporation 800 847-4176
　333 School Ln Telford (18969) *(G-18271)*
Case Mondern Work 717 785-1232
　2498 Iron Springs Rd Fairfield (17320) *(G-5765)*
Case Paper Co Inc 215 430-6400
　499 E Tioga St Philadelphia (19134) *(G-13510)*
Casework Cabinetry Cnstr 814 236-7601
　1382 Schofield Street Ext Curwensville (16833) *(G-3947)*
Caseworks Inc 724 522-5068
　203 Jayhawk Dr Jeannette (15644) *(G-8249)*
Cashel LLC 610 853-8227
　850 W Chester Pike # 200 Havertown (19083) *(G-7417)*
Casilio Concrete, Bethlehem *Also called Frank Casilio and Sons Inc* *(G-1518)*
Casket Shells Incorporated 570 876-2642
　432 1st St Eynon (18403) *(G-5754)*
Caskey Printing Inc (PA) 717 764-4500
　850 Vogelsong Rd York (17404) *(G-20420)*
Casner Fabrics 215 946-3334
　922 Woodbourne Rd Ste 244 Levittown (19057) *(G-9823)*
Cassel Vineyards Hershey LLC 717 533-2008
　80 Shetland Dr Hummelstown (17036) *(G-7905)*
Cassidys Brew Zoo 814 946-2739
　3415 Pleasant Valley Blvd # 48 Altoona (16602) *(G-487)*
Cast Pac Inc 610 264-8131
　206 Cascade Dr Allentown (18109) *(G-165)*
Cast-Rite Metal Company 610 582-1300
　101 Fairview Chapel Rd Birdsboro (19508) *(G-1691)*
Castec Inc (PA) 724 258-8700
　1462 Delberts Dr Monongahela (15063) *(G-11306)*
Castek Inc 570 759-3540
　23 River Rd Berwick (18603) *(G-1316)*
Castek Innovations Inc 717 267-2748
　4450 Sunset Pike Chambersburg (17202) *(G-2915)*
Castgrabber LLC 412 362-6802
　6507 Wilkins Ave Ste 212 Pittsburgh (15217) *(G-14825)*
Casting Headquarters Inc 215 922-2278
　740 Sansom St Ste 100 Philadelphia (19106) *(G-13511)*
Castle Builders Supply Inc 724 981-4212
　1325 Broadway Rd Hermitage (16148) *(G-7573)*
Castle Builders Supply Inc (PA) 724 658-5656
　1409 Moravia St New Castle (16101) *(G-12070)*
Castle Cheese Inc 724 368-3022
　525 William Penn Pl Fl 28 Pittsburgh (15219) *(G-14826)*
Castle Machine Company, Greencastle *Also called Antrim Machine Company* *(G-6597)*
Castle Mold & Tool Co Inc 724 652-4737
　3932 Wilmington Rd New Castle (16105) *(G-12071)*
Castor Printing Company Inc 215 535-1471
　6376 Castor Ave 80 Philadelphia (19149) *(G-13512)*
Castrol H D L, Warminster *Also called BP Lubricants USA Inc* *(G-18841)*
Castrol Industrial N Amer Inc 877 641-1600
　2201 Green Ln Levittown (19057) *(G-9824)*
Casturo Iron & Metal, McKeesport *Also called Charles Casturo* *(G-10662)*
Casual Living Unlimited LLC 717 351-7177
　172 Orlan Rd New Holland (17557) *(G-12231)*
Catalent Cts Inc 816 767-6013
　10381 Decatur Rd Philadelphia (19154) *(G-13513)*
Catalent Micron Tech Inc 610 251-7400
　333 Phoenixville Pike Malvern (19355) *(G-10200)*
Catalent Micron Tehcnologies, Malvern *Also called Catalent Micron Tech Inc* *(G-10200)*
Catalent Pharma Solutions Inc. 215 637-3565
　10381 Decatur Rd Philadelphia (19154) *(G-13514)*
Catalent Pharma Solutions Inc. 215 613-3001
　3031 Red Lion Rd Philadelphia (19114) *(G-13515)*
Catalogs By Design 610 337-9133
　590 N Gulph Rd King of Prussia (19406) *(G-8591)*
Catalus Corporation (PA) 814 781-7004
　286 Piper Rd Saint Marys (15857) *(G-16953)*
Catalus Corporation 814 435-6541
　1251 Route 6 W Galeton (16922) *(G-6238)*
Catalyst Crossroads LLC 412 969-2733
　210 Bower Hill Rd Rear Pittsburgh (15228) *(G-14827)*
Catalyst Energy Inc 412 325-4350
　424 S 27th St Pittsburgh (15203) *(G-14828)*
Catania Folk Instruments Inc 570 922-4487
　521 Paddy Mountain Rd Millmont (17845) *(G-11219)*
Caterpillar Globl Min Amer LLC (HQ) 724 743-1200
　2045 W Pike St Houston (15342) *(G-7869)*
Caterpillar Inc. 724 743-0566
　2045 W Pike St Houston (15342) *(G-7870)*
Caterpillar Inc. 717 751-5123
　600 Memory Ln York (17402) *(G-20421)*

Caterpillar URS Storeroom (PA)..........610 293-5576
100 W Matsonford Rd Radnor (19087) ***(G-16290)***
Cathedral Stained GL Studios..........215 379-5360
202 Franklin Ave Cheltenham (19012) ***(G-3027)***
Catherman's Home Made Candy, Lewisburg *Also called James A Marquette* ***(G-9913)***
Catholic Golden Age Inc..........570 586-1091
50 Pegula Ln Scott Township (18447) ***(G-17183)***
Catholic Light Publishing Co..........570 207-2229
330 Wyoming Ave 208 Scranton (18503) ***(G-17215)***
Catholic Register..........814 695-7563
927 S Logan Blvd Hollidaysburg (16648) ***(G-7643)***
Catholic Scl Svcs of Scranton (PA)..........570 207-2283
516 Fig St Scranton (18505) ***(G-17216)***
Catholic Scl Svcs of Scranton..........570 454-6693
240 S Poplar St Hazleton (18201) ***(G-7494)***
Cathys Creamery..........570 916-3386
25 Sylvan Ct Milton (17847) ***(G-11235)***
Catoris Candies Inc..........724 335-4371
981 5th Ave New Kensington (15068) ***(G-12333)***
Catridge World, LLC, Hanover *Also called Two Cousins Holdings LLC* ***(G-6963)***
Caulfield Associates Inc..........215 480-1940
243 Harvey Ave Doylestown (18901) ***(G-4290)***
Causco..........814 452-2004
944 W 26th St Erie (16508) ***(G-5223)***
Cava Intl MBL & Gran Inc..........215 732-7800
2000 Washington Ave Philadelphia (19146) ***(G-13516)***
Cawley Environmental Svcs Inc..........610 594-0101
637 Jeffers Cir Downingtown (19335) ***(G-4219)***
CB Excavating & Logging LLC..........570 756-2749
2108 Lakeview Rd Susquehanna (18847) ***(G-18178)***
Cbc Cabinetry & Home Services..........717 564-2521
1009 N Mountain Rd Harrisburg (17112) ***(G-7103)***
Cbc Latrobe Acquisition LLC..........724 532-5444
100 33rd St Latrobe (15650) ***(G-9462)***
Cbd Incorporated..........215 579-6337
10 W Center Ave Newtown (18940) ***(G-12500)***
Cbf Systems..........717 793-2941
3100 Farmtrail Rd York (17406) ***(G-20422)***
Cbh of Lancaster Company..........717 569-0485
311 W Stiegel St Manheim (17545) ***(G-10375)***
Cbmm North America Inc..........412 221-7008
1000 Omega Dr Ste 1110 Pittsburgh (15205) ***(G-14829)***
Ccf Industries, Apollo *Also called Clifton Custom Furn & Design* ***(G-670)***
Ccffg Inc..........570 270-3976
7 George Ave Wilkes Barre (18705) ***(G-19911)***
CCI, Holland *Also called Collegecart Innovations Inc* ***(G-7640)***
CCI, Harleysville *Also called Career Communications Inc* ***(G-7024)***
Cck Inc..........814 684-2270
Hc 220 Tyrone (16686) ***(G-18578)***
CCL Container, Hanover Township *Also called CCL Tube Inc* ***(G-6984)***
CCL Container (hermitage) Inc..........724 981-4420
1 Llodio Dr Hermitage (16148) ***(G-7574)***
CCL Container Corporation..........724 981-4420
1 Llodio Dr Hermitage (16148) ***(G-7575)***
CCL Containers, Hermitage *Also called CCL Container (hermitage) Inc* ***(G-7574)***
CCL Restoration LLC..........412 926-6156
310 N Linden Ave Pittsburgh (15208) ***(G-14830)***
CCL Tube Inc..........570 824-8485
1 Lasley Ave Hanover Township (18706) ***(G-6984)***
CCM, Carlisle *Also called Carlisle Construction Mtls LLC* ***(G-2694)***
Ccn America LP..........412 349-6300
300 Penn Center Blvd # 505 Pittsburgh (15235) ***(G-14831)***
Ccr Electronics..........317 469-4855
311 Old Clairton Rd Pittsburgh (15236) ***(G-14832)***
CCS Machining Inc..........724 668-7706
7728 Rte 22 W Greensburg (15601) ***(G-6657)***
CCT, Philadelphia *Also called Coating & Converting Tech Corp* ***(G-13554)***
CCT Manufacturing & Fulfillmen..........724 652-0818
203 Commerce Ave New Castle (16101) ***(G-12072)***
Ccx Inc..........724 224-6900
101 Braeburn Rd Lower Burrell (15068) ***(G-10105)***
CD Hardware, Harleysville *Also called V2r2 LLC* ***(G-7063)***
CD Technologies Inc..........215 619-2700
200 Precision Rd 150 Horsham (19044) ***(G-7801)***
CDF Industries, Quakertown *Also called Pump-Warehouse Co Inc* ***(G-16236)***
CDI Lawn Equipment & Grdn Sup..........610 489-3474
3474 Germantown Pike Collegeville (19426) ***(G-3371)***
CDI Printing Services Inc..........724 444-6160
Rr 910 Gibsonia (15044) ***(G-6330)***
CDK Perforating LLC..........724 222-8900
125 Museum Rd Washington (15301) ***(G-19155)***
CDK Perforating LLC..........570 358-3250
75 Stowell Ln Ulster (18850) ***(G-18598)***
Cdl Nuclear Technologies Inc..........724 933-5570
6400 Brooktree Ct Ste 320 Wexford (15090) ***(G-19794)***
Cdl Printing and Packaging, Harrisburg *Also called Corporate Distribution Ltd* ***(G-7109)***
CDM Holdings Inc..........215 724-8640
5013 Grays Ave Philadelphia (19143) ***(G-13517)***
Cdprintexpress LLC..........610 450-6176
2208 Periwinkle Ct Phoenixville (19460) ***(G-14539)***
Cdr Contracting..........814 536-7675
1208 Rebecca Dr Johnstown (15902) ***(G-8363)***
Cds Analytical LLC..........610 932-3636
465 Limestone Rd Oxford (19363) ***(G-13074)***
Cds Solutions Group, Lancaster *Also called Conestoga Data Services Inc* ***(G-8984)***
CE Ready Mix..........724 727-3331
185 N Washington Rd Apollo (15613) ***(G-667)***
Cecil Kilmer Flagstone, Nicholson *Also called Glenwood Stone Co Inc* ***(G-12614)***
Ceco Filters Inc (HQ)..........215 723-8155
700 Emlen Way Telford (18969) ***(G-18272)***
Cedar Craft..........610 273-9224
1113 Park Rd Honey Brook (19344) ***(G-7741)***
Cedar Forest Products Company (PA)..........815 946-3994
27 E Forge Rd Media (19063) ***(G-10917)***
Cedar Hollow Sales Inc..........610 644-2660
1101 Church Rd Malvern (19355) ***(G-10201)***
Cedar Lane Pallets..........717 365-4014
2253 Luxemburg Rd Lykens (17048) ***(G-10131)***
Cedar Ridge Furniture..........610 286-6225
112 Maxwell Hill Rd Morgantown (19543) ***(G-11519)***
Cedar Ridge Manufacturing LLC..........717 656-0404
255 Mascot Rd Ronks (17572) ***(G-16805)***
Cedars Wdwkg & Renovations LLC..........717 392-1736
630 W Fulton St Lancaster (17603) ***(G-8972)***
Cedars Woodworking & Intr Pntg, Lancaster *Also called Cedars Wdwkg & Renovations LLC* ***(G-8972)***
Cegelec Automation, Pittsburgh *Also called Alstom Grid LLC* ***(G-14689)***
Cei-Douglassville Inc..........610 385-9500
447 Old Swede Rd Douglassville (19518) ***(G-4172)***
Celebrity Jewelry, Philadelphia *Also called Norman Kivitz Co Inc* ***(G-14078)***
Celf Services LLC..........717 643-0039
1542 Buchanan Trl E Greencastle (17225) ***(G-6602)***
Cell-Con Inc (PA)..........800 771-7139
305 Commerce Dr Ste 300 Exton (19341) ***(G-5660)***
Cell-Con Inc..........814 623-7057
8468 Us Route 220 Bedford (15522) ***(G-1046)***
Cellar Tech LLC..........724 519-2139
4530 William Penn Hwy Murrysville (15668) ***(G-11849)***
Cellco Partnership..........610 431-5800
966 S Matlack St West Chester (19382) ***(G-19520)***
Cellcon Plastics Inc..........814 763-2195
17763 State Highway 198 Saegertown (16433) ***(G-16909)***
Cellmylight Inc..........800 575-5913
315 Municipal Dr Thorndale (19372) ***(G-18354)***
Cellomics Inc..........412 770-2500
100 Technology Dr Ste 100 # 100 Pittsburgh (15219) ***(G-14833)***
Cellucap Manufacturing Co (PA)..........800 523-3814
4626 N 15th St Philadelphia (19140) ***(G-13518)***
Cellular Concrete LLC..........610 398-7833
7020 Snowdrift Rd Allentown (18106) ***(G-166)***
Celsense Inc..........412 263-2870
603 Stanwix St Ste 390 Pittsburgh (15222) ***(G-14834)***
Cemex Cnstr Mtls ATL LLC..........724 535-4311
2001 Portland Park Wampum (16157) ***(G-18798)***
Cemline Corporation..........724 274-5430
808 Freeport Rd Cheswick (15024) ***(G-3104)***
Cenco Grinding Corporation..........610 434-5740
411 Business Park Ln Allentown (18109) ***(G-167)***
Cenprepavandcon..........215 778-6103
1926 Fleming Ave Willow Grove (19090) ***(G-20111)***
Centech Inc..........610 754-0720
2190 Colflesh Rd Perkiomenville (18074) ***(G-13300)***
Center City Pretzel Co..........215 463-5664
816 Washington Ave Philadelphia (19147) ***(G-13519)***
Center Edctn & Empymnt Law..........800 365-4900
370 Technology Dr Malvern (19355) ***(G-10202)***
Center Fashions Inc..........570 655-2861
216 Center St Ste 101 Dupont (18641) ***(G-4489)***
Center For Internal Change, Lancaster *Also called Team Approach Inc* ***(G-9213)***
Center For Orthtic and Prsthtc..........570 382-8208
1500 Main St Ste 2 Dickson Cty (18447) ***(G-4123)***
Center For RES & Tech Bristol, Bristol *Also called Solvay USA Inc* ***(G-2199)***
Center Hardwood LLC..........814 684-3600
14082 S Eagle Valley Rd Tyrone (16686) ***(G-18579)***
Center Independent Oil Company..........724 437-6607
1346 Connerville St Lemont Furnace (15456) ***(G-9734)***
Center Machine Company..........724 379-4066
And 136 Rr 906 Webster (15087) ***(G-19456)***
Center Rock Inc (PA)..........814 267-7100
118 Schrock Dr Berlin (15530) ***(G-1287)***
Centermoreland Concrete Pdts..........570 333-4944
12 Creamery Rd Tunkhannock (18657) ***(G-18533)***
Centerville Cabinet Shop..........717 351-0708
448 Centerville Rd Gordonville (17529) ***(G-6551)***
Centify LLC..........215 421-8375
204 Allison Rd Oreland (19075) ***(G-13019)***

Centocor Inc 215 325-2297
  800 Ridgeview Dr Horsham (19044) *(G-7802)*

Central Admxture Phrm Svcs Inc 215 706-4001
  253 Gibraltar Rd Horsham (19044) *(G-7803)*

Central Blair Electric Co 814 949-8280
  259 Lakemont Park Blvd Altoona (16602) *(G-488)*

Central Builders Supply Co 570 524-9147
  520 Saint Mary St Lewisburg (17837) *(G-9899)*

Central Concrete Co Inc 215 953-9736
  1066 Gravel Hill Rd Southampton (18966) *(G-17801)*

Central Concrete Supply Coinc 215 927-4686
  118 W Clarkson Ave Philadelphia (19120) *(G-13520)*

Central Distribution Co Inc (PA) 717 393-4851
  11b Meadow Ln Lancaster (17601) *(G-8973)*

Central Hydraulics Inc 814 224-0375
  366 Travelers Rd East Freedom (16637) *(G-4562)*

Central Machine Co Inc 215 536-5071
  27 S 4th St Quakertown (18951) *(G-16177)*

Central Manufacturing Company, Madera *Also called Eugene Zapsky* *(G-10163)*

Central Ohio Coal Company (HQ) 740 338-3100
  1000 Consol Energy Dr Canonsburg (15317) *(G-2558)*

Central Orthotic Prosthetic Co (PA) 814 535-8221
  725 Franklin St Johnstown (15901) *(G-8364)*

Central PA Wilbert Vault 717 248-3777
  201 6th Ave Burnham (17009) *(G-2359)*

Central Panel Inc 215 947-8500
  60 Tomlinson Rd Huntingdon Valley (19006) *(G-7968)*

Central Park West, Bernville *Also called Gloray If LLC* *(G-1299)*

Central Penn Distilling 717 808-7695
  25 Tamarack Dr Gettysburg (17325) *(G-6285)*

Central Penn Rig Service 814 342-4800
  540 Summit Hill Rd Morrisdale (16858) *(G-11547)*

Central Penn Wire and Cable 717 945-5540
  360 Steel Way A Lancaster (17601) *(G-8974)*

Central Penna Tool & Mfg Inc 717 932-1294
  450 Locust Rd New Cumberland (17070) *(G-12181)*

Central Pennsylvania 814 946-7411
  301 Cayuga Ave Altoona (16602) *(G-489)*

Central Road LLC 888 319-7778
  4607 Lib Rd Ste 220-303 Bethel Park (15102) *(G-1410)*

Central Sign Systems, Mechanicsburg *Also called Keystone Sign Systems Inc* *(G-10864)*

Central States Mfg Inc 814 239-2764
  402 Corporate Blvd Claysburg (16625) *(G-3202)*

Central Valley Aggregates, Pleasant Gap *Also called Glenn O Hawbaker Inc* *(G-15792)*

Centre Concrete Company 570 748-7747
  357 E Walnut St Lock Haven (17745) *(G-10085)*

Centre Concrete Company 570 433-3186
  307 Fairfield Rd Montoursville (17754) *(G-11435)*

Centre County Womens Journal 814 349-8202
  165 Main St Millheim (16854) *(G-11217)*

Centre Daily Times, State College *Also called Nittany Printing and Pubg Co* *(G-18000)*

Centre Glass Co, State College *Also called Neidighs Inc* *(G-17996)*

Centre of Web Inc 814 235-9592
  2026 Sandy Dr State College (16803) *(G-17949)*

Centre Pallets LLC 814 349-8693
  118 Pallet Dr Rebersburg (16872) *(G-16578)*

Centre Publications Inc 814 364-2000
  163 Mountainside Ln Centre Hall (16828) *(G-2840)*

Centreweb, State College *Also called Centre of Web Inc* *(G-17949)*

Centria Inc (HQ) 412 299-8000
  1005 Beaver Grade Rd # 2 Moon Township (15108) *(G-11483)*

Centria Inc 724 251-2300
  500 Perth Dr Ambridge (15003) *(G-612)*

Centria Inc 724 251-2208
  1005 Beaver Grade Rd # 2 Coraopolis (15108) *(G-3674)*

Centric Plastics LLC 215 309-1999
  925 Schwab Rd Ste 1 Hatfield (19440) *(G-7323)*

Centroid Corporation (PA) 814 353-9290
  159 Gates Rd Howard (16841) *(G-7886)*

Century Auto Parts, Philadelphia *Also called Century Motors Inc* *(G-13521)*

Century Buildings 814 336-1446
  17067 Townhouse Rd Saegertown (16433) *(G-16910)*

Century Motors Inc 215 724-8845
  3101 S 61st St Philadelphia (19153) *(G-13521)*

Century Packaging Co Inc 610 262-8860
  5217 Kemmerer St Whitehall (18052) *(G-19864)*

Century Propeller Corporation 814 677-7100
  687 Bucktail Rd Franklin (16323) *(G-6119)*

Cenveo Worldwide Limited 724 887-5400
  1001 Tech Dr Ste 1121 Mount Pleasant (15666) *(G-11691)*

Cenveo Worldwide Limited 717 285-9095
  3575 Hempland Rd Lancaster (17601) *(G-8975)*

Cephalon Inc 610 738-6410
  502 Brandywine Pkwy West Chester (19380) *(G-19521)*

Cephalon Inc (HQ) 610 344-0200
  41 Moores Rd Malvern (19355) *(G-10203)*

Cephalon Clinical Partners LP 610 883-5260
  145 Brandywine Pkwy West Chester (19380) *(G-19522)*

Cera-Met, Bethlehem *Also called Howmet Aluminum Casting Inc* *(G-1532)*

Cera-Met LLC 610 266-0270
  2175 Avenue C Bethlehem (18017) *(G-1481)*

Ceraln Corp (PA) 570 322-8400
  110 Reynolds St South Williamsport (17702) *(G-17790)*

Ceramic Art Company Inc 952 944-5600
  1414 Radcliffe St Fl 2 Bristol (19007) *(G-2124)*

Ceramic Color and Chem Mfg Co, New Brighton *Also called Ceramic Color and Chem Mfg Co* *(G-12032)*

Ceramic Color and Chem Mfg Co 724 846-4000
  13th St & 11th Ave New Brighton (15066) *(G-12032)*

Ceramic Services Inc 215 245-4040
  1060 Park Ave Bensalem (19020) *(G-1166)*

Ceratizit Usa Inc 724 694-8100
  5369 Rte 982 Latrobe (15650) *(G-9463)*

Cernostics Inc 412 315-7359
  1401 Forbes Ave Ste 302 Pittsburgh (15219) *(G-14835)*

Cerra Signs Inc 570 282-6283
  24 6th Ave Carbondale (18407) *(G-2670)*

Cerro Fabricated Products LLC 724 451-8202
  County Rd Brave (15316) *(G-2002)*

Cersell Company LLC 484 753-2655
  100 Woodledge Ln Exton (19341) *(G-5661)*

Certainteed Corporation (HQ) 610 893-5000
  20 Moores Rd Malvern (19355) *(G-10204)*

Certainteed Corporation 570 474-6731
  1220 Oak Hill Rd Mountain Top (18707) *(G-11754)*

Certainteed Corporation 610 651-8706
  18 Moores Rd Malvern (19355) *(G-10205)*

Certainteed Gypsum Inc (HQ) 610 893-6000
  20 Moores Rd Malvern (19355) *(G-10206)*

Certainteed Gypsum Mfg Inc (HQ) 813 286-3900
  750 E Swedesford Rd Wayne (19087) *(G-19312)*

Certainteed/Saint-Gobain, Malvern *Also called Certainteed Corporation* *(G-10205)*

Certech Inc 570 823-7400
  550 Stewart Rd Hanover Township (18706) *(G-6985)*

Certified Carpet Service Inc 717 393-3012
  932 High St Lancaster (17603) *(G-8976)*

Cervis, Warrendale *Also called Structured Mining Systems Inc* *(G-19098)*

Cessna Bros Lumber 814 767-9518
  150 Cessna Sawmill Rd Clearville (15535) *(G-3239)*

Cessna Industries 610 636-9282
  2188 Old Skippack Rd Harleysville (19438) *(G-7025)*

Cewa Technologies Inc 484 695-5489
  384 Kevin Dr Bethlehem (18017) *(G-1482)*

CF Textile Inc 215 817-5867
  39 Simons Way Huntingdon Valley (19006) *(G-7969)*

Cfb LLC 717 769-0857
  214 Dogwood Dr Elizabethtown (17022) *(G-4868)*

CFC Leola Properties Inc (HQ) 717 390-1978
  1301 Fulling Mill Rd # 3000 Middletown (17057) *(G-11050)*

CFC Manufacturing Co Inc 570 281-9605
  56 Dundaff St Carbondale (18407) *(G-2671)*

CFM Air Inc 814 539-6922
  84 Iron St Johnstown (15906) *(G-8365)*

CFM Designs Inc 610 520-7777
  840 W Lancaster Ave Bryn Mawr (19010) *(G-2318)*

Cgc, New Castle *Also called Consolidated Glass Corporation* *(G-12077)*

Cgi Products, Stroudsburg *Also called Craig Colabaugh Gunsmith Inc* *(G-18111)*

Cgm, Bensalem *Also called G M C Inc* *(G-1201)*

Cgm Incorporated 215 638-4400
  1445 Ford Rd Bensalem (19020) *(G-1167)*

Ch James G Thornton 412 207-2153
  25 Sheila Ct Pittsburgh (15227) *(G-14836)*

Chad Cross 570 549-3234
  19316 Route 6 Mansfield (16933) *(G-10412)*

Chadds Ford Cabinet Inc 610 388-6005
  1100 E Baltimore Pike Kennett Square (19348) *(G-8503)*

Chaddsford Winery Ltd (PA) 610 388-6221
  632 Baltimore Pike Chadds Ford (19317) *(G-2849)*

Chadwick Optical Inc 267 203-8665
  1557 Gehman Rd Harleysville (19438) *(G-7026)*

Chair Shoppe 570 353-2735
  132 Windsor Ln Morris (16938) *(G-11544)*

Challenger Fabrication 570 788-7911
  30 N Old Turnpike Rd B Drums (18222) *(G-4381)*

Challenger Manufacturing Ltd 215 968-6004
  16 Cricket Dr Southampton (18966) *(G-17802)*

Chalmur Bag LLC (PA) 215 455-1360
  4916 N 6th St Philadelphia (19120) *(G-13522)*

Chambers Group, Huntingdon Valley *Also called Copy Management Inc* *(G-7972)*

Chambersburg Machine Co Inc 717 264-7111
  250 Sunset Blvd W Chambersburg (17202) *(G-2916)*

Chambersburg Optical Service 717 263-4898
  227 Southgate Mall Chambersburg (17201) *(G-2917)*

Chambersburg Screen Print EMB 717 262-2111
  1495 Lincoln Way E # 105 Chambersburg (17202) *(G-2918)*

Chambord Et Cie Sarl 215 425-9300
  2633 Trenton Ave Philadelphia (19125) *(G-13523)*

A
L
P
H
A
B
E
T
I
C

Champ Printing Company Inc 412 269-0197
730 4th Ave Coraopolis (15108) *(G-3675)*
Champion Carrier Corporation (HQ) 724 981-3328
2755 Kirila Blvd Hermitage (16148) *(G-7576)*
Champion Choice Sports 814 236-2930
340 State St Curwensville (16833) *(G-3948)*
Champion Lumber Company Inc 724 455-3401
1195 Nebo Rd Champion (15622) *(G-3003)*
Chandler-White Publishing Co 312 907-3271
517 W Midvale Ave Philadelphia (19144) *(G-13524)*
Chango Inc 215 634-0400
1211 N 2nd St Philadelphia (19122) *(G-13525)*
Channel Veneer USA, Troy *Also called Oak Hill Veneer Inc* *(G-18524)*
Channellock Inc (PA) 814 337-9200
1306 S Main St Meadville (16335) *(G-10711)*
Chant Engineering Co Inc (PA) 215 230-4260
59 Industrial Dr New Britain (18901) *(G-12045)*
Chant Engineering Co Inc 215 230-4260
59 Industrial Dr New Britain (18901) *(G-12046)*
Chantelau Inc 215 723-1383
3225 Meetinghouse Rd Telford (18969) *(G-18273)*
Chapel Hill Mfg Co 215 884-3614
1807 Walnut Ave Oreland (19075) *(G-13020)*
Char-Mark Inc 570 754-7310
3084 Fair Rd Auburn (17922) *(G-815)*
Char-Val Candies 814 275-1602
1391 Route 66 New Bethlehem (16242) *(G-12025)*
Character Translation Inc 610 279-3970
501 W Washington St Ste 2 Norristown (19401) *(G-12644)*
Chargeitspot LLC 215 220-6600
111 S Independence Mall E Philadelphia (19106) *(G-13526)*
Charkit Chemical Company LLC 267 573-4062
301 Oxford Valley Rd Yardley (19067) *(G-20300)*
Charlene Crawford 215 432-7542
710 Martin Rd Elkins Park (19027) *(G-4901)*
Charles & Alice Inc 717 537-4700
2870 Yellow Goose Rd Lancaster (17601) *(G-8977)*
Charles A Henderson Prtg Svc 724 775-2623
101 Brighton Ave Rochester (15074) *(G-16783)*
Charles Beseler Co Inc 800 237-3537
2018 W Main St Stroudsburg (18360) *(G-18109)*
Charles Bond Company 610 593-5171
11 Green St Christiana (17509) *(G-3134)*
Charles Casturo 412 672-1407
750 W 5th Ave McKeesport (15132) *(G-10662)*
Charles Cracciolo Stl Met Yard 814 944-4051
1813 Old 6th Avenue Rd Altoona (16601) *(G-490)*
Charles Ernst's Sons Imports, Springfield *Also called Charles Ernsts Sons LLC* *(G-17910)*
Charles Ernsts Sons LLC 267 237-1271
74 S Hillcrest Rd Springfield (19064) *(G-17910)*
Charles F May Co 215 634-7257
3245 Amber St Ste 5 Philadelphia (19134) *(G-13527)*
Charles F Woodill 215 457-5858
5145 N 2nd St 47 Philadelphia (19120) *(G-13528)*
Charles Furriers, New Cumberland *Also called Charles L Simpson Sr* *(G-12182)*
Charles Ginty Associates Inc 610 347-1101
Pennsylvania 82 Unionville (19375) *(G-18647)*
Charles Hardy 610 366-9752
2908 Betz Ct Orefield (18069) *(G-13009)*
Charles Jacquin Et Cie Inc (PA) 215 425-9300
2633 Trenton Ave Philadelphia (19125) *(G-13529)*
Charles Jacquin Et Cie Inc 215 425-9300
2633 Trenton Ave Philadelphia (19125) *(G-13530)*
Charles Komar & Sons Inc 570 326-3741
801 Foresman St Williamsport (17701) *(G-19997)*
Charles L Simpson Sr 717 763-7023
333 Sharon Dr New Cumberland (17070) *(G-12182)*
Charles L Swenglish Sons Coal 724 437-3541
83 Swenglish Ln Smithfield (15478) *(G-17646)*
Charles Loose & Son, Myerstown *Also called BMC East LLC* *(G-11877)*
Charles Machine Inc 814 379-3706
10037 Olean Trl Summerville (15864) *(G-18157)*
Charles Navasky Co., Philipsburg *Also called Northside Manufacturing Inc* *(G-14521)*
Charles R Eckert Signs Inc 717 733-4601
291 Wabash Rd Ephrata (17522) *(G-5096)*
Charles R Kelley 717 840-0181
1295 Christensen Rd York (17402) *(G-20423)*
Charles Ritter Incorporated 215 320-5000
3333 S 3rd St Philadelphia (19148) *(G-13531)*
Charles S Smith McHning Draftg, Apollo *Also called Charles Smith* *(G-668)*
Charles Schillinger Co Inc 215 638-7200
1329 Ford Rd Bensalem (19020) *(G-1168)*
Charles Shavings Inc 570 458-4945
500 Sawmill Rd Benton (17814) *(G-1278)*
Charles Smith 724 727-3455
305 Woodland Rd Apollo (15613) *(G-668)*
Charles Steckman 724 789-7066
1009 Evans City Rd Renfrew (16053) *(G-16638)*
Charles W Romano Co 215 535-3800
2230 E Venango St Philadelphia (19134) *(G-13532)*

Charleston Marine Cntrs Inc (HQ) 843 745-0022
490 E Locust St Dallastown (17313) *(G-3973)*
Charlesworth Group (usa) Inc 215 922-1611
325 Chestnut St Ste 510 Philadelphia (19106) *(G-13533)*
Charlies Specialties Inc 724 346-2350
2500 Freeland Rd Hermitage (16148) *(G-7577)*
Charlies Tree Service 814 943-1131
611 N 6th Ave Altoona (16601) *(G-491)*
Charlotte Industries Inc 717 653-6721
630 Clay Aly Mount Joy (17552) *(G-11648)*
Charlotte Pipe and Foundry Co 570 546-7666
100 Industrial Park Rd Muncy (17756) *(G-11812)*
Charter Dura-Bar Inc 717 779-0807
90 Grumbacher Rd York (17406) *(G-20424)*
Charters Fabg Pwdr Coating LLC 412 203-5421
200 Main St Coraopolis (15108) *(G-3676)*
Chase Collection, The, State College *Also called Spectra Inc* *(G-18030)*
Chase Corporation 412 963-6285
201 Zeta Dr Pittsburgh (15238) *(G-14837)*
Chase Corporation 412 828-5470
201 Zeta Dr Pittsburgh (15238) *(G-14838)*
Chase Corporation 800 245-3209
128 1st St Blawnox (15238) *(G-1763)*
Chase Corporation 412 828-1500
201 Zeta Dr Pittsburgh (15238) *(G-14839)*
Chase Corporation 412 828-1500
201 Zeta Dr Pittsburgh (15238) *(G-14840)*
Chase Industries Inc 412 449-0160
1370 Old Frport Rd Ste 3b Pittsburgh (15238) *(G-14841)*
Chase Manufacturing 814 664-9069
9 Pennsylvania Ave Corry (16407) *(G-3747)*
Chase Specialty Coatings, Blawnox *Also called Chase Corporation* *(G-1763)*
Chatillon Scales Tester Co 215 745-3304
514 Knorr St Philadelphia (19111) *(G-13534)*
Chau Fresh Donuts 215 474-1533
5601 Market St Philadelphia (19139) *(G-13535)*
Chaucer Press Inc 570 825-2005
535 Stewart Rd Hanover Township (18706) *(G-6986)*
Chautauqua Mfg Corp 513 423-8840
80 Canal St Sharpsville (16150) *(G-17470)*
Checon Powder Met Contacts LLC 814 753-4466
600 Industrial Park Rd Kersey (15846) *(G-8554)*
Cheetah Chassis Corporation (PA) 570 752-2708
3rd & Oak Sts Berwick (18603) *(G-1317)*
Cheetah Technologies LP 412 928-7707
381 Mansfield Ave Ste 500 Pittsburgh (15220) *(G-14842)*
Cheetha, Berwick *Also called Cheetah Chassis Corporation* *(G-1317)*
Chef Specialties Inc 814 887-5652
411 W Water St Smethport (16749) *(G-17633)*
Chef'schoice, Avondale *Also called Edgecraft Corporation* *(G-851)*
Chefmaster East Division, Callery *Also called Byrnes and Kiefer Company* *(G-2468)*
Chefs Design Inc 215 763-5252
6711 Vandike St Philadelphia (19135) *(G-13536)*
Chelate Incorporated 717 203-0415
218 Ironstone Dr Lititz (17543) *(G-9997)*
Chelsea Building Products (HQ) 412 826-8077
565 Cedar Way Oakmont (15139) *(G-12914)*
Chelsea Partners Inc 215 603-7300
108 Arch St Ph 2 Philadelphia (19106) *(G-13537)*
Chelsea Plating Co, Philadelphia *Also called Scoopermarket Inc* *(G-14286)*
Chem and Lube, Allentown *Also called GTS Enterprises Inc* *(G-239)*
Chem Image Bio Threat LLC 412 241-7335
7301 Penn Ave Pittsburgh (15208) *(G-14843)*
Chem Service Inc 610 692-3026
660 Tower Ln West Chester (19380) *(G-19523)*
Chem-Clay Corporation 412 276-6333
24 Chestnut St Carnegie (15106) *(G-2765)*
Chem-Tainer Industries Inc 717 469-7316
187 S Meadow Ln Hummelstown (17036) *(G-7906)*
Chemalloy Company LLC (HQ) 610 527-3700
1301 Conshohocken Rd Conshohocken (19428) *(G-3527)*
Chemcoat Inc 570 368-8631
2790 Canfields Ln Montoursville (17754) *(G-11436)*
Chemcut Corporation 814 272-2800
500-1 Science Park Rd State College (16803) *(G-17950)*
Chemcut Holdings LLC 814 272-2800
500-1 Science Park Rd State College (16803) *(G-17951)*
Chemdaq Inc 412 787-0202
300 Business Center Dr # 330 Pittsburgh (15205) *(G-14844)*
Chemex Inc (PA) 610 398-6200
327 Burrell Blvd Allentown (18104) *(G-168)*
Chemgenex Pharmaceuticals Inc 650 804-7660
41 Moores Rd Malvern (19355) *(G-10207)*
Chemgro Fertilizer Co Inc 717 935-2185
316 Applehouse Rd Belleville (17004) *(G-1129)*
Chemical Equipment Labs of De, Newtown Square *Also called Chemical Equipment Labs VA Inc* *(G-12570)*
Chemical Equipment Labs VA Inc 610 497-9390
3920 Providence Rd A Newtown Square (19073) *(G-12570)*

Chemical Products Div, Erie *Also called Lord Corporation* **(G-5371)**

Chemical Service Philadelphia, Philadelphia *Also called Big 3 Packaging LLC* **(G-13459)**

Chemimage Corporation (PA).............................412 241-7335
7301 Penn Ave Pittsburgh (15208) **(G-14845)**

Chemimage Filter Tech LLC (PA).......................412 241-7335
7301 Penn Ave Pittsburgh (15208) **(G-14846)**

Cheminova Inc...919 474-6600
1735 Market St Philadelphia (19103) **(G-13538)**

Chemrock Corporation (HQ)............................610 667-6640
225 E City Ave Bala Cynwyd (19004) **(G-875)**

Chemstream Inc...814 629-7118
511 Railroad Ave Homer City (15748) **(G-7672)**

Chemstream Holdings Inc................................724 545-6222
301 Market St Kittanning (16201) **(G-8761)**

Chemtech Scientific, Holland *Also called Ajikabe Inc* **(G-7639)**

Chemtrade Chemicals Corp...............................814 965-4118
1224 E Center St Johnsonburg (15845) **(G-8344)**

Chep (usa) Inc..717 778-4279
3177 Biglerville Rd Biglerville (17307) **(G-1661)**

Cheri-Lee Inc...570 339-4195
1349 Scott St Kulpmont (17834) **(G-8822)**

Cherish Creamery, Reynoldsville *Also called Paula Keswick* **(G-16660)**

Chernay Printing Inc (PA)...............................610 282-3774
7483 S Main St Coopersburg (18036) **(G-3625)**

Cherokee Pharmaceuticals LLC..........................570 271-4195
100 Ave C Riverside (17868) **(G-16757)**

Cherokee Software Systems...............................717 932-5008
334 Hillcrest Dr New Cumberland (17070) **(G-12183)**

Cherry Steel Corp...215 340-2239
113 Willowbrook Dr Doylestown (18901) **(G-4291)**

Cherry Valley Vinyrd & Winery, Saylorsburg *Also called Sorrenti Orchards Inc* **(G-17108)**

Cherrydale Fundraising LLC..............................610 366-1606
1035 Mill Rd Allentown (18106) **(G-169)**

Cherryhill Manufacturing Corp...........................724 254-2185
3231 Laurel Run Rd Clymer (15728) **(G-3270)**

Cheryl Hewitt...814 943-7222
1321 Jefferson Ave Altoona (16602) **(G-492)**

Cheryl Nash Apparel LLC................................610 692-1919
210a Gale Ln Kennett Square (19348) **(G-8504)**

Chesapeake Del Brewing Co LLC.........................610 627-9000
30 E State St Media (19063) **(G-10918)**

Chester A Asher Inc (PA)...............................215 721-3000
80 Wambold Rd Souderton (18964) **(G-17729)**

Chester A Asher Inc.....................................717 248-8613
19 Susquehanna Ave Lewistown (17044) **(G-9925)**

Chester County Coating, Honey Brook *Also called Powder Coating Co* **(G-7756)**

Chester County Sports Products.........................610 327-4843
38 Glocker Way Pottstown (19465) **(G-15946)**

Chester Multi Copy Inc..................................610 876-1285
4007 Edgmont Ave Brookhaven (19015) **(G-2243)**

Chester Spirit, Chester *Also called Spirit Media Group Inc* **(G-3064)**

Chesterfield Special Cylinders...........................832 252-1082
55 Old Clairton Rd 205 Pittsburgh (15236) **(G-14847)**

Chestnut Acres Specialty.................................717 949-2875
156 W Reistville Rd Myerstown (17067) **(G-11879)**

Chestnut Group Inc (PA)................................610 688-3300
115 Bloomingdale Ave # 101 Wayne (19087) **(G-19313)**

Chestnut Hill Local.......................................215 248-8800
8434 Germantown Ave Ste 1 Philadelphia (19118) **(G-13539)**

Chestnut Rd Lumber & Dry Kiln..........................717 423-5941
90 Chestnut Rd Newburg (17240) **(G-12474)**

Chestnut Ridge Foam Inc................................724 537-9000
443 Warehouse Dr Latrobe (15650) **(G-9464)**

Chestnut Ridge LLC.....................................717 354-5741
475 Voganville Rd New Holland (17557) **(G-12232)**

Chestnut Vly Ctrl Systems LLC..........................717 330-2356
1470 S Colebrook Rd Manheim (17545) **(G-10376)**

Chests Unlimited, Morgantown *Also called David Esh* **(G-11521)**

Cheu Noodle Bar...267 639-4136
255 S 10th St Philadelphia (19107) **(G-13540)**

Chevron Ae Resources LLC..............................724 662-0300
101 Mcquiston Dr Jackson Center (16133) **(G-8226)**

Chevron USA Inc...412 262-2830
700 Cherrington Pkwy Coraopolis (15108) **(G-3677)**

CHI Signs & Designs Inc................................412 517-8691
387 Plum St Oakmont (15139) **(G-12915)**

Chiampi's Bakery, Scranton *Also called Pittston Baking Co Inc* **(G-17272)**

Chicago Rivet & Machine Co.............................814 684-2430
2728 Adams Ave Tyrone (16686) **(G-18580)**

Chick Machine Company LLC............................724 352-3330
118 Chick Ln Butler (16002) **(G-2388)**

Chick Wrkholding Solutions Inc.........................724 772-1644
500 Keystone Dr Warrendale (15086) **(G-19070)**

Chicopee Inc...800 835-2442
700 Mountain View Dr Smithfield (15478) **(G-17647)**

Chicopee Specialty Products, Smithfield *Also called Chicopee Inc* **(G-17647)**

Chief Fire..484 356-5316
1416 Phoenixville Pike West Chester (19380) **(G-19524)**

Chief Fire and Rescue, Downingtown *Also called Chief Technologies LLC* **(G-4220)**

Chief Technologies LLC..................................484 693-0750
3947 W Lincoln Hwy Downingtown (19335) **(G-4220)**

Child Evngelism Fellowship Inc..........................215 837-6324
4730 Chestnut St Philadelphia (19139) **(G-13541)**

Child Evngelism Fellowship Inc..........................724 463-1600
571 Felgar Rd Somerset (15501) **(G-17679)**

Child Evngelism Fellowship Inc..........................724 339-4825
Findley St Apollo (15613) **(G-669)**

Childcraft Education Corp................................717 653-7500
1156 Four Star Dr Mount Joy (17552) **(G-11649)**

Chilewski Flagstone.....................................570 756-3096
Lakeview Rd Susquehanna (18847) **(G-18179)**

Chill Frozen Desserts...................................724 695-8855
420 Penn Lincoln Dr Imperial (15126) **(G-8060)**

Chiltern International Inc................................484 679-2400
1016 W 9th Ave Ste 300 King of Prussia (19406) **(G-8592)**

Chima Inc (PA)..610 372-6508
1149 Bern Rd Reading (19610) **(G-16345)**

Chimneys Violin Shop....................................717 258-3203
614 Lerew Rd Fl 2 Boiling Springs (17007) **(G-1872)**

China Lenox Incorporated................................267 525-7800
1414 Radcliffe St Bristol (19007) **(G-2125)**

Chipblaster Inc..814 724-6278
13605 S Mosiertown Rd Meadville (16335) **(G-10712)**

Chippewa Twp Sewage Plant.............................724 846-3820
701 Constitution Blvd Beaver Falls (15010) **(G-998)**

Chitra Publications.....................................570 278-1984
2 Public Ave Montrose (18801) **(G-11462)**

Chiyoda America Inc.....................................610 286-3100
378 Thousand Oaks Blvd Morgantown (19543) **(G-11520)**

Chloe Textiles Incorporated.............................717 848-2800
135 N George St Ste 203 York (17401) **(G-20425)**

Choccobutter Inc..717 756-5590
1492 Maplewood Dr New Cumberland (17070) **(G-12184)**

Chocodiem...908 200-7044
325 Northampton St Easton (18042) **(G-4661)**

Chocolate Creations....................................724 774-7675
3465 Brodhead Rd Ste 4 Monaca (15061) **(G-11288)**

Chocolate Creations....................................570 383-9931
1520 Pennsylvania Ave Peckville (18452) **(G-13207)**

Chocolatecovers Ltd Inc................................717 534-1992
506 W Caracas Ave Hershey (17033) **(G-7606)**

Choice Auto Sales, Murrysville *Also called Murrysville Auto LLC* **(G-11860)**

Choice Cleangear LLC...................................610 497-9756
369 Turner Industrial Way Aston (19014) **(G-754)**

Choice Granite and Marble LLC..........................412 821-3900
803 Geyer Rd Ste 1 Pittsburgh (15212) **(G-14848)**

Choice Marketing Inc....................................610 494-1270
369 Turner Industrial Way Aston (19014) **(G-755)**

Choice Precision Machine Inc............................610 502-1111
4380 Commerce Dr Whitehall (18052) **(G-19865)**

Choice Therapeutics Inc.................................508 384-0425
2150 Cabot Blvd W Ste B Langhorne (19047) **(G-9284)**

Choice Tool...814 474-4656
483 Dorothy Ave Fairview (16415) **(G-5815)**

Choice Wood, Titusville *Also called Weaber Inc* **(G-18403)**

Choo R Choo Snacks Inc................................717 273-7499
1547 Joel Dr Lebanon (17046) **(G-9554)**

Choose Blackstone LLC..................................570 754-7800
285 Blue Mountain Rd Schuylkill Haven (17972) **(G-17152)**

Chop - Rite Two Inc....................................215 256-4620
531 Old Skippack Rd Harleysville (19438) **(G-7027)**

Chowns Fabrication Rigging Inc.........................610 584-0240
2053 Cressman Rd Skippack (19474) **(G-17595)**

Chris Candies Inc.......................................412 322-9400
1557 Spring Garden Ave Pittsburgh (15212) **(G-14849)**

Chris Machine Co Inc...................................215 348-1229
110 Doyle St Doylestown (18901) **(G-4292)**

Chris S Sensenig..717 423-5311
1033 Ridge Rd Shippensburg (17257) **(G-17522)**

Chrisber Corporation....................................800 872-7436
705 E Union St West Chester (19382) **(G-19525)**

Christian W Klay Winery Inc.............................724 439-3424
412 Fayette Springs Rd Chalk Hill (15421) **(G-2895)**

Christiansbrunn Die Fmlies Der..........................570 425-2548
75 Grove Rd Pitman (17964) **(G-14621)**

Christiansen Memorials, Montgomeryville *Also called Edward T Christiansen & Sons* **(G-11393)**

Christini Awd Mtcyc Mtn Bikes, Philadelphia *Also called Christini Technologies Inc* **(G-13542)**

Christini Technologies Inc................................215 351-9895
611 N 2nd St Philadelphia (19123) **(G-13542)**

Christman Awning Company, Pittsburgh *Also called Rose A Rupp* **(G-15496)**

Christmas City Printing Co Inc..........................610 868-5844
861 14th Ave Bethlehem (18018) **(G-1483)**

Christmas City Spirits LLC..............................484 893-0590
564 Main St Bethlehem (18018) **(G-1484)**

Christopher Co Ltd......................................215 331-8290
8701 Torresdale Ave Ste Q Philadelphia (19136) **(G-13543)**

A
L
P
H
A
B
E
T
I
C

Christopher Gans 610 353-8585
  2343 W Chester Pike Broomall (19008) *(G-2282)*
Christopher Resources Inc 724 430-9610
  682 W Main St Uniontown (15401) *(G-18620)*
Chroma Acrylics Inc 717 626-8866
  205 Bucky Dr Lititz (17543) *(G-9998)*
Chroma Graphics 724 693-9050
  1200 Mckee Rd Oakdale (15071) *(G-12896)*
Chromagen Vision LLC 610 628-2941
  326 W Cedar St Ste 1 Kennett Square (19348) *(G-8505)*
Chromaglass Inc 724 325-1437
  1201 Randall Ct Export (15632) *(G-5594)*
Chromalox Inc (HQ) 412 967-3800
  103 Gamma Dr Ste 2 Pittsburgh (15238) *(G-14850)*
Chromatan Corporation 617 529-0784
  727 Norristown Rd Bldg 3 Ambler (19002) *(G-573)*
Chrono-Log Corp 610 853-1130
  2 W Park Rd Havertown (19083) *(G-7418)*
Chrysler Encpsulated Seals Inc 570 319-1694
  11 Skyline Dr E Ste 1 S Abingtn Twp (18411) *(G-16891)*
Chucks Salsa 724 513-5708
  917 3rd St Baden (15005) *(G-870)*
Church & Dwight Co Inc 717 781-8800
  5197 Commerce Dr York (17408) *(G-20426)*
Church Communities PA Inc 724 329-8573
  Rr Box 381n Farmington (15437) *(G-5860)*
Church Publishing Incorporated 212 592-4229
  4475 Linglestown Rd Harrisburg (17112) *(G-7104)*
Churchtowne Cabinetry 717 354-6682
  281 Gehman Rd Narvon (17555) *(G-11918)*
Churchville Mech Assoc LLC 267 231-5968
  1080 Industrial Blvd # 1 Southampton (18966) *(G-17803)*
Ci Medical Technologies Inc (HQ) 724 537-9600
  149 Devereux Dr Latrobe (15650) *(G-9465)*
Cianflone Scientific LLC (PA) 412 787-3600
  135 Industry Dr Pittsburgh (15275) *(G-14851)*
Cibo Media Group LLC 215 732-6700
  1525 Locust St Ste 1201 Philadelphia (19102) *(G-13544)*
Cibrone B & Sons Bakery, Pittsburgh *Also called M Cibrone & Sons Bakery Inc (G-15244)*
Cicci Dance Supply Inc 724 348-7359
  2528 State Route 88 Finleyville (15332) *(G-5953)*
Cid Associates Inc 724 353-0300
  730 Ekastown Rd Sarver (16055) *(G-17066)*
Cider Press Woodworks LLC 215 804-1100
  585 Old Bethlehem Rd Quakertown (18951) *(G-16178)*
Cider Press Woodworks LLC 215 804-0880
  2320 Trumbauersville Rd Quakertown (18951) *(G-16179)*
Cieco Inc 412 262-5581
  2401 Hookstown Grade Rd Clinton (15026) *(G-3261)*
Cigar N More 717 541-1341
  3830 Union Deposit Rd Harrisburg (17109) *(G-7105)*
Cigarette Express, Erie *Also called Klafters Inc (G-5346)*
Cigas Machine Shop Inc 610 384-5239
  1245 Manor Rd Coatesville (19320) *(G-3296)*
Cima Labs Inc (HQ) 763 488-4700
  1090 Horsham Rd North Wales (19454) *(G-12795)*
Cima Labs Inc 763 315-4178
  1090 Horsham Rd North Wales (19454) *(G-12796)*
Cima Network Inc 267 308-0575
  121 New Britain Blvd Chalfont (18914) *(G-2866)*
Cima Technology Inc 724 733-2627
  480 Davidson Rd Pittsburgh (15239) *(G-14852)*
Cimarron Energy 724 801-8517
  1700 Sleepy Hollow Rd Indiana (15701) *(G-8086)*
Cimberio Valve Co Inc 610 560-0802
  100 Quaker Ln Malvern (19355) *(G-10208)*
Cincinnatus Group 724 600-0221
  305 S Maple Ave Fl 1 Greensburg (15601) *(G-6658)*
Cinemaplex Technologies Corp 610 935-8366
  238 Ridge Rd Spring City (19475) *(G-17857)*
Cingle Brothers Machine Shop 814 387-4994
  105 Dairy St Clarence (16829) *(G-3163)*
Cini Garment Sales Co, Plumsteadville *Also called Ed Cini Enterprises Inc (G-15809)*
Cinram Manufacturing 570 383-3291
  1400 E Lackawanna St Olyphant (18448) *(G-12986)*
Cintas Corporation No 2 ....440 352-4003
  4734 Pittsburgh Ave Erie (16509) *(G-5224)*
Cintas Corporation No 2 ....724 696-5640
  320 Westec Dr Mount Pleasant (15666) *(G-11692)*
Cipco Industries LLC 215 785-2976
  956 Washington Ave Croydon (19021) *(G-3913)*
Cir-Cut Corporation 215 324-1000
  4315 N 4th St Philadelphia (19140) *(G-13545)*
Cir-Q-Tek, Bristol *Also called Monach Associates Inc (G-2169)*
Circa Healthcare LLC 610 954-2340
  10 Valley Stream Pkwy # 201 Malvern (19355) *(G-10209)*
Circadiance LLC 724 858-2837
  1300 Rodi Rd Turtle Creek (15145) *(G-18562)*
Circle Manufacturing Company 570 585-2139
  995 Griffin Pond Rd S Abingtn Twp (18411) *(G-16892)*

Circuit Design Center, The, Wexford *Also called Pixel Innovations Inc (G-19821)*
Circuit Foil Trading Inc 215 887-7255
  115 E Glenside Ave Ste 8 Glenside (19038) *(G-6511)*
Ciright Automation LLC 855 247-4448
  7 Union Hill Rd Conshohocken (19428) *(G-3528)*
Cisco Systems Inc 814 789-2990
  30910 Dobie Ln Guys Mills (16327) *(G-6809)*
Cisco Systems Inc 610 695-6000
  301 Lindenwood Dr Ste 210 Malvern (19355) *(G-10210)*
Cisco Systems Inc 610 336-8500
  7540 Windsor Dr Allentown (18195) *(G-170)*
CIT, Hadley *Also called Component Intrtechnologies Inc (G-6816)*
Citadelle 610 777-8844
  400 Pennsylvania Ave Shillington (19607) *(G-17503)*
Citgo, Luzerne *Also called On Fuel (G-10128)*
Citgo, Danville *Also called On Fuel (G-4008)*
Citi Fuel Convenience Inc 215 724-2395
  6301 Dicks Ave Philadelphia (19142) *(G-13546)*
Citi Prepaid Services, Conshohocken *Also called Wirecard North America Inc (G-3617)*
Citizen 412 766-6679
  535 Citizens Way Pittsburgh (15202) *(G-14853)*
Citizen Publishing Company 570 454-5911
  262 N Cedar St Hazleton (18201) *(G-7495)*
Citizen Standard, Valley View *Also called The Scranton Times L P (G-18718)*
Citizens Voice, Wilkes Barre *Also called The Scranton Times L P (G-19965)*
Citizens Voice 570 821-2000
  75 N Washington St Wilkes Barre (18701) *(G-19912)*
Citterio U.S.A. Corporation, Freeland *Also called Euro Foods Inc (G-6194)*
City Brewing 724 532-5454
  100 33rd St Latrobe (15650) *(G-9466)*
City Btlg Co of New Kensington 724 335-3350
  1820 5th Ave New Kensington (15068) *(G-12334)*
City Engraving & Awards LLC 215 731-0200
  1220 Walnut St Philadelphia (19107) *(G-13547)*
City Limits Ice Cream, Titusville *Also called Steffees (G-18397)*
City of New Castle 724 654-1627
  110 E Washington St New Castle (16101) *(G-12073)*
City of Pittsburgh 412 255-2883
  414 Grant St Ste 301 Pittsburgh (15219) *(G-14854)*
City of Pittsburgh 412 255-2330
  414 Grant St Ste 502 Pittsburgh (15219) *(G-14855)*
City of Washington 724 225-4883
  25 Old Scales Rd Washington (15301) *(G-19156)*
City Paper, Scranton *Also called The Scranton Times L P (G-17299)*
City Paper of Baltimore, Scranton *Also called The Scranton Times L P (G-17298)*
City Shirt Co 570 874-4251
  242 Industrial Park Rd Frackville (17931) *(G-6104)*
City Sign Service Inc 800 523-4452
  424 Caredean Dr Ste A Horsham (19044) *(G-7804)*
City Suburban News 610 667-6623
  857 Montgomery Ave Fl 2 Penn Valley (19072) *(G-13234)*
Citywide Exclusive Newsppr Inc 215 467-8214
  732 Federal St Phila (19147) *(G-13309)*
Civic Mapper LLC 315 729-7869
  2014 Lacrosse St Pittsburgh (15218) *(G-14856)*
Civitas Media, Wilkes Barre *Also called Wilkes-Barre Publishing Co Inc (G-19977)*
Civitas Media LLC 570 829-7100
  90 E Market St Wilkes Barre (18701) *(G-19913)*
Ciw Enterprises Inc (PA) 800 233-8366
  24 Elmwood Ave Mountain Top (18707) *(G-11755)*
CJ Optical Holdings LLC 610 264-8537
  201 Lehigh Valley Mall Whitehall (18052) *(G-19866)*
CJ Packaging Inc 570 209-7836
  590 Rocky Glen Rd Avoca (18641) *(G-841)*
Cjc Contract Packaging Inc 570 209-7836
  590 Rocky Glen Rd Avoca (18641) *(G-842)*
CK Construction & Indus Inc (PA) 570 286-4128
  308 Valley Rd Pitman (17964) *(G-14622)*
CK Manufacturing LLC 717 442-8912
  330 Millwood Rd Lancaster (17603) *(G-8978)*
CK Replacement Stalls, Lancaster *Also called CK Manufacturing LLC (G-8978)*
CK Sportswear, Ephrata *Also called C K Sportwear Inc (G-5094)*
CK Stone LLC 570 903-5868
  69 Vago Rd Tunkhannock (18657) *(G-18534)*
CK Tool & Die Inc 814 836-9600
  3214 W 22nd St Erie (16506) *(G-5225)*
Ckl Augering Inc 724 479-0213
  129 Mazza St Homer City (15748) *(G-7673)*
CL Logging Inc 814 842-3725
  4255 Hyndman Rd Hyndman (15545) *(G-8048)*
Cla Industries Inc 724 858-7112
  1358 Poplar St Oakdale (15071) *(G-12897)*
Clair Bros Audio Entps Inc (PA) 717 626-4000
  1 Clair Blvd Manheim (17545) *(G-10377)*
Clair D Thompson & Sons Inc 570 398-1880
  400 Allegheny St Jersey Shore (17740) *(G-8311)*
Clairon News, Clarion *Also called Western PA Newsppr Co (G-3187)*

Clairton Slag Inc 412 384-8420
  1000 Madison Ave West Elizabeth (15088) *(G-19693)*

Clapper Enterprises Inc 570 368-3327
  701 1st Ste 101 Williamsport (17701) *(G-19998)*

Clapper Leon Plbg Htg Wtr Cond 570 629-2833
  425 Neyhart Rd Stroudsburg (18360) *(G-18110)*

Clarance J Venne Inc 215 547-7110
  6300 Mcpherson St Levittown (19057) *(G-9825)*

Clarcor Air Filtration Pdts 570 602-6274
  1001 Sathers Dr Pittston (18640) *(G-15745)*

Clarence J Venne LLC 215 547-7110
  7900 N Radcliffe St Ste 4 Bristol (19007) *(G-2126)*

Clarence Larkin Estate 215 576-5590
  2641 Mount Carmel Ave Glenside (19038) *(G-6512)*

Clarion Bathware Inc 814 782-3016
  16273 Route 208 Marble (16334) *(G-10435)*

Clarion Bathware Inc (PA) 814 226-5374
  44 Amsler Ave Shippenville (16254) *(G-17556)*

Clarion Bathware Inc 814 782-3016
  16273 Route 208 Marble (16334) *(G-10436)*

Clarion Boards, Shippenville *Also called Clarion Industries LLC (G-17558)*

Clarion Boards LLC 814 226-0851
  143 Fiberboard Rd Shippenville (16254) *(G-17557)*

Clarion Industries LLC (PA) 814 226-0851
  11120 Route 322 Shippenville (16254) *(G-17558)*

Clarion Laminates LLC 814 226-8032
  301 Fiberboard Rd Shippenville (16254) *(G-17559)*

Clarion Printing - Litho 814 226-9453
  645 Main St Clarion (16214) *(G-3173)*

Clarion River Brewing Co 814 297-8399
  600 Main St Clarion (16214) *(G-3174)*

Clarion Safety Systems LLC 570 296-5686
  190 Old Milford Rd Milford (18337) *(G-11157)*

Clarion Sintered Metals Inc 814 773-3124
  3472 Montmorenci Rd Ridgway (15853) *(G-16699)*

Clarivate Analytics (us) LLC (HQ) 215 386-0100
  1500 Spring Garden St # 400 Philadelphia (19130) *(G-13548)*

Clark Candies Inc 724 226-0866
  621 E 1st Ave Tarentum (15084) *(G-18239)*

Clark Deco Moldings Inc 412 363-9602
  1127 Washington Blvd Pittsburgh (15206) *(G-14857)*

Clark F Burger Inc 610 681-4762
  Off Rte 534 Kresgeville (18333) *(G-8820)*

Clark Filter Inc (HQ) 717 285-5941
  3649 Hempland Rd Lancaster (17601) *(G-8979)*

Clark H Ream Lumber 814 445-8185
  221 Salem Ave Somerset (15501) *(G-17680)*

Clark Industrial Supply Inc 610 705-3333
  301 W High St Pottstown (19464) *(G-15970)*

Clark Metal Products Inc 724 459-7550
  100 Serrell Dr Blairsville (15717) *(G-1719)*

Clark Traffic Control Inc 724 388-4023
  10125 Route 56 Hwy E Homer City (15748) *(G-7674)*

Clarke Container Inc 814 452-4848
  1513 Grimm Dr Erie (16501) *(G-5226)*

Clarke System 610 434-9889
  1857 W Walnut St Allentown (18104) *(G-171)*

Clarks Expert Sales & Service 570 321-8206
  1919 Lycoming Creek Rd Williamsport (17701) *(G-19999)*

Clarks Feed Mills Inc 570 648-4351
  19 Mountain Rd Shamokin (17872) *(G-17423)*

Clarkson Chemical Company Inc 570 323-3631
  213 Main St Williamsport (17702) *(G-20000)*

Classic Bedding Mfg Co Inc 800 810-0930
  10212 Old State Rd Conneaut Lake (16316) *(G-3470)*

Classic Brand Marketing, Philadelphia *Also called Bb and CC Inc (G-13448)*

Classic Caramel Co The, Ebensburg *Also called Lukas Confections Inc (G-4787)*

Classic Furniture (PA) 717 738-0088
  546c E 28th Division Hwy Lititz (17543) *(G-9999)*

Classic Ink USA LLC 724 482-1727
  556 S Benbrook Rd Butler (16001) *(G-2389)*

Classic Metal 724 991-2659
  311 Perry St Prospect (16052) *(G-16111)*

Classic Shotshell Co Inc 570 553-1651
  784 Turnpike Rd Friendsville (18818) *(G-6229)*

Classic Tool Inc 814 763-4805
  236 Grant St Saegertown (16433) *(G-16911)*

Classified Advertising 814 723-1400
  205 Pennsylvania Ave W Warren (16365) *(G-19016)*

Classroom Salon LLC 412 621-6287
  461 Melwood Ave Pittsburgh (15213) *(G-14858)*

Claudes Creamery 610 826-2663
  289 Delaware Ave Palmerton (18071) *(G-13103)*

Claylick Enterprises LLC 717 328-9876
  10278 Clay Lick Rd Mercersburg (17236) *(G-10983)*

Claylick Fabrication, Mercersburg *Also called Claylick Enterprises LLC (G-10983)*

Claypoole Hex Signs 610 562-8911
  227 Schock Rd Lenhartsville (19534) *(G-9757)*

Clayton Kendall Inc (PA) 412 798-7120
  167 Dexter Dr Monroeville (15146) *(G-11327)*

CLB Logging 814 784-3301
  323 Rock Hill Church Rd Clearville (15535) *(G-3240)*

Clean Concepts Group LLC 908 229-8812
  31 Beidler Dr Washington Crossing (18977) *(G-19254)*

Clean Energy Htg Systems LLC 888 519-2347
  625 Todd Rd Honey Brook (19344) *(G-7742)*

Clean Power Resources Inc 724 863-3768
  13031 State Route 30 Irwin (15642) *(G-8148)*

Clean World Industries Inc 724 962-0720
  4835 Anne Ln Hermitage (16148) *(G-7578)*

Clear Align LLC (PA) 484 956-0510
  2550 Boulevard Of The Gen Eagleville (19403) *(G-4512)*

Clear Creek Industries Inc 814 834-9880
  85 Stackpole St Saint Marys (15857) *(G-16954)*

Clear Gear, Norristown *Also called On Track Enterprises Inc (G-12699)*

Clear Lake Lumber Inc (PA) 800 237-1191
  409 Main St Spartansburg (16434) *(G-17847)*

Clear Microwave Inc 610 844-6421
  5 Great Valley Pkwy # 210 Malvern (19355) *(G-10211)*

Clear Visions Inc 717 236-4526
  2220 Chestnut St Apt 1 Harrisburg (17104) *(G-7106)*

Cleararmor Solutions Corp 610 816-0101
  519 Easton Rd Riegelsville (18077) *(G-16744)*

Clearcount Med Solutions Inc 412 931-7233
  101 Bellevue Rd Ste 300 Pittsburgh (15229) *(G-14859)*

Clearfield Energy Inc 610 293-0410
  101 E Matsonford Rd Conshohocken (19428) *(G-3529)*

Clearfield Machine Company 814 765-6544
  520 S 3rd St Clearfield (16830) *(G-3214)*

Clearfield Metal Tech Inc 814 765-7860
  114 Appalachian Dr Clearfield (16830) *(G-3215)*

Clearfield Ohio Holdings Inc (PA) 610 293-0410
  Radnor Corp Ctr Bdg5 40 Radnor (19087) *(G-16291)*

Clearkin Chemical Corp 215 426-7230
  Schiller & Allen Sts Philadelphia (19134) *(G-13549)*

Clearnav Instruments 610 925-0198
  256 Old Kennett Rd Kennett Square (19348) *(G-8506)*

Clearview Mirror and Glass 412 672-4122
  2801 5th Ave McKeesport (15132) *(G-10663)*

Cleftstone Works, The, Kutztown *Also called Princeton Trade Consulting Gro (G-8856)*

Clelan Industries Inc 717 248-5061
  600 Middle Rd Lewistown (17044) *(G-9926)*

Clemens Family Corporation (PA) 800 523-5291
  2700 Clemens Rd Hatfield (19440) *(G-7324)*

Clemens Food Group LLC (HQ) 215 368-2500
  2700 Clemens Rd Hatfield (19440) *(G-7325)*

Clemens Food Group LLC 215 368-2500
  4591 Colebrook Ave Emmaus (18049) *(G-5023)*

Clement Communications Inc (HQ) 610 497-6800
  3 Creek Pkwy Upper Chichester (19061) *(G-18658)*

Clementines 717 626-1378
  695 Sue Dr Lititz (17543) *(G-10000)*

Cleogeo Inc 610 868-7200
  21 E 3rd St Bethlehem (18015) *(G-1485)*

Cleveland Brothers Eqp Co Inc 717 564-2121
  5300 Paxton St Harrisburg (17111) *(G-7107)*

Cleveland Steel Container Corp 215 536-4477
  350 E Mill St Quakertown (18951) *(G-16180)*

Clever Advertising and Prtg, Waynesboro *Also called Clever Inc (G-19404)*

Clever Inc 717 762-7508
  809 S Potomac St Waynesboro (17268) *(G-19404)*

Clickcadence LLC 412 434-4911
  425 1st Ave Fl 1 Pittsburgh (15219) *(G-14860)*

Clickett,, Titusville *Also called Richard J Clickett Inc (G-18391)*

Clicks Document Management, Pittsburgh *Also called Marcus Uppe Inc (G-15254)*

Clicks Professional Copy Svc, Pittsburgh *Also called Marcus Uppe Inc (G-15253)*

Clifford Cnc Tling Surgeon LLC 717 528-4264
  1232 E Berlin Rd New Oxford (17350) *(G-12406)*

Cliffstar LLC 814 725-3801
  63 Wall St North East (16428) *(G-12735)*

Cliffstar North East, North East *Also called Cliffstar LLC (G-12735)*

Clifton Custom Furn & Design 724 727-2045
  4716 State Route 66 Apollo (15613) *(G-670)*

Clifton Machining Division, Lake City *Also called Great Lakes Automtn Svcs Inc (G-8901)*

Clifton Tube Cutting Inc 724 588-3241
  93 Werner Rd Greenville (16125) *(G-6739)*

Climatic Testing Systems Inc (PA) 215 773-9322
  2367 N Penn Rd Ste 100 Hatfield (19440) *(G-7326)*

Cline Oil Inc 814 368-5395
  1 Longfellow Ave Bradford (16701) *(G-1961)*

Clinical Supplies MGT LLC 215 596-4356
  300 Technology Dr Malvern (19355) *(G-10212)*

Clinton Controls Inc 570 748-4042
  860 Woodward Ave Lock Haven (17745) *(G-10086)*

Clinton County Cabinetry, Mill Hall *Also called Renningers Cabinetree Inc (G-11181)*

Clinton Industries Inc 717 848-2391
  525 E Market St York (17403) *(G-20427)*

Clinton Pallet Company Inc (PA) 570 753-3010
  51 Municipal Dr Jersey Shore (17740) *(G-8312)*

Clinton Press Inc.....................................814 455-9089
500 W 12th St Erie (16501) (G-5227)

Clipper Magazine LLC (HQ).....................717 569-5100
3708 Hempland Rd Mountville (17554) (G-11791)

Clipper Pipe & Service Inc.......................610 872-9067
11a Eddystone Indl Park Eddystone (19022) (G-4799)

Clln Directional Drilling Inc......................814 460-0248
37016 State Highway 77 Centerville (16404) (G-2833)

Clockwise Tees.......................................412 727-1602
400 N Lexington St Pittsburgh (15208) (G-14861)

Clore Enterprise.....................................724 745-0673
19 W Pike St Houston (15342) (G-7871)

Closet Cases..570 262-9092
44 Bluebell Ln Jim Thorpe (18229) (G-8338)

Closet City Ltd.......................................215 855-4400
352 Godshall Dr Ste A Harleysville (19438) (G-7028)

Closet Factory, Fleetwood Also called P A Office and Closet Systems (G-5977)

Closet Space...610 359-0583
2610 Oriole Rd Broomall (19008) (G-2283)

Closet Works Inc....................................215 675-6430
160 Commerce Dr Montgomeryville (18936) (G-11388)

Closet-Tier (PA)......................................412 421-7838
2811 Shady Ave Pittsburgh (15217) (G-14862)

Closets & Cabinetry By Closet, Harleysville Also called Closet City Ltd (G-7028)

Closson Press, Apollo Also called Marietta Closson (G-683)

Clothes-Pin..215 888-5784
2124 Spring St Philadelphia (19103) (G-13550)

Cloud Chemistry LLC...............................570 851-1680
4543 Milford Rd Ste 50 East Stroudsburg (18302) (G-4609)

Clover Farms Dairy Company (PA)..............610 921-9111
3300 Pottsville Pike Reading (19605) (G-16346)

Clover Farms Transportation Co................610 921-9111
3300 Pottsville Pike Reading (19612) (G-16347)

Clover Hill Enterprises Inc (PA)..................610 395-2468
9850 Newtown Rd Breinigsville (18031) (G-2012)

Clover Hill Vineyards & Winery, Breinigsville Also called Clover Hill Enterprises Inc (G-2012)

Clover Technologies Group LLC..................818 407-7500
301 National Rd Exton (19341) (G-5662)

Cloverleaf Alpacas (PA)...........................717 492-0504
1650 Cloverleaf Rd Mount Joy (17552) (G-11650)

Clp Publications Inc................................215 567-5080
2300 Chestnut St Ste 200 Philadelphia (19103) (G-13551)

Club Coin Boards Inc..............................570 473-0429
616 Susquehanna Trl Northumberland (17857) (G-12866)

Club, The, Sharon Also called Winner International Inc (G-17448)

Clymer Quality Hardwood.........................724 463-1827
15 Rayne Run Rd Clymer (15728) (G-3271)

CM Industries Inc...................................717 336-4545
158 Hamilton Rd Lancaster (17603) (G-8980)

CM Technologies Corporation....................412 262-0734
1026 4th Ave Coraopolis (15108) (G-3678)

CMA Refinishing Solutions Inc...................215 427-1141
1731 Tilghman St Philadelphia (19122) (G-13552)

CMC Defense Products, Chicora Also called Aht Inc (G-3125)

CMC Joist & Deck, New Columbia Also called C M C Steel Fabricators Inc (G-12173)

CMC Products, Easton Also called California Med Innovations LLC (G-4660)

CMCI, Dallastown Also called Charleston Marine Cntrs Inc (G-3973)

Cmd, West Grove Also called Custom Machine & Design Inc (G-19699)

Cmg Process Inc....................................724 962-8717
2659 Lake Rd Clark (16113) (G-3188)

CMI, Malvern Also called Copy Management Inc (G-10217)

CMI, Hadley Also called Controlled Molding Inc (G-6817)

CMI America Inc.....................................814 897-7000
5300 Knowledge Pkwy # 101 Erie (16510) (G-5228)

CMI Printgraphix Inc...............................717 697-4567
937 Nixon Dr Ste 2 Mechanicsburg (17055) (G-10827)

CMI Systems...215 596-0306
3601 Market St Unit 1605 Philadelphia (19104) (G-13553)

Cmmunications U Krienr-Ptthoff..................484 547-5261
6970 Beech Cir Macungie (18062) (G-10144)

Cmpressed A Zeks Solutions LLC................610 692-9100
1302 Goshen Pkwy West Chester (19380) (G-19526)

CMR USA Inc (PA)...................................724 452-2200
940 Riverside Pl Leetsdale (15056) (G-9689)

CMS East Inc (PA)..................................724 527-6700
400 Agnew Rd Jeannette (15644) (G-8250)

CMS Orthotic Lab LLC.............................717 329-9301
405 N East St Ste 110 Carlisle (17013) (G-2700)

Cmsjlp LLC...814 834-2817
103 Bridge St Ridgway (15853) (G-16700)

Cmu Robotics..412 681-6900
10 40th St Pittsburgh (15201) (G-14863)

Cmw Stainless, Telford Also called Cmw Technologies Inc (G-18274)

Cmw Technologies Inc.............................215 721-5824
841 Tech Dr Telford (18969) (G-18274)

Cnc Malting Company..............................570 954-4500
719 Clearfield Rd Fenelton (16034) (G-5944)

Cnc Manufacturing Inc.............................610 444-4437
131 Birch St Coatesville (19320) (G-3297)

Cnc Metalworks Inc.................................717 624-8436
45 Pine Run Rd New Oxford (17350) (G-12407)

Cnc Specialties Mfg Inc...........................724 727-5680
760 Pine Run Rd Apollo (15613) (G-671)

Cnc Technology Inc.................................610 444-4437
131 Birch St Coatesville (19320) (G-3298)

CNE Machinery Ltd..................................814 723-1685
4 E Harmar St Warren (16365) (G-19017)

CNG Mtor Fuels Clarion Cnty LP.................814 590-4498
5349 Route 36 Coolspring (15730) (G-3621)

CNG One Source Inc...............................814 673-4980
190 Oak Grove Cir Franklin (16323) (G-6120)

Cnh Inc..717 355-1121
500 Diller Ave New Holland (17557) (G-12233)

Cnh Industrial America LLC.......................262 636-6011
7100 Durand Ave Ste 300 Lancaster (17604) (G-8981)

Cnh Industrial America LLC.......................800 501-5711
535 500 Diller Ave New Holland (17557) (G-12234)

Cnh Industrial America LLC.......................717 355-1121
500 Diller Ave New Holland (17557) (G-12235)

Cnh Industrial America LLC.......................717 355-1902
200 George Delp Rd New Holland (17557) (G-12236)

Cnh Industrial Capital's, New Holland Also called Cnh Industrial America LLC (G-12234)

Cnhi LLC..814 781-1596
245 Brusselles St Saint Marys (15857) (G-16955)

Cni Inc...215 244-9650
1683b Winchester Rd Bensalem (19020) (G-1169)

CNT Fixture Company Inc.........................412 443-6260
1600 William Flynn Hwy Glenshaw (15116) (G-6484)

CNT Motion Systems Inc..........................412 244-5770
1600 William Flynn Hwy Glenshaw (15116) (G-6485)

Cnx Gas Company LLC (HQ).....................724 485-4000
1000 Consol Energy Dr Canonsburg (15317) (G-2559)

Cnx Gas Corporation (HQ)........................724 485-4000
1000 Consol Energy Dr Canonsburg (15317) (G-2560)

Cnx Land LLC..724 485-4000
1000 Consol Energy Dr Canonsburg (15317) (G-2561)

Cnx Resources Corporation (PA)................724 485-4000
1000 Consol Energy Dr Canonsburg (15317) (G-2562)

Co Optics Inc...610 478-1884
1802 Papermill Rd Reading (19610) (G-16348)

Co-Ax Valves Inc....................................215 757-3725
1518 Grundy Ln Bristol (19007) (G-2127)

Coach, Gettysburg Also called Gettysburg Village Factory Str (G-6294)

Coach Inc...215 659-6158
2500 W Mrland Rd Ste 2065 Willow Grove (19090) (G-20112)

Coach Built Press, Philadelphia Also called Michael Furman Photography (G-14020)

Coal Centrifuge Service...........................724 478-4205
700 Old State Rd Apollo (15613) (G-672)

Coal Contractors (1991) Inc......................570 450-5086
100 Hazle Brook Rd Hazle Township (18201) (G-7449)

Coal Contractors 1991, Hazle Township Also called Denis Bell Inc (G-7451)

Coal Innovations LLC..............................814 893-5790
1134 Stoystown Rd Friedens (15541) (G-6219)

Coal Loaders Inc....................................724 238-6601
210 E Main St Ligonier (15658) (G-9958)

Coalisland Cast Stone Inc........................610 476-1683
1670 Shefley Ln Collegeville (19426) (G-3372)

Coalview Recovery Group LLC...................814 443-6454
1166 Village Rd Somerset (15501) (G-17681)

Coastal Defense......................................570 858-1139
360 Proctor St Lock Haven (17745) (G-10087)

Coastal Forest Resources Co....................814 654-7111
43647 Fairview Rd Spartansburg (16434) (G-17848)

Coastal Treated Products Co.....................610 932-5100
385 Waterway Rd Oxford (19363) (G-13075)

Coates Electrographics Inc.......................570 675-1131
555 Country Club Rd Dallas (18612) (G-3960)

Coates Toners, Dallas Also called Toner Holdings LLC (G-3969)

Coatesville Scrap Ir Met Inc......................610 384-9230
1000 S 1st Ave Coatesville (19320) (G-3299)

Coatesvlle Coca Cola Btlg Wrks.................610 384-4343
299 Boot Rd Ste 200 Downingtown (19335) (G-4221)

Coating & Converting Tech Corp.................215 271-0610
80 E Morris St Philadelphia (19148) (G-13554)

Coating Concepts LLC.............................717 240-0010
405 N East St Ste 100 Carlisle (17013) (G-2701)

Coating Development Group Inc.................215 426-6216
Schiller & Allen St Philadelphia (19134) (G-13555)

Coating Innovations LLC..........................412 269-0100
900 Commerce Dr Ste 908 Coraopolis (15108) (G-3679)

Coating Technology Inc...........................610 296-7722
26 N Bacton Hill Rd B Malvern (19355) (G-10213)

Coax Incorporated..................................717 227-0045
4217 Fissels Church Rd Glen Rock (17327) (G-6454)

Cobalt Computers, Schnecksville Also called Element 27 Inc (G-17139)

Cobalt Computers Inc.............................610 395-3771
5960 Waterfowl Rd Schnecksville (18078) (G-17137)

Cobb & Dabaldo Printing Co 724 942-0544
110 Bremen Ln Canonsburg (15317) *(G-2563)*

Cobham Adv Elec Sol Inc (HQ) 215 996-2000
305 Richardson Rd Lansdale (19446) *(G-9351)*

Cobra Anchors Corp 610 929-5764
504 Mount Laurel Ave Temple (19560) *(G-18326)*

Cobra Wire & Cable Inc 215 674-8773
1800 Byberry Rd Ste 810 Huntingdon Valley (19006) *(G-7970)*

Coca Cola Refreshments US 814 357-8628
217 Aqua Penn Dr Howard (16841) *(G-7887)*

Coca- Cola 412 726-1482
2747 Race St Pittsburgh (15235) *(G-14864)*

Coca-Cola, Pittston *Also called Rochester Coca Cola Bottling* *(G-15782)*

Coca-Cola, Downingtown *Also called Coatesvlle Coca Cola Btlg Wrks* *(G-4221)*

Coca-Cola, Howard *Also called Coca Cola Refreshments US* *(G-7887)*

Coca-Cola, Lemoyne *Also called Rochester Coca Cola Bottling* *(G-9752)*

Coca-Cola, Lancaster *Also called Rochester Coca Cola Bottling* *(G-9190)*

Coca-Cola, Greensburg *Also called Rochester Coca Cola Bottling* *(G-6712)*

Coca-Cola, Ebensburg *Also called Rochester Coca Cola Bottling* *(G-4795)*

Coca-Cola, Erie *Also called Rochester Coca Cola Bottling* *(G-5465)*

Coca-Cola, Houston *Also called Rochester Coca Cola Bottling* *(G-7879)*

Coca-Cola Btlg Co of NY Inc 718 326-3334
725 E Erie Ave Philadelphia (19134) *(G-13556)*

Coca-Cola Btlg Co Pottsville 570 622-6991
243 Snyder Rd Reading (19605) *(G-16349)*

Coca-Cola Btlg of Lehigh Vly 610 866-8020
2150 Industrial Dr Bethlehem (18017) *(G-1486)*

Coca-Cola Company 610 530-3900
7551 Schantz Rd Allentown (18106) *(G-172)*

Coca-Cola Refreshments USA Inc 570 839-6706
Industrial Park Dr Mount Pocono (18344) *(G-11734)*

Cocalico Biologicals Inc 717 336-1990
449 Stevens Rd Reamstown (17567) *(G-16575)*

Cocco Bros 215 334-3816
2745 W Passyunk Ave Philadelphia (19145) *(G-13557)*

Cochecton Mills Inc 570 224-4144
18 Crestmont Dr Honesdale (18431) *(G-7707)*

Cocker-Weber Brush Co 215 723-3880
104 E Broad St Telford (18969) *(G-18275)*

Coder's Print Shop of Brockway, Brockway *Also called Guy Coder* *(G-2227)*

Codi Inc (PA) 717 540-1337
651 E Park Dr Ste 102 Harrisburg (17111) *(G-7108)*

Codi Direct, Harrisburg *Also called Codi Inc* *(G-7108)*

Cody Computer Services Inc 610 326-7476
1005 E High St Pottstown (19464) *(G-15971)*

Cody Well Service 814 726-3542
Block 1385 F Rr 1 Clarendon (16313) *(G-3168)*

Coeptis Pharmaceuticals Inc 724 290-1183
105 Bradford Rd Ste 420 Wexford (15090) *(G-19795)*

Coffee and Tea Exchange Corp 570 445-8778
406 Lackawanna Ave Olyphant (18447) *(G-12987)*

Coffee Cup Publishing 215 887-7365
99 Runnymede Ave Jenkintown (19046) *(G-8282)*

Coffee Cup Studio, Jenkintown *Also called Coffee Cup Publishing* *(G-8282)*

Coflex Inc 570 296-2100
851 Route 6 Shohola (18458) *(G-17578)*

Cogan Wind LLC 570 998-9554
623 Taylor Rd Trout Run (17771) *(G-18513)*

Cognition Therapeutics Inc 412 481-2210
2403 Sidney St Ste 261 Pittsburgh (15203) *(G-14865)*

Cognitive Oprtonal Systems LLC 908 672-4711
3733 Spruce St Rm 408 Philadelphia (19104) *(G-13558)*

COGNOS CORPORATION, Pittsburgh *Also called Cognos Corporation* *(G-14866)*

Cognos Corporation 412 490-9804
4 Penn Ctr W Ste 210 Pittsburgh (15276) *(G-14866)*

Coil Company LLC 610 408-8361
3223 Phoenixville Pike B Malvern (19355) *(G-10214)*

Coil Specialty Co Inc 814 234-7044
60 Decibel Rd Ste 108 State College (16801) *(G-17952)*

Coilplus Inc 215 331-5200
5135 Bleigh Ave Philadelphia (19136) *(G-13559)*

Coinco Inc (PA) 814 425-7407
23727 Us Highway 322 Cochranton (16314) *(G-3337)*

Coinco Inc 814 425-7476
125 High St Cochranton (16314) *(G-3338)*

Cola International LLC 267 977-6700
433 Brister Rd Bensalem (19020) *(G-1170)*

Colburn Orthopedics Inc 814 432-5252
302 Grant St Franklin (16323) *(G-6121)*

Cold Case Beverage LLC 570 388-2297
710 Apple Tree Rd Harding (18643) *(G-7010)*

Cold Comp, Pittsburgh *Also called Maiden Formats Inc* *(G-15248)*

Cold Spring Cabinetry Inc 215 348-8001
4050 Skyron Dr Ste G Doylestown (18902) *(G-4293)*

Cold Stone Creamery, Feasterville Trevose *Also called Bucks Creamery LLC* *(G-5895)*

Cold Stone Creamery, Scranton *Also called Icy Bites Inc* *(G-17242)*

Cole Construction Inc 570 888-5501
27315 Route 220 Milan (18831) *(G-11146)*

Colebrook Chocolate Co LLC 724 628-8383
830 Vanderbilt Rd Connellsville (15425) *(G-3492)*

Colebrook Supply 717 684-6287
1040 Prospect Rd Columbia (17512) *(G-3433)*

Coleman & Schmidt Inc 610 275-0796
843 Cherry St Norristown (19401) *(G-12645)*

Coleman Cable LLC 717 845-5100
160 S Hartman St York (17403) *(G-20428)*

Coleman Water Services 814 382-8004
14022 Coleman Rd Meadville (16335) *(G-10713)*

Colemans, Lebanon *Also called A Archery and Printing Place* *(G-9544)*

Coletech 814 474-3370
6950 Tow Rd Fairview (16415) *(G-5816)*

Colfab Industries LLC 215 768-2135
2522 State Rd Ste A Bensalem (19020) *(G-1171)*

Collective Intelligence Inc 717 545-9234
6 Kacey Ct Ste 203 Mechanicsburg (17055) *(G-10828)*

Colleen Klesh, Warminster *Also called Mk Precision* *(G-18924)*

College Town Inc (PA) 717 532-7354
73 W Burd St Shippensburg (17257) *(G-17523)*

College Town Inc 717 532-3034
17 W Burd St Shippensburg (17257) *(G-17524)*

Collegecart Innovations Inc 215 813-3900
20 Treeline Dr Holland (18966) *(G-7640)*

Collegian Inc 814 865-2531
123 S Burrowes St Ste 200 State College (16801) *(G-17953)*

Collegiate Furnishings Inc (PA) 814 234-1660
1199 E College Ave State College (16801) *(G-17954)*

Colletti, York *Also called Brewers Outlet* *(G-20413)*

Collins Deck Sealing 717 789-3322
121 Indiana Rd Landisburg (17040) *(G-9256)*

Collins Drilling LLC 814 489-3297
1050 Stillwater Rd Sugar Grove (16350) *(G-18144)*

Collins Harper Publishers 570 941-1557
53 Glnmura Nat Blvd 300 Moosic (18507) *(G-11504)*

Collins Pine Company 814 837-6941
W Of Kane Rr 6 Kane (16735) *(G-8461)*

Collins Tool Corporation 717 543-6070
3254 Old Stage Rd Lewistown (17044) *(G-9927)*

Colmetal Incorporated 215 225-1060
944 W Tioga St Philadelphia (19140) *(G-13560)*

Colonial Auto Supply Co (PA) 215 643-3699
135 Commerce Dr Fort Washington (19034) *(G-6065)*

Colonial Candlecrafters 570 524-4556
165 Brookpark Cir Lewisburg (17837) *(G-9900)*

Colonial Concrete Industries 610 279-2102
364 E Church Rd King of Prussia (19406) *(G-8593)*

Colonial Concrete Industries 610 279-2102
364 E Church Rd King of Prussia (19406) *(G-8594)*

Colonial Craft Kitchens Inc (PA) 717 867-1145
344 W Main St Annville (17003) *(G-645)*

Colonial Electric Supply Inc 610 935-2493
41 2nd Ave Phoenixville (19460) *(G-14540)*

Colonial EP LLC 844 376-9374
473 S Henderson Rd King of Prussia (19406) *(G-8595)*

Colonial Furniture Company 570 374-6016
St Frnt Front Freeburg (17827) *(G-6188)*

Colonial Hardwoods & Logging 814 583-5901
384 Evergreen Rd Luthersburg (15848) *(G-10121)*

Colonial Logging 814 583-5901
384 Evergreen Rd Luthersburg (15848) *(G-10122)*

Colonial Machine Company Inc 814 589-7033
140 W State St Pleasantville (16341) *(G-15798)*

Colonial Metal Products Inc 724 346-5550
2350 Quality Ln Hermitage (16148) *(G-7579)*

Colonial Metals Co (PA) 717 684-2311
217 Linden St Columbia (17512) *(G-3434)*

Colonial Press LLC 814 466-3380
500 Torrey Ln Boalsburg (16827) *(G-1865)*

Colonial Road Woodworks LLC 717 354-8998
285 Voganville Rd New Holland (17557) *(G-12237)*

Colonnial Generators, King of Prussia *Also called Colonial EP LLC* *(G-8595)*

Color House Company Ltd 215 322-4310
5 Charter Cir Warminster (18974) *(G-18845)*

Color Impressions Inc 717 872-2666
433 Brook View Dr Millersville (17551) *(G-11210)*

Color Scan LLC 814 949-2032
2000 7th Ave Altoona (16602) *(G-493)*

Coloratura Inc 717 867-1144
544 Louser Rd Lebanon (17042) *(G-9555)*

Colorcon Inc 215 256-7700
275 Ruth Rd Harleysville (19438) *(G-7029)*

Colorcon Inc (HQ) 215 699-7733
420 Moyer Blvd West Point (19486) *(G-19758)*

Colorcon Inc 267 695-7700
171 New Britain Blvd Chalfont (18914) *(G-2867)*

Colorfin LLC 484 646-9900
65 Willow St Kutztown (19530) *(G-8837)*

Colortech Inc 717 450-5416
232 S 9th St Lebanon (17042) *(G-9556)*

A
L
P
H
A
B
E
T
I
C

Colorworks Graphic Svcs Inc...............................610 367-7599
480 County Line Rd Gilbertsville (19525) **(G-6371)**
Colour Technologies, Downingtown *Also called Matthey Johnson Inc* **(G-4240)**
Colours Inc..814 542-4215
10 N Division St Mount Union (17066) **(G-11740)**
Colucci and Co..717 243-5562
200 S Ridge Rd Boiling Springs (17007) **(G-1873)**
Columbia Boiler Co, Schuylkill Haven *Also called Vari Corporation* **(G-17169)**
Columbia Boiler Company....................................610 323-9200
390 Old Reading Pike Pottstown (19464) **(G-15972)**
Columbia Heating Supply Co, Pottstown *Also called Columbia Boiler Company* **(G-15972)**
Columbia Industries Inc.....................................570 520-4048
930 Back Rd Berwick (18603) **(G-1318)**
Columbia Motor Parts Inc (PA)..............................717 684-2501
138 Lancaster Ave Columbia (17512) **(G-3435)**
Columbia Northwest Inc.....................................724 423-7440
1297 Kecksburg Rd Mount Pleasant (15666) **(G-11693)**
Columbia Organ Leathers, Columbia *Also called Columbia Organ Works Inc* **(G-3436)**
Columbia Organ Works Inc...................................717 684-3573
915 Lancaster Ave Columbia (17512) **(G-3436)**
Columbia Porch Shade Co....................................570 639-1223
583 Orange Rd Dallas (18612) **(G-3961)**
Columbia Research Labs Inc.................................610 872-3900
1925 Macdade Blvd Woodlyn (19094) **(G-20218)**
Columbia Silk Dyeing Company...............................215 739-2289
1726 N Howard St Philadelphia (19122) **(G-13561)**
Columbia Tape Mfg Div, Red Hill *Also called Mutual Industries North Inc* **(G-16583)**
Columbia Wood Industries Inc...............................570 458-4311
1000 State St Millville (17846) **(G-11224)**
Columbian Cutlery Company Inc..............................610 374-5762
440 Laurel St Reading (19602) **(G-16350)**
Colussy Enterprises Inc.....................................412 221-4750
336 Station St Ste 2 Bridgeville (15017) **(G-2057)**
Com Pros Inc..717 264-2769
584 W Loudon St Chambersburg (17201) **(G-2919)**
Comanche Manufacturing Inc.................................724 530-7278
3049 State Route 208 Volant (16156) **(G-18771)**
Combat Arms LLC..412 245-0824
871 Burnt House Rd Carlisle (17015) **(G-2702)**
Combined Systems Inc.......................................724 932-2177
388 Kinsman Rd Jamestown (16134) **(G-8235)**
Combined Tactical Systems, Jamestown *Also called Combined Systems Inc* **(G-8235)**
Combined Tactical Systems Inc..............................724 932-2177
388 Kinsman Rd Jamestown (16134) **(G-8236)**
Combustion Service & Eqp Co................................412 821-8900
2016 Babcock Blvd Pittsburgh (15209) **(G-14867)**
Comcast Spotlight..610 784-2560
4 Tower Brigde 200 Bar Conshohocken (19428) **(G-3530)**
Comdoc Inc...800 321-1009
900 Parish St Ste 100 Pittsburgh (15220) **(G-14868)**
Comfab Inc...724 339-1750
2095 Melwood Rd New Kensington (15068) **(G-12335)**
Comfort & Harmony, Exton *Also called C&H7 LLC* **(G-5658)**
Comfort Care Textiles, Parkesburg *Also called Jan Lew Textile Corp* **(G-13176)**
Comfort Products, Croydon *Also called Comfort Stump Sock Mfg Co* **(G-3915)**
Comfort Sportswear Inc.....................................215 781-0300
705 Linton Ave Croydon (19021) **(G-3914)**
Comfort Stump Sock Mfg Co..................................215 781-0300
931 River Rd Croydon (19021) **(G-3915)**
Commerce Drive Enterprises LLC.............................215 362-2766
101 Commerce Dr Montgomeryville (18936) **(G-11389)**
Commercial Asphalt Products, Connellsville *Also called Hanson Aggregates Bmc Inc* **(G-3498)**
Commercial Color Inc.......................................610 391-7444
6330 Farm Bureau Rd Frnt Allentown (18106) **(G-173)**
Commercial Flrg Professionals..............................717 576-7847
6029 Carlisle Pike Mechanicsburg (17050) **(G-10829)**
Commercial Job Printing Inc................................814 765-1925
2079 Turnpike Avenue Ext Clearfield (16830) **(G-3216)**
Commercial Metal Polishing.................................610 837-0267
369 Moorestown Dr Bath (18014) **(G-954)**
Commercial Precast...724 873-0708
116 Cancilla Dr Canonsburg (15317) **(G-2564)**
Commercial Printing & Off Sup, Clearfield *Also called Commercial Prtg & Off Suppy* **(G-3217)**
Commercial Prtg & Off Suppy................................814 765-4731
17 S 3rd St Clearfield (16830) **(G-3217)**
Commercial Stainless Inc...................................570 387-8980
955 Patterson Dr Bloomsburg (17815) **(G-1776)**
Commodore Corporation......................................814 226-9210
20898 Paint Blvd Clarion (16214) **(G-3175)**
Commonwealth Drilling Company..............................610 940-4015
525 Plymouth Rd Ste 320 Plymouth Meeting (19462) **(G-15839)**
Commonwealth Precast Inc...................................215 721-6005
694 Forman Rd Souderton (18964) **(G-17730)**
Commonwealth Press LLC.....................................412 431-4207
2020 Carey Way Pittsburgh (15203) **(G-14869)**

Commonwealth Utility Eqp Inc...............................724 283-8400
129 Pillow St Butler (16001) **(G-2390)**
Communication Automation Corp..............................610 692-9526
1171 Mcdermott Dr West Chester (19380) **(G-19527)**
Communication Graphics Inc.................................215 646-2225
1787 Sentry Pkwy W # 240 Blue Bell (19422) **(G-1821)**
Communication Svcs & Support...............................215 540-5888
850 Pnllyn Blue Bell Pike Blue Bell (19422) **(G-1822)**
Communimetrics Group LLC...................................215 260-5382
127 Watch Hill Ln Malvern (19355) **(G-10215)**
Community Express, East Stroudsburg *Also called Commuters Express Inc* **(G-4610)**
Community Light & Sound Inc................................610 876-3400
333 E 5th St Chester (19013) **(G-3043)**
Community Newspaper..814 683-4841
109 N Mercer St Linesville (16424) **(G-9979)**
Community Newspaper Group LLC..............................570 275-3235
200 Market St Sunbury (17801) **(G-18166)**
Community Prof Loudspeakers, Chester *Also called Community Light & Sound Inc* **(G-3043)**
Community Resource Svcs Inc................................717 338-9100
925 Johnson Dr Gettysburg (17325) **(G-6286)**
Community Services Group Inc...............................570 286-0111
330 N 2nd St Sunbury (17801) **(G-18167)**
Commuters Express Inc......................................570 476-0601
6002 Woodale Rd East Stroudsburg (18301) **(G-4610)**
Comor Inc..814 425-3943
23697 Us Highway 322 Cochranton (16314) **(G-3339)**
Compacting Tooling Inc.....................................412 751-3535
403 Wide Dr McKeesport (15135) **(G-10664)**
Compagnie Des Bxites De Guinee.............................412 235-0279
323 N Shore Dr Ste 510 Pittsburgh (15212) **(G-14870)**
Compass Group Usa Inc......................................717 569-2671
1640 Crooked Oak Dr Lancaster (17601) **(G-8982)**
Compass Group USA Investments..............................717 939-1200
3201 Fulling Mill Rd Middletown (17057) **(G-11051)**
Compass Ret Display Group Inc..............................215 744-2787
9250 Ashton Rd Unit 200 Philadelphia (19114) **(G-13562)**
Compass Sign Co LLC (PA)...................................215 639-6777
1505 Ford Rd Bensalem (19020) **(G-1172)**
Compass Welding LLC (PA)...................................570 928-7472
1524 Hayes Rd Dushore (18614) **(G-4508)**
Competitive Edge Dynamics USA, Orefield *Also called Charles Hardy* **(G-13009)**
Compleat Strategist Inc....................................610 265-8562
580 Shoemaker Rd King of Prussia (19406) **(G-8596)**
Complete Fluid Control Inc.................................570 382-3376
9 Skyline Dr E Ste 2 S Abingtn Twp (18411) **(G-16893)**
Complete Hand Assembly Finshg..............................215 634-7490
500 E Luzerne St Philadelphia (19124) **(G-13563)**
Complete Imaging Corp......................................610 827-1561
1924 Art School Rd Chester Springs (19425) **(G-3074)**
Complete Intrvnous Access Svcs.............................724 226-2618
828 Front St Rear Creighton (15030) **(G-3881)**
Completion Snubbing Servi..................................940 668-5109
158 Painter Rd Smithton (15479) **(G-17659)**
Complexa Inc...412 727-8727
1055 Westlakes Dr Ste 200 Berwyn (19312) **(G-1356)**
Complexx Gases Inc...610 969-6661
62 Mill Creek Rd East Stroudsburg (18301) **(G-4611)**
Component Enterprises Co Inc...............................610 272-7900
235 E Penn St Norristown (19401) **(G-12646)**
Component Intrtechnologies Inc (PA)........................724 253-3161
2426 Perry Hwy Hadley (16130) **(G-6816)**
Componentone Enterprises LLC...............................412 681-4343
201 S Highland Ave Fl 3 Pittsburgh (15206) **(G-14871)**
Comporto Communications, Philadelphia *Also called Comporto LLC* **(G-13564)**
Comporto LLC...215 595-6224
1500 Market St Ste Cc1 Philadelphia (19102) **(G-13564)**
Composidie Inc...717 764-2233
30 Willow Springs Cir York (17406) **(G-20429)**
Composidie Inc (PA)..724 845-8602
1295 Route 380 Apollo (15613) **(G-673)**
Composidie Inc...724 845-8602
River Rd Leechburg (15656) **(G-9643)**
Composidie Inc...724 845-8602
1159 Industrial Park Rd Vandergrift (15690) **(G-18723)**
Composiflex Inc..814 866-8616
8100 Hawthorne Dr Erie (16509) **(G-5229)**
Composing Room Inc (PA)....................................215 310-5559
2001 Market St Ste 2500 Philadelphia (19103) **(G-13565)**
Composite Pnels Innvations LLC.............................814 317-5023
485 Chimney Rocks Rd Hollidaysburg (16648) **(G-7644)**
Compost Films Inc..215 668-3001
307 W Brookhaven Rd Wallingford (19086) **(G-18782)**
Compost Science & Utilization, Emmaus *Also called J G Press Inc* **(G-5029)**
Compound Technology Inc....................................717 845-8646
609 E King St York (17403) **(G-20430)**
Compressed Air Specialists Co..............................814 835-2420
2022 Filmore Ave Ste 1 Erie (16506) **(G-5230)**
Compressed Air Systems Inc.................................215 340-1307
14 Appletree Ln Pipersville (18947) **(G-14613)**

(G-0000) Company's Geographic Section entry number

Compression Components Svc LLC 267 387-2000
364 Valley Rd Ste 100 Warrington (18976) ***(G-19111)***
Compression Polymers, Scranton *Also called CPI Scranton Inc* ***(G-17225)***
Compression Polymers 570 558-8000
888 N Keyser Ave Scranton (18504) ***(G-17217)***
Compton Flagstone Quarry 570 942-6359
909 Glenwood Rd Hop Bottom (18824) ***(G-7773)***
Compton Quarry 570 222-9489
565 Route 247 Greenfield Township (18407) ***(G-6643)***
Compu-Craft Fabricators Inc 215 646-2381
102d Park Dr Montgomeryville (18936) ***(G-11390)***
Compu-Tutor, Conshohocken *Also called Compututor Inc* ***(G-3531)***
Compudata Inc (PA) 215 969-1000
2701 Commerce Way Philadelphia (19154) ***(G-13566)***
Compunetics Inc (PA) 412 373-8110
700 Seco Rd Ste 5 Monroeville (15146) ***(G-11328)***
Compunetics Inc 724 519-4773
4060 Norbatrol Ct Murrysville (15668) ***(G-11850)***
Compunetix Inc 412 373-8110
700 Seco Rd Ste 2 Monroeville (15146) ***(G-11329)***
Compunetix Inc (PA) 412 373-8110
2420 Mosside Blvd Ste 1 Monroeville (15146) ***(G-11330)***
Computer Boss 215 444-9393
1111 Street Rd Ste 205 Southampton (18966) ***(G-17804)***
Computer Components Corp 215 676-7600
2751 Southampton Rd Philadelphia (19154) ***(G-13567)***
Computer Designs Inc (HQ) 610 261-2100
5235 W Coplay Rd Whitehall (18052) ***(G-19867)***
Computer Dev Systems LLC 717 591-0995
220 Cumberland Pkwy Ste 8 Mechanicsburg (17055) ***(G-10830)***
Computer Part and Technologies, York *Also called Print Happy LLC* ***(G-20639)***
Computer Print Inc 717 397-9174
2132 Oreville Rd Lancaster (17601) ***(G-8983)***
Computer Pwr Solutions PA Inc 724 898-2223
624 Route 228 Mars (16046) ***(G-10491)***
Computer Software Inc 215 822-9100
100 Highpoint Dr Ste 104 Chalfont (18914) ***(G-2868)***
Computer Talk Associates, Blue Bell *Also called Computertalk Associates Inc* ***(G-1823)***
Computertalk Associates Inc 610 825-7686
492 Norristown Rd Ste 160 Blue Bell (19422) ***(G-1823)***
Compututor Inc 610 260-0300
101 E 8th Ave Ste 102 Conshohocken (19428) ***(G-3531)***
Comtec Mfg Inc 814 834-9300
1012 Delaum Rd Saint Marys (15857) ***(G-16956)***
Comtech Industries Inc 724 884-0101
1301 Ashwood Dr Canonsburg (15317) ***(G-2565)***
Comtrol International 724 864-3800
500 Pennsylvania Ave Irwin (15642) ***(G-8149)***
Con Yeager Company (PA) 724 452-4120
144 Magill Rd Zelienople (16063) ***(G-20795)***
Con Yeager Spice, Zelienople *Also called Con Yeager Company* ***(G-20795)***
Con-Wald Corp 215 879-1400
5050 Parkside Ave Philadelphia (19131) ***(G-13568)***
Conagra Brands Inc 717 846-7773
2800 Black Bridge Rd York (17406) ***(G-20431)***
Conagra Brands Inc 570 742-7621
30 Marr St Milton (17847) ***(G-11236)***
Conagra Brands Inc 570 742-6607
50 Cameron Ave Milton (17847) ***(G-11237)***
Conagra Brands Inc 570 742-8910
60 N Industrial Park Rd Milton (17847) ***(G-11238)***
Conagra Redline, Red Lion *Also called Ardent Mills LLC* ***(G-16588)***
Conair Corporation 717 485-4871
1 Crystal Dr Mc Connellsburg (17233) ***(G-10563)***
Conair Group Inc 814 437-6861
455 Allegheny Blvd Franklin (16323) ***(G-6122)***
Conair Group Inc (HQ) 724 584-5500
200 W Kensinger Dr # 100 Cranberry Township (16066) ***(G-3811)***
Conant Corporation 215 557-7466
42 S 15th St Unit 905 Philadelphia (19102) ***(G-13569)***
Conant Printing & Copying, Philadelphia *Also called Conant Corporation* ***(G-13569)***
Concast Metal Products Company, Mars *Also called A Cubed Corporation* ***(G-10485)***
Concast Metal Products Company 724 538-4000
131 Myoma Rd Mars (16046) ***(G-10492)***
Concentrated Knowledge Corp 610 388-5020
511 School House Rd # 300 Kennett Square (19348) ***(G-8507)***
Concentric Machining Grinding 610 692-9450
510 E Barnard St Unit 29 West Chester (19382) ***(G-19528)***
Concept 1 County Furniture, Colmar *Also called Thomas Pennise Jr* ***(G-3421)***
Concept Engineering Group 412 826-8800
15 Plum St Ste 3 Verona (15147) ***(G-18753)***
Concept Products Corporation 610 722-0830
62 Five Points Rd Mertztown (19539) ***(G-11002)***
Concepts 717 600-2964
1150 N Sherman St Ste 600 York (17402) ***(G-20432)***
Concrete Concepts Inc 412 331-1500
1095 Thompson Ave Mc Kees Rocks (15136) ***(G-10606)***
Concrete Form Consultants Inc (PA) 570 281-9605
56 Dundaff St Carbondale (18407) ***(G-2672)***
Concrete Jungle 717 528-8851
7771 Carlisle Pike York Springs (17372) ***(G-20763)***
Concrete Pipe & Precast LLC 717 597-5000
401 S Carlisle St Greencastle (17225) ***(G-6603)***
Concrete Safety Systems LLC 717 933-4107
9190 Old Rte 22 Bethel (19507) ***(G-1394)***
Concrete Service Materials Co 610 825-1554
630 E Elm St Conshohocken (19428) ***(G-3532)***
Concrete Services Corporation 814 774-8807
3000 Blair Rd Fairview (16415) ***(G-5817)***
Concrete Simplicity Cons 814 857-7500
5635 Crone Rd Dover (17315) ***(G-4191)***
Concrete Step Units Inc 570 343-2458
3102 N Main Ave Scranton (18508) ***(G-17218)***
Concrete Texturing LLC 570 489-6025
45 Underwood Rd Throop (18512) ***(G-18357)***
Concrete Texturing Tool & Sup, Throop *Also called Concrete Texturing LLC* ***(G-18357)***
Concure Inc 610 497-0198
710 Trainer St Chester (19013) ***(G-3044)***
Condo's Welding, Mill Hall *Also called Condos Incorporated* ***(G-11174)***
Condoms Galore, Easton *Also called Gothic Inc* ***(G-4692)***
Condor Corporation 717 560-1882
124 W Airport Rd Lititz (17543) ***(G-10001)***
Condor Snack Company 303 333-6075
900 High St Hanover (17331) ***(G-6868)***
Condos Incorporated 570 748-9265
131 Draketown Rd Mill Hall (17751) ***(G-11174)***
Conductive Technologies Inc (PA) 717 764-6931
935 Borom Rd York (17404) ***(G-20433)***
Cone Guys Ltd 215 781-6996
925 Canal St Ste 3210 Bristol (19007) ***(G-2128)***
Conestoga Bookstore, Ephrata *Also called Grace Press Inc* ***(G-5107)***
Conestoga Co Inc 610 866-0777
323 Sumner Ave Allentown (18102) ***(G-174)***
Conestoga Data Services Inc 717 569-7728
46 E King St Lancaster (17602) ***(G-8984)***
Conestoga Dpi LLC 717 665-0298
181 E Stiegel St Ste 100 Manheim (17545) ***(G-10378)***
Conestoga Log Cabins, Lebanon *Also called Peak Industries Inc* ***(G-9617)***
Conestoga Log Cabins and Homes, Lebanon *Also called Peak Ventures Inc* ***(G-9618)***
Conestoga Mfg LLC 717 529-0199
1867 Kirkwood Pike Kirkwood (17536) ***(G-8745)***
Conestoga USA Inc 610 327-2882
300 Old Reading Pike # 3 Pottstown (19464) ***(G-15973)***
Conestoga Valley Cstm Kitchens 717 445-5415
2042 Turkey Hill Rd Narvon (17555) ***(G-11919)***
Conestoga Wood Machinery, New Holland *Also called John M Sensenig* ***(G-12255)***
Conestoga Wood Spc Corp (PA) 717 445-6701
245 Reading Rd East Earl (17519) ***(G-4540)***
Conestoga Wood Spc Corp 570 658-9663
441 W Market St Beavertown (17813) ***(G-1025)***
Conewago Ready Mix 717 633-5022
576 Edgegrove Rd Hanover (17331) ***(G-6869)***
Confer Logging, Ludlow *Also called James Confer* ***(G-10118)***
Confiseurs Inc 610 932-2706
461 Limestone Rd Oxford (19363) ***(G-13076)***
Conflow Inc 724 746-0200
270 Meadowlands Blvd Washington (15301) ***(G-19157)***
Confluense LLC 215 530-6461
7277 William Ave Unit 300 Allentown (18106) ***(G-175)***
Congoleum Corporation 609 584-3000
4401 Ridge Rd Marcus Hook (19061) ***(G-10439)***
Conicella-Fessler Dental Lab 610 622-3298
409 Shadeland Ave Drexel Hill (19026) ***(G-4362)***
Conicity Technologies LLC 412 601-1874
519 Braddock Ave Turtle Creek (15145) ***(G-18563)***
Conjelko Dairy & Ice Service 814 467-9997
518 Graham Ave Windber (15963) ***(G-20179)***
Conjelko's Ice Service, Windber *Also called Conjelko Dairy & Ice Service* ***(G-20179)***
Conn & Company LLC 814 723-7980
11 S Marion St Warren (16365) ***(G-19018)***
Connected Energy, Canonsburg *Also called Bpl Global LLC* ***(G-2550)***
Connectedsign LLC 717 490-6431
480 New Holland Ave # 6202 Lancaster (17602) ***(G-8985)***
Connectify Inc 215 854-8432
1429 Walnut St Fl 2 Philadelphia (19102) ***(G-13570)***
Connections Magazine 570 647-0085
3305 Lake Ariel Hwy Honesdale (18431) ***(G-7708)***
Connective Tssue Gene Tsts LLC 484 244-2900
6575 Snowdrift Rd 106 Allentown (18106) ***(G-176)***
Connectwo LLC 215 421-4225
121 Misty Meadow Ln Lansdale (19446) ***(G-9352)***
Conner Printing Co, Bloomsburg *Also called Dennis Albertson LLC* ***(G-1778)***
Conner Printing Inc 610 494-2222
2977 Dutton Mill Rd Aston (19014) ***(G-756)***
Connex Inc 814 474-4550
7660 Klier Dr N Fairview (16415) ***(G-5818)***
Connie Fogarty 610 647-3172
1151 Shadow Oak Dr Malvern (19355) ***(G-10216)***

ALPHABETIC

Connor Sign Group Ltd..215 741-1299
  101 Spring St Langhorne (19047) *(G-9285)*

Conoco Woodworking...717 536-3948
  99 Gideon Ln Blain (17006) *(G-1710)*

Conrad Enterprises Inc...717 274-5151
  200 Rexmont Rd Cornwall (17016) *(G-3738)*

Conrad Printing Co Inc...717 637-5414
  109 3rd St Rear Hanover (17331) *(G-6870)*

Conrader Valve, Erie *Also called R Conrader Company* *(G-5447)*

Conrex Pharmaceutical Corp................................610 355-2454
  1155 Phoenixvlle Pike 1 West Chester (19380) *(G-19529)*

Conroy Foods Inc..412 781-0977
  100 Chapel Harbor Dr # 2 Pittsburgh (15238) *(G-14872)*

Conshohocken Italian Bakery...............................610 825-9334
  79 Jones St Conshohocken (19428) *(G-3533)*

Conshohocken Steel Pdts Inc...............................215 283-9222
  301 Randolph Ave Ambler (19002) *(G-574)*

Considine Studios Inc...215 362-8922
  751 Maple Ave Unit B Lansdale (19446) *(G-9353)*

Consol Amonate Mining Co LLC...........................724 485-4000
  1000 Consol Energy Dr Canonsburg (15317) *(G-2566)*

Consol Coal Resources LP....................................724 485-3300
  1000 Consol Energy Dr Canonsburg (15317) *(G-2567)*

Consol Energy Inc...724 785-6242
  379 Alicia Rd East Millsboro (15433) *(G-4583)*

Consol Energy Inc (PA)...724 485-3300
  1000 Consol Energy Dr Canonsburg (15317) *(G-2568)*

Consol Energy Inc...412 854-6600
  1000 Consol Energy Dr Canonsburg (15317) *(G-2569)*

Consol Mining Company LLC.................................724 485-4000
  1000 Consol Energy Dr Canonsburg (15317) *(G-2570)*

Consol PA Coal Co LLC...724 485-4000
  1000 Consol Energy Dr Canonsburg (15317) *(G-2571)*

Consolidated Stor Companies Inc (PA)..................610 253-2775
  225 Main St Tatamy (18085) *(G-18256)*

Consoldated Stor Companies Inc...........................610 253-2775
  225 Main St Tatamy (18085) *(G-18257)*

Consoldtd Scrap Resources Inc (PA).....................717 843-0931
  120 Hokes Mill Rd York (17404) *(G-20434)*

Consoldtd Scrap Resources Inc.............................717 843-0660
  600 E Princess St York (17403) *(G-20435)*

Consoldtd Scrap Resources Inc.............................717 843-0931
  530 Vander Ave York (17403) *(G-20436)*

Consolidated Cigar, McAdoo *Also called Altadis USA Inc* *(G-10655)*

Consolidated Coatings Inc....................................215 949-1474
  8000 Bristol Pike Levittown (19057) *(G-9826)*

Consolidated Cont Holdings LLC...........................717 854-3454
  15 Lightner Rd York (17404) *(G-20437)*

Consolidated Container, Allentown *Also called Vanguard Manufacturing Inc* *(G-422)*

Consolidated Container Co LLC.............................724 658-4570
  221 Grove St New Castle (16101) *(G-12074)*

Consolidated Container Co LLC.............................724 658-4578
  221 Grove St New Castle (16101) *(G-12075)*

Consolidated Container Co LLC.............................412 828-1111
  601 Seldon Ave Verona (15147) *(G-18754)*

Consolidated Container Co LLC.............................724 658-0549
  221 Grove St New Castle (16101) *(G-12076)*

Consolidated Container Co LLC.............................717 267-3533
  1501 Orchard Dr Chambersburg (17201) *(G-2920)*

Consolidated Container Co LLC.............................570 759-0823
  910 Back Rd Berwick (18603) *(G-1319)*

Consolidated Container Co LLC.............................610 869-4021
  15 Lightner Rd York (17404) *(G-20438)*

Consolidated Container Co LP...............................814 676-5671
  15 Mineral St Oil City (16301) *(G-12943)*

Consolidated Containers, Oil City *Also called Consolidated Container Co LP* *(G-12943)*

Consolidated GL Holdings Inc (PA)........................866 412-6977
  500 Grant Ave Ste 201 East Butler (16029) *(G-4531)*

Consolidated Glass Corporation............................724 658-4541
  1150 N Cedar St New Castle (16102) *(G-12077)*

Consolidated Graphic Comm, Media *Also called Interform Corporation* *(G-10934)*

Consolidated Packaging LLC.................................215 968-6260
  304 Corporate Dr E Langhorne (19047) *(G-9286)*

Consolidated Printing Inc.....................................215 879-1400
  5050 Parkside Ave Philadelphia (19131) *(G-13571)*

Consolidated Steel Svcs Inc (PA)..........................814 944-5890
  632 Glendale Valley Blvd Fallentimber (16639) *(G-5851)*

Consolidated/Drake Press, Philadelphia *Also called Consolidated Printing Inc* *(G-13571)*

Consolidation Coal Company (HQ).........................740 338-3100
  1000 Consol Energy Dr Canonsburg (15317) *(G-2572)*

Conspec Controls Inc (HQ)...................................724 489-8450
  6 Guttman Blvd Charleroi (15022) *(G-3008)*

Constaflow Pump Company LLC............................610 515-1753
  626 Wirebach St Easton (18042) *(G-4662)*

Constantia Colmar LLC...215 997-6222
  92 County Line Rd Colmar (18915) *(G-3411)*

Constantia Colmar, Inc., Colmar *Also called Constantia Colmar LLC* *(G-3411)*

Construction Dynamics Inc...................................215 295-0777
  355 Newbold Rd Fairless Hills (19030) *(G-5775)*

Construction Equipment Guide (PA).......................215 885-2900
  470 Maryland Dr Ste 2 Fort Washington (19034) *(G-6066)*

Construction On Site Welding...............................610 367-1895
  945 N Reading Ave Boyertown (19512) *(G-1904)*

Construction Specialties Inc.................................570 546-2255
  6696 Route 405 Hwy Muncy (17756) *(G-11813)*

Construction Specialties Inc.................................570 546-5941
  6696 Route 405 Hwy Muncy (17756) *(G-11814)*

Construction Supply Center, West Chester *Also called Martin Limestone Inc* *(G-19597)*

Construction Tool Service Inc...............................814 231-3090
  2929 Stewart Dr A State College (16801) *(G-17955)*

Consumer Goods Manufacturing, Milford *Also called Edgell Communications* *(G-11159)*

Consumer Network Inc..215 235-2400
  3624 Market St Ste 200s Philadelphia (19104) *(G-13572)*

Consumer Products Division, Erie *Also called Plastek Industries Inc* *(G-5425)*

Consyst Inc...610 398-0752
  1610 Applewood Dr Orefield (18069) *(G-13010)*

Contact Technologies Inc.....................................814 834-9000
  229 West Creek Rd Saint Marys (15857) *(G-16957)*

Container Research Corporation (PA).....................610 459-2160
  2 New Rd Ste 1 Aston (19014) *(G-757)*

Containerboard & Paper Div, York *Also called Westrock Cp LLC* *(G-20709)*

Containment Solutions Inc....................................814 542-8621
  14489 Croghan Pike Mount Union (17066) *(G-11741)*

Contech Engnered Solutions LLC...........................717 597-2148
  600 N Washington St Greencastle (17225) *(G-6604)*

Contempory Pubg Group E LLC.............................215 953-8210
  1032 Millcreek Dr Feasterville Trevose (19053) *(G-5900)*

Contemprary Artisans Cabinetry...........................215 723-8803
  1020 Revenue Dr Telford (18969) *(G-18276)*

Contempri Kitchens, Scranton *Also called Custom Designs & Mfg Co* *(G-17226)*

Contine Corporation...814 899-0006
  1820 Nagle Rd Erie (16510) *(G-5231)*

Continental Apparel Corp......................................814 495-4625
  300 Grant St South Fork (15956) *(G-17773)*

Continental Auto Systems Inc...............................610 289-1390
  6755 Snowdrift Rd Allentown (18106) *(G-177)*

Continental Concrete Pdts Inc..............................610 327-3700
  1 S Grosstown Rd Pottstown (19464) *(G-15974)*

Continental Corporation..610 289-0488
  6755 Snowdrift Rd Allentown (18106) *(G-178)*

Continental Press Inc (PA)....................................717 367-1836
  520 E Bainbridge St Elizabethtown (17022) *(G-4869)*

Continental Seasoning, Bethlehem *Also called Newly Weds Foods Inc* *(G-1584)*

Continental Signs, York *Also called Laucks and Spaulding Inc* *(G-20562)*

Continental-Wirt Elec Corp (PA)...........................215 355-7080
  130 James Way Southampton (18966) *(G-17805)*

Continuous Metal Tech Inc....................................814 772-9274
  439 W Main St Ridgway (15853) *(G-16701)*

Contour Seats Inc...610 395-5144
  6530 Chapmans Rd Allentown (18106) *(G-179)*

Contrado BBH Holdings LLC.................................215 609-3400
  2929 Arch St Fl 27 Philadelphia (19104) *(G-13573)*

Contrail Systems Inc...724 353-1127
  199 Parker Rd Sarver (16055) *(G-17067)*

Contrast Metalworks LLC......................................484 624-5542
  301 S Keim St Pottstown (19464) *(G-15975)*

Control & Data Technologies, Coraopolis *Also called Tecnomasium Inc* *(G-3727)*

Control Chief Corporation.....................................814 362-6811
  200 Williams St Bradford (16701) *(G-1962)*

Control Chief Holdings Inc (PA).............................814 362-6811
  200 Williams St Bradford (16701) *(G-1963)*

Control Design Inc (PA)..412 788-2280
  211 Ridc Park West Dr Pittsburgh (15275) *(G-14873)*

Control Design Inc..814 833-4663
  4807 Atlantic Ave Erie (16506) *(G-5232)*

Control Dynamics Corporation..............................215 956-0700
  960 Louis Dr Warminster (18974) *(G-18846)*

Control Electronics Inc...610 942-3190
  148 Brandamore Rd Brandamore (19316) *(G-2001)*

Control Tech USA Ltd..570 529-6011
  22025 Route 14 Troy (16947) *(G-18519)*

Control Temp Insulation LLC.................................610 393-0943
  7113 Goldcris Ln Northampton (18067) *(G-12848)*

Controlled Molding Inc..724 253-3550
  3043 Perry Hwy Hadley (16130) *(G-6817)*

Controls Service & Repair.....................................412 487-7310
  1648 Butler Plank Rd Glenshaw (15116) *(G-6486)*

Controlsoft Inc...724 733-2000
  1 Technology Ln Ste 1 # 1 Export (15632) *(G-5595)*

Converging Sciences Tech Inc...............................215 626-5705
  1403 Old Jacksonville Rd Warminster (18974) *(G-18847)*

Converteam, Cranberry Township *Also called GE Enrgy Pwr Cnversion USA Inc* *(G-3820)*

Converter Accessory Corp.....................................610 863-6008
  201 Alpha Rd Wind Gap (18091) *(G-20168)*

Converter Pressure Sensitive, Olyphant *Also called Get It Right Tape Company Inc* *(G-12991)*

Converters Inc..215 355-5400
  1617 Republic Rd Huntingdon Valley (19006) *(G-7971)*

Conway-Phillips Holding LLC 412 315-7963
13a Talbot Ave Braddock (15104) (G-1943)
Cook & Frey Inc 717 336-1200
38 Wade Dr Lititz (17543) (G-10002)
Cook Forest Saw Mill Center (PA) 814 927-6655
Cooks Forest State Park Cooksburg (16217) (G-3620)
Cook Vandergrift Inc 724 845-8621
1186 Montgomery Ln Vandergrift (15690) (G-18724)
Cooke Tavern Ltd 814 422-7687
4158 Penns Valley Rd Spring Mills (16875) (G-17887)
Cooke Tavern Soups, Spring Mills Also called Cooke Tavern Ltd (G-17887)
Cookie Grams 814 942-4220
919 Logan Blvd Altoona (16602) (G-494)
Cookport Coal Co Inc 814 938-4253
425 E Market St Ste 1 Kittanning (16201) (G-8762)
Cooks Machine Work 814 589-5141
17283 Bugtown Rd Pleasantville (16341) (G-15799)
Cool Bio Inc 973 452-8309
1489 Lexington Ln Wayne (19087) (G-19314)
Coolspring Stone Supply Inc 724 437-8663
850 N Gallatin Avenue Ext Uniontown (15401) (G-18621)
Coolspring Stone Supply Inc (PA) 724 437-5200
1122 Jumonville Rd Uniontown (15401) (G-18622)
Coon Industries Inc 570 735-6852
30 Simon St Nanticoke (18634) (G-11899)
Coon Industries Inc 570 341-8033
200 Dunda Dr Dunmore (18512) (G-4471)
Cooney Manufacturing Co LLC 610 272-2100
313 Circle Of Progress Dr Pottstown (19464) (G-15976)
Cooper Bussmann LLC 724 553-5449
512 Daisy Ct Cranberry Township (16066) (G-3812)
Cooper Interconnect Inc 630 248-4007
620 Allendale Rd Ste 175 King of Prussia (19406) (G-8597)
Cooper Machine LLC 717 529-6155
245 Cooper Dr Kirkwood (17536) (G-8746)
Cooper Power Systems LLC 636 394-2877
122 Bethany Dr Canonsburg (15317) (G-2573)
Cooper Printing Inc 717 871-8856
2094 New Danville Pike Lancaster (17603) (G-8986)
Cooper Printing,, Lancaster Also called Cooper Printing Inc (G-8986)
Cooper Saws, Kirkwood Also called Cooper Machine LLC (G-8746)
Cooper Tire & Rubber Company 610 967-0860
8000 Quarry Rd Ste B Alburtis (18011) (G-51)
Cooper Wilbert Vault Co Inc 610 842-7782
1052 Waterloo Rd Berwyn (19312) (G-1357)
Cooperheat Mqs Proj 412 787-8690
4525 Campbells Run Rd Pittsburgh (15205) (G-14874)
Coopers 610 369-8992
813 S Reading Ave Bldg C Boyertown (19512) (G-1905)
Coopers Creek Chemical Corp 610 828-0375
884 River Rd Conshohocken (19428) (G-3534)
Coopersburg Associates Inc 610 282-1360
2600 Saucon Valley Rd Center Valley (18034) (G-2825)
Coopersburg Products LLC 610 282-1360
2600b Saucon Valley Rd Center Valley (18034) (G-2826)
Coopersburg Sports, Center Valley Also called Coopersburg Associates Inc (G-2825)
Coordinated Health Systems LLC 610 861-8080
2775 Schoenersville Rd Bethlehem (18017) (G-1487)
Copeland Lumber, Albion Also called David Copeland (G-42)
Copiers Inc 610 837-7400
102 W Northampton St Frnt Bath (18014) (G-955)
Copies For Less, Pittsburgh Also called Technosystems Service Corp (G-15602)
Copitech Associates 570 963-1391
336 Adams Ave Scranton (18503) (G-17219)
Copper Kettle Fudge Factory 412 824-1233
355 Lincoln Hwy Ste 16 North Versailles (15137) (G-12773)
Copperhead Chemical Co Inc 570 386-6123
120 River Rd Tamaqua (18252) (G-18209)
Coppers Inc 412 233-2137
436 7th Ave Pittsburgh (15219) (G-14875)
Copy Center Plus 724 547-5850
311 N Diamond St Mount Pleasant (15666) (G-11694)
Copy Corner Inc 570 992-4769
Old Rte 115 Mxvlle Vly Rd Saylorsburg (18353) (G-17104)
Copy Corner, The, Saylorsburg Also called Copy Corner Inc (G-17104)
Copy Management Inc 610 993-8686
147 Pnnsylvania Ave Ste 3 Malvern (19355) (G-10217)
Copy Management Inc (PA) 215 269-5000
447 Veit Rd Huntingdon Valley (19006) (G-7972)
Copy Right Printing & Graphics 814 838-6255
2827 W 26th St Ste A Erie (16506) (G-5233)
Copy Rite, Altoona Also called D L Dravis & Associates Inc (G-496)
Copy Rite 814 644-0360
105 Mount Vernon Ave Huntingdon (16652) (G-7941)
Copy Shop 724 654-6515
3447 Wilmington Rd New Castle (16105) (G-12078)
Copy Stop Inc 412 271-4444
2013 Noble St Swissvale (15218) (G-18191)

Copy Systems Group Inc 215 355-2223
1300 Industrial Blvd # 100 Southampton (18966) (G-17806)
Copycat Quick Print, Uniontown Also called Kwikticketscom Inc (G-18632)
Cor-Rite Inc 570 287-1718
195 Slocum St Swoyersville (18704) (G-18196)
Cor-Rite Corrugated Inc 570 287-1718
195 Slocum St Kingston (18704) (G-8714)
Cora Lee Cupcakes 724 681-5498
442 Violet Dr New Kensington (15068) (G-12336)
Coraopolis Light Metal Inc 412 264-2252
1221 3rd Ave Coraopolis (15108) (G-3680)
Corban Corporation 610 837-9700
Rr 248 Bath (18014) (G-956)
Corby Industries Inc 610 433-1412
812 N Gilmore St Allentown (18109) (G-180)
Corcoran Printing Inc 570 822-1991
641 N Pennsylvania Ave Wilkes Barre (18705) (G-19914)
CORD TEST, Westfield Also called Electri-Cord Manufacturing Co (G-19777)
Cordova 570 578-7413
3396 S 2nd St Whitehall (18052) (G-19868)
Cordray Corporation 610 644-6200
420 Feheley Dr Ste D King of Prussia (19406) (G-8598)
Core Color Graphics, Feasterville Trevose Also called Urban Enterprises T & M LLC (G-5936)
Core Covers, Allentown Also called Roberts Manufacturing LLC (G-376)
Core Essence Orthopedics Inc 215 660-5014
1000 Continental Dr # 240 King of Prussia (19406) (G-8599)
Core House 717 566-3810
34 Sweet Arrow Dr Hummelstown (17036) (G-7907)
Core Laboratories LP 412 884-9250
3915 Saw Mill Run Blvd Pittsburgh (15227) (G-14876)
Core Technology Group Inc 215 822-0120
140 Independence Ln Chalfont (18914) (G-2869)
Coreco Fiberglass Inc 724 463-3726
1698 Church St Indiana (15701) (G-8087)
Coren Metal Inc 215 244-4260
600 Center Ave Bensalem (19020) (G-1173)
Coren Metalcrafts Company 215 244-0532
600 Center Ave Bensalem (19020) (G-1174)
Coren-Indik Inc 267 288-1200
6300 Bristol Pike Levittown (19057) (G-9827)
Corestar International Corp 724 744-4094
1044 Sandy Hill Rd Irwin (15642) (G-8150)
Corestar International Corp (PA) 724 744-4094
1044 Sandy Hill Rd Irwin (15642) (G-8151)
Coretec, Richland Also called Delstar Technologies Inc (G-16686)
Coretec Plastics Inc 717 866-7472
308 Poplar St Richland (17087) (G-16684)
Coretech International Inc 908 454-7999
1237 Sesqui St Allentown (18103) (G-181)
Corey Associates Inc 570 676-4800
120 Corey Way Greentown (18426) (G-6733)
Cork Industries Inc (PA) 610 522-9550
500 Kaiser Dr Folcroft (19032) (G-6001)
Corle Building Systems Inc 814 276-9611
404 Sarah Furnace Rd Imler (16655) (G-8054)
Corles Printing 814 276-3775
210 Sound Ln Imler (16655) (G-8055)
Cornell Bros Inc (PA) 570 376-2471
1 Mill St Middlebury Center (16935) (G-11043)
Cornellcookson LLC 800 294-4358
24 Elmwood Ave Mountain Top (18707) (G-11756)
Cornellcookson Inc 570 474-6773
24 Elmwood Ave Mountain Top (18707) (G-11757)
Corner News, Scranton Also called MSP Corporation (G-17260)
Cornerstone Automation LLC 215 513-4111
112 Moyer Rd Telford (18969) (G-18277)
Cornerstone Printing Services 717 626-7895
160 Koser Rd Lititz (17543) (G-10003)
Cornerstone Woodworks LLC 717 866-0230
101 N Ramona Rd Myerstown (17067) (G-11880)
Corning Incorporated 570 883-9005
160 Research Dr Pittston (18640) (G-15746)
Cornwell Quality Tools Company 814 756-5484
14800 W Cherry Hill Rd Albion (16401) (G-41)
Corona Corporation 215 679-9538
820 Main St Red Hill (18076) (G-16580)
Coronet Books, Schwenksville Also called Trans Atlantic Publications (G-17180)
Coronet Books Inc 215 925-2762
311 Bainbridge St Philadelphia (19147) (G-13574)
Corporate Arts Inc 610 298-8374
7397 Gun Club Rd New Tripoli (18066) (G-12454)
Corporate Carpentry, Hatboro Also called Canalley Painting (G-7276)
Corporate Distribution Ltd 717 697-6900
3930 Chambers Hill Rd Harrisburg (17111) (G-7109)
Corporate Graphics Inc 570 424-0475
Rr 5 Box 5268 East Stroudsburg (18301) (G-4612)
Corporate Graphics Intl Inc 800 247-2751
101 E 9th St Waynesboro (17268) (G-19405)

A L P H A B E T I C

Corporate Images Company 610 439-7961
  1434 W Union St Allentown (18102) *(G-182)*

Corporate Print Solutions Inc 215 774-1119
  9 E Glenolden Ave Glenolden (19036) *(G-6472)*

Correvio LLC 610 833-6050
  3 Dickinson Dr Ste 101 Chadds Ford (19317) *(G-2850)*

Corro Therm, Feasterville Trevose *Also called Electrospray Incorporated (G-5904)*

Corro Therm, Feasterville Trevose *Also called Electrospray Incorporated (G-5905)*

Corrosion Technology Inc 610 429-1450
  125 Willowbrook Ln West Chester (19382) *(G-19530)*

Corrugated Services Corp (PA) 215 639-9540
  515 Pennsylvania Ave # 100 Fort Washington (19034) *(G-6067)*

Corrugated Specialties 814 337-5705
  10677 Mchenry St Meadville (16335) *(G-10714)*

Corrugated Specialties (PA) 814 337-5705
  10677 Mchenry St Meadville (16335) *(G-10715)*

Corry Contract Inc 814 665-8221
  21 Maple Ave Corry (16407) *(G-3748)*

Corry Forge Company (HQ) 814 664-9664
  441 E Main St Corry (16407) *(G-3749)*

Corry Forge Company 814 459-4495
  1533 E 12th St Erie (16511) *(G-5234)*

Corry Journal Inc 814 665-8291
  28 W South St Corry (16407) *(G-3750)*

Corry Laser Technology Inc 814 664-7212
  1530 Enterprise Rd Corry (16407) *(G-3751)*

Corry Manufacturing Company 814 664-9611
  320 W Main St Corry (16407) *(G-3752)*

Corry Metal Products Inc 814 664-7087
  46500 Route 6 Corry (16407) *(G-3753)*

Corry Micronics Inc (PA) 814 664-7728
  1 Plastics Rd Ste 1a Corry (16407) *(G-3754)*

Corry Opothecary 814 452-4220
  612 W Sweet St Corry (16407) *(G-3755)*

Corry Peat Products Co Inc 814 665-7101
  515 Turnpike Rd Corry (16407) *(G-3756)*

Corry Rubber Corporation 814 664-2313
  601 W Main St Corry (16407) *(G-3757)*

Corrylaser.com, Corry *Also called Corry Laser Technology Inc (G-3751)*

Corsa Coal Corp 724 754-0028
  4600 J Barry Ct Ste 220 Canonsburg (15317) *(G-2574)*

Cortape Ne Inc 610 997-7900
  2285 Avenue A Bethlehem (18017) *(G-1488)*

Cortendo AB Inc 610 254-9200
  900 Northbrook Dr Ste 200 Trevose (19053) *(G-18490)*

Cortineo Creative LLC 215 348-1100
  260 N Broad St Doylestown (18901) *(G-4294)*

Corvette America, Reedsville *Also called Auto Accessories America Inc (G-16621)*

Cory Reservoir Testing Inc 814 438-2006
  16450 Route 8 Union City (16438) *(G-18606)*

Cosma USA LLC 412 551-0708
  229 Huckleberry Ct Wexford (15090) *(G-19796)*

Cosolidated Drake Press, Philadelphia *Also called Con-Wald Corp (G-13568)*

Costa Industries LLC 412 384-8170
  600 Hayden Blvd Elizabeth (15037) *(G-4858)*

Costar Brewing Inc 412 401-8433
  919 N Saint Clair St Pittsburgh (15206) *(G-14877)*

Costumes Online, Hooversville *Also called Angelie Original (G-7770)*

Costys Energy Services 570 662-2752
  2329 S Main St Mansfield (16933) *(G-10413)*

Cott Beverages Wyomissing Inc 484 840-4800
  20 Aldan Ave Concordville (19331) *(G-3456)*

Cott Manufacturing Company 412 675-0101
  43 Allegheny Sq Glassport (15045) *(G-6410)*

Cott Manufacturing Company (PA) 724 625-3730
  43 Allegheny Sq Glassport (15045) *(G-6411)*

Cottage Communications Inc 610 678-7473
  718 N Church Rd Reading (19608) *(G-16351)*

Cottage Roads, New Hope *Also called Giving Tree Inc (G-12303)*

Cottage Woodworks, Harleysville *Also called Mike Steck (G-7048)*

Cotton Bureau 412 573-9041
  110 Torrens St Pittsburgh (15206) *(G-14878)*

Coudersport Precast Inc (PA) 814 274-9634
  30 W Hebron Rd Coudersport (16915) *(G-3780)*

Cougar Metals Inc (PA) 724 251-9030
  100 Washington St Leetsdale (15056) *(G-9690)*

Coulter Logging 814 236-2855
  456 Ridge Ave Curwensville (16833) *(G-3949)*

Counterflow Inc 814 734-9440
  6933 Route 6n Edinboro (16412) *(G-4810)*

Countertek Inc 717 336-2371
  1215 Ridge Ave Ephrata (17522) *(G-5097)*

Country Accents (PA) 570 478-4127
  615 Dunwoody Rd Williamsport (17701) *(G-20001)*

Country Acres Cider & Prod Inc 717 263-9349
  6540 Wayne Hwy Waynesboro (17268) *(G-19406)*

Country Additions Inc 610 404-2062
  420 Beacon St Birdsboro (19508) *(G-1692)*

Country Barns of Pittsburgh 412 221-1630
  1606 Bingham St 1 Pittsburgh (15203) *(G-14879)*

Country Butcher Shop (PA) 717 249-4691
  286 Mcallister Church Rd Carlisle (17015) *(G-2703)*

Country CLB Rest Pastry Shops, Philadelphia *Also called Country Club Restaurant (G-13575)*

Country Club Restaurant 215 722-0500
  1717 Cottman Ave Philadelphia (19111) *(G-13575)*

Country Creek Winery 215 723-6516
  133 Cressman Rd Telford (18969) *(G-18278)*

Country Creek Winery Orchards, Telford *Also called Country Creek Winery (G-18278)*

Country Cupboard Cookies Lt 724 325-3045
  947 Old Frankstown Rd G Pittsburgh (15239) *(G-14880)*

Country Cupola Ltd (PA) 717 866-8801
  53 N Ramona Rd Myerstown (17067) *(G-11881)*

Country Farm & Home Center, Mifflinburg *Also called Mifflinburg Farmers Exchange (G-11098)*

Country Flair Quarter Horses 724 822-8413
  214 Worthington S L Rd Worthington (16262) *(G-20229)*

Country Food LLC 717 506-0393
  937 Nixon Dr Ste D Mechanicsburg (17055) *(G-10831)*

Country Food USA, Mechanicsburg *Also called Country Food LLC (G-10831)*

Country Fresh Batter Inc (PA) 610 272-5751
  221 King Manor Dr Ste B King of Prussia (19406) *(G-8600)*

Country Fresh Pennsylvania LLC 215 855-2408
  2600 Richmond Rd Hatfield (19440) *(G-7327)*

Country Heirlooms Inc 610 869-9550
  3844 Gap Newport Pike West Grove (19390) *(G-19698)*

Country Impressions Inc 570 477-5000
  5724 Main Rd Hunlock Creek (18621) *(G-7931)*

Country Keepsakes 570 744-2246
  5232 Route 467 Rome (18837) *(G-16796)*

Country Lane Gazebos, New Holland *Also called Country Lane Woodworking LLC (G-12238)*

Country Lane Woodworking LLC 717 351-9250
  191 Jalyn Dr New Holland (17557) *(G-12238)*

Country Maid Bakery Foods, Bowmansville *Also called Hartings Bakery Inc (G-1887)*

Country Press Inc 610 565-8808
  10 S Pennell Rd Media (19063) *(G-10919)*

Country Print Shop, The, Middleburg *Also called Leon Spangler (G-11028)*

Country Tees & Grafx LLC 570 568-0973
  2794 Crossroads Dr Lewisburg (17837) *(G-9901)*

Country Traditions 570 386-3621
  2174 Sunny Rd New Ringgold (17960) *(G-12437)*

Country Value Woodworks LLC 717 786-7949
  2302 Beaver Valley Pike Quarryville (17566) *(G-16267)*

Country Woodcrafts 814 793-4417
  345 Windy Acres Ln Roaring Spring (16673) *(G-16763)*

Countryside Woodcrafts Inc 717 627-5641
  802 Scott Ln Lititz (17543) *(G-10004)*

County Delaware, The, Media *Also called Delaware County Pennsylvania (G-10920)*

County Line Fence Co 215 343-5085
  2051 County Line Rd Warrington (18976) *(G-19112)*

County Line Quarry Inc 717 252-1584
  740 S Front St Wrightsville (17368) *(G-20235)*

County Line Screenprinting 570 758-5397
  126 Melody Ln Dalmatia (17017) *(G-3984)*

County of Montgomery 215 234-4528
  2144 Snyder Rd Green Lane (18054) *(G-6586)*

County of Somerset 814 629-9460
  458 Mastillo Rd Hollsopple (15935) *(G-7657)*

Coupler Enterprises Inc 267 487-8982
  125 Titus Ave Ste 200 Warrington (18976) *(G-19113)*

Courier Express, Du Bois *Also called Tioga Publishing Company (G-4424)*

Courier Times Inc (HQ) 215 949-4011
  8400 Bristol Pike Levittown (19057) *(G-9828)*

Courier Times Inc 215 949-4219
  2 Geoffrey Dr Fairless Hills (19030) *(G-5776)*

Courier, The, Dillsburg *Also called Gannett Stllite Info Ntwrk LLC (G-4130)*

Courier-Express, Brookville *Also called Tioga Publishing Company (G-2273)*

Courtney Design, Lincoln University *Also called Courtney Metal Design (G-9973)*

Courtney Metal Design 610 932-6065
  458 Elkdale Rd Fl 3 Lincoln University (19352) *(G-9973)*

Courtside Document Svcs Inc 570 969-2991
  408 Spruce St Apt 1 Scranton (18503) *(G-17220)*

Courtyard Wineries LLC 814 725-0236
  10021 W Main Rd North East (16428) *(G-12736)*

Cove Stake & Wood Products GP 814 793-3257
  1434 Curryville Rd Martinsburg (16662) *(G-10522)*

Covenant Group of China Inc 610 660-7828
  2 Bala Plz Ste 300 Bala Cynwyd (19004) *(G-876)*

Coventry Pewter Inc 610 328-1557
  118 Lynbrooke Rd Springfield (19064) *(G-17911)*

Cover Lumber Co 814 750-2006
  108 Sawmill Ln Bedford (15522) *(G-1047)*

Covers All Canvas Products 412 653-6010
  5171 Brownsville Rd Pittsburgh (15236) *(G-14881)*

Covestro LLC (HQ) 412 413-2000
  1 Covestro Cir Pittsburgh (15205) *(G-14882)*

Covestro LLC 215 428-4400
  1 Progress Dr Morrisville (19067) *(G-11556)*

Covia Holdings Corporation 412 431-4777
  3810 S Water St Pittsburgh (15203) *(G-14883)*

Covington Plastic Molding 717 624-1111
  10 S Bolton St New Oxford (17350) *(G-12408)*

Cowboy Magic, Bethlehem *Also called Cummings Group Inc (G-1492)*

Cowz Leap Creamery LLC 717 653-1532
  369 Kelly Ave Mount Joy (17552) *(G-11651)*

Cox Machining Inc 814 642-5009
  479 Combs Creek Rd Port Allegany (16743) *(G-15892)*

Coxs Machine Shop 724 796-7815
  312 Eaton St Midway (15060) *(G-11090)*

Cozy Cabins LLC 717 354-3278
  455 Farmersville Rd New Holland (17557) *(G-12239)*

CP Food Stores Inc (PA) 412 831-7777
  2610 Lindenwood Dr Pittsburgh (15241) *(G-14884)*

CP Industries Holdings Inc 412 664-6604
  2214 Walnut St McKeesport (15132) *(G-10665)*

CP Precision Inc 267 364-0870
  1979 Stout Dr Unit 3 Warminster (18974) *(G-18848)*

CP Precision Inc 267 364-0870
  1979 Stout Dr Ste 3 Warminster (18974) *(G-18849)*

CPA Operations LLC 215 743-6860
  2917 Hedley St Philadelphia (19137) *(G-13576)*

Cpd Lighting LLC 215 361-6100
  66 Bethlehem Pike Colmar (18915) *(G-3412)*

Cpg International Holdings LP 570 558-8000
  888 N Keyser Ave Scranton (18504) *(G-17221)*

Cpg International I Inc (HQ) 570 346-8797
  801 E Corey St Scranton (18505) *(G-17222)*

Cpg International LLC 570 348-0997
  801 Corey Ave Scranton (18505) *(G-17223)*

Cpg International LLC 570 558-8000
  888 N Keyser Ave Scranton (18504) *(G-17224)*

CPI, Malvern *Also called Crane Payment Innovations Inc (G-10218)*

CPI Locus Microwave Inc 814 466-6275
  176 Technology Dr Ste 200 Boalsburg (16827) *(G-1866)*

CPI Scranton Inc 570 558-8000
  801 E Corey St Scranton (18505) *(G-17225)*

Cpk Manufacturing LLC (HQ) 814 839-4186
  214 Industrial Ln Alum Bank (15521) *(G-559)*

CPM Wolverine Proctor LLC (HQ) 215 443-5200
  251 Gibraltar Rd Horsham (19044) *(G-7805)*

Cpo 2 Inc 570 759-1233
  1437 Fairview Ave Berwick (18603) *(G-1320)*

Cpv Manufacturing, Kennett Square *Also called Admiral Valve LLC (G-8501)*

Craddock & Lerro Associates 610 543-0200
  1005 Pontiac Rd Ste 312 Drexel Hill (19026) *(G-4363)*

Crafco Inc 610 264-7541
  1680 E Race St Allentown (18109) *(G-183)*

Craft Lite Inc 717 359-7131
  100 Craftway Dr Littlestown (17340) *(G-10065)*

Craft Manufacturing Inc 724 532-2702
  315 Linden St Latrobe (15650) *(G-9467)*

Craft Metal Products Inc 570 829-2441
  1 Industrial Dr Sugar Notch (18706) *(G-18149)*

Craft Products Co Inc 412 821-8102
  2014b Babcock Blvd Pittsburgh (15209) *(G-14885)*

Craft-Bilt Manufacturing Co 215 721-7700
  53 Soderton Hatfield Pike Souderton (18964) *(G-17731)*

Craft-Maid Custom Kitchens, Reading *Also called Craft-Maid Kitchen Inc (G-16352)*

Craft-Maid Kitchen Inc 610 376-8686
  501 S 9th St Bldg C Reading (19602) *(G-16352)*

Craftbilt, Souderton *Also called Craft-Bilt Manufacturing Co (G-17731)*

Craftex By Victor, Blue Bell *Also called Craftex Mills Inc Pennsylvania (G-1824)*

Craftex Mills Inc Pennsylvania 610 941-1212
  450 Sentry Pkwy E Blue Bell (19422) *(G-1824)*

Craftweld Fabrication Co Inc 267 492-1100
  105 Park Dr Montgomeryville (18936) *(G-11391)*

Craig A Scholedice Inc 610 683-8910
  58 Willow St Kutztown (19530) *(G-8838)*

Craig Colabaugh Gunsmith Inc 570 992-4499
  4168 Gumm St Stroudsburg (18360) *(G-18111)*

Craig Hollern (PA) 814 539-2974
  1107 Cushon St Johnstown (15902) *(G-8366)*

Craig R Wickett 610 599-6882
  190 Washington Blvd Bangor (18013) *(G-910)*

Craig Sidleck 610 261-9580
  5988 Coplay Rd Whitehall (18052) *(G-19869)*

Craig Walters (PA) 570 645-3415
  348 E White St Summit Hill (18250) *(G-18159)*

Craigg Manufacturing Corp 610 678-8200
  700 Henry Cir Reading (19608) *(G-16353)*

Craigjill Inc 570 803-0234
  36 Hazleton St Ashley (18706) *(G-739)*

Cramco Dinettes, Philadelphia *Also called Cramco Inc (G-13577)*

Cramco Inc (PA) 215 427-9500
  2200 E Ann St Philadelphia (19134) *(G-13577)*

Cramer Bakery, Yardley *Also called Cramer Partnership (G-20301)*

Cramer Partnership 215 378-6024
  26 E Afton Ave Yardley (19067) *(G-20301)*

Cranberry Beverage Corp 814 437-7998
  689 Bucktail Rd Franklin (16323) *(G-6123)*

Cranberry Eagle, Cranberry Township *Also called Eagle Printing Company (G-3817)*

Crane Co 610 631-7700
  2650 Eisenhower Ave 100a Norristown (19403) *(G-12647)*

Crane Man Inc 215 996-1033
  237 Schoolhouse Rd Chalfont (18914) *(G-2870)*

Crane Payment Innovations Inc (HQ) 610 430-2700
  3222 Phoenixville Pike # 200 Malvern (19355) *(G-10218)*

Craneco LLC 610 948-1400
  490 1st Ave Royersford (19468) *(G-16847)*

Crave Cupcakes By Tamara LLC 610 417-4909
  4209 Windsor Dr Allentown (18104) *(G-184)*

Crawford Designs, West Newton *Also called Crawford Dzignes Inc (G-19750)*

Crawford Dzignes Inc 724 872-4644
  430 Turkeytown Rd West Newton (15089) *(G-19750)*

Crawford Education Plus, Elkins Park *Also called Charlene Crawford (G-4901)*

Cray Valley, Exton *Also called Total Ptrchemicals Ref USA Inc (G-5737)*

Cray Valley, West Chester *Also called Total Ptrchemicals Ref USA Inc (G-19667)*

Crayola Experience, The, Easton *Also called Crayola LLC (G-4663)*

Crayola Factory Discovery Ctr, Easton *Also called Crayola LLC (G-4665)*

Crayola LLC (HQ) 610 253-6272
  1100 Church Ln Easton (18040) *(G-4663)*

Crayola LLC 610 253-6271
  2869 Route 22 Fredericksburg (17026) *(G-6173)*

Crayola LLC 610 814-7681
  3025 Commerce Center Blvd Bethlehem (18015) *(G-1489)*

Crayola LLC 610 253-6272
  2035 Edgewood Ave Easton (18045) *(G-4664)*

Crayola LLC 610 515-8000
  30 Centre Sq Ste 2 Easton (18042) *(G-4665)*

Craze For Rayz Tanning Center 484 231-1164
  3333 Ridge Pike Apt 1 Norristown (19403) *(G-12648)*

Crazy Aaron Enterprises Inc 866 578-2845
  700 E Main St Fl 1rear Norristown (19401) *(G-12649)*

Crazy Aaron's Puttyworld, Norristown *Also called Crazy Aaron Enterprises Inc (G-12649)*

CRC, Aston *Also called Container Research Corporation (G-757)*

CRC Industries Inc 800 556-5074
  86 Railroad Dr Warminster (18974) *(G-18850)*

CRC Industries Inc (HQ) 215 674-4300
  800 Enterprise Rd Ste 101 Horsham (19044) *(G-7806)*

CRC Industries Inc 215 441-4380
  885 Louis Dr Warminster (18974) *(G-18851)*

CRC Manufacturing Inc 703 408-0645
  13358 Lincoln Hwy Everett (15537) *(G-5569)*

Creamery On Main 610 928-1500
  4665 Mill Rd Emmaus (18049) *(G-5024)*

Creation Cabinetry & Sign Co 717 246-3386
  3265 Cape Horn Rd Red Lion (17356) *(G-16591)*

Creative Apron, Havertown *Also called Davy Manufacturing Inc (G-7420)*

Creative Architectural Metals 215 638-1650
  1642 Woodhaven Dr Bensalem (19020) *(G-1175)*

Creative Awnings Inc 610 282-3305
  425 Springfield St Coopersburg (18036) *(G-3626)*

Creative Case Works, Pittsburgh *Also called Alumagraphics Inc (G-14694)*

Creative Ceramics 724 504-4318
  606 New Castle Rd Butler (16001) *(G-2391)*

Creative Characters 215 923-2679
  990 Spring Garden St # 401 Philadelphia (19123) *(G-13578)*

Creative Chemical Co 724 443-5010
  4609 Woodlake Dr Allison Park (15101) *(G-448)*

Creative Color Display, New Castle *Also called Interstate Cont New Castle LLC (G-12106)*

Creative Design & Machining 570 587-3077
  969 Griffin Pond Rd S Abingtn Twp (18411) *(G-16894)*

Creative Designs Intl Ltd 215 953-2800
  2450 Metropolitan Dr Trevose (19053) *(G-18491)*

Creative Embedments 717 299-0385
  1851 Wickersham Ln Lancaster (17603) *(G-8987)*

Creative Embroidery Designs 412 793-1923
  158 Random Rd Douglassville (19518) *(G-4173)*

Creative Energy Distributors 717 354-6090
  150 Jalyn Dr New Holland (17557) *(G-12240)*

Creative Engnred Solutions Inc 570 655-3399
  1 Freeport Rd Pittston (18640) *(G-15747)*

Creative Flavor Concepts Inc 949 705-6584
  350 Richardson Dr Lancaster (17603) *(G-8988)*

Creative Forge, Telford *Also called Carl E Reichert Corp (G-18269)*

Creative Graphics Inc 610 973-8300
  6620 Grant Way Allentown (18106) *(G-185)*

Creative Impressions Advg LLC 215 357-1228
  1209 Ridge Rd Ste B Langhorne (19053) *(G-9287)*

Creative Imprint Systems, Erie *Also called Ras Sports Inc (G-5457)*

Creative Kink LLC 610 506-9809
  12 Char Mar Ln Royersford (19468) *(G-16848)*

Creative Labworks Inc 724 667-4093
203 W Poland Ave Bessemer (16112) *(G-1390)*
Creative Logistics Ltd 724 458-6560
23 Tower Rd Grove City (16127) *(G-6782)*
Creative Management Svcs LLC 610 863-1900
521 W Babbitt Ave Pen Argyl (18072) *(G-13212)*
Creative Marketing Associates, Pittsburgh *Also called Berkman John A Display Sls Inc (G-14763)*
Creative Mountain Software LLC 814 383-2685
258 Hoy Rd Howard (16841) *(G-7888)*
Creative Nonfiction Foundation 412 688-0304
5119 Coral St Pittsburgh (15224) *(G-14886)*
Creative Printing & Graphics 724 222-8304
1250 Washington Rd Washington (15301) *(G-19158)*
Creative Printing Co 570 875-1811
430 S Hoffman Blvd Ashland (17921) *(G-729)*
Creative Pultrusions Inc (HQ) 814 839-4186
214 Industrial Ln Alum Bank (15521) *(G-560)*
Creative Services Dept, Easton *Also called Crayola LLC (G-4664)*
Creative Stitches By Dina Inc 724 863-4104
11380 State Route 30 Irwin (15642) *(G-8152)*
Creative Structures, Quakertown *Also called Sarik Corporation (G-16243)*
Creative Systems Usa LLC 610 450-6580
505 Second Ave Collegeville (19426) *(G-3373)*
Creative Thought Media LLC 267 270-5147
2301 N 9th St Ste 310 Philadelphia (19133) *(G-13579)*
Creative Touch Inc 215 856-9177
11500 Roosevelt Blvd B Philadelphia (19116) *(G-13580)*
Creavey Seal Co, Clarks Summit *Also called G F C Inc (G-3193)*
Creek View Manufacturing LLC 717 445-4922
1751 Mill Rd East Earl (17519) *(G-4541)*
Creekhill Cabinetry 717 656-7438
261 S Kinzer Rd Paradise (17562) *(G-13155)*
Creekside Springs LLC (PA) 724 266-9000
667 Merchant St Ambridge (15003) *(G-613)*
Creekside Springs LLC 724 266-9000
667 Merchant St Ambridge (15003) *(G-614)*
Creekside Structures LLC 717 627-5267
745 E Millport Rd Leola (17540) *(G-9775)*
Creekside Tanning, Conneaut Lake *Also called Tammy Williams (G-3481)*
Creekside Welding LLC 717 355-2008
137 Meadowcreek Rd New Holland (17557) *(G-12241)*
Crees Wldg & Fabrication Inc 717 795-8711
320 E Allen St Mechanicsburg (17055) *(G-10832)*
Creighton Printing Inc 724 224-0444
917 Freeport Rd Creighton (15030) *(G-3882)*
Creotech Industries LLC 724 267-3100
72 Little Creek Rd Marianna (15345) *(G-10456)*
Creperie Bechamel LLC 610 964-9700
11 Louella Ct Radnor (19087) *(G-16292)*
Creps United Publications Inc 724 463-9722
40 Christy Park Dr Indiana (15701) *(G-8088)*
Crescent Designed Metals, Philadelphia *Also called CDM Holdings Inc (G-13517)*
Crescent Industries Inc (PA) 717 235-3844
70 E High St New Freedom (17349) *(G-12203)*
Crescent Industries Inc 717 235-3844
70 E High St New Freedom (17349) *(G-12204)*
Crescent Paint Co, Philadelphia *Also called Sharp Coatings (G-14298)*
Cresline Plastic Pipe Co Inc 717 766-9262
264 Silver Spring Rd Mechanicsburg (17050) *(G-10833)*
Crespo & Diaz Industries LLC 484 895-7139
850 N 5th St Allentown (18102) *(G-186)*
Cressona Textile Waste Inc 570 385-4556
Front And Rail Rd St Cressona (17929) *(G-3903)*
Crest Advertising Co 724 774-4413
1529 Old Brodhead Rd Monaca (15061) *(G-11289)*
Creston E Lockbaum Inc 717 414-6885
89 Industrial Dr Chambersburg (17201) *(G-2921)*
Crestwood Membranes Inc 570 474-6741
755 Oak Hill Rd Mountain Top (18707) *(G-11758)*
Crete NYCE Co Inc 215 855-4628
Iron & 6th St # 6 Lansdale (19446) *(G-9354)*
Crew Systems Corporation 570 281-9221
10 Enterprise Carbondale (18407) *(G-2673)*
Crg Holding Inc 215 569-9900
1845 Walnut St Ste 800 Philadelphia (19103) *(G-13581)*
Crg Resources LLC 814 571-7190
214 Norris Rd Curwensville (16833) *(G-3950)*
Crichton Diversfd Ventures LLC 814 288-1561
636 Tire Hill Rd Johnstown (15905) *(G-8367)*
Cricket Communications LLC 267 687-5949
930 Washington Ave Philadelphia (19147) *(G-13582)*
Crighton Plastics, Coraopolis *Also called C & E Plastic East (G-3666)*
Crighton Plastics Inc 724 457-0594
392 Flaugherty Run Rd Coraopolis (15108) *(G-3681)*
Crile Consolidated Inds Inc 724 228-0880
1086 Jolly School Rd Washington (15301) *(G-19159)*
Crismor Machine Inc 717 292-9646
225 Blue Hill School Rd East Berlin (17316) *(G-4521)*

Crisp Control Inc 724 864-6777
200 Productivity Pl Irwin (15642) *(G-8153)*
Crispin Valve, Berwick *Also called Multiplex Manufacturing Co (G-1337)*
Crispin Valve LLC 570 752-4524
600 Fowler Ave Berwick (18603) *(G-1321)*
Critic Publications Inc 215 536-8884
1380 Masi Dr Quakertown (18951) *(G-16181)*
Critical Path Project Inc 215 545-2212
2062 Lombard St Philadelphia (19146) *(G-13583)*
Critical Systems LLC 570 643-6903
2369 Route 715 Tannersville (18372) *(G-18235)*
Crl, Pittsburgh *Also called Carnegie Robotics LLC (G-14819)*
Crncte LLC 610 648-0419
1013 W King Rd Malvern (19355) *(G-10219)*
Crockett Log Homes of PA Inc 717 697-6198
58 Sunset Dr Mechanicsburg (17050) *(G-10834)*
Croda Inc 570 893-7650
8 Croda Way Mill Hall (17751) *(G-11175)*
Crofchick Inc 570 287-3940
90 Owen St Swoyersville (18704) *(G-18197)*
Crogan Inc 814 944-3057
2109 9th Ave Altoona (16602) *(G-495)*
Cromaflow Inc 570 546-3557
143 Lumber Ln Montoursville (17754) *(G-11437)*
Cromie Machine Tool Co Inc (PA) 724 385-0729
4800 Harrison St Pittsburgh (15201) *(G-14887)*
Cronan Sheet Metal Inc 610 375-9230
141 Schiller St Reading (19601) *(G-16354)*
Cronimet Corporation (HQ) 724 375-5004
1 Pilarsky Way Aliquippa (15001) *(G-71)*
Cronimet Spcialty Mtls USA Inc (HQ) 724 347-2208
40 Council Ave Wheatland (16161) *(G-19835)*
Cropcare, Lititz *Also called Pbz LLC (G-10029)*
Cross Excavating, Mansfield *Also called Chad Cross (G-10412)*
Cross Works Embroidery Sp Inc 610 261-1690
129 S 2nd St Coplay (18037) *(G-3642)*
Crossing Vineyards and Winery 215 493-6500
1853 Wrightstown Rd Washington Crossing (18977) *(G-19255)*
Crossroads Beverage Group LLC 352 509-3127
1055 Crossroads Blvd Reading (19605) *(G-16355)*
Crosstex International Inc 724 347-0400
534 Vine Ave Sharon (16146) *(G-17431)*
Crouse Run Ventures Inc 412 491-5738
706 Timber Ln Sewickley (15143) *(G-17385)*
Crouses Pallet Service 717 577-9012
100 Redco Ave Red Lion (17356) *(G-16592)*
Crow Valley Pottery 360 376-4260
61 W Broadway Jim Thorpe (18229) *(G-8339)*
Crowell Metal Fabrication 814 486-2664
221 E 2nd St Emporium (15834) *(G-5054)*
Crown Americas LLC 215 698-5100
1 Crown Way Philadelphia (19154) *(G-13584)*
Crown Beverage Packaging LLC 215 698-5100
1 Crown Way Philadelphia (19154) *(G-13585)*
Crown Boiler Co 215 535-8900
3633 I St Philadelphia (19134) *(G-13586)*
Crown Boilers, Philadelphia *Also called Crown Boiler Co (G-13586)*
Crown Cork & Seal Company Inc 215 698-5100
770 Township Line Rd # 100 Yardley (19067) *(G-20302)*
Crown Cork & Seal Usa Inc (HQ) 215 698-5100
770 Township Line Rd # 100 Yardley (19067) *(G-20303)*
Crown Cork & Seal Usa Inc 215 322-5507
3100 Tremont Ave Feasterville Trevose (19053) *(G-5901)*
Crown Cork & Seal Usa Inc 215 698-5100
3070 Red Lion Rd Philadelphia (19114) *(G-13587)*
Crown Cork & Seal Usa Inc 724 626-0121
1840 Baldridge Ave Connellsville (15425) *(G-3493)*
Crown Cork & Seal Usa Inc 717 633-1163
1650 Broadway Hanover (17331) *(G-6871)*
Crown Cork Seal 610 687-2616
233 Plant Ave Wayne (19087) *(G-19315)*
Crown Equipment Corporation 724 696-3533
300 Westec Dr Mount Pleasant (15666) *(G-11695)*
Crown Food Carts Incorporated 610 628-9612
527 Sumner Ct Allentown (18102) *(G-187)*
Crown Hardwood West Inc 717 436-9677
26960 Route 75 N Mifflintown (17059) *(G-11112)*
Crown Holdings Inc 215 322-3533
3100 Tremont Ave Feasterville Trevose (19053) *(G-5902)*
Crown Holdings Inc (PA) 215 698-5100
770 Township Line Rd # 100 Yardley (19067) *(G-20304)*
Crown Intl Holdings Inc (HQ) 215 698-5100
770 Township Line Rd Yardley (19067) *(G-20305)*
Crown Lift Trucks, Mount Pleasant *Also called Crown Equipment Corporation (G-11695)*
Crown Molding 412 779-9209
2603 Old Washington Rd Pittsburgh (15241) *(G-14888)*
Crown Precious Metals 267 923-5263
859 Main St Pennsburg (18073) *(G-13247)*
Crown Scaffolding, Plymouth Meeting *Also called Spring Lock Scaffolding Eqp Co (G-15873)*

Crownwood Custom Cabinetry, Mc Alisterville *Also called Crownwood LLC* ***(G-10548)***
Crownwood LLC.......717 463-2942
1739 Main St Mc Alisterville (17049) ***(G-10548)***
Crp Inc.......610 970-7663
191 S Keim St Pottstown (19464) ***(G-15977)***
CRS, Gettysburg *Also called Community Resource Svcs Inc* ***(G-6286)***
Cru Group.......724 940-7100
2000 Corporate Dr Ste 410 Wexford (15090) ***(G-19797)***
Crudeaco, Callensburg *Also called Randy Larkin* ***(G-2465)***
Crumbs.......717 609-1120
101 Watts St Mount Holly Springs (17065) ***(G-11633)***
Crusader Precision Shtmtl Co.......610 485-4321
1581 Chichester Ave Marcus Hook (19061) ***(G-10440)***
Crw Graphics, Philadelphia *Also called Composing Room Inc* ***(G-13565)***
Cryo Technologies, Allentown *Also called Cryogenic Gas Technologies Inc* ***(G-188)***
Cryo Tempering Tech of Ne PA.......570 287-7443
189 River St Kingston (18704) ***(G-8715)***
Cryocal.......714 568-0201
767 Route 30 Imperial (15126) ***(G-8061)***
Cryogenic Gas Technologies Inc.......610 530-7288
241 N Cedar Crest Blvd Allentown (18104) ***(G-188)***
Cryognic Inds Svc Cmpanies LLC.......724 695-1910
767 State Route 30 Imperial (15126) ***(G-8062)***
Cryoguard Corporation.......215 712-9018
151 Discovery Dr Ste 107 Colmar (18915) ***(G-3413)***
Cryostar USA.......484 281-3261
5897 Colony Dr Bethlehem (18017) ***(G-1490)***
Cryovac Inc.......610 926-7500
4275 Reading Crest Ave Reading (19605) ***(G-16356)***
Cryovac Inc.......610 929-9190
1002 Patriot Pkwy Reading (19605) ***(G-16357)***
Crystal Inc - PMC (HQ).......215 368-1661
601 W 8th St Lansdale (19446) ***(G-9355)***
Crystal Custom Kitchens Inc.......610 683-8187
755 Crystal Cave Rd Kutztown (19530) ***(G-8839)***
Crystal Engineering Corp.......610 647-2121
1100 Cassatt Rd Berwyn (19312) ***(G-1358)***
Crystal Frms Refrigerated Dist.......570 425-2910
68 Spain Rd Klingerstown (17941) ***(G-8807)***
Crystal Imagery Inc.......888 440-6073
680 S Ridge Rd York Springs (17372) ***(G-20764)***
Crystal Metal Products Co Inc.......215 423-2500
2700 Castor Ave Philadelphia (19134) ***(G-13588)***
Crystal Palace, Lancaster *Also called Rob Kei Inc* ***(G-9189)***
Crystal Pure Bottled Water, Altoona *Also called Altoona Soft Water Company* ***(G-473)***
Crystal Shower Doors.......717 642-9689
13 Eagle Trl Fairfield (17320) ***(G-5766)***
Crystal Springs, Harrisburg *Also called Ds Services of America Inc* ***(G-7122)***
Crystaline Bus & Rail Inc.......570 645-3145
442 Industrial Rd Nesquehoning (18240) ***(G-12004)***
Crystalplex Corporation.......412 787-1525
1816 Parkway View Dr Pittsburgh (15205) ***(G-14889)***
Cs Trucking LLC (PA).......814 224-0395
366 Travelers Rd East Freedom (16637) ***(G-4563)***
CS&e, Pittsburgh *Also called Combustion Service & Eqp Co* ***(G-14867)***
Cs-B2 Investments Inc.......412 261-1300
814 Penn Ave Pittsburgh (15222) ***(G-14890)***
CSC Sugar LLC.......215 428-3670
80 Roebling Rd Fairless Hills (19030) ***(G-5777)***
Cse Corporation.......724 733-2247
825 Plum Industrial Park Pittsburgh (15239) ***(G-14891)***
Csg Bakery, Sunbury *Also called Community Services Group Inc* ***(G-18167)***
Csi Industries Inc.......814 474-9353
6910 W Ridge Rd Unit 1 Fairview (16415) ***(G-5819)***
Csl Behring LLC (HQ).......610 878-4000
1020 1st Ave King of Prussia (19406) ***(G-8601)***
Csl Plasma Inc.......717 767-2348
2430 Eastern Blvd York (17402) ***(G-20439)***
Cslb Holdings Inc (HQ).......610 878-4000
1020 1st Ave King of Prussia (19406) ***(G-8602)***
CSP Technologies Inc.......610 635-1202
2570 Blvd Of The Gen 215 Audubon (19403) ***(G-824)***
CSS, Blue Bell *Also called Communication Svcs & Support* ***(G-1822)***
CSS Industries Inc (PA).......610 729-3959
450 Plymouth Rd Ste 300 Plymouth Meeting (19462) ***(G-15840)***
CSS Industries Inc.......570 275-5241
350 Wall St Danville (17821) ***(G-3999)***
CSS International Corporation.......215 533-6110
2061 E Glenwood Ave Philadelphia (19124) ***(G-13589)***
Ctc, Greensburg *Also called Cardiac Telecom Corporation* ***(G-6656)***
Ctc Pressure Products LLC.......814 315-6427
2820 W 21st St Ste 1 Erie (16506) ***(G-5235)***
CTI King of Prussia LLC.......610 879-2868
400 Drew Ct King of Prussia (19406) ***(G-8603)***
Ctor Tipple, Clearfield *Also called Victor LLC* ***(G-3233)***
Ctp Carrera Inc (HQ).......724 539-6995
600 Depot St Latrobe (15650) ***(G-9468)***
Ctp Carrera Inc.......724 733-2994
6009 Enterprise Dr Export (15632) ***(G-5596)***
CTS Bulk Terminals.......610 759-8330
4677 Hanoverville Rd Bethlehem (18020) ***(G-1491)***
Cudd Energy Services, Lemont Furnace *Also called Cudd Pressure Control Inc* ***(G-9735)***
Cudd Pressure Control Inc.......570 250-9043
90 Brittany Ln Lemont Furnace (15456) ***(G-9735)***
Cudd Pressure Services, Canton *Also called Rpc Inc* ***(G-2667)***
Cueco, Butler *Also called Commonwealth Utility Eqp Inc* ***(G-2390)***
Cullari Vineyards & Winery Inc.......717 571-2376
2149 Sand Hill Rd Hershey (17033) ***(G-7607)***
Culligan, Star Junction *Also called Trilli Holdings Inc* ***(G-17938)***
Culpepper Corporation.......215 425-6532
1310 N 2nd St Philadelphia (19122) ***(G-13590)***
Culturenik Publishing Inc.......570 424-9848
1901 W Main St Stroudsburg (18360) ***(G-18112)***
Culver Hardwoods.......814 827-3202
13977 Windfall Rd Titusville (16354) ***(G-18377)***
Culver Industries Inc.......724 857-5770
1000 Industrial Blvd # 400 Aliquippa (15001) ***(G-72)***
Culver Tool & Die Inc.......717 932-2000
688 Yorktown Rd Ste E Lewisberry (17339) ***(G-9882)***
Culverts Inc.......412 262-3111
330 Pittsburgh Ave Coraopolis (15108) ***(G-3682)***
Cumberland Coal Resources LP (HQ).......724 852-5845
158 Portal Rd Waynesburg (15370) ***(G-19436)***
Cumberland Coal Resources LP.......724 627-7500
855 Kirby Rd Waynesburg (15370) ***(G-19437)***
Cumberland Contura LLC.......724 627-7500
158 Portal Rd Waynesburg (15370) ***(G-19438)***
Cumberland Farms Inc.......412 331-4419
2620 Neville Rd Pittsburgh (15225) ***(G-14892)***
Cumberland Printing Co, Mechanicsburg *Also called Minnich Limited* ***(G-10871)***
Cumberland Tool & Die Inc.......717 691-1125
6 Brenneman Cir Mechanicsburg (17050) ***(G-10835)***
Cumberland Valley Coop Assn.......717 532-2197
908 Mount Rock Rd Shippensburg (17257) ***(G-17525)***
Cumberland Valley Wldg & Repr.......717 249-1129
1129 Harrisburg Pike # 4 Carlisle (17013) ***(G-2704)***
Cumberland Woodcraft Co Inc.......717 243-0063
10 Stover Dr Carlisle (17015) ***(G-2705)***
Cummings Custom Saw Milling.......570 586-3277
109 Cummings Pond Rd Clarks Summit (18411) ***(G-3190)***
Cummings Group Inc.......714 237-1140
2020 Highland Ave Bethlehem (18020) ***(G-1492)***
Cummings Group Ltd.......814 774-8238
227 Hathaway St E Girard (16417) ***(G-6385)***
Cummings Veneer Products Inc.......570 995-1892
23189 Rte 14 N Troy (16947) ***(G-18520)***
Cummins - Allison Corp.......610 355-1400
630 Park Way Frnt 1a Broomall (19008) ***(G-2284)***
Cummins - Allison Corp.......215 245-8436
3260 Tillman Dr Bensalem (19020) ***(G-1176)***
Cummins Inc.......724 798-4511
483 Rehoboth Rd Belle Vernon (15012) ***(G-1085)***
Cummins Inc.......717 564-1344
4499 Lewis Rd Harrisburg (17111) ***(G-7110)***
Cummins Inc.......570 333-0360
24 Pine Ridge Rd Tunkhannock (18657) ***(G-18535)***
Cummins Inc.......215 785-6005
2727 Ford Rd Bristol (19007) ***(G-2129)***
Cummins Inc.......412 820-0330
3 Alpha Dr Pittsburgh (15238) ***(G-14893)***
Cummins-Wagner Company Inc.......717 367-8294
3 Meating Pl Elizabethtown (17022) ***(G-4870)***
Cupcake Momma.......724 516-5098
1170 Walton Rd Jeannette (15644) ***(G-8251)***
Cupoladua Oven LLC.......412 592-5378
137 Grand Ave Ste 1 Mars (16046) ***(G-10493)***
Curbell Inc.......724 772-6800
250 W Kensinger Dr # 100 Cranberry Township (16066) ***(G-3813)***
Curbs Plus Inc.......888 639-2872
208 N Division St Mount Union (17066) ***(G-11742)***
Curbs Plus Inc.......888 639-2872
208 N Division St Mount Union (17066) ***(G-11743)***
Curio Electrical Motor Repr Sp.......610 432-9923
825 S 5th St Allentown (18103) ***(G-189)***
Currency Inc.......814 509-6157
1700 Somerset Ave Windber (15963) ***(G-20180)***
Current Circuits Inc.......215 444-9295
375 Ivyland Rd Ste 21 Warminster (18974) ***(G-18852)***
Current History Inc.......610 772-5709
4225 Main St Philadelphia (19127) ***(G-13591)***
Current Therapeutics Inc.......610 644-5995
477 Howellville Rd Berwyn (19312) ***(G-1359)***
Curry Copy Center, Lancaster *Also called Jaren Enterprises Inc* ***(G-9072)***
Curry Flour Mills Inc.......717 838-2421
338 N Railroad St Palmyra (17078) ***(G-13119)***
Curry Lumber Co (PA).......724 438-1911
40 Buttermilk Ln Hopwood (15445) ***(G-7776)***

ALPHABETIC

Curry Printing & Copy 610 373-2890
712 Corporate Dr Reading (19605) *(G-16358)*

Curry Rail Services Inc 814 793-7245
1477 Degol Indl Dr Hollidaysburg (16648) *(G-7645)*

Curry Spectacle Shop Inc 814 899-6833
3202 Buffalo Rd Erie (16510) *(G-5236)*

Curtain Call Costumes, York *Also called Perform Group LLC* *(G-20624)*

Curtis and Son Oil Inc 814 489-7858
Lander Rd Sugargrove (16350) *(G-18150)*

Curtis and Sons Oil, Sugargrove *Also called Curtis Well Service Company* *(G-18151)*

Curtis Baker Lumber Inc 814 425-3020
751 Old Route 322 Cochranton (16314) *(G-3340)*

Curtis Glenchem Corp 610 876-9906
2000 Industrial Hwy Eddystone (19022) *(G-4800)*

Curtis Industries, Kittanning *Also called Curtis Sure-Grip Inc* *(G-8763)*

Curtis Leljedal Trading Loggn 570 924-3938
Pa Rt 154 N Forksville (18616) *(G-6056)*

Curtis Pharmaceutical Service 724 223-1114
36 Old Hickory Ridge Rd Washington (15301) *(G-19160)*

Curtis Sure-Grip Inc 724 545-8333
105 West Park Dr Kittanning (16201) *(G-8763)*

Curtis Well Service, Sugargrove *Also called Curtis and Son Oil Inc* *(G-18150)*

Curtis Well Service Company 814 489-7858
Rr 957 Sugargrove (16350) *(G-18151)*

Curtiss Laboratories Inc 215 245-8833
2510 State Rd Bensalem (19020) *(G-1177)*

Curtiss- Wright Nuclear Div, Freeport *Also called Curtiss-Wright Flow Control* *(G-6202)*

Curtiss-Wright Corporation 724 275-5277
205 Nebraska Dr New Kensington (15068) *(G-12337)*

Curtiss-Wright Corporation 215 721-1100
2701 Township Line Rd Hatfield (19440) *(G-7328)*

Curtiss-Wright Electro- (HQ) 724 275-5000
1000 Wright Way Cheswick (15024) *(G-3105)*

Curtiss-Wright Electro- 610 997-6400
1185 Feather Way Bethlehem (18015) *(G-1493)*

Curtiss-Wright Flow Control 724 295-6200
203 Armstrong Dr Freeport (16229) *(G-6202)*

Curto Toy Manufacturing Co 610 438-5241
425 S 15th St Easton (18042) *(G-4666)*

Curvebeam LLC 267 483-8081
2800 Bronze Dr Ste 110 Hatfield (19440) *(G-7329)*

Cusick Tool Inc 724 253-4455
19 Larimer Rd Hadley (16130) *(G-6818)*

Cussewago Truss LLC 814 763-3229
23416 Middle Rd Cambridge Springs (16403) *(G-2476)*

Custeads Sawmill Inc 814 425-3863
8950 Frenchtown Rd Guys Mills (16327) *(G-6810)*

Custer Ave Woodworking LLC 717 354-3999
868 S Custer Ave New Holland (17557) *(G-12242)*

Custom Aluminum Frame Fabg, Pittsburgh *Also called Caff Co* *(G-14799)*

Custom Bedframe Products 570 539-8770
49 Summer Breeze Ln Port Trevorton (17864) *(G-15911)*

Custom Bins Pallet Mfg 570 539-4158
64 Summer Breeze Ln Port Trevorton (17864) *(G-15912)*

Custom Blends Inc 215 934-7080
9951 Global Rd Philadelphia (19115) *(G-13592)*

Custom Built Products Inc 215 946-9555
760 Oxford Ave Bristol (19007) *(G-2130)*

Custom Cabinetry Unlimited LLC 717 656-9170
20 S Groffdale Rd Leola (17540) *(G-9776)*

Custom Carbioe Grinding 724 539-8826
303 State Route 217 Latrobe (15650) *(G-9469)*

Custom Carpet & Bedding Inc 570 344-7533
105 Corner St Dunmore (18512) *(G-4472)*

Custom Chill Inc 215 676-7600
2751 Southampton Rd Philadelphia (19154) *(G-13593)*

Custom Container Solutions LLC 570 524-7835
391 Wolfland Rd Lewisburg (17837) *(G-9902)*

Custom Container Vly Can LLC 724 253-2038
391 Wolfland Rd Lewisburg (17837) *(G-9903)*

Custom Corner Sportswear 724 588-1667
275 Main St Greenville (16125) *(G-6740)*

Custom Craft Cabinets 215 886-6105
1274 Thomson Rd Abington (19001) *(G-10)*

Custom Design 570 462-0041
144 Delaware Ave Shenandoah (17976) *(G-17493)*

Custom Designs & Mfg Co 570 207-4432
40 Poplar St Scranton (18509) *(G-17226)*

Custom Die Services Inc 717 867-5400
409 Ono Rd Annville (17003) *(G-646)*

Custom Doorcraft LLC 717 768-7613
2902 Miller Ln Bird In Hand (17505) *(G-1672)*

Custom Elevator Mfg Co Inc 215 766-3380
5191 Stump Rd Plumsteadville (18949) *(G-15807)*

Custom Engineering Co (PA) 814 898-1390
2800 Mcclelland Ave Erie (16510) *(G-5237)*

Custom Entryways & Millwork 814 798-2500
2989 Whistler Rd Stoystown (15563) *(G-18074)*

Custom Etch Inc 724 652-7117
1813 W State St Ste 1 New Castle (16101) *(G-12079)*

Custom Extruders Inc 570 345-6600
80 Roberts Rd Pine Grove (17963) *(G-14590)*

Custom Fab Inc 717 721-5008
596 W Trout Run Rd Ephrata (17522) *(G-5098)*

Custom Fab Co Inc 570 784-0874
1439 Millville Rd Ste 1 Bloomsburg (17815) *(G-1777)*

Custom Fab Trailers Inc 724 548-5529
12478 Us Route 422 Kittanning (16201) *(G-8764)*

Custom Finishing Inc 215 269-7500
7205 Hibbs Ln Levittown (19057) *(G-9829)*

Custom Graphic and Plates, Colmar *Also called Custom Platecrafters Inc* *(G-3414)*

Custom Heliarc Welding & Mch 570 897-0400
4136 Church St Mount Bethel (18343) *(G-11608)*

Custom Hydraulics Inc 724 729-3170
38 Steubenville Pike Burgettstown (15021) *(G-2344)*

Custom Industrial Processing 814 834-1883
336 State St Saint Marys (15857) *(G-16958)*

Custom Inserts, Glenmoore *Also called JP Betz Inc* *(G-6468)*

Custom Iron Works Welding 814 444-1315
570 Berlin Plank Rd Somerset (15501) *(G-17682)*

Custom Kitchens Inc 814 833-5338
3014 W 12th St Erie (16505) *(G-5238)*

Custom Laminating Corporation 570 897-8300
5000 River Rd Mount Bethel (18343) *(G-11609)*

Custom Linings Spray On Bed 570 779-4609
112 Narrows Rd Plymouth (18651) *(G-15816)*

Custom Machine & Design Inc 610 932-4717
21 Commerce Blvd West Grove (19390) *(G-19699)*

Custom Machined Spc Inc 814 938-1031
1356 N Main St Punxsutawney (15767) *(G-16130)*

Custom Manufactured Products 215 228-3830
1100 W Indiana Ave Philadelphia (19133) *(G-13594)*

Custom Manufacturing Corp 215 638-3888
2542 State Rd Bensalem (19020) *(G-1178)*

Custom McHining Great Bend Inc 570 879-2559
26122 State Route 11 Great Bend (18821) *(G-6581)*

Custom Metal Innovations Inc 724 965-3929
1 Church St Ext Wheatland (16161) *(G-19836)*

Custom Mfg & Indus Svcs LLC 412 621-2982
4821 Harrison St Pittsburgh (15201) *(G-14894)*

Custom Mil & Consulting Inc (PA) 610 926-0984
1246 Maidencreek Rd Fleetwood (19522) *(G-5969)*

Custom Molds Plastic 717 417-5639
165 S Orchard St Yoe (17313) *(G-20359)*

Custom Nuclear Fabrication CNF, Canonsburg *Also called Custom Nuclear Fabrication LLC* *(G-2575)*

Custom Nuclear Fabrication LLC 724 271-3006
50 Curry Ave Canonsburg (15317) *(G-2575)*

Custom Pack Inc 610 363-1900
662 Exton Cmns Exton (19341) *(G-5663)*

Custom Pallet Recycler 724 658-6086
1799 County Line Rd New Castle (16101) *(G-12080)*

Custom Particle Reduction Inc 215 766-9791
5189 Stump Rd Plumsteadville (18949) *(G-15808)*

Custom Plastic Specialties LLC 814 838-6471
5678 W Ridge Rd Erie (16506) *(G-5239)*

Custom Platecrafters Inc (PA) 215 997-1990
230 Bethlehem Pike Colmar (18915) *(G-3414)*

Custom Polishing and Finishing 215 331-0960
8301 Torresdale Ave # 23 Philadelphia (19136) *(G-13595)*

Custom Pool Coping Inc 215 822-9098
3210 Unionville Pike Hatfield (19440) *(G-7330)*

Custom Power Recycler, New Castle *Also called Custom Pallet Recycler* *(G-12080)*

Custom Printed Graphics Inc (PA) 412 881-8208
2933 Mary St Pittsburgh (15203) *(G-14895)*

Custom Printing Unlimited 724 339-3000
1515 5th Ave New Kensington (15068) *(G-12338)*

Custom Processing Services Inc (PA) 610 779-7001
2 Birchmont Dr Ste 3 Reading (19606) *(G-16359)*

Custom Products 814 453-6803
2250 W 23rd St Erie (16506) *(G-5240)*

Custom Riding Apparel, Souderton *Also called Total Equestrian Inc* *(G-17768)*

Custom Scientific Instruments 610 923-6500
1125 Conroy Pl Easton (18040) *(G-4667)*

Custom Seats Inc 570 602-7408
1212 Scott St Wilkes Barre (18705) *(G-19915)*

Custom Signs Inc 814 786-7232
1535 Millbrook Rd Grove City (16127) *(G-6783)*

Custom Sintered Specialties 814 834-5154
199 Ceramic St Saint Marys (15857) *(G-16959)*

Custom Stair Builders Inc 717 261-0551
1271 Candice Ln Chambersburg (17201) *(G-2922)*

Custom Steel Products Inc (PA) 412 215-9923
98 Vanadium Rd Ste 12 Bridgeville (15017) *(G-2058)*

Custom Stone Interiors Inc 814 548-0120
360 Rolling Ridge Dr Bellefonte (16823) *(G-1096)*

Custom Systems Technology Inc 215 822-2525
3075 Advance Ln Colmar (18915) *(G-3415)*

Custom Tool & Design Inc 814 838-9777
4962 Pittsburgh Ave Erie (16509) *(G-5241)*

Custom Tool & Grinding Inc 724 223-1555
2131 W Chestnut St Washington (15301) *(G-19161)*

Custom Tool and Die Inc 717 522-1440
103 S Manor St Mountville (17554) *(G-11792)*

Custom Truss, Greenville *Also called Oakes & McClelland Co* *(G-6761)*

Custom Turf Inc 412 384-4111
1900 Gill Hall Rd Finleyville (15332) *(G-5954)*

Custom Ultrasonics Inc 215 364-1477
144 Railroad Dr Ivyland (18974) *(G-8208)*

Custom Urethane Elastomers, Cranberry Township *Also called U E C Inc* *(G-3860)*

Custom Wood Crafters Inc 215 357-6677
135 Industrial Dr Warminster (18974) *(G-18853)*

Custom Wood Products, Pittsburgh *Also called Richard Riberich* *(G-15484)*

Custom Woodworking 610 273-2907
3400 Horseshoe Pike Honey Brook (19344) *(G-7743)*

Customers Choice Brand, Kingston *Also called M Robzen Inc* *(G-8723)*

Customfold Inc 724 376-8565
926 Fredonia Rd Stoneboro (16153) *(G-18068)*

Customized Envmtl Systems 412 380-2311
3930 Old William Penn Hwy # 302 Pittsburgh (15235) *(G-14896)*

Cutanea Life Sciences Inc 484 568-0100
1500 Liberty Ridge Dr # 3000 Chesterbrook (19087) *(G-3090)*

Cute Loops 484 318-7175
36 Independence Pl Chesterbrook (19087) *(G-3091)*

Cuthbert & Son Inc 717 657-1050
5706 Jonestown Rd Harrisburg (17112) *(G-7111)*

Cutix Inc 610 246-7518
585 E Swedes Rd Ste 200 Wayne (19080) *(G-19316)*

Cutler Hammer, Moon Township *Also called Eaton Corporation* *(G-11484)*

Cutler Hammer, Moon Township *Also called Eaton Electrical Inc* *(G-11485)*

Cutpasteandprint, Huntingdon Valley *Also called Newtown Business Forms Corp* *(G-8017)*

Cutting Edge Countertops 724 397-8605
10064 Route 119 Hwy N Marion Center (15759) *(G-10472)*

Cutting Edge Doors Inc 215 425-5921
3423 Melvale St Phila (19134) *(G-13310)*

Cutting Edge Embroidery Inc 412 732-9990
681 Union Avenue Ext Pittsburgh (15229) *(G-14897)*

Cutting Edge Knives Inc 412 279-9350
1728 Berkwood Dr Pittsburgh (15243) *(G-14898)*

Cutting Edge Machining 814 345-6690
75 Basin Run Rd Drifting (16834) *(G-4374)*

Cutting Sheet, Stroudsburg *Also called American Ribbon Manufacturers* *(G-18103)*

Cutts Group LLC 610 366-9620
847 Dorset Rd Allentown (18104) *(G-190)*

Cv Anglers Club 814 203-3861
354 Azelta Rd Westfield (16950) *(G-19776)*

Cvip Inc 610 967-1525
801 Broad St Emmaus (18049) *(G-5025)*

Cw Industries, Warminster *Also called Industrial Enterprises Inc* *(G-18897)*

Cw Thomas LLC 215 335-0200
8000 State Rd Philadelphia (19136) *(G-13596)*

Cwi Inc 610 652-2211
1827 County Line Rd Barto (19504) *(G-941)*

Cyanide Vs Xaneria 570 968-4522
124 N Washington St Orwigsburg (17961) *(G-13041)*

Cyb Machining Inc 814 938-8133
130 Brown Bridge Dr Punxsutawney (15767) *(G-16131)*

Cybel LLC 610 691-7012
1195 Pennsylvania Ave Bethlehem (18018) *(G-1494)*

Cyberink LLC 814 870-1600
205 W 12th St Erie (16534) *(G-5242)*

Cyberscan Technologies Inc 215 321-0447
17 Lookout Ln Washington Crossing (18977) *(G-19256)*

Cybersonics Inc 814 898-4734
5340 Fryling Rd Ste 101 Erie (16510) *(G-5243)*

Cybertech Inc 215 957-6220
935 Horsham Rd Ste I Horsham (19044) *(G-7807)*

Cycle Source Magazine 724 226-2867
118 Dellenbaugh Rd Tarentum (15084) *(G-18240)*

Cycle Venture, Exton *Also called Dynamic Team Sports Inc* *(G-5670)*

Cycling Sports Group Inc (HQ) 203 749-7000
16 Trowbridge Dr Bedford (15522) *(G-1048)*

Cygnus Manufacturing Co LLC 724 352-8000
491 Chantler Dr Saxonburg (16056) *(G-17082)*

Cygnus Technology Inc 570 424-5701
74 Broad St Delaware Water Gap (18327) *(G-4042)*

Cymatics Laboratories Corp 412 578-0280
425 N Craig St Ste 200 Pittsburgh (15213) *(G-14899)*

Cyoptics Inc (HQ) 484 397-2000
9999 Hamilton Blvd # 250 Breinigsville (18031) *(G-2013)*

Cypher Company Inc (PA) 412 661-4913
4790 Old Frankstown Rd Monroeville (15146) *(G-11331)*

Cyrus-Xp Inc 610 986-8408
9 Rittenhouse Pl Ardmore (19003) *(G-706)*

Czar Floors, Huntingdon Valley *Also called Czar Imports Inc* *(G-7973)*

Czar Imports Inc 800 577-2927
390 Pike Rd Unit 4 Huntingdon Valley (19006) *(G-7973)*

Czeck Tool, Saegertown *Also called John W Czech* *(G-16920)*

Czerw's Phila Provision Co, Philadelphia *Also called Philadelphia Provision Co* *(G-14151)*

D & A Associates 610 534-4840
864 Main St 66 Darby (19023) *(G-4017)*

D & A Business Services Inc 610 837-7748
460 Spruce Ln Nazareth (18064) *(G-11960)*

D & A Emergency Equipment Inc 610 691-6847
1655 Jeter Ave Bethlehem (18015) *(G-1495)*

D & A Printing, Darby *Also called D & A Associates* *(G-4017)*

D & B Services Inc 610 381-2848
Fiddletown Rd Kunkletown (18058) *(G-8832)*

D & D Machine 412 821-3725
5 Newland Ln Pittsburgh (15209) *(G-14900)*

D & D Sawmill Parts and Svc, Chambersburg *Also called Goshorn Industries LLC* *(G-2936)*

D & D Wood Sales Inc 814 948-8672
268 Amadei Rd Nicktown (15762) *(G-12620)*

D & F Tool Inc 814 899-6364
4370 Knoyle Rd Erie (16510) *(G-5244)*

D & G Machine 724 864-0043
367 Wendel Rd Irwin (15642) *(G-8154)*

D & H Inc (PA) 800 340-1001
2525 N 7th St Harrisburg (17110) *(G-7112)*

D & J Metal Tech, Kirkwood *Also called Ds Fabrication* *(G-8748)*

D & J Welding, Albion *Also called Doug Herhold* *(G-43)*

D & K Logging Inc 814 663-0210
1335 Cobb Rd Spartansburg (16434) *(G-17849)*

D & K Machine Company Inc 814 328-2382
23514 Route 949 Ridgway (15853) *(G-16702)*

D & M Precision Mfg Inc 724 727-3039
718 Pine Run Rd Apollo (15613) *(G-674)*

D & M Welding Co Inc 717 767-9353
1550 Trolley Rd York (17408) *(G-20440)*

D & N Enterprise Inc 215 238-9050
238 Market St Philadelphia (19106) *(G-13597)*

D & R Machine Co, Clairton *Also called D/R Machine & Weld Co Inc* *(G-3149)*

D & R Machine Co 215 526-2080
1330 Industrial Blvd Southampton (18966) *(G-17807)*

D & R Steel Construction Inc 570 265-6216
28463 Route 220 Milan (18831) *(G-11147)*

D & S Business Services Inc 724 545-3143
529 Butler Rd Kittanning (16201) *(G-8765)*

D & S Clothing Inc 856 383-3794
176 W Loudon St Fl 2 Philadelphia (19120) *(G-13598)*

D & S Fabricating & Welding 412 653-9185
678 Cochran Mill Rd Clairton (15025) *(G-3148)*

D & S Industrial Contg Inc 412 490-3215
3100 Casteel Dr Coraopolis (15108) *(G-3683)*

D & Sr Inc (PA) 717 569-3264
500 E Oregon Rd Lancaster (17601) *(G-8989)*

D & Z Printers 724 539-8922
1101 Ligonier St Latrobe (15650) *(G-9470)*

D A D Fabrication and Welding 814 781-1886
1009 Delaum Rd Saint Marys (15857) *(G-16960)*

D A R A Inc 717 274-1800
1650 N 7th St Lebanon (17046) *(G-9557)*

D A R Industrial Pdts Inc (PA) 610 825-4900
2 Union Hill Rd Bldg 1 Conshohocken (19428) *(G-3535)*

D A Tool and Machine Company 215 887-1673
415 W Glenside Ave Glenside (19038) *(G-6513)*

D and S Artistic Wdwkg LLC (PA) 973 495-7008
144 Salzer Way Henryville (18332) *(G-7566)*

D and S Artistic Wdwkg LLC 973 495-7008
1410 Spruce St Ste 116 Stroudsburg (18360) *(G-18113)*

D B Products Inc 215 628-0416
120 Keystone Dr Unit B Montgomeryville (18936) *(G-11392)*

D B T, Houston *Also called Caterpillar Globl Min Amer LLC* *(G-7869)*

D C Humphrys Co 215 307-3363
5000 Paschall Ave Philadelphia (19143) *(G-13599)*

D Cooper Works LLC 717 733-4220
100 Industrial Dr Ephrata (17522) *(G-5099)*

D D J Manufacturing Inc 814 378-7625
46 Shoff Ln Madera (16661) *(G-10162)*

D Dietrich Associates Inc 215 258-1071
9 Blue Rock Dr Sellersville (18960) *(G-17342)*

D E Errick Corporation 814 642-2589
24843 Route 6 Port Allegany (16743) *(G-15893)*

D E Gemill Inc 717 755-9794
10174 Chapel Church Rd Red Lion (17356) *(G-16593)*

D E Hyde Contracting 814 228-3685
2048 Kinney Rd Genesee (16923) *(G-6271)*

D F Stauffer Biscuit Co Inc (PA) 717 815-4600
360 S Belmont St York (17403) *(G-20441)*

D Flagstone, Hop Bottom *Also called Kenneth E Decker* *(G-7774)*

D G A Inc 717 249-8542
121 N Pitt St Carlisle (17013) *(G-2706)*

D G Woodworks LLC 215 368-8001
675 W 3rd St Lansdale (19446) *(G-9356)*

D G Yuengling and Son Inc (PA) 570 622-4141
5th & Mahantongo Sts Pottsville (17901) *(G-16075)*

A
L
P
H
A
B
E
T
I
C

D G Yuengling and Son Inc.................................570 622-0153
   310 Mill Creek Ave Pottsville (17901) *(G-16076)*

D Gillette Indus Svcs Inc..................................610 588-4939
   46 N Main St Bangor (18013) *(G-911)*

D I Furnace LLC..412 231-1200
   100 Sandusky St Pittsburgh (15212) *(G-14901)*

D J Precision Instrument Corp.............................570 836-2229
   149 Marcy Rd Tunkhannock (18657) *(G-18536)*

D K Gas Inc..814 365-5621
   3809 Cherry Aly Hawthorn (16230) *(G-7443)*

D K Hostetler Inc...717 667-3921
   5015 Old Us Hwy 322 Milroy (17063) *(G-11229)*

D K P -Hardy Inc..215 441-0383
   2015 Stout Dr Warminster (18974) *(G-18854)*

D L Carmody Holdings LLC.................................717 741-4863
   76 Acco Dr York (17402) *(G-20442)*

D L Dravis & Associates Inc (PA)..........................814 943-6155
   711 N 9th Ave Altoona (16601) *(G-496)*

D L Dravis & Associates Inc...............................814 944-5880
   1904 Union Ave Altoona (16601) *(G-497)*

D L Electronics Inc......................................215 742-2666
   6020 Palmetto St Philadelphia (19111) *(G-13600)*

D L Enterprise Inc..814 948-6060
   333 Main St Barnesboro (15714) *(G-939)*

D L George & Sons Mfg Inc.................................717 765-4700
   20 E 6th St Ste 201 Waynesboro (17268) *(G-19407)*

D L Machine LLC...724 627-7870
   134 Reservoir Hill Rd Jefferson (15344) *(G-8269)*

D L Martin Co (PA)..717 328-2141
   25 D L Martin Dr Mercersburg (17236) *(G-10984)*

D Luther Trucking...814 952-2136
   199 Jackson Run Rd Punxsutawney (15767) *(G-16132)*

D R Gaumer Metal Fabricating..............................610 395-5101
   589 Krocks Rd Wescosville (18106) *(G-19488)*

D R M Services Corporation................................610 789-2685
   443 W Chester Pike Havertown (19083) *(G-7419)*

D S Machine, Gordonville Also called Ds Machine LLC *(G-6552)*

D U E C O, Mountville Also called Terex Corporation *(G-11803)*

D W Machine Co Inc..215 672-3340
   220 Jacksonville Rd Hatboro (19040) *(G-7277)*

D&B Tailors Inc...610 356-9279
   3620 Chapel Rd Newtown Square (19073) *(G-12571)*

D&D Cigar & Cigarette Emporium............................570 722-4665
   2591 State Route 903 # 4 Albrightsville (18210) *(G-48)*

D&D Security Solutions LLC................................484 614-7024
   192 Sawmill Rd Landenberg (19350) *(G-9248)*

D&E Communications LLC...................................814 238-0000
   441 Science Park Rd State College (16803) *(G-17956)*

D&E Communications LLC...................................570 524-2200
   20 S 2nd St Lewisburg (17837) *(G-9904)*

D&E Machining Ltd..814 664-3531
   150 Industrial Dr Corry (16407) *(G-3758)*

D&J Pallet Services Inc...................................717 275-1064
   548 Landisburg Rd Landisburg (17040) *(G-9257)*

D&M Tool Inc..814 724-6743
   10976 Mchenry St Meadville (16335) *(G-10716)*

D&R Logging...570 345-4632
   49 Trumbo Rd Pine Grove (17963) *(G-14591)*

D&W Fine Pack LLC...215 362-1501
   1100 Schwab Rd Hatfield (19440) *(G-7331)*

D'Antonio-Klein Jewelers, Philadelphia Also called J & D Jewelers Inc *(G-13880)*

D'Orazio Paul Custom Uphl, Flourtown Also called Paul Dorazio Custom Furniture *(G-5989)*

D'Rocco & Sons, Philadelphia Also called S DRocco Upholstery *(G-14270)*

D-Electric Inc...215 529-6020
   2070 Quaker Pointe Dr Quakertown (18951) *(G-16182)*

D-K Trading Corporation Inc (PA).........................570 586-9662
   41 Marshwood Bnd Clarks Summit (18411) *(G-3191)*

D. J. Mfg Co, Tunkhannock Also called D J Precision Instrument Corp *(G-18536)*

D/R Machine & Weld Co Inc.................................412 655-4452
   668 Cochran Mill Rd Clairton (15025) *(G-3149)*

Dacar Chemical Company, Pittsburgh Also called Dacar Industries *(G-14902)*

Dacar Industries (PA).....................................412 921-3620
   1007 Mccartney St Pittsburgh (15220) *(G-14902)*

Dach Dime Manufacture.....................................814 336-2376
   15926 S Mosiertown Rd Meadville (16335) *(G-10717)*

Dacval LLC...215 331-9600
   7341 Tulip St Ste 101 Philadelphia (19136) *(G-13601)*

DAddario & Company Inc...................................856 217-4954
   421 N 7th St Philadelphia (19123) *(G-13602)*

Dade Paper Co...570 579-6780
   1119 N Church St Hazle Township (18202) *(G-7450)*

Daedal Group Inc..215 745-8718
   6136 Palmetto St 38 Philadelphia (19111) *(G-13603)*

Daffin's Candies, Sharon Also called Daffins Inc *(G-17432)*

Daffin's Candy Factory, Farrell Also called Daffins Inc *(G-5867)*

Daffins Inc (PA)..724 342-2892
   496 E State St Sharon (16146) *(G-17432)*

Daffins Inc...724 983-8336
   7 Spearman Ave Farrell (16121) *(G-5867)*

Dagus Machining Inc.......................................814 834-3491
   138 Station St Ridgway (15853) *(G-16703)*

Dahill Bottling Company Inc...............................215 699-6432
   135 Belle Cir Blue Bell (19422) *(G-1825)*

Dailey Manufacturing Co (PA)..............................215 659-0477
   700 Davisville Rd Willow Grove (19090) *(G-20113)*

Daily..610 384-0372
   2590 Strasburg Rd Coatesville (19320) *(G-3300)*

Daily American (HQ).......................................814 444-5900
   334 W Main St Somerset (15501) *(G-17683)*

DAILY COLLEGIAN, THE, State College Also called Collegian Inc *(G-17953)*

Daily Dove Care LLC.......................................215 316-5888
   1700 Market St Ste 1005 Philadelphia (19103) *(G-13604)*

Daily Grind Quarryville...................................717 786-0615
   221 W 4th St Quarryville (17566) *(G-16268)*

Daily Herald, Tyrone Also called Joseph F Biddle Publishing Co *(G-18585)*

Daily Informer LLC.......................................717 634-9087
   209 3rd St Apt A Hanover (17331) *(G-6872)*

Daily Item, Lewisburg Also called Local Media Group Inc *(G-9915)*

Daily Local News, Exton Also called Journal Register Company *(G-5704)*

Dairiconcepts LP...717 566-4500
   8190 Presidents Dr Hummelstown (17036) *(G-7908)*

Dairy Conveyor Corp.......................................717 431-3121
   2173 Embassy Dr Lancaster (17603) *(G-8990)*

Dairy Farmers America Inc................................717 691-4141
   4825 Old Gettysburg Rd Mechanicsburg (17055) *(G-10836)*

Dairy Farmers America Inc................................724 946-8729
   925 State Route 18 New Wilmington (16142) *(G-12465)*

Dairy Farmers America Inc................................724 946-8729
   82 North St West Middlesex (16159) *(G-19722)*

Dairy Farmers of America, Middlebury Center Also called Dietrichs Milk Products
LLC *(G-11044)*

Dairy Sales, Coatesville Also called L D Kallman Inc *(G-3312)*

Daisy Data Displays Inc..................................717 932-9999
   2850 Lewisberry Rd York Haven (17370) *(G-20756)*

Daisy Mae Prtg & Design LLC...............................610 467-1989
   119 S 3rd St Ste 1 Oxford (19363) *(G-13077)*

Dajr Enterprises Inc......................................215 949-0800
   8000 Bristol Pike Levittown (19057) *(G-9830)*

Dal-Tile Corporation......................................717 334-1181
   211 N 4th St Gettysburg (17325) *(G-6287)*

Dal-Tile Corporation......................................484 530-9066
   5105 Campus Dr Plymouth Meeting (19462) *(G-15841)*

Dale Property Services Penn LP............................724 705-0444
   1000 Town Center Way # 325 Canonsburg (15317) *(G-2576)*

Daleco Resources Corporation..............................570 795-4347
   929 S High St Ste 174 West Chester (19382) *(G-19531)*

Dallas - Morris Drilling Inc (PA)........................814 362-6493
   29 Morris Ln Bradford (16701) *(G-1964)*

Dallas - Morris Drilling Inc.............................814 362-6493
   103 S Kendall Ave Bradford (16701) *(G-1965)*

Dallas Machine Inc..610 799-2800
   4410 Park View Dr Schnecksville (18078) *(G-17138)*

Dallco Industries Inc (PA)................................717 854-7875
   463 S Albemarle St York (17403) *(G-20443)*

Dallice Precious Metals...................................570 501-0850
   216 W 21st St Hazleton (18201) *(G-7496)*

Dally Slate Company Inc...................................610 863-4172
   500 Railroad Ave Pen Argyl (18072) *(G-13213)*

Dalmo Optical Center, Pittsburgh Also called Dalmo Optical Corporation *(G-14903)*

Dalmo Optical Corporation (PA)............................412 521-2100
   5831 Forbes Ave Pittsburgh (15217) *(G-14903)*

Dalmo Optical Corporation.................................412 937-1112
   950 Greentree Rd 202 Pittsburgh (15220) *(G-14904)*

Dalos Bakery Inc..570 752-4519
   1201 Freas Ave Berwick (18603) *(G-1322)*

Daltech Inc...570 823-9911
   1420 Sans Souci Pkwy Hanover Township (18706) *(G-6987)*

Dalton Pavillions Inc.....................................215 721-1492
   3120 Commerce Dr Telford (18969) *(G-18279)*

Dalrymple Gravel and Contracti............................570 297-0340
   278 Elmira St Troy (16947) *(G-18521)*

DAmbrosio Bakery LLC (PA)................................610 560-4700
   1040 1st Ave Ste 435 King of Prussia (19406) *(G-8604)*

Dame Design LLC...610 458-3290
   710 Wheatland St Ste 107 Phoenixville (19460) *(G-14541)*

Damian Hntz Locomotive Svc Inc............................814 748-7222
   494 Twenty Row Rd Colver (15927) *(G-3453)*

Damin Printing Co LLC.....................................814 472-9530
   122 S Locust St Ebensburg (15931) *(G-4784)*

Damsel In Defense...215 262-3643
   1588 S Pennsylvania Ave Morrisville (19067) *(G-11557)*

Dan Ber Concrete & Supply, Danville Also called J A & W A Hess Inc *(G-4007)*

Dan Donahue...814 336-3262
   21717 Ryan Rd Meadville (16335) *(G-10718)*

Dan Dulls Specialty Wdwkg.................................724 843-6223
   1027 4th Ave New Brighton (15066) *(G-12033)*

Dan Orner Signs...610 876-6042
   1131 Mulberry St Chester (19015) *(G-3045)*

Dan Smith Candies Inc (PA) 814 849-8221
77 Barnett St Brookville (15825) *(G-2259)*

Dan-Beck Well Services Inc 724 538-1001
353 Railroad St Evans City (16033) *(G-5557)*

Dana Auto Systems Group LLC 610 323-4200
1040 Center Ave Pottstown (19464) *(G-15978)*

Dana Driveshaft Products LLC 610 323-4200
1040 Center Ave Pottstown (19464) *(G-15979)*

Dana Light Vehicle Driveline, Pottstown *Also called Dana Driveshaft Products LLC (G-15979)*

Danaher Corporation 610 692-2700
110 Westtown Rd West Chester (19382) *(G-19532)*

Danaken Designs Inc 570 445-9797
949 Adams Ave Scranton (18510) *(G-17227)*

Danchcks Extinguishers Svc Inc 570 589-1610
512 Northampton St Edwardsville (18704) *(G-4823)*

Danco Precision Inc (PA) 610 933-8981
601 Wheatland St Phoenixville (19460) *(G-14542)*

Danco Precision Inc 610 933-1090
354 Walnut St Phoenixville (19460) *(G-14543)*

Danco Precision Inc 610 933-8981
Morgan St Phoenixville (19460) *(G-14544)*

Danco Products, Greencastle *Also called Darco Inc (G-6605)*

Danfelt Paul Logging Contr, Mapleton Depot *Also called Paul Danfelt (G-10431)*

Dangelo Autobody and Towing, Kane *Also called Dangelos Custom Built Mfg LLC (G-8462)*

Dangelos Custom Built Mfg LLC 814 837-6053
2 Poplar St Kane (16735) *(G-8462)*

Daniel B Proffitt Jr 717 529-2194
195 Schoolhouse Rd Kirkwood (17536) *(G-8747)*

Daniel Baum Company 717 509-5724
1383 Arcadia Rd Ste 102 Lancaster (17601) *(G-8991)*

Daniel C Tanney Inc 215 639-3131
3268 Clive Ave Bensalem (19020) *(G-1179)*

Daniel D Esh 814 383-4579
147 Coder Ln Howard (16841) *(G-7889)*

Daniel G Berg 610 856-7095
477 Alleghenyville Rd Mohnton (19540) *(G-11261)*

Daniel Gerard Worldwide Inc (PA) 800 232-3332
34 Barnhart Dr Hanover (17331) *(G-6873)*

Daniel Gerard Worldwide Inc 717 630-3787
762 Wilson Ave Hanover (17331) *(G-6874)*

Daniel Gerard Worldwide Inc 717 637-3250
150 Factory St Hanover (17331) *(G-6875)*

Daniel Leo Olesnevich 724 352-3160
120 Equine Ln Butler (16002) *(G-2392)*

Daniel Parent 914 850-5473
102 Link Rd Milford (18337) *(G-11158)*

Daniel W Benedict 717 709-0149
4574 Altenwald Rd Waynesboro (17268) *(G-19408)*

Daniel Weaver Company Inc 717 274-6100
1415 Weavertown Rd Lebanon (17046) *(G-9558)*

Danieli Corporation 724 778-5400
600 Cranberry Woods Dr # 200 Cranberry Township (16066) *(G-3814)*

Daniels Electric Service 412 821-2594
329 Ohio St Pittsburgh (15209) *(G-14905)*

Danita Container Inc 570 448-3606
1338 Bethany Tpke Honesdale (18431) *(G-7709)*

Danmir Therapeutics LLC 610 896-8826
24 Dartmouth Ln Haverford (19041) *(G-7407)*

Dannic Energy Corporation 724 465-6663
134 Mill Run Dr Indiana (15701) *(G-8089)*

Dannunzio and Battistoni, Newtown Square *Also called D&B Tailors Inc (G-12571)*

Danowski 717 328-5057
111 N Main St Mercersburg (17236) *(G-10985)*

Dansk, Bristol *Also called Lenox Corporation (G-2159)*

Danskin 717 747-3051
305 N State St York (17403) *(G-20444)*

Dansway Incorporated 570 672-1550
159 Reed Rd Elysburg (17824) *(G-4973)*

Dant Enterprises 570 379-3121
226 Overlook Rd Nescopeck (18635) *(G-12000)*

Dante Defranco Printing 610 588-7300
4 Dante St Roseto (18013) *(G-16819)*

Danville News, Sunbury *Also called Community Newspaper Group LLC (G-18166)*

Danzer Lumber North Amer Inc 814 368-3701
444 High St Bradford (16701) *(G-1966)*

Danzer Services Inc 724 827-3700
119 Aid Dr Darlington (16115) *(G-4025)*

Danzer Veneer Americas Inc 570 322-4400
240 N Reach Rd Williamsport (17701) *(G-20002)*

Danzer Veneer Americas Inc (HQ) 724 827-8366
119 A I D Dr Darlington (16115) *(G-4026)*

Danzi Energy 814 723-8640
422 Crescent Park Warren (16365) *(G-19019)*

Darby Industries Inc 570 388-6173
2682 Sullivans Trl Falls (18615) *(G-5852)*

Darco Inc 717 597-7139
411 S Cedar Ln Greencastle (17225) *(G-6605)*

Daria Metal Fabricators Inc 215 453-2110
1507 W Park Ave Perkasie (18944) *(G-13271)*

Dark Star Alpacas LLC 610 235-6638
443 Mayberry Rd Schwenksville (19473) *(G-17175)*

Darkar Railway Equipment Inc 610 296-5712
641 Lancaster Ave # 1008 Malvern (19355) *(G-10220)*

Darkar Railway Supplies, Malvern *Also called Darkar Railway Equipment Inc (G-10220)*

Darling Blends LLC 215 630-2802
433 White Swan Way Langhorne (19047) *(G-9288)*

Darling Ingredients Inc 724 695-1212
3173 Potato Garden Run Rd Imperial (15126) *(G-8063)*

Darlings Locker Plant 570 945-5716
And 11 Rr 6 La Plume (18440) *(G-8869)*

Daron Northeast, Ashley *Also called Craigjill Inc (G-739)*

Darra Group Inc 724 684-6040
63 Overhill Dr Monessen (15062) *(G-11298)*

Dart Container Corp PA (PA) 717 656-2236
60 E Main St Leola (17540) *(G-9777)*

Dart Container Corp PA 717 397-1032
110 Pitney Rd Lancaster (17602) *(G-8992)*

Dartonya Manufacturing Inc 814 849-3240
243 Dartonya Ln Brookville (15825) *(G-2260)*

Dasco Inc 412 771-4140
3001 Grand Ave Pittsburgh (15225) *(G-14906)*

Dassault Systemes Americas, Radnor *Also called Quintiq Inc (G-16299)*

Data Center, Collegeville *Also called Glaxosmithkline LLC (G-3380)*

Data Display Systems, Philadelphia *Also called Decora Industries Inc (G-13614)*

Data Machine LLC 724 864-4370
140 Brush Creek Rd Irwin (15642) *(G-8155)*

Data Print 484 329-7553
147 Pennsylvania Ave Malvern (19355) *(G-10221)*

Data Tech Pos Inc 215 925-8888
702 N 3rd St Ste 100 Philadelphia (19123) *(G-13605)*

Datacap Systems Inc 215 997-8989
100 New Britain Blvd Chalfont (18914) *(G-2871)*

Datalogic Usa Inc 215 723-0981
511 School House Rd Telford (18969) *(G-18280)*

Datapath North America Inc 484 679-1553
2550 Blvd Of The Generals Norristown (19403) *(G-12650)*

Datatech Software Inc 717 652-4344
4800 Linglestown Rd # 201 Harrisburg (17112) *(G-7113)*

Datum Filing Systems Inc (PA) 717 764-6350
89 Church Rd Emigsville (17318) *(G-4986)*

Datum Storage Solutions, Emigsville *Also called Datum Filing Systems Inc (G-4986)*

Datumrite Corporation 215 407-4447
206 Avondale Dr North Wales (19454) *(G-12797)*

Daugherty Tool and Die Inc 412 754-0200
325 Industry Rd Buena Vista (15018) *(G-2341)*

Dauphin Precision Tool LLC 800 522-8665
200 Front St Millersburg (17061) *(G-11192)*

Davan Manufacturing Inc 724 228-0115
500 Crile Rd Washington (15301) *(G-19162)*

Davco Advertising Inc 717 442-4155
89 N Kinzer Rd Kinzers (17535) *(G-8736)*

Davco Pallet 570 837-5910
837 Hartman Rd Middleburg (17842) *(G-11024)*

Dave Fine Meat Packer Inc 724 352-1537
Butler Rd Saxonburg (16056) *(G-17083)*

Dave Zerbe Studio 610 376-0379
1135 N 5th St Reading (19601) *(G-16360)*

Dave's Counter Tops, Allentown *Also called David Walters (G-192)*

Daven Sharpe Machine Products 610 821-4022
817 N Gilmore St Allentown (18109) *(G-191)*

Davenmark Inc 484 461-8683
707 Long Ln Upper Darby (19082) *(G-18684)*

Daves Airport Shuttle LLC 215 288-1000
5915 Harbison Ave Philadelphia (19135) *(G-13606)*

Daves Boat Repair LLC 215 453-6904
3 Ridge Valley Rd Sellersville (18960) *(G-17343)*

Daves Pro Shop Inc 814 834-6116
83 Erie Ave Saint Marys (15857) *(G-16961)*

Daves Welding Shop 814 796-6520
1389 Old State Rd Waterford (16441) *(G-19261)*

David A Bierig 814 459-8001
11092 Freeport Ln North East (16428) *(G-12737)*

David A Smith Printing Inc 717 564-3719
742 S 22nd St Harrisburg (17104) *(G-7114)*

David B Lytle Products Inc 724 352-3322
920 N Pike Rd Cabot (16023) *(G-2454)*

David Bream 717 334-1513
449 W Middle St Gettysburg (17325) *(G-6288)*

David C Weigle 610 327-1616
800 Heritage Dr Ste 811 Pottstown (19464) *(G-15980)*

David City Manufacturing, Norristown *Also called Fargo Assembly of Pa Inc (G-12657)*

David Copeland 814 756-3250
10140 S Akerley Rd Albion (16401) *(G-42)*

David Craig Jewelers Ltd 215 968-8900
10 Summit Sq Shopg Ctr Shopping Ctr Langhorne (19047) *(G-9289)*

David Elliot Poultry Farm Inc......................................570 344-6348
  300 Breck St Scranton (18505) *(G-17228)*

David Esh...610 286-6225
  112 Maxwell Hill Rd Morgantown (19543) *(G-11521)*

David I Helfer Inc..412 281-6734
  717 Liberty Ave Ste 312 Pittsburgh (15222) *(G-14907)*

David J Hohenshilt Welding LLC...............................610 349-2937
  5628 Route 873 Neffs (18065) *(G-11998)*

David J Klein Inc...610 385-4888
  1343 Ben Franklin Hwy W Douglassville (19518) *(G-4174)*

David Jefferys LLC..215 977-9900
  1 Chester Rd Wallingford (19086) *(G-18783)*

David John Metal Artisan, Lahaska *Also called Oaklawn Metal Craft Shop Inc (G-8885)*

David Jonathan Wdwkg & Mfg Co.............................724 499-5225
  3250 Golden Oaks Rd Rogersville (15359) *(G-16795)*

David K Hart Co..610 527-0388
  9 Meadowood Rd Bryn Mawr (19010) *(G-2319)*

David Karr..814 669-4406
  6425 Barree Rd Alexandria (16611) *(G-63)*

David Kovalcik..724 539-3181
  922 Industrial Blvd Loyalhanna (15661) *(G-10110)*

David Lee Designs..814 725-4289
  107 Clay St Ste 1 North East (16428) *(G-12738)*

David Lee Furniture and Access, North East *Also called David Lee Designs (G-12738)*

David M Byler...717 667-6157
  157 Sawmill Rd Belleville (17004) *(G-1130)*

David M Oley...570 247-5599
  Rr 1 Box 285 Rome (18837) *(G-16797)*

David Michael & Co Inc (HQ)....................................215 632-3100
  10801 Decatur Rd Philadelphia (19154) *(G-13607)*

David Michael & Co Inc..909 887-3800
  10801 Decatur Rd Philadelphia (19154) *(G-13608)*

David Moscinski...215 271-6193
  1632 S 2nd St Philadelphia (19148) *(G-13609)*

David R Englehart...814 238-6734
  220 Regent Ct Ste D State College (16801) *(G-17957)*

David R Houser...610 505-5924
  10 Clyston Cir Norristown (19403) *(G-12651)*

David R Kipar..570 833-4068
  451 Mcgavin Rd Meshoppen (18630) *(G-11006)*

David R Webb Company Inc......................................570 322-7186
  3100 Reach Rd Williamsport (17701) *(G-20003)*

David S Stoltzsus...717 556-0462
  2441 Stumptown Rd Bird In Hand (17505) *(G-1673)*

David Seidel...610 921-8310
  4700 5th Street Hwy # 101 Temple (19560) *(G-18327)*

David Smith Printing Copy Ctrs, Harrisburg *Also called Print Works On Demand Inc (G-7202)*

David Trunk..570 247-2012
  486 West Rd Rome (18837) *(G-16798)*

David Tuttle...570 280-8441
  391 Belmont Tpke Waymart (18472) *(G-19286)*

David Walters...610 435-5433
  136 W Linden St Allentown (18101) *(G-192)*

David Weber Co Inc..215 426-3500
  3500 Richmond St Philadelphia (19134) *(G-13610)*

David Zerbe, Reading *Also called Dave Zerbe Studio (G-16360)*

Davids Bridal Inc..610 943-6210
  444 E North Ln Conshohocken (19428) *(G-3536)*

Davidson Supply Co Inc...412 635-2671
  4721 Mcknight Rd Ste 1 Pittsburgh (15237) *(G-14908)*

Davidsons Fabricating Inc.......................................610 544-9750
  511 Abbott Dr Broomall (19008) *(G-2285)*

Davies & Sons LLC..814 723-7430
  3200 Conewango Ave Warren (16365) *(G-19020)*

Davies Precision Machining Inc................................717 273-5495
  2400 Colebrook Rd Lebanon (17042) *(G-9559)*

Davinci Graphics Inc..215 441-8180
  433 Horsham Rd Horsham (19044) *(G-7808)*

Davis & Davis Gourmet Foods..................................412 487-7770
  3614 William Flynn Hwy Allison Park (15101) *(G-449)*

Davis Cookie Company...814 473-3125
  256 Baker St Rimersburg (16248) *(G-16749)*

Davis Feed of Bucks County.....................................215 257-2966
  140 N 7th St Perkasie (18944) *(G-13272)*

Davis Lamp & Shade Inc...215 426-2777
  4550 Melrose St Philadelphia (19124) *(G-13611)*

Davis Lattemann Inc...877 576-5885
  7 Stonier Rd Tunkhannock (18657) *(G-18537)*

Davis Machine Inc..724 265-2266
  967 Saxonburg Blvd Saxonburg (16056) *(G-17084)*

Davis Ne Company Inc..412 751-5122
  11000 Parker Dr Irwin (15642) *(G-8156)*

Davis Sign Service LLC (PA).....................................412 856-5535
  4112 Monroeville Blvd Monroeville (15146) *(G-11332)*

Davis Tool Company...215 368-0300
  1830 Tomlinson Rd Kulpsville (19443) *(G-8825)*

Davis Trophies & Sports Wear...................................610 455-0640
  1004 Plumly Rd West Chester (19382) *(G-19533)*

Davis Trophy & Sportswear, West Chester *Also called Davis Trophies & Sports Wear (G-19533)*

Davro Optical Systems Inc..215 362-3870
  500 N Cannon Ave Lansdale (19446) *(G-9357)*

Davy Manufacturing Inc...610 583-8240
  101 W Eagle Rd Ste A Havertown (19083) *(G-7420)*

Dawar Technologies Inc..412 322-9900
  1016 N Lincoln Ave Pittsburgh (15233) *(G-14909)*

Dawar Touch, Pittsburgh *Also called Dawar Technologies Inc (G-14909)*

Dawn Evening Inc...610 272-0518
  1410 Cortez Rd Blue Bell (19422) *(G-1826)*

Dawn Food Products Inc...717 840-0044
  3701 Concord Rd York (17402) *(G-20445)*

Dawson Performance Inc..717 261-1414
  5274 Sunset Pike Chambersburg (17202) *(G-2923)*

Dayco Inc...610 326-4500
  325 Circle Of Progress Dr Pottstown (19464) *(G-15981)*

Daye-Licious Baking...570 965-2491
  487 Hunsinger Rd Springville (18844) *(G-17928)*

Daynight Transport LLC..800 288-4996
  135 C St Carlisle (17013) *(G-2707)*

Days Beverage Inc..215 990-0983
  529 Guinevere Dr Newtown Square (19073) *(G-12572)*

Days Communication Inc...215 538-1240
  1208 Juniper St Quakertown (18951) *(G-16183)*

Dayto-Batco, Harrisburg *Also called Dayton Parts LLC (G-7115)*

Dayton Computer & Sign Inc.....................................814 257-8670
  107 N School St 3 Dayton (16222) *(G-4038)*

Dayton Parts LLC..717 255-8548
  3500 Industrial Rd Bldg 1 Harrisburg (17110) *(G-7115)*

Dayton Parts LLC (PA)..717 255-8500
  3500 Industrial Rd Bldg 1 Harrisburg (17110) *(G-7116)*

Dayton Superior Corporation....................................570 695-3163
  55 N Pine St Tremont (17981) *(G-18480)*

Dayton Superior Corporation....................................610 366-3890
  7130 Ambassador Dr Allentown (18106) *(G-193)*

Db & S Cabinets..814 437-2529
  1728 Keely Rd Franklin (16323) *(G-6124)*

Dbaza Inc...412 681-1180
  3401 Market St Ste 201 Philadelphia (19104) *(G-13612)*

Dbex Tek LLC..267 566-0354
  1105 William Penn Dr Bensalem (19020) *(G-1180)*

Dbi Inc...814 653-7625
  660 Longview Rd Fairmount City (16224) *(G-5808)*

Dbmotion Inc..412 605-1952
  600 Grant St Ste 22017 Pittsburgh (15219) *(G-14910)*

Dbmtion Inc..412 605-1952
  600 Grant St Ste 22017 Pittsburgh (15219) *(G-14911)*

Dbwave Technologies LLC...412 345-8081
  2009 Mackenzie Way # 100 Cranberry Township (16066) *(G-3815)*

DC Welding...717 361-9400
  643 Hereford Rd Elizabethtown (17022) *(G-4871)*

DCI, Burgettstown *Also called Dedicated Customs Inc (G-2345)*

DCI Products, Clifton Heights *Also called Designer Cabinets and Hdwr Co (G-3252)*

Dcm Slot Car Raceway..215 805-6887
  26 Thornbury Ln Newtown (18940) *(G-12501)*

DCS, Dayton *Also called Dayton Computer & Sign Inc (G-4038)*

Ddm Novastar Inc...610 337-3050
  212 Railroad Dr Warminster (18974) *(G-18855)*

Ddp Specialty Electronic MA (HQ).............................610 244-6000
  400 Arcola Rd Collegeville (19426) *(G-3374)*

De Alfredo Foods, Garnet Valley *Also called PCA Group Inc (G-6267)*

De Angelis Donut Shop, Rochester *Also called Deangelis Bros Inc (G-16784)*

De Limited Family Partnership...................................814 938-0800
  1406 N Main St Punxsutawney (15767) *(G-16133)*

De Lucas Draperys..610 284-2464
  195 N Springfield Rd Clifton Heights (19018) *(G-3251)*

De Marco Waste Dumpster Svc..................................412 904-4260
  229 Amanda Ave Pittsburgh (15210) *(G-14912)*

De Nora Water Technologies Inc................................412 494-4077
  1000 Cliffmine Rd Pittsburgh (15275) *(G-14913)*

De Nora Water Technologies Inc................................412 788-8300
  1000 Cliffmine Rd Ste 600 Pittsburgh (15275) *(G-14914)*

De Paul Concrete (PA)...610 832-8000
  409 Stenton Ave Flourtown (19031) *(G-5986)*

De Signs By Ben Pogue...724 592-5013
  230 Pumpkin Run Rd Jefferson (15344) *(G-8270)*

De Technologies Inc (PA)..610 337-2800
  100 Queens Dr King of Prussia (19406) *(G-8605)*

De Vore Tool Co Inc..814 425-2566
  136 S Smith St Cochranton (16314) *(G-3341)*

Deacon Industries, Washington *Also called Whitmore Manufacturing Company (G-19246)*

Dead Lightning Distillery...717 695-0927
  311 Bridge St New Cumberland (17070) *(G-12185)*

Dead Lightning Distillery LLC....................................717 798-2021
  233 Plum St Lemoyne (17043) *(G-9743)*

Deadsolid Simulations Inc..570 655-6500
  1192 Sathers Dr Pittston (18640) *(G-15748)*

Dean Barrett..........814 427-2586
630 Mill Rd Punxsutawney (15767) ***(G-16134)***
Dean Construction LLC..........814 887-8750
15884 Route 6 Smethport (16749) ***(G-17634)***
Dean Dairy Products Company..........724 962-7801
1690 Oneida Ln Sharpsville (16150) ***(G-17471)***
Dean Foods Company, Sharpsville *Also called Dean Dairy Products Company* ***(G-17471)***
Dean Foods Company..........717 522-5653
3800 Hempland Rd Mountville (17554) ***(G-11793)***
Dean Foods Company..........215 855-8205
880 Allentown Rd Lansdale (19446) ***(G-9358)***
Dean Foods Company..........724 962-7801
1858 Oneida Ln Sharpsville (16150) ***(G-17472)***
Dean Foods Company..........717 228-0445
2401 Walnut St Lebanon (17042) ***(G-9560)***
Dean Technology Inc..........724 479-3533
1000 Lucerne Rd Lucernemines (15754) ***(G-10117)***
Dean Technology Inc..........724 349-9440
2866 W Pike Rd Indiana (15701) ***(G-8090)***
Dean Transporation Inc..........570 385-1884
110 Manheim Rd Schuylkill Haven (17972) ***(G-17153)***
Dean W Brouse & Sons..........570 374-7695
E Main St Kreamer (17833) ***(G-8817)***
Deane Carbide Products Inc..........215 639-3333
2820 Momerton Rd Old Lincoln Trevose (19053) ***(G-18492)***
Deangelis Bros Inc..........724 775-1641
202 Pleasant St Rochester (15074) ***(G-16784)***
Deangelis Carbide Tooling Inc..........724 224-7280
1047 1st Ave Brackenridge (15014) ***(G-1938)***
Deanrosecrans, Newtown Square *Also called Ultravoice Ltd* ***(G-12595)***
Deasey Machine Tl & Die Works..........814 847-2728
339 Ott Town Rd Everett (15537) ***(G-5570)***
Debbie Dengler..........717 755-5226
4845 Fake Rd York (17406) ***(G-20446)***
Debenham Media Group..........412 264-2526
416 Mill St Coraopolis (15108) ***(G-3684)***
Debweld, Towanda *Also called Dennys Welding* ***(G-18423)***
Decal Specialties Inc..........610 644-9200
37 Industrial Blvd Ste D Paoli (19301) ***(G-13137)***
Decalcraft Corp..........215 822-0517
2750 Bethlehem Pike Hatfield (19440) ***(G-7332)***
Dechert Dynamics Corporation..........717 838-1326
713 W Main St Palmyra (17078) ***(G-13120)***
Decherts Machine Shop Inc..........717 838-1326
713 W Main St Palmyra (17078) ***(G-13121)***
Decilog Inc..........215 657-0817
2500 Maryland Rd Ste 302 Willow Grove (19090) ***(G-20114)***
Deck Machine Co..........570 879-2833
Liberty Park Rd Hallstead (18822) ***(G-6832)***
Deckman Electric Inc..........610 272-6944
49 W Front St Bridgeport (19405) ***(G-2034)***
Decon Laboratories Inc..........610 755-0800
460 Glennie Cir King of Prussia (19406) ***(G-8606)***
Decon Labs, King of Prussia *Also called Decon Laboratories Inc* ***(G-8606)***
Decopro Inc..........215 939-7983
300 E Godfrey Ave Ste 3 Philadelphia (19120) ***(G-13613)***
Decora Industries Inc (PA)..........215 698-2600
14001 Townsend Rd Philadelphia (19154) ***(G-13614)***
Dectile Harkus Construction..........724 789-7125
195 Kriess Rd Butler (16001) ***(G-2393)***
Dedicated Customs Inc..........724 678-6609
327 Meadow Rd Burgettstown (15021) ***(G-2345)***
Dee Paper Company Inc..........610 876-9285
100 Broomall St Chester (19013) ***(G-3046)***
Deely Custom Cabinetry..........267 566-5704
240 Woodstream Dr North Wales (19454) ***(G-12798)***
Deems Logging..........724 657-7384
223 Grange Hall Rd Volant (16156) ***(G-18772)***
Deepwell Energy Services LLC..........412 316-5243
207 Carlton Dr Eighty Four (15330) ***(G-4837)***
Deer Creek Malthouse LLC (PA)..........717 746-6258
1629 E Street Rd Glen Mills (19342) ***(G-6433)***
Deer Creek Malthouse LLC..........717 746-6258
1646 E Street Rd Glen Mills (19342) ***(G-6434)***
Deer Creek Winery LLC..........814 354-7392
3333 Soap Fat Rd Shippenville (16254) ***(G-17560)***
Deer Park Lumber Inc..........570 836-1133
3042 Sr 6 Tunkhannock (18657) ***(G-18538)***
Deetag USA Inc..........828 465-2644
1683 Opputunity Ave Chambersburg (17201) ***(G-2924)***
Def Medical Technologies LLC..........802 299-8457
4040 Locust St Philadelphia (19104) ***(G-13615)***
Default Servicing Inc..........502 968-1400
4 Penn Ctr W Pittsburgh (15276) ***(G-14915)***
Defence Sport, Allentown *Also called Sani-Brands Inc* ***(G-382)***
Defense Training Solutions LLC..........484 240-1188
3499 Gun Club Rd Nazareth (18064) ***(G-11961)***
Deffibaugh Butcher Supply..........814 944-1297
1200 N 6th Ave Altoona (16601) ***(G-498)***
Deffibaugh James W Butcher Sup, Altoona *Also called Deffibaugh Butcher Supply* ***(G-498)***
Deforest Signs & Lighting Inc..........717 564-6102
780 Elder St Harrisburg (17104) ***(G-7117)***
Degadan Corp..........610 940-1282
950 Colwell Ln Ste 2 Conshohocken (19428) ***(G-3537)***
Deihl Vault & Precast Inc..........570 458-6466
1786 State Route 254 Orangeville (17859) ***(G-13005)***
Dein-Verbit Associates Inc..........610 649-9674
337 E County Line Rd Ardmore (19003) ***(G-707)***
Deist Industries Inc..........800 233-0867
3547 Perry Hwy Hadley (16130) ***(G-6819)***
Dek Machine Co Inc..........215 794-5791
4794 Mechanicsville Rd Mechanicsville (18934) ***(G-10911)***
Del Electronic Co..........412 787-1177
1060 Saw Mill Run Blvd Pittsburgh (15220) ***(G-14916)***
Del Martin Screen Prtg & EMB..........717 597-5751
21 Sarah Susan Ln Greencastle (17225) ***(G-6606)***
Del Monte Foods, Bloomsburg *Also called Big Heart Pet Brands* ***(G-1772)***
Del Monte Foods Inc..........412 222-2200
375 N Shore Dr Ste 500 Pittsburgh (15212) ***(G-14917)***
Del Ren Assoc Inc..........215 467-7000
3310 S 20th St Philadelphia (19145) ***(G-13616)***
Del Val Flag Philadelphia Sp..........610 235-7179
407 Virginia Ln Aston (19014) ***(G-758)***
Del-Wood Kitchens Inc..........717 637-9320
1856 Dubs Church Rd Hanover (17331) ***(G-6876)***
Delavau LLC (HQ)..........215 671-1400
10101 Roosevelt Blvd Philadelphia (19154) ***(G-13617)***
Delavau Pharmaceutical Partner, Philadelphia *Also called Delavau LLC* ***(G-13617)***
Delaware County Pennsylvania..........610 891-4865
201 W Front St Frnt Media (19063) ***(G-10920)***
Delaware County Legal Journal..........717 337-9812
111 Baltimore St Rm 117 Gettysburg (17325) ***(G-6289)***
Delaware Electric Inc..........610 252-7803
2149 Bushkill Park Dr # 2 Easton (18040) ***(G-4668)***
Delaware Tool & Machine Co..........610 259-1810
544 Industrial Park Dr Yeadon (19050) ***(G-20352)***
Delaware Valley Con Co Inc (PA)..........215 675-8900
248 E County Line Rd Hatboro (19040) ***(G-7278)***
Delaware Valley Packg Group, Bensalem *Also called Delaware Valley Shipping & Pac* ***(G-1182)***
Delaware Valley Shippers Inc..........215 633-1535
3685 Marshall Ln Bensalem (19020) ***(G-1181)***
Delaware Valley Shippers Inc, Bensalem *Also called Delaware Valley Shippers Inc* ***(G-1181)***
Delaware Valley Shipping & Pac..........215 638-8900
1425 Wells Dr Bensalem (19020) ***(G-1182)***
Delco Mini Mix LLC..........610 809-0316
325 Ulrich St Chester (19013) ***(G-3047)***
Delco Pallets LLC..........267 438-1227
1916 Pershing Ave Morton (19070) ***(G-11591)***
Delco Trade Services Inc..........610 659-9978
235 Strafford Ave Wayne (19087) ***(G-19317)***
Delex Co..........724 938-2366
116 Blaine Rd Brownsville (15417) ***(G-2311)***
Delgrosso Foods Inc (PA)..........814 684-5880
632 Sauce Factory Dr Tipton (16684) ***(G-18374)***
Delicious Bite LLC..........610 701-4213
1128 Greenhill Rd West Chester (19380) ***(G-19534)***
Delktech Systems Inc..........267 341-8391
1213 Vine St Ste 232 Philadelphia (19107) ***(G-13618)***
Dell Perry Farms..........717 741-3485
90 Indian Rock Dam Rd York (17403) ***(G-20447)***
Dell Sunny Foods LLC..........610 932-5164
135 N 5th St Oxford (19363) ***(G-13078)***
Dellovade Fabricators Inc..........615 370-7000
18 Seneca Pl Avella (15312) ***(G-835)***
Delmar Enterprises Inc..........215 674-4534
995 Louis Dr Warminster (18974) ***(G-18856)***
Delp Family Powder Coatings..........724 287-3200
692 Glenwood Way Butler (16001) ***(G-2394)***
Delri Industrial Supplies Inc..........610 833-2070
1431 Chester Pike Crum Lynne (19022) ***(G-3936)***
Delstar Technologies Inc..........717 866-7472
308 Poplar St Richland (17087) ***(G-16685)***
Delstar Technologies Inc..........717 866-7472
308 Poplar St Richland (17087) ***(G-16686)***
Delta Analytical Instruments..........412 372-0739
108 Saunders Station Rd Trafford (15085) ***(G-18453)***
Delta Fabricating, Berwick *Also called Delta Mechanical Inc* ***(G-1323)***
Delta Galil USA Inc..........570 326-2451
1501 W 3rd St Williamsport (17701) ***(G-20004)***
Delta Information Systems Inc..........215 657-5270
300 Welsh Rd Bldg 3-120 Horsham (19044) ***(G-7809)***
Delta Mechanical Inc..........570 752-5511
325 S Eaton St Berwick (18603) ***(G-1323)***
Delta Usa Inc (HQ)..........412 429-3574
600 N Bell Ave Ste 180 Carnegie (15106) ***(G-2766)***
Delta/Ducon Conveying Techlgy..........610 695-9700
33 Sproul Rd Malvern (19355) ***(G-10222)***
Deltronic Labs Inc..........215 997-8616
120 Liberty Ln Chalfont (18914) ***(G-2872)***

ALPHABETIC

Deluxe Corporation 215 631-7500
　1180 Church Rd Ste A Lansdale (19446) *(G-9359)*

Delvania Indus Fabrication Inc 732 417-0333
　1535 Manatawny St Pine Forge (19548) *(G-14587)*

Delweld Industries Corp (PA) 814 535-2412
　149 Commerce Dr Stoystown (15563) *(G-18075)*

Demarchi John 724 547-6440
　150 Three Mile Hl Mount Pleasant (15666) *(G-11696)*

Demco Automation, Quakertown *Also called Demco Enterprises Inc (G-16184)*

Demco Enterprises Inc 888 419-3343
　300 Commerce Dr Quakertown (18951) *(G-16184)*

Demestia Baking Company LLC 215 896-2289
　402 Bonnie Ln Lansdale (19446) *(G-9360)*

Demet's Candy Company, Mohnton *Also called Star Brands North America Inc (G-11270)*

Democratic Print Shop 717 787-3307
　6 Technology Park Harrisburg (17110) *(G-7118)*

Demuth Steel Products Inc 717 653-2239
　25 Eby Chiques Rd Mount Joy (17552) *(G-11652)*

Denim Inc Division 215 627-1400
　414 South St Philadelphia (19147) *(G-13619)*

Denis Bell Inc 570 450-5086
　100 Hazle Brook Rd Hazle Township (18201) *(G-7451)*

Dennis Albertson LLC 570 784-1677
　1180 Old Berwick Rd Bloomsburg (17815) *(G-1778)*

Dennis Downing 724 598-0043
　2386 Eastbrook Rd New Castle (16105) *(G-12081)*

Dennis Filges Co Inc 724 287-3735
　238 Center Dr Chicora (16025) *(G-3126)*

Dennis Lumber and Concrete 724 329-5542
　4888 National Pike Markleysburg (15459) *(G-10480)*

Dennis Sanders 814 833-5497
　3030 W 25th St Erie (16506) *(G-5245)*

Dennis Snyder 570 682-9698
　66 Snyder Ln Hegins (17938) *(G-7540)*

Dennys Welding 570 265-8015
　207 N Main St Towanda (18848) *(G-18423)*

Denron Sign Co Inc 610 269-6622
　4214 W Lincoln Hwy Downingtown (19335) *(G-4222)*

Dens-A-Can International, Greensburg *Also called Stanko Products Inc (G-6717)*

Dent-Chew Brush LLC 610 520-9941
　10 Williams Rd Haverford (19041) *(G-7408)*

Dental Corp of America 610 344-7488
　889 S Matlack St West Chester (19382) *(G-19535)*

Dental Imaging Tech Corp (HQ) 215 997-5666
　2800 Crystal Dr Hatfield (19440) *(G-7333)*

Dentalez Inc (PA) 610 725-8004
　2 W Liberty Blvd Ste 160 Malvern (19355) *(G-10223)*

Dentalez Inc 717 291-1161
　1816 Colonial Village Ln Lancaster (17601) *(G-8993)*

Dentalez Integrated Solutions, Malvern *Also called Dentalez Inc (G-10223)*

Dente Classic and Exotic Stone, Oakmont *Also called Dente Pittsburgh Inc (G-12916)*

Dente Pittsburgh Inc 412 828-1772
　201a Ann St Oakmont (15139) *(G-12916)*

Dentsply Holding Company 717 845-7511
　221 W Philadelphia St # 60 York (17401) *(G-20448)*

Dentsply International Inc 717 767-8500
　1301 Smile Way York (17404) *(G-20449)*

Dentsply International Inc 717 487-0100
　500 W College Ave York (17401) *(G-20450)*

Dentsply LLC 800 323-0970
　1301 Smile Way York (17404) *(G-20451)*

Dentsply North America LLC 717 849-4229
　221 W Philadelphia St York (17401) *(G-20452)*

Dentsply Rinn, York *Also called Dentsply LLC (G-20451)*

Dentsply Sirona Inc 717 849-7747
　1800 Cloister Dr Lancaster (17601) *(G-8994)*

Dentsply Sirona Inc 717 699-4100
　1301 Smile Way York (17404) *(G-20453)*

Dentsply Sirona Inc (PA) 717 845-7511
　221 W Philadelphia St York (17401) *(G-20454)*

Dentsply Sirona Inc 717 845-7511
　470 W College Ave York (17401) *(G-20455)*

Dep Technologies LLC 800 578-7929
　1000 New Holland Ave Lancaster (17601) *(G-8995)*

Depuy Synthes Inc 610 647-9700
　1690 Russell Rd Paoli (19301) *(G-13138)*

Depuy Synthes Inc 610 701-7078
　108 Willowbrook Ln West Chester (19382) *(G-19536)*

Depuy Synthes Inc 610 738-4600
　1303 Goshen Pkwy West Chester (19380) *(G-19537)*

Depuy Synthes Inc 610 719-5000
　1303 Goshen Pkwy West Chester (19380) *(G-19538)*

Depuy Synthes Products Inc 610 719-5000
　1302 Wrights Ln E West Chester (19380) *(G-19539)*

Depuy Synthes Sales Inc 610 719-5000
　1302 Wrights Ln E West Chester (19380) *(G-19540)*

Depuy Synthes Sales Inc 610 738-4600
　1301 Goshen Pkwy West Chester (19380) *(G-19541)*

Derbyshire Marine Products LLC 267 222-8900
　100 Christopher Ln Harleysville (19438) *(G-7030)*

Dercher Enterprises Inc 610 734-2011
　6801 Ludlow St Upper Darby (19082) *(G-18685)*

Derma Medical, Kempton *Also called National Dermalogy Image Corp (G-8493)*

Dermamed Usa Inc 610 358-4447
　394 Parkmount Rd Lenni (19052) *(G-9761)*

Dermavance Pharmaceuticals Inc 610 727-3935
　1055 Westlakes Dr Berwyn (19312) *(G-1360)*

Dernier Cree Inc 917 287-7452
　15 Genoa Ln Shavertown (18708) *(G-17480)*

Derr Industries, Greenville *Also called James Derr (G-6750)*

Derrick Publishing Company (PA) 814 676-7444
　1510 W 1st St Oil City (16301) *(G-12944)*

Derrick Publishing Company 412 364-8202
　200 Mcknight Park Dr Pittsburgh (15237) *(G-14918)*

Derrick Publishing Company 814 226-7000
　860 S 5th Ave Clarion (16214) *(G-3176)*

Derry Construction Co Inc (PA) 724 539-7600
　527 State Route 217 Latrobe (15650) *(G-9471)*

Derry Stone & Lime Co, Latrobe *Also called Ligonier Stone & Lime Company (G-9500)*

Derry Stone & Lime Co Inc 724 459-3971
　523 State Route 217 Latrobe (15650) *(G-9472)*

Derse Inc 724 772-4853
　422 Keystone Dr Warrendale (15086) *(G-19071)*

Derstine's Custom Embroidery, Telford *Also called Ray Derstine (G-18311)*

Desavino & Sons Inc 570 383-3988
　1003 Underwood Rd Olyphant (18447) *(G-12988)*

Deshlers Machine Inc (PA) 610 588-5622
　120 N Main St Bangor (18013) *(G-912)*

Desi S Interstate Beer 814 528-5914
　2605 Evanston Ave Erie (16506) *(G-5246)*

Design Decorators 215 634-8300
　3076 Jasper St Philadelphia (19134) *(G-13620)*

Design Dynamics Inc 724 266-4826
　2920 Duss Ave Ambridge (15003) *(G-615)*

Design Options Holdings LLC 610 667-8180
　273 Montgomery Ave # 204 Bala Cynwyd (19004) *(G-877)*

Design Originals, East Petersburg *Also called Suza Inc (G-4592)*

Design Print, Scranton *Also called James Saks (G-17247)*

Design Scapes, Philadelphia *Also called Design Decorators (G-13620)*

Design Space Inpharmatics LLC 215 272-4275
　1209 Payne Rd Green Lane (18054) *(G-6587)*

Designed For Fun Inc 215 675-4718
　1800 Mearns Rd Ste G Warminster (18974) *(G-18857)*

Designer Cabinets and Hdwr Co 610 622-4455
　415 S Penn St Clifton Heights (19018) *(G-3252)*

Designer Fashions Plus 215 416-5062
　6100 City Ave Apt 512 Philadelphia (19131) *(G-13621)*

Designer Michael Todd LLC 215 376-0145
　1166 Timbergate Dr Jenkintown (19046) *(G-8283)*

Designing Wright, West Chester *Also called Blue Dog Printing & Design (G-19511)*

Designs By Lawrence Inc 215 698-4555
　12301 Mcnulty Rd Ste A Philadelphia (19154) *(G-13622)*

Designs In Stone Inc 800 878-6631
　163 E County Line Rd Hatboro (19040) *(G-7279)*

Designs Unlimited 717 367-4405
　160 S Poplar St Ste 101 Elizabethtown (17022) *(G-4872)*

Desmond Wholesale Distrs Inc 215 225-0300
　270 Geiger Rd Bldg C Philadelphia (19115) *(G-13623)*

Destech Publications Inc (PA) 717 290-1660
　439 N Duke St Ste 3 Lancaster (17602) *(G-8996)*

Destefanos Hardwood Lumber 724 483-6196
　19 Holly Dr Charleroi (15022) *(G-3009)*

Destiny Image Inc 717 532-3040
　167 Walnut Bottom Rd Shippensburg (17257) *(G-17526)*

Detayl Manufacturing Co Inc 610 754-7123
　303a Big Rd Zieglerville (19492) *(G-20832)*

Detroit Switch Inc 412 322-9144
　1025 Beaver Ave Ste 9 Pittsburgh (15233) *(G-14919)*

Detwiler Tool Co 215 257-5770
　720 Ridge Rd Sellersville (18960) *(G-17344)*

Deval Life Cycle Support LLC 865 786-8675
　7341 Tulip St Philadelphia (19136) *(G-13624)*

Devaltronix Inc 215 331-9600
　7341 Tulip St Philadelphia (19136) *(G-13625)*

Devault Foods, Devault *Also called Devault Packing Company Inc (G-4111)*

Devault Packing Company Inc 610 644-2536
　1 Devault Ln Devault (19432) *(G-4111)*

Devcom Manufacturing LLC (PA) 484 462-4907
　1434 Knox Ave Ste 104 Easton (18040) *(G-4669)*

Developed Resources Inc 724 274-6956
　21 Low Grade Rd Cheswick (15024) *(G-3106)*

Deversign 610 583-2312
　1400 Chester Pike Sharon Hill (19079) *(G-17456)*

Devido Ranier Stone Co 724 658-8518
　2619 New Butler Rd New Castle (16101) *(G-12082)*

Devilbiss Healthcare LLC (HQ) 814 443-4881
　100 Devilbiss Dr Somerset (15501) *(G-17684)*

Devon Energy Corporation 412 366-7474
　9805 Mcknight Rd Pittsburgh (15237) *(G-14920)*

Devon Health Services, King of Prussia *Also called Devon International Group Inc* ***(G-8607)***
Devon International Group Inc (PA)....866 312-3373
700 American Ave Ste 100 King of Prussia (19406) ***(G-8607)***
Devon It Inc....610 757-4220
700 American Ave Ste 100 King of Prussia (19406) ***(G-8608)***
Devonian Resources Inc....814 589-7061
15566 Tionesta Rd Pleasantville (16341) ***(G-15800)***
Devra Party Corp....718 522-7421
4343 G St Ste 1 Philadelphia (19124) ***(G-13626)***
Dew Electric Inc....724 628-9711
189 Enterprise Ln Connellsville (15425) ***(G-3494)***
Dewalt Industrial Tool, Philadelphia *Also called Black & Decker (us) Inc* ***(G-13467)***
Dewitt Fab Welding Co....215 538-9477
271 Scholls School Rd Quakertown (18951) ***(G-16185)***
Dex Media Inc....412 858-4800
1985 Lincoln Way Ste 23 White Oak (15131) ***(G-19854)***
Dexter Rosettes Inc....215 542-0118
1425 Township Line Rd Gwynedd Valley (19437) ***(G-6815)***
DFT Inc....610 363-8903
140 Sheree Blvd Exton (19341) ***(G-5664)***
Dg Services LLC....724 845-7300
1057 State Route 356 A Leechburg (15656) ***(G-9644)***
Dgh Koi Inc....717 582-7749
5055 Spring Rd Shermans Dale (17090) ***(G-17500)***
Dgh Technology Inc (PA)....610 594-9100
110 Summit Dr Ste B Exton (19341) ***(G-5665)***
Dghkoi Inc....610 594-9100
110 Summit Dr Ste B Exton (19341) ***(G-5666)***
Dgm Custom Plsg Finsg C....215 331-0960
8301 Torresdale Ave # 23 Philadelphia (19136) ***(G-13627)***
DH Steel Products LLC....814 459-2715
2420 W 15th St Erie (16505) ***(G-5247)***
Dharini LLC....215 595-3915
1471 Hidden Pond Dr Yardley (19067) ***(G-20306)***
Dhl Machine, Quakertown *Also called DHL Machine Co Inc* ***(G-16186)***
DHL Machine Co Inc (PA)....215 536-3591
2450 Milford Square Pike Quakertown (18951) ***(G-16186)***
Di Chem Concentrate Inc....717 938-8391
509 Fishing Creek Rd Lewisberry (17339) ***(G-9883)***
Dia Doce....610 476-5684
100 S High St Glenmoore (19343) ***(G-6465)***
Diabetic Pastry Chef Inc....412 260-6468
1438 Old Meadow Rd Pittsburgh (15241) ***(G-14921)***
Dial Machine Co, Bensalem *Also called Giordano Incorporated* ***(G-1205)***
Dialogue Institute....215 204-7520
1700 N Broad St Ste 315t Philadelphia (19121) ***(G-13628)***
Diamatic Management Services, Folcroft *Also called Global Polishing Solutions LLC* ***(G-6003)***
Diamond Awning Mfg Co....610 656-1924
618 Grant Rd Folcroft (19032) ***(G-6002)***
Diamond Drinks Inc....570 326-2003
600 Railway St Unit 1 Williamsport (17701) ***(G-20005)***
Diamond Fabrications Inc (PA)....724 228-8422
30 Stewart Ct Washington (15301) ***(G-19163)***
Diamond Graphics Inc....610 269-7335
456 Acorn Ln Downingtown (19335) ***(G-4223)***
Diamond Hvy Vhcl Solutions LLC....717 695-9378
7389 Paxton St Harrisburg (17111) ***(G-7119)***
Diamond Manufacturing Company (HQ)....570 693-0300
243 W Eigth St Wyoming (18644) ***(G-20275)***
Diamond Manufacturing Company....570 693-0300
243 W 8th St Wyoming (18644) ***(G-20276)***
Diamond Milling Company Inc (PA)....724 846-0920
313 5th Ave New Brighton (15066) ***(G-12034)***
Diamond Mt Inc....814 535-3505
213 Chestnut St Johnstown (15906) ***(G-8368)***
Diamond Power Intl Inc....484 875-1600
457 Creamery Way Exton (19341) ***(G-5667)***
Diamond Road Resawing LLC....717 738-3741
1635 Diamond Station Rd Ephrata (17522) ***(G-5100)***
Diamond Rock Productions....215 564-3401
2101 Brandywine St # 200 Philadelphia (19130) ***(G-13629)***
Diamond Tech Group Inc....814 445-8953
1012 S Center Ave Somerset (15501) ***(G-17685)***
Diamond Tool & Die, Inc, Townville *Also called Brian L Dewey* ***(G-18444)***
Diamond Trpcl Hardwoods Intl (PA)....215 257-2556
220 N Main St Sellersville (18960) ***(G-17345)***
Diamond Wear....610 433-2680
116 7th St Whitehall (18052) ***(G-19870)***
Diamond Wire Spring Company....412 821-2703
1901 Babcock Blvd Pittsburgh (15209) ***(G-14922)***
Diamondback Automotive ACC Inc....800 935-4002
354 Enterprise Dr Philipsburg (16866) ***(G-14510)***
Diamondback Truck Covers, Philipsburg *Also called Diamondback Automotive ACC Inc* ***(G-14510)***
Dianas Heavenly Cupcakes....412 628-0642
1007 Gaskill Ave Jeannette (15644) ***(G-8252)***
Diane A Walters....215 453-0890
615 Redwing Rd Perkasie (18944) ***(G-13273)***
Diatome U S Joint Venture....215 646-1478
1560 Industry Rd Hatfield (19440) ***(G-7334)***
Diatome-US, Hatfield *Also called Diatome U S Joint Venture* ***(G-7334)***
Diaz Stone and Pallet Inc....570 289-8760
7822 N Weston Rd Kingsley (18826) ***(G-8703)***
Diaz Stone and Pallet Inc (PA)....570 289-8760
7686 State Route 167 Kingsley (18826) ***(G-8704)***
Dibruno Bros Inc (PA)....215 665-9220
1730 Chestnut St Philadelphia (19103) ***(G-13630)***
Dices Creative Cakes....610 367-0107
30 N Reading Ave Boyertown (19512) ***(G-1906)***
Dick Rughs Aut PA & En REB, Uniontown *Also called Dick Rughs Auto Parts Inc* ***(G-18623)***
Dick Rughs Auto Parts Inc....724 438-3425
285 E Fayette St Uniontown (15401) ***(G-18623)***
Dick Warner Sales & Contg....814 683-4606
17385 Tighe Rd Linesville (16424) ***(G-9980)***
Dickinson's FDA Review, Camp Hill *Also called Ferdic Inc* ***(G-2497)***
Dickson Investment Hdwr Inc....610 272-0764
386 E Church Rd King of Prussia (19406) ***(G-8609)***
Die Botschaft....717 433-4417
420 Weaver Rd Millersburg (17061) ***(G-11193)***
Die Urglaawisch Sippschaft....215 499-1323
1817 Benson Pl Bristol (19007) ***(G-2131)***
Die-Quip Corporation....412 833-1662
5360 Enterprise Blvd Bethel Park (15102) ***(G-1411)***
Die-Tech Inc....717 938-6771
295 Sipe Rd York Haven (17370) ***(G-20757)***
Dieci United States LLC (PA)....724 215-7081
40851 Route 6 Wyalusing (18853) ***(G-20249)***
Dieffenbachs Potato Chips Inc....610 589-2385
51 Host Rd Womelsdorf (19567) ***(G-20206)***
Dielectric Sales LLC (PA)....724 543-2333
1655 Orr Ave Kittanning (16201) ***(G-8766)***
Dielectric Solutions LLC....724 543-2333
192 Devonwood Dr Pittsburgh (15241) ***(G-14923)***
Diesel ERA, Halifax *Also called Paul Withers* ***(G-6827)***
Diesel Pro Inc....717 235-4996
99 Manchester St Glen Rock (17327) ***(G-6455)***
Dietech Tool & Die Inc....814 834-2779
425 W Theresia Rd Saint Marys (15857) ***(G-16962)***
Dietrich Bros Dream Catchr Fly....717 267-0515
416 Cumberland Ave Chambersburg (17201) ***(G-2925)***
Dietrichs Milk Products LLC (HQ)....610 929-5736
100 Mckinley Ave Reading (19605) ***(G-16361)***
Dietrichs Milk Products LLC....570 376-2001
72 Milk Plant Rd Middlebury Center (16935) ***(G-11044)***
Dietz & Watson Inc (PA)....800 333-1974
5701 Tacony St Philadelphia (19135) ***(G-13631)***
Dig Family Business LLC....717 299-5703
451 Richardson Dr Lancaster (17603) ***(G-8997)***
Digestive Care Inc....610 882-5950
1120 Win Dr Bethlehem (18017) ***(G-1496)***
Digibuddha Design LLC....267 387-8165
237 Jacksonville Rd Hatboro (19040) ***(G-7280)***
Digiorgio Mushroom Corp (PA)....610 926-2139
1161 Park Rd Reading (19605) ***(G-16362)***
Digital Card Inc....215 275-7100
303 Corporate Dr E Langhorne (19047) ***(G-9290)***
Digital Card Media, Langhorne *Also called Digital Card Inc* ***(G-9290)***
Digital Care Sysytems Inc....215 946-7700
2000 Hartel Ave Levittown (19057) ***(G-9831)***
Digital Color Graphics Inc....215 942-7500
105 James Way Southampton (18966) ***(G-17808)***
Digital Concepts Inc....724 745-4000
8 Grandview Cir Canonsburg (15317) ***(G-2577)***
Digital Designed Solutions LLC....484 440-9665
96 E Lincoln St Media (19063) ***(G-10921)***
Digital Designs Inc....215 781-2525
37 Scarlet Oak Rd Levittown (19056) ***(G-9832)***
Digital Direct Tm Inc....215 491-1725
2445 Greensward N Warrington (18976) ***(G-19114)***
Digital Dsgns Grphics Sgns LLC....724 568-1626
12 Kelly Ct Gibsonia (15044) ***(G-6331)***
Digital Dynamics Audio Inc....412 434-1630
3383 Industrial Blvd # 5 Bethel Park (15102) ***(G-1412)***
Digital First Media Inc....215 504-4200
Lower Makefield Corpor Yardley (19067) ***(G-20307)***
Digital Grapes LLC....866 458-4226
1100 1st Ave Ste 200 King of Prussia (19406) ***(G-8610)***
Digital Impact LLC....610 623-1269
451 Penn St Yeadon (19050) ***(G-20353)***
Digital Machine Company Inc....215 672-6454
1055 Louis Dr Ste B Warminster (18974) ***(G-18858)***
Digital Media Solutions LLC....610 234-3834
1100 E Hector St Ste 210 Conshohocken (19428) ***(G-3538)***
Digital Plaza LLC....267 515-8000
741 Tennis Ave Ambler (19002) ***(G-575)***
Digital Plaza Direct, Ambler *Also called Digital Plaza LLC* ***(G-575)***
Digital Press Inc....610 758-9680
90 S Commerce Way Ste 340 Bethlehem (18017) ***(G-1497)***

ALPHABETIC

Digital Print & Design Inc................................570 347-6001
  536 Fallon St Old Forge (18518) **(G-12963)**

Digital Sign Id Corporation................................800 407-9188
  853 2nd Street Pike A111 Richboro (18954) **(G-16674)**

Digital-Ink Inc (PA)................................717 731-8890
  230 Gettysburg St Dillsburg (17019) **(G-4126)**

Diiulio Logging................................814 965-3183
  1797 Bendigo Rd Johnsonburg (15845) **(G-8345)**

Diken Machine Inc................................610 495-9995
  133 Possum Hollow Rd Pottstown (19464) **(G-15982)**

Dilullo Graphics Inc................................610 775-4360
  448 Imperial Dr Mohnton (19540) **(G-11262)**

Dilworth Manufacturing Co................................717 354-8956
  6051 Division Hwy Narvon (17555) **(G-11920)**

Dim Sum & Noodle................................215 515-3992
  2000 Hamilton St Philadelphia (19130) **(G-13632)**

Dimec Rail Service................................844 362-9221
  191 S Keim St Ste 212 Pottstown (19464) **(G-15983)**

Dimension Carbide................................814 789-2102
  25320 State St Saegertown (16433) **(G-16912)**

Dimension Data North Amer Inc................................484 362-2563
  301 Lindenwood Dr Ste 330 Malvern (19355) **(G-10224)**

Dimensions................................610 939-9900
  1801 N 12th St Reading (19604) **(G-16363)**

Dimesol Usa LLC................................717 938-0796
  509 Fishing Creek Rd Lewisberry (17339) **(G-9884)**

Dimetix USA, Chester Springs *Also called Laser-View Technologies Inc* **(G-3082)**

Dimpter Woodworking................................215 855-2335
  35 E Blaine St Lansdale (19446) **(G-9361)**

Dinardo Brothers Material Inc................................215 535-4645
  4455 Castor Ave Philadelphia (19124) **(G-13633)**

Dine-A-Heat, Phoenixville *Also called Le Jo Enterprises Incorporated* **(G-14559)**

Dine-Glow Dblo Fd Svc Fels LLC................................800 526-7583
  765 Pike Springs Rd Phoenixville (19460) **(G-14545)**

Dingmans Ferry Stone Inc................................570 828-2617
  432 Park Rd Dingmans Ferry (18328) **(G-4142)**

Dinneen & Son Inc................................412 241-2727
  7838 Kelly St Pittsburgh (15208) **(G-14924)**

Dinosaw Inc................................570 374-5531
  81 Universal Rd Selinsgrove (17870) **(G-17323)**

Dinsmore Wldg Fabrication Inc................................814 885-6407
  31 Innovative Dr Kersey (15846) **(G-8555)**

Diocese of Altoona Johnstown, Hollidaysburg *Also called Catholic Register* **(G-7643)**

Diocese of Scranton, The, Scranton *Also called Catholic Scl Svcs of Scranton* **(G-17216)**

Diox Water Hygiene, Conshohocken *Also called Klenzoid Inc* **(G-3570)**

Direct Digital Master Inc................................215 634-2235
  495 E Erie Ave Philadelphia (19134) **(G-13634)**

Direct Energy Products Inc................................216 255-7777
  13649 Route 36 Tionesta (16353) **(G-18370)**

Direct Line Productions Inc................................610 633-7082
  151 Creek Rd Glen Mills (19342) **(G-6435)**

Direct Mail Service & Press................................610 432-4538
  313 Sumner Ave Allentown (18102) **(G-194)**

Direct Mail Service Inc................................412 471-6300
  939 W North Ave Pittsburgh (15233) **(G-14925)**

Direct Marketing Publishers................................215 321-3068
  1304 University Dr Yardley (19067) **(G-20308)**

Direct Results Bsp Inc................................724 627-2040
  185 Wade St Waynesburg (15370) **(G-19439)**

Direct Wire & Cable Inc................................717 336-2842
  412 Oak St Denver (17517) **(G-4070)**

Directional Systems, Erie *Also called Fm2 Inc* **(G-5295)**

Direnzo Inc................................215 740-6166
  1426 Marielle Dr Warrington (18976) **(G-19115)**

Dirt Rag Magazine................................412 767-9910
  3483 Saxonburg Blvd Pittsburgh (15238) **(G-14926)**

Disc Hounds LLC................................610 696-8668
  323 E Gay St Ste 2 West Chester (19380) **(G-19542)**

Dischem Inc................................814 772-6603
  17295 Boot Jack Rd Ste A Ridgway (15853) **(G-16704)**

Disco, Philadelphia *Also called Cellucap Manufacturing Co* **(G-13518)**

Discovery Direct Inc................................610 252-3809
  335 Wedgewood Dr Easton (18045) **(G-4670)**

Discovery Machine Inc................................570 601-1966
  153 W 4th St Ste 1 Williamsport (17701) **(G-20006)**

Discovery Oil Gas LLC................................724 746-4004
  125 Technology Dr Ste 105 Canonsburg (15317) **(G-2578)**

Dispatch Printing, Fairview *Also called Kim Kraft Inc* **(G-5830)**

Dispatch Printing Inc (PA)................................814 870-9600
  917 Bacon St Erie (16511) **(G-5248)**

Dispersion Tech Systems LLC................................610 832-2040
  1002 W Ridge Pike Ste 100 Conshohocken (19428) **(G-3539)**

Display Design & Sales Co, Philadelphia *Also called Creative Touch Inc* **(G-13580)**

Display Source Alliance LLC................................717 534-0884
  1 W Chocolate Ave Ste 700 Hershey (17033) **(G-7608)**

Displays and Graphics Inc................................717 540-1481
  5321d Jaycee Ave Harrisburg (17112) **(G-7120)**

Disston Precision, Philadelphia *Also called Bangor Steel Erectors Inc* **(G-13443)**

Disston Precision Inc................................215 338-1200
  6795 New State Rd Philadelphia (19135) **(G-13635)**

Distinctive Outdoor Spaces LLC................................484 718-5050
  101 Everett Ct Parkesburg (19365) **(G-13173)**

Distribution Center, Fredericksburg *Also called Crayola LLC* **(G-6173)**

Dita Exchange Inc................................267 327-4889
  150 N Radnor Chester Rd Radnor (19087) **(G-16293)**

Ditech Group, York *Also called York Steel Rule Dies Inc* **(G-20750)**

Div-Forest Manor, Grampian *Also called Hepburnia Coal Company* **(G-6571)**

Dively Manufacture Co Inc................................814 239-5441
  1600 Locust Hollow Rd Claysburg (16625) **(G-3203)**

Diversatech Industrial LLC................................724 887-4199
  3234 Richey Rd Connellsville (15425) **(G-3495)**

Diverse Defense Solutions, Hanover *Also called Diverse Tchnical Solutions LLC* **(G-6877)**

Diverse Sales Company Inc................................215 317-1815
  311 Wyckford Dr Perkasie (18944) **(G-13274)**

Diverse Tchnical Solutions LLC................................717 630-8522
  72 Joshua Dr Hanover (17331) **(G-6877)**

Diversey Inc................................570 421-7850
  880 Crowe Rd East Stroudsburg (18301) **(G-4613)**

Diversified Air Systems Inc................................724 873-0884
  269 Meadowlands Blvd Washington (15301) **(G-19164)**

Diversified Coatings Inc................................814 772-3850
  224 River Rd Ridgway (15853) **(G-16705)**

Diversified Design & Mfg Inc................................610 337-1969
  161 Boro Line Rd King of Prussia (19406) **(G-8611)**

Diversified Designing & Mfg, King of Prussia *Also called Diversified Design & Mfg Inc* **(G-8611)**

Diversified Fabrications Inc................................814 344-8434
  514 Deveaux St Carrolltown (15722) **(G-2807)**

Diversified Logging................................724 228-4143
  440 Route 519 Unit 2 Eighty Four (15330) **(G-4838)**

Diversified Machine Inc................................717 397-5347
  430 N Franklin St Lancaster (17602) **(G-8998)**

Diversified Mech Svcs Inc................................215 368-3084
  618 Knapp Rd Lansdale (19446) **(G-9362)**

Diversified Metal Products Co................................215 423-8877
  2020 Frankford Ave Philadelphia (19125) **(G-13636)**

Diversified Mfg Systems................................814 455-2400
  421 W 12th St Ste 57 Erie (16501) **(G-5249)**

Diversified Modular Casework................................484 442-8007
  60 State Rd Ste A Media (19063) **(G-10922)**

Diversified Traffic Pdts Inc................................717 428-0222
  3846 Green Valley Rd Seven Valleys (17360) **(G-17377)**

Diversified Wear Products, Pittsburgh *Also called Trinity Mining Services Inc* **(G-15649)**

Division of Thermo Dynamics................................570 385-0731
  155 Route 61 S Schuylkill Haven (17972) **(G-17154)**

Division Seven Inc................................724 449-8400
  230 Laurel Ave Gibsonia (15044) **(G-6332)**

Dixie S Young Cleaning................................814 623-3015
  317 N Richard St Bedford (15522) **(G-1049)**

Dixie Seating Company, York *Also called Dsc2 Inc* **(G-20458)**

Dixon Tool & Die Inc................................814 684-0266
  2500 Adams Ave Tyrone (16686) **(G-18581)**

Dixon-Saunders Enterprises................................215 335-2150
  4504 Briar Hl W Lafayette Hill (19444) **(G-8878)**

Dixon-Saunders Printing, Lafayette Hill *Also called Dixon-Saunders Enterprises* **(G-8878)**

Diyshutters, Stowe *Also called Kestrel Shutters & Doors Inc* **(G-18072)**

Dj Machining LLC (PA)................................724 938-0812
  125 Theobold Ave Greensburg (15601) **(G-6659)**

Djf Print Xpress................................215 964-1258
  47 Locust Ln Levittown (19054) **(G-9833)**

Djk Properties LLC................................717 597-5965
  80 Commerce Ave Greencastle (17225) **(G-6607)**

Djquesne Bottling Company................................412 831-2779
  2555 Washington Rd Pittsburgh (15241) **(G-14927)**

Dl Truss LLC................................717 355-9813
  199 Quality Cir New Holland (17557) **(G-12243)**

Dl1 Processing LLC................................215 582-3263
  805b W 2nd St Chester (19013) **(G-3048)**

Dla Document Services................................717 605-3777
  5450 Crlsle Pike Bldg 410 Mechanicsburg (17055) **(G-10837)**

Dlubak Fabrication Inc................................724 224-5887
  1487 Saxonburg Rd Natrona Heights (15065) **(G-11938)**

Dlubak Glass Company (PA)................................724 226-1991
  1600 Saxonburg Rd Natrona Heights (15065) **(G-11939)**

Dlubak Glass Company................................724 224-5887
  1487 Saxonburg Rd Natrona Heights (15065) **(G-11940)**

Dm Coatings Inc................................717 561-1175
  6950 Chatham Dr Harrisburg (17111) **(G-7121)**

Dmand Energy................................970 201-4976
  901 N Pike Rd Cabot (16023) **(G-2455)**

DMC, Leola *Also called Dutchie Manufacturing LLC* **(G-9778)**

DMC Global Inc................................724 277-9710
  1138 Industrial Park Dr Mount Braddock (15465) **(G-11616)**

Dmi Companies, Charleroi *Also called Ductmate Industries Inc* **(G-3011)**

Dmi Locksmith Inc................................412 232-3000
  439 Wood St Pittsburgh (15222) **(G-14928)**

Dmm Woodworking 717 390-2828
  518 Fremont St Lancaster (17603) *(G-8999)*

DMS, Allentown *Also called Direct Mail Service & Press (G-194)*

DMS Computer Services Inc 412 835-3570
  91 Fort Couch Rd Pittsburgh (15241) *(G-14929)*

DMS Shredding Inc 570 819-3339
  9 Fellows Ave Rear Hanover Township (18706) *(G-6988)*

DMW Marine Group LLC 610 827-2032
  1123 Saint Matthews Rd Chester Springs (19425) *(G-3075)*

Dn Printer Solutions 717 606-6233
  175 E King St Bldg 6 Ephrata (17522) *(G-5101)*

Dnh Speakers Inc 484 494-5790
  900 Calcon Hook Rd Ste 16 Sharon Hill (19079) *(G-17457)*

Dnp Imagingcomm America Corp 724 696-7500
  1001 Technology Dr Mount Pleasant (15666) *(G-11697)*

Dnp IMS America Corporation, Mount Pleasant *Also called Dnp Imagingcomm America Corp (G-11697)*

Do It Best, Canonsburg *Also called Al Lorenzi Lumber Co Inc (G-2534)*

Do-Co Inc 814 382-8339
  560 Water St Conneaut Lake (16316) *(G-3471)*

Dobish Signs & Display Inc 724 375-3943
  3182 Green Garden Rd Aliquippa (15001) *(G-73)*

DOC Printing LLC 267 702-6196
  5156 Baynton St Philadelphia (19144) *(G-13637)*

Doc's Candies, Gillett *Also called Halls Candies LLC (G-6381)*

Dock Tool & Machine Inc 215 338-8989
  5200 Unruh Ave Ste E1 Philadelphia (19135) *(G-13638)*

Doctor Bart Ayurveda 717 524-4208
  108 Fair Ave Hanover (17331) *(G-6878)*

Doctor In The House Inc 610 277-1998
  1515 Dekalb Pike Ste 204 Blue Bell (19422) *(G-1827)*

Dodie Sable 610 756-3836
  593 Old 22 Lenhartsville (19534) *(G-9758)*

Dodson Bros Inc 412 793-0600
  164 Sandy Creek Rd Verona (15147) *(G-18755)*

Doellken- Woodtape Inc 610 929-1910
  141 Beacon Hill Rd Temple (19560) *(G-18328)*

Doerschner Machine 724 625-1350
  114 Grand Ave Mars (16046) *(G-10494)*

Dogs In Cast Stone 717 291-9696
  175 N Concord St Lancaster (17603) *(G-9000)*

Dolans Wldg Stl Fbrication Inc 814 749-8639
  118 Venture St Johnstown (15909) *(G-8369)*

Dolphin Group 610 640-7513
  537 Foxwood Ln Paoli (19301) *(G-13139)*

Domar Group Inc 714 674-0391
  108 Aragon Pl Finleyville (15332) *(G-5955)*

Dombach, C B & Son, Lancaster *Also called Tmu Inc (G-9220)*

Domenic Stangherlin 610 434-5624
  943 Kurtz St Allentown (18102) *(G-195)*

Dominion Energy Transm Inc 724 354-3433
  Rte 156 Rr 3 Rt 156 Shelocta (15774) *(G-17485)*

Dominion Exploration and Prod 724 349-4450
  303 Airport Rd Indiana (15701) *(G-8091)*

Dominion Powdered Metals 814 598-4684
  266 Battery St Saint Marys (15857) *(G-16963)*

Domtar Paper Company LLC 814 965-2521
  100 W Center St Johnsonburg (15845) *(G-8346)*

Domtar Paper Company LLC 814 371-0630
  377 Satterlee Rd Du Bois (15801) *(G-4387)*

Don Fooderte Food Market, Lykens *Also called S Don Food Market Inc (G-10135)*

Don Saylors Markets Inc 717 776-7551
  37 Carlisle Rd Newville (17241) *(G-12600)*

Don's Food Products, Schwenksville *Also called Aldon Food Corporation (G-17172)*

Don's Food Rite, Lykens *Also called Dons Lykens Food Market Inc (G-10132)*

Donahue's Classic Auto, Meadville *Also called Dan Donahue (G-10718)*

Donald B Remmey Inc (PA) 570 386-5379
  523 Mill Rd Lehighton (18235) *(G-9711)*

Donald B Remmey Inc 570 386-5379
  523 Mill Rd Lehighton (18235) *(G-9712)*

Donald B Smith Incorporated (PA) 717 632-2100
  450 W Chestnut St Hanover (17331) *(G-6879)*

Donald Beiswenger Inc 814 886-8341
  107 S Main St Gallitzin (16641) *(G-6245)*

Donald Blyler Offset Inc 717 949-6831
  2101 Fonderwhite Rd Lebanon (17042) *(G-9561)*

Donald Campbell 412 793-6068
  3262 Clements Rd Pittsburgh (15239) *(G-14930)*

Donald EBY 814 767-9406
  2301 Beans Cove Rd Clearville (15535) *(G-3241)*

Donald Greathouse 814 242-7624
  2966 Whistler Rd Stoystown (15563) *(G-18076)*

Donald Plants 412 384-5911
  3067 Scotia Hollow Rd West Elizabeth (15088) *(G-19694)*

Donald Trammell 484 238-5467
  935 W Main St Coatesville (19320) *(G-3301)*

Donald W Deitz 814 745-2857
  489 Lilac Ln Clarion (16214) *(G-3177)*

Donaldson Company Inc 215 396-8349
  85 Railroad Dr Warminster (18974) *(G-18859)*

Donaldson Supply & Eqp Co 724 745-5250
  40 Murdock St Canonsburg (15317) *(G-2579)*

Donart Electronics Inc 724 796-3011
  1005 Robinson Hwy Mc Donald (15057) *(G-10572)*

Donatucci Kitchens & Appls 215 545-5755
  1901 Washington Ave Philadelphia (19146) *(G-13639)*

Donawald Enterprises LLC 215 962-3635
  13 Independence Way Doylestown (18901) *(G-4295)*

Donbar Shea Butter Products, Coatesville *Also called Donald Trammell (G-3301)*

Doner Design Inc 717 786-4172
  2175 Beaver Valley Pike New Providence (17560) *(G-12433)*

Donjon Shipbuilding & Repr LLC 814 455-6442
  220 E Bayfront Pkwy Erie (16507) *(G-5250)*

Donlee Tool Corp 814 398-8215
  21 North St Cambridge Springs (16403) *(G-2477)*

Donna Karan Company LLC 610 625-4410
  77 Sands Blvd Bethlehem (18015) *(G-1498)*

Donna Karan Company LLC 717 299-1706
  801 Stanley K Tanger Blvd Lancaster (17602) *(G-9001)*

Donna Stanton 412 561-2661
  6365 Library Rd South Park (15129) *(G-17781)*

Donnelley Financial LLC 717 293-3725
  2 Braxton Way Fl 2 # 2 Glen Mills (19342) *(G-6436)*

Donnelley Jr Joseph 570 998-2541
  3835 State Route 973 W Cogan Station (17728) *(G-3359)*

Donohoe Corporation 724 850-2433
  593 Rugh St Ste 6 Greensburg (15601) *(G-6660)*

Donohue Railroad Equipment Inc 724 827-8104
  100 Hollow Rd Darlington (16115) *(G-4027)*

Donora Embroidery Service, Donora *Also called Donora Sportswear Company Inc (G-4151)*

Donora Sportswear Company Inc 724 929-2387
  585 Galiffa Dr Donora (15033) *(G-4151)*

Donovan Schoonover Lumber Co 814 697-7266
  Academy St Ext Shinglehouse (16748) *(G-17506)*

Dons Lykens Food Market Inc 717 453-7042
  672 Main St Lykens (17048) *(G-10132)*

Dons Machine Shop Inc 570 655-1950
  777 Ash St West Pittston (18643) *(G-19754)*

Donsco Inc (PA) 717 252-1561
  124 N Front St Wrightsville (17368) *(G-20236)*

Donsco Inc 717 653-1851
  100 S Jacob St Mount Joy (17552) *(G-11653)*

Donsco Inc 717 252-1561
  4381 Front Mountain Rd Belleville (17004) *(G-1131)*

Donut Connection 724 282-6214
  330 Center Ave Butler (16001) *(G-2395)*

Donut Shack 412 793-4222
  13041 Frankstown Rd Pittsburgh (15235) *(G-14931)*

Doodad Printing LLC 800 383-6973
  1842 Clnl Vlg Ln 101 Lancaster (17601) *(G-9002)*

Dooley Gasket and Seal Inc 610 328-2720
  838 Sussex Blvd Broomall (19008) *(G-2286)*

Dooner Ventures LLC 610 420-1100
  301 Highland Ln Bryn Mawr (19010) *(G-2320)*

Door Guard Inc 724 695-8936
  809 Parkway View Dr Pittsburgh (15205) *(G-14932)*

Door Stop Ltd 610 353-8707
  326 Overhill Rd Wayne (19087) *(G-19318)*

Doors Unlimited, Philadelphia *Also called Tri-State Door and Hardware (G-14408)*

Doppelhauer Manufacturing 724 691-0763
  125 Theobold Ave Greensburg (15601) *(G-6661)*

Dor-Mae Industries Inc 610 929-5003
  4001 Reading Crest Ave Reading (19605) *(G-16364)*

Dorado Solutions Inc 480 216-1056
  1185 Hampshire Pl West Chester (19382) *(G-19543)*

Doran & Associates Inc 412 344-5200
  200 Roessler Rd Pittsburgh (15220) *(G-14933)*

Dorchester Publishing Co Inc 212 725-8811
  100 W Matsonford Rd # 101 Wayne (19087) *(G-19319)*

Doremus Kitchens, Pennsburg *Also called Irving K Doremus Jr (G-13249)*

Doren Inc 724 535-4397
  2313 State Route 18 Wampum (16157) *(G-18799)*

Doren Inc Parkway 724 375-6637
  2321 Todd Rd Aliquippa (15001) *(G-74)*

Dorland Health Care Info, Philadelphia *Also called Dorland Healthcare Information (G-13640)*

Dorland Healthcare Information (HQ) 800 784-2332
  1500 Walnut St Ste 1000 Philadelphia (19102) *(G-13640)*

Dormakaba USA Inc (HQ) 717 336-3881
  100 Dorma Dr Reamstown (17567) *(G-16576)*

Dorman Products Inc (PA) 215 997-1800
  3400 E Walnut St Colmar (18915) *(G-3416)*

Dormont Manufacturing Company 724 327-7909
  6015 Enterprise Dr Export (15632) *(G-5597)*

Dorothy M Nelson 724 837-6210
  1181 Swede Hill Rd Greensburg (15601) *(G-6662)*

Dorothy's Candies, White Oak *Also called Robert W Gastel Jr (G-19858)*

Dorrance Publishing Co Inc 800 788-7654
  585 Alpha Dr Ste 103 Pittsburgh (15238) *(G-14934)*

Dorso LLC 724 934-7710
104 Bradford Rd Wexford (15090) (G-19798)

Dorwards Electric Corp 610 767-8148
450 W Church St Slatington (18080) (G-17605)

Dotted Quarter Music 724 541-4211
1563 English Dr Mechanicsburg (17055) (G-10838)

Double A Logging LLC 814 885-6844
5237 Boone Mountain Rd Kersey (15846) (G-8556)

Double D Service Center LLC 717 201-2800
1338 Johnson Mill Ln Columbia (17512) (G-3437)

Double D Sheet Metal Inc 610 987-3733
196 Main St Oley (19547) (G-12978)

Double DS Roadhouse Llc 814 395-3535
7966 Kingwood Rd Confluence (15424) (G-3464)

Double H Manufacturing Corp 215 674-4100
2548 W 26th St Warminster (18974) (G-18860)

Double H Manufacturing Corp (PA) 215 674-4100
50 W Street Rd Warminster (18974) (G-18861)

Double H Plastics, Warminster Also called Double H Manufacturing Corp (G-18860)

Double M Productions LLC 570 476-8000
N 1st St Bldg 8 Stroudsburg (18360) (G-18114)

Double Nickel Delivery LLC 412 721-0550
620 1st St Irwin (15642) (G-8157)

Double R Enterprises, Verona Also called Consolidated Container Co LLC (G-18754)

Doucette Industries Inc 717 845-8746
20 Leigh Dr York (17406) (G-20456)

Doug Herhold 814 756-5141
9901 Route 6n Albion (16401) (G-43)

Doug Pfers Deer Ctng Smoke Hse 724 758-7965
1685 Route 65 Ellwood City (16117) (G-4929)

Dough Nuts For Doughnuts LLC (PA) 610 642-6186
341 Lancaster Ave Ste 200 Haverford (19041) (G-7409)

Douglas Explosives Inc 814 342-0782
2052 Phlpsburg Bigler Hwy Philipsburg (16866) (G-14511)

Douglas Laboratories 412 494-0122
600 Boyce Rd Pittsburgh (15205) (G-14935)

Douglas Pharma Us Inc 267 317-2010
1035 Louis Dr Warminster (18974) (G-18862)

Doutt Tool Inc 814 398-2989
21879 Gravel Run Rd Venango (16440) (G-18740)

Dove Plastics Inc 610 562-2600
111 Valley Rd Hamburg (19526) (G-6837)

Dow Bar Roman House, Collegeville Also called Rohm and Haas Chemicals LLC (G-3391)

Dow Chemical Co 610 244-7101
4602 Merchant Square Pl Lansdale (19446) (G-9363)

Dow Chemical Company 215 641-7000
400 Arcola Rd Collegeville (19426) (G-3375)

Dow Chemical Company 215 785-8000
2900 River Rd Croydon (19021) (G-3916)

Dow Chemical Company 610 775-6640
3 Commerce Dr Reading (19607) (G-16365)

Dow Chemical Company 215 785-8000
200 Route 413 Bristol (19007) (G-2132)

Dow Chemical Company 215 592-3000
100 S Indpdnc Mall W Fl 5 Philadelphia (19106) (G-13641)

Dow Chemical Company 215 785-7000
310 Grge Pttrson Dr 100 Bristol (19007) (G-2133)

Down Home Rice Pudding 570 945-5744
1580 Aberdeen Rd Madison Township (18444) (G-10168)

Down River, Hazle Township Also called Signode Industrial Group LLC (G-7479)

Downey's Honey Butter, Manheim Also called Honey Butter Products Co Inc (G-10389)

Downhome Homemade Rice Pudding, Madison Township Also called Down Home Rice Pudding (G-10168)

Downing Enterprises Inc 610 873-0070
441 Boot Rd Ste 100 Downingtown (19335) (G-4224)

Downing Machines Inc 412 461-0580
467 W 8th Ave Homestead (15120) (G-7684)

Downing's Cab, New Castle Also called Dennis Downing (G-12081)

Doyle & Roth Mfg Co Inc 570 282-5010
1 Morse Ave Simpson (18407) (G-17592)

Doyle Design 215 456-9745
241 W Wyoming Ave Philadelphia (19140) (G-13642)

Doyle Equipment Company 724 837-4500
Rr 66 Box S Delmont (15626) (G-4050)

Dp Machining & Fabrication, Chambersburg Also called Dawson Performance Inc (G-2923)

Dp Millwork Inc 215 996-1179
2262 N Penn Rd Ste 200 Hatfield (19440) (G-7335)

Dpc Pet Specialties LLC 814 724-7710
18746 Mill St Meadville (16335) (G-10719)

Dpi Inc 215 953-9800
2800 Turnpike Dr Hatboro (19040) (G-7281)

DPR INDUSTRIES, Coatesville Also called Pacer Industries Inc (G-3320)

Dqe Communications (HQ) 412 393-1033
424 S 27th St Ste 220 Pittsburgh (15203) (G-14936)

Dr Controls Inc 570 622-7109
353 E Railroad St Pottsville (17901) (G-16077)

Dr Davies Products Inc 570 321-5423
1318 Commerce Park Dr Williamsport (17701) (G-20007)

Dr G H Michel Restor-Skin Co 724 526-5551
202 6th St East Brady (16028) (G-4529)

Dr Opalka's Office, Kittanning Also called Lens Contact Center (G-8777)

Dr Pepper Snapple Group 724 776-6111
125 E Kensinger Dr Cranberry Township (16066) (G-3816)

Dr Pepper's Snapple Drink, Aspers Also called Motts LLP (G-743)

Draeger Inc 215 721-5400
3135 Quarry Rd Telford (18969) (G-18281)

Draeger Inc 215 660-2252
3124 Commerce Dr Telford (18969) (G-18282)

Draeger Medical Systems Inc (HQ) 800 437-2437
3135 Quarry Rd Telford (18969) (G-18283)

Drafto, Cochranton Also called Zurex Corporation (G-3353)

Drafto Corporation 814 425-7445
100 Pressler Ave Cochranton (16314) (G-3342)

Dragonfly Pictures Inc 610 521-6115
600 W End Of 2nd St # 2 Essington (19029) (G-5542)

Drake Refrigeration Inc 215 638-5515
2900 Samuel Dr Bensalem (19020) (G-1183)

Drakenfeld Products, Washington Also called Ferro Color & Glass Corp (G-19175)

Draper Dbs Inc 215 257-3833
1803 N 5th St Perkasie (18944) (G-13275)

Draperies Plus, Camp Hill Also called Westerbrook Custom Made Drap (G-2525)

Drd Inc 215 879-1055
4916 Merion Ave Philadelphia (19131) (G-13643)

Drdavesbestbodies Inc 610 926-5728
1050 Maidencreek Rd Ste D Fleetwood (19522) (G-5970)

Dream Publishing 610 945-2017
1150 1st Ave Ste 501 King of Prussia (19406) (G-8612)

Dream World International Inc 215 320-0200
10073 Sandmeyer Ln Philadelphia (19116) (G-13644)

Dreamlike Entertainment 610 392-5614
2122 Mountain Rd Slatington (18080) (G-17606)

Dreamline 215 957-1411
905 Louis Dr Warminster (18974) (G-18863)

Dreamspring Institute 570 829-1378
9 Hutson St Wilkes Barre (18702) (G-19916)

Dreamspring Institute , The, Wilkes Barre Also called Dreamspring Institute (G-19916)

Drebo America Inc 724 938-0690
500 Technology Dr Coal Center (15423) (G-3275)

Dreistern Inc 215 799-0220
801 Tech Dr Telford (18969) (G-18284)

Dressel Welding Supply Inc 570 505-1994
4450 Lycoming Creek Rd Cogan Station (17728) (G-3360)

Dresser LLC 814 362-9200
41 Fisher Ave Bradford (16701) (G-1967)

Dresser-Rand Company 215 441-0400
203 Precision Rd Horsham (19044) (G-7810)

Dreumex USA Inc 717 767-6881
3445 Board Rd York (17406) (G-20457)

Drexel Bindery Inc 215 232-3808
3992 Rowena Dr Philadelphia (19114) (G-13645)

Drexel Foods Inc 215 425-9900
1705 N American St Philadelphia (19122) (G-13646)

Drexel University 215 590-8863
3219 Arch St Philadelphia (19104) (G-13647)

Drexler Associates Inc 724 888-2042
112 Olivia Ave Mars (16046) (G-10495)

Dri Machine Shop Inc 717 633-9306
145 Ram Dr Hanover (17331) (G-6880)

Driban Body Works Inc 215 468-6900
8950 State Rd Ste 2 Philadelphia (19136) (G-13648)

Drifton Precision Machining 570 636-1408
Rr 940 Drifton (18221) (G-4376)

Drill Management Inc 717 227-8189
3543 Ridge Rd Glen Rock (17327) (G-6456)

Drillmasters LLC 717 319-8657
712 Ridge Rd Telford (18969) (G-18285)

Drindustries 412 704-5840
1320 Renton Rd Pittsburgh (15239) (G-14937)

Drinkworks Corporation 800 825-5575
618 4th Ave Warren (16365) (G-19021)

Driveline Service Pittsburgh, Pittsburgh Also called Westmoreland Machine & Elc Co (G-15712)

Dronetti Upholstery Inc 610 435-2957
415 Auburn St Allentown (18103) (G-196)

Drs Laurel Technologies (HQ) 814 534-8900
246 Airport Rd Johnstown (15904) (G-8370)

Drs Printing Services Inc 717 502-1117
6 N Grantham Rd Dillsburg (17019) (G-4127)

Drt Medical LLC 215 997-2900
2342 N Penn Rd Hatfield (19440) (G-7336)

Drucker Company Intl Inc 814 342-6210
168 Bradford Dr Philipsburg (16866) (G-14512)

Drucker Company LLC 814 692-7661
200 Shady Ln Ste 170 Philipsburg (16866) (G-14513)

Drug Plastics and Glass Co (HQ) 610 367-5000
1 Bottle Dr Boyertown (19512) (G-1907)

Drug Plastics and Glass Co Inc 570 672-3215
  State Rd 4012 Elysburg (17824) *(G-4974)*

Drug Plastics and Glass Co Inc 724 548-5654
  104 West Park Dr Kittanning (16201) *(G-8767)*

Drug Plastics and Glass Co Inc 570 672-3215
  6 Bottle Dr Elysburg (17824) *(G-4975)*

Drug Plastics Closures Inc (HQ) 610 367-5000
  850 Montgomery Ave Boyertown (19512) *(G-1908)*

Drugdev Inc (PA) 888 650-1860
  1170 Devon Park Dr # 300 Wayne (19087) *(G-19320)*

Drumm & Oharah TI & Design Inc 814 476-1349
  8343 Edinboro Rd Erie (16509) *(G-5251)*

Drummond Scientific Company 610 353-0200
  500 Parkway Broomall (19008) *(G-2287)*

Drv Metal Fab LLC 717 968-9028
  3089 Berry Ridge Rd East Waterford (17021) *(G-4640)*

Ds Fabrication 717 529-2282
  834 Pumping Station Rd Kirkwood (17536) *(G-8748)*

Ds Inpharmatics, Green Lane Also called Design Space Inpharmatics LLC *(G-6587)*

Ds Machine LLC 717 768-3853
  238b Old Leacock Rd Gordonville (17529) *(G-6552)*

DS Services Group Corp 724 350-6429
  10 Chamber Plz Charleroi (15022) *(G-3010)*

Ds Services of America Inc 717 901-4620
  1890 Old Crooked Hill Rd Harrisburg (17110) *(G-7122)*

Ds Smith - Reading Mill, Reading Also called United Corrstack LLC *(G-16554)*

DSC Label, Perkasie Also called Diverse Sales Company Inc *(G-13274)*

Dsc2 Inc 980 223-2270
  586 Campbell Rd York (17402) *(G-20458)*

Dsg Pittsburgh, Pittsburgh Also called Sentage Corporation *(G-15525)*

DSI Underground Systems Inc 740 432-7302
  258 Kappa Dr Pittsburgh (15238) *(G-14938)*

DSI-Lang Geotech LLC 610 268-2221
  1263 Newark Rd Toughkenamon (19374) *(G-18418)*

Dsid, Richboro Also called Digital Sign Id Corporation *(G-16674)*

DSM Biomedical Inc (HQ) 484 713-2100
  735 Pennsylvania Dr Exton (19341) *(G-5668)*

DSM Biomedical Inc 610 321-2720
  735 Pennsylvania Dr Exton (19341) *(G-5669)*

DT Davis Enterprises Ltd 610 694-9600
  4482 Innovation Way Allentown (18109) *(G-197)*

Dti, Yeadon Also called Delaware Tool & Machine Co *(G-20352)*

Du Bois Div, Du Bois Also called Stella-Jones Corporation *(G-4421)*

Du Penn Inc 814 371-6280
  160 Barnoff Rd Du Bois (15801) *(G-4388)*

Du-Co Ceramics Company (PA) 724 352-1511
  155 S Rebecca St Saxonburg (16056) *(G-17085)*

Dual Core LLC (HQ) 800 233-0298
  148 E Stiegel St Manheim (17545) *(G-10379)*

Dualsun International Inc 412 421-7934
  5539 Fair Oaks St Pittsburgh (15217) *(G-14939)*

Duane Grant 412 856-1357
  1367 Foxwood Dr Monroeville (15146) *(G-11333)*

Dubel D H Mill & Lumber Co 717 993-2566
  15979 Sawmill Rd Stewartstown (17363) *(G-18060)*

Dubose Printing & Bus Svcs 215 877-9071
  7592a Haverford Ave Philadelphia (19151) *(G-13649)*

Dubose Printing and Bus Svcs, Philadelphia Also called Dubose Printing & Bus
Svcs *(G-13649)*

Dubrook Inc (PA) 814 371-3113
  40 Hoover Ave Du Bois (15801) *(G-4389)*

Dubrook Inc 724 538-3111
  600 S Washington St Evans City (16033) *(G-5558)*

Dubrook Inc 724 283-3111
  303 Bantam Ave Butler (16001) *(G-2396)*

Dubrook Inc 814 371-3111
  40 Parkway Dr Du Bois (15801) *(G-4390)*

Dubrook Inc 814 834-3111
  875 Theresia St Saint Marys (15857) *(G-16964)*

Duchesnay Usa Inc 484 380-2641
  919 Conestoga Rd 1-203 Bryn Mawr (19010) *(G-2321)*

Duckloe Frederick and Bros 570 897-6172
  513 Delaware Ave Portland (18351) *(G-15939)*

Duco Holdings LLC 215 942-6274
  116 Railroad Dr Ivyland (18974) *(G-8209)*

Duco Plastics and Supply, Ivyland Also called Duco Holdings LLC *(G-8209)*

Duct Shop USA Inc 412 231-2330
  625 Plum Industrial Park Pittsburgh (15239) *(G-14940)*

Ductmate Industries Inc 724 258-0500
  1502 Industrial Dr Monongahela (15063) *(G-11307)*

Ductmate Industries Inc (PA) 800 990-8459
  210 5th St Charleroi (15022) *(G-3011)*

Ductworks Inc 412 231-2330
  625 Plum Industrial Park Pittsburgh (15239) *(G-14941)*

Dudley Enterprises Inc 724 523-5522
  56 Millersdale Rd Jeannette (15644) *(G-8253)*

Dudlik Industries Inc 215 674-4383
  326 Jacksonville Rd Hatboro (19040) *(G-7282)*

Duerr Packaging Company Inc (PA) 724 947-1234
  892 Steubenville Pike Burgettstown (15021) *(G-2346)*

Duerr Packaging Company Inc 724 695-2226
  8152 Steubenville Pike Imperial (15126) *(G-8064)*

Duff AI Bag Screenprinting Co 717 249-8686
  254 E North St Carlisle (17013) *(G-2708)*

Duggan and Marcon, Allentown Also called Marcon & Boyer Inc *(G-307)*

Dukane Mining Products, Pittsburgh Also called Duquesne Mine Supply Company *(G-14944)*

Dukane Radiator Inc 412 233-3300
  1029 Transit Blvd Bethel Park (15102) *(G-1413)*

Dull Knife Terminator Inc 717 512-8596
  5005 Inverness Dr Mechanicsburg (17050) *(G-10839)*

Dumond Chemicals Inc (PA) 609 655-7700
  1475 Phnxvlle Pike Ste 18 West Chester (19380) *(G-19544)*

Dun Rite Window and Door 412 781-8200
  718 Main St Pittsburgh (15215) *(G-14942)*

Dunay Tool & Die Co 724 335-7972
  2027 Bakerstown Rd Tarentum (15084) *(G-18241)*

Dunbar Asphalt Products Inc 724 346-3594
  Ohio St Wheatland (16161) *(G-19837)*

Dunbar Asphalt Products Inc (HQ) 724 528-9310
  3766 New Castle Rd West Middlesex (16159) *(G-19723)*

Dunbar Machine Co Inc 724 277-8711
  75 Woodvale St Dunbar (15431) *(G-4439)*

Duncan Associates Inc 717 299-6940
  517 High St Lancaster (17603) *(G-9003)*

Duncan Land & Energy Inc 412 922-0135
  147 Noble Ave Ste 100 Pittsburgh (15205) *(G-14943)*

Duncannon Record, New Bloomfield Also called Advance Publications *(G-12029)*

Dunes Point Capital 610 666-1225
  98 Highland Ave Oaks (19456) *(G-12932)*

Dunhuntin Machine Shop Inc 724 794-5404
  799 W Liberty Rd Slippery Rock (16057) *(G-17619)*

Dunkin Donuts 610 992-0111
  251 W Dekalb Pike Apt 132 King of Prussia (19406) *(G-8613)*

Dunkin' Donuts, Philadelphia Also called J F M Philadelphia Donut Inc *(G-13883)*

Dunkin' Donuts, Altoona Also called Brinic Donuts Inc *(G-484)*

Dunkin' Donuts, Philadelphia Also called Howard Donuts Inc *(G-13836)*

Dunkin' Donuts, Norristown Also called Shree Swami Narayan Corp *(G-12713)*

Dunkin' Donuts, Carbondale Also called Fred Fairburn *(G-2675)*

Dunmore Corporation (HQ) 215 781-8895
  145 Wharton Rd Bristol (19007) *(G-2134)*

Dunmore International Corp (PA) 215 781-8895
  145 Wharton Rd Bristol (19007) *(G-2135)*

Dunnmorr Studio, Confluence Also called Robin Morris *(G-3469)*

Dunns Sawmill LLP 570 253-5217
  217 Navajo Rd Honesdale (18431) *(G-7710)*

Dupill Group, Leechburg Also called R E Dupill & Associates Ltd *(G-9651)*

Dupli Craft Printing Inc 570 344-8980
  1000 W Market St Scranton (18508) *(G-17229)*

Dupli Graphics Corporation 610 644-4188
  2533 Yellow Springs Rd # 1 Malvern (19355) *(G-10225)*

Dupli-Craft Printing, Scranton Also called Dupli Craft Printing Inc *(G-17229)*

Dupont, Avondale Also called E I Du Pont De Nemours & Co *(G-850)*

Dupont Elec & Communications, Towanda Also called Dupont Specialty Pdts USA
LLC *(G-18424)*

Dupont Specialty Pdts USA LLC 570 265-6141
  192 Patterson Blvd Towanda (18848) *(G-18424)*

Dupont Tool & Machine Co 570 655-1728
  311 Elm St Dupont (18641) *(G-4490)*

Duppstadt, Arthur G, Od, Leechburg Also called Leechburg Contact Lens Lab *(G-9648)*

Duquesne Beer Distributing, Indiana Also called Duquesne Distributing Co *(G-8092)*

Duquesne Distributing Co 724 465-6141
  1215 Maple St Indiana (15701) *(G-8092)*

Duquesne Mine Supply Company 412 821-2100
  2 Cross St Pittsburgh (15209) *(G-14944)*

Duquesne Univ of Holy Spirit 412 396-6610
  600 Forbes Ave Pittsburgh (15219) *(G-14945)*

Duquesne University Press, Pittsburgh Also called Duquesne Univ of Holy Spirit *(G-14945)*

Dura-Bar Services Div, York Also called Charter Dura-Bar Inc *(G-20424)*

Dura-Bilt Products Inc 570 596-2000
  17066 Berwick Tpke Gillett (16925) *(G-6380)*

Dura-Bond Coating Inc 412 436-2411
  5 N Linden St Duquesne (15110) *(G-4496)*

Dura-Bond Coating Inc (HQ) 724 327-0782
  2658 Puckety Dr Export (15632) *(G-5598)*

Dura-Bond Coating Inc 717 939-1079
  2716 S Front St Steelton (17113) *(G-18046)*

Dura-Bond Pipe LLC 412 672-0764
  301 4th Ave McKeesport (15132) *(G-10666)*

Dura-Bond Pipe LLC (HQ) 717 986-1100
  2716 S Front St Steelton (17113) *(G-18047)*

Dura-Bond Steel Corp 724 327-0280
  2658 Puckety Dr Export (15632) *(G-5599)*

Dura-Kan, Drifting Also called Pts Industries Corp *(G-4375)*

Durabond Pipes, Steelton Also called Dura-Bond Coating Inc *(G-18046)*

Duracart, Hanover Also called R & G Products Inc *(G-6940)*

A
L
P
H
A
B
E
T
I
C

Duracart Usa LLC 888 743-9957
  1300 Adams Ave Philadelphia (19124) *(G-13650)*
Duralife Inc 570 323-9743
  1255 Adams Ave Frnt Philadelphia (19124) *(G-13651)*
Duraloy Technologies Inc (HQ) 724 887-5100
  120 Bridge St Scottdale (15683) *(G-17190)*
Durant Excavating 724 583-9800
  18 N Ross St Masontown (15461) *(G-10535)*
Durawood Products Inc 717 336-0220
  18 Industrial Way Denver (17517) *(G-4071)*
Durex Coverings Inc (PA) 717 626-8566
  53 Industrial Dr Brownstown (17508) *(G-2307)*
Durham Press Inc 610 346-6133
  892 Durham Rd Durham (18039) *(G-4502)*
Duritzas Enterprises Inc (PA) 724 223-5494
  125 W Beau St Washington (15301) *(G-19165)*
Durrel, Clearville Also called EBY Sawmill *(G-3242)*
Duryea Technologies Inc 610 939-0480
  1060 Old Bernville Rd # 300 Reading (19605) *(G-16366)*
Dutch Cntry Soft Pretzels LLC 717 354-4493
  2758 Division Hwy Fl 1 New Holland (17557) *(G-12244)*
Dutch Gold Honey Inc (PA) 717 393-1716
  2220 Dutch Gold Dr Lancaster (17601) *(G-9004)*
Dutch Wood LLC 717 933-5133
  1317 Hilltop Rd Myerstown (17067) *(G-11882)*
Dutcher Brothers Inc 215 922-4555
  134 S 8th St Philadelphia (19107) *(G-13652)*
Dutchie Manufacturing LLC 717 656-2186
  21 School Rd Leola (17540) *(G-9778)*
Dutchland Inc 717 442-8282
  160 Route 41 Gap (17527) *(G-6249)*
Dutka Inc 717 285-5880
  1812 Stony Battery Rd Mountville (17554) *(G-11794)*
Duvall Lumber, Crystal Spring Also called Roderick Duvall *(G-3938)*
Duvinage LLC 717 283-6111
  11550 Molly Pitcher Hwy Greencastle (17225) *(G-6608)*
DVC, Hatboro Also called Delaware Valley Con Co Inc *(G-7278)*
Dvm Manufacturing LLC 215 839-3425
  315 W Street Rd Warminster (18974) *(G-18864)*
Dw Machine & Fabricating 570 788-8144
  109 Birch St Drums (18222) *(G-4382)*
DW Services LLC 484 241-8915
  1874 Catasauqua Rd # 335 Allentown (18109) *(G-198)*
Dwell America LLC 717 272-4666
  1349 Cumberland St Ste 1 Lebanon (17042) *(G-9562)*
Dwell America Holdings Inc (HQ) 717 272-4665
  1349 Cumberland St Ste 1 Lebanon (17042) *(G-9563)*
Dwight Lewis Lumber Co Inc 570 924-3507
  1895 Route 87 Hillsgrove (18619) *(G-7635)*
Dyco Inc 800 545-3926
  50 Naus Way Bloomsburg (17815) *(G-1779)*
Dye Works, Philadelphia Also called G J Littlewood & Son Inc *(G-13739)*
Dyeco Inc 717 545-1882
  2300 Academy Dr Harrisburg (17112) *(G-7123)*
Dyer Industries Inc 724 258-3400
  2013 Church Hollow Rd Bunola (15020) *(G-2343)*
Dyer Quarry Inc 610 582-6010
  1275 Rock Hollow Rd Birdsboro (19508) *(G-1693)*
Dyets Inc 610 868-7701
  2508 Easton Ave Bethlehem (18017) *(G-1499)*
Dykema Rubber Band 412 771-1955
  4075 Windgap Ave Bldg 5 Pittsburgh (15204) *(G-14946)*
Dymax Corporation 800 296-4146
  110 Marshall Dr Warrendale (15086) *(G-19072)*
Dymond Oil, Fayetteville Also called Dymonds Concrete Products *(G-5876)*
Dymonds Concrete Products 717 352-2321
  40 Dymond Ave Fayetteville (17222) *(G-5876)*
Dyna East Corporation 610 270-9900
  3620 Horizon Dr King of Prussia (19406) *(G-8614)*
Dyna-Tech Industries Ltd 717 274-3099
  120 N 25th St Lebanon (17042) *(G-9564)*
Dynacell Life Sciences LLC 215 813-8775
  19 Hendricks St Ambler (19002) *(G-576)*
Dynacut Inc 610 346-7386
  3425 Funks Mill Rd Springtown (18081) *(G-17926)*
Dynaflo Inc 610 200-8017
  10 Vanguard Dr Ste 20 Reading (19606) *(G-16367)*
Dynagherm Boiler, Quakertown Also called Prodex Inc *(G-16234)*
Dynalene Inc (PA) 610 262-9686
  5250 W Coplay Rd Whitehall (18052) *(G-19871)*
Dynamic Balancing Co Inc 610 337-2757
  831 Crooked Ln King of Prussia (19406) *(G-8615)*
Dynamic Business Systems 800 782-2946
  6420 Pleasant St South Park (15129) *(G-17782)*
Dynamic Ceramics Inc 724 353-9527
  265 N Pike Rd Sarver (16055) *(G-17068)*
Dynamic Concepts Mfg LLC 215 675-9006
  1836 Stout Dr Ste 8 Warminster (18974) *(G-18865)*
Dynamic Control Systems Inc 484 674-1408
  600 Clark Ave Ste 1 King of Prussia (19406) *(G-8616)*

Dynamic Creations Screen Prtg 724 229-1157
  600 W Chestnut St Washington (15301) *(G-19166)*
Dynamic Dies Inc 724 325-1514
  3251 Old Frankstown Rd E Pittsburgh (15239) *(G-14947)*
Dynamic Graphic Finishing Inc (HQ) 215 441-8880
  945 Horsham Rd Horsham (19044) *(G-7811)*
Dynamic Manufacturing LLC 724 295-4200
  156 Armstrong Dr Freeport (16229) *(G-6203)*
Dynamic Printing Inc 215 793-9453
  852 Burgdorf Dr Ambler (19002) *(G-577)*
Dynamic Sealing Systems LLC 724 537-6315
  5927 State Route 981 # 7 Latrobe (15650) *(G-9473)*
Dynamic Surfc Applications Ltd 570 546-6041
  373 Village Rd Pennsdale (17756) *(G-13262)*
Dynamic Systems 412 835-6100
  6420 Pleasant St Library (15129) *(G-9954)*
Dynamic Team Sports Inc 610 518-3300
  15 E Uwchlan Ave Ste 416 Exton (19341) *(G-5670)*
Dynatherm Boiler Mfg, Red Hill Also called Prodex Inc *(G-16584)*
Dynavox Inc 412 381-4883
  2100 Wharton St Ste 400 Pittsburgh (15203) *(G-14948)*
Dyneon LLC 610 497-8899
  50 Milton Dr Aston (19014) *(G-759)*
Dyno Nobel Inc 814 938-2035
  1132 Robertsville Rd Punxsutawney (15767) *(G-16135)*
Dyno Nobel Inc 724 379-8100
  1320 Galiffa Dr Donora (15033) *(G-4152)*
Dyvex Industries Inc 570 281-7141
  26 N Scott St Carbondale (18407) *(G-2674)*
E & C Africa, Pittsburgh Also called Equipment & Contrls Africa Inc *(G-14983)*
E & E Building Group LP 215 453-5124
  1104 N Bethlehem Pike Ambler (19002) *(G-578)*
E & E Logging & Sons 814 886-4440
  6721 Admiral Peary Hwy Loretto (15940) *(G-10102)*
E & E Metal Fabrications Inc 717 228-3727
  110 N 16th St Lebanon (17042) *(G-9565)*
E A Quirin Machine Shop Inc 570 429-0590
  W Hancock Saint Clair (17970) *(G-16937)*
E B Endres Inc 814 643-1860
  10630 Fairgrounds Rd Huntingdon (16652) *(G-7942)*
E Beiler Cabinetry 717 354-5515
  617 New Holland Rd New Holland (17557) *(G-12245)*
E C T Inc (PA) 610 239-5120
  401 E 4th St Ste 20 Bridgeport (19405) *(G-2035)*
E D I Enviro-Drill Inc 412 788-1046
  5000 Steubenville Pike Pittsburgh (15205) *(G-14949)*
E D Woodworks 610 857-1465
  215 Harry Rd Parkesburg (19365) *(G-13174)*
E E C, Landisville Also called Electron Energy Corporation *(G-9259)*
E E S Augering Company 724 397-8821
  687 Ambrose Rd Home (15747) *(G-7668)*
E E Zimmerman Company (HQ) 412 963-0949
  1370 Old Frport Rd Ste 2a Pittsburgh (15238) *(G-14950)*
E F E Laboratories Inc 215 672-2400
  420 Babylon Rd Ste A Horsham (19044) *(G-7812)*
E F Laudenslager Inc 610 395-1582
  3545 Route 309 Orefield (18069) *(G-13011)*
E F M, Kulpsville Also called Elements For Motion LLC *(G-8826)*
E F S, Erie Also called Erie Forge and Steel Inc *(G-5267)*
E G Emils and Son Inc 215 763-3311
  1344 N American St Philadelphia (19122) *(G-13653)*
E H Beiler Sawmill LLC 610 593-5989
  442 S Vintage Rd Paradise (17562) *(G-13156)*
E H Schwab Company 412 823-5003
  1281 Rodi Rd Turtle Creek (15145) *(G-18564)*
E H Woodworking 717 445-6595
  1763 Weaverland Rd East Earl (17519) *(G-4542)*
E I Du Pont De Nemours & Co 302 996-7165
  Chestnut Run Plz Avondale (19311) *(G-850)*
E I P, West Chester Also called Efficient Ip Inc *(G-19548)*
E I T Corporation Phoenix 570 286-7744
  Rr 61 Sunbury (17801) *(G-18168)*
E Instruments Group LLC 215 750-1212
  402 Middletown Blvd # 216 Langhorne (19047) *(G-9291)*
E J Bognar Inc 814 443-6000
  182 Bando Rd Somerset (15501) *(G-17686)*
E K Holdings Inc (HQ) 717 436-5921
  Rr 5 Mifflintown (17059) *(G-11113)*
E K L Machine Inc 215 639-0150
  500 Mill Rd Bensalem (19020) *(G-1184)*
E L W Manufacturing Inc 717 246-6600
  464 E Market Ave Dallastown (17313) *(G-3974)*
E M Brown Incorporated 814 765-7519
  329 Mount Joy Rd Clearfield (16830) *(G-3218)*
E M C, Telford Also called EMC Global Technologies Inc *(G-18287)*
E M United Wldg & Fabrication 570 595-0695
  7404 W Dogwood Ln Cresco (18326) *(G-3893)*
E O J Incorporated 570 943-2860
  2401 Summer Valley Rd New Ringgold (17960) *(G-12438)*

2019 Harris Pennsylvania
Manufacturers Directory

(G-0000) Company's Geographic Section entry number

E O S Group Inc..412 781-6023
18 Oakhurst Cir Pittsburgh (15215) *(G-14951)*

E P Bender Coal Company................................814 344-8063
198 S Main St Carrolltown (15722) *(G-2808)*

E P M, Saint Marys *Also called Engineered Pressed Materials (G-16972)*

E P M Corporation (PA)....................................814 825-6650
7337 Footemill Rd Erie (16509) *(G-5252)*

E R Kinley & Sons...570 323-6740
131 W 4th St Williamsport (17701) *(G-20008)*

E R Schantz Inc...610 272-3603
613 W Marshall St Norristown (19401) *(G-12652)*

E R Shantz, Norristown *Also called E R Schantz Inc (G-12652)*

E R Shaw Inc...412 212-4343
5312 Thoms Run Rd Bridgeville (15017) *(G-2059)*

E S C O, West Chester *Also called Effective Shielding Company (G-19547)*

E S E Machines, Coatesville *Also called Ewald A Stellrecht Inc (G-3302)*

E S F, Topton *Also called Electro-Space Fabricators Inc (G-18412)*

E S H Poultry...717 517-9535
2316 Norman Rd Ste 1 Lancaster (17601) *(G-9005)*

E S S Packaging Machinery.............................610 588-8579
305 Roseto Ave Roseto (18013) *(G-16820)*

E S Specialty Manufacturing............................215 635-0973
8470 Limekiln Pike B814 Wyncote (19095) *(G-20262)*

E Schneider & Sons Inc...................................610 435-3527
616-656 Sumner Ave Allentown (18102) *(G-199)*

E Victor Pesce...610 444-5903
611 W State St Kennett Square (19348) *(G-8508)*

E W Yost Co..215 699-4868
340 N Wales Rd Blue Bell (19422) *(G-1828)*

E Y Productions, Bala Cynwyd *Also called East Associates Inc (G-878)*

E Z Net Solutions Inc......................................215 887-7200
728 Rodman Ave Jenkintown (19046) *(G-8284)*

E Z Sensenig & Son..717 445-5580
895 Centerville Rd New Holland (17557) *(G-12246)*

E Z Storage Barns, Leola *Also called Elvin B Zimmerman (G-9780)*

E&J Construction...570 924-4455
1261 Masten Rd Canton (17724) *(G-2664)*

E&M Tile Restoration, Chester *Also called Eric Snow (G-3049)*

E&M Wholesale Foods......................................610 367-2299
105 Fortress Dr Boyertown (19512) *(G-1909)*

E-Carbon America LLC.....................................814 834-7777
806 Theresia St Saint Marys (15857) *(G-16965)*

E-Finity Dstrbted Gnration LLC.........................610 688-6212
161 Pennsylvania Ave Wayne (19087) *(G-19321)*

E-Harvest Systems...908 832-0400
5124 Erbs Bridge Rd Mechanicsburg (17050) *(G-10840)*

E-Lynxx Corporation...717 709-0990
1051 Sheffler Dr Ste W Chambersburg (17201) *(G-2926)*

E-Nanomedsys LLC..917 734-1462
746 E Mccormick Ave State College (16801) *(G-17958)*

E-Slinger LLC..412 848-1742
14527 State Highway 98 Meadville (16335) *(G-10720)*

E-Tech Industrial..570 297-1300
1 Skyline Dr Troy (16947) *(G-18522)*

E-Z Systems, Bethlehem *Also called Euthanex Corporation (G-1505)*

E.H.C. Industries, Mount Pleasant *Also called Ehc Industries Inc (G-11699)*

E.T.I., Peckville *Also called Equipment Technology Inc (G-13208)*

EA Fischione Instruments (PA).........................724 325-5444
9003 Corporate Cir Export (15632) *(G-5600)*

Eag Electronics Corp..814 836-8080
7700 Birkmire Dr Fairview (16415) *(G-5820)*

Eagle Bio Diesel Inc..814 773-3133
111 Metoxet St Ridgway (15853) *(G-16706)*

Eagle Design Group, Chester Springs *Also called Eagle Design Innovation LLC (G-3077)*

Eagle Design Group..610 321-2488
45 Senn Dr Chester Springs (19425) *(G-3076)*

Eagle Design Innovation LLC............................610 321-2488
45 Senn Dr Chester Springs (19425) *(G-3077)*

Eagle Displays LLC..724 335-8900
2112 River Rd North Apollo (15673) *(G-12726)*

Eagle Distrg, Hazleton *Also called Viking Signs Inc (G-7535)*

Eagle Energy Systems Ltd...............................610 444-3388
500 N Walnut Rd Kennett Square (19348) *(G-8509)*

Eagle Far East Inc...215 957-9333
816 Nina Way Warminster (18974) *(G-18866)*

Eagle Graphics Inc..717 867-5576
150 N Moyer St Annville (17003) *(G-647)*

Eagle Industrial Solutions.................................610 509-8275
2162 Michael Rd Nazareth (18064) *(G-11962)*

Eagle Line Corporation.....................................814 589-7724
Shamburg St Pleasantville (16341) *(G-15801)*

Eagle Metals Inc (PA)......................................610 926-4111
1243 Old Bernville Rd Leesport (19533) *(G-9661)*

Eagle Mfg & Design Corp.................................717 848-9767
1245 W Princess St York (17404) *(G-20459)*

Eagle Microsystems..610 323-2250
366 Circle Of Progress Dr Pottstown (19464) *(G-15984)*

Eagle Precision Tooling Inc...............................814 838-3515
4264 1 An A Hlf W 26th St 26 Th Erie (16506) *(G-5253)*

Eagle Printery Inc..724 287-0754
107 Bonnie Dr Butler (16002) *(G-2397)*

Eagle Printing Company (PA)............................724 282-8000
114 W Diamond St Butler (16001) *(G-2398)*

Eagle Printing Company....................................724 776-4270
20701 Route 19 Cranberry Township (16066) *(G-3817)*

Eagle Rock Winery...570 567-7715
414 W 4th St Apt 1 Williamsport (17701) *(G-20009)*

Eagle Rubber Products Inc...............................724 452-3200
306 Halstead Blvd Zelienople (16063) *(G-20796)*

Eagle Spinco Inc...412 434-3131
1 Ppg Pl Pittsburgh (15272) *(G-14952)*

Eagle Stainless Container, Warminster *Also called Eagle Far East Inc (G-18866)*

Eagle Tool & Die Co Inc..................................610 264-6011
183 Pennsylvania Ave Malvern (19355) *(G-10226)*

Eagle Woodworking LLC....................................484 764-7275
1229 Main St Northampton (18067) *(G-12849)*

Eaglerise E&E Inc..215 675-5953
320 Constance Dr Ste 1 Warminster (18974) *(G-18867)*

Eam-Mosca Corp (PA).....................................570 459-3426
675 Jaycee Dr Hazle Township (18202) *(G-7452)*

Eamco Corp...610 262-5731
5275 W Coplay Rd Whitehall (18052) *(G-19872)*

Earl E Knox Company (PA)...............................814 459-2754
1111 Bacon St Erie (16511) *(G-5254)*

Earl E Knox Company.......................................814 459-2754
550 Huron St Erie (16502) *(G-5255)*

Earl F Dean Inc...814 435-6581
766 Route 6 W Galeton (16922) *(G-6239)*

Earl Wenz Inc..610 395-2331
9038 Breinigsville Rd Breinigsville (18031) *(G-2014)*

Earl West Industries...717 656-6600
164 Butter Rd Leola (17540) *(G-9779)*

Early American Candle Supplies, Mount Pleasant *Also called Early American Pittsburgh Inc (G-11698)*

Early American Pittsburgh Inc...........................412 486-6757
402 E Main St Ste 100 Mount Pleasant (15666) *(G-11698)*

Early Corp of American Gas, Punxsutawney *Also called Eastern American Energy Corp (G-16136)*

Early Morning Donuts Corp...............................570 961-5150
511 Moosic St Scranton (18505) *(G-17230)*

Earlys Body Machine & Welding........................717 838-1663
917 N Forge Rd Palmyra (17078) *(G-13122)*

Earnest Industries Inc......................................412 323-1911
1013 Spring Garden Ave Pittsburgh (15212) *(G-14953)*

Earth & Turf Products LLC...............................717 355-2276
112 S Railroad Ave New Holland (17557) *(G-12247)*

Earth Friendly Compost Inc..............................570 760-4510
2015 Monkey Hollow Rd Harveys Lake (18618) *(G-7256)*

Earthgrains Distribution (HQ)............................215 672-8010
255 Business Center Dr Horsham (19044) *(G-7813)*

Earthware Corporation......................................412 563-1920
100 Oak Way Pittsburgh (15228) *(G-14954)*

East Asia Noodle Inc.......................................215 923-6838
212 N 11th St Philadelphia (19107) *(G-13654)*

East Associates Inc..610 667-3980
11 Union Ave Fl 1 Bala Cynwyd (19004) *(G-878)*

East Bank Machine Inc.....................................412 384-4721
1 Church St Finleyville (15332) *(G-5956)*

East Cast Erosion Blankets LLC (PA)...............610 488-8496
443 Bricker Rd Bernville (19506) *(G-1298)*

East Coast Atv Inc...267 733-7364
313 S 3rd St Coopersburg (18036) *(G-3627)*

East Coast Constructors Inc.............................610 532-3650
101 Talbot Ave Holmes (19043) *(G-7661)*

East Coast Control Systems..............................814 857-5420
Main St Bigler (16825) *(G-1658)*

East Coast Hoist Inc..215 646-2336
105 Keystone Dr Telford (18969) *(G-18286)*

East Coast Liquid Filling, King of Prussia *Also called Evergreen Synergies LLC (G-8617)*

East Coast Metals Inc......................................215 256-9550
171 Ruth Rd Ste C Harleysville (19438) *(G-7031)*

East Coast Partners LLC..................................215 207-9360
3225 N Smedley St Philadelphia (19140) *(G-13655)*

East Coast Sign Advg Co Inc...........................888 724-0380
5058 Rte 13 N Bristol (19007) *(G-2136)*

East Coast Threading Company.........................610 970-9933
1520 Manatawny Rd Pine Forge (19548) *(G-14588)*

East End Brewing Company Inc........................412 361-2848
6923 Susquehanna St Pittsburgh (15208) *(G-14955)*

East End Welding...570 726-7925
31 Welders Ln Mill Hall (17751) *(G-11176)*

East Falls Beverage LLC..................................215 844-5600
3343 445 Conrad St Philadelphia (19129) *(G-13656)*

East Hill Media, Lansdale *Also called East Hill Video Prod Co LLC (G-9364)*

East Hill Video Prod Co LLC............................215 855-4457
157 S Broad St Ste 103 Lansdale (19446) *(G-9364)*

East Indies Coffee & Tea 717 228-2000
7 Keystone Dr Lebanon (17042) *(G-9566)*

East Liberty Elcpltg Inc 412 487-4080
1126 Butler Plank Rd Glenshaw (15116) *(G-6487)*

East Loop Sand Company Inc 814 695-3082
210 River Rd Hollidaysburg (16648) *(G-7646)*

East Lycoming Shopper & News, Hughesville *Also called Ogden Newspapers Inc* *(G-7898)*

East Penn Container Dctg Inc 610 944-3227
19 W Poplar St Fleetwood (19522) *(G-5971)*

East Penn Manufacturing Co 412 793-0283
4 Commerce Dr Pittsburgh (15239) *(G-14956)*

East Penn Manufacturing Co 610 682-6361
50 W Jefferson St Topton (19562) *(G-18411)*

East Penn Manufacturing Co 610 929-4920
1002 Patriot Pkwy Reading (19605) *(G-16368)*

East Penn Manufacturing Co 610 682-6361
191 Willow St Kutztown (19530) *(G-8840)*

East Penn Publishing Co, Allentown *Also called Pencor Services Inc* *(G-346)*

East Penn Truck Eqp W Inc 724 342-1800
7298 W Market St Mercer (16137) *(G-10961)*

East Penn Truck Equipment Inc 610 694-9234
1100 Win Dr Bethlehem (18017) *(G-1500)*

East Penn Welding Inc 610 682-2290
110 S Maple St Kutztown (19530) *(G-8841)*

East Side Concrete Supply Co (PA) 814 944-8175
114 Old Mill Run Rd Altoona (16601) *(G-499)*

East West Component Inc 215 616-4414
442 Industrial Dr North Wales (19454) *(G-12799)*

East West Drilling Inc 570 966-7312
157 Buffalo Creek Rd Mifflinburg (17844) *(G-11093)*

East West Manufacturing A 412 207-7385
3849 Willow Ave Pittsburgh (15234) *(G-14957)*

East York Diagnostic Center 717 851-1850
2250 E Market St York (17402) *(G-20460)*

East-West Label Co Inc 610 825-0410
1000 E Hector St Conshohocken (19428) *(G-3540)*

Eastcoast Cutter Inc 717 933-5566
1940 Camp Swatara Rd Myerstown (17067) *(G-11883)*

Easter Unlimited Inc 814 542-8661
436 N Industrial Dr Mount Union (17066) *(G-11744)*

Eastern Adhesives Inc 215 348-0119
904 Crosskeys Dr Doylestown (18902) *(G-4296)*

Eastern Alloy Inc 724 379-5776
1138 Meldon Ave Donora (15033) *(G-4153)*

Eastern American Energy Corp 814 938-9000
725 Snyder Hill Rd Punxsutawney (15767) *(G-16136)*

Eastern American Energy Corp 724 463-8400
101 Heritage Run Ste 1 Indiana (15701) *(G-8093)*

Eastern Architectural Pdts LLC 724 513-1630
213 Front St Zelienople (16063) *(G-20797)*

Eastern Bakery Equipment Co 717 938-8278
475 Stevens Rd York Haven (17370) *(G-20758)*

Eastern Catalytic, Langhorne *Also called Eastern Manufacturing LLC* *(G-9293)*

Eastern Die Cutting & Finshg 610 917-9765
1000 Township Line Rd # 5 Phoenixville (19460) *(G-14546)*

Eastern Environmental Inds LLC 814 371-2221
4456 Route 219 Brockway (15824) *(G-2224)*

Eastern Exterior Wall 610 868-5522
645 Hamilton St Ste 300 Allentown (18101) *(G-200)*

Eastern Gauge & Regulator 215 443-5192
1825 Stout Dr Warminster (18974) *(G-18868)*

Eastern Industrial Pdts Inc 610 459-1212
830 Tryens Rd Aston (19014) *(G-760)*

Eastern Industries Inc (HQ) 610 866-0932
3724 Crescent Ct W 200 Whitehall (18052) *(G-19873)*

Eastern Industries Inc 610 683-7400
210 Hinterleiter Rd Kutztown (19530) *(G-8842)*

Eastern Industries Inc 570 265-9191
6154 Leisure Dr Towanda (18848) *(G-18425)*

Eastern Industries Inc 570 524-2251
220 Park Rd Winfield (17889) *(G-20199)*

Eastern Industries Inc 717 362-3388
3633 State Route 225 Elizabethville (17023) *(G-4893)*

Eastern Industries Inc 717 667-2015
475 Naginey Rd Milroy (17063) *(G-11230)*

Eastern Machine & Conveyers, Donora *Also called Eastern Machine & Convyrs Inc* *(G-4154)*

Eastern Machine & Convyrs Inc (PA) 724 379-4701
482 Gallifa Dr Donora Industrial Donora (15033) *(G-4154)*

Eastern Manufacturing LLC 215 702-3600
2151 Cabot Blvd W Langhorne (19047) *(G-9292)*

Eastern Manufacturing LLC (HQ) 215 702-3600
2151 Cabot Blvd W Langhorne (19047) *(G-9293)*

Eastern Millwork Ltd 570 344-7128
108 E Elm St Scranton (18505) *(G-17231)*

Eastern Oil Corporation 412 221-2911
98 Vanadium Rd Ste 3 Bridgeville (15017) *(G-2060)*

Eastern Pennsylvania Bus Jurnl, Bethlehem *Also called Press-Enterprise Inc* *(G-1604)*

Eastern Press Div, Pottsville *Also called Tor Industries Inc* *(G-16099)*

Eastern Production Division, Lancaster *Also called Nissin Foods USA Company Inc* *(G-9146)*

Eastern Rail Systems Inc 215 826-9980
2014 Ford Rd Ste G Bristol (19007) *(G-2137)*

Eastern Sintered Alloys Inc 814 834-1216
126 Access Rd Saint Marys (15857) *(G-16966)*

Eastern Sleep Products Company 610 582-7228
71 Vanguard Dr Reading (19606) *(G-16369)*

Eastern Surfaces Inc 610 266-3121
601 S 10th St Allentown (18103) *(G-201)*

Eastern Systems Management 717 391-9700
1860 Charter Ln Ste 207 Lancaster (17601) *(G-9006)*

Eastern Technologies Inc 610 286-2010
60 Thousand Oaks Blvd Morgantown (19543) *(G-11522)*

Eastern Tool Steel Service Inc 814 834-7224
1045 Delaum Rd Saint Marys (15857) *(G-16967)*

Eastman Chemical Company 412 384-2520
2200 State Rt 837 Jefferson Hills (15025) *(G-8274)*

Eastman Chemical Company 423 229-2000
200 Willcox Dr Jefferson Hills (15025) *(G-8275)*

Eastman Chemical Resins Inc 412 384-2520
2200 State Rte 837 Jefferson Hills (15025) *(G-8276)*

Easton Beer 215 884-1252
230 S Easton Rd Glenside (19038) *(G-6514)*

Easton Block & Supply, Easton *Also called H&K Group Inc* *(G-4694)*

Easton Furn & Upholstery, Easton *Also called Easton Upholstery Furn Mfg Co* *(G-4675)*

Easton Photoworks Inc 610 559-1998
429 Centre St Easton (18042) *(G-4671)*

Easton Pltg & Met Finshg Inc 610 252-9007
925 Conroy Pl Easton (18040) *(G-4672)*

Easton Publishing Company 610 258-7171
30 N 4th St Easton (18042) *(G-4673)*

Easton Salsa Company LLC 610 923-3692
50 N 18th St Easton (18042) *(G-4674)*

Easton Upholstery Furn Mfg Co 610 252-3169
512 Northampton St # 514 Easton (18042) *(G-4675)*

Easttmont Chemical, Monongahela *Also called Solutia Inc* *(G-11316)*

Easy Liner LLC 717 825-7962
1069 Kings Mill Rd York (17403) *(G-20461)*

Easy To Use Big Books 814 946-7442
301 Cayuga Ave Altoona (16602) *(G-500)*

Easy Use Air Tools Inc 412 486-2270
3876 William Flynn Hwy Allison Park (15101) *(G-450)*

Easy Walking Inc 215 654-1626
1478 Dillon Rd Maple Glen (19002) *(G-10429)*

Easygo Drinkware LLC 814 723-7600
618 4th Ave Warren (16365) *(G-19022)*

Easytousebigbooks.com, Altoona *Also called Easy To Use Big Books* *(G-500)*

Eat This 215 391-5807
75 Headquarters Rd Erwinna (18920) *(G-5538)*

Eaton Aerospace LLC (HQ) 610 522-4000
24 E Glenolden Ave Glenolden (19036) *(G-6473)*

Eaton Corporation 610 497-6100
7 Chelsea Pkwy Ste 700 Boothwyn (19061) *(G-1877)*

Eaton Corporation 724 773-1231
1 Tuscarawas Rd Beaver (15009) *(G-980)*

Eaton Corporation 412 893-3300
1000 Cherrington Pkwy Moon Township (15108) *(G-11484)*

Eaton Corporation 412 893-3300
1000 Cherrington Pkwy Coraopolis (15108) *(G-3685)*

Eaton Corporation 610 522-4059
24 E Glenolden Ave Glenolden (19036) *(G-6474)*

Eaton Electric Holdings LLC 717 755-2933
3990 E Market St York (17402) *(G-20462)*

Eaton Electric Holdings LLC 724 228-7333
2800 N Main St Washington (15301) *(G-19167)*

Eaton Electrical Inc (HQ) 412 893-3300
1000 Cherrington Pkwy Moon Township (15108) *(G-11485)*

Ebc, Blairsville *Also called Erie Bolt Corporation* *(G-1720)*

Eber & Wein Inc 717 759-8065
15727 Whitcraft Rd New Freedom (17349) *(G-12205)*

Eber & Wein Inc 717 759-8065
595 S Main St Shrewsbury (17361) *(G-17582)*

Eber & Wein Publishing, Shrewsbury *Also called Eber & Wein Inc* *(G-17582)*

Eberharts Cstm Embroidery Inc 215 639-9530
3448 Progress Dr Ste E Bensalem (19020) *(G-1185)*

Ebersole Engineering 215 675-0106
469b Oakdale Ave Hatboro (19040) *(G-7283)*

Ebinger Iron Works Inc 570 385-3460
38 Keystoker Ln Schuylkill Haven (17972) *(G-17155)*

Ebroker Software LLC (HQ) 717 540-3720
2600 Commerce Dr Harrisburg (17110) *(G-7124)*

Ebtech Industrial, Connellsville *Also called Uh Structures Inc* *(G-3509)*

EBY Company, Philadelphia *Also called EBY Group LLC* *(G-13657)*

EBY Group LLC 215 537-4700
4300 H St Philadelphia (19124) *(G-13657)*

EBY Sawmill 814 767-8060
2319 Beans Cove Rd Clearville (15535) *(G-3242)*

Ecad Division, Coraopolis *Also called CM Technologies Corporation* *(G-3678)*

Ecco Industries Inc...570 288-1226
  215 Courtdale Ave Kingston (18704) *(G-8716)*

Ecco/Gregory Inc...610 840-0390
  1199 Mcdermott Dr West Chester (19380) *(G-19545)*

Eccotrol LLC...877 322-6876
  111 Buck Rd Unit 307 Huntingdon Valley (19006) *(G-7974)*

Ecg Ellwood Crankshaft Group, Hermitage *Also called Ellwood Crankshaft and Mch Co (G-7581)*

Echo Delta Charlie Inc...267 278-7598
  458 N Locust Point Rd Mechanicsburg (17050) *(G-10841)*

Echo Pilot...717 597-2164
  29 Center Sq Greencastle (17225) *(G-6609)*

Echurchdepot, Camp Hill *Also called Zur Ltd (G-2528)*

Eclat Industries Inc...215 547-2684
  1604 Hanford St Levittown (19057) *(G-9834)*

Eclipse Electric, Franklin *Also called Gerald Boughner (G-6132)*

Eclipse Resources Holdings LP...814 308-9754
  2121 Old Gatesburg Rd # 110 State College (16803) *(G-17959)*

Eclipse Resources I LP (HQ)...814 308-9754
  2121 Old Gatesburg Rd # 110 State College (16803) *(G-17960)*

Eclipse Resources Oper LLC...814 308-9731
  2121 Old Gatesburg Rd # 110 State College (16803) *(G-17961)*

Eclipse Resources-Pa LP...814 409-7006
  2121 Old Gatesburg Rd # 110 State College (16803) *(G-17962)*

Ecm...724 347-0250
  2727 Freedland Rd Hermitage (16148) *(G-7580)*

Ecm Energy Services Inc...888 659-2413
  130 Court St Williamsport (17701) *(G-20010)*

Eco Fusions, Exton *Also called Focus Noise Ltd Liability Co (G-5680)*

Eco Product Group LLC...412 364-1792
  5700 Corporate Dr Ste 455 Pittsburgh (15237) *(G-14958)*

Eco Services Operations Corp (HQ)...610 251-9118
  300 Lindenwood Dr Malvern (19355) *(G-10227)*

Eco Solution Distributing LLC...724 941-4140
  2275 Swallow Hill Rd Pittsburgh (15220) *(G-14959)*

Ecobee Advanced Tech LLC...609 474-0010
  1531 Meetinghouse Rd Warminster (18974) *(G-18869)*

Ecolab Inc...610 521-1072
  1 Scott Way Philadelphia (19113) *(G-13314)*

Ecolution Energy LLC...908 707-1400
  565 Lake Dr Lehighton (18235) *(G-9713)*

Ecomm Life Safety Systems LLC...215 953-5858
  27 Steam Whistle Dr Ivyland (18974) *(G-8210)*

Econo Pak, Milford *Also called North American Packaging LLC (G-11165)*

Econo Trailer, Claysburg *Also called Dively Manufacture Co Inc (G-3203)*

Econoco...570 384-3000
  575 Oak Ridge Rd Hazle Township (18202) *(G-7453)*

Economy Industrial Corporation...724 266-5720
  2097 Duss Ave 2 Ambridge (15003) *(G-616)*

Economy Metal Inc...724 869-2887
  340 Dunlap Hill Rd Freedom (15042) *(G-6189)*

Economy Tooling Corp PA...724 266-4546
  1703 Ridge Road Ext Ambridge (15003) *(G-617)*

Econotool Inc...215 947-2404
  2971 Franks Rd Huntingdon Valley (19006) *(G-7975)*

Ecopax LLC...484 546-0700
  3600 Glover Rd Easton (18040) *(G-4676)*

Ecore International Inc (PA)...717 295-3400
  715 Fountain Ave Lancaster (17601) *(G-9007)*

Ecotech, Bethlehem *Also called Lightbox Inc (G-1561)*

Ecotech Inc...610 954-8480
  999 Postal Rd Ste 100 Allentown (18109) *(G-202)*

Ecotech Marine LLC...610 954-8480
  999 Postal Rd Ste 100 Allentown (18109) *(G-203)*

Ecowater Systems, West Chester *Also called Suburban Water Technology Inc (G-19648)*

Ed Cini Enterprises Inc...215 432-3855
  5611 Deer Path Rd Plumsteadville (18949) *(G-15809)*

Ed Fish Maching Co...724 224-0992
  2627 Butler Logan Rd Tarentum (15084) *(G-18242)*

Ed Jupiter Inc...888 367-6175
  614 S 4th St Ste 314 Philadelphia (19147) *(G-13658)*

Ed London Wreath Co, Philadelphia *Also called Red Bandana Co (G-14236)*

Ed Nicholson & Sons Lumber Co...724 628-4440
  2451 Springfield Pike Connellsville (15425) *(G-3496)*

Ed RE Invent...814 590-0771
  366 Carson Hill Rd Luthersburg (15848) *(G-10123)*

Edaptive Systems LLC...717 718-1230
  1246 Greensprings Dr York (17402) *(G-20463)*

Edas Premium Hard Candies, Philadelphia *Also called Adrenalation Inc (G-13346)*

Eddington Thread Mfg Co Inc (PA)...215 639-8900
  3222 Knights Rd Bensalem (19020) *(G-1186)*

Eden Inc...814 797-1160
  210 Miller St Knox (16232) *(G-8809)*

Eden Green Energy Inc...267 255-9462
  2405 Federal St Philadelphia (19146) *(G-13659)*

Eden Tool Company...717 235-7009
  157 E Main St New Freedom (17349) *(G-12206)*

Edenberg Welding Co, Hamburg *Also called Randy Brensinger (G-6851)*

Edens Ticketing...215 625-0314
  115 Chestnut St Philadelphia (19106) *(G-13660)*

Edgar Industries, New Kensington *Also called H R Edgar Machining & Fabg Inc (G-12344)*

Edge Building Products Inc...717 567-2311
  224 Market St Newport (17074) *(G-12489)*

Edge Rubber LLC...717 660-2353
  811 Progress Rd Chambersburg (17201) *(G-2927)*

Edge Rubber Recycling LLC...717 660-2353
  811 Progress Rd Chambersburg (17201) *(G-2928)*

Edgecraft Corporation...610 268-0500
  825 Southwood Rd Avondale (19311) *(G-851)*

Edgell Communications...570 296-8330
  134 Vandermark Dr Milford (18337) *(G-11159)*

Edgemarc Energy Holdings LLC (PA)...724 749-8466
  1800 Main St Ste 220 Canonsburg (15317) *(G-2580)*

Edgemate Inc (PA)...814 224-5717
  213 Smith Transport Rd Roaring Spring (16673) *(G-16764)*

Edgewood Welding & Fabrication...814 445-7746
  842 S Edgewood Ave Somerset (15501) *(G-17687)*

Edgmont Metallic Pigment Inc...610 429-1345
  203 Garfield Ave West Chester (19380) *(G-19546)*

Edi-USA, Bryn Mawr *Also called Executive Distributors Intl (G-2323)*

Edinboro Creations...412 462-0370
  1210 Commonwealth Ave Homestead (15120) *(G-7685)*

Edinboro Industries...814 734-1100
  4200 Route 6n Edinboro (16412) *(G-4811)*

Edinboro Redi Mix Concrete, Edinboro *Also called Meadville Redi-Mix Concrete (G-4816)*

Edison, Red Hill *Also called Corona Corporation (G-16580)*

Edison Quarry Inc...215 348-4382
  25 Quarry Rd Doylestown (18901) *(G-4297)*

Editorial Office, Honesdale *Also called Highlights For Children Inc (G-7714)*

Edlon Inc (HQ)...610 268-3101
  150 Pomeroy Ave Avondale (19311) *(G-852)*

Edlyn's Closet-Tier, Pittsburgh *Also called Closet-Tier (G-14862)*

EDM Co...717 626-2186
  302 Front St Lititz (17543) *(G-10005)*

EDM Services, Apollo *Also called Composidie Inc (G-673)*

Edmar Abrasive Company...610 544-4900
  1107 Sussex Blvd Broomall (19008) *(G-2288)*

Edmil Fuels Inc...717 249-4901
  501 Shatto Dr Carlisle (17013) *(G-2709)*

Edmiston Signs...814 742-8930
  809 N 6th St Bellwood (16617) *(G-1137)*

Edmund Burke Inc...724 932-5200
  2880 State Highway 18 Adamsville (16110) *(G-25)*

Edon Corporation...215 672-8050
  1160 Easton Rd Horsham (19044) *(G-7814)*

Edon Fiberglass, Horsham *Also called Edon Corporation (G-7814)*

Edro Engineering Inc...610 940-1993
  1027 Conshohocken Rd A Conshohocken (19428) *(G-3541)*

Edro Specialty Steel, Conshohocken *Also called Edro Engineering Inc (G-3541)*

Edsell & Edsell Logging...570 746-3203
  285 Herrickville Rd Wyalusing (18853) *(G-20250)*

Edt...724 217-4008
  110 Danko Ln Greensburg (15601) *(G-6663)*

Education MGT Solutions LLC...610 701-7002
  436 Creamery Way Ste 300 Exton (19341) *(G-5671)*

Edward A Shelly Vmd...610 826-2793
  2695 Little Gap Rd Palmerton (18071) *(G-13104)*

Edward C Rinck Associates Inc...610 397-1727
  462 Germantown Pike Ste 5 Lafayette Hill (19444) *(G-8879)*

Edward H Quay Welding Spc...610 326-8050
  948 Commerce Dr Pottstown (19464) *(G-15985)*

Edward Hecht Importers Inc...215 925-5520
  111 S Independence Mall E # 835 Philadelphia (19106) *(G-13661)*

Edward Hennessy Co Inc...215 426-4154
  3820 Pearson Ave Philadelphia (19114) *(G-13662)*

Edward J Deseta Co Inc...302 691-2040
  1510 Gehman Rd Harleysville (19438) *(G-7032)*

Edward M Arnold Drilling Contr, Douglassville *Also called Edward M Arnold Jr (G-4175)*

Edward M Arnold Jr...610 689-5636
  95 Pine Forge Rd Douglassville (19518) *(G-4175)*

Edward Marc Chocolatier, Pittsburgh *Also called Marc Edward Brands Inc (G-15250)*

Edward Oil Company...814 726-9576
  Brown Hl Youngsville (16371) *(G-20770)*

Edward T Christiansen & Sons...215 368-1001
  697 Bethlehem Pike Montgomeryville (18936) *(G-11393)*

Edward T Regina...570 223-8358
  5181 Milford Rd East Stroudsburg (18302) *(G-4614)*

Edward Thompson...717 442-4550
  825 Simmontown Rd Gap (17527) *(G-6250)*

Edwards Co...215 343-2133
  2124 Wodock Ave Warrington (18976) *(G-19116)*

Edwards Concrete...570 842-8438
  204 State Route 435 Elmhurst Township (18444) *(G-4957)*

Edwards Sand & Stone, Elmhurst Township *Also called GF Edwards Inc (G-4959)*

Edwards Sand & Stone, South Sterling *Also called GF Edwards Inc (G-17787)*

A L P H A B E T I C

Edwards Sherm Candies Inc (PA)....412 372-4331
509 Cavitt Ave Trafford (15085) ***(G-18454)***
Edwin Bell Cooperage Company....412 221-1830
697 Millers Run Rd Cuddy (15031) ***(G-3942)***
Edwin Johnson & Sons....570 458-4488
575 Eyersgrove Rd Bloomsburg (17815) ***(G-1780)***
Edwin L Heim Co (PA)....717 233-8711
1918 Greenwood St Harrisburg (17104) ***(G-7125)***
Edwin Ringer....724 746-3374
188 Dogwood St Westland (15378) ***(G-19782)***
EF Precision Inc....215 784-0861
2301 Computer Rd Ste A Willow Grove (19090) ***(G-20115)***
Efco Inc....814 455-3941
1253 W 12th St Erie (16501) ***(G-5256)***
Effective CD Llc....607 351-5949
51b Main St Lawrenceville (16929) ***(G-9541)***
Effective Plan Inc....717 428-6190
47 Cherry St Seven Valleys (17360) ***(G-17378)***
Effective Shielding Company....610 429-9449
817 Lincoln Ave West Chester (19380) ***(G-19547)***
Effective Software Products....717 267-2054
2038 Lincoln Way E Ste A Chambersburg (17202) ***(G-2929)***
Efficient Ip Inc....888 228-4655
1 S Church St Ste 400 West Chester (19382) ***(G-19548)***
Efflands Sawmill Repair S....717 369-2391
10521 Richmond Rd Fort Loudon (17224) ***(G-6058)***
Effort Enterprises Inc....610 837-7003
6982 Chrisphalt Dr Bath (18014) ***(G-957)***
Effort Foundry Inc....610 837-1837
6980 Chrisphalt Dr Bath (18014) ***(G-958)***
Effort Woodcraft Inc....570 629-1160
1 Evergreen Hollow Rd Effort (18330) ***(G-4825)***
Efi Connection LLC....814 566-0946
6586 Station Rd Erie (16510) ***(G-5257)***
Efs Plastics US Inc....570 455-0925
504 White Birch Rd Hazle Township (18202) ***(G-7454)***
EG Emils and Son Inc....800 228-3645
1345 Germantown Ave Philadelphia (19122) ***(G-13663)***
Egalet Corporation (PA)....610 833-4200
600 Lee Rd Ste 100 Wayne (19087) ***(G-19322)***
Egalet Ltd....484 875-3095
460 E Swedesford Rd Wayne (19087) ***(G-19323)***
Egalet US Inc....610 833-4200
600 Lee Rd Ste 100 Wayne (19087) ***(G-19324)***
Egg To Apples LLC....610 822-3670
355 Lancaster Ave Ste 111 Haverford (19041) ***(G-7410)***
Egglands Best Inc....610 265-6500
70 E Swedesford Rd # 150 Malvern (19355) ***(G-10228)***
Ego Construction, Williamsport *Also called Woodcraft Industries* ***(G-20098)***
Egr Ventures Inc....610 358-0500
1 Crozerville Rd Aston (19014) ***(G-761)***
Egw, Quakertown *Also called Evolution Gun Works Inc* ***(G-16191)***
Egypt Star Inc (PA)....610 434-8516
608 N Front St Allentown (18102) ***(G-204)***
Ehb Logisitics Inc....717 764-5800
40 Willow Springs Cir York (17406) ***(G-20464)***
Ehc Industries Inc....724 696-1212
319 Westec Dr Mount Pleasant (15666) ***(G-11699)***
Ehi Trading International, Philadelphia *Also called Edward Hecht Importers Inc* ***(G-13661)***
Ehmke Manufacturing Co Inc (PA)....215 324-4200
4200 Macalester St Philadelphia (19124) ***(G-13664)***
Ehst Custom Kitchens Inc....610 367-2074
1 Sweinhart Rd Boyertown (19512) ***(G-1910)***
Ei Detection & Imaging, Saxonburg *Also called Endicott Interconnect Tech* ***(G-17086)***
Ei Machine Inc....724 348-0296
3459 Washington Ave Finleyville (15332) ***(G-5957)***
Eic Solutions Inc....215 443-5190
700 Veterans Cir Ste 200 Warminster (18974) ***(G-18870)***
Eickhoff Corporation....724 218-1856
165 Temple Rd Georgetown (15043) ***(G-6275)***
Eidemiller Door Co....724 668-8294
176 Skyview Dr New Alexandria (15670) ***(G-12018)***
Eight Oaks Craft Distillers, New Tripoli *Also called Eight Oaks Craft Distillery Co* ***(G-12455)***
Eight Oaks Craft Distillery Co....484 387-5287
7189 Route 309 New Tripoli (18066) ***(G-12455)***
Eighteenth Century Hardware Co, Derry *Also called Simpson Manufacturing Inc* ***(G-4107)***
Eighty-Four Mining Company (HQ)....740 338-3100
1000 Consol Energy Dr Canonsburg (15317) ***(G-2581)***
Eis Inc....215 674-8773
1800 Byberry Rd Ste 810 Huntingdon Valley (19006) ***(G-7976)***
Eisenhardt Mills Inc....610 253-2791
1510 Richmond Rd Easton (18040) ***(G-4677)***
Eisenhower Tool Inc....215 538-9381
120 Pacific Dr Quakertown (18951) ***(G-16187)***
EJ Bognar Incorporated (PA)....412 344-9900
733 Washington Rd Fl 5 Pittsburgh (15228) ***(G-14960)***
Ej Usa Inc....412 795-6000
141 Dexter Dr Monroeville (15146) ***(G-11334)***
Eko Solutions Plus Inc....215 856-9517
7305 Old York Rd Ste 2 Elkins Park (19027) ***(G-4902)***
Ekopak Inc....412 264-9800
1120 Stevenson Mill Rd Coraopolis (15108) ***(G-3686)***
Eks Vinyl Structures....570 725-3439
816 E Valley Rd Loganton (17747) ***(G-10094)***
El Milagro....412 668-2627
1542 Beechview Ave Pittsburgh (15216) ***(G-14961)***
El Serrano Inc....717 397-6191
3410 E Market St Ste E York (17402) ***(G-20465)***
El Torero Spanish Newspaper....610 435-6608
505 N 7th St Allentown (18102) ***(G-205)***
El-Ana Collection Inc....215 953-8820
61 Buck Rd Huntingdon Valley (19006) ***(G-7977)***
Elbach & Johnson Inc....724 457-6180
1309 Main St Glenwillard (15046) ***(G-6546)***
Elbeco Incorporated (PA)....610 921-0651
4418 Pottsville Pike Reading (19605) ***(G-16370)***
Elby Bedding Inc....610 292-8700
1210 Stnbridge St Ste 800 Norristown (19401) ***(G-12653)***
Elc Manufacturing....570 655-3060
330 Philadelphia Ave West Pittston (18643) ***(G-19755)***
Elcam Tool & Die Inc (PA)....814 929-5831
479 Buena Vista Hwy Wilcox (15870) ***(G-19898)***
Elco Machine & Tool, Lebanon *Also called Patricia Morris* ***(G-9615)***
Elco Sintered Alloys Co Inc....814 885-8031
269 Fairview Rd Kersey (15846) ***(G-8557)***
Elderhorst Bells Inc....215 679-3264
875 Gravel Pike Palm (18070) ***(G-13094)***
Elec Const Jt....610 777-3150
20 Morgan Dr Reading (19608) ***(G-16371)***
Elecast Inc....570 587-5105
937 Griffin Pond Rd S Abingtn Twp (18411) ***(G-16895)***
Electra-Kool Division, Broomall *Also called Wayne Products Inc* ***(G-2305)***
Electri-Cord Manufacturing Co (PA)....814 367-2265
312 E Main St Westfield (16950) ***(G-19777)***
Electric City Baseball & Soft....570 955-0471
501 Wyoming Ave Scranton (18509) ***(G-17232)***
Electric City Yoga....570 558-9642
1120 Moosic St Scranton (18505) ***(G-17233)***
Electric Materials Company (HQ)....814 725-9621
50 S Washington St North East (16428) ***(G-12739)***
Electric Metering Corp USA....215 949-1900
202 William Leigh Dr Bristol (19007) ***(G-2138)***
Electric Motor & Supply Inc....814 946-0401
1000 50th St Altoona (16601) ***(G-501)***
Electric Motor Service Inc....724 348-6858
3755 Ann St Finleyville (15332) ***(G-5958)***
Electric Pepper Company LLC....812 340-4321
1716 Akeley Rd Russell (16345) ***(G-16880)***
Electric Rewind Co Inc....215 675-6912
706 Burbridge Rd Hatboro (19040) ***(G-7284)***
Electrical Design Developm....412 747-4970
1104 Parkway View Dr Pittsburgh (15205) ***(G-14962)***
Electrical Mechanical Products, Warminster *Also called Emp Industries Inc* ***(G-18871)***
Electrical Supply, Elkins Park *Also called Io Solutions & Controls* ***(G-4907)***
Electrichp USA Corp....724 678-5084
309 Merrifield Dr Venetia (15367) ***(G-18742)***
Electro Soft Inc....215 654-0701
113 Keystone Dr Montgomeryville (18936) ***(G-11394)***
Electro-Glass Products Inc....724 423-5000
3936 Rte 981 Norvelt (15674) ***(G-12878)***
Electro-Mec, Indiana *Also called Integrated Power Services LLC* ***(G-8108)***
Electro-Mechanical Division, Cheswick *Also called Curtiss-Wright Electro-* ***(G-3105)***
Electro-Optical Systems Inc....610 935-5838
1288 Valley Forge Rd # 49 Phoenixville (19460) ***(G-14547)***
Electro-Platers of York Inc....717 751-2712
100 B Lane York St 1 York (17402) ***(G-20466)***
Electro-Space Fabricators Inc....610 682-7181
300 W High St Topton (19562) ***(G-18412)***
Electro-Tech Systems Inc....215 887-2196
3101 Mount Carmel Ave Glenside (19038) ***(G-6515)***
Electrocell Systems Inc....610 438-2969
3320 Nazareth Rd Easton (18045) ***(G-4678)***
Electrochem Water Systems, Easton *Also called Electrocell Systems Inc* ***(G-4678)***
Electroline Corp....215 766-2229
6182 Easton Rd Pipersville (18947) ***(G-14614)***
Electromagnetic Liberation....724 568-2869
410 Harrison Ave Vandergrift (15690) ***(G-18725)***
Electromechanical North Amer, Irwin *Also called Parker-Hannifin Corporation* ***(G-8188)***
Electromenu, Aston *Also called Electrovue LLC* ***(G-762)***
Electron Energy Corporation (PA)....717 898-2294
924 Links Ave Landisville (17538) ***(G-9259)***
Electron Microscopy Sciences, Hatfield *Also called Ems Acquisition Corp* ***(G-7339)***
Electron Technology Division, Breinigsville *Also called Triton Services Inc* ***(G-2029)***
Electronic Assembly Co Inc....215 799-0600
150 S Front St Souderton (18964) ***(G-17732)***
Electronic Components & Mtls, Warren *Also called Osram Sylvania Inc* ***(G-19041)***
Electronic Concepts Inc....717 235-9450
223 W Main St New Freedom (17349) ***(G-12207)***

Electronic Imaging Svcs Inc 215 785-2284
  1501 Grundy Ln Bristol (19007) *(G-2139)*
Electronic Instrument Res Ltd 724 744-7028
  2231 Trolist Dr Irwin (15642) *(G-8158)*
Electronic Integration Inc 215 364-3390
  875 Pnnsylvnia Blvd Ste 4 Feasterville Trevose (19053) *(G-5903)*
Electronic Mfg Svcs Group Inc 717 764-0002
  951 Monocacy Rd York (17404) *(G-20467)*
Electronic Prototype Dev Inc 412 767-4111
  5 Acee Dr Natrona Heights (15065) *(G-11941)*
Electronic Service & Design 717 243-7743
  2118 Church Rd Hummelstown (17036) *(G-7909)*
Electronic Tech Systems Inc 724 295-6000
  2 Acee Dr Natrona Heights (15065) *(G-11942)*
Electronic Test Eqp Mfg Co 717 393-9653
  1370 Arcadia Rd Lancaster (17601) *(G-9008)*
Electronic Tool & Die Works 215 639-0730
  3156 Tucker Rd Bensalem (19020) *(G-1187)*
Electronics Boutique Amer Inc 610 518-5300
  40 Quarry Rd Ste H Downingtown (19335) *(G-4225)*
Electronics Instrs & Optics (PA) 215 245-6300
  Pennsylvnia Wicker Ave Bensalem (19020) *(G-1188)*
Electrospray Incorporated 215 322-5255
  175 Philmont Ave Feasterville Trevose (19053) *(G-5904)*
Electrospray Incorporated (PA) 215 322-5255
  175 Philmont Ave Feasterville Trevose (19053) *(G-5905)*
Electrostatics Inc 215 513-0850
  63 E Broad St Ste 6 Hatfield (19440) *(G-7337)*
Electrovue LLC 855 226-4430
  200 Turner Industrial Way Aston (19014) *(G-762)*
Elegant Furniture & Lighting 888 388-3390
  500-550 E Erie Ave Philadelphia (19134) *(G-13665)*
Elegant Lighting, Philadelphia *Also called Elegant Furniture & Lighting (G-13665)*
Elegant Marble Products Inc 717 939-0373
  416 Richardson Rd Middletown (17057) *(G-11052)*
Element 1 LLC 570 593-8177
  950 E Main St Schuylkill Haven (17972) *(G-17156)*
Element 27 Inc 610 502-2727
  5960 Waterfowl Rd Schnecksville (18078) *(G-17139)*
Element Granite & Quartz 215 437-9368
  4800 Ashburner St Philadelphia (19136) *(G-13666)*
Element Id Inc 610 419-8822
  520 Evans St Bethlehem (18015) *(G-1501)*
Element Roofing LLC 610 737-0641
  1909 Aripine Ave Bethlehem (18018) *(G-1502)*
Elemental 3 LLC 267 217-3592
  1701 Walnut St Philadelphia (19103) *(G-13667)*
Elements Direct LLC 903 343-5441
  913 6th St New Brighton (15066) *(G-12035)*
Elements For Motion LLC 215 768-1641
  1515 Gehman Rd Kulpsville (19443) *(G-8826)*
Elements Home Accents LLC 412 521-0724
  1010 Greenfield Ave Pittsburgh (15217) *(G-14963)*
Elements of Love 267 262-9796
  1051 Flanders Rd Philadelphia (19151) *(G-13668)*
Elements Skin Care LLC 814 254-4227
  1753 Lyter Dr Johnstown (15905) *(G-8371)*
Eles Bros Inc 412 824-6161
  1000 Thompson Run Rd Monroeville (15146) *(G-11335)*
Elevated Sign Solutions LLC 267 374-4758
  1377 Reservoir Ave Abington (19001) *(G-11)*
Elf Atochem 215 826-2600
  100 Route 413 Bristol (19007) *(G-2140)*
Elge Precision Machining Inc 610 376-5458
  360 Blair Ave Reading (19601) *(G-16372)*
Elge Spark Wheel Co, Reading *Also called Elge Precision Machining Inc (G-16372)*
Eli K Lapp Jr 717 768-0258
  84 Colonial Rd Gordonville (17529) *(G-6553)*
Elick Logging Inc 814 743-5546
  1434 Dogwood Rd Cherry Tree (15724) *(G-3032)*
Elite Cabinetry Inc 717 993-5269
  501 Marsteller Rd Ste 4 New Park (17352) *(G-12429)*
Elite Midstream Services Inc 412 220-3082
  3 Nicholson Dr Cuddy (15031) *(G-3943)*
Elite Oil Field Services Inc (PA) 724 627-6060
  99 E Main St Ste 1 Uniontown (15401) *(G-18624)*
Elite Sweets Inc (PA) 610 391-1719
  7150 Hamilton Blvd Trexlertown (18087) *(G-18510)*
Elite Timber Harvesting LLC 570 836-2453
  795 Bardwell Rd Factoryville (18419) *(G-5756)*
Elite Tool Company Inc 724 379-5800
  First & Wall Webster (15087) *(G-19457)*
Elite Vinyl Railings LLC (PA) 717 354-0524
  3431 Division Hwy New Holland (17557) *(G-12248)*
Elizabeth C Baker 610 566-0691
  10 W State St Media (19063) *(G-10923)*
Elizabeth Carbide Components 724 539-3574
  200 Monastery Dr Latrobe (15650) *(G-9474)*
Elizabeth Carbide Die Co 412 829-7700
  14559 State Route 30 Irwin (15642) *(G-8159)*

Elizabeth Carbide Die Co Inc (PA) 412 751-3000
  601 Linden St McKeesport (15132) *(G-10667)*
Elizabeth Carbide Die Co Inc 412 829-7700
  101 Peterson Dr Irwin (15642) *(G-8160)*
Elizabeth Hata International, Irwin *Also called Elizabeth Carbide Die Co Inc (G-8160)*
Elizabeth Milling Company LLC (PA) 724 872-9404
  608 Center St Smithton (15479) *(G-17660)*
Elizabeth-Hata International, Irwin *Also called Elizabeth Carbide Die Co (G-8159)*
Elizabethtown Advocate 717 361-0340
  9 S Market St Elizabethtown (17022) *(G-4873)*
Eljobo Inc 215 822-5544
  2800 Sterling Dr Hatfield (19440) *(G-7338)*
Elk County Designing, Saint Marys *Also called Elk County Machining (G-16969)*
Elk County Heat Treaters Inc 814 834-0056
  316 Battery St Saint Marys (15857) *(G-16968)*
Elk County Machining 814 781-3502
  177 West Creek Rd Saint Marys (15857) *(G-16969)*
Elk County Tool & Die Inc 814 834-1434
  1020 Graphite Rd Saint Marys (15857) *(G-16970)*
Elk Creek Redi-Mix, Fairview *Also called Concrete Services Corporation (G-5817)*
Elk Group International LLC 800 613-3261
  100 N 3rd St Easton (18042) *(G-4679)*
Elk Lake Services LLC 724 463-7303
  280 Indian Springs Rd Indiana (15701) *(G-8094)*
Elk Lighting, Easton *Also called Elk Group International LLC (G-4679)*
Elk Lighting Inc (PA) 610 767-0511
  40 3rd St Walnutport (18088) *(G-18791)*
Elk Lighting Inc 800 613-3261
  101 W White St Summit Hill (18250) *(G-18160)*
Elk Metals Inc 814 834-4959
  266 Battery St Saint Marys (15857) *(G-16971)*
Elk Premium Building Products 717 866-8300
  401 Weavertown Rd Myerstown (17067) *(G-11884)*
Elk River Logging Inc 814 787-4327
  3342 River Rd Weedville (15868) *(G-19458)*
Elk Systems Inc 717 884-9355
  303 Heck Hill Rd Lewisberry (17339) *(G-9885)*
Elkay Weaving Co Inc 570 822-5371
  701 E Northampton St Wilkes Barre (18702) *(G-19917)*
Elkay Wood Products Company 570 966-1076
  5 N 8th St Mifflinburg (17844) *(G-11094)*
Elkem Holding Inc (HQ) 412 299-7200
  Airport Office Park Bldg Coraopolis (15108) *(G-3687)*
Elkem Materials Inc 412 299-7200
  400 Rouser Rd Ste 600 Coraopolis (15108) *(G-3688)*
Elkem Materials Inc (HQ) 412 299-7200
  Airpo Offic Parl Bldg 24 Moon Township (15108) *(G-11486)*
Elkem Metal, Coraopolis *Also called Elkem Holding Inc (G-3687)*
Elkhorn Operating Company 814 723-4390
  15470 Route 6 Warren (16365) *(G-19023)*
Elkhorn Propane, Warren *Also called Elkhorn Operating Company (G-19023)*
Ellco Products Inc 724 758-3526
  107 Jamison Ave Ellwood City (16117) *(G-4930)*
Ellectralloy Division, Oil City *Also called G O Carlson Inc (G-12945)*
Ellectralloy Division, Titusville *Also called G O Carlson Inc (G-18378)*
Elliott Bros Steel Company 724 658-5561
  356 George Washington Rd Volant (16156) *(G-18773)*
Elliott Company 724 379-5440
  1250 Scott St Donora (15033) *(G-4155)*
Elliott Company (HQ) 724 527-2811
  901 N 4th St Jeannette (15644) *(G-8254)*
Elliott Lumber Company, Roulette *Also called C A Elliot Lumber Co Inc (G-16834)*
Elliott Machine Company 610 485-5345
  3345 Market St Upper Chichester (19014) *(G-18659)*
Elliott Printing Services LLC 610 614-1500
  3000 Portage Rd Bethlehem (18020) *(G-1503)*
Elliott Support Services, Jeannette *Also called Elliott Company (G-8254)*
Elliott Turbomachinery Co, Donora *Also called Elliott Company (G-4155)*
Ellis Machine 724 657-4519
  303 N Street Ext Pulaski (16143) *(G-16123)*
ELLIS PAINT COMPANY, Philadelphia *Also called Axalta Coating Systems Ltd (G-13433)*
Ellison Industrial Contrls LLC 724 483-0251
  19 State St Belle Vernon (15012) *(G-1086)*
Ellucian Support Inc 610 647-5930
  4 Country View Rd Malvern (19355) *(G-10229)*
Ellwood City Forge, New Castle *Also called Ellwood Group Inc (G-12084)*
Ellwood City Forge, Ellwood City *Also called Ellwood Group Inc (G-4931)*
Ellwood City Forge Company 724 202-5008
  700 Moravia St New Castle (16101) *(G-12083)*
Ellwood City Ledger, Beaver *Also called Beaver Newspapers Inc (G-979)*
Ellwood Crankshaft and Machine, Hermitage *Also called Ellwood Group Inc (G-7582)*
Ellwood Crankshaft and Mch Co 724 347-0250
  2727 Freedland Rd Hermitage (16148) *(G-7581)*
Ellwood Group Inc 724 658-3685
  712 Moravia St 10 New Castle (16101) *(G-12084)*
Ellwood Group Inc 724 752-0055
  800 Commercial Ave Ellwood City (16117) *(G-4931)*

A
L
P
H
A
B
E
T
I
C

Ellwood Group Inc 724 981-1012
   2727 Freedland Rd Hermitage (16148) *(G-7582)*

Ellwood Mill Products Company 724 752-0055
   710 Moravia St New Castle (16101) *(G-12085)*

Ellwood Mill Products Company (PA) 724 658-9632
   712 Moravia St New Castle (16101) *(G-12086)*

Ellwood Nat Crankshaft Svcs (HQ) 724 342-4965
   2727 Freedland Rd Hermitage (16148) *(G-7583)*

Ellwood National Crankshaft Co 814 563-7522
   1 Front St Irvine (16329) *(G-8139)*

Ellwood National Forge Company 814 563-7522
   1 Front St Irvine (16329) *(G-8140)*

Ellwood Quality Steels Company 724 658-6502
   700 Moravia St Ste 7 New Castle (16101) *(G-12087)*

Ellwood Safety Appliance Co 724 758-7538
   927 Beaver Ave Ellwood City (16117) *(G-4932)*

Ellwood Specialty Steel Co (HQ) 724 657-1160
   499 Honey Bee Ln New Castle (16105) *(G-12088)*

Elm Ave Car Wash 717 637-7392
   703 W Elm Ave Hanover (17331) *(G-6881)*

ELM Enterprises Inc 724 452-8699
   50 Halstead Blvd Ste 1 Zelienople (16063) *(G-20798)*

Elmark Graphics, West Chester *Also called MWM Graphics (G-19603)*

Elmark Sign & Graphics Inc 610 692-0525
   307 Westtown Rd Ste 1 West Chester (19382) *(G-19549)*

Elmark Sign & Graphics Inc 610 692-0525
   307 Westtown Rd Ste 1 West Chester (19382) *(G-19550)*

Elmwood 570 524-9663
   25 Cedar Dr Lewisburg (17837) *(G-9905)*

Elroy Turpentine Company (PA) 412 963-0949
   1370 Old Frport Rd Ste 2a Pittsburgh (15238) *(G-14964)*

Els Manufacturing LLC 717 442-8569
   5270 Amish Rd Kinzers (17535) *(G-8737)*

Elsevier Inc 215 239-3441
   1600 John F Kennedy Blvd # 1800 Philadelphia (19103) *(G-13669)*

Elsevier Inc 215 239-3900
   1600 John F Kennedy Blvd # 1800 Philadelphia (19103) *(G-13670)*

Elsie A Mundkowsky 814 922-3072
   14415 Ridge Rd West Springfield (16443) *(G-19767)*

Elsner Engineering Works Inc 717 637-5991
   475 Fame Ave Hanover (17331) *(G-6882)*

Elsol Latino Newspaper 215 424-1200
   198 W Chew Ave Philadelphia (19120) *(G-13671)*

Elster American Meter Co LLC 412 833-2550
   1725 Washington Rd Pittsburgh (15241) *(G-14965)*

Elvin B Zimmerman 717 656-9327
   275 W Farmersville Rd Leola (17540) *(G-9780)*

Elynxx Solutions, Chambersburg *Also called E-Lynxx Corporation (G-2926)*

Elyse Aion 215 663-8787
   820 Fox Chase Rd Jenkintown (19046) *(G-8285)*

Em Energy Employer LLC 412 564-1300
   601 Technology Dr Ste 300 Canonsburg (15317) *(G-2582)*

Em Energy Pennsylvania LLC 412 564-1300
   1800 Main St Ste 220 Canonsburg (15317) *(G-2583)*

Em-Bed-It & Co Inc 412 781-8585
   128 Green Commons Dr Pittsburgh (15243) *(G-14966)*

Em1 Services LLC 570 560-2561
   359 Clyde Rd Unityville (17774) *(G-18650)*

Emanuel K Fisher 570 547-2599
   1065 Bob Drick Rd Allenwood (17810) *(G-441)*

Emball Iso Inc 267 687-8570
   130 Keystone Dr Montgomeryville (18936) *(G-11395)*

Embassy Powdered Metals Inc 814 486-1011
   70 Airport Rd Emporium (15834) *(G-5055)*

Embedded Energy Technology LLC 412 254-3381
   1936 5th Ave Pittsburgh (15219) *(G-14967)*

Embroider Smith 570 961-8781
   1021 Lookout Dr Scranton (18504) *(G-17234)*

Embroidery Etc Inc 412 381-6884
   42 Terminal Way Pittsburgh (15219) *(G-14968)*

Embroidery Concepts 724 225-3644
   231 S College St Washington (15301) *(G-19168)*

Embroidery Factory Inc 570 654-7640
   137 Market St Pittston (18640) *(G-15749)*

Embroidery Just For You, Altoona *Also called Samfam Inc (G-546)*

Embroidery Plus, Carbondale *Also called Cerra Signs Inc (G-2670)*

Embroidery Systems Inc. 412 967-9271
   523 Dorseyville Rd Pittsburgh (15238) *(G-14969)*

EMC Corporation 484 322-1000
   80 E Germantown Pike Norristown (19401) *(G-12654)*

EMC Corporation 610 834-0471
   300 Conshohocken State Rd # 700 Conshohocken (19428) *(G-3542)*

EMC Fintech 814 230-9157
   34 E Harmar St Warren (16365) *(G-19024)*

EMC Global Technologies Inc 215 340-0650
   4059 Skyron Dr Doylestown (18902) *(G-4298)*

EMC Global Technologies Inc (PA) 267 347-5100
   1060 Revenue Dr Telford (18969) *(G-18287)*

EMC Metals Inc 412 299-7200
   400 Rouser Rd Ste 600 Coraopolis (15108) *(G-3689)*

EMC Technology LLC 814 728-8857
   22 Drumcliffe Dr Warren (16365) *(G-19025)*

Emcee Communication, Mountain Top *Also called Wireless Acquisition LLC (G-11781)*

Emcee Knitwear, Nesquehoning *Also called Taraco Sportswear Inc (G-12009)*

Emcom, State College *Also called API Cryptek Inc (G-17941)*

EMD Millipore Corporation 484 652-5600
   1 International Plz # 300 Philadelphia (19113) *(G-13315)*

EMD Performance Materials Corp (HQ) 888 367-3275
   1200 Intrepid Ave Ste 3 Philadelphia (19112) *(G-13672)*

Emeco Industries Inc (PA) 717 637-5951
   805 W Elm Ave Hanover (17331) *(G-6883)*

Emerald Art Glass Inc 412 381-2274
   2300 Josephine St Pittsburgh (15203) *(G-14970)*

Emerald Coal Resources LP 724 627-7500
   2071 Garards Fort Rd Waynesburg (15370) *(G-19440)*

Emerald Mine, Waynesburg *Also called Emerald Coal Resources LP (G-19440)*

Emerald Printing & Imaging 814 899-6959
   3212 Cherry St Erie (16508) *(G-5258)*

Emerald Windows Inc 215 236-6767
   2301 N 9th St Philadelphia (19133) *(G-13673)*

Emergensee Inc 610 804-9007
   1620 Minden Ln Malvern (19355) *(G-10230)*

Emerging Computer Technologies 717 761-4027
   3518 Hawthorne Dr Camp Hill (17011) *(G-2495)*

Emericks Maple Products 814 324-4536
   156 Ridge Rd Hyndman (15545) *(G-8049)*

Emericks Meat & Packing Co 814 842-6779
   552 Hyndman Rd Hyndman (15545) *(G-8050)*

Emerilware, Canonsburg *Also called All-Clad Metalcrafters LLC (G-2537)*

Emerson Company 310 940-1755
   3539 N 6th St Harrisburg (17110) *(G-7126)*

Emerson Electric Co 610 569-4023
   410 W Linfield Trappe Rd # 200 Royersford (19468) *(G-16849)*

Emerson Electric Co 215 638-8904
   855 Dunksferry Rd A Bensalem (19020) *(G-1189)*

Emerson Process Management (HQ) 412 963-4000
   200 Beta Dr Pittsburgh (15238) *(G-14971)*

Emig Machine and Tool, Warminster *Also called Timothy Emig (G-18982)*

Emil Rarick Fuel Delivery 570 345-8584
   250 Tremont Rd Side Pine Grove (17963) *(G-14592)*

Emilius, J A Sons, Cheltenham *Also called J A Emilius Sons Inc (G-3030)*

Emily J High 570 345-6268
   60 Martins Rd Pine Grove (17963) *(G-14593)*

Emka-Incorporated 717 986-1111
   1961 Fulling Mill Rd Middletown (17057) *(G-11053)*

Emma One Sock Inc 215 542-1082
   566 Cardinal Dr Dresher (19025) *(G-4354)*

Emp Industries Inc 215 357-5333
   153 Railroad Dr Warminster (18974) *(G-18871)*

Emp Sales Associates Inc 412 731-9899
   1445 Beulah Rd Pittsburgh (15235) *(G-14972)*

Emperor Aquatics Inc. 610 970-0440
   940 Crimson Ln Pottstown (19464) *(G-15986)*

Empire Building Products Inc (HQ) 610 926-0500
   2741 Bernville Rd Leesport (19533) *(G-9662)*

Empire Energy E&P LLC (PA) 724 483-2070
   380 Sthpinte Blvd Ste 130 Canonsburg (15317) *(G-2584)*

Empire Energy E&P LLC 814 365-5621
   Hc 28 Hawthorn (16230) *(G-7444)*

Empire Glove Inc 570 824-4400
   525 Scott St Wilkes Barre (18702) *(G-19918)*

Empire Kosher Poultry Inc (HQ) 717 436-5921
   Chicken Plant Rd Mifflintown (17059) *(G-11114)*

Empire Kosher Poultry Inc 570 374-0501
   2243 Route 522 Selinsgrove (17870) *(G-17324)*

Empire Surplus Home Center, Leesport *Also called Empire Building Products Inc (G-9662)*

Emporeum Plastics Corporation 610 698-6347
   1522 Golf Course Rd Birdsboro (19508) *(G-1694)*

Emporium Contractors Inc 814 562-0631
   Rich Valley Rd Rr 46 Emporium (15834) *(G-5056)*

Emporium Hardwoods Oper Co LLC 814 486-3764
   15970 Route 120 Emporium (15834) *(G-5057)*

Emporium Powdered Metal Inc 814 486-0136
   140 W 2nd St Ste 3 Emporium (15834) *(G-5058)*

Emporium Secondaries Inc 814 486-1881
   11769 Route 120 Emporium (15834) *(G-5059)*

Emporium Specialties Company 814 647-8661
   94 Foster St Austin (16720) *(G-833)*

Ems Acquisition Corp 215 412-8400
   1560 Industry Rd Hatfield (19440) *(G-7339)*

Ems Clothing & Novelty Inc 570 752-2896
   764 Knob Mountain Rd Berwick (18603) *(G-1324)*

Ems Engnred Mtls Solutions LLC 610 562-3841
   600 Valley Way Hamburg (19526) *(G-6838)*

Ems Surgical LP 570 374-0569
   801 N Old Trl Selinsgrove (17870) *(G-17325)*

Emsco Inc (PA) 814 774-3137
   607 Church St Girard (16417) *(G-6386)*

(G-0000) Company's Geographic Section entry number

Emsco Inc...814 774-3137
306 Shenango St Girard (16417) (G-6387)

Emsco Distributor Company.............................412 754-1236
11025 Parker Dr Irwin (15642) (G-8161)

Emsco Group, Girard Also called Emsco Inc (G-6386)

Emsg, York Also called Electronic Mfg Svcs Group Inc (G-20467)

Emw Inc..717 626-0248
10 W 2nd Ave Lititz (17543) (G-10006)

Enango Newspapers, The, Clarion Also called Derrick Publishing Company (G-3176)

Enchanted Acres Farm Group LLC.......................877 707-3833
200 N 8th St Ste 500 Reading (19601) (G-16373)

Enchanted Beauty, Glenside Also called Paul F Rothstein Inc (G-6532)

Enchlor Inc...215 453-2533
130 W Main St Silverdale (18962) (G-17591)

Enclosure Direct Corp..................................724 697-5191
4097 State Route 819 Avonmore (15618) (G-864)

Enclosures Direct Corporation..........................724 837-7600
141 Wilson Ave Greensburg (15601) (G-6664)

Encoat, Morrisville Also called Shawcor Pipe Protection LLC (G-11581)

Encompass Health Corporation..........................610 478-8797
1025 Berkshire Blvd # 500 Reading (19610) (G-16374)

Encor Coatings, Bath Also called Corban Corporation (G-956)

Encotech Inc (PA).......................................724 222-3334
1037 Route 519 Eighty Four (15330) (G-4839)

Endagraph Inc...724 327-9384
9000 Corporate Cir Export (15632) (G-5601)

Endeavor Lumber, Endeavor Also called Itl Corp (G-5079)

Endeavour Sky Inc......................................610 872-5694
3719 Arlington Ave Brookhaven (19015) (G-2244)

Endicott Interconnect Tech.............................724 352-6315
373 Saxonburg Blvd Saxonburg (16056) (G-17086)

Endless Mountain Stone Co, Susquehanna Also called Premier Bluestone Inc (G-18182)

Endless Mountains Specialties..........................570 432-4018
873 Old County Rd Montrose (18801) (G-11463)

Endnote, Philadelphia Also called Clarivate Analytics (us) LLC (G-13548)

Endo Finance Co..484 216-0000
1400 Atwater Dr Malvern (19355) (G-10231)

Endo Health Solutions Inc (HQ)........................484 216-0000
1400 Atwater Dr Malvern (19355) (G-10232)

Endo Pharmaceutical Inc................................484 216-2759
420 Babylon Rd Horsham (19044) (G-7815)

Endo Pharmaceuticals Inc (HQ).........................484 216-0000
1400 Atwater Dr Malvern (19355) (G-10233)

Endo Phrmcticals Solutions Inc (HQ)...................484 216-0000
1400 Atwater Dr Malvern (19355) (G-10234)

Endologix Inc...412 661-5877
5831 Alder St Pittsburgh (15232) (G-14973)

Endoscopic Laser Technologies.........................443 205-9340
20 W Pennsylvania Ave Stewartstown (17363) (G-18061)

Endress + Hauser Inc...................................317 535-7138
500 Horizon Dr Ste 502 Chalfont (18914) (G-2873)

Eneflux Armtek Magnetics Inc..........................215 443-5303
1775 Stout Dr Ste G Warminster (18974) (G-18872)

Enercorp Inc..814 345-6225
1310 Allport Cutoff Morrisdale (16858) (G-11548)

Enerflex Energy Systems Inc............................724 627-0751
106 Springfield Dr Canonsburg (15317) (G-2585)

Enerflex Energy Systems Inc............................570 726-0500
160 Logan Dr B Muncy (17756) (G-11815)

Energex Inc...717 436-2400
95 Energex Dr Mifflintown (17059) (G-11115)

Energex American Inc...................................717 436-2400
95 Energex Dr Mifflintown (17059) (G-11116)

Energex Corporation (PA)..............................717 436-2400
95 Energex Dr Mifflintown (17059) (G-11117)

Energize Inc..215 438-8342
5450 Wphickon Ave Ste C13 Philadelphia (19144) (G-13674)

Energizer Battery Co...................................215 572-0200
689 Pembroke Rd Jenkintown (19046) (G-8286)

Energy Construction Services, Lancaster Also called Rettew Field Services Inc (G-9187)

Energy Control Systems Inc.............................412 781-8500
100 Hafner Ave Ste 1 Pittsburgh (15223) (G-14974)

Energy Conversion Technology..........................412 835-0191
206 Locust Ln Pittsburgh (15241) (G-14975)

Energy Corporation of America.........................724 966-9000
205 Carmichaels Plz Carmichaels (15320) (G-2756)

Energy Field Services LLC..............................717 791-1018
39 S York Rd Ste A Dillsburg (17019) (G-4128)

Energy Innovation Ctr Inst Inc.........................412 894-9800
1435 Bedford Ave Pittsburgh (15219) (G-14976)

Energy Products & Technologies........................717 485-3137
433 Peach Orchard Rd Mc Connellsburg (17233) (G-10564)

Energy Services & Mfg, Du Bois Also called Staar Distributing Llc (G-4420)

Energy Worx Inc..321 610-4676
11 Vosburg St Mansfield (16933) (G-10414)

Energycap Inc..814 237-3744
2026 Sandy Dr State College (16803) (G-17963)

Enersys...724 223-4255
80 Stewart Ave Washington (15301) (G-19169)

Enersys...215 420-1000
375 Constance Dr Warminster (18974) (G-18873)

Enersys (PA)...610 208-1991
2366 Bernville Rd Reading (19605) (G-16375)

Enersys Advanced Systems Inc (HQ)....................215 674-3800
104 Rock Rd Horsham (19044) (G-7816)

Enersys Capital Inc (HQ)...............................610 208-1991
2366 Bernville Rd Reading (19605) (G-16376)

Enersys Delaware Inc...................................484 244-4150
7055 Ambassador Dr Allentown (18106) (G-206)

Enersys Delaware Inc (HQ).............................214 324-8990
2366 Bernville Rd Reading (19605) (G-16377)

Engdahl Manufacturing Inc.............................717 854-7114
190 Carlisle Ave York (17401) (G-20468)

Engine Cycle Inc.......................................717 214-4177
30 Vine St Highspire (17034) (G-7632)

Engineered Devices Corporation........................570 455-4897
125 Butler Dr Hazleton (18201) (G-7497)

Engineered Plastics, Philadelphia Also called Epc Inc (G-13675)

Engineered Plastics LLC................................814 452-6632
1241 Camphausen Ave Erie (16511) (G-5259)

Engineered Plastics LLC (PA)..........................814 774-2970
1040 Maple Ave Lake City (16423) (G-8899)

Engineered Pressed Materials..........................814 772-6127
1 Grant Rd Ridgway (15853) (G-16707)

Engineered Pressed Materials..........................814 834-3189
348 Center St Saint Marys (15857) (G-16972)

Engineering & Cnstr Dept, Pittsburgh Also called City of Pittsburgh (G-14854)

Engineering Animation, State College Also called Siemens Product Life Mgmt Sftw (G-18022)

Engineering Machining Ser, University Park Also called Pennsylvania State University (G-18652)

Enginred Arrsting Systems Corp (HQ)...................610 494-8000
2550 Market St Upper Chichester (19014) (G-18660)

Engle Online, Lancaster Also called Engle Printing & Pubg Co Inc (G-9009)

Engle Printing & Pubg Co Inc (PA).....................717 653-1833
1100 Corporate Blvd Lancaster (17601) (G-9009)

Engle Printing & Pubg Co Inc..........................717 892-6800
1100 Corporate Blvd Lancaster (17601) (G-9010)

Engle Printing & Pubg Co Inc..........................717 653-1833
1425 W Main St Mount Joy (17552) (G-11654)

Engle Publishing Co, Mount Joy Also called Alvin Engle Associates Inc (G-11645)

Englishs Model Railroad Supply, Montoursville Also called Bowser Manufacturing Co (G-11434)

Enhanced Sintered Products Inc........................814 834-2470
74 Pm St Saint Marys (15857) (G-16973)

Enhanced Systems & Products...........................215 794-6942
4700 Watson Dr Doylestown (18902) (G-4299)

Eni USA R & M Co Inc..................................724 352-4451
539 Marwood Rd Cabot (16023) (G-2456)

Enjet Aero Erie Inc.....................................814 860-3104
8127 Nathan Cir Erie (16509) (G-5260)

Enlightening Lrng Minds LLC............................412 880-9601
726 Garden City Dr Monroeville (15146) (G-11336)

Enpro Industries Inc....................................800 618-4701
1600 Industry Rd Hatfield (19440) (G-7340)

Enpro Industries Inc....................................215 946-0845
107 William Leigh Dr Bristol (19007) (G-2141)

Enquip Co..610 363-8275
365 Devon Dr Exton (19341) (G-5672)

Enrico Biscotti Company................................412 281-2602
2022 Penn Ave Pittsburgh (15222) (G-14977)

Enrico J Fiore...570 489-8430
9 Esther St Throop (18512) (G-18358)

Ensinger Inc...724 746-6050
365 Meadowlands Blvd Washington (15301) (G-19170)

Ensinger Industries Inc (HQ)..........................724 746-6050
365 Meadowlands Blvd Washington (15301) (G-19171)

Ensinger Penn Fibre Inc (HQ).........................215 702-9551
2434 Bristol Rd Bensalem (19020) (G-1190)

Ensinger Printing Service...............................717 484-4451
50 W Main St Adamstown (19501) (G-21)

Entec Polymers, Ambler Also called Ravago Americas LLC (G-601)

Entech Industries......................................724 244-9805
1038 N Cedar St New Castle (16102) (G-12089)

Entech Plastics Inc.....................................814 664-7205
1 Plastics Rd Ste 5 Corry (16407) (G-3759)

Enterprise Cloudworks Corp............................215 395-6311
1022 E Lancaster Ave Bryn Mawr (19010) (G-2322)

Enterprise Fashions....................................570 489-1863
116 Grant St Olyphant (18447) (G-12989)

Enterprise Machine.....................................215 679-7490
1341 Tagart Rd East Greenville (18041) (G-4567)

Enterprise Machine and Tool Co........................570 969-2587
229 Marion St Scranton (18509) (G-17235)

Enterprise Machine Co..................................215 855-0868
1370 Industry Rd Ste C Hatfield (19440) (G-7341)

Entrance Inc...610 926-0126
2651 Leiscczs Bridge Rd Leesport (19533) (G-9663)

A
L
P
H
A
B
E
T
I
C

Envelope Worx, Pittsburgh *Also called Printworx Inc* ***(G-15446)***
Envirnmntal Catalysts Tech Div, Wayne *Also called Matthey Johnson Inc* ***(G-19352)***
Envirnmntal Enrgy Slutions LLC 814 446-5625
10027 Route 403 Hwy S Seward (15954) ***(G-17381)***
Envirnmntal Protection PA Dept 570 621-3139
5 W Laurel Blvd Pottsville (17901) ***(G-16078)***
Envirodyne Systems Inc 717 763-0500
75 Zimmerman Dr Camp Hill (17011) ***(G-2496)***
Environmental Inc 412 394-2800
1000 Six Ppg Pl Pittsburgh (15222) ***(G-14978)***
Environmental Air Inc 412 922-8988
1100 Mccartney St Pittsburgh (15220) ***(G-14979)***
Environmental Chem & Lubr Co 610 923-6492
121 Blenheim Dr Easton (18045) ***(G-4680)***
Environmental Land Surveying &, Indiana *Also called Elk Lake Services LLC* ***(G-8094)***
Environmental Materials LLC 570 366-6460
98 Pheasant Run Rd Orwigsburg (17961) ***(G-13042)***
Environmental Solut World Inc (PA) 215 699-0730
200 Progress Dr Montgomeryville (18936) ***(G-11396)***
Environmental Stoneworks, Orwigsburg *Also called Environmental Materials LLC* ***(G-13042)***
Environmental Stoneworks LLC (PA) 570 366-6460
98 Pheasant Run Rd Orwigsburg (17961) ***(G-13043)***
Environmental Systems Research 909 793-2853
1325 Morris Dr Ste 201 Chesterbrook (19087) ***(G-3092)***
Environmental Tectonics Corp (PA) 215 355-9100
125 James Way Southampton (18966) ***(G-17809)***
Envirosafe Services of Ohio 717 354-1025
1046 Narvon Rd Narvon (17555) ***(G-11921)***
Envirotrol Inc 412 741-2030
670 Pennsylvania Ave Rochester (15074) ***(G-16785)***
Envision Products Inc 215 428-1791
1711 S Pennsylvania Ave Morrisville (19067) ***(G-11558)***
Envoy Lighting Inc 215 512-7000
4 Neshaminy Trevose (19053) ***(G-18493)***
Eog Resources Inc 724 745-9063
400 Sthpinte Blvd Ste 300 Canonsburg (15317) ***(G-2586)***
Eog Resources Inc 724 349-7620
2039 S 6th St Indiana (15701) ***(G-8095)***
EP Henry Corporation 610 495-8533
16 Anderson Rd Parker Ford (19457) ***(G-13168)***
Ep World Inc 814 361-3860
285 Ben Franklin Rd N Indiana (15701) ***(G-8096)***
Epc Inc 215 464-1440
2180 Bennett Rd Philadelphia (19116) ***(G-13675)***
EPC Powder Manufacturing Inc 814 725-2012
101 Loomis St North East (16428) ***(G-12740)***
Epd Electronics, Natrona Heights *Also called Electronic Prototype Dev Inc* ***(G-11941)***
Epe Industries Usa Inc 800 315-0336
1501 Distribution Dr Carlisle (17013) ***(G-2710)***
Epe Industries USA Harrisburg, Carlisle *Also called Epe Industries Usa Inc* ***(G-2710)***
Epex Soft Petals 717 848-8488
984 Loucks Rd York (17404) ***(G-20469)***
Epharmasolutions 610 832-2100
625 W Ridge Pike Ste E402 Conshohocken (19428) ***(G-3543)***
Ephraim L King 570 837-9470
636 Scholl Rd Winfield (17889) ***(G-20200)***
Ephrata Rview Susquehanna Prtg, Ephrata *Also called Lancaster County Weeklies* ***(G-5119)***
Epi Labelers, New Freedom *Also called ID Technology LLC* ***(G-12209)***
EPI of Cleveland Inc (HQ) 330 468-2872
1844 Ardmore Blvd Pittsburgh (15221) ***(G-14980)***
Epic Apparel LLC 412 350-9543
217 Mellon St West Mifflin (15122) ***(G-19736)***
Epic Industries Inc 570 586-0253
1133 S Abington Rd Unit 3 Clarks Summit (18411) ***(G-3192)***
Epic Litho 610 933-7400
751 Pike Springs Rd Phoenixville (19460) ***(G-14548)***
Epic Metals Corporation (PA) 412 351-3913
11 Talbot Ave Rankin (15104) ***(G-16305)***
Epic Pickles LLC 717 487-1323
165b S Orchard St Yoe (17313) ***(G-20360)***
Epilogue Systems LLC 281 249-5405
190 Woodstock Rd Villanova (19085) ***(G-18766)***
Epiroc USA LLC 717 552-9694
5105 Technology Ave Chambersburg (17201) ***(G-2930)***
Epiroc USA LLC 724 324-2391
201 Meadow Ridge Rd Mount Morris (15349) ***(G-11680)***
Eplans Inc 717 534-1183
2 Fox Chase Dr Hershey (17033) ***(G-7609)***
Epoxtal LLC 908 376-9825
3401 Market St Ste 200 Philadelphia (19104) ***(G-13676)***
Epps Manufacturing, Butler *Also called Larry J Epps* ***(G-2419)***
Eps Printing Services Inc 610 701-6403
1246 Upton Cir West Chester (19380) ***(G-19551)***
Epy Industries Inc 717 751-2712
100 Boxwood Ln Ste 2 York (17402) ***(G-20470)***
Eq Technologic Inc (PA) 215 891-9010
500 Office Center Dr # 400 Fort Washington (19034) ***(G-6068)***
Eqt Corporation (PA) 412 553-5700
625 Liberty Ave Ste 1700 Pittsburgh (15222) ***(G-14981)***
Eqt Corporation 412 395-2080
625 Liberty Ave Ste 1700 Pittsburgh (15222) ***(G-14982)***
Eqt Re LLC (HQ) 274 271-7200
2200 Rice Dr Canonsburg (15317) ***(G-2587)***
Equate Space-Time Tech LLC 814 838-3571
2545 W Grandview Blvd Erie (16506) ***(G-5261)***
Equine Specialty Feed Co 610 796-5670
122 W Lancaster Ave Reading (19607) ***(G-16378)***
Equinox Ltd 570 322-5900
1307 Park Ave Unit 14 Williamsport (17701) ***(G-20011)***
Equipment & Assembly Plant, Pittsburgh *Also called Calgon Carbon Corporation* ***(G-14804)***
Equipment & Contrls Africa Inc 412 489-3000
1721 Cochran Rd Pittsburgh (15220) ***(G-14983)***
Equipment Distributing, Hazleton *Also called Engineered Devices Corporation* ***(G-7497)***
Equipment Finance Advisor, Bryn Mawr *Also called Bryn Mawr Equipment Fin Inc* ***(G-2317)***
Equipment Technology Inc (PA) 570 489-8651
410 Cemetery St Peckville (18452) ***(G-13208)***
Equipto, Tatamy *Also called Consoldated Stor Companies Inc* ***(G-18256)***
Equipto, Tatamy *Also called Consoldated Stor Companies Inc* ***(G-18257)***
Equisol LLC 866 629-7646
200 Barr Harbor Dr # 400 Conshohocken (19428) ***(G-3544)***
Equivalent Prfmce Polymers, Eagleville *Also called James R Hanlon Inc* ***(G-4514)***
Er Carpentry, Lititz *Also called Carpenter Co* ***(G-9996)***
Eraseal Technologies LLC 215 350-3633
2970 Cowpath Rd Hatfield (19440) ***(G-7342)***
Erector Sets Inc 215 289-1505
4926 Benner St Philadelphia (19135) ***(G-13677)***
Ergogenic Technology Inc 215 766-8545
533 Junction Ln Quakertown (18951) ***(G-16188)***
Ergon Asphalt & Emulsions Inc 484 471-3999
153 Saxer Ave Springfield (19064) ***(G-17912)***
Ergon Asphalt & Emulsions Inc 610 921-0271
3847 Pottsville Pike Reading (19605) ***(G-16379)***
Ergonomic Mfg Group Inc 800 223-6430
591 Union Rd Quakertown (18951) ***(G-16189)***
Eric and Christopher LLC 215 257-2400
410 E Walnut St Ste 5 Perkasie (18944) ***(G-13276)***
Eric Herr 717 464-1829
2125 S View Rd Lancaster (17602) ***(G-9011)***
Eric L Socks 717 762-7488
4974 Orphanage Rd Waynesboro (17268) ***(G-19409)***
Eric Nemeyer Corporation 215 887-8880
107 E Glenside Ave A Glenside (19038) ***(G-6516)***
Eric Snow 267 602-3522
320 Townsend St Chester (19013) ***(G-3049)***
Erickson Corporation 814 371-4350
11 Clear Run Rd Du Bois (15801) ***(G-4391)***
Erie Asphalt Paving Co 814 898-4151
1902 Cherry St Erie (16502) ***(G-5262)***
Erie Bolt Corporation 814 456-4287
1325 Liberty St Blairsville (15717) ***(G-1720)***
Erie Bronze & Aluminum Company 814 838-8602
6300 W Ridge Rd Erie (16506) ***(G-5263)***
Erie Coke Corp 814 454-0177
925 E Bay Dr Erie (16507) ***(G-5264)***
Erie Coke Corporation 814 454-0177
Foot Of East Ave Erie (16512) ***(G-5265)***
Erie Custom Millwork, Erie *Also called Kitchens By Meade Inc* ***(G-5345)***
Erie Energy Products Inc 814 454-2828
1400 Irwin Dr Erie (16505) ***(G-5266)***
Erie Forge and Steel Inc 814 452-2300
1341 W 16th St Erie (16502) ***(G-5267)***
Erie Hard Chrome Inc 814 459-5114
1570 E 12th St Erie (16511) ***(G-5268)***
Erie Landmark, Columbia *Also called Paul W Zimmerman Foundries Co* ***(G-3446)***
Erie M & P Company Inc 814 454-1581
953 E 12th St Erie (16503) ***(G-5269)***
Erie Metal Basket Inc 814 833-1745
2643 W 17th St Erie (16505) ***(G-5270)***
Erie Mill and Press Company, Erie *Also called Erie M & P Company Inc* ***(G-5269)***
Erie OEM Inc 814 459-8024
1001 State St Ste 1300 Erie (16501) ***(G-5271)***
Erie Plating Company 814 453-7531
656 W 12th St Erie (16501) ***(G-5272)***
Erie Powder Coating, Girard *Also called Cummings Group Ltd* ***(G-6385)***
Erie Press Systems, Erie *Also called Efco Inc* ***(G-5256)***
Erie Protective Coatings Inc 814 833-0095
2646 W 14th St Erie (16505) ***(G-5273)***
Erie Sand & Gravel Co Inc (HQ) 412 995-5500
11 Stanwix St Fl 21 Pittsburgh (15222) ***(G-14984)***
Erie Specialty Products Inc 814 453-5611
645 W 11th St Erie (16501) ***(G-5274)***
Erie Strayer Company 814 456-7001
1851 Rudolph Ave Erie (16502) ***(G-5275)***
Erie Technical Systems Inc 814 899-2103
1239 Applejack Dr Erie (16509) ***(G-5276)***
Erie Technical Systems Inc 814 899-2103
4690 Iroquois Ave Erie (16511) ***(G-5277)***

Erie Times News, Erie *Also called Times Publishing Company* ***(G-5509)***
Erie Tool and Forge Inc.......814 587-2841
25035 N Center Rd Springboro (16435) ***(G-17895)***
Erie Tool Works, Erie *Also called Lakeview Forge Co* ***(G-5358)***
Erie Weld Products Inc.......814 899-6320
1709 Franklin Ave Erie (16510) ***(G-5278)***
Erie Wood Products LLC.......814 452-4961
1835 E 12th St Erie (16511) ***(G-5279)***
Eriez Magnetics, Erie *Also called Eriez Manufacturing Co* ***(G-5280)***
Eriez Manufacturing Co (PA).......814 835-6000
2200 Asbury Rd Erie (16506) ***(G-5280)***
Eriez Manufacturing Co.......814 520-8540
1901 Wager Rd Erie (16509) ***(G-5281)***
Eriks Na LLC (HQ).......412 787-2400
650 Washington Rd Ste 500 Pittsburgh (15228) ***(G-14985)***
Eriks North America, Pittsburgh *Also called Eriks Na LLC* ***(G-14985)***
Erisco Industries Inc.......814 459-2720
9565 New Rd North East (16428) ***(G-12741)***
Erivan Dairies, Oreland *Also called Paul Erivan* ***(G-13026)***
Erjo Services, Norristown *Also called Mawa Inc* ***(G-12679)***
Ernamatic Tool & Die Co, Philadelphia *Also called Robert I Oldfield* ***(G-14254)***
Ernest Hill Machine Co Inc.......215 467-7750
1434 Federal St Philadelphia (19146) ***(G-13678)***
Ernest Ricci.......412 490-9531
5888 Steubenville Pike # 1 Mc Kees Rocks (15136) ***(G-10607)***
Ernest W Parnell Burial Vaults, Monongahela *Also called Parnell Enterprises Inc* ***(G-11312)***
Ernie Saxton.......215 752-7797
1448 Hollywood Ave Langhorne (19047) ***(G-9294)***
Ernst Hoffmann Inc.......610 593-2280
806 Valley Ave Atglen (19310) ***(G-800)***
Ernst Timing Screw Company.......215 639-1438
1534 Bridgewater Rd Bensalem (19020) ***(G-1191)***
Eros Hosiery Co Del Vly Inc.......215 342-2121
1430 County Line Rd Huntingdon Valley (19006) ***(G-7978)***
Erp Software Consulting, Hummelstown *Also called First Supply Chain LLC* ***(G-7910)***
Ervin Amasteel Division, Butler *Also called Ervin Industries Inc* ***(G-2399)***
Ervin Industries Inc.......724 282-1060
681 E Butler Rd Butler (16002) ***(G-2399)***
Es & Son of Union I.......724 439-5589
999 N Gallatin Avenue Ext Uniontown (15401) ***(G-18625)***
ES Kluft & Co East LLC.......570 384-2800
412 Oak St Denver (17517) ***(G-4072)***
ES Kluft & Company Inc.......570 384-2800
1104 N Park Dr Hazle Township (18202) ***(G-7455)***
ESAB Group Inc.......717 637-8911
801 Wilson Ave Hanover (17331) ***(G-6884)***
ESAB Group Inc.......843 673-7700
1500 Karen Ln Hanover (17331) ***(G-6885)***
ESAB Group Inc.......717 637-8911
1500 Karen Ln Hanover (17331) ***(G-6886)***
ESAB Welding & Cutting Pdts, Hanover *Also called ESAB Group Inc* ***(G-6884)***
ESAB Welding & Cutting Pdts, Hanover *Also called ESAB Group Inc* ***(G-6885)***
ESAB Welding & Cutting Pdts, Hanover *Also called ESAB Group Inc* ***(G-6886)***
Esbenshade Farms, Mount Joy *Also called Esbenshade Inc* ***(G-11655)***
Esbenshade Inc (PA).......717 653-8061
220 Eby Chiques Rd Mount Joy (17552) ***(G-11655)***
Escalon Medical Corp (PA).......610 688-6830
435 Devon Park Dr Ste 100 Wayne (19087) ***(G-19325)***
Eschrich and Son Logging.......814 362-1371
20 Twin Buck Rd Lewis Run (16738) ***(G-9875)***
Esco Windber.......814 509-8927
214 Railroad St Windber (15963) ***(G-20181)***
Escort Lighting, Wernersville *Also called Hartman Design Inc* ***(G-19484)***
Esf Enterprise LLC.......610 334-2615
35 Queen St Reading (19608) ***(G-16380)***
Esilicon Corporation.......610 439-6800
1605 N Cedar Crest Blvd # 615 Allentown (18104) ***(G-207)***
Esm Group Inc.......724 538-8974
130 Myoma Rd Mars (16046) ***(G-10496)***
Esmark Inc (PA).......412 259-8868
100 Hazel Ln Ste 300 Sewickley (15143) ***(G-17386)***
Esmark Excalibur LLC.......724 371-3059
658 State Ave Beaver (15009) ***(G-981)***
Esmark Excalibur LLC (HQ).......814 382-5696
9723 Us Highway 322 Conneaut Lake (16316) ***(G-3472)***
Esmark Excalibur LLC.......814 382-5696
10730 Mchenry St Meadville (16335) ***(G-10721)***
Esmark Industrial Group LLC (HQ).......412 259-8868
100 Hazel Ln Ste 300 Sewickley (15143) ***(G-17387)***
Esoterix Genetic Labs LLC.......215 351-2331
833 Chestnut St Ste 1250 Philadelphia (19107) ***(G-13679)***
ESP, Doylestown *Also called Enhanced Systems & Products* ***(G-4299)***
ESP, Chambersburg *Also called Effective Software Products* ***(G-2929)***
Espresso Analysts.......724 541-2151
135 Stormer Rd Indiana (15701) ***(G-8097)***
Espresso Solutions.......412 326-0170
1200 Lebanon Rd West Mifflin (15122) ***(G-19737)***
Esquire Holdings, Lancaster *Also called Micro Precision Corporation* ***(G-9133)***
Esri, Chesterbrook *Also called Environmental Systems Research* ***(G-3092)***
Essay Precision Machining.......724 446-2422
233 W Newton Rd Madison (15663) ***(G-10165)***
Esschem Inc (HQ).......610 497-9000
4000 Columbia Ave Linwood (19061) ***(G-9989)***
Essence of Old Woods.......215 258-0852
2131 Old Woods Rd Green Lane (18054) ***(G-6588)***
Essential Images, Littlestown *Also called Rockafellow John* ***(G-10076)***
Essential Medical Inc.......610 557-1009
260 Sierra Dr Ste 120 Exton (19341) ***(G-5673)***
Essential Water Technologies.......570 317-2583
150 E 9th St 246-1 Bloomsburg (17815) ***(G-1781)***
Essentra Components, Erie *Also called Essentra Plastics LLC* ***(G-5282)***
Essentra Plastics LLC (HQ).......814 899-7671
3123 Station Rd Erie (16510) ***(G-5282)***
Essentra Porous Tech Corp.......814 898-3238
2614 Mcclelland Ave Erie (16510) ***(G-5283)***
Essex Engineering Corp.......215 322-5880
21 Industrial Dr Ste A Warminster (18974) ***(G-18874)***
Essity North America Inc.......610 499-3700
1510 Chester Pike Ste 500 Eddystone (19022) ***(G-4801)***
Essity North America Inc (HQ).......610 499-3700
2929 Arch St Ste 2600 Philadelphia (19104) ***(G-13680)***
Essroc Cement.......610 882-2498
5 Highland Ave Bethlehem (18017) ***(G-1504)***
Essroc Corp.......610 759-4211
401 W Prospect St Nazareth (18064) ***(G-11963)***
Essroc Corp (HQ).......610 837-6725
3251 Bath Pike Nazareth (18064) ***(G-11964)***
Essroc Italcementi Group, Nazareth *Also called Lehigh Hanson Ecc Inc* ***(G-11980)***
Esstech Inc.......610 521-3800
48 W Powhattan Ave Essington (19029) ***(G-5543)***
Estari Inc.......717 233-1518
1800 Paxton St Harrisburg (17104) ***(G-7127)***
Estech Division, Linwood *Also called Esschem Inc* ***(G-9989)***
Estee Lauder Companies Inc.......215 826-4247
300 Crossing Dr Bristol (19007) ***(G-2142)***
Estemerwalt Lumber Pdts LLC.......570 729-8572
505 Adams Pond Rd Honesdale (18431) ***(G-7711)***
Esten Lumber Products Inc.......215 536-4976
2015 Trumbauersville Rd Quakertown (18951) ***(G-16190)***
Esterly Concrete Co Inc.......610 376-2791
401 Elm St West Reading (19611) ***(G-19764)***
Esthers Sweet Shop Inc.......412 884-4224
1814 Brownsville Rd Pittsburgh (15210) ***(G-14986)***
Eta Industries Inc.......724 453-1722
1785 Route 68 New Brighton (15066) ***(G-12036)***
Etc, Southampton *Also called Environmental Tectonics Corp* ***(G-17809)***
Etched In Glass.......724 444-0808
5424 William Flynn Hwy Gibsonia (15044) ***(G-6333)***
Etched In Time.......717 334-3600
31 Buford Ave Gettysburg (17325) ***(G-6290)***
Etemco, Lancaster *Also called Electronic Test Eqp Mfg Co* ***(G-9008)***
Eternity Fashion Inc.......215 567-5571
1410 Chestnut St Philadelphia (19102) ***(G-13681)***
Ethan Horwitz Cabinet Mak.......610 948-4889
383 Circle Of Progress Dr Pottstown (19464) ***(G-15987)***
Ethel Maid, Schuylkill Haven *Also called Gardinier Associates Inc* ***(G-17157)***
Ethnic Gourmet Foods Inc.......610 692-2209
700 Old Fern Hill Rd West Chester (19380) ***(G-19552)***
Ethree, Philadelphia *Also called Elemental 3 LLC* ***(G-13667)***
Eti Closeco.......412 822-8250
2014a Babcock Blvd Pittsburgh (15209) ***(G-14987)***
Etsi, Natrona Heights *Also called Electronic Tech Systems Inc* ***(G-11942)***
Ettco Tool & Machine Co Inc.......717 792-1417
1600 6th Ave Ste 114 York (17403) ***(G-20471)***
Euclid Chemical Company.......610 438-2409
3 Adamson St Easton (18042) ***(G-4681)***
Euclid Technologies Inc.......610 515-1842
450 Milano Dr Easton (18040) ***(G-4682)***
Eugene Flynn Logging.......814 772-1219
856 Kemmer Rd Kersey (15846) ***(G-8558)***
Eugene Zapsky.......814 378-6157
266 Alexander Rd Madera (16661) ***(G-10163)***
Eurand Pharmaceuticals Inc.......937 898-9669
790 Township Line Rd Yardley (19067) ***(G-20309)***
Eureka Electrical Products.......814 725-9638
79 Clay St North East (16428) ***(G-12742)***
Eureka Foundry Co.......412 963-7881
4 Shadow Ln Pittsburgh (15238) ***(G-14988)***
Eureka Stone Quarry Inc (PA).......215 822-0593
Lower Stte Pickertown Rds Chalfont (18914) ***(G-2874)***
Eureka Stone Quarry Inc.......570 842-7694
35 Eureka Stone Quarry Rd Moscow (18444) ***(G-11596)***
Eureka Stone Quarry Inc.......570 689-2901
Rr 196 Sterling (18463) ***(G-18049)***
Eureka Stone Quarry Inc.......570 296-6632
460 Route 6 Milford (18337) ***(G-11160)***

ALPHABETIC

Eureka Stone Quarry Inc..215 723-9801
  451 E Reliance Rd Telford (18969) *(G-18288)*

Eureka Stone Quarry Inc..570 992-4444
  2443 Bush Ln Stroudsburg (18360) *(G-18115)*

Eureka Stone Quarry Inc..570 992-4210
  300 Keiser Rd Stroudsburg (18360) *(G-18116)*

Euro Foods Inc (HQ)..570 636-3171
  2008 State Route 940 Freeland (18224) *(G-6194)*

European & American Sausage Co............................215 232-1716
  1242 S American St Ste 46 Philadelphia (19147) *(G-13682)*

Eusa Pharma (usa) Inc (HQ)....................................215 867-4900
  1717 Langhorne Newtown Rd Langhorne (19047) *(G-9295)*

Euthanex Corporation...610 559-0159
  944 14th Ave Unit 1 Bethlehem (18018) *(G-1505)*

Eutsey Lumber Co Inc...724 887-8404
  Star Rte Scottdale (15683) *(G-17191)*

Ev Products Inc..724 352-5288
  143 Zehner School Rd Zelienople (16063) *(G-20799)*

Evans Candy LLC..717 295-7510
  2100 Willow Street Pike Lancaster (17602) *(G-9012)*

Evans Commercial Services LLC..............................412 573-9442
  2000 Fortune Ct Bridgeville (15017) *(G-2061)*

Evans Eagle Burial Vaults Inc (PA)...........................717 656-2213
  15 Graybill Rd Leola (17540) *(G-9781)*

Evans Heat Treating Company.................................215 938-8791
  360 Red Lion Rd Huntingdon Valley (19006) *(G-7979)*

Evans John Sons Incorporated................................215 368-7700
  1 Spring Ave Lansdale (19446) *(G-9365)*

Evans Machining Service Inc..................................412 233-3556
  314 State St Clairton (15025) *(G-3150)*

Evansburg Tool Corporation...................................610 489-7580
  16 Crosskeys Rd Collegeville (19426) *(G-3376)*

Evapco Alcoil Inc...717 347-7500
  3627 Sandhurst Dr York (17406) *(G-20472)*

Evaporated Coatings Inc.......................................215 659-3080
  2365 Maryland Rd Willow Grove (19090) *(G-20116)*

Evco Embouchure Visualizer Co..............................724 224-4817
  120 Evco Ln Tarentum (15084) *(G-18243)*

Evening Sun, The, Hanover *Also called Medianews Group Inc (G-6919)*

Evenlite Inc...215 244-4201
  2575 Metropolitan Dr Feasterville Trevose (19053) *(G-5906)*

Event Horizon LLC..717 557-1427
  810 Old W Chocolate Ave Hershey (17033) *(G-7610)*

Eveos Corporation..412 366-0159
  1888 Pioneer Dr Sewickley (15143) *(G-17388)*

Everclear Valley Inc (PA).......................................724 676-4703
  1820 Mulligan Rd New Florence (15944) *(G-12196)*

Everest Dental LLC...215 671-0188
  9892 Bustleton Ave # 302 Philadelphia (19115) *(G-13683)*

Everest Software LP...412 206-0005
  456 Washington Ave Ste 2 Bridgeville (15017) *(G-2062)*

Everfresh Juice Co Pgh...412 777-9660
  1 Sexton Rd Mc Kees Rocks (15136) *(G-10608)*

Evergreen Group Inc...610 799-2263
  4460 Bachman Dr Schnecksville (18078) *(G-17140)*

Evergreen Metallurgical LLC (HQ)............................724 431-2800
  679 E Butler Rd Butler (16002) *(G-2400)*

Evergreen Oilfld Solutions LLC...............................570 485-9998
  42751 Route 6 Wyalusing (18853) *(G-20251)*

Evergreen Pallet Company......................................717 463-3217
  2647 Free Spring Ch Rd Mc Alisterville (17049) *(G-10549)*

Evergreen Synergies LLC (PA)................................610 239-9425
  221 King Manor Dr King of Prussia (19406) *(G-8617)*

Evergreen Tank Solutions Inc.................................484 268-5168
  4601 Pearce St Philadelphia (19137) *(G-13684)*

Everight Position Tech Corp....................................856 727-9500
  114 Forrest Ave Ste 209 Narberth (19072) *(G-11910)*

Everite Door Co, Everett *Also called Howell Manufacturing Company (G-5573)*

Everite Door Company..814 652-5143
  122 Armory St Everett (15537) *(G-5571)*

Everlast Plastic Lumber Inc....................................610 562-8336
  1000 S 4th St Hamburg (19526) *(G-6839)*

Everpower Wind Holdings Inc (HQ)..........................412 253-9400
  1251 Waterfront Pl Fl 3 Pittsburgh (15222) *(G-14989)*

Everson Tesla Inc..610 746-1520
  614 Gremar Rd Nazareth (18064) *(G-11965)*

Everwine Machine Services, Leola *Also called C Everwine Machine LLC (G-9774)*

Everything Ice Inc (PA)..814 244-5477
  115 School St Salix (15952) *(G-17047)*

Everything Plastics, Philadelphia *Also called Total Plastics Inc (G-14399)*

Everything Postal Inc..610 367-7444
  828a N Route 100 Bechtelsville (19505) *(G-1032)*

Everything Prtg & Shipg Ctr, Bechtelsville *Also called Everything Postal Inc (G-1032)*

Evive Station LLC...724 972-6421
  236 Finley Rd Ste 20 Rostraver Township (15012) *(G-16825)*

Evolution Custom Coach, White Haven *Also called Asone Technologies Inc (G-19846)*

Evolution Energy Services LLC................................412 946-1371
  3935 Washington Rd # 1191 Mc Murray (15317) *(G-10644)*

Evolution Gun Works Inc..215 538-1012
  52 Belmont Ave Quakertown (18951) *(G-16191)*

Evolution Mlding Solutions Inc................................814 807-1982
  1099 Morgan Village Rd Meadville (16335) *(G-10722)*

Evolution Printing Systems.....................................814 724-5831
  217 North St Meadville (16335) *(G-10723)*

Evolve Guest Controls LLC.....................................855 750-9090
  827 Lincoln Ave Unit 2 West Chester (19380) *(G-19553)*

Evonik Corporation..610 990-8100
  1200 W Front St Chester (19013) *(G-3050)*

Evonik Corporation..800 345-3148
  7201 Hamilton Blvd Allentown (18195) *(G-208)*

Evonik Oil Additives Usa Inc (HQ)...........................215 706-5800
  723 Electronic Dr Horsham (19044) *(G-7817)*

Evoqua Water Technologies Corp (PA).......................724 772-0044
  210 6th Ave Ste 3300 Pittsburgh (15222) *(G-14990)*

Evoqua Water Technologies LLC.............................724 827-8181
  118 Park Rd Darlington (16115) *(G-4028)*

Evoqua Water Technologies LLC.............................215 638-7700
  258 Dunksferry Rd Bensalem (19020) *(G-1192)*

Evraz Inc NA...610 743-5970
  1290 Broadcasting Rd Reading (19610) *(G-16381)*

Ewald A Stellrecht Inc...610 363-1141
  21 S Caln Rd Coatesville (19320) *(G-3302)*

Ewt Holdings III Corp (PA).....................................724 772-0044
  210 6th Ave Ste 3300 Pittsburgh (15222) *(G-14991)*

Exact Machine Service Inc.....................................717 848-2121
  144 Roosevelt Ave York (17401) *(G-20473)*

Excalbur Mch Fbrction - Vnport, Beaver *Also called Esmark Excalibur LLC (G-981)*

Excel, Philadelphia *Also called Windle Mech Solutions Inc (G-14479)*

Excel Glass and Granite...724 523-6190
  103 Jayhawk Dr Jeannette (15644) *(G-8255)*

Excel Machine Co...215 624-8600
  6601 Marsden St Philadelphia (19135) *(G-13685)*

Excel Signworks..412 337-2966
  132 23rd St Pittsburgh (15215) *(G-14992)*

Excel Sportswear Inc..412 856-7616
  15 Forbes Rd Trafford (15085) *(G-18455)*

Excel-Pro...610 845-9752
  11 Mountain Rd Barto (19504) *(G-942)*

Excela Health Holding Co Inc..................................724 832-4450
  532 W Pittsburgh St Greensburg (15601) *(G-6665)*

Excell Cement Technologies, Sarver *Also called Harsco Minerals PA LLC (G-17071)*

Excellent Tool Inc..814 337-7705
  18879 E Cole Rd Meadville (16335) *(G-10724)*

Excelsior Blower Systems Inc (PA)..........................610 921-9558
  331 June Ave Blandon (19510) *(G-1753)*

Excl Inc..412 856-7616
  15 Forbes Rd Trafford (15085) *(G-18456)*

Excl Sportswear, Trafford *Also called Excl Inc (G-18456)*

Exclusive Supplements Inc.....................................412 787-2770
  1231 Elm Dr Oakdale (15071) *(G-12898)*

Exco Resources LLC (HQ)......................................724 720-2500
  13448 State Route 422 # 1 Kittanning (16201) *(G-8768)*

Execumold Inc...814 864-2535
  1649 Lee Rd Waterford (16441) *(G-19262)*

Executive Apparel Inc...215 464-5400
  2150 Kubach Rd Philadelphia (19116) *(G-13686)*

Executive Distributors Intl.....................................610 608-1664
  400 Morris Ave Bryn Mawr (19010) *(G-2323)*

Executive Print Solutions Inc..................................570 421-1437
  1250 N 9th St Unit 101 Stroudsburg (18360) *(G-18117)*

Executive Printing Company Inc..............................717 664-3636
  656 W Newport Rd Elm (17521) *(G-4956)*

Executool...814 836-1141
  941 Guetner Ave Erie (16505) *(G-5284)*

Executool Prcision Tooling Inc................................814 836-1141
  2727 W 16th St Erie (16505) *(G-5285)*

Exedyne Manufacturing Services.............................724 651-5100
  1527 Forestview Dr Pittsburgh (15234) *(G-14993)*

Exeter Architectural Products (PA)...........................570 693-4220
  243 W 8th St Wyoming (18644) *(G-20277)*

Exeter Printing, Reading *Also called Guy Hrezik (G-16397)*

Exhaust Track Inc (PA)..215 675-1021
  1011 Howard Rd Warminster (18974) *(G-18875)*

Exhibit G LLC...215 302-2260
  1701 Welsh Rd Philadelphia (19115) *(G-13687)*

Exhibits By Promotion Centre, York *Also called Promotion Centre Inc (G-20645)*

Exide Batteries, Downingtown *Also called Exide Technologies (G-4226)*

Exide Corporation Smelter......................................610 921-4003
  300 Spring Valley Rd Reading (19605) *(G-16382)*

Exide Technologies...717 464-2721
  829 Paramount Ave Lampeter (17537) *(G-8917)*

Exide Technologies...610 269-0429
  472 Boot Rd Downingtown (19335) *(G-4226)*

Exide Technologies...724 239-2006
  106 Simko Blvd Ste 106 # 106 Charleroi (15022) *(G-3012)*

Exide Technologies...610 921-4055
  3000 Montrose Ave Reading (19605) *(G-16383)*

Exide Technologies...304 345-5616
  236 Finley Rd Ste 15 Rostraver Township (15012) *(G-16826)*

Exigo Manufacturing Inc 484 285-0200
3486 Gun Club Rd Nazareth (18064) *(G-11966)*

Exim Steel & Shipbroking Inc 215 369-9746
1215 Knox Dr Yardley (19067) *(G-20310)*

Exit Store LLC 310 305-4646
303 W Lancaster Ave # 138 Wayne (19087) *(G-19326)*

Exone Company (PA) 724 863-9663
127 Industry Blvd North Huntingdon (15642) *(G-12769)*

Exotic Car Gear Inc 215 371-2855
533 S Sumneytown Pike North Wales (19454) *(G-12800)*

Expac Pre-Press Service Group, Downingtown *Also called Expert Pr-Press Consulting Ltd (G-4227)*

Expansion Seal Technologies 215 513-4300
334 Godshall Dr Harleysville (19438) *(G-7033)*

Expensewatch Inc 610 397-0532
620 W Germantown Pike Plymouth Meeting (19462) *(G-15842)*

Expert Pr-Press Consulting Ltd 484 401-9821
1030 Boot Rd Downingtown (19335) *(G-4227)*

Expert Process Systems LLC 570 424-0581
745 Main St Ste 202 Stroudsburg (18360) *(G-18118)*

Explorations Inc 814 365-2105
9590 Route 536 Punxsutawney (15767) *(G-16137)*

Export Boxing & Crating Inc 412 675-1000
18 Allegheny Sq Glassport (15045) *(G-6412)*

Export USA LLC 215 949-3380
103 Verdant Rd Levittown (19057) *(G-9835)*

Express Business Center, Trexlertown *Also called Valley Business Services Inc (G-18511)*

Express Business Center Inc 610 366-1970
5539 Stonecroft Ln Allentown (18106) *(G-209)*

Express Check Cashing, New Freedom *Also called Express Money Services Inc (G-12208)*

Express Money Services Inc 717 235-5993
16 Mccurley Dr New Freedom (17349) *(G-12208)*

Express Optical Laboratories, Brownsville *Also called Novotny Micheal (G-2313)*

Express Press Inc 412 824-1000
334 Penn Center Blvd Pittsburgh (15235) *(G-14994)*

Express Printing 215 357-7033
324 2nd Street Pike # 14 Southampton (18966) *(G-17810)*

Express Prtg & Graphics Inc 724 274-7700
1801 Pittsburgh St Cheswick (15024) *(G-3107)*

Express Screen Printing, Langhorne *Also called Express Screenprinting (G-9296)*

Express Screenprinting 215 579-8819
219 Shady Brook Dr Langhorne (19047) *(G-9296)*

Express Sign Outlet Inc 610 336-9636
4865 Hamilton Blvd 100 Wescosville (18106) *(G-19489)*

Express, The, Lock Haven *Also called Lock Haven Express (G-10090)*

Express-Times, Easton *Also called Penn Jersey Advance Inc (G-4742)*

Express-Times, The, Bethlehem *Also called Penn Jersey Advance Inc (G-1593)*

Expression Tees 631 523-5673
161 Philips Rd Exton (19341) *(G-5674)*

Expressway Printing Inc 215 244-0233
1800 Mearns Rd Ste V Warminster (18974) *(G-18876)*

Extec Eastern, Marcus Hook *Also called Screen Service Tech Inc (G-10454)*

Extech/Exterior Tech Inc 412 781-0991
200 Bridge St Pittsburgh (15223) *(G-14995)*

Exterran Energy Solutions LP 724 935-7660
12330 Perry Hwy Ste 220 Wexford (15090) *(G-19799)*

Extorr Inc 724 337-3000
307 Columbia Rd New Kensington (15068) *(G-12339)*

Extra Factors 717 859-1166
99 Locust Bend Rd Ephrata (17522) *(G-5102)*

Extramet Products LLC (PA) 724 532-3041
2890 Ligonier St Latrobe (15650) *(G-9475)*

Extrel Cms LLC 412 963-7530
575 Epsilon Dr Ste 2 Pittsburgh (15238) *(G-14996)*

Extreme Machine and Fabg Inc 724 342-4340
2340 Quality Ln Ste 1 West Middlesex (16159) *(G-19724)*

Extreme Manufacturing Inc 717 369-0044
9230 Mountain Brook Rd Saint Thomas (17252) *(G-17039)*

Extremity Imaging Partners 610 432-1055
3131 College Heights Blvd # 400 Allentown (18104) *(G-210)*

Extremity Imaging Partners (PA) 724 493-7452
4500 Brooktree Rd Ste 300 Wexford (15090) *(G-19800)*

Extrude Hone LLC (HQ) 724 863-5900
235 Industry Blvd Irwin (15642) *(G-8162)*

Extruded Plastic Solutions 610 756-6602
8891 Kings Hwy Kempton (19529) *(G-8491)*

Eye Catcher Graphics Inc 814 946-4080
2513 6th Ave Altoona (16602) *(G-502)*

Eye Catchers, Altoona *Also called Eye Catcher Graphics Inc (G-502)*

Eye Design LLC (PA) 610 409-1900
220 W 5th Ave Trappe (19426) *(G-18468)*

Eye-Bot Aerial Solutions LLC 724 904-7706
701 5th Ave Ste 108 New Kensington (15068) *(G-12340)*

Eyeland Optical 888 603-3937
769 E Main St Mount Joy (17552) *(G-11656)*

Eyeland Optical Corp (PA) 215 368-1600
1030 Arch St Ste 1 Philadelphia (19107) *(G-13688)*

Eyenavision Inc 412 456-2736
1501 Reedsdale St Ste 203 Pittsburgh (15233) *(G-14997)*

Eysters Machine and Wire Pdts, Shrewsbury *Also called Eysters Machine Shop Inc (G-17583)*

Eysters Machine Shop Inc 717 227-8400
50 W Clearview Dr Shrewsbury (17361) *(G-17583)*

EZ Garment Printing Inc 570 703-0961
501 Wyoming Ave Scranton (18509) *(G-17236)*

EZ Signs LLC 866 349-5444
10016 Bridle Rd Fl 1 Phila (19116) *(G-13311)*

EZ To Use Directories Inc (PA) 814 949-7100
1811 Valley View Blvd Altoona (16602) *(G-503)*

Ez-Flo Fertilizing Systems, Moon Township *Also called Ez-Flo Injection Systems Inc (G-11487)*

Ez-Flo Injection Systems Inc (PA) 412 996-2161
400 Lee Dr Apt 75 Moon Township (15108) *(G-11487)*

Ez-Plant Software Inc 814 421-6744
211 E Sample St Ebensburg (15931) *(G-4785)*

Ezeflow Usa Inc 724 658-3711
1400 New Butler Rd New Castle (16101) *(G-12090)*

Eznergy LLC 215 361-7332
411 Shipwrighter Way Lansdale (19446) *(G-9366)*

Ezy Products Co Inc 570 822-9600
530 Blackman St Wilkes Barre (18702) *(G-19919)*

F & D Coal Sales Co Inc 570 455-4745
803 S Church St Hazle Township (18201) *(G-7456)*

F & G Monument Lettering LLC 814 247-5032
517 Bridge St Hastings (16646) *(G-7260)*

F & H Wax Works Ltd 610 336-0308
6070 Eli Cir Macungie (18062) *(G-10145)*

F & M Designs Inc 717 564-8120
7412 Derry St Harrisburg (17111) *(G-7128)*

F & M Hat Company Inc 717 336-5505
103 Walnut St Denver (17517) *(G-4073)*

F & R Cargo Express LLC 610 351-9200
716 W Liberty St Allentown (18102) *(G-211)*

F & R Materials, Duncannon *Also called Furnley H Frisch (G-4445)*

F & S Tool Inc 814 838-7991
2300 Powell Ave Erie (16506) *(G-5286)*

F A Davis Company (PA) 215 568-2270
1915 Arch St Philadelphia (19103) *(G-13689)*

F and L Medical Products Co, Vandergrift *Also called Fred Foust (G-18727)*

F and T LP 215 355-2060
434 W Street Rd 436 Feasterville Trevose (19053) *(G-5907)*

F B F Inc 215 322-7110
1145 Industrial Blvd Southampton (18966) *(G-17811)*

F B F Industries Inc 215 322-7110
1145 Industrial Blvd Southampton (18966) *(G-17812)*

F C Young & Co Inc 215 788-9226
400 Howell St Bristol (19007) *(G-2143)*

F Creative Impressions Inc 215 743-7577
240 Lexington Ave Lansdowne (19050) *(G-9432)*

F Creative Impressions Inc 215 743-7577
240 Lexington Ave Philadelphia (19124) *(G-13690)*

F DEFrank& Son Custom Cabinets 724 430-1812
593 Industrial Park Rd Smock (15480) *(G-17665)*

F F Frickanisce Iron Works 724 568-2001
1124 Airport Rd Vandergrift (15690) *(G-18726)*

F F I, Aldan *Also called Foam Fair Industries Inc (G-59)*

F Ferrato Foods Company 412 431-1479
203 Boggs Ave Pittsburgh (15211) *(G-14998)*

F L W of PA, Malvern *Also called Flw of Pa Inc (G-10237)*

F M Browns Sons Incorporated 610 944-7654
118 W Main St Fleetwood (19522) *(G-5972)*

F M Browns Sons Incorporated (PA) 800 334-8816
205 Woodrow Ave Reading (19608) *(G-16384)*

F M Browns Sons Incorporated 610 582-2741
127 S Furnace St Birdsboro (19508) *(G-1695)*

F M I, Allentown *Also called Fragrance Manufacturing Inc (G-218)*

F M P Healthcare Products 800 611-7776
1018 Ryeland Ct Bridgeville (15017) *(G-2063)*

F M T, Lehighton *Also called Flow Measurement Technologies (G-9714)*

F P Engbert Discount Guns 724 465-9756
102b Adams Cir Indiana (15701) *(G-8098)*

F R Industries Inc 412 242-5903
557 Long Rd Pittsburgh (15235) *(G-14999)*

F R P Fabricators Inc 814 643-2525
10168 Frp Rd Huntingdon (16652) *(G-7943)*

F S Convergent 484 581-7065
460 E Swedesford Rd Wayne (19087) *(G-19327)*

F Tinker and Sons Company 412 781-3553
5665 Butler St Pittsburgh (15201) *(G-15000)*

F W B & Sons Welding Inc 610 543-0348
206 N State Rd Springfield (19064) *(G-17913)*

F W Echonhofer Company, Horsham *Also called Theodore Fazen (G-7858)*

F W Lang Co 267 401-8293
121 N Concord Ave Havertown (19083) *(G-7421)*

F X Smiths Sons Co 717 637-5232
372 North St Mc Sherrystown (17344) *(G-10650)*

F&F Machine Works 717 335-3008
23 Blue Jay Dr Stevens (17578) *(G-18050)*

A
L
P
H
A
B
E
T
I
C

F&M Surfaces Inc 717 267-3799
2295 Molly Pitcher Hwy Chambersburg (17202) *(G-2931)*

F&T Apparel LLC (HQ) 646 839-7000
4000 Chemical Rd Ste 500 Plymouth Meeting (19462) *(G-15843)*

F&T Apparel LLC 610 828-8400
4000 Chemical Rd Ste 500 Plymouth Meeting (19462) *(G-15844)*

F.I.R.E.S. Group, Levittown *Also called Super Can Industries Inc (G-9866)*

F/K Industries Inc 412 655-4982
506 Elaine Dr Pittsburgh (15236) *(G-15001)*

F2si, Pittsburgh *Also called Fidelity Flight Simulation Inc (G-15016)*

F3 Metalworx Inc (PA) 814 725-8637
12069 E Main Rd North East (16428) *(G-12743)*

Fab Dubrufaut Woodworking 215 533-4853
5635 Tulip St Philadelphia (19124) *(G-13691)*

Fab Tech Industries 717 597-4919
80 Commerce Ave Greencastle (17225) *(G-6610)*

Fab Tech V Industries Inc (PA) 717 597-4919
68 Commerce Ave Greencastle (17225) *(G-6611)*

Fab Universal Corp (PA) 412 621-0902
5001 Baum Blvd Ste 770 Pittsburgh (15213) *(G-15002)*

Fab-Rick Industries Inc 717 859-5633
28 Penn Sq Fl 1 Lancaster (17603) *(G-9013)*

Fab-TEC Industries Inc 412 262-1144
3500 University Blvd # 1 Coraopolis (15108) *(G-3690)*

Fabbco Steel Inc 717 792-4904
101 Mundis Race Rd York (17406) *(G-20474)*

Fabco Inc (HQ) 814 944-1631
1128 9th Ave Altoona (16602) *(G-504)*

Fabco Inc 814 944-1631
2111 Beale Ave Rear Altoona (16601) *(G-505)*

Fabcon East LLC 610 530-4470
1200 Morear Mahanoy City (17948) *(G-10173)*

Fabcote, York *Also called Fox Pool Lancaster Inc (G-20487)*

Faber Burner Company 570 748-4009
1000 E Bald Eagle St Lock Haven (17745) *(G-10088)*

Faber Fab, Lock Haven *Also called Faber Burner Company (G-10088)*

Fabri-Kal Corporation 570 501-2018
150 Lions Dr Hazle Township (18202) *(G-7457)*

Fabri-Kal Corporation 570 454-6672
955 Oak Hill Rd Mountain Top (18707) *(G-11759)*

Fabri-Weld LLC 814 490-7324
1133 W 18th St Erie (16502) *(G-5287)*

Fabric Development Inc 215 536-1420
1217 W Mill St Quakertown (18951) *(G-16192)*

Fabricated Components Inc 570 421-4110
2018 W Main St Stroudsburg (18360) *(G-18119)*

Fabricated Products, Bedford *Also called L B Foster Company (G-1060)*

Fabricated Products 570 588-1794
Milford Rd Bushkill (18324) *(G-2365)*

Fabricating Technology Inc 814 774-4403
409 Noble Rd Girard (16417) *(G-6388)*

Fabrication Store, The, Hazleton *Also called Kelly Iron Works Inc (G-7505)*

Fabrications Costume Co, Philadelphia *Also called David Moscinski (G-13609)*

Fabricon Inc 610 921-0203
4860 5th Street Hwy Temple (19560) *(G-18329)*

Fabrics For Industry Division, Huntingdon Valley *Also called Hydra-Matic Packing Co Inc (G-7995)*

Fabrifoam Products, Exton *Also called Applied Technology Intl Ltd (G-5645)*

Fabritech Inc 610 430-0027
935 Skyline Dr Chester Springs (19425) *(G-3078)*

Fabtech, Girard *Also called Fabricating Technology Inc (G-6388)*

Fabtex Inc (PA) 570 275-7500
29 Woodbine Ln Danville (17821) *(G-4000)*

Fabtex Inc 910 739-0019
29 Woodbine Ln Danville (17821) *(G-4001)*

Fabworks Inc 570 814-1515
Rr 3 Box 272-4 Dallas (18612) *(G-3962)*

Facchiano Ironworks Inc 610 865-1503
1762 Acker Ave Bethlehem (18015) *(G-1506)*

Facio Concepts LLC 717 945-8609
1564 Main St Ste 504 East Earl (17519) *(G-4543)*

Factor Medical LLC 215 862-5345
6542 Lower York Rd Ste A New Hope (18938) *(G-12301)*

Factor X Graffics 717 590-7402
145 Salem Church Rd Mechanicsburg (17050) *(G-10842)*

Factor X Graffics LLC 717 458-8336
145 Salem Church Rd Ste 2 Carlisle (17015) *(G-2711)*

Factory Linens Inc (PA) 610 825-2790
40 Portland Rd Conshohocken (19428) *(G-3545)*

Factory Unlocked LLC 724 882-9940
720 E Lacock St Pittsburgh (15212) *(G-15003)*

FAD Corporation 610 872-3844
2000 Industrial Hwy Ste 5 Eddystone (19022) *(G-4802)*

Faddis Concrete Products, Kutztown *Also called Hessian Co Ltd (G-8844)*

Faddis Concrete Products, Kutztown *Also called Hessian Co Ltd (G-8845)*

Faddis Concrete Products, Honey Brook *Also called Hessian Co Ltd (G-7747)*

Faddis Concrete Products, New Castle *Also called Hessian Co Ltd (G-12104)*

Fairchild Semiconductor Corp 570 474-6761
125 Crestwood Dr Mountain Top (18707) *(G-11760)*

Fairfax Precision Mfg 814 348-1184
13358 Lincoln Hwy Everett (15537) *(G-5572)*

Fairfield Confectionery 724 654-3888
2570 Blossom Ln New Castle (16105) *(G-12091)*

Fairfield Manufacturing Co Inc 570 368-8624
213 Streibeigh Ln Montoursville (17754) *(G-11438)*

Fairmans Roof Trusses Inc 724 349-6778
1020 Craig Rd Creekside (15732) *(G-3875)*

Fairmans Wood Processing Inc 724 349-6778
1020 Craig Rd Creekside (15732) *(G-3876)*

Fairmount Automation Inc 610 356-9840
10 Clipper Rd Conshohocken (19428) *(G-3546)*

Fairmount Minerals 724 873-9039
1432 Route 519 Eighty Four (15330) *(G-4840)*

Fairview Coal Co Inc 814 776-1158
324 Allenhurst Ave Ridgway (15853) *(G-16708)*

Fairview Manufacturing Corp 814 474-5581
2505 Avonia Rd Fairview (16415) *(G-5821)*

Fairview Swiss Cheese, Fredonia *Also called John Koller and Son Inc (G-6185)*

Fairway Building Products LLC (PA) 717 653-6777
53 Eby Chiques Rd Mount Joy (17552) *(G-11657)*

Fairwinds Manufacturing Inc 724 662-5210
68 Limber Rd Jackson Center (16133) *(G-8227)*

Fairylogue Press 717 713-5788
4173 Grouse Ct Apt 115 Mechanicsburg (17050) *(G-10843)*

Faivre Mch & Fabrication Inc 814 724-7160
1369 S Main St Meadville (16335) *(G-10725)*

Falcon Manufacturing Company 215 249-0212
107 High St Dublin (18917) *(G-4432)*

Falcon Plastics Inc 724 222-2620
250 W Wylie Ave Washington (15301) *(G-19172)*

Falcon Propane LLC 570 207-1711
1630 Main St Blakely (18447) *(G-1747)*

Fallene, Norristown *Also called Fallien Cosmeceuticals Ltd (G-12655)*

Fallien Cosmeceuticals Ltd 610 630-6800
2495 Blvd Of The Generals Norristown (19403) *(G-12655)*

Falls Creek Powdered Metals 814 265-8771
82 Industrial Park Dr Brockway (15824) *(G-2225)*

Falls Mfg Co 215 736-2557
129 Canal Rd Fairless Hills (19030) *(G-5778)*

Falosk Contract Machine Inc 724 228-0567
169 Vaneal Rd Washington (15301) *(G-19173)*

Falvey Steel Castings 484 678-2174
862 Maple Grove Rd Mohnton (19540) *(G-11263)*

Famco Manufacturing Div, Pittsburgh *Also called Allen Gauge & Tool Company (G-14684)*

Fame Manufacturing Inc (PA) 814 763-5645
329 Mill St Saegertown (16433) *(G-16913)*

Family Business Magazine, Philadelphia *Also called Family Business Publishing Co (G-13692)*

Family Business Publishing Co 215 567-3200
1845 Walnut St Ste 900 Philadelphia (19103) *(G-13692)*

Family Farm Creamery 412 418-2596
786 Western Ave Washington (15301) *(G-19174)*

Family First Sports Park 814 866-5425
8155 Oliver Rd Ste 1 Erie (16509) *(G-5288)*

Family Food Products Inc 215 633-1515
1271 Ford Rd Bensalem (19020) *(G-1193)*

Family Heir-Loom Weavers Inc 717 246-2431
775 Meadowview Dr Red Lion (17356) *(G-16594)*

Family Ready Labor Inc 717 615-4900
53 N Plum St Lancaster (17602) *(G-9014)*

Family-Life Media-Com Inc 724 543-6397
114 S Jefferson St Kittanning (16201) *(G-8769)*

Famous Forth Street Cookies Co, Philadelphia *Also called Bainbridge Group Inc (G-13442)*

Fangio Enterprises Inc 570 383-1030
416 Main St Unit 4 Dickson City (18519) *(G-4120)*

Fangio Enterprises Inc (PA) 570 383-1030
905 Stanton Rd Olyphant (18447) *(G-12990)*

Fangio Lighting, Dickson City *Also called Fangio Enterprises Inc (G-4120)*

Fangio Lighting, Olyphant *Also called Fangio Enterprises Inc (G-12990)*

Fantasy Printing Supplies LLC 215 569-3744
1243 Vine St Philadelphia (19107) *(G-13693)*

Farason Corporation 610 383-6224
855 Fox Chase Coatesville (19320) *(G-3303)*

Farel Corp 814 495-4625
300 Grant St South Fork (15956) *(G-17774)*

Fargo Assemblies 610 272-5726
800 W Washington St Norristown (19401) *(G-12656)*

Fargo Assembly of Pa Inc 717 866-5800
Apple & Curtis St Richland (17087) *(G-16687)*

Fargo Assembly of Pa Inc (PA) 610 272-6850
800 W Washington St Norristown (19401) *(G-12657)*

Farm Bilt, Gap *Also called Farm-Bilt Machine LLC (G-6251)*

Farm Journal Inc (PA) 215 557-8900
1600 Market St Ste 1530 Philadelphia (19103) *(G-13694)*

Farm Journal Media, Philadelphia *Also called Farm Journal Inc (G-13694)*

Farm-Bilt Machine LLC 717 442-5020
633 Quarry Rd Gap (17527) ***(G-6251)***
Farmco Manufacturing LP 717 768-7769
2937 Irishtown Rd Ronks (17572) ***(G-16806)***
Farmer Boy Ag Inc (PA) 717 866-7565
50 W Stoever Ave Myerstown (17067) ***(G-11885)***
Farmer's Friend, The, Towanda *Also called The Scranton Times L P* ***(G-18435)***
Farmer's Lumber & Supply Co., Media *Also called Cedar Forest Products Company* ***(G-10917)***
Farmers Co-Op, Reading *Also called Clover Farms Dairy Company* ***(G-16346)***
Farmers From Italy Foods LLC 484 480-3836
8 Creek Pkwy Fl 2 Upper Chichester (19061) ***(G-18661)***
Farmers Pride Inc (HQ) 717 865-6626
154 W Main St Fredericksburg (17026) ***(G-6174)***
Farmers Union Coop Assn 717 597-3191
30 E Walter Ave Greencastle (17225) ***(G-6612)***
Farmshine, Brownstown *Also called Krieg Dieter* ***(G-2308)***
Farnsworth Gowns and Fnrl Sups 412 881-4696
1806 Brownsville Rd Pittsburgh (15210) ***(G-15004)***
Faro Laser Division LLC 610 444-2300
222 Gale Ln Kennett Square (19348) ***(G-8510)***
Faro Technologies Inc 407 333-9911
290 National Rd Exton (19341) ***(G-5675)***
Faro Technologies Inc 412 559-7737
1216 Colescott St Pittsburgh (15205) ***(G-15005)***
Farrs Meat Processing 570 827-2241
367 Erickson Rd Lawrenceville (16929) ***(G-9542)***
Farzati Manufacturing Corp 724 836-3508
125 Theobold Ave Ste 2 Greensburg (15601) ***(G-6666)***
Fashion Optical Inc 724 339-4595
228 Buffalo Plz Sarver (16055) ***(G-17069)***
Fassett Mfg Co 724 446-7870
Wendel Herminie Rd Wendel (15691) ***(G-19480)***
Fassinger Products & Engraving 412 563-6226
3526 Willow Ave Pittsburgh (15234) ***(G-15006)***
Fast By Ferracci Inc 215 657-1276
1372 Edgewood Ave Abington (19001) ***(G-12)***
Fast Fill, Schuylkill Haven *Also called Vista Fuels LLC* ***(G-17170)***
Fast Ink Apparel 717 328-5057
111 N Main St Mercersburg (17236) ***(G-10986)***
Fast Ink Screen Prtg & EMB Co, Mercersburg *Also called Danowski* ***(G-10985)***
Fast Shelter Inc 610 415-0225
659 S 2nd Ave Phoenixville (19460) ***(G-14549)***
Fast Signs of Willow Grove 215 830-9960
707 Easton Rd Willow Grove (19090) ***(G-20117)***
Fast Signs of Wynnewood 484 278-4839
921 Montgomery Ave Penn Valley (19072) ***(G-13235)***
Fast Time Screen Printing 724 463-9007
2030 Shelly Dr Indiana (15701) ***(G-8099)***
Fastsigns, Montgomeryville *Also called Laurelind Corp* ***(G-11401)***
Fastsigns, Pittsburgh *Also called Krohmalys Printing Co* ***(G-15201)***
Fastsigns, Mechanicsburg *Also called B and B Signs and Graphics* ***(G-10821)***
Fastsigns, Fairless Hills *Also called Pls Signs LLC* ***(G-5791)***
Fastsigns, Lancaster *Also called Lancaster Sign Source Inc* ***(G-9106)***
Fastsigns, Penn Valley *Also called Fast Signs of Wynnewood* ***(G-13235)***
Fastsigns, Montgomeryville *Also called Laurelind Corp* ***(G-11402)***
Fastsigns, Harrisburg *Also called J & S Signco Inc* ***(G-7156)***
Fastsigns, Monroeville *Also called Raucmin Seven LLC* ***(G-11352)***
Fastsigns, Philadelphia *Also called Exhibit G LLC* ***(G-13687)***
Fastsigns, York *Also called Two Toys Inc* ***(G-20693)***
Fastsigns, Pittsburgh *Also called NMB Signs Inc* ***(G-15342)***
Fastsigns, Scranton *Also called Koroteo Investments Inc* ***(G-17252)***
Fastsigns, Erie *Also called Sign Here Inc* ***(G-5478)***
Fastsigns, Monroeville *Also called Star Organization Inc* ***(G-11359)***
Fastsigns, Allentown *Also called Jeff Enterprises Inc* ***(G-268)***
Fastsigns, Willow Grove *Also called Fast Signs of Willow Grove* ***(G-20117)***
Fastsigns 570 824-7446
763 Kidder St Wilkes Barre (18702) ***(G-19920)***
Fastsigns 610 280-6100
307 E Lincoln Hwy Exton (19341) ***(G-5676)***
Fastsigns 610 296-0400
257 Schuylkill Rd Phoenixville (19460) ***(G-14550)***
Fastsigns International Inc 717 840-6400
2801 E Market St York (17402) ***(G-20475)***
Fastsigns of Uniontown 724 430-7446
140 Morgantown St Uniontown (15401) ***(G-18626)***
Faull Fabricating Inc 724 458-7662
530 Courtney Mill Rd Grove City (16127) ***(G-6784)***
Fault Line Oil Corporation (PA) 814 368-5901
652 Derrick Rd Bradford (16701) ***(G-1968)***
Faux Arts Galleries, Oakmont *Also called Paul William Boyle* ***(G-12923)***
Fawn Embroidery Punching Svcs 717 382-4855
1537 Main St New Park (17352) ***(G-12430)***
Fawn Industries Inc 717 382-4855
1537 Main St New Park (17352) ***(G-12431)***
Fawnwood Energy Inc (PA) 724 753-2416
105 Daubenspeck Rd Bruin (16022) ***(G-2314)***
Fay Studios 215 672-2599
308 S Linden Ave Hatboro (19040) ***(G-7285)***
Fayette Springs Farm, Chalk Hill *Also called Christian W Klay Winery Inc* ***(G-2895)***
Fayette Steel Division, Scottdale *Also called Mlp Steel LLC* ***(G-17195)***
FB Leopold Company Inc 724 452-6300
227 S Division St Ste 1 Zelienople (16063) ***(G-20800)***
FB Shoemaker LLC 717 852-8029
2159 White St Ste 3 York (17404) ***(G-20476)***
FBC Chemical Corporation (PA) 724 625-3116
634 Route 228 Mars (16046) ***(G-10497)***
Fca LLC 309 792-3444
844 Route 6 Ste 3 Corry (16407) ***(G-3760)***
Fce LLC 215 947-7333
2600 Philmont Ave Huntingdon Valley (19006) ***(G-7980)***
FCG Inc 215 343-4617
222 Valley Rd Warrington (18976) ***(G-19117)***
Fci Electronics, Etters *Also called Fci USA LLC* ***(G-5548)***
Fci USA LLC (HQ) 717 938-7200
825 Old Trail Rd Etters (17319) ***(G-5548)***
Fclz Holdings Inc 412 788-4991
240 Vista Park Dr Pittsburgh (15205) ***(G-15007)***
Fd Pace, Whitehall *Also called Pace Environmental* ***(G-19885)***
Feast Mag LLC 484 343-5483
1210 W Wynnewood Rd Wynnewood (19096) ***(G-20267)***
FEC Technologies Inc 717 764-5959
700 Willow Springs Ln York (17406) ***(G-20477)***
Fedchem LLC 610 837-1808
275 Keystone Dr Bethlehem (18020) ***(G-1507)***
Fedchem LLC (HQ) 610 837-1808
275 Keystone Dr Bethlehem (18020) ***(G-1508)***
Fedco Manufacturing Inc 724 863-2252
11585 Rte 993 Larimer (15647) ***(G-9451)***
Fedegari Technologies Inc 215 453-0400
1228 Bethlehem Pike Sellersville (18960) ***(G-17346)***
Fedegari Technologies Inc 215 453-2180
1228 Bethlehem Pike Sellersville (18960) ***(G-17347)***
Federal Business Products Inc 570 454-2451
150 Jaycee Dr West Hazleton (18202) ***(G-19709)***
Federal Metal Products Inc 610 847-2077
174 Center Hill Rd Ferndale (18921) ***(G-5950)***
Federal Pretzel Baking Co 215 467-0505
636 Federal St Philadelphia (19147) ***(G-13695)***
Federal Prison Industries 570 524-0096
2400 Robert F Miller Dr Lewisburg (17837) ***(G-9906)***
Federal Prison Industries 570 544-7343
Interstate 81 & Route 901 Rt 901 Minersville (17954) ***(G-11254)***
Federal White Cement 814 946-8950
154 Woods Ln Altoona (16601) ***(G-506)***
Federal-Mogul Motorparts LLC 717 430-5021
20 Leo Ln York (17406) ***(G-20478)***
Federal-Mogul Motorparts LLC 717 430-5021
20 Leo Ln York (17406) ***(G-20479)***
Federal-Mogul Powertrain LLC 610 363-2600
241 Welsh Pool Rd Exton (19341) ***(G-5677)***
Fedex Corporation 412 441-2379
5996 Penn Cir S Ste D-102 Pittsburgh (15206) ***(G-15008)***
Fedex Office & Print Svcs Inc 412 856-8016
4010 William Penn Hwy Monroeville (15146) ***(G-11337)***
Fedex Office & Print Svcs Inc 215 386-5679
3535 Market St Ste 10b Philadelphia (19104) ***(G-13696)***
Fedex Office & Print Svcs Inc 412 788-0552
215 Summit Park Dr Pittsburgh (15275) ***(G-15009)***
Fedex Office & Print Svcs Inc 215 576-1687
636 Old York Rd Jenkintown (19046) ***(G-8287)***
Fedex Office & Print Svcs Inc 412 835-4005
1720 Washington Rd Pittsburgh (15241) ***(G-15010)***
Fedex Office & Print Svcs Inc 412 366-9750
4771 Mcknight Rd Pittsburgh (15237) ***(G-15011)***
Fedex Office Print & Ship, Pittsburgh *Also called Fedex Office & Print Svcs Inc* ***(G-15010)***
Fedinetz Co, Mc Donald *Also called Fedinetz Sawmill* ***(G-10573)***
Fedinetz Sawmill 724 796-9461
40 Belgium Hollow Rd Mc Donald (15057) ***(G-10573)***
Fedor Fabrication Inc 610 431-7150
207 Carter Dr Ste A West Chester (19382) ***(G-19554)***
Feedmobile Inc 717 626-8318
727 Furnace Hills Pike Lititz (17543) ***(G-10007)***
Fehl Awning Company Inc 717 776-3162
12 W Main St Walnut Bottom (17266) ***(G-18789)***
Fehl's Home & Garden, Temple *Also called K D Home & Garden Inc* ***(G-18331)***
Fejes Signs 724 527-7446
703 Bullitt Ave Jeannette (15644) ***(G-8256)***
Felchar Manufacturing Corp 607 723-4076
2323 Reach Rd Williamsport (17701) ***(G-20012)***
Feltch's Machine Shop, Hanover *Also called Wel-Mac Inc* ***(G-6974)***
Femco Holdings LLC (PA) 906 576-0418
754 S Main Street Ext Punxsutawney (15767) ***(G-16138)***

ALPHABETIC

Femco Machine Company LLC (PA) 814 938-9763
  754 S Main Street Ext Punxsutawney (15767) *(G-16139)*
Femmephrma Cnsmr Halthcare LLC 610 995-0801
  175 Strafford Ave Ste 275 Wayne (19087) *(G-19328)*
Fence Authority, West Chester *Also called The Adirondack Group Inc (G-19660)*
Fence City, Hatfield *Also called Prestige Fence Co Inc (G-7385)*
Fencor Graphics Inc 215 745-2266
  1505 Ford Rd Bensalem (19020) *(G-1194)*
Feng Shui Lighting Inc 215 393-5500
  1925 S Broad St Lansdale (19446) *(G-9367)*
Fenner Inc 717 665-2421
  311 W Stiegel St Manheim (17545) *(G-10380)*
Fenner Inc 717 665-2421
  1421 Arcadia Rd Lancaster (17601) *(G-9015)*
Fenner Inc 717 665-2421
  250 S Penn St Manheim (17545) *(G-10381)*
Fenner Inc (HQ) 717 665-2421
  311 W Stiegel St Manheim (17545) *(G-10382)*
Fenner Drives, Lancaster *Also called Fenner Inc (G-9015)*
Fenner Drives, Manheim *Also called Fenner Inc (G-10382)*
Fenner Dunlop Americas LLC 412 249-0692
  1400 Omega Dr Pittsburgh (15205) *(G-15012)*
Fenner Dunlop Americas LLC (HQ) 412 249-0700
  1000 Omega Dr Ste 1400 Pittsburgh (15205) *(G-15013)*
Fenner Dunlop Engineered, Pittsburgh *Also called Fenner Dunlop Americas LLC (G-15013)*
Fenner Precision Inc 800 327-2288
  250 S Penn St Manheim (17545) *(G-10383)*
Fenstemaker John 215 572-1444
  32 E Glenside Ave Glenside (19038) *(G-6517)*
Fentimans North America Inc 877 326-3248
  76 Passan Dr Wilkes Barre (18702) *(G-19921)*
Fenton Heat Treating Inc 412 466-3960
  3605 Hmestead Duquesne Rd West Mifflin (15122) *(G-19738)*
Fenton Welding LLC 570 746-9018
  41166 Route 6 Wyalusing (18853) *(G-20252)*
Ferag Inc 215 788-0892
  190 Rittenhouse Cir Bristol (19007) *(G-2144)*
Ferdic Inc (PA) 717 731-1426
  165 S 32nd St Camp Hill (17011) *(G-2497)*
Fergies Bait & Tackle 724 253-3655
  857 Georgetown Rd Sandy Lake (16145) *(G-17059)*
Ferguson and Hassler Inc 717 786-7301
  100 Townsedge Dr Quarryville (17566) *(G-16269)*
Ferguson Perforating Company 724 657-8703
  901 Commerce Ave New Castle (16101) *(G-12092)*
Ferguson Welding Inc 717 292-4179
  1030 Buck Rd Dover (17315) *(G-4192)*
Fermentec Inc 203 809-8078
  301 S 19th St Apt 8f Philadelphia (19103) *(G-13697)*
Ferncliff Meat Processing 724 592-6042
  276 Ferncliff Rd Rices Landing (15357) *(G-16669)*
Fero Vineyards and Winery LLC 570 568-0846
  758 Moores School Rd Lewisburg (17837) *(G-9907)*
Ferotec Friction Inc 717 492-9600
  150 Shellyland Rd Manheim (17545) *(G-10384)*
Ferrante Uphlstrng & Crptng 724 535-8866
  3384 State Route 18 Wampum (16157) *(G-18800)*
Ferrari Importing Company 412 323-0335
  200 Waterfront Dr Pittsburgh (15222) *(G-15014)*
Ferrato Fine Foods, Pittsburgh *Also called F Ferrato Foods Company (G-14998)*
Ferri Design 412 276-3700
  34 Woodridge Dr Carnegie (15106) *(G-2767)*
Ferro Color & Glass Corp (HQ) 724 223-5900
  251 W Wylie Ave Washington (15301) *(G-19175)*
Ferro Corporation 412 331-3550
  60 Greenway Dr Pittsburgh (15204) *(G-15015)*
Ferro Corporation 724 207-2152
  251 W Wylie Ave Washington (15301) *(G-19176)*
FERRO FILTER, Bristol *Also called S G Frantz Co Inc (G-2196)*
Ferro Plumbing & Heating, Upper Chichester *Also called Thomas E Ferro (G-18673)*
Fessler Machine Company 724 346-0878
  800 N Water Ave Sharon (16146) *(G-17433)*
Fessler Machine Company (PA) 412 367-3663
  800 N Water Ave Sharon (16146) *(G-17434)*
Fetchen Sheet Metal Inc 570 457-3560
  329 S Main St Rear Old Forge (18518) *(G-12964)*
Fetterolf Corporation 610 584-1500
  2021 Cressman Rd Skippack (19474) *(G-17596)*
Fetterolf Group Inc (HQ) 814 443-4688
  227 New Centerville Rd Somerset (15501) *(G-17688)*
Fey Steel Fabricating, Mars *Also called J W Steel Fabricating Co (G-10503)*
Fh, Quarryville *Also called Ferguson and Hassler Inc (G-16269)*
Fhritp Holdings LLC 215 675-4590
  309 Camars Dr Warminster (18974) *(G-18877)*
Fi-Hoff Concrete Products Inc 814 266-5834
  240 Bentwood Ave Johnstown (15904) *(G-8372)*
Fia, Mercer *Also called Mercer Forge Corporation (G-10968)*
Fiba Technologies Inc 215 679-7823
  1645 State St East Greenville (18041) *(G-4568)*

Fibematics Inc 215 226-2672
  3313 Stokley St Philadelphia (19140) *(G-13698)*
Fiber Optic Designs Inc 215 321-9750
  1790 Yardley Langhorne Rd Yardley (19067) *(G-20311)*
Fiber Optic Marketplace LLC 610 973-6000
  9999 Hamilton Blvd # 220 Breinigsville (18031) *(G-2015)*
Fiber Productions II Inc 267 546-7025
  2705 Old Rodgers Rd Bristol (19007) *(G-2145)*
Fiber Quest Composites LLC 610 419-0387
  1889 Jeanine Way Hellertown (18055) *(G-7555)*
Fiberamerica, Allentown *Also called Ne Fibers LLC (G-326)*
Fiberblade LLC 814 361-8730
  1150 Northbrook Dr # 150 Feasterville Trevose (19053) *(G-5908)*
Fiberglass Technologies Inc 215 943-4567
  1610 Hanford St Ste P Levittown (19057) *(G-9836)*
Fiberland Inc 215 744-5446
  384 Tomlinson Pl Philadelphia (19116) *(G-13699)*
Fiberlink Communications Corp (HQ) 215 664-1600
  1787 Sentry Pkwy W # 200 Blue Bell (19422) *(G-1829)*
Fiberoptic.com, Breinigsville *Also called Fiber Optic Marketplace LLC (G-2015)*
Fiberopticscom 215 499-8959
  1919 Sycamore Dr Quakertown (18951) *(G-16193)*
Fiberopticscom Inc 610 973-6000
  1 Tek Park Breinigsville (18031) *(G-2016)*
Fibertel Inc 570 714-7189
  576 W Main St Plymouth (18651) *(G-15817)*
Fibreflex Packing & Mfg Co 215 482-1490
  5101 Umbria St Philadelphia (19128) *(G-13700)*
Fibrocell Science Inc (PA) 484 713-6000
  405 Eagleview Blvd Exton (19341) *(G-5678)*
Fibrocell Technologies Inc 484 713-6000
  405 Eagleview Blvd Exton (19341) *(G-5679)*
Ficore Incorporated 717 735-9740
  3650 W Market St York (17404) *(G-20480)*
Fidelity Flight Simulation Inc 412 321-3280
  1815 Parkway View Dr Pittsburgh (15205) *(G-15016)*
Fidelity Graphics 610 586-9300
  238 Holmes Rd Holmes (19043) *(G-7662)*
Fidelity Technologies Corp (PA) 610 929-3330
  2501 Kutztown Rd Reading (19605) *(G-16385)*
Fieg Brothers Coal (PA) 814 893-5270
  3070 Stoystown Rd Stoystown (15563) *(G-18077)*
Fielco LLC 215 674-8700
  1957 Pioneer Rd Huntingdon Valley (19006) *(G-7981)*
Fielco Adhesives 267 282-5311
  1957 Pioneer Rd Huntingdon Valley (19006) *(G-7982)*
Fielco Industries Inc 215 674-8700
  1957 Pioneer Rd Huntingdon Valley (19006) *(G-7983)*
Fieseler Neon Sign Co 570 655-2976
  28 Industrial Dr Pittston (18640) *(G-15750)*
Fiesler Sand & Gravel LLC 814 899-6161
  3853 Knoyle Rd Erie (16510) *(G-5289)*
Fiftyone K LLC 908 222-8780
  4885 Mcknight Rd Ste 308a Pittsburgh (15237) *(G-15017)*
Fig Industries LLC 803 414-3950
  1411 Fieldstead Ln Lancaster (17603) *(G-9016)*
Fighters Quarters 334 657-4128
  725 N 15th St Allentown (18102) *(G-212)*
Fikes Dairy Inc 724 437-7931
  47 W Craig St Uniontown (15401) *(G-18627)*
Filippi Bros Inc 215 247-5973
  7722 Winston Rd Philadelphia (19118) *(G-13701)*
Filly Fabricating Inc 412 896-6452
  3916 Crooked Run Rd Ste A North Versailles (15137) *(G-12774)*
Filmet Color Lab Inc 724 275-1700
  1051 Russellton Rd Cheswick (15024) *(G-3108)*
Filmtech Corp 610 709-9999
  2121 31st St Sw Allentown (18103) *(G-213)*
Filmtech Group Sgma Plas Group, Allentown *Also called Filmtech Corp (G-213)*
Filmtronics Inc 724 352-3790
  675 Saxonburg Rd Butler (16002) *(G-2401)*
Filpro Corporation 215 699-4510
  810 Dickerson Rd Ste B North Wales (19454) *(G-12801)*
Filson Water Treatment Inc 717 240-0763
  11 Roadway Dr Ste A Carlisle (17015) *(G-2712)*
Filter & Water Technologies 267 450-4900
  162 Keystone Dr Montgomeryville (18936) *(G-11397)*
Filter Media Inc 570 874-2537
  Main St Gilberton (17934) *(G-6366)*
Filter Queen, Cranberry Township *Also called Filtrtion of Wstn Pnnsylvania (G-3818)*
Filter Service & Installation 724 274-5220
  600 Watercrest Way Cheswick (15024) *(G-3109)*
Filter Shine Inc 866 977-4463
  80 W Main St Reinholds (17569) *(G-16631)*
Filter Technology Inc 866 992-9490
  408 Conshohocken State Rd Gladwyne (19035) *(G-6407)*
Filterfab Manufacturing Corp 724 643-4000
  3847 Midland Beaver Rd Industry (15052) *(G-8136)*
Filtrtion of Wstn Pnnsylvania 412 855-7372
  1445 Market St Cranberry Township (16066) *(G-3818)*

Finance Dept, North Wales *Also called Teva Pharmaceuticals Usa Inc* ***(G-12835)***
Finch Flagstone....570 965-0982
1673 Sheldon Hill Rd Springville (18844) ***(G-17929)***
Finch Manufacturing & Tech LLC....570 655-2277
540 Montgomery Ave West Pittston (18643) ***(G-19756)***
Fine Grinding Corporation....610 828-7250
241 E Elm St Conshohocken (19428) ***(G-3547)***
Fine Life Media, Ardmore *Also called International Watch Magazine* ***(G-709)***
Fine Line Cabinets Inc (PA)....814 695-8133
737 S Logan Blvd Hollidaysburg (16648) ***(G-7647)***
Fine Line Homes (PA)....717 561-2040
7300 Derry St Harrisburg (17111) ***(G-7129)***
Fine Print Commercial Printers....814 337-7468
287 Chestnut St Meadville (16335) ***(G-10726)***
Fine Sign Designs Inc....610 277-9860
1848 Markley St Norristown (19401) ***(G-12658)***
Fine Thankyou, Jersey Shore *Also called P Stone Inc* ***(G-8319)***
Fine Trim Line LLC....717 642-9032
240 Valley View Ln Fairfield (17320) ***(G-5767)***
Fineline Circuits Inc (PA)....215 364-3311
1660 Loretta Ave Feasterville Trevose (19053) ***(G-5909)***
Finetex Rotary Engraving Inc....717 273-6841
1431 Willow St Lebanon (17046) ***(G-9567)***
Finetex Textile Group, Lebanon *Also called Finetex Rotary Engraving Inc* ***(G-9567)***
Finisar Corporation....267 803-3800
767 Electronic Dr Horsham (19044) ***(G-7818)***
Finish Carpenter, Phoenixville *Also called KB Woodcraft Inc* ***(G-14555)***
Finish Line Screen Prtg Inc....814 238-0122
1869 Park Forest Ave State College (16803) ***(G-17964)***
Finish Tech Corp....215 396-8800
184 Railroad Dr Warminster (18974) ***(G-18878)***
Finish Tech Corp (PA)....215 396-8800
90 Industrial Dr Warminster (18974) ***(G-18879)***
Finish Technology Inc....570 421-4110
2044 W Main St Stroudsburg (18360) ***(G-18120)***
Finish Thompson Inc....814 455-4478
921 Greengarden Rd Erie (16501) ***(G-5290)***
Finishing Associates LLC....517 371-2460
1119 Mearns Rd Warminster (18974) ***(G-18880)***
Fink & Stackhouse Inc (PA)....570 323-3475
515 Princeton Avenue Ext Williamsport (17701) ***(G-20013)***
Finmeccanica North America, Johnstown *Also called Oto Melara North America Inc* ***(G-8417)***
Finnaren & Haley Company, Lancaster *Also called Haley Paint Company* ***(G-9037)***
Finnegan Gas Corp....724 428-3688
229 Finnegan Rd Wind Ridge (15380) ***(G-20176)***
Fiore Precision Machine, Throop *Also called Enrico J Fiore* ***(G-18358)***
Fiorella Woodworking Inc....215 843-5870
20 E Herman St Philadelphia (19144) ***(G-13702)***
Fire 1st Defense Inc....610 296-7576
451 Cassatt Rd Berwyn (19312) ***(G-1361)***
Fire Station Resources Center, Beaver Falls *Also called Raceresq Inc* ***(G-1010)***
Fired Up....724 941-0302
4151 Washington Rd Canonsburg (15317) ***(G-2588)***
Firelock Fireproof Vaults, Kutztown *Also called Banc Technic Inc* ***(G-8836)***
Firewlkers Small Btch Dist LLC....610 737-7900
2296 Creekside Dr Coplay (18037) ***(G-3643)***
First Article Inc....267 382-0761
150 S Front St Ste B Souderton (18964) ***(G-17733)***
First Choice Radon Testing Co....215 947-1995
460 Newell Dr Huntingdon Valley (19006) ***(G-7984)***
First Class Energy LLC....724 548-2501
409 Butler Rd A Kittanning (16201) ***(G-8770)***
First Class Energy LLC (PA)....724 548-2501
409 Butler Rd Ste A Kittanning (16201) ***(G-8771)***
First Class Specialities, Herminie *Also called First Class Specialties* ***(G-7570)***
First Class Specialties....724 446-1000
218 Sewickley Ave Herminie (15637) ***(G-7570)***
First Defense Operations MGT, Monroeville *Also called Water Treatment Services Inc* ***(G-11363)***
First Level Inc....717 266-2450
3109 Espresso Way York (17406) ***(G-20481)***
First Line Coatings Inc....814 452-0046
901 W 12th St Ste 204 Erie (16501) ***(G-5291)***
First Quality Baby Pdts LLC....717 247-3516
97 Locust Rd Lewistown (17044) ***(G-9928)***
First Quality Enterprises Inc....570 384-1600
1 Oakridge Rd Hazleton (18202) ***(G-7498)***
First Quality Hygienic Inc (HQ)....570 769-6900
121 North Rd Mc Elhattan (17748) ***(G-10587)***
First Quality Products Inc....570 769-6900
121 North Rd Mc Elhattan (17748) ***(G-10588)***
First Quality Products Inc....610 265-5000
601 Allendale Rd King of Prussia (19406) ***(G-8618)***
First Quality Retail Svcs LLC (HQ)....610 265-5000
601 Allendale Rd King of Prussia (19406) ***(G-8619)***
First Quality Tissue LLC....570 748-1200
904 Woods Ave Lock Haven (17745) ***(G-10089)***
First Rate Met Fabrication LLC....724 515-7005
1 Penn St Manor (15665) ***(G-10410)***
First Regional Compost Auth....610 262-1000
6701 Weaversville Rd Northampton (18067) ***(G-12850)***
First Rspnse Ltg Solutions LLC....412 585-6220
3424 Babcock Blvd Pittsburgh (15237) ***(G-15018)***
First Shelburne Corporation....610 544-8660
162 Saxer Ave Ste 2 Springfield (19064) ***(G-17914)***
First State Sheet Metal Inc....215 766-9510
3 Appletree Ln Bedminster (18910) ***(G-1080)***
First State Sheet Metal Inc....302 521-1609
6263 Kellers Church Rd Pipersville (18947) ***(G-14615)***
First Supply Chain LLC....215 527-2264
1150 Chadwick Cir Hummelstown (17036) ***(G-7910)***
Firth Maple Products Inc....814 654-7265
22418 Firth Rd Spartansburg (16434) ***(G-17850)***
Fis Avantgard LLC (HQ)....800 468-7483
680 E Swedesford Rd Wayne (19087) ***(G-19329)***
Fis Avantgard LLC....215 413-4700
1500 Spring Garden St # 3 Philadelphia (19130) ***(G-13703)***
Fis Data Systems Inc (HQ)....484 582-2000
200 Campus Dr Collegeville (19426) ***(G-3377)***
Fis Sg LLC (HQ)....484 582-5400
680 E Swedesford Rd Wayne (19087) ***(G-19330)***
Fis Sg LLC....215 627-3800
510 Walnut St Ste 900 Philadelphia (19106) ***(G-13704)***
Fis Systems International LLC (HQ)....484 582-2000
200 Campus Dr Collegeville (19426) ***(G-3378)***
Fish Ed Machine, Tarentum *Also called Ed Fish Maching Co* ***(G-18242)***
Fish Wrapper, The, Myerstown *Also called Little Mountain Printing* ***(G-11892)***
Fisher & Ludlow Inc....859 282-7767
2000 Corporate Dr Ste 400 Wexford (15090) ***(G-19801)***
Fisher & Ludlow Inc....814 763-5914
607 Erie St Saegertown (16433) ***(G-16914)***
Fisher & Ludlow Inc....217 324-6106
2000 Corporate Dr Ste 400 Wexford (15090) ***(G-19802)***
Fisher & Ludlow Inc (HQ)....724 934-5320
2000 Corporate Dr Ste 400 Wexford (15090) ***(G-19803)***
Fisher Iron Works....717 687-7595
3260 E Gordon Rd Gordonville (17529) ***(G-6554)***
Fisher S Hand Made Quilts....717 392-5440
2713a Old Phila Pike Bird In Hand (17505) ***(G-1674)***
Fisher Safety, Pittsburgh *Also called Thermo Fisher Scientific Inc* ***(G-15613)***
Fisher Scientific Company LLC (HQ)....724 517-1500
300 Industry Dr Pittsburgh (15275) ***(G-15019)***
Fisher Structures....717 789-4569
183 Memory Ln Loysville (17047) ***(G-10114)***
Fisher Tank Company (PA)....610 494-7200
3131 W 4th St Chester (19013) ***(G-3051)***
Fisher Woodcraft....610 273-2076
1045 Compass Rd Honey Brook (19344) ***(G-7744)***
Fisher-Klosterman Inc....717 274-7280
200 N 7th St Ste 2 Lebanon (17046) ***(G-9568)***
Fishers Woodworking....570 725-2310
158 Country Ln Loganton (17747) ***(G-10095)***
Fishman & Tobin, Plymouth Meeting *Also called F&T Apparel LLC* ***(G-15843)***
Fishman and Tobin, Plymouth Meeting *Also called F&T Apparel LLC* ***(G-15844)***
Fit Engineering....717 432-2626
200 Mount Zion Rd Dillsburg (17019) ***(G-4129)***
Fit Fuel Foods LLC....267 342-1559
18 Oxford Ct Langhorne (19047) ***(G-9297)***
Fitz Security Co Inc....717 272-5020
2 Pershing Ave Lebanon (17042) ***(G-9569)***
Fitzkees Candies Inc....717 741-1031
2352 S Queen St York (17402) ***(G-20482)***
Fitzpatrick Container Company....215 699-3515
6923 Schantz Rd Allentown (18106) ***(G-214)***
Five Filer Brothers Company, Grove City *Also called Creative Logistics Ltd* ***(G-6782)***
Five Points Pet Supply LLC....724 857-6000
2061 Brodhead Rd Aliquippa (15001) ***(G-75)***
Five Star Associates Inc....610 588-7426
1 Blue Valley Dr Bangor (18013) ***(G-913)***
Five Star Group Inc....814 237-0241
26 Cricklewood Cir State College (16803) ***(G-17965)***
Five STS Dstlg Intl Sprits LLC....610 279-5364
129 E Main St Norristown (19401) ***(G-12659)***
Five Thousand Forms Inc (PA)....610 395-0900
8020 Mine St Fogelsville (18051) ***(G-5994)***
Fives N Amercn Combustn Inc....717 228-0714
819 Wheatfield Ln Lebanon (17042) ***(G-9570)***
Fives N Amercn Combustn Inc....610 996-8005
702 Mercers Mill Ln West Chester (19382) ***(G-19555)***
Fives N Amercn Combustn Inc....412 655-0101
526 E Bruceton Rd Ste 101 Pittsburgh (15236) ***(G-15020)***
Fizzano Bros Concrete Pdts Inc....610 363-6290
201 Phoenixville Pike Malvern (19355) ***(G-10235)***
Fizzano Bros Concrete Pdts Inc....215 355-6160
247 Sterner Mill Rd Langhorne (19053) ***(G-9298)***
Fizzano Bros Inc (PA)....610 833-1100
1776 Chester Pike Crum Lynne (19022) ***(G-3937)***

ALPHABETIC

Fizzano Bros Inc 215 355-6160
247 Sterner Mill Rd Feasterville Trevose (19053) ***(G-5910)***
FJ Performance Inc 724 681-7430
1022 Lexington Dr Export (15632) ***(G-5602)***
Flabeg Automotive US Corp 724 224-1800
851 3rd Ave Brackenridge (15014) ***(G-1939)***
Flabeg Solar US Corporation 724 899-4622
2201 Sweeney Dr Clinton (15026) ***(G-3262)***
Flags For All Seasons Inc 610 688-4235
230 Orchard Way Wayne (19087) ***(G-19331)***
Flagship By Bloksberg, Apollo *Also called Bloksberg Inc* ***(G-665)***
Flagship City Hardwoods 814 835-1178
1606 Harper Dr Erie (16505) ***(G-5292)***
Flagship Multimedia Inc 814 314-9364
1001 State St Ste 1315 Erie (16501) ***(G-5293)***
Flagstaff Industries Corp (PA) 215 638-9662
364 Dunksferry Rd Bensalem (19020) ***(G-1195)***
Flagstone Small Bus Vltons LLC 484 515-2621
714 Leibert St Bethlehem (18018) ***(G-1509)***
Flagzone LLC 610 367-9900
105a Industrial Dr Gilbertsville (19525) ***(G-6372)***
Flavor Pros, Allentown *Also called Flavorpros LLC* ***(G-215)***
Flavorpros LLC 610 435-4300
737 N 13th St Allentown (18102) ***(G-215)***
Flawless Lawncare, Bridgeville *Also called Colussy Enterprises Inc* ***(G-2057)***
Fleet Decal & Graphics Inc 570 779-4343
30 E Main St Plymouth (18651) ***(G-15818)***
Fleetwood Building Block Inc 610 944-8385
240 W Main St Fleetwood (19522) ***(G-5973)***
Fleming Steel Co 724 658-1511
2739 Pulaski Rd New Castle (16105) ***(G-12093)***
Flenniken & Flenniken PC 717 249-7777
30 State Ave Carlisle (17013) ***(G-2713)***
Fletcher's Sales and Service, Conneaut Lake *Also called T E Fletcher Snowmobiles* ***(G-3480)***
Fleur De Lait East, New Holland *Also called Savencia Cheese USA LLC* ***(G-12281)***
Fleur De Lait East LLC 717 355-8580
400 S Custer Ave New Holland (17557) ***(G-12249)***
Fleuri LLC 724 539-7566
105 Redwood Cir Latrobe (15650) ***(G-9476)***
Flex Com, Bath *Also called Flexible Compensators Inc* ***(G-959)***
Flex Rig Inc 215 638-5743
1935 Juniper Ln Bensalem (19020) ***(G-1196)***
Flex-Cell Precision 717 393-3335
833 2nd St Lancaster (17603) ***(G-9017)***
Flex-Cell Precision Inc 717 824-4086
1151 S Duke St Lancaster (17602) ***(G-9018)***
Flex-Y-Plan Industries Inc (PA) 814 881-3436
6960 W Ridge Rd Fairview (16415) ***(G-5822)***
Flexcut Tool Co Inc 814 864-7855
8105 Hawthorne Dr Erie (16509) ***(G-5294)***
Flexible Circuits, Warrington *Also called FCG Inc* ***(G-19117)***
Flexible Compensators Inc 610 837-3812
6864 Chrisphalt Dr Bath (18014) ***(G-959)***
Flexible Informatics LLC 215 253-8765
600 Germantown Pike B Lafayette Hill (19444) ***(G-8880)***
Flexicon Corporation (PA) 610 814-2400
2400 Emrick Blvd Bethlehem (18020) ***(G-1510)***
Flexlink Systems Inc (HQ) 610 973-8200
6580 Snowdrift Rd Ste 200 Allentown (18106) ***(G-216)***
Flexmove Americas LLC 267 203-8351
255 Schoolhouse Rd Souderton (18964) ***(G-17734)***
Flexospan Steel Buildings Inc 724 376-7221
253 Railroad St Sandy Lake (16145) ***(G-17060)***
Flexsteel Industries Inc 717 392-4161
107 Pitney Rd Lancaster (17602) ***(G-9019)***
Flexsteel Pipeline Tech Inc 570 505-3491
300 Streibeigh Ln Bldg D Montoursville (17754) ***(G-11439)***
Flexsys America LP 724 258-6200
829 Route 481 Monongahela (15063) ***(G-11308)***
Flextex, North Wales *Also called Plum Manufacturing Co Inc* ***(G-12825)***
Flextron Industries Inc 610 459-4600
720 Mount Rd Aston (19014) ***(G-763)***
Flextron Systems, Bensalem *Also called Flex Rig Inc* ***(G-1196)***
Flight Systems Inc (PA) 717 590-7330
207 Hempt Rd Mechanicsburg (17050) ***(G-10844)***
Flight Systems Auto Group LLC (HQ) 717 932-7000
505 Fishing Creek Rd Lewisberry (17339) ***(G-9886)***
Flight Systems Elec Group, Lewisberry *Also called Flight Systems Auto Group LLC* ***(G-9886)***
Flinchbaugh Company Inc (PA) 717 266-2202
245 Beshore School Rd Manchester (17345) ***(G-10356)***
Flinchbaugh Engineering Inc 717 755-1900
4387 Run Way York (17406) ***(G-20483)***
Flint Group US LLC 717 285-5454
3575 Hempland Rd Lancaster (17601) ***(G-9020)***
Flint Group US LLC 717 392-1953
216 Greenfield Rd Lancaster (17601) ***(G-9021)***
Flint Ink North America Div, Lancaster *Also called Flint Group US LLC* ***(G-9021)***
Flint Road Welding 717 535-5282
540 Center Rd Mifflintown (17059) ***(G-11118)***
Flintwood Metals, Lebanon *Also called Steel Plus Inc* ***(G-9634)***
Flintwood Metals Inc 717 274-9481
205 N 5th Ave Lebanon (17046) ***(G-9571)***
Flir Government Systems Pittsb 724 295-2880
183 Northpointe Blvd # 100 Freeport (16229) ***(G-6204)***
Flir Surveillance, Freeport *Also called Flir Government Systems Pittsb* ***(G-6204)***
Flir Systems Inc 412 423-2100
2240 William Pitt Way Pittsburgh (15238) ***(G-15021)***
Flo Ann Garments 717 445-5268
602 Gristmill Rd Ephrata (17522) ***(G-5103)***
Flontech USA LLC 866 654-2676
100 Thompson St Pittston (18640) ***(G-15751)***
Floral Mountain True Value, Markleysburg *Also called Dennis Lumber and Concrete* ***(G-10480)***
Florida Key West 717 208-3084
1308 Kelley Dr Lancaster (17601) ***(G-9022)***
Florig R & J Industrial Co Inc 610 825-6655
910 Brook Rd Conshohocken (19428) ***(G-3548)***
Florio Tooling Co, Saint Marys *Also called Florio Tooling Inc* ***(G-16974)***
Florio Tooling Inc 814 781-3973
1103 Aumadel Rd Saint Marys (15857) ***(G-16974)***
Flotran Exton Inc 610 640-4141
249 Planebrook Rd Ste 2 Malvern (19355) ***(G-10236)***
Flow Measurement Technologies 610 377-6050
1464 Lower Nis Hollow Dr Lehighton (18235) ***(G-9714)***
Flowers Baking Co Oxford Inc 610 932-2147
700 Lincoln St Oxford (19363) ***(G-13079)***
Flowers Foods Inc 717 528-4108
101 High St York Springs (17372) ***(G-20765)***
Flowline 724 658-3711
1400 Butter Rd New Castle (16101) ***(G-12094)***
Flowline Division, Zelienople *Also called Markovitz Enterprises Inc* ***(G-20810)***
Flowline Division, New Castle *Also called Ezeflow Usa Inc* ***(G-12090)***
Flowserve Corporation 570 451-2200
942 Griffin Pond Rd S Abingtn Twp (18411) ***(G-16896)***
Flowserve Corporation 908 859-7408
1480 Valley Center Pkwy Bethlehem (18017) ***(G-1511)***
Flowserve Corporation 570 451-2325
567 Rocky Glen Rd Moosic (18507) ***(G-11505)***
Flowserve Corporation 412 257-4600
1885 Mayview Rd Bridgeville (15017) ***(G-2064)***
FLS US Holdings Inc (HQ) 610 264-6011
2040 Avenue C Bethlehem (18017) ***(G-1512)***
Flsmidth Inc 610 264-6101
2040 Avenue C Bethlehem (18017) ***(G-1513)***
Flsmidth Inc 717 665-2224
236 S Cherry St Manheim (17545) ***(G-10385)***
Fluid Conditioning Pdts Inc 717 627-1550
101 Warwick St Lititz (17543) ***(G-10008)***
Fluid Dynamics Inc 215 699-8700
295 Dekalb Pike North Wales (19454) ***(G-12802)***
Fluid Energy Proc & Eqp Co (PA) 215 721-8990
4300 Bethlehem Pike Telford (18969) ***(G-18289)***
Fluid Energy Proc & Eqp Co 215 368-2510
2629 Penn St Hatfield (19440) ***(G-7343)***
Fluid Engineering, Erie *Also called Tm Industrial Supply Inc* ***(G-5510)***
Fluid Gear Products LLC 484 480-3923
115 Market St Marcus Hook (19061) ***(G-10441)***
Fluid Intelligence LLC 610 405-2698
641 Llewelyn Rd Berwyn (19312) ***(G-1362)***
Fluid Transfer, Philipsburg *Also called Lee Industries Inc* ***(G-14519)***
Fluidtechnik USA 610 321-2407
1699 Horseshoe Pile Glenmoore (19343) ***(G-6466)***
Fluoro-Plastics Inc 215 425-5500
3601 G St Philadelphia (19134) ***(G-13705)***
Fluorous Technologies Inc 267 225-5384
815 Copeland Way Pittsburgh (15232) ***(G-15022)***
Fluortek Inc 610 438-1800
12 Mcfadden Rd Easton (18045) ***(G-4683)***
Flurer Machine & Tool, Bethlehem *Also called Flurer Machine and Tool* ***(G-1514)***
Flurer Machine and Tool 610 759-6114
294 Nazareth Pike Bethlehem (18020) ***(G-1514)***
Flury Foundry Company 717 397-9080
1160 Elizabeth Ave Lancaster (17601) ***(G-9023)***
Flw of Pa Inc 610 251-9700
527 Lancaster Ave Malvern (19355) ***(G-10237)***
Fly Magazine 717 293-9772
2144 Kentwood Dr Lancaster (17601) ***(G-9024)***
Fly Mix Entertainment 215 722-6287
942 Borbeck Ave Philadelphia (19111) ***(G-13706)***
Flynn & OHara Uniforms Inc (PA) 800 441-4122
10905 Dutton Rd Philadelphia (19154) ***(G-13707)***
Fm2 Inc 814 874-0090
2250 W 23rd St Erie (16506) ***(G-5295)***
FMC Asia-Pacific Inc (HQ) 215 299-6000
2929 Walnut St Philadelphia (19104) ***(G-13708)***

FMC Corporation (PA) 215 299-6000
2929 Walnut St Philadelphia (19104) ***(G-13709)***
FMC Corporation 215 717-7500
1601 Market St Ste 910 Philadelphia (19103) ***(G-13710)***
FMC Corporation 800 526-3649
1735 Market St Fl 14 Philadelphia (19103) ***(G-13711)***
FMC Measurement Solutions, Erie *Also called FMC Technologies Measurement S* ***(G-5297)***
FMC Overseas Ltd 215 299-6000
1735 Market St Fl 14 Philadelphia (19103) ***(G-13712)***
FMC Technologies Inc 570 546-2441
320 Marcellus Dr Muncy (17756) ***(G-11816)***
FMC Technologies Inc 814 898-5000
1602 Wagner Ave Erie (16510) ***(G-5296)***
FMC Technologies Inc 215 822-4485
2750 Morris Rd Ste A100 Lansdale (19446) ***(G-9368)***
FMC Technologies Measurement S 281 591-4000
1648 Mcclelland Ave Erie (16510) ***(G-5297)***
FMR Industries Inc 215 536-2222
130 Penn Am Dr Quakertown (18951) ***(G-16194)***
Fmr Powder Coatings, Quakertown *Also called FMR Industries Inc* ***(G-16194)***
Foam Fabricators Inc 814 838-4538
6550 W Ridge Rd Erie (16506) ***(G-5298)***
Foam Fabricators Inc 570 752-7110
17 Industrial Dr Bloomsburg (17815) ***(G-1782)***
Foam Fair Industries Inc 610 622-4665
3 Merion Ter Aldan (19018) ***(G-59)***
Foambeak LLC 814 452-3626
4219 Knipper Ave Erie (16510) ***(G-5299)***
Foamex, Aston *Also called Fxi Inc* ***(G-766)***
Foamex, Corry *Also called Fxi Inc* ***(G-3762)***
Foamex International Inc 610 744-2300
1400 N Providence Rd Media (19063) ***(G-10924)***
Foamex LP (PA) 610 565-2374
1400 N Providence Rd # 2000 Media (19063) ***(G-10925)***
Focus Noise Ltd Liability Co 484 886-7242
705 Worthington Dr Exton (19341) ***(G-5680)***
Focus One Promotions Inc 610 459-7781
340 Turner Industrial Way Aston (19014) ***(G-764)***
Foerster Instruments Inc (HQ) 412 788-8976
140 Industry Dr Pittsburgh (15275) ***(G-15023)***
Fogle Forest Products 570 524-2580
521 Hoffa Mill Rd Lewisburg (17837) ***(G-9908)***
Fold Pak, Hazleton *Also called Westrock Rkt LLC* ***(G-7538)***
Folded Structures Company LLC 908 237-1955
1044 Durham Rd Newtown (18940) ***(G-12502)***
Folino Estate LLC 484 256-5300
340 Old Route 22 Kutztown (19530) ***(G-8843)***
Folino Estate Winery, Kutztown *Also called Folino Estate LLC* ***(G-8843)***
Follett Corporation, Easton *Also called Follett LLC* ***(G-4684)***
Follett LLC (HQ) 610 252-7301
801 Church Ln Easton (18040) ***(G-4684)***
Follett LLC 800 523-9361
157 N Commerce Way Bethlehem (18017) ***(G-1515)***
Folsom Tool & Mold Corp 610 358-5030
12 Mount Pleasant Rd Aston (19014) ***(G-765)***
Food Medication Interactions, Chester Springs *Also called Waza Inc* ***(G-3087)***
Footers Inc 610 437-2233
335 N 7th St Allentown (18102) ***(G-217)***
For Lenfest Institute (PA) 215 854-5600
1234 Market St Ste 1800 Philadelphia (19107) ***(G-13713)***
Foradora Welding & Machine 814 375-2176
904 Sandstone Dr Falls Creek (15840) ***(G-5853)***
Forallsecure Inc 412 256-8809
3710 Forbes Ave Fl 3 Pittsburgh (15213) ***(G-15024)***
Foranne Manufacturing Inc 215 357-4650
83 Steam Whistle Dr Warminster (18974) ***(G-18881)***
Force Inc (PA) 724 465-9399
1380 Route 286 Hwy E # 303 Indiana (15701) ***(G-8100)***
Force America Inc 610 495-4590
105 Jones Blvd 106 Pottstown (19464) ***(G-15988)***
Force Industries Inc 610 647-3575
28 Industrial Blvd Paoli (19301) ***(G-13140)***
Forcey Lumber Co Inc 814 857-5002
2020 Shiloh Rd Woodland (16881) ***(G-20211)***
Ford City Gun Workd 724 994-9501
502 Main St Ford City (16226) ***(G-6045)***
Ford City National Bakery 724 763-7684
821 5th Ave Ford City (16226) ***(G-6046)***
Foreign Policy Research Inst 215 732-3774
1528 Walnut St Ste 610 Philadelphia (19102) ***(G-13714)***
Forest City News Inc 570 785-3800
636 Main St Forest City (18421) ***(G-6053)***
Forest Devices Inc 724 612-1504
544 Miltenberger St Pittsburgh (15219) ***(G-15025)***
Forest Hill Manufacturing LLC 717 556-0363
240 Forest Hill Rd Leola (17540) ***(G-9782)***
Forest Hill Woodworking 717 806-0193
1985 Mine Rd Paradise (17562) ***(G-13157)***
Forest Resources, Oxford *Also called Coastal Treated Products Co* ***(G-13075)***
Forest Ridge Woodworking 717 442-3191
1733 Jack Russell Run Paradise (17562) ***(G-13158)***
Forest Scientific Corporation 814 463-5006
408 Emert Rd Tionesta (16353) ***(G-18371)***
Forever Christmas, Oxford *Also called Oxford Market Place Inc* ***(G-13086)***
Forging Parts & Machining Co 717 530-8810
150 Reading Rd Shippensburg (17257) ***(G-17527)***
Fork Creek Cabins LLC 717 442-1902
3351 Lincoln Hwy E Paradise (17562) ***(G-13159)***
Form Tech, York *Also called Form Tool Technology Inc* ***(G-20484)***
Form Tech Concrete Forms Inc 412 331-4500
2850 Kramer Rd Gibsonia (15044) ***(G-6334)***
Form Tool Technology Inc (PA) 717 792-3626
5174 Commerce Dr York (17408) ***(G-20484)***
Forman Sign Co 215 827-6500
10447 Drummond Rd Philadelphia (19154) ***(G-13715)***
Formex Business Printing 717 737-3430
328 Market St Lemoyne (17043) ***(G-9744)***
Formfast Powder Mtl Tech LLC 814 201-5292
2190 Montmorenci Rd Ridgway (15853) ***(G-16709)***
Formica Corporation 570 897-6319
1379 S Delaware Dr Mount Bethel (18343) ***(G-11610)***
Formica Surell, Mount Bethel *Also called Formica Corporation* ***(G-11610)***
Formit Metal Fabricators LLC 717 650-2895
101 Mundis Race Rd York (17406) ***(G-20485)***
Formit Steel Co, Red Lion *Also called Mas-Fab Inc* ***(G-16608)***
Forms and Surfaces Inc (PA) 412 781-9003
30 Pine St Pittsburgh (15223) ***(G-15026)***
Forms Graphics LLC 215 639-3504
1296 Adams Rd Ste 3 Bensalem (19020) ***(G-1197)***
Formtech Enterprises Inc 814 474-1940
7301 Klier Dr Fairview (16415) ***(G-5823)***
Formula Pharmaceuticals Inc 610 727-4172
1055 Westlakes Dr Ste 300 Berwyn (19312) ***(G-1363)***
Forney Holdings Inc (PA) 724 346-7400
1565 Broadway Rd Hermitage (16148) ***(G-7584)***
Forney LP 724 346-7400
2050 Jacksons Pointe Ct Zelienople (16063) ***(G-20801)***
Forrest Steel Corporation 412 884-5533
1000 Baldwin Rd Pittsburgh (15207) ***(G-15027)***
Forsht Concrete Pdts Co Inc 814 944-1617
616 Grandview Rd Altoona (16601) ***(G-507)***
Forsythe Marketing 717 764-9863
2575 Hepplewhite Dr York (17404) ***(G-20486)***
Fort Dearborn Company 814 686-7656
13985 S Eagle Valley Rd Tyrone (16686) ***(G-18582)***
Fort Washington Pharma LLC (PA) 800 279-7434
500 Office Center Dr # 400 Fort Washington (19034) ***(G-6069)***
Forta Corporation (PA) 724 458-5221
100 Forta Dr Grove City (16127) ***(G-6785)***
Fortmex Corporation 215 990-9688
249 Stoneway Ln Merion Station (19066) ***(G-10997)***
Fortney Packages Inc 717 243-1826
11 E High St Carlisle (17013) ***(G-2714)***
Fortney Printing 717 939-6422
512 Main St Harrisburg (17113) ***(G-7130)***
Fortune Electric Co Ltd (HQ) 724 346-2722
1965 Shenango Valley Fwy Hermitage (16148) ***(G-7585)***
Fortune Fabrics Inc 570 288-3666
315 Simpson St Kingston (18704) ***(G-8717)***
Forum Inc 412 781-5970
100 Chapel Harbor Dr # 1 Pittsburgh (15238) ***(G-15028)***
Forum Lighting, Pittsburgh *Also called Forum Inc* ***(G-15028)***
Fossil Rock LLC 724 355-3747
102 Kotchey Ln Harmony (16037) ***(G-7067)***
Foster's Monuments, Lewistown *Also called Gary Foster* ***(G-9932)***
Foster-Kmetz Woodworking 570 325-8222
165 W Broadway 167 Jim Thorpe (18229) ***(G-8340)***
Foster-Tobin, Meadville *Also called Fostermation Inc* ***(G-10727)***
Fostermation Inc 814 336-6211
200 Valleyview Dr Meadville (16335) ***(G-10727)***
Fostermation Inc (PA) 814 336-6211
200 Valleyview Dr Meadville (16335) ***(G-10728)***
Foto-Wear Inc (PA) 570 307-3600
473 Easton Tpke Ste D Lake Ariel (18436) ***(G-8888)***
Fotorecord Print Center Inc 724 837-0530
45 E Pittsburgh St Greensburg (15601) ***(G-6667)***
Foulk Equipment Leasing Inc 610 838-2260
1235 Easton Rd Bethlehem (18015) ***(G-1516)***
Foulk Warehousing, Bethlehem *Also called Foulk Equipment Leasing Inc* ***(G-1516)***
Foundation Print Solutions 717 330-0544
304 Dorchester Dr Lititz (17543) ***(G-10009)***
Foundation Surgery Center 215 628-4300
467 Pennsylvania Ave # 202 Fort Washington (19034) ***(G-6070)***
Foundry Div, Mount Joy *Also called Donsco Inc* ***(G-11653)***
Foundry Division, Sayre *Also called Ajax Xray Inc* ***(G-17109)***
Fountain Fabricating Co 570 682-9018
1657 E Main St Hegins (17938) ***(G-7541)***

ALPHABETIC

Four Guys Stnless Tank Eqp Inc................814 634-8373
230 Industrial Park Rd Meyersdale (15552) *(G-11010)*

Four Stars Pipe & Supply Inc......................724 746-2029
72 Wilson Rd Eighty Four (15330) *(G-4841)*

Four Three Energy Services LLC..................814 797-0021
7313 Route 338 Knox (16232) *(G-8810)*

Four Wheeling For Less LLC.........................724 287-7852
762 Route 422 E Butler (16002) *(G-2402)*

Four Winds Concrete Inc (PA)......................610 865-1788
925 Harvard Ave Bethlehem (18015) *(G-1517)*

Four Winds Concrete Inc...............................610 865-1788
4401 Camp Meeting Rd Center Valley (18034) *(G-2827)*

Four Winds Concrete Company, Center Valley *Also called Four Winds Concrete Inc (G-2827)*

Fourth Street Barbecue Inc..........................724 483-2000
3 Arentzen Blvd Charleroi (15022) *(G-3013)*

Foust Machine & Tool....................................717 766-7841
6380 Basehore Rd Mechanicsburg (17050) *(G-10845)*

Fowler Equipment Market, Wayne *Also called H B Fowler Co Inc (G-19334)*

Fowlers Logging...814 684-9883
309 Washington Ave Tyrone (16686) *(G-18583)*

Fox Bindery Inc...215 538-5380
2750 Morris Rd Lansdale (19446) *(G-9369)*

Fox Chapel Publishing Co Inc.......................800 457-9112
1970 Broad St East Petersburg (17520) *(G-4587)*

Fox Group Inc..215 538-5380
2750 Morris Rd Ste E1 Lansdale (19446) *(G-9370)*

Fox IV Technologies Inc...............................724 387-3500
6011 Enterprise Dr Export (15632) *(G-5603)*

Fox Meadows Creamery Inc...........................717 721-6455
2475 W Main St Ephrata (17522) *(G-5104)*

Fox Pool Lancaster Inc (HQ).........................717 718-1977
3490 Board Rd York (17406) *(G-20487)*

Fox Run Craftmen, Warminster *Also called Fox Run Holdings Inc (G-18882)*

Fox Run Craftsmen, Ivyland *Also called Fox Run Usa LLC (G-8211)*

Fox Run Holdings Inc (PA).............................215 675-7700
1907 Stout Dr Warminster (18974) *(G-18882)*

Fox Run Usa LLC (HQ)....................................215 675-7700
1907 Stout Dr Ivyland (18974) *(G-8211)*

Fox Specialties, Lansdale *Also called Fox Bindery Inc (G-9369)*

Fox Specialties Inc......................................215 822-5775
2750 Morris Rd Ste C Lansdale (19446) *(G-9371)*

Fox Welding Shop Inc...................................215 225-3069
1801 W Sedgley Ave Philadelphia (19132) *(G-13716)*

Foxburg Wine Cellars Inc.............................724 659-0021
65 Main St Foxburg (16036) *(G-6101)*

Foxcraft Cabinets...717 859-3261
224 Snyder Rd Ephrata (17522) *(G-5105)*

Foxcroft Equipment & Svcs Co......................610 942-2888
2101 Creek Rd Glenmoore (19343) *(G-6467)*

Foxpro Inc..717 248-2507
14 Fox Hollow Dr Lewistown (17044) *(G-9929)*

Foxs Country Sheds......................................717 626-9560
537 E 28th Division Hwy Lititz (17543) *(G-10010)*

FP Woll & Company.......................................215 934-5966
10060 Sandmeyer Ln Philadelphia (19116) *(G-13717)*

Fpd Company, Mc Murray *Also called Trigon Incorporated (G-10648)*

Fraccaro Industries Inc.................................610 367-2777
1032 N Reading Ave Boyertown (19512) *(G-1911)*

Fragrance Manufacturing Inc.......................610 266-7580
100 Cascade Dr Allentown (18109) *(G-218)*

Fralo Industries, Erie *Also called Victor Group Inc (G-5526)*

Frame Outlet Inc...412 351-7283
2314 Forest Dr Pittsburgh (15235) *(G-15029)*

Frame Up & Gallery.......................................724 627-0552
126 N Maiden St Waynesburg (15370) *(G-19441)*

Frameless Shower Doors...............................215 534-0021
2141 Chapman Cir Jamison (18929) *(G-8243)*

Frames & More...724 933-5557
100 Vip Dr Ste 104 Wexford (15090) *(G-19804)*

France Compressor Products, Bristol *Also called Enpro Industries Inc (G-2141)*

Franchise Bsness Opportunities...................412 831-2522
1155 Greenbriar Rd Bethel Park (15102) *(G-1414)*

Francis E, Sheriidan, Ephrata *Also called Morton Tool Company (G-5131)*

Francis J Nowalk..412 687-4017
4017 Liberty Ave Pittsburgh (15224) *(G-15030)*

Francis L Freas Glass Works.........................610 828-0430
148 E 9th Ave Conshohocken (19428) *(G-3549)*

Francis Latovich..570 339-1059
650 E 3rd St Mount Carmel (17851) *(G-11624)*

Francis Latovich Machine Shop, Mount Carmel *Also called Francis Latovich (G-11624)*

Franconia Plastics Corp................................215 723-8926
675 Forman Rd Souderton (18964) *(G-17735)*

Frank Bellace Welding..................................856 488-8099
3965 Snydertown Rd Danville (17821) *(G-4002)*

Frank Bryan Inc (PA)....................................412 331-1630
1263 Chartiers Ave Mc Kees Rocks (15136) *(G-10609)*

Frank Bryan Inc..412 431-2700
100 S 3rd St Pittsburgh (15219) *(G-15031)*

Frank Calandra Inc (PA)...............................412 963-9071
258 Kappa Dr Pittsburgh (15238) *(G-15032)*

Frank Casilio and Sons Inc (PA)....................610 867-5886
1035 Mauch Chunk Rd Bethlehem (18018) *(G-1518)*

Frank Casilio and Sons Inc...........................610 253-3558
1395 S 25th St Easton (18042) *(G-4685)*

Frank Custom Stainless Inc..........................412 784-0300
131 Cherry St Pittsburgh (15223) *(G-15033)*

Frank D Suppa Lumber Inc (PA).....................814 723-7360
740 Pleasant Dr Warren (16365) *(G-19026)*

Frank Daddario Wdwrkng...............................610 476-3414
1633 Sheridan Ln Audubon (19403) *(G-825)*

Frank Ferris Industries Inc (PA)....................724 352-9477
901 N Pike Rd Cabot (16023) *(G-2457)*

Frank Griffith..570 524-7175
2297 Pheasant Ridge Rd Lewisburg (17837) *(G-9909)*

Frank Griffith Remdlng/Cstm CB, Lewisburg *Also called Frank Griffith (G-9909)*

Frank J Butch Co Inc.....................................215 322-7399
5629 Tulip St Philadelphia (19124) *(G-13718)*

Frank J May Co Inc..215 923-3165
256 S 11th St Philadelphia (19107) *(G-13719)*

Frank Jones Sporting Goods, Norristown *Also called Hanford & Hockenbrock (G-12665)*

Frank Mance Plating Service.........................412 281-5748
2823 Penn Ave Pittsburgh (15222) *(G-15034)*

Frankenstein Builders Supplies, Zelienople *Also called Frankenstein Builders Supply (G-20802)*

Frankenstein Builders Supply.......................724 333-5260
404 Walnut St Zelienople (16063) *(G-20802)*

Frankensteins...814 938-2571
113 Shields Ave Punxsutawney (15767) *(G-16140)*

Frankford Candy LLC.....................................215 735-5200
9300 Ashton Rd Frnt Philadelphia (19114) *(G-13720)*

Frankford Plating Inc.....................................215 288-4518
2505 Orthodox St Philadelphia (19137) *(G-13721)*

Franklin Advanced Materials, Conshohocken *Also called American Ref & Biochem Inc (G-3520)*

Franklin Brine Treatment Corp (PA)...............814 437-3593
5148 Us 322 Franklin (16323) *(G-6125)*

Franklin Bronze & Alloy Co Inc.....................814 437-6891
655 Grant St Franklin (16323) *(G-6126)*

Franklin Bronze Precision Comp (HQ)............814 437-6891
655 Grant St Franklin (16323) *(G-6127)*

Franklin Clothing Company Inc.....................717 264-5768
5121 Innovation Way # 6 Chambersburg (17201) *(G-2932)*

Franklin Hill Vineyards Inc...........................610 332-9463
597 Main St Fl 2 Bethlehem (18018) *(G-1519)*

Franklin Hill Vineyards Inc (PA)....................610 588-8708
7833 Franklin Hill Rd Bangor (18013) *(G-914)*

Franklin Hill Vineyards Inc...........................610 559-8966
3625 Nazareth Rd Easton (18045) *(G-4686)*

Franklin Industries, Franklin *Also called Franklin Investment Corp (G-6130)*

Franklin Industries Co...................................814 437-3726
645 Atlantic Ave Franklin (16323) *(G-6128)*

Franklin Industries Inc..................................814 437-3726
600 Atlantic Ave Franklin (16323) *(G-6129)*

Franklin Instrument Co Inc............................215 355-7942
1187 Spencer Rd Warminster (18974) *(G-18883)*

Franklin Investment Corp..............................814 437-3726
645 Atlantic Ave Franklin (16323) *(G-6130)*

Franklin Penn Publishing Co.........................724 327-3471
4021 Old William Penn Hwy Murrysville (15668) *(G-11851)*

Franklin Potter Associates...........................215 345-0844
3681 Cold Spg Crmry Rd Doylestown (18902) *(G-4300)*

Franklin Shopper...717 263-0359
25 Penncraft Ave Ste 405 Chambersburg (17201) *(G-2933)*

Franklin Shopper, The, Chambersburg *Also called Franklin Shopper (G-2933)*

Franklin Steel Div, Franklin *Also called Franklin Industries Inc (G-6129)*

Franks Ice Service LLC..................................215 741-2026
3566 Hulmeville Rd Bensalem (19020) *(G-1198)*

Franks International LLC..............................724 943-3243
153 Dora Village Main St Greensboro (15338) *(G-6646)*

Franks Marble & Granite LLC.........................717 244-2685
125 Householder Ave Red Lion (17356) *(G-16595)*

Fraser Optics, Feasterville Trevose *Also called Fraser-Volpe LLC (G-5911)*

Fraser Optics LLC...215 443-5240
210 Andrews Rd Trevose (19053) *(G-18494)*

Fraser-Volpe LLC (PA)...................................215 443-5240
210 Andrews Rd Feasterville Trevose (19053) *(G-5911)*

Frazier Machine Company Inc......................717 632-1101
557 Centennial Ave Hanover (17331) *(G-6887)*

Frazier-Simplex Machine Co..........................724 222-5700
1720 N Main St Washington (15301) *(G-19177)*

Frb Machine Inc...724 867-0111
119 College Street Ext Emlenton (16373) *(G-5007)*

Freas Glass Works Inc..................................610 825-0430
401 E 4th St Ste 8f Bridgeport (19405) *(G-2036)*

Freckled Sage..610 888-2037
3245 Amber St Ste 6 Philadelphia (19134) *(G-13722)*

Fred Fairburn 570 282-3364
40 N Main St Carbondale (18407) (G-2675)

Fred Foust 724 845-7028
1129 Industrial Park Rd # 3 Vandergrift (15690) (G-18727)

Frederick Drilling Co & Sons 814 744-8581
18 Piper Ln Tylersburg (16361) (G-18573)

Frederick Wohlgemuth Inc 215 638-9672
3901 Bristol Pike Bensalem (19020) (G-1199)

Fredericks Company Inc 215 947-2500
2400 Philmont Ave Huntingdon Valley (19006) (G-7985)

Frediani Printing Company 412 281-8533
1719 Liberty Ave Pittsburgh (15222) (G-15035)

Freds Signs 412 741-3153
22 Spruce St Pittsburgh (15202) (G-15036)

Free Energy Systems Inc 610 583-2640
17 S Macdade Blvd 101-1 Collingdale (19023) (G-3404)

Free-Col Laboratories, Meadville Also called Modern Industries Inc (G-10765)

Freedman Seating Company 610 265-3610
150 Gordon Dr Exton (19341) (G-5681)

Freedom Components Inc 717 242-0101
262 Roundhouse Rd Lewistown (17044) (G-9930)

Freedom Corrugated LLC 570 384-7500
595 Oak Ridge Rd Hazle Township (18202) (G-7458)

Freedom Cyber Marketing LLC (PA) 717 654-2392
660 Blossom Hill Ln Dallastown (17313) (G-3975)

Freedom Management Svcs LLC 215 328-9111
440 Horsham Rd Ste 2 Horsham (19044) (G-7819)

Freedom Metals Mfg Inc (PA) 814 224-4438
185 Commerce Dr Duncansville (16635) (G-4451)

Freedom Millwork Corp 215 642-2213
5110 Applebutter Rd Pipersville (18947) (G-14616)

Freedom Technologies Inc 717 242-0101
855 Roundhouse Rd Lewistown (17044) (G-9931)

Freedom Welding 717 437-0943
816 E Freedom Ave Burnham (17009) (G-2360)

Freeland Machine Co, Freeland Also called Stephen R Lechman (G-6196)

Freeland's Fine Woodfinishings, West Springfield Also called Freelands Fine Wood
Finishings (G-19768)

Freelands Fine Wood Finishings 814 922-7101
14315 Underridge Rd West Springfield (16443) (G-19768)

Freespiritjeans Co, Philadelphia Also called Freespiritjeanscom Inc (G-13723)

Freespiritjeanscom Inc 302 319-9313
1735 Market St Ste 3750 Philadelphia (19103) (G-13723)

Freeze Thaw Cycles 814 272-0178
109 S Allen St State College (16801) (G-17966)

Freight Car Division, Johnstown Also called Johnstown America Corporation (G-8388)

Fremer Moulding Inc 814 265-0671
22 Sawmill Dr Brockway (15824) (G-2226)

Fremor Orchards Custom Mchs, York Also called Charles R Kelley (G-20423)

French Creek Offset Inc 610 582-3241
127 N Mill St Birdsboro (19508) (G-1696)

French Creek Woodworking Inc 610 286-9295
392 Trythall Rd Elverson (19520) (G-4963)

French Quaters 724 845-7387
1140 State Route 356 Leechburg (15656) (G-9645)

Frenchcreek Production Inc 814 437-1808
100 N 13th St Franklin (16323) (G-6131)

Freno Jr A J Mining 814 845-2286
4707 Gipsy Rd Glen Campbell (15742) (G-6424)

Fres-Co Systems Usa Inc (HQ) 215 721-4600
3005 State Rd Telford (18969) (G-18290)

Fresenius Kabi Usa Inc 724 772-6900
770 Commonwealth Dr Warrendale (15086) (G-19073)

Fresh Donuts 717 273-8886
1202 Cumberland St Lebanon (17042) (G-9572)

Fresh Express Mid-Atlantic LLC 717 561-2900
7505 Grayson Rd Harrisburg (17111) (G-7131)

Fresh Food Manufacturing Co 412 963-6200
101 Kappa Dr Pittsburgh (15238) (G-15037)

Fresh Foods Manufacturing 724 683-3639
2500 Lovi Rd Freedom (15042) (G-6190)

Fresh Link Industrial Ltd 724 779-6880
511 Thomson Park Dr Cranberry Township (16066) (G-3819)

Fresh Made Inc 215 725-9013
810 Bleigh Ave Philadelphia (19111) (G-13724)

Fresh Pet, Bethlehem Also called Freshpet Inc (G-1520)

Fresh Press LLC 717 504-9223
112 Savannah Dr Hummelstown (17036) (G-7911)

Fresh Roasted Coffee LLC 570 743-9228
200 N River Ave Sunbury (17801) (G-18169)

Fresh Start Vend & Cof Svc LLC 215 322-8647
86 Green Valley Dr Southampton (18966) (G-17813)

Fresh Tofu Inc 610 433-4711
1101 Harrison St Allentown (18103) (G-219)

Freshpet Inc 610 997-7192
176 N Commerce Way Bethlehem (18017) (G-1520)

Freshtemp LLC 844 370-1782
6739 Reynolds St Pittsburgh (15206) (G-15038)

Fretz Corporation (PA) 215 671-8300
4050 S 26th St Ste 100 Philadelphia (19112) (G-13725)

Frew Mill Die Crafts Inc 724 658-9026
311 W Grant St New Castle (16101) (G-12095)

Frey Group LLC 717 786-2146
372 Puseyville Rd Quarryville (17566) (G-16270)

Frey Lumber Company Inc 724 564-1888
2883 Morgantown Rd Smithfield (15478) (G-17648)

Frey Lutz Corp 717 394-4635
1195 Ivy Dr Lancaster (17601) (G-9025)

Frey Pallet Corporation 724 564-1888
2883 Morgantown Rd Smithfield (15478) (G-17649)

Freys Farm Dairy LLC 717 860-8015
1587 Newcomer Rd Chambersburg (17202) (G-2934)

Freys Research Inc (PA) 724 586-5659
463 Brownsdale Rd 1 Renfrew (16053) (G-16639)

Friendly City Box Co Inc 814 266-6287
520 Oakridge Dr Johnstown (15904) (G-8373)

Friendly Fuel 717 254-1932
156 Newville Rd Newburg (17240) (G-12475)

Friendly Organic LLC 609 709-2924
821 N Hancock St Philadelphia (19123) (G-13726)

Friends Boarding Ho Buc Qua ME 215 968-3346
50 S Congress St Newtown (18940) (G-12503)

Friends Journal, Philadelphia Also called Friends Publishing Corp (G-13727)

Friends Publishing Corp 215 563-8629
1216 Arch St Ste 2a Philadelphia (19107) (G-13727)

Friesens Welding 570 523-3580
3266 Col John Kelly Rd Lewisburg (17837) (G-9910)

Friesens Welding & Mfg, Lewisburg Also called Friesens Welding (G-9910)

Friskies Pet Care Factory, Allentown Also called Nestle Purina Petcare Company (G-329)

Frito-Lay North America Inc 570 323-6175
220 N Reach Rd Williamsport (17701) (G-20014)

Frito-Lay North America Inc 717 624-4206
140 Enterprise Dr Ste A New Oxford (17350) (G-12409)

Frito-Lay North America Inc 717 792-2611
3553 Gillespie Dr York (17404) (G-20488)

Fritz Logging 814 623-6011
620 S Richard St Bedford (15522) (G-1050)

Fritz Tastee Creme 570 925-2404
372 Distillery Hill Rd Benton (17814) (G-1279)

Fritzsche Organ Co Inc 610 797-2510
505 E Emmaus Ave Allentown (18103) (G-220)

Frog Creek Socks 215 997-6104
779 N Limekiln Pike Chalfont (18914) (G-2875)

Frog Switch and Mfg Co 717 243-2454
600 E High St Carlisle (17013) (G-2715)

Frogurt LLC 724 263-4299
507 Pinoak Dr Monroeville (15146) (G-11338)

Froio's Lawn & Landscape, West Chester Also called Hopper Lawn & Ldscp MGT
LLC (G-19563)

From Heart 570 278-6343
2 Public Ave Montrose (18801) (G-11464)

Fromm Elc Sup Corp Rding Penna 570 387-9711
1877 Columbia Blvd Bloomsburg (17815) (G-1783)

Frontage Laboratories Inc (PA) 610 232-0100
700 Pennsylvania Dr Exton (19341) (G-5682)

Frontage Laboratories Inc 610 232-0100
75 E Uwchlan Ave Ste 100 Exton (19341) (G-5683)

Fronti Fabrications Inc 610 900-6160
1145a Little Gap Rd Palmerton (18071) (G-13105)

Frontida Biopharm Inc 215 288-6500
7722 Dungan Rd Philadelphia (19111) (G-13728)

Frontida Biopharm Inc (PA) 610 232-0112
1100 Orthodox St Philadelphia (19124) (G-13729)

Frontier LLC 570 265-2500
67 Campbell Rd Towanda (18848) (G-18426)

Frontier Wood Products Inc 215 538-2330
500 E Pumping Station Rd Quakertown (18951) (G-16195)

Frontline Graphics Inc (PA) 610 941-2750
200 Barr Harbor Dr # 400 Conshohocken (19428) (G-3550)

Frosted Fantasia Cupcakes LLC 724 601-9440
1309 Rebecca Ct Oakdale (15071) (G-12899)

Frosty Hollow Hardwoods 724 568-2406
1127 Frosty Hollow Ln Vandergrift (15690) (G-18728)

Frox (PA) 215 822-9011
17 N 7th St Perkasie (18944) (G-13277)

Frp Architectural Doors, Bensalem Also called Frp Door Concepts Inc (G-1200)

Frp Door Concepts Inc 215 604-1545
2424 State Rd Ste 8 Bensalem (19020) (G-1200)

Fruehauf Manufacturing 412 771-4200
2069 New Castle Rd Portersville (16051) (G-15927)

Fry & 146 Cast Division 570 546-2109
3700 Clarkstown Rd Muncy (17756) (G-11817)

Fry Communications Inc (PA) 717 766-0211
800 W Church Rd Mechanicsburg (17055) (G-10846)

Fry International LLC 215 847-6359
715 Martin Rd Ofc Elkins Park (19027) (G-4903)

Fs-Elliott Co LLC (PA) 724 387-3200
5710 Mellon Rd Export (15632) (G-5604)

Fs-North America Inc (PA)..................724 387-3200
  5710 Mellon Rd Export (15632) **(G-5605)**
FSI Industries Inc..................215 295-0552
  8 Nancia Dr Levittown (19054) **(G-9837)**
Fsm Tools (PA)..................717 867-5359
  255 N Ulrich St Annville (17003) **(G-648)**
Ft Pitt Acquisition Corp..................412 269-2950
  400 Chess St Coraopolis (15108) **(G-3691)**
Fti, Erie Also called Finish Thompson Inc **(G-5290)**
Fts International LLC..................724 873-1021
  6000 Town Center Blvd Canonsburg (15317) **(G-2589)**
Fuchs Grafo Colloids Division, Emlenton Also called Fuchs Lubricants Co **(G-5008)**
Fuchs Lubricants Co..................724 867-5000
  105 8th St Emlenton (16373) **(G-5008)**
Fudgiewudgie, Pittsburgh Also called Three Rivers Confections LLC **(G-15618)**
Fuel..................215 468-3835
  1917 E Passyunk Ave Philadelphia (19148) **(G-13730)**
Fuel..................215 922-3835
  1225 Walnut St Philadelphia (19107) **(G-13731)**
Fuel & Save Inc..................814 857-5356
  Rr 879 Bigler (16825) **(G-1659)**
Fuel Cell Inc..................610 759-0143
  5879 Sullivan Trl Nazareth (18064) **(G-11967)**
Fuel Doctor Inc..................904 521-9889
  85 Tucker Dr Ronks (17572) **(G-16807)**
Fuel ME Green LLC..................267 825-7193
  1010 Race St Apt 6a Philadelphia (19107) **(G-13732)**
Fuel On Whitehaven LLC..................570 443-8830
  601 Church St White Haven (18661) **(G-19847)**
Fuel One Gas Cnvenience Str LLC..................551 208-3490
  17 Red Coat Ln Mountain Top (18707) **(G-11761)**
Fuel Recharge Yourself Inc 3..................215 468-3835
  1650 Arch St Philadelphia (19103) **(G-13733)**
Fuel Treatment Solutions LLC..................215 914-1006
  48 Lee Lynn Ln Huntingdon Valley (19006) **(G-7986)**
Fuel7 Inc..................267 980-7888
  13 Summit Square Ctr Langhorne (19047) **(G-9299)**
Fuelone Gas Cnvenience Str LLC..................570 443-8830
  601 Church St White Haven (18661) **(G-19848)**
Fuels & Lubes Technologies LLC..................724 282-8264
  152 Mclafferty Rd Fenelton (16034) **(G-5945)**
Full Strut Logging LLC..................814 323-5292
  20065 Hammond Rd Corry (16407) **(G-3761)**
Full Throttle Industries LLC..................724 926-2140
  328 E Lincoln Ave Mc Donald (15057) **(G-10574)**
Full-On Filters..................610 970-4701
  517 W Vine St Pottstown (19464) **(G-15989)**
Fulmer, Export Also called Lemm Liquidating Company LLC **(G-5615)**
Fulmer Company Inc..................724 325-7140
  3004 Vent Ct Westmrelnd I Export (15632) **(G-5606)**
Fulton County News..................717 485-4513
  417 E Market St Mc Connellsburg (17233) **(G-10565)**
Fulton County Reporter..................717 325-0079
  50 Hillside Ests Mc Connellsburg (17233) **(G-10566)**
Fulton Forest Products..................814 782-3448
  683 Fulton Rd Shippenville (16254) **(G-17561)**
Fulton Precision Inds Inc..................717 485-5158
  300 Success Dr Mc Connellsburg (17233) **(G-10567)**
Fun-Time International Inc..................215 925-1450
  433 W Girard Ave Philadelphia (19123) **(G-13734)**
Function Inc..................570 317-0737
  236 Parrs Mill Rd Catawissa (17820) **(G-2818)**
Function of Beauty, Catawissa Also called Function Inc **(G-2818)**
Funks Drilling Incorporated..................717 423-6688
  30 Myers Rd Newville (17241) **(G-12601)**
Funky Signs of Doylestown, Doylestown Also called A Funky Little Sign Shop **(G-4266)**
Furman Foods Inc..................570 473-3516
  770 Cannery Rd Northumberland (17857) **(G-12867)**
Furmano Foods, Northumberland Also called Furman Foods Inc **(G-12867)**
Furniture Connection, The, Saint Marys Also called Printing Plus+ Inc **(G-17009)**
Furniture Factory, Meyersdale Also called Maple Mountain Industries Inc **(G-11015)**
Furnley H Frisch..................717 957-3261
  291 Sawmill Rd Duncannon (17020) **(G-4445)**
Fusion Coatings Inc..................610 693-5886
  932 W Penn Ave Robesonia (19551) **(G-16773)**
Fusion Five USA LLC..................267 507-6127
  1735 Market St Ste 3750 Philadelphia (19103) **(G-13735)**
Futernal Order Police Lodge..................610 655-6116
  815 Washington St Reading (19601) **(G-16386)**
Futura Identities Inc..................215 333-3337
  6909 Frankford Ave Philadelphia (19135) **(G-13736)**
Future Building of America Co, Farrell Also called Somerset Enterprises Inc **(G-5874)**
Future Foam Inc..................215 736-8611
  259 Canal Rd Fairless Hills (19030) **(G-5779)**
Future Generation Ag LLC..................844 993-3311
  20 Keystone Ct Ste 20 # 20 Leola (17540) **(G-9783)**
Future Home Technology, Mechanicsburg Also called Cappelli Enterprises Inc **(G-10826)**
Future-All Inc..................412 279-2670
  Hammond Gregg St Bldg 21 Carnegie (15106) **(G-2768)**

Fuzion Technologies Inc..................724 545-2223
  114 West Park Dr Kittanning (16201) **(G-8772)**
Fx Express Publications Inc..................267 364-5811
  310 Floral Vale Blvd Yardley (19067) **(G-20312)**
Fxg Fine and Label, Mechanicsburg Also called Factor X Graffics **(G-10842)**
Fxi Inc..................610 245-2800
  120 Concord Rd Aston (19014) **(G-766)**
Fxi Inc..................814 664-7771
  466 S Shady Ave Corry (16407) **(G-3762)**
Fxi Inc (HQ)..................610 744-2300
  1400 N Providence Rd # 2000 Media (19063) **(G-10926)**
Fxi Building Products Corp..................610 744-2230
  1400 N Providence Rd # 2000 Media (19063) **(G-10927)**
Fxi Foamex Innovations, Media Also called Fxi Holdings Inc **(G-10928)**
Fxi Holdings Inc (PA)..................610 744-2300
  1400 N Providence Rd # 2000 Media (19063) **(G-10928)**
Fyda Energy Solutions, Canonsburg Also called Fyda Frghtliner Pittsburgh Inc **(G-2590)**
Fyda Frghtliner Pittsburgh Inc..................724 514-2055
  20 Fyda Dr Canonsburg (15317) **(G-2590)**
G & B Specialties Inc..................570 752-5901
  535 W 3rd St Berwick (18603) **(G-1325)**
G & D Erectors Inc..................724 587-0590
  1552 Avella Rd Avella (15312) **(G-836)**
G & F Products Inc..................215 781-6222
  920 Levick St Philadelphia (19111) **(G-13737)**
G & H Contracting, Palmerton Also called G and H Contracting Inc **(G-13106)**
G & K Watterson Company..................724 827-2800
  507 2nd Ave New Brighton (15066) **(G-12037)**
G & L Designs..................610 868-1381
  4406 Easton Ave Unit 1 Bethlehem (18020) **(G-1521)**
G & M Co Inc..................610 779-7812
  1250 Roosevelt Ave Reading (19606) **(G-16387)**
G & M Sales, Reynoldsville Also called Ralph McClure **(G-16662)**
G & R Machine Company, Warren Also called Boekeloo Inc **(G-19014)**
G & S Foods Inc (PA)..................717 259-5323
  101 Sutton Rd Abbottstown (17301) **(G-4)**
G & S Metal Products Inc..................412 462-7000
  173 Pinchtown Rd Pittsburgh (15236) **(G-15039)**
G & W Instruments Inc..................570 282-7352
  277 Brooklyn St Carbondale (18407) **(G-2676)**
G A, Philadelphia Also called Graphic Arts Incorporated **(G-13782)**
G Adasavage LLC..................215 355-3105
  110 Pike Cir Huntingdon Valley (19006) **(G-7987)**
G and H Contracting Inc..................610 826-7542
  316 Columbia Ave Palmerton (18071) **(G-13106)**
G B Well Service..................412 221-3102
  533 Wshington Ave Ste 200 Bridgeville (15017) **(G-2065)**
G Beswick Enterprises Inc..................412 829-3068
  1719 Howell St North Versailles (15137) **(G-12775)**
G C Carl Klemmer Inc (PA)..................215 329-4100
  4401 N Philip St Philadelphia (19140) **(G-13738)**
G C Wyant Fine Jewelry, Indiana Also called G C Wyant Ltd **(G-8101)**
G C Wyant Ltd..................724 357-8000
  716 Philadelphia St Indiana (15701) **(G-8101)**
G Case Inc..................717 737-5000
  11 Devonshire Sq Mechanicsburg (17050) **(G-10847)**
G D C Manufacturing Inc..................724 864-5000
  12591 State Route 30 Irwin (15642) **(G-8163)**
G E S I, Washington Also called Greenbank Energy Solutions Inc **(G-19179)**
G E T, Allentown Also called Global Environmental Tech **(G-234)**
G F C Inc..................570 587-4588
  91 Quinton Rd Clarks Summit (18411) **(G-3193)**
G F Edwards Inc..................570 842-8438
  204 State Route 435 Elmhurst Township (18444) **(G-4958)**
G F Goodman & Son Inc (PA)..................215 672-8810
  2 Ivybrook Blvd Warminster (18974) **(G-18884)**
G G Greene Enterprises Inc (PA)..................814 723-5700
  21610 Route 6 Warren (16365) **(G-19027)**
G G S, York Also called Ggs Information Services Inc **(G-20499)**
G G Schmitt & Sons Inc (PA)..................717 394-3701
  2821 Old Tree Dr Lancaster (17603) **(G-9026)**
G H Forbes Screw Machine Pdts..................215 884-4343
  115 E Glenside Ave Ste A Glenside (19038) **(G-6518)**
G H Lainez Manufacturing Inc..................610 776-0778
  314 N 12th St Allentown (18102) **(G-221)**
G I Electric Company..................570 323-6147
  944 Sheridan St Rear Williamsport (17701) **(G-20015)**
G I S Inc..................412 771-8860
  23 Furnace Street Ext Mc Kees Rocks (15136) **(G-10610)**
G J Bear Company, Pottsville Also called William A Fraser Inc **(G-16102)**
G J Littlewood & Son Inc..................215 483-3970
  4045 Main St Philadelphia (19127) **(G-13739)**
G L Laub Surplus, Mc Clure Also called Gerald Laub **(G-10558)**
G L R Mining Inc..................724 254-4043
  410 Franklin St Clymer (15728) **(G-3272)**
G M C Inc..................215 638-4400
  1445 Ford Rd Bensalem (19020) **(G-1201)**
G M M, Rydal Also called Global Machine and Maint LLC **(G-16885)**

G M P, Trevose *Also called General Machine Pdts Kt LLC (G-18496)*

G N F Produts Inc 215 781-6222
1025 Washington Ave Croydon (19021) *(G-3917)*

G O Carlson Inc 814 678-4100
675 Colbert Ave Oil City (16301) *(G-12945)*

G O Carlson Inc 610 384-2800
350 Marshallton Thorndale Downingtown (19335) *(G-4228)*

G O Carlson Inc 814 678-4168
2456 Petroleum Center Rd Titusville (16354) *(G-18378)*

G R G Technologies LLC 610 325-6701
3954 Miller Rd Newtown Square (19073) *(G-12573)*

G R Graphics 814 774-9592
321 Mechanic St Girard (16417) *(G-6389)*

G S I, Kelton *Also called Gourmet Specialty Imports (G-8488)*

G S K, Philadelphia *Also called Glaxosmithkline LLC (G-13766)*

G S P Signs & Banners Inc 610 430-7000
553 E Gay St West Chester (19380) *(G-19556)*

G Scudese Consultants Inc 610 250-7800
373 Little Creek Dr Nazareth (18064) *(G-11968)*

G T Watts Inc 717 732-1111
108 Altoona Ave Enola (17025) *(G-5080)*

G V D Inc 724 537-5586
1305 Spring St Latrobe (15650) *(G-9477)*

G W Becker Inc 724 983-1000
2600 Kirila Blvd Hermitage (16148) *(G-7586)*

G Wb European Treasures 610 275-4395
401 E 4th St Ste 12a Bridgeport (19405) *(G-2037)*

G Weston Bakeries 570 455-2066
325 Kiwanis Blvd West Hazleton (18202) *(G-19710)*

G&M Bandsaw Inc 570 547-2386
6124 Us Highway 15 Montgomery (17752) *(G-11369)*

G&R Designs LLC 717 697-4538
102a W Main St Unit A Mechanicsburg (17055) *(G-10848)*

G&U Sand Svcs 717 246-6724
50 3rd St Windsor (17366) *(G-20196)*

G&W PA Laboratories LLC (HQ) 215 799-5333
650 Cathill Rd Sellersville (18960) *(G-17348)*

G&W Solutions Inc 610 704-6959
121 Main St Emmaus (18049) *(G-5026)*

G-O-Metric Incorporated 814 376-6940
415 N 2nd St Philipsburg (16866) *(G-14514)*

G-S Hydraulics Inc 814 938-2862
406 G And S Rd Punxsutawney (15767) *(G-16141)*

G-S Products, Somerset *Also called Gsp Marketing Inc (G-17692)*

G-Vox, Philadelphia *Also called Lyrrus Inc (G-13979)*

G. V. M. Company, Titusville *Also called Grand Valley Manufacturing Co (G-18379)*

G.I. Jobs, Coraopolis *Also called Victory Media Inc (G-3731)*

G2 Diesel Products Inc 717 525-8709
3990 Paxton St Harrisburg (17111) *(G-7132)*

Gaadt Perspectives LLC 610 388-7641
251 S Fairville Rd Chadds Ford (19317) *(G-2851)*

Gaberseck Bros 814 274-0763
141 Troupe Rd Coudersport (16915) *(G-3781)*

Gable Printing 724 443-3444
5499 William Flynn Hwy Gibsonia (15044) *(G-6335)*

Gablers Beverage Distributors 717 532-2241
29 N Seneca St Shippensburg (17257) *(G-17528)*

GAF Materials Corporation, New Columbia *Also called Standard Industries Inc (G-12176)*

Gai-Tronics Corporation (HQ) 610 777-1374
3030 Kutztown Rd Reading (19605) *(G-16388)*

Gaia Enterprises Inc 800 783-7841
103 Roy Ln Huntingdon Valley (19006) *(G-7988)*

Gail Dagowitz 610 642-7634
1130 Rock Creek Rd Gladwyne (19035) *(G-6408)*

Gaines Company 814 435-2332
Long Run Rd Gaines (16921) *(G-6236)*

Gaintenna 724 654-9900
3804 Wilmington Rd New Castle (16105) *(G-12096)*

Galaxy Brushes, Avoca *Also called Galaxy Mfg Company Inc (G-843)*

Galaxy Fans & Heaters, West Chester *Also called Lasko Products LLC (G-19588)*

Galaxy Global Products LLC (PA) 610 692-7400
820 Lincoln Ave West Chester (19380) *(G-19557)*

Galaxy Mfg Company Inc 570 457-5199
500 Gleason Dr Avoca (18641) *(G-843)*

Galaxy Products 215 426-8640
317 Avon St Philadelphia (19116) *(G-13740)*

Galaxy Silkscreening, Philadelphia *Also called Galaxy Products (G-13740)*

Galaxy Wire and Cable Inc 215 957-8714
903 Sheehy Dr Ste E Horsham (19044) *(G-7820)*

Galbar Couture, Upper Darby *Also called Atkins Kareemah (G-18682)*

Gale Mining Co 570 622-2524
1441 Oak Rd Pottsville (17901) *(G-16079)*

Galer Estates Vinyrd & Winery 484 899-8013
700 Folly Hill Rd Kennett Square (19348) *(G-8511)*

Galeron Consulting LLC 267 293-9230
507 Windsor Ct Apt B3 Bensalem (19020) *(G-1202)*

Gallagher Printing Inc 717 838-1527
601 W Main St Ste 3 Palmyra (17078) *(G-13123)*

Galliker Dairy Company (PA) 814 266-8702
143 Donald Ln Johnstown (15904) *(G-8374)*

Galliker Dairy Company 814 944-8193
819 9th Ave Altoona (16602) *(G-508)*

Galliker Dairy Company 814 623-8597
170 Transport St Bedford (15522) *(G-1051)*

Galliker Dairy Company 717 258-6199
1513 Commerce Ave Carlisle (17015) *(G-2716)*

Galliker's Quality Chekd, Johnstown *Also called Galliker Dairy Company (G-8374)*

Gallimed Sciences Inc 814 777-2973
3500 E College Ave # 1000 State College (16801) *(G-17967)*

Gallo Design Group 724 628-0198
232 N 7th St Connellsville (15425) *(G-3497)*

Gallop Printing 215 542-0887
1227 Thomas Dr Fort Washington (19034) *(G-6071)*

Galomb Inc 610 434-3283
523 N 22nd St Allentown (18104) *(G-222)*

Galvtech, Pittsburgh *Also called Techs Industries Inc (G-15603)*

Galway Pumps, North East *Also called C W S Inc (G-12734)*

Gamajet Cleaning Systems Inc 610 408-9940
604 Jeffers Cir Exton (19341) *(G-5684)*

Gambal Printing & Design 570 265-8968
1038 Golden Mile Rd Towanda (18848) *(G-18427)*

Gambone Steel Company Inc 610 539-6505
545 Foundry Rd Norristown (19403) *(G-12660)*

Game Call, Bradford *Also called Quaker Boy Inc (G-1988)*

Gamefreaks101 Inc 215 587-9787
100 S Broad St Ste 623 Philadelphia (19110) *(G-13741)*

Gamers Vault 609 781-0938
411 Doylestown Rd G Montgomeryville (18936) *(G-11398)*

Gamesa Energy Usa Inc 215 665-9810
1150 Northbrook Dr # 150 Trevose (19053) *(G-18495)*

Gamesa Wind, Feasterville Trevose *Also called Siemens Gamesa Renewable (G-5930)*

Gamesa Wind Pa LLC (HQ) 215 665-9810
1801 Market St Ste 2700 Philadelphia (19103) *(G-13742)*

Gamlet Inc 717 852-9200
1750 Toronita St York (17402) *(G-20489)*

Gamma Irradiator Service LLC 570 925-5681
337 Distillery Hill Rd Benton (17814) *(G-1280)*

Gamma Technologies, Pittsburgh *Also called Ferrari Importing Company (G-15014)*

Gampe Machine & Tool Co Inc 814 696-6206
1224 Route 22 Hollidaysburg (16648) *(G-7648)*

Gamry Instruments Inc 215 682-9330
734 Louis Dr Warminster (18974) *(G-18885)*

Gamut Enterprises Inc 717 627-5282
219 E Main St Lititz (17543) *(G-10011)*

Ganesco Incorporated 931 284-9033
2624 Thorntree Dr Pittsburgh (15241) *(G-15040)*

Ganesh Donuts Inc 215 351-9370
1113 Market St Philadelphia (19107) *(G-13743)*

Gannett Co Inc 724 778-3388
770 Commonwealth Dr Ste 1 Warrendale (15086) *(G-19074)*

Gannett Stllite Info Ntwrk Inc 215 679-9561
501 Graber Aly Red Hill (18076) *(G-16581)*

Gannett Stllite Info Ntwrk LLC 703 854-6185
507 Harrisburg Pike Dillsburg (17019) *(G-4130)*

Gannons Gourmet 610 439-8949
526 N Saint Cloud St Allentown (18104) *(G-223)*

Ganoe Paving Inc 717 597-2567
1455 Buchanan Trl W Greencastle (17225) *(G-6613)*

Gant Media Llc 814 765-5256
219 S 2nd St Clearfield (16830) *(G-3219)*

Gantrex Inc 412 347-0300
6000 Town Center Blvd # 240 Canonsburg (15317) *(G-2591)*

Gantrex Crane Rail I Installat 412 655-1400
6000 Town Center Blvd Canonsburg (15317) *(G-2592)*

Gap Pollution & Envmtl Ctrl 814 266-9469
100 Gapvax Ln Johnstown (15904) *(G-8375)*

Gap Ridge Contractors LLC 717 442-4386
5206 Old Strasburg Rd Kinzers (17535) *(G-8738)*

Gap Stamping LLC 610 759-7820
3717 Lyndon St Bethlehem (18020) *(G-1522)*

Gar-Ren Tool & Machine Co Inc 610 534-1897
705 Chester Pike Prospect Park (19076) *(G-16114)*

Garda CL Technical Svcs Inc 610 926-7400
500 Corporate Dr Bldg 5 Reading (19605) *(G-16389)*

Gardan Manufacturing Company 724 652-8171
171 State Route 18 # 16142 New Wilmington (16142) *(G-12466)*

Garden Craft, New Holland *Also called Ridge Craft (G-12279)*

Garden Pond Promotions Inc 814 695-4325
1000 Whitetail Ct Duncansville (16635) *(G-4452)*

Gardencraft Mfg 717 354-3430
2909 Lincoln Hwy E Gordonville (17529) *(G-6555)*

Gardinier Associates Inc 570 385-2721
202 E Liberty St Schuylkill Haven (17972) *(G-17157)*

Gardner Associate Enterprises 717 624-2003
2776 Oxford Rd New Oxford (17350) *(G-12410)*

Gardner Cryogenics Inc 610 264-4523
2136 City Line Rd Bethlehem (18017) *(G-1523)*

A
L
P
H
A
B
E
T
I
C

Gardner Denver Holdings Inc..814 742-9600
    150 Enterprise Campus Dr Altoona (16601) *(G-509)*
Gardner Denver Nash LLC..724 239-1522
    200 Simko Blvd Charleroi (15022) *(G-3014)*
Gardner Denver Nash LLC..203 459-3923
    200 Simko Blvd Charleroi (15022) *(G-3015)*
Gardner S Construction...610 395-6614
    6613 Saint Peters Rd Macungie (18062) *(G-10146)*
Garl Machine & Fabrication Inc.....................................610 929-7886
    1000 Midway Ave Temple (19560) *(G-18330)*
Garlits Industries Inc...215 736-2121
    30 N Pennsylvania Ave Morrisville (19067) *(G-11559)*
Garlits Printing, Morrisville Also called Garlits Industries Inc *(G-11559)*
Garlock Lubri Kup Division, Williamsport Also called Garlock Sealing Tech LLC *(G-20016)*
Garlock Sealing Tech LLC..570 323-9409
    208 Rose St Williamsport (17701) *(G-20016)*
Garment Dimensions Inc..610 838-0484
    1760 Wyndham Ter Bethlehem (18015) *(G-1524)*
Garnes Park E Jr..757 502-3381
    78 Big Spring Ter Newville (17241) *(G-12602)*
Garnon Mobility Vehicles, Erie Also called Garnon Truck Equipment Inc *(G-5300)*
Garnon Truck Equipment Inc...814 833-6000
    1617 Peninsula Dr Erie (16505) *(G-5300)*
Garrett & Co Inc..800 748-4608
    804 Montclair Dr New Kensington (15068) *(G-12341)*
Garrett Liners Inc..215 295-0200
    295 Lower Morrisville Rd Levittown (19054) *(G-9838)*
Garrett Precision LLC...717 779-1384
    55 S Fayette St Ste 4 York (17404) *(G-20490)*
Garretts Fabricating..724 528-8193
    2646 Mrcer W Middlesex Rd West Middlesex (16159) *(G-19725)*
Garrow's Draft Service, Greensburg Also called Tuna Enterprises *(G-6722)*
Garth Groft...717 819-9479
    2164 Southbrook Dr York (17403) *(G-20491)*
Gary Edward Soden..215 723-5964
    133 Winding Way Telford (18969) *(G-18291)*
Gary Fike Logging..724 329-7175
    192 Fike Hollow Rd Farmington (15437) *(G-5861)*
Gary Foster..717 248-5322
    702 W 4th St Lewistown (17044) *(G-9932)*
Gary Gioia Coal Co..412 754-0994
    319 Karen Dr Elizabeth (15037) *(G-4859)*
Gary James Designs..814 623-2477
    3759 Business 220 Ste 205 Bedford (15522) *(G-1052)*
Gary Murelle...570 888-7006
    109 S Elmer Ave Sayre (18840) *(G-17114)*
Gary N Snyder...215 735-5656
    251 S 17th St Philadelphia (19103) *(G-13744)*
Gary T Rossman...814 837-7017
    326 Birch St Kane (16735) *(G-8463)*
Gary's Putter Golf, Coudersport Also called Lionette Enterprises *(G-3784)*
Gas & Air Systems Inc..610 838-9625
    1304 Whitaker St Hellertown (18055) *(G-7556)*
Gas & Oil Management Assoc...814 563-4601
    80 Dillon Dr Youngsville (16371) *(G-20771)*
Gas Analytical Services Inc...724 349-8133
    130 Airport Rd Indiana (15701) *(G-8102)*
Gas Breaker Inc..610 407-7200
    17 Lee Blvd Ste D Malvern (19355) *(G-10238)*
Gas Field Specialists Inc (PA).......................................814 698-2122
    2107 State Route 44 S Shinglehouse (16748) *(G-17507)*
Gas N Go Washington...724 228-2850
    98 Murtland Ave Washington (15301) *(G-19178)*
Gas Processing Tech Group, West Chester Also called Matthey Johnson Inc *(G-19599)*
Gas Well Services 24-7 LLC...570 398-7879
    515 Joes Run Rd Jersey Shore (17740) *(G-8313)*
Gasbarre Products Inc..814 236-3108
    159 Mckee Rd Olanta (16863) *(G-12960)*
Gasbarre Products Inc (PA)...814 371-3015
    590 Division St Du Bois (15801) *(G-4392)*
Gasbarre Products Inc..814 834-2200
    310 State St Saint Marys (15857) *(G-16975)*
Gasket Resources Inc (PA)..610 363-5800
    280 Boot Rd Downingtown (19335) *(G-4229)*
Gaslite America, Springdale Also called American Gas Lamp Works LLC *(G-17898)*
Gatan Inc...724 779-2572
    780 Commonwealth Dr Warrendale (15086) *(G-19075)*
Gate 7 LLC...717 593-0204
    1098 Armada Dr Greencastle (17225) *(G-6614)*
Gateco Inc...610 433-2100
    805 Harrison St Allentown (18103) *(G-224)*
Gatehouse, Honesdale Also called Carbondale News *(G-7705)*
Gatehouse Media LLC...570 253-3055
    220 8th St Ofc Honesdale (18431) *(G-7712)*
Gatehouse Media LLC...570 742-9671
    21 N Arch St Milton (17847) *(G-11239)*
Gates Corporation...717 267-7000
    1675 Orchard Dr Chambersburg (17201) *(G-2935)*

Gates Logging LLC...814 353-1238
    304 Gates Mountain Rd Howard (16841) *(G-7890)*
Gateway Industrial Services, Allentown Also called Gateco Inc *(G-224)*
Gateway Newspapers, Tarentum Also called Tribune-Review Publishing Co *(G-18251)*
Gateway Newspapers...412 856-7400
    460 Rodi Rd Pittsburgh (15235) *(G-15041)*
Gateway Packaging Corp...724 327-7400
    2240 Boyd Rd Export (15632) *(G-5607)*
Gateway Paint & Chemical Co..412 261-6642
    2929 Smallman St Pittsburgh (15201) *(G-15042)*
Gateway Press, Monroeville Also called Gateway Publications *(G-11339)*
Gateway Publications (PA)...412 856-7400
    610 Beatty Rd Ste 2 Monroeville (15146) *(G-11339)*
Gateway Publications...412 856-7400
    5500 Stbnvlle Pike Ste 1a Mckees Rocks (15136) *(G-10660)*
Gatto Moto LLC..412 487-3377
    1463 Glenn Ave Glenshaw (15116) *(G-6488)*
Gaumer Tool Machine Co Inc...717 266-0273
    230 Industrial Rd York (17406) *(G-20492)*
Gautier Steel Ltd..814 535-9200
    80 Clinton St Johnstown (15901) *(G-8376)*
Gaven Industries Inc..724 352-8100
    6655 N Noah Dr Saxonburg (16056) *(G-17087)*
Gaydos Equipment LLC...724 272-6951
    5060 Willow Wood Dr Gibsonia (15044) *(G-6336)*
Gazebo Room Salad Dressing, Lewisberry Also called Best Dressed Associates Inc *(G-9881)*
Gazette Printers, Indiana Also called Indiana Printing and Pubg Co *(G-8106)*
Gazette Two DOT O...412 458-1526
    706 Broadway Ave Mc Kees Rocks (15136) *(G-10611)*
Gb Biosciences Corporation...713 453-7281
    3959 Welsh Rd 369 Willow Grove (19090) *(G-20118)*
Gby Corporation..724 539-1626
    1001 Lloyd Ave Latrobe (15650) *(G-9478)*
Gc Enterprises LLC..570 655-5543
    457 N Main St Pittston (18640) *(G-15752)*
Gck US Processing, King of Prussia Also called Glaxosmithkline LLC *(G-8622)*
Gcl Inc..724 282-2221
    685 Glenwood Way Butler (16001) *(G-2403)*
Gcl Inc (PA)...724 933-7260
    2559 Brandt School Rd # 201 Wexford (15090) *(G-19805)*
Gda Corp...814 237-4060
    301 Science Park Rd # 112 State College (16803) *(G-17968)*
Gdc Fine Jewelry, Irwin Also called G D C Manufacturing Inc *(G-8163)*
Gdc/Keystone Wire Cloth, Hanover Also called Daniel Gerard Worldwide Inc *(G-6875)*
Gdp Space Systems, Horsham Also called Delta Information Systems Inc *(G-7809)*
GE Betz International Inc (HQ)..215 957-2200
    4636 Somerton Rd Langhorne (19053) *(G-9300)*
GE Enrgy Pwr Cnversion USA Inc (HQ)..............................412 967-0765
    100 E Kensinger Dr # 500 Cranberry Township (16066) *(G-3820)*
GE Infrastructure Sensing (HQ).......................................617 926-1749
    4636 Somerton Rd Feasterville Trevose (19053) *(G-5912)*
GE Infrastructure Sensing Inc..814 834-5506
    967 Windfall Rd Saint Marys (15857) *(G-16976)*
GE Oil & Gas, Muncy Also called Vetco Gray Inc *(G-11837)*
GE Sensing & Inspection Tech, Saint Marys Also called Amphenol Thermometrics Inc *(G-16948)*
GE Transportation Sys, Emporium Also called Alstom Signaling Operation LLC *(G-5048)*
GE Transportation Systems, Erie Also called Alstom Signaling Operation LLC *(G-5184)*
GE Water & Process Tech, Feasterville Trevose Also called GE Infrastructure Sensing *(G-5912)*
Ge-Hitachi Nuclear Energy...724 743-0270
    50 Curry Ave Canonsburg (15317) *(G-2593)*
Gea Systems North America Llc.......................................717 767-6411
    3475 Board Rd York (17406) *(G-20493)*
Gear 1, South Fork Also called Continental Apparel Corp *(G-17773)*
Gear Racewear Inc...724 458-6336
    517 Erie St Grove City (16127) *(G-6786)*
Geared Apparel, Morton Also called Amrit Works LLC *(G-11589)*
Gearmakers Inc...215 703-0390
    704 Forman Rd Souderton (18964) *(G-17736)*
GEC Enterprises Inc...570 662-8898
    15491 Route 6 Mansfield (16933) *(G-10415)*
Gecco Inc..570 945-3568
    Rr 407 Fleetville (18420) *(G-5966)*
Geemacher LLC...484 524-8251
    331 Circle Of Progress Dr Pottstown (19464) *(G-15990)*
Geh, Canonsburg Also called Ge-Hitachi Nuclear Energy *(G-2593)*
Gehret Wire Works Inc..215 236-3322
    437 N 11th St Philadelphia (19123) *(G-13745)*
Geissele Automatics LLC...610 272-2060
    800 N Wales Rd North Wales (19454) *(G-12803)*
Geitz Machine Inc..215 257-6752
    4422 Bethlehem Pike Telford (18969) *(G-18292)*
Gelateria...484 466-4228
    550 S Oak Ave Primos (19018) *(G-16108)*
Gelest Inc..215 547-1015
    1 Progress Dr Morrisville (19067) *(G-11560)*

Gelest Inc (PA) 215 547-1015
 11 Steel Rd E Morrisville (19067) *(G-11561)*
Gelest Realty Inc 215 547-1015
 11 Steel Rd E Morrisville (19067) *(G-11562)*
Gelest Technologies Inc 215 547-1015
 11 Steel Rd E Morrisville (19067) *(G-11563)*
Gellner Industrial LLC (PA) 570 668-8800
 105 Tide Rd Tamaqua (18252) *(G-18210)*
Gem Boutique, York *Also called Meighen Jinjou (G-20585)*
Gem Refrigerator Co (PA) 877 436-7374
 1339 Chestnut St Fl 16 Philadelphia (19107) *(G-13746)*
Gemanias Jeans Collection Inc 610 776-1777
 625 N 7th St Allentown (18102) *(G-225)*
Gemel Precision Tool Inc 215 355-2174
 31 Industrial Dr Warminster (18974) *(G-18886)*
Gemini Bakery Equipment Co 215 673-3520
 9990 Gantry Rd Philadelphia (19115) *(G-13747)*
Gemini Machining Company Inc 610 746-5000
 610 Bangor Rd Easton (18040) *(G-4687)*
Gemini Plastics Inc 215 736-1313
 7 Headley Pl Levittown (19054) *(G-9839)*
Gemini Precision Products Ltd 724 452-8700
 104 Isleworth Way Gibsonia (15044) *(G-6337)*
Gems Services Inc 215 399-8932
 5856 Penn St Philadelphia (19149) *(G-13748)*
Genco-Atc, Cranberry Township *Also called Atc Technology Corporation (G-3806)*
Gendx Products Inc 443 543-5254
 1349 Pennsridge Pl Downingtown (19335) *(G-4230)*
Gene Forrey Millwork 717 285-4046
 312 Druid Hill Dr Mountville (17554) *(G-11795)*
Gene Sanes & Associates 412 471-8224
 1645 Penn Ave Pittsburgh (15222) *(G-15043)*
Gene Szczurek S Quarterly P R 215 887-7377
 26 North Ave Wyncote (19095) *(G-20263)*
Gene Transcription Tech, Malvern *Also called Lifesensors Inc (G-10268)*
Genentech 717 572-8001
 5 Meadowbrook Ln Lititz (17543) *(G-10012)*
General Air Division, Erie *Also called Psb Industries Inc (G-5442)*
General Air Products, Exton *Also called Air Products Corporation (G-5637)*
General Air Products Inc 610 524-8950
 118 Summit Dr Exton (19341) *(G-5685)*
General Anesthetic Services 412 851-4390
 1900 Sleepy Hollow Rd South Park (15129) *(G-17783)*
General Blower Company, Exton *Also called General Air Products Inc (G-5685)*
General Cable Corporation 570 321-7750
 409 Reighard Ave Williamsport (17701) *(G-20017)*
General Cable Industries Inc 814 944-5002
 3101 Pleasant Valley Blvd Altoona (16602) *(G-510)*
General Carbide Corporation 724 836-3000
 1151 Garden St Greensburg (15601) *(G-6668)*
General Civil Company Inc 484 571-1998
 56a Concord Rd Aston (19014) *(G-767)*
General Doors, Bristol *Also called Mil-Del Corporation (G-2168)*
General Doors Corporation (PA) 215 788-9277
 1 Monroe St Bristol (19007) *(G-2146)*
General Dynamics Corporation 412 432-2200
 2730 Sidney St Ste 310 Pittsburgh (15203) *(G-15044)*
General Dynamics Corporation 570 340-1136
 156 Cedar Ave Scranton (18505) *(G-17237)*
General Dynamics Mission 412 488-8605
 2730 Sidney St Ste 310 Pittsburgh (15203) *(G-15045)*
General Dynamics Ots PA Inc 570 342-7801
 156 Cedar Ave Scranton (18505) *(G-17238)*
General Dynamics Ots PA Inc 717 244-4551
 200 E High St Red Lion (17356) *(G-16596)*
General Dynamics Ots PA Inc (HQ) 717 246-8208
 200 E High St Red Lion (17356) *(G-16597)*
General Dynmics Stcom Tech Inc 814 238-2700
 60 Decibel Rd Ste 200 State College (16801) *(G-17969)*
General Ecology Inc 610 363-7900
 151 Sheree Blvd Exton (19341) *(G-5686)*
General Electric Company 412 469-6080
 4930 Buttermilk Hollow Rd West Mifflin (15122) *(G-19739)*
General Electric Company 814 875-2234
 2901 E Lake Rd Erie (16531) *(G-5301)*
General Electric Company 724 450-1887
 1503 W Main Street Ext Grove City (16127) *(G-6787)*
General Electric Company 646 682-5601
 101 N Campus Dr Imperial (15126) *(G-8065)*
General Electric Company 610 770-1881
 404 Union Blvd Allentown (18109) *(G-226)*
General Electric Company 610 876-2200
 301 Saville Ave Eddystone (19022) *(G-4803)*
General Electric Company 215 289-0400
 1040 E Erie Ave Philadelphia (19124) *(G-13749)*
General Exterminating Co, Erie *Also called Specialized Svcs Promotions Inc (G-5487)*
General Fabricating Svcs LLC 412 262-1131
 1 Lewis Ave Coraopolis (15108) *(G-3692)*
General Foam Fabricators, Wilkes Barre *Also called M B Bedding Co (G-19939)*

General Foundry LLC 610 997-8660
 2350 Spring Valley Rd Bethlehem (18015) *(G-1525)*
General Graphics 724 337-1470
 1608 Leishman Ave New Kensington (15068) *(G-12342)*
General Lighting Division, Saint Marys *Also called Osram Sylvania Inc (G-16999)*
General Machine & Mfg Co 570 383-0990
 50 Pine St Peckville (18452) *(G-13209)*
General Machine Pdts Kt LLC 215 357-5500
 3111 Old Lincoln Hwy Trevose (19053) *(G-18496)*
General Machine Works Inc 717 848-2713
 515 E Prospect St York (17403) *(G-20494)*
General Manufacturing Co 412 833-4300
 3249 Industrial Blvd # 2 Bethel Park (15102) *(G-1415)*
General Medical Mfg LLC 610 599-0961
 519 Pennsylvania Ave Bangor (18013) *(G-915)*
General Metal Company Inc 215 638-3242
 1286 Adams Rd Bensalem (19020) *(G-1203)*
General Mills Inc 717 838-7600
 350 N Lingle Ave Palmyra (17078) *(G-13124)*
General Mills Inc 215 784-5100
 200 Dryden Rd E Ste 3000 Dresher (19025) *(G-4355)*
General Nuclear Corp 724 925-3565
 1651 New Stanton Hunker (15639) *(G-7928)*
General Nutrition Centers Inc (HQ) 412 288-4600
 300 6th Ave Fl 2 Pittsburgh (15222) *(G-15046)*
General Partition Company Inc 215 785-1000
 916 Washington Ave Croydon (19021) *(G-3918)*
General Partitions Mfg Corp (PA) 814 833-1154
 1702 Peninsula Dr Erie (16505) *(G-5302)*
General Plastics Inc 215 423-8200
 701 Kingston St Philadelphia (19134) *(G-13750)*
General Polymeric Corporation 610 374-5171
 1136 Morgantown Rd Reading (19607) *(G-16390)*
General Press Corporation (PA) 724 224-3500
 110 Allegheny Dr Natrona Heights (15065) *(G-11943)*
General Regulator Corp 717 848-5960
 517 E Prospect St York (17403) *(G-20495)*
General Rubber Corporation 412 424-0270
 200 Commerce Dr Ste 212 Coraopolis (15108) *(G-3693)*
General Services Fleet MGT, Pittsburgh *Also called City of Pittsburgh (G-14855)*
General Technical Plastics 610 363-5480
 424 Creamery Way Exton (19341) *(G-5687)*
General Transervice Inc (HQ) 610 857-1900
 211 Stewart Huston Dr Coatesville (19320) *(G-3304)*
General Welding & Machine Co 570 889-3776
 Bridge St Ringtown (17967) *(G-16753)*
General Weldments Inc 724 744-2105
 585 Pleasant Valley Rd Irwin (15642) *(G-8164)*
General Wire Spring Company 412 771-6300
 1101 Thompson Ave Mc Kees Rocks (15136) *(G-10612)*
Generation Stoneworks, McKeesport *Also called Prada Company Inc (G-10678)*
Generator and Mtr Svcs PA LLC 412 829-7500
 601 Braddock Ave Turtle Creek (15145) *(G-18565)*
Genergy Power LLC 717 584-0375
 1812 Olde Homestead Ln Lancaster (17601) *(G-9027)*
Generic Slides, Glenshaw *Also called Accu-Turn Tool Company Inc (G-6478)*
Generics International US Inc (HQ) 256 859-2575
 1400 Atwater Dr Malvern (19355) *(G-10239)*
Genesee River Trading Company 724 533-5354
 395 Brenneman Rd Volant (16156) *(G-18774)*
Genesis Alkali Wyoming LP 215 299-6904
 1735 Market St Philadelphia (19103) *(G-13751)*
Genesis Alkali Wyoming LP 215 845-4500
 1735 Market St Philadelphia (19103) *(G-13752)*
Genesis Hearing Systems 610 759-0459
 169 Spring St Nazareth (18064) *(G-11969)*
Genesis Packaging Technologies, Exton *Also called R-V Industries Inc (G-5726)*
Genesis Packaging Technologies, Exton *Also called Abps, Inc. (G-5635)*
Genesis Specialty Alkali LLC (HQ) 215 845-4550
 1735 Market St Fl 24 Philadelphia (19103) *(G-13753)*
Genesis Worldwide II Inc 724 538-3180
 130 Main St Callery (16024) *(G-2469)*
Genesys Controls Corporation 717 291-1116
 1908 Mcfarland Dr Landisville (17538) *(G-9260)*
Genesys Controls Corporation 717 291-1116
 1917 Olde Homestead Ln Landisville (17538) *(G-9261)*
Geneva Roth International LLC 724 887-8771
 3 Moyer Ave Scottdale (15683) *(G-17192)*
Genie Electronics Co Inc 717 244-1099
 3090 Cape Horn Rd Red Lion (17356) *(G-16598)*
Genie Electronics Co Inc (PA) 717 244-1099
 3090 Cape Horn Rd Red Lion (17356) *(G-16599)*
Genie Electronics Co Inc 717 840-6999
 1087 Valley View Rd York (17406) *(G-20496)*
Genilogix LLC 412 444-0554
 800 Waterfront Dr Ste 1 Pittsburgh (15222) *(G-15047)*
Genisphere LLC 215 996-3002
 2801 Sterling Dr Hatfield (19440) *(G-7344)*
Genoa Healthcare LLC 215 426-1007
 166 W Lehigh Ave Philadelphia (19133) *(G-13754)*

A
L
P
H
A
B
E
T
I
C

Genomind LLC 877 895-8658
  100 Highpoint Dr Ste 102 Chalfont (18914) *(G-2876)*

Genpore, Reading *Also called General Polymeric Corporation (G-16390)*

Gentell Inc 215 788-2700
  2701 Bartram Rd Bristol (19007) *(G-2147)*

Gentex Corporation (PA) 570 282-3550
  324 Main St Simpson (18407) *(G-17593)*

Gentherm Incorporated 215 362-9191
  215 Musket Cir Lansdale (19446) *(G-9372)*

Gentle Giant Brewing Co, Philadelphia *Also called AR Tart LLC (G-13404)*

Gentle Revolution Press 215 233-2050
  8801 Stenton Ave Glenside (19038) *(G-6519)*

Genuine Parts Company 215 968-4266
  42 Richboro Newtown Rd Newtown (18940) *(G-12504)*

Genus Lifesciences Inc 610 782-9780
  514 N 12th St Allentown (18102) *(G-227)*

Genx Sustainable Solutions Inc 484 244-7016
  1275 Glenlivet Dr Ste 100 Allentown (18106) *(G-228)*

Genzyme Corporation 610 594-8590
  115 Summit Dr Ste 3 Exton (19341) *(G-5688)*

Geo Fuels LLC 570 331-0800
  36 S Mountain Blvd Mountain Top (18707) *(G-11762)*

Geo Specialty Chemicals Inc 215 773-9280
  300 Brookside Ave Ambler (19002) *(G-579)*

Geo Specialty Chemicals Inc 215 773-9280
  903 Sheehy Dr Ste E Horsham (19044) *(G-7821)*

Geo Specialty Chemicals Inc 610 433-6331
  2409 N Cedar Crest Blvd Allentown (18104) *(G-229)*

Georg Fischer Harvel LLC (HQ) 610 252-7355
  300 Kuebler Rd Easton (18040) *(G-4688)*

Georg Fischer Harvel LLC 610 252-7355
  300 Kuebler Rd Easton (18040) *(G-4689)*

George Farms 570 275-0239
  33 Pottsgrove Rd Danville (17821) *(G-4003)*

George Fischer Harvel, Easton *Also called Georg Fischer Harvel LLC (G-4689)*

George I Reitz & Sons Inc (PA) 814 849-2308
  17214 Route 36 Brookville (15825) *(G-2261)*

George I Reitz & Sons Inc 412 824-9976
  805 Wood St East Pittsburgh (15112) *(G-4595)*

George J Anderton 814 382-9201
  9908 Louderman Rd Conneaut Lake (16316) *(G-3473)*

George J Bush Kitchen Center 724 694-9533
  1309 W 4th Ave Derry (15627) *(G-4101)*

George Kranich 610 295-2039
  201 E 10th St Marcus Hook (19061) *(G-10442)*

George L Wilson & Co Inc A 412 321-3217
  156 N Washington Rd Apollo (15613) *(G-675)*

George Nkashima Woodworker S A 215 862-2272
  1847 Aquetong Rd New Hope (18938) *(G-12302)*

George Skebeck 814 674-8169
  146 Sugar Ln Patton (16668) *(G-13188)*

George Skebeck Construction, Patton *Also called George Skebeck (G-13188)*

George T Bisel Co Inc 215 922-5760
  710 S Washington Sq Philadelphia (19106) *(G-13755)*

George T Faraghan Studios 215 928-0499
  940 N Delaware Ave Ste 2 Philadelphia (19123) *(G-13756)*

George Taylor Forklift Repair 412 221-7206
  108 Blythe Rd Morgan (15064) *(G-11517)*

George Weston Bakeries, Horsham *Also called Arnold Foods Company Inc (G-7788)*

George's Meats, Danville *Also called George Farms (G-4003)*

George-Ko Industries Inc 814 838-6992
  4861 W 23rd St Erie (16506) *(G-5303)*

Georgeos Water Ice Inc (PA) 610 494-4975
  409 Green St Marcus Hook (19061) *(G-10443)*

Georgetown Sand & Gravel Inc 724 573-9518
  3rd Rd Ext Georgetown (15043) *(G-6276)*

Georgia Web Inc (PA) 215 887-6600
  115 Lismore Ave Glenside (19038) *(G-6520)*

Georgia-Pacific Bldg Pdts LLC 814 778-6000
  147 Temple Dr Kane (16735) *(G-8464)*

Georgia-Pacific LLC 610 250-1400
  605 Kuebler Rd Easton (18040) *(G-4690)*

Georgia-Pacific LLC 215 538-7549
  3000 Am Dr Quakertown (18951) *(G-16196)*

Georgia-Pacific LLC 610 250-7402
  2410 Northampton St Easton (18042) *(G-4691)*

Georgia-Pacific LLC 717 266-3621
  25 Walnut St Mount Wolf (17347) *(G-11747)*

Georgia-Pacific LLC 814 778-6000
  149 Temple Dr Kane (16735) *(G-8465)*

Georgia-Pacific LLC 814 368-8700
  1 Owens Way Bradford (16701) *(G-1969)*

Geosonics Inc (PA) 724 934-2900
  359 Northgate Dr Ste 200 Warrendale (15086) *(G-19076)*

Gepharts Furniture 814 276-3357
  199 Dorchester Rd Alum Bank (15521) *(G-561)*

Gerald Boughner 814 432-3519
  508 Buffalo St Franklin (16323) *(G-6132)*

Gerald King Lumber Co Inc 724 887-3688
  1720 State Route 981 Ruffs Dale (15679) *(G-16872)*

Gerald Laub 570 658-2609
  Specht St Mc Clure (17841) *(G-10558)*

Gerald Maier 215 744-9999
  4332 Factory St Philadelphia (19124) *(G-13757)*

Gerald S Stillman 610 377-7650
  3440 Lehigh St Allentown (18103) *(G-230)*

Gerard Daniel Worldwide, Hanover *Also called Daniel Gerard Worldwide Inc (G-6873)*

Gerber Chair Mates Inc 814 266-6588
  1171 Ringling Ave Johnstown (15902) *(G-8377)*

Gerber Fabrics, Harrisburg *Also called Samuel Gerber Inc (G-7212)*

Gerdau Ameristeel US Inc 717 751-6898
  2870 Eastern Blvd York (17402) *(G-20497)*

Gerdau Ameristeel US Inc 717 846-7865
  1700 7th Ave York (17403) *(G-20498)*

Gerding Corp 215 441-0900
  809 Nina Way Warminster (18974) *(G-18887)*

Gerenser's Exotic Ice Cream, New Hope *Also called Robert Gerenser (G-12314)*

Gerg Tool & Die Inc 814 834-3888
  356 West Creek Rd Saint Marys (15857) *(G-16977)*

Gerhard Bilek, Cranesville *Also called Triple Creek (G-3872)*

Gerhart Coffee Co 717 397-8788
  224 Wohlsen Way Lancaster (17603) *(G-9028)*

Gerhart Systems & Contrls Corp (PA) 610 264-2800
  754 Roble Rd Ste 140 Allentown (18109) *(G-231)*

Germantown Tool & Mfg, Huntingdon Valley *Also called Germantown Tool Machine Sp Inc (G-7989)*

Germantown Tool and Machine, Huntingdon Valley *Also called Schiller Grounds Care Inc (G-8035)*

Germantown Tool Machine Sp Inc 215 322-4970
  1681 Republic Rd Huntingdon Valley (19006) *(G-7989)*

Germantown Welding Co 215 843-2643
  25 E Price St Philadelphia (19144) *(G-13758)*

Germantown Winery LLC 814 241-8458
  3586 Frankstown Rd Portage (15946) *(G-15917)*

Gerome Manufacturing Co Inc 724 438-8544
  80 Laurel View Dr Smithfield (15478) *(G-17650)*

Gerrity Markets, Scranton *Also called Gerritys Super Market Inc (G-17239)*

Gerritys Super Market Inc 570 961-9030
  320 Meadow Ave Scranton (18505) *(G-17239)*

Gerson Associates PC (PA) 215 637-6800
  2837 Southampton Rd Philadelphia (19154) *(G-13759)*

Gertrude Hawk Chocolates Inc (PA) 570 342-7556
  901 Keystone Indus Park Dunmore (18512) *(G-4473)*

Geryville Eye Associates PC 215 679-3500
  430 Pottstown Ave Pennsburg (18073) *(G-13248)*

Ges Automation Technology 717 236-8733
  2020 Greenwood St Harrisburg (17104) *(G-7133)*

Ges Graphite 205 838-0820
  2 Penn West Way Emlenton (16373) *(G-5009)*

Gesco Inc 724 846-8700
  711 4th St Beaver Falls (15010) *(G-999)*

Gessner Logging & Sawmill Inc 717 365-3883
  496 Luxemburg Rd Lykens (17048) *(G-10133)*

Gessner Products, Ambler *Also called New Thermo-Serv Ltd (G-594)*

Gesualdi Printing 215 785-3960
  2225 Farragut Ave Bristol (19007) *(G-2148)*

Get Hip Inc 412 231-4766
  R.J Casey Industrial Park Pittsburgh (15233) *(G-15048)*

Get It Right Tape Company Inc 570 383-6960
  1118 Mid Valley Dr Olyphant (18447) *(G-12991)*

Get-A-Grip Chafing Pans 724 443-6037
  2361 Banks School Rd Gibsonia (15044) *(G-6338)*

Getaways On Display Inc 717 653-8070
  147 Arrowhead Dr Manheim (17545) *(G-10386)*

Gettysburg Concrete Co Inc 717 334-1494
  1625 Baltimore Pike Gettysburg (17325) *(G-6291)*

Gettysburg Times Pubg LLC 717 253-9403
  1570 Fairfield Rd Gettysburg (17325) *(G-6292)*

Gettysburg Transformer Corp 717 334-2191
  1380 Old Harrisburg Rd Gettysburg (17325) *(G-6293)*

Gettysburg Village Factory Str 717 334-2332
  1863 Gettysburg Vlg Dr Gettysburg (17325) *(G-6294)*

Getz Paving 570 629-3007
  1038 Scenic Dr Kunkletown (18058) *(G-8833)*

Gexpro 570 265-2420
  151 Liberty Ln Towanda (18848) *(G-18428)*

Geyer & Son Inc 412 431-5231
  316 Poplargrove St Pittsburgh (15210) *(G-15049)*

GF Edwards Inc (PA) 570 842-8438
  204 State Route 435 Elmhurst Township (18444) *(G-4959)*

GF Edwards Inc 570 676-3200
  Rr 191 South Sterling (18460) *(G-17787)*

GF Harvel, Easton *Also called Georg Fischer Harvel LLC (G-4688)*

GFS, Coraopolis *Also called General Fabricating Svcs LLC (G-3692)*

Gfs LLC 412 262-1131
  1 Lewis Ave Coraopolis (15108) *(G-3694)*

Ggs Information Services Inc (PA) 717 764-2222
  3265 Farmtrail Rd York (17406) *(G-20499)*

Gh Holdings Inc (HQ) 610 666-4000
  Madison & Van Buren Ave Valley Forge (19482) *(G-18707)*

Gh Silver Asset Corp 404 432-3707
  1100 Vine St Apt C5 Philadelphia (19107) *(G-13760)*

Gharda Chemicals Limited 215 968-9474
  760 Newtown Yardley Rd # 110 Newtown (18940) *(G-12505)*

Ghp II LLC 724 775-0010
  400 9th St Monaca (15061) *(G-11290)*

Ghx Industrial LLC 410 687-7900
  151 N Washington St Greencastle (17225) *(G-6615)*

Gianna Skin & Laser Ltd 610 356-7870
  4667 West Chester Pike Newtown Square (19073) *(G-12574)*

Giant Eagle 724 772-1030
  20111 Route 19 Ste 35 Cranberry Township (16066) *(G-3821)*

Gibbons Brewing Co, Wilkes Barre *Also called Lion Brewery Inc (G-19936)*

Gibbys Ice Cream Inc 215 547-7253
  20 Candle Rd Levittown (19057) *(G-9840)*

Gibson Graphics Group Inc (PA) 717 755-7192
  4527 Cherry Ln Hellam (17406) *(G-7550)*

Gibson Journal 717 656-2582
  41 N Hershey Ave Leola (17540) *(G-9784)*

Gibson Stainless Specialty Inc 724 838-8320
  223 Donohoe Rd Greensburg (15601) *(G-6669)*

Gichner Shelter Systems, Dallastown *Also called Gichner Systems Group Inc (G-3976)*

Gichner Systems Group Inc (HQ) 877 520-1773
  490 E Locust St Dallastown (17313) *(G-3976)*

Gichner Systems Group LLC 717 244-7611
  490 E Locust St Dallastown (17313) *(G-3977)*

Gichner Systems Intl Inc (HQ) 717 244-7611
  490 E Locust St Dallastown (17313) *(G-3978)*

Gideon B Stoltzfus 717 656-4903
  2613 Stumptown Rd Bird In Hand (17505) *(G-1675)*

Giesler Engineering Inc 800 428-8616
  2881 Mount Rd Aston (19014) *(G-768)*

Giffin Interior & Fixture Inc 412 221-1166
  500 Scotti Dr Bridgeville (15017) *(G-2066)*

Gift Is In You Llc 267 974-3376
  13109 Bustleton Ave A17 Philadelphia (19116) *(G-13761)*

Gift Lumber Co Inc 610 689-9483
  7487 Boyertown Pike Douglassville (19518) *(G-4176)*

Gigantes Bakery, Masontown *Also called William Aupperle (G-10538)*

Gil Prebelli 215 281-0300
  10900 Dutton Rd Philadelphia (19154) *(G-13762)*

Gilbert Logging and Supply 717 528-4919
  1440 Cranberry Rd York Springs (17372) *(G-20766)*

Gilbert Printing Services 215 483-7772
  5635 Ridge Ave Philadelphia (19128) *(G-13763)*

Gilberton Coal, Gilberton *Also called R & R Energy Corp (G-6369)*

Gilberton Coal Company 570 874-1602
  10 Gilberton Rd Gilberton (17934) *(G-6367)*

Gilberton Energy Corporation (PA) 570 874-1602
  10 Gilberton Rd Gilberton (17934) *(G-6368)*

Gilead Enterprises Inc 717 733-2003
  15 Pleasure Rd Ephrata (17522) *(G-5106)*

Gill Powder Coating Inc 215 639-5486
  1384 Byberry Rd Bensalem (19020) *(G-1204)*

Gill Quarries Incorporated 610 584-6061
  3201 Potshop Rd East Norriton (19403) *(G-4584)*

Gill Rock Drill Company Inc 717 272-3861
  903 Cornwall Rd 905 Lebanon (17042) *(G-9573)*

Gillens Logging Inc 814 236-3999
  92 Patty Ln Curwensville (16833) *(G-3951)*

Gillespie Printing Inc 610 264-1863
  709 Roble Rd Unit 1 Allentown (18109) *(G-232)*

Gilliland Lumber, New Wilmington *Also called Gilliland Pallet Company Inc (G-12467)*

Gilliland Pallet Company Inc 724 946-2222
  71 Auction Rd New Wilmington (16142) *(G-12467)*

Gillo Brothers 724 254-4845
  7015 Rte 33 Hwy Clymer (15728) *(G-3273)*

Gilmore & Assoc Inc 215 345-4330
  65 E Butler Ave Ste 100 Doylestown (18901) *(G-4301)*

Gilson Boards LLC 570 798-9102
  62 Mountain View Rd Winfield (17889) *(G-20201)*

Gingrich Memorials Inc 717 272-0901
  424 Maple St 434 Lebanon (17046) *(G-9574)*

Ginty, Charles Cabinetmaker, Unionville *Also called Charles Ginty Associates Inc (G-18647)*

Giordano Incorporated 215 632-3470
  840 Mill Rd Bensalem (19020) *(G-1205)*

Giorgio Foods, Reading *Also called Digiorgio Mushroom Corp (G-16362)*

Giorgio Foods Inc (HQ) 610 926-2139
  1161 Park Rd Reading (19605) *(G-16391)*

Giovanni Demarco 724 898-7239
  271 Glade Mills Rd Valencia (16059) *(G-18697)*

Girard Coal, Girardville *Also called Girard Estate Fee (G-6405)*

Girard Estate Fee 570 276-1404
  Rr 54 Girardville (17935) *(G-6405)*

Gis, Emmaus *Also called Global Inserting Systems LLC (G-5027)*

Gish Logging Inc (PA) 717 369-2783
  4980 Path Valley Rd Fort Loudon (17224) *(G-6059)*

Gitman Bros, Ashland *Also called Hancock Company (G-731)*

Gittens Corp 215 945-0944
  1415 Hardy St Levittown (19057) *(G-9841)*

Giuntas Fine Woodworking 610 287-1749
  107 Yerger Rd Schwenksville (19473) *(G-17176)*

Givemefive.com, Fogelsville *Also called Five Thousand Forms Inc (G-5994)*

Giving Tree Inc 215 968-2487
  130 Heather Dr New Hope (18938) *(G-12303)*

Gjv Pharma LLC 267 880-6375
  995 Ferry Rd Doylestown (18901) *(G-4302)*

Gk Inc (PA) 215 223-7207
  2914 N 16th St Philadelphia (19132) *(G-13764)*

GK Flagstone Inc 570 942-4393
  405 State Route 374 Nicholson (18446) *(G-12613)*

Gkld Corp (PA) 215 643-6950
  794 Pnllyn Blue Bell Pike Blue Bell (19422) *(G-1830)*

GKN Instruments, Du Bois *Also called GKN Sinter Metals - Dubois Inc (G-4393)*

GKN Saint Marys, Kersey *Also called GKN Sinter Metals LLC (G-8561)*

GKN Sinter Metals LLC 814 486-3314
  1 Airport Rd Emporium (15834) *(G-5060)*

GKN Sinter Metals LLC 814 486-9234
  15420 Route 120 Emporium (15834) *(G-5061)*

GKN Sinter Metals LLC 814 885-8053
  319 Uhl Rd Kersey (15846) *(G-8559)*

GKN Sinter Metals LLC 814 781-6500
  104 Fairview Rd Kersey (15846) *(G-8560)*

GKN Sinter Metals LLC 814 781-6500
  104 Fairview Rd Kersey (15846) *(G-8561)*

GKN Sinter Metals - Dubois Inc 814 375-0938
  1 Tom Mix Dr Du Bois (15801) *(G-4393)*

GL Trade Capitl Mkts Solutions (HQ) 484 530-4400
  595 E Swedesford Rd 300 Wayne (19087) *(G-19332)*

Glacial Sand & Gravel Co (HQ) 724 548-8101
  1 Glade Dr Kittanning (16201) *(G-8773)*

Glades Pike Winery Inc 814 445-3753
  2208 Glades Pike Somerset (15501) *(G-17689)*

Gladstone Candies, Hummelstown *Also called Hiddie Kitchen Inc (G-7913)*

Glamorise Foundations Inc 570 322-7806
  2729 Reach Rd Williamsport (17701) *(G-20018)*

Glasgow Inc (PA) 215 884-8800
  104 Willow Grove Ave Glenside (19038) *(G-6521)*

Glasgow Inc 610 251-0760
  660 N Morehall Rd Malvern (19355) *(G-10240)*

Glasgow Inc 610 279-6840
  550 E Church Rd King of Prussia (19406) *(G-8620)*

Glasgow Hauling Inc 215 884-8800
  104 Willow Grove Ave Glenside (19038) *(G-6522)*

Glass Machinery Works LLC 724 473-0666
  594 Chapel Dr Ellwood City (16117) *(G-4933)*

Glass Molders Pottry Plstc 814 756-4042
  8751 Crossingville Rd Albion (16401) *(G-44)*

Glass Sports Cylinder Works, Charleroi *Also called Tri-State Hydraulics Inc (G-3022)*

Glass U LLC (PA) 855 687-7423
  4015 Chestnut St Philadelphia (19104) *(G-13765)*

Glassautomatic Inc 724 547-7500
  402 E Main St Ste 200 Mount Pleasant (15666) *(G-11700)*

Glasslight Inc 610 469-9066
  3611 Saint Peters Rd Saint Peters (19470) *(G-17034)*

Glatfelter Holdings LLC 717 225-2772
  96 S George St Ste 500 York (17401) *(G-20500)*

Glaxo Smith Kline, Philadelphia *Also called Glaxosmithkline PLC (G-13767)*

Glaxosmithkline 717 426-6644
  325 N Bridge St Marietta (17547) *(G-10462)*

Glaxosmithkline Consumer 717 268-0110
  105 Willow Springs Ln York (17406) *(G-20501)*

Glaxosmithkline LLC (HQ) 215 751-4000
  5 Crescent Dr Philadelphia (19112) *(G-13766)*

Glaxosmithkline LLC 610 223-9089
  345 W Walnut Tree Dr Blandon (19510) *(G-1754)*

Glaxosmithkline LLC 717 898-6853
  2937 Hearthside Ln Lancaster (17601) *(G-9029)*

Glaxosmithkline LLC 610 917-4085
  129 Buckwalter Rd Royersford (19468) *(G-16850)*

Glaxosmithkline LLC 610 270-5836
  570 Centre Ct Harleysville (19438) *(G-7034)*

Glaxosmithkline LLC 610 962-7548
  1440 Bernard Ave Willow Grove (19090) *(G-20119)*

Glaxosmithkline LLC 814 243-0366
  151 Raymond Dr Johnstown (15909) *(G-8378)*

Glaxosmithkline LLC 412 860-5475
  1042 Lexington Dr Export (15632) *(G-5608)*

Glaxosmithkline LLC 412 726-6041
  1207 Balsam Dr Imperial (15126) *(G-8066)*

Glaxosmithkline LLC 717 268-0319
  105 Willow Springs Ln York (17406) *(G-20502)*

Glaxosmithkline LLC 412 398-2600
  5547 Bartlett St Pittsburgh (15217) *(G-15050)*

Glaxosmithkline LLC 610 270-7125
  801 River Rd King of Prussia (19406) *(G-8621)*

A
L
P
H
A
B
E
T
I
C

Glaxosmithkline LLC...610 270-4692
709 Swedeland Rd King of Prussia (19406) *(G-8622)*

Glaxosmithkline LLC...610 917-4941
1250 S Collegeville Rd Collegeville (19426) *(G-3379)*

Glaxosmithkline LLC...610 768-3150
820 3rd Ave King of Prussia (19406) *(G-8623)*

Glaxosmithkline LLC...610 779-4774
42 Golfview Ln Reading (19606) *(G-16392)*

Glaxosmithkline LLC...610 270-4800
709 Swedeland Rd King of Prussia (19406) *(G-8624)*

Glaxosmithkline LLC...610 270-4800
893 River Rd Conshohocken (19428) *(G-3551)*

Glaxosmithkline LLC...814 935-5693
48 Sir William Dr Newville (17241) *(G-12603)*

Glaxosmithkline LLC...610 917-3493
1000 Black Rock Rd Collegeville (19426) *(G-3380)*

Glaxosmithkline PLC...215 336-0824
5 Crescent Dr Philadelphia (19112) *(G-13767)*

Glaxosmithkline Upsu, Marietta *Also called Glaxosmithkline (G-10462)*

Gleen...570 457-3858
523 Orchard St Moosic (18507) *(G-11506)*

Gleepet Inc..347 607-7850
1631 Loretta Ave Ste D Trevose (19053) *(G-18497)*

Glen Blooming Contractors Inc...............................717 566-3711
1 Old Farm Rd Hummelstown (17036) *(G-7912)*

Glen Carbide Inc...412 279-7500
1054 Campbells Run Rd Carnegie (15106) *(G-2769)*

Glen Carbonic Gas Co...570 779-1226
665 E Main St Plymouth (18651) *(G-15819)*

Glen Gery Brick, Reading *Also called Glen-Gery Corporation (G-16393)*

Glen Gery Brick Setter, Allentown *Also called Glen-Gery Corporation (G-233)*

Glen L Myers Inc...717 352-0035
1211 Knob Hill Rd Fayetteville (17222) *(G-5877)*

Glen Mills Sand & Gravel Inc...............................610 459-4988
5400 Pennell Rd Media (19063) *(G-10929)*

Glen-Gery Brick Center, York *Also called Glen-Gery Corporation (G-20503)*

Glen-Gery Brick Center, Watsontown *Also called Glen-Gery Corporation (G-19274)*

Glen-Gery Corporation (HQ)...................................610 374-4011
1166 Spring St Reading (19610) *(G-16393)*

Glen-Gery Corporation...610 374-4011
423 S Pottsville Pike Shoemakersville (19555) *(G-17570)*

Glen-Gery Corporation...814 856-2171
12637 Harrison St Summerville (15864) *(G-18158)*

Glen-Gery Corporation...717 854-8802
1090 E Boundary Ave York (17403) *(G-20503)*

Glen-Gery Corporation...484 240-4000
1960 Weaversville Rd Allentown (18109) *(G-233)*

Glen-Gery Corporation...717 848-2589
1090 E Boundary Ave York (17403) *(G-20504)*

Glen-Gery Corporation...570 742-4721
423 Susquehanna Trl Watsontown (17777) *(G-19274)*

Glen-Gery Corporation...814 857-7688
24 Pine Top Rd Bigler (16825) *(G-1660)*

Glen-Gery Corporation...717 939-6061
2750 Commerce Dr Middletown (17057) *(G-11054)*

Glen-Gery Hanley Plant, Summerville *Also called Glen-Gery Corporation (G-18158)*

Glendale Valley Winery...814 687-3438
2599 Glendale Valley Blvd Flinton (16640) *(G-5983)*

Glenfield Manufacturing, Pittsburgh *Also called Glenfield Supply Company Inc (G-15051)*

Glenfield Supply Company Inc.................................412 781-8188
1935 Main St Pittsburgh (15215) *(G-15051)*

Glenn A Hissim Woodworking LLC...........................610 847-8961
4770 Route 212 Kintnersville (18930) *(G-8727)*

Glenn Machine Co...724 457-7750
422 Flaugherty Run Rd Coraopolis (15108) *(G-3695)*

Glenn O Hawbaker Inc (PA).....................................814 237-1444
1952 Waddle Rd Ste 203 State College (16803) *(G-17970)*

Glenn O Hawbaker Inc...814 642-7869
1724 Champlin Hill Rd Turtlepoint (16750) *(G-18571)*

Glenn O Hawbaker Inc...814 359-3411
118 Bedrock Ln Pleasant Gap (16823) *(G-15792)*

Glenn O Hawbaker Inc...724 458-0991
106 Hawbaker Blvd Grove City (16127) *(G-6788)*

Glenn Shutter...717 867-2589
387 Palmyra Bellegrove Rd Annville (17003) *(G-649)*

Glens Dumpster Service LLC.................................202 521-1493
1613 W High St Pottstown (19464) *(G-15991)*

Glenshaw Distributors Inc.....................................412 753-0231
3114 William Flynn Hwy # 101 Allison Park (15101) *(G-451)*

Glenside Ready Mix Concrete Co.............................215 659-1500
147 E 4th St Erie (16507) *(G-5304)*

Glenwood Stone Co Inc...570 942-6420
Rr 1 Box 1130 Nicholson (18446) *(G-12614)*

Glicks Woodcraft LLC...717 536-3670
321 Meadowlark Ln Loysville (17047) *(G-10115)*

Glicks Woodworking...717 768-8958
4019 Old Phladelphia Pike Gordonville (17529) *(G-6556)*

Glidden Professional Paint Ctr, Downingtown *Also called PPG Architectural Finishes Inc (G-4250)*

Global Incorporated...814 445-9671
160 Cannery Rd Somerset (15501) *(G-17690)*

Global / Sfc Valve, Somerset *Also called Sfc Valve Corporation (G-17704)*

Global Advanced Metals USA Inc.............................610 367-2181
1223 County Line Rd Boyertown (19512) *(G-1912)*

Global Capital Corp (PA)..610 857-1900
140 Stewart Huston Dr Coatesville (19320) *(G-3305)*

Global Ceramic Services Inc...................................724 545-7224
238 North Park Dr Kittanning (16201) *(G-8774)*

Global Chem Feed Solutions LLC.............................215 675-2777
2015 Stout Dr Warminster (18974) *(G-18888)*

Global Custom...844 782-2653
101 Sycamore Ave Ofc 101 # 101 Folsom (19033) *(G-6023)*

Global Custom Decorating Inc.................................814 236-2110
82 Water St Curwensville (16833) *(G-3952)*

Global Data Consultants LLC.................................717 697-7500
4700 Westport Dr Mechanicsburg (17055) *(G-10849)*

Global Environmental Tech (PA)...............................610 821-4901
1001 S 10th St 1003 Allentown (18103) *(G-234)*

Global Epp Inc...412 580-4780
7038 Front River Rd Pittsburgh (15225) *(G-15052)*

Global Fabrication Inc...814 372-1500
235 Beaver Dr Du Bois (15801) *(G-4394)*

Global Home Automation LLC.................................484 686-7374
7250 Hollywood Rd Ste 4 Fort Washington (19034) *(G-6072)*

Global Indus Ltg Solutions LLC...............................215 671-2029
12401 Mcnulty Rd Philadelphia (19154) *(G-13768)*

Global Inserting Systems LLC...............................610 217-3019
88 Chestnut Hill Rd Emmaus (18049) *(G-5027)*

Global Institute For Strgc Inv.................................215 300-0907
1127 N Orianna St Philadelphia (19123) *(G-13769)*

Global Machine and Maint LLC...............................215 356-3077
1131 Delene Rd Rydal (19046) *(G-16885)*

Global Medical Solutions Inc (PA)............................215 440-7701
1116 South St Philadelphia (19147) *(G-13770)*

Global Metal Powders LLC...................................724 654-9171
315 Green Ridge Rd Ste H3 New Castle (16105) *(G-12097)*

Global Metal Products Inc.....................................814 834-2214
230 Stackpole St Saint Marys (15857) *(G-16978)*

Global Monitoring LLC...610 604-0760
491 Baltimore Pike # 421 Springfield (19064) *(G-17915)*

Global Packaging Solutions Inc...............................717 653-2345
1160 E Main St Mount Joy (17552) *(G-11658)*

Global Passive Safety Systems...............................267 297-2340
761 W Sproul Rd Ste 208 Springfield (19064) *(G-17916)*

Global Pharmaceuticals, Fort Washington *Also called Impax Laboratories Inc (G-6075)*

Global Polishing Solutions LLC...............................619 295-0893
622 Grant Rd Folcroft (19032) *(G-6003)*

Global Rubber LLC...610 878-9200
303 W Lancaster Ave Frnt Wayne (19087) *(G-19333)*

Global Trade Links LLC..888 777-1577
2610 Rockledge Ct Chester Springs (19425) *(G-3079)*

Global Traveler, Yardley *Also called Fx Express Publications Inc (G-20312)*

Global Tungsten & Powders Corp.............................570 268-5000
1 Hawes St Towanda (18848) *(G-18429)*

Global Utility Structures LLC.................................570 788-0826
39 Aristocrat Cir Sugarloaf (18249) *(G-18153)*

Globalcomm Suppliers, Philadelphia *Also called Mobile Outfitters LLC (G-14030)*

Globalsubmit Inc...215 253-7471
123 S Broad St Ste 1850 Philadelphia (19109) *(G-13771)*

Globe Canvas Products Company, Philadelphia *Also called 549 Industrial Holdings Inc (G-13320)*

Globe Color, Hazleton *Also called Globe Print Shop (G-7499)*

Globe Data Systems Inc..215 443-7960
300 Constance Dr Warminster (18974) *(G-18889)*

Globe Dye Works...215 288-4554
4500 Worth St Philadelphia (19124) *(G-13772)*

Globe Electric Company Inc...................................412 781-2671
200 23rd St Pittsburgh (15215) *(G-15053)*

Globe Metal Manufacturing Co.................................215 763-1024
2150 N 10th St Philadelphia (19122) *(G-13773)*

Globe Print Shop...570 454-8031
18 N Locust St Hazleton (18201) *(G-7499)*

Globe Ticket, Warminster *Also called Globe Data Systems Inc (G-18889)*

Globus Medical Inc...610 930-1800
2550 General Armistead Av Norristown (19403) *(G-12661)*

Globus Medical Inc (PA)..610 930-1800
2560 Gen Armistead Ave Audubon (19403) *(G-826)*

Gloninger Brothers Inc...215 456-5100
176 W Loudon St Philadelphia (19120) *(G-13774)*

Gloray If LLC...610 921-3300
104 Jefferson Ct Bernville (19506) *(G-1299)*

Gloroy Inc..610 435-7800
2001 Hamilton St Allentown (18104) *(G-235)*

Glory Fibers...610 444-5646
293 W Street Rd Kennett Square (19348) *(G-8512)*

Glossners Concrete Inc..570 962-2564
515 Laurel Run Rd Beech Creek (16822) *(G-1082)*

Glow Mfg 814 798-2215
2891 Whistler Rd Stoystown (15563) *(G-18078)*
Glunz & Jensen Inc 574 272-9950
500 Commerce Dr Quakertown (18951) *(G-16197)*
Glunz & Jensen K&F Inc 267 227-3493
500 Commerce Dr Quakertown (18951) *(G-16198)*
Glutalor Medical Inc 610 492-5710
436 Creamery Way Ste 200 Exton (19341) *(G-5689)*
Gluten Free Food Group LLC 570 689-9694
360 J J Rd Moscow (18444) *(G-11597)*
Glw Global Inc 412 664-7946
3009 Boyd St McKeesport (15132) *(G-10668)*
Glycol Technologies Inc 724 776-3554
140 Commonwealth Dr Warrendale (15086) *(G-19077)*
GM Home Inc 888 352-3442
1111 Street Rd Ste 304 Southampton (18966) *(G-17814)*
GM Homes of Florida Inc, Southampton *Also called GM Home Inc* *(G-17814)*
GM&s Coal Corp 814 629-5661
5815 Penn Ave Stoystown (15563) *(G-18079)*
Gma Garnet (usa) Corp 215 736-1868
25 Sorrels Rd Fairless Hills (19030) *(G-5780)*
Gma Manufacturing, Huntingdon Valley *Also called G Adasavage LLC* *(G-7987)*
Gma Manufacturing Inc 215 355-3105
110 Pike Cir Huntingdon Valley (19006) *(G-7990)*
Gma Tooling Company 215 355-3107
110 Pike Cir Huntingdon Valley (19006) *(G-7991)*
Gmp Nutraceuticals Inc 484 924-9042
711 1st Ave Ste B King of Prussia (19406) *(G-8625)*
GNC, Pittsburgh *Also called General Nutrition Centers Inc* *(G-15046)*
GNC Corporation (HQ) 412 288-4600
300 6th Ave Fl 2 Pittsburgh (15222) *(G-15054)*
GNC Parent LLC (HQ) 412 288-4600
300 6th Ave Fl 2 Pittsburgh (15222) *(G-15055)*
Gnk Sinter Metals - St Marys 1, Kersey *Also called GKN Sinter Metals LLC* *(G-8560)*
Gnosis USA Inc 215 340-7960
4259 W Swamp Rd Ste 305 Doylestown (18902) *(G-4303)*
Go Main Domains LLC 480 624-2500
334 Darby Ter Darby (19023) *(G-4018)*
Go Tell It Inc 212 769-3220
350 N Church St Rear Offc Robesonia (19551) *(G-16774)*
Go2power LLC 215 244-4202
2575 Metropolitan Dr Feasterville Trevose (19053) *(G-5913)*
Go2products, Reedsville *Also called Tip Top Resources LLC* *(G-16628)*
Goc Property Holdings LLC 814 678-4193
61 Main St Rouseville (16344) *(G-16836)*
Goc Property Holdings LLC 814 678-4127
175 Main St Oil City (16301) *(G-12946)*
Godfreys Custom Printing 717 530-8818
253 Walnut St Shippensburg (17257) *(G-17529)*
Godin Bros Inc 814 629-5117
377 Twin Hills Rd Friedens (15541) *(G-6220)*
Godino West Mtn Stone Quar 570 342-4340
703 Newton Rd Scranton (18504) *(G-17240)*
Godinos West Mtn Stone Quar, Scranton *Also called Godino West Mtn Stone Quar* *(G-17240)*
Godiva Chocolatier Inc 610 779-3797
650 E Neversink Rd Reading (19606) *(G-16394)*
Gods Country Creamery 814 848-7262
439 Pushersiding Rd Ulysses (16948) *(G-18602)*
Godshall Woodcraft 610 530-9386
10022 Allison Dr Breinigsville (18031) *(G-2017)*
Goebel Cabinetry 610 363-8970
308 Commerce Dr Exton (19341) *(G-5690)*
Goebelwood Industries Inc 610 532-4644
100 Sycamore Ave Folsom (19033) *(G-6024)*
Goerie.com, Erie *Also called Cyberink LLC* *(G-5242)*
Gog Paintball USA 724 520-8690
100 Station St Loyalhanna (15661) *(G-10111)*
Gogreenapu LLC 814 943-9948
1052 Neil Run Rd Altoona (16601) *(G-511)*
Gohn Mfg 717 426-3875
18 N Pine St Marietta (17547) *(G-10463)*
Gohrs On Demand, Erie *Also called Mvp Prnting Prmtional Pdts LLC* *(G-5400)*
Goji Systems Inc 267 309-2000
107 W Township Line Rd Norristown (19403) *(G-12662)*
Gokaaf International Inc 267 343-3075
7029 Rutland St Philadelphia (19149) *(G-13775)*
Gold Bug Exchange 724 770-9008
474 3rd St Beaver (15009) *(G-982)*
Gold Leaf The, King of Prussia *Also called Papyrus Inc* *(G-8659)*
Gold Medal Products Co 412 787-1030
519 Parkway View Dr Pittsburgh (15205) *(G-15056)*
Gold Metal Pittsburgh, Pittsburgh *Also called Gold Medal Products Co* *(G-15056)*
Gold Rush Inc 717 484-2424
920 Stone Hill Rd Denver (17517) *(G-4074)*
Goldcrafters Corner 717 412-4616
5301 Jonestown Rd Ste 101 Harrisburg (17112) *(G-7134)*
Golden Bone Pet Resort Inc 412 661-7001
6890 5th Ave Pittsburgh (15208) *(G-15057)*
Golden Brothers Inc 570 714-5002
263 Schuyler Ave Kingston (18704) *(G-8718)*
Golden Brothers Inc (PA) 570 457-0867
401 Bridge St Old Forge (18518) *(G-12965)*
Golden Eagle Construction Co (PA) 724 437-6495
850 N Gallatin Avenue Ext Uniontown (15401) *(G-18628)*
Golden Path LLC 215 290-1582
6514 Hasbrook Ave Philadelphia (19111) *(G-13776)*
Golden Specialties Ltd 717 273-9731
604 Cornwall Rd Lebanon (17042) *(G-9575)*
Golden Technologies, Kingston *Also called Golden Brothers Inc* *(G-8718)*
Golden Technologies, Old Forge *Also called Golden Brothers Inc* *(G-12965)*
Golden Technologies Inc 570 451-7477
401 Bridge St Old Forge (18518) *(G-12966)*
Goldfam Inc 215 379-6433
301 Ryers Ave Cheltenham (19012) *(G-3028)*
Goldsborough & Vansant Inc (PA) 724 782-0393
6116 Brownsville Road Ext # 108 Finleyville (15332) *(G-5959)*
Goldsborough & Vansant Inc 724 287-5590
1200 Railroad St East Butler (16029) *(G-4532)*
Goldsmith's, Glenside *Also called Fenstemaker John* *(G-6517)*
Goliath Development LLC (PA) 310 748-6288
136 Route 247 Jermyn (18433) *(G-8306)*
Golis Machine Inc 570 278-1963
92 Industrial Dr Montrose (18801) *(G-11465)*
Golob Concrete, Harrisburg *Also called John Stephen Golob* *(G-7158)*
Gonnella Frozen Products LLC 570 455-3194
301 Parkview Rd Hazle Township (18202) *(G-7459)*
Gooch Thermal Mfg Inc 610 285-2496
4631 S Church St Whitehall (18052) *(G-19874)*
Good 717 271-2917
1247 N Reading Rd Stevens (17578) *(G-18051)*
Good Catch, Newtown *Also called Seaco Foods International* *(G-12547)*
Good Crop Inc 585 944-7982
8 Lee Blvd Ste 3 Malvern (19355) *(G-10241)*
Good Food Inc 610 273-3776
4960 Horseshoe Pike Honey Brook (19344) *(G-7745)*
Good Health Natural Pdts Inc 570 655-0823
162 Commerce Rd Pittston (18640) *(G-15753)*
Good Health Natural Pdts Inc (HQ) 336 285-0735
900 High St Hanover (17331) *(G-6888)*
Good Ideas Inc 814 774-8231
10047 Keystone Dr Lake City (16423) *(G-8900)*
Good Lad Co 215 739-0200
431 E Tioga St Philadelphia (19134) *(G-13777)*
Good Neighbors Inc 610 444-1860
224 E Street Rd Ste 2 Kennett Square (19348) *(G-8513)*
Good Scents Candle Co Inc 814 349-5848
115 E Main St Millheim (16854) *(G-11218)*
Good Shepherd Thrift Store, Allentown *Also called Shepherd Good Work Services* *(G-388)*
GOOD TIME ICE, York *Also called York Ice Co Inc* *(G-20739)*
Good Time Ice 717 234-1479
1621 N 7th St Harrisburg (17102) *(G-7135)*
Good's Distribution Center, Boyertown *Also called Ralph Good Inc* *(G-1925)*
Good's Potato Chips, Adamstown *Also called Ralph Good Inc* *(G-23)*
Goodhart Sons Inc 717 656-2404
2515 Horseshoe Rd Lancaster (17601) *(G-9030)*
Goodie Bar Ice-Cream Co Inc 412 828-2840
828 3rd St Oakmont (15139) *(G-12917)*
Goods From Woods 215 699-6866
326 Washington Ave North Wales (19454) *(G-12804)*
Goodson Holding Company 215 370-6069
2100 Frost Rd Bristol (19007) *(G-2149)*
Goodstate Inc 215 366-2030
722 Avondale Rd Glenside (19038) *(G-6523)*
Goodway Graphics Inc 215 887-5700
261 York Rd Ste 930 Jenkintown (19046) *(G-8288)*
Goodwest Industries LLC (PA) 215 340-3100
48 Quarry Rd Douglassville (19518) *(G-4177)*
Goose Bros Inc 717 477-0010
81 Walnut Bottom Rd Shippensburg (17257) *(G-17530)*
Gorden Inc (PA) 610 644-4476
201 Inspiration Blvd # 400 Reading (19607) *(G-16395)*
Gordon Industries 516 354-8888
771 Indian Springs Rd Indiana (15701) *(G-8103)*
Gordon Laboratories, Upper Darby *Also called Dercher Enterprises Inc* *(G-18685)*
Gordon Seaver 724 356-2313
29 Hidden Acres Ln Hickory (15340) *(G-7628)*
Gordon Terminal Service Co PA (PA) 412 331-9410
1000 Ella St Mckees Rocks (15136) *(G-10661)*
Gordon's Hearing Aid Lab, Harrisburg *Also called Scott Gordon* *(G-7213)*
Goshen Sign Products, West Chester *Also called G S P Signs & Banners Inc* *(G-19556)*
Goshorn Industries LLC 717 369-3654
3911 Jack Rd Chambersburg (17202) *(G-2936)*
Gosiger Inc 724 778-3220
549a Keystone Dr Warrendale (15086) *(G-19078)*
Gosnell Logging 814 776-2038
6484 Grant Rd Ridgway (15853) *(G-16710)*

ALPHABETIC

Goss Inc (PA) 412 486-6100
1511 William Flynn Hwy Glenshaw (15116) *(G-6489)*

Gotcha Covered Pretzels LLC 215 253-3176
2411 Continental Dr Warrington (18976) *(G-19118)*

Gothic Inc 610 923-9180
370 Larry Holmes Dr Easton (18042) *(G-4692)*

Gotta Have It For Less, Honesdale *Also called Trashcans Unlimited LLC (G-7730)*

Gottlieb & Gottlieb, Huntingdon Valley *Also called Multi-Flow Dispensers LP (G-8014)*

Gottscho Printing Systems Inc 267 387-3005
740 Veterans Cir Warminster (18974) *(G-18890)*

Gouldey Welding & Fabrications 215 721-9522
84 Allentown Rd Souderton (18964) *(G-17737)*

Goulds Pumps LLC 570 875-2660
500 E Centre St Ashland (17921) *(G-730)*

Gourmail Inc (PA) 610 522-2650
816 Newtown Rd Berwyn (19312) *(G-1364)*

Gourmet Restaurant Apparel, Philadelphia *Also called Executive Apparel Inc (G-13686)*

Gourmet Specialty Imports 610 345-1113
171 Jennersville Rd Kelton (19346) *(G-8488)*

Gourmet Vinegars By Linda Lu 724 353-2026
116 Orchard Dr Sarver (16055) *(G-17070)*

Gow-Mac Instrument Co (PA) 610 954-9000
277 Brodhead Rd Bethlehem (18017) *(G-1526)*

GP Cabinets LLC 814 933-8902
604 S Moshannon Ave Snow Shoe (16874) *(G-17669)*

GP Metal Fabrication 570 494-1002
1827 Liberty Dr Williamsport (17701) *(G-20019)*

Gpc Capital Corp II 717 849-8500
2401 Pleasant Valley Rd York (17402) *(G-20505)*

Gpsa, Pittsburgh *Also called Greater Pitts Speciality (G-15061)*

Gra-Ter Industries Inc 570 658-7652
131 S Orange St Beavertown (17813) *(G-1026)*

Graber Letterin Inc 610 369-1112
58 School House Rd Boyertown (19512) *(G-1913)*

Grace Filter Company Inc 610 664-5790
2251 Fraley St Ste 8 Philadelphia (19137) *(G-13778)*

Grace Industries Inc (PA) 724 962-9231
305 Bend Hill Rd Fredonia (16124) *(G-6180)*

Grace Press Inc 717 354-0475
2175 Division Hwy Ephrata (17522) *(G-5107)*

Grace Winery LLC 610 459-4711
50 Sweetwater Rd Glen Mills (19342) *(G-6437)*

Graco High Pressure Eqp Inc 800 289-7447
2955 W 17th St Erie (16505) *(G-5305)*

Graco Inc 412 771-5774
10 Thomas St Mc Kees Rocks (15136) *(G-10613)*

Graffius Burial Vault Co, Reading *Also called Milroy Enterprises Inc (G-16444)*

Grafika Commercial Prtg Inc 610 678-8630
710 Johnston St Reading (19608) *(G-16396)*

Graftech Usa LLC 814 781-2478
800 Theresia St Saint Marys (15857) *(G-16979)*

Graham Architectural Pdts Corp (PA) 717 849-8100
1551 Mount Rose Ave York (17403) *(G-20506)*

Graham Engineering Corporation 717 848-3755
1203 Eden Rd York (17402) *(G-20507)*

Graham International Inc 203 838-3355
1528 Walnut St Ste 1601 Philadelphia (19102) *(G-13779)*

Graham Machine Inc 814 437-7190
1581 Pittsburgh Rd Franklin (16323) *(G-6133)*

Graham Packaging Co Europe LLC 209 572-5187
2401 Pleasant Valley Rd # 2 York (17402) *(G-20508)*

Graham Packaging Company LP 814 362-3861
105 Bolivar Dr Bradford (16701) *(G-1970)*

Graham Packaging Company LP 717 849-8700
500 Windsor St York (17403) *(G-20509)*

Graham Packaging Company LP 717 849-1800
2401 Pleasant Valley Rd # 99 York (17402) *(G-20510)*

Graham Packaging Company LP 717 849-8500
2401 Pleasant Valley Rd # 2 York (17402) *(G-20511)*

Graham Packaging Company LP 570 454-8261
360 Maplewood Dr Hazle Township (18202) *(G-7460)*

Graham Packaging Company Inc (HQ) 717 849-8500
700 Indian Springs Dr # 100 Lancaster (17601) *(G-9031)*

Graham Paining Co 215 447-8552
1501 Auburn Dr Bensalem (19020) *(G-1206)*

Graham Recycling Company LP 717 852-7744
505 Windsor St York (17403) *(G-20512)*

Graham Sign Company 814 765-7199
290 Wolf Run Rd Clearfield (16830) *(G-3220)*

Graham Tech Inc 814 807-1778
9245 Williamson Rd Meadville (16335) *(G-10729)*

Graham Thermal Products LLC 724 658-0500
105 Mahoning Ave New Castle (16102) *(G-12098)*

Grahams Welding 724 627-6082
1775 Oak Forest Rd Waynesburg (15370) *(G-19442)*

Grammaton Research LLC 410 703-9237
1005 Cherimoya St York (17404) *(G-20513)*

Grammeco Inc 610 352-4400
6430 Market St Upper Darby (19082) *(G-18686)*

Gran Enterprises 215 634-2883
3609 N 5th St Fl 1 Philadelphia (19140) *(G-13780)*

Grand Finale Desserts 610 864-3824
442 Hilltop Rd Paoli (19301) *(G-13141)*

Grand Openings Inc 724 325-2029
3075 Carson Ave Murrysville (15668) *(G-11852)*

Grand Valley Manufacturing Co (PA) 814 728-8760
701 E Spring St Unit 8 Titusville (16354) *(G-18379)*

Grand Valley Manufacturing Co 814 728-8760
1000 Pennsylvania Ave W Warren (16365) *(G-19028)*

Grandshare LLC 919 308-5115
2008 S 6th St Philadelphia (19148) *(G-13781)*

Grandview Manufacturing Co. 724 887-0631
2391 State Route 981 Alverton (15612) *(G-564)*

Grandville Hollow Pottery Inc 814 355-7928
1090 Railroad Ave Julian (16844) *(G-8455)*

Grange Lime & Stone, Coolspring *Also called Original Fuels Inc (G-3622)*

Granite Gllria Fabrication Inc 215 283-0341
425 Delaware Dr Ste C Fort Washington (19034) *(G-6073)*

Grannas Bros Contracting Co, Hollidaysburg *Also called Grannas Bros Stone Asp Co Inc (G-7649)*

Grannas Bros Stone Asp Co Inc 814 695-5021
157 Grannas Rd Hollidaysburg (16648) *(G-7649)*

Grant Belcher 814 853-9640
120 Clinton St Greenville (16125) *(G-6741)*

Grant Mfg & Alloying Inc (PA) 610 404-1380
200c N Furnace St Birdsboro (19508) *(G-1697)*

Grant's Tool Company, Monroeville *Also called Duane Grant (G-11333)*

Grape Fiberglass Inc 814 938-8118
100 Sutton St Punxsutawney (15767) *(G-16142)*

Grape Fiberglass Products, Punxsutawney *Also called Grape Fiberglass Inc (G-16142)*

Grape Spot, Easton *Also called Franklin Hill Vineyards Inc (G-4686)*

Graphcom Inc (PA) 800 699-1664
1219 Chambersburg Rd Gettysburg (17325) *(G-6295)*

Graphcom Creative, Gettysburg *Also called Graphcom Inc (G-6295)*

Graphex Inc 610 524-9525
301 National Rd Ste 400 Exton (19341) *(G-5691)*

Graphic Art Imaging, Malvern *Also called Graphic Arts Camera Service (G-10242)*

Graphic Arts Incorporated 215 382-5500
2867 E Allegheny Ave Philadelphia (19134) *(G-13782)*

Graphic Arts Camera Service 610 647-6395
1 Golfview Ln Malvern (19355) *(G-10242)*

Graphic Communications Inc 215 441-5335
793 Nina Way Warminster (18974) *(G-18891)*

Graphic Connections 814 948-5810
813 Front St 2 Cresson (16630) *(G-3898)*

Graphic Display Systems 717 274-3954
308 S 1st St Lebanon (17042) *(G-9576)*

Graphic Fine Color, Philadelphia *Also called Sun Chemical Corporation (G-14354)*

Graphic Garage 724 274-4930
1415 Pittsburgh St Cheswick (15024) *(G-3110)*

Graphic Impressions of America 610 296-3939
179 Lancaster Ave Malvern (19355) *(G-10243)*

Graphic Packaging Intl LLC 610 935-4000
1035 Longford Rd Phoenixville (19460) *(G-14551)*

Graphic Packaging Intl LLC 610 725-9840
1035 Longford Rd Phoenixville (19460) *(G-14552)*

Graphic Print Solutions L 610 845-0280
1892 County Line Rd Barto (19504) *(G-943)*

Graphic Products Inc 724 935-6600
320 Northgae Dr Ste B Warrendale (15086) *(G-19079)*

Graphic Search Associates 610 344-0644
1075 Powderhorn Dr Glen Mills (19342) *(G-6438)*

Graphic Services, Harrisburg *Also called Paxton Herald (G-7190)*

Graphics 22 Signs Inc 412 422-1125
5212 Lytle St Pittsburgh (15207) *(G-15058)*

Graphics Concepts Division, Erie *Also called Lemac Packaging Inc (G-5362)*

Graphite Electrode Mfg Fcilty, Saint Marys *Also called Graftech Usa LLC (G-16979)*

Graphite Machining Inc (PA) 610 682-0080
240 N Main St Topton (19562) *(G-18413)*

Graphite Machining Inc 610 682-0080
70 E Meadow Ave Robesonia (19551) *(G-16775)*

Graphtech, Harrisburg *Also called WM Enterprises Inc (G-7248)*

Graphtek LLC 724 564-9211
219 Hope Rd Smithfield (15478) *(G-17651)*

Grassroots Unwired Inc 215 788-1210
10 Canal St Ste 235 Bristol (19007) *(G-2150)*

Grate Clip Company Inc 215 230-8015
212 Decatur St Doylestown (18901) *(G-4304)*

Grattons Fabricating & Mfg 724 527-5681
198 Main St Adamsburg (15611) *(G-18)*

Gratz Industries LLC 215 739-7373
1108 Shackamaxon St Philadelphia (19125) *(G-13783)*

Grauch Enterprises Inc 814 342-7320
1878 Port Matilda Hwy Philipsburg (16866) *(G-14515)*

Gravel 215 675-3960
52 Horseshoe Ln Hatboro (19040) *(G-7286)*

Gravel Bar Inc 724 568-3518
2274 River Rd Vandergrift (15690) *(G-18729)*

Gray Bridge Software Inc 412 401-1045
2353 Westgate Dr Pittsburgh (15237) *(G-15059)*

Gray Sign Advertising 724 224-5008
1300 Metz Rd Tarentum (15084) *(G-18244)*

Gray Space Defense 814 475-2749
1461 Salco Rd Berlin (15530) *(G-1288)*

Gray Wldg Fabrication Svcs Inc 412 271-6900
19 Talbot Ave Braddock (15104) *(G-1944)*

Gray's Pallets, Mifflintown Also called Albert Gray *(G-11109)*

Graybill Farms Inc 717 361-8455
389 Heisey Quarry Rd Elizabethtown (17022) *(G-4874)*

Graybill Machines Inc 717 626-5221
221 W Lexington Rd Lititz (17543) *(G-10013)*

Grayco Controls LLC 724 545-2300
719 Tarrtown Rd Adrian (16210) *(G-29)*

Graymont Inc (HQ) 814 353-4613
375 Graymont Rd Bellefonte (16823) *(G-1097)*

Graymont Inc 814 359-2313
980 E College Ave Bellefonte (16823) *(G-1098)*

Graymont Inc 814 357-4500
375 Graymont Rd Bellefonte (16823) *(G-1099)*

Grays Automotive Speed Eqp 717 436-8777
713 Washington Ave Mifflintown (17059) *(G-11119)*

Grc Holding Inc (HQ) 610 667-6640
1 Bala Ave Ste 310 Bala Cynwyd (19004) *(G-879)*

Gre Mining Company (HQ) 814 226-6911
1062 E Main St Clarion (16214) *(G-3178)*

Gre Ventures Inc 814 226-6911
1062 E Main St Clarion (16214) *(G-3179)*

Great Additions Inc 570 675-0852
265 Charles St Luzerne (18709) *(G-10124)*

Great American Popcorn Works, Telford Also called Specialty Snacks Inc *(G-18317)*

Great American Printer Inc 570 752-7341
525 E 2nd St Berwick (18603) *(G-1326)*

Great American Weaving Corp 610 845-9200
20 N Front St Ste 3 Bally (19503) *(G-903)*

Great Atlantic Graphics Inc 610 296-8711
2750 Morris Rd Ste A120 Lansdale (19446) *(G-9373)*

Great Coasters Intl Inc (PA) 570 286-9330
2627 State Route 890 Sunbury (17801) *(G-18170)*

Great Dane LLC 570 437-3141
891 Strick Rd Danville (17821) *(G-4004)*

Great Dane LLC 717 492-0057
1155 Four Star Dr Mount Joy (17552) *(G-11659)*

Great Dane Trailers, Danville Also called Great Dane LLC *(G-4004)*

Great Dane Trailers Inc 570 221-6920
207 Progress Rd Elysburg (17824) *(G-4976)*

Great Day Improvements LLC 412 304-0089
4777 Streets Run Rd Ste 2 Pittsburgh (15236) *(G-15060)*

Great Display Company, Manheim Also called Getaways On Display Inc *(G-10386)*

Great Eastern Seating Co 610 366-8132
416 Arrowhead Ln Breinigsville (18031) *(G-2018)*

Great Lakes Automtn Machining, Mc Kean Also called Great Lakes Automtn Svcs Inc *(G-10591)*

Great Lakes Automtn Svcs Inc (PA) 814 476-7710
8835 Walmer Dr Mc Kean (16426) *(G-10591)*

Great Lakes Automtn Svcs Inc 814 774-3144
9937 Sampson Ave Lake City (16423) *(G-8901)*

Great Lakes Case & Cab Co Inc 814 663-6015
18433 Sciota Rd Corry (16407) *(G-3763)*

Great Lakes Case & Cab Co Inc (PA) 814 734-7303
4193 Route 6n Edinboro (16412) *(G-4812)*

Great Lakes Cast Stone Inc 814 402-1055
711 Beaver Rd Girard (16417) *(G-6390)*

Great Lakes Custom Graphics 814 723-0110
221 Pennsylvania Ave W Warren (16365) *(G-19029)*

Great Lakes Finishes LLC 814 438-2518
7724 Route 97 Union City (16438) *(G-18607)*

Great Lakes Framing LLC 724 399-0220
116 N River Ave Parker (16049) *(G-13165)*

Great Lakes Manufacturing Inc 814 734-2436
1521 Enterprise Rd Corry (16407) *(G-3764)*

Great Lakes Metal Finishing 814 452-1886
1113 W 18th St Erie (16502) *(G-5306)*

Great Lakes Power Products Inc 724 266-4000
450 Riverport Dr Leetsdale (15056) *(G-9691)*

Great Lakes Wellhead Inc 570 723-8995
81 Central Ave Wellsboro (16901) *(G-19463)*

Great Meadows Sawmill Frm Inc 724 329-7771
673 Nelson Rd Farmington (15437) *(G-5862)*

Great Northern Corporation 610 706-0910
Westpark Buss Ctr Ii 7220 Allentown (18106) *(G-236)*

Great Northern Foam 610 791-3356
2571 Mitchell Ave Allentown (18103) *(G-237)*

Great Northern Press of Wilkes 570 822-3147
173 Gilligan St Wilkes Barre (18702) *(G-19922)*

Great Oak Energy Inc 412 828-2900
637 Allegheny Ave Oakmont (15139) *(G-12918)*

Great Plains Oilfld Rentl LLC 570 882-7700
40 Lamoka Rd Sayre (18840) *(G-17115)*

Great Signs, Bird In Hand Also called Gregory Troyer *(G-1676)*

Great Socks, Reading Also called Lmt Corp of Pennsylvania *(G-16432)*

Great Valley Automotive 412 829-8904
1408 Greensburg Pike North Versailles (15137) *(G-12776)*

Great Valley Publishing Co 610 948-7639
3801 Schuylkill Rd Spring City (19475) *(G-17858)*

Greater Pitts Speciality 412 821-5976
1610 Babcock Blvd Pittsburgh (15209) *(G-15061)*

Greater Pttsbrgh Spcialty Advg 412 821-5976
112 Lincoln Ave Millvale (15209) *(G-11223)*

Greater Reading Merchandiser, Reading Also called Kapp Advertising Services Inc *(G-16418)*

Greco Apparel, Ambler Also called Greco International Inc *(G-580)*

Greco International Inc (PA) 215 628-2557
921a N Bethlehem Pike # 2 Ambler (19002) *(G-580)*

Green Business Forms, Gibsonia Also called Williams Business Forms Ltd *(G-6359)*

Green Filter, Mount Braddock Also called Ground Force Marketing Co *(G-11618)*

Green Filter Usa Inc 724 430-2050
714 Braddock View Dr Mount Braddock (15465) *(G-11617)*

Green Garden Inc 814 623-2735
1088 Greengarden Ln Bedford (15522) *(G-1053)*

Green Hills Software LLC 215 862-9474
325 Brownsburg Rd New Hope (18938) *(G-12304)*

Green Lighting Led, Erie Also called Jcr Sales & Mfg LLC *(G-5335)*

Green n Grow Compost LLC 717 284-5710
300 Douts Hill Rd Holtwood (17532) *(G-7667)*

Green Prosthetics & Orthotics (PA) 814 833-2311
2241 Peninsula Dr Erie (16506) *(G-5307)*

Green Prosthetics & Orthotics 814 833-2311
2241 Peninsula Dr Erie (16506) *(G-5308)*

Green Prosthetics & Orthotics 814 337-1159
279 North St Meadville (16335) *(G-10730)*

Green Scenes Landscape Inc 610 566-3154
520 S Old Middletown Rd Media (19063) *(G-10930)*

Green Tree Times 412 481-7830
420 Sulgrave Rd Pittsburgh (15211) *(G-15062)*

Greenbank Energy Solutions Inc 724 229-4454
185 Plumpton Ave Washington (15301) *(G-19179)*

Greenbank Group Inc (PA) 724 229-1180
185 Plumpton Ave Washington (15301) *(G-19180)*

Greenbriar Indus Systems Inc 814 474-1400
7800 Maple St Fairview (16415) *(G-5824)*

Greenbriar Plastics, Fairview Also called Greenbriar Indus Systems Inc *(G-5824)*

Greencastle Bronze & Granite, Greencastle Also called Richard Freeman *(G-6630)*

Greendesign LLC 215 242-0700
8434 Germantown Ave Philadelphia (19118) *(G-13784)*

Greene Tweed & Co Inc (PA) 215 256-9521
2075 Detwiler Rd Kulpsville (19443) *(G-8827)*

Greene County Drilling Co Inc 724 627-3393
155 Dark Hollow Rd Waynesburg (15370) *(G-19443)*

Greene County Gas & Oil Co 724 627-3393
155 Dark Hollow Rd Waynesburg (15370) *(G-19444)*

Greene Tweed, Kulpsville Also called Gt Services LLC *(G-8829)*

Greenerways LLC (PA) 215 280-7658
668 Stony Hill Rd Ste 143 Yardley (19067) *(G-20313)*

Greensaver, Waynesburg Also called Direct Results Bsp Inc *(G-19439)*

Greenetech Mfg Co Inc 724 228-2400
470 Crile Rd Washington (15301) *(G-19181)*

Greenfield Basket Factory Inc 814 725-3419
11423 Wilson Rd North East (16428) *(G-12744)*

Greenfield Mfg Co Inc 215 535-4141
9800 Bustleton Ave Philadelphia (19115) *(G-13785)*

Greenheat LP 724 545-6540
125 Pence Rd Cowansville (16218) *(G-3796)*

Greenhouse Winery 412 892-9017
3825 Saw Mill Run Blvd Pittsburgh (15227) *(G-15063)*

Greenkeepers Inc 215 464-7540
2170 Bennett Rd Fl 1 Philadelphia (19116) *(G-13786)*

Greenlane Park, Green Lane Also called County of Montgomery *(G-6586)*

Greenleaf Corporation (PA) 814 763-2915
18695 Greenleaf Dr Saegertown (16433) *(G-16915)*

Greenley Engery Holdings of PA (PA) 724 238-8177
153 Wilson St Central City (15926) *(G-2838)*

Greenline Foods Inc 717 630-9200
26 Industrial Dr Hanover (17331) *(G-6889)*

Greenray Industries Inc 717 766-0223
840 W Church Rd Mechanicsburg (17055) *(G-10850)*

Greensburg Location, Pittsburgh Also called Ductworks Inc *(G-14941)*

Greensburg Mch & Driveline LLC 724 837-8233
145 Talbot Ave Greensburg (15601) *(G-6670)*

Greenstar Allentown LLC 610 262-6988
799 Smith Ln Northampton (18067) *(G-12851)*

Greenstar Recycling-Allentown, Northampton Also called Greenstar Allentown LLC *(G-12851)*

Greentree Lumber 814 257-9878
26 Wolf Rd Smicksburg (16256) *(G-17638)*

A
L
P
H
A
B
E
T
I
C

Greentree Machine Works 717 786-4047
113a Greentree Rd Quarryville (17566) *(G-16271)*

Greentree Printing and Signs, Pittsburgh *Also called Greentree Printing Inc* *(G-15064)*

Greentree Printing Inc 412 921-5570
2351 Noblestown Rd Ste 10 Pittsburgh (15205) *(G-15064)*

Greenville Metals Inc 724 509-1861
99 Crestview Drive Ext Transfer (16154) *(G-18465)*

Greenville Record Argus Inc 724 588-5000
10 Penn Ave Greenville (16125) *(G-6742)*

Greenville Wood Products Inc 724 646-1193
425 Crestview Dr Greenville (16125) *(G-6743)*

Greenwood Business Printing 610 337-8887
950 W Valley Forge Rd # 1 King of Prussia (19406) *(G-8626)*

Greenwood Enterprises 412 429-6800
313 W Main St 315 Carnegie (15106) *(G-2770)*

Greenwood Products 717 337-2050
975 Marsh Creek Rd Gettysburg (17325) *(G-6296)*

Greenwood Township 570 458-0212
90 Shed Rd Millville (17846) *(G-11225)*

Greg Kiser 814 425-1678
1458 Frenchcreek Rd Utica (16362) *(G-18696)*

Greg Kline 610 367-4060
217 Old State Rd Boyertown (19512) *(G-1914)*

Greg Norton 724 625-3426
209 Oakland Ave Mars (16046) *(G-10498)*

Greg Speece 717 838-8365
24 N Chestnut St Ste 4 Palmyra (17078) *(G-13125)*

Gregg Lane LLC 215 269-9900
386 Lincoln Hwy Fairless Hills (19030) *(G-5781)*

Gregg Shirtmakers Inc 215 329-7700
4830 N Front St Philadelphia (19120) *(G-13787)*

Gregory Racing Fabrications 610 759-8217
314 Industrial Park Rd Nazareth (18064) *(G-11970)*

Gregory Troyer 717 393-0233
2688 Old Phladelphia Pike Bird In Hand (17505) *(G-1676)*

Gregory W Moyer Defibrillato 570 421-9993
819 Ann St Stroudsburg (18360) *(G-18121)*

Greif Inc 610 485-8148
3033 Market St Upper Chichester (19014) *(G-18662)*

Greif Inc 570 459-9075
95 Jaycee Dr West Hazleton (18202) *(G-19711)*

Greif Inc 215 956-9049
695 Louis Dr Warminster (18974) *(G-18892)*

Greiner Industries Inc 717 653-8111
1650 Steel Way Mount Joy (17552) *(G-11660)*

Greiner Packaging Corp 570 602-3900
225 Enterprise Way Pittston (18640) *(G-15754)*

Grelin Press 724 334-8240
1040 5th Ave New Kensington (15068) *(G-12343)*

Gretchen Maser 717 295-9426
142 Cliff Ave Lancaster (17602) *(G-9032)*

Gretz Machine Products 215 247-2495
52 W Gowen Ave Philadelphia (19119) *(G-13788)*

Greystone Materials BT 814 748-7652
272 Interpower Dr Colver (15927) *(G-3454)*

Greystone Materials BT (PA) 570 244-2082
617 Urban Rd Herndon (17830) *(G-7598)*

Greystone Quarries Inc 610 987-8055
329 Oysterdale Rd Boyertown (19512) *(G-1915)*

Grid Company LLC 610 341-7307
750 E Swedesford Rd Valley Forge (19482) *(G-18708)*

Grid Division, Coraopolis *Also called American Bridge Mfg Co* *(G-3655)*

Grid Elc & Solar Solutions LLC 717 885-5249
320 Loucks Rd Ste 202 York (17404) *(G-20514)*

Grid Electric Inc 610 466-7030
8 Steven Way Coatesville (19320) *(G-3306)*

Grid Sign Systems, Coatesville *Also called Grid Electric Inc* *(G-3306)*

Griff & Associates, Levittown *Also called Griff and Associates LP* *(G-9842)*

Griff and Associates LP (PA) 215 428-1075
275 Lower Morrisville Rd Levittown (19054) *(G-9842)*

Griffin Industries LLC 610 273-7014
97 Westbrook Dr Honey Brook (19344) *(G-7746)*

Griffin Sealing LLC 267 328-6600
900 Forty Foot Rd Kulpsville (19443) *(G-8828)*

Griffith Inc (HQ) 215 322-8100
458 Pike Rd Huntingdon Valley (19006) *(G-7992)*

Griffith Advertising, Oreland *Also called Griffith Pottery House Inc* *(G-13021)*

Griffith Pottery House Inc 215 887-2222
100 Lorraine Ave Oreland (19075) *(G-13021)*

Griffiths Printing, Lansdowne *Also called Griffiths Printing Co* *(G-9433)*

Griffiths Printing Co 610 623-3822
404 E Baltimore Ave Lansdowne (19050) *(G-9433)*

Grimm Industries Inc (PA) 814 474-2648
7070 W Ridge Rd Fairview (16415) *(G-5825)*

Grimm Machine & Model 724 228-2133
95 Statement St Washington (15301) *(G-19182)*

Grimm's Awnings, Sharon *Also called Grimms Inc* *(G-17435)*

Grimms Inc 724 346-4952
1017 Myrtle Pl Sharon (16146) *(G-17435)*

Grims Plastics 717 526-7980
6691 Allentown Blvd Harrisburg (17112) *(G-7136)*

Grinders On Go 717 712-0977
3605 Kohler Pl Camp Hill (17011) *(G-2498)*

Grinding Engineering & Svcs Co, Beaver Falls *Also called Gesco Inc* *(G-999)*

Grip-Flex Corp 215 743-7492
2245 E Ontario St Philadelphia (19134) *(G-13789)*

Grit Commercial Printing Inc 570 368-8021
80 Choate Cir Montoursville (17754) *(G-11440)*

Groff Tractor & Equipment LLC 814 353-8400
210 Rolling Ridge Dr Bellefonte (16823) *(G-1100)*

Groffdale Machine Co Inc 717 656-3249
194 S Groffdale Rd Leola (17540) *(G-9785)*

Groffs Candies 717 872-2845
3587 Blue Rock Rd Lancaster (17603) *(G-9033)*

Groffs Printing Company 717 786-1511
22 E State St Frnt Quarryville (17566) *(G-16272)*

Grokas Inc 610 565-1498
722 Hemlock Rd Media (19063) *(G-10931)*

Groll Ornamental Ir Works LLC 412 431-4444
1201 Becks Run Rd Pittsburgh (15210) *(G-15065)*

Groman Restoration Inc 724 235-5000
519 Sugar Run Rd New Florence (15944) *(G-12197)*

Gross Bros Wldg Fbrication Inc 814 443-1130
1344 Berlin Plank Rd Somerset (15501) *(G-17691)*

Gross Machine Inc 215 491-7077
1760 Costner Dr Ste 1 Warrington (18976) *(G-19119)*

Grothouse Lumber Company 610 767-6515
6104 Buckery Rd Germansville (18053) *(G-6278)*

Grotto 610 570-9060
2203 Union Blvd Allentown (18109) *(G-238)*

Grotto Pizza Delivery, Wilkes Barre *Also called Pizza Associates Incorporated* *(G-19957)*

Ground 34 LLC 914 299-7212
6024 Broad St Fl 2 Pittsburgh (15206) *(G-15066)*

Ground Force Marketing Co 724 430-2068
714 Braddock View Dr Mount Braddock (15465) *(G-11618)*

Group Optical, Pittsburgh *Also called Sosniak Opticians* *(G-15561)*

Grouse Hunt Farms Inc 570 573-2868
458 Fairview St Tamaqua (18252) *(G-18211)*

Grove Investors Inc 717 597-8121
1542 Buchanan Trl E Greencastle (17225) *(G-6616)*

Grove Printing Inc 814 355-2197
152 Raspberry Ln Bellefonte (16823) *(G-1101)*

Grove US LLc 717 597-8121
1565 Buchanan Trl E Shady Grove (17256) *(G-17420)*

Grove Worldwide LLC 717 597-8121
1565 Buchanan Trl E Shady Grove (17256) *(G-17421)*

Grovedale Winery & Vinyard (PA) 570 746-1400
119 Grovedale Ln Wyalusing (18853) *(G-20253)*

Growmark Fs LLC 814 359-2725
552 Feidler Rd Bellefonte (16823) *(G-1102)*

Growmark Fs LLC 724 543-1101
656 Tarrtown Rd Adrian (16210) *(G-30)*

Growmark Fs LLC 610 926-6339
119 E Wall St Leesport (19533) *(G-9664)*

Growmark Fs LLC 717 854-3818
980 Loucks Mill Rd York (17402) *(G-20515)*

Gruber Con Specialists Inc 610 760-0925
6638 Jefferson Ct New Tripoli (18066) *(G-12456)*

Grued Corporation 610 644-1300
63 Lancaster Ave Malvern (19355) *(G-10244)*

Gruma Corporation 570 474-6890
15 Elmwood Ave Mountain Top (18707) *(G-11763)*

Grundy Industries LLC 570 609-5487
944 Shoemaker Ave Wyoming (18644) *(G-20278)*

Gryphin Elements LLC 215 694-7727
5500 Wissahickon Ave A Philadelphia (19144) *(G-13790)*

Gs Design, Palmyra *Also called Greg Speece* *(G-13125)*

Gs Fuel Inc 484 751-5414
1399 Skippack Pike Blue Bell (19422) *(G-1831)*

Gsg Manufacturing Inc 814 336-4287
18544 Cussewago Rd Meadville (16335) *(G-10731)*

Gsi 610 667-4271
627 Moreno Rd Penn Valley (19072) *(G-13236)*

Gsk Technical Sourcing, King of Prussia *Also called Glaxosmithkline LLC* *(G-8624)*

GSM Hold Co 412 487-7140
3812 William Flynn Hwy # 2 Allison Park (15101) *(G-452)*

GSM Industrial Inc 717 207-8985
3249 Hempland Rd Lancaster (17601) *(G-9034)*

Gsp Marketing Inc 814 445-5866
322 Lavansville Rd Somerset (15501) *(G-17692)*

Gt Services LLC 215 256-9521
1510 Gehman Rd Kulpsville (19443) *(G-8829)*

Gtf Corporation 717 752-3631
103 Blair St 111 Berwick (18603) *(G-1327)*

Gtf Worldwide LLC 610 873-3663
454 Acorn Ln Downingtown (19335) *(G-4231)*

Gti, Bensalem *Also called Gyrotron Technology Inc* *(G-1207)*

Gtp, Towanda *Also called Global Tungsten & Powders Corp* *(G-18429)*

2019 Harris Pennsylvania
Manufacturers Directory

(G-0000) Company's Geographic Section entry number

Gtr Industries Incorporated 610 705-5900
　2113 Sanatoga Station Rd Pottstown (19464) *(G-15992)*

GTS Enterprises Inc 610 798-9922
　1801 S 12th St Ste 7 Allentown (18103) *(G-239)*

GTS-Welco, Allentown *Also called Praxair Dist Mid-Atlantic LLC (G-355)*

Gty Inc 717 764-8969
　2075 Loucks Rd York (17408) *(G-20516)*

Guardian Auto Glass, Lewistown *Also called Guardian Industries LLC (G-9933)*

Guardian CSC Corporation (PA) 717 848-2540
　6000 Susquehanna Plaza Dr Hellam (17406) *(G-7551)*

Guardian Filtration Pdts LLC 724 646-0450
　451 2nd St Greenville (16125) *(G-6744)*

Guardian Industries LLC 717 242-2571
　6395 State Route 103 N # 35 Lewistown (17044) *(G-9933)*

Guardian Tactical Inc 814 558-6761
　205 S Maple St Emporium (15834) *(G-5062)*

Guards Plus, Williamsport *Also called Jeff Hills (G-20029)*

Gudebrod Inc 610 327-4050
　274 Shoemaker Rd Pottstown (19464) *(G-15993)*

Guenther & Sons Enterprises 570 676-0585
　Rr 507 Box N Gouldsboro (18424) *(G-6568)*

Guida Inc (PA) 215 727-2222
　7 Chelsea Pkwy Ste 705 Marcus Hook (19061) *(G-10444)*

Guiding Technologies Corp 609 605-9273
　1500 Jfk Blvd Ste 1825 Philadelphia (19102) *(G-13791)*

Guildcraft Inc 717 854-3888
　401 S Sherman St York (17403) *(G-20517)*

Guildford Performance Textiles, Pine Grove *Also called Lear Corporation (G-14598)*

Gulden Ophthalmics Inc 215 884-8105
　225 Cadwalader Ave Elkins Park (19027) *(G-4904)*

Gulden, R. O. & Co, Elkins Park *Also called Gulden Ophthalmics Inc (G-4904)*

Gulf, Pittsburgh *Also called Cumberland Farms Inc (G-14892)*

Gunsmiths Stainless Clg Rods 215 256-9208
　431 Gruber Rd Harleysville (19438) *(G-7035)*

Gupta Permold Corporation 412 793-3511
　234 Lott Rd Pittsburgh (15235) *(G-15067)*

Gurpreet Fuel Company Llc 215 493-6322
　536 W Roosevelt Blvd Philadelphia (19120) *(G-13792)*

Guru Technologies Inc 610 572-2086
　121 S Broad St Fl 11 Philadelphia (19107) *(G-13793)*

Gutchess Lumber Co Inc 724 537-6447
　185 Devereux Dr Latrobe (15650) *(G-9479)*

Gutenberg Inc 570 488-9820
　677 Roosevelt Hwy Ste 2 Waymart (18472) *(G-19287)*

Guth Laboratories Inc 717 564-5470
　590 N 67th St Harrisburg (17111) *(G-7137)*

Gutierrez Machine Corporation 570 888-6088
　1069 Front St Athens (18810) *(G-811)*

Guy Coder 814 265-0519
　1701 Bond St Brockway (15824) *(G-2227)*

Guy Hrezik 610 779-7609
　3209 Oley Turnpike Rd Reading (19606) *(G-16397)*

Guy Sexton Timber Mgmt 717 548-3422
　1148 Pilgrims Pathway Peach Bottom (17563) *(G-13197)*

Guyasuta Printing Co 412 782-0112
　807 Main St Pittsburgh (15215) *(G-15068)*

Guyers Superior Walls 814 725-8575
　9391 W Main Rd North East (16428) *(G-12745)*

Guyon Industries Inc 717 528-0154
　100 Auction Dr York Springs (17372) *(G-20767)*

Guys Round Brewing Company 215 368-2640
　324 W Main St Lansdale (19446) *(G-9374)*

Guzzardo Mach Prodts, Folsom *Also called Allcams Machine Co (G-6022)*

Gvm Inc (PA) 717 677-6197
　374 Heidlersburg Rd Biglerville (17307) *(G-1662)*

Gwiz Products 724 864-0200
　870 Main St Irwin (15642) *(G-8165)*

Gwynedd Manufacturing Inc 610 272-2060
　800 N Wales Rd North Wales (19454) *(G-12805)*

Gwynn-E-Co Inc 215 423-6400
　2810 E Victoria St 28 Philadelphia (19134) *(G-13794)*

Gymboree Play & Music, Easton *Also called Hayes Enterprises Inc (G-4697)*

Gyrotron Technology Inc 215 244-4740
　3412 Progress Dr Bensalem (19020) *(G-1207)*

H & B Enterprises Inc 814 345-6416
　Int 80 Exit 21 St I Kylertown (16847) *(G-8865)*

H & C Ggrove Mills, Lewisburg *Also called Bessie Grove (G-9898)*

H & C Giamo Inc 610 941-0909
　200 Center St Conshohocken (19428) *(G-3552)*

H & F Manufacturing Corp 215 355-0250
　116 Railroad Dr Ivyland (18974) *(G-8212)*

H & G Diners Corp 610 494-5107
　3305 W 2nd St Marcus Hook (19061) *(G-10445)*

H & H Castings Inc 717 751-0064
　4300 Lincoln Hwy York (17406) *(G-20518)*

H & H Construction, Spring Grove *Also called H & H General Excavating Co (G-17877)*

H & H General Excavating Co (PA) 717 225-4669
　660 Old Hanover Rd Spring Grove (17362) *(G-17877)*

H & H Graphics Inc (PA) 717 393-3941
　854 N Prince St Lancaster (17603) *(G-9035)*

H & H Graphics Inc 717 393-3941
　1893 Commerce Park E Lancaster (17601) *(G-9036)*

H & H Manufacturing Co Inc 610 532-1250
　2 Horne Dr Folcroft (19032) *(G-6004)*

H & H Materials Inc 724 376-2834
　190 Canon Rd Stoneboro (16153) *(G-18069)*

H & H Precision Wire LLC 717 567-9600
　50 Red Hill Ct Newport (17074) *(G-12490)*

H & H Print Shop, Bradford *Also called Hounds & Hunting Publishing (G-1973)*

H & H Wholesale LLC 724 733-8338
　3251 Old Frankstown Rd D Pittsburgh (15239) *(G-15069)*

H & K Equipment Inc (PA) 412 490-5300
　4200 Casteel Dr Coraopolis (15108) *(G-3696)*

H & L Concrete 610 562-8273
　470 Main St Virginville (19564) *(G-18770)*

H & L Concrete Service, Virginville *Also called H & L Concrete (G-18770)*

H & M Diversified Entps Inc (PA) 717 277-0680
　981 Mount Zion Rd Lebanon (17046) *(G-9577)*

H & M Diversified Entps Inc 717 531-3490
　1712r E Chocolate Ave Hershey (17033) *(G-7611)*

H & M Glass, Lebanon *Also called H & M Diversified Entps Inc (G-9577)*

H & M Glass, Hershey *Also called H & M Diversified Entps Inc (G-7611)*

H & M Lumber 717 535-5080
　35 Petersheim Dr Mifflintown (17059) *(G-11120)*

H & M Net Works 484 344-2161
　3 Valley Sq Ste 200 Blue Bell (19422) *(G-1832)*

H & P Manufacturing 610 565-7344
　41 S New Middletown Rd Media (19063) *(G-10932)*

H & R Block, Warren *Also called H&R Block Inc (G-19030)*

H & R Neon Service Inc 724 222-6115
　1942 Jefferson Ave Washington (15301) *(G-19183)*

H & S Electronics 717 354-2200
　331 E Main St New Holland (17557) *(G-12250)*

H & W Global Industries Inc 724 459-5316
　414 Innovation Dr Blairsville (15717) *(G-1721)*

H & Z Auto LLC 610 419-8012
　2450 Catasauqua Rd Bethlehem (18018) *(G-1527)*

H and H Foundry Machine Co 724 863-3251
　1570 Rte 993 Manor (15665) *(G-10411)*

H and H Tool 814 333-4677
　384 Clark Rd Meadville (16335) *(G-10732)*

H and K Tool and Mch Co Inc 215 322-0380
　125 Pike Cir Huntingdon Valley (19006) *(G-7993)*

H B Fowler Co Inc 610 688-0567
　250 Conestoga Rd Wayne (19087) *(G-19334)*

H B Instrument Co 610 489-5500
　102 W 7th Ave Trappe (19426) *(G-18469)*

H B Mellott Estate Inc 301 678-2050
　424 Pigeon Cove Rd Warfordsburg (17267) *(G-18812)*

H B South Printing 412 751-1300
　428 Eden Park Blvd McKeesport (15132) *(G-10669)*

H C Harding, Philadelphia *Also called International Chemical Company (G-13865)*

H D Sampey Inc 215 723-3471
　115 S Main St Telford (18969) *(G-18293)*

H Edward Quay Welding, Pottstown *Also called Edward H Quay Welding Spc (G-15985)*

H H Fluorescent Parts Inc 215 379-2750
　104 Beecher Ave Cheltenham (19012) *(G-3029)*

H H Robertson Floor Systems, Coraopolis *Also called Centria Inc (G-3674)*

H H Seiferth Associates Inc 412 281-4983
　2800 Smallman St Pittsburgh (15222) *(G-15070)*

H J Heinz Company LP (HQ) 412 237-5757
　357 6th Ave Pittsburgh (15222) *(G-15071)*

H J Heinz Company Brands LLC 412 456-5700
　1 Ppg Pl Pittsburgh (15222) *(G-15072)*

H M Spencer Wire 570 726-7495
　1004 Ridge Rd Mill Hall (17751) *(G-11177)*

H M W Enterprises Inc 717 765-4690
　207 N Franklin St Waynesboro (17268) *(G-19410)*

H P Cadwallader Inc 215 256-6651
　175 Ruth Rd Harleysville (19438) *(G-7036)*

H P Gazzam Machine Company 412 471-6647
　3200 Penn Ave Pittsburgh (15201) *(G-15073)*

H P I, Telford *Also called Hpi Processes Inc (G-18294)*

H P I, Gibsonia *Also called Handling Products Inc (G-6339)*

H R Clutches, Bensalem *Also called H R Sales Inc (G-1208)*

H R Edgar Machining & Fabg Inc 724 339-6694
　931 Merwin Rd New Kensington (15068) *(G-12344)*

H R Sales Inc 215 639-7150
　3977 Bristol Pike Ste 1 Bensalem (19020) *(G-1208)*

H Troxel Cemetery Service Inc 610 489-4426
　1806 W James St Norristown (19403) *(G-12663)*

H V L, Pittsburgh *Also called V L H Inc (G-15688)*

H W Nicholson Wldg & Mfg Inc 724 727-3461
　3899 State Route 66 Apollo (15613) *(G-676)*

H Y K Construction Co Inc (PA) 610 489-2646
　430 Rahns Rd Collegeville (19426) *(G-3381)*

H Y K Construction Co Inc.....610 282-2300
7700 Keewayden St Coopersburg (18036) ***(G-3628)***
H&K Group Inc.....570 347-1800
950 Dunham Dr Dunmore (18512) ***(G-4474)***
H&K Group Inc.....610 705-0500
392 N Sanatoga Rd Pottstown (19465) ***(G-15947)***
H&K Group Inc (PA).....610 584-8500
2052 Lucon Rd Skippack (19474) ***(G-17597)***
H&K Group Inc.....570 646-3324
Hc 87 Box 282 Pocono Lake (18347) ***(G-15880)***
H&K Group Inc.....610 494-5364
414 W Knowlton Rd Media (19063) ***(G-10933)***
H&K Group Inc.....717 867-0701
155 Syner Rd Annville (17003) ***(G-650)***
H&K Group Inc.....610 250-7700
5137 Lower Mud Run Rd Easton (18040) ***(G-4693)***
H&K Group Inc.....717 445-0961
470 Yellow Hill Rd Narvon (17555) ***(G-11922)***
H&K Group Inc.....610 250-7703
5135 Lower Mud Run Rd Easton (18040) ***(G-4694)***
H&K Group Inc.....717 548-2147
303 Quarry Rd Peach Bottom (17563) ***(G-13198)***
H&R Block Inc.....814 723-3001
229 Pennsylvania Ave W A Warren (16365) ***(G-19030)***
H&R Signs, Washington *Also called H & R Neon Service Inc* ***(G-19183)***
H-D Advanced Manufacturing Co (PA).....724 759-2850
2200 Georgetown Dr # 300 Sewickley (15143) ***(G-17389)***
H-V Industries, Feasterville Trevose *Also called Crown Holdings Inc* ***(G-5902)***
H. A. Storage Systems, Audubon *Also called High Avlblity Stor Systems Inc* ***(G-827)***
H2o Degree, Bensalem *Also called Wellspring Wireless Inc* ***(G-1271)***
HA Harper Sons Inc (PA).....610 485-4776
2800 Chichester Ave Upper Chichester (19061) ***(G-18663)***
Haas Architectural Mllwk Inc.....717 840-4227
3750 E Market St York (17402) ***(G-20519)***
Haas Chem Managment of Mexico (HQ).....610 656-7454
1646 W Chester Pike 4-6 West Chester (19382) ***(G-19558)***
Haas Group.....484 564-4500
1475 Phoenixville Pike West Chester (19380) ***(G-19559)***
Haas Printing Co Inc.....717 761-0277
1000 Hummel Ave Lemoyne (17043) ***(G-9745)***
Haberle Steel Inc (PA).....215 723-8848
1946 E Cherry Ln Ste A Souderton (18964) ***(G-17738)***
Haberle Upholstery.....215 679-8195
6024 Palm Rd Zionsville (18092) ***(G-20835)***
Habsco Inc.....724 337-9498
Schreiber Industrial Dst New Kensington (15068) ***(G-12345)***
Hadco Aluminum & Metal Corp PA.....215 695-2705
2811 Charter Rd Philadelphia (19154) ***(G-13795)***
Haddad and Brooks Inc (PA).....724 228-8811
30 E Beau St Ste 700 Washington (15301) ***(G-19184)***
Haemer/Wright Tool & Die Inc.....814 763-6076
19990 State Highway 198 Saegertown (16433) ***(G-16916)***
Haemonetics Corporation.....412 741-7399
Avenue C Bldg 18 Leetsdale (15056) ***(G-9692)***
Hagerty Precision Tool.....814 734-8668
12250 Eureka Rd Edinboro (16412) ***(G-4813)***
Hahn Universal.....724 941-6444
163 Orchard Dr Canonsburg (15317) ***(G-2594)***
Hailiang America Corporation.....877 515-4522
1001 James Dr Ste B38 Leesport (19533) ***(G-9665)***
Hain Pure Protein Corporation (HQ).....717 865-2136
220 N Center St Fredericksburg (17026) ***(G-6175)***
Hain Pure Protein Corporation.....717 624-2191
304 S Water St New Oxford (17350) ***(G-12411)***
Haines Printing Co.....814 725-1955
10575 W Main Rd North East (16428) ***(G-12746)***
Hains Pattern Shop Inc.....717 273-6351
521 S 14th Ave Lebanon (17042) ***(G-9578)***
Hajoca Corporation.....610 432-0551
1801 Union Blvd Ste 104 Allentown (18109) ***(G-240)***
Hajoca Corporation.....215 657-0700
3155 Terwood Rd Willow Grove (19090) ***(G-20120)***
Hal Ben Mining Co.....724 748-4528
389 Irishtown Rd Grove City (16127) ***(G-6789)***
Hal-Jo Corp.....215 885-4747
261 York Rd Jenkintown (19046) ***(G-8289)***
Halco, Verona *Also called T J Corporation* ***(G-18763)***
Halco (mining) Inc (PA).....412 235-0265
323 N Shore Dr Pittsburgh (15212) ***(G-15074)***
Haldex Brake Products Corp.....717 939-5928
2700 Commerce Dr Middletown (17057) ***(G-11055)***
Haldex Midland, Middletown *Also called Haldex Brake Products Corp* ***(G-11055)***
Halex Corporation.....909 622-3537
352 Newbold Rd Fairless Hills (19030) ***(G-5782)***
Haley Paint Company (PA).....717 299-6771
194 Greenfield Rd Lancaster (17601) ***(G-9037)***
Half Pint Creamery LLC.....717 634-5459
3780 Centennial Rd Hanover (17331) ***(G-6890)***
Half Pint Creamery LLC.....717 420-2110
1101 Biglerville Rd Gettysburg (17325) ***(G-6297)***
Half Plus Half Inc Enterprise.....800 252-4545
7800 Temple Rd Philadelphia (19150) ***(G-13796)***
Halferty Metals Company Inc.....724 694-5280
294 Bergman Rd Derry (15627) ***(G-4102)***
Halkett Woodworking Inc.....215 721-9331
50 Schoolhouse Rd Souderton (18964) ***(G-17739)***
Hall Foods Inc.....412 257-9877
3249 Washington Pike Bridgeville (15017) ***(G-2067)***
Hall Industries Incorporated (PA).....724 752-2000
514 Mecklem Rd Ellwood City (16117) ***(G-4934)***
Hall Industries Incorporated.....724 758-5522
1 Uss Industrial Park Ellwood City (16117) ***(G-4935)***
Hall Industries & Eqp Div, Ellwood City *Also called Standard Tool & Machine Co* ***(G-4950)***
Hall Technical Services LLC.....724 752-2000
514 Mecklem Ln Ellwood City (16117) ***(G-4936)***
Hall-Woolford Wood Tank Co Inc.....215 329-9022
5500 N Water St Philadelphia (19120) ***(G-13797)***
Hallelujah Ink.....215 510-1152
2048 E Ann St Philadelphia (19134) ***(G-13798)***
Haller Energy Services LLC.....717 721-9560
1976 Bowmansville Rd Adamstown (19501) ***(G-22)***
Halliburton Company.....570 547-5800
343 Riddell Rd Montgomery (17752) ***(G-11370)***
Halliburton Energy Services, Montgomery *Also called Halliburton Company* ***(G-11370)***
Halls Candies LLC.....570 596-2267
3426 Thunder Rd Gillett (16925) ***(G-6381)***
Halls Ice Cream Inc.....717 589-3290
861 Raccoon Valley Rd Millerstown (17062) ***(G-11204)***
Halo Labs, Philadelphia *Also called Optofluidics Inc* ***(G-14100)***
Halsey Inc.....570 278-3610
State Route 706 W Montrose (18801) ***(G-11466)***
Halsit Holdings LLC.....814 724-6440
13680 S Mosiertown Rd Meadville (16335) ***(G-10733)***
Haltemans Hardwood Products.....814 745-2519
236 Halteman Ln Sligo (16255) ***(G-17615)***
Hamamatsu Corporation.....724 935-3600
2593 Wexford Bayne Rd # 305 Sewickley (15143) ***(G-17390)***
Hamburg Area Item.....610 367-6041
24 N Hanover St Pottstown (19464) ***(G-15994)***
Hamburg Item, Pottstown *Also called Berks-Mont Newspapers Inc* ***(G-15966)***
Hamburg Manufacturing Inc (PA).....610 562-2203
221 S 4th St Hamburg (19526) ***(G-6840)***
Hamburger Color Company Inc.....610 279-6450
555 E Church Rd King of Prussia (19406) ***(G-8627)***
Hamfab Products, Lehighton *Also called Ica Inc* ***(G-9716)***
Hamill Manufacturing Company.....724 744-2131
500 Pleasant Valley Rd Trafford (15085) ***(G-18457)***
Hamilton Awning Co.....724 774-7644
488 Buffalo St Beaver (15009) ***(G-983)***
Hamilton High Heat Inc.....814 635-4131
1951 Lytle Ln Saxton (16678) ***(G-17101)***
Hamilton L Fisher L C.....412 490-8300
2000 Park Ln Pittsburgh (15275) ***(G-15075)***
Hamilton Tool Co Inc.....814 382-3419
13887 Middle Rd Meadville (16335) ***(G-10734)***
Hamiltonian Systems Inc.....412 327-7204
117 Hunters Run Dr Coraopolis (15108) ***(G-3697)***
Hammaker East, Pittsburgh *Also called Russell Standard Corporation* ***(G-15504)***
Hammaker East.....717 263-0434
118 Siloam Rd Chambersburg (17201) ***(G-2937)***
Hammaker East (HQ).....412 221-7300
285 Kappa Dr Ste 300 Pittsburgh (15238) ***(G-15076)***
Hammaker East Emulsions LLC.....412 449-0700
285 Kappa Dr Ste 300 Pittsburgh (15238) ***(G-15077)***
Hammertek Corporation.....717 898-7665
2400 Emrick Blvd Bethlehem (18020) ***(G-1528)***
Hammond Group Inc.....610 327-1400
10 S Grosstown Rd Pottstown (19464) ***(G-15995)***
Hammond Lead Product, Pottstown *Also called Hammond Group Inc* ***(G-15995)***
Hammond Press Inc.....412 821-4100
404 North Ave Pittsburgh (15209) ***(G-15078)***
Hammond Pretzel Bakery Inc.....717 392-7532
716 S West End Ave Rear Lancaster (17603) ***(G-9038)***
Hammond's Old Fashnd Hnd Made, Lancaster *Also called Hammond Pretzel Bakery Inc* ***(G-9038)***
Hamot Breast Health Center, Erie *Also called Hamot Imaging Facility* ***(G-5309)***
Hamot Imaging Facility.....814 877-5381
3406 Peach St Erie (16508) ***(G-5309)***
Hampden Papers Inc.....610 255-4166
3 Meadow Wood Ln Landenberg (19350) ***(G-9249)***
Hampshire Paper Company.....570 759-7245
2015 W Front St Berwick (18603) ***(G-1328)***
Hampsons Farm & Garden Inc (PA).....570 724-3012
1 E Delmar Mdws Wellsboro (16901) ***(G-19464)***
Hampton Cabinet Shop.....717 898-7806
2730 Shenck Rd Manheim (17545) ***(G-10387)***
Hampton Concrete Products Inc.....724 443-7205
1435 Pittsburgh Rd Valencia (16059) ***(G-18698)***

1102
2019 Harris Pennsylvania Manufacturers Directory
(G-0000) Company's Geographic Section entry number

Hampton Controls Inc (PA) 724 861-0150
  Wendel Rd Wendel (15691) *(G-19481)*
Hampton Controls, Optics Div., Wendel Also called Hampton Controls Inc *(G-19481)*
Hampton Machining Inc 717 734-2497
  3 Hampton Ln East Waterford (17021) *(G-4641)*
Hampton's, Manheim Also called Hampton Cabinet Shop *(G-10387)*
Hancock Company 570 875-3100
  2309 Chestnut St Ashland (17921) *(G-731)*
Hand Crafted Furniture Co Inc (PA) 717 630-0036
  237 Ridge Ave Hanover (17331) *(G-6891)*
Hand In Hand Soap LLC 267 714-4168
  1646 S 12th St Ste 202 Philadelphia (19148) *(G-13799)*
Handbooks & Healthcare, Newtown Also called Associates In Medical Mktg Co *(G-12497)*
Handelok Bag Company Inc 215 362-3400
  701 W 5th St Ste A Lansdale (19446) *(G-9375)*
Handicapped Product Post Cards, Horsham Also called J L Communications Inc *(G-7826)*
Handling Products Inc (PA) 724 443-1100
  3151 Seneca Ct Gibsonia (15044) *(G-6339)*
Handrail Design Inc 717 285-4088
  3905 Continental Dr Columbia (17512) *(G-3438)*
Handwerks Welding & Fabg, Northampton Also called Terry L Handwerk *(G-12862)*
Handy & Harman Tube Co Inc 610 539-3900
  701 W Township Line Rd Norristown (19403) *(G-12664)*
Handy Tube Company, Norristown Also called Handy & Harman Tube Co Inc *(G-12664)*
Handygas Corporation (PA) 717 428-2506
  7927 Player Blvd Seven Valleys (17360) *(G-17379)*
Hanel Storage Systems 412 788-0509
  121 Industry Dr Pittsburgh (15275) *(G-15079)*
Hanes Erie Inc 814 474-1999
  7601 Klier Dr N Fairview (16415) *(G-5826)*
Hanesbrands Inc 610 970-5767
  18 W Lightcap Rd Ste 1153 Pottstown (19464) *(G-15996)*
Hanesbrands Inc 336 519-8080
  1519 Franklin Mills Cir Philadelphia (19154) *(G-13800)*
Hanford & Hockenbrock 610 275-5373
  1735 Markley St Norristown (19401) *(G-12665)*
Hang Xing Fa Inc 646 250-7175
  911 W Linden St 921 Allentown (18101) *(G-241)*
Hanger Inc 877 442-6437
  176 S Wilkes Barre Blvd Wilkes Barre (18702) *(G-19923)*
Hanger Inc 724 836-4949
  4000 Hempfield Plaza Blvd # 904 Greensburg (15601) *(G-6671)*
Hanger Clinic, Uniontown Also called Hanger Prsthetcs & Ortho Inc *(G-18629)*
Hanger Clinic, Bradford Also called Hanger Prsthetcs & Ortho Inc *(G-1971)*
Hanger Clinic, Greensburg Also called Hanger Prsthetcs & Ortho Inc *(G-6672)*
Hanger P & O, East Stroudsburg Also called Hanger Prsthetcs & Ortho Inc *(G-4615)*
Hanger Prsthetcs & Ortho Inc 724 438-4582
  211 Easy St Ste 120 Uniontown (15401) *(G-18629)*
Hanger Prsthetcs & Ortho Inc 215 365-1532
  3015 Island Ave Philadelphia (19153) *(G-13801)*
Hanger Prsthetcs & Ortho Inc 714 774-0637
  500 Market St Ste 105 West Bridgewater (15009) *(G-19491)*
Hanger Prsthetcs & Ortho Inc 814 368-3702
  900 Chestnut Street Ext Bradford (16701) *(G-1971)*
Hanger Prsthetcs & Ortho Inc 717 731-8181
  3514 Trindle Rd Camp Hill (17011) *(G-2499)*
Hanger Prsthetcs & Ortho Inc 724 836-4949
  4000 Hempfield Plaza Blvd Greensburg (15601) *(G-6672)*
Hanger Prsthetcs & Ortho Inc 724 285-1284
  108 Evans Rd Butler (16001) *(G-2404)*
Hanger Prsthetcs & Ortho Inc 570 421-8221
  423 Normal St East Stroudsburg (18301) *(G-4615)*
Hanger Prsthetcs & Ortho Inc 717 264-7117
  765 5th Ave Ste D Chambersburg (17201) *(G-2938)*
Hanger Prsthetcs & Ortho Inc 717 564-4521
  989 E Park Dr Harrisburg (17111) *(G-7138)*
Hanger Prsthetcs & Ortho Inc 724 981-5775
  165 N Hermitage Rd Hermitage (16148) *(G-7587)*
Hanger Prsthetcs & Ortho Inc 717 767-6667
  1603 Rodney Rd York (17408) *(G-20520)*
Hanks Beverage Company 215 396-2809
  969 Street Rd Southampton (18966) *(G-17815)*
Hannahoe Pallets, Reading Also called Hannahoes Pallets & Skids *(G-16398)*
Hannahoes Pallets & Skids 610 926-4699
  39 Riverside Dr Reading (19605) *(G-16398)*
Hannmann Machinery Systems Inc 610 583-6900
  930 Henderson Blvd Folcroft (19032) *(G-6005)*
Hannon Company 724 266-2712
  2940 Duss Ave Ambridge (15003) *(G-618)*
Hannon Electric, Ambridge Also called Hannon Company *(G-618)*
HANOVER ARCHITECTURA, Hanover Also called Hanover Prest-Paving Company *(G-6900)*
Hanover Architectural Products, Hanover Also called Hanover Prest Paving Company *(G-6899)*
Hanover Brick and Block Co 717 637-0500
  240 Bender Rd Hanover (17331) *(G-6892)*
Hanover Concrete, Gettysburg Also called Gettysburg Concrete Co Inc *(G-6291)*
Hanover Concrete Co 717 637-2288
  2000 Carlisle Pike Hanover (17331) *(G-6893)*

Hanover Foods Corporation (PA) 717 632-6000
  1486 York St Hanover (17331) *(G-6894)*
Hanover Foods Corporation 814 364-1482
  3008 Penns Valley Pike Centre Hall (16828) *(G-2841)*
Hanover Foods Corporation 717 665-2002
  1000 W College Ave York (17404) *(G-20521)*
Hanover Foods Corporation 717 843-0738
  1120 Zinns Quarry Rd York (17404) *(G-20522)*
Hanover Foods Corporation 800 888-4646
  1550 York St Hanover (17331) *(G-6895)*
Hanover Ice Co Inc 717 637-9137
  1904 Yingling Dr Spring Grove (17362) *(G-17878)*
Hanover Iron Works Inc 717 632-5624
  463 Gitts Run Rd Hanover (17331) *(G-6896)*
Hanover Paper Box Company Inc 215 432-5033
  1122 Hamilton St Allentown (18101) *(G-242)*
Hanover Pen Corp 717 637-3729
  14 Industrial Dr Hanover (17331) *(G-6897)*
Hanover Potato Products Inc 717 632-0700
  60 Black Rock Rd Hanover (17331) *(G-6898)*
Hanover Prest Paving Company 717 637-0500
  240 Bender Rd Hanover (17331) *(G-6899)*
Hanover Prest-Paving Company 717 637-0500
  5000 Hanover Rd Hanover (17331) *(G-6900)*
Hanover Publishing Co 717 637-3736
  135 Baltimore St Hanover (17331) *(G-6901)*
Hanover Quarry, Hanover Also called Legacy Vulcan LLC *(G-6913)*
Hanover Wire Cloth 717 637-3795
  500 E Middle St Hanover (17331) *(G-6902)*
Hanson Aggregates Bmc Inc 610 847-5211
  262 Quarry Rd Ottsville (18942) *(G-13062)*
Hanson Aggregates Bmc Inc 724 229-5840
  339 Somerset Dr Eighty Four (15330) *(G-4842)*
Hanson Aggregates Bmc Inc 724 626-0080
  2200 Springfield Pike Connellsville (15425) *(G-3498)*
Hanson Aggregates LLC 724 459-6031
  311 Quarry Rd Blairsville (15717) *(G-1722)*
Hanson Aggregates PA LLC 610 269-1710
  499 Quarry Rd Downingtown (19335) *(G-4232)*
Hanson Aggregates PA LLC 570 992-4951
  5804 Cherry Valley Rd Stroudsburg (18360) *(G-18122)*
Hanson Aggregates PA LLC (HQ) 610 366-4626
  7660 Imperial Way Allentown (18195) *(G-243)*
Hanson Aggregates PA LLC 570 368-2481
  503 Quarry Rd Jersey Shore (17740) *(G-8314)*
Hanson Aggregates PA LLC 570 584-2153
  1918 Lime Bluff Rd Muncy (17756) *(G-11818)*
Hanson Aggregates PA LLC 570 324-2514
  Blossburg Mtns Rr 15 Blossburg (16912) *(G-1807)*
Hanson Aggregates PA LLC 570 437-4068
  3 Quarry Rd Milton (17847) *(G-11240)*
Hanson Aggregates PA LLC 570 726-4511
  Rr 477 Salona (17767) *(G-17049)*
Hanson Aggregates PA LLC 570 322-6737
  3485 W 4th St Williamsport (17701) *(G-20020)*
Hanson Aggregates PA LLC 570 784-1640
  800 Paper Mill Rd Bloomsburg (17815) *(G-1784)*
Hanson Aggregates PA LLC 570 784-2888
  Rural Dr 4 Rte 42 N Bloomsburg (17815) *(G-1785)*
Hanson Aggregates PA LLC 814 355-4226
  1394 Forest Ave Bellefonte (16823) *(G-1103)*
Hanson Aggregates PA LLC 814 466-5101
  850 Boalsburg Rd Boalsburg (16827) *(G-1867)*
Hanson Aggrgates Southeast Inc 570 784-2888
  Rr 4 Bloomsburg (17815) *(G-1786)*
Hanson Lehigh Inc 610 366-4600
  7660 Imperial Way Ste 200 Allentown (18195) *(G-244)*
Hanson Ready Mix Inc 814 238-1781
  123 Hawbaker Indus Dr State College (16803) *(G-17971)*
Hanson Ready Mix Inc 814 269-9600
  248 Solomon Run Rd Johnstown (15904) *(G-8379)*
Hanson Ready Mix Inc 412 431-6001
  2220 2nd Ave Pittsburgh (15219) *(G-15080)*
Hanson Ready Mix Inc (HQ) 610 837-6725
  3251 Bath Pike Nazareth (18064) *(G-11971)*
Hapeman Electronics Inc (PA) 724 475-2033
  761 N Cottage Rd Mercer (16137) *(G-10962)*
Happening's Magazine, Clarks Summit Also called J P R Publications Inc *(G-3196)*
Happy Baking Co 412 621-4020
  5 Bayard Rd Pittsburgh (15213) *(G-15081)*
Happy Valley Blended Pdts LLC 814 548-7090
  660 Axemann Rd Pleasant Gap (16823) *(G-15793)*
Happy Valley Com 814 238-8066
  1669 N Atherton St State College (16803) *(G-17972)*
Happy Vly Vinyrd & Winery LLC 814 308-8756
  576 S Foxpointe Dr State College (16801) *(G-17973)*
Hapsco Design and Prtg Svcs 717 564-2323
  4750 Lindle Rd Harrisburg (17111) *(G-7139)*
Haraeuc Inc Cermalloy Div 610 825-8387
  24 Union Hill Rd Conshohocken (19428) *(G-3553)*

ALPHABETIC

Harbisnwlker Intl Holdings Inc (PA) 412 375-6600
　1305 Cherrington Pkwy Moon Township (15108) *(G-11488)*

Harbison Walker 215 364-5555
　4667 Somerton Rd Trevose (19053) *(G-18498)*

Harbisonwalker Intl Foundation 412 375-6600
　1305 Cherrington Pkwy # 100 Moon Township (15108) *(G-11489)*

Harbisonwalker Intl Inc 412 469-3880
　1001 Pittsbrg Mckeesp Blv West Mifflin (15122) *(G-19740)*

Harbisonwalker Intl Inc (HQ) 412 375-6600
　1305 Cherrington Pkwy # 100 Moon Township (15108) *(G-11490)*

Harbisonwalker Intl Inc 814 239-2111
　2926 Quarry Rd Claysburg (16625) *(G-3204)*

Harbor Bay Group Inc 610 566-5290
　660 13th Ave Ste 4 Prospect Park (19076) *(G-16115)*

Harbor Orthodontic Services 724 654-3599
　699 Kings Chapel Rd Ste A New Castle (16105) *(G-12099)*

Harbor Steel Inc 724 658-7748
　1980 Bnjmin Franklin Pkwy New Castle (16101) *(G-12100)*

Harbortouch, Allentown Also called Shift4 Payments LLC *(G-389)*

Hard Metal Tooling, Pleasant Unity Also called Jim Conrath *(G-15796)*

Hards Welding & Fabricating, Seneca Also called Bill Hards *(G-17364)*

Hardwoods Millworking 814 395-5474
　300 Whites Creek Rd Confluence (15424) *(G-3465)*

Hardy Machine Inc 215 822-9359
　2326 N Penn Rd Hatfield (19440) *(G-7345)*

Harford Stone Company 570 434-9141
　1060 Bartholomew Rd Kingsley (18826) *(G-8705)*

Hari Jayanti News Inc 215 546-1350
　230 S Broad St Philadelphia (19102) *(G-13802)*

Harlan Electric 717 243-4600
　1213 Paxton Church Rd Harrisburg (17110) *(G-7140)*

Harleysville Materials LLC 856 768-8493
　460 Indian Creek Rd Harleysville (19438) *(G-7037)*

Harliss Specialties Corp 724 863-0321
　Biddle Rd Irwin (15642) *(G-8166)*

Harman Beach Corporation 717 652-0556
　6700 Allentown Blvd Harrisburg (17112) *(G-7141)*

Harmonic Rays Mfg Group Inc 267 761-9558
　1116 Buttonwood St Unit A Philadelphia (19123) *(G-13803)*

Harmony Biosciences LLC 847 715-0500
　630 W Germantown Pike Plymouth Meeting (19462) *(G-15845)*

Harmony Designs Inc 610 869-4234
　129 E Harmony Rd West Grove (19390) *(G-19700)*

Harmony Flagstone LLC 570 727-2077
　21188 State Route 171 Susquehanna (18847) *(G-18180)*

Harmony Hill Forestry 570 247-2676
　1441 Harmony Hill Rd Rome (18837) *(G-16799)*

Harmony Labels Inc 570 664-6700
　114 Progress St East Stroudsburg (18301) *(G-4616)*

Harmony LL Plastics Inc 215 943-8888
　100 Main St Ste 2c Bristol (19007) *(G-2151)*

Harmony Paper Company LLC 724 991-1110
　352 Fanker Rd Harmony (16037) *(G-7068)*

Harmony Plus Woodworks Inc 717 432-0372
　300 Old Cabin Hollow Rd Dillsburg (17019) *(G-4131)*

Harmony Press Inc (PA) 610 559-9800
　717 W Berwick St Easton (18042) *(G-4695)*

Harmony Products Inc 717 767-2779
　20 Church Rd Emigsville (17318) *(G-4987)*

Harners Auto Body Inc 610 385-3825
　422e524 Ben Franklin Hwy Birdsboro (19508) *(G-1698)*

Harnish Production Machine 717 866-4562
　360 King St Myerstown (17067) *(G-11886)*

Harold Beck & Sons Inc (PA) 215 968-4600
　11 Terry Dr Newtown (18940) *(G-12506)*

Harold Graves Trucking 814 654-7836
　45332 Sundback Rd Spartansburg (16434) *(G-17851)*

Harold M Horst Inc 717 354-5815
　340 W Main St New Holland (17557) *(G-12251)*

Harper Collins, Moosic Also called Collins Harper Publishers *(G-11504)*

Harper Printing Service 412 884-2666
　2640 Library Rd Pittsburgh (15234) *(G-15082)*

Harpercollins Publishers LLC 570 941-1500
　53 Glnmura Nat Blvd 300 Moosic (18507) *(G-11507)*

Harpercollins Publishers LLC 800 242-7737
　53 Glnmura Nat Blvd St300 Moosic (18507) *(G-11508)*

Harpoint Holdings Inc (PA) 717 692-2113
　200 Front St Millersburg (17061) *(G-11194)*

Harrier Mfg Corp 814 838-9957
　904 Wilkins Rd Erie (16505) *(G-5310)*

Harrington Hoists Inc (HQ) 717 665-2000
　401 W End Ave Manheim (17545) *(G-10388)*

Harrington Machine and Tool Co 814 432-7339
　1027 Chestnut St Franklin (16323) *(G-6134)*

Harris Graphics & Detailing 610 532-0209
　122 Chester Pike Norwood (19074) *(G-12880)*

Harris Manufacturing Company (PA) 609 393-3717
　37 Rotterdam Rd E Southampton (18966) *(G-17816)*

Harris Rebar Atlantic Inc 610 882-1401
　1700 Riverside Dr Unit 1 Bethlehem (18015) *(G-1529)*

Harris Woodworking 610 932-2646
　120 Oxford St Oxford (19363) *(G-13080)*

Harrisburg Building Units, Middletown Also called York Building Products Co Inc *(G-11086)*

Harrisburg Dairies Inc 717 233-8701
　2001 Herr St Harrisburg (17103) *(G-7142)*

Harrisburg Field Office, Harrisburg Also called Surface Mining Reclamation Off *(G-7224)*

Harrisburg Magazine Inc 717 233-0109
　3400 N 6th St Harrisburg (17110) *(G-7143)*

Harrisburg Stamp & Stencil Co 717 236-9000
　3362 Paxton St Harrisburg (17111) *(G-7144)*

Harrison Custom Cabinets 215 548-2450
　125357 E Chelten Ave Philadelphia (19138) *(G-13804)*

Harrison Electronic Systems 570 639-5695
　1167 N Washington St Wilkes Barre (18705) *(G-19924)*

Harrison House Inc 918 523-5700
　167 Walnut Bottom Rd Shippensburg (17257) *(G-17531)*

Harrison House Publishers, Shippensburg Also called Harrison House Inc *(G-17531)*

Harrison Manufacturing, Philadelphia Also called Harrison Custom Cabinets *(G-13804)*

Harrison Systems, Wilkes Barre Also called Harrison Electronic Systems *(G-19924)*

Harro Hofliger Packg Systems, Doylestown Also called Harro Hofliger Packg
Systems *(G-4305)*

Harro Hofliger Packg Systems 215 345-4256
　350 S Main St Ste 315 Doylestown (18901) *(G-4305)*

Harrowgate Fine Foods Inc 717 823-6855
　2322 Hancock Dr Lancaster (17601) *(G-9039)*

Harry J Lawall & Son Inc (PA) 215 338-6611
　8028 Frankford Ave Philadelphia (19136) *(G-13805)*

Harry Rhoades 814 474-1099
　7395 Market Rd Fairview (16415) *(G-5827)*

Harry's Wood Shop, Tunkhannock Also called Recon Enterprises *(G-18548)*

Harrys Famous Pudding 484 494-6400
　5 1/2 N Bartram Ave Glenolden (19036) *(G-6475)*

Harsco Corporation 570 421-7500
　155 Burson St East Stroudsburg (18301) *(G-4617)*

Harsco Corporation 215 295-8675
　905 Steel Rd S Fairless Hills (19030) *(G-5783)*

Harsco Corporation 724 287-4791
　Rr 8 Box S Butler (16001) *(G-2405)*

Harsco Corporation 570 421-7500
　155 Burson St East Stroudsburg (18301) *(G-4618)*

Harsco Corporation 717 506-2071
　5020 Ritter Rd Ste 205 Mechanicsburg (17055) *(G-10851)*

Harsco Indus Patterson-Kelly, East Stroudsburg Also called Harsco Corporation *(G-4618)*

Harsco Minerals PA LLC 717 506-7157
　905 Steel Rd S Fairless Hills (19030) *(G-5784)*

Harsco Minerals PA LLC 724 352-0066
　357 N Pike Rd 9 Sarver (16055) *(G-17071)*

Hart McHncl-Lctrcal Contrs Inc 215 257-1666
　1200 N Ridge Rd Perkasie (18944) *(G-13278)*

Harte Hanks Inc 570 826-0414
　165 New Commerce Blvd Hanover Township (18706) *(G-6989)*

Harte-Hanks Direct Marketing, Hanover Township Also called Harte Hanks Inc *(G-6989)*

Harter Precision 724 459-5060
　Hwy 982 & Rte 22 Rt 22 Blairsville (15717) *(G-1723)*

Hartings Bakery Inc 717 445-5644
　1212 Reading Rd Rr 625 Bowmansville (17507) *(G-1887)*

Hartleys Potato Chip Mfg 717 248-0526
　2157 Back Maitland Rd Lewistown (17044) *(G-9934)*

Hartman Design Inc 610 670-2517
　51 N Elm St Wernersville (19565) *(G-19484)*

Hartman, Warren G, Clearfield Also called Warren C Hartman Contracting *(G-3237)*

Hartronics 717 597-3931
　3354 Conococheague Ln Greencastle (17225) *(G-6617)*

Hartstrings LLC 610 326-8221
　18 W Lightcap Rd Ste 723 Pottstown (19464) *(G-15997)*

Hartzell Machine Works Inc 610 485-3502
　3354 Market St Upper Chichester (19014) *(G-18664)*

Harvel Plastics Inc 610 252-7355
　300 Kuebler Rd Easton (18040) *(G-4696)*

Harvest Moon Woodworking 717 521-4204
　360 Fairview Ave Mc Sherrystown (17344) *(G-10651)*

Harvest Structures, Ronks Also called Johnathan Stoltzfus *(G-16808)*

Harvestmore Inc 814 725-5258
　10028 W Main Rd North East (16428) *(G-12747)*

Harvey Bell 215 634-4900
　1706 Frankford Ave Philadelphia (19125) *(G-13806)*

Harvey Leon 570 337-2665
　2117 Harvard Ave South Williamsport (17702) *(G-17791)*

Harvey M Stern & Co 610 649-1728
　431 Haverford Rd Wynnewood (19096) *(G-20268)*

Harvey-Robert's, Haverford Also called Robert H Berenson *(G-7414)*

Harvil Inc 412 682-1500
　1029 Mccartney St Pittsburgh (15220) *(G-15083)*

Has-Mor Industries Inc 570 383-0185
　503 Maplewood Dr Olyphant (18447) *(G-12992)*

Hassinger Diesel Service LLC 570 837-3412
　75 Diesel Rd Middleburg (17842) *(G-11025)*

Hastings Machine Company Inc 814 247-6562
192 Haida Ave Hastings (16646) *(G-7261)*
Hastings Machine Company Inc (HQ) 814 533-5777
111 Roosevelt Blvd Johnstown (15906) *(G-8380)*
Hatcrafters Inc 610 623-2620
20 N Springfield Rd Ste 1 Clifton Heights (19018) *(G-3253)*
Hatfield Manufacturing Inc 215 368-9574
1447 Leas Way Hatfield (19440) *(G-7346)*
Hatfield Quality Meats, Emmaus *Also called Clemens Food Group LLC (G-5023)*
Hatfield Rubber Company, Hatfield *Also called Surco Inc (G-7397)*
Hauck Manufacturing Company (HQ) 717 272-3051
235 W Penn Ave Cleona (17042) *(G-3244)*
Hauck Mfg Kromschroder Contrls, Cleona *Also called Hauck Manufacturing Company (G-3244)*
Haugh Woodworking 724 894-2205
119 Oak Hill Rd West Sunbury (16061) *(G-19770)*
Haulmark of Pennsylavania, McAdoo *Also called Universal Trlr Crgo Group Inc (G-10659)*
Hauser Estate Inc 717 334-4888
410 Cashtown Rd Biglerville (17307) *(G-1663)*
Hauser Estate Inc (PA) 717 334-4888
28 W Middle St Gettysburg (17325) *(G-6298)*
Hauser Estate Winery, The, Biglerville *Also called Hauser Estate Inc (G-1663)*
Hauser Estate Winery, The, Gettysburg *Also called Hauser Estate Inc (G-6298)*
Hausser Scientific Company 215 675-7769
935 Horsham Rd Ste C Horsham (19044) *(G-7822)*
Havaco Technologies Inc 814 878-5509
3058 W 22nd St Erie (16506) *(G-5311)*
Haveco Div of Ace Mobility 717 558-4301
7917 Derry St Ste 124 Harrisburg (17111) *(G-7145)*
Haveco Inc 717 558-4301
7917 Derry St Ste 124 Harrisburg (17111) *(G-7146)*
Haven Homes Inc (HQ) 410 694-0091
555 Croton Rd Ste 200 King of Prussia (19406) *(G-8628)*
Haverstick Bros Inc 717 392-5722
2111 Stone Mill Rd Lancaster (17603) *(G-9040)*
Havis Inc 215 354-3280
40 Indian Dr Warminster (18974) *(G-18893)*
Havpack 814 452-4989
1507 Wayne St Erie (16503) *(G-5312)*
Hawk Construction Products 610 873-8658
7 Martins Ln Downingtown (19335) *(G-4233)*
Hawk Grips 484 351-8050
1495 Alan Wood Rd Ste 201 Conshohocken (19428) *(G-3554)*
Hawk Industrial Services LLC 717 658-4332
4593 Coontown Rd Chambersburg (17202) *(G-2939)*
Hawk Industries Inc 717 359-4138
1880 White Hall Rd Littlestown (17340) *(G-10066)*
Hawk Mountain Art Papers, Leesport *Also called Hawk Mountain Editions Ltd (G-9666)*
Hawk Mountain Editions Ltd 484 220-0524
314 Ziegler Rd Leesport (19533) *(G-9666)*
Hawk Precision Components 814 371-0184
409 3rd St Falls Creek (15840) *(G-5854)*
Hawke Aerospace Holdings LLC 610 372-5141
128 W Apron Dr Reading (19605) *(G-16399)*
Hawke Aerospace Holdings LLC (PA) 610 372-5191
189a Twin County Rd Morgantown (19543) *(G-11523)*
Hawkeye-Jensen Inc 610 488-8500
203 Oak Ln Bernville (19506) *(G-1300)*
Hawkins Metal 215 538-9668
2020 Emerson Dr Quakertown (18951) *(G-16199)*
Hawstone Hollow Winery LLC 717 953-9613
11 Hawstone Rd Lewistown (17044) *(G-9935)*
Haycarb Usa Inc 281 292-8678
100 Willow Ave Oakdale (15071) *(G-12900)*
Hayden Printing Co 610 642-2105
206 E Lancaster Ave Ardmore (19003) *(G-708)*
Hayes Enterprises Inc (PA) 610 252-2530
306 S Watson St Easton (18045) *(G-4697)*
Hayes Industries Inc 484 624-5314
41 Robinson St A Pottstown (19464) *(G-15998)*
Hayes Metal Fabrication LLC 724 694-5280
294 Bergman Rd Derry (15627) *(G-4103)*
Hayes-Ivy Mfg Inc 610 767-3865
6273 Route 309 New Tripoli (18066) *(G-12457)*
Hayloft Candles 717 656-9463
99 S Groffdale Rd Leola (17540) *(G-9786)*
Haymark, Oakdale *Also called Haycarb Usa Inc (G-12900)*
Haysite Reinforced Plas LLC 814 868-3691
5599 Perry Hwy Erie (16509) *(G-5313)*
Hayward Laboratories Inc 570 424-9512
1921 Paradise Trl East Stroudsburg (18301) *(G-4619)*
Hazardous Materials Mgt Team 215 968-4044
418 Washington Ave Newtown (18940) *(G-12507)*
Hazards Distillery Inc 717 994-4860
241 Nicholson Dr Mifflintown (17059) *(G-11121)*
Hazel and Ash Organics LLC 717 521-9593
14 Spaulding Ave Coatesville (19320) *(G-3307)*
Hazle Park Packing Co 570 455-7571
260 Washington Ave Hazle Township (18202) *(G-7461)*
Hazleton Casting Company (PA) 570 453-0199
Rear 225 N Cedar St Hazleton (18201) *(G-7500)*
Hazleton Custom Metal Pdts Inc 570 455-0450
5057 Old Airport Rd Hazle Township (18202) *(G-7462)*
Hazleton Custom Metal Products 570 455-0450
Rr 4 Hazleton (18202) *(G-7501)*
Hazleton Iron Works Inc 570 455-0445
154 N Cedar St Hazleton (18201) *(G-7502)*
Hazleton Pumps, Hazleton *Also called Weir Hazleton Inc (G-7537)*
Hazleton Shaft Corporation 570 450-0900
414 Shaft Rd Hazleton (18201) *(G-7503)*
HB Fuller Company 610 688-1234
547 Saint Davids Ave Wayne (19087) *(G-19335)*
HB Hardware, Kylertown *Also called H & B Enterprises Inc (G-8865)*
HB Instrment Div Bel-Art Produ 610 489-5500
102 W 7th Ave Trappe (19426) *(G-18470)*
HB Sportswear Inc (PA) 717 354-2306
494 W Broad St New Holland (17557) *(G-12252)*
HB Trading LLC 610 212-4565
37 Briar Rd Wayne (19087) *(G-19336)*
Hbc Packaging, Lansdale *Also called Handelok Bag Company Inc (G-9375)*
Hbg-Upper Saucon Inc 215 491-7736
2500 York Rd Jamison (18929) *(G-8244)*
Hc Hoodco Inc 814 355-4003
649 E Rolling Ridge Dr Bellefonte (16823) *(G-1104)*
Hc Quality Doors LLC 717 768-7038
48 Queen Rd Ste 1 Gordonville (17529) *(G-6557)*
Hci Direct, Trevose *Also called Sculptz Inc (G-18503)*
Hcl Liquidation Ltd (PA) 724 251-4200
100 Washington St Leetsdale (15056) *(G-9693)*
Hd Laser Engrv & Etching LLC 724 924-9241
3374 Princeton Rd New Castle (16101) *(G-12101)*
Hd Surgical, Bristol *Also called Tecomet Inc (G-2204)*
Hdi Railings, Columbia *Also called Handrail Design Inc (G-3438)*
Hds Marketing Inc 412 279-1600
633 Napor Blvd Pittsburgh (15205) *(G-15084)*
Head & The Hand Press LLC 856 562-8545
2312 Emerald St Philadelphia (19125) *(G-13807)*
Head To Toe Sportswear 814 371-5119
128 W Long Ave Apt A Du Bois (15801) *(G-4395)*
Healey Welding Co Inc 570 655-9437
3 Cemetery St Pittston (18640) *(G-15755)*
Healing Environments Intl Inc 215 758-2107
7123 Cresheim Rd Philadelphia (19119) *(G-13808)*
Health Care Council Western PA (PA) 724 776-6400
500 Commonwealth Dr Warrendale (15086) *(G-19080)*
Health Chem, Emigsville *Also called Hercon Laboratories Inc (G-4990)*
Health Connection Center, Philadelphia *Also called New Visions Magazine (G-14069)*
Health Market Science Inc 610 940-4002
2700 Horizon Dr King of Prussia (19406) *(G-8629)*
Health Solutions Inc 610 379-0300
1001 Mahoning St Unit 3a Lehighton (18235) *(G-9715)*
Health Tree, Wynnewood *Also called Impilo LLC (G-20269)*
Health-Chem Corporation (PA) 717 764-1191
101 Sinking Springs Ln Emigsville (17318) *(G-4988)*
Healthcare Information Corp 724 776-9411
500 Commonwealth Dr Warrendale (15086) *(G-19081)*
HealthSouth, Reading *Also called Encompass Health Corporation (G-16374)*
Healthstratica LLC 412 956-1000
315 Pasadena Dr S Pittsburgh (15215) *(G-15085)*
Healthy Alternative Pet Diets 210 745-1493
1016 E Underhill Dr Tamiment (18371) *(G-18233)*
Healthy Home Resources 412 431-4449
227 N Neville St Pittsburgh (15213) *(G-15086)*
Healthy Pet Foods Inc 610 918-4702
505 Legion Dr West Chester (19380) *(G-19560)*
Healy Glass Artistry LLC 484 241-0989
3930 Bigal Ct Bethlehem (18020) *(G-1530)*
Hearing Lab Technology LLC 215 785-5437
806 Beaver St Bristol (19007) *(G-2152)*
Heart Masters Diagnsostics LLC 267 503-3803
413 E Allegheny Ave Philadelphia (19134) *(G-13809)*
Heart of The Home, Mars *Also called Primrose Consulting Inc (G-10510)*
Hearth & Home Technologies LLC 717 362-9080
352 Mountain House Rd Halifax (17032) *(G-6826)*
Heartland Fabrication LLC 724 785-2575
1800 Paul Thomas Blvd Brownsville (15417) *(G-2312)*
Heartland Kitchens & Bath 814 744-8266
1758 Anderson Dr Leeper (16233) *(G-9655)*
Heartsine Technologies LLC (HQ) 215 860-8100
121 Friends Ln Ste 400 Newtown (18940) *(G-12508)*
Heartsine Technologies, Inc., Newtown *Also called Heartsine Technologies LLC (G-12508)*
Heat Siphon, Latrobe *Also called United States Thermoamp Inc (G-9526)*
Heated Hunts 570 575-5080
515 Leach St S Abingtn Twp (18411) *(G-16897)*
Heatha Henrys LLC 215 968-2080
103 Penns Trl Unit B Newtown (18940) *(G-12509)*

ALPHABETIC

Heathen Mfg 724 887-0337
657 Spruce Hollow Rd White (15490) *(G-19844)*

Heathers Cupcakes N Things LLC 717 329-2324
421 Friendship Rd Harrisburg (17111) *(G-7147)*

Heatron Inc 814 868-8554
8135 Nathan Cir Erie (16509) *(G-5314)*

Heatron Inc 814 868-8554
8135 Nathan Cir Erie (16509) *(G-5315)*

Hecla Machinery & Equipment Co 570 385-4783
401 Route 61 S Schuylkill Haven (17972) *(G-17158)*

Heclyn Precision Gear Company 215 739-7094
1112 E Berks St Philadelphia (19125) *(G-13810)*

Hectrio, Pottstown Also called *Specialty Chemical Systems Inc* *(G-16050)*

Hedlund Glass & Auto, Erie Also called *Auto Seat Cover Company* *(G-5196)*

Heeter Direct, Canonsburg Also called *Heeter Printing Company Inc* *(G-2595)*

Heeter Printing Company Inc 724 746-8900
441 Technology Dr Canonsburg (15317) *(G-2595)*

Heffner Printing, Fleetwood Also called *Hoffman Enterprises Inc* *(G-5974)*

Hefner Machine & Tool Inc 215 721-5900
3003 Unionville Pike Hatfield (19440) *(G-7347)*

Hegedus Aluminum Industries, Oil City Also called *New Hegedus Aluminum Co Inc* *(G-12953)*

Hegins Valley Farm, Hegins Also called *Wenger Feeds LLC* *(G-7546)*

HEI-Way LLC 724 353-2700
290 N Pike Rd Sarver (16055) *(G-17072)*

Heilig Defense LLC 717 490-6833
171 Eshelman Rd Lancaster (17601) *(G-9041)*

Heilman Pavement Specialties 724 353-2700
290 N Pike Rd Sarver (16055) *(G-17073)*

Heim Company, Harrisburg Also called *Edwin L Heim Co* *(G-7125)*

Heimer Enterprises Inc 814 234-7446
228 S Allen St State College (16801) *(G-17974)*

Heinnickel Farms Inc. 724 837-9254
2207 State Route 119 Greensburg (15601) *(G-6673)*

Heintz Storage Center 412 931-3444
161 Rochester Rd Pittsburgh (15229) *(G-15087)*

Heinz Frozen Food Company 412 237-5700
357 6th Ave Pittsburgh (15222) *(G-15088)*

Heinz North America, Pittsburgh Also called *H J Heinz Company LP* *(G-15071)*

Heirloom Cabinetry PA Inc. 717 436-8091
977 Nelson Rd Mifflintown (17059) *(G-11122)*

Heirloom Engraving LLC 717 336-8451
179 E Church St Stevens (17578) *(G-18052)*

Heisey Machine Co Inc 717 293-1373
78 Pitney Rd Lancaster (17602) *(G-9042)*

Heister House Millworks Inc 570 539-2611
1937 Troup Valley Rd Mount Pleasant Mills (17853) *(G-11725)*

Helcrist LLC 215 727-2050
4643 Paschall Ave Philadelphia (19143) *(G-13811)*

Helen's Pure Foods, Cheltenham Also called *Goldfam Inc* *(G-3028)*

Helena Agri-Enterprises LLC 814 632-5177
2413 Pennington Rd Warriors Mark (16877) *(G-19142)*

Helena Chemical Company 724 538-3304
312 Seneca Ln Evans City (16033) *(G-5559)*

Helene Batoff Interiors 215 879-7727
7573 Haverford Ave Philadelphia (19151) *(G-13812)*

Helfran Glass 570 287-8105
416 Northampton St Kingston (18704) *(G-8719)*

Helicopter Tech Inc 610 272-8090
452 Swedeland Rd King of Prussia (19406) *(G-8630)*

Helius Medical Tech Inc (PA) 215 944-6100
642 Newtown Yardley Rd # 100 Newtown (18940) *(G-12510)*

Helix Inc 215 679-7924
436 Adams St Red Hill (18076) *(G-16582)*

Helix Scientific Inc 215 953-2072
129 Frog Hollow Rd Southampton (18966) *(G-17817)*

Hellenic News of America Inc 484 427-7446
26 W Chester Pike Havertown (19083) *(G-7422)*

Helm & Hahn Co Inc 412 854-4367
1738 N Highland Rd 105b Pittsburgh (15241) *(G-15089)*

Helm Fencing Inc 215 822-5595
2021 Bethlehem Pike Hatfield (19440) *(G-7348)*

Helmerich & Payne Intl Drlg Co 814 353-3450
912 N Eagle Valley Rd Howard (16841) *(G-7891)*

Help Every Addict Live 484 598-3285
3816 Berry Ave Drexel Hill (19026) *(G-4364)*

Helping Hnds For Wnded Vterans 724 600-4965
1641 Lincoln Way White Oak (15131) *(G-19855)*

Hemlock Oil & Gas Co Inc 814 368-6261
83 Rutherford Run Bradford (16701) *(G-1972)*

Hempt Bros Inc 717 486-5111
4700 Carlisle Rd Gardners (17324) *(G-6260)*

Hempt Bros Inc (PA) 717 774-2911
205 Creek Rd Camp Hill (17011) *(G-2500)*

Hems, Huntingdon Also called *Huntingdon Elc Mtr Svc Inc* *(G-7944)*

Henderson Bernard Furn Ardison 215 930-0400
150 Green Ln Philadelphia (19127) *(G-13813)*

Henderson Construction Fabrics 724 368-1145
753 Perry Hwy Harmony (16037) *(G-7069)*

Henderson Industries, Bethlehem Also called *C G S Enterprises Inc* *(G-1477)*

Henderson Resource Group LLC 814 203-3226
121 Dewey Ave Hazel Hurst (16733) *(G-7445)*

Hendersons Printing Inc (PA) 814 944-0855
Green Ave & Ninth St 9th Altoona (16601) *(G-512)*

Hendersons Tarpaulin Covers 717 944-5865
8 Ann St Side Middletown (17057) *(G-11056)*

Hendrick Manufacturing Company (PA) 570 282-1010
17th Ave Carbondale (18407) *(G-2677)*

Hendricks Welding Service Inc 215 757-5369
293 Hulmeville Rd Langhorne (19047) *(G-9301)*

Hendricks' Woodworking, Kempton Also called *Historic Doors LLC* *(G-8492)*

Henkel Corp 267 424-5645
20 Bricks Way Sellersville (18960) *(G-17349)*

Henkel US Operations Corp 570 455-9980
125 Jaycee Dr West Hazleton (18202) *(G-19712)*

Hennecke Inc 724 271-3686
1000 Energy Dr Bridgeville (15017) *(G-2068)*

Hennecke USA, Bridgeville Also called *Hennecke Inc* *(G-2068)*

Hennemuth Metal Fabricators 724 693-9605
101 N Branch Rd Oakdale (15071) *(G-12901)*

Hennemuth Metal Fabricators (PA) 724 693-9605
255 W State St Oakdale (15071) *(G-12902)*

Henry Company LLC 610 933-8888
336 Cold Stream Rd Kimberton (19442) *(G-8573)*

Henry H Ottens Mfg Co Inc (HQ) 215 365-7800
7800 Holstein Ave Philadelphia (19153) *(G-13814)*

Henry H Ross & Son Inc 717 626-6268
121 Koser Rd Lititz (17543) *(G-10014)*

Henry Jack Water On Wheels 724 925-1727
124 Ash Brook Ln New Stanton (15672) *(G-12448)*

Henry Margu Inc 610 622-0515
540 Commerce Dr Lansdowne (19050) *(G-9434)*

Henry S Esh 717 627-2585
95 W Newport Rd Lititz (17543) *(G-10015)*

Henry William Orna Ir Works, Willow Grove Also called *William Henry Orna Ir Works* *(G-20149)*

Henrys Welding Inc 717 548-2460
1537 River Rd Drumore (17518) *(G-4378)*

Henshell Corp 215 225-7755
2922 N 19th St Philadelphia (19132) *(G-13815)*

Henson Company Inc 800 486-2788
8 Corporate Blvd Reading (19608) *(G-16400)*

Hep Pennsylvania Gathering LLC 210 298-2229
36 Fox Chase Dr Towanda (18848) *(G-18430)*

Hepburnia Coal Company (PA) 814 236-0473
Haytown Rd Grampian (16838) *(G-6571)*

Hepco Quarries Inc. 484 844-5024
820 E Washington St West Chester (19380) *(G-19561)*

Hepco Quarries Incorporated 570 955-8545
418 Montrose St New Milford (18834) *(G-12396)*

Heraclitean Corporation 215 862-5518
Phillips Mill Rd New Hope (18938) *(G-12305)*

Heraeus Group, Yardley Also called *Heraeus Prcous Mtls N Amer LLC* *(G-20316)*

Heraeus Incorporated (HQ) 215 944-9981
770 Township Line Rd # 300 Yardley (19067) *(G-20314)*

Heraeus Incorporated 480 961-9200
770 Township Line Rd # 300 Yardley (19067) *(G-20315)*

Heraeus Incorporated Hic 610 825-6050
24 Union Hill Rd Conshohocken (19428) *(G-3555)*

Heraeus Kulzer LLC 215 944-9968
1 Summit Square Ctr # 403 Langhorne (19047) *(G-9302)*

Heraeus Prcous Mtls N Amer LLC 562 921-7464
770 Township Line Rd Yardley (19067) *(G-20316)*

Heraeus Precious Metals Nor 610 825-6050
24 Union Hill Rd Conshohocken (19428) *(G-3556)*

Heraeus Quartz America LLC (HQ) 512 703-9000
770 Township Line Rd # 300 Yardley (19067) *(G-20317)*

Heraeus Quartz America LLC 512 251-2027
770 Township Line Rd # 300 Yardley (19067) *(G-20318)*

Heraeus Sensor Tech USA LLC 732 940-4400
770 Township Line Rd # 300 Yardley (19067) *(G-20319)*

Herald Newspapers Company Inc 412 782-2121
402 Loop St Pittsburgh (15215) *(G-15090)*

Herald Products, Philadelphia Also called *J Carlton Jones & Associates* *(G-13881)*

Herald Standard, Uniontown Also called *Uniontown Newspapers Inc* *(G-18644)*

Herald Standard 724 626-8345
175 Arch Bridge Rd Dunbar (15431) *(G-4440)*

Herb & Lous LLC 267 626-7913
1710 Walton Rd Ste 207 Blue Bell (19422) *(G-1833)*

Herb Kilmer & Sons Flagstone 570 434-2060
11308 State Route 106 Kingsley (18826) *(G-8706)*

Herb Kreckman Antennas, Cresco Also called *Kreco Antennas* *(G-3894)*

Herb Penn Co Ltd (PA) 215 632-6100
10601 Decatur Rd Ste 200 Philadelphia (19154) *(G-13816)*

Herb Sheet Metal Inc 717 273-8001
630 N 5th St Lebanon (17046) *(G-9579)*

Herbal Extracts Plus 215 245-5055
350 Camer Dr Bensalem (19020) *(G-1209)*

Herbalife Distributor, Luthersburg *Also called Colonial Hardwoods & Logging* ***(G-10121)***
Herbert Cooper Company Inc......814 228-3417
121 Main St Genesee (16923) ***(G-6272)***
Hercon Laboratories Corp......717 764-1191
101 Sinking Springs Ln Emigsville (17318) ***(G-4989)***
Hercon Laboratories Inc......717 764-1191
101 Sinking Springs Ln Emigsville (17318) ***(G-4990)***
Hercon Pharmaceuticals LLC......717 764-1191
101 Sinking Springs Ln Emigsville (17318) ***(G-4991)***
Hercules Cement Company LP......610 759-6300
501 Hercules Dr Stockertown (18083) ***(G-18065)***
Herculite Products, Emigsville *Also called Aberdeen Road Company* ***(G-4983)***
Here and Now Brewing Co LLC......570 647-6085
645 Main St Honesdale (18431) ***(G-7713)***
Here Own By Bryan Materials, Pittsburgh *Also called Quality Concrete Inc* ***(G-15460)***
Herff Jones LLC......717 526-4373
6470 Huntsmen Dr Harrisburg (17111) ***(G-7148)***
Herff Jones LLC......215 638-2490
654 Street Rd Bensalem (19020) ***(G-1210)***
Herff Jones LLC......717 697-0649
5502 Gloucester St Unit B Mechanicsburg (17055) ***(G-10852)***
Herfurth Brothers Inc......610 681-4515
Rr 209 Gilbert (18331) ***(G-6361)***
Heritage Box Co......724 728-0200
3204 Industrial Dr Aliquippa (15001) ***(G-76)***
Heritage Fence & Deck LLC......610 476-0003
3890 Skippack Pike Skippack (19474) ***(G-17598)***
Heritage Fence Company......610 584-6710
Skippack Pike Skippack (19474) ***(G-17599)***
Heritage Gallery of Lace & Int......717 359-4121
1897 Hanover Pike Littlestown (17340) ***(G-10067)***
Heritage Industries Inc......412 435-0091
600 Fountain St Pittsburgh (15238) ***(G-15091)***
Heritage Maintenance Pdts LLC......610 277-5070
1537 Gehman Rd Harleysville (19438) ***(G-7038)***
Heritage Metalworks Ltd......610 518-3999
2089 Bondsville Rd Downingtown (19335) ***(G-4234)***
Heritage Screen Printing Inc (PA)......215 672-2382
3625 Daviscilla 2 Warrington (18976) ***(G-19120)***
Heritage Screen Printing Inc......215 672-2382
331 York Rd Warminster (18974) ***(G-18894)***
Heritage Stone & Marble Inc......610 222-0856
1045 Archer Ln Lansdale (19446) ***(G-9376)***
Heritage Truck Equipment LLC......215 256-0951
201 Ruth Rd Harleysville (19438) ***(G-7039)***
Heritage Wine Cellars, North East *Also called Bostwick Enterprises Inc* ***(G-12733)***
Heritage Wine Cellars......724 748-5070
1911 Leesburg Grove Cy Rd Grove City (16127) ***(G-6790)***
Heritage Wine Cellars Inc......814 725-8015
12162 E Main Rd North East (16428) ***(G-12748)***
Heritage Wood Products LLC......814 629-9265
216 Pelesky Rd Boswell (15531) ***(G-1882)***
Herkules USA Corporation (HQ)......724 763-2066
101 River St Ford City (16226) ***(G-6047)***
Herkules USA Corporation......724 763-2066
208-209 Mac Industrial Pa Ford City (16226) ***(G-6048)***
Herkys Food Products Inc......412 683-8511
4507 Minerva St Pittsburgh (15224) ***(G-15092)***
Herley Industries Inc......717 397-2777
3061 Industry Dr Lancaster (17603) ***(G-9043)***
Herley Industries Inc......717 397-2779
3061 Industry Dr Lancaster (17603) ***(G-9044)***
Herlocher Foods Inc......814 237-0134
415 E Calder Way State College (16801) ***(G-17975)***
Herman Geer Communications Inc......724 652-0511
2100 Wilmington Rd New Castle (16105) ***(G-12102)***
Herman Iron Works Inc......215 727-1127
1452 Grays Ferry Ave 54 Philadelphia (19143) ***(G-13817)***
Hermance Machine Company......570 326-9156
178 Campbell St Williamsport (17701) ***(G-20021)***
Hermes Press, New Castle *Also called Herman Geer Communications Inc* ***(G-12102)***
Hermetics Inc......215 848-9522
6122 N 21st St Philadelphia (19138) ***(G-13818)***
Hermexpo, Havertown *Also called Hellenic News of America Inc* ***(G-7422)***
Herndon Reload Company......570 758-2597
386 Pennsylvania Ave Herndon (17830) ***(G-7599)***
Hero Bx, Erie *Also called Lake Erie Biofuels LLC* ***(G-5353)***
Herr Foods Incorporated (PA)......610 932-9330
20 Herr Dr Nottingham (19362) ***(G-12882)***
Herr Foods Incorporated......610 395-6200
6810 Tilghman St Allentown (18106) ***(G-245)***
Herr Foods Incorporated......215 934-7144
2800 Comly Rd Philadelphia (19154) ***(G-13819)***
Herr Foods Incorporated......215 492-5990
7548 Brewster Ave Philadelphia (19153) ***(G-13820)***
Herr Foods Incorporated......610 932-9330
273 Old Baltimore Pike Nottingham (19362) ***(G-12883)***
Herr Industrial Inc (PA)......717 569-6619
610 E Oregon Rd Lititz (17543) ***(G-10016)***
Herr's Potato Chip Factory, Nottingham *Also called Herr Foods Incorporated* ***(G-12883)***
Herrmann Printing & Litho Inc......412 243-4100
1709 Douglas Dr Pittsburgh (15221) ***(G-15093)***
Herrmann Unlimited, Pittsburgh *Also called Herrmann Printing & Litho Inc* ***(G-15093)***
Hersehy Veterinary Hospital......717 534-2244
1016 Cocoa Ave Hershey (17033) ***(G-7612)***
Hersh Imports Inc......215 627-1128
721 Sansom St Philadelphia (19106) ***(G-13821)***
Hershey Company (PA)......717 534-4200
100 Crystal A Dr Hershey (17033) ***(G-7613)***
Hershey Company......717 534-4100
925 Reese Ave Hershey (17033) ***(G-7614)***
Hershey Company......717 509-9795
400 Running Pump Rd Lancaster (17603) ***(G-9045)***
Hershey Company......717 534-4200
1033 W Chocolate Ave Hershey (17033) ***(G-7615)***
Hershey Company......570 384-3271
2 Scotch Pine Dr Hazle Township (18202) ***(G-7463)***
Hershey Creamery Company (PA)......717 238-8134
301 S Cameron St Harrisburg (17101) ***(G-7149)***
Hershey Digital......717 431-9602
234 Peach Bottom Rd Willow Street (17584) ***(G-20151)***
Hershey Foods Corporation - MA......717 534-6799
100 Crystal A Dr Unit 8 Hershey (17033) ***(G-7616)***
Hershey's Ice Cream, Harrisburg *Also called Hershey Creamery Company* ***(G-7149)***
Hertz Machine & Fabrication......610 874-7848
3751 Clearwater Ln Brookhaven (19015) ***(G-2245)***
Herwin Inc......724 446-2000
2995 Clay Pike Rillton (15678) ***(G-16746)***
Hesford Keystone Printing Co......814 942-2911
221 Parrish St Altoona (16602) ***(G-513)***
Heslin-Steel Fab Inc......724 745-8282
7 Four Coins Dr Canonsburg (15317) ***(G-2596)***
Hess C & Sons Cabinets Inc......717 597-3295
2361 Buchanan Trl E Greencastle (17225) ***(G-6618)***
Hess Commercial Printing Inc......724 652-6802
703 Wilmington Ave New Castle (16101) ***(G-12103)***
Hess Embroidery & Uniforms LLC......610 816-5234
694 Reading Ave Reading (19611) ***(G-16401)***
Hess Machine International......717 733-0005
1040b S State St Ephrata (17522) ***(G-5108)***
Hess Readi-Mix, Schuylkill Haven *Also called J A & W A Hess Inc* ***(G-17160)***
Hess Ready Mix Inc......570 385-0300
2 Coal St Schuylkill Haven (17972) ***(G-17159)***
Hess S Ornamental Iron......717 927-9160
1754 Raub Rd Red Lion (17356) ***(G-16600)***
Hess Sand & Stone, Hazleton *Also called J A & W A Hess Inc* ***(G-7504)***
Hess Wood Recycling Inc......610 614-9070
2357 Newlins Mill Rd Easton (18045) ***(G-4698)***
Hessian Co Ltd......610 683-5464
210 Hinterleiter Rd Kutztown (19530) ***(G-8844)***
Hessian Co Ltd......610 683-0067
210 Hinterleiter Rd Kutztown (19530) ***(G-8845)***
Hessian Co Ltd (PA)......610 269-4685
2206 Horseshoe Pike Honey Brook (19344) ***(G-7747)***
Hessian Co Ltd......610 683-0067
210 Hinterleiter Rd Kutztown (19530) ***(G-8846)***
Hessian Co Ltd......724 658-6638
205 W Washington St New Castle (16101) ***(G-12104)***
Hessinger Group Inc......814 480-8912
216 E 8th St Erie (16503) ***(G-5316)***
Hetran-B Inc......570 366-1411
70 Pinedale Industrial Rd Orwigsburg (17961) ***(G-13044)***
Hetrick Mfg Inc......724 335-0455
210 Reimer St Lower Burrell (15068) ***(G-10106)***
Heucotech Ltd A NJ Ltd Partnr (HQ)......215 736-0712
99 Newbold Rd Fairless Hills (19030) ***(G-5785)***
Hewey Welding......717 867-5222
1045 Wampler Ln Lebanon (17042) ***(G-9580)***
Hewlett Manufacturing Co......814 683-4762
7343 Harmonsburg Rd Linesville (16424) ***(G-9981)***
Hey Girl Inc......610 945-6138
5105 Cornerstone Dr Newtown Square (19073) ***(G-12575)***
Heyco Metals Inc (PA)......610 926-4131
1069 Stinson Dr Reading (19605) ***(G-16402)***
Hf Group LLC......215 368-7308
63 E Broad St Ste 6 Hatfield (19440) ***(G-7349)***
Hf Group LLC......215 855-2293
63 E Broad St Ste 6 Hatfield (19440) ***(G-7350)***
Hg Energy LLC......724 935-8952
2200 Georgetown Dr # 501 Sewickley (15143) ***(G-17391)***
Hg Smith Crematory, Stroudsburg *Also called Hg Smith Wilbert Vault Company* ***(G-18123)***
Hg Smith Wilbert Vault Company......570 420-9599
2120 N 5th St Stroudsburg (18360) ***(G-18123)***
HH Brown Shoe Company Inc......814 793-3786
107 Highland St Martinsburg (16662) ***(G-10523)***
HH Brown Shoe Company Inc......814 793-3786
107 Highland St Martinsburg (16662) ***(G-10524)***
Hh Robertsons Flooring, Ambridge *Also called Centria Inc* ***(G-612)***

ALPHABETIC

HI Tech Plating Co Inc....................................814 455-4231
    1015 W 18th St Erie (16502) *(G-5317)*
Hi-LI Company Division, Schuylkill Haven *Also called Alpha Mills Corporation (G-17145)*
Hi-TEC Custom Painting Inc...............................724 932-2631
    3543 E State Rd Jamestown (16134) *(G-8237)*
Hi-TEC Magnetics Inc......................................484 681-4265
    109 Walker Ln King of Prussia (19406) *(G-8631)*
HI-Tech Color Inc..724 463-8522
    1163 Water St Indiana (15701) *(G-8104)*
Hi-Tech Nutraceuticals LLC (PA)........................717 667-2142
    5135 Old Us Highway 322 Reedsville (17084) *(G-16623)*
Hiatt Thompson Corporation.............................708 496-8585
    159 Conneaut Lake Rd Greenville (16125) *(G-6745)*
Hibachi Grill Supreme Buffet.............................215 728-7222
    2051 Cottman Ave Philadelphia (19149) *(G-13822)*
Hibbs Awning Company Inc...............................724 437-1494
    63 E Fayette St Uniontown (15401) *(G-18630)*
Hickman Lumber Company (PA)..........................724 867-9441
    501 Main St Emlenton (16373) *(G-5010)*
Hickman Lumber Company.................................814 797-0555
    4478 Route 38 Emlenton (16373) *(G-5011)*
Hicks Signs..717 328-3300
    8941 Oellig Rd Mercersburg (17236) *(G-10987)*
Hidden Still Inc..717 270-1753
    435 Willow St Lebanon (17046) *(G-9581)*
Hiddie Kitchen Inc..717 566-2211
    120 W 2nd St Hummelstown (17036) *(G-7913)*
Hidensee Inc...614 465-3375
    203 Beaumont Dr Wallingford (19086) *(G-18784)*
HIG Capital LLC..610 495-7011
    640 N Lewis Rd Royersford (19468) *(G-16851)*
Higgins Saw Mill..717 235-4189
    6549 Hokes Rd Glen Rock (17327) *(G-6457)*
High Avlblity Stor Systems Inc...........................610 254-5090
    820 Adams Ave Ste 200 Audubon (19403) *(G-827)*
High Chemical Company, Levittown *Also called National Generic Distributors (G-9852)*
High Concrete Group LLC (HQ)...........................717 336-9300
    125 Denver Rd Denver (17517) *(G-4075)*
High Concrete Structures, Denver *Also called High Concrete Group LLC (G-4075)*
High Country Motors LLC.................................814 886-9375
    6512 Admiral Peary Hwy Loretto (15940) *(G-10103)*
High Energy Corp..610 593-2800
    Lower Valley Rd Parkesburg (19365) *(G-13175)*
High Fidelity Screen Printing, Warminster *Also called Thomas A Laskowski (G-18981)*
High Industries Inc (PA)...................................717 293-4444
    1853 William Penn Way Lancaster (17601) *(G-9046)*
High Performance Formulas, Yardley *Also called Hpf LLC (G-20321)*
High Point Tool & Die Company, Wattsburg *Also called Rick Leasure (G-19282)*
High Pressure Equipment Co Inc.........................800 289-7447
    2955 W 17th St Erie (16505) *(G-5318)*
High Printing & Graphics Inc.............................610 693-5399
    231 E Penn Ave Robesonia (19551) *(G-16776)*
High Steel Structures Div, Lancaster *Also called High Steel Structures LLC (G-9049)*
High Steel Structures LLC.................................717 390-4227
    144 Greenfield Rd Lancaster (17601) *(G-9047)*
High Steel Structures LLC.................................570 326-9051
    3501 W 4th St Williamsport (17701) *(G-20022)*
High Steel Structures LLC (HQ)...........................717 299-5211
    1915 Old Phladelphia Pike Lancaster (17602) *(G-9048)*
High Steel Structures LLC.................................717 299-5211
    1915 Old Phladelphia Pike Lancaster (17602) *(G-9049)*
High Tech Aquatics Inc...................................570 546-3557
    104 Chas Rd Muncy (17756) *(G-11819)*
High Tech Machine, Punxsawney *Also called Quality Gear & Machine Inc (G-16157)*
High View Inc..814 886-7171
    517 Vale Wood Rd Loretto (15940) *(G-10104)*
High Voltage Solutions Sls Inc...........................412 523-0238
    359 Vine Ave Sharon (16146) *(G-17436)*
Highland Carbide Tool Co.................................724 863-7151
    741 Northeast Dr Irwin (15642) *(G-8167)*
Highland Forest Resources Inc...........................814 927-2226
    237 Highland Dr Marienville (16239) *(G-10457)*
Highland Forest Resources Inc (HQ).....................814 837-6760
    Rr 6 Box 84 Kane (16735) *(G-8466)*
Highland Hosiery Mills Inc.................................215 249-3934
    174 S Main St Dublin (18917) *(G-4433)*
Highland Tank, Manheim *Also called Bigbee Steel and Tank Company (G-10370)*
Highland Tank and Mfg Co (PA).........................814 893-5701
    1 Highland Rd Stoystown (15563) *(G-18080)*
Highland Tool & Die Company............................215 426-4116
    2127 E Ann St Philadelphia (19134) *(G-13823)*
Highlands of Donegal LLC................................717 653-2048
    650 Pinkerton Rd Mount Joy (17552) *(G-11661)*
Highlights For Children Inc...............................570 253-1080
    803 Church St Honesdale (18431) *(G-7714)*
Highline Polycarbonate LLC..............................267 847-0056
    2327 Lombard St Philadelphia (19146) *(G-13824)*
Highpoint Tool & Machine Inc...........................814 763-5453
    17380 State Highway 198 Saegertown (16433) *(G-16917)*

Highpoint Tool and Machine, Saegertown *Also called Highpoint Tool & Machine Inc (G-16917)*
Highpoint Woodworks LLC................................610 346-7739
    1387 Parkland Rd Coopersburg (18036) *(G-3629)*
Highway Manor Brewing...................................717 743-0613
    2238 Gettysburg Rd Camp Hill (17011) *(G-2501)*
Highway Materials Inc (PA)................................610 832-8000
    409 Stenton Ave Flourtown (19031) *(G-5987)*
Highway Materials Inc....................................610 647-5902
    29 Morehall Rd Malvern (19355) *(G-10245)*
Highway Materials Inc....................................717 626-8571
    859 Woodcrest Ave Lititz (17543) *(G-10017)*
Highway Materials Inc....................................215 234-4522
    1128 Crusher Rd Perkiomenville (18074) *(G-13301)*
Highway Materials Inc....................................610 828-4300
    500 Stenton Ave Plymouth Meeting (19462) *(G-15846)*
Highway Materials Inc....................................215 225-7020
    3870 N 2nd St Blue Bell (19422) *(G-1834)*
Highway Materials Inc....................................610 828-9525
    5100 Joshua Rd Conshohocken (19428) *(G-3557)*
Highway Materials Inc....................................717 252-3636
    740 S Front St Wrightsville (17368) *(G-20237)*
Highwood Usa LLC.......................................570 668-6113
    87 Tide Rd Tamaqua (18252) *(G-18212)*
Higley Enterprises...610 693-4039
    1339 Oakland Ave Levittown (19056) *(G-9843)*
Hii Holding Corporation....................................610 666-0219
    945 Madison Ave Norristown (19403) *(G-12666)*
Hilden Enterprises Inc (PA)...............................412 257-8459
    1377 Mclaughlin Run Rd Pittsburgh (15241) *(G-15094)*
Hilex Poly Co LLC...814 355-7410
    606 Old Curtin Rd Milesburg (16853) *(G-11151)*
Hill John M Machine Co Inc..............................610 562-8690
    233 Farview Rd Hamburg (19526) *(G-6841)*
Hill Crest Laminating LLC................................570 437-3357
    911 Strawberry Ridge Rd Danville (17821) *(G-4005)*
Hill Laboratories Co.......................................610 644-2867
    3 N Bacton Hill Rd Malvern (19355) *(G-10246)*
Hill Precision Manufacturing..............................814 827-4333
    10978 Skyline Dr Titusville (16354) *(G-18380)*
Hill Tool and Die, Titusville *Also called Hill Precision Manufacturing (G-18380)*
Hill Woodworks, Brogue *Also called R & C Foltz LLC (G-2239)*
Hill's Creek Truss Co, Blossburg *Also called Seals of Blossburg (G-1809)*
Hillandale Farms of Pa Inc...............................717 229-0601
    3910 Oxford Rd Gettysburg (17325) *(G-6299)*
Hillandale-Gettysburg LP.................................717 334-1973
    3910 Oxford Rd Gettysburg (17325) *(G-6300)*
Hillcrest Tool & Die Inc...................................814 827-1296
    10978 Skyline Dr Titusville (16354) *(G-18381)*
Hillendale Peat Moss Inc.................................610 444-5591
    519 Hillendale Rd Avondale (19311) *(G-853)*
Hillock Anodizing Inc.....................................215 535-8090
    5101 Comly St Ste 7 Philadelphia (19135) *(G-13825)*
Hills Machine Shop..570 645-8787
    1 Dock St Lansford (18232) *(G-9447)*
Hills Micro Weld Inc.......................................814 336-4511
    1134 Water St Meadville (16335) *(G-10735)*
Hills Qulty Seafood Mkts Inc..............................610 359-1888
    3605 West Chester Pike Newtown Square (19073) *(G-12576)*
Hillshire Brands Company.................................724 772-3440
    215 Commerce Park Dr Cranberry Township (16066) *(G-3822)*
Hillside Custom Mac Wel & Fab.........................610 942-3093
    2500 Chestnut Tree Rd Honey Brook (19344) *(G-7748)*
Hillside Enterprise...724 479-3678
    1274 Brush Creek Rd Homer City (15748) *(G-7675)*
Hillside Equity Inc...484 707-9012
    535 Wood St Unit 437 Bethlehem (18016) *(G-1531)*
Hillside Horse Sew-It.....................................717 548-2293
    345 Little Britain Rd S Peach Bottom (17563) *(G-13199)*
Hilltop Tank & Supply......................................814 658-3915
    19940 Raystown Rd James Creek (16657) *(G-8234)*
Hilltop The, Northumberland *Also called Mayberry Hospitality LLC (G-12871)*
Hilltop Tower Leasing Inc.................................814 942-1888
    400 Highland Ave Altoona (16602) *(G-514)*
Hilltop Woodshop Inc.....................................724 697-4506
    1269 School Rd Avonmore (15618) *(G-865)*
Hilltown Services..215 249-3694
    614 Dublin Pike Apt C Dublin (18917) *(G-4434)*
Hilmarr Rubber Co Inc....................................215 426-3628
    2168 E Firth St 70 Philadelphia (19125) *(G-13826)*
Hilsher Graphics Flp......................................570 326-9159
    1626 Riverside Dr Williamsport (17702) *(G-20023)*
Hiltz Propane Systems Inc................................717 799-4322
    693 W Market St Marietta (17547) *(G-10464)*
Himalayan International Instit (PA).......................570 253-5551
    952 Bethany Tpke Bldg 1 Honesdale (18431) *(G-7715)*
Himalayan Intl Ins of Yoga Ins...........................570 634-5168
    952 Bethany Tpke Bldg 1 Honesdale (18431) *(G-7716)*
Himes Machine Inc..724 927-6850
    9842 Espy Rd Linesville (16424) *(G-9982)*

Hindle Power Inc 610 330-9000
1075 Saint John St Easton (18042) *(G-4699)*

Hines Flask Div Bckeye Alnimum 814 683-4420
5906 W Center Rd Linesville (16424) *(G-9983)*

Hines Industries Inc 610 264-1656
2820 Lehigh St Whitehall (18052) *(G-19875)*

Hines Water Pumps, Shickshinny *Also called Ronald Hines (G-17502)*

Hings Lai Fashion 215 530-0348
231 E Allegheny Ave Philadelphia (19134) *(G-13827)*

Hinkel-Hofmann Supply Co Inc 412 231-3131
1910 Cochran Rd Ste 110 Pittsburgh (15220) *(G-15095)*

Hinkle & Co, Pittsburgh *Also called Pro Thermal Inc (G-15450)*

Hipple Signs, New Oxford *Also called W J Strickler Signs Inc (G-12425)*

Hipps Sons Coins Precious Mtls 215 550-6854
408 S State St Ste 5 Newtown (18940) *(G-12511)*

Hipps Tool & Design 814 236-3600
146 Bridgeport Rd Curwensville (16833) *(G-3953)*

Hirschmann Electronics Inc 717 217-2200
1665 Orchard Dr Chambersburg (17201) *(G-2940)*

Hirt Powersports LLC 717 834-9126
11 Kamp St Duncannon (17020) *(G-4446)*

His Light Kingdom LLC 267 777-3866
5320 Webster St Philadelphia (19143) *(G-13828)*

Hispanic Media LLC 215 424-1200
2800 Tyson Ave Philadelphia (19149) *(G-13829)*

Histand Brothers Inc 215 348-4121
114 Poplar St Ambler (19002) *(G-581)*

Historic Doors LLC 610 756-6187
67 Vole Hollow Rd Kempton (19529) *(G-8492)*

Historic York Inc 717 843-0320
25 N Duke St Ste 102 York (17401) *(G-20523)*

Historical Documents Co 215 533-4500
2555 Orthodox St Philadelphia (19137) *(G-13830)*

Historical Souvenirs, Philadelphia *Also called Historical Documents Co (G-13830)*

History Washer Inc 717 275-3101
33 Ridge Ln Elliottsburg (17024) *(G-4920)*

Hit, Bristol *Also called Holo Image Technology Inc (G-2153)*

Hitachi Rail STS Usa Inc (HQ) 412 688-2400
1000 Technology Dr Pittsburgh (15219) *(G-15096)*

Hitchcock E & R & Sons Lbr Inc 814 229-9402
69 Hitchcock Ln Strattanville (16258) *(G-18097)*

Hiwassee Acres LLC 717 334-1381
25 Chambersburg St Ste 1 Gettysburg (17325) *(G-6301)*

Hj Financial Group, Plymouth Meeting *Also called P H A Finance Inc (G-15862)*

Hj Heinz Innovation Center, Warrendale *Also called Kraft Heinz Foods Company (G-19085)*

Hkp Metals Inc 412 751-0500
301 Wide Dr McKeesport (15135) *(G-10670)*

Hlc Industries Inc 610 668-9112
4 E Montgomery Ave Bala Cynwyd (19004) *(G-880)*

Hli Rail & Rigging LLC 215 277-5558
511 Spring Ave Elkins Park (19027) *(G-4905)*

HLS Therapeutics (usa) Inc 844 457-8900
919 Conestoga Rd 3-310 Bryn Mawr (19010) *(G-2324)*

HMC Enterprises LLC 215 464-6800
831 E Cayuga St Philadelphia (19124) *(G-13831)*

Hmi, Hamburg *Also called Hamburg Manufacturing Inc (G-6840)*

Hmmt Environmental, Newtown *Also called Hazardous Materials Mgt Team (G-12507)*

Hmp Cmmunications Holdings LLC (PA) 610 560-0500
83 General Warren Blvd Malvern (19355) *(G-10247)*

Hmp Communications LLC 610 560-0500
70 E Swedesford Rd # 100 Malvern (19355) *(G-10248)*

Hmp Publications, Malvern *Also called Hmp Communications LLC (G-10248)*

HMS Industries Inc 724 459-5090
1256 Route 22 Hwy W Blairsville (15717) *(G-1724)*

Hn Automotive Inc 570 724-5191
9728 Route 287 Ste 10 Wellsboro (16901) *(G-19465)*

Hobart Corporation 717 397-5100
165 Independence Ct Lancaster (17601) *(G-9050)*

Hobart Sales and Service Inc 301 733-6560
2917 Wayne St Harrisburg (17111) *(G-7150)*

Hocking Printing Co Inc 717 738-1151
615 E Main St Ephrata (17522) *(G-5109)*

Hodge Electric Motors Inc 724 834-8420
524 Tremont Ave Ste 1 Greensburg (15601) *(G-6674)*

Hodge Foundry Inc 724 588-4100
42 Leech Rd Greenville (16125) *(G-6746)*

Hodge Tool Co Inc 717 393-5543
2831 Old Tree Dr Lancaster (17603) *(G-9051)*

Hodgsons Quick Printing 215 362-1356
1510 Franklin St Kulpsville (19443) *(G-8830)*

Hoeganaes Corporation 570 538-3587
4330 Paradise Rd Watsontown (17777) *(G-19275)*

Hoehl Assoc 412 741-4170
508 Grove St Sewickley (15143) *(G-17392)*

Hoff Enterprises Inc 814 535-8371
151 Freidhoff Ln Johnstown (15902) *(G-8381)*

Hoff Industries LLC 215 516-9849
362 Winslow Dr Souderton (18964) *(G-17740)*

Hoff Machining, Johnstown *Also called Joel Freidhoff (G-8387)*

Hoff Woodworking 717 259-6040
200 College Ave East Berlin (17316) *(G-4522)*

Hoffman Bros Speed 610 760-6274
5661 Route 100 New Tripoli (18066) *(G-12458)*

Hoffman Brothers Lumber Inc 717 694-3340
118 Sand Valley Rd Richfield (17086) *(G-16679)*

Hoffman Diamond Products Inc 814 938-7600
121 Cedar St Punxsutawney (15767) *(G-16143)*

Hoffman Enterprises Inc 610 944-8481
562 Blandon Rd Ste 1 Fleetwood (19522) *(G-5974)*

Hoffman Machine, Milton *Also called Hoffmans Machine Shop Inc (G-11241)*

Hoffman Manufacturing Inc 610 821-4222
2010 Sunset Dr Fogelsville (18051) *(G-5995)*

Hoffman Materials LLC 717 243-2011
321 Cherry St Carlisle (17013) *(G-2717)*

Hoffman Materials Inc 717 243-2011
321 Cherry St Carlisle (17013) *(G-2718)*

Hoffman Powder Coating 610 845-1422
221 Benfield Rd Macungie (18062) *(G-10147)*

Hoffman, Catherine, Emporium *Also called Art & Ink (G-5049)*

Hoffman-Kane Distributors Inc (PA) 412 653-6886
1143 Cochrans Mill Rd Pittsburgh (15236) *(G-15097)*

Hoffmann Tool & Die, Souderton *Also called Shed-Shop Incorporated (G-17763)*

Hoffmans Machine Shop Inc 570 437-2788
330 Limestone Rd Milton (17847) *(G-11241)*

Hofmann Industries Inc 610 678-8051
3145 Shillington Rd Reading (19608) *(G-16403)*

Hogg, Robert Treate Cab Mkr Sp, Oxford *Also called Robert Trate Hogg Cbinetmakers (G-13088)*

Hohmann & Barnard Inc 610 873-0070
1985 Ticonderoga Blvd # 15 Chester Springs (19425) *(G-3080)*

Holan Inc 724 744-1660
1048 Sandy Hill Rd Irwin (15642) *(G-8168)*

Holbrook Tool & Molding Inc 814 336-4113
10696 Perry Hwy Meadville (16335) *(G-10736)*

Holcim (us) Inc 724 226-1449
445 Grantham St Tarentum (15084) *(G-18245)*

Holden Precision Machine 814 968-3833
102 Horton Ave Sheffield (16347) *(G-17482)*

Holdrens Precision Machining 570 358-3377
23931 Route 220 Ulster (18850) *(G-18599)*

Holistic Horse Inc 215 249-1965
84 Irish Meetinghouse Rd Perkasie (18944) *(G-13279)*

Hollander Sleep Products LLC 570 874-2114
32 Industrial Park Rd Frackville (17931) *(G-6105)*

Hollinger Tchncal Pblctons Inc 717 755-8800
2550 Kingston Rd Ste 221 York (17402) *(G-20524)*

Hollow Ball Group LLC 215 822-3380
2280 Amber Dr Hatfield (19440) *(G-7351)*

Hollowell Aluminum 717 597-0826
14471 Hollowell Church Rd Waynesboro (17268) *(G-19411)*

Holly Label Company Inc 570 222-9000
1656 Maloney Hill Rd Nicholson (18446) *(G-12615)*

Holly Metals Inc 610 692-4989
892 Fernhill Rd West Chester (19380) *(G-19562)*

Holly Woodcrafters Inc 717 486-5862
Mill St Mount Holly Springs (17065) *(G-11634)*

Hollyfrntier Lubr Spcalty Pdts, Plymouth Meeting *Also called Hollyfrontier Corporation (G-15848)*

Hollyfrontier Corporation 800 456-4786
660 W Germantown Pike # 1 Plymouth Meeting (19462) *(G-15847)*

Hollyfrontier Corporation 800 395-2786
401 Plymouth Rd Ste 350 Plymouth Meeting (19462) *(G-15848)*

Hollys Embroidery 717 599-5975
500 Lesentier Ln Harrisburg (17112) *(G-7151)*

Holmes Dental Company 215 675-2877
50 S Penn St Ste 6a Hatboro (19040) *(G-7287)*

Holo Image Technology Inc 215 946-2190
101 William Leigh Dr Bristol (19007) *(G-2153)*

Holt & Bugbee Hardwoods, Mount Braddock *Also called Holt and Bugbee Company (G-11619)*

Holt and Bugbee Company 724 277-8510
1162 Industrial Park Dr Mount Braddock (15465) *(G-11619)*

Holt Le Grinding Service 724 864-6865
Maple St Rillton (15678) *(G-16747)*

Holt Precision Tool Co 814 342-3595
1422 Wllaceton Bigler Hwy West Decatur (16878) *(G-19688)*

Holtec International 215 646-5842
1838 Howe Ln Maple Glen (19002) *(G-10430)*

Holtrys LLC 717 532-7261
10948 Roxbury Rd Roxbury (17251) *(G-16838)*

Holy Rosary Church, Hazleton *Also called Catholic Scl Svcs of Scranton (G-7494)*

Home Grown Inc 610 642-3601
393 Lancaster Ave Haverford (19041) *(G-7411)*

Home Mag The, Doylestown *Also called Seapoint Enterprises Inc (G-4337)*

Home Service Beverage, Williamsport *Also called Wheeland Inc (G-20091)*

Home Town Sports, Pittsburgh *Also called Youre Putting ME On Inc (G-15731)*

A L P H A B E T I C

Home Town Sports Inc 412 672-2242
  3213 Orchard St McKeesport (15132) *(G-10671)*

Home Woodwork 570 295-2185
  180 Flanders Rd Port Trevorton (17864) *(G-15913)*

Homeland Mfg Svcs Inc 814 862-9103
  2591 Clyde Ave Ste 2 State College (16801) *(G-17976)*

Homeopathic Natural Healing 412 646-4151
  3824 Northern Pike Monroeville (15146) *(G-11340)*

Homer City Automation Inc 724 479-4503
  699 State Park Rd New Alexandria (15670) *(G-12019)*

Homer City Coal Proc Corp (HQ) 724 348-4800
  6108 Brownsville Road Ext # 201 Finleyville (15332) *(G-5960)*

Homer Group , The, Norristown *Also called Homer Reproductions Inc (G-12667)*

Homer Optical Company Inc 717 843-1822
  60 Hokes Mill Rd York (17404) *(G-20525)*

Homer Optics, York *Also called Homer Optical Company Inc (G-20525)*

Homer Reproductions Inc 610 539-8400
  2605 Egypt Rd Ste 100 Norristown (19403) *(G-12667)*

Homerwood Hardwood Flooring Co 814 827-3855
  1026 Industrial Park Titusville (16354) *(G-18382)*

Homescapers 814 353-0507
  421 Valentine Hill Rd Bellefonte (16823) *(G-1105)*

Homestat Farm Ltd 717 939-0407
  201 Race St Highspire (17034) *(G-7633)*

Homestead Automotive Supply 412 462-4467
  4704 Little St Homestead (15120) *(G-7686)*

Homestead Custom Cabinetry 717 859-8788
  120 S 11th St Akron (17501) *(G-35)*

Homestead Inspection Service 717 691-1586
  2471 Cope Dr Mechanicsburg (17055) *(G-10853)*

Homestead Valve Mfg Co 610 770-1100
  160 W Walnut St Allentown (18102) *(G-246)*

Homewood Energy Services Corp 256 882-2796
  820 Washington Blvd Pittsburgh (15206) *(G-15098)*

Homewood Products Corporation 412 665-2700
  820 Washington Blvd Pittsburgh (15206) *(G-15099)*

Hondels Machine Shop 814 677-7768
  2222 Horsecreek Rd Oil City (16301) *(G-12947)*

Hone Alone Inc 610 495-5832
  119 Alackness Rd Spring City (19475) *(G-17859)*

Honest Amish, Greenville *Also called Honest Industries LLC (G-6747)*

Honest Industries LLC 724 588-1540
  14 Louisa Ave Greenville (16125) *(G-6747)*

Honey Brook Cstm Cabinets Inc 610 273-2436
  5166 Horseshoe Pike Honey Brook (19344) *(G-7749)*

Honey Brook Woodcrafts 610 273-2928
  630 White School Rd Honey Brook (19344) *(G-7750)*

Honey Butter Products Co Inc 717 665-9323
  103 S Heintzelman St Manheim (17545) *(G-10389)*

Honey Sandts Co 610 252-6511
  714 Wagener Ln Easton (18040) *(G-4700)*

Honey-Creek Stone Co (HQ) 724 654-5538
  Rte 551 Rr 422 Rt 551 Edinburg (16116) *(G-4822)*

Honeybrook Woods 610 380-7108
  22 Martins Corner Rd Coatesville (19320) *(G-3308)*

Honeybrook Woodworks 610 593-6884
  98 Williams Run Rd Christiana (17509) *(G-3135)*

Honeywell Authorized Dealer, Erie *Also called Russo Heating & Cooling Inc (G-5468)*

Honeywell Authorized Dealer, Orefield *Also called E F Laudenslager Inc (G-13011)*

Honeywell Authorized Dealer, Chambersburg *Also called McCleary Heating & Cooling LLC (G-2959)*

Honeywell Authorized Dealer, Fleetwood *Also called Advanced Enviromation Inc (G-5967)*

HONEYWELL AUTHORIZED DEALER, Atglen *Also called Summers & Zims Inc (G-809)*

Honeywell Authorized Dealer, Lancaster *Also called Frey Lutz Corp (G-9025)*

Honeywell Authorized Dealer, Allentown *Also called Yeagers Field (G-439)*

Honeywell Authorized Dealer, Reading *Also called Optimum Controls Corporation (G-16459)*

Honeywell Authorized Dealer, Windber *Also called Marc-Service Inc (G-20189)*

Honeywell International Inc 570 621-6000
  98 Westwood Rd Pottsville (17901) *(G-16080)*

Honeywell International Inc 215 533-3000
  2501 Margaret St Philadelphia (19137) *(G-13832)*

Honeywell International Inc 724 452-1300
  195 Hartzell School Rd Fombell (16123) *(G-6031)*

Honeywell International Inc 717 771-8100
  525 E Market St York (17403) *(G-20526)*

Honeywell International Inc 717 741-3799
  383 Holyoke Dr York (17402) *(G-20527)*

Honeywell International Inc 814 432-2118
  1345 15th St Franklin (16323) *(G-6135)*

Honeywell Resins & Chem LLC 215 533-3000
  4698 Bermuda St Philadelphia (19137) *(G-13833)*

Hood & Son Inc 215 822-5750
  31 Maple Ave Line Lexington (18932) *(G-9976)*

Hoodco Inc 215 236-0951
  1024 Drexel Ave Drexel Hill (19026) *(G-4365)*

Hooke Mfg LLC 570 876-6787
  432 1st St Eynon (18403) *(G-5755)*

Hootboard LLC 610 844-2423
  2 Spring Ln Yardley (19067) *(G-20320)*

Hoover Cnvyor Fabrication Corp (PA) 814 634-5431
  262 Industrial Park Rd Meyersdale (15552) *(G-11011)*

Hoover Design & Manufacturing 717 767-9555
  1410 Harley Davidson Dr York (17402) *(G-20528)*

Hoover Precision Machine Works 717 445-9190
  1981 N Churchtown Rd East Earl (17519) *(G-4544)*

Hoover Pump Works 717 733-0630
  222 Conestoga Creek Rd Ephrata (17522) *(G-5110)*

Hoover Treated Wood Pdts Inc 800 220-6046
  385 Waterway Rd Oxford (19363) *(G-13081)*

Hoovers Stone Quarry LLC 724 639-9813
  3497 State Route 981 Saltsburg (15681) *(G-17051)*

HOP Millwork Inc 724 934-3880
  10539 Perry Hwy Wexford (15090) *(G-19806)*

Hope Good Animal Clinic 717 766-5535
  6108 Carlisle Pike # 120 Mechanicsburg (17050) *(G-10854)*

Hope Good Hardwoods Inc 610 350-1556
  1627 New London Rd Landenberg (19350) *(G-9250)*

Hope Hosiery Mills, Lancaster *Also called CM Industries Inc (G-8980)*

Hope Paige Designs LLC 610 234-0093
  100 Front St Ste 300 Conshohocken (19428) *(G-3558)*

Hope Uniform & Security Pdts, Bangor *Also called Hope Uniform Co Inc (G-916)*

Hope Uniform Co Inc 908 496-4899
  201 Roseto Ave Bangor (18013) *(G-916)*

Hope's Cookies, King of Prussia *Also called Country Fresh Batter Inc (G-8600)*

Hopewell Manufacturing Inc 717 593-9400
  217 N Franklin St Waynesboro (17268) *(G-19412)*

Hopewell Non-Ferrous Foundry 610 385-6747
  2261 E Main St Douglassville (19518) *(G-4178)*

Hopkins Logging 814 827-1681
  313 Davis Pl Titusville (16354) *(G-18383)*

Hopper Lawn & Ldscp MGT LLC 610 692-3879
  1306 Pottstown Pike West Chester (19380) *(G-19563)*

Hopper T and J Building Sups 724 443-2222
  5975 Station Hill Rd Gibsonia (15044) *(G-6340)*

Hordis Doors Inc 215 957-9585
  1250 Woodbrook Ln Warminster (18974) *(G-18895)*

Horeb Inc 610 285-1917
  927 Sage Rd West Chester (19382) *(G-19564)*

Horiba Instruments Inc 724 457-2424
  1002 Harvest Ct Coraopolis (15108) *(G-3698)*

Horix Manufacturing Company (PA) 412 771-1111
  1384 Island Ave Mc Kees Rocks (15136) *(G-10614)*

Horizon Electric Lighting LLC 267 288-5353
  998 2nd Street Pike Richboro (18954) *(G-16675)*

Horizon House Inc 610 532-7423
  418 Franklin St Darby (19023) *(G-4019)*

Horizon Lamps Inc 610 829-4220
  2 Danforth Dr Easton (18045) *(G-4701)*

Horizon Publication, Punxsutawney *Also called Spirit Publishing Company (G-16163)*

Horizon Signs LLC 215 538-2600
  1520 Allentown Rd Quakertown (18951) *(G-16200)*

Horizon Software Solutions 610 225-0989
  223 Knott 6th St Reading (19601) *(G-16404)*

Horizon Technology Inc 814 834-4004
  293 Battery St Saint Marys (15857) *(G-16980)*

Horizontal Wireline Svcs LLC (HQ) 724 382-5012
  381 Colonial Manor Rd Irwin (15642) *(G-8169)*

Horlacher & Sherwood 570 836-6298
  108 Sr 92 S Tunkhannock (18657) *(G-18539)*

Hormann Flexon LLC 724 385-9150
  117 Starpointe Blvd Burgettstown (15021) *(G-2347)*

Horn Linda Collectibles & Co 570 998-8401
  8837 Rose Valley Rd Trout Run (17771) *(G-18514)*

Horn Textile Inc 814 827-3606
  600 N Brown St Titusville (16354) *(G-18384)*

Horner Lumber Company 814 629-5861
  764 N Fork Dam Rd Boswell (15531) *(G-1883)*

Horning Manufacturing LLC 717 354-5040
  301 Twin Springs Ct New Holland (17557) *(G-12253)*

Horning Manufacturing LLC 717 354-5040
  1647 Union Grove Rd East Earl (17519) *(G-4545)*

Hornings Pallet Forks 570 966-1025
  370 Stahl Rd Mifflinburg (17844) *(G-11095)*

Hornings Woodcraft 717 949-3524
  4574 Stiegel Pike Newmanstown (17073) *(G-12477)*

Horoschuck Inc 814 860-3104
  8127 Nathan Cir Erie (16509) *(G-5319)*

Horse Systems Inc 724 544-9686
  151 Greenwood Rd Fombell (16123) *(G-6032)*

Horsehead Corporation 610 826-2111
  900 Delaware Ave Palmerton (18071) *(G-13107)*

Horsepower Logging 814 274-2236
  207 A Frame Rd Coudersport (16915) *(G-3782)*

Horsepower Wood Products 814 447-5662
  Hwy Contract Rt 60 Orbisonia (17243) *(G-13006)*

Horsey Darden Enterprises LLC 215 309-3139
  1354 W Girard Ave Philadelphia (19123) *(G-13834)*

Horst Signs 717 866-8899
　400 W Lincoln Ave Myerstown (17067) *(G-11887)*

Horst, H M, New Holland *Also called Harold M Horst Inc (G-12251)*

Horstcraft Millworks LLC 717 694-9222
　272 Mill Rd Richfield (17086) *(G-16680)*

Horsts Handpainting 717 336-7098
　1070 W Swartzville Rd Reinholds (17569) *(G-16632)*

Horton Printing 717 938-2777
　336 Valley Rd Etters (17319) *(G-5549)*

Horty Springer & Mattern 412 687-7677
　4614 5th Ave Ste 200 Pittsburgh (15213) *(G-15100)*

Hosch Company LP (HQ) 724 695-3002
　1002 International Dr Oakdale (15071) *(G-12903)*

Hosmer Supply Company Inc 412 892-2525
　384 Old Curry Hollow Rd Pittsburgh (15236) *(G-15101)*

Hostetler Truck Bodies & Trlrs, Milroy *Also called D K Hostetler Inc (G-11229)*

Hostvedt Pavoni Inc 215 489-7300
　30 S Pine St Doylestown (18901) *(G-4306)*

Hot Frog Print Media LLC 717 697-2204
　118 W Allen St Mechanicsburg (17055) *(G-10855)*

Hot Jams Dj Service 814 246-8144
　200 Horatio St Punxsutawney (15767) *(G-16144)*

Hot Off Press Inc 610 473-5700
　200 N Washington St Boyertown (19512) *(G-1916)*

Hot Rod Fabrications LLP 717 774-6302
　2 Pine Tree Dr New Cumberland (17070) *(G-12186)*

Hot Sauce Spot LLC 717 341-7573
　9 Owl Hill Rd Lititz (17543) *(G-10018)*

Hot Shot Tactical, Lancaster *Also called Black Bear Associates LLC (G-8956)*

Hot Sticks, Fort Loudon *Also called Gish Logging Inc (G-6059)*

Hotlineglass-Usa LLC 800 634-9252
　295 Delwood Rd Butler (16001) *(G-2406)*

Hotronix LLC 800 727-8520
　1 Paisley Park Carmichaels (15320) *(G-2757)*

Hotwash 610 351-2119
　2069 28th St Sw Allentown (18103) *(G-247)*

Houck Printing Company Inc 717 233-5205
　4150 Industrial Rd Harrisburg (17110) *(G-7152)*

Houghton Chemical Corporation 800 777-2466
　705 Davis St Scranton (18505) *(G-17241)*

Houghton International Inc (HQ) 888 459-9844
　945 Madison Ave Norristown (19403) *(G-12668)*

Hound Dog Corp 215 355-6424
　1612 Bonnie Brae Dr Huntingdon Valley (19006) *(G-7994)*

Hounds & Hunting Publishing 812 820-1588
　554 Bolivar Dr Bradford (16701) *(G-1973)*

House of Candles 570 629-1953
　Rr 715 Henryville (18332) *(G-7567)*

House of Price Inc 724 625-3415
　177 Brickyard Rd Mars (16046) *(G-10499)*

House of Printing 814 723-3701
　716 Pennsylvania Ave E # 2 Warren (16365) *(G-19031)*

House of Wings Foods LLC 570 627-6116
　102 Bradford St Sayre (18840) *(G-17116)*

House Wood Products Co 570 662-3868
　1 Lutes Ave Mansfield (16933) *(G-10416)*

Household Metals Inc 215 634-2800
　645 E Erie Ave Philadelphia (19134) *(G-13835)*

Houseknecht Precision Mch Sp, Muncy *Also called Houseknechts Mch & Tl Co
Inc (G-11820)*

Houseknechts Mch & Tl Co Inc (PA) 570 584-3010
　1064 Old Cement Rd Muncy (17756) *(G-11820)*

Houser's Mouthpiece Works, Norristown *Also called David R Houser (G-12651)*

Houston and Funds, Enon Valley *Also called Quick Clamp 2 (G-5087)*

Houston Screen Printing, Houston *Also called Tom Russell (G-7882)*

Hovertech International, Allentown *Also called DT Davis Enterprises Ltd (G-197)*

Howanitz Associates Inc 570 629-3388
　3414 Route 611 Bartonsville (18321) *(G-946)*

Howard & Son Meatpacking 724 662-3700
　8392 Sharon Mercer Rd Mercer (16137) *(G-10963)*

Howard Donuts Inc 215 634-7750
　2437 Aramingo Ave Philadelphia (19125) *(G-13836)*

Howard Drilling Inc 814 778-5820
　11 Bridge St Ste 4 Mount Jewett (16740) *(G-11642)*

Howard Industries Inc (PA) 814 833-7000
　6400 Howard Dr Fairview (16415) *(G-5828)*

Howard McCray, Philadelphia *Also called HMC Enterprises LLC (G-13831)*

Howard Productions, Mount Jewett *Also called Howard Drilling Inc (G-11642)*

Howden Compressors Inc 610 313-9800
　1850 Gravers Rd Ste 2 Plymouth Meeting (19462) *(G-15849)*

Howe Scale, Pittsburgh *Also called Libra Scale (G-15229)*

Howe Wood Products Inc 717 266-9855
　3107 Espresso Way York (17406) *(G-20529)*

Howell Craft Inc 412 751-6861
　591 Simpson Howell Rd Elizabeth (15037) *(G-4860)*

Howell Craft Memorials, Elizabeth *Also called Howell Craft Inc (G-4860)*

Howell Manufacturing Company 814 652-5143
　122 Armory St Everett (15537) *(G-5573)*

Howetts Custom Screen Printing 610 932-3697
　113 S 3rd St Oxford (19363) *(G-13082)*

Howmedica Osteonics Corp 610 760-7007
　5702 Route 873 Neffs (18065) *(G-11999)*

Howmet Aluminum Casting Inc 610 266-0270
　2175 Avenue C Bethlehem (18017) *(G-1532)*

Howmet Castings & Services Inc 973 361-2310
　201 Isabella St Pittsburgh (15212) *(G-15102)*

Hoy Redi-Mix, Waynesburg *Also called Hoys Construction Company Inc (G-19445)*

Hoyes Outdoor Products 570 275-2953
　134 Oak St Danville (17821) *(G-4006)*

Hoys Construction Company Inc 724 852-1112
　165 Rolling Meadows Rd Waynesburg (15370) *(G-19445)*

Hoyt Inc 570 326-9426
　220 Curtin St South Williamsport (17702) *(G-17792)*

Hoyt Wire Cloth Div, Lancaster *Also called Lumsden Corporation (G-9117)*

HP Hood LLC 215 855-9074
　711 N Brick St Allentown (18102) *(G-248)*

HP Hood LLC 215 637-2507
　10975 Dutton Rd Philadelphia (19154) *(G-13837)*

HP Inc 412 928-4978
　651 Holiday Dr Ste 5 Pittsburgh (15220) *(G-15103)*

Hpc Global, Hanover *Also called Hanover Pen Corp (G-6897)*

Hpf LLC 215 321-8170
　2001 Makefield Rd Yardley (19067) *(G-20321)*

Hpi Plastics Incorporated 610 273-7113
　373 Poplar Rd Honey Brook (19344) *(G-7751)*

Hpi Processes Inc 215 799-0450
　1030 Revenue Dr Telford (18969) *(G-18294)*

Hpkd Inc 412 922-7600
　1029 Mccartney St Pittsburgh (15220) *(G-15104)*

Hpt Pharma LLC 215 792-0020
　364 Valley Rd Unit 100 Warrington (18976) *(G-19121)*

Hr Pharmaceuticals Inc 877 302-1110
　2600 Eastern Blvd Ste 201 York (17402) *(G-20530)*

Hranec Sheet Metal Inc 724 437-2211
　763 Rte 21 Uniontown (15401) *(G-18631)*

Hrdq, West Chester *Also called Organization Design & Dev Inc (G-19612)*

Hri Inc 570 437-4315
　653 Narehood Rd Milton (17847) *(G-11242)*

Hri Inc 570 322-6737
　81 Fitness Dr 1 Muncy (17756) *(G-11821)*

Hri Networks Inc 267 515-5880
　170 S Independence Mall Philadelphia (19106) *(G-13838)*

HRP Metals Inc 412 741-6781
　207 Overlook Dr Ste 8 Sewickley (15143) *(G-17393)*

Hsk Manufacturing Inc 610 404-1940
　200 N Furnace St Ste J Birdsboro (19508) *(G-1699)*

Hsm of America LLC 610 918-4894
　419 Boot Rd Downingtown (19335) *(G-4235)*

Hub LLC (PA) 215 561-8090
　30 S 17th St Fl 14 Philadelphia (19103) *(G-13839)*

Hub Parking Technology USA Inc (PA) 724 772-2400
　761 Commonwealth Dr # 204 Warrendale (15086) *(G-19082)*

Hub USA, Warrendale *Also called Hub Parking Technology USA Inc (G-19082)*

Hubbard Feeds, Lancaster *Also called Ridley USA Inc (G-9188)*

Hubbell Incorporated Delaware 574 234-7151
　100 E Wyomissing Ave Mohnton (19540) *(G-11264)*

Huckstein Printing 724 452-5777
　107 E New Castle St Ste A Zelienople (16063) *(G-20803)*

Hudson Anthracite Inc 570 823-0531
　220 S River St Ste 1 Plains (18705) *(G-15785)*

Hudson Anthracite Inc 570 655-4151
　641 Main St Avoca (18641) *(G-844)*

Huepenbecker Enterprises Inc 717 393-3941
　854 N Prince St Lancaster (17603) *(G-9052)*

Hughes Network Systems LLC 610 363-1427
　184 Exton Square Mall Exton (19341) *(G-5692)*

Hughes Network Systems LLC 717 792-2987
　2115 Bannister St York (17404) *(G-20531)*

Hullihens Printery 570 288-6804
　45 Summit St Wilkes Barre (18704) *(G-19925)*

Hullvac Pump Corp 215 355-3995
　95 Pine Run Dr Southampton (18966) *(G-17818)*

Human Resource Executive, Horsham *Also called Lrp Publications Inc (G-7832)*

Humanistic Robotics Inc 215 922-7803
　251 Saint Josephs Way Philadelphia (19106) *(G-13840)*

Humanistic Robotics Inc 267 515-5880
　170 S Independence Philadelphia (19106) *(G-13841)*

Humanistic Robotics Inc 267 515-5880
　123 S Broad St Ste 2170 Philadelphia (19109) *(G-13842)*

Humble Elephant LLC 814 434-1743
　333 Beverly Dr Erie (16505) *(G-5320)*

Humphry's Textile Products, Philadelphia *Also called D C Humphrys Co (G-13599)*

Humphrys Flag Company Inc 215 922-0510
　374 Laurel St Pottstown (19464) *(G-15999)*

Huna Designs Ltd 570 522-9800
　1000 Buffalo Rd Lewisburg (17837) *(G-9911)*

A
L
P
H
A
B
E
T
I
C

Hunlock Sand & Gravel Company 570 256-3036
2437 Southmoore Dr Bath (18014) *(G-960)*

Hunsinger Plastics 610 845-9111
20 N Front St Bally (19503) *(G-904)*

Hunt Stained Glass Studios 412 391-1796
1756 W Carson St Pittsburgh (15219) *(G-15105)*

Hunter Engineering Company 610 330-9024
2745 Knollwood Way Easton (18040) *(G-4702)*

Hunter Highway Inc 570 454-8161
30 Lauren Ln Lattimer Mines (18234) *(G-9530)*

Hunter Kitchen & Bath LLC 570 926-0777
212 Philips Rd Exton (19341) *(G-5693)*

Hunter Mudler Inc 215 229-5470
2638 W Gordon St Philadelphia (19132) *(G-13843)*

Hunter Russell Group 724 445-7228
758 Christopher Ln Chicora (16025) *(G-3127)*

Hunter Sales Corporation 412 341-2444
3338 Industrial Blvd Bethel Park (15102) *(G-1416)*

Hunter Valley Winery 717 444-7211
3 Orchard Rd Liverpool (17045) *(G-10078)*

Huntingdon Elc Mtr Svc Inc 814 643-3921
Penn & 7th St # 7 Huntingdon (16652) *(G-7944)*

Huntingdon Fiberglass Pdts LLC 814 641-8129
1200 Susquehanna Ave Huntingdon (16652) *(G-7945)*

Huntingdon Offset Printing Co 814 641-7310
1431 Oneida St Huntingdon (16652) *(G-7946)*

Huntingdon Yarn Mills Inc 215 425-5656
3114 E Thompson St Philadelphia (19134) *(G-13844)*

Huntley & Huntley Inc 412 380-2355
2660 Monroeville Blvd Monroeville (15146) *(G-11341)*

Hunts Promotions 814 623-2751
782 W Pitt St Bedford (15522) *(G-1054)*

Hurdles Inc 814 467-8787
640 Main St Windber (15963) *(G-20182)*

Hurlock Bros Co Inc 610 659-8153
547 Forrest Ave Drexel Hill (19026) *(G-4366)*

Hurry Hill Maple Syrup 814 734-1358
11380 Fry Rd Edinboro (16412) *(G-4814)*

Hurst Engineering, Myerstown *Also called Richard Hurst (G-11897)*

Hussey Copper, Leetsdale *Also called Libertas Copper LLC (G-9697)*

Hussey Fabricated Products, Leetsdale *Also called Hcl Liquidation Ltd (G-9693)*

Hussey Marine Alloys Ltd 724 251-4200
100 Washington St Leetsdale (15056) *(G-9694)*

Hussey Performance LLC 724 318-8292
2601 Duss Ave Ambridge (15003) *(G-619)*

Huston National Printing Co 412 431-5335
209 Bausman St Pittsburgh (15210) *(G-15106)*

Hutchinson & Gunter Inc 724 837-3200
715 Grove St Greensburg (15601) *(G-6675)*

Hutspah Shirts, Philadelphia *Also called Gregg Shirtmakers Inc (G-13787)*

Hutton Metalcrafts Inc 570 646-7778
1812 Route 940 Bldg 1 Pocono Pines (18350) *(G-15881)*

Hutts Glass Co Inc 610 369-1028
3186 N Charlotte St Gilbertsville (19525) *(G-6373)*

Hv2 Enterprises Inc 610 330-9300
842 Line St Easton (18042) *(G-4703)*

Hvl LLC 412 494-9600
112 Technology Dr Ste 100 Pittsburgh (15275) *(G-15107)*

HW Marston & Co 610 328-6669
206 Cheshire Cir West Chester (19380) *(G-19565)*

HWI Intermediate 1 Inc 412 375-6800
1305 Cherrington Pkwy # 100 Moon Township (15108) *(G-11491)*

Hwp Fabrications 814 487-5507
5013 Clear Shade Dr Windber (15963) *(G-20183)*

Hy-Tech Machine (HQ) 724 776-6800
25 Leonb Rd Mashu Indus P K A Industrial P Cranberry Township (16066) *(G-3823)*

Hy-Tech Machine Inc 724 776-2400
25 Leonberg Rd Cranberry Township (16066) *(G-3824)*

Hydac Corp 610 266-0100
2280 City Line Rd Bethlehem (18017) *(G-1533)*

Hydac Technology Corp (HQ) 205 520-1220
2260 Cy Line Rd Ste 2280 Bethlehem (18017) *(G-1534)*

Hydac Technology Corp 610 266-3143
2204 Avenue C Bethlehem (18017) *(G-1535)*

Hyde Marine, Coraopolis *Also called Calgon Carbon Corporation (G-3668)*

Hyde Marine, Coraopolis *Also called Calgon Carbon Uv Tech LLC (G-3670)*

Hyde Special Tools, Saegertown *Also called Lon Hyde (G-16922)*

Hyde Special Tools 814 763-4140
16380 State Highway 86 Saegertown (16433) *(G-16918)*

Hydra Service Inc 724 852-2423
500 Jefferson Rd Waynesburg (15370) *(G-19446)*

Hydra-Matic Packing Co Inc (PA) 215 676-2992
2992 Franks Rd Huntingdon Valley (19006) *(G-7995)*

Hydra-Tech Pumps, Nesquehoning *Also called Whittco Inc (G-12011)*

Hydra-Tech Pumps Inc 570 645-3779
167 Stock St Nesquehoning (18240) *(G-12005)*

Hydratron, Pittsburgh *Also called Chesterfield Special Cylinders (G-14847)*

Hydro Carbide Inc (HQ) 724 539-9701
4439 State Route 982 Latrobe (15650) *(G-9480)*

Hydro Dynamics, Reading *Also called Tricorn Inc (G-16550)*

Hydro Extruder LLC 570 474-5935
330 Elmwood Ave Mountain Top (18707) *(G-11764)*

Hydro Extruder LLC (HQ) 412 299-7600
Airport Offc Park Moon Township (15108) *(G-11492)*

Hydro Extruder LLC 570 474-5935
330 Elmwood Ave Mountain Top (18707) *(G-11765)*

Hydro Extrusion Usa LLC 877 966-7272
400 Rouser Rd Ste 300 Moon Township (15108) *(G-11493)*

Hydro Extrusion Usa LLC 318 878-9703
53 Pottsville St Cressona (17929) *(G-3904)*

Hydro Instruments Inc 215 799-0980
600 Emlen Way Telford (18969) *(G-18295)*

Hydro Lazer Inc 724 295-9100
134 Armstrong Dr Freeport (16229) *(G-6205)*

Hydro Partners LLC 717 825-1332
1800 W King St York (17404) *(G-20532)*

Hydro-Pac Inc 814 474-1511
7470 Market Rd Fairview (16415) *(G-5829)*

Hydrocoil Power Inc 610 745-1990
1164 Saint Andrews Rd Bryn Mawr (19010) *(G-2325)*

Hydroflex Systems Inc 717 480-4200
1009 Silver Lake Rd Lewisberry (17339) *(G-9887)*

Hydroflow Pennsylvania LLC 814 643-7135
4020 Tadpole Rd Pennsylvania Furnace (16865) *(G-13263)*

Hydrogen Electrics LLC 267 334-3155
1022 Frederick Rd Jenkintown (19046) *(G-8290)*

Hydrojet Services Inc 610 375-7500
450 Gateway Dr Reading (19601) *(G-16405)*

Hydrol Chemical Company Inc 610 622-3603
520 Commerce Dr Yeadon (19050) *(G-20354)*

Hydromotion Inc 610 948-4150
85 E Bridge St Spring City (19475) *(G-17860)*

Hydrosource 570 676-8500
Rr 390 Canadensis (18325) *(G-2530)*

Hydrotherm, Boyertown *Also called Advanced Thermal Hydronics (G-1894)*

Hydrotrack, Middletown *Also called Hydroworx International Inc (G-11057)*

Hydroworx International Inc 717 902-1923
1420 Stoneridge Dr Ste C Middletown (17057) *(G-11057)*

Hygrade Acquisition Corp (PA) 610 866-2441
1990 Highland Ave Bethlehem (18020) *(G-1536)*

Hygrade Components, Bethlehem *Also called Hygrade Mtal Moulding Mfg Corp (G-1538)*

Hygrade Components 610 866-2441
1990 Highland Ave Bethlehem (18020) *(G-1537)*

Hygrade Mtal Moulding Mfg Corp (HQ) 610 866-2441
1990 Highland Ave Bethlehem (18020) *(G-1538)*

Hyma Devore Lumber Co, Youngsville *Also called Hyma Devore Lumber Mill Inc (G-20772)*

Hyma Devore Lumber Mill Inc 814 563-4646
Rt Youngsville (16371) *(G-20772)*

Hyponex Corporation 610 932-4200
311 Reedville Rd Oxford (19363) *(G-13083)*

Hyproca Nutrition USA Inc 416 565-4364
71 Mcmurray Rd Ste 104 Pittsburgh (15241) *(G-15108)*

Hyq Research Solutions LLC 717 439-9320
1258 Jill Dr Hummelstown (17036) *(G-7914)*

Hyq Resonance Systems, Hummelstown *Also called Hyq Research Solutions LLC (G-7914)*

Hyrdogen Corp 412 405-1000
2 Juniper St McKeesport (15132) *(G-10672)*

Hytech Tool & Design Co (PA) 814 734-6000
12076 Edinboro Rd Edinboro (16412) *(G-4815)*

Hytron Electric Products Div, Meadville *Also called Trojan Inc (G-10804)*

Hyundai Rotem USA Corporation 215 227-6836
1300 Virginia Dr Ste 103 Fort Washington (19034) *(G-6074)*

Hyvac Products Inc (PA) 484 901-4100
1265 Ridge Rd Pottstown (19465) *(G-15948)*

I & I Sling Inc (PA) 800 874-3539
205 Bridgewater Rd Aston (19014) *(G-769)*

I & J Manufacturing LLC 717 442-9451
10 S New Holland Rd Ste 2 Gordonville (17529) *(G-6558)*

I 2 M, Mountain Top *Also called Crestwood Membranes Inc (G-11758)*

I A Construction Western PA, Franklin *Also called IA Construction Corporation (G-6137)*

I A S, Canonsburg *Also called Integrted Assembly Systems Inc (G-2597)*

I C A, Allentown *Also called Insulation Corporation America (G-262)*

I C S, Wind Gap *Also called Innovative Control Systems Inc (G-20169)*

I C S, West Chester *Also called Infinite Control Systems Inc (G-19570)*

I Cat, Hatfield *Also called Imaging Sciences Intl LLC (G-7353)*

I D S I Fabrication Machining, Sewickley *Also called Interlocking Deck Systems Inte (G-17395)*

I D Technologies Inc 610 652-2418
3186 N Charlotte St Gilbertsville (19525) *(G-6374)*

I D Tek Inc 215 699-8888
297 Dekalb Pike North Wales (19454) *(G-12806)*

I Design, Pittsburgh *Also called 2820 Associates Inc (G-14625)*

I F H Industries Inc 215 699-9344
522 Chestnut St Royersford (19468) *(G-16852)*

I Fuel 570 524-6851
71 Walter Dr Lewisburg (17837) *(G-9912)*

I G I, Titusville *Also called International Group Inc* **(G-18385)**

I H Rissler Mfg LLC 717 484-0551
  448 Orchard Rd Mohnton (19540) **(G-11265)**

I L Geer and Sons 814 723-7569
  14232 Route 6 Clarendon (16313) **(G-3169)**

I Optical City 412 881-3090
  1225 Brownsville Rd Pittsburgh (15210) **(G-15109)**

I P D, Hanover Township *Also called Integrated Power Designs Inc* **(G-6990)**

I P E P, Pittsburgh *Also called Institute Prof Envmtl Practice* **(G-15130)**

I P Graphics Inc 215 673-2600
  11601 Caroline Rd Philadelphia (19154) **(G-13845)**

I S M, Erie *Also called Industrial Sales & Mfg Inc* **(G-5324)**

I T C Industrial Tube Cleaning (PA) 724 752-3100
  416 Pittsburgh Cir Ellwood City (16117) **(G-4937)**

I T V, Jackson Center *Also called Interntional Timber Veneer LLC* **(G-8228)**

I2r Electronics Inc 610 928-1045
  7448 Industrial Park Way Macungie (18062) **(G-10148)**

IA Construction Corporation (HQ) 814 432-3184
  24 Gibb Rd Franklin (16323) **(G-6136)**

IA Construction Corporation 724 368-2140
  62 Old City Franklin Rd Franklin (16323) **(G-6137)**

IA Construction Corporation 724 479-9690
  Old Rte 119 Homer City (15748) **(G-7676)**

Iag Distribution Center, Chambersburg *Also called Tom James Company* **(G-2986)**

Ial Assoc LLC 215 887-5114
  890 Serpentine Ln Elkins Park (19027) **(G-4906)**

Iam Robotics LLC 412 636-7425
  31 Newgate Rd Pittsburgh (15202) **(G-15110)**

Iberdrola Renewable (PA) 610 254-9800
  100 W Matsonford Rd Radnor (19087) **(G-16294)**

Ibis Tek Inc (HQ) 724 431-3000
  912 Pittsburgh Rd Butler (16002) **(G-2407)**

Ibis Tek Apparel LLC 724 586-2179
  912 Pittsburgh Rd Butler (16002) **(G-2408)**

Ibis Tek Holdings Inc (PA) 724 431-3000
  912 Pittsburgh Rd Butler (16002) **(G-2409)**

IBM, Wayne *Also called International Bus Mchs Corp* **(G-19339)**

Ic Mechanics Inc 412 682-5560
  425 N Craig St Ste 500 Pittsburgh (15213) **(G-15111)**

IC&s Distributing Co 717 391-6250
  1833 William Penn Way Lancaster (17601) **(G-9053)**

Ica Inc (PA) 610 377-6100
  500 S 9th St Lehighton (18235) **(G-9716)**

Icb Acquisitions LLC 412 682-7400
  3340 Liberty Ave Pittsburgh (15201) **(G-15112)**

Icbridal LLC 570 409-6333
  322 Broad St Milford (18337) **(G-11161)**

ICC Ammo, Reynoldsville *Also called International Cartridge Corp* **(G-16657)**

Ice, Lawrence *Also called Industrial Controls & Eqp Inc* **(G-9537)**

Ice Butler 610 644-3243
  44 Malin Rd Malvern (19355) **(G-10249)**

Ice Cream World, Emmaus *Also called JAS Wholesale & Supply Co Inc* **(G-5031)**

Ice Qube Inc 724 837-7600
  141 Wilson Ave Greensburg (15601) **(G-6676)**

Ice Qube Cooling Systems, Greensburg *Also called Ice Qube Inc* **(G-6676)**

Ice River Springs Usa Inc 828 391-6900
  734 Roble Rd Allentown (18109) **(G-249)**

Ice/Stations, Mount Pleasant *Also called Integration Tech Systems Inc* **(G-11701)**

Iceblox Inc 717 697-1900
  1405 Brandton Rd Mechanicsburg (17055) **(G-10856)**

Iceutica Inc 267 546-1400
  3602 Horizon Dr Ste 160 King of Prussia (19406) **(G-8632)**

ICO Polymers North America Inc 610 398-5900
  6355 Farm Bureau Rd Allentown (18106) **(G-250)**

Icon Identity Solutions, Bristol *Also called East Coast Sign Advg Co Inc* **(G-2136)**

Icon Lgacy Cstm Mdlar Hmes LLC 570 374-3280
  246 Sand Hill Rd Selinsgrove (17870) **(G-17326)**

Icon Marketing LLC 610 356-4050
  2215 Anthony Ave Fl 3 Broomall (19008) **(G-2289)**

Icon Screenprinting Inc 814 454-0086
  1710 French St Erie (16501) **(G-5321)**

Icon/Information Concepts Inc 215 545-6700
  1 Oxford Vly Ste 312 Langhorne (19047) **(G-9303)**

ICP Industries LLC 888 672-2123
  200 N Furnace St Birdsboro (19508) **(G-1700)**

Icreate Automation Inc 610 443-1758
  964 Marcon Blvd Ste 120 Allentown (18109) **(G-251)**

Ictv Holdings Inc (HQ) 484 598-2300
  489 Devon Park Dr Ste 315 Wayne (19087) **(G-19337)**

Icu Medical Sales Inc 610 265-9100
  920 E 8th Ave King of Prussia (19406) **(G-8633)**

Icy Bites Inc 570 558-5558
  2603 Stafford Ave Scranton (18505) **(G-17242)**

Icy Feet Inc 610 462-3887
  2629 Augusta Dr Whitehall (18052) **(G-19876)**

Icy Ice Co, Butler *Also called Michalski Refrigeration Inc* **(G-2423)**

ID Technology LLC 717 235-8345
  1145 E Wellspring Rd New Freedom (17349) **(G-12209)**

ID Technology LLC 717 848-3875
  391 Greendale Rd York (17403) **(G-20533)**

Idac Corporation 570 534-4400
  207 Johnson Ct Ste B Sciota (18354) **(G-17181)**

Iddings Quarry Inc (PA) 570 966-1551
  900 Chestnut St Mifflinburg (17844) **(G-11096)**

Idea Group Inc 717 533-3673
  701 E Chocolate Ave # 100 Hershey (17033) **(G-7617)**

Ideal Aerosmith Inc 412 963-1495
  232 Alpha Dr Pittsburgh (15238) **(G-15113)**

Ideal Building Fasteners Inc 412 299-6199
  920 2nd Ave Ste 2 Coraopolis (15108) **(G-3699)**

Ideal Manufacturing LLC 717 629-3751
  10 S New Holland Rd 1 Gordonville (17529) **(G-6559)**

Ideal Products, Du Bois *Also called Prosco Inc* **(G-4414)**

Ideal Products America LP 484 320-6194
  3239 Phoenixville Pike Malvern (19355) **(G-10250)**

Ideal Prtg Co Lancaster Inc 717 299-2643
  1136 Elizabeth Ave Lancaster (17601) **(G-9054)**

Ideal Sleeves Intl LLC 570 823-8456
  182 Courtright St Wilkes Barre (18702) **(G-19926)**

Ideal-Pmt Machine Inc 570 879-2165
  1 Tannery St Great Bend (18821) **(G-6582)**

Idemia America Corp 610 524-2410
  523 James Hance Ct Exton (19341) **(G-5694)**

Identicard Systems Worldwide, Manheim *Also called Dual Core LLC* **(G-10379)**

Identification Systems Inc 814 774-9656
  10043 Peach St Girard (16417) **(G-6391)**

Identity Group 610 767-4700
  4 N Walnut St Slatington (18080) **(G-17607)**

Idera Pharmaceuticals Inc 484 348-1600
  505 Eagleview Blvd # 212 Exton (19341) **(G-5695)**

Idlewild Ski Shop Inc 570 222-4200
  7471 State Route 374 Clifford Township (18470) **(G-3248)**

Idlewood Industries Inc 724 624-1499
  17 Georgetown Ln Beaver (15009) **(G-984)**

Idn Global Inc 215 698-8155
  2815 Southampton Rd Philadelphia (19154) **(G-13846)**

Idp Association Management, Palmer *Also called Innovative Designs & Pubg* **(G-13098)**

Idreco USA Ltd 610 701-9944
  24 Hagerty Blvd Ste 9 West Chester (19382) **(G-19566)**

IDS USA, Orefield *Also called Interntnal Def Systems USA LLC* **(G-13012)**

Idsi LLC 717 227-9055
  888 Far Hills Dr Ste 200 New Freedom (17349) **(G-12210)**

Idsi LLC (HQ) 717 235-5474
  888 Far Hills Dr Ste 200 New Freedom (17349) **(G-12211)**

Iehle Enterprises Inc 717 859-1113
  1305 Manheim Pike Ste 2 Lancaster (17601) **(G-9055)**

Ifco Enterprises Inc (PA) 610 651-0999
  14 Lee Blvd 46 Malvern (19355) **(G-10251)**

Iff, Philadelphia *Also called Interntnal Flvors Frgrnces Inc* **(G-13869)**

Iff Ottens, Philadelphia *Also called Henry H Ottens Mfg Co Inc* **(G-13814)**

Ifm Efector Inc 610 524-2000
  2007 Running Deer Dr Auburn (17922) **(G-816)**

Ifm Efector Inc (HQ) 800 441-8246
  1100 Atwater Dr Malvern (19355) **(G-10252)**

Ifs Industries Inc (PA) 610 378-1381
  400 Orton Ave Reading (19603) **(G-16406)**

Igb Tool & Machine Inc 215 338-1420
  7363 Melrose St Philadelphia (19136) **(G-13847)**

Igi Global, Hershey *Also called Idea Group Inc* **(G-7617)**

Igi Printing, Jenkintown *Also called Goodway Graphics Inc* **(G-8288)**

Igm Carbon, Du Bois *Also called Du Penn Inc* **(G-4388)**

Igneous Rock Gallery 717 774-4074
  4702 Carlisle Pike Ste 25 Mechanicsburg (17050) **(G-10857)**

Igs Industries Inc 724 222-5800
  200 Country Club Rd Meadow Lands (15347) **(G-10690)**

Iheadbones Inc 888 866-0807
  1636 Wrightstown Rd Newtown (18940) **(G-12512)**

Ii-VI Incorporated (PA) 724 352-4455
  375 Saxonburg Blvd Saxonburg (16056) **(G-17088)**

Ii-VI Laser Enterprise Inc 724 352-4455
  375 Saxonburg Blvd Saxonburg (16056) **(G-17089)**

Ii-VI Optical Systems Inc 215 842-3675
  2710 Commerce Way Philadelphia (19154) **(G-13848)**

Ik Stotzfus Service Corp 717 397-3503
  1896 Auction Rd Manheim (17545) **(G-10390)**

Ikan Industries Inc 412 670-6026
  905 Powers Run Rd Pittsburgh (15238) **(G-15114)**

IKEA Indirect Mtl & Svcs LLC 610 834-0150
  400 Alan Wood Rd Conshohocken (19428) **(G-3559)**

Ikor Industries Inc 302 456-0280
  103 Indian Springs Rd Kennett Square (19348) **(G-8514)**

Ilera Healthcare LLC (PA) 610 440-8443
  420 Plymouth Rd Plymouth Meeting (19462) **(G-15850)**

Ilkem Marble and Granite, Allentown *Also called Signline LLC* **(G-391)**

Illadelph Glass Inc 215 483-1801
  128 Leverington Ave Philadelphia (19127) **(G-13849)**

Illinois Tool Works Inc...215 822-2171
2257 N Penn Rd Hatfield (19440) *(G-7352)*
Illinois Tool Works Inc...215 855-8450
130 Commerce Dr Montgomeryville (18936) *(G-11399)*
Ilsco Extrusions Inc..724 589-5888
93 Werner Rd Bldg A Greenville (16125) *(G-6748)*
Ilsemann Corp...610 323-4143
398 Circle Of Progrepa Dr Pottstown (19464) *(G-16000)*
Ilva USA, Lancaster *Also called IC&s Distributing Co (G-9053)*
Ima North America Inc..215 826-8500
211 Sinclair Rd Bristol (19007) *(G-2154)*
Imac Systems Inc..215 946-2200
90 Main St Bristol (19007) *(G-2155)*
Image 360, Flourtown *Also called Pike Graphics Inc (G-5990)*
Image 360..717 317-9147
3950 Tecport Dr Harrisburg (17111) *(G-7153)*
Image Components Inc...215 739-3599
2502 Edgemont St Philadelphia (19125) *(G-13850)*
Image Connections, Lansdowne *Also called Artistworks Wholesale Inc (G-9430)*
Image Makers Art Inc...610 722-5807
62 Central Ave Apt A Berwyn (19312) *(G-1365)*
Image Net Ventures LLC...610 240-0800
1140 Mcdermott Dr Ste 200 West Chester (19380) *(G-19567)*
Image Signs Inc..814 946-4663
1720 Margaret Ave B Altoona (16601) *(G-515)*
Imagenet/Docstar, West Chester *Also called Image Net Ventures LLC (G-19567)*
Imagewear International Inc....................................724 335-2425
4491 Hilty Rd Murrysville (15668) *(G-11853)*
Imagewear Ltd...704 999-9979
2 Maplecroft Ave Easton (18045) *(G-4704)*
Imagineered Signs & Display....................................717 846-6114
1890 W Market St Ste 1 York (17404) *(G-20534)*
Imaging Fx Inc...484 223-3311
1801 W Tilghman St Allentown (18104) *(G-252)*
Imaging Sciences International, Hatfield *Also called Dental Imaging Tech Corp (G-7333)*
Imaging Sciences Intl LLC.......................................215 997-5666
1910 N Penn Rd Hatfield (19440) *(G-7353)*
Imex Pa LLC...607 343-3160
14 Merrill St Hallstead (18822) *(G-6833)*
Imf Printing LLC (PA)..844 463-2726
840 W Linden St Allentown (18101) *(G-253)*
IMI, Chambersburg *Also called International Marketing Inc (G-2942)*
Imler's, Ken Garage, East Freedom *Also called Ken Imler (G-4564)*
Immersion Research Inc (PA)..................................814 395-9191
808 Oden St Confluence (15424) *(G-3466)*
Immunocore...484 534-5261
181 Washington St Conshohocken (19428) *(G-3560)*
Immunome Inc...610 716-3599
665 Stockton Dr Ste 300 Exton (19341) *(G-5696)*
Immunotek Bio Centers LLC...................................570 300-7940
1838 N Township Blvd Pittston (18640) *(G-15756)*
Immunotek Bio Centers LLC...................................484 408-6376
1587 Lehigh St Allentown (18103) *(G-254)*
Immunotek Bio Centers LLC...................................814 283-6421
5901 6th Ave Altoona (16602) *(G-516)*
Immunotope Inc..215 489-4945
3805 Old Easton Rd Doylestown (18902) *(G-4307)*
IMO, Philadelphia *Also called Interntonal Mar Outfitting LLC (G-13871)*
Imod Oil Production LLC..814 589-7539
15852 Pleasant Valley Dr Pleasantville (16341) *(G-15802)*
Imp Inc...610 458-1533
232 W Gay St West Chester (19380) *(G-19568)*
Impac Technology Inc...610 430-1400
967 S Matlack St West Chester (19382) *(G-19569)*
Impact Colors Inc...302 224-8310
201 E Elm St Conshohocken (19428) *(G-3561)*
Impact Energy Services, Eighty Four *Also called Select Energy Services LLC (G-4848)*
Impact Guard LLC...724 318-8800
31 Leetsdale Indus Dr Leetsdale (15056) *(G-9695)*
Impact Innovative Products LLC................................724 864-8440
127 Industry Blvd Irwin (15642) *(G-8170)*
Impact Printing and Embroidery...............................814 857-7246
4199 Clearfield Wdlnd Hwy Woodland (16881) *(G-20212)*
Impax Laboratories Inc...215 289-2220
602 W Office Center Dr # 200 Fort Washington (19034) *(G-6075)*
Impax Laboratories LLC..215 558-4300
602 W Office Center Dr # 200 Fort Washington (19034) *(G-6076)*
Impecca USA, Wilkes Barre *Also called Luzerne Trading Company Inc (G-19938)*
Imperial Bakery..570 343-4537
416 S Hyde Park Ave Scranton (18504) *(G-17243)*
Imperial Beverage Systems Inc................................717 238-6870
1201 S 20th St Harrisburg (17104) *(G-7154)*
Imperial Counter Top Company................................610 435-4803
211 W Turner St 213 Allentown (18101) *(G-255)*
Imperial Dough Company Inc..................................724 695-3625
103a International Dr Oakdale (15071) *(G-12904)*
Imperial Eagle Products Inc...................................717 252-1573
319 Cool Creek Rd Wrightsville (17368) *(G-20238)*

Imperial Newbould Inc...814 337-8155
15256 Harmonsburg Rd Meadville (16335) *(G-10737)*
Imperial Specialty Inc...610 323-4531
1153 Sembling Ave Pottstown (19464) *(G-16001)*
Imperial Systems Inc..724 662-2801
7320 W Market St Mercer (16137) *(G-10964)*
Imperial Tool Co..215 947-7650
78 Tomlinson Rd Ste E Huntingdon Valley (19006) *(G-7996)*
Imperial Truck Body & Eqp......................................724 695-3165
934 Santiago Rd Imperial (15126) *(G-8067)*
Impilo LLC...610 662-2867
307 Violet Ln Wynnewood (19096) *(G-20269)*
Implant Research Center...215 571-4345
3401 Market St Ste 345 Philadelphia (19104) *(G-13851)*
Imposters LLC...412 781-3443
12 Brilliant Ave Pittsburgh (15215) *(G-15115)*
Impression Technology Inc......................................412 318-4437
2987 Babcock Blvd 201 Pittsburgh (15237) *(G-15116)*
Impressions Media...570 829-7140
90 E Market St Wilkes Barre (18701) *(G-19927)*
Impressions Printing & Pubg.....................................717 436-2034
5196 W River Rd Mifflintown (17059) *(G-11123)*
Impressive Signs Inc..717 848-9305
351 N East St York (17403) *(G-20535)*
Imprintables Warehouse LLC.....................................724 966-8599
1 Posley Pike Carmichaels (15320) *(G-2758)*
Imprinted Promotions...215 342-7226
8529 Bustleton Ave Philadelphia (19152) *(G-13852)*
Imprints Unlimited...215 879-9484
4950 Parkside Ave Ste 400 Philadelphia (19131) *(G-13853)*
Imprints USA, Feasterville Trevose *Also called Penn Emblem Company (G-5926)*
IMS, Horsham *Also called International Mill Service (G-7824)*
IMS, Houston *Also called Tms International LLC (G-7881)*
Imtech, Pittsburgh *Also called Impression Technology Inc (G-15116)*
In A Week Guaranteed Inc.......................................610 965-7700
2701 Sickle Cir Emmaus (18049) *(G-5028)*
In Speck Corporation...610 272-9500
208 E Penn St Norristown (19401) *(G-12669)*
In Stitches Embroidery...570 368-5525
317 Broad St Ste 2 Montoursville (17754) *(G-11441)*
In-Tec Inc (PA)...570 342-8464
1 Kennedy Creek Rd Waverly (18471) *(G-19285)*
Incyte Chemicals, Wayne *Also called Drugdev Inc (G-19320)*
Incyte Corporation..302 498-6700
109 Diane Dr Broomall (19008) *(G-2290)*
Indeck Keystone Energy LLC..................................814 452-6421
5340 Fryling Rd Ste 200 Erie (16510) *(G-5322)*
Independent Concepts Inc.......................................412 741-7903
109 Priscilla Dr Sewickley (15143) *(G-17394)*
Independent Fbrc, Bensalem *Also called Men of Steel Enterprises LLC (G-1226)*
Independent Graphics Inc..570 609-5267
242 W 8th St Wyoming (18644) *(G-20279)*
Independent Hose Co..570 544-9528
16 Sunshine St Pottsville (17901) *(G-16081)*
Independent Pattern Shop.......................................814 459-2591
1919 Reed St Ste 1 Erie (16503) *(G-5323)*
Independent Tool & Mfg...814 336-5168
422 Park Ave Meadville (16335) *(G-10738)*
Independent Tool and Die, Freeport *Also called Oberg Industries Inc (G-6210)*
Independent-Observer (PA)......................................724 887-7400
228 Pittsburgh St Scottdale (15683) *(G-17193)*
Independent-Observer...724 238-2111
112 W Main St Ligonier (15658) *(G-9959)*
Independent-Observer...724 547-5722
127 W Apple St Connellsville (15425) *(G-3499)*
Indian Head TI Cutter Grinding, Waterford *Also called Indian Head TI Cutter
Grinding (G-19263)*
Indian Head TI Cutter Grinding..................................814 796-4954
802 Walnut St N Waterford (16441) *(G-19263)*
Indian Lake Marina Inc..814 754-4774
234 S Shore Trl Central City (15926) *(G-2839)*
Indian Valley Printing Co Inc....................................215 723-7884
16 Harbor Pl Souderton (18964) *(G-17741)*
Indiana Gazette, Indiana *Also called Indiana Printing and Pubg Co (G-8105)*
Indiana Printing and Pubg Co (PA)............................724 465-5555
899 Water St Indiana (15701) *(G-8105)*
Indiana Printing and Pubg Co...................................724 349-3434
775 Indian Springs Rd Indiana (15701) *(G-8106)*
Indiana Tool & Die LLC...724 463-0386
207 Nibert Rd Indiana (15701) *(G-8107)*
Indocarb AC LLC...412 928-4970
651 Holiday Dr Ste 300 Pittsburgh (15220) *(G-15117)*
Indoor City Granite & MBL Inc.................................717 393-3931
1284 Loop Rd Lancaster (17601) *(G-9056)*
Indoor Sky LLC...570 220-1903
2401 Reach Rd Williamsport (17701) *(G-20024)*
Indspec Chemical Corporation (HQ)...........................724 756-2370
133 Main St Petrolia (16050) *(G-13305)*

Indspec Chemical Corporation 412 826-3666
　1010 William Pitt Way Pittsburgh (15238) *(G-15118)*

Indus Graphics Inc 215 443-7773
　445 York Rd Warminster (18974) *(G-18896)*

Industrial Brake Company Inc 724 625-0010
　300 Clay Ave Mars (16046) *(G-10500)*

Industrial Composites Inc 412 221-2662
　373 Carol Ave Bridgeville (15017) *(G-2069)*

Industrial Consortium Inc 610 775-5760
　40 S Church St Mohnton (19540) *(G-11266)*

Industrial Consortium Inc (PA) 610 777-1653
　40 S Church St Mohnton (19540) *(G-11267)*

Industrial Control & Elec Inc 610 859-9272
　4009 Market St Unit J Upper Chichester (19014) *(G-18665)*

Industrial Controls & Eqp Inc 724 746-3705
　2 Park Dr Lawrence (15055) *(G-9537)*

Industrial Controls Inc 717 697-7555
　837 W Trindle Rd Mechanicsburg (17055) *(G-10858)*

Industrial Ctrl Concepts Inc 412 464-1905
　278 Mifflin St Homestead (15120) *(G-7687)*

Industrial Ctrl Concepts Inc (PA) 412 464-1905
　209 Frank St Homestead (15120) *(G-7688)*

Industrial Data Exchange Inc 717 653-1833
　1425 W Main St Mount Joy (17552) *(G-11662)*

Industrial Diesel Power Inc 215 781-2378
　933 Washington Ave Croydon (19021) *(G-3919)*

Industrial Division, Willow Grove *Also called Ogontz Corporation* *(G-20131)*

Industrial Enterprises Inc (HQ) 215 355-7080
　130 James Way Southampton (18966) *(G-17819)*

Industrial Enterprises Inc 215 355-7080
　550 Davisville Rd Warminster (18974) *(G-18897)*

Industrial Eqp Fabricators Inc 724 752-8819
　2 Early St Ellwood City (16117) *(G-4938)*

Industrial Floor Corporation (PA) 215 886-1800
　261 Old York Rd Ste 612 Jenkintown (19046) *(G-8291)*

Industrial Food Truck LLC 215 596-0010
　5200 Grays Ave Philadelphia (19143) *(G-13854)*

Industrial Harness Company Inc (PA) 717 477-0100
　100 Outlook Ln Shippensburg (17257) *(G-17532)*

Industrial Heating Magazine, Pittsburgh *Also called BNP Media Inc* *(G-14777)*

Industrial Instrs & Sups Inc 215 396-0822
　865 Cherry Ln Wycombe (18980) *(G-20260)*

Industrial Learning Systems 412 512-8257
　4244 Yarmouth Dr Allison Park (15101) *(G-453)*

Industrial Machine Inc 724 452-7730
　1870 Route 588 Ste 1 Zelienople (16063) *(G-20804)*

Industrial Machine Designs Inc 724 981-2707
　30 Ohio St Wheatland (16161) *(G-19838)*

Industrial Machine Works Inc 412 782-5055
　Grant St Pittsburgh (15219) *(G-15119)*

Industrial Metal Plating Inc 610 374-5107
　153 Wagner Ln Reading (19601) *(G-16407)*

Industrial Nameplate Inc 215 322-1111
　29 Indian Dr Warminster (18974) *(G-18898)*

Industrial Packaging Supplies 724 459-8299
　285 Westinghouse Rd Blairsville (15717) *(G-1725)*

Industrial Pallet, Greencastle *Also called American Fibertech Corporation* *(G-6595)*

Industrial Plas Fabrication 610 524-7090
　151 Philips Rd Exton (19341) *(G-5697)*

Industrial Polsg & Grinding 717 854-9001
　390 N Eberts Ln York (17403) *(G-20536)*

Industrial Pump & Mtr Repr Inc 412 369-5060
　1648 Butler Plank Rd Glenshaw (15116) *(G-6490)*

Industrial Rubber Products Co, Meadow Lands *Also called Rubber Rolls Inc* *(G-10692)*

Industrial Sales & Mfg Inc 814 833-9876
　2609 W 12th St Erie (16505) *(G-5324)*

Industrial Scientific Corp (HQ) 412 788-4353
　1 Life Way Pittsburgh (15205) *(G-15120)*

Industrial Service Co Ltd 484 373-0410
　720 Sheridan Dr Easton (18045) *(G-4705)*

Industrial Services 610 437-1453
　2300 Eberhart Rd Whitehall (18052) *(G-19877)*

Industrial Services and Pdts, Pittsburgh *Also called Industrial Systems & Process C* *(G-15122)*

Industrial Shipping Pdts Isp 724 423-6533
　2404 State Route 130 Latrobe (15650) *(G-9481)*

Industrial Svc Instllation Inc 717 767-1129
　290 Emig Rd Emigsville (17318) *(G-4992)*

Industrial Systems & Controls 412 638-4977
　317 S Main St Pittsburgh (15220) *(G-15121)*

Industrial Systems & Process C 412 279-4750
　1058 Larchdale Dr Pittsburgh (15243) *(G-15122)*

Industrial Terminal Systems 724 335-9837
　100 Logans Ferry Rd New Kensington (15068) *(G-12346)*

Industrial Vision Systems Inc 215 393-5300
　436 Morris Ave Bryn Mawr (19010) *(G-2326)*

Industrial Welding & Fabg, Leetsdale *Also called Industrial Welding and Fabg* *(G-9696)*

Industrial Welding and Fabg (PA) 724 266-2887
　80 Leetsdale Indus Dr Leetsdale (15056) *(G-9696)*

Industry Weapon Inc 877 344-8450
　900 Parish St Pittsburgh (15220) *(G-15123)*

Industrybuilt Software Ltd 866 788-1086
　1275 Glenlivet Dr Ste 100 Allentown (18106) *(G-256)*

Indutex Inc (PA) 724 935-1482
　528 Eden Park Blvd McKeesport (15132) *(G-10673)*

Inert Products LLC 570 341-3751
　100 Powderly Ct Scranton (18504) *(G-17244)*

Infacare Pharmaceutical Corp 267 515-5850
　8 Neshaminy Interplex Dr # 221 Trevose (19053) *(G-18499)*

Inferno Sports & Athletics LLC 610 633-0919
　492 Orchard Cir Exton (19341) *(G-5698)*

Infineon Tech Americas Corp 408 503-2655
　1110 American Pkwy Ne Allentown (18109) *(G-257)*

Infineon Tech Americas Corp 610 712-7100
　1110 American Pkwy Ne Allentown (18109) *(G-258)*

Infinera Corporation 408 572-5200
　7584 Morris Ct Allentown (18106) *(G-259)*

Infinera Corporation 484 866-4600
　7360 Windsor Dr Allentown (18106) *(G-260)*

Infinite Control Systems Inc 610 696-8600
　320 Turner Ln West Chester (19380) *(G-19570)*

Infinite Quest Cabinetry Corp 301 222-3592
　560 Boundary Ave Red Lion (17356) *(G-16601)*

Infinity Ltl, Morrisville *Also called Ltl Color Compounders LLC* *(G-11570)*

Infinity Marketing Inc 610 296-0653
　1065 S Wisteria Dr Malvern (19355) *(G-10253)*

Infinity Oilfield Services LLC 570 327-8114
　1500 Sycamore Rd Montoursville (17754) *(G-11442)*

Infinity Print Graphics, Carlisle *Also called D G A Inc* *(G-2706)*

Infinity Publishing (PA) 610 941-9999
　1094 New Dehaven St Conshohocken (19428) *(G-3562)*

Inflection Energy 303 531-2343
　49 E 4th St Williamsport (17701) *(G-20025)*

Infloor, Jenkintown *Also called Industrial Floor Corporation* *(G-8291)*

Infoline, Lewistown *Also called Lewistown Sentinel Inc* *(G-9939)*

Infomat Associates Inc 610 668-8306
　215 Forrest Ave Narberth (19072) *(G-11911)*

Infonxx, Bethlehem *Also called Kgb Usa Inc* *(G-1552)*

Infor (us) Inc 678 319-8000
　40 General Warren Blvd # 110 Malvern (19355) *(G-10254)*

Information Builders Inc 610 940-0790
　620 W Germantown Pike # 410 Plymouth Meeting (19462) *(G-15851)*

Information Conservation, Hatfield *Also called Library Bindery Co of PA Inc* *(G-7365)*

Information Mktg Group Inc 508 626-8682
　1000 Transit Blvd 1 Bethel Park (15102) *(G-1417)*

Informing Design Inc 412 465-0047
　216 Green St Pittsburgh (15221) *(G-15124)*

Infotechnologies Inc 717 285-7105
　306 Primrose Ln Mountville (17554) *(G-11796)*

Inframark LLC (PA) 215 646-9201
　220 Gibraltar Rd Ste 200 Horsham (19044) *(G-7823)*

Inframark LLC 215 822-2258
　3000 Advance Ln Colmar (18915) *(G-3417)*

Infrascan Inc 215 387-6784
　3508 Market St Ste 128 Philadelphia (19104) *(G-13855)*

Infrastructure H Environmental (PA) 866 629-7646
　200 Barr Harbor Dr # 400 Conshohocken (19428) *(G-3563)*

Ingaglio Welding and Ir Works, Hop Bottom *Also called Raphael A Ingaglio* *(G-7775)*

Ingenuware Ltd 724 843-3140
　1610 6th Ave Beaver Falls (15010) *(G-1000)*

Ingersoll Rand Co 215 345-4470
　245 Saddle Dr Furlong (18925) *(G-6231)*

Ingersoll-Rand Co 717 530-1160
　328 E Burd St Shippensburg (17257) *(G-17533)*

Ingersoll-Rand Co 610 882-8800
　1495 Valley Center Pkwy # 200 Bethlehem (18017) *(G-1539)*

Ingersoll-Rand Company 410 238-0542
　16 Northbrook Ln Shrewsbury (17361) *(G-17584)*

Ingersoll-Rand Company 717 532-9181
　1280 Superior Ave Chambersburg (17201) *(G-2941)*

Ingham's Powder Coating, Denver *Also called Inghams Regrooving Service Inc* *(G-4076)*

Ingham's Powder Coating, Stevens *Also called Inghams Regrooving Service Inc* *(G-18053)*

Inghams Regrooving Service Inc 717 336-8473
　22 Industrial Way Denver (17517) *(G-4076)*

Inghams Regrooving Service Inc (PA) 717 336-8473
　1860 N Reading Rd Stevens (17578) *(G-18053)*

Ingmar Medical Ltd 412 441-8228
　5940 Baum Blvd Ste 6 Pittsburgh (15206) *(G-15125)*

Ingrain Construction LLC (PA) 717 205-1475
　735 Lafayette St Lancaster (17603) *(G-9057)*

Ingrain Construction LLC 717 205-1475
　845 Wright St Columbia (17512) *(G-3439)*

Ingretec Ltd 717 273-0711
　1500 Lehman St Lebanon (17046) *(G-9582)*

Ink Division LLC 412 381-1104
　218 Braddock Ave Braddock (15104) *(G-1945)*

Ink RE Phill 717 840-0835
　1833 Shawan Ln York (17406) *(G-20537)*

Ink Spot Printing...570 743-7979
6821 Park Rd Selinsgrove (17870) *(G-17327)*

Ink Spot Printing & Copy Ctr............................610 647-0776
14 Church Rd Malvern (19355) *(G-10255)*

Ink Spot, The, Connellsville *Also called Karen Holbrook (G-3500)*

Ink Star, Beaver Falls *Also called J A Mitch Printing & Copy Ctr (G-1002)*

Ink Toner Store, West Chester *Also called Itc Supplies LLC (G-19574)*

Ink Vault...724 355-8616
310 Center Ave Butler (16001) *(G-2410)*

Inksewn USA...570 534-5199
128 Leverington Ave Philadelphia (19127) *(G-13856)*

Inkster Prints...267 886-0021
530 S 4th St 2 Philadelphia (19147) *(G-13857)*

Inlet Tools Inc..814 382-3511
11694 Dicksonburg Rd Conneautville (16406) *(G-3483)*

Inmetco, Ellwood City *Also called Interntnal Mtal Rclaiming Corp (G-4939)*

Innaventure LLC...570 371-9390
7 S Main St Ste 271 Wilkes Barre (18701) *(G-19928)*

Innochem Inc...610 323-0730
400 Old Reading Pike B202 Pottstown (19464) *(G-16002)*

Innocoll Inc...484 406-5200
3803 West Chester Pike Newtown Square (19073) *(G-12577)*

Innocor Foam Tech - Acp Inc...........................570 876-4544
103 Power Blvd Archbald (18403) *(G-687)*

Innocor Foam Tech - Acp Inc...........................570 876-4544
103 Power Blvd Archbald (18403) *(G-688)*

Innodyn LLC..814 339-7328
156 Nearhoof Ln Osceola Mills (16666) *(G-13055)*

Innofoods Usa Inc...412 854-9012
71 Mcmurray Rd Ste 104 Pittsburgh (15241) *(G-15126)*

Innogreen Group, State College *Also called Innogreen USA LLC (G-17977)*

Innogreen USA LLC...814 880-4493
200 Innovation Blvd # 257 State College (16803) *(G-17977)*

Innotech Industries Inc.....................................215 533-6400
3908 Frankford Ave Philadelphia (19124) *(G-13858)*

Innovalgae LLC...412 996-2556
113 Rabold Dr Wexford (15090) *(G-19807)*

Innovate Software Inc.......................................724 935-1790
106 Forest Rd Bradfordwoods (15015) *(G-1998)*

Innovation Plus Llc..610 272-2600
3630 Horizon Dr King of Prussia (19406) *(G-8634)*

Innovation Prtg Communications, Philadelphia *Also called Phoenix Lithographing Corp (G-14170)*

Innovation Prtg Communications, Philadelphia *Also called I P Graphics Inc (G-13845)*

Innovative Advertising & Mktg.........................717 788-1385
12178 Country Club Rd Waynesboro (17268) *(G-19413)*

Innovative Advg Vend Svcs LLC.......................814 528-7204
7790 Clark Rd Erie (16510) *(G-5325)*

Innovative Building Systems, L (PA)................717 458-1400
4900 Ritter Rd Ste 130 Mechanicsburg (17055) *(G-10859)*

Innovative Carbide Inc (PA).............................412 751-6900
11040 Parker Dr Irwin (15642) *(G-8171)*

Innovative Control Systems Inc.......................610 881-8061
3370 Fox Hill Rd Easton (18045) *(G-4706)*

Innovative Control Systems Inc (PA)...............610 881-8000
1349 Jacobsburg Rd Wind Gap (18091) *(G-20169)*

Innovative Custom Cabinetry...........................724 624-0164
118 Snyder Dr Rochester (15074) *(G-16786)*

Innovative Design Inc (PA)...............................717 202-1306
210 Weidman St Lebanon (17046) *(G-9583)*

Innovative Designs Inc (PA).............................412 799-0350
124 Cherry St Pittsburgh (15223) *(G-15127)*

Innovative Designs Inc......................................412 799-0350
124 Cherry St Pittsburgh (15223) *(G-15128)*

Innovative Designs & Pubg (PA).......................610 923-8000
3245 Freemansburg Ave Palmer (18045) *(G-13098)*

Innovative Displays...570 386-8121
1768 W Penn Pike New Ringgold (17960) *(G-12439)*

Innovative Exhibit Productions.........................610 770-9833
841 N Fenwick St Allentown (18109) *(G-261)*

Innovative Finishers Inc....................................215 536-2222
130 Penn Am Dr Quakertown (18951) *(G-16201)*

Innovative Finishers Inc....................................215 536-2222
871 Tech Dr Telford (18969) *(G-18296)*

Innovative Machining Tech Inc.........................610 473-5600
1090 N Reading Ave Boyertown (19512) *(G-1917)*

Innovative Machining Tech Inc.........................610 473-5600
8 Rowell Rd Boyertown (19512) *(G-1918)*

Innovative Manufacturing Svcs........................610 583-4883
777 Hnderson Blvd Ste 1/2 Folcroft (19032) *(G-6006)*

Innovative Office Products LLC (HQ)...............610 559-6369
100 Kuebler Rd Easton (18040) *(G-4707)*

Innovative Pharmacy Services, Warrington *Also called Coupler Enterprises Inc (G-19113)*

Innovative Plastics of PA LLC..........................717 529-2699
1084 Noble Rd Christiana (17509) *(G-3136)*

Innovative Pressure Tech LLC..........................814 833-5200
4922 Pittsburgh Ave Erie (16509) *(G-5326)*

Innovative Services USA, Erie *Also called Innovative Advg Vend Svcs LLC (G-5325)*

Innovative Sintered Metals Inc........................814 781-1033
1037 Delaum Rd Saint Marys (15857) *(G-16981)*

Innovative Tech In Print, Elizabethtown *Also called Itp of Usa Inc (G-4875)*

Innovtive Print Mdia Group Inc (PA)...............610 489-4800
500 Schell Ln Phoenixville (19460) *(G-14553)*

Innovtive Slutions Support Inc (PA)................610 646-9800
720 Pennsylvania Dr Exton (19341) *(G-5699)*

Inofast Manufacturing Inc................................215 996-9963
2880 Bergey Rd Ste R Hatfield (19440) *(G-7354)*

Inolex Group Inc (PA)..215 271-0800
2101 S Swanson St Philadelphia (19148) *(G-13859)*

Inquirer & Daily News Fed CU (PA)..................610 292-6762
800 River Rd Conshohocken (19428) *(G-3564)*

Insaco Incorporated..215 536-3500
1365 Canary Rd Quakertown (18951) *(G-16202)*

Insert Molding Tech Inc.....................................814 406-7033
36 Clark St Warren (16365) *(G-19032)*

Inserta Products Inc..215 643-0192
534 Township Line Rd Blue Bell (19422) *(G-1835)*

Inservio3 LLC...310 343-3486
650 Smithfield St # 1810 Pittsburgh (15222) *(G-15129)*

Insinger Machine Company................................215 624-4800
6245 State Rd Philadelphia (19135) *(G-13860)*

Inspire Closing Services LLC............................412 348-8367
420 Rouser Rd Moon Township (15108) *(G-11494)*

Inspro Technologies Corp (PA).........................484 654-2200
1510 Chester Pike Ste 400 Eddystone (19022) *(G-4804)*

Inspyr Apparel Co LLC......................................267 784-3036
1206 Susan Cir Oreland (19075) *(G-13022)*

Insta-Mold Products Inc....................................610 935-7270
640 Hollow Rd Oaks (19456) *(G-12933)*

Instant Impressions & More, Pittsburgh *Also called L G Graphics Inc (G-15208)*

Instant Print..724 261-5153
454 S Main St Greensburg (15601) *(G-6677)*

Instant Response Inc..215 322-1271
111 Buck Rd Unit 600 Huntingdon Valley (19006) *(G-7997)*

Instant Web Inc..952 474-0961
65 Steamboat Dr Warminster (18974) *(G-18899)*

Instech Laboratories Inc...................................610 941-0132
450 Gravers Rd Ste 100 Plymouth Meeting (19462) *(G-15852)*

Instech Solomon, Plymouth Meeting *Also called Instech Laboratories Inc (G-15852)*

Institute of Physics Pubg, Philadelphia *Also called Iop Publishing Incorporated (G-13872)*

Institute Prof Envmtl Practice..........................412 396-1703
600 Forbes Ave Pittsburgh (15219) *(G-15130)*

Instrument & Valve Services Co.......................724 205-3348
204 Brandywine Dr Irwin (15642) *(G-8172)*

Instrumental Associates....................................610 992-3300
1220 Valley Forge Rd # 28 Phoenixville (19460) *(G-14554)*

Instrumentation Industries Inc.........................412 854-1133
2990 Industrial Blvd Bethel Park (15102) *(G-1418)*

Insty-Prints, Allentown *Also called Allegra Print Imaging (G-125)*

Insul-Board Inc..814 833-7400
2120 Colonial Ave Erie (16506) *(G-5327)*

Insulation Corporation America........................610 791-4200
2571 Mitchell Ave Allentown (18103) *(G-262)*

Insulation Products, Glenshaw *Also called Ipi Co Inc (G-6491)*

Insulboot Division, Quakertown *Also called Plastic Dip Moldings Inc (G-16229)*

Intact Vascular Inc..484 253-1048
1285 Drummers Ln Ste 200 Wayne (19087) *(G-19338)*

Intech P/M Stainless Inc...................................814 776-6150
7028 Ridgway St Marys Rd Ridgway (15853) *(G-16711)*

Intect Metals, Ridgway *Also called Intech P/M Stainless Inc (G-16711)*

Integra Graphics, Lititz *Also called Cornerstone Printing Services (G-10003)*

Integra Graphics Synergy, Lititz *Also called Integra Graphix Inc (G-10019)*

Integra Graphix Inc...717 626-7895
160 Koser Rd Lititz (17543) *(G-10019)*

Integrated Cnstr Systems Inc (PA)..................724 528-9310
3766 New Castle Rd West Middlesex (16159) *(G-19726)*

Integrated Envmtl Tech Inc...............................412 298-5845
124 Edgewood Dr Washington (15301) *(G-19185)*

Integrated Fabrication Mch Inc........................724 962-3526
639 Keystone Rd Greenville (16125) *(G-6749)*

Integrated Machine Company............................814 835-4949
3952 W 12th St Erie (16505) *(G-5328)*

Integrated Metal Products Inc..........................717 824-4052
2016 Single Tree Ln Lancaster (17602) *(G-9058)*

Integrated Myers Systems LLC.........................814 937-3958
500 Church St Gallitzin (16641) *(G-6246)*

Integrated Power Designs Inc..........................570 824-4666
300 Stewart Rd Hanover Township (18706) *(G-6990)*

Integrated Power Services LLC.........................724 479-9066
4470 Lucerne Rd Indiana (15701) *(G-8108)*

Integrated Power Services LLC.........................724 225-2900
320 Reliance Dr Washington (15301) *(G-19186)*

Integrated Power Services LLC.........................215 365-1500
3240 S 78th St Philadelphia (19153) *(G-13861)*

Integrated SEC Communications, Plymouth Meeting *Also called Integrated Securty & Communctn (G-15853)*

Integrated Securty & Communctn 610 397-0988
  4110 Butler Pike Ste B100 Plymouth Meeting (19462) *(G-15853)*

Integrated Software Services 717 534-1480
  1171 Jill Dr Ste 104 Hershey (17033) *(G-7618)*

Integrated Tech Svcs Intl LLC 814 262-7332
  633 Napoleon St Johnstown (15901) *(G-8382)*

Integration Tech Systems Inc 724 696-3000
  271 Westec Dr Mount Pleasant (15666) *(G-11701)*

Integritas Inc 814 941-7006
  1331 12th Ave Altoona (16601) *(G-517)*

Integritas Inc (HQ) 800 411-6281
  40 24th St Fl 5 Pittsburgh (15222) *(G-15131)*

Integrted Assembly Systems Inc (PA) 724 746-6532
  3 Four Coins Dr Ste 400 Canonsburg (15317) *(G-2597)*

Integrted Productivity Systems 215 646-1374
  1037 Hickory Dr Blue Bell (19422) *(G-1836)*

Intel Corporation 908 894-6035
  1110 American Pkwy Ne F100 Allentown (18109) *(G-263)*

Intel Homes Ltd Liability Co 570 872-9559
  6518 Moschella Ct East Stroudsburg (18302) *(G-4620)*

Intel Network Systems Inc 610 973-5566
  1110 American Pkwy Ne Allentown (18109) *(G-264)*

Inteligistics Inc 412 826-0379
  410 William Pitt Way Pittsburgh (15238) *(G-15132)*

Intelipc 610 534-8268
  1572 Chester Pike Folcroft (19032) *(G-6007)*

Intellidrives Inc 215 728-6804
  8510 Bustleton Ave Philadelphia (19152) *(G-13862)*

Intelligent Direct Inc 570 724-7355
  10 1st St Wellsboro (16901) *(G-19466)*

Intelligent Micro Systems Ltd 610 664-1207
  4401 Parkview Dr Haverford (19041) *(G-7412)*

Intelomed Inc 412 536-7661
  6041 Wallace Road Ext # 110 Wexford (15090) *(G-19808)*

Intents Mfg 215 527-6441
  200 W 4th St East Greenville (18041) *(G-4569)*

Inteprod LLC 610 650-9002
  2583 Industry Ln Norristown (19403) *(G-12670)*

Inter Media Outdoors 717 695-8171
  6385 Flank Dr Harrisburg (17112) *(G-7155)*

Inter Tech Supplies Inc 610 435-1333
  802 E Fairmont St Allentown (18109) *(G-265)*

Inter-State Treated Material, Mount Morris *Also called Arrison H B West Virginia
Inc (G-11678)*

Interactive Worldwide Corp 906 370-7609
  7601 Edmund St Philadelphia (19136) *(G-13863)*

Intercon Printer & Consultants 724 837-5428
  412 Willow Crossing Rd Greensburg (15601) *(G-6678)*

Intercounty Newspaper Group, Bristol *Also called Goodson Holding Company (G-2149)*

Intercourse Pretzel Factory 717 768-3432
  3614 Old Phila Pike Intercourse (17534) *(G-8137)*

Interface Solutions Inc 717 824-8009
  216 Wohlsen Way Lancaster (17603) *(G-9059)*

Interforest Corp (HQ) 724 827-8366
  119 Aid Dr Darlington (16115) *(G-4029)*

Interforest Penn Beaver Div, Darlington *Also called Interforest Corp (G-4029)*

Interform Corporation (HQ) 412 221-7321
  1901 Mayview Rd Bridgeville (15017) *(G-2070)*

Interform Corporation 610 566-1515
  7046 Snow Drift Rd Media (19063) *(G-10934)*

Interform Solutions, Bridgeville *Also called Interform Corporation (G-2070)*

Interior Creations Inc 215 425-9390
  700 E Erie Ave Frnt Frnt Philadelphia (19134) *(G-13864)*

Interior Motives Inc 814 672-3100
  1168 Maple Rd Coalport (16627) *(G-3283)*

Interlectric Corporation (HQ) 814 723-6061
  1401 Lexington Ave Warren (16365) *(G-19033)*

Interlock Industries Inc 570 366-2020
  29 Pinedale Industrial Rd Orwigsburg (17961) *(G-13045)*

Interlocking Deck Systems Inte 412 682-3041
  921 Beaver St Sewickley (15143) *(G-17395)*

Intermec Technologies Corp 724 218-1444
  237 Roanoke Way Imperial (15126) *(G-8068)*

Intermetro Industries Corp (HQ) 570 825-2741
  651 N Washington St Wilkes Barre (18705) *(G-19929)*

International Bakery 814 452-3435
  610 W 18th St Erie (16502) *(G-5329)*

International Bus Mchs Corp 610 578-2017
  650 E Swedesford Rd # 200 Wayne (19087) *(G-19339)*

International Cartridge Corp 814 938-6820
  2273 Route 310 Reynoldsville (15851) *(G-16657)*

International Chemical Company 215 739-2313
  2628 N Mascher St 48 Philadelphia (19133) *(G-13865)*

International Conveyor Rbr LLC 724 343-4225
  72 Industrial Park Rd Blairsville (15717) *(G-1726)*

International Gate Devices 610 461-0811
  101 Sycamore Ave Ofc 101 # 101 Folsom (19033) *(G-6025)*

International Group Inc (HQ) 814 827-4900
  1007 E Spring St Titusville (16354) *(G-18385)*

International Heat Transf Assn, Wexford *Also called Narsa (G-19814)*

International Marketing Inc (PA) 717 264-5819
  3183 Black Gap Rd Chambersburg (17202) *(G-2942)*

International Mfg Corp 215 925-7558
  712 Chestnut St Fl 3 Philadelphia (19106) *(G-13866)*

International Mill Service 215 956-5500
  1155 Bus Ctr Dr Ste 200 Horsham (19044) *(G-7824)*

International Paper, Cranberry Township *Also called Veritiv Operating Company (G-3863)*

International Paper Company 717 677-8121
  136 E York St Biglerville (17307) *(G-1664)*

International Paper Company 570 384-3251
  533 Forest Rd Hazle Township (18202) *(G-7464)*

International Paper Company 724 745-2288
  10 Wilson Rd Eighty Four (15330) *(G-4843)*

International Paper Company 717 391-3400
  801 Fountain Ave Lancaster (17601) *(G-9060)*

International Paper Company 814 454-9001
  32 E 14th St Erie (16501) *(G-5330)*

International Paper Company 570 339-1611
  2164 Locust Gap Hwy Mount Carmel (17851) *(G-11625)*

International Paper Company 610 268-5456
  1270 Old Baltimore Park Toughkenamon (19374) *(G-18419)*

International Publications Svc, Philadelphia *Also called Taylor & Francis Inc (G-14378)*

International Raw Mtls Ltd (PA) 215 928-1010
  600 Chestnut St Ste 800 Philadelphia (19106) *(G-13867)*

International Road Dynamics 717 264-2077
  1002 S Main St Chambersburg (17201) *(G-2943)*

International Salt, Fairless Hills *Also called Morton Salt Inc (G-5789)*

International Trailers Inc 814 634-1922
  8535 Mason Dixon Hwy Meyersdale (15552) *(G-11012)*

International Union-Elevator 570 842-5430
  16 Park St Sprng Brk Twp (18444) *(G-17932)*

International Vectors Ltd 717 767-4008
  310 Emig Rd Emigsville (17318) *(G-4993)*

International Watch Magazine 484 417-2122
  65 Saint James Pl Ardmore (19003) *(G-709)*

International Waxes Inc 814 827-3609
  1007 E Spring St Titusville (16354) *(G-18386)*

Internet Pipeline Inc (PA) 484 348-6555
  222 Valley Creek Blvd # 300 Exton (19341) *(G-5700)*

Internet Probation and 610 701-8921
  1562 Mcdaniel Dr West Chester (19380) *(G-19571)*

Interntional Timber Veneer LLC 724 662-0880
  75 Mcquiston Dr Jackson Center (16133) *(G-8228)*

Interntional Track Systems Inc 724 658-5970
  221 E Cherry St New Castle (16102) *(G-12105)*

Interntnal Def Systems USA LLC 610 973-2228
  2867 Post Rd Orefield (18069) *(G-13012)*

Interntnal Flvors Frgrnces Inc 215 365-7800
  7800 Holstein Ave Philadelphia (19153) *(G-13868)*

Interntnal Flvors Frgrnces Inc 215 365-7800
  12285 Mcnulty Rd Philadelphia (19154) *(G-13869)*

Interntnal Lthers of Phldlphia 610 793-1140
  1073 Squire Cheney Dr West Chester (19382) *(G-19572)*

Interntnal Mtal Rclaiming Corp 724 758-5515
  1 Inmetco Dr Ellwood City (16117) *(G-4939)*

Interntnal Soc of Nurovirology 215 707-9788
  Merb 3500 Rm 740 Philadelphia (19140) *(G-13870)*

Interntonal Mar Outfitting LLC 215 875-9911
  321 S 17th St Philadelphia (19103) *(G-13871)*

Interphase Materials Inc 814 282-8119
  370 William Pitt Way Pittsburgh (15238) *(G-15133)*

Intersource Inc 724 940-2220
  946 Route 228 Mars (16046) *(G-10501)*

Interstate Building Mtls Inc 570 655-8496
  3000 N Township Blvd Pittston (18640) *(G-15757)*

Interstate Building Mtls Inc (PA) 570 655-2811
  3000 N Township Blvd Pittston (18640) *(G-15758)*

Interstate Chemical Co Inc (PA) 724 981-3771
  2797 Freedland Rd Hermitage (16148) *(G-7588)*

Interstate Chemical Co Inc 724 813-2576
  1432 Chestnut St Erie (16502) *(G-5331)*

Interstate Chemical Co Inc 724 774-1669
  725 Riverside Dr Beaver (15009) *(G-985)*

Interstate Cont Brunswick LLC 610 208-9300
  100 Grace St Reading (19611) *(G-16408)*

Interstate Cont New Castle LLC 724 657-3650
  792 Commerce Ave New Castle (16101) *(G-12106)*

Interstate Cont Reading LLC 800 822-2002
  100 Grace St Reading (19611) *(G-16409)*

Interstate Equipment Corp 412 563-5556
  929 Park Ave Pittsburgh (15234) *(G-15134)*

Interstate Foundry Products 814 456-4202
  1432 Chestnut St Erie (16502) *(G-5332)*

Interstate Paper Supply Co Inc 724 938-2218
  103 Good St Roscoe (15477) *(G-16817)*

Interstate Safety Service Inc 570 563-1161
  1301 Winola Rd Clarks Summit (18411) *(G-3194)*

Interstate Self Storage 724 662-1186
  410 N Cottage Rd Mercer (16137) *(G-10965)*

Interstate Window & Door Co, Pittston *Also called Interstate Building Mtls Inc (G-15758)*

A L P H A B E T I C

Interstock Premium Cabinetry, Levittown *Also called Solid Wood Cabinet Company LLC (G-9864)*

Intervala LLC 412 829-4800
700 Braddock Ave East Pittsburgh (15112) *(G-4596)*

Intervideo Inc 717 435-9433
35 E Orange St Lancaster (17602) *(G-9061)*

Intra Corporation 215 672-7003
433 Caredean Dr Ste D Horsham (19044) *(G-7825)*

Intricate Edm LLC 717 392-8244
2970 Old Tree Dr Lancaster (17603) *(G-9062)*

Intricate Precision Mfg, Lancaster *Also called Intricate Edm LLC (G-9062)*

Intricate Precision Mfg LLC 717 392-8244
2970 Old Tree Dr Lancaster (17603) *(G-9063)*

Intuidex Inc 484 851-3423
1892 Mill Run Ct Hellertown (18055) *(G-7557)*

Invensys Energy Metering Corp 814 371-3011
805 Liberty Blvd Du Bois (15801) *(G-4396)*

Inventure Foods Inc (HQ) 623 932-6200
900 High St Hanover (17331) *(G-6903)*

Invibio Inc 484 342-6004
300 Conshohocken State Rd # 120 Conshohocken (19428) *(G-3565)*

Invitations Plus 412 421-7778
1406 S Negley Ave Pittsburgh (15217) *(G-15135)*

Inweld, Coplay *Also called Robinson Technical Pdts Corp (G-3647)*

Inweld Corporation (PA) 610 261-1900
3962 Portland St Coplay (18037) *(G-3644)*

Io Solutions & Controls 215 635-4480
864 Township Line Rd Elkins Park (19027) *(G-4907)*

Iobbi Shellac, Feasterville Trevose *Also called A I Floor Products (G-5881)*

Ion Technologies Inc 814 772-0440
324 Servidea Dr Ridgway (15853) *(G-16712)*

Ionx LLC 484 653-2600
515 S Franklin St Ste 200 West Chester (19382) *(G-19573)*

Iop Publishing Incorporated 215 627-0880
190 N Independence Mall W Philadelphia (19106) *(G-13872)*

Iota Communications Inc (PA) 855 743-6478
540 Union Square Dr New Hope (18938) *(G-12306)*

Ip Lasso LLC 484 352-2029
1045 First Ave Ste 120 King of Prussia (19406) *(G-8635)*

IPA Systems Inc 215 425-6607
2745 Amber St Philadelphia (19134) *(G-13873)*

Ipeg Inc 814 437-6861
455 Allegheny Blvd Franklin (16323) *(G-6138)*

Ipeg Inc 814 437-6861
455 Allegheny Blvd Franklin (16323) *(G-6139)*

Ipeg Inc 814 437-6861
455 Allegheny Blvd Franklin (16323) *(G-6140)*

Ipf, Exton *Also called Industrial Plas Fabrication (G-5697)*

Ipi Co Inc 412 487-3995
517 Glenhaven Dr Glenshaw (15116) *(G-6491)*

Ipipeline, Exton *Also called Internet Pipeline Inc (G-5700)*

Ippc Technologies, West Chester *Also called Internet Probation and (G-19571)*

Ipsco, Roscoe *Also called Interstate Paper Supply Co Inc (G-16817)*

Ipsco Koppel Tubulars LLC (HQ) 724 847-6389
6403 6th Ave Koppel (16136) *(G-8814)*

Ipsco Koppel Tubulars Llc 724 266-8830
2225 Duss Ave Ambridge (15003) *(G-620)*

Ipsco Tubulars Inc 724 251-2539
2300 Duss Ave Ambridge (15003) *(G-621)*

Ipsen Inc 215 723-8125
1946 E Cherry Ln Ste B Souderton (18964) *(G-17742)*

Ipsi, Blue Bell *Also called Integrted Productivity Systems (G-1836)*

Iqe Inc 610 861-6930
119 Technology Dr Bethlehem (18015) *(G-1540)*

Iqe Rf LLC 732 271-5990
119 Technology Dr Bethlehem (18015) *(G-1541)*

Iqe Usa Inc 610 861-6930
119 Technology Dr Bethlehem (18015) *(G-1542)*

Ira G Steffy and Son Inc 717 626-6500
460 Wenger Dr Ephrata (17522) *(G-5111)*

Ira Middleswarth and Son Inc 717 248-3093
520 Princeton St Lewistown (17044) *(G-9936)*

Iridium Industries Inc (PA) 570 476-8800
147 Forge Rd East Stroudsburg (18301) *(G-4621)*

Irish Edition 215 836-4900
1506 Walnut Ave Oreland (19075) *(G-13023)*

Irish Network Philadelphia 215 690-1353
7 S Cedar Ln Upper Darby (19082) *(G-18687)*

IRM, Philadelphia *Also called International Raw Mtls Ltd (G-13867)*

Iroko Intermediate Holdings 267 546-3003
1 Crescent Dr Ste 400 Philadelphia (19112) *(G-13874)*

Iroko Pharmaceuticals Inc 267 546-3003
1 Kew Pl 150 Rouse Blvd St 1 Kew Pla Philadelphia (19112) *(G-13875)*

Iroko Pharmaceuticals LLC (PA) 267 546-3003
1 Kew Pl 150 Rouse Blvd St 1 Kew Pla Philadelphia (19112) *(G-13876)*

Iron Art, Danville *Also called Frank Bellace Welding (G-4002)*

Iron City Brewing Company, Pittsburgh *Also called Icb Acquisitions LLC (G-15112)*

Iron Compass Map Company 717 295-1194
313 W Liberty St Ste 239 Lancaster (17603) *(G-9064)*

Iron Hill Brewery & Restaurant, Media *Also called Chesapeake Del Brewing Co LLC (G-10918)*

Iron Hose Company LLC 877 277-9035
844 E Columbus Ave Corry (16407) *(G-3765)*

Iron Lung LLC 412 291-8928
4609 Liberty Ave Pittsburgh (15224) *(G-15136)*

Ironmaster LLC 412 554-6705
401 Revere Ln Export (15632) *(G-5609)*

Ironridge 800 227-9523
7250 Hollywood Rd Ste 6 Fort Washington (19034) *(G-6077)*

Ironshore Marine LLC 484 941-3914
1713 Sawmill Rd Spring City (19475) *(G-17861)*

Ironstone Creamery 610 952-2748
3500 Coventryville Rd Pottstown (19465) *(G-15949)*

Ironstone Mills Inc 717 656-4539
334 Quarry Rd Leola (17540) *(G-9787)*

Ironwood Learning LLC 412 784-1384
101 Brilliant Ave 200 Pittsburgh (15215) *(G-15137)*

Irp Group Inc 412 276-6400
726 Trumbull Dr Pittsburgh (15205) *(G-15138)*

Irvin G Tyson & Son Inc 610 754-0930
6 Simmons Rd Perkiomenville (18074) *(G-13302)*

Irvin Plant, West Mifflin *Also called United States Steel Corp (G-19746)*

Irving K Doremus Jr 215 679-6653
2025 Ziegler Rd Pennsburg (18073) *(G-13249)*

Irvins Corp 570 539-8200
101 Cedar Ln Mount Pleasant Mills (17853) *(G-11726)*

Irwin Automation Inc 724 834-7160
715 Cleveland St Greensburg (15601) *(G-6679)*

Irwin Car & Equipment Inc 724 864-5170
9933 Broadway St Irwin (15642) *(G-8173)*

Irwin Car & Equipment Inc (PA) 724 864-8900
9953 Broadway St Irwin (15642) *(G-8174)*

Irwin Car and Equipment, Blairsville *Also called Balco Inc (G-1714)*

Irwin Concrete Co 724 863-1848
185 N Washington Rd Apollo (15613) *(G-677)*

Irwin Printing, Emlenton *Also called James Irwin (G-5012)*

IS&S, Exton *Also called Innovtive Slutions Support Inc (G-5699)*

Isaac Stephens & Assoc Inc 215 576-5414
214 Paper Mill Rd Oreland (19075) *(G-13024)*

Isabelles Kitchen Inc 215 256-7987
417 Main St Harleysville (19438) *(G-7040)*

Ishman Plastic & Wood Cutting 814 849-9961
67 S White St Brookville (15825) *(G-2262)*

Isimac Machine Company Inc (PA) 610 926-6400
Excelsr Indl Park June Av Blandon (19510) *(G-1755)*

Isimac Machine Company Inc 610 926-6400
June Ave Blandon (19510) *(G-1756)*

Ising LLC 610 216-2644
3140b W Tilghman St # 190 Allentown (18104) *(G-266)*

Islamic Communication Network 215 227-0640
2451 N 19th St Philadelphia (19132) *(G-13877)*

Island Fragrances Inc 570 793-1680
1129 Sunset Dr Pittston (18640) *(G-15759)*

Islip Transformer and Metal Co 814 272-2700
1900 W College Ave State College (16801) *(G-17978)*

Ism Enterprises Inc 800 378-3430
629 E Butler Rd Butler (16002) *(G-2411)*

Ismystuffreal.com, Pottstown *Also called Ark Ideaz Inc (G-15943)*

Isola Services Inc 724 547-5142
207 Cedar St Mount Pleasant (15666) *(G-11702)*

Isolation Technologies, Danielsville *Also called Shock Solutions Inc (G-3995)*

Isotrol Systems, Exton *Also called Bender Electronics Inc (G-5652)*

Isp Minerals, Blue Ridge Summit *Also called Specialty Granules Inc (G-1861)*

Istil (usa) Milton Inc 570 742-7420
230 Lower Market St Milton (17847) *(G-11243)*

It Sell, Sellersville *Also called Sell-It (G-17358)*

It Takes A Village To Feed 888 702-9610
112 Kearney Pl Ridley Park (19078) *(G-16739)*

Italcementi Group, Nazareth *Also called Lehigh Hanson Ecc Inc (G-11978)*

Italian Mutual Benefit Society 412 221-0751
414 Market St Bridgeville (15017) *(G-2071)*

Itc Supplies LLC 610 430-1300
1043 Andrew Dr Ste B West Chester (19380) *(G-19574)*

ITCC, Eddystone *Also called Inspro Technologies Corp (G-4804)*

Item Publications, Plymouth Meeting *Also called Robar Industries Inc (G-15868)*

Itf Pharma Inc (PA) 484 328-4964
850 Cassatt Rd Ste 350 Berwyn (19312) *(G-1366)*

ITI, Meyersdale *Also called International Trailers Inc (G-11012)*

ITI Inmate Telephone Inc 814 944-0405
5000 6th Ave Ste 1 Altoona (16602) *(G-518)*

ITI Trailers & Trck Bodies Inc 814 634-0080
8535 Mason Dixon Hwy Meyersdale (15552) *(G-11013)*

Itl Corp 814 463-7701
Russell St Rr 666 Endeavor (16322) *(G-5079)*

ITOH Denki USA Inc (HQ) 570 820-8811
2 Great Valley Blvd Wilkes Barre (18706) *(G-19930)*

Itp of Usa Inc 717 367-3670
200 S Chestnut St Elizabethtown (17022) *(G-4875)*

Its Only Cupcakes LLC 717 421-6646
90 Drummers Ln Wayne (19087) *(G-19340)*

Itsi-Biosciences, Johnstown *Also called Integrated Tech Svcs Intl LLC (G-8382)*

ITT Awt F B Leopold, Zelienople *Also called Xylem Wtr Sltons Zlienople LLC (G-20830)*

ITT Corporation 717 262-2945
1425 Excel Ave Chambersburg (17201) *(G-2944)*

ITT Corporation 717 509-2200
33 Centerville Rd Lancaster (17603) *(G-9065)*

ITT Engineered Valves LLC 717 509-2200
33 Centerville Rd Lancaster (17603) *(G-9066)*

ITT LLC 215 218-7400
1 Crescent Dr Ste 304 Philadelphia (19112) *(G-13878)*

ITT Water & Wastewater USA Inc 610 647-6620
2330 Yellow Springs Rd Malvern (19355) *(G-10256)*

ITW, Hatfield *Also called Simco Industrial Static Cntrl (G-7396)*

Iusa Wire Inc (HQ) 610 926-4141
74 Tube Dr Reading (19605) *(G-16410)*

Ivan C Dutterer Inc 717 637-8977
115 Ann St Hanover (17331) *(G-6904)*

Ivax Pharmaceuticals LLC 215 591-3000
1090 Horsham Rd North Wales (19454) *(G-12807)*

Ivd LLC (HQ) 949 664-5500
10101 Roosevelt Blvd Philadelphia (19154) *(G-13879)*

Ividix Software Inc 484 580-9601
1401 Reiner Rd Eagleville (19403) *(G-4513)*

Ivvi Media, Bryn Mawr *Also called Dooner Ventures LLC (G-2320)*

Ivy Graphics Inc 215 396-9446
29 Indian Dr Warminster (18974) *(G-18900)*

Ivy Steel & Wire Inc 570 450-2090
503a Forest Rd Hazle Township (18202) *(G-7465)*

Iwi Us Inc 717 695-2081
1441 Stoneridge Dr Middletown (17057) *(G-11058)*

Iwm International LLC (HQ) 717 637-3795
500 E Middle St Hanover (17331) *(G-6905)*

Iwm International LLC 800 323-5585
408 E Philadelphia St York (17403) *(G-20538)*

Iwom Outerwear LLC 814 272-5400
1981 Pine Hall Rd State College (16801) *(G-17979)*

Izzo Embroidery & Screen Prtg 724 843-2334
517 2nd Ave E Beaver Falls (15010) *(G-1001)*

J & Ak Inc 412 787-9750
5350 Campbells Run Rd Pittsburgh (15205) *(G-15139)*

J & B Blending & Technologies 412 331-2850
163 Nichol Ave Mc Kees Rocks (15136) *(G-10615)*

J & B Printing 570 587-4427
400 S State St Ste 1 Clarks Summit (18411) *(G-3195)*

J & D Jewelers Inc 215 592-8956
726 Sansom St Ste 1 Philadelphia (19106) *(G-13880)*

J & E Flagstone 570 869-2718
2512 Whitney Rd Laceyville (18623) *(G-8871)*

J & E Industries Inc 570 876-1361
201 S Washington Ave Jermyn (18433) *(G-8307)*

J & F Ready Mix, Williamsport *Also called Wolyniec Construction Inc (G-20097)*

J & H Concrete Co 570 824-3565
84 Scott St Wilkes Barre (18702) *(G-19931)*

J & J Carbide Tool Co Inc 570 538-9283
1199 Matthew St Watsontown (17777) *(G-19276)*

J & J Consulting Corp 610 678-6611
421 N Church Rd Wernersville (19565) *(G-19485)*

J & J Pallet Co Inc 570 489-7705
1000 Marshwood Rd Throop (18512) *(G-18359)*

J & J Precision Tech LLC 717 625-0130
10 W 2nd Ave Lititz (17543) *(G-10020)*

J & J Specialties of PA 717 838-7220
101 N Harrison St Palmyra (17078) *(G-13126)*

J & J Truck Bodies and Trlrs, Somerset *Also called Somerset Welding & Steel Inc (G-17710)*

J & J Truck Equipment, Somerset *Also called Somerset Welding & Steel Inc (G-17711)*

J & K Hydraulic Hose, Grove City *Also called J & K Industrial Sales (G-6791)*

J & K Industrial Sales 724 458-7670
Rr 58 Box E Grove City (16127) *(G-6791)*

J & L Building Materials Inc (PA) 610 644-6311
600 Lancaster Ave Malvern (19355) *(G-10257)*

J & L Logging 717 687-8096
46b Hartman Bridge Rd Lancaster (17602) *(G-9067)*

J & L Precision Machine Co Inc 610 691-8411
102 N Commerce Way Bethlehem (18017) *(G-1543)*

J & L Professional Sales Inc 412 788-4927
200 Meteor Cir Mc Kees Rocks (15136) *(G-10616)*

J & M Custom Powdr Coating LLC 717 445-4869
245 S Muddy Creek Rd Denver (17517) *(G-4077)*

J & M Industrial Coatings Inc 570 547-1825
163 Bower St Montgomery (17752) *(G-11371)*

J & M Pallet LLC 717 463-9205
506 Oak Dr Mifflintown (17059) *(G-11124)*

J & M Printing, Waynesboro *Also called Mercersburg Printing Inc (G-19418)*

J & M Woodworks, Christiana *Also called Jake Stoltzfus (G-3140)*

J & P Incorporated 610 759-2378
68 S Main St Frnt Nazareth (18064) *(G-11972)*

J & P Men's & Boy's, Nazareth *Also called J & P Incorporated (G-11972)*

J & R Beck Inc 724 981-5220
309 Penn Ave Sharon (16146) *(G-17437)*

J & R Emerick Inc 724 752-1251
140 Petrie Rd Ellwood City (16117) *(G-4940)*

J & R Metal Products LLC 717 656-6241
52 Hess Rd Leola (17540) *(G-9788)*

J & R Slaw Inc 610 852-2020
438 Riverview Rd Lehighton (18235) *(G-9717)*

J & R Wire Inc 570 342-3193
943 Sanderson Ave Scranton (18509) *(G-17245)*

J & S Fabrication Inc 717 469-1409
9330 Allentown Blvd Grantville (17028) *(G-6574)*

J & S Grinding Co Inc 814 776-1113
224 River Rd Ridgway (15853) *(G-16713)*

J & S Machining Corp 717 653-6358
3491 Back Run Rd Manheim (17545) *(G-10391)*

J & S Pizza, Natrona Heights *Also called Biagio Schiano Di Cola Debora (G-11935)*

J & S Signco Inc 717 657-3800
4315 Jonestown Rd Harrisburg (17109) *(G-7156)*

J A & W A Hess Inc (PA) 570 454-3731
10 Hess Rd Hazleton (18202) *(G-7504)*

J A & W A Hess Inc 570 271-0227
57 Old Valley School Rd Danville (17821) *(G-4007)*

J A & W A Hess Inc 570 385-0300
Coal St Schuylkill Haven (17972) *(G-17160)*

J A Brown Company 610 832-0400
1013 Conshohocken Rd # 213 Conshohocken (19428) *(G-3566)*

J A Emilius Sons Inc 215 379-6162
537 Woodland Ave Cheltenham (19012) *(G-3030)*

J A K Machine Co 610 346-6906
4740 Lehnenberg Rd Kintnersville (18930) *(G-8728)*

J A Kohlepp and Sons Stone (PA) 814 371-5200
650 Dubois St Du Bois (15801) *(G-4397)*

J A Kohlhepp Sons Inc (PA) 814 371-5200
650 Dubois St Du Bois (15801) *(G-4398)*

J A Mitch Printing & Copy Ctr 724 847-2940
2243 Darlington Rd Beaver Falls (15010) *(G-1002)*

J A Reinhardt & Co Inc 570 595-7491
3319 Spruce Cabin Rd Mountainhome (18342) *(G-11787)*

J A Smith Inc 724 295-1133
709 Market St Freeport (16229) *(G-6206)*

J and B Precision Machine Co 215 822-1400
3020 Bethlehem Pike Hatfield (19440) *(G-7355)*

J and D Custom Strings 717 252-4078
118 Brook Ln Wrightsville (17368) *(G-20239)*

J B Booth and Co (PA) 724 452-8400
1761 Rt 588 Zelienople (16063) *(G-20805)*

J B Booth and Co 724 452-1313
1761 Rte 588 W Zelienople (16063) *(G-20806)*

J B Cooper and Cooper Co Inc 724 573-9860
232 Silver Slipper Rd Hookstown (15050) *(G-7769)*

J B Kreider Co Inc 412 246-0343
1800 Columbus Ave Ste 37 Pittsburgh (15233) *(G-15140)*

J Baur Machining Inc 724 625-2680
241 Clay Avenue Ext Mars (16046) *(G-10502)*

J Benson Corp (PA) 610 678-2692
2201 Reading Ave Reading (19609) *(G-16411)*

J Brown Machine LLC 724 543-4044
991 Butler Rd Kittanning (16201) *(G-8775)*

J C H Associates Inc 610 367-5000
2204 Farmington Ave Boyertown (19512) *(G-1919)*

J C K Services 814 755-7772
Hc 1 Tionesta (16353) *(G-18372)*

J C Moore Industries Inc (PA) 724 475-3185
152 2nd St Fredonia (16124) *(G-6181)*

J C Moore Industries Sales 724 475-3185
152 2nd St Fredonia (16124) *(G-6182)*

J C Moore Sales Corp 724 475-4605
152 2nd St Fredonia (16124) *(G-6183)*

J C Penney Optical Center, West Mifflin *Also called Usv Optical Inc (G-19747)*

J C Snavely & Sons Inc (PA) 717 898-2241
150 Main St Landisville (17538) *(G-9262)*

J C Snavely & Sons Inc 717 291-8989
3149 Hempland Rd Lancaster (17601) *(G-9068)*

J C& Well Services Inc 724 475-4881
1554 N Perry Hwy Fredonia (16124) *(G-6184)*

J Carlton Jones & Associates 267 538-5009
4329 Paul St Philadelphia (19124) *(G-13881)*

J Clem Kline & Son Inc 610 258-6071
2824 Freemansburg Ave Easton (18045) *(G-4708)*

J D Enterprise-Mp LLC 215 855-4003
427 W Main St Ste 1 Lansdale (19446) *(G-9377)*

J D Kauffman Machine Sp Inc (PA) 610 593-2033
414 Newport Ave Christiana (17509) *(G-3137)*

J D Kauffman Machine Sp Inc 610 593-2033
414 Newport Ave Christiana (17509) *(G-3138)*

J D Lohr Woodworking Inc 610 287-7802
242 N Limerick Rd Schwenksville (19473) **(G-17177)**

J D M, Huntingdon Valley *Also called JDM Materials* **(G-8003)**

J D Printing Inc 724 327-0006
1811 Route 286 Pittsburgh (15239) **(G-15141)**

J D R Fixtures Inc 610 323-6599
264 Shoemaker Rd Pottstown (19464) **(G-16003)**

J Davis Printing LLC 215 483-1006
7109 Ridge Ave Philadelphia (19128) **(G-13882)**

J E M Manufacturing, Renfrew *Also called James McAtee* **(G-16640)**

J F Burns Machine, Export *Also called J F Burns Machine Co Inc* **(G-5610)**

J F Burns Machine Co Inc 724 327-2870
4583 School Rd S Export (15632) **(G-5610)**

J F Chobert Associates Inc 610 431-2200
112 Lemonton Way Wayne (19087) **(G-19341)**

J F M Philadelphia Donut Inc 215 676-0700
9834 Bustleton Ave Philadelphia (19115) **(G-13883)**

J F Rohrbaugh & Co 800 800-4353
1030 Wilson Ave Hanover (17331) **(G-6906)**

J G McGinness Prosthetics 610 278-1866
1445 Dekalb St Norristown (19401) **(G-12671)**

J G Mundy Machine LLC 610 583-1200
1224 Macdade Blvd Collingdale (19023) **(G-3405)**

J G Mundy Machine Shop, Collingdale *Also called J G Mundy Machine LLC* **(G-3405)**

J G Press Inc 610 967-4135
419 State Ave Ste 1 Emmaus (18049) **(G-5029)**

J H C Fabrications Inc 570 277-6150
2 Pine St New Philadelphia (17959) **(G-12432)**

J H R Inc 412 221-1617
533 Wshington Ave Ste 200 Bridgeville (15017) **(G-2072)**

J H Zerbey Newspapers Inc 570 622-3456
111 Mahantongo St Pottsville (17901) **(G-16082)**

J Halligan and Son, Broomall *Also called Lansdowne Ice & Coal Co Inc* **(G-2293)**

J Harris & Sons Co (PA) 412 391-5532
50 26th St Pittsburgh (15222) **(G-15142)**

J Hats, Scranton *Also called Jacobson Hat Co Inc* **(G-17246)**

J I T Tool & Die Inc 814 265-0257
7294 Route 219 Brockport (15823) **(G-2221)**

J J C L Inc 570 619-7347
6 Mountain Rd Reeders (18352) **(G-16619)**

J J Cacchio Enterprises 610 399-9750
1515 W Chester Pike A6 West Chester (19382) **(G-19575)**

J K J Tool Co 570 322-1411
2102 Marydale Ave Williamsport (17701) **(G-20026)**

J K Miller Corp 412 922-5070
80 Wabash St Pittsburgh (15220) **(G-15143)**

J K Tool Inc 724 727-2490
321 N Washington Rd Apollo (15613) **(G-678)**

J K Tool Die Co 724 339-1858
148 Prominence Dr New Kensington (15068) **(G-12347)**

J Kinderman & Sons Inc 215 271-7600
2900 S 20th St Unit 1 Philadelphia (19145) **(G-13884)**

J L Communications Inc 215 675-9133
415 Horsham Rd Horsham (19044) **(G-7826)**

J L G, Mc Connellsburg *Also called Jlg Industries Inc* **(G-10568)**

J L Logging, Ickesburg *Also called Justin L Zehr* **(G-8052)**

J L Machine & Tool, Pottstown *Also called Jay-Ell Industries Inc* **(G-16005)**

J L Screen Printing 724 696-5630
Rr 31 Ruffs Dale (15679) **(G-16873)**

J L W Ventures Incorporated 814 765-9648
290 Bigler Ave Clearfield (16830) **(G-3221)**

J M Caldwell Co Inc 610 436-9997
322 Turner Ln West Chester (19380) **(G-19576)**

J M S Fabricated Systems Inc 724 832-3640
647 Donohoe Rd Latrobe (15650) **(G-9482)**

J M Schmidt Precision Tool Co 610 436-5010
931 Newcomen Rd Chester Springs (19425) **(G-3081)**

J M Smucker Company 724 228-6633
946 Manifold Rd Washington (15301) **(G-19187)**

J M Smucker PA Inc 814 275-1323
300 Keck Ave New Bethlehem (16242) **(G-12026)**

J M T Machine Company 215 934-7600
2115 Byberry Rd Huntingdon Valley (19006) **(G-7998)**

J M Wood Products 717 483-6700
Hc 61 Allensville (17002) **(G-108)**

J Marcus Company, Pittsburgh *Also called Marcus J Wholesalers Inc* **(G-15252)**

J Margulis Inc 215 739-9100
50 Belmont Ave Apt 803 Bala Cynwyd (19004) **(G-881)**

J Mastrocola Hauling Inc 610 631-1773
2828 Breckenridge Blvd Norristown (19403) **(G-12672)**

J Maze Corp 717 329-8350
85 Overview Dr Hummelstown (17036) **(G-7915)**

J Meyer & Sons Inc (PA) 215 699-7003
Jones Ave & Chestnut St West Point (19486) **(G-19759)**

J Meyer & Sons Inc 215 324-4440
4321 N 4th St Philadelphia (19140) **(G-13885)**

J N B Screen Printing, Alburtis *Also called Jnb Screen Printing Inc* **(G-52)**

J P Cerini Technologies Inc 215 457-7337
4600 N Fairhill St Philadelphia (19140) **(G-13886)**

J P R Publications Inc 570 587-3532
115 N State St Clarks Summit (18411) **(G-3196)**

J P Tees Inc 215 634-2348
2930 Richmond St Philadelphia (19134) **(G-13887)**

J P Tine Tool Co 724 863-0332
2751 Hahntown Wendel Rd Irwin (15642) **(G-8175)**

J Penner Corporation 215 340-9700
17 Weldon Dr Doylestown (18901) **(G-4308)**

J R B Printing 570 689-9114
302 Wimmers Rd Jefferson Township (18436) **(G-8278)**

J R Finio & Sons Inc 610 623-5800
555 Baily Rd Lansdowne (19050) **(G-9435)**

J R Kline Butchery LLC 570 220-4229
3302 Route 220 New Albany (18833) **(G-12012)**

J R Kline Butchery LLC 570 220-4229
3302 Route 220 New Albany (18833) **(G-12013)**

J R M Machinery Inc 570 544-9505
14 Coal Ln Pottsville (17901) **(G-16083)**

J R Peters Inc 610 395-7104
6656 Grant Way Allentown (18106) **(G-267)**

J R Ramos Dental Lab Inc 717 272-5821
21 S 7th St Lebanon (17042) **(G-9584)**

J R Resources L P 814 365-5821
18 J R Resources Dr Ringgold (15770) **(G-16751)**

J R Young 717 935-2919
76 S Penn St Belleville (17004) **(G-1132)**

J Russel Tooling Co 724 423-2766
Poplar St Calumet (15621) **(G-2472)**

J Rybnick Mech Contr Inc 570 222-2544
1087 State Route 2035 Nicholson (18446) **(G-12616)**

J S H Enterprises Inc 814 486-3939
547 E Allegany Ave 1 Emporium (15834) **(G-5063)**

J S H Industries LLC 717 267-3566
5110 Technology Ave Chambersburg (17201) **(G-2945)**

J S Paluch Co Inc 724 772-8850
316 Thomson Park Dr Cranberry Township (16066) **(G-3825)**

J S Zimmerman Co 717 232-6842
2701 Elm St Harrisburg (17103) **(G-7157)**

J T Ltd Custom Woodworking, Exton *Also called Turner John* **(G-5740)**

J Thomas Ltd 717 397-3483
300 Richardson Dr Lancaster (17603) **(G-9069)**

J W Hoist and Crane LLC 814 696-0350
3269 Route 764 Duncansville (16635) **(G-4453)**

J W Steel Fabricating Co (PA) 724 625-1355
100 Fey Ln Mars (16046) **(G-10503)**

J W T Holding Corp (PA) 814 532-5600
124 Laurel Ave Johnstown (15906) **(G-8383)**

J W Zaprazny Inc 570 943-2860
2401 Summer Valley Rd New Ringgold (17960) **(G-12440)**

J Walker & Associates LLC 717 755-7142
3521 Thunderhill Rd York (17402) **(G-20539)**

J&B Outdoor Center 814 848-3838
1600 White Knoll Rd Ulysses (16948) **(G-18603)**

J&B Tree Service 570 282-1193
47 Pearl St Carbondale (18407) **(G-2678)**

J&J Carriers Inc 814 285-0217
754 Winegardner Rd Schellsburg (15559) **(G-17132)**

J&J Snack Foods Corp/Mia 570 457-7431
Rocky Glenn Industrial Pa Moosic (18507) **(G-11509)**

J&M Fluidics Inc 888 539-1731
851 Tech Dr Telford (18969) **(G-18297)**

J&R Cad Enterprise LLC 724 695-4279
400 Chelsea Dr Imperial (15126) **(G-8069)**

J-Air, Johnstown *Also called CFM Air Inc* **(G-8365)**

J-M Manufacturing Company Inc 814 432-2166
315 Grant St Franklin (16323) **(G-6141)**

J-M Manufacturing Company Inc 814 337-7675
15661 Delano Rd Cochranton (16314) **(G-3343)**

J-Mar Metal Fabricating Co 215 785-6521
1025 Washington Ave Croydon (19021) **(G-3920)**

J. C. Vinyl Siding, Carbondale *Also called JC Vinyl Fence Rail & Deck* **(G-2680)**

J.A. Reinhardt, Mountainhome *Also called B/E Aerospace Inc* **(G-11785)**

J/M Fence & Deck Company 610 488-7382
2209 Shartlesville Rd Mohrsville (19541) **(G-11276)**

Jaak Holdings LLC 267 462-4092
12 E Butler Ave Ste 119 Ambler (19002) **(G-582)**

Jaboa Enterprises Inc 610 703-5185
202 S 6th St Emmaus (18049) **(G-5030)**

Jabtek LLC 724 796-5656
450 Industrial Blvd New Kensington (15068) **(G-12348)**

Jack Burnley Son Stair Contrs 610 948-4166
405 Reitnour Rd Spring City (19475) **(G-17862)**

Jack Garner & Sons Inc 717 367-8866
1901 Landis Rd Mount Joy (17552) **(G-11663)**

Jack Murray Design 610 845-9154
20 Birch Dr Barto (19504) **(G-944)**

Jack OReilly Tuxedos (PA) 610 929-9409
1501 Rockland St Reading (19604) **(G-16412)**

Jack Pressman 610 668-8847
301 Montgomery Ave Bala Cynwyd (19004) **(G-882)**

(G-0000) Company's Geographic Section entry number

Jack Williams Tire Co Inc 610 437-4651
2157 Macarthur Rd Whitehall (18052) *(G-19878)*

Jack's 6 Pack Bottle Shop, State College Also called Happy Valley Com *(G-17972)*

Jackburn Corporation 814 774-3573
438 Church St Girard (16417) *(G-6392)*

Jackburn Mfg Inc 814 774-3573
438 Church St Girard (16417) *(G-6393)*

Jackie L Trout Septic 717 244-6640
57 Church Ave Felton (17322) *(G-5940)*

Jackson & Sons Machine Co 724 744-2116
104 Johntown St Harrison City (15636) *(G-7249)*

Jackson Farms Dairy 724 246-7010
6718 National Pike New Salem (15468) *(G-12445)*

Jacob B Kauffman 717 529-6522
315 Bell Rd Christiana (17509) *(G-3139)*

Jacob Casting Division, Pottstown Also called Jacob Pattern Works Inc *(G-16004)*

Jacob E Leisenring Lumber 570 672-9793
1145 Bear Gap Rd Elysburg (17824) *(G-4977)*

Jacob Gerger & Sons Inc 215 491-4659
2546 Park Rd Warrington (18976) *(G-19122)*

Jacob Holtz Company LLC (PA) 215 423-2800
10 Industrial Hwy Ste Ms6 Philadelphia (19113) *(G-13316)*

Jacob Pattern Works Inc 610 326-1100
449 Old Reading Pike Pottstown (19464) *(G-16004)*

Jacob Schmidt & Son Inc 215 234-4641
1936 Sumneytown Pike Harleysville (19438) *(G-7041)*

Jacob Siegel LP (HQ) 610 828-8400
625 W Ridge Pike Ste B105 Conshohocken (19428) *(G-3567)*

Jacobs Tool & Mfg Inc 717 630-0083
210 N Blettner Ave Ste 5 Hanover (17331) *(G-6907)*

Jacobson Hat Co Inc (PA) 570 342-7887
1301 Ridge Row Scranton (18510) *(G-17246)*

Jacobsons Farm Syrup Co 814 367-2880
234 Cooper Rd Westfield (16950) *(G-19778)*

Jacoby Transportation Inc 717 677-7733
2350 Biglerville Rd Gettysburg (17325) *(G-6302)*

Jadco Manufacturing Inc (PA) 724 452-5252
167 Evergreen Mill Rd Harmony (16037) *(G-7070)*

Jadden Inc 724 212-3715
1542 Constitution Blvd New Kensington (15068) *(G-12349)*

Jade, Huntingdon Valley Also called Pb Holdings Inc *(G-8021)*

Jade Apparel, Philadelphia Also called Jade Fashion Corporation *(G-13888)*

Jade Equipment Corporation (HQ) 215 947-3333
3063 Philmont Ave Huntingdon Valley (19006) *(G-7999)*

Jade Fashion Corporation 215 922-3953
1017 Race St Fl 4 Philadelphia (19107) *(G-13888)*

Jade Holdings Inc 215 947-3333
3063a Philmont Ave Huntingdon Valley (19006) *(G-8000)*

Jade Industries Inc 610 828-4830
101 Washington St Conshohocken (19428) *(G-3568)*

Jade Prcsion Med Cmponents LLC 215 947-5762
3063 Philmont Ave Huntingdon Valley (19006) *(G-8001)*

Jade Yoga, Conshohocken Also called Jade Industries Inc *(G-3568)*

Jadeite Foods LLC 267 522-8193
3684 Marshall Ln Bensalem (19020) *(G-1211)*

Jaeco Fluid Solutions Inc 610 407-7207
100 Quaker Ln Malvern (19355) *(G-10258)*

Jaeco Fluid Systems, Malvern Also called Jaeco Fluid Solutions Inc *(G-10258)*

Jag Fabrication LLC 724 457-2347
392 Flaugherty Run Rd Moon Township (15108) *(G-11495)*

Jaindls Incorporated 610 395-3333
3150 Coffeetown Rd Orefield (18069) *(G-13013)*

Jake Stoltzfus 717 529-4082
1644 Georgetown Rd Christiana (17509) *(G-3140)*

Jalite Inc 570 491-2205
202 7th St Matamoras (18336) *(G-10539)*

Jam Works LLC 570 972-1562
889 Route 6 Mayfield (18433) *(G-10541)*

Jamaica Way Limited 267 593-9724
2900 Island Ave Ste 2930 Philadelphia (19153) *(G-13889)*

Jamarco 814 833-3159
3316 W 22nd St Erie (16506) *(G-5333)*

James A & Paulette M Berry 814 486-2323
34 N Cherry St Emporium (15834) *(G-5064)*

James A Marquette 570 523-3873
209 N Front St Lewisburg (17837) *(G-9913)*

James A Schultz 814 763-5561
18879 Schultz Dr Saegertown (16433) *(G-16919)*

James Abbott 215 426-8070
2105 E Wishart St Philadelphia (19134) *(G-13890)*

James Austin Company (PA) 724 625-1535
115 Downieville Rd Mars (16046) *(G-10504)*

James B Carty Jr MD 610 527-0897
Bryn Mawr Medical Bryn Mawr (19010) *(G-2327)*

James C Richards 724 758-9032
380 Stamm Hollow Rd Ellwood City (16117) *(G-4941)*

James Confer 814 945-7013
37 Church St Ludlow (16333) *(G-10118)*

James Craft & Son Inc (PA) 717 266-6629
2780 York Haven Rd York Haven (17370) *(G-20759)*

James D Morrissey Inc 267 554-7946
1200 Veterans Hwy Bristol (19007) *(G-2156)*

James Derr 724 475-2094
201 Oniontown Rd Greenville (16125) *(G-6750)*

James E Krack 724 864-4150
214 Cameron Dr Irwin (15642) *(G-8176)*

James E Roth Inc 724 776-1910
9043 Marshall Rd Cranberry Township (16066) *(G-3826)*

James Eagen Sons Company 570 693-2100
200 W 8th St Wyoming (18644) *(G-20280)*

James F Geibel 724 287-1964
416 Chicora Rd Butler (16001) *(G-2412)*

James F Kemp Inc 412 233-8166
709 Miller Ave Clairton (15025) *(G-3151)*

James F Sargent 570 549-2168
6350 Route 549 Millerton (16936) *(G-11215)*

James G Beaver 570 799-0388
251 Airport Rd Catawissa (17820) *(G-2819)*

James G Bohn 717 597-1901
2205 Pikeside Dr Greencastle (17225) *(G-6619)*

James Irwin 724 867-6083
170 De Ly Bro Rd Emlenton (16373) *(G-5012)*

James J Tuzzi Jr 570 752-2704
504 Washington St Berwick (18603) *(G-1329)*

James Jesse & Co Inc 610 419-9880
950 Jennings St Unit 1b Bethlehem (18017) *(G-1544)*

James K Reisinger 717 275-2124
2877 Dobbs Rd Loysville (17047) *(G-10116)*

James K Wallick 717 471-8152
25 Dickinson Ave Lancaster (17603) *(G-9070)*

James Kirkpatrick 610 869-4412
553 S Guernsey Rd West Grove (19390) *(G-19701)*

James May Costume Co 610 532-3430
450 Macdade Blvd Folsom (19033) *(G-6026)*

James May Enterprises, Folsom Also called James May Costume Co *(G-6026)*

James McAtee 724 789-9078
101 Eckstein Dr Renfrew (16053) *(G-16640)*

James P Wolfley 570 541-0414
7718 Old Stage Rd Mc Clure (17841) *(G-10559)*

James R Hanlon Inc 610 631-9999
2550 Boulevard Of The Eagleville (19403) *(G-4514)*

James Richard Woodworking 717 397-4790
727 W Vine St Lancaster (17603) *(G-9071)*

James Saks 570 343-8150
731 Saginaw St Scranton (18505) *(G-17247)*

James Shoe Store, Waynesboro Also called Three Soles Corp *(G-19428)*

James Sluga 814 778-5100
8 Boyd St Mount Jewett (16740) *(G-11643)*

James Van Etten Furn By Design, Perkasie Also called Van Etten James *(G-13297)*

James W Quandel & Sons Inc 570 544-2261
9 Schaeffers Hill Rd Minersville (17954) *(G-11255)*

James Wood Company, Williamsport Also called Selectrim Corporation *(G-20071)*

Jameson Publishing, Erie Also called Vert Markets Inc *(G-5525)*

Jamesons Candy Inc 724 658-7441
3451 Wilmington Rd New Castle (16105) *(G-12107)*

Jamico Materials, Pocono Lake Also called H&K Group Inc *(G-15880)*

Jamies Courtside Spt & Spirits 717 757-7689
18 S Belmont St York (17403) *(G-20540)*

Jamison Bsmnt Wterproofing Inc 215 885-2424
150 Roesch Ave Oreland (19075) *(G-13025)*

Jan & Dans Jewelry (PA) 814 452-3336
28 W 8th St Erie (16501) *(G-5334)*

Jan Lew Textile Corp 610 857-8050
102d Shamrock Ln Parkesburg (19365) *(G-13176)*

Jan-Stix LLC 267 918-9561
2346 Fairway Rd Huntingdon Valley (19006) *(G-8002)*

Janatics USA Inc 610 443-2400
2004 Eberhart Rd Whitehall (18052) *(G-19879)*

Janette Jewelers 717 632-9478
25 York St Hanover (17331) *(G-6908)*

Jankensteph Inc 412 446-2777
1597 Wash Pike Ste A38 Bridgeville (15017) *(G-2073)*

Janoski Gus, Pittston Also called Tri-Our Brands *(G-15783)*

Jansen Greetings, Elysburg Also called Rekord Printing Co *(G-4980)*

Janssen Biotech Inc 610 407-0194
260 Great Valley Pkwy Malvern (19355) *(G-10259)*

Janssen Biotech Inc 610 651-6000
200 Great Valley Pkwy Malvern (19355) *(G-10260)*

Janssen Biotech Inc 610 651-7200
184 Bayberry Dr Royersford (19468) *(G-16853)*

Janssen Biotech Inc (HQ) 610 651-6000
800 Ridgeview Dr Horsham (19044) *(G-7827)*

Janssen Biotech Inc 215 325-4250
155 Great Valley Pkwy Malvern (19355) *(G-10261)*

Janssen Biotech Inc 610 651-6000
52 Great Valley Pkwy Malvern (19355) *(G-10262)*

Janssen Research & Dev LLC 610 458-2192
665 Stockton Dr Ste 104 Exton (19341) *(G-5701)*

A L P H A B E T I C

Janssen Research & Dev LLC 215 628-5000
  Welsh And Mckean Rds Spring House (19477) *(G-17882)*
Janus Biogenics LLC 814 215-3013
  330 N Point Dr Clarion (16214) *(G-3180)*
Janzer Corporation 215 757-1168
  5898 Tibby Rd Bensalem (19020) *(G-1212)*
Jara, Butler *Also called John A Romeo & Associates Inc (G-2413)*
Jarcandlestorecom 412 758-8855
  1316 Hillsdale Ave Pittsburgh (15216) *(G-15144)*
Jarden Corporation 717 667-2131
  20 Plastics Ave Reedsville (17084) *(G-16624)*
Jarden Plastic Solution, Reedsville *Also called Jarden Corporation (G-16624)*
Jarden Plastic Solutions, Reedsville *Also called Alltrista Plastics Corporation (G-16620)*
Jaren Enterprises Inc 717 394-2671
  155 E King St Lancaster (17602) *(G-9072)*
Jarex Enterprises 215 855-2149
  1141 W 8th St Lansdale (19446) *(G-9378)*
Jarmens Fashion 215 441-5242
  1207 Wedgewood Dr Warminster (18974) *(G-18901)*
Jarrett Machine Co (PA) 814 362-2755
  1061 Lafferty Ln Bradford (16701) *(G-1974)*
Jarrett Machine Co 814 362-2755
  20 Roberts St Bradford (16701) *(G-1975)*
JAS Precision Inc 215 239-7299
  355 Ramsey Rd Yardley (19067) *(G-20322)*
JAS Wholesale & Supply Co Inc 610 967-0663
  4501 Colebrook Ave Emmaus (18049) *(G-5031)*
Jasinski Dental Lab Inc 215 699-8861
  1141 Smile Ln Lansdale (19446) *(G-9379)*
Jason A Kreinbrook 724 493-6202
  1117 Carlisle St Natrona Heights (15065) *(G-11944)*
Jasper Steel Fabrication Inc 570 329-3330
  701 1st St Ste 101 Williamsport (17701) *(G-20027)*
Jat Creative Pdts Div Lafrance, Concordville *Also called La France Corp (G-3457)*
Jatco Machine & Tool Co Inc 412 761-4344
  4429 Ohio River Blvd Pittsburgh (15202) *(G-15145)*
Jaworski Sign Company, Scranton *Also called Tjaws LLC (G-17304)*
Jaws Inc 215 423-2234
  2148 E Tucker St Philadelphia (19125) *(G-13891)*
Jay Design Inc 412 683-1184
  4603 Butler St Pittsburgh (15201) *(G-15146)*
Jay Weiss Corporation 610 834-8585
  600 Germantown Pike Ste 1 Lafayette Hill (19444) *(G-8881)*
Jay Weller 215 257-4859
  119 3 Mile Run Rd Sellersville (18960) *(G-17350)*
Jay Zimmerman 717 445-7246
  859 Broad St East Earl (17519) *(G-4546)*
Jay-Ell Industries Inc 610 326-0921
  815 South St Pottstown (19464) *(G-16005)*
Jay-Mari Company, Latrobe *Also called G V D Inc (G-9477)*
Jaybird Manufacturing Inc 814 364-1800
  135 Summer Ln Centre Hall (16828) *(G-2842)*
Jayco Grafix Inc 610 678-2640
  16 Buck Run Reinholds (17569) *(G-16633)*
Jaymar Tool, Erie *Also called Lisa Mikolajczak (G-5367)*
Jays Railing & Fabrication Co 717 933-9244
  9630 Old Rte 22 Bethel (19507) *(G-1395)*
Jaz Forms 610 272-0770
  318 W Main St Norristown (19401) *(G-12673)*
Jazz Pharmaceuticals 215 832-3750
  2005 Market St Fl 21 Philadelphia (19103) *(G-13892)*
Jazz Pharmaceuticals (HQ) 215 867-4900
  1717 Langhorne Newtown Rd Langhorne (19047) *(G-9304)*
JB Anderson & Son Inc 724 523-9610
  115 Railroad St Irwin (15642) *(G-8177)*
JB Machine Inc 570 824-2003
  398 N Pennsylvania Ave Wilkes Barre (18702) *(G-19932)*
JB Mill & Fabricating Inc 724 202-6814
  2851 Eastbrook Volant Rd New Castle (16105) *(G-12108)*
JB Racing Inc 814 922-3523
  4097 Scott Rd East Springfield (16411) *(G-4599)*
JB Services of Indiana LLC 215 862-2515
  6931 Ely Rd New Hope (18938) *(G-12307)*
Jbm Metalcraft Corp 814 241-0448
  2309 Shannon Way Johnstown (15905) *(G-8384)*
Jbr Associates Inc 215 362-1318
  200 W Mount Vernon St Lansdale (19446) *(G-9380)*
Jbs, Philadelphia *Also called Jumpbutton Studio LLC (G-13914)*
Jbs Packerland Inc 215 723-5559
  741 Souder Rd Souderton (18964) *(G-17743)*
Jbs Souderton Inc (HQ) 215 723-5555
  249 Allentown Rd Souderton (18964) *(G-17744)*
Jbs Woodwork Shop 570 374-4883
  631 Lumber Hill Rd Port Trevorton (17864) *(G-15914)*
JC Printing 570 282-1187
  176 N Scott St Carbondale (18407) *(G-2679)*
JC Vinyl Fence Rail & Deck (PA) 570 282-2222
  128 Pike St Carbondale (18407) *(G-2680)*

JC Woodworking Inc (PA) 215 651-2049
  2150 Rosedale Rd Quakertown (18951) *(G-16203)*
JC Woodworking Inc 215 651-2049
  98 Tower Rd Sellersville (18960) *(G-17351)*
Jcm Audio Inc 570 323-9014
  900 Washington Blvd Williamsport (17701) *(G-20028)*
Jcpds International Centre (PA) 610 325-9814
  12 Campus Blvd Newtown Square (19073) *(G-12578)*
Jcr Sales & Mfg LLC 814 897-8870
  1133 W 18th St Ste 200 Erie (16502) *(G-5335)*
Jcs Oilfield Services LLC 814 665-4008
  111 Shady Ave Corry (16407) *(G-3766)*
JD Delta Company Inc 484 320-7600
  136 Pennsylvania Ave Malvern (19355) *(G-10263)*
JD Product Solutions LLC 570 234-9421
  3115 Route 611 Bartonsville (18321) *(G-947)*
Jd's Carribean Spice, Bartonsville *Also called JD Product Solutions LLC (G-947)*
Jdh Pacific Inc 562 926-8088
  4201 Pottsville Pike Reading (19605) *(G-16413)*
Jdl Equipment Co 215 489-0134
  107 E Court St Ste 2 Doylestown (18901) *(G-4309)*
JDM Materials (PA) 215 357-5505
  851 County Line Rd Huntingdon Valley (19006) *(G-8003)*
Jdn Block Inc 215 723-5506
  711 N County Line Rd Souderton (18964) *(G-17745)*
Jdp Therapeutics Inc 215 661-8557
  823 Jays Dr Lansdale (19446) *(G-9381)*
Je Logging 724 455-5723
  788 Clinton By Pass Rd Normalville (15469) *(G-12623)*
JE Lyons Construction Inc 724 686-3967
  174 Smiths Hill Rd Latrobe (15650) *(G-9483)*
Jean Alexander Cosmetics Inc 412 331-6069
  815 7th St Mc Kees Rocks (15136) *(G-10617)*
Jeannette Machine & Die, Manor *Also called H and H Foundry Machine Co (G-10411)*
Jeannette Shade and Novelty Co 724 523-5567
  215 N 4th St Jeannette (15644) *(G-8257)*
Jeannette Specialty Glass, Jeannette *Also called Jeannette Shade and Novelty Co (G-8257)*
Jeannette Steel & Supply Div, Greensburg *Also called Multi-Metals Co Inc (G-6691)*
Jedco Products Inc 724 453-3490
  155 Zehner School Rd Zelienople (16063) *(G-20807)*
Jeddo-Highland Coal Company (HQ) 570 825-8700
  46 Public Sq Ste 600 Wilkes Barre (18701) *(G-19933)*
Jefco Awning Manufacturing, Wynnewood *Also called Jefco Manufacturing Inc (G-20270)*
Jefco Manufacturing Inc 215 334-3220
  432 Owen Rd Wynnewood (19096) *(G-20270)*
Jeff Enterprises Inc 610 434-7353
  700 N 13th St Allentown (18102) *(G-268)*
Jeff Hills 570 322-4536
  1827 Liberty Dr Williamsport (17701) *(G-20029)*
Jeffers & Leek Electric Inc 724 384-0315
  438 Constitution Blvd New Brighton (15066) *(G-12038)*
Jefferson Memorial Park Inc (PA) 412 655-4500
  401 Curry Hollow Rd Pittsburgh (15236) *(G-15147)*
Jeffersonian Democrats, Brookville *Also called Mpc Liquidation Inc (G-2266)*
Jeffery Faust 610 759-1951
  583 Nazareth Pike Nazareth (18064) *(G-11973)*
Jeffrey L Roberts 724 627-4600
  107 E Oakland Ave Waynesburg (15370) *(G-19447)*
Jeffrey R Knudsen 717 529-4011
  6150 Street Rd Kirkwood (17536) *(G-8749)*
Jeffrey Shepler 724 537-7411
  10 W 2nd Ave Latrobe (15650) *(G-9484)*
Jeglinski Group Inc 814 807-0681
  18075 Woodland Dr Meadville (16335) *(G-10739)*
Jeld-Wen Inc 570 628-5317
  1162 Keystone Blvd Pottsville (17901) *(G-16084)*
Jeld-Wen Inc 570 889-3173
  700 W Main St Ringtown (17967) *(G-16754)*
Jeld-Wen Inc 570 265-9121
  825 Shiner Rd Towanda (18848) *(G-18431)*
Jeld-Wen Doors, Pottsville *Also called Jeld-Wen Inc (G-16084)*
Jeld-Wen Windows, Ringtown *Also called Jeld-Wen Inc (G-16754)*
Jem Graphics LLC 412 220-0290
  3189 Washington Pike Bridgeville (15017) *(G-2074)*
Jem Industries LLC 412 818-2606
  14 Sedgwick St Pittsburgh (15209) *(G-15148)*
Jem Pallets 717 532-5304
  11742 Weaver Rd Orrstown (17244) *(G-13032)*
Jemson Cabinetry Inc 717 733-0540
  1060 S State St Ste A Ephrata (17522) *(G-5112)*
Jenard Corporation 610 622-3600
  451 Penn St Lansdowne (19050) *(G-9436)*
Jeneral Machine Company 610 837-5206
  6070 Route 209 Stroudsburg (18360) *(G-18124)*
Jenkins Competition, Malvern *Also called William T Jenkins (G-10346)*
Jenkins Machine Inc 610 837-6723
  5901 Colony Dr Bethlehem (18017) *(G-1545)*
Jenkintown Electric Company, Jenkintown *Also called Leslie S Geissel (G-8294)*
Jennies Gluten Free Bakery, Moosic *Also called Red Mill Farms LLC (G-11513)*

Jennifers Cards & Gifts 412 462-8505
3411 Main St Ste 1 Homestead (15120) *(G-7689)*
Jennison Corporation 412 429-0500
54 Arch St Carnegie (15106) *(G-2771)*
Jennison Ice LLC 412 596-5914
54 Arch St Carnegie (15106) *(G-2772)*
Jennison Manufacturing Group, Carnegie *Also called Jennison Corporation (G-2771)*
Jennison Precision Machine Inc 412 279-3007
54 Arch St Carnegie (15106) *(G-2773)*
Jennmar Corp of West Virginia (HQ) 412 963-9071
258 Kappa Dr Pittsburgh (15238) *(G-15149)*
Jennmar Corporation 814 886-4121
Rr 53 Box S Cresson (16630) *(G-3899)*
Jennmar of Kentucky Inc (HQ) 412 963-9071
258 Kappa Dr Pittsburgh (15238) *(G-15150)*
Jennmar of Pennsylvania LLC (HQ) 412 963-9071
258 Kappa Dr Pittsburgh (15238) *(G-15151)*
Jenny Lee Swirl Breads, Mc Kees Rocks *Also called 5 Generation Bakers LLC (G-10597)*
Jenny Products Inc (PA) 814 445-3400
850 N Pleasant Ave Somerset (15501) *(G-17693)*
Jenny Tools, Pipersville *Also called Electroline Corp (G-14614)*
Jens Flowers & More 570 898-3176
618 N 8th St Shamokin (17872) *(G-17424)*
Jensen Machine Co Inc 724 568-3787
403 Jackson Ave Vandergrift (15690) *(G-18730)*
Jensen Manufacturing Co Inc 800 525-5245
700 Arlington Ave Jeannette (15644) *(G-8258)*
Jensen Steam Engine Mfg, Jeannette *Also called Jensen Manufacturing Co Inc (G-8258)*
Jepson Precision Tool Inc 814 756-4806
9437 State Rd Cranesville (16410) *(G-3867)*
Jeraco Enterprises Inc 570 742-9688
135 Sodom Rd Milton (17847) *(G-11244)*
Jerden Industries Inc 814 375-7822
24 W Washington Ave Du Bois (15801) *(G-4399)*
Jeremiah Junction Inc 215 529-6430
2410 Milford Square Pike Quakertown (18951) *(G-16204)*
Jerico Bolt Co 215 721-9567
381 Moyer Rd Souderton (18964) *(G-17746)*
Jerith Manufacturing LLC 215 676-4068
14400 Mcnulty Rd Philadelphia (19154) *(G-13893)*
Jerome W Sinclair 215 477-3996
888 N Lex St Philadelphia (19104) *(G-13894)*
Jerrdan Corporation 717 597-7111
Molly Pitcher Hwy Greencastle (17225) *(G-6620)*
Jerry D Watson Jr 814 355-7104
329 Old 220 Rd 220th Milesburg (16853) *(G-11152)*
Jerry G Martin 814 395-5475
1427 Sugar Loaf Rd Confluence (15424) *(G-3467)*
Jerry James Trdng As Mnls BSC 425 255-0199
4104 Fountain Green Rd Lafayette Hill (19444) *(G-8882)*
Jerry Lister Custom Upholsteri (PA) 215 639-3880
2075 Byberry Rd Ste 108 Bensalem (19020) *(G-1213)*
Jerry Lister Custom Upholsteri 215 639-3882
111 Buck Rd Unit 900 Huntingdon Valley (19006) *(G-8004)*
Jersey Chrome Plating Co 412 681-7044
144 46th St Pittsburgh (15201) *(G-15152)*
Jersey Ink, Reading *Also called Susan Becker (G-16531)*
Jersey Shore Steel Company (PA) 570 753-3000
70 Maryland Ave Jersey Shore (17740) *(G-8315)*
Jersey Shore Steel Company 570 368-2601
2800 Canfields Ln Montoursville (17754) *(G-11443)*
Jess Miller Machine Shop Inc 610 692-2193
325 Westtown Rd Ste 6 West Chester (19382) *(G-19577)*
Jesse James Beads, Bethlehem *Also called James Jesse & Co Inc (G-1544)*
Jessica Kingsley Publishers 215 922-1161
400 Market St Ste 400e Philadelphia (19106) *(G-13895)*
Jessop Steel LLC 724 222-4000
500 Green St Washington (15301) *(G-19188)*
Jet Industries LLC 724 758-5601
700 2nd St Ellwood City (16117) *(G-4942)*
Jet Industries Inc 724 452-5780
416 Halstead Blvd Zelienople (16063) *(G-20808)*
Jet Metals Inc 814 781-7399
412 Grotzinger Rd Saint Marys (15857) *(G-16982)*
Jet Plastica Industries Inc 800 220-5381
1100 Schwab Rd Hatfield (19440) *(G-7356)*
Jet Plate Inc 610 373-6600
1840 Cotton St Reading (19606) *(G-16414)*
Jet Stream Manufacturing Inc 610 532-6632
125 S Front St Darby (19023) *(G-4020)*
Jet Tool and Die, Albion *Also called Jet Tool Company Inc (G-45)*
Jet Tool Company Inc 814 756-3169
25 Euclid St Albion (16401) *(G-45)*
Jetnet Corporation (PA) 412 741-0100
505 North Dr Sewickley (15143) *(G-17396)*
Jewelstik, Linesville *Also called Hewlett Manufacturing Co (G-9981)*
Jewish Chronicle, Pittsburgh *Also called Pittsburgh Jewish Publication (G-15399)*
Jewish Chronicle 412 687-1000
5915 Beacon St Pittsburgh (15217) *(G-15153)*
Jewish Exponent Inc 215 832-0700
2100 Arch St Fl 4 Philadelphia (19103) *(G-13896)*
Jewish Publication Soc of Amer 215 832-0600
2100 Arch St Fl 2 Philadelphia (19103) *(G-13897)*
Jewish Publishing Group, Philadelphia *Also called Jewish Exponent Inc (G-13896)*
Jex Manufacturing Inc 412 292-5516
648 Chestnut St Bridgeville (15017) *(G-2075)*
JF Mill and Lumber Co 724 654-9542
1032 N Cedar St New Castle (16102) *(G-12109)*
Jfi Redi-Mix LLC 215 428-3560
18 Steel Rd W Morrisville (19067) *(G-11564)*
Jfs Welding 717 687-6554
4 Quarry Rd Paradise (17562) *(G-13160)*
JG Seating, Exton *Also called Ussc Group Inc (G-5743)*
JGM Fabricators & Constrs LLC 484 698-6201
1201 Valley Rd Coatesville (19320) *(G-3309)*
JGM Welding & Fabg Svcs Inc 610 873-0081
1201 Valley Rd Coatesville (19320) *(G-3310)*
Jiba LLC 215 739-9644
1300 Adams Ave Ste 1 Philadelphia (19124) *(G-13898)*
Jiffy Printing Inc 814 452-2067
947 W 26th St Erie (16508) *(G-5336)*
Jigging Tech LLC DBA Atoll 814 619-5187
950 Riders Rd Johnstown (15906) *(G-8385)*
Jigging Technologies LLC 814 254-4376
1008 Club Dr Johnstown (15905) *(G-8386)*
Jim Airgood Pressure Washer 814 837-7626
22 Old Mill Rd Kane (16735) *(G-8467)*
Jim Borden 570 965-2505
1325 Sheldon Hill Rd Springville (18844) *(G-17930)*
Jim Conrath 724 423-6363
2136 Route 130 Pleasant Unity (15676) *(G-15796)*
Jim E Dooley, Broomall *Also called Dooley Gasket and Seal Inc (G-2286)*
Jim Mannello 610 681-6467
1356 Route 209 Gilbert (18331) *(G-6362)*
Jim Neidermyer Poultry 717 738-1036
324 Tamarack Dr Denver (17517) *(G-4078)*
Jimmi News 215 988-9095
1234 Market St Philadelphia (19107) *(G-13899)*
Jims Soft Pretzel Bakery LLC 215 431-1045
27 Sienna Cir Ivyland (18974) *(G-8213)*
Jioios Italian Corner Inc 724 837-4576
132 Mount Odin Dr Greensburg (15601) *(G-6680)*
Jit Global Enterprises LLC 724 478-1135
2025 Shady Plain Rd Apollo (15613) *(G-679)*
Jit Silicones Plus, Oakdale *Also called Sensible Components LLC (G-12911)*
Jj Bucher Producing Corp 814 697-6593
2568 Bells Run Rd Shinglehouse (16748) *(G-17508)*
Jj Kennedy Inc (PA) 724 452-6260
1790 Route 588 Fombell (16123) *(G-6033)*
Jj Kennedy Inc 724 783-6081
10373 State Route 85 Kittanning (16201) *(G-8776)*
Jj Kennedy Inc 814 226-6320
19929 Paint Blvd Shippenville (16254) *(G-17562)*
Jj Kennedy Inc 724 357-9696
8690 Route 422 Hwy E Penn Run (15765) *(G-13228)*
Jj Kennedy Inc 724 368-8660
120 Fisher Rd Portersville (16051) *(G-15928)*
Jka Inc (PA) 412 741-9288
1718 Mount Nebo Rd Sewickley (15143) *(G-17397)*
Jklm Energy LLC 561 826-3620
2200 Georgetown Dr # 500 Sewickley (15143) *(G-17398)*
Jkr Prolift 724 547-5955
256 Brook Hollow Rd Mount Pleasant (15666) *(G-11703)*
Jl Cabinet Company 412 931-8580
128 Brookview Ln Pittsburgh (15237) *(G-15154)*
JL Clark LLC 717 392-4125
303 N Plum St Lancaster (17602) *(G-9073)*
Jl Hartman Stainless LLC 724 646-1150
903 Brentwood Dr Greenville (16125) *(G-6751)*
Jle Industries LLC (PA) 724 603-2228
119 Icmi Rd Ste 100 Dunbar (15431) *(G-4441)*
Jlg Industries Inc 717 530-9000
560 Walnut Bottom Rd Shippensburg (17257) *(G-17534)*
Jlg Industries Inc 814 623-2156
450 Sunnyside Rd Bedford (15522) *(G-1055)*
Jlg Industries Inc (HQ) 717 485-5161
1 J L G Dr Mc Connellsburg (17233) *(G-10568)*
Jlg Industries Inc 814 623-0045
441 Weber Ln Bedford (15522) *(G-1056)*
Jlg Industries Inc 717 485-5161
221 Success Dr Mc Connellsburg (17233) *(G-10569)*
Jlg Industries Inc 717 485-6464
220 Success Dr Mc Connellsburg (17233) *(G-10570)*
Jli Electronics Inc 215 256-3200
2080 Detwiler Rd Ste 2a Harleysville (19438) *(G-7042)*
Jls Automation LLC 717 505-3800
20 Innovation Dr York (17402) *(G-20541)*
JM Automation Services 215 675-0125
1800 Mearns Rd Warminster (18974) *(G-18902)*

ALPHABETIC

JM Daugherty Industries LLC 412 835-2135
3003 S Park Rd Bethel Park (15102) (G-1419)

JM Enterprise LLC 814 758-5998
634 Elm St Tionesta (16353) (G-18373)

JM Fabrications LLC 267 354-1741
220 N Main St B Sellersville (18960) (G-17352)

JM Industries Inc 724 452-6060
232 E Lancaster Rd Harmony (16037) (G-7071)

JM Smuckers Foodservice, Washington Also called J M Smucker Company (G-19187)

JM Steel, Pittsburgh Also called Frank Calandra Inc (G-15032)

JM Welding Company Inc 610 872-2049
916 Lamokin St Chester (19013) (G-3052)

Jma Group 724 444-0004
4790 W Flynn Hwy 27 Allison Park (15101) (G-454)

JMB Signs LLC 814 933-9725
616 Old Farm Ln State College (16803) (G-17980)

Jmc Engraving Inc 610 759-0140
802 Colonna Ln Nazareth (18064) (G-11974)

Jmd Company, Bethel Park Also called Johnston-Morehouse-Dickey Co (G-1421)

Jmd Ersion Ctrl Instlltons Inc 412 833-7100
5401 Progress Blvd Bethel Park (15102) (G-1420)

Jmg Inc 215 659-4087
1851 Fairview Ave Willow Grove (19090) (G-20121)

Jmh Trailers, Hamburg Also called Hill John M Machine Co Inc (G-6841)

JMJ Finishing 814 838-4050
2640 W 17th St Erie (16505) (G-5337)

Jml Industries Inc 570 453-1201
400 Jaycee Dr Hazle Township (18202) (G-7466)

Jna Materials LLC 215 233-0121
254 S Main St Ambler (19002) (G-583)

Jnb Industrial Supply Inc 412 455-5170
114 Riverview Ave Blawnox (15238) (G-1764)

Jnb Screen Printing Inc 610 845-7680
699 Huffs Church Rd Alburtis (18011) (G-52)

Jo Jan Sportsequip Co Inc 724 225-5582
W Pointe Dr Bldg 3 Washington (15301) (G-19189)

Jo MI Pallet Co Inc 570 875-3540
615 Market St Ashland (17921) (G-732)

Jo Suzy Donuts 610 279-1350
49 E 4th St Bridgeport (19405) (G-2038)

Jo-An Inc 610 664-8777
133 Montgomery Ave Bala Cynwyd (19004) (G-883)

Joan Vadyak Printing Inc 570 645-5507
321 W Ridge St Lansford (18232) (G-9448)

JOB Logging Inc 814 772-0513
3915 Montmorenci Rd Ridgway (15853) (G-16714)

Job Training Systems Inc 610 444-0868
410 Dean Dr Kennett Square (19348) (G-8515)

Job-Fab Inc 724 225-8225
295 Meadow Ave Washington (15301) (G-19190)

Jobco Mfg & Stl Fabrication 724 266-3210
800 Keystone Rd Ambridge (15003) (G-622)

Jobomax Global Ltd 215 253-3691
1229 Chestnut St 153 Philadelphia (19107) (G-13900)

Jobson Medical Information LLC 610 492-1000
11 Campus Blvd Ste 100 Newtown Square (19073) (G-12579)

Jod Contracting Inc 724 323-2124
1250 Connellsville Rd Fayette City (15438) (G-5875)

Joe Bento Construction Co Inc 215 969-1505
806 Regina St Philadelphia (19116) (G-13901)

Joe Gigliotti & Sons Ornament 610 775-3532
1530 Lancaster Ave Rear Reading (19607) (G-16415)

Joe Grow Inc 814 355-2878
442 E Linn St Bellefonte (16823) (G-1106)

Joe Jurgielewicz & Son Ltd (PA) 610 562-3825
189 Cheese Ln Hamburg (19526) (G-6842)

Joe Kuperavage 570 622-8080
916 Park Ave Port Carbon (17965) (G-15897)

Joe's Used Auto Parts Div, New Ringgold Also called J W Zaprazny Inc (G-12440)

Joel Alan, Wilkes Barre Also called Joel Mfg Co Inc (G-19934)

Joel Freidhoff 814 536-6458
151 Freidhoff Ln Johnstown (15902) (G-8387)

Joel Mfg Co Inc 570 822-1182
219 S Washington St 221 Wilkes Barre (18701) (G-19934)

Joes Welding Repairs 570 546-5223
645 Allen Dr Muncy (17756) (G-11822)

John A Manning Jr 215 233-0976
709 Bethlehem Pike Ste 2 Glenside (19038) (G-6524)

John A Romeo & Associates Inc 724 586-6961
890 Pittsburgh Rd Ste 7 Butler (16002) (G-2413)

JOHN ANTHONY JEWELERS, Bala Cynwyd Also called Jo-An Inc (G-883)

John Bachman Hvac 610 266-3877
739 2nd St Catasauqua (18032) (G-2815)

John Bean Technologies Corp 215 822-4600
400 Highpoint Dr Chalfont (18914) (G-2877)

John Beirs Studio 215 627-1410
225 Race St Fl 1 Philadelphia (19106) (G-13902)

John Carvell Logging 717 354-8136
417 E Main St New Holland (17557) (G-12254)

John Deere Authorized Dealer, Leetsdale Also called Great Lakes Power Products Inc (G-9691)

John Dibble Tree Service 814 825-4543
9470 Wattsburg Rd Erie (16509) (G-5338)

John E Stiles Jr 215 947-5571
2450a Huntingdon Pike Huntingdon Valley (19006) (G-8005)

John Eppler Machine Works 215 624-3400
206 N Washington St Orwigsburg (17961) (G-13046)

John F Biel 814 945-6306
6 Willow Ln Ludlow (16333) (G-10119)

John F Kraft 570 516-1092
1489 Bearcat Cv Auburn (17922) (G-817)

John F Martin & Sons, Stevens Also called John F Martin & Sons LLC (G-18054)

John F Martin & Sons LLC 717 336-2804
55 Lower Hillside Rd Stevens (17578) (G-18054)

John Galt Bndery Publ Svcs Inc 724 733-1439
2251 Woodmont Dr Export (15632) (G-5611)

John H Bricker Welding 717 263-5588
1354 Sollenberger Rd Chambersburg (17202) (G-2946)

John Hunt Logging 814 967-4464
33229 Terrill Rd Townville (16360) (G-18445)

John J Kelley Associates Ltd 215 545-0939
1528 Walnut St Ste 1801 Philadelphia (19102) (G-13903)

John J Peachey 717 667-9373
209 Sawmill Rd Reedsville (17084) (G-16625)

John Jost Jr Inc 610 395-5461
4344 Hamilton Blvd Allentown (18103) (G-269)

John Kegges Jr 412 821-5535
4845 Harrison St Rear Pittsburgh (15201) (G-15155)

John Koller and Son Inc 724 475-4154
1734 Perry Hwy Fredonia (16124) (G-6185)

John L Luchs Logging 814 772-5767
508 Olson St Ridgway (15853) (G-16715)

John L Mary D Shaffer 814 427-2894
186 Route 410 Punxsutawney (15767) (G-16145)

John L Stopay LLC (PA) 570 562-6541
354 N Main St Taylor (18517) (G-18259)

John M Fink Lumber 570 435-0362
77 Lumber Ln Montoursville (17754) (G-11444)

John M Rohrbaugh Co Inc 717 244-2895
237 N Church Ln Red Lion (17356) (G-16602)

John M Sensenig 717 445-4669
887 Centerville Rd New Holland (17557) (G-12255)

John Middleton Co 804 274-2000
418 W Church Rd King of Prussia (19406) (G-8636)

John O Machine Co 215 228-1155
415 W Pike St Philadelphia (19140) (G-13904)

John Pasquarello 610 825-3069
147 W 3rd Ave Conshohocken (19428) (G-3569)

John Prosock Machine Inc 215 804-0321
2250 Trumbauersville Rd Quakertown (18951) (G-16205)

John R Armstrong 717 464-3239
200 Radcliff Rd Willow Street (17584) (G-20152)

John R Bromiley Company Inc 215 822-7723
105 Bristol Rd Chalfont (18914) (G-2878)

John R Holt 814 837-8687
5531 Highland Rd Kane (16735) (G-8468)

John R Novak & Son Inc 724 285-6802
107 E Quarry St Butler (16001) (G-2414)

John R Wald Company Inc 814 643-3908
10576 Fairgrounds Rd Huntingdon (16652) (G-7947)

John Reeves & Sons Awning, Jermyn Also called Reeves Awning Inc (G-8309)

John Rock Inc 610 857-8080
500 Independence Way Coatesville (19320) (G-3311)

John Schmidt Printing Co 215 624-2945
4721 Longshore Ave Philadelphia (19135) (G-13905)

John Stephen Golob 717 469-7931
895 Shawnee Dr Harrisburg (17112) (G-7158)

John Stortz and Son Inc 215 627-3855
210 Vine St Philadelphia (19106) (G-13906)

John V Potero Enterprises Inc 215 537-3320
2100 Byberry Rd Ste 108 Philadelphia (19116) (G-13907)

John W Burdge 814 259-3901
20577 Van Buren Rd Blairs Mills (17213) (G-1711)

John W Czech 814 763-4470
17741 Brookhouser Rd Saegertown (16433) (G-16920)

John W Keplinger & Son 610 666-6191
2789 Egypt Rd Norristown (19403) (G-12674)

John W Thrower Inc (PA) 724 352-9421
409 Saxonburg Blvd Saxonburg (16056) (G-17090)

John Wall Inc 724 966-9255
440 W Greene St Carmichaels (15320) (G-2759)

John Wallace 814 374-4619
693 Bradleytown Rd Cooperstown (16317) (G-3637)

John's Custom Gluing, Quarryville Also called Stoltzfus John (G-16281)

Johnathan Stoltzfus 717 768-7922
3104 Harvest Dr Ronks (17572) (G-16808)

Johnnie Lustigs Hotdogs LLC 484 661-8333
835 N New St Bethlehem (18018) (G-1546)

Johnny Appleseeds Inc 800 546-4554
220 Hickory St Warren (16366) *(G-19034)*

Johnnys Discount Furniture 717 564-1898
3440 Derry St Harrisburg (17111) *(G-7159)*

Johns Cstm Stairways Mllwk Co 215 463-1211
2115 S 8th St Philadelphia (19148) *(G-13908)*

Johns Custom Leather 724 459-6802
523 S Liberty St Blairsville (15717) *(G-1727)*

Johns Custom Stairways & Mllwk, Philadelphia *Also called Johns Cstm Stairways Mllwk Co (G-13908)*

Johns Manville Corporation 570 455-5340
600 Jaycee Dr Hazle Township (18202) *(G-7467)*

Johns Welding Shop 814 643-4564
10321 Fairgrounds Rd Huntingdon (16652) *(G-7948)*

Johnson & Johnson 215 273-7000
7050 Camp Hill Rd Philadelphia (19118) *(G-13909)*

Johnson & Johnson Consumer Inc 717 207-3500
1838 Colonial Village Ln Lancaster (17601) *(G-9074)*

Johnson & Son Stone Works 570 278-9385
Rr 4 Montrose (18801) *(G-11467)*

Johnson Bros Machine 610 749-2313
231 Red Bridge Rd Riegelsville (18077) *(G-16745)*

Johnson Communications Inc 215 474-7411
6253 Pine St Philadelphia (19143) *(G-13910)*

Johnson Contrls Authorized Dlr, Plymouth Meeting *Also called C S Fuller Inc (G-15837)*

Johnson Contrls Authorized Dlr, Mechanicsburg *Also called Industrial Controls Inc (G-10858)*

Johnson Contrls Authorized Dlr, Pittsburgh *Also called A M Parts Inc (G-14630)*

Johnson Contrls Authorized Dlr, Alburtis *Also called Johnstone Supply (G-53)*

Johnson Controls 717 610-8100
195 Limekiln Rd New Cumberland (17070) *(G-12187)*

Johnson Controls 610 398-7260
6330 Hedgewood Dr Ste 250 Allentown (18106) *(G-270)*

Johnson Controls Inc 717 765-2461
100 Cumberland Valley Ave Waynesboro (17268) *(G-19414)*

Johnson Controls Inc 610 276-3700
550 Blair Mill Rd Ste 110 Horsham (19044) *(G-7828)*

Johnson Controls Inc 717 771-7890
631 S Richland Ave York (17403) *(G-20542)*

Johnson Controls Inc 717 771-7890
631 S Richland Ave York (17403) *(G-20543)*

Johnson Controls Inc 800 877-9675
950 Forge Ave Audubon (19403) *(G-828)*

Johnson Controls Inc 717 531-5371
500 University Dr Hershey (17033) *(G-7619)*

Johnson Controls Inc 717 815-4200
1499 E Philadelphia St York (17403) *(G-20544)*

Johnson Industries, Sharpsville *Also called Limpach Industries Inc (G-17473)*

Johnson Jerry Flagstone Quarry, Stevensville *Also called Johnson Quarries Inc (G-18059)*

Johnson Machine & Prod Inc 570 724-2042
70 Woodland Ave Wellsboro (16901) *(G-19467)*

Johnson Machine Co, Clearfield *Also called J L W Ventures Incorporated (G-3221)*

Johnson March Systems Inc 215 364-2500
220 Railroad Dr Warminster (18974) *(G-18903)*

Johnson Memorial Co (PA) 814 634-0622
20 Salisbury St Meyersdale (15552) *(G-11014)*

Johnson Pattern & Machine Shop 724 697-4079
46 Stewart St Salina (15680) *(G-17043)*

Johnson Quarries Inc 570 744-1284
15962 Route 467 Stevensville (18845) *(G-18059)*

Johnson Sawmill Logging 717 532-7784
10441 Tim Rd Orrstown (17244) *(G-13033)*

Johnson's Pharmacy, West Mifflin *Also called Johnsons Pharmaceuticals (G-19741)*

Johnson, Edwin & Sons Saw Mill, Bloomsburg *Also called Edwin Johnson & Sons (G-1780)*

Johnsonburg Press Inc 814 965-2503
517 Market St Johnsonburg (15845) *(G-8347)*

Johnsonburg Press Ofc, Johnsonburg *Also called Johnsonburg Press Inc (G-8347)*

Johnsons Frog & Rail Wldg Inc 724 475-2305
111 Shearer Rd Greenville (16125) *(G-6752)*

Johnsons Pharmaceuticals 412 655-2151
2000 Clairton Rd West Mifflin (15122) *(G-19741)*

Johnston Auto Body, Parkesburg *Also called Mega Enterprises Inc (G-13179)*

Johnston Dandy Company, The, Mill Hall *Also called H M Spencer Wire (G-11177)*

Johnston Meat Processing 814 225-3495
74 Larabee Rd B Eldred (16731) *(G-4853)*

Johnston-Morehouse-Dickey Co (PA) 412 833-7100
5401 Progress Blvd Bethel Park (15102) *(G-1421)*

Johnston-Morehouse-Dickey Co 814 684-0916
5582 E Pleasant Vly Blvd Tyrone (16686) *(G-18584)*

Johnstone Supply 610 967-9900
8000 Quarry Rd Ste A Alburtis (18011) *(G-53)*

Johnstone Supply Inc 484 765-1160
200 Boulder Dr Ste 200 # 200 Breinigsville (18031) *(G-2019)*

Johnstown America Corporation (HQ) 877 739-2006
129 Industrial Park Rd Johnstown (15904) *(G-8388)*

Johnstown Foundry Castings Inc 814 539-8840
548 Horner St Johnstown (15902) *(G-8389)*

Johnstown McHning Fbrction Inc 814 539-2209
210 Iolite Ave Johnstown (15901) *(G-8390)*

Johnstown Specialty Castings 814 535-9002
545 Central Ave Johnstown (15902) *(G-8391)*

Johnstown Tribune Democrat, Johnstown *Also called Newspaper Holding Inc (G-8412)*

Johnstown Tube Laser LLC 814 532-4121
195 Jari Dr Ste 300 Johnstown (15904) *(G-8392)*

Johnstown Wire Tech Inc 814 532-5600
124 Laurel Ave Johnstown (15906) *(G-8393)*

Johnstown Wire Technologies, Johnstown *Also called J W T Holding Corp (G-8383)*

Johnstown Wldg Fabrication Inc (PA) 800 225-9353
84 Iron St Johnstown (15906) *(G-8394)*

Joint Ammunition and Tech Inc 703 926-5509
300 Market St Johnstown (15901) *(G-8395)*

Joint Venture Between, Philadelphia *Also called Philadelphia Energy Solutions (G-14144)*

Jokers Coal & Building Sups (PA) 570 724-4912
368 Tioga St Wellsboro (16901) *(G-19468)*

Joliett Coal Co 717 647-9628
837 E Grand Ave Tower City (17980) *(G-18438)*

Jomarr Products, Dunmore *Also called Jomarr Safety Systems Inc (G-4475)*

Jomarr Safety Systems Inc 570 346-5330
1000 Meade St Dunmore (18512) *(G-4475)*

Jon Swan Inc (PA) 412 264-9000
929 2nd Ave Coraopolis (15108) *(G-3700)*

Jonas Home, Philadelphia *Also called John Beirs Studio (G-13902)*

Jonathan Fallos Cabinetmaker 610 253-4063
1158 Stones Crossing Rd Easton (18045) *(G-4709)*

Jonathan Spoon, Kempton *Also called Spoonwood Inc (G-8495)*

Jonathans Woodcraft 610 857-1359
6649 N Moscow Rd Parkesburg (19365) *(G-13177)*

Joneric Products Inc (PA) 215 441-9669
400 Babylon Rd Ste D Horsham (19044) *(G-7829)*

Jones Brewing Company Inc 724 872-2337
260 Second St Smithton (15479) *(G-17661)*

Jones Crafts Inc 610 346-6247
1860 Stony Garden Rd Kintnersville (18930) *(G-8729)*

Jones Machine Racing Products 610 847-2028
72 Annawanda Rd Ottsville (18942) *(G-13063)*

Jones Manufacturing, York *Also called Steve Jones (G-20680)*

Jones Performance Products Inc 724 528-3569
1 Jones Way West Middlesex (16159) *(G-19727)*

Jones Stone & Marble Inc 724 838-7625
1580 Woodward Drive Ext Greensburg (15601) *(G-6681)*

Jones, L H & Associates, Allentown *Also called Lloyd Jones (G-298)*

Joni Britton Logging 814 887-9920
232 Bloomster Holw Smethport (16749) *(G-17635)*

Jonny T Fletcher 814 724-6687
10921 Murray Rd Ste 540 Meadville (16335) *(G-10740)*

Joo Young Inc 267 298-0054
1823 Davisville Rd Side A Willow Grove (19090) *(G-20122)*

Jordan Acquisition Group LLC 724 733-2000
1 Technology Ln Export (15632) *(G-5612)*

Jordan David, Horsham *Also called Joneric Products Inc (G-7829)*

Jordan Draft Service 412 382-4299
1002 Oak St Clairton (15025) *(G-3152)*

Jordans Bear Den 814 938-4081
112 Ewing Rd Northpoint (15763) *(G-12864)*

Jos Pallets 570 278-8935
5495 Davis Rd Montrose (18801) *(G-11468)*

Joseph F Biddle Publishing Co 814 684-4000
1067 Pennsylvania Ave Tyrone (16686) *(G-18585)*

Joseph F Mariani Contrs Inc 610 358-9746
10 Mount Pleasant Rd Aston (19014) *(G-770)*

Joseph H Tees & Son Inc 215 638-3368
1450 Bridgewater Rd Bensalem (19020) *(G-1214)*

Joseph Jenkins Inc 814 786-9085
143 Forest Ln Grove City (16127) *(G-6792)*

Joseph Lagrua 814 274-7163
557 State Route 49 Coudersport (16915) *(G-3783)*

Joseph Lee & Son Inc 610 825-1944
38 Scarlet Oak Dr Lafayette Hill (19444) *(G-8883)*

Joseph Machine Company Inc 717 432-3442
595 Range End Rd Dillsburg (17019) *(G-4132)*

Joseph McCormick Cnstr Co Inc (PA) 814 899-3111
3340 Pearl Ave Erie (16510) *(G-5339)*

Joseph Mikstas 215 271-2419
2419 S 7th St 21 Philadelphia (19148) *(G-13911)*

Joseph Nedorezov 215 661-0600
504 Louise Ln North Wales (19454) *(G-12808)*

Joseph Nedorezov (PA) 610 278-9325
1365 Horseshoe Dr Blue Bell (19422) *(G-1837)*

Joseph Piazza 610 593-3053
398 Bryson Rd Atglen (19310) *(G-801)*

Joseph Riepole Construction 412 833-6611
2728 Gould Dr Library (15129) *(G-9955)*

Joseph T Ryerson & Son Inc 215 736-8970
20 Steel Rd S Morrisville (19067) *(G-11565)*

Josh Early Candies Inc (PA) 610 395-4321
4640 W Tilghman St Allentown (18104) *(G-271)*

A
L
P
H
A
B
E
T
I
C

Joshi Bharkatkumar 610 861-7733
1124 Linden St Frnt Bethlehem (18018) *(G-1547)*

Jost Iron Works, Allentown *Also called John Jost Jr Inc (G-269)*

Jostens Inc 814 237-5771
401 Science Park Rd State College (16803) *(G-17981)*

Journal Herald, White Haven *Also called Journal Newspapers Inc (G-19849)*

Journal Newspapers Inc 570 443-9131
211 Main St White Haven (18661) *(G-19849)*

Journal of Economic Literature, Pittsburgh *Also called American Economic Association (G-14702)*

JOURNAL OF ECUMENICAL STUDIES, Philadelphia *Also called Dialogue Institute (G-13628)*

Journal Register Company 610 323-3000
390 Eagleview Blvd Exton (19341) *(G-5702)*

Journal Register Company 610 280-2295
390 Eagleview Blvd Exton (19341) *(G-5703)*

Journal Register Company 215 368-6976
307 Derstine Ave Lansdale (19446) *(G-9382)*

Journal Register Company 610 696-1775
390 Eagleview Blvd Exton (19341) *(G-5704)*

Journals, Philadelphia *Also called Taylor & Francis Group LLC (G-14377)*

Jowitt & Rodgers Company (PA) 215 824-0401
9400 State Rd Philadelphia (19114) *(G-13912)*

Joy Cone Co (PA) 724 962-5747
3435 Lamor Rd Hermitage (16148) *(G-7589)*

Joy Dog Food, Oakdale *Also called Best Feeds & Farm Supplies Inc (G-12894)*

Joy Global Inc 814 432-1202
120 Liberty St Franklin (16323) *(G-6142)*

Joy Global Underground Min LLC 724 873-4200
2101 W Pike St Houston (15342) *(G-7872)*

Joy Global Underground Min LLC 814 676-8531
Rr 8 Box North Franklin (16323) *(G-6143)*

Joy Global Underground Min LLC 724 915-2200
601 Lucerne Rd Homer City (15748) *(G-7677)*

Joy Global Underground Min LLC 724 873-4200
2101 W Pike St Houston (15342) *(G-7873)*

Joy Global Underground Min LLC (HQ) 724 779-4500
40 Pennwood Pl Ste 100 Warrendale (15086) *(G-19083)*

Joy Global Underground Min LLC 814 432-1647
325 Buffalo St Franklin (16323) *(G-6144)*

Joy Global Underground Min LLC 814 437-5731
120 Liberty St Franklin (16323) *(G-6145)*

Joy Mining, Franklin *Also called Joy Global Inc (G-6142)*

Joy Mining Machinery, Houston *Also called Joy Global Underground Min LLC (G-7872)*

Joy Mining Machinery, Franklin *Also called Joy Global Underground Min LLC (G-6145)*

Joyce Inc 206 937-4633
38 Southern Ave Ste 1 Pittsburgh (15211) *(G-15156)*

Joyce Langelier 610 659-8859
463 N Mill Rd Kennett Square (19348) *(G-8516)*

Joyce Stair Corp 570 345-8000
23 Roberts Rd Pine Grove (17963) *(G-14594)*

JP Betz Inc 610 458-8787
18 Normandy Cir Glenmoore (19343) *(G-6468)*

Jpa Printing 610 270-8855
1716 Glenn Ln Blue Bell (19422) *(G-1838)*

JPK Secure Healthcare Solution, Paoli *Also called Tcg Document Solutions LLC (G-13150)*

Jpms Manufacturing LLC 610 373-1007
237 Buttonwood St Reading (19601) *(G-16416)*

Jpmw Partners LLC 484 888-8558
3127 Lower Valley Rd Parkesburg (19365) *(G-13178)*

Jpw Design & Manufacturing Inc 570 995-5025
6080 State Route 14 Trout Run (17771) *(G-18515)*

Jr Machine & Tool Inc 610 873-4100
1100 Bondsville Rd Downingtown (19335) *(G-4236)*

Jr Metal, Leola *Also called J & R Metal Products LLC (G-9788)*

Jr Ramos Recording, Lebanon *Also called J R Ramos Dental Lab Inc (G-9584)*

JRKN Industries LLC 717 324-3996
2765 Pilgrim Rd York (17406) *(G-20545)*

Jrm Pallets Inc 717 926-6812
212 E Mill Ave Myerstown (17067) *(G-11888)*

Jrt Calibration Services Inc 610 327-9610
581b W High St Pottstown (19464) *(G-16006)*

JS Little Publication 412 343-5288
2120 Greentree Rd Apt 310 Pittsburgh (15220) *(G-15157)*

JS&d Graphics Inc 717 397-3440
1770 Hempstead Rd Lancaster (17601) *(G-9075)*

Jskc LLC 724 933-5575
2602 Fountain Hills Dr Wexford (15090) *(G-19809)*

Jsp International Group Ltd (HQ) 610 651-8600
1285 Drummers Ln Ste 301 Wayne (19087) *(G-19342)*

Jsp International LLC (HQ) 610 651-8600
1285 Drummers Ln Ste 301 Wayne (19087) *(G-19343)*

Jsp International LLC 724 477-5100
150 Eastbrook Ln Butler (16002) *(G-2415)*

Jsp Resins LLC 610 651-8600
1285 Drummers Ln Ste 301 Wayne (19087) *(G-19344)*

Jst Corporation 717 920-7700
1501 Fulling Mill Rd Middletown (17057) *(G-11059)*

Jt Industries, Meadville *Also called Jonny T Fletcher (G-10740)*

Jt-Mesh Diagnostics LLC 610 299-7482
900 Merrybell Ln Kennett Square (19348) *(G-8517)*

Jtm Foods LLC 814 899-0886
2126 E 33rd St Erie (16510) *(G-5340)*

Judge Excavating and Pav Ink, Collegeville *Also called William J Judge (G-3400)*

Judson A Smith Company 610 367-2021
857-863 Sweinhart Rd Boyertown (19512) *(G-1920)*

Judy Raymond Corporation 814 677-4058
10 Myers St Rouseville (16344) *(G-16837)*

Juergensen Defense Corporation 814 395-9509
1448 Polk Hill Rd Addison (15411) *(G-27)*

Juice Merchant 215 483-8888
4330 Main St Philadelphia (19127) *(G-13913)*

Jujama Inc 570 209-7670
600 Jefferson Ave Scranton (18510) *(G-17248)*

Julabo Usa Inc 610 231-0250
884 Marcon Blvd Allentown (18109) *(G-272)*

Julabo West Inc 610 231-0250
754 Roble Rd Ste 180 Allentown (18109) *(G-273)*

Juline-Titans LLC 412 352-4744
32 39th St Pittsburgh (15201) *(G-15158)*

Jumpbutton Studio LLC 267 407-7535
4738 Meridian St Philadelphia (19136) *(G-13914)*

Jumpers Shoe Service 717 766-3422
106 E Main St Frnt Mechanicsburg (17055) *(G-10860)*

Juniata Concrete Co (PA) 717 436-2176
721 Smith Rd Mifflintown (17059) *(G-11125)*

Juniata Concrete Co 717 567-3183
2320 Keystone Way Newport (17074) *(G-12491)*

Juniata Concrete Co 717 248-9677
2 Silversand Ave Lewistown (17044) *(G-9937)*

Juniata Fabrics Inc 814 944-9381
1301 Broadway Altoona (16601) *(G-519)*

Juniata Packing Co, Tyrone *Also called Cck Inc (G-18578)*

Junior Coal Contracting Inc 814 342-2012
2330 Six Mile Rd Philipsburg (16866) *(G-14516)*

Just Born Inc (PA) 610 867-7568
1300 Stefko Blvd Bethlehem (18017) *(G-1548)*

Just Born Inc 215 335-4500
7701 State Rd Philadelphia (19136) *(G-13915)*

Just Born Quality Confections, Bethlehem *Also called Just Born Inc (G-1548)*

Just Kidstuff Inc 610 336-9200
6520 Stonegate Dr Ste 160 Allentown (18106) *(G-274)*

Just Normlicht Inc 267 852-2200
2000 Cabot Blvd W Ste 120 Langhorne (19047) *(G-9305)*

Just Play 215 953-1208
6 Terry Dr Ste 300 Newtown (18940) *(G-12513)*

Justfroyo Inc 215 355-7555
70 E Street Rd Feasterville Trevose (19053) *(G-5914)*

Justi Group Inc (PA) 484 318-7158
804 Old Lancaster Rd Berwyn (19312) *(G-1367)*

Justick & Justick Inc 570 840-0187
888 State Route 307 Sprng Brk Twp (18444) *(G-17933)*

Justin L Zehr 717 582-6436
68 Reisinger Rd Ickesburg (17037) *(G-8052)*

JV Manufacturing Co Inc 724 224-1704
1603 Burtner Rd Natrona Heights (15065) *(G-11945)*

JW Aluminum Company 570 323-4430
2475 Trenton Ave Williamsport (17701) *(G-20030)*

Jwf Defense Systems LLC 814 539-6922
84 Iron St Johnstown (15906) *(G-8396)*

Jwf Industries, Johnstown *Also called Johnstown Wldg Fabrication Inc (G-8394)*

Jwi Architectural Millwork Inc 717 328-5880
209 Oregon St Mercersburg (17236) *(G-10988)*

Jyoti N Stand 215 843-5354
176 W Chelten Ave Philadelphia (19144) *(G-13916)*

Jyoti Natural Foods, Berwyn *Also called Gourmail Inc (G-1364)*

K & A Tool Co 814 835-1405
5208 Laurelwood Ct Erie (16506) *(G-5341)*

K & B Aqua Express Co LLC 215 343-2247
3169 County Line Rd Chalfont (18914) *(G-2879)*

K & B Outfitters Inc 724 266-1133
514 Merchant St Ambridge (15003) *(G-623)*

K & C Machine 724 266-1737
3086 Sylvan Rd Ambridge (15003) *(G-624)*

K & C Machining Company Inc 610 588-6749
2132 Lake Minsi Dr Bangor (18013) *(G-917)*

K & F Printing Systems Intl, Quakertown *Also called Glunz & Jensen K&F Inc (G-16198)*

K & H Cabinet Company Inc 717 949-6551
320 Stricklerstown Rd Newmanstown (17073) *(G-12478)*

K & H Die and Mold Inc 814 445-9584
648 W Bakersville Edie Rd Somerset (15501) *(G-17694)*

K & H Industrial Filtration, Green Lane *Also called Matthew McKeon (G-6589)*

K & H Pharma LLC 267 893-6578
3805 Old Easton Rd Ofc 20 Doylestown (18902) *(G-4310)*

K & I Sheet Metal Inc 412 781-8111
2010 Chapman St Pittsburgh (15215) *(G-15159)*

K & J Magnetics Inc 215 766-8055
18 Appletree Ln Pipersville (18947) *(G-14617)*

K & K Coal Company 570 622-0210
133 Valley Furnace Ave Port Carbon (17965) *(G-15898)*

K & K Mine Products Inc 724 463-5000
200 Airport Rd Indiana (15701) *(G-8109)*

K & K Precision Enterprises 215 364-4120
6109 Haring Rd Perkasie (18944) *(G-13280)*

K & K Precision Grinding Co 215 333-1276
6795 State Rd Rear Philadelphia (19135) *(G-13917)*

K & L Feeds, Selinsgrove Also called Empire Kosher Poultry Inc *(G-17324)*

K & L Machining Inc 717 656-0948
50 Trinity Dr Leola (17540) *(G-9789)*

K & L Operating Co 215 646-0760
155 N Ridge Ave Ambler (19002) *(G-584)*

K & L Woodworking Inc 610 372-0738
440 N 4th St Reading (19601) *(G-16417)*

K & M Wood Products 814 967-4613
36529 Tryonville Rd Centerville (16404) *(G-2834)*

K & N Enterprises Inc 724 334-0698
112 Sunny Ridge Ln New Kensington (15068) *(G-12350)*

K & N Machine Shop LLC 717 624-3403
925 Kohler Mill Rd New Oxford (17350) *(G-12412)*

K & R Skids, Hamburg Also called Timber Pallet & Lumber Co Inc *(G-6853)*

K & S Castings Inc 717 272-9775
402 Schaeffer Rd Lebanon (17042) *(G-9585)*

K & S Tool & Die Inc 814 336-6932
15256 Harmonsburg Rd Meadville (16335) *(G-10741)*

K B D, Philadelphia Also called Joseph Mikstas *(G-13911)*

K B Offset Printing Inc 814 238-8445
3500 E College Ave # 1000 State College (16801) *(G-17982)*

K C I, Ardmore Also called Kane Communications Inc *(G-711)*

K C Stoves & Fireplaces Inc 610 966-3556
120 N Main St Alburtis (18011) *(G-54)*

K Castings Inc. 724 539-9753
523 Lloyd Ave Latrobe (15650) *(G-9485)*

K D & T Metals, Pottstown Also called Kendred F Hunt *(G-16007)*

K D Graphics, New Cumberland Also called Karl Dodson *(G-12188)*

K D Home & Garden Inc 610 929-5794
5369 Allentown Pike Temple (19560) *(G-18331)*

K D Machine Inc 724 652-8833
600 Gilmore Rd New Castle (16102) *(G-12110)*

K Diamond Incorporated 570 346-4684
900 Battle St Scranton (18508) *(G-17249)*

K H Controls Inc 724 459-7474
75 Innovation Dr Blairsville (15717) *(G-1728)*

K Heeps Inc 610 434-4312
721 N 17th St Allentown (18104) *(G-275)*

K J Shaffer Milled Products 570 698-8650
136 Wallace Rd Lake Ariel (18436) *(G-8889)*

K M B Inc 215 643-7999
822 Bell Ln Ambler (19002) *(G-585)*

K M E, Nesquehoning Also called Kovatch Corp *(G-12006)*

K Machine & Tool Inc 717 272-2241
554 E Walnut St Lebanon (17042) *(G-9586)*

K Matkem of Morrisville LP (HQ) 215 428-3664
6612 Snowdrift Rd Allentown (18106) *(G-276)*

K Matkem of Morrisville LP 215 295-4158
120 Enterprise Ave Morrisville (19067) *(G-11566)*

K N M, Warminster Also called Knm Machine and Tool Inc *(G-18905)*

K S A, Pittsburgh Also called Koppers Industries Del Inc *(G-15191)*

K S M Enterprises Inc 717 463-2383
224 White Pine Ln Mifflintown (17059) *(G-11126)*

K S Manufacturing Co LP (PA) 412 931-5365
4561 Peoples Rd Pittsburgh (15237) *(G-15160)*

K S Tooling Inc 717 764-5817
535 Willow Springs Ln York (17406) *(G-20546)*

K T & Co 610 520-0221
841 1/2 W Lancaster Ave Bryn Mawr (19010) *(G-2328)*

K Tool Inc 717 624-3866
99 Enterprise Dr New Oxford (17350) *(G-12413)*

K V Inc 215 322-4044
1458 County Line Rd Ste B Huntingdon Valley (19006) *(G-8006)*

K Wagner Machine Inc 610 485-3831
701 Chestnut St Marcus Hook (19061) *(G-10446)*

K&C Machine Inc 724 375-3633
310 Steel St Aliquippa (15001) *(G-77)*

K&J Machine Shop 814 364-1101
195 Sand Mountain Rd Spring Mills (16875) *(G-17888)*

K&L Machining, Leola Also called K & L Machining Inc *(G-9789)*

K&L Plating Company Inc 717 397-9819
524 E Mifflin St Lancaster (17602) *(G-9076)*

K&L Services 610 349-1358
215 N 8th St Allentown (18102) *(G-277)*

K&S Interconnect Inc (HQ) 267 256-1725
1005 Virginia Dr Fort Washington (19034) *(G-6078)*

K- Flo Butterfly 570 752-4524
600 Fowler Ave Berwick (18603) *(G-1330)*

K-B Lighting Manufacturing Co (PA) 215 953-6663
2515 Metropolitan Dr Feasterville Trevose (19053) *(G-5915)*

K-Fab Inc 570 759-8411
1408 N Vine St Berwick (18603) *(G-1331)*

K-R-K Paving LLC 267 602-7715
6631 Gillespie St Philadelphia (19135) *(G-13918)*

K-Systems Inc 717 795-7711
2104 Aspen Dr Mechanicsburg (17055) *(G-10861)*

K-Tool Inc 717 632-3015
1045 Storms Store Rd Gettysburg (17325) *(G-6303)*

K.T. Originals, Bryn Mawr Also called K T & Co *(G-2328)*

K12systems Inc 610 366-9540
7540 Windsor Dr Ste 314 Allentown (18195) *(G-278)*

K2 Concepts Inc 717 207-0820
114 Prince St Lancaster (17603) *(G-9077)*

Kaast Machine Tools Inc 224 216-8886
194 Midfield Rd Ardmore (19003) *(G-710)*

Kabar Tack and Feed 717 416-0069
35 Cashman Rd New Oxford (17350) *(G-12414)*

Kabinet Koncepts Inc 724 327-7737
4482 William Penn Hwy Murrysville (15668) *(G-11854)*

Kabrita, Pittsburgh Also called Hyproca Nutrition USA Inc *(G-15108)*

Kada Energy Resources LLC 215 839-9159
1441 S Bouvier St Philadelphia (19146) *(G-13919)*

Kadco Ceramics LLC 610 252-5424
1175 Conroy Pl Easton (18040) *(G-4710)*

Kadmon Pharmaceuticals Inc 724 778-6100
119 Commonwealth Dr Warrendale (15086) *(G-19084)*

Kaf-Tech Industries Inc 724 523-2343
1010 Harrison Ave Jeannette (15644) *(G-8259)*

Kahle Ruud, Huntingdon Valley Also called Ruud Kahle Master Goldsmith *(G-8032)*

Kahles Kitchens Inc 814 744-9388
7422 Route 36 Leeper (16233) *(G-9656)*

Kahn Lucas, Mountville Also called Kahn-Lucas-Lancaster Inc *(G-11797)*

Kahn-Lucas-Lancaster Inc (PA) 717 537-4140
306 Primrose Ln Mountville (17554) *(G-11797)*

Kahr Arms, Greeley Also called Saeilo Inc *(G-6583)*

Kaiser Mulch 610 588-8111
6 Flicksville Rd Bangor (18013) *(G-918)*

Kajevi Services LLC 215 722-0711
7229 Rising Sun Ave Philadelphia (19111) *(G-13920)*

Kal-Cameron Manufacturing 814 486-3394
221 E 2nd St Emporium (15834) *(G-5065)*

Kalamata Farms Llc 570 972-1021
1330 S Race St Allentown (18103) *(G-279)*

Kalas Mfg Inc (PA) 717 336-5575
167 Greenfield Rd Lancaster (17601) *(G-9078)*

Kalas Mfg Inc 717 335-0193
80 Denver Rd Denver (17517) *(G-4079)*

Kalco Metals, Wheatland Also called PM Kalco Inc *(G-19841)*

Kaleidas Machining Inc 814 398-4337
24195 State Highway 99 Cambridge Springs (16403) *(G-2478)*

Kalil Printing Inc 610 948-9330
241 Vaughn Rd Royersford (19468) *(G-16854)*

Kalnin Graphics Inc 215 887-3203
261 York Rd Ste A30 Jenkintown (19046) *(G-8292)*

Kalumetals Inc 724 694-2800
116 Pittsburgh St Derry (15627) *(G-4104)*

Kamila Farm LLC 570 427-8318
174 Dulcey Rd Weatherly (18255) *(G-19454)*

Kampel Enterprises Inc 717 432-9688
8930 Carlisle Rd Wellsville (17365) *(G-19478)*

Kampus Klothes Inc 215 357-0892
164 Railroad Dr Warminster (18974) *(G-18904)*

Kanawha Scales & Systems Inc 724 258-6650
579a Park Way Monongahela (15063) *(G-11309)*

Kane Communications Inc 610 645-6940
10 E Athens Ave Ste 208 Ardmore (19003) *(G-711)*

Kane Detention Products, Erie Also called Kane Innovations Inc *(G-5342)*

Kane Innovations Inc (PA) 814 838-7731
2250 Powell Ave Erie (16506) *(G-5342)*

Kane Innovations Inc 814 838-7731
226 Chestnut St Kane (16735) *(G-8469)*

Kane Republican 814 837-6000
200 N Fraley St Kane (16735) *(G-8470)*

Kapanick Construction Inc 814 763-3681
17547 State Highway 98 Meadville (16335) *(G-10742)*

Kaplan's New Model Gold Medal, Philadelphia Also called Kaplans New Model Baking
Co *(G-13921)*

Kaplans New Model Baking Co 215 627-5288
901 N 3rd St Philadelphia (19123) *(G-13921)*

Kapothanasis Group Inc 207 939-5680
2720 Walnut St Harrisburg (17103) *(G-7160)*

Kapp Advertising Services Inc (PA) 717 270-2742
100 E Cumberland St Lebanon (17042) *(G-9587)*

Kapp Advertising Services Inc 610 670-2595
4239 Penn Ave Ste 11 Reading (19608) *(G-16418)*

Kapp Advertising Services Inc 717 632-8303
300 High St Hanover (17331) *(G-6909)*

Kapp Alloy & Wire Inc 814 676-0613
1 Klein St Oil City (16301) *(G-12948)*

(PA)=Parent Co (HQ)=Headquarters (DH)=Div Headquarters

Kappa Books, Blue Bell *Also called Kappa Graphics L P* ***(G-1840)***
Kappa Books Publishers LLC 215 643-6385
6198 Butler Pike Ste 200 Blue Bell (19422) ***(G-1839)***
Kappa Graphics L P 215 542-2800
6198 Butler Pike Ste 200 Blue Bell (19422) ***(G-1840)***
Kappa Graphics L P (PA) 570 655-9681
50 Rock St Hughestown (18640) ***(G-7893)***
Kappa Map Group LLC (HQ) 215 643-5800
6198 Butler Pike Blue Bell (19422) ***(G-1841)***
Kappa Media LLC (PA) 215 643-5800
40 Skippack Pike Fort Washington (19034) ***(G-6079)***
Kappa Media Group Inc (PA) 215 643-5800
40 Skippack Pike Fort Washington (19034) ***(G-6080)***
Kappa Publishing Group Inc (PA) 215 643-6385
6198 Butler Pike Ste 200 Blue Bell (19422) ***(G-1842)***
Kappa Publishing Group Inc 215 643-6385
6198 Butler Pike Ste 200 Blue Bell (19422) ***(G-1843)***
Kappa Publishing Group Inc 215 643-6385
7002 W Butler Pike # 100 Ambler (19002) ***(G-586)***
Kappa Publishing Group Inc 215 643-6385
7002 W Butler Pike # 100 Ambler (19002) ***(G-587)***
Kappa Publishing Group Inc 215 643-6385
7002 W Butler Pike # 100 Ambler (19002) ***(G-588)***
Karadon Corporation 724 676-5790
4125 Route 22 Hwy E Blairsville (15717) ***(G-1729)***
Kardex Systems Inc (HQ) 610 296-9730
25 Industrial Blvd Paoli (19301) ***(G-13142)***
Karel Construction, Ashland *Also called Carol Fetterolf* ***(G-728)***
Karen Holbrook 724 628-3858
411 E Youghiogheny Ave Connellsville (15425) ***(G-3500)***
Karen Wrigley Dr 215 563-8440
1919 Chestnut St Lbby 105 Philadelphia (19103) ***(G-13922)***
Kares Krafted Kitchen Inc 610 694-0180
535 Washington St Freemansburg (18017) ***(G-6197)***
Karl Dodson 717 938-6132
464 Big Spring Rd New Cumberland (17070) ***(G-12188)***
Karma Industrial Services LLC 717 814-7101
275 Herman St York (17404) ***(G-20547)***
Karp Excavating Ltd 570 840-9026
100 Schlesser Rd Factoryville (18419) ***(G-5757)***
Kartri Sales Company Inc (PA) 570 785-3365
100 Delaware St Forest City (18421) ***(G-6054)***
Kasgro Rail Corp (PA) 724 658-9061
121 Rundle Rd New Castle (16102) ***(G-12111)***
Kasmark & Marshall Inc 570 287-3663
354 Sorbertown Hl Hunlock Creek (18621) ***(G-7932)***
Kassa Coal Co, Wilkes Barre *Also called Silverbrook Anthracite Inc* ***(G-19963)***
Kasunick Welding & Fabg Co Inc 412 321-2722
1476 Spring Garden Ave Pittsburgh (15212) ***(G-15161)***
Kat, Emporium *Also called Keystone Automatic Tech Inc* ***(G-5066)***
Katz Imports Inc 215 238-0197
723 Sansom St Fl 1 Philadelphia (19106) ***(G-13923)***
Katz Media Group Inc 215 567-5166
1880 Jfk Blvd Ste 703 Philadelphia (19103) ***(G-13924)***
Katz Radio, Philadelphia *Also called Katz Media Group Inc* ***(G-13924)***
Kaufer Associates Inc 814 756-4997
142 Main St E Ste 1 Girard (16417) ***(G-6394)***
Kauffman Controls, Wrightsville *Also called Kauffman Elec Contrls & Contg* ***(G-20240)***
Kauffman Elec Contrls & Contg 717 252-3667
1058 Cool Creek Rd Wrightsville (17368) ***(G-20240)***
Kauffman Woodwork, Christiana *Also called Jacob B Kauffman* ***(G-3139)***
Kauffmans Animal Health Inc 717 274-3676
21 Keystone Dr Lebanon (17042) ***(G-9588)***
Kauffmans Upholstery Inc 610 262-8298
100 Main St Northampton (18067) ***(G-12852)***
Kauffmans Welding Iron Wo 717 361-9844
3111 Sunnyside Rd Manheim (17545) ***(G-10392)***
Kauffmantreatscom LLC 717 715-6409
33 S Weavertown Rd Ronks (17572) ***(G-16809)***
Kawneer Commercial Windows LLC 724 776-7000
71 Progress Ave Cranberry Township (16066) ***(G-3827)***
Kawneer Company Inc 570 784-8000
500 E 12th St Bloomsburg (17815) ***(G-1787)***
Kawneer Company Inc 570 784-8000
201 Isabella St Pittsburgh (15212) ***(G-15162)***
Kay Core, New Kensington *Also called Rock-Built Inc* ***(G-12372)***
Kaylin Mfg Co 610 820-6224
1701 Union Blvd Ste 201 Allentown (18109) ***(G-280)***
Kaytee Products Incorporated 570 385-1530
55 N Sillyman St Cressona (17929) ***(G-3905)***
KB Alloys Holdings LLC 484 582-3520
435 Devon Park Dr Ste 200 Wayne (19087) ***(G-19345)***
KB Systems Inc 610 588-7788
90 Jacktown Rd Bangor (18013) ***(G-919)***
KB Woodcraft Inc 502 533-2773
128 Jackson St Phoenixville (19460) ***(G-14555)***
Kba North America Inc (HQ) 717 505-1150
3900 E Market St York (17402) ***(G-20548)***
Kbm Industries Inc 717 938-2870
1065b Pines Rd Etters (17319) ***(G-5550)***
Kc Signs Co, Aston *Also called Kgc Enterprises Inc* ***(G-771)***
Kc-13 LLC 484 887-8900
900 Airport Rd Ste 3b West Chester (19380) ***(G-19578)***
Kca Enterprises 724 880-2534
122 W Apple St Connellsville (15425) ***(G-3501)***
Kcf Technologies Inc 814 867-4097
336 S Fraser St State College (16801) ***(G-17983)***
KCS Energy Inc 814 723-4672
201 Wetmore St Warren (16365) ***(G-19035)***
Kdc Engineering 267 203-8487
500 Emlen Way Telford (18969) ***(G-18298)***
Kdl Industries 814 398-1555
27360 Zilhaver Rd Cambridge Springs (16403) ***(G-2479)***
Kdl Pharmaceutical Co Ltd 215 259-3024
606 Edwin Ln Hatfield (19440) ***(G-7357)***
Ke Custom PC Mfg 215 228-6437
3933 Germantown Ave Philadelphia (19140) ***(G-13925)***
Keamco Industries Inc 215 938-6050
1043 Hilton Ave Feasterville Trevose (19053) ***(G-5916)***
Keane Frac LP (HQ) 570 302-4050
14235 Route 6 Mansfield (16933) ***(G-10417)***
Keane Frac Tx LLC 570 302-4050
14235 Route 6 Mansfield (16933) ***(G-10418)***
Keane Group Holdings LLC 570 302-4050
14235 Route 6 Mansfield (16933) ***(G-10419)***
Kebb Inc 610 859-0907
213 Meetinghouse Rd Upper Chichester (19014) ***(G-18666)***
Kebeico Inc 610 241-8163
6 Dickinson Dr Ste 114 Chadds Ford (19317) ***(G-2852)***
Keebar Enterprises Inc 610 873-0150
1514 Machinery Rd West Chester (19380) ***(G-19579)***
Keebler Company 717 790-9886
5045 Ritter Rd Mechanicsburg (17055) ***(G-10862)***
Keebler Company 215 752-4010
100 Witmer Rd Ste 300 Horsham (19044) ***(G-7830)***
Keeler Instruments Inc 610 353-4359
3222 Phoenixville Pike # 100 Malvern (19355) ***(G-10264)***
Keenan and Meier LLC 215 766-3010
5191 Stump Rd Plumsteadville (18949) ***(G-15810)***
Keenan Cnstr & Excvtg Inc 610 724-4157
171 Dilworthtown Rd West Chester (19382) ***(G-19580)***
Keenan Construction & Excvtg, West Chester *Also called Keenan Cnstr & Excvtg Inc* ***(G-19580)***
Keener Coatings Inc 717 764-9412
3711 Board Rd York (17406) ***(G-20549)***
Keener Electric Motors Inc 717 272-7686
705 State Dr Lebanon (17042) ***(G-9589)***
Keeney Printing Group Inc 215 855-6116
816 W 2nd St Lansdale (19446) ***(G-9383)***
Keffer Development Svcs LLC 724 458-5289
24 Village Park Dr Grove City (16127) ***(G-6793)***
Kegges Cabinets, Pittsburgh *Also called John Kegges Jr* ***(G-15155)***
Keims Machine & Tool Co Inc 570 758-2605
454 Jackson Twp Rd Herndon (17830) ***(G-7600)***
Keiper Tech LLC 717 938-1674
30 Bridle Ct Etters (17319) ***(G-5551)***
Keith Bush Associates Inc 215 968-5255
1709 Langhorne Newtown Rd # 4 Langhorne (19047) ***(G-9306)***
Keiths Cabinet Company 814 793-2614
2181 Curryville Rd Martinsburg (16662) ***(G-10525)***
Keiths Truck Service 814 696-6008
124 Repair Rd Duncansville (16635) ***(G-4454)***
Keller Enterprises Inc 866 359-6828
507 Washington Ave Northampton (18067) ***(G-12853)***
Keller-Charles of Philadelphia, Philadelphia *Also called L & L K Incorporated* ***(G-13948)***
Kellers Creamery LLC (HQ) 215 256-8871
855 Maple Ave Harleysville (19438) ***(G-7043)***
Kelley 412 833-4559
5999 Baptist Rd Pittsburgh (15236) ***(G-15163)***
Kelley-Tron Machine Company 717 545-8814
115 Aster Dr Harrisburg (17112) ***(G-7161)***
Kellner Millwork Co Inc 412 784-1414
6301 Butler St Pittsburgh (15201) ***(G-15164)***
Kellogg Company 717 898-0161
2050 State Rd Lancaster (17601) ***(G-9079)***
Kellogg Company 570 546-0200
572 Industrial Park Rd Muncy (17756) ***(G-11823)***
Kelloggs Snacks 412 787-1183
3 Penn Ctr W Ste 120 Pittsburgh (15276) ***(G-15165)***
Kelly Custom Furn & Cabinetry 412 781-3997
5239 Butler St Pittsburgh (15201) ***(G-15166)***
Kelly Dry Ice 412 766-1555
590 Jacks Run Rd Pittsburgh (15202) ***(G-15167)***
Kelly Fuel Co Inc 610 444-5055
615 S Broad St Kennett Square (19348) ***(G-8518)***
Kelly Iron Works Inc 610 872-5436
270 S Pine St Unit 1 Hazleton (18201) ***(G-7505)***

Kelly Line Inc 570 527-6822
500 S Centre St Pottsville (17901) **(G-16085)**

Kelly Machine Works 717 273-0303
604 N 22nd St Lebanon (17046) **(G-9590)**

Kelly Precision Machining Co 717 396-8622
1895 Commerce Park E Lancaster (17601) **(G-9080)**

Kelly Printing Co, Pottsville *Also called Kelly Line Inc* **(G-16085)**

Kellys Trophies 610 626-3300
3621 Garrett Rd Drexel Hill (19026) **(G-4367)**

Kelman Bottles LLC 412 486-9100
1101 William Flynn Hwy Glenshaw (15116) **(G-6492)**

Kelman Holdings Llc 412 486-9100
1101 William Flynn Hwy Glenshaw (15116) **(G-6493)**

Keltrol Enterprises Inc 717 764-5940
140 Rose Ct York (17406) **(G-20550)**

Kemet Investment Ltd Partnr 215 822-1550
200 Highpoint Dr Ste 215 Chalfont (18914) **(G-2880)**

Kemet Investments Inc 215 822-1550
200 Highpoint Dr Ste 215 Chalfont (18914) **(G-2881)**

Kemko Industries Inc 267 613-8651
5105 Lilac Ct Upper Gwynedd (19446) **(G-18695)**

Kemosabe Inc 412 961-0190
1010 Glenn Ave Glenshaw (15116) **(G-6494)**

Kempf Building Materials, King of Prussia *Also called Sfk Ventures Inc* **(G-8672)**

Ken F Smith Custom Shtmtl LLC 717 624-4214
25 Walker Dr New Oxford (17350) **(G-12415)**

Ken Hall Machine Shop Inc 724 637-3273
384 Thompsontown Rd West Sunbury (16061) **(G-19771)**

Ken Imler 814 695-1310
795 Mountain Rd East Freedom (16637) **(G-4564)**

Ken Leaman Signs 717 295-4531
2060 Lincoln Hwy E Lancaster (17602) **(G-9081)**

Ken Weaver Meats Inc 717 502-0118
47 North St Wellsville (17365) **(G-19479)**

Ken-Co Company Inc 724 887-7070
1009 Water St Scottdale (15683) **(G-17194)**

Ken-Fab & Weld Inc (PA) 724 283-8815
145 Valvoline Rd East Butler (16029) **(G-4533)**

Ken-Fab & Weld Inc 724 283-8815
145 Valvoline Rd East Butler (16029) **(G-4534)**

Ken-Tex Corp 570 374-4476
599 S High St Selinsgrove (17870) **(G-17328)**

Kena Corporation 717 292-7097
5420 Old Carlisle Rd Dover (17315) **(G-4193)**

Kenai Associates Inc 412 655-2079
5248 Becky Dr Pittsburgh (15236) **(G-15168)**

Kenbern Storm Doors 412 678-7210
2801 5th Ave McKeesport (15132) **(G-10674)**

Kenco Construction Pdts Inc 724 238-3387
170 State Route 271 Ligonier (15658) **(G-9960)**

Kenco Fabricating, Scottdale *Also called Ken-Co Company Inc* **(G-17194)**

Kendall Healthcare Products, King of Prussia *Also called First Quality Products Inc* **(G-8618)**

Kendalls Kreations 814 427-2517
223 W Main St Big Run (15715) **(G-1656)**

Kendred F Hunt (PA) 610 327-4131
471 N Charlotte St Pottstown (19464) **(G-16007)**

Kenexa Learning Inc (HQ) 610 971-9171
650 E Swedesford Rd 2nd Wayne (19087) **(G-19346)**

Kenic Gas & Oil Company 724 445-7701
443 Donaldson Rd Fenelton (16034) **(G-5946)**

Kennametal Inc (PA) 412 248-8000
600 Grant St Ste 5100 Pittsburgh (15219) **(G-15169)**

Kennametal Inc 814 623-2711
442 Chalybeate Rd Bedford (15522) **(G-1057)**

Kennametal Inc 412 539-5000
Rr 981 Box S Latrobe (15650) **(G-9486)**

Kennametal Inc 814 624-2406
550 Sunnyside Rd Bedford (15522) **(G-1058)**

Kennametal Inc 276 646-0080
442 Chalybeate Rd Bedford (15522) **(G-1059)**

Kennametal Inc 724 864-5900
1576 Arona Rd Irwin (15642) **(G-8178)**

Kennametal Inc 724 657-1967
599 Northgate Cir New Castle (16105) **(G-12112)**

Kennebec Inc 412 278-2040
2140 Greentree Rd Pittsburgh (15220) **(G-15170)**

Kennedy Beverage LLC 724 302-0123
1523 Kennedy Blvd Aliquippa (15001) **(G-78)**

Kennedy Concrete Inc 570 875-2780
570 Dutchtown Rd Ashland (17921) **(G-733)**

Kennedy Fuels Inc 412 721-7404
223 4th Ave Ste 400 Pittsburgh (15222) **(G-15171)**

Kennedy Printing Co Inc 215 474-5150
5534 Baltimore Ave Philadelphia (19143) **(G-13926)**

Kennedy Tool & Die, Birdsboro *Also called Kw Inc* **(G-1702)**

Kennedy Tubular Products Inc 724 658-5508
430 S Cascade St New Castle (16101) **(G-12113)**

Kennedys Powder Coating 717 866-6747
410 E Lincoln Ave Myerstown (17067) **(G-11889)**

Kenneth E Decker 570 677-3710
3724 Forest St Hop Bottom (18824) **(G-7774)**

Kennett Advance Printing House 610 444-5840
101 S Walnut St Kennett Square (19348) **(G-8519)**

Kennett Square Specialties LLC 610 444-8122
546 Creek Rd Kennett Square (19348) **(G-8520)**

Kennett Steak and Mushroom, Kennett Square *Also called Kennett Square Specialties LLC* **(G-8520)**

Kenney Press, Southampton *Also called Express Printing* **(G-17810)**

Kensey Nash Corporation, Exton *Also called DSM Biomedical Inc* **(G-5668)**

Kensington High Prfmce Pdts, Vandergrift *Also called Kensington Hpp Inc* **(G-18731)**

Kensington Home Fashions, Bath *Also called Lincoln Textile Pdts Co Inc* **(G-965)**

Kensington Hpp Inc 866 318-6628
1136 Industrial Park Rd Vandergrift (15690) **(G-18731)**

Kensington Lighting Company, Greensburg *Also called Donohoe Corporation* **(G-6660)**

Kenson Plastics Inc 724 776-6820
2835 Darlington Rd Beaver Falls (15010) **(G-1003)**

Kent Studios 610 534-7777
190 Fairview Rd Woodlyn (19094) **(G-20219)**

Kentucky Berwind Land Company (HQ) 215 563-2800
1500 Market St Ste 3000w Philadelphia (19102) **(G-13927)**

Kenum Distribution LLC 814 383-2626
229 Hecla Rd Mingoville (16856) **(G-11256)**

Kenway Composites, Alum Bank *Also called Cpk Manufacturing LLC* **(G-559)**

Kepco Plant Service & Engrg Co 412 374-3410
1000 Westinghouse Dr Cranberry Township (16066) **(G-3828)**

Kepner-Scott Shoe Co 570 366-0229
209 N Liberty St Orwigsburg (17961) **(G-13047)**

Ker Communications 412 310-1973
6520 Ventura Dr Pittsburgh (15236) **(G-15172)**

Ker Custom Molders Inc 610 582-0967
5 Riga Ln Birdsboro (19508) **(G-1701)**

Kercher Enterprises Inc 717 273-2111
920 Mechanic St Lebanon (17046) **(G-9591)**

Kercher Industries, Lebanon *Also called Kercher Machine Works Inc* **(G-9593)**

Kercher Industries Inc 717 273-2111
920 Mechanic St Lebanon (17046) **(G-9592)**

Kercher Machine Works, Lebanon *Also called Kercher Enterprises Inc* **(G-9591)**

Kercher Machine Works Inc 717 273-2111
920 Mechanic St Lebanon (17046) **(G-9593)**

Kerex Inc 814 735-3838
1106 S Breezewood Rd Breezewood (15533) **(G-2003)**

Kermitool Liquidation Company 717 846-8665
401 Manor St York (17401) **(G-20551)**

Kern Brothers Lumber Inc 814 893-5042
3075 Whistler Rd Stoystown (15563) **(G-18081)**

Kern Industries Inc 814 691-4211
16 Rachael Rd Dover (17315) **(G-4194)**

Kerotest Industries Inc (PA) 412 521-4200
5500 2nd Ave Pittsburgh (15207) **(G-15173)**

Kerotest Manufacturing Corp (HQ) 412 521-4200
5500 2nd Ave Pittsburgh (15207) **(G-15174)**

Kerr Group LLC (HQ) 812 424-2904
1846 Charter Ln Ste 209 Lancaster (17601) **(G-9082)**

Kerr Group LLC 812 424-2904
1846 Charter Ln Ste 209 Lancaster (17601) **(G-9083)**

Kerr Light Manufacturing Inc 724 309-6598
761 Old State Rd Apollo (15613) **(G-680)**

Kerrico Corporation 570 374-9831
2254 Route 522 Selinsgrove (17870) **(G-17329)**

Kerry Coal Company Inc 724 535-1311
309 Industrial Park Dr Wampum (16157) **(G-18801)**

Kerry Company Inc 412 486-3388
3003 Wildwood Sample Rd Allison Park (15101) **(G-455)**

Kersey Tool and Die Co Inc 814 885-8045
272 Fairview Rd Kersey (15846) **(G-8562)**

Kerygma Inc 412 344-6062
20 Russell Blvd E Bradford (16701) **(G-1976)**

Kerygma Program, Bradford *Also called Kerygma Inc* **(G-1976)**

Keslar Lumber Co 724 455-3210
884 Buchanan Rd White (15490) **(G-19845)**

Kesser Baking Co 215 878-8080
7555 Haverford Ave Philadelphia (19151) **(G-13928)**

Kessler Industries LLC 570 590-2333
360 S 3rd St Frackville (17931) **(G-6106)**

Kestner Wood Products Inc 724 368-3605
330 Levis Rd Portersville (16051) **(G-15929)**

Kestone Digital Press 484 318-7017
37 Industrial Blvd Ste A Paoli (19301) **(G-13143)**

Kestrel Growth Brands Inc 484 932-8447
1041 W Bridge St Ste 100 Phoenixville (19460) **(G-14556)**

Kestrel Shutters & Doors Inc 610 326-6679
9 E Race St Stowe (19464) **(G-18072)**

Kettle Creek Corporation 800 527-7848
33 Sunset Dr Ottsville (18942) **(G-13064)**

Keurig Dr Pepper Inc 610 264-5151
2172 City Line Rd Bethlehem (18017) **(G-1549)**

Keurig Dr Pepper Inc 570 547-0777
121 State Route 54 Montgomery (17752) **(G-11372)**

A
L
P
H
A
B
E
T
I
C

Keurig Dr Pepper Inc 717 677-7121
45 Aspers North Rd Aspers (17304) (G-741)

Kevin OBrien Studio Inc 215 923-6378
1412 S Broad St Philadelphia (19146) (G-13929)

Kevins Wholesale LLC 570 344-9055
710 Capouse Ave Scranton (18509) (G-17250)

Kevins Worldwide, Scranton Also called Kevins Wholesale LLC (G-17250)

Kevro Precision Components Inc 814 834-5387
1273 Brusselles St Saint Marys (15857) (G-16983)

Key Dies Inc 717 838-5200
22 Landings Dr Annville (17003) (G-651)

Key Energy Services Inc 878 302-3333
2154 Greensburg Rd Ste 1 New Kensington (15068) (G-12351)

Key Ingredient Market LLC 484 281-3900
7289 Park Dr Bath (18014) (G-961)

Key Instruments, Langhorne Also called World Wide Plastics Inc (G-9336)

Key Septic Tank Company, Butler Also called James F Geibel (G-2412)

Keys Wholesale Distributors 610 626-4787
417 Lyndhurst Dr Broomall (19008) (G-2291)

Keyscripts LLC 866 446-2848
1970 Technology Pkwy Mechanicsburg (17050) (G-10863)

Keystone Abrasives Co 610 939-1060
621 Hiesters Ln Reading (19605) (G-16419)

Keystone Anthracite Co Inc 570 276-6480
259 N 2nd St Girardville (17935) (G-6406)

Keystone Automatic Tech Inc 814 486-0513
1 S Maple St Emporium (15834) (G-5066)

Keystone Automotive Inds Inc 814 467-5531
320 Dobson St Windber (15963) (G-20184)

Keystone Automotive Inds Inc 610 866-0313
3658 Route 378 Bethlehem (18015) (G-1550)

Keystone Automotive Inds Inc 717 843-8927
275a Cross Farm Ln York (17406) (G-20552)

Keystone Bolt, Pittsburgh Also called Jennmar Corp of West Virginia (G-15149)

Keystone Bolt Division, Cresson Also called Jennmar Corporation (G-3899)

Keystone Brewers, Pittsburgh Also called Pittsburgh Brewing Company (G-15388)

Keystone Cap Co Inc 717 684-3716
927 Blunstone St Columbia (17512) (G-3440)

Keystone Casework Inc 814 941-7250
2101 Beale Ave Altoona (16601) (G-520)

Keystone Cement Co 610 837-1881
557 W Uwchlan Ave Exton (19341) (G-5705)

Keystone Cement Company 610 837-1881
6507 N Bath Blvd Bath (18014) (G-962)

KEYSTONE CHARGE, Telford Also called Cornerstone Automation LLC (G-18277)

Keystone Coal Mining Corp 740 338-3100
1000 Consol Energy Dr Canonsburg (15317) (G-2598)

Keystone Coating LLC 717 440-5922
419 Glenn Ave Boiling Springs (17007) (G-1874)

Keystone Collections, Myerstown Also called Martins Wood Products LLC (G-11893)

Keystone Con Block Sup Co Inc (PA) 570 346-7701
600 Glenn St Scranton (18509) (G-17251)

Keystone Containers Inc 603 888-1315
4201 Pottsville Pike # 2 Reading (19605) (G-16420)

Keystone Containment Contrs LP 412 921-2070
250 Bilmar Dr Pittsburgh (15205) (G-15175)

Keystone Controls Company 215 355-7080
130 James Way Southampton (18966) (G-17820)

Keystone Converting Inc 215 661-9004
108 Park Dr Montgomeryville (18936) (G-11400)

Keystone Cooperage, Jefferson Also called Wilson Global Inc (G-8272)

Keystone Crystal Corporation 724 282-1506
140 Green Manor Dr Butler (16002) (G-2416)

Keystone Cstm Fabricators Inc 412 384-9131
108 Atlantic Ave Elizabeth (15037) (G-4861)

Keystone Dehorner 610 857-9728
49 Chestnut St Pomeroy (19367) (G-15890)

Keystone Diamond Blades Inc 570 942-4526
363 State Route 374 Nicholson (18446) (G-12617)

Keystone Displays Corporation 717 612-0340
230 S 2nd St Lemoyne (17043) (G-9746)

Keystone Electronics Inc 717 747-5900
2315 S Queen St York (17402) (G-20553)

Keystone Expressions Ltd 570 648-5785
583 N Oak St Coal Township (17866) (G-3279)

Keystone Fabricating Inc 610 868-0900
1220 Win Dr Bethlehem (18017) (G-1551)

Keystone Filler & Mfg Co 570 546-3148
214 Railroad St Muncy (17756) (G-11824)

Keystone Findings Inc 215 723-4600
Emlen Way Telford (18969) (G-18299)

Keystone Fire Apparatus Inc 412 771-7722
1751 Mckees Rocks Rd Mc Kees Rocks (15136) (G-10618)

Keystone Fire Co Apparatus 610 587-3859
240 N Walnut St Boyertown (19512) (G-1921)

Keystone Flashing Co 215 329-8500
5119 N 2nd St Fl 1 Philadelphia (19120) (G-13930)

Keystone Food Products Inc 610 258-2706
3767 Hecktown Rd Easton (18045) (G-4711)

Keystone Forging Company 570 473-3524
215 Duke St Northumberland (17857) (G-12868)

Keystone Foundation Service 215 968-2955
910 Creamery Rd Newtown (18940) (G-12514)

Keystone Frewrks Specialty Sls 724 277-4294
High St Ext Dunbar (15431) (G-4442)

Keystone Fuels LLC 724 357-1710
175 Cornell Rd Ste 1 Blairsville (15717) (G-1730)

Keystone Fur Dressing Inc 717 677-4553
1495 Carlisle Rd Aspers (17304) (G-742)

Keystone Granite Tile Inc 717 394-4972
1905 Olde Homestead Ln Lancaster (17601) (G-9084)

Keystone Honing Corporation 814 827-9641
11663 Mckinney Rd Titusville (16354) (G-18387)

Keystone Industries 717 866-7571
52 King St Myerstown (17067) (G-11890)

Keystone Koating LLC (HQ) 717 738-2148
295 Wood Corner Rd Lititz (17543) (G-10021)

Keystone Koating LLC 717 436-2056
583 E Industrial Dr Mifflintown (17059) (G-11127)

Keystone Leather Distrs LLC 570 329-3780
2100 Reach Rd Frnt Williamsport (17701) (G-20031)

Keystone Lime Company (PA) 814 662-2025
1156 Christner Hollow Rd Springs (15562) (G-17925)

Keystone Machine Inc 717 359-9256
115 Newark St Littlestown (17340) (G-10068)

Keystone Machinery Corporation 717 859-4977
20 Cocalico Creek Rd Ephrata (17522) (G-5113)

Keystone Metal Structures LLC 717 816-3631
792 Coble Rd Chambersburg (17202) (G-2947)

Keystone Nap LLC 215 280-6614
150 Roebling Rd Fairless Hills (19030) (G-5786)

Keystone Nitewear Co Inc (PA) 717 336-7534
550 W Route 897 Reinholds (17569) (G-16634)

Keystone North Inc 570 662-3882
310 S Main St Mansfield (16933) (G-10420)

Keystone Pallet and Recycl LLC 570 279-7236
13 Industrial Park Rd # 4 Milton (17847) (G-11245)

Keystone Pine Machine Inc Co 215 425-0605
2130 E Somerset St Philadelphia (19134) (G-13931)

Keystone Potato Products LLC 570 695-0909
2317 Shermans Mtn Rd Hegins (17938) (G-7542)

Keystone Powdered Metal Co (HQ) 814 781-1591
251 State St Saint Marys (15857) (G-16984)

Keystone Powdered Metal Co 814 368-5320
8 Hanley Dr Lewis Run (16738) (G-9876)

Keystone Powdered Metal Co 814 834-9140
967 Windfall Rd Saint Marys (15857) (G-16985)

Keystone Precast Inc 570 837-1864
3671 Paxtonville Rd Middleburg (17842) (G-11026)

Keystone Precision Inc 814 336-2187
1379 S Main St Meadville (16335) (G-10743)

Keystone Precision Machining 215 699-5553
403 Elm Ave North Wales (19454) (G-12809)

Keystone Pretzels, Lititz Also called Condor Corporation (G-10001)

Keystone Printed Spc Co LLC 570 457-8334
1001 Moosic Rd Ste 1 Old Forge (18518) (G-12967)

Keystone Printing Co 570 622-4377
11 W Savory St Pottsville (17901) (G-16086)

Keystone Printing Ink Co (PA) 215 228-8100
2700 Roberts Ave Philadelphia (19129) (G-13932)

Keystone Printing Services 215 675-6464
445 Jacksonville Rd Hatboro (19040) (G-7288)

Keystone Printing Services (PA) 215 675-6464
445 Jacksonville Rd Hatboro (19040) (G-7289)

Keystone Prtg & Graphics Inc 570 648-5785
583 N Oak St Coal Township (17866) (G-3280)

Keystone Quality Products LLC 717 354-2762
83 S Groffdale Rd Leola (17540) (G-9790)

Keystone Rail Recovery LLC 865 567-2166
70 Maryland Ave Jersey Shore (17740) (G-8316)

Keystone Ridge Designs Inc 724 284-1213
670 Mercer Rd Butler (16001) (G-2417)

Keystone Rustproofing Inc (PA) 724 339-7588
1901 Dr Thomas Blvd Ste 1 New Kensington (15068) (G-12352)

Keystone Scrw Corp 215 657-7100
535 Davisville Rd Willow Grove (19090) (G-20123)

Keystone Sftwr Solutions Inc 610 685-2111
844 Centre Ave Reading (19601) (G-16421)

Keystone Sign Service, Mount Holly Springs Also called Keystone Signs (G-11635)

Keystone Sign Systems Inc 717 319-2265
703 W Simpson St Ste 1 Mechanicsburg (17055) (G-10864)

Keystone Signs 717 486-5381
88 Cedar St Mount Holly Springs (17065) (G-11635)

Keystone Spike 717 270-2700
255 N Lincoln Ave Lebanon (17046) (G-9594)

Keystone Sporting Arms Llc 570 742-2066
155 Sodom Rd Milton (17847) (G-11246)

Keystone Spring Service Inc (PA) 412 621-4800
112 35th St Pittsburgh (15201) (G-15176)

Keystone Structures Inc 610 444-9525
705 Terminal Way Kennett Square (19348) *(G-8521)*

Keystone Surgical Systems Inc 717 412-4383
4949 Queen St Ste 104 Harrisburg (17109) *(G-7162)*

Keystone Technologies LLC (PA) 215 283-2600
1390 Welsh Rd North Wales (19454) *(G-12810)*

Keystone Test Solutions Inc 814 733-4490
2164 Lincoln Hwy Schellsburg (15559) *(G-17133)*

Keystone Truck & Trailer LLC 570 903-1902
4171 Quicktown Rd Madison Township (18444) *(G-10169)*

Keystone Truck Caps LLC 570 836-4322
3444 Sr 6 Tunkhannock (18657) *(G-18540)*

Keystone Typewriter Company 814 539-6077
1268 Oconnor St Johnstown (15905) *(G-8397)*

Keystone Uniform Cap LP 215 821-3434
2251 Fraley St Ste 8 Philadelphia (19137) *(G-13933)*

Keystone Weaving, Lebanon Also called Dwell America Holdings Inc *(G-9563)*

Keystone Welding & Fabricaton, Mansfield Also called Keystone North Inc *(G-10420)*

Keystone Wire and Cable, Bristol Also called Lynn Electronics Corp *(G-2163)*

Keystone Wireline Inc (PA) 814 362-0230
344 High St Bradford (16701) *(G-1977)*

Keystone Wood Specialties Inc 717 299-6288
2225 Old Phladelphia Pike Lancaster (17602) *(G-9085)*

Keystone Wood Turning 717 354-2435
230 S Fairmount Rd Ephrata (17522) *(G-5114)*

Keytronics Inc 814 272-2700
1900 W College Ave State College (16801) *(G-17984)*

Keywell Metals LLC 412 462-5555
890 Noble Dr West Mifflin (15122) *(G-19742)*

Keyword Communications Inc 717 481-2960
788 Winding Ln Harrisburg (17111) *(G-7163)*

Kfw Automation Inc 610 266-5731
795 Roble Rd Unit 3 Allentown (18109) *(G-281)*

Kgb Usa Inc (HQ) 610 997-1000
3864 Courtney St Ste 411 Bethlehem (18017) *(G-1552)*

Kgc Enterprises Inc (PA) 610 497-0111
142 Conchester Hwy Aston (19014) *(G-771)*

Kgm Gaming LLC 215 430-0388
4250 Wissahickon Ave Philadelphia (19129) *(G-13934)*

Khs Corp 215 947-4010
2693 Philmont Ave Rear Huntingdon Valley (19006) *(G-8007)*

Kibbes Concrete 814 334-5537
4617 State Route 49 W Mills (16937) *(G-11222)*

Kickaway, Williamsport Also called Delta Galil USA Inc *(G-20004)*

Kickup LLC 610 256-1004
31 N 2nd St 2 Philadelphia (19106) *(G-13935)*

Kiczan Manufacturing Inc 412 678-0980
3916 Crooked Run Rd North Versailles (15137) *(G-12777)*

Kidde Fire Fighting, West Chester Also called Kidde Fire Protection Inc *(G-19581)*

Kidde Fire Protection Inc (HQ) 610 363-1400
350 E Union St West Chester (19382) *(G-19581)*

Kidron Division, Montgomery Also called VT Hackney Inc *(G-11381)*

Kidsbrigade, Norristown Also called Titan Group Ltd *(G-12719)*

Kidstuff Coupon Books, Allentown Also called Just Kidstuff Inc *(G-274)*

Kiefer Coal and Supply Co 412 835-7900
5088 W Library Ave Bethel Park (15102) *(G-1422)*

Kiefer Pallet 610 599-0971
9766 N Delaware Dr Bangor (18013) *(G-920)*

Kies, Harry M Moving, Easton Also called William H Kies Jr *(G-4776)*

Kilbane Wood Creations 814 664-0563
9 Putnam St Union City (16438) *(G-18608)*

Kilimanjaro Distillery 484 661-2488
995 Postal Rd Allentown (18109) *(G-282)*

Killeen Printing Co 412 381-4090
537 E Carson St Pittsburgh (15203) *(G-15177)*

Kilolabs.com, Hatboro Also called Sentinel Process Systems Inc *(G-7304)*

Kim Kraft Inc (HQ) 814 870-9600
6485 Fairoaks Cir Fairview (16415) *(G-5830)*

Kimberly A Spickler 814 627-2316
11637 Redstone Ridge Rd Hesston (16647) *(G-7627)*

Kimberly-Clark Corporation 610 874-4331
1 Avenue Of The States Chester (19013) *(G-3053)*

Kime Cider Mill 717 677-7539
171 Church St Bendersville (17306) *(G-1139)*

Kimenski Burial Vaults 724 223-0364
1703 E Maiden St Washington (15301) *(G-19191)*

Kimjohn Industries Inc 610 436-8600
905 Fernhill Rd West Chester (19380) *(G-19582)*

Kimkopy Printing Inc 814 454-6635
2040 W 8th St Erie (16505) *(G-5343)*

Kimmels Coal and Packaging Inc 717 453-7151
401 Machamer Ave Wiconisco (17097) *(G-19895)*

Kimre Inc 305 233-4249
501 Cambria Ave # 108112 Bensalem (19020) *(G-1215)*

Kimzey Casing Service LLC 724 225-0529
1000 Sheffield St Washington (15301) *(G-19192)*

Kin-Tech Manufacturing Inc 724 446-0777
2766 Clay Pike Irwin (15642) *(G-8179)*

Kincaid Manufacturing Inc 412 795-9811
201 Sandy Creek Rd Verona (15147) *(G-18756)*

Kindle Creations Inc 215 997-6878
4355 County Line Rd Chalfont (18914) *(G-2882)*

Kinesis Software LLC 610 353-4150
2600 Andrew Rd Broomall (19008) *(G-2292)*

Kinetic 814 603-1131
2 E Maloney Rd Du Bois (15801) *(G-4400)*

Kinetic Buildings LLC 203 858-0813
4028 Filbert St Philadelphia (19104) *(G-13936)*

Kinetic Ceramics LLC 510 264-2140
4050 S 26th St Ste 200 Philadelphia (19112) *(G-13937)*

Kinetic Concepts Inc 717 558-0985
4400 Lewis Rd Harrisburg (17111) *(G-7164)*

Kinetics Hydro Inc 717 532-6016
108 E Orange St Shippensburg (17257) *(G-17535)*

Kinetigear LLC 412 810-0049
7800 Susquehanna St Pittsburgh (15208) *(G-15178)*

King Airline Tooling Co, Pittsburgh Also called Kasunick Welding & Fabg Co Inc *(G-15161)*

King Associates Ltd 717 556-5673
62 Industrial Cir Lancaster (17601) *(G-9086)*

King Coal Sales Inc (PA) 814 342-6610
602 N Centre St Philipsburg (16866) *(G-14517)*

King Coatings LLC 610 435-1212
929 N 9th St Allentown (18102) *(G-283)*

King Coils Manufacturing Inc 484 645-4054
201 Water St Boyertown (19512) *(G-1922)*

King Koil Sleep Products, Old Forge Also called Pennsylvania Bedding Inc *(G-12974)*

King Logging and Sawmill 717 365-3341
200 Joss Ln Spring Glen (17978) *(G-17873)*

King Precision Solutions LLC 877 312-3858
2200 Colonial Ave Ste 2 Erie (16506) *(G-5344)*

King Printing and Pubg Inc 814 238-2536
1305 W College Ave State College (16801) *(G-17985)*

King Publications 610 395-4074
126 N 37th St Allentown (18104) *(G-284)*

King Strength Mfg., Allentown Also called King Coatings LLC *(G-283)*

King Tester Corporation 610 279-6010
300 Schell Ln Ste 308 Phoenixville (19460) *(G-14557)*

King Tester Corporation 610 279-6010
308 Schell Ln Phoenixville (19460) *(G-14558)*

King's Country Korner, Gordonville Also called Kings Kountry Korner LLC *(G-6560)*

Kingdom Exposure Ltd 215 621-8291
4633 State Rd Drexel Hill (19026) *(G-4368)*

Kingpin Production Vans Inc 305 772-0687
6341 Memorial Rd Germansville (18053) *(G-6279)*

Kings Kountry Korner LLC (PA) 717 768-3425
101 Centerville Rd Gordonville (17529) *(G-6560)*

Kings Potato Chip Company 717 445-4521
1451 Reading Rd Mohnton (19540) *(G-11268)*

Kings Quality Foods, Mohnton Also called Kings Potato Chip Company *(G-11268)*

Kings Red Barn, Hatfield Also called Peter Mamienski *(G-7381)*

Kings Woodwork Shop 717 768-7721
181 Snake Ln Kinzers (17535) *(G-8739)*

Kingsbury Inc (PA) 215 824-4000
10385 Drummond Rd Philadelphia (19154) *(G-13938)*

Kingsbury Inc 215 824-4000
10385 Drummond Rd Philadelphia (19154) *(G-13939)*

Kingsbury Inc 215 824-4000
3615 Davisville Rd Ste 4 Hatboro (19040) *(G-7290)*

Kingsly Compression Inc (PA) 724 524-1840
3750 S Noah Dr Saxonburg (16056) *(G-17091)*

Kingston Brick Co, Pittsburgh Also called Union Min Co of Allegheny Cnty *(G-15669)*

Kinkisharyo USA Inc 724 778-0100
2100 Garden Dr Ste 201 Seven Fields (16046) *(G-17375)*

Kinloch Woodworking Ltd 610 347-2070
Rr 82 Unionville (19375) *(G-18648)*

Kinseys Archery Products Inc (PA) 717 653-9074
1660 Steel Way Mount Joy (17552) *(G-11664)*

Kinsley Concrete, York Also called Kinsley Construction Inc *(G-20554)*

Kinsley Construction Inc 717 846-6711
629 Loucks Mill Rd York (17403) *(G-20554)*

Kinsley Incorporated 215 348-7723
901 Crosskeys Dr Doylestown (18902) *(G-4311)*

Kinteco Inc 610 921-1494
4434 Kutztown Rd Temple (19560) *(G-18332)*

Kinteco Screen Printing, Temple Also called Kinteco Inc *(G-18332)*

Kinton Carbide Inc 724 327-3141
3000 Venture Ct Export (15632) *(G-5613)*

Kio Logging LLC 570 584-0283
654 Beaver Lake Rd Hughesville (17737) *(G-7895)*

Kirby Agri Inc (PA) 717 299-2541
500 Running Pump Rd Lancaster (17601) *(G-9087)*

Kirkland Printing Inc 215 706-2399
526 York Rd Willow Grove (19090) *(G-20124)*

Kirkwood Electric 814 467-7171
902 Wissinger Rd Windber (15963) *(G-20185)*

Kisel Printing Service Inc 570 489-7666
424 Boulevard Ave Dickson City (18519) *(G-4121)*

Kiser Construction, Utica *Also called Greg Kiser* ***(G-18696)***
Kish Lumber Co, Belleville *Also called David M Byler* ***(G-1130)***
Kish Printing, Burnham *Also called Semler Enterprises Inc* ***(G-2361)***
Kiski Precision Industries LLC...724 845-2799
531 Hyde Park Rd Leechburg (15656) ***(G-9646)***
Kistler & Dinapoli Inc...215 428-4740
364 W Trenton Ave Ste 4 Morrisville (19067) ***(G-11567)***
Kistler Printing Co Inc...570 421-2050
109 Prospect St East Stroudsburg (18301) ***(G-4622)***
Kitchen and Bath Concepts, West View *Also called Archetype Design Studio LLC* ***(G-19773)***
Kitchen Craft, East Earl *Also called Jay Zimmerman* ***(G-4546)***
Kitchen Express Inc...570 693-0285
55 W 7th St Wyoming (18644) ***(G-20281)***
Kitchen Express of Wyoming...570 693-0285
55 W 7th St Wyoming (18644) ***(G-20282)***
Kitchen Gallery Inc...724 838-0911
626 Alwine Curry Rd Greensburg (15601) ***(G-6682)***
Kitchens By Meade Inc...814 453-4888
2035 W 12th St Erie (16505) ***(G-5345)***
Kitchenview Custom Cabinets...717 687-6740
37 Mount Pleasant Rd Paradise (17562) ***(G-13161)***
Kitco Tool Inc...570 726-6190
21 Water St Mill Hall (17751) ***(G-11178)***
Kite Tables, Drums *Also called ABF USA Ltd* ***(G-4380)***
Kitko Wood Products Inc...814 672-3606
6098 Glen Hope Blvd Glen Hope (16645) ***(G-6426)***
Kitron Inc (PA)...814 619-0523
160 Jari Dr Ste 160 # 160 Johnstown (15904) ***(G-8398)***
Kitron Holding USA Inc (HQ)...814 467-9060
345 Pomroys Dr Windber (15963) ***(G-20186)***
Kitron Technologies Inc...814 474-4300
345 Pomroys Dr Windber (15963) ***(G-20187)***
Kittaning Paper, Kittanning *Also called Family-Life Media-Com Inc* ***(G-8769)***
Kittatinny Manufacturing Svcs...717 530-1242
160 Reading Rd Shippensburg (17257) ***(G-17536)***
KKR & Co LP...717 741-4863
76 Acco Dr York (17402) ***(G-20555)***
Klafters Inc...814 833-7444
2663 W 8th St Erie (16505) ***(G-5346)***
Klapec Excavating Inc...814 678-3478
201 Deer Run Trl Oil City (16301) ***(G-12949)***
Klaric Forge & Machine Inc (PA)...814 382-6290
10 Fruit Ave Farrell (16121) ***(G-5868)***
Kleen Line Service Co Inc...412 466-6277
524 Washington Ave Dravosburg (15034) ***(G-4351)***
Kleen-Line Parts Clr Svc Co, Dravosburg *Also called Kleen Line Service Co Inc* ***(G-4351)***
Klein Electric Advertising Inc...215 657-6984
242 Duffield St Willow Grove (19090) ***(G-20125)***
Klein Plating Works Inc...814 452-3793
2020 Greengarden Rd Erie (16502) ***(G-5347)***
Klenzoid Inc...610 825-9494
912 Spring Mill Ave Conshohocken (19428) ***(G-3570)***
Klimek Molding Corp...814 774-4051
321 Mechanic St Girard (16417) ***(G-6395)***
Kline Bros...717 469-0699
10083 Allentown Blvd Grantville (17028) ***(G-6575)***
Kline Construction, Boyertown *Also called Greg Kline* ***(G-1914)***
Klinge Corporation (PA)...717 840-4500
4075 E Market St York (17402) ***(G-20556)***
Klinger Machinery Co Inc...717 362-8656
333 N Church St Elizabethville (17023) ***(G-4894)***
Klingler Family Sawmill...717 677-4957
875 Narrows Rd Biglerville (17307) ***(G-1665)***
Klingler Incorporated...717 535-5151
12039 William Penn Hwy Thompsontown (17094) ***(G-18347)***
Klk Welding Inc...717 637-0080
15 Barnhart Dr Hanover (17331) ***(G-6910)***
Klocek Burial Vault Co...724 547-2865
153 S Quarry St Mount Pleasant (15666) ***(G-11704)***
Kloeckner Metals Corporation...717 755-1923
420 Memory Ln York (17402) ***(G-20557)***
Kloeckner Metals Corporation...215 245-3300
555 State Rd Bensalem (19021) ***(G-1216)***
Klondike Block and Masonry Sup, Smithfield *Also called Klondike Block Masnry Sups Inc* ***(G-17652)***
Klondike Block Masnry Sups Inc...724 439-3888
331 Shoaf Rd Smithfield (15478) ***(G-17652)***
Klosterman Baking Co...412 564-1023
98 Vanadium Rd Ste 2 Bridgeville (15017) ***(G-2076)***
Klt Group Inc...215 525-0902
557 Kulp Rd Pottstown (19465) ***(G-15950)***
Klx Energy Services LLC...570 835-0149
18355 Route 287 Tioga (16946) ***(G-18363)***
Km Custom Pack, Philadelphia *Also called Select Medical Systems Inc* ***(G-14293)***
Kme Fire Apparatus, Nesquehoning *Also called Kovatch Mobile Equipment Corp* ***(G-12007)***
Kmi Surgical Ltd...610 518-7110
110 Hopewell Rd Ste 2d Downingtown (19335) ***(G-4237)***
Kmn Associates, Reading *Also called Kmn Packaging Inc* ***(G-16422)***
Kmn Packaging Inc...610 376-3606
1610 Meadowlark Rd Reading (19610) ***(G-16422)***
Kms, Shippensburg *Also called Kittatinny Manufacturing Svcs* ***(G-17536)***
Kms Fab LLC...570 338-0200
100 Parry St Luzerne (18709) ***(G-10125)***
Kms of Pennsylvania, Luzerne *Also called Kms Fab LLC* ***(G-10125)***
Kmz Enterprises LLC...215 659-8400
2885 Terwood Rd Willow Grove (19090) ***(G-20126)***
Knauss Inc...215 536-4220
625 E Broad St Quakertown (18951) ***(G-16206)***
Kneppco Equipment LLC...814 483-0108
465 Log House Rd Berlin (15530) ***(G-1289)***
Knepper Press Corporation...724 899-4200
2251 Sweeney Dr Clinton (15026) ***(G-3263)***
Kneppers Kleen Water...717 264-9715
2793 Wiles Rd Chambersburg (17202) ***(G-2948)***
KNex Industries Inc...215 997-7722
2990 Bergey Rd Hatfield (19440) ***(G-7358)***
KNex Ltd Partnership Group...215 997-7722
2990 Bergey Rd Hatfield (19440) ***(G-7359)***
Knf Corporation (PA)...570 386-3550
734 W Penn Pike Tamaqua (18252) ***(G-18213)***
Knf Flexpak Corporation...570 386-3550
734 W Penn Pike Tamaqua (18252) ***(G-18214)***
Knight Corporation (PA)...610 853-2161
2138 Darby Rd Havertown (19083) ***(G-7423)***
Knight Ridder Inc...570 829-7100
15 N Main St Wilkes Barre (18701) ***(G-19935)***
Knittle & Frey AG-Center Inc...570 323-7554
2101 Sweeley Ave Williamsport (17701) ***(G-20032)***
Knm Machine and Tool Inc...215 443-9660
1800 Mearns Rd Ste H Warminster (18974) ***(G-18905)***
Knock On Woodwork...717 579-8179
320 Contemdra Dr Mechanicsburg (17055) ***(G-10865)***
Knoll Inc...215 988-1788
130 N 18th St Philadelphia (19103) ***(G-13940)***
Knoll Inc...484 224-3760
7132 Daniels Dr Allentown (18106) ***(G-285)***
Knoll Inc (PA)...215 679-7991
1235 Water St East Greenville (18041) ***(G-4570)***
Knoll Inc...215 679-1218
329 Railroad St East Greenville (18041) ***(G-4571)***
Knouse Foods Cooperative Inc (PA)...717 677-8181
800 Pach Glen Idaville Rd Peach Glen (17375) ***(G-13205)***
Knouse Foods Cooperative Inc...717 263-9177
421 Grant St Chambersburg (17201) ***(G-2949)***
Knouse Foods Cooperative Inc...717 642-8291
1505 Orrtanna Rd Orrtanna (17353) ***(G-13036)***
Knouse Foods Cooperative Inc...717 328-3065
9332 Heisey Rd Mercersburg (17236) ***(G-10989)***
Knouse Foods Cooperative Inc...717 677-9115
53 E Hanover St Biglerville (17307) ***(G-1666)***
Knowledge In A Nut Shell Inc...412 765-2020
1420 Centre Ave Apt 2213 Pittsburgh (15219) ***(G-15179)***
Knowledge MGT & Tech Corp...412 503-3657
269 N Main St Washington (15301) ***(G-19193)***
Knox Western, Erie *Also called Earl E Knox Company* ***(G-5255)***
Knox Western Gas Compressors, Erie *Also called Knox-Western Inc* ***(G-5348)***
Knox Western Gas Comprsr Div, Erie *Also called Earl E Knox Company* ***(G-5254)***
Knox-Western Inc...814 459-2754
1111 Bacon St Erie (16511) ***(G-5348)***
Knudsen's Woodworking, Kirkwood *Also called Jeffrey R Knudsen* ***(G-8749)***
Koaxis Inc...610 222-0154
2081 Lucon Rd Schwenksville (19473) ***(G-17178)***
Kobold Instruments Inc...412 490-4806
1801 Parkway View Dr Pittsburgh (15205) ***(G-15180)***
Koch Filter Corporation...215 679-3135
1653 State St East Greenville (18041) ***(G-4572)***
Koch Industries Inc...717 949-3469
Rr 501 Box South Schaefferstown (17088) ***(G-17128)***
Koch Industries Inc...814 453-5444
1710 Greengarden Rd Erie (16501) ***(G-5349)***
Koch S Custom Woodworking...610 261-2607
3557 Howertown Rd Northampton (18067) ***(G-12854)***
Koch's Turkey Farm, Tamaqua *Also called Lewistown Valley Entps Inc* ***(G-18218)***
Kochmer Graphics...570 222-5713
82 Main St Clifford (18413) ***(G-3246)***
Kochmer Graphics & Auto Svc, Clifford *Also called Kochmer Graphics* ***(G-3246)***
Kochs Portable Sawmill & Lbr...717 776-7961
4354 Enola Rd Newville (17241) ***(G-12604)***
Kocks Pittsburgh Corporation...412 367-4174
504 Mcknight Park Dr Pittsburgh (15237) ***(G-15181)***
Kodabow Inc (PA)...484 947-5471
1126 Greenhill Rd West Chester (19380) ***(G-19583)***
Kodyn Products Company, Loyalhanna *Also called David Kovalcik* ***(G-10110)***
Koehler-Bright Star LLC...570 825-1900
380 Stewart Rd Hanover Township (18706) ***(G-6991)***
Kohlepp Stone Center, Du Bois *Also called J A Kohlepp and Sons Stone* ***(G-4397)***
Kohlhepp Stone Center, Du Bois *Also called J A Kohlhepp Sons Inc* ***(G-4398)***

Kol Industries Inc 717 630-0600
  635 Maple Ave Hanover (17331) *(G-6911)*

Kold Draft International LLC 814 453-6761
  1525 E Lake Rd Ste 700 Erie (16511) *(G-5350)*

Kold-Draft, Erie Also called Kold Draft International LLC *(G-5350)*

Koller Concrete Inc 610 865-5034
  900 Marshall St Bethlehem (18017) *(G-1553)*

Kollman Label and Packg Group, Yardley Also called Prime Packaging LLC *(G-20333)*

Kone Cranes Inc 814 878-8070
  1351 W 12th St Erie (16501) *(G-5351)*

Konecranes Inc 814 237-2663
  200 Shady Ln Ste 150 Philipsburg (16866) *(G-14518)*

Konecranes Inc 610 321-2900
  371 Circle Of Progress Dr Pottstown (19464) *(G-16008)*

Konecranes Inc 814 878-8070
  1351 W 12th St Erie (16501) *(G-5352)*

Kongsberg Integrated Tactical 814 269-5700
  210 Industrial Park Rd # 105 Johnstown (15904) *(G-8399)*

Kongsberg Protech Systems (HQ) 814 269-5700
  210 Industrial Park Rd Johnstown (15904) *(G-8400)*

Konhaus Farms Inc 717 731-9456
  3544 Gettysburg Rd Camp Hill (17011) *(G-2502)*

Konhaus Print & Marketing, Camp Hill Also called Konhaus Farms Inc *(G-2502)*

Kono Co 724 462-3333
  13517a Broadway Meadville (16335) *(G-10744)*

Konsep Co, Manchester Also called Allegheny-York Co *(G-10354)*

Kontrol Automation Inc (PA) 610 284-4106
  528 Mildred Ave Secane (19018) *(G-17317)*

Kontron America Incorporated 412 921-3322
  750 Holiday Dr Ste 560 Pittsburgh (15220) *(G-15182)*

Kool Dri Rainwear, Reinholds Also called Keystone Nitewear Co Inc *(G-16634)*

Kool Stuff 4 Kids, Levittown Also called Higley Enterprises *(G-9843)*

Kop-Coat Inc (HQ) 412 227-2426
  3040 William Pitt Way Pittsburgh (15238) *(G-15183)*

Kop-Coat Inc 412 826-3387
  3020 William Pitt Way Pittsburgh (15238) *(G-15184)*

Kopenitz Lumber Co 570 544-2131
  89 Woodside Rd Pottsville (17901) *(G-16087)*

Koppel Steel, Ambridge Also called Ipsco Koppel Tubulars Llc *(G-620)*

Koppers Asia LLC 412 227-2001
  436 7th Ave Pittsburgh (15219) *(G-15185)*

Koppers Concrete Products Inc 412 227-2001
  436 7th Ave Pittsburgh (15219) *(G-15186)*

Koppers Holdings Inc (PA) 412 227-2001
  436 7th Ave Pittsburgh (15219) *(G-15187)*

Koppers Inc (HQ) 412 227-2001
  436 7th Ave Pittsburgh (15219) *(G-15188)*

Koppers Industries Inc 412 227-2001
  436 7th Ave Ste 2026 Pittsburgh (15219) *(G-15189)*

Koppers Industries Inc 570 547-1651
  50 Koppers Ln Montgomery (17752) *(G-11373)*

Koppers Industries Inc 412 826-3970
  1005 William Pitt Way Pittsburgh (15238) *(G-15190)*

Koppers Industries Del Inc (HQ) 412 227-2001
  436 7th Ave Ste 2026 Pittsburgh (15219) *(G-15191)*

Koppers Industries Inc 724 684-1000
  345 Donner Ave Monessen (15062) *(G-11299)*

Koppers Performance Chem Inc 412 227-2001
  436 7th Ave Pittsburgh (15219) *(G-15192)*

Koppers Technical Center, Pittsburgh Also called Koppers Industries Inc *(G-15190)*

Koppers Utility Indus Pdts Inc 412 620-6238
  707 Grant St Ste 2307 Pittsburgh (15219) *(G-15193)*

Kord King Company, Lancaster Also called King Associates Ltd *(G-9086)*

Kore Mart Ltd 610 562-5900
  7 Hill Dr Hamburg (19526) *(G-6843)*

Korea Daily News Inc 215 277-1112
  1135 W Cheltenham Ave # 100 Elkins Park (19027) *(G-4908)*

Korea Week Inc 215 782-8883
  273 Woodcock Ln Ambler (19002) *(G-589)*

Korean Phila Time Inc 215 663-2400
  103 Township Line Rd 2a Rockledge (19046) *(G-16791)*

Koren Publications 267 498-0071
  777-K Schwab Rd Philadelphia (19019) *(G-13941)*

Koren Publications Inc 267 498-0071
  777 Schwab Rd Ste K Hatfield (19440) *(G-7360)*

Korns Galvanizing Company Inc 814 535-3293
  75 Bridge St Johnstown (15902) *(G-8401)*

Koroteo Investments Inc 570 342-4422
  205 Scrnton Crbondale Hwy Scranton (18508) *(G-17252)*

Korsak Glass & Aluminum Inc 610 987-9888
  809 Hill Church Rd Boyertown (19512) *(G-1923)*

Korte & Co Inc 610 253-9141
  364 E Berwick St Easton (18042) *(G-4712)*

Koryak Consulting Inc 412 364-6600
  2003 Kinvara Dr Pittsburgh (15237) *(G-15194)*

Kos & Associates Inc 412 367-7444
  Mc Knight Park Dr Ste 203 Pittsburgh (15237) *(G-15195)*

Kosko Wood Products Inc 814 427-2499
  Rr 119 Stump Creek (15863) *(G-18143)*

Kottcamp Sheet Metal 717 845-7616
  145 Roosevelt Ave York (17401) *(G-20558)*

Kountry Kraft Kitchens Inc 610 589-4575
  291 S Sheridan Rd Newmanstown (17073) *(G-12479)*

Kountry Kustom Kitchens 717 768-3091
  338 N Ronks Rd Bird In Hand (17505) *(G-1677)*

Kovacs Machine Co, Southampton Also called Kovacs Manufacturing Inc *(G-17821)*

Kovacs Manufacturing Inc 215 355-1985
  67 Heather Rd Southampton (18966) *(G-17821)*

Kovalchick Corporation (PA) 724 349-3300
  1060 Wayne Ave Indiana (15701) *(G-8110)*

Kovalick Lumber Co 814 263-4928
  24338 Shawville Frenchvll Frenchville (16836) *(G-6217)*

Kovatch Corp 570 669-5130
  1 Industrial Complex Nesquehoning (18240) *(G-12006)*

Kovatch Mobile Equipment Corp (HQ) 570 669-9461
  1 Industrial Complex Nesquehoning (18240) *(G-12007)*

Kowalewski Quarries 570 465-7025
  3886 E Lake Rd New Milford (18834) *(G-12397)*

Kozik Bros Inc 724 443-2230
  213 Executive Dr Ste 300 Cranberry Township (16066) *(G-3829)*

Kozmer Technologies Ltd 610 358-4099
  950 Beverly Ln Newtown Square (19073) *(G-12580)*

Kpc Direct Mail, Philadelphia Also called Kennedy Printing Co Inc *(G-13926)*

KPM Herkules, Ford City Also called Herkules USA Corporation *(G-6047)*

Krack Sales Co, Irwin Also called James E Krack *(G-8176)*

Kraemer Properties Inc 717 246-0208
  1 Vulcan Ln Ste 1 # 1 Red Lion (17356) *(G-16603)*

Kraemer Textiles Inc 610 759-4030
  240 S Main St Nazareth (18064) *(G-11975)*

Kraemer Yarn Shop, Nazareth Also called Kraemer Textiles Inc *(G-11975)*

Kraft and Jute Incorporated 814 969-8121
  273 S Main St Cambridge Springs (16403) *(G-2480)*

Kraft Concrete Products Inc 814 677-3019
  304 Duncomb St Oil City (16301) *(G-12950)*

Kraft Foods, Wilkes Barre Also called Mondelez Global LLC *(G-19945)*

Kraft Foods, Camp Hill Also called Nestle Pizza Company Inc *(G-2506)*

Kraft Heinz Company (PA) 412 456-5700
  1 Ppg Pl Fl 34 Pittsburgh (15222) *(G-15196)*

Kraft Heinz Foods Company (HQ) 412 456-5700
  1 Ppg Pl Fl 34 Pittsburgh (15222) *(G-15197)*

Kraft Heinz Foods Company 412 237-5868
  704 Bristlecone Dr Gibsonia (15044) *(G-6341)*

Kraft Heinz Foods Company 724 778-5700
  1000 Ericsson Dr Warrendale (15086) *(G-19085)*

Kraft Heinz Foods Company 412 456-2482
  121 Wright Brothers Dr Moon Township (15108) *(G-11496)*

Kraft Heinz Foods Company 610 430-1536
  1247 Wrights Ln West Chester (19380) *(G-19584)*

Kraft Heinz Foods Company 412 237-5757
  1062 Progress St Pittsburgh (15212) *(G-15198)*

Kraft Heinz Foods Company 412 237-5715
  86 Pilgrim St Carnegie (15106) *(G-2774)*

Kraft Heinz Foods Company 412 456-5773
  1062 Progress St Pittsburgh (15212) *(G-15199)*

Kraft Home Solutions LLC 717 819-2690
  352 Westwood Dr York (17404) *(G-20559)*

Kras Corporation 610 566-0271
  2 Old Mill Ln Media (19063) *(G-10935)*

Kras Worldwide, Media Also called Kras Corporation *(G-10935)*

Krause C W & Son Lumber 814 378-8919
  515 David St Houtzdale (16651) *(G-7883)*

Krauss S E Tool & Die Co 215 957-1517
  1843 Stout Dr Warminster (18974) *(G-18906)*

Krauss Tool & Die, Warminster Also called Krauss S E Tool & Die Co *(G-18906)*

Kravitch Machine, Pittsburgh Also called Nick Charles Kravitch *(G-15340)*

Kravitch Machine Co, Pittsburgh Also called Nick Charles Kravitch *(G-15339)*

Kreamer Feed Inc 570 374-8148
  215 Kreamer Ave Kreamer (17833) *(G-8818)*

Kreckel Enterprises Inc 814 834-1874
  1044 Windfall Rd Saint Marys (15857) *(G-16986)*

Kreco Antennas 570 595-2212
  3340 Spruce Cabin Rd Cresco (18326) *(G-3894)*

Krehling Industries Inc 717 232-7936
  1399 Hagy Way Harrisburg (17110) *(G-7165)*

Kreico LLC 717 228-7312
  609 S 4th St Lebanon (17042) *(G-9595)*

Kreider Digital Communications 412 446-2784
  2100 Babcock Blvd Pittsburgh (15209) *(G-15200)*

Kreider Foods Inc 717 898-3372
  1555 Sylvan Rd Lancaster (17601) *(G-9088)*

Kreider Printing, Pittsburgh Also called J B Kreider Co Inc *(G-15140)*

Kreiders Canvas Service Inc 717 656-7387
  73 W Main St Leola (17540) *(G-9791)*

Kreiders Mulch 717 871-9177
  356 Penn St Washington Boro (17582) *(G-19250)*

Kreiser Fuel Service Inc 570 455-0418
  128 W Green St Hazleton (18201) *(G-7506)*

Kreitz Wldg & Fabrication Inc 610 678-6010
788 Fritztown Rd Reading (19608) *(G-16423)*

Krem Cars/Racing Inc 814 336-6619
10204 Perry Hwy Meadville (16335) *(G-10745)*

Krem Speed Equipment Inc 814 724-4806
10204 Perry Hwy Meadville (16335) *(G-10746)*

Kremers Urban Pharmaceuticals 609 936-5940
13200 Townsend Rd Philadelphia (19154) *(G-13942)*

Kremers Urban Phrmcuticals Inc 609 936-5940
13200 Townsend Rd Philadelphia (19154) *(G-13943)*

Krengel Quaker City Corp 215 969-9800
12285 Mcnulty Rd Ste 103 Philadelphia (19154) *(G-13944)*

Kress Manufacturing Inc 724 864-5056
378 Main St Irwin (15642) *(G-8180)*

Kretchmar Bakery Inc 724 774-2324
664 3rd St Beaver (15009) *(G-986)*

Kreutz Creek Vineyards, West Grove Also called James Kirkpatrick *(G-19701)*

Krg Enterprises Inc 215 708-2811
9901 Blue Grass Rd Philadelphia (19114) *(G-13945)*

Kriebel Gas Inc (PA) 814 226-4160
633 Mayfield Rd Clarion (16214) *(G-3181)*

Kriebel Gas Inc 814 938-2010
193 Yoder Rd Punxsutawney (15767) *(G-16146)*

Kriebel Minerals Inc 814 226-4160
633 Mayfield Rd Clarion (16214) *(G-3182)*

Kriebel Wells 814 226-4160
633 Mayfield Rd Clarion (16214) *(G-3183)*

Krieg Dieter 717 656-8050
3 W Main St Brownstown (17508) *(G-2308)*

Krimes Industrial and Mech Inc 717 628-1301
633 W Liton Ave Bldg N0 7 Ephrata (17522) *(G-5115)*

Krimes Machine Shop Inc 717 733-1271
509 W Main St Ephrata (17522) *(G-5116)*

Krishna Protects Cows Inc 717 527-4101
534 Gita Nagari Rd Port Royal (17082) *(G-15910)*

Krispy Kreme, Scranton Also called Early Morning Donuts Corp *(G-17230)*

Krispy Kreme Doughnuts 724 228-1800
14 Trinity Point Dr Washington (15301) *(G-19194)*

Kroesen Tool Co Inc 717 653-1392
43 Eby Chiques Rd Mount Joy (17552) *(G-11665)*

Krohmalys Printing Co 412 271-4234
7425 Washington Ave Pittsburgh (15218) *(G-15201)*

Kromek, Zelienople Also called Ev Products Inc *(G-20799)*

Kronos Incorporated 724 772-2400
555 Keystone Dr Warrendale (15086) *(G-19086)*

Kronos Incorporated 724 742-3142
8050 Rowan Rd Ste 600 Cranberry Township (16066) *(G-3830)*

Kronos Incorporated 610 567-2127
2704 Noble Way Royersford (19468) *(G-16855)*

Krosaki Mgnsita Rfrctories LLC 717 793-5536
425 S Salem Church Rd York (17408) *(G-20560)*

Kross Cabinets 724 375-7504
2313 W Main St Aliquippa (15001) *(G-79)*

Kruppko Inc 610 489-2334
44 W Ridge Pike Royersford (19468) *(G-16856)*

Krystal Biotech Inc 412 586-5830
2100 Wharton St Ste 701 Pittsburgh (15203) *(G-15202)*

KS Krafts 717 764-7033
2923 Balsa St York (17404) *(G-20561)*

Kt Zimmerman Lumber & Logging 570 345-2542
21 Zimmerman Ln Pine Grove (17963) *(G-14595)*

Kt-Grant Inc (PA) 724 468-4700
3073 Route 66 Export (15632) *(G-5614)*

Kt-Grants, Export Also called Kt-Grant Inc *(G-5614)*

Ktc, Mount Joy Also called Kroesen Tool Co Inc *(G-11665)*

Kubota Equipment, Apollo Also called Artman Equipment Company Inc *(G-662)*

Kufen Electric Motors Inc 215 672-5250
27 York Rd Warminster (18974) *(G-18907)*

Kufen Motor and Pump Tech 215 672-5250
27 York Rd Warminster (18974) *(G-18908)*

Kuhcoon, Moosic Also called Andrew Torba *(G-11503)*

Kuhn Auto Electric 717 632-4197
215 Linden Ave R Hanover (17331) *(G-6912)*

Kuhn Tool & Die Co 814 336-2123
21371 Blooming Valley Rd Meadville (16335) *(G-10747)*

Kuhns Bros Lumber Co Inc 570 568-1412
434 Swartz Rd Lewisburg (17837) *(G-9914)*

Kulicke & Soffa, Fort Washington Also called Kulicke and Soffa Inds Inc *(G-6081)*

Kulicke and Soffa Inds Inc (PA) 215 784-6000
1005 Virginia Dr Fort Washington (19034) *(G-6081)*

Kulp Foundry Inc 610 881-8093
1349 Jacobsburg Rd Wind Gap (18091) *(G-20170)*

Kunsman Aggregates 610 882-1455
1080 Win Dr Bethlehem (18017) *(G-1554)*

Kunz Business Products Inc 814 643-4320
1600 Penn St Huntingdon (16652) *(G-7949)*

Kunzler & Company Inc (PA) 717 299-6301
652 Manor St Lancaster (17603) *(G-9089)*

Kuper Technologies LLC 610 358-5120
6 Rigby Ct Garnet Valley (19060) *(G-6266)*

Kuperavage Coal Company, Port Carbon Also called Joe Kuperavage *(G-15897)*

Kuperavage Enterprises Inc 570 668-1633
Old Rte 209 Middleport (17953) *(G-11045)*

Kurt J Lesker, Jefferson Hills Also called Kurt J Lesker Company *(G-8277)*

Kurt J Lesker Company (PA) 412 387-9200
1925 Route 51 Ste 1 Jefferson Hills (15025) *(G-8277)*

Kurt Lebo 610 682-4071
230 Schweitz Rd Fleetwood (19522) *(G-5975)*

Kurts Making Whoopie 570 888-9102
122 S Hopkins St Sayre (18840) *(G-17117)*

Kurtz Bros (PA) 814 765-6561
400 Reed St Clearfield (16830) *(G-3222)*

Kurtzs Machining LLC 717 899-6125
56 Flower Dr Mc Veytown (17051) *(G-10653)*

Kurz-Hastings Inc 215 632-2300
10901 Dutton Rd Philadelphia (19154) *(G-13946)*

Kuss Enterprises LLC 412 583-0206
3608 Spring Garden Rd Pittsburgh (15212) *(G-15203)*

Kustom Cards International 215 233-1678
1018 E Willow Grove Ave Glenside (19038) *(G-6525)*

Kustom Komponents 484 671-3076
2670 Leisczs Bridge Rd # 300 Leesport (19533) *(G-9667)*

Kutz Fabricating Inc 412 771-4161
4000 Windgap Ave Pittsburgh (15204) *(G-15204)*

Kutz Farm Equipment Inc 570 345-4882
72 Kutz Rd Pine Grove (17963) *(G-14596)*

Kutzner Manufacturing Inds Inc 215 721-1712
3255 Meetinghouse Rd Telford (18969) *(G-18300)*

Kutztown Bottling Works Inc 610 683-7377
78 S Whiteoak St 80 Kutztown (19530) *(G-8847)*

Kutztown Optical Corp 610 683-5544
126 W Main St Kutztown (19530) *(G-8848)*

Kutztown Publishing Co Inc 610 683-7341
7036 Snowdrift Rd Ste 110 Allentown (18106) *(G-286)*

Kutztown Publishing Company 610 683-7341
7036 Snowdrift Rd Ste 110 Allentown (18106) *(G-287)*

Kutztown Quarry, East Earl Also called New Enterprise Stone Lime Inc *(G-4551)*

Kutztown Woodworking Company, Kutztown Also called Craig A Scholedice Inc *(G-8838)*

Kvaerner Philadelphia Shi 215 875-2725
2100 Kitty Hawk Ave Philadelphia (19112) *(G-13947)*

Kvk-Tech Inc 215 579-1842
100 Campus Dr Newtown (18940) *(G-12515)*

Kvk-Tech Inc (PA) 215 579-1842
110 Terry Dr Newtown (18940) *(G-12516)*

Kw Inc 610 582-8735
325 W Main St Birdsboro (19508) *(G-1702)*

Kw Container, Allentown Also called Kw Plastics *(G-288)*

Kw Plastics 334 566-1563
7529 Morris Ct Allentown (18106) *(G-288)*

Kwik Goal Ltd 800 531-4252
140 Pacific Dr Quakertown (18951) *(G-16207)*

Kwik Kerb of Valley 610 419-8854
4980 Long Dr Bethlehem (18020) *(G-1555)*

Kwik Quality Press Inc 717 273-0005
732 Locust St Lebanon (17042) *(G-9596)*

Kwikticketscom Inc 724 438-7712
109 S Mount Vernon Ave Uniontown (15401) *(G-18632)*

Kyjs Bakery (PA) 610 494-9400
2702 W 3rd St Chester (19013) *(G-3054)*

Kykayke Inc 610 522-0106
500 Pine St Ste 3a Holmes (19043) *(G-7663)*

Kyles Auto Tags & Insurance (PA) 610 429-1447
529 E Gay St West Chester (19380) *(G-19585)*

Kynectiv Inc 484 899-0746
1820 Masters Way Chadds Ford (19317) *(G-2853)*

Kyron International, Bensalem Also called Kyron Naval Architecture *(G-1217)*

Kyron Naval Architecture 516 304-1769
111 Royal Mews Bensalem (19020) *(G-1217)*

L & D Cabinetry 717 484-1272
700 Stone Hill Rd Denver (17517) *(G-4080)*

L & D Stoneworks Inc 570 553-1670
Rr 5 Box 112m Montrose (18801) *(G-11469)*

L & G Manufacturing 570 876-1550
100 S Main St Frnt Archbald (18403) *(G-689)*

L & H Signs Inc 610 374-2748
425 N 3rd St Reading (19601) *(G-16424)*

L & L Industrial Chemical Inc 215 368-7813
115 Hemlock Dr North Wales (19454) *(G-12811)*

L & L K Incorporated 215 732-2614
2413 Federal St 27 Philadelphia (19146) *(G-13948)*

L & L Special Furnace Co Inc 610 459-9216
20 Kent Rd Aston (19014) *(G-772)*

L & M Construction 610 326-9970
498 Lower Fricks Lock Rd Pottstown (19465) *(G-15951)*

L & M Engines Inc 215 675-8485
246 E County Line Rd 7b Hatboro (19040) *(G-7291)*

L & M Fabrication and Mch Inc 610 837-1848
6814 Chrisphalt Dr Bath (18014) *(G-963)*

L & M Lawn Care, Pittsburgh *Also called Jefferson Memorial Park Inc* ***(G-15147)***
L & M Machine Inc 724 733-2283
947 Old Frankstown Rd Pittsburgh (15239) ***(G-15205)***
L & P Machine Shop Inc 610 262-7356
177 S Front St Coplay (18037) ***(G-3645)***
L & R Lumber Inc 717 463-3411
5374 Mountain Rd Mc Alisterville (17049) ***(G-10550)***
L & S Fireplace Shoppe, Chambersburg *Also called L&S Stone LLC* ***(G-2950)***
L A Card and Gift, Reading *Also called L A Draperies Inc* ***(G-16425)***
L A Draperies Inc 610 375-2224
101 Newport Ave Reading (19611) ***(G-16425)***
L A Welte Inc 412 341-9400
535 Mcneilly Rd Pittsburgh (15226) ***(G-15206)***
L and J Equipment Co Inc 724 437-5405
682 W Main St Uniontown (15401) ***(G-18633)***
L B Foster Company (PA) 412 928-3400
415 Holiday Dr Ste 1 Pittsburgh (15220) ***(G-15207)***
L B Foster Company 814 623-6101
202 Weber Ln Bedford (15522) ***(G-1060)***
L B G Machine Inc 610 770-2550
744 E Highland St Allentown (18109) ***(G-289)***
L B Taxin, Wyncote *Also called E S Specialty Manufacturing* ***(G-20262)***
L B Toney Co 814 375-9974
153 Beaver Dr Du Bois (15801) ***(G-4401)***
L C S, Scott Township *Also called Laboratory Control Systems Inc* ***(G-17184)***
L D H Printing Ltd Inc 609 924-4664
30 N Pennsylvania Ave Morrisville (19067) ***(G-11568)***
L D Kallman Inc 610 384-1200
1001 E Chestnut St Coatesville (19320) ***(G-3312)***
L D Wood Designs, Dushore *Also called Seasons Specialties Inc* ***(G-4510)***
L E Holt Grinding Service Inc 724 446-0977
452 Maple St Rillton (15678) ***(G-16748)***
L G Graphics Inc 412 421-6330
1886 Shaw Ave Pittsburgh (15217) ***(G-15208)***
L I, Mercersburg *Also called Loudon Industries Inc* ***(G-10991)***
L L B Group, Glenside *Also called Leon L Berkowitz Co* ***(G-6527)***
L L Brown Inc 717 766-1885
348 Sample Bridge Rd Enola (17025) ***(G-5081)***
L M I, New Castle *Also called Lee Michael Industries Inc* ***(G-12115)***
L M Robbins Co (PA) 610 760-8301
5757 Oakwood Ln Slatington (18080) ***(G-17608)***
L M Stevenson Company Inc 724 458-7510
2600 Kirila Blvd Hermitage (16148) ***(G-7590)***
L P Aero Plastics Inc 724 744-4448
1086 Boquet Rd Jeannette (15644) ***(G-8260)***
L R M Inc 215 721-4840
215 N Main St Souderton (18964) ***(G-17747)***
L Rand Incorporated 215 490-8090
2300 Pine St Apt 7 Philadelphia (19103) ***(G-13949)***
L Richard Sensenig Co 717 733-0364
183 S Market St Ephrata (17522) ***(G-5117)***
L S I Controls, Waynesboro *Also called LSI Controls Inc* ***(G-19415)***
L S Martin LLC 717 859-3073
891 Rettew Mill Rd Ephrata (17522) ***(G-5118)***
L S Wimmer Machine Co Inc 215 257-3006
115 Ridge Ave Perkasie (18944) ***(G-13281)***
L V T, Allentown *Also called Genus Lifesciences Inc* ***(G-227)***
L W Green Frames 610 432-3726
1584 Alley Close Hill Rd Westfield (16950) ***(G-19779)***
L W M, Whitehall *Also called Lightweight Manufacturing Inc* ***(G-19883)***
L&D Millwork Inc 570 285-3200
161 Eley St Kingston (18704) ***(G-8720)***
L&S Stone LLC 717 264-3559
462 Gateway Ave Chambersburg (17201) ***(G-2950)***
L&S Tool and Machine, York *Also called T-Bird McHning Fabrication LLC* ***(G-20683)***
L'Nard, Philadelphia *Also called Restorative Care America Inc* ***(G-14241)***
L-3 SPD Electrical Systems, Philadelphia *Also called SPD Electrical Systems Inc* ***(G-14331)***
L-One Inc (PA) 717 938-6771
295 Sipe Rd York Haven (17370) ***(G-20760)***
L. Myers Associates, Harrisburg *Also called Larry Myers* ***(G-7169)***
L3 Electron Devices Inc 570 326-3561
1035 Westminster Dr Williamsport (17701) ***(G-20033)***
L3 Technologies Inc 267 545-7000
1515 Grundy Ln Bristol (19007) ***(G-2157)***
L3 Technologies Inc 412 967-7700
615 Epsilon Dr Pittsburgh (15238) ***(G-15209)***
L3 Telemetry & Rf Products, Bristol *Also called L3 Technologies Inc* ***(G-2157)***
La Cronica Newspaper 484 357-2903
34 N 12th St Allentown (18101) ***(G-290)***
La France Corp (PA) 610 361-4300
1 Lafrance Way Concordville (19331) ***(G-3457)***
La Gourmandine LLC 412 682-2210
4605 Butler St Pittsburgh (15201) ***(G-15210)***
La Gourmandine LLC 412 200-7969
300 Cochran Rd Pittsburgh (15228) ***(G-15211)***
La Gourmandine LLC (PA) 412 291-8146
5013 2nd Ave Hazelwood (15207) ***(G-7446)***
La Perla LLC 717 561-1257
806 S 29th St Bldg C Harrisburg (17111) ***(G-7166)***
La Plume Country Market, La Plume *Also called Darlings Locker Plant* ***(G-8869)***
La Prima Expresso Co (PA) 412 565-7070
20th And Smallman Pittsburgh (15222) ***(G-15212)***
La Rue Meat Processing, Somerset *Also called Louis G Sredy* ***(G-17696)***
La Salle Products Inc 412 488-1585
1250 Brookline Blvd Pittsburgh (15226) ***(G-15213)***
Labb Machine, Philadelphia *Also called William J Labb Sons Inc* ***(G-14474)***
Labchem Inc 412 826-5230
1010 Jacksons Pointe Ct Zelienople (16063) ***(G-20809)***
Label Converters Inc 215 675-6900
4 Ivybrook Blvd Ivyland (18974) ***(G-8214)***
Labelcom 814 362-3252
400 Chestnut Street Ext Bradford (16701) ***(G-1978)***
Labelcraft Press Inc 215 257-6368
304 S 4th St Perkasie (18944) ***(G-13282)***
Labelpack Automation Inc (PA) 814 362-1528
20 Russell Blvd Bldg E Bradford (16701) ***(G-1979)***
Labels By Pulizzi Inc 570 326-1244
3325 Wahoo Dr Williamsport (17701) ***(G-20034)***
Labelworx Inc 215 945-5645
51 Runway Dr Levittown (19057) ***(G-9844)***
Laboratory Control Systems Inc 570 487-2490
91 Quinton Rd Scott Township (18447) ***(G-17184)***
Laboratory Testing Inc 215 997-9080
2331 Topaz Dr Hatfield (19440) ***(G-7361)***
Labriola Joseph Sausage Co, Pittsburgh *Also called Labriola Sausage Co* ***(G-15214)***
Labriola Sausage Co 412 281-5966
2614 Penn Ave Pittsburgh (15222) ***(G-15214)***
Labue Printing Inc 814 371-5059
140 Mccracken Run Rd Du Bois (15801) ***(G-4402)***
Lacasa Narcisi Winery 724 444-4744
4578 Gibsonia Rd Gibsonia (15044) ***(G-6342)***
Laceyville Lumber Inc 570 869-1212
227 Main St Laceyville (18623) ***(G-8872)***
Lachina Drapery Company Inc 412 665-4900
5750 Baum Blvd Ste 1 Pittsburgh (15206) ***(G-15215)***
Lackawanna Distributor Corp 570 342-8245
60 Keystone Industrial Pa Dunmore (18512) ***(G-4476)***
Lackawanna Printing Co 570 342-0528
902 Capouse Ave Scranton (18509) ***(G-17253)***
Ladie & Friends Inc 215 453-8200
220 N Main St Sellersville (18960) ***(G-17353)***
Ladisch Corporation Inc 267 313-4189
292 Baldy Hill Rd Alburtis (18011) ***(G-55)***
Ladmac Services 724 679-8047
205 Freeport Rd Butler (16002) ***(G-2418)***
Ladyfingers Sewing Studio 610 689-0068
6375 Oley Turnpike Rd Oley (19547) ***(G-12979)***
Laessig Associates 610 353-3543
833 Malin Rd Newtown Square (19073) ***(G-12581)***
Lafarge North America Inc 610 262-7831
5160 Main St Whitehall (18052) ***(G-19880)***
Lafarge North America Inc 412 461-1163
4810 Buttermilk Hollow Rd Pittsburgh (15122) ***(G-15216)***
Lafarge Rd Marking Inc 570 547-1621
79 Montgomery St Montgomery (17752) ***(G-11374)***
Lafayette Interior Fashions, Harrisburg *Also called Lafayette Venetian Blind Inc* ***(G-7167)***
Lafayette Supply, Phoenixville *Also called R & G Gorr Enterprises Inc* ***(G-14573)***
Lafayette Venetian Blind Inc 717 652-3750
5700 Lingstown Rd Ste D Harrisburg (17112) ***(G-7167)***
Lafayette Welding Inc 610 489-3529
64 W Ridge Pike Royersford (19468) ***(G-16857)***
Lagonda Machine LLC 724 222-2710
2410 Park Ave Washington (15301) ***(G-19195)***
Lagos Inc (PA) 215 925-1693
441 N 5th St Fl 4 Philadelphia (19123) ***(G-13950)***
Lagos Design, Philadelphia *Also called Lagos Inc* ***(G-13950)***
Lagrew Printing Co, Coudersport *Also called Joseph Lagrua* ***(G-3783)***
Laird Technologies Inc 570 424-8510
Shielding Way Delaware Water Gap (18327) ***(G-4043)***
Lake Ariel Wood Products, Lake Ariel *Also called K J Shaffer Milled Products* ***(G-8889)***
Lake City Power Systems LLC 814 774-2034
2170 Rice Ave Lake City (16423) ***(G-8902)***
Lake Cy Manufactured Hsing Inc (PA) 814 774-2033
10068 Keystone Dr Lake City (16423) ***(G-8903)***
Lake Erie Biofuels LLC (HQ) 814 528-9200
1670 E Lake Rd Erie (16511) ***(G-5353)***
Lake Erie Molded Plastics, Fairview *Also called Harry Rhoades* ***(G-5827)***
Lake Erie Regional Center For 814 725-4601
662 Cemetery Rd North East (16428) ***(G-12749)***
Lake Erie Rubber & Mfg LLC 814 835-0170
6410 W Ridge Rd Erie (16506) ***(G-5354)***
Lake Erie Rubber Works Inc 814 835-0170
6410 W Ridge Rd Erie (16506) ***(G-5355)***
Lake Paper Products Inc 570 836-8815
2722 Sr 6 Tunkhannock (18657) ***(G-18541)***

A
L
P
H
A
B
E
T
I
C

Lake Region Medical Inc................610 489-0300
 200 W 7th Ave Trappe (19426) *(G-18471)*
Lake Shore Charcoal, Pittston *Also called Milazzo Industries Inc (G-15767)*
Lake Shore Industries Inc................814 456-4277
 1817 Poplar St Erie (16502) *(G-5356)*
Lake Tool Inc................814 374-4401
 190 Howard St Ste 400 Franklin (16323) *(G-6146)*
Lakeland Industries Inc................610 775-0505
 5 Dutch Ct Ste C Reading (19608) *(G-16426)*
Lakeland Precision Inc................814 382-6811
 13236 Phelps Rd Conneaut Lake (16316) *(G-3474)*
Lakeland Precision Tool, Conneaut Lake *Also called Lakeland Precision Inc (G-3474)*
Lakeland Sand & Gravel Inc................724 588-7020
 11203 Ellion Rd Conneaut Lake (16316) *(G-3475)*
Lakeshore Isotopes LLC................814 836-0207
 2727 W 21st St Erie (16506) *(G-5357)*
Lakeside Stop-N-Go LLC................814 213-0202
 12211 Lakeside Dr Conneaut Lake (16316) *(G-3476)*
Lakeview Forge Co................814 454-4518
 735 W 12th St Erie (16501) *(G-5358)*
Lamagna Cheese, Verona *Also called Mrckl Closeco Inc (G-18758)*
Lambert-Jones Rubber Co................412 781-8100
 319 Butler St Ste 1 Pittsburgh (15223) *(G-15217)*
Lamberti Usa Incorporated................610 862-1400
 161 Wshington St Ste 1000 Conshohocken (19428) *(G-3571)*
Lamens Furniture................814 733-4537
 145 Sugar Camp Rd Schellsburg (15559) *(G-17134)*
Laminar Flow Inc................215 672-0232
 102 Richard Rd Warminster (18974) *(G-18909)*
Laminated Materials Corp................215 425-4100
 625 Winks Ln Bensalem (19020) *(G-1218)*
Laminations Inc................570 876-8199
 101 Power Blvd Archbald (18403) *(G-690)*
Laminators Incorporated (PA)................215 723-5285
 3255 Penn St Hatfield (19440) *(G-7362)*
Lamjen Inc................814 459-5277
 2254 E 30th St Erie (16510) *(G-5359)*
Lammers Micro Drill, Kutztown *Also called William Lammers (G-8863)*
Lamms Machine Inc................610 797-2023
 3216 Berger St Allentown (18103) *(G-291)*
Lampire Biological Labs Inc (PA)................215 795-2838
 3599 Farm School Rd Ottsville (18942) *(G-13065)*
Lamtec Corporation................570 897-8200
 5010 River Rd Mount Bethel (18343) *(G-11611)*
Lancaster Artificial Eye, Lancaster *Also called Lancaster Contact Lens Inc (G-9092)*
Lancaster Brewing Company................717 391-6258
 302 N Plum St Lancaster (17602) *(G-9090)*
Lancaster Cabinet Company LLC................717 556-8420
 584 Gibbons Rd Bird In Hand (17505) *(G-1678)*
Lancaster Composite................717 872-8999
 131 Stable Dr Lancaster (17603) *(G-9091)*
Lancaster Composite Inc................717 872-8999
 1000 Houston St Columbia (17512) *(G-3441)*
Lancaster Contact Lens Inc................717 569-7386
 700 Eden Rd Ste 2 Lancaster (17601) *(G-9092)*
Lancaster Container Inc................717 285-3312
 100 Bridge St Columbia (17512) *(G-3442)*
Lancaster Country Winery, Willow Street *Also called Lancaster County Winery Ltd (G-20153)*
Lancaster County Weeklies................717 626-2191
 1 E Main St Ephrata (17522) *(G-5119)*
Lancaster County Winery Ltd................717 464-3555
 799 Rawlinsville Rd Willow Street (17584) *(G-20153)*
Lancaster Extrusion Inc................717 392-9622
 212 Hazel St Lancaster (17603) *(G-9093)*
Lancaster Farming, Ephrata *Also called Lnp Media Group Inc (G-5121)*
Lancaster Fine Foods Inc................717 397-9578
 501 Richardson Dr Ste 100 Lancaster (17603) *(G-9094)*
Lancaster Fuels................717 687-5390
 902 Strasburg Pike Strasburg (17579) *(G-18090)*
Lancaster General Svcs Bus Tr (HQ)................717 544-5474
 607 N Duke St Lancaster (17602) *(G-9095)*
Lancaster General Svcs Bus Tr................800 341-2121
 555 N Duke St Lancaster (17602) *(G-9096)*
Lancaster Leaf Tob Co PA Inc (HQ)................717 394-2676
 198 W Liberty St Lancaster (17603) *(G-9097)*
Lancaster Leaf Tob Co PA Inc................717 291-1528
 207 Pitney Rd Lancaster (17601) *(G-9098)*
Lancaster Leaf Tob Co PA Inc................717 393-1526
 850 N Water St Lancaster (17603) *(G-9099)*
Lancaster Lime Works................717 207-7014
 1630 Millersville Pike Lancaster (17603) *(G-9100)*
Lancaster Log Cabins LLC................717 445-5522
 1370 Reading Rd Denver (17517) *(G-4081)*
Lancaster Maid Cabinets Inc................717 336-0111
 45 Lincoln Ave Reinholds (17569) *(G-16635)*
Lancaster Metal Mfg Inc................717 293-4480
 1548 Fruitville Pike Lancaster (17601) *(G-9101)*
Lancaster Metals, Lancaster *Also called JL Clark LLC (G-9073)*

Lancaster Metals Science Corp................717 299-9709
 826 N Queen St Lancaster (17603) *(G-9102)*
Lancaster Parts & Eqp Inc................717 299-3721
 2008 Horseshoe Rd Lancaster (17602) *(G-9103)*
Lancaster Propane Gas Inc (PA)................717 898-0800
 2860 Yellow Goose Rd Lancaster (17601) *(G-9104)*
Lancaster Pump................717 397-3521
 1340 Manheim Pike Lancaster (17601) *(G-9105)*
Lancaster Pump & Water Trtmnt, Lancaster *Also called C-B Tool Co (G-8967)*
Lancaster Pump & Water Trtmnt, Lancaster *Also called Lancaster Pump (G-9105)*
Lancaster Reprographics, Lancaster *Also called Mjjm Enterprises Inc (G-9137)*
Lancaster Sign Co Inc................717 284-3500
 1334 Rawlinsville Rd New Providence (17560) *(G-12434)*
Lancaster Sign Source Inc................717 569-7606
 121 Centerville Rd Lancaster (17603) *(G-9106)*
Lancaster Truck Bodies, Lancaster *Also called Mid Atlantic Municipal LLC (G-9134)*
Lancaster Tube Plant, Lancaster *Also called Caraustar Industrial and Con (G-8970)*
Lancer Systems LP................610 973-2600
 2800 Milford Square Pike Quakertown (18951) *(G-16208)*
Lanchester Woodworking................717 355-2184
 935 Churchtown Rd Narvon (17555) *(G-11923)*
Lanco Industries................717 949-3435
 2605 Prescott Rd Lebanon (17042) *(G-9597)*
Lanco Manufacturing Company................717 556-4143
 2740 Stumptown Rd Bird In Hand (17505) *(G-1679)*
Lanco Sheds Inc................717 351-7100
 150 Commerce Dr New Holland (17557) *(G-12256)*
Land OLakes Inc................717 486-7000
 405 Park Dr Carlisle (17015) *(G-2719)*
Landau, A Co, Warminster *Also called A Landau Diamond Co (G-18815)*
Landes Bioscience................512 637-6050
 530 Walnut St Ste 850 Philadelphia (19106) *(G-13951)*
Landfried Paving Inc................724 646-2505
 172 Crestview Dr Greenville (16125) *(G-6753)*
Landis Block & Concrete, Souderton *Also called Jdn Block Inc (G-17745)*
Landis Neon Sign Co Inc................717 397-0588
 425 Rohrerstown Rd Lancaster (17603) *(G-9107)*
Landmark Casting Co, Dover *Also called Barkby Group Inc (G-4185)*
Landons Car Wash and Laundry................570 673-4188
 51 S Center St Canton (17724) *(G-2665)*
Lane Cherry Manufacturing................717 687-9059
 2849 Lincoln Hwy E Ronks (17572) *(G-16810)*
Lane Construction Corporation................412 838-0251
 290 Bilmar Dr Pittsburgh (15205) *(G-15218)*
Lane Display Inc................610 361-1110
 210 Wilmington W Chadds Ford (19317) *(G-2854)*
Lane Enterprises Inc (PA)................717 761-8175
 3905 Hartzdale Dr Ste 514 Camp Hill (17011) *(G-2503)*
Lane Enterprises Inc................610 272-4531
 377 Crooked Ln King of Prussia (19406) *(G-8637)*
Lane Enterprises Inc................724 652-7747
 8271 Mercer St Pulaski (16143) *(G-16124)*
Lane Enterprises Inc................814 623-1191
 682 Quaker Valley Rd Bedford (15522) *(G-1061)*
Lane Enterprises Inc................717 249-8342
 1244 Claremont Rd Carlisle (17015) *(G-2720)*
Lane Enterprises Inc................717 532-5959
 34 Strohm Rd Shippensburg (17257) *(G-17537)*
Lane Holdings LLC................412 279-1234
 12 Noblestown Rd Carnegie (15106) *(G-2775)*
Lane Metal Products, Bedford *Also called Lane Enterprises Inc (G-1061)*
Lane Signs, Chadds Ford *Also called Lane Display Inc (G-2854)*
Laneko Roll Form Inc................215 822-1930
 3003 Unionville Pike Hatfield (19440) *(G-7363)*
Laneys Feed Mill Inc................814 643-3211
 850 Ice Plant Rd Huntingdon (16652) *(G-7950)*
Lang Filter Media LP................570 459-7005
 603 S Church St Hazleton (18201) *(G-7507)*
Lang Speciality Trailers LLC................724 972-6590
 321 Cherry Hills Dr Latrobe (15650) *(G-9487)*
Langelier Designs, Kennett Square *Also called Joyce Langelier (G-8516)*
Langeloth Metallurgical Co LLC................724 947-2201
 10 Langeloth Plant Dr Langeloth (15054) *(G-9270)*
Langhorne Carpet Company Inc................215 757-5155
 201 W Lincoln Hwy Penndel (19047) *(G-13239)*
Langhorne Metal Spinning Inc................215 497-8876
 1095 Wood Ln Langhorne (19047) *(G-9307)*
Lannett Company Inc (PA)................215 333-9000
 9000 State Rd Philadelphia (19136) *(G-13952)*
Lannett Company Inc................215 333-9000
 9001 Torresdale Ave Philadelphia (19136) *(G-13953)*
Lansberry Stone & Wood, Woodland *Also called Stone & Wood Inc (G-20214)*
Lansdale Ice, Harleysville *Also called Lansdale Packaged Ice Inc (G-7044)*
Lansdale Packaged Ice Inc................215 256-8808
 2080 Detwiler Rd Ste 4 Harleysville (19438) *(G-7044)*
Lansdowne Ice & Coal Co Inc................610 353-6500
 610 Park Way Ste A Broomall (19008) *(G-2293)*

ALPHABETIC SECTION
Laurelind Corp (PA)

Lantica Software LLC ... 215 598-8419
100 Jericho Valley Dr Newtown (18940) *(G-12517)*
Lantz Structures LLC ... 717 656-9418
162 Newport Rd Leola (17540) *(G-9792)*
Lanum Metal Products LLC ... 215 329-5010
4100 N 16th St Philadelphia (19140) *(G-13954)*
Lanxess, Pittsburgh *Also called Verichem Inc (G-15692)*
Lanxess Corporation (HQ) ... 800 526-9377
111 Ridc Park West Dr Pittsburgh (15275) *(G-15219)*
Lanxess Corporation ... 412 809-4735
8 Morgan Rd Burgettstown (15021) *(G-2348)*
Lanxess Solutions US Inc ... 724 756-2210
100 Sonneborn Ln Petrolia (16050) *(G-13306)*
Lap Distributors Inc ... 215 744-4000
3515 Amber St Philadelphia (19134) *(G-13955)*
Lap-O-Valve, Pittsburgh *Also called United States Products Co (G-15675)*
Lapp John ... 717 442-8583
5459 Buena Vista Rd Gap (17527) *(G-6252)*
Lapp Lumber Co ... 717 442-4116
1640 Mine Rd Paradise (17562) *(G-13162)*
Lapp's Pallet Repair, Quarryville *Also called Lapps Pallet Repair LLC (G-16273)*
Lapps Logging ... 814 642-7949
92 Volney St Port Allegany (16743) *(G-15894)*
Lapps Pallet Repair LLC ... 717 806-5348
1315 Georgetown Rd Quarryville (17566) *(G-16273)*
Lapps Woodworking, Gordonville *Also called Eli K Lapp Jr (G-6553)*
Lapsley Print Shop, Philadelphia *Also called Lapsley Printing Inc (G-13956)*
Lapsley Printing Inc ... 215 332-7451
4612 Wellington St Philadelphia (19135) *(G-13956)*
Laran Bronze Inc ... 610 874-4414
310 E 6th St Chester (19013) *(G-3055)*
Laret Sign Co ... 814 695-4455
121 Justice St Hollidaysburg (16648) *(G-7650)*
Larimer & Norton Inc ... 814 757-4532
2 Cable Hollow Rd Russell (16345) *(G-16881)*
Larimer & Norton Inc ... 814 723-1778
1163 Scandia Rd Warren (16365) *(G-19036)*
Larimer & Norton Inc ... 814 435-2202
91 West St Galeton (16922) *(G-6240)*
Lark Enterprises Inc (PA) ... 724 657-2001
315 Green Ridge Rd Ste A1 New Castle (16105) *(G-12114)*
Larkin C Company Inc ... 610 696-9096
510 E Barnard St Unit D10 West Chester (19382) *(G-19586)*
Laron Pharma Inc ... 267 575-1470
500 Office Center Dr # 400 Fort Washington (19034) *(G-6082)*
Larry Arnold ... 717 236-0080
1025 Miller Ln Harrisburg (17110) *(G-7168)*
Larry D Baumgardner Coal Co ... 814 345-6404
421 Knox Run Rd Lanse (16849) *(G-9446)*
Larry D Mays (PA) ... 814 833-7988
4726 Pittsburgh Ave Erie (16509) *(G-5360)*
Larry Darling ... 215 677-1452
10156 Ferndale St Philadelphia (19116) *(G-13957)*
Larry Gilman, Philadelphia *Also called Lawrence R Gilman LLC (G-13960)*
Larry J Epps ... 724 712-1156
507 Dodds Rd Butler (16002) *(G-2419)*
Larry Myers ... 717 564-8300
3901 Derry St Ste A Harrisburg (17111) *(G-7169)*
Larry Paige ... 570 374-5650
45 Top Flight Ln Middleburg (17842) *(G-11027)*
Larry Paul Casting Co Inc ... 215 928-1644
720 Sansom St Fl 1 Philadelphia (19106) *(G-13958)*
Larson Enterprises Inc ... 814 345-5101
Larson Rd Kylertown (16847) *(G-8866)*
Larson-Juhl US LLC ... 215 638-5940
1574 Bridgewater Rd Bensalem (19020) *(G-1219)*
Larue Optical, Dover *Also called Prairie Products Inc (G-4200)*
Lasco Fittings Inc ... 570 301-1170
500 Keystone Ave Pittston (18640) *(G-15760)*
Laser Center of Central PA ... 814 867-1852
428 Windmere Dr Ste 100 State College (16801) *(G-17986)*
Laser Creations, Girard *Also called Identification Systems Inc (G-6391)*
Laser Hair Enhancemen ... 724 591-5670
748 Spring St Harmony (16037) *(G-7072)*
Laser Imaging Systems Inc ... 717 266-1700
2100 State Rd Lancaster (17601) *(G-9108)*
Laser Lab Inc ... 717 738-3333
1438 W Main St Ste A Ephrata (17522) *(G-5120)*
Laser Tool Inc ... 814 763-2032
17763 State Highway 198 Saegertown (16433) *(G-16921)*
Laser Vginal Rejuvenation Inst ... 610 584-0584
2017 Cedars Hill Rd Lansdale (19446) *(G-9384)*
Laser Wizard, Schwenksville *Also called Teeco Associates Inc (G-17179)*
Laser-View Technologies Inc ... 610 497-8910
205 Byers Rd Chester Springs (19425) *(G-3082)*
Laserfab Inc ... 717 272-0060
26 Lebanon Valley Pkwy Lebanon (17042) *(G-9598)*
Lasermation Inc ... 215 228-7900
2629 N 15th St Philadelphia (19132) *(G-13959)*
Lasersense Inc ... 856 207-5701
230 N Monroe St Media (19063) *(G-10936)*
Lasertek Tner Crtrdge Rchrging ... 412 244-9505
315 Unity Center Rd Pittsburgh (15239) *(G-15220)*
Lasko Group Inc (PA) ... 610 692-7400
820 Lincoln Ave West Chester (19380) *(G-19587)*
Lasko Products LLC (HQ) ... 610 692-7400
820 Lincoln Ave West Chester (19380) *(G-19588)*
Lasting Expressions ... 724 776-3953
9103 Marshall Rd Cranberry Township (16066) *(G-3831)*
Laticrete International Inc ... 610 326-9970
412 Laurel St Pottstown (19464) *(G-16009)*
Latona Mining LLC ... 570 654-3525
620 S Main St Pittston (18640) *(G-15761)*
Latrobe Associates Inc ... 724 539-1612
135 Gertrude St Latrobe (15650) *(G-9488)*
Latrobe Bulletin, Latrobe *Also called Latrobe Printing and Pubg Co (G-9493)*
Latrobe Foundry Mch & Sup Co (PA) ... 724 537-3341
5655 State Route 981 Latrobe (15650) *(G-9489)*
Latrobe Foundry Mch & Sup Co ... 724 423-4210
120 Augusta Ln Whitney (15693) *(G-19894)*
Latrobe Glass & Mirror Inc ... 724 539-2431
4915 State Route 982 Latrobe (15650) *(G-9490)*
Latrobe Pallet Inc ... 724 537-9636
1284 State Route 981 Latrobe (15650) *(G-9491)*
Latrobe Pattern Co ... 724 539-9753
523 Lloyd Ave Latrobe (15650) *(G-9492)*
Latrobe Printing and Pubg Co ... 724 537-3351
1211 Ligonier St Latrobe (15650) *(G-9493)*
Latrobe Specialty Mtls Co LLC (HQ) ... 724 537-7711
2626 Ligonier St Latrobe (15650) *(G-9494)*
Latrobe Specialty Mtls Co LLC ... 814 432-8575
1680 Debence Dr Franklin (16323) *(G-6147)*
Laucks and Spaulding Inc ... 717 845-3312
350 S Albemarle St York (17403) *(G-20562)*
Laudermilch Meats Inc ... 717 867-1251
724 W Main St Annville (17003) *(G-652)*
Laura J Designs ... 610 213-1082
109 Walsh Rd Lansdowne (19050) *(G-9437)*
Laurel Aggregates Inc ... 724 564-5099
2480 Springhill Frnc Rd Uniontown (15401) *(G-18634)*
Laurel Awning Company, Apollo *Also called Laurel Industrial Fabric Entps (G-681)*
Laurel Carbide Inc ... 724 537-4810
920 Lloyd Ave Latrobe (15650) *(G-9495)*
Laurel Energy LP ... 724 537-5731
1 Energy Pl Ste 7500 Latrobe (15650) *(G-9496)*
Laurel Fence and Railing, Hunker *Also called Marietta Fence Experts LLC (G-7929)*
Laurel Group Newspapers, Scottdale *Also called Independent-Observer (G-17193)*
Laurel Group Newspapers, Ligonier *Also called Independent-Observer (G-9959)*
Laurel Highlands Finishing ... 724 537-9850
319 Unity St Latrobe (15650) *(G-9497)*
Laurel Holdings Inc (PA) ... 814 533-5777
111 Roosevelt Blvd Johnstown (15906) *(G-8402)*
Laurel Industrial Fabric Entps (PA) ... 724 567-5689
1573 Hancock Ave Apollo (15613) *(G-681)*
Laurel Machine Inc ... 724 438-8661
119 Commerce Dr Mount Braddock (15465) *(G-11620)*
Laurel Mountain Energy, Pittsburgh *Also called Laurel Mountain Production LLC (G-15221)*
Laurel Mountain Production LLC ... 412 595-8700
61 Mcmurray Rd Ste 300 Pittsburgh (15241) *(G-15221)*
Laurel Mountain Stone Works, Vanderbilt *Also called Miller and Roebuck Inc (G-18720)*
Laurel Mountain Vineyard, Falls Creek *Also called Nordberg John (G-5856)*
Laurel Parcel Services Inc ... 724 850-6245
645 E Pittsburgh St Greensburg (15601) *(G-6683)*
Laurel Printing (PA) ... 724 459-7554
48 W Market St Blairsville (15717) *(G-1731)*
Laurel Printing & Copy, Blairsville *Also called Laurel Printing (G-1731)*
Laurel Printing & Graphics, Duquesne *Also called Marlo Enterprises Inc (G-4498)*
Laurel Products LLC ... 610 286-2534
47 Park Ave Elverson (19520) *(G-4964)*
Laurel Ridge Resawing ... 814 629-5026
561 N Fork Dam Rd Boswell (15531) *(G-1884)*
Laurel Run Mining Company LLC ... 412 831-4000
1000 Consol Energy Dr Canonsburg (15317) *(G-2599)*
Laurel Run Pallet Company LLC ... 717 436-5428
975 Billyville Rd Mifflintown (17059) *(G-11128)*
Laurel Valley Farms Inc ... 610 268-2074
705 Penn Green Rd Landenberg (19350) *(G-9251)*
Laurel Valley Graphics Inc ... 724 539-4545
1511 Monastery Dr Latrobe (15650) *(G-9498)*
Laurel Valley Metals LLC ... 724 990-8189
4200 Route 22 Hwy E Blairsville (15717) *(G-1732)*
Laurel Valley Soils, Landenberg *Also called Laurel Valley Farms Inc (G-9251)*
Laurel Valley Soils ... 610 268-5555
705 Penn Green Rd Avondale (19311) *(G-854)*
Laureldale Tool Co Inc ... 610 929-5406
3215 Holtry St Reading (19605) *(G-16427)*
Laurelind Corp (PA) ... 215 368-5800
724 Bethlehem Pike Montgomeryville (18936) *(G-11401)*

ALPHABETIC

Laurelind Corp..215 230-4737
   411 Doylestown Rd Montgomeryville (18936) *(G-11402)*

Laurell Technologies Corp....................................215 699-7278
   441 Industrial Dr North Wales (19454) *(G-12812)*

Laurence Ronald Entps Inc..................................215 677-3801
   300 Constance Dr Warminster (18974) *(G-18910)*

Lavale Wilbert Vault Division, Blairsville *Also called Blairsville Wilbert Burial Vlt (G-1717)*

Laveings Mobility..724 368-9417
   368 Heinz Camp Rd Portersville (16051) *(G-15930)*

Lavender Badge LLC...610 994-9476
   840 First Ave Ste 200 King of Prussia (19406) *(G-8638)*

Lawco Inc...717 691-6965
   383 Sample Bridge Rd Enola (17025) *(G-5082)*

Lawless Assoc Pipe Organ Inc.............................717 593-0398
   501 S Cedar Ln Ste 2 Greencastle (17225) *(G-6621)*

Lawn & Garden...724 458-6141
   410 Erie St Grove City (16127) *(G-6794)*

Lawrence Printing Service....................................215 799-2332
   28 N 3rd St Souderton (18964) *(G-17748)*

Lawrence R Gilman LLC......................................215 432-2733
   2417 Welsh Rd Ste 21-252 Philadelphia (19114) *(G-13960)*

Lawrence R McGuigan..724 493-9175
   7 Hemlock St Warren (16365) *(G-19037)*

Lawrence Schiff Silk Mills Inc.............................215 536-5460
   1409 W Broad St Quakertown (18951) *(G-16209)*

Lawrence Schiff Silk Mills Inc.............................717 776-4073
   15 Railroad Ave Newville (17241) *(G-12605)*

Lawrie Technology Inc...814 402-1208
   227 Hathaway St E Girard (16417) *(G-6396)*

Lawruk Machine & Tool Co Inc............................814 943-6136
   302 E 6th Ave Altoona (16602) *(G-521)*

Lawson Labs Inc...610 725-8800
   3217 Phoenixville Pike Malvern (19355) *(G-10265)*

Lawson Pallet Co, Russell *Also called Wayne Lawson (G-16882)*

LAY Machine and Tool Inc....................................610 469-0928
   1751 Pottstown Pike Pottstown (19465) *(G-15952)*

Layke Tool & Manufacturing Co...........................814 333-1169
   23877 State Highway 77 Meadville (16335) *(G-10748)*

Lazerfit Smart Soles, Cranberry Township *Also called Three Dimensions Systems Inc (G-3852)*

LB Bohle LLC..215 957-1240
   700 Veterans Cir Ste 100 Warminster (18974) *(G-18911)*

Lb Full Circle Canine Fitness...............................267 825-7755
   180 W Girard Ave Philadelphia (19123) *(G-13961)*

Lb Woodworking LLC...570 729-0000
   621 River Rd Beach Lake (18405) *(G-974)*

Lbfoster, Pittsburgh *Also called L B Foster Company (G-15207)*

Lblock Transportation Inc.....................................347 533-0943
   362 W Princess St York (17401) *(G-20563)*

Lbp Manufacturing LLC..570 291-5463
   7 Alberigi Dr Jessup (18434) *(G-8330)*

Lccm Solar LLC..717 514-0751
   3029 N Front St Ste 201 Harrisburg (17110) *(G-7170)*

LD Davis Industries Inc (PA)................................800 883-6199
   1725 The Fairway Jenkintown (19046) *(G-8293)*

Ldh Printing Unlimited, Morrisville *Also called L D H Printing Ltd Inc (G-11568)*

Ldp Inc (PA)..570 455-8511
   75 Kiwanis Blvd West Hazleton (18202) *(G-19713)*

Ldp Inc...717 657-8500
   4807 Jonestown Rd Ste 251 Harrisburg (17109) *(G-7171)*

LDS Machine Shop, Newville *Also called Melvin Leid (G-12606)*

Le Bus Bakery Inc (PA).......................................610 337-1444
   480 Shoemaker Rd King of Prussia (19406) *(G-8639)*

Le Grand Assoc of Pittsburgh (PA).......................215 496-1307
   1601 Walnut St Ste 616 Philadelphia (19102) *(G-13962)*

Le Jo Enterprises Incorporated............................484 921-9000
   765 Pike Springs Rd Phoenixville (19460) *(G-14559)*

Leader Publishing Co., Coudersport *Also called Tioga Publishing Company (G-3789)*

Leader Services, Harrisburg *Also called Ldp Inc (G-7171)*

Leader Vindicator, New Bethlehem *Also called McLean Publishing Co (G-12027)*

Leader-Times Daily Newspaper, Kittanning *Also called Trib Total Media LLC (G-8800)*

Leading Edge Composites Inc...............................610 932-9055
   645 Sands Ct Ste 101 Coatesville (19320) *(G-3313)*

Leading Edge Tooling Inc.....................................215 953-9717
   1840 County Line Rd # 103 Huntingdon Valley (19006) *(G-8008)*

Leading Technologies Inc.....................................724 842-3400
   1153 Industrial Pk Rd Leechburg (15656) *(G-9647)*

Leahmarlin Corp...610 692-7378
   501 Hannum Ave West Chester (19380) *(G-19589)*

Leanfm Technologies Inc......................................412 818-5167
   100 S Commons Pittsburgh (15212) *(G-15222)*

Lear Corporation...570 345-6725
   141 Wideawake St Pine Grove (17963) *(G-14597)*

Lear Corporation...570 345-2611
   1 Penn Dye St Pine Grove (17963) *(G-14598)*

Learjet Inc..215 246-3454
   1500 Market St Philadelphia (19102) *(G-13963)*

Lease More..814 796-4047
   2160 Elk Creek Rd Waterford (16441) *(G-19264)*

Leatex Chemical Co...215 739-2000
   2722 N Hancock St Philadelphia (19133) *(G-13964)*

Leathersmith Inc...717 933-8084
   417 Frystown Rd Myerstown (17067) *(G-11891)*

Lebanon Daily News...717 272-5615
   718 Poplar St Lebanon (17042) *(G-9599)*

Lebanon Gasket & Seal, Lebanon *Also called Lebanon Gasket and Seal Inc (G-9600)*

Lebanon Gasket and Seal Inc...............................717 274-3684
   2380 Colebrook Rd Lebanon (17042) *(G-9600)*

Lebanon Machine & Mfg Co LLC...........................717 274-3636
   2380 Colebrook Rd Lebanon (17042) *(G-9601)*

Lebanon Materials, Annville *Also called H&K Group Inc (G-650)*

Lebanon Parts Service Inc....................................717 272-0181
   335 S 9th St Lebanon (17042) *(G-9602)*

Lebanon Pattern Shop Inc....................................717 273-8159
   504 E Canal St Lebanon (17046) *(G-9603)*

Lebanon Tool Co Inc..717 273-3711
   330 N 7th Ave Lebanon (17046) *(G-9604)*

Lebanon Valley Engraving Inc (PA)........................717 273-7913
   1245 Chestnut St Lebanon (17042) *(G-9605)*

Lebanon Valley Engraving Co, Lebanon *Also called Lebanon Valley Engraving Inc (G-9605)*

Lebanon Valley Enterprises...................................717 866-2030
   14 Martin Rd Newmanstown (17073) *(G-12480)*

Lebanon Water Treatment Plant.............................717 865-2191
   12 E Behney St Lebanon (17046) *(G-9606)*

Leber Mining Company Inc....................................717 367-1453
   36 S Market St Fl 2 Elizabethtown (17022) *(G-4876)*

Leboeuf Industries Inc...814 796-9000
   14960 Willy Rd Waterford (16441) *(G-19265)*

Leclerc Foods Usa Inc...570 547-6295
   44 Park Dr Montgomery (17752) *(G-11375)*

Leco Corporation...814 355-7903
   1150 Blanchard St Bellefonte (16823) *(G-1107)*

Lectromat Inc..724 625-3502
   Mars Valencia Rd Mars (16046) *(G-10505)*

Led Living Technologies Inc..................................215 633-1558
   211 Sinclair Rd Ste 100 Bristol (19007) *(G-2158)*

Led Saving Solutions LLC (PA).............................484 588-5401
   487 Devon Park Dr Ste 204 Wayne (19087) *(G-19347)*

Led Tube USA..724 650-0691
   1693 Merchant St Ambridge (15003) *(G-625)*

Ledger Newspapers...610 444-6590
   250 N Bradford Ave West Chester (19382) *(G-19590)*

Ledonne Brothers Bakery, Roseto *Also called Robert Bath (G-16822)*

Lee Antenna & Line Service Inc...........................610 346-7999
   3050 Route 212 Springtown Springtown (18081) *(G-17927)*

Lee Concrete Products...814 467-4470
   648 Seanor Rd Windber (15963) *(G-20188)*

Lee Engraving Services Inc...................................412 788-4224
   318 Virginia Dr Oakdale (15071) *(G-12905)*

Lee Enterprises Inc Sentinel (HQ)........................717 240-7135
   327 B St Carlisle (17013) *(G-2721)*

Lee High Valley Bakers LLC (PA)..........................610 868-2392
   957 Minsi Trail St Bethlehem (18018) *(G-1556)*

Lee Industries Inc...814 342-0460
   50 W Pine St Philipsburg (16866) *(G-14519)*

Lee Metals Inc..412 331-8630
   102 Freedom Ct Coraopolis (15108) *(G-3701)*

Lee Michael Industries Inc....................................724 656-0890
   124 E Long Ave New Castle (16101) *(G-12115)*

Lee Publication Inc..717 240-7167
   457 E North St Carlisle (17013) *(G-2722)*

Lee Regional Health System Inc...........................814 254-4716
   1236 Scalp Ave Johnstown (15904) *(G-8403)*

Lee Rj Group Inc (PA)..800 860-1775
   350 Hochberg Rd Monroeville (15146) *(G-11342)*

Lee Sandusky Corporation (PA).............................717 359-4111
   80 Keystone St Littlestown (17340) *(G-10069)*

Lee's Hoagie House, Quakertown *Also called R E B Inc (G-16240)*

Leech Inc..814 724-5454
   1085 Lamont Dr Meadville (16335) *(G-10749)*

Leech Carbide, Meadville *Also called Leech Inc (G-10749)*

Leechburg Advance, Vandergrift *Also called Wysocki-Cole Enterprises Inc (G-18738)*

Leechburg Contact Lens Lab.................................724 845-7777
   84 2nd St Leechburg (15656) *(G-9648)*

Leedom Welding & Fabricating (PA).......................215 757-8787
   434 Penn St Newtown (18940) *(G-12518)*

Leefson Tool & Die Company................................610 461-7772
   850 Henderson Blvd Folcroft (19032) *(G-6008)*

Lees Mister Noodle Bar.......................................610 829-2799
   325 Northampton St Easton (18042) *(G-4713)*

Lees Orntal Gourmet Foods Inc............................570 462-9505
   99 E Washington St Shenandoah (17976) *(G-17494)*

Leese & Co Inc (PA)...724 834-5810
   768 Old State Route 66 Greensburg (15601) *(G-6684)*

Lefever Logging...717 587-7889
   147 Fort Henry Rd Bethel (19507) *(G-1396)*

Legacy Mark LLC..800 444-9260
   284 Overhill Dr Chambersburg (17202) *(G-2951)*

Legacy Polymer Products Inc 570 344-5019
500 Mill St Dunmore (18512) ***(G-4477)***
Legacy Printing and Pubg Co 724 567-5657
340 Chestnut St Vandergrift (15690) ***(G-18732)***
Legacy Restoration LLC 716 239-0695
3237 Amber St Philadelphia (19134) ***(G-13965)***
Legacy Service USA LLC 215 675-7770
95 James Way Ste 100 Southampton (18966) ***(G-17822)***
Legacy Vulcan LLC 717 637-7121
875 Oxford Ave Hanover (17331) ***(G-6913)***
Legacy Vulcan LLC 717 792-6996
322 N Baker Rd York (17408) ***(G-20564)***
Legal Sifter Inc 724 221-7438
1251 Waterfront Pl # 200 Pittsburgh (15222) ***(G-15223)***
Legend Spine LLC 267 566-3273
300 Old Reading Pike 3a Pottstown (19464) ***(G-16010)***
Leggett & Platt Incorporated 724 748-3057
966 Perry Hwy Mercer (16137) ***(G-10966)***
Leggett & Platt Incorporated 570 824-6622
1655 Sans Souci Pkwy Hanover Township (18706) ***(G-6992)***
Leggett & Platt 0071, Hanover Township *Also called Leggett & Platt Incorporated* ***(G-6992)***
Leggett & Platt 0383, Berwick *Also called Leggett & Platt Incorporated* ***(G-1332)***
Leggett & Platt Incorporated 570 542-4171
515 Salem Blvd Berwick (18603) ***(G-1332)***
Leggs Hanes Bali Factory Otlt 717 392-2511
104 Stanley K Tanger Blvd Lancaster (17602) ***(G-9109)***
Legnini RC Architectural Mllwk 610 640-1227
46 Pennsylvania Ave Malvern (19355) ***(G-10266)***
Legrand Associates, Philadelphia *Also called Le Grand Assoc of Pittsburgh* ***(G-13962)***
Legrand Home Systems Inc (HQ) 717 702-2532
301 Fulling Mill Rd Ste G Middletown (17057) ***(G-11060)***
Legrand Home Systems Inc 717 702-2532
1001 Aip Dr Middletown (17057) ***(G-11061)***
Lehigh Anthracite LP 570 668-9060
1233 E Broad St Tamaqua (18252) ***(G-18215)***
Lehigh Anthracite Coal LLC 814 446-6700
224 Grange Hall Rd Armagh (15920) ***(G-724)***
Lehigh Asphalt Pav & Cnstr Co (HQ) 570 668-2040
1314 E Broad St Tamaqua (18252) ***(G-18216)***
Lehigh Cement Company LLC 610 926-1024
537 Evansville Rd Fleetwood (19522) ***(G-5976)***
Lehigh Cement Company LLC 717 843-0811
200 Hokes Mill Rd York (17404) ***(G-20565)***
Lehigh Cement Company LLC 610 366-4600
7660 Imperial Way Ste 400 Allentown (18195) ***(G-292)***
Lehigh Cement Company LLC 610 837-6725
3251 Bath Pike Nazareth (18064) ***(G-11976)***
Lehigh Cement Company LLC 610 759-2222
3938 Easton Nazareth Hwy Nazareth (18064) ***(G-11977)***
Lehigh Cement Company LLC 724 378-2232
100 Woodlawn Rd Aliquippa (15001) ***(G-80)***
Lehigh Cement Company LLC 610 562-3000
204 Windsor Ave Hamburg (19526) ***(G-6844)***
Lehigh Cement Company LLC 610 366-0500
1718 Spring Creek Rd Macungie (18062) ***(G-10149)***
Lehigh Consumer Products LLC 484 232-7100
2834 Schoeneck Rd Macungie (18062) ***(G-10150)***
Lehigh Electric Products Co 610 395-3386
6265 Hamilton Blvd # 106 Allentown (18106) ***(G-293)***
Lehigh Fabrication LLC 908 791-4800
1139 Lehigh Ave Ste 500 Whitehall (18052) ***(G-19881)***
Lehigh Gap Seamless Gutter LLC 610 824-4888
380 Sand Quarry Rd Ste 1 Palmerton (18071) ***(G-13108)***
Lehigh Gasket, Bath *Also called Staver Hydraulics Co Inc* ***(G-970)***
Lehigh Gasket Inc 610 837-1818
7709 Beth Bath Pike Bath (18014) ***(G-964)***
Lehigh Group The, Macungie *Also called Lehigh Consumer Products LLC* ***(G-10150)***
Lehigh Hanson Ecc Inc (HQ) 610 837-6725
3251 Bath Pike Nazareth (18064) ***(G-11978)***
Lehigh Hanson Ecc Inc 610 837-3312
3162 Bath Pike 1 Nazareth (18064) ***(G-11979)***
Lehigh Hanson Ecc Inc 610 759-2222
3938 Easton Nazareth Hwy Nazareth (18064) ***(G-11980)***
Lehigh Heavy Forge Corporation 610 332-8100
275 Emery St Bethlehem (18015) ***(G-1557)***
Lehigh Machine Tools Inc 215 493-6446
201 Dean Sievers Pl Morrisville (19067) ***(G-11569)***
Lehigh Masonry Cement, Allentown *Also called Hanson Aggregates PA LLC* ***(G-243)***
Lehigh Print & Data LLC 610 421-8891
16 Lehigh St Macungie (18062) ***(G-10151)***
Lehigh Services Inc 610 966-2525
142 W Main St Ste 3 Macungie (18062) ***(G-10152)***
Lehigh Specialty Melting Inc 724 537-7731
107 Gertrude St Latrobe (15650) ***(G-9499)***
Lehigh Surfaces, Macungie *Also called Leo Taur Technology Group Inc* ***(G-10153)***
Lehigh Valley Chronicle 610 965-1636
49 N 6th St Emmaus (18049) ***(G-5032)***
Lehigh Valley Dairies, Lansdale *Also called Tuscan/Lehigh Dairies Inc* ***(G-9420)***
Lehigh Valley Magazine, Bethlehem *Also called Benchmark Group Media Inc* ***(G-1459)***
Lehigh Valley Plastics Inc 484 893-5500
187 N Commerce Way Bethlehem (18017) ***(G-1558)***
Lehigh Valley Printing LLC (PA) 610 905-5686
1314 Lorain Ave Bethlehem (18018) ***(G-1559)***
Lehigh Valley Sign & Service 610 760-8590
5812 Walter Rd Germansville (18053) ***(G-6280)***
Lehigh Valley Venom Basbal CLB 610 262-1750
4556 Cairo Dr Whitehall (18052) ***(G-19882)***
Lehighton Electronics Inc (PA) 610 377-5990
208 Memorial Dr Lehighton (18235) ***(G-9718)***
Lehle Enterprises, Lancaster *Also called lehle Enterprises Inc* ***(G-9055)***
Lehman Cabinetry 717 432-5014
16 S Fileys Rd Dillsburg (17019) ***(G-4133)***
Lehman Scientific LLC 717 244-7540
85 Surrey Dr Wrightsville (17368) ***(G-20241)***
Lehr Design & Manufacturing 717 428-1828
12 Valley Rd Jacobus (17407) ***(G-8230)***
Leibys Ichr LLC 570 778-0108
848 W Penn Pike Tamaqua (18252) ***(G-18217)***
Leica Imaging Systems, Exton *Also called Leica Microsystems Inc* ***(G-5706)***
Leica Microsystems Inc 610 321-0434
410 Eagleview Blvd # 107 Exton (19341) ***(G-5706)***
Leico Manufacturing Corp 610 376-8288
981 River Rd Reading (19601) ***(G-16428)***
Leidys Inc (HQ) 215 723-4606
266 W Cherry Ln Souderton (18964) ***(G-17749)***
Leidys Custom Woodworking 717 328-9323
11427 Church Hill Rd Mercersburg (17236) ***(G-10990)***
Leiphart Enterprises LLC 717 938-4100
688 Yorktown Rd Ste A Lewisberry (17339) ***(G-9888)***
Leiss Tool & Die 814 444-1444
801 N Pleasant Ave Somerset (15501) ***(G-17695)***
Leister Machine 814 623-5992
1170 Dogwood Rd Bedford (15522) ***(G-1062)***
Leisters Furniture Inc 717 632-8177
433 Ridge Ave Hanover (17331) ***(G-6914)***
Leisure Books Division, Wayne *Also called Dorchester Publishing Co Inc* ***(G-19319)***
Leisure Graphics Inc 610 692-9872
808 Lauber Rd West Chester (19382) ***(G-19591)***
Leisure Line Stove Co, Berwick *Also called Black Rock Manufacturing Co* ***(G-1314)***
Leljedal Fencing, Forksville *Also called Curtis Leljedal Trading Loggn* ***(G-6056)***
Lem Products Inc 800 220-2400
147 Keystone Dr Montgomeryville (18936) ***(G-11403)***
Lema Novelty Co Inc 610 754-7242
309 Glenway Rd Glenside (19038) ***(G-6526)***
Lemac Packaging Inc (PA) 814 453-7652
2121 Mckinley Ave Erie (16503) ***(G-5361)***
Lemac Packaging Inc 814 866-7469
645 W 32nd St Erie (16508) ***(G-5362)***
Leman Machine Company 814 736-9696
1049 S Railroad Ave Portage (15946) ***(G-15918)***
Lemar Mast 610 286-0258
219 Mill Rd Morgantown (19543) ***(G-11524)***
Lemco Tool Corporation 570 494-0620
1850 Metzger Ave Cogan Station (17728) ***(G-3361)***
Lemm Liquidating Company LLC (HQ) 724 325-7140
3004 Venture Ct Export (15632) ***(G-5615)***
Lemos Labs LLC 724 519-2936
329 Pillow St Butler (16001) ***(G-2420)***
Len Dick Signs, Gettysburg *Also called Leonard Dick* ***(G-6304)***
Len Sabatine Automotive 610 258-8020
5238 S Delaware Dr Easton (18040) ***(G-4714)***
Lenape Castings, Perkasie *Also called Mervine Corp* ***(G-13284)***
Lenape Forged Products Corp 610 793-5090
1334 Lenape Rd West Chester (19382) ***(G-19592)***
Lenape Tooling Inc 215 257-0431
7 E Walnut St Perkasie (18944) ***(G-13283)***
Lengyel Electric 724 475-2045
1657 Mercer Rd Fredonia (16124) ***(G-6186)***
Lenny's Automotive, Mohrsville *Also called Leonard Leibensperger* ***(G-11277)***
Lennys Machine Company 814 490-4407
10047 Keystone Dr 200 Lake City (16423) ***(G-8904)***
Lennys Machine Company 814 474-5510
7900 Middle Rd Fairview (16415) ***(G-5831)***
Lenox Collections, Bristol *Also called Ceramic Art Company Inc* ***(G-2124)***
Lenox Corporation 610 954-7590
77 Sands Blvd Ste 223 Bethlehem (18015) ***(G-1560)***
Lenox Corporation (PA) 267 525-7800
1414 Radcliffe St Fl 1 Bristol (19007) ***(G-2159)***
Lenox Instrument Co Inc 215 322-9990
265 Andrews Rd Trevose (19053) ***(G-18500)***
Lenox Machine Inc 717 394-8760
833 2nd St Ste I Lancaster (17603) ***(G-9110)***
Lens Contact Center 724 543-2702
131 N Mckean St Kittanning (16201) ***(G-8777)***
Lensco, Philadelphia *Also called CPA Operations LLC* ***(G-13576)***
Lenscrafters, Monroeville *Also called Luxottica of America Inc* ***(G-11344)***
Lenscrafters, Springfield *Also called Luxottica of America Inc* ***(G-17918)***

ALPHABETIC

Lenscrafters, King of Prussia *Also called Luxottica of America Inc* **(G-8647)**

Lenscrafters, Erie *Also called Luxottica of America Inc* **(G-5375)**

Lenscrafters, Lancaster *Also called Luxottica of America Inc* **(G-9118)**

Leo Taur Technology Group Inc 610 966-3484
111 Lehigh St Macungie (18062) **(G-10153)**

Leon L Berkowitz Co 215 654-0800
2832 Mount Carmel Ave Glenside (19038) **(G-6527)**

Leon Miller & Company Ltd 412 281-8498
800 Penn Ave Ste 700 Pittsburgh (15222) **(G-15224)**

Leon O'Berholtzer, Lititz *Also called Rocky Ridge Steel LLC* **(G-10042)**

Leon Spangler 570 837-7903
44 N Shuman St Middleburg (17842) **(G-11028)**

Leona Meat Plant Inc 570 297-3574
1961 Leona Rd Troy (16947) **(G-18523)**

Leonard Anderson 724 463-3615
190 Anderson Rd Indiana (15701) **(G-8111)**

Leonard Block Company Inc 570 398-3376
560 Old Us Highway 220 Jersey Shore (17740) **(G-8317)**

Leonard Dick 717 334-8992
3000 York Rd Gettysburg (17325) **(G-6304)**

Leonard Forest Products 724 329-4703
114 Mudd Pike Rd Markleysburg (15459) **(G-10481)**

Leonard Leibensperger 610 926-7491
26 Railroad Rd Mohrsville (19541) **(G-11277)**

Leonards Auto Tag Service 570 489-4777
1500 Main St Ste 4 Dickson Cty (18447) **(G-4124)**

Leonards Auto Tag Service 570 693-0122
635 Luzerne St Ste 4 Scranton (18504) **(G-17254)**

Leonetti Food Distributors Inc 215 729-4200
5935 Woodland Ave Philadelphia (19143) **(G-13966)**

Leonetti Frozen Food, Philadelphia *Also called Leonetti Food Distributors Inc* **(G-13966)**

Leonhardt Manufacturing Co Inc 717 632-4150
800 High St Hanover (17331) **(G-6915)**

Lepko J D Finishing 215 538-9717
118 N Hellertown Ave Quakertown (18951) **(G-16210)**

Leprino Foods Company 570 888-9658
217 Yanuzzi Dr Sayre (18840) **(G-17118)**

Lerko Products 570 473-3501
103 Terrace St Northumberland (17857) **(G-12869)**

Lerner Laboratories, Pittsburgh *Also called Thermo Shandon Inc* **(G-15615)**

Leroy M Sensenig Inc 717 354-4756
115 S Railroad Ave New Holland (17557) **(G-12257)**

Lerro Candy Co 610 461-8886
601 Columbia Ave Darby (19023) **(G-4021)**

Lesher Inc 717 944-4431
2400 Swatara Creek Rd Middletown (17057) **(G-11062)**

Lesher Machine Shop Inc 717 263-0673
5522 Wayne Rd Chambersburg (17202) **(G-2952)**

Lesher Metal Stone and Tiles, Middletown *Also called Lesher Inc* **(G-11062)**

Lesjofors Springs America Inc 800 551-0298
250 Research Dr Pittston (18640) **(G-15762)**

Lesko Enterprises Inc 814 756-4030
21 Euclid St Albion (16401) **(G-46)**

Lesleh Precision Inc 724 823-0901
430 Jonathan Willey Rd Rostraver Township (15012) **(G-16827)**

Leslie S Geissel 215 884-1050
220 York Rd Jenkintown (19046) **(G-8294)**

Lester Water Inc 610 444-4660
920 S Union St Kennett Square (19348) **(G-8522)**

Letica Corporation 570 654-2451
2 Commerce Rd Pittston (18640) **(G-15763)**

Letica Corporation 570 883-0299
20 Commerce Rd Pittston (18640) **(G-15764)**

Lets Get Personal 412 829-0975
2526 Mnrvlle Blvd Ste 102 Monroeville (15146) **(G-11343)**

Letterco Inc 215 721-9010
108 Clarion Dr Souderton (18964) **(G-17750)**

Letterpress Shop 412 231-2282
R J Casey Industial Park Pittsburgh (15233) **(G-15225)**

Lettuce Turnip The Beet 412 334-8631
3008 Amy Dr South Park (15129) **(G-17784)**

Lettuce Turnip The Beet Csga, South Park *Also called Lettuce Turnip The Beet* **(G-17784)**

Level-Lok, Pittsburgh *Also called Brutis Enterprises Inc* **(G-14795)**

Leverwood Knife, Red Lion *Also called Leverwood Machine Works Inc* **(G-16604)**

Leverwood Machine Works Inc 717 246-4105
100 Redco Ave Ste D Red Lion (17356) **(G-16604)**

Levi Strauss & Co 610 337-0388
640 W Dekalb Pike # 1216 King of Prussia (19406) **(G-8640)**

Levine & Co, Robert T, Pittsburgh *Also called Levine Design Incorporated* **(G-15226)**

Levine Design Incorporated 412 288-0220
401 Amberson Ave Apt 103 Pittsburgh (15232) **(G-15226)**

Levis Only Stores Inc 717 337-1294
1863 Gettysburg Vlg Dr Gettysburg (17325) **(G-6305)**

Levittown Printing Inc 215 945-8156
1433 Haines Rd Levittown (19057) **(G-9845)**

Levroil LLC (PA) 412 722-9849
855 Lindsay Rd Pittsburgh (15242) **(G-15227)**

Lew-Hoc Wood Products Inc 814 486-0359
4725 Rich Valley Rd Emporium (15834) **(G-5067)**

Lewis & Hockenberry Inc (PA) 814 486-0359
4725 Rich Valley Rd Emporium (15834) **(G-5068)**

Lewis Bawol Welding, Erie *Also called Lewis Welding Services Inc* **(G-5363)**

Lewis Emmil Ornamental Iron Co, Coraopolis *Also called Ronald E Koller Welding* **(G-3724)**

Lewis Lumber & Supply Co Inc 412 828-3810
364 Plum St Oakmont (15139) **(G-12919)**

Lewis Lumber Products Inc 570 584-6167
30 S Main St Picture Rocks (17762) **(G-14585)**

Lewis Welding & Xcavating 570 353-7301
331 Plank Rd Morris (16938) **(G-11545)**

Lewis Welding Services Inc 814 838-1074
3308 W 22nd St Erie (16506) **(G-5363)**

Lewistown Cabinet Center Inc 717 667-2121
20 Water St Milroy (17063) **(G-11231)**

Lewistown Manufacturing Inc 717 242-1468
1 Belle Ave Bldg 1 # 1 Lewistown (17044) **(G-9938)**

Lewistown Sentinel Inc 717 248-6741
375 6th St Lewistown (17044) **(G-9939)**

Lewistown Valley Entps Inc 570 668-2089
416 Valley Rd Tamaqua (18252) **(G-18218)**

Lewrene Interiors 717 263-8300
110 Industrial Dr Chambersburg (17201) **(G-2953)**

Lexicon International Corp 215 639-8220
1400 Adams Rd Ste A Bensalem (19020) **(G-1220)**

Lexmark International Inc 610 966-8283
7631 Victoria Ln Coopersburg (18036) **(G-3630)**

Lexmarusa Inc 412 896-9266
627 Market St McKeesport (15132) **(G-10675)**

Lexyline Millwork 267 895-1733
196 W Ashland St Doylestown (18901) **(G-4312)**

Leybold USA Inc (HQ) 724 327-5700
5700 Mellon Rd Export (15632) **(G-5616)**

Lge Coachworks Inc 814 434-0856
10190 W Main Rd North East (16428) **(G-12750)**

Lia Diagnostics Inc 267 362-9670
737 Bainbridge St Philadelphia (19147) **(G-13967)**

Libertas Copper LLC (PA) 724 251-4200
100 Washington St Leetsdale (15056) **(G-9697)**

Liberty Atlantic, Bethlehem *Also called Cameron Supply Corporation* **(G-1478)**

Liberty Bell Beverages, Allentown *Also called Liberty Bell Bottling Co Inc* **(G-294)**

Liberty Bell Beverages 610 799-6600
4041 Route 309 Unit 2 Schnecksville (18078) **(G-17141)**

Liberty Bell Bottling Co Inc 610 820-6020
718 N 13th St Allentown (18102) **(G-294)**

Liberty Bell Steak Co 215 537-4797
3457 Janney St Philadelphia (19134) **(G-13968)**

Liberty Coca-Cola Bevs LLC (PA) 215 427-4500
725 E Erie Ave Philadelphia (19134) **(G-13969)**

Liberty Craftsmen Inc 717 871-0125
202 Springdale Ln Millersville (17551) **(G-11211)**

Liberty Electronics 814 676-0600
191 Howard St Reno (16343) **(G-16646)**

Liberty Electronics Inc 814 432-7505
189 Howard St Franklin (16323) **(G-6148)**

Liberty Homes Inc 717 656-2381
21 S Groffdale Rd Leola (17540) **(G-9793)**

Liberty Polyglas Pultrusions, West Mifflin *Also called Advanced Pultrusions LLC* **(G-19735)**

Liberty Press LLC 215 943-3788
4510 New Falls Rd Levittown (19056) **(G-9846)**

Liberty Pressed Metals LLC 814 885-6277
151 Irishtown Rd Kersey (15846) **(G-8563)**

Liberty Products Group Inc 215 631-1700
1500 Industry Rd Ste S Hatfield (19440) **(G-7364)**

Liberty Spring Company Inc 484 652-1100
109 Willows Ave Collingdale (19023) **(G-3406)**

Liberty Spring Usa LLC 484 652-1100
109 Willows Ave Darby (19023) **(G-4022)**

Liberty Throwing Company 570 287-1114
214 Pringle St Kingston (18704) **(G-8721)**

Liberty Uplink Inc 215 964-5222
2547 Yellow Springs Rd Malvern (19355) **(G-10267)**

Liberty Vhcl Ltg & Safety Sup 610 356-5320
700 Moore Industrial Park Prospect Park (19076) **(G-16116)**

Liberty View Creamery LLC 717 359-8206
467 Orphanage Rd Littlestown (17340) **(G-10070)**

Liberty Welding Co 412 661-1776
1235 Washington Blvd Pittsburgh (15206) **(G-15228)**

Libra Scale 412 782-0611
1601 Marys Ave Ste 6 Pittsburgh (15215) **(G-15229)**

Libra Three Inc 610 217-9992
2235 Little Gap Rd Palmerton (18071) **(G-13109)**

Librandi Machine Shop Inc 717 944-9442
93 Airport Dr Middletown (17057) **(G-11063)**

Librandi's Plating, Middletown *Also called Librandi Machine Shop Inc* **(G-11063)**

Library Bindery Co of PA Inc 215 855-2293
63 E Broad St Ste 6 Hatfield (19440) **(G-7365)**

Library Bindery of PA, Hatfield *Also called Hf Group LLC* **(G-7350)**

Library Video Company (PA) 610 645-4000
300 Barr Harbor Dr # 700 Conshohocken (19428) **(G-3572)**

Lids Corporation..814 868-1944
    654 Mllcreek Mall Ste 525 Erie (16565) *(G-5364)*

Life Support International..................................215 785-2870
    2250 Cabot Blvd W Ste 255 Langhorne (19047) *(G-9308)*

Life Tree Pharmacy Svcs LLC.............................610 522-2010
    800 Chester Pike Sharon Hill (19079) *(G-17458)*

Lifeaire Systems LLC.......................................484 224-3042
    1275 Glenlivet Dr Ste 100 Allentown (18106) *(G-295)*

Lifegas, Sewickley Also called Linde Gas North America LLC *(G-17399)*

Lifeguard Health Networks Inc............................484 584-4071
    993 Old Eagle School Rd Wayne (19087) *(G-19348)*

Lifescan Inc (HQ)..800 227-8862
    965 Chesterbrook Blvd Chesterbrook (19087) *(G-3093)*

Lifescan Global Corporation (PA)........................800 227-8862
    965 Chesterbrook Blvd Chesterbrook (19087) *(G-3094)*

Lifesensors Inc...610 644-8845
    271 Great Valley Pkwy Malvern (19355) *(G-10268)*

Lifestyle Evolution Inc (PA).............................412 828-4115
    520 2nd St Oakmont (15139) *(G-12920)*

Lifestyle Furniture USA, Pennsylvania Furnace Also called Sam Mannino Enterprises
LLC *(G-13264)*

Lifetime Bathtub Enclosures.............................215 228-2500
    2409 W Westmoreland St Philadelphia (19129) *(G-13970)*

Lifewatch Services Inc (HQ).............................847 720-2100
    1000 Cedar Hollow Rd # 102 Malvern (19355) *(G-10269)*

Lifewear Inc..610 327-2884
    284 N Hanover St Pottstown (19464) *(G-16011)*

Lifewear Inc (PA)..610 327-9938
    1280 Laurelwood Rd Pottstown (19465) *(G-15953)*

Lift-Tech Inc (PA)...717 898-6615
    1909 Mcfarland Dr Landisville (17538) *(G-9263)*

Liftex Corporation (PA)...................................800 478-4651
    48 Vincent Cir Ste D Ivyland (18974) *(G-8215)*

Light By Hutton, Pocono Pines Also called Hutton Metalcrafts Inc *(G-15881)*

Light My Fiber LLC...888 428-4454
    882 S Matlack St Ste 109 West Chester (19382) *(G-19593)*

Light Tool and Machine Inc...............................814 684-2755
    108 Enterprise Dr Tyrone (16686) *(G-18586)*

Lightbox Inc..610 954-8480
    532 E 4th St Bethlehem (18015) *(G-1561)*

Lighthouse Electric Contrls Co...........................814 835-2348
    1307 Lowell Ave Erie (16505) *(G-5365)*

Lighthouse Enrgy Solutions LLC..........................610 269-0113
    601 Ridgeview Dr Morgantown (19543) *(G-11525)*

Lighthouse Studios Inc....................................717 394-1300
    439 E Ross St Lancaster (17602) *(G-9111)*

Lighting Accents Inc.......................................412 761-5000
    3946 Oswald St Pittsburgh (15212) *(G-15230)*

Lighting By Led LLC..412 600-3132
    105 Berwyn Rd Pittsburgh (15237) *(G-15231)*

Lightning Gaming Inc (PA)................................610 494-5534
    23 Creek Cir Ste 400 Boothwyn (19061) *(G-1878)*

Lightning Group Inc (PA)..................................717 834-3031
    722 N Market St Duncannon (17020) *(G-4447)*

Lights Welding Inc...717 838-3931
    2628 Brandt Rd Annville (17003) *(G-653)*

Lightweight Manufacturing.................................610 435-4720
    1139 Sumner Ave Ste 1 Whitehall (18052) *(G-19883)*

Lignetics New England Inc...............................814 563-4358
    1055 Matthews Run Rd Youngsville (16371) *(G-20773)*

Lignitech Inc...814 474-9590
    8000c Middle Rd Fairview (16415) *(G-5832)*

Lignitech Limited, Fairview Also called Lignitech Inc *(G-5832)*

Ligonier Newsstand, Ligonier Also called Ligonier Outfitters Newsstands *(G-9961)*

Ligonier Outfitters Newsstands...........................724 238-4900
    127 W Main St Ligonier (15658) *(G-9961)*

Ligonier Stone & Lime Company...........................724 537-6023
    117 Marcia St Latrobe (15650) *(G-9500)*

Ligus Electric Mtr & Pump Svc............................570 287-1272
    340 Union St Luzerne (18709) *(G-10126)*

Lillie, Julie E Od, Erie Also called West Penn Optical Inc *(G-5528)*

Lilliput Play Homes Inc (PA)..............................724 348-7071
    6114 Brownsville Road Ext Finleyville (15332) *(G-5961)*

Lilly Pulitzer, King of Prussia Also called Sugartown Worldwide LLC *(G-8682)*

Lily Kay Doll Clothes LLC................................724 814-2210
    402 Hidden Meadow Dr Cranberry Township (16066) *(G-3832)*

Lilys LLC..814 938-9419
    535 E Mahoning St Punxsutawney (15767) *(G-16147)*

Lima Quick Print, Media Also called Country Press Inc *(G-10919)*

Limb Technologies Inc (PA)...............................215 781-8454
    2925 Veterans Hwy Bristol (19007) *(G-2160)*

Lime Kiln AG LLC...610 589-4302
    37 Weiser Ln Womelsdorf (19567) *(G-20207)*

Lime Rock Gazebos LLC....................................717 625-4066
    33 Limerock Rd Lititz (17543) *(G-10022)*

Lime Sportswear...484 461-7000
    164 S Bishop Ave Secane (19018) *(G-17318)*

Limeco, Cranesville Also called Liquid Meter Company Inc *(G-3868)*

Limestone Mobile Concrete...............................570 437-2640
    122 Strick Rd Milton (17847) *(G-11247)*

Limestone Products & Supply Co.........................412 221-5120
    260 Millers Run Rd Bridgeville (15017) *(G-2077)*

Limeville Quarry, East Earl Also called Martin Limestone Inc *(G-4548)*

Limeville Quarry, Gap Also called New Enterprise Stone Lime Inc *(G-6254)*

Limitless Longevity LLC...................................215 279-8376
    1429 Walnut St Ste 1101 Philadelphia (19102) *(G-13971)*

Limpach Industries Inc....................................724 646-4011
    6774 Orangeville Rd Sharpsville (16150) *(G-17473)*

Limpet Inc..610 273-7155
    1355 Walnut Rd Honey Brook (19344) *(G-7752)*

Lin Kay Associates Inc.....................................610 469-6833
    2132 Robin Ln Pottstown (19465) *(G-15954)*

Linbob LLC..610 375-7446
    82 Commerce Dr Reading (19610) *(G-16429)*

Lincoln Contg & Eqp Co Inc (HQ).........................814 629-6641
    2478 Lincoln Hwy Stoystown (15563) *(G-18082)*

Lincoln Fabricating Co Inc.................................412 361-2400
    1920 Lincoln Rd Pittsburgh (15235) *(G-15232)*

Lincoln Foundry Inc.......................................814 833-1514
    1600 Industrial Dr Erie (16505) *(G-5366)*

Lincoln Industrial Chemical Co............................610 375-4596
    600 S 9th St Reading (19602) *(G-16430)*

Lincoln Stone, Thomasville Also called York Building Products Co Inc *(G-18344)*

Lincoln Textile Pdts Co Inc................................484 281-3999
    900 Conroy Pl Bath (18014) *(G-965)*

Linda K Woodward Inc.....................................610 791-3694
    2310 26th St Sw Allentown (18103) *(G-296)*

Lindas Stuff Inc...215 956-9190
    330 S Warminster Rd # 340 Hatboro (19040) *(G-7292)*

Lindberg Tool, Waterford Also called Brent A Lindberg *(G-19260)*

Linde Corporation...570 299-5700
    118 Armstrong Rd Pittston (18640) *(G-15765)*

Linde Engineering N Amer Inc............................610 834-0300
    5 Sentry Pkwy E Ste 300 Blue Bell (19422) *(G-1844)*

Linde Gas North America LLC.............................610 539-6510
    2570 Blvd Of The Generals Norristown (19403) *(G-12675)*

Linde Gas North America LLC.............................412 741-6613
    503 North Dr Sewickley (15143) *(G-17399)*

Lindenmuth Saw Mill.......................................570 875-3546
    Taylorsville Rd Ashland (17921) *(G-734)*

Lindner Wood Technology Inc.............................610 820-8310
    1411 W Linden St Allentown (18102) *(G-297)*

Lindstrom Machine Shop..................................717 848-2983
    1420 Orange St Rear York (17404) *(G-20566)*

Line Tool Co, Allentown Also called Domenic Stangherlin *(G-195)*

Line-X of Cumberland County, Mechanicsburg Also called Wendells Prfmce Trck Sp
LLC *(G-10906)*

Linear Acoustic Inc..717 735-6142
    108 Foxshire Dr Lancaster (17601) *(G-9112)*

Linear Technology LLC.....................................215 638-9667
    3220 Tillman Dr Ste 120 Bensalem (19020) *(G-1221)*

Lineman & Sons...814 677-7215
    447 Mcpherson Rd Oil City (16301) *(G-12951)*

Linen Sand Supplies.......................................610 399-8305
    15 Bolingbroke Rd West Chester (19382) *(G-19594)*

Linett Co Inc..412 826-8531
    390 Fountain St Pittsburgh (15238) *(G-15233)*

Lingenfelter Awning.......................................814 696-4353
    Rr 764 Duncansville (16635) *(G-4455)*

Link Group Inc..215 957-6061
    341 Ivyland Rd Warminster (18974) *(G-18912)*

Link Software Corp...717 399-3023
    815 E Madison St Lancaster (17602) *(G-9113)*

Lintel Plant, York Also called York Building Products Co Inc *(G-20729)*

Lion Brewery Inc (PA).....................................570 823-8801
    700 N Pennsylvania Ave Wilkes Barre (18705) *(G-19936)*

Lion Energy Co LLC..724 444-7501
    5636 N Montour Rd Gibsonia (15044) *(G-6343)*

Lion Industrial Knife Co Inc...............................717 244-8195
    107 E High St Red Lion (17356) *(G-16605)*

Lion Ribbon Company LLC................................570 752-5934
    2015 W Front St Berwick (18603) *(G-1333)*

Lionette Enterprises.......................................814 274-9401
    156 Cherry Springs Rd Coudersport (16915) *(G-3784)*

Lionheart Holdings LLC (PA)..............................215 283-8400
    54 Friends Ln Ste 125 Newtown (18940) *(G-12519)*

Lionheart Industrial Group LLC...........................215 283-8400
    54 Friends Ln Ste 125 Newtown (18940) *(G-12520)*

Lionheart Ventures, Newtown Also called Lionheart Holdings LLC *(G-12519)*

Lions World Media LLC.....................................917 645-7590
    1498 Pine Rdg Bushkill (18324) *(G-2366)*

Lionshare Media Services.................................724 837-9700
    530 Pellis Rd Ste 8000a Greensburg (15601) *(G-6685)*

Lip Strippers, Yardley Also called Long Island Pllution Strippers *(G-20323)*

Lipella Pharmaceuticals Inc...............................412 901-0315
    400 N Lexington St # 103 Pittsburgh (15208) *(G-15234)*

Lipinski Logging and Lbr Inc 814 385-4101
 3731 State Route 208 Kennerdell (16374) *(G-8498)*

Lipkin's Bakery, Philadelphia *Also called Nawalany-Franciotti LLC (G-14059)*

Lippincott Williams & Wilkin, Philadelphia *Also called Wolters Kluwer Health Inc (G-14482)*

Lippincott Williams & Wilkins 215 521-8300
 530 Walnut St Fl 7 Philadelphia (19106) *(G-13972)*

Liquent Inc (HQ) 215 957-6401
 101 Gibraltar Rd Ste 200 Horsham (19044) *(G-7831)*

Liquid Container, York *Also called Graham Packaging Co Europe LLC (G-20508)*

Liquid Fence Co Inc (HQ) 570 722-8165
 5683 Route 115 Blakeslee (18610) *(G-1748)*

Liquid Ion Solutions LLC 412 275-0919
 1816 Parkway View Dr Pittsburgh (15205) *(G-15235)*

Liquid Meter Company Inc 814 756-5602
 10512 Crosby Cir Cranesville (16410) *(G-3868)*

Liquid Tech Tank Systems Inc 717 796-7056
 125 Old Orchard Rd Dillsburg (17019) *(G-4134)*

Liquid X Printed Metals Inc 412 426-3521
 252 Parkwest Dr Pittsburgh (15275) *(G-15236)*

Liquor Control Board PA 570 383-5248
 1512 Scrnton Crbndale Hwy Scranton (18508) *(G-17255)*

Lis, Lancaster *Also called Laser Imaging Systems Inc (G-9108)*

Lisa Leleu Studios Inc 215 345-1233
 100 Mechanics St Ste 1 Doylestown (18901) *(G-4313)*

Lisa Little Inc 814 697-7500
 262 Route 44 Shinglehouse (16748) *(G-17509)*

Lisa Mikolajczak 814 898-4700
 119 Lake Cliff Dr Erie (16511) *(G-5367)*

Lisa Thomas 724 748-3600
 1046 Perry Hwy Mercer (16137) *(G-10967)*

Lister Uphlstring Win Fashions, Bensalem *Also called Jerry Lister Custom Upholsteri (G-1213)*

Lite Fibers LLC 724 758-0123
 812 Marion Ave Ellwood City (16117) *(G-4943)*

Lite Tech Inc 610 650-8690
 975 Madison Ave Norristown (19403) *(G-12676)*

Litescaping LLC 814 833-6200
 2225 Colonial Ave Erie (16506) *(G-5368)*

Lithium Technology Corporation 888 776-0942
 5115 Campus Dr Plymouth Meeting (19462) *(G-15854)*

Lititz Flooring Company, Lititz *Also called Capri Cork LLC (G-9995)*

Lititz Planing Mill Co, Lititz *Also called EDM Co (G-10005)*

Lititz Record Express Inc 717 626-2191
 22 E Main St Lititz (17543) *(G-10023)*

Lititz Sign Company 717 626-7715
 400 N Cedar St Rear Lititz (17543) *(G-10024)*

Litter Quick, Irwin *Also called Sageking Inc (G-8199)*

Little Bear Creek Alpacas 814 788-0971
 971 Ogrin Rd Kane (16735) *(G-8471)*

Little Bits, Mechanicsburg *Also called G&R Designs LLC (G-10848)*

Little Earth Productions Inc 412 471-0909
 2400 Josephine St Ste 1 Pittsburgh (15203) *(G-15237)*

Little Johns Woodshop 724 924-9029
 2671 Copper Rd New Castle (16101) *(G-12116)*

Little Mountain Printing 717 933-8091
 234 E Rosebud Rd Myerstown (17067) *(G-11892)*

Little Partners Inc 318 220-7005
 501 S 9th St Reading (19602) *(G-16431)*

Little Pine Resources 814 765-6300
 2 E Market St Ste 1 Clearfield (16830) *(G-3223)*

Little Printing Co Inc (PA) 724 437-4831
 110 S Beeson Ave Uniontown (15401) *(G-18635)*

Little Round Industries LLC 215 361-1456
 2800 Richmond Rd Hatfield (19440) *(G-7366)*

Little Sheet Metal Inc 215 946-9970
 413 River Rd Bldg 90-1 Bristol (19007) *(G-2161)*

Little Souls Inc 610 278-0500
 222 Berkley Rd Devon (19333) *(G-4113)*

Little Wash Fabricators Inc 717 768-7356
 52 Mill St Christiana (17509) *(G-3141)*

Livent Corporation 215 299-6000
 2929 Walnut St Philadelphia (19104) *(G-13973)*

Lizzie BS Bakery 717 817-1791
 4250 Krebs Rd Glenville (17329) *(G-6545)*

Lizzie High Collection, Sellersville *Also called Ladie & Friends Inc (G-17353)*

LLC Armstrong Power 724 354-5300
 2313 State Route 156 Shelocta (15774) *(G-17486)*

LLC Snyder Gates 877 621-0195
 2339 Highland Rd Millerstown (17062) *(G-11205)*

Llc, Dentsply, Lancaster *Also called Dentsply Sirona Inc (G-8994)*

Lloyd Concrete Products, Tarentum *Also called Stacy Lloyd (G-18247)*

Lloyd Industries Inc (PA) 215 367-5863
 231 Commerce Dr Montgomeryville (18936) *(G-11404)*

Lloyd Jones 610 395-3386
 6265 Hamilton Blvd Allentown (18106) *(G-298)*

Lls Graphics 610 435-9055
 632 N 8th St Allentown (18102) *(G-299)*

Lmc-Plasticsource, Bensalem *Also called Laminated Materials Corp (G-1218)*

LMS, Lancaster *Also called Lancaster Metals Science Corp (G-9102)*

LMS Stampings, Bethlehem *Also called Smoyer L M Brass Products Inc (G-1620)*

Lmt Corp of Pennsylvania 610 921-3926
 205 E Bellevue Ave Reading (19605) *(G-16432)*

Lnp Media Group Inc 717 733-6397
 1 E Main St Ephrata (17522) *(G-5121)*

Load Control Technologies, King of Prussia *Also called Innovation Plus Llc (G-8634)*

Local Media Group Inc 570 421-3000
 511 Lenox St Stroudsburg (18360) *(G-18125)*

Local Media Group Inc 724 458-5010
 201 Erie St Ste A Grove City (16127) *(G-6795)*

Local Media Group Inc 570 524-2261
 328 Market St Ste 4 Lewisburg (17837) *(G-9915)*

Local Pages Publishing LLC 610 579-3809
 2811 W Crossing Cir Norristown (19403) *(G-12677)*

Localedge Media Inc 716 875-9100
 3715 Zimmerman Rd Erie (16510) *(G-5369)*

Lochs Maple Fiber Mill Inc 570 965-2679
 143 Cokely Rd Springville (18844) *(G-17931)*

Lock 3 Company 724 258-7773
 1469 Delberts Dr Monongahela (15063) *(G-11310)*

Lock and Mane 215 221-2131
 30 W Bridge St Ste 2 New Hope (18938) *(G-12308)*

Lock Haven Express 570 748-6791
 9 W Main St Lock Haven (17745) *(G-10090)*

Lockcrete Bauer 800 419-9255
 119 Ruth Hill Rd Worthington (16262) *(G-20230)*

Locker Plant LLC 814 652-2714
 422 E South St Everett (15537) *(G-5574)*

Lockhart Chemical Company (PA) 724 444-1900
 2873 W Hardies Rd Gibsonia (15044) *(G-6344)*

Lockhart Company (PA) 724 444-1900
 2873 W Hardies Rd Ste 1 Gibsonia (15044) *(G-6345)*

Lockhart Gene Canvas Awnings, Philadelphia *Also called Canvas Awnings Inc (G-13498)*

Lockhart Holdings Inc (HQ) 724 444-1900
 2873 W Hardies Rd Ste 1 Gibsonia (15044) *(G-6346)*

Lockhart Industries, Gibsonia *Also called Lockhart Company (G-6345)*

Lockheed Martin Aeroparts 814 262-3000
 211 Industrial Park Rd Johnstown (15904) *(G-8404)*

Lockheed Martin Corporation 610 337-9560
 2111 Yellow Springs Rd Malvern (19355) *(G-10270)*

Lockheed Martin Corporation 570 307-1590
 1270 Mid Valley Dr Jessup (18434) *(G-8331)*

Lockheed Martin Corporation 717 267-5796
 Advantage Ave Bldg 13 Chambersburg (17201) *(G-2954)*

Lockheed Martin Corporation 610 382-3200
 230 Mall Blvd King of Prussia (19406) *(G-8641)*

Lockheed Martin Corporation 610 354-7782
 900 Forge Ave Audubon (19403) *(G-829)*

Lockheed Martin Corporation 610 354-3083
 230 Mall Blvd King of Prussia (19406) *(G-8642)*

Lockheed Martin Corporation 610 531-7400
 230 Mall Blvd King of Prussia (19406) *(G-8643)*

Lockheed Martin Corporation 610 962-4954
 230 Mall Blvd King of Prussia (19406) *(G-8644)*

Lockheed Martin Corporation 610 531-7400
 7000 Geerdes Blvd King of Prussia (19406) *(G-8645)*

Lockheed Martin Corporation 570 876-2132
 459 Kennedy Dr Archbald (18403) *(G-691)*

Lockheed Martin Corporation 610 962-2264
 700 American Ave Ste 101 King of Prussia (19406) *(G-8646)*

Lockheed Martin Corporation 610 531-5640
 590 Lancaster Ave Malvern (19355) *(G-10271)*

Lockheed Martin Corporation 814 262-3000
 211 Industrial Park Rd Johnstown (15904) *(G-8405)*

Loco Yoco 570 331-4529
 26 Pierce St Kingston (18704) *(G-8722)*

Locus Pharmaceuticals Inc (PA) 215 358-2000
 512 Township Line Rd Blue Bell (19422) *(G-1845)*

Locust Ridge Quarry, Skippack *Also called H&K Group Inc (G-17597)*

Locust Ridge Woodworks LLC 610 350-6029
 56 Schoolhouse Rd Kirkwood (17536) *(G-8750)*

Locust Run Pallet LLC 717 535-5883
 299 Jonestown Rd Thompsontown (17094) *(G-18348)*

Loeffler Corporation 215 757-2404
 201 E Lincoln Hwy Langhorne (19047) *(G-9309)*

Log Cabin Embroidery Inc 724 327-5929
 3941 William Penn Hwy # 3 Murrysville (15668) *(G-11855)*

Log Hard Premium Pellets Inc 814 654-2100
 44939 Old Route 77 Spartansburg (16434) *(G-17852)*

Logo Depot Inc 610 543-3890
 627 Park Way Broomall (19008) *(G-2294)*

Logo Wearhouse, Broomall *Also called Logo Depot Inc (G-2294)*

Logue Industries Inc 570 368-2639
 120 S Arch St Montoursville (17754) *(G-11445)*

Loh Enterprises LLC 570 737-4143
 318 Davis St Ste 1 Clarks Summit (18411) *(G-3197)*

Loh Medical, Clarks Summit *Also called Loh Enterprises LLC (G-3197)*

Lollipop HM Halthcare Svcs LLC 570 286-9460
204 N Front St Sunbury (17801) *(G-18171)*

Lombardo Industries 412 264-4588
1813 Madison Dr Coraopolis (15108) *(G-3702)*

Lombardo Quarry, Wyalusing *Also called Tony Bennett Flagstone (G-20259)*

Lomed Inc 800 477-0239
553 Geigel Hill Rd Ottsville (18942) *(G-13066)*

Lomma Investments 570 346-5555
305 Cherry St Scranton (18505) *(G-17256)*

Lomma Investments Citrus Div, Scranton *Also called Lomma Investments (G-17256)*

Lon Hyde 814 763-4140
16380 State Highway 86 Saegertown (16433) *(G-16922)*

London Wreath Co Inc 215 739-6440
2014 E Orleans St Philadelphia (19134) *(G-13974)*

Lone Star Western Beef Inc 484 509-2093
115 Little Rock Rd Reading (19605) *(G-16433)*

Lonergan Pump Systems Inc 610 770-2050
127 N Lumber St Allentown (18102) *(G-300)*

Lonestar, Stockertown *Also called Buzzi Unicem USA Inc (G-18064)*

Long Drop Games LLC 814 460-7961
2110 Knoll Ave Erie (16510) *(G-5370)*

Long Island Pllution Strippers 215 752-2709
484 Franklin Cir Yardley (19067) *(G-20323)*

Long Trout Enterprises Inc 570 366-6443
84 Fork Mountain Rd Auburn (17922) *(G-818)*

Longacres Modern Dairy Inc 610 845-7551
1445 Rte 100 Barto (19504) *(G-945)*

Longevity Brands LLC 484 373-3600
610 Uhler Rd Easton (18040) *(G-4715)*

Longevity Coatings 610 871-1427
221 Evergreen Ct Saylorsburg (18353) *(G-17105)*

Longevity Prmier Ntraceuticals 877 529-1118
325 Chestnut St Fl 8 Philadelphia (19106) *(G-13975)*

Longos Bakery Inc 570 233-0558
138 W 21st St Hazleton (18201) *(G-7508)*

Longs Hardwoods Inc 814 472-4740
Hc 3 Ebensburg (15931) *(G-4786)*

Longs Horseradish 717 872-9343
2192 W Ridge Dr Lancaster (17603) *(G-9114)*

Longs Water Technol 610 398-3737
State Rt 309 Orefield (18069) *(G-13014)*

Longwall Mining Services Inc 724 816-7871
9862 Old Kummer Rd Allison Park (15101) *(G-456)*

Longwall Services Inc 724 228-9898
63 S Country Club Rd Meadow Lands (15347) *(G-10691)*

Longwood Manufacturing Corp 610 444-4200
816 E Baltimore Pike Kennett Square (19348) *(G-8523)*

Lontex Corporation 610 272-5040
8 Dekalb St Fl 4 Norristown (19401) *(G-12678)*

Lonza Inc 570 321-3900
3500 Trenton Ave Williamsport (17701) *(G-20035)*

Loomis Products Company 215 547-2121
5500 Bristol Emilie Rd Levittown (19057) *(G-9847)*

Loranger International Corp (PA) 814 723-2250
817 4th Ave Warren (16365) *(G-19038)*

Lord Corporation 814 868-0924
2455 Robison Rd W Erie (16509) *(G-5371)*

Lord Corporation 814 763-2345
601 South St Saegertown (16433) *(G-16923)*

Lord Corporation 814 398-4641
124 Grant St Cambridge Springs (16403) *(G-2481)*

Lord Corporation 724 260-5541
267 Arrowhead Ln Eighty Four (15330) *(G-4844)*

Lord Corporation 814 868-3180
2455 Robison Rd W Erie (16509) *(G-5372)*

Lord Corporation 877 275-5673
2455 Robison Rd W Erie (16509) *(G-5373)*

Lord Industrial Products, Erie *Also called Lord Corporation (G-5373)*

Lore's Chocolate, Philadelphia *Also called Wfc & C Inc (G-14471)*

Lorenzo Fst Flw Cylinder Heads 215 750-8324
112 Reetz Ave Langhorne (19047) *(G-9310)*

Lost Creek Mining 724 335-8780
212 Gabrielle Dr New Kensington (15068) *(G-12353)*

Lost Creek Shoe Shop Inc 717 463-3117
643 Oakland Rd Mifflintown (17059) *(G-11129)*

Lost Tavern Brewing LLC 484 851-3980
782 Main St Hellertown (18055) *(G-7558)*

Lot Made Gallery LLC 717 458-8716
43 W Main St Mechanicsburg (17055) *(G-10866)*

Loudon Industries Inc (PA) 717 328-9808
140 Landis Dr Mercersburg (17236) *(G-10991)*

Louis Berkman Company (PA) 740 283-3722
600 Grant St Ste 3230 Pittsburgh (15219) *(G-15238)*

Louis Emmel Co 412 859-6781
821 Branchton Rd Boyers (16020) *(G-1889)*

Louis Fliszar 610 865-6494
3721 Amherst Ct Bethlehem (18020) *(G-1562)*

Louis G Sredy 814 445-7229
1908 Water Level Rd Somerset (15501) *(G-17696)*

Louis Mattes Jr (PA) 412 653-1266
1231 Gill Hall Rd Clairton (15025) *(G-3153)*

Louis Nardello Company 215 467-1420
124 Cornerstone Dr Newtown Square (19073) *(G-12582)*

Louis Neibauer Co Inc 215 322-6200
20 Industrial Dr Warminster (18974) *(G-18913)*

Louis P Canuso Inc 610 366-7914
7522 Morris Ct Ste 1 Allentown (18106) *(G-301)*

Louise Grace Publishing 610 781-6874
2368 High St Reading (19605) *(G-16434)*

Louisville Ladder Inc 215 638-8904
855 Dunksferry Rd Bensalem (19020) *(G-1222)*

Louston International Inc 610 859-9860
168 E Ridge Rd Ste 202 Marcus Hook (19061) *(G-10447)*

Lovell Strouble Inc 570 326-5561
312 South St Williamsport (17701) *(G-20036)*

Loveshaw Corporation 570 937-4921
2206 Easton Tpke South Canaan (18459) *(G-17769)*

Lowlander Corporation 412 221-1240
105 4th St Apt 306 Monaca (15061) *(G-11291)*

Loyal Gaming Rewards LLC 814 822-2008
139 Stadium Dr Altoona (16601) *(G-522)*

Lozier Corporation 570 658-8111
48 E Ohio St Mc Clure (17841) *(G-10560)*

Lpg Industries Inc 610 622-2900
307 N Sycamore Ave Clifton Heights (19018) *(G-3254)*

LPI, Rostraver Township *Also called Lesleh Precision Inc (G-16827)*

LPT Trucking, North Bend *Also called Thompson Logging and Trckg Inc (G-12727)*

Lpw Racing Products Inc 717 394-7432
632 E Marion St Lancaster (17602) *(G-9115)*

Lpw Technology Inc 844 480-7663
110 S Campus Dr Imperial (15126) *(G-8070)*

LRG Corporation 724 523-3131
210 Magee Ave Jeannette (15644) *(G-8261)*

Lrp Magazine Group 215 784-0860
747 Dresher Rd Ste 500 Dresher (19025) *(G-4356)*

Lrp Publications Inc 215 784-0941
747 Dresher Rd Ste 500 Horsham (19044) *(G-7832)*

Lrt Sensors Inc 877 299-8595
71 Sunflower Way Huntingdon Valley (19006) *(G-8009)*

Ls Steel Inc 717 669-4581
1318 W Kings Hwy Coatesville (19320) *(G-3314)*

Ls Zittle Company, Philadelphia *Also called Wade Technology Incorporated (G-14456)*

Lsc Acquistion Company Inc 412 795-6400
100 Herman Dr Pittsburgh (15239) *(G-15239)*

Lsc Communications Us LLC 717 392-4074
1375 Harrisburg Pike Lancaster (17601) *(G-9116)*

Lsc Company, Pittsburgh *Also called Lsc Acquistion Company Inc (G-15239)*

Lsc Equipment, Lancaster *Also called Lancaster Parts & Eqp Inc (G-9103)*

LSI Controls Inc 717 762-2191
11664 Orchard Rd Waynesboro (17268) *(G-19415)*

Lt, Hatfield *Also called Laboratory Testing Inc (G-7361)*

Ltc, Lebanon *Also called Lebanon Tool Co Inc (G-9604)*

LTI, Williamsport *Also called Lundy Warehousing Inc (G-20037)*

LTI Orthotic Prosthetic Center, Bristol *Also called Limb Technologies Inc (G-2160)*

Ltl Color Compounders LLC 215 736-1126
20 Progress Dr Morrisville (19067) *(G-11570)*

Ltlprints.com, Philadelphia *Also called Rockpetz Ventures LLC (G-14256)*

Lu-Mac Inc 724 763-3750
2021 State Route 66 Ford City (16226) *(G-6049)*

Lube Center 717 848-4885
1195 Loucks Rd York (17404) *(G-20567)*

Lube Systems Company 724 335-4050
416 Utopia Rd Apollo (15613) *(G-682)*

Lubedealercom 814 521-9625
417 Yonai Rd Berlin (15530) *(G-1290)*

Lubiniecki Welding & Equipment, Meadville *Also called Lwe Inc (G-10751)*

Lubrite LLC (HQ) 814 337-4234
18649 Brake Shoe Rd Meadville (16335) *(G-10750)*

Lubrite Technologies, Meadville *Also called Lubrite LLC (G-10750)*

Luccis 903 600-5848
101 N York Rd Hatboro (19040) *(G-7293)*

Luccis Bakery 570 876-3830
171 S Main St Archbald (18403) *(G-692)*

Luchs John L Logging, Ridgway *Also called John L Luchs Logging (G-16715)*

Lucifer Furnaces Inc 215 343-0411
2048 Bunnell Rd Warrington (18976) *(G-19123)*

Lucisano Bros Inc 215 945-2700
665 River Rd Ste 1 Bristol (19007) *(G-2162)*

Lucks Upper Bucks Gym LLC 610 847-2392
542 Cafferty Hill Rd Upper Black Eddy (18972) *(G-18655)*

Lucky Sign Shop Inc 610 459-5825
1348 Middletown Rd Glen Mills (19342) *(G-6439)*

Lucky Vitamin LLC 412 741-2598
Ave B And Ferry St Bldg 8 Leetsdale (15056) *(G-9698)*

Luckyvitamin.com, Leetsdale *Also called Lucky Vitamin LLC (G-9698)*

Lucy's Foods, Latrobe *Also called Zappone Bros Foods (G-9529)*

Luftrol Inc 215 355-0532
  550 Concord Rd Warminster (18974) **(G-18914)**
Lug-All Co Inc 610 286-9884
  604 Hemlock Rd Morgantown (19543) **(G-11526)**
Luhv Food, Hatboro *Also called Luccis* **(G-7293)**
Luicana Industries Inc 570 325-9699
  99 Packer Hl Jim Thorpe (18229) **(G-8341)**
Lukas Confections Inc 717 843-0921
  310 N Locust St Ebensburg (15931) **(G-4787)**
Lukens Inc 610 383-2000
  50 S 1st Ave Coatesville (19320) **(G-3315)**
Lukens Steel, Coatesville *Also called Lukens Inc* **(G-3315)**
Lukjan Supply & Manufacturing (PA) 814 838-1328
  4364 W Ridge Rd Erie (16506) **(G-5374)**
Lumber and Things Inc 717 848-1622
  1850 Lemon St York (17404) **(G-20568)**
Lumenoptix LLC 215 671-2029
  203 Progress Dr Montgomeryville (18936) **(G-11405)**
Lumi Trak Inc 717 235-2863
  230 Orwig Rd New Freedom (17349) **(G-12212)**
Luminite Products Corporation 814 817-1420
  148 Commerce Dr Bradford (16701) **(G-1980)**
Lumsden Corporation (PA) 717 394-6871
  10 Abraso St Lancaster (17601) **(G-9117)**
Luna Collison Ltd 412 466-8866
  316 Grant Ave Duquesne (15110) **(G-4497)**
Lunacor Inc 610 328-6150
  616 Sheffield Dr Springfield (19064) **(G-17917)**
Lunchera LLC 787 607-8914
  5930 Walnut St Apt C3 Pittsburgh (15232) **(G-15240)**
Lundy Warehousing Inc 570 327-4541
  25 W 3rd St Ste 504 Williamsport (17701) **(G-20037)**
Lung Hing Noodle Company Inc 215 829-1988
  928 Ridge Ave Philadelphia (19107) **(G-13976)**
Luposello Enterprises 570 994-2500
  107 Bull Run N Milford (18337) **(G-11162)**
Lusch Frames For Upholstering, Philadelphia *Also called Lusch Frames LLC* **(G-13977)**
Lusch Frames LLC 215 739-6264
  1127 E Dunton St Philadelphia (19123) **(G-13977)**
Luscious Layers 724 967-2357
  140 Garden Ave Grove City (16127) **(G-6796)**
Lusitania Bakery, Bethlehem *Also called Lee High Valley Bakers LLC* **(G-1556)**
Luson Drums LLC 412 867-9404
  5328 Forbes Ave Pittsburgh (15217) **(G-15241)**
Lustra-Line LLC 412 766-5757
  2901 Brighton Rd Pittsburgh (15212) **(G-15242)**
Lutech Inc 717 898-9150
  127 W Main St Ste B Salunga (17538) **(G-17054)**
Lutron Electronics Co Inc 610 282-6617
  8240 Spring Creek Rd Alburtis (18011) **(G-56)**
Lutron Electronics Co Inc 610 282-6268
  6540 Stonegate Dr Allentown (18106) **(G-302)**
Lutz and Associates (PA) 724 776-9800
  20232 Route 19 Ste 5 Cranberry Township (16066) **(G-3833)**
Lux Ornamental Iron Works Inc 412 481-5677
  1815 S 18th St Pittsburgh (15203) **(G-15243)**
Luxcelis Technologies LLC 724 424-1800
  45 Bay Hill Dr Latrobe (15650) **(G-9501)**
Luxfer Magtech Inc 570 668-0001
  1415 E Broad St Tamaqua (18252) **(G-18219)**
Luxottica of America Inc 412 373-2200
  370 Monroeville Mall Monroeville (15146) **(G-11344)**
Luxottica of America Inc 610 543-8622
  910 E Woodland Ave Rear A Springfield (19064) **(G-17918)**
Luxottica of America Inc 610 962-5945
  160 N Gulph Rd Ste 1065 King of Prussia (19406) **(G-8647)**
Luxottica of America Inc 814 868-7502
  200 Millcreek Plz Erie (16565) **(G-5375)**
Luxottica of America Inc 717 295-3001
  1158 Park City Ctr Lancaster (17601) **(G-9118)**
Luxtech LLC 888 340-4266
  325 Chestnut St Ste 1212 Philadelphia (19106) **(G-13978)**
Luxury Electronics LLC 215 847-0937
  660 Bayberry Ln Yardley (19067) **(G-20324)**
LUZERNE COUNTY BAR ASSOCIATION, Wilkes Barre *Also called Wilkes Barre Law & Lib Assn* **(G-19975)**
Luzerne Iron Works, Luzerne *Also called Luzerne Ironworks Inc* **(G-10127)**
Luzerne Ironworks Inc 570 288-1950
  300 Sly St Luzerne (18709) **(G-10127)**
Luzerne Optical Laboratories 570 822-3183
  180 N Wilkes Barre Blvd Wilkes Barre (18702) **(G-19937)**
Luzerne Trading Company Inc 866 954-4440
  8 W Market St Ste 930 Wilkes Barre (18701) **(G-19938)**
Lwb Holding Company 717 792-3611
  425 S Salem Church Rd York (17408) **(G-20569)**
Lwb Holding Company (HQ) 717 792-3611
  425 S Salem Church Rd York (17408) **(G-20570)**
Lwb Refractories Co, York *Also called Magnesita Refractories Company* **(G-20572)**

Lwe Inc 814 336-3553
  17071 Cussewago Rd Meadville (16335) **(G-10751)**
Lyco I LLC 570 784-0903
  147 W 4th St Bloomsburg (17815) **(G-1788)**
Lycoming Bakery, South Williamsport *Also called Hoyt Inc* **(G-17792)**
Lycoming Burial Vault Co Inc 570 368-8642
  350 Spruce St Montoursville (17754) **(G-11446)**
Lycoming Concrete Septic Tanks, Montoursville *Also called Lycoming Burial Vault Co Inc* **(G-11446)**
Lycoming Screen Printing Co 570 326-3301
  1 Maynard St Williamsport (17701) **(G-20038)**
Lydall Performance Mtls US Inc 717 207-6000
  310 Running Pump Rd Lancaster (17603) **(G-9119)**
Lydall Performance Mtls US Inc 717 207-6025
  320 Running Pump Rd Lancaster (17603) **(G-9120)**
Lydall Performance Mtls US Inc (HQ) 717 390-1886
  216 Wohlsen Way Lancaster (17603) **(G-9121)**
Lykens Corporation 814 375-9961
  336 Aspen Way Du Bois (15801) **(G-4403)**
Lynar Corporation 610 395-3155
  6837 Patterson Ct Allentown (18106) **(G-303)**
Lyndan Cabinets Inc 724 626-9630
  27 Wills Rd Connellsville (15425) **(G-3502)**
Lyndan Designs Inc 724 626-9630
  27 Wills Rd Connellsville (15425) **(G-3503)**
Lynn Electronics Corp (PA) 215 355-8200
  154 Railroad Dr Ivyland (18974) **(G-8216)**
Lynn Electronics Corp 215 826-9600
  171 Rittenhouse Cir Bristol (19007) **(G-2163)**
Lynn Electronics Corp 954 977-3800
  154 Railroad Dr Warminster (18974) **(G-18915)**
Lynn Parker Associates LLC 561 406-6472
  14 Forest View Rd Rose Valley (19086) **(G-16818)**
Lynx Specialty Tapes Inc 215 348-1382
  4264 Southview Ln Doylestown (18902) **(G-4314)**
Lyondell Chemical Company 610 359-2360
  3801 West Chester Pike Newtown Square (19073) **(G-12583)**
Lyons Electric Motor Service 814 456-7127
  1427 E 10th St Erie (16503) **(G-5376)**
Lyons Industries Inc 814 472-9770
  3912 Admiral Peary Hwy Ebensburg (15931) **(G-4788)**
Lyrrus Inc 215 922-0880
  1080 N Delaware Ave Fl 8 Philadelphia (19125) **(G-13979)**
Lzk Manufacturing Inc 717 891-5792
  28 Onion Blvd Shrewsbury (17361) **(G-17585)**
M & A Coatings LLC 724 267-2868
  1508 Amity Ridge Rd Washington (15301) **(G-19196)**
M & B Machine Inc 717 766-7879
  10 Long Ln Ste 102 Mechanicsburg (17050) **(G-10867)**
M & C Lumber Co Inc 717 573-2200
  4693 Great Cove Rd Warfordsburg (17267) **(G-18813)**
M & C Specialties Co 215 322-7441
  90 James Way Southampton (18966) **(G-17823)**
M & D Industries Inc 814 723-2381
  251 S Main St Clarendon (16313) **(G-3170)**
M & G Packaging Corp 610 363-7455
  602 Jeffers Cir Ste 120 Exton (19341) **(G-5707)**
M & J Sales, Cranberry Township *Also called Lasting Expressions* **(G-3831)**
M & M Cabinets LLC 412 220-9663
  3265 Millers Run Rd Cecil (15321) **(G-2822)**
M & M Creative Laminates Inc 412 781-4700
  4 5th St Aspinwall (15215) **(G-746)**
M & M Displays Inc 800 874-7171
  3301 Maiden Ln Philadelphia (19145) **(G-13980)**
M & M Industries Inc (PA) 610 447-0663
  800 W Front St Ste 2a Chester (19013) **(G-3056)**
M & M Lime Co Inc 724 297-3958
  215 Nichola Rd Worthington (16262) **(G-20231)**
M & M Manufacturing Co 724 274-0767
  460 Nixon Rd Cheswick (15024) **(G-3111)**
M & M Quick Print, Springfield *Also called First Shelburne Corporation* **(G-17914)**
M & M Salt & Pallet 717 845-4039
  235 Sheffield Dr Dallastown (17313) **(G-3979)**
M & M Sheet Metal Inc 570 326-4655
  2104 Marydale Ave Williamsport (17701) **(G-20039)**
M & M Shtmtl & Fabricators, Williamsport *Also called M & M Sheet Metal Inc* **(G-20039)**
M & M Tool & Die Inc (PA) 717 359-7178
  10 E King St Littlestown (17340) **(G-10071)**
M & M Tool & Die Inc 717 359-7178
  10 E King St Littlestown (17340) **(G-10072)**
M & M Welding & Fabricating 724 794-2045
  124 Smith Rd Slippery Rock (16057) **(G-17620)**
M & M Wood Products Inc 570 638-2234
  159 Lake St Morris Run (16939) **(G-11546)**
M & P Refinishing Co 724 527-6360
  212 S 5th St Jeannette (15644) **(G-8262)**
M & Q Plastic Products Co (PA) 484 369-8906
  542 N Lewis Rd Ste 206 Limerick (19468) **(G-9969)**
M & R Electric Inc 412 831-6101
  2025 Milford Dr Bethel Park (15102) **(G-1423)**

M & R Woodworks Inc 724 378-7677
  412 Chapel Rd Apt C Aliquippa (15001) *(G-81)*

M & S Centerless Grinding Inc 215 675-4144
  258 E County Line Rd Hatboro (19040) *(G-7294)*

M & S Conversion Company Inc 570 368-1991
  248 Streibeigh Ln Montoursville (17754) *(G-11447)*

M & T Industries LLC 724 216-5256
  1265 Brinkerton Rd Greensburg (15601) *(G-6686)*

M A Hanna Color 610 317-3300
  2513 Highland Ave Bethlehem (18020) *(G-1563)*

M A S Printing & Storage, Williamsport *Also called Michael Anthony Salvatori (G-20041)*

M and M Pallet LLC 717 845-4039
  1601 W King St Ste 1 York (17404) *(G-20571)*

M and P Custom Design Inc 610 444-0244
  510 S Walnut St Kennett Square (19348) *(G-8524)*

M B Bedding Co 570 822-2491
  526 S Main St Unit 1 Wilkes Barre (18701) *(G-19939)*

M B Graphics 717 246-9000
  608 Nottingham Way Red Lion (17356) *(G-16606)*

M B Mumma Inc 610 372-6962
  503 Penn St Ste 2 Reading (19601) *(G-16435)*

M C E Development Inc 412 952-0918
  27 Renaissance Dr Irwin (15642) *(G-8181)*

M C Enterprises, Irwin *Also called M C E Development Inc (G-8181)*

M C M Machine & Tool Inc 570 897-5472
  2561 N Delaware Dr Mount Bethel (18343) *(G-11612)*

M C Tool & Die Inc 814 944-8654
  3387 Colonel Drake Hwy Altoona (16601) *(G-523)*

M Cibrone & Sons Bakery Inc 412 885-6200
  1231 Grove Rd Pittsburgh (15234) *(G-15244)*

M D Cline Metal Fabg Inc 724 459-8968
  832 Penn View Rd Blairsville (15717) *(G-1733)*

M D Pharma Connection LLC 814 371-7726
  102 E Long Ave Du Bois (15801) *(G-4404)*

M Dobron & Sons Inc 215 297-5331
  7273 Ferry Rd Point Pleasant (18950) *(G-15887)*

M E Enterprise Services Inc 570 457-5221
  325 Bridge St Old Forge (18518) *(G-12968)*

M E I, Jenkintown *Also called Managing Editor Inc (G-8295)*

M E Inc 610 820-5250
  133 Mickley Rd Whitehall (18052) *(G-19884)*

M E Kmachine 570 636-0710
  450 Ridge St Freeland (18224) *(G-6195)*

M G Industries 814 238-5092
  1348 Benner Pike State College (16801) *(G-17987)*

M G S Trailers, Denver *Also called Mgs Inc (G-4083)*

M Glosser & Sons Inc 412 751-4700
  1 Douglas St Mc Keesport (15134) *(G-10642)*

M H EBY Inc (PA) 800 292-4752
  1194 Main St Blue Ball (17506) *(G-1811)*

M I P Inc 724 643-5114
  1066 Midland Ave Midland (15059) *(G-11087)*

M J M Industries 724 368-8400
  1 Good Pl Ste A Portersville (16051) *(G-15931)*

M J Stranko Inc 610 929-8080
  2413 Hampden Blvd Reading (19604) *(G-16436)*

M K Crafts 717 786-6080
  450 Walnut Run Rd Strasburg (17579) *(G-18091)*

M L Scott & Sons 610 847-5671
  8537 Easton Rd Revere (18953) *(G-16653)*

M L T U S, New Castle *Also called Magnetic Lifting Tech US LLC (G-12118)*

M P N Inc (PA) 215 289-9480
  3675 Amber St Philadelphia (19134) *(G-13981)*

M Robzen Inc 570 283-1226
  734 Milford Dr Kingston (18704) *(G-8723)*

M S & M Manufacturing Co Inc 215 743-3930
  7707 Dungan Rd Philadelphia (19111) *(G-13982)*

M S A, Cranberry Township *Also called Mine Safety Appliances Co LLC (G-3836)*

M S S I Inc 412 771-5533
  264 Valley Brook Rd Canonsburg (15317) *(G-2600)*

M Shanken Communications Inc 610 967-1083
  167 Main St Emmaus (18049) *(G-5033)*

M Simon Zook Co (PA) 610 273-3776
  4960 Horseshoe Pike Honey Brook (19344) *(G-7753)*

M Squared Electronics Inc 215 945-6658
  1610 Manning Blvd Ste C Levittown (19057) *(G-9848)*

M T C, Erie *Also called Winston & Duke Inc (G-5529)*

M T D, New Castle *Also called Molinaro Tool & Die Inc (G-12121)*

M T L, Jessup *Also called Material Tech & Logistics Inc (G-8332)*

M W Gary and Associates 724 206-0071
  470 Johnson Rd Ste 220 Washington (15301) *(G-19197)*

M&B Enterprises Inc 814 454-4461
  209 E 21st St Erie (16503) *(G-5377)*

M&M Stone Co 215 723-1177
  2840 Clymer Ave Ste 100 Telford (18969) *(G-18301)*

M&Q Holdings LLC (PA) 570 385-4991
  3 Earl Ave Schuylkill Haven (17972) *(G-17161)*

M&Z Anodizing, Dallastown *Also called Anodizing Plus Inc (G-3971)*

M-B Companies Inc 570 547-1621
  95 Blessing Dr Muncy (17756) *(G-11825)*

M/D Gas Inc 724 548-2501
  409 Butler Rd Ste A Kittanning (16201) *(G-8778)*

M3 Media LLC 215 463-6348
  440 Brown St Philadelphia (19123) *(G-13983)*

M3 Printing, Philadelphia *Also called M3 Media LLC (G-13983)*

M4I Inc 717 566-1610
  8176 Presidents Dr Ste M Hummelstown (17036) *(G-7916)*

Mac Beverage Inc 215 474-2024
  6120 Vine St Philadelphia (19139) *(G-13984)*

Mac Carty & Sons, Bryn Mawr *Also called Undercoveralls Inc (G-2336)*

Mac Clay Leather, East Petersburg *Also called Mac Inc (G-4588)*

Mac Hydraulics, Brookhaven *Also called Mac Machine LLC (G-2246)*

Mac Inc 717 560-0612
  1986 New St East Petersburg (17520) *(G-4588)*

Mac Kitchens, Allentown *Also called Macson Company (G-305)*

Mac Machine LLC 610 583-3055
  4901 Chester Creek Rd Brookhaven (19015) *(G-2246)*

Mac Millan Poultry, Philadelphia *Also called Mac Millan William Company (G-13985)*

Mac Millan William Company 215 627-3273
  416 Vine St Philadelphia (19106) *(G-13985)*

Mac Sign Systems Inc 570 347-7446
  232 S Sherman Ave Scranton (18504) *(G-17257)*

Mac Tool & Die Inc 814 337-9105
  18836 Cussewago Rd Meadville (16335) *(G-10752)*

Mac-It Corporation 717 397-3535
  275 E Liberty St Lancaster (17602) *(G-9122)*

Mach-Dynamics, Susquehanna *Also called Mark Gingerella (G-18181)*

Macherey-Nagel Inc 484 821-0984
  2850 Emrick Blvd Bethlehem (18020) *(G-1564)*

Machine Fabg & Weight Eqp S, Uniontown *Also called Machine Fabg & Weight Eqp Sp (G-18636)*

Machine Fabg & Weight Eqp Sp 724 439-1222
  267 Coolspring St Uniontown (15401) *(G-18636)*

Machine Rebuilders 724 694-3190
  5722 Route 982 New Derry (15671) *(G-12191)*

Machine Shop, Hadley *Also called Cusick Tool Inc (G-6818)*

Machine Specialties 717 264-0061
  600 Paper Mill Rd Chambersburg (17201) *(G-2955)*

Machine TI Rebuild Specialists 717 423-6073
  299 Shippensburg Rd Shippensburg (17257) *(G-17538)*

Machined Products Company 717 299-3757
  82 Pitney Rd Lancaster (17602) *(G-9123)*

Machinery & Industrial Eqp Co 412 781-8053
  1850 Chapman St Pittsburgh (15215) *(G-15245)*

Machining America Inc 717 249-8635
  1257 Claremont Rd Carlisle (17015) *(G-2723)*

Machining Center 724 530-7212
  85 State Route 956 Slippery Rock (16057) *(G-17621)*

Machining Concepts Inc 814 838-8896
  1304 Industrial Dr Erie (16505) *(G-5378)*

Machining Solutions 412 798-6590
  4000 Saltsburg Rd Murrysville (15668) *(G-11856)*

Machining Technology Inc 570 459-3440
  1324 Harwood Rd Hazle Township (18202) *(G-7468)*

Macinnis Group LLC 814 695-2016
  8180 Woodbury Pike Roaring Spring (16673) *(G-16765)*

Mack Defense LLC 484 387-5911
  7310 Tilghman St Ste 600 Allentown (18106) *(G-304)*

Mack Information Systems Inc 215 884-8123
  25 South Ave Wyncote (19095) *(G-20264)*

Mack Trucks Inc 717 939-1338
  2800 Commerce Dr Middletown (17057) *(G-11064)*

Mack Trucks Inc 610 966-8800
  7000 Alburtis Rd Macungie (18062) *(G-10154)*

Mack's Bill Ice Cream, Dover *Also called Bill Macks Ice Cream (G-4188)*

Mackissic Inc 610 495-7181
  1189 Old Schuylkill Rd Parker Ford (19457) *(G-13169)*

Maclean Saegertown LLC (HQ) 814 763-2655
  1 Crawford St Saegertown (16433) *(G-16924)*

Macnificent Pages 610 323-6253
  155 E High St Ste 360 Pottstown (19464) *(G-16012)*

Macorp Print Group, Souderton *Also called Magagna Associates Inc (G-17751)*

Macris Sports Inc 724 654-6065
  3132 Wilmington Rd Ste 2 New Castle (16105) *(G-12117)*

Macs Donut Shop Inc (PA) 724 375-6776
  2698 Brodhead Rd Aliquippa (15001) *(G-82)*

Macson Company (PA) 610 264-7733
  2500 Schoenersville Rd Allentown (18109) *(G-305)*

Maculogix Inc 717 982-6751
  3721 Tecport Dr Ste 301 Harrisburg (17111) *(G-7172)*

Madame Alexander Doll Co LLC (HQ) 717 537-4140
  306 Primrose Ln Mountville (17554) *(G-11798)*

Madera Cabinets 412 793-5850
  13035 Frankstown Rd Pittsburgh (15235) *(G-15246)*

Madhavan Inc 610 534-2600
  900 Ashland Ave Folcroft (19032) *(G-6009)*

Madison Inds Holdings LLC 717 762-3151
360 S Church St Waynesboro (17268) *(G-19416)*

Madrigal Pharmaceuticals Inc 484 380-9263
200 Barr Harbor Dr # 400 Conshohocken (19428) *(G-3573)*

Mae-Eitel Inc..570 366-0585
97 Pinedale Industrial Rd Orwigsburg (17961) *(G-13048)*

Maeva Usa Inc 215 461-2453
100 S Broad St Ste 1400a Philadelphia (19110) *(G-13986)*

Mag, Philadelphia *Also called Mecaer Aviation Group Inc (G-14002)*

Magagna Associates 610 213-2335
261 Schoolhouse Rd Ste 8 Souderton (18964) *(G-17751)*

Magdic Precision Tooling Inc 412 824-6661
1070 3rd St North Versailles (15137) *(G-12778)*

Magee and Magee Inc 814 966-3623
1441 Looker Mountain Trl Rixford (16745) *(G-16759)*

Magee Plastics Company 724 776-2220
303 Brush Creek Rd Warrendale (15086) *(G-19087)*

Magic Sleeper Bedding Co, Pottstown *Also called Magic Sleeper Inc (G-16013)*

Magic Sleeper Inc (PA) 610 327-2322
125 E 4th St Pottstown (19464) *(G-16013)*

Magiseal Services 724 327-3068
3825 Wiestertown Rd Export (15632) *(G-5617)*

Maglio Bros Inc (PA) 215 465-3902
3632 S 3rd St Philadelphia (19148) *(G-13987)*

Maglio Sausage, Philadelphia *Also called Maglio Bros Inc (G-13987)*

Magna Graphics Inc 412 687-0500
369 Coltart Ave Pittsburgh (15213) *(G-15247)*

Magne Rod, Elverson *Also called Skotz Manufacturing Inc (G-4966)*

Magnesita Refractories Company (HQ) 717 792-3611
425 S Salem Church Rd York (17408) *(G-20572)*

Magnesita Refractories Company 717 792-4216
2580 W Philadelphia St York (17404) *(G-20573)*

Magnesita Refractories Company 717 792-3611
425 S Salem Church Rd York (17408) *(G-20574)*

Magnesium Elektron 570 668-0001
1415 E Broad St Tamaqua (18252) *(G-18220)*

Magnetic Lifting Tech US LLC (PA) 412 490-5300
4200 Casteel Dr Coraopolis (15108) *(G-3703)*

Magnetic Lifting Tech US LLC 724 202-7987
3877 Wilmington Rd New Castle (16105) *(G-12118)*

Magnetic Specialties, Telford *Also called Solar Transformers Inc (G-18316)*

Magnetic Windings Company Inc 610 253-2751
2711 Freemansburg Ave Easton (18045) *(G-4716)*

Magnetics Div, State College *Also called Keytronics Inc (G-17984)*

Magnetics International, Inc., Pittsburgh *Also called Ssw International Inc (G-15572)*

Magneticsgroup, Bethlehem *Also called National Magnetics Group Inc (G-1578)*

Magnetizer Industrial Tech 215 766-9150
2880 Bergey Rd Ste D Hatfield (19440) *(G-7367)*

Magnum Carbide LLC 717 762-7181
225 E 9th St Waynesboro (17268) *(G-19417)*

Magnum Model Concepts Inc 717 529-0912
886 King Pen Rd Kirkwood (17536) *(G-8751)*

Magnum Screening 570 489-2902
214 Jackson St Olyphant (18447) *(G-12993)*

Magnus Group Inc 717 764-5908
2013 Mount Zion Rd York (17406) *(G-20575)*

Magritek Inc 855 667-6835
103 Great Valley Pkwy Malvern (19355) *(G-10272)*

Maguire Products Inc (PA) 610 459-4300
11 Crozerville Rd Aston (19014) *(G-773)*

Maguire Products Inc 610 494-6566
400 W Knowlton Rd Media (19063) *(G-10937)*

Mahogany and More Inc 610 666-6500
1620 East Dr Oaks (19456) *(G-12934)*

Mahoning Outdoor Furnace Inc 814 277-6675
208 Whiskey Run Rd Mahaffey (15757) *(G-10171)*

Maid-Rite Specialty Foods LLC 570 346-3572
151 Cedar Ave Scranton (18505) *(G-17258)*

MAID-RITESTEAKCO, Dunmore *Also called Polarized Meat Co Inc (G-4481)*

Maiden Formats Inc 412 884-4716
91 Green Glen Dr Pittsburgh (15227) *(G-15248)*

Maidwell-Glamorise, Williamsport *Also called Glamorise Foundations Inc (G-20018)*

Maier's Bakery, York *Also called Bimbo Bakeries Usa Inc (G-20406)*

Maier's Bakery, Reading *Also called Bimbo Bakeries Usa Inc (G-16332)*

Maier's Bakery, Easton *Also called Bimbo Bakeries USA Inc (G-4656)*

Maier's Bakery, Aston *Also called Bimbo Bakeries Usa Inc (G-752)*

Mail Center At Marathon Prtg, Philadelphia *Also called Marathon Printing Inc (G-13991)*

Main Engine Builders & Svc Ctr, Old Forge *Also called Main Engines & Service Center (G-12969)*

Main Engines & Service Center 570 457-7081
325 Bridge St Old Forge (18518) *(G-12969)*

Main Line Center For Skin Surg 610 664-1414
191 Presidential Blvd Bala Cynwyd (19004) *(G-884)*

Main Line Concrete & Sup Inc 610 269-5556
1001 Boot Rd Downingtown (19335) *(G-4238)*

Main Line Print Shop Inc 610 688-7782
25 West Ave Wayne (19087) *(G-19349)*

Main St Prtg & Copy Ctr Inc 570 424-0800
408 Main St Unit 1 Stroudsburg (18360) *(G-18126)*

Main St Stop N Go 570 424-5505
1650 W Main St Stroudsburg (18360) *(G-18127)*

Main Steel LLC 724 453-3000
6 Whitney Dr Harmony (16037) *(G-7073)*

Main Steel - Harmony 6010, Harmony *Also called Main Steel LLC (G-7073)*

Main Technologies, Old Forge *Also called M E Enterprise Services Inc (G-12968)*

Mainline Biosciences LLC 610 643-4881
40 Lloyd Ave Ste 309 Malvern (19355) *(G-10273)*

Mainline Environmental LLC 215 651-6635
605 Elmwood Ave Trevose (19053) *(G-18501)*

Mainline Newspapers 814 472-4110
975 Rowena Dr Ebensburg (15931) *(G-4789)*

Mainstream Industries 610 488-1148
7340 Bernville Rd Bernville (19506) *(G-1301)*

Mainstream Swimsuits Inc 484 373-3600
610 Uhler Rd Easton (18040) *(G-4717)*

Maintain It All, Eagleville *Also called Maintain-It (G-4515)*

Maintain-It 484 684-6766
18 W Mount Kirk Ave Eagleville (19403) *(G-4515)*

Mainville AG Services Inc 570 784-6922
360 Main-Mifflin Rd Bloomsburg (17815) *(G-1789)*

Maiolatesi Wine Cellar 570 254-9977
210 Green Grove Rd Scott Township (18447) *(G-17185)*

Majer Brand Company Inc (PA) 717 632-1320
557 Centennial Ave Hanover (17331) *(G-6916)*

Majestic Athletic, Easton *Also called Maroco Ltd (G-4719)*

Majestic Athletic Intl Ltd 610 746-7494
2320 Newlins Mill Rd Easton (18045) *(G-4718)*

Majestic Creations Inc 215 968-5411
31 Cottonwood Dr Southampton (18966) *(G-17824)*

Majestic Fire Apparel Inc 610 377-6273
255 Wagner St Lehighton (18235) *(G-9719)*

Majestic Flyers, Chambersburg *Also called Majestic Windsocks (G-2956)*

Majestic Windsocks 717 264-3113
2690 Williamsburg Cir Chambersburg (17202) *(G-2956)*

Majesty Marble and Granite Inc 610 859-8181
2939 Dutton Mill Rd Aston (19014) *(G-774)*

Major League Screen Prtg & EMB 717 270-9511
19 S 5th Ave Lebanon (17042) *(G-9607)*

Majr Products Corporation 814 763-3211
780 South St Saegertown (16433) *(G-16925)*

Makefield Collection Inc 610 496-4649
6028 Old Hickory Rd Coopersburg (18036) *(G-3631)*

Makes Scents LLC 717 824-3094
336 N Charlotte St # 100 Lancaster (17603) *(G-9124)*

Makteam Software Ltd Co 814 504-1283
3519 Anne Marie Dr Erie (16506) *(G-5379)*

Mal Parts Financial, Sutersville *Also called Netmercatus LLC (G-18184)*

Mal-Ber Manufacturing Company 215 672-6440
2115 Byberry Rd Huntingdon Valley (19006) *(G-8010)*

Malatesta Enterprises 570 752-2516
201 E 2nd St Berwick (18603) *(G-1334)*

Maldonado T Norberto, Philadelphia *Also called Casting Headquarters Inc (G-13511)*

Malek Ham 610 691-7600
151 W 4th St Bethlehem (18015) *(G-1565)*

MALL SILKS, Pittsburgh *Also called Plantscape Inc (G-15415)*

Mallard Contracting Co Inc 570 339-2930
122 Wilburton Rd Mount Carmel (17851) *(G-11626)*

Mallet and Company Inc (HQ) 412 276-9000
51 Arch St Carnegie (15106) *(G-2776)*

Mallinckrodt LLC 570 824-8980
300 Laird St Ste C Wilkes Barre (18702) *(G-19940)*

Malmark Incorporated 215 766-7200
5712 Easton Rd Plumsteadville (18949) *(G-15811)*

Malmark Bellcraftsmen, Plumsteadville *Also called Malmark Incorporated (G-15811)*

Malone & Blunt Inc 215 563-1368
10300 Drummond Rd Philadelphia (19154) *(G-13988)*

Maloney Plastics Inc 814 337-8417
10890 Mercer Pike Meadville (16335) *(G-10753)*

Maloney Tool & Mold Inc 814 337-8407
10890 Mercer Pike Meadville (16335) *(G-10754)*

Malsom Logging 570 840-1044
443 Spring Hill Rd Moscow (18444) *(G-11598)*

Malvern Scale Data Systems (PA) 610 296-9642
81 Lancaster Ave Ste 216 Malvern (19355) *(G-10274)*

Malvern Systems, Malvern *Also called Malvern Scale Data Systems (G-10274)*

Mam Software Inc 610 336-9045
512 Township Line Rd # 220 Blue Bell (19422) *(G-1846)*

Mama DS Buns Inc 724 752-1700
2555 River Rd Ellwood City (16117) *(G-4944)*

Mama Nardone Baking Co Inc 570 825-3421
138 W 21st St Hazleton (18201) *(G-7509)*

Mama Nardone Pizza, Hazleton *Also called Mama Nardone Baking Co Inc (G-7509)*

Mamaux Supply Co 412 782-3456
1700 S Canal St Pittsburgh (15215) *(G-15249)*

Mammoth Materials 570 385-4232
44 Keystoker Ln Schuylkill Haven (17972) *(G-17162)*

Man Pan LLC 724 942-9500
309 Buffalo Ridge Rd Mc Murray (15317) *(G-10645)*
Manac Trailers Inc 724 294-0007
1001 Lyn Rd Freeport (16229) *(G-6207)*
Managing Editor Inc 215 517-5116
610 Old York Rd Ste 250 Jenkintown (19046) *(G-8295)*
Manatawny Still Works 484 624-8271
320 Circle Of Progress Dr Pottstown (19464) *(G-16014)*
Manayunk Brewing Company, Philadelphia *Also called Philadelphia Beer Works Inc (G-14142)*
Mance Plating Co 724 695-0550
255 Main St Imperial (15126) *(G-8071)*
Manchester Hydraulics Inc 717 764-5226
3775 N George Street Ext Manchester (17345) *(G-10357)*
Manchester Industries Inc 717 764-1161
10 Grumbacher Rd York (17406) *(G-20576)*
Manchester Industries Inc VA 570 822-9308
175 Stewart Rd Hanover Township (18706) *(G-6993)*
Manchester Township 717 779-0297
3200 Farmtrail Rd York (17406) *(G-20577)*
Mancinci Metal Specialty Inc 215 529-5800
2015 Grant Rd Quakertown (18951) *(G-16211)*
Mancino Manufacturing Co Inc 800 338-6287
1180 Church Rd Ste 400 Lansdale (19446) *(G-9385)*
Mancor-Pa Inc 610 398-2300
160 Olin Way Allentown (18106) *(G-306)*
Mandelbroks 814 813-5555
16226 Conneaut Lake Rd Meadville (16335) *(G-10755)*
Mangar Industries Inc 215 230-0300
97 Britain Dr New Britain (18901) *(G-12047)*
Mangar Medical Inc 215 230-0300
97 Britain Dr New Britain (18901) *(G-12048)*
Mangar Medical Packaging, New Britain *Also called Mangar Industries Inc (G-12047)*
Manhattan Bagel, Downingtown *Also called Northwest Bagel Corporation (G-4245)*
Manheim Specialty Machine 717 665-5400
76 W End Dr Manheim (17545) *(G-10393)*
Manischewitz Shelzer Company, Newtown Square *Also called Days Beverage Inc (G-12572)*
Manitowoc Crane Group, Shady Grove *Also called Grove US LLc (G-17420)*
Manley Fence Co 610 842-8833
301 Reeceville Rd Coatesville (19320) *(G-3316)*
Manncorp Inc (PA) 215 830-1200
1610 Republic Rd Huntingdon Valley (19006) *(G-8011)*
Manni's Frank Sales & Service, New Kensington *Also called Mannis Wash Systems (G-12354)*
Manning Farm Dairy 570 563-2016
Manning Rd Dalton (18414) *(G-3987)*
Mannings USA Inc 412 816-1264
501 Mosside Blvd North Versailles (15137) *(G-12779)*
Mannings USA 863 619-8099
501 Mosside Blvd North Versailles (15137) *(G-12780)*
Mannis Wash Systems 724 337-8255
1131 Greensburg Rd New Kensington (15068) *(G-12354)*
Manns Home Medical Products, White Oak *Also called Manns Sickroom Service Inc (G-19856)*
Manns Sickroom Service Inc (PA) 412 672-5680
1101 Lincoln Way White Oak (15131) *(G-19856)*
Manor House Publishing Co Inc 215 259-1700
880 Louis Dr Warminster (18974) *(G-18916)*
Mansco Products Inc 215 674-4395
34 Richard Rd Warminster (18974) *(G-18917)*
Manuals-Basic Business Forms, Lafayette Hill *Also called Jerry James Trdng As Mnls BSC (G-8882)*
Manufactured Rubber Pdts Co 215 533-3600
4501 Tacony St Philadelphia (19124) *(G-13989)*
Manufacturing, Warminster *Also called Specialty Vhcl Solutions LLC (G-18972)*
Manufacturing Enterprises, Whitehall *Also called M E Inc (G-19884)*
Manufacturing Jewelers, Erie *Also called Jan & Dans Jewelry (G-5334)*
Manufacturing Pallets, Factoryville *Also called Northern Pallet Inc (G-5759)*
Manufctring Technical Svcs Inc 610 857-3500
Greenbelt Dr Sadsburyville (19369) *(G-16905)*
Manufcturer Electronic Contrls, Carnegie *Also called Phase Guard Co Inc (G-2778)*
Manugraph Americas Inc 717 362-3243
158 Damhill Rd Millersburg (17061) *(G-11195)*
Manugraph Dgm, Millersburg *Also called Manugraph Americas Inc (G-11195)*
Maple Craft USA, Girard *Also called Kaufer Associates Inc (G-6394)*
Maple Donuts Inc (PA) 717 757-7826
3455 E Market St York (17402) *(G-20578)*
Maple Donuts Inc 717 843-4276
970 Loucks Rd Ste A York (17404) *(G-20579)*
Maple Donuts Inc 814 774-3131
10307 Hall Ave Lake City (16423) *(G-8905)*
Maple Donuts Erie, Lake City *Also called Maple Donuts Inc (G-8905)*
Maple Grove Enterprises Inc 814 473-6272
1873 Flick Rd Rimersburg (16248) *(G-16750)*
Maple Mountain, New Florence *Also called Everclear Valley Inc (G-12196)*
Maple Mountain Equipment, Mansfield *Also called Maple Mountain Industries Inc (G-10421)*
Maple Mountain Homes, New Florence *Also called Maple Mountain Industries Inc (G-12198)*
Maple Mountain Industries Inc 724 439-1234
655 Pittsburgh Rd Uniontown (15401) *(G-18637)*
Maple Mountain Industries Inc 814 634-0674
150 6th Ave Meyersdale (15552) *(G-11015)*
Maple Mountain Industries Inc 570 662-3200
845 Route 660 Mansfield (16933) *(G-10421)*
Maple Mountain Industries Inc (PA) 724 676-4703
1820 Mulligan Hill Rd New Florence (15944) *(G-12198)*
Maple Press Company (PA) 717 764-5911
480 Willow Springs Ln York (17406) *(G-20580)*
Maple-Vail, York *Also called Maple Press Company (G-20580)*
Mapleton, Mapleton Depot *Also called U S Silica Company (G-10432)*
Mar Cor Purification Inc (HQ) 800 633-3080
4450 Township Line Rd Skippack (19474) *(G-17600)*
Mar-Van Industries Inc 215 249-3336
117 Middle Rd Dublin (18917) *(G-4435)*
Marando Industries Inc 610 621-2536
90 Water St Reading (19605) *(G-16437)*
Marathon Embroidery 215 627-8848
719 S 7th St Philadelphia (19147) *(G-13990)*
Marathon Metal, Freeport *Also called J A Smith Inc (G-6206)*
Marathon Oil, Tarentum *Also called Tri-State Petroleum Corp (G-18249)*
Marathon Printing Inc 215 238-1100
9 N 3rd St Philadelphia (19106) *(G-13991)*
Marble Crafters Inc 610 497-6000
11 Nealy Blvd Marcus Hook (19061) *(G-10448)*
Marble Crafters USA, Marcus Hook *Also called Marble Crafters Inc (G-10448)*
Marble Source Inc 610 847-5694
87 Brownstone Rd Ottsville (18942) *(G-13067)*
Marc Edward Brands Inc (PA) 412 380-0888
55 38th St Pittsburgh (15201) *(G-15250)*
Marc Publishing Company, Lafayette Hill *Also called Jay Weiss Corporation (G-8881)*
Marc Williams Goldsmith Inc (PA) 570 322-4248
430 William St Williamsport (17701) *(G-20040)*
Marc-Service Inc 814 467-8611
135 5th St Ste 3 Windber (15963) *(G-20189)*
Marcan Advertising Inc 717 270-6929
537 E Maple St Cleona (17042) *(G-3245)*
Marcegaglia Usa Inc 412 462-2185
1001 E Waterfront Dr Munhall (15120) *(G-11844)*
Marcellus Shale Coalition 412 706-5160
24 Summit Park Dr Ste 200 Pittsburgh (15275) *(G-15251)*
Marcho Farms Inc 215 721-7131
176 Orchard Ln Harleysville (19438) *(G-7045)*
Marcies Homemade Ice Cream (PA) 814 336-1749
18 Forest Ave Meadville (16335) *(G-10756)*
Marco Manufacturing Co Inc 215 463-2332
1701 S 26th St 15 Philadelphia (19145) *(G-13992)*
Marco Products, Fairless Hills *Also called Marking Device Mfg Co Inc (G-5787)*
Marcom Group Ltd 610 859-8989
20 Creek Pkwy Upper Chichester (19061) *(G-18667)*
Marcon & Boyer Inc (PA) 610 866-5959
645 Hamilton St Ste 300 Allentown (18101) *(G-307)*
Marcus J Wholesalers Inc 412 261-3315
1728 Smallman St Pittsburgh (15222) *(G-15252)*
Marcus Hook Pharmacy, Marcus Hook *Also called Mrlrx LLC (G-10450)*
Marcus Uppe Inc 412 261-4233
411 7th Ave Ste 350 Pittsburgh (15219) *(G-15253)*
Marcus Uppe Inc (PA) 412 391-1218
320 Fort Duquesne Blvd # 300 Pittsburgh (15222) *(G-15254)*
Mardinly Enterprises LLC 610 544-9490
701 Park Way Ste 2 Broomall (19008) *(G-2295)*
Marg Inc (HQ) 724 703-3020
1 Willow Ave Oakdale (15071) *(G-12906)*
Margaret Mary Music Publishing 570 282-3503
161 Belmont St Carbondale (18407) *(G-2681)*
Margraf Dental Mfg Inc 215 884-0369
611 Harper Ave Jenkintown (19046) *(G-8296)*
Margro, Lancaster *Also called Kirby Agri Inc (G-9087)*
Marguerite Davison, West Chester *Also called Spencer Graphics Inc (G-19643)*
Mariani Metal Fabricators Usa 717 432-9241
325 Beaver Creek Rd Dillsburg (17019) *(G-4135)*
Mariano Welding Corp 610 626-0975
Baltimore & Marple Ave Clifton Heights (19018) *(G-3255)*
Marie Chomicki 717 432-3456
31 S Baltimore St Dillsburg (17019) *(G-4136)*
Marietta Closson 724 337-4482
257 Delilah St Apollo (15613) *(G-683)*
Marietta Fence Experts LLC 724 925-6100
126 Emerald Dr Hunker (15639) *(G-7929)*
Marilake Winery LLC 570 536-6575
209 Main St Childs (18407) *(G-3131)*
Marilyn Cohen Designs 610 664-6219
1121 Hillcrest Rd Penn Valley (19072) *(G-13237)*
Marilyn Strawser Beauty Salon 717 463-2804
Rr 1 Thompsontown (17094) *(G-18349)*

ALPHABETIC

Marine Acquisition US Inc..............................610 495-7011
640 N Lewis Rd Limerick (19468) *(G-9970)*
Marine Division, Pittsburgh *Also called Kop-Coat Inc (G-15183)*
Marine Information Tech LLC..........................610 429-5180
104 Willowbrook Ln West Chester (19382) *(G-19595)*
Marine Ingredients LLC (HQ).........................570 260-6900
794 Sunrise Blvd Mount Bethel (18343) *(G-11613)*
Marine Performance Products, Marcus Hook *Also called George Kranich (G-10442)*
Marine Sheet Metal Works..............................814 455-9700
1447 E 10th St Erie (16503) *(G-5380)*
Marine Tech Wire and Cable Inc.....................717 854-1992
631 S Richland Ave York (17403) *(G-20581)*
Marino Indus Systems Svcs Inc.......................610 872-3630
805 W 2nd St Ste A Chester (19013) *(G-3057)*
Marinus Pharmaceuticals Inc (PA)..................267 440-4200
100 W Matsonford Rd 3-304 Radnor (19087) *(G-16295)*
Mario Dinardo Jr Custom WD Wkg...................610 495-7010
103 Lightcap Rd Pottstown (19464) *(G-16015)*
Marion Center Supply Inc (PA)........................724 397-5505
517 Church St Marion Center (15759) *(G-10473)*
Marion Center Supply Inc................................724 354-2143
10680 Route 422 Hwy W Shelocta (15774) *(G-17487)*
Marion's Kitchen, Pittsburgh *Also called Innofoods Usa Inc (G-15126)*
Marionette Company Inc.................................570 644-1936
401 S Pearl St Shamokin (17872) *(G-17425)*
Marios Tree Service Inc...................................610 637-1405
453 Crooked Ln King of Prussia (19406) *(G-8648)*
Mark A Kulka...814 726-7331
6 Mader Dr Warren (16365) *(G-19039)*
Mark Case Logging..570 729-8856
108 Logger Rd Beach Lake (18405) *(G-975)*
Mark Gingerella...570 213-5603
494 Main St Susquehanna (18847) *(G-18181)*
Mark Grim...724 758-2270
705 Lawrence Ave Ste 2 Ellwood City (16117) *(G-4945)*
Mark Hershey Farms Inc..................................717 867-4624
479 Horseshoe Pike Lebanon (17042) *(G-9608)*
Mark Im Com...724 282-0997
115 N Main St Butler (16001) *(G-2421)*
Mark IV Office Supply, Uniontown *Also called Little Printing Co Inc (G-18635)*
Mark Metal Division, Reading *Also called Rose Corporation (G-16505)*
Mark R Stairs..814 634-0871
4914 Brush Creek Rd Meyersdale (15552) *(G-11016)*
Mark Rioux Pallets...610 562-7030
1100 Pennsylvania 61 Hamburg (19526) *(G-6845)*
Mark Tk Welding Inc......................................724 545-2001
11771 State Route 85 Kittanning (16201) *(G-8779)*
Mark-A-Hydrant LLC......................................888 399-5532
2863 Edgemont Dr Allentown (18103) *(G-308)*
Markel Corp...610 272-8960
435 School Ln Plymouth Meeting (19462) *(G-15855)*
Market Service Corp.......................................610 696-1884
1244 W Chester Pike # 402 West Chester (19382) *(G-19596)*
Market Service Corp.......................................610 644-6211
641 S Warren Ave Malvern (19355) *(G-10275)*
Marking Device Mfg Co Inc..............................215 632-9583
225 Lincoln Hwy Bldg Es Fairless Hills (19030) *(G-5787)*
Marko Radiator Inc (PA).................................570 462-2281
725 W Coal St Shenandoah (17976) *(G-17495)*
Markovitz Enterprises Inc (PA).......................724 452-4500
100 Badger Dr Zelienople (16063) *(G-20810)*
Markovitz Enterprises Inc...............................412 381-2305
1207 Muriel St Pittsburgh (15203) *(G-15255)*
Markovitz Enterprises Inc................................724 658-6575
597 Commerce Ave New Castle (16101) *(G-12119)*
Markowski International Pubg...........................717 566-0468
1 Oakglade Cir Hummelstown (17036) *(G-7917)*
Markraft Company..724 733-3654
104 Artman Ln Murrysville (15668) *(G-11857)*
Markwest Hydrocarbon Inc.............................724 514-4398
1084 Western Ave Washington (15301) *(G-19198)*
Markwest Liberty Midstream............................724 514-4401
800 Western Ave Washington (15301) *(G-19199)*
Marlan Tool Inc..814 382-2744
13385 Denny Rd Meadville (16335) *(G-10757)*
Marley Cooling Technologies, York *Also called SPX Cooling Technologies Inc (G-20677)*
Marlin A Inch...570 374-1106
201 W Pine St Selinsgrove (17870) *(G-17330)*
Marlo Enterprises Inc....................................412 678-3800
32 S Linden St Duquesne (15110) *(G-4498)*
Marlowes Metal Fabricating.............................717 292-7360
2111 Palomino Rd Dover (17315) *(G-4195)*
Maro Electronics Inc......................................215 788-7919
1246 Hayes Blvd Bristol (19007) *(G-2164)*
Maroco Ltd (HQ)..610 746-6800
2320 Newlins Mill Rd Easton (18045) *(G-4719)*
Maronda Systems Inc Florida (HQ)...................724 695-1200
11 Timberglen Dr Imperial (15126) *(G-8072)*
Marquee Graphx LLC......................................215 538-2992
243 W Broad St Quakertown (18951) *(G-16212)*

Marquip Ward United......................................570 742-7859
318 Yocum Rd Milton (17847) *(G-11248)*
Marquise Mining Corp.....................................724 459-5775
3889 Menoher Blvd Johnstown (15905) *(G-8406)*
Mars Incorporated...717 367-1500
295 S Brown St Elizabethtown (17022) *(G-4877)*
Mars Chocolate North Amer LLC.......................717 367-1500
295 S Brown St Elizabethtown (17022) *(G-4878)*
Mars Lumber Inc..724 625-2224
1084 Mars Evans City Rd Mars (16046) *(G-10506)*
Mars Mineral, Mars *Also called Woodward Inc (G-10516)*
Marsh Creek Signs Inc....................................610 458-5503
240 Little Conestoga Rd Downingtown (19335) *(G-4239)*
Marsh Laboratories...412 271-3060
2437 Waverly St Pittsburgh (15218) *(G-15256)*
Marsh Planing Company, Titusville *Also called Marsh Planing Inc (G-18388)*
Marsh Planing Inc..814 827-9947
5034 State Route 8 Titusville (16354) *(G-18388)*
Marshall Flp LP...570 465-3817
70 Mitchell St New Milford (18834) *(G-12398)*
Marshall Wood Works, Pittsburgh *Also called Marshall Woodworks Ltd (G-15257)*
Marshall Woodworks Ltd.................................412 321-1685
1500 Spring Garden Ave Pittsburgh (15212) *(G-15257)*
Marshmallowmba...703 340-7157
35 East Ave Red Lion (17356) *(G-16607)*
Marstellar Concrete Inc..................................717 834-6200
2011 State Rd Duncannon (17020) *(G-4448)*
Marston Records, West Chester *Also called HW Marston & Co (G-19565)*
Marstrand Industries Inc................................412 921-1511
12 Rutgers Rd Pittsburgh (15205) *(G-15258)*
Martec-A Division of Busch, Wexford *Also called Busch Company (G-19792)*
Martech Medical Products Inc (PA)...................215 256-8833
1500 Delp Dr Harleysville (19438) *(G-7046)*
Martek Power Laser Drive LLC........................805 383-5548
620 William Pitt Way Pittsburgh (15238) *(G-15259)*
Martell Sales & Service Inc.............................814 765-6557
1509 Washington Ave Hyde (16843) *(G-8047)*
Martell Sales and Services, Hyde *Also called Martell Sales & Service Inc (G-8047)*
Martellis Mtal Fabrication Inc...........................215 957-9700
4 Louise Dr Ivyland (18974) *(G-8217)*
Martin Amr LLC...908 313-2459
3709 Beale Ave Altoona (16601) *(G-524)*
Martin Associates Ephrata LLC.......................717 733-7968
280 Pleasant Valley Rd Ephrata (17522) *(G-5122)*
Martin Burial Vault Co, Pittsburgh *Also called Harvil Inc (G-15083)*
Martin Communications Inc.............................412 498-0157
1639 Pine Hollow Rd Ste C Mc Kees Rocks (15136) *(G-10619)*
Martin Custom Cabinets LLC..........................717 721-1859
1564 Main St Ste 504 East Earl (17519) *(G-4547)*
Martin Design Group LLC................................717 633-9214
850 Vogelsong Rd Hanover (17331) *(G-6917)*
Martin Fabricating Inc.....................................610 435-5700
601 S 10th St Allentown (18103) *(G-309)*
Martin Limestone Inc (HQ)..............................717 335-4500
3580 Division Hwy East Earl (17519) *(G-4548)*
Martin Limestone Inc.....................................717 354-1340
621 Martindale Rd Ephrata (17522) *(G-5123)*
Martin Limestone Inc.....................................717 354-1200
828 E Earl Rd New Holland (17557) *(G-12258)*
Martin Limestone Inc.....................................717 335-4523
74 Kurtz Rd Denver (17517) *(G-4082)*
Martin Limestone Inc.....................................814 224-6837
820 E Washington St West Chester (19380) *(G-19597)*
Martin Limestone Inc.....................................717 354-1298
875 E Earl Rd New Holland (17557) *(G-12259)*
Martin Limestone Inc.....................................717 354-1370
3580 Division Hwy East Earl (17519) *(G-4549)*
Martin Marietta Materials Inc...........................724 573-9518
3rd St Ext Georgetown (15043) *(G-6277)*
Martin Metal Works Inc...................................717 292-5691
6711 Davidsburg Rd East Berlin (17316) *(G-4523)*
Martin Rawdin Od (PA)....................................610 323-8007
1630 E High St Bldg 4 Pottstown (19464) *(G-16016)*
Martin Rollison Inc (PA)..................................570 253-4141
120 Sunrise Ave Honesdale (18431) *(G-7717)*
Martin Sprocket & Gear Inc............................610 837-1841
3376 Delps Rd Danielsville (18038) *(G-3994)*
Martin Truck Bodies Inc.................................814 793-3353
279 Cross Roads Ln Martinsburg (16662) *(G-10526)*
Martin Weaver R...717 354-8970
192 Amishtown Rd New Holland (17557) *(G-12260)*
Martin's Ice, Ephrata *Also called Martin Associates Ephrata LLC (G-5122)*
Martin-Baker America Inc...............................814 262-9325
169 Jari Dr Johnstown (15904) *(G-8407)*
Martina Guerra Goldsmith...............................570 398-1833
1102 Allegheny St Jersey Shore (17740) *(G-8318)*
Martindale Lumber Co Inc................................814 736-3032
1047 Puritan Rd Portage (15946) *(G-15919)*

Martindale Welding LLC...717 445-4666
977 Martindale Rd Ephrata (17522) ***(G-5124)***
Martino Fuel...484 802-2183
122 Beechtree Dr Broomall (19008) ***(G-2296)***
Martino Signs Inc (PA)...610 622-7446
453 Penn St Yeadon (19050) ***(G-20355)***
Martino Signs Inc...610 355-9269
101 Mulberry Ln Newtown Square (19073) ***(G-12584)***
Martinos Delicatessen Inc...814 432-2525
1218 15th St Franklin (16323) ***(G-6149)***
Martins Buildings...717 733-6689
1825 W Main St Ephrata (17522) ***(G-5125)***
Martins Draperies & Interiors...717 239-0501
1520 Commerce Dr Lancaster (17601) ***(G-9125)***
Martins Feed Mill Inc...814 349-8787
534 Main St Coburn (16832) ***(G-3333)***
Martins Fmous Pstry Shoppe Inc (PA)...717 263-9580
1000 Potato Roll Ln Chambersburg (17202) ***(G-2957)***
Martins Fmous Pstry Shoppe Inc...717 263-9580
1000 Potato Roll Ln Chambersburg (17202) ***(G-2958)***
Martins Furniture LLC...717 354-5657
230 S Fairmount Rd Ephrata (17522) ***(G-5126)***
Martins Potato Chips Inc (PA)...717 792-3065
5847 Lincoln Hwy W Thomasville (17364) ***(G-18341)***
Martins Potato Chips Inc...610 777-3643
7 Morgan Dr Reading (19608) ***(G-16438)***
Martins Pretzel Bakery...717 859-1272
1229 Diamond St Akron (17501) ***(G-36)***
Martins Starter Service...814 398-2496
27749 Oregon Corners Rd Cambridge Springs (16403) ***(G-2482)***
Martins Steel LLC...570 966-3775
2050 Swengle Rd Mifflinburg (17844) ***(G-11097)***
Martins Wood Products LLC...717 933-5115
650 Houtztown Rd Myerstown (17067) ***(G-11893)***
Martra LLC...610 444-9469
206 Gale Ln Kennett Square (19348) ***(G-8525)***
Marty's Welding Service, North Versailles *Also called Martys Muffler & Weld Shop* ***(G-12781)***
Martys Muffler & Weld Shop...412 673-4141
3433 5th Ave North Versailles (15137) ***(G-12781)***
Martz Chassis Inc...814 623-9501
646 Imlertown Rd Bedford (15522) ***(G-1063)***
Marula Oil Holdings LLC...310 559-8600
40 E Montgomery Ave Ardmore (19003) ***(G-712)***
Marula Pure Beauty Oil, Ardmore *Also called Marula Oil Holdings LLC* ***(G-712)***
Marvel Manufacturing Company...570 421-6221
40 N 2nd St Stroudsburg (18360) ***(G-18128)***
Marvel Manufacturing Company (PA)...570 421-6221
40 N 2nd St Stroudsburg (18360) ***(G-18129)***
Marvel Marking Products...412 381-0700
3000 Jane St Pittsburgh (15203) ***(G-15260)***
Marvin Dale Slaymaker...717 684-5050
146 Penn St Washington Boro (17582) ***(G-19251)***
Marwood Machine Company Inc...724 352-2646
557 Marwood Rd Cabot (16023) ***(G-2458)***
Mary Ann Pensiero Inc...717 545-8289
3514 Ridgeway Rd Harrisburg (17109) ***(G-7173)***
Mary Hail Rubber Co Inc...215 343-1955
803 Monaco Dr Warrington (18976) ***(G-19124)***
Mary J Backaroo...570 819-4809
107 Wyoming Valley Mall Wilkes Barre (18702) ***(G-19941)***
Marzonies...814 695-2931
164 Patchway Rd Duncansville (16635) ***(G-4456)***
Marzucco Enterprises, West Conshohocken *Also called Aluminum Athletic Equipment Co* ***(G-19684)***
Mas Engineering LLC...724 652-1367
2008 County Line Rd New Castle (16101) ***(G-12120)***
Mas-Fab Inc...717 244-4561
775 Lombard Rd Red Lion (17356) ***(G-16608)***
Masco Cabinetry LLC...570 882-8565
217 Lamoka Rd Athens (18810) ***(G-812)***
Masco Communications Inc...215 625-8501
505 S 4th St Philadelphia (19147) ***(G-13993)***
Mashan Inc...724 397-4008
20 Minich Rd Home (15747) ***(G-7669)***
Maslo Company Inc (PA)...610 540-9000
11 Lee Blvd Malvern (19355) ***(G-10276)***
Mason Crest Publishers Inc (PA)...610 543-6200
450 Park Way Ste 206 Broomall (19008) ***(G-2297)***
Mason Dickson Distilleri, Gettysburg *Also called Central Penn Distilling* ***(G-6285)***
Mason Dixon Sand and Gravel, York *Also called York Building Products Co Inc* ***(G-20728)***
Mason East Inc...631 254-2240
2 Neshaminy Interplex Dr # 205 Feasterville Trevose (19053) ***(G-5917)***
Mason Hill Logging...814 546-2478
5838 Mason Hill Rd Driftwood (15832) ***(G-4377)***
Mason Jars Company...877 490-5565
1001 State St Ste 1220 Erie (16501) ***(G-5381)***
Mason Rubber Co Inc...215 355-3440
1819 2nd St Ste A Feasterville Trevose (19053) ***(G-5918)***
Mason-Dixon Bbq Services, Greencastle *Also called Celf Services LLC* ***(G-6602)***
Mason-Dixon Distillery...717 314-2070
331 E Water St Gettysburg (17325) ***(G-6306)***
Masonite Corporation...570 473-3557
980 Point Township Dr Northumberland (17857) ***(G-12870)***
Masons Mark Stone Veneer Corp...724 635-0082
106 Sewickley St New Stanton (15672) ***(G-12449)***
Mass Industrial Control...610 678-8228
19 Woodrow Ave Reading (19608) ***(G-16439)***
Mass Machine & Fabricating Co...724 225-1125
595 Meadow Ave Washington (15301) ***(G-19200)***
Mass Storage Newsletter, Erie *Also called R M G Enterprises Inc* ***(G-5448)***
Master Machine and Mfg...412 262-1550
1220 2nd Ave Coraopolis (15108) ***(G-3704)***
Master Machine Co Inc...814 495-4900
310 River St South Fork (15956) ***(G-17775)***
Master Replicas Group Inc...610 652-2265
313 Big Rd Zieglerville (19492) ***(G-20833)***
Master Solutions Inc...717 243-6849
20 Wolfs Bridge Rd Carlisle (17013) ***(G-2724)***
Master Terrazzo Technologies, Levittown *Also called Consolidated Coatings Inc* ***(G-9826)***
Master Tool and Mold Inc...717 757-3671
4075 E Market St Ste 30 York (17402) ***(G-20582)***
Master Water Conditioning Corp...610 323-8358
224 Shoemaker Rd Pottstown (19464) ***(G-16017)***
Master Woodcraft Corporation...724 225-5530
100 Stationvue Washington (15301) ***(G-19201)***
Master-Lee Engineered Products...724 537-6002
5631 State Route 981 Latrobe (15650) ***(G-9502)***
Masterbrand Cabinets Inc...717 359-4131
219 Allen Rd Carlisle (17013) ***(G-2725)***
Mastercraft Printing & Design, Fogelsville *Also called Placemat Printers Inc* ***(G-5996)***
Mastercraft Woodworking Co Inc...610 926-1500
681 Mohrsville Rd Shoemakersville (19555) ***(G-17571)***
Masterflo Pump Inc...724 443-1122
23 Dewey Ln Ste A Gibsonia (15044) ***(G-6347)***
Mastermix Inc...610 346-8723
1800 Shale Rd Quakertown (18951) ***(G-16213)***
Masteros Homestyle Foods Inc...215 551-2530
1511 Packer Ave Philadelphia (19145) ***(G-13994)***
Masterpiece Kitchens, Perkasie *Also called Shawn Harr* ***(G-13292)***
Masters Concrete...570 798-2680
Main St Lakewood (18439) ***(G-8915)***
Masters Ink Corporation...724 745-1122
617 Giffin Ave Ste A Canonsburg (15317) ***(G-2601)***
Masters Ready Mix Concrete Co, Montrose *Also called Masters RMC Inc* ***(G-11470)***
Masters RMC Inc...570 278-3258
Off Route 106 Montrose (18801) ***(G-11470)***
Masthof Press, Morgantown *Also called Lemar Mast* ***(G-11524)***
Mastowski Lumber Company Inc...724 455-7502
Foxburg Rd Normalville (15469) ***(G-12624)***
Mastro Ice Inc...412 681-4423
835 Herron Ave Pittsburgh (15219) ***(G-15261)***
Mastrorocco Machine...724 539-4511
Rr 2 Latrobe (15650) ***(G-9503)***
Mat Penn Company Inc...724 837-7060
612 S Urania Ave Greensburg (15601) ***(G-6687)***
Matachana USA Corp...484 873-2763
300 N Pottstown Pike Exton (19341) ***(G-5708)***
Matamatic Inc...724 696-5678
181 Westec Dr Mount Pleasant (15666) ***(G-11705)***
Matangos Candies Inc...717 234-0882
1501 Catherine St Harrisburg (17104) ***(G-7174)***
Material Tech & Logistics Inc...570 487-6162
1325 Veterans Memorial Dr Jessup (18434) ***(G-8332)***
Materion Brush Inc...610 562-2211
230 Shoemakersville Rd Shoemakersville (19555) ***(G-17572)***
Maternity Club, Philadelphia *Also called Matthew Cole Inc* ***(G-13995)***
Matheson Tri-Gas Inc...724 379-4104
1 Nitrous Ln Donora (15033) ***(G-4156)***
Matheson Tri-Gas Inc...814 453-5637
1313 Chestnut St Erie (16501) ***(G-5382)***
Matheson Tri-Gas Inc...814 781-6990
203 West Creek Rd Saint Marys (15857) ***(G-16987)***
Matheson Tri-Gas Inc...215 641-2700
166 Keystone Dr Montgomeryville (18936) ***(G-11406)***
Matreya LLC...814 355-1030
2178 High Tech Rd State College (16803) ***(G-17988)***
Matric Group LLC (PA)...814 677-0716
2099 Hill City Rd Seneca (16346) ***(G-17366)***
Matrix Atm...215 661-2916
210 S Center St North Wales (19454) ***(G-12813)***
Matrix Publishing Services Inc...717 764-9673
36 N Highland Ave York (17404) ***(G-20583)***
Matrix Solutions LLC...412 697-3000
1 Allegheny Sq Ste 500 Pittsburgh (15212) ***(G-15262)***
Matson Industries Inc (PA)...814 849-5334
132 Main St Brookville (15825) ***(G-2263)***
Matson Lumber Company (HQ)...814 849-5334
132 Main St Brookville (15825) ***(G-2264)***

ALPHABETIC

Matson Wood Products, Brookville *Also called Matson Lumber Company* **(G-2264)**
Matt Kilmer Flagstone LLC 570 756-2591
13763 State Route 92 South Gibson (18842) **(G-17779)**
Matt Machine & Mfg Inc 412 793-6020
820 Unity Center Rd Pittsburgh (15239) **(G-15263)**
Matt Nabeja 412 787-2876
3193 Old Oakdale Rd Mc Donald (15057) **(G-10575)**
Matterns Hatchery, Mifflintown *Also called Empire Kosher Poultry Inc* **(G-11114)**
Matteson Logging Inc 814 848-9863
843 Bingham Center Rd Genesee (16923) **(G-6273)**
Matthew Cole Inc 215 425-6606
500 E Luzerne St Ste 1 Philadelphia (19124) **(G-13995)**
Matthew McKeon 215 234-8505
120 Hausman Rd Green Lane (18054) **(G-6589)**
Matthewas Auto Supplies 610 797-3729
2336 S 12th St Allentown (18103) **(G-310)**
Matthews International Corp (PA) 412 442-8200
2 N Shore Ctr Ste 200 Pittsburgh (15212) **(G-15264)**
Matthews International Corp 412 665-2500
6515 Penn Ave Pittsburgh (15206) **(G-15265)**
Matthews International Corp 412 571-5500
1315 W Liberty Ave Pittsburgh (15226) **(G-15266)**
Matthews International Corp 717 854-9566
2880 Black Bridge Rd York (17406) **(G-20584)**
Matthews International Corp 412 665-2500
101 Fairview Ave Pittsburgh (15238) **(G-15267)**
Matthey Johnson Holdings Inc (HQ) 610 971-3000
435 Devon Park Dr Ste 600 Wayne (19087) **(G-19350)**
Matthey Johnson Inc (HQ) 610 971-3000
435 Devon Park Dr Ste 600 Wayne (19087) **(G-19351)**
Matthey Johnson Inc 610 648-8000
1401 King Rd West Chester (19380) **(G-19598)**
Matthey Johnson Inc 610 341-8300
436 Devon Park Dr Wayne (19087) **(G-19352)**
Matthey Johnson Inc 484 320-2223
900 Forge Ave Audubon (19403) **(G-830)**
Matthey Johnson Inc 610 292-4300
900 Schuylkill River Rd Conshohocken (19428) **(G-3574)**
Matthey Johnson Inc 610 232-1900
1397 King Rd West Chester (19380) **(G-19599)**
Matthey Johnson Inc 610 873-3200
498 Acorn Ln Downingtown (19335) **(G-4240)**
Matthey Johnson Inc 724 564-7200
605 Mountain View Dr Smithfield (15478) **(G-17653)**
Matthey Johnson Inc 610 341-8300
456 Devon Park Dr Wayne (19087) **(G-19353)**
Mauell Corporation 717 432-8686
31 Old Cabin Hollow Rd Dillsburg (17019) **(G-4137)**
Maugus Manufacturing Inc (PA) 717 299-5681
505 E Fulton St Lancaster (17602) **(G-9126)**
Maugus Manufacturing Inc 717 481-4823
708 E Walnut St Lancaster (17602) **(G-9127)**
Mauser Usa LLC 610 258-2700
7 Mcfadden Rd Easton (18045) **(G-4720)**
Maverick Steel Company LLC 412 271-1620
98 Antisbury St Braddock (15104) **(G-1946)**
Mawa Inc 610 539-5007
15 Woodlyn Ave Norristown (19403) **(G-12679)**
Max Intrntional Converters Inc 717 898-0147
2360 Dairy Rd Lancaster (17601) **(G-9128)**
Max Levy Autograph Inc 215 842-3675
2710 Commerce Way Philadelphia (19154) **(G-13996)**
Max Machine LLC 717 361-8744
39 Industrial Rd Elizabethtown (17022) **(G-4879)**
Maxi Phase, Stevens *Also called W M S Phase Converters* **(G-18057)**
Maxima Tech & Systems Inc 717 569-5713
1090 N Charlotte St Lancaster (17603) **(G-9129)**
Maxima Tech & Systems LLC (HQ) 717 581-1000
1090 N Charlotte St # 101 Lancaster (17603) **(G-9130)**
Maximal Art Inc 484 840-0600
1606 S 8th St Philadelphia (19148) **(G-13997)**
Maximum Graphics Corporation 215 639-6700
1408 Ford Rd Bensalem (19020) **(G-1223)**
Maxpower Inc (PA) 215 256-4575
141 Christopher Ln Harleysville (19438) **(G-7047)**
Maxpro Technologies Inc (PA) 814 474-9191
7728 Klier Dr S Fairview (16415) **(G-5833)**
Maxwell Canby Fuel Oil Co 610 269-0288
8301 Lansdowne Ave Upper Darby (19082) **(G-18688)**
Maxwell Truck & Equipment LLC 814 359-2672
689 E College Ave Pleasant Gap (16823) **(G-15794)**
Maxwell Welding and Mch Inc 724 729-3160
11 Starck Dr Burgettstown (15021) **(G-2349)**
Maxx-Flex, Sharpsburg *Also called Paragon America LLC* **(G-17467)**
Maya Devi Inc 717 420-7060
1980 Biglerville Rd Gettysburg (17325) **(G-6307)**
Mayberry Hardwoods, Volant *Also called Mayberry Supply Company Inc* **(G-18775)**
Mayberry Hospitality LLC 570 275-9292
143 King St Northumberland (17857) **(G-12871)**

Mayberry Supply Company Inc 724 652-6008
629 State Route 956 Volant (16156) **(G-18775)**
Mayer Brothers Construction Co 814 452-3748
1902 Cherry St Erie (16502) **(G-5383)**
Mayer Electric Supply Co Inc 814 765-7531
1145 Fullerton St Clearfield (16830) **(G-3224)**
Mayport Cottons & Quilt Shop 814 365-2212
68 Paradise Rd Mayport (16240) **(G-10546)**
Mays Sporting Gds & Award Ctr, Erie *Also called Larry D Mays* **(G-5360)**
Mazak Corporation 610 481-0850
1275 Glenlivet Dr Ste 145 Allentown (18106) **(G-311)**
Mazza Chautauqua Cellars LLC (PA) 814 725-8695
11580 Lake Rd North East (16428) **(G-12751)**
Mazza Vineyards, North East *Also called Robert Mazza Inc* **(G-12759)**
Mazza Vineyards Inc (PA) 717 665-7021
2775 Lebanon Rd Manheim (17545) **(G-10394)**
Mazzolis Ice Cream 717 533-2252
72 W Governor Rd Hershey (17033) **(G-7620)**
MBA Design & Display Pdts Corp (HQ) 610 524-7590
35 E Uwchlan Ave Ste 310 Exton (19341) **(G-5709)**
MBI, Harrisburg *Also called Mold-Base Industries Inc* **(G-7180)**
Mbm Industries Inc 215 844-2490
4717 Stenton Ave Philadelphia (19144) **(G-13998)**
Mbpj Corporation (PA) 814 461-9120
420 E Bayfront Pkwy Erie (16507) **(G-5384)**
MBR Inc 570 386-8820
720 Laurel St Reading (19602) **(G-16440)**
Mbr2 Graphic Services LLC 610 490-8996
2550 Industry Ln Ste 103 Norristown (19403) **(G-12680)**
Mc Crackens Feed Mill Inc (PA) 717 665-2186
63 New Charlotte St Manheim (17545) **(G-10395)**
Mc Cullough Machine Inc 724 694-8485
116 Atlantic Rd New Derry (15671) **(G-12192)**
Mc Dowell Implement Company 814 786-7955
1433 Sandy Lake Rd Grove City (16127) **(G-6797)**
Mc Gear Co Inc 412 767-5502
969 Route 910 Pittsburgh (15238) **(G-15268)**
Mc Grew Welding and Fabg Inc 724 379-9303
30 S Washington St Donora (15033) **(G-4157)**
Mc Iron Works Inc 610 837-9444
7230 Beth Tach Pike Bath (18014) **(G-966)**
Mc Ironworks, Bath *Also called Michelmn-Cncllere Irnworks Inc* **(G-967)**
Mc Kruit Meat Packing 724 352-2988
1011 Bear Creek Rd Cabot (16023) **(G-2459)**
Mc Mahon Welding Inc 215 794-0260
5248 Mechanicsville Rd Mechanicsville (18934) **(G-10912)**
Mc Norton Cabinet Co 724 538-5680
311 Plains Church Rd Cranberry Township (16066) **(G-3834)**
Mc Square, Pen Argyl *Also called Creative Management Svcs LLC* **(G-13212)**
McAdoo & Allen Inc 215 536-3520
201 S Hellertown Ave Quakertown (18951) **(G-16214)**
McAdoo Machine Company 570 929-3717
51 4th St Kelayres (18231) **(G-8487)**
McArdle Surgical, Pittsburgh *Also called McKnight Surgical Inc* **(G-15270)**
McAvoy Brick Company 610 933-2932
75 Mcavoy Ln Phoenixville (19460) **(G-14560)**
McBrothers Inc 215 675-3003
665 Mary St Warminster (18974) **(G-18918)**
McC, Pittsburgh *Also called Multilingual Communications* **(G-15307)**
McC Holdings Company LLC 724 745-0300
110 Centrifugal Ct Mc Donald (15057) **(G-10576)**
McC International Inc 724 745-0300
110 Centrifugal Ct Mc Donald (15057) **(G-10577)**
McCabes Custom Leather 814 414-1442
125 Byron Ave Altoona (16602) **(G-525)**
McCahans Pharmacy Inc 814 635-2911
813 Lower Main St Saxton (16678) **(G-17102)**
McCarls Inc 724 581-5409
56 Blessing Dr Muncy (17756) **(G-11826)**
McCarty Printing Corp (PA) 814 454-4561
246 E 7th St Erie (16503) **(G-5385)**
McClarin Plastics Llc (PA) 717 637-2241
15 Industrial Dr Hanover (17331) **(G-6918)**
McCleary Heating & Cooling LLC 717 263-3833
198 Sunset Blvd E Chambersburg (17202) **(G-2959)**
McCloy Awning Company 412 271-4044
2029 Noble St Swissvale (15218) **(G-18192)**
McClure Enterprises Inc (PA) 570 562-1180
3 E Mcclure St Old Forge (18518) **(G-12970)**
McClure's Pies & Salads, Gap *Also called McClures Pie and Salad Inc* **(G-6253)**
McClures Pie and Salad Inc 717 442-4461
18 Newport Rd Gap (17527) **(G-6253)**
McConway & Torley LLC (HQ) 412 622-0494
109 48th St Pittsburgh (15201) **(G-15269)**
McConway & Torley LLC 610 683-7351
230 Railroad St Kutztown (19530) **(G-8849)**
McCourt Label Cabinet Company 800 458-2390
20 Egbert Ln Lewis Run (16738) **(G-9877)**
McCourt Label Company, Lewis Run *Also called McCourt Label Cabinet Company* **(G-9877)**

McCullough Banner Company, Strasburg *Also called McCullough Manufacturing Inc* **(G-18092)**
McCullough Manufacturing Inc....717 687-8784
27 Miller St Strasburg (17579) **(G-18092)**
McDal Corporation (PA)....800 626-2325
475 E Church Rd King of Prussia (19406) **(G-8649)**
McDanel Advnced Crmic Tech LLC....724 843-8300
510 9th Ave Beaver Falls (15010) **(G-1004)**
McDonald Sand & Gravel Inc....814 774-8149
11425 Neiger Rd Girard (16417) **(G-6397)**
McElroy Coal Company (HQ)....724 485-4000
1000 Consol Energy Dr Canonsburg (15317) **(G-2602)**
McFadden Machine & Mfg Co....724 459-9278
160 Hill Rd Blairsville (15717) **(G-1734)**
McGee Industries Inc....610 459-1890
9 Crozerville Rd Aston (19014) **(G-775)**
McGinness Group LLC....610 278-1866
1445 Dekalb St Norristown (19401) **(G-12681)**
McGivern Bindery Inc....610 770-9611
747 Pittston St Ste 2 Allentown (18103) **(G-312)**
McGregor Industries Inc....570 343-2436
46 Line St Dunmore (18512) **(G-4478)**
McGrory Inc....610 444-1512
576 Rosedale Rd Kennett Square (19348) **(G-8526)**
McHugh Locomotive and Crane Co, Fairless Hills *Also called McHugh Railroad Maint Eqp* **(G-5788)**
McHugh Railroad Maint Eqp (PA)....215 949-0430
225 Lincoln Hwy Fairless Hills (19030) **(G-5788)**
McInnes Rolled Rings, Erie *Also called T S K Partners Inc* **(G-5503)**
McKay & Gould Drilling Inc....724 436-6823
267 Taggert Rd Darlington (16115) **(G-4030)**
McKean County Miner, Bradford *Also called Bradford Journal Miner* **(G-1959)**
McKee Drilling....814 427-2444
770 Bonner Rd Rossiter (15772) **(G-16823)**
McKees Rock Forging, Mc Kees Rocks *Also called Standard Forged Products LLC* **(G-10637)**
McKees Rocks Forgings Inc....412 778-2020
75 Nichol Ave Mc Kees Rocks (15136) **(G-10620)**
McKennas Woodworking....570 836-3652
88 Shupp Hill Rd Tunkhannock (18657) **(G-18542)**
McKenzie Sports Products LLC....717 731-9920
460 Sterling St Ste 3 Camp Hill (17011) **(G-2504)**
McKesson Ptent Care Sltons Inc....814 860-8160
14 Millcreek Sq Erie (16565) **(G-5386)**
McKinley Blacksmith Limited....610 459-2730
2011 Foulk Rd Boothwyn (19060) **(G-1879)**
McKinney Drilling Company LLC....724 468-4139
Rr 22 Delmont (15626) **(G-4051)**
McKnight Surgical Inc....412 821-9000
2171 Babcock Blvd Pittsburgh (15209) **(G-15270)**
McKruit Hide & Glove, Cabot *Also called Mc Kruit Meat Packing* **(G-2459)**
McLanahan Corporation (PA)....814 695-9807
200 Wall St Hollidaysburg (16648) **(G-7651)**
McLaughlin Distillery....315 486-1372
3799 Blackburn Rd Sewickley (15143) **(G-17400)**
McLean Packaging Corporation....610 759-3550
Easton Rd Mp Mp Broad St Amp Amp Nazareth (18064) **(G-11981)**
McLean Publishing Co....814 275-3131
435 Broad St New Bethlehem (16242) **(G-12027)**
McLube, Aston *Also called McGee Industries Inc* **(G-775)**
McM Architectural Products LLC....240 416-2809
1410 Wayne Ave Ste A Indiana (15701) **(G-8112)**
McM Vaccine Co....570 957-7187
1 Discovery Dr Swiftwater (18370) **(G-18188)**
McMahon's Welding, Mechanicsville *Also called Mc Mahon Welding Inc* **(G-10912)**
McMillan Music Co LLC....215 441-0212
15 Britain Dr New Britain (18901) **(G-12049)**
McMillen Welding Inc....724 745-4507
2415 W Pike St Houston (15342) **(G-7874)**
McMullens Furniture Store....814 942-1202
601 N 2nd St Altoona (16601) **(G-526)**
McNaughton Book Service, Williamsport *Also called Brodart Co* **(G-19995)**
McNear Charles & Associates....215 514-9431
1431 Dondill Pl Philadelphia (19122) **(G-13999)**
McNeil Consmr Pharmaceuticals (HQ)....215 273-7700
7050 Camp Hill Rd Fort Washington (19034) **(G-6083)**
McNeilus Company, Morgantown *Also called McNeilus Truck and Mfg Inc* **(G-11527)**
McNeilus Truck and Mfg Inc....610 286-0400
941 Hemlock Rd Morgantown (19543) **(G-11527)**
McNs Technologies LLC....610 269-2891
608 Chadds Ford Dr # 300 Chadds Ford (19317) **(G-2855)**
McNulty Tool Die....215 957-9900
36 Vincent Cir Ste A Warminster (18974) **(G-18919)**
MCS Inc....412 429-8991
Bldg 16 Carnegie (15106) **(G-2777)**
McShane Welding Company Inc....814 459-3797
12 Port Access Rd Ste 1 Erie (16507) **(G-5387)**
McVeys Logging & Lumbe....814 542-2776
320 Mcvey Rd Mount Union (17066) **(G-11745)**
Mdbel Inc....215 738-3383
123 Hayhurst Ct Southampton (18966) **(G-17825)**
Mdc Machine Incorporated....814 372-2345
335 Aspen Way Du Bois (15801) **(G-4405)**
MDC Romani Inc....724 349-5533
2860 W Pike Rd Indiana (15701) **(G-8113)**
Mdg Associates....215 969-6623
1865 Welsh Rd Philadelphia (19115) **(G-14000)**
Mdi Membrane Technologies Inc....717 412-0943
5340 Jaycee Ave Ste A Harrisburg (17112) **(G-7175)**
Mdl Lighting LLC....267 968-3611
2800 Comly Rd Philadelphia (19154) **(G-14001)**
Mdl Manufacturing Inds Inc (PA)....814 623-0888
15 Commerce Ct Bedford (15522) **(G-1064)**
Mds Associated Companies Inc (PA)....724 548-2501
409 Butler Rd Ste A Kittanning (16201) **(G-8780)**
Mds Energy Development LLC....724 548-2501
409 Butler Rd Ste A Kittanning (16201) **(G-8781)**
Mds Energy Partners Gp LLC....724 548-2501
409 Butler Rd Ste A Kittanning (16201) **(G-8782)**
Mds Securities LLC....724 548-2501
409 Butler Rd Ste A Kittanning (16201) **(G-8783)**
Mds Well Holdings LLC....724 548-2501
409 Butler Rd Ste A Kittanning (16201) **(G-8784)**
Me Ken + Jen Crative Svcs LLC....215 997-2355
303 Nottingham Pl Chalfont (18914) **(G-2883)**
ME 5 Cents LLC....570 574-4701
1429 Sans Souci Pkwy Hanover Township (18706) **(G-6994)**
Meadow Burke Products, Hazle Township *Also called Merchants Metals LLC* **(G-7469)**
Meadowcreek Welding LLC....717 354-7533
221 Jalyn Dr New Holland (17557) **(G-12261)**
Meadville Forging Company LP (HQ)....814 332-8200
15309 Baldwin Street Ext Meadville (16335) **(G-10758)**
Meadville Forging Company LP....814 398-2203
440 Mcclellan St Cambridge Springs (16403) **(G-2483)**
Meadville New Products Inc....814 336-2174
15850 Conneaut Lake Rd Meadville (16335) **(G-10759)**
Meadville Plant, Cochranton *Also called J-M Manufacturing Company Inc* **(G-3343)**
Meadville Plating Company Inc....814 724-1084
10775 Franklin Pike Meadville (16335) **(G-10760)**
Meadville Redi-Mix Concrete....814 734-1644
26269 Blicestone Rd Edinboro (16412) **(G-4816)**
Meadville Tool & Manufacturing....814 337-7555
696 Hickory St Meadville (16335) **(G-10761)**
Meadville Tool Grinding Inc....814 382-1201
570 State St Conneaut Lake (16316) **(G-3477)**
Meadville Tribune, Meadville *Also called Newspaper Holding Inc* **(G-10769)**
Mears Tool & Die Inc....814 425-8304
24668 Us Highway 322 Cochranton (16314) **(G-3344)**
Measurement Specialties Inc....610 971-9893
460 E Swedesford Rd # 3005 Wayne (19087) **(G-19354)**
Mecaer Aviation Group Inc....301 790-3645
9800 Ashton Rd Ste 1 Philadelphia (19114) **(G-14002)**
Mecco....412 548-3549
1153 Southvale Rd Pittsburgh (15237) **(G-15271)**
Mecco Marking & Traceability, Cranberry Township *Also called Mecco Partners LLC* **(G-3835)**
Mecco Partners LLC....724 779-9555
290 Executive Dr Ste 200 Cranberry Township (16066) **(G-3835)**
Mechancal Fbrication Group Inc....717 351-0437
100 E Franklin St New Holland (17557) **(G-12262)**
Mechanical Piping Solutions, Morrisville *Also called Accu-Fire Fabrication Inc* **(G-11550)**
Mechanical Safety Equipment....215 676-7828
2070 Bennett Rd Philadelphia (19116) **(G-14003)**
Mechanical Service Co Inc....610 351-1655
710 N Jefferson St Allentown (18102) **(G-313)**
Mechanical Service Company....570 654-2445
1145 Oak St Pittston (18640) **(G-15766)**
Mechantech Inc....570 389-1039
162 Little Mountain Rd Catawissa (17820) **(G-2820)**
Mechling Associates Inc....724 287-2120
124 Evans Rd Butler (16001) **(G-2422)**
Mechling Bookbindery, Butler *Also called Mechling Associates Inc* **(G-2422)**
Meck Manufacturing....610 756-6284
30 Donat Rd Lenhartsville (19534) **(G-9759)**
Meckleys Limestone Pdts Inc (PA)....570 758-3011
1543 State Route 225 Herndon (17830) **(G-7601)**
Meckleys Limestone Pdts Inc....570 837-5228
2401 Quarry Rd Beavertown (17813) **(G-1027)**
Med-Fast Pharmacy LP (PA)....866 979-7378
2003 Sheffield Rd Aliquippa (15001) **(G-83)**
Med-Pak Division, Boyertown *Also called Self-Seal Cont Corp Del Vly* **(G-1929)**
Medalist, Reading *Also called Performance Sports Apparel Inc* **(G-16468)**
Medarbor LLC....732 887-6111
200 Rittenhouse Cir 5e Bristol (19007) **(G-2165)**
Medarbor Pharma, Bristol *Also called Medarbor LLC* **(G-2165)**

ALPHABETIC

Medart Inc..724 752-3555
199 Clyde St Ellwood City (16117) *(G-4946)*

Medchive LLC...215 688-7475
211 Brown St Unit 8 Philadelphia (19123) *(G-14004)*

Medco Process Inc (HQ).....................................717 453-7298
Coaldale Rd Wiconisco (17097) *(G-19896)*

Medcomp Technologies Inc................................814 504-3328
12220 Main St East Springfield (16411) *(G-4600)*

Medcontrol Technologies LLC...........................508 479-8109
6617 Jackson St Pittsburgh (15206) *(G-15272)*

Medeast Post-Op & Surgical Inc........................888 629-2030
2591 Baglyos Cir Ste C43 Bethlehem (18020) *(G-1566)*

Media Advantage Inc..800 985-5596
3741 Ridgeview Rd Huntingdon Valley (19006) *(G-8012)*

Media Copy, Media *Also called Portico Group LLC (G-10943)*

Media Div, Watsontown *Also called Xylem Wtr Sltons Zlienople LLC (G-19281)*

Media Highway...610 647-2255
850 Cassatt Rd Ste 350 Berwyn (19312) *(G-1368)*

Media Management Services Inc (PA)................800 523-5948
105 Terry Dr Ste 120 Newtown (18940) *(G-12521)*

Media Quarry Co Inc..610 566-6667
500 Beatty Rd Media (19063) *(G-10938)*

Media Rooms Inc..610 719-8500
20 Hagerty Blvd Ste 5 West Chester (19382) *(G-19600)*

Medianews Group Inc..717 637-3736
135 Baltimore St Hanover (17331) *(G-6919)*

Mediaonepa, York *Also called Texas-New Mxico Newspapers LLC (G-20686)*

Medical Alarm Concepts LLC............................877 639-2929
200 W Church Rd Ste 2 King of Prussia (19406) *(G-8650)*

Medical Creative Technologies...........................267 347-4436
2404 Milford Square Pike Quakertown (18951) *(G-16215)*

Medical Device Bus Svcs Inc.............................724 933-0288
7500 Brooktree Rd Ste 101 Wexford (15090) *(G-19810)*

Medical Precision Plastics Inc...........................215 441-4800
447 Ivyland Rd Warminster (18974) *(G-18920)*

Medical Products Labs Inc.................................215 677-2700
9990 Global Rd Philadelphia (19115) *(G-14005)*

Medicalabbreviations, Warminster *Also called Neil M Davis (G-18928)*

Medicapture Inc (PA)..610 238-0700
2250 Hickory Rd Ste 200 Plymouth Meeting (19462) *(G-15856)*

Medicine Shoppe..717 208-3415
625 S Duke St Lancaster (17602) *(G-9131)*

Medico Industries Inc (PA).................................570 825-7711
1500 Highway 315 Blvd Wilkes Barre (18702) *(G-19942)*

Medico Industries Inc..570 208-3140
1060 Hanover St Hanover Township (18706) *(G-6995)*

Medico Industries Inc..570 825-7711
1060 Hanover St Hanover Township (18706) *(G-6996)*

Medico International Inc.....................................610 253-7009
440 Allentown Dr Allentown (18109) *(G-314)*

Medihill Inc..215 464-7016
3466 Progress Dr Ste 111 Bensalem (19020) *(G-1224)*

Medimmune..240 751-5625
104 Rosemont Ln Royersford (19468) *(G-16858)*

Medimmune LLC..215 501-1300
3600 Marshall Ln Bensalem (19020) *(G-1225)*

Medina Wells Servicing Limited, Bradford *Also called Fault Line Oil Corporation (G-1968)*

Medipendant, King of Prussia *Also called Medical Alarm Concepts LLC (G-8650)*

Medisox, Newville *Also called Garnes Park E Jr (G-12602)*

Medisurg Ltd..610 277-3937
100 W Fornance St Norristown (19401) *(G-12682)*

Medl Tool & Die Inc..215 443-5457
1800 Mearns Rd Ste B Warminster (18974) *(G-18921)*

Medplast Engineered Pdts Inc...........................814 367-2246
115 Pritchard Hollow Rd Westfield (16950) *(G-19780)*

Medplast Westfield, LLC, Warminster *Also called Viant Westfield LLC (G-18994)*

Medrad Incorporated Ohara...............................412 967-9700
271 Kappa Dr Pittsburgh (15238) *(G-15273)*

Medshifts Inc...856 834-0074
1500 Market St Philadelphia (19102) *(G-14006)*

Medtronic Monitoring Inc...................................610 257-3640
111 Presidential Blvd # 102 Bala Cynwyd (19004) *(G-885)*

Medtronic Usa Inc...724 933-8100
1603 Carmody Ct Ste 401 Wexford (15090) *(G-19811)*

Medtronic Usa Inc...717 657-6140
4230 Crums Mill Rd # 201 Harrisburg (17112) *(G-7176)*

Medunik Usa Inc..484 380-2641
919 Conestoga Rd Bryn Mawr (19010) *(G-2329)*

Meeco Inc...215 343-6600
250 Titus Ave Warrington (18976) *(G-19125)*

Meeco Manufacturing Targe................................412 653-1323
5905 Brownsville Rd Pittsburgh (15236) *(G-15274)*

Mefiag Filtration, Telford *Also called Ceco Filters Inc (G-18272)*

Mega Enterprises Inc...610 380-0255
37 E Highland Rd Parkesburg (19365) *(G-13179)*

Mega Motion LLC...800 800-8586
182 Susquehanna Ave Exeter (18643) *(G-5583)*

Megagrafix, Erie *Also called Hessinger Group Inc (G-5316)*

Megan Sweet Baking Company.........................267 288-5080
234 Holland Rd Holland (18966) *(G-7641)*

Megaphase LLC..570 424-8400
122 Banner Rd Stroudsburg (18360) *(G-18130)*

Megator Corporation...412 963-9200
1721 Main St Pittsburgh (15215) *(G-15275)*

Megger, Norristown *Also called Avo Multi-AMP Corporation (G-12638)*

Meighen Jinjou...717 846-5600
1243 E Market St Frnt York (17403) *(G-20585)*

Meinert Holdings Inc..412 835-2727
5309 Enterprise Blvd Bethel Park (15102) *(G-1424)*

Meiserville Milling Co..570 539-8855
127 Mill Rd Ofc Rte 104 Mount Pleasant Mills (17853) *(G-11727)*

Meke Corp..717 354-6353
1282 E Earl Rd East Earl (17519) *(G-4550)*

Melinessence LLC..717 668-3730
1875 Church Rd York (17408) *(G-20586)*

Melitta Usa Inc...215 355-5581
1394 Hiview Dr Southampton (18966) *(G-17826)*

Mellinger Manufacturing Co Inc.........................717 464-3318
367 Millwood Rd Willow Street (17584) *(G-20154)*

Mellott Wood Preserving Inc (PA).....................717 573-2519
1398 Sawmill Rd Needmore (17238) *(G-11996)*

Melrath Gasket Inc...215 223-6000
1500 John F Kennedy Blvd # 200 Philadelphia (19102) *(G-14007)*

Melt Enterprises LLC..570 244-2970
9 Wichita Ct Gouldsboro (18424) *(G-6569)*

Melvin Leid...717 776-4940
237 Green Hill Rd Newville (17241) *(G-12606)*

Melvin Stoltzfus...717 656-3520
S State St Talmage (17580) *(G-18207)*

Memory Makers Ltd...215 679-3636
2528 Quakertown Rd Pennsburg (18073) *(G-13250)*

Memrs Inc...724 589-5567
203 S Summit Rd Greenville (16125) *(G-6754)*

Men of Steel Enterprises Inc.............................609 871-2000
555 State Rd 101 Bensalem (19020) *(G-1226)*

Menasha Packaging Company LLC....................570 243-5512
2086 Corporate Ctr Dr W Tobyhanna (18466) *(G-18407)*

Menasha Packaging Company LLC....................630 236-4925
4000 Miller Cir N Bethlehem (18020) *(G-1567)*

Menasha Packaging Company LLC....................717 776-2900
954 Centerville Rd # 100 Newville (17241) *(G-12607)*

Menasha Packaging Company LLC....................800 477-8746
30 Grumbacher Rd York (17406) *(G-20587)*

Menasha Packaging Company LLC....................800 477-8746
3301 Barwood Rd York (17406) *(G-20588)*

Menasha Packaging Company LLC....................717 520-5990
245 W Chocolate Ave Hershey (17033) *(G-7621)*

Menasha Packaging Company LLC....................800 245-2486
567 Waltz Mill Rd Ruffs Dale (15679) *(G-16874)*

Menasha Packaging Company LLC....................215 426-7110
601 E Erie Ave Philadelphia (19134) *(G-14008)*

Menasha Packaging Company LLC....................215 426-7110
601 E Erie Ave Philadelphia (19134) *(G-14009)*

Menasha Packaging Company LLC....................800 783-4563
131 Menasha Ln Latrobe (15650) *(G-9504)*

Mendel Steel & Orna Ir Co.................................412 341-7778
3017 S Park Rd Bethel Park (15102) *(G-1425)*

Mendit Chemical Inc...610 239-5120
401 E 4th St Ste 20 Bridgeport (19405) *(G-2039)*

Menghini's Truss Systems, Hazle Township *Also called V Menghini & Sons Inc (G-7489)*

Meniscus Limited...610 567-2725
18 Elizabeth St Ste 100 Conshohocken (19428) *(G-3575)*

Mensco Inc...610 863-9233
125 W West St Ste A Wind Gap (18091) *(G-20171)*

Menu For Less..215 240-1582
2 Park Ln Ste 107 Feasterville Trevose (19053) *(G-5919)*

Menu Mon.net, Willow Grove *Also called Menu World Inc (G-20127)*

Menu World Inc..267 784-8515
726 Fitzwatertown Rd # 9 Willow Grove (19090) *(G-20127)*

Meow Mix Company (HQ)...................................412 222-2200
375 N Shore Dr Pittsburgh (15212) *(G-15276)*

Meppi, Warrendale *Also called Mitsubishi Elc Pwr Pdts Inc (G-19088)*

Mercer Co...724 347-4534
200 Stewart Way Sharon (16146) *(G-17438)*

Mercer Forge Corporation (HQ)........................724 662-2750
315 S Erie St Ste E Mercer (16137) *(G-10968)*

Mercer Lime Company (HQ)..............................412 220-0316
50 Abele Rd Ste 1006 Bridgeville (15017) *(G-2078)*

Mercer Spring & Wire LLC.................................814 967-2545
15715 Mercer Rd Townville (16360) *(G-18446)*

Mercer Spring and Wire Div, Monroeville *Also called Union Spring & Mfg Corp (G-11361)*

Mercer Valve Co Inc..412 859-0300
1616 Parkway View Dr Pittsburgh (15205) *(G-15277)*

Mercersburg Journal...717 485-3162
115 Lincoln Way E Ste A Mc Connellsburg (17233) *(G-10571)*

Mercersburg Journal...717 328-3223
11 S Main St Mercersburg (17236) *(G-10992)*

Mercersburg Printing Inc (PA) 717 328-3902
9964 Buchanan Trl W Mercersburg (17236) *(G-10993)*

Mercersburg Printing Inc 717 762-8204
114 Walnut St Ste 1 Waynesboro (17268) *(G-19418)*

Merchandiser, Hanover *Also called Kapp Advertising Services Inc* *(G-6909)*

Merchandiser, The, Lebanon *Also called Kapp Advertising Services Inc* *(G-9587)*

Merchandiser, The, Mount Joy *Also called Alvin Engle Associates Inc* *(G-11646)*

Merchandising Methods Inc 215 262-4842
800 W State St Doylestown (18901) *(G-4315)*

Merchandising Solutions Inc 717 898-1800
2882 Yellow Goose Rd Lancaster (17601) *(G-9132)*

Merchants Metals LLC 570 384-3063
565 Oak Ridge Rd Hazle Township (18202) *(G-7469)*

Merck & Co Inc 215 652-5000
351 N Sumneytown Pike North Wales (19454) *(G-12814)*

Merck and Company Inc 215 993-1616
502 Louise Ln North Wales (19454) *(G-12815)*

Merck Sharp & Dohme Corp 215 652-6777
770 Sumneytown Pike West Point (19486) *(G-19760)*

Merck Sharp & Dohme Corp 215 652-5000
351 N Sumneytown Pike North Wales (19454) *(G-12816)*

Merck Sharp & Dohme Corp 215 652-8368
770 Sumneytown Pike West Point (19486) *(G-19761)*

Merck Sharp & Dohme Corp 484 344-2493
10 Sentry Pkwy Blue Bell (19422) *(G-1847)*

Merck Sharp & Dohme Corp 267 305-5000
351 N Sumneytown Pike North Wales (19454) *(G-12817)*

Merck Sharp & Dohme Corp 215 631-5000
770 Sumneytown Pike West Point (19486) *(G-19762)*

Merck Sharp & Dohme Corp 215 397-2541
1227 Independence Way Hatfield (19440) *(G-7368)*

Merck Sharp & Dohme Corp 215 652-5000
770 Sumneytown Pike West Point (19486) *(G-19763)*

Merck Sharp Dhme Argentina Inc 215 996-3806
333 S Broad St Lansdale (19446) *(G-9386)*

Mercurios Mulberry Creamery 412 621-6220
5523 Walnut St Pittsburgh (15232) *(G-15278)*

Mercury Electronics, Seven Valleys *Also called Diversified Traffic Pdts Inc* *(G-17377)*

Mercury Systems Inc 215 245-0546
2182 Lillian Dr Bensalem (19020) *(G-1227)*

Mercury, The, Exton *Also called Journal Register Company* *(G-5702)*

Meredith Banzhoff LLC (PA) 717 919-5074
2308 Stumpstown Rd Mechanicsburg (17055) *(G-10868)*

Mergtech Inc 570 584-3388
48 N Main St Hughesville (17737) *(G-7896)*

Meridian Precision Inc 570 345-6600
80 Roberts Rd Pine Grove (17963) *(G-14599)*

Meridian Products Inc 717 355-7700
124 Earland Dr New Holland (17557) *(G-12263)*

Merien Music, King of Prussia *Also called Theodore Presser Company* *(G-8687)*

Merisol Antioxidants LLC 814 677-2028
292 State Route 8 Oil City (16301) *(G-12952)*

Merit Entertainment, Bristol *Also called AMI Entertainment Network Inc* *(G-2106)*

Merit Manufacturing Corp 610 327-4000
319 Circle Of Progress Dr Pottstown (19464) *(G-16018)*

Merit Medical 610 651-5000
65 Great Valley Pkwy Malvern (19355) *(G-10277)*

Merit Press, West Chester *Also called R Graphics Inc* *(G-19625)*

Merkin Body and Hoist Company 610 258-6179
1539 Church St Easton (18042) *(G-4721)*

Merlin Machine & Tool Co Inc 215 493-6322
17 S Macdade Blvd Collingdale (19023) *(G-3407)*

Merlot Graphics, Verona *Also called Merlot Trpulin Sidekit Mfg Inc* *(G-18757)*

Merlot Trpulin Sidekit Mfg Inc 412 828-7664
10 Plum St Verona (15147) *(G-18757)*

Merrigan Corporation 610 317-6300
950 Jennings St Unit 3 Bethlehem (18017) *(G-1568)*

Merrill Corporation 215 405-8443
2000 Market St Ste 760 Philadelphia (19103) *(G-14010)*

Merrill Y Landis Ltd 215 723-8177
20 S 3rd St Telford (18969) *(G-18302)*

Merry Maid Inc 800 360-3836
25 W Messinger Street Ext Bangor (18013) *(G-921)*

Merry Maid Novelties 610 599-4104
25 W Messinger Street Ext Bangor (18013) *(G-922)*

Mersen USA Bn Corp 814 781-1234
215 Stackpole St Saint Marys (15857) *(G-16988)*

Mersen USA St Marys-PA Corp (HQ) 814 781-1234
215 Stackpole St Saint Marys (15857) *(G-16989)*

Mersen USA St Marys-PA Corp 814 781-1234
215 Stackpole St Saint Marys (15857) *(G-16990)*

Mervine Corp 215 257-0431
7 E Walnut St Perkasie (18944) *(G-13284)*

Meshnet Inc 215 237-7712
206 N 22nd St Unit B Philadelphia (19103) *(G-14011)*

Meshoppen Stone Incorporated 570 833-2767
131 Frantz Rd Meshoppen (18630) *(G-11007)*

Mesko Glass and Mirror Co Inc 570 457-1700
100 Glendale Rd Avoca (18641) *(G-845)*

Messer Gt & S 717 232-3173
2551 Paxton St Harrisburg (17111) *(G-7177)*

Messer LLC 610 317-8500
1011 E Market St Bethlehem (18017) *(G-1569)*

Messer LLC 412 351-4580
1000 Washington Ave Braddock (15104) *(G-1947)*

Messer LLC 484 281-3261
5897 Colony Dr Bethlehem (18017) *(G-1570)*

Messinger Bearings, Philadelphia *Also called Kingsbury Inc* *(G-13939)*

Mesta Electronics Inc 412 754-3000
11020 Parker Dr Irwin (15642) *(G-8182)*

Mestek Inc 570 746-1888
450 Riverside Dr Wyalusing (18853) *(G-20254)*

Met Fab Division, Montoursville *Also called Jersey Shore Steel Company* *(G-11443)*

Met-Fin Co Inc 215 699-3505
S 4th St & Railroad Ave North Wales (19454) *(G-12818)*

Met-Pro Technologies LLC 215 822-1963
700 Emlen Way Telford (18969) *(G-18303)*

Met-Pro Technologies LLC 215 723-4700
700 Emlen Way Telford (18969) *(G-18304)*

Met-Pro Technologies LLC 215 723-8155
700 Emlen Way Telford (18969) *(G-18305)*

Metabloc Inc 717 764-4937
120 Rose Ct York (17406) *(G-20589)*

Metadyne Inc (PA) 570 265-6963
Fox Chase Dr Towanda (18848) *(G-18432)*

Metal Bulletin Holdings LLC 412 765-2580
1 Gateway Ctr Ste 1375 Pittsburgh (15222) *(G-15279)*

Metal Crafters Inc 215 491-9925
1409 Easton Rd Ste 1 Warrington (18976) *(G-19126)*

Metal Exchange Corporation 724 373-8471
93 Werner Rd Greenville (16125) *(G-6755)*

Metal Fabricating Co 717 442-4729
5425 W Lincoln Hwy Parkesburg (19365) *(G-13180)*

Metal Fence Supply, Slippery Rock *Also called Machining Center* *(G-17621)*

Metal Finishing Corporation 215 788-9246
2979 State Rd Bristol (19007) *(G-2166)*

Metal Finishing Industries 724 836-1003
1166 Garden St Greensburg (15601) *(G-6688)*

Metal Finishing Systems Inc 610 524-9336
240 Welsh Pool Rd Exton (19341) *(G-5710)*

Metal Group 215 438-6156
740 E Vernon Rd Philadelphia (19119) *(G-14012)*

Metal Integrity Inc 814 234-7399
341 Airport Rd State College (16801) *(G-17989)*

Metal Integrity LLC 570 281-2303
47 N Scott St Carbondale (18407) *(G-2682)*

Metal Light Manufacturing 215 430-7200
1100 W Indiana Ave Philadelphia (19133) *(G-14013)*

Metal Litho and Laminating LLC 724 646-1222
242 Reynolds Indus Pk Dr Greenville (16125) *(G-6756)*

Metal Menders LLC 412 580-8625
230 Saunders Station Rd Trafford (15085) *(G-18458)*

Metal Peddler Inc 724 476-1061
110 Miller School Ln West Sunbury (16061) *(G-19772)*

Metal Photo Service Inc 412 829-2992
465 Wall Ave Wall (15148) *(G-18779)*

Metal Powder Pdts Ridgway Div, Ridgway *Also called O Alpine Pressed Metals Inc* *(G-16721)*

Metal Powder Products LLC 814 834-2886
150 Ford Rd Saint Marys (15857) *(G-16991)*

Metal Powder Products LLC 814 834-7261
879 Washington St Saint Marys (15857) *(G-16992)*

Metal Powder Products LLC 814 776-2141
310 Tanner St Ridgway (15853) *(G-16716)*

Metal Sales Manufacturing Corp 570 366-2020
29 Pinedale Industrial Rd Orwigsburg (17961) *(G-13049)*

Metal Service, Temple *Also called David Seidel* *(G-18327)*

Metal Service Company Inc (PA) 724 567-6500
210 1st St Vandergrift (15690) *(G-18733)*

Metal Services LLC (HQ) 610 347-0444
148 W State St Ste 301 Kennett Square (19348) *(G-8527)*

Metal Tech Machine Company 412 833-3239
1065 Grandview Farms Dr Bethel Park (15102) *(G-1426)*

Metal USA Plates and Shapes 724 266-1283
81 Century Dr Ambridge (15003) *(G-626)*

Metaldyne Sintered Ridgway LLC 814 776-1141
1149 Rocky Rd Ridgway (15853) *(G-16717)*

Metaldyne Snterforged Pdts LLC 814 834-1222
197 West Creek Rd Saint Marys (15857) *(G-16993)*

Metalife Industries Inc 814 676-5661
141 Mong Way Reno (16343) *(G-16647)*

Metalkraft Industries Inc 570 724-6800
1944 Shumway Hill Rd Wellsboro (16901) *(G-19469)*

Metallurg Inc (HQ) 610 293-2501
435 Devon Park Dr Ste 200 Wayne (19087) *(G-19355)*

Metallurg Holdings Inc (HQ) 610 293-2501
435 Devon Park Dr Ste 200 Wayne (19087) *(G-19356)*

Metallurgical Products Company 610 696-6770
810 Lincoln Ave West Chester (19380) *(G-19601)*

A
L
P
H
A
B
E
T
I
C

Metalor Electronics USA Corp (HQ)..........724 733-8332
1003 Corporate Ln Export (15632) ***(G-5618)***
Metals Usa Inc..........215 540-8004
1300 Virginia Dr Ste 320 Fort Washington (19034) ***(G-6084)***
Metals Usa Inc..........215 540-8004
1300 Virginia Dr Ste 320 Fort Washington (19034) ***(G-6085)***
Metalsa SA De CV..........610 371-7000
1100 Weiser St Reading (19601) ***(G-16441)***
Metaltech..........412 464-5000
2400 2nd Ave Pittsburgh (15219) ***(G-15280)***
Metaltech Inc..........814 375-9399
3547 Watson Hwy Du Bois (15801) ***(G-4406)***
Metalwerks Inc..........724 378-9020
401 Steel St Aliquippa (15001) ***(G-84)***
Metalworking Machinery Co Inc (PA)..........724 625-3181
700 Constitution Blvd New Kensington (15068) ***(G-12355)***
Metalzed Ceramics For Elec Inc..........724 287-5752
119 Grant Ave East Butler (16029) ***(G-4535)***
Metamora Products Corp Elkland..........814 258-7122
112 Industrial Pkwy Elkland (16920) ***(G-4916)***
Metaphase Lighting, Bristol *Also called Metaphase Technologies Inc* ***(G-2167)***
Metaphase Technologies Inc..........215 639-8699
211 Sinclair Rd Ste 100k Bristol (19007) ***(G-2167)***
Metavis Technologies Inc..........484 288-2990
256 Eagleview Blvd # 258 Exton (19341) ***(G-5711)***
Metco Industries Inc..........814 781-3630
1241 Brusselles St Saint Marys (15857) ***(G-16994)***
Metco Manufacturing Co Inc (PA)..........215 518-7400
3035 Franks Rd Huntingdon Valley (19006) ***(G-8013)***
Metcure Inc..........813 601-3533
18 Campus Blvd Ste 100 Newtown Square (19073) ***(G-12585)***
Method Automation Services Inc..........724 337-9064
1801 5th Ave New Kensington (15068) ***(G-12356)***
Metkote Laminated Products Inc..........570 562-0107
1151 Union St Taylor (18517) ***(G-18260)***
Metlab, Glenside *Also called Podcon Inc* ***(G-6533)***
Metplas Inc..........724 295-5200
3 Acee Dr Natrona Heights (15065) ***(G-11946)***
Metpro Fybroc Division, Telford *Also called Strobic Air Corporation* ***(G-18321)***
Metro Building Services..........412 221-1284
379 Rockhill Rd Pittsburgh (15243) ***(G-15281)***
Metro Corp (HQ)..........215 564-7700
170 S Independence Mall Philadelphia (19106) ***(G-14014)***
Metro Corp..........215 564-7700
170 S Independence Mall W # 200 Philadelphia (19106) ***(G-14015)***
Metro Corp Holdings Inc (PA)..........215 564-7700
170 S Independence Mall W # 200 Philadelphia (19106) ***(G-14016)***
Metro International Corp..........570 825-2741
651 N Washington St Wilkes Barre (18705) ***(G-19943)***
Metro Magazines, Philadelphia *Also called Metro Corp Holdings Inc* ***(G-14016)***
Metro Manufacturing & Supply (PA)..........610 891-1899
524 N Providence Rd Media (19063) ***(G-10939)***
Metro News Gifts..........610 734-2262
6901 Market St Upper Darby (19082) ***(G-18689)***
Metro Ready Mix and Supplies, Philadelphia *Also called Dinardo Brothers Material Inc* ***(G-13633)***
Metroplitan Communications Inc..........610 874-7100
940 Eddystone Ave Eddystone (19022) ***(G-4805)***
Metropolitan Flag & Banner, West Chester *Also called S & H Ltd* ***(G-19633)***
Metroweek Corp..........215 735-8444
1845 Walnut St Ste 900 Philadelphia (19103) ***(G-14017)***
Metso Automation USA Inc..........215 393-3900
2750 Morris Rd Ste A100 Lansdale (19446) ***(G-9387)***
Metso Automation USA Inc (HQ)..........215 393-3947
2750 Morris Rd Ste A100 Lansdale (19446) ***(G-9388)***
Metso Minerals Industries Inc..........717 843-8671
2715 Pleasant Valley Rd York (17402) ***(G-20590)***
Metso Minerals Industries Inc..........717 843-8671
2715 Pleasant Valley Rd York (17402) ***(G-20591)***
Metso Minerals Industries Inc..........210 491-9521
42 Leech Rd Greenville (16125) ***(G-6757)***
Metvac Inc..........215 541-4495
7178 Pine Tree Rd Hereford (18056) ***(G-7568)***
Mexico Heat Treating..........717 535-5034
Rr 2 Mifflintown (17059) ***(G-11130)***
Meyer Machine Company Inc..........724 368-3711
2647 Perry Hwy Portersville (16051) ***(G-15932)***
Meyer Products, Pittsburgh *Also called Louis Berkman Company* ***(G-15238)***
MFC, Meadville *Also called Meadville Forging Company LP* ***(G-10758)***
MFC Valve, Somerset *Also called Global Incorporated* ***(G-17690)***
Mfg Plant-Shipping, Reading *Also called Sfs Group Usa Inc* ***(G-16513)***
Mfg Water Treat Prod..........814 438-3959
55 4th Ave Union City (16438) ***(G-18609)***
Mg Development America Inc..........412 288-9959
187 36th St Pittsburgh (15201) ***(G-15282)***
Mg Financial Services Inc..........215 364-7555
575 Virginia Dr Ste D Fort Washington (19034) ***(G-6086)***
Mg Industrial Products Inc..........814 255-2471
1248 Laurelview Dr Johnstown (15905) ***(G-8408)***
Mg Industries Erie Inc..........814 806-6826
2103 E 33rd St Ste W-5 Erie (16510) ***(G-5388)***
Mg Industries Inc (PA)..........724 694-8290
515 W 3rd Ave Derry (15627) ***(G-4105)***
Mg Welding & Fabrication..........717 292-5206
7070 Bull Rd Dover (17315) ***(G-4196)***
Mgi Seagull Inc (PA)..........610 380-6470
520 Lincoln Ave Ste 300 Downingtown (19335) ***(G-4241)***
Mgk Produce Co..........610 853-3678
610 Industrial Park Dr Lansdowne (19050) ***(G-9438)***
Mgk Technologies Inc..........814 849-3061
57 Cooper Ave Homer City (15748) ***(G-7678)***
Mgs Inc (PA)..........717 336-7528
178 Muddy Creek Church Rd Denver (17517) ***(G-4083)***
Mgs04 Corporation..........267 249-2372
1700 Market St Ste 1105 Philadelphia (19103) ***(G-14018)***
Mgtf Paper Company LLC..........412 316-3342
650 Smithfield St # 2200 Pittsburgh (15222) ***(G-15283)***
Mh EBY Trailers, Blue Ball *Also called M H EBY Inc* ***(G-1811)***
Mhp Industries Inc..........717 450-4753
2402 E Cumberland St Lebanon (17042) ***(G-9609)***
Ml Metals Inc..........717 692-4851
1517 Rte 209 Millersburg (17061) ***(G-11196)***
Ml Products, Allentown *Also called Valco Investment Corporation* ***(G-419)***
Ml Swaco..........724 820-3306
4600 Jbarry Ct Ste 200 Canonsburg (15317) ***(G-2603)***
Ml Windows and Doors Inc (HQ)..........717 365-3300
650 W Market St Gratz (17030) ***(G-6578)***
Ml Windows and Doors Inc..........717 362-8196
4314 State Route 209 Elizabethville (17023) ***(G-4895)***
Ml Windows and Doors Inc..........717 365-3300
760 W Market St Route 25 Gratz (17030) ***(G-6579)***
Ml Windows and Doors Inc..........570 682-1206
79 Park Ln Hegins (17938) ***(G-7543)***
Ml Windows and Doors LLC..........717 365-3300
650 W Market St Gratz (17030) ***(G-6580)***
Mi-Jo Enterprises, Forest City *Also called Kartri Sales Company Inc* ***(G-6054)***
Mi-Kee-Tro Metal Mfg Inc..........717 764-9090
460 Grim Ln Ste 2 York (17406) ***(G-20592)***
Mi-Llon Sales Associates, Easton *Also called Brown Jr Merritt* ***(G-4658)***
Mia Products Company (HQ)..........570 457-7431
4 Rocky Glen Rd Avoca (18641) ***(G-846)***
MIC Industries Inc..........814 266-8226
137 Bronze Dr Elton (15934) ***(G-4960)***
Micale Fabricators Inc..........814 368-7133
85 Forman St Bradford (16701) ***(G-1981)***
Micfralip Inc..........215 338-3293
4625 Knorr St Philadelphia (19135) ***(G-14019)***
Michael Anthony Salvatori..........570 326-9222
116 Emery St Williamsport (17701) ***(G-20041)***
Michael Boyle, Pittsburgh *Also called Derrick Publishing Company* ***(G-14918)***
Michael Bryan..........610 273-2535
749 Poplar Rd Honey Brook (19344) ***(G-7754)***
Michael Cain..........814 333-1852
576 Washington St Meadville (16335) ***(G-10762)***
Michael Dahma Associates..........412 607-1151
558 Carroll Dr Irwin (15642) ***(G-8183)***
Michael Eldridge, Westfield *Also called Sunrise Maple* ***(G-19781)***
Michael Furman Photography..........215 925-4233
16 S 3rd St Philadelphia (19106) ***(G-14020)***
Michael J Doyle..........215 587-1000
5918 Hammond Ave Philadelphia (19120) ***(G-14021)***
Michael J Zellers..........610 562-2825
611 1st Street Ext Hamburg (19526) ***(G-6846)***
Michael Meyer Pallets..........814 781-1107
1022 S Michael St Saint Marys (15857) ***(G-16995)***
Michael Mootz Candies Inc..........570 823-8272
1246 Sans Souci Pkwy Hanover Township (18706) ***(G-6997)***
Michael N Sullenberger..........724 725-5285
126 Penn St Point Marion (15474) ***(G-15886)***
Michael P Hoover Company Inc..........717 757-7842
3775 Starview Dr York (17402) ***(G-20593)***
Michael P Hoover Excavating, York *Also called Michael P Hoover Company Inc* ***(G-20593)***
Michael R Skrip Excavating..........610 965-5331
420 S 6th St Emmaus (18049) ***(G-5034)***
Michael S Cwalina..........412 341-1606
250 Mount Lebanon Blvd # 322 Pittsburgh (15234) ***(G-15284)***
Michael Z Gehman..........814 483-0488
184 Marts Rd Friedens (15541) ***(G-6221)***
Michaels Glass Co, Philadelphia *Also called Micfralip Inc* ***(G-14019)***
Michalman Cancelliere Ir Works, Bath *Also called Mc Iron Works Inc* ***(G-966)***
Michalski Refrigeration Inc..........724 352-1666
368 Dinnerbell Rd Butler (16002) ***(G-2423)***
Michelin North America Inc..........301 641-0121
100 Northpointe Cir Seven Fields (16046) ***(G-17376)***
Michelman Steel Entps LLC..........610 395-3472
6338 Farm Bureau Rd Allentown (18106) ***(G-315)***
Michelmn-Cncllere Irnworks Inc..........610 837-9914
7230 Beth Bath Pike Bath (18014) ***(G-967)***

Michels Bakery Inc 215 742-3900
5698 Rising Sun Ave Philadelphia (19120) (G-14022)

Michels Corporation 724 249-2065
2155 Park Ave Washington (15301) (G-19202)

Michels Hearing Aid Center (PA) 570 622-9151
459 N Claude A Lord Blvd Pottsville (17901) (G-16088)

Michels Pipeline, Washington Also called Michels Corporation (G-19202)

Micheners Engraving Inc 717 738-9630
307 N State St Ephrata (17522) (G-5127)

Mick Brothers Lumber Inc 814 664-8700
12242 Lovell Rd Corry (16407) (G-3767)

Mickelson Mfg Inds Inc 215 529-5442
550 California Rd Ste 5 Quakertown (18951) (G-16216)

Micor Inc 412 487-1113
824 12th Ave Bethlehem (18018) (G-1571)

Micro Dimensional Products 610 239-7940
199 W Spruce St Norristown (19401) (G-12683)

Micro Facture LLC 717 285-9700
200 N Donnerville Rd Mountville (17554) (G-11799)

Micro Machine Design Inc 717 274-3500
1555 Joel Dr Lebanon (17046) (G-9610)

Micro Matic Usa Inc 610 625-4464
4601 Saucon Creek Rd Center Valley (18034) (G-2828)

Micro Miniature Manufacturing 724 481-1033
506 Pittsburgh Rd Butler (16002) (G-2424)

Micro Mold Co Inc (PA) 814 838-3404
4820 Pittsburgh Ave Erie (16509) (G-5389)

Micro Oscillator Inc 610 617-8682
118 Cornell Rd Bala Cynwyd (19004) (G-886)

Micro Plastics Inc 814 337-0781
13561 Broadway Ste A Meadville (16335) (G-10763)

Micro Plating Inc 814 866-0073
8110 Hawthorne Dr Erie (16509) (G-5390)

Micro Precision Corporation 717 393-4100
200 Centerville Rd Lancaster (17603) (G-9133)

Micro Tool Company 610 882-3740
284 Brodhead Rd Bethlehem (18017) (G-1572)

Micro-Coax Inc (HQ) 610 495-4438
206 Jones Blvd Pottstown (19464) (G-16019)

Micro-Fusion LLC 717 244-4648
536 Boundary Ave Red Lion (17356) (G-16609)

Micro-Trap Corporation 215 295-8208
1300 Steel Rd E Ste 2 Morrisville (19067) (G-11571)

Microbiology Lab Co 570 800-5795
300 Mulberry St Scranton (18503) (G-17259)

Microchip Technology Inc 610 630-0556
2490 Genl Armistd Ave 2 Norristown (19403) (G-12684)

Microcomputer Task Group, York Also called Garth Groft (G-20491)

Microcut Inc 717 848-4150
1758 S Queen St York (17403) (G-20594)

Microgenics 412 490-8365
2000 Park Ln Pittsburgh (15275) (G-15285)

Microimage Video Systems, Bechtelsville Also called World Video Sales Co Inc (G-1038)

Microlite Corporation 724 375-6711
2315 Mill St Aliquippa (15001) (G-85)

Micromechatronics Inc 814 861-5688
200 Innovation Blvd # 155 State College (16803) (G-17990)

Micromed LLC 480 236-4705
224 S Maple St Ambler (19002) (G-590)

Micron Research Corporation 814 486-2444
13746 Route 120 Emporium (15834) (G-5069)

Micronic 484 480-3372
210 Bridgewater Rd Ste 3 Aston (19014) (G-776)

Micronic America LLC 484 483-8075
210 Bridgewater Rd Ste 3 Aston (19014) (G-777)

Micronic Manufacturingusa LLC 484 483-8075
210 Bridgewater Rd Ste 3 Aston (19014) (G-778)

Microprocess Technolgies LLC 570 778-0925
1862 Tollgate Rd Unit D Palm (18070) (G-13095)

Microsemi Corp 610 929-7142
2136 N 13th St Ste D Reading (19604) (G-16442)

Microsemi Corp - High 717 486-3411
100 Watts St Mount Holly Springs (17065) (G-11636)

Microsemi Corp - Mntgmeryville 215 631-9840
140 Commerce Dr Montgomeryville (18936) (G-11407)

Microsemi Stor Solutions Inc 610 289-5200
3500 Winchester Rd # 400 Allentown (18104) (G-316)

Microsilver Wear LLC 215 917-7203
593 Nottingham Dr Yardley (19067) (G-20325)

Microsoft Corporation 484 754-7600
160 N Gulph Rd Ste 1644 King of Prussia (19406) (G-8651)

Microsoft Corporation 412 323-6700
30 Isabella St Ste 2 Pittsburgh (15212) (G-15286)

Microsoft Corporation 610 240-7000
45 Liberty Blvd Ste 210 Malvern (19355) (G-10278)

Microsonic Inc (PA) 724 266-2031
2960 Duss Ave Ambridge (15003) (G-627)

Microsphere Inc 610 444-3450
455 Birch St Kennett Square (19348) (G-8528)

Micross Components, Hatfield Also called Premier Semiconductor Svcs LLC (G-7384)

Micross Components, Hatfield Also called NORTH PENN TECHNOLOGY INC (G-7374)

Micross Components Inc 215 997-3200
2294 N Penn Rd Hatfield (19440) (G-7369)

Microtrac Inc (HQ) 215 619-9920
215 Keystone Dr Montgomeryville (18936) (G-11408)

Microtrac Inc 717 843-4433
3230 N Susquehanna Trl York (17406) (G-20595)

Microtrac Inc 717 843-4433
3230 N Susquehanna Trl York (17406) (G-20596)

Microwave Measurement Systems, State College Also called MMS Technologies LLC (G-17993)

Mid Atlantic Municipal LLC 717 394-2647
310 Richardson Dr Lancaster (17603) (G-9134)

Mid Atlantic Retractable 610 496-8062
641 Lancaster Ave # 1011 Malvern (19355) (G-10279)

Mid Atlntic Stl Fbrication LLC 717 687-0292
14 N Ronks Rd Ronks (17572) (G-16811)

Mid Mon Valley Pub 724 314-0030
996 Donner Ave Monessen (15062) (G-11300)

Mid Valley Bottling Co, Jessup Also called C S M Bottling Inc (G-8328)

Mid-Atlantic Circuit Inc 215 672-8480
1001 Pulinski Rd Ste B Warminster (18974) (G-18922)

Mid-Atlantic Events Magazine, Huntingdon Valley Also called Tri-State Events Magazine Inc (G-8044)

Mid-Atlantic Tech Publications 610 783-6100
10 Gay St Valley Forge (19481) (G-18709)

Mid-Atlntic Bldg Solutions LLC 484 532-7269
650 Sentry Pkwy Ste 1 Blue Bell (19422) (G-1848)

Mid-Life Stone Works LLC 570 928-8802
111 Kocher Rd Dushore (18614) (G-4509)

Mid-State Awning Inc 814 355-8979
113 Musser Ln Bellefonte (16823) (G-1108)

Mid-State Electric, Osceola Mills Also called Nearhoof Machine Inc (G-13056)

Middleburg Pre Cast LLC 570 837-1463
Rr 522 Box N Middleburg (17842) (G-11029)

Middleburg Yarn Processing Co 570 374-1284
909 Orange St Selinsgrove (17870) (G-17331)

Middlecreek Pallet 570 658-7667
13274 Route 235 Beaver Springs (17812) (G-1019)

Middlecreek Welding & Mfg 315 853-3936
201 Hopeland Rd Newmanstown (17073) (G-12481)

Middleport Materials Inc 570 277-0335
730 Mountain Rd Middleport (17953) (G-11046)

Middlesales Manufacturing, Orwigsburg Also called Interlock Industries Inc (G-13045)

Middleswarth and Son Inc (PA) 570 837-1431
250 Furnace Rd Middleburg (17842) (G-11030)

Middleswarth Potato Chip, Harrisburg Also called Cuthbert & Son Inc (G-7111)

Midgard Inc (PA) 215 536-3174
1255 Nursery Rd Green Lane (18054) (G-6590)

Midgard Plastics, Green Lane Also called Midgard Inc (G-6590)

Midlantic Pallet LLC 717 266-0300
35 N Marshall St York (17402) (G-20597)

Midnight Madness Distlg LLC 215 268-6071
2300 Trumbauersville Rd Trumbauersville (18970) (G-18532)

Midnight Oil Express 215 933-9690
203 N Ambler St Quakertown (18951) (G-16217)

Midvale Paper Box Company 610 649-6992
409 Richard Knl Haverford (19041) (G-7413)

Midvale Paper Box Company (HQ) 570 824-3577
19 Bailey St Plains (18705) (G-15786)

Midway Automotive & Indus Mch 570 339-2411
23 State St Mount Carmel (17851) (G-11627)

Midway Performance Warehouse, Mount Carmel Also called Midway Automotive & Indus Mch (G-11627)

Midwest Material Inds Inc (HQ) 610 882-5000
100 Brodhead Rd Ste 230 Bethlehem (18017) (G-1573)

Miesse Candies Corp 717 299-5427
118 N Water St Ste 102 Lancaster (17603) (G-9135)

Mifflin Press Inc 717 684-2253
336 Locust St Columbia (17512) (G-3443)

Mifflin Valley Inc 610 775-0505
31 S Sterley St Reading (19607) (G-16443)

Mifflin Valley Reflective AP, Reading Also called Mifflin Valley Inc (G-16443)

Mifflinburg Farmers Exchange 570 966-4030
Rr 45 Box E Mifflinburg (17844) (G-11098)

Mifflinburg Telegraph Inc 570 966-2255
358 Walnut St Mifflinburg (17844) (G-11099)

Mighty Fine Donuts, Erie Also called Mighty Fine Inc (G-5391)

Mighty Fine Inc 814 455-6408
2612 Parade St Erie (16504) (G-5391)

Migu Press Inc (PA) 215 957-9763
260 Ivyland Rd Warminster (18974) (G-18923)

Mike Barta and Sons Inc 215 757-1162
1036 Woodbourne Rd Langhorne (19047) (G-9311)

Mike Dupuy Hawk Food 570 837-1551
4552 Troxelville Rd Middleburg (17842) (G-11031)

Mike Steck 610 287-3518
868 Skippack Rd Harleysville (19438) (G-7048)

Mike Woodshop..724 272-0259
205 Hespenheide Rd Mars (16046) (G-10507)

Mikes Packing Company........................724 222-5476
1600 Weirich Ave Washington (15301) (G-19203)

Mikey Gs..717 820-4053
3 Old Route 22 Trlr 2 Jonestown (17038) (G-8450)

Mikron Valve & Mfr Inc............................814 453-2337
1282 W 12th St Erie (16501) (G-5392)

Mil-Del Corporation (PA).........................215 788-9277
1 Monroe St Bristol (19007) (G-2168)

Milan Energy LLC....................................724 933-0140
106 Isabella St Pittsburgh (15212) (G-15287)

Milan Printing..570 325-2649
1012 North St Jim Thorpe (18229) (G-8342)

Milazzo Industries Inc (PA)....................570 722-0522
1609 River Rd Pittston (18640) (G-15767)

Milco Industries Inc (PA)........................570 784-0400
550 E 5th St Bloomsburg (17815) (G-1790)

Milder Office Inc (PA).............................215 717-7027
1901 S 9th St Ste 204 Philadelphia (19148) (G-14023)

Milestone Quarry, Greenfield Township *Also called Compton Quarry* (G-6643)

Milford Enterprises Inc (PA)...................215 538-2778
450 Commerce Dr Quakertown (18951) (G-16218)

Milford Fertilizer, Leesport *Also called Growmark Fs LLC* (G-9664)

Milford Sportswear Inc...........................215 529-9316
2023 Emerson Dr Quakertown (18951) (G-16219)

Military and Coml Fas Corp (PA).............717 767-6856
11 Grumbacher Rd York (17406) (G-20598)

Mill Hall Clay Products Inc......................570 726-6752
2 Homestead Dr Mill Hall (17751) (G-11179)

Mill Professional Services.......................724 335-4625
1562 Fairmont Dr New Kensington (15068) (G-12357)

Mill Run Carriage....................................717 438-3149
355 Lyons Rd Millerstown (17062) (G-11206)

Mill Services Corp (HQ)...........................412 678-6141
12 Monongahela Ave Glassport (15045) (G-6413)

Millcraft Corporation...............................724 743-3400
95 W Beau St Ste 600 Washington (15301) (G-19204)

Millcraft Industries Inc..........................412 281-7675
222 5th Ave Pittsburgh (15222) (G-15288)

Millcraft Industries Inc (PA)..................724 229-8800
95 W Beau St Ste 600 Washington (15301) (G-19205)

Millcraft SMS Services LLC.....................724 222-5000
750 Manifold Rd Washington (15301) (G-19206)

Millcreek Metal Finishing Inc..................814 833-9045
2401 W 15th St Erie (16505) (G-5393)

Millcreek Metals Inc................................814 764-3708
58 Mcm Ln Strattanville (16258) (G-18098)

Millcreek Structures................................717 656-2797
429 Hess Rd Leola (17540) (G-9794)

Millenium Medical Educational...............215 230-1960
1980 S Easton Rd Ste 240 Doylestown (18901) (G-4316)

Millennium Circuits Limited....................717 558-5975
7703 Derry St Harrisburg (17111) (G-7178)

Millennium Machining Spc.......................570 501-2002
34 N Conahan Dr Hazleton (18201) (G-7510)

Millennium Manufacturing Inc...............215 536-3006
130d Penn Am Dr Quakertown (18951) (G-16220)

Millennium Packaging Svc Inc.................570 282-2990
100 Enterprise Carbondale (18407) (G-2683)

Miller and Roebuck Inc..........................724 398-3054
256 Virgin Run Rd Vanderbilt (15486) (G-18720)

Miller and Son Paving Inc......................215 598-7801
887 Mill Creek Rd Rushland (18956) (G-16879)

Miller Burial Vault Co.............................570 386-5479
17 Dorset Rd New Ringgold (17960) (G-12441)

Miller By Honeywell, Franklin *Also called Sperian Fall Protection Inc* (G-6163)

Miller Casket Company Inc (PA)..............570 876-3872
21 Franklin St Jermyn (18433) (G-8308)

Miller Centrifugal Casting, Mc Donald *Also called McC Holdings Company LLC* (G-10576)

Miller Centrifugal Casting Co, Mc Donald *Also called McC International Inc* (G-10577)

Miller Chemical & Fert Corp...................717 632-8921
120 Radio Rd Hanover (17331) (G-6920)

Miller Country Craft................................717 336-1318
309 Lausch Rd Denver (17517) (G-4084)

Miller Edge Inc (PA)...............................610 869-4422
300 N Jennersville Rd West Grove (19390) (G-19702)

Miller Electric Service & Sup..................814 942-9943
2701 Washington Ave Altoona (16601) (G-527)

Miller Fabrication Inc.............................717 359-4433
13130 Worleytown Rd Greencastle (17225) (G-6622)

Miller Fabrication Solutions, Brookville *Also called Miller Welding and Machine Co* (G-2265)

Miller Inds Towing Eqp Inc......................724 981-3328
2755 Kirila Blvd Hermitage (16148) (G-7591)

Miller J Walter Company Inc....................717 392-7428
411 E Chestnut St Lancaster (17602) (G-9136)

Miller Machine Shop Inc..........................814 834-2114
1030 Brusselles St Ste C Saint Marys (15857) (G-16996)

Miller Metalcraft Inc..............................717 399-8100
113 E Charlotte St Millersville (17551) (G-11212)

Miller News Stand, Philadelphia *Also called Jyoti N Stand* (G-13916)

Miller Plastic Products Inc.....................724 947-5000
24 Todd Dr Burgettstown (15021) (G-2350)

Miller Printing Inc..................................717 626-5800
336 N Reading Rd Ephrata (17522) (G-5128)

Miller Printing & Publishing....................814 425-7272
Perry Hwy Rr 19 Cochranton (16314) (G-3345)

Miller Process Coatingmiller...................724 274-5880
309 S Main St Pittsburgh (15215) (G-15289)

Miller Quarries, Rushland *Also called Miller and Son Paving Inc* (G-16879)

Miller Screen & Design Inc....................724 625-1870
449 Mars Valencia Rd Mars (16046) (G-10508)

Miller Welding and Machine Co (PA)........814 849-3061
111 2nd St Brookville (15825) (G-2265)

Miller Welding Service.............................814 238-2950
1831 W College Ave State College (16801) (G-17991)

Miller Wholesale Paper Co Div, Allentown *Also called Penn State Paper & Box Co Inc* (G-349)

Millers Fabricating..................................717 733-9311
1156 Steinmetz Rd Ephrata (17522) (G-5129)

Millers Publishing and Prtg, Cochranton *Also called Area Shopper* (G-3335)

Millers Welding & Repair..........................610 593-6112
54 Christiana Pike Christiana (17509) (G-3142)

Millersville University PA........................717 871-4636
Student Memrl Ctr Mu 18 Millersville (17551) (G-11213)

Millet Plastics Inc..................................717 277-7404
21 Lebanon Valley Pkwy Lebanon (17042) (G-9611)

Millheim Small Engine Inc......................814 349-5007
4857 Penns Valley Rd Spring Mills (16875) (G-17889)

Milli-Switch Manufacturing Co.................610 270-9222
61 E 4th St Ste 2 Bridgeport (19405) (G-2040)

Milliken Nonwovens LLC (HQ).................610 544-7117
370 Reed Rd Ste 200 Broomall (19008) (G-2298)

Million Dollar Machining Inc....................814 834-9224
930 S Saint Marys St Saint Marys (15857) (G-16997)

Millstat LLC..610 783-0181
26 Ridge Rd Phoenixville (19460) (G-14561)

Millvale Vault Co, Glenshaw *Also called Kemosabe Inc* (G-6494)

Millwood Inc...610 421-6230
8018 Quarry Rd Alburtis (18011) (G-57)

Millwood Inc...724 266-7030
200 Leetsdale Indus Blvd Leetsdale (15056) (G-9699)

Millwood Inc...717 790-9118
435 Independence Ave Mechanicsburg (17055) (G-10869)

Millwood Inc...570 836-9280
5530 Sr 6 Tunkhannock (18657) (G-18543)

Millwood Wood Working, Gap *Also called Lapp John* (G-6252)

Millwork For Less, Hummelstown *Also called M4I Inc* (G-7916)

Millwork Solutions Inc.............................814 446-4009
450 Route 711 Hwy Seward (15954) (G-17382)

Millwork Specialties................................610 261-2878
159 W Laubach Ave Northampton (18067) (G-12855)

Milner Enterprises Inc.............................610 252-0700
115 Kuebler Rd Easton (18040) (G-4722)

Milnor Auto Parts, Philadelphia *Also called Dock Tool & Machine Inc* (G-13638)

Milroy Enterprises Inc.............................610 678-4537
100 Park Ave Reading (19608) (G-16444)

Milton Daily Standard..............................570 742-9077
21 Arch St Montgomery (17752) (G-11376)

Milton Home Systems Inc........................800 533-4402
55 Patton Dr Milton (17847) (G-11249)

Milton Roy LLC (HQ)................................215 441-0800
201 Ivyland Rd Ivyland (18974) (G-8218)

Milton Roy LLC..215 293-0401
201 Ivyland Rd Ivyland (18974) (G-8219)

Milton Roy Americas, Ivyland *Also called Milton Roy LLC* (G-8218)

Mimco Equipment Inc..............................610 494-7400
1509 Chichester Ave Linwood (19061) (G-9990)

Mimco Products LLC (PA).......................724 258-8208
731 E Main St Monongahela (15063) (G-11311)

Minahan Corporation...............................814 288-1561
636 Tire Hill Rd Johnstown (15905) (G-8409)

Minahan Sign, Johnstown *Also called Crichton Diversfd Ventures LLC* (G-8367)

Minahan Signs, Johnstown *Also called Minahan Corporation* (G-8409)

Minard Run Oil Company (PA)..................814 362-3531
609 South Ave Bradford (16701) (G-1982)

Minard Run Oil Company..........................814 368-4931
Music Mtn Bradford (16701) (G-1983)

Minco Tool & Mold Inc.............................814 724-1376
370 Linden St Meadville (16335) (G-10764)

Mincorp Inc (HQ)....................................814 443-4668
Rr 281 Friedens (15541) (G-6222)

Mind Matrix, Pittsburgh *Also called Mindmatrix Inc* (G-15291)

Mindful Brewing Company LLC...............412 965-8428
3759 Library Rd Pittsburgh (15234) (G-15290)

Mindmatrix Inc...412 381-0230
2403 Sidney St Ste 150 Pittsburgh (15203) (G-15291)

Mindy Inc 215 739-0432
2552 N 3rd St Philadelphia (19133) *(G-14024)*

Mine Drilling Services LL 814 765-1075
615 Tipple Ln Clearfield (16830) *(G-3225)*

Mine Safety Appliance Company, Murrysville *Also called MSA Safety Incorporated* *(G-11859)*

Mine Safety Appliances Co LLC (HQ) 724 776-8600
1000 Cranberry Woods Dr Cranberry Township (16066) *(G-3836)*

Mine Vision Systems Inc 412 626-7461
5877 Commerce St Ste 118 Pittsburgh (15206) *(G-15292)*

Mineral Manufacturing Corp 814 643-0410
10627 Hartslog Valley Rd Huntingdon (16652) *(G-7951)*

Mineral Processing Spc Inc 724 339-8630
1 Industrial Park Blvd New Kensington (15068) *(G-12358)*

Minerals Technologies, Easton *Also called Specialty Minerals Inc* *(G-4755)*

Minerals Technologies, Bethlehem *Also called Specialty Minerals Inc* *(G-1626)*

Mines and Meadows LLC 724 535-6026
1307 Old Route 18 Wampum (16157) *(G-18802)*

Mingo Creek Craft Distillers 724 503-4014
68 W Maiden St Washington (15301) *(G-19207)*

Mini-Golf Inc 570 489-8623
202 Bridge St Jessup (18434) *(G-8333)*

Minichi Inc 570 654-8332
453 Ziegler St Dupont (18641) *(G-4491)*

Minichi Energy, Dupont *Also called Minichi Inc* *(G-4491)*

Minichi Energy LLC 570 654-8332
453 Ziegler St Dupont (18641) *(G-4492)*

Mining, Erie *Also called Fiesler Sand & Gravel LLC* *(G-5289)*

Mining Clamps Fasteners & More 724 324-2430
117 Little Shannon Run Rd Mount Morris (15349) *(G-11681)*

Mining Joy Machinery, Warrendale *Also called Joy Global Underground Min LLC* *(G-19083)*

Minit Rubber Stamps 610 352-8600
6425 Market St Upper Darby (19082) *(G-18690)*

Minitab LLC (PA) 814 238-3280
1829 Pine Hall Rd State College (16801) *(G-17992)*

Minleon Intl USA Ltd LLC 717 991-1432
4902 Carlisle Pike Mechanicsburg (17050) *(G-10870)*

Minnich Limited 717 697-2204
4 W Allen St Mechanicsburg (17055) *(G-10871)*

Minnotte Manufacturing Corp 412 373-5270
1000 Commerce Cir Trafford (15085) *(G-18459)*

Minteq International Inc 610 250-3000
640 N 13th St Easton (18042) *(G-4723)*

Minteq International Inc 724 794-3000
395 Grove City Rd Slippery Rock (16057) *(G-17622)*

Minteq International Inc (HQ) 724 794-3000
35 Highland Ave Bethlehem (18017) *(G-1574)*

Minton Holdings LLC 412 787-5912
1525 Park Manor Blvd Pittsburgh (15205) *(G-15293)*

Minusnine Technologies, Birdsboro *Also called ICP Industries LLC* *(G-1700)*

Minusnine Technologies Inc 215 704-9396
2211 Christian St Philadelphia (19146) *(G-14025)*

Minuteman Press, Philadelphia *Also called Virgo Investment LLC* *(G-14449)*

Minuteman Press, Allentown *Also called Imaging Fx Inc* *(G-252)*

Minuteman Press, Stroudsburg *Also called Executive Print Solutions LLC* *(G-18117)*

Minuteman Press, Ambler *Also called Jaak Holdings LLC* *(G-582)*

Minuteman Press, Doylestown *Also called Vocam Corp* *(G-4344)*

Minuteman Press, Allison Park *Also called Jma Group* *(G-454)*

Minuteman Press, Smithton *Also called Bodrie Inc* *(G-17658)*

Minuteman Press, Butler *Also called Vernon Printing Inc* *(G-2447)*

Minuteman Press, North Versailles *Also called Rancatore & Lavender Inc* *(G-12782)*

Minuteman Press, Bethlehem *Also called Pikewood Inc* *(G-1597)*

Minuteman Press, Bala Cynwyd *Also called Jack Pressman* *(G-882)*

Minuteman Press, Cranberry Township *Also called Boltz Printing Company LLC* *(G-3809)*

Minuteman Press, Lansdale *Also called J D Enterprise-Mp LLC* *(G-9377)*

Minuteman Press, Morrisville *Also called Kistler & Dinapoli Inc* *(G-11567)*

Minuteman Press, Lancaster *Also called Carol Fanelli* *(G-8971)*

Minuteman Press 412 621-7456
1963 Wharton Sq Pittsburgh (15203) *(G-15294)*

Minuteman Press 724 346-1105
3170 E State St Hermitage (16148) *(G-7592)*

Minuteman Press 610 272-6220
545 Swede St Ste 102 Norristown (19401) *(G-12685)*

Minuteman Press 724 236-0261
541 Hyde Park Rd Leechburg (15656) *(G-9649)*

Minuteman Press 724 846-9740
920 7th Ave Beaver Falls (15010) *(G-1005)*

Minuteman Press 215 538-2200
39 Trumbauersville Rd Quakertown (18951) *(G-16221)*

Minuteman Press Inc 610 923-9266
2473 Hay St Easton (18042) *(G-4724)*

Minuteman Press International 610 539-6707
2938 W Main St Ste 100 Norristown (19403) *(G-12686)*

Minuteman Press Intl Inc 610 902-0203
489 Devon Park Dr Ste 307 Wayne (19087) *(G-19357)*

Minuteman Press of Glenside 267 626-2706
359 N Easton Rd Glenside (19038) *(G-6528)*

Minuteman Press of Hanover 717 632-5400
955 Carlisle St Ofc Ofc Hanover (17331) *(G-6921)*

Minuteman Press South Hills 412 531-0809
74 Markham Dr Pittsburgh (15228) *(G-15295)*

Mio Mechanical Corporation 215 613-8189
2020 Bennett Rd Philadelphia (19116) *(G-14026)*

Mipc LLC 610 364-8660
4101 Post Rd Marcus Hook (19061) *(G-10449)*

Mirada Energy Inc 717 730-9412
3920 Market St Camp Hill (17011) *(G-2505)*

Mirador Global LP 302 983-3430
148 W State St Ste 303 Kennett Square (19348) *(G-8529)*

Mirage Advertising Inc 412 372-4181
206 Monroe St Monroeville (15146) *(G-11345)*

Mirage Marcom, Monroeville *Also called Mirage Advertising Inc* *(G-11345)*

Miroglyphics 215 224-2486
5615 N Fairhill St Philadelphia (19120) *(G-14027)*

Misco Products Corporation 610 926-4106
1048 Stinson Dr Reading (19605) *(G-16445)*

Miscreation Brewing 717 698-3666
6 Center Sq Hanover (17331) *(G-6922)*

Misko Inc 610 524-1881
171 Philips Rd Exton (19341) *(G-5712)*

Missiles and Fire Control, Chambersburg *Also called Lockheed Martin Corporation* *(G-2954)*

Missing Piece 610 759-4033
462 Bushkill Center Rd Nazareth (18064) *(G-11982)*

Mission Critical Solutions LLC 814 839-2078
271 Industrial Ln Alum Bank (15521) *(G-562)*

Mission Foods, Mountain Top *Also called Gruma Corporation* *(G-11763)*

Mister Bobbin Embroidery Inc 717 838-5841
1525 N State Route 934 Annville (17003) *(G-654)*

Misterplexi 724 759-7500
10475 Perry Hwy Ste 105g Wexford (15090) *(G-19812)*

Mistras Group Inc 610 497-0400
5 Nealy Blvd Trainer (19061) *(G-18463)*

Mitchco Inc 717 843-3345
15 E Philadelphia St York (17401) *(G-20599)*

Mitchel Loading Crew 570 837-5907
45 Black Bear Dr Middleburg (17842) *(G-11032)*

Mitchell & Westerman, Cabot *Also called Frank Ferris Industries Inc* *(G-2457)*

Mitchell Apx Machine Shop Inc 717 597-2157
11550 Molly Pitcher Hwy Greencastle (17225) *(G-6623)*

Mitchell Aviation Ltd 717 232-7575
1310 Crooked Hill Rd # 100 Harrisburg (17110) *(G-7179)*

Mitchell Hardwood 814 796-4925
13926 Flatts Rd Waterford (16441) *(G-19266)*

Mitchell Machine Shop, Greencastle *Also called Mitchell Apx Machine Shop Inc* *(G-6623)*

Mitcheltree Bros 814 665-4019
18700 Conelway Rd Corry (16407) *(G-3768)*

Mitcheltree Bros Logging & Lbr 724 598-7885
8485 Mercer St Pulaski (16143) *(G-16125)*

Miti, Hatfield *Also called Magnetizer Industrial Tech* *(G-7367)*

Mitigation Technologies, Chambersburg *Also called Mititech LLC* *(G-2960)*

Mitigator Inc 717 576-9589
198 Rose Hill Dr New Cumberland (17070) *(G-12189)*

Mititech LLC 410 309-9447
40 N 2nd St Chambersburg (17201) *(G-2960)*

Mito Biopharm 215 767-9700
170 N Radnor Chester Rd # 350 Radnor (19087) *(G-16296)*

Mito Industries, New Kensington *Also called Mito Insulation Company* *(G-12359)*

Mito Insulation Company 724 335-8551
1290 3rd Ave New Kensington (15068) *(G-12359)*

Mitre Wright Inc 717 812-1000
160 E 9th Ave York (17404) *(G-20600)*

Mitsubishi Chemical Advncd Mtr (HQ) 610 320-6600
2120 Fairmont Ave Reading (19605) *(G-16446)*

Mitsubishi Elc Pwr Pdts Inc 724 772-2555
110 Commerce Dr Freedom (15042) *(G-6191)*

Mitsubishi Elc Pwr Pdts Inc (HQ) 724 772-2555
530 Keystone Dr Warrendale (15086) *(G-19088)*

Mitsubishi Elc Pwr Pdts Inc 724 778-5112
520 Keystone Dr Warrendale (15086) *(G-19089)*

Mittal Steel USA Steelton, Steelton *Also called Arcelormittal USA LLC* *(G-18045)*

Mivatek Global LLC 610 358-5120
6 Dickinson Dr Ste 215 Chadds Ford (19317) *(G-2856)*

Mix Earl 610 444-3245
131 Knoxlyn Farm Dr Kennett Square (19348) *(G-8530)*

Mjjm Enterprises Inc 717 392-1711
19 Prestige Ln Lancaster (17603) *(G-9137)*

MJM Ices LLC 412 401-4610
10101 Edgewood Ct North Huntingdon (15642) *(G-12770)*

Mjs LLC 215 732-3501
124 S 13th St Philadelphia (19107) *(G-14028)*

Mk Precision 215 675-4590
1621 Mearns Rd Ste 206 Warminster (18974) *(G-18924)*

Mk Solutions Inc 860 760-0438
75 Acco Dr Ste A-3 York (17402) *(G-20601)*

Mkj Creative, Chalfont *Also called Me Ken + Jen Crative Svcs LLC* *(G-2883)*

Mkt Metal Manufacturing 717 764-9090
460 Grim Ln Ste 2 York (17406) *(G-20602)*

Mlp Steel LLC 724 887-7720
800 Brown St Everson (15631) *(G-5580)*

Mlp Steel LLC (PA) 724 887-8100
18 Mount Pleasant Rd Scottdale (15683) *(G-17195)*

Mlr Holdings LLC 215 567-3200
1845 Walnut St Ste 900 Philadelphia (19103) *(G-14029)*

Mlre LLC 724 514-1800
1500 Corporate Dr Ste 400 Canonsburg (15317) *(G-2604)*

Mm USA Holdings LLC (PA) 267 685-2300
780 Township Line Rd Yardley (19067) *(G-20326)*

Mmi, Burgettstown *Also called Multifab & Machine Inc (G-2351)*

MMS Education, Newtown *Also called Media Management Services Inc (G-12521)*

MMS Technologies LLC 814 238-2323
2597 Clyde Ave Ste 2 State College (16801) *(G-17993)*

Mmscc-2 LLC 610 266-8990
515 Hamilton St Ste 200 Allentown (18101) *(G-317)*

Mmscc2, Allentown *Also called Mmscc-2 LLC (G-317)*

Mnw, Mount Pocono *Also called Monadnock Non-Wovens LLC (G-11735)*

Moa Instrumentation Inc (PA) 609 352-9329
1606 Manning Blvd Ste 1 Levittown (19057) *(G-9849)*

Moai Technologies Inc (PA) 412 454-5550
100 1st Ave Ste 1101 Pittsburgh (15222) *(G-15296)*

Moberg Research Inc 215 283-0860
224 S Maple Way Ambler (19002) *(G-591)*

Mobile Concepts By Scotty Inc 724 542-7640
480 Bessemer Rd Mount Pleasant (15666) *(G-11706)*

Mobile Medical Innovations 724 646-2200
700 Coolspring Church Rd Mercer (16137) *(G-10969)*

Mobile Mini, Philadelphia *Also called Evergreen Tank Solutions Inc (G-13684)*

Mobile Mini Inc 484 540-9072
1960 Weaversville Rd Allentown (18109) *(G-318)*

Mobile Mini Inc 412 220-4477
981 Steen Rd Bridgeville (15017) *(G-2079)*

Mobile Mini Inc 484 540-9073
10 Industrial Hwy Bldg E Essington (19029) *(G-5544)*

Mobile Outfitters LLC (PA) 215 325-0747
3901b Main St Ste 106 Philadelphia (19127) *(G-14030)*

Mobile Technology Graphics LLC 610 838-8075
3984 Lower Saucon Rd Hellertown (18055) *(G-7559)*

Mobile Video Corporation 215 863-1072
501 Abbott Dr Ste 4 Broomall (19008) *(G-2299)*

Mobile Video Devices Inc 610 921-5720
156 Madison Ave Reading (19605) *(G-16447)*

Mobile Wash Power Wash Inc 814 327-3820
124 Finland Rd Bedford (15522) *(G-1065)*

Mobile Welding & Boiler Repair 610 253-9688
500 Industrial Dr Easton (18042) *(G-4725)*

Mobilia Fruit Farm Inc 814 725-4077
12073 E Main Rd North East (16428) *(G-12752)*

Mobility and Access Inc 724 695-1590
1003 International Dr Oakdale (15071) *(G-12907)*

Mobinol Fuel Company 484 432-9007
119 Hunt Club Dr Collegeville (19426) *(G-3382)*

Mobius Acquisition LLC (HQ) 412 281-7000
1000 Mcknight Park Dr Pittsburgh (15237) *(G-15297)*

Modern Blending Tech Inc 267 580-1000
2061 Hartel Ave Levittown (19057) *(G-9850)*

Modern Cabinet and Cnstr Co 814 942-1000
110 Frankstown Rd Altoona (16602) *(G-528)*

Modern Industries Inc 814 885-8514
129 Green Rd Kersey (15846) *(G-8564)*

Modern Industries Inc (PA) 814 455-8061
613 W 11th St Erie (16501) *(G-5394)*

Modern Industries Inc 814 724-6242
16285 Conneaut Lake Rd # 99 Meadville (16335) *(G-10765)*

Modern Manufacturing Co, Glenside *Also called Moore Push Pin Company (G-6531)*

Modern Manufacturing Co Inc 215 659-4820
680 Davisville Rd Willow Grove (19090) *(G-20128)*

Modern Mushroom Farms Inc 610 268-3535
1330 Newark Rd Toughkenamon (19374) *(G-18420)*

Modern Plastics Corp (PA) 570 822-1124
152 Horton St Wilkes Barre (18702) *(G-19944)*

Modern Precast Concrete Inc 484 548-6200
3900 Glover Rd Easton (18040) *(G-4726)*

Modern Reproductions Inc 412 488-7700
127 Mckean St Pittsburgh (15219) *(G-15298)*

Modern Specialties Inc 814 643-0410
10627 Hartslog Valley Rd Huntingdon (16652) *(G-7952)*

Moderne Glass Company Inc (PA) 724 857-5700
1000 Industrial Blvd Aliquippa (15001) *(G-86)*

Modevity LLC 610 251-0700
20 Valley Stream Pkwy # 265 Malvern (19355) *(G-10280)*

Modular International Inc 412 734-9000
3941 California Ave Pittsburgh (15212) *(G-15299)*

Modzori LLC 215 833-3618
157 Justice Dr Newtown (18940) *(G-12522)*

Moen Incorporated 570 345-8021
12 Roberts Rd Pine Grove (17963) *(G-14600)*

Moglabs Usa LLC 814 251-4363
419 14th St Huntingdon (16652) *(G-7953)*

Mognet Industries LLC 814 418-0864
265 Wess Rd Mineral Point (15942) *(G-11252)*

Mohawk Flush Doors (HQ) 570 473-3557
980 Point Township Dr Northumberland (17857) *(G-12872)*

Mohawk Inc 717 243-9231
400 Creek Rd Carlisle (17013) *(G-2726)*

Mohawk Industries Inc 215 977-2871
2300 Chestnut St Philadelphia (19103) *(G-14031)*

Mohn's Lumber Mill, Waynesboro *Also called Richard K Mohn (G-19423)*

Mohney Fabricating & Mfg LLC 724 349-6136
320 Chestnut Ridge Rd Penn Run (15765) *(G-13229)*

Moishe's Addison Bakery, Philadelphia *Also called Addison Baking Company (G-13344)*

Mol Communications & Elec 570 383-3658
821 Enterprise St Dickson City (18519) *(G-4122)*

Mold 911 LLC 267 312-1432
635 Wyndrise Dr Blue Bell (19422) *(G-1849)*

Mold-Base Industries Inc 717 564-7960
7501 Derry St Harrisburg (17111) *(G-7180)*

Moldamatic LLC 215 785-2356
3911 Nebraska Ave Levittown (19056) *(G-9851)*

Moldcraft Co 610 399-1404
503 School House Rd Kennett Square (19348) *(G-8531)*

Molded Acstcal Pdts Easton Inc 610 250-6738
500 Industrial Dr Easton (18042) *(G-4727)*

Molded Fiber Glass Companies 814 438-3841
55 4th Ave Union City (16438) *(G-18610)*

Molded Fiber Glass Companies 814 683-4500
6175 Us Highway 6 Linesville (16424) *(G-9984)*

Molded Products Division, Shrewsbury *Also called Te Connectivity Corporation (G-17588)*

Moldex Tool & Design Corp 814 337-3190
823 Bessemer St Meadville (16335) *(G-10766)*

Molecular Devices LLC 610 873-5610
402 Boot Rd Downingtown (19335) *(G-4242)*

Molecular Finishing Systems 724 695-0554
1270 Mccaslin Rd Imperial (15126) *(G-8073)*

Molek Brothers 717 248-8032
250 High Dump Rd Yeagertown (17099) *(G-20357)*

Molinaro Tool & Die Inc 724 654-5141
Shenango Commrce Prk Comr New Castle (16101) *(G-12121)*

Molloy Associates Inc 610 293-1300
919 Conestoga Rd 3-213 Bryn Mawr (19010) *(G-2330)*

Molly Pitcher Brewing Company 717 609-0969
10 E South St Carlisle (17013) *(G-2727)*

Moltec Heating and AC (PA) 215 755-2169
120 Wharton St Ste 124 Philadelphia (19147) *(G-14032)*

Molyneux Industries Inc 724 695-3406
621 Cliff Mine Rd Coraopolis (15108) *(G-3705)*

Mom's Bake At Home Pizza, Newtown *Also called Rockfish Venture LLP (G-12545)*

Moms Wholesale Foods Inc (PA) 724 856-3049
930 Cass St Ste 3 New Castle (16101) *(G-12122)*

Mon River Supply LLC 412 382-7178
120 First St West Elizabeth (15088) *(G-19695)*

Mon Valley Independent 724 314-0030
111 Fallowfield Ave Charleroi (15022) *(G-3016)*

Mon Valley Signs, Charleroi *Also called DS Services Group Corp (G-3010)*

Mona Lisa Fashions 610 770-0806
650 E Green St Allentown (18109) *(G-319)*

Monach Associates Inc (PA) 888 849-0149
2210 E Farragut Ave Bristol (19007) *(G-2169)*

Monadnock Non-Wovens LLC 570 839-9210
5110 Park Ct Mount Pocono (18344) *(G-11735)*

Monalisa Fashions, Allentown *Also called Mona Lisa Fashions (G-319)*

Monarch Brands, Philadelphia *Also called Monarch Global Brands Inc (G-14033)*

Monarch Global Brands Inc (PA) 215 482-6100
11350 Norcom Rd Philadelphia (19154) *(G-14033)*

Monarch Precast Concrete Corp 610 435-6746
425 N Dauphin St Allentown (18109) *(G-320)*

Mondelez Global LLC 215 673-4800
12000 Roosevelt Blvd Philadelphia (19116) *(G-14034)*

Mondelez Global LLC 570 820-1200
50 New Commerce Blvd Wilkes Barre (18762) *(G-19945)*

Mondlak Printery 570 654-9871
5 Ambrose St Pittston (18640) *(G-15768)*

Mondo Usa Inc (HQ) 610 834-3835
1100 E Hector St Ste 160 Conshohocken (19428) *(G-3576)*

Mong Fabrication & Machine 724 745-8370
112 Acme Rd Canonsburg (15317) *(G-2605)*

Mongoose Products Inc 215 887-6600
115 Lismore Ave Glenside (19038) *(G-6529)*

Monitor Data Corp 215 887-8343
3 Limekiln Pike Ste 3g Glenside (19038) *(G-6530)*

Monocacy Fabs Inc (PA) 610 866-7311
1122 Browntown Rd Pen Argyl (18072) *(G-13214)*

Monoflex, Bechtelsville *Also called Campbell Manufacturing Inc (G-1030)*

Monomer-Polymer and Dajac Labs 215 364-1155
340 Mathers Rd Ambler (19002) *(G-592)*

Monroe Energy LLC (HQ)..610 364-8000
   4101 Post Rd Trainer (19061) *(G-18464)*

Monroe Press Inc..215 778-7868
   4668 Canton St Philadelphia (19127) *(G-14035)*

Monroe Scale Company Inc.......................................412 793-8134
   424 Regency Dr Pittsburgh (15239) *(G-15300)*

Monroeville Ink Refills Inc..412 374-1700
   2671 Monroeville Blvd Monroeville (15146) *(G-11346)*

Montauk Energy Holdings LLC..................................412 747-8700
   680 Andersen Dr·Ste 100 Pittsburgh (15220) *(G-15301)*

Montbrite, Conshohocken *Also called Montgomery Chemicals LLC (G-3577)*

Montco Advertising Spc Inc.......................................610 270-9800
   9 S Forrest Ave Unit B Norristown (19403) *(G-12687)*

Montco Enterprises Ltd..610 948-5316
   500 S Main St Spring City (19475) *(G-17863)*

Montco Industries..610 233-1081
   100 Ross Rd Ste 203 King of Prussia (19406) *(G-8652)*

Montco Manufacturing Co Inc...................................215 822-1291
   1610 Bethlehem Pike Hatfield (19440) *(G-7370)*

Montco Packaging Co Inc...610 935-9545
   400 Taylor St Phoenixville (19460) *(G-14562)*

Montco Scientific Inc..215 699-8057
   565 W 3rd St Lansdale (19446) *(G-9389)*

Montdale Farm Dairy..570 254-6511
   453 Montdale Rd Scott Township (18447) *(G-17186)*

Monterey Mushrooms Inc...610 929-1961
   1108 Beaumont Ave Temple (19560) *(G-18333)*

Monterey Shop, Bird In Hand *Also called Stoltzfus Ephram (G-1682)*

Montgmrys Atomtn Parts Sls Svc...............................724 368-3001
   100 Fisher Rd Portersville (16051) *(G-15933)*

Montgomery Block Works Inc....................................724 735-2931
   4275 William Flynn Hwy Harrisville (16038) *(G-7253)*

Montgomery Chemicals LLC (PA)...............................610 567-0877
   901 Conshohocken Rd Conshohocken (19428) *(G-3577)*

Montgomery Cnty Womans Newsppr, Telford *Also called Gary Edward Soden (G-18291)*

Montgomery County Record, Levittown *Also called Calkins Media Incorporated (G-9822)*

Montgomery Laboratories Inc.....................................570 752-7712
   355 Bowers Rd Berwick (18603) *(G-1335)*

Montgomery Products Ltd..610 933-2500
   30 S 2nd Ave Phoenixville (19460) *(G-14563)*

Montgomery Signs Inc...610 834-5400
   539 Ford St Ste C Conshohocken (19428) *(G-3578)*

Montgomery Truss & Panel Inc (PA)...........................724 458-7500
   803 W Main St Grove City (16127) *(G-6798)*

Monticello Granite Ltd...215 677-1000
   101 Cherry Tree Blvd Collegeville (19426) *(G-3383)*

Montour Creek Mining Co...717 582-7526
   2302 Shermans Valley Rd Elliottsburg (17024) *(G-4921)*

Montrose Machine Works Inc (PA)..............................570 278-7655
   Rr 29 Box S Montrose (18801) *(G-11471)*

Monument Sign Mfg LLC..570 366-9505
   804 N Warren St Orwigsburg (17961) *(G-13050)*

Monumental Express..570 501-1009
   764 Alter St Hazleton (18201) *(G-7511)*

Monumental Touch..484 226-7277
   4557 Lehigh Dr Walnutport (18088) *(G-18792)*

Moody Corporation..724 453-9470
   1688 Route 288 Zelienople (16063) *(G-20811)*

Moog Components Group, Springfield *Also called Moog Inc (G-17919)*

Moog Inc...610 328-4000
   750 W Sproul Rd Springfield (19064) *(G-17919)*

Moon Dancer Vineyards & Winery..............................717 252-9463
   1282 Klines Run Rd Wrightsville (17368) *(G-20242)*

Moon Shine Camo, Mount Pleasant Mills *Also called Shine Moon L P (G-11732)*

Moon Township Office, Coraopolis *Also called Eaton Corporation (G-3685)*

Moonlight Graphics Studio...570 322-6570
   2310 Lycoming Creek Rd Williamsport (17701) *(G-20042)*

Moonshine Mine Distillery Inc....................................814 749-3038
   2046 Cardiff Rd Nanty Glo (15943) *(G-11906)*

Moore & Morford Inc (PA)..724 834-1100
   1030 Broad St Greensburg (15601) *(G-6689)*

Moore Bends, Philadelphia *Also called C F Moores Co Inc (G-13490)*

Moore Business Forms, Johnstown *Also called R R Donnelley & Sons Company (G-8428)*

Moore Design Inc...215 627-3379
   54 N 2nd St Philadelphia (19106) *(G-14036)*

Moore Document Solutions, Lewisburg *Also called R R Donnelley & Sons Company (G-9918)*

Moore Performance Pwr Pdts LLC..............................610 507-2344
   1199 Ashbourne Dr Reading (19605) *(G-16448)*

Moore Push Pin Company..215 233-5700
   1300 E Mermaid Ln Glenside (19038) *(G-6531)*

Moore Wallace North America, Breinigsville *Also called R R Donnelley & Sons Company (G-2025)*

Moore Welding..814 328-2399
   1790 Sugar Hill Rd Brockway (15824) *(G-2228)*

Mooretown Sawmill & Supply, Sweet Valley *Also called Brian O Keffe (G-18187)*

Moorhouse Stair...610 367-9275
   2009 Weisstown Rd Bechtelsville (19505) *(G-1033)*

Mopac, Souderton *Also called Jbs Souderton Inc (G-17744)*

MOr Saw Service Center Inc.......................................215 333-0441
   7353 State Rd Philadelphia (19136) *(G-14037)*

Morabito Baking Co Inc (PA).....................................610 275-5419
   757 Kohn St Norristown (19401) *(G-12688)*

Morabito Baking Company, Norristown *Also called Morabito Baking Co Inc (G-12688)*

Morantz Inc...215 969-0266
   9984 Gantry Rd Philadelphia (19115) *(G-14038)*

Morco, Cochranton *Also called Coinco Inc (G-3337)*

Morco, Cochranton *Also called Coinco Inc (G-3338)*

Morehouse Instrument Company.................................717 843-0081
   1742 6th Ave York (17403) *(G-20603)*

Moreno Welding Service...717 646-0000
   320 Maple Ave Hanover (17331) *(G-6923)*

Morey General Contracting..570 759-2021
   20 Maplewood Rd Berwick (18603) *(G-1336)*

Morgan Advanced Ceramics Inc.................................724 537-7791
   580 Monastery Dr Latrobe (15650) *(G-9505)*

Morgan Advanced Ceramics Inc.................................610 366-7100
   7331 William Ave Allentown (18106) *(G-321)*

Morgan Advanced Mtls Tech Inc.................................814 274-6132
   1118 E 2nd St Coudersport (16915) *(G-3785)*

Morgan Advanced Mtls Tech Inc.................................570 421-9921
   100 Mill Creek Rd East Stroudsburg (18301) *(G-4623)*

Morgan Advanced Mtls Tech Inc (HQ)..........................814 781-1573
   441 Hall Ave Saint Marys (15857) *(G-16998)*

Morgan AM&t, Coudersport *Also called Morgan Advanced Mtls Tech Inc (G-3785)*

Morgan AM&t, Saint Marys *Also called Morgan Advanced Mtls Tech Inc (G-16998)*

Morgan Brothers Company...724 843-7485
   1401 10th Ave Beaver Falls (15010) *(G-1006)*

Morgan Printing Company..215 784-0966
   2365 Wyandotte Rd Willow Grove (19090) *(G-20129)*

Morgan Signs Inc (PA)..814 238-5051
   403 S Allen St Ste 200 State College (16801) *(G-17994)*

Morgan Technical Ceramics, Hanover Township *Also called Certech Inc (G-6985)*

Morgan Truck Body LLC..717 733-8644
   485 Wenger Dr Ephrata (17522) *(G-5130)*

Morgantown Eye Care Center.....................................610 286-0206
   105 Moreview Blvd Morgantown (19543) *(G-11528)*

Morgantown Technical Services..................................724 324-5433
   303 Meadow Ridge Rd Mount Morris (15349) *(G-11682)*

Morgardshammar Inc..724 778-5400
   600 Cranberry Woods Dr # 200 Cranberry Township (16066) *(G-3837)*

Moritz Aerospace Inc..215 249-1300
   123 N Main St Ste 257-258 Dublin (18917) *(G-4436)*

Moritz Embroidery Works Inc.....................................570 839-9600
   405 Industrial Park Dr Mount Pocono (18344) *(G-11736)*

Moritz Machine & Repairs LLC..................................717 677-6838
   211 E York St Biglerville (17307) *(G-1667)*

Morlatton Post Card Club...717 263-1638
   806 Stanley Ave Chambersburg (17201) *(G-2961)*

Morlin Inc..814 454-5559
   2044 W 20th St Erie (16502) *(G-5395)*

Morning Call LLC (HQ)..610 820-6500
   101 N 6th St Allentown (18101) *(G-322)*

Morning Call LLC..610 379-3200
   179 Interchange Rd Lehighton (18235) *(G-9720)*

Morning Call Inc..610 861-3600
   515 Main St Unit 1 Bethlehem (18018) *(G-1575)*

Morning Times, Sayre *Also called Sample News Group LLC (G-17122)*

Morningstar Corporation (PA).....................................267 685-0500
   8 Pheasant Run Newtown (18940) *(G-12523)*

Morningstar Credit Ratings LLC..................................800 299-1665
   220 Gibraltar Rd Ste 300 Horsham (19044) *(G-7833)*

Morocco Welding LLC...814 444-9353
   133 Morocco St Somerset (15501) *(G-17697)*

Morris Coupling Company (PA)...................................814 459-1741
   2240 W 15th St Erie (16505) *(G-5396)*

Morris Millwork LLC...215 667-1889
   241 W Wyoming Ave Philadelphia (19140) *(G-14039)*

Morris Millwork LLC...215 736-0708
   82 Sutphin Pnes Yardley (19067) *(G-20327)*

Morris Print Management...610 408-8922
   632 Contention Ln Berwyn (19312) *(G-1369)*

Morris Printing Company..412 881-8626
   5220 Elmwood Dr Pittsburgh (15227) *(G-15302)*

Morris Twnship Spervisors Barn..................................724 627-3096
   1317 Browns Creek Rd Sycamore (15364) *(G-18201)*

Morrison Consulting Inc...717 268-8201
   190 Canal Road Ext York (17406) *(G-20604)*

Morrisons Cove Herald Inc...814 793-2144
   113 N Market St Martinsburg (16662) *(G-10527)*

Morrow Bros Countertop LP.......................................724 327-8980
   104 Technology Ln Export (15632) *(G-5619)*

Morrow Brother's Countertops, Export *Also called Morrow Bros Countertop LP (G-5619)*

Morton Buildings Inc...717 624-8000
   3370 York Rd Gettysburg (17325) *(G-6308)*

Morton Buildings Inc...814 364-9500
   2789 Earlystown Rd Centre Hall (16828) *(G-2843)*

Morton Buildings Inc 724 542-7930
615 Valley Ln Mount Pleasant (15666) *(G-11707)*

Morton International LLC (HQ) 989 636-1000
400 Arcola Rd Collegeville (19426) *(G-3384)*

Morton Salt Inc 215 428-2012
12 Roebling Rd Fairless Hills (19030) *(G-5789)*

Morton Tool Company 717 824-1723
87 Fieldcrest Ln Ephrata (17522) *(G-5131)*

Mosaic Engineering Inc 406 544-7902
210 W Hamilton Ave # 290 State College (16801) *(G-17995)*

Mosaic Entertainment House 215 353-1729
700 W Tabor Rd Ste 1 Philadelphia (19120) *(G-14040)*

Moscow Villager, The, Honesdale *Also called Carbondale News (G-7706)*

Mosebach Manufacturing Company 412 220-0200
1417 Mclaughlin Run Rd # 2 Pittsburgh (15241) *(G-15303)*

Moshes Foods LLC 215 291-8333
301 W Hunting Park Ave Philadelphia (19140) *(G-14041)*

Moss Machine & Design LLC 570 724-9119
1121 Route 362 Wellsboro (16901) *(G-19470)*

Mosse Blocks Inc 717 624-2597
140 Enterprise Dr Ste C New Oxford (17350) *(G-12416)*

Mostollers Mfg & Distrg 814 445-7281
1207 Stoystown Rd Friedens (15541) *(G-6223)*

Mother Nature Corporation 412 798-3911
200 Carriage Blvd Pittsburgh (15239) *(G-15304)*

Motivos LLC 267 283-1733
220 Belgrade St Philadelphia (19125) *(G-14042)*

Moto Tees, Grove City *Also called Gear Racewear Inc (G-6786)*

Motor Actuator Specialties Inc 215 919-1437
20 Vivian Dr Coatesville (19320) *(G-3317)*

Motor Fuels Management, King of Prussia *Also called American Auto Wash Inc (G-8580)*

Motor Technology Inc 717 266-4045
515 Willow Springs Ln York (17406) *(G-20605)*

Motorama Assoc 717 359-4310
100 Speedway Ln Hanover (17331) *(G-6924)*

Motorola Mobility LLC 215 674-4800
101 Tournament Dr Horsham (19044) *(G-7834)*

Motorola Mobility LLC 610 238-0109
450 Plymouth Rd Ste 102 Plymouth Meeting (19462) *(G-15857)*

Motorola Solutions Inc 724 837-3030
515 New Alexandria Rd Greensburg (15601) *(G-6690)*

Motorsport Green Engineer 570 386-8600
2040 W Penn Pike New Ringgold (17960) *(G-12442)*

Motorsports Sponship Mktg News, Langhorne *Also called Ernie Saxton (G-9294)*

Motson Graphics Inc (PA) 215 233-0500
1717 Bethlehem Pike Flourtown (19031) *(G-5988)*

Motto Graphics Inc 570 639-5555
469 Orange Rd Dallas (18612) *(G-3963)*

Motts LLP 717 677-7121
45 Aspers North Rd Aspers (17304) *(G-743)*

Mount Hope Estate & Winery, Manheim *Also called Mazza Vineyards Inc (G-10394)*

Mount Hope Lumber 814 789-4953
29749 State Highway 27 Guys Mills (16327) *(G-6811)*

Mount Joy Wire Corporation 717 653-1461
1000 E Main St Mount Joy (17552) *(G-11666)*

Mount Lebanon Magazine, Pittsburgh *Also called Mount Lebanon Municipality (G-15305)*

Mount Lebanon Municipality 412 343-3400
710 Washington Rd Ste 1 Pittsburgh (15228) *(G-15305)*

Mount Pleasant Journal, Connellsville *Also called Independent-Observer (G-3499)*

Mount Plsnt Twnshp-Wshngtn CNT 724 356-7974
31 Mccarrell Rd Hickory (15340) *(G-7629)*

Mount Svage Spclty Rfrractories 814 236-8370
4882 Curwensville Curwensville (16833) *(G-3954)*

Mountain Brook Industrial Coat 717 369-4040
9226 Mountain Brook Rd Saint Thomas (17252) *(G-17040)*

Mountain City Cabinets Inc 814 652-3977
1595 Raystown Rd Everett (15537) *(G-5575)*

Mountain Energy Inc 724 428-5200
1593 Aleppo Rd Aleppo (15310) *(G-61)*

Mountain Lake Winery LLC 267 664-6343
391 Bailey Rd Towanda (18848) *(G-18433)*

Mountain Man Deer Processing 717 532-7295
10125 Mountain Rd Orrstown (17244) *(G-13034)*

Mountain Meadows Cheese Mfrs, Richfield *Also called Quaker Valley Specialties (G-16681)*

Mountain Metal Studio Inc 724 329-0238
190 Thomas Rd Markleysburg (15459) *(G-10482)*

Mountain Mouldings 814 535-8563
112 Schneider St Johnstown (15906) *(G-8410)*

Mountain Pure Water Systems, Mifflintown *Also called Ultra Pure Products Inc (G-11139)*

Mountain Resources Inc 814 734-1496
12321 Culbertson Dr Edinboro (16412) *(G-4817)*

Mountain Ridge Metals LLC 717 692-4851
1517 Rte 209 Millersburg (17061) *(G-11197)*

Mountain Side Scrn Prnt/Desgn 570 539-2400
309 Leister Ln Mount Pleasant Mills (17853) *(G-11728)*

Mountain Side Supply LLC 814 201-2525
400 E Pleasant Vly Blvd Altoona (16602) *(G-529)*

Mountain Top Distillery 570 745-2227
150 Bennardi Dev Rd Williamsport (17702) *(G-20043)*

Mountain Top Foam Co., Mountain Top *Also called Tempur Production Usa LLC (G-11778)*

Mountain Top Welding & Repair 570 888-7174
3894 Centerville Rd Gillett (16925) *(G-6382)*

Mountain View Rendering Co (PA) 215 723-5555
249 Allentown Rd Souderton (18964) *(G-17752)*

Mountain Vly Mold Solution LLC 570 460-6592
515 Queen St Stroudsburg (18360) *(G-18131)*

Mountain-Valley Services LLC 814 594-3167
6584 Ridgway St Marys Rd Ridgway (15853) *(G-16718)*

Mountaineer Mining Corporation 814 445-5806
1010 Garrett Shortcut Rd Berlin (15530) *(G-1291)*

Mountaineer Publishing 724 880-3753
601 Pisgah Ridge Rd Waynesburg (15370) *(G-19448)*

Mountainside Log Homes 570 745-2388
105 Mountainstone Ln Williamsport (17702) *(G-20044)*

Mountainside Wood Products 717 935-5753
3559 Front Mountain Rd Belleville (17004) *(G-1133)*

Mountaintop Anthracite Inc 570 474-1222
1550 Crestwood Dr Mountain Top (18707) *(G-11766)*

Mountaintop Eagle Inc 570 474-6397
85 S Main Rd Wilkes Barre (18707) *(G-19946)*

Mountaintop Welding 814 387-9353
1262 Ridge Rd Clarence (16829) *(G-3164)*

Mountainview Graphics 610 939-1471
201 E Bellevue Ave Reading (19605) *(G-16449)*

Mounts Equipment Co Inc 724 225-0460
Berry Rd Washington (15301) *(G-19208)*

Mousley Consulting Inc 610 539-0150
447 Alexandra Dr Norristown (19403) *(G-12689)*

Movad LLC 215 638-2679
5166 Campus Dr Plymouth Meeting (19462) *(G-15858)*

Moving Out 724 794-6831
118 And A Half Frnklin St Slippery Rock (16057) *(G-17623)*

Moxham Lumber Co 814 536-5186
150 Dupont St Johnstown (15902) *(G-8411)*

Moyco Precision, Montgomeryville *Also called Saint-Gobain Abrasives Inc (G-11416)*

Moyer & Son Inc (PA) 215 799-2000
113 E Reliance Rd Souderton (18964) *(G-17753)*

Moyer Music Test Inc 717 566-8778
4 Meadowood Dr Hummelstown (17036) *(G-7918)*

Moyer Specialty Foods LLC 215 703-0100
20 S 2nd St Souderton (18964) *(G-17754)*

Moyers Sawmill Company 610 488-1462
361 Pearl Rd Bernville (19506) *(G-1302)*

Moyers Service Co 267 205-1105
4409 Somers Ave Feasterville Trevose (19053) *(G-5920)*

Mp Machinery and Testing LLC 814 234-8860
260 Pantops Parade Port Matilda (16870) *(G-15902)*

Mpc Industries LLC 717 393-4100
200 Centerville Rd Lancaster (17603) *(G-9138)*

Mpc Liquidation Inc 814 849-6737
301 Main St Brookville (15825) *(G-2266)*

Mpe Machine Tool Inc 814 664-4822
27 W Washington St Corry (16407) *(G-3769)*

Mpi Supply Incorporated 412 664-9320
25 Allegheny Sq Glassport (15045) *(G-6414)*

Mpm Holdings Inc 610 678-8131
7 Bristol Ct Reading (19610) *(G-16450)*

Mpower Software Services LLC (PA) 215 497-9730
115 Pheasant Run Ste 110 Newtown (18940) *(G-12524)*

Mpp Ford Road Division, Saint Marys *Also called Metal Powder Products LLC (G-16991)*

Mpp Washington Street Division, Saint Marys *Also called Metal Powder Products LLC (G-16992)*

MPS Techline of PA, Willow Grove *Also called Techline Technologies Inc (G-20146)*

MPW Industrial Services Inc 412 233-4060
400 State St Clairton (15025) *(G-3154)*

Mr Kotula, Scranton *Also called Straz (G-17294)*

Mr Luck Inc 570 766-8734
1609 Route 507 Greentown (18426) *(G-6734)*

Mr Moo Cow LLC 570 235-1061
1280 Highway 315 Blvd Wilkes Barre (18702) *(G-19947)*

Mr Printer Inc 215 354-5533
855 Bustleton Pike Richboro (18954) *(G-16676)*

Mr Rebuildables Inc 610 767-2100
4800 Lehigh Dr Walnutport (18088) *(G-18793)*

Mr Smoothie (PA) 412 630-9065
1000 Ross Park Mall Dr Vc13 Pittsburgh (15237) *(G-15306)*

Mr Spouting 814 692-4880
301 S Main St Port Matilda (16870) *(G-15903)*

Mr TS Sixpack 814 226-8890
540 Main St Clarion (16214) *(G-3184)*

Mr ZS Food Mart 570 421-7070
1070 N 9th St Stroudsburg (18360) *(G-18132)*

Mr. Shrinkwrap, Prospect Park *Also called Harbor Bay Group Inc (G-16115)*

Mr.pastie, Pen Argyl *Also called Real English Foods Inc (G-13215)*

MRC Electric 267 988-4370
145 Railroad Dr Ste C Warminster (18974) *(G-18925)*

Mrckl Closeco Inc 412 828-6112
1 Lamagna Dr Verona (15147) *(G-18758)*

Mrg Food LLC 412 482-7430
  800 Manning Ave McKeesport (15132) *(G-10676)*
Mri Flexible Packaging Company 800 448-8183
  181 Rittenhouse Cir Bristol (19007) *(G-2170)*
Mri Flexible Packaging Company (HQ) 215 860-7676
  181 Rittenhouse Cir Bristol (19007) *(G-2171)*
Mri Flexible Packaging Company 215 860-7676
  660 Newtown Yardley Rd Newtown (18940) *(G-12525)*
Mrlrx LLC 610 485-7750
  46 E 10th St Marcus Hook (19061) *(G-10450)*
MRS and Son LLC 215 750-7828
  765 Old Bristol Pike Morrisville (19067) *(G-11572)*
Mrs Resslers Food Products Co (PA) 215 744-4700
  5501 Tabor Ave Philadelphia (19120) *(G-14043)*
Mrs. T'S, Shenandoah *Also called Ateeco Inc (G-17492)*
Ms Wheelchair PA Program 814 331-1722
  18 Woodlawn Ave Bradford (16701) *(G-1984)*
MSA Advanced Detection LLC ((HQ) 724 776-8600
  1000 Cranberry Woods Dr Cranberry Township (16066) *(G-3838)*
MSA Pittsburgh Dist Ctr 724 742-8090
  1750 Shenango Rd New Galilee (16141) *(G-12221)*
MSA Safety Incorporated (PA) 724 776-8600
  1000 Cranberry Woods Dr Cranberry Township (16066) *(G-3839)*
MSA Safety Incorporated 724 733-9100
  3880 Meadowbrook Rd Murrysville (15668) *(G-11858)*
MSA Safety Incorporated 724 776-7700
  1100 Cranberry Woods Dr Cranberry Township (16066) *(G-3840)*
MSA Safety Incorporated 724 733-9100
  3880 Meadowbrook Rd Murrysville (15668) *(G-11859)*
MSA Safety Sales LLC 724 776-8600
  1000 Cranberry Woods Dr Cranberry Township (16066) *(G-3841)*
MSA Worldwide, Murrysville *Also called MSA Safety Incorporated (G-11858)*
Msci, Allentown *Also called Mechanical Service Co Inc (G-313)*
MSE - PA, Exton *Also called Clover Technologies Group LLC (G-5662)*
Msf Management LLC 724 371-3059
  685 State Ave Beaver (15009) *(G-987)*
Msgo Manufacturing Company, Lansdale *Also called Scatton Bros Mfg Co (G-9409)*
Msh Industries 814 866-0777
  9640 Lake Pleasant Rd Erie (16509) *(G-5397)*
Mshar Power Train Specialists 717 231-3900
  3525 N 6th Side 4 Harrisburg (17110) *(G-7181)*
MSI Acquisition Corp (HQ) 717 397-2777
  3061 Industry Dr Ste 200 Lancaster (17603) *(G-9139)*
MSI Technologies LLC 215 968-5068
  1267 Fountain Rd Newtown (18940) *(G-12526)*
Msjc Inc 717 930-0718
  643 Southward St Middletown (17057) *(G-11065)*
Msk Industries LLC 570 485-4908
  232 Rocky Top Ln Rome (18837) *(G-16800)*
Msl Oil & Gas Corp 814 362-6891
  Marshburg Rd Rr 59 Lewis Run (16738) *(G-9878)*
MSP Corporation 570 344-7670
  1055 Blair Ave Scranton (18508) *(G-17260)*
MSP Distribution Svcs C LLC 215 652-6160
  351 N Sumneytown Pike North Wales (19454) *(G-12819)*
Mspi Enterprises LLC 814 258-7500
  10726 Route 249 Knoxville (16928) *(G-8812)*
Mssi Refractory LLC 412 771-5533
  2 John St Mc Kees Rocks (15136) *(G-10621)*
Mt Chemical Company LLC 570 474-2200
  1050 Crestwood Dr Mountain Top (18707) *(G-11767)*
Mt Displays LLC 201 636-4144
  1081 Hanover St Hanover Township (18706) *(G-6998)*
Mt Holly Sprng Specialty Ppr 717 486-8500
  1 Mountain St Mount Holly Springs (17065) *(G-11637)*
Mt Lebanon Awning, Presto *Also called Mt Lebanon Awning & Tent Co (G-16104)*
Mt Lebanon Awning & Tent Co 412 221-2233
  5309 Thoms Run Rd Presto (15142) *(G-16104)*
Mt Pleasant Mine Service, Mount Pleasant *Also called Demarchi John (G-11696)*
Mt. Cydonia Plant I, Fayetteville *Also called Valley Quarries Inc (G-5879)*
Mtekka LLC 610 619-3555
  124 Knoxlyn Farm Dr Kennett Square (19348) *(G-8532)*
Mtg Sign, Hellertown *Also called Mobile Technology Graphics LLC (G-7559)*
MTI Dental, Coatesville *Also called MTI Precision Products LLC (G-3318)*
MTI Precision Products LLC 610 679-5280
  131 Birch St Coatesville (19320) *(G-3318)*
Mtl Holdings Inc 570 343-7921
  101 Power Blvd Archbald (18403) *(G-693)*
Mto Battery, Red Lion *Also called Battery Builders Inc (G-16590)*
Mtr Fuel LLC 609 610-0783
  117 Osborne Ave Morrisville (19067) *(G-11573)*
MTS Forge, Sadsburyville *Also called Manufctring Technical Svcs Inc (G-16905)*
Mudhook Brewing Company LLC 717 747-3605
  34 N Cherry Ln York (17401) *(G-20606)*
Mueller Industries Inc 215 699-5801
  287 Wissahickon Ave North Wales (19454) *(G-12820)*
Mukies/Mccarty Seal Coating C 717 684-2799
  913 Chestnut St Columbia (17512) *(G-3444)*

Mulch Barn 215 703-0300
  10 Schoolhouse Rd Ste 2 Souderton (18964) *(G-17755)*
Mulch Works Recycling Inc 888 214-4628
  22 Mount Pleasant Rd Aston (19014) *(G-779)*
Muldoon Window Door & Awning 570 347-9453
  1230 Sanderson Ave Scranton (18509) *(G-17261)*
Mulkerrin Burial Vaults, Oakdale *Also called Ron Mulkerrin (G-12910)*
Muller Inc 215 676-7575
  2800 Grant Ave Philadelphia (19114) *(G-14044)*
Muller Martini Mailroom (HQ) 610 266-7000
  4444 Innovation Way Allentown (18109) *(G-323)*
Mulligan Mining Inc 412 831-1787
  5945 Pudding Stone Ln Bethel Park (15102) *(G-1427)*
Mulligan Printing Corporation 570 278-3271
  110 E Harrison St Tunkhannock (18657) *(G-18544)*
Multi Flex Plating, Collingdale *Also called Multiflex Plating Company Inc (G-3408)*
Multi-Color Corporation 717 266-9675
  405 Willow Springs Ln York (17406) *(G-20607)*
Multi-Copy Printing, Brookhaven *Also called Chester Multi Copy Inc (G-2243)*
Multi-Flow Dispensers LP (PA) 215 322-1800
  1434 County Line Rd Huntingdon Valley (19006) *(G-8014)*
Multi-Flow Industries LLC (HQ) 215 322-1800
  1434 County Line Rd Huntingdon Valley (19006) *(G-8015)*
Multi-Metals Co Inc (PA) 724 836-2720
  1941 State Route 66 Greensburg (15601) *(G-6691)*
Multi-Plastics Extrusions Inc (HQ) 570 455-2021
  600 Dietrich Ave Hazleton (18201) *(G-7512)*
Multicell North Inc 610 683-9000
  240 Broad St Kutztown (19530) *(G-8850)*
Multicolor Corp 610 262-8420
  52 N 2nd St Ste 2 Coplay (18037) *(G-3646)*
Multifab & Machine Inc 724 947-7700
  670 Steubenville Pike Burgettstown (15021) *(G-2351)*
Multiflex Plating Company Inc 610 461-7700
  109 Willows Ave Collingdale (19023) *(G-3408)*
Multilingual Communications 412 621-7450
  3603 Bates St Pittsburgh (15213) *(G-15307)*
Multimedia Training Systems 412 341-2185
  370 Broadmoor Ave Pittsburgh (15228) *(G-15308)*
Multiple Metal Processing Inc 570 620-7254
  1906 Silver Maple Rd Effort (18330) *(G-4826)*
Multiplex Manufacturing Co 570 752-4524
  600 Fowler Ave Berwick (18603) *(G-1337)*
Multiscope Dcment Slutions Inc 724 743-1083
  300 Bursca Dr Ste 307 Bridgeville (15017) *(G-2080)*
Multiscope Dgital Offset Print, Canonsburg *Also called Multiscope Incorporated (G-2606)*
Multiscope Incorporated 724 743-1083
  135 Technology Dr Ste 402 Canonsburg (15317) *(G-2606)*
Multisorb Tech Intl LLC 412 521-3685
  6422 Monitor St Pittsburgh (15217) *(G-15309)*
Multitherm Heat Transfer 610 408-8361
  11 General Warren Blvd Malvern (19355) *(G-10281)*
Mumps Audiofax Inc 610 293-2160
  744 W Lancaster Ave # 250 Wayne (19087) *(G-19358)*
Muncy Homes 570 546-2261
  1567 Route 442 Hwy Muncy (17756) *(G-11827)*
Muncy Industries LLC 570 649-5188
  5820 Susquehanna Trl Turbotville (17772) *(G-18554)*
Muncy Luminary 570 584-0111
  1025 Route 405 Hwy Hughesville (17737) *(G-7897)*
Muncy Machine & Tool Co Inc 570 649-5188
  5820 Susquehanna Trl Turbotville (17772) *(G-18555)*
Mundorf Sign Co 717 854-3071
  29 Overbrook Ave York (17404) *(G-20608)*
Municipal Board, Slippery Rock *Also called Borough of Slippery Rock (G-17618)*
Municipal Fire Equipment Inc 412 366-8180
  1038 Perry Hwy Ste 201 Pittsburgh (15237) *(G-15310)*
Municipal Publications 724 397-9812
  1369 Wrigden Run Rd Marion Center (15759) *(G-10474)*
Municpl Athrty of the Brgh of, Shenandoah *Also called Shenandoah Water Trtmnt Plant (G-17496)*
Munot Plastics Inc (PA) 814 838-7721
  2935 W 17th St Erie (16505) *(G-5398)*
Munot Plastics Inc 814 838-7721
  2935 W 17th St Erie (16505) *(G-5399)*
Munro Prtg Graphic Design LLC 610 485-1966
  815 Market St Marcus Hook (19061) *(G-10451)*
Munroe Incorporated (HQ) 412 231-0600
  1820 N Franklin St Pittsburgh (15233) *(G-15311)*
Munroe Incorporated 412 231-0600
  12 Century Dr Ambridge (15003) *(G-628)*
Murazzi Provision Co 570 344-2285
  1262 Providence Rd Scranton (18508) *(G-17262)*
Murdick Auto Parts & Racg Sups 724 482-2177
  576 Evans City Rd Butler (16001) *(G-2425)*
Murlin Chemical Inc 610 825-1165
  10 Balligomingo Rd Ste Q Conshohocken (19428) *(G-3579)*
Murphy Printing Free Press 724 927-2222
  1887 State Highway 285 Linesville (16424) *(G-9985)*

A
L
P
H
A
B
E
T
I
C

Murrelle Printing Co Inc......570 888-2244
206 S Keystone Ave Sayre (18840) ***(G-17119)***
Murrelle, Joe Press, Sayre *Also called Gary Murelle* ***(G-17114)***
Murry's Plant, Lebanon *Also called Murrys of Maryland Inc* ***(G-9612)***
Murrys of Maryland Inc......301 420-6400
1501 Willow St Lebanon (17046) ***(G-9612)***
Murrysville Auto LLC......724 387-1607
4765 Old William Penn Hwy Murrysville (15668) ***(G-11860)***
Murslack Welding Inc......412 364-5554
484 Lowries Run Rd 2 Pittsburgh (15237) ***(G-15312)***
Muscle Gauge Nutrition LLC......484 840-8006
893 S Matlack St Ste 150 West Chester (19382) ***(G-19602)***
Muscle Products Corporation......814 786-0166
752 Kilgore Rd Jackson Center (16133) ***(G-8229)***
Musgraves Elc Mtr Repr Svc, Greenville *Also called Memrs Inc* ***(G-6754)***
Musselman Lumber - US Lbm LLC......717 354-4321
200 Brimmer Ave New Holland (17557) ***(G-12264)***
Musser Manufacturing......717 271-2321
1235 W Route 897 Denver (17517) ***(G-4085)***
Mustang Trailer Mfg......724 628-1000
402 S Arch St Connellsville (15425) ***(G-3504)***
Musumeci Santo......215 467-2158
1306 Jackson St Philadelphia (19148) ***(G-14045)***
Mutual Industries North Inc......215 679-7682
625 Washington St Red Hill (18076) ***(G-16583)***
Mutual Industries North Inc (PA)......215 927-6000
707 W Grange Ave Ste 1 Philadelphia (19120) ***(G-14046)***
Mutual Pharmaceutical Co Inc (HQ)......215 288-6500
1100 Orthodox St Philadelphia (19124) ***(G-14047)***
Mutual Pharmaceutical Co Inc......215 807-1312
7722 Dungan Rd Philadelphia (19111) ***(G-14048)***
Mutual Press Cliping, Harrisburg *Also called Burrells Information Services* ***(G-7101)***
Mvc Industries Inc......610 650-0500
2675 Eisenhower Ave Norristown (19403) ***(G-12690)***
Mvd, Reading *Also called Mobile Video Devices Inc* ***(G-16447)***
Mvp Prnting Prmtional Pdts LLC......814 520-8392
4734 Pittsburgh Ave Erie (16509) ***(G-5400)***
Mvp Sports & Games Co......302 250-4836
50 Redwood Dr Lancaster (17603) ***(G-9140)***
Mvs Saegertown, Saegertown *Also called Maclean Saegertown LLC* ***(G-16924)***
Mw/Td Inspired LLC......724 741-0473
750 Commonwealth Dr Warrendale (15086) ***(G-19090)***
Mwi Service......717 578-2324
6182 Hill Top Dr E Spring Grove (17362) ***(G-17879)***
MWM Graphics......610 692-0525
307 Westtown Rd Ste 1 West Chester (19382) ***(G-19603)***
Mxl Industries Inc......717 569-8711
1764 Rohrerstown Rd Lancaster (17601) ***(G-9141)***
Mxstrategies LLC......610 241-2099
1003 Saber Rd West Chester (19382) ***(G-19604)***
My Aunties Candies......610 269-0919
1419 Price Ln Downingtown (19335) ***(G-4243)***
My Biblical Perception LLC......267 450-9655
2304 Applewood Ct Perkasie (18944) ***(G-13285)***
My Instant Benefits......724 465-6075
1707 Warren Rd Indiana (15701) ***(G-8114)***
My Jewel Shop Inc......215 887-3881
411 Old York Rd Jenkintown (19046) ***(G-8297)***
Mybiani LLC......267 253-1866
197 Fairhill St Willow Grove (19090) ***(G-20130)***
Myers Cabinet Co......724 887-4070
312 Mount Pleasant Rd Scottdale (15683) ***(G-17196)***
Myers Canning Co......610 929-8644
3721 Pottsville Pike Reading (19605) ***(G-16451)***
Myers Drugstore Inc......610 233-3300
48 E Main St Norristown (19401) ***(G-12691)***
Myers Electrical Repairs......717 334-8105
1785 Biglerville Rd Gettysburg (17325) ***(G-6309)***
Myers Power Products Inc......610 868-3500
44 S Commerce Way Bethlehem (18017) ***(G-1576)***
Myers Sheet Metal Division, Wellsville *Also called Kampel Enterprises Inc* ***(G-19478)***
Myers Steel Works Inc......717 502-0266
10 Big Oak Rd Dillsburg (17019) ***(G-4138)***
Myers Vacuum Repair Svcs Inc (PA)......724 545-8331
1155 Myers Ln Kittanning (16201) ***(G-8785)***
Myers Wldg & Fabrication Inc......717 502-7473
10 Big Oak Rd Dillsburg (17019) ***(G-4139)***
Myers/Abacus, Bethlehem *Also called Myers Power Products Inc* ***(G-1576)***
Myerstown Sheds......717 866-7644
513 King St Apt E Lebanon (17042) ***(G-9613)***
Myerstown Sheds and Fencing......717 866-7015
694 E Lincoln Ave Myerstown (17067) ***(G-11894)***
Myexposome Inc......610 668-0145
1024 Spruce St Apt A Philadelphia (19107) ***(G-14049)***
Mylan Inc (HQ)......724 514-1800
1000 Mylan Blvd Canonsburg (15317) ***(G-2607)***
Mylan Pharmaceuticals Inc......724 514-1800
1000 Mylan Blvd Canonsburg (15317) ***(G-2608)***
Myoderm Medical Supply, Norristown *Also called Myers Drugstore Inc* ***(G-12691)***
Mystic Assembly & Dctg Co......215 957-0280
19 Vincent Cir Warminster (18974) ***(G-18926)***
Mystic Lanes LLC......724 898-2960
1318 Pittsburgh Rd Valencia (16059) ***(G-18699)***
Mystic Screen Printing and EMB......570 628-3520
1108 S Centre St Pottsville (17901) ***(G-16089)***
Mytamed Inc......877 444-6982
274 Lancaster Ave Ste 208 Malvern (19355) ***(G-10282)***
Mzp Kiln Services Inc......724 318-8653
328 14th St Ambridge (15003) ***(G-629)***
Mzp Kiln Services Inc......412 825-5100
201 Penn Center Blvd Pittsburgh (15235) ***(G-15313)***
N & N Drilling Supply, Jessup *Also called Angelo Nieto Inc* ***(G-8326)***
N A Petroleum Corp......610 438-5463
2911 Old Nazareth Rd Easton (18045) ***(G-4728)***
N B Garber Inc......267 387-6225
1520 Campus Dr Ste H Warminster (18974) ***(G-18927)***
N Barsky & Sons......215 925-8639
724 Sansom St Philadelphia (19106) ***(G-14050)***
N C B Technologies Inc......724 658-5544
1220 Frew Mill Rd New Castle (16101) ***(G-12123)***
N C Stauffer & Sons Inc......570 945-3047
309 Vail Rd Factoryville (18419) ***(G-5758)***
N D C, Warminster *Also called Neu Dynamics Corp* ***(G-18929)***
N E D LLC......610 442-1017
2225 Park Pl Slatington (18080) ***(G-17609)***
N E Prestressed Products, Cressona *Also called Northeast Prestressed Pdts LLC* ***(G-3906)***
N F C Industries Inc (PA)......215 766-8890
6124 Potters Ln Plumsteadville (18949) ***(G-15812)***
N F String & Son Inc......717 234-2441
1380 Howard St Harrisburg (17104) ***(G-7182)***
N H I, Windber *Also called National Hybrid Inc* ***(G-20190)***
N H Laboratories Inc......717 545-3221
6940 Allentown Blvd Harrisburg (17112) ***(G-7183)***
N H Morgan Inc......412 561-1046
3241 W Liberty Ave Ste 1 Pittsburgh (15216) ***(G-15314)***
N I W, Huntingdon Valley *Also called Northern Iron Works Inc* ***(G-8018)***
N J K Lettering......724 356-2583
928 Old Ridge Rd Avella (15312) ***(G-837)***
N K I, Pittsburgh *Also called Neuro Kinetics Inc* ***(G-15329)***
N M A......814 453-6787
1525 E Lake Rd Ste C Erie (16511) ***(G-5401)***
N P I, Feasterville Trevose *Also called Natures Pillows Inc* ***(G-5921)***
N P S, Washington *Also called Network Products & Services* ***(G-19210)***
N Pgh Imaging Specialists......724 935-6200
6001 Stonewood Dr Ste 100 Wexford (15090) ***(G-19813)***
N R I, Philadelphia *Also called National Refrigerants Inc* ***(G-14056)***
N T M Inc......717 567-9374
222 Red Hill Rd Newport (17074) ***(G-12492)***
N Vision Group Inc......610 278-1900
1 N Morton Ave Morton (19070) ***(G-11592)***
N-Jay Machines......724 232-0110
355 Fredericksburg Rd Karns City (16041) ***(G-8481)***
N-Zyme Scientifics LLC......267 218-1098
3805 Old Easton Rd Doylestown (18902) ***(G-4317)***
N.A. Hoganas, Hollsopple *Also called North American Hoganas Company* ***(G-7658)***
N/S Corporation......610 436-5552
1230 Wrights Ln West Chester (19380) ***(G-19605)***
N3 Oceanic Inc......215 541-1073
404 Main St Pennsburg (18073) ***(G-13251)***
N3zn Keys LLC......412 389-7797
74 Green Meadow Ct Pittsburgh (15239) ***(G-15315)***
Naamans Creek Co Inc......610 268-3833
353 Indian Run Rd Avondale (19311) ***(G-855)***
Nabco Inc (PA)......724 746-9617
1001 Corporate Dr Ste 205 Canonsburg (15317) ***(G-2609)***
Nabco Systems LLC......724 746-9617
171 Hillpointe Dr Ste 303 Canonsburg (15317) ***(G-2610)***
Nabi Genmed LLC......610 258-5627
12 Starlite Dr Easton (18045) ***(G-4729)***
Nabisco, Philadelphia *Also called Mondelez Global LLC* ***(G-14034)***
Nabisco Brands Inc......570 820-1669
50 New Commerce Blvd Wilkes Barre (18762) ***(G-19948)***
Nabors Drilling Tech USA......814 768-4640
143 Cresswood Dr Clearfield (16830) ***(G-3226)***
Nabriva Therapeutics Us Inc......610 816-6640
1000 Continental Dr # 600 King of Prussia (19406) ***(G-8653)***
Nac Carbon Products Inc......814 938-7450
Elk Run Ave Punxsutawney (15767) ***(G-16148)***
Nac Joint Venture Pipline......814 938-7450
314 Elk Run Ave Punxsutawney (15767) ***(G-16149)***
Nacah Tech LLC......412 833-0687
37 Mcmurray Rd Ste 203 Pittsburgh (15241) ***(G-15316)***
Nacci Printing Inc......610 434-1224
1327 N 18th St Allentown (18104) ***(G-324)***
NACE, Bethlehem *Also called National Assn Cllges Employers* ***(G-1577)***
Naceville Materials JV......215 453-8933
2001 Ridge Rd Sellersville (18960) ***(G-17354)***

Nadine Corporation 412 795-5100
  184 Sandy Creek Rd Verona (15147) *(G-18759)*

Nail Central 717 664-5051
  605 Goldfinch Ln Manheim (17545) *(G-10396)*

Nailed It II LLC 215 803-2060
  314 W Lincoln Hwy Ste 2 Langhorne (19047) *(G-9312)*

Najafi Companies LLC 570 383-3291
  1400 E Lackawanna St Olyphant (18448) *(G-12994)*

Nak International Corp 724 774-9200
  1729 Penn Ave Ste 7 Monaca (15061) *(G-11292)*

Nalco Chemical, Pittsburgh *Also called Nalco Company LLC (G-15317)*

Nalco Company LLC 412 278-8600
  650 Trumbull Dr Pittsburgh (15205) *(G-15317)*

Nalco Wtr Prtrtment Sltons LLC 610 358-0717
  2 New Rd Aston (19014) *(G-780)*

Names 'n Things, East Earl *Also called Aunt Barbies (G-4537)*

Nammo Pocal Inc (PA) 570 961-1999
  100 Electric St Scranton (18509) *(G-17263)*

Nammo Pocal Inc 570 842-2288
  Rr 435 Moscow (18444) *(G-11599)*

Namsco Plastics Inds Inc 724 339-3591
  100 Hunt Valley Rd New Kensington (15068) *(G-12360)*

Namsco Plastics Industries 724 339-3100
  1035 Hunt Valley Cir New Kensington (15068) *(G-12361)*

Nanogriptech Inc 412 224-2136
  91 43rd St Ste 240 Pittsburgh (15201) *(G-15318)*

Nanohorizons Inc 814 355-4700
  270 Rolling Ridge Dr Bellefonte (16823) *(G-1109)*

Nanomagnetics Instrs USA LLC 610 417-3857
  15 S Bank St Loft 6 Easton (18042) *(G-4730)*

Nanopack Inc 484 367-7015
  985 Old Eagle School Rd # 501 Wayne (19087) *(G-19359)*

Nanoscan Imaging LLC 215 699-1703
  2250 Berks Rd Lansdale (19446) *(G-9390)*

Nao Inc (PA) 215 743-5300
  1284 E Sedgley Ave Philadelphia (19134) *(G-14051)*

NAPA Auto Parts, Selinsgrove *Also called Snyder County Automotive Inc (G-17335)*

NAPA Auto Parts, Newtown *Also called Genuine Parts Company (G-12504)*

Napoletano Pasta, Springfield *Also called Springfield Pasta (G-17923)*

Napotnik Welding Inc 814 446-4500
  4225 Power Plant Rd New Florence (15944) *(G-12199)*

Nardone Bros, Hanover Township *Also called Nardone Brothers Baking Co (G-6999)*

Nardone Brothers Baking Co 570 823-0141
  420 New Commerce Blvd Hanover Township (18706) *(G-6999)*

Narsa 724 799-8415
  3000 Village Run Rd # 103 Wexford (15090) *(G-19814)*

Nartak Media Group 412 276-4000
  2275 Swallow Hill Rd # 100 Pittsburgh (15220) *(G-15319)*

Narvon Construction LLC 717 989-2026
  247 S Pool Forge Rd Narvon (17555) *(G-11924)*

Nascent Energy Systems LLC 203 722-1101
  712 Filbert St Apt 2 Pittsburgh (15232) *(G-15320)*

Nash Engineering, Charleroi *Also called Gardner Denver Nash LLC (G-3015)*

Nash Printing LLC 215 855-4267
  1617 N Line St Apt A Lansdale (19446) *(G-9391)*

Nass Inc 717 846-3685
  501 E King St York (17403) *(G-20609)*

Natawill Industries Inc 610 574-8226
  1118 Almond Dr Phoenixville (19460) *(G-14564)*

Nation Ruskin Holdings Inc (PA) 267 654-4000
  206 Progress Dr Montgomeryville (18936) *(G-11409)*

Nation-Wide Sign Service Inc 888 234-5300
  3015 Garrett Rd Drexel Hill (19026) *(G-4369)*

National Airoil Burner Co Inc 215 743-5300
  1284 E Sedgley Ave Philadelphia (19134) *(G-14052)*

National Artificial Limb Co 412 608-9910
  5740 Baum Blvd Ste 1 Pittsburgh (15206) *(G-15321)*

National Assn Cllges Employers 610 868-1421
  62 Highland Ave Bethlehem (18017) *(G-1577)*

National Bakery Inc (PA) 570 343-1609
  1100 Capouse Ave Scranton (18509) *(G-17264)*

National Basic Sensor Corp 215 322-4700
  455 Veit Rd Huntingdon Valley (19006) *(G-8016)*

National Bearings Company, Manheim *Also called Cbh of Lancaster Company (G-10375)*

National Beef Packing Co LLC 570 743-4420
  1811 N Old Trl Hummels Wharf (17831) *(G-7900)*

National Carbide Saw Co, Philadelphia *Also called MOr Saw Service Center Inc (G-14037)*

National Center For Def (PA) 724 539-8811
  486 Cornell Rd Ste 2 Blairsville (15717) *(G-1735)*

National Chemical Labs PA Inc 215 922-1200
  401 N 10th St Philadelphia (19123) *(G-14053)*

National Contact Lens, Philadelphia *Also called Karen Wrigley Dr (G-13922)*

National Crane Corporation 717 597-8121
  1565 Buchanan Trl E Shady Grove (17256) *(G-17422)*

National Cthlic Bthics Ctr Inc (PA) 215 877-2660
  6399 Drexel Rd Philadelphia (19151) *(G-14054)*

National Decal Craft Corp (PA) 215 822-0517
  2750 Bethlehem Pike Hatfield (19440) *(G-7371)*

National Dermalogy Image Corp 610 756-0065
  253 Quaker City Rd Kempton (19529) *(G-8493)*

National Dumpster Service LLC 484 949-1060
  116 Country Run Dr Coatesville (19320) *(G-3319)*

National Elec Carbn Pdts Inc 570 476-9004
  100 Mills Rd East Stroudsburg (18301) *(G-4624)*

National Embroidery 610 323-4400
  429 E Moyer Rd Pottstown (19464) *(G-16020)*

National Engineering and Mfg, Feasterville Trevose *Also called Nemco (G-5922)*

National Film Converting Inc 800 422-6651
  106 W 11th St Berwick (18603) *(G-1338)*

National Foam Inc (PA) 610 363-1400
  350 E Union St West Chester (19382) *(G-19606)*

National Foam Inc 610 363-1400
  350 E Union St West Chester (19382) *(G-19607)*

National Forest Products Ltd 814 927-5622
  S Forest St Marienville (16239) *(G-10458)*

National Fuel Gas Dist Corp 814 837-9585
  5405 Highland Rd Kane (16735) *(G-8472)*

National Furniture Assoc Inc (PA) 814 342-2007
  219 N Front St Philipsburg (16866) *(G-14520)*

National Furniture Wholesaler, Philipsburg *Also called National Furniture Assoc Inc (G-14520)*

National Generic Distributors 215 788-3113
  3901 Nebraska Ave Ste A Levittown (19056) *(G-9852)*

National Hot Rod Association 717 584-1200
  2420 Gehman Ln Ste 200 Lancaster (17602) *(G-9142)*

National Hybrid Inc 814 467-9060
  345 Pomroys Dr Windber (15963) *(G-20190)*

National Hydraulic Systems LLC 724 628-4010
  915 W Crawford Ave Connellsville (15425) *(G-3505)*

National Hydraulics Inc (PA) 724 547-9222
  1558 Mt Plsant Connell Rd Mount Pleasant (15666) *(G-11708)*

National Hydraulics Inc 724 887-3850
  1000 Water St Scottdale (15683) *(G-17197)*

National Imprint Corporation (HQ) 814 239-8141
  William Ward Indus Park Claysburg (16625) *(G-3205)*

National Imprint Corporation 814 239-5116
  114 Ward Dr Claysburg (16625) *(G-3206)*

National Limestone Quarry 570 837-1635
  3499 Quarry Rd Middleburg (17842) *(G-11033)*

National Magnetics Group Inc (PA) 610 867-7600
  1210 Win Dr Bethlehem (18017) *(G-1578)*

National Magnetics Group Inc 610 867-7600
  1210 Win Dr Bethlehem (18017) *(G-1579)*

National Magnetics Group Inc 610 867-7600
  1210 Win Dr Bethlehem (18017) *(G-1580)*

National Magnetics Group Inc 610 867-7600
  1210 Win Dr Bethlehem (18017) *(G-1581)*

National Magnetics Group Inc 610 867-6003
  1210 Win Dr Bethlehem (18017) *(G-1582)*

National Mail Graphics Corp 610 524-1600
  300 Old Mill Ln Exton (19341) *(G-5713)*

National Material LP 724 337-6551
  2001 Dr Thomas Blvd New Kensington (15068) *(G-12362)*

National Metalcrafters, Philadelphia *Also called Xynatech Mfg Co (G-14496)*

National Ministries, King of Prussia *Also called American Baptst HM Mission Soc (G-8581)*

National Molding LLC 724 266-8770
  2305 Duss Ave Bldg 4 Ambridge (15003) *(G-630)*

National Oilwell Varco Inc 724 745-6005
  100 Alpha Dr Canonsburg (15317) *(G-2611)*

National Oilwell Varco Inc 724 947-4581
  1132 Route 18 Burgettstown (15021) *(G-2352)*

National Oilwell Varco Inc 814 427-2555
  257 Caroline St Punxsutawney (15767) *(G-16150)*

National Oilwell Varco Inc 318 243-5910
  850 Wilmington St Washington (15301) *(G-19209)*

National Oilwell Varco LP 570 862-2548
  201 Center Ave Leetsdale (15056) *(G-9700)*

National Paperbox, Jenkintown *Also called Simkins Corporation (G-8301)*

National Plas Acquisition LLC 610 250-7800
  11 Mcfadden Rd Easton (18045) *(G-4731)*

National Plastics 610 252-6172
  212 E Broad St Bethlehem (18018) *(G-1583)*

National Polymers Inc 724 483-9300
  9 Guttman Blvd Charleroi (15022) *(G-3017)*

National Printing Company, Pittsburgh *Also called Huston National Printing Co (G-15106)*

National Publishing Company 215 676-1863
  11311 Roosevelt Blvd Philadelphia (19154) *(G-14055)*

National Refrigerants Inc (PA) 215 698-6620
  11401 Roosevelt Blvd Philadelphia (19154) *(G-14056)*

National Refrigeration Pdts, Langhorne *Also called National Rfrgn & AC Pdts Inc (G-9313)*

National Refrigeration Pdts, Bensalem *Also called National Rfrgn & AC Pdts Inc (G-1228)*

National Rfrgn & AC Pdts Inc 215 638-8909
  985 Wheeler Way Langhorne (19047) *(G-9313)*

National Rfrgn & AC Pdts Inc (PA) 215 244-1400
  539 Dunksferry Rd Bensalem (19020) *(G-1228)*

National Rubber Corporation 412 831-6100
  367 Morganza Rd Canonsburg (15317) *(G-2612)*

National Scientific Company......................................215 536-2577
　205 E Paletown Rd Quakertown (18951) *(G-16222)*
National Signs Inc...724 375-3083
　2003 Sheffield Rd Aliquippa (15001) *(G-87)*
National Ticket Company (PA)...............................570 672-2900
　5562 Snyderton Rd Paxinos (17860) *(G-13190)*
National Towelette Company.................................215 245-7300
　1726 Woodhaven Dr Bensalem (19020) *(G-1229)*
National Uniforms, Reading *Also called Roeberg Enterprises Inc (G-16503)*
National Woodwork Mfg, Bethlehem *Also called Merrigan Corporation (G-1568)*
National Woodworks LLC.......................................412 431-7071
　4075 Windgap Ave Bldg 20 Pittsburgh (15204) *(G-15322)*
Nationwide Recyclers Inc.....................................215 698-5100
　1 Crown Way Philadelphia (19154) *(G-14057)*
Native Flatbreads, Hershey *Also called Native Foods LLC (G-7622)*
Native Foods LLC...717 298-6157
　434 Maple Ave Hershey (17033) *(G-7622)*
Natrona Bottling Company, Natrona Heights *Also called Natrona Bottling Works Inc (G-11947)*
Natrona Bottling Works Inc..................................724 224-9224
　91 River Ave Natrona Heights (15065) *(G-11947)*
Natstone LLC..570 278-1611
　631 State Route 1039 Montrose (18801) *(G-11472)*
Natural Marketing Inst Inc.....................................215 513-7300
　272 Ruth Rd Fl 1 Harleysville (19438) *(G-7049)*
Natural Oil & Gas Corp..814 362-6890
　5 Fairway Dr Bradford (16701) *(G-1985)*
Natural Soil Products Company.............................570 695-2211
　200 E Main St Tremont (17981) *(G-18481)*
Natural Textiles Solutions LLC.............................484 660-4085
　3648 Gehman Rd Macungie (18062) *(G-10155)*
Naturally Yours Whl Foods, Fairview *Also called Ames Enterprises Inc (G-5813)*
Nature Flooring Industries Inc..............................610 280-9800
　40 Lloyd Ave Ste 306 Malvern (19355) *(G-10283)*
Nature Soy LLC..215 765-3289
　713 N 10th St Philadelphia (19123) *(G-14058)*
Nature's Wonderland, Philadelphia *Also called Herb Penn Co Ltd (G-13816)*
Natures Best Cbd PA LLC......................................724 568-4657
　700 Hancock Ave Vandergrift (15690) *(G-18734)*
Natures Blend Wood Pdts Inc...............................724 763-7057
　717 1st Ave Ford City (16226) *(G-6050)*
Natures Bounty Co..570 384-2270
　10 Simmons Dr Hazle Township (18202) *(G-7470)*
Natures Pillows Inc...215 633-9801
　2607 Nshminy Interplex Dr Feasterville Trevose (19053) *(G-5921)*
Natures Way Prwter Systems Inc...........................570 655-7755
　164 Commerce Rd Pittston (18640) *(G-15769)*
Natures Way Pure Water..800 407-7873
　900 Sathers Dr Pittston (18640) *(G-15770)*
Naughton Energy Corporation...............................570 646-0422
　1898 Route 940 Pocono Pines (18350) *(G-15882)*
Naura Akrion Inc (HQ)...610 391-9200
　6330 Hedgewood Dr Ste 150 Allentown (18106) *(G-325)*
Nautica of Lancaster...717 396-9414
　35 S Willowdale Dr # 105 Lancaster (17602) *(G-9143)*
Naval Company Inc..215 348-8982
　4747 Cold Spg Crmry Rd Doylestown (18902) *(G-4318)*
Naval Foundry Propeller Center, Philadelphia *Also called United States Dept of Navy (G-14423)*
Navarro Spring Company..610 259-3177
　550 Commerce Dr Lansdowne (19050) *(G-9439)*
Navistar Inc...717 767-3800
　105 Steam Boat Blvd Manchester (17345) *(G-10358)*
Navistar Inc...610 375-4230
　1200 Brdcstg Rd Ste 102 Reading (19610) *(G-16452)*
Navitek Group Inc..814 474-2312
　8305 Middle Rd Fairview (16415) *(G-5834)*
Navitor Inc...717 765-3121
　725 Clayton Ave Waynesboro (17268) *(G-19419)*
Nawalany-Franciotti LLC.......................................215 342-3005
　8013 Castor Ave Philadelphia (19152) *(G-14059)*
Naylor Candies Inc..717 266-2706
　289 Chestnut St Mount Wolf (17347) *(G-11748)*
Nazareth Industrial Corp.......................................610 759-9776
　595 E Lawn Rd Nazareth (18064) *(G-11983)*
Nazareth Key Youngs Press..................................610 759-5000
　127 E High St Frnt Nazareth (18064) *(G-11984)*
Nazareth Pallet Co Inc..610 262-9799
　800 Held Dr Northampton (18067) *(G-12856)*
NC Industries Inc (PA)..248 528-5200
　150 S 5th St Reynoldsville (15851) *(G-16658)*
NC Industries Antiq Auto Parts.............................570 888-6216
　301 S Thomas Ave Sayre (18840) *(G-17120)*
Ncbc, Philadelphia *Also called National Cthlic Bthics Ctr Inc (G-14054)*
Ncc Automated Systems Inc................................215 721-1900
　255 Schoolhouse Rd Ste 2 Souderton (18964) *(G-17756)*
Ncc Wholesome Foods Inc...................................724 652-3440
　809 Sampson St New Castle (16101) *(G-12124)*

NCM Barge Maintence...724 469-0083
　1231 Rostraver Rd Rostraver Township (15012) *(G-16828)*
Ncn Data Networks LLC..570 213-8300
　586 Main St Stroudsburg (18360) *(G-18133)*
Ncri Inc (HQ)...724 654-7711
　3909 Station Rd New Castle (16101) *(G-12125)*
Ncrx Optical Solutions Inc....................................724 745-1011
　106 Commerce Blvd Lawrence (15055) *(G-9538)*
Nds Holdings LP..610 408-0500
　3811 West Chester Pike Newtown Square (19073) *(G-12586)*
Ne, Bensalem *Also called Northstern Precision Pdts Corp (G-1232)*
Ne Fibers LLC..570 445-2086
　157 Passan Dr Bldg 2 2 Bldng Wilkes Barre (18702) *(G-19949)*
Ne Fibers LLC..610 366-8600
　7072 Snowdrift Rd Allentown (18106) *(G-326)*
Ne Foods Inc...814 725-4835
　1640 Freeport Rd North East (16428) *(G-12753)*
Neac Compressor Svcs USA Inc............................814 437-3711
　191 Howard St Ste 204 Franklin (16323) *(G-6150)*
Neapco Components LLC (HQ)..............................610 323-6000
　740 Queen St Pottstown (19464) *(G-16021)*
Near By Eggs, Gettysburg *Also called Hillandale Farms of Pa Inc (G-6299)*
Nearhoof Machine Inc...814 339-6621
　156 Nearhoof Ln Osceola Mills (16666) *(G-13056)*
Neat Company Inc..215 382-4283
　1500 Jf Kennedy Blvd # 700 Philadelphia (19102) *(G-14060)*
Neater Pet Brands, Malvern *Also called Towerstar Pets LLC (G-10334)*
Neatreceipts, Philadelphia *Also called Neat Company Inc (G-14060)*
Neatsfoot Oil Refineries Corp................................215 739-1291
　2925 E Ontario St Philadelphia (19134) *(G-14061)*
Neco Equipment Company.....................................215 721-2200
　458 E King Rd Ste 1 Malvern (19355) *(G-10284)*
Neco Pumping Systems, Malvern *Also called Neco Equipment Company (G-10284)*
Nedco, Irwin *Also called Davis Ne Company Inc (G-8156)*
Needle and Pin..412 207-9724
　3271 W Liberty Ave Pittsburgh (15216) *(G-15323)*
Neely By Vnb, King of Prussia *Also called Lavender Badge LLC (G-8638)*
Neenah Northeast LLC...215 536-4600
　45 N 4th St Quakertown (18951) *(G-16223)*
Neenah Northeast LLC...610 926-1996
　220 Corporate Dr Reading (19605) *(G-16453)*
Neff Specialties LLC..814 247-8887
　1505 Main St Hastings (16646) *(G-7262)*
Nefra Communication Center.................................717 509-1430
　3011 Columbia Ave Lancaster (17603) *(G-9144)*
Nefra Communications Center, Lancaster *Also called Nefra Communication Center (G-9144)*
Neh Inc (PA)..412 299-7200
　400 Rouser Rd 6airport Coraopolis (15108) *(G-3706)*
Neibauer Press, Warminster *Also called Louis Neibauer Co Inc (G-18913)*
Neidighs Inc..814 237-3985
　1121 W College Ave State College (16801) *(G-17996)*
Neighborhood Publications Inc.............................412 481-0266
　813 E Warrington Ave Pittsburgh (15210) *(G-15324)*
Neil M Davis..215 442-7430
　605 Louis Dr Ste 508b Warminster (18974) *(G-18928)*
Neilly, S W Air Notching, Bradford *Also called Scott Neilly (G-1991)*
Neillys Food LLC...717 428-6431
　75 Acco Dr Ste A-12 York (17402) *(G-20610)*
Nelipak Healthcare Packaging, Whitehall *Also called Computer Designs Inc (G-19867)*
Nelmark Electric Inc...724 290-0314
　335 Beacon Rd Renfrew (16053) *(G-16641)*
Nelson Bridge Inc...908 996-6646
　6103 Upper York Rd New Hope (18938) *(G-12309)*
Nelson Company..724 652-6681
　301 Mahoning Ave New Castle (16102) *(G-12126)*
Nelson Company Inc..717 593-0600
　113 Commerce Ave Greencastle (17225) *(G-6624)*
Nelson Steel Products Inc.....................................215 721-9449
　3051 Penn Ave Hatfield (19440) *(G-7372)*
Nelson Stud Welding Inc......................................610 873-0012
　260 Boot Rd Downingtown (19335) *(G-4244)*
Nelson Wire Rope Corporation..............................215 721-9449
　3051 Penn St Hatfield (19440) *(G-7373)*
Nelson Wrap Dispenser Inc...................................814 623-1317
　2406 Younts Rd Bedford (15522) *(G-1066)*
Nelson's Ice Cream, Plymouth Meeting *Also called Nelsons Creamery LLC (G-15859)*
Nelsons Arrows, Greensburg *Also called Dorothy M Nelson (G-6662)*
Nelsons Competition Engines...............................724 538-5282
　121 Pebble Creek Ln Zelienople (16063) *(G-20812)*
Nelsons Creamery LLC...610 948-3000
　600 W Germantown Pike Plymouth Meeting (19462) *(G-15859)*
Nem-Pak Llc...215 785-6430
　1117 Cedar Ave Croydon (19021) *(G-3921)*
Nema Food Co, McKeesport *Also called Rendulic Packing Company (G-10679)*
Nema Usa Inc (PA)...412 678-9541
　2535 Washington Rd # 1121 Pittsburgh (15241) *(G-15325)*
Nemco..215 355-2100
　900 Pennsylvania Blvd Feasterville Trevose (19053) *(G-5922)*

Neo Lights Holdings Inc (PA) 215 831-7700
700 Ramona Ave Philadelphia (19120) ***(G-14062)***
Neo-Solutions Inc 724 728-7360
1340 Brighton Rd Beaver (15009) ***(G-988)***
Neon Doctor LLC 412 885-7075
4658 Cook Ave Pittsburgh (15236) ***(G-15326)***
Neon Moon 814 332-0302
891 Market St Meadville (16335) ***(G-10767)***
Neon Trading 610 530-2988
1324 Sherman St Rear Allentown (18109) ***(G-327)***
Neopost USA Inc 717 939-2700
1201 Fulling Mill Rd Middletown (17057) ***(G-11066)***
Neopost USA Inc 717 939-2700
3100 Horizon Dr Ste 100 King of Prussia (19406) ***(G-8654)***
Neosystemsusa Inc 717 586-5040
19 W Railroad Ave Shrewsbury (17361) ***(G-17586)***
Nepa Carton & Carrier Co., Moosic *Also called Northeastern PA Carton Co Inc* ***(G-11510)***
Neptune Pump Manufacturing Co 484 901-4100
1265 Ridge Rd Pottstown (19465) ***(G-15955)***
Neptune-Benson Inc (HQ) 724 772-0044
210 6th Ave Ste 3300 Pittsburgh (15222) ***(G-15327)***
Nerites, Exton *Also called DSM Biomedical Inc* ***(G-5669)***
Nesglo Products Division, Warren *Also called Interlectric Corporation* ***(G-19033)***
Neshaminy Valley Millwork 215 604-0251
773 American Dr Bensalem (19020) ***(G-1230)***
Nest 215 545-6378
1301 Locust St Philadelphia (19107) ***(G-14063)***
Nestle Ocean Spray Alliance, Breinigsville *Also called Ocean Spray Cranberries Inc* ***(G-2022)***
Nestle Pizza Company Inc 717 737-7268
1177 Shoreham Rd Camp Hill (17011) ***(G-2506)***
Nestle Purina Factory, Mechanicsburg *Also called Nestle Purina Petcare Company* ***(G-10872)***
Nestle Purina Petcare Company 717 795-5454
6509 Brandy Ln Mechanicsburg (17050) ***(G-10872)***
Nestle Purina Petcare Company 610 398-4667
2050 Pope Rd Allentown (18104) ***(G-328)***
Nestle Purina Petcare Company 610 395-3301
2050 Pope Rd Allentown (18104) ***(G-329)***
Nestle Usa Inc 610 391-7900
555 Nestle Way Breinigsville (18031) ***(G-2020)***
Nestle Usa Inc 818 549-6000
3000 Horizon Dr King of Prussia (19406) ***(G-8655)***
Nestle Waters 484 221-0876
305 Nestle Way Breinigsville (18031) ***(G-2021)***
Nestor Systems International 610 767-5000
4347 2nd St Treichlers (18086) ***(G-18477)***
Nestor's Iron Works, Tamaqua *Also called Nestors Welding Co* ***(G-18221)***
Nestors Welding Co 570 668-3401
431 E Broad St Tamaqua (18252) ***(G-18221)***
Net Reach Technologies LLC 215 283-2300
124 S Maple Way Ste 210 Ambler (19002) ***(G-593)***
Net Synergy, Woodlyn *Also called Ace Sports Inc* ***(G-20216)***
Netbeez Inc 412 465-0638
5124b Penn Ave Pittsburgh (15224) ***(G-15328)***
Netco, State College *Also called Nittany Extraction Tech LLC* ***(G-17999)***
Netgear Inc 724 941-5748
107 Scenery Cir Canonsburg (15317) ***(G-2613)***
Nethercraft Incorporated 248 224-1963
580 Mayer St Bridgeville (15017) ***(G-2081)***
Netmercatus LLC 646 822-7900
1784 Mars Hill Rd Sutersville (15083) ***(G-18184)***
Netreach, Ambler *Also called Net Reach Technologies LLC* ***(G-593)***
Netshape Technologies LLC 814 371-0184
409 3rd St Falls Creek (15840) ***(G-5855)***
Network Products & Services 724 229-0332
41 Stone Marker Dr Washington (15301) ***(G-19210)***
Netzsch Pumps North Amer LLC (HQ) 610 363-8010
119 Pickering Way Exton (19341) ***(G-5714)***
Neu, Philadelphia *Also called Glass U LLC* ***(G-13765)***
Neu Dynamics Corp 215 355-2460
110 Steam Whistle Dr Warminster (18974) ***(G-18929)***
Neuro Kinetics Inc 412 963-6649
128 Gamma Dr Pittsburgh (15238) ***(G-15329)***
Neurodx Development LLC 609 865-4426
115 E Ferry Rd Yardley (19067) ***(G-20328)***
Neuroflow Inc 347 881-6306
1635 Market St Ste 1600 Philadelphia (19103) ***(G-14064)***
Neurohabilitation Corporation 215 809-2018
642 Newtown Yardley Rd # 100 Newtown (18940) ***(G-12527)***
Neurointerventions, Pittsburgh *Also called Neurontrvntnal Thrapeutics Inc* ***(G-15330)***
Neurokine Therapeutics LLC 609 937-0409
3711 Market St Fl 8 Philadelphia (19104) ***(G-14065)***
Neurologix Technologies Inc 512 914-7941
297 Shepherd Rd Cherry Tree (15724) ***(G-3033)***
Neuronetics Inc 610 640-4202
3222 Phoenixville Pike # 300 Malvern (19355) ***(G-10285)***
Neurontrvntnal Thrapeutics Inc 412 726-3111
2403 Sidney St Ste 200 Pittsburgh (15203) ***(G-15330)***
Neuropedic LLC 570 501-7713
115 Rotary Dr Ste 1 West Hazleton (18202) ***(G-19714)***
Neuxpower Inc 267 238-3833
1800 Jfk Blvd Ste 300 Philadelphia (19103) ***(G-14066)***
Nevco Service Co LLC 717 626-1479
102 Chestnut St Lititz (17543) ***(G-10025)***
Neville Galvanizing Inc 412 771-9799
3005 Grand Ave Pittsburgh (15225) ***(G-15331)***
Neville Grating LLC 412 771-6973
3001 Grand Ave Pittsburgh (15225) ***(G-15332)***
Neville Island RR Holdings Inc 724 981-4100
American Way Sharon (16146) ***(G-17439)***
New Age Examiner, Tunkhannock *Also called Wyoming County Press Inc* ***(G-18553)***
New Alexandria Tractor Supply, New Alexandria *Also called Rt 66 Tractor Supply* ***(G-12020)***
New Bern Pbg Pepsi 570 320-3324
1320 Dewey Ave Williamsport (17701) ***(G-20045)***
New Berry Inc 724 452-8040
2408 Evans City Rd Harmony (16037) ***(G-7074)***
New Bethlehem Burial Service (PA) 814 275-3333
171 Theas Farms Rd New Bethlehem (16242) ***(G-12028)***
New Busch Co Inc 724 940-2326
10431 Perry Hwy Ste 210 Wexford (15090) ***(G-19815)***
New Castle Battery Mfg Co 724 658-5501
3601 Wilmington Rd New Castle (16105) ***(G-12127)***
New Castle Company Inc 724 658-4516
3812 Wilmington Rd New Castle (16105) ***(G-12128)***
New Castle Industries Inc 724 656-5600
925 Industrial St New Castle (16102) ***(G-12129)***
New Castle News, New Castle *Also called Newspaper Holding Inc* ***(G-12131)***
New Castle Refactories Co In 724 654-7711
606 Mccleary Ave New Castle (16101) ***(G-12130)***
New Centervill, Rockwood *Also called Svonavec Inc* ***(G-16793)***
New Centuries LLC 724 347-3030
1540 E State St Hermitage (16148) ***(G-7593)***
New Century Energy Inc 724 693-9266
1851 North Rd Oakdale (15071) ***(G-12908)***
New Concept Manufacturing LLC 717 741-0840
320 Busser Rd Emigsville (17318) ***(G-4994)***
New Concept Technology Inc 717 741-0840
320 Busser Rd Emigsville (17318) ***(G-4995)***
New Enterprise Stone Lime Inc (PA) 814 224-6883
3912 Brumbaugh Rd New Enterprise (16664) ***(G-12194)***
New Enterprise Stone Lime Inc 610 374-5131
80 Willow St Kutztown (19530) ***(G-8851)***
New Enterprise Stone Lime Inc 717 349-2412
18746 Dry Run Rd W Dry Run (17220) ***(G-4384)***
New Enterprise Stone Lime Inc 814 224-2121
301 Plum Creek Rd Roaring Spring (16673) ***(G-16766)***
New Enterprise Stone Lime Inc 814 652-5121
526 Ashcom Rd Everett (15537) ***(G-5576)***
New Enterprise Stone Lime Inc 814 472-4717
235 Rubisch Rd Ebensburg (15931) ***(G-4790)***
New Enterprise Stone Lime Inc 814 443-6494
1100 S Edgewood Ave Somerset (15501) ***(G-17698)***
New Enterprise Stone Lime Inc 610 683-3302
3580 Division Hwy East Earl (17519) ***(G-4551)***
New Enterprise Stone Lime Inc 610 678-1913
1119 Snyder Rd Reading (19609) ***(G-16454)***
New Enterprise Stone Lime Inc 610 374-5131
167 New Enterprise Dr Leesport (19533) ***(G-9668)***
New Enterprise Stone Lime Inc 814 342-7096
1556 Clearfield St West Decatur (16878) ***(G-19689)***
New Enterprise Stone Lime Inc 570 823-0531
220 S River St Ste 1 Plains (18705) ***(G-15787)***
New Enterprise Stone Lime Inc 814 684-4905
1 Mile S Of Tyrone Rt 453 Tyrone (16686) ***(G-18587)***
New Enterprise Stone Lime Inc 814 796-1413
14341 Route 19 Ste 2 Cambridge Springs (16403) ***(G-2484)***
New Enterprise Stone Lime Inc 814 754-4921
417 Sandplant Rd Cairnbrook (15924) ***(G-2463)***
New Enterprise Stone Lime Inc 610 374-5131
5050 Crackersport Rd Allentown (18104) ***(G-330)***
New Enterprise Stone Lime Inc 717 442-4148
520 Lime Quarry Rd Gap (17527) ***(G-6254)***
New Enterprise Stone Lime Inc 610 678-1913
Rte 73 Rr 61 Leesport (19533) ***(G-9669)***
New Frontier Industries Inc (HQ) 814 337-4234
18649 Brake Shoe Rd Meadville (16335) ***(G-10768)***
New Gear Brands LLC 407 674-6850
214 W Harford St Unit 2 Milford (18337) ***(G-11163)***
New Germany Wood Products Inc 814 495-5923
1444 New Germany Rd Summerhill (15958) ***(G-18154)***
New Growth Resources Inc 814 837-2206
51 Gregory Dr Kane (16735) ***(G-8473)***
New Harrisburg Truck Body Co 717 766-7651
408 Sheely Ln Mechanicsburg (17050) ***(G-10873)***
New Hegedus Aluminum Co Inc 814 676-5635
312 State Route 428 Oil City (16301) ***(G-12953)***

ALPHABETIC

New Heights LLC..717 768-0070
  49 Eagle Dr Leola (17540) *(G-9795)*

New Holland Concrete, Denver *Also called Martin Limestone Inc (G-4082)*

New Holland Concrete, New Holland *Also called Martin Limestone Inc (G-12259)*

New Holland Fence LLC..717 355-2204
  917 Walnut St New Holland (17557) *(G-12265)*

New Holland North America....................................717 354-4514
  300 Diller Ave New Holland (17557) *(G-12266)*

New Holland North America (PA).............................717 355-1121
  300 Diller Ave New Holland (17557) *(G-12267)*

New Holland North America....................................717 355-1121
  300 Diller Ave New Holland (17557) *(G-12268)*

New Home Window Shade Co Inc...........................570 346-2047
  106 Greenbrier Dr Clarks Green (18411) *(G-3189)*

New Hope Crushed Stone Lime Co.........................215 862-5295
  6970 Phillips Mill Rd New Hope (18938) *(G-12310)*

New Hope Dealer Services, Thornton *Also called Savemypixcom Inc (G-18355)*

New Hope Industries LLC......................................570 994-6391
  206 Welford Ct Bushkill (18324) *(G-2367)*

New Hudson Facades LLC (PA)..............................610 494-8100
  815 Columbia Ave Upper Chichester (19061) *(G-18668)*

New Jersey Shell Casting Corp..............................717 426-1835
  21 S Decatur St Marietta (17547) *(G-10465)*

New Kensington Green Sheet, Pittsburgh *Also called Hammond Press Inc (G-15078)*

New Liberty Distillery..800 996-0595
  1431 N Cadwallader St Philadelphia (19122) *(G-14067)*

New Look Kitchens, Lock Haven *Also called Wagner Masters Custom Wdwkg (G-10093)*

New Look Uniform & Embroidery.............................814 944-5515
  800 S 20th St Altoona (16602) *(G-530)*

New Lycoming Bakery Inc.....................................570 326-9426
  220 Curtin St Williamsport (17702) *(G-20046)*

New Mainstream Press Inc....................................610 617-8800
  167 Old Belmont Ave 200 Bala Cynwyd (19004) *(G-887)*

New Ngc Inc...570 538-2531
  2586 Old Route 15 New Columbia (17856) *(G-12174)*

New Ngc Inc...724 643-3440
  168 Shippingport Hill Rd Shippingport (15077) *(G-17567)*

New Oxford Tool & Die Inc....................................717 624-8441
  186 Poplar Rd New Oxford (17350) *(G-12417)*

New Pittsburgh Courier Pubg Co............................412 481-8302
  315 E Carson St Pittsburgh (15219) *(G-15333)*

New Precision Technology Inc................................412 596-5948
  7800 Susquehanna St Pittsburgh (15208) *(G-15334)*

New Promise Farms, Lenhartsville *Also called Dodie Sable (G-9758)*

New Republic..814 634-8321
  688 Creek Rd Meyersdale (15552) *(G-11017)*

New Republic Newspaper, Meyersdale *Also called Victorian Publishing Co Inc (G-11020)*

New Standard Corporation (PA).............................717 757-9450
  74 Commerce Way York (17406) *(G-20611)*

New Standard Corporation....................................717 757-9450
  170 New Haven St Mount Joy (17552) *(G-11667)*

New Standard Corporation....................................717 764-2409
  3310 Connelly Rd Emigsville (17318) *(G-4996)*

New Stanton Machining Tooling, Irwin *Also called Corestar International Corp (G-8150)*

New Stanton Machining Tooling, Irwin *Also called Corestar International Corp (G-8151)*

New Stars LLC..215 962-4239
  1603 N 5th St Philadelphia (19122) *(G-14068)*

New Tech Dental Training Ctr, Lansdale *Also called Jasinski Dental Lab Inc (G-9379)*

New Thermo-Serv Ltd...215 646-7667
  241 N Main St Ambler (19002) *(G-594)*

New View Gifts & ACC Ltd (PA).............................610 627-0190
  311 E Baltimore Ave # 300 Media (19063) *(G-10940)*

New Virtus Pharmaceuticals, Langhorne *Also called Virtus Pharmaceuticals LLC (G-9331)*

New Vision Lens Lab LLC......................................610 351-7376
  1918 W Tilghman St Allentown (18104) *(G-331)*

New Visions Magazine (PA)...................................215 627-0102
  530 S 2nd St Ste 106 Philadelphia (19147) *(G-14069)*

New Wave Custom Wdwkg Inc................................570 251-8218
  214 6th St Honesdale (18431) *(G-7718)*

New Way Air Bearings, Aston *Also called New Way Machine Components Inc (G-781)*

New Way Homes...570 967-2187
  425 Gontarski Rd Hallstead (18822) *(G-6834)*

New Way Machine Components Inc.........................610 494-6700
  50 Mcdonald Blvd Aston (19014) *(G-781)*

New Way Packaging Machinery..............................717 637-2133
  210 N Blettner Ave Ste 1 Hanover (17331) *(G-6925)*

New Werner Holding Co Inc (HQ)...........................724 588-2000
  93 Werner Rd Greenville (16125) *(G-6758)*

New York Bagelry...610 678-6420
  2720 Penn Ave Reading (19609) *(G-16455)*

New York Wire, Hanover *Also called Wire Company Holdings Inc (G-6977)*

New York Wire Company.......................................717 637-3795
  500 E Middle St Hanover (17331) *(G-6926)*

New York Wire Company.......................................717 266-5626
  152 N M St Mount Wolf (17347) *(G-11749)*

Newage Industries Inc...215 526-2151
  145 James Way Southampton (18966) *(G-17827)*

Newage Testing Instruments (HQ)..........................215 355-6900
  205 Keith Valley Rd Horsham (19044) *(G-7835)*

Newburg Woodcrafts (PA)....................................717 530-8823
  8915 Rowe Run Rd Shippensburg (17257) *(G-17539)*

Newco Industries...717 566-9560
  25 S Landis St Hummelstown (17036) *(G-7919)*

Newcrete Products, Roaring Spring *Also called New Enterprise Stone Lime Inc (G-16766)*

Newell Brands Inc...814 278-6771
  2568 Park Center Blvd State College (16801) *(G-17997)*

Newly Weds Foods Inc...610 758-9100
  23 S Commerce Way Bethlehem (18017) *(G-1584)*

Newman & Company Inc.......................................215 333-8700
  6101 Tacony St Philadelphia (19135) *(G-14070)*

Newman Wine & Spirits Gp LLC.............................610 476-3964
  1079 Baron Dr Bryn Mawr (19010) *(G-2331)*

Newmetro Design LLC...814 696-2550
  141 Nac Dr Duncansville (16635) *(G-4457)*

Newpark Mats Intgrted Svcs LLC...........................570 323-4970
  573 E 3rd St Williamsport (17701) *(G-20047)*

Newport Aggregate Inc...570 736-6612
  31 N Market St Nanticoke (18634) *(G-11900)*

Newport Fabricators Inc.......................................215 234-4400
  432 Walnut St Green Lane (18054) *(G-6591)*

News Chronicle Co Inc (PA)...................................717 532-4101
  1011 Ritner Hwy Shippensburg (17257) *(G-17540)*

News Eagle (PA)...570 226-4547
  220 8th St Honesdale (18431) *(G-7719)*

News Eagle...570 296-4547
  301 E Harford St Milford (18337) *(G-11164)*

News Item Cin 5..570 644-0891
  707 N Rock St Shamokin (17872) *(G-17426)*

News Letters Ink, Lancaster *Also called Two Letters Ink (G-9225)*

News of Delaware County, Ardmore *Also called Acme Newspapers Inc (G-699)*

News of Delaware County......................................610 583-4432
  639 S Chester Rd Swarthmore (19081) *(G-18185)*

Newshams Woodshop Inc.....................................610 622-5800
  Merion Ave Bldg 2 Clifton Heights (19018) *(G-3256)*

Newsletters Ink Corp..717 393-1000
  700 Eden Rd Ste 2 Lancaster (17601) *(G-9145)*

Newsline Publishing Inc..610 337-1050
  661 Moore Rd Ste 100 King of Prussia (19406) *(G-8656)*

Newspaper Guild of Philadelphi.............................215 928-0118
  1329 Buttonwood St Philadelphia (19123) *(G-14071)*

Newspaper Holding Inc (HQ).................................814 532-5102
  425 Locust St Johnstown (15901) *(G-8412)*

Newspaper Holding Inc...724 981-6100
  52 S Dock St Sharon (16146) *(G-17440)*

Newspaper Holding Inc...814 724-6370
  947 Federal Ct Ste 49 Meadville (16335) *(G-10769)*

Newspaper Holding Inc...724 654-6651
  27 N Mercer St New Castle (16101) *(G-12131)*

Newspaper Networks Inc......................................610 853-2121
  8600 W Chester Pike # 206 Upper Darby (19082) *(G-18691)*

Newstech PA LP..315 955-6710
  6 Horwith Dr Northampton (18067) *(G-12857)*

Newswanger Woods Specialties.............................717 355-9274
  313 Gristmill Rd New Holland (17557) *(G-12269)*

Newterra Inc...610 631-7700
  2650 Eisenhower Ave 100a Norristown (19403) *(G-12692)*

Newtown Business Forms Corp..............................215 364-3898
  1908 County Line Rd Huntingdon Valley (19006) *(G-8017)*

Newtown Gazette..215 702-3405
  341 Rumpf Ave Langhorne (19047) *(G-9314)*

Newtown Mfg & Bldg Sup Corp (PA).......................570 825-3675
  247 Old River Rd Wilkes Barre (18702) *(G-19950)*

Newtown Printing Corp...215 968-6876
  358 S Lincoln Ave Newtown (18940) *(G-12528)*

Newtown-Slocomb Mfg Inc (PA).............................570 825-3675
  767 Sans Souci Pkwy Hanover Township (18706) *(G-7000)*

Newtown-Slocomb Mfg Inc....................................570 825-3675
  767 Sans Souci Pkwy Hanover Township (18706) *(G-7001)*

Newville Print Shop...717 776-7673
  35 S High St Newville (17241) *(G-12608)*

Nexans Aerospace USA LLC.................................252 236-4311
  132 White Oak Rd New Holland (17557) *(G-12270)*

Nexans USA Inc..717 354-6200
  132 White Oak Rd New Holland (17557) *(G-12271)*

Nexarc Inc..570 458-6990
  76 Guys Ln Bloomsburg (17815) *(G-1791)*

Nexgen Ats..717 779-9580
  115 Timber Dr Mountville (17554) *(G-11800)*

Nexgen Industrial Contractors, Rices Landing *Also called Nexgen Industrial Services Inc (G-16670)*

Nexgen Industrial Services Inc..............................724 592-5133
  125 Long St Rices Landing (15357) *(G-16670)*

Next Generation Filtration.....................................412 548-1659
  3000 Mcknight East Dr Pittsburgh (15237) *(G-15335)*

Next Generation Software.....................................215 361-2754
  30 E Main St Ste 2 Lansdale (19446) *(G-9392)*

Next Rev Distribution Inc....................................717 576-9050
337 W Chocolate Ave Hershey (17033) *(G-7623)*

Nextech, Turtle Creek Also called *Techs Industries Inc* *(G-18570)*

Nexus Inc..412 391-2444
810 Penn Ave Ste 700 Pittsburgh (15222) *(G-15336)*

NF&m, Monaca Also called *Nak International Corp* *(G-11292)*

Ngc Industries, Shippingport Also called *New Ngc Inc* *(G-17567)*

Nhra Northeast Division, Lancaster Also called *National Hot Rod Association* *(G-9142)*

Niagara Bottling LLC.......................................610 562-2176
316 Front St Hamburg (19526) *(G-6847)*

Niagara Cutter, Reynoldsville Also called *NC Industries Inc* *(G-16658)*

Niagara Cutter PA Inc.....................................814 653-8211
150 S 5th St Reynoldsville (15851) *(G-16659)*

Niagara Holdings Inc.......................................610 651-4200
300 Lindenwood Dr Malvern (19355) *(G-10286)*

Niagara Machine Inc (PA)................................814 455-8838
325 W Front St Erie (16507) *(G-5402)*

Niagara Manufacturing Co...............................814 838-4511
2725 W 17th St Erie (16505) *(G-5403)*

Niagara Piston Ring Works Inc.........................716 782-2307
18455 Sciota St Corry (16407) *(G-3770)*

Niagara Plastics...814 464-8169
7090 Edinboro Rd Erie (16509) *(G-5404)*

Nian-Crae Inc...732 545-5881
2200 Benjamin Franklin Pk Philadelphia (19130) *(G-14072)*

Nice Threads International................................610 259-0788
4 Rockbourne Rd Ste 501 Clifton Heights (19018) *(G-3257)*

Nicewonger Awning Co....................................724 837-5920
512 Euclid Ave Greensburg (15601) *(G-6692)*

Niche Electronics Tech Inc..............................717 532-6620
201 Dykeman Rd Shippensburg (17257) *(G-17541)*

Nicholas Caputo...570 454-8280
190 S Pine St Hazleton (18201) *(G-7513)*

Nicholas Custom Interiors, Uniontown Also called *Nicholas Meyokovich* *(G-18638)*

Nicholas Meat LLC..570 725-3511
508 E Valley Rd Loganton (17747) *(G-10096)*

Nicholas Meat Packing Co...............................570 725-3511
508 E Valley Rd Loganton (17747) *(G-10097)*

Nicholas Meyokovich......................................724 439-0955
62 Easy St Uniontown (15401) *(G-18638)*

Nicholas Shea Co Inc......................................610 296-9036
3353 Perkiomen Ave Reading (19606) *(G-16456)*

Nicholas Smith Trains, Broomall Also called *Christopher Gans* *(G-2282)*

Nicholas Wohlfarth...412 373-6811
1370 Frey Rd Pittsburgh (15235) *(G-15337)*

Nichols Electronics Inc....................................724 668-2526
187 Kennan Dr Greensburg (15601) *(G-6693)*

Nichols Welding Service Inc.............................412 362-8855
1309 Washington Blvd Pittsburgh (15206) *(G-15338)*

Nichols4nickels..215 317-6717
6038 Master St Philadelphia (19151) *(G-14073)*

Nick Charles Kravitch (PA)..............................412 341-7265
3706 Rebecca St Pittsburgh (15234) *(G-15339)*

Nick Charles Kravitch.....................................412 882-6262
50 Mcneilly Rd Pittsburgh (15226) *(G-15340)*

Nick Mulone & Son...724 274-3221
109 S Highland Ave Cheswick (15024) *(G-3112)*

Nick-Of-Time Textiles Ltd................................610 395-4641
1701 Union Blvd Ste 301 Allentown (18109) *(G-332)*

Nickel Cobalt Battery LLC...............................412 567-6828
2364 Eldridge St Pittsburgh (15217) *(G-15341)*

Nickles Industries..724 422-7211
1425 Olson Rd Marion Center (15759) *(G-10475)*

Nicole Lynn Inc..717 292-6130
6451 Clearview Rd Dover (17315) *(G-4197)*

Nicole M Reasner...814 259-3827
22389 Decorum Rd Neelyton (17239) *(G-11997)*

Nicomatic LP...215 444-9580
450 Progress Dr Horsham (19044) *(G-7836)*

Nicomatic North America, Horsham Also called *Nicomatic LP* *(G-7836)*

Night Vision Devices Inc.................................610 395-9743
542 Kemmerer Ln Allentown (18104) *(G-333)*

Nightlife & Clothing Co...................................718 415-6391
7415 Brockton Rd Unit 1 Philadelphia (19151) *(G-14074)*

Nikal Imaging Products In...............................215 887-1319
1108 Arboretum Rd Wyncote (19095) *(G-20265)*

Nike Inc..412 922-3660
3000 Gsk Dr Ste 300 Coraopolis (15108) *(G-3707)*

Nikon Precision Inc...610 439-6203
1544 Hamilton St Ste 205 Allentown (18102) *(G-334)*

Nilfisk Inc..800 645-3475
740 Hemlock Rd Ste 100 Morgantown (19543) *(G-11529)*

Nilfisk Industrial Vacuums, Morgantown Also called *Nilfisk Inc* *(G-11529)*

Nine 2 Five Ceo...919 729-2536
806 Wynnewood Rd Philadelphia (19151) *(G-14075)*

Nine Energy Service, Ulster Also called *CDK Perforating LLC* *(G-18598)*

Nippon Panel Inc..570 326-4258
124 Reynolds St Williamsport (17702) *(G-20048)*

Niramaya Inc...267 799-2120
212 Moore Rd Wallingford (19086) *(G-18785)*

Nissin Foods USA Company Inc........................717 291-5901
2901 Hempland Rd Lancaster (17601) *(G-9146)*

Nissley Vineyards, Bainbridge Also called *A & R Nissley Inc* *(G-871)*

Nissley Vineyards Wine Shop, Harrisburg Also called *A & R Nissley Inc* *(G-7078)*

Nite Lite Sign Co..570 649-5825
1359 Schuyler Rd Turbotville (17772) *(G-18556)*

Nitebrite Ltd..215 493-9361
1126 Taylorsville Rd Washington Crossing (18977) *(G-19257)*

Nitrogen...440 208-7474
800 Township Line Rd Yardley (19067) *(G-20329)*

Nitrogen (was Dorland)..................................215 928-2727
1 S Broad St Fl 11 Philadelphia (19107) *(G-14076)*

Nittany Coatings Inc.......................................724 588-1898
309 3rd St Greenville (16125) *(G-6759)*

Nittany EMB & Digitizing.................................814 359-0905
153 S Allen St State College (16801) *(G-17998)*

Nittany Extraction Tech LLC............................814 571-4776
149 W Fairmount Ave State College (16801) *(G-17999)*

Nittany Paper Mills Inc....................................888 288-7907
6395 State Route 103 N Lewistown (17044) *(G-9940)*

Nittany Printing and Pubg Co..........................814 238-5000
3400 E College Ave State College (16801) *(G-18000)*

Nittany Valley Offset, State College Also called *21st Century Media Newsppr LLC* *(G-17939)*

Nitterhouse Concrete Pdts Inc.........................717 207-7837
2655 Molly Pitcher Hwy Chambersburg (17202) *(G-2962)*

Nitterhouse Masonry Pdts LLC.........................717 268-4137
859 Cleveland Ave Chambersburg (17201) *(G-2963)*

Nix Optical Co Inc..724 483-6527
216 Lincoln Avenue Ext # 1 Charleroi (15022) *(G-3018)*

Nk Graphics Inc...717 838-8324
18 W Main St Palmyra (17078) *(G-13127)*

Nlmk Pennsylvania LLC...................................724 983-6464
15 Roemer Blvd Farrell (16121) *(G-5869)*

NMB Signs Inc...412 344-5700
2831 Banksville Rd Pittsburgh (15216) *(G-15342)*

Nmg, Exton Also called *National Mail Graphics Corp* *(G-5713)*

Nnbc, Lancaster Also called *Maugus Manufacturing Inc* *(G-9126)*

No Fear Inc...484 527-8000
99 Great Valley Pkwy Malvern (19355) *(G-10287)*

No Pallett, Leesport Also called *Noll Pallet Inc* *(G-9671)*

Noah F Boyle Cabinets...................................717 944-1007
3043 Steinruck Rd Elizabethtown (17022) *(G-4880)*

Noah Shirk Sawmill..717 354-0192
220 Covered Bridge Rd Ephrata (17522) *(G-5132)*

Nobility Alpacas..484 332-1499
99 Heffner Rd Wernersville (19565) *(G-19486)*

Noble Biomaterials Inc (PA)............................570 955-1800
300 Palm St Scranton (18505) *(G-17265)*

Noble Metals, West Chester Also called *Matthey Johnson Inc* *(G-19598)*

Noble Road Woodworks LLC............................610 593-5122
732 Noble Rd Christiana (17509) *(G-3143)*

Noblemd, Bryn Mawr Also called *Noblemedical LLC* *(G-2332)*

Noblemedical LLC..917 750-9605
364 Thornbrook Ave Bryn Mawr (19010) *(G-2332)*

Noblesoft Solutions Inc...................................713 480-7510
405 Executive Dr Langhorne (19047) *(G-9315)*

Noco Distribution LLC.....................................866 946-3927
20 Gillis Ave Ridgway (15853) *(G-16719)*

Nocopi Technologies Inc (PA)..........................610 834-9600
480 Shoemaker Rd Ste 104 King of Prussia (19406) *(G-8657)*

Noel Interactive Group LLC.............................732 991-1484
1789 Rhine Dr Easton (18045) *(G-4732)*

Noftz Sheet Metal Inc.....................................412 471-1983
2737 Penn Ave Pittsburgh (15222) *(G-15343)*

Noga Logging..724 224-6369
4825 Garvers Ferry Rd New Kensington (15068) *(G-12363)*

Noise Solutions (usa) Inc................................724 308-6901
420 Vine Ave Sharon (16146) *(G-17441)*

Nolatron Inc..717 564-3398
1259 2nd St Harrisburg (17113) *(G-7184)*

Noll Pallet & Lumber Co (PA)..........................610 926-3502
61 Cider Mill Run Leesport (19533) *(G-9670)*

Noll Pallet Inc..610 926-2500
61 Cider Mill Run Leesport (19533) *(G-9671)*

Nolt Bros Inc...717 733-8761
121 Valley View Dr Ephrata (17522) *(G-5133)*

Nolt Cabinet Shop, East Earl Also called *Paul H Nolt Woodworking* *(G-4552)*

Nolt Services LLC...717 738-1066
728 Rettew Mill Rd Lititz (17543) *(G-10026)*

Nolt's Services, Lititz Also called *Nolt Services LLC* *(G-10026)*

Noltpak LLC..717 725-9862
319 Conowingo Rd Quarryville (17566) *(G-16274)*

Non Mtallic Machining Assembly......................814 453-6787
1525 E Lake Rd Ste C Erie (16511) *(G-5405)*

Non-Sport Update, Harrisburg Also called *Roxanne Toser Non-Sport Entps* *(G-7209)*

Nonlethal Technologies Inc..............................724 479-5100
9419 Route 286 Hwy W Homer City (15748) *(G-7679)*

Noodle 88 ....215 721-0888
664 E Broad St Souderton (18964) *(G-17757)*

Noodle King 717 299-2799
216 N Duke St Lancaster (17602) *(G-9147)*

Noor Furniture Inc 215 533-0703
6304 Roosevelt Blvd Philadelphia (19149) *(G-14077)*

Norcom Systems Inc 610 592-0167
1055 W Germantown Pike # 4 Norristown (19403) *(G-12693)*

Norcorp Inc 814 445-2523
610 N Center Ave Somerset (15501) *(G-17699)*

Nordberg John 814 371-2217
1754 Old Grade Rd Falls Creek (15840) *(G-5856)*

Nordic Ice, Hatfield *Also called Temperatsure LLC (G-7401)*

Nordic Tool & Die Co 570 889-5650
76 Main Blvd Ringtown (17967) *(G-16755)*

Nordson Corporation 610 829-4240
2 Danforth Frive Easton (18045) *(G-4733)*

Norfab, Norristown *Also called Amatex Corporation (G-12632)*

Norfab Corporation 610 275-7270
1310 Stanbridge St Norristown (19401) *(G-12694)*

Norfolk Southern Corporation 814 949-1551
200 N 4th Ave Altoona (16601) *(G-531)*

Norghern Liberty Press, Philadelphia *Also called Old City Publishing (G-14093)*

Nori Medical Group (PA) 717 532-3040
167 Walnut Bottom Rd Shippensburg (17257) *(G-17542)*

Norma Pennsylvania Inc 724 639-3571
3582 Tunnelton Rd Saltsburg (15681) *(G-17052)*

Norman Hoover Welding LLC 717 445-5333
750 Gristmill Rd Ephrata (17522) *(G-5134)*

Norman Kivitz Co Inc 215 922-3038
731 Sansom St Fl 1 Philadelphia (19106) *(G-14078)*

Normandy Industries Inc (PA) 412 826-1825
1150 Freeport Rd Pittsburgh (15238) *(G-15344)*

Normandy Products, Pittsburgh *Also called Normandy Industries Inc (G-15344)*

Normandy Products Company (HQ) 412 826-1825
1150 Freeport Rd Pittsburgh (15238) *(G-15345)*

Norplas Industries Inc 724 705-7483
292 E Maiden St Washington (15301) *(G-19211)*

Norquay Technology Inc 610 874-4330
800 W Front St Chester (19013) *(G-3058)*

Norse Paddle Co 814 422-8844
121 Penn Field Ln Spring Mills (16875) *(G-17890)*

Norshel Industries Inc 215 788-2200
2933 River Rd Croydon (19021) *(G-3922)*

Norstone Incorporated 484 684-6986
315 E 4th St Bridgeport (19405) *(G-2041)*

Nortech Energy Solutions LLC 570 323-3060
75 Palmer Industrial Rd Williamsport (17701) *(G-20049)*

Nortek Global Hvac LLC 814 938-1408
400 N Walnut St Punxsutawney (15767) *(G-16151)*

North Amer Hoganas High Alloys 814 361-6800
101 Bridge St Johnstown (15902) *(G-8413)*

North American Arms Inc (PA) 610 940-1668
600 W Germantown Pike # 4 Plymouth Meeting (19462) *(G-15860)*

North American Compounding 814 899-0621
4680 Iroquois Ave Erie (16511) *(G-5406)*

North American Display 412 209-9988
300 Camp Horne Rd Pittsburgh (15202) *(G-15346)*

North American Drillers LLC (HQ) 304 291-0175
130 Madow Ridge Rd Ste 22 Mount Morris (15349) *(G-11683)*

North American Fencing Corp 412 362-3900
1005 Pittsburgh St Cheswick (15024) *(G-3113)*

North American Forgemasters Co 724 656-6440
710 Moravia St New Castle (16101) *(G-12132)*

North American Hoganas Company 814 479-3500
111 Hoganas Way Hollsopple (15935) *(G-7658)*

North American Mfg Co 570 348-1163
1074 Barring Ave Scranton (18508) *(G-17266)*

North American Packaging LLC 570 296-4200
535 Route 6 And 209 Ste A Milford (18337) *(G-11165)*

North American Powder Coatings, Erie *Also called North American Compounding (G-5406)*

North American Stl & Wire Inc 724 431-0626
629 E Butler Rd Butler (16002) *(G-2426)*

North American Tooling Inc 814 486-3700
6834 Beechwood Rd Ste 2 Emporium (15834) *(G-5070)*

North American Wire LLC 724 431-0626
629 E Butler Rd Butler (16002) *(G-2427)*

North Amrcn Communications Inc 814 696-3553
141 Nac Dr Duncansville (16635) *(G-4458)*

North Amrcn Hgnas Holdings Inc (HQ) 814 479-2551
111 Hoganas Way Hollsopple (15935) *(G-7659)*

North Amrcn Specialty Pdts LLC (HQ) 484 253-4545
993 Old Eagle School Rd Wayne (19087) *(G-19360)*

North Branch Industries, Catawissa *Also called James G Beaver (G-2819)*

North Central Sight Svcs Inc 570 323-9401
2121 Reach Rd Williamsport (17701) *(G-20050)*

North Coast Plastics Inc 814 838-1343
2114 Loveland Ave Erie (16506) *(G-5407)*

North Coast Tool Inc 814 836-7685
9843 Martin Ave Lake City (16423) *(G-8906)*

North Country Woodworking Inc 570 549-8105
9646 N Elk Run Rd Mansfield (16933) *(G-10422)*

North East Louvers Inc 717 436-5300
481 E Industrial Park Dr Mifflintown (17059) *(G-11131)*

North East Plant, North East *Also called Welch Foods Inc A Cooperative (G-12766)*

North East Print Supplies, Pittston *Also called Gc Enterprises LLC (G-15752)*

North End Electric Service Inc 570 342-6740
1225 N Keyser Ave Scranton (18504) *(G-17267)*

North Hills Monthly Magazine, Cranberry Township *Also called Lutz and Associates (G-3833)*

North Jckson Specialty Stl LLC (HQ) 412 257-7600
600 Mayer St Bridgeville (15017) *(G-2082)*

North Jckson Specialty Stl LLC 412 257-7600
600 Mayer St Bridgeville (15017) *(G-2083)*

North Mountain Butcher Shop, Carlisle *Also called Country Butcher Shop (G-2703)*

North Mountain Structures LLC 717 369-3400
9035 Fort Mccord Rd Chambersburg (17202) *(G-2964)*

North Penn Art Inc 215 362-2494
720 S Broad St Lansdale (19446) *(G-9393)*

North Penn Industries Corp 215 453-9775
410 E Walnut St Ste 7 Perkasie (18944) *(G-13286)*

North Penn Machine Works, Perkasie *Also called North Penn Industries Corp (G-13286)*

North Penn Polishing and Pltg 215 257-4945
40 W Park Ave Sellersville (18960) *(G-17355)*

NORTH PENN TECHNOLOGY INC 215 997-3200
2294 N Penn Rd Ste A Hatfield (19440) *(G-7374)*

North Pittsburgh Steel, Mercer *Also called Lisa Thomas (G-10967)*

North Pittsburgh Upper Cervica 724 553-8526
8050 Rowan Rd Ste 400 Cranberry Township (16066) *(G-3842)*

North Side Foods, New Kensington *Also called Smithfield Packaged Meats Corp (G-12378)*

North Star Aggregates Inc 814 637-5599
Rr 255 Box N Penfield (15849) *(G-13222)*

North Star Leasing Inc (PA) 814 629-6999
147 Mine Rd Friedens (15541) *(G-6224)*

North Warren BP, Warren *Also called Triangle Petroleum Inc (G-19052)*

Northampton Herald 215 702-3405
341 Rumpf Ave Langhorne (19047) *(G-9316)*

Northeast Building Pdts Corp (HQ) 215 535-7110
4280 Aramingo Ave Philadelphia (19124) *(G-14079)*

Northeast Building Pdts Corp 215 331-2400
4926 Benner St Philadelphia (19135) *(G-14080)*

Northeast Cabinet Center Inc 570 226-5005
2591 Route 6 Ste 102 Hawley (18428) *(G-7434)*

Northeast Contracting, Waymart *Also called Northeastern Foam and Fiber (G-19288)*

Northeast Dental Laboratories 215 725-0950
914 Stratford Ave Elkins Park (19027) *(G-4909)*

Northeast Discount Printing 215 742-3111
2630 Welsh Rd Apt A3 Philadelphia (19152) *(G-14081)*

Northeast Energy Co Inc 570 823-1719
254 Johnson St Wilkes Barre (18702) *(G-19951)*

Northeast Energy MGT Inc 724 465-7958
127 College Lodge Rd Indiana (15701) *(G-8115)*

Northeast Fabricators Inc 570 883-0936
490 N Main St Ste 101 Pittston (18640) *(G-15771)*

Northeast Fence & Ir Works Inc 215 335-1681
8451 Hegerman St Philadelphia (19136) *(G-14082)*

Northeast Foods Inc 215 638-2400
2945 Samuel Dr Bensalem (19020) *(G-1231)*

Northeast Geotechnical Sup LLC 570 307-1283
1505 E Lackawanna St # 3 Olyphant (18447) *(G-12995)*

Northeast Glass Co 267 991-0054
1913 Conwell Ave Philadelphia (19115) *(G-14083)*

Northeast Indus Batteries Inc 215 788-8000
2300 David Dr Ste 6 Bristol (19007) *(G-2172)*

Northeast Industrial Mfg 724 253-3110
191 Pearson Rd Hadley (16130) *(G-6820)*

Northeast Industrial Mfg Inc 724 588-7711
640 Keystone Rd Greenville (16125) *(G-6760)*

Northeast Laminated Glass Corp 570 489-6421
14 Alberigi Dr Jessup (18434) *(G-8334)*

Northeast Plastics Supply, Bensalem *Also called Total Plastics Resources LLC (G-1261)*

Northeast Prestressed Pdts LLC 570 385-2352
121 River St Cressona (17929) *(G-3906)*

Northeast Print, Philadelphia *Also called Northeast Discount Printing (G-14081)*

Northeast Products & Svcs Inc 610 899-0286
130 W High St Topton (19562) *(G-18414)*

Northeast Specialty Packaging, Parkesburg *Also called Jpmw Partners LLC (G-13178)*

Northeast Spring Inc 610 374-8508
506 S 5th St Reading (19602) *(G-16457)*

Northeast Wood Products, Rome *Also called David M Oley (G-16797)*

Northeastern Envelope Company (PA) 800 233-4285
2 Maxson Dr Old Forge (18518) *(G-12971)*

Northeastern Foam and Fiber 570 488-6859
Owego Tpke Waymart (18472) *(G-19288)*

Northeastern Hydro-Seeding Inc 570 668-1108
411 Claremont Ave Tamaqua (18252) *(G-18222)*

Northeastern PA Carton Co Inc 570 457-7711
4820 Birney Ave Moosic (18507) *(G-11510)*

(G-0000) Company's Geographic Section entry number

Northeimer Engineering & Mfg, Leesport *Also called Northeimer Manufacturing* ***(G-9672)***

Northeimer Manufacturing 610 926-1136
2670 Leisczs Bridge Rd Leesport (19533) ***(G-9672)***

Northern Connection Magazine, Wexford *Also called Swanson Publishing Company Inc* ***(G-19830)***

Northern Crafts, East Stroudsburg *Also called Amanda Reiche* ***(G-4605)***

Northern Engrg Plas Corp PR 724 658-9019
1902 New Butler Rd New Castle (16101) ***(G-12133)***

Northern Hardwoods Inc 814 274-8060
17 S Main St Coudersport (16915) ***(G-3786)***

Northern Hot Shot Services LLC 724 664-5477
126 N Jefferson St Kittanning (16201) ***(G-8786)***

Northern Iron Works Inc 215 947-1867
2955 Franks Rd Huntingdon Valley (19006) ***(G-8018)***

Northern Lehigh Erectors Corp (PA) 610 791-4200
2571 Mitchell Ave Allentown (18103) ***(G-335)***

Northern Liberty Press LLC 215 634-3000
1223 N Mascher St 31 Philadelphia (19122) ***(G-14084)***

Northern Millwork Inc 215 393-7242
505 N Mitchell Ave Lansdale (19446) ***(G-9394)***

Northern Pallet Inc 570 945-3920
151 Creek Rd Factoryville (18419) ***(G-5759)***

Northern Powdered Metals Inc 814 772-0882
439b W Main St Ridgway (15853) ***(G-16720)***

Northern Son Inc 724 548-1137
1022 Treasure Lk Du Bois (15801) ***(G-4407)***

Northern Tier Inc 814 465-2299
24 Northland Rd Rew (16744) ***(G-16654)***

Northern Tier Beverage Inc 570 662-2523
133 N Main St Mansfield (16933) ***(G-10423)***

Northern Winding Inc 724 776-4983
270 Myoma Rd Mars (16046) ***(G-10509)***

Northside Manufacturing Inc 814 342-4638
300 Shady Ln Philipsburg (16866) ***(G-14521)***

Northstar Sales 215 364-5540
963 Street Rd 2 Southampton (18966) ***(G-17828)***

Northstern Cnsld Enrgy Prtners 412 491-6660
2570 Matterhorn Dr Wexford (15090) ***(G-19816)***

Northstern Precision Pdts Corp 215 245-6300
2230 Pennsylvania Ave Bensalem (19020) ***(G-1232)***

Northtec LLC 215 781-2731
150 Rittenhouse Cir Bristol (19007) ***(G-2173)***

Northtec LLC (PA) 215 781-1600
411 Sinclair Rd Bristol (19007) ***(G-2174)***

Northway Industries Inc 570 837-1564
434 Paxtonville Rd Middleburg (17842) ***(G-11034)***

Northwest Bagel Corporation 610 237-0586
546 Lancaster Ct Downingtown (19335) ***(G-4245)***

Northwest Hardwoods, Titusville *Also called Weyerhaeuser Company* ***(G-18404)***

Northwest Logging LLC 814 598-1350
326 Birch St Kane (16735) ***(G-8474)***

Northwest PA Burial Service 814 425-2436
22996 Us Highway 322 Cochranton (16314) ***(G-3346)***

Northwest Synergy Corp 814 726-0543
1438 Stone Hill Rd Warren (16365) ***(G-19040)***

Northwest Tool & Die Inc 814 763-5087
22973 Cannon Hollow Rd Saegertown (16433) ***(G-16926)***

Northwestern Energy Corp 814 277-9935
1214 Mcgees Mills Rd Mahaffey (15757) ***(G-10172)***

Northwestern Manufacturing, Lake City *Also called Northwestern Welding & Mch Co* ***(G-8907)***

Northwestern Welding & Mch Co 814 774-2866
9704 Martin Ave Lake City (16423) ***(G-8907)***

Northwoods Ppr Converting Inc 570 424-8786
830 Crowe Rd East Stroudsburg (18301) ***(G-4625)***

Norton Oglebay Company (HQ) 412 995-5500
11 Stanwix St Fl 21 Pittsburgh (15222) ***(G-15347)***

Norton Oglebay Specialty Mnrl 412 995-5500
11 Stanwix St Fl 21 Pittsburgh (15222) ***(G-15348)***

Norton Pulpstones Incorporated (PA) 610 964-0544
604 Lindsay Cir Villanova (19085) ***(G-18767)***

Nortons Building Supply Inc 814 697-6351
112 Water St Shinglehouse (16748) ***(G-17510)***

Norwin Mfg Inc 724 515-7092
1061 Main St Ste 18 Irwin (15642) ***(G-8184)***

Norwood Manufacture Co LLC 724 652-0698
224 E Cherry St New Castle (16102) ***(G-12134)***

Nosco Inc 215 788-1105
1504 Grundy Ln Bristol (19007) ***(G-2175)***

Not For Radio LLC 484 437-9962
2750 Shenck Rd Manheim (17545) ***(G-10397)***

Notaries Equipment Co 215 563-8190
2021 Arch St Fl 2 Philadelphia (19103) ***(G-14085)***

Notations Inc (PA) 215 259-2000
539 Jacksonville Rd Warminster (18974) ***(G-18930)***

Notations Clothing Co, Warminster *Also called Notations Inc* ***(G-18930)***

Nov Fluid Control, Leetsdale *Also called National Oilwell Varco LP* ***(G-9700)***

Nova Aurora Corp 817 467-7567
781 Station St Pittsburgh (15235) ***(G-15349)***

Nova Chemicals Inc (HQ) 412 490-4000
1555 Coraopolis Hts Rd Moon Township (15108) ***(G-11497)***

Nova Chemicals Inc 724 770-5542
400 Frankfort Rd Monaca (15061) ***(G-11293)***

Nova Global Inc 619 822-2465
1518 Walnut St Philadelphia (19102) ***(G-14086)***

Nova Molding 610 767-7858
8867 N Loop Rd Slatington (18080) ***(G-17610)***

Nova Precision Casting Corp 570 366-2679
12 Hickory Dr Auburn (17922) ***(G-819)***

Novacare Prosthetics Orthotics, Washington *Also called Benchmark Orthot & Prosth Inc* ***(G-19154)***

Novapak, Hazle Township *Also called Pvc Container Corporation* ***(G-7476)***

Novapak Corporation 717 266-6687
1 Devco Dr Manchester (17345) ***(G-10359)***

Novares US LLC 717 244-0151
12367 Mount Olivet Rd Felton (17322) ***(G-5941)***

Novares US LLC 717 244-4581
12367 Mount Olivet Rd Felton (17322) ***(G-5942)***

Novartis Corporation 215 255-4200
1717 Arch St Fl 28 Philadelphia (19103) ***(G-14087)***

Novartis Pharmaceuticals Corp 717 901-1916
300 Salem Church Rd Mechanicsburg (17050) ***(G-10874)***

Novasentis Inc 814 238-7400
200 Innovation Blvd # 237 State College (16803) ***(G-18001)***

Novasentis Inc 814 238-7400
200 Innovation Blvd # 237 State College (16803) ***(G-18002)***

Novatech LLC (PA) 484 812-6000
1720 Molasses Way Quakertown (18951) ***(G-16224)***

Novatech Industries Inc 610 584-8996
1221 Bridge Rd Skippack (19474) ***(G-17601)***

Novative Designs Inc 215 794-3380
275 Norristown Rd Blue Bell (19422) ***(G-1850)***

Novavax Execoffice 484 913-1200
508 Lapp Rd Malvern (19355) ***(G-10288)***

Novelli Inc 215 739-3538
2011 Frankford Ave Philadelphia (19125) ***(G-14088)***

Novelty Concepts, Bensalem *Also called Afab Industrial Services Inc* ***(G-1145)***

Novelty Concepts Inc 215 245-5570
350 Camer Dr Bensalem (19020) ***(G-1233)***

Novinger Welding Repair Inc 570 758-6592
126 Tulpehocken Path Rd Herndon (17830) ***(G-7602)***

Novipax LLC 570 644-0314
1123 W Valley Ave Paxinos (17860) ***(G-13191)***

Novocellars, New Wilmington *Also called Novosel LLC* ***(G-12468)***

Novosel Instrument Shop Inc 814 359-2249
264 Commerce St Pleasant Gap (16823) ***(G-15795)***

Novosel LLC 724 230-6686
5253 Old Pulaski Rd New Wilmington (16142) ***(G-12468)***

Novotny Micheal 724 785-2160
18 Bridge St Brownsville (15417) ***(G-2313)***

Novus X-Ray LLC (HQ) 215 962-3171
726 Boehms Church Rd Blue Bell (19422) ***(G-1851)***

Nowalk Lighting, Pittsburgh *Also called Francis J Nowalk* ***(G-15030)***

Nowinski Pierogies, North East *Also called Rae Foods Inc* ***(G-12755)***

NP, Lewistown *Also called Nittany Paper Mills Inc* ***(G-9940)***

NP Precision Inc 610 586-5100
5 Horne Dr Folcroft (19032) ***(G-6010)***

Npc Inc (PA) 814 239-8787
13710 Dunnings Hwy Claysburg (16625) ***(G-3207)***

Npc Acquisition Inc (HQ) 215 946-2000
100 Main St Bristol (19007) ***(G-2176)***

Nrf US Inc (PA) 814 947-1378
105 E Germantown Pike Plymouth Meeting (19462) ***(G-15861)***

NRG Texas Power LLC 412 655-4134
2351 Century Dr West Mifflin (15122) ***(G-19743)***

Nri Data and Business Products, Springfield *Also called Aserdiv Inc* ***(G-17907)***

NS Corporation - Eastern Off, West Chester *Also called N/S Corporation* ***(G-19605)***

NTC, Bensalem *Also called National Towelette Company* ***(G-1229)***

Ntec Inc 215 768-0261
12 Penns Trl Ste 102 Newtown (18940) ***(G-12529)***

Nth Solutions LLC 610 594-2191
15 E Uwchlan Ave Ste 412 Exton (19341) ***(G-5715)***

NTI, Clifton Heights *Also called Nice Threads International* ***(G-3257)***

Nu Tech Inc 215 297-8889
5985 Carversville Rd Doylestown (18902) ***(G-4319)***

Nu-Art Graphics Inc 610 436-4336
899 Fernhill Rd Ste A West Chester (19380) ***(G-19608)***

Nu-Chem Corp 610 770-2000
747 N Fenwick St Allentown (18109) ***(G-336)***

Nu-TEC Tooling Co 570 538-2571
13115 State Route 405 Watsontown (17777) ***(G-19277)***

Nu-U Laser Center 717 718-7880
1600 6th Ave Ste 117 York (17403) ***(G-20612)***

Nuchem, Allentown *Also called Nu-Chem Corp* ***(G-336)***

Nuclear Systems Group, Malvern *Also called Siemens Med Solutions USA Inc* ***(G-10315)***

Nucor Corporation 717 735-7766
201 Granite Run Dr # 280 Lancaster (17601) ***(G-9148)***

Nucor Grating 724 934-5320
2000 Corporate Dr Ste 400 Wexford (15090) *(G-19817)*

Nufeeds Inc (PA) 570 278-3767
200 Jackson St Montrose (18801) *(G-11473)*

Nufeeds Inc 570 836-2866
16 Sr 1006 Tunkhannock (18657) *(G-18545)*

Nugo Nutrition, Oakmont *Also called Lifestyle Evolution Inc (G-12920)*

Null Machine Shop Inc 717 597-3330
95 Commerce Ave Greencastle (17225) *(G-6625)*

Numonics, Montgomeryville *Also called Commerce Drive Enterprises LLC (G-11389)*

Nupak Printing LLC 717 244-4041
177 E Walnut St Red Lion (17356) *(G-16610)*

Nupathe Inc 610 232-0800
41 Moores Rd Malvern (19355) *(G-10289)*

Nupp Printing Company, Sykesville *Also called Premier Graphics LLC (G-18202)*

Nurelm Inc 724 430-0490
128 N Highland Ave # 201 Pittsburgh (15206) *(G-15350)*

Nurture Inc (PA) 610 989-0945
28 S Waterloo Rd Ste 100 Devon (19333) *(G-4114)*

Nushield Inc 215 500-6426
2110 S Eagle Rd Ste 400 Newtown (18940) *(G-12530)*

Nuss Printing Inc 610 853-3005
1225 W Chester Pike Havertown (19083) *(G-7424)*

Nutech LLC 215 361-0373
2705 Clemens Rd Ste 101b Hatfield (19440) *(G-7375)*

Nutech Hydronic Specialty Pdts, Hatfield *Also called Nutech LLC (G-7375)*

Nutek Disposables Inc (HQ) 570 769-6900
121 North Rd Mc Elhattan (17748) *(G-10589)*

Nutra-Soils Inc 610 869-7645
324 E Baltimore Pike West Grove (19390) *(G-19703)*

Nutricia Mfg USA Inc 412 288-4600
300 6th Ave Pittsburgh (15222) *(G-15351)*

Nutrient Control Systems Inc 717 261-5711
130 Industrial Dr Chambersburg (17201) *(G-2965)*

Nutrition Inc (PA) 724 978-2100
580 Wendel Rd Ste 100 Irwin (15642) *(G-8185)*

Nutrition Inc 814 382-3656
580 Wendel Rd 100 Irwin (15642) *(G-8186)*

Nuts & Such Ltd 215 708-8500
8845 Torresdale Ave Philadelphia (19136) *(G-14089)*

Nuts About Granola LLC 717 814-9648
9 W Philadelphia St York (17401) *(G-20613)*

Nuts About Ice Cream, Bethlehem *Also called Joshi Bharkatkumar (G-1547)*

Nuvanna LLC 844 611-2324
225 Wilmington W Chester Chadds Ford (19317) *(G-2857)*

Nuvu Services, Irwin *Also called Nutrition Inc (G-8186)*

Nuwave Technologies Inc 610 584-8428
1221 Quarry Hall Rd Norristown (19403) *(G-12695)*

Nuweld Inc 570 505-1500
2600 Reach Rd Williamsport (17701) *(G-20051)*

NY Bagel Bakery, Philadelphia *Also called Kesser Baking Co (G-13928)*

Nydia Cake Nuggets, Willow Grove *Also called Mybiani LLC (G-20130)*

Nye Technical Sales 610 639-9985
1501 Eagle Ridge Dr Downingtown (19335) *(G-4246)*

Nyes Machine and Design 717 533-9514
90 S Wilson Ave Elizabethtown (17022) *(G-4881)*

Nyes Machine and Design (PA) 717 533-9514
1153 Roush Rd Hummelstown (17036) *(G-7920)*

Nylacast LLC (HQ) 717 270-5600
6951 Allentown Blvd Ste K Harrisburg (17112) *(G-7185)*

Nylomatic, Levittown *Also called Adventek Corporation (G-9813)*

Nyp Corp (frmr Ny-Pters Corp) 717 656-0299
10 Site Rd Leola (17540) *(G-9796)*

Nytef Plastics Ltd 215 244-6950
633 Dunksferry Rd Bensalem (19020) *(G-1234)*

Nzinganet Inc 877 709-6459
500 Office Ct Dr Ste 400 Fort Washington (19034) *(G-6087)*

Nzk Plastics LLC 412 823-8630
1210 Airbrake Ave Turtle Creek (15145) *(G-18566)*

O & B Communications 610 647-8585
3 Paoli Plz Ste 1a Paoli (19301) *(G-13144)*

O & N Arcft Modification Inc 570 945-3769
210 Windsock Ln 9n Factoryville (18419) *(G-5760)*

O & P Benchmark Holdings Inc (HQ) 610 644-7824
855 Springdale Dr Ste 200 Exton (19341) *(G-5716)*

O & S Machine Co Inc 724 539-9431
718 Ashland Dr Latrobe (15650) *(G-9506)*

O Alpine Pressed Metals Inc 814 776-2141
310 Tanner St Ridgway (15853) *(G-16721)*

O and P Svetz Inc (PA) 724 834-1448
600 S Main St Greensburg (15601) *(G-6694)*

O C Tanner Company 610 458-1245
74 Pottstown Pike # 1006 Chester Springs (19425) *(G-3083)*

O G Industries, Drexel Hill *Also called Ogi Inc (G-4370)*

O K Automation, Reading *Also called Universal Pen & Pencil Co Inc (G-16555)*

O K McCloyawnings Inc 412 271-4044
2029 Noble St Swissvale (15218) *(G-18193)*

O Land Lakes 717 845-8076
365 Emig Rd York (17406) *(G-20614)*

O S A Global LLC (PA) 724 698-7042
2700 Highland Ave Ste 6 New Castle (16105) *(G-12135)*

O S I Software 215 606-0612
1700 Market St Ste 2200 Philadelphia (19103) *(G-14090)*

O'Donnell, B T Goldsmith, Lebanon *Also called Golden Specialties Ltd (G-9575)*

O-N Minerals Chemstone Company (HQ) 412 995-5500
11 Stanwix St Fl 21 Pittsburgh (15222) *(G-15352)*

O-N Minerals Company (ohio) (HQ) 412 995-5500
11 Stanwix St Fl 21 Pittsburgh (15222) *(G-15353)*

O-N Minerals Luttrell Company (HQ) 412 995-5500
11 Stanwix St Fl 21 Pittsburgh (15222) *(G-15354)*

O-N Minerals Michigan Company (HQ) 412 995-5500
11 Stanwix St Fl 21 Pittsburgh (15222) *(G-15355)*

O-N Minerals Portage Co LLC 412 995-5500
11 Stanwix St Fl 21 Pittsburgh (15222) *(G-15356)*

O-Z/Gedney Co Inc 610 926-3645
150 Birch Hill Rd Shoemakersville (19555) *(G-17573)*

O2s LLC 215 299-8500
1500 Spring Garden St Philadelphia (19130) *(G-14091)*

Oa Systems Llc 888 347-7950
2559 Brandt School Rd # 102 Wexford (15090) *(G-19818)*

Oak Bows, Chambersburg *Also called South Penn Restoration Shop (G-2977)*

Oak Crest Industries Inc 610 246-9177
500 Oakcrest Ln Wallingford (19086) *(G-18786)*

Oak Hill Controls LLC (PA) 610 967-3985
3433 Oak Hill Rd Emmaus (18049) *(G-5035)*

Oak Hill Controls LLC 610 758-9500
22 S Commerce Way Ste 9 Bethlehem (18017) *(G-1585)*

Oak Hill Veneer Inc 570 297-4137
23189 Rte 14 Troy (16947) *(G-18524)*

Oak Management, Harrisburg *Also called Image 360 (G-7153)*

Oak Park Cabinetry Inc 717 561-4216
4220 Paxton St Harrisburg (17111) *(G-7186)*

Oak Ridge Logging LLC 717 687-8168
3166 White Oak Rd Quarryville (17566) *(G-16275)*

Oak Shade Cheese LLC 717 529-6049
286 Reath Rd Kirkwood (17536) *(G-8752)*

Oak Spring Enterprises Inc 570 622-2001
130 W Bacon St Pottsville (17901) *(G-16090)*

Oak Spring Winery Incorporated (PA) 814 946-3799
2401 E Pleasant Vly Blvd Altoona (16601) *(G-532)*

Oak Systems, Fort Washington *Also called Mg Financial Services Inc (G-6086)*

Oakes & McClelland Co 724 588-6400
1505 Arlington Dr Greenville (16125) *(G-6761)*

Oakes Gas Co Inc 814 837-7972
47 E Brick Yard Rd Kane (16735) *(G-8475)*

Oaklawn Metal Craft Shop Inc 215 794-7387
5752 York Rd Lahaska (18931) *(G-8885)*

Oaks Industrial Supply Inc 610 539-7008
1055 W Germantown Pike # 3 Norristown (19403) *(G-12696)*

Oaks Poultry Co Inc 814 798-3631
172 Folly Ln Stoystown (15563) *(G-18083)*

Oaks Welding LLC 570 527-7328
50 Dutchtown Rd Ashland (17921) *(G-735)*

Oakwood Bindery 717 396-9559
1133 Manheim Pike Lancaster (17601) *(G-9149)*

Oakwood Controls Corporation 717 801-1515
159 Industrial Rd Glen Rock (17327) *(G-6458)*

Oakworks Inc 717 227-0516
923 E Wellspring Rd New Freedom (17349) *(G-12213)*

Obadiah School, Bethel *Also called Assemblies of Yahweh (G-1392)*

Oberg Arizona, Sarver *Also called Oberg Industries Inc (G-17074)*

Oberg Carbide Punch & Die 724 295-2118
604 Oberg Dr Freeport (16229) *(G-6208)*

Oberg Industries, Freeport *Also called Oberg Carbide Punch & Die (G-6208)*

Oberg Industries Inc (PA) 724 295-2121
2301 Silverville Rd Freeport (16229) *(G-6209)*

Oberg Industries Inc 724 353-9700
275 N Pike Rd Sarver (16055) *(G-17074)*

Oberg Industries Inc 724 295-5151
604 Oberg Dr Freeport (16229) *(G-6210)*

Oberg Industries Inc 724 353-9700
275 N Pike Rd Sarver (16055) *(G-17075)*

Oberg Industries Inc 724 353-9700
275 N Pike Rd Sarver (16055) *(G-17076)*

Oberg Medical, Freeport *Also called Oberg Industries Inc (G-6209)*

Oberg Sarver, Sarver *Also called Oberg Industries Inc (G-17076)*

Oberg Stamping & Tech Center, Sarver *Also called Oberg Industries Inc (G-17075)*

Oberon Inc 814 867-2312
1315 S Allen St Ste 410 State College (16801) *(G-18003)*

Oberthur Card Systems Inc 610 280-2707
523 James Hance Ct Exton (19341) *(G-5717)*

Obh Enterprises LLC 610 436-0796
205 Gypsie Ln West Chester (19380) *(G-19609)*

Observer Publishing Company (PA) 724 222-2200
122 S Main St Washington (15301) *(G-19212)*

Observer Publishing Company 724 852-2602
32 S Church St Fl 1 Waynesburg (15370) *(G-19449)*

Observer Publishing Company 724 941-7725
395 Valley Brook Rd Canonsburg (15317) *(G-2614)*

Observer-Reporter, Washington *Also called Observer Publishing Company (G-19212)*

Oc Canvas Studio LLC 717 510-4847
15 S 20th St Harrisburg (17104) *(G-7187)*

Occidental Chemical Corp 610 327-4145
375 Armand Hammer Blvd Pottstown (19464) *(G-16022)*

Occuped Orthotics 717 949-2377
439 Sunnyside Rd Newmanstown (17073) *(G-12482)*

Ocean King Enterprises Inc 215 365-2500
7831 Bartram Ave Philadelphia (19153) *(G-14092)*

Ocean Spray Cranberries Inc 609 298-0905
151 Boulder Dr Breinigsville (18031) *(G-2022)*

Ocean Spray Cranberries Inc 508 946-1000
151 Boulder Dr Breinigsville (18031) *(G-2023)*

Ocean Thermal Energy Corp (PA) 717 299-1344
800 S Queen St Lancaster (17603) *(G-9150)*

Ocello Inc 717 866-5778
300 Poplar St Richland (17087) *(G-16688)*

Oci, North Wales *Also called Omnispread Communications Inc (G-12821)*

OConnell Hardwood Inc 814 796-2297
5636 Route 97 Waterford (16441) *(G-19267)*

Ocp Inc 814 827-3661
45619 State Highway 27 Titusville (16354) *(G-18389)*

October 6 2011 .... 814 422-8810
119 Cooper St Spring Mills (16875) *(G-17891)*

Odellick Baking LLC 814 515-1337
4209 5th Ave Altoona (16602) *(G-533)*

Odhner and Odhner Fine Wdwkg 610 258-9300
3405 William N Hwy Easton (18042) *(G-4734)*

Odhner Corporation 610 364-3200
400 W Knowlton Rd Media (19063) *(G-10941)*

ODonnell Metal Fabricators 610 279-8810
315 W Germantown Pike Norristown (19403) *(G-12697)*

OEM Group East Inc 610 282-0105
416 S 4th St Coopersburg (18036) *(G-3632)*

OEM Shades Inc 724 763-3600
141 Singleton Rd Sarver (16055) *(G-17077)*

OEM Technology News, Bala Cynwyd *Also called Technology Data Exchange Inc (G-894)*

Oerlikon Leybold Vacuum USA, Export *Also called Leybold USA Inc (G-5616)*

Oerlikon Management USA Inc 412 967-7016
615 Epsilon Dr Pittsburgh (15238) *(G-15357)*

Oesterling Feed & Farm Sups, Grove City *Also called Lawn & Garden (G-6794)*

Oesterlings Concrete Co Inc 724 282-8556
690 Glenwood Way Butler (16001) *(G-2428)*

Oesterlings Feed 724 283-1819
3035 Old Route 422 E Fenelton (16034) *(G-5947)*

Oesterlings Sndblst & Pntg, Butler *Also called Oesterlings Sndblst & Pntg Inc (G-2429)*

Oesterlings Sndblst & Pntg Inc 724 282-1391
686 Glenwood Way Butler (16001) *(G-2429)*

Oesterlngs Grnding Mxing Feeds, Fenelton *Also called Oesterlings Feed (G-5947)*

Ofcg Inc 570 655-0804
243 Lidy Rd Dupont (18641) *(G-4493)*

Office Mats Inc 717 359-9571
51 N Queen St Littlestown (17340) *(G-10073)*

Officelogic Inc 215 752-3069
2452 Williamson Ct Bensalem (19020) *(G-1235)*

Offset Paperback 570 602-1316
10 Passan Dr Wilkes Barre (18702) *(G-19952)*

Offset Paperback Mfrs Inc (HQ) 570 675-5261
2211 Memorial Hwy Dallas (18612) *(G-3964)*

Ogden, Pittsburgh *Also called Chromalox Inc (G-14850)*

Ogden Brothers Incorporated 610 789-1258
213 N Ormond Ave Havertown (19083) *(G-7425)*

Ogden Brothers Office Supply, Havertown *Also called Ogden Brothers Incorporated (G-7425)*

Ogden Directories PA Inc 814 946-7404
301 Cayuga Ave Altoona (16602) *(G-534)*

Ogden Newspapers Inc 814 946-7411
301 Cayuga Ave Altoona (16602) *(G-535)*

Ogden Newspapers Inc 570 584-2134
1025 Route 405 Hwy Hughesville (17737) *(G-7898)*

Ogden Newspapers of PA 717 248-6741
352 6th St Lewistown (17044) *(G-9941)*

Ogi Inc 610 623-6747
4219 Garrett Rd Drexel Hill (19026) *(G-4370)*

Ogontz Corporation (PA) 215 657-4770
2835 Terwood Rd Willow Grove (19090) *(G-20131)*

OH Little Town Cupcakes LLC 484 353-9709
1731 W Market St Bethlehem (18018) *(G-1586)*

OH Ryans Irish Potatoes 610 494-7123
168 E Ridge Rd Ste 201 Marcus Hook (19061) *(G-10452)*

Ohio Mat Lcnsing Cmpnnts Group 570 715-7200
25 Elmwood Ave Mountain Top (18707) *(G-11768)*

Ohio Valley Indus Svcs Inc (PA) 412 269-0020
530 Moon Clinton Rd Ste B Moon Township (15108) *(G-11498)*

Ohio Valley Indus Svcs Inc 412 335-5237
620 Moon Clinton Rd Coraopolis (15108) *(G-3708)*

Ohiopyle Prints Inc 724 329-4652
410 Dinner Bell Rd Ohiopyle (15470) *(G-12939)*

OHM- Labs Inc 412 431-0640
611 E Carson St Pittsburgh (15203) *(G-15358)*

Oil & Gas Management Inc 724 925-1568
114 Oil Ln Hunker (15639) *(G-7930)*

Oil & Vinegar 724 840-9656
350 Bryce Ln Chicora (16025) *(G-3128)*

Oil City Tube Div, Oil City *Also called Webco Industries Inc (G-12959)*

Oil Creek Plastics, Titusville *Also called Ocp Inc (G-18389)*

Oil Process Systems Inc 610 437-4618
602 Tacoma St Allentown (18109) *(G-337)*

Oil States Energy Services LLC 570 538-1623
449 E 8th St Bldg 11 Watsontown (17777) *(G-19278)*

Oil States Energy Services LLC 724 746-1168
255 Johnson Rd Canonsburg (15317) *(G-2615)*

Oil States Energy Services LLC 814 290-6755
15106 Clrfld Shwvlle Hwy Clearfield (16830) *(G-3227)*

Oilfield LLC 814 623-8125
264 Reynoldsdale Rd Bedford (15522) *(G-1067)*

Oilfield Supply Company, Bedford *Also called Oilfield LLC (G-1067)*

Ois LLC 717 447-0265
10 S Jefferson St Mount Union (17066) *(G-11746)*

OJacks Inc 814 225-4755
45 Railroad Ave Eldred (16731) *(G-4854)*

Okumus Enterprises Ltd 215 295-3340
42 Newbold Rd Fairless Hills (19030) *(G-5790)*

Old Bedford Village Inc 814 623-1156
220 Sawblade Rd Bedford (15522) *(G-1068)*

Old Candle Barn Gift Shop, Intercourse *Also called Old Candle Barn Inc (G-8138)*

Old Candle Barn Inc 717 768-3231
3551 Main St Intercourse (17534) *(G-8138)*

Old City Publishing 215 925-4390
628 N 2nd St Philadelphia (19123) *(G-14093)*

Old Epp Inc 570 430-9089
150 Lawson Ln Tunkhannock (18657) *(G-18546)*

Old Glory Corp 724 423-3580
4150 State Route 981 Mount Pleasant (15666) *(G-11709)*

Old Ladder Co (PA) 888 523-3371
93 Werner Rd Greenville (16125) *(G-6762)*

Old News, Salunga *Also called Susquehanna Times & Magazine (G-17056)*

Old Time Games Inc 215 538-5422
1915 Fawn Ln Quakertown (18951) *(G-16225)*

Old Town Woodworking Inc 570 562-2117
209 Dunn Ave Old Forge (18518) *(G-12972)*

Old York Road Printing LLC 215 957-6200
905 Louis Dr Warminster (18974) *(G-18931)*

Old York Road Publishing Co, Warminster *Also called Baltimore Corp (G-18835)*

Oldcastle Apg Northeast Inc 484 240-2176
1960 Weaversville Rd Allentown (18109) *(G-338)*

Oldcastle Industrial Minerals, Thomasville *Also called Pennsy Supply Inc (G-18342)*

Oldcastle Materials Inc 717 898-2278
1 Clear Spring Rd Annville (17003) *(G-655)*

Oldcastle Prcast Modular Group, Telford *Also called Oldcastle Precast Inc (G-18306)*

Oldcastle Precast Inc 484 548-6200
3900 Glover Rd Easton (18040) *(G-4735)*

Oldcastle Precast Inc 888 965-3227
1900 Pennsylvania Ave Croydon (19021) *(G-3923)*

Oldcastle Precast Inc 215 257-8081
200 Keystone Dr Telford (18969) *(G-18306)*

Oldcastle Precast Inc 215 257-2255
200 Keystone Dr Telford (18969) *(G-18307)*

Oldcastle Precast Inc 215 736-9576
1381 S Pennsylvania Ave Morrisville (19067) *(G-11574)*

Oldco Ep Inc 484 768-1000
15 Milton Dr Aston (19014) *(G-782)*

Oldco Ep Inc (HQ) 888 314-9356
1601 Dutton Mill Rd Aston (19014) *(G-783)*

Olde Mill Cabinet Co 717 866-6504
103 E Main Ave Myerstown (17067) *(G-11895)*

Olde Mill Lighting Limited 717 299-7240
833 2nd St Ste E Lancaster (17603) *(G-9151)*

Olde Mill Lighting Ltd Shop, Lancaster *Also called Olde Mill Lighting Limited (G-9151)*

Olde Recipe Foods Inc 724 654-5779
120 Adams Ln Portersville (16051) *(G-15934)*

Olde Slate Mtn Color Co Inc 570 421-8910
248 Lackawanna Ave East Stroudsburg (18301) *(G-4626)*

Olde Town Grove City 724 458-0301
118 S Center St Grove City (16127) *(G-6799)*

Oldskool Produxions Inc 215 638-4804
2100 Bristol Pike Bensalem (19020) *(G-1236)*

Olek Belts, Bensalem *Also called A Olek & Son Inc (G-1141)*

Olenicks Prtg & Photography Sp 814 342-2853
122 N Front St Fl 1 Philipsburg (16866) *(G-14522)*

Olesnevich Fabg & Trck Repr, Butler *Also called Daniel Leo Olesnevich (G-2392)*

Oleson Saw Technology, Emigsville *Also called York Saw & Knife Company Inc (G-5003)*

Oleum Exploration LLC 855 912-6200
108 Switzgabel Dr Brodheadsville (18322) *(G-2237)*

A
L
P
H
A
B
E
T
I
C

Olifant USA Inc 916 996-6207
3507 Market St Ste 102 Camp Hill (17011) *(G-2507)*

Olio Fresca Olive Oil Company 585 820-8400
217 Irving Ave Ridgway (15853) *(G-16722)*

Olive Kastania Oil 610 347-6736
759 Northbrook Rd Kennett Square (19348) *(G-8533)*

Olive Oakmont Oil Company 412 435-6912
640 Allegheny River Blvd Oakmont (15139) *(G-12921)*

Olive Olio Oils and Balsamics 717 627-0088
41 S Broad St B Lititz (17543) *(G-10027)*

Oliver Healthcare Packaging, New Britain Also called Oliver Products Company *(G-12050)*

Oliver Products Company 215 230-0300
97 Britain Dr New Britain (18901) *(G-12050)*

Oliver T Korb & Sons Inc 814 371-4545
15 E Park Ave Du Bois (15801) *(G-4408)*

Oliver-Tlas Hlthcare Packg Inc 215 322-7900
905 Pennsylvania Blvd Feasterville Trevose (19053) *(G-5923)*

Oliveros Vineyard LLC 717 856-4566
1271 Troyer Rd Mc Alisterville (17049) *(G-10551)*

Olmsted Inc 412 384-2161
Madison Ave West Elizabeth (15088) *(G-19696)*

Olson Technologies Inc (PA) 610 770-1100
160 W Walnut St Allentown (18102) *(G-339)*

Olympia Chimney Supply Inc 570 496-8890
600 Sanders St Ste 2 Scranton (18505) *(G-17268)*

Olympian Athletics 717 765-8615
55 W Main St Waynesboro (17268) *(G-19420)*

Olympic Mill Services Division, Glassport Also called Tms International LLC *(G-6419)*

Olympic Steel Inc 717 709-1515
1599 Nitterhouse Dr Chambersburg (17201) *(G-2966)*

Olympic Tool & Machine Corp 610 494-1600
2100 Bridgewater Rd Aston (19014) *(G-784)*

Olympus Advanced Tech LLC 814 838-3571
2545 W Grandview Blvd Erie (16506) *(G-5408)*

OMalley Wood Products Inc 717 677-6550
465 Upper Bermudian Rd Gardners (17324) *(G-6261)*

Omco Cast Metals Inc 724 222-7006
259 S College St Washington (15301) *(G-19213)*

Omega Design, Exton Also called Beta Industries Inc *(G-5655)*

Omega Design Corporation 610 363-6555
211 Philips Rd Exton (19341) *(G-5718)*

Omega Fence Co 215 729-7474
5709 Whitby Ave Philadelphia (19143) *(G-14094)*

Omega Flex Inc (PA) 610 524-7272
451 Creamery Way Exton (19341) *(G-5719)*

Omega Logging Inc 724 342-5430
21 Council Ave Wheatland (16161) *(G-19839)*

Omega Piezo Technologies Inc 814 861-4160
2591 Clyde Ave Ste 3 State College (16801) *(G-18004)*

Omega Plastics LLC 814 452-4989
1507 Wayne St Erie (16503) *(G-5409)*

Omega Transworld Ltd 724 966-5183
877 Garards Fort Rd Waynesburg (15370) *(G-19450)*

Omg, Franklin Also called Borchers Americas Inc *(G-6117)*

Omni Fab Inc 724 334-8851
822 Anderson St New Kensington (15068) *(G-12364)*

Omni One Group of Pennsylvania, Lyndora Also called Sr Jan Fisher *(G-10136)*

Omni Precast Products Inc 724 316-1582
339 Industrial Park Dr Wampum (16157) *(G-18803)*

Omni Publlishing Eastern PA 610 626-8819
615 Penn St Lansdowne (19050) *(G-9440)*

Omnia LLC 717 259-1633
301 Pleasant St Abbottstown (17301) *(G-5)*

Omnimax International Inc 215 355-1200
805 Pennsylvania Blvd Feasterville Trevose (19053) *(G-5924)*

Omnimax International Inc 717 299-3711
450 Richardson Dr Lancaster (17603) *(G-9152)*

Omnimax International Inc 717 397-2741
3449 Hempland Rd Lancaster (17601) *(G-9153)*

Omnipress Inc 610 631-2171
2562 Industry Ln Norristown (19403) *(G-12698)*

Omnispread Communications Inc 215 654-9900
809 Bethlehem Pike North Wales (19454) *(G-12821)*

Omnitech Automation Inc 610 965-3279
316 Wood St Emmaus (18049) *(G-5036)*

Omnitech Partners Inc (HQ) 724 295-2880
108 Kountz Ln Freeport (16229) *(G-6211)*

Omnova Solutions Inc 724 523-5441
1001 Chambers Ave Jeannette (15644) *(G-8263)*

Omnova Solutions Inc. 570 366-1051
95 Hickory Dr Auburn (17922) *(G-820)*

Ompi of America Inc 267 757-8747
41 University Dr Ste 400 Newtown (18940) *(G-12531)*

Omya PCC USA Inc (HQ) 814 965-3400
499 Glen Ave Johnsonburg (15845) *(G-8348)*

On Demand Printing 610 696-2258
1210 Nottingham Dr West Chester (19380) *(G-19610)*

On Fire Promotions, Shamokin Dam Also called Trautman Associates Inc *(G-17429)*

On Fuel 570 288-5805
360 Main St Luzerne (18709) *(G-10128)*

On Fuel 570 784-5320
711 Market St Bloomsburg (17815) *(G-1792)*

On Fuel 814 837-1017
159 Fraley St Kane (16735) *(G-8476)*

On Fuel 570 275-0170
614 E Market St Danville (17821) *(G-4008)*

On Line Publishers Inc 717 285-1350
3912 Abel Dr Columbia (17512) *(G-3445)*

On Line Publishers Inc 717 285-1350
808 Paddington Dr Lancaster (17601) *(G-9154)*

On Q Home, Middletown Also called Legrand Home Systems Inc *(G-11060)*

On Q Home, Middletown Also called Legrand Home Systems Inc *(G-11061)*

On Semiconductor 570 475-6030
125 Crestwood Dr Mountain Top (18707) *(G-11769)*

On Semiconductor Corp 602 244-6600
768 N Bethlehem Pike # 301 Ambler (19002) *(G-595)*

On Semiconductor Corporation 215 654-9700
768 N Bethlehem Pike Ambler (19002) *(G-596)*

On The Edge, Butler Also called John R Novak & Son Inc *(G-2414)*

On The Edge Mfg Inc 724 285-6802
107 E Quarry St Butler (16001) *(G-2430)*

On Track Enterprises Inc 610 277-4995
1219 W Main St Norristown (19401) *(G-12699)*

Ona Corporation 610 378-1381
400 Orton Ave Reading (19603) *(G-16458)*

Oncoceutics Inc 678 897-0563
3675 Market St Ste 200 Philadelphia (19104) *(G-14095)*

Onconova Therapeutics Inc (PA) 267 759-3680
375 Pheasant Run Newtown (18940) *(G-12532)*

Oncore Biopharma Inc 215 589-6378
3805 Old Easton Rd Doylestown (18902) *(G-4320)*

One Brew At A Time 267 797-5437
229 Plaza Blvd Morrisville (19067) *(G-11575)*

One Brilliant, Pittsburgh Also called Imposters LLC *(G-15115)*

One Day Baths Inc 570 402-2337
2241 Suburban Ln Effort (18330) *(G-4827)*

One Outboard, West Sunbury Also called Blackbird Industries Inc *(G-19769)*

One Sign Inc 412 478-6809
219 Chinkapin Dr Natrona Heights (15065) *(G-11948)*

Oneida Instant Log 814 336-2125
300 Allegheny St Meadville (16335) *(G-10770)*

Oneill Industries Inc 215 533-2101
5101 Comly St Ste 1 Philadelphia (19135) *(G-14096)*

ONeils Custom Cab & Design 412 422-4723
5233 Gertrude St Pittsburgh (15207) *(G-15359)*

Onexia Inc 610 431-7271
750 Springdale Dr Exton (19341) *(G-5720)*

Onexia Brass Inc 610 431-3271
1220 American Blvd West Chester (19380) *(G-19611)*

Online Data Systems Inc 610 967-5821
22 S 2nd St Emmaus (18049) *(G-5037)*

Onlyboth Inc 412 303-8798
1110 S Negley Ave Pittsburgh (15217) *(G-15360)*

Ono Industries Inc (PA) 717 865-6619
Rr 22 Box W Ono (17077) *(G-13004)*

Onsite Sterilization LLC 484 624-8566
1200 E High St Ste 306 Pottstown (19464) *(G-16023)*

Ontelaunee Farms Inc 610 929-5753
5379 Allentown Pike Temple (19560) *(G-18334)*

Onyx Optical 570 951-7750
113 S Washington St Wilkes Barre (18701) *(G-19953)*

Ooh Lala Salad 215 769-1006
1238 W Girard Ave Philadelphia (19123) *(G-14097)*

OP Schuman & Sons Inc 215 343-1530
817 Nina Way Warminster (18974) *(G-18932)*

Opco Inc 724 537-9300
205 W Harrison Ave Latrobe (15650) *(G-9507)*

Open Flow Gas Supply Corp 814 371-2228
90 Beaver Dr Ste 110b Du Bois (15801) *(G-4409)*

Open Solution 646 696-8686
631 Saw Creek Est Bushkill (18324) *(G-2368)*

Operating Room Safety LLC 866 498-6882
960 Brook Rd Ste 2 Conshohocken (19428) *(G-3580)*

Opertech Bio Inc 215 456-8765
5501 Old York Rd Philadelphia (19141) *(G-14098)*

Ophthalmic Associates PC 215 368-1646
1000 N Broad St Ste 2 Lansdale (19446) *(G-9395)*

Opi Holdings Inc 610 857-2000
1001 Moosic Rd Ste 1 Old Forge (18518) *(G-12973)*

Opinionmeter International Ltd 888 676-3837
44 E Broad St Fl 1 Bethlehem (18018) *(G-1587)*

Oppenheimer Precision Pdts Inc 215 674-9100
163-175 Gibralter Rd Horsham (19044) *(G-7837)*

Ops, Salunga Also called Ortho Depot LLC *(G-17055)*

Opsec Security Inc (HQ) 717 293-4110
1857 Colonial Village Ln Lancaster (17601) *(G-9155)*

Optical Crosslinks Inc 610 444-9469
206 Gale Ln Kennett Square (19348) *(G-8534)*

Optical Filters USA LLC 814 333-2222
13447 S Mosiertown Rd A Meadville (16335) *(G-10771)*

Optical Guidance Systems, Huntingdon Valley *Also called John E Stiles Jr (G-8005)*

Optical Interlinks, Kennett Square *Also called Martra LLC (G-8525)*

Optical Systems Technology.............................724 295-2880
183 Northpointe Blvd # 100 Freeport (16229) *(G-6212)*

Opticscampcom...888 978-5330
422 Louisa St Williamsport (17701) *(G-20052)*

Optilumen Inc...717 547-5417
167 Market St Pillow (17080) *(G-14586)*

Optima Plus International LLC..........................717 207-9037
436 Mahogany Dr Lancaster (17602) *(G-9156)*

Optima Technology Assoc Inc...........................717 932-5877
515 Fishing Creek Rd Lewisberry (17339) *(G-9889)*

Optimized Markets Inc..................................412 654-5994
830 Amberson Ave Pittsburgh (15232) *(G-15361)*

Optimum Controls Corporation..........................610 375-0990
1044 Macarthur Rd Reading (19605) *(G-16459)*

Optimus Technologies Inc...............................412 727-8228
6901 Lynn Way Pittsburgh (15208) *(G-15362)*

Optinose Inc (PA).......................................267 364-3500
1020 Stony Hill Rd # 300 Yardley (19067) *(G-20330)*

Optium Corporation (HQ)................................215 675-3105
200 Precision Rd Horsham (19044) *(G-7838)*

Optixtal Inc...215 254-5225
1901 S 54th St Philadelphia (19143) *(G-14099)*

Optofluidics Inc (PA)..................................215 253-5777
3675 Market St Apt 1 Philadelphia (19104) *(G-14100)*

Optotech Optical Machinery Inc.........................215 679-2091
1862 Tollgate Rd Palm (18070) *(G-13096)*

Optotherm Inc..724 940-7600
2591 Wexford Bayne Rd Sewickley (15143) *(G-17401)*

or Safety, Conshohocken *Also called Operating Room Safety LLC (G-3580)*

Oracle America Inc......................................412 859-6051
1550 Coraopls Hgts Rd 4 Coraopolis (15108) *(G-3709)*

Oracle America Inc......................................610 647-8530
400 Chesterfield Pkwy Malvern (19355) *(G-10290)*

Oracle America Inc......................................717 730-5501
645 N 12th St Ste 101 Lemoyne (17043) *(G-9747)*

Oracle Corporation.....................................610 667-8600
300 Barr Harbor Dr # 400 Conshohocken (19428) *(G-3581)*

Oracle Corporation.....................................717 234-5858
403 N 2nd St Harrisburg (17101) *(G-7188)*

Oracle Systems Corporation............................412 262-5200
1550 Coraopls Hts Rd 400 Coraopolis (15108) *(G-3710)*

Oracle Systems Corporation............................610 729-3600
300 Barr Harbor Dr # 400 Conshohocken (19428) *(G-3582)*

Oracle Systems Corporation............................610 260-9000
100 4 Falls Corp Ctr # 515 Conshohocken (19428) *(G-3583)*

Orahealth International 610 971-9600
407 E Lancaster Ave Wayne (19087) *(G-19361)*

Oram Transport Co Inc.................................702 559-4067
238 Peach St Allentown (18102) *(G-340)*

Orange Products Inc (PA)...............................610 791-9711
1929 Vultee St Allentown (18103) *(G-341)*

Orasure Technologies Inc (PA).........................610 882-1820
220 E 1st St Bethlehem (18015) *(G-1588)*

Orasure Technologies Inc..............................610 882-1820
150 Webster St Bethlehem (18015) *(G-1589)*

Orasure Technologies Inc..............................610 882-1820
1745 Eaton Ave Bethlehem (18018) *(G-1590)*

Orbel Corporation......................................610 829-5000
2 Danforth Dr Easton (18045) *(G-4736)*

Orbisonia Rockhill Joint.................................814 447-5414
843 Elliot St Ste 1 Orbisonia (17243) *(G-13007)*

Orbit Advanced Tech Inc...............................215 674-5100
650 Louis Dr Ste 100 Warminster (18974) *(G-18933)*

Orbit Software Inc.....................................484 941-0820
424 King St Pottstown (19464) *(G-16024)*

Orbit/Fr Inc (HQ)......................................215 674-5100
650 Louis Dr Ste 100 Warminster (18974) *(G-18934)*

Orchard Coal Company.................................570 695-2301
214 Vaux Ave Tremont (17981) *(G-18482)*

Orchem Pumps Inc.....................................215 743-6352
4434 Salmon St Ste 36 Philadelphia (19137) *(G-14101)*

Ordie Price Sawmill Inc.................................570 222-3986
7025 State Route 92 South Gibson (18842) *(G-17780)*

Ordnance Research Inc................................717 738-6941
121 Valley View Dr Ephrata (17522) *(G-5135)*

Ordnance Research Co., Ephrata *Also called Ordnance Research Inc (G-5135)*

Ore Enterprises Inc....................................814 898-3933
4725a Iroquois Ave Erie (16511) *(G-5410)*

Oregon Metallurgical LLC (HQ)........................541 967-9000
1000 Six Ppg Pl Pittsburgh (15222) *(G-15363)*

Oreland Sheet Metal, Conshohocken *Also called Schatzie Ltd (G-3604)*

Organ Historical Society.................................804 353-9226
330 N Spring Mill Rd Villanova (19085) *(G-18768)*

Organic Climbing LLC.................................651 245-1079
256 Enterprise Dr Philipsburg (16866) *(G-14523)*

Organic Mechanics Soil Co LLC.........................484 557-2961
12 Union St Rear Warehouse Modena (19358) *(G-11258)*

Organic Unlimited Inc..................................610 593-2995
120 Liberty St Atglen (19310) *(G-802)*

Organization Design & Dev Inc.........................610 279-2202
827 Lincoln Ave Unit B-10 West Chester (19380) *(G-19612)*

Original Fuels Inc......................................814 938-5171
91 Coolspring Rd Coolspring (15730) *(G-3622)*

Original Horse Tack Company, New Oxford *Also called Kabar Tack and Feed (G-12414)*

Original Little Pepis Inc...............................215 822-9650
2866 Sandstone Dr 70 Hatfield (19440) *(G-7376)*

Original Philly Holdings Inc (HQ)......................215 423-3333
31 Trailwood Dr Southampton (18966) *(G-17829)*

Orion Safety Products, Croydon *Also called Standard Fusee Corporation (G-3929)*

Orion Systems Inc....................................215 346-8200
1800 Byberry Rd Ste 1300 Huntingdon Valley (19006) *(G-8019)*

Orkist LLC..412 346-8316
322 N Shore Dr Pittsburgh (15212) *(G-15364)*

Orlotronics Corporation................................610 239-8200
401 E 4th St Ste 4 Bridgeport (19405) *(G-2042)*

Ormsbees Pro Shop, Reading *Also called Terre Trophy Co (G-16536)*

Ornamental Iron Works, Marcus Hook *Also called Guida Inc (G-10444)*

ORourke & Sons Inc..................................610 436-0932
992 S Bolmar St West Chester (19382) *(G-19613)*

Orr Screw Machine Products............................724 668-2256
190 Orr Dr Greensburg (15601) *(G-6695)*

Orrco, Greensburg *Also called Orr Screw Machine Products (G-6695)*

Ortho Depot LLC......................................800 992-9999
127 W Main St Salunga (17538) *(G-17055)*

Orthopli Corp...215 671-1000
10061 Sandmeyer Ln Philadelphia (19116) *(G-14102)*

Orthovita Inc..610 640-1775
45 Great Valley Pkwy Malvern (19355) *(G-10291)*

Orville Bronze and Alum LLC............................330 948-1231
18649 Brake Shoe Rd Meadville (16335) *(G-10772)*

Orwin Lathe & Dowel..................................717 647-4397
50 Snyder Ave Tower City (17980) *(G-18439)*

Oscar & Banks LLC....................................701 922-1005
110 Maple Dr Ligonier (15658) *(G-9962)*

Oscar Daniels & Company Inc..........................610 678-8144
35 Queen St Reading (19608) *(G-16460)*

OSheas Candies (PA)..................................814 536-4800
1118 Solomon St Johnstown (15902) *(G-8414)*

OSheas Candies.......................................814 266-7041
2451 Bedford St Johnstown (15904) *(G-8415)*

Oshikiri Corporation America............................215 637-6005
10425 Drummond Rd Philadelphia (19154) *(G-14103)*

OSI Industries...412 741-3630
101 Sonie Dr Sewickley (15143) *(G-17402)*

Osisoft LLC...215 606-0700
1700 Market St Ste 2200 Philadelphia (19103) *(G-14104)*

Oskis Woodworks......................................215 444-0523
31 Dorsett Cir Warminster (18974) *(G-18935)*

Ospcom LLC..267 356-7124
350 S Main St Ste 107 Doylestown (18901) *(G-4321)*

Osram Sylvania Inc.....................................814 834-1800
835 Washington St Saint Marys (15857) *(G-16999)*

Osram Sylvania Inc.....................................814 726-6600
816 Lexington Ave Warren (16365) *(G-19041)*

Osram Sylvania Inc.....................................717 854-3499
835 Washington St Saint Marys (15857) *(G-17000)*

Osram Sylvania Inc.....................................814 269-1418
224 W Oakmont Blvd Johnstown (15904) *(G-8416)*

Osram Sylvania Inc.....................................570 724-8200
1 Jackson St Wellsboro (16901) *(G-19471)*

Osram Sylvania Inc.....................................412 856-2111
9001 Rico Rd Monroeville (15146) *(G-11347)*

Osspray Inc...866 238-9902
301 Pleasant St Abbottstown (17301) *(G-6)*

Osterwalder Inc.......................................570 325-2500
1825 Franklin St Ste A Northampton (18067) *(G-12858)*

Osti Startron, Freeport *Also called Optical Systems Technology (G-6212)*

Ostrom Stone Co, Coudersport *Also called Pennsylvanin Flagstone Inc (G-3787)*

Oswald & Associates Inc...............................814 627-0300
10517 Raystown Rd Ste A Huntingdon (16652) *(G-7954)*

Oswaldsmill Inc.......................................610 298-3271
7002 Gun Club Rd New Tripoli (18066) *(G-12459)*

Ot Medical LLC.......................................484 588-2063
100 Springhouse Dr # 108 Collegeville (19426) *(G-3385)*

Otex Specialty Narrow Fabrics..........................570 538-5990
204 E 7th St Watsontown (17777) *(G-19279)*

Othera Pharmaceuticals Inc.............................484 879-2800
200 Barr Harbor Dr # 400 Conshohocken (19428) *(G-3584)*

Otis Elevator Company.................................814 452-2703
1001 State St Ste 319 Erie (16501) *(G-5411)*

Oto Melara North America Inc...........................314 707-4223
246 Airport Rd Johnstown (15904) *(G-8417)*

Oto Tech, Bristol *Also called Ototech Inc (G-2177)*

Otoole Plastic Surgery Dr...............................412 345-1615
5830 Ellsworth Ave # 300 Pittsburgh (15232) *(G-15365)*

A
L
P
H
A
B
E
T
I
C

Ototech Inc 215 781-7987
  806 Beaver St Bristol (19007) (G-2177)
Otte Gear LLC 917 923-6230
  6542a Lower York Rd 41 New Hope (18938) (G-12311)
Otten Flavors, Philadelphia Also called Interntnal Flvors Frgrnces Inc (G-13868)
Otterbine Barebo Inc 610 965-6018
  3840 Main Rd E Emmaus (18049) (G-5038)
Ottinger Machine Co Inc 610 933-2101
  1138 Spring City Rd Phoenixville (19460) (G-14565)
Otto Design Casefixture Inc (PA) 412 824-3580
  7341 Sandy Ln Greenock (15047) (G-6645)
Otto Design Casefixture Inc 412 378-6460
  14581 Josephine St Irwin (15642) (G-8187)
Ottocase, Greenock Also called Otto Design Casefixture Inc (G-6645)
Otw Tool Co 724 539-8952
  939 Donohoe Rd Latrobe (15650) (G-9508)
Otx Logistics Inc 412 567-8821
  1730 Route 30 Clinton (15026) (G-3264)
Our Town 814 269-9704
  500 Galleria Dr Ste 198 Johnstown (15904) (G-8418)
Out of Site Stump Removal LLC 610 692-9907
  27 Patrick Ave West Chester (19380) (G-19614)
Out On A Limb Creations 570 287-3778
  140 Center St Forty Fort (18704) (G-6098)
Outback Trading Company Ltd 610 932-5314
  39 S 3rd St Ste 1 Oxford (19363) (G-13084)
Outcast Studios LLC 267 242-1332
  2409 Cedar St 2417 Philadelphia (19125) (G-14105)
Outlaw Performance Inc 724 697-4876
  136 Nelson Rd Avonmore (15618) (G-866)
Outlook Printing Solutions Inc 215 680-4014
  2279 Shelly Rd Harleysville (19438) (G-7050)
Oven Industries Inc 717 766-0721
  434 Railroad Ave Camp Hill (17011) (G-2508)
Overdrive Holdings Inc 724 452-1500
  22073 Perry Hwy Zelienople (16063) (G-20813)
Overend & Krill Lumber Inc 724 348-7511
  3800 Baltimore St Finleyville (15332) (G-5962)
Overhead Crane Sales Svc LLC 724 335-1415
  2644 Leechburg Rd Lower Burrell (15068) (G-10107)
Overhead Door Corporation 717 248-0131
  23 Industrial Park Rd Lewistown (17044) (G-9942)
Overhead Door Corporation 570 326-7325
  3200 Reach Rd Williamsport (17701) (G-20053)
Overhead Door Corporation 215 368-8700
  1441 Industry Rd Lansdale (19446) (G-9396)
Overly Door Company (PA) 724 834-7300
  574 W Otterman St Greensburg (15601) (G-6696)
Overly Manufacturing Company 724 834-7300
  1551 Woodward Drive Ext Greensburg (15601) (G-6697)
Overtime Tool Inc 814 734-0848
  6020 Crane Rd Edinboro (16412) (G-4818)
Owen St Bakers, Swoyersville Also called Crofchick Inc (G-18197)
Owens Brockway Glass, Brockport Also called Owens-Illinois Inc (G-2222)
Owens Corning Sales LLC 570 339-3374
  1024 Locust Gap Hwy Mount Carmel (17851) (G-11628)
Owens Monumental Company 610 588-3370
  245 S 1st St Bangor (18013) (G-923)
Owens-Brockway Glass Cont Inc 814 226-0500
  151 Grand Ave Clarion (16214) (G-3185)
Owens-Brockway Glass Cont Inc 814 461-5100
  316 W 16th St Erie (16502) (G-5412)
Owens-Brockway Glass Cont Inc 814 849-4265
  1082 Route 28 Brookville (15825) (G-2267)
Owens-Brockway Glass Cont Inc 814 261-6284
  Cherry St Brockway (15824) (G-2229)
Owens-Illinois Inc 814 261-5200
  3831 Route 219 Brockport (15823) (G-2222)
Owl Testing Software, Pittsburgh Also called Prismatic Consulting LLC (G-15449)
Ox Paper Tube and Core Inc (PA) 800 414-2476
  600 W Elm Ave Hanover (17331) (G-6927)
Ox Paperboard LLC (PA) 304 725-2076
  331 Maple Ave Hanover (17331) (G-6928)
Oxbow Activated Carbon LLC 724 791-2411
  3539 Oneida Valley Rd Emlenton (16373) (G-5013)
Oxford Area Sewer Authority 610 932-3493
  14 S 3rd St Oxford (19363) (G-13085)
Oxford Cabinetry LLC 610 932-3793
  209 Glen Roy Rd Nottingham (19362) (G-12884)
Oxford Construction PA Inc 215 809-2245
  1715 Rittenhouse Sq Philadelphia (19103) (G-14106)
Oxford Daily LLC 215 533-5656
  5759 Oxford Ave Philadelphia (19149) (G-14107)
Oxford Market Place Inc 610 998-9080
  180 Limestone Rd Oxford (19363) (G-13086)
Oxicool Inc (PA) 215 462-2665
  508 Lapp Rd Malvern (19355) (G-10292)
Oz World Media LLC 202 470-6757
  1100 H St Nw Ste M Devon (19333) (G-4115)

P & C Tool Inc 814 425-7050
  8111 Pettis Rd Meadville (16335) (G-10773)
P & H Lumber Millwork Co Inc 215 699-9365
  1616 Rose Ln North Wales (19454) (G-12822)
P & L Sportswear Inc 717 359-9000
  950 Bulk Plant Rd Littlestown (17340) (G-10074)
P & M Precision Machining Inc 215 357-3313
  65 Buck Rd Huntingdon Valley (19006) (G-8020)
P & N Coal Co Inc (PA) 814 938-7660
  240 W Mahoning St Punxsutawney (15767) (G-16152)
P & N Holdings Inc (PA) 570 455-3636
  25 N Wyoming St Hazleton (18201) (G-7514)
P & N Packing Inc 570 746-1974
  180 Rr 2 Wyalusing (18853) (G-20255)
P & P Stone LLC 570 967-2279
  239 Franklin Hill Rd Hallstead (18822) (G-6835)
P & R Engine Rebuilders 724 837-7590
  952 W Pittsburg St Greensburg (15601) (G-6698)
P & R United Welding and Fabg 610 375-9928
  316 Franklin St 322 Reading (19602) (G-16461)
P & S Pallet Inc 570 655-4628
  40 Tompkins St Pittston (18640) (G-15772)
P & S Ravioli Co (PA) 215 465-8888
  2001 S 26th St Philadelphia (19145) (G-14108)
P & S Ravioli Co 215 339-9929
  1722 W Oregon Ave Philadelphia (19145) (G-14109)
P & S Sportswear Inc 215 455-7133
  176 W Loudon St Philadelphia (19120) (G-14110)
P A C, Boyertown Also called Premier Applied Coatings Inc (G-1924)
P A Hutchison Company 570 876-4560
  400 Penn Ave Mayfield (18433) (G-10542)
P A M P, Bellefonte Also called Patrick Mc Cool (G-1110)
P A Office and Closet Systems 610 944-1333
  7 Willow Street Indus Par Fleetwood (19522) (G-5977)
P B S, Middleburg Also called Professional Bldg Systems Inc (G-11036)
P C S, Ridgway Also called PC Systems Inc (G-16724)
P D Plastics 724 941-3930
  609 E Mcmurray Rd Canonsburg (15317) (G-2616)
P D Q Instant Print Center, Kingston Also called PDQ Print Center (G-8724)
P D Q Pest Control Inc 814 774-8882
  8799 Ridge Rd Girard (16417) (G-6398)
P D Q Tooling Inc 412 751-2214
  940 Grnock Buena Vista Rd Mckeesport (15135) (G-10677)
P E, Ivyland Also called Power & Energy Inc (G-8221)
P E H Inc 610 845-9111
  20 N Front St Bally (19503) (G-905)
P E P R O, Oil City Also called Pioneer Energy Products LLC (G-12954)
P F P, Pennsburg Also called Precision Filtration Pdts Inc (G-13252)
P G A Machine Co Inc 610 874-1335
  914 Simpson St Eddystone (19022) (G-4806)
P G E, Warren Also called Pennsylvania Gen Enrgy Corp (G-19043)
P G Recycling Incorporated 814 696-6000
  155 Rossman Rd Tyrone (16686) (G-18588)
P H A Finance Inc 610 272-4700
  1000 Germantown Pike E3 Plymouth Meeting (19462) (G-15862)
P H B Molding, Fairview Also called Phb Inc (G-5838)
P H Glatfelter Company (PA) 717 225-4711
  96 S George St Ste 520 York (17401) (G-20615)
P J Electronics Inc 412 793-3912
  575 Davidson Rd Pittsburgh (15239) (G-15366)
P K B Inc 215 826-1988
  570 Otter St Bristol (19007) (G-2178)
P K Choppers Mobile 570 458-6983
  1205 State Route 254 Millville (17846) (G-11226)
P M C, Hanover Also called Penn Mar Castings Inc (G-6935)
P M I, Montgomeryville Also called Penn Manufacturing Inds Inc (G-11411)
P M I, Norristown Also called Positran Manufacturing Inc (G-12704)
P M L C, Hanover Township Also called Pocono Mountain Leather Co (G-7004)
P M P, Denver Also called Roechling Med Lancaster LLC (G-4092)
P M Supply Co Inc (PA) 814 472-4430
  136 Lazor Rd Ebensburg (15931) (G-4791)
P P G Coatings & Resins Group, Springdale Also called PPG Industries Inc (G-17899)
P P G Coatings & Resins R & D, Allison Park Also called PPG Industries Inc (G-459)
P P S, Latrobe Also called Premium Plastics Solutions LLC (G-9511)
P Q, Conshohocken Also called PQ Corporation (G-3591)
P R Finishing Inc 610 565-0378
  5 Horne Dr Folcroft (19032) (G-6011)
P R L Inc (PA) 717 273-2470
  64 Rexmont Rd Cornwall (17016) (G-3739)
P R X 570 578-0136
  1065 Hanover St Hanover Township (18706) (G-7002)
P S A, Aston Also called Egr Ventures Inc (G-761)
P S Composites Inc 724 329-4413
  311 Friendsville Rd Markleysburg (15459) (G-10483)
P S S Company Fax, Girard Also called Pennside Machining LLC (G-6399)
P Stone Inc 570 745-7166
  1430 Route 880 Hwy Jersey Shore (17740) (G-8319)

2019 Harris Pennsylvania
Manufacturers Directory

(G-0000) Company's Geographic Section entry number

P T S, Rochester *Also called Pittsbrgh Tubular Shafting Inc* **(G-16787)**

P V C, Fairless Hills *Also called Gregg Lane LLC* **(G-5781)**

P Varnish Contractors, Johnstown *Also called Parrish R Varnish* **(G-8419)**

P/M National Inc 814 781-1960
201 Grotzinger Rd Saint Marys (15857) **(G-17001)**

P/S Printing & Copy Services 814 623-7033
133 Mann St Ste 3 Bedford (15522) **(G-1069)**

PA & Implant Surgery LLC 814 375-0500
90 Beaver Dr Du Bois (15801) **(G-4410)**

PA Artificial Limb & Brace Co 724 588-6860
111 N Main St Ste 101 Greenville (16125) **(G-6763)**

PA Biodiesel Supply, Hummelstown *Also called J Maze Corp* **(G-7915)**

PA Mining Professional 717 761-4646
704 Lisburn Rd Camp Hill (17011) **(G-2509)**

PA Outdoor Times 814 946-7400
301 Cayuga Ave Altoona (16602) **(G-536)**

PA Packing Products & Svcs Inc 717 486-8100
433 Zion Rd Carlisle (17015) **(G-2728)**

PA Pallet Exchange, Columbia *Also called Rick Degeorge* **(G-3449)**

PA Pellets LLC 814 848-9970
958 State Route 49 W Ulysses (16948) **(G-18604)**

PA Vault Co, Johnstown *Also called Richard Rhodes* **(G-8430)**

Paar Precision Industries 610 807-9230
93 Market St Freemansburg (18017) **(G-6198)**

Pabcor Inc 724 652-1930
925 N Cedar St New Castle (16102) **(G-12136)**

Pac Strapping Products Inc 610 363-8805
307 National Rd Exton (19341) **(G-5721)**

Paccar Inc 717 397-4111
3001 Industry Dr Lancaster (17603) **(G-9157)**

Pace Environmental 610 262-3818
5240 W Coplay Rd Whitehall (18052) **(G-19885)**

Pace Industries LLC 724 539-4527
1004 Industrial Blvd Loyalhanna (15661) **(G-10112)**

Pace Precisions Products Inc 814 371-6201
21 Ohio Ave Du Bois (15801) **(G-4411)**

Pace Resources Inc (PA) 717 852-1300
140 E Market St Fl 2 York (17401) **(G-20616)**

Pacemaker Press PP&s Inc 301 696-9629
4999 Zane A Miller Dr Waynesboro (17268) **(G-19421)**

Pacer Industries Inc 610 383-4200
200 Red Rd Coatesville (19320) **(G-3320)**

Pacer Pumps, Lancaster *Also called Asm Industries Inc* **(G-8945)**

Pacer Pumps, Lancaster *Also called Service Filtration Corp* **(G-9194)**

Pacific Process Systems Inc 724 993-4445
1385 Washington Rd # 105 Washington (15301) **(G-19214)**

Pack Nano, Wayne *Also called Nanopack Inc* **(G-19359)**

Pack Pro Technologies LLC 717 517-9065
204 Bucky Dr Ste A Lititz (17543) **(G-10028)**

Packaging Coordinators Inc 215 613-3600
3001 Red Lion Rd Philadelphia (19114) **(G-14111)**

Packaging Corp O 717 293-2877
1530 Fruitville Pike Lancaster (17601) **(G-9158)**

Packaging Corporation America 301 497-9090
435 Gitts Run Rd Hanover (17331) **(G-6929)**

Packaging Corporation America 610 366-6501
7451 Cetronia Rd Allentown (18106) **(G-342)**

Packaging Corporation America 610 366-6500
7451 Cetronia Rd Allentown (18106) **(G-343)**

Packaging Corporation America 610 916-3200
173 Tuckerton Rd Reading (19605) **(G-16462)**

Packaging Corporation America 724 275-3700
499 Nixon Rd Cheswick (15024) **(G-3114)**

Packaging Corporation America 717 624-2122
104 Commerce St New Oxford (17350) **(G-12418)**

Packaging Corporation America 717 632-4800
401 Moulstown Rd Hanover (17331) **(G-6930)**

Packaging Corporation America 717 632-4727
201 S College St New Oxford (17350) **(G-12419)**

Packaging Corporation America 717 397-3591
1530 Fruitville Pike Lancaster (17601) **(G-9159)**

Packaging Corporation America 717 637-3758
435 Gitts Run Rd Hanover (17331) **(G-6931)**

Packaging Corporation America 717 653-0420
109 Arrowhead Dr Bldg 2 Manheim (17545) **(G-10398)**

Packaging Enterprises Inc 215 379-1234
12 N Penn Ave Jenkintown (19046) **(G-8298)**

Packaging Equipment Sales, Warrington *Also called Ameripak* **(G-19107)**

Packaging Progressions Inc 610 489-9096
261 Schoolhouse Rd Ste 7 Souderton (18964) **(G-17758)**

Packaging Science Inc 610 992-9991
105 Town Center Rd Ste 7 King of Prussia (19406) **(G-8658)**

Packaging Stratagies, West Chester *Also called BNP Media Inc* **(G-19512)**

Packer Avenue Foods Inc 215 271-0300
700 Packer Ave Ste R2 Philadelphia (19148) **(G-14112)**

Paco Winders Mfg LLC 215 673-6265
2040 Bennett Rd Philadelphia (19116) **(G-14113)**

Pactiv LLC 610 269-1776
461 Boot Rd Downingtown (19335) **(G-4247)**

Padc 1 (HQ) 215 781-1600
411 Sinclair Rd Bristol (19007) **(G-2179)**

Padc 1 .... 215 322-3300
2595 Metropolitan Dr Feasterville Trevose (19053) **(G-5925)**

Paddycake Bakery 412 621-4477
4763 Liberty Ave Pittsburgh (15224) **(G-15367)**

Paeonia Arts & Literature LLC 267 520-4572
525 Wharton St Philadelphia (19147) **(G-14114)**

Page 1 Publishers Inc 610 380-8264
341 E Lancaster Ave Ste 3 Downingtown (19335) **(G-4248)**

Pagnotti Enterprises Inc (PA) 570 825-8700
46 Public Sq Ste 600 Wilkes Barre (18701) **(G-19954)**

Pagoda Industries, Reading *Also called Pagoda Products Inc* **(G-16463)**

Pagoda Products Inc 610 678-8096
777 Commerce St Reading (19608) **(G-16463)**

Painted Truffle 215 996-0606
105 Guinness Ln North Wales (19454) **(G-12823)**

Painter Meat Processing 814 258-7283
408 E River St Elkland (16920) **(G-4917)**

Pak Innovations Inc 215 723-0498
206 Diamond St Souderton (18964) **(G-17759)**

Pak-It Displays Inc 215 638-7510
1324 Adams Rd Bensalem (19020) **(G-1237)**

Pak-Rapid Inc 610 828-3511
1050 Colwell Ln Ste F Conshohocken (19428) **(G-3585)**

Palace Foods Inc (PA) 610 939-0631
194 Mill St Wilkes Barre (18705) **(G-19955)**

Palace Foods Inc 610 775-9947
100 Cleveland Ave Reading (19605) **(G-16464)**

Palace Industries 215 442-5508
605 Louis Dr Ste 501c Warminster (18974) **(G-18936)**

Palace Packaging Machines Inc 610 873-7252
4102 Edges Mill Rd Downingtown (19335) **(G-4249)**

Palcon LLC (PA) 570 546-9032
1759 Lime Bluff Rd Muncy (17756) **(G-11828)**

Palcon LLC 570 546-9032
1759 Lime Bluff Rd Muncy (17756) **(G-11829)**

Palermo Metal Products Inc 610 253-6230
3760 Nicholas St Easton (18045) **(G-4737)**

Paletti Usa LLC 267 289-0020
145 Keystone Dr Montgomeryville (18936) **(G-11410)**

Pall Corporation 610 458-9500
770 Pnnsylvnia Dr Ste 100 Exton (19341) **(G-5722)**

Palladino Martial Arts, Oakdale *Also called Cla Industries Inc* **(G-12897)**

Palladino Mtal Fabrication Inc (PA) 610 323-9439
337 W High St Pottstown (19464) **(G-16025)**

Pallet Connection 570 963-1432
120 N Van Buren Ave Scranton (18504) **(G-17269)**

Pallet Express Inc 610 258-8846
2906 William Penn Hwy # 503 Easton (18045) **(G-4738)**

Pallet Outlet, Biglerville *Also called Chep (usa) Inc* **(G-1661)**

Pallets Unlimited Inc 717 755-3691
1721 Eberts Ln York (17406) **(G-20617)**

Palmer International Inc (PA) 610 584-4241
2036 Lucon Rd Skippack (19474) **(G-17602)**

Palmer International Inc 610 584-3204
2955 Skippack Pike Worcester (19490) **(G-20225)**

Palmer Plastics Inc 610 330-9900
2906 William Penn Hwy # 505 Easton (18045) **(G-4739)**

Palmer Snyder Furniture, Conneautville *Also called PS Furniture Inc* **(G-3486)**

Palmyra Bologna Company (PA) 717 838-6336
230 N College St Palmyra (17078) **(G-13128)**

Palmyra Bologna Company 717 273-9581
1035 Willow St Lebanon (17046) **(G-9614)**

Palram 2000, Kutztown *Also called Palram Americas Inc* **(G-8853)**

Palram 2000 Inc 610 285-9918
9735 Commerce Cir Kutztown (19530) **(G-8852)**

Palram Americas Inc 610 285-9918
9735 Commerce Cir Kutztown (19530) **(G-8853)**

Palram Industries 1990, Kutztown *Also called Palram Panels Inc* **(G-8854)**

Palram Panels Inc 610 285-9918
9735 Commerce Cir Kutztown (19530) **(G-8854)**

Palumbo's Meat Market, Du Bois *Also called Palumbos Meats Dubois Inc* **(G-4412)**

Palumbos Meats Dubois Inc 814 371-2150
326 W Long Ave Du Bois (15801) **(G-4412)**

Pan Saver, Limerick *Also called M & Q Plastic Products Co* **(G-9969)**

Panache Plus 717 812-8999
403 W Market St York (17401) **(G-20618)**

Panagraphics Inc 717 292-5606
4690 Raycom Rd Dover (17315) **(G-4198)**

Pandalai Coatings Company Inc 724 224-5600
837 6th Ave Brackenridge (15014) **(G-1940)**

Panel Prints, Old Forge *Also called W M Abene Co* **(G-12977)**

Panel Solutions Inc 570 459-3490
100 E Diamond Ave Hazleton (18201) **(G-7515)**

Panel Technologies Inc 215 538-7055
550 California Rd Ste 2 Quakertown (18951) **(G-16226)**

Pannebaker Holdings Inc 717 463-3615
758 Johnstown Rd Thompsontown (17094) **(G-18350)**

A L P H A B E T I C

Pannell Mfg Corp...610 268-2012
  1780 Baltimore Pike Avondale (19311) *(G-856)*
Pannier Corporation (PA).....................................412 323-4900
  207 Sandusky St Pittsburgh (15212) *(G-15368)*
Pannier Corporation...724 265-4900
  345 Oak Rd Gibsonia (15044) *(G-6348)*
Pannier Corporation...412 492-1400
  1130 Butler Plank Rd Glenshaw (15116) *(G-6495)*
Panthera Products Inc..724 532-3362
  5055 Center Dr Latrobe (15650) *(G-9509)*
Paoli Print & Copy Inc..610 644-7471
  45 E Lancaster Ave Paoli (19301) *(G-13145)*
Pap Technologies Inc..717 399-3333
  1813 Colonial Village Ln Lancaster (17601) *(G-9160)*
Papco Inc (PA)..814 726-2130
  213 W 3rd Ave Rm 304 Warren (16365) *(G-19042)*
Paper and Ink of Pa LLC.......................................717 709-0533
  1050 Superior Ave Chambersburg (17201) *(G-2967)*
Paper Converting Machine Co................................814 695-5521
  899 Plank Rd Ste 1 Duncansville (16635) *(G-4459)*
Paper Exchange Inc..412 325-7075
  2504 College Park Rd Allison Park (15101) *(G-457)*
Paper Magic Group Inc (HQ)..................................570 961-3863
  54 Glenmra Ntl Blvd Moosic (18507) *(G-11511)*
Paper Magic Group Inc...570 644-0842
  210 Industrial Park Rd Elysburg (17824) *(G-4978)*
Paper Plant, New Columbia *Also called New Ngc Inc (G-12174)*
Paper Preserve, Philadelphia *Also called Mbm Industries Inc (G-13998)*
Paper Recovery Systems Inc..................................215 423-6624
  3287 Chatham St Philadelphia (19134) *(G-14115)*
Paperia..215 247-8521
  8521 Germantown Ave Philadelphia (19118) *(G-14116)*
Paperworks Industries Inc (HQ)............................215 984-7000
  40 Monument Rd Ste 200 Bala Cynwyd (19004) *(G-888)*
Pappajohn Woodworking Inc.................................215 289-8625
  4355 Orchard St Philadelphia (19124) *(G-14117)*
Papyrus Inc...610 354-9480
  160 N Gulph Rd Ste 2650 King of Prussia (19406) *(G-8659)*
Par Pharmaceutical 2 Inc....................................484 216-7741
  1400 Atwater Dr Malvern (19355) *(G-10293)*
Para Science International, Harrisburg *Also called Larry Arnold (G-7168)*
Parabo Press LLC...484 843-1230
  4040 Locust St Philadelphia (19104) *(G-14118)*
Parade Strapping & Baling LLC............................215 537-9473
  3300 Tulip St Philadelphia (19134) *(G-14119)*
Paradies Pleasant News LL...................................610 521-2936
  100 Putcan Ave Essington (19029) *(G-5545)*
Paradigm Corporation..215 675-9488
  409 Lincoln Ave Hatboro (19040) *(G-7295)*
Paradigm Dgital Color Graphics, Southampton *Also called Digital Color Graphics
Inc (G-17808)*
Paradigm Labs Inc...570 345-2600
  7 Roberts Rd Pine Grove (17963) *(G-14601)*
Paradigm Tool and Mfg, Hatboro *Also called Paradigm Corporation (G-7295)*
Paradise Pillow LLC..215 225-8700
  2207 W Glenwood Ave Philadelphia (19132) *(G-14120)*
Paradocx Vineyard LLC.......................................610 255-5684
  1833 Flint Hill Rd Landenberg (19350) *(G-9252)*
Paragon America LLC...412 408-3447
  111 3rd St Sharpsburg (15215) *(G-17467)*
Paragon Development Corp...................................724 254-1551
  4748 Route 403 Hwy N Penn Run (15765) *(G-13230)*
Paragon Print Systems Inc..................................814 456-8331
  2021 Paragon Dr Erie (16510) *(G-5413)*
Paragon Technologies Inc (PA).............................610 252-7321
  101 Larry Holmes Dr # 500 Easton (18042) *(G-4740)*
Paragon Welding Company Inc..............................215 634-7300
  2134 E Lippincott St Philadelphia (19134) *(G-14121)*
Paramount Die Corporation...................................814 734-6999
  4180 Route 6n Edinboro (16412) *(G-4819)*
Paramount Games Inc..800 282-5766
  30 Mill St Wheatland (16161) *(G-19840)*
Paratek Pharmaceuticals Inc...............................484 751-4920
  1000 1st Ave Ste 200 King of Prussia (19406) *(G-8660)*
Paravano Company Inc.......................................215 659-4600
  2557 Wyandotte Rd Ste C Willow Grove (19090) *(G-20132)*
Parc Productions...724 283-3300
  112 Hollywood Dr Ste 202 Butler (16001) *(G-2431)*
Pardee Resources Company (PA)...........................215 405-1260
  1717 Arch St Ste 4010 Philadelphia (19103) *(G-14122)*
Pardees Jewelry & Accessories.............................814 282-1172
  664 Tremont St Meadville (16335) *(G-10774)*
Pardoes Perky Peanuts Inc.................................570 524-9595
  143 Center St Montandon (17850) *(G-11366)*
Parent Co Is Sig Holdg USA, Chester *Also called Sig Combibloc Inc (G-3062)*
Parent Company Is Selmax, Selinsgrove *Also called Ken-Tex Corp (G-17328)*
Parent Metal Products, Bensalem *Also called Pickell Enterprises Inc (G-1243)*
Park & Park Norristown Inc.................................267 346-0932
  409 W Main St Norristown (19401) *(G-12700)*

Park Corporation...412 472-0500
  210 Airside Dr Coraopolis (15108) *(G-3711)*
Park Place Pa LLC..717 336-2846
  412 Oak St Denver (17517) *(G-4086)*
Park Place Transmission Inc..................................717 859-2998
  65 N Church St Ephrata (17522) *(G-5136)*
Park Press Inc..724 465-5812
  333 Elm St Indiana (15701) *(G-8116)*
Parker Autoclave, Erie *Also called Autoclave Engineers (G-5197)*
Parker Industries Inc..412 561-6902
  3585 Valley Dr Pittsburgh (15234) *(G-15369)*
Parker Machine and Fabrication.............................570 673-4160
  Road 1 Route 14 S Canton (17724) *(G-2666)*
Parker Machine Company......................................814 772-0135
  1 Grant Rd Ridgway (15853) *(G-16723)*
Parker Plastics, Pittsburgh *Also called Parker Industries Inc (G-15369)*
Parker Precision Molding Inc...............................724 930-8099
  129 Landmark Ln Rostraver Township (15012) *(G-16829)*
Parker Service Center, Chambersburg *Also called Parker-Hannifin Corporation (G-2968)*
Parker Snap-Tite Qdv Assembly.............................814 438-3821
  74 S Main St Union City (16438) *(G-18611)*
Parker White Metal Company.................................814 474-5511
  7900 W Ridge Rd Fairview (16415) *(G-5835)*
Parker-Hannifin Corporation.................................610 926-1115
  1018 Stinson Dr Reading (19605) *(G-16465)*
Parker-Hannifin Corporation.................................814 438-3821
  201 Titusville Rd Union City (16438) *(G-18612)*
Parker-Hannifin Corporation.................................814 866-4100
  8325 Hessinger Dr Erie (16509) *(G-5414)*
Parker-Hannifin Corporation.................................215 723-4000
  245 Township Line Rd Hatfield (19440) *(G-7377)*
Parker-Hannifin Corporation.................................724 861-8200
  1140 Sandy Hill Rd Irwin (15642) *(G-8188)*
Parker-Hannifin Corporation.................................814 860-5700
  6424 W Ridge Rd Erie (16506) *(G-5415)*
Parker-Hannifin Corporation.................................717 263-5099
  1201a Sheffler Dr Chambersburg (17201) *(G-2968)*
Parker-Hannifin Corporation.................................814 866-4100
  8325 Hessinger Dr Erie (16509) *(G-5416)*
Parker-Majestic Div, Sarver *Also called Penn United Technologies Inc (G-17078)*
Parkin Chemical Corporation.................................412 828-7355
  516 Allegheny River Blvd Oakmont (15139) *(G-12922)*
Parkland Bindery Inc..610 433-6153
  2232 Walbert Ave Allentown (18104) *(G-344)*
Parks Design & Ink..814 643-1120
  719 Washington St Huntingdon (16652) *(G-7955)*
Parkside Creamery LLC.......................................412 372-1110
  1 Forbes Rd Trafford (15085) *(G-18460)*
Parkside Graphics Inc..215 453-1123
  160 E Walnut St Sellersville (18960) *(G-17356)*
Parkway Industries, Pittsburgh *Also called Achieva (G-14641)*
Parkway Industries, Bridgeville *Also called Achieva (G-2052)*
Parkway Printing...610 928-3433
  326 S 2nd St Emmaus (18049) *(G-5039)*
Parkwood Resources Inc.....................................724 479-4090
  301 Market St Kittanning (16201) *(G-8787)*
Parma Sausage Products Inc.................................412 261-2532
  1734 Penn Ave Pittsburgh (15222) *(G-15370)*
Parmer Metered Concrete Inc..............................717 533-3344
  2981 Elizabethtown Rd Hershey (17033) *(G-7624)*
Parnell Enterprises Inc...724 258-3320
  787 Dry Run Rd Monongahela (15063) *(G-11312)*
Parodi Holdings LLC...570 344-8566
  200 Keystone Industrial P Dunmore (18512) *(G-4479)*
Parrish R Varnish..814 242-1786
  602 Demuth St Johnstown (15904) *(G-8419)*
Parrot Graphics...570 746-1745
  807 Iron Bridge Rd New Albany (18833) *(G-12014)*
Parsons Garage, Shade Gap *Also called Wood Mizer (G-17418)*
Parthenon, Bensalem *Also called Janzer Corporation (G-1212)*
Particle Sciences Inc..610 861-4701
  3894 Courtney St Bethlehem (18017) *(G-1591)*
Particle Size Technology Inc..................................215 529-9771
  1930 Kumry Rd Quakertown (18951) *(G-16227)*
Partners Press Inc...610 666-7960
  98 Highland Ave 18 Oaks (19456) *(G-12935)*
Partridge Wirth Company Inc.................................570 344-8514
  523 Wyoming Ave Scranton (18509) *(G-17270)*
Parts Now, Middletown *Also called Phxco LLC (G-11069)*
Parts To Your Door LP..610 916-5380
  800 Corporate Dr Reading (19605) *(G-16466)*
Party Time Manufacturing Co................................800 346-3847
  421 Parsonage St Hughestown (18640) *(G-7894)*
Pasadena Scientific Inc..717 227-1220
  5125 Pine View Dr Glen Rock (17327) *(G-6459)*
Pasadena Scientific Industries, Glen Rock *Also called Pasadena Scientific Inc (G-6459)*
Paser Inc...814 623-7221
  1804 Fleegle Rd Bedford (15522) *(G-1070)*

Pasta Acquisition Corp 559 485-8110
85 Shannon Rd Harrisburg (17112) ***(G-7189)***
Pat Garrett Western Wear, Strausstown *Also called Sickafus Sheepskins* ***(G-18100)***
Pat Landgraf 412 221-0347
260 Millers Run Rd Ste 1 Bridgeville (15017) ***(G-2084)***
Pat Stinely Ceramic & Stone, Erie *Also called Patrick G Stinely* ***(G-5417)***
Patel, Satyn & Pragness, Lansdale *Also called Best Bakery Inc* ***(G-9345)***
Pathfinders Travel Inc 215 438-2140
6325 Germantown Ave Philadelphia (19144) ***(G-14123)***
Pathfinders Travel Magazine, Philadelphia *Also called Pathfinders Travel Inc* ***(G-14123)***
Pathfnder Eqine Pblcations LLC 610 488-1282
243 N Garfield Rd Mohrsville (19541) ***(G-11278)***
Pati Petite Butter Cookies Inc 412 221-4033
1785 Mayview Rd Bridgeville (15017) ***(G-2085)***
Pati Petite Cookies, Bridgeville *Also called Pati Petite Butter Cookies Inc* ***(G-2085)***
Patio Concepts, Bradfordwoods *Also called Ski Haus LLC* ***(G-1999)***
Patiova LLC 610 857-1359
6649 N Moscow Rd Parkesburg (19365) ***(G-13181)***
Patricia Morris 717 272-5594
21 Lehman St Lebanon (17046) ***(G-9615)***
Patrick Aiello Cabinetry LLC 610 681-7167
225 Berger St Kunkletown (18058) ***(G-8834)***
Patrick Custom Vynals, Mount Joy *Also called Patrick Industries Inc* ***(G-11668)***
Patrick Donovan 724 238-9038
105 Deerfield Rd Ligonier (15658) ***(G-9963)***
Patrick G Stinely 814 528-3832
952 W 28th St Erie (16508) ***(G-5417)***
Patrick Industries Inc 717 653-2086
20 Eby Chiques Rd Mount Joy (17552) ***(G-11668)***
Patrick Mc Cool (PA) 814 359-2447
136 S Harrison Rd Bellefonte (16823) ***(G-1110)***
Patriot Armory & Coatings LLC 215 723-7228
1000 Revenue Dr Telford (18969) ***(G-18308)***
Patriot Exploration 724 593-4427
1384 State Route 711 Stahlstown (15687) ***(G-17936)***
Patriot Exploration Corp 724 282-2339
202 Sunset Dr Butler (16001) ***(G-2432)***
Patriot Kutztown Area 610 367-6041
24 N Hanover St Pottstown (19464) ***(G-16026)***
Patriot Metal Products Inc 570 759-3634
1005 N Vine St Berwick (18603) ***(G-1339)***
Patriot Pharmaceuticals LLC 215 325-7676
200 Tournament Dr Horsham (19044) ***(G-7839)***
Patriot Sensors & Contrls Corp 336 449-3400
215 Keith Valley Rd Horsham (19044) ***(G-7840)***
Patriot-News Co (PA) 717 255-8100
2020 Tech Pkwy Ste 300 Mechanicsburg (17050) ***(G-10875)***
Patriot-News Co 717 255-8100
1900 Patriot Dr Mechanicsburg (17050) ***(G-10876)***
Patriot-News Co 717 243-1758
101 Noble Blvd Ste 103 Carlisle (17013) ***(G-2729)***
Patternmaster Chokes LLC 877 388-2259
1102 W Loop Rd Hollidaysburg (16648) ***(G-7652)***
Patterson Furniture Co 412 771-0600
701 Yunker St Mc Kees Rocks (15136) ***(G-10622)***
Patterson Lumber Co Inc 814 435-2210
95 West St Galeton (16922) ***(G-6241)***
Patterson Plastics & Mfg 215 736-3020
253 Lower Morrisville Rd Levittown (19054) ***(G-9853)***
Patton Picture Company 717 796-1508
207 Lynndale Ct Mechanicsburg (17050) ***(G-10877)***
Patton Wall Decor, Mechanicsburg *Also called Patton Picture Company* ***(G-10877)***
Patwell Phrm Solutions LLC 610 380-7101
555 Fox Chase Ste 102 Coatesville (19320) ***(G-3321)***
Paul Danfelt 814 448-2592
Rr 1 Mapleton Depot (17052) ***(G-10431)***
Paul Dorazio Custom Furniture 215 836-1057
1410 Bethlehem Pike Flourtown (19031) ***(G-5989)***
Paul Downs Cabinet Makers Inc 610 239-0142
401 E 4th St Ste 4 Bridgeport (19405) ***(G-2043)***
Paul Dry Books Inc 215 231-9939
1700 Sansom St Ste 700 Philadelphia (19103) ***(G-14124)***
Paul E Seymour Tool & Die LLC 814 725-5170
11416 Wilson Rd North East (16428) ***(G-12754)***
Paul Erivan 215 887-2009
105 Allison Rd Oreland (19075) ***(G-13026)***
Paul F Rothstein Inc 215 884-4720
39 S Easton Rd Glenside (19038) ***(G-6532)***
Paul Family Farms LLC 570 772-2420
377 Paul Hollow Rd Galeton (16922) ***(G-6242)***
Paul G Benedum Jr 412 288-0280
223 4th Ave Ste 1500 Pittsburgh (15222) ***(G-15371)***
Paul Groth & Sons Inc 724 843-8086
101 Blockhouse Run Rd New Brighton (15066) ***(G-12039)***
Paul H Nolt Woodworking 717 445-4972
795 Terre Hill Rd East Earl (17519) ***(G-4552)***
Paul Morelli Design Inc 215 922-7392
1118 Walnut St Philadelphia (19107) ***(G-14125)***
Paul Morelli Studio, Philadelphia *Also called Paul Morelli Design Inc* ***(G-14125)***
Paul Scalese 814 743-5121
2353 Cherry Tree Rd Cherry Tree (15724) ***(G-3034)***
Paul W Zimmerman Foundries Co 717 285-5253
637 Hempfield Hill Rd Columbia (17512) ***(G-3446)***
Paul William Boyle 412 828-0883
610 Allegheny River Blvd Oakmont (15139) ***(G-12923)***
Paul Withers 717 896-3173
528 Dunkel School Rd Halifax (17032) ***(G-6827)***
Paula Keswick 574 298-2022
2771 Paradise Rd Reynoldsville (15851) ***(G-16660)***
Paulhus and Associates Inc 717 274-5621
8 Keystone Dr Lebanon (17042) ***(G-9616)***
Pauls Chrome Plating Inc 724 538-3367
90 Pattison St Evans City (16033) ***(G-5560)***
Paulson Brands, Broomall *Also called Icon Marketing LLC* ***(G-2289)***
Paulsonbilt Ltd 610 384-6112
1000 W 11th Ave Coatesville (19320) ***(G-3322)***
Paulus & Son Cabinet Co 717 896-3610
110 S 2nd St Halifax (17032) ***(G-6828)***
Pavlish Beverage Co Inc 610 866-7722
2800 Easton Ave Bethlehem (18017) ***(G-1592)***
Pavlish Ice Company, Bethlehem *Also called Pavlish Beverage Co Inc* ***(G-1592)***
Paxson Lightning Rods Inc 610 696-8290
620 W Union St West Chester (19382) ***(G-19615)***
Paxton Herald 717 545-9868
101 Lincoln St Harrisburg (17112) ***(G-7190)***
Paxton Precast LLC 717 692-5686
725 Paxton Dr Dalmatia (17017) ***(G-3985)***
Payal News 215 625-3699
1101 Market St Philadelphia (19107) ***(G-14126)***
Payco, Harrisburg *Also called Fine Line Homes* ***(G-7129)***
Payloadz Inc 609 510-3074
3 Richards Rdg Newtown Square (19073) ***(G-12587)***
Payne Engineering Sales, Telford *Also called Scott H Payne* ***(G-18313)***
Payne Prcsion Clor Lithography, Dallas *Also called Payne Printery Inc* ***(G-3965)***
Payne Printery Inc 570 675-1147
3235 Memorial Hwy Dallas (18612) ***(G-3965)***
Payserv Inc 610 524-3251
104 W Front St Media (19063) ***(G-10942)***
Pb Heat LLC (HQ) 610 845-6100
131 S Church St Bally (19503) ***(G-906)***
Pb Holdings Inc (PA) 215 947-3333
3063 Philmont Ave Huntingdon Valley (19006) ***(G-8021)***
Pbg Johnstown 814 262-1125
167 Allenbill Dr Johnstown (15904) ***(G-8420)***
Pbg Philadelphia 2120 ....215 676-6401
11701 Roosevelt Blvd Philadelphia (19154) ***(G-14127)***
PBM Inc 724 863-0550
1070 Sandy Hill Rd Irwin (15642) ***(G-8189)***
PBM Valve, Irwin *Also called PBM Inc* ***(G-8189)***
Pbs Coals, Friedens *Also called Roxcoal Inc* ***(G-6226)***
Pbs Coals Inc (HQ) 814 443-4668
4600 J Barry Ct Ste 220 Canonsburg (15317) ***(G-2617)***
Pbz LLC 800 578-1121
295 Wood Corner Rd Lititz (17543) ***(G-10029)***
PC Network Inc (PA) 267 236-0015
1315 Walnut St Ste 1402 Philadelphia (19107) ***(G-14128)***
PC Systems Inc 814 772-6359
288 Servidea Dr Ridgway (15853) ***(G-16724)***
PC Workshop, Bridgeville *Also called Pat Landgraf* ***(G-2084)***
PCA, Hanover *Also called Packaging Corporation America* ***(G-6930)***
PCA, New Oxford *Also called Packaging Corporation America* ***(G-12419)***
PCA Corrugated and Display LLC 800 572-6061
148 Penn St Hanover (17331) ***(G-6932)***
PCA Corrugated and Display LLC 717 624-3500
201 S College St New Oxford (17350) ***(G-12420)***
PCA Corrugated and Display LLC 800 572-6061
148 Penn St Hanover (17331) ***(G-6933)***
PCA Corrugated and Display LLC 800 572-6061
401 Moulstown Rd Hanover (17331) ***(G-6934)***
PCA Corrugated and Display LLC 717 624-2122
104 Commerce St New Oxford (17350) ***(G-12421)***
PCA Corrugated and Display LLC 610 489-8740
5 Iron Bridge Dr Collegeville (19426) ***(G-3386)***
PCA Group Inc 610 558-2802
3060 Plaza Dr Ste 108 Garnet Valley (19060) ***(G-6267)***
PCA Supply Services 302, Manheim *Also called Packaging Corporation America* ***(G-10398)***
Pca/Baltimore, 306, Hanover *Also called Packaging Corporation America* ***(G-6929)***
Pca/Cheswick 379, Cheswick *Also called Packaging Corporation America* ***(G-3114)***
Pca/Hanover 331, Hanover *Also called Packaging Corporation America* ***(G-6931)***
Pca/Lancaster 344, Lancaster *Also called Packaging Corporation America* ***(G-9159)***
Pca/Northeast Area, Allentown *Also called Packaging Corporation America* ***(G-342)***
Pca/Reading 389, Reading *Also called Packaging Corporation America* ***(G-16462)***
Pca/Trexlertown 388, Allentown *Also called Packaging Corporation America* ***(G-343)***
PCC Aerostructure, Wilkes Barre *Also called Unison Engine Components Inc* ***(G-19967)***
PCC Arostructures Wilkes-Barre, Wilkes Barre *Also called Precision Castparts Corp* ***(G-19959)***

ALPHABETIC

PCC Forged Products, Transfer *Also called Greenville Metals Inc* **(G-18465)**
PCC Forged Products, Wilkes Barre *Also called Wyman-Gordon Pennsylvania LLC* **(G-19978)**
PCC SPS Fastener Division, Jenkintown *Also called SPS Technologies LLC* **(G-8302)**
PCI, Philadelphia *Also called Mrs Resslers Food Products Co* **(G-14043)**
PCI, Phoenixville *Also called Printing Consulting Inc* **(G-14571)**
PCI, Waltersburg *Also called Piccolomini Contractors Inc* **(G-18795)**
PCI Labs, Bangor *Also called Performnce Ctngs Intl Labs LLC* **(G-924)**
PCI Pharma Services, Philadelphia *Also called Packaging Coordinators Inc* **(G-14111)**
Pcm Contracting Inc 215 675-8846
 537 E County Line Rd Hatboro (19040) **(G-7296)**
Pcm Paving & Sealcoating, Hatboro *Also called Pcm Contracting Inc* **(G-7296)**
Pcmc 814 934-3262
 899 Plank Rd Duncansville (16635) **(G-4460)**
Pcn, Philadelphia *Also called PC Network Inc* **(G-14128)**
Pcs Ferguson Inc 412 264-6000
 1191 Route 36 Brookville (15825) **(G-2268)**
Pcs Technologies, Philadelphia *Also called Progressive Computer Svcs Inc* **(G-14207)**
Pcxpert Company Inc 717 792-0005
 1370 Sven Vlleys Rd Ste 2 York (17408) **(G-20619)**
PDC Machines Inc 215 443-9442
 1875 Stout Dr Warminster (18974) **(G-18937)**
PDC Spas, Williamsport *Also called Plastic Development Company PA* **(G-20058)**
Pdir Inc 215 794-5011
 2101 Potshop Ln Norristown (19403) **(G-12701)**
PDQ Pest Control, Girard *Also called P D Q Pest Control Inc* **(G-6398)**
PDQ Print Center, Taylor *Also called United Partners Ltd* **(G-18265)**
PDQ Print Center 570 283-0995
 502 Market St Kingston (18704) **(G-8724)**
PDQ Printing, Norristown *Also called Jaz Forms* **(G-12673)**
PDQ Printing Services 717 691-4777
 325 Hemlock Rd Mechanicsburg (17055) **(G-10878)**
Pdqtooling.com, Mckeesport *Also called P D Q Tooling Inc* **(G-10677)**
PDS INDUSTRIES, Irwin *Also called Precision Defense Services Inc* **(G-8193)**
Pds Paint Inc 717 393-5838
 334 Mill St Lancaster (17603) **(G-9161)**
Peace Products Co Inc 610 296-4222
 143 Pnnsylvania Ave Ste 2 Malvern (19355) **(G-10294)**
Peach Bottom Transport LLC 717 278-8055
 2663 Robert Fulton Hwy Peach Bottom (17563) **(G-13200)**
Peaches Wood Products, Reedsville *Also called John J Peachey* **(G-16625)**
Peachey-Yoder LP 570 658-8371
 3782 Sawmill Rd Beaver Springs (17812) **(G-1020)**
Peacheys Sawmill Inc 717 483-6336
 122 Sunnyside Ln Belleville (17004) **(G-1134)**
Peachtree City Foamcraft Inc 610 769-0661
 4215 Independence Dr Schnecksville (18078) **(G-17142)**
Peacock Printing 814 336-5009
 205 W 12th St Erie (16534) **(G-5418)**
Peak Beam Systems Inc 610 353-8505
 3938 Miller Rd Newtown Square (19073) **(G-12588)**
Peak Industries Inc 717 306-4490
 246 N Lincoln Ave Lebanon (17046) **(G-9617)**
Peak Precision Inc 215 799-1929
 3195 Penn St Hatfield (19440) **(G-7378)**
Peak Ventures Inc 717 306-4490
 246 N Lincoln Ave Lebanon (17046) **(G-9618)**
Pear Tree Mfg 610 273-9281
 1275 Beaver Dam Rd Honey Brook (19344) **(G-7755)**
Pearce Lumber Co, Smicksburg *Also called Robert Pearce & Sons* **(G-17639)**
Peca, Philadelphia *Also called Professional Electronic Compon* **(G-14205)**
Peca Labs Inc 412 589-9847
 4424 Penn Ave Ste 201 Pittsburgh (15224) **(G-15372)**
Pecks Graphics LLC 717 963-7588
 1310 Crooked Hill Rd # 200 Harrisburg (17110) **(G-7191)**
Pecora Corporation 215 723-6051
 165 Wambold Rd Harleysville (19438) **(G-7051)**
Pedagology, Philadelphia *Also called Kickup LLC* **(G-13935)**
Pedco-Hill Inc 215 942-5193
 91 Steam Whistle Dr Warminster (18974) **(G-18938)**
Pediatrix Medical Group PA PC 717 782-3127
 111 S Front St Harrisburg (17101) **(G-7192)**
Pedline, Norristown *Also called Montco Advertising Spc Inc* **(G-12687)**
Peeco, Fairview *Also called Automation Devices Inc* **(G-5814)**
Peeco, Aston *Also called Philadelphia Electrical Eqp Co* **(G-786)**
Peei, Mount Pleasant *Also called Pittsburgh Electric Engs Inc* **(G-11711)**
Peerless Chain Company 800 395-2445
 1558 Mount Pleasant Conne Mount Pleasant (15666) **(G-11710)**
Peerless Hardware Mfg Co 717 684-2889
 210 Chestnut St Columbia (17512) **(G-3447)**
Peerless Paper Specialty Inc 215 657-3460
 349 York Rd Ste 2 Willow Grove (19090) **(G-20133)**
Peerless Printery, Bethlehem *Also called SYN Apparel LLC* **(G-1636)**
Peerless Printery 610 258-5226
 1211 Butler St Easton (18042) **(G-4741)**

Peerless Publications Inc (HQ) 610 323-3000
 24 N Hanover St Pottstown (19464) **(G-16027)**
Peerless Publications Inc 610 970-3210
 21 N Hanover St Pottstown (19464) **(G-16028)**
Peerless Tool Division, Hanover *Also called CAM Industries Inc* **(G-6866)**
Pegasus Print & Copy Centers 610 356-8787
 2501 W Chester Pike Broomall (19008) **(G-2300)**
Pei Genesis International, Philadelphia *Also called Pei/Genesis Inc* **(G-14129)**
Pei/Genesis Inc 215 638-1645
 651 Winks Ln Bensalem (19020) **(G-1238)**
Pei/Genesis Inc (PA) 215 464-1410
 2180 Hornig Rd Ste 2 Philadelphia (19116) **(G-14129)**
Peifer Welding Inc 717 687-7581
 715 Georgetown Rd Ronks (17572) **(G-16812)**
Peifer Welding Water Jet Cutng, Ronks *Also called Peifer Welding Inc* **(G-16812)**
Peiffer Machine Division, Mount Aetna *Also called Ressler Enterprises Inc* **(G-11605)**
Pelets Welding Inc 610 384-5048
 19 N 12th Ave Coatesville (19320) **(G-3323)**
Pella Corporation 610 648-0922
 555 Lancaster Ave Ste B Berwyn (19312) **(G-1370)**
Pella Corporation 610 648-0922
 555 Lancaster Ave Ste B Berwyn (19312) **(G-1371)**
Pella Corporation 610 648-0922
 555 Lancaster Ave Ste B Berwyn (19312) **(G-1372)**
Pella Corporation 717 334-0099
 2000 Proline Pl Gettysburg (17325) **(G-6310)**
Pella Window Door, Berwyn *Also called Pella Corporation* **(G-1370)**
Pella Window Door, Berwyn *Also called Pella Corporation* **(G-1371)**
Pella Window Door, Berwyn *Also called Pella Corporation* **(G-1372)**
Pellheat Inc 724 850-8169
 928 Country Club Dr Greensburg (15601) **(G-6699)**
Pelmor Laboratories Inc 215 968-3334
 401 Lafayette St Newtown (18940) **(G-12533)**
Pelonis Technologies Inc 888 546-0524
 444 Creamery Way Ste 500 Exton (19341) **(G-5723)**
Pelseal Technologies LLC 215 245-0581
 3161 State Rd Ste G Bensalem (19020) **(G-1239)**
Pemcor Printing Company LLC (HQ) 717 898-1555
 330 Eden Rd Lancaster (17601) **(G-9162)**
Pen Dor Manufacturing Inc 724 863-7180
 1 Biddle Ave Westmoreland City (15692) **(G-19784)**
Pen Fabricators, Emigsville *Also called International Vectors Ltd* **(G-4993)**
Pen Pal LLC 917 882-1441
 1045 Webster Ave Allentown (18103) **(G-345)**
Penco Products Inc 800 562-1000
 2024 Cressman Rd Skippack (19474) **(G-17603)**
Pencor Services Inc 570 668-1250
 200 E Broad St Tamaqua (18252) **(G-18223)**
Pencor Services Inc (PA) 610 826-2115
 613 3rd Street Palmerton Palmerton (18071) **(G-13110)**
Pencor Services Inc 570 386-2660
 594 Blakeslee Blvd Dr W Lehighton (18235) **(G-9721)**
Pencor Services Inc 610 740-0944
 1633 N 26th St Ste 102 Allentown (18104) **(G-346)**
Pencoyd Iron Works Inc 610 522-5000
 4 School Ln Folcroft (19032) **(G-6012)**
Pendant Systems, Bensalem *Also called Pendants Systems Mfg Co* **(G-1240)**
Pendants Systems Mfg Co 215 638-8552
 1670 Winchester Rd Bensalem (19020) **(G-1240)**
Pendu Manufacturing Inc 717 354-4348
 718 N Shirk Rd New Holland (17557) **(G-12272)**
Penflex Corporation 610 367-2260
 105b Industrial Dr Gilbertsville (19525) **(G-6375)**
Penford Carolina LLC 570 218-4321
 920 E 7th St Berwick (18603) **(G-1340)**
Penguin Logistics Holdings LLC 724 772-9800
 4500 Brooktree Rd Ste 200 Wexford (15090) **(G-19819)**
Penlin Fabricators LLC 610 837-6667
 335 Moorestown Dr Bath (18014) **(G-968)**
Penn A Caster Loft Offices 412 471-3285
 3030 Penn Ave Pittsburgh (15201) **(G-15373)**
Penn Arms Inc 814 938-5279
 388 Kinsman Rd Jamestown (16134) **(G-8238)**
Penn Assurance Software LLC 610 996-6124
 32 Venuti Dr Aston (19014) **(G-785)**
Penn Big Bed Slate Co Inc 610 767-4601
 8450 Brown St Slatington (18080) **(G-17611)**
Penn Blind Manufacturing Inc 610 770-1700
 1301 Union Blvd Allentown (18109) **(G-347)**
Penn Brewery, Pittsburgh *Also called Pennsylvania Brewing Company* **(G-15375)**
Penn Central Spring Corp 717 564-6792
 1451 Stoneridge Dr Middletown (17057) **(G-11067)**
Penn Cheese, Winfield *Also called Vetch LLC* **(G-20204)**
Penn Cheese Corporation 570 524-7700
 7199 County Line Rd Winfield (17889) **(G-20202)**
Penn Chrome, Pittsburgh *Also called Industrial Machine Works Inc* **(G-15119)**
Penn Cigar Machines Inc (PA) 570 740-1112
 1 Line St Nanticoke (18634) **(G-11901)**

2019 Harris Pennsylvania Manufacturers Directory
(G-0000) Company's Geographic Section entry number

Penn Color Inc (PA) 215 345-6550
400 Old Dublin Pike Doylestown (18901) ***(G-4322)***
Penn Color Inc 215 997-9206
2801 Richmond Rd Hatfield (19440) ***(G-7379)***
Penn Color Inc 215 997-2221
2755 Bergey Rd Hatfield (19440) ***(G-7380)***
Penn Crossing Limited 724 744-7725
492 Mnr Harrison City Rd Harrison City (15636) ***(G-7250)***
Penn Dairy LLC 570 524-7700
7199 County Line Rd Winfield (17889) ***(G-20203)***
Penn Drill Manufacturing, Imperial *Also called Pennsylvania Drilling Company* ***(G-8074)***
Penn Drill Manufacturing, Mc Kees Rocks *Also called Pennsylvania Drilling Company* ***(G-10623)***
Penn Electric Motor Company, Philadelphia *Also called Willier Elc Mtr Repr Co Inc* ***(G-14477)***
Penn Emblem Company (PA) 215 632-7800
2577 Neshaminy Interplex # 100 Feasterville Trevose (19053) ***(G-5926)***
Penn Engineering & Mfg Corp (HQ) 215 766-8853
5190 Old Easton Rd Danboro (18916) ***(G-3991)***
Penn Engineering & Mfg Corp 215 766-8853
5190 Old Easton Rd Danboro (18916) ***(G-3992)***
Penn Engineering & Mfg Corp 215 766-8853
5190 Old Easton Rd Danboro (18916) ***(G-3993)***
Penn Equipment Corporation 570 622-9933
15 Main St Port Carbon (17965) ***(G-15899)***
Penn Erie Manufacturing Div, Erie *Also called Triangle Tool Company Inc* ***(G-5517)***
Penn Fabrication LLC 610 292-1980
220 E Washington St D Norristown (19401) ***(G-12702)***
Penn Fan Inc 724 452-4570
22329 Perry Hwy Zelienople (16063) ***(G-20814)***
Penn Fasteners Inc 215 674-2772
220 Jacksonville Rd Hatboro (19040) ***(G-7297)***
Penn Fibre Inc 800 662-7366
2434 Bristol Rd Bensalem (19020) ***(G-1241)***
Penn Fibre & Specialty Co 215 702-9551
2434 Bristol Rd Bensalem (19020) ***(G-1242)***
Penn Fishing Tackle Mfg Co (HQ) 215 227-1087
3028 W Hunting Park Ave Philadelphia (19132) ***(G-14130)***
Penn Foam Corporation 610 797-7500
2625 Mitchell Ave Allentown (18103) ***(G-348)***
Penn Forged, Upper Chichester *Also called Pennsylvania Machine Works Inc* ***(G-18669)***
Penn Fuel Gas Incorporated 814 353-0404
109 Rishel Hill Rd Bellefonte (16823) ***(G-1111)***
Penn Gold Hughes 724 735-2121
540 County Line Rd Harrisville (16038) ***(G-7254)***
Penn Graphics Equipment Inc 610 488-7414
139 Mill Hill Rd Hamburg (19526) ***(G-6848)***
Penn Iron Works Inc 610 777-7656
700 Old Fritztown Rd Reading (19608) ***(G-16467)***
Penn Jersey Advance Inc (PA) 610 258-7171
18 Centre Sq Easton (18042) ***(G-4742)***
Penn Jersey Advance Inc 610 258-7171
531 Main St Bethlehem (18018) ***(G-1593)***
Penn Jersey Farms Inc 610 488-7003
162 Talbert Rd Bethel (19507) ***(G-1397)***
Penn Kleen Ex-Its Inc (PA) 717 792-3608
2607 W Market St York (17404) ***(G-20620)***
Penn Lock Corp 570 288-5547
21 Noyes Ave Kingston (18704) ***(G-8725)***
Penn Machine Company 724 459-0302
310 Innovation Dr Blairsville (15717) ***(G-1736)***
Penn Machine Company (HQ) 814 288-1547
106 Station St Johnstown (15905) ***(G-8421)***
Penn Mag Incorporated 724 545-2300
719 Tarrtown Rd Adrian (16210) ***(G-31)***
Penn Manufacturing 717 626-8879
393 W Lexington Rd Lititz (17543) ***(G-10030)***
Penn Manufacturing LLC 724 845-4682
634 Pleasant Valley Rd New Kensington (15068) ***(G-12365)***
Penn Manufacturing Inds Inc 215 362-1217
506 Stump Rd Montgomeryville (18936) ***(G-11411)***
Penn Mar Castings Inc 717 632-4165
500 Broadway Hanover (17331) ***(G-6935)***
Penn Medical Education LLC 215 524-2785
2865 S Eagle Rd B354 Newtown (18940) ***(G-12534)***
Penn Metal Stamping Inc 814 834-7171
130 Sunset Rd Kersey (15846) ***(G-8565)***
Penn Pallet Inc 814 857-2988
553 Independent Rd Woodland (16881) ***(G-20213)***
Penn Pallet Inc (PA) 814 834-1700
675 Fillmore Rd Saint Marys (15857) ***(G-17002)***
Penn Panel & Box Company 610 586-2700
Willows Ave Collingdale (19023) ***(G-3409)***
Penn Power Group LLC 570 208-1192
1081 Hanover St Hanover Township (18706) ***(G-7003)***
Penn Power Systems, Hanover Township *Also called Penn Power Group LLC* ***(G-7003)***
Penn Print & Graphics 724 239-5849
200 Main St Bentleyville (15314) ***(G-1273)***
Penn Pro Manufacturing Inc 724 222-6450
1561 Hillcrest St Washington (15301) ***(G-19215)***
Penn Production Group LLC 724 349-6690
418 Gompers Ave Indiana (15701) ***(G-8117)***
Penn Protective Coatings Corp 215 355-0708
470 Veit Rd B Huntingdon Valley (19006) ***(G-8022)***
Penn Public Services, Altoona *Also called Penn Public Truck & Equipment* ***(G-537)***
Penn Public Truck & Equipment 814 944-5314
714 11th St Altoona (16602) ***(G-537)***
Penn Quaker Site Contrs Inc 610 614-0401
267 Daniels Rd B Nazareth (18064) ***(G-11985)***
Penn Recycling Inc 570 326-9041
2525 Trenton Ave Williamsport (17701) ***(G-20054)***
Penn Reel, Philadelphia *Also called Penn Fishing Tackle Mfg Co* ***(G-14130)***
Penn Run Quarry Spruce Mine 724 465-0272
590 Spruce Grove Rd Penn Run (15765) ***(G-13231)***
Penn Sauna Corp (PA) 610 932-5700
601 Lincoln St Oxford (19363) ***(G-13087)***
Penn Sauna Corp 610 932-5700
1604 E Lancaster Ave Paoli (19301) ***(G-13146)***
Penn Scale Manufacturing Co, Philadelphia *Also called Jiba LLC* ***(G-13898)***
Penn Scientific Products Co (PA) 888 238-6710
1000 Old York Rd Abington (19001) ***(G-13)***
Penn Separator Corp 814 849-7328
5 S Pickering St Brookville (15825) ***(G-2269)***
Penn Shadecrafters Inc 570 342-3193
941 Sanderson Ave Scranton (18509) ***(G-17271)***
Penn Sheet Metal, Allentown *Also called PSMLV Inc* ***(G-363)***
Penn Sign Company 717 732-8900
650 S Enola Rd Enola (17025) ***(G-5083)***
Penn State Cnstr J&D LLC 717 953-9200
27 State St Lewistown (17044) ***(G-9943)***
Penn State Paper & Box Co Inc 610 433-7468
323 Sumner Ave Allentown (18102) ***(G-349)***
Penn State Special Metals LLC 724 847-4623
7544 State Rte 18 Big Bea Koppel (16136) ***(G-8815)***
Penn Steel Fabrication Inc 267 878-0705
805 N Wilson Ave Ste 206 Bristol (19007) ***(G-2180)***
Penn Trafford News, Murrysville *Also called Franklin Penn Publishing Co* ***(G-11851)***
Penn Troy Manufacturing Inc 570 297-2125
182 Railroad St Troy (16947) ***(G-18525)***
Penn United Carbide, Saxonburg *Also called Penn United Technologies Inc* ***(G-17092)***
Penn United Technologies Inc 724 431-2482
300 N Pike Rd Sarver (16055) ***(G-17078)***
Penn United Technologies Inc 724 352-5151
196 Alwine Rd Saxonburg (16056) ***(G-17092)***
Penn United Technologies Inc (PA) 724 352-1507
799 N Pike Rd Cabot (16023) ***(G-2460)***
Penn Valley Paint, Levittown *Also called Dajr Enterprises Inc* ***(G-9830)***
Penn Valley Printing Company, Selinsgrove *Also called Marlin A Inch* ***(G-17330)***
Penn Valley Printing Company 215 295-5755
1320 Bristol Pike Morrisville (19067) ***(G-11576)***
Penn Veterinary Supply Inc 717 656-4121
53 Industrial Cir Lancaster (17601) ***(G-9163)***
Penn Weld Inc 814 332-3682
1057 French St Meadville (16335) ***(G-10775)***
Penn West Homes, Emlenton *Also called Tcc Pennwest LLC* ***(G-5015)***
Penn West Trading Co Inc 814 664-7649
Scotts Crossing Rd Corry (16407) ***(G-3771)***
Penn Wind Energy LLC 814 288-8064
3212 Ben Franklin Hwy Ebensburg (15931) ***(G-4792)***
Penn Wire Products Corporation 717 664-4411
280 S Penn St Manheim (17545) ***(G-10399)***
Penn Wire Products Corporation (PA) 717 393-2352
481 Richardson Dr Lancaster (17603) ***(G-9164)***
Penn Wire Working Equipment, Glenside *Also called John A Manning Jr* ***(G-6524)***
Penn Wood Products Inc (PA) 717 259-9551
102 Locust St East Berlin (17316) ***(G-4524)***
Penn-American Inc 570 649-5173
6840 Susquehanna Trl Muncy (17756) ***(G-11830)***
Penn-Central Industries Inc 814 371-3211
210 Ohio Ave Du Bois (15801) ***(G-4413)***
Penn-Century Inc 215 843-6540
7327 Bryan St Philadelphia (19119) ***(G-14131)***
Penn-Elkco Inc 814 834-4304
1017 Delaum Rd Saint Marys (15857) ***(G-17003)***
Penn-Erie Division, Erie *Also called Plastek Industries Inc* ***(G-5423)***
Penn-Gold Ice Cream Company, Harrisville *Also called Penn Gold Hughes* ***(G-7254)***
Penn-MO Fire Brick Co Inc 717 234-4504
825 Paxton St Harrisburg (17104) ***(G-7193)***
Penn-Sylvan International Inc 724 932-5200
2880 State Highway 18 Adamsville (16110) ***(G-26)***
Penn-Sylvan International Inc (PA) 814 654-7111
43647 Fairview Rd Spartansburg (16434) ***(G-17853)***
Penn-Union Corp (HQ) 814 734-1631
229 Waterford St Edinboro (16412) ***(G-4820)***
Penna Flame Industries Inc 724 452-8750
1856 Route 588 Zelienople (16063) ***(G-20815)***

ALPHABETIC

Pennatronics Corporation 724 938-1800
  75 Technology Dr California (15419) *(G-2464)*
Pennco Tool & Die Inc 814 336-5035
  99 Mead Ave Meadville (16335) *(G-10776)*
Penncraft Cabinet Co 724 379-7040
  151 Donora Rd Monongahela (15063) *(G-11313)*
Penndel Hydraulic Sls & Svc Co 215 757-2000
  77 W Lincoln Hwy Langhorne (19047) *(G-9317)*
Penneco Oil Company (PA) 724 468-8232
  Penneco 6608 Rr 22 Delmont (15626) *(G-4052)*
Pennengineering, Danboro Also called Penn Engineering & Mfg Corp *(G-3993)*
Pennergy Solutions LLC 484 393-1539
  7 Buckwalter Cir Royersford (19468) *(G-16859)*
Pennex Aluminum Company LLC 724 373-8471
  93 Werner Rd Bldg B Greenville (16125) *(G-6764)*
Penngear LLC 215 968-2403
  2305 Waterford Rd Yardley (19067) *(G-20331)*
Pennheat LLC 814 282-6774
  360 Chestnut St Meadville (16335) *(G-10777)*
Pennico Oil Co Inc 724 468-8232
  6608 State Route 22 Delmont (15626) *(G-4053)*
Pennmark Technologies Corp 570 255-5000
  1170 Lower Demunds Rd Dallas (18612) *(G-3966)*
Pennram Diversified Mfg, Williamsport Also called Pennram Diversified Mfg Corp *(G-20055)*
Pennram Diversified Mfg Corp 570 327-2802
  1315 W 3rd St Williamsport (17701) *(G-20055)*
Penns Creek Raceway Park 570 473-9599
  185 16th St Northumberland (17857) *(G-12873)*
Penns Valley Publishers 215 855-4948
  154 E Main St Ste 1 Lansdale (19446) *(G-9397)*
Pennsbury Enterprises Inc 215 741-5960
  569 Hulmeville Ave Ste B Penndel (19047) *(G-13240)*
Pennside Machining LLC 814 774-2075
  18 Elk Creek Ave Girard (16417) *(G-6399)*
Pennstar LLC 484 275-7990
  6 Horwith Dr Northampton (18067) *(G-12859)*
Pennstress, Roaring Spring Also called Macinnis Group LLC *(G-16765)*
Pennswood Manufacturing, Oil City Also called Titan Boards Inc *(G-12958)*
Pennsy Supply Inc 570 833-4497
  15644 State Route 267 Montrose (18801) *(G-11474)*
Pennsy Supply Inc 717 569-2623
  2743 Lancaster Rd Manheim (17545) *(G-10400)*
Pennsy Supply Inc 717 397-0391
  1060 Manheim Pike Lancaster (17601) *(G-9165)*
Pennsy Supply Inc 570 471-7358
  7 Regulators Ln Ste 4 Avoca (18641) *(G-847)*
Pennsy Supply Inc 717 792-2631
  550 S Biesecker Rd Thomasville (17364) *(G-18342)*
Pennsy Supply Inc 570 868-6936
  51 Small Mountain Rd Wapwallopen (18660) *(G-18808)*
Pennsy Supply Inc 717 274-3661
  201 Prescott Rd Ste A Lebanon (17042) *(G-9619)*
Pennsy Supply Inc 717 486-5414
  Mountain View Rd Mount Holly Springs (17065) *(G-11638)*
Pennsy Supply Inc 570 654-3462
  300 Armstrong Rd Pittston (18640) *(G-15773)*
Pennsy Supply Inc 570 754-7508
  2225 Fair Rd Schuylkill Haven (17972) *(G-17163)*
Pennsy Supply Inc 717 867-5925
  1 Clear Spring Rd Annville (17003) *(G-656)*
Pennsy Supply Inc 717 566-0222
  39 Hersey Park Dr Hummelstown (17036) *(G-7921)*
Pennsy Supply Inc 717 766-7676
  5450 Carlisle Pike Mechanicsburg (17050) *(G-10879)*
Pennsylvania Academy of Pet Gr, Indiana Also called MDC Romani Inc *(G-8113)*
Pennsylvania Agri-Fuel Inc 717 733-1050
  820 Hilltop Rd Ephrata (17522) *(G-5137)*
Pennsylvania Aluminum 570 752-2666
  2637 W Front St Berwick (18603) *(G-1341)*
Pennsylvania American Water - 412 884-5113
  380 Becks Run Rd Pittsburgh (15210) *(G-15374)*
Pennsylvania Art Glass Company, New Kensington Also called K & N Enterprises Inc *(G-12350)*
Pennsylvania Avenue Sports 610 533-4133
  405 Pennsylvania Ave Roseto (18013) *(G-16821)*
Pennsylvania Bedding Inc 570 457-0933
  301 1st St Old Forge (18518) *(G-12974)*
Pennsylvania Brewing Company 412 237-9400
  800 Vinial St Ste 1 Pittsburgh (15212) *(G-15375)*
Pennsylvania Carbon Pdts LLC 724 564-9211
  219 Hope Rd Smithfield (15478) *(G-17654)*
Pennsylvania Carbon Products, Smithfield Also called Graphtek LLC *(G-17651)*
Pennsylvania Drilling Company (PA) 412 771-2110
  281 Route 30 Imperial (15126) *(G-8074)*
Pennsylvania Drilling Company 412 771-2110
  500 Thompson Ave Mc Kees Rocks (15136) *(G-10623)*
Pennsylvania Dry Mix 717 509-3520
  499 Running Pump Rd # 102 Lancaster (17601) *(G-9166)*
Pennsylvania Dutch Candies, Camp Hill Also called Warrell Corporation *(G-2523)*

Pennsylvania Equestrian 717 509-9800
  336 E Orange St Lancaster (17602) *(G-9167)*
Pennsylvania Fireman Inc 717 397-9174
  632 E Roegon Rd Lititz (17543) *(G-10031)*
Pennsylvania Gazette, Philadelphia Also called Trustees of The Univ of PA *(G-14413)*
Pennsylvania Gen Enrgy Corp (PA) 814 723-3230
  120 Market St Warren (16365) *(G-19043)*
Pennsylvania Grains Proc LLC 877 871-0774
  250 Technology Dr Clearfield (16830) *(G-3228)*
Pennsylvania Insert Corp 610 474-0112
  490 1st Ave Royersford (19468) *(G-16860)*
Pennsylvania Institute of CPA (PA) 215 496-9272
  1801 Market St Fl 24 Philadelphia (19103) *(G-14132)*
Pennsylvania Insulating Glass 717 247-0560
  6395 State Route 103 N Lewistown (17044) *(G-9944)*
Pennsylvania Intl Trlr, Pine Grove Also called Kutz Farm Equipment Inc *(G-14596)*
Pennsylvania Legislative Svcs 717 236-6984
  240 N 3rd St Ste 1100 Harrisburg (17101) *(G-7194)*
Pennsylvania Machine Works Inc (PA) 610 497-3300
  201 Bethel Ave Upper Chichester (19014) *(G-18669)*
Pennsylvania Monument Co 570 454-2621
  Rr 924 Box Humboldt Hazleton (18201) *(G-7516)*
Pennsylvania Motor Truck Assn 717 761-7122
  910 Linda Ln Camp Hill (17011) *(G-2510)*
Pennsylvania Patterns 717 533-4188
  25 Trinidad Ave Hershey (17033) *(G-7625)*
Pennsylvania Perlite Corp York (PA) 610 868-0992
  1428 Mauch Chunk Rd Bethlehem (18018) *(G-1594)*
Pennsylvania Perlite Corp York 717 755-6206
  125 Stonewood Rd York (17402) *(G-20621)*
Pennsylvania Powdered Mtls Inc 814 834-9565
  1066 Trout Run Rd Saint Marys (15857) *(G-17004)*
Pennsylvania Production Svcs 724 463-0729
  1032 Brown Rd Indiana (15701) *(G-8118)*
Pennsylvania Promotions Inc 800 360-2800
  256 Eagleview Blvd Exton (19341) *(G-5724)*
Pennsylvania Rail Car Co, Mercer Also called Rail Car Service Co *(G-10970)*
Pennsylvania Scale Co, Lancaster Also called A H Emery Company *(G-8918)*
Pennsylvania Sewing Res Co 570 344-4000
  1321 E Drinker St Dunmore (18512) *(G-4480)*
Pennsylvania Sintered Mtls Inc 814 486-1768
  2950 Whittimore Rd Emporium (15834) *(G-5071)*
Pennsylvania Sling Co (HQ) 717 657-7700
  421 Amity Rd Ste C Harrisburg (17111) *(G-7195)*
Pennsylvania Stair Lifts Inc 215 914-0800
  2727 Philmont Ave Ste 310 Huntingdon Valley (19006) *(G-8023)*
Pennsylvania State University 814 865-4963
  102 Engineering Unit E University Park (16802) *(G-18652)*
Pennsylvania State University 814 863-3764
  110 Rackley Bldg University Park (16802) *(G-18653)*
Pennsylvania State University 814 865-1327
  820 N University Dr University Park (16802) *(G-18654)*
Pennsylvania State University 215 682-4000
  995 Newtown Dr Warminster (18974) *(G-18939)*
Pennsylvania Steel Company 610 432-4541
  1139 Lehigh Ave Ste 500 Whitehall (18052) *(G-19886)*
Pennsylvania Supply Inc 717 567-3197
  1001 Paxton St Harrisburg (17104) *(G-7196)*
Pennsylvania Tool & Gages Inc 814 336-3136
  16906 Pa Tool & Gauge Dr Meadville (16335) *(G-10778)*
Pennsylvania Trans Tech Inc (PA) 724 873-2100
  30 Curry Ave Ste 2 Canonsburg (15317) *(G-2618)*
Pennsylvania Wiping Mtl Co, Reading Also called Oscar Daniels & Company Inc *(G-16460)*
Pennsylvanin Flagstone Inc 814 544-7575
  307 E Oak St Coudersport (16915) *(G-3787)*
Pennsylvania Precision Cast P 717 273-3338
  521 N 3rd Ave Lebanon (17046) *(G-9620)*
Pennsylvnia Precision Pdts Inc 724 568-4397
  309 Walnut St Vandergrift (15690) *(G-18735)*
Pennsylvania Pure Dstlries LLC 412 486-8666
  1101 William Flynn Hwy Glenshaw (15116) *(G-6496)*
Pennsylvnia Soc Newsppr Editor 717 703-3000
  3899 N Front St Fl 1 Harrisburg (17110) *(G-7197)*
Penntech - Sp Scientific, Warminster Also called S P Industries Inc *(G-18958)*
Penntecq Inc 724 646-4250
  106 Kuder Dr Greenville (16125) *(G-6765)*
Penntex Industries Inc (PA) 717 266-8762
  202 Plaza Dr Manchester (17345) *(G-10360)*
Pennwood, East Berlin Also called Penn Wood Products Inc *(G-4524)*
Penny Mansfield Saver Inc (PA) 570 662-3277
  98 N Main St Mansfield (16933) *(G-10424)*
Penny Power Ltd 610 282-4808
  202 S 3rd St Ste 6 Coopersburg (18036) *(G-3633)*
Penny Press of York Inc 717 843-4078
  53 S Adams St Ste 1 York (17404) *(G-20622)*
Penny Saver, Tunkhannock Also called Mulligan Printing Corporation *(G-18544)*
Pennypack Supply Company (PA) 215 338-2200
  8047 Craig St Philadelphia (19136) *(G-14133)*
Pennysaver, Greensburg Also called Trib Total Media LLC *(G-6720)*

(G-0000) Company's Geographic Section entry number

Pennysaver, Tarentum Also called Weekly Shopper **(G-18254)**
Pennzoil-Quaker State Company 724 756-0110
  138 Petrolia St Karns City (16041) **(G-8482)**
Pensionpro Software LLC 717 545-6060
  940 E Park Dr Ste 100 Harrisburg (17111) **(G-7198)**
Pentavision LLC 215 628-6550
  321 Norristown Rd Ste 150 Ambler (19002) **(G-597)**
Pentec Health Inc 800 223-4376
  4 Creek Pkwy Upper Chichester (19061) **(G-18670)**
Pentec Health Inc 610 494-8700
  9 Creek Pkwy Upper Chichester (19061) **(G-18671)**
Pentec Health Inc (PA) 610 494-8700
  50 Applied Card Way Glen Mills (19342) **(G-6440)**
Peoplejoy Inc 267 603-7726
  22 N 3rd St Philadelphia (19106) **(G-14134)**
PeopleSoft, Pittsburgh Also called Kos & Associates Inc **(G-15195)**
Pepper Italian Bistro 717 392-3000
  486 Royer Dr Lancaster (17601) **(G-9168)**
Pepperell Braiding Company Inc 814 368-4454
  548 High St Bradford (16701) **(G-1986)**
Pepperidge Farm Incorporated 610 356-0553
  2058 Sproul Rd Broomall (19008) **(G-2301)**
Pepperidge Farm Incorporated 717 336-8500
  2195 N Reading Rd Denver (17517) **(G-4087)**
Pepperidge Farm Thrift Store, Broomall Also called Pepperidge Farm Incorporated **(G-2301)**
Peppers Performance Eyeware 412 688-8555
  3001 Pulawski Way Pittsburgh (15219) **(G-15376)**
Pepsi Beverages Company 412 778-4552
  400 Graham St Mc Kees Rocks (15136) **(G-10624)**
Pepsi Co Inc 717 792-2935
  3553 Gillespie Dr York (17404) **(G-20623)**
Pepsi-Cola Btlg Co of Scranton 570 344-1159
  290 Research Dr Pittston (18640) **(G-15774)**
Pepsi-Cola Metro Btlg Co Inc 570 344-1159
  290 Research Dr Pittston (18640) **(G-15775)**
Pepsi-Cola Metro Btlg Co Inc 814 266-9556
  166 Allenbill Dr Johnstown (15904) **(G-8422)**
Pepsi-Cola Metro Btlg Co Inc 215 937-6102
  3245 S 78th St Philadelphia (19153) **(G-14135)**
Pepsi-Cola Metro Btlg Co Inc 814 834-5700
  854 S Saint Marys St Saint Marys (15857) **(G-17005)**
Pepsi-Cola Metro Btlg Co Inc 412 331-6775
  400 Graham St Mc Kees Rocks (15136) **(G-10625)**
Pepsi-Cola Metro Btlg Co Inc 570 326-9086
  1450 Dewey Ave Williamsport (17701) **(G-20056)**
Pepsico, Philadelphia Also called Pbg Philadelphia 2120 **(G-14127)**
Pepsico, York Also called Pepsi Co Inc **(G-20623)**
Pepsico, Mc Kees Rocks Also called Pepsi-Cola Metro Btlg Co Inc **(G-10625)**
Pepsico Inc 814 266-6005
  429 Industrial Park Rd Johnstown (15904) **(G-8423)**
Pequea Planter LLC 717 442-4406
  561 White Horse Rd Gap (17527) **(G-6255)**
Pequea Storage Sheds LLC 717 768-8980
  211 S New Holland Rd Kinzers (17535) **(G-8740)**
Pequignot Logging 570 659-5251
  526 E Hill Rd Covington (16917) **(G-3792)**
Per Midstream LLC 412 275-3200
  1000 Commerce Dr Ste 400 Pittsburgh (15275) **(G-15377)**
Perakis Frames Inc 215 627-7700
  18 S Bank St Philadelphia (19106) **(G-14136)**
Perdue Farms Inc 717 426-1961
  1609 River Rd Marietta (17547) **(G-10466)**
Perdue Farms Inc 610 388-1385
  314 Kennett Pike Chadds Ford (19317) **(G-2858)**
Peregrine Surgical Ltd 215 348-0456
  51 Britain Dr Doylestown (18901) **(G-4323)**
Perennial Pleasures LLC 484 318-8376
  1604 E Lancaster Ave Paoli (19301) **(G-13147)**
Perfect Impression 610 444-9493
  340 N Mill Rd Ste 1 Kennett Square (19348) **(G-8535)**
Perfect Precision 610 461-3625
  19 S Macdade Blvd Darby (19023) **(G-4023)**
Perfect Stride Ltd 412 221-1722
  1857 Tilton Dr Pittsburgh (15241) **(G-15378)**
Perfectdata Corporation (PA) 800 973-7332
  1323 Conshohocken Rd Plymouth Meeting (19462) **(G-15863)**
Perfection Foods Company Inc 215 455-5400
  3901 Old York Rd Philadelphia (19140) **(G-14137)**
Perfomance Castings LLC 814 454-1243
  6101 Bridlewood Dr Fairview (16415) **(G-5836)**
Perform Group LLC (PA) 717 852-6950
  333 E 7th Ave Ste 2 York (17404) **(G-20624)**
Perform Group LLC 717 252-1578
  5130 E Prospect Rd York (17406) **(G-20625)**
Perform Group Mfg, York Also called Perform Group LLC **(G-20625)**
Performa Forsythe Marketing, York Also called Forsythe Marketing **(G-20486)**
Performance Additives LLC 215 321-4388
  33 S Delaware Ave Ste 204 Yardley (19067) **(G-20332)**

Performance Coatings Corp 610 525-1190
  1610 Manning Blvd Ste A Levittown (19057) **(G-9854)**
Performance Controls Inc (HQ) 215 619-4920
  151 Domorah Dr Montgomeryville (18936) **(G-11412)**
Performance Inspired Nutrition, Warrendale Also called Mw/Td Inspired LLC **(G-19090)**
Performance Machining Inc 724 864-2499
  79 Pennsylvania Ave Irwin (15642) **(G-8190)**
Performance Materials Division, Allentown Also called Evonik Corporation **(G-208)**
Performance Metals, Bechtelsville Also called Scicast International Inc **(G-1036)**
Performance Metals Inc 610 369-3060
  650 N Route 100 Bechtelsville (19505) **(G-1034)**
Performance Proc Ventures LLC 724 704-8827
  660 Martin Luther King Farrell (16121) **(G-5870)**
Performance Sports Apparel Inc 508 384-8036
  2607 Keiser Blvd Ste 205 Reading (19610) **(G-16468)**
Performnce Ctngs Intl Labs LLC 610 588-7900
  600 Murray St Bangor (18013) **(G-924)**
Perfusion Management Group 717 392-4112
  555 N Duke St Lancaster (17602) **(G-9169)**
Pergamon Corp 610 239-0721
  380 Crooked Ln Ste 3 King of Prussia (19406) **(G-8661)**
Perkasie Container Corporation 215 257-3683
  801 Pine St Perkasie (18944) **(G-13287)**
Perkasie Industries Corp 215 257-6581
  499 Constitution Ave Perkasie (18944) **(G-13288)**
Perkinelmer Inc 215 368-6900
  221 Commerce Dr Montgomeryville (18936) **(G-11413)**
Perkins Family Restaurant, Erie Also called Travaglini Enterprises Inc **(G-5515)**
Perkins Family Restaurant, Hermitage Also called Travaglini Enterprises Inc **(G-7596)**
Perkiomen Valley Printing Inc 215 679-4000
  114 Main St East Greenville (18041) **(G-4573)**
Perkiomenville Quarry, Perkiomenville Also called Highway Materials Inc **(G-13301)**
Perma Cast LLC 724 325-1662
  9002 Corporate Cir Export (15632) **(G-5620)**
Perma-Column East 610 562-7161
  65 Penn St Lenhartsville (19534) **(G-9760)**
Permabond Engrg Adhesives, Pottstown Also called Permabond LLC **(G-16029)**
Permabond LLC 732 868-1372
  14 Robinson St Pottstown (19464) **(G-16029)**
Permanent Sign & Display 610 736-3222
  1141 Penn Ave Rear Reading (19610) **(G-16469)**
Permegear Inc 484 851-3688
  1815 Leithsville Rd Hellertown (18055) **(G-7560)**
Peroxychem LLC (HQ) 267 422-2400
  1 Commerce Sq 2005 Mark Philadelphia (19103) **(G-14138)**
Perpetual Enterprises Inc (PA) 412 299-6356
  2511 Beaver Grade Rd Coraopolis (15108) **(G-3712)**
Perpetual Enterprises Inc 412 299-6356
  701 4th Ave Coraopolis (15108) **(G-3713)**
Perpetual Enterprises Inc 814 437-3705
  190 Howard St Ste 406 Franklin (16323) **(G-6151)**
Perpetual Powder Coating, Franklin Also called Powderco Inc **(G-6153)**
Perrotte Wood Finishing Co 412 322-2592
  19 35th St Pittsburgh (15201) **(G-15379)**
Perry C Ritter 215 699-7079
  685 Jones Ave Lansdale (19446) **(G-9398)**
Perry Ercolino Inc 215 348-5885
  51 E Oakland Ave Doylestown (18901) **(G-4324)**
Perry Pallet Inc 717 589-3345
  5124 Sugar Run Rd Millerstown (17062) **(G-11207)**
Perry Printing 215 256-8074
  776 Moccasin Dr Harleysville (19438) **(G-7052)**
Perry Printing Company 717 582-2838
  51 Church St New Bloomfield (17068) **(G-12030)**
Perry S Swanson Logging 814 837-7020
  421 Haines St Kane (16735) **(G-8477)**
Perry Screw Machine Co Inc 814 452-3095
  1043 E 20th St Erie (16503) **(G-5419)**
Perrydell Farm Dairy, York Also called Dell Perry Farms **(G-20447)**
Perryman Company 724 745-7272
  149 S Johnson Rd Houston (15342) **(G-7875)**
Perryman Company (PA) 724 743-4239
  213 Vandale Dr Houston (15342) **(G-7876)**
Perryman Company 724 746-9390
  625 Technology Dr Coal Center (15423) **(G-3276)**
Perseon Corporation 201 486-5924
  102 Weatherburn Way Newtown Square (19073) **(G-12589)**
Personlytics LLC 484 929-0853
  763 Wesley Ct West Chester (19382) **(G-19616)**
Perspectives, Export Also called B L Tees Inc **(G-5591)**
Pertetual Powder Coting, Franklin Also called Perpetual Enterprises Inc **(G-6151)**
Pet Feed and Supply, Manheim Also called Mc Crackens Feed Mill Inc **(G-10395)**
Pete Rickard Co, Galeton Also called Protektor Model **(G-6244)**
Pete Rickard Company 518 234-3758
  1 Bridge St Galeton (16922) **(G-6243)**
Pete's Partners, Philadelphia Also called Good Lad Co **(G-13777)**
Peter Mamienski 215 822-3293
  2333 Bethlehem Pike Hatfield (19440) **(G-7381)**

Peter Sheims Cow Mattress 717 786-2918
972 Dry Wells Rd Quarryville (17566) *(G-16276)*

Peters Equipment Corp 215 364-9147
65 Buck Rd Huntingdon Valley (19006) *(G-8024)*

Peters Heat Treating Inc (PA) 814 333-1782
215 Race St Meadville (16335) *(G-10779)*

Peters James & Son Inc 215 739-9500
1934 N Front St 1936 Philadelphia (19122) *(G-14139)*

Petersen Machine Shop Inc 412 233-8077
1014 Neng Hollow Rd Clairton (15025) *(G-3155)*

Petes Beverage 814 563-7374
29100 Route 6 Youngsville (16371) *(G-20774)*

Petnet Solutions Inc 865 218-2000
398-406 Industrial Dr North Wales (19454) *(G-12824)*

Petnovations Inc 610 994-2103
1100 Schell Ln Ste 101 Phoenixville (19460) *(G-14566)*

Petrex Inc 814 723-2050
2349 Dorcon Rd Warren (16365) *(G-19044)*

Petrified Forest, Blandon *Also called Steve Day (G-1760)*

Petrillos Appliance 215 491-9400
1111 Easton Rd Ste 6 Warrington (18976) *(G-19127)*

Petroleum Products Corp 412 264-8242
520 Narrows Run Rd Coraopolis (15108) *(G-3714)*

Petroleum Service Partners 724 349-1536
1460 Old Route 119 Hwy N Indiana (15701) *(G-8119)*

Petronorth Ltd 814 368-6992
510 W Green St Smethport (16749) *(G-17636)*

Petrunak & Company Inc 814 467-7860
819 Horner St Windber (15963) *(G-20191)*

Petrunak Paving, Windber *Also called Petrunak & Company Inc (G-20191)*

Petruzzi Pizza Mfg Inc 570 454-5887
138 W 21st St Hazleton (18201) *(G-7517)*

Petruzzis Home Dlvry Pizzeria, Hazleton *Also called Petruzzis Manufacturing Inc (G-7518)*

Petruzzis Manufacturing Inc 570 459-5957
34 W 9th St Hazleton (18201) *(G-7518)*

Pets United LLC 570 384-5555
1 Maplewood Dr Hazle Township (18202) *(G-7471)*

Petta Enterprises 607 857-5915
299 S Main St Mansfield (16933) *(G-10425)*

Pexco LLC 215 736-2553
16 Progress Dr Morrisville (19067) *(G-11577)*

Peyty Construction 570 764-5995
741 Poplar St B Bloomsburg (17815) *(G-1793)*

Pfa Inc 717 664-4216
280 Hostetter Rd Manheim (17545) *(G-10401)*

Pfaltzgraff Factory Stores Inc (HQ) 717 848-5500
140 E Market St York (17401) *(G-20626)*

Pfizer Global Supply, Carlisle *Also called Alacer Corp (G-2688)*

Pfizer Inc 717 932-3701
543 Industrial Dr B Lewisberry (17339) *(G-9890)*

Pfizer Inc 484 865-5000
500 Arcola Rd Collegeville (19426) *(G-3387)*

Pfizer Inc 717 627-2211
400 W Lincoln Ave Lititz (17543) *(G-10032)*

Pfizer Inc 484 865-0288
200 Campus Dr Collegeville (19426) *(G-3388)*

Pfizer Inc 717 932-3701
543 Industrial Dr Ste B Lewisberry (17339) *(G-9891)*

Pfm Enterprises, Downingtown *Also called Asr Enterprises Inc (G-4211)*

Pfnonwovens LLC (HQ) 570 384-1600
101 Green Mountain Rd Hazle Township (18202) *(G-7472)*

Pg Publishing Company 412 263-1100
2201 Sweeney Dr Clinton (15026) *(G-3265)*

Pge, Oakmont *Also called Precision Grit Etching & Engrv (G-12924)*

Pgw, Pittsburgh *Also called Pittsburgh Glass Works LLC (G-15398)*

Pgw Division 5, Cochranton *Also called Pittsburgh Glass Works LLC (G-3347)*

PH Tool LLC (PA) 267 203-1600
6021 Easton Rd Pipersville (18947) *(G-14618)*

PH Tool Reference Standards, Pipersville *Also called PH Tool LLC (G-14618)*

Phablab, Carnegie *Also called Ferri Design (G-2767)*

Pharma Acumen LLC 215 885-1029
947 Frog Hollow Rd Rydal (19046) *(G-16886)*

Pharma Innvtion Srcing Ctr LLC 203 314-8095
105 Perry Ln Newtown (18940) *(G-12535)*

Pharma Rep Training 215 369-1719
34 Jonathan Way Washington Crossing (18977) *(G-19258)*

Pharma Tech Pro LLC 570 412-4008
95 Erin Dr Danville (17821) *(G-4009)*

Pharmaceutical Procurement 610 680-7708
324 Martingale Cir Coatesville (19320) *(G-3324)*

Pharmaloz Manufacturing Inc 717 274-9800
500 N 15th Ave Lebanon (17046) *(G-9621)*

Pharmceutical Mfg RES Svcs Inc 267 960-3300
202 Precision Rd Horsham (19044) *(G-7841)*

Pharmctcal Stffing Sltons Inc 215 322-5392
130 Almshouse Rd Richboro (18954) *(G-16677)*

Phase Guard Co Inc 412 276-3415
400 Logan St Carnegie (15106) *(G-2778)*

Phasebio Pharmaceuticals Inc 610 981-6500
1 Great Valley Pkwy # 30 Malvern (19355) *(G-10295)*

Phasetek Inc 215 536-6648
550 California Rd Ste 11 Quakertown (18951) *(G-16228)*

Phaztech Inc 814 834-3262
40 S Saint Marys St Saint Marys (15857) *(G-17006)*

Phb Inc (PA) 814 474-5511
7900 W Ridge Rd Fairview (16415) *(G-5837)*

Phb Inc 814 474-2683
8152 W Ridge Rd Fairview (16415) *(G-5838)*

Phb Inc 814 474-1552
8150 W Ridge Rd Fairview (16415) *(G-5839)*

Phb Die Casting, Fairview *Also called Parker White Metal Company (G-5835)*

Phb Machining Div, Fairview *Also called Phb Inc (G-5839)*

Phb Tool and Die Division, Fairview *Also called Phb Inc (G-5837)*

Pheasant & Shearer Contractors, Johnstown *Also called Shearer Elbie (G-8434)*

Phenomenex 484 680-0678
341 Indian Run Rd Avondale (19311) *(G-857)*

Phibro Animal Health Corp 201 329-7300
3048 Research Dr State College (16801) *(G-18005)*

Phil Skrzat 215 257-8583
311 N 8th St Ste 1 Perkasie (18944) *(G-13289)*

Phil Stupp Furs, Jenkintown *Also called Hal-Jo Corp (G-8289)*

Phila Legnds of Jazz Orchestra 215 763-2819
1436 N 25th St Philadelphia (19121) *(G-14140)*

Philadelphia Animal Health LLC 215 573-4503
3401 Grays Ferry Ave Philadelphia (19146) *(G-14141)*

Philadelphia Beer Works Inc 215 482-8220
4120 Main St Philadelphia (19127) *(G-14142)*

Philadelphia Business Services, Philadelphia *Also called C3 Media LLC (G-13492)*

Philadelphia Carbide Co Inc 215 885-0770
1451 Anderson Ave Oreland (19075) *(G-13027)*

Philadelphia Chrome 267 988-5834
3945 N Reese St Philadelphia (19140) *(G-14143)*

Philadelphia City Paper, Philadelphia *Also called Metroweek Corp (G-14017)*

Philadelphia Custom Millwork, Fort Washington *Also called Cantwell Woodworking LLC (G-6064)*

Philadelphia Electrical Eqp Co 484 840-0860
14 Mount Pleasant Rd Aston (19014) *(G-786)*

Philadelphia Energy Solutions (PA) 267 238-4300
1735 Market St Fl 11 Philadelphia (19103) *(G-14144)*

Philadelphia Energy Solutions 215 339-1200
3144 W Passyunk Ave Philadelphia (19145) *(G-14145)*

Philadelphia Eyeglass Labs, Philadelphia *Also called Eyeland Optical Corp (G-13688)*

Philadelphia Gay News, Philadelphia *Also called Masco Communications Inc (G-13993)*

Philadelphia Gear, King of Prussia *Also called Timken Gears & Services Inc (G-8689)*

Philadelphia Inquirer, Philadelphia *Also called Phildelphia-Newspapers-Llc (G-14167)*

Philadelphia Inquirer, Philadelphia *Also called Philadelphia Media Network Pbc (G-14147)*

Philadelphia Instrs & Contrls 215 329-8828
4401 N 6th St Philadelphia (19140) *(G-14146)*

Philadelphia Macaroni Company 215 441-5220
40 Jacksonville Rd Warminster (18974) *(G-18940)*

Philadelphia Magazine, Philadelphia *Also called Metro Corp (G-14014)*

Philadelphia Magazine, Philadelphia *Also called Metro Corp (G-14015)*

Philadelphia Media Network Pbc 610 292-6389
1150 Schuylkill River Rd Conshohocken (19428) *(G-3586)*

Philadelphia Media Network Pbc (PA) 215 854-2000
801 Market St Ste 300 Philadelphia (19107) *(G-14147)*

Philadelphia Newspapers Inc 610 292-6200
800 River Rd Conshohocken (19428) *(G-3587)*

Philadelphia Photo Arts Center 215 232-5678
1400 N American St # 103 Philadelphia (19122) *(G-14148)*

Philadelphia Photo Review 215 364-9185
140 E Richardson Ave # 3 Langhorne (19047) *(G-9318)*

Philadelphia Pipe Bending Co (PA) 215 225-8955
4135 To 4165 N Fifth St Philadelphia (19140) *(G-14149)*

Philadelphia Poultry Inc 215 574-0343
346 N Front St Philadelphia (19106) *(G-14150)*

Philadelphia Provision Co 215 423-1707
3370 Tilton St Philadelphia (19134) *(G-14151)*

Philadelphia Public Record 215 755-2000
1323 S Broad St Philadelphia (19147) *(G-14152)*

Philadelphia Regalia Co 610 237-9757
529 Chester Pike Ste B Prospect Park (19076) *(G-16117)*

Philadelphia Rust Proof Co (PA) 215 425-3000
2086 E Willard St Philadelphia (19134) *(G-14153)*

Philadelphia Safety Devices 215 245-7554
10 Canal St Ste 205 Bristol (19007) *(G-2181)*

Philadelphia Scientific LLC 215 616-0390
207 Progress Dr Montgomeryville (18936) *(G-11414)*

Philadelphia Security Pdts Inc 610 521-4400
5 Poulson Ave Essington (19029) *(G-5546)*

Philadelphia Ship Repair LLC 215 339-1026
5195 S 19th St Philadelphia (19112) *(G-14154)*

Philadelphia Shutter Company 610 685-2344
4700 5th Street Hwy # 100 Temple (19560) *(G-18335)*

Philadelphia Skating Club A 610 642-8700
220 Holland Ave Ardmore (19003) *(G-713)*

Philadelphia Soft Pretzels.......215 324-4315
4315 N 3rd St Philadelphia (19140) *(G-14155)*
Philadelphia Style Mag LLC.......215 468-6670
141 League St Philadelphia (19147) *(G-14156)*
Philadelphia Sun Group Inc.......215 848-7864
6661 Germantown Ave Philadelphia (19119) *(G-14157)*
Philadelphia Sunday Sun, Philadelphia *Also called Philadelphia Sun Group Inc (G-14157)*
Philadelphia Toboggan Coaster.......215 799-2155
3195 Penn St Hatfield (19440) *(G-7382)*
Philadelphia Tribune Company.......215 893-5356
520 S 16th St Philadelphia (19146) *(G-14158)*
Philadelphia Valve Company Inc.......570 669-9461
1 Industrial Complex Nesquehoning (18240) *(G-12008)*
Philadelphia Window Washers.......215 742-3875
1202 Ripley St Philadelphia (19111) *(G-14159)*
Philadelphia Woodworks LLC.......267 331-5880
4901 Umbria St Ste C Philadelphia (19128) *(G-14160)*
Philadlphia Enrgy Slutions LLC (PA).......267 238-4300
3144 W Passyunk Ave Philadelphia (19145) *(G-14161)*
Philadlphia Media Holdings LLC.......215 854-2000
400 N Broad St Philadelphia (19130) *(G-14162)*
Philadlphia Mtal Rsrce Rcovery.......215 423-4800
2200 E Somerset St Philadelphia (19134) *(G-14163)*
Philadlphia Mxing Slutions Ltd (HQ).......717 832-2800
1221 E Main St Palmyra (17078) *(G-13129)*
Philadlphia Pr-Coked Steak Inc.......215 426-4949
4001 N American St Philadelphia (19140) *(G-14164)*
Philadlphia Reg Prtg Prcrement, Southampton *Also called Publishing Office US Gvernment (G-17832)*
Philadlphia Tramrail Entps Inc (PA).......215 743-4359
2207 E Ontario St Philadelphia (19134) *(G-14165)*
Philapack LLC.......215 322-2122
1840 County Line Rd Huntingdon Valley (19006) *(G-8025)*
Philarx Pharmacy Inc (PA).......267 324-5231
2102 S Broad St Philadelphia (19145) *(G-14166)*
Phildelphia-Newspapers-Llc (PA).......215 854-2000
801 Market St Ste 300 Philadelphia (19107) *(G-14167)*
Phildelphia-Newspapers-Llc.......610 292-6200
800 River Rd Conshohocken (19428) *(G-3588)*
Philip Cooke.......717 854-4081
1900 Orange St York (17404) *(G-20627)*
Philip J Stofanak Inc.......610 759-9311
176 Nazareth Pike Bethlehem (18020) *(G-1595)*
Philip Reese Coal Co Inc.......814 263-4231
3513 Main St Karthaus (16845) *(G-8483)*
Philips, Murrysville *Also called Respironics Inc (G-11865)*
Philips Respironics, Mount Pleasant *Also called Respironics Inc (G-11714)*
Philips Respironics, Monroeville *Also called Respironics Inc (G-11354)*
Philips Ultrasound Inc.......717 667-5000
1 Echo Dr Reedsville (17084) *(G-16626)*
Philips-Hadco.......717 359-7131
100 Craftway Dr Littlestown (17340) *(G-10075)*
Philipsburg Journal.......814 342-1320
216 E Presqueisle St Philipsburg (16866) *(G-14524)*
Phillips & Dart Oil Field Svc.......814 465-2292
3502 Route 646 Gifford (16732) *(G-6360)*
Phillips Drilling Company (HQ).......724 479-1135
190 Thorn Hill Rd Warrendale (15086) *(G-19091)*
Phillips Drilling Company.......724 479-1135
598 Lutz School Rd Indiana (15701) *(G-8120)*
Phillips Exploration LLC.......724 772-3500
502 Keystone Dr Warrendale (15086) *(G-19092)*
Phillips Graphic Finishing LLC.......717 653-4565
150 Arrowhead Dr Manheim (17545) *(G-10402)*
Phillips Tank & Structure, Braddock *Also called Conway-Phillips Holding LLC (G-1943)*
Phillips Wood Products Inc.......570 726-3515
479 Sugar Run Rd Mill Hall (17751) *(G-11180)*
Philly Banner Express LLC.......267 385-5451
236 E Hunting Park Ave Philadelphia (19124) *(G-14168)*
Philly Case Co, Philadelphia *Also called Tre-Ray Cases Inc (G-14404)*
Philly Designs, Philadelphia *Also called Gerald Maier (G-13757)*
Philly Fades Inc.......678 672-9727
200 Bridge St Phoenixville (19460) *(G-14567)*
Philly Originals.......724 728-3011
478 3rd St Beaver (15009) *(G-989)*
Philly Pretzel Factory (PA).......215 962-5593
7368 Frankford Ave Philadelphia (19136) *(G-14169)*
Phillyrubber.com, Philadelphia *Also called Manufactured Rubber Pdts Co (G-13989)*
Phillys Best Steak Company Inc.......610 259-6000
619 Indl Park Dr Lansdowne (19050) *(G-9441)*
Phillystran Inc.......215 368-6611
151 Commerce Dr Montgomeryville (18936) *(G-11415)*
Phillyvoice.com, Philadelphia *Also called Wwb Holdings LLC (G-14493)*
Philosophical Publishing Co, Quakertown *Also called Beverly Hall Co (G-16172)*
Phl Collective LLC.......610 496-7758
544 Virginia Ave Havertown (19083) *(G-7426)*
Phlexglobal Inc.......484 324-7921
400 Chesterfield Pkwy Malvern (19355) *(G-10296)*
Phoenix Avs LLC.......610 910-6251
501 Abbott Dr Side E Broomall (19008) *(G-2302)*
Phoenix Awning Company, Philadelphia *Also called Charles F Woodill (G-13528)*
Phoenix Bronze Resources LLC.......724 857-2225
100 Steel St Aliquippa (15001) *(G-88)*
Phoenix Cabinetry Inc.......484 831-5741
98 Highland Ave Phoenixville (19460) *(G-14568)*
Phoenix Cfb Inc.......215 957-0500
971 Mearns Rd Warminster (18974) *(G-18941)*
Phoenix Coach Works Inc.......610 495-2266
39 Sheridan Ln Pottstown (19464) *(G-16030)*
Phoenix Combustion Inc.......610 495-5800
15 Airport Rd Pottstown (19464) *(G-16031)*
Phoenix Contact Dev & Mfg Inc (PA).......717 944-1300
586 Fulling Mill Rd Middletown (17057) *(G-11068)*
Phoenix Corporation.......215 295-9510
600 Dean Sievers Pl Morrisville (19067) *(G-11578)*
Phoenix Data Inc.......570 547-1665
8813 State Route 405 Montgomery (17752) *(G-11377)*
Phoenix Design & Print Inc.......412 264-4895
614 5th Ave Coraopolis (15108) *(G-3715)*
Phoenix Energy Marketing, Freeport *Also called Phoenix Energy Productions (G-6213)*
Phoenix Energy Productions.......724 295-9220
419 Riverside Dr Freeport (16229) *(G-6213)*
Phoenix Fine Dining, Erie *Also called Schultz Mktg & Communications (G-5469)*
Phoenix Forge Group LLC (PA).......800 234-8665
1020 Macarthur Rd Reading (19605) *(G-16470)*
Phoenix Forging Company Inc.......610 530-8249
7550 Walker Way Allentown (18106) *(G-350)*
Phoenix Forging Company Inc (PA).......610 264-2861
800 Front St Catasauqua (18032) *(G-2816)*
Phoenix Glass Co The, Monaca *Also called Ghp II LLC (G-11290)*
Phoenix Hotform, Allentown *Also called Phoenix Forging Company Inc (G-350)*
Phoenix Hotform, Catasauqua *Also called Phoenix Forging Company Inc (G-2816)*
Phoenix Laboratories Inc.......215 295-5222
1a Headley Pl Levittown (19054) *(G-9855)*
Phoenix Lithographing Corp.......215 969-4600
11601 Caroline Rd Philadelphia (19154) *(G-14170)*
Phoenix Lithographing Corp (PA).......215 698-9000
11631 Caroline Rd Ste A Philadelphia (19154) *(G-14171)*
Phoenix Lock Company, West Chester *Also called Onexia Brass Inc (G-19611)*
Phoenix Metals, Morrisville *Also called Phoenix Corporation (G-11578)*
Phoenix Metals of Pa Inc.......724 282-0679
308 Mitchell Hill Rd Butler (16002) *(G-2433)*
Phoenix Mold and Machine LLC.......215 355-1985
42 Steam Whistle Dr Warminster (18974) *(G-18942)*
Phoenix Printers Inc.......610 427-3069
665 Nutt Rd Phoenixville (19460) *(G-14569)*
Phoenix Services, Kennett Square *Also called Metal Services LLC (G-8527)*
Phoenix Sintered Metals LLC.......814 268-3455
921 Clark St Brockway (15824) *(G-2230)*
Phoenix Trim Works Inc.......570 320-0322
2211 Reach Rd Williamsport (17701) *(G-20057)*
Phoenix Tube Co Inc.......610 865-5337
1185 Win Dr Bethlehem (18017) *(G-1596)*
Phoenix Woodworking Inc.......610 209-9030
211 Reading Rd East Earl (17519) *(G-4553)*
Phoenixx Intl Resources Inc.......412 782-7060
111 Delafield Rd Pittsburgh (15215) *(G-15380)*
Phonetics Inc.......610 558-2700
901 Tryens Rd Aston (19014) *(G-787)*
Photo Process Screen Mfg Co.......215 426-5473
179 W Berks St Philadelphia (19122) *(G-14172)*
Photo Review, The, Langhorne *Also called Philadelphia Photo Review (G-9318)*
Photomedex Inc.......215 619-3286
2300 Computer Rd Ste G26 Willow Grove (19090) *(G-20134)*
Photomedex Inc.......215 619-3235
2300 Computer Rd Ste G26 Willow Grove (19090) *(G-20135)*
Photonis Defense Inc (HQ).......717 295-6000
1000 New Holland Ave Lancaster (17601) *(G-9170)*
Photonis Digital Imaging LLC.......972 987-1460
1000 New Holland Ave Lancaster (17601) *(G-9171)*
Photonis USA Pennsylvania Inc, Lancaster *Also called Photonis Defense Inc (G-9170)*
Photosonix Medical Inc.......215 641-4909
23 Brookline Ct Ambler (19002) *(G-598)*
Phresh Prints Ink LLC.......267 687-7483
2825 N 22nd St Philadelphia (19132) *(G-14173)*
Phufar.......215 483-0487
6190 Ridge Ave Philadelphia (19128) *(G-14174)*
Phxco LLC.......608 203-1500
1451 Stoneridge Dr Ste B Middletown (17057) *(G-11069)*
Physical Graffi-Tees.......610 439-3344
1951 W Tilghman St Allentown (18104) *(G-351)*
Physician Transformations LLC.......484 420-4407
17 Bishop Hollow Rd Ste C Newtown Square (19073) *(G-12590)*
Physiic LLC.......424 653-6410
320 Main St Irwin (15642) *(G-8191)*
Phytogenx Inc.......610 286-0111
35 Thousand Oaks Blvd Morgantown (19543) *(G-11530)*

ALPHABETIC

Piad Cast Precision, Greensburg *Also called Piad Precision Casting Corp* ***(G-6700)***
Piad Precision Casting Corp 724 838-5500
112 Industrial Park Rd Greensburg (15601) ***(G-6700)***
Pic Mobile Advertising LLC 570 208-1459
550 Anderson St Wilkes Barre (18702) ***(G-19956)***
Piccolo Group Inc 610 738-7733
1204 Waterford Rd West Chester (19380) ***(G-19617)***
Piccolomini Contractors Inc 724 437-7946
1790 Pittsburgh Rd Waltersburg (15488) ***(G-18795)***
Pickar Brothers Inc 610 582-0967
5 Riga Ln Birdsboro (19508) ***(G-1703)***
Pickell Enterprises Inc 215 244-7800
1345 Bridgewater Rd Bensalem (19020) ***(G-1243)***
Pickering Winery 570 247-7269
27697 Pennsylvania 187 Wysox (18854) ***(G-20290)***
Pickett Quarries Inc 570 869-1817
167 River Ln Laceyville (18623) ***(G-8873)***
Picoma Industries, Waynesboro *Also called Bitrekpasub Inc* ***(G-19401)***
Picpa, Philadelphia *Also called Pennsylvania Institute of CPA* ***(G-14132)***
Picwell Inc 215 563-0976
2200 Arch St Ste 1a Philadelphia (19103) ***(G-14175)***
Pidilite Usa Inc 800 424-3596
100 E Diamond Ave Hazleton (18201) ***(G-7519)***
Pieces By Pallets LLC 717 872-7238
210 S Lime St Quarryville (17566) ***(G-16277)***
Pierce Pen Design Limited, Williamsport *Also called Country Accents* ***(G-20001)***
Pieri Creations LLC 215 634-4000
100 W Oxford St Philadelphia (19122) ***(G-14176)***
Pierre's Costumes, Philadelphia *Also called Williamson Costume Company* ***(G-14476)***
Piezo Kinetics Inc (HQ) 814 355-1593
660 E Rolling Ridge Dr Bellefonte (16823) ***(G-1112)***
Pignuts Inc 610 530-8788
6853 Ruppsville Rd Allentown (18106) ***(G-352)***
Piht LLC 814 781-6262
118 Access Rd Saint Marys (15857) ***(G-17007)***
Pik-A-Boo Photos LLC 267 334-6379
6344 N 8th St Apt G7 Philadelphia (19126) ***(G-14177)***
Pike County Concrete Inc 570 775-7880
N Rte 434 Rr 739 Hawley (18428) ***(G-7435)***
Pike County Dispatch Inc 570 296-2611
105 W Catherine St Milford (18337) ***(G-11166)***
Pike Creek Salt Company 570 585-8818
43 Marshwood Bnd Clarks Summit (18411) ***(G-3198)***
Pike Graphics Inc 215 836-9120
1200 E Mermaid Ln Flourtown (19031) ***(G-5990)***
Pikes Creek Raceway Park Inc 570 477-2226
111 Croop Rd Hunlock Creek (18621) ***(G-7933)***
Pikewood Inc 610 974-8000
123 E Broad St Bethlehem (18018) ***(G-1597)***
Piles Concrete Products Co Inc 814 445-6619
115 Pickett Ln Friedens (15541) ***(G-6225)***
Pilling Company 215 643-2600
420 Delaware Dr Fort Washington (19034) ***(G-6088)***
Pillings FRP (PA) 570 538-9202
Old Rte 15 New Columbia (17856) ***(G-12175)***
Pillsbury Company LLC 610 593-5133
Lower Valley Rd Rr 2 Parkesburg (19365) ***(G-13182)***
Pilot-Run Stamping Company 440 255-8821
715 Spring St Corry (16407) ***(G-3772)***
Pima LLC 412 770-8130
1605 Middle Rd Glenshaw (15116) ***(G-6497)***
Pin Hsun Kuo 717 795-7297
1041 Brookwood Dr Mechanicsburg (17055) ***(G-10880)***
Pinch Road Sawmill 717 665-1096
2770 Pinch Rd Manheim (17545) ***(G-10403)***
Pindar Set Inc 610 731-2921
2201 Renaissance Blvd King of Prussia (19406) ***(G-8662)***
Pine Creek Construction LLC 717 362-6974
6140 State Route 225 Elizabethville (17023) ***(G-4896)***
Pine Creek Lumber, Co, Mill Hall *Also called Bingaman & Son Lumber Inc* ***(G-11173)***
Pine Electronics Inc 724 458-6391
101 Industrial Dr Grove City (16127) ***(G-6800)***
Pine Grove Mnfctured Homes Inc 570 345-2011
2 Pleasant Valley Rd Pine Grove (17963) ***(G-14602)***
Pine Hill Manufacturing LLC 717 288-2443
2969 Lincoln Hwy E Gordonville (17529) ***(G-6561)***
Pine Instrument Company (PA) 724 458-6391
101 Industrial Dr Grove City (16127) ***(G-6801)***
Pine Valley Supply Corporation 215 676-8100
225 Geiger Rd Fl 2 Philadelphia (19115) ***(G-14178)***
Pinecreek Quarry, Jersey Shore *Also called Hanson Aggregates PA LLC* ***(G-8314)***
Pinehurst Tool & Die, Conneaut Lake *Also called George J Anderton* ***(G-3473)***
Pinnacle Climate Tech Inc 215 891-8460
1602 William Leigh Dr Bristol (19007) ***(G-2182)***
Pinnacle Performace Group, Philadelphia *Also called Atlantic Alliance Pubg Co* ***(G-13421)***
Pinnacle Precision Co 412 678-6816
37 Allegheny Sq Glassport (15045) ***(G-6415)***
Pinnacle Products Intl Inc 215 302-1417
1602 William Leigh Dr Bristol (19007) ***(G-2183)***
Pinnacle Ridge Winery 610 756-4481
407 Old Route 22 Kutztown (19530) ***(G-8855)***
Pinnacle Systems 412 262-3950
2504 State Ave Coraopolis (15108) ***(G-3716)***
Pinnacle Textile Inds LLC 800 901-4784
440 Drew Ct King of Prussia (19406) ***(G-8663)***
Pinter Industries Inc 717 898-9517
3152 Woodridge Dr Landisville (17538) ***(G-9264)***
Pioneer Aggregates, Plains *Also called New Enterprise Stone Lime Inc* ***(G-15787)***
Pioneer Burial Vault Co Inc 215 766-2943
Crosskeys Rd Rr 611 Doylestown (18901) ***(G-4325)***
Pioneer Drilling Services Ltd 724 592-6707
1083 N 88 Rd Rices Landing (15357) ***(G-16671)***
Pioneer Electric Supply Co Inc (PA) 814 437-1342
405 Allegheny Blvd Franklin (16323) ***(G-6152)***
Pioneer Energy Products LLC 814 676-5688
671 Colbert Ave Oil City (16301) ***(G-12954)***
Pioneer Enterprises Inc 717 938-9388
1008 Pinetown Rd Lewisberry (17339) ***(G-9892)***
Pioneer Machine & Tooling LLC 610 623-3908
515 Mildred Ave Secane (19018) ***(G-17319)***
Pioneer Supply Company Inc 856 314-8299
660 E Pittsburgh St Ste 1 Greensburg (15601) ***(G-6701)***
Pioneer Tool & Forge Inc 724 337-4700
101 6th St New Kensington (15068) ***(G-12366)***
Pioneer Tool & Mold Division, Erie *Also called Plastek Industries Inc* ***(G-5422)***
Pioneer Woodcrafts LLC 717 656-0776
35 Graybill Rd Leola (17540) ***(G-9797)***
PIP Printing, Erie *Also called Copy Right Printing & Graphics* ***(G-5233)***
PIP Printing, Lancaster *Also called Ideal Prtg Co Lancaster Inc* ***(G-9054)***
PIP Printing, King of Prussia *Also called Greenwood Business Printing* ***(G-8626)***
Pipe & Precast Cnstr Pdts Inc 610 644-7338
Old Phoenixville Pike Devault (19432) ***(G-4112)***
Pipe Dreams Plumbing Sup Inc 215 741-0889
579 Heatons Mill Dr Langhorne (19047) ***(G-9319)***
Pipe Supports Group, Donora *Also called Carpenter & Paterson Inc* ***(G-4150)***
Pipes Skate Park 724 327-4247
215 Obey St Pittsburgh (15205) ***(G-15381)***
Piramal Critical Care Inc (HQ) 800 414-1901
3950 Schelden Cir Bethlehem (18017) ***(G-1598)***
Piramal Critical Care Inc 610 974-9760
3950 Schelden Cir Bethlehem (18017) ***(G-1599)***
Piramal Healthcare, Bethlehem *Also called Piramal Critical Care Inc* ***(G-1599)***
Piramal Healthcare Inc (PA) 610 974-9760
3950 Schelden Cir Bethlehem (18017) ***(G-1600)***
Piscis 412 464-5181
4501 Main St Homestead (15120) ***(G-7690)***
Pita Pita LLC 267 440-7482
1932 Liacouras Walk Philadelphia (19122) ***(G-14179)***
Pitcal Inc 412 433-1121
600 Grant St Ste 3214 Pittsburgh (15219) ***(G-15382)***
Pitney Bowes Inc 717 884-1882
2405 Park Dr Ste 100 Harrisburg (17110) ***(G-7199)***
Pitney Bowes Inc 412 689-6639
800 Vinial St Ste B201 Pittsburgh (15212) ***(G-15383)***
Pitney Bowes Inc 215 751-9800
2000 Hamilton St Ste C01 Philadelphia (19130) ***(G-14180)***
Pitney Bowes Inc 215 946-2863
42 Runway Dr Levittown (19057) ***(G-9856)***
Pitsburghfudge.com, North Versailles *Also called Copper Kettle Fudge Factory* ***(G-12773)***
Pitt News, Pittsburgh *Also called University of Pittsburgh* ***(G-15683)***
Pitt Oil Service Inc 412 771-6950
3498 Grand Ave Pittsburgh (15225) ***(G-15384)***
Pitt Penn Oil Co LLC 813 968-9635
426 Freeport Rd Creighton (15030) ***(G-3883)***
Pittman Bros Lumber 814 652-6396
184 Pine Hollow Rd Everett (15537) ***(G-5577)***
Pitts Doggn It LLC 412 687-1440
260 Atwood St Pittsburgh (15213) ***(G-15385)***
Pittsbrgh Tubular Shafting Inc (PA) 724 774-7212
Cleveland St Kentucky Ave Rochester (15074) ***(G-16787)***
Pittsbrgh Tubular Shafting Inc 724 774-7212
611 Connecticut Ave Rochester (15074) ***(G-16788)***
Pittsburgh Advertising Spc Co, Pittsburgh *Also called Callery Sr John* ***(G-14805)***
Pittsburgh Aluminum Co LLC 724 452-5900
100 Evergreen Ave Pittsburgh (15209) ***(G-15386)***
Pittsburgh Anodizing Co 724 265-5110
41 Blue Rd Russellton (15076) ***(G-16884)***
Pittsburgh Bakery Equipment Co 724 533-2158
1118 State Route 956 Volant (16156) ***(G-18776)***
Pittsburgh Binding 412 481-8108
2538 Mission St Pittsburgh (15203) ***(G-15387)***
Pittsburgh Bolt Company LLC 724 935-6844
114 Vip Dr Wexford (15090) ***(G-19820)***
Pittsburgh Brewing Company 412 682-7400
3340 Liberty Ave Pittsburgh (15201) ***(G-15388)***
Pittsburgh Business Times 412 481-6397
45 S 23rd St Pittsburgh (15203) ***(G-15389)***

Pittsburgh Carbide Die Co LLC.....412 384-5785
254 Lovedale Rd Elizabeth (15037) ***(G-4862)***
Pittsburgh Casing Co, Pittsburgh *Also called Pittsburgh Spice Seasoning Co **(G-15408)***
Pittsburgh Catholic Pubg Assoc.....412 471-1252
135 1st Ave Ste 200 Pittsburgh (15222) ***(G-15390)***
Pittsburgh City Paper Inc.....412 316-3342
650 Smithfield St # 2200 Pittsburgh (15222) ***(G-15391)***
Pittsburgh Corning LLC (HQ).....724 327-6100
800 Presque Isle Dr Pittsburgh (15239) ***(G-15392)***
Pittsburgh Design Services Inc.....412 276-3000
Hammond & Gregg Sts Carnegie (15106) ***(G-2779)***
Pittsburgh Digital.....412 431-6008
2530 Josephine St Pittsburgh (15203) ***(G-15393)***
Pittsburgh Distilling Co LLC.....412 224-2827
2401 Smallman St Pittsburgh (15222) ***(G-15394)***
Pittsburgh Elc Mtr Repr Inc.....724 443-2333
4790 William Flynn Hwy # 24 Allison Park (15101) ***(G-458)***
Pittsburgh Electric Engs Inc.....724 547-9170
402 E Main St Ste 800 Mount Pleasant (15666) ***(G-11711)***
Pittsburgh Electric Mtr & Repr, Allison Park *Also called Pittsburgh Elc Mtr Repr Inc **(G-458)***
Pittsburgh Fabrication Mch Inc.....412 771-1400
3000 Grand Ave Ste 2 Pittsburgh (15225) ***(G-15395)***
Pittsburgh Fence Co Inc.....724 775-6550
551 E Main St Carnegie (15106) ***(G-2780)***
Pittsburgh File & Box Co.....412 431-5465
51 S 14th St Pittsburgh (15203) ***(G-15396)***
Pittsburgh Flatroll Company.....412 237-2260
1200 Reedsdale St Ste 3 Pittsburgh (15233) ***(G-15397)***
Pittsburgh Foam Products, Hickory *Also called Gordon Seaver **(G-7628)***
Pittsburgh Gear Company, Pittsburgh *Also called Brad Foote Gear Works Inc **(G-14789)***
Pittsburgh Glass Works LLC.....419 683-2400
150 Ferry St Creighton (15030) ***(G-3884)***
Pittsburgh Glass Works LLC.....814 336-4411
5123 Victory Blvd Cochranton (16314) ***(G-3347)***
Pittsburgh Glass Works LLC.....814 684-2300
4408 E Pleasant Vly Blvd Tyrone (16686) ***(G-18589)***
Pittsburgh Glass Works LLC (HQ).....412 995-6500
30 Isabella St Ste 500 Pittsburgh (15212) ***(G-15398)***
Pittsburgh Jet Center.....724 452-4719
1859 Route 588 Zelienople (16063) ***(G-20816)***
Pittsburgh Jewish Publication.....412 687-1000
5915 Beacon St Pittsburgh (15217) ***(G-15399)***
Pittsburgh Magazine, Pittsburgh *Also called Wmpm LLC **(G-15721)***
Pittsburgh Magazine.....412 622-1360
4802 5th Ave Pittsburgh (15213) ***(G-15400)***
Pittsburgh Medical Device.....724 325-1869
1008 Summer Ridge Ct Murrysville (15668) ***(G-11861)***
Pittsburgh Metal Processing Co.....412 781-8053
1850 Chapman St Pittsburgh (15215) ***(G-15401)***
Pittsburgh Mfrs & Installers, Homestead *Also called PMI Stainless **(G-7691)***
Pittsburgh Mobile Concrete Inc.....412 486-0186
1933 Babcock Blvd Pittsburgh (15209) ***(G-15402)***
Pittsburgh Photon Studio LLC.....724 263-6502
393 Vanadium Rd Pittsburgh (15243) ***(G-15403)***
Pittsburgh Plug and Pdts Corp (PA).....724 538-4022
101 3rd St Evans City (16033) ***(G-5561)***
Pittsburgh Plug and Pdts Corp.....724 538-4022
700 S Washington St Evans City (16033) ***(G-5562)***
Pittsburgh Post Gazette, Clinton *Also called Pg Publishing Company **(G-3265)***
Pittsburgh Post Gazette.....724 266-2701
144 Ferry St Leetsdale (15056) ***(G-9701)***
Pittsburgh Poster, Ambridge *Also called Design Dynamics Inc **(G-615)***
Pittsburgh Postgazette.....412 858-1850
2350 Eldo Rd Monroeville (15146) ***(G-11348)***
Pittsburgh Powder Coat.....412 419-8434
4273 Fnleyville Elrama Rd Finleyville (15332) ***(G-5963)***
Pittsburgh Powder Coat L.....724 348-8434
621 Mclaughlin Run Rd Bridgeville (15017) ***(G-2086)***
Pittsburgh Precision.....412 712-1111
100 Herman Dr Pittsburgh (15239) ***(G-15404)***
Pittsburgh Professional Magazi.....412 221-2992
1885 Tilton Dr Pittsburgh (15241) ***(G-15405)***
Pittsburgh Prtg Solutions LLC.....412 977-2026
1020 Timber Ridge Dr Pittsburgh (15239) ***(G-15406)***
Pittsburgh Shed Company Inc.....724 745-4422
2544 Washington Rd Canonsburg (15317) ***(G-2619)***
Pittsburgh Special-T Dairy LLC (HQ).....412 881-1409
1614 Brownsville Rd Pittsburgh (15210) ***(G-15407)***
Pittsburgh Specialty, Evans City *Also called Helena Chemical Company **(G-5559)***
Pittsburgh Spice Seasoning Co.....412 288-5036
1235 Clairhaven St Pittsburgh (15205) ***(G-15408)***
Pittsburgh Stage Inc.....412 534-4500
2 South Ave Sewickley (15143) ***(G-17403)***
Pittsburgh Stained GL Studio.....412 921-2500
160 Warden St Pittsburgh (15220) ***(G-15409)***
Pittsburgh Stained GL Studios, Pittsburgh *Also called Pittsburgh Stained GL Studio **(G-15409)***
Pittsburgh Tank Corporation.....724 258-0200
1500 Industrial Dr Monongahela (15063) ***(G-11314)***
Pittsburgh Technologies Inc.....724 339-0900
1035 Hunt Valley Cir New Kensington (15068) ***(G-12367)***
Pittsburgh Technology Council.....412 687-2700
2000 Tech Dr Ste 100 Pittsburgh (15219) ***(G-15410)***
Pittsburgh Trane Parts Center, Pittsburgh *Also called Trane US Inc **(G-15636)***
Pittsburgh Tribune Review, Tarentum *Also called Trib Total Media LLC **(G-18250)***
Pittsburgh Trophy Company Inc.....412 261-4376
3225 Penn Ave Pittsburgh (15201) ***(G-15411)***
Pittsburgh Tube Company, Wexford *Also called Ptc Alliance Corp **(G-19823)***
Pittsburgh Welding & Forge Div, Zelienople *Also called J B Booth and Co **(G-20805)***
Pittsburgh Window & Door, Pittsburgh *Also called Pittsburgh Aluminum Co LLC **(G-15386)***
Pittsburgh Winery.....412 566-1000
2815 Penn Ave Pittsburgh (15222) ***(G-15412)***
Pittsburgh Wool Co Inc.....412 642-0606
2401 Smallman St Pittsburgh (15222) ***(G-15413)***
Pittston Baking Co Inc.....570 343-2102
2646 Pittston Ave Scranton (18505) ***(G-17272)***
Pittston Lumber & Mfg Co.....570 654-3328
234 N Main St Pittston (18640) ***(G-15776)***
Pixcontroller Inc.....724 733-0970
1001 Corporate Ln Ste 100 Export (15632) ***(G-5621)***
Pixel Innovations Inc.....724 935-8366
11676 Perry Hwy Ste 3202 Wexford (15090) ***(G-19821)***
Pixelle Spcialty Solutions LLC (PA).....717 225-4711
228 S Main St Spring Grove (17362) ***(G-17880)***
Pizza Associates Incorporated.....570 822-6600
337 Wyoming Valley Mall Wilkes Barre (18702) ***(G-19957)***
Pizza Hut, Carlisle *Also called Atlantic Dev Corp of PA **(G-2690)***
Pjr Printing Inc.....724 283-2666
229 S Main St Butler (16001) ***(G-2434)***
Pkt Technologies.....412 494-5600
114 Technology Dr Pittsburgh (15275) ***(G-15414)***
Pl Bath Products, Bristol *Also called Robern Inc **(G-2195)***
Placemat Printers Inc.....610 285-2255
10195 Old Rt 22 Fogelsville (18051) ***(G-5996)***
Plain & Fancy Custom Cabinetry, Schaefferstown *Also called Plain n Fancy Kitchens Inc **(G-17129)***
Plain n Fancy Kitchens Inc (PA).....717 949-6571
2550 Stiegel Pike Schaefferstown (17088) ***(G-17129)***
Plains Lpg Services.....717 376-0830
2397 Quentin Rd Ste A Lebanon (17042) ***(G-9622)***
Plan B Consultants LLC.....215 638-0767
475 Veit Rd Huntingdon Valley (19006) ***(G-8026)***
Plan B Engineering, Huntingdon Valley *Also called Plan B Consultants LLC **(G-8026)***
Plan Management Corporation.....610 359-5870
5 Radnor Corp Ctr Ste 450 Wayne (19087) ***(G-19362)***
Planet Ryo.....717 938-8860
116 Newberry Pkwy Etters (17319) ***(G-5552)***
Plant, Philadelphia *Also called United Color Manufacturing Inc **(G-14420)***
Plant, Bethlehem *Also called Bethlehem Pre-Cast Inc **(G-1462)***
Plant 7, Turtlepoint *Also called Glenn O Hawbaker Inc **(G-18571)***
Plant Growers Workshop Inc.....724 473-1079
106 Center St Bldg 3 Callery (16024) ***(G-2470)***
Plantarium Living Envirom.....215 338-2008
5101 Cottman Ave Philadelphia (19135) ***(G-14181)***
Plantation Candies Inc.....215 723-6810
4224 Bethlehem Pike Telford (18969) ***(G-18309)***
Plants and Goodwin Inc.....814 697-6330
1034 Route 44 Shinglehouse (16748) ***(G-17511)***
Plantscape Inc (PA).....412 281-6352
3101 Liberty Ave Pittsburgh (15201) ***(G-15415)***
Plasma Automation Incorporated.....814 333-2181
10346 Mercer Pike Meadville (16335) ***(G-10780)***
Plasma Source.....215 942-6370
649 2nd Street Pike Ste B Southampton (18966) ***(G-17830)***
Plastek Group, The, Erie *Also called Plastek Industries Inc **(G-5420)***
Plastek Industries Inc (PA).....814 878-4400
2425 W 23rd St Erie (16506) ***(G-5420)***
Plastek Industries Inc.....814 878-4741
2200 Yoder Dr Erie (16506) ***(G-5421)***
Plastek Industries Inc.....814 878-4719
3230 W 22nd St Erie (16506) ***(G-5422)***
Plastek Industries Inc.....814 878-4601
2315 W 23rd St Erie (16506) ***(G-5423)***
Plastek Industries Inc.....814 878-4466
2425 W 23rd St Erie (16506) ***(G-5424)***
Plastek Industries Inc.....814 878-4515
2310 Pittsburgh Ave Erie (16502) ***(G-5425)***
Plasti-Coat Corp.....475 235-2761
3225 State Rd Sellersville (18960) ***(G-17357)***
Plastic Components Inc.....215 235-5550
1526 N American St Philadelphia (19122) ***(G-14182)***
Plastic Development Company PA.....800 451-1420
75 Palmer Industrial Rd Williamsport (17701) ***(G-20058)***
Plastic Dip Moldings Inc (PA).....215 766-2020
2345 Milford Square Pike Quakertown (18951) ***(G-16229)***
Plastic Fabricators Inc.....717 843-4222
1450 W College Ave York (17404) ***(G-20628)***

ALPHABETIC

Plastic Lumber Yard LLC 610 277-3900
  227 Isabella St Plymouth Meeting (19462) *(G-15864)*
Plastic Options LLC (PA) 724 730-5225
  2704 Mercer Rd New Castle (16105) *(G-12137)*
Plastic Packaging & Print Co, Honesdale Also called St Clair Graphics Inc *(G-7726)*
Plastic Profiles LLC 717 593-9200
  48 S Antrim Way Greencastle (17225) *(G-6626)*
Plastic Solutions Inc 215 968-3242
  424 Mahogany Walk Newtown (18940) *(G-12536)*
Plastic System Packaging Mille 717 277-7404
  17 Lebanon Valley Pkwy Lebanon (17042) *(G-9623)*
Plasticoncentrates Inc (PA) 215 243-4143
  4548 Market St Philadelphia (19139) *(G-14183)*
Plastics Services Network, Erie Also called Advanced Solutions Network LLC *(G-5175)*
Plastics Services Network 814 898-6317
  5451 Mrwin Ln Knwldge Par Knowledge Prk Erie (16510) *(G-5426)*
Plastikos Inc 814 868-1656
  8165 Hawthorne Dr Erie (16509) *(G-5427)*
Plastinetics Inc 570 384-4832
  613 Oak Ridge Rd Hazle Township (18202) *(G-7473)*
Plastrac Inc (PA) 610 356-3000
  3928 Miller Rd Edgemont (19028) *(G-4807)*
Plate Rite, Folcroft Also called P R Finishing Inc *(G-6011)*
Plating Unlimited LLC 814 952-3135
  201 Rockland Ave Punxsutawney (15767) *(G-16153)*
Platt Robert E Machine Pdts, Springtown Also called Dynacut Inc *(G-17926)*
Platypus LLC 412 979-4629
  2010 Smallman St Pittsburgh (15222) *(G-15416)*
Playpower Inc 570 522-9800
  1000 Buffalo Rd Lewisburg (17837) *(G-9916)*
Playword, Lewisburg Also called Playworld Systems Incorporated *(G-9917)*
Playworld, Lewisburg Also called Playpower Inc *(G-9916)*
Playworld Systems Incorporated (HQ) 570 522-5435
  1000 Buffalo Rd Lewisburg (17837) *(G-9917)*
Pleasant Luck Corp 215 968-2080
  46 Blacksmith Rd Newtown (18940) *(G-12537)*
Pleasant Mount Welding Inc 570 282-6164
  45 Dundaff St Carbondale (18407) *(G-2684)*
Pleasant Valley Homes Inc 570 345-2011
  100 Hammersmith Dr Pine Grove (17963) *(G-14603)*
Pleasant Valley Modular Homes, Pine Grove Also called Pleasant Valley Homes
Inc *(G-14603)*
Pleasant Valley Saw Mill 814 767-9016
  422 Beans Cove Rd Clearville (15535) *(G-3243)*
Pleasantview Welding, Honey Brook Also called Aaron King *(G-7735)*
Pleiger Plastics Company 724 228-2244
  498 Crile Rd Washington (15301) *(G-19216)*
Plouse Machine Shop Inc 717 558-8530
  401 Aviation Way Highspire (17034) *(G-7634)*
Plouse Precision Manufacturing, Highspire Also called Plouse Machine Shop Inc *(G-7634)*
Plow Shop At Lafayette Welding, Royersford Also called Lafayette Welding Inc *(G-16857)*
Pls Signs LLC 215 269-1400
  463 S Oxford Valley Rd Fairless Hills (19030) *(G-5791)*
Plum Corporation 724 836-7261
  1534 Woodward Drive Ext Greensburg (15601) *(G-6702)*
Plum Enterprises Inc 610 783-7377
  500 Freedom View Ln Valley Forge (19481) *(G-18710)*
Plum Manufacturing Co Inc 215 520-2236
  101 Colettes Ct North Wales (19454) *(G-12825)*
Plumpy's Homemade, Jessup Also called Plumpys Pierogies Inc *(G-8335)*
Plumpys Pierogies Inc 570 489-5520
  515 Delaware St Ste 1 Jessup (18434) *(G-8335)*
Plumriver LLC (PA) 781 577-9575
  1257 E College Ave State College (16801) *(G-18006)*
Plurogen Therapeutics LLC 610 539-3670
  2495 Gen Armistead Ave Norristown (19403) *(G-12703)*
Plymouth Blind Co Inc 412 771-8569
  7 Crawford St Mc Kees Rocks (15136) *(G-10626)*
Plymouth Graphics Inc 570 779-9645
  411 W Main St Plymouth (18651) *(G-15820)*
Plymouth Interiors, Mc Kees Rocks Also called Plymouth Blind Co Inc *(G-10626)*
Plymouth Interiors, Mc Kees Rocks Also called Acacia Corp *(G-10600)*
Plymouth Interiors LP 412 771-8569
  7 Crawford St Mc Kees Rocks (15136) *(G-10627)*
PM Kalco Inc 724 347-2208
  40 Council Ave Wheatland (16161) *(G-19841)*
PMC, Johnstown Also called Penn Machine Company *(G-8421)*
Pmdi Signs Inc 215 526-0898
  10 Council Rock Dr Ivyland (18974) *(G-8220)*
PMF Industries Inc 570 323-9944
  2601 Reach Rd Williamsport (17701) *(G-20059)*
PMI Inc 814 455-8085
  1655 W 20th St Erie (16502) *(G-5428)*
PMI Stainless 412 461-1463
  Forest & West 8th Ave Homestead (15120) *(G-7691)*
Pmp, Berwick Also called Patriot Metal Products Inc *(G-1339)*
Pmrs, Horsham Also called Pharmceutical Mfg RES Svcs Inc *(G-7841)*

Pmt Machining Inc 570 329-0349
  200 Fleming St Williamsport (17702) *(G-20060)*
PMTA, Camp Hill Also called Pennsylvania Motor Truck Assn *(G-2510)*
PNC Equity Partners LP (PA) 412 914-0175
  620 Liberty Ave Pittsburgh (15222) *(G-15417)*
Pneu-Dart Inc 570 323-2710
  15223 State Route 87 Williamsport (17701) *(G-20061)*
Pocket Cross Inc 724 745-1140
  10 Cherry Ave Ste 100 Houston (15342) *(G-7877)*
Pocono Candle Works Inc (PA) 570 421-1832
  2712 Wigwam Park Rd East Stroudsburg (18301) *(G-4627)*
Pocono Hydrponic Solutions LLC 570 730-4544
  3280 Route 611 Bartonsville (18321) *(G-948)*
Pocono Industries Inc 570 421-3889
  Hickory Valley Rd Stroudsburg (18360) *(G-18134)*
Pocono Land & Homes Magazine P 570 424-1000
  1929 N 5th St Stroudsburg (18360) *(G-18135)*
Pocono Mountain Creamery LLC 570 443-9868
  501 Main St White Haven (18661) *(G-19850)*
Pocono Mountain Leather Co (PA) 570 814-6672
  44 E Saint Marys Rd Hanover Township (18706) *(G-7004)*
Pocono Pistol Club LLC 570 424-2940
  85 N 1st St Stroudsburg (18360) *(G-18136)*
Pocono Pool Products Inc 570 839-9291
  117 Carlton Rd Swiftwater (18370) *(G-18189)*
Pocono Protech 610 681-3550
  732 Gilbert Rd Gilbert (18331) *(G-6363)*
Pocono Record, Stroudsburg Also called Local Media Group Inc *(G-18125)*
Pocono Screen Supply LLC 570 253-6375
  908 E Elm St Scranton (18505) *(G-17273)*
Pocono Times 570 421-4800
  96 S Courtland St East Stroudsburg (18301) *(G-4628)*
Pocono Transcrete Incorporated (PA) 570 646-2662
  179 Burger Rd Blakeslee (18610) *(G-1749)*
Pocono Transcrete Incorporated 570 655-9166
  160 Brown Rd Pittston (18640) *(G-15777)*
Pocono Water Centers Inc 570 839-8012
  307 Rr 502 Moscow (18444) *(G-11600)*
Pocopson Industries Inc 610 793-0344
  919 Pocopson Rd West Chester (19382) *(G-19618)*
Podcon Inc 215 233-2600
  1000 E Mermaid Ln Glenside (19038) *(G-6533)*
Poff Sheet Metal Inc 717 845-9622
  736 Vander Ave York (17403) *(G-20629)*
Pohl Railroad Mtls Corp LLC 610 916-7645
  5662 Leesport Ave Reading (19605) *(G-16471)*
Poiesis Informatics Inc 412 327-8766
  1710 Murray Ave Ste 1 Pittsburgh (15217) *(G-15418)*
Point 2 Point Wireless Inc 347 543-5227
  6690 Hauser Rd Apt K203 Macungie (18062) *(G-10156)*
Point Blank Defense LLC 717 801-2632
  2956 Woodshead Ter York (17403) *(G-20630)*
Point of View LLC 215 340-1725
  24 N Main St Doylestown (18901) *(G-4326)*
Point Spring Company 724 658-9076
  1001 Harbor St New Castle (16101) *(G-12138)*
Pointer Hill Pet Products, Bechtelsville Also called Pointer Hill Pets Inc *(G-1035)*
Pointer Hill Pets Inc 610 754-7830
  625 Hoffmansville Rd # 1 Bechtelsville (19505) *(G-1035)*
Polar Blox Inc 814 629-7397
  650 Gilbert Hollow Rd Hollsopple (15935) *(G-7660)*
Polar Manufacturing Co Inc 215 535-6940
  2046 Castor Ave Philadelphia (19134) *(G-14184)*
Polar Peach LLC 717 517-9497
  2481 Lincoln Hwy E Ste 3 Lancaster (17602) *(G-9172)*
Polar Tech Industries Inc 800 423-2749
  1017 W Valley Ave Elysburg (17824) *(G-4979)*
Polarized Meat Co Inc (PA) 570 347-3396
  107 Keystone Indus Park Dunmore (18512) *(G-4481)*
Police Shield Corp 215 788-3489
  323 Otter St Bristol (19007) *(G-2184)*
Policymap Inc (HQ) 866 923-6277
  1315 Walnut St Ste 1500 Philadelphia (19107) *(G-14185)*
Policymap, LLC, Philadelphia Also called Policymap Inc *(G-14185)*
Polish This Inc 484 269-9450
  3006 Gateway Dr Royersford (19468) *(G-16861)*
Polish Water Ice, West Chester Also called TLC Refreshments Inc *(G-19665)*
Polkabla Industries LLC 724 322-7740
  16 1st St Smock (15480) *(G-17666)*
Pollock Advertising 724 794-6857
  118 1/2 Franklin St Slippery Rock (16057) *(G-17624)*
Pollyodd 215 271-1161
  1908 E Passyunk Ave Philadelphia (19148) *(G-14186)*
Polonier Corporation 267 994-1698
  225 Lincoln Hwy Ste H8 Fairless Hills (19030) *(G-5792)*
Polvac Corp 610 625-1505
  2442 Emrick Blvd Bethlehem (18020) *(G-1601)*
Poly Creations, Palmerton Also called Architectural Polymers Inc *(G-13102)*
Poly Grower Greenhouse Co, Muncy Also called Poly-Growers Inc *(G-11831)*

Poly Lite Windshield Repr Sups 717 845-1596
   1952 Stanton St York (17404) *(G-20631)*

Poly Sat Inc 215 332-7700
   7240 State Rd Philadelphia (19135) *(G-14187)*

Poly-Caster, Willow Street *Also called Rotation Dynamics Corporation (G-20156)*

Poly-Growers Inc 570 546-3216
   161 Fairground St Muncy (17756) *(G-11831)*

Poly-TEC Products Inc 215 547-3366
   697 Main St Bristol (19007) *(G-2185)*

Polychemy, Taylor *Also called Taylor Chemical Inc (G-18262)*

Polycube Company LLC 215 946-2823
   30a Runway Dr Levittown (19057) *(G-9857)*

Polycycle Industrial Pdts Inc 412 747-1101
   5501 Campbells Run Rd Pittsburgh (15205) *(G-15419)*

Polyfab Corporation 610 926-3245
   94 Dries Rd 222a Reading (19605) *(G-16472)*

Polyflo Inc 570 429-2340
   2 Tension Way St Saint Clair (17970) *(G-16938)*

Polyglass USA Inc 570 384-1230
   555 Oak Ridge Rd Hazle Township (18202) *(G-7474)*

Polymer Div of Wyomissing Spc 610 488-0981
   231 E 2nd St Bernville (19506) *(G-1303)*

Polymer Enterprises Inc (PA) 724 838-2340
   4731 State Route 30 # 401 Greensburg (15601) *(G-6703)*

Polymer Instrumentation & C (PA) 814 357-5860
   2215 High Tech Rd State College (16803) *(G-18007)*

Polymer Molding Inc 800 344-7584
   1655 W 20th St Erie (16502) *(G-5429)*

Polymer Surface Systems LLC 724 222-6544
   307 Roupe Rd Eighty Four (15330) *(G-4845)*

Polymer Tennessee Holdings (HQ) 724 838-2340
   1600 Washington St Indiana (15701) *(G-8121)*

Polymeric Extruded Products 215 943-1288
   6000 Hibbs Ln Levittown (19057) *(G-9858)*

Polymeric Systems Inc 610 286-2500
   47 Park Ave Elverson (19520) *(G-4965)*

Polymics, State College *Also called Polymer Instrumentation & C (G-18007)*

Polyone Corporation 570 474-7770
   855 Oak Hill Rd Mountain Top (18707) *(G-11770)*

Polyone Corporation 610 317-3300
   2513 Highland Ave Bethlehem (18020) *(G-1602)*

Polyports, Berwick *Also called Pennsylvania Aluminum (G-1341)*

Polysciences Inc (PA) 215 343-6484
   400 Valley Rd Warrington (18976) *(G-19128)*

Polysciences Inc 215 520-9358
   1981 County Line Rd Warrington (18976) *(G-19129)*

Polytek Development Corp (PA) 610 559-8620
   55 Hilton St Easton (18042) *(G-4743)*

Polyvisions Holdings Inc (PA) 717 266-3031
   25 Devco Dr Manchester (17345) *(G-10361)*

Poma GL Specialty Windows Inc 215 538-9424
   480 California Rd Quakertown (18951) *(G-16230)*

Pomco Graphics Inc 215 455-9500
   4411-27 Whitaker Ave Philadelphia (19120) *(G-14188)*

Pompa Trssler Chiropractic LLC 724 327-5665
   4905 William Penn Hwy Monroeville (15146) *(G-11349)*

Pompanette LLC 717 569-2300
   595 E Oregon Rd Lititz (17543) *(G-10033)*

Pomps Tire Service Inc 814 623-6764
   550 Sunnyside Rd Ste 201 Bedford (15522) *(G-1071)*

Pond Hockey Brewing Co LLC 814 429-9846
   508 Outer Dr State College (16801) *(G-18008)*

Pond Hockey Brewing Company, State College *Also called Pond Hockey Brewing Co LLC (G-18008)*

Ponfeigh Distillery Inc 919 606-0526
   3954 Brush Creek Rd Meyersdale (15552) *(G-11018)*

Pool and Spa Living, Warminster *Also called Manor House Publishing Co Inc (G-18916)*

Poolpak Inc 717 757-2648
   3491 Industrial Hwy York (17402) *(G-20632)*

Poolpak LLC 717 757-2648
   3491 Industrial Hwy York (17402) *(G-20633)*

Poonam International Inc 215 968-1555
   104 Justice Dr Newtown (18940) *(G-12538)*

Poormans Wldg Fabrication Inc 814 349-5893
   168 Kramer Rd Aaronsburg (16820) *(G-1)*

Popcorn Alley Inc 877 292-5611
   1 Popcorn Ln Dover (17315) *(G-4199)*

Popcorn Buddha Inc 570 476-5676
   266 River Rd Ste 104e East Stroudsburg (18301) *(G-4629)*

Popit Inc 215 752-8410
   250 Woodbourne Rd Langhorne (19047) *(G-9320)*

Popit Inc 215 945-5201
   922 Woodbourne Rd 333 Levittown (19057) *(G-9859)*

Poppi Als Inc 717 652-6263
   7750 Allentown Blvd Frnt Harrisburg (17112) *(G-7200)*

Popultion Hlth Innovations LLC 717 735-8105
   313 W Liberty St Lancaster (17603) *(G-9173)*

Porosky Lumber Company Inc 570 798-2326
   1903 Crosstown Hwy Preston Park (18455) *(G-16105)*

Port Augustus Glass Co LLC 412 486-9100
   1101 William Flynn Hwy Glenshaw (15116) *(G-6498)*

Port Erie Plastics Inc (PA) 814 899-7602
   909 Troupe Rd Harborcreek (16421) *(G-7008)*

Port Erie Plastics Inc 814 899-7602
   1350 Troupe Rd Harborcreek (16421) *(G-7009)*

Port Pittsburgh Distillery LLC 412 294-8071
   1330 Akehurst Rd Pittsburgh (15220) *(G-15420)*

Port Richman Holdings LLC 212 777-1178
   2701 E Tioga St Philadelphia (19134) *(G-14189)*

Port Richmond Millwork 215 423-4803
   2909 Salmon St Philadelphia (19134) *(G-14190)*

Port Richmond Tool & Die Inc 215 426-2287
   2839 E Tioga St Philadelphia (19134) *(G-14191)*

Porter Ao Co 570 366-1387
   Rr 2 Auburn (17922) *(G-821)*

Porter Instrument 215 723-4000
   235 Township Line Rd Hatfield (19440) *(G-7383)*

Portico Group LLC 610 566-8499
   11 E State St Ste 1 Media (19063) *(G-10943)*

Portico Printing LLC 215 717-5151
   1310 Sansom St Philadelphia (19107) *(G-14192)*

Porto Exim Usa LLC (PA) 412 406-8442
   780 Route 910 Ste 100 Cheswick (15024) *(G-3115)*

Portzlines Pallets 717 694-3951
   Laurel Hill Rd Mount Pleasant Mills (17853) *(G-11729)*

Positively Pasta 484 945-1007
   115 E High St Pottstown (19464) *(G-16032)*

Positran Manufacturing Inc 610 277-0500
   800 E Main St Norristown (19401) *(G-12704)*

Post Gazette 412 854-9722
   2892 Oneill Dr Bethel Park (15102) *(G-1428)*

Post Gazette 412 965-6738
   26 Ridgewood Dr Mc Donald (15057) *(G-10578)*

Post Precision Castings Inc 610 488-1011
   21 Walnut St Strausstown (19559) *(G-18099)*

Post Service, Tamaqua *Also called Northeastern Hydro-Seeding Inc (G-18222)*

Postal History Society Inc 717 624-5941
   869 Bridgewater Dr New Oxford (17350) *(G-12422)*

Posties Beverages Inc 570 929-2464
   55 S Manning St McAdoo (18237) *(G-10656)*

PostNet, Scranton *Also called Red Gravel Partners LLC (G-17278)*

Postupack Oil, McAdoo *Also called Postupack Russell Culm Corp (G-10657)*

Postupack Russell Culm Corp 570 929-1699
   109 Silverbrook Rd McAdoo (18237) *(G-10657)*

Potoeski Decal Aplicat Svcs, Millmont *Also called Thomas Henry Potoeski (G-11220)*

Potomac Bakery Inc 412 531-5066
   1419 Potomac Ave Pittsburgh (15216) *(G-15421)*

Pots By Deperrot 717 627-6789
   201 S Locust St Lititz (17543) *(G-10034)*

Potter Distributing Co 724 495-3189
   112 Mowry Rd Monaca (15061) *(G-11294)*

Potters Holdings II LP 610 651-4200
   300 Lindenwood Dr Malvern (19355) *(G-10297)*

Potters Industries LLC (HQ) 610 651-4700
   300 Lindenwood Dr Malvern (19355) *(G-10298)*

Potters Industries LLC 610 651-4600
   280 Cedar Grove Rd Conshohocken (19428) *(G-3589)*

Pottsgrove Metal Finishers 610 323-7004
   1533 W High St Pottstown (19464) *(G-16033)*

Pottstown Mercury, The, Pottstown *Also called Peerless Publications Inc (G-16027)*

Pottstown Trap Rock Quarries (PA) 610 326-4843
   394 S Sanatoga Rd Pottstown (19464) *(G-16034)*

Pottstown Trap Rock Quarries 610 326-5921
   1 Quarry Rd Douglassville (19518) *(G-4179)*

Pottsville Fuel Stop Inc 570 429-2970
   1471 Route 61 Hwy N Pottsville (17901) *(G-16091)*

Pottsville Republican Inc (PA) 570 622-3456
   111 Mahantongo St Pottsville (17901) *(G-16092)*

Poux Plastics Inc 814 425-2100
   5605 State Highway 173 Cochranton (16314) *(G-3348)*

Poward Plastics Incorporated 484 660-3690
   725 Hex Hwy Hamburg (19526) *(G-6849)*

Powder City LLC 717 745-4795
   408 Willeta Ct York (17402) *(G-20634)*

Powder Coating 570 837-3325
   148 Pitzer Rd Middleburg (17842) *(G-11035)*

Powder Coating Co (PA) 610 273-9007
   5177 Horseshoe Pike Honey Brook (19344) *(G-7756)*

Powder Coating Specialists LLC 717 968-1479
   40 Leigh Dr York (17406) *(G-20635)*

Powder Metal Products Inc 814 834-7261
   879 Washington St Saint Marys (15857) *(G-17008)*

Powderco Inc 814 437-3705
   190 Howard St Ste 406 Franklin (16323) *(G-6153)*

Powdersize LLC 215 536-5605
   20 Pacific Dr Quakertown (18951) *(G-16231)*

Powell Electro Systems LLC 610 869-8393
   5 Briar Dr West Grove (19390) *(G-19704)*

A L P H A B E T I C

Power & Energy Inc 215 942-4600
106 Railroad Dr Ivyland (18974) **(G-8221)**

Power & Industrial Svcs Corp (PA) 800 676-7116
95 Washington St Donora (15033) **(G-4158)**

Power Ign Cntrls Applachia LLC 724 746-3700
2 Park Dr Lawrence (15055) **(G-9539)**

Power Line Packaging Inc 610 239-7088
1304 Conshohocken Rd Conshohocken (19428) **(G-3590)**

Power Mechanical Corp 570 823-8824
Pethick Rd Rr 315 Wilkes Barre (18705) **(G-19958)**

Power One Inc 267 429-0374
532 W Market St Perkasie (18944) **(G-13290)**

Power Pipe Supports Inc 724 379-5212
484 Galiffa Dr Donora (15033) **(G-4159)**

Power Products Inc 610 532-3880
950 Calcon Hook Rd Ste 5 Sharon Hill (19079) **(G-17459)**

Power Systems Specialists Inc 570 296-4573
103 Route 6 Milford (18337) **(G-11167)**

Powercast Corporation 412 455-5800
620 Alpha Dr Ste 1 Pittsburgh (15238) **(G-15422)**

Powerex Inc 724 925-7272
200 E Hillis St Youngwood (15697) **(G-20781)**

Powerex Inc (PA) 724 925-7272
173 Pavilion Ln Youngwood (15697) **(G-20782)**

Powerhouse Generator Inc (PA) 717 759-8535
454 N Constitution Ave New Freedom (17349) **(G-12214)**

Powerrail Distribution, Duryea *Also called Powerrail Holdings Inc* **(G-4505)**

Powerrail Distribution Inc 570 883-7005
205 Clark Rd Duryea (18642) **(G-4504)**

Powerrail Holdings Inc (PA) 570 883-7005
205 Clark Rd Duryea (18642) **(G-4505)**

Powers Stone Inc 570 553-4276
Stuart Rd Montrose (18801) **(G-11475)**

Powersafe Inc 717 436-5380
4311 William Penn Hwy Mifflintown (17059) **(G-11132)**

Powertrack International LLC (PA) 412 787-4444
4605 Campbells Run Rd Pittsburgh (15205) **(G-15423)**

Powertrack International LLC 412 787-4444
4625 Campbells Run Rd Pittsburgh (15205) **(G-15424)**

Powsus Inc 610 296-2237
14 Woodstream Dr Chesterbrook (19087) **(G-3095)**

PP&I, Coatesville *Also called Pharmaceutical Procurement* **(G-3324)**

PPAC, Philadelphia *Also called Philadelphia Photo Arts Center* **(G-14148)**

Ppcp, Lebanon *Also called Pennsylvannia Precision Cast P* **(G-9620)**

PPG Architectural Finishes Inc 610 380-6200
255 S Bailey Rd Downingtown (19335) **(G-4250)**

PPG Glass Technology Ctr - GL, Cheswick *Also called PPG Industries Inc* **(G-3116)**

PPG Industries Inc (PA) 412 434-3131
1 Ppg Pl Pittsburgh (15272) **(G-15425)**

PPG Industries Inc 724 274-7900
125 Colfax St Springdale (15144) **(G-17899)**

PPG Industries Inc 215 873-8940
444 N 2nd St Philadelphia (19123) **(G-14193)**

PPG Industries Inc 717 218-5400
24 W South St Carlisle (17013) **(G-2730)**

PPG Industries Inc 724 224-6500
150 Ferry St Creighton (15030) **(G-3885)**

PPG Industries Inc 717 763-1030
1039 Columbus Ave Lemoyne (17043) **(G-9748)**

PPG Industries Inc 610 544-1925
160 Baltimore Pike Springfield (19064) **(G-17920)**

PPG Industries Inc 888 774-1010
2001 Centre Ave Reading (19605) **(G-16473)**

PPG Industries Inc 412 820-8116
400 Park Dr Carlisle (17015) **(G-2731)**

PPG Industries Inc 412 820-8500
400 Guys Run Rd Cheswick (15024) **(G-3116)**

PPG Industries Inc 412 276-1922
416 Washington Ave Carnegie (15106) **(G-2781)**

PPG Industries Inc 412 434-4463
1 Ppg Pl Pittsburgh (15272) **(G-15426)**

PPG Industries Inc 724 772-0005
20804 Route 19 Ste 2 Cranberry Township (16066) **(G-3843)**

PPG Industries Inc 724 863-4473
10739 State Route 30 Irwin (15642) **(G-8192)**

PPG Industries Inc 412 487-4500
4325 Rosanna Dr Allison Park (15101) **(G-459)**

PPG Industries Inc 724 327-3000
440 College Park Dr Monroeville (15146) **(G-11350)**

PPG Industries Foundation 412 434-3131
1 Ppg Pl Pittsburgh (15272) **(G-15427)**

PPG Pittsburgh Paints, Philadelphia *Also called PPG Industries Inc* **(G-14193)**

PPG Pittsburgh Paints, Carlisle *Also called PPG Industries Inc* **(G-2730)**

Ppi Imaging, Monroeville *Also called R A Palmer Products Company* **(G-11351)**

Ppi-Erie, Fairview *Also called Precise Plastics Inc* **(G-5840)**

Ppk Animal Healthcare LLC 718 288-4318
416 Vandine Rd Montoursville (17754) **(G-11448)**

Ppp, Evans City *Also called Pittsburgh Plug and Pdts Corp* **(G-5561)**

Ppt Research Inc 610 434-0103
515 Business Park Ln Allentown (18109) **(G-353)**

Pptp, Pittsburgh *Also called Pittsburgh Precision* **(G-15404)**

PQ Corporation (HQ) 610 651-4200
300 Lindenwood Dr Malvern (19355) **(G-10299)**

PQ Corporation 610 447-3900
1201 W Front St Chester (19013) **(G-3059)**

PQ Corporation 610 651-4600
280 Cedar Grove Rd Conshohocken (19428) **(G-3591)**

PQ Export Company 610 651-4200
300 Lindenwood Dr Malvern (19355) **(G-10300)**

PQ Group Holdings Inc (PA) 610 651-4400
300 Lindenwood Dr Malvern (19355) **(G-10301)**

PQ Holding Inc (HQ) 610 651-4400
300 Lindenwood Dr Malvern (19355) **(G-10302)**

PQ International, Inc., Malvern *Also called PQ Export Company* **(G-10300)**

PR Hoffman Machine Pdts Inc 717 243-9900
1517 Commerce Ave Carlisle (17015) **(G-2732)**

Practical Machine Solutions 717 949-3345
300 E Main St Schaefferstown (17088) **(G-17130)**

Practicom 267 979-5446
604 S Washington Sq # 2002 Philadelphia (19106) **(G-14194)**

Prada Company Inc 412 751-4900
2000 Donner St McKeesport (15135) **(G-10678)**

Prairie Dog Tech LLC 215 558-4975
1500 John F Kennedy Blvd Philadelphia (19102) **(G-14195)**

Prairie Products Inc 717 292-0421
4660 Raycom Rd Dover (17315) **(G-4200)**

Prantl's Bakery, Pittsburgh *Also called Prantls of Shadyside LLC* **(G-15428)**

Prantls of Shadyside LLC 412 621-2092
5100 5th Ave Apt 311 Pittsburgh (15232) **(G-15428)**

Pratt & Whitney Americon Inc 717 546-0220
181 Fulling Mill Rd Ste 1 Middletown (17057) **(G-11070)**

Pratt Industries USA Inc 610 967-6027
726 Broad St Emmaus (18049) **(G-5040)**

Pratt Rock Solid Displays LLC 610 929-4800
184 Tuckerton Rd Reading (19605) **(G-16474)**

Praxair Inc 215 721-9099
2929 E Township Line Rd Souderton (18964) **(G-17760)**

Praxair Inc 610 691-2474
145 Shimersville Rd Bethlehem (18015) **(G-1603)**

Praxair Inc 610 759-3923
90 Commerce Way Stockertown (18083) **(G-18066)**

Praxair Inc 610 530-3885
7355 William Ave Ste 200 Allentown (18106) **(G-354)**

Praxair Dist Mid-Atlantic LLC 610 398-2211
5275 Tilghman St Allentown (18104) **(G-355)**

Praxair Distribution Inc 570 655-3721
114 Brown Rd Pittston (18640) **(G-15778)**

Praxair Distribution Inc 717 393-3681
1311-15 Harrisburg Pike Lancaster (17603) **(G-9174)**

Praxair Distribution Inc 412 781-6273
28 Mccandless Ave Pittsburgh (15201) **(G-15429)**

Praxair Distribution Inc 610 398-2211
5275 Tilghman St Allentown (18104) **(G-356)**

Praxair Distribution Inc 814 238-5092
1348 Benner Pike State College (16801) **(G-18009)**

Praxair Distribution Inc 215 736-8005
1 Steel Rd E Morrisville (19067) **(G-11579)**

Praxair Distribution Inc 610 921-9230
1800 N 11th St Reading (19604) **(G-16475)**

Prb Mfg Representatives 814 466-2161
436 Bailey Ln Boalsburg (16827) **(G-1868)**

PRC - Desoto International Inc 412 434-3131
1 Ppg Pl Pittsburgh (15272) **(G-15430)**

Prco America Inc 412 837-2798
8150 Perry Hwy Ste 105 Pittsburgh (15237) **(G-15431)**

Pre Cast Systems LLC 717 369-3773
5877 Bullitt Rd Greencastle (17225) **(G-6627)**

Pre-Blend Products Inc 215 295-6004
100 Ben Fairless Dr Fairless Hills (19030) **(G-5793)**

Pre-Mach Inc 717 757-5685
4365 Run Way York (17406) **(G-20636)**

Prebelli Industries, Philadelphia *Also called Gil Prebelli* **(G-13762)**

Prebola Enterprises Inc 570 693-3036
206 W 6th St Wyoming (18644) **(G-20283)**

Precast Services Inc 330 425-2880
51 Thsand Oaks Blvd Ste A Morgantown (19543) **(G-11531)**

Precast Systems LLC 717 267-4500
859 Cleveland Ave Chambersburg (17201) **(G-2969)**

Precious Metal Plating Co Inc 610 586-1500
21 S Chester Pike Glenolden (19036) **(G-6476)**

Precise Graphic Products Inc 412 481-0952
311 Smallwood Dr Coraopolis (15108) **(G-3717)**

Precise Graphix LLC 610 965-9400
2310 26th St Sw Allentown (18103) **(G-357)**

Precise Medical 215 345-6729
3140 Cloverly Dr Furlong (18925) **(G-6232)**

Precise Plastics Inc 814 474-5504
7700 Middle Rd Fairview (16415) **(G-5840)**

Precise Polish 814 453-4220
1405 W 21st St Erie (16502) **(G-5430)**
Precise Tool & Die Inc 724 845-1285
1711 Piper Rd Leechburg (15656) **(G-9650)**
Precisian Inc 610 861-0844
Merchants Plz 9 Rte 611 Tannersville (18372) **(G-18236)**
Precision Assembly Inc 215 784-0861
2301 Computer Rd Willow Grove (19090) **(G-20136)**
Precision Automatic Machine Co 724 339-2360
134 Prominence Dr New Kensington (15068) **(G-12368)**
Precision Bushing Inc 717 264-6461
1151 Sheffler Dr Chambersburg (17201) **(G-2970)**
Precision Carbide Inc 215 355-4220
325 Philmont Ave Ste 1 Feasterville Trevose (19053) **(G-5927)**
Precision Carbide Tooling Inc 717 244-4771
267 Cherry St Western Red Lion (17356) **(G-16611)**
Precision Castparts Corp 570 825-4544
120 Hazle St Wilkes Barre (18702) **(G-19959)**
Precision Castparts Corp 570 474-6371
701 Crestwood Dr Mountain Top (18707) **(G-11771)**
Precision Cmpcted Cmpnents LLC 814 929-5805
317 Buena Vista Hwy Wilcox (15870) **(G-19899)**
Precision Coating Tech Mfg Inc 717 336-5030
245 S Muddy Creek Rd Denver (17517) **(G-4088)**
Precision Components Group LLC 717 848-1126
500 Lincoln St York (17401) **(G-20637)**
Precision Controls LLC 267 337-9812
47 Crystal Pl Levittown (19057) **(G-9860)**
Precision Cstm Components LLC 717 848-1126
500 Lincoln St York (17401) **(G-20638)**
Precision Cuntertops Mllwk Inc 215 598-7161
301a Lincoln Ave Hatboro (19040) **(G-7298)**
Precision Custom Ammunition 717 274-8762
373 Acorn Cir Lebanon (17042) **(G-9624)**
Precision Cut Industries Inc (PA) 717 632-2550
115 Ram Dr Hanover (17331) **(G-6936)**
Precision Defense Services Inc 724 863-1100
1 Quality Way Irwin (15642) **(G-8193)**
Precision Devices Facility, Reading *Also called Alcon Research Ltd* **(G-16317)**
Precision Dimension Inc 814 684-4150
121 Cherry Ave Tyrone (16686) **(G-18590)**
Precision Drilling Oilfld Svcs 570 329-5100
2640 Reach Rd Williamsport (17701) **(G-20062)**
Precision Fabg Group LLC 610 438-3156
1 Adamson St Easton (18042) **(G-4744)**
Precision Fbrction Contrls Inc 814 368-7320
195 Chestnut St Bradford (16701) **(G-1987)**
Precision Feedscrews Inc 724 654-9676
373 Commerce Ave New Castle (16101) **(G-12139)**
Precision Filtration Pdts Inc 215 679-6645
3770 Layfield Rd Pennsburg (18073) **(G-13252)**
Precision Finishing Inc (PA) 215 257-6862
1800 Am Dr Quakertown (18951) **(G-16232)**
Precision Glass, Oreland *Also called Spectrocell Inc* **(G-13030)**
Precision Glass Products Co 215 885-0145
143 Montgomery Ave Oreland (19075) **(G-13028)**
Precision Glass Technologies 610 323-2825
3110 W Ridge Pike Sanatoga (19464) **(G-17058)**
Precision Grit Etching & Engrv 412 828-5790
930 3rd St Oakmont (15139) **(G-12924)**
Precision Industries Inc (PA) 724 222-2100
99 Berry Rd Washington (15301) **(G-19217)**
Precision Kidd Steel Co Inc (PA) 724 695-2216
1 Quality Way Aliquippa (15001) **(G-89)**
Precision Kidd Steel Co Inc 724 695-2216
Lncln Hy & Mtchtt Rr 30 Clinton (15026) **(G-3266)**
Precision Laser and Instr Inc (PA) 724 266-1600
85 11th St Ambridge (15003) **(G-631)**
Precision Matthews McHy Co, Coraopolis *Also called Quality Machine Tools LLC* **(G-3720)**
Precision Medical Inc 610 262-6090
300 Held Dr Northampton (18067) **(G-12860)**
Precision Medical Devices Inc 717 795-9480
5020 Ritter Rd Ste 211 Mechanicsburg (17055) **(G-10881)**
Precision Metal Crafters Ltd 724 837-2511
220 Huff Ave Ste 700 Greensburg (15601) **(G-6704)**
Precision Metal Pdts Co Inc 724 758-5555
1010 Shady Ln Ellwood City (16117) **(G-4947)**
Precision Millwork & Cabinetry 814 445-9669
731 E Bakersville Edie Rd Somerset (15501) **(G-17700)**
Precision Pallets & Lumber Inc 814 395-5351
3593 Listonburg Rd Addison (15411) **(G-28)**
Precision Parts & Machine Co 412 824-9367
510 Braddock Ave Turtle Creek (15145) **(G-18567)**
Precision Pattern & Wdwkg 724 588-2224
303 Methodist Rd Greenville (16125) **(G-6766)**
Precision Plastic Balls, Reno *Also called Business Applications Ltd* **(G-16645)**
Precision Plating Co Inc 724 652-2393
407 Summit View Dr New Castle (16105) **(G-12140)**
Precision Plus Machine Shop, Warren *Also called Lawrence R McGuigan* **(G-19037)**
Precision Polymer Processors 570 344-9916
2400 Stafford Ave Ste 700 Scranton (18505) **(G-17274)**
Precision Polymer Products Inc 610 326-0921
815 South St Pottstown (19464) **(G-16035)**
Precision Polymers Inc 814 838-9288
1425 Selinger Ave Erie (16505) **(G-5431)**
Precision Production Turning 610 872-8557
1128 Chestnut St Chester (19013) **(G-3060)**
Precision Products Ltd 215 538-1795
2365 Milford Square Pike Quakertown (18951) **(G-16233)**
Precision Profiles LLC 814 827-9887
45727 State Highway 27 Titusville (16354) **(G-18390)**
Precision Rebuilding Division, Reading *Also called Parker-Hannifin Corporation* **(G-16465)**
Precision Rehab Manufacturing 814 899-8731
5325 Kuhl Rd Erie (16510) **(G-5432)**
Precision Roll Grinders Inc (PA) 610 395-6966
6356 Chapmans Rd Allentown (18106) **(G-358)**
Precision Runners LLC 330 240-5988
140 W Shenango St B Sharpsville (16150) **(G-17474)**
Precision Secondary Machining 814 885-6572
157 Dagus Mines Rd Kersey (15846) **(G-8566)**
Precision Sheet Metal LLC 570 254-6670
1226 Heart Lake Rd Scott Township (18433) **(G-17187)**
Precision Sign & Awning 412 281-0330
1021 5th Ave Pittsburgh (15219) **(G-15432)**
Precision Steel Services Inc 724 347-2770
650 M L King Jr Blvd # 111 Farrell (16121) **(G-5871)**
Precision Technical Sales LLC 610 282-4541
1876 Salem Rd Coopersburg (18036) **(G-3634)**
Precision Technology, Douglassville *Also called Wolf Technologies LLC* **(G-4182)**
Precision Technology Assoc Inc 412 881-8006
1203 Edgebrook Ave Pittsburgh (15226) **(G-15433)**
Precision Tl & Die Mfg Co Inc 814 676-1864
651 N Seneca St Oil City (16301) **(G-12955)**
Precision Tool & Die Co Inc 814 676-1864
651 N Seneca St Oil City (16301) **(G-12956)**
Precision Tool & Mfg Corp 717 767-6454
70 Church Rd Emigsville (17318) **(G-4997)**
Precision Tool and Machine Co 570 868-3920
1698 Stairville Rd Mountain Top (18707) **(G-11772)**
Precision Transmission Inc (PA) 215 822-8300
159 Discovery Dr Colmar (18915) **(G-3418)**
Precision Tube Company Inc 215 699-5801
287 Wissahickon Ave North Wales (19454) **(G-12826)**
Precision Wire Products Inc 724 459-5601
207 E Brown St Blairsville (15717) **(G-1737)**
Precision Wood Works 814 793-9900
356 Spring Farm Rd Martinsburg (16662) **(G-10528)**
Precision Woodworking & C 215 317-3533
1365 Barness Dr Warminster (18974) **(G-18943)**
Precision-Marshall Steel Co, Washington *Also called Precision Industries Inc* **(G-19217)**
Precisioneering Inc 724 423-2472
5420 Pleasant Unity Rd Latrobe (15650) **(G-9510)**
Precisionform Incorporated 717 560-7610
148 W Airport Rd Lititz (17543) **(G-10035)**
Precisions Signs and Awning (PA) 412 278-0400
3 Glass St Carnegie (15106) **(G-2782)**
Preferred Meal Systems Inc 570 457-8311
4135 Birney Ave Moosic (18507) **(G-11512)**
Preferred Proppants LLC 610 834-1969
100 W Matsonford Rd # 101 Radnor (19087) **(G-16297)**
Preferred Rocks LLC 484 684-1221
100 W Matsonford Rd # 101 Wayne (19087) **(G-19363)**
Preferred Sands LLC (PA) 610 834-1969
100 W Matsonford Rd # 1 Radnor (19087) **(G-16298)**
Preferred Sheet Metal Inc 717 732-7100
4417 Valley St Enola (17025) **(G-5084)**
Preferred Sportswear Inc 484 494-3067
520 Pusey Ave Ste 260 Darby (19023) **(G-4024)**
Preform Specialties Inc 724 459-0808
176 Cherry St Blairsville (15717) **(G-1738)**
Preformance Products Div, Eighty Four *Also called Washington Penn Plastic Co Inc* **(G-4851)**
Premax Tool Machine Inc 610 326-3860
76 Robinson St Pottstown (19464) **(G-16036)**
Premier Applied Coatings Inc 610 367-2635
326 S Franklin St Boyertown (19512) **(G-1924)**
Premier Automotive 570 966-0363
925 Grand Valley Rd Mifflinburg (17844) **(G-11100)**
Premier Bluestone Inc 570 465-7200
5212 Brushville Rd Susquehanna (18847) **(G-18182)**
Premier Brnds Group Hldngs LLC 212 835-3672
180 Rittenhouse Cir Bristol (19007) **(G-2186)**
Premier Brnds Group Hldngs LLC 215 785-4000
180 Rittenhouse Cir Bristol (19007) **(G-2187)**
Premier Brnds Group Hldngs LLC 212 642-3860
180 Rittenhouse Cir Bristol (19007) **(G-2188)**
Premier Chemicals LLC 610 420-7500
120 Marshall Bridge Rd Kennett Square (19348) **(G-8536)**

ALPHABETIC

Premier Conduit Inc (PA) 814 451-0898
 1409 S Shore Dr Erie (16505) *(G-5433)*
Premier Conduit Inc 814 451-0898
 3200 W 22nd St Erie (16506) *(G-5434)*
Premier Dental Products Co (PA) 610 239-6000
 1710 Romano Dr Plymouth Meeting (19462) *(G-15865)*
Premier Dental Products Co Inc 215 676-9090
 10090 Sandmeyer Ln Philadelphia (19116) *(G-14196)*
Premier Fence & Iron Works Inc 267 567-2078
 5856 Penn St Philadelphia (19149) *(G-14197)*
Premier Graphics LLC 814 894-2467
 5 E Main St Sykesville (15865) *(G-18202)*
Premier Hydraulics LLC 724 342-6506
 10 Fruit Ave Farrell (16121) *(G-5872)*
Premier Ink Systems Inc 570 459-2300
 103 Rotary Dr Ste 1 West Hazleton (18202) *(G-19715)*
Premier Magnesia LLC (PA) 610 828-6929
 1275 Drummers Ln Ste 102 Wayne (19087) *(G-19364)*
Premier Magnesia LLC 717 677-7313
 1305 Center Mills Rd Aspers (17304) *(G-744)*
Premier Medical Products, Plymouth Meeting *Also called Premier Dental Products
Co (G-15865)*
Premier Pan Company Inc 724 457-4220
 33 Mcgovern Blvd Crescent (15046) *(G-3887)*
Premier Printing Services Inc 724 588-5577
 275 Main St Greenville (16125) *(G-6767)*
Premier Printing Solutions LLC 570 426-1570
 405 Airport Rd East Stroudsburg (18301) *(G-4630)*
Premier Screen Printing Inc 717 560-9088
 519b Airport Rd Lititz (17543) *(G-10036)*
Premier Semiconductor Svcs LLC (HQ) 267 954-0130
 2294 N Penn Rd Hatfield (19440) *(G-7384)*
Premier Spouting Design LLC 717 336-1205
 50 Willow St Reinholds (17569) *(G-16636)*
Premise Maid Candies Inc 610 395-3221
 10860 Hamilton Blvd Breinigsville (18031) *(G-2024)*
Premium Molding Inc 724 424-7000
 294 Bergman Rd Derry (15627) *(G-4106)*
Premium Pet Division 215 364-0211
 325 Andrews Rd Langhorne (19053) *(G-9321)*
Premium Plastics Solutions LLC 724 424-7000
 59 Bay Hill Dr Latrobe (15650) *(G-9511)*
Premium Tool Co Inc 570 753-5070
 1082 Penn Ave Jersey Shore (17740) *(G-8320)*
Prepped Delivery, Langhorne *Also called Fit Fuel Foods LLC (G-9297)*
Preptech Inc (PA) 724 727-3439
 4412 State Route 66 Apollo (15613) *(G-684)*
Presco Sheet Metal Fabricators 215 672-7200
 355 Constance Dr Warminster (18974) *(G-18944)*
Preseeder, New Holland *Also called ATI Corporation (G-12229)*
Preservation Technologies LP (PA) 724 779-2111
 111 Thomson Park Dr Cranberry Township (16066) *(G-3844)*
Presque Isle Medical Tech, Erie *Also called Presque Isle Orthpd Lab Inc (G-5435)*
Presque Isle Orthpd Lab Inc 814 838-0002
 2440 W 8th St Erie (16505) *(G-5435)*
Press & Journal Publications, Middletown *Also called Press and Journal (G-11071)*
Press and Journal 717 944-4628
 20 S Union St Middletown (17057) *(G-11071)*
Press Bistro 814 254-4835
 110 Franklin St Ste 110 # 110 Johnstown (15901) *(G-8424)*
Press Box Printing, Altoona *Also called Crogan Inc (G-495)*
Press Box Printing 814 944-3057
 2109 9th Ave Altoona (16602) *(G-538)*
Press Craft Printers Inc 412 761-8200
 532 California Ave 34 Pittsburgh (15202) *(G-15434)*
Press Enterprise Coml Prtg Div, Bloomsburg *Also called Press-Enterprise Inc (G-1795)*
Press Start Games 267 253-0595
 70 Sedgwick Dr East Berlin (17316) *(G-4525)*
Press-Enterprise Inc 570 752-3645
 3185 Lackawanna Ave Bloomsburg (17815) *(G-1794)*
Press-Enterprise Inc 610 807-9619
 65 E Elizabeth Ave # 700 Bethlehem (18018) *(G-1604)*
Press-Enterprise Inc (PA) 570 784-2121
 3185 Lackawanna Ave Bloomsburg (17815) *(G-1795)*
Pressure Chemical Co 412 682-5882
 3419 Smallman St Pittsburgh (15201) *(G-15435)*
Pressure Dynamic Consultants, Warminster *Also called PDC Machines Inc (G-18937)*
Pressure Innovators LLC 215 431-6520
 1800 Mearns Rd Bldg 4 Warminster (18974) *(G-18945)*
Pressure Technology Inc 215 674-8844
 415 Patricia Dr Warminster (18974) *(G-18946)*
Pressure Water Systems of PA 412 668-0878
 130 Amabell St Pittsburgh (15211) *(G-15436)*
Pressure-Tech Inc 717 597-1868
 120 E Grant St Greencastle (17225) *(G-6628)*
Presta Contractor Supply Inc 814 833-0655
 2669 W 16th St Erie (16505) *(G-5436)*
Presti Group Inc 215 340-2870
 200 Hyde Park Doylestown (18902) *(G-4327)*

Prestige Fence Co Inc 215 362-8200
 3434 Unionville Pike Hatfield (19440) *(G-7385)*
Prestige Gift Box Systems 610 865-6768
 16 S Commerce Way Bethlehem (18017) *(G-1605)*
Prestige Institute For Plastic 215 275-1011
 79 Bittersweet Dr Doylestown (18901) *(G-4328)*
Presto Dyechem Co Inc 215 627-1863
 60 N Front St Philadelphia (19106) *(G-14198)*
Presto Packaging Inc (PA) 215 822-9598
 1795 Keystone Dr Hatfield (19440) *(G-7386)*
Presto Packaging Inc 215 646-7514
 155 N Ridge Ave Ambler (19002) *(G-599)*
Pretium Packaging LLC 717 266-6687
 1 Devco Dr Manchester (17345) *(G-10362)*
Pretzel Lady 717 632-7046
 113 S Blettner Ave Hanover (17331) *(G-6937)*
Pretzel Shop 412 431-2574
 2316 E Carson St Pittsburgh (15203) *(G-15437)*
Pretzels Plus 724 228-9785
 1500 W Chestnut St # 266 Washington (15301) *(G-19218)*
Pretzelworks Inc 215 288-4002
 5331 Oxford Ave Philadelphia (19124) *(G-14199)*
PRI International Inc 610 436-8292
 404 Price St West Chester (19382) *(G-19619)*
Price C L Lumber LLC (PA) 814 349-5505
 319 Tattletown Rd Aaronsburg (16820) *(G-2)*
Price Chopper Oper Co of PA 570 223-2410
 4547 Milford Rd East Stroudsburg (18302) *(G-4631)*
Price CL Lumber Mill, Aaronsburg *Also called Price C L Lumber LLC (G-2)*
Price Lumber Company 814 231-0260
 Meeks Ln Port Matilda (16870) *(G-15904)*
Price Machine Tool Repair 215 631-9440
 422 W 6th St Lansdale (19446) *(G-9399)*
Price Tool Inc 814 763-4410
 514 Broad St Saegertown (16433) *(G-16927)*
Priceless Times 267 538-5723
 3538 Cottman Ave Philadelphia (19149) *(G-14200)*
Pricetown Ephrata Gas &F 610 939-1701
 3123 Pricetown Rd Fleetwood (19522) *(G-5978)*
Pride Garden Products, Ridley Park *Also called Pride Group Inc (G-16740)*
Pride Garden Products, Ridley Park *Also called Pride Group Inc (G-16741)*
Pride Group Inc 484 540-8059
 500 W Sellers Ave Ridley Park (19078) *(G-16740)*
Pride Group Inc 484 540-8059
 500 W Sellers Ave Ridley Park (19078) *(G-16741)*
Pride Mobility Products Corp 570 655-5574
 401 York Ave Pittston (18642) *(G-15779)*
Priest Enterprises 724 658-7692
 11 Irishtown Rd Grove City (16127) *(G-6802)*
Prieto Machine Co Inc 215 675-6061
 1785 Stout Dr Ste D Warminster (18974) *(G-18947)*
Primarc Uv Technology, Easton *Also called Horizon Lamps Inc (G-4701)*
Primaxx Inc 610 336-0314
 7377 William Ave Unit 800 Allentown (18106) *(G-359)*
Prime Contract Pkg Svcs Corp 570 876-2300
 299 Main St Fl 2 Olyphant (18447) *(G-12996)*
Prime Image Delaware Inc (PA) 215 822-1561
 200 Highpoint Dr Ste 215 Chalfont (18914) *(G-2884)*
Prime Metal and Alloys, Homer City *Also called Prime Metals Acquisition LLC (G-7680)*
Prime Metals Acquisition LLC 724 479-4155
 101 Innovation Dr Homer City (15748) *(G-7680)*
Prime Packaging LLC (PA) 215 499-0446
 1000 Garey Dr Yardley (19067) *(G-20333)*
Prime Plastics Inc 724 250-7172
 100 Detroit Ave Washington (15301) *(G-19219)*
Prime Ribbon Inc (PA) 412 761-4470
 1239 Woodland Ave Pittsburgh (15212) *(G-15438)*
Prime Turbines LLC 724 586-0124
 485 Airport Rd Butler (16002) *(G-2435)*
Primetals Technologies USA LLC 724 514-8500
 501 Technology Dr Canonsburg (15317) *(G-2620)*
Primitive Country Tole 570 247-2719
 185 Edsell Rd Rome (18837) *(G-16801)*
Primitives By Kathy Inc 717 394-4220
 1817 William Penn Way Lancaster (17601) *(G-9175)*
Primrose Consulting Inc 724 816-5769
 125 Majestic Dr Mars (16046) *(G-10510)*
Primrose Press, New Hope *Also called Heraclitean Corporation (G-12305)*
Primus Technologies Corp (PA) 570 326-6591
 2333 Reach Rd Williamsport (17701) *(G-20063)*
Prince Company Inc 717 526-2200
 85 Shannon Rd Harrisburg (17112) *(G-7201)*
Prince Printing 412 233-3555
 517 Saint Clair Ave Clairton (15025) *(G-3156)*
Princeton Security Tech LLC 609 915-9700
 2925 State Rd Croydon (19021) *(G-3924)*
Princeton Trade Consulting Gro 610 683-9348
 760 Seem Dr Kutztown (19530) *(G-8856)*
Print & Copy Center Inc 412 828-2205
 731 Allegheny River Blvd Verona (15147) *(G-18760)*

Print 'n Copy Center, Philadelphia *Also called AMD Graphics Inc* ***(G-13377)***
Print A Tooth Inc....610 647-6990
155 Planebrook Rd Malvern (19355) ***(G-10303)***
Print and Graphics Scholrship....412 741-6860
301 Brush Creek Rd Warrendale (15086) ***(G-19093)***
Print and Sew Inc....215 281-3909
10960 Dutton Rd Ste B Philadelphia (19154) ***(G-14201)***
Print Box Inc....212 741-1381
3947 W Lincoln Hwy Downingtown (19335) ***(G-4251)***
Print Charming Design....412 519-5226
1391 Peterson Dr Clairton (15025) ***(G-3157)***
Print City Graphics Inc....610 495-5524
680 Hollow Rd Ste 3 Phoenixville (19460) ***(G-14570)***
Print Copy Design Solutions, Trappe *Also called B O H I C A Inc* ***(G-18467)***
Print Craft Studio, Pittsburgh *Also called N H Morgan Inc* ***(G-15314)***
Print Escape LLC....888 524-8690
5886 Hobart St Pittsburgh (15217) ***(G-15439)***
Print Factory....570 961-2111
1807 Luzerne St Unit 1 Scranton (18504) ***(G-17275)***
Print Happy LLC....717 699-4465
1805 Loucks Rd Ste 100 York (17408) ***(G-20639)***
Print Shop....215 788-1883
945 Washington Ave Croydon (19021) ***(G-3925)***
Print Shop....570 327-9005
421 Washington Blvd Frnt Williamsport (17701) ***(G-20064)***
Print Shop Inc....570 784-4020
3820 Old Berwick Rd Bloomsburg (17815) ***(G-1796)***
Print Shop , The, Lancaster *Also called Lancaster General Svcs Bus Tr* ***(G-9095)***
Print Shop Inc....610 692-1810
705 E Union St West Chester (19382) ***(G-19620)***
Print Solutions Ltd....484 538-3938
512 Thomas St Coopersburg (18036) ***(G-3635)***
Print Tech Western PA (PA)....412 963-1500
250 Alpha Dr Pittsburgh (15238) ***(G-15440)***
Print Tech Western PA....412 963-1500
250 Alpha Dr Pittsburgh (15238) ***(G-15441)***
Print Works On Demand Inc (PA)....717 545-5215
5630 Allentown Blvd Harrisburg (17112) ***(G-7202)***
Print-O-Stat Inc....724 742-9811
230 Executive Dr Ste 108 Cranberry Township (16066) ***(G-3845)***
Print-O-Stat Inc (HQ)....717 812-9476
1011 W Market St York (17404) ***(G-20640)***
Print-O-Stat Inc....717 795-9255
5040 Louise Dr Mechanicsburg (17055) ***(G-10882)***
Print-O-Stat Inc....610 265-5470
489 Shoemaker Rd Ste 109 King of Prussia (19406) ***(G-8664)***
Print2finish LLC....215 369-5494
835 Hudson Dr Yardley (19067) ***(G-20334)***
Printaway Inc....717 263-1839
29 S Main St Chambersburg (17201) ***(G-2971)***
Printbiz LLC....412 881-3318
4611 W Lawnview Ave Pittsburgh (15227) ***(G-15442)***
Printcompass LLC....610 541-6763
451 Alliston Rd Springfield (19064) ***(G-17921)***
Printdropper Inc....412 657-6170
945 Vista Park Dr Pittsburgh (15205) ***(G-15443)***
Printed Ink LLC....215 355-1683
1840 County Line Rd # 301 Huntingdon Valley (19006) ***(G-8027)***
Printers Edge....570 454-4803
17 S Hazle Brook Rd Hazleton (18201) ***(G-7520)***
Printers Parts Store Inc....610 279-6660
21 Depot St Bridgeport (19405) ***(G-2044)***
Printers Printer Inc....610 454-0102
14 Iron Bridge Dr Collegeville (19426) ***(G-3389)***
Printex LLC....412 371-6667
201 N Braddock Ave Pittsburgh (15208) ***(G-15444)***
Printfly Corporation (PA)....800 620-1233
2727 Commerce Way Philadelphia (19154) ***(G-14202)***
Printforce Inc....610 797-6455
2361 Sunshine Rd Allentown (18103) ***(G-360)***
Printfresh Studio LLC....215 426-1661
2930 Jasper St Unit 408 Philadelphia (19134) ***(G-14203)***
Printing, Bensalem *Also called Forms Graphics LLC* ***(G-1197)***
Printing & Quick Copy, Philadelphia *Also called Bonnie Kaiser* ***(G-13471)***
Printing 4u....610 377-0111
1895 Indian Hill Rd Lehighton (18235) ***(G-9722)***
Printing Concepts Inc....814 833-8080
4982 Pacific Ave Erie (16506) ***(G-5437)***
Printing Consulting Inc....610 933-9311
200 Lincoln Ave Ste 105 Phoenixville (19460) ***(G-14571)***
Printing Craftsmen Inc....570 646-2121
112 Print Shop Rd Pocono Pines (18350) ***(G-15883)***
Printing Express Inc....717 600-1111
3460 Industrial Hwy York (17402) ***(G-20641)***
Printing Inds Amer Foundation....412 741-6860
301 Brush Creek Rd Warrendale (15086) ***(G-19094)***
Printing Mas....570 326-9222
116 Emery St Williamsport (17701) ***(G-20065)***
Printing Plus+ Inc (PA)....814 834-1000
207 Stackpole St Ste 1 Saint Marys (15857) ***(G-17009)***
Printing Post LLC....412 367-7468
3458 Babcock Blvd Ste 2 Pittsburgh (15237) ***(G-15445)***
Printing Press....412 264-3355
246 Moon Clinton Rd # 101 Coraopolis (15108) ***(G-3718)***
Printing Services Unlimited, Pittsburgh *Also called Michael S Cwalina* ***(G-15284)***
Printing Works....215 357-5609
975 Jaymor Rd Ste 2 Southampton (18966) ***(G-17831)***
Printmark Industries Inc....570 501-0547
600 S Poplar St Ste 2 Hazleton (18201) ***(G-7521)***
Prints & More By Holly....814 453-5548
621 Indiana Dr Erie (16505) ***(G-5438)***
Printwearonline....267 987-6118
510 Heritage Oak Dr Yardley (19067) ***(G-20335)***
Printworks & Company Inc (PA)....215 721-8500
1617 N Line St Apt A Lansdale (19446) ***(G-9400)***
Printworx Inc....412 939-6004
159 Cemetery Ln Pittsburgh (15237) ***(G-15446)***
Prion Manufacturing Co Inc....724 693-0200
1 Prion Dr Oakdale (15071) ***(G-12909)***
Priscilla of Boston Inc (HQ)....610 943-5000
1001 Washington St Conshohocken (19428) ***(G-3592)***
Prism Engineering LLC (HQ)....215 784-0800
655 Business Center Dr # 100 Horsham (19044) ***(G-7842)***
Prism Fiber Optics Inc....412 802-0750
4514 Plummer St Pittsburgh (15201) ***(G-15447)***
Prism Graphics Inc....215 782-1600
7804 Montgomery Ave Ste 7 Elkins Park (19027) ***(G-4910)***
Prism Performance, Crescent *Also called Prism Powder Coating Services* ***(G-3888)***
Prism Plastics Inc....814 724-8222
1045 French St Meadville (16335) ***(G-10781)***
Prism Powder Coating Services....724 457-2836
1232 Mckee St Crescent (15046) ***(G-3888)***
Prism Technologies Inc....412 751-3090
1011 Lovedale Rd 1 Elizabeth (15037) ***(G-4863)***
Prisma Inc....412 503-4006
790 Holiday Dr Ste 11 Pittsburgh (15220) ***(G-15448)***
Prismatic Consulting LLC....412 915-9072
1484 Washington Rd Pittsburgh (15228) ***(G-15449)***
Pritts Feed & Supply, Smithton *Also called Elizabeth Milling Company LLC* ***(G-17660)***
Private Zone Productions Corp (PA)....267 592-5447
1601 Cherry St 130016th Philadelphia (19102) ***(G-14204)***
Prizer-Painter Stove Works Inc....610 376-7479
328 June Ave Blandon (19510) ***(G-1757)***
Prl Industries Inc....717 273-6787
64 Rexmont Rd Cornwall (17016) ***(G-3740)***
Pro Action Inc (PA)....724 846-9055
3611 8th Ave Beaver Falls (15010) ***(G-1007)***
Pro Active Sports Inc....814 943-4651
5910 California Ave Altoona (16602) ***(G-539)***
Pro America Premium Tools, Emporium *Also called Kal-Cameron Manufacturing* ***(G-5065)***
Pro Barrier Engineering LLC....717 944-6056
228 Grandview Rd Hummelstown (17036) ***(G-7922)***
Pro Cel Inc....215 322-9883
39 Steam Whistle Dr Warminster (18974) ***(G-18948)***
Pro Dyne Corporation....610 789-0606
136 Green Tree Rd Ste 100 Phoenixville (19460) ***(G-14572)***
Pro Guard Coatings Inc....717 336-7900
1 Industrial Way Denver (17517) ***(G-4089)***
Pro Hardware 12923, York *Also called Standard Concrete Products Co* ***(G-20679)***
Pro Knitwear, Pittsburgh *Also called La Salle Products Inc* ***(G-15213)***
Pro Pac Inc....717 646-9555
254 Obrien Ln Hanover (17331) ***(G-6938)***
Pro Pak Containers Inc....412 741-0549
103 Chateau Ct Sewickley (15143) ***(G-17404)***
Pro Pallet LLC....717 292-5510
1730 Butter Rd Dover (17315) ***(G-4201)***
Pro Pallet Partners....717 741-2418
460 Chestnut Ln York (17403) ***(G-20642)***
Pro Printing & Office LLC....814 834-3006
969 Brusselles St Saint Marys (15857) ***(G-17010)***
Pro Signs, Downingtown *Also called Upper Darby Sign Company* ***(G-4259)***
Pro Tech Machining Inc....814 587-3200
21382 N Norrisville Rd Conneautville (16406) ***(G-3484)***
Pro Thermal Inc....412 203-1588
114 Lamar Rd Pittsburgh (15241) ***(G-15450)***
Pro Tool Industries Inc....484 945-5001
337 W High St Pottstown (19464) ***(G-16037)***
Pro Tube Inc....717 765-9400
4872 Zane A Miller Dr Zullinger (17272) ***(G-20838)***
Pro Vision, Whitehall *Also called CJ Optical Holdings LLC* ***(G-19866)***
Pro-Action Suspension, Beaver Falls *Also called Pro Action Inc* ***(G-1007)***
Pro-Con, Hazle Township *Also called Progressive Converting Inc* ***(G-7475)***
Pro-Fab Associates, Manheim *Also called Pfa Inc* ***(G-10401)***
Pro-Machine LLC....724 342-9895
83 Main St Wheatland (16161) ***(G-19842)***
Pro-Mic Corp....610 783-7901
20135 Valley Forge Cir King of Prussia (19406) ***(G-8665)***
Pro-Sltons For Chropractic Inc....724 942-4284
370 Sthpinte Blvd Ste 100 Canonsburg (15317) ***(G-2621)***

ALPHABETIC

Probee Safety LLC..302 893-0258
320 N Main St Telford (18969) *(G-18310)*

Probes Unlimited Inc..267 263-0400
836 W 8th St Lansdale (19446) *(G-9401)*

Proceq USA Inc (HQ)..724 512-0330
117 Corporation Dr Aliquippa (15001) *(G-90)*

Process Automation, Warminster *Also called ABB Inc (G-18818)*

Process Constractors, Conshohocken *Also called J A Brown Company (G-3566)*

Process Control Spc Inc....................................570 753-5799
1854 Dutch Hollow Rd Jersey Shore (17740) *(G-8321)*

Process Development & Ctrl LLC.........................724 695-3440
1075 Montour West Ind Par Coraopolis (15108) *(G-3719)*

Process Instruments Inc...................................412 431-4600
615 E Carson St Pittsburgh (15203) *(G-15451)*

Process Masters Corporation.............................610 683-5674
940 Krumsville Rd Kutztown (19530) *(G-8857)*

Process Reproductions Inc.................................412 321-3120
939 W North Ave Pittsburgh (15233) *(G-15452)*

Process Science & Innovation............................717 428-3511
2807 Godfrey Rd Glen Rock (17327) *(G-6460)*

Process Sltions Consulting Inc............................610 248-2002
8009 George Rd New Tripoli (18066) *(G-12460)*

Process Tech & Packg LLC.................................570 587-8326
102 Life Science Dr Scott Township (18447) *(G-17188)*

Process Technologies Inc..................................412 771-8555
1641 Pine Hollow Rd Mc Kees Rocks (15136) *(G-10628)*

Process Technology of PA.................................215 628-2222
25 Tennis Ave Ambler (19002) *(G-600)*

Prochemtech International Inc (PA)......................814 265-0959
51 Pro Chem Tech Dr Brockway (15824) *(G-2231)*

Proconveyor LLC..717 887-5897
251 Herman St York (17404) *(G-20643)*

Procopy Inc (PA)..814 231-1256
434 W Aaron Dr Ste 200 State College (16803) *(G-18010)*

Procter & Gamble Company................................570 833-5141
Rr 87 Box S Tunkhannock (18657) *(G-18547)*

Procter & Gamble Paper Pdts Co.........................570 833-5141
Rr 87 Mehoopany (18629) *(G-10957)*

Prodex Inc (PA)...215 679-2405
436 Adams St Rear Red Hill (18076) *(G-16584)*

Prodex Inc...215 536-4078
43 E Cherry Rd Quakertown (18951) *(G-16234)*

Product Design and Development, York *Also called York Tool & Die Inc (G-20752)*

Product Design and Development (PA)...................717 741-4844
2603 Keyway Dr York (17402) *(G-20644)*

Production Abrasives Inc...................................814 938-5490
46 Sheesley Way Hamilton (15744) *(G-6858)*

Production Components Corp...............................215 368-7416
701 W 5th St Ste D Lansdale (19446) *(G-9402)*

Production Department, Scranton *Also called The Scranton Times L P (G-17297)*

Production Plus Steel Inc..................................724 376-3634
21 A Pine Tree Dr Sandy Lake (16145) *(G-17061)*

Production Systems Automtn LLC (PA)..................610 358-0500
1 Crozerville Rd Aston (19014) *(G-788)*

Production Systems Automtn LLC.........................570 602-4200
201 Clark Rd Duryea (18642) *(G-4506)*

Products Finishing Inc.....................................814 452-4887
2002 Greengarden Rd Erie (16502) *(G-5439)*

Professional Bldg Systems Inc (PA).....................570 837-1424
72 E Market St Middleburg (17842) *(G-11036)*

Professional Duplicating Inc (PA).......................610 891-7979
33 E State St Media (19063) *(G-10944)*

Professional Electronic Compon...........................215 245-1550
100 S Broad St Ste 707 Philadelphia (19110) *(G-14205)*

Professional Graphic Co...................................724 318-8530
2260 Big Swckly Crk Rd Sewickley (15143) *(G-17405)*

Professional Health Pdts S W, Pittsburgh *Also called Nova Aurora Corp (G-15349)*

Professional Hearing Aid Svc (PA).......................724 548-4801
141 S Jefferson St Kittanning (16201) *(G-8788)*

Profi Vision Inc...610 530-2025
1150 Glenlivet Dr Ste C41 Allentown (18106) *(G-361)*

Profile Shop Inc (PA).......................................215 633-3461
3300 Tillman Dr Ste 101 Bensalem (19020) *(G-1244)*

Profile Shop, The, Bensalem *Also called Profile Shop Inc (G-1244)*

Profiners Inc..215 997-1060
2299 Amber Dr Ste 100 Hatfield (19440) *(G-7387)*

Profit Engine LLC..412 848-8187
5500 Brooktree Rd Ste 104 Wexford (15090) *(G-19822)*

Proform Powdered Metals Inc.............................814 938-7411
700 Martha St Punxsutawney (15767) *(G-16154)*

Proforma Graphic Impressions...........................610 759-2430
161 Heyer Rd Nazareth (18064) *(G-11986)*

Profresh International Corp................................800 610-5110
4900 S Broad St Ste LI00 Philadelphia (19112) *(G-14206)*

Progeny Systems Corporation............................724 239-3939
106 Simko Blvd Ste 100 Charleroi (15022) *(G-3019)*

Progress For Industry Inc..................................814 763-3707
201 Grant St Saegertown (16433) *(G-16928)*

Progress News..724 867-2435
410 Main St Emlenton (16373) *(G-5014)*

Progress Rail Services Corp...............................610 779-2039
211 Emerald Ave Reading (19606) *(G-16476)*

Progressive Bus Publications, Reading *Also called American Future Systems Inc (G-16319)*

Progressive Computer Svcs Inc...........................215 226-2220
4250 Wissahickon Ave Philadelphia (19129) *(G-14207)*

Progressive Converting Inc................................570 384-2979
109 Maplewood Dr Hazle Township (18202) *(G-7475)*

Progressive Door Corporation.............................724 733-4636
3075 Carson Ave Murrysville (15668) *(G-11862)*

Progressive Gifts & Incentives, Malvern *Also called American Future Systems Inc (G-10186)*

Progressive Information Tech, York *Also called Magnus Group Inc (G-20575)*

Progressive Machine Works Inc...........................610 562-2281
100 S 2nd St Hamburg (19526) *(G-6850)*

Progressive Machining......................................610 469-6204
473 Pughtown Rd Spring City (19475) *(G-17864)*

Progressive Power Tech LLC..............................724 452-6064
100 Precision Dr Harmony (16037) *(G-7075)*

Progressive Publishing Company (PA)...................814 765-5051
615 Elm Ave Clearfield (16830) *(G-3229)*

Progressive Tool & Die Inc................................814 333-2992
13693 Broadway Ste A Meadville (16335) *(G-10782)*

Project Enterprise..717 933-9517
82 Deck Rd Womelsdorf (19567) *(G-20208)*

Project One Inc...267 901-7906
3230 Market St Ste 410 Philadelphia (19104) *(G-14208)*

Projectile Tube Cleaning Inc...............................724 763-7633
110 Valley View Dr Ford City (16226) *(G-6051)*

Proline Composites Corp...................................814 536-8491
883 Ragers Hill Rd South Fork (15956) *(G-17776)*

Promachining and Technology............................814 796-3254
627 Walnut St Waterford (16441) *(G-19268)*

Promark Industries Inc.....................................724 356-4060
45 Casey Rd Mc Donald (15057) *(G-10579)*

Promedia Publishing, Bensalem *Also called Bcmi Ad Concepts Inc (G-1154)*

Prominent Fluid Controls Inc (HQ)......................412 787-2484
136 Industry Dr Pittsburgh (15275) *(G-15453)*

Promo Gear...570 775-4078
693 Route 739 Ste 4 Hawley (18428) *(G-7436)*

Promostitch, Pittsburgh *Also called Hds Marketing Inc (G-15084)*

Promote ME Printing......................................412 486-2504
134 Ridgewood Rd Pittsburgh (15237) *(G-15454)*

Promotion Centre Inc......................................717 843-1582
701 Hay St York (17403) *(G-20645)*

Promotional Printing Assoc................................215 639-1662
2025 State Rd Bensalem (19020) *(G-1245)*

Prompton Tool Inc...570 253-4141
120 Sunrise Ave Ste 2 Honesdale (18431) *(G-7720)*

Proofreaders LLC...215 295-9400
842 Durham Rd Ste 427 Penns Park (18943) *(G-13243)*

Proper Brewing Company, The, Quakertown *Also called Wilbos Inc (G-16259)*

Proper Nutrition Inc..610 692-2060
439 S Bolmar St West Chester (19382) *(G-19621)*

Property Preservers..267 975-3990
7126 Vandike St Philadelphia (19135) *(G-14209)*

Prophase Labs Inc (PA)....................................215 345-0919
621 N Shady Retreat Rd Doylestown (18901) *(G-4329)*

Propipe..610 518-6320
1025 Boot Rd Downingtown (19335) *(G-4252)*

Proplastix International Inc.................................717 692-4733
1519 State Route 209 Millersburg (17061) *(G-11198)*

Proportal LLC...215 923-7100
124 Chestnut St Philadelphia (19106) *(G-14210)*

Prosco Inc...814 375-0484
1122 S Main St Du Bois (15801) *(G-4414)*

Proshort Stamping Services Inc...........................814 371-9633
6025 Route 219 Brockway (15824) *(G-2232)*

Prosit LLC...610 430-1470
1554 Paoli Pike West Chester (19380) *(G-19622)*

Prosit Print & Copy, West Chester *Also called Prosit LLC (G-19622)*

Prosoft Clinical, Wayne *Also called Prosoft Software Inc (G-19365)*

Prosoft Harris School Solution, Bethel Park *Also called Prosoft Technologies Inc (G-1429)*

Prosoft Software Inc.......................................484 580-8162
996 Old Eagle School Rd # 1106 Wayne (19087) *(G-19365)*

Prosoft Technologies Inc (HQ)............................412 835-6217
2000 Oxford Dr Ste 610 Bethel Park (15102) *(G-1429)*

Prosource of Lancaster.....................................717 299-5680
2969 Old Tree Dr Lancaster (17603) *(G-9176)*

Prospect Aggregates, Landisville *Also called Prospect Concrete Inc (G-9265)*

Prospect Concrete Inc......................................717 898-2277
1591 Quarry Rd Landisville (17538) *(G-9265)*

Prosthetic Arts Inc...570 842-2929
440 N Main St Moscow (18444) *(G-11601)*

Prosthetic Artworks LLC...................................570 828-6177
123 Orchid Dr Dingmans Ferry (18328) *(G-4143)*

Prosthetic Cad-CAM Tech Inc............................814 763-1151
21150 Peters Rd Saegertown (16433) *(G-16929)*

Prosthtic Orthtic Sltions Intl, Horsham *Also called Freedom Management Svcs LLC (G-7819)*

(G-0000) Company's Geographic Section entry number

Protarga Inc 610 260-4000
2200 Renaissance Blvd # 200 King of Prussia (19406) *(G-8666)*

Protech Powder Coatings 814 456-1243
361 W 11th St Erie (16501) *(G-5440)*

Protech Powder Coatings Inc 717 767-6996
939 Monocacy Rd York (17404) *(G-20646)*

Protech Powder Coatings Inc 814 899-7628
939 Monocacy Rd York (17404) *(G-20647)*

Protechs LLC 717 768-0800
2724 Division Hwy New Holland (17557) *(G-12273)*

Protect Machining Inc 814 587-3200
21382 N Norrisville Rd Conneautville (16406) *(G-3485)*

Protect-A-Board, York *Also called Caraustar Industries Inc (G-20418)*

Protection Services, Cambridge Springs *Also called New Enterprise Stone Lime Inc (G-2484)*

Protective Industries Inc 814 868-3671
7090 Edinboro Rd Erie (16509) *(G-5441)*

Protective Packaging Corp 610 398-2229
6813b Ruppsville Rd Allentown (18106) *(G-362)*

Protektor Model 814 435-2442
1 Bridge St 11 Galeton (16922) *(G-6244)*

Proteus Optics LLC 215 204-5241
4 Locust Ln Media (19063) *(G-10945)*

Protherics Inc 615 327-1027
300 Barr Harbor Dr # 800 Conshohocken (19428) *(G-3593)*

Protica Inc (PA) 610 832-2000
1002 Macarthur Rd Whitehall (18052) *(G-19887)*

Protica Research, Whitehall *Also called Protica Inc (G-19887)*

Proto Fab Technologies 570 682-2000
924 W Maple St Valley View (17983) *(G-18716)*

Proto-Cast LLC 610 326-1723
1460 Ben Franklin Hwy E Douglassville (19518) *(G-4180)*

Protos Foods Inc (PA) 724 836-1802
449 Glenmeade Rd Greensburg (15601) *(G-6705)*

Protostar Technologies 484 988-0964
202 S Deer Run Dr Lincoln University (19352) *(G-9974)*

Prototype Precision, Bunola *Also called Dyer Industries Inc (G-2343)*

Prova Inc 412 278-3010
1703 E Railroad St Carnegie (15106) *(G-2783)*

Provance Truss LLC 724 437-0585
119 Republic St Lemont Furnace (15456) *(G-9736)*

Provell Pharmaceuticals LLC 610 942-8970
1801 Horseshoe Pike Ste 1 Honey Brook (19344) *(G-7757)*

Provident Marketing, Langhorne *Also called Premium Pet Division (G-9321)*

Provost Display, Norristown *Also called Character Translation Inc (G-12644)*

Proweld 724 836-0207
1100 Swede Hill Rd Greensburg (15601) *(G-6706)*

Pruftechnik Inc 844 242-6296
7821 Bartram Ave Ste 3 Philadelphia (19153) *(G-14211)*

Pruftechnik Service Inc 856 401-3095
7821 Bartram Ave Ste 3 Philadelphia (19153) *(G-14212)*

Prwt Services Inc 570 275-2220
100 Avenue C Riverside (17868) *(G-16758)*

Prysmian Cbles Systems USA LLC 570 385-4381
1 Tamaqua Blvd Schuylkill Haven (17972) *(G-17164)*

PS & QS Inc 215 592-0888
820 South St Philadelphia (19147) *(G-14213)*

PS Furniture Inc 814 587-6313
801 High St Conneautville (16406) *(G-3486)*

Psb Industries Inc (PA) 814 453-3651
1202 W 12th St Erie (16501) *(G-5442)*

PSC Publishing 570 443-9749
1220 Vine St White Haven (18661) *(G-19851)*

Psg Controls Inc 215 257-3621
11401 Roosevelt Blvd Philadelphia (19154) *(G-14214)*

PSI, Elverson *Also called Polymeric Systems Inc (G-4965)*

PSI, Glen Rock *Also called Process Science & Innovation (G-6460)*

PSI Container Inc 570 929-1600
1057 Tresckow Rd McAdoo (18237) *(G-10658)*

PSI Industries, Connellsville *Also called PSI Packaging Services Inc (G-3506)*

PSI Packaging Services Inc 724 626-0100
2245 Industrial Dr Connellsville (15425) *(G-3506)*

PSI Pharma Support America Inc 267 464-2500
875 1st Ave King of Prussia (19406) *(G-8667)*

PSM Brownco, Emporium *Also called Pennsylvania Sintered Mtls Inc (G-5071)*

PSMLV Inc 610 395-8214
18106 Schantz Rd Allentown (18104) *(G-363)*

Psnergy LLC 724 581-3845
5368 Kuhl Rd Erie (16510) *(G-5443)*

PST Fuel Inc 215 676-3545
413 Hendrix St Phila (19116) *(G-13312)*

Pt Industries Inc 717 755-1679
807 Arbor Ln York (17406) *(G-20648)*

Ptb Rice Noodle 717 569-0330
401 Parkwynne Rd Lancaster (17601) *(G-9177)*

Ptc Alliance Corp (HQ) 412 299-7900
6051 Wallace Road Ext # 200 Wexford (15090) *(G-19823)*

Ptc Alliance Corp 724 847-7137
4400 W 3rd Ave Beaver Falls (15010) *(G-1008)*

Ptc Group Holdings Corp 724 847-7137
4400 W 3rd Ave Beaver Falls (15010) *(G-1009)*

Ptc Group Holdings Corp (PA) 412 299-7900
6051 Wallace Road Ext # 2 Wexford (15090) *(G-19824)*

Ptc Holdings I Corp 412 299-7900
6051 Wallace Road Ext # 200 Wexford (15090) *(G-19825)*

Ptc Inc 724 219-2600
41 W Otterman St Ste 310 Greensburg (15601) *(G-6707)*

Ptc-In-Liquidation Inc 814 763-2000
606 Erie St Saegertown (16433) *(G-16930)*

Pti Machine Inc 410 452-8855
23 Mccall Rd Delta (17314) *(G-4062)*

Ptr Baler and Compactor Co 215 533-5100
2207 E Ontario St Philadelphia (19134) *(G-14215)*

Ptr Paving, Pottstown *Also called Pottstown Trap Rock Quarries (G-16034)*

Ptr Tool & Plastics LLC 814 724-6979
150 Baldwin Street Ext Meadville (16335) *(G-10783)*

Pts Industries Corp 814 345-5200
506 Firehouse Rd Drifting (16834) *(G-4375)*

Ptubes Inc 201 560-7127
84 4th St Ste 1 Honesdale (18431) *(G-7721)*

PTX - Pentronix Inc 734 667-2897
590 Division St Du Bois (15801) *(G-4415)*

PTX Pentronix, Du Bois *Also called PTX - Pentronix Inc (G-4415)*

Public Image Printing Inc 215 677-4088
11972 Dumont Rd Philadelphia (19116) *(G-14216)*

Publication Connexion LLC 215 944-9400
6 Terry Dr Newtown (18940) *(G-12539)*

Publiccharters.com, Avoca *Also called Aviation Technologies Inc (G-840)*

Publicsource 412 315-0264
6300 5th Ave Pittsburgh (15232) *(G-15455)*

Publishers Survey Associate, Williamsport *Also called Sovereign Media Company Inc (G-20073)*

Publishing Office US Gvernment 215 364-6465
928 Jaymor Rd Ste A190 Southampton (18966) *(G-17832)*

Puchalski Inc 570 842-0361
46 Kosinski Rd Covington Township (18444) *(G-3793)*

Pudliner Packing, Johnstown *Also called Pudliners Packing (G-8425)*

Pudliners Packing 814 539-5422
167 Norton Rd Johnstown (15906) *(G-8425)*

Pulakos Chocolates, Erie *Also called 926 Partners Inc (G-5163)*

Pulse Ruggedized Solutions, Bristol *Also called Pulser LLC (G-2189)*

Pulse Ruggedized Solutions, Bristol *Also called Pulser LLC (G-2190)*

Pulse Technologies Inc 267 733-0200
2000 Am Dr Quakertown (18951) *(G-16235)*

Pulsemetrics LLC 412 656-5776
3911 Ash Dr Allison Park (15101) *(G-460)*

Pulser LLC 215 781-6400
2 Pearl Buck Ct Bristol (19007) *(G-2189)*

Pulser LLC 215 781-6400
311 Sinclair Rd Bristol (19007) *(G-2190)*

Pulva Corporation 724 898-3000
105 Industrial Dr W Valencia (16059) *(G-18700)*

Pulverman, Dallas *Also called Pennmark Technologies Corp (G-3966)*

Pump Shop Inc 610 431-6570
823 Lincoln Ave Ste 2 West Chester (19380) *(G-19623)*

Pump Station 2, York *Also called Manchester Township (G-20577)*

Pump Station Ridgway 814 772-3251
12230 Waterworks Rd Ridgway (15853) *(G-16725)*

Pump-Warehouse Co Inc 215 536-0500
359 New St Ste 2 Quakertown (18951) *(G-16236)*

Punxsutawney Finshg Works Inc 814 938-9164
701 Martha St Punxsutawney (15767) *(G-16155)*

Punxsutawney Glass Tile, Punxsutawney *Also called Punxsutawney Tile & Glass Inc (G-16156)*

Punxsutawney Tile & Glass Inc 814 938-4200
220 Lane Ave Punxsutawney (15767) *(G-16156)*

Pup E Luv LLC 610 458-5280
112 Magnolia Dr Chester Springs (19425) *(G-3084)*

Puraglobe Florida LLC (PA) 813 247-1754
435 Devon Park Dr Wayne (19087) *(G-19366)*

Purblu Beverages Inc 412 281-9808
1 Oxford Ctr Ste 820 Pittsburgh (15219) *(G-15456)*

Purcell Company 717 838-5611
6021 Colebrook Rd Palmyra (17078) *(G-13130)*

Pure Fishing America Inc 215 229-9415
3028 W Hunting Park Ave Philadelphia (19132) *(G-14217)*

Pure Flow Water Co 215 723-0237
101 W Broad St Ste A Souderton (18964) *(G-17761)*

Pure Hospitality LLC 724 935-1515
119 Neely School Rd Wexford (15090) *(G-19826)*

Pure Power 412 673-5285
515 Mckee Rd White Oak (15131) *(G-19857)*

Pure Screenprinting Inc 412 246-2048
428 Bingham St Pittsburgh (15203) *(G-15457)*

Pureland Supply LLC 610 444-0590
210 Gale Ln Kennett Square (19348) *(G-8537)*

A
L
P
H
A
B
E
T
I
C

Pureoptix Led LLC...610 301-9767
  6986 Periwinkle Ct Macungie (18062) *(G-10157)*

Puricore, Malvern *Also called Realm Therapeutics Inc (G-10308)*

Purina Animal Nutrition LLC...........................717 737-4581
  475 Saint Johns Church Rd Camp Hill (17011) *(G-2511)*

Purina Animal Nutrition LLC...........................717 393-1361
  3029 Hempland Rd Lancaster (17601) *(G-9178)*

Purina Mills LLC..717 737-4581
  475 Saint Johns Church Rd Camp Hill (17011) *(G-2512)*

Purina Mills LLC..717 393-1299
  3029 Hempland Rd Lancaster (17601) *(G-9179)*

Purity Candy Co (PA)......................................570 538-9502
  18047 Us Route 15 Allenwood (17810) *(G-442)*

Purolite Company, Philadelphia *Also called Purolite Corporation (G-14218)*

Purolite Corporation (PA).................................610 668-9090
  150 Monument Rd Ste 202 Bala Cynwyd (19004) *(G-889)*

Purolite Corporation.......................................610 668-9090
  3620 G St Philadelphia (19134) *(G-14218)*

Purple Cow Creamery Ltd.................................610 252-5544
  290 Raubsville Rd Easton (18042) *(G-4745)*

Purple Cow Winery..570 854-6969
  281 Welliversville Rd Bloomsburg (17815) *(G-1797)*

Purple Deck Media Inc.....................................717 884-9529
  3583 Scotland Rd Scotland (17254) *(G-17182)*

Purpose 1 LLC...717 232-9077
  309 S 10th St Lemoyne (17043) *(G-9749)*

Purtech Inc...570 424-1669
  124 Progress St East Stroudsburg (18301) *(G-4632)*

Pushcart USA Inc...570 622-2479
  104 Pottsville St Port Carbon (17965) *(G-15900)*

Pvc Container Corporation................................570 384-3930
  605 Oak Ridge Rd Hazle Township (18202) *(G-7476)*

Pvc Container Corporation................................717 266-9100
  50 Devco Dr Manchester (17345) *(G-10363)*

PVS Steel Services Inc....................................412 929-0177
  Fster Plz Ste 7661 Pittsburgh (15220) *(G-15458)*

Pyco LLC..215 757-3704
  600 E Lincoln Hwy Penndel (19047) *(G-13241)*

Pyle Machine Manufacturing Inc........................814 443-3171
  343 Bromm Rd Somerset (15501) *(G-17701)*

Pyramed Health Systems, Berwyn *Also called Media Highway (G-1368)*

Pyrogenics Group, Easton *Also called Minteq International Inc (G-4723)*

Pyromet, Aston *Also called Pyropure Inc (G-789)*

Pyropure Inc...610 497-1743
  5 Commerce Dr Aston (19014) *(G-789)*

Pyrotek Incorporated......................................717 249-2075
  1285 Claremont Rd Carlisle (17015) *(G-2733)*

Pyxidis..267 614-8348
  1050 Crosskeys Dr Doylestown (18902) *(G-4330)*

Pzp, Philadelphia *Also called Private Zone Productions Corp (G-14204)*

Q A Technology, Hatfield *Also called Quick Assembly Inc (G-7388)*

Q Aluminum LLC..570 966-2800
  10 Willow Pond Rd New Berlin (17855) *(G-12021)*

Q C M Corporation..610 586-4770
  116 Darby Commons Ct Folcroft (19032) *(G-6013)*

Q Company LLC...570 966-1017
  809 Market St New Berlin (17855) *(G-12022)*

Q D F Inc..610 670-2090
  2530 Penn Ave Reading (19609) *(G-16477)*

Q S I, Chester Springs *Also called Quality Systems Integrators (G-3085)*

Q-Cast Inc..724 728-7440
  630 New York Ave Rochester (15074) *(G-16789)*

Q-E Manufacturing Company............................570 966-1017
  809 Market St New Berlin (17855) *(G-12023)*

Q-Linx Inc..610 941-2756
  200 Barr Harbor Dr Ste 40 Conshohocken (19428) *(G-3594)*

Q-R-S Music Rolls, Seneca *Also called Qrs Music Inc (G-17367)*

Qbc Diagnostics LLC.......................................814 342-6210
  168 Bradford Dr Port Matilda (16870) *(G-15905)*

Qbc Dianostics, Philipsburg *Also called Drucker Company LLC (G-14513)*

Qcast Aluminum, New Berlin *Also called Q Aluminum LLC (G-12021)*

Qdp Inc..610 828-2324
  4110 Butler Pike Ste F101 Plymouth Meeting (19462) *(G-15866)*

Qfix, Avondale *Also called Anholt Technologies Inc (G-848)*

Qg LLC...414 208-2700
  4581 Lower Valley Rd Atglen (19310) *(G-803)*

Qg Printing II Corp...610 593-1445
  4581 Lower Valley Rd Atglen (19310) *(G-804)*

Qg Printing II Corp...717 642-5871
  100 N Miller St Fairfield (17320) *(G-5768)*

Qilu Pharma Inc..484 443-2935
  101 Lindenwood Dr Ste 225 Malvern (19355) *(G-10304)*

Qlf Inc...717 445-6225
  947 E Earl Rd New Holland (17557) *(G-12274)*

Qmac-Quality Machining Inc............................814 548-2000
  622 E Rolling Ridge Dr Bellefonte (16823) *(G-1113)*

Qohal, Philadelphia *Also called Quality Health and Life Inc (G-14219)*

Qol Meds..724 602-0532
  112 Hillvue Dr Butler (16001) *(G-2436)*

Qortek Inc (PA)..570 322-2700
  1965 Lycoming Creek Rd # 205 Williamsport (17701) *(G-20066)*

Qovalent...610 269-3075
  1030 Boot Rd Downingtown (19335) *(G-4253)*

Qrs Music Inc (PA)...239 597-5888
  269 Quaker Dr Seneca (16346) *(G-17367)*

Qrs Music Technologies Inc (HQ).......................814 676-6683
  269 Quaker Dr Seneca (16346) *(G-17368)*

Qtd Plastics Inc...814 724-1641
  21398 Blooming Valley Rd Meadville (16335) *(G-10784)*

Qtg Qu Trop Gat9084......................................570 474-9995
  750 Oak Hill Rd Rear Mountain Top (18707) *(G-11773)*

Quad Graphics, Fairfield *Also called Qg Printing II Corp (G-5768)*

Quad Tron Inc..215 441-9303
  303 Camars Dr Warminster (18974) *(G-18949)*

Quad/Graphics Inc..215 541-2729
  2512 Quakertown Rd Pennsburg (18073) *(G-13253)*

Quad/Graphics Inc..570 459-5700
  Humboldt Indus Park Rr 92 Hazleton (18202) *(G-7522)*

Quadax Valves Inc..713 429-5458
  1518 Grundy Ln Bristol (19007) *(G-2191)*

Quadrant Holding Inc......................................570 558-6000
  900 N South Rd Scranton (18504) *(G-17276)*

Quadrant Holding Inc......................................724 468-7062
  201 Industrial Dr Delmont (15626) *(G-4054)*

Quaker Boy Inc..814 362-7073
  20 Russell Blvd Bradford (16701) *(G-1988)*

Quaker Chemical Corporation (PA).....................610 832-4000
  901 E Hector St Conshohocken (19428) *(G-3595)*

Quaker City Mfg Co, Folcroft *Also called Q C M Corporation (G-6013)*

Quaker City Stamp & Stencil, Philadelphia *Also called Krengel Quaker City Corp (G-13944)*

Quaker Color Div, Quakertown *Also called McAdoo & Allen Inc (G-16214)*

Quaker Hardwoods Company..............................215 538-0401
  992 E Cherry Rd Quakertown (18951) *(G-16237)*

Quaker Maid Meats Inc....................................610 376-1500
  610 Morgantown Rd Reading (19611) *(G-16478)*

Quaker Maid Meats Inc....................................610 376-1500
  521 Carroll St Reading (19611) *(G-16479)*

Quaker Oats Company......................................570 474-3800
  750 Oak Hill Rd Mountain Top (18707) *(G-11774)*

Quaker Plastics, Schuylkill Haven *Also called Cardinal Systems Inc (G-17151)*

Quaker Safety Products Corp.............................215 536-2991
  1121 Richland Commrce Dr A Quakertown (18951) *(G-16238)*

Quaker Sales Corporation (PA)..........................814 536-7541
  Rear 83 Cooper Ave Johnstown (15906) *(G-8426)*

Quaker Sales Corporation.................................814 539-1376
  2 Asphalt Rd Johnstown (15907) *(G-8427)*

Quaker State Farms, Klingerstown *Also called Crystal Frms Refrigerated Dist (G-8807)*

Quaker State Tube Mfg Corp.............................610 287-8841
  1303 Gravel Pike Rt 29 Zieglerville (19492) *(G-20834)*

Quaker Valley Specialties.................................717 694-3999
  2383 Quaker Run Rd Richfield (17086) *(G-16681)*

Quakermaid Cabinets Inc.................................570 207-4432
  40 Poplar St Scranton (18509) *(G-17277)*

Qual Krom Great Lakes, Erie *Also called Ore Enterprises Inc (G-5410)*

Quala-Die Inc..814 781-6280
  1250 Brusselles St Saint Marys (15857) *(G-17011)*

Qualastat Electronics Inc (PA)...........................717 253-9301
  1270 Fairfield Rd Ste 50 Gettysburg (17325) *(G-6311)*

Qualitest Pharmaceuticals, Malvern *Also called Generics International US Inc (G-10239)*

Qualitox Laboratories LLC.................................412 458-5431
  109 William Cir Mc Kees Rocks (15136) *(G-10629)*

Quality Aggregates Inc....................................724 924-2198
  552 Many Springs Farm Rd Portersville (16051) *(G-15935)*

Quality Aggregates Inc (PA)..............................412 777-6704
  4955 Steubenville Pike Pittsburgh (15205) *(G-15459)*

Quality Aluminum Casting Co............................717 484-4545
  603 Lauschtown Rd Denver (17517) *(G-4090)*

Quality Box Company, Nazareth *Also called McLean Packaging Corporation (G-11981)*

Quality Brand Printing Inc................................724 864-1731
  12120 State Route 30 # 210 Irwin (15642) *(G-8194)*

Quality Canvas...724 329-1571
  148 Mae West Rd Confluence (15424) *(G-3468)*

Quality Canvas...814 695-8343
  411 2nd Ave Duncansville (16635) *(G-4461)*

Quality Compacted Metals Inc...........................814 486-1500
  513 E 2nd St Emporium (15834) *(G-5072)*

Quality Components, Ridgway *Also called Cmsjlp LLC (G-16700)*

Quality Concrete Inc.......................................412 922-0200
  1051 Mccartney St Pittsburgh (15220) *(G-15460)*

Quality Crrctons Inspctons Inc (PA)....................814 696-3737
  611 Gildea Dr Duncansville (16635) *(G-4462)*

Quality Crrections Inspections, Duncansville *Also called Quality Crrctons Inspctons Inc (G-4462)*

Quality Custom Cabinetry Inc (PA)......................717 656-2721
  125 Peters Rd New Holland (17557) *(G-12275)*

(G-0000) Company's Geographic Section entry number

Quality Custom Cabinetry Inc 717 661-6565
  295 E Main St Leola (17540) *(G-9798)*

Quality Die Makers Inc 724 325-1264
  831 Oak Ave Turtle Creek (15145) *(G-18568)*

Quality Dispersions Inc 814 781-7927
  1413 Million Dollar Hwy Kersey (15846) *(G-8567)*

Quality Fencing & Supply 717 355-7112
  622 N Shirk Rd New Holland (17557) *(G-12276)*

Quality Gear & Machine Inc 814 938-5552
  188 Blose Rd Punxsutawney (15767) *(G-16157)*

Quality Health and Life Inc 866 547-8447
  2927 N Stillman St Philadelphia (19132) *(G-14219)*

Quality Hose Div, New Castle *Also called Summers Acquisition Corp (G-12156)*

Quality Laser Alternatives 610 373-0788
  1615 Crowder Ave Reading (19607) *(G-16480)*

Quality Machine Inc 610 942-2488
  8 Andover Rd Glenmoore (19343) *(G-6469)*

Quality Machine Tools, Mc Donald *Also called Matt Nabeja (G-10575)*

Quality Machine Tools LLC 412 787-2876
  1060 Montour West Ind Par Coraopolis (15108) *(G-3720)*

Quality Machined Pdts Mfg Inc 724 339-2360
  134 Prominence Dr New Kensington (15068) *(G-12369)*

Quality Metal Coatings Inc 814 781-6161
  122 Access Rd Saint Marys (15857) *(G-17012)*

Quality Metal Products Inc 570 333-4248
  718 Orange Rd Dallas (18612) *(G-3967)*

Quality Metal Works Inc 717 367-2120
  385 Anchor Rd Elizabethtown (17022) *(G-4882)*

Quality Millwork Inc 412 831-3500
  6299 State Route 88 Finleyville (15332) *(G-5964)*

Quality Mold Inc 814 459-1084
  1302 Irwin Dr Erie (16505) *(G-5444)*

Quality Mold Inc (PA) 814 866-2255
  8130 Hawthorne Dr Erie (16509) *(G-5445)*

Quality Mould Inc 724 532-3678
  110 Dill Ln Bldg 2 Latrobe (15650) *(G-9512)*

Quality Pasta Company LLC 855 878-9630
  100 Chamber Plz Charleroi (15022) *(G-3020)*

Quality Penn Products Inc 215 430-0117
  2015 W Allegheny Ave Philadelphia (19132) *(G-14220)*

Quality Perforating Inc 570 267-2092
  166 Dundaff St Carbondale (18407) *(G-2685)*

Quality Print Shop Inc 570 473-1122
  123 Duke St Northumberland (17857) *(G-12874)*

Quality Process Services 724 455-1687
  216 Indian Creek Vly Rd Normalville (15469) *(G-12625)*

Quality Stamping 724 459-5060
  9177 Route 22 Blairsville (15717) *(G-1739)*

Quality Steel Fabricators 724 646-0500
  106 Mortensen Rd Greenville (16125) *(G-6768)*

Quality Systems Associates (PA) 215 345-5575
  100 Mechanics St Ste 2 Doylestown (18901) *(G-4331)*

Quality Systems Integrators 610 458-0539
  148 Magnolia Dr Chester Springs (19425) *(G-3085)*

Quality Tool & Die Enterprises 814 834-2384
  967 Cherry Hill Rd Saint Marys (15857) *(G-17013)*

Quality Tool & Die Inc 814 336-6364
  21398 Blooming Valley Rd Meadville (16335) *(G-10785)*

Quality Tooling & Repair Inc 724 522-1555
  139 Penn Manor Rd Irwin (15642) *(G-8195)*

Quality Trailer Products LP 717 354-7070
  170 Commerce Dr New Holland (17557) *(G-12277)*

Quality Wire Forming 717 656-4478
  120 Brick Church Rd Leola (17540) *(G-9799)*

Qualtek Molecular Laboratories 215 504-7402
  300 Pheasant Run Newtown (18940) *(G-12540)*

Quanotech Inc 610 658-0116
  428 Ballytore Cir Wynnewood (19096) *(G-20271)*

Quanta Technologies Inc 610 644-7101
  1036 New Holland Ave Lancaster (17601) *(G-9180)*

Quanta Technologies Inc 610 644-7101
  1004 New Holland Ave Lancaster (17601) *(G-9181)*

Quantam Software Solutions 610 373-4770
  4228 Saint Lawrence Ave B Reading (19606) *(G-16481)*

Quantam Business Services, Reading *Also called Quantam Software Solutions (G-16481)*

Quantum Connection 814 333-9398
  10553 Shaffer Rd Meadville (16335) *(G-10786)*

Quantum Engineered Pdts Inc 724 352-5100
  438 Saxonburg Blvd Saxonburg (16056) *(G-17093)*

Quantum Global Tech LLC (HQ) 215 892-9300
  1900 Am Dr Ste 200 Quakertown (18951) *(G-16239)*

Quantum Leap Engnered Pdts LLC 814 289-1476
  330 High St Somerset (15501) *(G-17702)*

Quantum Mfg Services Inc 570 785-9716
  20 Anderson Ln Waymart (18472) *(G-19289)*

Quantum One 412 432-5234
  2 Hot Metal St Ste 135 Pittsburgh (15203) *(G-15461)*

Quantum Plating Inc 814 835-9213
  4300 W Ridge Rd Erie (16506) *(G-5446)*

Quantum Qube Inc 412 767-0506
  2629 Syracuse Ct Sewickley (15143) *(G-17406)*

Quantum Restoration LLC 215 259-3402
  539 Ford St Conshohocken (19428) *(G-3596)*

Quantum Vortex Inc 814 325-0148
  200 Innovation Blvd # 254 State College (16803) *(G-18011)*

Quantumclean, Quakertown *Also called Quantum Global Tech LLC (G-16239)*

Quarkermaid, Scranton *Also called Quakermaid Cabinets Inc (G-17277)*

Quarry Management LLC 646 599-5893
  237 Masthope Plank Rd Lackawaxen (18435) *(G-8876)*

Quartz Tubing Inc 215 638-0909
  2273 New York Ave Bensalem (19020) *(G-1246)*

Qube Global Software Americas 610 431-9080
  105 E Evans St West Chester (19380) *(G-19624)*

Queen of Hearts Catering, Malvern *Also called Queen of Hearts Inc (G-10305)*

Queen of Hearts Inc 610 889-0477
  189 Pennsylvania Ave Malvern (19355) *(G-10305)*

Quehanna Millwork 814 263-4145
  22792 Shawville Frenchvil Frenchville (16836) *(G-6218)*

Quentin Wood, Newmanstown *Also called Shane Hostetter (G-12483)*

Quest Systems & Technology, West Hazleton *Also called Ldp Inc (G-19713)*

Questa Petroleum Co 724 832-7297
  255 Lancewood Pl Greensburg (15601) *(G-6708)*

Questa Petroleum Company 412 220-9210
  1580 Mclaughlin Run Rd Pittsburgh (15241) *(G-15462)*

Questar Corporation (PA) 215 862-5277
  6204 Ingham Rd New Hope (18938) *(G-12312)*

Quick Assembly Inc 215 361-4100
  1500 Industry Rd Ste E Hatfield (19440) *(G-7388)*

Quick Clamp 2 .... 724 336-5719
  533 Enon Rd Enon Valley (16120) *(G-5087)*

Quick Field, Warren *Also called United Refining Company (G-19056)*

Quick Print Center PA 717 637-2838
  16 Centennial Ave Hanover (17331) *(G-6939)*

Quickandeasy.com, Harrisburg *Also called Datatech Software Inc (G-7113)*

Quickel International Corp 215 862-1313
  65 Chapel Rd New Hope (18938) *(G-12313)*

Quiet Core Inc 610 694-9190
  1440 Schoenersville Rd Bethlehem (18018) *(G-1606)*

Quiet Valley Printing LLC 908 400-3689
  421 Quiet Valley Rd Mount Bethel (18343) *(G-11614)*

Quietflex Manufacturing 570 883-9019
  220 Research Dr Pittston (18640) *(G-15780)*

Quigley Motor Company Inc 717 266-5631
  100 Sunset Dr Manchester (17345) *(G-10364)*

Quigley Nutraceuticals LLC 646 499-5100
  64 E Uwchlan Ave Ste 443 Exton (19341) *(G-5725)*

Quik Piks & Paks Inc 570 459-3099
  218 Laurel Mall Hazle Township (18202) *(G-7477)*

Quikrete Companies Inc 570 672-1063
  3 Industrial Park 9 Paxinos (17860) *(G-13192)*

Quikrete Companies LLC 724 539-6600
  519 Red Barn Ln Latrobe (15650) *(G-9513)*

Quikrete/Pittsburgh, Latrobe *Also called Quikrete Companies LLC (G-9513)*

Quilting Stone House 610 495-8762
  30 Hershey Dr Pottstown (19465) *(G-15956)*

Quiltpatch Fabric Furn & Gifts, Littlestown *Also called Heritage Gallery of Lace & Int (G-10067)*

Quinlan Scenic Studio Inc 610 859-9130
  203 E 10th St Marcus Hook (19061) *(G-10453)*

Quinnova Pharmaceuticals Inc 215 860-6263
  2500 York Rd Ste 210 Jamison (18929) *(G-8245)*

Quintech Elec Cmmnications Inc 724 349-1412
  250 Airport Rd Indiana (15701) *(G-8122)*

Quintiq Inc 610 964-8111
  201 King Of Prussia Rd # 500 Radnor (19087) *(G-16299)*

Quire LLC 267 935-9777
  23 Taylor Ave Doylestown (18901) *(G-4332)*

Quirk Books, Philadelphia *Also called Quirk Productions Inc (G-14221)*

Quirk Productions Inc 215 627-3581
  215 Church St Ste 1 Philadelphia (19106) *(G-14221)*

Quotient Biodiagnostics Inc (PA) 215 497-8820
  301 S State St Ste S204 Newtown (18940) *(G-12541)*

Quotient Sciences - Phila 610 485-4270
  3 Chelsea Pkwy Ste 305 Boothwyn (19061) *(G-1880)*

R & C Foltz LLC 717 927-9771
  2270 Delta Rd Brogue (17309) *(G-2239)*

R & D Americas Best Packaging 610 435-4300
  737 N 13th St Allentown (18102) *(G-364)*

R & D Assembly Inc 610 770-0700
  1660 E Race St Allentown (18109) *(G-365)*

R & D Coatings Inc 412 771-8110
  1320 Island Ave Mc Kees Rocks (15136) *(G-10630)*

R & D Lab, Pittsburgh *Also called Kop-Coat Inc (G-15184)*

R & D Machine Controls Inc (PA) 267 205-5976
  806 Branagan Dr Bristol (19007) *(G-2192)*

R & D Packaging PA Inc 570 235-2310
  458 S Empire St Unit A Wilkes Barre (18702) *(G-19960)*

R & D Pallett Co 610 944-9484
  Breazy Ind Park Rr 73 Blandon (19510) *(G-1758)*

R & D Raceway Inc 724 258-8754
  1054 State Route 917 Bentleyville (15314) *(G-1274)*

R & E International Inc (HQ) 610 664-5637
  136 Broome Ln Merion Station (19066) *(G-10998)*

R & G Gorr Enterprises Inc 610 356-8500
  1000 Schell Ln Phoenixville (19460) *(G-14573)*

R & G Products Inc 717 633-0011
  33 Amy Way Hanover (17331) *(G-6940)*

R & H Jewelers 215 928-1240
  740 Sansom St Ste 402 Philadelphia (19106) *(G-14222)*

R & H Manufacturing Inc 570 288-6648
  105 Woodward Hill Rd Edwardsville (18704) *(G-4824)*

R & J Logging Inc 717 933-5646
  300 Schneck St Bethel (19507) *(G-1398)*

R & J Trophy 570 345-2277
  36 S Tulpehocken St Pine Grove (17963) *(G-14604)*

R & K Neon Inc 724 834-8570
  731 Santone Dr Greensburg (15601) *(G-6709)*

R & K Wettlaufer Logging Inc 570 924-4752
  3326 Dushore Overton Rd A 1 New Albany (18833) *(G-12015)*

R & M Apparel Inc 814 886-9272
  790 Clark St Gallitzin (16641) *(G-6247)*

R & M Equipment Company, Spring City Also called Tri Bms LLC *(G-17870)*

R & M Ship Tech USA Inc (HQ) 352 403-8365
  4619 S Broad St Philadelphia (19112) *(G-14223)*

R & M Targets Inc 814 774-0160
  227 Hathaway St E Ste E Girard (16417) *(G-6400)*

R & R Automotive Machine Shop 717 732-5521
  59 S Enola Dr Enola (17025) *(G-5085)*

R & R Briggs Inc 215 357-3413
  1067 Churchville Rd Southampton (18966) *(G-17833)*

R & R Components Inc 717 792-4641
  76 Bowman Rd York (17408) *(G-20649)*

R & R Energy Corp 570 874-1602
  10 Gilberton Rd Gilberton (17934) *(G-6369)*

R & R Eyewear Imports Inc 215 393-5895
  311 W Moreland Rd Willow Grove (19090) *(G-20137)*

R & R Heat Treating Inc 570 424-8750
  28 Mill Creek Rd East Stroudsburg (18301) *(G-4633)*

R & R Provision Co (PA) 610 258-5366
  1240 Pine St Easton (18042) *(G-4746)*

R & R Retail Outlet, Easton Also called R & R Provision Co *(G-4746)*

R & R Wood Products Inc 215 723-3470
  645 Fretz Rd Mainland (19451) *(G-10175)*

R & S Machine Inc 814 938-7540
  7707 Porter Rd Punxsutawney (15767) *(G-16158)*

R A Egan Sign & Awng Co Inc 610 777-3795
  1100 Berkshire Blvd Reading (19610) *(G-16482)*

R A Palmer Products Company 412 823-5971
  2808 Broadway Blvd Monroeville (15146) *(G-11351)*

R A S Industries Inc 215 541-4627
  2452 Quakertown Rd # 100 Pennsburg (18073) *(G-13254)*

R and C Logging 814 590-4422
  1964 Shale Pit Rd Reynoldsville (15851) *(G-16661)*

R and M Machining Company Inc 724 532-0890
  2412 Raymond Ave Latrobe (15650) *(G-9514)*

R and R Glass Inc 215 443-7010
  30 Steam Whistle Dr Warminster (18974) *(G-18950)*

R C Kletzing Inc 215 357-1788
  1325 Industrial Blvd # 1 Southampton (18966) *(G-17834)*

R C Paper Company 610 821-9610
  374 Auburn St Allentown (18103) *(G-366)*

R C Print Specialist 814 942-1204
  810 S 12th St Altoona (16602) *(G-540)*

R C Silivis & Sons 814 257-8401
  565 State Route 1037 Dayton (16222) *(G-4039)*

R C Southwell 814 723-7182
  59 Scientific Rd Warren (16365) *(G-19045)*

R C'S Print Specialists, Altoona Also called R C Print Specialist *(G-540)*

R Conrader Company 814 898-2727
  749 E 18th St Erie (16503) *(G-5447)*

R E B Bloxham Inc 570 222-4693
  4344 State Route 106 Clifford Township (18470) *(G-3249)*

R E B Inc (PA) 215 538-7875
  228 S West End Blvd Quakertown (18951) *(G-16240)*

R E Dupill & Associates Ltd 724 845-7300
  1057 State Route 356 Leechburg (15656) *(G-9651)*

R E M Automotive Parts Inc 717 838-4242
  20 Landings Dr Annville (17003) *(G-657)*

R E Wildes Sheet Metal Inc 570 501-3828
  253 W 32nd St Hazle Township (18202) *(G-7478)*

R F Circuits & Cad Services 215 368-6483
  1500 Breckenridge Pl Harleysville (19438) *(G-7053)*

R F Fager Company 717 564-1166
  3901 Derry St Harrisburg (17111) *(G-7203)*

R F Specialties Pennsylvania 814 472-2000
  619 Industrial Park Rd # 200 Ebensburg (15931) *(G-4793)*

R Fritz Enterprises Inc 814 267-4204
  326 Vanyo Rd Berlin (15530) *(G-1292)*

R G B Business Tech Solutions 215 745-3646
  7948 Oxford Ave Philadelphia (19111) *(G-14224)*

R G Johnson Company Inc (PA) 724 222-6810
  25 S College St Washington (15301) *(G-19220)*

R G Johnson Company Inc 724 225-4969
  75 Shady Ln Washington (15301) *(G-19221)*

R G S Machine Inc 610 532-1850
  101 Sycamore Ave Ste 109 Folsom (19033) *(G-6027)*

R G Steel Corp 724 656-1722
  8301 Mercer St Pulaski (16143) *(G-16126)*

R Graphics Inc 610 918-0373
  1313 W Chester Pike West Chester (19382) *(G-19625)*

R H Benedix Contracting 610 889-7472
  77 N Bacton Hill Rd Malvern (19355) *(G-10306)*

R H Carbide & Epoxy Inc 724 356-2277
  107 Main St Ste 3 Hickory (15340) *(G-7630)*

R H Fink Inc 717 266-1054
  3945 N Susquehanna Trl York (17404) *(G-20650)*

R H Sheppard Co Inc (HQ) 717 637-3751
  101 Philadelphia St Hanover (17331) *(G-6941)*

R H Sheppard Co Inc 717 633-4106
  447 E Middle St Hanover (17331) *(G-6942)*

R I Lampus Company (PA) 412 362-3800
  816 R I Lampus Ave Springdale (15144) *(G-17900)*

R Illig Machining 814 344-6202
  314 Deveaux St Carrolltown (15722) *(G-2809)*

R J & Sons Hoffman 570 539-2428
  1144 Buckwheat Valley Rd Mount Pleasant Mills (17853) *(G-11730)*

R J Brunner & Company 717 285-3534
  3540 Marietta Ave Silver Spring (17575) *(G-17590)*

R J Evercrest Polymers Inc 610 647-1555
  1234 Wrights Ln West Chester (19380) *(G-19626)*

R J Junk 717 734-3838
  1165 Mccoysville Rd Honey Grove (17035) *(G-7768)*

R J Machine Co Inc 610 494-8107
  3353 Market St Upper Chichester (19014) *(G-18672)*

R J Reynolds Tobacco Company 215 244-9071
  3580 Progress Dr Ste B2 Bensalem (19020) *(G-1247)*

R J Reynolds Tobacco Company 570 654-0770
  420 N Main St Pittston (18640) *(G-15781)*

R J S Wood Products Inc 570 689-7630
  308 Sawmill Rd Lake Ariel (18436) *(G-8890)*

R K L Controls Div, Carnegie Also called Red Valve Company Inc *(G-2785)*

R K Neon Company 724 539-9605
  410 Unity St Latrobe (15650) *(G-9515)*

R L Holliday Company Inc (PA) 412 561-7620
  525 Mcneilly Rd Pittsburgh (15226) *(G-15463)*

R L Kingsley Lumber Company 570 596-3575
  3404 Milan Rd Milan (18831) *(G-11148)*

R L Sgath McHining Fabrication 724 327-3895
  1111 Spring Hill Rd Murrysville (15668) *(G-11863)*

R L Sipes Locker Plant 814 652-2714
  14 S St Ext Everett (15537) *(G-5578)*

R L Snelbecker Inc 717 292-4971
  90 S Main St Dover (17315) *(G-4202)*

R M Frantz Inc 570 421-3020
  909 Mill Aly Stroudsburg (18360) *(G-18137)*

R M G Enterprises Inc 814 866-2247
  4003 Wood St Erie (16509) *(G-5448)*

R M Kerner Co (PA) 814 898-2000
  2208 E 33rd St Erie (16510) *(G-5449)*

R M Kerner Co 814 898-2000
  2000 E 36th St Erie (16510) *(G-5450)*

R M Metals Inc 717 656-8737
  32 Industrial Cir Lancaster (17601) *(G-9182)*

R M Palmer Company 610 582-5551
  40 Dennis Dr Reading (19606) *(G-16483)*

R M Palmer Company 610 374-5224
  800 Van Reed Rd Wyomissing (19610) *(G-20287)*

R M S Graphics Inc 215 322-6000
  1601 Republic Rd Ste 100 Huntingdon Valley (19006) *(G-8028)*

R P M Nittany Printing Service, Altoona Also called RPM Nittany Printing *(G-545)*

R P Neese & Sons LLC 724 465-5718
  2425 Tanoma Rd Marion Center (15759) *(G-10476)*

R PS Machinery Sales Inc 570 398-7456
  175 Old Rt 220 Hwy Jersey Shore (17740) *(G-8322)*

R Q I Inc 724 209-4100
  807 E Mcmurray Rd Ste 202 Venetia (15367) *(G-18743)*

R R Donnelley, Wayne Also called R R Donnelley & Sons Company *(G-19367)*

R R Donnelley, Lancaster Also called R R Donnelley & Sons Company *(G-9183)*

R R Donnelley, Philadelphia Also called R R Donnelley & Sons Company *(G-14226)*

R R Donnelley, Breinigsville Also called R R Donnelley & Sons Company *(G-2026)*

R R Donnelley, Allentown Also called RR Donnelley & Sons Company *(G-380)*

R R Donnelley, Lancaster Also called R R Donnelley & Sons Company *(G-9184)*

R R Donnelley & Sons Company 570 524-2224
  1601 Industrial Blvd Lewisburg (17837) *(G-9918)*

R R Donnelley & Sons Company 610 688-9090
440 E Swedesford Rd # 480 Wayne (19087) *(G-19367)*

R R Donnelley & Sons Company 610 391-3900
700 Nestle Way Ste 200 Breinigsville (18031) *(G-2025)*

R R Donnelley & Sons Company 717 295-4002
391 Steel Way Lancaster (17601) *(G-9183)*

R R Donnelley & Sons Company 215 671-9500
9985 Gantry Rd Philadelphia (19115) *(G-14225)*

R R Donnelley & Sons Company 814 266-6031
334 Bloomfield St Johnstown (15904) *(G-8428)*

R R Donnelley & Sons Company 215 564-3220
2 Logan Sq Ste 1800 Philadelphia (19103) *(G-14226)*

R R Donnelley & Sons Company 610 391-0203
700 Nestle Way Ste 200 Breinigsville (18031) *(G-2026)*

R R Donnelley & Sons Company 717 209-7700
1905 Horseshoe Rd Lancaster (17602) *(G-9184)*

R R Donnelley Financial, Pittsburgh *Also called RR Donnelley & Sons Company (G-15501)*

R R Pankratz Inc 610 696-1043
1241 Wrights Ln West Chester (19380) *(G-19627)*

R S Carlin Inc (PA) 814 387-4190
951 Fountain Rd Snow Shoe (16874) *(G-17670)*

R S Machine & Tool Inc 610 857-1644
Valley E Industrial Park Sadsburyville (19369) *(G-16906)*

R S Myers Welding 717 532-4714
402 S Washington St Shippensburg (17257) *(G-17543)*

R S Quality Products Inc 610 266-1916
719 Roboe Rd Ste 103 Allentown (18109) *(G-367)*

R S T, Friendsville *Also called Classic Shotshell Co Inc (G-6229)*

R S W Enterprises Inc 570 888-2184
1 Railroad St Milan (18831) *(G-11149)*

R Scheinert & Son Inc 215 673-9800
10092 Sandmeyer Ln Philadelphia (19116) *(G-14227)*

R T Callahan Machine Pdts Inc 215 256-8765
230 Stahl Rd Harleysville (19438) *(G-7054)*

R T Grim Co 717 761-4113
3925 Trindle Rd Camp Hill (17011) *(G-2513)*

R T I, Titusville *Also called Roser Technologies Inc (G-18393)*

R T R Business Products Inc 724 733-7373
5110 Old William Penn Hwy Export (15632) *(G-5622)*

R Vbridendolph & Sons Inc 717 328-3650
14144 Buchanan Trl W Mercersburg (17236) *(G-10994)*

R W Hartnett Company 215 969-9190
2055 Bennett Rd Philadelphia (19116) *(G-14228)*

R W Pefferle Inc 724 265-2764
91 Pennsylvania Ave Oakmont (15139) *(G-12925)*

R W Sidley Inc 724 794-4451
715 New Castle Rd Slippery Rock (16057) *(G-17625)*

R W Sidley Incorporated 724 755-0205
88 E Hillis St Youngwood (15697) *(G-20783)*

R W Sidley Incorporated 724 794-4451
715 New Castle Rd Slippery Rock (16057) *(G-17626)*

R Way Gasket & Supply Company 215 743-1650
1950 E Sedgley Ave Philadelphia (19124) *(G-14229)*

R&D Circuits Inc 610 443-2299
1660 E Race St Allentown (18109) *(G-368)*

R&D Interconnect Solutions, Allentown *Also called R&D Sockets Inc (G-369)*

R&D Sockets Inc 610 443-2299
1660 E Race St Unit B Allentown (18109) *(G-369)*

R&F Pallet Co 717 463-3560
Rr 1 Mifflintown (17059) *(G-11133)*

R&M American Marine Pdts Inc 352 345-4866
2100 Kitty Hawk Ave Philadelphia (19112) *(G-14230)*

R&M International, Pipersville *Also called Rwb Special Services Corp (G-14619)*

R&N Manufacturing LLC 412 778-4103
3500 Neville Rd Pittsburgh (15225) *(G-15464)*

R&R Machine Inc 724 286-9507
1440 Watering Trough Rd Rochester Mills (15771) *(G-16790)*

R&S Ventures LLC 610 532-2950
1015 Lincoln Ave Prospect Park (19076) *(G-16118)*

R-A-S Industries, Coatesville *Also called Saha Industries Inc (G-3325)*

R-G-T Plastics Company 814 683-2161
600 Penn St Linesville (16424) *(G-9986)*

R-V Industries Inc (PA) 610 273-2457
584 Poplar Rd Honey Brook (19344) *(G-7758)*

R-V Industries Inc 800 552-9980
435 Creamery Way Ste 100 Exton (19341) *(G-5726)*

R. J. Corman Railpower, Erie *Also called Railpower LLC (G-5453)*

R/W Connection Inc (HQ) 717 898-5257
936 Links Ave Landisville (17538) *(G-9266)*

R/W Connection Inc 717 767-3660
30 Aberdeen Rd Emigsville (17318) *(G-4998)*

Rabe Environmental Systems Inc 814 456-5374
2300 W 23rd St Erie (16506) *(G-5451)*

Racechairs LLC 267 632-5003
312 Harriet Dr Perkasie (18944) *(G-13291)*

Raceresq Inc 724 891-3473
1001 15th St Beaver Falls (15010) *(G-1010)*

Racetronics, Nazareth *Also called Gregory Racing Fabrications (G-11970)*

Raceway Beverage Center 724 695-3130
1242 Route 30 Imperial (15126) *(G-8075)*

Rackem Mfg LLC 570 226-6093
1301 Purdytown Tpke Hawley (18438) *(G-7442)*

Rackware Inc 408 430-5821
580 W Main St Ste D Trappe (19426) *(G-18472)*

Raco International LP 412 835-5744
3350 Industrial Blvd Bethel Park (15102) *(G-1430)*

Racoh Products Inc 814 486-3288
1751 Rich Valley Rd Emporium (15834) *(G-5073)*

RAD Mfg LLC (PA) 570 752-4514
531 Maple St Nescopeck (18635) *(G-12001)*

RAD Mfg LLC 570 752-4514
Maple St Nescopeck (18635) *(G-12002)*

Radiance 717 290-1517
9 W Grant St Lancaster (17603) *(G-9185)*

Radiancy Inc (HQ) 845 398-1647
2300 Computer Rd Ste G26 Willow Grove (19090) *(G-20138)*

Radiant Steel Products Company 570 322-7828
205 Locust St Williamsport (17701) *(G-20067)*

Radical Wine Company 610 365-7969
511 Mahoning Dr E Ste 1 Lehighton (18235) *(G-9723)*

Radio Communications, Eddystone *Also called Metroplitan Communications Inc (G-4805)*

Radio Parts Company 412 963-6202
650 Alpha Dr Pittsburgh (15238) *(G-15465)*

Radio-TV Interview Report, Broomall *Also called Bradley Communications Corp (G-2281)*

Radioshack, New Holland *Also called H & S Electronics (G-12250)*

Radius Corporation 484 646-9122
40 Willow St Kutztown (19530) *(G-8858)*

Radius Systems LLC 610 388-9940
101 Ponds Edge Dr Ste 201 Chadds Ford (19317) *(G-2859)*

Rado Enterprises Inc 570 759-0303
4441 Red Rock Rd Benton (17814) *(G-1281)*

Rae Foods Inc 716 326-7437
8719 Windy Ln North East (16428) *(G-12755)*

RAF Industries Inc (PA) 215 572-0738
165 Township Line Rd # 2100 Jenkintown (19046) *(G-8299)*

Raff Printing Inc 412 431-4044
2201 Mary St Pittsburgh (15203) *(G-15466)*

Rage Bulk Systems Ltd 215 489-5373
607 Airport Blvd Doylestown (18902) *(G-4333)*

Ragnasoft Inc 866 471-2001
117 S West End Ave Ste 12 Lancaster (17603) *(G-9186)*

Rahn's Construction Material, Coopersburg *Also called H Y K Construction Co Inc (G-3628)*

Rahns Construction Material Co 610 584-8500
430 Rahns Rd Collegeville (19426) *(G-3390)*

Rail Car Service Co (PA) 724 662-3660
584 Fairground Rd Mercer (16137) *(G-10970)*

Rail Ryder LLC (PA) 814 873-1623
2155 Norcross Rd Erie (16510) *(G-5452)*

Rail Transit Products Inc 724 527-2386
901 S Railroad St Penn (15675) *(G-13227)*

Railpower LLC 814 835-2212
2011 Peninsula Dr Erie (16506) *(G-5453)*

Railway Specialties Corp 215 788-9242
2979 State Rd Croydon (19021) *(G-3926)*

Rainbow Awnings Inc 610 534-5380
620 Grant Rd Folcroft (19032) *(G-6014)*

Rainbow Graphics Inc 724 228-3007
105 Dolson St Bentleyville (15314) *(G-1275)*

Rainbow Mills, Pittsburgh *Also called Dualsun International Inc (G-14939)*

Rainbow Vision Stained GL Ctr 717 657-9737
3105 Walnut St Harrisburg (17109) *(G-7204)*

Raineater LLC 814 806-3100
2420 W 23rd St Erie (16506) *(G-5454)*

Rajant Corporation (PA) 484 595-0233
200 Chesterfield Pkwy Malvern (19355) *(G-10307)*

Rakoczy Industries Inc 412 389-3123
125 W Pike St Ste 3 Canonsburg (15317) *(G-2622)*

Ralph A Hiller Company 724 325-1200
6005 Enterprise Dr Export (15632) *(G-5623)*

Ralph Good Inc (PA) 717 484-4884
306 E Main St Adamstown (19501) *(G-23)*

Ralph Good Inc 610 367-2253
860 Sweinhart Rd Boyertown (19512) *(G-1925)*

Ralph McClure 610 738-1440
1500 Mcdaniel Dr Reynoldsville (15851) *(G-16662)*

Ralph Stuck Lumber Company 570 539-8666
684 Maneval Rd Mount Pleasant Mills (17853) *(G-11731)*

Rals Run Ranch, Tionesta *Also called Anderson Family Farm Inc (G-18369)*

Ralston Shop Inc 610 268-3829
Old Rte 1 And Rte 41 Avondale (19311) *(G-858)*

Ram Cat Farms, Confluence *Also called Jerry G Martin (G-3467)*

Ram Forest Products Inc 814 697-7185
Honeoye Rd Shinglehouse (16748) *(G-17512)*

Ram Industrial Services LLC 717 232-4414
2850 Appleton St Ste D Camp Hill (17011) *(G-2514)*

Ram Instrumentation, Union City *Also called Cory Reservior Testing Inc (G-18606)*

A
L
P
H
A
B
E
T
I
C

Ram Precision Inc 215 674-0663
405 Caredean Dr Ste A Horsham (19044) **(G-7843)**

Ram Technologies Inc 215 654-8810
275 Commerce Dr Ste 100 Fort Washington (19034) **(G-6089)**

Ram Tool Co Inc 814 382-1842
195 N 3rd St Conneaut Lake (16316) **(G-3478)**

Ram-Wood Custom Cabinetry LLC 717 242-6357
6395 Belle Ave Ste 1 Lewistown (17044) **(G-9945)**

Ramac Industries Inc 814 456-6159
1624 Cranberry St Erie (16502) **(G-5455)**

Rampmaster, Coatesville *Also called General Transervice Inc* **(G-3304)**

Rampmaster, Coatesville *Also called Global Capital Corp* **(G-3305)**

Ramsay Machine Development 610 395-4764
4017 Hampshire Ct Allentown (18104) **(G-370)**

Ranbar Electrical Mtls LLC 724 864-8200
408 Mnr Harrison City Rd Harrison City (15636) **(G-7251)**

Rancatore & Lavender Inc 412 829-7456
1727 Lincoln Hwy North Versailles (15137) **(G-12782)**

Rand 2339 Haverford LP 215 620-6993
50 Hood Rd Ardmore (19003) **(G-714)**

Randall A Reese 570 748-6528
7 E Main St Lock Haven (17745) **(G-10091)**

Randall Inds Ltd Liablility Co 814 743-6630
4565 Hemlock Rd Cherry Tree (15724) **(G-3035)**

Randall Industries LLC 412 281-6901
1801 Centre Ave Ste 300 Pittsburgh (15219) **(G-15467)**

Randall Lesso 724 746-2100
123 S Main St Houston (15342) **(G-7878)**

Randall Publications 610 871-1427
6047 Adams Ln Allentown (18109) **(G-371)**

Randolph Manufacturing Corp 610 253-9626
4 Danforth Dr Easton (18045) **(G-4747)**

Randy Brensinger 610 562-2184
149 Pine St Hamburg (19526) **(G-6851)**

Randy George Wdwkg Cstm Signs 724 514-7201
227 Smithfield St Canonsburg (15317) **(G-2623)**

Randy Larkin 814 358-2508
217 Main St Callensburg (16213) **(G-2465)**

Range Operating Co, Scottdale *Also called Range Rsurces - Appalachia LLC* **(G-17198)**

Range Operating Company, Yatesboro *Also called Range Rsurces - Appalachia LLC* **(G-20348)**

Range Resources 570 858-1200
80 Hillside Ave Bradford (16701) **(G-1989)**

Range Rsurces - Appalachia LLC 724 887-5715
156 Mill Ln Scottdale (15683) **(G-17198)**

Range Rsurces - Appalachia LLC 724 783-7144
150 4th Ave N Yatesboro (16263) **(G-20348)**

Range Rsurces - Appalachia LLC (HQ) 724 743-6700
3000 Town Center Blvd Canonsburg (15317) **(G-2624)**

Range Rsurces - Appalachia LLC 817 870-2601
1369 Cochranton Rd Carlton (16311) **(G-2753)**

Ransome Idealease LLC 215 639-4300
2975 Galloway Rd Bensalem (19020) **(G-1248)**

Raphael A Ingaglio 570 289-5000
87 Greenwood St Hop Bottom (18824) **(G-7775)**

Rapid Granulator Inc (HQ) 724 584-5220
555 W Park Rd Leetsdale (15056) **(G-9702)**

Rapid Granulator Inc 814 437-6861
455 Allegheny Blvd Franklin (16323) **(G-6154)**

Rapid Learning Institute 877 792-2172
435 Devon Park Dr Ste 510 Wayne (19087) **(G-19368)**

Rapid Mold Solutions Inc (PA) 814 833-2721
4820 Pacific Ave Erie (16506) **(G-5456)**

Rapid Pathogen Screening Inc 718 288-4318
416 Vandine Rd Montoursville (17754) **(G-11449)**

Rapid Reaction Inc 814 432-9832
1618 Debence Dr Franklin (16323) **(G-6155)**

Rapid Recycling Inc (HQ) 610 650-0737
5 Brower Ave Oaks (19456) **(G-12936)**

Rapid Tag & Wire Co 724 452-7760
133 Eckert Stop Rd Fombell (16123) **(G-6034)**

Rapid Tpc LLC 412 450-0482
6945 Lynn Way Pittsburgh (15208) **(G-15468)**

Ras Sports Inc 814 833-9111
2670 W 11th St Erie (16505) **(G-5457)**

Raser Industries Inc 610 320-5130
1630 N 9th St Ste 1 Reading (19604) **(G-16484)**

Rasley Enterprise 610 588-9520
905 Lower South Main St Bangor (18013) **(G-925)**

Raster Manufacturing LLC 724 837-7354
609 Richfield Ct Greensburg (15601) **(G-6710)**

Ratchet Rake LLC 717 249-1228
405 N East St Carlisle (17013) **(G-2734)**

Raucmin Seven LLC 412 374-1420
4051 William Penn Hwy Monroeville (15146) **(G-11352)**

Rausch Creek Land LP (PA) 570 682-4600
978 Gap St Valley View (17983) **(G-18717)**

Ravago Americas LLC 215 591-9641
554 Ellington Ct Ambler (19002) **(G-601)**

Raven Industries Inc 724 539-8230
5049 Center Dr Latrobe (15650) **(G-9516)**

Ravine Inc 814 946-5006
610 7th St Altoona (16602) **(G-541)**

Rawlee Fuels LLC 724 349-3320
555 Philadelphia St Indiana (15701) **(G-8123)**

Ray Burial Vault Company Inc 814 684-0104
N3 N 3 Miles Rr 220 Tyrone (16686) **(G-18591)**

Ray Derstine 215 723-6573
76 Hunsberger Rd Telford (18969) **(G-18311)**

Ray-Guard International Ltd (PA) 215 543-3849
280 N Hanover St Pottstown (19464) **(G-16038)**

Rayco Process Services Inc 717 464-2572
3551 Willow Street Pike N Willow Street (17584) **(G-20155)**

Raycom Electronics Inc (HQ) 717 292-3641
1 Raycom Rd Dover (17315) **(G-4203)**

Raymond Dunn 412 734-2135
109 Seville Ave Pittsburgh (15214) **(G-15469)**

Raymond Sherman Co Inc 610 272-4640
1304 Conshohocken Rd # 160 Conshohocken (19428) **(G-3597)**

Raytec LLC (PA) 717 445-0510
544 Gristmill Rd Ephrata (17522) **(G-5138)**

Raytec Fabricating LLC 717 355-5333
3340 Division Hwy New Holland (17557) **(G-12278)**

Raytec Manufacturing, Ephrata *Also called Raytec LLC* **(G-5138)**

Raytheon Company 717 267-4200
1 Letterkenny Army Depot Chambersburg (17201) **(G-2972)**

Raytheon Company 814 278-2256
302 Science Park Rd State College (16803) **(G-18012)**

Razzy Fresh Frz Yogurt Forbes 412 586-5270
3533 Forbes Ave Pittsburgh (15213) **(G-15470)**

RB Concepts LLC 484 351-8211
1100 E Hector St Ste 220 Conshohocken (19428) **(G-3598)**

RB Distribution Inc 215 997-1800
3400 E Walnut St Colmar (18915) **(G-3419)**

RB Farms Inc 570 842-7246
Sandy Beach Rd Moscow (18444) **(G-11602)**

Rbna Fluid Exchange Inc 717 840-0678
10 Innovation Dr York (17402) **(G-20651)**

Rbs Fab Inc 717 566-9513
230 N Hoernerstown Rd Hummelstown (17036) **(G-7923)**

RBS Impex Inc 412 566-2488
717 Liberty Ave Ste 414 Pittsburgh (15222) **(G-15471)**

Rbw Technologies, Evans City *Also called Spadre Investments Inc* **(G-5564)**

RC & Design Company 484 626-1216
180 James Ln Lehighton (18235) **(G-9724)**

RC Cement Co Inc 610 866-4400
100 Brodhead Rd Ste 230 Bethlehem (18017) **(G-1607)**

RC Concrete Inc 724 947-9005
N Of Burgettstown Rr 18 Burgettstown (15021) **(G-2353)**

RC Lonestar Inc (HQ) 610 882-5000
100 Brodhead Rd Ste 230 Bethlehem (18017) **(G-1608)**

RC Machine, Titusville *Also called Ronald Copeland* **(G-18392)**

Rcd Technology Inc 215 529-9440
670 Pineville Rd Newtown (18940) **(G-12542)**

RCP, New Castle *Also called Richardson Coolg Packages LLC* **(G-12142)**

Rdp Technologies Inc 610 650-9900
960 Brook Rd Ste 8 Conshohocken (19428) **(G-3599)**

Rdy Gutters Plus LLC 610 488-5666
60 Paddock Dr Bernville (19506) **(G-1304)**

RE Gas Development LLC 814 278-7267
366 Walker Dr State College (16801) **(G-18013)**

RE Pack Inc 215 699-9252
500 N Cannon Ave Lansdale (19446) **(G-9403)**

RE Uptegraff Mfg Co LLC 724 887-7700
120 Uptegraff Dr Scottdale (15683) **(G-17199)**

Re2 Inc 412 681-6382
4925 Harrison St Pittsburgh (15201) **(G-15472)**

REA Jobber Inc (PA) 814 226-9552
204 Grand Ave Clarion (16214) **(G-3186)**

Reaction Chemicals 610 838-5496
3767 Elm Ter Hellertown (18055) **(G-7561)**

Reaction Nutrition LLC 412 276-7800
230 E Main St Carnegie (15106) **(G-2784)**

Reaction Orthotics 717 609-2361
405 N East St Ste 110 Carlisle (17013) **(G-2735)**

Readco Kurimoto LLC 717 848-2801
460 Grim Ln York (17406) **(G-20652)**

Reading Alloys Inc 610 693-5822
220 Old West Penn Ave Robesonia (19551) **(G-16777)**

Reading Anthracite Company (PA) 570 622-5150
200 Mahantongo St Pottsville (17901) **(G-16093)**

Reading Bakery Systems Inc (PA) 610 693-5816
380 Old West Penn Ave Robesonia (19551) **(G-16778)**

Reading Box Company Inc 610 374-2080
250 Blair Ave Reading (19601) **(G-16485)**

Reading City Police Department, Reading *Also called Futernal Order Police Lodge* **(G-16386)**

Reading Coml Heat Treating Co 610 376-3994
320 Greenwich St Reading (19601) **(G-16486)**

Reading Draft Birch Co 610 372-2565
614 Gregg Ave Reading (19611) *(G-16487)*
Reading Eagle Company (PA) 610 371-5000
345 Penn St Reading (19601) *(G-16488)*
Reading Eagle Company 610 371-5180
340 Court St Reading (19601) *(G-16489)*
Reading Eagle Press, Reading *Also called Reading Eagle Company (G-16488)*
Reading Eagle Press, Reading *Also called Reading Eagle Company (G-16489)*
Reading Electric Motor Svc Inc 610 929-5777
80 Witman Rd Reading (19605) *(G-16490)*
Reading Equipment & Dist LLC 717 445-6746
1704 Rockwell Rd Abington (19001) *(G-14)*
Reading Fracture Inc 570 628-2308
200 Mahantongo St Pottsville (17901) *(G-16094)*
Reading Plastic Machining & FA, Reading *Also called Polyfab Corporation (G-16472)*
Reading Plastic Products Inc 610 779-3128
101 Elm St Reading Station (19606) *(G-16573)*
Reading Precast Inc 610 926-5000
5494 Pottsville Pike Leesport (19533) *(G-9673)*
Reading Reading Books LLC 757 329-4224
508 Quaker Hill Rd Morgantown (19543) *(G-11532)*
Reading Refractories Company 610 375-4422
1 Bala Ave Ste 310 Bala Cynwyd (19004) *(G-890)*
Reading Soda Works & Carbonic 610 372-2565
614 Gregg Ave Reading (19611) *(G-16491)*
Reading Thermal Systems Inc 610 678-5890
7 Corporate Blvd Reading (19608) *(G-16492)*
Reading Truck Body LLC (HQ) 610 775-3301
201 Hancock Blvd Reading (19611) *(G-16493)*
Ready Aim Fire, Philadelphia *Also called Tafisco Inc (G-14368)*
Ready Food Products Inc 215 824-2800
10975 Dutton Rd Philadelphia (19154) *(G-14231)*
Ready Set Live Inc 215 953-1509
15 E Myrtle Ave Feasterville Trevose (19053) *(G-5928)*
Ready Training Inc 717 366-4253
222 Old Hershey Rd Elizabethtown (17022) *(G-4883)*
Ready Training Online, Elizabethtown *Also called Ready Training Inc (G-4883)*
Real Automotive Pc Inc 609 876-7450
73 Chestnut Rd Paoli (19301) *(G-13148)*
Real English Foods Inc 610 863-9091
10 E Bell Ave Pen Argyl (18072) *(G-13215)*
Real Estate Book South Cent 814 943-8110
206 6th Ave Altoona (16602) *(G-542)*
Real Estate Marketing Services, Easton *Also called Easton Photoworks Inc (G-4671)*
Real Scent 717 692-0527
667 Wert Rd Millersburg (17061) *(G-11199)*
Realco Diversified Inc 814 638-0800
3688 Bailey Rd Cochranton (16314) *(G-3349)*
Realm Therapeutics Inc (PA) 484 321-2700
267 Great Valley Pkwy Malvern (19355) *(G-10308)*
Ream Printing Co Inc 717 764-5663
515 Farmbrook Ln York (17406) *(G-20653)*
Rear Dock, Irwin *Also called Crisp Control Inc (G-8153)*
Rearden Steel Fabrication Inc 717 503-1989
100 Market St Lemoyne (17043) *(G-9750)*
Rearick Tooling Inc/Jit, Apollo *Also called Jit Global Enterprises LLC (G-679)*
Reaxis Inc 412 517-6070
941 Robinson Hwy Mc Donald (15057) *(G-10580)*
Rebco Inc 814 885-8035
650 Brandy Camp Rd Kersey (15846) *(G-8568)*
Rebco Machining Inc 215 957-5133
403 Lincoln Ave Hatboro (19040) *(G-7299)*
Rebecca J'S Gourmet, Glenshaw *Also called Remarkable Designs Inc (G-6499)*
Rebecca Wilson Ltd Lblty Co 973 670-7089
2159 White St Ste 3 York (17404) *(G-20654)*
Rebel Indian Smoke Shop 610 499-1711
4101 Edgmont Ave Brookhaven (19015) *(G-2247)*
Rebling Plastics, Warrington *Also called Rocal Corporation (G-19132)*
Rebs Pallet Co Inc 570 386-5516
645 Pine Hill Rd Andreas (18211) *(G-640)*
Rebtech Corporation 570 421-6616
140 N 2nd St Stroudsburg (18360) *(G-18138)*
Rebus Inc 610 459-1597
595 Dilworthtown Rd West Chester (19382) *(G-19628)*
Recathco LLC 412 487-1482
2855 Oxford Blvd Allison Park (15101) *(G-461)*
Reccare Incorporated 215 886-0880
923 E Ellet St Philadelphia (19150) *(G-14232)*
Recirculation Technologies LLC 215 682-7099
550 Pinetown Rd Ste 210 Fort Washington (19034) *(G-6090)*
Reckitt Benckiser LLC 717 506-0165
360 Independence Ave Mechanicsburg (17055) *(G-10883)*
Reclamation Inc 814 265-2564
1915 Fermantown Rd Brockway (15824) *(G-2233)*
Reclamation Brewing Company 724 282-0831
221 S Main St Butler (16001) *(G-2437)*
Reclamere Inc 814 684-5505
905 Pennsylvania Ave Tyrone (16686) *(G-18592)*

Recognition Engraving (PA) 717 242-1166
100 S Main St Lewistown (17044) *(G-9946)*
Recoil Inc 814 623-3921
170 Transport St Bedford (15522) *(G-1072)*
Recon Enterprises 570 836-1179
3971 Sr 6 Tunkhannock (18657) *(G-18548)*
Recon Publications 215 843-4256
431 W Rittenhouse St Philadelphia (19144) *(G-14233)*
Record Herald Publishing Co (HQ) 717 762-2151
30 Walnut St Waynesboro (17268) *(G-19422)*
Recovery Environment Inc 717 625-0040
324 North Ln Lititz (17543) *(G-10037)*
Recovery Networks Inc 215 809-1300
4747 S Broad St Ste 232 Philadelphia (19112) *(G-14234)*
Recreation Resource Usa LLC 610 444-4402
425 Mcfarlan Rd Ste 100 Kennett Square (19348) *(G-8538)*
Recro Pharma Inc (PA) 484 395-2470
490 Lapp Rd Malvern (19355) *(G-10309)*
Recycled Oil 610 250-8747
1600 S 25th St Easton (18042) *(G-4748)*
Recycled Pallets 717 754-3114
224 Blue Mountain Rd Schuylkill Haven (17972) *(G-17165)*
Recycled Pallets Inc 724 657-6978
1603 Hanna St New Castle (16102) *(G-12141)*
Recycling Tech Intl LLC 717 633-9008
76 Acco Dr York (17402) *(G-20655)*
Red, Bedford *Also called Revoltnary Elctrnic Design LLC (G-1073)*
Red Associates 215 722-4895
605 Allengrove St Philadelphia (19120) *(G-14235)*
Red Bandana Co (PA) 215 744-3144
3801 Castor Ave Philadelphia (19124) *(G-14236)*
Red Bank Welding 570 966-0695
53 Red Bank Rd Mifflinburg (17844) *(G-11101)*
Red Devil Brakes Inc 724 696-3744
1378 Old State Route 119 Mount Pleasant (15666) *(G-11712)*
Red Flag Media Inc 215 625-9850
1032 Arch St Fl 3 Philadelphia (19107) *(G-14237)*
Red Gravel Partners LLC 570 445-3553
219 N Main St Scranton (18504) *(G-17278)*
Red Hill Grinding Wheel Corp 215 679-7964
335 Dotts St Pennsburg (18073) *(G-13255)*
Red Lion Manufacturing Inc 717 767-6511
20 Willow Springs Cir York (17406) *(G-20656)*
Red Mill Farms LLC 570 457-2400
591 Rocky Glen Rd Moosic (18507) *(G-11513)*
RED Orthodontic Lab 610 237-1100
906 Mitchell Farm Ln Kennett Square (19348) *(G-8539)*
Red Orthodontic Laboratories, Kennett Square *Also called RED Orthodontic Lab (G-8539)*
Red Rose Cabinetry 717 625-4456
740 Rothsville Rd Lititz (17543) *(G-10038)*
Red Rose Screen Prtg Awrds Inc 717 625-1581
30 Wright Ave Lititz (17543) *(G-10039)*
Red Square Corp 412 422-8631
1722 Murray Ave Fl 2 Pittsburgh (15217) *(G-15473)*
Red Strings Holographics, Warminster *Also called Finish Tech Corp (G-18878)*
Red Strings Holographics, Warminster *Also called Finish Tech Corp (G-18879)*
Red Valve Company Inc (HQ) 412 279-0044
600 N Bell Ave Ste 300 Carnegie (15106) *(G-2785)*
Red Valve Company Inc 412 279-0044
500 N Bell Ave Carnegie (15106) *(G-2786)*
Redco Foods Inc (HQ) 800 556-6674
1 Hansen Is Bethlehem (18017) *(G-1609)*
Reddog Industries Inc (PA) 814 898-4321
2012 E 33rd St Erie (16510) *(G-5458)*
Redland Brick Inc 412 828-8046
230 Rich Hill Rd Cheswick (15024) *(G-3117)*
Redland Brick Inc Harmar Plant, Cheswick *Also called Redland Brick Inc (G-3117)*
Redmonds Ready Mix Inc 814 776-1437
Johnsonburg Rd Ridgway (15853) *(G-16726)*
Redner's Warehouse Market 85, Allentown *Also called Redners Markets Inc (G-372)*
Redners Markets Inc 610 678-2900
4870 Penn Ave Reading (19608) *(G-16494)*
Redners Markets Inc 610 776-2726
1201 Airport Rd Allentown (18109) *(G-372)*
Redstar Ironworks LLC 412 821-3630
2 Sedgwick St Pittsburgh (15209) *(G-15474)*
Redstone Corporation 321 213-2135
469 Airport Rd Hngr 9 Johnstown (15904) *(G-8429)*
Redstone International Inc 724 439-1500
1200 E National Pike Scenery Hill (15360) *(G-17125)*
Reece Lighting & Prod LLC 215 460-8560
245 Radcliffe St Fl 2 Bristol (19007) *(G-2193)*
Reecon North America LLC 412 850-8001
2515 Liberty Ave Pittsburgh (15222) *(G-15475)*
Reed & Witting Company 412 682-1000
2900 Sassafras Way Pittsburgh (15201) *(G-15476)*
Reed Associates Inc 215 256-9572
1500 Industry Rd Ste P Hatfield (19440) *(G-7389)*
Reed Drabick Inc 215 794-2068
3771 Sablewood Dr Doylestown (18902) *(G-4334)*

ALPHABETIC

Reed Drabick Publishers, Doylestown *Also called Reed Drabick Inc* **(G-4334)**
Reed Manufacturing Company (PA) 814 452-3691
1425 W 8th St Erie (16502) **(G-5459)**
Reed Micro Automation Inc 814 941-0225
3900 Industrial Park Dr # 6 Altoona (16602) **(G-543)**
Reed Minerals, Mechanicsburg *Also called Harsco Corporation* **(G-10851)**
Reed Minerals 215 295-8675
905 Steel Rd S Fairless Hills (19030) **(G-5794)**
Reed Sign Company 215 679-5066
1050 Main St Pennsburg (18073) **(G-13256)**
Reed Tech & Info Svcs Inc (HQ) 215 441-6400
7 Walnut Grove Dr Horsham (19044) **(G-7844)**
Reed Tool & Die Inc 724 547-3500
1643 Pleasant Valley Rd Mount Pleasant (15666) **(G-11713)**
Reefer Parts, York *Also called Klinge Corporation* **(G-20556)**
Reese Daryl C Wallpapering 717 597-2532
9984 Browns Mill Rd Greencastle (17225) **(G-6629)**
Reese's Print Shop, Lock Haven *Also called Randall A Reese* **(G-10091)**
Reeser Bros 717 266-6644
905 Pleasant Grove Rd York Haven (17370) **(G-20761)**
Reeser Bros Concrete, York Haven *Also called Reeser Bros* **(G-20761)**
Reeves Awning Inc 570 876-0350
623 Lincoln Ave Jermyn (18433) **(G-8309)**
Refined Outoor Lvng Envirnmnts 412 635-8440
2130 Reis Run Rd Pittsburgh (15237) **(G-15477)**
Refined Pallet 570 238-9455
1406 Breon Rd Middleburg (17842) **(G-11037)**
Refractory Machining Services 724 285-7674
610 E Butler Rd Butler (16002) **(G-2438)**
Refresco Beverages US Inc 484 840-4800
20 Aldan Ave Glen Mills (19342) **(G-6441)**
Refrigeration Care & Ice, Canonsburg *Also called Refrigeration Care Inc* **(G-2625)**
Refrigeration Care Inc 724 746-1525
111 Orchard Ave Canonsburg (15317) **(G-2625)**
Regal Cast Inc 717 270-1888
307 N 9th Ave Lebanon (17046) **(G-9625)**
Regal Sales and Marketing, Ardmore *Also called Rgl Distributors LLC* **(G-715)**
Regasol, Stroudsburg *Also called Ritter Group Usa Inc* **(G-18140)**
Regency Energy Partners LP 610 687-8900
100 W Matsonford Rd 3-301 Wayne (19087) **(G-19369)**
Regency Infographics, Philadelphia *Also called Regency Typographic Svcs Inc* **(G-14238)**
Regency Plus Inc 570 339-1390
2000 Locust Gap Hwy Mount Carmel (17851) **(G-11629)**
Regency Typographic Svcs Inc 215 425-8810
2867 E Allegheny Ave Philadelphia (19134) **(G-14238)**
Regenex Corporation 724 528-5900
1 New St West Middlesex (16159) **(G-19728)**
Regina Farms, East Stroudsburg *Also called Edward T Regina* **(G-4614)**
Registry For Excellence, Wrightsville *Also called Donsco Inc* **(G-20236)**
Rego Precision Machine LLC 610 434-1582
671 E Allen St Allentown (18109) **(G-373)**
Regupol America LLC (HQ) 717 675-2198
11 Ritter Way Lebanon (17042) **(G-9626)**
Reh Holdings Inc (PA) 717 843-0021
150 S Sumner St York (17404) **(G-20657)**
Reha Technology Usa Inc 267 419-8690
5209 Militia Hill Rd # 102 Plymouth Meeting (19462) **(G-15867)**
Rehmeyer Precision Mllwk Inc 717 235-0607
6 Onion Blvd Shrewsbury (17361) **(G-17587)**
Rehoboth Signs 717 458-8520
5221 Simpson Ferry Rd Mechanicsburg (17050) **(G-10884)**
Rehrig Pacific Company 814 455-8023
1738 W 20th St Erie (16502) **(G-5460)**
Reichdrill LLC 814 342-5500
99 Troy Hawk Run Hwy Philipsburg (16866) **(G-14525)**
Reid S Tannery 610 929-4403
2052 Lucon Rd Reading (19605) **(G-16495)**
Reidler Decal Corporation 800 628-7770
264 Industrial Park Rd Saint Clair (17970) **(G-16939)**
Reiff & Nestor Company (PA) 717 453-7113
50 Reiff St W Lykens (17048) **(G-10134)**
Reiff Metal Fabrications 717 445-7050
451 Weaverland Valley Rd East Earl (17519) **(G-4554)**
Reilly Finishing Technologies, Nanticoke *Also called Reilly Plating Company Inc* **(G-11902)**
Reilly Foam Corp (PA) 610 834-1900
751 5th Ave King of Prussia (19406) **(G-8668)**
Reilly Plating Company Inc 570 735-7777
130 Alden Rd Nanticoke (18634) **(G-11902)**
Reiner Associates Inc 717 647-7454
22 S Yohe St Tower City (17980) **(G-18440)**
Reinert & Sons Inc 215 781-8311
5800 Elwood Ave Ste A Bristol (19007) **(G-2194)**
Reinhardt Awning Co 610 965-2544
550 Dalton St Emmaus (18049) **(G-5041)**
Reining Force Products, Beach Lake *Also called W J Reining & Sons Inc* **(G-976)**
Reino's Design Print Mail, Malvern *Also called No Fear Inc* **(G-10287)**
Reisingers Precision Polsg LLC 814 763-2226
19881 S Mosiertown Rd Saegertown (16433) **(G-16931)**

Reist Popcorn Company (PA) 717 653-8078
113 Manheim St Mount Joy (17552) **(G-11669)**
Reist Precision Machine Inc 717 606-3166
156 N Donnerville Rd Mountville (17554) **(G-11801)**
Reitnouer Inc 610 929-4856
5 E Point Dr Birdsboro (19508) **(G-1704)**
Reitnouer Trailers, Birdsboro *Also called Reitnouer Inc* **(G-1704)**
Rejniaks Alpaca 724 265-4062
1187 Logan Rd Gibsonia (15044) **(G-6349)**
Rekord Printing Co 570 648-3231
1 Madison Ave Elysburg (17824) **(G-4980)**
Rel-Tek Corporation 412 373-4417
4185 Old William Penn Hwy Monroeville (15146) **(G-11353)**
Relay Shoe Company LLC 610 970-6450
18 W Lightcap Rd Pottstown (19464) **(G-16039)**
Reliable Equipment Mfg, Warminster *Also called Reliable Equipment Mfg Co* **(G-18951)**
Reliable Equipment Mfg Co 215 357-7015
101 Steam Whistle Dr Warminster (18974) **(G-18951)**
Reliable Products Inc 215 860-2011
110 Terry Dr Ste 200 Newtown (18940) **(G-12543)**
Reliable Products Intl LLC 717 261-1291
218 N Main St Mercersburg (17236) **(G-10995)**
Reliable Rubber Products Co, Bensalem *Also called C E Conover & Co Inc* **(G-1164)**
Reliable Sign & Striping Inc 610 767-8090
301 Chestnut St Slatington (18080) **(G-17612)**
Reliance Packaging & Supply Co 724 468-8849
2963 Route 66 Export (15632) **(G-5624)**
Reliance Paragon Paper Box 215 743-1231
2070 Wheatsheaf Ln Philadelphia (19124) **(G-14239)**
Reliance Well Services LLC (PA) 814 454-1644
510 Cranberry St Ste 230 Erie (16507) **(G-5461)**
Relianology International Ltd 412 607-1503
3421 Chapel Hill Ct Export (15632) **(G-5625)**
Reliant Molding Inc 814 756-5522
10525 Crosby Cir Cranesville (16410) **(G-3869)**
Reliant Systems LLC 412 496-2580
6 3rd St Irwin (15642) **(G-8196)**
Reliefband Technologies LLC 877 735-2263
220 Gibraltar Rd Fl 2 Horsham (19044) **(G-7845)**
Religious Theological Abstract 717 866-6734
100 W Park Ave Myerstown (17067) **(G-11896)**
Relx Inc 610 964-4516
201 King Of Prussia Rd Radnor (19087) **(G-16300)**
Relyence Corporation 724 433-1909
145 Weavers Rd Greensburg (15601) **(G-6711)**
Remanufacturing Center, Middletown *Also called Mack Trucks Inc* **(G-11064)**
Remanufacturing Division, Hanover *Also called R H Sheppard Co Inc* **(G-6942)**
Remarkable Designs Inc 412 512-6564
1216 Willow St Glenshaw (15116) **(G-6499)**
Remcal Products Corporation 215 343-5500
2068 Bunnell Rd Warrington (18976) **(G-19130)**
Remcon Plastics Inc 610 376-2666
208 Chestnut St Reading (19602) **(G-16496)**
Remilux LLC 717 737-7120
2500 Gettysburg Rd # 101 Camp Hill (17011) **(G-2515)**
Remindermedia, King of Prussia *Also called Digital Grapes LLC* **(G-8610)**
Remington Lamp Company, Camp Hill *Also called Remilux LLC* **(G-2515)**
Remington Pallets & Crates 814 749-7557
1452 Pyer Rd Vintondale (15961) **(G-18769)**
Remmey Pallet Co 570 658-7575
3685 Sawmill Rd Beaver Springs (17812) **(G-1021)**
Remmey The Pallet Company, Lehighton *Also called Donald B Remmey Inc* **(G-9711)**
Remmey The Pallet Company, Lehighton *Also called Donald B Remmey Inc* **(G-9712)**
Remote Remotes 215 420-7934
420 Dresher Rd Ste 400 Horsham (19044) **(G-7846)**
Renaissance Art Gallery, Berwyn *Also called Image Makers Art Inc* **(G-1365)**
Renaissance Conservators, Leola *Also called Advanced Building Products* **(G-9766)**
Renaissance Glassworks Inc 724 969-9009
3311 Washington Rd Canonsburg (15317) **(G-2626)**
Renaissance Nutrition Inc (PA) 814 793-2113
339 Frederick Rd Roaring Spring (16673) **(G-16767)**
Renaissance Press Inc 717 534-0708
1071 Stoney Run Rd Hummelstown (17036) **(G-7924)**
Renaissance Ssa LLC 267 685-0340
411 S State St Ste E100 Newtown (18940) **(G-12544)**
Renal Ntrtn Intrathecal Pumps, Upper Chichester *Also called Pentec Health Inc* **(G-18670)**
Renal Solutions Inc (HQ) 724 772-6900
770 Commonwealth Dr Warrendale (15086) **(G-19095)**
Renaptys Vaccines LLC 917 620-2256
113 W Chestnut Hill Ave # 9 Philadelphia (19118) **(G-14240)**
Rendulic Packing Company 412 678-9541
800 Morange Ave McKeesport (15132) **(G-10679)**
Renee Awad ND 717 875-3056
259 N 6th St Columbia (17512) **(G-3448)**
Reneer Films, Auburn *Also called Omnova Solutions Inc* **(G-820)**
Renees Cold Cut Hut 570 215-0057
103 Berwick St White Haven (18661) **(G-19852)**

2019 Harris Pennsylvania
Manufacturers Directory

(G-0000) Company's Geographic Section entry number

Renegade Winery LLC 570 664-6626
600 Main St Stroudsburg (18360) ***(G-18139)***
Renerva LLC 412 841-7966
217 Vine St Pittsburgh (15218) ***(G-15478)***
Renewal Kombucha LLC 484 525-3575
200 Leaman St Lititz (17543) ***(G-10040)***
Renewal Processing Inc 570 838-3838
10705 State Route 44 Watsontown (17777) ***(G-19280)***
Renmatix Inc (PA) 484 681-9246
660 Allendale Rd King of Prussia (19406) ***(G-8669)***
Renningers Cabinetree Inc 570 726-6494
225 Long Run Rd Mill Hall (17751) ***(G-11181)***
Renovo Rail Industries LLC (PA) 570 923-2093
504 Erie Ave Renovo (17764) ***(G-16649)***
Rent-A-Center Inc 724 845-1070
397 Hyde Park Rd Ste B Leechburg (15656) ***(G-9652)***
Rental World, Royersford *Also called Kruppko Inc* ***(G-16856)***
Renu Labs Inc 215 675-5227
1836 Stout Dr Ste 5 Warminster (18974) ***(G-18952)***
REO & Sons Fuels LLC 267 374-6400
690 Mine Rd Quakertown (18951) ***(G-16241)***
Replica I, Philadelphia *Also called S G Business Services Inc* ***(G-14271)***
Replicant Metals 717 626-1618
330 Snavely Mill Rd Lititz (17543) ***(G-10041)***
Reporter, The, Lansdale *Also called Journal Register Company* ***(G-9382)***
Repperts Candy 610 689-9200
2708 W Philadelphia Ave Oley (19547) ***(G-12980)***
Reprint Management Services, York *Also called Ficore Incorporated* ***(G-20480)***
Repro Center, Philadelphia *Also called Brilliant Inc* ***(G-13482)***
Repsol Oil & Gas Usa LLC 724 814-5300
50 Pennwood Pl Warrendale (15086) ***(G-19096)***
Republic Lens Co Inc 610 588-7867
1683 Valley View Dr Bangor (18013) ***(G-926)***
Republican Herald, Pottsville *Also called Pottsville Republican Inc* ***(G-16092)***
RES Coal LLC (PA) 814 765-7525
51 Airport Rd Clearfield (16830) ***(G-3230)***
RES Coal LLC 814 765-0352
1128 3rd Level Rd West Decatur (16878) ***(G-19690)***
RES-Q, Pennsburg *Also called N3 Oceanic Inc* ***(G-13251)***
Resco Group Inc 412 494-4491
1 Robinson Plz 300 Pittsburgh (15205) ***(G-15479)***
Resco Products, New Castle *Also called Shenango Advanced Ceramics LLC* ***(G-12149)***
Resdel Corporation 215 343-2400
150 Franklin Dr Warrington (18976) ***(G-19131)***
Research & Technology Center, Homestead *Also called United States Steel Corp* ***(G-7694)***
Research and Technology Centre, Homestead *Also called United States Steel Corp* ***(G-7695)***
Resolve Rooter, Warminster *Also called Resolve Trnchless Slutions Inc* ***(G-18953)***
Resolve Trnchless Slutions Inc 215 441-5544
216 W Bristol Rd Ste A Warminster (18974) ***(G-18953)***
Resource Dynamics Incorporated 412 369-7760
1549 Field Club Dr Pittsburgh (15237) ***(G-15480)***
Respiratory Products Division, Somerset *Also called Vcp Mobility Inc* ***(G-17715)***
Respironics Inc 724 387-5200
174 Tech Center Dr # 100 Mount Pleasant (15666) ***(G-11714)***
Respironics Inc 724 733-0200
1001 Murry Ridge Ln Murrysville (15668) ***(G-11864)***
Respironics Inc 724 387-4270
1740 Golden Mile Hwy Monroeville (15146) ***(G-11354)***
Respironics Inc 724 771-7837
174 Tech Center Dr # 100 Mount Pleasant (15666) ***(G-11715)***
Respironics Inc (HQ) 724 387-5200
1001 Murry Ridge Ln Murrysville (15668) ***(G-11865)***
Respironics Inc 724 733-5803
137 Gary Dr Sewickley (15143) ***(G-17407)***
Respironics Inc 724 334-3100
312 Alvin Dr New Kensington (15068) ***(G-12370)***
Response Electric Inc 215 799-2400
6301 Fifth St Green Lane (18054) ***(G-6592)***
Responselogix Inc 215 256-1700
220 Stahl Rd Harleysville (19438) ***(G-7055)***
Ressler Enterprises Inc 717 933-5611
7650 Lancaster Ave Mount Aetna (19544) ***(G-11605)***
Restorative Care America Inc 215 592-8880
27 N 3rd St Philadelphia (19106) ***(G-14241)***
Resun Modspace Inc 610 232-1200
1200 W Swedesford Rd Berwyn (19312) ***(G-1373)***
Retal Pa LLC 724 705-3975
55 S Washington St Donora (15033) ***(G-4160)***
Retrohair Inc 412 278-2383
427 Jane St Carnegie (15106) ***(G-2787)***
Retrolinear Inc 215 699-8000
401 Elm Ave North Wales (19454) ***(G-12827)***
Retrolite Corporation America 215 443-9370
89 Steam Whistle Dr Warminster (18974) ***(G-18954)***
Rettew Field Services Inc (PA) 717 697-3551
3020 Columbia Ave Lancaster (17603) ***(G-9187)***
Reubes Machine & Tool Co Inc 215 368-0200
1239 Welsh Rd Lansdale (19446) ***(G-9404)***
Reubes Plastics Co Inc 215 368-3010
1001 W Orvilla Rd Hatfield (19440) ***(G-7390)***
Reuss Industries Inc 724 722-3300
195 Waltz Mill Flat Rd Madison (15663) ***(G-10166)***
Revel Capewell Inc 610 272-8075
303 W Oak St Norristown (19401) ***(G-12705)***
Revelations Perfume Cosmt Inc 215 396-7286
2800 Turnpike Dr Ste B Hatboro (19040) ***(G-7300)***
Review of Ophthalmology, Newtown Square *Also called Jobson Medical Information LLC* ***(G-12579)***
Review Publishing Ltd Partnr (PA) 215 563-7400
1617 Jfk Blvd Ste 1005 Philadelphia (19103) ***(G-14242)***
Revoltnary Elctrnic Design LLC 814 977-9546
7127 Lincoln Hwy Bedford (15522) ***(G-1073)***
Revonah Pretzel LLC 717 632-4477
1250 York St Hanover (17331) ***(G-6943)***
Revtur Welding Company LLC 215 672-8233
1836 Stout Dr Ste 9 Warminster (18974) ***(G-18955)***
Rex Energy Corporation 724 814-3230
600 Cranberry Woods Dr # 250 Cranberry Township (16066) ***(G-3846)***
Rex Energy Corporation (PA) 814 278-7267
366 Walker Dr State College (16801) ***(G-18014)***
Rex Energy IV LLC 814 278-7267
366 Walker Dr State College (16801) ***(G-18015)***
Rex Energy Operating Corp (HQ) 814 278-7267
366 Walker Dr State College (16801) ***(G-18016)***
Rex Heat Treat -Lansdale Inc (PA) 215 855-1131
951 W 8th St Lansdale (19446) ***(G-9405)***
Rex Heat Treat -Lansdale Inc 814 623-1701
7 Corporate Dr Bedford (15522) ***(G-1074)***
Rex Medical Inc 610 940-0665
555 E North Ln Ste 5035 Conshohocken (19428) ***(G-3600)***
Reyna Foods Inc 412 904-1242
2031 Penn Ave Ste 3 Pittsburgh (15222) ***(G-15481)***
Reynolds & Reynolds Elec Inc 484 221-6381
2501 Baglyos Cir Bethlehem (18020) ***(G-1610)***
Reynolds Building Systems Inc 724 646-0771
205 Arlington Dr Greenville (16125) ***(G-6769)***
Reynolds Iron Works Inc 570 323-4663
157 Palmer Industrial Rd Williamsport (17701) ***(G-20068)***
Reynolds Machine Co Inc 724 925-1982
229 Potoka Mine Rd Ruffs Dale (15679) ***(G-16875)***
Reynolds Manufacturing Co Inc 724 697-4522
621 Railroad Ave Avonmore (15618) ***(G-867)***
Reynolds Metals Company LLC 412 343-5020
573 Audubon Ave Pittsburgh (15228) ***(G-15482)***
Reynolds Presto Products Inc 866 254-3310
201 Isabella St Pittsburgh (15212) ***(G-15483)***
Reynolds Sales Co Inc 412 461-7877
462 W 7th Ave Homestead (15120) ***(G-7692)***
Reynolds Services Inc (PA) 724 646-2600
860 Brentwood Dr Greenville (16125) ***(G-6770)***
Reynoldsville Casket Company (HQ) 814 653-9666
560 Myrtle St Reynoldsville (15851) ***(G-16663)***
Reznor LLC 724 662-4400
150 Mckinley Ave Mercer (16137) ***(G-10971)***
Rfc Sharon, Farrell *Also called Roll Forming Corp - Sharon* ***(G-5873)***
Rfcircuits Inc 215 364-2450
1840 County Line Rd # 207 Huntingdon Valley (19006) ***(G-8029)***
Rfhero, Greensburg *Also called Nichols Electronics Inc* ***(G-6693)***
Rfsj Inc 724 547-4457
654 W Main St Mount Pleasant (15666) ***(G-11716)***
RG Group, York *Also called RG Industries Inc* ***(G-20658)***
RG Industries Inc 717 849-0345
15 Flour Mill Rd York (17406) ***(G-20658)***
Rgb Duct Cleaning, Bloomsburg *Also called Robert G Dent Heating & AC* ***(G-1798)***
Rgl Distributors LLC 610 207-9000
2517 Huntingdon Ln Ardmore (19003) ***(G-715)***
Rgm Hardwoods Inc 570 842-4533
Rr 7 Box 7190 Moscow (18444) ***(G-11603)***
Rgm Watch Company 717 653-9799
801 W Main St Mount Joy (17552) ***(G-11670)***
Rhino Inc 215 442-1504
451 Oakdale Ave Hatboro (19040) ***(G-7301)***
Rhkg Holdings Inc 814 337-8407
10890 Mercer Pike Meadville (16335) ***(G-10787)***
Rhoades Logging 814 757-4711
781 White Rd Sugar Grove (16350) ***(G-18145)***
Rhoads Industries Inc 267 728-6544
5100 S 16th St Philadelphia (19112) ***(G-14243)***
Rhoads Industries Inc (PA) 267 728-6300
1900 Kitty Hawk Ave Philadelphia (19112) ***(G-14244)***
Rhoads Marine Industries, Philadelphia *Also called Rhoads Industries Inc* ***(G-14244)***
Rhoads Sign Systems 717 776-7309
225 Farm Rd Newville (17241) ***(G-12609)***
Rhodes & Hammers Printing 724 852-1457
54 S Church St Waynesburg (15370) ***(G-19451)***
Rhotau Pharma Services LLC 484 437-2654
920 Sassafras Cir West Chester (19382) ***(G-19629)***

ALPHABETIC

Ribarchik John....215 547-8901
1606 Unit C2 Levittown 2 C Levittown (19055) *(G-9861)*
Ribbon Factory Outlet, Titusville *Also called Horn Textile Inc (G-18384)*
Ribbon Renu, Pittsburgh *Also called Prime Ribbon Inc (G-15438)*
Ribbons and More, Collingdale *Also called Free Energy Systems Inc (G-3404)*
Ribonova Inc....610 801-2541
100 E Lancaster Ave R133 Wynnewood (19096) *(G-20272)*
Ricci Italian Sausage, Mc Kees Rocks *Also called Ernest Ricci (G-10607)*
Rice Aesthetics LLC....814 503-8540
90 Beaver Dr Du Bois (15801) *(G-4416)*
Rice Drilling B LLC....274 281-7200
2200 Rice Dr Canonsburg (15317) *(G-2627)*
Rice Drilling D LLC....274 281-7200
400 Woodcliff Dr Canonsburg (15317) *(G-2628)*
Rice Electric Company....724 225-4180
30 Linnwood Rd Eighty Four (15330) *(G-4846)*
Rice Olympus Midstream LLC....724 746-6720
400 Woodcliff Dr Canonsburg (15317) *(G-2629)*
Rice Poseidon Midstream LLC....724 746-6720
400 Woodcliff Dr Canonsburg (15317) *(G-2630)*
Rich and Sons, Seminole *Also called Richard Shilling Jr (G-17363)*
Rich Industrial Services Inc....610 534-0195
2230 Forrester Ave Holmes (19043) *(G-7664)*
Rich Reenie Inc....610 439-7962
1434 W Union St Allentown (18102) *(G-374)*
Rich-Art Sign Co Inc....215 922-1539
1305 Vine St Philadelphia (19107) *(G-14245)*
Richard Baringer....610 346-7661
1868 California Rd Richlandtown (18955) *(G-16690)*
Richard E Krall Inc....717 432-4179
60 Yeager Rd Rossville (17358) *(G-16824)*
Richard Freeman....717 597-4580
400 N Antrim Way Greencastle (17225) *(G-6630)*
Richard Hurst....717 866-2343
516 S Cherry St Myerstown (17067) *(G-11897)*
Richard J Clickett Inc....814 827-7548
708 N Perry St Titusville (16354) *(G-18391)*
Richard J McMenamin Inc....215 673-1200
11000 Roosevelt Blvd Philadelphia (19116) *(G-14246)*
Richard J Summons Sculpture....610 223-9013
172 Mail Route Rd Reading (19608) *(G-16497)*
Richard James Woodworking, Lancaster *Also called James Richard Woodworking (G-9071)*
Richard K Mohn....717 762-7646
10375 Old Forge Rd Waynesboro (17268) *(G-19423)*
Richard Meyers....814 359-4340
270 Commerce St Bellefonte (16823) *(G-1114)*
Richard Rhodes....814 535-3633
846 Benshoff Hill Rd Johnstown (15906) *(G-8430)*
Richard Riberich....412 271-8427
1027 Wilkins Ave Pittsburgh (15221) *(G-15484)*
Richard Scofield Hstorc Lghtng....860 767-7032
2089 Bondsville Rd Downingtown (19335) *(G-4254)*
Richard Shilling Jr....814 319-4326
209 Chestnut Ave Seminole (16253) *(G-17363)*
Richard Zerbe Ltd....717 564-2024
3109 Paul Dr Harrisburg (17109) *(G-7205)*
Richards and Danielson LLC....610 435-4300
737 N 13th St Allentown (18102) *(G-375)*
Richardsapex Inc (PA)....215 487-1100
4202 Main St 24 Philadelphia (19127) *(G-14247)*
Richardson Coolg Packages LLC....724 698-2302
1900 New Butler Rd New Castle (16101) *(G-12142)*
Richardson Paint Co Inc....215 535-4500
4821 Garden St Philadelphia (19137) *(G-14248)*
Richart Graphics, Philadelphia *Also called Rich-Art Sign Co Inc (G-14245)*
Richland Manufacturing, Richland *Also called Fargo Assembly of Pa Inc (G-16687)*
Richland Plastics & Engraving....814 266-3002
624 Lamberd Ave Johnstown (15904) *(G-8431)*
Richlyn Manufacturing Inc....814 833-8925
3017 W 15th St Erie (16505) *(G-5462)*
Richman Industries Inc....717 561-1766
810 S 31st St Harrisburg (17111) *(G-7206)*
Richter Precision Inc (PA)....717 560-9990
1021 Commercial Ave East Petersburg (17520) *(G-4589)*
Rick Degeorge....717 684-4555
2560 Ironville Pike Columbia (17512) *(G-3449)*
Rick Leasure....814 739-9521
11355 Backus Rd Wattsburg (16442) *(G-19282)*
Rick Radvansky & Sons....724 335-7411
1578 Fairmont Dr New Kensington (15068) *(G-12371)*
Rick Weyand Signs....814 893-5524
4277 Lincoln Hwy Stoystown (15563) *(G-18084)*
Ricks Custom Wood Design Inc....717 627-2701
10 Lauber Rd Akron (17501) *(G-37)*
Ricks Quick Printing Inc....412 571-0333
2239 Banksville Rd Pittsburgh (15216) *(G-15485)*
Ricky E Shaffer....814 328-2318
873 Jim Town Rd Brookville (15825) *(G-2270)*
Ricochet Manufacturing Corp....888 462-1999
4700 Wissahickon Ave # 112 Philadelphia (19144) *(G-14249)*
Rideltin Powder Metal Inc....412 788-0956
221 Waterford Dr Mc Kees Rocks (15136) *(G-10631)*
Ridg-U-Rak Inc (PA)....814 725-8751
120 S Lake St North East (16428) *(G-12756)*
Ridg-U-Rak Inc....814 725-8751
4800 Loomis St North East (16428) *(G-12757)*
Ridg-U-Rak Inc....814 725-8751
12340 Gay Rd North East (16428) *(G-12758)*
Ridge Craft....717 355-2254
280 Commerce Dr New Holland (17557) *(G-12279)*
Ridge Machine Shop Inc....717 896-8348
158c Hoffman Rd Halifax (17032) *(G-6829)*
Ridge Tool Company....814 454-2461
1501 Cherry St Erie (16502) *(G-5463)*
Ridge Woodworking....814 839-0151
329 Ferguson Rd Schellsburg (15559) *(G-17135)*
Ridgeview Forest Products LLC....717 423-6465
550 Ridge Rd Shippensburg (17257) *(G-17544)*
Ridgeview Mdlar Hsing Group LP....570 837-2333
7172 Route 522 Middleburg (17842) *(G-11038)*
Ridgeview Woodwork, Shippensburg *Also called Ridgeview Forest Products LLC (G-17544)*
Ridgewood Winery....484 509-0100
2039 Philadelphia Ave Birdsboro (19508) *(G-1705)*
Ridgway Industries Inc....610 259-5534
6250 Baltimore Ave Ste 22 Lansdowne (19050) *(G-9442)*
Ridgway Mfg Facility, Ridgway *Also called Metaldyne Sintered Ridgway LLC (G-16717)*
Ridgway Powdered Metals Inc....814 772-5551
6931 Ridgway St Marys Rd Ridgway (15853) *(G-16727)*
Ridgway Record....814 773-3161
325 Main St Ste A Ridgway (15853) *(G-16728)*
Ridgway Waterworks, Ridgway *Also called Pump Station Ridgway (G-16725)*
Ridgways Inc....215 735-8055
3751 Island Ave Ste 200 Philadelphia (19153) *(G-14250)*
Ridley USA Inc....717 509-1078
3349 Hempland Rd Lancaster (17601) *(G-9188)*
Rieck's Printing, Reading *Also called Riecks Letter Service Inc (G-16498)*
Riecks Letter Service Inc....610 375-8581
101 S 1st Ave Reading (19611) *(G-16498)*
Riecks Publishing....610 685-1222
101 S 1st Ave Reading (19611) *(G-16499)*
Riehl Quality Stor Barns LLC....717 442-8655
4940 Lincoln Hwy Kinzers (17535) *(G-8741)*
Rieker Electronics Inc....610 500-2000
34 Mount Pleasant Rd Aston (19014) *(G-790)*
Rieker Instrument Company Inc....610 500-2000
34 Mount Pleasant Rd Aston (19014) *(G-791)*
Riethmiller Lumber Mfg Corp....724 946-8608
171 Riethmiller Rd New Wilmington (16142) *(G-12469)*
Riggans Advg Specialty Co....724 654-5741
2934 Mercer Rd New Castle (16105) *(G-12143)*
Riggeals Performance Fibrgls....717 677-4167
1741 Goldenville Rd Gettysburg (17325) *(G-6312)*
Riggs Industries Inc (PA)....814 629-5621
2478 Lincoln Hwy Stoystown (15563) *(G-18085)*
Right Reason Technologies LLC....570 234-0324
430 Sterling Rd Tobyhanna (18466) *(G-18408)*
Right Reason Technologies LLC....484 898-1967
3864 Adler Pl Ste 200 Bethlehem (18017) *(G-1611)*
Righters Associat Ferry....610 667-6767
600 Righters Ferry Rd Bala Cynwyd (19004) *(G-891)*
Rightnour Machining....814 383-4176
229 Hale Ln Bellefonte (16823) *(G-1115)*
Rightnour Manufacturing Co Inc....800 326-9113
229 Hecla Rd Mingoville (16856) *(G-11257)*
Rightscreen, Elizabethville *Also called MI Windows and Doors Inc (G-4895)*
Rigidply Rafters Inc....717 866-6581
701 E Linden St Richland (17087) *(G-16689)*
Riise Inc....724 528-3305
9 Carbaugh St West Middlesex (16159) *(G-19729)*
Rijuven Corp....412 404-6292
10475 Perry Hwy Ste 104 Wexford (15090) *(G-19827)*
Riley Tool Incorporated....814 425-4140
18908 Adamsville Rd Cochranton (16314) *(G-3350)*
Riley Welding and Fabg Inc....717 637-6014
234 Poplar St Hanover (17331) *(G-6944)*
Rin Tin Tim Inc....412 403-5378
1172 Jefferson Heights Rd Pittsburgh (15235) *(G-15486)*
Ringtown Concrete Products, Ringtown *Also called Ringtown Wilbert Vault Works (G-16756)*
Ringtown Wilbert Vault Works....570 889-3153
710 W Main St Ringtown (17967) *(G-16756)*
Rio Brands LLC....610 629-6200
100 Front St Ste 1350 Conshohocken (19428) *(G-3601)*
Risco Industries Inc....412 767-0349
971 Route 910 Pittsburgh (15238) *(G-15487)*
Rising Spring Meat Company, Spring Mills *Also called October 6 2011 (G-17891)*
Rissler Conveyors....717 336-2244
1275 Indiantown Rd Stevens (17578) *(G-18055)*

Rissler Custom Kitchens......717 656-6101
90 Brethren Church Rd Leola (17540) ***(G-9800)***
Rissler E Manufacturing LLC......814 766-2246
2794 Brumbaugh Rd New Enterprise (16664) ***(G-12195)***
Ristau Drilling Co......814 723-4858
100 Kamp St Warren (16365) ***(G-19046)***
Ritcheys Dairy Inc......814 793-2157
2130 Cross Cove Rd Martinsburg (16662) ***(G-10529)***
Rite Envelope and Graphics Inc......610 518-1601
250 Boot Rd Downingtown (19335) ***(G-4255)***
Ritescreen Company LLC (PA)......717 362-7483
4314 State Route 209 Elizabethville (17023) ***(G-4897)***
Ritner Engraved Stationary, Philadelphia *Also called Novelli Inc* ***(G-14088)***
Ritner Steel Inc......717 249-1449
131 Stover Dr Carlisle (17015) ***(G-2736)***
Rittenhouse Instant Press......215 854-0505
1811 Sansom St Philadelphia (19103) ***(G-14251)***
Ritter Group Usa Inc......570 517-5380
105 Fetherman Rd Stroudsburg (18360) ***(G-18140)***
Ritter Industries Inc......724 225-6563
46 Route 519 Eighty Four (15330) ***(G-4847)***
Ritter Precision Machining......610 377-2011
839 Blakeslee Blvd Dr E Lehighton (18235) ***(G-9725)***
Ritters Fuel Delivery LLC......717 957-4477
4335 Valley Rd Shermans Dale (17090) ***(G-17501)***
Ritztex, Montrose *Also called Shen Manufacturing Company Inc* ***(G-11476)***
River City Venom......724 316-5886
225 Kilgallen Rd Butler (16002) ***(G-2439)***
River Hill Coal Co Inc (PA)......814 345-5642
S Second St Kylertown (16847) ***(G-8867)***
River Hill Coal Co Inc......814 263-4506
Hwy 879 Karthaus (16845) ***(G-8484)***
River Hill Coal Co Inc......814 263-4506
Hauseman Dr Karthaus (16845) ***(G-8485)***
River Hill Coal Co Inc......814 263-4341
Potter St Karthaus (16845) ***(G-8486)***
River Run Foods Inc......570 701-1192
50 Blue Hl Northumberland (17857) ***(G-12875)***
River Street Pedorthics Inc......570 299-5472
881 Bear Lake Rd Gouldsboro (18424) ***(G-6570)***
River Supply Inc......717 927-1555
2555 Delta Rd Brogue (17309) ***(G-2240)***
Riverbed Technology Inc......610 648-3819
5 Great Valley Pkwy Malvern (19355) ***(G-10310)***
Riverbend Foods LLC......412 442-6989
1080 River Ave Pittsburgh (15212) ***(G-15488)***
Riverdale Global LLC......610 358-2900
11 Crozerville Rd Aston (19014) ***(G-792)***
Riverside Builders Supply......412 264-8835
889 Pennsylvania Ave Coraopolis (15108) ***(G-3721)***
Riverside Cement Company, Coraopolis *Also called Riverside Builders Supply* ***(G-3721)***
Riverside Materials Inc......215 426-7299
2870 E Allegheny Ave # 1 Philadelphia (19134) ***(G-14252)***
Riverview Block Inc......570 752-7191
1507 Salem Blvd Berwick (18603) ***(G-1342)***
Riverview Orthotics......570 270-6231
220 S River St Ste 2 Plains (18705) ***(G-15788)***
Riverview Orthtics Prosthetics......570 743-1414
2 Atrium Ct Ste B Selinsgrove (17870) ***(G-17332)***
Riverview Orthtics Prosthetics......570 284-4291
957 Bloom Rd Danville (17821) ***(G-4010)***
Riverwoods Cabinetry......724 991-0097
177 Schmidt Rd Grove City (16127) ***(G-6803)***
Riverwoods Cabinetry LLC......724 807-1045
139 Barkey Hoffman Rd Harrisville (16038) ***(G-7255)***
Riviana Foods Inc......717 526-2200
85 Shannon Rd Harrisburg (17112) ***(G-7207)***
Rixie Paper Products Inc......610 323-9220
10 Quinter St Pottstown (19464) ***(G-16040)***
Rizworks......570 226-7611
605 Church St Ste A Hawley (18428) ***(G-7437)***
Rizzo & Sons Industrial Svc Co......814 948-5381
9965 Rte 221 Hwy Pittsburgh (15229) ***(G-15489)***
Rj Custom Products Llc......717 246-2693
33 W Maple St Dallastown (17313) ***(G-3980)***
Rj Evercrests Inc......610 431-4200
1234 Wrights Ln West Chester (19380) ***(G-19630)***
Rj Foods, York *Also called Rebecca Wilson Ltd Lblty Co* ***(G-20654)***
Rjb Well Services Inc......814 368-9570
557 Interstate Pkwy Bradford (16701) ***(G-1990)***
Rjc Kohl Inc......814 948-5903
1927 Killen School Rd Nicktown (15762) ***(G-12621)***
Rjc Manufacturing Services LLC......724 836-3636
7590 Us 30 Irwin (15642) ***(G-8197)***
Rjf Enterprises Inc......570 383-1030
905 Stanton Rd Olyphant (18447) ***(G-12997)***
Rjj Mobile LLC......215 796-1935
5815 Wayne Ave Philadelphia (19144) ***(G-14253)***
Rjj Wayne LLC......215 796-1935
9223 Eagleview Dr Lafayette Hill (19444) ***(G-8884)***
Rjw Hired Hands Inc......412 341-1477
505 Mcneilly Rd Ste 1 Pittsburgh (15226) ***(G-15490)***
RLB Ventures Inc......717 964-1111
10 Industrial Way Denver (17517) ***(G-4091)***
RLC Electronic Systems Inc......610 898-4902
10 Corporate Blvd Reading (19608) ***(G-16500)***
Rle Millwork, Warminster *Also called Laurence Ronald Entps Inc* ***(G-18910)***
Rle Systems LLC......610 518-3751
1155 Phoenixville Pike 104a West Chester (19380) ***(G-19631)***
Rm Battery Doctors LLC......570 441-9184
67 Reese Ln Millville (17846) ***(G-11227)***
RM Benney Technical Sls Inc......724 935-0150
207 Pine Creek Rd Ste 202 Wexford (15090) ***(G-19828)***
Rmb Specialtees LLC......570 578-8258
85 Broad St Beaver Meadows (18216) ***(G-1017)***
RMH Image Group LLC......610 731-0050
950 Colwell Ln Ste 2 Conshohocken (19428) ***(G-3602)***
RMS Kunkle Inc......717 564-8829
631 S 17th St Harrisburg (17104) ***(G-7208)***
RMS Omega Tech Grouping......610 917-0472
406 Westridge Dr Phoenixville (19460) ***(G-14574)***
RMS Systems Inc......724 458-7580
1850 Mercer Grove City Rd Mercer (16137) ***(G-10972)***
RNS Services Inc......814 472-5202
354 Rubisch Rd Ebensburg (15931) ***(G-4794)***
RNS Services Inc (HQ)......570 638-3322
7 Riverside Plz Blossburg (16912) ***(G-1808)***
Roach & Associates Inc......412 344-9310
615 Washington Rd Ste 404 Pittsburgh (15228) ***(G-15491)***
Road Ready LLC......717 647-7902
469 E Market St Williamstown (17098) ***(G-20103)***
Road Runner Race Fuels LLC......717 587-1693
2645 Welsh Rd Mohnton (19540) ***(G-11269)***
Roadsafe Traffic Systems Inc......412 559-1396
1623 Middle Road Ext Gibsonia (15044) ***(G-6350)***
Roadsafe Traffic Systems Inc......904 350-0080
1011 Mumma Rd Ste 101 Lemoyne (17043) ***(G-9751)***
Roadside PA LLC......412 464-1452
5747 Interboro Ave Pittsburgh (15207) ***(G-15492)***
Roadside Products Inc......412 220-9694
124 Hickory Heights Dr Bridgeville (15017) ***(G-2087)***
Roaring Spring Blank Book Co (PA)......814 224-2306
740 Spang St Roaring Spring (16673) ***(G-16768)***
Roaring Spring Blank Book Co......814 793-3744
270 Martin Ln Martinsburg (16662) ***(G-10530)***
Roaring Spring Blank Book Co......814 224-2222
301 Cove Lane Rd Roaring Spring (16673) ***(G-16769)***
Roaring Spring Blank Book Co......717 334-8080
1325 Hanover Rd Gettysburg (17325) ***(G-6313)***
Roaring Spring Bottling Co, Gettysburg *Also called Roaring Spring Blank Book Co* ***(G-6313)***
Roaring Spring Paper Products, Roaring Spring *Also called Roaring Spring Blank Book Co* ***(G-16768)***
Roaring Spring Water......814 942-9844
420 Water St Roaring Spring (16673) ***(G-16770)***
Roast-A-Matic, Lebanon *Also called Schnupps Grain Roasting LLC* ***(G-9627)***
Rob Kei Inc......717 293-8991
142 Park City Ctr Lancaster (17601) ***(G-9189)***
Rob Rand Enterprises Inc......724 927-6844
7299 Snodgrass Rd Jamestown (16134) ***(G-8239)***
Robanco......412 795-7444
415 Mower Dr Pittsburgh (15239) ***(G-15493)***
Robar Industries Inc (PA)......484 688-0300
1000 Germantown Pike F2 Plymouth Meeting (19462) ***(G-15868)***
Robbie Holland......610 495-5441
44 Church Rd Royersford (19468) ***(G-16862)***
Robbie Holland Welding, Royersford *Also called Robbie Holland* ***(G-16862)***
Robbins Concrete Block Mfg, Cambridge Springs *Also called A A Robbins Inc* ***(G-2473)***
Robbins Logging & Lumber......814 236-3384
2365 Zion Rd Olanta (16863) ***(G-12961)***
Robern Inc......215 826-0280
701 N Wilson Ave Bristol (19007) ***(G-2195)***
Robert A Crooks......724 541-2746
1485 Pollock Rd Marion Center (15759) ***(G-10477)***
Robert Aguglia......412 487-6511
1515 William Flynn Hwy Glenshaw (15116) ***(G-6500)***
Robert Bath......610 588-0423
314 Garibaldi Ave Roseto (18013) ***(G-16822)***
Robert Boone Company......215 362-2577
806 W 5th St Lansdale (19446) ***(G-9406)***
Robert Bosch LLC......610 694-8200
2315 City Line Rd Bethlehem (18017) ***(G-1612)***
Robert D Rennick......570 429-0784
2 Overlook Dr Saint Clair (17970) ***(G-16940)***
Robert G Dent Heating & AC......570 784-6721
1140 Main St Bloomsburg (17815) ***(G-1798)***
Robert Gerenser......215 646-1853
22 S Main St New Hope (18938) ***(G-12314)***
Robert H Berenson......610 642-9380
104 Woodside Rd Apt C206 Haverford (19041) ***(G-7414)***

ALPHABETIC

Robert I Oldfield..215 533-5860
  4717 Duffield St Philadelphia (19124) **(G-14254)**
Robert J Brown...814 486-1768
  228 W 4th St Emporium (15834) **(G-5074)**
Robert J Fleig Inc..215 702-7676
  750 Parker St Langhorne (19047) **(G-9322)**
Robert J Quinn Jr...570 622-4420
  146 W Savory St Pottsville (17901) **(G-16095)**
Robert John Enterprises Inc (PA)........................814 944-0187
  3500 6th Ave Altoona (16602) **(G-544)**
Robert Johnson..570 746-1287
  Lime Hill Rd Wyalusing (18853) **(G-20256)**
Robert L Baker..443 617-0164
  975 Wayne Ave Chambersburg (17201) **(G-2973)**
Robert Mazza Inc (PA).......................................814 725-8695
  11815 Lake Rd North East (16428) **(G-12759)**
Robert Mrvel Plastic Mulch LLC..........................717 838-0976
  2425 Horseshoe Pike Annville (17003) **(G-658)**
Robert P Williams..814 563-7660
  29030 Route 6 Youngsville (16371) **(G-20775)**
Robert Pearce & Sons.......................................724 286-9757
  7416 Route 210 Hwy Smicksburg (16256) **(G-17639)**
Robert Trate Hogg Cbinetmakers........................717 529-2522
  5650 Homeville Rd Oxford (19363) **(G-13088)**
Robert Urda Jr...724 775-9333
  1990 Beaver Ave Monaca (15061) **(G-11295)**
Robert W Gastel Jr..412 678-2723
  1228 Long Run Rd White Oak (15131) **(G-19858)**
Robert W Turner...610 372-8863
  425 Carsonia Ave Reading (19606) **(G-16501)**
Robert Water Technologies, Media *Also called Roberts Filter Holding Company* **(G-10946)**
Robert Williams Truck Sales, Youngsville *Also called Robert P Williams* **(G-20775)**
Robert Wirth..724 947-3615
  60 Center Ave Burgettstown (15021) **(G-2354)**
Robert Wooler Company.....................................215 542-7600
  1755 Susquehanna Rd Dresher (19025) **(G-4357)**
Roberta Weissburg Leathers (PA).........................412 681-8188
  5415 Walnut St Pittsburgh (15232) **(G-15494)**
Roberts Filter Holding Company (PA)....................610 583-3131
  214 N Jackson St Media (19063) **(G-10946)**
Roberts Manufacturing LLC................................855 763-7450
  1801 Union Blvd Ste E Allentown (18109) **(G-376)**
Roberts Orthotics Prosthetics, Waynesburg *Also called Jeffrey L Roberts* **(G-19447)**
Robertson Manufacturing Inc..............................610 869-9600
  112 Woodland Ave West Grove (19390) **(G-19705)**
Robertsons Flrg & Countertops, Erie *Also called Robertsons Inc* **(G-5464)**
Robertsons Inc...814 838-2313
  4101 W 12th St Erie (16505) **(G-5464)**
Robin Morris..814 395-9555
  255 Paddlers Ln Confluence (15424) **(G-3469)**
Robindale Energy, Latrobe *Also called Robindale Export LLC* **(G-9517)**
Robindale Export LLC.......................................724 879-4264
  11 Lloyd Ave Ste 200 Latrobe (15650) **(G-9517)**
Robinson Fans Inc (HQ)....................................863 646-5270
  400 Robinson Dr Zelienople (16063) **(G-20817)**
Robinson Fans Holdings Inc (PA)........................724 452-6121
  400 Robinson Dr Zelienople (16063) **(G-20818)**
Robinson Sawmill Works....................................570 559-7454
  450 Route 434 Shohola (18458) **(G-17579)**
Robinson Technical Pdts Corp............................610 261-1900
  3962 Portland St Coplay (18037) **(G-3647)**
Robinson Vacuum Tanks Inc..............................814 355-4474
  306 Runville Rd Bellefonte (16823) **(G-1116)**
Robisons Cabinet Studio....................................717 677-9828
  33 Prospect St Aspers (17304) **(G-745)**
Robo Construction LLC......................................570 494-1028
  2700 Lycoming Creek Rd Williamsport (17701) **(G-20069)**
Robotic Services Inc (PA)..................................215 550-1823
  3401 Grays Ferry Ave Philadelphia (19146) **(G-14255)**
Robroy Industries Inc (PA)................................412 828-2100
  10 River Rd Verona (15147) **(G-18761)**
Robvon Backing Ring Co Inc..............................570 945-3800
  Ring Rd 1 Factoryville (18419) **(G-5761)**
ROC Service Company Ltd.................................724 745-3319
  125 Technology Dr Ste 200 Canonsburg (15317) **(G-2631)**
Rocal Corporation..215 343-2400
  150 Franklin Dr Warrington (18976) **(G-19132)**
Roccas Italian Foods Inc...................................724 654-3344
  520 S Mill St New Castle (16101) **(G-12144)**
Roch Grande Gst Waffles LLC.............................484 840-9179
  50 Applied Card Way Glen Mills (19342) **(G-6442)**
Rocher Incorporated...717 637-9320
  1856 Dubs Church Rd Hanover (17331) **(G-6945)**
Rochester Alloy Casting Co................................724 452-5659
  2 Brookview Ct Zelienople (16063) **(G-20819)**
Rochester Coca Cola Bottling (HQ)......................570 655-2874
  300 Oak St Pittston (18640) **(G-15782)**
Rochester Coca Cola Bottling..............................717 730-2100
  230 S 10th St Ste A Lemoyne (17043) **(G-9752)**

Rochester Coca Cola Bottling..............................717 209-4411
  1428 Manheim Pike Lancaster (17601) **(G-9190)**
Rochester Coca Cola Bottling..............................724 834-2700
  Rr 12 Box 289 Greensburg (15601) **(G-6712)**
Rochester Coca Cola Bottling..............................814 472-6113
  108 Barefoot Rd Ebensburg (15931) **(G-4795)**
Rochester Coca Cola Bottling..............................610 916-3996
  243 Snyder Rd Reading (19605) **(G-16502)**
Rochester Coca Cola Bottling..............................814 833-0101
  2209 W 50th St Erie (16506) **(G-5465)**
Rochester Coca Cola Bottling..............................412 787-3610
  300 Vandale Dr Houston (15342) **(G-7879)**
Rochester Machine Corporation...........................724 843-7820
  1300 Allegheny St New Brighton (15066) **(G-12040)**
Rochester Pharmaceuticals................................215 345-4880
  43 S Main St Doylestown (18901) **(G-4335)**
Rochling Machined Plastics.................................724 696-5200
  161 Westec Dr Mount Pleasant (15666) **(G-11717)**
Rock Creek Lumber..570 756-2909
  232 State Route 2036 Thompson (18465) **(G-18346)**
Rock Hill Materials Company (PA).........................610 264-5586
  339 School St Ste 3 Catasauqua (18032) **(G-2817)**
Rock Hill Materials Company...............................610 852-2314
  Rr 248 Parryville (18244) **(G-13186)**
Rock It Printwear..717 697-3983
  416 Ricky Rd Mechanicsburg (17055) **(G-10885)**
Rock Lake Inc...570 465-2986
  4412 State Route 848 New Milford (18834) **(G-12399)**
Rock Proof Boats..717 957-3282
  407 Mountain Rd Marysville (17053) **(G-10532)**
Rock Run Enterprises LLC.................................814 938-8778
  264 Sunny Acres Ln Punxsutawney (15767) **(G-16159)**
Rock Run Recreation Area.................................814 674-6026
  1228 Saint Lawrence Rd Patton (16668) **(G-13189)**
Rock Star Quarries LLC.....................................570 721-1426
  75 Johnson Hill Ln Wyalusing (18853) **(G-20257)**
Rock-Built Inc..878 302-3978
  1170 2nd Ave New Kensington (15068) **(G-12372)**
Rock-Tenn Paperboard Products, Delaware Water Gap *Also called Westrock Rkt LLC* **(G-4045)**
Rockafellow John...717 359-4276
  382 Schottie Rd Littlestown (17340) **(G-10076)**
Rocket Cloud Inc..484 948-0327
  116 Research Dr Bethlehem (18015) **(G-1613)**
Rocket Shopper, Wyalusing *Also called Rocket-Courier Newspaper* **(G-20258)**
Rocket-Courier Newspaper.................................570 746-1217
  302 State St Wyalusing (18853) **(G-20258)**
Rockfield Partitions, Erie *Also called General Partitions Mfg Corp* **(G-5302)**
Rockfish Venture LLP (PA)..................................215 968-5054
  156 N State St Newtown (18940) **(G-12545)**
Rockland Inc...814 623-1115
  152 Weber Ln Bedford (15522) **(G-1075)**
Rockland Coach Works LLC................................610 682-2830
  24 High View Ln Mertztown (19539) **(G-11003)**
Rockland Embroidery Inc...................................610 682-5042
  125 Centre Ave Topton (19562) **(G-18415)**
Rockland Immunochemicals Inc............................484 791-3823
  321 Jones Blvd Pottstown (19464) **(G-16041)**
Rockland Manufacturing Company, Bedford *Also called Rockland Inc* **(G-1075)**
Rockland Signs, Fleetwood *Also called Kurt Lebo* **(G-5975)**
Rockler Woodworking Hardware, Williamsport *Also called Hermance Machine Company* **(G-20021)**
Rockpetz Ventures LLC......................................610 608-2788
  34 N Front St Lowr Level Philadelphia (19106) **(G-14256)**
Rockport, Pottstown *Also called Relay Shoe Company LLC* **(G-16039)**
Rocksolid Installation Inc...................................717 548-8700
  2030 Robert Fulton Hwy Peach Bottom (17563) **(G-13201)**
Rocktemn, Lancaster *Also called Southern Container Corp* **(G-9203)**
Rockwell American, New Holland *Also called Quality Trailer Products LP* **(G-12277)**
Rockwell Automation, Washington *Also called Integrated Power Services LLC* **(G-19186)**
Rockwell Automation Inc...................................717 747-8240
  390 Saint Charles Way York (17402) **(G-20659)**
Rockwell Automation Inc...................................610 650-6840
  2650 Eisenhower Ave 108b Norristown (19403) **(G-12706)**
Rockwell Automation Inc...................................724 741-4000
  510 Lindbergh Dr Coraopolis (15108) **(G-3722)**
Rockwell Automation Inc...................................412 375-4700
  510 Lindbergh Dr Coraopolis (15108) **(G-3723)**
Rockwell Collins Inc...610 925-5844
  503 School House Rd Kennett Square (19348) **(G-8540)**
Rockwell Interior Services, Mountainhome *Also called J A Reinhardt & Co Inc* **(G-11787)**
Rockwell Lumber Co Inc....................................717 597-7428
  3865 Buchanan Trl W Greencastle (17225) **(G-6631)**
Rockwell Venture Capital (PA)............................412 281-4620
  960 Penn Ave Ste 800 Pittsburgh (15222) **(G-15495)**
Rockwells Feed Farm & Pet Sup..........................877 797-4575
  1943 Shumway Hill Rd Wellsboro (16901) **(G-19472)**

Rockwood Manufacturing Company 814 926-2026
300 Main St Rockwood (15557) *(G-16792)*

Rockwood Pigments Na Inc 610 279-6450
555 Church St King of Prussia (19406) *(G-8670)*

Rocky Mountain Air Purifiers, Mercersburg *Also called Reliable Products Intl LLC (G-10995)*

Rocky Ridge Steel LLC 717 626-0153
1501 E Newport Rd Lititz (17543) *(G-10042)*

Rococo, Southampton *Also called Tlr Redwood Inc (G-17841)*

Rocwel Industries Inc 610 459-5490
277 Conchester Hwy Concordville (19331) *(G-3458)*

Rod Quellette 814 274-8812
707 N Main St Coudersport (16915) *(G-3788)*

Rod's Welding, Coudersport *Also called Rod Quellette (G-3788)*

Rodale Inc 610 398-2255
6461 Snowdrift Rd Allentown (18106) *(G-377)*

Rodale Institute (PA) 610 683-6009
611 Siegfriedale Rd Kutztown (19530) *(G-8859)*

Rodale Press Distribution Ctr, Allentown *Also called Rodale Inc (G-377)*

Roddy Products 610 623-7040
3 Merion Ter Aldan (19018) *(G-60)*

Roderick Duvall 814 735-4969
2190 S Valley Rd Crystal Spring (15536) *(G-3938)*

Rodon Group 215 822-5544
2800 Sterling Dr Hatfield (19440) *(G-7391)*

Roe Fabricators Inc 610 485-4990
3304 W 2nd St Chester (19013) *(G-3061)*

Roeberg Enterprises Inc (PA) 800 523-8197
1700 Fairview St Reading (19606) *(G-16503)*

Roechling Med Lancaster LLC (HQ) 717 335-3700
44 Denver Rd Denver (17517) *(G-4092)*

Roffler, Coraopolis *Also called Ft Pitt Acquisition Corp (G-3691)*

Roger S Wright Furniture Ltd 215 257-5700
911 S Perkasie Rd Blooming Glen (18911) *(G-1765)*

Rogers & Deturck Printing Inc 412 828-8868
467 Wildwood Ave Ste 1 Verona (15147) *(G-18762)*

Rogers Foam Corporation 215 295-8720
150 E Post Rd Morrisville (19067) *(G-11580)*

Rogerson & Associates 724 943-3934
500 Walnut Hill Rd Dilliner (15327) *(G-4125)*

Rogue Audio Inc 570 992-9901
545 Jenna Dr Brodheadsville (18322) *(G-2238)*

Rohm and Haas Chemicals LLC 215 592-3696
100 S Indpdnc Mall W Fl 5 Philadelphia (19106) *(G-14257)*

Rohm and Haas Chemicals LLC (HQ) 989 636-1000
400 Arcola Rd Collegeville (19426) *(G-3391)*

Rohm and Haas Company (HQ) 989 636-1000
400 Arcola Rd Collegeville (19426) *(G-3392)*

Rohm and Haas Powder Coatings, Collegeville *Also called Morton International LLC (G-3384)*

Rohmax Additives GMBH LLC 215 706-5800
100 N Independence Mall W Philadelphia (19106) *(G-14258)*

Rohmax USA, Philadelphia *Also called Rohmax Additives GMBH LLC (G-14258)*

Rohrer's Concrete, Lititz *Also called Rohrers Quarry Inc (G-10043)*

Rohrers Quarry Inc (PA) 717 626-9760
70 Lititz Rd Lititz (17543) *(G-10043)*

Rohrers Quarry Inc 717 626-9756
16 Lititz Rd Lititz (17543) *(G-10044)*

Rokat Machine 610 432-1830
351 Star Rd Allentown (18106) *(G-378)*

Roland Lynagh Associates LLC 570 467-2528
830 Barnesville Dr Barnesville (18214) *(G-940)*

Rolands Special Millwork Inc 215 885-5588
3119 Pennsylvania Ave Glenside (19038) *(G-6534)*

Rolf Glass, Mount Pleasant *Also called Glassautomatic Inc (G-11700)*

Roll Former Corporation 215 997-2511
140 Independence Ln Chalfont (18914) *(G-2885)*

Roll Forming Corp - Sharon 724 982-0400
250 Martin Luther King Farrell (16121) *(G-5873)*

Roll Your Own 215 420-7441
207 N York Rd Hatboro (19040) *(G-7302)*

Rolled Steel Products Corp PA 610 647-6264
511 Old Lancaster Rd # 9 Berwyn (19312) *(G-1374)*

Roller Derby Skate Corp 610 593-6931
401 Zion Hill Rd Atglen (19310) *(G-805)*

Roller Printing Company Inc 717 632-1433
2 Industrial Dr Hanover (17331) *(G-6946)*

Rolling Ridge Metals LLC 724 588-2375
366 Kinsman Rd Greenville (16125) *(G-6771)*

Rolling Rock Bldg Stone Inc 610 987-6226
40 Rolling Rock Rd Boyertown (19512) *(G-1926)*

Rollock Company (PA) 814 893-6421
3179 Lincoln Hwy Stoystown (15563) *(G-18086)*

Rolls Technology Inc 724 697-4533
400 Railroad Ave Avonmore (15618) *(G-868)*

Roltite Capper, Doylestown *Also called Kinsley Incorporated (G-4311)*

Roma Aluminum Co Inc 215 545-5700
1924 Washington Ave Philadelphia (19146) *(G-14259)*

Roma Therm Window Systems Plus, Philadelphia *Also called Roma Aluminum Co Inc (G-14259)*

Roman Press Inc 215 997-9650
142 Upper Stump Rd Chalfont (18914) *(G-2886)*

Romano Service, Philadelphia *Also called Charles W Romano Co (G-13532)*

Romans Precision Machining 724 774-6444
327 S Walnut Ln Beaver (15009) *(G-990)*

Romar Textile Co Inc 724 535-7787
1605 Old Route 18 Unit 3 Wampum (16157) *(G-18804)*

Romax Hose Inc 570 869-0860
Rr 367 Laceyville (18623) *(G-8874)*

Rome At Home 412 361-3782
233 Auburn St East Liberty (15206) *(G-4579)*

Romolo Chocolates Inc 814 452-1933
1525 W 8th St Erie (16505) *(G-5466)*

Ron Andrus Logging 814 435-6484
8317 Leetonia Rd Gaines (16921) *(G-6237)*

Ron Anthony Wood Products Inc 724 459-7620
9488 Route 22 Blairsville (15717) *(G-1740)*

Ron Eppley Pioneer Enterprises, Lewisberry *Also called Pioneer Enterprises Inc (G-9892)*

Ron Francis Wire Works, Chester *Also called Wire Works Enterprises Inc (G-3069)*

Ron Lee Inc 570 784-6020
4065 Old Berwick Rd Bloomsburg (17815) *(G-1799)*

Ron Mulkerrin 724 693-8920
401 Cottonwood Dr Oakdale (15071) *(G-12910)*

Ronal Tool Company Inc 717 741-0880
99 Hokes Mill Rd York (17404) *(G-20660)*

Ronald Copeland 814 827-3968
933 Meadville Rd Titusville (16354) *(G-18392)*

Ronald D Jones Financial Svc 724 352-5020
101 Alwine Rd Ste 210 Saxonburg (16056) *(G-17094)*

Ronald E Koller Welding 412 859-6781
33 Evelyn Dr Coraopolis (15108) *(G-3724)*

Ronald Hines 570 256-3355
75 Park Ridge Dr Shickshinny (18655) *(G-17502)*

Ronald J Stidmon 724 336-0501
214 Little Beaver Rd Enon Valley (16120) *(G-5088)*

Ronald Kauffman 717 589-3789
100 Owl Hollow Rd Millerstown (17062) *(G-11208)*

Ronco Machine Inc 570 319-1832
11 Skyline Dr E Ste 3&4 S Abingtn Twp (18411) *(G-16898)*

Ronnas Ruff Bark Trucking Inc 814 221-4410
2928 Knight Town Rd Shippenville (16254) *(G-17563)*

Roo Tees Inc 412 279-9889
300 Noblestown Rd Ste 1 Carnegie (15106) *(G-2788)*

Rooftop Equipment Inc 724 946-9999
4617 New Castle Rd New Wilmington (16142) *(G-12470)*

Rooster Anodizing, Russellton *Also called Pittsburgh Anodizing Co (G-16884)*

Roovers Inc 570 455-7548
125 Butler Dr Hazleton (18201) *(G-7523)*

Roppa Industries LLC 412 749-9250
698 Avenue C Leetsdale (15056) *(G-9703)*

Ropro Design Inc 724 630-1976
530 Bradys Ridge Rd Beaver (15009) *(G-991)*

Rorabaugh Lumber Co 814 845-2277
Rr 219 Box 321 Burnside (15721) *(G-2363)*

Rosalind Candy Castle Inc 724 843-1144
1301 5th Ave New Brighton (15066) *(G-12041)*

Rosati Italian Water Ice, Clifton Heights *Also called SR Rosati Inc (G-3258)*

Rosciolis Bakery 570 961-1151
716 Court St Scranton (18508) *(G-17279)*

Rose A Rupp 412 622-6827
4328 Butler St Rear Pittsburgh (15201) *(G-15496)*

Rose Corporation (PA) 610 376-5004
401 N 8th St Reading (19601) *(G-16504)*

Rose Corporation 610 921-9647
2100 Adams St Reading (19605) *(G-16505)*

Rose Network Solutions 610 563-1958
109 Acorn Way Honey Brook (19344) *(G-7759)*

Rose Plastic Usa Lllp 724 938-8530
525 Technology Dr Coal Center (15423) *(G-3277)*

Rose Tree Corporate Center II, Media *Also called Fxi Inc (G-10926)*

Rose Wild Inc 570 835-4329
17288 Route 287 Tioga (16946) *(G-18364)*

Rosebud Coal Sales Inc 724 545-6222
301 Market St Kittanning (16201) *(G-8789)*

Rosebud Mining Co 814 948-6390
6314 Route 403 Hwy S Heilwood (15745) *(G-7548)*

Rosebud Mining Co 814 749-5208
776 Plank Rd Twin Rocks (15960) *(G-18572)*

Rosebud Mining Company 724 354-4050
4460 Mccreight Rd Shelocta (15774) *(G-17488)*

Rosebud Mining Company (PA) 724 545-6222
301 Market St Kittanning (16201) *(G-8790)*

Rosebud Mining Company 724 459-4970
1878 Saltsburg Rd Clarksburg (15725) *(G-3199)*

Roselon Industries Inc (PA) 215 536-3275
35 S 5th St Quakertown (18951) *(G-16242)*

Rosemount Inc 412 788-1160
  3 Robinson Plz Ste 330 Pittsburgh (15205) *(G-15497)*

Rosemount Inc 724 746-3400
  2 Park Dr Lawrence (15055) *(G-9540)*

Rosenau Beck Inc (PA) 215 364-1714
  1310 Industrial Blvd # 201 Southampton (18966) *(G-17835)*

Rosenberger N Amer Akron LLC 717 859-8900
  309 Colonial Dr Akron (17501) *(G-38)*

Rosenberger's Ice, Hatfield *Also called Rosenbergers Cold Storage (G-7392)*

Rosenbergers Cold Storage 215 721-0700
  2525 Bergey Rd Hatfield (19440) *(G-7392)*

Rosenberry Bros Lumber Co 717 349-7196
  6827 Path Valley Rd Fannettsburg (17221) *(G-5858)*

Rosenberry Septic Tank Service 717 532-4026
  8885 Pineville Rd Shippensburg (17257) *(G-17545)*

Roser Technologies Inc (PA) 814 827-7717
  701 E Spring St Unit 3 Titusville (16354) *(G-18393)*

Roser Technologies Inc 814 589-7031
  347 E Industrial Dr Titusville (16354) *(G-18394)*

Rosewood Company A Partnership 717 349-2289
  7446 Path Valley Rd Fort Loudon (17224) *(G-6060)*

Rosewood Kitchens Inc 717 436-9878
  12 Industrial Cir Mifflintown (17059) *(G-11134)*

Roseys Creations Inc 610 704-8591
  1466 Hampton Rd Allentown (18104) *(G-379)*

Rosie's Butterkins, Philadelphia *Also called Larry Darling (G-13957)*

Rosini Coal Inc 570 874-2879
  236 S Ballard Frackville (17931) *(G-6107)*

Ross Mc Donnell Optical 570 348-0464
  217 E Drinker St Unit 1 Dunmore (18512) *(G-4482)*

Ross Enterprises Inc (PA) 215 968-3334
  401 Lafayette St Newtown (18940) *(G-12546)*

Ross Feeds Inc (PA) 570 289-4388
  6 Mill St Kingsley (18826) *(G-8707)*

Ross Mould LLC (PA) 724 222-7006
  259 S College St Washington (15301) *(G-19222)*

Ross Products Division, Harrisburg *Also called Abbott Laboratories (G-7080)*

Ross Sand Casting 724 222-7006
  259 S College St Washington (15301) *(G-19223)*

Ross Security Systems LLC 717 656-2200
  104 N Maple Ave Leola (17540) *(G-9801)*

Rossi Bros, Philadelphia *Also called Rossi Brothers Cabinet Makers (G-14260)*

Rossi Brothers Cabinet Makers 215 426-9960
  1805 N Howard St Philadelphia (19122) *(G-14260)*

Rossi Excavating Company 570 455-9607
  10 Centtown Rd Beaver Meadows (18216) *(G-1018)*

Rossi Precision Inc 724 667-9334
  250 Reed Rd New Castle (16102) *(G-12145)*

Rossi Welding Co, Reading *Also called P & R United Welding and Fabg (G-16461)*

Rossman, Gary Logging, Kane *Also called Gary T Rossman (G-8463)*

Rosss Custom Butchering 570 634-3571
  44 Ross Rd Trout Run (17771) *(G-18516)*

Rosuco Inc 724 297-5610
  1503 Butler Rd Worthington (16262) *(G-20232)*

Rotadyne Company, Leola *Also called Rotation Dynamics Corporation (G-9802)*

Rotary and Mission Systems, King of Prussia *Also called Lockheed Martin Corporation (G-8641)*

Rotation Dynamics Corporation 717 464-2724
  2 Brooks Ave Willow Street (17584) *(G-20156)*

Rotation Dynamics Corporation 717 656-4252
  21 Zimmerman Rd Leola (17540) *(G-9802)*

Rotech, Berwick *Also called Cpo 2 Inc (G-1320)*

Roth Woodworking LLC 717 476-8609
  107 S Water St New Oxford (17350) *(G-12423)*

Rothman Awning Co Inc 412 589-9974
  44 W Elizabeth St Pittsburgh (15207) *(G-15498)*

Rothrocks Silversmiths Inc 570 253-1990
  3361 Lake Ariel Hwy Honesdale (18431) *(G-7722)*

Rotondo Weirich Entps Inc 215 256-7940
  1240 S Broad St Ste 120 Lansdale (19446) *(G-9407)*

Rough Stone Software LLC 412 444-4295
  200 Fleet St Ste 1200 Pittsburgh (15220) *(G-15499)*

Round River Woodworking 717 776-5876
  457 Meadows Rd Newville (17241) *(G-12610)*

Route 422 Buisness Advisor, Pottstown *Also called Macnificent Pages (G-16012)*

Route One Furniture, Philadelphia *Also called Noor Furniture Inc (G-14077)*

Rovi Corporation 610 293-8561
  550 E Swedesford Rd # 350 Wayne (19087) *(G-19370)*

Rowa Corporation 609 567-8600
  110 Phyllis Ave Croydon (19021) *(G-3927)*

Rowe Printing Shop 717 249-5485
  350 E High St Carlisle (17013) *(G-2737)*

Rowe Screen Print Inc 717 774-8920
  1605 Elm St New Cumberland (17070) *(G-12190)*

Rowe Sprinkler Systems Inc 570 837-7647
  7993 Route 522 Middleburg (17842) *(G-11039)*

Rowland Group, Phoenixville *Also called Rowland Printing Inc (G-14575)*

Rowland Printing Inc 610 933-7400
  751 Pike Springs Rd Phoenixville (19460) *(G-14575)*

Rowman & Littlefield Publish 717 794-3800
  15200 Nbn Way Blue Ridge Summit (17214) *(G-1859)*

Rowman & Littlefield Publs Inc 717 794-3800
  15200 Nbn Way Blue Ridge Summit (17214) *(G-1860)*

Roxanne Toser Non-Sport Entps 717 238-1936
  4019 Green St Harrisburg (17110) *(G-7209)*

Roxcoal Inc 814 443-4668
  1576 Stoystown Rd Friedens (15541) *(G-6226)*

Royal Bake Shop 570 654-2011
  1701 Wyoming Ave Frnt 1 Exeter (18643) *(G-5584)*

Royal Chemical Company Ltd 570 421-7850
  1336 Crowe Rd East Stroudsburg (18301) *(G-4634)*

Royal Graphics, Allentown *Also called Gloroy Inc (G-235)*

Royal Hydraulic Svc & Mfg Inc 724 945-6800
  2 Washington St Cokeburg (15324) *(G-3364)*

Royal Karina Air Service Inc 215 321-3981
  504 Aspen Woods Dr Yardley (19067) *(G-20336)*

Royal Oil & Gas Corporation (PA) 724 463-0246
  1 Indian Springs Rd Indiana (15701) *(G-8124)*

Royal Plastic Lockers, Clifford Township *Also called Bidwell Machining Inc (G-3247)*

Royal Powdered Metals, Palmerton *Also called United Sttes Metal Powders Inc (G-13113)*

Royal Production Company Inc 724 463-0246
  1 Indian Springs Rd Indiana (15701) *(G-8125)*

Royal Service, Center Valley *Also called Shamaseen Hamzah (G-2830)*

Royal T'S, Furlong *Also called Royalty Promotions Inc (G-6233)*

Royal Welsh Winery 724 396-7560
  125 W Main St Ligonier (15658) *(G-9964)*

Royalton Press Inc 610 929-4040
  351 Martingale Dr Camp Hill (17011) *(G-2516)*

Royalton Tool and Die Inc 717 944-5838
  412 Wyoming St Middletown (17057) *(G-11072)*

Royalty Promotions Inc 215 794-2707
  1970 Swamp Rd Furlong (18925) *(G-6233)*

Royco Logistics, Royersford *Also called Royersford Spring Co (G-16863)*

Royco Packaging Inc 215 322-8082
  3979 Mann Rd Huntingdon Valley (19006) *(G-8030)*

Royer Quality Castings Inc 610 367-1390
  380 S Reading Ave Boyertown (19512) *(G-1927)*

Royersford Fndry & Mch Co Inc 610 935-7200
  835 Township Line Rd Phoenixville (19460) *(G-14576)*

Royersford Spring Co 610 948-4440
  98 Main St Royersford (19468) *(G-16863)*

Rozema Printing LLC 717 564-4143
  4790 Derry St Harrisburg (17111) *(G-7210)*

Rpc Inc 570 673-5965
  2897 Route 414 Canton (17724) *(G-2667)*

RPC Bramlage-Wiko-Usa Inc 610 286-0805
  1075 Hemlock Rd Morgantown (19543) *(G-11533)*

RPM Industries LLC 724 228-5130
  1660 Jefferson Ave Washington (15301) *(G-19224)*

RPM Nittany Printing 814 941-7775
  404 27th Ave Altoona (16601) *(G-545)*

Rpw Group Inc 215 493-7456
  503 Jenny Dr Yardley (19067) *(G-20337)*

RR Donnelley & Sons Company 412 241-8200
  218 N Braddock Ave Pittsburgh (15208) *(G-15500)*

RR Donnelley & Sons Company 412 281-7401
  210 6th Ave Ste 3600 Pittsburgh (15222) *(G-15501)*

RR Donnelley & Sons Company 610 391-8825
  7108 Daniels Dr Allentown (18106) *(G-380)*

RR Enterprises Inc 610 266-9600
  1885 Weaversville Rd Allentown (18109) *(G-381)*

Rs Asphalt Maintenance Inc 717 367-4914
  99 Cassell Rd Elizabethtown (17022) *(G-4884)*

RSC Worldwide (us) Inc 215 966-6206
  3711 Market St Ste 800 Philadelphia (19104) *(G-14261)*

RSI, Greenville *Also called Reynolds Services Inc (G-6770)*

RSI Silicon Products LLC 610 258-3100
  3700 Glover Rd Easton (18040) *(G-4749)*

Rsj Technologies LLC 570 673-4173
  184 S Minnequa Ave Canton (17724) *(G-2668)*

RSR Industries Inc 215 543-3350
  315 W Street Rd Warminster (18974) *(G-18956)*

Rss Optometry LLC 610 933-2177
  523 Kimberton Rd Ste 11c Phoenixville (19460) *(G-14577)*

Rt 66 Tractor Supply 724 668-2000
  1855 Lions Club Rd New Alexandria (15670) *(G-12020)*

Rtb Products Inc 724 861-2080
  1061 Main St Ste 2g Irwin (15642) *(G-8198)*

Rtcsnacks LLC 570 234-7266
  225 Sundance Rd Effort (18330) *(G-4828)*

RTD Embedded Technologies Inc 814 234-8087
  103 Innovation Blvd State College (16803) *(G-18017)*

Rtj Inc A Close Corporation 215 943-9220
  1601 Harmer St Ste C Levittown (19057) *(G-9862)*

Rtm Vital Signs LLC 215 643-1286
  439 Dreshertown Rd Fort Washington (19034) *(G-6091)*

Rtr Manufacturing Co 412 665-1500
204 Auburn St East Liberty (15206) *(G-4580)*

RTS Packaging LLC 724 489-4495
98 3rd St Charleroi (15022) *(G-3021)*

Rubber Rolls Inc (PA) 412 276-6400
726 Trumbull Dr Pittsburgh (15205) *(G-15502)*

Rubber Rolls Inc 724 225-9240
50 Rockwood Dr Meadow Lands (15347) *(G-10692)*

Rubber Technology Inc (HQ) 724 838-2340
Berkshire Ctr Ste 401 Greensburg (15601) *(G-6713)*

Rubbermaid Commercial Pdts LLC 570 622-7715
1400 Laurel Blvd Pottsville (17901) *(G-16096)*

Rubertones Casting Division 215 922-1314
740 Sansom St Ste 306 Philadelphia (19106) *(G-14262)*

Ruby Custom Woodcraft Inc 570 698-7741
138 Deacon Hill Rd Lake Ariel (18436) *(G-8891)*

Ruch Carbide Burs Inc 215 657-3660
2750 Terwood Rd Willow Grove (19090) *(G-20139)*

Ruck Engineering Inc 412 835-2408
1246 Plantation Dr Bethel Park (15102) *(G-1431)*

Ruckus Wireless Inc 215 323-1000
101 Tournament Dr Horsham (19044) *(G-7847)*

Ruckus Wireless Inc 215 209-6160
2 Logan Sq Ste 1810 Philadelphia (19103) *(G-14263)*

Ruckus Wireless Inc 814 231-3710
270 Walker Dr State College (16801) *(G-18018)*

Rudy Art Glass Studio, York Also called Mitchco Inc *(G-20599)*

Rudys Fabricating & Mch Inc 724 377-1425
40 Fishpot Run Rd Fredericktown (15333) *(G-6178)*

Ruffcutt Timber LLC 724 626-7306
132 E End Rd Connellsville (15425) *(G-3507)*

Rugani & Rugani LLC 412 223-6472
64a Locust St Mc Kees Rocks (15136) *(G-10632)*

Running Press Book Publishers, Philadelphia Also called Clp Publications Inc *(G-13551)*

Runway Liquidation LLC 401 351-4994
1925 Chestnut St Philadelphia (19103) *(G-14264)*

Runwell Solutions Inc 610 376-7773
575 Van Reed Rd Reading (19610) *(G-16506)*

Ruscomb Tool & Machine Co Inc 215 455-1301
600 W Ruscomb St Philadelphia (19120) *(G-14265)*

Rush Archtectural Met Erectors, Washington Also called A M E R Inc *(G-19143)*

Rush Order Tees 215 677-9200
2727 Commerce Way Philadelphia (19154) *(G-14266)*

Rushimprint, Monroeville Also called Clayton Kendall Inc *(G-11327)*

Rushland Rdge Vineyards Winery 215 598-0251
2665 Rushland Rd Jamison (18929) *(G-8246)*

Rusmar Incorporated 610 436-4314
216 Garfield Ave West Chester (19380) *(G-19632)*

Russ Industrial Solutions LLC 724 736-2580
3285 Pittsburgh Rd Perryopolis (15473) *(G-13304)*

Russell Ribbon & Trim Co 215 938-8550
1100 Jefferson Ln Huntingdon Valley (19006) *(G-8031)*

Russell Rolls Inc 412 321-6623
2217 Preble Ave Pittsburgh (15233) *(G-15503)*

Russell Standard Corporation (PA) 412 449-0700
285 Kappa Dr Ste 300 Pittsburgh (15238) *(G-15504)*

Russell Standard Corporation 724 625-1505
171 7th Ave Valencia (16059) *(G-18701)*

Russell Standard Corporation 724 748-3700
12 Penn Perry Hwy Mercer (16137) *(G-10973)*

Russell Stone Products Inc 814 236-2449
2640 Greenville Pike Grampian (16838) *(G-6572)*

Russell Upholstery Co Inc 814 455-9021
1923 W 26th St Erie (16508) *(G-5467)*

Russo Heating & Cooling Inc 814 454-6263
1406 E 28th St Erie (16504) *(G-5468)*

Russo Machine Works 215 634-1630
3341 D St Philadelphia (19134) *(G-14267)*

Rusticraft Fence Co 610 644-6770
439 E King Rd Malvern (19355) *(G-10311)*

Rustys Oil and Propane Inc 814 497-4423
275 Spring St Houtzdale (16651) *(G-7884)*

Rutter Bros Dairy Inc (PA) 717 848-9827
2100 N George St York (17404) *(G-20661)*

Rutter Bros Dairy Inc 717 388-1665
2800 Vine St Middletown (17057) *(G-11073)*

Rutter's Dairy, York Also called Rutter Bros Dairy Inc *(G-20661)*

Rutts Machine Inc 717 367-3011
300 Jonlyn Dr Elizabethtown (17022) *(G-4885)*

Ruud Kahle Master Goldsmith 215 947-5050
2535 Huntingdon Pike Huntingdon Valley (19006) *(G-8032)*

Rwb Special Services Corp 215 766-4800
6250 Kellers Church Rd Pipersville (18947) *(G-14619)*

Rwe Holding Company 724 752-9082
535 Rundle Rd New Castle (16107) *(G-12146)*

Rwg Company 215 552-9541
333 Lancaster Ave Apt 804 Malvern (19355) *(G-10312)*

Ryan Foster Inc 215 769-0118
7118 Germantown Ave Philadelphia (19119) *(G-14268)*

Ryan Kanaskie 717 248-9822
306 Country Club Rd Lewistown (17044) *(G-9947)*

Ryder Graphics 717 697-0187
701 W Simpson St Mechanicsburg (17055) *(G-10886)*

Ryder Rock, New Wilmington Also called Tervo Masonry Llc *(G-12471)*

Ryders Aluminum Welding, Chambersburg Also called Ryders Welding LLC *(G-2974)*

Ryders Welding LLC 717 369-5198
3959 Warm Spring Rd Chambersburg (17202) *(G-2974)*

Ryerson Thypin Steel, Morrisville Also called Joseph T Ryerson & Son Inc *(G-11565)*

Ryno Linesets, Honesdale Also called Ptubes Inc *(G-7721)*

Rynone Manufacturing Corp (PA) 570 888-5272
N Thomas Ave Sayre (18840) *(G-17121)*

S & B Foundry Co 570 784-2047
3825 Columbia Blvd Bloomsburg (17815) *(G-1800)*

S & D Welding Inc 570 546-8772
1754 John Brady Dr Muncy (17756) *(G-11832)*

S & G Corrugated Packaging Inc 570 287-1718
195 Slocum St Swoyersville (18704) *(G-18198)*

S & G Water Conditioning Inc 215 672-2030
525 York Rd Warminster (18974) *(G-18957)*

S & H Hardware & Supply Co (PA) 215 745-9375
6700 Castor Ave Philadelphia (19149) *(G-14269)*

S & H Hardware & Supply Co 267 288-5950
2146-2150 County Line Rd Huntingdon Valley (19006) *(G-8033)*

S & H Logging LLC 570 966-8958
745 White Springs Rd Mifflinburg (17844) *(G-11102)*

S & H Ltd 215 426-2775
620 Oakbourne Rd West Chester (19382) *(G-19633)*

S & K Scope Mounts 814 489-3091
70 Swede Hollow Rd Sugar Grove (16350) *(G-18146)*

S & K Vending 570 675-5180
5843 Main Rd Hunlock Creek (18621) *(G-7934)*

S & L Motors Inc 570 342-9718
200 S 7th Ave Scranton (18505) *(G-17280)*

S & M Machine Company 724 339-2035
1500 Queensburg Rd New Kensington (15068) *(G-12373)*

S & N Industries LLC (PA) 724 406-0322
871 New Castle Rd Slippery Rock (16057) *(G-17627)*

S & R Woodworking 717 354-8628
3841 Yost Rd Gordonville (17529) *(G-6562)*

S & S Electric Motors Inc 717 263-1919
125 Falling Spring Rd Chambersburg (17202) *(G-2975)*

S & S Fasteners Inc 724 251-9288
2501a Duss Ave Ambridge (15003) *(G-632)*

S & S Loggs Inc 814 339-7375
2030 Eagle Eye Rd West Decatur (16878) *(G-19691)*

S & S Machine & Tool Company 610 265-1582
150 W Church Rd King of Prussia (19406) *(G-8671)*

S & S Packaging Products Inc 800 633-0272
10549 Crosby Cir Cranesville (16410) *(G-3870)*

S & S Precision Tool Inc 717 244-1600
380 Boxwood Rd Red Lion (17356) *(G-16612)*

S & S Processing Inc 724 535-3110
478 Beaver Rd West Pittsburg (16160) *(G-19752)*

S & S Refractories, Mars Also called Intersource Inc *(G-10501)*

S & S Sbsrface Invstgtions Inc 610 738-8762
24 Hagerty Blvd Ste 11 West Chester (19382) *(G-19634)*

S & S Slides Inc 724 545-2001
11771 State Route 85 Kittanning (16201) *(G-8791)*

S & T Service & Supply, Pleasantville Also called S & T Supply Co *(G-15803)*

S & T Supply Co 814 589-7025
15267 Tionesta Rd Pleasantville (16341) *(G-15803)*

S & W Metal Products Inc 610 473-2400
441 County Line Rd Gilbertsville (19525) *(G-6376)*

S & W Race Cars Components Inc 610 948-7303
11 Mennonite Church Rd Spring City (19475) *(G-17865)*

S & W Wire, Cranberry Township Also called Stimple and Ward Company *(G-3851)*

S B I Inc 610 595-3300
528 9th Ave Prospect Park (19076) *(G-16119)*

S Corporation, Ephrata Also called Laser Lab Inc *(G-5120)*

S D & R, Ridgway Also called Secondary Development & Res *(G-16729)*

S D L Custom Cabinetry Inc 215 355-8188
4570 E Bristol Rd Langhorne (19053) *(G-9323)*

S Don Food Market Inc 717 453-7470
672 Main St Lykens (17048) *(G-10135)*

S DRocco Upholstery 215 745-2869
7217 Montour St Philadelphia (19111) *(G-14270)*

S E Hagarman Designs LLC 717 633-5336
207 Eichelberger St Hanover (17331) *(G-6947)*

S E Moulding Inc 717 385-4119
155 Garfield Dr Carlisle (17015) *(G-2738)*

S F Spector Inc 717 236-0805
608 Brook St Harrisburg (17110) *(G-7211)*

S F U LLC 610 473-0730
136 Pinehurst Way Gilbertsville (19525) *(G-6377)*

S Frey Pallets 717 284-9937
984 Buck Heights Rd Quarryville (17566) *(G-16278)*

S G Business Services Inc 215 567-7107
35 S 18th St Philadelphia (19103) *(G-14271)*

S G Frantz Co Inc...215 943-2930
  1507 Branagan Dr Bristol (19007) **(G-2196)**
S H Bath, Huntingdon Valley *Also called S & H Hardware & Supply Co* **(G-8033)**
S H Sharpless & Son Inc...570 454-6685
  61 N Pine St Hazleton (18201) **(G-7524)**
S I A M, Philadelphia *Also called Society For Industrial & Appli* **(G-14320)**
S J A Concrete, Philadelphia *Also called S J A Construction Inc* **(G-14272)**
S J A Construction Inc...856 985-3400
  3600 S 26th St Philadelphia (19145) **(G-14272)**
S K I, King of Prussia *Also called Sheen Kleen Inc* **(G-8673)**
S K P Company...570 344-0561
  710 E Mountain Rd Scranton (18505) **(G-17281)**
S M E Foods LLC..717 852-8515
  70 Aberdeen Rd York (17406) **(G-20662)**
S M I, Carlisle *Also called Superior Metalworks Inc* **(G-2740)**
S M P, Red Lion *Also called Specilty Mtallurgical Pdts Inc* **(G-16614)**
S Morantz Inc..215 969-0266
  9984 Gantry Rd Philadelphia (19115) **(G-14273)**
S Morantz, Inc, Philadelphia *Also called Morantz Inc* **(G-14038)**
S P Industries Inc...215 396-2200
  103 Steam Whistle Dr Warminster (18974) **(G-18958)**
S P Industries Inc (HQ)..215 672-7800
  935 Mearns Rd Warminster (18974) **(G-18959)**
S P Kinney Engineers Inc (PA)..................................412 276-4600
  143 1st Ave Carnegie (15106) **(G-2789)**
S P Printing..610 562-8551
  620 Franklin St Shoemakersville (19555) **(G-17574)**
S R Sloan Inc..570 366-8934
  87 Pinedale Industrial Rd Orwigsburg (17961) **(G-13051)**
S S Salvage Recycling Inc.......................................717 444-0008
  600 Susquehanna Trl Liverpool (17045) **(G-10079)**
S Schiff Restaurant Svc Inc.....................................570 343-1294
  3410 N Main Ave Scranton (18508) **(G-17282)**
S SM, Philadelphia *Also called Ssm Industries Inc* **(G-14337)**
S T G, Monessen *Also called Santelli Tempered Glass Inc* **(G-11301)**
S T I Creative Division, Erie *Also called Parker-Hannifin Corporation* **(G-5415)**
S T M Co, Ellwood City *Also called Standard Tool & Machine Co* **(G-4951)**
S T M Heavy Duty Electric Inc..................................610 967-3810
  7601 Chestnut St Zionsville (18092) **(G-20836)**
S W Machine..717 336-2699
  401 Stevens Rd Stevens (17578) **(G-18056)**
S W U Automotive Machinery LLC..............................570 457-4299
  4961 Birney Ave R Moosic (18507) **(G-11514)**
S Wenger Feed Mill Inc..717 361-4223
  26 Linden Ave Elizabethtown (17022) **(G-4886)**
S&K Pallet LLC...717 667-0001
  684 Old Three Cent Ln Reedsville (17084) **(G-16627)**
S&L Motor Service, Scranton *Also called S & L Motors Inc* **(G-17280)**
S&N Energy, Pocono Pines *Also called Sean Naughton* **(G-15884)**
S&P Global Inc..215 430-6000
  2001 Market St Philadelphia (19103) **(G-14274)**
S&S Custom Sawing..717 694-3248
  31 Saw Mill Ln Richfield (17086) **(G-16682)**
S-Bond Technologies LLC..215 631-7114
  2299 Amber Dr Ste 120 Hatfield (19440) **(G-7393)**
S-L Snacks Real Estate Inc......................................717 632-4477
  1250 York St Hanover (17331) **(G-6948)**
S. C. S., Nazareth *Also called Software Consulting Svcs LLC* **(G-11988)**
S.E. Firestone Associates, Bridgeport *Also called Norstone Incorporated* **(G-2041)**
S.O.M.A., Philadelphia *Also called Support McRcomputers Assoc Inc* **(G-14359)**
S.P.I. Supplies, West Chester *Also called Structure Probe Inc* **(G-19646)**
Sa-Fe Windows Inc...717 464-9605
  206 W Kendig Rd Willow Street (17584) **(G-20157)**
Saba Holding Company Inc......................................717 737-3431
  2001 State Rd Camp Hill (17011) **(G-2517)**
Sabic Innovative Plas US LLC...................................610 363-4500
  475 Creamery Way Exton (19341) **(G-5727)**
Sabic Innovative Plas US LLC...................................610 383-8900
  475 Creamery Way Exton (19341) **(G-5728)**
Sabina Mfg., Carnegie *Also called Supply Technologies LLC* **(G-2797)**
Sable Calibration Services, Harleysville *Also called Scs Inc* **(G-7057)**
Sabold Design Inc..610 401-4086
  242 Grandview Rd Bernville (19506) **(G-1305)**
Sabre Equipment Inc...412 262-3080
  802 Pennsylvania Ave Coraopolis (15108) **(G-3725)**
Sabre Tblar Strctures - PA LLC.................................724 201-9968
  700 2nd St Ellwood City (16117) **(G-4948)**
Sabrosa Salt Company LLC......................................610 250-9002
  4030 Lantern Pl W Easton (18045) **(G-4750)**
Sac Industries Inc..412 787-7500
  137 Industry Dr Pittsburgh (15275) **(G-15505)**
Sac Manufacturing, Pittsburgh *Also called Sac Industries Inc* **(G-15505)**
Sadies Salads..717 768-3774
  4021b Old Phila Pike Gordonville (17529) **(G-6563)**
Saegar Machine and Welding, Harleysville *Also called Saeger Machine Inc* **(G-7056)**
Saeger Machine Inc..215 256-8754
  531 Old Skippack Rd Harleysville (19438) **(G-7056)**

Saegertown Hardware, Saegertown *Also called Fame Manufacturing Inc* **(G-16913)**
Saegertown Manufacturing Corp................................814 763-2655
  1 Crawford St Saegertown (16433) **(G-16932)**
Saeilo Inc (HQ)...845 735-4500
  105 Kahr Ave Greeley (18425) **(G-6583)**
Saeilo Enterprises Inc (PA)......................................845 735-6500
  105 Kahr Ave Greeley (18425) **(G-6584)**
Saeilo Manufacturing Inds, Greeley *Also called SMI IL Inc* **(G-6585)**
Safari Tools Inc...717 350-9869
  383 N Perry Hwy Mercer (16137) **(G-10974)**
Safc Biosciences Inc...610 750-8801
  5 Dutch Ct Reading (19608) **(G-16507)**
Safe Pac Pasteurization LLC.....................................267 324-5631
  2712 Grays Ferry Ave Philadelphia (19146) **(G-14275)**
Safe Paw, Huntingdon Valley *Also called Gaia Enterprises Inc* **(G-7988)**
Safe-TEC Clinical Products LLC..................................215 364-5582
  142 Railroad Dr Warminster (18974) **(G-18960)**
Safeguard Business Systems Inc.................................215 631-7500
  1180 Church Rd Ste A Lansdale (19446) **(G-9408)**
Safeguard By Innovative, Phoenixville *Also called Innovtive Print Mdia Group Inc* **(G-14553)**
Safeguard Products Inc..717 354-4586
  2710 Division Hwy New Holland (17557) **(G-12280)**
Safeguard Scientifics Inc (PA)..................................610 293-0600
  170 N Radnor Chester Rd # 200 Radnor (19087) **(G-16301)**
Safeguard Systems, Philadelphia *Also called Softboss Corp* **(G-14321)**
Safety Guard Steel Fabg Co......................................412 821-1177
  220 Lincoln Ave McKnight (15237) **(G-10688)**
Safety House Inc..610 344-0637
  99 Alda Ave Glen Mills (19342) **(G-6443)**
Safety Rail Source LLC...610 539-9535
  2570 Blvd Of The Gen 20 Norristown (19403) **(G-12707)**
Safety Sling Company Inc..412 231-6684
  919 Fulton St Pittsburgh (15233) **(G-15506)**
Safetydecals.net, Greencastle *Also called Gate 7 LLC* **(G-6614)**
Safeware Inc..215 354-1401
  1601 Republic Rd Ste 105 Huntingdon Valley (19006) **(G-8034)**
Safeware Willow Grove, Huntingdon Valley *Also called Safeware Inc* **(G-8034)**
Safran Brothers Inc..724 266-9758
  2910 Duss Ave Ambridge (15003) **(G-633)**
Sageking Inc..717 540-0525
  4395 Sage Ln Irwin (15642) **(G-8199)**
Saha Industries Inc..610 383-5070
  717 E Chestnut St Coatesville (19320) **(G-3325)**
SAI Hydraulics Inc..610 497-0190
  168 E Ridge Rd Ste 106 Linwood (19061) **(G-9991)**
Saint Lukes Hosp Bethlehem PA..................................610 954-3531
  4379 Easton Ave Ste 103 Bethlehem (18020) **(G-1614)**
Saint-Gobain, Malvern *Also called Certainteed Corporation* **(G-10204)**
Saint-Gobain Abrasives Inc......................................215 855-4300
  200 Commerce Dr Montgomeryville (18936) **(G-11416)**
Saint-Gobain Abrasives Inc......................................267 218-7100
  200 Commerce Dr Montgomeryville (18936) **(G-11417)**
Saint-Gobain Ceramics Plas Inc..................................570 383-3261
  1401 E Lackawanna St Olyphant (18447) **(G-12998)**
Saint-Gobain Ceramics Plas Inc..................................724 539-6000
  4702 Route 982 Latrobe (15650) **(G-9518)**
Saint-Gobain Ceramics Plas Inc (HQ)............................508 795-5000
  750 E Swedesford Rd Valley Forge (19482) **(G-18711)**
Saint-Gobain Corporation (HQ)..................................610 893-6000
  20 Moores Rd Malvern (19355) **(G-10313)**
Saint-Gobain Crystals, Valley Forge *Also called Saint-Gobain Ceramics Plas Inc* **(G-18711)**
Saint-Gobain Delaware Corp (HQ)...............................610 341-7000
  750 E Swedesford Rd Valley Forge (19482) **(G-18712)**
Saint-Gobain Vetrotex Amer Inc (HQ)...........................610 893-6000
  20 Moores Rd Valley Forge (19482) **(G-18713)**
Saj Publishing..814 445-9695
  113 S Center Ave Ste 1 Somerset (15501) **(G-17703)**
Saj Publishing..610 544-5484
  100 Harned Dr Springfield (19064) **(G-17922)**
Sakala Stone Products...724 339-2224
  7230 Guyer Rd New Kensington (15068) **(G-12374)**
Salad Specialty, Harleysville *Also called Isabelles Kitchen Inc* **(G-7040)**
Saladax Biomedical Inc..610 419-6731
  116 Research Dr Bethlehem (18015) **(G-1615)**
Salem Antiquities...724 309-1781
  1 W Pittsburgh St Delmont (15626) **(G-4055)**
Salem Hardwood, Adamsville *Also called Penn-Sylvan International Inc* **(G-26)**
Salem Hardwood, Inc., Adamsville *Also called Edmund Burke Inc* **(G-25)**
Salem Millwork Inc...724 468-5701
  100 Industrial Dr Delmont (15626) **(G-4056)**
Salem Printing Inc..724 468-8604
  506 Athena Dr Delmont (15626) **(G-4057)**
Salem Supply Co, Warminster *Also called Delmar Enterprises Inc* **(G-18856)**
Salem Tube Inc...724 646-4301
  951 4th St Greenville (16125) **(G-6772)**
Sales Marketing Group Inc.......................................412 928-0422
  300 Cedar Ridge Dr # 310 Pittsburgh (15205) **(G-15507)**

Salimetrics LLC 814 234-7748
  101 Innovation Blvd # 302 State College (16803) *(G-18019)*

Salix Cabinetry Inc 814 266-4181
  307 Bellwood Dr Salix (15952) *(G-17048)*

Sallack Well Services Inc 814 938-8179
  304 Hidden Hollow Ln Punxsutawney (15767) *(G-16160)*

Salmen Tech Co Inc 412 854-1822
  533 N St Bethel Park (15102) *(G-1432)*

Salmon Pillowmakers 717 767-4978
  2076 Church Rd York (17408) *(G-20663)*

Salt Box, The, Lancaster Also called American Period Lighting Inc *(G-8931)*

Salt Fctry By Snow Ice MGT Inc 412 321-7669
  2220 Palmer St Pittsburgh (15218) *(G-15508)*

Salter's Industries, Collegeville Also called Unisource Associates Inc *(G-3398)*

Salus Security Devices LLC 610 388-6387
  459 Chambers Ln West Chester (19382) *(G-19635)*

Sam Andrew 724 224-5445
  588 Meander Ln Tarentum (15084) *(G-18246)*

Sam Beachy & Sons 814 662-2220
  381 Niverton Rd Salisbury (15558) *(G-17045)*

Sam Beiler 717 442-8990
  3533 Lincoln Hwy E Kinzers (17535) *(G-8742)*

Sam King 610 273-7979
  450 Beaver Dam Rd Honey Brook (19344) *(G-7760)*

Sam Mannino Enterprises LLC 814 692-4100
  191 Anaconda Dr Ste 100 Pennsylvania Furnace (16865) *(G-13264)*

Sam's Pop and Beer Shop, New Kensington Also called City Btlg Co of New Kensington *(G-12334)*

Samco Inc 814 495-4632
  Rr 869 Saint Michael (15951) *(G-17032)*

Samfam Inc 814 941-1915
  3614 6th Ave Altoona (16602) *(G-546)*

Samir Corp 412 647-6000
  200 Lothrop St Pittsburgh (15213) *(G-15509)*

Sample News Group LLC (PA) 814 665-8291
  28 W South St Corry (16407) *(G-3773)*

Sample News Group LLC 814 774-7073
  142 Main St E Ste 3 Girard (16417) *(G-6401)*

Sample News Group LLC 570 888-9643
  201 N Lehigh Ave Sayre (18840) *(G-17122)*

Samples News Group, Corry Also called Corry Journal Inc *(G-3750)*

Samson Paper Co Inc 610 630-9090
  2554 Industry Ln Ste 300 Norristown (19403) *(G-12708)*

Samuel Son & Co (usa) Inc 412 865-4444
  4990 Grand Ave Pittsburgh (15225) *(G-15510)*

Samuel C Rizzo Jr 814 725-3047
  23 S Lake St North East (16428) *(G-12760)*

Samuel Deans Associates, Ardmore Also called Dein-Verbit Associates Inc *(G-707)*

Samuel Gerber Inc 717 761-0250
  6802 Clubhouse Dr Apt L Harrisburg (17111) *(G-7212)*

Samuel Grossi & Sons Inc 215 638-4470
  2526 State Rd Bensalem (19020) *(G-1249)*

Samuel Stamping Tech LLC 724 981-5042
  1760 Broadway Rd Hermitage (16148) *(G-7594)*

Samuel Yellin Metalworkers Co 610 527-2334
  721 Moore Ave Bryn Mawr (19010) *(G-2333)*

Samuelson Leather LLC 484 328-3273
  2309 Woodview Way Malvern (19355) *(G-10314)*

Samuelson Leather LLC (PA) 610 719-7391
  638 Metro Ct West Chester (19380) *(G-19636)*

San-Fab Co Inc 570 385-2551
  319 Saint Charles St Schuylkill Haven (17972) *(G-17166)*

Sanatoga Water Cond Inc 610 326-9803
  80 N Charlotte St Pottstown (19464) *(G-16042)*

Sanavita Medical LLC 267 517-3220
  551 E Church Ave Telford (18969) *(G-18312)*

Sand Castle Winery 484 924-9530
  236 Bridge St Phoenixville (19460) *(G-14578)*

Sand Castle Winery (PA) 610 294-9181
  755 River Rd Erwinna (18920) *(G-5539)*

Sand Patch Mill LLC 814 634-9772
  134 Deal Rd Meyersdale (15552) *(G-11019)*

Sanda Corporation 502 510-8782
  19 W Third St Media (19063) *(G-10947)*

Sanders Saws & Blades Inc 610 273-3733
  2470 Conestoga Ave Honey Brook (19344) *(G-7761)*

Sanders Tool Co, Erie Also called Dennis Sanders *(G-5245)*

Sandlex Corporation 570 820-8568
  84 Beekman St Wilkes Barre (18702) *(G-19961)*

Sandrose Trophies, Chester Also called Bob Allen & Sons Inc *(G-3040)*

Sandt Printing Co Inc 610 258-7445
  2333 Northwood Ave Easton (18045) *(G-4751)*

Sandt's Honey, Easton Also called Honey Sandts Co *(G-4700)*

Sandvik Inc 570 585-7500
  982 Griffin Pond Rd S Abingtn Twp (18411) *(G-16899)*

Sandvik Inc 724 246-2901
  6701 National Pike Brier Hill (15415) *(G-2101)*

Sandvik Mining and Cnstr 215 245-0280
  777 American Dr Bensalem (19020) *(G-1250)*

Sandvik Mining and Tunneling, Brier Hill Also called Sandvik Inc *(G-2101)*

Sandvik Pubg Interactive Inc 203 205-0188
  9 South Dr Yardley (19067) *(G-20338)*

Sandys Fashion Jewelry LLC 814 938-4356
  400 Sutton St Apt 4 Punxsutawney (15767) *(G-16161)*

Sandys Nail 215 848-0299
  3726 Midvale Ave Philadelphia (19129) *(G-14276)*

Saner Architecture Millwork 717 786-2014
  310 Park Ave Quarryville (17566) *(G-16279)*

Sanes, Gene Upholstery, Pittsburgh Also called Gene Sanes & Associates *(G-15043)*

Sanfelice Wldg Fabrication LLC 610 337-4125
  620 W Washington St Norristown (19401) *(G-12709)*

Sanford Miller Inc 724 479-5090
  150 Ross Rd Homer City (15748) *(G-7681)*

Sanguis LLC 267 228-7502
  3711 Market St Ste 800 Philadelphia (19104) *(G-14277)*

Sani-Brands Inc 610 841-1599
  1636 N Cedar Crest Blvd Allentown (18104) *(G-382)*

Sanitary Process Systems Inc 717 627-6630
  945 Fruitville Pike Lititz (17543) *(G-10045)*

Sanitation Billing Office, New Castle Also called City of New Castle *(G-12073)*

Sankey, Ellwood City Also called Ellwood Safety Appliance Co *(G-4932)*

Sanofi Pasteur Inc (HQ) 570 839-7187
  1 Discovery Dr Swiftwater (18370) *(G-18190)*

Sanofi Pasteur Inc 570 957-7187
  50 Stauffer Industrial Pa Taylor (18517) *(G-18261)*

Sansom Quilting & EMB Co 215 627-6990
  511 Spring Garden St Philadelphia (19123) *(G-14278)*

Sansom Street Soft Pretzel Fac 215 569-3988
  1532 Sansom St Philadelphia (19102) *(G-14279)*

Sansom Tool & Die Inc 814 967-4985
  37414 Bowmaster Rd Centerville (16404) *(G-2835)*

Santana Lamination, Archbald Also called Mtl Holdings Inc *(G-693)*

Santarelli Ready Mixed Con, Wyoming Also called Santarelli Vibrated Block LLC *(G-20284)*

Santarelli Vibrated Block LLC 570 693-2200
  966 Shoemaker Ave Wyoming (18644) *(G-20284)*

Santees Love 215 821-9679
  5353 Akron St Philadelphia (19124) *(G-14280)*

Santelli Tempered Glass Inc 724 684-4144
  240 Riverview Dr Monessen (15062) *(G-11301)*

Santucci Process Development (PA) 412 787-0747
  121 Beaver Grade Rd Mc Kees Rocks (15136) *(G-10633)*

Sanyo Chemical & Resins LLC 412 384-5700
  2200 St Hwy 837 West Elizabeth (15088) *(G-19697)*

Sapa Extruder LLC, Moon Township Also called Hydro Extruder LLC *(G-11492)*

Sapa Extrusions Inc 870 235-2609
  335 Camer Dr Bensalem (19020) *(G-1251)*

Sapa Industrial Extrusions, Cressona Also called Hydro Extrusion Usa LLC *(G-3904)*

Sapa North America Inc 877 922-7272
  53 Pottsville St Cressona (17929) *(G-3907)*

Sapa Precision Tubing LLC (HQ) 412 893-1300
  400 Rouser Rd Ste 300 Moon Township (15108) *(G-11499)*

Sapient Automation LLC 877 451-4044
  2398 N Penn Rd Hatfield (19440) *(G-7394)*

Sapling Inc 215 322-6063
  670 Louis Dr Warminster (18974) *(G-18961)*

Sapling Press 412 681-1003
  4618 Friendship Ave Pittsburgh (15224) *(G-15511)*

Sapor Food Group LLC 267 714-4382
  30 N 41st St Ste 570 Philadelphia (19104) *(G-14281)*

Sapphire Software, Allentown Also called K12systems Inc *(G-278)*

Sappi Fine Paper North America, Allentown Also called Sappi North America Inc *(G-383)*

Sappi North America Inc 610 398-8400
  1340 Hickory Ln Allentown (18106) *(G-383)*

Sarah Lynn Fashions, Allentown Also called Sarah Lynn Sportswear Inc *(G-384)*

Sarah Lynn Sportswear Inc 610 770-1702
  707 N 4th St Fl 2 Allentown (18102) *(G-384)*

Sarclad (north America) LP 412 466-2000
  30 S Linden St Duquesne (15110) *(G-4499)*

Sardello Inc 724 375-4101
  1000 Corporation Dr Aliquippa (15001) *(G-91)*

Sardello Inc 724 827-8835
  407 Cannelton Rd Darlington (16115) *(G-4031)*

Sardello's, Aliquippa Also called Sardello Inc *(G-91)*

Sargent Art, Hazleton Also called Pidilite Usa Inc *(G-7519)*

Sargent Art, Inc., Hazleton Also called Sargent Realty Inc *(G-7525)*

Sargent Realty Inc 570 454-3596
  100 E Diamond Ave Hazleton (18201) *(G-7525)*

Sarik Corporation 215 538-2269
  420 Station Rd Ste 3 Quakertown (18951) *(G-16243)*

Sarris Candies Inc 724 745-4042
  511 Adams Ave Canonsburg (15317) *(G-2632)*

Sarro Signs Inc 610 444-2020
  116 W Street Rd Kennett Square (19348) *(G-8541)*

Sartomer Americas Division, Exton Also called Arkema Inc *(G-5646)*

Sartomer Company Divison Total 610 692-8401
  610 S Bolmar St West Chester (19382) *(G-19637)*

Sarver Hardware Co Inc 724 295-5131
551 S Pike Rd Sarver (16055) *(G-17079)*

Sasol Chemicals (usa) LLC 814 677-2028
292 State Route 8 Oil City (16301) *(G-12957)*

Satcom Digital Networks LLC 724 824-1699
20 Leonberg Rd Ste E Cranberry Township (16066) *(G-3847)*

Saturnalian N Y A 215 271-9181
1811 S 2nd St Philadelphia (19148) *(G-14282)*

Saucon Source LLC 610 442-3370
612 N Hoffert St Fountain Hill (18015) *(G-6100)*

Saucy Noodle 412 440-0432
300 Munt Lbnon Blvd Ste 5 Pittsburgh (15234) *(G-15512)*

Sauder Fuel, Adamstown *Also called Haller Energy Services LLC (G-22)*

Sauders Nursery 717 354-9851
1210 E Earl Rd East Earl (17519) *(G-4555)*

Sauer Industries Inc (PA) 412 687-4100
30 51st St Pittsburgh (15201) *(G-15513)*

Sauereisen Inc 412 963-0303
160 Gamma Dr Pittsburgh (15238) *(G-15514)*

Saupp Signs Co LLC 814 342-2100
220 New Liberty Rd Philipsburg (16866) *(G-14526)*

Sauquoit Industries LLC 570 348-2751
300 Palm St Scranton (18505) *(G-17283)*

Savello USA Incorporated 570 822-9743
1265 Sans Souci Pkwy Hanover Township (18706) *(G-7005)*

Savemypixcom Inc 800 535-6299
82 Stirrup Ln Thornton (19373) *(G-18355)*

Savencia Cheese USA LLC (HQ) 717 355-8500
400 S Custer Ave New Holland (17557) *(G-12281)*

Savor Street Foods Inc (PA) 610 320-7800
1 Park Plz Wyomissing (19610) *(G-20288)*

Saw Horse Woodworking, Kutztown *Also called Saw Rocking Horse (G-8860)*

Saw Rocking Horse 610 683-8075
83 Sieger Rd Kutztown (19530) *(G-8860)*

Sawcom Tech Inc 610 433-7900
3676 Crescent Ct E Whitehall (18052) *(G-19888)*

Saxon Office Technology Inc 215 736-2620
225 Lincoln Hwy Fairless Hills (19030) *(G-5795)*

Saxon Turf Equipment, Lower Burrell *Also called Wolfe Metal Fab Inc (G-10108)*

Say Plastics Inc 717 633-6333
165 Oak Ln Mc Sherrystown (17344) *(G-10652)*

Say Plastics Inc 717 624-3222
2259 Oxford Rd New Oxford (17350) *(G-12424)*

Say-Core Inc 814 736-8018
132 Block Rd Portage (15946) *(G-15920)*

Saybolt LP 412 464-7380
1200 Lebanon Rd Ste 1 West Mifflin (15122) *(G-19744)*

Saylor Industries Inc 814 479-4964
757 Tire Hill Rd Johnstown (15905) *(G-8432)*

Saylors Farm & Wood Products 814 745-2306
17319 Route 68 Sligo (16255) *(G-17616)*

Saylorsburg Metal Works, Saylorsburg *Also called Saylorsburg Stl Fbricators Inc (G-17106)*

Saylorsburg Stl Fbricators Inc 610 381-4444
1281 Princess Run Rd Saylorsburg (18353) *(G-17106)*

Sb Distribution Center Inc 215 717-2600
30 S 15th St Graham Bldg Philadelphia (19102) *(G-14283)*

Sb Global Foods Inc 215 361-9500
2940 Turnpike Dr Ste 15 Hatboro (19040) *(G-7303)*

Sb New York Inc 215 717-2600
30 S 15th St Fl 14 Philadelphia (19102) *(G-14284)*

Sb Specialty Metals LLC 814 337-8804
99 W Poplar St Meadville (16335) *(G-10788)*

Sbi Survivor Corporation (PA) 215 997-8900
3810 Clover Dr Center Valley (18034) *(G-2829)*

Sbn Holding LLC 724 756-2210
100 Sonneborn Ln Petrolia (16050) *(G-13307)*

Sca Personal Care, Eddystone *Also called Essity North America Inc (G-4801)*

Scaffs Enterprises Inc 570 725-3497
2550 E Valley Rd Loganton (17747) *(G-10098)*

Scale Watcher North Amer Inc 610 932-6888
345 Lincoln St Oxford (19363) *(G-13089)*

Scalese Mill Works, Cherry Tree *Also called Paul Scalese (G-3034)*

Scaletron Industries Ltd 215 766-2670
53 Apple Tree Ln Plumsteadville (18949) *(G-15813)*

Scalpy Hollow Timber Service 717 284-2862
1147 Scalpy Hollow Rd Drumore (17518) *(G-4379)*

Scandura.com, Haverford *Also called Intelligent Micro Systems Ltd (G-7412)*

Scanmaster 215 208-4732
375 Lemon St Warminster (18974) *(G-18962)*

Scantron Corporation 717 684-4600
3975 Continental Dr Columbia (17512) *(G-3450)*

Scatton Bros Mfg Co 215 362-6830
1680 Bridle Path Dr Lansdale (19446) *(G-9409)*

Scenic Ridge Company 717 768-7522
48 Queen Rd Gordonville (17529) *(G-6564)*

Scenic Ridge Contruction, Gordonville *Also called Scenic Ridge Company (G-6564)*

Scenic Road Manufacturing 717 768-7300
3539 Scenic Rd Gordonville (17529) *(G-6565)*

Scenic View Leather Shop, Howard *Also called Daniel D Esh (G-7889)*

Scents Krafts & Stitches 610 770-0204
1071 Hill Dr Allentown (18103) *(G-385)*

Scepter Signs and Electric, Pottstown *Also called Scepter Signs Inc (G-16043)*

Scepter Signs Inc 610 326-7446
431 W Vine St Pottstown (19464) *(G-16043)*

Schaefer Fireworks, Ronks *Also called Schaefer Pyrotechnics Inc (G-16814)*

Schaefer Machine Inc 724 796-7755
727 Robinson Hwy Mc Donald (15057) *(G-10581)*

Schaefer Paint Company 717 687-7017
730 Georgetown Rd Ronks (17572) *(G-16813)*

Schaefer Pyrotechnics Inc 717 687-0647
376 Hartman Bridge Rd Ronks (17572) *(G-16814)*

Schafco Packaging Co, Ronks *Also called Schaefer Paint Company (G-16813)*

Schaffner Manufacturing Co (PA) 412 761-9902
21 Herron Ave Pittsburgh (15202) *(G-15515)*

Schake Industries Inc 814 677-9333
3467 State Route 257 Seneca (16346) *(G-17369)*

Schalow Visual Concepts Inc 570 336-2714
347 Hurley St Benton (17814) *(G-1282)*

Schank Printing Inc 610 828-1623
520 Wells St Conshohocken (19428) *(G-3603)*

Schatzie Ltd 610 834-1240
601 Washington St Conshohocken (19428) *(G-3604)*

Scheerer Bearing Corporation (PA) 215 443-5252
645 Davisville Rd Willow Grove (19090) *(G-20140)*

Scheerer Bearing Corporation 215 443-5252
436 Caredean Dr Horsham (19044) *(G-7848)*

Scheirer Machine Company Inc 412 833-6500
2857 Tischler Rd Bethel Park (15102) *(G-1433)*

Schermerhorn Bros Co 610 284-7402
610 Industrial Park Dr Lansdowne (19050) *(G-9443)*

Schetler Lumber - Sawmill 814 590-9592
3727 Route 410 Punxsutawney (15767) *(G-16162)*

Schiel Inc 570 970-4460
30 Hanover St Wilkes Barre (18702) *(G-19962)*

Schiel's Family Market, Wilkes Barre *Also called Schiel Inc (G-19962)*

Schiff's Cash & Carry, Scranton *Also called S Schiff Restaurant Svc Inc (G-17282)*

Schiffer Publishing Ltd 610 593-1777
4880 Lower Valley Rd Atglen (19310) *(G-806)*

Schiller Grounds Care Inc 215 355-9700
1028 Street Rd Southampton (18966) *(G-17836)*

Schiller Grounds Care Inc 215 322-4970
1681 Republic Rd Huntingdon Valley (19006) *(G-8035)*

Schlessinger Media, Conshohocken *Also called Library Video Company (G-3572)*

Schlotter Precision Pdts Inc (PA) 215 354-3280
40 Indian Dr Warminster (18974) *(G-18963)*

Schlumberger Technology Corp 814 220-1900
147 Industrial Park Rd Brookville (15825) *(G-2271)*

Schmalbch-Lubeca Plastic Cntrs, Allentown *Also called Amcor Rigid Plastics Usa LLC (G-131)*

Schmidt Feintechnik, Cranberry Township *Also called Schmidt Technology Corporation (G-3848)*

Schmidt Technology Corporation 724 772-4600
280 Executive Dr Ste 1 Cranberry Township (16066) *(G-3848)*

Schmitt Aluminum Foundry Inc 717 299-5651
2485 Old Phladelphia Pike Smoketown (17576) *(G-17668)*

Schmitt Mar Stering Wheels Inc 717 431-2316
1001 Ranck Mill Rd Lancaster (17602) *(G-9191)*

Schmitt Walter H and Assoc 724 872-5007
580 Plummer School Rd West Newton (15089) *(G-19751)*

Schneck Art Optical Co 610 965-4066
720 Harrison St Emmaus (18049) *(G-5042)*

Schneder Elc Bldngs Amrcas Inc 215 441-4389
125 Rock Rd Horsham (19044) *(G-7849)*

Schneider Dairy, Pittsburgh *Also called Schneiders Dairy Holdings Inc (G-15517)*

Schneider Electric It Corp 215 230-7270
3853 E Brandon Way Doylestown (18902) *(G-4336)*

Schneider Electric It Corp 717 948-1200
201 Fulling Mill Rd Middletown (17057) *(G-11074)*

Schneiders Dairy Inc (HQ) 412 881-3525
726 Frank St Pittsburgh (15227) *(G-15516)*

Schneiders Dairy Holdings Inc (PA) 412 881-3525
726 Frank St Pittsburgh (15227) *(G-15517)*

Schnoch Corporation 570 326-4700
229 W 4th St 231 Williamsport (17701) *(G-20070)*

Schnupps Grain Roasting LLC 717 865-6611
416 Union Rd Lebanon (17046) *(G-9627)*

Schnure Manufacturing Co Inc 610 273-3352
102 Suplee Rd Honey Brook (19344) *(G-7762)*

School Bus Parts, Plumsteadville *Also called N F C Industries Inc (G-15812)*

School Colors Inc 570 561-2632
507 New York St Scranton (18509) *(G-17284)*

School Gate Guardian Inc 800 805-3808
301 Science Park Rd # 123 State College (16803) *(G-18020)*

Schott North America Inc 717 228-4200
30 Lebanon Valley Pkwy Lebanon (17042) *(G-9628)*

Schott North America Inc 570 457-7485
400 York Ave Ste B Duryea (18642) *(G-4507)*

Schott Pharmaceutical Packg, Lebanon *Also called Schott North America Inc* **(G-9628)**

Schrage Box & Design Inc 215 604-0800
2511 State Rd Bensalem (19020) **(G-1252)**

Schramm Inc 610 696-2500
800 E Virginia Ave Ste 3 West Chester (19380) **(G-19638)**

Schrantz Indus Electricians 610 435-8255
13 W Tilghman St Allentown (18102) **(G-386)**

Schreiber & Goldberg Ltd 570 344-4000
1321 E Drinker St Dunmore (18512) **(G-4483)**

Schreiber Foods Inc 717 530-5000
208 Dykeman Rd Shippensburg (17257) **(G-17546)**

Schroeder Industries LLC 724 318-1100
580 W Park Rd Leetsdale (15056) **(G-9704)**

Schroth Industries Inc 724 465-5701
145 Martin Rd Indiana (15701) **(G-8126)**

Schroth Lumber, Indiana *Also called Schroth Industries Inc* **(G-8126)**

Schubert Custom Cabinetry Inc (PA) 610 372-5559
39 Moss St Reading (19601) **(G-16508)**

Schubert Plastics Inc 610 358-4920
245 Lundgreen Rd Lenni (19052) **(G-9762)**

Schubert's Cabinet Shop, Reading *Also called Schubert Custom Cabinetry Inc* **(G-16508)**

Schuibbeo Holdings Inc 610 268-2825
568 Baltimore Pike Avondale (19311) **(G-859)**

Schulmerich Bells LLC 215 257-2771
11 Church Rd Hatfield (19440) **(G-7395)**

Schultz Industries, Saegertown *Also called James A Schultz* **(G-16919)**

Schultz Mktg & Communications 814 455-4772
317 W 6th St Erie (16507) **(G-5469)**

Schultz Precision Tooling 724 334-4491
111 Kathleen Rd Leechburg (15656) **(G-9653)**

Schultz Richard Design & Mfg 215 679-2222
1235 Water St East Greenville (18041) **(G-4574)**

Schultz Water Systems, Nazareth *Also called Jeffery Faust* **(G-11973)**

SCHUMAN PARTNERS DBA, Pittsburgh *Also called All ADS Up* **(G-14673)**

Schutte Koerting Acquisition (PA) 215 639-0900
2510 Metropolitan Dr Trevose (19053) **(G-18502)**

Schutte Woodworking & Mfg Co 814 453-5110
2831 Zimmerman Rd Erie (16510) **(G-5470)**

Schuylkill Coal Processing 570 875-3123
Duhctown Ex 116off Rte901 Ashland (17921) **(G-736)**

Schuylkill Printing Plant, Conshohocken *Also called Philadelphia Media Network Pbc* **(G-3586)**

Schuylkill Valley Sports Inc 717 627-0417
701 S Broad St Ste B Lititz (17543) **(G-10046)**

Schuylkill Vly Spt Trappe Ctr 877 711-8100
118 Industrial Dr Ste 1 Pottstown (19464) **(G-16044)**

Schwartz Technical Plastics, Pittsburgh *Also called T P Schwartz Inc* **(G-15594)**

Schwartz, Louis W MD, Lansdale *Also called Ophthalmic Associates PC* **(G-9395)**

Schwebel Baking Co of PA Inc 412 751-4080
4315 Walnut St McKeesport (15132) **(G-10680)**

Schwebel Baking Co PA, McKeesport *Also called Schwebel Baking Co of PA Inc* **(G-10680)**

Schwebel Baking Company 814 333-2498
813 Water St Meadville (16335) **(G-10789)**

Schwebel Baking Company 412 257-6067
111 Southpointe Dr Bridgeville (15017) **(G-2088)**

Schwenk Custom Machining Inc 610 367-1777
7a Rowell Rd Boyertown (19512) **(G-1928)**

Scicast International Inc 610 369-3060
650 N Route 100 Bechtelsville (19505) **(G-1036)**

Science Products, Berwyn *Also called Captek Inc* **(G-1355)**

Scientific Development Co, State College *Also called Cannon Instrument Company* **(G-17948)**

Scientific Tool Inc 724 446-9311
596 Middletown Rd New Stanton (15672) **(G-12450)**

Scitech Assoc Holdings Inc 201 218-3777
232 Woodland Dr State College (16803) **(G-18021)**

Sciullo Machine Shop & Tool Co 412 466-9571
854 Forest Ave Homestead (15120) **(G-7693)**

Sciullo Machine Shop & Tool Co (PA) 412 462-1604
1061 Kentucky Blue Dr West Mifflin (15122) **(G-19745)**

Scoop USA, Philadelphia *Also called Horsey Darden Enterprises LLC* **(G-13834)**

Scooperman Water Ice Inc 267 623-8494
4603 Conshohocken Ave Philadelphia (19131) **(G-14285)**

Scoopermarket Inc 215 925-1132
920 Pine St Philadelphia (19107) **(G-14286)**

Scoopy's Cone Co, Hermitage *Also called Joy Cone Co* **(G-7589)**

Scorecast Medical LLC 877 475-1001
123 S Broad St Ste 1830 Philadelphia (19109) **(G-14287)**

Scorpion Signs, Philadelphia *Also called Stephanie McClain* **(G-14345)**

Scot Lubricants, Northampton *Also called Pennstar LLC* **(G-12859)**

Scott Smith G 724 378-2880
2116 Sheffield Rd Aliquippa (15001) **(G-92)**

Scott Gordon 717 652-2828
6091 Linglestown Rd Harrisburg (17112) **(G-7213)**

Scott H Payne (PA) 215 723-0510
26 Orchard Cir Telford (18969) **(G-18313)**

Scott Metals Inc 412 279-7021
730 Superior St Ste 2 Carnegie (15106) **(G-2790)**

Scott Neilly 814 362-4443
350 Minard Run Rd Bradford (16701) **(G-1991)**

Scott R Mix 570 220-5887
112 Richmond Rd Bellefonte (16823) **(G-1117)**

Scott Zimmerman Logging Inc 814 965-5070
59 East Branch Dam Rd Wilcox (15870) **(G-19900)**

Scotts Company LLC 215 538-0191
2385 John Fries Hwy Quakertown (18951) **(G-16244)**

Scotts Company LLC 610 268-3006
944 Newark Rd Avondale (19311) **(G-860)**

Scotts- Hyponex, Oxford *Also called Hyponex Corporation* **(G-13083)**

Scotty's Porta-Potty's, Friedens *Also called Piles Concrete Products Co Inc* **(G-6225)**

Scottys Fashion of Lehighton (PA) 610 377-3032
315 W Pennsylvania Ave Pen Argyl (18072) **(G-13216)**

Scraders Dairy Queen, Jeannette *Also called Dudley Enterprises Inc* **(G-8253)**

Scranton Craftsmen Excvtg Inc 800 775-1479
930 Dunmore St Throop (18512) **(G-18360)**

Scranton Craftsmen Inc 570 347-5125
930 Dunmore St Throop (18512) **(G-18361)**

Scranton Grinder & Hardware 570 344-2520
1020 Hemlock St Scranton (18505) **(G-17285)**

Scranton Materials LLC 570 961-8586
819 Newton Rd Scranton (18504) **(G-17286)**

Scranton Products Inc 570 558-8000
801 E Corey St Scranton (18505) **(G-17287)**

Scranton Sheet Metal Inc 570 342-2904
240 E Elm St Unit 2 Scranton (18505) **(G-17288)**

Scranton Times-Tribune 570 348-9100
149 Penn Ave Ste 1 Scranton (18503) **(G-17289)**

Scranton Wilbert Vault Inc 570 489-5065
1260 Mid Valley Dr Jessup (18434) **(G-8336)**

Scrapbook Station 724 287-4311
168 Point Plz Butler (16001) **(G-2440)**

Scratch Cupcakes 717 271-2466
378 Jeff Ave Ephrata (17522) **(G-5139)**

Scream Graphix Inc 215 638-3900
230 Nauldo Rd Philadelphia (19154) **(G-14288)**

Screen Images Inc 610 926-3061
392a Five Locks Rd Shoemakersville (19555) **(G-17575)**

Screen Printing USA, Halifax *Also called Screenprinted Grafix Inc* **(G-6830)**

Screen Service Tech Inc 610 497-3555
22 Nealy Blvd Marcus Hook (19061) **(G-10454)**

Screening Room Inc 610 363-5405
305 Commerce Dr Ste 100 Exton (19341) **(G-5729)**

Screenprinted Grafix Inc 717 564-7464
245 Hershey Rd Halifax (17032) **(G-6830)**

Scribe Inc 215 336-5095
7540 Windsor Dr Ste 200b Allentown (18195) **(G-387)**

Scribe Inc (PA) 215 336-5094
842 S 2nd St Philadelphia (19147) **(G-14289)**

Scripture Union 610 935-2807
1485 Valley Forge Rd Valley Forge (19481) **(G-18714)**

Scritchfield Controls LLC 717 887-5992
210 S 2nd St Wrightsville (17368) **(G-20243)**

Scroll Publishing Co 717 349-7033
22012 Indian Spring Trl Doylesburg (17219) **(G-4265)**

Scrub Daddy Inc 610 583-4883
6 Horne Dr Folcroft (19032) **(G-6015)**

Scs Inc 866 727-4436
1523 Gehman Rd Harleysville (19438) **(G-7057)**

Scullin Group Inc 215 640-3330
2005 Market St Ste 3120 Philadelphia (19103) **(G-14290)**

Scully Enterprises Inc (PA) 814 835-0173
6410 W Ridge Rd Erie (16506) **(G-5471)**

Sculpted Ice Works Inc 570 226-6246
311 Purdytown Tpke Lakeville (18438) **(G-8913)**

Sculptz Inc (PA) 215 494-2900
1150 Northbrook Dr # 300 Trevose (19053) **(G-18503)**

SDC Building Center, Somerset *Also called Somerset Door and Column Co* **(G-17708)**

SDC Nutrition Inc 412 276-7800
230 E Main St Carnegie (15106) **(G-2791)**

Sdi Custom Decow 570 685-7278
1777 Route 590 Hawley (18428) **(G-7438)**

Sea Group Graphics Inc 215 805-0290
1590 Huntingdon Rd Huntingdon Valley (19006) **(G-8036)**

Sea Mar Tackle Co Inc 610 769-0755
4440 Spring Hill Dr Schnecksville (18078) **(G-17143)**

Seaco Foods International 844 579-1133
2110 S Eagle Rd Newtown (18940) **(G-12547)**

Seafood America, Warminster *Also called Seafood Enterprises LP* **(G-18964)**

Seafood Enterprises LP 215 672-2211
645 Mearns Rd Warminster (18974) **(G-18964)**

Seagate Technology LLC 412 918-7000
1251 Waterfront Pl Fl 1 Pittsburgh (15222) **(G-15518)**

Seahorse Oilfield Services LLC 724 597-2039
2400 Ansys Dr Ste 102 Canonsburg (15317) **(G-2633)**

Seak Inc 215 288-7209
604 W York St Philadelphia (19133) **(G-14291)**

Seal Glove Mfg Inc 717 692-4837
525 North St Millersburg (17061) **(G-11200)**
Seal Science Inc 610 868-2800
1160 Win Dr Bethlehem (18017) **(G-1616)**
Seal Science East, Bethlehem Also called Seal Science Inc **(G-1616)**
Seal-Master Manufacturing, Hillsville Also called Sealmaster Pennsylvania Inc **(G-7636)**
Sealed Air Corporation 717 637-5905
260 N Blettner Ave Hanover (17331) **(G-6949)**
Sealed Air Corporation 610 926-7517
4275 Reading Crest Ave Reading (19605) **(G-16509)**
Sealed Air Corporation 610 384-2650
22 Meredith Rd Modena (19358) **(G-11259)**
Sealed Air Corporation 610 375-4281
450 Riverfront Dr Reading (19602) **(G-16510)**
Sealguard Inc 724 625-4550
1015 Foggy Hollow Rd Gibsonia (15044) **(G-6351)**
Sealmark Manufacturing Corp (PA) 724 379-4442
480 Galiffa Dr Donora (15033) **(G-4161)**
Sealmaster, Allentown Also called Pignuts Inc **(G-352)**
Sealmaster Pennsylvania Inc 724 667-0444
4551w State 3 Hillsville (16132) **(G-7636)**
Sealmor Industries, Factoryville Also called Teflex Inc **(G-5762)**
Seals of Blossburg 570 638-2161
329 N Williamson Rd Blossburg (16912) **(G-1809)**
Sealy Component Group, Mountain Top Also called Ohio Mat Lcnsing Cmpnnts Group **(G-11768)**
Sean Naughton 570 646-0422
Rr 940 Pocono Pines (18350) **(G-15884)**
Sean S Zuniga 215 757-2676
227 E Maple Ave Langhorne (19047) **(G-9324)**
Seapoint Enterprises Inc 215 230-6933
199 Washington St Doylestown (18901) **(G-4337)**
Seaquay Archtctural Mllwk Corp 610 279-1201
55 E Front St Ste C221 Bridgeport (19405) **(G-2045)**
Search Live Today LLC 610 805-7734
530 Waller Way Norristown (19403) **(G-12710)**
Searer Solutions Inc 302 475-6944
1315 Walnut St Ste 815 Philadelphia (19107) **(G-14292)**
Sears Carpet and Uphl Care Inc 412 821-5200
1601 Marys Ave Ste 10 Sharpsburg (15215) **(G-17468)**
Seasons Specialties Inc 570 928-9522
178 Carpenter St Dushore (18614) **(G-4510)**
Seastar Solutions, Limerick Also called Marine Acquisition US Inc **(G-9970)**
Seastar Solutions 610 495-7011
640 N Lewis Rd Limerick (19468) **(G-9971)**
Seaway Manufacturing Corp (PA) 814 898-2255
2250 E 33rd St Erie (16510) **(G-5472)**
Seay Custom Woodworking 814 422-8986
106 Windy Way Spring Mills (16875) **(G-17892)**
Sebastian Brothers 717 930-8797
4189 E Harrisburg Pike Middletown (17057) **(G-11075)**
Sebastian Management LLC 412 203-1273
1016 Greentree Rd Ste 102 Pittsburgh (15220) **(G-15519)**
Sebastiani Concrete, Middletown Also called Sebastian Brothers **(G-11075)**
Secant Group LLC (HQ) 877 774-2835
551 E Church St Telford (18969) **(G-18314)**
Secant Group LLC 215 538-9601
195 Oneill Rd Quakertown (18951) **(G-16245)**
Sechler Family Foods Inc (PA) 717 865-6626
154 W Main St Fredericksburg (17026) **(G-6176)**
Sechrist Bros Inc 717 244-2975
32 E Main St Dallastown (17313) **(G-3981)**
Seco/Vacuum Technologies LLC 814 332-8520
180 Mercer St Meadville (16335) **(G-10790)**
Seco/Warwick Corporation 814 332-8400
180 Mercer St Meadville (16335) **(G-10791)**
Second Century Media LLC 610 948-9500
3801 Schuylkill Rd Spring City (19475) **(G-17866)**
Second Play LLC 267 229-8033
6 Terry Dr Newtown (18940) **(G-12548)**
Secondary Development & Res 814 772-3882
219 Servidea Dr Ridgway (15853) **(G-16729)**
Secrets of Big Dogs 814 696-0469
506 Allegheny St Ste 2 Hollidaysburg (16648) **(G-7653)**
Secure Components LLC 610 551-3475
1000 E Main St Norristown (19401) **(G-12711)**
Secure Rhbltition Vctonal Entps, Monroeton Also called Serve Inc **(G-11320)**
Security Resource Management, Greensburg Also called Srm-Avant Inc **(G-6716)**
Sedco Manufacturing 570 323-1232
10823 Route 864 Hwy Hughesville (17737) **(G-7899)**
Seder Gaming Inc 814 736-3611
3135 New Germany Rd # 43 Ebensburg (15931) **(G-4796)**
See-Line, Houston Also called Pocket Cross Inc **(G-7877)**
Seegrid Corporation 412 379-4500
216 Ridc Park West Dr Pittsburgh (15275) **(G-15520)**
Seel Tool & Die Inc 814 834-4561
421 N Michael St Saint Marys (15857) **(G-17014)**
Sehrer Mill & Hardware, Gallitzin Also called Donald Beiswenger Inc **(G-6245)**

Seiberts Computers 717 349-7859
10850 Back Rd Fannettsburg (17221) **(G-5859)**
Seiders Printing Co Inc 570 622-0570
110 E Arch St Pottsville (17901) **(G-16097)**
Seiferth Signs, Pittsburgh Also called H H Seiferth Associates Inc **(G-15070)**
Sein Organizing Solutions 215 932-8837
4621 E Mill Hill Rd East Greenville (18041) **(G-4575)**
Seitz Tech LLC 610 268-2228
1041 Hickory Hill Rd Oxford (19363) **(G-13090)**
Sekisui Diagnostics LLC 610 594-8590
102 Pickering Way Ste 501 Exton (19341) **(G-5730)**
Sekisui Polymr Innovations LLC (HQ) 570 387-6997
6685 Lowe St Bloomsburg (17815) **(G-1801)**
Sekisui SPI, Bloomsburg Also called Sekisui Polymr Innovations LLC **(G-1801)**
Seko Dosing Systems Corp 215 945-0125
913 William Leigh Dr Bristol (19007) **(G-2197)**
Sekula Sign Corporation 814 371-4650
811 S Brady St Du Bois (15801) **(G-4417)**
Selah Publshng Co Inc 412 886-1020
4055 Cloverlea St Pittsburgh (15227) **(G-15521)**
Selas Heat Technology Co LLC 215 646-6600
54 Friends Ln Ste 125 Newtown (18940) **(G-12549)**
Selco Publications, West Chester Also called Marine Information Tech LLC **(G-19595)**
Select Dismantling Corp 724 861-6004
137 Sycamore St Wendel (15691) **(G-19482)**
Select Energy Services LLC 724 239-2056
100 Gallaway Dr Eighty Four (15330) **(G-4848)**
Select Industries Inc (PA) 724 654-7747
420 S Cascade St New Castle (16101) **(G-12147)**
Select Medical Systems Inc 215 207-9003
1800 W Indiana Ave Philadelphia (19132) **(G-14293)**
Select Tissue Pennsylvania LLC 570 785-2000
939 Main St Vandling (18421) **(G-18739)**
Select Veal Feeds Inc (PA) 215 721-7131
519 Allentown Rd Souderton (18964) **(G-17762)**
Select-Tron Industries Inc 814 459-0847
1946 E 12th St Erie (16511) **(G-5473)**
Selectrim Corporation 570 326-3662
140 Catawissa Ave Williamsport (17701) **(G-20071)**
Selectrode Industries Inc 724 378-6351
100 Commerce Way Aliquippa (15001) **(G-93)**
Self-Powered Lighting Inc (PA) 484 595-9130
31 Waterloo Ave Berwyn (19312) **(G-1375)**
Self-Seal Cont Corp Del Vly 610 275-2300
315 329 E 2nd St Boyertown (19512) **(G-1929)**
Selinsgrove Instnl Csework LLC 570 374-1176
100 E Sherman St Selinsgrove (17870) **(G-17333)**
Sell-It 215 453-8937
1214 Ridge Rd Sellersville (18960) **(G-17358)**
Sellars Nonwovens 610 593-5145
808 Valley Ave Atglen (19310) **(G-807)**
Selmax Corp 570 374-2833
599 S High St Selinsgrove (17870) **(G-17334)**
Seltzer's Smokehouse Meats, Palmyra Also called Palmyra Bologna Company **(G-13128)**
Seltzers Bologna, Lebanon Also called Palmyra Bologna Company **(G-9614)**
Semi-Mounts Inc 412 422-7988
1618 Murdoch Rd Pittsburgh (15217) **(G-15522)**
Semicndctor Ozone Slutions LLC 541 936-0844
36 Lake Rd Fleetwood (19522) **(G-5979)**
Semilab USA LLC 610 377-5990
208 Memorial Dr Lehighton (18235) **(G-9726)**
Semler Enterprises Inc 717 242-0322
20 Windmill Hl Ste 2 Burnham (17009) **(G-2361)**
Sen Dec Corp 585 425-3390
8031 Avonia Rd Fairview (16415) **(G-5841)**
Senapes Bakery Inc 570 454-0839
222 W 17th St Hazleton (18201) **(G-7526)**
Senate Coal Mines (PA) 724 537-2062
1 Energy Pl Ste 5100 Latrobe (15650) **(G-9519)**
Sencillo Systems Inc 610 340-2848
966 Argyle Rd Warrington (18976) **(G-19133)**
Sendec Corp (HQ) 585 425-3390
345 Pomroys Dr Windber (15963) **(G-20192)**
Sender Ornamental Iron Works 814 536-5139
742 Cooper Ave Johnstown (15906) **(G-8433)**
Seneca Enterprises Inc (PA) 814 432-7890
1642 Debence Dr Franklin (16323) **(G-6156)**
Seneca Foods Corporation 717 675-2074
30 Keystone Dr Lebanon (17042) **(G-9629)**
Seneca Hardwood Lumber Co Inc 814 498-2241
212 Seneca Hardwood Rd Cranberry (16319) **(G-3797)**
Seneca Mineral Co Inc 814 476-0076
8431 Edinboro Rd Erie (16509) **(G-5474)**
Seneca Mineral Company 814 476-0076
8431 Edinboro Rd Erie (16509) **(G-5475)**
Seneca Printing & Label Inc 814 437-5364
191 Howard St Ste 302 Franklin (16323) **(G-6157)**
Seneca Printing Express & Dist, Franklin Also called Seneca Printing & Label Inc **(G-6157)**
Seneca Printing Express Inc 814 437-5364
191 Howard St Ste 302 Franklin (16323) **(G-6158)**

2019 Harris Pennsylvania
Manufacturers Directory

(G-0000) Company's Geographic Section entry number

Seneca Resources Company LLC 412 548-2500
  5800 Corporate Dr Ste 300 Pittsburgh (15237) *(G-15523)*

Sengenuity, Mount Holly Springs *Also called Vectron International Inc* *(G-11640)*

Senior Craftsmens Shop 570 344-7089
  232 Wyoming Ave Scranton (18503) *(G-17290)*

Senoret Chemical Company 717 626-2125
  69 N Locust St Lititz (17543) *(G-10047)*

Sensaphone, Aston *Also called Phonetics Inc* *(G-787)*

Sense Technology Inc 724 733-2277
  1033 Matamoras Rd Halifax (17032) *(G-6831)*

Sensenich Propeller Company 717 560-3711
  519 Airport Rd Lititz (17543) *(G-10048)*

Sensenig Chair Shop 717 463-3480
  Rr 1 Thompsontown (17094) *(G-18351)*

Sensenig's Feed Mill, New Holland *Also called Leroy M Sensenig Inc* *(G-12257)*

Sensenig's Woodworking, Shippensburg *Also called Chris S Sensenig* *(G-17522)*

Sensenig, E Z Harness & Son, New Holland *Also called E Z Sensenig & Son* *(G-12246)*

Sensenigs Spouting 717 627-6886
  265 E Meadow Valley Rd Lititz (17543) *(G-10049)*

Sensenigs Wood Shavings 717 336-2047
  375 Lausch Rd Denver (17517) *(G-4093)*

Sensible Components LLC 855 548-7587
  5 Industrial Park Dr Oakdale (15071) *(G-12911)*

Sensible Organics Inc 724 891-4560
  3740 W 4th Ave Beaver Falls (15010) *(G-1011)*

Sensible Portions, Mountville *Also called World Gourmet Acquisition LLC* *(G-11804)*

Sensible Portions 717 898-7131
  3775 Hempland Rd Mountville (17554) *(G-11802)*

Sensing Devices LLC 717 295-4735
  625 2nd St Lancaster (17603) *(G-9192)*

Sensing Devices Inc 717 295-4735
  625 2nd St Lancaster (17603) *(G-9193)*

Sensitron Associates Inc 610 779-0939
  223 Seidel St Reading (19606) *(G-16511)*

Sensor Corporation 724 887-4080
  303 Scottdale Ave Scottdale (15683) *(G-17200)*

Sensor Networks Inc 814 466-7207
  176 Technology Dr Ste 500 Boalsburg (16827) *(G-1869)*

Sensor Networks Inc 814 441-2476
  171 Technology Dr Ste 500 Boalsburg (16827) *(G-1870)*

Sensor Networks Corporation 717 466-7207
  171 Technology Dr Ste 500 Boalsburg (16827) *(G-1871)*

Sensortex Inc 302 444-2383
  948 Wawaset Rd Kennett Square (19348) *(G-8542)*

Sensoryeffects Inc 610 582-2170
  61 Vanguard Dr Reading (19606) *(G-16512)*

Sensus Metering Systems, Du Bois *Also called Sensus USA Inc* *(G-4418)*

Sensus Metering Systems, Uniontown *Also called Sensus USA Inc* *(G-18640)*

Sensus Metering Systems-North 724 439-7700
  450 N Gallatin Ave Uniontown (15401) *(G-18639)*

Sensus USA Inc 814 375-8354
  805 Liberty Blvd Du Bois (15801) *(G-4418)*

Sensus USA Inc 724 439-7700
  450 N Gallatin Ave Uniontown (15401) *(G-18640)*

Sensus USA Inc 800 375-8875
  805 Liberty Blvd Du Bois (15801) *(G-4419)*

Sensus USA Inc 724 430-3956
  1501 Ardmore Blvd Pittsburgh (15221) *(G-15524)*

Sentage Corporation 412 431-3353
  600 Old Clairton Rd Pittsburgh (15236) *(G-15525)*

Sentech Inc 215 887-8665
  2851 Limekiln Pike Glenside (19038) *(G-6535)*

Sentinel Connector System, York *Also called Sentinel Holding Inc* *(G-20665)*

Sentinel Connector Systems Inc 717 843-4240
  1953 Stanton St York (17404) *(G-20664)*

Sentinel Holding Inc 717 843-4240
  1953 Stanton St York (17404) *(G-20665)*

Sentinel Power Inc 724 925-8181
  922 Middletown Rd New Stanton (15672) *(G-12451)*

Sentinel Process Systems Inc (PA) 215 675-5700
  3265 Sunset Ln Hatboro (19040) *(G-7304)*

Sentinel, The, Carlisle *Also called Lee Enterprises Inc Sentinel* *(G-2721)*

Sentry Buildings, Greenville *Also called Reynolds Building Systems Inc* *(G-6769)*

Sentry Fire Protection Inc 717 843-4973
  277 Rose Ave York (17401) *(G-20666)*

Sentry Wellhead Systems LLC 724 422-8108
  100 Beta Dr Canonsburg (15317) *(G-2634)*

Separation Technologies (PA) 724 325-4546
  20 Claridge Rd Export (15632) *(G-5626)*

Sepco Erie 814 864-0311
  1221 Robison Rd W Erie (16509) *(G-5476)*

Septa, Malvern *Also called Southeastern PA Trnsp Auth* *(G-10323)*

Septic Surgeons LLC 570 224-4822
  57 Lester Rd Bldg B Equinunk (18417) *(G-5160)*

Serendib Imports Inc 610 203-3070
  116 Moore Dr Media (19063) *(G-10948)*

Sergood Corp (HQ) 724 772-5600
  1235 Freedom Rd Cranberry Township (16066) *(G-3849)*

Serigraph Factory 570 647-0644
  2 Chapel St Honesdale (18431) *(G-7723)*

Serv-I-Quip Inc 610 873-7010
  127 Wallace Ave Downingtown (19335) *(G-4256)*

Servant PC Resources Inc 570 748-2800
  220 Woodward Ave Ste 1 Lock Haven (17745) *(G-10092)*

Serve Inc (PA) 570 265-3119
  22 Chiola Ln Monroeton (18832) *(G-11320)*

Servedio A Elc Mtr Svc Inc 724 658-8041
  634 E Washington St New Castle (16101) *(G-12148)*

Service Construction Co Inc 610 377-2111
  701 Bridge St Ste 102 Lehighton (18235) *(G-9727)*

Service Die Cutng & Packg Corp 215 739-8809
  3250 Boudinot St Philadelphia (19134) *(G-14294)*

Service Filtration Corp 717 656-2161
  41 Industrial Cir Lancaster (17601) *(G-9194)*

Service Rite 814 774-8716
  9045 Miller Rd Cranesville (16410) *(G-3871)*

Services Unlimited Mstr Prtg 610 891-7877
  451 W Baltimore Ave Media (19063) *(G-10949)*

Servo Repair International 412 492-8116
  3812 William Flynn Hwy # 7 Allison Park (15101) *(G-462)*

SES Inc 484 767-3280
  4483 Sarah Marie Ct Nazareth (18064) *(G-11987)*

Sesco, Waynesboro *Also called Souders Industries Inc* *(G-19424)*

Sesco, Mont Alto *Also called Souders Industries Inc* *(G-11365)*

Sesha Anti Oxdent Skin Therapy, West Chester *Also called Conrex Pharmaceutical Corp* *(G-19529)*

Sethco, Telford *Also called Met-Pro Technologies LLC* *(G-18305)*

Seths Auto Machine Shop 570 658-2886
  19362 Route 522 Beaver Springs (17812) *(G-1022)*

Sett 215 322-9301
  1633 Republic Rd Huntingdon Valley (19006) *(G-8037)*

Seven D Industries LP (HQ) 814 317-4077
  1001 W Loop Rd Hollidaysburg (16648) *(G-7654)*

Seven D Truss LP (PA) 814 317-4077
  3229 Pleasant Valley Blvd Altoona (16602) *(G-547)*

Seven Sisters Mining Company (PA) 724 468-8232
  200 Route 22 Delmont (15626) *(G-4058)*

Seven Sons Roofing, Greenville *Also called Grant Belcher* *(G-6741)*

Seven Trees Woodworking LLC 717 351-6300
  939 E Earl Rd New Holland (17557) *(G-12282)*

Seventy-Three Mfg Co Inc 610 845-7823
  136 Stauffer Rd Bechtelsville (19505) *(G-1037)*

Severn Trent Services, Pittsburgh *Also called De Nora Water Technologies Inc* *(G-14914)*

Sew Be It, Prospect Park *Also called S B I Inc* *(G-16119)*

Sew Special 724 438-1765
  73 W Main St Uniontown (15401) *(G-18641)*

Sewell Logging 814 837-7136
  6014 Jacobs Ave Harrisburg (17112) *(G-7214)*

Sewickley Creek Greenhouse 724 935-8500
  2639 Big Swckly Crk Rd Sewickley (15143) *(G-17408)*

Sewickley Herald 412 324-1403
  504 Beaver St Sewickley (15143) *(G-17409)*

Sewickley Village Fuel and Svc 412 741-9972
  590 Beaver St Sewickley (15143) *(G-17410)*

Sewing Equipment Co Inc 610 825-2581
  3030 Warrior Rd Plymouth Meeting (19462) *(G-15869)*

Sewsations LLC 484 842-1024
  3405 Half Mile Post N Garnet Valley (19060) *(G-6268)*

Seybert Castings Inc 215 364-7115
  1840 County Line Rd # 108 Huntingdon Valley (19006) *(G-8038)*

Seymore Bros Inc 814 944-2074
  4221 6th Ave Altoona (16602) *(G-548)*

Sez Sew Stitching Inc 814 339-6734
  105 Elizabeth St Osceola Mills (16666) *(G-13057)*

Sfa Therapeutics LLC 267 584-1080
  610 Old York Rd Ste 400 Jenkintown (19046) *(G-8300)*

Sfc Global Supply Chain Inc 610 327-5074
  255 South St Pottstown (19464) *(G-16045)*

Sfc Valve Corporation 814 445-9671
  160 Cannery Rd Somerset (15501) *(G-17704)*

Sfk Ventures Inc 610 825-5151
  381 Brooks Rd King of Prussia (19406) *(G-8672)*

Sfpc, Franklin *Also called Specialty Fabrication and Powd* *(G-6161)*

Sfs, Franklin *Also called Specialty Fitness Systems LLC* *(G-6162)*

Sfs Group Usa Inc 610 376-5751
  41 Dennis Dr Reading (19606) *(G-16513)*

Sgl LLC 610 670-4040
  796 Fritztown Rd Reading (19608) *(G-16514)*

Sgo Designer Glass, Spring House *Also called Art Glass Sgo Inc* *(G-17881)*

Sgrignoli Brothers 717 766-2812
  97 Texaco Rd Mechanicsburg (17050) *(G-10887)*

Sgws of PA, King of Prussia *Also called Southern Glazer s Wine and Sp* *(G-8678)*

Sh Quints Sons Company (PA) 215 533-1988
  3725 Castor Ave Philadelphia (19124) *(G-14295)*

Sha Co Welding & Fabrication 724 588-0993
  53 Canal St Greenville (16125) *(G-6773)*

Shaco, Greenville *Also called Sha Co Welding & Fabrication* ***(G-6773)***
Shade Gap Farm Supplies....814 259-3258
21963 Croghan Pike Shade Gap (17255) ***(G-17416)***
Shade Lumber Company Inc....570 658-2425
3627 Sawmill Rd Beaver Springs (17812) ***(G-1023)***
Shade Mountain Countertops....717 463-2729
75 Steves Woods Dr Mc Alisterville (17049) ***(G-10552)***
Shade Mountain Winery Inc (PA)....570 837-3644
16140 Route 104 Middleburg (17842) ***(G-11040)***
Shades of Country....570 297-3327
5103 Route 6 Troy (16947) ***(G-18526)***
Shadlure Tackle, West Elizabeth *Also called Donald Plants* ***(G-19694)***
Shadowfax Inc (PA)....610 373-5177
141 S 7th St Reading (19602) ***(G-16515)***
Shady Acres Saddlery Inc....412 963-9454
595 Dorseyville Rd Pittsburgh (15238) ***(G-15526)***
Shady Elms Sawmill LLC....724 356-2594
50 Caldwell Rd Hickory (15340) ***(G-7631)***
Shady Grove Cabinet Shop Inc....717 597-0825
3030 Buchanan Trl E Greencastle (17225) ***(G-6632)***
Shady Grove Woodworking....610 273-7038
622 Buchland Rd Narvon (17555) ***(G-11925)***
Shady Hill Hardwood Inc....717 463-9475
Rr 2 Box 1225 Mifflintown (17059) ***(G-11135)***
Shady Lane Wagons, New Holland *Also called Martin Weaver R* ***(G-12260)***
Shaffer Desouza Brown Inc....610 449-6400
17 Mifflin Ave Ste 1 Havertown (19083) ***(G-7427)***
Shaffer Block and Con Pdts Inc....814 445-4414
951 S Edgewood Ave Somerset (15501) ***(G-17705)***
Shaffer Brothers Lumber Co....814 842-3996
5927 Kennells Mill Rd Hyndman (15545) ***(G-8051)***
Shaffer Logging....814 827-1729
13955 State Highway 8 Titusville (16354) ***(G-18395)***
Shaffer Products LLC....717 597-2688
13062 Grant Shook Rd Greencastle (17225) ***(G-6633)***
Shaffers Fabg & Diesl Svc, Masontown *Also called Shaffers Fabricating Inc* ***(G-10536)***
Shaffers Fabricating Inc (PA)....724 583-2833
417 N Water St Masontown (15461) ***(G-10536)***
Shaffers Feed Service Inc....570 265-3300
8 Dalpiaz Dr Monroeton (18832) ***(G-11321)***
Shake and Twist Chartiers Ave....412 331-9606
1238 Chartiers Ave Mc Kees Rocks (15136) ***(G-10634)***
Shale Tank Solutions LLC....724 823-0953
98 E 1st St Donora (15033) ***(G-4162)***
Shallenberger Construction Inc (PA)....724 628-8408
195 Enterprise Ln Connellsville (15425) ***(G-3508)***
Shallenberger Lumber Co, Millerstown *Also called Ronald Kauffman* ***(G-11208)***
Shalmet Corporation (HQ)....570 366-1414
116 Pinedale Indus Rd Orwigsburg (17961) ***(G-13052)***
Shamaseen Hamzah....484 557-5051
6137 Main St Center Valley (18034) ***(G-2830)***
Shammy Solutions....412 871-0939
344 Pennoak Dr Pittsburgh (15235) ***(G-15527)***
Shamokin Carbons, Coal Township *Also called Shamokin Filler Co Inc* ***(G-3281)***
Shamokin Filler Co Inc....570 644-0437
453-455 Venn Access Rd Coal Township (17866) ***(G-3281)***
Shamokin News Item, Shamokin *Also called The Scranton Times L P* ***(G-17427)***
Shamrock Building Services Inc....412 279-2800
535 Forest Ave Carnegie (15106) ***(G-2792)***
Shamrock Concrete, Paxinos *Also called Shamrock Metered Concrete Inc* ***(G-13193)***
Shamrock Metered Concrete Inc....570 672-3223
129 Rose Dr Paxinos (17860) ***(G-13193)***
Shane Candies, Philadelphia *Also called Shane Candy Co* ***(G-14296)***
Shane Candy Co....215 922-1048
110 Market St Philadelphia (19106) ***(G-14296)***
Shane Hostetter....717 949-6563
307 Old Mill Rd Newmanstown (17073) ***(G-12483)***
Shangri La Productions....610 838-5188
2425 Apple St Hellertown (18055) ***(G-7562)***
Shangri-La Beverage LLC....724 222-2222
1601 Park Ave Washington (15301) ***(G-19225)***
Shank Pallet Recyclers, Waynesboro *Also called Aj Pallet LLC* ***(G-19395)***
Shank Pallet Recyclers Inc (PA)....717 597-3545
1620 Buchanan Trl E Greencastle (17225) ***(G-6634)***
Shank Pallet Recyclers Inc....717 597-3545
13132 Gearhart Rd Greencastle (17225) ***(G-6635)***
Shanks Portable Sawmills....717 334-0352
540 Buchanan Valley Rd Orrtanna (17353) ***(G-13037)***
Shannons Kandy Kitchen (PA)....724 662-5211
225 N Erie St Mercer (16137) ***(G-10975)***
Shape TEC Ltd....610 689-8940
860 Limekiln Rd Limekiln (19535) ***(G-9968)***
Shared Financial Services....412 968-1178
200 Alpha Dr Pittsburgh (15238) ***(G-15528)***
Shared Services, Moon Township *Also called Hydro Extrusion Usa LLC* ***(G-11493)***
Sharedxpertise Media LLC....215 606-9520
123 S Broad St Ste 1930 Philadelphia (19109) ***(G-14297)***
Sharon Coating LLC....724 983-6464
277 N Sharpsville Ave Sharon (16146) ***(G-17442)***
Sharon Commercial Printing, Sharon *Also called J & R Beck Inc* ***(G-17437)***
Sharon Herald, Sharon *Also called Newspaper Holding Inc* ***(G-17440)***
Sharon McGuigan Inc....610 361-8100
35 Mount Pleasant Rd Aston (19014) ***(G-793)***
Sharp & Wily LLC....717 893-2970
1012 Smallbrook Ln York (17403) ***(G-20667)***
Sharp Coatings....215 324-8500
162 E Courtland St Philadelphia (19120) ***(G-14298)***
Sharp Tool and Die Inc....814 763-1133
25947 Plank Rd Guys Mills (16327) ***(G-6812)***
Sharper Embroidery Inc....570 714-3617
1081 Main St Swoyersville (18704) ***(G-18199)***
Sharpsville Container Corp....724 962-1100
600 W Main St Sharpsville (16150) ***(G-17475)***
Sharretts Plating Co Inc....717 767-6702
3315 Connelly Rd Emigsville (17318) ***(G-4999)***
Shasta Inc (HQ)....724 378-8280
300 Steel St Aliquippa (15001) ***(G-94)***
Shasta Holdings Company (PA)....724 378-8280
300 Steel St Aliquippa (15001) ***(G-95)***
Shaw Industries Group Inc....724 266-0315
780 Brickworks Dr Leetsdale (15056) ***(G-9705)***
Shaw Industries Inc....814 432-0954
561 Allegheny Blvd Franklin (16323) ***(G-6159)***
Shaw Mack Sales & Service-Div, Kylertown *Also called W W Engine and Supply Inc* ***(G-8868)***
Shawcor Pipe Protection LLC....215 736-1111
21 Steel Rd S Morrisville (19067) ***(G-11581)***
Shawn Harr....215 258-5434
1831 Three Mile Run Rd Perkasie (18944) ***(G-13292)***
Shawn Paul Zimmerman Kevin Joh....814 594-1371
24670 Bennetts Valley Hwy Weedville (15868) ***(G-19459)***
Shawnee Optical, Hermitage *Also called Bruce N Pelsh Inc* ***(G-7572)***
Shawnee Ready Mix Con & Asp Co (PA)....570 779-9586
715 E Main St Plymouth (18651) ***(G-15821)***
Shawnee Structures....814 623-8212
6231 Lincoln Hwy Bedford (15522) ***(G-1076)***
Sheaffer Signs, Lewisberry *Also called Leiphart Enterprises LLC* ***(G-9888)***
Shearer Elbie....814 266-7548
204 Atlantic St Johnstown (15904) ***(G-8434)***
Shearers Fods Canonsburg Plant....724 746-1162
42 Swihart Rd Canonsburg (15317) ***(G-2635)***
Shearers Welding Inc....717 361-9196
240 Heisey Quarry Rd Elizabethtown (17022) ***(G-4887)***
Shed-Shop Incorporated....215 723-4209
203 E Chestnut St 50 Souderton (18964) ***(G-17763)***
Shedaker Metal Arts Inc....215 788-3383
519 Browns Ln Croydon (19021) ***(G-3928)***
Shedio Logging & Lumber (PA)....724 794-1321
114 Silver Dr Renfrew (16053) ***(G-16642)***
Sheds Unlimited Inc....717 442-3281
2025 Valley Rd Morgantown (19543) ***(G-11534)***
Sheen Kleen Inc....610 337-3969
3000 Valley Forge Cir G9 King of Prussia (19406) ***(G-8673)***
Sheep Thrills....724 465-2617
244 Lower Twolick Dr Indiana (15701) ***(G-8127)***
Sheerlund Products LLC....484 248-2650
740 Corporate Dr Reading (19605) ***(G-16516)***
Sheet Metal Specialists LLC....717 910-7000
1731 S 19th St Harrisburg (17104) ***(G-7215)***
Sheet Metal Wkrs Local Un 19....215 952-1999
1301 S Columbus Blvd Philadelphia (19147) ***(G-14299)***
Sheffield Container Corp....814 968-3287
311 Horton Ave Sheffield (16347) ***(G-17483)***
Sheinman Provision Co Inc....305 592-0300
4192 Viola St 96 Philadelphia (19104) ***(G-14300)***
Shell Containers Inc PA, Ambler *Also called Allflex Packaging Products Inc* ***(G-566)***
Shelly & Son Fenstermacher Div, Bethlehem *Also called Shelly Enterprises -US Lbm LLC* ***(G-1617)***
Shelly Building Supply, Kimberton *Also called Shelly Enterprises -US Lbm LLC* ***(G-8574)***
Shelly Enterprises -US Lbm LLC (HQ)....215 723-5108
3110 Old State Rd Telford (18969) ***(G-18315)***
Shelly Enterprises -US Lbm LLC....610 432-4511
6410 Airport Rd Bethlehem (18017) ***(G-1617)***
Shelly Enterprises -US Lbm LLC....610 933-1116
629 Pike Spgs Rd Kimberton (19442) ***(G-8574)***
Shelter Structures Inc....267 239-5906
2043 Locust St Fl 2b Philadelphia (19103) ***(G-14301)***
Sheltons Pallet Company....610 932-3182
102 Oaks Rd Oxford (19363) ***(G-13091)***
Shemco Corp....412 831-6022
100 Skylark Cir Pittsburgh (15234) ***(G-15529)***
Shen Manufacturing Company Inc....570 278-3707
S Main St Montrose (18801) ***(G-11476)***
Shenandoah Water Trtmnt Plant....570 462-4918
Raven Run Rd Shenandoah (17976) ***(G-17496)***
Shenango Advanced Ceramics LLC (HQ)....724 652-6668
606 Mccleary Ave New Castle (16101) ***(G-12149)***

Shenango Auto Mall LLC 724 698-7304
2515 Ellwood Rd New Castle (16101) ***(G-12150)***
Shenango Group Inc 412 771-4400
200 Neville Rd Ste 8 Pittsburgh (15225) ***(G-15530)***
Shenango Incorporated 412 771-4400
200 Neville Rd Unit 5 Pittsburgh (15225) ***(G-15531)***
Shenango Operating Inc 724 657-3650
792 Commerce Ave New Castle (16101) ***(G-12151)***
Shenango Valley Quik Print, Hermitage *Also called New Centuries LLC* ***(G-7593)***
Shenango Valley Sand and Grav 724 932-5600
172 Shine Rd Jamestown (16134) ***(G-8240)***
Shenango Vallley Sand & Gravel, Jamestown *Also called Shenango Valley Sand and Grav* ***(G-8240)***
Shenk Athletic Equipment Co (PA) 717 766-6600
5010 E Trindle Rd Ste 203 Mechanicsburg (17050) ***(G-10888)***
Shenk Company, Mechanicsburg *Also called Shenk Athletic Equipment Co* ***(G-10888)***
Shenks Foods Inc 717 393-4240
1980 New Danville Pike Lancaster (17603) ***(G-9195)***
Shepherd Good Work Services 610 776-8353
1901 Lehigh St Allentown (18103) ***(G-388)***
Shepherd Press Inc 570 379-2015
437 S River St Wapwallopen (18660) ***(G-18809)***
Shereen Fuel Inc 215 632-2160
9998 Frankford Ave Philadelphia (19114) ***(G-14302)***
Sheridan Construction Group 717 948-0507
950 Swatara Creek Rd Middletown (17057) ***(G-11076)***
Sheridan Group Inc (HQ) 717 632-3535
450 Fame Ave Hanover (17331) ***(G-6950)***
Sheridan Press Inc 717 632-3535
450 Fame Ave Hanover (17331) ***(G-6951)***
Sheridan Supply Company Inc 610 589-4361
7 Furnace Rd Newmanstown (17073) ***(G-12484)***
Sherman & Gosweiler Inc 610 270-0825
401 E 4th St Ste 8e Bridgeport (19405) ***(G-2046)***
Sherman Coal Company Inc 570 695-2690
Rr 81 Elysburg (17824) ***(G-4981)***
Sherman Tool & Gage, Erie *Also called Ramac Industries Inc* ***(G-5455)***
Sherpa Mining Contractors Inc 814 754-5560
337 Benny Rd Hooversville (15936) ***(G-7771)***
Sherpa Software Partners, Bridgeville *Also called Everest Software LP* ***(G-2062)***
Sherwin-Williams Company 610 975-0126
317 W Lancaster Ave Wayne (19087) ***(G-19371)***
Sherwood Valve LLC (HQ) 724 225-8000
100 Business Center Dr # 400 Pittsburgh (15205) ***(G-15532)***
Sheth International Inc 610 584-8670
2844 Highview Dr Norristown (19403) ***(G-12712)***
Shetler Lumber Company Inc 814 796-0303
2850 Route 6 Waterford (16441) ***(G-19269)***
Shetler Memorials Inc 814 288-1087
935 Tire Hill Rd Johnstown (15905) ***(G-8435)***
Shetron Manufacturing LLC 717 532-4400
103 Hammond Rd Shippensburg (17257) ***(G-17547)***
Shetron Trailer Sales, Shippensburg *Also called Shetron Manufacturing LLC* ***(G-17547)***
Shetron Wldg & Fabrication Inc 717 776-4344
1100 Remmington Dr Shippensburg (17257) ***(G-17548)***
Shields Embroidery By Design 412 531-2321
4156 Library Rd Ste 2 Pittsburgh (15234) ***(G-15533)***
Shields Logging LLC 814 778-6183
8592 Route 6 Kane (16735) ***(G-8478)***
Shift4 Payments LLC (HQ) 800 201-0461
2202 N Irving St Allentown (18109) ***(G-389)***
Shiloh Industries 717 779-7654
3656 Kortni Dr Dover (17315) ***(G-4204)***
Shine Moon L P 570 539-8602
10594 Route 35 Mount Pleasant Mills (17853) ***(G-11732)***
Shingle Belting Inc 610 825-5500
420 Drew Ct Ste A King of Prussia (19406) ***(G-8674)***
Shippensburg Pump Co Inc 717 532-7321
1 Schwenk Dr Shippensburg (17257) ***(G-17549)***
Shire Holdings US AG (HQ) 484 595-8800
725 Chesterbrook Blvd Chesterbrook (19087) ***(G-3096)***
Shire Pharmaceuticals LLC (HQ) 484 595-8800
1200 Morris Dr Chesterbrook (19087) ***(G-3097)***
Shire US Manufacturing Inc (HQ) 484 595-8800
1200 Morris Dr Chesterbrook (19087) ***(G-3098)***
Shire Viropharma Incorporated 610 644-9929
730 Stockton Dr Exton (19341) ***(G-5731)***
Shirk AG Supply, Narvon *Also called Shirk Manufacturing* ***(G-11926)***
Shirk Manufacturing 717 445-9353
2100 Turkey Hill Rd Narvon (17555) ***(G-11926)***
Shirks Custom Wood Turning 717 656-6295
1155 Short Rd New Holland (17557) ***(G-12283)***
Shirks Saw Mill 717 776-7083
2033 Ritner Hwy Shippensburg (17257) ***(G-17550)***
Shirleys Cookie Company Inc 814 239-2208
153 William Ward Dr Claysburg (16625) ***(G-3208)***
Shirt Gallery Inc 215 364-1212
200 Elmwood Ave Ste A Feasterville Trevose (19053) ***(G-5929)***
Shivkanta Corporation 610 376-3515
1905 N 5th Street Hwy Reading (19605) ***(G-16517)***
Shock Solutions Inc 610 767-7090
3807 Cinnamon Dr Danielsville (18038) ***(G-3995)***
Shoemaker Mfg Solutions Inc 215 723-5567
302 Leidy Rd Souderton (18964) ***(G-17764)***
Shojoberry Magazine 814 736-3210
805 Sherman St Portage (15946) ***(G-15921)***
Shook Specialty Welding Inc 724 368-8419
3968 State Route 488 Portersville (16051) ***(G-15936)***
Shop Vac Corporation 570 673-5145
2323 Reach Rd Williamsport (17701) ***(G-20072)***
Shopmuse, Philadelphia *Also called Twenty61 LLC* ***(G-14415)***
Shopper Report, The, Philadelphia *Also called Consumer Network Inc* ***(G-13572)***
Shoppers Guide 724 349-0336
899 Water St Indiana (15701) ***(G-8128)***
Shopping News of Lncaster Cnty, Ephrata *Also called Hocking Printing Co Inc* ***(G-5109)***
Shoprite of Oxford & Levick, Philadelphia *Also called Wakefern Food Corp* ***(G-14457)***
Shore Chemical Co, Pittsburgh *Also called Shore Corporation* ***(G-15534)***
Shore Corporation 412 471-3330
2917 Spruce Way Pittsburgh (15201) ***(G-15534)***
Shorts Tool & Mfg Inc 814 763-2401
18927 Reservoir Rd Saegertown (16433) ***(G-16933)***
Showmark LLC 610 458-0304
410 Eagleview Blvd # 102 Exton (19341) ***(G-5732)***
Showtex Logistics LLC 570 218-0054
404 E 10th St Berwick (18603) ***(G-1343)***
Shred Patrol, West Chester *Also called Wiggins Shredding Inc* ***(G-19677)***
Shredstation Express of Montgo 215 723-1694
535 Hagey Rd Franconia (18924) ***(G-6110)***
Shree Swami Narayan Corp 610 272-8404
1882 Markley St Norristown (19401) ***(G-12713)***
Shrewsbury Concrete Co, Shrewsbury *Also called Trenton Group Inc* ***(G-17589)***
Shrock Fabrication 717 397-9500
229 Maple Ave Bird In Hand (17505) ***(G-1680)***
Shs Drinks Us LLC 412 854-9012
71 Mcmurray Rd Ste 104 Pittsburgh (15241) ***(G-15535)***
Shubandit LLC 610 916-8313
133 Penrose Ave Blandon (19510) ***(G-1759)***
Shuler Woodworking 724 679-5222
300 Cornetti Rd Fenelton (16034) ***(G-5948)***
Shultz Food Company, Hanover *Also called Todds Snax Inc* ***(G-6961)***
Shumars Welding & Mch Svc Inc 724 246-8095
414 Stone Church Rd Grindstone (15442) ***(G-6779)***
Shutter Tech Inc 610 696-9322
1155 Phoenixville Pike # 105 West Chester (19380) ***(G-19639)***
Shvarts, Roman, Southampton *Also called Majestic Creations Inc* ***(G-17824)***
Shydas Services Inc 717 274-8676
2360 Colebrook Rd Frnt Lebanon (17042) ***(G-9630)***
Si Novelties, Bensalem *Also called Novelty Concepts Inc* ***(G-1233)***
Siberian Coolers, Folsom *Also called Global Custom* ***(G-6023)***
Sic Marking Usa Inc 412 487-1165
137 Delta Dr Pittsburgh (15238) ***(G-15536)***
Sichel Sleep Products, Norristown *Also called Elby Bedding Inc* ***(G-12653)***
Sickafus Sheepskins 610 488-1782
Exit 19 Rr 78 Strausstown (19559) ***(G-18100)***
Sickley Hollow Sawyer, Waynesboro *Also called Wilmer R EBY* ***(G-19430)***
Sicom Systems Inc (HQ) 215 489-2500
1684 S Broad St Ste 300 Lansdale (19446) ***(G-9410)***
Sid Global Solutions LLC 484 218-0021
407 W Lincoln Hwy Ste 500 Exton (19341) ***(G-5733)***
Sidehill Copper Works Inc 814 451-0400
12 Port Access Rd Ste 2 Erie (16507) ***(G-5477)***
Sidelinger Bros Tool & Die 814 885-8001
500 Main St Kersey (15846) ***(G-8569)***
Sidelinger Brothers Tool & Die, Kersey *Also called Sidelinger Bros Tool & Die* ***(G-8569)***
Sidleck Welding & Fabricating, Whitehall *Also called Craig Sidleck* ***(G-19869)***
Siegwerk Ink Packaging, Drums *Also called Siegwerk USA Inc* ***(G-4383)***
Siegwerk USA Inc 570 708-0267
80 Hillside Dr Drums (18222) ***(G-4383)***
Sieling and Jones Inc 717 235-7931
127 Pleasant Ave New Freedom (17349) ***(G-12215)***
Siem Tool Company Inc 724 520-1904
131 Turnberry Cir Latrobe (15650) ***(G-9520)***
Siemens Energy, Spring House *Also called Siemens Industry Inc* ***(G-17883)***
Siemens Gamesa Renewable (HQ) 215 710-3100
1150 Northbrook Dr # 300 Feasterville Trevose (19053) ***(G-5930)***
Siemens Gamesa Renewable 215 665-9810
1801 Market St Ste 2700 Philadelphia (19103) ***(G-14303)***
Siemens Industry Inc 610 921-3135
4201 Pottsville Pike Reading (19605) ***(G-16518)***
Siemens Industry Inc 215 712-0280
100 Highpoint Dr Ste 101 Chalfont (18914) ***(G-2887)***
Siemens Industry Inc 412 829-7511
664 Linden Ave East Pittsburgh (15112) ***(G-4597)***
Siemens Industry Inc 215 646-7400
1201 Sumneytown Pike Spring House (19477) ***(G-17883)***

Siemens Industry Inc 724 339-9500
500 Hunt Valley Rd New Kensington (15068) *(G-12375)*

Siemens Industry Inc 724 772-0044
181 Thorn Hill Rd Warrendale (15086) *(G-19097)*

Siemens Industry Inc 724 743-5913
100 Southpointe Blvd Canonsburg (15317) *(G-2636)*

Siemens Industry Inc 724 733-2569
100 Sagamore Hill Rd Murrysville (15668) *(G-11866)*

Siemens Industry Inc 215 654-8040
1450 Union Meeting Rd Blue Bell (19422) *(G-1852)*

Siemens Med Solutions USA Inc 610 834-1220
5168 Campus Dr Plymouth Meeting (19462) *(G-15870)*

Siemens Med Solutions USA Inc (HQ) 888 826-9702
40 Liberty Blvd Malvern (19355) *(G-10315)*

Siemens Product Life Mgmt Sftw 717 299-1846
301 Post Oak Rd Lancaster (17603) *(G-9196)*

Siemens Product Life Mgmt Sftw 814 237-4999
100 Walker Dr State College (16801) *(G-18022)*

Siemens Product Life Mgmt Sftw 814 861-1651
330 Innovation Blvd # 202 State College (16803) *(G-18023)*

Sierra Media Services Inc 412 722-1701
2 Robinson Plz Ste 300 Pittsburgh (15205) *(G-15537)*

Sig Combibloc Inc 610 546-4200
2501 Seaport Dr Ste Rf100 Chester (19013) *(G-3062)*

Sigbet Manufacturing 724 459-7920
3994 Chestnut Ridge Rd Blairsville (15717) *(G-1741)*

Sigelock Systems LLC 814 673-2791
191 Howard St Ste 318 Franklin (16323) *(G-6160)*

Sigma Biologics Inc 215 741-1523
24203 Cornerstone Dr Yardley (19067) *(G-20339)*

Sigma Controls Inc 215 257-3412
217 S 5th St Perkasie (18944) *(G-13293)*

Sigma Instruments Inc 724 776-9500
506 Thomson Park Dr Cranberry Township (16066) *(G-3850)*

Sigma Technology Systems LLC 717 569-2926
1148 Elizabeth Ave Ste 6 Lancaster (17601) *(G-9197)*

Sigmapharm Laboratories LLC 215 352-6655
3375 Progress Dr Bensalem (19020) *(G-1253)*

Sign Concepts Inc 610 586-7070
106 Swarthmore Ave Ste 1 Folsom (19033) *(G-6028)*

Sign Crafters, West Homestead *Also called Sign Creators Inc (G-19720)*

Sign Creators Inc 412 461-3567
345 Cherry St West Homestead (15120) *(G-19720)*

Sign Design Associates Inc 610 791-9301
510 S Fawn St Allentown (18103) *(G-390)*

Sign Factory, Bethlehem *Also called G & L Designs (G-1521)*

Sign Fuel 989 245-6284
4618 Mary Ann Cir Coplay (18037) *(G-3648)*

Sign Guy 724 483-2200
770 E Main St Monongahela (15063) *(G-11315)*

Sign Here Inc 814 453-6711
144 W 12th St Ste A Erie (16501) *(G-5478)*

Sign Here Sign Co Inc 845 858-6366
808 Pennsylvania Ave Matamoras (18336) *(G-10540)*

Sign Innovation, Zelienople *Also called ELM Enterprises Inc (G-20798)*

Sign Maker Inc 215 676-6711
6909 Frankford Ave Philadelphia (19135) *(G-14304)*

Sign ME Up LLC 814 931-0933
224 Woodlawn Ter Hollidaysburg (16648) *(G-7655)*

Sign Medix Inc 717 396-9749
2153 Columbia Ave Lancaster (17603) *(G-9198)*

Sign O Rama Inc 215 784-9494
215 Easton Rd Willow Grove (19090) *(G-20141)*

Sign Services Inc 412 996-0824
306 North Ave East Pittsburgh (15112) *(G-4598)*

Sign Shop of The Poconos Inc 347 972-1775
196 W Moorestown Rd Wind Gap (18091) *(G-20172)*

Sign Shop, The, Mansfield *Also called GEC Enterprises Inc (G-10415)*

Sign Spot 570 455-7775
420 W 9th St Hazleton (18201) *(G-7527)*

Sign Stop 814 238-3338
426 S Atherton St State College (16801) *(G-18024)*

Sign-A-Rama, Monroeville *Also called Tomdel Inc (G-11360)*

Sign-A-Rama, Lancaster *Also called Signarama (G-9199)*

Sign-A-Rama, Reading *Also called Linbob LLC (G-16429)*

Sign-A-Rama, Norristown *Also called Fine Sign Designs Inc (G-12658)*

Sign-A-Rama, Philadelphia *Also called D & N Enterprise Inc (G-13597)*

Sign-A-Rama, Philadelphia *Also called Futura Identities Inc (G-13736)*

Sign-A-Rama, Sharon Hill *Also called Deversign (G-17456)*

Sign-A-Rama, Allison Park *Also called West Signs Inc (G-467)*

Sign-A-Rama, Willow Grove *Also called Sign O Rama Inc (G-20141)*

Sign-A-Rama, Feasterville Trevose *Also called F and T LP (G-5907)*

Sign-A-Rama, Philadelphia *Also called Sign Maker Inc (G-14304)*

Signage Unlimited Inc 610 647-6962
197 Pennsylvania Ave Malvern (19355) *(G-10316)*

Signal Graphics Printing, Canonsburg *Also called Steel City Graphics Inc (G-2640)*

Signal Item, Mckees Rocks *Also called Gateway Publications (G-10660)*

Signal Machine Co 717 354-9994
150 King Ct New Holland (17557) *(G-12284)*

Signarama 717 397-3173
1748 Columbia Ave Ste 1 Lancaster (17603) *(G-9199)*

Signature 2000, Erie *Also called Precision Rehab Manufacturing (G-5432)*

Signature Building Systems Inc 570 774-1000
1004 Springbrook Ave Moosic (18507) *(G-11515)*

Signature Building Systems Inc (PA) 570 774-1000
1004 Springbrook Ave Moosic (18507) *(G-11516)*

Signature Building Systems PA, Moosic *Also called Signature Building Systems Inc (G-11516)*

Signature Custom Cabinetry Inc 717 738-4884
434 Springville Rd Ephrata (17522) *(G-5140)*

Signature Door Inc 814 949-2770
401 Priority St Altoona (16602) *(G-549)*

Signature Flags, Ambridge *Also called K & B Outfitters Inc (G-623)*

Signature Gallery 610 792-5399
50 1st Ave Royersford (19468) *(G-16864)*

Signature Stone Inc 717 397-2364
1005 Willow Street Pike Lancaster (17602) *(G-9200)*

Signature Structures LLC 610 882-9030
312 E Broad St Bethlehem (18018) *(G-1618)*

Signature Vacuum Systems Inc 814 333-1110
10358 Harmonsburg Rd Harmonsburg (16422) *(G-7064)*

Significant Developments LLC 724 348-5277
1710 Wheatland Ct Moon Township (15108) *(G-11500)*

Signline LLC 610 973-3600
997 Postal Rd Allentown (18109) *(G-391)*

Signode Industrial Group LLC 570 450-0123
450 Jaycee Dr Hazle Township (18202) *(G-7479)*

Signode Industrial Group LLC 570 937-4921
2206 Easton Tpke South Canaan (18459) *(G-17770)*

Signode Industrial Group LLC 570 937-4921
2206 Easton Trpke South Canaan (18459) *(G-17771)*

Signs & More In 24, Harrisburg *Also called RMS Kunkle Inc (G-7208)*

Signs By Design 717 626-6212
2273 Lititz Pike Lancaster (17601) *(G-9201)*

Signs By Renee 814 763-4206
16520 State Highway 198 Saegertown (16433) *(G-16934)*

Signs By Rick Inc 724 287-3887
217 Freeport Rd Butler (16002) *(G-2441)*

Signs By Sam 724 752-3711
106 Elizabeth Way Ellwood City (16117) *(G-4949)*

Signs By Tomorrow, Morton *Also called Surf & Turf Enterprises (G-11593)*

Signs By Tomorrow, Allentown *Also called 13 Big Bears Inc (G-109)*

Signs By Tomorrow, Monroeville *Also called Davis Sign Service LLC (G-11332)*

Signs By Tomorrow 717 757-4909
2260 Industrial Hwy York (17402) *(G-20668)*

Signs By Tomorrow 724 838-9060
422 E Pittsburgh St Greensburg (15601) *(G-6714)*

Signs By Tomorrow 484 356-0707
1609 Margo Ln West Chester (19380) *(G-19640)*

Signs By Tomorrow Inc 717 975-2456
333 S Front St Lemoyne (17043) *(G-9753)*

Signs By Tomorrow USA Inc 484 592-0404
130 E Lancaster Ave Rear Ardmore (19003) *(G-716)*

Signs Now 717 633-5864
643 Frederick St Hanover (17331) *(G-6952)*

Signs Now 814 453-6564
2232 W 23rd St Erie (16506) *(G-5479)*

Signs of Excellence Inc 724 325-7446
4225 Old William Penn Hwy Murrysville (15668) *(G-11867)*

Signs Service & Crane Inc 724 515-5272
165 Leger Rd Irwin (15642) *(G-8200)*

Signstat 724 527-7475
412 Harrison Ave Jeannette (15644) *(G-8264)*

Sikkens Inc 610 337-8710
310 Hansen Access Rd King of Prussia (19406) *(G-8675)*

Sikorsky Concrete Product LLC 610 826-3676
760 Little Gap Rd Palmerton (18071) *(G-13111)*

Sil Kemp Concrete Inc (PA) 215 295-0777
355 Newbold Rd Fairless Hills (19030) *(G-5796)*

Sil-Base Company Inc 412 751-2314
4 Juniper St McKeesport (15132) *(G-10681)*

Silarx Pharmaceuticals Inc 845 225-1500
13200 Townsend Rd Philadelphia (19154) *(G-14305)*

Silbaugh Vault and Burial Svc 724 437-3002
4 Speedway Blvd Uniontown (15401) *(G-18642)*

Silber Brush Manufacturing Co 215 634-4063
1342 E Montgomery Ave Philadelphia (19125) *(G-14306)*

Silberine Manufacturing 570 668-8361
4905 W Tilghman St Allentown (18104) *(G-392)*

Silberline Holding Co (PA) 570 668-6050
130 Lincoln Dr Tamaqua (18252) *(G-18224)*

Silberline Mfg Co Inc (PA) 570 668-6050
130 Lincoln Dr Tamaqua (18252) *(G-18225)*

Silberline Mfg Co Inc 570 668-6050
201 Dock St Lansford (18232) *(G-9449)*

Silcotek Corp....814 353-1778
225 Penntech Dr Bellefonte (16823) ***(G-1118)***
Silgan Containers Corporation....484 223-3189
8201 Industrial Blvd Breinigsville (18031) ***(G-2027)***
Silgan Containers Mfg Corp....610 337-2203
620 Freedom Business Ctr King of Prussia (19406) ***(G-8676)***
Silgan Ipec Corporation....724 658-3004
185 Northgate Cir New Castle (16105) ***(G-12152)***
Silgan Ipec Corporation (HQ)....724 658-3004
185 Northgate Cir New Castle (16105) ***(G-12153)***
Silgan Plastics, Langhorne *Also called Sean S Zuniga* ***(G-9324)***
Silgan Plastics LLC....215 727-2676
121 Wheeler Ct Langhorne (19047) ***(G-9325)***
Silgan White Cap Corporation....570 455-7781
350 Jaycee Dr Hazle Township (18202) ***(G-7480)***
Silhol Builders Supply Co Inc....412 221-7400
100 Union St Bridgeville (15017) ***(G-2089)***
Silicon Power Corporation (PA)....610 407-4700
280 Great Valley Pkwy Malvern (19355) ***(G-10317)***
Silk Screen Printers....717 761-1121
3814 Seneca Ave Camp Hill (17011) ***(G-2518)***
Silver Charm Clothing Company....484 274-6796
930 N 4th St Allentown (18102) ***(G-393)***
Silver Creek, Bloomsburg *Also called Bloomsburg Carpet Inds Inc* ***(G-1775)***
Silver Creek Services Inc....724 710-0440
601 Technology Dr Ste 310 Canonsburg (15317) ***(G-2637)***
Silver Springs Farm Inc....215 256-4321
640 Meetinghouse Rd Harleysville (19438) ***(G-7058)***
Silver Star Meats Inc (PA)....412 771-5539
1720 Middletown Rd Mc Kees Rocks (15136) ***(G-10635)***
Silver Vly Drlg & Blastg Inc....570 992-1125
Rr 4 Saylorsburg (18353) ***(G-17107)***
Silverbrook Anthracite Inc....570 654-3560
1 Market St Wilkes Barre (18702) ***(G-19963)***
Silverline Screen Printing....570 275-8866
275 Mill St Danville (17821) ***(G-4011)***
Silvi Concrete Products, Fairless Hills *Also called Construction Dynamics Inc* ***(G-5775)***
Silvi Concrete Products Inc....215 295-0777
355 Newbold Rd Fairless Hills (19030) ***(G-5797)***
Silvi of Englishtown, Fairless Hills *Also called Sil Kemp Concrete Inc* ***(G-5796)***
Silvine Inc....215 657-2345
1843 Fairview Ave Willow Grove (19090) ***(G-20142)***
Simco Graphics, Collingdale *Also called Simco Sign Studios Inc* ***(G-3410)***
Simco Industrial Static Cntrl....215 822-2171
2257 N Penn Rd Hatfield (19440) ***(G-7396)***
Simco Sign Studios Inc....610 534-5550
50 Jackson Ave Collingdale (19023) ***(G-3410)***
Simkar LLC (HQ)....215 831-7700
700 Ramona Ave Philadelphia (19120) ***(G-14307)***
Simkins Corporation (PA)....215 739-4033
1636 Valley Rd Jenkintown (19046) ***(G-8301)***
Simms Abrasives....610 327-1877
122 E 4th St Pottstown (19464) ***(G-16046)***
Simon Candy Co, Lebanon *Also called Pharmaloz Manufacturing Inc* ***(G-9621)***
Simon of Bolivar Enterprises....814 697-7891
1140 State Route 44 S Shinglehouse (16748) ***(G-17513)***
Simona America Inc (HQ)....570 579-1300
101 Power Blvd Archbald (18403) ***(G-694)***
Simone Associates Inc....717 274-3621
845 Cumberland St Lebanon (17042) ***(G-9631)***
Simons Bros Company....215 426-9901
2424 E Sergeant St Philadelphia (19125) ***(G-14308)***
Simple Treat Bakery....412 681-0303
4734 Liberty Ave Pittsburgh (15224) ***(G-15538)***
Simplex Industries Inc....570 495-4333
1180 Line St Sunbury (17801) ***(G-18172)***
Simplex Industries Inc (PA)....570 346-5113
1 Simplex Dr Scranton (18504) ***(G-17291)***
Simplex Paper Box Corp....717 757-3611
100 S Friendship Ave Hellam (17406) ***(G-7552)***
Simplicity Creative Corp....800 653-7301
450 Plymouth Rd Ste 300 Plymouth Meeting (19462) ***(G-15871)***
Simplr Technologies LLC....814 883-6463
1754 Cambridge Dr State College (16803) ***(G-18025)***
Simply Automated Llc....412 343-0348
190a Industry Dr Pittsburgh (15275) ***(G-15539)***
Simply Business LLC....814 241-7113
1016 New Germany Rd Summerhill (15958) ***(G-18155)***
Simply Good Jars, Philadelphia *Also called Sapor Food Group LLC* ***(G-14281)***
Simpson Manufacturing Inc....724 694-2708
131 E 3rd St Derry (15627) ***(G-4107)***
Simpson Reinforcing Inc (PA)....412 362-6200
2001 Dr Thomas Blvd New Kensington (15068) ***(G-12376)***
Simpson Staff Reinfofrcement, New Kensington *Also called Simpson Reinforcing Inc* ***(G-12376)***
Simpson Technical Sales Inc....724 375-7133
212 University Dr Aliquippa (15001) ***(G-96)***
Simtech Industrial Pdts Inc....215 547-0444
47 Runway Dr Ste A Levittown (19057) ***(G-9863)***

Simulation Live Fire Training....412 787-2832
4853 Campbells Run Rd Pittsburgh (15205) ***(G-15540)***
Sinacom North America Inc....610 337-2250
1020 W 8th Ave King of Prussia (19406) ***(G-8677)***
Sinclair Technologies LLC....610 296-8259
200 E State St Ste 301 Media (19063) ***(G-10950)***
Sinfully Sweet....412 523-1887
10114 Saltsburg Rd Pittsburgh (15239) ***(G-15541)***
Sing Out Magazine, Bethlehem *Also called Sing-Out Corporation* ***(G-1619)***
Sing-Out Corporation....610 865-5366
360 16th Ave Bethlehem (18018) ***(G-1619)***
Singerman Laboratories....412 798-0447
4091 Saltsburg Rd Ste F Murrysville (15668) ***(G-11868)***
Singing Dog Vanilla, Phoenixville *Also called Kestrel Growth Brands Inc* ***(G-14556)***
Sinking Ship Premium Juice LLC....570 855-2316
102 E Main St Glen Lyon (18617) ***(G-6427)***
Sinking Ship Vapors, Glen Lyon *Also called Sinking Ship Premium Juice LLC* ***(G-6427)***
Sinnott Industries Inc....215 677-7793
2060 Bennett Rd Philadelphia (19116) ***(G-14309)***
Sinocom North America, King of Prussia *Also called Sinacom North America Inc* ***(G-8677)***
Sinterfire Inc....814 885-6672
200 Indl Pk Rd Kersey (15846) ***(G-8570)***
Sintergy Inc....814 653-9640
2130 Indl Blvd Reynoldsville (15851) ***(G-16664)***
Sinterite Furnace Division, Du Bois *Also called Gasbarre Products Inc* ***(G-4392)***
Sinterite Products, Saint Marys *Also called C I Hayes Inc* ***(G-16951)***
Sintermet LLC....724 548-7631
222 North Park Dr Ste 1 Kittanning (16201) ***(G-8792)***
Sip Bulletin LLC....267 235-3359
1920 S 23rd St Philadelphia (19145) ***(G-14310)***
Sippel Co Inc....724 266-9800
101 Port Ambridge Dr Ambridge (15003) ***(G-634)***
Sippel Co Inc (PA)....724 266-9800
21 Century Dr Ambridge (15003) ***(G-635)***
Sippel Steel Fab, Ambridge *Also called Sippel Co Inc* ***(G-634)***
Sippel Steel Fab, Ambridge *Also called Sippel Co Inc* ***(G-635)***
Sir James Prtg & Bus Forms Inc....724 339-2122
864 4th Ave New Kensington (15068) ***(G-12377)***
Sir Speedy, Lancaster *Also called H & H Graphics Inc* ***(G-9035)***
Sir Speedy, Lancaster *Also called Huepenbecker Enterprises Inc* ***(G-9052)***
Sir Speedy, Newtown *Also called Heatha Henrys LLC* ***(G-12509)***
Sir Speedy, King of Prussia *Also called A J Printing* ***(G-8575)***
Sir Speedy, Havertown *Also called D R M Services Corporation* ***(G-7419)***
Sir Speedy, West Chester *Also called A Stuart Morton Inc* ***(G-19492)***
Sir Speedy, Lancaster *Also called H & H Graphics Inc* ***(G-9036)***
Sir Speedy, Reading *Also called Q D F Inc* ***(G-16477)***
Sir Speedy, Butler *Also called Pjr Printing Inc* ***(G-2434)***
Sir Speedy, Newtown *Also called Pleasant Luck Corp* ***(G-12537)***
Sir Speedy, Warminster *Also called Indus Graphics Inc* ***(G-18896)***
Sir Speedy Inc....215 877-8888
7573 Haverford Ave Philadelphia (19151) ***(G-14311)***
Sir Speedy 7108 Inc....412 787-9898
4573 Campbells Run Rd Pittsburgh (15205) ***(G-15542)***
Sir Speedy Printing and Mktg, Pittsburgh *Also called Sir Speedy 7108 Inc* ***(G-15542)***
Sir Speedy Printing Center....412 687-0500
369 Coltart Ave Pittsburgh (15213) ***(G-15543)***
Sire Press LLC....267 909-9233
3237 Amber St Ste 2 Philadelphia (19134) ***(G-14312)***
Sirtris Pharmaceuticals Inc....585 275-5774
1250 S Collegeville Rd Collegeville (19426) ***(G-3393)***
SIS Software LLC....888 844-6599
4955 Steubenville Pike Pittsburgh (15205) ***(G-15544)***
Sitka Enterprises Inc....610 393-6708
2490 Lantern Ct S Macungie (18062) ***(G-10158)***
Siu King....215 769-9863
1024 Buttonwood St Philadelphia (19123) ***(G-14313)***
Siw, Scranton *Also called Standard Iron Works* ***(G-17293)***
Six Pack Creamery LLC....267 261-2727
226 Oak Hill Dr Hatboro (19040) ***(G-7305)***
Six Pak Shack....724 593-2401
339 State Route 711 Jones Mills (15646) ***(G-8448)***
Sixth Wheel Inc....610 647-0880
23 Deer Run Ln Malvern (19355) ***(G-10318)***
Sixty Ninth St Coml Prtrs, Norristown *Also called 69th St Commercial Printers* ***(G-12627)***
Sjm Manufacturing Inc....724 478-5580
119 Florida Ave Bldg 1 Apollo (15613) ***(G-685)***
Sk, Leola *Also called Swing Kingdom LLC* ***(G-9807)***
Sk Sales Company Inc....570 474-5600
980 Crestwood Dr Mountain Top (18707) ***(G-11775)***
Sk Wood Working, Honey Brook *Also called Sam King* ***(G-7760)***
Skaffl LLC....484 809-9351
4283 Elm Dr Allentown (18103) ***(G-394)***
Skantra Diagnostics Inc....215 990-0381
825 Hollow Rd Radnor (19087) ***(G-16302)***
Skc Inc (PA)....724 260-0741
863 Valley View Rd Eighty Four (15330) ***(G-4849)***

ALPHABETIC

Skc Gulf Coast Inc 724 677-0340
75 Colonial Ave Smock (15480) **(G-17667)**

Skee-Ball Amusement Games, Center Valley *Also called Sbi Survivor Corporation* **(G-2829)**

SKF Hanover, Hanover *Also called SKF USA Inc* **(G-6953)**

SKF Motion Technologies LLC (HQ) 267 436-6000
890 Forty Foot Rd Ste 105 Lansdale (19446) **(G-9411)**

SKF USA Inc 717 637-8981
20 Industrial Dr Hanover (17331) **(G-6953)**

SKF USA Inc 610 954-7000
6580 Snowdrift Rd Ste 200 Allentown (18106) **(G-395)**

Ski Haus LLC 412 760-7547
716 Woodland Rd Bradfordwoods (15015) **(G-1999)**

Skias Chuck Wldg & Fabricators 610 375-0912
322 Blair Ave Reading (19601) **(G-16519)**

Skinner Power Systems, Polk *Also called Time Machine Inc* **(G-15889)**

Skitco Iron Works, Hazle Township *Also called Skitco Manufacturing Inc* **(G-7481)**

Skitco Manufacturing Inc 570 929-2100
1478 S Church St Hazle Township (18201) **(G-7481)**

Skm Industries Inc (PA) 570 383-3062
1012 Underwood Rd Olyphant (18447) **(G-12999)**

Skotz Manufacturing Inc (PA) 610 286-0710
2676 Ridge Rd Elverson (19520) **(G-4966)**

Skovira Fabrication Mch Sp Inc 717 323-0056
101 Watts St Mount Holly Springs (17065) **(G-11639)**

Skovira Machine Company 724 887-4896
146 Catalina Farm Rd Scottdale (15683) **(G-17201)**

Skrapits Concrete Company (PA) 610 262-8830
2650 Howertown Rd 3 Northampton (18067) **(G-12861)**

Skrapits Concrete Company 610 442-5355
2550 Quarry St Coplay (18037) **(G-3649)**

Skunkwirkz LLC 814 602-8936
2672 Hannon Rd Erie (16510) **(G-5480)**

Skuta Signs of All Kinds (PA) 724 863-6159
10649 State Route 30 Irwin (15642) **(G-8201)**

Sky Fuel Inc 215 343-3825
318 Evening Walk Ln Warrington (18976) **(G-19134)**

Sky Fuel Inc 215 257-5392
501 Route 313 Perkasie (18944) **(G-13294)**

Sky Haven Coal Inc 814 765-1665
5510 State Park Rd Penfield (15849) **(G-13223)**

Sky Oxygen Inc 412 278-3001
2790 Idlewood Ave Carnegie (15106) **(G-2793)**

Sky Point Crane LLC 724 471-5710
188 Wren St Indiana (15701) **(G-8129)**

Sky Top Coal Company Inc 570 773-2000
State Hwy New Boston Mahanoy City (17948) **(G-10174)**

Skydive Store Inc 856 629-4600
354 Brentwood Dr Bushkill (18324) **(G-2369)**

Skyline Auto Supply LLC 484 365-4040
2571 Nazareth Rd Easton (18045) **(G-4752)**

Skyline Beauty Supply Inc 215 468-1888
505 Washington Ave Philadelphia (19147) **(G-14314)**

Skyline Champion Corporation 717 656-2071
99 Horseshoe Rd Leola (17540) **(G-9803)**

Skyline Homes, Leola *Also called Skyline Champion Corporation* **(G-9803)**

Skyline Technology Inc 610 296-7501
44 Pennsylvania Ave Malvern (19355) **(G-10319)**

Skylon Inc 814 489-3622
12210 Jackson Run Rd Sugar Grove (16350) **(G-18147)**

Skyroc LLC 215 840-5466
122 N Lambert St Philadelphia (19103) **(G-14315)**

Skytop Machine & Tool Inc 814 234-3430
1263 Skytop Mountain Rd Port Matilda (16870) **(G-15906)**

Slate and Copper Sales Co 814 455-7430
436 W 12th St Erie (16501) **(G-5481)**

Slate Belt Printers Inc 610 863-6752
115 W Pennsylvania Ave Pen Argyl (18072) **(G-13217)**

Slate Belt Woodworkers Inc 610 588-1922
729 1/2 S Main St Bangor (18013) **(G-927)**

Slate Lick Printing Inc 724 295-2053
944 Freeport Rd Freeport (16229) **(G-6214)**

Slate Pharmaceuticals Inc 484 321-5900
1400 Atwater Dr Malvern (19355) **(G-10320)**

Slate Road Supply LLC 717 445-5222
150 Slate Rd Ephrata (17522) **(G-5141)**

Slatedale Aggregate Mtls Inc 610 767-4601
8452 Brown St Slatington (18080) **(G-17613)**

Slater Electric & Sons 724 306-1060
1115 New Castle Rd Prospect (16052) **(G-16112)**

Slates Enterprises Inc 814 695-2851
1147 3rd Ave Duncansville (16635) **(G-4463)**

Slates Salvage 814 448-3218
22380 Waterfall Rd Three Springs (17264) **(G-18356)**

Slavia Printing Co Inc 412 343-4444
157 Mcneilly Rd Pittsburgh (15226) **(G-15545)**

Slavic Group Inc 724 437-6756
1189 Connellsville Rd Lemont Furnace (15456) **(G-9737)**

Slaw Precast, Lehighton *Also called J & R Slaw Inc* **(G-9717)**

Slawko Racing Heads Inc 610 286-1822
171 Twin County Rd Morgantown (19543) **(G-11535)**

Slaymaker Group, Washington Boro *Also called Marvin Dale Slaymaker* **(G-19251)**

SLC Sales and Service Inc 724 238-7692
132 Presidents Dr Ligonier (15658) **(G-9965)**

Sleep Specialists LLC 610 304-6408
150 Monument Rd Bala Cynwyd (19004) **(G-892)**

Slippery Rock Materials Inc 724 530-7472
704 Golf Course Rd Volant (16156) **(G-18777)**

Sloan Equipment Sales Co Inc (PA) 215 784-0771
1677 Tuckerstown Rd Dresher (19025) **(G-4358)**

Sloan Valve Company 717 387-3959
5031 Richard Ln Ste 101 Mechanicsburg (17055) **(G-10889)**

Slocomb Windows & Doors, Hanover Township *Also called Newtown-Slocomb Mfg Inc* **(G-7001)**

Slothower Machine Shop LLC 717 846-3409
1700 Toronita St York (17402) **(G-20669)**

Sluga Logging, Mount Jewett *Also called James Sluga* **(G-11643)**

Slygt, Malvern *Also called ITT Water & Wastewater USA Inc* **(G-10256)**

Smales Printery Inc 610 323-7775
785 N Charlotte St Pottstown (19464) **(G-16047)**

Small Arms Manufacturing Co., Bridgeville *Also called E R Shaw Inc* **(G-2059)**

Small Parts Machine Inc 724 452-6116
252 Mercer Rd Harmony (16037) **(G-7076)**

Smart Avionics Inc 717 928-4360
186 Airport Rd Marietta (17547) **(G-10467)**

Smart Fertilizer LLC 814 880-8873
932 E Mccormick Ave State College (16801) **(G-18026)**

Smart Fuels LLC 717 645-8983
2145 Canterbury Dr Mechanicsburg (17055) **(G-10890)**

Smart Ops, Pittsburgh *Also called Smartops Corporation* **(G-15548)**

Smart Potato LLC 215 380-5050
512 Marks Rd Oreland (19075) **(G-13029)**

Smart Print Technologies Inc 412 771-8307
312 Thompson Ave Mc Kees Rocks (15136) **(G-10636)**

Smart Systems Inc 412 323-2128
R.J Casey Industrial Park Pittsburgh (15233) **(G-15546)**

Smart Systems Enterprises Inc 412 323-2128
1800 Preble Ave Pittsburgh (15233) **(G-15547)**

Smart-Hose Technologies, Folcroft *Also called Zena Associates Llc* **(G-6021)**

Smarterfuel Inc (PA) 570 972-4727
591 Male Rd Wind Gap (18091) **(G-20173)**

Smartops Corporation (PA) 412 231-0115
1251 Waterfront Pl # 301 Pittsburgh (15222) **(G-15548)**

Smartshake 724 396-7947
307 Cola St Pittsburgh (15203) **(G-15549)**

SMC, Saegertown *Also called Saegertown Manufacturing Corp* **(G-16932)**

SMC Direct LLC 800 521-1635
143 Wagner Rd Evans City (16033) **(G-5563)**

SMC Industries Inc (PA) 610 647-5687
3239 Phnxvlle Pike Bldg 1 Malvern (19355) **(G-10321)**

Sme Sales and Service Inc 724 384-1159
328 Aley Hill Rd Beaver Falls (15010) **(G-1012)**

Smeal Ltc LLC 717 918-1806
68 Cocalico Creek Rd Ephrata (17522) **(G-5142)**

Smg Fab Inc 717 556-8263
129 Ashmore Dr Leola (17540) **(G-9804)**

Smg-Global Circuits Inc (PA) 724 229-3200
120 Stationvue Washington (15301) **(G-19226)**

SMI IL Inc 847 228-0090
105 Kahr Ave Greeley (18425) **(G-6585)**

SMI Incorprated, Bethlehem *Also called Specialty Measurements Inc* **(G-1623)**

Smit Corporation 215 396-2200
103 Steam Whistle Dr Warminster (18974) **(G-18965)**

Smith & Nephew Inc 412 914-1190
300 Bursca Dr Ste 308 Bridgeville (15017) **(G-2090)**

Smith Auto Service 215 788-2401
3112 Hilltop Ave Bristol (19007) **(G-2198)**

Smith Concrete Products 724 349-5858
Old Rte 119 N Homer City (15748) **(G-7682)**

Smith Group Inc (PA) 215 957-7800
816 Nina Way Warminster (18974) **(G-18966)**

Smith Lawton Millwork 570 934-2544
Rr 706 Montrose (18801) **(G-11477)**

Smith Logging 814 371-2698
887 Sterrett Rd Reynoldsville (15851) **(G-16665)**

Smith Lumber Co 570 923-0188
12476 Renovo Rd Renovo (17764) **(G-16650)**

Smith Micro Software Inc (PA) 412 837-5300
5800 Corporate Dr Ste 500 Pittsburgh (15237) **(G-15550)**

Smith Paint Products, Harrisburg *Also called Brunner Industrial Group Inc* **(G-7100)**

Smith Prints Inc 215 997-8077
74 Park Ave Ste G2 Chalfont (18914) **(G-2888)**

Smith Provision Co Inc (PA) 814 459-4974
1300 Cranberry St Erie (16501) **(G-5482)**

Smith Provision Co Inc 814 459-4974
1890 W 20th St Erie (16502) **(G-5483)**

Smith Wilbert Vault Co, Bangor *Also called Smiths Wilbert Vault Company* **(G-929)**

SMITH'S, Erie *Also called Smith Provision Co Inc* **(G-5482)**

Smith, C Leslie, Allentown *Also called C Leslie Smith Inc* **(G-160)**

Smith-Freeman & Associates 610 929-5728
　4900 Kutztown Rd Ste Frnt Temple (19560) *(G-18336)*

Smith-Koch Co, Aston *Also called Eastern Industrial Pdts Inc (G-760)*

Smithfield Foods Inc 215 752-1090
　370 Maple Rd Middletown (17057) *(G-11077)*

Smithfield Global Product, Middletown *Also called Smithfield Foods Inc (G-11077)*

Smithfield Packaged Meats Corp 724 335-5800
　2200 Rivers Edge Dr New Kensington (15068) *(G-12378)*

Smithkline Beecham Corporation 215 751-4000
　1 Franklin Sq Philadelphia (19106) *(G-14316)*

Smiths Wilbert Vault Company (PA) 610 588-5259
　8 Wildon Dr Bangor (18013) *(G-928)*

Smiths Wilbert Vault Company 610 588-5259
　882 Lower South Main St Bangor (18013) *(G-929)*

Smiths Aerospace Components I 570 474-3011
　701 Crestwood Dr Mountain Top (18707) *(G-11776)*

Smiths Group North America Inc (HQ) 772 286-9300
　101 Lindenwood Dr Ste 125 Malvern (19355) *(G-10322)*

Smithton Raceway LLC 724 797-1822
　425 Fitz Henry Rd Smithton (15479) *(G-17662)*

SMK & Son Inc 215 455-7867
　4252 Rising Sun Ave Philadelphia (19140) *(G-14317)*

Smoke Town LLC 570 383-7833
　594 Burke Byp Ste C Olyphant (18447) *(G-13000)*

Smoker Logging Inc 814 486-2570
　Rich Vly Rr 1 Emporium (15834) *(G-5075)*

Smoker Manufacturing 717 529-6915
　415 Jackson School Rd Oxford (19363) *(G-13092)*

Smokers Outlet 814 827-1104
　302 E Central Ave Titusville (16354) *(G-18396)*

Smokers Sports, Ronks *Also called Smokers Sports Store (G-16815)*

Smokers Sports Store 717 687-9445
　247 Gap Rd Ste B Ronks (17572) *(G-16815)*

Smokers Stop 717 232-5206
　11 Kline Vlg Harrisburg (17104) *(G-7216)*

Smokey Mountain Woodworking 717 445-5120
　170 Sensenig Rd Ephrata (17522) *(G-5143)*

Smooth Line Inc 412 828-3599
　780 Route 910 Ste 400 Cheswick (15024) *(G-3118)*

Smooth-On Inc (PA) 610 252-5800
　5600 Lower Macungie Rd Macungie (18062) *(G-10159)*

Smouse Trucks & Vans Inc 724 887-7777
　207 Smouse Rd Mount Pleasant (15666) *(G-11718)*

Smoyer L M Brass Products Inc 610 867-5011
　1209 W Lehigh St Bethlehem (18018) *(G-1620)*

SMS Demag Inc 412 231-1200
　100 Sandusky St Pittsburgh (15212) *(G-15551)*

SMS Group Inc (HQ) 412 231-1200
　100 Sandusky St Pittsburgh (15212) *(G-15552)*

Smt Manufacturing Group LLC 717 767-4900
　60 S Prospect St Ste 100 York (17406) *(G-20670)*

Smucker Management Corporation 717 768-1501
　2715 Old Phladelphia Pike Bird In Hand (17505) *(G-1681)*

Smuckers Harness Shop Inc 717 445-5956
　2016 Main St Narvon (17555) *(G-11927)*

Smuckers Salad 267 757-0944
　2150 S Eagle Rd Newtown (18940) *(G-12550)*

Smuckers Sales & Services LLC 717 354-4158
　643 Peters Rd New Holland (17557) *(G-12285)*

Snack Shack 570 270-2929
　750 Wilkes Barre Townshp Wilkes Barre (18702) *(G-19964)*

Snakable Inc 347 449-3378
　709 16th Ave Fl 2 Prospect Park (19076) *(G-16120)*

Snake Creek Lasers LLC 570 553-1120
　26741 State Route 267 # 2 Friendsville (18818) *(G-6230)*

Snap Kitchen 3 LLC 215 845-0001
　1901 Callowhill St Philadelphia (19130) *(G-14318)*

Snap Tite Qd & V, Union City *Also called Parker-Hannifin Corporation (G-18612)*

Snapcab, Warrington *Also called Bostock Company Inc (G-19110)*

Snapper Cane LLC 516 770-3569
　1021 Hidden Hollow Ln West Chester (19380) *(G-19641)*

Snapper, The, Millersville *Also called Millersville University PA (G-11213)*

Snaptex International LLC 215 283-0152
　111a Park Dr Montgomeryville (18936) *(G-11418)*

Snavelys Mill Inc (PA) 717 626-6256
　333 Snavely Mill Rd Lititz (17543) *(G-10050)*

Snavelys Mill Inc 570 726-4747
　22 Fishing Creek Rd Mill Hall (17751) *(G-11182)*

Snb Publishing Inc 215 464-2500
　9908 Roosevelt Blvd Philadelphia (19115) *(G-14319)*

Snellbaker Printing Inc 215 885-0674
　128 S Keswick Ave Glenside (19038) *(G-6536)*

Snitz Creek Cabinet Shop LLC 717 273-9861
　2020 Cornwall Rd Lebanon (17042) *(G-9632)*

Snoblox-Snojax, Mechanicsburg *Also called Iceblox Inc (G-10856)*

Snooks Rhine & Arnold 570 658-3410
　113 Log Ln Mc Clure (17841) *(G-10561)*

Snow Shoe Refractories LLC 814 387-6811
　895 Clarence Rd Clarence (16829) *(G-3165)*

Snowberger Embroidery 814 696-6499
　2239 Maple Hollow Rd Duncansville (16635) *(G-4464)*

Snowtop LLC 724 297-5491
　1 Moonlight Dr Worthington (16262) *(G-20233)*

Snyder & Sons Tree Surgeons 610 932-2966
　480 Mount Hope Rd Lincoln University (19352) *(G-9975)*

Snyder Assod Companies Inc (PA) 724 548-8101
　1 Glade Park Dr Kittanning (16201) *(G-8793)*

Snyder Brothers Inc (HQ) 724 548-8101
　1 Glade Dr Kittanning (16201) *(G-8794)*

Snyder Coal Co, Hegins *Also called Dennis Snyder (G-7540)*

Snyder Contractors, Bala Cynwyd *Also called Reading Refractories Company (G-890)*

Snyder County Automotive Inc 570 374-2072
　808 N Market St Selinsgrove (17870) *(G-17335)*

Snyder County Times 570 837-6065
　405 E Main St Middleburg (17842) *(G-11041)*

Snyder Enterprises Inc 724 548-8101
　1 Glade Dr Kittanning (16201) *(G-8795)*

Snyder Exploration Co 724 548-8101
　1 Glade Dr Kittanning (16201) *(G-8796)*

Snyder Graphics, Bristol *Also called Bucks County Off Svcs & Prtg (G-2121)*

Snyder of Berlin, Altoona *Also called Birds Eye Foods Inc (G-478)*

Snyder of Berlin, Berlin *Also called Birds Eye Foods LLC (G-1285)*

Snyder Optical Co., Philadelphia *Also called Gary N Snyder (G-13744)*

Snyder Potato Chips, Berlin *Also called Birds Eye Foods Inc (G-1284)*

Snyder Printing & Promotional 215 358-3178
　714 N Bethlehem Pike # 201 Ambler (19002) *(G-602)*

Snyder Welding LLC 610 657-4916
　7747 Harbor Ct Slatington (18080) *(G-17614)*

Snyder's Associated Co, Kittanning *Also called Snyder Exploration Co (G-8796)*

Snyders Hanover Mfg Inc 800 233-7125
　1350 York St Hanover (17331) *(G-6954)*

Snyders-Lance Inc 724 929-6270
　230 Finley Rd Rostraver Township (15012) *(G-16830)*

Snyders-Lance Inc 717 632-4477
　1250 York St Hanover (17331) *(G-6955)*

Soap Alchemy LLC 412 671-4278
　317 Walker Rd New Galilee (16141) *(G-12222)*

Soap Plant Inc 724 656-3601
　765 Commerce Ave New Castle (16101) *(G-12154)*

Soaphies 814 861-7627
　244 E Calder Way State College (16801) *(G-18027)*

Social Still LLC 610 625-4585
　530 E 3rd St Bethlehem (18015) *(G-1621)*

Society For Industrial & Appli (PA) 215 382-9800
　3600 Market St Fl 6 Philadelphia (19104) *(G-14320)*

Society Hill Snacks, Philadelphia *Also called Nuts & Such Ltd (G-14089)*

Society of Clinical 215 822-8644
　530 W Butler Ave Ste 2 Chalfont (18914) *(G-2889)*

Society of Good Shepherd 717 349-7033
　22012 Indian Spring Trl Amberson (17210) *(G-565)*

Society Printers, Womelsdorf *Also called Amherst Corporation (G-20205)*

Socra, Chalfont *Also called Society of Clinical (G-2889)*

Soda Rental Service, Philadelphia *Also called Carbonator Rental Service Inc (G-13500)*

Sodium Systems LLC 800 821-8962
　1100 N Hartley St Ste 300 York (17404) *(G-20671)*

Soft Pretzels Franchise System (PA) 215 338-4606
　1525 Ford Rd Bensalem (19020) *(G-1254)*

Softboss Corp (PA) 215 563-7488
　1735 Market St Ste A459 Philadelphia (19103) *(G-14321)*

Softkog Inc 717 490-1091
　691 Sumneytown Pike Ste G Harleysville (19438) *(G-7059)*

Softstuf Inc 215 627-8850
　333 Bainbridge St Fl 2 Philadelphia (19147) *(G-14322)*

Software Consulting Svcs LLC 610 746-7700
　630 Municipal Dr Ste 420 Nazareth (18064) *(G-11988)*

Software Engineering Assoc 570 803-0535
　1 Export Ln Archbald (18403) *(G-695)*

Soh, Hanover *Also called S-L Snacks Real Estate Inc (G-6948)*

Solar Atmospheres Inc (PA) 215 721-1502
　1969 Clearview Rd Souderton (18964) *(G-17765)*

Solar Atmospheres Mfg Inc (PA) 267 384-5040
　1983 Clearview Rd Souderton (18964) *(G-17766)*

Solar Atmospheres Wstn PA Inc 742 982-0660
　30 Industrial Rd Hermitage (16148) *(G-7595)*

Solar Cool Coatings 267 664-3667
　117 Elm Ave Apt 5 Glenside (19038) *(G-6537)*

Solar Fuel Co Inc 814 443-2646
　1134 Stoystown Rd Friedens (15541) *(G-6227)*

Solar Innovations Inc 570 915-1500
　31 Roberts Rd Pine Grove (17963) *(G-14605)*

Solar Laundry & Dry Cleaning 610 323-2121
　1503 W High St Pottstown (19464) *(G-16048)*

Solar Light Company Inc 215 517-8700
　100 E Glenside Ave Glenside (19038) *(G-6538)*

Solar Manufacturing, Souderton *Also called Solar Atmospheres Mfg Inc (G-17766)*

Solar Power Solutions LLC 724 379-2002
　13 Airport Rd Belle Vernon (15012) *(G-1087)*

Solar Technology Inc 610 391-8600
7620 Cetronia Rd Allentown (18106) *(G-396)*

Solar Technology Solutions 610 916-0864
2670 Leisczs Bridge Rd # 100 Leesport (19533) *(G-9674)*

Solar Transformers Inc 267 384-5231
174 Keystone Dr Telford (18969) *(G-18316)*

Solar Turbines Incorporated 724 759-7800
2200 Georgetown Dr # 601 Sewickley (15143) *(G-17411)*

Solarian US 610 550-6350
2617 Saint Davids Ln Ardmore (19003) *(G-717)*

Solaris Select 267 987-2082
18 Sandy Dr Morrisville (19067) *(G-11582)*

Solcon USA LLC 724 728-2100
1050 Rico Rd Monroeville (15146) *(G-11355)*

Sole Artisan Ales Llc 570 977-0053
45 N 2nd St Apt 203 Easton (18042) *(G-4753)*

Solenoid Solutions Inc 814 838-3190
2251 Manchester Rd Erie (16506) *(G-5484)*

Soleo Health, Sharon Hill *Also called Biomed Healthcare Inc (G-17453)*

Soleo Health Holdings Inc (PA) 888 244-2340
950 Calcon Hook Rd Ste 19 Sharon Hill (19079) *(G-17460)*

Soleo Health Inc (HQ) 888 244-2340
950 Calcon Hook Rd Ste 19 Sharon Hill (19079) *(G-17461)*

Solid State Ceramics Inc 570 322-2700
341 Science Park Rd # 105 State College (16803) *(G-18028)*

Solid State Eqp Holdings LLC 215 328-0700
185 Gibraltar Rd Horsham (19044) *(G-7850)*

Solid Steel Buildings Inc 800 377-6543
1 Forestwood Dr Ste 101 Pittsburgh (15237) *(G-15553)*

Solid Wood Cabinet Company LLC (PA) 267 288-1200
6300 Bristol Pike Levittown (19057) *(G-9864)*

Solidays Millwork 717 274-2841
36 Weidman St Lebanon (17046) *(G-9633)*

Sollenberger Silos LLC 717 264-9588
2216 Wayne Rd Chambersburg (17202) *(G-2976)*

Solo Soundz LLC 610 931-8448
1714 N 61st St Philadelphia (19151) *(G-14323)*

Soltech Solutions LLC 484 821-1001
520 Evans St 4 Bethlehem (18015) *(G-1622)*

Soltrace Inc 215 765-5700
910 Fairmount Ave 950 Philadelphia (19123) *(G-14324)*

Solts Sawmill Inc 610 682-6179
33 S Park Ave Mertztown (19539) *(G-11004)*

Solutia Inc 724 258-6200
829 Route 481 Monongahela (15063) *(G-11316)*

Solution People Inc 215 750-2694
675 Eagle Rd Newtown (18940) *(G-12551)*

Solution Systems Inc 610 668-4620
201 Sabine Ave Ste 500 Narberth (19072) *(G-11912)*

Solvay 412 423-2030
2180 William Pitt Way Pittsburgh (15238) *(G-15554)*

Solvay USA Inc 609 860-4000
2180 William Pitt Way Pittsburgh (15238) *(G-15555)*

Solvay USA Inc 570 748-4450
400 W Brown St Castanea (17726) *(G-2811)*

Solvay USA Inc 215 781-6001
350 George Patterson Dr Bristol (19007) *(G-2199)*

Somat Company 717 397-5100
165 Independence Ct Lancaster (17601) *(G-9202)*

Somerset Consolidated Inds Inc (PA) 814 445-7927
809 S Edgewood Ave Somerset (15501) *(G-17706)*

Somerset Door & Column Company 814 444-9427
174 Sagamore St Somerset (15501) *(G-17707)*

Somerset Door and Column Co 814 445-9608
1123 S Edgewood Ave Somerset (15501) *(G-17708)*

Somerset Enterprises Inc 724 734-9497
212 Idaho St Farrell (16121) *(G-5874)*

Somerset Foundry & Mch Co Div, Somerset *Also called Somerset Consolidated Inds Inc (G-17706)*

Somerset Plastics, Somerset *Also called Diamond Tech Group Inc (G-17685)*

Somerset Sand & Stone Co Div, Somerset *Also called E J Bognar Inc (G-17686)*

Somerset Welding & Steel Inc 814 444-7000
422 Riggs Rd Somerset (15501) *(G-17709)*

Somerset Welding & Steel Inc (HQ) 814 443-2671
10558 Somerset Pike Somerset (15501) *(G-17710)*

Somerset Welding & Steel Inc 814 444-7000
422 Riggs Rd Somerset (15501) *(G-17711)*

Something Wicked Brewing LLC 717 316-5488
34 Broadway Hanover (17331) *(G-6956)*

Somni Scientific LLC 412 851-4390
1900 Sleepy Hollow Rd South Park (15129) *(G-17785)*

Sonco Fence, Bristol *Also called Sonco Worldwide Inc (G-2200)*

Sonco Worldwide Inc 215 337-9651
805 N Wilson Ave Ste 205 Bristol (19007) *(G-2200)*

Songbird Sanctuary LLC 412 780-1270
1234 Oak Hill Dr Pittsburgh (15239) *(G-15556)*

Songer Steel Services, Washington *Also called Sssi Inc (G-19228)*

Sonic Energy Services USA Inc 724 782-0560
405 Longleaf Dr Venetia (15367) *(G-18744)*

Sonic Systems Inc 267 803-1964
204 Railroad Dr Warminster (18974) *(G-18967)*

Sonic Tronics Inc 215 635-6520
7865 Mill Rd Elkins Park (19027) *(G-4911)*

Sonneborn LLC 724 756-9337
100 Sonneborn Ln Petrolia (16050) *(G-13308)*

Sonobond Ultrasonics Inc 610 696-4710
1191 Mcdermott Dr West Chester (19380) *(G-19642)*

Sonoco Consumer Products, Hanover *Also called Sonoco Products Company (G-6957)*

Sonoco Display & Packaging LLC 717 757-2683
200 Boxwood Ln York (17402) *(G-20672)*

Sonoco Products Company 717 637-2103
310 Pine St Hanover (17331) *(G-6957)*

Sonoco Products Company 610 693-5804
30 W Meadow Ave Robesonia (19551) *(G-16779)*

Sonoco Products Company 610 323-9221
10 Quinter St Pottstown (19464) *(G-16049)*

Sonoco Prtective Solutions Inc 215 643-3555
161 Corporate Dr Montgomeryville (18936) *(G-11419)*

Sonoco Prtective Solutions Inc 800 377-2692
7218 Church Ave Pittsburgh (15202) *(G-15557)*

Sonoco Prtective Solutions Inc 412 415-1462
7218 Church Ave Pittsburgh (15202) *(G-15558)*

Sonoco Prtective Solutions Inc 412 415-3784
7218 Church Ave Pittsburgh (15202) *(G-15559)*

Sonus-USA, Pittsburgh *Also called West Penn Ear Nose and Throat (G-15709)*

Sony Music Holdings Inc 724 794-8500
1137 Branchton Rd Boyers (16016) *(G-1890)*

Sooner Pipe LLC 570 368-4590
150 S Loyalsock Ave Montoursville (17754) *(G-11450)*

Sophisticakes Inc 610 626-9991
4624 Drexelbrook Dr Drexel Hill (19026) *(G-4371)*

Sorbent, Warrendale *Also called Renal Solutions Inc (G-19095)*

Soroka Sales Inc 412 381-7700
138 S 25th St Pittsburgh (15203) *(G-15560)*

Sorrelli Inc 610 894-9857
125 W Main St Kutztown (19530) *(G-8861)*

Sorrelli Jewelry Co, Kutztown *Also called Sorrelli Inc (G-8861)*

Sorrenti Orchards Inc 570 992-2255
130 Lower Cherry Vly Rd Saylorsburg (18353) *(G-17108)*

SOS Products Company Inc 215 679-6262
401 W 4th St East Greenville (18041) *(G-4576)*

Sosko Manufacturing Inc 724 879-4117
410 Unity St Ste 500 Latrobe (15650) *(G-9521)*

Sosniak Opticians (PA) 412 281-9199
208 5th Ave Pittsburgh (15222) *(G-15561)*

Souders Industries Inc 717 271-4975
6806 Anthony Hwy Waynesboro (17268) *(G-19424)*

Souders Industries Inc (PA) 717 749-3900
19 Ash St Mont Alto (17237) *(G-11365)*

Soul Customs Metal Works 610 881-4300
320 W Main St Pen Argyl (18072) *(G-13218)*

Soumaya & Sons Bakery LLC 610 432-0405
264 Fullerton Ave Whitehall (18052) *(G-19889)*

Sound Technology Inc (HQ) 814 234-4377
401 Science Park Rd State College (16803) *(G-18029)*

Soundhorse Technologies LLC 610 347-0453
82 N Lanefield Rd Unionville (19375) *(G-18649)*

Sour Junkie LLC 412 612-6860
921 Clarissa St Pittsburgh (15219) *(G-15562)*

Source Halthcare Analytics LLC 602 381-9500
1001 E Hector St Ste 400 Conshohocken (19428) *(G-3605)*

Souriau Usa Inc 717 718-8810
150 Farm Ln Ste 100 York (17402) *(G-20673)*

South Bend Lime Stone Co, Delmont *Also called Pennico Oil Co Inc (G-4053)*

South Bend Limestone Company (PA) 724 468-8232
6608 State Route 22 # 205 Delmont (15626) *(G-4059)*

South Erie Production Co Inc 814 864-0311
1221 Robison Rd W Erie (16509) *(G-5485)*

South Fork Hardware Company 814 248-3375
115 Haynes St Johnstown (15901) *(G-8436)*

South Fork News Agency 814 495-9394
403 Main St South Fork (15956) *(G-17777)*

South Franklin Township Garage, Washington *Also called City of Washington (G-19156)*

South Greensburg Printing Co 724 834-0295
409 Coulter Ave Ste A Greensburg (15601) *(G-6715)*

South Hills Brewing Supply 412 937-0773
2526 Mosside Blvd Monroeville (15146) *(G-11356)*

South Hills Printing, Pittsburgh *Also called Abboud Samar (G-14634)*

South Morgan Technologies LLC 814 774-2000
227 Hathaway St E Girard (16417) *(G-6402)*

South Penn Resources LLC (PA) 724 880-5882
334 Livinggood Hollow Rd Mc Clellandtown (15458) *(G-10556)*

South Penn Restoration Shop 717 264-2602
122 Ramsey Ave Chambersburg (17201) *(G-2977)*

South Pittsburgh Reporter, The, Pittsburgh *Also called Neighborhood Publications Inc (G-15324)*

South Pole Magnetics 412 537-5625
225 Waldorf St Pittsburgh (15214) *(G-15563)*

South Schuylkill Prtg & Pubg, Schuylkill Haven *Also called Call Newspapers Inc* **(G-17150)**
South Tamaqua Coal Pockets 570 386-5445
804 W Penn Pike Tamaqua (18252) **(G-18226)**
Southco Inc (HQ) 610 459-4000
210 N Brinton Lake Rd Concordville (19331) **(G-3459)**
Southco Inc 267 957-9260
1025 Louis Dr Warminster (18974) **(G-18968)**
Southco Inc 215 957-9260
1025 Louis Dr Warminster (18974) **(G-18969)**
Southco Counterbalance, Warminster *Also called Southco Inc* **(G-18969)**
Southco Counterbalance Div FL, Warminster *Also called Southco Inc* **(G-18968)**
Southco Cunterbalance Div - PA 267 957-9260
1025 Louis Dr Warminster (18974) **(G-18970)**
Southeastern PA Trnsp Auth 215 580-7800
32 Sproul Rd Malvern (19355) **(G-10323)**
Southern Alleghenies Advg Inc 814 472-8593
517 W Lloyd St Ebensburg (15931) **(G-4797)**
Southern Container Corp 717 393-0436
500 Richardson Dr Lancaster (17603) **(G-9203)**
Southern Glazer s Wine and Sp (HQ) 610 265-6800
460 American Ave King of Prussia (19406) **(G-8678)**
Southern Graphic Systems LLC 215 843-2243
2781 Roberts Ave Philadelphia (19129) **(G-14325)**
Southern Ohio Coal Company 740 338-3100
1000 Consol Energy Dr Canonsburg (15317) **(G-2638)**
Southern Stretch Forming & 724 256-8474
300 Mitchell Hill Rd Butler (16002) **(G-2442)**
Southside Brew-Thru LLC 814 254-4828
114 Bridge St Johnstown (15902) **(G-8437)**
Southside Holdings Inc 412 431-8300
1501 Reedsdale St # 2008 Pittsburgh (15233) **(G-15564)**
Southwell Oil Co 814 723-5178
381 Hillcrest Dr Warren (16365) **(G-19047)**
Southwest Vinyl Windows Inc 610 626-8826
6250 Baltimore Ave Ste 7 Lansdowne (19050) **(G-9444)**
Southwind Studios Ltd 610 664-4110
901 Beechwood Rd Lower Merion (19083) **(G-10109)**
Southwire Company LLC 717 266-2004
1500 Bartlett Dr York (17406) **(G-20674)**
Souto Mould 570 596-3128
1283 Laurel Hill Rd Milan (18831) **(G-11150)**
Sovana Bistro Inc 610 444-5600
696 Unionville Rd Ste 8 Kennett Square (19348) **(G-8543)**
Sovereign Media Company Inc 570 322-7848
2406 Reach Rd Williamsport (17701) **(G-20073)**
Sovereign Services Inc 412 331-6704
4201 Grand Ave Pittsburgh (15225) **(G-15565)**
Sovereign Steel Mfg LLC 610 797-2800
2027 S 12th St Bldg 507 Allentown (18103) **(G-397)**
Sp Environmental Inc 724 935-1300
1718 Mount Nebo Rd Sewickley (15143) **(G-17412)**
Sp Scientific, Warminster *Also called S P Industries Inc* **(G-18959)**
Space 1026 ....215 574-7630
1026 Arch St Philadelphia (19107) **(G-14326)**
Space Age Plastics Inc 570 630-6060
581 Cortez Rd Jefferson Township (18436) **(G-8279)**
Space U Rent, Rankin *Also called Epic Metals Corporation* **(G-16305)**
Spadone Machine Inc 215 396-8005
601 Davisville Rd Willow Grove (19090) **(G-20143)**
Spadre Investments Inc (PA) 724 452-8440
433 Hartmann Rd Evans City (16033) **(G-5564)**
Spahr-Evans Printers 215 886-4057
2816 Limekiln Pike Glenside (19038) **(G-6539)**
Spalding Automotive Inc (PA) 215 638-3334
4529 Adams Cir Bensalem (19020) **(G-1255)**
Spang & Company (PA) 412 963-9363
110 Delta Dr Pittsburgh (15238) **(G-15566)**
Spang & Company 724 376-7515
5241 Lake St Sandy Lake (16145) **(G-17062)**
Spang & Company 412 963-9363
110 Delta Dr Pittsburgh (15238) **(G-15567)**
Spang Power Electronic, Sandy Lake *Also called Spang & Company* **(G-17062)**
Spang Power Electronics, Pittsburgh *Also called Spang & Company* **(G-15566)**
Spare Time Bowling 570 668-3210
17 Tide Rd Tamaqua (18252) **(G-18227)**
Spark Technologies Inc 724 295-3860
150 Railroad St Schenley (15682) **(G-17136)**
Spark Therapeutics Inc (PA) 888 772-7560
3737 Market St Ste 1300 Philadelphia (19104) **(G-14327)**
Sparks Belting Company Inc 717 767-1490
66 Leigh Dr York (17406) **(G-20675)**
Sparks Custom Retail LLC (HQ) 215 602-8100
2828 Charter Rd Philadelphia (19154) **(G-14328)**
Sparks Exhbits Envrnments Corp (HQ) 215 676-1100
2828 Charter Rd Philadelphia (19154) **(G-14329)**
Sparks Exhibits Holding Corp (HQ) 215 676-1100
2828 Charter Rd Philadelphia (19154) **(G-14330)**
Spartan Motors Usa Inc 605 582-4000
64 Cocalico Creek Rd Ephrata (17522) **(G-5144)**

Sparton Aydin LLC (HQ) 610 404-7400
1 Riga Ln Birdsboro (19508) **(G-1706)**
SPD Electrical Systems Inc 215 698-6426
13500 Roosevelt Blvd Philadelphia (19116) **(G-14331)**
Speakman Company 302 764-7100
51 Lacrue Ave Glen Mills (19342) **(G-6444)**
Spears Manufacturing Co 570 384-4832
613 Oak Ridge Rd Hazle Township (18202) **(G-7482)**
Spears Manufacturing Co 717 938-8844
590 Industrial Dr Ste 100 Lewisberry (17339) **(G-9893)**
Spec Adv Spec Prod Grp, Fairview *Also called Spectrum Microwave Inc* **(G-5847)**
Spec Fab, Honey Brook *Also called Turf Teq LLC* **(G-7767)**
Spec Industries Inc. 610 497-4220
101 Engle St 103 Chester (19013) **(G-3063)**
Spec Sciences Inc 607 972-3159
758 Thornton St Sharon (16146) **(G-17443)**
Spec-TEC, Saint Clair *Also called Spector Manufacturing Inc* **(G-16941)**
Specac Inc (HQ) 215 793-4044
414 Commerce Dr Ste 175 Fort Washington (19034) **(G-6092)**
Specgas Inc 215 355-2405
86 Vincent Cir Warminster (18974) **(G-18971)**
Special Electric Motor Company 724 378-4200
148 Davidson Ln Aliquippa (15001) **(G-97)**
Special Machine Operations, Houston *Also called Randall Lesso* **(G-7878)**
Special T Design & Mfg Co, Reading *Also called Specialty Design & Mfg Co Inc* **(G-16520)**
Special T Electronic LLC 412 635-4997
9329 Doral Dr Pittsburgh (15237) **(G-15568)**
Special-Lite Products LLC 724 537-4711
1634 Latrobe Derry Rd Loyalhanna (15661) **(G-10113)**
Speciality Firms, Wayne *Also called Jsp International LLC* **(G-19343)**
Speciality Precast Company 724 865-9255
830 Unionville Rd Prospect (16052) **(G-16113)**
Specialized Desanders USA Inc 412 535-3396
24 Summit Park Dr Pittsburgh (15275) **(G-15569)**
Specialized Welding Inc 724 733-7801
205 Mamont Dr Export (15632) **(G-5627)**
Specialty Adhesives Inc 484 524-5324
535 Misty Patch Rd Coatesville (19320) **(G-3326)**
Specialty Alloy Proc Co Inc 724 339-0464
14th St New Kensington (15068) **(G-12379)**
Specialty Automation Inc 215 453-0817
614 Hillcrest Dr Perkasie (18944) **(G-13295)**
Specialty Bakers LLC 717 626-8002
450 S State Rd Marysville (17053) **(G-10533)**
Specialty Bar Products Company (HQ) 724 459-0544
200 Martha St Blairsville (15717) **(G-1742)**
Specialty Building Systems 610 954-0595
484 S Nulton Ave Easton (18045) **(G-4754)**
Specialty Chemical Systems Inc 610 323-2716
243 Shoemaker Rd Pottstown (19464) **(G-16050)**
Specialty Conduit & Mfg LLC 724 439-9371
760 Bradockview Dr Mount Braddock (15465) **(G-11621)**
Specialty Design & Mfg Co Inc 610 779-1357
2000 Friedensburg Rd Reading (19606) **(G-16520)**
Specialty Emulsions Inc 717 849-5020
1194 Zinns Quarry Rd York (17404) **(G-20676)**
Specialty Extrusion Inc 610 792-3800
135 1st Ave Royersford (19468) **(G-16865)**
Specialty Fabrication and Powd 814 432-6406
455 Allegheny Blvd Franklin (16323) **(G-6161)**
Specialty Fitness Systems LLC 814 432-6406
455 Allegheny Blvd Franklin (16323) **(G-6162)**
Specialty Glass Products, Willow Grove *Also called Kmz Enterprises LLC* **(G-20126)**
Specialty Granules Inc 717 794-2184
1455 Old Waynesboro Rd Blue Ridge Summit (17214) **(G-1861)**
Specialty Group Printing Inc (PA) 814 425-3061
126 E Adams St Cochranton (16314) **(G-3351)**
Specialty Holdings Corp (PA) 610 779-1357
2000 Friedensburg Rd Reading (19606) **(G-16521)**
Specialty Ice 724 283-7000
229 Cecelia St Rear Butler (16001) **(G-2443)**
Specialty Industries Inc (HQ) 717 246-1661
175 E Walnut St Red Lion (17356) **(G-16613)**
Specialty Machine & Hydraulic 814 589-7381
1736 Shreve Rd Pleasantville (16341) **(G-15804)**
Specialty Measurements Inc 908 534-1500
2420 Emrick Blvd Bethlehem (18020) **(G-1623)**
Specialty Millworks Inc (PA) 610 682-6334
130 W High St Topton (19562) **(G-18416)**
Specialty Minerals Inc 860 824-5435
1 Highland Ave Bethlehem (18017) **(G-1624)**
Specialty Minerals Inc 610 250-3000
640 N 13th St Easton (18042) **(G-4755)**
Specialty Minerals Inc 610 861-3400
9 Highland Ave Bethlehem (18017) **(G-1625)**
Specialty Minerals Inc 212 878-1800
5 Highland Ave Bethlehem (18017) **(G-1626)**
Specialty Paints Coatings Inc 717 249-5523
608 Alexander Spring Rd Carlisle (17015) **(G-2739)**

**A
L
P
H
A
B
E
T
I
C**

Specialty Phrm Pdts LLC....215 321-5836
1 Harlow Ct Yardley (19067) ***(G-20340)***
Specialty Products & Insul Co....717 569-3900
1097 Commercial Ave East Petersburg (17520) ***(G-4590)***
Specialty Products Company....570 729-7192
362 Tryon St Honesdale (18431) ***(G-7724)***
Specialty Products Inc....814 455-6978
938 E 12th St Erie (16503) ***(G-5486)***
Specialty Resin Systems, Chester *Also called Evonik Corporation* ***(G-3050)***
Specialty Retail Fabricators (PA)....215 477-5977
901 N Penn St Apt P402 Philadelphia (19123) ***(G-14332)***
Specialty Roller and Mch Inc....570 759-1278
233 Columbia Ave Berwick (18603) ***(G-1344)***
Specialty Seal Group Inc....724 539-1626
1001 Lloyd Ave Latrobe (15650) ***(G-9522)***
Specialty Snacks Inc....215 721-0414
336 W Broad St Telford (18969) ***(G-18317)***
Specialty Steel Supply Co Inc....215 949-8800
225 Lincoln Hwy Fairless Hills (19030) ***(G-5798)***
Specialty Support Systems Inc....215 945-1033
2100 Hartel Ave Levittown (19057) ***(G-9865)***
Specialty Surfaces Intl Inc....877 686-8873
660 American Ave Ste 101 King of Prussia (19406) ***(G-8679)***
Specialty Tank & Wldg Co Inc....215 949-2939
7900 N Rdcliffe St Ste 11 Bristol (19007) ***(G-2201)***
Specialty Trading Co, Bridgeport *Also called Veterinary Tag Supply Co Inc* ***(G-2048)***
Specialty Tstg & Dev Co Inc....717 428-0186
21 Church St Seven Valleys (17360) ***(G-17380)***
Specialty Vermiculite Corp (HQ)....610 660-8840
1 Bala Ave Ste 310 Bala Cynwyd (19004) ***(G-893)***
Specialty Vhcl Solutions LLC....609 882-1900
1540 Campus Dr Ste B Warminster (18974) ***(G-18972)***
Specilized Svcs Promotions Inc....814 864-4984
2204 W 38th St Erie (16506) ***(G-5487)***
Specilty Mtallurgical Pdts Inc....717 246-0385
25 Pleasant Ave Red Lion (17356) ***(G-16614)***
Spectacular Fire Works USA....570 465-2100
1541 Oliver Rd New Milford (18834) ***(G-12400)***
Spector Manufacturing Inc....570 429-2510
158 Industrial Park Rd Saint Clair (17970) ***(G-16941)***
Spectra Inc....814 238-6332
2625 Carolean Indus Dr State College (16801) ***(G-18030)***
Spectra Hardware Inc....724 863-7527
1150 First St Westmoreland City (15692) ***(G-19785)***
Spectra-Kote Corporation....717 334-3177
301 E Water St Gettysburg (17325) ***(G-6314)***
Spectragenetics Inc....412 488-9350
2403 Sidney St Ste 255 Pittsburgh (15203) ***(G-15570)***
Spectrasonics Imaging, Wayne *Also called Spectrasonics Inc* ***(G-19372)***
Spectrasonics Inc....610 964-9637
440 Woodcrest Rd Wayne (19087) ***(G-19372)***
Spectrim Building Products LLC....267 223-1030
3433 Marshall Ln Bensalem (19020) ***(G-1256)***
Spectrocell Inc....215 572-7605
143 Montgomery Ave Oreland (19075) ***(G-13030)***
Spectrodyne Inc....215 804-1044
2036 Emerson Dr 577 Quakertown (18951) ***(G-16246)***
Spectrum Automated Inc....610 433-7755
701 E Congress St Allentown (18109) ***(G-398)***
Spectrum Control Inc (HQ)....814 474-2207
8061 Avonia Rd Fairview (16415) ***(G-5842)***
Spectrum Control Inc....814 272-2700
1900 W College Ave State College (16801) ***(G-18031)***
Spectrum Control Inc....814 474-1571
8061 Avonia Rd Fairview (16415) ***(G-5843)***
Spectrum Control Inc....814 835-4000
8061 Avonia Rd Fairview (16415) ***(G-5844)***
Spectrum Control Inc....814 272-2700
1900 W College Ave State College (16801) ***(G-18032)***
Spectrum Control Inc....814 474-4315
8031 Avonia Rd Fairview (16415) ***(G-5845)***
Spectrum Control Tech Inc....814 474-2207
8031 Avonia Rd Fairview (16415) ***(G-5846)***
Spectrum Devices Corporation....215 997-7870
3009a Old State Rd Telford (18969) ***(G-18318)***
Spectrum Healthcare Inc....888 210-5576
20 Eagleville Rd Eagleville (19403) ***(G-4516)***
Spectrum Microwave, Philadelphia *Also called API Technologies Corp* ***(G-13399)***
Spectrum Microwave Inc (HQ)....814 474-4300
8061 Avonia Rd Fairview (16415) ***(G-5847)***
Spectrum Microwave Inc....215 464-0586
2707 Black Lake Pl Philadelphia (19154) ***(G-14333)***
Spectrum Microwave Inc....814 272-2700
1900 W College Ave State College (16801) ***(G-18033)***
Spectrum Molding Division, Erie *Also called Plastek Industries Inc* ***(G-5424)***
Spectrum Power MGT Systems, State College *Also called Spectrum Control Inc* ***(G-18032)***
Spectrum Printing, East Petersburg *Also called Stauffer Acquisition Corp* ***(G-4591)***
Spectrum Software Innovations....610 779-6974
4 Saint Andrews Ct Reading (19606) ***(G-16522)***
Speed Partz LLC....513 874-2034
198 Black Gap Rd Trlr 145 Fayetteville (17222) ***(G-5878)***
Speed Raceway....215 672-6128
200 Blair Mill Rd Horsham (19044) ***(G-7851)***
Speedbear Fasteners....724 695-3696
103 Enlow Rd Imperial (15126) ***(G-8076)***
SpeeDee Shirts.com, Clairton *Also called Prince Printing* ***(G-3156)***
Speedwell Garage....607 434-2376
689 Salem Rd Klingerstown (17941) ***(G-8808)***
Spektra Manufacturing Inc....814 454-6879
2002 Evanston Ave Erie (16506) ***(G-5488)***
Spencer Graphics Inc....610 793-2348
711 Haines Mill Rd West Chester (19382) ***(G-19643)***
Spencer Industries Inc....570 969-9931
1014-1016 Sanderson Ave Scranton (18509) ***(G-17292)***
Spencer Industries Inc....215 634-2700
80 Red Lion Rd Philadelphia (19115) ***(G-14334)***
Spencer Printing Inc....570 253-2001
216 Willow Ave Honesdale (18431) ***(G-7725)***
Spencer Printing and Graphics, Honesdale *Also called Spencer Printing Inc* ***(G-7725)***
Speranza Specialty Machining....724 733-8045
2226 Boyd Rd Export (15632) ***(G-5628)***
Sperian Fall Protection Inc....814 432-2118
1345 15th St Franklin (16323) ***(G-6163)***
Sperry Graphic Inc....610 534-8585
4 Horne Dr Folcroft (19032) ***(G-6016)***
Spicer Wldg & Fabrication Inc....814 355-7046
123 Spicer Ln Bellefonte (16823) ***(G-1119)***
Spicer Wldg & Fabrication Inc....814 355-7046
1593 S Eagle Valley Rd Julian (16844) ***(G-8456)***
Spices Inc....570 509-2340
463 Industrial Park Rd Elysburg (17824) ***(G-4982)***
Spider Venom Racing Pdts LLC....484 547-1400
1805 Willow Ln East Texas (18046) ***(G-4639)***
Spiders Den Inc....724 445-7450
120 Paradise Ln Chicora (16025) ***(G-3129)***
Spigelmyer Wood Products Inc....717 248-6555
2316 Hawstone Rd Lewistown (17044) ***(G-9948)***
Spilltech Environmental Inc....814 247-8566
233 Haida Ave Hastings (16646) ***(G-7263)***
Spin-A-Latte Tm....215 285-1567
642 Cowpath Rd 292 Lansdale (19446) ***(G-9412)***
Spin-A-Latte Tm Laundry, Lansdale *Also called Spin-A-Latte Tm* ***(G-9412)***
Spin-Works, North East *Also called Spinworks International Corp* ***(G-12762)***
Spinal Acoustics LLC....724 846-3600
1104 Darlington Rd Beaver Falls (15010) ***(G-1013)***
Spinlon Industries, Quakertown *Also called Roselon Industries Inc* ***(G-16242)***
Spinworks LLC....814 725-1188
10093 W Main Rd North East (16428) ***(G-12761)***
Spinworks International Corp....814 725-1188
10093 W Main Rd North East (16428) ***(G-12762)***
Spiral Stairs of America LLC....800 422-3700
4201 Bell St Ste 2 Erie (16511) ***(G-5489)***
Spiral Tool Corporation....570 409-1331
761 Route 6 Shohola (18458) ***(G-17580)***
Spirax Sarco Inc....610 807-3500
4647 Saucon Creek Rd Center Valley (18034) ***(G-2831)***
Spirit Media Group Inc....610 447-8484
1109 Remington St Chester (19013) ***(G-3064)***
Spirit Publishing Company....814 938-8740
510 Pine St Punxsutawney (15767) ***(G-16163)***
Spitz Inc....610 459-5200
700 Brandywine Dr Chadds Ford (19317) ***(G-2860)***
Spitzenburg Cider House LLC....484 357-2058
67 Kempton Rd Kempton (19529) ***(G-8494)***
SPM Flow Control Inc....570 546-1005
76 Odell Rd Muncy (17756) ***(G-11833)***
Spm Global Services Inc (PA)....610 340-2828
2501 Seaport Dr Ste Sh103 Chester (19013) ***(G-3065)***
Spohn Performance Inc....717 866-6033
494 E Lincoln Ave Myerstown (17067) ***(G-11898)***
Spomin Metals Inc....724 924-9718
2975 New Butler Rd New Castle (16101) ***(G-12155)***
Sponge-Jet Inc....570 278-4563
1230 Bare Valley Rd Montrose (18801) ***(G-11478)***
Spoonful Mag, Wynnewood *Also called Feast Mag LLC* ***(G-20267)***
Spoonwood Inc (PA)....610 756-6464
3716 Route 737 Kempton (19529) ***(G-8495)***
Sport and Equipment, Dillsburg *Also called Fit Engineering* ***(G-4129)***
Sport Manufacturing Group Inc....718 575-1801
1840 County Line Rd # 111 Huntingdon Valley (19006) ***(G-8039)***
Sportin My Stuff....724 457-7005
148 Mcgovern Blvd Crescent (15046) ***(G-3889)***
Sporting Goods Intelligence, Glen Mills *Also called Sports Management News Inc* ***(G-6445)***
Sporting Valley Feeds LLC....717 665-6122
934 Junction Rd Manheim (17545) ***(G-10404)***
Sports Factory Promotions Inc....724 847-2684
917 3rd Ave New Brighton (15066) ***(G-12042)***

Sports Images International 412 851-1610
1725 Washington Rd # 200 Pittsburgh (15241) *(G-15571)*

Sports Management News Inc 610 459-4040
442 Featherbed Ln Glen Mills (19342) *(G-6445)*

Sportsmansliquidationcom LLC 717 263-6000
2201 N Front St Harrisburg (17110) *(G-7217)*

Spray Products Corporation (PA) 610 277-1010
1323 Conshohocken Rd Plymouth Meeting (19462) *(G-15872)*

Spray-Tek Inc 610 814-2922
3010 Avenue B Bethlehem (18017) *(G-1627)*

Spreng Machine Co Inc 724 352-9467
190 Pittsburgh St Saxonburg (16056) *(G-17095)*

Spring City Electrical Mfg Co (PA) 610 948-4000
1 S Main St Spring City (19475) *(G-17867)*

Spring City Electrical Mfg Co 610 948-4000
Hall & Main St Spring City (19475) *(G-17868)*

Spring City Foundry Co, Spring City *Also called Spring City Electrical Mfg Co* *(G-17867)*

Spring Cove Container, Roaring Spring *Also called Roaring Spring Blank Book Co* *(G-16769)*

Spring Ford Castings Inc 610 489-2600
25 W 5th Ave Trappe (19426) *(G-18473)*

Spring Gate Vineyard 717 599-5574
5790 Devonshire Rd Harrisburg (17112) *(G-7218)*

Spring Glen Fresh Foods Inc (HQ) 717 733-2201
314 Spring Glen Dr Ephrata (17522) *(G-5145)*

Spring Health Products Inc 610 630-8024
705 General Washington Av Norristown (19403) *(G-12714)*

Spring Hill Laser Services 570 689-0970
6 Industrial Park Rd A Lake Ariel (18436) *(G-8892)*

Spring Hill Woodworks 724 762-0111
625 Arcadia Rd Cherry Tree (15724) *(G-3036)*

Spring House Specialty, Zieglerville *Also called Quaker State Tube Mfg Corp* *(G-20834)*

Spring Lock Scaffolding Eqp Co 215 426-5727
901 Artis Rd Plymouth Meeting (19462) *(G-15873)*

Spring Mill Woodworking 610 286-7051
217 S Red School Rd Morgantown (19543) *(G-11536)*

Spring Mill Woodworks 267 408-9469
837 Penn Ave Glenside (19038) *(G-6540)*

Spring Mills Manufacturing Inc 814 422-8892
1 Streamside Pl E Spring Mills (16875) *(G-17893)*

Spring Tool & Die Co Inc 814 224-5173
408 E Main St Roaring Spring (16673) *(G-16771)*

Spring Valley Millwork Inc 610 927-0144
108 S Hull St Reading (19608) *(G-16523)*

Spring Valley Mulch Brian 717 292-7945
2770 Mill Creek Rd Dover (17315) *(G-4205)*

Spring Vly Altrntive Fuels LLC 814 587-3002
21810 Palmer Rd Conneautville (16406) *(G-3487)*

Springdale Specialty Plas Inc 724 274-4144
997 Sherosky Way Springdale (15144) *(G-17901)*

Springer Adis Us LLC 215 574-2201
400 Market St Ste 700 Philadelphia (19106) *(G-14335)*

Springer Pumps LLC 484 949-2900
861 Tech Dr Telford (18969) *(G-18319)*

Springfield Meat Co, Richlandtown *Also called Richard Baringer* *(G-16690)*

Springfield Pasta 610 543-5687
186 Saxer Ave Springfield (19064) *(G-17923)*

Springhill Well Service Inc 724 447-2449
669 Deep Valley Rd New Freeport (15352) *(G-12218)*

Springs Window Fashions LLC 570 547-6671
8467 Route 405 Hwy S Montgomery (17752) *(G-11378)*

Sprint Print Inc 570 586-5947
322 Northern Blvd Chinchilla (18410) *(G-3132)*

Sprinturf, King of Prussia *Also called Specialty Surfaces Intl Inc* *(G-8679)*

Sproule Mfg., Malvern *Also called SMC Industries Inc* *(G-10321)*

Sprung Instant Structures Inc 610 391-9553
5000 W Tilghman St # 155 Allentown (18104) *(G-399)*

SPS Technologies LLC (HQ) 215 572-3000
301 Highland Ave Jenkintown (19046) *(G-8302)*

SPS Technologies LLC 215 572-3000
301 Highland Ave Jenkintown (19046) *(G-8303)*

Spts Technologies, Allentown *Also called Primaxx Inc* *(G-359)*

Spw Warehouse, Sharon *Also called Wheatland Tube LLC* *(G-17446)*

SPX Cooling Technologies Inc 717 845-4830
1670 Toronita St York (17402) *(G-20677)*

SPX Corporation 814 476-5800
5620 West Rd Mc Kean (16426) *(G-10592)*

SPX Corporation 724 746-4240
100 Commerce Dr 40 Washington (15301) *(G-19227)*

SPX Flow Us LLC 814 476-5842
5620 West Rd Mc Kean (16426) *(G-10593)*

SPX Flow Us LLC 814 476-5800
5620 West Rd Mc Kean (16426) *(G-10594)*

SPX Heat Transfer LLC 610 250-1146
95 Highland Ave Ste 210 Bethlehem (18017) *(G-1628)*

SPX Valves & Controls, Mc Kean *Also called SPX Flow Us LLC* *(G-10594)*

Spyware 215 444-0405
227 York Rd Warminster (18974) *(G-18973)*

Sqp, Bethlehem *Also called Superior Quartz Products Inc* *(G-1634)*

Square Tool and Die Corp Inc 570 489-8657
934 Sanderson St Throop (18512) *(G-18362)*

Square Wheel Inc 610 921-8561
80 Irish Mountain Rd Temple (19560) *(G-18337)*

Squibb Alvah M Company Inc 412 751-2301
637 Long Run Rd McKeesport (15132) *(G-10682)*

Squibb Custom Machine Inc 610 258-0923
4200 Kesslersville Rd Easton (18040) *(G-4756)*

Squid Wire LLC 484 235-5155
1950 Butler Pike Pmb 231 Conshohocken (19428) *(G-3606)*

Sr Jan Fisher 724 841-0508
716 Hansen Ave Lyndora (16045) *(G-10136)*

SR Rosati Inc 610 626-1818
201 E Madison Ave Clifton Heights (19018) *(G-3258)*

SRC Elastomerics Inc (PA) 215 335-2049
4749 Tolbut St Philadelphia (19136) *(G-14336)*

Srd Design Corp 717 699-0005
207 S Sumner St Frnt York (17404) *(G-20678)*

Srm Entertainment Group LLC (PA) 610 825-1039
4030 Skyron Dr Ste C Doylestown (18902) *(G-4338)*

Srm-Avant Inc 724 537-0300
4727 State Route 30 # 204 Greensburg (15601) *(G-6716)*

SSC Distributors, Chester *Also called Sykes-Scholtz-Collins Lbr Inc* *(G-3066)*

Ssi, Narberth *Also called Solution Systems Inc* *(G-11912)*

Sskj Enterprises Inc 412 494-3308
2812 Idlewood Ave Carnegie (15106) *(G-2794)*

Ssm Industries Inc 215 288-7777
5238 Comly St Philadelphia (19135) *(G-14337)*

SSS, Beaver Falls *Also called Standard Steel Specialty Co* *(G-1014)*

Sssi Inc (PA) 724 743-5815
2755a Park Ave Washington (15301) *(G-19228)*

Ssw International Inc (HQ) 412 922-9100
661 Andersen Dr Ste 7 Pittsburgh (15220) *(G-15572)*

St Benjamins Brewing Co 215 232-4305
1710 N 5th St Philadelphia (19122) *(G-14338)*

St Clair Graphics Inc 570 253-6692
406 Erie St Honesdale (18431) *(G-7726)*

St Clair Precast Concrete Inc 412 221-2577
601 4th Ave Bridgeville (15017) *(G-2091)*

St Croix Alumina LLC 412 553-4545
201 Isabella St Pittsburgh (15212) *(G-15573)*

St Laurent Apartments, Philadelphia *Also called Mdg Associates* *(G-14000)*

St Lukes Hsptl St Lukes, Bethlehem *Also called Saint Lukes Hosp Bethlehem PA* *(G-1614)*

St Martin America Inc 570 593-8596
87 Schuylkill St Cressona (17929) *(G-3908)*

St Marys Box Company 814 834-3819
109 Jeep Rd Saint Marys (15857) *(G-17015)*

St Marys Carbon Co Inc (PA) 814 781-7333
259 Eberl St Saint Marys (15857) *(G-17016)*

St Marys Carbon Co Inc 814 781-7333
259 Eberl St Saint Marys (15857) *(G-17017)*

St Marys Carbon Co Inc 814 781-7333
259 Eberl St Saint Marys (15857) *(G-17018)*

St Marys Metal Finishing Inc 814 834-6500
1057 Trout Run Rd Saint Marys (15857) *(G-17019)*

St Marys Pressed Metals Inc 814 772-7455
2 Bark St Ridgway (15853) *(G-16730)*

St Marys Spring Co 814 834-2460
630 Lehner Ave Saint Marys (15857) *(G-17020)*

St Marys Tool & Die Co Inc 814 834-7420
1003 Trout Run Rd Saint Marys (15857) *(G-17021)*

St Thomas Development Inc 717 369-3030
8153b Lincoln Way W Saint Thomas (17252) *(G-17041)*

St, Martin Cabinetry, Cressona *Also called St Martin America Inc* *(G-3908)*

St. Marys Mfg Facility, Saint Marys *Also called Metaldyne Snterforged Pdts LLC* *(G-16993)*

Staab Typographic, Emlenton *Also called Progress News* *(G-5014)*

Staar Distributing Llc (PA) 814 612-2115
560 Myrtle St Reynoldsville (15851) *(G-16666)*

Staar Distributing Llc 814 371-3500
130a Satterlee Rd Du Bois (15801) *(G-4420)*

Stabler Companies Inc (HQ) 717 236-9307
635 Lucknow Rd Harrisburg (17110) *(G-7219)*

Stabler Companies Inc 610 799-2421
2500 Quarry St Coplay (18037) *(G-3650)*

Stackpole Inc 717 796-0411
15200 Nbn Way Blue Ridge Summit (17214) *(G-1862)*

Stacy Lloyd 724 265-3445
1612 Saxonburg Blvd Tarentum (15084) *(G-18247)*

Stadium Solutions Inc 724 287-5330
108 Elliott Dr Butler (16001) *(G-2444)*

Stagestep Inc 267 672-2900
4701 Bath St Ste 46b Philadelphia (19137) *(G-14339)*

Staggert Disposal 570 547-6150
147 James Rd Montgomery (17752) *(G-11379)*

Stagno Italian Accent, Pittsburgh *Also called Stagnos Bakery Inc* *(G-15574)*

Stagno's Italian Accent, East Liberty *Also called Stagnos Bakery Inc* *(G-4581)*

Stagnos Bakery Inc (PA) 412 441-3485
233 Auburn St East Liberty (15206) *(G-4581)*

A
L
P
H
A
B
E
T
I
C

Stagnos Bakery Inc 412 361-2093
  1747 Chislett St Pittsburgh (15206) *(G-15574)*

Stahl's Hotronix, Masontown *Also called Stahls Special Projects Inc (G-10537)*

Stahls Hotronix 724 966-5996
  1 Posley Park Carmichaels (15320) *(G-2760)*

Stahls Special Projects Inc 724 583-1176
  1 Stahls Dr Masontown (15461) *(G-10537)*

Staiman Recycling Corporation (PA) 717 646-0951
  201 Hepburn St Williamsport (17701) *(G-20074)*

Stained Glass Creations 570 629-5070
  2736 Route 611 Tannersville (18372) *(G-18237)*

Stainless Distributors Inc 215 369-9746
  1215 Knox Dr Yardley (19067) *(G-20341)*

Stainless Steel Services Inc 215 831-1471
  4330 Sepviva St Philadelphia (19124) *(G-14340)*

Stainless Systems Service, Danville *Also called Agri Welding Service Inc (G-3996)*

Stainless Technolgy, Bethlehem *Also called Abec Inc (G-1442)*

Stair Pak Products Co, Pine Grove *Also called Joyce Stair Corp (G-14594)*

Stairworks Inc 215 703-0823
  811 Tech Dr Telford (18969) *(G-18320)*

Stallion Littlefield Services 724 966-2272
  12 Industrial Park Rd Carmichaels (15320) *(G-2761)*

Stallion Oilfield Services Ltd 724 743-4801
  300 Woodcliff Dr Ste 201 Canonsburg (15317) *(G-2639)*

Stallion Oilfield Services Ltd 570 494-0760
  297 Beautys Run Rd Cogan Station (17728) *(G-3362)*

Stallion Oilfield Services Ltd 724 222-9059
  2699 Jefferson Ave Washington (15301) *(G-19229)*

Stalnaker Lumber 724 447-2248
  138 Renner Creek Rd New Freeport (15352) *(G-12219)*

Stambaugh Metal Inc 717 632-5957
  802 High St Hanover (17331) *(G-6958)*

Stampede Industries LLC 724 239-2104
  1019 Route 519 Eighty Four (15330) *(G-4850)*

Stan Bender 610 759-4021
  890 Lahr Rd Nazareth (18064) *(G-11989)*

Stan Clark Military Books 717 337-1728
  915 Fairview Ave Gettysburg (17325) *(G-6315)*

Standard & Custom LLC 412 345-7901
  6901 Lynn Way Pittsburgh (15208) *(G-15575)*

Standard Artifical Limb, Exton *Also called Cape Prosthetics-Orthotics (G-5659)*

Standard Awnings & Aluminum 570 824-3535
  799 Hazle St Hanover Township (18706) *(G-7006)*

Standard Bent Glass LLC (HQ) 724 287-3747
  136 Lincoln Ave East Butler (16029) *(G-4536)*

Standard Car Truck Company 412 782-7300
  1 Mccandless Ave Pittsburgh (15201) *(G-15576)*

Standard Ceramic Supply Co, Carnegie *Also called Chem-Clay Corporation (G-2765)*

Standard Concrete Products Co 717 843-8074
  700 N Sherman St York (17402) *(G-20679)*

Standard Forged Products LLC 412 778-2020
  75 Nichol Ave Mc Kees Rocks (15136) *(G-10637)*

Standard Fusee Corporation 215 788-3001
  2975 State Rd Croydon (19021) *(G-3929)*

Standard Horse Nail Corp 724 846-4660
  1415 5th Ave Ste 2 New Brighton (15066) *(G-12043)*

Standard Industries Inc. 570 568-7230
  2093 Old Route 15 New Columbia (17856) *(G-12176)*

Standard Ink & Color Corp 570 424-5214
  Airport Rd East Stroudsburg (18301) *(G-4635)*

Standard Iron Works 570 347-2058
  990 N South Rd Ste 1 Scranton (18504) *(G-17293)*

Standard Journal, Montgomery *Also called Milton Daily Standard (G-11376)*

Standard Journal Newspapers, Milton *Also called Gatehouse Media LLC (G-11239)*

Standard Metal Industries LLC 610 377-5400
  500 S 9th St Lehighton (18235) *(G-9728)*

Standard Offset Prtg Co Inc (PA) 610 375-6174
  433 Pearl St Reading (19602) *(G-16524)*

Standard Pattern Works Inc 814 455-5145
  549 Huron St Erie (16502) *(G-5490)*

Standard Pennant Company Inc 814 427-2066
  109 Main St Big Run (15715) *(G-1657)*

Standard Precision Mfg Inc 814 724-1202
  13617 Broadway Meadville (16335) *(G-10792)*

Standard Speaker Newspaper, Hazleton *Also called Times-Shamrock (G-7531)*

Standard Steel (HQ) 717 242-4615
  500 N Walnut St Burnham (17009) *(G-2362)*

Standard Steel Specialty Co 724 846-7600
  100 Jamison St Beaver Falls (15010) *(G-1014)*

Standard Tool & Machine Co (PA) 724 758-5522
  514 Mecklem Ln Ellwood City (16117) *(G-4950)*

Standard Tool & Machine Co 724 758-5522
  1 Uss Industrial Park Ellwood City (16117) *(G-4951)*

Staneco Corporation 215 672-6500
  901 Sheehy Dr Horsham (19044) *(G-7852)*

Stanho, New Brighton *Also called Standard Horse Nail Corp (G-12043)*

Stanhope Microworks 717 796-9000
  614 Apple Dr Mechanicsburg (17055) *(G-10891)*

Stanko Products Inc 724 834-8080
  278 Donohoe Rd Greensburg (15601) *(G-6717)*

Stanley Access Tech LLC 570 368-1435
  270 Dogwood Ridge Rd Montgomery (17752) *(G-11380)*

Stanley Access Tech LLC 800 722-2377
  135 Plum Industrial Park Pittsburgh (15239) *(G-15577)*

Stanley Black & Decker Inc 215 710-9300
  2000 Cabot Blvd W Langhorne (19047) *(G-9326)*

Stanley Industrial & Auto LLC 800 523-9462
  11 Grammes Rd Allentown (18103) *(G-400)*

Stanley Security Solution, Langhorne *Also called Stanley Black & Decker Inc (G-9326)*

Stanley Security Solutions, Pittsburgh *Also called Stanley Access Tech LLC (G-15577)*

Stanley Security Solutions Inc 877 476-4968
  2350 Eldo Rd Ste B Monroeville (15146) *(G-11357)*

Stanley Security Solutions Inc 888 265-0412
  2350 Eldo Rd Ste B Monroeville (15146) *(G-11358)*

Stanley Storage Systems Inc 610 797-6600
  11 Grammes Rd Allentown (18103) *(G-401)*

Stanley Vidmar (HQ) 610 797-6600
  11 Grammes Rd Allentown (18103) *(G-402)*

Stans Dental Service, Nazareth *Also called Stan Bender (G-11989)*

Stansons Kitchens & Vanities 570 648-4660
  729 S 5th St Coal Township (17866) *(G-3282)*

Stanton Dynamics Inc 814 849-6255
  11575 Route 36 Brookville (15825) *(G-2272)*

Stapf Energy Services 610 831-1500
  5 Center Ave Ste A Trappe (19426) *(G-18474)*

Star Brands North America Inc 610 775-4100
  11 Main St Mohnton (19540) *(G-11270)*

Star Continuous Card Systems 800 458-1413
  140 Chalfant Rd Glenmoore (19343) *(G-6470)*

Star Energy Inc 814 257-8485
  1009 State Route 839 Dayton (16222) *(G-4040)*

Star Iron Works, Punxsutawney *Also called National Oilwell Varco Inc (G-16150)*

Star Label Products, Fairless Hills *Also called Okumus Enterprises Ltd (G-5790)*

Star Organization Inc 412 374-1420
  4051 William Penn Hwy Monroeville (15146) *(G-11359)*

Star Printing Company 717 456-5692
  811 Main St Delta (17314) *(G-4063)*

Star Surplus One 215 654-9237
  1164 Limekiln Pike Ambler (19002) *(G-603)*

Star-H Corporation 717 826-7587
  48-50 W Chestnut St Lancaster (17603) *(G-9204)*

Starfire Corporation (PA) 814 948-5164
  682 Cole Rd Carrolltown (15722) *(G-2810)*

Starfire Corporation 814 948-5164
  617 Philadelphia Ave Northern Cambria (15714) *(G-12863)*

Starflite Systems Inc 724 789-9200
  116 Dogwood Ln Connoquenessing (16027) *(G-3513)*

Starke Millwork Inc 610 759-1753
  671 Bangor Rd Nazareth (18064) *(G-11990)*

Starkist Co (HQ) 412 323-7400
  225 N Shore Dr Ste 400 Pittsburgh (15212) *(G-15578)*

Starline Busway Systems, Canonsburg *Also called Universal Electric Corporation (G-2652)*

Starlite Group Inc 814 333-1377
  246 Race St Meadville (16335) *(G-10793)*

Starlite Industries Inc 610 527-1300
  1111 E Lancaster Ave # 2 Bryn Mawr (19010) *(G-2334)*

Starliteindustries, Bryn Mawr *Also called Starlite Industries Inc (G-2334)*

Starn Tool & Manufacturing Co (PA) 814 724-1057
  20524 Blooming Valley Rd Meadville (16335) *(G-10794)*

Starprint Publications Inc (PA) 814 736-9666
  722 Dulancey Dr Portage (15946) *(G-15922)*

Starr Financial Group Inc (PA) 814 236-0910
  861 Bailey Rd Curwensville (16833) *(G-3955)*

Starrhock Silicones Inc 610 837-4883
  6854b Chrisphalt Dr Bath (18014) *(G-969)*

Stasik Custom Cabinetry 215 357-7277
  410 Clearview Ave Ste H Feasterville Trevose (19053) *(G-5931)*

State Industries Inc (HQ) 724 548-8101
  1 Glade Dr Kittanning (16201) *(G-8797)*

State Line Fencing 610 932-9352
  161 Stoney Ln Nottingham (19362) *(G-12885)*

State Line Supply Company 814 362-7433
  1333 E Main St Bradford (16701) *(G-1992)*

State of ARC Wldg & Fabg LLC (PA) 610 216-6862
  800 Rutt Rd Bangor (18013) *(G-930)*

State of Art Inc 814 355-2714
  2470 Fox Hill Rd State College (16803) *(G-18034)*

State of Art Prosthetics 215 914-1222
  2910 Franks Rd Ste 2 Huntingdon Valley (19006) *(G-8040)*

State Street Copy and Press 717 232-6684
  500 N 3rd St Fl 1 Harrisburg (17101) *(G-7220)*

Stateasy 412 437-8287
  111 N Whitfield St Pittsburgh (15206) *(G-15579)*

Statement Walls LLC 267 266-0869
  1045 W Glenwood Ave Philadelphia (19133) *(G-14341)*

Statementwalls.com, Philadelphia *Also called Statement Walls LLC (G-14341)*

Stationary Engravers Inc 215 739-3538
2011 Frankford Ave Philadelphia (19125) *(G-14342)*

Statler Body Works, Marion Also called Wade Holdings LLC *(G-10470)*

Statler Body Works Inc 717 261-5936
1266 N Franklin St Chambersburg (17201) *(G-2978)*

Statlers Repair Shop 717 263-5074
1053 Paper Mill Rd Chambersburg (17202) *(G-2979)*

Status Label Corporation 215 443-0124
2910 Turnpike Dr Hatboro (19040) *(G-7306)*

Staudt Machine Company 215 598-7225
16 Martindell Dr Newtown (18940) *(G-12552)*

Stauffer Acquisition Corp 717 569-3200
1160 Enterprise Ct East Petersburg (17520) *(G-4591)*

Stauffer Compressor N Machine 717 733-4128
49 Pleasant Valley Rd Ephrata (17522) *(G-5146)*

Stauffer Con Pdts & Excvtg Inc 570 629-1977
Rr 534 Kunkletown (18058) *(G-8835)*

Stauffer Frames 570 374-7100
460 Lumber Hill Rd Port Trevorton (17864) *(G-15915)*

Stauffer Manufacturing LLC 717 445-6122
1058 Martindale Rd Ephrata (17522) *(G-5147)*

Stauffer Wood Products 717 647-4372
221 Clarks Valley Rd Tower City (17980) *(G-18441)*

Stauffers Mini Barns 724 479-0760
1082 Myers Rd Indiana (15701) *(G-8130)*

Staurowsky Woodworking 610 489-0770
3454 Germantown Pike Collegeville (19426) *(G-3394)*

Staurowsky, Gary F Woodworking, Collegeville Also called Staurowsky
Woodworking *(G-3394)*

Staver Hydraulics Co Inc 610 837-1818
7709 Beth Bath Pike Bath (18014) *(G-970)*

Staychilled Usa LLC 215 284-6018
13 Laurence Pl Plymouth Meeting (19462) *(G-15874)*

STC Industries, Shohola Also called Spiral Tool Corporation *(G-17580)*

Steadman Tool & Die Inc 814 967-4333
32883 State Highway 408 Townville (16360) *(G-18447)*

Stealth Composites Inc (PA) 215 919-7584
313 Johnson St Pottstown (19464) *(G-16051)*

Steam Mad Carpet Cleaners Inc 215 283-9833
558 Coach Rd Horsham (19044) *(G-7853)*

Steckel Printing Inc 717 898-1555
2100 State Rd Lancaster (17601) *(G-9205)*

Steckman, C K Memorials, Renfrew Also called Charles Steckman *(G-16638)*

Stediwatt, Chambersburg Also called Advanced Electronics Systems *(G-2897)*

Steel City Chromium Plating Co 610 838-8441
320 Front St Hellertown (18055) *(G-7563)*

Steel City Controls Inc 412 851-8566
3672 Maplevue Dr Bethel Park (15102) *(G-1434)*

Steel City Graphics Inc 724 942-5699
3529 Washington Rd Canonsburg (15317) *(G-2640)*

Steel City Optronics LLC 412 501-3849
5149 Prince Phillip Ct Gibsonia (15044) *(G-6352)*

Steel City Plate Company, Conneaut Lake Also called Esmark Excalibur LLC *(G-3472)*

Steel City Plate Company, Meadville Also called Esmark Excalibur LLC *(G-10721)*

Steel Consulting Services LLC 412 727-6645
58 Ridge Rd Pittsburgh (15221) *(G-15580)*

Steel Fab Enterprises LLC 717 464-0330
623 Baumgardner Rd Lancaster (17603) *(G-9206)*

Steel Fabricators LLC 610 775-3532
1530 Lancaster Ave Rear Reading (19607) *(G-16525)*

Steel Factory Corp 412 771-2944
200 Bradley St Mc Kees Rocks (15136) *(G-10638)*

Steel Fitness Premier LLC 610 973-1500
250 Cetronia Rd Ste 100 Allentown (18104) *(G-403)*

Steel Plus Inc 717 274-9481
205 N 5th Ave Lebanon (17046) *(G-9634)*

Steel Shield Technologies Inc 412 479-0024
3351 Industrial Blvd Bethel Park (15102) *(G-1435)*

Steel Stone Manufacturing Co 610 837-9966
6693 Ruch Rd Lehigh Valley (18002) *(G-9707)*

Steel Systems Installation Inc 717 786-1264
175 N Lime St Quarryville (17566) *(G-16280)*

Steel Valley Casting LLC 724 777-4025
1784a Route 68 New Brighton (15066) *(G-12044)*

Steel Will, Huntingdon Valley Also called Sport Manufacturing Group Inc *(G-8039)*

Steele Print Inc 724 758-6178
420 Wampum Ave Ellwood City (16117) *(G-4952)*

Steelway Cellar Doors LLC 610 277-9988
290 E Church Rd King of Prussia (19406) *(G-8680)*

Steelway Custom Cellar Doors, King of Prussia Also called Steelway Cellar Doors
LLC *(G-8680)*

Steer Machine Tool & Die Corp 570 253-5152
3113 Lake Ariel Hwy Honesdale (18431) *(G-7727)*

Stefanelli's Candies, Erie Also called 4sis LLC *(G-5162)*

Stefanos Printing Inc 724 277-8374
266 Furnace Hill Rd Dunbar (15431) *(G-4443)*

Steffan Industries Inc 412 751-4484
950 E Smithfield St McKeesport (15135) *(G-10683)*

Steffees 814 827-4332
4219 State Route 8 Titusville (16354) *(G-18397)*

Steffy Printing Inc 717 859-5040
103 Zooks Mill Rd Brownstown (17508) *(G-2309)*

Steffys Pattern Shop 717 656-6032
297 E Main St Leola (17540) *(G-9805)*

Steigrwalds Kitchens Baths Inc 724 458-0280
120 S Broad St Ste C Grove City (16127) *(G-6804)*

Steimer and Co Inc 610 933-7450
157 E 7 Stars Rd Phoenixville (19460) *(G-14579)*

Stein Seal Company (PA) 215 256-0201
1500 Industrial Blvd Kulpsville (19443) *(G-8831)*

Steinmetz Inc 570 842-6161
660 Spencer Rd Roaring Brook Twp (18444) *(G-16760)*

Steinmetz Polymers, Roaring Brook Twp Also called Steinmetz Inc *(G-16760)*

Steins Generator & Starter Svc, Philadelphia Also called Steins Pasco Battery
Starter *(G-14343)*

Steins Pasco Battery Starter 215 969-6900
10069 Sandmeyer Ln Philadelphia (19116) *(G-14343)*

Stel Life Inc 610 724-3688
1 S Broad St Ste 1010 Philadelphia (19107) *(G-14344)*

Stelkast Inc 888 273-1583
200 Hidden Valley Rd Mc Murray (15317) *(G-10646)*

Stella-Jones Corporation 717 721-3113
206 Kimberly Ln Ephrata (17522) *(G-5148)*

Stella-Jones Corporation 814 371-7331
392 Larkeytown Rd Du Bois (15801) *(G-4421)*

Stella-Jones Corporation (HQ) 412 325-0202
1000 Cliffmine Rd Ste 500 Pittsburgh (15275) *(G-15581)*

Stella-Jones US Holding Corp (HQ) 304 372-2211
603 Stanwix St Pittsburgh (15222) *(G-15582)*

Stellar Images Imges Dcrtv GLS 717 367-6500
204 S Market St Elizabethtown (17022) *(G-4888)*

Stellar Industries Inc 724 335-5525
Schreiber Industrial Park New Kensington (15068) *(G-12380)*

Stellar Machine Incorporated 570 718-1733
250 Railroad St Nanticoke (18634) *(G-11903)*

Stellar Prcsion Components Ltd 724 523-5559
1201 Rankin Ave Jeannette (15644) *(G-8265)*

Stello Foods Inc 814 938-8764
551 E Mahoning St Punxsutawney (15767) *(G-16164)*

Stemmetry 678 770-6781
1529 Brimfield Dr Sewickley (15143) *(G-17413)*

Stengels Welding Shop Inc 610 444-4110
810 E Baltimore Pike Kennett Square (19348) *(G-8544)*

Stephan Enterprises, Horsham Also called Davinci Graphics Inc *(G-7808)*

Stephanie McClain 267 820-9273
600 Hermitage St Philadelphia (19128) *(G-14345)*

Stephen Gould Corporation 724 933-1400
8000 Brooktree Rd Ste 110 Wexford (15090) *(G-19829)*

Stephen R Lechman 570 636-3159
1113 Cunnius St Freeland (18224) *(G-6196)*

Stephens Excavating Svc LLC 484 888-1010
115 Corman Dr Kennett Square (19348) *(G-8545)*

Steppin' Out, Warren Also called House of Printing *(G-19031)*

Steq America LLC 267 644-5477
1456 Ferry Rd Ste 501 Doylestown (18901) *(G-4339)*

Stereo Shoppe, Williamsport Also called Jcm Audio Inc *(G-20028)*

Steril-Sil Co LLC 617 739-2970
1241 Grants Pl Denver (17517) *(G-4094)*

Sterilzer Rfurbishing Svcs Inc 814 882-4116
1039 W 11th St Erie (16502) *(G-5491)*

Sterilzer Rfurbishing Svcs Inc (PA) 814 456-2616
1039 W 11th St Erie (16502) *(G-5492)*

Steris Barrier Pdts Solutions 215 763-8200
3000 Henderson Dr Sharon Hill (19079) *(G-17462)*

Steris Corporation 215 763-8200
1725 N 6th St Philadelphia (19122) *(G-14346)*

Sterling Compress Gas, Minersville Also called Alig LLC *(G-11253)*

Sterling Computer Sales LLC 610 255-0198
11 Laetitia Ln Landenberg (19350) *(G-9253)*

Sterling Division, Sterling Also called Eureka Stone Quarry Inc *(G-18049)*

Sterling Dula Architectural 814 838-7731
2250 Powell Ave Erie (16506) *(G-5493)*

Sterling Finishing 267 682-0844
1300 E Mermaid Ln Glenside (19038) *(G-6541)*

Sterling Forest Products 570 226-4233
136 Wenonah Rd Tafton (18464) *(G-18205)*

Sterling Machine Tech Inc 717 838-1234
220 Kreider Rd Palmyra (17078) *(G-13131)*

Sterling Paper Company 215 744-5350
2155 Castor Ave Philadelphia (19134) *(G-14347)*

Sterling Quarry, Chalfont Also called Eureka Stone Quarry Inc *(G-2874)*

Sterling Technologies Inc 814 774-2500
10047 Keystone Dr Lake City (16423) *(G-8908)*

Sterling-Fleischman Inc 610 647-1717
198 Martins Run Media (19063) *(G-10951)*

Sterns Soft Serve LLC 724 349-4118
477 Indiana Rd Creekside (15732) *(G-3877)*

Steve A Vitelli 570 937-4546
  347 Tisdel Rd Lake Ariel (18436) *(G-8893)*

Steve Day 610 916-1317
  663 Gulden Rd Blandon (19510) *(G-1760)*

Steve Eversoll 717 768-3298
  604 Gault Rd Gap (17527) *(G-6256)*

Steve Goldberg Company 215 322-0615
  145 Meadowfield Dr Southampton (18966) *(G-17837)*

Steve Jones 717 845-7700
  948 Elm St York (17403) *(G-20680)*

Steve Schwartz Associates Inc 412 765-3400
  1700 Forbes Ave Pittsburgh (15219) *(G-15583)*

Steve Shannon Tire Company Inc 570 675-8473
  4090 Memorial Hwy Dallas (18612) *(G-3968)*

Steven E Tachoir 814 726-1572
  977 Watson Farm Rd Marienville (16239) *(G-10459)*

Steven Laucks 717 244-6310
  675 Blouse Rd Red Lion (17356) *(G-16615)*

Stevens Clogging Supplies Inc 724 662-0808
  49 Franklin Rd Mercer (16137) *(G-10976)*

Stevens Woodworks 412 487-4408
  4437 Birchwood Ln Allison Park (15101) *(G-463)*

Stevenson Machine Shop, Mechanicsburg *Also called Weskem Technologies Inc (G-10907)*

Stevenson-Cooper Inc 215 223-2600
  1039 W Venango St Philadelphia (19140) *(G-14348)*

Stevensons, Hermitage *Also called L M Stevenson Company Inc (G-7590)*

Steves Refacing 724 274-4740
  731 Pittsburgh St Springdale (15144) *(G-17902)*

Steves Ventures 717 808-2501
  19 Sunflower Dr Ephrata (17522) *(G-5149)*

Stewart Connector, Glen Rock *Also called Bel Connector Inc (G-6452)*

Stewart Warner, Lancaster *Also called Maxima Tech & Systems Inc (G-9129)*

Stewart Warner Electronics, Lancaster *Also called Herley Industries Inc (G-9044)*

Stewart Welding & Fabg Inc 717 252-3948
  6287 Lincoln Hwy Wrightsville (17368) *(G-20244)*

Stewart-Amos Steel Inc 717 564-3931
  4400 Paxton St Harrisburg (17111) *(G-7221)*

Stewarts Fabrication Inc 610 921-1600
  4927 Commerce St Temple (19560) *(G-18338)*

STI, Whitehall *Also called Sawcom Tech Inc (G-19888)*

STI Pharma LLC 215 710-3270
  32 Blacksmith Rd Newtown (18940) *(G-12553)*

Stickman Brews 484 938-5900
  326 N Lewis Rd Royersford (19468) *(G-16866)*

Stickman Brews 856 912-4372
  431 Woodhill Rd Wayne (19087) *(G-19373)*

Stiltz Inc 610 443-2282
  57 S Commerce Way Ste 300 Bethlehem (18017) *(G-1629)*

Stimple and Ward Company (PA) 412 364-5200
  3400 Babcock Blvd Pittsburgh (15237) *(G-15584)*

Stimple and Ward Company 724 772-0049
  45a Progress Ave Cranberry Township (16066) *(G-3851)*

Stineman Management Corp 814 495-4686
  128 Ribbon Ln South Fork (15956) *(G-17778)*

Stineman Ribbon Company, South Fork *Also called Stineman Management Corp (G-17778)*

Stines Equipment & Maintenance 717 432-4374
  680 Ridge Rd Dillsburg (17019) *(G-4140)*

Sting Free Company, West Chester *Also called Stingfree Technologies Company (G-19644)*

Stingfree Technologies Company 610 444-2806
  1851 Huntsman Ln West Chester (19382) *(G-19644)*

Stitch Art Custom Embroidery 814 382-2702
  14058 Conneaut Lake Rd Conneaut Lake (16316) *(G-3479)*

Stitch Crazy 610 526-0154
  360 Arden Rd Conshohocken (19428) *(G-3607)*

Stitch U S A Inc 215 699-0123
  436 Industrial Dr North Wales (19454) *(G-12828)*

Stitch Wizards Inc 412 264-9973
  1009 4th Ave Coraopolis (15108) *(G-3726)*

Stitches Embroidery Inc 412 781-7046
  1600 Marys Ave Pittsburgh (15215) *(G-15585)*

Stk LLC (PA) 724 430-2477
  2282 University Dr Ste 1 Lemont Furnace (15456) *(G-9738)*

Stm Heavyduty Electric, Zionsville *Also called S T M Heavy Duty Electric Inc (G-20836)*

Stockton Anthracite, Hazle Township *Also called Coal Contractors (1991) Inc (G-7449)*

Stockwatch, Wernersville *Also called J & J Consulting Corp (G-19485)*

Stockwell Elastomerics, Philadelphia *Also called SRC Elastomerics Inc (G-14336)*

Stoltz Mfg LLC 610 286-5146
  121 Morgan Way Morgantown (19543) *(G-11537)*

Stoltzfoos Layers (PA) 717 826-0371
  1003 Gap Rd Kinzers (17535) *(G-8743)*

Stoltzfus Cabinet Shop, Talmage *Also called Melvin Stoltzfus (G-18207)*

Stoltzfus Custom Welding 717 477-8200
  11738 Weaver Rd Orrstown (17244) *(G-13035)*

Stoltzfus Enterprises Ltd 610 273-9266
  34 Lauver Cir Honey Brook (19344) *(G-7763)*

Stoltzfus Ephram 717 656-0513
  339 Monterey Rd Bird In Hand (17505) *(G-1682)*

Stoltzfus John 717 786-2481
  918 Valley Rd Quarryville (17566) *(G-16281)*

Stoltzfus Manufacturing Inc 610 273-3603
  540 White School Rd Honey Brook (19344) *(G-7764)*

Stoltzfus Rv's & Marine, West Chester *Also called Stoltzfus Trailer Sales Inc (G-19645)*

Stoltzfus Spreaders, Morgantown *Also called Stoltz Mfg LLC (G-11537)*

Stoltzfus Steel Manufacturing 570 524-7835
  391 Wolfland Rd Lewisburg (17837) *(G-9919)*

Stoltzfus Structures 610 593-7700
  5075 Lower Valley Rd Atglen (19310) *(G-808)*

Stoltzfus Sylvan Lee 570 682-9755
  85 Maple Dr Hegins (17938) *(G-7544)*

Stoltzfus Trailer Sales Inc 610 399-0628
  1335 Wilmington Pike West Chester (19382) *(G-19645)*

Stoltzfus Woodturning 717 687-8237
  264 Paradise Ln Ronks (17572) *(G-16816)*

Stoltzfus Woodworking 717 656-4823
  324 Willow Rd Lancaster (17601) *(G-9207)*

Stolzfus Transport, Lewisburg *Also called Stoltzfus Steel Manufacturing (G-9919)*

Stone & Co, Connellsville *Also called Wendell H Stone Company Inc (G-3510)*

Stone & Co, Greensburg *Also called Wendell H Stone Company Inc (G-6729)*

Stone & Co, Monroeville *Also called Wendell H Stone Company Inc (G-11364)*

Stone & Company, Charleroi *Also called Wendell H Stone Company Inc (G-3025)*

Stone & Company, Connellsville *Also called Wendell H Stone Company Inc (G-3511)*

Stone & Wood Inc 814 857-7621
  Rr 2 Woodland (16881) *(G-20214)*

Stone Breaker LLC 312 203-5632
  10 E Athens Ave Ste 209 Ardmore (19003) *(G-718)*

Stone County Specialties 570 467-2850
  458 Fairview St Tamaqua (18252) *(G-18228)*

Stone Creek Hunds Hunting Sups, Hesston *Also called Kimberly A Spickler (G-7627)*

Stone Edge Technologies Inc 484 927-4804
  1100 Schell Ln Ste 104 Phoenixville (19460) *(G-14580)*

Stone Hedge Farms, Dover *Also called Burkey Acquisition Inc (G-4189)*

Stone House Logistics, Red Lion *Also called Steven Laucks (G-16615)*

Stone Mill Rug Co 215 744-2331
  1250 Adams Ave Ste 2 Philadelphia (19124) *(G-14349)*

Stone Silo Foods Inc 570 676-0809
  Rr 191 South Sterling (18460) *(G-17788)*

Stone Supply Inc 570 434-2076
  2432 Orphan School Rd Kingsley (18826) *(G-8708)*

Stone Valley Welding LLC 814 667-2046
  11582 Guyer Rd Huntingdon (16652) *(G-7956)*

Stonebraker John 724 238-6466
  946 Bridlewood Ln Ligonier (15658) *(G-9966)*

Stonebraker's Jewelers, Ligonier *Also called Stonebraker John (G-9966)*

Stonemak Enterprises Inc 570 752-3209
  5 Glennwood St Berwick (18603) *(G-1345)*

Stoner Graphix Inc 717 469-7716
  163 S Meadow Ln Hummelstown (17036) *(G-7925)*

Stoner Incorporated (PA) 717 786-7355
  1070 Robert Fulton Hwy Quarryville (17566) *(G-16282)*

Stoner Incorporated 800 227-5538
  1813 William Penn Way Lancaster (17601) *(G-9208)*

Stoney Lonesome Quarry Inc 570 434-2509
  1475 Orphan School Rd Kingsley (18826) *(G-8709)*

Stoney's Brewing Company, Smithton *Also called Jones Brewing Company Inc (G-17661)*

Stony Hill Woodworks 717 786-8358
  332 Stony Hill Rd Quarryville (17566) *(G-16283)*

Stony Run Winery, Kempton *Also called Spitzenburg Cider House LLC (G-8494)*

Stonybrook Shooting Supplies 717 757-1088
  3755 E Market St Ste 18 York (17402) *(G-20681)*

Stop N Go Signs 570 374-3939
  18 Lenker Ave Selinsgrove (17870) *(G-17336)*

Stopay, Jon L Candies, Taylor *Also called John L Stopay LLC (G-18259)*

Stopper Construction Co Inc 570 322-5947
  339 Washington Blvd Williamsport (17701) *(G-20075)*

Store Fixtures Unlimited, Gilbertsville *Also called S F U LLC (G-6377)*

Stored Energy Concepts Inc 610 469-6543
  3250b St Peters Rd Saint Peters (19470) *(G-17035)*

Storeflex LLC 856 498-0079
  603 Creeks Edge Cir New Hope (18938) *(G-12315)*

Story & Clark Piano's, Seneca *Also called Qrs Music Technologies Inc (G-17368)*

Stott Publications Inc 814 632-6700
  2314 Pennington Rd Tyrone (16686) *(G-18593)*

Stoudt Brewing Company 717 484-4386
  Rr 272 Box 880 Adamstown (19501) *(G-24)*

Stouffer's Paving, Mount Pleasant *Also called Stouffers Asphalt Construction (G-11719)*

Stouffers Asphalt Construction 724 527-0917
  1320 W Laurel Cir Mount Pleasant (15666) *(G-11719)*

Stout Logging, Somerset *Also called Stout Lumber Company (G-17712)*

Stout Lumber Company 814 443-9920
  246 Stout Ln Somerset (15501) *(G-17712)*

Stownsee, Wallingford *Also called Hidensee Inc (G-18784)*

Stoystown Tank & Steel Co 814 893-5133
  235 Reading Mine Rd Stoystown (15563) *(G-18087)*

Strahman Industries Inc 484 893-5080
  2801 Baglyos Cir Bethlehem (18020) *(G-1630)*

Strahman Valves Inc (PA) 877 787-2462
  2801 Baglyos Cir Bethlehem (18020) *(G-1631)*

Straight Arrow Products Inc (PA) 610 882-9606
  2020 Highland Ave Bethlehem (18020) *(G-1632)*

Straight Arrow Products Inc 610 882-9606
  2655 Brodhead Rd Bethlehem (18020) *(G-1633)*

Straightline Saw Mill Inc 724 639-3090
  207 Lucky Ln Saltsburg (15681) *(G-17053)*

Strainsense Enterprises Inc 412 751-3055
  1080 Long Run Rd McKeesport (15132) *(G-10684)*

Strainsert Company 610 825-3310
  12 Union Hill Rd Conshohocken (19428) *(G-3608)*

Strait Steel Inc 717 597-3125
  8400 Molly Pitcher Hwy Greencastle (17225) *(G-6636)*

Straits Door Co, Pittsburgh *Also called B & L Manufacturing Corp* *(G-14745)*

Strasburg Creamery LLC 717 456-7497
  4850 Delta Rd Delta (17314) *(G-4064)*

Strasburg Lawn Structures LLC 717 687-8210
  909 Strasburg Pike Strasburg (17579) *(G-18093)*

Strasburg Pallet Co Inc 717 687-8131
  2940 White Oak Rd Strasburg (17579) *(G-18094)*

Strassheim Grphic Dsign & Pres 215 525-5134
  1500 Spring Garden St Philadelphia (19130) *(G-14350)*

Strassheim Printing Co Inc 610 446-3637
  754 Lawson Ave Havertown (19083) *(G-7428)*

Strat-O-Span Buildings Inc 717 334-4606
  2020 Chambersburg Rd Gettysburg (17325) *(G-6316)*

Strata Products Worldwide LLC 724 745-5030
  130 Technology Dr Canonsburg (15317) *(G-2641)*

Strata Skin Sciences Inc (PA) 215 619-3200
  5 Walnut Grove Dr Ste 140 Horsham (19044) *(G-7854)*

Stratagem Consoles, South Williamsport *Also called Ceraln Corp* *(G-17790)*

Strategic Defense Unit LLC 267 591-0725
  3460 Joyce St Philadelphia (19134) *(G-14351)*

Strategic Medicine Inc 814 659-5450
  231 Deepdale Dr Kennett Square (19348) *(G-8546)*

Strategic Mfg Tech LLC 610 269-0054
  505 Trestle Pl Downingtown (19335) *(G-4257)*

Strategic Reports Inc 610 370-5640
  2645 Perkiomen Ave Reading (19606) *(G-16526)*

Straub Industries Inc 814 364-9789
  234 Goodhart Rd Centre Hall (16828) *(G-2844)*

Strauss Eng Co, Huntingdon Valley *Also called Strauss Engineering Company* *(G-8041)*

Strauss Engineering Company 215 947-1083
  80 Tracey Rd Huntingdon Valley (19006) *(G-8041)*

Straz 570 344-1513
  1006 Pittston Ave Scranton (18505) *(G-17294)*

Stream-Flo USA LLC 724 349-6090
  1410 Wayne Ave Ste C Indiana (15701) *(G-8131)*

Streamlight Inc 610 631-0600
  30 Eagleville Rd Ste 100 Eagleville (19403) *(G-4517)*

Streamline Energy Services LLC 610 415-1220
  1220 Valley Rd Ste 25 Valley Forge (19482) *(G-18715)*

Streamline Propane Llc 215 919-4500
  35 Schultz Rd Green Lane (18054) *(G-6593)*

Stretch Devices Inc 215 739-3000
  3401 I St Ste 1 Philadelphia (19134) *(G-14352)*

Strick Corporation (PA) 215 949-3600
  225 Lincoln Hwy Fairless Hills (19030) *(G-5799)*

Strine Corrugated Products 717 764-4800
  150 Emig Rd Emigsville (17318) *(G-5000)*

Strishock Coal Co 814 375-1245
  220 Hillcrest Dr Du Bois (15801) *(G-4422)*

Strobel Machine Inc 724 297-3441
  1442 Butler Rd Worthington (16262) *(G-20234)*

Strobic Air Corporation 215 723-4700
  700 Emlen Way Telford (18969) *(G-18321)*

Stroehmann Bakeries, Altoona *Also called Bimbo Bakeries Usa Inc* *(G-477)*

Stroehmann Bakeries 20, Williamsport *Also called Bimbo Bakeries Usa Inc* *(G-19993)*

Stroehmann Bakeries 34, Leetsdale *Also called Bimbo Bakeries Usa Inc* *(G-9684)*

Stroehmann Bakeries 75, Reading *Also called Bimbo Bakeries Usa Inc* *(G-16333)*

Stroehmann Maiers Bakeries, Bethlehem *Also called Bimbo Bakeries Usa Inc* *(G-1466)*

Strong Body Care Products Inc 717 786-8947
  1 Lakeside Dr New Providence (17560) *(G-12435)*

Strong Industries Inc (PA) 570 275-2700
  3204 Point Township Dr Northumberland (17857) *(G-12876)*

Strong Pools, Northumberland *Also called Strong Industries Inc* *(G-12876)*

Strongbridge Biopharma PLC (PA) 610 254-9200
  900 Northbrook Dr Ste 200 Trevose (19053) *(G-18504)*

Strube Inc 717 426-1906
  629 W Market St Marietta (17547) *(G-10468)*

Strubles Fire and Safety 814 594-0840
  185 Struble Rd Kersey (15846) *(G-8571)*

Structural Fiberglass Inc 814 623-0458
  4766 Business 220 Bedford (15522) *(G-1077)*

Structural Glulam LLC 717 355-9813
  199 Quality Cir New Holland (17557) *(G-12286)*

Structural Services Inc 610 282-5810
  7001 N Route 309 Ste 169 Coopersburg (18036) *(G-3636)*

Structure Manufacturing Work 570 271-2880
  5 Walnut St Danville (17821) *(G-4012)*

Structure Probe Inc 610 436-5400
  206 Garfield Ave West Chester (19380) *(G-19646)*

Structured Mining Systems Inc 724 741-9000
  170 Thorn Hill Rd Warrendale (15086) *(G-19098)*

Strunk Concrete Blocks, Reading *Also called C Strunk Inc* *(G-16339)*

Strutz Fabricators Inc 724 625-1501
  440 Mars Valencia Rd Valencia (16059) *(G-18702)*

Stryker Orthobiologics, Malvern *Also called Orthovita Inc* *(G-10291)*

Stryker Orthobiologics 610 407-5259
  67 Great Valley Pkwy Malvern (19355) *(G-10324)*

Stuart Kranzel 717 737-7223
  415 Bosler Ave Lemoyne (17043) *(G-9754)*

Stucco Code Inc 610 348-3905
  918 Shadeland Ave Drexel Hill (19026) *(G-4372)*

Studio 8 .... 610 372-7065
  832 Franklin St Reading (19602) *(G-16527)*

Studio Print Group, Dallas *Also called Offset Paperback Mfrs Inc* *(G-3964)*

Studio Technology, Kennett Square *Also called Advantage Millwork Inc* *(G-8502)*

Studio Technology, Malvern *Also called Legnini RC Architectural Mllwk* *(G-10266)*

Sturdevant Signs 814 723-3361
  20980 Route 6 Warren (16365) *(G-19048)*

Sturdy Built Manufacturing LLC 717 484-2233
  260 S Muddy Creek Rd Denver (17517) *(G-4095)*

Sturgis Pretzel Company, Lititz *Also called Tshudy Snacks Inc* *(G-10055)*

Stutz Candy Company (PA) 215 675-2630
  400 S Warminster Rd Hatboro (19040) *(G-7307)*

Stv Rental, Mount Pleasant *Also called Smouse Trucks & Vans Inc* *(G-11718)*

Stx Industries 412 513-6689
  245 Amboy St Pittsburgh (15224) *(G-15586)*

Style-Rite Industries, Penn *Also called A B N A Inc* *(G-13226)*

Subcon TI/Cctool Mch Group Inc 814 456-7797
  5301 Iroquois Ave Erie (16511) *(G-5494)*

Subterranean Tech Inc 610 517-0995
  109 Ashton Way West Chester (19380) *(G-19647)*

Suburban Advertiser 610 363-2815
  575 Exton Cmns Exton (19341) *(G-5734)*

Suburban Audiology Balance Ctr 610 647-3710
  11 Industrial Blvd # 102 Paoli (19301) *(G-13149)*

Suburban Deer Defense Llc 717 632-8844
  1196 Moulstown Rd N Hanover (17331) *(G-6959)*

Suburban Marble LLC 215 734-9100
  1010 Pulinski Rd Warminster (18974) *(G-18974)*

Suburban News, Hunlock Creek *Also called Country Impressions Inc* *(G-7931)*

Suburban Newspaper of America 215 513-4145
  304 Morgan Way Harleysville (19438) *(G-7060)*

Suburban Precison Mold Company 814 337-3413
  19370 Cochranton Rd Meadville (16335) *(G-10795)*

Suburban Publications,, Exton *Also called Journal Register Company* *(G-5703)*

Suburban Pump and Mch Co Inc 412 221-2823
  98 Vanadium Rd Bldg B Bridgeville (15017) *(G-2092)*

Suburban Tool & Die Co Inc 814 833-4882
  4940 Pacific Ave Erie (16506) *(G-5495)*

Suburban Water Technology Inc 610 696-1495
  300 E Evans St West Chester (19380) *(G-19648)*

Suburbia Systems-Div, Wilkes Barre *Also called Unifilt Corporation* *(G-19966)*

Subway 814 368-2576
  48 Davis St Bradford (16701) *(G-1993)*

Sucursal Espana, York *Also called El Serrano Inc* *(G-20465)*

Sue N Doug Inc 717 838-6341
  1218 E Main St Palmyra (17078) *(G-13132)*

Suez Water Tech & Solutions, Trevose *Also called Suez Wts Usa Inc* *(G-18506)*

Suez Wts Systems Usa Inc (HQ) 781 359-7000
  4636 Somerton Rd Trevose (19053) *(G-18505)*

Suez Wts Systems Usa Inc 724 743-0270
  30 Curry Ave Canonsburg (15317) *(G-2642)*

Suez Wts Usa Inc (HQ) 215 355-3300
  4636 Somerton Rd Trevose (19053) *(G-18506)*

Suffolk McHy & Pwr TI Corp 631 289-7153
  Rr 219 Box N Brockway (15824) *(G-2234)*

Sugar Creek Candles LLC 724 261-1927
  40 Carpenter Ln Irwin (15642) *(G-8202)*

Sugar Magnolia Inc 610 649-9462
  637 Loraine St Ardmore (19003) *(G-719)*

Sugar Shack 814 425-2220
  29950 Lake Creek Rd Cochranton (16314) *(G-3352)*

Sugar Valley Collar Shop Inc 570 725-3499
  18 Wagon Wheel Ln Loganton (17747) *(G-10099)*

Sugaright LLC 215 295-4709
  200 Rock Run Rd Fairless Hills (19030) *(G-5800)*

Sugartown Worldwide LLC 610 265-7607
  160 N Gulph Rd Ste 2333 King of Prussia (19406) *(G-8681)*

Sugartown Worldwide LLC (HQ) 610 878-5550
  800 3rd Ave King of Prussia (19406) *(G-8682)*

ALPHABETIC

Suit-Kote Corporation 814 337-1171
　10965 Mchenry St Meadville (16335) *(G-10796)*

Suitable, Philadelphia *Also called Meshnet Inc* *(G-14011)*

Sukup Steel Structures LLC 724 266-6484
　360 14th St Ambridge (15003) *(G-636)*

Sullis Wldg & Pipe Fitting LLC 814 445-9147
　1217 Glades Pike Somerset (15501) *(G-17713)*

Sullivan Review 570 928-8403
　101 N Main St Dushore (18614) *(G-4511)*

Sullivan's Scrap Metals, Hatboro *Also called Rhino Inc (G-7301)*

Sumitomo Shi Crygnics Amer Inc (HQ) 610 791-6700
　1833 Vultee St Allentown (18103) *(G-404)*

Summer Music Festival 570 343-7271
　224 Prospect St Dunmore (18512) *(G-4484)*

Summer Valley EMB 570 386-3711
　2704 Summer Valley Rd New Ringgold (17960) *(G-12443)*

Summerill Tube Corporation 724 887-9700
　220 Franklin St Koppel (16136) *(G-8816)*

Summerill Tube Corporation 724 887-9700
　220 Franklin St Scottdale (15683) *(G-17202)*

Summers & Zims Inc 610 593-2420
　403 Valley Ave Atglen (19310) *(G-809)*

Summers Acquisition Corp 724 652-4673
　1101 N Liberty St New Castle (16102) *(G-12156)*

Summers Construction 724 924-1700
　2196 Copper Rd New Castle (16101) *(G-12157)*

Summers Laboratories Inc 610 454-1471
　103 G P Clement Dr Collegeville (19426) *(G-3395)*

Summit Aerospace Machining, Mount Pocono *Also called Summit Aerospace USA*
Inc (G-11737)

Summit Aerospace USA Inc 570 839-8615
　137 Market Way Mount Pocono (18344) *(G-11737)*

Summit Apparel, Allentown *Also called Apex Apparel Inc (G-140)*

Summit Architectural Metals, Chambersburg *Also called Robert L Baker (G-2973)*

Summit Contracting Svcs Inc 570 943-2232
　1329 Red Dale Rd Orwigsburg (17961) *(G-13053)*

Summit Control Panels 814 431-4402
　10190 Tiger Lily Ln Waterford (16441) *(G-19270)*

Summit Forest Resources Inc 724 329-3314
　5441 National Pike Markleysburg (15459) *(G-10484)*

Summit Materials LLC 412 260-8048
　1274 Oakridge Rd Mc Donald (15057) *(G-10582)*

Summit Packaging LLC (PA) 570 622-5150
　200 Mahantongo St Pottsville (17901) *(G-16098)*

Summit Steel & Mfg Inc 610 921-1119
　1005 Patriot Pkwy Reading (19605) *(G-16528)*

Summit Storage Solutions, Reading *Also called Summit Steel & Mfg Inc (G-16528)*

Summit Trailer Sales Inc 570 754-3511
　1 Summit Plz Summit Station (17979) *(G-18161)*

Summitville Woodworking 717 355-5337
　855 S Custer Ave New Holland (17557) *(G-12287)*

Sun and Shade Inc 610 409-0366
　704 E 4th St Ste 4 Boyertown (19512) *(G-1930)*

Sun Chemical Corporation 215 223-8220
　3301 W Hunting Park Ave Philadelphia (19132) *(G-14353)*

Sun Chemical Corporation 215 223-8220
　3301 W Hunting Park Ave Philadelphia (19132) *(G-14354)*

Sun Energy Services LLC 724 473-0687
　719 W New Castle St Zelienople (16063) *(G-20820)*

Sun Energy Services LLC (PA) 724 473-0687
　307 W New Castle St Zelienople (16063) *(G-20821)*

Sun Kee Tofu Food Co 215 625-3818
　448 N 12th St Philadelphia (19123) *(G-14355)*

Sun Laboratories Inc 215 659-1111
　319 Davisville Rd Willow Grove (19090) *(G-20144)*

Sun Litho Print Inc 570 421-3250
　421 N Courtland St East Stroudsburg (18301) *(G-4636)*

Sun Microsystems, Coraopolis *Also called Oracle America Inc (G-3709)*

Sun Microsystems, Malvern *Also called Oracle America Inc (G-10290)*

Sun Microsystems, Lemoyne *Also called Oracle America Inc (G-9747)*

Sun Precast Company 570 658-8000
　4051 Ridge Rd Beaver Springs (17812) *(G-1024)*

Sun Prime Energy LLC 215 962-4196
　1100 Horizon Cir Chalfont (18914) *(G-2890)*

Sun Star Inc 724 537-5990
　4427 State Route 982 Latrobe (15650) *(G-9523)*

Sun Valley Film Wash Inc 610 497-1743
　5 Commerce Dr Aston (19014) *(G-794)*

Sun-Gazette Company 570 326-1551
　252 W 4th St Williamsport (17701) *(G-20076)*

Sun-RE Cheese Corp 570 286-1511
　178 Lenker Ave Sunbury (17801) *(G-18173)*

Sunbeam Morrisville Inc 215 736-9991
　395 W Trenton Ave Morrisville (19067) *(G-11583)*

Sunbelt Drilling Services Inc 215 764-9544
　651 E Township Line Rd # 1345 Blue Bell (19422) *(G-1853)*

Sunburst Electronics, Erie *Also called Tsrubnus Liquidation Inc (G-5520)*

Sunbury Controls Inc 570 274-7847
　1030 Walnut St Sunbury (17801) *(G-18174)*

Sunbury Press 717 254-7274
　50 W Main St Mechanicsburg (17055) *(G-10892)*

Sunday Review 570 265-2151
　116 Main St Ste 5 Towanda (18848) *(G-18434)*

Sunday Topic Korean News 215 935-1111
　7300 Old York Rd Ste 210 Elkins Park (19027) *(G-4912)*

Sunday Topic News, Elkins Park *Also called Sunday Topic Korean News (G-4912)*

Sunflower Graphics 412 369-7769
　337 Rochester Rd Pittsburgh (15237) *(G-15587)*

Sungard, Wayne *Also called Fis Avantgard LLC (G-19329)*

Sungard, Collegeville *Also called Fis Systems International LLC (G-3378)*

Sungard, Wayne *Also called Fis Sg LLC (G-19330)*

Sungard, Philadelphia *Also called Fis Sg LLC (G-13704)*

Sungard AR Financing LLC 484 582-2000
　680 E Swedesford Rd Wayne (19087) *(G-19374)*

Sungard Asset MGT Systems Inc (HQ) 610 251-6500
　200 Campus Dr Collegeville (19426) *(G-3396)*

Sungard Availability Service, Philadelphia *Also called Fis Avantgard LLC (G-13703)*

Sungard Availability Services, Wayne *Also called Sungard AR Financing LLC (G-19374)*

Sungard Capital Corp II (HQ) 484 582-2000
　680 E Swedesford Rd Wayne (19087) *(G-19375)*

Sungard Holdco LLC 484 582-2000
　680 E Swedesford Rd Wayne (19087) *(G-19376)*

Sungard Holding Corp (HQ) 888 332-2564
　680 E Swedesford Rd Wayne (19087) *(G-19377)*

Sunkee Tofu, Philadelphia *Also called Sun Kee Tofu Food Co (G-14355)*

Sunny's Music Studio, Philadelphia *Also called Paeonia Arts & Literature LLC (G-14114)*

Sunnyburn Welding 717 862-3878
　32 W Telegraph Rd Airville (17302) *(G-32)*

Sunnys Fashions 724 527-1800
　410 Clay Ave Jeannette (15644) *(G-8266)*

Sunnys Sweeping Service Inc 570 785-5564
　948 Creek Dr Prompton (18456) *(G-16110)*

Sunnyside Supply Inc 724 947-9966
　1830 Route 18 Slovan (15078) *(G-17630)*

Sunnyway Food Market, Greencastle *Also called Sunnyway Foods Inc (G-6637)*

Sunnyway Foods 2, Chambersburg *Also called Sunnyway Foods Inc (G-2980)*

Sunnyway Foods Inc (PA) 717 597-7121
　212 N Antrim Way Greencastle (17225) *(G-6637)*

Sunnyway Foods Inc 717 264-6001
　49 Warm Spring Rd Chambersburg (17202) *(G-2980)*

Sunoco, Blairsville *Also called Black Lick Stake Plant (G-1716)*

Sunoco Inc (HQ) 215 977-3000
　3801 West Chester Pike Newtown Square (19073) *(G-12591)*

Sunoco Inc 717 564-1440
　80 S 40th St Harrisburg (17111) *(G-7222)*

Sunoco Inc (R&m) 610 859-1000
　Cavern 5 Hewes Post Rd Marcus Hook (19061) *(G-10455)*

Sunoco (R&m) LLC (HQ) 215 977-3000
　3801 West Chester Pike Newtown Square (19073) *(G-12592)*

Sunoco (R&m) LLC 215 339-2000
　3144 W Passyunk Ave Philadelphia (19145) *(G-14356)*

Sunoco, Inc. R&M, Newtown Square *Also called Sunoco (R&m) LLC (G-12592)*

Sunquest Metal Rollforming, Friedens *Also called Michael Z Gehman (G-6221)*

Sunrise Designs, Philadelphia *Also called Musumeci Santo (G-14045)*

Sunrise Maple 814 628-3110
　5695 Route 349 Westfield (16950) *(G-19781)*

Sunrise Mulch, Malvern *Also called B V Landscape Supplies Inc (G-10191)*

Sunrise Naturals LLC 717 350-6169
　420 Weaver Rd Millersburg (17061) *(G-11201)*

Sunrise Publishing & Distrg 724 946-9057
　7500 Seneca Rd Sharpsville (16150) *(G-17476)*

Sunrise Technologies, Warminster *Also called N B Garber Inc (G-18927)*

Suns Manufacturing Inc (PA) 610 837-0798
　8318 Airport Rd Bath (18014) *(G-971)*

Sunsational Signs Win Tinting 610 277-4344
　234 W Johnson Hwy Norristown (19401) *(G-12715)*

Sunset Creations 717 768-7663
　203 Churchtown Rd Narvon (17555) *(G-11928)*

Sunset Ice Cream 570 326-3902
　1849 Lycoming Creek Rd Williamsport (17701) *(G-20077)*

Sunset Tees 717 737-9919
　2236 Gettysburg Rd Ste 2 Camp Hill (17011) *(G-2519)*

Sunset Valley Structures 570 758-2840
　1936 Mahantongo Creek Rd Dalmatia (17017) *(G-3986)*

Sunshine Biologies Inc 484 494-0818
　501 Elmwood Ave Sharon Hill (19079) *(G-17463)*

Sunshine Plastics Inc. 215 943-8888
　100 Main St Unit 2 Bristol (19007) *(G-2202)*

Sunshine Polishing Systems 610 828-6197
　379 New Dehaven St Conshohocken (19428) *(G-3609)*

Sunshine Screen Print 610 678-9034
　2411 Lasalle Dr Reading (19609) *(G-16529)*

Sunsweet Growers Inc 610 944-1005
　105 S Buttonwood St Fleetwood (19522) *(G-5980)*

Suntuf 2000 Inc 610 285-6968
　9735 Commerce Cir Kutztown (19530) *(G-8862)*

Sunworks Etc LLC 717 473-3743
2612 Brandt Rd Annville (17003) *(G-659)*

Super Can Industries Inc (PA) 215 945-1075
6913 Bristol Pike Levittown (19057) *(G-9866)*

Super Sonic Air Knife, Allison Park Also called Easy Use Air Tools Inc *(G-450)*

Superbolt Inc 412 279-1149
1000 Gregg St Carnegie (15106) *(G-2795)*

Supercleanscom Inc 412 429-1640
969 Bell Ave Carnegie (15106) *(G-2796)*

Superfit Inc 215 391-4380
211 N 13th St Fl 9 Philadelphia (19107) *(G-14357)*

Superior Applchian Ppeline LLC 724 746-6744
4000 Town Center Blvd # 202 Canonsburg (15317) *(G-2643)*

Superior Autoglass LLC 724 452-9870
22056 Perry Hwy Zelienople (16063) *(G-20822)*

Superior Bronze Corporation 814 452-3474
1901 Poplar St Erie (16502) *(G-5496)*

Superior Cabinet Co 724 569-9581
701 Old Frame Rd Smithfield (15478) *(G-17655)*

Superior Cabinet Company 215 536-5228
2075 Baumans Rd Quakertown (18951) *(G-16247)*

Superior Coal Prep Coop LLC 570 682-3246
184 Schwenks Rd Hegins (17938) *(G-7545)*

Superior Custom Designs Inc 412 744-0110
Allegheny Ave Bldg 42 Glassport (15045) *(G-6416)*

Superior Dual Laminates Inc 610 965-9061
750 Broad St Emmaus (18049) *(G-5043)*

Superior Energy Resources LLC 814 265-1080
2691 Route 219 Brockway (15824) *(G-2235)*

Superior Energy Resources LLC (HQ) 814 265-1080
2691 Route 219 Brockway (15824) *(G-2236)*

Superior Flrcvgs Kitchens LLC 717 264-9096
254 E King St Chambersburg (17201) *(G-2981)*

Superior Forge & Steel Corp 412 431-8250
1207 Muriel St Pittsburgh (15203) *(G-15588)*

Superior Fundations of Rockies, Glassport Also called Superior Walls of Colorado *(G-6417)*

Superior Group Inc (PA) 610 397-2040
100 Front St Ste 525 Conshohocken (19428) *(G-3610)*

Superior Hose & Fittings, Brockway Also called Superior Energy Resources LLC *(G-2235)*

Superior Hose & Fittings, Brockway Also called Superior Energy Resources LLC *(G-2236)*

Superior Lumber Inc 814 684-3420
2432 Ridge Rd Tyrone (16686) *(G-18594)*

Superior Machining Inc 814 372-2270
317 Aspen Way Du Bois (15801) *(G-4423)*

Superior Metal Products Co 610 326-0607
116 Berks St Pottstown (19464) *(G-16052)*

Superior Metalworks Inc 717 245-2446
1779 W Trindle Rd Ste B Carlisle (17015) *(G-2740)*

Superior Packaging Inc (PA) 570 824-3577
19 Bailey St Plains (18705) *(G-15789)*

Superior Pallet LLC 717 789-9525
1616 Valentine Rd Ickesburg (17037) *(G-8053)*

Superior Pasta Company Inc 215 627-3306
905 Christian St Fl 1 Philadelphia (19147) *(G-14358)*

Superior Plastic Products Inc (PA) 717 355-7100
260 Jalyn Dr New Holland (17557) *(G-12288)*

Superior Plastic Products LLC 717 556-3240
33 Hess Rd Leola (17540) *(G-9806)*

Superior Powder Coating Inc 412 221-8250
785 Millers Run Rd Mc Donald (15057) *(G-10583)*

Superior Printing & Engraving 610 352-1966
6425 Market St Upper Darby (19082) *(G-18692)*

Superior Quartz Products Inc 610 317-3450
2701 Baglyos Cir Bethlehem (18020) *(G-1634)*

Superior Respiratory Home Care 717 560-7806
1505 Rohrerstown Rd Lancaster (17601) *(G-9209)*

Superior Sign, Elizabethtown Also called Burkhart & Quinn Sign Co Inc *(G-4867)*

Superior Surgical Ltd Lblty Co 877 669-7646
321 Jones Blvd Ste 112 Pottstown (19464) *(G-16053)*

Superior Tech Inc 717 569-3359
266 Tobacco Rd Ephrata (17522) *(G-5150)*

Superior Tire & Rubber Corp (PA) 814 723-2370
40 Scientific Rd Warren (16365) *(G-19049)*

Superior Tire & Rubber Corp 814 723-2370
1818 Pennsylvania Ave W Warren (16365) *(G-19050)*

Superior Tool and Die Co 215 638-1904
3170 Tucker Rd Bensalem (19020) *(G-1257)*

Superior Tooling Tech Inc 814 486-9498
12027 Route 120 Emporium (15834) *(G-5076)*

Superior Transparent Noise 610 715-1969
220 Golfview Rd Ardmore (19003) *(G-720)*

Superior Trophy & Engraving Co 570 343-4087
965 Providence Rd Scranton (18508) *(G-17295)*

Superior Trusses LLC 717 721-2411
465 N Reading Rd Ephrata (17522) *(G-5151)*

Superior Value Beverage Center, Phoenixville Also called Superior Value Beverage Co *(G-14581)*

Superior Value Beverage Co 610 935-3111
701 Wheatland St Phoenixville (19460) *(G-14581)*

Superior Walls of Colorado 412 664-7788
25 Allegheny Sq Glassport (15045) *(G-6417)*

Superior Welding Co 570 344-4212
870 Providence Rd Scranton (18508) *(G-17296)*

Superior Window Mfg Inc 412 793-3500
7903 Saltsburg Rd Pittsburgh (15239) *(G-15589)*

Superior Woodcraft Inc 215 348-9942
160 N Hamilton St Doylestown (18901) *(G-4340)*

Supermedia LLC 814 833-2121
1600 Peninsula Dr Ste 4 Erie (16505) *(G-5497)*

Supermedia LLC 610 317-5500
252 Brodhead Rd Ste 300 Bethlehem (18017) *(G-1635)*

Supermedia LLC 717 540-6500
4000 Crums Mill Rd # 204 Harrisburg (17112) *(G-7223)*

Superpac Inc 215 322-1010
1220 Industrial Blvd Southampton (18966) *(G-17838)*

Supervisors' Barn, Sycamore Also called Morris Twnship Spervisors Barn *(G-18201)*

Suplee Envelope Co Inc 610 352-2900
1743 Ashbrooke Ave Garnet Valley (19060) *(G-6269)*

Supply Technologies LLC 724 745-8877
1200 Arch St Ste 1 Carnegie (15106) *(G-2797)*

Supplyone Holdings Company Inc (PA) 484 582-5005
11 Campus Blvd Ste 150 Newtown Square (19073) *(G-12593)*

Support McRcomputers Assoc Inc 215 496-0303
1819 John F Kennedy Blvd # 460 Philadelphia (19103) *(G-14359)*

Supra Office Solutions Inc 267 275-8888
5070 Parkside Ave # 3200 Philadelphia (19131) *(G-14360)*

Suprawater 717 528-9949
20 Seneca Dr York Springs (17372) *(G-20768)*

Supreme - DSC Dredge LLC 724 376-4368
327 Billy Boyd Rd Stoneboro (16153) *(G-18070)*

Supreme Corq LLC 610 408-0500
3811 West Chester Pike # 200 Newtown Square (19073) *(G-12594)*

Supreme Manufacturing Inc 724 376-4110
327 Billy Boyd Rd Stoneboro (16153) *(G-18071)*

Supreme Mid-Atlantic Corp (HQ) 717 865-0031
411 Jonestown Rd Jonestown (17038) *(G-8451)*

Supreme Trading Ltd 215 739-2237
431 E Tioga St Fl 3 Philadelphia (19134) *(G-14361)*

Supreme Zipper Industries 570 226-9501
1076 Purdytown Tpke Lakeville (18438) *(G-8914)*

Surco Inc 215 855-9551
271 W Broad St Hatfield (19440) *(G-7397)*

Surco Portable Sanitation Pdts, Pittsburgh Also called Surco Products Inc *(G-15590)*

Surco Products Inc 412 252-7000
292 Alpha Dr Pittsburgh (15238) *(G-15590)*

Sure Fold Co Inc 215 634-7480
600 E Erie Ave Bldg 4 Philadelphia (19134) *(G-14362)*

Sure-Lok Inc 610 814-0300
400 S Greenwood Ave 302 Easton (18045) *(G-4757)*

Sureflow Corporation 412 828-5900
3 Mcduff Industrial Park Pittsburgh (15238) *(G-15591)*

Surf & Turf Enterprises 610 338-0274
1 Kedron Ave Ste K3 Morton (19070) *(G-11593)*

Surf Chemical, Easton Also called Milner Enterprises Inc *(G-4722)*

Surface Mining Reclamation Off 717 782-4036
415 Market St Ste 3c Harrisburg (17101) *(G-7224)*

Surgeoneering LLC 412 292-2816
423 Heights Dr Gibsonia (15044) *(G-6353)*

Surgical Institute Reading LP 610 378-8800
2752 Century Blvd Reading (19610) *(G-16530)*

Surgical Laser Tech Inc 215 619-3600
147 Keystone Dr Montgomeryville (18936) *(G-11420)*

Surgical Specialties Corp 610 404-1000
1100 Berkshire Blvd # 308 Wyomissing (19610) *(G-20289)*

Surtech Industries Inc 717 767-6808
915 Borom Rd York (17404) *(G-20682)*

Surtreat Holding LLC (PA) 412 281-1202
437 Grant St Ste 1210 Pittsburgh (15219) *(G-15592)*

Susan Becker 610 378-7844
1601 N 9th St Apt 1 Reading (19604) *(G-16531)*

Susan Reabuck 610 797-7014
2848 Klein St Allentown (18103) *(G-405)*

Suscon Inc 570 326-2003
600 Railway St Unit 2 Williamsport (17701) *(G-20078)*

Susini Specialty Steels Inc 724 295-6511
Highlands Industr Park 11 Park Nds Industrial Natrona Heights (15065) *(G-11949)*

Susquehanna Capitl Acquisition (HQ) 800 942-7538
216 Wohlsen Way Lancaster (17603) *(G-9210)*

Susquehanna Fishing Mag LLC 570 441-4606
13 York Rd Bloomsburg (17815) *(G-1802)*

Susquehanna Games & Bingo Sups 570 322-9941
25 W 2nd Ave Ste 5 Williamsport (17702) *(G-20079)*

Susquehanna Glass Co 717 684-2155
731 Avenue H Columbia (17512) *(G-3451)*

Susquehanna Grdn Concepts LLC 717 826-5144
20 Breezy Park Dr Fleetwood (19522) *(G-5981)*

Susquehanna Independent Wkndr 570 278-6397
231 Church St Montrose (18801) *(G-11479)*

Susquehanna Life Magazine 570 522-0149
217 Market St Lewisburg (17837) *(G-9920)*
Susquehanna Sales, Williamsport Also called Susquehanna Games & Bingo Sups *(G-20079)*
Susquehanna Services LLC 570 288-5269
1204 Main St Swoyersville (18704) *(G-18200)*
Susquehanna Times & Magazine 717 898-9207
3 W Brandt Blvd Salunga (17538) *(G-17056)*
Susquehanna Transcript Inc 570 853-3134
36 Exchange St Susquehanna (18847) *(G-18183)*
Susquehanna Trl, Northumberland Also called Club Coin Boards Inc *(G-12866)*
Susquehanna Valley Prosthetics, Selinsgrove Also called Riverview Orthtics
Prosthetics *(G-17332)*
Susquehanna Valley Prosthetics 570 743-1414
2 Atrium Ct Ste B Selinsgrove (17870) *(G-17337)*
Susquehnna Vly Woodcrafters Inc 717 898-7564
131 W Main St Salunga (17538) *(G-17057)*
Susquhnna Wire Rope Rgging Inc 814 772-4766
112 South St Ridgway (15853) *(G-16731)*
Sussex Wire Inc (PA) 610 250-7750
4 Danforth Dr Easton (18045) *(G-4758)*
Sustrana LLC 610 651-2870
15 N Devon Blvd Ste 200 Devon (19333) *(G-4116)*
Sutherland Baskets 610 438-8233
410 S 16th St Easton (18042) *(G-4759)*
Sutherland Hardwoods, Burgettstown Also called Sutherland Lumber Co *(G-2355)*
Sutherland Lumber Co 724 947-3388
1664 Langeloth Rd Burgettstown (15021) *(G-2355)*
Sutley Tool Co 814 789-4332
25439 Plank Rd Guys Mills (16327) *(G-6813)*
Sutton Brothers, Marysville Also called Allen P Sutton *(G-10531)*
Suza Inc 817 877-0067
1970 Broad St East Petersburg (17520) *(G-4592)*
Suzannes Choclat & Confections 570 753-8545
Rr 150 Avis (17721) *(G-838)*
Suzie BS Pretzeltown Inc 814 868-8443
527 Millcreek Mall Erie (16565) *(G-5498)*
Svc Manufacturing Inc 623 907-1822
750 Oak Hill Rd Mountain Top (18707) *(G-11777)*
Svm2 Pharma Inc 717 369-4636
4495 Lincoln Way W Saint Thomas (17252) *(G-17042)*
Svonavec Inc 814 926-2815
2555 New Centerville Rd Rockwood (15557) *(G-16793)*
Svpo Inc 570 743-1414
3120 N Old Trl Shamokin Dam (17876) *(G-17428)*
Svt Inc 215 245-5055
350 Camer Dr Bensalem (19020) *(G-1258)*
SW Philadelphia Review, Philadelphia Also called Review Publishing Ltd Partnr *(G-14242)*
Swab Wagon Company 717 362-8151
44 S Callowhill St Elizabethville (17023) *(G-4898)*
Swagelok, Erie Also called Innovative Pressure Tech LLC *(G-5326)*
Swagelok Allentown, Schnecksville Also called Swagelok Company *(G-17144)*
Swagelok Company 610 799-9001
4245 Independence Dr Schnecksville (18078) *(G-17144)*
Swampy Hollow Mfg LLC 610 273-0157
16 Westbrook Dr Honey Brook (19344) *(G-7765)*
Swan Label & Tag Co, Coraopolis Also called Jon Swan Inc *(G-3700)*
Swaney Truck & Equip Co, Monroeville Also called Ben Swaney *(G-11325)*
Swanson Assembly Systems, Erie Also called Swanson-Erie Corporation *(G-5500)*
Swanson Erie, Erie Also called Swanson Systems Inc *(G-5499)*
Swanson Publishing Company Inc 724 940-2444
6600 Brooktree Rd # 1600 Wexford (15090) *(G-19830)*
Swanson Systems Inc (PA) 814 453-5841
814 E 8th St Erie (16503) *(G-5499)*
Swanson-Anaheim, Erie Also called Automation Products Inc *(G-5199)*
Swanson-Erie Corporation 814 453-5841
814 E 8th St Erie (16503) *(G-5500)*
Swarovski Botique, King of Prussia Also called Swarovski US Holding Limited *(G-8683)*
Swarovski North America Ltd 412 833-3708
301 S Hills Vlg Spc 1045a Pittsburgh (15241) *(G-15593)*
Swarovski North America Ltd 215 752-3198
2300 E Lincoln Hwy Langhorne (19047) *(G-9327)*
Swarovski Retail Ventures Ltd 215 659-3649
2500 W Moreland Rd Willow Grove (19090) *(G-20145)*
Swarovski US Holding Limited 610 992-9661
160 N Gulph Rd King of Prussia (19406) *(G-8683)*
Swartfager Welding Inc 814 797-0394
199 Boyle Memorial Dr Knox (16232) *(G-8811)*
Swedenborg Foundation Inc 610 430-3222
320 N Church St West Chester (19380) *(G-19649)*
Sweeper City Inc 724 283-0859
156 Point Plz Butler (16001) *(G-2445)*
Sweet Jubilee Gourmet 717 691-9782
275 Mulberry Dr Mechanicsburg (17050) *(G-10893)*
Sweet Roll Studio Llc 209 559-8219
504 N 39th St Unit 1 Philadelphia (19104) *(G-14363)*
Sweet Salvation Truffle 610 220-4157
10 Coopertown Rd Haverford (19041) *(G-7415)*

Sweet Sanctions 717 222-1859
323 Bricker Ln Lebanon (17042) *(G-9635)*
Sweet Tammy's Bakery, Pittsburgh Also called Tsb Group LLC *(G-15659)*
Sweet Water Woodworks LLC 610 273-1270
6430 Emery Rd Narvon (17555) *(G-11929)*
Sweetdreams Brusters LLC 717 261-1484
500 Gateway Ave Chambersburg (17201) *(G-2982)*
Sweethearts Bridal Formalwear 610 750-5087
4631 Penn Ave Ste 2 Reading (19608) *(G-16532)*
Sweetwater 100, Chester Springs Also called Sweetwater Natural Pdts LLC *(G-3086)*
Sweetwater Natural Pdts LLC (PA) 610 321-1900
976 Pottstown Pike Chester Springs (19425) *(G-3086)*
Sweetzels Foods LLC 610 278-8700
1166 Dekalb Pike Blue Bell (19422) *(G-1854)*
Swf Industrial, Wrightsville Also called Stewart Welding & Fabg Inc *(G-20244)*
Swick Ornamental Iron 412 487-5755
4785 Josephine Dr Gibsonia (15044) *(G-6354)*
Swimtech Distributing Inc 570 595-7680
191 Rr 390 Cresco (18326) *(G-3895)*
Swing Kingdom LLC 717 656-4449
36 Glenbrook Rd Leola (17540) *(G-9807)*
Swirling Silks Inc 610 584-5595
310 Broad St Ste H Harleysville (19438) *(G-7061)*
Swisher Concrete Products Inc 814 765-9502
9428 Clearfield Cwnvl Hwy Clearfield (16830) *(G-3231)*
Swisher Contracting Inc 814 765-6006
Mt Joy Rd Clearfield (16830) *(G-3232)*
Swiss Chocolatier , The, Oxford Also called Confiseurs Inc *(G-13076)*
Swiss Premium Dairy, Lebanon Also called Dean Foods Company *(G-9560)*
Swissaero Inc 814 796-4166
802 Walnut St Waterford (16441) *(G-19271)*
Swope & Bartholomew Inc 610 264-2672
925 Front St Whitehall (18052) *(G-19890)*
Sws Vidmarlista, Allentown Also called Black & Decker (us) Inc *(G-154)*
Sy-Con Systems Inc 610 253-0900
1700 Northampton St Ste 6 Easton (18042) *(G-4760)*
Sy-Con Technology, Easton Also called Sy-Con Systems Inc *(G-4760)*
Sycamore Partners MGT LP 724 748-0052
1911 Leesburg Grove Cy Rd Grove City (16127) *(G-6805)*
Sykes-Scholtz-Collins Lbr Inc 610 494-2700
3130 W 4th St Chester (19013) *(G-3066)*
Sylish, Newtown Also called Modzori LLC *(G-12522)*
Sylray Manufacturing LLC 570 640-0689
639 E Allen St Allentown (18109) *(G-406)*
Sylvan, Kittanning Also called Snyder Assod Companies Inc *(G-8793)*
Sylvan Bio Inc 724 543-3900
90 Glade Dr Kittanning (16201) *(G-8798)*
Sylvan Bioproducts, Inc., Kittanning Also called Sylvan Bio Inc *(G-8798)*
Sylvan Corporation 724 864-9350
612 Cedar St Irwin (15642) *(G-8203)*
Sylvan Fiberoptics, Irwin Also called Sylvan Corporation *(G-8203)*
Symbol Mattress, Reading Also called Eastern Sleep Products Company *(G-16369)*
Symbol Technologies LLC 610 834-8900
450 Plymouth Rd Ste 202 Plymouth Meeting (19462) *(G-15875)*
Symmco Inc 814 894-2461
40 S Park St Sykesville (15865) *(G-18203)*
Symmco Group Inc (PA) 814 894-2461
40 S Park St Sykesville (15865) *(G-18204)*
Symphony Brewing Systems LLC 215 493-0430
173 N Main St Yardley (19067) *(G-20342)*
SYN Apparel LLC (PA) 484 821-3664
18 W 3rd St Bethlehem (18015) *(G-1636)*
Synatek LP 888 408-5433
737 Hagey Center Dr A Souderton (18964) *(G-17767)*
Synchrgnix Info Strategies Inc 302 892-4800
5 Great Valley Pkwy # 359 Malvern (19355) *(G-10325)*
Synchrony Medical LLC 484 947-5003
2 W Market St Fl 5 Flr 5 Kennett Square (19348) *(G-8547)*
Syncom Specialty Inc (PA) 215 322-9708
16 Arbor Rd Southampton (18966) *(G-17839)*
Syncom Specialty Inc 215 322-9708
110 Pike Cir Huntingdon Valley (19006) *(G-8042)*
Synergistic Systems Inc 814 796-4217
2800 White Oak Dr Waterford (16441) *(G-19272)*
Synergy Applications Inc 814 454-8803
1341 W 12th St Erie (16501) *(G-5501)*
Synergy Business Forms Inc 814 833-3344
3802 W Lake Rd Erie (16505) *(G-5502)*
Synergy Contracting Svcs LLC 724 349-0855
1380 Route 286 Hwy E # 221 Indiana (15701) *(G-8132)*
Synergy Core Elements 267 885-5832
560 Union Square Dr New Hope (18938) *(G-12316)*
Synergy Electrical Sales Inc 215 428-1130
95 Canal Rd Fairless Hills (19030) *(G-5801)*
Synergy Health Systems Inc 570 473-7506
173 Pint Twnship Dr Ste 2 Northumberland (17857) *(G-12877)*
Synergy Industries LLC 215 699-4045
407 Elm Ave North Wales (19454) *(G-12829)*

Synergy Metal Solutions Inc 215 699-7060
407 Elm Ave 120 North Wales (19454) *(G-12830)*

Synergy Print Design, Prospect Park *Also called R&S Ventures LLC (G-16118)*

Synergy Print Design LLC 610 532-2950
1015 Lincoln Ave Prospect Park (19076) *(G-16121)*

Synthes Inc (HQ) 610 647-9700
1302 Wrights Ln E West Chester (19380) *(G-19650)*

Synthes Spine Inc 610 695-2424
1380 Enterprise Dr West Chester (19380) *(G-19651)*

Synthes Technical Center, West Chester *Also called Depuy Synthes Sales Inc (G-19541)*

Synthes Usa LLC (HQ) 610 719-5000
1302 Wrights Ln E West Chester (19380) *(G-19652)*

Synthes USA Products LLC 610 719-5000
1302 Wrights Ln E West Chester (19380) *(G-19653)*

Synthex Organics LLC 814 941-8375
4601 Cortland Ave Altoona (16601) *(G-550)*

Synygy, Chester *Also called Spm Global Services Inc (G-3065)*

Systematic Filing Products, Danville *Also called Tele-Media Sfp LLC (G-4014)*

Systematics Inc 610 696-9040
1025 Saunders Ln West Chester (19380) *(G-19654)*

Szoke Iron Works Inc 610 760-9565
1115 Riverview Dr Walnutport (18088) *(G-18794)*

T & B Logging Inc 570 561-4847
530 E Avery Station Rd Tunkhannock (18657) *(G-18549)*

T & J Bowling Products Corp 717 428-0100
250 N Main St Jacobus (17407) *(G-8231)*

T & L Pierogie Incorporated 570 454-3198
127 W Chestnut St Hazleton (18201) *(G-7528)*

T & L Welding 724 354-3538
162 Farster Rd Kittanning (16201) *(G-8799)*

T & N Excavating LLC 717 801-5525
1365 Valley Rd Etters (17319) *(G-5553)*

T & P Bagels Inc 610 867-8695
2910 Easton Ave Unit 10 Bethlehem (18017) *(G-1637)*

T & T Machine & Welding Co 814 845-9054
26529 Route 286 Hwy E Glen Campbell (15742) *(G-6425)*

T & T Prtg T & Symbol T Printi 724 938-9495
1875 Main St Allenport (15412) *(G-105)*

T & W Traffic Control, Lancaster *Also called Superior Respiratory Home Care (G-9209)*

T A E Ltd 215 925-7860
233 Church St Philadelphia (19106) *(G-14364)*

T B W Industries Inc 215 794-8070
2389 Forest Grove Rd Furlong (18925) *(G-6234)*

T Baird McIlvain Company 717 630-0025
370 Poplar St Hanover (17331) *(G-6960)*

T Bruce Campbell Cnstr Co Inc 724 528-9944
3658 New Castle Rd West Middlesex (16159) *(G-19730)*

T Bruce Sales Inc (PA) 724 528-9961
9 Carbaugh St West Middlesex (16159) *(G-19731)*

T C B Displays Inc (PA) 610 983-0500
200 Lincoln Ave Ste 200 # 200 Phoenixville (19460) *(G-14582)*

T C Redi Mix Youngstown Inc 724 652-7878
203 W Washington St New Castle (16101) *(G-12158)*

T C Redi-Mix, New Castle *Also called T C Redi Mix Youngstown Inc (G-12158)*

T C S Industries Inc 717 657-7032
4326 Crestview Rd Harrisburg (17112) *(G-7225)*

T C Specialties Company, Coudersport *Also called Northern Hardwoods Inc (G-3786)*

T D Landis Air Flow Design 215 679-4395
3232 Hillegass Rd Pennsburg (18073) *(G-13257)*

T E Fletcher Snowmobiles 724 253-3225
10492 Mohawk Rd Conneaut Lake (16316) *(G-3480)*

T E S I, Norristown *Also called Tech Equipment Sales Inc (G-12716)*

T Foster & Co Inc 215 493-1044
7 W Afton Ave Yardley (19067) *(G-20343)*

T G Faust Inc 610 375-8549
544 Minor St Reading (19602) *(G-16533)*

T Gear, Allentown *Also called Anthony Hauze (G-137)*

T H E M Services Inc 610 559-9341
647 Garr Rd Easton (18040) *(G-4761)*

T Helbling LLC 724 601-9819
119 Highlandwood Dr Beaver (15009) *(G-992)*

T J Corporation 724 929-7300
723 E Railroad Ave Verona (15147) *(G-18763)*

T K Plastics Inc 724 443-6760
4390 Gibsonia Rd Ste 1 Gibsonia (15044) *(G-6355)*

T L King Cabinetmaker 610 869-4220
155 Hood Rd Cochranville (19330) *(G-3356)*

T M Fitzgerald & Assoc Inc (PA) 610 853-2008
850 W Chester Pike # 303 Havertown (19083) *(G-7429)*

T M P Refining Corporation 484 318-8285
23 Long Ln Malvern (19355) *(G-10326)*

T N T Manufacturing 724 745-6242
1 Caley Dr Canonsburg (15317) *(G-2644)*

T P Schwartz Inc 724 266-7045
7038 Front River Rd Pittsburgh (15225) *(G-15594)*

T R, New Eagle *Also called Therm-O-Rock East Inc (G-12193)*

T S Beh Trucking Services 267 918-0493
230 Buckley St Bristol (19007) *(G-2203)*

T S K Partners Inc (PA) 814 459-4495
1533 E 12th St Erie (16511) *(G-5503)*

T Shirt Loft 724 452-4380
420 S Main St Zelienople (16063) *(G-20823)*

T Shirt Printer 717 367-1167
251 Poplar Ln Elizabethtown (17022) *(G-4889)*

T T M Contacts Corporation 215 497-1078
7 Garrison Pl Newtown (18940) *(G-12554)*

T&G Logging 814 589-1731
Rr 1 Grand Valley (16420) *(G-6573)*

T&T Buttas LLC 833 251-1357
6616 N 20th St Philadelphia (19138) *(G-14365)*

T-3, Burgettstown *Also called National Oilwell Varco Inc (G-2352)*

T-Bird McHning Fabrication LLC 717 384-8362
710 Willow Springs Ln York (17406) *(G-20683)*

T-M-T Gravel and Contg Inc 570 537-2647
8792 Route 549 Millerton (16936) *(G-11216)*

T-R Associates Inc 570 876-4067
1 Export Ln Archbald (18403) *(G-696)*

T-TEC, Quakertown *Also called Thermocouple Technology LLC (G-16252)*

T-Town Sheds & Supply 570 836-5686
100 Dymond Ter Tunkhannock (18657) *(G-18550)*

T.F.campbell Co., Pittsburgh *Also called Precision Technology Assoc Inc (G-15433)*

T/A Reborn Pallets 484 841-3085
428 Grouse Dr Bath (18014) *(G-972)*

Taba Labels Company 215 455-9977
210 W Mentor St Philadelphia (19120) *(G-14366)*

Tabacos USA Inc 610 438-2005
4500 William Penn Hwy Easton (18045) *(G-4762)*

Tactical Technologies Inc 610 522-0106
500 Pine St Ste 3a Holmes (19043) *(G-7665)*

Tactile Design Group LLC 215 732-2311
109 S 13th St Ste 3n Philadelphia (19107) *(G-14367)*

Tactile Group, The, Philadelphia *Also called Tactile Design Group LLC (G-14367)*

Tadford, Harrisburg *Also called Supermedia LLC (G-7223)*

Tafisco Inc 215 493-3167
7932 State Rd Philadelphia (19136) *(G-14368)*

Taggart Printing Corporation 610 431-2500
323 S Matlack St West Chester (19382) *(G-19655)*

Tagline Inc 610 594-9300
253 Welsh Pool Rd Exton (19341) *(G-5735)*

Tags Processing 724 345-8279
320 Lynn Portal Rd Washington (15301) *(G-19230)*

Taif Inc 610 534-0669
20 E Sellers Ave Ridley Park (19078) *(G-16742)*

Taif Inc (PA) 610 522-0122
600 Kaiser Dr Ste A Folcroft (19032) *(G-6017)*

Tailgate Master Truck Steps, Moon Township *Also called Significant Developments LLC (G-11500)*

Tait Towers Inc 717 626-9571
9 Wynfield Dr Lititz (17543) *(G-10051)*

Tait Towers Manufacturing LLC 717 626-9571
401 W Lincoln Ave Lititz (17543) *(G-10052)*

Take Away Refuse 717 490-9258
810 Pinetree Way Lancaster (17601) *(G-9211)*

Take Six 814 237-4350
100 W College Ave State College (16801) *(G-18035)*

Takraf Usa Inc 215 822-4485
2750 Morris Rd Ste A120 Lansdale (19446) *(G-9413)*

Taktl LLC 412 486-1600
503 Braddock Ave Turtle Creek (15145) *(G-18569)*

Tal Technologies Inc 215 496-0222
2101 Brandywine St # 102 Philadelphia (19130) *(G-14369)*

Talaris Inc 215 674-2882
417 Caredean Dr Horsham (19044) *(G-7855)*

Talbar Inc 814 337-8400
10991 Liberty St Meadville (16335) *(G-10797)*

Talbot, Millersburg *Also called Dauphin Precision Tool LLC (G-11192)*

Talbot Holdings LLC 717 692-2113
200 Front St Millersburg (17061) *(G-11202)*

Talexmedical LLC 888 327-2221
5 Great Valley Pkwy # 210 Malvern (19355) *(G-10327)*

Talk Express 412 977-1786
1503 Donnelville Rd Natrona Heights (15065) *(G-11950)*

Talkin Stick Game Calls Inc 724 758-3869
1285 Fairlane Dr Ellwood City (16117) *(G-4953)*

Talking Phone Book, Erie *Also called Localedge Media Inc (G-5369)*

Tall Oak Energy Inc 724 636-0621
317 W Tall Oak Ln Boyers (16020) *(G-1891)*

Tall Pines Distillery LLC 814 442-2245
9224 Mason Dixon Hwy Salisbury (15558) *(G-17046)*

Tallman Supply Company 717 647-2123
114 E Church St Tower City (17980) *(G-18442)*

Taltech, Philadelphia *Also called Tal Technologies Inc (G-14369)*

Tama Mfg Co Inc (PA) 610 231-3100
100 Cascade Dr A Allentown (18109) *(G-407)*

Tamaqua Truck & Trailer Inc 570 386-5994
794 W Penn Pike Tamaqua (18252) *(G-18229)*

Tamarack Packaging Ltd 814 724-2860
    11124 Mercer Pike Meadville (16335) *(G-10798)*
Tamco Inc 724 258-6622
    1466 Delberts Dr Monongahela (15063) *(G-11317)*
Tamini Transformers USA LLC 412 534-4275
    518 Broad St Ste 1 Sewickley (15143) *(G-17414)*
Tamis Corporation 412 241-7161
    10700 Frankstown Rd # 105 Pittsburgh (15235) *(G-15595)*
Tammy M Tibbens 717 979-3063
    6103 Blue Grass Ave Apt B Harrisburg (17112) *(G-7226)*
Tammy Williams 814 654-7127
    10509 Mohawk Rd Conneaut Lake (16316) *(G-3481)*
Tan Clothing Co Inc 215 625-2536
    1017 Race St Ste 3 Philadelphia (19107) *(G-14370)*
Tancredi Machining Inc 215 679-8985
    20 N Front St Ste 9 Bally (19503) *(G-907)*
Tandemheart, Pittsburgh Also called Cardiacassist Inc *(G-14808)*
Tangent Rail Corporation (HQ) 412 325-0202
    603 Stanwix St Ste 1000 Pittsburgh (15222) *(G-15596)*
Tangent Rail Products Inc (HQ) 412 325-0202
    101 W Station Square Dr # 600 Pittsburgh (15219) *(G-15597)*
Tangled Manes 717 581-0600
    5313 Main St East Petersburg (17520) *(G-4593)*
Tank Heads, Langhorne Also called Bristol Tank & Welding Co Inc *(G-9282)*
Tapco Tube Company 814 336-2201
    10748 S Water Street Ext Meadville (16335) *(G-10799)*
Tapestration 215 536-0977
    1395 Doylestown Pike Quakertown (18951) *(G-16248)*
Tapeworks, Bethlehem Also called Cortape Ne Inc *(G-1488)*
TApp Technology LLC 800 288-3184
    120-124 E Lancaster Ave Ardmore (19003) *(G-721)*
Tapptek, Ardmore Also called TApp Technology LLC *(G-721)*
Tar Hunt Custom Rifles Inc 570 784-6368
    101 Dogtown Rd Bloomsburg (17815) *(G-1803)*
Taraco Sportswear Inc 570 669-9004
    258 W Columbus Ave Nesquehoning (18240) *(G-12009)*
Tarco Inc 717 597-1876
    8650 Molly Pitcher Hwy Greencastle (17225) *(G-6638)*
Tarco Roofing Materials, Greencastle Also called Tarco Inc *(G-6638)*
Targa Energy LP (HQ) 412 489-0006
    1000 Commerce Dr Ste 400 Pittsburgh (15275) *(G-15598)*
Targa Pipeline Oper Partnr LP (HQ) 412 489-0006
    1845 Walnut St Philadelphia (19103) *(G-14371)*
Targa Pipeline Partners GP LLC 215 546-5005
    1845 Walnut St Ste 1000 Philadelphia (19103) *(G-14372)*
Target Drilling Inc 724 633-3927
    1112 Glacier Rd Smithton (15479) *(G-17663)*
Target Industrial Products 412 486-2627
    969 William Flynn Hwy Glenshaw (15116) *(G-6501)*
Target Precision 814 382-3000
    10314 Harmonsburg Rd Harmonsburg (16422) *(G-7065)*
Target Tool Inc 717 949-2407
    450 W Main St Schaefferstown (17088) *(G-17131)*
Targeted Pet Treats LLC 814 406-7351
    151 Struthers St Warren (16365) *(G-19051)*
Tarod Roll Forming Div, West Chester Also called Kimjohn Industries Inc *(G-19582)*
Tarp America Inc 724 339-4771
    588 State Route 380 Murrysville (15668) *(G-11869)*
Tarpon Energy Services LLC 570 547-0442
    1901 Mayview Rd Ste 10 Bridgeville (15017) *(G-2093)*
Tarr's Ready Mix Concrete, Washington Also called Tarrs Concrete & Supplies *(G-19231)*
Tarrs Concrete & Supplies 724 438-4114
    45 Arden Rd Washington (15301) *(G-19231)*
Tarsa Therapeutics Inc 267 273-7940
    8 Penn Ctr 1628 John F Philadelphia (19103) *(G-14373)*
Tartan News, The, Pittsburgh Also called Carnegie Mellon University *(G-14818)*
Tasman Pharma Inc 267 317-2010
    1035 Louis Dr Warminster (18974) *(G-18975)*
Tasseron Sensors Inc 570 601-1971
    140 Choate Cir Montoursville (17754) *(G-11451)*
Taste of Puebla 484 467-8597
    201 Birch St Kennett Square (19348) *(G-8548)*
Tastepoint By Iff, Philadelphia Also called David Michael & Co Inc *(G-13607)*
Tasty Baking Company (HQ) 215 221-8500
    4300 S 26th St Philadelphia (19112) *(G-14374)*
Tasty Baking Company 717 295-2530
    1127 Elizabeth Ave Lancaster (17601) *(G-9212)*
Tasty Baking Company 717 651-0307
    493 Blue Eagle Ave Harrisburg (17112) *(G-7227)*
Tasty Baking Company 570 961-8211
    120 Monahan Ave Ste 3 Dunmore (18512) *(G-4485)*
Tasty Baking Company 215 221-8500
    4300 S 26th St Philadelphia (19112) *(G-14375)*
Tasty Fries Inc 610 941-2109
    650 Sentry Pkwy Ste 1 Blue Bell (19422) *(G-1855)*
Tasty Kake, Philadelphia Also called Tasty Baking Company *(G-14374)*
Tasty Twisters Inc 215 487-7828
    5002 Umbria St Philadelphia (19128) *(G-14376)*
Tastykake, Dunmore Also called Tasty Baking Company *(G-4485)*

Tastykake Lancaster Dist Ctr, Lancaster Also called Tasty Baking Company *(G-9212)*
Tastysnack Quality Foods Inc 717 259-6961
    105 Sutton Rd Abbottstown (17301) *(G-7)*
Tata America Intl Corp 717 737-4737
    50 Utley Dr Ste 100 Camp Hill (17011) *(G-2520)*
Tatano Wire and Steel Inc (PA) 724 746-3118
    2 Iron St Canonsburg (15317) *(G-2645)*
Tatano Wire and Steel Inc 724 746-3118
    224 Jackson St Houston (15342) *(G-7880)*
Tate Access Floors Inc 717 244-4071
    52 Spring Bale Rd Red Lion (17356) *(G-16616)*
Tate Access Floors Inc 717 244-4071
    52 Springvale Rd Red Lion (17356) *(G-16617)*
Tate Jones Inc 412 771-4200
    2069 New Castle Rd Portersville (16051) *(G-15937)*
Tate Lyle Ingrdnts Amricas LLC 215 295-5011
    E Post Rd Morrisville (19067) *(G-11584)*
Taty Bug Inc 814 856-3323
    8631 Route 28 Mayport (16240) *(G-10547)*
Taurus Holdings, East Brady Also called Dr G H Michel Restor-Skin Co *(G-4529)*
Tavo Packaging Inc 215 428-0900
    2 Canal Rd Fairless Hills (19030) *(G-5802)*
Taylor & Francis Group LLC 215 625-8900
    530 Walnut St Ste 850 Philadelphia (19106) *(G-14377)*
Taylor & Francis Inc (HQ) 215 625-8900
    530 Walnut St Ste 850 Philadelphia (19106) *(G-14378)*
Taylor Chemical Inc 570 562-7771
    10 Stauffer Industrial Pa Taylor (18517) *(G-18262)*
Taylor Communications Inc 610 688-9090
    440 E Swedesford Rd # 3045 Wayne (19087) *(G-19378)*
Taylor Communications Inc 412 594-2800
    209 9th St Ste 700 Pittsburgh (15222) *(G-15599)*
Taylor Communications Inc 717 755-1051
    121 Mount Zion Rd York (17402) *(G-20684)*
Taylor Logging 814 642-2788
    36 E Vine St Port Allegany (16743) *(G-15895)*
Taylor Made Smiles 724 212-3167
    2300 Freeport Rd Ste 1b New Kensington (15068) *(G-12381)*
Taylor Run 610 436-1369
    795 Downingtown Pike West Chester (19380) *(G-19656)*
Taylor Tool Inc 814 967-4642
    29914 State Highway 408 Townville (16360) *(G-18448)*
Taylor-Backes Inc 610 367-4600
    0 2nd And Washington St Boyertown (19512) *(G-1931)*
Taylor-Wharton Intl LLC 717 763-5060
    4718 Old Gettysburg Rd # 300 Mechanicsburg (17055) *(G-10894)*
Taylored Building Solutions 570 898-5361
    9 Stauffer Industrial Par Taylor (18517) *(G-18263)*
Taylormaid Custom Cabinetry 717 865-6598
    87 Crooked Rd Annville (17003) *(G-660)*
Tb Woods Incorporated (HQ) 717 264-7161
    440 5th Ave Chambersburg (17201) *(G-2983)*
Tbj Incorporated 717 261-9700
    1671 Orchard Dr Chambersburg (17201) *(G-2984)*
TBM Hardwoods, Hanover Also called T Baird McIlvain Company *(G-6960)*
TC Millwork Inc 215 245-4210
    3433 Marshall Ln Bensalem (19020) *(G-1259)*
Tcc Pennwest LLC 724 867-0047
    4 Penn West Way Emlenton (16373) *(G-5015)*
Tcg Document Solutions LLC (PA) 215 957-0600
    447 Veit Rd Huntingdon Valley (19006) *(G-8043)*
Tcg Document Solutions LLC 610 356-4700
    16 Industrial Blvd Paoli (19301) *(G-13150)*
Tcp Printing Company, Pittsburgh Also called TP (old) LLC *(G-15634)*
Tcw Technologies LLC 610 928-3420
    2955 Main Rd E Emmaus (18049) *(G-5044)*
Td & Company 610 637-6100
    780 Ranck Rd Morgantown (19543) *(G-11538)*
Td's, Smithton Also called Target Drilling Inc *(G-17663)*
Tdc Manufacturing Inc 570 385-0731
    155 Route 61 S Schuylkill Haven (17972) *(G-17167)*
Tdy Industries LLC (HQ) 412 394-2896
    1000 Six Ppg Pl Pittsburgh (15222) *(G-15600)*
Te Connectivity Corporation (HQ) 610 893-9800
    1050 Westlakes Dr Berwyn (19312) *(G-1376)*
Te Connectivity Corporation 717 564-0100
    3101 Fulling Mill Rd # 128 Middletown (17057) *(G-11078)*
Te Connectivity Corporation 717 986-3028
    2801 Fulling Mill Rd Middletown (17057) *(G-11079)*
Te Connectivity Corporation 717 492-2000
    209 Shellyland Rd Manheim (17545) *(G-10405)*
Te Connectivity Corporation 717 564-0100
    2100 Paxton St Harrisburg (17111) *(G-7228)*
Te Connectivity Corporation 717 762-9186
    627 N Grant St Waynesboro (17268) *(G-19425)*
Te Connectivity Corporation 717 227-4400
    50 W Clearview Dr Shrewsbury (17361) *(G-17588)*
Te Connectivity Corporation 717 898-4302
    1590 Kauffman Rd Landisville (17538) *(G-9267)*

Te Connectivity Corporation 717 861-5000
3155 State Route 72 Jonestown (17038) ***(G-8452)***
Te Connectivity Corporation 717 492-1000
30 S Jacob St Mount Joy (17552) ***(G-11671)***
Te Connectivity Corporation 866 743-6440
2800 Fulling Mill Rd Middletown (17057) ***(G-11080)***
Te Connectivity Corporation 717 986-3743
2900 Fulling Mill Rd Middletown (17057) ***(G-11081)***
Te Connectivity Corporation 717 762-9186
627 N Grant St Waynesboro (17268) ***(G-19426)***
Te Connectivity Corporation 717 691-5842
1311 S Market St Mechanicsburg (17055) ***(G-10895)***
Te Connectivity Corporation 717 653-8151
1250 E Main St Mount Joy (17552) ***(G-11672)***
Te Connectivity Corporation 717 564-0100
2901 Fulling Mill Rd Middletown (17057) ***(G-11082)***
Te Connectivity Corporation 717 564-0100
449 Eisenhower Blvd Harrisburg (17111) ***(G-7229)***
Te Connectivity Foundation 717 810-2987
1050 Westlakes Dr Berwyn (19312) ***(G-1377)***
Te Stone Products LLC 570 335-4921
301 Whitmore Ave Mayfield (18433) ***(G-10543)***
Team Approach Inc 847 259-0005
2174 Old Philadelphia Pik Lancaster (17602) ***(G-9213)***
Team Biondi LLC 570 503-7087
248 Easton Tpke Lake Ariel (18436) ***(G-8894)***
Team Laminates Co, Pittsburgh *Also called Earnest Industries Inc* ***(G-14953)***
Team Oil Tools LP 724 301-2659
109 N Madison Ave Grove City (16127) ***(G-6806)***
Team Ten LLC 814 684-1610
1600 Pennsylvania Ave Tyrone (16686) ***(G-18595)***
Teamwork Graphic Inc 570 368-2360
227 Streibeigh Ln Montoursville (17754) ***(G-11452)***
TEC Fab, New Freedom *Also called Technical Fabrication Inc* ***(G-12216)***
Tech Cycle Performance Pdts 215 702-8324
169 W Lincoln Hwy Ste 1 Langhorne (19047) ***(G-9328)***
Tech Equipment Sales Inc 610 279-0370
1200 Markley St Norristown (19401) ***(G-12716)***
Tech Group North America Inc 570 326-7673
2921 Reach Rd Williamsport (17701) ***(G-20080)***
Tech Group North America Inc 480 281-4500
530 Herman O West Dr Exton (19341) ***(G-5736)***
Tech Manufacturing Corporation 610 586-0620
801 Chester Pike Sharon Hill (19079) ***(G-17464)***
Tech Met Inc 412 678-8277
15 Allegheny Sq Glassport (15045) ***(G-6418)***
Tech Modem CB Comcast 267 288-5661
55 Industrial Dr Warminster (18974) ***(G-18976)***
Tech Molded Plastics, Meadville *Also called Prism Plastics Inc* ***(G-10781)***
Tech Packaging Inc 570 759-7717
20 Cinnamon Oak Dr Hazle Township (18202) ***(G-7483)***
Tech Sheet Metal Company Inc 724 539-3763
133 Center St Bradenville (15620) ***(G-1952)***
Tech Support Screen P 412 697-0171
1441 Meteor Cir Ste 2 Pittsburgh (15241) ***(G-15601)***
Tech Tag & Label Inc 215 822-2400
1901 N Penn Rd Hatfield (19440) ***(G-7398)***
Tech Tube Inc 610 491-8000
750 Vandenburg Rd King of Prussia (19406) ***(G-8684)***
Tech-Seal Products Inc 847 805-6400
460 E Swedesford Rd # 3000 Wayne (19087) ***(G-19379)***
Techline Technologies Inc 215 657-1909
668 Davisville Rd Willow Grove (19090) ***(G-20146)***
Techna-Plastic Services Inc (PA) 570 386-2732
164 Seneca Rd Lehighton (18235) ***(G-9729)***
Technetics 215 855-9916
1600 Industry Rd Hatfield (19440) ***(G-7399)***
Techni-Forms Inc 215 345-0333
601 Airport Blvd Doylestown (18902) ***(G-4341)***
Technical Applications Inc 610 353-0722
610 Park Way Ste B Broomall (19008) ***(G-2303)***
Technical Fabrication Inc 717 227-0909
15842 Elm Dr Ste 1 New Freedom (17349) ***(G-12216)***
Technical Precision Inc 724 253-2800
2343 Perry Hwy Hadley (16130) ***(G-6821)***
Technical Process & Engrg Inc 570 386-4777
892 Blakeslee Blvd Dr W Lehighton (18235) ***(G-9730)***
Technical Vision Inc 215 205-6084
74 Stagecoach Rd Pipersville (18947) ***(G-14620)***
Technically Media Inc 215 821-8745
601 Walnut St Ste 1200 Philadelphia (19106) ***(G-14379)***
Technicolor HM Entrmt Svcs Inc 570 383-3291
1400 E Lackawanna St Olyphant (18448) ***(G-13001)***
Technicolor Usa Inc 717 295-6100
1002 New Holland Ave Lancaster (17601) ***(G-9214)***
Technipfmc US Holdings Inc 303 217-2030
1602 Wagner Ave Erie (16510) ***(G-5504)***
Technipfmc US Holdings Inc 724 459-7350
451 Innovation Dr Blairsville (15717) ***(G-1743)***
Technipfmc US Holdings Inc 570 546-2380
320 Marcellus Dr Muncy (17756) ***(G-11834)***
Technipfmc US Holdings Inc 724 820-5023
1001 Corporate Dr Ste 260 Canonsburg (15317) ***(G-2646)***
Technique Architectural Pdts 412 241-1644
815 Penn Ave Wilkinsburg (15221) ***(G-19981)***
Techniserv Inc 570 759-2315
351 S Eaton St Berwick (18603) ***(G-1346)***
Techniservice, Kennett Square *Also called Textured Yarn Co Inc* ***(G-8549)***
Technitrol Inc 215 355-2900
1210 Northbrook Dr Feasterville Trevose (19053) ***(G-5932)***
Technology Data Exchange Inc 610 668-4717
721 Yale Rd Bala Cynwyd (19004) ***(G-894)***
Technology Development Corp (PA) 610 631-5043
1055 W Germantown Pike Norristown (19403) ***(G-12717)***
Technology Dynamics Inc 888 988-3243
489 Devon Park Dr Ste 318 Wayne (19087) ***(G-19380)***
Technology Fabricators, Montgomeryville *Also called Environmental Solut World Inc* ***(G-11396)***
Technology Fabricators Inc 215 699-0731
200 Progress Dr Montgomeryville (18936) ***(G-11421)***
Technology Publishing Company, Pittsburgh *Also called Southside Holdings Inc* ***(G-15564)***
Technosystems Service Corp 412 288-2525
804 Penn Ave Pittsburgh (15222) ***(G-15602)***
Techo-Bloc (ne) Corp 610 863-2300
852 W Pennsylvania Ave Pen Argyl (18072) ***(G-13219)***
Techo-Bloc Corp 610 326-3677
23 Quarry Rd Douglassville (19518) ***(G-4181)***
Techo-Bloc Corp (PA) 610 863-2300
852 W Pennsylvania Ave Pen Argyl (18072) ***(G-13220)***
Techs Industries Inc 412 464-5000
300 Braddock Ave Turtle Creek (15145) ***(G-18570)***
Techs Industries Inc 412 464-5000
300 Mifflin Rd Pittsburgh (15207) ***(G-15603)***
Techs Industries Inc (HQ) 412 464-5000
2400 2nd Ave Pittsburgh (15219) ***(G-15604)***
Techs, The, Pittsburgh *Also called Techs Industries Inc* ***(G-15604)***
Techsource Engineering Inc 814 459-2150
2101 W 12th St Erie (16505) ***(G-5505)***
Techspec Inc 724 694-2716
718 Y St Derry (15627) ***(G-4108)***
Tecklane Manufacturing Inc (PA) 724 274-9464
200 Hoeveler St Springdale (15144) ***(G-17903)***
Tecnomasium Inc 412 264-7364
105 Bertley Ridge Dr Coraopolis (15108) ***(G-3727)***
Teco Mfg Co, Christiana *Also called J D Kauffman Machine Sp Inc* ***(G-3137)***
Tecomet Inc 215 826-8250
1507 Clyde Waite Dr Ste 2 Bristol (19007) ***(G-2204)***
Ted J Tedesco 215 316-8303
473 Linville Rd Media (19063) ***(G-10952)***
Ted Venesky Co Inc 724 224-7992
5746 Bull Creek Rd Tarentum (15084) ***(G-18248)***
Tedd Wood LLC 717 463-3615
758 Johnstown Rd Thompsontown (17094) ***(G-18352)***
Teddico, Pittsburgh *Also called Electrical Design Developm* ***(G-14962)***
Teddy Wears 610 273-3234
1469 Telegraph Rd Honey Brook (19344) ***(G-7766)***
Tedesco & Son Products, Media *Also called Ted J Tedesco* ***(G-10952)***
Tee & Gee Pallets, Allentown *Also called Gerald S Stillman* ***(G-230)***
Tee Printing Inc 717 394-2978
124 College Ave Lancaster (17603) ***(G-9215)***
Tee-To-Green 570 275-8335
2011 Montour Blvd Danville (17821) ***(G-4013)***
Teeco Associates Inc 610 539-4708
63 Tanglewood Dr Schwenksville (19473) ***(G-17179)***
Teeship LLC 717 497-2970
409 Pleasant View Rd Hummelstown (17036) ***(G-7926)***
Teeter Enterprises Inc 717 732-5994
49 Sherwood Cir Enola (17025) ***(G-5086)***
Tef - Cap Industries Inc 610 692-2576
1155 Phoenixville Pike # 103 West Chester (19380) ***(G-19657)***
Teflex Inc 570 945-9185
101 College Ave Factoryville (18419) ***(G-5762)***
Tegrant Corporation 215 643-3555
161 Corporate Dr Montgomeryville (18936) ***(G-11422)***
Tegrant Thermosare Brands, Montgomeryville *Also called Tegrant Corporation* ***(G-11422)***
Tek ID 215 699-8888
297 Dekalb Pike North Wales (19454) ***(G-12831)***
Tek Products & Services Inc 610 376-0690
530 Crestmont St Reading (19611) ***(G-16534)***
Tek-Temp Instruments Inc 215 788-5528
401 Magnolia Ave Croydon (19021) ***(G-3930)***
Tekgard Inc 717 854-0005
3390 Farmtrail Rd York (17406) ***(G-20685)***
Tekni-Plex Inc (PA) 484 690-1520
460 E Swedesford Rd # 3000 Wayne (19087) ***(G-19381)***
Tekniplex Co, Wayne *Also called Tekni-Plex Inc* ***(G-19381)***
Tel Tin 717 259-9004
45 Cherry Ln Abbottstown (17301) ***(G-8)***

ALPHABETIC

Telamon Corporation...800 945-8800
45 Runway Dr Ste A Levittown (19057) ***(G-9867)***
Telan Corporation...215 822-1234
2880 Bergey Rd Ste G Hatfield (19440) ***(G-7400)***
Tele-Media Sfp LLC...570 271-0810
701 Montour Blvd Danville (17821) ***(G-4014)***
Teledyne Defense Elec LLC...814 238-3450
328 Innovation Blvd # 100 State College (16803) ***(G-18036)***
Teledyne Instruments Inc...814 234-7311
349 Science Park Rd State College (16803) ***(G-18037)***
Teledyne Judson Technologies, Montgomeryville *Also called Teledyne Scientific Imaging LLC* ***(G-11423)***
Teledyne Paradise Datacom, State College *Also called Teledyne Defense Elec LLC* ***(G-18036)***
Teledyne Scientific Imaging LLC...215 368-6900
221 Commerce Dr Montgomeryville (18936) ***(G-11423)***
Teledyne Ssi, State College *Also called Teledyne Instruments Inc* ***(G-18037)***
Telefactor Robotics LLC...610 940-6040
1094 New Dehaven St Conshohocken (19428) ***(G-3611)***
Teleflex, Wayne *Also called Arrow International Inc* ***(G-19303)***
Teleflex Incorporated (PA)...610 225-6800
550 E Swedesford Rd # 400 Wayne (19087) ***(G-19382)***
Teleflex Incorporated...610 495-7011
640 N Lewis Rd Royersford (19468) ***(G-16867)***
Teleflex Marine, Royersford *Also called HIG Capital LLC* ***(G-16851)***
Telepole Manufacturing Inc...570 546-3699
1975 John Brady Dr Muncy (17756) ***(G-11835)***
Telesis Therapeutics LLC...215 848-4773
3711 Market St Ste 800 Philadelphia (19104) ***(G-14380)***
Teletrix Corp...412 798-3636
2000 Golden Mile Hwy C Pittsburgh (15239) ***(G-15605)***
Teletronics Technology Corp...267 352-2020
15 Terry Dr Newtown (18940) ***(G-12555)***
Telex Metals LLC...215 781-6335
105 Phyllis Ave Croydon (19021) ***(G-3931)***
Telikin, Hatfield *Also called Venture 3 Systems LLC* ***(G-7405)***
Tell Doors & Windows LLC...717 625-2990
18 Richard Dr Lititz (17543) ***(G-10053)***
Tell Manufacturing Inc (PA)...717 625-2990
18 Richard Dr Lititz (17543) ***(G-10054)***
Tellus Three Sixty...717 628-1866
603 E Main St Palmyra (17078) ***(G-13133)***
Telstar North America Inc...215 826-0770
1504 Grundy Ln Bristol (19007) ***(G-2205)***
Tem Pres Division, Bellefonte *Also called Leco Corporation* ***(G-1107)***
Temco, North East *Also called Electric Materials Company* ***(G-12739)***
Temco Industries Inc...412 831-5620
670 Steubenville Pike Burgettstown (15021) ***(G-2356)***
Temperatsure LLC (PA)...775 358-1999
2705 Clemens Rd Ste 103 Hatfield (19440) ***(G-7401)***
Temperature Ctrl Professionals...215 295-1616
225 Lincoln Hwy Bldg As-6 Fairless Hills (19030) ***(G-5803)***
Temple Aluminum Foundry Inc...610 926-2125
1145 Park Rd Blandon (19510) ***(G-1761)***
Tempur Production Usa LLC...570 715-7200
25 Elmwood Ave Mountain Top (18707) ***(G-11778)***
Tempus Transport, White Oak *Also called Wolenski Enterprises Inc* ***(G-19859)***
Temtek Solutions Inc...724 980-4270
264 Valley Brook Rd Canonsburg (15317) ***(G-2647)***
Tena, Philadelphia *Also called Essity North America Inc* ***(G-13680)***
Tenex Systems Inc (PA)...610 239-9988
2011 Renaissance Blvd # 100 King of Prussia (19406) ***(G-8685)***
Tennant Wilbert, Mount Morris *Also called Blairsville Wilbert Burial Vlt* ***(G-11679)***
Tennessee Tubebending Division, Erie *Also called Morris Coupling Company* ***(G-5396)***
Tennett Manufacturing Inc...215 721-3803
3205 Meetinghouse Rd Telford (18969) ***(G-18322)***
Tension Envelope Corporation...570 429-1444
1 Tension Way Saint Clair (17970) ***(G-16942)***
Tensitron, Pittsburgh *Also called Cianflone Scientific LLC* ***(G-14851)***
Terex Corporation...717 840-0226
180a N Donnerville Rd Mountville (17554) ***(G-11803)***
Teris Deli & Bakery LLC...570 785-7007
104 Main St Forest City (18421) ***(G-6055)***
Termac Corp...610 863-5356
65 Constitution Ave Wind Gap (18091) ***(G-20174)***
Termaco USA Inc...610 916-2600
171 Tuckerton Rd Reading (19605) ***(G-16535)***
Termalock, Telford *Also called Fres-Co Systems Usa Inc* ***(G-18290)***
Termini Brothers Bakery, Philadelphia *Also called Termini Brothers Inc* ***(G-14381)***
Termini Brothers Inc (PA)...215 334-1816
1523 S 8th St 25 Philadelphia (19147) ***(G-14381)***
Terra Essential Scents Sy...412 213-3600
4361 William Flynn Hwy Allison Park (15101) ***(G-464)***
Terra Group Corp...610 821-7003
735 Pittston St Allentown (18103) ***(G-408)***
Terra-Glo Lighting Corporation...267 430-1259
59 Steam Whistle Dr Ivyland (18974) ***(G-8222)***
Terraglo Lighting, Ivyland *Also called Terra-Glo Lighting Corporation* ***(G-8222)***
Terrain Merchandising LLC...310 709-8784
5000 S Broad St Philadelphia (19112) ***(G-14382)***
Terranettis Italian Bakery...717 697-5434
844 W Trindle Rd Mechanicsburg (17055) ***(G-10896)***
Terrasource Global Corporation...610 544-7200
1400 N Providence Rd # 3000 Media (19063) ***(G-10953)***
Terraviz Geospatial Inc (PA)...717 938-3591
1 W Elm St Ste 400 Conshohocken (19428) ***(G-3612)***
Terraviz Geospatial Inc...717 512-9658
60 Maplewood Dr Etters (17319) ***(G-5554)***
Terre Hill Concrete...717 738-9164
400 W Main St Ste 5 Ephrata (17522) ***(G-5152)***
Terre Hill Concrete Products, Terre Hill *Also called Terre Hill Silo Company Inc* ***(G-18339)***
Terre Hill Silo Company Inc (PA)...717 445-3100
485 Weaverland Valley Rd Terre Hill (17581) ***(G-18339)***
Terre Trophy Co...610 777-2050
965 New Holland Rd Reading (19607) ***(G-16536)***
Terry Baker...717 263-5942
2045 Country Rd Chambersburg (17202) ***(G-2985)***
Terry D Miles...814 686-1997
6096 Tyrone Pike Tyrone (16686) ***(G-18596)***
Terry L Handwerk (PA)...610 262-0986
1522 Lincoln Ave Northampton (18067) ***(G-12862)***
Tervo Masonry Llc...724 944-6179
117 James St New Wilmington (16142) ***(G-12471)***
TESCO, Erie *Also called Transportation Eqp Sup Co* ***(G-5514)***
Tescor, Warminster *Also called Link Group Inc* ***(G-18912)***
Tescor Inc...215 957-6061
341 Ivyland Rd Warminster (18974) ***(G-18977)***
Tesla Inc...484 235-5858
160 N Gulph Rd Ste 1926 King of Prussia (19406) ***(G-8686)***
Test Boring Services Inc...724 267-4649
140 Mong Rd Scenery Hill (15360) ***(G-17126)***
Testa Machine Company Inc...724 947-9397
28 Baird Ave Slovan (15078) ***(G-17631)***
Testlink Corp (PA)...267 743-2956
73 W Mechanic St New Hope (18938) ***(G-12317)***
Tetra Tech Inc-Harrisburg, Harrisburg *Also called Tetra Technologies Inc* ***(G-7230)***
Tetra Technologies Inc...717 545-3580
2400 Park Dr Harrisburg (17110) ***(G-7230)***
Tetra Technologies Inc...610 853-1679
900 N Eagle Rd Havertown (19083) ***(G-7430)***
Tetra Technologies Inc...570 659-5357
2467 S Main St Mansfield (16933) ***(G-10426)***
Tetra Tool Company...814 833-6127
1425 Industrial Dr Erie (16505) ***(G-5506)***
Tetralgic Pharmaceuticals Corp (PA)...610 889-9900
343 Phoenixville Pike Malvern (19355) ***(G-10328)***
Tetratec Corp...215 396-8349
85 Railroad Dr Warminster (18974) ***(G-18978)***
Teufel & Sons, Chambersburg *Also called Hanger Prsthetcs & Ortho Inc* ***(G-2938)***
Teufles, Camp Hill *Also called Hanger Prsthetcs & Ortho Inc* ***(G-2499)***
Teutech LLC...814 486-1896
227 Barton St Emporium (15834) ***(G-5077)***
Teva, North Wales *Also called Barr Laboratories Inc* ***(G-12790)***
Teva Bopharmaceuticals USA Inc...240 821-9000
145 Brandywine Pkwy West Chester (19380) ***(G-19658)***
Teva Branded Phrm Pdts R&D Inc...215 591-3000
145 Brandywine Pkwy West Chester (19380) ***(G-19659)***
Teva Branded Phrm Pdts R&D Inc (HQ)...215 591-3000
41 Moores Rd Malvern (19355) ***(G-10329)***
Teva Neuroscience...215 591-6309
1090 Horsham Rd Horsham (19044) ***(G-7856)***
Teva North America, North Wales *Also called Teva Pharmaceuticals Usa Inc* ***(G-12834)***
Teva Pharmaceutical Fin Co LLC...215 591-3000
1090 Horsham Rd North Wales (19454) ***(G-12832)***
Teva Pharmaceutical Fin IV LLC...215 591-3000
1090 Horsham Rd North Wales (19454) ***(G-12833)***
Teva Pharmaceuticals Usa Inc (HQ)...215 591-3000
1090 Horsham Rd North Wales (19454) ***(G-12834)***
Teva Pharmaceuticals Usa Inc...215 591-3000
1090 Horsham Rd North Wales (19454) ***(G-12835)***
Teva Pharmaceuticals Usa Inc...240 821-9000
1090 Horsham Rd North Wales (19454) ***(G-12836)***
Teva Pharmaceuticals Usa Inc...215 591-3000
650 Cathill Rd Sellersville (18960) ***(G-17359)***
Teva Pharmaceuticals Usa Inc...215 591-3000
425 Privet Rd Horsham (19044) ***(G-7857)***
Teva Pharmaceuticals Usa Inc...215 591-3000
111 New Britain Blvd Chalfont (18914) ***(G-2891)***
Teva Respiratory LLC...610 344-0200
41 Moores Rd Malvern (19355) ***(G-10330)***
Tex Styles LLC...610 562-4939
392 Five Locks Rd Ste 4 Shoemakersville (19555) ***(G-17576)***
Tex Visions LLC...717 240-0213
10 Pine Hill Dr Carlisle (17013) ***(G-2741)***
Texan Corporation...215 441-8967
355 Ivyland Rd Warminster (18974) ***(G-18979)***

Texas Ces Inc 412 490-9200
2 Penn Ctr W Ste 227 Pittsburgh (15276) (G-15606)

Texas Hose Products, Pittsburgh Also called Powertrack International LLC (G-15423)

Texas Instrs Lehigh Vly Inc 610 849-5100
116 Research Dr Bethlehem (18015) (G-1638)

Texas Instruments Incorporated 610 849-5100
116 Research Dr Bethlehem (18015) (G-1639)

Texas Keystone Inc (PA) 412 435-6555
333 Allegheny Ave Ste 201 Oakmont (15139) (G-12926)

Texas-New Mxico Newspapers LLC 717 767-3554
1891 Loucks Rd York (17408) (G-20686)

Textbook LLC 717 779-7101
1911 E Market St York (17402) (G-20687)

Textemp LLC 215 322-9670
3788 Sterner Mill Rd Quakertown (18951) (G-16249)

Textron Inc 570 323-6181
652 Oliver St Williamsport (17701) (G-20081)

Textron Lycoming, Williamsport Also called Textron Inc (G-20081)

Textured Yarn Co Inc 610 444-5400
738 W Cypress St Kennett Square (19348) (G-8549)

TFC LLC 412 979-1670
851 3rd Ave Brackenridge (15014) (G-1941)

Tfi, Montgomeryville Also called Technology Fabricators Inc (G-11421)

TG Marcis Wire Designs LLC 412 391-5532
50 26th St Pittsburgh (15222) (G-15607)

Tgb I LLC 724 431-3090
220 S Noah Dr Saxonburg (16056) (G-17096)

TGI, Philadelphia Also called Todays Graphics Inc (G-14394)

Tha Inc 215 804-0220
121 Park Ave Quakertown (18951) (G-16250)

Thackray Inc 800 245-4387
2071 Byberry Rd Philadelphia (19116) (G-14383)

Thai Chef, West Chester Also called Ethnic Gourmet Foods Inc (G-19552)

Thal, David, Malvern Also called Woodshop LLC (G-10348)

Thales Transport & SEC Inc (HQ) 412 366-8814
5500 Corporate Dr Ste 500 Pittsburgh (15237) (G-15608)

Thar Pharmaceuticals Inc (HQ) 412 963-6800
150 Gamma Dr Pittsburgh (15238) (G-15609)

Thar Process Inc 412 968-9180
150 Gamma Dr Pittsburgh (15238) (G-15610)

Thats True Media LLC 215 437-3292
744 South St Ste 40 Philadelphia (19147) (G-14384)

Thd Contracting Service LLC 215 626-1548
1921 N 54th St Philadelphia (19131) (G-14385)

The Adirondack Group Inc (PA) 610 431-4343
100 Colonial Way West Chester (19382) (G-19660)

The Area Shopper, Cochranton Also called Miller Printing & Publishing (G-3345)

The Cs Group, Muncy Also called Construction Specialties Inc (G-11814)

The Evening Sun, Hanover Also called Hanover Publishing Co (G-6901)

The Graphic Garage, Cheswick Also called Bubco Enterprise Inc (G-3102)

The Ink Spot, Malvern Also called Ink Spot Printing & Copy Ctr (G-10255)

The Keystone Friction Hinge Co (PA) 570 321-0693
520 Matthews Blvd Williamsport (17702) (G-20082)

The Lincoln Company, Reading Also called Lincoln Industrial Chemical Co (G-16430)

The M & A Journal Inc 215 238-0506
1008 Spruce St Apt 2r Philadelphia (19107) (G-14386)

The Old Glenshaw Glass, Glenshaw Also called Port Augustus Glass Co LLC (G-6498)

The Penny Pincher, Pottstown Also called Peerless Publications Inc (G-16028)

The Perfect Present, Gladwyne Also called Gail Dagowitz (G-6408)

The Reynolds and Reynolds Co 717 767-5264
York County Industrial Pa Emigsville (17318) (G-5001)

THE REYNOLDS AND REYNOLDS COMPANY (INC), Emigsville Also called The Reynolds
and Reynolds Co (G-5001)

The Scranton Times L P 570 348-9146
149 Scranton Times Bldg Scranton (18503) (G-17297)

The Scranton Times L P (PA) 570 348-9100
149 Penn Ave Ste 1 Scranton (18503) (G-17298)

The Scranton Times L P 570 644-6397
707 N Rock St Shamokin (17872) (G-17427)

The Scranton Times L P 570 821-2095
75 N Washington St Wilkes Barre (18701) (G-19965)

The Scranton Times L P 410 523-2300
149 Penn Ave Ofc C Scranton (18503) (G-17299)

The Scranton Times L P 570 682-9081
104 W Main St Valley View (17983) (G-18718)

The Scranton Times L P 570 265-2151
116 N Main St Towanda (18848) (G-18435)

The Sentinel, Lewistown Also called Ogden Newspapers of PA (G-9941)

The Sign Factory, State College Also called Heimer Enterprises Inc (G-17974)

The Swedish Pastry Shop, Collegeville Also called Anthony Mieczkowski (G-3369)

Thebathoutlet LLC 877 256-1645
1953 W Point Pike Lansdale (19446) (G-9414)

Thefire Store.com, Coatesville Also called Witmer Public Safety Group Inc (G-3331)

Then Defense Group 717 465-0584
1480 Highland Avenue Rd Gettysburg (17325) (G-6317)

Theodore Fazen 215 672-1122
426 Horsham Rd Horsham (19044) (G-7858)

Theodore Presser Company (HQ) 610 592-1222
588 N Gulph Rd Ste B King of Prussia (19406) (G-8687)

Theodore W Styborski 814 337-8535
10246 Mercer Pike Meadville (16335) (G-10800)

Theorem Clinical Research, King of Prussia Also called Chiltern International Inc (G-8592)

Theory LLC 610 326-5040
18 W Lightcap Rd Ste 425 Pottstown (19464) (G-16054)

Theotek Corporation 610 336-9191
5934 Armstrong St Orefield (18069) (G-13015)

Thepaperframercom 570 239-1444
75 Mary St Ashley (18706) (G-740)

Theprinterscom Inc 814 238-8445
3500 E College Ave # 1000 State College (16801) (G-18038)

Therm-Coil Mfg Co, West Newton Also called Schmitt Walter H and Assoc (G-19751)

Therm-O-Rock East Inc (PA) 724 258-3670
1 Pine St New Eagle (15067) (G-12193)

Therm-O-Rock East Inc 724 379-8604
85 Washington St Donora (15033) (G-4163)

Therm-Omega-Tech Inc (PA) 877 379-8258
353 Ivyland Rd Warminster (18974) (G-18980)

Therma-Fab Inc 814 664-9429
256 Eagle St Corry (16407) (G-3774)

Therma-Fab Inc (PA) 814 827-9455
109 W Central Ave Titusville (16354) (G-18398)

Therma-Tek Range Corp 570 455-3000
115 Rotary Dr West Hazleton (18202) (G-19716)

Thermablaster, Pittsburgh Also called Reecon North America LLC (G-15475)

Thermacore International Inc 717 569-6551
780 Eden Rd Ofc Lancaster (17601) (G-9216)

Thermal Care Inc 724 584-5500
455 Allegheny Blvd Franklin (16323) (G-6164)

Thermal Engrg Intl USA Inc 610 948-5400
155 S Limerick Rd 200 Royersford (19468) (G-16868)

Thermal Industries Inc (HQ) 724 325-6100
3700 Haney Ct Murrysville (15668) (G-11870)

Thermal Industries Inc 814 944-4534
810 S 12th St Altoona (16602) (G-551)

Thermal Instrument Co Inc 215 355-8400
217 Sterner Mill Rd Trevose (19053) (G-18507)

Thermal Product Solutions, New Columbia Also called Tps LLC (G-12177)

Thermal Solutions Products LLC 717 239-7642
1175 Manheim Pike Ste 7 Lancaster (17601) (G-9217)

Thermal Transfer Corporation 412 460-4004
50 N Linden St Duquesne (15110) (G-4500)

Thermal Windows & Doors LLC 724 325-6100
3700 Haney Ct Murrysville (15668) (G-11871)

Thermal-Gard, Punxsutawney Also called Nortek Global Hvac LLC (G-16151)

Thermablade LLC (PA) 570 995-1425
775 Christian Camp Rd Muncy Valley (17758) (G-11843)

Thermigate LLC 610 931-1023
617 Glenwood Ave Lansdowne (19050) (G-9445)

Thermistors Unlimited Inc 814 781-5920
1028 Graphite Rd Saint Marys (15857) (G-17022)

Thermo Electric Company Inc (PA) 610 692-7990
1193 Mcdermott Dr West Chester (19380) (G-19661)

Thermo Electric Pa Inc 610 692-7990
1193 Mcdermott Dr West Chester (19380) (G-19662)

Thermo Electron, Bellefonte Also called Thermo Hypersil-Keystone LLC (G-1121)

Thermo Fisher Scientific Inc 610 837-5091
6771 Silver Crest Rd Nazareth (18064) (G-11991)

Thermo Fisher Scientific Inc 717 692-2104
163 Research Ln Millersburg (17061) (G-11203)

Thermo Fisher Scientific Inc 561 688-8725
195 Shearer Ln Stahlstown (15687) (G-17937)

Thermo Fisher Scientific Inc 412 490-8000
600 Business Center Dr Pittsburgh (15205) (G-15611)

Thermo Fisher Scientific Inc 814 353-2300
320 Rolling Ridge Dr Bellefonte (16823) (G-1120)

Thermo Fisher Scientific Inc 215 964-6020
1601 Cherry St Ste 1200 Philadelphia (19102) (G-14387)

Thermo Fisher Scientific Inc 412 770-2326
100 Technology Dr Ste 100 # 100 Pittsburgh (15219) (G-15612)

Thermo Fisher Scientific Inc 412 490-8300
300 Industry Dr Pittsburgh (15275) (G-15613)

Thermo Fisher Scientific Inc 412 490-8000
600 Business Center Dr Pittsburgh (15205) (G-15614)

Thermo Hypersil-Keystone LLC 814 353-2300
320 Rolling Ridge Dr Bellefonte (16823) (G-1121)

Thermo Scientific, Pittsburgh Also called Cellomics Inc (G-14833)

Thermo Shandon Inc (HQ) 412 788-1133
171 Industry Dr Pittsburgh (15275) (G-15615)

Thermo-Electric Co 724 695-2774
549 Route 30 Imperial (15126) (G-8077)

Thermo-Twin Industries Inc (PA) 412 826-1000
1155 Allegheny Ave Oakmont (15139) (G-12927)

Thermoclad Company (PA) 814 456-1243
361 W 11th St Erie (16501) (G-5507)

Thermoclad Company 814 899-7628
4690 Iroquois Ave Erie (16511) (G-5508)

Thermocouple Technologies Inc..................................215 529-9394
350 New St Quakertown (18951) *(G-16251)*

Thermocouple Technology LLC...............................215 529-9394
350 New St Quakertown (18951) *(G-16252)*

Thermolite Inc...570 969-1957
950 N South Rd Ste 3 Scranton (18504) *(G-17300)*

Thermosafe, Montgomeryville *Also called Sonoco Prtective Solutions Inc (G-11419)*

Thermtrend Inc..215 752-0711
480 State Rd Ste B Bensalem (19020) *(G-1260)*

Thespiderfriends Com LLC.......................................412 257-2346
434 Pine Valley Dr Bridgeville (15017) *(G-2094)*

Thg Health Products, Oxford *Also called Thg/Paradigm Health Intl Inc (G-13093)*

Thg/Paradigm Health Intl Inc..................................610 998-1080
54 N 4th St Oxford (19363) *(G-13093)*

Thin Film Industries Inc..267 316-9999
1300 Steel Rd E Ste 9 Morrisville (19067) *(G-11585)*

Thin Labs Inc...215 269-3322
225 Lincoln Hwy Ste 178 Fairless Hills (19030) *(G-5804)*

Third Dimension Graphics Group, Scranton *Also called Third Dimension Spc LLC (G-17301)*

Third Dimension Spc LLC...570 969-0623
856 Capouse Ave Scranton (18509) *(G-17301)*

This Life Forever Inc...707 733-0383
106 W Ridge St Lansford (18232) *(G-9450)*

This Week In Poconos Magazine, Pocono Pines *Also called Printing Craftsmen Inc (G-15883)*

This Week's Ad, Elkins Park *Also called Fry International LLC (G-4903)*

Thistlethwaite Vineyards..724 883-3372
151 Thistlewaite Ln Jefferson (15344) *(G-8271)*

Thoma Meat Market Inc...724 352-2020
748 Dinnerbell Rd Saxonburg (16056) *(G-17097)*

Thoman Logging...570 265-4993
662 Main St Le Raysville (18829) *(G-9543)*

Thomas...717 642-6600
3245 Fairfield Rd Gettysburg (17325) *(G-6318)*

Thomas & Betts, Mercer *Also called ABB Installation Products Inc (G-10958)*

Thomas & Muller Systems Ltd...................................215 541-1961
80 Gravel Pike Red Hill (18076) *(G-16585)*

Thomas A Laskowski..215 957-1544
239 Madison Ave Ste D Warminster (18974) *(G-18981)*

Thomas Catanese & Co..610 277-6230
324 Knoll Rd Plymouth Meeting (19462) *(G-15876)*

Thomas E Ferro...610 485-1356
2124 Vernon Ave Upper Chichester (19061) *(G-18673)*

Thomas E Siegel..814 226-7421
208 Woodland Rd Shippenville (16254) *(G-17564)*

Thomas Fetterman Inc...215 355-8849
1680 Hillside Rd Southampton (18966) *(G-17840)*

Thomas Gross Woodworking....................................724 593-7044
135 Greenbriar Dr Ligonier (15658) *(G-9967)*

Thomas Henry Potoeski...570 922-3361
17355 Old Turnpike Rd Millmont (17845) *(G-11220)*

Thomas Hontz Associates, Quakertown *Also called Tha Inc (G-16250)*

Thomas Magnetix Inc...570 879-4363
350 New York Ave Hallstead (18822) *(G-6836)*

Thomas Miller & Co Inc...215 822-3118
3101 E Walnut St Colmar (18915) *(G-3420)*

Thomas Nay LLC..215 613-8367
3332 Red Lion Rd Philadelphia (19114) *(G-14388)*

Thomas Pennise Jr...215 822-1832
2522 Lenhart Rd Colmar (18915) *(G-3421)*

Thomas Sales Inc...717 597-9366
124 S Washington St Greencastle (17225) *(G-6639)*

Thomas Spinning Lures Inc......................................570 226-4011
316 Wayne Ave Hawley (18428) *(G-7439)*

Thomas Timberland Enterprises...............................814 359-2890
244 Breons Ln Bellefonte (16823) *(G-1122)*

Thomas W Springer Inc...610 274-8400
227 Buttonwood Rd Landenberg (19350) *(G-9254)*

Thomaston Manufacturing LLC (PA).........................215 576-6352
135 Greenwood Ave Wyncote (19095) *(G-20266)*

Thompson Gear & Machine Co.................................724 468-5625
135 Cupp Way Delmont (15626) *(G-4060)*

Thompson Logging and Trckg Inc.............................570 923-2590
Po Box 264 North Bend (17760) *(G-12727)*

Thompson Machine Company Inc.............................814 941-4982
1128 N 4th Ave Altoona (16601) *(G-552)*

Thompson Maple Products Inc.................................814 664-7717
175 Sample Flats Rd Corry (16407) *(G-3775)*

Thompson's Packing Co, Jersey Shore *Also called Clair D Thompson & Sons Inc (G-8311)*

Thompsons Candle Co..814 641-7490
328 Allegheny St Huntingdon (16652) *(G-7957)*

Thomson Candies..610 268-8337
201 Pennsylvania Ave Avondale (19311) *(G-861)*

Thomson Consumer Electronics, Lancaster *Also called Technicolor Usa Inc (G-9214)*

Thoren Caging Systems Inc (PA)..............................570 454-3517
815 W 7th St Hazleton (18201) *(G-7529)*

Thoren Industries, Hazleton *Also called Thoren Caging Systems Inc (G-7529)*

Thoren Industries Inc..570 454-3514
325 W 7th St Hazleton (18201) *(G-7530)*

Thorn Hill Printing Inc...724 774-4700
155 Commerce Dr Freedom (15042) *(G-6192)*

Thorn Hill Vineyards..717 517-7839
2076 Fruitville Pike Lancaster (17601) *(G-9218)*

Thorndale Press Inc...610 384-3363
3947 W Lincoln Hwy Downingtown (19335) *(G-4258)*

Thornton Industries...814 756-3578
14200 Route 226 Albion (16401) *(G-47)*

Thoroughcare Inc...412 737-7332
100 S Commons Ste 102 Pittsburgh (15212) *(G-15616)*

Thorsens Precision Grinding....................................717 765-9090
20 E 6th St Ste 216 Waynesboro (17268) *(G-19427)*

Thread International Pbc Inc....................................814 876-9999
7800 Susquehanna St Pittsburgh (15208) *(G-15617)*

Three Bakers, Moscow *Also called Gluten Free Food Group LLC (G-11597)*

Three Belle Cheese...570 713-8722
137 Dice Rd Mifflinburg (17844) *(G-11103)*

Three Bridges Media LLC...717 695-2621
2601 N Front St Ste 101 Harrisburg (17110) *(G-7231)*

Three Brothers Publishing LLC................................412 656-3905
579 E Lafayette St Norristown (19401) *(G-12718)*

Three Dimensions Systems Inc.................................724 779-3890
210 W Kensinger Dr # 400 Cranberry Township (16066) *(G-3852)*

Three M Tool and Die Corp (PA)..............................717 854-6379
1038 Elm St York (17403) *(G-20688)*

Three Rivers Aluminum Company.............................800 837-7002
71 Progress Ave Cranberry Township (16066) *(G-3853)*

Three Rivers Confections LLC..................................412 402-0388
3530 Smallman St Pittsburgh (15201) *(G-15618)*

Three Rivers Gamma Service....................................724 947-9020
1132 Route 18 Ste A Burgettstown (15021) *(G-2357)*

Three Rivers Harley-Davidson, Glenshaw *Also called Gatto Moto LLC (G-6488)*

Three Rivers Mothers Milk Bank..............................412 281-4400
3127 Penn Ave Pittsburgh (15201) *(G-15619)*

Three Rivers Optical Company.................................412 928-2020
260 Bilmar Dr Pittsburgh (15205) *(G-15620)*

Three Rivers Orthotics Prsthti..................................412 371-2318
305 Overdale Rd Pittsburgh (15221) *(G-15621)*

Three Soles Corp...717 762-1945
76 W Main St Frnt Waynesboro (17268) *(G-19428)*

Threeway Pattern Enterprises..................................610 929-2889
3144 Marion St Reading (19605) *(G-16537)*

Thresher Pharmaceuticals.......................................215 826-0227
1200 Veterans Hwy Ste 827 Bristol (19007) *(G-2206)*

Threshold Rhblitation Svcs Inc (PA).........................610 777-7691
1000 Lancaster Ave Reading (19607) *(G-16538)*

Thrifty Dumpster Inc...215 688-1774
3037 Griffith Rd Eagleville (19403) *(G-4518)*

Thrifty Pallet, Coatesville *Also called Annalee Wood Products Inc (G-3288)*

Thrifty Pallet Co, West Chester *Also called Annalee Wood Products Inc (G-19499)*

Thru Tubing Solutions Inc..412 787-8060
100 S Campus Dr Imperial (15126) *(G-8078)*

Thru Tubing Solutions Inc..570 546-0323
243 Grey Fox Dr Ste 3 Montoursville (17754) *(G-11453)*

Thruways Door Systems Inc.....................................412 781-4030
400 Poplar St Pittsburgh (15223) *(G-15622)*

Thunder Basin Corporation (HQ)..............................610 962-3770
555 Croton Rd Ste 200 King of Prussia (19406) *(G-8688)*

Thyssenkrupp Elevator Corp....................................412 364-2624
539 Rochester Rd Pittsburgh (15237) *(G-15623)*

Thyssenkrupp Elevator Corp....................................610 366-0161
5925 Tilghman St Ste 100 Allentown (18104) *(G-409)*

Thyssnkrupp Indus Slutions USA.............................412 257-8277
1370 Washington Pike Bridgeville (15017) *(G-2095)*

TI Lighting Co, Bensalem *Also called Electronic Tool & Die Works (G-1187)*

TI Oregon Inc (HQ)..412 394-2800
1000 Six Ppg Pl Pittsburgh (15222) *(G-15624)*

Tiadaghton Embroidery..570 398-4477
110 Charles St Jersey Shore (17740) *(G-8323)*

Tiberi Gun Shop..724 245-6151
47 Pala Ave Fairbank (15435) *(G-5764)*

Tiberi Service, Fairbank *Also called Tiberi Gun Shop (G-5764)*

Tiburon Waterjet Services, Lebanon *Also called Lebanon Machine & Mfg Co LLC (G-9601)*

Ticket Counter...717 536-3092
4902 Carlisle Pike Mechanicsburg (17050) *(G-10897)*

Ties Magazine, Philadelphia *Also called Drexel University (G-13647)*

Tiffany Tiffany Designers Inc....................................215 297-0550
27 Cafferty Rd Point Pleasant (18950) *(G-15888)*

Tiger Brand Jack Post Co...814 333-4302
10721 S Water Street Ext Meadville (16335) *(G-10801)*

Tiger Enterprises Inc...717 786-5441
2052 White Oak Rd Strasburg (17579) *(G-18095)*

Tiger Optics LLC..215 343-6600
250 Titus Ave Warrington (18976) *(G-19135)*

Tiger PC Defense..888 531-1530
502 Jefferson St Whitehall (18052) *(G-19891)*

Tiger Power, Lebanon *Also called Dyna-Tech Industries Ltd (G-9564)*

Tiger Printing Group LLC...215 799-0500
65 W Madison Ave Telford (18969) *(G-18323)*

Tigereye Enterprise Inc.....724 443-7810
100 Allegheny Dr Ste 100 # 100 Warrendale (15086) ***(G-19099)***
Tigg Corporation, Oakdale *Also called Marg Inc* ***(G-12906)***
Tiki Kevs.....267 718-4527
3462 Limekiln Pike Chalfont (18914) ***(G-2892)***
Tilden Manufacturing Inc.....610 562-4682
229 Lowland Rd Hamburg (19526) ***(G-6852)***
Tilo Industries.....570 524-9990
2738 Buffalo Rd Lewisburg (17837) ***(G-9921)***
Tilsit Corporation.....610 681-5951
Rr 209 Gilbert (18331) ***(G-6364)***
Tim Brennan's Heavy Equipment, Carbondale *Also called Timothy R Brennan Jr* ***(G-2686)***
Timac Agro Usa Inc.....610 375-7272
153 Angstadt Ln Reading (19607) ***(G-16539)***
Timbar Packaging & Display, Hanover *Also called PCA Corrugated and Display LLC* ***(G-6934)***
Timber Hollow Woodworking, Hegins *Also called Stoltzfus Sylvan Lee* ***(G-7544)***
Timber Mill Woodcraft LLC.....717 597-7433
556 Buchanan Trl W Greencastle (17225) ***(G-6640)***
Timber Pallet & Lumber Co Inc.....610 562-8442
1008 Mountain Rd Hamburg (19526) ***(G-6853)***
Timber Skate Shop.....570 492-6063
257 Market St Sunbury (17801) ***(G-18175)***
Timberhaven Log Homes LLC.....570 568-1422
434a Swartz Rd Lewisburg (17837) ***(G-9922)***
Timberlane Inc.....215 616-0600
150 Domorah Dr Montgomeryville (18936) ***(G-11424)***
Timberstrong LLC.....484 357-8730
441 Mountain Rd Kempton (19529) ***(G-8496)***
Time Machine Inc (PA).....814 432-5281
1746 Pittsburgh Rd Polk (16342) ***(G-15889)***
Time Man Jr Corporation.....856 244-1485
5253 Roosevelt Blvd Philadelphia (19124) ***(G-14389)***
Time Tech Industries Inc.....412 670-5498
226 Field Club Cir Mc Kees Rocks (15136) ***(G-10639)***
Time Zone, Ardmore *Also called Calconix Inc* ***(G-705)***
Time's News, The, Tamaqua *Also called Pencor Services Inc* ***(G-18223)***
Timely Impressions, Elkins Park *Also called Weisman Novelty Co Inc* ***(G-4914)***
Times Leader, Wilkes Barre *Also called Civitas Media LLC* ***(G-19913)***
Times Leader Circulation, Wilkes Barre *Also called Impressions Media* ***(G-19927)***
Times News, The, Palmerton *Also called Pencor Services Inc* ***(G-13110)***
Times Partner LLC.....570 348-9100
149 Penn Ave Scranton (18503) ***(G-17302)***
Times Printing, Taylor *Also called United Partners Ltd* ***(G-18264)***
Times Pubg Newspapers Inc.....215 702-3405
341 Rumpf Ave Langhorne (19047) ***(G-9329)***
Times Publishing Company (HQ).....814 453-4691
205 W 12th St Erie (16534) ***(G-5509)***
Times Shamrock Newspaper Group.....570 348-9100
149 Penn Ave Scranton (18503) ***(G-17303)***
Times Tribune Co, Altoona *Also called Hendersons Printing Inc* ***(G-512)***
Times-Shamrock.....570 501-0278
21 N Wyoming St Hazleton (18201) ***(G-7531)***
Timet, Morgantown *Also called Titanium Metals Corporation* ***(G-11539)***
Timinski Logging Co.....570 457-2641
5 Timinski Rd Sprng Brk Twp (18444) ***(G-17934)***
Timken Company.....215 654-7606
7 Great Valley Pkwy # 140 Malvern (19355) ***(G-10331)***
Timken Gears & Services Inc (HQ).....610 265-3000
901 E 8th Ave Ste 100 King of Prussia (19406) ***(G-8689)***
Timm Medical Technologies Inc.....484 321-5900
500 Office Center Dr # 400 Fort Washington (19034) ***(G-6093)***
Timothy A Musser & Co Inc.....610 433-6380
213 N 14th St Allentown (18102) ***(G-410)***
Timothy Emig.....215 443-7810
2031 Stout Dr Ste 4 Warminster (18974) ***(G-18982)***
Timothy R Brennan Jr.....570 281-9504
Rr 1 Box 1357 Carbondale (18407) ***(G-2686)***
Tims Electric Motor Repair Co.....814 445-5078
220 S Ankeny Ave Somerset (15501) ***(G-17714)***
Tims Printing Inc.....215 208-0699
148 W Ashdale St Philadelphia (19120) ***(G-14390)***
Tin Cup Inc.....570 322-1115
972 2nd St Williamsport (17701) ***(G-20083)***
Tin Lizzy Inc.....724 836-0281
909 Rolling Meadows Dr D Greensburg (15601) ***(G-6718)***
Tin Man Sweets.....724 432-3930
205 S Main St Zelienople (16063) ***(G-20824)***
Tin Roof Enterprises LLC.....610 659-3989
342 W Second St Media (19063) ***(G-10954)***
Tin Technology and Ref LLC.....610 430-2225
905 Fernhill Rd West Chester (19380) ***(G-19663)***
Tin Tinker.....215 230-9619
3781 Dogwood Ln Doylestown (18902) ***(G-4342)***
Tindall Virgin Timbers Clnl WD.....717 548-2435
700 Nottingham Rd Peach Bottom (17563) ***(G-13202)***
Tine, J P Tool Mfg, Irwin *Also called J P Tine Tool Co* ***(G-8175)***
Tinicum Magnetics Inc.....717 530-2424
345 Baltimore Rd Shippensburg (17257) ***(G-17551)***
Tinicum Research Company (PA).....610 294-9390
17 Roaring Rocks Rd Erwinna (18920) ***(G-5540)***
Tinicum Research Company.....215 766-7277
67 Appletree Ln Plumsteadville (18949) ***(G-15814)***
Tioga Publishing Company.....814 371-4200
500 Jeffers St Du Bois (15801) ***(G-4424)***
Tioga Publishing Company.....814 274-8044
6 W 2nd St Coudersport (16915) ***(G-3789)***
Tioga Publishing Company.....814 849-6737
301 Main St Brookville (15825) ***(G-2273)***
Tioga Publishing Company (HQ).....570 724-2287
25 East Ave Frnt Ste Wellsboro (16901) ***(G-19473)***
Tip Top Resources LLC (PA).....407 818-6937
837 Green Ln Reedsville (17084) ***(G-16628)***
Tirechain.com, Johnstown *Also called South Fork Hardware Company* ***(G-8436)***
Tiros Machine & Tool Company.....215 322-9965
285 Andrews Rd Feasterville Trevose (19053) ***(G-5933)***
Tita Machine & Tool Inc.....724 535-4988
229 Industrial Park Dr Wampum (16157) ***(G-18805)***
Titan Abrasive Systems LLC.....215 310-5055
35 Steam Whistle Dr Ivyland (18974) ***(G-8223)***
Titan Boards Inc.....814 516-1899
1798 State Route 157 Oil City (16301) ***(G-12958)***
Titan Co2 Inc.....814 669-4544
5559 William Penn Hwy Alexandria (16611) ***(G-64)***
Titan Group Ltd.....610 631-0831
2566 Industry Ln Norristown (19403) ***(G-12719)***
Titan Manufacturing Inc (PA).....610 935-8203
1 Rapps Run Dr Malvern (19355) ***(G-10332)***
Titan Manufacturing Inc.....781 767-1963
1 Rapps Run Dr Malvern (19355) ***(G-10333)***
Titan Metal & Machine Co Inc.....724 747-9528
46 E Wheeling St Washington (15301) ***(G-19232)***
Titan Robotics Inc.....724 986-6737
2516 Jane St Pittsburgh (15203) ***(G-15625)***
Titan Security Group LLC.....914 474-2221
79 Millrace Dr Lancaster (17603) ***(G-9219)***
Titan Technologies Inc (PA).....888 671-6649
2543 Washington Rd # 900 Pittsburgh (15241) ***(G-15626)***
Titan Tool Company.....814 474-1583
7410 W Ridge Rd Fairview (16415) ***(G-5848)***
Titan Wireline Service Inc.....724 354-2629
717 State Route 210 Shelocta (15774) ***(G-17489)***
Titanium 40 LLC.....610 338-0446
539 Riverview Rd Swarthmore (19081) ***(G-18186)***
Titanium Brkg Solutions LLC.....267 506-6642
1003 W Duncannon Ave Philadelphia (19141) ***(G-14391)***
Titanium Finishing Co.....215 679-4181
248 Main St East Greenville (18041) ***(G-4577)***
Titanium Foundation.....717 668-8423
1550 Elm Dr New Freedom (17349) ***(G-12217)***
Titanium Metals Corporation.....702 564-2544
900 Hemlock Rd Morgantown (19543) ***(G-11539)***
Titanium Wealth Advisors LLC.....610 429-1700
1217 W Chester Pike Ste A West Chester (19382) ***(G-19664)***
Titus Company.....610 913-9100
36 Mountain View Rd Morgantown (19543) ***(G-11540)***
Titusville Dairy Products Co.....814 827-1833
217 S Washington St Titusville (16354) ***(G-18399)***
Titusville Enterprises Inc (PA).....412 826-8140
700 Blaw Ave Ste 300 Pittsburgh (15238) ***(G-15627)***
Titusville Fabricators, Pittsburgh *Also called Titusville Enterprises Inc* ***(G-15627)***
Titusville Fabricators Inc.....814 432-2551
191 Howard St Ste 203 Franklin (16323) ***(G-6165)***
Titusville Herald, Titusville *Also called Titusville Herald Inc* ***(G-18400)***
Titusville Herald Inc.....814 827-3634
209 W Spring St Titusville (16354) ***(G-18400)***
Titusville Laundry Center.....814 827-9127
117 Diamond St Titusville (16354) ***(G-18401)***
TJ Cope Inc.....215 961-2570
11500 Norcom Rd Philadelphia (19154) ***(G-14392)***
Tj Manufacturing LLC.....717 575-0675
10313 Plank Rd Narvon (17555) ***(G-11930)***
Tjaws LLC.....570 344-2117
913 S Main Ave Scranton (18504) ***(G-17304)***
Tk Beer Inc.....610 446-2337
8794 W Chester Pike Upper Darby (19082) ***(G-18693)***
Tkd Mfg Inc.....717 266-3156
3945 N Susquehanna Trl York (17404) ***(G-20689)***
Tlb Industries Inc.....570 729-7192
292 Dunn Rd Honesdale (18431) ***(G-7728)***
TLC Refreshments Inc.....610 429-4124
797 Tree Ln West Chester (19380) ***(G-19665)***
Tlr Redwood Inc.....215 322-1005
265 2nd Street Pike Southampton (18966) ***(G-17841)***
Tm Industrial Supply Inc.....814 453-5014
1432 Walnut St Erie (16502) ***(G-5510)***

A
L
P
H
A
B
E
T
I
C

Tm Systems Inc 814 272-2700
  1900 W College Ave State College (16801) *(G-18039)*
TMC Candies LLC 814 623-1545
  106 E Pitt St Bedford (15522) *(G-1078)*
Tmf, Havertown Also called T M Fitzgerald & Assoc Inc *(G-7429)*
Tmf Corporation 610 853-3080
  850 W Chester Pike # 303 Havertown (19083) *(G-7431)*
TMI International LLC (HQ) 412 787-9750
  5350 Campbells Run Rd Pittsburgh (15205) *(G-15628)*
Tmk-Ipsco, Koppel Also called Ipsco Koppel Tubulars LLC *(G-8814)*
Tms International LLC (HQ) 412 678-6141
  12 Monongahela Ave Glassport (15045) *(G-6419)*
Tms International LLC 724 658-2004
  208 Rundle Rd New Castle (16102) *(G-12159)*
Tms International LLC 814 535-1911
  240 Parkhill Dr Johnstown (15945) *(G-8438)*
Tms International LLC 412 271-4430
  1300 Braddock Ave Braddock (15104) *(G-1948)*
Tms International LLC 610 208-3293
  101 Bern St Reading (19601) *(G-16540)*
Tms International LLC 724 746-5377
  Western Ave Houston (15342) *(G-7881)*
Tms International LLC 412 885-3600
  516 Delwar Rd Pittsburgh (15236) *(G-15629)*
Tms International LLC 215 956-5500
  1155 Buss Ctr Dr Ste 200 Horsham (19044) *(G-7859)*
Tms International LLC 412 257-1083
  600 Mayer St Bridgeville (15017) *(G-2096)*
Tms International LLC 814 535-5081
  240 Parkhill Dr Johnstown (15945) *(G-8439)*
Tms International LLC 724 929-4515
  891 Mills Ln Belle Vernon (15012) *(G-1088)*
Tms International Corp 215 956-5500
  1155 Business Pa Ctr Dr Horsham (19044) *(G-7860)*
Tms International Corp (PA) 412 678-6141
  12 Monongahela Ave Glassport (15045) *(G-6420)*
Tms International Corporation (HQ) 412 675-8251
  12 Monongahela Ave Glassport (15045) *(G-6421)*
Tms Precision Machining Inc 215 547-6070
  5 Fox Dr Bldg Jc5 Jc Bristol (19007) *(G-2207)*
Tmu Inc 717 392-0578
  252 N Prince St Side Lancaster (17603) *(G-9220)*
TMW Associates Inc 215 624-3940
  7352 Melrose St Philadelphia (19136) *(G-14393)*
Tmw Products LLC 215 997-9687
  630 Broad St Perkasie (18944) *(G-13296)*
TN TS 717 248-2278
  9210 Us Highway 522 S Lewistown (17044) *(G-9949)*
Tna Doors 570 484-5858
  243 Matterhorn Dr Effort (18330) *(G-4829)*
TNT, Barnesville Also called Roland Lynagh Associates LLC *(G-940)*
TNT Disposal 570 297-0101
  Rr 3 Troy (16947) *(G-18527)*
To Get It Now Print, Harrisburg Also called Rozema Printing LLC *(G-7210)*
Toad-Ally Snax Inc 215 788-7500
  1410 Farragut Ave Bristol (19007) *(G-2208)*
Toastmasters International 215 355-4838
  30 Remington Pl Warminster (18974) *(G-18983)*
Tobacco Plus Cash Checking 267 585-3802
  8612 New Falls Rd Levittown (19054) *(G-9868)*
Tobii Dynavox LLC (HQ) 412 381-4883
  2100 Wharton St Ste 400 Pittsburgh (15203) *(G-15630)*
Tocono Shopper, Scranton Also called Twanda Printing *(G-17307)*
Todays Graphics Inc 215 634-6200
  4848 Island Ave Philadelphia (19153) *(G-14394)*
Todays Hospitalist, Chalfont Also called Roman Press Inc *(G-2886)*
Todd A Forsythe 814 512-1457
  22949 Bennetts Valley Hwy Weedville (15868) *(G-19460)*
Todd Curyto 215 906-8097
  120 Merion Ave Narberth (19072) *(G-11913)*
Todd Lengle & Co Inc 610 777-0731
  50 S Brobst St Reading (19607) *(G-16541)*
Todd Smith Logging Inc 814 887-2183
  120 W Green St Smethport (16749) *(G-17637)*
Todd Weikel 610 779-5508
  3100 Saint Lawrence Ave Reading (19606) *(G-16542)*
Todds Snax Inc 717 637-5931
  680 W Chestnut St Hanover (17331) *(G-6961)*
Tohickon Corp (PA) 267 450-5020
  60 Noble St Sellersville (18960) *(G-17360)*
Tohickon Glass Eyes, Sellersville Also called Tohickon Corp *(G-17360)*
Tohickon Tool & Die Co 215 766-8285
  4130 Stump Rd Doylestown (18902) *(G-4343)*
Tokarick Printing Services 570 385-4639
  419 Hess St Schuylkill Haven (17972) *(G-17168)*
Toledo Tickets, Cochranville Also called Butts Ticket Company Inc *(G-3355)*
Tolino Vineyards LLC (PA) 610 588-9463
  280 Mount Pleasant Rd Bangor (18013) *(G-931)*
Tolino Vineyards Bangor, Bangor Also called Tolino Vineyards LLC *(G-931)*

Tollgrade Communications Inc (HQ) 724 720-1400
  260 Executive Dr Ste 150 Cranberry Township (16066) *(G-3854)*
Tom Cesarino Lumber 724 329-0467
  433 Camp Riamo Rd Farmington (15437) *(G-5863)*
Tom Hester Hiesters Ho Raceway 610 796-0490
  256 Old Lancaster Pike Reading (19607) *(G-16543)*
Tom James Company 570 875-3100
  2309 Chestnut St Ashland (17921) *(G-737)*
Tom James Company 412 642-2797
  412-414 Strawberry Way Pittsburgh (15219) *(G-15631)*
Tom James Company 717 264-5768
  5121 Innovation Way Chambersburg (17201) *(G-2986)*
Tom Russell 724 746-5029
  18 W Pike St Houston (15342) *(G-7882)*
Tom Sturgis Pretzels Inc 610 775-0335
  2267 Lancaster Pike Reading (19607) *(G-16544)*
Tom's Bagel Cafe', Bethlehem Also called T & P Bagels Inc *(G-1637)*
Toma Inc 717 597-7194
  853 Buchanan Trl E Greencastle (17225) *(G-6641)*
Toma Inc (PA) 717 597-7194
  212 Locust St Ste 500 Harrisburg (17101) *(G-7232)*
Toma Concrete & Materials, Harrisburg Also called Toma Inc *(G-7232)*
Tomanetti Food Products Inc 412 828-3040
  625 Allegheny Ave Oakmont (15139) *(G-12928)*
Tomanetti Pizza, Oakmont Also called Tomanetti Food Products Inc *(G-12928)*
Tomark-Worthen LLC 610 978-1889
  64 Watkin Ave Chadds Ford (19317) *(G-2861)*
Tomayko Group LLC (PA) 412 481-0600
  2403 Sidney St Ste 220 Pittsburgh (15203) *(G-15632)*
Tomdel Inc 724 519-2697
  4901 Old William Penn Hwy Monroeville (15146) *(G-11360)*
Tompkins Manufacturing Co 724 287-4927
  190 Oak Ridge Dr Butler (16002) *(G-2446)*
Tomtec Sales, Doylestown Also called Wkw Associates LLC *(G-4346)*
Tonda Inc 570 454-3323
  1127 Harwood Rd Hazle Township (18202) *(G-7484)*
Toner Holdings LLC 570 675-1131
  555 Country Club Rd Dallas (18612) *(G-3969)*
Tonnard Manufacturing Corp 814 664-7794
  715 Spring St Corry (16407) *(G-3776)*
Tonnard Manufacturing Corp 715, Corry Also called Tonnard Manufacturing Corp *(G-3776)*
Tony Bennett Flagstone 570 746-6015
  3657 Old Stagecoach Rd Wyalusing (18853) *(G-20259)*
Tony L Stec Lumber Company 814 563-9002
  Hosmer Run Rd Garland (16416) *(G-6263)*
Tookan Graphics & Screen Prtg, Beaver Falls Also called Tookan Screening & Design
Inc *(G-1015)*
Tookan Screening & Design Inc 724 846-2264
  2305 6th Ave Beaver Falls (15010) *(G-1015)*
Tool & Die Productions 814 838-3304
  5424 W Ridge Rd Erie (16506) *(G-5511)*
Tool City Welding LLC 814 333-9353
  280 Baldwin Street Ext Meadville (16335) *(G-10802)*
Tool O Matic Inc 724 776-3232
  3016 Unionville Rd Cranberry Township (16066) *(G-3855)*
Tool Tec Inc 610 688-9086
  900 W Valley Rd Ste 504 Wayne (19087) *(G-19383)*
Tool-All Inc 814 898-3917
  2053 E 30th St Erie (16510) *(G-5512)*
Tool-Rite Inc 814 587-3151
  14136 W Center Rd Springboro (16435) *(G-17896)*
Toolco Inc 724 337-9119
  4020 Leechburg Rd New Kensington (15068) *(G-12382)*
Tooling Dynamics LLC 717 764-8873
  905 Vogelsong Rd York (17404) *(G-20690)*
Tooling Specialists Inc (PA) 724 539-2534
  433 Fayette St Latrobe (15650) *(G-9524)*
Tooling Specialists Inc 724 837-0433
  Alexandria Rd Latrobe (15650) *(G-9525)*
Tootsie Roll Industries Inc 570 455-2975
  490 Forest Rd Hazle Township (18202) *(G-7485)*
Top Box Inc 724 258-8966
  1428 Delberts Dr Monongahela (15063) *(G-11318)*
Top Circle Hosiery Mills Co 610 379-0470
  329 Franklin St Weissport (18235) *(G-19461)*
Top Flight Wings, Middleburg Also called Larry Paige *(G-11027)*
Top Gun Tool Inc 814 454-4849
  421 W 12th St Erie (16501) *(G-5513)*
Top Hats Drum and Baton Co 724 339-7861
  451 Longvue Dr New Kensington (15068) *(G-12383)*
Top Line Process Equipment, Lewis Run Also called Bradford Allegheny
Corporation *(G-9871)*
Top Line Process Equipment 814 362-4626
  Valley Hunt Dr Bradford (16701) *(G-1994)*
Top Notch Cnc Machining Inc 570 658-3725
  543 W Market St Ste 2 Beavertown (17813) *(G-1028)*
Top Notch Distributors Inc 800 233-4210
  80 4th St Honesdale (18431) *(G-7729)*

Top Notch Products Inc 724 475-2341
109 2nd St Fredonia (16124) *(G-6187)*

Top of Line Auto Svc II LLC 215 727-6958
919 S 53rd St Philadelphia (19143) *(G-14395)*

Top Shop 610 622-6101
1220 Wolf St Philadelphia (19148) *(G-14396)*

Top-Notch Trucking Inc 267 456-1744
7766b Penrose Ave Elkins Park (19027) *(G-4913)*

Topflight Corporation (PA) 717 227-5400
277 Commerce Dr Glen Rock (17327) *(G-6461)*

Tophole Drilling LLC 724 272-1932
2900 S Noah Dr Saxonburg (16056) *(G-17098)*

Topit Toppings LLC 267 263-2590
1535 Gehman Rd Harleysville (19438) *(G-7062)*

Topos Mondial Corp (PA) 610 970-2270
600 Queen St Pottstown (19464) *(G-16055)*

Toppan Interamerica Inc 610 286-3100
378 Thsnd Oks Bld Crp Ctr Morgantown (19543) *(G-11541)*

Topps Chewing Gum, Scranton *Also called Topps Company Inc (G-17305)*

Topps Company Inc 570 346-5874
50 Poplar St Scranton (18509) *(G-17305)*

Topps Company Inc 570 471-7649
1001 Moosic Rd Old Forge (18518) *(G-12975)*

Tops Friendly Markets 650, Sayre *Also called Tops Markets LLC (G-17123)*

Tops Markets LLC 570 882-9188
1006 N Elmira St Sayre (18840) *(G-17123)*

Topsmal Dairy LLC 814 880-3724
2289 Jacksonville Rd Bellefonte (16823) *(G-1123)*

Tor Industries Inc 570 622-7370
2067 W Market St Pottsville (17901) *(G-16099)*

Torchbearer Sauces LLC 717 697-3568
1110 E Powderhorn Rd Mechanicsburg (17050) *(G-10898)*

Torcomp Usa LLC 717 261-1530
1690 Opportunity Ave Chambersburg (17201) *(G-2987)*

Torcup Inc 610 250-5800
1025 Conroy Pl Easton (18040) *(G-4763)*

Torgeman Gabi 215 563-0882
42 S 11th St Philadelphia (19107) *(G-14397)*

Tornier Inc 610 585-2111
801 Wagonwheel Ln West Chester (19380) *(G-19666)*

Torpedo Specialty Wire Inc 814 563-7505
Rr 2 Pittsfield (16340) *(G-15739)*

Torquato Drilling ACC Inc 570 457-8565
533 S Main St Old Forge (18518) *(G-12976)*

Torrent Pharma Inc 215 949-3711
2091 Hartel Ave Levittown (19057) *(G-9869)*

Torresdale Pharmacy 215 612-5400
3998 Red Lion Rd Ste 105 Philadelphia (19114) *(G-14398)*

Tortel Products 267 477-1805
2880 Bergey Rd Ste C Hatfield (19440) *(G-7402)*

Torvac, Imperial *Also called Darling Ingredients Inc (G-8063)*

Tory Leather Co, Williamsport *Also called Dr Davies Products Inc (G-20007)*

Tory Tool Inc (PA) 814 772-5439
1906 Bucktail Rd Saint Marys (15857) *(G-17023)*

Tory Tool Inc 814 772-5439
6955 Ridgeway St Marys Rd Ridgway (15853) *(G-16732)*

Torytown Sculpture 215 458-8092
701 Canal St Bristol (19007) *(G-2209)*

Toshiba International Corp 215 830-3340
200 Dryden Rd E Dresher (19025) *(G-4359)*

Toss Machine Components Inc 610 759-8883
539 S Main St Ste 1 Nazareth (18064) *(G-11992)*

Total Document Resource Inc 717 648-6234
19 Prestige Ln Lancaster (17603) *(G-9221)*

Total Equestrian Inc 215 721-1247
38 Green St Souderton (18964) *(G-17768)*

Total Mobility Services Inc (PA) 814 629-9935
4785 Penn Ave Boswell (15531) *(G-1885)*

Total Plastics Inc 877 677-8872
444 N 2nd St Philadelphia (19123) *(G-14399)*

Total Plastics Resources LLC 215 637-2221
633 Dunksferry Rd Bensalem (19020) *(G-1261)*

Total Ptrchemicals Ref USA Inc 877 871-2729
665 Stockton Dr Exton (19341) *(G-5737)*

Total Ptrchemicals Ref USA Inc 610 692-8401
610 S Bolmar St West Chester (19382) *(G-19667)*

Total Scope Inc 484 490-2100
17 Creek Pkwy Upper Chichester (19061) *(G-18674)*

Total Systems Technology Inc (PA) 412 653-7690
65 Terence Dr Pittsburgh (15236) *(G-15633)*

Totem Pole Ranch and Winery 717 448-8370
940 Cranes Gap Rd Carlisle (17013) *(G-2742)*

Tottser Tool & Manufacturing, Southampton *Also called Tottser Tool and Die Shop Inc (G-17843)*

Tottser Tool and Die Shop Inc (PA) 215 357-7600
935 Jaymor Rd Southampton (18966) *(G-17842)*

Tottser Tool and Die Shop Inc 215 357-7600
935 Jaymor Rd Southampton (18966) *(G-17843)*

Touch Pro, Garnet Valley *Also called Accustar Inc (G-6264)*

Touchpoint Inc (PA) 610 459-4000
210 N Brinton Lake Rd Concordville (19331) *(G-3460)*

Touchstone Home Products Inc 510 782-1282
611 Jeffers Cir Exton (19341) *(G-5738)*

Touchtown Inc 412 826-0460
931 3rd St Ste 100 Oakmont (15139) *(G-12929)*

Tour Skate Company, Atglen *Also called Roller Derby Skate Corp (G-805)*

Towanda Metadyne, Towanda *Also called Metadyne Inc (G-18432)*

Towanda Printing Co Inc 570 297-4158
778 Canton St Troy (16947) *(G-18528)*

Towanda Printing Co (PA) 570 265-2151
116 N Main St Towanda (18848) *(G-18436)*

Tower 23, Meadville *Also called Michael Cain (G-10762)*

Tower Hill Berery 267 308-8992
237 W Butler Ave Chalfont (18914) *(G-2893)*

Towerstar Pets LLC 610 296-4970
2350 Yellow Springs Rd # 2 Malvern (19355) *(G-10334)*

Towerview Health Inc 715 771-9831
2001 Market St Ste 2500 Philadelphia (19103) *(G-14400)*

Town & Country Fuel LLC 717 252-2152
1082 Letort Rd Conestoga (17516) *(G-3461)*

Town & Country Newspaper, Red Hill *Also called Gannett Stllite Info Ntwrk Inc (G-16581)*

Town Square Software LLC 610 374-7900
24 Club Ln Reading (19607) *(G-16545)*

Town Talk Newspapers Inc 610 583-4432
1914 Parker Ave Holmes (19043) *(G-7666)*

Toxicity Assssors Globl PA LLC 215 921-6972
5070 Parkside Ave # 2103 Philadelphia (19131) *(G-14401)*

Toyo Denki Usa Inc 724 774-1760
2507 Lovi Rd Bldg 3 Freedom (15042) *(G-6193)*

TP (old) LLC 412 488-1600
2403 Sidney St Ste 500 Pittsburgh (15203) *(G-15634)*

Tpl Plastic Engraving 412 771-3773
265 Forest Grove Rd Coraopolis (15108) *(G-3728)*

Tps LLC (HQ) 570 538-7200
2821 Old Route 15 New Columbia (17856) *(G-12177)*

Tq Electronics Inc 570 320-1760
1965 Lycoming Creek Rd # 205 Williamsport (17701) *(G-20084)*

Tr Technology Solutions, Archbald *Also called Software Engineering Assoc (G-695)*

Trac Fabrication Inc 717 862-8722
111 Arrowhead Dr Ste D Slippery Rock (16057) *(G-17628)*

Trac Products Inc (PA) 610 789-7853
1509 Lynnewood Dr Havertown (19083) *(G-7432)*

Tracey, Philadelphia *Also called Soltrace Inc (G-14324)*

Track Trail Search Rescue Inc 814 715-5608
26 Cherry St Brookville (15825) *(G-2274)*

Traco, Cranberry Township *Also called Kawneer Commercial Windows LLC (G-3827)*

Traco Delaware Inc (HQ) 724 776-7000
71 Progress Ave Cranberry Township (16066) *(G-3856)*

Traction Motor Service, Irwin *Also called Irwin Car & Equipment Inc (G-8173)*

Traction Software Inc 401 528-1145
513 Redwood St Harrisburg (17109) *(G-7233)*

Trademark Specialties 412 353-3752
700 Watercrest Way # 740 Cheswick (15024) *(G-3119)*

Trademark Threads, Cheswick *Also called Trademark Specialties (G-3119)*

Trafcon Industries Inc 717 691-8007
81 Texaco Rd Mechanicsburg (17050) *(G-10899)*

Traffic & Safety Signs Inc 610 925-1990
703 Terminal Way Kennett Square (19348) *(G-8550)*

Traffic Control Eqp & Sups Co 412 882-2012
979 State Route 917 Bentleyville (15314) *(G-1276)*

Traffic Maintenance Attenuator 215 997-1272
1610 Bethlehem Pike Hatfield (19440) *(G-7403)*

Trailgate Tailgate Systems 724 321-6558
1012 Fells Church Rd Rostraver Township (15012) *(G-16831)*

Trailway Speedway, Hanover *Also called Motorama Assoc (G-6924)*

Training Resource Corporation 717 652-3100
5 Miller Rd Harrisburg (17109) *(G-7234)*

Trak Ceramics Inc 610 867-7600
1210 Win Dr Bethlehem (18017) *(G-1640)*

Tran Hoang 215 833-0923
4938 N 5th St Philadelphia (19120) *(G-14402)*

Trane US Inc 412 747-3000
400 Business Center Dr # 1 Pittsburgh (15205) *(G-15635)*

Trane US Inc 412 394-9021
3042 New Beaver Ave Pittsburgh (15233) *(G-15636)*

Trane US Inc 412 963-9021
2501 Smallman St Pittsburgh (15222) *(G-15637)*

Trane US Inc 717 561-5400
3909 Tecport Dr Harrisburg (17111) *(G-7235)*

Tranquilities, Ephrata *Also called Gilead Enterprises Inc (G-5106)*

Trans American Tool Company 610 948-4411
305 S Main St Spring City (19475) *(G-17869)*

Trans Atlantic Publications 215 925-2762
33 Ashley Dr Schwenksville (19473) *(G-17180)*

Trans Energy Inc (HQ) 304 684-7053
625 Liberty Ave Ste 1790 Pittsburgh (15222) *(G-15638)*

Trans Western Polymers Inc 570 668-5690
31 Progress Ave Tamaqua (18252) *(G-18230)*

(PA)=Parent Co (HQ)=Headquarters (DH)=Div Headquarters

A
L
P
H
A
B
E
T
I
C

Trans-Tech Technologies Inc................724 327-6600
  3247 Old Frankstown Rd C Pittsburgh (15239) *(G-15639)*

Transcelerate Biopharma................484 539-1236
  1001 Cnshohocken State Rd Conshohocken (19428) *(G-3613)*

Transco Railway Products Inc................570 322-3411
  2483 Trenron Ave Williamsport (17701) *(G-20085)*

Transcontinental US LLC................570 384-4674
  3 Maplewood Dr Hazle Township (18202) *(G-7486)*

Transfer Junction (PA)................814 942-4434
  442 Polecat Hollow Rd Williamsburg (16693) *(G-19982)*

Transicoil LLC (HQ)................484 902-1100
  9 Iron Bridge Dr Collegeville (19426) *(G-3397)*

Transol Corporation (PA)................610 527-0234
  604 Hemlock Rd Ste 1 Morgantown (19543) *(G-11542)*

Transparent Protection Syst................215 638-0800
  633 Dunksferry Rd Bensalem (19020) *(G-1262)*

Transporeon Group Americas Inc................267 281-1555
  500 Office Center Dr # 400 Fort Washington (19034) *(G-6094)*

Transport Custom Designs LLC................570 368-1403
  240 Streibeigh Ln Montoursville (17754) *(G-11454)*

Transport For Christ Inc (PA)................717 426-9977
  1525 River Rd Marietta (17547) *(G-10469)*

Transport For Christ Intl, Marietta *Also called Transport For Christ Inc (G-10469)*

Transportation Eqp Sup Co................814 866-1952
  8106 Hawthorne Dr Erie (16509) *(G-5514)*

Transportation PA Dept................717 787-2304
  1101 S Front St Harrisburg (17104) *(G-7236)*

Transtar Industries Inc................412 441-7353
  6550 Hamilton Ave Pittsburgh (15206) *(G-15640)*

Transwall Corp................610 429-1400
  1220 Wilson Dr West Chester (19380) *(G-19668)*

Transwall Office Systems Inc................610 429-1400
  1220 Wilson Dr West Chester (19380) *(G-19669)*

Trashcans Unlimited LLC................800 279-3615
  1114 Texas Palmyra Hwy Honesdale (18431) *(G-7730)*

Trau & Loevner Inc................412 361-7700
  838 Braddock Ave Braddock (15104) *(G-1949)*

TRAU & LOEVNER OPERATING CO, Braddock *Also called Trau & Loevner Inc (G-1949)*

Trautman Associates Inc (PA)................570 743-0430
  2832 N Susquehanna Trl Shamokin Dam (17876) *(G-17429)*

Trautners Well Drilling & Svc, Cogan Station *Also called Andrew E Trautner & Sons Inc (G-3358)*

Travaglini Enterprises Inc................814 898-1212
  4334 Buffalo Rd Erie (16510) *(G-5515)*

Travaglini Enterprises Inc................724 342-3334
  2945 E State St Hermitage (16148) *(G-7596)*

Travaini Pumps USA Inc................757 988-3930
  530 Foundry Rd Norristown (19403) *(G-12720)*

Tray-Pak Corporation (PA)................888 926-1777
  4216 Reading Crest Ave Reading (19605) *(G-16546)*

Tray-Pak Corporation................484 509-0046
  251 Tuckerton Rd Reading (19605) *(G-16547)*

Trbz Ink LLC................267 918-2242
  2435 N Park Ave Ste 100 Philadelphia (19132) *(G-14403)*

TRC Services, Reading *Also called Rose Corporation (G-16504)*

Tre Graphics Etc Inc................610 821-8508
  5012 Med Ctr Cir Ste 3 Allentown (18106) *(G-411)*

Tre-Ray Cases Inc................215 551-6811
  2409 S Water St Philadelphia (19148) *(G-14404)*

Treasures Inc................412 920-5421
  2180 Noblestown Rd Pittsburgh (15205) *(G-15641)*

Treco Incorporated................215 226-0908
  3313 Stokley St Philadelphia (19140) *(G-14405)*

Treco-Fibematics, Philadelphia *Also called Treco Incorporated (G-14405)*

Treco-Fibematics, Philadelphia *Also called Fibematics Inc (G-13698)*

Tredegar Corporation................570 544-7600
  30 S Maple Ave Pottsville (17901) *(G-16100)*

Tredegar Film Products, Pottsville *Also called Tredegar Corporation (G-16100)*

Tree Equipment Design Inc................570 386-3515
  1392 W Penn Pike New Ringgold (17960) *(G-12444)*

Treehouse Foods Inc................814 725-5696
  11160 Parkway Dr North East (16428) *(G-12763)*

Treehouse Private Brands Inc................610 589-4526
  336 Hill Rd Womelsdorf (19567) *(G-20209)*

Treen Box & Pallet Corp (PA)................717 535-5800
  400 Center Rd Mifflintown (17059) *(G-11136)*

Trega Corporation................610 562-5558
  625 Valley Rd Hamburg (19526) *(G-6854)*

Tremco Incorporated................717 944-9702
  46 Hillcrest Dr Middletown (17057) *(G-11083)*

Trench Shoring Services................412 331-8118
  1200 Neville Rd Pittsburgh (15225) *(G-15642)*

Trent Inc................215 482-5000
  201 Leveringtion Ave Philadelphia (19127) *(G-14406)*

Trenton Group Inc (PA)................717 637-2288
  2000 Carlisle Pike Hanover (17331) *(G-6962)*

Trenton Group Inc................717 235-3807
  35 Constitution Ave Shrewsbury (17361) *(G-17589)*

Trenwyth Industries Inc (HQ)................717 767-6868
  1 Connelly Rd Emigsville (17318) *(G-5002)*

Tresco Concrete Products Inc................724 468-4640
  1 Plant Rd Export (15632) *(G-5629)*

Tresco Paving Corporation (PA)................412 793-0651
  415 Unity Center Rd Pittsburgh (15239) *(G-15643)*

Trevena Inc................610 354-8840
  955 Chesterbrook Blvd # 200 Chesterbrook (19087) *(G-3099)*

Trexler Industries Inc................610 974-9800
  95 Southland Dr Bethlehem (18017) *(G-1641)*

Treyco Manufacturing Inc................717 273-6504
  1500 Chestnut St Lebanon (17042) *(G-9636)*

Tri Bms LLC (PA)................610 495-9700
  501 S Main St Ste 106 Spring City (19475) *(G-17870)*

Tri City Aluminum Company (HQ)................724 799-8917
  71 Progress Ave Cranberry Township (16066) *(G-3857)*

Tri City Marble Inc................610 481-0177
  4724 Springside Ct Allentown (18104) *(G-412)*

Tri County Record................610 970-3218
  24 N Hanover St Pottstown (19464) *(G-16056)*

Tri County Sports Inc................717 394-9169
  2007 Lincoln Hwy E Lancaster (17602) *(G-9222)*

Tri County Transit Service Inc................610 495-5640
  110 Industrial Pkwy Pottstown (19464) *(G-16057)*

Tri Max Manufacturing Co Inc................724 898-1400
  103 Mcfann Rd Valencia (16059) *(G-18703)*

Tri Star Precision Mfg................215 443-8610
  375 Ivyland Rd Ste 28 Warminster (18974) *(G-18984)*

Tri State Filter Mfg Co................412 621-8491
  744 Edmond St Pittsburgh (15224) *(G-15644)*

Tri State Golf Inc................215 200-7000
  2421 S Philip St Philadelphia (19148) *(G-14407)*

Tri State Kitchens and Baths................
  139 Possum Hollow Rd Pottstown (19464) *(G-16058)*

Tri State Metal Cleaning Inc................814 898-3933
  4725 Iroquois Ave Erie (16511) *(G-5516)*

Tri State Scales LLC................610 779-5361
  28 Basket Rd Reading (19606) *(G-16548)*

Tri- Med Laboratories Inc................732 249-6363
  2159 White St Ste 3 York (17404) *(G-20691)*

Tri-Ad Litho Inc................412 795-3110
  1385 Frey Rd Pittsburgh (15235) *(G-15645)*

Tri-Boro Construction Sups Inc (PA)................717 246-3095
  465 E Locust St Dallastown (17313) *(G-3982)*

Tri-Boro Construction Sups Inc................717 249-6448
  1490 Ritner Hwy Carlisle (17013) *(G-2743)*

Tri-City Marble LLC................610 481-0177
  4724 Springside Ct Allentown (18104) *(G-413)*

Tri-Com Inc................610 259-7400
  359 E Madison Ave Clifton Heights (19018) *(G-3259)*

Tri-County News, Slippery Rock *Also called Pollock Advertising (G-17624)*

Tri-Dim Filter Corporation................610 481-9926
  7036 Snowdrift Rd Allentown (18106) *(G-414)*

Tri-Form Inc................724 334-0237
  2104 Constitution Blvd New Kensington (15068) *(G-12384)*

Tri-Kris Co Inc................215 855-5183
  1001 Walnut St Lansdale (19446) *(G-9415)*

Tri-Kris Company................215 855-5183
  1001 Walnut St Lansdale (19446) *(G-9416)*

Tri-Our Brands................570 655-1512
  400 Pollock Dr Pittston (18640) *(G-15783)*

Tri-Rivers Electric Inc................412 290-6525
  35 W Prospect Ave Pittsburgh (15205) *(G-15646)*

Tri-State Blueprinting, Pittsburgh *Also called Tristate Blue Printing Inc (G-15653)*

Tri-State Container Corp................215 638-1311
  1440 Bridgewater Rd Bensalem (19020) *(G-1263)*

Tri-State Door and Hardware................215 455-2100
  318 W Hunting Park Ave Philadelphia (19140) *(G-14408)*

Tri-State Envelope Corporation (PA)................570 875-0433
  20th Market St Ashland (17921) *(G-738)*

Tri-State Events Magazine Inc................215 947-8600
  1800 Byberry Rd Ste 901 Huntingdon Valley (19006) *(G-8044)*

Tri-State Hydraulics Inc................724 483-1790
  1250 Mckean Ave Charleroi (15022) *(G-3022)*

Tri-State Petroleum Corp................724 226-0135
  100 E 7th Ave Tarentum (15084) *(G-18249)*

Tri-State Plastics Inc................724 457-2847
  392 Flaugherty Run Rd Coraopolis (15108) *(G-3729)*

Tri-State Rebar Company................412 824-4000
  1558 Mt Pleasnt Cnl Rd # 72 Mount Pleasant (15666) *(G-11720)*

Tri-State Reprographics Inc................412 281-3538
  2934 Smallman St Pittsburgh (15201) *(G-15647)*

Tri-State River Products Inc................724 775-2221
  334 Insurance St Beaver (15009) *(G-993)*

Tri-State Tubular Rivet Co................610 644-6060
  382 Lancaster Ave Malvern (19355) *(G-10335)*

Tri-State Welding Corp................610 374-0321
  126 Carpenter St Reading (19602) *(G-16549)*

Tri-Tech, Edinboro *Also called Hytech Tool & Design Co (G-4815)*

Tri-Tech Injection Molding Inc 814 476-7748
8556 Edinboro Rd Mc Kean (16426) *(G-10595)*
Tri-Vet Design Fabrication LLC 570 462-4941
301 E Washington St Shenandoah (17976) *(G-17497)*
Tri-Way Metalworkers Inc 570 462-4941
301 E Washington St Shenandoah (17976) *(G-17498)*
Triad Isotopes Inc 717 558-8640
4400 Lewis Rd Ste A Harrisburg (17111) *(G-7237)*
Triad Truck Equipment 484 614-7349
3380 W Ridge Pike Pottstown (19464) *(G-16059)*
Triangle Petroleum Inc 908 380-2685
107 Jackson Run Rd Warren (16365) *(G-19052)*
Triangle Poster and Prtg Co 412 371-0774
2119 Robinson Blvd Pittsburgh (15221) *(G-15648)*
Triangle Press Inc 717 541-9315
6720 Allentown Blvd Frnt Harrisburg (17112) *(G-7238)*
Triangle Printing & Packg Co, York *Also called Triangle Printing Company Inc (G-20692)*
Triangle Printing Company Inc 717 854-1521
1000 E Boundary Ave York (17403) *(G-20692)*
Triangle Spring, Du Bois *Also called Triangle Sspension Systems Inc (G-4425)*
Triangle Sspension Systems Inc (HQ) 814 375-7211
47 E Maloney Rd Du Bois (15801) *(G-4425)*
Triangle Tool Company Inc (PA) 814 878-4400
3230 W 22nd St Erie (16506) *(G-5517)*
Triangle Tool Company Inc 814 878-4400
2425 W 23rd St Erie (16506) *(G-5518)*
Triangle Tool Company Inc 814 878-4603
2315 W 23rd St Erie (16506) *(G-5519)*
Triaxial Structures Inc 215 248-0380
507 E Roumfort Rd Philadelphia (19119) *(G-14409)*
Trib Total Media Inc 724 684-5200
622 Cabin Hill Dr Greensburg (15601) *(G-6719)*
Trib Total Media LLC (PA) 412 321-6460
622 Cabin Hill Dr Greensburg (15601) *(G-6720)*
Trib Total Media LLC 724 543-1303
1270 N Water St Kittanning (16201) *(G-8800)*
Trib Total Media LLC 412 871-2301
210 Wood St Tarentum (15084) *(G-18250)*
Trib Total Media LLC 724 834-1151
622 Cabin Hill Dr Greensburg (15601) *(G-6721)*
Tribology Systems (PA) 610 466-7547
239-K Madison Ave Warminster (18974) *(G-18985)*
Triboro Banner 570 348-9185
149 Penn Ave Scranton (18503) *(G-17306)*
Tribune-Review Publishing Co 724 779-8742
210 Wood St Tarentum (15084) *(G-18251)*
Trickling Springs Creamery LLC 717 709-0711
2330 Molly Pitcher Hwy Chambersburg (17202) *(G-2988)*
Trico Welding Company 724 722-1300
100 Acorn Ln Yukon (15698) *(G-20785)*
Tricor Industries Inc 610 265-1111
636 Markley St Norristown (19401) *(G-12721)*
Tricorn Inc 610 777-6823
333 Trout Ln Reading (19607) *(G-16550)*
Tricounty Printers Ltd 215 886-3737
222 Roesch Ave Oreland (19075) *(G-13031)*
Trident Emergency Products LLC 215 293-0700
2940 Turnpike Dr Ste 9 Hatboro (19040) *(G-7308)*
Trident Engineering Plastics, Bristol *Also called Trident Plastics Inc (G-2210)*
Trident Plastics Inc (PA) 215 443-7147
1029 Pulinski Rd Warminster (18974) *(G-18986)*
Trident Plastics Inc 215 946-3999
7900 N Radcliffe St Ste 7 Bristol (19007) *(G-2210)*
Trident Tpi Holdings Inc 484 690-1520
460 E Swedesford Rd # 3000 Wayne (19087) *(G-19384)*
Tridex Technology Ltd 484 388-5000
4125 Whitaker Ave Philadelphia (19124) *(G-14410)*
Trigon Holding Inc (PA) 724 941-5540
124 Hidden Valley Rd Mc Murray (15317) *(G-10647)*
Trigon Incorporated 724 941-5540
124 Hidden Valley Rd Mc Murray (15317) *(G-10648)*
Trijay Systems Inc 215 997-5833
10 Maple Ave Line Lexington (18932) *(G-9977)*
Trilion Quality Systems LLC (PA) 215 710-3000
651 Park Ave King of Prussia (19406) *(G-8690)*
Trilli Holdings Inc 724 736-8000
228 Church St Star Junction (15482) *(G-17938)*
Trillion Source Inc 631 949-2304
1438 Chestnut St Unit 4 Emmaus (18049) *(G-5045)*
Trim Line Foundations, South Fork *Also called Farel Corp (G-17774)*
Trim P A C LLC 717 375-2366
2823 Molly Pitcher Hwy Chambersburg (17202) *(G-2989)*
Trim Tech Inc 215 321-0841
1055 Little Rd Newtown (18940) *(G-12556)*
Trimach LLC 610 252-8983
1350 Sullivan Trl Ste C Easton (18040) *(G-4764)*
Trimetric Enterprises Inc 610 670-2099
250 Holland St Wernersville (19565) *(G-19487)*
Trimetric Mold & Design, Wernersville *Also called Trimetric Enterprises Inc (G-19487)*
Trimline Windows Inc 215 672-5233
Gingko Industrial K Industrial Pr Ivyland (18974) *(G-8224)*
Trimmaster, Temple *Also called Fabricon Inc (G-18329)*
Trims 215 541-1946
2123 Berry Ln East Greenville (18041) *(G-4578)*
Trinity Fibrgls Composites LLC 412 855-3398
1000 Gregg St Carnegie (15106) *(G-2798)*
Trinity Glass Intl Inc 610 395-2030
8014 Industrial Blvd # 200 Breinigsville (18031) *(G-2028)*
Trinity Highway Rentals Inc 570 380-2856
900 Patterson Dr Bloomsburg (17815) *(G-1804)*
Trinity Industries 724 588-7000
100 York St Greenville (16125) *(G-6774)*
Trinity Manufacturing Tech, Allentown *Also called Artman and Artman Inc (G-143)*
Trinity Mining Services Inc 412 605-0612
109 48th St Pittsburgh (15201) *(G-15649)*
Trinity Partners LLC 610 233-1210
301 E Germantown Pike East Norriton (19401) *(G-4585)*
Trinity Plastics Inc 717 242-2355
13 Industrial Park Rd Lewistown (17044) *(G-9950)*
Trinity Sup & Installation LLC 412 331-3044
288a Corliss St Pittsburgh (15220) *(G-15650)*
Trinseo LLC (HQ) 610 240-3200
1000 Chesterbrook Blvd # 300 Berwyn (19312) *(G-1378)*
Trinseo Materials Finance Inc 610 240-3200
1000 Chesterbrook Blvd Berwyn (19312) *(G-1379)*
Trinseo S A (PA) 610 240-3200
1000 Chesterbrook Blvd Berwyn (19312) *(G-1380)*
Trio Motion Technology LLC 724 472-4100
187 Northpointe Blvd # 105 Freeport (16229) *(G-6215)*
Trio Plastics Inc 814 724-1640
21398 Blooming Valley Rd Meadville (16335) *(G-10803)*
Triomi Inc 215 756-2771
1317 S 10th St Philadelphia (19147) *(G-14411)*
Triple C Motor Accessories, York *Also called Philip Cooke (G-20627)*
Triple Creek 814 756-4500
9225 Fillinger Rd Cranesville (16410) *(G-3872)*
Triple D Screen Printing 215 788-4877
2854 Veterans Hwy Bristol (19007) *(G-2211)*
Triple D Truss LLC 570 726-7092
168 Sunrise Ln Mill Hall (17751) *(G-11183)*
Triple Play Sports 215 923-5466
827 S 9th St Philadelphia (19147) *(G-14412)*
Triple Trophy Products Inc 412 781-8801
1102 N Canal St Ste E Pittsburgh (15215) *(G-15651)*
Triple W Enterprises Inc 610 865-0071
1230 Illicks Mill Rd Bethlehem (18017) *(G-1642)*
Tripwire Operations Group LLC 717 648-2792
1685 Baltimore Pike Ste C Gettysburg (17325) *(G-6319)*
Trireme Energy Development LLC 412 253-9400
1251 Waterfront Pl Fl 3 Pittsburgh (15222) *(G-15652)*
Tristar Lighting Company 215 245-3400
1349 Ford Rd Bensalem (19020) *(G-1264)*
Tristate Blue Printing Inc 412 281-3538
2934 Smallman St Pittsburgh (15201) *(G-15653)*
Tristate Golf Carts, Scranton *Also called North End Electric Service Inc (G-17267)*
Tristate Precast Products Div, Jeannette *Also called CMS East Inc (G-8250)*
Tritech Applied Sciences Inc 215 362-6890
650 N Cannon Ave 20 Lansdale (19446) *(G-9417)*
Triton Services Inc 484 851-3883
9999 Hamilton Blvd # 350 Breinigsville (18031) *(G-2029)*
Triton Signs Incorporated 610 495-4747
133a Possum Hollow Rd Pottstown (19464) *(G-16060)*
Triumph Aerospace Systems Grp (HQ) 610 251-1000
899 Cassatt Rd Ste 210 Berwyn (19312) *(G-1381)*
Triumph Aviations Inc 610 251-1000
899 Cassatt Rd Ste 210 Berwyn (19312) *(G-1382)*
Triumph Controls LLC (HQ) 215 699-4861
205 Church Rd North Wales (19454) *(G-12837)*
Triumph Controls- North Wales, North Wales *Also called Triumph Controls LLC (G-12837)*
Triumph Group Inc (PA) 610 251-1000
899 Cassatt Rd Ste 210 Berwyn (19312) *(G-1383)*
Triumph Group Acquisition Corp (HQ) 610 251-1000
899 Cassatt Rd Ste 210 Berwyn (19312) *(G-1384)*
Triumph Group Holdings - Mexic (PA) 610 251-1000
899 Cassatt Rd Ste 210 Berwyn (19312) *(G-1385)*
Triumph Group Operations Inc (HQ) 610 251-1000
899 Cassatt Rd Ste 210 Berwyn (19312) *(G-1386)*
Triumph Insulation Systems LLC 610 251-1000
899 Cassatt Rd Ste 210 Berwyn (19312) *(G-1387)*
Triumph Sales Inc 412 781-0950
51 Bridge St Ste 100 Pittsburgh (15223) *(G-15654)*
Triumph Structures - E Texas 610 251-1000
899 Cassatt Rd Ste 210 Berwyn (19312) *(G-1388)*
Triune Color Corporation 856 829-5600
1625 Terwood Rd Huntingdon Valley (19006) *(G-8045)*
Trivagory Enterprises 570 474-6520
89 S Main St Mountain Top (18707) *(G-11779)*
TRM Emergency Vehicles LLC 610 689-0702
41 Spring Rd Boyertown (19512) *(G-1932)*

ALPHABETIC

Troemel Landscaping 215 783-3150
  2027 Wentz Church Rd Lansdale (19446) *(G-9418)*

Trofi Idoni Specialty Baking 484 892-0876
  421 Central Blvd Bethlehem (18018) *(G-1643)*

Trojan Inc 814 336-4468
  114 W Poplar St Meadville (16335) *(G-10804)*

Trojan Boiler Service, Muncy *Also called Trojan Tube Sls & Fabrications* *(G-11836)*

Trojan Tube Sls & Fabrications 570 546-8860
  161 W Water St Muncy (17756) *(G-11836)*

Tronox Specialty Alkali Corp, Philadelphia *Also called Genesis Specialty Alkali LLC (G-13753)*

Trophy Works 412 279-0111
  1001 Campbells Run Rd Carnegie (15106) *(G-2799)*

Trotter Industries 610 369-9473
  30 S Jefferson St Boyertown (19512) *(G-1933)*

Trotwood Manor 724 635-3057
  612 Woodmere Dr New Stanton (15672) *(G-12452)*

Trout Run Secondary 814 834-0075
  1105 Monroe Rd Saint Marys (15857) *(G-17024)*

Troutman Machine Shop Inc 610 363-5480
  424 Creamery Way Exton (19341) *(G-5739)*

Troy Gazette Register, Troy *Also called Bradco Printers Inc (G-18517)*

Troy Healthcare LLC 570 453-5252
  130 Lions Dr Hazle Township (18202) *(G-7487)*

Troy Manufacturing Co Inc 570 453-5252
  130 Lions Dr Hazle Township (18202) *(G-7488)*

Troy Penny Saver, Troy *Also called Towanda Printing Co Inc (G-18528)*

Troyer Inc 724 746-1162
  42 Swihart Rd Canonsburg (15317) *(G-2648)*

Troyer Farms, Canonsburg *Also called Troyer Inc (G-2648)*

Troyer Pallet Company 717 535-4499
  81 Center Rd Mifflintown (17059) *(G-11137)*

Troyer Rope Co 814 587-3879
  20785 Morris Rd Conneautville (16406) *(G-3488)*

Troyer's Wholesome Foods, New Castle *Also called Ncc Wholesome Foods Inc (G-12124)*

Trs Technologies Inc (HQ) 814 238-7485
  2820 E College Ave State College (16801) *(G-18040)*

Trs Welding & Fabrication Inc 610 369-0897
  500 County Line Rd Gilbertsville (19525) *(G-6378)*

Tru Tech Valve LLC (PA) 724 916-4805
  3287 Perry Hwy New Castle (16101) *(G-12160)*

Tru Temp Sensors Inc 215 396-1550
  495 Morgan Ct Southampton (18966) *(G-17844)*

Tru-Gas Inc 814 723-9260
  Rd 1 Rr 6 Clarendon (16313) *(G-3171)*

Tru-Lite International Inc 724 443-6821
  5311 William Flynn Hwy Gibsonia (15044) *(G-6356)*

Tru-Tech Industries Inc (PA) 724 776-1020
  9025 Marshall Rd Cranberry Township (16066) *(G-3858)*

Truck Lite Co Inc 716 664-3519
  107 Industrial Park Rd Beech Creek (16822) *(G-1083)*

Truck-Lite Co LLC 570 769-7231
  786 Mcelhattan Rd Mc Elhattan (17748) *(G-10590)*

Truck-Lite Co LLC 814 274-5400
  100 Market St Coudersport (16915) *(G-3790)*

Truckcraft Corporation 717 375-2900
  5751 Molly Pitcher Hwy Chambersburg (17202) *(G-2990)*

True Cut Sawmills Inc 814 694-2192
  40021 Dorn Rd Centerville (16404) *(G-2836)*

True Form Plastics LLC 717 875-4521
  904c Strasburg Pike Strasburg (17579) *(G-18096)*

True Position Inc 724 444-0300
  3919 Chessrown Ave Gibsonia (15044) *(G-6357)*

True Precision Plastics LLC 717 358-9251
  310 Running Pump Rd Lancaster (17603) *(G-9223)*

Trufood Mfg Inc 412 963-6600
  106 Gamma Dr Pittsburgh (15238) *(G-15655)*

Trufood Mfg Inc (PA) 412 963-2330
  610 Alpha Dr Pittsburgh (15238) *(G-15656)*

Trugen3 LLC 412 668-3831
  733 Wshington Rd Ste 211 Pittsburgh (15228) *(G-15657)*

Trulite GL Alum Solutions LLC 724 274-9050
  100 Business Center Dr Cheswick (15024) *(G-3120)*

Trulite GL Alum Solutions LLC 570 282-6711
  Clidco Dr Carbondale (18407) *(G-2687)*

Trumco Inc 814 382-7767
  3324 Mcmaster Rd Atlantic (16111) *(G-814)*

Truss-Tech Inc 717 436-9778
  98 E Industrial Dr Mifflintown (17059) *(G-11138)*

Trust Franklin Press Co 412 481-6442
  516 Bingham St Pittsburgh (15203) *(G-15658)*

Trustees of The Univ of PA 215 898-5555
  3533 Locust Walk Philadelphia (19104) *(G-14413)*

Try Tek Machine Works Inc 717 428-1477
  250 N Main St Jacobus (17407) *(G-8232)*

Tryone Forge Limestone, Tyrone *Also called New Enterprise Stone Lime Inc (G-18587)*

TS McCorry Heating and Cooling 215 379-2800
  1035 Kipling Rd Rydal (19046) *(G-16887)*

Tsb Group LLC 412 224-2306
  2119 Murray Ave Pittsburgh (15217) *(G-15659)*

Tsb Nclear Enrgy USA Group Inc 412 374-4111
  1000 Westinghouse Dr Cranberry Township (16066) *(G-3859)*

Tsg Finishing 828 850-4381
  1400 Welsh Rd North Wales (19454) *(G-12838)*

Tshudy Snacks Inc 717 626-4354
  219 E Main St Lititz (17543) *(G-10055)*

Tsi Associates Inc (PA) 610 375-4371
  1031q Macarthur Rd Reading (19605) *(G-16551)*

Tsi Competition Engines, Easton *Also called T H E M Services Inc (G-4761)*

Tsi Titanium, Derry *Also called Techspec Inc (G-4108)*

Tsitouch Inc 802 874-0123
  1 Millennium Dr 1 # 1 Uniontown (15401) *(G-18643)*

TSO of Ohio Inc 724 452-6161
  115 West Rd Fombell (16123) *(G-6035)*

Tsrubnus Liquidation Inc 814 461-9120
  420 E Bayfront Pkwy Erie (16507) *(G-5520)*

TSS Industries Inc 717 821-6570
  404 Oak Grove Rd Pine Grove (17963) *(G-14606)*

TST, Pittsburgh *Also called Total Systems Technology Inc (G-15633)*

TT&I, Hatfield *Also called Tech Tag & Label Inc (G-7398)*

TTI, Holmes *Also called Kykayke Inc (G-7663)*

TTI Metals, Wayne *Also called Tool Tec Inc (G-19383)*

Tube Laser Industries, Johnstown *Also called Johnstown Tube Laser LLC (G-8392)*

Tube Methods Inc 610 279-7700
  416 Depot St Bridgeport (19405) *(G-2047)*

Tubro Company Inc 800 673-7887
  30 Council Rock Dr Warminster (18974) *(G-18987)*

Tucker Indus Lquid Catings Inc 717 259-8339
  407 N Avenue E Berlin East Berlin (17316) *(G-4526)*

Tucker Industries Incorporated 215 638-1900
  3170 Tucker Rd Bensalem (19020) *(G-1265)*

Tuckey Metal Fabricators Inc 717 249-8111
  150 Stover Dr Carlisle (17015) *(G-2744)*

Tudor Design 215 638-3366
  2205 Lillian Dr Bensalem (19020) *(G-1266)*

Tuff Temp, Quakertown *Also called Textemp LLC (G-16249)*

Tukes Tearoff (PA) 570 695-3171
  57 E Main St Tremont (17981) *(G-18483)*

Tulip Biolabs Inc 610 584-2706
  2031 N Broad St Ste 139 Lansdale (19446) *(G-9419)*

Tumacs Corp (PA) 412 653-1188
  50 Terence Dr Pittsburgh (15236) *(G-15660)*

Tumbling With Jojo 267 574-5074
  970 Pulaski Dr King of Prussia (19406) *(G-8691)*

Tuna Enterprises 724 205-6535
  1811 S Broad Street Ext Greensburg (15601) *(G-6722)*

Tunefly LLC 570 392-9239
  371 State St Nanticoke (18634) *(G-11904)*

Tung Yee Restaurant Supply, Philadelphia *Also called Siu King (G-14313)*

Turbo Software LLC 215 490-6806
  5450 Wissahickon Ave 553b Philadelphia (19144) *(G-14414)*

Turbo Start Battery, New Castle *Also called New Castle Battery Mfg Co (G-12127)*

Turck Engineered Packaging 717 421-7371
  806 Crosby St Harrisburg (17112) *(G-7239)*

Turf Teq LLC 484 798-6300
  699 Todd Rd Honey Brook (19344) *(G-7767)*

Turkey Hill LP 717 872-5461
  2601 River Rd Conestoga (17516) *(G-3462)*

Turkey Hill Dairy, Conestoga *Also called Turkey Hill LP (G-3462)*

Turner Dairy Farms Inc (PA) 412 372-7155
  1049 Jefferson Rd Pittsburgh (15235) *(G-15661)*

Turner John 610 524-2050
  305 Commerce Dr Ste 200 Exton (19341) *(G-5740)*

Turner Knit Products, Reading *Also called Robert W Turner (G-16501)*

Turner Tool & Die Inc 570 378-3233
  Orchard Dr Lake Winola (18625) *(G-8912)*

Turner White Cmmunications Inc 610 975-4541
  339 Millbank Rd Bryn Mawr (19010) *(G-2335)*

Turning Solutions Inc 814 723-1134
  34 E Harmar St Ste 3 Warren (16365) *(G-19053)*

Turnings By Edric 412 833-5127
  240 Graeser Ave Bethel Park (15102) *(G-1436)*

Turnitin LLC 724 272-7250
  160 N Craig St Pittsburgh (15213) *(G-15662)*

Turnmatic 717 898-3200
  2878 Yellow Goose Rd Lancaster (17601) *(G-9224)*

Turri Associates Incorporated 717 795-9936
  327 W Allen St Mechanicsburg (17055) *(G-10900)*

Turtle Creek Sportswear, Pittsburgh *Also called Nicholas Wohlfarth (G-15337)*

Turtle Moon Gardens 814 639-0287
  303 Lower Julian Pike Port Matilda (16870) *(G-15907)*

Tuscan/Lehigh Dairies Inc 215 855-8205
  880 Allentown Rd Lansdale (19446) *(G-9420)*

Tuscan/Lehigh Dairies Inc 610 434-9666
  711 N Brick St Allentown (18102) *(G-415)*

Tuscarora Coal Company, Middleport *Also called Kuperavage Enterprises Inc (G-11045)*

ALPHABETIC SECTION Ultimate Tool Inc

Tuscarora Electric Mfg Co 570 836-2101
41 Hilltop Dr Tunkhannock (18657) ***(G-18551)***
Tuscarora Hardwoods Inc 717 582-4122
2240 Shermans Valley Rd Elliottsburg (17024) ***(G-4922)***
Tuscarora Structures Inc 717 436-5591
152 Tuscarora Ln Mifflin (17058) ***(G-11091)***
Tuscarora Usa Inc 717 491-2861
1626 Majestic Dr Chambersburg (17202) ***(G-2991)***
Tutorgen Inc 704 710-8445
505 Linden Ct Mars (16046) ***(G-10511)***
Tuxedos By Jack O'Reilly, Reading *Also called Jack OReilly Tuxedos* ***(G-16412)***
Tuzzi Bakery, Berwick *Also called James J Tuzzi Jr* ***(G-1329)***
TV Guide Distribution Inc 610 293-8500
100 W Matsonford Rd Ste 1 Wayne (19087) ***(G-19385)***
TV Guide Magazine LLC 212 852-7500
100 W Matsonford Rd Ste 1 Radnor (19087) ***(G-16303)***
TVC Communications LLC (HQ) 717 838-3790
800 Airport Rd Annville (17003) ***(G-661)***
TW Metals LLC (HQ) 610 458-1300
760 Constitution Dr # 204 Exton (19341) ***(G-5741)***
Twanda Printing 570 421-4800
149 Penn Ave Scranton (18503) ***(G-17307)***
Twenty First Century Tool Co 724 423-5357
176 County Line Rd Acme (15610) ***(G-17)***
Twenty61 LLC 215 370-7076
812 S Saint Bernard St # 3 Philadelphia (19143) ***(G-14415)***
Twin Brook Coal Co 724 254-4030
410 Franklin St Clymer (15728) ***(G-3274)***
Twin County Machine, Gap *Also called Edward Thompson* ***(G-6250)***
Twin Pines Manufacturing, Clarksburg *Also called Twin Pines Manuifacturing Corp* ***(G-3200)***
Twin Pines Manuifacturing Corp 724 459-3850
5779 Newport Rd Clarksburg (15725) ***(G-3200)***
Twin Specialties Corporation 610 834-7900
15 E Ridge Pike Ste 210 Conshohocken (19428) ***(G-3614)***
Twisted Tmber Deadwood Log Inc 215 541-4140
521 W 5th St Pennsburg (18073) ***(G-13258)***
Twisted Vine Winery 814 512-4330
13106 Route 948 Kane (16735) ***(G-8479)***
Two Cousins Holdings LLC 717 637-1311
1000 Carlisle St Ste 1350 Hanover (17331) ***(G-6963)***
Two Letters Ink 717 393-8989
700 Eden Rd Ste 2 Lancaster (17601) ***(G-9225)***
Two M Electric Inc 215 530-9964
109 Camars Dr Warminster (18974) ***(G-18988)***
Two Paperdolls LLC 610 293-4933
163 E Lancaster Ave Wayne (19087) ***(G-19386)***
Two Rivers Olives Oil Company 724 775-2748
428 3rd St Beaver (15009) ***(G-994)***
Two Technologies Inc 215 441-5305
419 Sargon Way Ste A Horsham (19044) ***(G-7861)***
Two Togethers Inc 814 838-1234
5539 Peach St Erie (16509) ***(G-5521)***
Two Toys Inc 717 840-6400
2801 E Market St York (17402) ***(G-20693)***
Ty-Gard 2000, Bensalem *Also called Walnut Industries Inc* ***(G-1268)***
Ty-Pak Inc 570 835-5269
9 Fish St Tioga (16946) ***(G-18365)***
Tyber Medical LLC 303 717-5060
83 S Commerce Way Ste 310 Bethlehem (18017) ***(G-1644)***
Tybot LLC 412 756-3360
3812 William Flynn Hwy Allison Park (15101) ***(G-465)***
Tyco Elec Latin Amer Holdg LLC (HQ) 610 893-9800
1050 Westlakes Dr Berwyn (19312) ***(G-1389)***
Tyco Electronics, Mount Joy *Also called Te Connectivity Corporation* ***(G-11672)***
Tyco Fire Products LP (HQ) 215 362-0700
1400 Pennbrook Pkwy Lansdale (19446) ***(G-9421)***
Tyco Fire Products LP 256 238-0579
1411 Lancaster Ave Columbia (17512) ***(G-3452)***
Tyco Fire Protection Products, Columbia *Also called Tyco Fire Products LP* ***(G-3452)***
Tyco Fire Sppression Bldg Pdts, Lansdale *Also called Tyco Fire Products LP* ***(G-9421)***
Tye Bar LLC 412 896-1376
1050 Ohio Ave Glassport (15045) ***(G-6422)***
Tygart Steel Division, Mc Keesport *Also called M Glosser & Sons Inc* ***(G-10642)***
Tyger Construction 814 467-9342
217 Cameron Ct Windber (15963) ***(G-20193)***
Tyk America Inc (HQ) 412 384-4259
301 Brickyard Rd Clairton (15025) ***(G-3158)***
Tyoga Container, Tioga *Also called Ty-Pak Inc* ***(G-18365)***
Tyoga Container Company Inc (PA) 570 835-5295
9 Fish St Tioga (16946) ***(G-18366)***
Type & Print Inc (PA) 412 241-6070
2251 Sweeney Dr Clinton (15026) ***(G-3267)***
Type Set Print 570 542-5910
310 Hartman Rd Hunlock Creek (18621) ***(G-7935)***
Typecraft Press Inc 412 488-1600
2403 Sidney St 500 Pittsburgh (15203) ***(G-15663)***
Tyrone Bureau Water Department, Tyrone *Also called Borough of Tyrone* ***(G-18577)***
Tyson 717 755-4782
440 Steinfelt Rd Red Lion (17356) ***(G-16618)***
Tyson Foods Inc 717 653-8326
455 Ridge Run Rd Mount Joy (17552) ***(G-11673)***
Tyson Foods Inc 412 257-3224
1344 Greystone Dr Pittsburgh (15241) ***(G-15664)***
Tyson Foods Inc 717 354-4211
403 S Custer Ave New Holland (17557) ***(G-12289)***
TYT LLC 800 511-2009
177 Mikron Rd Ste 1 Bethlehem (18020) ***(G-1645)***
U B R LLC 717 432-3490
4 Barlo Cir Ste G Dillsburg (17019) ***(G-4141)***
U C S, South Park *Also called United Commercial Supply LLC* ***(G-17786)***
U E C Inc 724 772-5225
11 Leonberg Rd Cranberry Township (16066) ***(G-3860)***
U G L, Scranton *Also called United Gilsonite Laboratories* ***(G-17308)***
U R I Compressors Inc (PA) 484 223-3265
405 Allentown Dr Unit A Allentown (18109) ***(G-416)***
U S Durum Products Limited 717 293-8698
1812 William Penn Way Lancaster (17601) ***(G-9226)***
U S Plastic Coatings Corp 215 257-5300
3225 State Rd Sellersville (18960) ***(G-17361)***
U S Silica Company 814 542-2561
1885 Rte 1 Mapleton Depot (17052) ***(G-10432)***
U S Textile Corp 828 733-9244
1150 Northbrook Dr # 300 Feasterville Trevose (19053) ***(G-5934)***
U S Textile Corp (HQ) 803 283-6800
1150 Northbrook Dr # 300 Feasterville Trevose (19053) ***(G-5935)***
U S Weatherford L P 724 745-7050
121 Hillpointe Dr Canonsburg (15317) ***(G-2649)***
U Squared Interactive LLC 214 770-7437
339 6th Ave Ste 1100 Pittsburgh (15222) ***(G-15665)***
U-Haul, Greenville *Also called Arthur K Miller* ***(G-6738)***
U-Haul, Mercer *Also called Interstate Self Storage* ***(G-10965)***
U. S. Steel, Braddock *Also called United States Steel Corp* ***(G-1950)***
U. S. Steel, Fairless Hills *Also called United States Steel Corp* ***(G-5805)***
U. S. Steel, Uniontown *Also called United States Steel Corp* ***(G-18645)***
U.S. Energy Exploration Group, Rural Valley *Also called US Energy Expl Corp* ***(G-16878)***
U.S. Heat Treaters, Kersey *Also called Modern Industries Inc* ***(G-8564)***
U.S. Liner Company, Cranberry Township *Also called American Made LLC* ***(G-3803)***
U.S.webcon, Paxinos *Also called US Web Converting McHy Corp* ***(G-13194)***
Uae Coalcorp Associates 570 339-4090
1 Harmony Rd Mount Carmel (17851) ***(G-11630)***
Uav Aviation Services 717 691-8882
827 W Trindle Rd Mechanicsburg (17055) ***(G-10901)***
Ubedesktop, Fort Washington *Also called Nzinganet Inc* ***(G-6087)***
Uber Advance Technologies Ctr, Pittsburgh *Also called Uber Atc* ***(G-15666)***
Uber Atc 412 587-2986
91 43rd St Ste 220 Pittsburgh (15201) ***(G-15666)***
Ucg Georgia LLC 610 515-8589
3001 Emrick Blvd Ste 320 Bethlehem (18020) ***(G-1646)***
Uct Inc 215 781-9255
2500 Pearl Buck Rd Bristol (19007) ***(G-2212)***
Uct Inc (PA) 215 781-9255
2731 Bartram Rd Bristol (19007) ***(G-2213)***
Uct LLC 215 781-9255
2731 Bartram Rd Bristol (19007) ***(G-2214)***
Uds Home Medical Equipment LLC 717 665-1490
2270 Erin Ct Lancaster (17601) ***(G-9227)***
Ue Lifesciences Inc 631 980-8340
3711 Market St Philadelphia (19104) ***(G-14416)***
Ufc Aerospace 610 485-4704
18 Creek Pkwy Upper Chichester (19061) ***(G-18675)***
Ufp Eastern Division Inc 724 399-2992
116 N River Ave Parker (16049) ***(G-13166)***
Ufp Gordon LLC 570 875-2811
1 Royer St Gordon (17936) ***(G-6547)***
Ufp Parker LLC 724 399-2992
116 N River Ave Parker (16049) ***(G-13167)***
Ufp Stockertown LLC 610 759-8536
33 Rr 191 Stockertown (18083) ***(G-18067)***
UGI Europe Inc (PA) 610 337-1000
460 N Gulph Rd King of Prussia (19406) ***(G-8692)***
UGI Newco LLC 610 337-7000
460 N Gulph Rd King of Prussia (19406) ***(G-8693)***
UGm Precision Machining Inc 215 957-6175
239-P Madison Ave Ste P Warminster (18974) ***(G-18989)***
Uh Structures Inc 724 628-6100
2241 Industrial Dr Ste A Connellsville (15425) ***(G-3509)***
Uhl Technologies LLC 814 437-6346
127 Lamberton St Franklin (16323) ***(G-6166)***
Uhl's Ayrshire Dairy, Saint Marys *Also called Ayrshire Dairy* ***(G-16950)***
Uhuru Mfg LLC 717 345-3366
622 Farmersville Rd New Holland (17557) ***(G-12290)***
Ukani Brothers Enterprise 412 269-0499
2900 Banksville Rd Pittsburgh (15216) ***(G-15667)***
Ultimate Screw Machine Pdts 610 565-1565
641 Painter St Media (19063) ***(G-10955)***
Ultimate Tool Inc 814 835-2291
2001 Peninsula Dr Ste 12 Erie (16506) ***(G-5522)***

ALPHABETIC

Ultra Chem LLC 215 778-5967
  665a Catherine St Warminster (18974) *(G-18990)*
Ultra Lite Brakes An C...724 696-3743
  1378 Old State Route 119 Mount Pleasant (15666) *(G-11721)*
Ultra Precision Incorporated 724 295-5161
  2220 Silverville Rd Freeport (16229) *(G-6216)*
Ultra Pure Products Inc 717 589-7001
  46 N Main St Mifflintown (17059) *(G-11139)*
Ultra Tech Frac Services, Mansfield *Also called Keane Frac LP (G-10417)*
Ultra-Mold Corporation 215 493-9840
  301 Oxford Valley Rd 504a Yardley (19067) *(G-20344)*
Ultra-Poly Corporation (PA) 570 897-7500
  102 Demi Rd Portland (18351) *(G-15940)*
Ultra-Poly Corporation 570 784-1586
  480 W 5th St Bloomsburg (17815) *(G-1805)*
Ultraflex Systems Inc 610 906-1410
  237 South St Ste 200 Pottstown (19464) *(G-16061)*
Ultramet Heat Treating Inc 814 781-7215
  258 Church St Saint Marys (15857) *(G-17025)*
Ultraoptics Inc 724 838-7155
  507 New Haven Dr Greensburg (15601) *(G-6723)*
Ultrasound Division, Plymouth Meeting *Also called Siemens Med Solutions USA*
Inc (G-15870)
Ultravoice Ltd 610 356-6443
  90 S Newtown Street Rd # 14 Newtown Square (19073) *(G-12595)*
Ultronix Inc 215 822-8206
  2880 Bergey Rd Ste M Hatfield (19440) *(G-7404)*
Umoja Erectors LLC 215 235-7662
  926 N 19th St Philadelphia (19130) *(G-14417)*
Una Biologicals LLC 412 889-9746
  4322 Butler St Pittsburgh (15201) *(G-15668)*
Unami Ridge Winery 215 804-5445
  2144 Kumry Rd Quakertown (18951) *(G-16253)*
Uncle Charleys Sausage Co LLC 724 845-3302
  1135 Industrial Park Rd Vandergrift (15690) *(G-18736)*
Uncle Henrys Handmade Pretzels, Bowmansville *Also called Uncle Henrys Pretzel*
Bakery (G-1888)
Uncle Henrys Pretzel Bakery 717 445-4698
  1550 Bowmansville Rd Bowmansville (17507) *(G-1888)*
Unclecharleyssausage.com, Vandergrift *Also called Uncle Charleys Sausage Co*
LLC (G-18736)
Under Armour Inc 717 393-7671
  35 S Willowdale Dr # 207 Lancaster (17602) *(G-9228)*
Under Pressure Connections LLC...........................570 326-1117
  825 Us Highway 15 South Williamsport (17702) *(G-17793)*
Undercoveralls Inc 610 519-0858
  815 E Railroad Ave Bryn Mawr (19010) *(G-2336)*
Undernet Gaming Incorporated 484 544-8943
  1005 Brittany Blvd Harrisburg (17109) *(G-7240)*
Unek Designs EMB & Sew Sp LLC 610 563-6676
  1108 W Lincoln Hwy Coatesville (19320) *(G-3327)*
Unequal Technologies Company 610 444-5900
  10 Lacrue Ave Glen Mills (19342) *(G-6446)*
Unequal Technologies Company 610 444-5900
  10 Lacrue Ave Glen Mills (19342) *(G-6447)*
Ungerer & Company, Bethlehem *Also called Ungerer Industries Inc (G-1647)*
Ungerer Industries Inc 610 868-7266
  110 N Commerce Way Bethlehem (18017) *(G-1647)*
UNI-Pro Inc (PA) 610 668-9191
  7330 Tulip St Philadelphia (19136) *(G-14418)*
UNI-Ref United Refractories Co (PA) 724 941-9390
  264 Valley Brook Rd Canonsburg (15317) *(G-2650)*
Unicast Inc 610 559-9998
  17 Mcfadden Rd Easton (18045) *(G-4765)*
Unicast Company 610 366-8836
  241 N Washington St Boyertown (19512) *(G-1934)*
Unicast Company 610 366-8836
  1653 Hausman Rd Allentown (18104) *(G-417)*
Unicor, Lewisburg *Also called Federal Prison Industries (G-9906)*
Unicor, Minersville *Also called Federal Prison Industries (G-11254)*
Unified Orthopedics, Bethlehem *Also called Tyber Medical LLC (G-1644)*
Unifilt Corporation (PA) 717 823-0313
  375 Johnson St Wilkes Barre (18702) *(G-19966)*
Uniflex Holdings Inc 516 932-2000
  2900 Grant Ave Philadelphia (19114) *(G-14419)*
Uniform Tubes Division, Trappe *Also called Lake Region Medical Inc (G-18471)*
Unigraphics Communications 717 697-8132
  1 Jeffrey Rd Mechanicsburg (17050) *(G-10902)*
Unilever 717 776-2180
  954 Centerville Rd Newville (17241) *(G-12611)*
Unimach Manufacturing 724 285-5505
  1652 Route 422 E Fenelton (16034) *(G-5949)*
Unimove LLC 610 826-7855
  1145c Little Gap Rd Palmerton (18071) *(G-13112)*
Union Apparel Inc 724 423-4900
  Main St Norvelt (15674) *(G-12879)*
Union Chill Mat Co (PA) 724 452-6400
  160 Dean Ln Zelienople (16063) *(G-20825)*

Union City Non-Ferrous Inc..................................937 968-5460
  259 S College St Washington (15301) *(G-19233)*
Union Electric Akers, Avonmore *Also called Akers National Roll Company (G-862)*
Union Electric Company 814 452-0587
  1712 Greengarden Rd Erie (16501) *(G-5523)*
Union Electric Drive, Burgettstown *Also called Union Electric Steel Corp (G-2358)*
Union Electric Steel Corp (HQ) 412 429-7655
  726 Bell Ave Ste 101 Carnegie (15106) *(G-2800)*
Union Electric Steel Corp 724 947-9595
  31 Union Electric Rd Burgettstown (15021) *(G-2358)*
Union Min Co of Allegheny Cnty 412 344-9900
  31 Moffett St Pittsburgh (15243) *(G-15669)*
Union News 570 343-4958
  1256 Oneill Hwy Dunmore (18512) *(G-4486)*
Union Orthotics Prosthetics Co, Greensburg *Also called Union Orthotics Prosthetics*
Co (G-6724)
Union Orthotics Prosthetics Co, Pittsburgh *Also called Union Orthotics Prosthetics*
Co (G-15670)
Union Orthotics Prosthetics Co 724 836-6656
  3 Gibralter Way Greensburg (15601) *(G-6724)*
Union Orthotics Prosthetics Co 412 943-1950
  5704 Brownsville Rd Pittsburgh (15236) *(G-15670)*
Union Orthotics Prosthetics Co 412 621-2698
  6301 Northumberland St Pittsburgh (15217) *(G-15671)*
Union Packaging LLC 610 572-7265
  6250 Baltimore Ave Ste 1 Yeadon (19050) *(G-20356)*
Union Quarries At Bonny Brook, Carlisle *Also called Union Quarries Inc (G-2745)*
Union Quarries Inc 717 249-5012
  102 Bonnybrook Rd Carlisle (17013) *(G-2745)*
Union Roofing & Sheet Metal, Altoona *Also called Union Roofing and Shtmtl Co (G-553)*
Union Roofing and Shtmtl Co 814 946-0824
  430 7th Ave Altoona (16602) *(G-553)*
Union Sealants LLC 610 473-2892
  35 Ashley Cir Gilbertsville (19525) *(G-6379)*
Union Spring & Mfg Corp 814 967-2545
  15715 Mercer Rd Townville (16360) *(G-18449)*
Union Spring & Mfg Corp (PA) 412 843-5900
  4268 N Pike Ste 1 Monroeville (15146) *(G-11361)*
Union Square Frog LLC 717 561-0623
  3911 Union Deposit Rd Harrisburg (17109) *(G-7241)*
Union Switch and Signal 412 688-2400
  68 Renova St Pittsburgh (15207) *(G-15672)*
Union Tank Car Company 814 944-4523
  Chestnut Ave And Sixth St Altoona (16601) *(G-554)*
Unione Italian Newspaper, Pittsburgh *Also called Frediani Printing Company (G-15035)*
Uniontown Newspapers Inc (HQ) 724 439-7500
  8 E Church St Ste 18 Uniontown (15401) *(G-18644)*
Unipack Inc (PA) 724 733-7381
  3253 Old Frankstown Rd Pittsburgh (15239) *(G-15673)*
Unipak Inc 610 436-6600
  715 E Washington St West Chester (19380) *(G-19670)*
Unipak Products Company, West Chester *Also called Unipak Inc (G-19670)*
Unipaper Recycling Company (HQ) 412 429-8522
  73 Noblestown Rd Ste D Carnegie (15106) *(G-2801)*
Unipar Inc 717 667-3354
  130 Royal St Reedsville (17084) *(G-16629)*
Unique Desserts By Anne Louise, Reading *Also called Unique Desserts Inc (G-16552)*
Unique Desserts Inc 610 372-7879
  530 Grape St Reading (19611) *(G-16552)*
Unique Fabrication LLC 814 227-2627
  19059 Paint Blvd Ste 2 Shippenville (16254) *(G-17565)*
Unique Machine & Tool 412 331-2717
  365 Munson Ave Mc Kees Rocks (15136) *(G-10640)*
Unique Machine Co 215 368-8550
  131 Commerce Dr Montgomeryville (18936) *(G-11425)*
Unique Pretzel Bakery Inc 610 929-3172
  215 E Bellevue Ave Reading (19605) *(G-16553)*
Unique Systems Inc 610 499-1463
  221 Stanford Dr Wallingford (19086) *(G-18787)*
Unique Technologies Inc 610 775-9191
  111 Chestnut St Mohnton (19540) *(G-11271)*
Unique Wood Creation LLC 717 687-8843
  609 Strasburg Rd Paradise (17562) *(G-13163)*
Unique Wood Creation LLC 717 687-7900
  609 Strasburg Rd Paradise (17562) *(G-13164)*
Uniquely Diamonds 610 356-5025
  3513 West Chester Pike # 1 Newtown Square (19073) *(G-12596)*
Unison Engine Components Inc 570 825-4544
  120 Hazle St Wilkes Barre (18702) *(G-19967)*
Unisource Associates Inc 610 489-5799
  105 G P Clement Dr Collegeville (19426) *(G-3398)*
Unisteel LLC 724 657-1160
  499 Honey Bee Ln New Castle (16105) *(G-12161)*
Unistress Corp 610 395-5930
  5071 Bridlepath Dr Macungie (18062) *(G-10160)*
United Ammunition Container (PA) 610 658-0888
  101h Cherry Ln Wynnewood (19096) *(G-20273)*
United Brass Works Inc 814 456-4296
  944 W 12th St Erie (16501) *(G-5524)*

United Bronze of Pittsburgh 724 226-8500
344 W 6th Ave Tarentum (15084) *(G-18252)*

United Color Manufacturing Inc (PA) 215 860-2165
660 Newtown Yardley Rd # 205 Newtown (18940) *(G-12557)*

United Color Manufacturing Inc 215 423-2527
2940 E Tioga St Philadelphia (19134) *(G-14420)*

United Commercial Supply LLC 412 835-2690
6348 Lib Rd Bldg 1 Ste 2 South Park (15129) *(G-17786)*

United Coolair Corporation 717 845-8685
491 E Princess St York (17403) *(G-20694)*

United Corrstack LLC 610 374-3000
720 Laurel St Reading (19602) *(G-16554)*

United Electric Supply Co Inc 717 632-7640
550 W Elm Ave Hanover (17331) *(G-6964)*

United Enrgy Plus Trminals LLC 610 774-5151
2 N 9th St Allentown (18101) *(G-418)*

United Envelope LLC 570 839-1600
1200 Industrial Park Mount Pocono (18344) *(G-11738)*

United Fabricating Inc (PA) 724 663-5891
4522 State Route 40 Claysville (15323) *(G-3209)*

United Fence Supply Company 570 307-0782
1105 Mid Valley Dr Olyphant (18447) *(G-13002)*

United Foundry Company Inc 814 539-8840
548 Horner St Johnstown (15902) *(G-8440)*

United Gilsonite Laboratories (PA) 570 344-1202
1396 Jefferson Ave Scranton (18509) *(G-17308)*

United Hydrogen Group Inc 866 942-7763
1900 Main St Ste 223 Canonsburg (15317) *(G-2651)*

United Industrial Electro 814 539-6115
163 Cramer Pike Johnstown (15906) *(G-8441)*

United Industrial Group Inc 724 746-4700
290 Meadowlands Blvd Washington (15301) *(G-19234)*

United Laminations Inc 570 876-1360
1311 Lackawanna Ave Mayfield (18433) *(G-10544)*

United Metal Products Corp 570 226-3084
516 Keystone St Hawley (18428) *(G-7440)*

United Metal Traders Inc 215 288-6555
5240 Comly St Philadelphia (19135) *(G-14421)*

United Offset 215 721-2251
429 Harleysville Pike Franconia (18924) *(G-6111)*

United Oil Company Corp 412 231-1269
1800 N Franklin St Pittsburgh (15233) *(G-15674)*

United Panel Inc 610 588-6871
8 Wildon Dr Mount Bethel (18343) *(G-11615)*

United Partners Ltd 570 288-7603
27 Stauffer Industrial Pa Taylor (18517) *(G-18264)*

United Partners Ltd (PA) 570 283-0995
27 Stauffer Industrial Pa Taylor (18517) *(G-18265)*

United Phosphorus Inc., King of Prussia Also called Upl NA Inc *(G-8694)*

United Plastics Machinery Inc 610 363-0990
131 S Whitford Rd Exton (19341) *(G-5742)*

United Precision Mfg Co Inc 215 938-5890
85 Tomlinson Rd Huntingdon Valley (19006) *(G-8046)*

United Refining Inc (HQ) 814 723-1500
15 Bradley St Warren (16365) *(G-19054)*

United Refining Company, Warren Also called United Refining Inc *(G-19054)*

United Refining Company 724 274-0885
13 Mellon Springdale (15144) *(G-17904)*

United Refining Company (HQ) 814 723-1500
15 Bradley St Warren (16365) *(G-19055)*

United Refining Company 814 723-6511
2351 Market St Warren (16365) *(G-19056)*

United Research Labs Inc (HQ) 215 535-7460
1100 Orthodox St Philadelphia (19124) *(G-14422)*

United Service Co, New Tripoli Also called Hayes-Ivy Mfg Inc *(G-12457)*

United States Dept of Navy 215 897-3537
1701 Kitty Hawk Ave Philadelphia (19112) *(G-14423)*

United States Gypsum Company 724 857-4300
1 Woodlawn Rd Aliquippa (15001) *(G-98)*

United States Hardmetal 724 834-8381
857 S Main St Greensburg (15601) *(G-6725)*

United States Hardware Mfg Inc (PA) 724 222-5110
79 Stewart Ave Washington (15301) *(G-19235)*

United States Products Co 412 621-2130
518 Melwood Ave Pittsburgh (15213) *(G-15675)*

United States Steel Corp 412 675-7459
1 Camp Hollow Rd West Mifflin (15122) *(G-19746)*

United States Steel Corp 412 433-1121
1268 Camp Hollow Rd Pittsburgh (15122) *(G-15676)*

United States Steel Corp (PA) 412 433-1121
600 Grant St Ste 468 Pittsburgh (15219) *(G-15677)*

United States Steel Corp 412 273-7000
1300 Braddock Ave Braddock (15104) *(G-1950)*

United States Steel Corp 412 433-1121
600 Grant St Ste 468 Pittsburgh (15219) *(G-15678)*

United States Steel Corp 215 736-4600
Penne Ave S Fairless Hills (19030) *(G-5805)*

United States Steel Corp 412 810-0286
800 E Waterfront Dr Homestead (15120) *(G-7694)*

United States Steel Corp 215 736-4600
400 Berdis Blvd Fairless Hills (19030) *(G-5806)*

United States Steel Corp 412 433-7215
800 E Waterfront Dr Homestead (15120) *(G-7695)*

United States Steel Corp 724 439-1116
751 Mcclellandtown Rd Uniontown (15401) *(G-18645)*

United States Steel Corp 412 433-1419
1509 Muriel St Pittsburgh (15203) *(G-15679)*

United States Thermoamp Inc 724 537-3500
1223 Heat Siphon Ln Latrobe (15650) *(G-9526)*

United Sttes Metal Powders Inc (PA) 908 782-5454
K Clive Ramsey Bldg Palmerton (18071) *(G-13113)*

United Technologies Corp 800 227-7437
303 Mount Pleasant Rd Scottdale (15683) *(G-17203)*

United Theatrical Services 215 242-2134
16 E Hartwell Ln Philadelphia (19118) *(G-14424)*

United Tool & Die Inc 814 763-1133
275 Terrace Street Ext Meadville (16335) *(G-10805)*

United Wldg & Fabrication Inc 814 266-3598
246 Seanor Rd Windber (15963) *(G-20194)*

United-Erie Division, Hermitage Also called Interstate Chemical Co Inc *(G-7588)*

Unitex Group Usa LLC 864 846-8700
48 Vincent Cir Ste D Warminster (18974) *(G-18991)*

Uniti Titanium LLC 412 424-0440
400 Industry Dr Ste 220 Pittsburgh (15275) *(G-15680)*

Unitrac Railroad Materials Inc 570 923-1514
100 Industrial Park Rd Renovo (17764) *(G-16651)*

Unity Fabrication Tech Inc 724 423-7500
1235 Marguerite Lake Rd Greensburg (15601) *(G-6726)*

Unity Marble and Granite Inc 412 793-4220
3201 Universal Rd Pittsburgh (15235) *(G-15681)*

Unity Printing Company Inc 724 537-5800
5848 State Route 981 Latrobe (15650) *(G-9527)*

Univar USA Inc 717 944-7471
532 E Emaus St Ste 1 Middletown (17057) *(G-11084)*

Universal, Bangor Also called Windjammer Corporation Inc *(G-935)*

Universal Awnings & Signs Inc 215 634-7150
3119 Boudinot St Philadelphia (19134) *(G-14425)*

Universal Carnegie Mfg 800 867-9554
66a Arch St Carnegie (15106) *(G-2802)*

Universal Concrete Pdts Corp (HQ) 610 323-0700
400 Old Reading Pike A100 Stowe (19464) *(G-18073)*

Universal Display Corporation 609 671-0980
2005 Trowbridge Dr Newtown (18940) *(G-12558)*

Universal Electric Corporation 724 597-7800
168 Georgetown Rd Canonsburg (15317) *(G-2652)*

Universal Fire Protection, Philadelphia Also called UNI-Pro Inc *(G-14418)*

Universal Fluids Inc 267 639-2238
3010 E Ontario St Philadelphia (19134) *(G-14426)*

Universal Forest Products, Parker Also called Great Lakes Framing LLC *(G-13165)*

Universal Forest Products, Stockertown Also called Ufp Stockertown LLC *(G-18067)*

Universal Forest Products, Gordon Also called Ufp Gordon LLC *(G-6547)*

Universal Glass Cnstr Inc 570 390-4900
95 Purdytown Tpke Lake Ariel (18436) *(G-8895)*

Universal Machine & Engrg, Pottstown Also called Universal Mch Co Pottstown
Inc *(G-16062)*

Universal Manufacturing Corp 724 452-8300
550 W New Castle St Zelienople (16063) *(G-20826)*

Universal Mch Co Pottstown Inc 610 323-1810
645 Old Reading Pike Pottstown (19464) *(G-16062)*

Universal Network Technologies 412 490-0990
100 Urick Ct Monroeville (15146) *(G-11362)*

Universal Pen & Pencil Co Inc (PA) 610 670-4720
776 Fritztown Rd Reading (19608) *(G-16555)*

Universal Pioneers LLC 570 239-3950
67 Nottingham St Plymouth (18651) *(G-15822)*

Universal Polly Products, New Holland Also called Quality Fencing & Supply *(G-12276)*

Universal Pressure Pumping Inc 814 373-3226
18360 Technology Dr Meadville (16335) *(G-10806)*

Universal Printing Company LLC 570 342-1243
1205 Oneill Hwy Dunmore (18512) *(G-4487)*

Universal Protective Packg Inc (PA) 717 766-1578
61 Texaco Rd Mechanicsburg (17050) *(G-10903)*

Universal Publishing, Waymart Also called Gutenberg Inc *(G-19287)*

Universal Ready Mix & Supply 724 529-2950
400 Dawson Scottdale Rd Dawson (15428) *(G-4033)*

Universal Refractories Inc (PA) 724 535-4374
915 Clyde St Wampum (16157) *(G-18806)*

Universal Refractories Inc 412 787-7220
500 Beaver Grade Rd Coraopolis (15108) *(G-3730)*

Universal Services Assoc Inc (PA) 610 461-0300
5 Horne Dr Folcroft (19032) *(G-6018)*

Universal Specialties, Wampum Also called Universal Refractories Inc *(G-18806)*

Universal Stainless, Bridgeville Also called North Jckson Specialty Stl LLC *(G-2082)*

Universal Stainless & Alloy (PA) 412 257-7600
600 Mayer St Bridgeville (15017) *(G-2097)*

Universal STAinless& Alloy 814 827-9723
121 Caldwell St Titusville (16354) *(G-18402)*

Universal Transfers Inc 215 744-6227
  3800 Jasper St Philadelphia (19124) *(G-14427)*
Universal Trlr Crgo Group Inc 570 929-3761
  6 Banks Ave McAdoo (18237) *(G-10659)*
Universal Well Services Inc 724 430-6201
  2198 University Dr Lemont Furnace (15456) *(G-9739)*
Universal Well Services Inc 814 938-5327
  324 Meter St Punxsutawney (15767) *(G-16165)*
Universal Well Services Inc 570 321-5302
  250 Arch St Williamsport (17701) *(G-20086)*
Universal Well Services Inc (HQ) 814 337-1983
  13549 S Mosiertown Rd Meadville (16335) *(G-10807)*
Universal Well Services Inc 814 333-2656
  18360 Technology Dr 4 Meadville (16335) *(G-10808)*
Universal Well Services Inc 814 938-2051
  114 Universal Dr Punxsutawney (15767) *(G-16166)*
Universal Well Services Inc 814 368-6175
  18360 Technology Dr Meadville (16335) *(G-10809)*
University City Review Inc 215 222-2846
  3927 Walnut St Fl 3 Philadelphia (19104) *(G-14428)*
University Copy Service Inc 215 898-5574
  5070 Parkside Ave Unit 66 Philadelphia (19131) *(G-14429)*
University of Pittsburgh 412 383-2456
  3400 4th Ave Fl 5 Eureka B Flr 5 Pittsburgh (15260) *(G-15682)*
University of Pittsburgh 412 648-7980
  434 William Pitt Un Pittsburgh (15260) *(G-15683)*
University of Pittsburgh Press, Pittsburgh *Also called University of Pittsburgh (G-15682)*
University Pittsburgh Med Ctr 412 647-8762
  200 Lothrop St Pittsburgh (15213) *(G-15684)*
University Rifle Club Inc 610 927-1810
  590 Schoffers Rd Reading (19606) *(G-16556)*
University Services, Philadelphia *Also called Gerson Associates PC (G-13759)*
Unlimited Mobility 484 620-9587
  39-5 Mint Tier Ct Reading (19606) *(G-16557)*
Unlocked Entertainment Tech 267 507-6028
  1735 Market St Ste 3750 Philadelphia (19103) *(G-14430)*
Up-Front Footwear Inc 717 492-1875
  33 N Market St Mount Joy (17552) *(G-11674)*
Upinya Beverages LLC 717 398-7309
  22 Centennial St Fairfield (17320) *(G-5769)*
Upl NA Inc (HQ) 610 491-2800
  630 Freedom Business Ctr King of Prussia (19406) *(G-8694)*
Upper Bucks Publishing Company, Allentown *Also called Morning Call LLC (G-322)*
Upper Case Living 724 229-8190
  475 Mankey Rd Washington (15301) *(G-19236)*
Upper Darby Sign Company 610 518-5881
  251 Boot Rd Downingtown (19335) *(G-4259)*
Upper Delaware Valley ID 570 251-8040
  54 Miller Dr Bethany (18431) *(G-1391)*
Upper Milford Western Dst Fire 610 966-3541
  6341 Chestnut St Zionsville (18092) *(G-20837)*
Upper Moreland 215 773-9880
  204 Fair Oaks Ave Horsham (19044) *(G-7862)*
Upper Perk Robotics 215 541-1654
  1005 Jodie Ct Pennsburg (18073) *(G-13259)*
Upper Perk Shoppers Guide Inc 215 679-4133
  878 Main St Pennsburg (18073) *(G-13260)*
Upper Perk Sportswear Inc 215 541-3211
  343 Main St Pennsburg (18073) *(G-13261)*
Upper Providence Township 610 933-8179
  1286 Clack Rock Rd Oaks (19456) *(G-12937)*
Upper Room Inc 724 437-5815
  311 Dixon Blvd Uniontown (15401) *(G-18646)*
Upper Room Tees, Uniontown *Also called Upper Room Inc (G-18646)*
Upreach Inc 215 536-8758
  2118 Nrthmpton St Ste 100 Easton (18042) *(G-4766)*
UPS, Pittsburgh *Also called Minton Holdings LLC (G-15293)*
UPS Store Inc 724 934-1088
  3000 Village Run Rd # 103 Wexford (15090) *(G-19831)*
UPS Store 6410 ....484 816-0252
  4920 Pennell Rd Aston (19014) *(G-795)*
UPS Store, The, York *Also called FB Shoemaker LLC (G-20476)*
UPS Stores, The, Greensburg *Also called Laurel Parcel Services Inc (G-6683)*
Upson-Walton Company 570 649-5188
  5820 Susquehanna Trl Turbotville (17772) *(G-18557)*
Upstate Niagara Coop Inc 570 326-2021
  1860 E 3rd St Williamsport (17701) *(G-20087)*
Urania Engineering Co Inc 570 455-0776
  198 S Poplar St Hazleton (18201) *(G-7532)*
Urban Enterprises T & M LLC 215 485-5209
  535 Andrews Rd Ste 100 Feasterville Trevose (19053) *(G-5936)*
Urban Outfitters Wholesale Inc (HQ) 215 454-5500
  5000 S Broad St Philadelphia (19112) *(G-14431)*
Urban Tees Inc DBA Soho G 646 295-8923
  2741 E Country Club Rd Philadelphia (19131) *(G-14432)*
Urgent Denture Repair LLC 412 714-8157
  1201 Broughton Rd Pittsburgh (15236) *(G-15685)*
Urick Foundry, Erie *Also called Ridge Tool Company (G-5463)*
Url Distribution, Philadelphia *Also called United Research Labs Inc (G-14422)*

Url Pharma, Philadelphia *Also called Mutual Pharmaceutical Co Inc (G-14047)*
Url Pharma Inc (HQ) 215 288-6500
  1100 Orthodox St Philadelphia (19124) *(G-14433)*
Urns & Ivy, Chambersburg *Also called F&M Surfaces Inc (G-2931)*
Ursa Mjor Drctnal Crssings LLC 866 410-9719
  102 Bartleson Deer Trl Greentown (18426) *(G-6735)*
Ursoft Inc 724 452-2150
  134 S Main St Ste A Zelienople (16063) *(G-20827)*
Ursus Medical LLC 412 779-4016
  100 Sandune Dr Pittsburgh (15239) *(G-15686)*
US Axle Inc 610 323-3800
  275 Shoemaker Rd Pottstown (19464) *(G-16063)*
US Boiler 215 535-8900
  3633 I St Philadelphia (19134) *(G-14434)*
US Boiler Company Inc 717 397-4701
  1548 Fruitville Pike Lancaster (17601) *(G-9229)*
US Bronze Foundry & Mch Inc (PA) 814 337-4234
  18649 Brake Shoe Rd Meadville (16335) *(G-10810)*
US Concrete Inc 610 532-6290
  1401 Calcon Hook Rd Sharon Hill (19079) *(G-17465)*
US Corrugated Inc (PA) 724 345-2050
  95 W Beau St Ste 430 Washington (15301) *(G-19237)*
US Crossings Unlimited LLC 888 359-1115
  20436 Route 19 620-244 Cranberry Township (16066) *(G-3861)*
US Custom Wiring LLC 856 905-0250
  1501 N 18th St Philadelphia (19121) *(G-14435)*
US Energy 724 783-7532
  145 Valley Rd Rural Valley (16249) *(G-16877)*
US Energy Expl Corp 724 783-7624
  145 Valley Rd Rural Valley (16249) *(G-16878)*
US Municipal Supply Inc (PA) 610 292-9450
  10583 Raystown Rd Huntingdon (16652) *(G-7958)*
US PHARMACEUTICALS, Pittsburgh *Also called Unipack Inc (G-15673)*
US Resistor Inc 814 834-9369
  1016 Delaum Rd Saint Marys (15857) *(G-17026)*
US Specialty Formulations LLC 610 849-5030
  116 Research Dr Bethlehem (18015) *(G-1648)*
US Steel Holdings Inc 412 433-1121
  600 Grant St Fl 1 Pittsburgh (15219) *(G-15687)*
US Web Converting McHy Corp 570 644-1401
  138 Miles Rd Paxinos (17860) *(G-13194)*
USA, Wayne *Also called Cool Bio Inc (G-19314)*
USA All Pro Auto Salon Inc 267 230-7442
  869 W Street Rd Unit B Warminster (18974) *(G-18992)*
USA Coil & Air Inc (PA) 610 296-9668
  11 General Warren Blvd # 2 Malvern (19355) *(G-10336)*
USA Coil and Air, Malvern *Also called USA Coil & Air Inc (G-10336)*
USA Embroidery & Silkscre 570 837-7700
  317 W Mulberry Aly Beavertown (17813) *(G-1029)*
USA Media LLC 215 571-9241
  756 Taylor Dr Folcroft (19032) *(G-6019)*
USA Medical, Folcroft *Also called Universal Services Assoc Inc (G-6018)*
USA Optical Inc (PA) 717 757-5632
  2553 E Market St York (17402) *(G-20695)*
USA Pork Packers Inc 570 501-7675
  328 S Wyoming St Hazleton (18201) *(G-7533)*
USA Precision 724 924-2838
  1957 Shaffer Rd Ellwood City (16117) *(G-4954)*
USA Spares Inc 717 241-9222
  1729 W Trindle Rd Carlisle (17015) *(G-2746)*
Usafrica Journal, Folcroft *Also called USA Media LLC (G-6019)*
Usironline, New Hope *Also called Quickel International Corp (G-12313)*
Usm Aerostructures Corp 570 613-1234
  74 W 6th St Wyoming (18644) *(G-20285)*
Usma, Wyoming *Also called Usm Aerostructures Corp (G-20285)*
Usnr LLC 724 929-8405
  212 State St Ste 1 Belle Vernon (15012) *(G-1089)*
Usnr LLC 724 929-8405
  212 State St Belle Vernon (15012) *(G-1090)*
USS Irvin Works Plant, Pittsburgh *Also called United States Steel Corp (G-15676)*
Ussc Group Inc (PA) 610 265-3610
  101 Gordon Dr Ste 1 Exton (19341) *(G-5743)*
Ussc LLC 610 265-3610
  101 Gordon Dr Ste 1 Exton (19341) *(G-5744)*
Usv Optical Inc 412 655-8311
  3075 Clairton Rd Ste 100 West Mifflin (15123) *(G-19747)*
UTC Fire SEC Americas Corp Inc 717 569-5797
  40 Citation Ln Lititz (17543) *(G-10056)*
Utcras Inc 610 328-1100
  501 Highland Ave Morton (19070) *(G-11594)*
Utcras LLC 610 328-1100
  501 Highland Ave Morton (19070) *(G-11595)*
Uticom Systems Inc 610 857-2655
  109 Independence Way Coatesville (19320) *(G-3328)*
Utilities & Industries Inc (HQ) 814 653-8269
  1995 Reynoldsville Reynoldsville (15851) *(G-16667)*
Utilities and Industries, Fairmount City *Also called Dbi Inc (G-5808)*
Utility Service Group Inc 717 737-6092
  1304 Slate Hill Rd Camp Hill (17011) *(G-2521)*

Utra Precision, Freeport *Also called Ultra Precision Incorporated* ***(G-6216)***
Utz Quality Foods Inc.....570 368-8050
90 Choate Cir Montoursville (17754) ***(G-11455)***
Utz Quality Foods Inc.....717 637-6644
900 High St Hanover (17331) ***(G-6965)***
Utz Quality Foods Inc.....717 637-5666
1437 Broadway Hanover (17331) ***(G-6966)***
Utz Quality Foods LLC (PA).....800 367-7629
900 High St Hanover (17331) ***(G-6967)***
Utz Quality Foods LLC.....717 698-4032
25 Wyndfield Dr Hanover (17331) ***(G-6968)***
V & S Lebanon Galvanizing, Jonestown *Also called Voigt & Schweitzer LLC* ***(G-8454)***
V and S Lbanon Galvanizing LLC.....717 861-7777
153 Micro Dr Jonestown (17038) ***(G-8453)***
V Boxes, Philadelphia *Also called Michael J Doyle* ***(G-14021)***
V C I Quality Masonry Contrs, Julian *Also called Village Craft Iron & Stone Inc* ***(G-8457)***
V I P Machining Inc (PA).....814 665-1840
18381 Sciota St Corry (16407) ***(G-3777)***
V I P Machining Inc.....814 665-1840
18381 Sciota St Corry (16407) ***(G-3778)***
V L H Inc (HQ).....800 245-4440
600 Boyce Rd Pittsburgh (15205) ***(G-15688)***
V Menghini & Sons Inc.....570 455-6315
1052 S Church St Hazle Township (18201) ***(G-7489)***
V P L Inc (PA).....814 652-6767
100 Masters Ave Everett (15537) ***(G-5579)***
V R Machine Co Inc.....717 846-9203
257a N Duke St York (17401) ***(G-20696)***
V-Factor Technologies, Pittsburgh *Also called Cheetah Technologies LP* ***(G-14842)***
V2r2 LLC.....215 277-2181
672 Main St Ste D Harleysville (19438) ***(G-7063)***
Vacon LLC.....717 261-5000
1500 Nitterhouse Dr Chambersburg (17201) ***(G-2992)***
Vacu-Braze Inc.....215 453-0414
2200 Kumry Rd Quakertown (18951) ***(G-16254)***
Vacuum Works LLC.....570 202-8407
370 N Courtland St East Stroudsburg (18301) ***(G-4637)***
Vacuumet Div, The, Pittsburgh *Also called F Tinker and Sons Company* ***(G-15000)***
Vag USA LLC.....978 544-2511
9025 Marshall Rd Cranberry Township (16066) ***(G-3862)***
Vai, Malvern *Also called Veltek Associates Inc* ***(G-10338)***
Vai Pomini Inc.....610 921-9101
4201 Pottsville Pike Reading (19605) ***(G-16558)***
Val Products Inc.....717 354-4586
2710 Division Hwy New Holland (17557) ***(G-12291)***
Val Products Inc (HQ).....717 392-3978
2599 Old Phladelphia Pike Bird In Hand (17505) ***(G-1683)***
Val-Co Companies, New Holland *Also called Safeguard Products Inc* ***(G-12280)***
Valco.....610 691-3205
1410 Stonewood Dr Bethlehem (18017) ***(G-1649)***
Valco Investment Corporation.....610 770-1881
404 Union Blvd Allentown (18109) ***(G-419)***
Valco Tool Co, Bethlehem *Also called Valco* ***(G-1649)***
Valdez Foods Inc.....215 634-6106
1815 N 2nd St Philadelphia (19122) ***(G-14436)***
Vale Wood Farms, Loretto *Also called High View Inc* ***(G-10104)***
Valerio Coffee Roasters Inc.....610 676-0034
2675 Eisenhower Ave Audubon (19403) ***(G-831)***
Valero Service Inc.....724 468-1010
2718 Route 66 Delmont (15626) ***(G-4061)***
Validity LLC.....610 768-8042
101 Lindenwood Dr Ste 225 Malvern (19355) ***(G-10337)***
Validus Inc.....215 822-2525
3075 Advance Ln Colmar (18915) ***(G-3422)***
Valier Coal Yard.....814 938-5171
Cool Spring Rd Valier (15780) ***(G-18706)***
Valira LLC.....973 216-5803
1300 Fayette St Apt 100 Conshohocken (19428) ***(G-3615)***
Valk Manufacturing Company.....717 766-0711
66 E Main St New Kingstown (17072) ***(G-12394)***
Valley Broom Inc.....717 349-2614
25591 Horse Valley Rd East Waterford (17021) ***(G-4642)***
Valley Business Services Inc (PA).....610 366-1970
6900 Hamilton Blvd # 285 Trexlertown (18087) ***(G-18511)***
Valley Can Inc.....724 253-2038
1264 Fredonia Rd Hadley (16130) ***(G-6822)***
Valley Can Custom Container, Lewisburg *Also called Custom Container Vly Can LLC* ***(G-9903)***
Valley Custom Cabinetry.....717 957-2819
109 Tower Rd Marysville (17053) ***(G-10534)***
Valley Enterprise Cont Inc.....570 962-2194
111 Eagleville Rd Blanchard (16826) ***(G-1750)***
Valley Enterprise Cont LLC.....570 962-2194
111 Eagleville Rd Blanchard (16826) ***(G-1751)***
Valley Enterprises, Levittown *Also called Gittens Corp* ***(G-9841)***
Valley Extrusions LLC.....610 266-8550
795 Roble Rd Unit 1 Allentown (18109) ***(G-420)***
Valley Farm LLC, Williamsport *Also called Upstate Niagara Coop Inc* ***(G-20087)***
Valley Forge Instrument Co.....610 933-1806
210 Buckwalter Rd Phoenixville (19460) ***(G-14583)***
Valley Forge Tape Label Co Inc.....610 524-8900
119 Summit Dr Exton (19341) ***(G-5745)***
Valley Grinding & Mfg, Dupont *Also called Dupont Tool & Machine Co* ***(G-4490)***
Valley Instant Printing.....610 439-4122
2291 Bobby Ct Orefield (18069) ***(G-13016)***
Valley Instrument Co Inc.....610 363-2650
491 Clover Mill Rd Exton (19341) ***(G-5746)***
Valley Litho Inc.....610 437-5122
504 Spruce St Whitehall (18052) ***(G-19892)***
Valley Machine and Tool Co.....814 637-5621
48 Mill Run Rd Penfield (15849) ***(G-13224)***
Valley Machine Ltd.....814 259-3624
11210 Dlg Dr Shade Gap (17255) ***(G-17417)***
Valley Mirror.....412 462-0626
3315 Main St Ste A Homestead (15120) ***(G-7696)***
Valley Mirror The, Homestead *Also called Valley Mirror* ***(G-7696)***
Valley Plastics Inc.....570 287-7964
124 Welles St Forty Fort (18704) ***(G-6099)***
Valley Precision LLC.....215 536-0676
195 Penn Am Dr Quakertown (18951) ***(G-16255)***
Valley Precision Tl & Tech Inc.....717 647-7550
20 Clarks Valley Rd Tower City (17980) ***(G-18443)***
Valley Press Inc.....610 664-7770
5 E Montgomery Ave Ste 3 Bala Cynwyd (19004) ***(G-895)***
Valley Printing and Design Co.....814 536-5990
667 Main St Ste 667 # 667 Johnstown (15901) ***(G-8442)***
Valley Printing Co, Johnstown *Also called Valley Printing and Design Co* ***(G-8442)***
Valley Proteins Inc.....717 445-6890
693 Wide Hollow Rd East Earl (17519) ***(G-4556)***
Valley Proteins Inc.....717 436-0004
687 Cleck Rd Mifflintown (17059) ***(G-11140)***
Valley Quarries Inc.....717 334-3281
1575 Baltimore Pike Gettysburg (17325) ***(G-6320)***
Valley Quarries Inc.....717 263-9186
3593 Stone Quarry Rd Chambersburg (17202) ***(G-2993)***
Valley Quarries Inc (HQ).....717 267-2244
297 Quarry Rd Chambersburg (17202) ***(G-2994)***
Valley Quarries Inc.....717 532-4161
472 Newville Rd Shippensburg (17257) ***(G-17552)***
Valley Quarries Inc.....717 264-4178
3587 Stone Quarry Rd Chambersburg (17202) ***(G-2995)***
Valley Quarries Inc.....717 264-5811
2921 Stone Quarry Rd Chambersburg (17202) ***(G-2996)***
Valley Quarries Inc.....717 532-4456
470 Newville Rd Shippensburg (17257) ***(G-17553)***
Valley Quarries Inc.....717 642-8535
3805 Bullfrog Rd Fairfield (17320) ***(G-5770)***
Valley Quarries Inc.....814 766-2211
1071 Mount Cydonia Rd Fayetteville (17222) ***(G-5879)***
Valley Retreading Inc (PA).....724 489-4483
15 Mckean Ave Charleroi (15022) ***(G-3023)***
Valley Retreading of Charleroi, Charleroi *Also called Valley Retreading Inc* ***(G-3023)***
Valley Silk Screening Inc.....724 962-5255
412 W Main St Sharpsville (16150) ***(G-17477)***
Valley Spring, New Castle *Also called Point Spring Company* ***(G-12138)***
Valley Times Star, The, Shippensburg *Also called News Chronicle Co Inc* ***(G-17540)***
Valley Transit Mix, Chambersburg *Also called Valley Quarries Inc* ***(G-2994)***
Valley Transit Mix Div, Shippensburg *Also called Valley Quarries Inc* ***(G-17552)***
Valley Vending, Parker Ford *Also called West Dairy Inc* ***(G-13170)***
Valley Voice Inc.....610 838-2066
1188 Main St Hellertown (18055) ***(G-7564)***
Valley Wholesale & Supply.....724 783-6531
10307 Ste Rte 85 Kittanning (16201) ***(G-8801)***
Vallorbs Jewel Company.....717 392-3978
2599 Old Phladelphia Pike Bird In Hand (17505) ***(G-1684)***
Vallos Bakery LLC.....610 866-1012
1800 Broadway Bethlehem (18015) ***(G-1650)***
Vallos Baking Company, Bethlehem *Also called Vallos Bakery LLC* ***(G-1650)***
Valmet Inc.....570 587-5111
987 Griffin Pond Rd S Abingtn Twp (18411) ***(G-16900)***
Valmet Inc.....570 587-5111
987 Griffin Pond Rd S Abingtn Twp (18411) ***(G-16901)***
Valmont Newmark Inc.....570 454-8730
225 Kiwanis Blvd West Hazleton (18202) ***(G-19717)***
Valos Candy, New Kensington *Also called Valos House of Candy* ***(G-12385)***
Valos House of Candy.....724 339-2669
1726 5th Ave New Kensington (15068) ***(G-12385)***
Valtech Corporation (PA).....610 705-5900
2113 Sanatoga Station Rd Pottstown (19464) ***(G-16064)***
Value Recharge Service, Ellwood City *Also called Mark Grim* ***(G-4945)***
Valumax International Inc.....610 336-0101
848 Hausman Rd Allentown (18104) ***(G-421)***
Valves Inc.....724 378-0600
1291 Airport Rd Aliquippa (15001) ***(G-99)***
Van Air Inc (PA).....814 774-2631
2950 Mechanic St Lake City (16423) ***(G-8909)***

ALPHABETIC

Van Bennett Food Co Inc 610 374-8348
  62 Shea Dr Mohnton (19540) *(G-11272)*
Van Eerden Coatings Company 484 368-3073
  60 Flourtown Rd Plymouth Meeting (19462) *(G-15877)*
Van Etten James 215 453-8228
  124 N 6th St Perkasie (18944) *(G-13297)*
Van Hampton Gas & Oil Inc 814 589-7061
  15566 Tionesta Rd Pleasantville (16341) *(G-15805)*
Van Heyneker Fine Woodworking 610 388-1772
  1005 Brintons Bridge Rd West Chester (19382) *(G-19671)*
Van Industries Inc 610 582-1118
  2 Industrial Dr Birdsboro (19508) *(G-1707)*
Van Maanen Albert 610 373-7292
  706 Wayne Ave Reading (19611) *(G-16559)*
Van Mar Manufacturing 717 733-8948
  445 Hahnstown Rd Ephrata (17522) *(G-5153)*
Van Tongeren America LLC 717 450-3835
  518 S 8th St Lebanon (17042) *(G-9637)*
Van Varick Inc 610 588-9997
  530 S Main St Bangor (18013) *(G-932)*
Vanadium Enterprises Corp (PA) 412 206-2990
  100 Emerson Ln Ste 1513 Bridgeville (15017) *(G-2098)*
Vanadium Group, Bridgeville *Also called Vanadium Enterprises Corp (G-2098)*
Vanalstine Manufacturing Co 610 489-7670
  27 Cherry Ave Trappe (19426) *(G-18475)*
Vanco, Hughesville *Also called Sedco Manufacturing (G-7899)*
Vanderslice Machine Company 215 659-0429
  2557a Wyandotte Rd Bldg A Willow Grove (19090) *(G-20147)*
Vanguard ID Systems, West Chester *Also called Vanguard Identification (G-19672)*
Vanguard Identification 610 719-0700
  1210 American Blvd West Chester (19380) *(G-19672)*
Vanguard Manufacturing Inc 610 481-0655
  6831 Ruppsville Rd Allentown (18106) *(G-422)*
Vangura Iron Inc 412 461-7825
  1020 Neng Hollow Rd Clairton (15025) *(G-3159)*
Vangura Kitchen Tops Inc 412 824-0772
  14431 Vangura Ln Irwin (15642) *(G-8204)*
Vangura Surfacing Products, Irwin *Also called Vangura Kitchen Tops Inc (G-8204)*
Vangura Tool Inc 412 233-6401
  440 Waddell Ave Clairton (15025) *(G-3160)*
Vanicek Precision Machining Co 814 774-9012
  9192 Middle Rd Lake City (16423) *(G-8910)*
Vanquish Fencing Incorporated 215 295-2863
  1900 S Pennsylvania Ave Morrisville (19067) *(G-11586)*
Vanroden Inc 717 509-2600
  747 Flory Mill Rd Lancaster (17601) *(G-9230)*
Vans Inc 215 632-2481
  1455 Franklin Mills Cir Philadelphia (19154) *(G-14437)*
Vans Inc 717 291-8936
  569 Park City Ctr Lancaster (17601) *(G-9231)*
Vantage Energy LLC 724 746-6720
  2200 Rice Dr Canonsburg (15317) *(G-2653)*
Vantage Foods PA LP 717 691-4728
  2700 Yetter Ct Camp Hill (17011) *(G-2522)*
Vantage Learning Usa LLC (PA) 800 230-2213
  6805 Route 202 New Hope (18938) *(G-12318)*
Vantage Learning Usa LLC 800 230-2213
  444 Oxford Valley Rd Langhorne (19047) *(G-9330)*
Vantage Online Store LLC 267 756-1155
  6805 Route 202 New Hope (18938) *(G-12319)*
Vanzel Inc 215 223-1000
  2900 N 18th St Philadelphia (19132) *(G-14438)*
Varchettis Furniture 814 733-4318
  163 Fochtman Rd Berlin (15530) *(G-1293)*
Vargo Outdoors Incorporated 570 437-0990
  214 Market St Rear Lewisburg (17837) *(G-9923)*
Vari Corporation (PA) 570 385-0731
  155 Route 61 S Schuylkill Haven (17972) *(G-17169)*
Varinel Inc 610 256-3119
  929 S High St Ste 159 West Chester (19382) *(G-19673)*
Varitronics Inc 610 356-3995
  620 Park Way Ste 4 Broomall (19008) *(G-2304)*
Varsal LLC 215 957-5880
  363 Ivyland Rd Warminster (18974) *(G-18993)*
Vaughens Price Pubg Co Inc 412 367-5100
  809 Oak Rd Bradfordwoods (15015) *(G-2000)*
Vault Clothing Store 570 871-4135
  721 Scrnton Crbondale Hwy Scranton (18508) *(G-17309)*
Vault Clothing Store Inc 570 780-8240
  335 Bailey St S Abingtn Twp (18411) *(G-16902)*
Vault My Keys LLC 267 575-0506
  2710 Laurel Ln Glenside (19038) *(G-6542)*
Vault Services 814 282-8143
  22237 Stull Rd Saegertown (16433) *(G-16935)*
Vautid North America Inc 412 429-0800
  554 Washington Ave Ste 3 Carnegie (15106) *(G-2803)*
Vb Fabricators Inc 412 486-6385
  1467 Glenn Ave Glenshaw (15116) *(G-6502)*
Vbbc, Easton *Also called Victor-Balata Belting Company (G-4772)*

Vci Coatings LLC 412 281-1202
  437 Grant St Ste 1210 Pittsburgh (15219) *(G-15689)*
VCM Salvage, Sandy Lake *Also called Vista Custom Millwork Inc (G-17063)*
Vcp Mobility Inc 814 443-4881
  100 Devilbiss Dr Somerset (15501) *(G-17715)*
Vcw Enterprises Inc (HQ) 610 847-5112
  210 Durham Rd Ottsville (18942) *(G-13068)*
Vector Aerospace Usa Inc 610 559-2191
  3314 Sturbridge Ave Easton (18045) *(G-4767)*
Vectron International Inc (HQ) 603 598-0070
  100 Watts St Mount Holly Springs (17065) *(G-11640)*
Veeco Precision Surfc Proc LLC 215 328-0700
  185 Gibraltar Rd Horsham (19044) *(G-7863)*
Veeco Psp, Horsham *Also called Veeco Precision Surfc Proc LLC (G-7863)*
Veeder-Root Company 814 695-4476
  2709 Route 764 Duncansville (16635) *(G-4465)*
Veeva Systems Inc 215 422-3356
  601 Office Center Dr # 100 Fort Washington (19034) *(G-6095)*
Vega Applications Development 610 892-1812
  176 S New Middletown Rd # 204 Media (19063) *(G-10956)*
Vegely Welding Inc 412 469-9808
  600 Duquesne Blvd Duquesne (15110) *(G-4501)*
Veka Holdings Inc (HQ) 724 452-1000
  100 Veka Dr Fombell (16123) *(G-6036)*
Veka Inc 800 654-5589
  100 Veka Dr Fombell (16123) *(G-6037)*
Veka Innovations, Fombell *Also called Veka Holdings Inc (G-6036)*
Veka West Inc (HQ) 724 452-1000
  100 Veka Dr Fombell (16123) *(G-6038)*
Vektron Corporation 215 354-0300
  83 Blaises Gate Dr Southampton (18966) *(G-17845)*
Velicept Therapeutics Inc 484 318-2988
  640 Lee Rd Ste 119 Wayne (19087) *(G-19387)*
Velocity Color Inc 717 431-2591
  841 N Prince St Lancaster (17603) *(G-9232)*
Velocity Eqp Solutions LLC (PA) 800 521-1368
  2618 W State St New Castle (16101) *(G-12162)*
Velocity Magnetics Inc 724 657-8290
  200 Green Ridge Rd New Castle (16105) *(G-12163)*
Velocity Munitions Inc 724 966-2140
  480 Jacobs Ferry Rd Carmichaels (15320) *(G-2762)*
Velocity Powder Coating LLC 704 287-1024
  2618 W State St New Castle (16101) *(G-12164)*
Velocity Robotics 412 254-3011
  100 S Commons Ste 102 Pittsburgh (15212) *(G-15690)*
Veltek Associates Inc 610 644-8335
  15 Lee Blvd Malvern (19355) *(G-10338)*
Venango County Notary 814 677-2216
  3537 State Rt 357 Seneca (16346) *(G-17370)*
Venango Innovative Services, Seneca *Also called Venango Training & Dev Ctr Inc (G-17371)*
Venango Machine Company Inc 814 739-2211
  14118 Route 8 89 Wattsburg (16442) *(G-19283)*
Venango Machine Products Inc 814 676-5741
  702 Walnut St Reno (16343) *(G-16648)*
Venango Newspaper, Oil City *Also called Derrick Publishing Company (G-12944)*
Venango Steel Inc 814 437-9353
  1655 Pittsburgh Rd Franklin (16323) *(G-6167)*
Venango Training & Dev Ctr Inc (PA) 814 676-5755
  239 Quaker Dr Seneca (16346) *(G-17371)*
Venator Americas LLC 610 279-6450
  555 E Church Rd King of Prussia (19406) *(G-8695)*
Venatorx Pharmaceuticals Inc 610 644-8935
  30 Spring Mill Dr Malvern (19355) *(G-10339)*
Vend Natural of Western PA 724 518-6594
  309 W 11th St Donora (15033) *(G-4164)*
Vendors 1st Choice Inc 215 804-1011
  2455 Willow Stream Dr Quakertown (18951) *(G-16256)*
Venom Power Sports 717 467-5190
  90 S Main St Dover (17315) *(G-4206)*
Ventana USA 724 325-3400
  6001 Enterprise Dr Export (15632) *(G-5630)*
Ventasia Inc 412 661-6600
  6108 Howe St Pittsburgh (15206) *(G-15691)*
Ventura Foods LLC 215 223-8700
  650 W Sedgley Ave Philadelphia (19140) *(G-14439)*
Ventura Foods LLC 717 263-6900
  1501 Orchard Dr Chambersburg (17201) *(G-2997)*
Venture 3 Systems LLC 267 954-0100
  2805 Sterling Dr Hatfield (19440) *(G-7405)*
Venture Precision Tool Inc 717 566-6496
  241 E 2nd St Hummelstown (17036) *(G-7927)*
Ventwell Inc 717 683-1477
  78 Willow Springs Cir York (17406) *(G-20697)*
Venus Machines & Tool 570 421-4564
  64 N 3rd St Stroudsburg (18360) *(G-18141)*
Venus Nail & Spa 610 660-6180
  219 Haverford Ave Narberth (19072) *(G-11914)*
Venus Video 215 937-1545
  6301 Passyunk Ave Philadelphia (19153) *(G-14440)*

Vepar LLC....610 462-4545
900 W Bridge St Spring City (19475) *(G-17871)*
Verail Technologies Inc....513 454-8192
650 N Cannon Ave Lansdale (19446) *(G-9422)*
Verallia....814 642-2521
1 Glass Pl Port Allegany (16743) *(G-15896)*
Verder Scientific Inc....267 757-0351
11 Penns Trl Ste 300 Newtown (18940) *(G-12559)*
Vere Inc....724 335-5530
3 Schreiber Industrial Pa New Kensington (15068) *(G-12386)*
Vergona Outdoors LLC....814 967-4844
12391 Leboeuf Trail Rd Centerville (16404) *(G-2837)*
Verichem Inc....412 331-2616
3499 Grand Ave Pittsburgh (15225) *(G-15692)*
Veritas Press Inc....717 519-1974
1805 Olde Homestead Ln Lancaster (17601) *(G-9233)*
Veritiv Operating Company....724 776-3122
41 Progress Ave Ste A Cranberry Township (16066) *(G-3863)*
Verizon, Erie *Also called Supermedia LLC (G-5497)*
Verizon, West Chester *Also called Cellco Partnership (G-19520)*
Verizon Communications Inc....570 387-3840
5 W 3rd St Bloomsburg (17815) *(G-1806)*
Verizon Pennsylvania Inc....215 879-7898
4860 W Jefferson St Philadelphia (19131) *(G-14441)*
Verls Salads Inc....717 865-2771
Rr 343 Fredericksburg (17026) *(G-6177)*
Vermiculite Association Inc....717 238-9902
2207 Forest Hills Dr Harrisburg (17112) *(G-7242)*
Verners Paint Center Inc....724 224-7445
711 E 2nd Ave Tarentum (15084) *(G-18253)*
Vernon Printing Inc....724 283-9242
112 Hollywood Dr Ste 103 Butler (16001) *(G-2447)*
Verrica Pharmaceuticals Inc....484 453-3300
10 N High St Fl 2 West Chester (19380) *(G-19674)*
Versa-Fab Inc....724 889-0137
270 Hunt Valley Rd New Kensington (15068) *(G-12387)*
Versalift East LLC (HQ)....610 866-1400
2706 Brodhead Rd Bethlehem (18020) *(G-1651)*
Versalot Enterprises LLC....610 213-1017
3540 Alyssa Ct New Tripoli (18066) *(G-12461)*
Versalot Sales & Specialty Sup, New Tripoli *Also called Versalot Enterprises LLC (G-12461)*
Versatech Incorporated....724 327-8324
6012 Enterprise Dr Export (15632) *(G-5631)*
Versatek Enterprises LLC....717 626-6390
508 Front St Lititz (17543) *(G-10057)*
Versatex Building Products LLC....724 857-1111
400 Steel St Aliquippa (15001) *(G-100)*
Versatile Credit Inc....800 851-1281
4900 Ritter Rd Ste 100 Mechanicsburg (17055) *(G-10904)*
Versico Incorporated....717 960-4024
1285 Ritner Hwy Carlisle (17013) *(G-2747)*
Versitex of America Ltd....610 948-4442
3545 Schuylkill Rd Spring City (19475) *(G-17872)*
Versum Materials Us LLC....610 481-3946
1919 Vultee St Allentown (18103) *(G-423)*
Versum Materials Us LLC....570 467-2981
357 Marian Ave Tamaqua (18252) *(G-18231)*
Vert Markets Inc....814 897-9000
5340 Fryling Rd Ste 300 Erie (16510) *(G-5525)*
Vert Markets Inc (PA)....215 675-1800
101 Gibraltar Rd Ste 100 Horsham (19044) *(G-7864)*
Vertech International Inc....215 529-0300
420 Station Rd Quakertown (18951) *(G-16257)*
Vertees....570 630-0678
324 Spruce St Hawley (18428) *(G-7441)*
Vertellus DWG LLC....800 344-3426
Rr 611 Delaware Water Gap (18327) *(G-4044)*
Vertex Image Products Inc....724 722-3400
173 Spring St Yukon (15698) *(G-20786)*
Vertical Access Solutions LLC (HQ)....412 787-9102
4465 Campbells Run Rd Pittsburgh (15205) *(G-15693)*
Vertical Access Solutions LLC....412 787-9102
120 N Lime St Lancaster (17602) *(G-9234)*
Vertical Energy, Sugar Grove *Also called Vertical Resources Inc (G-18148)*
Vertical Resources Inc....814 489-3931
44 Valley Park Dr Sugar Grove (16350) *(G-18148)*
Vertirack Manufacturing Co....484 971-7341
74 Pleasant Dr Bernville (19506) *(G-1306)*
Verus Sports Inc (PA)....215 283-0153
1300 Virginia Dr Ste 401 Fort Washington (19034) *(G-6096)*
Vestcom Retail Solutions, Bristol *Also called Electronic Imaging Svcs Inc (G-2139)*
Vesuvius U S A Corporation....215 708-7404
8701 Torresdale Ave Philadelphia (19136) *(G-14442)*
Vesuvius U S A Corporation....412 276-1750
250 Parkwest Dr Pittsburgh (15275) *(G-15694)*
Vesuvius U S A Corporation....419 986-5126
4604 Campbells Run Rd Pittsburgh (15205) *(G-15695)*
Vesuvius U S A Corporation....412 788-4441
4604 Campbells Run Rd Pittsburgh (15205) *(G-15696)*
Vesuvius U S A Corporation....814 387-6811
895 Clarence Rd Snow Shoe (16874) *(G-17671)*
Vesuvius U S A Corporation....412 429-1800
250 Parkwest Dr Pittsburgh (15275) *(G-15697)*
Vetch LLC....570 524-7700
7199 County Line Rd Winfield (17889) *(G-20204)*
Vetco Gray Inc....570 435-8027
321 Marcellus Dr Muncy (17756) *(G-11837)*
Veteran Pallet Remanufacturing, Spring City *Also called Vepar LLC (G-17871)*
Veterinary Tag Supply Co Inc....610 649-1550
401 E 4th St Ste 2 Bridgeport (19405) *(G-2048)*
Vetmed Communications Inc....610 361-0555
37 Paul Ln Glen Mills (19342) *(G-6448)*
Vetpack Enterprises LLC....215 680-8637
113 Winchester Rd Merion Station (19066) *(G-10999)*
Vetstreet Incorporated (HQ)....267 685-2400
3800 Horizon Blvd Ste 201 Feasterville Trevose (19053) *(G-5937)*
Vexcon, Philadelphia *Also called Poly Sat Inc (G-14187)*
Vexcon Chemicals Inc....215 332-7709
7240 State Rd Philadelphia (19135) *(G-14443)*
Veyko Design Inc....215 928-1349
1600 N Amrcn St Phldlphia Philadelphia Philadelphia (19122) *(G-14444)*
Vf Imagewear Inc....610 746-6800
2320 Newlins Mill Rd Easton (18045) *(G-4768)*
Vf Imagewer Majestic, Easton *Also called Majestic Athletic Intl Ltd (G-4718)*
Vf Outdoor LLC....610 327-1734
18 W Lightcap Rd Ste 599 Pottstown (19464) *(G-16065)*
Vf Outdoor LLC....610 323-6575
18 W Lightcap Rd Pottstown (19464) *(G-16066)*
Vf Outdoor LLC....610 265-2193
690 W Dekalb Pike # 2049 King of Prussia (19406) *(G-8696)*
Vgx Pharmaceuticals, Blue Bell *Also called Viral Genomix Inc (G-1856)*
Vgx Pharmaceuticals LLC (HQ)....215 542-5912
660 W Germantown Pike # 110 Plymouth Meeting (19462) *(G-15878)*
Vh Service LLC....267 808-9745
102 E Pennsylvania Blvd Feasterville Trevose (19053) *(G-5938)*
Via Design & Technologies....215 579-5730
12 Penns Trl Ste 125 Newtown (18940) *(G-12560)*
Via Veneto Italian Ice Inc....610 630-3355
2564 Industry Ln Ste 100 Norristown (19403) *(G-12722)*
Viant Westfield LLC....215 675-4653
631 Catherine St Warminster (18974) *(G-18994)*
Vibro Industries Inc....717 527-2094
Main St Fogelsville (18051) *(G-5997)*
Vibroplating Inc....215 638-4413
353 Camer Dr Bensalem (19020) *(G-1267)*
Vic Auto Tech Place....215 969-2083
10100 Bustleton Ave Philadelphia (19116) *(G-14445)*
Vicious Cycle Works Llc....724 662-0581
1684 Pulaski Mercer Rd Mercer (16137) *(G-10977)*
Vicjah Corporation....610 826-7475
450 Delaware Ave Palmerton (18071) *(G-13114)*
Vicksburg Buggy Shop....570 966-3658
1400 Beaver Run Rd Mifflinburg (17844) *(G-11104)*
Vicor Technologies Inc....570 897-5797
399 Autumn Dr Bangor (18013) *(G-933)*
Vics Time, Palmerton *Also called Vicjah Corporation (G-13114)*
Victaulic LLC....610 559-3300
4901 Kesslersville Rd Easton (18040) *(G-4769)*
Victaulic Company (PA)....610 559-3300
4901 Kesslersville Rd Easton (18040) *(G-4770)*
Victaulic Company of America, Easton *Also called Victaulic Company (G-4770)*
Victaulic Company of America....610 966-3966
8023 Quarry Rd Alburtis (18011) *(G-58)*
Victaulic Company of America....610 614-1261
2860 Bath Pike Nazareth (18064) *(G-11993)*
Victaulic Holding Company LLC....610 559-3300
4901 Kesslersville Rd Easton (18040) *(G-4771)*
Victor LLC....814 765-5681
3056 Washington Ave Clearfield (16830) *(G-3233)*
Victor Associates Inc....215 393-5437
453 Country Club Dr Lansdale (19446) *(G-9423)*
Victor Group Inc....814 899-1079
1651 E 12th St Erie (16511) *(G-5526)*
Victor Metals....570 925-2618
70 Mchenry St Stillwater (17878) *(G-18062)*
Victor Printing Inc (PA)....724 342-2106
1 Victor Way Sharon (16146) *(G-17444)*
Victor Sun Ctrl of Philadelphia....215 743-0800
4101 G St Philadelphia (19124) *(G-14446)*
Victor-Balata Belting Company....610 258-2010
2779 Ohio St Easton (18045) *(G-4772)*
Victoria Leather Company, Harleysville *Also called Softkog Inc (G-7059)*
Victoria Orchard LLC....610 873-2848
1403 Dodd Dr Downingtown (19335) *(G-4260)*
Victoria Precision Inc....215 355-7576
410 Clearview Ave Ste C Feasterville Trevose (19053) *(G-5939)*
Victorian Backyard, Bird In Hand *Also called David S Stoltzsus (G-1673)*

ALPHABETIC

Victorian Lighting Works Inc 814 364-9577
251 S Pennsylvania Ave Centre Hall (16828) *(G-2845)*
Victorian Publishing Co Inc 814 634-8321
145 Center St Meyersdale (15552) *(G-11020)*
Victorias Candies Inc (PA) 570 455-6341
51 N Laurel St Frnt Hazleton (18201) *(G-7534)*
Victorias Candies Inc 570 455-6345
Airport Hwy Rd Laurel West Hazleton (18201) *(G-19718)*
Victory Athletics 814 886-4866
324 Laurel Ave Cresson (16630) *(G-3900)*
Victory Brewing Company LLC (PA) 610 873-0881
420 Acorn Ln Downingtown (19335) *(G-4261)*
Victory Energy Corporation 724 349-6366
220 Airport Rd Indiana (15701) *(G-8133)*
Victory Media Inc 412 269-1663
420 Rouser Rd Ste 101 Coraopolis (15108) *(G-3731)*
Victory Parkesburg 610 574-4000
3127 Lower Valley Rd Parkesburg (19365) *(G-13183)*
Video Display Corporation 770 938-2080
276 Spearing St Howard (16841) *(G-7892)*
Video Tech, Bensalem *Also called Svt Inc* *(G-1258)*
Video Visions Inc (PA) 215 942-6642
3600 Boundbrook Ave Trevose (19053) *(G-18508)*
Videon Central Inc 814 235-1111
2171 Sandy Dr State College (16803) *(G-18041)*
Videoray LLC 610 458-3000
212 E High St Ste 201 Pottstown (19464) *(G-16067)*
Videotek Inc 610 327-2292
243 Shoemaker Rd Pottstown (19464) *(G-16068)*
Vidmar, Allentown *Also called Stanley Industrial & Auto LLC* *(G-400)*
View Thru Technologies Inc 215 703-0950
1765 Walnut Ln Quakertown (18951) *(G-16258)*
View Works Inc 724 226-9773
944 Lincoln Ave Springdale (15144) *(G-17905)*
Vigon International Inc 877 844-6639
127 Airport Rd East Stroudsburg (18301) *(G-4638)*
Viking LLC 570 645-3633
512 Industrial Rd Nesquehoning (18240) *(G-12010)*
Viking Electronic Services 610 992-0400
620 Allendale Rd Ste 175 King of Prussia (19406) *(G-8697)*
Viking Importing Co 610 690-2900
1260 E Wdlnd Ave Ste 15 Springfield (19064) *(G-17924)*
Viking Plastics, Corry *Also called VPI Acquisition LLC* *(G-3779)*
Viking Signs Inc 570 455-4369
175 Carleton Ave Hazleton (18201) *(G-7535)*
Viking Tool & Gage Inc 814 382-8691
11210 State Highway 18 Conneaut Lake (16316) *(G-3482)*
Viking Vee Inc 724 789-9194
839 Evans City Rd Renfrew (16053) *(G-16643)*
Viking Woodworking Llc 412 381-5171
201 E Carson St Pittsburgh (15219) *(G-15698)*
Viking-Spirit Trailers, Renfrew *Also called Viking Vee Inc* *(G-16643)*
Vilimia Inc (PA) 570 654-6735
131 Brown Rd Yatesville (18640) *(G-20349)*
Village At Overlook LLC 570 538-9167
99 Park Dr New Columbia (17856) *(G-12178)*
Village Craft Iron & Stone Inc 814 353-1777
4725 S Eagle Valley Rd Julian (16844) *(G-8457)*
Village Farm Market 717 733-5340
1520 Division Hwy Ephrata (17522) *(G-5154)*
Village Hndcrfted Cbinetry Inc 215 393-3040
200 W 8th St Lansdale (19446) *(G-9424)*
Village Idiot Designs 724 545-7477
12157 Us Route 422 Kittanning (16201) *(G-8802)*
Village Pretzels 215 674-5070
36 S York Rd Ste 1 Hatboro (19040) *(G-7309)*
Village Publishing Operations 215 794-0202
73 Valley Dr Furlong (18925) *(G-6235)*
Village Wood Shop, Lansdale *Also called Village Hndcrfted Cbinetry Inc* *(G-9424)*
Villanova Cheese Shop Inc 610 495-8343
181 Ppaum Hollow Rd Ste A Pottstown (19464) *(G-16069)*
Vincent Giordano Corp 215 467-6629
2600 Washington Ave Philadelphia (19146) *(G-14447)*
Vincent Giordano Prosciutto, Philadelphia *Also called Vincent Giordano Corp* *(G-14447)*
Vincent Lohuvey 724 527-2994
123 Laskoski Rd Greensburg (15601) *(G-6727)*
Vincents Welding, West Elizabeth *Also called BJ REO Inc* *(G-19692)*
Vinces Gas & Welding Supply Co, Carnegie *Also called Sky Oxygen Inc* *(G-2793)*
Vinegar Hill Picture Works 724 596-0023
65 Bradley Ct Indiana (15701) *(G-8134)*
Vineyard At Grandview LLC 717 653-4825
1489 Grandview Rd Mount Joy (17552) *(G-11675)*
Vineyard Oil & Gas Company 814 725-8742
10299 W Main Rd North East (16428) *(G-12764)*
Vink & Beri LLC 215 654-5252
140 Domorah Dr Montgomeryville (18936) *(G-11426)*
Vinomis Laboratories LLC 877 484-6664
841 23rd St Ste 2 Aliquippa (15001) *(G-101)*

Vinoski Winery LLC 724 872-3333
333 Castle Dr Rostraver Township (15012) *(G-16832)*
Vintage Color Graphics Inc 215 646-6589
1218 Joseph Rd Ambler (19002) *(G-604)*
Vintage Pharmaceuticals LLC (HQ) 256 859-2222
1400 Atwater Dr Malvern (19355) *(G-10340)*
Vinyl Dizzign 267 246-7725
1106 Elm St Lansdale (19446) *(G-9425)*
Vinyl Graphics Unlimited 814 226-7887
9912 Route 322 Shippenville (16254) *(G-17566)*
Vinyl Window Wells LLC 717 768-0618
229 S Groffdale Rd Gordonville (17529) *(G-6566)*
VIP Advertising & Printing 570 251-7897
Main And Elizabeth Honesdale (18431) *(G-7731)*
VIP Tech LLC 267 582-1554
2900 Hedley St Philadelphia (19137) *(G-14448)*
Viper Holsters, Atglen *Also called Joseph Piazza* *(G-801)*
Viper Network Systems Inc 855 758-4737
40 Center Ave West View (15229) *(G-19774)*
Viral Genomix Inc 267 440-4200
450 Sentry Pkwy E Blue Bell (19422) *(G-1856)*
Virgo Investment LLC 215 339-1596
1717 S Broad St Philadelphia (19148) *(G-14449)*
Viridor Global 202 360-1617
733 Winton St Philadelphia (19148) *(G-14450)*
Virtic Industries LLC 610 246-9428
504 Woodland Ct Wayne (19087) *(G-19388)*
Virtix Consulting LLC 412 440-4835
228 Fox Meadow Dr Wexford (15090) *(G-19832)*
Virtus Pharmaceuticals LLC 267 938-4850
310 George Patterson Dr Bristol (19007) *(G-2215)*
Virtus Pharmaceuticals LLC (HQ) 267 938-4850
2050 Cabot Blvd W Ste 200 Langhorne (19047) *(G-9331)*
Virtus Pharmaceuticals LLC 813 283-1344
12 Penns Trl Ste A Newtown (18940) *(G-12561)*
Virtus Phrmctcals Holdings LLC (PA) 267 938-4850
2050 Cabot Blvd W Ste 200 Langhorne (19047) *(G-9332)*
Virtus Phrmcticals Opco II LLC (HQ) 267 938-4850
2050 Cabot Blvd W Ste 200 Langhorne (19047) *(G-9333)*
Visco 215 420-7437
65 Richard Rd Warminster (18974) *(G-18995)*
Viscogliosi Brothers Venture, Morrisville *Also called Avanta Orthopaedics Inc* *(G-11555)*
Visconti Garment Hangers Inc (PA) 570 366-7745
1140 Centre Tpke Ste A Orwigsburg (17961) *(G-13054)*
Vishay Intertechnology Inc (PA) 610 644-1300
63 Lancaster Ave Malvern (19355) *(G-10341)*
Vishay Precision Foil Inc (HQ) 484 321-5300
3 Great Valley Pkwy # 150 Malvern (19355) *(G-10342)*
Vishay Precision Group Inc (PA) 484 321-5300
3 Great Valley Pkwy # 150 Malvern (19355) *(G-10343)*
Vishay Siliconix LLC 408 567-8177
63 Lancaster Ave Malvern (19355) *(G-10344)*
Vision Custom Tooling Inc 610 582-1640
5 Riga Ln Birdsboro (19508) *(G-1708)*
Vision Denim, The, Philadelphia *Also called Denim Inc Division* *(G-13619)*
Vision Design, Winfield *Also called Ephraim L King* *(G-20200)*
Vision Grinding & Tool Co 215 744-5069
4572 Ditman St Philadelphia (19124) *(G-14451)*
Vision Optics 267 639-5773
2658 Germantown Ave Philadelphia (19133) *(G-14452)*
Vision Products Inc 724 274-0767
460 Nixon Rd Ste 100 Cheswick (15024) *(G-3121)*
Vision Products Ic, Cheswick *Also called M & M Manufacturing Co* *(G-3111)*
Vision Quality Components Inc 814 765-1903
1433 Industrial Park Rd Clearfield (16830) *(G-3234)*
Vision Quest Inc 570 448-2845
2065 Great Bend Tpke Honesdale (18431) *(G-7732)*
Vision Technology UHS LLC 717 465-0694
513 Highland Ave Hanover (17331) *(G-6969)*
Vision Tool & Manufacturing 814 724-6363
10670 Mercer Pike Meadville (16335) *(G-10811)*
Vision Warehousing and Dist 717 762-5912
144 Cleveland Ave Waynesboro (17268) *(G-19429)*
Visplay, Inc., Allentown *Also called Vitra Retail Inc* *(G-425)*
Vista Custom Millwork Inc 724 376-4093
4843 Sndy Lk Grenville Rd Sandy Lake (16145) *(G-17063)*
Vista Fuels LLC 570 385-7274
356 Center Ave Schuylkill Haven (17972) *(G-17170)*
Vista Manufacturing Inc (PA) 724 495-6860
1201 State Route 18 Aliquippa (15001) *(G-102)*
Vista Manufacturing Inc 724 495-6860
728 Railroad Ave Midland (15059) *(G-11088)*
Vista Mercer County, Pittsburgh *Also called Vista Resources Inc* *(G-15699)*
Vista Metals Inc (PA) 412 751-4600
1024 E Smithfield St McKeesport (15135) *(G-10685)*
Vista Metals Inc. 724 545-7750
189 Nolpe Dr Kittanning (16201) *(G-8803)*
Vista Optical 724 458-0333
15 Pine Grove Sq Grove City (16127) *(G-6807)*

(G-0000) Company's Geographic Section entry number

Vista Resources Inc (PA) 412 833-8884
61 Mcmurray Rd Ste 300 Pittsburgh (15241) *(G-15699)*

Vistappliances 215 600-1232
437 W Bridge St Morrisville (19067) *(G-11587)*

Visual Display Products LLC 570 271-0815
701b Montour Blvd Danville (17821) *(G-4015)*

Visual Information Services (PA) 800 777-3565
105 Hawk C Corporate Ctr Denver (17517) *(G-4096)*

Visual Marketing, Folsom *Also called Sign Concepts Inc (G-6028)*

Visual Merchandising LLC 610 353-7550
832 Hunt Rd Newtown Square (19073) *(G-12597)*

Visual Resources LLC 484 351-8100
1950 Butler Pike Ste 225 Conshohocken (19428) *(G-3616)*

Visualize Digitized LLC 610 494-9504
603 Taylor Ave Upper Chichester (19061) *(G-18676)*

Vita-Line Products Inc 570 450-0192
1111 N Park Dr Hazle Township (18202) *(G-7490)*

Vitabru Embroidery 610 296-0181
115 Great Valley Pkwy Malvern (19355) *(G-10345)*

Vital Signs, Carnegie *Also called Sskj Enterprises Inc (G-2794)*

Vitaltrax LLC 610 864-0211
3401 Market St Ste 200 Philadelphia (19104) *(G-14453)*

Vitols Tool & Machine Corp 215 464-8240
10082 Sandmeyer Ln Philadelphia (19116) *(G-14454)*

Vitra Inc 610 391-9780
7528 Walker Way Ste 200 Allentown (18106) *(G-424)*

Vitra Retail Inc 610 366-1658
7528 Walker Way Allentown (18106) *(G-425)*

Vitro Architectural Glass, Cheswick *Also called Vitro Flat Glass LLC (G-3122)*

Vitro Architectural Glass, Carlisle *Also called Vitro Flat Glass LLC (G-2748)*

Vitro Flat Glass LLC (HQ) 412 820-8500
400 Guys Run Rd Cheswick (15024) *(G-3122)*

Vitro Flat Glass LLC 717 486-3366
400 Park Dr Carlisle (17015) *(G-2748)*

Vivid Apparel, Warminster *Also called Vivid Products LLC (G-18996)*

Vivid Glass, Pittsburgh *Also called Forms and Surfaces Inc (G-15026)*

Vivid Products LLC 215 394-0235
622 Mary St Ste 3-B Warminster (18974) *(G-18996)*

Vivid Publishing Inc 570 567-7808
924 Funston Ave Apt 1 Williamsport (17701) *(G-20088)*

Vivino Selections Inc 412 920-1336
24 Woodville Ave 2 Pittsburgh (15220) *(G-15700)*

Viwinco Inc 610 286-8884
851 Hemlock Rd Morgantown (19543) *(G-11543)*

Vizinex LLC 215 529-9440
6343 Winside Dr Bethlehem (18017) *(G-1652)*

Vizinex Rfid, Bethlehem *Also called Vizinex LLC (G-1652)*

Vizinex Rfid, Newtown *Also called Rcd Technology Inc (G-12542)*

Vmd Machine Co Inc 215 723-7782
4304 Bethlehem Pike Telford (18969) *(G-18324)*

Vmf Inc 570 575-0997
415 Walnut St Scranton (18509) *(G-17310)*

Vocam Corp 215 348-7115
451 N Main St Ste A Doylestown (18901) *(G-4344)*

Voci Technologies Incorporated 412 621-9310
6301 Forbes Ave Ste 120 Pittsburgh (15217) *(G-15701)*

Vocollect Inc (HQ) 412 829-8145
703 Rodi Rd Pittsburgh (15235) *(G-15702)*

Vocollect Healthcare Systems 412 829-8145
701 Rodi Rd Ste 102 Pittsburgh (15235) *(G-15703)*

Vodka Brands Corp 412 681-7777
554 33rd St Pittsburgh (15201) *(G-15704)*

Vodvarka Springs 724 695-3268
1251 Route 30 Clinton (15026) *(G-3268)*

Voegele Company Inc (PA) 412 781-0940
200 Bridge St Pittsburgh (15223) *(G-15705)*

Vogan Mfg Inc 717 354-9954
316 Voganville Rd New Holland (17557) *(G-12292)*

Vogel Carton LLC 215 957-0612
670 Louis Dr Warminster (18974) *(G-18997)*

Voicestar Inc 267 514-0000
1315 Walnut St Ste 1532 Philadelphia (19107) *(G-14455)*

Voicestars Inc 305 902-9666
214 N 5th St Apt 2 Emmaus (18049) *(G-5046)*

Voigt & Schweitzer LLC 717 861-7777
153 Micro Dr Jonestown (17038) *(G-8454)*

Voith Digital Solutions Inc 717 792-7000
760 E Berlin Rd York (17408) *(G-20698)*

Voith Hydro Inc (HQ) 717 792-7000
760 E Berlin Rd York (17408) *(G-20699)*

Voith It Solutions Inc., York *Also called Voith Digital Solutions Inc (G-20698)*

Voith Paper Fabric and Roll Sy (HQ) 717 792-7000
760 E Berlin Rd York (17408) *(G-20700)*

Volant Enterprises Ltd (PA) 724 533-2500
550 Main St Volant (16156) *(G-18778)*

Volant Mills, Volant *Also called Volant Enterprises Ltd (G-18778)*

Volian Enterprises Inc 724 335-3744
122 Kerr Rd Ste 4 New Kensington (15068) *(G-12388)*

Volleyball Corner, Lancaster *Also called Tri County Sports Inc (G-9222)*

Vollman Pershing H Inc 215 956-1971
301 Camars Dr Warminster (18974) *(G-18998)*

Vollmer of America Corp (HQ) 412 278-0655
105 Broadway St Carnegie (15106) *(G-2804)*

Vollmer Patterns Inc 610 562-7920
389 Creamery Rd Hamburg (19526) *(G-6855)*

Vollmer Tar & Chip Inc 814 834-1332
1069 Trout Run Rd Saint Marys (15857) *(G-17027)*

Vollmer Tar and Chip Asp Pav, Saint Marys *Also called Vollmer Tar & Chip Inc (G-17027)*

Von Machine Co 412 276-4505
338 Logan St Carnegie (15106) *(G-2805)*

Von-Crete, Hanover Township *Also called Wilkes Barre Burial Vault (G-7007)*

Vornhold Wallpapers Inc 215 757-6641
501 Main St Langhorne (19047) *(G-9334)*

Vorteq Coil Finishers LLC 610 797-5200
2233 26th St Sw Allentown (18103) *(G-426)*

Vorteq Coil Finishers LLC 724 898-1511
125 Mcfann Rd Valencia (16059) *(G-18704)*

Vortx United Inc 570 742-7859
318 Yocum Rd Milton (17847) *(G-11250)*

Vossloh Track Material Inc (HQ) 610 926-5400
5662a Leesport Ave Reading (19605) *(G-16560)*

Vpak Technology 610 458-8600
638 Perimeter Dr Downingtown (19335) *(G-4262)*

Vpg, Malvern *Also called Vishay Precision Group Inc (G-10343)*

VPI Acquisition LLC (PA) 814 664-8671
1 Viking St Corry (16407) *(G-3779)*

Vr Enterprises Llc 215 932-1113
1170 Troxel Rd Lansdale (19446) *(G-9426)*

VSC Services Division, Bensalem *Also called Lexicon International Corp (G-1220)*

VSI Meter Services Inc 484 482-2480
2900 Dutton Mill Rd 200 Aston (19014) *(G-796)*

VSI Sales LLC (PA) 724 625-4060
416 Johns Ave Hazleton (18201) *(G-7536)*

Vsmpo-Tirus US Inc 724 251-9400
401 Riverport Dr Leetsdale (15056) *(G-9706)*

VT Hackney Inc 570 547-1681
914 Saegers Station Rd Montgomery (17752) *(G-11381)*

Vtg Tanktainer North Amer Inc 610 429-5440
109 E Evans St Ste C West Chester (19380) *(G-19675)*

Vue-More Manufacturing, Allentown *Also called RR Enterprises Inc (G-381)*

Vulcan Industries Inc 412 269-7655
701 4th Ave Coraopolis (15108) *(G-3732)*

Vulcan Materials, York *Also called Legacy Vulcan LLC (G-20564)*

Vulcan Oilfield Services LLC 724 698-1008
418 S Cascade St Ste 1 New Castle (16101) *(G-12165)*

VWR Corporation (HQ) 610 386-1700
Radnor Corp Ctr 1 200 Radnor (19087) *(G-16304)*

VWR Scientific Inc 412 487-1983
3830 Mount Royal Blvd Allison Park (15101) *(G-466)*

Vynecrest LLC 610 398-7525
172 Arrowhead Ln Breinigsville (18031) *(G-2030)*

Vynecrest LLC 610 398-7525
172 Arrowhead Ln Breinigsville (18031) *(G-2031)*

Vynecrest Winery, Breinigsville *Also called Vynecrest LLC (G-2031)*

Vynex Window Systems Inc 412 681-3800
1083 3rd St Ste 1 North Versailles (15137) *(G-12783)*

W & H Machine Shop Co LLC 814 834-6258
1051 Trout Run Rd Saint Marys (15857) *(G-17028)*

W & H Machine Shop Inc 814 834-6258
1051 Trout Run Rd Saint Marys (15857) *(G-17029)*

W & K Steel LLC 412 271-0540
98 Antisbury St Braddock (15104) *(G-1951)*

W & W Welding Inc 717 336-4314
530a Swamp Church Rd Reinholds (17569) *(G-16637)*

W B Mason Co Inc 888 926-2766
966 Postal Rd 100 Allentown (18109) *(G-427)*

W B Mason Co Inc 888 926-2766
1640 E Pleasant Valley Bl Altoona (16602) *(G-555)*

W C H Inc 814 725-8431
10832 Lake Rd North East (16428) *(G-12765)*

W C S, West Chester *Also called Wire and Cable Specialties Inc (G-19679)*

W C Wolff Company 610 359-9600
40 Bishop Hollow Rd Newtown Square (19073) *(G-12598)*

W D Pattern Company, Trappe *Also called Spring Ford Castings Inc (G-18473)*

W D Zwicky & Son Inc 484 248-5300
220 Buena Vista Rd Fleetwood (19522) *(G-5982)*

W E Keller Machining Welding 724 337-8327
327 Phillips Ln Leechburg (15656) *(G-9654)*

W Graphics Digital Services 610 252-3565
18 N 4th St 20 Easton (18042) *(G-4773)*

W H Cooke & Co Inc 717 630-2222
6868 York Rd Hanover (17331) *(G-6970)*

W J Reining & Sons Inc 570 729-7325
1257 Beach Lake Hwy Beach Lake (18405) *(G-976)*

W J Strickler Signs Inc (PA) 717 624-8450
3999 Carlisle Pike New Oxford (17350) *(G-12425)*

W L Fegley & Son Inc 610 779-0277
2701 Perkiomen Ave Reading (19606) *(G-16561)*

A
L
P
H
A
B
E
T
I
C

W L Gore & Associates Inc 610 268-1864
380 Starr Rd Landenberg (19350) *(G-9255)*

W M Abene Co 570 457-8334
1001 Moosic Rd Ste 2 Old Forge (18518) *(G-12977)*

W M Machine Tool, Pottstown *Also called William A Moddrel (G-15957)*

W M S Phase Converters 717 336-6566
187 E Church St Stevens (17578) *(G-18057)*

W O Hickok Manufacturing Co 717 234-8041
900 Cumberland St Harrisburg (17103) *(G-7243)*

W R Meadows Inc 717 792-2627
2150 Monroe St York (17404) *(G-20701)*

W R Meadows of Pennsylvannia, York *Also called W R Meadows Inc (G-20701)*

W Rose Inc 610 583-4125
1300 Elmwood Ave Sharon Hill (19079) *(G-17466)*

W S Display 717 460-3485
6 Pine Hill Dr Carlisle (17013) *(G-2749)*

W S Lee & Sons LP 814 317-5010
3000 7th Ave Altoona (16602) *(G-556)*

W T, Birdsboro *Also called Wunsch Technologies Corp (G-1709)*

W T Storey Inc 570 923-2400
96 Little Italy Rd North Bend (17760) *(G-12728)*

W V Fabricating & Welding Inc 724 266-3000
2197 Duss Ave Ambridge (15003) *(G-637)*

W W Engine and Supply Inc (PA) 814 345-5693
Old Route 53 Kylertown (16847) *(G-8868)*

W W McFarland Inc 724 946-9663
1103 Pulaski Mercer Rd New Wilmington (16142) *(G-12472)*

W W Pallet Co 717 362-9388
1318 Mountain Rd Elizabethville (17023) *(G-4899)*

W W Patterson Company 412 322-2012
870 Riversea Rd Pittsburgh (15233) *(G-15706)*

W. G. Malden, New Holland *Also called Protechs LLC (G-12273)*

W.C. Weil Company, Allison Park *Also called GSM Hold Co (G-452)*

WA Dehart Inc 570 568-1551
1130 Old Route 15 New Columbia (17856) *(G-12179)*

Wabtec, Wilmerding *Also called Westinghouse A Brake Tech Corp (G-20163)*

Wabtec Corporation (HQ) 412 825-1000
1001 Airbrake Ave Wilmerding (15148) *(G-20160)*

Wabtec Global Services, Wilmerding *Also called Wabtec Corporation (G-20160)*

Wabtec Investments Limited LLC 412 825-1000
1001 Airbrake Ave Wilmerding (15148) *(G-20161)*

Wabtec Rubber Products, Greensburg *Also called Westinghouse A Brake Tech Corp (G-6730)*

Wacker Chemical Corporation 610 336-2700
6870 Tilghman St Allentown (18106) *(G-428)*

Wade Holdings LLC 717 375-2251
5573 Main St Marion (17235) *(G-10470)*

Wade Technology Incorporated 215 765-2478
445 N 11th St Philadelphia (19123) *(G-14456)*

Waggoner Fbrction Mllwrght LLC 717 486-7533
30 Woodcraft Dr Mount Holly Springs (17065) *(G-11641)*

Wagman Manufacturing Inc 717 266-5616
215 Beshore School Rd Manchester (17345) *(G-10365)*

Wagman Metal Products Inc 717 854-2120
400 S Albemarle St York (17403) *(G-20702)*

Wagner & Sons Machine Shop 610 434-6640
420 Business Park Ln Allentown (18109) *(G-429)*

Wagner Industries Inc 570 874-4400
6 Starter Dr Frackville (17931) *(G-6108)*

Wagner Masters Custom Wdwkg 570 748-9424
700 Maple St Lock Haven (17745) *(G-10093)*

Wagner Tarps Inc 814 849-3422
244 Indl Park Rd Brookville (15825) *(G-2275)*

Wakeem Inc 610 258-2311
2045 Fairview Ave Easton (18042) *(G-4774)*

Wakefern Food Corp 215 744-9500
6301 Oxford Ave Philadelphia (19111) *(G-14457)*

Wakefield Dairy LLC 717 548-2179
125 Warfel Rd Peach Bottom (17563) *(G-13203)*

Wakefield Steel & Welding LLC 717 548-2172
1989 Lancaster Pike Peach Bottom (17563) *(G-13204)*

Wakefield Steel and Welding, Peach Bottom *Also called Wakefield Steel & Welding LLC (G-13204)*

Wakefoose Office Supply & Prtg 814 623-5742
240 W Penn St Bedford (15522) *(G-1079)*

Wakins Food Corporation 215 785-3420
218 Us Highway 13 Rear Bristol (19007) *(G-2216)*

Walco Fabricating Inc 570 628-4523
501 W Bacon St Pottsville (17901) *(G-16101)*

Walco Label & Packaging, Erie *Also called McCarty Printing Corp (G-5385)*

Waldrich GMBH Inc 724 763-3889
101 River St Ford City (16226) *(G-6052)*

Walker Fabricating 724 847-5111
712 7th St Beaver Falls (15010) *(G-1016)*

Walker Lumber Co Inc 814 857-7642
148 Tipple Ln Woodland (16881) *(G-20215)*

Walker Printer, Kittanning *Also called Butter Milk Falls Inc (G-8759)*

Walker Wood Products Inc 717 436-2105
1060 Smith Rd Mifflintown (17059) *(G-11141)*

Wall Firma Inc 724 258-6873
733 E Main St Monongahela (15063) *(G-11319)*

Wallace Brothers Mfg Co 570 822-3808
275 Mundy St Ste 103 Wilkes Barre (18702) *(G-19968)*

Wallace Cranes, Malvern *Also called B E Wallace Products Corp (G-10190)*

Wallace Moving & Storage 724 568-2411
210 Washington Ave Vandergrift (15690) *(G-18737)*

Wallace Pharmaceuticals Inc 732 564-2700
1000 Mylan Blvd Canonsburg (15317) *(G-2654)*

Wallquest Inc 610 293-1330
465 Devon Park Dr Wayne (19087) *(G-19389)*

Walman Optical Company 717 767-5193
150 Rose Ct York (17406) *(G-20703)*

Walnut Burl Woodmill 717 259-8479
87 N Ridge Rd Thomasville (17364) *(G-18343)*

Walnut Industries Inc 215 638-7847
1356 Adams Rd Bensalem (19020) *(G-1268)*

Walnut Uniforms and Embroidery, Johnstown *Also called Lee Regional Health System Inc (G-8403)*

Walsh Sheet Metal Inc 570 344-3495
818 Meadow Ave Scranton (18505) *(G-17311)*

Walsh Tool Company Inc 570 823-1375
33 Hanover St Wilkes Barre (18702) *(G-19969)*

Waltco Inc 724 625-3110
1100 Mars Evans City Rd Mars (16046) *(G-10512)*

Walter and Jackson Inc 610 593-5195
44 Gay St Christiana (17509) *(G-3144)*

Walter B Staller Inc 570 385-5386
106 Tennis Ave Schuylkill Haven (17972) *(G-17171)*

Walter E Lee Inc 215 443-0271
601 High Ave Hatboro (19040) *(G-7310)*

Walter Long Mfg Co Inc 724 348-6631
86 Walter Long Rd Finleyville (15332) *(G-5965)*

Walter McClelland Jr LLC 814 378-7434
102 Mcclelland Dr Madera (16661) *(G-10164)*

Walter Progner, Lebanon *Also called East Indies Coffee & Tea (G-9566)*

Walter R Erle - Mrrisville LLC 215 736-1708
14 Steel Rd E Morrisville (19067) *(G-11588)*

Walter S Custom Cabinetry 570 420-9800
1410 Spruce St Stroudsburg (18360) *(G-18142)*

Walters Electric Co, Latrobe *Also called Jeffrey Shepler (G-9484)*

Walters Mlding Fabrication LLC 724 662-4836
339 Stonepile Rd Mercer (16137) *(G-10978)*

Walters Monument Co, Summit Hill *Also called Craig Walters (G-18159)*

Waltersdorf Manufacturing Inc 717 630-0036
237 Ridge Ave Hanover (17331) *(G-6971)*

Waltersdorff Mfg Co, Hanover *Also called Hand Crafted Furniture Co Inc (G-6891)*

Walton Paint Company Inc (PA) 724 932-3101
108 Main St Jamestown (16134) *(G-8241)*

Walton Paint Company Inc 814 774-3042
710 Beaver Rd Girard (16417) *(G-6403)*

Wampum Hardware Co (PA) 724 336-4501
636 Paden Rd New Galilee (16141) *(G-12223)*

Wampum Hardware Co 814 893-5470
533 Old Lincoln Hwy Stoystown (15563) *(G-18088)*

Wanner Road Woodcraft 717 768-0207
6011 Wanner Rd Narvon (17555) *(G-11931)*

Ward Fabricating Inc 814 345-6707
1930 Palestine Rd Morrisdale (16858) *(G-11549)*

Ward Manufacturing LLC (HQ) 570 638-2131
117 Gulick St Blossburg (16912) *(G-1810)*

Warehouse, Bethlehem *Also called Bethlehem Apparatus Co Inc (G-1461)*

Warehouse, Phoenixville *Also called Danco Precision Inc (G-14544)*

Wargo Interior Systems Inc 215 723-6200
416 School House Rd 1 Telford (18969) *(G-18325)*

Warminster Fiberglass, Southampton *Also called WFC Company Inc (G-17846)*

Warner Music Inc 570 383-3291
1400 E Lackawanna St Olyphant (18448) *(G-13003)*

Warner-Crivellaro Stained Glas 610 264-1100
603 8th St Whitehall (18052) *(G-19893)*

Warners Candies 215 639-1615
3518 Bristol Pike Bensalem (19020) *(G-1269)*

Warners Innvtive Solutions Inc 814 201-2429
1304 11th Ave Altoona (16601) *(G-557)*

Waroquier Coal Inc (PA) 814 765-5681
Rr 879 Clearfield (16830) *(G-3235)*

Waroquier Coal Inc 814 765-5681
3056 Washington Ave Clearfield (16830) *(G-3236)*

Warp Processing Inc 570 655-1275
95 Stevens Ln Exeter (18643) *(G-5585)*

Warrell Corporation (PA) 717 761-5440
1250 Slate Hill Rd Camp Hill (17011) *(G-2523)*

Warren Associates, Pittsburgh *Also called Lustra-Line Inc (G-15242)*

Warren C Hartman Contracting 814 765-8842
5003 Bigler Rd Clearfield (16830) *(G-3237)*

Warren Controls Inc 610 317-0800
2600 Emrick Blvd Bethlehem (18020) *(G-1653)*

Warren Electric Motor Service....................814 723-2045
900 Pennsylvania Ave W Warren (16365) *(G-19057)*

Warren Industrial Solutions.......................814 728-8500
21890 Route 6 Warren (16365) *(G-19058)*

Warren Industries Inc (PA)........................814 723-2050
2349 Crescent Park Ext Warren (16365) *(G-19059)*

Warren Industries Incorporated (PA)............215 464-9300
2045 Bennett Rd Philadelphia (19116) *(G-14458)*

Warren Industries Incorporated.................215 969-5011
2045 Bennett Rd Philadelphia (19116) *(G-14459)*

Warren Installations Inc..........................717 517-9321
1842 William Penn Way Lancaster (17601) *(G-9235)*

Warren Knight Instr Co Div, Philadelphia *Also called Warren Industries Incorporated* *(G-14458)*

Warren Machine Co Inc............................215 491-5500
429 Easton Rd Ste A Warrington (18976) *(G-19136)*

Warren Machine Technology Inc.................215 491-5500
429 Easton Rd Ste A Warrington (18976) *(G-19137)*

Warren Plastics Mfg...............................814 726-9511
123 Elm St Warren (16365) *(G-19060)*

Warren Products Inc...............................570 655-4596
530 Exeter Ave West Pittston (18643) *(G-19757)*

Warren Railcar Service Inc.......................814 723-2500
51 Railcar Rd Warren (16365) *(G-19061)*

Warren Scrap, Sharon *Also called Mercer Co* *(G-17438)*

Warren Sheet Metal Inc...........................814 726-5777
21 S Irvine St Warren (16365) *(G-19062)*

Warren Times Observer...........................814 723-8200
205 Pennsylvania Ave W Warren (16365) *(G-19063)*

Warren's Honda, Bethlehem *Also called Triple W Enterprises Inc* *(G-1642)*

Warrington Equipment Mfg Co....................215 343-1714
2051 Bunnell Rd Warrington (18976) *(G-19138)*

Warrington Pastry Shop...........................215 343-1946
1380 Easton Rd Ste 3 Warrington (18976) *(G-19139)*

Warrior Energy Services Corp....................814 637-5191
10865 Bennetts Valley Hwy Penfield (15849) *(G-13225)*

Warrior Fashions Inc..............................215 925-7905
513 South St Frnt Philadelphia (19147) *(G-14460)*

Warrior Roofing Mfg Inc..........................717 709-0323
323 Development Ave Chambersburg (17201) *(G-2998)*

Warrior Wiper Wraps LLC.........................720 577-9499
3608 Woodhaven Rd Apt 1 Philadelphia (19154) *(G-14461)*

Warwick Machine & Tool Company...............717 892-6814
1917 Mcfarland Dr Landisville (17538) *(G-9268)*

Wash n Grind LLC.................................814 383-4707
366 Aspen Ridge Way Bellefonte (16823) *(G-1124)*

Washington Fabricators, Philadelphia *Also called Donatucci Kitchens & Appls* *(G-13639)*

Washington Greene County Blind.................724 228-0770
566 E Maiden St Washington (15301) *(G-19238)*

Washington Penn Mexico Holding.................724 228-1260
450 Racetrack Rd Washington (15301) *(G-19239)*

Washington Penn Plastic Co Inc (HQ)............724 228-1260
450 Racetrack Rd Washington (15301) *(G-19240)*

Washington Penn Plastic Co Inc.................724 228-1260
2080 N Main St Washington (15301) *(G-19241)*

Washington Penn Plastic Co Inc.................724 206-2120
1500 Weirich Ave Washington (15301) *(G-19242)*

Washington Penn Plastic Co Inc.................724 228-3709
136 Mitchell Rd Eighty Four (15330) *(G-4851)*

Washington Radio Reports Inc (PA)..............717 334-0668
1588 Fairfield Rd Gettysburg (17325) *(G-6321)*

Washington Radio Reports Inc....................717 334-0668
1588 Fairfield Rd Gettysburg (17325) *(G-6322)*

Washington Rotating Control.....................724 228-8889
63 Springfield Ave Washington (15301) *(G-19243)*

Washington Shop N Save, Washington *Also called Duritzas Enterprises Inc* *(G-19165)*

Washington Steel Products, Washington *Also called Acrelormittal Us LLC* *(G-19144)*

Washita Valley Enterprises Inc...................724 437-1593
1152 National Pike Hopwood (15445) *(G-7777)*

WAsnyder An Son LLC............................724 260-0695
107 Lexington Dr Canonsburg (15317) *(G-2655)*

Waste Gas Fabricating Co Inc....................215 736-9240
450 Newbold Rd Fairless Hills (19030) *(G-5807)*

Waste Management & Processors.................570 874-2003
51 Eleanor Ave Frackville (17931) *(G-6109)*

Waste Recovery Designed Pdts...................724 926-5713
2936 Industrial Blvd Bethel Park (15102) *(G-1437)*

Watch My Net Inc.................................267 625-6000
317 W Glenside Ave Glenside (19038) *(G-6543)*

Watch U Want Inc................................954 961-1445
166 E Levering Mill Rd # 100 Bala Cynwyd (19004) *(G-896)*

Watchword Worldwide.............................814 366-2770
1001 Merchant St Ambridge (15003) *(G-638)*

Water Gem Inc.....................................717 561-4440
818 S 28th St Harrisburg (17111) *(G-7244)*

Water Master Inc..................................717 561-4440
818 S 28th St Harrisburg (17111) *(G-7245)*

Water Treatment By Design LLC..................717 938-0670
730 Seitz Dr Lewisberry (17339) *(G-9894)*

Water Treatment Services Inc....................800 817-5116
203 Townsend Dr Monroeville (15146) *(G-11363)*

Waterford Precast & Sales Inc (PA)..............814 864-4956
8260 E Johnson Rd Erie (16509) *(G-5527)*

Waterford Sand & Gravel Co......................814 796-6250
15871 Sturgis Rd Union City (16438) *(G-18613)*

Waterfront Embroidery............................412 337-9269
233 W 8th Ave Homestead (15120) *(G-7697)*

Waterloo Structures................................610 857-2170
3898 W Lincoln Hwy Parkesburg (19365) *(G-13184)*

Waterloo Woodcraft...............................724 221-0438
4474 Route 217 Hwy N Blairsville (15717) *(G-1744)*

Watermark Usa LLC..............................610 983-0500
408 Conshohocken State Rd Gladwyne (19035) *(G-6409)*

Waters Corporation...............................412 967-5665
307 23rd Street Ext Pittsburgh (15215) *(G-15707)*

Waters Corporation...............................484 344-5404
5205 Militia Hill Rd # 100 Plymouth Meeting (19462) *(G-15879)*

Watson Industries Inc (PA).......................724 275-1000
616 Hite Rd Harwick (15049) *(G-7257)*

Watson Laboratories Inc..........................951 493-5300
1090 Horsham Rd North Wales (19454) *(G-12839)*

Watson McDaniel Company (HQ).................610 495-5131
428 Jones Blvd Pottstown (19464) *(G-16070)*

Watson McDaniel Company........................610 367-7191
813 S Reading Ave Bldg 6 Boyertown (19512) *(G-1935)*

Watson Metal Products Corp (PA)................908 276-2202
731 Martha Ave Lancaster (17601) *(G-9236)*

Watson Standard Adhesives Co...................724 274-5014
616 Hite Rd Harwick (15049) *(G-7258)*

Watson Standard Company (HQ)..................724 275-1000
616 Hite Rd Harwick (15049) *(G-7259)*

Watt Enterprises Inc...............................570 698-8081
1117 Easton Tpke Lake Ariel (18436) *(G-8896)*

Watt Fuel Cell Corp (PA)..........................724 547-9170
402 E Main St Ste 800 Mount Pleasant (15666) *(G-11722)*

Watts Brothers Tool Works Inc....................412 823-7877
760 Airbrake Ave Wilmerding (15148) *(G-20162)*

Watts Welding Shop LLC..........................570 398-1184
11282 W Route 973 Hwy Jersey Shore (17740) *(G-8324)*

Wattsburg Lumber Co LLC........................814 739-2770
9723 Jamestown St Wattsburg (16442) *(G-19284)*

Waugaman Awnings...............................724 837-1239
115 Laird St Greensburg (15601) *(G-6728)*

Waupaca Foundry Inc.............................570 724-5191
18986 Route 287 Tioga (16946) *(G-18367)*

Waupaca Foundry Inc.............................570 827-3245
18986 Route 287 Tioga (16946) *(G-18368)*

Wausau Paper Corp (HQ)..........................866 722-8675
2929 Arch St Ste 2600 Philadelphia (19104) *(G-14462)*

Wave, Malvern *Also called Worthington Armstrong Venture* *(G-10351)*

Wave Central LLC.................................717 503-7157
99 Garden Pkwy Ste C Carlisle (17013) *(G-2750)*

Wave Swimmer Inc................................215 367-3778
116 E Athens Ave Ardmore (19003) *(G-722)*

Waveline Direct Llc................................717 795-8830
192 Hempt Rd Mechanicsburg (17050) *(G-10905)*

Waverly Partners Inc..............................610 687-7867
175 Strafford Ave Wayne (19087) *(G-19390)*

Wayne Abel Repairs..............................610 857-1708
1934 Valley Rd Parkesburg (19365) *(G-13185)*

Wayne Automation Corporation..................610 630-8900
605 General Wash Ave Norristown (19403) *(G-12723)*

Wayne Concrete, Shinglehouse *Also called Lisa Little Inc* *(G-17509)*

Wayne Concrete Inc...............................814 697-7500
262 Route 44 Shinglehouse (16748) *(G-17514)*

Wayne County Ready Mix Inc....................570 253-4341
397 Grimms Rd Honesdale (18431) *(G-7733)*

Wayne Fueling Systems...........................215 257-1046
1000 E Walnut St Perkasie (18944) *(G-13298)*

Wayne Independent, Honesdale *Also called Gatehouse Media LLC* *(G-7712)*

Wayne Lawson..................................814 757-8424
110 Creek Rd Russell (16345) *(G-16882)*

Wayne Mills Company Inc (HQ)..................215 842-2134
130 W Berkley St Philadelphia (19144) *(G-14463)*

Wayne Products Inc..............................800 255-5665
888 Sussex Blvd Ste 3 Broomall (19008) *(G-2305)*

Wayneco Inc.....................................717 225-4413
800 Hanover Rd York (17408) *(G-20704)*

Waynesburg Milling Co............................724 627-6137
387 S Washington St Waynesburg (15370) *(G-19452)*

Waza Inc...610 827-7800
19 Red Rock Ln Chester Springs (19425) *(G-3087)*

Wbe, Pittsburgh *Also called Dasco Inc* *(G-14906)*

Wc Welding Services.............................570 798-2300
162 Beaver Hollow Rd Lakewood (18439) *(G-8916)*

Wc Wolff Company, Newtown Square *Also called W C Wolff Company* *(G-12598)*

Wced News Talk..................................814 372-1420
12 W Long Ave Du Bois (15801) *(G-4426)*

Wcr Inc 215 447-8152
  4080 Blanche Rd Bensalem (19020) *(G-1270)*

WD Services Inc 610 970-7946
  300 Old Reading Pike # 10 Pottstown (19464) *(G-16071)*

Wdt, Mars Also called Woodings Doweling Tech Inc *(G-10514)*

We, Kennerdell Also called Witherup Fbrction Erection Inc *(G-8499)*

We Care Screen Printing, Philadelphia Also called Jerome W Sinclair *(G-13894)*

We Love Wood, Altoona Also called Cheryl Hewitt *(G-492)*

We-Ef Lighting USA LLC 724 742-0027
  410 Keystone Dr Warrendale (15086) *(G-19100)*

Weaber Inc (HQ) 717 867-2212
  1231 Mount Wilson Rd Lebanon (17042) *(G-9638)*

Weaber Inc 814 827-4621
  11117 Skyline Dr Titusville (16354) *(G-18403)*

Weaber Hardwoods, Lebanon Also called Weaber Inc *(G-9638)*

Weaber Lumber, Lebanon Also called Wt Hardwoods Group Inc *(G-9639)*

Weahterford Manufacturing 724 239-1404
  100 Vista Dr Charleroi (15022) *(G-3024)*

Wearable Health Solutions Inc (HQ) 877 639-2929
  200 W Church Rd Ste B King of Prussia (19406) *(G-8698)*

Wearforce North America LLC 215 996-1770
  69 Bristol Rd Chalfont (18914) *(G-2894)*

Wearing Products, Mc Connellsburg Also called Conair Corporation *(G-10563)*

Weather Shield Mfg Inc 717 761-7131
  1401 Slate Hill Rd Camp Hill (17011) *(G-2524)*

Weathered Vineyards LLC 484 560-1528
  7670 Carpet Rd New Tripoli (18066) *(G-12462)*

Weatherford Artificia 570 308-3400
  25 Energy Dr Muncy (17756) *(G-11838)*

Weatherford International LLC 570 326-2754
  25 Energy Dr Muncy (17756) *(G-11839)*

Weatherford International LLC 570 546-0745
  306 Industrial Park Rd Muncy (17756) *(G-11840)*

Weatherford International LLC 724 745-7050
  121 Hillpointe Dr Ste 300 Canonsburg (15317) *(G-2656)*

Weatherly Casting and Mch Co 570 427-8611
  300 Commerce St Weatherly (18255) *(G-19455)*

Weave Hub LLC 215 809-2082
  41 University Dr Ste 400 Newtown (18940) *(G-12562)*

Weaver Glen A & Son LLC 814 432-3013
  823 Congress Hill Rd Franklin (16323) *(G-6168)*

Weaver Bros Pallets, Beaver Springs Also called Peachey-Yoder LP *(G-1020)*

Weaver Carriage Shop 717 445-7191
  361 Iron Bridge Rd East Earl (17519) *(G-4557)*

Weaver Industries Inc 717 336-7507
  425 S 4th St Denver (17517) *(G-4097)*

Weaver Machine & Hardware LLC 717 445-9927
  385 Reading Rd East Earl (17519) *(G-4558)*

Weaver Metal Fab LLC 717 466-6601
  150 Industrial Dr Ephrata (17522) *(G-5155)*

Weaver Mulch LLC 610 383-6818
  3186 Strasburg Rd Coatesville (19320) *(G-3329)*

Weaver Pallet Company 717 463-3037
  2107 Free Springs Ch Rd Mifflintown (17059) *(G-11142)*

Weaver Pallet Company LLC 717 463-2770
  2107 Free Spring Ch Rd Mc Alisterville (17049) *(G-10553)*

Weaver Sawmill 570 539-8420
  305 Sawmill Rd Liverpool (17045) *(G-10080)*

Weaver Screen Printing Inc 717 632-9158
  24 Baltimore St Hanover (17331) *(G-6972)*

Weaver Sheet Metal LLC 717 733-4763
  200 S Market St Ephrata (17522) *(G-5156)*

Weaver Wood Specialties 610 589-5889
  36 Host Rd Womelsdorf (19567) *(G-20210)*

Weaverland Quarry, East Earl Also called Martin Limestone Inc *(G-4549)*

Weaverline LLC 717 445-6724
  180 Boot Jack Rd Narvon (17555) *(G-11932)*

Weavers Famous Lebanon Bologna, Lebanon Also called Daniel Weaver Company Inc *(G-9558)*

WEAVERS OF WELLSVILLE, Wellsville Also called Ken Weaver Meats Inc *(G-19479)*

Weavertown Coach Shop 717 768-3299
  3007 Old Phladelphia Pike Bird In Hand (17505) *(G-1685)*

Web Age Solutions Inc 215 517-6540
  744 Yorkway Pl Jenkintown (19046) *(G-8304)*

Web Paint Inc 570 208-2528
  152 Horton St Wilkes Barre (18702) *(G-19970)*

Web Press Div, York Also called Kba North America Inc *(G-20548)*

Webb Communications Inc 570 326-7634
  1719 W Main St Plymouth (18651) *(G-15823)*

Webb Communications Inc 570 326-7634
  301 W Main St Plymouth (18651) *(G-15824)*

Webb Communications Inc 570 779-9543
  180 W Main St Plymouth (18651) *(G-15825)*

Webb Communications Inc (PA) 570 326-7634
  1 Maynard St Williamsport (17701) *(G-20089)*

Webb Weekly 570 326-9322
  280 Kane St Ste 2 Williamsport (17702) *(G-20090)*

Webb-Mason Inc 724 935-1770
  12330 Perry Hwy Ste 240 Wexford (15090) *(G-19833)*

Webbs Super-Gro Products Inc 570 726-4525
  30 Pennsylvania Ave Mill Hall (17751) *(G-11184)*

Webco Inc 215 942-9366
  7 Legacy Oaks Dr Richboro (18954) *(G-16678)*

Webco Industries Inc 814 678-1325
  363 Seneca St Oil City (16301) *(G-12959)*

Weber Display & Packaging, Philadelphia Also called David Weber Co Inc *(G-13610)*

Weber Electmotor Service 717 436-8120
  310 Henry St Mifflintown (17059) *(G-11143)*

Webtrans Limited LLC 215 260-3313
  701 W 5th St Ste D Lansdale (19446) *(G-9427)*

Wec, Pittsburgh Also called Westinghouse Electric Co LLC *(G-15710)*

Wedj/Three CS Inc 717 845-8685
  491 E Princess St York (17403) *(G-20705)*

Weeds Inc (PA) 610 358-9430
  250 Bodley Rd Aston (19014) *(G-797)*

Weekend Directional Services 800 494-4954
  22 Georgetown Ln A Beaver (15009) *(G-995)*

Weekender 570 831-7320
  90 E Market St Wilkes Barre (18701) *(G-19971)*

Weekenders, Uniontown Also called Ad Star Inc *(G-18614)*

Weekly Bargain Bulletin Inc 724 654-5529
  1576 Sunrise Dr New Castle (16105) *(G-12166)*

Weekly Piper Ltd 717 341-3726
  112 S Spruce St Lititz (17543) *(G-10058)*

Weekly Press, Philadelphia Also called University City Review Inc *(G-14428)*

Weekly Shopper (HQ) 412 243-4215
  210 Wood St Tarentum (15084) *(G-18254)*

Wegco Welding Inc 412 833-7020
  3180 Industrial Blvd # 2 Bethel Park (15102) *(G-1438)*

Wege Pretzel Co Inc 717 843-0738
  116 N Blettner Ave Hanover (17331) *(G-6973)*

Wehrungs Specialty Woods 610 847-6002
  8422 Rte 611 Ottsville (18942) *(G-13069)*

Weichert Machining Inc 717 235-6761
  97 Manchester St Glen Rock (17327) *(G-6462)*

Weidenhammer Systems Corp 610 317-4000
  951 Marcon Blvd Allentown (18109) *(G-430)*

Weidenhammer Systems Corp (PA) 610 378-1149
  935 Berkshire Blvd Reading (19610) *(G-16562)*

Weidenhammer Systems Corp 610 378-1149
  25 N Queen St Ste 501 Lancaster (17603) *(G-9237)*

Weidenhammer Systems Corp 610 687-0037
  1787 Sentry Pkwy W 305 Blue Bell (19422) *(G-1857)*

Weikel's Sportswear, Reading Also called Todd Weikel *(G-16542)*

Weiler Corporation (PA) 570 595-7495
  1 Weiler Dr Cresco (18326) *(G-3896)*

Weinman Eye Center, Kutztown Also called Kutztown Optical Corp *(G-8848)*

Weinrich Bakery 215 659-7062
  55 Easton Rd Willow Grove (19090) *(G-20148)*

Weinrichs Bakery A Konditorei, Willow Grove Also called Weinrich Bakery *(G-20148)*

Weinstein Sup - Willow Grove, Willow Grove Also called Hajoca Corporation *(G-20120)*

Weir Hazleton Inc 570 455-7711
  225 N Cedar St Hazleton (18201) *(G-7537)*

Weir Kitchens 717 292-6829
  350 S Winding Rd Dover (17315) *(G-4207)*

Weir Welding Company Inc 610 974-8140
  1745 Eaton Ave Ste 2 Bethlehem (18018) *(G-1654)*

Weis Markets Inc 570 724-6364
  11798 Route 6 Wellsboro (16901) *(G-19474)*

Weiser Group LLC 724 452-6535
  122 Beahm Crest Ln Evans City (16033) *(G-5565)*

Weisman Novelty Co Inc 215 635-0147
  608 Webb Rd Elkins Park (19027) *(G-4914)*

Wel Instrument Co 724 625-9041
  106 Camp Trees Rd Mars (16046) *(G-10513)*

Wel-Mac Inc 717 637-6921
  231 Baltimore St Hanover (17331) *(G-6974)*

Welch Foods Inc A Cooperative 814 725-4577
  139 S Lake St North East (16428) *(G-12766)*

Weld Tek Ltd 717 367-0666
  69 Industrial Rd Elizabethtown (17022) *(G-4890)*

Weld Tooling Corporation (PA) 412 331-1776
  280 Technology Dr Canonsburg (15317) *(G-2657)*

Weld Tooling Corporation 412 331-1776
  280 Technology Dr Canonsburg (15317) *(G-2658)*

Welded Shtmtl Specialty Co 412 331-3534
  745 Greenway Dr Pittsburgh (15204) *(G-15708)*

Welding & Thermal Technologies 610 678-4847
  44 Woodrow Ave Reading (19608) *(G-16563)*

Welding Alloys USA 724 202-7497
  759 Northgate Cir New Castle (16105) *(G-12167)*

Welding Technologies, North Wales Also called Joseph Nedorezov *(G-12808)*

Welding Technologies, Blue Bell Also called Joseph Nedorezov *(G-1837)*

Welding Technologies Inc 814 432-0954
  561 Allegheny Blvd Franklin (16323) *(G-6169)*

Weldon Machine Tool Inc 717 846-4000
425 E Berlin Rd York (17408) *(G-20706)*

Weldon Solutions, York *Also called Weldon Machine Tool Inc (G-20706)*

Weldsale Company LLC 215 739-7474
2151 Dreer St Philadelphia (19125) *(G-14464)*

Weldship Industries Inc (PA) 610 861-7330
225 W 2nd St Unit 2 Bethlehem (18015) *(G-1655)*

Well Testing, Clearfield *Also called Oil States Energy Services LLC (G-3227)*

Wellborn Holdings Inc 717 351-1700
215 Diller Ave New Holland (17557) *(G-12293)*

Weller Wood Works, Sellersville *Also called Jay Weller (G-17350)*

Wellfboro Gazette, Wellsboro *Also called Tioga Publishing Company (G-19473)*

Wellington's Best Foods, Aston *Also called Sharon McGuigan Inc (G-793)*

Wellm Dyna Mach and Asse Inc 717 764-8855
706 Willow Springs Ln York (17406) *(G-20707)*

Wells Technology Inc 215 672-7000
31 Commerce Dr Warminster (18974) *(G-18999)*

Wellsboro Advertiser, Mansfield *Also called Penny Mansfield Saver Inc (G-10424)*

Wellspring Gift Lancaster, Lancaster *Also called Vanroden Inc (G-9230)*

Wellspring Wireless Inc 215 788-8485
3580 Progress Dr Ste L Bensalem (19020) *(G-1271)*

Wellsville Foundry Inc 330 532-2995
24939 State St Meadville (16335) *(G-10812)*

Welltec Inc 724 553-5922
212 Commerce Park Dr Cranberry Township (16066) *(G-3864)*

Welltech Products Inc 610 417-8928
7823 Sweetwood Dr Macungie (18062) *(G-10161)*

Wellvue365, Horsham *Also called Addaren Holdings LLC (G-7779)*

Welsh Mountain Woodworking, Gap *Also called Steve Eversoll (G-6256)*

Welte Roofing, Pittsburgh *Also called L A Welte Inc (G-15206)*

Wemco Inc 570 869-9660
3087 State Route 367 Laceyville (18623) *(G-8875)*

Wendell August Forge Inc (PA) 724 748-9500
111 Amercian Way Mercer (16137) *(G-10979)*

Wendell H Stone and Company 412 331-1944
149 Nichol Ave Mc Kees Rocks (15136) *(G-10641)*

Wendell H Stone Company Inc (PA) 724 836-1400
606 Mccormick Ave Connellsville (15425) *(G-3510)*

Wendell H Stone Company Inc 724 483-6571
201 2nd St Charleroi (15022) *(G-3025)*

Wendell H Stone Company Inc 724 224-7688
606 Mccormick Ave Connellsville (15425) *(G-3511)*

Wendell H Stone Company Inc 724 836-1400
1718 Roseytown Rd Greensburg (15601) *(G-6729)*

Wendell H Stone Company Inc 412 373-6235
4135 Old William Penn Hwy Monroeville (15146) *(G-11364)*

Wendells Prfmce Trck Sp LLC 717 458-8404
5253 Simpson Ferry Rd Mechanicsburg (17050) *(G-10906)*

Wendt Dunnington Company, Royersford *Also called Winterthur Wendt Usa Inc (G-16869)*

Wenger Corporate Services LLC 800 692-6008
101 W Harrisburg Ave Rheems (17570) *(G-16668)*

Wenger Feeds Inc 717 367-1195
6829 Route 405 Hwy Muncy (17756) *(G-11841)*

Wenger Feeds LLC 717 367-1195
Rr 25 Spring Glen (17978) *(G-17874)*

Wenger Feeds LLC 717 367-1195
3579 Hempland Rd Lancaster (17601) *(G-9238)*

Wenger Feeds LLC 717 367-1195
230 S Market Ave Mount Joy (17552) *(G-11676)*

Wenger Feeds LLC 570 682-8812
824 Church Rd Hegins (17938) *(G-7546)*

Wenger Feeds LLC 717 367-1195
1122 Mount Rock Rd Shippensburg (17257) *(G-17554)*

Wenger Systems, New Holland *Also called Aaron Wenger (G-12225)*

Wengerd Pallet Company 717 463-3274
1824 Rockland Rd Mifflintown (17059) *(G-11144)*

Wenning Entertainment LLC 412 292-8776
1354 Wilmerding Ave East Mc Keesport (15035) *(G-4582)*

Wenturine Bros Lumber Inc 814 948-6050
Rr 553 Box 66 Nicktown (15762) *(G-12622)*

Wentzel Fabrication Inc 610 987-6909
52 Legion Dr Oley (19547) *(G-12981)*

Wenz Co Inc 610 434-6157
1928 Hamilton St Allentown (18104) *(G-431)*

Wenzco Supplies 610 434-6157
1928 Hamilton St Allentown (18104) *(G-432)*

Wepco Inc (PA) 570 368-8184
101 Armstrong Rd Pittston (18640) *(G-15784)*

Weppco, Allentown *Also called Aetna Felt Corp (G-117)*

WER Corporation (PA) 610 678-8023
4601 Penn Ave Reading (19608) *(G-16564)*

Werner Co (HQ) 724 588-2000
93 Werner Rd Greenville (16125) *(G-6775)*

Werner Extruded Products, Greenville *Also called Old Ladder Co (G-6762)*

Werner Holding Co Inc 888 523-3371
93 Werner Rd Greenville (16125) *(G-6776)*

Werner Welding LLC 724 379-4240
475 W Newton Rd Elizabeth (15037) *(G-4864)*

Wert Bookbinding Inc 717 469-0626
9975 Allentown Blvd Grantville (17028) *(G-6576)*

Werther Partners LLC (PA) 215 677-5200
9990 Global Rd Philadelphia (19115) *(G-14465)*

Wertner Signs 717 597-4502
8002 Stone Bridge Rd Greencastle (17225) *(G-6642)*

Werzalit of America Inc 814 362-3881
40 Holley Ave Bradford (16701) *(G-1995)*

Wescho Company Inc 610 436-5866
924 S Concord Rd West Chester (19382) *(G-19676)*

Wesco Distribution Inc 724 772-5000
780 Commonwealth Dr Warrendale (15086) *(G-19101)*

Wescott Steel Inc 215 364-3636
425 Andrews Rd Langhorne (19053) *(G-9335)*

Wesel Manufacturing Company 570 586-8978
710 Layton Rd S Abingtn Twp (18411) *(G-16903)*

Weskem Technologies Inc 717 697-8228
49 Texaco Rd Mechanicsburg (17050) *(G-10907)*

West Collection 570 762-8844
1 Freedom Valley Dr Oaks (19456) *(G-12938)*

West Dairy Inc 610 495-0100
2492 Schuylkill Rd Parker Ford (19457) *(G-13170)*

West End Beer Mart 814 536-1846
119 Fairfield Ave Johnstown (15906) *(G-8443)*

West End Electric Inc 570 682-9292
896 E Mountain Rd Hegins (17938) *(G-7547)*

West End Precision 570 695-3911
196 S Tremont St Tremont (17981) *(G-18484)*

West End Printing, Gilbert *Also called Jim Mannello (G-6362)*

West Hanover Winery Inc 717 652-3711
7646 Jonestown Rd Harrisburg (17112) *(G-7246)*

West Hills Specialty Dntl Lab, Carnegie *Also called West Hills Specialty Supply Co (G-2806)*

West Hills Specialty Supply Co 412 279-6766
312 2nd Ave Carnegie (15106) *(G-2806)*

West Moreland Precision Tool 724 537-6558
151 Kingston St Latrobe (15650) *(G-9528)*

West Penn Ear Nose and Throat 412 621-2656
4815 Liberty Ave Ste 443 Pittsburgh (15224) *(G-15709)*

West Penn Energy Services LLC (PA) 724 354-4118
865 State Route 210 Shelocta (15774) *(G-17490)*

West Penn Mfg Tech LLC 814 886-4100
1027 Front St Cresson (16630) *(G-3901)*

West Penn Optical Inc (PA) 814 833-1194
2576 W 8th St Erie (16505) *(G-5528)*

West Penn Printing 724 546-2020
103 Riverpark Dr New Castle (16101) *(G-12168)*

West Pharmaceutical Services D (PA) 610 594-2900
530 Herman O West Dr Exton (19341) *(G-5747)*

West Pharmaceutical Svcs Inc (PA) 610 594-2900
530 Herman O West Dr Exton (19341) *(G-5748)*

West Pharmaceutical Svcs Inc 570 398-5411
347 Oliver St Jersey Shore (17740) *(G-8325)*

West Pharmaceutical Svcs Inc 717 560-8460
179 W Airport Rd Lititz (17543) *(G-10059)*

West Pharmaceutical Svcs Inc 610 853-3200
8647 W Chester Pike Upper Darby (19082) *(G-18694)*

West Phila Bronze Co Inc 610 874-1454
500 Concord Ave Chester (19013) *(G-3067)*

West Philadelphia Mch Works, Elverson *Also called Wpmw Inc (G-4970)*

West Phrm Svcs Del Inc (HQ) 610 594-2900
530 Herman O West Dr Exton (19341) *(G-5749)*

West Point Acquisition LLC (HQ) 724 222-2354
95 W Beau St Ste 400 Washington (15301) *(G-19244)*

West Point Mining Corp 570 339-5259
2811 Lincoln Hwy Stoystown (15563) *(G-18089)*

West Point Products, Washington *Also called West Point Acquisition LLC (G-19244)*

West Salisbury Fndry Mch Inc 814 662-2809
700 Tub Mill Run Rd West Salisbury (15565) *(G-19765)*

West Shore Prtg & Dist Corp 717 691-8282
304 Mulberry Dr Mechanicsburg (17050) *(G-10908)*

West Side Tool and Die Company 570 331-7016
93 John St Wilkes Barre (18702) *(G-19972)*

West Side Wood Products Inc (PA) 610 562-8166
157 State St Hamburg (19526) *(G-6856)*

West Signs Inc 724 443-5588
3130 Westwind Dr Allison Park (15101) *(G-467)*

Westbrook Window Washers LLC 610 873-0245
1510 Waimea Dr Downingtown (19335) *(G-4263)*

Westcom Wireless Inc 412 228-5507
1025 Lysle Blvd McKeesport (15132) *(G-10686)*

Wester Burlap Bag & Supply Co 412 835-4314
3446 S Park Rd Bethel Park (15102) *(G-1439)*

Westerbrook Custom Made Drap 717 737-8185
4 Amherst Dr Camp Hill (17011) *(G-2525)*

Westerly Incorporated 610 693-8866
17 E Meadow Ave Robesonia (19551) *(G-16780)*

Western PA Newsppr Co 814 226-7000
860 S 5th Ave Ste 4 Clarion (16214) *(G-3187)*

Western PA Stl Fabg Inc 724 658-8575
550 Honey Bee Ln New Castle (16105) *(G-12169)*

A
L
P
H
A
B
E
T
I
C

Western PA Weather LLC.................................814 341-5086
557 Russell Ave Johnstown (15902) *(G-8444)*

Westerwald Corp of America.............................724 945-6000
40 Pottery Ln Scenery Hill (15360) *(G-17127)*

Westerwald Pottery, Scenery Hill *Also called Westerwald Corp of America (G-17127)*

Westfalia Technologies Inc...............................717 764-1115
3655 Sandhurst Dr York (17406) *(G-20708)*

Westinghouse A Brake Tech Corp.......................724 838-1317
269 Donohoe Rd Greensburg (15601) *(G-6730)*

Westinghouse A Brake Tech Corp (PA)................412 825-1000
1001 Airbrake Ave Wilmerding (15148) *(G-20163)*

Westinghouse Electric Co LLC (HQ)....................412 374-2020
1000 Westinghouse Dr Cranberry Township (16066) *(G-3865)*

Westinghouse Electric Co LLC...........................412 374-4252
5000 Ericsson Dr Warrendale (15086) *(G-19102)*

Westinghouse Electric Co LLC...........................412 256-1085
1332 Beulah Rd Pittsburgh (15235) *(G-15710)*

Westinghouse Electric Company (HQ)..................866 442-7873
20 Stanwix St Pittsburgh (15222) *(G-15711)*

Westinghouse Industry Products........................412 374-2020
1000 Westinghouse Dr Cranberry Township (16066) *(G-3866)*

Westinghouse Lighting Corp (PA).......................215 671-2000
12401 Mcnulty Rd Philadelphia (19154) *(G-14466)*

Westinghouse Plasma Center, Mount Pleasant *Also called Westinghouse Plasma Corp (G-11723)*

Westinghouse Plasma Corp...............................724 722-7053
221 Westec Dr Mount Pleasant (15666) *(G-11723)*

Westlab Distribution Inc..................................800 699-0301
1050 Broad St Ste 5 Montoursville (17754) *(G-11456)*

Westlake Chemical Partners LP.........................484 253-4545
993 Old Eagle School Rd Wayne (19087) *(G-19391)*

Westlake Plastics Company (PA)........................610 459-1000
490 Lenni Rd Lenni (19052) *(G-9763)*

Westlake United Corporation (PA)......................570 876-0222
91 Hickory St Mayfield (18433) *(G-10545)*

Westmoreland Advanced Mtls Inc.......................724 684-5902
501 Mckean Ave Ste 3 Charleroi (15022) *(G-3026)*

Westmoreland Contract Fur..............................724 838-7748
1572 Woodward Drive Ext Greensburg (15601) *(G-6731)*

Westmoreland Insurance Svcs, New Kensington *Also called Burrell Group Inc (G-12328)*

Westmoreland Iron and Met LLC........................724 523-8151
2571 Radebaugh Rd Jeannette (15644) *(G-8267)*

Westmoreland Machine & Elc Co........................412 784-1991
5212 Butler St Pittsburgh (15201) *(G-15712)*

Westmoreland Plastics Company, Latrobe *Also called Latrobe Associates Inc (G-9488)*

Westmoreland Regional Hospital, Greensburg *Also called Excela Health Holding Co Inc (G-6665)*

Westmrland Stl Fabrication Inc...........................724 446-0555
371 Middletown Rd Madison (15663) *(G-10167)*

Weston Commercial Group Inc...........................215 717-9675
6020 Spruce St Philadelphia (19139) *(G-14467)*

Westport Allentown, Breinigsville *Also called Westport Axle (G-2032)*

Westport Axle...610 366-2900
650 Boulder Dr Ste 100a Breinigsville (18031) *(G-2032)*

Westrock Company.......................................215 826-2497
3001 State Rd Croydon (19021) *(G-3932)*

Westrock Cp LLC...904 751-6400
423 Kings Mill Rd York (17401) *(G-20709)*

Westrock Cp LLC...610 485-8700
100 Mcdonald Blvd Aston (19014) *(G-798)*

Westrock Cp LLC...215 699-4444
500 Church Rd North Wales (19454) *(G-12840)*

Westrock Cp LLC...215 984-7000
5000 Flat Rock Rd Philadelphia (19127) *(G-14468)*

Westrock Packaging Inc (HQ)............................215 785-3350
3001 State Rd Croydon (19021) *(G-3933)*

Westrock Rkt LLC..570 476-0120
1 Paper Mill Rd Delaware Water Gap (18327) *(G-4045)*

Westrock Rkt LLC..570 454-0433
33 Powell Dr Hazleton (18201) *(G-7538)*

Westrock Rkt LLC..717 393-0436
500 Richardson Dr Lancaster (17603) *(G-9239)*

Westrock Rkt Company...................................717 520-7600
10 W Chocolate Ave # 101 Hershey (17033) *(G-7626)*

Westrock Rkt Company...................................717 790-1596
300 Salem Church Rd Mechanicsburg (17050) *(G-10909)*

Westrock Usc Inc...724 938-3020
400 Technology Dr Coal Center (15423) *(G-3278)*

Westside Weekly, Philadelphia *Also called Johnson Communications Inc (G-13910)*

Westway Feed Products LLC.............................215 425-3707
2900 E Allegheny Ave Philadelphia (19134) *(G-14469)*

Westway Terminal Company, Philadelphia *Also called Westway Feed Products LLC (G-14469)*

Westwood Precision LLC.................................610 264-7020
1530 E Race St Allentown (18109) *(G-433)*

Wesworld Fabrications Inc...............................215 455-5015
3441 Old York Rd Philadelphia (19140) *(G-14470)*

Wet Paint T Shirts Inc....................................570 822-2221
152 Horton St Wilkes Barre (18702) *(G-19973)*

Wexco Incorporated (PA)................................717 764-8585
3490 Board Rd York (17406) *(G-20710)*

Wexford Beer, Wexford *Also called Jskc LLC (G-19809)*

Weyand Sign Company, Stoystown *Also called Rick Weyand Signs (G-18084)*

Weyerbacher Brewing Co.................................610 559-5561
905 Line St Ste G Easton (18042) *(G-4775)*

Weyerhaeuser Company..................................814 827-4621
10589 Campbell Rd Titusville (16354) *(G-18404)*

Weyerhaeuser Company..................................814 371-0630
377 Satterlee Rd Du Bois (15801) *(G-4427)*

Wfc, Mount Pleasant *Also called Watt Fuel Cell Corp (G-11722)*

Wfc & C Inc...215 627-3233
34 S 7th St Philadelphia (19106) *(G-14471)*

WFC Company Inc (PA)..................................215 953-1260
725 County Line Rd Southampton (18966) *(G-17846)*

Wg Products Pittsburgh LLC............................412 795-7177
8031 Saltsburg Rd Pittsburgh (15239) *(G-15713)*

Wgm Gas Company Inc...................................724 397-9600
37 Copper Valley Rd Creekside (15732) *(G-3878)*

Wgs Equipment & Controls..............................610 459-8800
3060 Plaza Dr Ste 110 Garnet Valley (19060) *(G-6270)*

Wharton School Univ of PA..............................215 746-7846
3620 Locust Walk Rm 305 Philadelphia (19104) *(G-14472)*

Wheatland Steel Processing Co.........................724 981-4242
1700 Broadway Ave Wheatland (16161) *(G-19843)*

Wheatland Tube, Sharon *Also called Zekelman Industries Inc (G-17451)*

Wheatland Tube LLC.....................................724 981-5200
134 Mill St Sharon (16146) *(G-17445)*

Wheatland Tube LLC.....................................724 342-6851
1169 N Sharpsville Ave Sharon (16146) *(G-17446)*

Wheatland Tube Company, Sharon *Also called Wheatland Tube LLC (G-17445)*

Wheaton & Son's Iron Works, McKeesport *Also called Wheaton & Sons Inc (G-10687)*

Wheaton & Sons Inc.....................................412 351-0405
2121 5th Ave McKeesport (15132) *(G-10687)*

Wheel & Axel Division, Colver *Also called Damian Hntz Locomotive Svc Inc (G-3453)*

Wheel Collision Center, Bath *Also called Advanced Machine Systems Inc (G-949)*

Wheeland Inc...570 323-3237
419 5th Ave Williamsport (17701) *(G-20091)*

Wheeland Lumber Co Inc.................................570 324-6042
3558 Williamson Trl Liberty (16930) *(G-9952)*

Wheeler Bros Inc...814 443-3269
501 Drum Ave Somerset (15501) *(G-17716)*

Wheeler Bros Inc (HQ)...................................814 443-7000
384 Drum Ave Somerset (15501) *(G-17717)*

Wheeler Brothers, Somerset *Also called Wheeler Bros Inc (G-17717)*

Wheeler Brothers, Somerset *Also called Wheeler Bros Inc (G-17716)*

Wheeler Enterprises Inc..................................610 975-9230
175 Strafford Ave Ste 1 Wayne (19087) *(G-19392)*

Wheeler Tool Co..570 888-2275
215 Wheelock Ave Athens (18810) *(G-813)*

Whemco - Steel Castings Inc............................724 643-7001
1 12th St Midland (15059) *(G-11089)*

Whemco - Steel Castings Inc (HQ).....................412 390-2700
5 Hot Metal St Ste 300 Pittsburgh (15203) *(G-15714)*

Whemco Inc (HQ)..412 390-2700
5 Hot Metal St Ste 300 Pittsburgh (15203) *(G-15715)*

Whemco-Steel Castings Inc.............................724 643-7001
601 W 7th Ave Homestead (15120) *(G-7698)*

Where Philadelphia, Philadelphia *Also called Abardia Media (G-13333)*

Wherleys Trailer Inc......................................717 624-2268
6480 York Rd New Oxford (17350) *(G-12426)*

Wheyclean, Washington Crossing *Also called Clean Concepts Group LLC (G-19254)*

Whiff Roasters, Lititz *Also called Gamut Enterprises Inc (G-10011)*

Whipple Bros Inc (PA)...................................570 836-6262
34 Pine Tree Rd Mountain Top (18707) *(G-11780)*

Whipples Building Mtls Ctr, Mountain Top *Also called Whipple Bros Inc (G-11780)*

Whirl Magazine, Pittsburgh *Also called Whirl Publishing (G-15716)*

Whirl Publishing..412 431-7888
2549 Penn Ave Ste 2 Pittsburgh (15222) *(G-15716)*

Whirled Peace Inc..484 318-7735
111 E Lancaster Ave Paoli (19301) *(G-13151)*

Whirley Drinkworks, Warren *Also called Whirley Industries Inc (G-19065)*

Whirley Industries Inc (PA)..............................814 723-7600
618 4th Ave Warren (16365) *(G-19064)*

Whirley Industries Inc....................................814 723-7600
140 W Harmar St Warren (16365) *(G-19065)*

Whirley-Drinkworks, Warren *Also called Whirley Industries Inc (G-19064)*

Whiskey Dicks..570 342-9824
308 N Washington Ave Scranton (18503) *(G-17312)*

Whisky Advocate, Emmaus *Also called M Shanken Communications Inc (G-5033)*

Whispering Leaf Inc......................................267 437-2991
5835 Stockton Rd Philadelphia (19138) *(G-14473)*

Whispering Oaks Vineyard..............................570 495-4054
1306 State Route 61 Sunbury (17801) *(G-18176)*

Whispering Pine Woodworking..........................570 922-4530
235 Diehl Rd Mifflinburg (17844) *(G-11105)*

Whistle Pig Pumpkin Patch	570 298-0962
3369 Sr 29 S Noxen (18636) *(G-12886)*	
Whitaker Corporation	724 334-7000
1030 Hunt Valley Cir New Kensington (15068) *(G-12389)*	
White Box Systems LLC	717 612-9911
418 Plum St Lemoyne (17043) *(G-9755)*	
White Castle Services LLC	484 560-5961
9174 Briar Edge Rd New Tripoli (18066) *(G-12463)*	
White Deer Woodworking	570 547-1664
16150 S State Route 44 Allenwood (17810) *(G-443)*	
White Engrg Surfaces Corp	215 968-5021
1 Pheas Run Newto Busin Newtown (18940) *(G-12563)*	
White Hawk Beef, Eldred Also called OJacks Inc *(G-4854)*	
White Horse Machine LLC	717 768-8313
5566 Old Phladelphia Pike Gap (17527) *(G-6257)*	
White Light Productions	610 518-0644
505 Reeds Rd Downingtown (19335) *(G-4264)*	
White Mane Publishing Co Inc	717 532-2237
63 W Burd St Shippensburg (17257) *(G-17555)*	
White Oak Farms Inc	814 257-8485
1009 State Route 839 Dayton (16222) *(G-4041)*	
White Oak Group Inc	717 291-2222
1180 Dillerville Rd Lancaster (17601) *(G-9240)*	
White Oak Ice Company LLC (PA)	717 354-5322
106 Conestoga Ave New Holland (17557) *(G-12294)*	
White Oak Mills Inc (PA)	717 367-1525
419 W High St Elizabethtown (17022) *(G-4891)*	
White Oak Woodcraft	717 665-4738
2407 Newport Rd Manheim (17545) *(G-10406)*	
White Refrigeration Inc	570 265-7335
13838 Route 220 Towanda (18848) *(G-18437)*	
White The, Bensalem Also called White Trophy Co Inc *(G-1272)*	
White Trophy Co Inc	215 638-9134
2248 Bristol Pike Bensalem (19020) *(G-1272)*	
White-Brook Inc	814 849-8441
1 Sylvania St Brookville (15825) *(G-2276)*	
Whitebrier, Robesonia Also called Adelphi Kitchens Inc *(G-16772)*	
Whitehall Specialties	724 368-3959
2850 Perry Hwy Slippery Rock (16057) *(G-17629)*	
Whitehead Eagle Corporation	724 346-4280
191 N Sharpsville Ave Sharon (16146) *(G-17447)*	
Whitehead Tool & Design Inc	814 967-3064
27014 State Highway 77 Guys Mills (16327) *(G-6814)*	
Whitehill Mfg Corp	610 494-2378
2540 Green St Ste 1 Chester (19013) *(G-3068)*	
Whiteman Tower Inc	800 748-3891
600 Baltimore Dr Wilkes Barre (18702) *(G-19974)*	
Whites Machine Inc	570 345-1142
114 Covered Bridge Rd Pine Grove (17963) *(G-14607)*	
Whitewave Foods, Du Bois Also called Wwf Operating Company *(G-4429)*	
Whitford Corporation (HQ)	610 286-3500
47 Park Ave Elverson (19520) *(G-4967)*	
Whitford Worldwide Company LLC (HQ)	610 286-3500
47 Park Ave Elverson (19520) *(G-4968)*	
Whitley East LLC (HQ)	717 656-2081
64 Hess Rd Leola (17540) *(G-9808)*	
Whitmore Manufacturing Company	724 225-4151
63 W Point Rd Washington (15301) *(G-19245)*	
Whitmore Manufacturing Company	724 225-8008
1 W Point Rd Washington (15301) *(G-19246)*	
Whittco Inc	570 645-3779
167 Stock St Nesquehoning (18240) *(G-12011)*	
Whole House Cabinetry	610 286-2901
30 Chrisman Dr Elverson (19520) *(G-4969)*	
Wholesale Linens Supply Inc	814 886-7000
720 2nd St Cresson (16630) *(G-3902)*	
Wick Copy Center	814 942-8040
503 E Plank Rd Altoona (16602) *(G-558)*	
Wicked Cool Toys Holdings LLC (PA)	267 536-9186
10 Canal St Ste 327 Bristol (19007) *(G-2217)*	
Wickett & Craig America Inc	814 236-2220
120 Cooper Rd Curwensville (16833) *(G-3956)*	
Wicks Kitchen, Marcus Hook Also called H & G Diners Corp *(G-10445)*	
Wicktek Inc	513 474-4518
360 Frmington Ohiopyle Rd Farmington (15437) *(G-5864)*	
Widmer Sign Company Inc	570 343-0319
2209 Amelia Ave Scranton (18509) *(G-17313)*	
Wierman Diller Inc	717 637-3871
20 W Park Ave Hanover (17331) *(G-6975)*	
Wiest Asphalt Products and Pav	724 282-6913
310 Mitchell Hill Rd Butler (16002) *(G-2448)*	
Wiggins Shredding Inc	610 692-8327
1301 W Chester Pike West Chester (19382) *(G-19677)*	
Wigle Whiskey, Pittsburgh Also called Pittsburgh Distilling Co LLC *(G-15394)*	
Wikoff Color Corporation	484 681-4065
445 Hillview Rd King of Prussia (19406) *(G-8699)*	
Wilbert Vault Co	724 459-8400
100 N East Ln Blairsville (15717) *(G-1745)*	
Wilbos Inc	267 490-5168
117 W Broad St Quakertown (18951) *(G-16259)*	
Wilbur Enterprises Inc	724 625-8010
446 Four Lakes Dr Gibsonia (15044) *(G-6358)*	
Wild Asaph Outfitters	570 724-5155
71 Main St Wellsboro (16901) *(G-19475)*	
Wild Birds Unlimited	610 366-1725
4251 W Tilghman St Allentown (18104) *(G-434)*	
Wild Cat Publishing LLC	570 966-1120
229 E Chestnut St Mifflinburg (17844) *(G-11106)*	
Wild Well Control Inc	724 873-5083
380 Southpointe Blvd Canonsburg (15317) *(G-2659)*	
Wilder Diamond Blades Inc	570 222-9590
5638 State Route 92 Kingsley (18826) *(G-8710)*	
Wildfowl Carving & Collecting, Blue Ridge Summit Also called Stackpole Inc *(G-1862)*	
Wiley Electric Sign Service	610 759-8167
2232 Whitehead Rd Nazareth (18064) *(G-11994)*	
Wilhelm Winery Inc (PA)	724 253-3700
590 Georgetown Rd Hadley (16130) *(G-6823)*	
Wilke Enginuity Inc	717 632-5937
250 Obrien Ln Hanover (17331) *(G-6976)*	
Wilkes Barre Burial Vault	570 824-8268
628 Nanticoke St Hanover Township (18706) *(G-7007)*	
Wilkes Barre Law & Lib Assn	570 822-6712
200 N River St Rm 23 Wilkes Barre (18711) *(G-19975)*	
Wilkes Pool Corp	570 759-0317
Interstate 80 Exit 242 Mifflinville (18631) *(G-11145)*	
Wilkes-Barre Materials LLC	570 829-1181
130 Ridgewood Rd Plains (18702) *(G-15790)*	
Wilkes-Barre Publishing Co	570 829-7100
15 N Main St Wilkes Barre (18701) *(G-19976)*	
Wilkes-Barre Publishing Co Inc (HQ)	570 829-7100
15 N Main St Wilkes Barre (18701) *(G-19977)*	
Wilkinsburg Penn Joint Wtr	412 243-6254
7603 Tyler Rd Verona (15147) *(G-18764)*	
Willamsport Dies & Cuts Inc	570 323-8351
5 Hoover Rd Williamsport (17701) *(G-20092)*	
Willard Agri Service of Marion, Marion Also called Willard Agri-Service Inc *(G-10471)*	
Willard Agri-Service Inc	717 375-2229
5325 3rd St Marion (17235) *(G-10471)*	
Willard Burial Service Inc	724 528-9965
3955 New Cstl Rd Rr 18 West Middlesex (16159) *(G-19732)*	
William A Fraser Inc	717 766-1126
5521 Carlisle Pike Mechanicsburg (17050) *(G-10910)*	
William A Fraser Inc	570 622-7347
442 N C A Lord Blvd 3/4 Pottsville (17901) *(G-16102)*	
William A Moddrel	610 327-8296
888 Scholl Rd Pottstown (19465) *(G-15957)*	
William Aupperle	724 583-8310
1892 Mcclellandtown Rd Masontown (15461) *(G-10538)*	
William Bender Trimming	570 922-4274
1290 Shirk Rd Millmont (17845) *(G-11221)*	
William Cottage	724 266-2961
311 Creese St Ambridge (15003) *(G-639)*	
William Deleeuw Co	570 296-2694
102 Schocopee Ct Milford (18337) *(G-11168)*	
William Elston Incorporated	570 689-2203
481 Cortez Rd Jefferson Township (18436) *(G-8280)*	
William F and Kathy A Yeager	717 665-6964
62 Doe Run Rd Manheim (17545) *(G-10407)*	
William F Kempf & Son Inc	610 532-2000
900 Ashland Ave Folcroft (19032) *(G-6020)*	
William H Hammonds & Bros	610 489-7924
21 Crosskeys Rd Collegeville (19426) *(G-3399)*	
William H Kies Jr	610 252-6261
1928 Jefferson St Easton (18042) *(G-4776)*	
William Henry Orna Ir Works	215 659-1887
524 Davisville Rd Willow Grove (19090) *(G-20149)*	
William J Dixon Company	610 524-1131
756 Springdale Dr Exton (19341) *(G-5750)*	
William J Judge	610 348-8070
3938 Ridge Pike Ste 6 Collegeville (19426) *(G-3400)*	
William J Koshinskie	570 742-4969
100 Hepburn St Milton (17847) *(G-11251)*	
William J Labb Sons Inc	215 289-3450
4617 Milnor St Philadelphia (19137) *(G-14474)*	
William Klein Signs Inc	610 374-5371
938 Walnut St Reading (19601) *(G-16565)*	
William Kleinberger & Sons (PA)	570 347-9331
217 Reese St Rear Scranton (18508) *(G-17314)*	
William Kleinberger & Sons	570 347-9331
1039 Quincy Ave Scranton (18510) *(G-17315)*	
William Lammers	610 894-9502
973 Saucony Rd Kutztown (19530) *(G-8863)*	
William Penn Printing Company	412 322-3660
1800 Preble Ave Pittsburgh (15233) *(G-15717)*	
William Plange	215 303-0069
4507 N Broad St Unit 1 Philadelphia (19140) *(G-14475)*	
William Richter Lumber	814 926-4608
367 Fox Rd Rockwood (15557) *(G-16794)*	
William Sport Crane & Rigging	570 433-3300
214 Brushy Ridge Rd Montoursville (17754) *(G-11457)*	

A
L
P
H
A
B
E
T
I
C

William T Jenkins 610 644-7052
460 E King Rd Malvern (19355) *(G-10346)*

Williams & Sons Slate & Tile 610 863-4161
6596 Sullivan Trl Wind Gap (18091) *(G-20175)*

Williams and Sons Lumber Co (PA) 814 735-4295
12142 Old 126 Crystal Spring (15536) *(G-3939)*

Williams Business Forms Ltd 724 444-6771
Middle Rd Ext Rr 910 Gibsonia (15044) *(G-6359)*

Williams Companies Inc 717 490-6857
1848 Charter Ln Lancaster (17601) *(G-9241)*

Williams Company Limited 610 409-0520
256 Freeland Dr Collegeville (19426) *(G-3401)*

Williams Field Services 570 965-7643
310 Sr 29 N Tunkhannock (18657) *(G-18552)*

Williams Fresh Scents LLC 484 838-0147
501 W Highland Ter Nazareth (18064) *(G-11995)*

Williams Garden Center Inc 570 842-7277
516 Drinker Tpke Covington Township (18424) *(G-3794)*

Williams Machining Co 814 734-3121
2171 Route 6n Edinboro (16412) *(G-4821)*

Williams Metalfinishing Inc 610 670-1077
870 Commerce St Reading (19608) *(G-16566)*

Williams Richard H Pharmacist 717 393-6708
1405 Center Rd Lancaster (17603) *(G-9242)*

Williamsigns 610 530-0300
6346 Farm Bureau Rd Allentown (18106) *(G-435)*

Williamson Costume Company 215 925-7121
211 N 3rd St Philadelphia (19106) *(G-14476)*

Williamson Gear & Machine, Philadelphia Also called Heclyn Precision Gear
Company *(G-13810)*

Williamsport Foundry Co Inc 570 323-6216
164 Maynard St Williamsport (17701) *(G-20093)*

Williamsport Orthopedic 570 322-5277
613 E 3rd St Ste 1 Williamsport (17701) *(G-20094)*

Williamsport Steel Cont Corp 570 323-9473
360 Arch St Williamsport (17701) *(G-20095)*

Williamsport Sun-Gazette, Williamsport Also called Sun-Gazette Company *(G-20076)*

Willier Elc Mtr Repr Co Inc 215 426-9920
3080 Emerald St Philadelphia (19134) *(G-14477)*

Willow Grove Auto Top Inc 215 659-3276
43 York Rd Willow Grove (19090) *(G-20150)*

Willow Terrace 215 951-8500
1 Penn Blvd Philadelphia (19144) *(G-14478)*

Wilmand Labglass 215 672-7800
935 Mearns Rd Warminster (18974) *(G-19000)*

Wilmer R EBY 717 597-1090
15640 Oak Rd Waynesboro (17268) *(G-19430)*

Wilmington Die Inc 724 946-8020
Maple St Ext New Wilmington (16142) *(G-12473)*

Wilmington Metalcraft 717 442-9834
1406 W Kings Hwy Gap (17527) *(G-6258)*

Wilmoth Interests Inc 724 397-5558
550 Hastings Rd Marion Center (15759) *(G-10478)*

Wilsey Tool Company Inc 215 538-0800
140 Penn Am Dr Quakertown (18951) *(G-16260)*

Wilson & Mc Cracken Inc 412 784-1772
5255 Butler St Pittsburgh (15201) *(G-15718)*

Wilson Candy Co Inc (PA) 724 523-3151
408 Harrison Ave Jeannette (15644) *(G-8268)*

Wilson Creek Energy LLC 814 619-4600
334 Budfield St Ste 180 Johnstown (15904) *(G-8445)*

Wilson Creek Energy LLC (PA) 724 754-0028
4600 J Barry Ct Ste 220 Canonsburg (15317) *(G-2660)*

Wilson Creek Energy LLC 814 443-4668
1576 Stoystown Rd Friedens (15541) *(G-6228)*

Wilson Global Inc 724 883-4952
1216 Jefferson Rd Jefferson (15344) *(G-8272)*

Wilson Hardwoods Inc 814 827-0277
10951 Johnson Rd Titusville (16354) *(G-18405)*

Wilson Paving Inc 717 249-3227
480 W Old York Rd Carlisle (17015) *(G-2751)*

Wilson Pdts Compressed Gas Co 610 253-9608
3411 Northwood Ave Easton (18045) *(G-4777)*

Wilson, I L Company, Philadelphia Also called Gloninger Brothers Inc *(G-13774)*

Wilsons Outdoor Services LLC 724 503-4261
456 Craft Rd Washington (15301) *(G-19247)*

Win Tron Technologies, Howard Also called Video Display Corporation *(G-7892)*

Win-Holt Equipment Corp 516 222-0335
7028 Snowdrift Rd Allentown (18106) *(G-436)*

Windermere Motion, Exeter Also called Mega Motion LLC *(G-5583)*

Windgate Vineyards Inc 814 257-8797
1998 Hemlock Acres Rd Smicksburg (16256) *(G-17640)*

Windglo Manufacturing Co 717 859-2932
1 Lauber Rd Akron (17501) *(G-39)*

Windjammer Corporation Inc (PA) 610 588-0626
525 N Main St Bangor (18013) *(G-934)*

Windjammer Corporation Inc 610 588-0626
Quarry Rd Bangor (18013) *(G-935)*

Windjammer Corporation Inc 610 588-2137
519 Pnnsylvnia Ave Fl 1 Flr 1 Bangor (18013) *(G-936)*

Windkits LLC 610 530-5704
7346 Penn Dr Unit 2 Allentown (18106) *(G-437)*

Windle Mech Solutions Inc 215 624-8600
6601 Marsden St Philadelphia (19135) *(G-14479)*

Windover Fabricators, Perkasie Also called Phil Skrzat *(G-13289)*

Windridge Design Inc 610 692-1919
319 Westtown Rd Ste J West Chester (19382) *(G-19678)*

Windridge/Cheryl Nash, West Chester Also called Windridge Design Inc *(G-19678)*

Windsor Barrel Works, Ottsville Also called Kettle Creek Corporation *(G-13064)*

Windsor Beach Technologies Inc 814 474-4900
7321 Klier Dr Fairview (16415) *(G-5849)*

Windsor Service Trucking Corp 610 929-0716
2415 Kutztown Rd Reading (19605) *(G-16567)*

Windsor-Press Inc 610 562-3624
6 N 3rd St Hamburg (19526) *(G-6857)*

Windstax Inc 412 235-7907
155 Plum Industrial Park Pittsburgh (15239) *(G-15719)*

Windstax Wind Power Systems, Pittsburgh Also called Windstax Inc *(G-15719)*

Windtree Therapeutics Inc (PA) 215 488-9300
2600 Kelly Rd Ste 100 Warrington (18976) *(G-19140)*

Windurance 814 678-1318
2099 Hill City Rd Seneca (16346) *(G-17372)*

Windurance LLC 412 424-8900
1300 Commerce Dr Coraopolis (15108) *(G-3733)*

Windview Truck & Trlr Repr LLC 570 374-8077
94 Windview Ln Port Trevorton (17864) *(G-15916)*

Windy Hill Concrete Inc 717 464-3889
1760 Windy Hill Rd Lancaster (17602) *(G-9243)*

Windy Hill Furniture, Alexandria Also called David Karr *(G-63)*

Wine & Spirits Shoppe 3502, Scranton Also called Liquor Control Board PA *(G-17255)*

Wine Concrete Products Inc 724 266-9500
1000 Big Swckly Crk Rd Sewickley (15143) *(G-17415)*

Winery At Wilcox Inc 412 490-9590
1940 Stlers Ridge Ctr Dr Pittsburgh (15205) *(G-15720)*

Winery At Wilcox Inc (PA) 814 929-5598
1867 Mefferts Run Rd Wilcox (15870) *(G-19901)*

Winery of Wilcox 814 375-4501
5522 Shaffer Rd Unit 122 Du Bois (15801) *(G-4428)*

Winfield Lime & Stone Co Inc (PA) 724 352-3596
340 Fisher Rd Cabot (16023) *(G-2461)*

Winfield Winery LLC 724 352-9589
1026 Winfield Rd Cabot (16023) *(G-2462)*

Winfosoft Inc 717 226-1299
910 S George St York (17403) *(G-20711)*

Wing Dynamics 570 275-5502
59 Clark Rd Danville (17821) *(G-4016)*

Winn-Marion Barber LLC 412 319-7392
200 Old Pond Rd Ste 106 Bridgeville (15017) *(G-2099)*

Winner International Inc 724 981-1152
32 W State St Sharon (16146) *(G-17448)*

Winola Ice Co 570 378-2726
Rd Lowr Lower Dalton (18414) *(G-3988)*

Winola Industrial Inc 570 378-3808
Rr 1 Box 1070 Factoryville (18419) *(G-5763)*

Winston & Duke Inc 814 456-0582
2008 W 16th St Erie (16505) *(G-5529)*

Winston & Duke Inc 814 456-0582
2008 W 16th St Erie (16505) *(G-5530)*

Winston Industries Inc 215 394-8178
29 Richard Rd Warminster (18974) *(G-19001)*

Winter Gardens Qulty Foods Inc 717 624-4911
304 Commerce St New Oxford (17350) *(G-12427)*

Winter Transfer Company, West Elizabeth Also called Clairton Slag Inc *(G-19693)*

Wintercorp LLC 717 848-3425
847 Galtee Ct York (17402) *(G-20712)*

Winterhouse Furniture Inc 215 249-3410
112 Maple Ave Dublin (18917) *(G-4437)*

Winters Lumber Co 570 435-2231
6765 Pleasant Valley Rd Cogan Station (17728) *(G-3363)*

Winters Performance Pdts Inc 717 764-9844
1580 Trolley Rd York (17408) *(G-20713)*

Winterthur Wendt Usa Inc 610 495-2850
546 Enterprise Dr Royersford (19468) *(G-16869)*

Wintronics Inc 724 981-5770
191 Pitt St Sharon (16146) *(G-17449)*

Wipro Enterprises Inc 717 496-8877
1101 Sheffler Dr Chambersburg (17201) *(G-2999)*

Wire and Cable Specialties Inc (PA) 610 466-6200
440 Highland Blvd Coatesville (19320) *(G-3330)*

Wire and Cable Specialties Inc 610 692-7551
205 Carter Dr West Chester (19382) *(G-19679)*

Wire Company Holdings Inc 717 637-3795
500 E Middle St Hanover (17331) *(G-6977)*

Wire Crafters 610 296-2538
3119 Phnxvlle Pike Unit 2 Malvern (19355) *(G-10347)*

Wire Mesh Products Inc (PA) 717 848-3620
501 E King St Ste 1 York (17403) *(G-20714)*

Wire Mesh Sales LLC 724 245-9577
1015 New Salem Rd New Salem (15468) *(G-12446)*

Wire Rope, Trafford *Also called Wireco Worldgroup Inc* **(G-18461)**

Wire Tech & Tool Inc 814 333-3175
350 Linden St Meadville (16335) **(G-10813)**

Wire Works Enterprises Inc 610 485-1981
200 Keystone Rd Ste 1 Chester (19013) **(G-3069)**

Wirecard North America Inc 610 234-4410
555 E North Ln Ste 5040 Conshohocken (19428) **(G-3617)**

WireCo World Group, Montgomeryville *Also called Phillystran Inc* **(G-11415)**

Wireco Worldgroup Inc 412 373-6122
2500 Commerce Cir Trafford (15085) **(G-18461)**

Wireless Acquisition LLC 602 315-9979
395 Oak Hill Rd Mountain Top (18707) **(G-11781)**

Wireless Experience of PA Inc 215 340-1382
4341 W Swamp Rd Doylestown (18902) **(G-4345)**

Wirerope Works Inc 570 327-4229
100 Maynard St Williamsport (17701) **(G-20096)**

Wirerope Works Inc 570 286-0115
880 S 2nd St Sunbury (17801) **(G-18177)**

Wirthmore Pdts & Svc Co Inc 610 430-0300
1330 Green Hill Ave West Chester (19380) **(G-19680)**

Wise Business Forms Inc 724 789-0010
150 Kriess Rd Butler (16001) **(G-2449)**

Wise Electronic Systems Inc 717 244-0111
1362 Craley Rd Windsor (17366) **(G-20197)**

Wise Foods Inc (HQ) 888 759-4401
228 Rasely St Berwick (18603) **(G-1347)**

Wise Foods Employees Chrtble E 570 759-4095
228 Rasely St Berwick (18603) **(G-1348)**

Wise Intervention Svcs USA Inc 724 405-6660
146 Painter Rd Smithton (15479) **(G-17664)**

Wise Machine Co Inc 724 287-2705
244 S Cliff St Butler (16001) **(G-2450)**

Wise Plastics 847 697-2840
7253 Huntingdon St Harrisburg (17111) **(G-7247)**

Wise Printing Co Inc 717 741-2751
2449 S Queen St Rear Rear York (17402) **(G-20715)**

Wismarq Valencia LLC 724 898-1511
125 Mcfann Rd Valencia (16059) **(G-18705)**

Wismer Machine Company Inc 215 257-5081
1006 Old Bethlehem Pike Sellersville (18960) **(G-17362)**

Wissahickon Brewing Company 267 239-6596
7524 Lawn St Philadelphia (19128) **(G-14480)**

Wissahickon Stone Quarry LLC 215 887-3330
1 Waverly Rd Glenside (19038) **(G-6544)**

Wist Enterprises Inc 724 283-7230
201 Pillow St Butler (16001) **(G-2451)**

Wistex II LLC 215 328-9100
1730 Stout Dr Ste 1 Warminster (18974) **(G-19002)**

Witherup Fbrction Erection Inc (PA) 814 385-6601
431 Kennerdell Rd Kennerdell (16374) **(G-8499)**

Witmer Motor Service 717 336-2949
187 E Church St Stevens (17578) **(G-18058)**

Witmer Public Safety Group Inc (PA) 800 852-6088
104 Independence Way Coatesville (19320) **(G-3331)**

Wittmans Pure Maple Syrup LLC 814 781-7523
214 N Saint Marys St Saint Marys (15857) **(G-17030)**

Wixons Bakery Inc 610 777-6056
332 S Wyomissing Ave Reading (19607) **(G-16568)**

WJM Coal Co Inc 724 354-2922
8955 Rte 422 W Shelocta (15774) **(G-17491)**

Wkw Associates LLC 215 348-1257
206 Oneida Ln Doylestown (18901) **(G-4346)**

Wlek Inc 800 772-8247
645 W 11th St Erie (16501) **(G-5531)**

Wlh Enterprise 814 498-2040
5939 Route 38 Emlenton (16373) **(G-5016)**

WM A SCHMIDT & SONS, Chester *Also called Byrne Chiarlone LP* **(G-3042)**

Wm C Haldeman 215 324-2400
4713 N Broad St Philadelphia (19141) **(G-14481)**

WM Enterprises Inc 717 238-5751
1310 Crooked Hill Rd # 800 Harrisburg (17110) **(G-7248)**

Wm Industries Inc 215 822-2525
3075 Advance Ln Colmar (18915) **(G-3423)**

Wm Robots, LLC 215 822-2525
3075 Advance Ln Colmar (18915) **(G-3424)**

Wm S Long Inc 724 538-3775
127 Breakneck St Callery (16024) **(G-2471)**

Wm T Spaeder Co Inc (PA) 814 456-7014
1602 E 18th St Erie (16510) **(G-5532)**

Wmi Group, Colmar *Also called Custom Systems Technology Inc* **(G-3415)**

Wmi Group Inc 215 822-2525
3075 Advance Ln Colmar (18915) **(G-3425)**

Wmma, Philadelphia *Also called Wood Machinery Mfrs Amer* **(G-14483)**

Wmpm LLC 303 662-5231
600 Waterfront Dr Ste 100 Pittsburgh (15222) **(G-15721)**

WMS Metals - Welding Alloys 412 231-3811
1501 Reedsdale St Pittsburgh (15233) **(G-15722)**

Wodrig Logging Corporation 570 435-0783
9763 Route 864 Hwy Muncy (17756) **(G-11842)**

Wojanis Supply Company (PA) 724 695-1415
1001 Montour West Ind Par Coraopolis (15108) **(G-3734)**

Wolbert Welding Inc 814 437-2870
191 Howard St Ste 330 Franklin (16323) **(G-6170)**

Wolenski Enterprises Inc 205 307-9862
1415 Pittsbugh Rd White Oak (15131) **(G-19859)**

Wolf Lumber and Millwork Inc 814 317-5111
1984 Maple Hollow Rd Duncansville (16635) **(G-4466)**

Wolf Printing 717 755-1560
1200 Haines Rd York (17402) **(G-20716)**

Wolf Printing & Copy Center, York *Also called Wolf Printing* **(G-20716)**

Wolf Rock Furniture, Kinzers *Also called Sam Beiler* **(G-8742)**

Wolf Technologies LLC 610 385-6091
551 Old Swede Rd Douglassville (19518) **(G-4182)**

Wolfe Dye and Bleach Works Inc 610 562-7639
25 Ridge Rd Shoemakersville (19555) **(G-17577)**

Wolfe Metal Fab Inc (PA) 724 339-7790
299 Greensburg Rd Lower Burrell (15068) **(G-10108)**

Wolfe Tool & Machine Company 717 848-6375
210 Lafayette St York (17401) **(G-20717)**

Wolfgang Candy Company, York *Also called Wolfgang Operations LLC* **(G-20718)**

Wolfgang Operations LLC (PA) 717 843-5536
50 E 4th Ave York (17404) **(G-20718)**

Wolfgang Operations LLC 717 843-5536
122 North St York (17403) **(G-20719)**

Wolfington Body Company Inc (PA) 610 458-8501
N Off Pa Tpk Exit Rr 100 Exton (19341) **(G-5751)**

Wolodymyr Zin, DDS, Philadelphia *Also called Everest Dental LLC* **(G-13683)**

Wolters Kluwer Health Inc (HQ) 215 521-8300
2001 Market St Ste 5 Philadelphia (19103) **(G-14482)**

Wolverine Enterprise LLC 570 463-4103
2740 S Main St Mansfield (16933) **(G-10427)**

Wolverine Plastics Inc 724 856-5610
516 Mecklem Ln Ellwood City (16117) **(G-4955)**

Wolyniec Construction Inc 570 322-8634
294 Freedom Rd Williamsport (17701) **(G-20097)**

Wombat Security Tech Inc (HQ) 412 621-1484
3030 Penn Ave Fl 2 Pittsburgh (15201) **(G-15723)**

Womens Yellw Pages Gtr Phil 610 446-4747
117 N Concord Ave Havertown (19083) **(G-7433)**

Wondering Canvas Tattoos 717 244-8260
40 W Main St Dallastown (17313) **(G-3983)**

Wood Craft, Burgettstown *Also called Robert Wirth* **(G-2354)**

Wood Creations LLC 717 445-7007
125 W Main St Terre Hill (17581) **(G-18340)**

Wood Fabricators Inc 717 284-4849
938 Lancaster Pike Quarryville (17566) **(G-16284)**

Wood Group Usa Inc 724 514-1600
4600 Jbarry Ct Ste 210 Canonsburg (15317) **(G-2661)**

Wood Hollow Crafts LLC 215 428-0870
561 Gordon Dr Yardley (19067) **(G-20345)**

Wood Machinery Mfrs Amer 215 564-3484
100 N 20th St Fl 4 Philadelphia (19103) **(G-14483)**

Wood Mizer (PA) 814 259-9976
22638 Croghan Pike Shade Gap (17255) **(G-17418)**

Wood Moulding and Millwork 215 324-8400
316 W Hunting Park Ave Philadelphia (19140) **(G-14484)**

Wood Racing Products LLC 717 454-7003
146 Nut Grove Rd Pine Grove (17963) **(G-14608)**

Wood Specialty Company Inc 610 539-6384
2606 Mann Rd Norristown (19403) **(G-12724)**

Wood Ya Like Cabinets 570 725-2523
2455 E Valley Rd Loganton (17747) **(G-10100)**

Wood-Metal Industries, Selinsgrove *Also called Selinsgrove Instnl Csework LLC* **(G-17333)**

Wood-Mizer Holdings Inc 814 259-9976
22638 Croghan Pike Shade Gap (17255) **(G-17419)**

Wood-Mizer Resharp, Shade Gap *Also called Wood-Mizer Holdings Inc* **(G-17419)**

Wood-Mode Incorporated (PA) 570 374-2711
1 Second St Kreamer (17833) **(G-8819)**

Wood-Mode Incorporated 570 374-1176
100 E Sherman St Selinsgrove (17870) **(G-17338)**

Woodbine Properties (PA) 814 443-4688
227 New Centerville Rd Somerset (15501) **(G-17718)**

Woodcraft Industries 570 323-4458
647 E 3rd St Williamsport (17701) **(G-20098)**

Woodcraft Industries Inc 724 638-4044
62 Grant Rd Greenville (16125) **(G-6777)**

Woodcraft Products Co Inc (PA) 215 329-2793
241 W Wyoming Ave Philadelphia (19140) **(G-14485)**

Woodcraft Products Co Inc 215 426-6123
4057 G St Philadelphia (19124) **(G-14486)**

Woode Mode, Selinsgrove *Also called Wood-Mode Incorporated* **(G-17338)**

Wooden Door Winery LLC 724 889-7244
4087 Greenwood Rd New Kensington (15068) **(G-12390)**

Wooden Nickel Sales, Philadelphia *Also called Charles F May Co* **(G-13527)**

Wooden Nickels LLC 484 408-4901
117 Hillside Ln Pottstown (19465) **(G-15958)**

Woodhouse Post & Beam 570 549-6232
Rr 549 Mansfield (16933) **(G-10428)**

Woodings Doweling Tech Inc 724 625-3131
218 Clay Avenue Ext Mars (16046) *(G-10514)*
Woodings Industrial, Harmony *Also called Progressive Power Tech LLC (G-7075)*
Woodings Industrial Corp (PA) 724 625-3131
218 Clay Ave Mars (16046) *(G-10515)*
Woodland Pavarn, Mayport *Also called Taty Bug Inc (G-10547)*
Woodline Productions Inc 814 362-5397
317 W Corydon St Bradford (16701) *(G-1996)*
Woodlore Builders Studio, Harrisburg *Also called Clear Visions Inc (G-7106)*
Woodmasters Cabinetry Inc 717 949-3937
204 Rod And Gun Rd Newmanstown (17073) *(G-12485)*
Woodpeckers Woodcraft Inc 814 397-2282
4040 Stanton St Erie (16510) *(G-5533)*
Woodruff Corporation 570 675-0890
1540 Huntsville Rd Shavertown (18708) *(G-17481)*
Woods Company Inc 717 263-6524
2121 Carbaugh Ave Chambersburg (17201) *(G-3000)*
Woods Wings 610 417-5684
85 Traugers Crossing Rd Kintnersville (18930) *(G-8730)*
Woodshop LLC 610 647-4190
214 N Warren Ave Malvern (19355) *(G-10348)*
Woodside Glueing 814 349-5646
210 Back Rd Rebersburg (16872) *(G-16579)*
Woodstock Mfg Services Inc 814 336-4426
831 Mulberry St Meadville (16335) *(G-10814)*
Woodstream Corporation (HQ) 717 626-2125
69 N Locust St Lititz (17543) *(G-10060)*
Woodward Inc 724 538-3110
128 Myoma Rd Mars (16046) *(G-10516)*
Woodward McCoach Inc (PA) 610 692-9526
1171 Mcdermott Dr West Chester (19380) *(G-19681)*
Woody Associates Inc 717 843-3975
844 E South St York (17403) *(G-20720)*
Wool Concrete Block 570 322-1943
525 Poplar St Williamsport (17701) *(G-20099)*
Woolf Steel Inc 717 944-1423
170 Fulling Mill Rd Middletown (17057) *(G-11085)*
Woolrich Inc (HQ) 570 769-6464
2 Mill St Woolrich (17779) *(G-20220)*
Woolrich Inc 570 769-7401
1 Mill St Woolrich (17779) *(G-20221)*
Workcenter 570 320-7444
1100 Grampian Blvd Williamsport (17701) *(G-20100)*
Workmaster Inc 866 476-9217
284 Three Tun Rd Malvern (19355) *(G-10349)*
Workrite Packaged Cement Pdts, Thomasville *Also called York Building Products Co Inc (G-18345)*
Works27, Tyrone *Also called Pittsburgh Glass Works LLC (G-18589)*
Worktask Media Inc 610 762-9014
7511 Richard Ln Bath (18014) *(G-973)*
Workzone LLC 610 275-9861
16 W Township Line Rd Norristown (19401) *(G-12725)*
World Chronicle Inc 724 745-3808
105 William St Mc Donald (15057) *(G-10584)*
World Elec Sls & Svc Inc (PA) 610 939-9800
3000 Kutztown Rd Reading (19605) *(G-16569)*
World Energy Harrisburg LLC 717 412-0374
2850 Appleton St Ste E Camp Hill (17011) *(G-2526)*
World Flavors Inc 215 672-4400
76 Louise Dr Warminster (18974) *(G-19003)*
World Gourmet Acquisition LLC 717 285-1884
3775 Hempland Rd Mountville (17554) *(G-11804)*
World Manufacturing Inc 215 426-0500
3000 C St Philadelphia (19134) *(G-14487)*
World Marketing of America (PA) 814 643-6500
12256 William Penn Hwy Mill Creek (17060) *(G-11169)*
World Motorsports Inc 610 929-1982
3000 Kutztown Rd Reading (19605) *(G-16570)*
World of Wheels Inc 814 676-5721
2572 State Route 257 Seneca (16346) *(G-17373)*
World Poetry Inc 215 309-3722
1906 Rittenhouse Sq Philadelphia (19103) *(G-14488)*
World Resources Company 570 622-4747
170 Walnut Ln Pottsville (17901) *(G-16103)*
World Video Sales Co Inc 610 754-6800
625 Hoffmansville Rd # 4 Bechtelsville (19505) *(G-1038)*
World Wide Plastics Inc (PA) 215 357-0893
250 Andrews Rd Langhorne (19053) *(G-9336)*
Worldcolor Atglen, Atglen *Also called Qg LLC (G-803)*
Worldwide EDM Graphite Inc 814 781-6939
1215 Million Dollar Hwy Kersey (15846) *(G-8572)*
Worldwide Fabricating Ltd (PA) 215 455-2266
171 E Hunting Park Ave Philadelphia (19124) *(G-14489)*
Worldwide Refractories Inc 724 224-8800
Sixth & Center Sts Tarentum (15084) *(G-18255)*
Worldwide Turbine LLC 610 821-9500
350 Union Blvd Allentown (18109) *(G-438)*
Worldwide Window Fashions, Philadelphia *Also called Worldwide Fabricating Ltd (G-14489)*
Worthington Armstrong Intl LLC (HQ) 610 722-1200
9 Old Lincoln Hwy Ste 200 Malvern (19355) *(G-10350)*
Worthington Armstrong Venture (PA) 610 722-1200
101 Lindenwood Dr Ste 350 Malvern (19355) *(G-10351)*
Worthington Stowe Fine Woodwor (PA) 215 504-5500
1108 Wrightstown Rd Newtown (18940) *(G-12564)*
Worthington Trailers LP 570 567-7921
333 Rose St Williamsport (17701) *(G-20101)*
Wortman Controls Inc 814 834-1299
207 Stackpole St Saint Marys (15857) *(G-17031)*
Wound Care Concepts Inc 215 788-2700
2701 Bartram Rd Bristol (19007) *(G-2218)*
Wov Inc 412 261-3791
111 Ryan Ct Ste 200 Pittsburgh (15205) *(G-15724)*
Woxall Woodcraft Inc 215 234-8774
115 Walnut St Green Lane (18054) *(G-6594)*
Wpi Solutions, Ellwood City *Also called Wolverine Plastics Inc (G-4955)*
Wpmw Inc 610 286-5071
50 Shop Dr Elverson (19520) *(G-4970)*
Wpp Dough Company Inc 814 539-7799
1280 Saint Clair Rd Johnstown (15905) *(G-8446)*
Wrapmaster Usa LLC 215 782-2285
7401 Old York Rd Elkins Park (19027) *(G-4915)*
Wright Appellate Services LLC 215 733-9870
1015 Chestnut St Ste 517 Philadelphia (19107) *(G-14490)*
Wright Linear Pump Inc 724 695-0800
103 International Dr Oakdale (15071) *(G-12912)*
Wright Meat Packing Co Inc 724 368-8571
689 N Camp Run Rd Fombell (16123) *(G-6039)*
Wsg & Solutions Inc 267 638-3000
160 Commerce Dr Ste 100 Montgomeryville (18936) *(G-11427)*
Wsp Solvay, Castanea *Also called Solvay USA Inc (G-2811)*
Wt Hardwoods Group Inc (PA) 717 867-2212
1231 Mount Wilson Rd Lebanon (17042) *(G-9639)*
Wtk Holdings Inc 724 695-3440
1075 Montour West Ind Par Coraopolis (15108) *(G-3735)*
Wundies 570 322-7245
1501 W 3rd St Williamsport (17701) *(G-20102)*
Wunsch Technologies Corp 610 207-0628
471 Fairview Chapel Rd Birdsboro (19508) *(G-1709)*
Wuxi Apptec Inc 215 334-1380
4000 S 26th St Philadelphia (19112) *(G-14491)*
Wuxi Apptec Inc 215 218-5500
4701 League Island Blvd Philadelphia (19112) *(G-14492)*
WW Henry Company LP (HQ) 704 203-5000
400 Ardex Park Dr Aliquippa (15001) *(G-103)*
Wwb Holdings LLC 267 519-4500
1431 Walnut St Philadelphia (19102) *(G-14493)*
Wwf Operating Company 814 590-8511
2592 Oklahoma Salem Rd Du Bois (15801) *(G-4429)*
Www.deutzboyz.com, Roxbury *Also called Holtrys LLC (G-16838)*
Wyatt Incorporated 724 684-7060
112 Riverview Dr Monessen (15062) *(G-11302)*
Wyatt Woodworking 717 246-8740
11931 Mount Olivet Rd Felton (17322) *(G-5943)*
Wychocks Mountaintop Beverage 570 474-5577
75 S Mountain Blvd Mountain Top (18707) *(G-11782)*
Wycon Mold & Tool Inc 215 675-2945
1756 Stout Dr Warminster (18974) *(G-19004)*
Wyeth, Collegeville *Also called Pfizer Inc (G-3387)*
Wyeth LLC 610 696-3100
611 E Nields St West Chester (19382) *(G-19682)*
Wyman Gordon - Mountain Top, Mountain Top *Also called Wyman-Gordon Pennsylvania LLC (G-11783)*
Wyman-Gordon Pennsylvania LLC (HQ) 570 474-6371
701 Crestwood Dr Mountain Top (18707) *(G-11783)*
Wyman-Gordon Pennsylvania LLC 570 474-3059
1141 Highway 315 Blvd Wilkes Barre (18702) *(G-19978)*
Wyoming Casing Service Inc 570 363-2883
4713 Route 220 N New Albany (18833) *(G-12016)*
Wyoming County Press Inc 570 348-9185
16 E Tioga St Tunkhannock (18657) *(G-18553)*
Wyoming Valley Pallets Inc 570 655-3640
240 Slocum Ave Exeter (18643) *(G-5586)*
Wyoming Valley Times Jurnl Inc 570 288-8362
16 Bidlack St Kingston (18704) *(G-8726)*
Wyoming Vly Prsthtic Orthotics 570 283-3835
300 Avenue A Wilkes Barre (18704) *(G-19979)*
Wyoming Weavers, Kingston *Also called Fortune Fabrics Inc (G-8717)*
Wyomissing Structures LLC 610 374-2370
223 Refton Rd New Providence (17560) *(G-12436)*
Wysocki-Cole Enterprises Inc (PA) 724 567-5656
143 Washington Ave Vandergrift (15690) *(G-18738)*
Wysox S&G Inc 570 265-6760
22448 Route 187 Wysox (18854) *(G-20291)*
Wysox Sand and Gravel, Wysox *Also called Wysox S&G Inc (G-20291)*
Wyss-Gallifent Corporation 215 343-3974
2123 Longview Rd Warrington (18976) *(G-19141)*

X F Enterprises Inc 717 859-1166
  99 Locust Bend Rd Ephrata (17522) **(G-5157)**

X Material Processing Company 717 968-8765
  200 Innovation Blvd State College (16803) **(G-18042)**

X-Act Technology Incorporated 814 824-6811
  2154 Norcross Rd Erie (16510) **(G-5534)**

X-Bar Diagnostics Systems Inc 610 388-2071
  77 Deer Path Kennett Square (19348) **(G-8551)**

X-Cell Molding Inc 814 836-0202
  2125 Filmore Ave Erie (16506) **(G-5535)**

X-Cell Tool and Mold Inc 814 474-9100
  7701 Klier Dr S Fairview (16415) **(G-5850)**

X-Deco LLC 412 257-9755
  633 Napor Blvd Pittsburgh (15205) **(G-15725)**

X-Mark/Cdt Inc 724 228-7373
  2001 N Main St Washington (15301) **(G-19248)**

XA Fishing Inc 610 356-0340
  88 Cherry Hill Ln Broomall (19008) **(G-2306)**

Xact Metal Inc 814 777-7727
  200 Innovation Blvd # 257 State College (16803) **(G-18043)**

Xaloy Superior Holdings Inc 724 656-5600
  1399 County Line Rd New Castle (16101) **(G-12170)**

Xcell Automation Inc 717 755-6800
  20 Innovation Dr York (17402) **(G-20721)**

Xecol Corporation 412 262-5222
  200 Marshall Dr Fl 2 Coraopolis (15108) **(G-3736)**

Xensor Corporation 610 284-2508
  4000 Bridge St Drexel Hill (19026) **(G-4373)**

Xerothera Inc 610 525-9916
  763 Applegate Ln Bryn Mawr (19010) **(G-2337)**

Xerox Corporation 412 506-4000
  8 Penn Ctr W Ste 200 Pittsburgh (15276) **(G-15726)**

Xf Enterprises, Ephrata Also called Extra Factors **(G-5102)**

Xfe Products, Ephrata Also called X F Enterprises Inc **(G-5157)**

Xgen LLC 877 450-9436
  201 Precision Rd Horsham (19044) **(G-7865)**

Xgen Products, Horsham Also called Xgen LLC **(G-7865)**

Xiii Touches Printing 484 754-6504
  1150 First Ave Ste 530 King of Prussia (19406) **(G-8700)**

Xl Precision Technologies 610 696-6800
  19 Hagerty Blvd Ste C West Chester (19382) **(G-19683)**

Xode Inc 610 683-8777
  15519 Kutztown Rd Kutztown (19530) **(G-8864)**

Xodus Medical Inc 724 337-5500
  204 Myles Dr New Kensington (15068) **(G-12391)**

Xodus Medical Inc 724 337-5500
  702 Prominence Dr New Kensington (15068) **(G-12392)**

Xomox Corporation (PA) 570 824-3577
  19 Bailey St Wilkes Barre (18705) **(G-19980)**

Xperia, Emmaus Also called Online Data Systems Inc **(G-5037)**

Xpert Machining Inc 724 694-0123
  501 S Bank St Derry (15627) **(G-4109)**

Xpogo LLC 717 650-5232
  1256 Franklin Ave Pittsburgh (15221) **(G-15727)**

Xpress Energy 610 935-9200
  383 Schuylkill Rd Phoenixville (19460) **(G-14584)**

Xray Eyewear 215 545-3361
  215 S Broad St Ste 203 Philadelphia (19107) **(G-14494)**

Xser Coatings Llc 732 754-9887
  3711 Spring Garden St Philadelphia (19104) **(G-14495)**

Xto Energy Inc 570 368-8920
  1050 Broad St Montoursville (17754) **(G-11458)**

Xto Energy Inc 540 772-3220
  230 Hicks Rd Renfrew (16053) **(G-16644)**

Xto Energy Inc 724 772-3500
  190 Thorn Hill Rd Warrendale (15086) **(G-19103)**

Xtreme Hunting Products 610 967-4588
  4972 Chestnut St Emmaus (18049) **(G-5047)**

Xtreme Wear, Du Bois Also called Lykens Corporation **(G-4403)**

Xylem Water Solutions USA Inc 724 452-6300
  227 S Division St Zelienople (16063) **(G-20828)**

Xylem Wtr Sltons Zlienople LLC 724 452-6300
  610 W Beaver St Zelienople (16063) **(G-20829)**

Xylem Wtr Sltons Zlienople LLC (HQ) 724 452-6300
  227 S Division St Ste 1 Zelienople (16063) **(G-20830)**

Xylem Wtr Sltons Zlienople LLC 570 538-2260
  Glen Gery Rd Off 8th St Watsontown (17777) **(G-19281)**

Xynatech Mfg Co (PA) 215 423-0804
  1405 E Oxford St Philadelphia (19125) **(G-14496)**

Y B Welding Inc 717 267-0104
  990 Progress Rd Chambersburg (17201) **(G-3001)**

Y H Newspaper Inc 215 546-0372
  1531 Locust St Philadelphia (19102) **(G-14497)**

Y T & A Inc 717 854-3806
  7 E 7th Ave York (17404) **(G-20722)**

Y&Q Home Plus LLC 412 642-6708
  1739 Liberty Ave Pittsburgh (15222) **(G-15728)**

Yardcraft Products LLC 866 210-9273
  191 Jalyn Dr New Holland (17557) **(G-12295)**

Yarde Metals Inc 610 495-7545
  1200 Enterprise Dr Limerick (19468) **(G-9972)**

Yardley Products LLC 215 493-2700
  10 W College Ave Yardley (19067) **(G-20346)**

Yardley Products Corp., Yardley Also called Yardley Products LLC **(G-20346)**

Yarger Precision Machining 814 364-1961
  2848 Earlystown Rd Centre Hall (16828) **(G-2846)**

Yarmouth Construction 267 592-1432
  4938 N 11th St Philadelphia (19141) **(G-14498)**

Yarrington Mills Corporation 215 674-5125
  412 S Warminster Rd Hatboro (19040) **(G-7311)**

Yates Division, Fairview Also called Formtech Enterprises Inc **(G-5823)**

Yazoo Mills Incorporated 717 624-8993
  305 Commerce St New Oxford (17350) **(G-12428)**

Yb, Chambersburg Also called Y B Welding Inc **(G-3001)**

Ybc Holdings Inc (PA) 215 634-2600
  500 Spring Garden St Philadelphia (19123) **(G-14499)**

Ye Logging Veneer 814 387-6503
  Rr 53 Box P Moshannon (16859) **(G-11604)**

Ye Olde Village Workshop 570 595-2593
  And Golf Dr Rr 390 Mountainhome (18342) **(G-11788)**

Yeager Wire Works Inc 570 752-2769
  620 Broad St Berwick (18603) **(G-1349)**

Yeagers Field 610 434-1516
  1431 W Green St Allentown (18102) **(G-439)**

Yellow Goat Design, West Chester Also called Carey Schuster LLC **(G-19519)**

Yellow Pages Group LLC 610 825-7720
  1 Sentry Pkwy E Ste 7000 Blue Bell (19422) **(G-1858)**

Yerecic Label Co Inc 724 334-3300
  701 Hunt Valley Rd New Kensington (15068) **(G-12393)**

Yes Towels Inc (PA) 215 538-5230
  1139 Red Barn Ln Quakertown (18951) **(G-16261)**

Yesco Handyman Services 724 206-9541
  1250 W Wylie Ave Washington (15301) **(G-19249)**

Yesco Hndyman Remodelling Svcs, Washington Also called Yesco Handyman
Services **(G-19249)**

Yesco New Castle Elec Sup 724 656-0911
  218 Old Youngstown Rd New Castle (16101) **(G-12171)**

Yesco Pittsburgh Inc 330 747-8593
  1290 Western Ave Pittsburgh (15233) **(G-15729)**

Ygs Group Inc (PA) 717 505-9701
  3650 W Market St York (17404) **(G-20723)**

Ygs Group Inc 425 251-5005
  3650 W Market St York (17404) **(G-20724)**

Ygs Group, The, York Also called York Graphic Services Co **(G-20738)**

Ygs West LLC 425 251-5005
  3650 W Market St York (17404) **(G-20725)**

Yingli Green Enrgy Amricas Inc 212 609-4909
  2 Logan Sq Ste 1900 Philadelphia (19103) **(G-14500)**

Yingli Solar, Philadelphia Also called Yingli Green Enrgy Amricas Inc **(G-14500)**

Ymc, Hatboro Also called Yarrington Mills Corporation **(G-7311)**

Yoder Industries LLC 717 656-6770
  83 S Groffdale Rd Leola (17540) **(G-9809)**

Yoder Lumber Co Inc 717 463-9253
  114 Yoder Ln Mc Alisterville (17049) **(G-10554)**

Yoga International, Honesdale Also called Himalayan Intl Ins of Yoga Ins **(G-7716)**

Yogo Factories 215 230-9646
  73 Old Dublin Pike Doylestown (18901) **(G-4347)**

Yoh Industrial LLC 215 656-2650
  1500 Spring Garden St # 500 Philadelphia (19130) **(G-14501)**

Yonish Disposal Company 814 839-4797
  300 Mountain Rd Alum Bank (15521) **(G-563)**

York Building Products Co Inc (PA) 717 848-2831
  950 Smile Way York (17404) **(G-20726)**

York Building Products Co Inc 717 944-1488
  325 Fulling Mill Rd Middletown (17057) **(G-11086)**

York Building Products Co Inc 717 845-5333
  915 Loucks Mill Rd York (17402) **(G-20727)**

York Building Products Co Inc 717 324-2379
  950 Smile Way Ste A York (17404) **(G-20728)**

York Building Products Co Inc 717 764-5996
  900 N Hartley St York (17404) **(G-20729)**

York Building Products Co Inc 717 792-9922
  Rr 30 Thomasville (17364) **(G-18344)**

York Building Products Co Inc 717 792-4700
  5799 Lincoln Hwy W Thomasville (17364) **(G-18345)**

York Building Products Co Inc 717 792-1200
  542 N West St York (17404) **(G-20730)**

York Casket Company 717 854-9566
  2880 Black Bridge Rd York (17406) **(G-20731)**

York Concrete Company 717 843-8746
  400 Girard Ave York (17403) **(G-20732)**

York Container Company 717 757-7611
  138 Mount Zion Rd York (17402) **(G-20733)**

York Corrugating Company (PA) 717 845-3512
  120 S Adams St York (17404) **(G-20734)**

York County Womens Journal 717 634-1658
  545 Quaker Dr York (17402) **(G-20735)**

A
L
P
H
A
B
E
T
I
C

York Daily Record Sunday News 717 771-2000
  1891 Loucks Rd York (17408) *(G-20736)*

York Electro-Mechanical Corp 717 764-5262
  120 Rose Ct York (17406) *(G-20737)*

York Glass Etching, Red Lion *Also called Atlantic Glass Etching Inc (G-16589)*

York Graphic Services Co 717 505-9701
  3650 W Market St York (17404) *(G-20738)*

York Haven Fabricators Inc 717 932-4000
  2850 Lewisberry Rd York Haven (17370) *(G-20762)*

York Ice Co Inc 717 848-2639
  281 Kings Mill Rd York (17401) *(G-20739)*

York II, Felton *Also called Novares US LLC (G-5942)*

York Imperial Plastics Inc 717 428-3939
  718 Country Rd York (17403) *(G-20740)*

York Industrial Tool Inc 717 200-1149
  491 Maryland Ave York (17404) *(G-20741)*

York Industries Inc 717 764-8855
  706 Willow Springs Ln York (17406) *(G-20742)*

York Integra PA Inc 717 840-3438
  3670 Concord Rd York (17402) *(G-20743)*

York International Corporation 414 524-1200
  950 Forge Ave Unit 110 Audubon (19403) *(G-832)*

York International Corporation 814 479-4005
  395 Industrial Park Rd Johnstown (15904) *(G-8447)*

York International Corporation 717 815-4200
  1499 E Philadelphia St York (17403) *(G-20744)*

York International Corporation 717 762-1440
  100 C V Ave Waynesboro (17268) *(G-19431)*

York International Corporation (HQ) 717 771-7890
  631 S Richland Ave York (17403) *(G-20745)*

York International Corporation 717 762-2121
  100 Cumberland Valley Ave Waynesboro (17268) *(G-19432)*

York Newspaper Company 717 767-6397
  1891 Loucks Rd York (17408) *(G-20746)*

York Newspapers Inc 717 767-6397
  1891 Loucks Rd York (17408) *(G-20747)*

York P-B Truss Inc 717 779-0327
  3487 N Susquehanna Trl York (17406) *(G-20748)*

York Precision 717 764-8855
  706 Willow Springs Ln York (17406) *(G-20749)*

York Products, York *Also called York Casket Company (G-20731)*

York Saw & Knife Company Inc 717 767-6402
  295 Emig Rd Emigsville (17318) *(G-5003)*

York Sheet Metal, York *Also called Apx York Sheet Metal Inc (G-20382)*

York Steel Rule Dies Inc 717 846-6002
  630 Loucks Mill Rd Ste 8 York (17403) *(G-20750)*

York Sunday News, The, York *Also called York Newspapers Inc (G-20747)*

York Tent & Awning, York *Also called Y T & A Inc (G-20722)*

York Textile Products Inc 717 764-2528
  2110 Brougher Ln York (17408) *(G-20751)*

York Tool & Die Inc 717 741-4844
  2603 Keyway Dr York (17402) *(G-20752)*

York Towne Embroidery Works 717 854-0006
  220 W Philadelphia St York (17401) *(G-20753)*

York Wallcoverings Inc (PA) 717 846-4456
  750 Linden Ave York (17404) *(G-20754)*

York-Seaway Indus Pdts Inc 814 774-7080
  9843 Martin Ave Lake City (16423) *(G-8911)*

Yorkaire Inc 717 755-2836
  1877 Whiteford Rd York (17402) *(G-20755)*

Yorkaire Group, The, York *Also called Yorkaire Inc (G-20755)*

Yorkshire Lead Glass Company 215 694-2727
  7128 N Radcliffe St Bristol (19007) *(G-2219)*

Yorktowne Cabinets, Mifflinburg *Also called Elkay Wood Products Company (G-11094)*

Yost Drilling LLC 724 324-2253
  313 Steel Hill Rd Mount Morris (15349) *(G-11684)*

Youghiogheny Opalescent GL Inc 724 628-3000
  300 S 1st St Connellsville (15425) *(G-3512)*

Young and Brothers Constuction 215 852-5398
  5952 Warrington Ave Philadelphia (19143) *(G-14502)*

Young Face 412 928-2676
  651 Holiday Dr Pittsburgh (15220) *(G-15730)*

Young Windows Inc 610 828-5036
  680 Colwell Ln Conshohocken (19428) *(G-3618)*

Youngcraft, Bristol *Also called F C Young & Co Inc (G-2143)*

Youngs Truck Repair LLC 570 329-3571
  44 Steinbacher Ln South Williamsport (17702) *(G-17794)*

Youngstown Alloy & Chain Corp 724 347-1920
  364 Yankee Ridge Rd Mercer (16137) *(G-10980)*

Youngtron Inc 215 822-7866
  2873 Sterling Dr Hatfield (19440) *(G-7406)*

Your Building Centers Inc 570 962-2129
  109 Industrial Park Rd Beech Creek (16822) *(G-1084)*

Your Community Phonebook, Blue Bell *Also called Yellow Pages Group LLC (G-1858)*

Your Private Printer, Harrisburg *Also called Tammy M Tibbens (G-7226)*

Your Town Magazine, Coatesville *Also called Z Publication LLC (G-3332)*

Youre Putting ME On Inc 412 655-9666
  275 Curry Hollow Rd Pittsburgh (15236) *(G-15731)*

Youth Services Agency 215 752-7050
  120 Bellevue Ave Penndel (19047) *(G-13242)*

Youth Services of Bucks County, Penndel *Also called Youth Services Agency (G-13242)*

YS Manufacturing Inc 610 444-4832
  101 Blue Spruce Dr Kennett Square (19348) *(G-8552)*

Yuasa Battery Inc 610 929-5781
  2901 Montrose Ave Reading (19605) *(G-16571)*

Yuengling Brewing, Pottsville *Also called D G Yuengling and Son Inc (G-16075)*

Yuengling Brewing, Pottsville *Also called D G Yuengling and Son Inc (G-16076)*

Yum Yum Bake Shops Inc 215 675-9874
  500 W Street Rd Warminster (18974) *(G-19005)*

Yum-Yum Bakers, Colmar *Also called Yum-Yum Colmar Inc (G-3426)*

Yum-Yum Colmar Inc 215 822-9468
  100 Bethlehem Pike Colmar (18915) *(G-3426)*

Yurchak Printing Inc 717 399-0209
  920 Links Ave Landisville (17538) *(G-9269)*

Yurchak Printing Inc 717 399-9551
  1781 Hidden Ln Lancaster (17603) *(G-9244)*

Z & F USA 412 257-8575
  700 Old Pond Rd Ste 606 Bridgeville (15017) *(G-2100)*

Z & Z Machine Inc 717 428-0354
  12 Valley Rd Jacobus (17407) *(G-8233)*

Z Publication LLC 484 574-5321
  143 Milbury Rd Coatesville (19320) *(G-3332)*

Z Weldco 610 689-8773
  24 Covered Bridge Rd Oley (19547) *(G-12982)*

Z Wood Products Co Inc 215 423-9891
  400 W Glenwood Ave Philadelphia (19140) *(G-14503)*

Z-Axis Connector Company 267 803-9000
  345 Ivyland Rd Warminster (18974) *(G-19006)*

Z-Band Technologies LLC 717 249-2606
  848 N Hanover St Ste B Carlisle (17013) *(G-2752)*

Zachary R Marella 724 557-1671
  1178 Walnut Hill Rd Smithfield (15478) *(G-17656)*

Zakes Cakes 215 654-7600
  444 S Bethlehem Pike Fort Washington (19034) *(G-6097)*

Zakes Cakes & Cafe, Fort Washington *Also called Zakes Cakes (G-6097)*

Zama Petroleum Inc 360 321-6160
  225 Ross St Ste 4 Pittsburgh (15219) *(G-15732)*

Zambelli Fireworks Mfg Co 724 652-1156
  782 Garner Rd New Castle (16101) *(G-12172)*

Zambotti Collision & Wldg Ctr 724 545-2305
  138 Zambotti St Kittanning (16201) *(G-8804)*

Zampell Refractories Inc 215 788-3000
  125 Phyllis Ave Croydon (19021) *(G-3934)*

Zappone Bros Foods 724 539-1430
  408 Longs Rd Latrobe (15650) *(G-9529)*

Zareba Systems Inc (HQ) 763 551-1125
  69 N Locust St Lititz (17543) *(G-10061)*

Zausner Foods Corp (HQ) 717 355-8505
  400 S Custer Ave New Holland (17557) *(G-12296)*

Zavante Therapeutics Inc 610 816-6640
  1000 Continental Dr # 600 King of Prussia (19406) *(G-8701)*

Zaveta Millwork Spc Inc 215 489-4065
  4030 Skyron Dr Ste H Doylestown (18902) *(G-4348)*

Zavillas Oil Co 724 445-3702
  1479 State Route 4011 Chicora (16025) *(G-3130)*

Zeb Machine Co Inc 610 926-4766
  331 Kindt Corner Rd Leesport (19533) *(G-9675)*

Zehrco-Giancola Composites Inc 814 406-7033
  36 Clark St Warren (16365) *(G-19066)*

Zeigler Bros Inc (PA) 717 677-6181
  400 Gardners Station Rd Gardners (17324) *(G-6262)*

Zeiglers Beverages LLC 215 855-5161
  1513 N Broad St Lansdale (19446) *(G-9428)*

Zeiglers Machine Shop 570 374-5535
  650 E Hollow Rd Middleburg (17842) *(G-11042)*

Zeiglers Packing and Crating (PA) 814 238-4021
  938 Meeks Ln Port Matilda (16870) *(G-15908)*

Zekelman Industries Inc 610 889-3337
  2304 Westfield Ct Newtown Square (19073) *(G-12599)*

Zekelman Industries Inc 724 342-6851
  700 S Dock St Sharon (16146) *(G-17450)*

Zekelman Industries Inc 724 342-6851
  700 S Dock St Sharon (16146) *(G-17451)*

Zell Manufacturing Co Inc 724 327-4771
  213 Pfeffer Rd Export (15632) *(G-5632)*

Zellner Welding, Whitehall *Also called Hines Industries Inc (G-19875)*

Zemco Tool & Die Inc 717 647-7151
  113 S West St Williamstown (17098) *(G-20104)*

Zena Associates Llc 215 730-9000
  701a Ashland Ave Ste 1 Folcroft (19032) *(G-6021)*

Zenco Machine & Tool Co Inc 215 345-6262
  205 N Broad St Doylestown (18901) *(G-4349)*

Zenescope Entertainment Inc 215 442-9094
  433 Caredean Dr Ste C Horsham (19044) *(G-7866)*

Zentis North America LLC (HQ) 215 676-3900
  1741 Tomlinson Rd Philadelphia (19116) *(G-14504)*

Zenzel III Michael 570 752-2666
  2637 W Front St Berwick (18603) *(G-1350)*

2019 Harris Pennsylvania
Manufacturers Directory

(G-0000) Company's Geographic Section entry number

Zeolyst International (PA) 610 651-4200
300 Lindenwood Dr Malvern (19355) *(G-10352)*

Zeomedix Inc 610 517-7818
26 Ashlawn Cir Malvern (19355) *(G-10353)*

Zep Inc 610 295-1360
860 Nestle Way Ste 200 Breinigsville (18031) *(G-2033)*

Zep Manufacturing, Breinigsville *Also called Zep Inc (G-2033)*

Zerbe Manufacturing 570 640-1528
245 Sweet Arrow Lake Rd Pine Grove (17963) *(G-14609)*

Zero Error Racing Inc 724 588-5898
660 Keystone Rd A Greenville (16125) *(G-6778)*

Zero Ice Corporation 717 264-7912
42 Siloam Rd Chambersburg (17201) *(G-3002)*

Zero Restriction, York *Also called Red Lion Manufacturing Inc (G-20656)*

Zero Technologies LLC 215 244-0823
7 Neshaminy Interplex Dr # 116 Trevose (19053) *(G-18509)*

Zero Water, Trevose *Also called Zero Technologies LLC (G-18509)*

Zeyon Inc 814 899-3311
3408 Mcclelland Ave Erie (16510) *(G-5536)*

Zia-Tech Gear Mfg Inc 412 321-0770
2131 N Charles St Pittsburgh (15214) *(G-15733)*

Ziamatic Corp (PA) 215 493-2777
10 W College Ave Yardley (19067) *(G-20347)*

Zico Safety Products, Yardley *Also called Ziamatic Corp (G-20347)*

Ziel Technologies LLC 717 951-7485
590 Sylvan Rd Ste 341 Lancaster (17601) *(G-9245)*

Zielke Orthotics & Prosthetics, York *Also called Hanger Prsthetcs & Ortho Inc (G-20520)*

Zimm-O-Matic LLC 717 445-6432
1216 Muddy Creek Rd Denver (17517) *(G-4098)*

Zimmerman Chair Shop 717 273-2706
1486 Colebrook Rd Lebanon (17042) *(G-9640)*

Zimmerman Deisel, Lewisburg *Also called Allen Zimmmerman (G-9896)*

Zimmerman Industries Inc 717 733-6166
196 Wabash Rd Ephrata (17522) *(G-5158)*

Zinc Corporation America Div, Palmerton *Also called Horsehead Corporation (G-13107)*

Zinc Plating Specialists, Punxsutawney *Also called Punxsutawney Finshg Works Inc (G-16155)*

Zip-Net Inc 610 939-9762
801 William Ln Reading (19604) *(G-16572)*

Zipcorp Inc (PA) 814 368-2700
33 Barbour St Bradford (16701) *(G-1997)*

Zipf Associates Inc 610 667-1717
25 Bala Ave Ste 201 Bala Cynwyd (19004) *(G-897)*

Zippercord Llc 610 797-6564
1801 S 12th St Allentown (18103) *(G-440)*

Zippo Manufacturing Company, Bradford *Also called Zipcorp Inc (G-1997)*

Zircon Corp 215 757-7156
348 Main St Langhorne (19047) *(G-9337)*

Zitner Candy Corp 215 229-4990
3120 N 17th St Philadelphia (19132) *(G-14505)*

Zodiac Arresting Systems Amer, Upper Chichester *Also called Enginred Arrsting Systems Corp (G-18660)*

Zodiac Printing Corporation 570 474-9220
395 Oak Hill Rd Mountain Top (18707) *(G-11784)*

Zoetis Inc 908 901-1116
812 Springdale Dr Exton (19341) *(G-5752)*

Zoetis LLC 717 932-3702
543 Industrial Dr Lewisberry (17339) *(G-9895)*

Zoll 717 761-1842
2001 Clarendon St Camp Hill (17011) *(G-2527)*

Zoll Lifevest, Cheswick *Also called Zoll Medical Corporation (G-3124)*

Zoll Manufacturing Corporation (PA) 412 968-3333
121 Gamma Dr Pittsburgh (15238) *(G-15734)*

Zoll Manufacturing Corporation 412 968-3333
1000 Commerce Dr Cheswick (15024) *(G-3123)*

Zoll Medical Corporation 800 543-3267
121 Gamma Dr Pittsburgh (15238) *(G-15735)*

Zoll Medical Corporation 412 968-3333
1001 Commerce Dr Cheswick (15024) *(G-3124)*

Zoll Services LLC 412 968-3333
121 Gamma Dr Pittsburgh (15238) *(G-15736)*

Zondervan Corporation LLC 570 941-1366
1000 Keystone Indus Park Dunmore (18512) *(G-4488)*

Zook Molasses Co, Honey Brook *Also called M Simon Zook Co (G-7753)*

Zooks Pallets Inc 717 935-5030
10 State St Belleville (17004) *(G-1135)*

Zooks Pallets LLC 717 667-9077
149 Sawmill Rd Belleville (17004) *(G-1136)*

Zooks Pallets LLC 717 899-5212
260 Riverside Dr Mc Veytown (17051) *(G-10654)*

Zooks Sawmill LLC 610 593-1040
1205 Smyrna Rd Christiana (17509) *(G-3145)*

Zooks Woodworking 570 758-3579
713 Smeltz Rd Dornsife (17823) *(G-4165)*

Zoom Room, Philadelphia *Also called Lb Full Circle Canine Fitness (G-13961)*

Zoombang Protective Gear, Irwin *Also called Impact Innovative Products LLC (G-8170)*

Zottola Fab A PA Bus Tr 412 221-4488
5 Mcclane St Cuddy (15031) *(G-3944)*

Zottola Steel Corporation 412 362-5577
900 Washington Blvd Pittsburgh (15206) *(G-15737)*

Zrile Brothers Packing Inc 724 528-9246
4129 Longview Rd West Middlesex (16159) *(G-19733)*

Zrm Enterprises LLC 724 437-3116
1178 Walnut Hill Rd Smithfield (15478) *(G-17657)*

Zubek Inc 814 443-4441
173 House Coal Rd Berlin (15530) *(G-1294)*

Zukay Live Foods LLC 610 286-3077
1904 Tollgate Rd Palm (18070) *(G-13097)*

Zur Ltd 717 761-7044
75 Utley Dr Camp Hill (17011) *(G-2528)*

Zurenko Welding & Fabricating 724 254-1131
2902 Hemlock Rd Commodore (15729) *(G-3455)*

Zurex Corporation (PA) 814 425-7445
100 Pressler Ave Cochranton (16314) *(G-3353)*

Zurn Aluminum Products Co 814 774-2681
10884 Ridge Rd Girard (16417) *(G-6404)*

Zurn Industries LLC (HQ) 814 455-0921
1801 Pittsburgh Ave Erie (16502) *(G-5537)*

Zurn Industries LLC 215 946-0216
37 Runway Dr Levittown (19057) *(G-9870)*

Zuzek Lumber, Kane *Also called Carol Zuzek (G-8460)*

Zwicky Processing & Recycling, Fleetwood *Also called W D Zwicky & Son Inc (G-5982)*

Zylux America Inc (HQ) 412 221-5530
225 Library Rd Pmb 500 500 Pmb Bethel Park (15102) *(G-1440)*

Zynerba Pharmaceuticals Inc 484 581-7505
80 Lancaster Ave Ste 300 Devon (19333) *(G-4117)*

Zynitech Medical Inc 610 592-0755
347 N Pottstown Pike Exton (19341) *(G-5753)*

Zynnie Bakes 610 905-6283
211 Mercer St Philadelphia (19125) *(G-14506)*

A L P H A B E T I C

PRODUCT INDEX

• Product categories are listed in alphabetical order.

A

ABRASIVE SCOURING MATERIALS
ABRASIVES
ABRASIVES: Coated
ABRASIVES: Diamond Powder
ABRASIVES: Silicon Carbide
ABRASIVES: Synthetic
ABRASIVES: Tungsten Carbide
ACADEMIC TUTORING SVCS
ACCELERATION INDICATORS & SYSTEM COMPONENTS: Aerospace
ACCELERATORS: Electrostatic Particle
ACCOUNTING MACHINES & CASH REGISTERS
ACCOUNTING SVCS, NEC
ACETONE: Synthetic
ACID RESIST: Etching
ACIDS
ACIDS: Hydrocyanic
ACIDS: Inorganic
ACIDS: Sulfuric, Oleum
ACOUSTICAL BOARD & TILE
ACRYLIC RESINS
ACRYLIC RUBBERS: Polyacrylate
ACTOR
ACTUATORS: Indl, NEC
ADDRESSING SVCS
ADHESIVES
ADHESIVES & SEALANTS
ADHESIVES: Adhesives, paste
ADHESIVES: Epoxy
ADVERTISING AGENCIES
ADVERTISING AGENCIES: Consultants
ADVERTISING CURTAINS
ADVERTISING DISPLAY PRDTS
ADVERTISING MATERIAL DISTRIBUTION
ADVERTISING REPRESENTATIVES: Electronic Media
ADVERTISING REPRESENTATIVES: Magazine
ADVERTISING REPRESENTATIVES: Media
ADVERTISING REPRESENTATIVES: Newspaper
ADVERTISING REPRESENTATIVES: Printed Media
ADVERTISING SPECIALTIES, WHOLESALE
ADVERTISING SVCS: Billboards
ADVERTISING SVCS: Direct Mail
ADVERTISING SVCS: Display
ADVERTISING SVCS: Outdoor
ADVERTISING SVCS: Poster, Outdoor
ADVOCACY GROUP
AERIAL WORK PLATFORMS
AGENTS, BROKERS & BUREAUS: Personal Service
AGRICULTURAL DISINFECTANTS
AGRICULTURAL EQPT: BARN, SILO, POULTRY, DAIRY/LIVESTOCK MACH
AGRICULTURAL EQPT: Clippers, Animal, Hand Or Electric
AGRICULTURAL EQPT: Dusters, Mechanical
AGRICULTURAL EQPT: Fertilizing Machinery
AGRICULTURAL EQPT: Fertilizng, Sprayng, Dustng/Irrigatn Mach
AGRICULTURAL EQPT: Fillers & Unloaders, Silo
AGRICULTURAL EQPT: Grade, Clean & Sort Machines, Fruit/Veg
AGRICULTURAL EQPT: Greens Mowing Eqpt
AGRICULTURAL EQPT: Harvesters, Fruit, Vegetable, Tobacco
AGRICULTURAL EQPT: Loaders, Manure & General Utility
AGRICULTURAL EQPT: Planting Machines
AGRICULTURAL EQPT: Soil Preparation Mach, Exc Turf & Grounds
AGRICULTURAL EQPT: Tractors, Farm
AGRICULTURAL EQPT: Trailers & Wagons, Farm
AGRICULTURAL EQPT: Transplanters
AGRICULTURAL EQPT: Turf & Grounds Eqpt
AGRICULTURAL EQPT: Turf Eqpt, Commercial
AGRICULTURAL EQPT: Weeding Machines
AGRICULTURAL MACHINERY & EQPT REPAIR
AGRICULTURAL MACHINERY & EQPT: Wholesalers
AIR CLEANING SYSTEMS
AIR CONDITIONERS: Motor Vehicle
AIR CONDITIONING & VENTILATION EQPT & SPLYS: Wholesales

AIR CONDITIONING EQPT
AIR CONDITIONING EQPT, WHOLE HOUSE: Wholesalers
AIR CONDITIONING REPAIR SVCS
AIR CONDITIONING UNITS: Complete, Domestic Or Indl
AIR COOLERS: Metal Plate
AIR CURTAINS
AIR DUCT CLEANING SVCS
AIR MATTRESSES: Plastic
AIR PURIFICATION EQPT
AIR TRAFFIC CONTROL SYSTEMS & EQPT
AIR, WATER & SOLID WASTE PROGRAMS ADMINISTRATION SVCS
AIRCRAFT & AEROSPACE FLIGHT INSTRUMENTS & GUIDANCE SYSTEMS
AIRCRAFT & HEAVY EQPT REPAIR SVCS
AIRCRAFT ASSEMBLY PLANTS
AIRCRAFT AUTOMATIC PILOT SYSTEMS
AIRCRAFT CONTROL SYSTEMS:
AIRCRAFT CONTROL SYSTEMS: Electronic Totalizing Counters
AIRCRAFT ENGINES & ENGINE PARTS: Air Scoops
AIRCRAFT ENGINES & ENGINE PARTS: Airfoils
AIRCRAFT ENGINES & PARTS
AIRCRAFT EQPT & SPLYS WHOLESALERS
AIRCRAFT FLIGHT INSTRUMENT REPAIR SVCS
AIRCRAFT FLIGHT INSTRUMENTS
AIRCRAFT LIGHTING
AIRCRAFT MAINTENANCE & REPAIR SVCS
AIRCRAFT PARTS & AUXILIARY EQPT: Accumulators, Propeller
AIRCRAFT PARTS & AUXILIARY EQPT: Aircraft Training Eqpt
AIRCRAFT PARTS & AUXILIARY EQPT: Arresting Device Systems
AIRCRAFT PARTS & AUXILIARY EQPT: Assys, Subassemblies/Parts
AIRCRAFT PARTS & AUXILIARY EQPT: Body & Wing Assys & Parts
AIRCRAFT PARTS & AUXILIARY EQPT: Gears, Power Transmission
AIRCRAFT PARTS & AUXILIARY EQPT: Landing Assemblies & Brakes
AIRCRAFT PARTS & AUXILIARY EQPT: Military Eqpt & Armament
AIRCRAFT PARTS & AUXILIARY EQPT: Research & Development, Mfr
AIRCRAFT PARTS & AUXILIARY EQPT: Seat Ejector Devices
AIRCRAFT PARTS & AUXILIARY EQPT: Tanks, Fuel
AIRCRAFT PARTS & EQPT, NEC
AIRCRAFT PARTS/AUX EQPT: Airframe Assy, Exc Guided Missiles
AIRCRAFT SEATS
AIRCRAFT TURBINES
AIRCRAFT: Airplanes, Fixed Or Rotary Wing
AIRCRAFT: Research & Development, Manufacturer
AIRFRAME ASSEMBLIES: Guided Missiles
ALARM SYSTEMS WHOLESALERS
ALARMS: Burglar
ALARMS: Fire
ALCOHOL, ETHYL: For Beverage Purposes
ALCOHOL: Ethyl & Ethanol
ALKALIES & CHLORINE
ALL-TERRAIN VEHICLE DEALERS
ALLOYS: Additive, Exc Copper Or Made In Blast Furnaces
ALTERNATORS & GENERATORS: Battery Charging
ALTERNATORS: Automotive
ALUMINUM
ALUMINUM PRDTS
ALUMINUM: Coil & Sheet
ALUMINUM: Rolling & Drawing
AMMUNITION
AMMUNITION: Components
AMMUNITION: Cores, Bullet, 30 mm & Below
AMMUNITION: Detonators, Ammunition Over 30 mm
AMMUNITION: Mortar Shells, Over 30 mm
AMMUNITION: Pellets & BB's, Pistol & Air Rifle
AMMUNITION: Small Arms
AMPLIFIERS: Parametric
AMPLIFIERS: RF & IF Power

AMUSEMENT & REC SVCS: Attractions, Concessions & Rides
AMUSEMENT & REC SVCS: Skating Instruction, Ice Or Roller
AMUSEMENT & RECREATION SVCS: Amusement Ride
AMUSEMENT & RECREATION SVCS: Arts & Crafts Instruction
AMUSEMENT & RECREATION SVCS: Exposition Operation
AMUSEMENT & RECREATION SVCS: Gun Club, Membership
AMUSEMENT & RECREATION SVCS: Hot Air Balloon Rides
AMUSEMENT & RECREATION SVCS: Outfitters, Recreation
AMUSEMENT & RECREATION SVCS: Recreation Center
AMUSEMENT & RECREATION SVCS: School, Hockey Instruction
AMUSEMENT & RECREATION SVCS: Shooting Range
AMUSEMENT & RECREATION SVCS: Tourist Attraction, Commercial
AMUSEMENT & RECREATION SVCS: Yoga Instruction
AMUSEMENT MACHINES: Coin Operated
AMUSEMENT PARK DEVICES & RIDES
ANALGESICS
ANALYZERS: Coulometric, Exc Indl Process
ANALYZERS: Coulometric, Indl Process
ANALYZERS: Electrical Testing
ANALYZERS: Moisture
ANALYZERS: Network
ANALYZERS: Respiratory
ANESTHESIA EQPT
ANIMAL BASED MEDICINAL CHEMICAL PRDTS
ANIMAL FEED & SUPPLEMENTS: Livestock & Poultry
ANIMAL FEED: Wholesalers
ANIMAL FOOD & SUPPLEMENTS: Bird Food, Prepared
ANIMAL FOOD & SUPPLEMENTS: Cat
ANIMAL FOOD & SUPPLEMENTS: Chicken Feeds, Prepared
ANIMAL FOOD & SUPPLEMENTS: Dog
ANIMAL FOOD & SUPPLEMENTS: Dog & Cat
ANIMAL FOOD & SUPPLEMENTS: Feed Premixes
ANIMAL FOOD & SUPPLEMENTS: Feed Supplements
ANIMAL FOOD & SUPPLEMENTS: Livestock
ANIMAL FOOD & SUPPLEMENTS: Mineral feed supplements
ANIMAL FOOD & SUPPLEMENTS: Pet, Exc Dog & Cat, Dry
ANIMAL FOOD & SUPPLEMENTS: Poultry
ANIMAL FOOD/SUPPLEMENTS: Feeds Fm Meat/Meat/Veg Combnd Meals
ANNEALING: Metal
ANODIZING EQPT
ANODIZING SVC
ANTENNAS: Receiving
ANTHRACITE PREPARATION PLANTS
ANTIBIOTICS
ANTIBIOTICS, PACKAGED
ANTIFREEZE
ANTIMONY ORE MINING
ANTIQUE & CLASSIC AUTOMOBILE RESTORATION
ANTIQUE FURNITURE RESTORATION & REPAIR
ANTIQUE REPAIR & RESTORATION SVCS, EXC FURNITURE & AUTOS
ANTIQUE SHOPS
APPAREL ACCESS STORES
APPAREL DESIGNERS: Commercial
APPLIANCE CORDS: Household Electrical Eqpt
APPLIANCES, HOUSEHOLD: Kitchen, Major, Exc Refrigs & Stoves
APPLIANCES, HOUSEHOLD: Sewing Machines & Attchmnts, Domestic
APPLIANCES: Household, NEC
APPLIANCES: Major, Cooking
APPLIANCES: Small, Electric
APPLICATIONS SOFTWARE PROGRAMMING
AQUARIUM DESIGN & MAINTENANCE SVCS
AQUARIUMS & ACCESS: Glass
AQUARIUMS & ACCESS: Plastic
ARCHITECTURAL PANELS OR PARTS: Porcelain Enameled
ARCHITECTURAL SVCS
ARCHITECTURAL SVCS: Engineering
ARMATURE REPAIRING & REWINDING SVC
ARMORED CAR SVCS
AROMATIC CHEMICAL PRDTS
ART & ORNAMENTAL WARE: Pottery

INDEX

ART DEALERS & GALLERIES
ART DESIGN SVCS
ART GALLERIES
ART GOODS, WHOLESALE
ART MARBLE: Concrete
ART NEEDLEWORK, MADE FROM PURCHASED MATERIALS
ART RESTORATION SVC
ART SPLY STORES
ARTIFICIAL FLOWER SHOPS
ARTIFICIAL FLOWERS & TREES
ARTIST'S MATERIALS & SPLYS
ARTISTS' AGENTS & BROKERS
ARTISTS' MATERIALS, WHOLESALE
ARTISTS' MATERIALS: Eraser Guides & Shields
ARTISTS' MATERIALS: Frames, Artists' Canvases
ARTISTS' MATERIALS: Ink, Drawing, Black & Colored
ARTWORK: Framed
ASBESTOS PRDTS: Insulating Materials
ASBESTOS PRDTS: Roofing, Felt Roll
ASBESTOS PRODUCTS
ASBESTOS REMOVAL EQPT
ASPHALT & ASPHALT PRDTS
ASPHALT COATINGS & SEALERS
ASPHALT MINING & BITUMINOUS STONE QUARRYING SVCS
ASPHALT MIXTURES WHOLESALERS
ASPHALT PLANTS INCLUDING GRAVEL MIX TYPE
ASSEMBLING & PACKAGING SVCS: Cosmetic Kits
ASSEMBLING SVC: Plumbing Fixture Fittings, Plastic
ASSOCIATION FOR THE HANDICAPPED
ASSOCIATIONS: Bar
ASSOCIATIONS: Business
ASSOCIATIONS: Real Estate Management
ASSOCIATIONS: Trade
ATHLETIC CLUB & GYMNASIUMS, MEMBERSHIP
ATOMIZERS
ATTENUATORS
AUDIO & VIDEO EQPT, EXC COMMERCIAL
AUDIO COMPONENTS
AUDIO ELECTRONIC SYSTEMS
AUDIO-VISUAL PROGRAM PRODUCTION SVCS
AUDIOLOGICAL EQPT: Electronic
AUDIOLOGISTS' OFFICES
AUTO & HOME SUPPLY STORES: Auto & Truck Eqpt & Parts
AUTO & HOME SUPPLY STORES: Auto Air Cond Eqpt, Sell/Install
AUTO & HOME SUPPLY STORES: Automotive Access
AUTO & HOME SUPPLY STORES: Automotive parts
AUTO & HOME SUPPLY STORES: Batteries, Automotive & Truck
AUTO & HOME SUPPLY STORES: Trailer Hitches, Automotive
AUTO & HOME SUPPLY STORES: Truck Eqpt & Parts
AUTOCLAVES: Indl
AUTOMATED TELLER MACHINE NETWORK
AUTOMATED TELLER MACHINE OR ATM REPAIR SVCS
AUTOMATIC REGULATING CNTRLS: Flame Safety, Furnaces & Boiler
AUTOMATIC REGULATING CNTRLS: Steam Press, Residential/ Comm
AUTOMATIC REGULATING CONTROL: Building Svcs Monitoring, Auto
AUTOMATIC REGULATING CONTROLS: AC & Refrigeration
AUTOMATIC REGULATING CONTROLS: Hardware, Environmental Reg
AUTOMATIC REGULATING CONTROLS: Hydronic Pressure Or Temp
AUTOMATIC REGULATING CONTROLS: Incinerator, Residential/Comm
AUTOMATIC REGULATING CONTROLS: Pneumatic Relays, Air-Cond
AUTOMATIC REGULATING CTRLS: Damper, Pneumatic Or Electric
AUTOMATIC TELLER MACHINES
AUTOMATIC VENDING MACHINES: Mechanisms & Parts
AUTOMOTIVE & TRUCK GENERAL REPAIR SVC
AUTOMOTIVE BATTERIES WHOLESALERS
AUTOMOTIVE BODY SHOP
AUTOMOTIVE BODY, PAINT & INTERIOR REPAIR & MAINTENANCE SVC
AUTOMOTIVE BRAKE REPAIR SHOPS
AUTOMOTIVE CUSTOMIZING SVCS, NONFACTORY BASIS
AUTOMOTIVE EXTERIOR REPAIR SVCS
AUTOMOTIVE GLASS REPLACEMENT SHOPS
AUTOMOTIVE LETTERING SVCS

AUTOMOTIVE PARTS, ACCESS & SPLYS
AUTOMOTIVE PARTS: Plastic
AUTOMOTIVE RADIATOR REPAIR SHOPS
AUTOMOTIVE REPAIR SHOPS: Alternators/Generator, Rebuild/Rpr
AUTOMOTIVE REPAIR SHOPS: Auto Brake Lining, Installation
AUTOMOTIVE REPAIR SHOPS: Diesel Engine Repair
AUTOMOTIVE REPAIR SHOPS: Electrical Svcs
AUTOMOTIVE REPAIR SHOPS: Engine Rebuilding
AUTOMOTIVE REPAIR SHOPS: Engine Repair
AUTOMOTIVE REPAIR SHOPS: Frame & Front End Repair Svcs
AUTOMOTIVE REPAIR SHOPS: Machine Shop
AUTOMOTIVE REPAIR SHOPS: Sound System Svc & Installation
AUTOMOTIVE REPAIR SHOPS: Springs, Rebuilding & Repair
AUTOMOTIVE REPAIR SHOPS: Trailer Repair
AUTOMOTIVE REPAIR SHOPS: Truck Engine Repair, Exc Indl
AUTOMOTIVE REPAIR SHOPS: Turbocharger & Blower Repair
AUTOMOTIVE REPAIR SVC
AUTOMOTIVE REPAIR SVCS, MISCELLANEOUS
AUTOMOTIVE SPLYS & PARTS, NEW, WHOLESALE: Engines/Eng Parts
AUTOMOTIVE SPLYS & PARTS, NEW, WHOLESALE: Filters, Air & Oil
AUTOMOTIVE SPLYS & PARTS, NEW, WHOLESALE: Pumps, Oil & Gas
AUTOMOTIVE SPLYS & PARTS, NEW, WHOLESALE: Splys
AUTOMOTIVE SPLYS & PARTS, NEW, WHOLESALE: Trailer Parts
AUTOMOTIVE SPLYS & PARTS, USED, WHOLESALE
AUTOMOTIVE SPLYS & PARTS, USED, WHOLESALE: Access, NEC
AUTOMOTIVE SPLYS & PARTS, USED, WHOLESALE: Engines
AUTOMOTIVE SPLYS & PARTS, WHOLESALE, NEC
AUTOMOTIVE SPLYS/PART, NEW, WHOL: Spring, Shock Absorb/Strut
AUTOMOTIVE SPLYS/PARTS, NEW, WHOL: Body Rpr/Paint Shop Splys
AUTOMOTIVE SVCS, EXC REPAIR & CARWASHES: Insp & Diagnostic
AUTOMOTIVE SVCS, EXC REPAIR & CARWASHES: Lubrication
AUTOMOTIVE SVCS, EXC REPAIR & CARWASHES: Maintenance
AUTOMOTIVE SVCS, EXC REPAIR & CARWASHES: Trailer Maintenance
AUTOMOTIVE SVCS, EXC REPAIR: Carwash, Automatic
AUTOMOTIVE SVCS, EXC REPAIR: Carwash, Self-Service
AUTOMOTIVE SVCS, EXC REPAIR: Washing & Polishing
AUTOMOTIVE SVCS, EXC RPR/CARWASHES: High Perf Auto Rpr/Svc
AUTOMOTIVE TOWING SVCS
AUTOMOTIVE UPHOLSTERY SHOPS
AUTOMOTIVE WELDING SVCS
AUTOMOTIVE: Bodies
AUTOMOTIVE: Seating
AUTOTRANSFORMERS: Electric
AWNING REPAIR SHOP
AWNINGS & CANOPIES
AWNINGS & CANOPIES: Awnings, Fabric, From Purchased Matls
AWNINGS: Fiberglass
AWNINGS: Metal
AWNINGS: Wood
AXLES: Rolled Or Forged, Made In Steel Mills
Ammunition Loading & Assembling Plant

B

BACKHOES
BADGES, WHOLESALE
BADGES: Identification & Insignia
BAFFLES
BAGS & CONTAINERS: Textile, Exc Sleeping
BAGS: Canvas
BAGS: Cellophane
BAGS: Duffle, Canvas, Made From Purchased Materials
BAGS: Food Storage & Frozen Food, Plastic
BAGS: Laundry, Garment & Storage
BAGS: Paper
BAGS: Plastic
BAGS: Plastic & Pliofilm

BAGS: Plastic, Made From Purchased Materials
BAGS: Shopping, Made From Purchased Materials
BAGS: Tea, Fabric, Made From Purchased Materials
BAGS: Textile
BAGS: Wardrobe, Closet Access, Made From Purchased Materials
BAKERIES, COMMERCIAL: On Premises Baking Only
BAKERIES: On Premises Baking & Consumption
BAKERY FOR HOME SVC DELIVERY
BAKERY MACHINERY
BAKERY PRDTS: Bagels, Fresh Or Frozen
BAKERY PRDTS: Bakery Prdts, Partially Cooked, Exc frozen
BAKERY PRDTS: Biscuits, Baked, Baking Powder & Raised
BAKERY PRDTS: Biscuits, Dry
BAKERY PRDTS: Bread, All Types, Fresh Or Frozen
BAKERY PRDTS: Buns, Bread Type, Fresh Or Frozen
BAKERY PRDTS: Cakes, Bakery, Exc Frozen
BAKERY PRDTS: Cakes, Bakery, Frozen
BAKERY PRDTS: Cones, Ice Cream
BAKERY PRDTS: Cookies
BAKERY PRDTS: Cookies & crackers
BAKERY PRDTS: Croissants, Exc Frozen
BAKERY PRDTS: Doughnuts, Exc Frozen
BAKERY PRDTS: Dry
BAKERY PRDTS: Frozen
BAKERY PRDTS: Pies, Exc Frozen
BAKERY PRDTS: Pretzels
BAKERY PRDTS: Rolls, Bread Type, Fresh Or Frozen
BAKERY PRDTS: Wholesalers
BAKERY: Wholesale Or Wholesale & Retail Combined
BALANCES EXC LABORATORY WHOLESALERS
BALANCING SVC
BALERS
BALLOONS: Hot Air
BALLOONS: Novelty & Toy
BALLOONS: Toy & Advertising, Rubber
BALLS: Rubber, Exc Athletic
BANDS: Copper & Copper Alloy
BANDS: Plastic
BANISTERS: Metal Pipe
BANK & TURN INDICATORS & COMPONENTS
BANNERS: Fabric
BANQUET HALL FACILITIES
BAR
BAR FIXTURES: Wood
BAR JOISTS & CONCRETE REINFORCING BARS: Fabricated
BARBECUE EQPT
BARGES BUILDING & REPAIR
BARRELS: Shipping, Metal
BARRICADES: Metal
BARS, COLD FINISHED: Steel, From Purchased Hot-Rolled
BARS, PIPES, PLATES & SHAPES: Lead/Lead Alloy Bars, Pipe
BARS: Concrete Reinforcing, Fabricated Steel
BARS: Iron, Made In Steel Mills
BASEMENT WINDOW AREAWAYS: Concrete
BASES, BEVERAGE
BASKETS, GIFT, WHOLESALE
BASKETS, WHOLESALE
BATCHING PLANTS: Aggregate Concrete & Bulk Cement
BATCHING PLANTS: Bituminous
BATH SALTS
BATHING SUIT STORES
BATHMATS: Rubber
BATHROOM FIXTURES: Plastic
BATTERIES, EXC AUTOMOTIVE: Wholesalers
BATTERIES: Dry
BATTERIES: Lead Acid, Storage
BATTERIES: Rechargeable
BATTERIES: Storage
BATTERIES: Wet
BATTERY CASES: Plastic Or Plastics Combination
BATTERY CHARGERS
BATTERY REPAIR & SVCS
BATTS & BATTING: Cotton
BAUXITE MINING
BEADS, WHOLESALE
BEADS: Unassembled
BEARINGS
BEARINGS & PARTS Ball
BEARINGS: Ball & Roller
BEARINGS: Plastic
BEAUTY & BARBER SHOP EQPT
BEAUTY SALONS

BEDDING, BEDSPREAD, BLANKET/SHEET: Pillowcase, Purchd Mtrl
BEDS & ACCESS STORES
BEDSPREADS & BED SETS, FROM PURCHASED MATERIALS
BEDSPREADS, FROM SILK OR MANMADE FIBER
BEEKEEPERS' SPLYS
BEEKEEPERS' SPLYS: Bee Smokers
BEEKEEPERS' SPLYS: Honeycomb Foundations
BEER & ALE WHOLESALERS
BEER & ALE, WHOLESALE: Beer & Other Fermented Malt Liquors
BEER, WINE & LIQUOR STORES
BEER, WINE & LIQUOR STORES: Beer, Packaged
BEER, WINE & LIQUOR STORES: Wine
BELLOWS
BELTING: Rubber
BELTING: Transmission, Rubber
BELTS & BELT PRDTS
BELTS: Conveyor, Made From Purchased Wire
BELTS: Money
BENTONITE MINING
BERYLLIUM
BEVERAGE BASES & SYRUPS
BEVERAGE POWDERS
BEVERAGE PRDTS: Brewers' Grain
BEVERAGE PRDTS: Malt Syrup
BEVERAGE STORES
BEVERAGE, NONALCOHOLIC: Iced Tea/Fruit Drink, Bottled/Canned
BEVERAGES, ALCOHOLIC: Ale
BEVERAGES, ALCOHOLIC: Beer
BEVERAGES, ALCOHOLIC: Beer & Ale
BEVERAGES, ALCOHOLIC: Brandy & Brandy Spirits
BEVERAGES, ALCOHOLIC: Cordials
BEVERAGES, ALCOHOLIC: Cordials & Premixed Cocktails
BEVERAGES, ALCOHOLIC: Distilled Liquors
BEVERAGES, ALCOHOLIC: Liquors, Malt
BEVERAGES, ALCOHOLIC: Near Beer
BEVERAGES, ALCOHOLIC: Neutral Spirits, Exc Fruit
BEVERAGES, ALCOHOLIC: Vodka
BEVERAGES, ALCOHOLIC: Wines
BEVERAGES, MALT
BEVERAGES, NONALCOHOLIC: Bottled & canned soft drinks
BEVERAGES, NONALCOHOLIC: Carbonated
BEVERAGES, NONALCOHOLIC: Carbonated, Canned & Bottled, Etc
BEVERAGES, NONALCOHOLIC: Cider
BEVERAGES, NONALCOHOLIC: Flavoring extracts & syrups, nec
BEVERAGES, NONALCOHOLIC: Fruit Drnks, Under 100% Juice, Can
BEVERAGES, NONALCOHOLIC: Soft Drinks, Canned & Bottled, Etc
BEVERAGES, NONALCOHOLIC: Tea, Iced, Bottled & Canned, Etc
BEVERAGES, WINE & DISTILLED ALCOHOLIC, WHOLESALE: Wine
BEVERAGES, WINE/DISTILLED ALCOHOLIC, WHOL: Bttlg Wine/Liquor
BICYCLE SHOPS
BICYCLES, PARTS & ACCESS
BILLETS: Steel
BILLING & BOOKKEEPING SVCS
BINDING SVC: Books & Manuals
BINDING SVC: Pamphlets
BINDING SVC: Trade
BINS: Prefabricated, Sheet Metal
BIOLOGICAL PRDTS: Bacterial Vaccines
BIOLOGICAL PRDTS: Blood Derivatives
BIOLOGICAL PRDTS: Exc Diagnostic
BIOLOGICAL PRDTS: Extracts
BIOLOGICAL PRDTS: Vaccines
BIOLOGICAL PRDTS: Vaccines & Immunizing
BIOLOGICAL PRDTS: Venoms
BIOLOGICAL PRDTS: Veterinary
BIRTH CONTROL DEVICES: Rubber
BITUMINOUS & LIGNITE COAL LOADING & PREPARATION
BITUMINOUS LIMESTONE QUARRYING SVCS
BLACKBOARDS & CHALKBOARDS
BLACKBOARDS: Slate
BLADES: Knife
BLADES: Saw, Hand Or Power
BLANKBOOKS & LOOSELEAF BINDERS
BLANKBOOKS: Albums

BLANKBOOKS: Albums, Record
BLANKBOOKS: Passbooks, Bank, Etc
BLANKBOOKS: Scrapbooks
BLANKETS & BLANKETING, COTTON
BLANKETS: Horse
BLAST FURNACE & RELATED PRDTS
BLASTING SVC: Sand, Metal Parts
BLINDS & SHADES: Porch, Wood Slat
BLINDS & SHADES: Vertical
BLINDS : Window
BLINDS, WOOD
BLOCKS & BRICKS: Concrete
BLOCKS: Glazed Face, Concrete
BLOCKS: Hat
BLOCKS: Landscape Or Retaining Wall, Concrete
BLOCKS: Paving
BLOCKS: Paving, Concrete
BLOCKS: Paving, Cut Stone
BLOCKS: Pillow, With Plain Bearings
BLOCKS: Plinth, Precast Terrazzo
BLOCKS: Radiation-Proof, Concrete
BLOCKS: Standard, Concrete Or Cinder
BLOOD RELATED HEALTH SVCS
BLOWERS & FANS
BLOWERS & FANS
BLUEPRINTING SVCS
BLUESTONE: Dimension
BOARDS: Stove, Sheet Metal
BOAT BUILDING & REPAIR
BOAT BUILDING & REPAIRING: Fiberglass
BOAT BUILDING & REPAIRING: Houseboats
BOAT BUILDING & REPAIRING: Jet Skis
BOAT BUILDING & REPAIRING: Kayaks
BOAT DEALERS
BOAT DEALERS: Marine Splys & Eqpt
BOAT DEALERS: Motor
BOAT YARD: Boat yards, storage & incidental repair
BODIES: Truck & Bus
BODY PARTS: Automobile, Stamped Metal
BOILER & HEATING REPAIR SVCS
BOILER GAGE COCKS
BOILER REPAIR SHOP
BOILERS & BOILER SHOP WORK
BOILERS: Low-Pressure Heating, Steam Or Hot Water
BOLTS: Metal
BOLTS: Wooden, Hewn
BONDERIZING: Bonderizing, Metal Or Metal Prdts
BOOK STORES
BOOK STORES: Religious
BOOKS, WHOLESALE
BOOTHS: Spray, Sheet Metal, Prefabricated
BOOTS: Men's
BOOTS: Women's
BOTTLE CAPS & RESEALERS: Plastic
BOTTLED GAS DEALERS: Propane
BOTTLED WATER DELIVERY
BOTTLES: Plastic
BOULDER: Crushed & Broken
BOUTIQUE STORES
BOWLING EQPT & SPLY STORES
BOWLING EQPT & SPLYS
BOX & CARTON MANUFACTURING EQPT
BOXES & CRATES: Rectangular, Wood
BOXES & SHOOK: Nailed Wood
BOXES: Corrugated
BOXES: Filing, Paperboard Made From Purchased Materials
BOXES: Junction, Electric
BOXES: Mail Or Post Office, Collection/Storage, Sheet Metal
BOXES: Outlet, Electric Wiring Device
BOXES: Packing & Shipping, Metal
BOXES: Paperboard, Folding
BOXES: Paperboard, Set-Up
BOXES: Plastic
BOXES: Solid Fiber
BOXES: Wirebound, Wood
BOXES: Wooden
BRAKE LININGS
BRAKES & BRAKE PARTS
BRAKES: Metal Forming
BRASS & BRONZE PRDTS: Die-casted
BRASS FOUNDRY, NEC
BRASS GOODS, WHOLESALE
BRAZING SVCS
BRAZING: Metal
BREECHINGS
BRICK & SHAPES: Dolomite Or Dolomite, Magnesite

BRICK, STONE & RELATED PRDTS WHOLESALERS
BRICKS : Paving, Clay
BRICKS: Clay
BRICKS: Concrete
BRIDAL SHOPS
BRIDGE COMPONENTS: Bridge sections, prefabricated, highway
BROADCASTING & COMMS EQPT: Antennas, Transmitting/Comms
BROADCASTING & COMMS EQPT: Rcvr-Transmitter Unt, Transceiver
BROADCASTING & COMMUNICATION EQPT: Transmit-Receiver, Radio
BROADCASTING & COMMUNICATIONS EQPT: Transmitting, Radio/TV
BROKERS & DEALERS: Securities
BROKERS' SVCS
BROKERS: Commodity Contracts
BROKERS: Contract Basis
BROKERS: Food
BROKERS: Mortgage, Arranging For Loans
BROKERS: Printing
BROKERS: Security
BRONZE FOUNDRY, NEC
BROOMS & BRUSHES
BROOMS & BRUSHES: Household Or Indl
BROOMS & BRUSHES: Street Sweeping, Hand Or Machine
BRUCITE MINING
BRUSH BLOCKS: Carbon Or Molded Graphite
BRUSHES & BRUSH STOCK CONTACTS: Electric
BUCKETS: Plastic
BUFFET
BUILDING & OFFICE CLEANING SVCS
BUILDING & STRUCTURAL WOOD MBRS: Timbers, Struct, Lam Lumber
BUILDING & STRUCTURAL WOOD MEMBERS
BUILDING BOARD & WALLBOARD, EXC GYPSUM, NEC
BUILDING CLEANING & MAINTENANCE SVCS
BUILDING COMPONENTS: Structural Steel
BUILDING EXTERIOR CLEANING SVCS
BUILDING ITEM REPAIR SVCS, MISCELLANEOUS
BUILDING MAINTENANCE SVCS, EXC REPAIRS
BUILDING PRDTS & MATERIALS DEALERS
BUILDING PRDTS: Concrete
BUILDING PRDTS: Stone
BUILDING STONE, ARTIFICIAL: Concrete
BUILDINGS & COMPONENTS: Prefabricated Metal
BUILDINGS: Farm & Utility
BUILDINGS: Farm, Prefabricated Or Portable, Wood
BUILDINGS: Portable
BUILDINGS: Prefabricated, Metal
BUILDINGS: Prefabricated, Wood
BUILDINGS: Prefabricated, Wood
BULLETIN BOARDS: Cork
BULLETPROOF VESTS
BUMPERS: Motor Vehicle
BUOYS: Metal
BUOYS: Plastic
BURGLAR ALARM MAINTENANCE & MONITORING SVCS
BURIAL VAULTS: Concrete Or Precast Terrazzo
BURNERS: Oil, Domestic Or Indl
BURNT WOOD ARTICLES
BUS BARS: Electrical
BUSHINGS & BEARINGS
BUSHINGS: Cast Steel, Exc Investment
BUSINESS ACTIVITIES: Non-Commercial Site
BUSINESS FORMS WHOLESALERS
BUSINESS FORMS: Printed, Continuous
BUSINESS FORMS: Printed, Manifold
BUSINESS MACHINE REPAIR, ELECTRIC
BUSINESS SUPPORT SVCS
BUSINESS TRAINING SVCS

C

CABINETS & CASES: Show, Display & Storage, Exc Wood
CABINETS: Bathroom Vanities, Wood
CABINETS: Entertainment
CABINETS: Entertainment Units, Household, Wood
CABINETS: Factory
CABINETS: Filing, Wood
CABINETS: Kitchen, Metal
CABINETS: Kitchen, Wood
CABINETS: Office, Metal
CABINETS: Office, Wood
CABINETS: Show, Display, Etc, Wood, Exc Refrigerated
CABINETS: Stereo, Wood

INDEX

CABLE TELEVISION
CABLE TELEVISION PRDTS
CABLE WIRING SETS: Battery, Internal Combustion Engines
CABLE: Coaxial
CABLE: Fiber
CABLE: Fiber Optic
CABLE: Nonferrous, Shipboard
CABLE: Noninsulated
CABLE: Ropes & Fiber
CABLE: Steel, Insulated Or Armored
CABS: Indl Trucks & Tractors
CAFES
CAGES: Wire
CALCULATING & ACCOUNTING EQPT
CALENDARS: Framed
CALIBRATING SVCS, NEC
CALIPERS & DIVIDERS
CALLIGRAPHER
CAMERA & PHOTOGRAPHIC SPLYS STORES
CAMERA & PHOTOGRAPHIC SPLYS STORES: Cameras
CAMERA & PHOTOGRAPHIC SPLYS STORES: Photo-
  graphic Splys
CAMERAS & RELATED EQPT: Photographic
CANDLE SHOPS
CANDLES
CANDLES: Wholesalers
CANDY & CONFECTIONS: Candy Bars, Including Chocolate
  Covered
CANDY & CONFECTIONS: Chocolate Candy, Exc Solid
  Chocolate
CANDY & CONFECTIONS: Chocolate Covered Dates
CANDY & CONFECTIONS: Fudge
CANDY & CONFECTIONS: Licorice
CANDY & CONFECTIONS: Nuts, Candy Covered
CANDY & CONFECTIONS: Popcorn Balls/Other Trtd Popcorn
  Prdts
CANDY, NUT & CONFECTIONERY STORES: Candy
CANDY, NUT & CONFECTIONERY STORES: Confectionery
CANDY, NUT & CONFECTIONERY STORES: Nuts
CANDY, NUT & CONFECTIONERY STORES: Produced For
  Direct Sale
CANDY: Chocolate From Cacao Beans
CANDY: Hard
CANDY: Soft
CANNED SPECIALTIES
CANOE BUILDING & REPAIR
CANS & TUBES: Ammunition, Board Laminated With Metal
  Foil
CANS: Aluminum
CANS: Beer, Metal
CANS: Composite Foil-Fiber, Made From Purchased Materials
CANS: Garbage, Stamped Or Pressed Metal
CANS: Metal
CANS: Tin
CANVAS PRDTS
CANVAS PRDTS: Convertible Tops, Car/Boat, Fm Purchased
  Mtrl
CAPACITORS & CONDENSERS
CAPACITORS: Fixed Or Variable
CAPACITORS: NEC
CAPS & TOPS: Bottle, Stamped Metal
CAPS: Plastic
CAR LOADING SVCS
CAR WASH EQPT
CAR WASH EQPT & SPLYS WHOLESALERS
CAR WASHES
CARBIDES
CARBON & GRAPHITE PRDTS, NEC
CARBON BLACK
CARBON PAPER & INKED RIBBONS
CARBON SPECIALTIES Electrical Use
CARBONS: Electric
CARDIOVASCULAR SYSTEM DRUGS, EXC DIAGNOSTIC
CARDS: Greeting
CARDS: Identification
CARPET & RUG CLEANING & REPAIRING PLANTS
CARPET & UPHOLSTERY CLEANING SVCS
CARPETS, RUGS & FLOOR COVERING
CARPETS: Hand & Machine Made
CARPETS: Wilton
CARPORTS: Prefabricated Metal
CARRIAGES: Horse Drawn
CARRIERS: Infant, Textile
CARTONS: Egg, Molded Pulp, Made From Purchased Materi-
  als
CARTS: Grocery

CASEMENTS: Aluminum
CASES, WOOD
CASES: Attache'
CASES: Carrying
CASES: Carrying, Clothing & Apparel
CASES: Nonrefrigerated, Exc Wood
CASES: Packing, Nailed Or Lock Corner, Wood
CASES: Plastic
CASES: Shipping, Nailed Or Lock Corner, Wood
CASH REGISTER REPAIR SVCS
CASINGS: Storage, Missile & Missile Components
CASKETS & ACCESS
CASKETS WHOLESALERS
CAST STONE: Concrete
CASTERS
CASTINGS GRINDING: For The Trade
CASTINGS: Aerospace Investment, Ferrous
CASTINGS: Aerospace, Aluminum
CASTINGS: Aerospace, Nonferrous, Exc Aluminum
CASTINGS: Aluminum
CASTINGS: Brass, Bronze & Copper
CASTINGS: Brass, NEC, Exc Die
CASTINGS: Bronze, NEC, Exc Die
CASTINGS: Commercial Investment, Ferrous
CASTINGS: Copper & Copper-Base Alloy, NEC, Exc Die
CASTINGS: Die, Aluminum
CASTINGS: Die, Copper & Copper Alloy
CASTINGS: Die, Nonferrous
CASTINGS: Die, Zinc
CASTINGS: Ductile
CASTINGS: Gray Iron
CASTINGS: Machinery, Aluminum
CASTINGS: Machinery, Brass
CASTINGS: Machinery, Nonferrous, Exc Die or Aluminum
  Copper
CASTINGS: Precision
CASTINGS: Steel
CASTINGS: Titanium
CASTINGS: Zinc
CATALOG & MAIL-ORDER HOUSES
CATALOG SALES
CATALOG SHOWROOMS
CATALYSTS: Chemical
CATERERS
CATTLE WHOLESALERS
CAULKING COMPOUNDS
CEILING SYSTEMS: Luminous, Commercial
CEMENT & CONCRETE RELATED PRDTS & EQPT: Bitumi-
  nous
CEMENT ROCK: Crushed & Broken
CEMENT, EXC LINOLEUM & TILE
CEMENT: High Temperature, Refractory, Nonclay
CEMENT: Hydraulic
CEMENT: Masonry
CEMENT: Natural
CEMENT: Portland
CEMETERIES: Real Estate Operation
CEMETERY ASSOCIATION
CEMETERY MEMORIAL DEALERS
CERAMIC FIBER
CERAMIC FLOOR & WALL TILE WHOLESALERS
CERAMIC SCHOOLS
CHAIN: Tire, Made From Purchased Wire
CHAIN: Wire
CHALK MINING: Crushed & Broken
CHANDELIERS: Commercial
CHANGE MAKING MACHINES
CHARCOAL
CHARCOAL: Activated
CHART & GRAPH DESIGN SVCS
CHASSIS: Automobile Trailer
CHASSIS: Motor Vehicle
CHASSIS: Travel Trailer
CHECK CASHING SVCS
CHEESE WHOLESALERS
CHEESECLOTH
CHEMICAL CLEANING SVCS
CHEMICAL ELEMENTS
CHEMICAL PROCESSING MACHINERY & EQPT
CHEMICAL SPLYS FOR FOUNDRIES
CHEMICALS & ALLIED PRDTS WHOLESALERS, NEC
CHEMICALS & ALLIED PRDTS, WHOL: Chemical, Organic,
  Synthetic
CHEMICALS & ALLIED PRDTS, WHOL: Noncorrosive
  Prdts/Matls
CHEMICALS & ALLIED PRDTS, WHOLESALE: Adhesives

CHEMICALS & ALLIED PRDTS, WHOLESALE: Aerosols
CHEMICALS & ALLIED PRDTS, WHOLESALE: Alcohols
CHEMICALS & ALLIED PRDTS, WHOLESALE: Alkalines &
  Chlorine
CHEMICALS & ALLIED PRDTS, WHOLESALE: Anti-Corro-
  sion Prdts
CHEMICALS & ALLIED PRDTS, WHOLESALE: Aromatic
CHEMICALS & ALLIED PRDTS, WHOLESALE: Calcium
  Chloride
CHEMICALS & ALLIED PRDTS, WHOLESALE: Carbon Black
CHEMICALS & ALLIED PRDTS, WHOLESALE: Chemical Ad-
  ditives
CHEMICALS & ALLIED PRDTS, WHOLESALE: Chemicals,
  Indl
CHEMICALS & ALLIED PRDTS, WHOLESALE: Chemicals,
  Indl & Heavy
CHEMICALS & ALLIED PRDTS, WHOLESALE: Concrete Ad-
  ditives
CHEMICALS & ALLIED PRDTS, WHOLESALE: Indl Gases
CHEMICALS & ALLIED PRDTS, WHOLESALE: Plastics Film
CHEMICALS & ALLIED PRDTS, WHOLESALE: Plastics Ma-
  terials, NEC
CHEMICALS & ALLIED PRDTS, WHOLESALE: Plastics
  Prdts, NEC
CHEMICALS & ALLIED PRDTS, WHOLESALE: Plastics
  Sheets & Rods
CHEMICALS & ALLIED PRDTS, WHOLESALE: Plastics,
  Basic Shapes
CHEMICALS & ALLIED PRDTS, WHOLESALE: Polyurethane
  Prdts
CHEMICALS & ALLIED PRDTS, WHOLESALE: Resins
CHEMICALS & ALLIED PRDTS, WHOLESALE: Resins, Plas-
  tics
CHEMICALS & ALLIED PRDTS, WHOLESALE: Spec
  Clean/Sanitation
CHEMICALS & ALLIED PRDTS, WHOLESALE: Syn Resin,
  Rub/Plastic
CHEMICALS & ALLIED PRDTS, WHOLESALE: Waxes, Exc
  Petroleum
CHEMICALS & OTHER PRDTS DERIVED FROM COKING
CHEMICALS, AGRICULTURE: Wholesalers
CHEMICALS: Agricultural
CHEMICALS: Alkali Metals, Lithium, Cesium, Francium/Rubid-
  ium
CHEMICALS: Aluminum Oxide
CHEMICALS: Aluminum Sulfate
CHEMICALS: Bauxite, Refined
CHEMICALS: Bleaching Powder, Lime Bleaching Compounds
CHEMICALS: Brine
CHEMICALS: Calcium & Calcium Compounds
CHEMICALS: Calcium Chloride
CHEMICALS: Chromates & Bichromates
CHEMICALS: Cyanides
CHEMICALS: Fire Retardant
CHEMICALS: Fuel Tank Or Engine Cleaning
CHEMICALS: High Purity Grade, Organic
CHEMICALS: High Purity, Refined From Technical Grade
CHEMICALS: Hydrogen Peroxide
CHEMICALS: Inorganic, NEC
CHEMICALS: Lithium Compounds, Inorganic
CHEMICALS: Magnesium Compounds Or Salts, Inorganic
CHEMICALS: Medicinal
CHEMICALS: Medicinal, Organic, Uncompounded, Bulk
CHEMICALS: Mercury, Redistilled
CHEMICALS: NEC
CHEMICALS: Nonmetallic Compounds
CHEMICALS: Organic, NEC
CHEMICALS: Phenol
CHEMICALS: Phosphates, Defluorinated/Ammoniated, Exc
  Fertlr
CHEMICALS: Reagent Grade, Refined From Technical Grade
CHEMICALS: Silica Compounds
CHEMICALS: Soda Ash
CHEMICALS: Sodium Bicarbonate
CHEMICALS: Sodium Silicate
CHEMICALS: Sodium/Potassium Cmpnds,Exc Bleach,Alka-
  lies/Alum
CHEMICALS: Sulfur, Incl Rcvrd/Refined, Fm Sour Natural Gas
CHEMICALS: Tin, Stannic/Stannous, Compounds/Salts, Inor-
  ganic
CHEMICALS: Water Treatment
CHESTS: Bank, Metal
CHICKEN SLAUGHTERING & PROCESSING
CHILD DAY CARE SVCS
CHINA & GLASS REPAIR SVCS
CHINA & GLASS: Decalcomania Work

CHINA: Fired & Decorated
CHINAWARE STORES
CHINAWARE WHOLESALERS
CHIROPRACTORS' OFFICES
CHLORINE
CHOCOLATE, EXC CANDY FROM BEANS: Chips, Powder, Block, Syrup
CHOCOLATE, EXC CANDY FROM PURCH CHOC: Chips, Powder, Block
CHRISTMAS NOVELTIES, WHOLESALE
CHRISTMAS TREE LIGHTING SETS: Electric
CHRISTMAS TREES WHOLESALERS
CHROMATOGRAPHY EQPT
CHRONOGRAPHS, SPRING WOUND
CHUTES & TROUGHS
CHUTES: Coal, Sheet Metal, Prefabricated
CIGARETTE & CIGAR PRDTS & ACCESS
CIGARETTE LIGHTERS
CIGARETTE STORES
CIRCUIT BOARDS, PRINTED: Television & Radio
CIRCUIT BOARDS: Wiring
CIRCUIT BREAKERS
CIRCUIT BREAKERS: Air
CIRCUITS: Electronic
CIRCULAR KNIT FABRICS DYEING & FINISHING
CIVIL SVCS TRAINING SCHOOL
CLAIMS ADJUSTING SVCS
CLAMPS & COUPLINGS: Hose
CLAMPS: Metal
CLAY MINING, COMMON
CLEANERS: Boiler Tube
CLEANERS: Paintbrush
CLEANING & DESCALING SVC: Metal Prdts
CLEANING & DYEING PLANTS, EXC RUGS
CLEANING COMPOUNDS: Rifle Bore
CLEANING EQPT: Blast, Dustless
CLEANING EQPT: Commercial
CLEANING EQPT: Floor Washing & Polishing, Commercial
CLEANING EQPT: High Pressure
CLEANING OR POLISHING PREPARATIONS, NEC
CLEANING PRDTS: Ammonia, Household
CLEANING PRDTS: Degreasing Solvent
CLEANING PRDTS: Deodorants, Nonpersonal
CLEANING PRDTS: Dusting Cloths, Chemically Treated
CLEANING PRDTS: Floor Waxes
CLEANING PRDTS: Laundry Preparations
CLEANING PRDTS: Paint & Wallpaper
CLEANING PRDTS: Polishing Preparations & Related Prdts
CLEANING PRDTS: Sanitation Preparations
CLEANING PRDTS: Sanitation Preps, Disinfectants/Deodorants
CLEANING PRDTS: Shoe Polish Or Cleaner
CLEANING PRDTS: Specialty
CLEANING PRDTS: Window Cleaning Preparations
CLEANING SVCS
CLEANING SVCS: Industrial Or Commercial
CLIPS & FASTENERS, MADE FROM PURCHASED WIRE
CLOSURES: Closures, Stamped Metal
CLOSURES: Plastic
CLOTHING & ACCESS, WOMEN, CHILD & INFANT, WHOL: Scarves
CLOTHING & ACCESS, WOMEN, CHILD & INFANT, WHSLE: Sportswear
CLOTHING & ACCESS, WOMEN, CHILDREN & INFANT, WHOL: Handbags
CLOTHING & ACCESS, WOMEN, CHILDREN & INFANT, WHOL: Sweaters
CLOTHING & ACCESS, WOMEN, CHILDREN & INFANT, WHOL: Uniforms
CLOTHING & ACCESS, WOMEN, CHILDREN/INFANT, WHOL: Outerwear
CLOTHING & ACCESS, WOMEN, CHILDREN/INFANT, WHOL: Underwear
CLOTHING & ACCESS: Costumes, Masquerade
CLOTHING & ACCESS: Costumes, Theatrical
CLOTHING & ACCESS: Handicapped
CLOTHING & ACCESS: Men's Miscellaneous Access
CLOTHING & ACCESS: Regalia
CLOTHING & APPAREL STORES: Custom
CLOTHING & FURNISHINGS, MEN'S & BOYS', WHOLE-SALE: Caps
CLOTHING & FURNISHINGS, MEN'S & BOYS', WHOLE-SALE: Coats
CLOTHING & FURNISHINGS, MEN'S & BOYS', WHOLE-SALE: Gloves

CLOTHING & FURNISHINGS, MEN'S & BOYS', WHOLE-SALE: Hats
CLOTHING & FURNISHINGS, MEN'S & BOYS', WHOLE-SALE: Shirts
CLOTHING & FURNISHINGS, MEN'S & BOYS', WHOLE-SALE: Sweaters
CLOTHING & FURNISHINGS, MEN'S & BOYS', WHOLE-SALE: Uniforms
CLOTHING & FURNISHINGS, MENS & BOYS, WHOL: Sportswear/Work
CLOTHING & FURNISHINGS, MENS & BOYS, WHOLE-SALE: Lined
CLOTHING STORES, NEC
CLOTHING STORES: Caps & Gowns
CLOTHING STORES: Designer Apparel
CLOTHING STORES: Dresses, Knit, Made To Order
CLOTHING STORES: Formal Wear
CLOTHING STORES: Leather
CLOTHING STORES: Shirts, Custom Made
CLOTHING STORES: T-Shirts, Printed, Custom
CLOTHING STORES: Uniforms & Work
CLOTHING STORES: Unisex
CLOTHING: Access
CLOTHING: Access, Women's & Misses'
CLOTHING: Aprons, Harness
CLOTHING: Aprons, Work, Exc Rubberized & Plastic, Men's
CLOTHING: Athletic & Sportswear, Men's & Boys'
CLOTHING: Athletic & Sportswear, Women's & Girls'
CLOTHING: Blouses, Women's & Girls'
CLOTHING: Blouses, Womens & Juniors, From Purchased Mtrls
CLOTHING: Brassieres
CLOTHING: Bridal Gowns
CLOTHING: Burial
CLOTHING: Capes & Jackets, Women's & Misses'
CLOTHING: Children & Infants'
CLOTHING: Children's, Girls'
CLOTHING: Coats & Jackets, Leather & Sheep-Lined
CLOTHING: Coats & Suits, Men's & Boys'
CLOTHING: Coats, Hunting & Vests, Men's
CLOTHING: Coats, Leatherette, Oiled Fabric, Etc, Mens & Boys
CLOTHING: Coats, Tailored, Mens/Boys, From Purchased Mtls
CLOTHING: Costumes
CLOTHING: Disposable
CLOTHING: Dresses
CLOTHING: Foundation Garments, Women's
CLOTHING: Garments, Indl, Men's & Boys
CLOTHING: Gloves & Mittens, Knit
CLOTHING: Gowns & Dresses, Wedding
CLOTHING: Hats & Caps, NEC
CLOTHING: Hats & Caps, Uniform
CLOTHING: Hats, Harvest, Straw
CLOTHING: Hosiery, Pantyhose & Knee Length, Sheer
CLOTHING: Hospital, Men's
CLOTHING: Jackets, Field, Military
CLOTHING: Jogging & Warm-Up Suits, Knit
CLOTHING: Knit Underwear & Nightwear
CLOTHING: Leather
CLOTHING: Maternity
CLOTHING: Men's & boy's underwear & nightwear
CLOTHING: Neckwear
CLOTHING: Outerwear, Knit
CLOTHING: Outerwear, Lthr, Wool/Down-Filled, Men, Youth/Boy
CLOTHING: Outerwear, Women's & Misses' NEC
CLOTHING: Overcoats & Topcoats, Men/Boy, Purchased Materials
CLOTHING: Pants, Work, Men's, Youths' & Boys'
CLOTHING: Raincoats, Exc Vulcanized Rubber, Purchased Matls
CLOTHING: Robes & Dressing Gowns
CLOTHING: Rubber, Vulcanized Or Rubberized Fabric
CLOTHING: Sheep-Lined
CLOTHING: Shirts
CLOTHING: Shirts & T-Shirts, Knit
CLOTHING: Shirts, Dress, Men's & Boys'
CLOTHING: Shirts, Sports & Polo, Men & Boy, Purchased Mtrl
CLOTHING: Shirts, Sports & Polo, Men's & Boys'
CLOTHING: Shirts, Uniform, From Purchased Materials
CLOTHING: Shirts, Women's & Juniors', From Purchased Mtrls
CLOTHING: Skirts
CLOTHING: Slacks & Shorts, Dress, Men's, Youths' & Boys'
CLOTHING: Socks

CLOTHING: Sportswear, Women's
CLOTHING: Suits, Men's & Boys', From Purchased Materials
CLOTHING: Sweaters & Sweater Coats, Knit
CLOTHING: Sweaters, Men's & Boys'
CLOTHING: Sweatshirts & T-Shirts, Men's & Boys'
CLOTHING: Swimwear, Men's & Boys'
CLOTHING: Swimwear, Women's & Misses'
CLOTHING: T-Shirts & Tops, Knit
CLOTHING: T-Shirts & Tops, Women's & Girls'
CLOTHING: Tailored Dress/Sport Coats, Mens & Boys
CLOTHING: Tailored Suits & Formal Jackets
CLOTHING: Ties, Neck & Bow, Men's & Boys'
CLOTHING: Trousers & Slacks, Men's & Boys'
CLOTHING: Tuxedos, From Purchased Materials
CLOTHING: Underwear, Knit
CLOTHING: Underwear, Women's & Children's
CLOTHING: Uniforms & Vestments
CLOTHING: Uniforms, Ex Athletic, Women's, Misses' & Juniors'
CLOTHING: Uniforms, Men's & Boys'
CLOTHING: Uniforms, Policemen's, From Purchased Materials
CLOTHING: Uniforms, Team Athletic
CLOTHING: Uniforms, Work
CLOTHING: Vests
CLOTHING: WarmUp, Jogging & Sweat Suits, Girls' & Children's
CLOTHING: Waterproof Outerwear
CLOTHING: Work Apparel, Exc Uniforms
CLOTHING: Work, Men's
CLOTHS: Dish, Textile, Nonwoven, From Purchased Materials
CLOTHS: Dust, Made From Purchased Materials
COAL & OTHER MINERALS & ORES WHOLESALERS
COAL LIQUEFACTION
COAL MINING EXPLORATION & TEST BORING SVC
COAL MINING EXPLORATION SVCS: Bituminous Or Lignite
COAL MINING SERVICES
COAL MINING SVCS: Bituminous, Contract Basis
COAL MINING: Anthracite
COAL MINING: Anthracite, Strip
COAL MINING: Anthracite, Underground
COAL MINING: Bituminous & Lignite Surface
COAL MINING: Bituminous Coal & Lignite-Surface Mining
COAL MINING: Bituminous Underground
COAL MINING: Bituminous, Auger
COAL MINING: Bituminous, Strip
COAL MINING: Bituminous, Surface, NEC
COAL MINING: Lignite, Strip
COAL MINING: Underground, Subbituminous
COAL PREPARATION PLANT: Bituminous or Lignite
COAL TAR PRDTS
COAL, MINERALS & ORES, WHOLESALE: Coal
COAL, MINERALS & ORES, WHOLESALE: Coal & Coke
COATED OR PLATED PRDTS
COATING COMPOUNDS: Tar
COATING OR WRAPPING SVC: Steel Pipe
COATING SVC
COATING SVC: Aluminum, Metal Prdts
COATING SVC: Hot Dip, Metals Or Formed Prdts
COATING SVC: Metals & Formed Prdts
COATING SVC: Metals, With Plastic Or Resins
COATING SVC: Rust Preventative
COATINGS: Epoxy
COATINGS: Polyurethane
COCKTAIL LOUNGE
COFFEE SVCS
COILS & TRANSFORMERS
COILS: Electric Motors Or Generators
COILS: Pipe
COIN COUNTERS
COIN OPERATED LAUNDRIES & DRYCLEANERS
COIN-OPERATED LAUNDRY
COKE: Petroleum
COKE: Produced In Chemical Recovery Coke Ovens
COLD REMEDIES
COLLATING MACHINES:Printing Or Bindery
COLOR LAKES OR TONERS
COLOR PIGMENTS
COLORING & FINISHING SVC: Aluminum Or Formed Prdts
COLORS: Pigments, Inorganic
COLORS: Pigments, Organic
COLUMNS, FRACTIONING: Metal Plate
COMB MOUNTINGS
COMBINATION UTILITIES, NEC
COMBS, EXC HARD RUBBER

COMFORTERS & QUILTS, FROM MANMADE FIBER OR SILK
COMMERCIAL & INDL SHELVING WHOLESALERS
COMMERCIAL & LITERARY WRITINGS
COMMERCIAL & OFFICE BUILDINGS RENOVATION & REPAIR
COMMERCIAL ART & GRAPHIC DESIGN SVCS
COMMERCIAL ART & ILLUSTRATION SVCS
COMMERCIAL CONTAINERS WHOLESALERS
COMMERCIAL EQPT & SPLYS, WHOLESALE: Hotel
COMMERCIAL EQPT WHOLESALERS, NEC
COMMERCIAL EQPT, WHOLESALE: Bakery Eqpt & Splys
COMMERCIAL EQPT, WHOLESALE: Comm Cooking & Food Svc Eqpt
COMMERCIAL EQPT, WHOLESALE: Parking Meters
COMMERCIAL EQPT, WHOLESALE: Restaurant, NEC
COMMERCIAL EQPT, WHOLESALE: Scales, Exc Laboratory
COMMERCIAL EQPT, WHOLESALE: Store Fixtures & Display Eqpt
COMMERCIAL PHOTOGRAPHIC STUDIO
COMMERCIAL PRINTING & NEWSPAPER PUBLISHING COMBINED
COMMODITY INVESTORS
COMMON SAND MINING
COMMUNICATION HEADGEAR: Telephone
COMMUNICATIONS CARRIER: Wired
COMMUNICATIONS EQPT & SYSTEMS, NEC
COMMUNICATIONS EQPT REPAIR & MAINTENANCE
COMMUNICATIONS EQPT WHOLESALERS
COMMUNICATIONS EQPT: Microwave
COMMUNICATIONS SVCS
COMMUNICATIONS SVCS: Cellular
COMMUNICATIONS SVCS: Data
COMMUNICATIONS SVCS: Facsimile Transmission
COMMUNICATIONS SVCS: Internet Connectivity Svcs
COMMUNICATIONS SVCS: Internet Host Svcs
COMMUNICATIONS SVCS: Online Svc Providers
COMMUNICATIONS SVCS: Signal Enhancement Network Svcs
COMMUNICATIONS SVCS: Telephone, Data
COMMUNICATIONS SVCS: Telephone, Local
COMMUNICATIONS SVCS: Telephone, Local & Long Distance
COMMUNITY CENTERS: Adult
COMMUNITY CENTERS: Youth
COMMUNITY DEVELOPMENT GROUPS
COMMUTATORS: Electronic
COMPACT DISCS OR CD'S, WHOLESALE
COMPACT LASER DISCS: Prerecorded
COMPACTORS: Trash & Garbage, Residential
COMPOST
COMPRESSORS, AIR CONDITIONING: Wholesalers
COMPRESSORS: Air & Gas
COMPRESSORS: Air & Gas, Including Vacuum Pumps
COMPRESSORS: Refrigeration & Air Conditioning Eqpt
COMPRESSORS: Repairing
COMPRESSORS: Wholesalers
COMPUTER & COMPUTER SOFTWARE STORES
COMPUTER & COMPUTER SOFTWARE STORES: Peripheral Eqpt
COMPUTER & COMPUTER SOFTWARE STORES: Personal Computers
COMPUTER & COMPUTER SOFTWARE STORES: Printers & Plotters
COMPUTER & COMPUTER SOFTWARE STORES: Software & Access
COMPUTER & COMPUTER SOFTWARE STORES: Software, Bus/Non-Game
COMPUTER & COMPUTER SOFTWARE STORES: Software, Computer Game
COMPUTER & DATA PROCESSING EQPT REPAIR & MAINTENANCE
COMPUTER & OFFICE MACHINE MAINTENANCE & REPAIR
COMPUTER & SFTWR STORE: Modem, Monitor, Terminal/Disk Drive
COMPUTER FACILITIES MANAGEMENT SVCS
COMPUTER FORMS
COMPUTER GRAPHICS SVCS
COMPUTER INTERFACE EQPT: Indl Process
COMPUTER PAPER TAPE EQPT: Punches, Readers, Etc
COMPUTER PAPER WHOLESALERS
COMPUTER PERIPHERAL EQPT REPAIR & MAINTENANCE
COMPUTER PERIPHERAL EQPT, NEC
COMPUTER PERIPHERAL EQPT, WHOLESALE

COMPUTER PERIPHERAL EQPT: Decoders
COMPUTER PERIPHERAL EQPT: Encoders
COMPUTER PERIPHERAL EQPT: Graphic Displays, Exc Terminals
COMPUTER PERIPHERAL EQPT: Input Or Output
COMPUTER PERIPHERAL EQPT: Output To Microfilm Units
COMPUTER PHOTOGRAPHY OR PORTRAIT SVC
COMPUTER PLOTTERS
COMPUTER PROCESSING SVCS
COMPUTER PROGRAMMING SVCS
COMPUTER PROGRAMMING SVCS: Custom
COMPUTER RELATED MAINTENANCE SVCS
COMPUTER SERVICE BUREAU
COMPUTER SOFTWARE DEVELOPMENT
COMPUTER SOFTWARE DEVELOPMENT & APPLICATIONS
COMPUTER SOFTWARE SYSTEMS ANALYSIS & DESIGN: Custom
COMPUTER SOFTWARE WRITERS
COMPUTER SOFTWARE WRITERS: Freelance
COMPUTER STORAGE DEVICES, NEC
COMPUTER STORAGE UNITS: Auxiliary
COMPUTER SYSTEM SELLING SVCS
COMPUTER SYSTEMS ANALYSIS & DESIGN
COMPUTER TERMINALS
COMPUTER-AIDED DESIGN SYSTEMS SVCS
COMPUTER-AIDED MANUFACTURING SYSTEMS SVCS
COMPUTERS, NEC
COMPUTERS, NEC, WHOLESALE
COMPUTERS, PERIPH & SOFTWARE, WHLSE: Personal & Home Entrtn
COMPUTERS, PERIPHERALS & SOFTWARE, WHOLESALE: Printers
COMPUTERS, PERIPHERALS & SOFTWARE, WHOLESALE: Software
COMPUTERS, PERIPHERALS & SOFTWARE, WHOLESALE: Terminals
COMPUTERS: Indl, Process, Gas Flow
COMPUTERS: Mainframe
COMPUTERS: Personal
CONCENTRATES, DRINK
CONCRETE BUILDING PRDTS WHOLESALERS
CONCRETE CURING & HARDENING COMPOUNDS
CONCRETE MIXERS
CONCRETE PLANTS
CONCRETE PRDTS
CONCRETE PRDTS, PRECAST, NEC
CONCRETE REINFORCING MATERIAL
CONCRETE: Asphaltic, Not From Refineries
CONCRETE: Bituminous
CONCRETE: Dry Mixture
CONCRETE: Ready-Mixed
CONDENSERS & CONDENSING UNITS: Air Conditioner
CONDENSERS: Heat Transfer Eqpt, Evaporative
CONDENSERS: Steam
CONDUITS & FITTINGS: Electric
CONFECTIONERY PRDTS WHOLESALERS
CONFECTIONS & CANDY
CONNECTORS & TERMINALS: Electrical Device Uses
CONNECTORS: Cord, Electric
CONNECTORS: Electrical
CONNECTORS: Electronic
CONSTRUCTION & MINING MACHINERY WHOLESALERS
CONSTRUCTION EQPT REPAIR SVCS
CONSTRUCTION EQPT: Airport
CONSTRUCTION EQPT: Attachments
CONSTRUCTION EQPT: Attachments, Snow Plow
CONSTRUCTION EQPT: Backhoes, Tractors, Cranes & Similar Eqpt
CONSTRUCTION EQPT: Blade, Grader, Scraper, Dozer/Snow Plow
CONSTRUCTION EQPT: Buckets, Excavating, Clamshell, Etc
CONSTRUCTION EQPT: Crane Carriers
CONSTRUCTION EQPT: Cranes
CONSTRUCTION EQPT: Hammer Mills, Port, Incl Rock/Ore Crush
CONSTRUCTION EQPT: Rakes, Land Clearing, Mechanical
CONSTRUCTION EQPT: Roofing Eqpt
CONSTRUCTION EQPT: SCRAPERS, GRADERS, ROLLERS & SIMILAR EQPT
CONSTRUCTION EQPT: Spreaders, Aggregates
CONSTRUCTION EQPT: Tractors
CONSTRUCTION EQPT: Trucks, Off-Highway
CONSTRUCTION EQPT: Wrecker Hoists, Automobile
CONSTRUCTION MATERIALS, WHOL: Concrete/Cinder Bldg Prdts

CONSTRUCTION MATERIALS, WHOLESALE: Aggregate
CONSTRUCTION MATERIALS, WHOLESALE: Architectural Metalwork
CONSTRUCTION MATERIALS, WHOLESALE: Asphalt Felts & coating
CONSTRUCTION MATERIALS, WHOLESALE: Awnings
CONSTRUCTION MATERIALS, WHOLESALE: Block, Concrete & Cinder
CONSTRUCTION MATERIALS, WHOLESALE: Blocks, Building, NEC
CONSTRUCTION MATERIALS, WHOLESALE: Brick, Exc Refractory
CONSTRUCTION MATERIALS, WHOLESALE: Building Stone
CONSTRUCTION MATERIALS, WHOLESALE: Building Stone, Granite
CONSTRUCTION MATERIALS, WHOLESALE: Building Stone, Marble
CONSTRUCTION MATERIALS, WHOLESALE: Building, Exterior
CONSTRUCTION MATERIALS, WHOLESALE: Building, Interior
CONSTRUCTION MATERIALS, WHOLESALE: Cement
CONSTRUCTION MATERIALS, WHOLESALE: Concrete Mixtures
CONSTRUCTION MATERIALS, WHOLESALE: Door Frames
CONSTRUCTION MATERIALS, WHOLESALE: Fiberglass Building Mat
CONSTRUCTION MATERIALS, WHOLESALE: Glass
CONSTRUCTION MATERIALS, WHOLESALE: Guardrails, Metal
CONSTRUCTION MATERIALS, WHOLESALE: Hardboard
CONSTRUCTION MATERIALS, WHOLESALE: Limestone
CONSTRUCTION MATERIALS, WHOLESALE: Metal Buildings
CONSTRUCTION MATERIALS, WHOLESALE: Millwork
CONSTRUCTION MATERIALS, WHOLESALE: Pallets, Wood
CONSTRUCTION MATERIALS, WHOLESALE: Paneling, Wood
CONSTRUCTION MATERIALS, WHOLESALE: Paving Materials
CONSTRUCTION MATERIALS, WHOLESALE: Paving Mixtures
CONSTRUCTION MATERIALS, WHOLESALE: Plastering Materials
CONSTRUCTION MATERIALS, WHOLESALE: Prefabricated Structures
CONSTRUCTION MATERIALS, WHOLESALE: Roof, Asphalt/Sheet Metal
CONSTRUCTION MATERIALS, WHOLESALE: Roofing & Siding Material
CONSTRUCTION MATERIALS, WHOLESALE: Sand
CONSTRUCTION MATERIALS, WHOLESALE: Septic Tanks
CONSTRUCTION MATERIALS, WHOLESALE: Siding, Exc Wood
CONSTRUCTION MATERIALS, WHOLESALE: Stone, Crushed Or Broken
CONSTRUCTION MATERIALS, WHOLESALE: Stucco
CONSTRUCTION MATERIALS, WHOLESALE: Tile & Clay Prdts
CONSTRUCTION MATERIALS, WHOLESALE: Tile, Clay/Other Ceramic
CONSTRUCTION MATERIALS, WHOLESALE: Trim, Sheet Metal
CONSTRUCTION MATERIALS, WHOLESALE: Veneer
CONSTRUCTION MATERIALS, WHOLESALE: Windows
CONSTRUCTION MATLS, WHOL: Composite Board Prdts, Woodboard
CONSTRUCTION MATLS, WHOL: Lumber, Rough, Dressed/Finished
CONSTRUCTION MATLS, WHOLESALE: Soil Erosion Cntrl Fabrics
CONSTRUCTION MATLS, WHOLESALE: Struct Assy, Prefab, NonWood
CONSTRUCTION MTRLS, WHOL: Exterior Flat Glass, Plate/Window
CONSTRUCTION MTRLS, WHOL: Interior Flat Glass, Plate/Window
CONSTRUCTION SAND MINING
CONSTRUCTION SITE PREPARATION SVCS
CONSTRUCTION: Agricultural Building
CONSTRUCTION: Athletic & Recreation Facilities
CONSTRUCTION: Athletic & Recreation Facilities
CONSTRUCTION: Bridge
CONSTRUCTION: Commercial & Institutional Building
CONSTRUCTION: Commercial & Office Building, New

CONSTRUCTION: Dams, Waterways, Docks & Other Marine
CONSTRUCTION: Drainage System
CONSTRUCTION: Electric Power Line
CONSTRUCTION: Farm Building
CONSTRUCTION: Foundation & Retaining Wall
CONSTRUCTION: Guardrails, Highway
CONSTRUCTION: Heavy Highway & Street
CONSTRUCTION: Indl Building & Warehouse
CONSTRUCTION: Indl Building, Prefabricated
CONSTRUCTION: Indl Buildings, New, NEC
CONSTRUCTION: Indl Plant
CONSTRUCTION: Irrigation System
CONSTRUCTION: Land Preparation
CONSTRUCTION: Manhole
CONSTRUCTION: Marine
CONSTRUCTION: Mausoleum
CONSTRUCTION: Natural Gas Compressor Station
CONSTRUCTION: Nonresidential Buildings, Custom
CONSTRUCTION: Oil & Gas Pipeline Construction
CONSTRUCTION: Parking Lot
CONSTRUCTION: Pipeline, NEC
CONSTRUCTION: Power & Communication Transmission
  Tower
CONSTRUCTION: Railroad & Subway
CONSTRUCTION: Refineries
CONSTRUCTION: Residential, Nec
CONSTRUCTION: Roads, Gravel or Dirt
CONSTRUCTION: School Building
CONSTRUCTION: Sewer Line
CONSTRUCTION: Single-Family Housing
CONSTRUCTION: Single-family Housing, New
CONSTRUCTION: Stadium
CONSTRUCTION: Steel Buildings
CONSTRUCTION: Street Surfacing & Paving
CONSTRUCTION: Svc Station
CONSTRUCTION: Transmitting Tower, Telecommunication
CONSTRUCTION: Truck & Automobile Assembly Plant
CONSTRUCTION: Utility Line
CONSTRUCTION: Waste Disposal Plant
CONSTRUCTION: Water & Sewer Line
CONSTRUCTION: Water Main
CONSULTING SVC: Business, NEC
CONSULTING SVC: Chemical
CONSULTING SVC: Computer
CONSULTING SVC: Educational
CONSULTING SVC: Engineering
CONSULTING SVC: Executive Placement & Search
CONSULTING SVC: Financial Management
CONSULTING SVC: Management
CONSULTING SVC: Marketing Management
CONSULTING SVC: Online Technology
CONSULTING SVC: Sales Management
CONSULTING SVC: Telecommunications
CONSULTING SVCS, BUSINESS: Environmental
CONSULTING SVCS, BUSINESS: Indl Development Planning
CONSULTING SVCS, BUSINESS: Lighting
CONSULTING SVCS, BUSINESS: Publishing
CONSULTING SVCS, BUSINESS: Safety Training Svcs
CONSULTING SVCS, BUSINESS: Sys Engnrg, Exc Com-
  puter/Prof
CONSULTING SVCS, BUSINESS: Systems Analysis & Engi-
  neering
CONSULTING SVCS, BUSINESS: Systems Analysis Or De-
  sign
CONSULTING SVCS, BUSINESS: Testing, Educational Or
  Personnel
CONSULTING SVCS, BUSINESS: Traffic
CONSULTING SVCS: Geological
CONSULTING SVCS: Nuclear
CONSULTING SVCS: Oil
CONSULTING SVCS: Scientific
CONSUMER ELECTRONICS STORE: Video & Disc
  Recorder/Player
CONTACT LENSES
CONTACTS: Electrical
CONTAINERS, GLASS: Food
CONTAINERS, GLASS: Medicine Bottles
CONTAINERS, GLASS: Packers' Ware
CONTAINERS, GLASS: Water Bottles
CONTAINERS: Air Cargo, Metal
CONTAINERS: Cargo, Wood
CONTAINERS: Corrugated
CONTAINERS: Foil, Bakery Goods & Frozen Foods
CONTAINERS: Food & Beverage
CONTAINERS: Food, Folding, Made From Purchased Materi-
  als

CONTAINERS: Glass
CONTAINERS: Laminated Phenolic & Vulcanized Fiber
CONTAINERS: Liquid Tight Fiber, From Purchased Materials
CONTAINERS: Metal
CONTAINERS: Plastic
CONTAINERS: Plywood & Veneer, Wood
CONTAINERS: Sanitary, Food
CONTAINERS: Shipping & Mailing, Fiber
CONTAINERS: Shipping, Bombs, Metal Plate
CONTAINERS: Shipping, Wood
CONTAINERS: Wood
CONTRACT FOOD SVCS
CONTRACTOR: Framing
CONTRACTOR: Rigging & Scaffolding
CONTRACTORS: Acoustical & Ceiling Work
CONTRACTORS: Acoustical & Insulation Work
CONTRACTORS: Airwave Shielding Installation, Computer
  Rooms
CONTRACTORS: Artificial Turf Installation
CONTRACTORS: Asbestos Removal & Encapsulation
CONTRACTORS: Asphalt
CONTRACTORS: Awning Installation
CONTRACTORS: Blasting, Exc Building Demolition
CONTRACTORS: Boiler & Furnace
CONTRACTORS: Boiler Maintenance Contractor
CONTRACTORS: Boring, Building Construction
CONTRACTORS: Bowling Alley Installation & Svc
CONTRACTORS: Building Eqpt & Machinery Installation
CONTRACTORS: Building Fireproofing
CONTRACTORS: Building Sign Installation & Mntnce
CONTRACTORS: Building Site Preparation
CONTRACTORS: Cable Laying
CONTRACTORS: Caisson Drilling
CONTRACTORS: Carpentry Work
CONTRACTORS: Carpentry, Cabinet & Finish Work
CONTRACTORS: Carpentry, Cabinet Building & Installation
CONTRACTORS: Carpentry, Finish & Trim Work
CONTRACTORS: Carpet Laying
CONTRACTORS: Central Vacuum Cleaning System Installa-
  tion
CONTRACTORS: Closet Organizers, Installation & Design
CONTRACTORS: Coating, Caulking & Weather, Water & Fire
CONTRACTORS: Commercial & Office Building
CONTRACTORS: Communications Svcs
CONTRACTORS: Computerized Controls Installation
CONTRACTORS: Concrete
CONTRACTORS: Concrete Block Masonry Laying
CONTRACTORS: Concrete Breaking, Street & Highway
CONTRACTORS: Concrete Pumping
CONTRACTORS: Concrete Reinforcement Placing
CONTRACTORS: Concrete Repair
CONTRACTORS: Concrete Structure Coating, Plastic
CONTRACTORS: Corrosion Control Installation
CONTRACTORS: Countertop Installation
CONTRACTORS: Demolition, Building & Other Structures
CONTRACTORS: Directional Oil & Gas Well Drilling Svc
CONTRACTORS: Drapery Track Installation
CONTRACTORS: Driveway
CONTRACTORS: Drywall
CONTRACTORS: Earthmoving
CONTRACTORS: Electric Power Systems
CONTRACTORS: Electrical
CONTRACTORS: Electronic Controls Installation
CONTRACTORS: Excavating
CONTRACTORS: Excavating Slush Pits & Cellars Svcs
CONTRACTORS: Exterior Concrete Stucco
CONTRACTORS: Fence Construction
CONTRACTORS: Fiber Optic Cable Installation
CONTRACTORS: Fiberglass Work
CONTRACTORS: Fire Sprinkler System Installation Svcs
CONTRACTORS: Floor Laying & Other Floor Work
CONTRACTORS: Flooring
CONTRACTORS: Food Svcs Eqpt Installation
CONTRACTORS: Foundation Building
CONTRACTORS: Garage Doors
CONTRACTORS: Gas Detection & Analysis Svcs
CONTRACTORS: Gas Field Svcs, NEC
CONTRACTORS: General Electric
CONTRACTORS: Geothermal Drilling
CONTRACTORS: Glass Tinting, Architectural & Automotive
CONTRACTORS: Glass, Glazing & Tinting
CONTRACTORS: Grave Excavation
CONTRACTORS: Gutters & Downspouts
CONTRACTORS: Heating & Air Conditioning
CONTRACTORS: Heating Systems Repair & Maintenance
  Svc

CONTRACTORS: Highway & Street Construction, General
CONTRACTORS: Highway & Street Paving
CONTRACTORS: Home & Office Intrs Finish, Furnish/Re-
  model
CONTRACTORS: Hot Shot Svcs
CONTRACTORS: Hotel, Motel/Multi-Family Home
  Renovtn/Remodel
CONTRACTORS: Hydraulic Eqpt Installation & Svcs
CONTRACTORS: Hydraulic Well Fracturing Svcs
CONTRACTORS: Indl Building Renovation, Remodeling &
  Repair
CONTRACTORS: Insulation Installation, Building
CONTRACTORS: Kitchen & Bathroom Remodeling
CONTRACTORS: Kitchen Cabinet Installation
CONTRACTORS: Lighting Syst
CONTRACTORS: Lightweight Steel Framing Installation
CONTRACTORS: Machine Rigging & Moving
CONTRACTORS: Machinery Dismantling
CONTRACTORS: Machinery Installation
CONTRACTORS: Maintenance, Parking Facility Eqpt
CONTRACTORS: Mantel Work
CONTRACTORS: Marble Installation, Interior
CONTRACTORS: Masonry & Stonework
CONTRACTORS: Mechanical
CONTRACTORS: Millwrights
CONTRACTORS: Office Furniture Installation
CONTRACTORS: Oil & Gas Aerial Geophysical Exploration
  Svcs
CONTRACTORS: Oil & Gas Building, Repairing & Dismantling
  Svc
CONTRACTORS: Oil & Gas Field Fire Fighting Svcs
CONTRACTORS: Oil & Gas Field Geological Exploration
  Svcs
CONTRACTORS: Oil & Gas Field Geophysical Exploration
  Svcs
CONTRACTORS: Oil & Gas Field Salt Water Impound/Storing
  Svc
CONTRACTORS: Oil & Gas Field Tools Fishing Svcs
CONTRACTORS: Oil & Gas Well Casing Cement Svcs
CONTRACTORS: Oil & Gas Well Drilling Svc
CONTRACTORS: Oil & Gas Well Foundation Grading Svcs
CONTRACTORS: Oil & Gas Well On-Site Foundation Building
  Svcs
CONTRACTORS: Oil & Gas Well Plugging & Abandoning
  Svcs
CONTRACTORS: Oil & Gas Well reworking
CONTRACTORS: Oil & Gas Wells Pumping Svcs
CONTRACTORS: Oil & Gas Wells Svcs
CONTRACTORS: Oil Field Haulage Svcs
CONTRACTORS: Oil Field Mud Drilling Svcs
CONTRACTORS: Oil/Gas Well Construction, Rpr/Dismantling
  Svcs
CONTRACTORS: On-Site Welding
CONTRACTORS: Ornamental Metal Work
CONTRACTORS: Painting & Wall Covering
CONTRACTORS: Painting, Commercial
CONTRACTORS: Painting, Commercial, Interior
CONTRACTORS: Painting, Indl
CONTRACTORS: Painting, Residential
CONTRACTORS: Parking Lot Maintenance
CONTRACTORS: Patio & Deck Construction & Repair
CONTRACTORS: Pavement Marking
CONTRACTORS: Pipe & Boiler Insulating
CONTRACTORS: Pipe Laying
CONTRACTORS: Plastering, Plain or Ornamental
CONTRACTORS: Plumbing
CONTRACTORS: Pole Cutting
CONTRACTORS: Pollution Control Eqpt Installation
CONTRACTORS: Power Generating Eqpt Installation
CONTRACTORS: Precast Concrete Struct Framing & Panel
  Placing
CONTRACTORS: Prefabricated Window & Door Installation
CONTRACTORS: Refractory or Acid Brick Masonry
CONTRACTORS: Refrigeration
CONTRACTORS: Roofing
CONTRACTORS: Roustabout Svcs
CONTRACTORS: Safety & Security Eqpt
CONTRACTORS: Sandblasting Svc, Building Exteriors
CONTRACTORS: Seismograph Survey Svcs
CONTRACTORS: Septic System
CONTRACTORS: Sheet Metal Work, NEC
CONTRACTORS: Sheet metal Work, Architectural
CONTRACTORS: Ship Joinery
CONTRACTORS: Shoring & Underpinning
CONTRACTORS: Siding
CONTRACTORS: Single-family Home General Remodeling

INDEX

CONTRACTORS: Solar Energy Eqpt
CONTRACTORS: Sound Eqpt Installation
CONTRACTORS: Special Trades, NEC
CONTRACTORS: Stone Masonry
CONTRACTORS: Storage Tank Erection, Metal
CONTRACTORS: Structural Iron Work, Structural
CONTRACTORS: Structural Steel Erection
CONTRACTORS: Svc Station Eqpt Installation, Maint & Repair
CONTRACTORS: Svc Well Drilling Svcs
CONTRACTORS: Tile Installation, Ceramic
CONTRACTORS: Tuck Pointing & Restoration
CONTRACTORS: Underground Utilities
CONTRACTORS: Ventilation & Duct Work
CONTRACTORS: Warm Air Heating & Air Conditioning
CONTRACTORS: Water Intake Well Drilling Svc
CONTRACTORS: Water Well Drilling
CONTRACTORS: Water Well Servicing
CONTRACTORS: Waterproofing
CONTRACTORS: Well Bailing, Cleaning, Swabbing & Treating Svc
CONTRACTORS: Well Casings Perforating Svcs
CONTRACTORS: Well Logging Svcs
CONTRACTORS: Well Surveying Svcs
CONTRACTORS: Window Treatment Installation
CONTRACTORS: Windows & Doors
CONTRACTORS: Wood Floor Installation & Refinishing
CONTRACTORS: Wrecking & Demolition
CONTROL CIRCUIT DEVICES
CONTROL EQPT: Electric
CONTROL EQPT: Noise
CONTROL PANELS: Electrical
CONTROLS & ACCESS: Indl, Electric
CONTROLS & ACCESS: Motor
CONTROLS: Access, Motor
CONTROLS: Automatic Temperature
CONTROLS: Crane & Hoist, Including Metal Mill
CONTROLS: Electric Motor
CONTROLS: Environmental
CONTROLS: Fan, Temperature Responsive
CONTROLS: Hydronic
CONTROLS: Marine & Navy, Auxiliary
CONTROLS: Nuclear Reactor
CONTROLS: Positioning, Electric
CONTROLS: Relay & Ind
CONTROLS: Thermostats
CONTROLS: Thermostats, Exc Built-in
CONTROLS: Truck, Indl Battery
CONTROLS: Voice
CONVENIENCE STORES
CONVENTION & TRADE SHOW SVCS
CONVERTERS: Data
CONVERTERS: Frequency
CONVERTERS: Power, AC to DC
CONVEYOR SYSTEMS
CONVEYOR SYSTEMS: Belt, General Indl Use
CONVEYOR SYSTEMS: Bucket Type
CONVEYOR SYSTEMS: Bulk Handling
CONVEYOR SYSTEMS: Pneumatic Tube
CONVEYOR SYSTEMS: Robotic
CONVEYORS & CONVEYING EQPT
CONVEYORS: Overhead
COOKING & FOOD WARMING EQPT: Commercial
COOKING & FOODWARMING EQPT: Coffee Brewing
COOKING EQPT, HOUSEHOLD: Ranges, Electric
COOKWARE, STONEWARE: Coarse Earthenware & Pottery
COOLING TOWERS: Metal
COPINGS: Concrete
COPPER PRDTS: Refined, Primary
COPPER: Bars, Primary
COPPER: Rolling & Drawing
CORD & TWINE
CORES: Magnetic
CORK & CORK PRDTS
CORRECTION FLUID
CORRECTIONAL INSTITUTIONS
CORRECTIONAL INSTITUTIONS, GOVERNMENT: Federal
CORRUGATED PRDTS: Boxes, Partition, Display Items, Sheet/Pad
COSMETIC PREPARATIONS
COSMETICS & TOILETRIES
COSMETOLOGY & BEAUTY SCHOOLS
COSTUME JEWELRY & NOVELTIES: Apparel, Exc Precious Metals
COSTUME JEWELRY & NOVELTIES: Exc Semi & Precious

COSTUME JEWELRY & NOVELTIES: Rosaries & Sm Religious Items
COSTUME JEWELRY STORES
COUGH MEDICINES
COUNTER & SINK TOPS
COUNTERS & COUNTING DEVICES
COUNTERS OR COUNTER DISPLAY CASES, WOOD
COUNTING DEVICES: Controls, Revolution & Timing
COUNTING DEVICES: Electromechanical
COUNTING DEVICES: Registers
COUNTING DEVICES: Tachometer, Centrifugal
COUNTING DEVICES: Vehicle Instruments
COUPLINGS, EXC PRESSURE & SOIL PIPE
COUPLINGS: Hose & Tube, Hydraulic Or Pneumatic
COUPLINGS: Pipe
COUPLINGS: Shaft
COURIER SVCS: Air
COVERS: Automobile Seat
COVERS: Automotive, Exc Seat & Tire
COVERS: Canvas
COVERS: Metal Plate
CRADLES: Aircraft Engine
CRADLES: Drum
CRANE & AERIAL LIFT SVCS
CRANES & MONORAIL SYSTEMS
CRANES: Indl Plant
CRANES: Overhead
CRANKSHAFTS & CAMSHAFTS: Machining
CRATES: Fruit, Wood Wirebound
CRAYONS
CREDIT CARD SVCS
CREDIT INST, SHORT-TERM BUSINESS: Financing Dealers
CREMATORIES
CROWNS & CLOSURES
CRUCIBLES
CRUDE PETROLEUM & NATURAL GAS PRODUCTION
CRUDE PETROLEUM & NATURAL GAS PRODUCTION
CRUDE PETROLEUM PRODUCTION
CRUDES: Cyclic, Organic
CRYOGENIC COOLING DEVICES: Infrared Detectors, Masers
CRYSTALS
CRYSTALS & CRYSTAL ASSEMBLIES: Radio
CRYSTALS: Piezoelectric
CULVERTS: Sheet Metal
CUPS & PLATES: Foamed Plastics
CUPS: Paper, Made From Purchased Materials
CUPS: Plastic Exc Polystyrene Foam
CURBING: Granite Or Stone
CURTAIN & DRAPERY FIXTURES: Poles, Rods & Rollers
CURTAIN WALLS: Building, Steel
CURTAINS: Shower
CURTAINS: Window, From Purchased Materials
CUSHIONS & PILLOWS
CUSHIONS & PILLOWS: Bed, From Purchased Materials
CUSHIONS: Carpet & Rug, Foamed Materials
CUSTOM COMPOUNDING OF RUBBER MATERIALS
CUT STONE & STONE PRODUCTS
CUTLERY
CUTTING SVC: Paper, Exc Die-Cut
CUTTING SVC: Paperboard
CYCLE CONDENSATE PRODUCTION
CYCLIC CRUDES & INTERMEDIATES
CYCLO RUBBERS: Natural
CYLINDER & ACTUATORS: Fluid Power
CYLINDERS: Pressure
CYLINDERS: Pump

D

DAIRY EQPT
DAIRY PRDTS STORE: Cheese
DAIRY PRDTS STORE: Ice Cream, Packaged
DAIRY PRDTS STORES
DAIRY PRDTS WHOLESALERS: Fresh
DAIRY PRDTS: Butter
DAIRY PRDTS: Buttermilk, Cultured
DAIRY PRDTS: Cheese
DAIRY PRDTS: Condensed Milk
DAIRY PRDTS: Custard, Frozen
DAIRY PRDTS: Dairy Based Desserts, Frozen
DAIRY PRDTS: Dietary Supplements, Dairy & Non-Dairy Based
DAIRY PRDTS: Dips & Spreads, Cheese Based
DAIRY PRDTS: Dips & Spreads, Sour Cream Based
DAIRY PRDTS: Dried Nonfat Milk
DAIRY PRDTS: Evaporated Milk

DAIRY PRDTS: Farmers' Cheese
DAIRY PRDTS: Fermented & Cultured Milk Prdts
DAIRY PRDTS: Frozen Desserts & Novelties
DAIRY PRDTS: Ice Cream & Ice Milk
DAIRY PRDTS: Ice Cream, Bulk
DAIRY PRDTS: Ice Cream, Packaged, Molded, On Sticks, Etc.
DAIRY PRDTS: Ice milk, Bulk
DAIRY PRDTS: Milk, Chocolate
DAIRY PRDTS: Milk, Condensed & Evaporated
DAIRY PRDTS: Milk, Fluid
DAIRY PRDTS: Milk, Processed, Pasteurized, Homogenized/Btld
DAIRY PRDTS: Natural Cheese
DAIRY PRDTS: Powdered Milk
DAIRY PRDTS: Processed Cheese
DAIRY PRDTS: Spreads, Cheese
DAIRY PRDTS: Whey Butter
DAIRY PRDTS: Whey, Powdered
DAIRY PRDTS: Whipped Topping, Exc Frozen Or Dry Mix
DAIRY PRDTS: Yogurt, Exc Frozen
DAIRY PRDTS: Yogurt, Frozen
DAMAGED MERCHANDISE SALVAGING, SVCS ONLY
DATA ENTRY SVCS
DATA PROCESSING & PREPARATION SVCS
DATA PROCESSING SVCS
DATABASE INFORMATION RETRIEVAL SVCS
DECORATIVE WOOD & WOODWORK
DEFENSE SYSTEMS & EQPT
DEGREASING MACHINES
DEHYDRATION EQPT
DEICING OR DEFROSTING FLUID
DELIVERY SVCS, BY VEHICLE
DENTAL EQPT
DENTAL EQPT & SPLYS
DENTAL EQPT & SPLYS WHOLESALERS
DENTAL EQPT & SPLYS: Dental Hand Instruments, NEC
DENTAL EQPT & SPLYS: Dental Materials
DENTAL EQPT & SPLYS: Enamels
DENTAL EQPT & SPLYS: Hand Pieces & Parts
DENTAL EQPT & SPLYS: Impression Materials
DENTAL EQPT & SPLYS: Laboratory
DENTAL EQPT & SPLYS: Metal
DENTAL EQPT & SPLYS: Orthodontic Appliances
DENTAL EQPT & SPLYS: Teeth, Artificial, Exc In Dental Labs
DENTAL EQPT & SPLYS: Tools, NEC
DENTAL INSTRUMENT REPAIR SVCS
DENTISTS' OFFICES & CLINICS
DEODORANTS: Personal
DEPARTMENT STORES: Country General
DERMATOLOGICALS
DERRICKS
DESIGN SVCS, NEC
DESIGN SVCS: Commercial & Indl
DESIGN SVCS: Computer Integrated Systems
DESIGN SVCS: Hand Tools
DESIGNS SVCS: Scenery, Theatrical
DETECTION APPARATUS: Electronic/Magnetic Field, Light/Heat
DETECTION EQPT: Aeronautical Electronic Field
DETECTION EQPT: Magnetic Field
DETECTORS: Water Leak
DETINNING: Cans & Scrap
DIAGNOSTIC SUBSTANCES
DIAGNOSTIC SUBSTANCES OR AGENTS: Blood Derivative
DIAGNOSTIC SUBSTANCES OR AGENTS: Enzyme & Isoenzyme
DIAGNOSTIC SUBSTANCES OR AGENTS: In Vitro
DIAGNOSTIC SUBSTANCES OR AGENTS: In Vivo
DIAGNOSTIC SUBSTANCES OR AGENTS: Microbiology & Virology
DIAGNOSTIC SUBSTANCES OR AGENTS: Radioactive
DIAMONDS, GEMS, WHOLESALE
DIAPERS: Disposable
DIATOMACEOUS EARTH MINING SVCS
DIE CUTTING SVC: Paper
DIE SETS: Presses, Metal Stamping
DIES & TOOLS: Special
DIES: Cutting, Exc Metal
DIES: Extrusion
DIES: Plastic Forming
DIES: Steel Rule
DIFFERENTIAL ASSEMBLIES & PARTS
DIODES: Light Emitting
DIODES: Solid State, Germanium, Silicon, Etc
DIORITE: Crushed & Broken

DIRECT SELLING ESTABLISHMENTS, NEC
DIRECT SELLING ESTABLISHMENTS: Cosmetic, House-To-House
DIRECT SELLING ESTABLISHMENTS: Food Svcs
DIRECT SELLING ESTABLISHMENTS: Lunch Wagon
DISCS & TAPE: Optical, Blank
DISHWASHING EQPT: Commercial
DISK & DISKETTE CONVERSION SVCS
DISK DRIVES: Computer
DISKS & DRUMS Magnetic
DISPENSERS: Soap
DISPENSING EQPT & PARTS, BEVERAGE: Beer
DISPENSING EQPT & PARTS, BEVERAGE: Cold, Exc Coin-Operated
DISPENSING EQPT & PARTS, BEVERAGE: Coolers, Milk/Water, Elec
DISPENSING EQPT & PARTS, BEVERAGE: Fountain/Other Beverage
DISPENSING EQPT & PARTS, BEVERAGE: Fountains, Parts/Access
DISPLAY CASES, REFRIGERATED: Wholesalers
DISPLAY FIXTURES: Wood
DISPLAY ITEMS: Corrugated, Made From Purchased Materials
DISPLAY ITEMS: Solid Fiber, Made From Purchased Materials
DISPLAY LETTERING SVCS
DISPLAY STANDS: Merchandise, Exc Wood
DISTANCE MEASURING EQPT OR DME: Aeronautical
DOCKS: Prefabricated Metal
DOCUMENT DESTRUCTION SVC
DOCUMENTATION CENTER
DOLLIES: Industrial
DOLOMITE: Crushed & Broken
DOOR & WINDOW REPAIR SVCS
DOOR FRAMES: Wood
DOOR OPERATING SYSTEMS: Electric
DOORS & WINDOWS WHOLESALERS: All Materials
DOORS & WINDOWS: Screen & Storm
DOORS & WINDOWS: Storm, Metal
DOORS: Combination Screen & Storm, Wood
DOORS: Fiberglass
DOORS: Garage, Overhead, Metal
DOORS: Garage, Overhead, Wood
DOORS: Glass
DOORS: Rolling, Indl Building Or Warehouse, Metal
DOORS: Screen, Metal
DOORS: Wooden
DOWELS & DOWEL RODS
DOWNSPOUTS: Sheet Metal
DRAFTING SPLYS WHOLESALERS
DRAFTING SVCS
DRAPERIES & CURTAINS
DRAPERIES & DRAPERY FABRICS, COTTON
DRAPERIES: Plastic & Textile, From Purchased Materials
DRAPERY & UPHOLSTERY STORES: Draperies
DRAPES & DRAPERY FABRICS, FROM MANMADE FIBER
DRESSES WHOLESALERS
DRIED FRUITS WHOLESALERS
DRILL BITS
DRILLING MACHINERY & EQPT: Oil & Gas
DRILLING MACHINERY & EQPT: Water Well
DRILLS & DRILLING EQPT: Mining
DRILLS: Core
DRILLS: Rock, Portable
DRINKING FOUNTAINS: Mechanically Refrigerated
DRINKING PLACES: Alcoholic Beverages
DRINKING PLACES: Beer Garden
DRINKING PLACES: Tavern
DRINKING WATER COOLERS WHOLESALERS: Mechanical
DRIVE SHAFTS
DRUG STORES
DRUG TESTING KITS: Blood & Urine
DRUGS & DRUG PROPRIETARIES, WHOLESALE
DRUGS & DRUG PROPRIETARIES, WHOLESALE: Druggists' Sundries
DRUGS & DRUG PROPRIETARIES, WHOLESALE: Medicinals/Botanicals
DRUGS & DRUG PROPRIETARIES, WHOLESALE: Pharmaceuticals
DRUGS & DRUG PROPRIETARIES, WHOLESALE: Vitamins & Minerals
DRUGS ACTING ON THE CENTRAL NERVOUS SYSTEM & SENSE ORGANS
DRUGS AFFECTING NEOPLASMS & ENDOCRINE SYSTEMS

DRUGS: Parasitic & Infective Disease Affecting
DRUMS: Fiber
DRUMS: Magnetic
DRYCLEANING & LAUNDRY SVCS: Commercial & Family
DRYCLEANING PLANTS
DRYCLEANING SVC: Collecting & Distributing Agency
DRYERS & REDRYERS: Indl
DUCTING: Metal Plate
DUCTS: Sheet Metal
DUMBWAITERS
DUMPSTERS: Garbage
DURABLE GOODS WHOLESALERS, NEC
DUST OR FUME COLLECTING EQPT: Indl
DYEING & FINISHING: Wool Or Similar Fibers
DYES & PIGMENTS: Organic
DYES OR COLORS: Food, Synthetic
DYES: Acid, Synthetic

E

EARTH SCIENCE SVCS
EATING PLACES
EDITORIAL SVCS
EDUCATIONAL PROGRAMS ADMINISTRATION SVCS
EDUCATIONAL SVCS
EDUCATIONAL SVCS, NONDEGREE GRANTING: Continuing Education
EGG WHOLESALERS
ELASTOMERS
ELECTRIC FENCE CHARGERS
ELECTRIC MOTOR & GENERATOR AUXILIARY PARTS
ELECTRIC MOTOR REPAIR SVCS
ELECTRIC SERVICES
ELECTRIC SVCS, NEC Power Broker
ELECTRIC SVCS, NEC: Power Generation
ELECTRICAL APPARATUS & EQPT WHOLESALERS
ELECTRICAL APPLIANCES, TELEVISIONS & RADIOS WHOLESALERS
ELECTRICAL CURRENT CARRYING WIRING DEVICES
ELECTRICAL DISCHARGE MACHINING, EDM
ELECTRICAL EQPT & SPLYS
ELECTRICAL EQPT FOR ENGINES
ELECTRICAL EQPT REPAIR & MAINTENANCE
ELECTRICAL EQPT REPAIR SVCS
ELECTRICAL EQPT REPAIR SVCS: High Voltage
ELECTRICAL EQPT: Automotive, NEC
ELECTRICAL GOODS, WHOLESALE: Alarms & Signaling Eqpt
ELECTRICAL GOODS, WHOLESALE: Batteries, Dry Cell
ELECTRICAL GOODS, WHOLESALE: Batteries, Storage, Indl
ELECTRICAL GOODS, WHOLESALE: Boxes & Fittings
ELECTRICAL GOODS, WHOLESALE: Burglar Alarm Systems
ELECTRICAL GOODS, WHOLESALE: Connectors
ELECTRICAL GOODS, WHOLESALE: Electrical Appliances, Major
ELECTRICAL GOODS, WHOLESALE: Electronic Parts
ELECTRICAL GOODS, WHOLESALE: Facsimile Or Fax Eqpt
ELECTRICAL GOODS, WHOLESALE: Fire Alarm Systems
ELECTRICAL GOODS, WHOLESALE: Fittings & Construction Mat
ELECTRICAL GOODS, WHOLESALE: Garbage Disposals
ELECTRICAL GOODS, WHOLESALE: Generators
ELECTRICAL GOODS, WHOLESALE: Household Appliances, NEC
ELECTRICAL GOODS, WHOLESALE: Insulators
ELECTRICAL GOODS, WHOLESALE: Light Bulbs & Related Splys
ELECTRICAL GOODS, WHOLESALE: Lighting Fixtures, Comm & Indl
ELECTRICAL GOODS, WHOLESALE: Lighting Fixtures, Residential
ELECTRICAL GOODS, WHOLESALE: Modems, Computer
ELECTRICAL GOODS, WHOLESALE: Motor Ctrls, Starters & Relays
ELECTRICAL GOODS, WHOLESALE: Motors
ELECTRICAL GOODS, WHOLESALE: Paging & Signaling Eqpt
ELECTRICAL GOODS, WHOLESALE: Security Control Eqpt & Systems
ELECTRICAL GOODS, WHOLESALE: Semiconductor Devices
ELECTRICAL GOODS, WHOLESALE: Signaling, Eqpt
ELECTRICAL GOODS, WHOLESALE: Sound Eqpt
ELECTRICAL GOODS, WHOLESALE: Switches, Exc Electronic, NEC
ELECTRICAL GOODS, WHOLESALE: Telephone & Telegraphic Eqpt

ELECTRICAL GOODS, WHOLESALE: Transformer & Transmission Eqpt
ELECTRICAL GOODS, WHOLESALE: Video Eqpt
ELECTRICAL GOODS, WHOLESALE: Wire & Cable
ELECTRICAL GOODS, WHOLESALE: Wire & Cable, Electronic
ELECTRICAL GOODS, WHOLESALE: Wire & Cable, Power
ELECTRICAL MEASURING INSTRUMENT REPAIR & CALIBRATION SVCS
ELECTRICAL SPLYS
ELECTRICAL SUPPLIES: Porcelain
ELECTRODES: Thermal & Electrolytic
ELECTROMEDICAL EQPT
ELECTROMEDICAL EQPT WHOLESALERS
ELECTROMETALLURGICAL PRDTS
ELECTRON TUBES
ELECTRONIC COMPONENTS
ELECTRONIC DETECTION SYSTEMS: Aeronautical
ELECTRONIC DEVICES: Solid State, NEC
ELECTRONIC EQPT REPAIR SVCS
ELECTRONIC LOADS & POWER SPLYS
ELECTRONIC PARTS & EQPT WHOLESALERS
ELECTRONIC SHOPPING
ELECTRONIC TRAINING DEVICES
ELECTROPLATING & PLATING SVC
ELEMENTARY & SECONDARY PRIVATE DENOMINATIONAL SCHOOLS
ELEVATORS & EQPT
ELEVATORS WHOLESALERS
ELEVATORS: Installation & Conversion
EMBALMING FLUID
EMBLEMS: Embroidered
EMBOSSING SVC: Paper
EMBROIDERING & ART NEEDLEWORK FOR THE TRADE
EMBROIDERING SVC
EMBROIDERING SVC: Schiffli Machine
EMBROIDERY ADVERTISING SVCS
EMERGENCY ALARMS
EMPLOYMENT AGENCY SVCS
ENAMELING SVC: Metal Prdts, Including Porcelain
ENCLOSURES: Electronic
ENCLOSURES: Screen
ENCODERS: Digital
ENCRYPTION EQPT & DEVICES
ENERGY MEASUREMENT EQPT
ENGINE PARTS & ACCESS: Internal Combustion
ENGINE REBUILDING: Diesel
ENGINE REBUILDING: Gas
ENGINEERING SVCS
ENGINEERING SVCS: Acoustical
ENGINEERING SVCS: Building Construction
ENGINEERING SVCS: Civil
ENGINEERING SVCS: Construction & Civil
ENGINEERING SVCS: Electrical Or Electronic
ENGINEERING SVCS: Energy conservation
ENGINEERING SVCS: Heating & Ventilation
ENGINEERING SVCS: Industrial
ENGINEERING SVCS: Machine Tool Design
ENGINEERING SVCS: Mechanical
ENGINEERING SVCS: Pollution Control
ENGINEERING SVCS: Professional
ENGINEERING SVCS: Structural
ENGINES & ENGINE PARTS: Guided Missile
ENGINES & ENGINE PARTS: Guided Missile, Research & Develpt
ENGINES: Diesel & Semi-Diesel Or Duel Fuel
ENGINES: Internal Combustion, NEC
ENGINES: Marine
ENGRAVING SVC, NEC
ENGRAVING SVC: Jewelry & Personal Goods
ENGRAVING SVCS
ENGRAVING SVCS: Tombstone
ENGRAVINGS: Currency
ENGRAVINGS: Plastic
ENVELOPES
ENVELOPES WHOLESALERS
EPOXY RESINS
EQUIPMENT & VEHICLE FINANCE LEASING COMPANIES
EQUIPMENT: Pedestrian Traffic Control
EQUIPMENT: Rental & Leasing, NEC
ESCALATORS: Passenger & Freight
ETCHING & ENGRAVING SVC
ETCHING SVC: Metal
ETHANOLAMINES
ETHYLENE
EXCAVATING EQPT

INDEX

EXCAVATING MACHINERY & EQPT WHOLESALERS
EXHAUST SYSTEMS: Eqpt & Parts
EXPLORATION, METAL MINING
EXPLOSIVES
EXPLOSIVES, EXC AMMO & FIREWORKS WHOLESALERS
EXPLOSIVES, FUSES & DETONATORS: Primary explosives
EXPLOSIVES: Cartridges For Concussion Forming Of Metal
EXPLOSIVES: Emulsions
EXTENSION CORDS
EXTRACTS, FLAVORING
EXTRUDED SHAPES, NEC: Copper & Copper Alloy
EYEGLASS CASES
EYEGLASSES
EYEGLASSES: Sunglasses
EYES: Artificial
Ethylene Glycols

F

FABRIC STORES
FABRICATED METAL PRODUCTS, NEC
FABRICS & CLOTH: Quilted
FABRICS: Alpacas, Cotton
FABRICS: Alpacas, Mohair, Woven
FABRICS: Apparel & Outerwear, Broadwoven
FABRICS: Apparel & Outerwear, Cotton
FABRICS: Bags & Bagging, Cotton
FABRICS: Broad Woven, Goods, Cotton
FABRICS: Broadwoven, Cotton
FABRICS: Broadwoven, Synthetic Manmade Fiber & Silk
FABRICS: Broadwoven, Wool
FABRICS: Canvas
FABRICS: Coated Or Treated
FABRICS: Coutil, Cotton
FABRICS: Decorative Trim & Specialty, Including Twist Weave
FABRICS: Denims
FABRICS: Dishcloths
FABRICS: Fiberglass, Broadwoven
FABRICS: Furniture Denim
FABRICS: Jacquard Woven, From Manmade Fiber Or Silk
FABRICS: Lace & Decorative Trim, Narrow
FABRICS: Lacings, Textile
FABRICS: Laminated
FABRICS: Manmade Fiber, Narrow
FABRICS: Marquisettes, From Manmade Fiber
FABRICS: Metallized
FABRICS: Nonwoven
FABRICS: Nylon, Broadwoven
FABRICS: Oilcloth
FABRICS: Press Cloth
FABRICS: Rayon, Narrow
FABRICS: Resin Or Plastic Coated
FABRICS: Rubberized
FABRICS: Shirting, Cotton
FABRICS: Specialty Including Twisted Weaves, Broadwoven
FABRICS: Spunbonded
FABRICS: Table Cover, Cotton
FABRICS: Tricot
FABRICS: Trimmings
FABRICS: Trimmings, Textile
FABRICS: Tubing, Seamless, Cotton
FABRICS: Tubing, Textile, Varnished
FABRICS: Upholstery, Cotton
FABRICS: Wall Covering, From Manmade Fiber Or Silk
FABRICS: Weft Or Circular Knit
FABRICS: Wool, Broadwoven
FABRICS: Woven Wire, Made From Purchased Wire
FABRICS: Woven, Narrow Cotton, Wool, Silk
FABRICS: Yarn-Dyed, Cotton
FACILITIES SUPPORT SVCS
FACSIMILE COMMUNICATION EQPT
FAMILY CLOTHING STORES
FANS, BLOWING: Indl Or Commercial
FANS, EXHAUST: Indl Or Commercial
FANS, VENTILATING: Indl Or Commercial
FANS: Ceiling
FARM & GARDEN MACHINERY WHOLESALERS
FARM BUREAUS
FARM MACHINERY REPAIR SVCS
FARM PRDTS, RAW MATERIAL, WHOLESALE: Tobacco & Tobacco Prdts
FARM PRDTS, RAW MATERIALS, WHOLESALE: Fibers, Vegetable
FARM PRDTS, RAW MATERIALS, WHOLESALE: Sugar
FARM SPLY STORES
FARM SPLYS WHOLESALERS
FARM SPLYS, WHOLESALE: Equestrian Eqpt

FARM SPLYS, WHOLESALE: Feed
FARM SPLYS, WHOLESALE: Fertilizers & Agricultural Chemicals
FARM SPLYS, WHOLESALE: Greenhouse Eqpt & Splys
FARM SPLYS, WHOLESALE: Harness Eqpt
FASTENERS WHOLESALERS
FASTENERS: Brads, Alum, Brass/Other Nonferrous Metal/Wire
FASTENERS: Metal
FASTENERS: Metal
FASTENERS: Notions, NEC
FATTY ACID ESTERS & AMINOS
FEATHERS & FEATHER PRODUCTS
FELT PARTS
FELTS: Saturated
FENCE POSTS: Iron & Steel
FENCES & FENCING MATERIALS
FENCES OR POSTS: Ornamental Iron Or Steel
FENCING DEALERS
FENCING MADE IN WIREDRAWING PLANTS
FENCING MATERIALS: Docks & Other Outdoor Prdts, Wood
FENCING MATERIALS: Plastic
FENCING MATERIALS: Wood
FERRALLOY ORES, EXC VANADIUM
FERRITES
FERROALLOYS
FERROALLOYS: Produced In Blast Furnaces
FERROMOLYBDENUM
FERROUS METALS: Reclaimed From Clay
FERTILIZER MINERAL MINING
FERTILIZER, AGRICULTURAL: Wholesalers
FERTILIZERS: NEC
FERTILIZERS: Nitrogen Solutions
FERTILIZERS: Nitrogenous
FERTILIZERS: Phosphatic
FIBER & FIBER PRDTS: Cigarette Tow Cellulosic
FIBER & FIBER PRDTS: Elastomeric
FIBER & FIBER PRDTS: Organic, Noncellulose
FIBER & FIBER PRDTS: Synthetic Cellulosic
FIBER OPTICS
FIBER PRDTS: Pressed, Wood Pulp, From Purchased Materials
FIBERS: Carbon & Graphite
FILE FOLDERS
FILLING SVCS: Pressure Containers
FILM & SHEET: Unsuppported Plastic
FILM: Motion Picture
FILTER ELEMENTS: Fluid & Hydraulic Line
FILTERING MEDIA: Pottery
FILTERS
FILTERS & SOFTENERS: Water, Household
FILTERS & STRAINERS: Pipeline
FILTERS: Air
FILTERS: Air Intake, Internal Combustion Engine, Exc Auto
FILTERS: General Line, Indl
FILTRATION DEVICES: Electronic
FINANCIAL SVCS
FINDINGS & TRIMMINGS Shoulder Straps, Women's Undergarments
FINDINGS & TRIMMINGS: Apparel
FINDINGS & TRIMMINGS: Fabric
FINISHING AGENTS: Textile
FIRE ARMS, SMALL: Guns Or Gun Parts, 30 mm & Below
FIRE ARMS, SMALL: Pellet & BB guns
FIRE ARMS, SMALL: Pistols Or Pistol Parts, 30 mm & below
FIRE ARMS, SMALL: Rifles Or Rifle Parts, 30 mm & below
FIRE ARMS, SMALL: Shotguns Or Shotgun Parts, 30 mm & Below
FIRE CLAY MINING
FIRE DETECTION SYSTEMS
FIRE ESCAPES
FIRE EXTINGUISHER SVC
FIRE EXTINGUISHERS: Portable
FIRE OR BURGLARY RESISTIVE PRDTS
FIRE PROTECTION EQPT
FIREARMS & AMMUNITION, EXC SPORTING, WHOLESALE
FIREARMS: Large, Greater Than 30mm
FIREARMS: Small, 30mm or Less
FIREBRICK: Clay
FIREFIGHTING APPARATUS
FIREPLACE & CHIMNEY MATERIAL: Concrete
FIREPLACE EQPT & ACCESS
FIREPLACE LOGS: Electric
FIREWOOD, WHOLESALE
FIREWORKS
FIREWORKS DISPLAY SVCS

FIREWORKS SHOPS
FIREWORKS: Wholesalers
FISH & SEAFOOD MARKETS
FISH & SEAFOOD PROCESSORS: Canned Or Cured
FISH & SEAFOOD PROCESSORS: Fresh Or Frozen
FISH & SEAFOOD WHOLESALERS
FISH FOOD
FISHING EQPT: Lures
FISHING EQPT: Nets & Seines
FITTINGS & ASSEMBLIES: Hose & Tube, Hydraulic Or Pneumatic
FITTINGS & SPECIALTIES: Steam
FITTINGS: Pipe
FITTINGS: Pipe, Fabricated
FIXTURES & EQPT: Kitchen, Metal, Exc Cast Aluminum
FIXTURES & EQPT: Kitchen, Porcelain Enameled
FLAGPOLES
FLAGS: Fabric
FLAGSTONE: Dimension
FLAGSTONES
FLAKES: Metal
FLAT GLASS: Cathedral
FLAT GLASS: Construction
FLAT GLASS: Float
FLAT GLASS: Laminated
FLAT GLASS: Optical, Transparent, Exc Lenses
FLAT GLASS: Picture
FLAT GLASS: Skylight
FLAT GLASS: Strengthened Or Reinforced
FLAT GLASS: Tempered
FLAT GLASS: Window, Clear & Colored
FLAVORS OR FLAVORING MATERIALS: Synthetic
FLOOR CLEANING & MAINTENANCE EQPT: Household
FLOOR COVERING STORES
FLOOR COVERING STORES: Carpets
FLOOR COVERING STORES: Floor Tile
FLOOR COVERING STORES: Linoleum
FLOOR COVERING STORES: Vinyl Covering
FLOOR COVERING: Plastic
FLOOR COVERINGS WHOLESALERS
FLOOR COVERINGS: Rubber
FLOOR COVERINGS: Twisted Paper, Grass, Reed, Coir, Etc
FLOORING & GRATINGS: Open, Construction Applications
FLOORING & SIDING: Metal
FLOORING: Baseboards, Wood
FLOORING: Cellular Steel
FLOORING: Hard Surface
FLOORING: Hardwood
FLOORING: Parquet, Hardwood
FLOORING: Rubber
FLOORING: Tile
FLORIST: Plants, Potted
FLORISTS
FLOWER ARRANGEMENTS: Artificial
FLOWERS & FLORISTS' SPLYS WHOLESALERS
FLOWERS & NURSERY STOCK, WHOLESALE
FLOWERS: Artificial & Preserved
FLUE LINING: Clay
FLUID METERS & COUNTING DEVICES
FLUID POWER PUMPS & MOTORS
FLUID POWER VALVES & HOSE FITTINGS
FLUMES: Sheet Metal
FLUXES
FOAM CHARGE MIXTURES
FOAM RUBBER
FOAM RUBBER, WHOLESALE
FOIL & LEAF: Metal
FOIL: Magnesium & Magnesium-Base Alloy
FOOD CASINGS: Plastic
FOOD COLORINGS
FOOD PRDTS, BREAKFAST: Cereal, Rice: Cereal Breakfast Food
FOOD PRDTS, CANNED OR FRESH PACK: Fruit Juices
FOOD PRDTS, CANNED, NEC
FOOD PRDTS, CANNED: Applesauce
FOOD PRDTS, CANNED: Baby Food
FOOD PRDTS, CANNED: Barbecue Sauce
FOOD PRDTS, CANNED: Catsup
FOOD PRDTS, CANNED: Chili Sauce, Tomato
FOOD PRDTS, CANNED: Ethnic
FOOD PRDTS, CANNED: Fruit Butters
FOOD PRDTS, CANNED: Fruit Juices, Fresh
FOOD PRDTS, CANNED: Fruits
FOOD PRDTS, CANNED: Fruits
FOOD PRDTS, CANNED: Fruits & Fruit Prdts
FOOD PRDTS, CANNED: Italian

FOOD PRDTS, CANNED: Jams, Jellies & Preserves
FOOD PRDTS, CANNED: Macaroni
FOOD PRDTS, CANNED: Marmalade
FOOD PRDTS, CANNED: Mexican, NEC
FOOD PRDTS, CANNED: Mushrooms
FOOD PRDTS, CANNED: Puddings, Exc Meat
FOOD PRDTS, CANNED: Spaghetti & Other Pasta Sauce
FOOD PRDTS, CANNED: Tomato Sauce.
FOOD PRDTS, CANNED: Tomatoes
FOOD PRDTS, CANNED: Vegetables
FOOD PRDTS, CANNED: Vegetables
FOOD PRDTS, CONFECTIONERY, WHOLESALE: Candy
FOOD PRDTS, CONFECTIONERY, WHOLESALE: Corn Chips
FOOD PRDTS, CONFECTIONERY, WHOLESALE: Nuts, Salted/Roasted
FOOD PRDTS, CONFECTIONERY, WHOLESALE: Potato Chips
FOOD PRDTS, CONFECTIONERY, WHOLESALE: Pretzels
FOOD PRDTS, CONFECTIONERY, WHOLESALE: Snack Foods
FOOD PRDTS, DAIRY, WHOLESALE: Frozen Dairy Desserts
FOOD PRDTS, DAIRY, WHOLESALE: Milk & Cream, Fluid
FOOD PRDTS, FISH & SEAFOOD, WHOLESALE: Fresh
FOOD PRDTS, FISH & SEAFOOD, WHOLESALE: Seafood
FOOD PRDTS, FISH & SEAFOOD: Fish, Frozen, Prepared
FOOD PRDTS, FISH & SEAFOOD: Fresh, Prepared
FOOD PRDTS, FISH & SEAFOOD: Fresh/Frozen Chowder, Soup/Stew
FOOD PRDTS, FISH & SEAFOOD: Prepared Cakes & Sticks
FOOD PRDTS, FISH & SEAFOOD: Seafood, Frozen, Prepared
FOOD PRDTS, FROZEN, WHOLESALE: Dinners
FOOD PRDTS, FROZEN, WHOLESALE: Vegetables & Fruit Prdts
FOOD PRDTS, FROZEN: Ethnic Foods, NEC
FOOD PRDTS, FROZEN: Fruit Juice, Concentrates
FOOD PRDTS, FROZEN: Fruits
FOOD PRDTS, FROZEN: Fruits, Juices & Vegetables
FOOD PRDTS, FROZEN: NEC
FOOD PRDTS, FROZEN: Pizza
FOOD PRDTS, FROZEN: Potato Prdts
FOOD PRDTS, FROZEN: Snack Items
FOOD PRDTS, FROZEN: Soups
FOOD PRDTS, FROZEN: Vegetables, Exc Potato Prdts
FOOD PRDTS, FRUITS & VEGETABLES, FRESH, WHOLESALE: Vegetable
FOOD PRDTS, MEAT & MEAT PRDTS, WHOLESALE: Brokers
FOOD PRDTS, MEAT & MEAT PRDTS, WHOLESALE: Cured Or Smoked
FOOD PRDTS, MEAT & MEAT PRDTS, WHOLESALE: Fresh
FOOD PRDTS, MEAT & MEAT PRDTS, WHOLESALE: Lard
FOOD PRDTS, POULTRY, WHOLESALE: Live/Dressed/Frozen, Unpkgd
FOOD PRDTS, POULTRY, WHOLESALE: Poultry Prdts, NEC
FOOD PRDTS, WHOLESALE: Beverages, Exc Coffee & Tea
FOOD PRDTS, WHOLESALE: Breakfast Cereals
FOOD PRDTS, WHOLESALE: Chocolate
FOOD PRDTS, WHOLESALE: Coffee & Tea
FOOD PRDTS, WHOLESALE: Coffee, Green Or Roasted
FOOD PRDTS, WHOLESALE: Cooking Oils & Shortenings
FOOD PRDTS, WHOLESALE: Diet
FOOD PRDTS, WHOLESALE: Dog Food
FOOD PRDTS, WHOLESALE: Dried or Canned Foods
FOOD PRDTS, WHOLESALE: Flavorings & Fragrances
FOOD PRDTS, WHOLESALE: Flour
FOOD PRDTS, WHOLESALE: Grain Elevators
FOOD PRDTS, WHOLESALE: Grains
FOOD PRDTS, WHOLESALE: Honey
FOOD PRDTS, WHOLESALE: Juices
FOOD PRDTS, WHOLESALE: Molasses, Indl
FOOD PRDTS, WHOLESALE: Pasta & Rice
FOOD PRDTS, WHOLESALE: Pizza Splys
FOOD PRDTS, WHOLESALE: Rice, Polished
FOOD PRDTS, WHOLESALE: Salt, Edible
FOOD PRDTS, WHOLESALE: Sandwiches
FOOD PRDTS, WHOLESALE: Sauces
FOOD PRDTS, WHOLESALE: Shortening, Vegetable
FOOD PRDTS, WHOLESALE: Soybeans
FOOD PRDTS, WHOLESALE: Specialty
FOOD PRDTS, WHOLESALE: Spices & Seasonings
FOOD PRDTS, WHOLESALE: Syrups, Exc Fountain Use
FOOD PRDTS, WHOLESALE: Tea
FOOD PRDTS, WHOLESALE: Water, Mineral Or Spring, Bottled

FOOD PRDTS: Animal & marine fats & oils
FOOD PRDTS: Baking Powder, Soda, Yeast & Leavenings
FOOD PRDTS: Bread Crumbs, Exc Made In Bakeries
FOOD PRDTS: Breakfast Bars
FOOD PRDTS: Cereals
FOOD PRDTS: Cheese Curls & Puffs
FOOD PRDTS: Chicken, Processed, Cooked
FOOD PRDTS: Chicken, Processed, Frozen
FOOD PRDTS: Chicken, Processed, NEC
FOOD PRDTS: Chicken, Slaughtered & Dressed
FOOD PRDTS: Chocolate Bars, Solid
FOOD PRDTS: Chocolate Coatings & Syrup
FOOD PRDTS: Chocolate Liquor
FOOD PRDTS: Chocolate, Baking
FOOD PRDTS: Coffee
FOOD PRDTS: Coffee Extracts
FOOD PRDTS: Coffee Roasting, Exc Wholesale Grocers
FOOD PRDTS: Coffee, Ground, Mixed With Grain Or Chicory
FOOD PRDTS: Cole Slaw, Bulk
FOOD PRDTS: Cooking Oils, Refined Vegetable, Exc Corn
FOOD PRDTS: Corn Chips & Other Corn-Based Snacks
FOOD PRDTS: Corn Oil, Refined
FOOD PRDTS: Corn Syrup, Dried Or Unmixed
FOOD PRDTS: Dessert Mixes & Fillings
FOOD PRDTS: Dips, Exc Cheese & Sour Cream Based
FOOD PRDTS: Dough, Pizza, Prepared
FOOD PRDTS: Doughs, Frozen Or Refrig From Purchased Flour
FOOD PRDTS: Dressings, Salad, Raw & Cooked Exc Dry Mixes
FOOD PRDTS: Dried & Dehydrated Fruits, Vegetables & Soup Mix
FOOD PRDTS: Eggs, Processed
FOOD PRDTS: Eggs, Processed, Frozen
FOOD PRDTS: Emulsifiers
FOOD PRDTS: Fish Oil
FOOD PRDTS: Flavored Ices, Frozen
FOOD PRDTS: Flour
FOOD PRDTS: Flour & Other Grain Mill Products
FOOD PRDTS: Flour Mixes & Doughs
FOOD PRDTS: Fruit Juices
FOOD PRDTS: Fruits & Vegetables, Pickled
FOOD PRDTS: Fruits, Dehydrated Or Dried
FOOD PRDTS: Fruits, Dried Or Dehydrated, Exc Freeze-Dried
FOOD PRDTS: Granola & Energy Bars, Nonchocolate
FOOD PRDTS: Honey
FOOD PRDTS: Ice, Blocks
FOOD PRDTS: Ice, Cubes
FOOD PRDTS: Instant Coffee
FOOD PRDTS: Lozenges, Non-Medicated
FOOD PRDTS: Macaroni, Noodles, Spaghetti, Pasta, Etc
FOOD PRDTS: Malt
FOOD PRDTS: Margarine, Including Imitation
FOOD PRDTS: Mixes, Bread & Roll From Purchased Flour
FOOD PRDTS: Mixes, Cake, From Purchased Flour
FOOD PRDTS: Mixes, Flour
FOOD PRDTS: Mixes, Pancake From Purchased Flour
FOOD PRDTS: Mixes, Sauces, Dry
FOOD PRDTS: Molasses
FOOD PRDTS: Mustard, Prepared
FOOD PRDTS: Noodles, Uncooked, Packaged W/Other Ingredients
FOOD PRDTS: Nuts & Seeds
FOOD PRDTS: Oil, Hydrogenated, Edible
FOOD PRDTS: Olive Oil
FOOD PRDTS: Onions, Pickled
FOOD PRDTS: Oriental Noodles
FOOD PRDTS: Pasta, Rice/Potatoes, Uncooked, Pkgd
FOOD PRDTS: Pasta, Uncooked, Packaged With Other Ingredients
FOOD PRDTS: Peanut Butter
FOOD PRDTS: Pickles, Vinegar
FOOD PRDTS: Pizza, Refrigerated
FOOD PRDTS: Popcorn, Popped
FOOD PRDTS: Popcorn, Unpopped
FOOD PRDTS: Pork Rinds
FOOD PRDTS: Potato & Corn Chips & Similar Prdts
FOOD PRDTS: Potato Chips & Other Potato-Based Snacks
FOOD PRDTS: Potatoes, Dried
FOOD PRDTS: Potatoes, Fresh Cut & Peeled
FOOD PRDTS: Poultry, Processed, Fresh
FOOD PRDTS: Poultry, Slaughtered & Dressed
FOOD PRDTS: Preparations
FOOD PRDTS: Prepared Meat Sauces Exc Tomato & Dry
FOOD PRDTS: Prepared Sauces, Exc Tomato Based

FOOD PRDTS: Prepared Seafood Sauces Exc Tomato & Dry
FOOD PRDTS: Relishes, Vinegar
FOOD PRDTS: Salads
FOOD PRDTS: Sausage, Poultry
FOOD PRDTS: Seasonings & Spices
FOOD PRDTS: Soup Mixes
FOOD PRDTS: Soup Mixes, Dried
FOOD PRDTS: Soups, Dehydrated
FOOD PRDTS: Soybean Flour & Grits
FOOD PRDTS: Spices, Including Ground
FOOD PRDTS: Spreads, Garlic
FOOD PRDTS: Sugar, Cane
FOOD PRDTS: Sugar, Liquid Sugar Beet
FOOD PRDTS: Sugar, Maple, Indl
FOOD PRDTS: Sugar, Refined Cane, Purchased Raw Sugar/Syrup
FOOD PRDTS: Syrup, Maple
FOOD PRDTS: Tea
FOOD PRDTS: Tofu, Exc Frozen Desserts
FOOD PRDTS: Tortilla Chips
FOOD PRDTS: Tortillas
FOOD PRDTS: Turkey, Processed, Cooked
FOOD PRDTS: Turkey, Processed, NEC
FOOD PRDTS: Vegetable Oil Mills, NEC
FOOD PRDTS: Vegetable Shortenings, Exc Corn Oil
FOOD PRDTS: Vinegar
FOOD PRDTS: Wheat Flour
FOOD PRODUCTS MACHINERY
FOOD STORES: Convenience, Chain
FOOD STORES: Convenience, Independent
FOOD STORES: Cooperative
FOOD STORES: Delicatessen
FOOD STORES: Grocery, Independent
FOOD STORES: Supermarkets
FOOD STORES: Supermarkets, Chain
FOOD STORES: Supermarkets, Independent
FOOTWEAR, WHOLESALE: Shoes
FOOTWEAR: Cut Stock
FOOTWEAR: Except Rubber, NEC
FORESTRY EQPT WHOLESALERS
FORGES: Fan
FORGINGS
FORGINGS: Aircraft, Ferrous
FORGINGS: Aluminum
FORGINGS: Automotive & Internal Combustion Engine
FORGINGS: Bearing & Bearing Race, Nonferrous
FORGINGS: Construction Or Mining Eqpt, Ferrous
FORGINGS: Gear & Chain
FORGINGS: Iron & Steel
FORGINGS: Machinery, Ferrous
FORGINGS: Machinery, Nonferrous
FORGINGS: Metal , Ornamental, Ferrous
FORGINGS: Nonferrous
FORGINGS: Nuclear Power Plant, Ferrous
FORGINGS: Pump & Compressor, Ferrous
FORMS: Concrete, Sheet Metal
FOUNDRIES: Aluminum
FOUNDRIES: Brass, Bronze & Copper
FOUNDRIES: Gray & Ductile Iron
FOUNDRIES: Iron
FOUNDRIES: Nonferrous
FOUNDRIES: Steel
FOUNDRIES: Steel Investment
FOUNDRY FACINGS: Ground Or Otherwise Treated
FOUNDRY MACHINERY & EQPT
FOUNDRY SAND MINING
FRAMES & FRAMING WHOLESALE
FRANCHISES, SELLING OR LICENSING
FREIGHT TRANSPORTATION ARRANGEMENTS
FRICTION MATERIAL, MADE FROM POWDERED METAL
FRITS
FRUIT STANDS OR MARKETS
FRUITS & VEGETABLES WHOLESALERS: Fresh
FUEL ADDITIVES
FUEL DEALERS, NEC
FUEL DEALERS: Coal
FUEL OIL DEALERS
FUEL TREATING
FUELS: Diesel
FUELS: Ethanol
FUELS: Jet
FUELS: Oil
FUNDRAISING SVCS
FUNERAL HOMES & SVCS
FUNGICIDES OR HERBICIDES
FUR APPAREL STORES: Made To Custom Order

INDEX

FUR STRIPPING
FUR: Apparel
FUR: Coats
FURNACE CASINGS: Sheet Metal
FURNACES & OVENS: Indl
FURNACES & OVENS: Vacuum
FURNACES: Indl, Electric
FURNACES: Indl, Fuel-Fired, Metal Melting
FURNISHINGS: Bridge Sets, Cloth/Napkin, From Purchased Matls
FURNITURE & CABINET STORES: Cabinets, Custom Work
FURNITURE & CABINET STORES: Custom
FURNITURE & FIXTURES Factory
FURNITURE PARTS: Metal
FURNITURE REFINISHING SVCS
FURNITURE STOCK & PARTS: Carvings, Wood
FURNITURE STOCK & PARTS: Chair Seats, Hardwood
FURNITURE STOCK & PARTS: Dimension Stock, Hardwood
FURNITURE STOCK & PARTS: Frames, Upholstered Furniture, Wood
FURNITURE STOCK & PARTS: Hardwood
FURNITURE STOCK & PARTS: Squares, Hardwood
FURNITURE STORES
FURNITURE STORES: Cabinets, Kitchen, Exc Custom Made
FURNITURE STORES: Custom Made, Exc Cabinets
FURNITURE STORES: Office
FURNITURE STORES: Outdoor & Garden
FURNITURE STORES: Unfinished
FURNITURE WHOLESALERS
FURNITURE, HOUSEHOLD: Wholesalers
FURNITURE, OFFICE: Wholesalers
FURNITURE, OUTDOOR & LAWN: Wholesalers
FURNITURE, WHOLESALE: Beds
FURNITURE, WHOLESALE: Chairs
FURNITURE, WHOLESALE: Shelving
FURNITURE: Altars, Cut Stone
FURNITURE: Bed Frames & Headboards, Wood
FURNITURE: Bedroom, Wood
FURNITURE: Beds, Household, Incl Folding & Cabinet, Metal
FURNITURE: Bedsprings, Assembled
FURNITURE: Bookcases, Office, Wood
FURNITURE: Bookcases, Wood
FURNITURE: Bowling Establishment
FURNITURE: Box Springs, Assembled
FURNITURE: Cabinets & Filing Drawers, Office, Exc Wood
FURNITURE: Cabinets & Vanities, Medicine, Metal
FURNITURE: Chair Beds
FURNITURE: Chairs, Folding
FURNITURE: Chairs, Household Upholstered
FURNITURE: Chairs, Household Wood
FURNITURE: Chairs, Office Exc Wood
FURNITURE: Chests, Cedar
FURNITURE: Church
FURNITURE: Couches, Sofa/Davenport, Upholstered Wood Frames
FURNITURE: Cut Stone
FURNITURE: Desks & Tables, Office, Exc Wood
FURNITURE: Desks & Tables, Office, Wood
FURNITURE: Desks, Household, Wood
FURNITURE: Desks, Wood
FURNITURE: Dining Room, Wood
FURNITURE: Foundations & Platforms
FURNITURE: Garden, Metal
FURNITURE: Garden, Wood
FURNITURE: Hospital
FURNITURE: Household, Metal
FURNITURE: Household, Upholstered On Metal Frames
FURNITURE: Household, Upholstered, Exc Wood Or Metal
FURNITURE: Household, Wood
FURNITURE: Institutional, Exc Wood
FURNITURE: Juvenile, Metal
FURNITURE: Juvenile, Wood
FURNITURE: Juvenile, Wood
FURNITURE: Kitchen & Dining Room
FURNITURE: Kitchen & Dining Room, Metal
FURNITURE: Laboratory
FURNITURE: Lawn & Garden, Except Wood & Metal
FURNITURE: Lawn & Garden, Metal
FURNITURE: Lawn, Wood
FURNITURE: Living Room, Upholstered On Wood Frames
FURNITURE: Mattresses & Foundations
FURNITURE: Mattresses, Box & Bedsprings
FURNITURE: Mattresses, Innerspring Or Box Spring
FURNITURE: NEC
FURNITURE: Novelty, Wood
FURNITURE: Office Panel Systems, Exc Wood

FURNITURE: Office Panel Systems, Wood
FURNITURE: Office, Exc Wood
FURNITURE: Office, Wood
FURNITURE: Outdoor, Wood
FURNITURE: Pews, Church
FURNITURE: Picnic Tables Or Benches, Park
FURNITURE: Restaurant
FURNITURE: School
FURNITURE: Stools, Household, Wood
FURNITURE: Storage Chests, Household, Wood
FURNITURE: Table Tops, Marble
FURNITURE: Tables & Table Tops, Wood
FURNITURE: Television, Wood
FURNITURE: Unfinished, Wood
FURNITURE: Upholstered
FURNITURE: Vehicle
FURRIERS
FUSES: Electric
Furs

G

GAME MACHINES, COIN-OPERATED, WHOLESALE
GAMES & TOYS: Bingo Boards
GAMES & TOYS: Board Games, Children's & Adults'
GAMES & TOYS: Craft & Hobby Kits & Sets
GAMES & TOYS: Darts & Dart Games
GAMES & TOYS: Doll Clothing
GAMES & TOYS: Dollhouses & Furniture
GAMES & TOYS: Dolls, Exc Stuffed Toy Animals
GAMES & TOYS: Electronic
GAMES & TOYS: Engines, Miniature
GAMES & TOYS: Miniature Dolls, Collectors'
GAMES & TOYS: Models, Airplane, Toy & Hobby
GAMES & TOYS: Models, Railroad, Toy & Hobby
GAMES & TOYS: Trains & Eqpt, Electric & Mechanical
GARAGES: Portable, Prefabricated Metal
GARBAGE CONTAINERS: Plastic
GARBAGE DISPOSERS & COMPACTORS: Commercial
GARNET MINING SVCS
GAS & OIL FIELD EXPLORATION SVCS
GAS & OIL FIELD SVCS, NEC
GAS FIELD MACHINERY & EQPT
GAS PRODUCTION & DISTRIBUTION
GAS PRODUCTION & DISTRIBUTION: Coke Oven
GAS STATIONS
GASES & LIQUIFIED PETROLEUM GASES
GASES: Carbon Dioxide
GASES: Hydrogen
GASES: Indl
GASES: Neon
GASES: Nitrogen
GASES: Oxygen
GASKET MATERIALS
GASKETS
GASKETS & SEALING DEVICES
GASOLINE BLENDING PLANT
GASOLINE FILLING STATIONS
GATES: Ornamental Metal
GAUGES
GAUGES: Pressure
GEARS
GEARS: Power Transmission, Exc Auto
GENERATING APPARATUS & PARTS: Electrical
GENERATION EQPT: Electronic
GENERATOR REPAIR SVCS
GENERATORS: Storage Battery Chargers
GENERATORS: Ultrasonic
GIFT SHOP
GIFT, NOVELTY & SOUVENIR STORES: Artcraft & carvings
GIFT, NOVELTY & SOUVENIR STORES: Gift Baskets
GIFT, NOVELTY & SOUVENIR STORES: Gifts & Novelties
GIFTS & NOVELTIES: Wholesalers
GIFTWARE: Brass
GIFTWARE: Copper
GLASS & GLASS CERAMIC PRDTS, PRESSED OR BLOWN: Tableware
GLASS FABRICATORS
GLASS PRDTS, FROM PURCHASED GLASS: Art
GLASS PRDTS, FROM PURCHASED GLASS: Enameled
GLASS PRDTS, FROM PURCHASED GLASS: Glass Beads, Reflecting
GLASS PRDTS, FROM PURCHASED GLASS: Glassware
GLASS PRDTS, FROM PURCHASED GLASS: Insulating
GLASS PRDTS, FROM PURCHASED GLASS: Mirrored
GLASS PRDTS, FROM PURCHASED GLASS: Sheet, Bent
GLASS PRDTS, FROM PURCHASED GLASS: Silvered

GLASS PRDTS, FROM PURCHD GLASS: Strengthened Or Reinforced
GLASS PRDTS, PRESSED OR BLOWN: Blocks & Bricks
GLASS PRDTS, PRESSED OR BLOWN: Furnishings & Access
GLASS PRDTS, PRESSED OR BLOWN: Glassware, Art Or Decorative
GLASS PRDTS, PRESSED OR BLOWN: Glassware, Novelty
GLASS PRDTS, PRESSED OR BLOWN: Lighting Eqpt Parts
GLASS PRDTS, PRESSED OR BLOWN: Optical
GLASS PRDTS, PRESSED OR BLOWN: Scientific Glassware
GLASS PRDTS, PRESSED OR BLOWN: Vases
GLASS PRDTS, PRESSED/BLOWN: Glassware, Art, Decor/Novelty
GLASS PRDTS, PRESSED/BLOWN: Lenses, Lantern, Flshlght, Etc
GLASS PRDTS, PURCHASED GLASS: Glassware, Scientific/Tech
GLASS PRDTS, PURCHSD GLASS: Ornamental, Cut, Engraved/Décor
GLASS STORE: Leaded Or Stained
GLASS STORES
GLASS, AUTOMOTIVE: Wholesalers
GLASS: Fiber
GLASS: Flat
GLASS: Indl Prdts
GLASS: Insulating
GLASS: Leaded
GLASS: Pressed & Blown, NEC
GLASS: Safety
GLASS: Stained
GLASS: Tempered
GLASSWARE STORES
GLASSWARE WHOLESALERS
GLASSWARE, NOVELTY, WHOLESALE
GLASSWARE: Cut & Engraved
GLASSWARE: Indl
GLASSWARE: Laboratory
GLASSWARE: Laboratory & Medical
GLOBAL POSITIONING SYSTEMS & EQPT
GLOVES: Fabric
GLOVES: Leather
GLOVES: Work
GLUE
GOLF CARTS: Wholesalers
GOLF COURSES: Public
GOLF EQPT
GOLF GOODS & EQPT
GOURMET FOOD STORES
GOVERNMENT, EXECUTIVE OFFICES: City & Town Managers' Offices
GOVERNMENT, EXECUTIVE OFFICES: Mayors'
GOVERNMENT, GENERAL: Administration
GOVERNORS: Diesel Engine, Pump
GRAIN & FIELD BEANS WHOLESALERS
GRANITE: Crushed & Broken
GRANITE: Cut & Shaped
GRANITE: Dimension
GRANITE: Dimension
GRAPHIC ARTS & RELATED DESIGN SVCS
GRATINGS: Open Steel Flooring
GRATINGS: Tread, Fabricated Metal
GRAVEL MINING
GREASE TRAPS: Concrete
GREASES & INEDIBLE FATS, RENDERED
GREENHOUSES: Prefabricated Metal
GREETING CARD SHOPS
GRILLES & REGISTERS: Ornamental Metal Work
GRILLS & GRILLWORK: Woven Wire, Made From Purchased Wire
GRINDING SAND MINING
GRINDING SVC: Precision, Commercial Or Indl
GRINDING SVCS: Ophthalmic Lens, Exc Prescription
GRIPS OR HANDLES: Rubber
GRITS: Crushed & Broken
GROCERIES WHOLESALERS, NEC
GROCERIES, GENERAL LINE WHOLESALERS
GUARD SVCS
GUARDRAILS
GUARDS: Machine, Sheet Metal
GUARDS: Metal Pipe
GUIDED MISSILES & SPACE VEHICLES
GUIDED MISSILES & SPACE VEHICLES: Research & Development
GUIDED MISSILES/SPACE VEHICLE PARTS/AUX EQPT: Research/Devel

GUM & WOOD CHEMICALS
GUN PARTS MADE TO INDIVIDUAL ORDER
GUN SVCS
GUNNING MIXES: Nonclay
GUNSMITHS
GUTTERS: Sheet Metal
GYPSUM & CALCITE MINING SVCS
GYPSUM BOARD
GYPSUM PRDTS

H

HAIR & HAIR BASED PRDTS
HAIR CARE PRDTS: Hair Coloring Preparations
HAMPERS: Shipping, Vulcanized Fiber, From Purchased Matls
HAMPERS: Solid Fiber, Made From Purchased Materials
HAND TOOLS, NEC: Wholesalers
HANDBAGS
HANDBAGS: Women's
HANDCUFFS & LEG IRONS
HANDLES: Brush Or Tool, Plastic
HANGERS: Garment, Home & Store, Wooden
HANGERS: Garment, Plastic
HARD RUBBER PRDTS, NEC
HARDWARE
HARDWARE & BUILDING PRDTS: Plastic
HARDWARE & EQPT: Stage, Exc Lighting
HARDWARE CLOTH: Woven Wire, Made From Purchased Wire
HARDWARE STORES
HARDWARE STORES: Builders'
HARDWARE STORES: Tools
HARDWARE STORES: Tools, Hand
HARDWARE WHOLESALERS
HARDWARE, WHOLESALE: Bolts
HARDWARE, WHOLESALE: Builders', NEC
HARDWARE, WHOLESALE: Garden Tools, Hand
HARDWARE, WHOLESALE: Padlocks
HARDWARE, WHOLESALE: Power Tools & Access
HARDWARE, WHOLESALE: Screws
HARDWARE, WHOLESALE: Security Devices, Locks
HARDWARE: Builders'
HARDWARE: Cabinet
HARDWARE: Furniture
HARDWARE: Furniture, Builders' & Other Household
HARDWARE: Harness
HARDWARE: Luggage
HARDWARE: Plastic
HARDWARE: Rubber
HARNESS ASSEMBLIES: Cable & Wire
HARNESS REPAIR SHOP
HARNESSES, HALTERS, SADDLERY & STRAPS
HATS: Paper, Novelty, Made From Purchased Paper
HEADPHONES: Radio
HEALTH AIDS: Exercise Eqpt
HEALTH FOOD & SUPPLEMENT STORES
HEALTH SYSTEMS AGENCY
HEARING AID REPAIR SVCS
HEARING AIDS
HEAT EXCHANGERS
HEAT EXCHANGERS: After Or Inter Coolers Or Condensers, Etc
HEAT TREATING: Metal
HEATER RADIANTS: Clay
HEATERS: Space, Exc Electric
HEATERS: Swimming Pool, Electric
HEATERS: Swimming Pool, Oil Or Gas
HEATING & AIR CONDITIONING EQPT & SPLYS WHOLE-SALERS
HEATING & AIR CONDITIONING UNITS, COMBINATION
HEATING EQPT & SPLYS
HEATING EQPT: Complete
HEATING EQPT: Induction
HEATING PADS: Nonelectric
HEATING SYSTEMS: Radiant, Indl Process
HEATING UNITS & DEVICES: Indl, Electric
HEATING UNITS: Gas, Infrared
HELICOPTERS
HELMETS: Athletic
HELMETS: Steel
HIGH ENERGY PARTICLE PHYSICS EQPT
HOBBY & CRAFT SPLY STORES
HOBBY GOODS, WHOLESALE
HOBBY SUPPLIES, WHOLESALE
HOBBY, TOY & GAME STORES: Arts & Crafts & Splys
HOBBY, TOY & GAME STORES: Ceramics Splys

HOBBY, TOY & GAME STORES: Dolls & Access
HOBBY, TOY & GAME STORES: Toys & Games
HOISTING SLINGS
HOISTS
HOLDING COMPANIES: Investment, Exc Banks
HOLDING COMPANIES: Personal, Exc Banks
HOLDING COMPANIES: Public Utility
HOLLOWARE, SILVER
HOME CENTER STORES
HOME ENTERTAINMENT EQPT: Electronic, NEC
HOME FURNISHINGS WHOLESALERS
HOME HEALTH CARE SVCS
HOMEFURNISHING STORE: Bedding, Sheet, Blanket,Spread/Pillow
HOMEFURNISHING STORES: Beddings & Linens
HOMEFURNISHING STORES: Closet organizers & shelving units
HOMEFURNISHING STORES: Lighting Fixtures
HOMEFURNISHING STORES: Pictures, Wall
HOMEFURNISHING STORES: Pottery
HOMEFURNISHING STORES: Wicker, Rattan, Or Reed
HOMEFURNISHING STORES: Window Furnishings
HOMEFURNISHING STORES: Window Shades, NEC
HOMEFURNISHINGS & SPLYS, WHOLESALE: Decorative
HOMEFURNISHINGS, WHOLESALE: Blinds, Venetian
HOMEFURNISHINGS, WHOLESALE: Blinds, Vertical
HOMEFURNISHINGS, WHOLESALE: Carpets
HOMEFURNISHINGS, WHOLESALE: Draperies
HOMEFURNISHINGS, WHOLESALE: Kitchenware
HOMEFURNISHINGS, WHOLESALE: Pillowcases
HOMEFURNISHINGS, WHOLESALE: Towels
HOMEFURNISHINGS, WHOLESALE: Window Covering Parts & Access
HOMEFURNISHINGS, WHOLESALE: Window Shades
HOMES, MODULAR: Wooden
HOMES: Log Cabins
HONEYCOMB CORE & BOARD: Made From Purchased Materials
HOODS: Range, Sheet Metal
HOPPERS: End Dump
HORMONE PREPARATIONS
HORSE & PET ACCESSORIES: Textile
HORSE ACCESS: Harnesses & Riding Crops, Etc, Exc Leather
HORSE DRAWN VEHICLE REPAIR SVCS
HORSESHOES
HOSE: Air Line Or Air Brake, Rubber Or Rubberized Fabric
HOSE: Fire, Rubber
HOSE: Flexible Metal
HOSE: Garden, Plastic
HOSE: Plastic
HOSE: Pneumatic, Rubber Or Rubberized Fabric, NEC
HOSE: Rubber
HOSES & BELTING: Rubber & Plastic
HOSPITALS: Medical & Surgical
HOT TUBS
HOUSEHOLD APPLIANCE STORES
HOUSEHOLD APPLIANCE STORES: Air Cond Rm Units, Self-Contnd
HOUSEHOLD APPLIANCE STORES: Electric Household, Major
HOUSEHOLD ARTICLES, EXC FURNITURE: Cut Stone
HOUSEHOLD ARTICLES: Metal
HOUSEHOLD FURNISHINGS, NEC
HOUSEKEEPING & MAID SVCS
HOUSEWARES, ELECTRIC: Blenders
HOUSEWARES, ELECTRIC: Cooking Appliances
HOUSEWARES, ELECTRIC: Fans, Exhaust & Ventilating
HOUSEWARES, ELECTRIC: Heaters, Space
HOUSEWARES, ELECTRIC: Heating Units, Electric Appliances
HOUSEWARES, ELECTRIC: Lighters, Cigar
HOUSEWARES, ELECTRIC: Massage Machines, Exc Beauty/Barber
HOUSEWARES: Dishes, Earthenware
HOUSEWARES: Dishes, Plastic
HUMIDIFIERS & DEHUMIDIFIERS
HYDRAULIC EQPT REPAIR SVC
HYDRAULIC FLUIDS: Synthetic Based
HYDROPONIC EQPT
Hard Rubber & Molded Rubber Prdts

I

ICE
ICE BOXES: Indl
ICE CREAM & ICES WHOLESALERS

IDENTIFICATION PLATES
IDENTIFICATION TAGS, EXC PAPER
IGNEOUS ROCK: Crushed & Broken
IGNITION APPARATUS & DISTRIBUTORS
IGNITION SYSTEMS: Internal Combustion Engine
INCENSE
INCINERATORS
INDL & PERSONAL SVC PAPER WHOLESALERS
INDL & PERSONAL SVC PAPER, WHOL: Bags, Paper/Disp Plastic
INDL & PERSONAL SVC PAPER, WHOL: Boxes, Corrugtd/Solid Fiber
INDL & PERSONAL SVC PAPER, WHOL: Boxes, Paperbrd/Plastic
INDL & PERSONAL SVC PAPER, WHOL: Cups, Disp, Plastic/Paper
INDL & PERSONAL SVC PAPER, WHOLESALE: Boxes & Containers
INDL & PERSONAL SVC PAPER, WHOLESALE: Disposable
INDL & PERSONAL SVC PAPER, WHOLESALE: Shipping Splys
INDL CONTRACTORS: Exhibit Construction
INDL EQPT CLEANING SVCS
INDL EQPT SVCS
INDL GASES WHOLESALERS
INDL MACHINERY & EQPT WHOLESALERS
INDL MACHINERY REPAIR & MAINTENANCE
INDL PATTERNS: Foundry Cores
INDL PATTERNS: Foundry Patternmaking
INDL PROCESS INSTRUMENTS: Analyzers
INDL PROCESS INSTRUMENTS: Chromatographs
INDL PROCESS INSTRUMENTS: Control
INDL PROCESS INSTRUMENTS: Controllers, Process Variables
INDL PROCESS INSTRUMENTS: Digital Display, Process Variables
INDL PROCESS INSTRUMENTS: Fluidic Devices, Circuit & Systems
INDL PROCESS INSTRUMENTS: Indl Flow & Measuring
INDL PROCESS INSTRUMENTS: Level & Bulk Measuring
INDL PROCESS INSTRUMENTS: Manometers
INDL PROCESS INSTRUMENTS: Moisture Meters
INDL PROCESS INSTRUMENTS: Temperature
INDL PROCESS INSTRUMENTS: Thermistors
INDL PROCESS INSTRUMENTS: Water Quality Monitoring/Cntrl Sys
INDL SPLYS WHOLESALERS
INDL SPLYS, WHOL: Fasteners, Incl Nuts, Bolts, Screws, Etc
INDL SPLYS, WHOLESALE: Abrasives
INDL SPLYS, WHOLESALE: Adhesives, Tape & Plasters
INDL SPLYS, WHOLESALE: Bearings
INDL SPLYS, WHOLESALE: Brushes, Indl
INDL SPLYS, WHOLESALE: Electric Tools
INDL SPLYS, WHOLESALE: Fasteners & Fastening Eqpt
INDL SPLYS, WHOLESALE: Filters, Indl
INDL SPLYS, WHOLESALE: Gaskets
INDL SPLYS, WHOLESALE: Gaskets & Seals
INDL SPLYS, WHOLESALE: Hydraulic & Pneumatic Pistons/Valves
INDL SPLYS, WHOLESALE: Knives, Indl
INDL SPLYS, WHOLESALE: Mill Splys
INDL SPLYS, WHOLESALE: Pipeline Wrappings, Anti-Corrosive
INDL SPLYS, WHOLESALE: Power Transmission, Eqpt & Apparatus
INDL SPLYS, WHOLESALE: Rope, Exc Wire
INDL SPLYS, WHOLESALE: Rubber Goods, Mechanical
INDL SPLYS, WHOLESALE: Seals
INDL SPLYS, WHOLESALE: Springs
INDL SPLYS, WHOLESALE: Tanks, Pressurized
INDL SPLYS, WHOLESALE: Textile Printers' Splys
INDL SPLYS, WHOLESALE: Tools
INDL SPLYS, WHOLESALE: Tools, NEC
INDL SPLYS, WHOLESALE: Valves & Fittings
INDL TOOL GRINDING SVCS
INDL TRUCK REPAIR SVCS
INDUSTRIAL & COMMERCIAL EQPT INSPECTION SVCS
INFANTS' WEAR STORES
INFORMATION RETRIEVAL SERVICES
INGOT, EXTRUSION: Extrusion ingot, aluminum: rolling mills
INGOT: Aluminum
INK OR WRITING FLUIDS
INK: Duplicating
INK: Gravure
INK: Letterpress Or Offset
INK: Lithographic

INK: Printing
INNER TUBES: Indl
INSECTICIDES & PESTICIDES
INSPECTION & TESTING SVCS
INSTRUMENTS & ACCESSORIES: Surveying
INSTRUMENTS & METERS: Measuring, Electric
INSTRUMENTS, LAB: Spectroscopic/Optical Properties Measuring
INSTRUMENTS, LABORATORY: Analyzers, Thermal
INSTRUMENTS, LABORATORY: Blood Testing
INSTRUMENTS, LABORATORY: Infrared Analytical
INSTRUMENTS, LABORATORY: Mass Spectrometers
INSTRUMENTS, LABORATORY: Spectrographs
INSTRUMENTS, LABORATORY: Spectrometers
INSTRUMENTS, LABORATORY: Titrimeters
INSTRUMENTS, MEASURING & CNTRG: Plotting, Drafting/Map Rdg
INSTRUMENTS, MEASURING & CNTRL: Gauges, Auto, Computer
INSTRUMENTS, MEASURING & CNTRL: Radiation & Testing, Nuclear
INSTRUMENTS, MEASURING & CNTRL: Tester, Acft Hydc Ctrl Test
INSTRUMENTS, MEASURING & CNTRL: Testing, Abrasion, Etc
INSTRUMENTS, MEASURING & CNTRLG: Aircraft & Motor Vehicle
INSTRUMENTS, MEASURING & CNTRLG: Fatigue Test, Indl, Mech
INSTRUMENTS, MEASURING & CNTRLG: Tensile Strength Testing
INSTRUMENTS, MEASURING & CNTRLG: Thermometers/Temp Sensors
INSTRUMENTS, MEASURING & CONTROLLING: Breathalyzers
INSTRUMENTS, MEASURING & CONTROLLING: Coal Testing Apparatus
INSTRUMENTS, MEASURING & CONTROLLING: Gas Detectors
INSTRUMENTS, MEASURING & CONTROLLING: Leak Detection, Liquid
INSTRUMENTS, MEASURING & CONTROLLING: Polygraph
INSTRUMENTS, MEASURING & CONTROLLING: Torsion Testing
INSTRUMENTS, MEASURING & CONTROLLING: Transits, Surveyors'
INSTRUMENTS, MEASURING & CONTROLLING: Ultrasonic Testing
INSTRUMENTS, MEASURING & CONTROLLING: Weather Tracking
INSTRUMENTS, MEASURING/CNTRL: Gauging, Ultrasonic Thickness
INSTRUMENTS, MEASURING/CNTRL: Testing/Measuring, Kinematic
INSTRUMENTS, MEASURING/CNTRLNG: Med Diagnostic Sys, Nuclear
INSTRUMENTS, OPTICAL: Cinetheodolites
INSTRUMENTS, OPTICAL: Elements & Assemblies, Exc Ophthalmic
INSTRUMENTS, OPTICAL: Lenses, All Types Exc Ophthalmic
INSTRUMENTS, OPTICAL: Magnifying, NEC
INSTRUMENTS, OPTICAL: Metallographs
INSTRUMENTS, OPTICAL: Mirrors
INSTRUMENTS, OPTICAL: Reflectors
INSTRUMENTS, OPTICAL: Sighting & Fire Control
INSTRUMENTS, OPTICAL: Test & Inspection
INSTRUMENTS, SURGICAL & MED: Cleaning Eqpt, Ultrasonic Med
INSTRUMENTS, SURGICAL & MEDI: Knife Blades/Handles, Surgical
INSTRUMENTS, SURGICAL & MEDICAL: Blood & Bone Work
INSTRUMENTS, SURGICAL & MEDICAL: Blood Pressure
INSTRUMENTS, SURGICAL & MEDICAL: Cannulae
INSTRUMENTS, SURGICAL & MEDICAL: Catheters
INSTRUMENTS, SURGICAL & MEDICAL: IV Transfusion
INSTRUMENTS, SURGICAL & MEDICAL: Inhalation Therapy
INSTRUMENTS, SURGICAL & MEDICAL: Knives
INSTRUMENTS, SURGICAL & MEDICAL: Lasers, Surgical
INSTRUMENTS, SURGICAL & MEDICAL: Muscle Exercise, Ophthalmic
INSTRUMENTS, SURGICAL & MEDICAL: Ophthalmic
INSTRUMENTS, SURGICAL & MEDICAL: Plates & Screws, Bone
INSTRUMENTS, SURGICAL & MEDICAL: Rifles, Hypodermic, Animal

INSTRUMENTS: Analytical
INSTRUMENTS: Colonoscopes, Electromedical
INSTRUMENTS: Combustion Control, Indl
INSTRUMENTS: Differential Pressure, Indl
INSTRUMENTS: Elec Lab Stds, Resist, Inductance/Capacitance
INSTRUMENTS: Electrocardiographs
INSTRUMENTS: Electrolytic Conductivity, Laboratory
INSTRUMENTS: Electron Test Tube
INSTRUMENTS: Electronic, Analog-Digital Converters
INSTRUMENTS: Endoscopic Eqpt, Electromedical
INSTRUMENTS: Eye Examination
INSTRUMENTS: Flow, Indl Process
INSTRUMENTS: Frequency Meters, Electrical, Mech & Electronic
INSTRUMENTS: Galvanometers
INSTRUMENTS: Humidity, Indl Process
INSTRUMENTS: Indl Process Control
INSTRUMENTS: Laser, Scientific & Engineering
INSTRUMENTS: Liquid Level, Indl Process
INSTRUMENTS: Measurement, Indl Process
INSTRUMENTS: Measuring & Controlling
INSTRUMENTS: Measuring Electricity
INSTRUMENTS: Measuring, Electrical Power
INSTRUMENTS: Measuring, Electrical Quantities
INSTRUMENTS: Medical & Surgical
INSTRUMENTS: Meteorological
INSTRUMENTS: Microwave Test
INSTRUMENTS: Optical, Analytical
INSTRUMENTS: Particle Size Analyzers
INSTRUMENTS: Pressure Measurement, Indl
INSTRUMENTS: Radio Frequency Measuring
INSTRUMENTS: Seismographs
INSTRUMENTS: Temperature Measurement, Indl
INSTRUMENTS: Test, Digital, Electronic & Electrical Circuits
INSTRUMENTS: Test, Electrical, Engine
INSTRUMENTS: Test, Electronic & Electric Measurement
INSTRUMENTS: Test, Electronic & Electrical Circuits
INSTRUMENTS: Thermal Conductive, Indl
INSTRUMENTS: Thermal Property Measurement
INSTRUMENTS: Transducers, Volts, Amperes, Watts, VARs & Freq
INSULATING BOARD, CELLULAR FIBER
INSULATING BOARD, HARD PRESSED
INSULATING COMPOUNDS
INSULATION & CUSHIONING FOAM: Polystyrene
INSULATION & ROOFING MATERIALS: Wood, Reconstituted
INSULATION MATERIALS WHOLESALERS
INSULATION: Fiberglass
INSULATORS & INSULATION MATERIALS: Electrical
INSULATORS, GLASS MADE IN GLASS PLANTS: Electrical
INSULATORS, PORCELAIN: Electrical
INSURANCE AGENTS, NEC
INSURANCE BROKERS, NEC
INSURANCE CARRIERS: Life
INSURANCE CARRIERS: Property & Casualty
INSURANCE: Agents, Brokers & Service
INTEGRATED CIRCUITS, SEMICONDUCTOR NETWORKS, ETC
INTERCOMMUNICATIONS SYSTEMS: Electric
INTERIOR DECORATING SVCS
INTERIOR DESIGN SVCS, NEC
INTERIOR DESIGNING SVCS
INTERIOR REPAIR SVCS
INVENTOR
INVERTERS: Nonrotating Electrical
INVERTERS: Rotating Electrical
INVESTMENT FUNDS, NEC
INVESTMENT FUNDS: Open-Ended
INVESTMENT RESEARCH SVCS
INVESTORS: Real Estate, Exc Property Operators
IRON & STEEL PRDTS: Hot-Rolled
IRON ORE BENEFICIATING
IRON ORE MINING
IRON ORES
IRON OXIDES
IRRADIATION EQPT: Gamma Ray

J

JACKETS: Indl, Metal Plate
JACKS: Hydraulic
JANITORIAL & CUSTODIAL SVCS
JANITORIAL EQPT & SPLYS WHOLESALERS
JARS: Plastic
JEWELERS' FINDINGS & MATERIALS: Bearings, Synthetic

JEWELERS' FINDINGS/MTRLS: Gem Prep, Settings, Real/Imitation
JEWELRY & PRECIOUS STONES WHOLESALERS
JEWELRY APPAREL
JEWELRY FINDINGS & LAPIDARY WORK
JEWELRY REPAIR SVCS
JEWELRY STORES
JEWELRY STORES: Precious Stones & Precious Metals
JEWELRY STORES: Silverware
JEWELRY, PRECIOUS METAL: Bracelets
JEWELRY, PRECIOUS METAL: Cigar & Cigarette Access
JEWELRY, PRECIOUS METAL: Mountings & Trimmings
JEWELRY, PRECIOUS METAL: Pearl, Natural Or Cultured
JEWELRY, PRECIOUS METAL: Pins
JEWELRY, PRECIOUS METAL: Rings, Finger
JEWELRY, PRECIOUS METAL: Settings & Mountings
JEWELRY, WHOLESALE
JEWELRY: Decorative, Fashion & Costume
JEWELRY: Precious Metal
JIGS & FIXTURES
JIGS: Welding Positioners
JOB PRINTING & NEWSPAPER PUBLISHING COMBINED
JOB TRAINING & VOCATIONAL REHABILITATION SVCS
JOB TRAINING SVCS
JOINTS & COUPLINGS
JOINTS: Expansion
JOINTS: Expansion, Pipe
JOISTS: Long-Span Series, Open Web Steel

K

KAOLIN & BALL CLAY MINING
KEYBOARDS: Computer Or Office Machine
KEYS, KEY BLANKS
KEYS: Machine
KILNS & FURNACES: Ceramic
KILNS: Calcining
KITCHEN & COOKING ARTICLES: Pottery
KITCHEN CABINET STORES, EXC CUSTOM
KITCHEN CABINETS WHOLESALERS
KITCHEN UTENSILS: Wooden
KITCHENWARE STORES
KITCHENWARE: Plastic
KNIT GOODS, WHOLESALE
KNIVES: Agricultural Or indl

L

LABELS: Cotton, Printed
LABELS: Paper, Made From Purchased Materials
LABOR UNION
LABORATORIES, TESTING: Forensic
LABORATORIES, TESTING: Metallurgical
LABORATORIES, TESTING: Pollution
LABORATORIES, TESTING: Product Testing
LABORATORIES, TESTING: Product Testing, Safety/Performance
LABORATORIES: Biological Research
LABORATORIES: Biotechnology
LABORATORIES: Dental
LABORATORIES: Dental & Medical X-Ray
LABORATORIES: Dental Orthodontic Appliance Production
LABORATORIES: Dental, Artificial Teeth Production
LABORATORIES: Dental, Denture Production
LABORATORIES: Electronic Research
LABORATORIES: Medical
LABORATORIES: Medical Bacteriological
LABORATORIES: Noncommercial Research
LABORATORIES: Physical Research, Commercial
LABORATORIES: Testing
LABORATORIES: Testing
LABORATORY APPARATUS & FURNITURE
LABORATORY APPARATUS & FURNITURE: Worktables
LABORATORY APPARATUS, EXC HEATING & MEASURING
LABORATORY APPARATUS: Calibration Tapes, Phy Testing Mach
LABORATORY APPARATUS: Dryers
LABORATORY APPARATUS: Particle Size Reduction
LABORATORY APPARATUS: Physics, NEC
LABORATORY APPARATUS: Sample Preparation Apparatus
LABORATORY APPARATUS: Time Interval Measuring, Electric
LABORATORY CHEMICALS: Organic
LABORATORY EQPT, EXC MEDICAL: Wholesalers
LABORATORY EQPT: Centrifuges
LABORATORY EQPT: Chemical
LABORATORY EQPT: Clinical Instruments Exc Medical
LABORATORY EQPT: Distilling

INDEX

MACHINE TOOLS, METAL CUTTING: Tool Replacement & Rpr Parts
MACHINE TOOLS, METAL CUTTING: Vertical Turning & Boring
MACHINE TOOLS, METAL FORMING: Electroforming
MACHINE TOOLS, METAL FORMING: Marking
MACHINE TOOLS, METAL FORMING: Mechanical, Pneumatic Or Hyd
MACHINE TOOLS, METAL FORMING: Presses, Hyd & Pneumatic
MACHINE TOOLS, METAL FORMING: Pressing
MACHINE TOOLS, METAL FORMING: Rebuilt
MACHINE TOOLS, METAL FORMING: Spinning, Spline Rollg/Windg
MACHINE TOOLS: Metal Cutting
MACHINE TOOLS: Metal Forming
MACHINERY & EQPT FINANCE LEASING
MACHINERY & EQPT, AGRICULTURAL, WHOLESALE: Dairy
MACHINERY & EQPT, AGRICULTURAL, WHOLESALE: Lawn
MACHINERY & EQPT, AGRICULTURAL, WHOLESALE: Lawn & Garden
MACHINERY & EQPT, AGRICULTURAL, WHOLESALE: Tractors
MACHINERY & EQPT, INDL, WHOL: Controlling Instruments/Access
MACHINERY & EQPT, INDL, WHOLESALE: Alcoholic Beverage Mfrg
MACHINERY & EQPT, INDL, WHOLESALE: Chemical Process
MACHINERY & EQPT, INDL, WHOLESALE: Conveyor Systems
MACHINERY & EQPT, INDL, WHOLESALE: Cranes
MACHINERY & EQPT, INDL, WHOLESALE: Crushing
MACHINERY & EQPT, INDL, WHOLESALE: Dairy Prdts Manufacturing
MACHINERY & EQPT, INDL, WHOLESALE: Drilling, Exc Bits
MACHINERY & EQPT, INDL, WHOLESALE: Engines & Parts, Diesel
MACHINERY & EQPT, INDL, WHOLESALE: Engines, Gasoline
MACHINERY & EQPT, INDL, WHOLESALE: Engs & Parts, Air-Cooled
MACHINERY & EQPT, INDL, WHOLESALE: Fans
MACHINERY & EQPT, INDL, WHOLESALE: Food Manufacturing
MACHINERY & EQPT, INDL, WHOLESALE: Fuel Injection Systems
MACHINERY & EQPT, INDL, WHOLESALE: Hydraulic Systems
MACHINERY & EQPT, INDL, WHOLESALE: Indl Machine Parts
MACHINERY & EQPT, INDL, WHOLESALE: Instruments & Cntrl Eqpt
MACHINERY & EQPT, INDL, WHOLESALE: Machine Tools & Access
MACHINERY & EQPT, INDL, WHOLESALE: Machine Tools & Metalwork
MACHINERY & EQPT, INDL, WHOLESALE: Measure/Test, Electric
MACHINERY & EQPT, INDL, WHOLESALE: Packaging
MACHINERY & EQPT, INDL, WHOLESALE: Petroleum Industry
MACHINERY & EQPT, INDL, WHOLESALE: Plastic Prdts Machinery
MACHINERY & EQPT, INDL, WHOLESALE: Pneumatic Tools
MACHINERY & EQPT, INDL, WHOLESALE: Processing & Packaging
MACHINERY & EQPT, INDL, WHOLESALE: Propane Conversion
MACHINERY & EQPT, INDL, WHOLESALE: Safety Eqpt
MACHINERY & EQPT, INDL, WHOLESALE: Sawmill
MACHINERY & EQPT, INDL, WHOLESALE: Sewing
MACHINERY & EQPT, INDL, WHOLESALE: Tanks, Storage
MACHINERY & EQPT, INDL, WHOLESALE: Tapping Attachments
MACHINERY & EQPT, INDL, WHOLESALE: Textile
MACHINERY & EQPT, INDL, WHOLESALE: Trailers, Indl
MACHINERY & EQPT, INDL, WHOLESALE: Water Pumps
MACHINERY & EQPT, INDL, WHOLESALE: Woodworking
MACHINERY & EQPT, WHOLESALE: Concrete Processing
MACHINERY & EQPT, WHOLESALE: Construction, Cranes
MACHINERY & EQPT, WHOLESALE: Construction, General
MACHINERY & EQPT, WHOLESALE: Crushing, Pulverizng & Screeng
MACHINERY & EQPT, WHOLESALE: Masonry
MACHINERY & EQPT, WHOLESALE: Oil Field Eqpt

MACHINERY & EQPT: Electroplating
MACHINERY & EQPT: Farm
MACHINERY & EQPT: Gas Producers, Generators/Other Rltd Eqpt
MACHINERY & EQPT: Liquid Automation
MACHINERY & EQPT: Metal Finishing, Plating Etc
MACHINERY & EQPT: Petroleum Refinery
MACHINERY BASES
MACHINERY CLEANING SVCS
MACHINERY, COMM LAUNDRY: Rug Cleaning, Drying Or Napping
MACHINERY, COMMERCIAL LAUNDRY & Drycleaning: Pressing
MACHINERY, EQPT & SUPPLIES: Parking Facility
MACHINERY, FLOOR SANDING: Commercial
MACHINERY, FOOD PRDTS: Chocolate Processing
MACHINERY, FOOD PRDTS: Confectionery
MACHINERY, FOOD PRDTS: Dairy, Pasteurizing
MACHINERY, FOOD PRDTS: Distillery
MACHINERY, FOOD PRDTS: Food Processing, Smokers
MACHINERY, FOOD PRDTS: Grinders, Commercial
MACHINERY, FOOD PRDTS: Mixers, Commercial
MACHINERY, FOOD PRDTS: Ovens, Bakery
MACHINERY, FOOD PRDTS: Pasta
MACHINERY, FOOD PRDTS: Potato Peelers, Electric
MACHINERY, FOOD PRDTS: Processing, Poultry
MACHINERY, FOOD PRDTS: Roasting, Coffee, Peanut, Etc.
MACHINERY, FOOD PRDTS: Sausage Stuffers
MACHINERY, FOOD PRDTS: Slicers, Commercial
MACHINERY, FOOD PRDTS: Sugar Plant
MACHINERY, LUBRICATION: Automatic
MACHINERY, MAILING: Mailing
MACHINERY, MAILING: Postage Meters
MACHINERY, METALWORKING: Assembly, Including Robotic
MACHINERY, METALWORKING: Coilers, Metalworking
MACHINERY, METALWORKING: Cutting & Slitting
MACHINERY, METALWORKING: Draw Benches
MACHINERY, OFFICE: Embossing, Store Or Office
MACHINERY, OFFICE: Perforators
MACHINERY, OFFICE: Time Clocks &Time Recording Devices
MACHINERY, PACKAGING: Packing & Wrapping
MACHINERY, PACKAGING: Wrapping
MACHINERY, PAPER INDUSTRY: Converting, Die Cutting & Stampng
MACHINERY, PAPER INDUSTRY: Paper Mill, Plating, Etc
MACHINERY, PAPER INDUSTRY: Pulp Mill
MACHINERY, PRINTING TRADES: Bronzing Or Dusting
MACHINERY, PRINTING TRADES: Copy Holders
MACHINERY, PRINTING TRADES: Galleys Or Chases
MACHINERY, PRINTING TRADES: Plates
MACHINERY, SERVICING: Coin-Operated, Exc Dry Clean & Laundry
MACHINERY, SEWING: Sewing & Hat & Zipper Making
MACHINERY, TEXTILE: Braiding
MACHINERY, TEXTILE: Embroidery
MACHINERY, TEXTILE: Frames, Double & Twisting
MACHINERY, TEXTILE: Printing
MACHINERY, TEXTILE: Shearing
MACHINERY, TEXTILE: Silk Screens
MACHINERY, WOODWORKING: Cabinet Makers'
MACHINERY, WOODWORKING: Furniture Makers
MACHINERY/EQPT, INDL, WHOL: Cleaning, High Press, Sand/Steam
MACHINERY: Ammunition & Explosives Loading
MACHINERY: Assembly, Exc Metalworking
MACHINERY: Automobile Garage, Frame Straighteners
MACHINERY: Automotive Maintenance
MACHINERY: Automotive Related
MACHINERY: Banking
MACHINERY: Blasting, Electrical
MACHINERY: Bottling & Canning
MACHINERY: Brewery & Malting
MACHINERY: Brick Making
MACHINERY: Bridge Or Gate, Hydraulic
MACHINERY: Cement Making
MACHINERY: Centrifugal
MACHINERY: Coin Wrapping
MACHINERY: Concrete Prdts
MACHINERY: Construction
MACHINERY: Cryogenic, Industrial
MACHINERY: Custom
MACHINERY: Desalination Eqpt
MACHINERY: Die Casting
MACHINERY: Drill Presses
MACHINERY: Electrical Discharge Erosion

MACHINERY: Electronic Component Making
MACHINERY: Electronic Teaching Aids
MACHINERY: Extruding
MACHINERY: Gear Cutting & Finishing
MACHINERY: Glassmaking
MACHINERY: Grinding
MACHINERY: Ice Making
MACHINERY: Industrial, NEC
MACHINERY: Kilns
MACHINERY: Kilns, Cement
MACHINERY: Kilns, Lumber
MACHINERY: Knitting
MACHINERY: Labeling
MACHINERY: Marking, Metalworking
MACHINERY: Metalworking
MACHINERY: Milling
MACHINERY: Mining
MACHINERY: Nuclear Reactor Control Rod & Drive Mechanism
MACHINERY: Optical Lens
MACHINERY: Packaging
MACHINERY: Paint Making
MACHINERY: Paper Industry Miscellaneous
MACHINERY: Pharmaciutical
MACHINERY: Plastic Working
MACHINERY: Printing Presses
MACHINERY: Recycling
MACHINERY: Riveting
MACHINERY: Road Construction & Maintenance
MACHINERY: Robots, Molding & Forming Plastics
MACHINERY: Rubber Working
MACHINERY: Semiconductor Manufacturing
MACHINERY: Separation Eqpt, Magnetic
MACHINERY: Separators, Mineral
MACHINERY: Service Industry, NEC
MACHINERY: Sheet Metal Working
MACHINERY: Specialty
MACHINERY: Stone Working
MACHINERY: Textile
MACHINERY: Tire Shredding
MACHINERY: Wire Drawing
MACHINERY: Woodworking
MACHINES: Forming, Sheet Metal
MACHINISTS' TOOLS: Measuring, Precision
MACHINISTS' TOOLS: Precision
MACHINISTS' TOOLS: Scales, Measuring, Precision
MAGAZINE STAND
MAGAZINES, WHOLESALE
MAGNESITE MINING
MAGNETIC INK & OPTICAL SCANNING EQPT
MAGNETIC INK RECOGNITION DEVICES
MAGNETIC RESONANCE IMAGING DEVICES: Nonmedical
MAGNETIC SHIELDS, METAL
MAGNETIC TAPE, AUDIO: Prerecorded
MAGNETS: Ceramic
MAGNETS: Permanent
MAIL-ORDER HOUSE, NEC
MAIL-ORDER HOUSES: Automotive Splys & Eqpt
MAIL-ORDER HOUSES: Book & Record Clubs
MAIL-ORDER HOUSES: Clothing, Exc Women's
MAIL-ORDER HOUSES: Computer Software
MAIL-ORDER HOUSES: Food
MAIL-ORDER HOUSES: General Merchandise
MAIL-ORDER HOUSES: Magazines
MAIL-ORDER HOUSES: Women's Apparel
MAILBOX RENTAL & RELATED SVCS
MAILING & MESSENGER SVCS
MAILING LIST: Brokers
MAILING MACHINES WHOLESALERS
MAILING SVCS, NEC
MANAGEMENT CONSULTING SVCS: Automation & Robotics
MANAGEMENT CONSULTING SVCS: Business
MANAGEMENT CONSULTING SVCS: Business Planning & Organizing
MANAGEMENT CONSULTING SVCS: Construction Project
MANAGEMENT CONSULTING SVCS: Distribution Channels
MANAGEMENT CONSULTING SVCS: Hospital & Health
MANAGEMENT CONSULTING SVCS: Industrial
MANAGEMENT CONSULTING SVCS: Industrial & Labor
MANAGEMENT CONSULTING SVCS: Industry Specialist
MANAGEMENT CONSULTING SVCS: Information Systems
MANAGEMENT CONSULTING SVCS: Manufacturing
MANAGEMENT CONSULTING SVCS: Planning
MANAGEMENT CONSULTING SVCS: Public Utilities
MANAGEMENT CONSULTING SVCS: Restaurant & Food

MANAGEMENT CONSULTING SVCS: Retail Trade Consultant

MANAGEMENT CONSULTING SVCS: Training & Development

MANAGEMENT SERVICES

MANAGEMENT SVCS, FACILITIES SUPPORT: Environ Remediation

MANAGEMENT SVCS: Business

MANAGEMENT SVCS: Construction

MANAGEMENT SVCS: Restaurant

MANHOLES & COVERS: Metal

MANHOLES COVERS: Concrete

MANICURE PREPARATIONS

MANUFACTURING INDUSTRIES, NEC

MAPMAKING SVCS

MARBLE, BUILDING: Cut & Shaped

MARINE CARGO HANDLING SVCS

MARINE HARDWARE

MARINE RELATED EQPT

MARINE RELATED EQPT: Cranes, Ship

MARKERS

MARKETS: Meat & fish

MARKING DEVICES

MARKING DEVICES: Canceling Stamps, Hand, Rubber Or Metal

MARKING DEVICES: Date Stamps, Hand, Rubber Or Metal

MARKING DEVICES: Embossing Seals & Hand Stamps

MARKING DEVICES: Figures, Metal

MARKING DEVICES: Irons, Marking Or Branding

MARKING DEVICES: Printing Dies, Marking Mach, Rubber/Plastic

MARKING DEVICES: Seal Presses, Notary & Hand

MASKS: Gas

MASQUERADE OR THEATRICAL COSTUMES STORES

MASTS: Cast Aluminum

MATERIAL GRINDING & PULVERIZING SVCS NEC

MATERIALS HANDLING EQPT WHOLESALERS

MATS OR MATTING, NEC: Rubber

MATS, MATTING & PADS: Door, Paper, Grass, Reed, Coir, Etc

MATS, MATTING & PADS: Nonwoven

MATTRESS RENOVATING & REPAIR SHOP

MATTRESS STORES

MEAT & MEAT PRDTS WHOLESALERS

MEAT CUTTING & PACKING

MEAT MARKETS

MEAT PRDTS: Bacon, Side & Sliced, From Purchased Meat

MEAT PRDTS: Bacon, Slab & Sliced, From Slaughtered Meat

MEAT PRDTS: Beef Stew, From Purchased Meat

MEAT PRDTS: Bologna, From Purchased Meat

MEAT PRDTS: Boneless Meat, From Purchased Meat

MEAT PRDTS: Boxed Beef, From Slaughtered Meat

MEAT PRDTS: Corned Beef, From Purchased Meat

MEAT PRDTS: Cured Meats, From Purchased Meat

MEAT PRDTS: Dried Beef, From Purchased Meat

MEAT PRDTS: Frozen

MEAT PRDTS: Hams & Picnics, From Slaughtered Meat

MEAT PRDTS: Head Cheese, From Purchased Meat

MEAT PRDTS: Lamb, From Slaughtered Meat

MEAT PRDTS: Luncheon Meat, From Purchased Meat

MEAT PRDTS: Meat By-Prdts, From Slaughtered Meat

MEAT PRDTS: Pork, From Slaughtered Meat

MEAT PRDTS: Prepared Beef Prdts From Purchased Beef

MEAT PRDTS: Roast Beef, From Purchased Meat

MEAT PRDTS: Sausage Casings, Natural

MEAT PRDTS: Sausages & Related Prdts, From Purchased Meat

MEAT PRDTS: Sausages, From Purchased Meat

MEAT PRDTS: Smoked

MEAT PRDTS: Snack Sticks, Incl Jerky, From Purchased Meat

MEAT PRDTS: Veal, From Slaughtered Meat

MEAT PROCESSED FROM PURCHASED CARCASSES

MEATS, PACKAGED FROZEN: Wholesalers

MEDIA: Magnetic & Optical Recording

MEDICAL & HOSPITAL EQPT WHOLESALERS

MEDICAL & HOSPITAL SPLYS: Radiation Shielding Garments

MEDICAL & SURGICAL SPLYS: Abdominal Support, Braces/Trusses

MEDICAL & SURGICAL SPLYS: Autoclaves

MEDICAL & SURGICAL SPLYS: Bandages & Dressings

MEDICAL & SURGICAL SPLYS: Braces, Orthopedic

MEDICAL & SURGICAL SPLYS: Canes, Orthopedic

MEDICAL & SURGICAL SPLYS: Clothing, Fire Resistant & Protect

MEDICAL & SURGICAL SPLYS: Cosmetic Restorations

MEDICAL & SURGICAL SPLYS: Dressings, Surgical

MEDICAL & SURGICAL SPLYS: Extension Shoes, Orthopedic

MEDICAL & SURGICAL SPLYS: Hosiery, Support

MEDICAL & SURGICAL SPLYS: Iron Lungs

MEDICAL & SURGICAL SPLYS: Limbs, Artificial

MEDICAL & SURGICAL SPLYS: Orthopedic Appliances

MEDICAL & SURGICAL SPLYS: Personal Safety Eqpt

MEDICAL & SURGICAL SPLYS: Prosthetic Appliances

MEDICAL & SURGICAL SPLYS: Respiratory Protect Eqpt, Personal

MEDICAL & SURGICAL SPLYS: Socks, Stump

MEDICAL & SURGICAL SPLYS: Space Helmets

MEDICAL & SURGICAL SPLYS: Sponges

MEDICAL & SURGICAL SPLYS: Stretchers

MEDICAL & SURGICAL SPLYS: Supports, Abdominal, Ankle, Etc

MEDICAL & SURGICAL SPLYS: Sutures, Non & Absorbable

MEDICAL & SURGICAL SPLYS: Swabs, Sanitary Cotton

MEDICAL & SURGICAL SPLYS: Technical Aids, Handicapped

MEDICAL & SURGICAL SPLYS: Trusses, Orthopedic & Surgical

MEDICAL & SURGICAL SPLYS: Walkers

MEDICAL & SURGICAL SPLYS: Welders' Hoods

MEDICAL CENTERS

MEDICAL EQPT REPAIR SVCS, NON-ELECTRIC

MEDICAL EQPT: CAT Scanner Or Computerized Axial Tomography

MEDICAL EQPT: Defibrillators

MEDICAL EQPT: Diagnostic

MEDICAL EQPT: Electromedical Apparatus

MEDICAL EQPT: Electrotherapeutic Apparatus

MEDICAL EQPT: Heart & Lung

MEDICAL EQPT: Heart-Lung Machines, Exc Iron Lungs

MEDICAL EQPT: Laser Systems

MEDICAL EQPT: MRI/Magnetic Resonance Imaging Devs, Nuclear

MEDICAL EQPT: Pacemakers

MEDICAL EQPT: Patient Monitoring

MEDICAL EQPT: Sterilizers

MEDICAL EQPT: Ultrasonic Scanning Devices

MEDICAL EQPT: Ultrasonic, Exc Cleaning

MEDICAL EQPT: X-Ray Apparatus & Tubes, Therapeutic

MEDICAL FIELD ASSOCIATION

MEDICAL HELP SVCS

MEDICAL INSURANCE CLAIM PROCESSING: Contract Or Fee Basis

MEDICAL TRAINING SERVICES

MEDICAL X-RAY MACHINES & TUBES WHOLESALERS

MEDICAL, DENTAL & HOSPITAL EQPT, WHOL: Dentists' Prof Splys

MEDICAL, DENTAL & HOSPITAL EQPT, WHOL: Hospital Eqpt & Splys

MEDICAL, DENTAL & HOSPITAL EQPT, WHOL: Hosptl Eqpt/Furniture

MEDICAL, DENTAL & HOSPITAL EQPT, WHOL: Surgical Eqpt & Splys

MEDICAL, DENTAL & HOSPITAL EQPT, WHOLESALE: Hearing Aids

MEDICAL, DENTAL & HOSPITAL EQPT, WHOLESALE: Med Eqpt & Splys

MEDICAL, DENTAL & HOSPITAL EQPT, WHOLESALE: Medical Lab

MEDICAL, DENTAL & HOSPITAL EQPT, WHOLESALE: Orthopedic

MEDICAL, DENTAL & HOSPITAL EQPT, WHOLESALE: Safety

MEDICAL, DENTAL & HOSPITAL EQPT, WHOLESALE: Therapy

MEDICAL, DENTAL/HOSPITAL EQPT, WHOL: Veterinarian Eqpt/Sply

MEMBERSHIP ORGANIZATIONS, NEC: Charitable

MEMBERSHIP ORGANIZATIONS, NEC: Historical Club

MEMBERSHIP ORGANIZATIONS, PROF: Education/Teacher Assoc

MEMBERSHIP ORGANIZATIONS, PROFESSIONAL: Accounting Assoc

MEMBERSHIP ORGANIZATIONS, PROFESSIONAL: Health Association

MEMBERSHIP ORGANIZATIONS, REL: Churches, Temples & Shrines

MEMBERSHIP ORGANIZATIONS, RELIGIOUS: Baptist Church

MEMBERSHIP ORGANIZATIONS, RELIGIOUS: Catholic Church

MEMBERSHIP ORGANIZATIONS, RELIGIOUS: Lutheran Church

MEMBERSHIP ORGANIZATIONS, RELIGIOUS: Religious Instruction

MEMORIALS, MONUMENTS & MARKERS

MEN'S & BOYS' CLOTHING ACCESS STORES

MEN'S & BOYS' CLOTHING STORES

MEN'S & BOYS' CLOTHING WHOLESALERS, NEC

MEN'S & BOYS' HATS STORES

MEN'S & BOYS' HOSIERY WHOLESALERS

MEN'S & BOYS' SPORTSWEAR CLOTHING STORES

MEN'S & BOYS' SPORTSWEAR WHOLESALERS

MEN'S & BOYS' UNDERWEAR WHOLESALERS

MEN'S SUITS STORES

MERCHANDISING MACHINE OPERATORS: Vending

MESH, REINFORCING: Plastic

METAL & STEEL PRDTS: Abrasive

METAL COMPONENTS: Prefabricated

METAL CUTTING SVCS

METAL DETECTORS

METAL FABRICATORS: Architechtural

METAL FABRICATORS: Plate

METAL FABRICATORS: Sheet

METAL FABRICATORS: Structural, Ship

METAL FABRICATORS: Structural, Ship

METAL FINISHING SVCS

METAL MINING SVCS

METAL ORES, NEC

METAL RESHAPING & REPLATING SVCS

METAL SERVICE CENTERS & OFFICES

METAL SPINNING FOR THE TRADE

METAL STAMPING, FOR THE TRADE

METAL STAMPINGS: Perforated

METAL TREATING COMPOUNDS

METAL TREATING: Cryogenic

METAL, TITANIUM: Sponge & Granules

METAL: Battery

METALS SVC CENTERS & WHOL: Structural Shapes, Iron Or Steel

METALS SVC CENTERS & WHOLESALERS: Bars, Metal

METALS SVC CENTERS & WHOLESALERS: Cable, Wire

METALS SVC CENTERS & WHOLESALERS: Copper Prdts

METALS SVC CENTERS & WHOLESALERS: Forgings, Ferrous

METALS SVC CENTERS & WHOLESALERS: Iron & Steel Prdt, Ferrous

METALS SVC CENTERS & WHOLESALERS: Lead

METALS SVC CENTERS & WHOLESALERS: Misc Nonferrous Prdts

METALS SVC CENTERS & WHOLESALERS: Nonferrous Sheets, Etc

METALS SVC CENTERS & WHOLESALERS: Piling, Iron & Steel

METALS SVC CENTERS & WHOLESALERS: Pipe & Tubing, Steel

METALS SVC CENTERS & WHOLESALERS: Rails & Access

METALS SVC CENTERS & WHOLESALERS: Rope, Wire, Exc Insulated

METALS SVC CENTERS & WHOLESALERS: Sheets, Metal

METALS SVC CENTERS & WHOLESALERS: Steel

METALS SVC CENTERS & WHOLESALERS: Steel Decking

METALS SVC CENTERS & WHOLESALERS: Tubing, Metal

METALS SVC CENTERS/WHOL: Forms, Steel Concrete Construction

METALS SVC CNTRS & WHOL: Metal Wires, Ties, Cables/Screening

METALS SVC CTRS & WHOLESALERS: Aluminum Bars, Rods, Etc

METALS: Antifriction Bearing, Lead-Base

METALS: Precious NEC

METALS: Precious, Secondary

METALS: Primary Nonferrous, NEC

METALWORK: Miscellaneous

METALWORK: Ornamental

METALWORKING MACHINERY WHOLESALERS

METERING DEVICES: Gas Meters, Domestic & Large Cap, Indl

METERING DEVICES: Integrating & Totalizing, Gas & Liquids

METERING DEVICES: Positive Displacement Meters

METERING DEVICES: Rotary Type

METERING DEVICES: Water Quality Monitoring & Control Systems

METERS: Elasped Time

METERS: Hydrometers, Indl Process

METERS: Magnetic Flow, Indl Process

MGMT CONSULTING SVCS: Matls, Incl Purch, Handle & Invntry
MGT SVCS, FACIL SUPPT: Base Maint Or Provide Personnel
MICROCIRCUITS, INTEGRATED: Semiconductor
MICROFILM EQPT
MICROFILM SVCS
MICROPROCESSORS
MICROSCOPES
MICROSCOPES: Electron & Proton
MICROWAVE COMPONENTS
MILITARY GOODS & REGALIA STORES
MILITARY INSIGNIA
MILITARY INSIGNIA, TEXTILE
MILL PRDTS: Structural & Rail
MILLINERY SUPPLIES: Veils & Veiling, Bridal, Funeral, Etc
MILLING: Cereal Flour, Exc Rice
MILLING: Chemical
MILLING: Grains, Exc Rice
MILLS: Bar
MILLS: Ferrous & Nonferrous
MILLWORK
MIMEOGRAPHING SVCS
MINE & QUARRY SVCS: Nonmetallic Minerals
MINE PREPARATION SVCS
MINE PUMPING OR DRAINING SVCS: Nonmetallic Minerals
MINE SHAFT OR TUNNEL PREPARATION SVCS: Anthracite
MINE SHAFT OR TUNNEL PREPARATION SVCS: Bituminous Or Lignite
MINE SHAFT SINKING SVCS: Nonmetallic Minerals
MINERAL MINING: Nonmetallic
MINERAL WOOL
MINERALS: Ground Or Otherwise Treated
MINERALS: Ground or Treated
MINIATURE GOLF COURSES
MINIATURES
MINING EXPLORATION & DEVELOPMENT SVCS
MINING MACHINERY & EQPT WHOLESALERS
MINING MACHINES & EQPT: Augers
MINING MACHINES & EQPT: Bits, Rock, Exc Oil/Gas Field Tools
MINING MACHINES & EQPT: Cleaning, Mineral
MINING MACHINES & EQPT: Crushers, Stationary
MINING MACHINES & EQPT: Flotation
MINING MACHINES & EQPT: Grinders, Stone, Stationary
MINING MACHINES & EQPT: Mineral Beneficiation
MINING MACHINES & EQPT: Pellet Mills
MINING MACHINES & EQPT: Pulverizers, Stone, Stationary
MINING MACHINES & EQPT: Rock Crushing, Stationary
MINING MACHINES & EQPT: Shuttle Cars, Underground
MINING MACHINES/EQPT: Mine Car, Plow, Loader, Feeder/Eqpt
MINING SVCS, NEC: Anthracite
MINING SVCS, NEC: Lignite
MINING: Sand & Shale Oil
MIRRORS: Motor Vehicle
MISCELLANEOUS FINANCIAL INVEST ACT: Oil/Gas Lease Brokers
MIXING EQPT
MIXTURES & BLOCKS: Asphalt Paving
MOBILE COMMUNICATIONS EQPT
MOBILE HOME & TRAILER REPAIR
MOBILE HOME DEALERS: Mobile Home Parts & Access
MOBILE HOME FRAMES
MOBILE HOMES
MOBILE HOMES, EXC RECREATIONAL
MODELS
MODELS: General, Exc Toy
MOLDED RUBBER PRDTS
MOLDING COMPOUNDS
MOLDING SAND MINING
MOLDINGS & TRIM: Metal, Exc Automobile
MOLDINGS & TRIM: Wood
MOLDINGS: Picture Frame
MOLDS: Indl
MOLDS: Plastic Working & Foundry
MONORAIL SYSTEMS
MONUMENTS & GRAVE MARKERS, EXC TERRAZZO
MONUMENTS: Concrete
MONUMENTS: Cut Stone, Exc Finishing Or Lettering Only
MOPS: Floor & Dust
MOTION PICTURE & VIDEO PRODUCTION SVCS
MOTION PICTURE & VIDEO PRODUCTION SVCS: Indl
MOTION PICTURE & VIDEO PRODUCTION SVCS: Training
MOTOR & GENERATOR PARTS: Electric
MOTOR HOMES
MOTOR REBUILDING SVCS, EXC AUTOMOTIVE

MOTOR REPAIR SVCS
MOTOR VEHICLE ASSEMBLY, COMPLETE: Autos, Incl Specialty
MOTOR VEHICLE ASSEMBLY, COMPLETE: Bus/Large Spclty Vehicles
MOTOR VEHICLE ASSEMBLY, COMPLETE: Buses, All Types
MOTOR VEHICLE ASSEMBLY, COMPLETE: Cars, Armored
MOTOR VEHICLE ASSEMBLY, COMPLETE: Fire Department Vehicles
MOTOR VEHICLE ASSEMBLY, COMPLETE: Military Motor Vehicle
MOTOR VEHICLE ASSEMBLY, COMPLETE: Mobile Lounges
MOTOR VEHICLE ASSEMBLY, COMPLETE: Motor Homes, Self Contain
MOTOR VEHICLE ASSEMBLY, COMPLETE: Reconnaissance Cars
MOTOR VEHICLE ASSEMBLY, COMPLETE: Snow Plows
MOTOR VEHICLE ASSEMBLY, COMPLETE: Truck & Tractor Trucks
MOTOR VEHICLE ASSEMBLY, COMPLETE: Truck Tractors, Highway
MOTOR VEHICLE ASSEMBLY, COMPLETE: Universal Carriers, Mil
MOTOR VEHICLE ASSEMBLY, COMPLETE: Wreckers, Tow Truck
MOTOR VEHICLE DEALERS: Automobiles, New & Used
MOTOR VEHICLE DEALERS: Cars, Used Only
MOTOR VEHICLE PARTS & ACCESS: Acceleration Eqpt
MOTOR VEHICLE PARTS & ACCESS: Bearings
MOTOR VEHICLE PARTS & ACCESS: Body Components & Frames
MOTOR VEHICLE PARTS & ACCESS: Booster Cables, Jump-Start
MOTOR VEHICLE PARTS & ACCESS: Clutches
MOTOR VEHICLE PARTS & ACCESS: Cylinder Heads
MOTOR VEHICLE PARTS & ACCESS: Engines & Parts
MOTOR VEHICLE PARTS & ACCESS: Fuel Pumps
MOTOR VEHICLE PARTS & ACCESS: Gears
MOTOR VEHICLE PARTS & ACCESS: Hoods
MOTOR VEHICLE PARTS & ACCESS: Instrument Board Assemblies
MOTOR VEHICLE PARTS & ACCESS: Lubrication Systems & Parts
MOTOR VEHICLE PARTS & ACCESS: Mufflers, Exhaust
MOTOR VEHICLE PARTS & ACCESS: Pickup Truck Bed Liners
MOTOR VEHICLE PARTS & ACCESS: Propane Conversion Eqpt
MOTOR VEHICLE PARTS & ACCESS: Tops
MOTOR VEHICLE PARTS & ACCESS: Transmission Housings Or Parts
MOTOR VEHICLE PARTS & ACCESS: Transmissions
MOTOR VEHICLE PARTS & ACCESS: Universal Joints
MOTOR VEHICLE PARTS & ACCESS: Windshield Frames
MOTOR VEHICLE PARTS & ACCESS: Wipers, Windshield
MOTOR VEHICLE PARTS & ACCESS: Wiring Harness Sets
MOTOR VEHICLE RACING & DRIVER SVCS
MOTOR VEHICLE SPLYS & PARTS WHOLESALERS: New
MOTOR VEHICLE SPLYS & PARTS WHOLESALERS: Used
MOTOR VEHICLE: Hardware
MOTOR VEHICLE: Radiators
MOTOR VEHICLE: Wheels
MOTOR VEHICLES & CAR BODIES
MOTOR VEHICLES, WHOLESALE: Commercial
MOTOR VEHICLES, WHOLESALE: Fire Trucks
MOTOR VEHICLES, WHOLESALE: Trailers for passenger vehicles
MOTOR VEHICLES, WHOLESALE: Trailers, Truck, New & Used
MOTOR VEHICLES, WHOLESALE: Truck bodies
MOTOR VEHICLES, WHOLESALE: Truck tractors
MOTOR VEHICLES, WHOLESALE: Trucks, Noncommercial
MOTOR VEHICLES, WHOLESALE: Trucks, commercial
MOTORCYCLE & BICYCLE PARTS: Frames
MOTORCYCLE ACCESS
MOTORCYCLE DEALERS
MOTORCYCLE DEALERS
MOTORCYCLE PARTS & ACCESS DEALERS
MOTORCYCLE PARTS: Wholesalers
MOTORCYCLE RACING
MOTORCYCLE REPAIR SHOPS
MOTORCYCLES & RELATED PARTS
MOTORS: Electric
MOTORS: Generators
MOUTHWASHES
MOWERS & ACCESSORIES

MULTI-SVCS CENTER
MUSEUMS & ART GALLERIES
MUSIC BROADCASTING SVCS
MUSIC SCHOOLS
MUSICAL INSTRUMENT PARTS & ACCESS, WHOLESALE
MUSICAL INSTRUMENT REPAIR
MUSICAL INSTRUMENTS & ACCESS: Carrying Cases
MUSICAL INSTRUMENTS & ACCESS: NEC
MUSICAL INSTRUMENTS & ACCESS: Pipe Organs
MUSICAL INSTRUMENTS & PARTS: String
MUSICAL INSTRUMENTS & SPLYS STORES
MUSICAL INSTRUMENTS & SPLYS STORES: Keyboards
MUSICAL INSTRUMENTS: Bells
MUSICAL INSTRUMENTS: Carillon Bells
MUSICAL INSTRUMENTS: Electric & Electronic
MUSICAL INSTRUMENTS: Guitars & Parts, Electric & Acoustic
MUSICAL INSTRUMENTS: Harpsichords
MUSICAL INSTRUMENTS: Mouthpieces
MUSICAL INSTRUMENTS: Music Rolls, Perforated
MUSICAL INSTRUMENTS: Organs
MUSICAL INSTRUMENTS: Synthesizers, Music
MUSICAL INSTRUMENTS: Violins & Parts

N

NAME PLATES: Engraved Or Etched
NAMEPLATES
NATIONAL SECURITY FORCES
NATURAL GAS COMPRESSING SVC, On-Site
NATURAL GAS DISTRIBUTION TO CONSUMERS
NATURAL GAS LIQUID FRACTIONATING SVC
NATURAL GAS LIQUIDS PRODUCTION
NATURAL GAS LIQUIDS PRODUCTION
NATURAL GAS PRODUCTION
NATURAL GAS TRANSMISSION
NATURAL GASOLINE PRODUCTION
NATURAL PROPANE PRODUCTION
NAVIGATIONAL SYSTEMS & INSTRUMENTS
NETS: Laundry
NETTING: Elastic, Meat
NEWS DEALERS & NEWSSTANDS
NEWSPAPER COLUMN WRITING SVCS
NEWSSTAND
NICKEL ALLOY
NONCURRENT CARRYING WIRING DEVICES
NONFERROUS: Rolling & Drawing, NEC
NONMETALLIC MINERALS: Support Activities, Exc Fuels
NOTARIES PUBLIC
NOTIONS: Pins & Needles
NOVELTIES
NOVELTIES & SPECIALTIES: Metal
NOVELTIES, PAPER, WHOLESALE
NOVELTIES: Leather
NOVELTIES: Paper, Made From Purchased Materials
NOVELTIES: Plastic
NOVELTY SHOPS
NOZZLES & SPRINKLERS Lawn Hose
NURSERIES & LAWN & GARDEN SPLY STORE, RET: Lawn/Garden Splys
NURSERIES & LAWN & GARDEN SPLY STORES, RETAIL
NURSERIES & LAWN & GARDEN SPLY STORES, RETAIL: Fertilizer
NURSERIES & LAWN & GARDEN SPLY STORES, RETAIL: Lawn Ornament
NURSERIES & LAWN/GARDEN SPLY STORE, RET: Lawnmowers/Tractors
NURSERIES & LAWN/GARDEN SPLY STORES, RET: Garden Splys/Tools
NURSERIES/LAWN/GARDEN SPLY STORES, RET: Hydroponic Eqpt/Sply
NURSERY & GARDEN CENTERS
NUTRITION SVCS
NUTS: Metal
NYLON FIBERS
NYLON RESINS

O

OAKUM
OFFICE EQPT WHOLESALERS
OFFICE EQPT, WHOLESALE: Blueprinting
OFFICE EQPT, WHOLESALE: Micrographic
OFFICE EQPT, WHOLESALE: Photocopy Machines
OFFICE SPLY & STATIONERY STORES: Office Forms & Splys
OFFICE SPLY & STATIONERY STORES: Writing Splys
OFFICE SPLYS, NEC, WHOLESALE

OFFICES & CLINICS OF DENTISTS: Dental Clinic
OFFICES & CLINICS OF DOCTORS OF MEDICINE: Surgeon
OFFICES & CLINICS OF DRS OF MEDICINE: Physician, Orthopedic
OFFICES & CLINICS OF HEALTH PRACTITIONERS: Nutrition
OFFICES & CLINICS OF OPTOMETRISTS: Specialist, Optometrists
OIL & GAS FIELD MACHINERY
OIL BURNER REPAIR SVCS
OIL FIELD MACHINERY & EQPT
OIL FIELD SVCS, NEC
OILS & ESSENTIAL OILS
OILS & GREASES: Blended & Compounded
OILS & GREASES: Lubricating
OILS: Acid
OILS: Core Or Binders
OILS: Cutting
OILS: Essential
OILS: Lubricating
OILS: Lubricating
OINTMENTS
OLEFINS
ON-LINE DATABASE INFORMATION RETRIEVAL SVCS
ONYX MARBLE: Dimension
OPERATIVE BUILDERS: Condominiums
OPERATOR: Apartment Buildings
OPERATOR: Nonresidential Buildings
OPHTHALMIC GOODS
OPHTHALMIC GOODS WHOLESALERS
OPHTHALMIC GOODS, NEC, WHOLESALE: Frames
OPHTHALMIC GOODS, NEC, WHOLESALE: Lenses
OPHTHALMIC GOODS: Frames & Parts, Eyeglass & Spectacle
OPHTHALMIC GOODS: Lenses, Ophthalmic
OPHTHALMIC GOODS: Mountings, Eyeglass & Spectacle
OPHTHALMIC GOODS: Protectors, Eye
OPTICAL GOODS STORES
OPTICAL GOODS STORES: Contact Lenses, Prescription
OPTICAL GOODS STORES: Eyeglasses, Prescription
OPTICAL GOODS STORES: Opticians
OPTICAL INSTRUMENT REPAIR SVCS
OPTICAL INSTRUMENTS & APPARATUS
OPTICAL INSTRUMENTS & LENSES
OPTOMETRIC EQPT & SPLYS WHOLESALERS
OPTOMETRISTS' OFFICES
ORAL PREPARATIONS
ORDNANCE
ORGAN TUNING & REPAIR SVCS
ORGANIZATIONS: Civic & Social
ORGANIZATIONS: Educational Research Agency
ORGANIZATIONS: Medical Research
ORGANIZATIONS: Professional
ORGANIZATIONS: Religious
ORGANIZATIONS: Research Institute
ORGANIZATIONS: Scientific Research Agency
ORGANIZERS, CLOSET & DRAWER Plastic
ORNAMENTS: Lawn
OSCILLATORS
OSICIZERS: Inorganic
OUTLETS: Electric, Convenience
OVENS: Cremating
OVENS: Laboratory
OVERBURDEN REMOVAL, METAL MINING

P

PACKAGE DESIGN SVCS
PACKAGED FROZEN FOODS WHOLESALERS, NEC
PACKAGING & LABELING SVCS
PACKAGING MATERIALS, INDL: Wholesalers
PACKAGING MATERIALS, WHOLESALE
PACKAGING MATERIALS: Paper
PACKAGING MATERIALS: Paper, Coated Or Laminated
PACKAGING MATERIALS: Paper, Thermoplastic Coated
PACKAGING MATERIALS: Plastic Film, Coated Or Laminated
PACKAGING MATERIALS: Polystyrene Foam
PACKAGING: Blister Or Bubble Formed, Plastic
PACKING & CRATING SVC
PACKING & CRATING SVCS: Containerized Goods For Shipping
PACKING MATERIALS: Mechanical
PACKING SVCS: Shipping
PACKING: Metallic
PACKING: Rubber
PADDING: Foamed Plastics
PADS: Mattress

PAGING SVCS
PAINT STORE
PAINTING SVC: Metal Prdts
PAINTS & ADDITIVES
PAINTS & ALLIED PRODUCTS
PAINTS & VARNISHES: Plastics Based
PAINTS, VARNISHES & SPLYS, WHOLESALE: Colors & Pigments
PAINTS, VARNISHES & SPLYS, WHOLESALE: Paints
PAINTS: Asphalt Or Bituminous
PAINTS: Marine
PAINTS: Oil Or Alkyd Vehicle Or Water Thinned
PAINTS: Waterproof
PALLET REPAIR SVCS
PALLETS
PALLETS & SKIDS: Wood
PALLETS: Corrugated
PALLETS: Metal
PALLETS: Plastic
PALLETS: Solid Fiber, Made From Purchased Materials
PALLETS: Wood & Metal Combination
PALLETS: Wooden
PANEL & DISTRIBUTION BOARDS & OTHER RELATED APPARATUS
PANEL & DISTRIBUTION BOARDS: Electric
PANELS & SECTIONS: Prefabricated, Concrete
PANELS, FLAT: Plastic
PANELS: Building, Metal
PANELS: Building, Plastic, NEC
PANELS: Building, Wood
PANELS: Cardboard, Die-Cut, Made From Purchased Materials
PANELS: Wood
PAPER & BOARD: Die-cut
PAPER & PAPER PRDTS: Crepe, Made From Purchased Materials
PAPER CONVERTING
PAPER MANUFACTURERS: Exc Newsprint
PAPER PRDTS
PAPER PRDTS: Book Covers
PAPER PRDTS: Cleansing Tissues, Made From Purchased Material
PAPER PRDTS: Feminine Hygiene Prdts
PAPER PRDTS: Infant & Baby Prdts
PAPER PRDTS: Molded Pulp Prdts
PAPER PRDTS: Sanitary
PAPER PRDTS: Sanitary Tissue Paper
PAPER PRDTS: Toilet Paper, Made From Purchased Materials
PAPER PRDTS: Toweling Tissue
PAPER PRDTS: Towels, Napkins/Tissue Paper, From Purchd Mtrls
PAPER PRDTS: Wrappers, Blank, Made From Purchased Materials
PAPER, WHOLESALE: Fine
PAPER, WHOLESALE: Printing
PAPER: Adhesive
PAPER: Art
PAPER: Bank Note
PAPER: Book
PAPER: Bristols
PAPER: Building, Insulation
PAPER: Business Form
PAPER: Card
PAPER: Cardboard
PAPER: Cloth, Lined, Made From Purchased Materials
PAPER: Coated & Laminated, NEC
PAPER: Coated, Exc Photographic, Carbon Or Abrasive
PAPER: Envelope
PAPER: Fine
PAPER: Gift Wrap
PAPER: Insulation Siding
PAPER: Offset
PAPER: Packaging
PAPER: Parchment
PAPER: Poster & Art
PAPER: Printer
PAPER: Specialty
PAPER: Specialty Or Chemically Treated
PAPER: Tablet
PAPER: Tissue
PAPER: Uncoated
PAPER: Wallpaper
PAPER: Wrapping & Packaging
PAPERBOARD
PAPERBOARD CONVERTING

PAPERBOARD PRDTS: Building Insulating & Packaging
PAPERBOARD PRDTS: Container Board
PAPERBOARD PRDTS: Folding Boxboard
PAPERBOARD PRDTS: Pressboard
PAPERBOARD PRDTS: Setup Boxboard
PAPERBOARD: Boxboard
PAPERBOARD: Corrugated
PARACHUTES
PARTICLEBOARD
PARTICLEBOARD: Laminated, Plastic
PARTITIONS & FIXTURES: Except Wood
PARTITIONS WHOLESALERS
PARTITIONS: Nonwood, Floor Attached
PARTITIONS: Solid Fiber, Made From Purchased Materials
PARTITIONS: Wood & Fixtures
PARTS: Metal
PARTY & SPECIAL EVENT PLANNING SVCS
PASTES: Metal
PATENT OWNERS & LESSORS
PATIENT MONITORING EQPT WHOLESALERS
PATTERNS: Indl
PAVERS
PAVING MATERIALS: Prefabricated, Concrete
PAVING MIXTURES
PEARLS, WHOLESALE
PENCILS & PENS WHOLESALERS
PENHOLDERS & PARTS
PENNANTS
PENS & PARTS: Ball Point
PENS & PARTS: Cartridges, Refill, Ball Point
PERFUMES
PERISCOPES
PERLITE MINING SVCS
PERLITE: Processed
PERSONAL & HOUSEHOLD GOODS REPAIR, NEC
PERSONAL CARE FACILITY
PEST CONTROL SVCS
PESTICIDES
PESTICIDES WHOLESALERS
PET & PET SPLYS STORES
PET COLLARS, LEASHES, MUZZLES & HARNESSES: Leather
PET FOOD WHOLESALERS
PET SPLYS
PET SPLYS WHOLESALERS
PETROLATUMS: Nonmedicinal
PETROLEUM & PETROLEUM PRDTS, WHOLESALE Engine Fuels & Oils
PETROLEUM & PETROLEUM PRDTS, WHOLESALE Fuel Oil
PETROLEUM & PETROLEUM PRDTS, WHOLESALE Petroleum Terminals
PETROLEUM & PETROLEUM PRDTS, WHOLESALE: Bulk Stations
PETROLEUM BULK STATIONS & TERMINALS
PETROLEUM PRDTS WHOLESALERS
PEWTER WARE
PHARMACEUTICAL PREPARATIONS: Adrenal
PHARMACEUTICAL PREPARATIONS: Druggists' Preparations
PHARMACEUTICAL PREPARATIONS: Emulsions
PHARMACEUTICAL PREPARATIONS: Medicines, Capsule Or Ampule
PHARMACEUTICAL PREPARATIONS: Penicillin
PHARMACEUTICAL PREPARATIONS: Pills
PHARMACEUTICAL PREPARATIONS: Pituitary Gland
PHARMACEUTICAL PREPARATIONS: Powders
PHARMACEUTICAL PREPARATIONS: Proprietary Drug PRDTS
PHARMACEUTICAL PREPARATIONS: Solutions
PHARMACEUTICAL PREPARATIONS: Tablets
PHARMACEUTICAL PREPARATIONS: Tranquilizers Or Mental Drug
PHARMACEUTICALS
PHARMACEUTICALS: Medicinal & Botanical Prdts
PHARMACIES & DRUG STORES
PHONOGRAPH RECORDS WHOLESALERS
PHONOGRAPH RECORDS: Prerecorded
PHOTOCOPY MACHINES
PHOTOCOPYING & DUPLICATING SVCS
PHOTOELECTRIC DEVICES: Magnetic
PHOTOENGRAVING SVC
PHOTOFINISHING LABORATORIES
PHOTOFINISHING LABORATORIES
PHOTOGRAMMATIC MAPPING SVCS

INDEX

PHOTOGRAPHIC EQPT & SPLY: Sound Recordg/Reprod Eqpt, Motion
PHOTOGRAPHIC EQPT & SPLYS
PHOTOGRAPHIC EQPT & SPLYS WHOLESALERS
PHOTOGRAPHIC EQPT & SPLYS, WHOLESALE: Project, Motion/Slide
PHOTOGRAPHIC EQPT & SPLYS: Cameras, Aerial
PHOTOGRAPHIC EQPT & SPLYS: Cameras, Still & Motion Pictures
PHOTOGRAPHIC EQPT & SPLYS: Developers, Not Chemical Plants
PHOTOGRAPHIC EQPT & SPLYS: Graphic Arts Plates, Sensitized
PHOTOGRAPHIC EQPT & SPLYS: Printing Eqpt
PHOTOGRAPHIC EQPT & SPLYS: Printing Frames
PHOTOGRAPHIC EQPT & SPLYS: Processing Eqpt
PHOTOGRAPHIC EQPT & SPLYS: Toners, Prprd, Not Chem Plnts
PHOTOGRAPHIC EQPT & SPLYS: Washers, Print & Film
PHOTOGRAPHIC EQPT/SPLYS, WHOL: Cameras/Projectors/Eqpt/Splys
PHOTOGRAPHY SVCS: Commercial
PHOTOGRAPHY SVCS: Passport
PHOTOGRAPHY SVCS: Portrait Studios
PHOTOGRAPHY SVCS: School
PHOTOGRAPHY SVCS: Still Or Video
PHOTOGRAPHY: Aerial
PHOTOTYPESETTING SVC
PHOTOVOLTAIC Solid State
PHYSICAL EXAMINATION & TESTING SVCS
PHYSICAL EXAMINATION SVCS, INSURANCE
PHYSICAL FITNESS CENTERS
PHYSICIANS' OFFICES & CLINICS: Medical doctors
PICTURE FRAMES: Metal
PICTURE FRAMES: Wood
PICTURE FRAMING SVCS, CUSTOM
PICTURE PROJECTION EQPT
PIECE GOODS & NOTIONS WHOLESALERS
PIECE GOODS, NOTIONS & DRY GOODS, WHOL: Textiles, Woven
PIECE GOODS, NOTIONS & DRY GOODS, WHOLESALE: Fabrics, Knit
PIECE GOODS, NOTIONS & OTHER DRY GOODS, WHOL: Flags/Banners
PIECE GOODS, NOTIONS & OTHER DRY GOODS, WHOLESALE: Buttons
PIECE GOODS, NOTIONS & OTHER DRY GOODS, WHOLESALE: Fabrics
PIECE GOODS, NOTIONS & OTHER DRY GOODS, WHOLESALE: Ribbons
PIECE GOODS, NOTIONS & OTHER DRY GOODS, WHOLESALE: Zippers
PIECE GOODS, NOTIONS/DRY GOODS, WHOL: Drapery Mtrl, Woven
PIGMENTS, INORGANIC: Metallic & Mineral, NEC
PIGMENTS, INORGANIC: Zinc Oxide, Zinc Sulfide
PINS
PINS: Cotter
PINS: Spring
PIPE & FITTING: Fabrication
PIPE & FITTINGS: Cast Iron
PIPE & TUBES: Aluminum
PIPE & TUBES: Copper & Copper Alloy
PIPE FITTINGS: Plastic
PIPE SECTIONS, FABRICATED FROM PURCHASED PIPE
PIPE, SEWER: Concrete
PIPE: Plastic
PIPE: Plate Fabricated, Large Diameter
PIPE: Seamless Steel
PIPE: Sheet Metal
PIPE: Water, Cast Iron
PIPELINE & POWER LINE INSPECTION SVCS
PIPELINE TERMINAL FACILITIES: Independent
PIPELINES: Crude Petroleum
PIPELINES: Natural Gas
PIPELINES: Refined Petroleum
PIPES & FITTINGS: Fiber, Made From Purchased Materials
PIPES & TUBES
PIPES & TUBES: Steel
PIPES & TUBES: Welded
PIPES OR FITTINGS: Sewer, Clay
PIPES: Tobacco
PISTONS & PISTON RINGS
PLANING MILL, NEC
PLANING MILLS: Millwork
PLANTS, POTTED, WHOLESALE

PLANTS: Artificial & Preserved
PLAQUES: Picture, Laminated
PLASMAS
PLASTER WORK: Ornamental & Architectural
PLASTIC COLORING & FINISHING
PLASTIC PRDTS
PLASTIC PRDTS REPAIR SVCS
PLASTIC WOOD
PLASTICIZERS, ORGANIC: Cyclic & Acyclic
PLASTICS FILM & SHEET
PLASTICS FILM & SHEET: Polyethylene
PLASTICS FILM & SHEET: Polypropylene
PLASTICS FILM & SHEET: Polyvinyl
PLASTICS FILM & SHEET: Vinyl
PLASTICS FINISHED PRDTS: Laminated
PLASTICS FOAM, WHOLESALE
PLASTICS MATERIAL & RESINS
PLASTICS MATERIALS, BASIC FORMS & SHAPES WHOLESALERS
PLASTICS PROCESSING
PLASTICS SHEET: Packing Materials
PLASTICS: Blow Molded
PLASTICS: Cast
PLASTICS: Extruded
PLASTICS: Finished Injection Molded
PLASTICS: Injection Molded
PLASTICS: Molded
PLASTICS: Polystyrene Foam
PLASTICS: Thermoformed
PLATE WORK: For Nuclear Industry
PLATE WORK: Metalworking Trade
PLATEMAKING SVC: Color Separations, For The Printing Trade
PLATENS, EXC PRINTERS': Rubber, Solid Or Covered
PLATES
PLATES: Plastic Exc Polystyrene Foam
PLATES: Steel
PLATFORMS: Cargo
PLATING & POLISHING SVC
PLATING SVC: Chromium, Metals Or Formed Prdts
PLATING SVC: Electro
PLATING SVC: NEC
PLAYGROUND EQPT
PLEATING & STITCHING FOR THE TRADE: Decorative & Novelty
PLEATING & STITCHING SVC
PLUMBING & HEATING EQPT & SPLY, WHOL: Htg Eqpt/Panels, Solar
PLUMBING & HEATING EQPT & SPLY, WHOLESALE: Hydronic Htg Eqpt
PLUMBING & HEATING EQPT & SPLYS WHOLESALERS
PLUMBING & HEATING EQPT & SPLYS, WHOL: Pipe/Fitting, Plastic
PLUMBING & HEATING EQPT & SPLYS, WHOL: Plumbing Fitting/Sply
PLUMBING & HEATING EQPT & SPLYS, WHOL: Plumbng/Heatng Valves
PLUMBING & HEATING EQPT & SPLYS, WHOL: Water Purif Eqpt
PLUMBING & HEATING EQPT & SPLYS, WHOLESALE: Boilers, Steam
PLUMBING & HEATING EQPT & SPLYS, WHOLESALE: Pwr Indl Boiler
PLUMBING & HEATING EQPT, WHOLESALE: Water Heaters/Purif
PLUMBING & HEATING EQPT/SPLYS, WHOL: Boilers, Hot Water Htg
PLUMBING FIXTURES
PLUMBING FIXTURES: Plastic
POINT OF SALE DEVICES
POLE LINE HARDWARE
POLES & POSTS: Concrete
POLISHING SVC: Metals Or Formed Prdts
POLITICAL ACTION COMMITTEES
POLYCARBONATE RESINS
POLYESTERS
POLYETHYLENE RESINS
POLYMETHYL METHACRYLATE RESINS: Plexiglas
POLYPROPYLENE RESINS
POLYSTYRENE RESINS
POLYSULFIDES
POLYTETRAFLUOROETHYLENE RESINS
POLYURETHANE RESINS
POLYVINYL CHLORIDE RESINS
PORCELAIN ENAMELED PRDTS & UTENSILS
POSTERS

POTTERY
POTTERY: Laboratory & Indl
POTTING SOILS
POULTRY & POULTRY PRDTS WHOLESALERS
POULTRY & SMALL GAME SLAUGHTERING & PROCESSING
POULTRY SLAUGHTERING & PROCESSING
POWDER: Aluminum Atomized
POWDER: Iron
POWDER: Metal
POWDER: Silver
POWDERS, FLAVORING, EXC DRINK
POWER DISTRIBUTION BOARDS: Electric
POWER GENERATORS
POWER SUPPLIES: All Types, Static
POWER SUPPLIES: Transformer, Electronic Type
POWER TOOL REPAIR SVCS
POWER TOOLS, HAND: Drills & Drilling Tools
POWER TRANSMISSION EQPT WHOLESALERS
POWER TRANSMISSION EQPT: Mechanical
PRECAST TERRAZZO OR CONCRETE PRDTS
PRECIOUS METALS
PRECIOUS METALS WHOLESALERS
PRECIOUS STONES WHOLESALERS
PREFABRICATED BUILDING DEALERS
PREPARING SHAFTS OR TUNNELS, METAL MINING
PRERECORDED TAPE, COMPACT DISC & RECORD STORES: Compact Disc
PRESCHOOL CENTERS
PRESSED FIBER & MOLDED PULP PRDTS, EXC FOOD PRDTS
PRESSES
PRESTRESSED CONCRETE PRDTS
PRIMARY METAL PRODUCTS
PRIMARY ROLLING MILL EQPT
PRINT CARTRIDGES: Laser & Other Computer Printers
PRINTED CIRCUIT BOARDS
PRINTERS & PLOTTERS
PRINTERS' SVCS: Folding, Collating, Etc
PRINTERS: Computer
PRINTERS: Magnetic Ink, Bar Code
PRINTING & BINDING: Books
PRINTING & BINDING: Pamphlets
PRINTING & BINDING: Textbooks
PRINTING & EMBOSSING: Plastic Fabric Articles
PRINTING & ENGRAVING: Card, Exc Greeting
PRINTING & ENGRAVING: Financial Notes & Certificates
PRINTING & ENGRAVING: Invitation & Stationery
PRINTING & ENGRAVING: Poster & Decal
PRINTING & ENGRAVING: Rolls, Textile Printing
PRINTING & STAMPING: Fabric Articles
PRINTING & WRITING PAPER WHOLESALERS
PRINTING INKS WHOLESALERS
PRINTING MACHINERY
PRINTING MACHINERY, EQPT & SPLYS: Wholesalers
PRINTING TRADES MACHINERY & EQPT REPAIR SVCS
PRINTING, COMMERCIAL Newspapers, NEC
PRINTING, COMMERCIAL: Announcements, NEC
PRINTING, COMMERCIAL: Bags, Plastic, NEC
PRINTING, COMMERCIAL: Business Forms, NEC
PRINTING, COMMERCIAL: Calendars, NEC
PRINTING, COMMERCIAL: Catalogs, NEC
PRINTING, COMMERCIAL: Decals, NEC
PRINTING, COMMERCIAL: Directories, Exc Telephone, NEC
PRINTING, COMMERCIAL: Envelopes, NEC
PRINTING, COMMERCIAL: Invitations, NEC
PRINTING, COMMERCIAL: Labels & Seals, NEC
PRINTING, COMMERCIAL: Letterpress & Screen
PRINTING, COMMERCIAL: Literature, Advertising, NEC
PRINTING, COMMERCIAL: Magazines, NEC
PRINTING, COMMERCIAL: Menus, NEC
PRINTING, COMMERCIAL: Periodicals, NEC
PRINTING, COMMERCIAL: Promotional
PRINTING, COMMERCIAL: Publications
PRINTING, COMMERCIAL: Schedules, Transportation, NEC
PRINTING, COMMERCIAL: Screen
PRINTING, COMMERCIAL: Stationery, NEC
PRINTING, COMMERCIAL: Tickets, NEC
PRINTING, LITHOGRAPHIC: Advertising Posters
PRINTING, LITHOGRAPHIC: Billheads
PRINTING, LITHOGRAPHIC: Calendars
PRINTING, LITHOGRAPHIC: Catalogs
PRINTING, LITHOGRAPHIC: Circulars
PRINTING, LITHOGRAPHIC: Color
PRINTING, LITHOGRAPHIC: Coupons
PRINTING, LITHOGRAPHIC: Decals

PRINTING, LITHOGRAPHIC: Fashion Plates
PRINTING, LITHOGRAPHIC: Forms & Cards, Business
PRINTING, LITHOGRAPHIC: Forms, Business
PRINTING, LITHOGRAPHIC: Letters, Circular Or Form
PRINTING, LITHOGRAPHIC: Offset & photolithographic printing
PRINTING, LITHOGRAPHIC: On Metal
PRINTING, LITHOGRAPHIC: Post Cards, Picture
PRINTING, LITHOGRAPHIC: Posters & Decals
PRINTING, LITHOGRAPHIC: Promotional
PRINTING, LITHOGRAPHIC: Publications
PRINTING, LITHOGRAPHIC: Tickets
PRINTING, LITHOGRAPHIC: Transfers, Decalcomania Or Dry
PRINTING: Books
PRINTING: Books
PRINTING: Checkbooks
PRINTING: Commercial, NEC
PRINTING: Engraving & Plate
PRINTING: Flexographic
PRINTING: Gravure, Business Form & Card
PRINTING: Gravure, Calendar & Card, Exc Business
PRINTING: Gravure, Certificates, Security
PRINTING: Gravure, Coupons
PRINTING: Gravure, Envelopes
PRINTING: Gravure, Forms, Business
PRINTING: Gravure, Invitations
PRINTING: Gravure, Labels
PRINTING: Gravure, Promotional
PRINTING: Gravure, Publications
PRINTING: Gravure, Rotogravure
PRINTING: Gravure, Seals
PRINTING: Laser
PRINTING: Letterpress
PRINTING: Lithographic
PRINTING: Manmade Fiber & Silk, Broadwoven Fabric
PRINTING: Offset
PRINTING: Pamphlets
PRINTING: Photo-Offset
PRINTING: Screen, Broadwoven Fabrics, Cotton
PRINTING: Screen, Fabric
PRINTING: Screen, Manmade Fiber & Silk, Broadwoven Fabric
PRINTING: Thermography
PROFESSIONAL EQPT & SPLYS, WHOLESALE: Analytical Instruments
PROFESSIONAL EQPT & SPLYS, WHOLESALE: Engineers', NEC
PROFESSIONAL EQPT & SPLYS, WHOLESALE: Optical Goods
PROFESSIONAL INSTRUMENT REPAIR SVCS
PROFILE SHAPES: Unsupported Plastics
PROGRAMMERS: Indl Process
PROMOTION SVCS
PROPELLERS: Boat & Ship, Cast
PROPRIETARY STORES, NON-PRESCRIPTION MEDICINE
PROTECTION EQPT: Lightning
PUBLISHERS: Art Copy
PUBLISHERS: Art Copy & Poster
PUBLISHERS: Book
PUBLISHERS: Books, No Printing
PUBLISHERS: Catalogs
PUBLISHERS: Directories, NEC
PUBLISHERS: Directories, Telephone
PUBLISHERS: Guides
PUBLISHERS: Magazines, No Printing
PUBLISHERS: Maps
PUBLISHERS: Miscellaneous
PUBLISHERS: Music Book
PUBLISHERS: Music, Sheet
PUBLISHERS: Newsletter
PUBLISHERS: Newspaper
PUBLISHERS: Newspapers, No Printing
PUBLISHERS: Pamphlets, No Printing
PUBLISHERS: Periodical Statistical Reports, No Printing
PUBLISHERS: Periodical, With Printing
PUBLISHERS: Periodicals, Magazines
PUBLISHERS: Periodicals, No Printing
PUBLISHERS: Sheet Music
PUBLISHERS: Shopping News
PUBLISHERS: Technical Manuals
PUBLISHERS: Technical Manuals & Papers
PUBLISHERS: Technical Papers
PUBLISHERS: Telephone & Other Directory
PUBLISHERS: Textbooks, No Printing
PUBLISHERS: Trade journals, No Printing
PUBLISHING & BROADCASTING: Internet Only

PUBLISHING & PRINTING: Art Copy
PUBLISHING & PRINTING: Book Music
PUBLISHING & PRINTING: Books
PUBLISHING & PRINTING: Catalogs
PUBLISHING & PRINTING: Comic Books
PUBLISHING & PRINTING: Directories, NEC
PUBLISHING & PRINTING: Directories, Telephone
PUBLISHING & PRINTING: Guides
PUBLISHING & PRINTING: Magazines: publishing & printing
PUBLISHING & PRINTING: Music, Book
PUBLISHING & PRINTING: Newsletters, Business Svc
PUBLISHING & PRINTING: Newspapers
PUBLISHING & PRINTING: Pamphlets
PUBLISHING & PRINTING: Periodical Statistical Reports
PUBLISHING & PRINTING: Shopping News
PUBLISHING & PRINTING: Television Schedules
PUBLISHING & PRINTING: Textbooks
PUBLISHING & PRINTING: Trade Journals
PULP MILLS
PULP MILLS: Chemical & Semichemical Processing
PULP MILLS: Mechanical & Recycling Processing
PULSE FORMING NETWORKS
PUMP JACKS & OTHER PUMPING EQPT: Indl
PUMPS
PUMPS & PARTS: Indl
PUMPS & PUMPING EQPT REPAIR SVCS
PUMPS & PUMPING EQPT WHOLESALERS
PUMPS, HEAT: Electric
PUMPS: Domestic, Water Or Sump
PUMPS: Fluid Power
PUMPS: Hydraulic Power Transfer
PUMPS: Measuring & Dispensing
PUMPS: Oil Well & Field
PUMPS: Vacuum, Exc Laboratory
PUNCHES: Forming & Stamping
PUPPETS & MARIONETTES
PURIFICATION & DUST COLLECTION EQPT
PURIFIERS: Centrifugal
PUSHCARTS

Q

QUARTZ CRYSTALS: Electronic
QUILTING SVC & SPLYS, FOR THE TRADE

R

RACETRACKS
RACETRACKS: Auto
RACEWAYS
RACKS: Display
RACKS: Garment, Exc Wood
RACKS: Garment, Wood
RACKS: Luggage, Car Top
RACKS: Trash, Metal Rack
RADIO & TELEVISION COMMUNICATIONS EQUIPMENT
RADIO BROADCASTING & COMMUNICATIONS EQPT
RADIO BROADCASTING STATIONS
RADIO COMMUNICATIONS: Airborne Eqpt
RADIO PRODUCERS
RADIO RECEIVER NETWORKS
RADIO REPAIR SHOP, NEC
RADIO, TELEVISION & CONSUMER ELECTRONICS STORES: Eqpt, NEC
RADIO, TV & CONSUMER ELECTRONICS: VCR & Access
RADIO, TV/CONSUMER ELEC STORES: Antennas, Satellite Dish
RAIL & STRUCTURAL SHAPES: Aluminum rail & structural shapes
RAILINGS: Prefabricated, Metal
RAILINGS: Wood
RAILROAD CAR CUSTOMIZING SVCS
RAILROAD CAR REPAIR SVCS
RAILROAD CARGO LOADING & UNLOADING SVCS
RAILROAD CROSSINGS: Steel Or Iron
RAILROAD EQPT
RAILROAD EQPT & SPLYS WHOLESALERS
RAILROAD EQPT, EXC LOCOMOTIVES
RAILROAD EQPT: Brakes, Air & Vacuum
RAILROAD EQPT: Cars & Eqpt, Dining
RAILROAD EQPT: Cars & Eqpt, Interurban
RAILROAD EQPT: Cars & Eqpt, Rapid Transit
RAILROAD EQPT: Cars & Eqpt, Train, Freight Or Passenger
RAILROAD EQPT: Cars, Maintenance
RAILROAD EQPT: Cars, Rebuilt
RAILROAD EQPT: Cars, Tank Freight & Eqpt
RAILROAD EQPT: Locomotives & Parts, Electric Or Nonelectric

RAILROAD FREIGHT AGENCY
RAILROAD MAINTENANCE & REPAIR SVCS
RAILROAD RELATED EQPT
RAILROAD RELATED EQPT: Ballast Distributors
RAILROAD RELATED EQPT: Laying Eqpt, Rail
RAILROAD RELATED EQPT: Railway Track
RAILROAD TIES: Concrete
RAILROAD TIES: Wood
RAILROADS: Long Haul
RAILS: Copper & Copper Alloy
RAILS: Elevator, Guide
RAILS: Rails, rolled & drawn, aluminum
RAILS: Steel Or Iron
RAZORS, RAZOR BLADES
REAL ESTATE AGENCIES & BROKERS
REAL ESTATE AGENCIES: Residential
REAL ESTATE AGENTS & MANAGERS
REAL ESTATE INVESTMENT TRUSTS
REAL ESTATE OPERATORS, EXC DEVELOPERS: Commercial/Indl Bldg
REAL ESTATE OPERATORS, EXC DEVELOPERS: Property, Retail
REAMERS
REBABBITTING SVCS
RECLAIMED RUBBER: Reworked By Manufacturing Process
RECORD BLANKS: Phonographic
RECORDING & PLAYBACK HEADS: Magnetic
RECORDING HEADS: Speech & Musical Eqpt
RECORDS & TAPES: Prerecorded
RECORDS OR TAPES: Masters
RECOVERY SVC: Iron Ore, From Open Hearth Slag
RECOVERY SVCS: Anthracite, Culm Bank
RECOVERY SVCS: Metal
RECREATIONAL CAMPS
RECREATIONAL DEALERS: Campers/Pickup Coaches Truck Mounted
RECREATIONAL VEHICLE DEALERS
RECREATIONAL VEHICLE PARKS & CAMPGROUNDS
RECREATIONAL VEHICLE PARTS & ACCESS STORES
RECREATIONAL VEHICLE REPAIRS
RECTIFIERS: Electronic, Exc Semiconductor
RECTIFIERS: Mercury Arc, Electrical
RECYCLABLE SCRAP & WASTE MATERIALS WHOLESALERS
RECYCLING: Paper
REELS: Cable, Metal
REELS: Wood
REFINERS & SMELTERS: Copper
REFINERS & SMELTERS: Copper, Secondary
REFINERS & SMELTERS: Nonferrous Metal
REFINERS & SMELTERS: Platinum Group Metal Refining, Primary
REFINERS & SMELTERS: Platinum Group Metals, Secondary
REFINERS & SMELTERS: Tin, Primary
REFINERS & SMELTERS: Zinc, Primary, Including Slabs & Dust
REFINERS & SMELTERS: Zinc, Primary, Including Zinc Residue
REFINING LUBRICATING OILS & GREASES, NEC
REFINING: Petroleum
REFRACTORIES: Alumina Fused
REFRACTORIES: Brick
REFRACTORIES: Castable, Clay
REFRACTORIES: Cement
REFRACTORIES: Cement, nonclay
REFRACTORIES: Clay
REFRACTORIES: Foundry, Clay
REFRACTORIES: Glasshouse
REFRACTORIES: Graphite, Carbon Or Ceramic Bond
REFRACTORIES: Nonclay
REFRACTORY CASTABLES
REFRACTORY MATERIALS WHOLESALERS
REFRIGERATION & HEATING EQUIPMENT
REFRIGERATION EQPT & SPLYS WHOLESALERS
REFRIGERATION EQPT & SPLYS, WHOLESALE: Beverage Dispensers
REFRIGERATION EQPT & SPLYS, WHOLESALE: Ice Making Machines
REFRIGERATION EQPT: Complete
REFRIGERATION REPAIR SVCS
REFRIGERATION SVC & REPAIR
REFUSE SYSTEMS
REGULATE, LICENSE & INSPECT, GOVT: Alcoholic Bev Control Bd
REGULATORS: Generator Voltage
REGULATORS: Power

INDEX

REGULATORS: Transmission & Distribution Voltage
REHABILITATION SVCS
RELAYS & SWITCHES: Indl, Electric
RELAYS: Control Circuit, Ind
RELAYS: Electronic Usage
RELAYS: Vacuum
RELIGIOUS SCHOOL
REMOVERS & CLEANERS
REMOVERS: Paint
RENDERING PLANT
RENTAL CENTERS: Furniture
RENTAL SVCS: Aircraft
RENTAL SVCS: Business Machine & Electronic Eqpt
RENTAL SVCS: Floor Maintenance Eqpt
RENTAL SVCS: Personal Items, Exc Recreation & Medical
RENTAL SVCS: Propane Eqpt
RENTAL SVCS: Sign
RENTAL SVCS: Sound & Lighting Eqpt
RENTAL SVCS: Stores & Yards Eqpt
RENTAL SVCS: Tent & Tarpaulin
RENTAL SVCS: Trailer
RENTAL SVCS: Tuxedo
RENTAL SVCS: Work Zone Traffic Eqpt, Flags, Cones, Etc
RENTAL: Portable Toilet
REPAIR SERVICES, NEC
REPRODUCTION SVCS: Video Tape Or Disk
RESEARCH & DEVELOPMENT SVCS, COMMERCIAL: Engineering Lab
RESEARCH, DEV & TESTING SVCS, COMM: Chem Lab, Exc Testing
RESEARCH, DEVELOPMENT & TEST SVCS, COMM: Cmptr Hardware Dev
RESEARCH, DEVELOPMENT & TEST SVCS, COMM: Research, Exc Lab
RESEARCH, DEVELOPMENT & TESTING SVCS, COMM: Agricultural
RESEARCH, DEVELOPMENT & TESTING SVCS, COMM: Natural Resource
RESEARCH, DEVELOPMENT & TESTING SVCS, COMM: Research Lab
RESEARCH, DEVELOPMENT & TESTING SVCS, COMM: Sociological
RESEARCH, DEVELOPMENT & TESTING SVCS, COMMERCIAL: Business
RESEARCH, DEVELOPMENT & TESTING SVCS, COMMERCIAL: Education
RESEARCH, DEVELOPMENT & TESTING SVCS, COMMERCIAL: Energy
RESEARCH, DEVELOPMENT & TESTING SVCS, COMMERCIAL: Medical
RESEARCH, DEVELOPMENT & TESTING SVCS, COMMERCIAL: Physical
RESEARCH, DEVELOPMENT SVCS, COMMERCIAL: Indl Lab
RESEARCH, DVLPT & TEST SVCS, COMM: Mkt Analysis or Research
RESEARCH, DVLPT & TESTING SVCS, COMM: Mkt, Bus & Economic
RESIDENTIAL REMODELERS
RESINS: Custom Compound Purchased
RESISTORS
RESISTORS: Networks
RESORCINOL
RESPIRATORS
RESPIRATORY SYSTEM DRUGS
RESTAURANT EQPT: Carts
RESTAURANT EQPT: Food Wagons
RESTAURANT EQPT: Sheet Metal
RESTAURANTS:Full Svc, American
RESTAURANTS:Full Svc, Diner
RESTAURANTS:Full Svc, Family
RESTAURANTS:Full Svc, Family, Chain
RESTAURANTS:Full Svc, Family, Independent
RESTAURANTS:Full Svc, German
RESTAURANTS:Full Svc, Indian-Pakistan
RESTAURANTS:Full Svc, Italian
RESTAURANTS:Full Svc, Mexican
RESTAURANTS:Full Svc, Vietnamese
RESTAURANTS:Limited Svc, Coffee Shop
RESTAURANTS:Limited Svc, Ice Cream Stands Or Dairy Bars
RESTAURANTS:Limited Svc, Lunch Counter
RESTAURANTS:Limited Svc, Pizza
RESTAURANTS:Limited Svc, Pizzeria, Chain
RESTAURANTS:Limited Svc, Pizzeria, Independent

RESTAURANTS:Limited Svc, Sandwiches & Submarines Shop
RESTAURANTS:Limited Svc, Snow Cone Stand
RETAIL BAKERY: Bagels
RETAIL BAKERY: Bread
RETAIL BAKERY: Cakes
RETAIL BAKERY: Cookies
RETAIL BAKERY: Doughnuts
RETAIL BAKERY: Pastries
RETAIL BAKERY: Pretzels
RETAIL LUMBER YARDS
RETAIL STORES, NEC
RETAIL STORES: Artificial Limbs
RETAIL STORES: Audio-Visual Eqpt & Splys
RETAIL STORES: Awnings
RETAIL STORES: Banners
RETAIL STORES: Business Machines & Eqpt
RETAIL STORES: Canvas Prdts
RETAIL STORES: Children's Furniture, NEC
RETAIL STORES: Christmas Lights & Decorations
RETAIL STORES: Cleaning Eqpt & Splys
RETAIL STORES: Concrete Prdts, Precast
RETAIL STORES: Cosmetics
RETAIL STORES: Drafting Eqpt & Splys
RETAIL STORES: Educational Aids & Electronic Training Mat
RETAIL STORES: Electronic Parts & Eqpt
RETAIL STORES: Engine & Motor Eqpt & Splys
RETAIL STORES: Engines & Parts, Air-Cooled
RETAIL STORES: Farm Eqpt & Splys
RETAIL STORES: Farm Machinery, NEC
RETAIL STORES: Fire Extinguishers
RETAIL STORES: Flags
RETAIL STORES: Hair Care Prdts
RETAIL STORES: Hearing Aids
RETAIL STORES: Hospital Eqpt & Splys
RETAIL STORES: Ice
RETAIL STORES: Medical Apparatus & Splys
RETAIL STORES: Monuments, Finished To Custom Order
RETAIL STORES: Motors, Electric
RETAIL STORES: Orthopedic & Prosthesis Applications
RETAIL STORES: Pet Splys
RETAIL STORES: Photocopy Machines
RETAIL STORES: Picture Frames, Ready Made
RETAIL STORES: Plumbing & Heating Splys
RETAIL STORES: Police Splys
RETAIL STORES: Rubber Stamps
RETAIL STORES: Sauna Eqpt & Splys
RETAIL STORES: Swimming Pools, Above Ground
RETAIL STORES: Telephone & Communication Eqpt
RETAIL STORES: Telephone Eqpt & Systems
RETAIL STORES: Toilet Preparations
RETAIL STORES: Water Purification Eqpt
RETAIL STORES: Welding Splys
RETREADING MATERIALS: Tire
REUPHOLSTERY SVCS
RIBBONS & BOWS
RIBBONS, NEC
RIBBONS: Machine, Inked Or Carbon
RIFLES: Recoilless
RIVETS: Metal
ROAD CONSTRUCTION EQUIPMENT WHOLESALERS
ROAD MATERIALS: Bituminous, Not From Refineries
ROBOTS: Assembly Line
ROD & BAR: Aluminum
RODS: Extruded, Aluminum
RODS: Plastic
RODS: Steel & Iron, Made In Steel Mills
RODS: Welding
ROLL COVERINGS: Rubber
ROLL FORMED SHAPES: Custom
ROLLED OR DRAWN SHAPES, NEC: Copper & Copper Alloy
ROLLING MACHINERY: Steel
ROLLING MILL EQPT: Rod Mills
ROLLING MILL MACHINERY
ROLLING MILL ROLLS: Cast Iron
ROLLING MILL ROLLS: Cast Steel
ROLLS & BLANKETS, PRINTERS': Rubber Or Rubberized Fabric
ROLLS & ROLL COVERINGS: Rubber
ROLLS: Rubber, Solid Or Covered
ROOF DECKS
ROOFING GRANULES
ROOFING MATERIALS: Asphalt
ROOFING MATERIALS: Sheet Metal
ROOFING MEMBRANE: Rubber
ROPE

ROTORS: Motor
RUBBER
RUBBER BANDS
RUBBER PRDTS
RUBBER PRDTS: Appliance, Mechanical
RUBBER PRDTS: Mechanical
RUBBER PRDTS: Reclaimed
RUBBER PRDTS: Sheeting
RUBBER PRDTS: Silicone
RUBBER PRDTS: Sponge
RUBBER STAMP, WHOLESALE
RUGS : Braided & Hooked
RUST PROOFING SVC: Hot Dipping, Metals & Formed Prdts
RUST REMOVERS
RUST RESISTING

S

SADDLERY STORES
SAFE DEPOSIT BOXES
SAFES & VAULTS: Metal
SAFETY EQPT & SPLYS WHOLESALERS
SAFETY INSPECTION SVCS
SAILS
SALES PROMOTION SVCS
SALT
SALT & SULFUR MINING
SAND & GRAVEL
SAND LIME PRDTS
SAND MINING
SAND: Hygrade
SAND: Silica
SANDBLASTING EQPT
SANDSTONE: Crushed & Broken
SANDSTONE: Dimension
SANITARY SVCS: Dumps, Operation Of
SANITARY SVCS: Environmental Cleanup
SANITARY SVCS: Hazardous Waste, Collection & Disposal
SANITARY SVCS: Refuse Collection & Disposal Svcs
SANITARY SVCS: Waste Materials, Recycling
SANITATION CHEMICALS & CLEANING AGENTS
SASHES: Door Or Window, Metal
SATELLITE COMMUNICATIONS EQPT
SATELLITES: Communications
SAUNA ROOMS: Prefabricated
SAW BLADES
SAWDUST & SHAVINGS
SAWING & PLANING MILLS
SAWING & PLANING MILLS: Custom
SAWMILL MACHINES
SAWS & SAWING EQPT
SAWS: Hand, Metalworking Or Woodworking
SAWS: Portable
SCAFFOLDS: Mobile Or Stationary, Metal
SCALE REPAIR SVCS
SCALES & BALANCES, EXC LABORATORY
SCALES: Counting
SCALES: Indl
SCALP TREATMENT SVCS
SCANNING DEVICES: Optical
SCHOOL BUS SVC
SCHOOL SPLYS, EXC BOOKS: Wholesalers
SCHOOLS & EDUCATIONAL SVCS, NEC
SCHOOLS: Elementary & Secondary
SCIENTIFIC EQPT REPAIR SVCS
SCRAP & WASTE MATERIALS, WHOLESALE: Ferrous Metal
SCRAP & WASTE MATERIALS, WHOLESALE: Junk & Scrap
SCRAP & WASTE MATERIALS, WHOLESALE: Metal
SCRAP & WASTE MATERIALS, WHOLESALE: Nonferrous Metals Scrap
SCRAP & WASTE MATERIALS, WHOLESALE: Plastics Scrap
SCREENS: Door, Metal Covered Wood
SCREENS: Projection
SCREENS: Window, Metal
SCREENS: Window, Wood Framed
SCREENS: Woven Wire
SCREW MACHINE PRDTS
SCREW MACHINES
SCREWS: Metal
SEALANTS
SEALING COMPOUNDS: Sealing, synthetic rubber or plastic
SEALS: Hermetic
SEARCH & DETECTION SYSTEMS, EXC RADAR
SEARCH & NAVIGATION SYSTEMS
SEATING: Stadium
SEATING: Transportation

SPORTING GOODS
SPORTING GOODS STORES, NEC
SPORTING GOODS STORES: Archery Splys
SPORTING GOODS STORES: Firearms
SPORTING GOODS STORES: Fishing Eqpt
SPORTING GOODS STORES: Hunting Eqpt
SPORTING GOODS STORES: Playground Eqpt
SPORTING GOODS STORES: Skiing Eqpt
SPORTING GOODS STORES: Soccer Splys
SPORTING GOODS STORES: Specialty Sport Splys, NEC
SPORTING GOODS STORES: Team sports Eqpt
SPORTING GOODS STORES: Water Sport Eqpt
SPORTING GOODS: Archery
SPORTING GOODS: Hammocks & Other Net Prdts
SPORTING GOODS: Sleeping Bags
SPORTING/ATHLETIC GOODS: Gloves, Boxing, Handball, Etc
SPORTS APPAREL STORES
SPORTS PROMOTION SVCS
SPORTS TEAMS & CLUBS: Basketball
SPOUTING: Plastic & Fiberglass Reinforced
SPOUTS: Sheet Metal
SPRAYING EQPT: Agricultural
SPRINGS: Automobile
SPRINGS: Gun, Precision
SPRINGS: Hot Formed
SPRINGS: Hot Wound, Exc Wire
SPRINGS: Leaf, Automobile, Locomotive, Etc
SPRINGS: Mechanical, Precision
SPRINGS: Precision
SPRINGS: Steel
SPRINGS: Torsion Bar
SPRINGS: Wire
SPRINKLING SYSTEMS: Fire Control
SPROCKETS: Power Transmission
STAGE LIGHTING SYSTEMS
STAINLESS STEEL
STAIR TREADS: Rubber
STAIRCASES & STAIRS, WOOD
STAMPED ART GOODS FOR EMBROIDERING
STAMPING SVC: Book, Gold
STAMPING: Fabric Articles
STAMPINGS: Automotive
STAMPINGS: Metal
STANDPIPES
STARTERS & CONTROLLERS: Motor, Electric
STARTERS: Motor
STATIONARY & OFFICE SPLYS, WHOLESALE: Inked Ribbons
STATIONARY & OFFICE SPLYS, WHOLESALE: Laser Printer Splys
STATIONARY & OFFICE SPLYS, WHOLESALE: Manifold Business Form
STATIONARY & OFFICE SPLYS, WHOLESALE: Office Filing Splys
STATIONARY & OFFICE SPLYS, WHOLESALE: Stationers, Commercial
STATIONARY & OFFICE SPLYS, WHOLESALE: Stationery
STATIONERY & OFFICE SPLYS WHOLESALERS
STATIONERY ARTICLES: Pottery
STATIONERY PRDTS
STATIONERY: Made From Purchased Materials
STATORS REWINDING SVCS
STATUARY GOODS, EXC RELIGIOUS: Wholesalers
STEEL & ALLOYS: Tool & Die
STEEL FABRICATORS
STEEL MILLS
STEEL SHEET: Cold-Rolled
STEEL WOOL
STEEL, COLD-ROLLED: Sheet Or Strip, From Own Hot-Rolled
STEEL, COLD-ROLLED: Strip NEC, From Purchased Hot-Rolled
STEEL, COLD-ROLLED: Strip Or Wire
STEEL: Cold-Rolled
STEEL: Galvanized
STEEL: Laminated
STENCILS
STERILIZERS, BARBER & BEAUTY SHOP
STITCHING SVCS: Custom
STOCK SHAPES: Plastic
STONE: Cast Concrete
STONE: Crushed & Broken, NEC
STONE: Dimension, NEC
STONE: Quarrying & Processing, Own Stone Prdts
STONEWARE CLAY MINING

STONEWARE PRDTS: Pottery
STORE FIXTURES, EXC REFRIGERATED: Wholesalers
STORE FIXTURES: Wood
STORE FRONTS: Prefabricated, Metal
STORES: Auto & Home Supply
STORES: Drapery & Upholstery
STOVES: Wood & Coal Burning
STRAIGHTENERS
STRAINERS: Line, Piping Systems
STRAPPING
STRAPS: Bindings, Textile
STRAPS: Cotton Webbing
STRAPS: Elastic Webbing
STRAPS: Webbing, Woven
STRIPS: Copper & Copper Alloy
STRUCTURAL SUPPORT & BUILDING MATERIAL: Concrete
STUCCO
STUDIOS: Artist
STUDIOS: Sculptor's
STUDS & JOISTS: Sheet Metal
STYLING SVCS: Wigs
SUBDIVIDERS & DEVELOPERS: Real Property, Cemetery Lots Only
SUBMARINE BUILDING & REPAIR
SUBSCRIPTION FULFILLMENT SVCS: Magazine, Newspaper, Etc
SUNDRIES & RELATED PRDTS: Medical & Laboratory, Rubber
SUNROOMS: Prefabricated Metal
SUPERMARKETS & OTHER GROCERY STORES
SURFACE ACTIVE AGENTS
SURFACE ACTIVE AGENTS: Processing Assistants
SURFACERS: Concrete Grinding
SURGICAL & MEDICAL INSTRUMENTS WHOLESALERS
SURGICAL APPLIANCES & SPLYS
SURGICAL APPLIANCES & SPLYS
SURGICAL EQPT: See Also Instruments
SURGICAL IMPLANTS
SURGICAL INSTRUMENT REPAIR SVCS
SURVEYING & MAPPING: Land Parcels
SURVEYING SVCS: Aerial Digital Imaging
SUSPENSION SYSTEMS: Acoustical, Metal
SVC ESTABLISHMENT EQPT & SPLYS WHOLESALERS
SVC ESTABLISHMENT EQPT, WHOL: Concrete Burial Vaults & Boxes
SVC ESTABLISHMENT EQPT, WHOL: Funeral Director's Eqpt/Splys
SVC ESTABLISHMENT EQPT, WHOLESALE: Beauty Parlor Eqpt & Sply
SVC ESTABLISHMENT EQPT, WHOLESALE: Carpet Installation Eqpt
SVC ESTABLISHMENT EQPT, WHOLESALE: Engraving Eqpt & Splys
SVC ESTABLISHMENT EQPT, WHOLESALE: Firefighting Eqpt
SVC ESTABLISHMENT EQPT, WHOLESALE: Locksmith Eqpt & Splys
SVC ESTABLISHMENT EQPT, WHOLESALE: Shredders, Indl & Comm
SVC ESTABLISHMENT EQPT, WHOLESALE: Sprinkler Systems
SVC ESTABLISHMENT EQPT, WHOLESALE: Vending Machines & Splys
SWEEPING COMPOUNDS
SWIMMING POOL ACCESS: Leaf Skimmers Or Pool Rakes
SWIMMING POOL EQPT: Filters & Water Conditioning Systems
SWIMMING POOL SPLY STORES
SWIMMING POOLS, EQPT & SPLYS: Wholesalers
SWITCHBOARDS & PARTS: Power
SWITCHES
SWITCHES: Electric Power, Exc Snap, Push Button, Etc
SWITCHES: Electronic
SWITCHES: Electronic Applications
SWITCHES: Silicon Control
SWITCHES: Stepping
SWITCHGEAR & SWITCHBOARD APPARATUS
SWITCHGEAR & SWITCHGEAR ACCESS, NEC
SYNTHETIC RESIN FINISHED PRDTS, NEC
SYRUPS, DRINK
SYRUPS: Pharmaceutical
SYSTEMS ENGINEERING: Computer Related
SYSTEMS INTEGRATION SVCS
SYSTEMS INTEGRATION SVCS: Local Area Network
SYSTEMS INTEGRATION SVCS: Office Computer Automation

SYSTEMS SOFTWARE DEVELOPMENT SVCS

T

TABLE OR COUNTERTOPS, PLASTIC LAMINATED
TABLES: Lift, Hydraulic
TABLETS & PADS
TABLETS & PADS: Book & Writing, Made From Purchased Material
TABLETS & PADS: Newsprint, Made From Purchased Materials
TABLETS: Bronze Or Other Metal
TABLEWARE: Vitreous China
TACKS: Steel, Wire Or Cut
TAGS & LABELS: Paper
TAGS: Paper, Blank, Made From Purchased Paper
TALLOW: Animal
TANK COMPONENTS: Military, Specialized
TANK REPAIR SVCS
TANKS & OTHER TRACKED VEHICLE CMPNTS
TANKS: Cryogenic, Metal
TANKS: For Tank Trucks, Metal Plate
TANKS: Fuel, Including Oil & Gas, Metal Plate
TANKS: Lined, Metal
TANKS: Military, Including Factory Rebuilding
TANKS: Plastic & Fiberglass
TANKS: Standard Or Custom Fabricated, Metal Plate
TANKS: Water, Metal Plate
TANKS: Wood
TANNERIES: Leather
TANNING SALONS
TAPE DRIVES
TAPE: Instrumentation Type, Blank
TAPES: Insulating
TAPES: Pressure Sensitive
TAPES: Tie, Woven Or Braided
TAPS
TAR
TARPAULINS
TARPAULINS, WHOLESALE
TAX RETURN PREPARATION SVCS
TAXIDERMISTS
TECHNICAL WRITING SVCS
TELECOMMUNICATION EQPT REPAIR SVCS, EXC TELEPHONES
TELECOMMUNICATION SYSTEMS & EQPT
TELECOMMUNICATIONS CARRIERS & SVCS: Wireless
TELEMARKETING BUREAUS
TELEMETERING EQPT
TELEPHONE CENTRAL OFFICE EQPT: Dial Or Manual
TELEPHONE EQPT INSTALLATION
TELEPHONE EQPT: Modems
TELEPHONE EQPT: NEC
TELEPHONE EQPT: PBX, Manual & Automatic
TELEPHONE SWITCHING EQPT
TELEPHONE: Fiber Optic Systems
TELEPHONE: Headsets
TELESCOPES
TELEVISION BROADCASTING & COMMUNICATIONS EQPT
TELEVISION BROADCASTING STATIONS
TELEVISION FILM PRODUCTION SVCS
TELEVISION: Closed Circuit Eqpt
TEN PIN CENTERS
TENT REPAIR SHOP
TENTS: All Materials
TERMINAL BOARDS
TEST BORING SVCS: Nonmetallic Minerals
TESTERS: Battery
TESTERS: Environmental
TESTERS: Gas, Exc Indl Process
TESTERS: Hardness
TESTERS: Integrated Circuit
TESTERS: Liquid, Exc Indl Process
TESTERS: Physical Property
TESTERS: Sewage
TESTERS: Water, Exc Indl Process
TESTING SVCS
TEXTILE & APPAREL SVCS
TEXTILE CONVERTERS: Knit Goods
TEXTILE DESIGNERS
TEXTILE FABRICATORS
TEXTILE FINISHING: Bleaching, Broadwoven, Cotton
TEXTILE FINISHING: Bleaching, Man Fiber & Silk, Broadwoven
TEXTILE FINISHING: Cloth Mending, For The Trade
TEXTILE FINISHING: Dyeing, Finishing & Printng, Linen Fabric

TEXTILE FINISHING: Dyeing, Manmade Fiber & Silk, Broad-
woven
TEXTILE FINISHING: Preshrinking, Cotton
TEXTILE PRDTS: Hand Woven & Crocheted
TEXTILE: Finishing, Cotton Broadwoven
TEXTILE: Finishing, Raw Stock NEC
TEXTILE: Goods, NEC
TEXTILES
TEXTILES: Carbonized Rags
TEXTILES: Fibers, Textile, Rcvrd From Mill Waste/Rags
TEXTILES: Linen Fabrics
TEXTILES: Linings, Carpet, Exc Felt
TEXTILES: Mill Waste & Remnant
TEXTILES: Scouring & Combing
THEATRICAL LIGHTING SVCS
THEATRICAL PRODUCERS & SVCS
THEATRICAL SCENERY
THERMISTORS, EXC TEMPERATURE SENSORS
THERMOCOUPLES
THERMOCOUPLES: Indl Process
THERMOELECTRIC DEVICES: Solid State
THERMOMETERS: Indl
THERMOPLASTIC MATERIALS
THERMOPLASTICS
THERMOSETTING MATERIALS
THREAD, ELASTIC: Fabric Covered
THREAD: All Fibers
THREAD: Embroidery
THREAD: Natural Fiber
THREAD: Sewing
THREAD: Thread, From Manmade Fiber
TIES, FORM: Metal
TILE: Brick & Structural, Clay
TILE: Clay, Drain & Structural
TILE: Clay, Roof
TILE: Mosaic, Ceramic
TILE: Partition, Clay
TILE: Quarry, Clay
TILE: Structural Clay
TILE: Wall, Fiberboard
TIMBER PRDTS WHOLESALERS
TIMING DEVICES: Electronic
TIN
TINSEL
TIRE & INNER TUBE MATERIALS & RELATED PRDTS
TIRE CORD & FABRIC: Fuel Cells, Reinforcing
TIRE DEALERS
TIRE RECAPPING & RETREADING
TIRE SUNDRIES OR REPAIR MATERIALS: Rubber
TIRES & INNER TUBES
TIRES: Cushion Or Solid Rubber
TIRES: Indl Vehicles
TITANIUM MILL PRDTS
TOBACCO & PRDTS, WHOLESALE: Smoking
TOBACCO & TOBACCO PRDTS WHOLESALERS
TOBACCO LEAF PROCESSING
TOBACCO STORES & STANDS
TOBACCO: Chewing & Snuff
TOBACCO: Cigarettes
TOBACCO: Cigars
TOILET PREPARATIONS
TOILETRIES, COSMETICS & PERFUME STORES
TOILETRIES, WHOLESALE: Razor Blades
TOMBSTONES: Cut Stone, Exc Finishing Or Lettering Only
TOOL & DIE STEEL
TOOL REPAIR SVCS
TOOLS & EQPT: Used With Sporting Arms
TOOLS: Carpenters', Including Levels & Chisels, Exc Saws
TOOLS: Hand
TOOLS: Hand, Carpet Layers
TOOLS: Hand, Engravers'
TOOLS: Hand, Hammers
TOOLS: Hand, Masons'
TOOLS: Hand, Mechanics
TOOLS: Hand, Power
TOOTHBRUSHES: Exc Electric
TOPS: Automobile, Stamped Metal
TOURIST LODGINGS
TOWELETTES: Premoistened
TOWELS: Indl
TOWELS: Linen & Linen & Cotton Mixtures
TOWELS: Paper
TOWERS, SECTIONS: Transmission, Radio & Television
TOYS
TOYS & HOBBY GOODS & SPLYS, WHOLESALE:
Arts/Crafts Eqpt/Sply

TOYS & HOBBY GOODS & SPLYS, WHOLESALE: Toys,
NEC
TOYS: Dolls, Stuffed Animals & Parts
TOYS: Rubber
TRADE SHOW ARRANGEMENT SVCS
TRADERS: Commodity, Contracts
TRAILER COACHES: Automobile
TRAILERS & CHASSIS: Camping
TRAILERS & PARTS: Truck & Semi's
TRAILERS & TRAILER EQPT
TRAILERS OR VANS: Horse Transportation, Fifth-Wheel Type
TRAILERS: Bodies
TRAILERS: Demountable Cargo Containers
TRAILERS: Semitrailers, Truck Tractors
TRAILERS: Truck, Chassis
TRANSDUCERS: Electrical Properties
TRANSDUCERS: Pressure
TRANSFORMERS: Airport Lighting
TRANSFORMERS: Control
TRANSFORMERS: Distribution
TRANSFORMERS: Distribution, Electric
TRANSFORMERS: Electric
TRANSFORMERS: Electronic
TRANSFORMERS: Meters, Electronic
TRANSFORMERS: Power Related
TRANSFORMERS: Rectifier
TRANSFORMERS: Specialty
TRANSISTORS
TRANSLATION & INTERPRETATION SVCS
TRANSMISSIONS: Motor Vehicle
TRANSPORTATION AGENTS & BROKERS
TRANSPORTATION EPQT & SPLYS, WHOL: Aeronautical
Eqpt & Splys
TRANSPORTATION EQPT & SPLYS WHOLESALERS, NEC
TRANSPORTATION EQUIPMENT, NEC
TRANSPORTATION PROGRAM REGULATION & ADMIN
GOVT: Local
TRANSPORTATION SVCS: Airport
TRANSPORTATION SVCS: Railroad Terminals
TRANSPORTATION SVCS: Railroads, Interurban
TRANSPORTATION: Air, Scheduled Passenger
TRANSPORTATION: Great Lakes Domestic Freight
TRANSPORTATION: Transit Systems, NEC
TRAP ROCK: Crushed & Broken
TRAP ROCK: Dimension
TRAPS: Crab, Steel
TRAPS: Stem
TRAVEL AGENCIES
TRAVEL TRAILER DEALERS
TRAVEL TRAILERS & CAMPERS
TRAVELER ACCOMMODATIONS, NEC
TRAYS: Greenhouse Flats, Wood
TRAYS: Plastic
TRIM: Window, Wood
TROPHIES, NEC
TROPHIES, PEWTER
TROPHIES, PLATED, ALL METALS
TROPHIES, WHOLESALE
TROPHIES: Metal, Exc Silver
TROPHY & PLAQUE STORES
TRUCK & BUS BODIES: Automobile Wrecker Truck
TRUCK & BUS BODIES: Beverage Truck
TRUCK & BUS BODIES: Bus Bodies
TRUCK & BUS BODIES: Car Carrier
TRUCK & BUS BODIES: Cement Mixer
TRUCK & BUS BODIES: Dump Truck
TRUCK & BUS BODIES: Garbage Or Refuse Truck
TRUCK & BUS BODIES: Motor Vehicle, Specialty
TRUCK & BUS BODIES: Stake Platform Truck
TRUCK & BUS BODIES: Truck Cabs, Motor Vehicles
TRUCK & BUS BODIES: Truck Tops
TRUCK & BUS BODIES: Truck, Motor Vehicle
TRUCK & BUS BODIES: Utility Truck
TRUCK BODIES: Body Parts
TRUCK BODY SHOP
TRUCK GENERAL REPAIR SVC
TRUCK PAINTING & LETTERING SVCS
TRUCK PARTS & ACCESSORIES: Wholesalers
TRUCKING & HAULING SVCS: Contract Basis
TRUCKING & HAULING SVCS: Draying, Local, Without Stor-
age
TRUCKING & HAULING SVCS: Heavy Machinery, Local
TRUCKING & HAULING SVCS: Heavy, NEC
TRUCKING & HAULING SVCS: Lumber & Log, Local
TRUCKING & HAULING SVCS: Steel, Local
TRUCKING & HAULING SVCS: Timber, Local

TRUCKING, AUTOMOBILE CARRIER
TRUCKING: Except Local
TRUCKING: Local, Without Storage
TRUCKS & TRACTORS: Industrial
TRUCKS, INDL: Wholesalers
TRUCKS: Forklift
TRUCKS: Indl
TRUNKS
TRUSSES: Wood, Floor
TRUSSES: Wood, Roof
TUB CONTAINERS: Plastic
TUBE & TUBING FABRICATORS
TUBES: Boiler, Wrought
TUBES: Electron, Indl
TUBES: Light Sensing & Emitting
TUBES: Mailing
TUBES: Paper
TUBES: Paper Or Fiber, Chemical Or Electrical Uses
TUBES: Photomultiplier
TUBES: Steel & Iron
TUBES: Vacuum
TUBES: Welded, Aluminum
TUBES: Wrought, Welded Or Lock Joint
TUBING, COLD-DRAWN: Mech Or Hypodermic Sizes, Stain-
less
TUBING: Copper
TUBING: Plastic
TUBING: Rubber
TUBING: Seamless
TUMBLERS: Plastic
TUNGSTEN CARBIDE
TUNGSTEN CARBIDE POWDER
TUNGSTEN MILL PRDTS
TURBINE GENERATOR SET UNITS: Hydraulic, Complete
TURBINES & TURBINE GENERATOR SET UNITS: Gas,
Complete
TURBINES & TURBINE GENERATOR SETS
TURBINES & TURBINE GENERATOR SETS & PARTS
TURBINES: Gas, Mechanical Drive
TURBINES: Hydraulic, Complete
TURBINES: Steam
TURKEY PROCESSING & SLAUGHTERING
TURNKEY VENDORS: Computer Systems
TWINE
TWINE PRDTS
TWINE: Binder & Baler
TYPE: Rubber
TYPESETTING SVC
TYPESETTING SVC: Computer
TYPOGRAPHY

U

ULTRASONIC EQPT: Cleaning, Exc Med & Dental
UNDERCOATINGS: Paint
UNIFORM SPLY SVCS: Indl
UNIFORM STORES
UNISEX HAIR SALONS
UNIVERSITY
UPHOLSTERERS' EQPT & SPLYS WHOLESALERS
UPHOLSTERY FILLING MATERIALS
UPHOLSTERY MATERIAL
UPHOLSTERY MATERIALS, BROADWOVEN
UPHOLSTERY WORK SVCS
URINALS: Vitreous China
USED CAR DEALERS
UTENSILS: Household, Cooking & Kitchen, Metal
UTENSILS: Household, Metal, Exc Cast
UTILITY TRAILER DEALERS

V

VACUUM CLEANER REPAIR SVCS
VACUUM CLEANER STORES
VACUUM CLEANERS: Household
VACUUM CLEANERS: Indl Type
VACUUM PUMPS & EQPT: Laboratory
VACUUM SYSTEMS: Air Extraction, Indl
VALUE-ADDED RESELLERS: Computer Systems
VALVE REPAIR SVCS, INDL
VALVES
VALVES & PARTS: Gas, Indl
VALVES & PIPE FITTINGS
VALVES & REGULATORS: Pressure, Indl
VALVES: Aerosol, Metal
VALVES: Control, Automatic
VALVES: Electrohydraulic Servo, Metal
VALVES: Engine

INDEX

VALVES: Fire Hydrant
VALVES: Fluid Power, Control, Hydraulic & pneumatic
VALVES: Gas Cylinder, Compressed
VALVES: Indl
VALVES: Plumbing & Heating
VALVES: Regulating & Control, Automatic
VALVES: Regulating, Process Control
VALVES: Water Works
VAN CONVERSIONS
VARNISHES, NEC
VASES: Pottery
VAULTS & SAFES WHOLESALERS
VEGETABLES, FROZEN: Wholesaler
VEHICLES: All Terrain
VEHICLES: Recreational
VENDING MACHINE OPERATORS: Candy & Snack Food
VENDING MACHINE OPERATORS: Sandwich & Hot Food
VENDING MACHINES & PARTS
VENETIAN BLINDS & SHADES
VENTILATING EQPT: Sheet Metal
VENTURE CAPITAL COMPANIES
VERMICULITE MINING SVCS
VETERINARY PHARMACEUTICAL PREPARATIONS
VETERINARY PRDTS: Instruments & Apparatus
VIALS: Glass
VIDEO & AUDIO EQPT, WHOLESALE
VIDEO EQPT
VIDEO TAPE PRODUCTION SVCS
VIDEO TRIGGERS EXC REMOTE CONTROL TV DEVICES
VINYL RESINS, NEC
VISES: Machine
VISUAL COMMUNICATIONS SYSTEMS
VITAMINS: Natural Or Synthetic, Uncompounded, Bulk
VITAMINS: Pharmaceutical Preparations
VOCATIONAL OR TECHNICAL SCHOOLS, PUBLIC
VOCATIONAL REHABILITATION AGENCY
VOCATIONAL TRAINING AGENCY

W

WALLBOARD: Decorated, Made From Purchased Materials
WALLPAPER & WALL COVERINGS
WALLPAPER: Made From Purchased Paper
WAREHOUSING & STORAGE FACILITIES, NEC
WAREHOUSING & STORAGE, REFRIGERATED: Cold Storage Or Refrig
WAREHOUSING & STORAGE, REFRIGERATED: Frozen Or Refrig Goods
WAREHOUSING & STORAGE: Bulk St & Termnls, Hire, Petro/Chem
WAREHOUSING & STORAGE: General
WAREHOUSING & STORAGE: General
WAREHOUSING & STORAGE: Refrigerated
WAREHOUSING & STORAGE: Self Storage
WARM AIR HEAT & AC EQPT & SPLYS, WHOLESALE Fan, Heat & Vent
WARM AIR HEATING & AC EQPT & SPLYS, WHOL: Dust Collecting
WARM AIR HEATING & AC EQPT & SPLYS, WHOL: Elec Heating Eqpt
WARM AIR HEATING & AC EQPT & SPLYS, WHOLESALE Heat Exchgrs
WARM AIR HEATING/AC EQPT/SPLYS, WHOL Warm Air Htg Eqpt/Splys
WASHERS
WASHERS: Spring, Metal
WATCH REPAIR SVCS
WATCHES
WATCHES & PARTS, WHOLESALE
WATER HEATERS
WATER PURIFICATION EQPT: Household
WATER PURIFICATION PRDTS: Chlorination Tablets & Kits
WATER SOFTENER SVCS
WATER SUPPLY
WATER TREATMENT EQPT: Indl
WATER: Mineral, Carbonated, Canned & Bottled, Etc
WATER: Pasteurized & Mineral, Bottled & Canned
WATER: Pasteurized, Canned & Bottled, Etc

WATERPROOFING COMPOUNDS
WAXES: Mineral, Natural
WAXES: Petroleum, Not Produced In Petroleum Refineries
WEAVING MILL, BROADWOVEN FABRICS: Wool Or Similar Fabric
WEIGHING MACHINERY & APPARATUS
WELDING & CUTTING APPARATUS & ACCESS, NEC
WELDING EQPT
WELDING EQPT & SPLYS WHOLESALERS
WELDING EQPT & SPLYS: Electrodes
WELDING EQPT & SPLYS: Gas
WELDING EQPT & SPLYS: Resistance, Electric
WELDING EQPT REPAIR SVCS
WELDING EQPT: Electric
WELDING EQPT: Electrical
WELDING MACHINES & EQPT: Ultrasonic
WELDING REPAIR SVC
WELDING SPLYS, EXC GASES: Wholesalers
WELDMENTS
WET CORN MILLING
WHEEL & CASTER REPAIR SVCS
WHEELBARROWS
WHEELCHAIR LIFTS
WHEELCHAIRS
WHEELS & BRAKE SHOES: Railroad, Cast Iron
WHEELS & GRINDSTONES, EXC ARTIFICIAL: Abrasive
WHEELS & PARTS
WHEELS: Abrasive
WHEELS: Disc, Wheelbarrow, Stroller, Etc, Stamped Metal
WHEELS: Iron & Steel, Locomotive & Car
WHEELS: Railroad Car, Cast Steel
WHEELS: Rolled, Locomotive
WHIRLPOOL BATHS: Hydrotherapy
WHISTLES
WHITING MINING: Crushed & Broken
WIGS & HAIRPIECES
WIGS, WHOLESALE
WINCHES
WINDINGS: Coil, Electronic
WINDMILLS: Electric Power Generation
WINDOW & DOOR FRAMES
WINDOW CLEANING SVCS
WINDOW FRAMES & SASHES: Plastic
WINDOW FRAMES, MOLDING & TRIM: Vinyl
WINDOW FURNISHINGS WHOLESALERS
WINDOW SCREENING: Plastic
WINDOWS: Frames, Wood
WINDOWS: Wood
WINDSHIELD WIPER SYSTEMS
WINDSHIELDS: Plastic
WINE & DISTILLED ALCOHOLIC BEVERAGES WHOLESALERS
WINE CELLARS, BONDED: Wine, Blended
WIRE
WIRE & CABLE: Aluminum
WIRE & CABLE: Aluminum
WIRE & CABLE: Nonferrous, Building
WIRE & WIRE PRDTS
WIRE CLOTH & WOVEN WIRE PRDTS, MADE FROM PURCHASED WIRE
WIRE CLOTH: Fourdrinier, Made From Purchased Wire
WIRE FABRIC: Welded Steel
WIRE FENCING & ACCESS WHOLESALERS
WIRE MATERIALS: Aluminum
WIRE MATERIALS: Copper
WIRE MATERIALS: Steel
WIRE PRDTS: Ferrous Or Iron, Made In Wiredrawing Plants
WIRE PRDTS: Steel & Iron
WIRE ROPE CENTERS
WIRE WHOLESALERS
WIRE: Communication
WIRE: Mesh
WIRE: Nonferrous
WIRE: Nonferrous, Appliance Fixture
WIRE: Steel, Insulated Or Armored
WIRE: Wire, Ferrous Or Iron
WIRING DEVICES WHOLESALERS

WOMEN'S & CHILDREN'S CLOTHING WHOLESALERS, NEC
WOMEN'S & GIRLS' SPORTSWEAR WHOLESALERS
WOMEN'S CLOTHING STORES
WOMEN'S CLOTHING STORES: Ready-To-Wear
WOMEN'S FULL & KNEE LENGTH HOSIERY DYEING & FINISHING
WOMEN'S KNITWEAR STORES
WOMEN'S SPORTSWEAR STORES
WOOD CARVINGS, WHOLESALE
WOOD CHIPS, PRODUCED AT THE MILL
WOOD FENCING WHOLESALERS
WOOD PRDTS
WOOD PRDTS: Applicators
WOOD PRDTS: Barrel Heading, Sawn or split
WOOD PRDTS: Barrels & Barrel Parts
WOOD PRDTS: Baskets, Fruit & Veg, Round Stave, Till, Etc
WOOD PRDTS: Beekeeping Splys
WOOD PRDTS: Engraved
WOOD PRDTS: Handles, Tool
WOOD PRDTS: Laundry
WOOD PRDTS: Logs Of Sawdust & Wood Particles, Pressed
WOOD PRDTS: Moldings, Unfinished & Prefinished
WOOD PRDTS: Mulch Or Sawdust
WOOD PRDTS: Mulch, Wood & Bark
WOOD PRDTS: Novelties, Fiber
WOOD PRDTS: Oars & Paddles
WOOD PRDTS: Outdoor, Structural
WOOD PRDTS: Panel Work
WOOD PRDTS: Porch Columns
WOOD PRDTS: Rulers & Yardsticks
WOOD PRDTS: Shoe Trees
WOOD PRDTS: Signboards
WOOD PRDTS: Spars
WOOD PRDTS: Stepladders
WOOD PRDTS: Survey Stakes
WOOD PRDTS: Trim
WOOD PRDTS: Yard Sticks
WOOD PRODUCTS: Reconstituted
WOOD TREATING: Bridges
WOOD TREATING: Creosoting
WOOD TREATING: Flooring, Block
WOOD TREATING: Millwork
WOOD TREATING: Railroad Cross Bridges & Switch Ties
WOOD TREATING: Structural Lumber & Timber
WOOD TREATING: Wood Prdts, Creosoted
WOODWORK & TRIM: Exterior & Ornamental
WOODWORK & TRIM: Interior & Ornamental
WOODWORK: Carved & Turned
WOODWORK: Interior & Ornamental, NEC
WOODWORK: Ornamental, Cornices, Mantels, Etc.
WOOL PULLING SVC
WOOLEN & WORSTED YARNS, WHOLESALES
WOVEN WIRE PRDTS, NEC
WRENCHES
WRITING FOR PUBLICATION SVCS

X

X-RAY EQPT & TUBES

Y

YARN & YARN SPINNING
YARN MILLS: Texturizing
YARN MILLS: Texturizing, Throwing & Twisting
YARN MILLS: Throwing
YARN MILLS: Winding
YARN: Knitting, Spun
YARN: Manmade & Synthetic Fiber, Spun
YARN: Specialty & Novelty
YARN: Weaving, Spun
YARNS & ROVING: Coir
YARNS & ROVING: Flax

Z

ZIRCONIUM

PRODUCT SECTION

Product category — **BOXES: Folding**
Edgar & Son Paperboard ....G....... 999 999-9999
   Yourtown *(G-11480)*
Ready Box Co ....E....... 999 999-9999
   Anytown *(G-7097)*
City —

Indicates approximate employment figure
A = Over 500 employees, B = 251-500
C = 101-250, D = 51-100, E = 20-50
F = 10-19, G = 3-9
Business phone
Geographic Section entry number where full
company information appears.

See footnotes for symbols and codes identification.
- Refer to the Industrial Product Index preceding this section to locate product headings.

ABRASIVE SCOURING MATERIALS

Confluense LLC ....G....... 215 530-6461
  Allentown *(G-175)*

ABRASIVES

Associated Ceramics & Tech ....D....... 724 353-1585
  Sarver *(G-17065)*
Dynacut Inc ....G....... 610 346-7386
  Springtown *(G-17926)*
Elge Precision Machining Inc ....F....... 610 376-5458
  Reading *(G-16372)*
Hewlett Manufacturing Co ....G....... 814 683-4762
  Linesville *(G-9981)*
Norstone Incorporated ....G....... 484 684-6986
  Bridgeport *(G-2041)*
Ppt Research Inc ....G....... 610 434-0103
  Allentown *(G-353)*
Precision Finishing Inc ....E....... 215 257-6862
  Quakertown *(G-16232)*
Production Abrasives Inc ....E....... 814 938-5490
  Hamilton *(G-6858)*
Saint-Gobain Abrasives Inc ....E....... 215 855-4300
  Montgomeryville *(G-11416)*
Saint-Gobain Abrasives Inc ....E....... 267 218-7100
  Montgomeryville *(G-11417)*
Saint-Gobain Delaware Corp ....G....... 610 341-7000
  Valley Forge *(G-18712)*
T B W Industries Inc ....F....... 215 794-8070
  Furlong *(G-6234)*
United States Products Co ....G....... 412 621-2130
  Pittsburgh *(G-15675)*
Weiler Corporation ....B....... 570 595-7495
  Cresco *(G-3896)*
Winterthur Wendt Usa Inc ....C....... 610 495-2850
  Royersford *(G-16869)*

ABRASIVES: Coated

Ervin Industries Inc ....D....... 724 282-1060
  Butler *(G-2399)*
Keystone Abrasives Co ....F....... 610 939-1060
  Reading *(G-16419)*

ABRASIVES: Diamond Powder

Penn Scientific Products Co ....F....... 888 238-6710
  Abington *(G-13)*

ABRASIVES: Silicon Carbide

Morgan Advanced Mtls Tech Inc ....C....... 814 781-1573
  Saint Marys *(G-16998)*

ABRASIVES: Synthetic

Extramet Products LLC ....F....... 724 532-3041
  Latrobe *(G-9475)*
Innovative Carbide Inc ....D....... 412 751-6900
  Irwin *(G-8171)*
Laurel Carbide Inc ....G....... 724 537-4810
  Latrobe *(G-9495)*

ABRASIVES: Tungsten Carbide

Basic Carbide Corporation ....E....... 724 446-1630
  Irwin *(G-8146)*
Basic Carbide Corporation ....D....... 412 754-0060
  Elizabeth *(G-4856)*
Basic Carbide Corporation ....D....... 412 751-3774
  Buena Vista *(G-2340)*
Carbide Metals Inc ....F....... 724 459-6355
  Blairsville *(G-1718)*

Ceratizit Usa Inc ....F....... 724 694-8100
  Latrobe *(G-9463)*
Global Tungsten & Powders Corp ....B....... 570 268-5000
  Towanda *(G-18429)*

ACADEMIC TUTORING SVCS

Charlene Crawford ....G....... 215 432-7542
  Elkins Park *(G-4901)*

ACCELERATION INDICATORS & SYSTEM COMPONENTS: Aerospace

Advanced Acoustic Concepts LLC ....D....... 724 434-5100
  Lemont Furnace *(G-9732)*
Cobham Adv Elec Sol Inc ....B....... 215 996-2000
  Lansdale *(G-9351)*
Discovery Machine Inc ....F....... 570 601-1966
  Williamsport *(G-20006)*
Enjet Aero Erie Inc ....C....... 814 860-3104
  Erie *(G-5260)*

ACCELERATORS: Electrostatic Particle

Solid State Eqp Holdings LLC ....G....... 215 328-0700
  Horsham *(G-7850)*

ACCOUNTING MACHINES & CASH REGISTERS

Beaver Valley Cash Register Co ....G....... 724 728-0800
  New Brighton *(G-12031)*

ACCOUNTING SVCS, NEC

Charles Komar & Sons Inc ....C....... 570 326-3741
  Williamsport *(G-19997)*
Donald W Deitz ....G....... 814 745-2857
  Clarion *(G-3177)*

ACETONE: Synthetic

Braskem America Inc ....E....... 412 208-8100
  Pittsburgh *(G-14790)*
Braskem America Inc ....C....... 610 497-8378
  Marcus Hook *(G-10438)*
Braskem America Inc ....C....... 215 841-3100
  Philadelphia *(G-13478)*

ACID RESIST: Etching

Langeloth Metallurgical Co LLC ....C....... 724 947-2201
  Langeloth *(G-9270)*
Nanohorizons Inc ....E....... 814 355-4700
  Bellefonte *(G-1109)*
Parkin Chemical Corporation ....G....... 412 828-7355
  Oakmont *(G-12922)*

ACIDS

Advanced Skin Technologies Inc ....G....... 610 488-7643
  Bernville *(G-1295)*
Dimesol Usa LLC ....F....... 717 938-0796
  Lewisberry *(G-9884)*

ACIDS: Hydrocyanic

Arkema Inc ....C....... 610 582-1551
  Birdsboro *(G-1686)*

ACIDS: Inorganic

Ssw International Inc ....E....... 412 922-9100
  Pittsburgh *(G-15572)*

ACIDS: Sulfuric, Oleum

Eco Services Operations Corp ....D....... 610 251-9118
  Malvern *(G-10227)*

ACOUSTICAL BOARD & TILE

Armstrong World Industries Inc ....A....... 717 397-0611
  Lancaster *(G-8942)*
Keith Bush Associates Inc ....G....... 215 968-5255
  Langhorne *(G-9306)*
Panel Solutions Inc ....E....... 570 459-3490
  Hazleton *(G-7515)*

ACRYLIC RESINS

APT Advanced Polymer Tech Corp ......D....... 724 452-1330
  Harmony *(G-7066)*
Custom Kitchens Inc ....G....... 814 833-5338
  Erie *(G-5238)*
Poly Sat Inc ....E....... 215 332-7700
  Philadelphia *(G-14187)*

ACRYLIC RUBBERS: Polyacrylate

Sartomer Company Divison Total ....E....... 610 692-8401
  West Chester *(G-19637)*

ACTOR

Wenning Entertainment LLC ....F....... 412 292-8776
  East Mc Keesport *(G-4582)*

ACTUATORS: Indl, NEC

Auma Actuators Inc ....G....... 714 247-1250
  Canonsburg *(G-2546)*
Harold Beck & Sons Inc ....C....... 215 968-4600
  Newtown *(G-12506)*
Novasentis Inc ....F....... 814 238-7400
  State College *(G-18001)*
Seventy-Three Mfg Co Inc ....E....... 610 845-7823
  Bechtelsville *(G-1037)*

ADDRESSING SVCS

Great Atlantic Graphics Inc ....D....... 610 296-8711
  Lansdale *(G-9373)*

ADHESIVES

Accu Bond Corporation ....F....... 610 269-8433
  Downingtown *(G-4208)*
ACE Company ....G....... 215 234-4615
  Harleysville *(G-7012)*
Acrymax Technologies Inc ....F....... 610 566-7470
  Media *(G-10913)*
Adhesives Research Inc ....B....... 717 235-7979
  Glen Rock *(G-6449)*
Adhesives Specialists Inc ....E....... 610 266-8910
  Allentown *(G-116)*
Adlamco Inc ....G....... 717 292-1577
  York *(G-20367)*
Air Products and Chemicals Inc ....A....... 610 481-4911
  Allentown *(G-119)*
Air Products and Chemicals Inc ....E....... 724 266-1563
  Leetsdale *(G-9677)*
Arkema Delaware Inc ....A....... 610 205-7000
  King of Prussia *(G-8582)*
Cardolite Corporation ....E....... 609 436-0902
  Bristol *(G-2123)*
DSM Biomedical Inc ....G....... 610 321-2720
  Exton *(G-5669)*
Eastern Adhesives Inc ....F....... 215 348-0119
  Doylestown *(G-4296)*

P R O D U C T

Fielco Adhesives...............................G...... 267 282-5311
Huntingdon Valley *(G-7982)*

Fielco Industries Inc.......................E...... 215 674-8700
Huntingdon Valley *(G-7983)*

HB Fuller Company...........................E...... 610 688-1234
Wayne *(G-19335)*

LD Davis Industries Inc....................E...... 800 883-6199
Jenkintown *(G-8293)*

Lord Corporation.............................C...... 724 260-5541
Eighty Four *(G-4844)*

Lord Corporation.............................C...... 814 763-2345
Saegertown *(G-16923)*

Lutech Inc......................................G...... 717 898-9150
Salunga *(G-17054)*

Lynx Specialty Tapes Inc..................G...... 215 348-1382
Doylestown *(G-4314)*

Morton International LLC...................C...... 989 636-1000
Collegeville *(G-3384)*

PPG Industries Inc...........................E...... 412 487-4500
Allison Park *(G-459)*

Saint-Gobain Corporation..................A...... 610 893-6000
Malvern *(G-10313)*

Specialty Adhesives Inc...................G...... 484 524-5324
Coatesville *(G-3326)*

Versum Materials Us LLC..................F...... 610 481-3946
Allentown *(G-423)*

Versum Materials Us LLC..................G...... 570 467-2981
Tamaqua *(G-18231)*

Vilimia Inc......................................F...... 570 654-6735
Yatesville *(G-20349)*

WW Henry Company LP......................E...... 704 203-5000
Aliquippa *(G-103)*

ADHESIVES & SEALANTS

American Cnsld Mfg Co Inc.................E...... 610 825-2630
Conshohocken *(G-3519)*

Arkema Inc......................................C...... 215 826-2600
Bristol *(G-2109)*

Bemis Packaging Inc.........................E...... 717 279-5000
Lebanon *(G-9547)*

C P Converters Inc..........................D...... 717 764-1193
York *(G-20415)*

Carlisle Construction Mtls LLC...........B...... 717 245-7000
Carlisle *(G-2695)*

Concrete Service Materials Co............G...... 610 825-1554
Conshohocken *(G-3532)*

Covestro LLC..................................A...... 412 413-2000
Pittsburgh *(G-14882)*

Ddp Specialty Electronic MA...............G...... 610 244-6000
Collegeville *(G-3374)*

Fres-Co Systems Usa Inc...................B...... 215 721-4600
Telford *(G-18290)*

Fuchs Lubricants Co.........................E...... 724 867-5000
Emlenton *(G-5008)*

Hahn Universal................................G...... 724 941-6444
Canonsburg *(G-2594)*

Haraeuc Inc Cermalloy Div................G...... 610 825-8387
Conshohocken *(G-3553)*

Harsco Corporation..........................G...... 215 295-8675
Fairless Hills *(G-5783)*

Heraeus Incorporated Hic..................C...... 610 825-6050
Conshohocken *(G-3555)*

Laticrete International Inc..................G...... 610 326-9970
Pottstown *(G-16009)*

Lord Corporation.............................B...... 814 868-0924
Erie *(G-5371)*

Lord Corporation.............................A...... 877 275-5673
Erie *(G-5373)*

Modern Blending Tech Inc..................F...... 267 580-1000
Levittown *(G-9850)*

Nanogriptech Inc.............................G...... 412 224-2136
Pittsburgh *(G-15318)*

Oneida Instant Log...........................E...... 814 336-2125
Meadville *(G-10770)*

Pelmor Laboratories Inc....................E...... 215 968-3334
Newtown *(G-12533)*

Pelseal Technologies LLC..................F...... 215 245-0581
Bensalem *(G-1239)*

Performance Coatings Corp................F...... 610 525-1190
Levittown *(G-9854)*

Permabond LLC...............................G...... 732 868-1372
Pottstown *(G-16029)*

Polytek Development Corp..................E...... 610 559-8620
Easton *(G-4743)*

Rohm and Haas Company...................A...... 989 636-1000
Collegeville *(G-3392)*

Saint-Gobain Delaware Corp...............G...... 610 341-7000
Valley Forge *(G-18712)*

Sauereisen Inc................................E...... 412 963-0303
Pittsburgh *(G-15514)*

Sensible Components LLC..................F...... 855 548-7587
Oakdale *(G-12911)*

Wall Firma Inc.................................F...... 724 258-6873
Monongahela *(G-11319)*

Whitford Corporation........................D...... 610 286-3500
Elverson *(G-4967)*

Whitford Worldwide Company LLC.......D...... 610 286-3500
Elverson *(G-4968)*

ADHESIVES: Adhesives, paste

Berwind Consumer Products LLC.........A...... 215 563-2800
Philadelphia *(G-13458)*

ADHESIVES: Epoxy

Concure Inc....................................G...... 610 497-0198
Chester *(G-3044)*

R H Carbide & Epoxy Inc...................G...... 724 356-2277
Hickory *(G-7630)*

ADVERTISING AGENCIES

Adcomm Inc....................................F...... 610 820-8565
Allentown *(G-115)*

Altris Incorporated...........................G...... 724 259-8338
Greensburg *(G-6649)*

Altus Group Inc...............................F...... 215 977-9900
Philadelphia *(G-13374)*

B & D Advertising Inc.......................D...... 717 852-6950
York *(G-20394)*

Berm Studios Incorporated................D...... 610 622-2100
Garnet Valley *(G-6265)*

Borris Information Group Inc...............G...... 717 285-9141
Mountville *(G-11790)*

Centre Publications Inc.....................G...... 814 364-2000
Centre Hall *(G-2840)*

Chelsea Partners Inc........................E...... 215 603-7300
Philadelphia *(G-13537)*

Jayco Grafix Inc..............................D...... 610 678-2640
Reinholds *(G-16633)*

Lionshare Media Services...................G...... 724 837-9700
Greensburg *(G-6685)*

Mbr2 Graphic Services LLC................G...... 610 490-8996
Norristown *(G-12680)*

Me Ken + Jen Crative Svcs LLC...........G...... 215 997-2355
Chalfont *(G-2883)*

Minuteman Press.............................G...... 215 538-2200
Quakertown *(G-16221)*

Mirage Advertising Inc......................G...... 412 372-4181
Monroeville *(G-11345)*

Noel Interactive Group LLC................G...... 732 991-1484
Easton *(G-4732)*

Observer Publishing Company.............E...... 724 941-7725
Canonsburg *(G-2614)*

Pindar Set Inc.................................C...... 610 731-2921
King of Prussia *(G-8662)*

Printing Post Inc..............................G...... 412 367-7468
Pittsburgh *(G-15445)*

York Daily Record Sunday News...........F...... 717 771-2000
York *(G-20736)*

ADVERTISING AGENCIES: Consultants

American Future Systems Inc.............D...... 610 695-8600
Malvern *(G-10186)*

ARA Corporation.............................G...... 724 843-5378
Koppel *(G-8813)*

Creative Labworks Inc......................G...... 724 667-4093
Bessemer *(G-1390)*

Innovative Advertising & Mktg.............G...... 717 788-1385
Waynesboro *(G-19413)*

Localedge Media Inc.........................E...... 716 875-9100
Erie *(G-5369)*

Morgan Signs Inc.............................E...... 814 238-5051
State College *(G-17994)*

ADVERTISING CURTAINS

Matthey Johnson Inc........................B...... 610 341-8300
Wayne *(G-19352)*

Shaffer Block and Con Pdts Inc...........E...... 814 445-4414
Somerset *(G-17705)*

ADVERTISING DISPLAY PRDTS

Azar International Inc........................G...... 570 288-0786
Kingston *(G-8712)*

Baar Products Company.....................G...... 610 873-4591
Downingtown *(G-4214)*

Chestnut Group Inc..........................G...... 610 688-3300
Wayne *(G-19313)*

Creative Touch Inc...........................E...... 215 856-9177
Philadelphia *(G-13580)*

Eagle Displays LLC...........................F...... 724 335-8900
North Apollo *(G-12726)*

Sparks Exhbits Envrnments Corp.........D...... 215 676-1100
Philadelphia *(G-14329)*

World Manufacturing Inc....................E...... 215 426-0500
Philadelphia *(G-14487)*

ADVERTISING MATERIAL DISTRIBUTION

D & A Associates.............................G...... 610 534-4840
Darby *(G-4017)*

Getaways On Display Inc...................F...... 717 653-8070
Manheim *(G-10386)*

ADVERTISING REPRESENTATIVES: Electronic Media

Andrew Torba.................................G...... 570 209-1622
Moosic *(G-11503)*

Beye LLC..G...... 484 581-1840
Wayne *(G-19305)*

Creative Thought Media LLC...............G...... 267 270-5147
Philadelphia *(G-13579)*

ADVERTISING REPRESENTATIVES: Magazine

Islamic Communication Network..........G...... 215 227-0640
Philadelphia *(G-13877)*

ADVERTISING REPRESENTATIVES: Media

Farm Journal Inc.............................E...... 215 557-8900
Philadelphia *(G-13694)*

Millenium Medical Educational............E...... 215 230-1960
Doylestown *(G-4316)*

ADVERTISING REPRESENTATIVES: Newspaper

Ad Star Inc.....................................F...... 724 439-5519
Uniontown *(G-18614)*

Journal Register Company..................D...... 610 323-3000
Exton *(G-5702)*

Pike County Dispatch Inc...................F...... 570 296-2611
Milford *(G-11166)*

ADVERTISING REPRESENTATIVES: Printed Media

Times-Shamrock..............................D...... 570 501-0278
Hazleton *(G-7531)*

ADVERTISING SPECIALTIES, WHOLESALE

American Calendar Inc......................F...... 215 743-3834
Philadelphia *(G-13382)*

American Future Systems Inc.............D...... 610 695-8600
Malvern *(G-10186)*

Awards & More................................G...... 724 444-1040
Gibsonia *(G-6325)*

Callery Sr John...............................G...... 412 344-9010
Pittsburgh *(G-14805)*

Clever Inc......................................G...... 717 762-7508
Waynesboro *(G-19404)*

Collegian Inc...................................E...... 814 865-2531
State College *(G-17953)*

Craig Hollern..................................E...... 814 539-2974
Johnstown *(G-8366)*

D G A Inc.......................................G...... 717 249-8542
Carlisle *(G-2706)*

Danowski.......................................G...... 717 328-5057
Mercersburg *(G-10985)*

Davco Advertising Inc.......................E...... 717 442-4155
Kinzers *(G-8736)*

First Class Specialties......................F...... 724 446-1000
Herminie *(G-7570)*

Five Thousand Forms Inc...................F...... 610 395-0900
Fogelsville *(G-5994)*

Hds Marketing.................................E...... 412 279-1600
Pittsburgh *(G-15084)*

Iehle Enterprises Inc.........................E...... 717 859-1113
Lancaster *(G-9055)*

Kemko Industries Inc........................G...... 267 613-8651
Upper Gwynedd *(G-18695)*

Kinteco Inc.....................................G...... 610 921-1494
Temple *(G-18332)*

Larry D Mays..................................F...... 814 833-7988
Erie *(G-5360)*

Montco Advertising Spc Inc..............E...... 610 270-9800
Norristown *(G-12687)*
Musumeci Santo ....G...... 215 467-2158
Philadelphia *(G-14045)*
New Look Uniform & Embroidery..........F...... 814 944-5515
Altoona *(G-530)*
Nittany EMB & Digitizing.....................F...... 814 359-0905
State College *(G-17998)*
Pennsylvania Promotions Inc...............F...... 800 360-2800
Exton *(G-5724)*
Physical Graffi-Tees...........................G...... 610 439-3344
Allentown *(G-351)*
Precision Sign & Awning.....................G...... 412 281-0330
Pittsburgh *(G-15432)*
Ras Sports Inc ....E...... 814 833-9111
Erie *(G-5457)*
Riggans Advg Specialty Co ....F...... 724 654-5741
New Castle *(G-12143)*
Southern Alleghenies Advg Inc............G...... 814 472-8593
Ebensburg *(G-4797)*
Stefanos Printing Inc ....G...... 724 277-8374
Dunbar *(G-4443)*
Steve Schwartz Associates Inc ....E...... 412 765-3400
Pittsburgh *(G-15583)*
Trautman Associates Inc ....F...... 570 743-0430
Shamokin Dam *(G-17429)*

ADVERTISING SVCS: Billboards

Adams Outdoor Advg Ltd Partnr..........E...... 610 266-9461
Bethlehem *(G-1444)*
Graham Sign Company ....G...... 814 765-7199
Clearfield *(G-3220)*
Morgan Signs Inc ....E...... 814 238-5051
State College *(G-17994)*
Saupp Signs Co LLC ....G...... 814 342-2100
Philipsburg *(G-14526)*

ADVERTISING SVCS: Direct Mail

A Link Prtg & Promotions LLC ....G...... 412 220-0290
Bridgeville *(G-2049)*
Acumark Inc......................................G...... 570 883-1800
West Pittston *(G-19753)*
Choice Marketing Inc..........................E...... 610 494-1270
Aston *(G-755)*
Creative Characters............................G...... 215 923-2679
Philadelphia *(G-13578)*
Direct Mail Service Inc ....D...... 412 471-6300
Pittsburgh *(G-14925)*
Everything Postal Inc ....G...... 610 367-7444
Bechtelsville *(G-1032)*
Goodway Graphics Inc........................B...... 215 887-5700
Jenkintown *(G-8288)*
Graphcom Inc....................................C...... 800 699-1664
Gettysburg *(G-6295)*
Interform Corporation ....C...... 412 221-7321
Bridgeville *(G-2070)*
Jem Graphics LLC ....G...... 412 220-0290
Bridgeville *(G-2074)*
Kirkland Printing Inc...........................G...... 215 706-2399
Willow Grove *(G-20124)*
North Amrcn Communications Inc........A...... 814 696-3553
Duncansville *(G-4458)*
RB Concepts LLC ....G...... 484 351-8211
Conshohocken *(G-3598)*
Sir Speedy 7108 Inc ....F...... 412 787-9898
Pittsburgh *(G-15542)*
Stagestep Inc....................................F...... 267 672-2900
Philadelphia *(G-14339)*
VIP Advertising & Printing ....G...... 570 251-7897
Honesdale *(G-7731)*
Webb Communications Inc..................E...... 570 326-7634
Plymouth *(G-15823)*
Webb Communications Inc..................D...... 570 326-7634
Williamsport *(G-20089)*

ADVERTISING SVCS: Display

Madera Cabinets ....F...... 412 793-5850
Pittsburgh *(G-15246)*
Purpose 1 LLC ....G...... 717 232-9077
Lemoyne *(G-9749)*
View Works Inc..................................G...... 724 226-9773
Springdale *(G-17905)*

ADVERTISING SVCS: Outdoor

Derse Inc..D...... 724 772-4853
Warrendale *(G-19071)*
Sign Spot ....G...... 570 455-7775
Hazleton *(G-7527)*

ADVERTISING SVCS: Poster, Outdoor

Pecks Graphics LLC ....G...... 717 963-7588
Harrisburg *(G-7191)*

ADVOCACY GROUP

American Soc For Deaf Children..........G...... 717 909-5577
Camp Hill *(G-2486)*

AERIAL WORK PLATFORMS

G W Becker Inc ....D...... 724 983-1000
Hermitage *(G-7586)*
Jlg Industries Inc ....C...... 717 530-9000
Shippensburg *(G-17534)*
Jlg Industries Inc ....A...... 717 485-5161
Mc Connellsburg *(G-10568)*
Jlg Industries Inc ....E...... 717 485-6464
Mc Connellsburg *(G-10570)*

AGENTS, BROKERS & BUREAUS: Personal Service

Carleton Inc ....E...... 215 230-8900
Doylestown *(G-4289)*
Ggs Information Services Inc ....C...... 717 764-2222
York *(G-20499)*
Great Atlantic Graphics Inc..................D...... 610 296-8711
Lansdale *(G-9373)*
Sodium Systems LLC ....G...... 800 821-8962
York *(G-20671)*
United Commercial Supply LLC ....G...... 412 835-2690
South Park *(G-17786)*

AGRICULTURAL DISINFECTANTS

Koch Industries Inc ....G...... 717 949-3469
Schaefferstown *(G-17128)*
Koch Industries Inc ....F...... 814 453-5444
Erie *(G-5349)*

AGRICULTURAL EQPT: BARN, SILO, POULTRY, DAIRY/LIVESTOCK MACH

Morris Twnship Spervisors Barn..........G...... 724 627-3096
Sycamore *(G-18201)*
Raytec LLC ....E...... 717 445-0510
Ephrata *(G-5138)*
Taty Bug Inc......................................G...... 814 856-3323
Mayport *(G-10547)*

AGRICULTURAL EQPT: Clippers, Animal, Hand Or Electric

Keystone Dehorner.............................G...... 610 857-9728
Pomeroy *(G-15890)*

AGRICULTURAL EQPT: Dusters, Mechanical

Horning Manufacturing LLC ....F...... 717 354-5040
East Earl *(G-4545)*

AGRICULTURAL EQPT: Fertilizing Machinery

Gvm Inc..D...... 717 677-6197
Biglerville *(G-1662)*
Pannell Mfg Corp ....G...... 610 268-2012
Avondale *(G-856)*
Superior Tech Inc ....G...... 717 569-3359
Ephrata *(G-5150)*

AGRICULTURAL EQPT: Fertilizng, Sprayng, Dustng/Irrigatn Mach

Ez-Flo Injection Systems Inc ....G...... 412 996-2161
Moon Township *(G-11487)*

AGRICULTURAL EQPT: Fillers & Unloaders, Silo

Angell Industries Inc...........................G...... 412 269-2956
Coraopolis *(G-3658)*

AGRICULTURAL EQPT: Grade, Clean & Sort Machines, Fruit/Veg

Andritz Inc ....B...... 570 546-1253
Muncy *(G-11806)*
AZS Brusher Equipment LLC ....G...... 717 733-2584
Ephrata *(G-5092)*

AGRICULTURAL EQPT: Greens Mowing Eqpt

Richard Shilling Jr..............................G...... 814 319-4326
Seminole *(G-17363)*

AGRICULTURAL EQPT: Harvesters, Fruit, Vegetable, Tobacco

Harvestmore Inc.................................F...... 814 725-5258
North East *(G-12747)*

AGRICULTURAL EQPT: Loaders, Manure & General Utility

Els Manufacturing LLC ....F...... 717 442-8569
Kinzers *(G-8737)*

AGRICULTURAL EQPT: Planting Machines

Pequea Planter LLC ....F...... 717 442-4406
Gap *(G-6255)*

AGRICULTURAL EQPT: Soil Preparation Mach, Exc Turf & Grounds

ATI Corporation ....E...... 717 354-8721
New Holland *(G-12229)*

AGRICULTURAL EQPT: Tractors, Farm

Kennedys Powder Coating ....F...... 717 866-6747
Myerstown *(G-11889)*

AGRICULTURAL EQPT: Trailers & Wagons, Farm

Aaron Wenger ....G...... 717 656-9876
New Holland *(G-12225)*
Farmco Manufacturing LP....................G...... 717 768-7769
Ronks *(G-16806)*
Mill Run Carriage ....G...... 717 438-3149
Millerstown *(G-11206)*
Smouse Trucks & Vans Inc ....G...... 724 887-7777
Mount Pleasant *(G-11718)*
Tuscarora Electric Mfg Co ....G...... 570 836-2101
Tunkhannock *(G-18551)*

AGRICULTURAL EQPT: Transplanters

Tree Equipment Design Inc..................G...... 570 386-3515
New Ringgold *(G-12444)*

AGRICULTURAL EQPT: Turf & Grounds Eqpt

Synatek LP..D...... 888 408-5433
Souderton *(G-17767)*

AGRICULTURAL EQPT: Turf Eqpt, Commercial

Wolfe Metal Fab Inc ....G...... 724 339-7790
Lower Burrell *(G-10108)*

AGRICULTURAL EQPT: Weeding Machines

Weeds Inc ....E...... 610 358-9430
Aston *(G-797)*

AGRICULTURAL MACHINERY & EQPT REPAIR

Lancaster Parts & Eqp Inc ....F....... 717 299-3721
Lancaster *(G-9103)*
Lwe Inc...G...... 814 336-3553
Meadville *(G-10751)*

AGRICULTURAL MACHINERY & EQPT: Wholesalers

Andrew E Reken.................................G...... 724 783-7878
Dayton *(G-4034)*
Artman Equipment Company Inc ....F...... 724 337-3700
Apollo *(G-662)*
Lancaster Parts & Eqp Inc ....F...... 717 299-3721
Lancaster *(G-9103)*
Nutrient Control Systems Inc ....G...... 717 261-5711
Chambersburg *(G-2965)*
Rt 66 Tractor Supply ....G...... 724 668-2000
New Alexandria *(G-12020)*
Somerset Welding & Steel Inc ....E...... 814 444-7000
Somerset *(G-17709)*

PRODUCT

AIR CLEANING SYSTEMS

Aircon Filter Sales & Svc Co..............E 215 922-7727
Philadelphia *(G-13359)*

Lifeaire Systems LLC......................G....... 484 224-3042
Allentown *(G-295)*

Met-Pro Technologies LLC................D..... 215 723-8155
Telford *(G-18305)*

AIR CONDITIONERS: Motor Vehicle

American Cooling Tech Inc..............F 717 767-2775
York *(G-20373)*

AIR CONDITIONING & VENTILATION EQPT & SPLYS: Wholesales

486 Associates Inc........................E 717 691-7077
Mechanicsburg *(G-10815)*

AIR CONDITIONING EQPT

Capital Coil & Air LLC.....................G..... 484 498-6880
West Chester *(G-19518)*

Cni Inc...E 215 244-9650
Bensalem *(G-1169)*

Eic Solutions Inc...........................E 215 443-5190
Warminster *(G-18870)*

Havaco Technologies Inc ....G 814 878-5509
Erie *(G-5311)*

Honeywell International Inc ....A 215 533-3000
Philadelphia *(G-13832)*

Time Tech Industries Inc ....G 412 670-5498
Mc Kees Rocks *(G-10639)*

York International Corporation.........F 814 479-4005
Johnstown *(G-8447)*

AIR CONDITIONING EQPT, WHOLE HOUSE: Wholesalers

Crystaline Bus & Rail Inc ....F 570 645-3145
Nesquehoning *(G-12004)*

AIR CONDITIONING REPAIR SVCS

Building Inspectors Contrs Inc..............G....... 215 481-0606
Glenside *(G-6509)*

AIR CONDITIONING UNITS: Complete, Domestic Or Indl

Carrier Corporation........................E 610 834-1717
Plymouth Meeting *(G-15838)*

Grokas Inc....................................F 610 565-1498
Media *(G-10931)*

Oxicool Inc...................................G...... 215 462-2665
Malvern *(G-10292)*

United Coolair Corporation..............C 717 845-8685
York *(G-20694)*

USA Coil & Air Inc ....E 610 296-9668
Malvern *(G-10336)*

York International Corporation.............A 717 771-7890
York *(G-20745)*

AIR COOLERS: Metal Plate

Brumbaugh Body Co Inc.................G...... 814 696-9552
Duncansville *(G-4450)*

Nrf US Inc.....................................G...... 814 947-1378
Plymouth Meeting *(G-15861)*

Solar Cool Coatings.......................G...... 267 664-3667
Glenside *(G-6537)*

Thermal Engrg Intl USA Inc ....E 610 948-5400
Royersford *(G-16868)*

AIR CURTAINS

Berner International LLC....................E 724 658-3551
New Castle *(G-12063)*

AIR DUCT CLEANING SVCS

D & R Steel Construction Inc..............F 570 265-6216
Milan *(G-11147)*

Robert G Dent Heating & AC................F 570 784-6721
Bloomsburg *(G-1798)*

AIR MATTRESSES: Plastic

CCL Tube Inc.................................D...... 570 824-8485
Hanover Township *(G-6984)*

Greif Inc.......................................E 570 459-9075
West Hazleton *(G-19711)*

Newtown-Slocomb Mfg Inc ....G..... 570 825-3675
Hanover Township *(G-7001)*

AIR PURIFICATION EQPT

Advanced Industrial Tech Corp ....F 201 483-7235
Langhorne *(G-9273)*

Calgon Carbon Corporation................C..... 412 787-6700
Moon Township *(G-11482)*

Calgon Carbon Corporation................B..... 412 787-6700
Pittsburgh *(G-14803)*

Luftrol Inc ....G...... 215 355-0532
Warminster *(G-18914)*

New Busch Co Inc ....G...... 724 940-2326
Wexford *(G-19815)*

Penn Fan Inc ....G...... 724 452-4570
Zelienople *(G-20814)*

AIR TRAFFIC CONTROL SYSTEMS & EQPT

Nexgen Ats ....G....... 717 779-9580
Mountville *(G-11800)*

AIR, WATER & SOLID WASTE PROGRAMS ADMINISTRATION SVCS

County of Somerset.......................G...... 814 629-9460
Hollsopple *(G-7657)*

Envirnmntal Protection PA Dept............F 570 621-3139
Pottsville *(G-16078)*

AIRCRAFT & AEROSPACE FLIGHT INSTRUMENTS & GUIDANCE SYSTEMS

Acutronic Company........................G....... 412 926-1200
Pittsburgh *(G-14647)*

Acutronic USA Inc ....G....... 412 926-1200
Pittsburgh *(G-14648)*

Innovtive Slutions Support Inc............D..... 610 646-9800
Exton *(G-5699)*

Teletronics Technology Corp ....C 267 352-2020
Newtown *(G-12555)*

Tortel Products.............................G...... 267 477-1805
Hatfield *(G-7402)*

Ufc Aerospace ....G...... 610 485-4704
Upper Chichester *(G-18675)*

AIRCRAFT & HEAVY EQPT REPAIR SVCS

General Transervice Inc ....E 610 857-1900
Coatesville *(G-3304)*

J R Young ....G...... 717 935-2919
Belleville *(G-1132)*

Mike Barta and Sons Inc ....G 215 757-1162
Langhorne *(G-9311)*

O & N Arcft Modification Inc ....E 570 945-3769
Factoryville *(G-5760)*

Tri-State Hydraulics Inc ....E 724 483-1790
Charleroi *(G-3022)*

Vector Aerospace Usa Inc................G...... 610 559-2191
Easton *(G-4767)*

Vr Enterprises Llc ....G 215 932-1113
Lansdale *(G-9426)*

AIRCRAFT ASSEMBLY PLANTS

Boeing Company ....D...... 610 828-7764
Lafayette Hill *(G-8877)*

Bombardier Transportation..................F 412 655-0325
Pittsburgh *(G-14781)*

Learjet Inc ....A 215 246-3454
Philadelphia *(G-13963)*

Lockheed Martin Corporation............G...... 610 337-9560
Malvern *(G-10270)*

Pittsburgh Jet Center ....F 724 452-4719
Zelienople *(G-20816)*

Textron Inc...................................D...... 570 323-6181
Williamsport *(G-20081)*

Usm Aerostructures Corp ....E 570 613-1234
Wyoming *(G-20285)*

AIRCRAFT AUTOMATIC PILOT SYSTEMS

Tcw Technologies LLC ....G 610 928-3420
Emmaus *(G-5044)*

AIRCRAFT CONTROL SYSTEMS:

Triumph Controls LLC ....C 215 699-4861
North Wales *(G-12837)*

Triumph Group Inc.........................C 610 251-1000
Berwyn *(G-1383)*

AIRCRAFT CONTROL SYSTEMS: Electronic Totalizing Counters

Honeywell International Inc ....A 215 533-3000
Philadelphia *(G-13832)*

L3 Technologies Inc........................C 267 545-7000
Bristol *(G-2157)*

Smiths Group North America Inc ....F 772 286-9300
Malvern *(G-10322)*

AIRCRAFT ENGINES & ENGINE PARTS: Air Scoops

Cnc Metalworks Inc........................G...... 717 624-8436
New Oxford *(G-12407)*

Mecaer Aviation Group Inc.................E 301 790-3645
Philadelphia *(G-14002)*

AIRCRAFT ENGINES & ENGINE PARTS: Airfoils

Pratt & Whitney Americon Inc ....C 717 546-0220
Middletown *(G-11070)*

Precision Castparts Corp..................B 570 474-6371
Mountain Top *(G-11771)*

AIRCRAFT ENGINES & PARTS

Acutec Precision Aerospace Inc ....B 814 336-2214
Meadville *(G-10695)*

Ametek Inc....................................D...... 267 933-2121
Harleysville *(G-7018)*

Ametek Inc....................................E 267 933-2121
Harleysville *(G-7019)*

Avco Corporation...........................C 570 323-6181
Williamsport *(G-19990)*

Corry Manufacturing Company ....C 814 664-9611
Corry *(G-3752)*

Eaton Aerospace LLC......................D...... 610 522-4000
Glenolden *(G-6473)*

Holtec International ....G...... 215 646-5842
Maple Glen *(G-10430)*

Honeywell International Inc ....D...... 724 452-1300
Fombell *(G-6031)*

Honeywell International Inc ....A 717 741-3799
York *(G-20527)*

Honeywell International Inc ....C 814 432-2118
Franklin *(G-6135)*

Innodyn LLC ....G...... 814 339-7328
Osceola Mills *(G-13055)*

Lionheart Holdings LLC...................D...... 215 283-8400
Newtown *(G-12519)*

Lockheed Martin Aeroparts ....C 814 262-3000
Johnstown *(G-8404)*

Lord Corporation............................B 814 868-0924
Erie *(G-5371)*

Netmercatus LLC ....G...... 646 822-7900
Sutersville *(G-18184)*

Precision Castparts Corp..................C 570 825-4544
Wilkes Barre *(G-19959)*

Prime Turbines LLC ....G...... 724 586-0124
Butler *(G-2435)*

Stein Seal Company ....C 215 256-0201
Kulpsville *(G-8831)*

Summit Aerospace USA Inc ....F 570 839-8615
Mount Pocono *(G-11737)*

Teledyne Scentific Imaging LLC.........F 215 368-6900
Montgomeryville *(G-11423)*

Triumph Group Inc.........................C 610 251-1000
Berwyn *(G-1383)*

Triumph Group Operations Inc............F 610 251-1000
Berwyn *(G-1386)*

Unison Engine Components Inc............C 570 825-4544
Wilkes Barre *(G-19967)*

AIRCRAFT EQPT & SPLYS WHOLESALERS

Mitchell Aviation Ltd ....G....... 717 232-7575
Harrisburg *(G-7179)*

AIRCRAFT FLIGHT INSTRUMENT REPAIR SVCS

Willier Elc Mtr Repr Co Inc................G...... 215 426-9920
Philadelphia *(G-14477)*

AIRCRAFT FLIGHT INSTRUMENTS

Aircraft Instruments Company ....G...... 215 348-5274
Doylestown *(G-4269)*

Blue Avionics Inc ....F 310 433-9431
Chester Springs (G-3072)
Strube Inc ....F 717 426-1906
Marietta (G-10468)

AIRCRAFT LIGHTING

B/E Aerospace Inc ....G 570 595-7491
Mountainhome (G-11785)

AIRCRAFT MAINTENANCE & REPAIR SVCS

Mecaer Aviation Group Inc................E 301 790-3645
Philadelphia (G-14002)

AIRCRAFT PARTS & AUXILIARY EQPT: Accumulators, Propeller

Bridge Acpuncture Natural Hlth ....G 215 348-8058
Doylestown (G-4281)

AIRCRAFT PARTS & AUXILIARY EQPT: Aircraft Training Eqpt

Environmental Tectonics Corp ....C 215 355-9100
Southampton (G-17809)

AIRCRAFT PARTS & AUXILIARY EQPT: Arresting Device Systems

Victor-Balata Belting Company ....E 610 258-2010
Easton (G-4772)

AIRCRAFT PARTS & AUXILIARY EQPT: Assys, Subassemblies/Parts

O & N Arcft Modification Inc ....E 570 945-3769
Factoryville (G-5760)
Triumph Aerospace Systems Grp ....E 610 251-1000
Berwyn (G-1381)
Triumph Aviations Inc............................G 610 251-1000
Berwyn (G-1382)

AIRCRAFT PARTS & AUXILIARY EQPT: Body & Wing Assys & Parts

Triumph Group Inc ....C 610 251-1000
Berwyn (G-1383)
Triumph Insulation Systems LLC ....G 610 251-1000
Berwyn (G-1387)

AIRCRAFT PARTS & AUXILIARY EQPT: Gears, Power Transmission

Eaton Aerospace LLC.........................D 610 522-4000
Glenolden (G-6473)
Eaton Corporation ....C 610 522-4059
Glenolden (G-6474)
H-D Advanced Manufacturing Co ....G 724 759-2850
Sewickley (G-17389)

AIRCRAFT PARTS & AUXILIARY EQPT: Landing Assemblies & Brakes

Acutec Precision Aerospace Inc ....B 814 336-2214
Meadville (G-10695)
Enginred Arrsting Systems Corp ....C 610 494-8000
Upper Chichester (G-18660)

AIRCRAFT PARTS & AUXILIARY EQPT: Military Eqpt & Armament

Bsm Enterprises Company Inc.............F 215 257-2231
Perkasie (G-13268)
Sgrignoli Brothers ....G 717 766-2812
Mechanicsburg (G-10887)

AIRCRAFT PARTS & AUXILIARY EQPT: Research & Development, Mfr

Gogreenapu LLC................................G 814 943-9948
Altoona (G-511)
Titan Robotics Inc ....G 724 986-6737
Pittsburgh (G-15625)

AIRCRAFT PARTS & AUXILIARY EQPT: Seat Ejector Devices

Martin-Baker America Inc ....C 814 262-9325
Johnstown (G-8407)

AIRCRAFT PARTS & AUXILIARY EQPT: Tanks, Fuel

Mike Barta and Sons Inc ....G 215 757-1162
Langhorne (G-9311)

AIRCRAFT PARTS & EQPT, NEC

Air Parts of Lock Haven ....F 570 748-0823
Lock Haven (G-10083)
Alvord-Polk Inc ....G 800 925-2126
Millersburg (G-11187)
American Sun Inc ....F 610 497-2210
Aston (G-751)
Ametek Inc ....D 267 933-2121
Harleysville (G-7018)
Ametek Inc ....E 267 933-2121
Harleysville (G-7019)
Amies Airparts LLC ....G 570 871-7991
Clifton Twp (G-3260)
Anholt Technologies Inc ....F 610 268-2758
Avondale (G-848)
B/E Aerospace Inc ....G 570 595-7491
Mountainhome (G-11785)
Blue Avionics Inc ....F 310 433-9431
Chester Springs (G-3072)
Carson Helicopters Inc.......................D 215 249-3535
Perkasie (G-13270)
Enersys Advanced Systems Inc ....D 215 674-3800
Horsham (G-7816)
Foranne Manufacturing Inc ....G 215 357-4650
Warminster (G-18881)
Helicopter Tech Inc ....F 610 272-8090
King of Prussia (G-8630)
J A Reinhardt & Co Inc ....C 570 595-7491
Mountainhome (G-11787)
L P Aero Plastics Inc..........................C 724 744-4448
Jeannette (G-8260)
Lockheed Martin Aeroparts ....C 814 262-3000
Johnstown (G-8404)
Lockheed Martin Corporation..............B 814 262-3000
Johnstown (G-8405)
Magee Plastics Company ....D 724 776-2220
Warrendale (G-19087)
Mitchell Aviation Ltd ....G 717 232-7575
Harrisburg (G-7179)
Moritz Aerospace Inc ....B 215 249-1300
Dublin (G-4436)
Olympic Tool & Machine Corp ....D 610 494-1600
Aston (G-784)
Pratt & Whitney Americon Inc ....C 717 546-0220
Middletown (G-11070)
Redstone Corporation ....G 321 213-2135
Johnstown (G-8429)
Smiths Aerospace Components I.........G 570 474-3011
Mountain Top (G-11776)
Strube Inc ....F 717 426-1906
Marietta (G-10468)
Transicoil LLC ....C 484 902-1100
Collegeville (G-3397)
Trigon Holding Inc ....E 724 941-5540
Mc Murray (G-10647)
Trigon Incorporated ....D 724 941-5540
Mc Murray (G-10648)
Triumph Group Acquisition Corp ....G 610 251-1000
Berwyn (G-1384)
Triumph Group Holdings - Mexic ....D 610 251-1000
Berwyn (G-1385)
Triumph Structures - E Texas ....A 610 251-1000
Berwyn (G-1388)
Usm Aerostructures Corp ....E 570 613-1234
Wyoming (G-20285)

AIRCRAFT PARTS/AUX EQPT: Airframe Assy, Exc Guided Missiles

Brenner Aerostructures LLC ....E 215 638-3884
Bensalem (G-1161)

AIRCRAFT SEATS

B/E Aerospace Inc ....G 570 595-7491
Mountainhome (G-11785)
Enginred Arrsting Systems Corp ....C 610 494-8000
Upper Chichester (G-18660)

AIRCRAFT TURBINES

Honeywell International Inc ....A 215 533-3000
Philadelphia (G-13832)
Vector Aerospace Usa Inc ....G 610 559-2191
Easton (G-4767)

AIRCRAFT: Airplanes, Fixed Or Rotary Wing

Boeing Company ....G 610 591-1978
Ridley Park (G-16734)
Boeing Company ....A 610 591-2121
Ridley Park (G-16737)

AIRCRAFT: Research & Development, Manufacturer

Dragonfly Pictures Inc ....F 610 521-6115
Essington (G-5542)
General Electric Company ....G 610 770-1881
Allentown (G-226)
Lockheed Martin Corporation..............B 610 531-5640
Malvern (G-10271)

AIRFRAME ASSEMBLIES: Guided Missiles

G Adasavage LLC ....E 215 355-3105
Huntingdon Valley (G-7987)

ALARM SYSTEMS WHOLESALERS

Willow Grove Auto Top Inc...................G 215 659-3276
Willow Grove (G-20150)

ALARMS: Burglar

Big Brother Hd Ltd Lblty Co ....G 201 355-8166
Tamiment (G-18232)
Harrison Electronic Systems ....F 570 639-5695
Wilkes Barre (G-19924)

ALARMS: Fire

Keystone Fire Co Apparatus ....F 610 587-3859
Boyertown (G-1921)

ALCOHOL, ETHYL: For Beverage Purposes

Mac Beverage Inc ....G 215 474-2024
Philadelphia (G-13984)

ALCOHOL: Ethyl & Ethanol

Bionol Clearfield LLC ....F 814 913-3100
Clearfield (G-3213)

ALKALIES & CHLORINE

Arkema Inc ....B 610 878-6500
King of Prussia (G-8583)
FMC Corporation...............................B 800 526-3649
Philadelphia (G-13711)
Occidental Chemical Corp ....F 610 327-4145
Pottstown (G-16022)
PPG Industries Inc ....A 412 434-3131
Pittsburgh (G-15425)
Univar USA Inc ....D 717 944-7471
Middletown (G-11084)

ALL-TERRAIN VEHICLE DEALERS

East Coast Atv Inc ....F 267 733-7364
Coopersburg (G-3627)

ALLOYS: Additive, Exc Copper Or Made In Blast Furnaces

General Electric Company ....G 646 682-5601
Imperial (G-8065)
Greenville Metals Inc ....D 724 509-1861
Transfer (G-18465)
Metallurg Inc ....G 610 293-2501
Wayne (G-19355)
Metallurg Holdings Inc ....F 610 293-2501
Wayne (G-19356)

ALTERNATORS & GENERATORS: Battery Charging

Chargeitspot LLC ....C 215 220-6600
Philadelphia (G-13526)
Steins Pasco Battery Starter................G 215 969-6900
Philadelphia (G-14343)

ALTERNATORS: Automotive

Penntex Industries Inc........................G 717 266-8762
Manchester (G-10360)
S T M Heavy Duty Electric Inc..............F 610 967-3810
Zionsville (G-20836)

PRODUCT

ALUMINUM

Alcoa USA Corp ....G....... 212 518-5400
Pittsburgh (G-14666)
Alcoa USA Corp ....G....... 412 553-4545
Pittsburgh (G-14667)
Alumax LLC ....C....... 412 553-4545
Pittsburgh (G-14695)
Alumisource Corporation ....F....... 412 250-0360
Monessen (G-11296)
Arconic Mexico Holdings LLC ....A....... 412 553-4545
Pittsburgh (G-14719)
Custom Manufacturing Corp ....E....... 215 638-3888
Bensalem (G-1178)
Hollowell Aluminum ....G....... 717 597-0826
Waynesboro (G-19411)
Old Ladder Co ....A....... 888 523-3371
Greenville (G-6762)

ALUMINUM PRDTS

Accuride Erie LP ....B....... 814 480-6400
Erie (G-5170)
All-Clad Metalcrafters LLC ....D....... 724 745-8300
Canonsburg (G-2537)
Alloy America LLC ....F....... 412 828-8270
Cheswick (G-3100)
Alumax LLC ....C....... 412 553-4545
Pittsburgh (G-14695)
Aluminum & Carbon Plus Inc ....G....... 724 368-9200
Portersville (G-15924)
AMG Aluminum North America LLC .....F....... 610 293-2501
Wayne (G-19297)
Associated Ceramics & Tech ....D....... 724 353-1585
Sarver (G-17065)
Ballews Aluminum Products Inc ....F....... 717 492-8956
Manheim (G-10369)
Bristol Aluminum Co ....E....... 215 946-1566
Levittown (G-9820)
Construction Specialties Inc ....B....... 570 546-2255
Muncy (G-11813)
Craft-Bilt Manufacturing Co ....D....... 215 721-7700
Souderton (G-17731)
Hydro Extruder LLC ....C....... 570 474-5935
Mountain Top (G-11764)
Hydro Extruder LLC ....C....... 412 299-7600
Moon Township (G-11492)
Hydro Extruder LLC ....C....... 570 474-5935
Mountain Top (G-11765)
Hydro Extrusion Usa LLC ....E....... 877 966-7272
Moon Township (G-11493)
Hydro Extrusion Usa LLC ....C....... 318 878-9703
Cressona (G-3904)
Ilsco Extrusions Inc ....G....... 724 589-5888
Greenville (G-6748)
KB Alloys Holdings LLC ....F....... 484 582-3520
Wayne (G-19345)
Matthews International Corp ....B....... 412 571-5500
Pittsburgh (G-15266)
MI Metals Inc ....F....... 717 692-4851
Millersburg (G-11196)
Mountain Ridge Metals LLC ....C....... 717 692-4851
Millersburg (G-11197)
Railway Specialties Corp ....E....... 215 788-9242
Croydon (G-3926)
Ralph McClure ....G....... 610 738-1440
Reynoldsville (G-16662)
Reitnouer Inc ....E....... 610 929-4856
Birdsboro (G-1704)
Rockwood Manufacturing Company ....C....... 814 926-2026
Rockwood (G-16792)
Sapa Extrusions Inc ....G....... 870 235-2609
Bensalem (G-1251)
Sapa North America Inc ....B....... 877 922-7272
Cressona (G-3907)
Sapa Precision Tubing LLC ....F....... 412 893-1300
Moon Township (G-11499)
Specilty Mtallurgical Pdts Inc ....F....... 717 246-0385
Red Lion (G-16614)
Traco Delaware Inc ....F....... 724 776-7000
Cranberry Township (G-3856)
Tredegar Corporation ....C....... 570 544-7600
Pottsville (G-16100)
Tri City Aluminum Company ....A....... 724 799-8917
Cranberry Township (G-3857)
Tyk America Inc ....E....... 412 384-4259
Clairton (G-3158)
Victor Sun Ctrl of Phladelphia ....E....... 215 743-0800
Philadelphia (G-14446)

ALUMINUM: Coil & Sheet

Ampco-Pittsburgh Corporation ....D....... 412 456-4400
Carnegie (G-2763)
Evapco Alcoil Inc ....E....... 717 347-7500
York (G-20472)
JW Aluminum Company ....C....... 570 323-4430
Williamsport (G-20030)

ALUMINUM: Rolling & Drawing

Alcoa Business Park LLC ....G....... 412 553-4545
Pittsburgh (G-14660)
Alcoa Corporation ....G....... 412 553-4001
Pittsburgh (G-14661)
Alcoa Corporation ....E....... 412 315-2900
Pittsburgh (G-14662)
Alcoa Remediation MGT LLC ....G....... 412 553-4545
Pittsburgh (G-14663)
Alcoa South Carolina Inc ....G....... 412 553-4545
Pittsburgh (G-14664)
Alcoa Technical Center LLC ....G....... 724 337-5300
New Kensington (G-12322)
Alcoa Technical Center LLC ....G....... 412 553-4545
Pittsburgh (G-14665)
Alcoa Warrick LLC ....F....... 412 553-4545
Pittsburgh (G-14668)
Alcoa Wenatchee LLC ....G....... 412 553-4545
Pittsburgh (G-14669)
Aluminum Company of America ....G....... 412 553-4545
Pittsburgh (G-14696)
Badin Business Park LLC ....G....... 412 553-4545
Pittsburgh (G-14748)
C F Moores Co Inc ....F....... 215 248-1250
Philadelphia (G-13490)
H & M Diversified Entps Inc ....E....... 717 277-0680
Lebanon (G-9577)
Inweld Corporation ....F....... 610 261-1900
Coplay (G-3644)
Panel Technologies Inc ....G....... 215 538-7055
Quakertown (G-16226)
Southwire Company LLC ....F....... 717 266-2004
York (G-20674)
St Croix Alumina LLC ....G....... 412 553-4545
Pittsburgh (G-15573)
Torpedo Specialty Wire Inc ....E....... 814 563-7505
Pittsfield (G-15739)
Trulite GL Alum Solutions LLC ....F....... 724 274-9050
Cheswick (G-3120)

AMMUNITION

3si Security Systems Holdg Inc ....G....... 610 280-2000
Malvern (G-10177)
Combined Systems Inc ....C....... 724 932-2177
Jamestown (G-8235)
General Dynamics Ots PA Inc ....C....... 717 244-4551
Red Lion (G-16596)
General Dynamics Ots PA Inc ....G....... 717 246-8208
Red Lion (G-16597)
General Dynamics Ots PA Inc ....C....... 570 342-7801
Scranton (G-17238)
Lockheed Martin Corporation ....B....... 570 876-2132
Archbald (G-691)
Medico Industries Inc ....C....... 570 825-7711
Wilkes Barre (G-19942)
Medico Industries Inc ....E....... 570 825-7711
Hanover Township (G-6996)
Nonlethal Technologies Inc ....E....... 724 479-5100
Homer City (G-7679)

AMMUNITION: Components

Action Manufacturing Company ....B....... 267 540-4041
Bristol (G-2103)

AMMUNITION: Cores, Bullet, 30 mm & Below

Steel Valley Casting LLC ....G....... 724 777-4025
New Brighton (G-12044)

AMMUNITION: Detonators, Ammunition Over 30 mm

Action Manufacturing Company ....D....... 610 593-1800
Atglen (G-799)

AMMUNITION: Mortar Shells, Over 30 mm

Nammo Pocal Inc ....E....... 570 961-1999
Scranton (G-17263)
Nammo Pocal Inc ....F....... 570 842-2288
Moscow (G-11599)

AMMUNITION: Pellets & BB's, Pistol & Air Rifle

Precision Custom Ammunition ....G....... 717 274-8762
Lebanon (G-9624)

AMMUNITION: Small Arms

Ballistic Scientific Usa LLC ....G....... 267 282-6666
Corry (G-3744)
Combined Tactical Systems Inc ....C....... 724 932-2177
Jamestown (G-8236)
Ford City Gun Workd ....G....... 724 994-9501
Ford City (G-6045)
G G Greene Enterprises Inc ....E....... 814 723-5700
Warren (G-19027)
International Cartridge Corp ....F....... 814 938-6820
Reynoldsville (G-16657)
Joint Ammunition and Tech Inc ....F....... 703 926-5509
Johnstown (G-8395)
Nonlethal Technologies Inc ....E....... 724 479-5100
Homer City (G-7679)
Pocono Pistol Club LLC ....G....... 570 424-2940
Stroudsburg (G-18136)
Velocity Munitions Inc ....E....... 724 966-2140
Carmichaels (G-2762)

AMPLIFIERS: Parametric

Performance Controls Inc ....D....... 215 619-4920
Montgomeryville (G-11412)

AMPLIFIERS: RF & IF Power

Amplifier Research Corp ....C....... 215 723-8181
Souderton (G-17724)
Amplifier Solutions Corp ....F....... 215 799-2561
Telford (G-18267)
Spectrum Control Inc ....B....... 814 474-2207
Fairview (G-5842)
Spectrum Control Inc ....G....... 814 474-4315
Fairview (G-5845)

AMUSEMENT & REC SVCS: Attractions, Concessions & Rides

Old Bedford Village Inc ....G....... 814 623-1156
Bedford (G-1068)

AMUSEMENT & REC SVCS: Skating Instruction, Ice Or Roller

Philadelphia Skating Club A ....F....... 610 642-8700
Ardmore (G-713)

AMUSEMENT & RECREATION SVCS: Amusement Ride

Great Coasters Intl Inc ....F....... 570 286-9330
Sunbury (G-18170)

AMUSEMENT & RECREATION SVCS: Arts & Crafts Instruction

Cook Forest Saw Mill Center ....F....... 814 927-6655
Cooksburg (G-3620)

AMUSEMENT & RECREATION SVCS: Exposition Operation

Park Corporation ....G....... 412 472-0500
Coraopolis (G-3711)

AMUSEMENT & RECREATION SVCS: Gun Club, Membership

C&G Arms LLC ....G....... 724 858-2856
Natrona Heights (G-11937)

AMUSEMENT & RECREATION SVCS: Hot Air Balloon Rides

Air Ventures Balloon Rides ....G....... 610 827-2138
Chester Springs (G-3070)

AMUSEMENT & RECREATION SVCS: Outfitters, Recreation

Aeo Management Co ....G....... 724 776-4857
Warrendale (G-19067)

Aeo Management Co ....F...... 412 432-3300
Pittsburgh **(G-14654)**

AMUSEMENT & RECREATION SVCS: Recreation Center

Swing Kingdom LLC ....F...... 717 656-4449
Leola **(G-9807)**

AMUSEMENT & RECREATION SVCS: School, Hockey Instruction

Pond Hockey Brewing Co LLC ....G...... 814 429-9846
State College **(G-18008)**

AMUSEMENT & RECREATION SVCS: Shooting Range

A & S Firearm Supplies Inc ....G...... 724 925-1212
Youngwood **(G-20776)**

AMUSEMENT & RECREATION SVCS: Tourist Attraction, Commercial

Mazza Vineyards Inc ....E...... 717 665-7021
Manheim **(G-10394)**

AMUSEMENT & RECREATION SVCS: Yoga Instruction

Electric City Yoga.................................G...... 570 558-9642
Scranton **(G-17233)**
Himalayan International Instit................E...... 570 253-5551
Honesdale **(G-7715)**

AMUSEMENT MACHINES: Coin Operated

AMI Entertainment Network Inc............E...... 215 826-1400
Bristol **(G-2106)**
Lightning Gaming Inc ....F...... 610 494-5534
Boothwyn **(G-1878)**
Marc Edward Brands Inc ....D...... 412 380-0888
Pittsburgh **(G-15250)**
Pinter Industries Inc ....G...... 717 898-9517
Landisville **(G-9264)**

AMUSEMENT PARK DEVICES & RIDES

Filter Technology Inc ....G...... 866 992-9490
Gladwyne **(G-6407)**
Hayes Enterprises Inc ....G...... 610 252-2530
Easton **(G-4697)**
Industrial Consortium Inc ....G...... 610 775-5760
Mohnton **(G-11266)**
Mines and Meadows LLC ....G...... 724 535-6026
Wampum **(G-18802)**
Philadelphia Toboggan Coaster ....F...... 215 799-2155
Hatfield **(G-7382)**
Sbi Survivor Corporation ....C...... 215 997-8900
Center Valley **(G-2829)**
Stahls Hotronix ....G...... 724 966-5996
Carmichaels **(G-2760)**

ANALGESICS

Endo Health Solutions Inc ....B...... 484 216-0000
Malvern **(G-10232)**
Troy Healthcare LLC ....G...... 570 453-5252
Hazle Township **(G-7487)**

ANALYZERS: Coulometric, Exc Indl Process

Specialty Tstg & Dev Co Inc.................G...... 717 428-0186
Seven Valleys **(G-17380)**

ANALYZERS: Coulometric, Indl Process

Pro-Mic Corp ....G...... 610 783-7901
King of Prussia **(G-8665)**

ANALYZERS: Electrical Testing

RLC Electronic Systems Inc ....E...... 610 898-4902
Reading **(G-16500)**

ANALYZERS: Moisture

Mitigator Inc......................................G...... 717 576-9589
New Cumberland **(G-12189)**

ANALYZERS: Network

Eko Solutions Plus Inc ....G...... 215 856-9517
Elkins Park **(G-4902)**
Keystone Nap LLC ....G...... 215 280-6614
Fairless Hills **(G-5786)**

ANALYZERS: Respiratory

Cpo 2 Inc ....Cpo 2... 570 759-1233
Berwick **(G-1320)**

ANESTHESIA EQPT

Draeger Inc ....F...... 215 721-5400
Telford **(G-18281)**
Draeger Inc ....F...... 215 660-2252
Telford **(G-18282)**
Draeger Medical Systems Inc ....C...... 800 437-2437
Telford **(G-18283)**
Loh Enterprises LLC ....E...... 570 737-4143
Clarks Summit **(G-3197)**

ANIMAL BASED MEDICINAL CHEMICAL PRDTS

Kauffmans Animal Health Inc ....G...... 717 274-3676
Lebanon **(G-9588)**

ANIMAL FEED & SUPPLEMENTS: Livestock & Poultry

Bedford Farm Bureau Coop Assn ....F...... 814 793-2721
Curryville **(G-3945)**
Bessie Grove......................................G...... 570 524-2436
Lewisburg **(G-9898)**
Cargill Incorporated ....E...... 717 530-7778
Shippensburg **(G-17521)**
Cargill Incorporated ....G...... 570 524-4777
Winfield **(G-20198)**
Cargill Incorporated ....A...... 814 793-2137
Martinsburg **(G-10521)**
Cargill Incorporated ....F...... 717 273-1133
Lebanon **(G-9552)**
Cochecton Mills Inc ....E...... 570 224-4144
Honesdale **(G-7707)**
Cornell Bros Inc ....F...... 570 376-2471
Middlebury Center **(G-11043)**
Davis Feed of Bucks County ....G...... 215 257-2966
Perkasie **(G-13272)**
Dyets Inc ....G...... 610 868-7701
Bethlehem **(G-1499)**
Equine Specialty Feed Co ....F...... 610 796-5670
Reading **(G-16378)**
Kreamer Feed Inc ....E...... 570 374-8148
Kreamer **(G-8818)**
Lawn & Garden...................................G...... 724 458-6141
Grove City **(G-6794)**
Leroy M Sensenig Inc ....E...... 717 354-4756
New Holland **(G-12257)**
M Simon Zook Co ....C...... 610 273-3776
Honey Brook **(G-7753)**
Mark Hershey Farms Inc ....E...... 717 867-4624
Lebanon **(G-9608)**
Mike Dupuy Hawk Food.......................G...... 570 837-1551
Middleburg **(G-11031)**
Nestle Purina Petcare Company...........C...... 717 795-5454
Mechanicsburg **(G-10872)**
Nufeeds Inc..G...... 570 836-2866
Tunkhannock **(G-18545)**
Occidental Chemical Corp ....F...... 610 327-4145
Pottstown **(G-16022)**
Organic Unlimited Inc ....G...... 610 593-2995
Atglen **(G-802)**
Purina Animal Nutrition LLC ....D...... 717 737-4581
Camp Hill **(G-2511)**
Purina Animal Nutrition LLC ....G...... 717 393-1361
Lancaster **(G-9178)**
Purina Mills LLC ....F...... 717 737-4581
Camp Hill **(G-2512)**
Purina Mills LLC.................................G...... 717 393-1299
Lancaster **(G-9179)**
Renaissance Nutrition Inc ....E...... 814 793-2113
Roaring Spring **(G-16767)**
Renewal Processing Inc.......................E...... 570 838-3838
Watsontown **(G-19280)**
Ross Feeds Inc...................................F...... 570 289-4388
Kingsley **(G-8707)**
S Wenger Feed Mill Inc ....G...... 717 361-4223
Elizabethtown **(G-4886)**
Shade Gap Farm Supplies ....G...... 814 259-3258
Shade Gap **(G-17416)**

Sporting Valley Feeds LLC....................E...... 717 665-6122
Manheim **(G-10404)**
Valley Proteins LLC.............................D...... 717 445-6890
East Earl **(G-4556)**
Waynesburg Milling Co ....G...... 724 627-6137
Waynesburg **(G-19452)**
Wenger Corporate Services LLC...........G...... 800 692-6008
Rheems **(G-16668)**
Wenger Feeds LLC ....E...... 717 367-1195
Spring Glen **(G-17874)**
Wenger Feeds LLC ....E...... 717 367-1195
Mount Joy **(G-11676)**
Wenger Feeds LLC ....E...... 570 682-8812
Hegins **(G-7546)**
Westway Feed Products LLC.................F...... 215 425-3707
Philadelphia **(G-14469)**
White Oak Mills Inc ....E...... 717 367-1525
Elizabethtown **(G-4891)**
X F Enterprises Inc ....E...... 717 859-1166
Ephrata **(G-5157)**

ANIMAL FEED: Wholesalers

Davis Feed of Bucks County ....G...... 215 257-2966
Perkasie **(G-13272)**
Equine Specialty Feed Co ....F...... 610 796-5670
Reading **(G-16378)**
Moyer & Son Inc.................................C...... 215 799-2000
Souderton **(G-17753)**
Renaissance Nutrition Inc ....E...... 814 793-2113
Roaring Spring **(G-16767)**
Shade Gap Farm Supplies ....G...... 814 259-3258
Shade Gap **(G-17416)**
Shaffers Feed Service Inc ....F...... 570 265-3300
Monroeton **(G-11321)**

ANIMAL FOOD & SUPPLEMENTS: Bird Food, Prepared

F M Browns Sons Incorporated............D...... 800 334-8816
Reading **(G-16384)**
Kaytee Products Incorporated..............E...... 570 385-1530
Cressona **(G-3905)**
Songbird Sanctuary LLC ....G...... 412 780-1270
Pittsburgh **(G-15556)**
Wild Birds Unlimited...........................G...... 610 366-1725
Allentown **(G-434)**

ANIMAL FOOD & SUPPLEMENTS: Cat

Dpc Pet Specialties LLC.......................E...... 814 724-7710
Meadville **(G-10719)**
Meow Mix Company.............................E...... 412 222-2200
Pittsburgh **(G-15276)**
Nestle Purina Petcare Company............D...... 610 398-4667
Allentown **(G-328)**

ANIMAL FOOD & SUPPLEMENTS: Chicken Feeds, Prepared

Clarks Feed Mills Inc ....E...... 570 648-4351
Shamokin **(G-17423)**

ANIMAL FOOD & SUPPLEMENTS: Dog

Ainsworth Pet Ntrtn Parent LLC............G...... 814 724-7710
Meadville **(G-10697)**
Ainsworth Pet Nutrition LLC.................F...... 814 724-7710
Meadville **(G-10698)**
Ainsworth Pet Nutrition LLC.................C...... 814 724-7710
Meadville **(G-10699)**
Annamaet Pet Foods Inc ....G...... 215 453-0381
Sellersville **(G-17340)**
Best Feeds & Farm Supplies Inc ....C...... 724 693-9417
Oakdale **(G-12894)**
Big Heart Pet Brands ....C...... 570 389-7650
Bloomsburg **(G-1772)**
Big Heart Pet Brands ....C...... 570 784-8200
Bloomsburg **(G-1773)**
Nestle Usa Inc ....C...... 818 549-6000
King of Prussia **(G-8655)**
Oscar & Banks LLC ....G...... 701 922-1005
Ligonier **(G-9962)**

ANIMAL FOOD & SUPPLEMENTS: Dog & Cat

Freshpet Inc.......................................F...... 610 997-7192
Bethlehem **(G-1520)**
Healthy Alternative Pet Diets ....G...... 210 745-1493
Tamiment **(G-18233)**
Nestle Purina Petcare Company............C...... 717 795-5454
Mechanicsburg **(G-10872)**

PRODUCT

Nestle Purina Petcare Company............C...... 610 395-3301
　Allentown (G-329)
Pup E Luv LLC...D...... 610 458-5280
　Chester Springs (G-3084)
Valley Proteins Inc..................................D...... 717 445-6890
　East Earl (G-4556)
X F Enterprises Inc..................................E...... 717 859-1166
　Ephrata (G-5157)

ANIMAL FOOD & SUPPLEMENTS: Feed Premixes

Chestnut Ridge LLC ....G...... 717 354-5741
　New Holland (G-12232)
Select Veal Feeds Inc..............................F....... 215 721-7131
　Souderton (G-17762)

ANIMAL FOOD & SUPPLEMENTS: Feed Supplements

Extra Factors...F....... 717 859-1166
　Ephrata (G-5102)
J Maze Corp...G...... 717 329-8350
　Hummelstown (G-7915)
Shaffers Feed Service Inc ....F....... 570 265-3300
　Monroeton (G-11321)

ANIMAL FOOD & SUPPLEMENTS: Livestock

Albrights Mill LLC ....E...... 610 756-6022
　Kempton (G-8489)
Bedford Farm Bureau Coop Assn ....F....... 814 623-6194
　Bedford (G-1040)
F M Browns Sons Incorporated.............E...... 610 582-2741
　Birdsboro (G-1695)
Farmers Union Coop Assn.....................F....... 717 597-3191
　Greencastle (G-6612)
Hampsons Farm & Garden Inc ....G...... 570 724-3012
　Wellsboro (G-19464)
Laneys Feed Mill Inc...............................F....... 814 643-3211
　Huntingdon (G-7950)
Martins Feed Mill Inc..............................F....... 814 349-8787
　Coburn (G-3333)
Ridley USA Inc ....F....... 717 509-1078
　Lancaster (G-9188)
Zeigler Bros Inc ....E...... 717 677-6181
　Gardners (G-6262)

ANIMAL FOOD & SUPPLEMENTS: Mineral feed supplements

Cargill Incorporated...............................E...... 814 793-3701
　Martinsburg (G-10520)
Mw/Td Inspired LLC................................G...... 724 741-0473
　Warrendale (G-19090)
Qlf Inc..E...... 717 445-6225
　New Holland (G-12274)

ANIMAL FOOD & SUPPLEMENTS: Pet, Exc Dog & Cat, Dry

Benebone LLC..G...... 610 366-3718
　Macungie (G-10142)
Nestle Purina Petcare Company............D...... 610 398-4667
　Allentown (G-328)
Vita-Line Products Inc ....C...... 570 450-0192
　Hazle Township (G-7490)

ANIMAL FOOD & SUPPLEMENTS: Poultry

Cumberland Valley Coop Assn.............E...... 717 532-2197
　Shippensburg (G-17525)
Esbenshade Inc.......................................C...... 717 653-8061
　Mount Joy (G-11655)
Mc Crackens Feed Mill Inc ....F....... 717 665-2186
　Manheim (G-10395)
Meiserville Milling Co ....G...... 570 539-8855
　Mount Pleasant Mills (G-11727)
Nufeeds Inc..G...... 570 278-3767
　Montrose (G-11473)
Wenger Feeds LLC ....G...... 717 367-1195
　Muncy (G-11841)
Wenger Feeds LLC ....B...... 717 367-1195
　Lancaster (G-9238)
Wenger Feeds LLC ....C...... 717 367-1195
　Shippensburg (G-17554)

ANIMAL FOOD/SUPPLEMENTS: Feeds Fm Meat/Meat/Veg Combnd Meals

Rockwells Feed Farm & Pet Sup ....G....... 877 797-4575
　Wellsboro (G-19472)

ANNEALING: Metal

Aht Inc ....D....... 724 445-2155
　Chicora (G-3125)

ANODIZING EQPT

Ntec Inc ....G....... 215 768-0261
　Newtown (G-12529)

ANODIZING SVC

A L Finishing Co Inc ....F 215 855-9422
　Hatfield (G-7313)
Anodizing Plus Inc.................................G...... 717 246-0584
　Dallastown (G-3971)
Erie Protective Coatings Inc ....G...... 814 833-0095
　Erie (G-5273)
Hillock Anodizing Inc.............................E...... 215 535-8090
　Philadelphia (G-13825)
Industrial Metal Plating Inc ....D...... 610 374-5107
　Reading (G-16407)
Jaws Inc ....G...... 215 423-2234
　Philadelphia (G-13891)
Klein Plating Works Inc ....D...... 814 452-3793
　Erie (G-5347)
Pittsburgh Anodizing Co ....G...... 724 265-5110
　Russellton (G-16884)

ANTENNAS: Receiving

Apogee Labs Inc ....E...... 215 699-2060
　North Wales (G-12788)
Snakable Inc ....G...... 347 449-3378
　Prospect Park (G-16120)
Wunsch Technologies Corp....................E...... 610 207-0628
　Birdsboro (G-1709)

ANTHRACITE PREPARATION PLANTS

Filter Media Inc ....G 570 874-2537
　Gilberton (G-6366)
Kuperavage Enterprises Inc ....E...... 570 668-1633
　Middleport (G-11045)
R & R Energy Corp..................................E...... 570 874-1602
　Gilberton (G-6369)
Sky Top Coal Company Inc....................G...... 570 773-2000
　Mahanoy City (G-10174)
South Tamaqua Coal Pockets................F...... 570 386-5445
　Tamaqua (G-18226)

ANTIBIOTICS

Lampire Biological Labs Inc ....E...... 215 795-2838
　Ottsville (G-13065)
Nabriva Therapeutics Us Inc.................F....... 610 816-6640
　King of Prussia (G-8653)
Venatorx Pharmaceuticals Inc..............G...... 610 644-8935
　Malvern (G-10339)

ANTIBIOTICS, PACKAGED

Catalent Micron Tech Inc........................D...... 610 251-7400
　Malvern (G-10200)
Glaxosmithkline LLC ....E...... 717 898-6853
　Lancaster (G-9029)

ANTIFREEZE

Dynalene Inc..F....... 610 262-9686
　Whitehall (G-19871)
Houghton Chemical Corporation ....G...... 800 777-2466
　Scranton (G-17241)

ANTIMONY ORE MINING

Jigging Technologies LLC ....G...... 814 254-4376
　Johnstown (G-8386)

ANTIQUE & CLASSIC AUTOMOBILE RESTORATION

Ore Enterprises Inc................................G...... 814 898-3933
　Erie (G-5506)
South Penn Restoration Shop ....G...... 717 264-2602
　Chambersburg (G-2977)
Tri State Metal Cleaning Inc ....G...... 814 898-3933
　Erie (G-5516)

ANTIQUE FURNITURE RESTORATION & REPAIR

Goods From Woods....................................G...... 215 699-6866
　North Wales (G-12804)
Groman Restoration Inc ....G...... 724 235-5000
　New Florence (G-12197)

ANTIQUE REPAIR & RESTORATION SVCS, EXC FURNITURE & AUTOS

Arcman Corporation ....G...... 570 489-6402
　Dunmore (G-4467)

ANTIQUE SHOPS

Historic York Inc.....................................G...... 717 843-0320
　York (G-20523)

APPAREL ACCESS STORES

Bollman Industries Inc ....C...... 717 484-4361
　Adamstown (G-20)

APPAREL DESIGNERS: Commercial

Nelson Bridge Inc ....G...... 908 996-6646
　New Hope (G-12309)
Windridge Design Inc ....F....... 610 692-1919
　West Chester (G-19678)

APPLIANCE CORDS: Household Electrical Eqpt

Battery Zone ....F....... 800 371-5033
　Bethlehem (G-1458)

APPLIANCES, HOUSEHOLD: Kitchen, Major, Exc Refrigs & Stoves

Fretz Corporation ....E...... 215 671-8300
　Philadelphia (G-13725)
Leslie S Geissel.......................................G...... 215 884-1050
　Jenkintown (G-8294)
Petrillos Appliance.................................G...... 215 491-9400
　Warrington (G-19127)
Rent-A-Center Inc ....G...... 724 845-1070
　Leechburg (G-9652)
Therma-Tek Range Corp ....E...... 570 455-3000
　West Hazleton (G-19716)
Versalot Enterprises LLC ....G...... 610 213-1017
　New Tripoli (G-12461)

APPLIANCES, HOUSEHOLD: Sewing Machines & Attchmnts, Domestic

Sewing Equipment Co Inc......................G...... 610 825-2581
　Plymouth Meeting (G-15869)

APPLIANCES: Household, NEC

Clearnav Instruments ....G...... 610 925-0198
　Kennett Square (G-8506)
Merkin Body and Hoist Company.........G...... 610 258-6179
　Easton (G-4721)

APPLIANCES: Major, Cooking

Breeo LLC...F....... 800 413-9848
　Kinzers (G-8733)

APPLIANCES: Small, Electric

Conair Corporation ....D...... 717 485-4871
　Mc Connellsburg (G-10563)
Heatron Inc ....E...... 814 868-8554
　Erie (G-5315)
Munroe Incorporated ....D...... 412 231-0600
　Pittsburgh (G-15311)
Powerex Inc ....E...... 724 925-7272
　Youngwood (G-20781)

APPLICATIONS SOFTWARE PROGRAMMING

Accion Labs Us Inc ....E...... 724 260-5139
　Bridgeville (G-2051)
Cleararmor Solutions Corp ....G...... 610 816-0101
　Riegelsville (G-16744)
Fab Universal Corp.................................F....... 412 621-0902
　Pittsburgh (G-15002)
Sungard AR Financing LLC ....G...... 484 582-2000
　Wayne (G-19374)

Veeva Systems Inc..................G........ 215 422-3356
  Fort Washington (G-6095)
VIP Tech LLC..........................G........ 267 582-1554
  Philadelphia (G-14448)

AQUARIUM DESIGN & MAINTENANCE SVCS

Laurence Ronald Entps Inc..................F....... 215 677-3801
  Warminster (G-18910)

AQUARIUMS & ACCESS: Glass

Glassautomatic Inc..........................E....... 724 547-7500
  Mount Pleasant (G-11700)

AQUARIUMS & ACCESS: Plastic

Emperor Aquatics Inc ....F....... 610 970-0440
  Pottstown (G-15986)

ARCHITECTURAL PANELS OR PARTS: Porcelain Enameled

Robert L Baker ....F....... 443 617-0164
  Chambersburg (G-2973)
United Panel Inc ....E....... 610 588-6871
  Mount Bethel (G-11615)

ARCHITECTURAL SVCS

Eastern Architectural Pdts LLC.............G....... 724 513-1630
  Zelienople (G-20797)
Joseph Jenkins Inc ....G....... 814 786-9085
  Grove City (G-6792)
Kebb Inc..........................G....... 610 859-0907
  Upper Chichester (G-18666)
Nelson Bridge Inc ....G....... 908 996-6646
  New Hope (G-12309)
Werzalit of America Inc..........................D....... 814 362-3881
  Bradford (G-1995)

ARCHITECTURAL SVCS: Engineering

Moore Design Inc ....G....... 215 627-3379
  Philadelphia (G-14036)
Wilson & Mc Cracken Inc ....E....... 412 784-1772
  Pittsburgh (G-15718)

ARMATURE REPAIRING & REWINDING SVC

Allegheny Mfg & Elec Svc Inc ....E....... 814 288-1597
  Johnstown (G-8350)
General Electric Company ....D....... 412 469-6080
  West Mifflin (G-19739)
General Electric Company ....D....... 215 289-0400
  Philadelphia (G-13749)
Integrated Power Services LLC ....E....... 724 479-9066
  Indiana (G-8108)
Royal Hydraulic Svc & Mfg Inc ....E....... 724 945-6800
  Cokeburg (G-3364)

ARMORED CAR SVCS

Garda CL Technical Svcs Inc ....D....... 610 926-7400
  Reading (G-16389)

AROMATIC CHEMICAL PRDTS

Turtle Moon Gardens ....G....... 814 639-0287
  Port Matilda (G-15907)

ART & ORNAMENTAL WARE: Pottery

Aud-A-Bud Ceramics ....G....... 717 898-7537
  Landisville (G-9258)
Bakers Lawn Ornaments ....F....... 814 445-7028
  Somerset (G-17678)
Campania International Inc ....D....... 215 541-4627
  Pennsburg (G-13246)
Fired Up ....G....... 724 941-0302
  Canonsburg (G-2588)

ART DEALERS & GALLERIES

Crow Valley Pottery ....G....... 360 376-4260
  Jim Thorpe (G-8339)

ART DESIGN SVCS

A Messinger Arch ....G....... 610 896-7227
  Penn Valley (G-13232)
Great Atlantic Graphics Inc..........................D....... 610 296-8711
  Lansdale (G-9373)
Pecks Graphics LLC ....G....... 717 963-7588
  Harrisburg (G-7191)

T C B Displays Inc..........................E....... 610 983-0500
  Phoenixville (G-14582)

ART GALLERIES

Lot Made Gallery LLC ....G....... 717 458-8716
  Mechanicsburg (G-10866)

ART GOODS, WHOLESALE

Artistworks Wholesale Inc ....G....... 610 622-9940
  Lansdowne (G-9430)
Greg Speece ....G....... 717 838-8365
  Palmyra (G-13125)

ART MARBLE: Concrete

Wenzco Supplies ....F....... 610 434-6157
  Allentown (G-432)

ART NEEDLEWORK, MADE FROM PURCHASED MATERIALS

Hub LLC ....G....... 215 561-8090
  Philadelphia (G-13839)

ART RESTORATION SVC

ART Research Enterprises..........................E....... 717 290-1303
  Lancaster (G-8944)

ART SPLY STORES

Hawk Mountain Editions Ltd..........................G....... 484 220-0524
  Leesport (G-9666)

ARTIFICIAL FLOWER SHOPS

Lasting Expressions..........................G....... 724 776-3953
  Cranberry Township (G-3831)

ARTIFICIAL FLOWERS & TREES

Plantscape Inc..........................D....... 412 281-6352
  Pittsburgh (G-15415)
Seasons Specialties Inc ....F....... 570 928-9522
  Dushore (G-4510)

ARTIST'S MATERIALS & SPLYS

Sargent Realty Inc..........................D....... 570 454-3596
  Hazleton (G-7525)

ARTISTS' AGENTS & BROKERS

John L Luchs Logging ....G....... 814 772-5767
  Ridgway (G-16715)

ARTISTS' MATERIALS, WHOLESALE

Kent Studios ....E....... 610 534-7777
  Woodlyn (G-20219)

ARTISTS' MATERIALS: Eraser Guides & Shields

Odhner Corporation..........................G....... 610 364-3200
  Media (G-10941)

ARTISTS' MATERIALS: Frames, Artists' Canvases

Kent Studios ....E....... 610 534-7777
  Woodlyn (G-20219)
Statement Walls LLC ....G....... 267 266-0869
  Philadelphia (G-14341)

ARTISTS' MATERIALS: Ink, Drawing, Black & Colored

Nocopi Technologies Inc..........................G....... 610 834-9600
  King of Prussia (G-8657)

ARTWORK: Framed

Frames & More ....G....... 724 933-5557
  Wexford (G-19804)
Paeonia Arts & Literature LLC..........................G....... 267 520-4572
  Philadelphia (G-14114)
West Collection ....G....... 570 762-8844
  Oaks (G-12938)

ASBESTOS PRDTS: Insulating Materials

Control Temp Insulation LLC..........................G....... 610 393-0943
  Northampton (G-12848)

ASBESTOS PRDTS: Roofing, Felt Roll

Certainteed Corporation..........................B....... 610 893-5000
  Malvern (G-10204)
Certainteed Corporation..........................G....... 610 651-8706
  Malvern (G-10205)

ASBESTOS PRODUCTS

Abmech Acquisitions LLC ....E....... 412 462-7440
  West Homestead (G-19719)
Cdr Contracting..........................G....... 814 536-7675
  Johnstown (G-8363)

ASBESTOS REMOVAL EQPT

Safety House Inc ....F....... 610 344-0637
  Glen Mills (G-6443)

ASPHALT & ASPHALT PRDTS

A-One Asphalt Paving ....G....... 215 658-1616
  Philadelphia (G-13331)
American Asphalt Paving Co..........................C....... 570 696-1181
  Shavertown (G-17478)
Bituminous Pav Mtls York Inc..........................G....... 717 632-8919
  Hanover (G-6863)
Clairton Slag Inc..........................F....... 412 384-8420
  West Elizabeth (G-19693)
Cole Construction Inc..........................G....... 570 888-5501
  Milan (G-11146)
Crafco Inc..........................G....... 610 264-7541
  Allentown (G-183)
Eastern Industries Inc ....E....... 570 265-9191
  Towanda (G-18425)
Eureka Stone Quarry Inc ....E....... 215 822-0593
  Chalfont (G-2874)
Glenn O Hawbaker Inc..........................D....... 814 237-1444
  State College (G-17970)
Glenn O Hawbaker Inc..........................C....... 724 458-0991
  Grove City (G-6788)
H&K Group Inc..........................C....... 610 705-0500
  Pottstown (G-15947)
Hammaker East ....E....... 412 221-7300
  Pittsburgh (G-15076)
Hanson Aggregates PA LLC ....F....... 570 322-6737
  Williamsport (G-20020)
Highway Materials Inc ....G....... 717 626-8571
  Lititz (G-10017)
Highway Materials Inc ....G....... 717 252-3636
  Wrightsville (G-20237)
IA Construction Corporation ....E....... 724 368-2140
  Franklin (G-6137)
IA Construction Corporation ....G....... 724 479-9690
  Homer City (G-7676)
Joseph McCormick Cnstr Co Inc..........................E....... 814 899-3111
  Erie (G-5339)
Lehigh Asphalt Pav & Cnstr Co ....F....... 570 668-2040
  Tamaqua (G-18216)
M&M Stone Co..........................D....... 215 723-1177
  Telford (G-18301)
New Enterprise Stone Lime Inc ....E....... 610 678-1913
  Reading (G-16454)
New Enterprise Stone Lime Inc ....G....... 610 678-1913
  Leesport (G-9669)
Pennsy Supply Inc ....F....... 717 867-5925
  Annville (G-656)
Pottstown Trap Rock Quarries ....F....... 610 326-4843
  Pottstown (G-16034)
Quaker Sales Corporation ....F....... 814 536-7541
  Johnstown (G-8426)
Riverside Materials Inc ....F....... 215 426-7299
  Philadelphia (G-14252)
Russell Standard Corporation ....G....... 724 748-3700
  Mercer (G-10973)
Russell Standard Corporation ....E....... 724 625-1505
  Valencia (G-18701)
Stopper Construction Co Inc ....E....... 570 322-5947
  Williamsport (G-20075)
Suit-Kote Corporation ....D....... 814 337-1171
  Meadville (G-10796)
Valley Quarries Inc..........................F....... 717 267-2244
  Chambersburg (G-2994)
Wiest Asphalt Products and Pav ....F....... 724 282-6913
  Butler (G-2448)
Wilkes-Barre Materials LLC ....E....... 570 829-1181
  Plains (G-15790)

Employee Codes: A=Over 500 employees, B=251-500
C=101-250, D=51-100, E=20-50, F=10-19, G=3-9

2019 Harris Pennsylvania
Manufacturers Directory

1299

PRODUCT

Wilson Paving Inc ....E 717 249-3227
Carlisle **(G-2751)**

ASPHALT COATINGS & SEALERS

Atlas Minerals & Chemicals Inc..............E 800 523-8269
Mertztown **(G-11000)**
Atlas Roofing Corporation ....E 717 760-5460
Camp Hill **(G-2492)**
Chase Corporation.............................G 412 828-5470
Pittsburgh **(G-14838)**
Choose Blackstone LLC ....G 570 754-7800
Schuylkill Haven **(G-17152)**
Dally Slate Company Inc ....D 610 863-4172
Pen Argyl **(G-13213)**
Dectile Harkus Construction...................E 724 789-7125
Butler **(G-2393)**
Fairmans Roof Trusses Inc ....E 724 349-6778
Creekside **(G-3875)**
Henry Company LLC ....B 610 933-8888
Kimberton **(G-8573)**
Kunsman Aggregates..........................G 610 882-1455
Bethlehem **(G-1554)**
Maintain-It ....E 484 684-6766
Eagleville **(G-4515)**
Omnova Solutions Inc ....B 724 523-5441
Jeannette **(G-8263)**
Penn Big Bed Slate Co Inc ....D 610 767-4601
Slatington **(G-17611)**
Performance Coatings Corp ....F 610 525-1190
Levittown **(G-9854)**
Polyglass USA Inc ....E 570 384-1230
Hazle Township **(G-7474)**
Russell Standard Corporation..................E 724 625-1505
Valencia **(G-18701)**
Tangent Rail Corporation ....G 412 325-0202
Pittsburgh **(G-15596)**
Versico Incorporated ....E 717 960-4024
Carlisle **(G-2747)**

ASPHALT MINING & BITUMINOUS STONE QUARRYING SVCS

Allegheny Mineral Corporation...............E 724 735-2088
Harrisville **(G-7252)**
Harleysville Materials LLC ....F 856 768-8493
Harleysville **(G-7037)**

ASPHALT MIXTURES WHOLESALERS

Ergon Asphalt & Emulsions Inc ....G 610 921-0271
Reading **(G-16379)**

ASPHALT PLANTS INCLUDING GRAVEL MIX TYPE

Glenn O Hawbaker Inc.........................F 814 642-7869
Turtlepoint **(G-18571)**

ASSEMBLING & PACKAGING SVCS: Cosmetic Kits

Northtec LLC ....F 215 781-2731
Bristol **(G-2173)**
Northtec LLC ....E 215 781-1600
Bristol **(G-2174)**

ASSEMBLING SVC: Plumbing Fixture Fittings, Plastic

Certainteed Corporation.......................B 610 893-5000
Malvern **(G-10204)**
Certainteed Corporation.......................G 610 651-8706
Malvern **(G-10205)**

ASSOCIATION FOR THE HANDICAPPED

Cambria County Asso ....B 814 536-3531
Johnstown **(G-8360)**
Cambria County Asso ....C 814 472-5077
Ebensburg **(G-4782)**

ASSOCIATIONS: Bar

Wilkes Barre Law & Lib Assn.................G 570 822-6712
Wilkes Barre **(G-19975)**

ASSOCIATIONS: Business

Construction Equipment Guide.............E 215 885-2900
Fort Washington **(G-6066)**

Health Care Council Western PA.............F 724 776-6400
Warrendale **(G-19080)**
Technology Data Exchange Inc ....G 610 668-4717
Bala Cynwyd **(G-894)**

ASSOCIATIONS: Real Estate Management

Gorden Inc ....G 610 644-4476
Reading **(G-16395)**

ASSOCIATIONS: Trade

Pennsylvania Motor Truck Assn............G 717 761-7122
Camp Hill **(G-2510)**
Pittsburgh Technology Council ....E 412 687-2700
Pittsburgh **(G-15410)**

ATHLETIC CLUB & GYMNASIUMS, MEMBERSHIP

Steel Fitness Premier LLC ....E 610 973-1500
Allentown **(G-403)**

ATOMIZERS

Acutronic Company ....G 412 926-1200
Pittsburgh **(G-14647)**
Acutronic USA Inc ....G 412 926-1200
Pittsburgh **(G-14648)**
American Mfg & Integration LLC ....F 724 861-2080
North Huntingdon **(G-12767)**
Ameripak.......................................E 215 343-1530
Warrington **(G-19107)**
Bri-Mar Manufacturing LLC...................E 717 263-6116
Chambersburg **(G-2913)**
Chemcut Corporation ....B 814 272-2800
State College **(G-17950)**
Custom Nuclear Fabrication LLC ....G 724 271-3006
Canonsburg **(G-2575)**
Doppelhauer Manufacturing ....G 724 691-0763
Greensburg **(G-6661)**
Entech Industries ....G 724 244-9805
New Castle **(G-12089)**
Eti Closeco ....G 412 822-8250
Pittsburgh **(G-14987)**
Meadville Tool Grinding Inc ....F 814 382-1201
Conneaut Lake **(G-3477)**
Penn Fibre Inc ....G 800 662-7366
Bensalem **(G-1241)**
Premier Brnds Group Hldngs LLC ....E 212 835-3672
Bristol **(G-2186)**
Rearden Steel Fabrication Inc ....F 717 503-1989
Lemoyne **(G-9750)**
Simplex Industries Inc.........................G 570 495-4333
Sunbury **(G-18172)**
Sovereign Steel Mfg LLC......................G 610 797-2800
Allentown **(G-397)**

ATTENUATORS

Bliley Technologies Inc ....C 814 838-3571
Erie **(G-5214)**
Powercast Corporation ....G 412 455-5800
Pittsburgh **(G-15422)**
Traffic Maintenance Attenuator ....G 215 997-1272
Hatfield **(G-7403)**

AUDIO & VIDEO EQPT, EXC COMMERCIAL

All American Installs............................G 215 888-0046
Penndel **(G-13238)**
Altec Lansing Inc ....F 570 296-4434
Milford **(G-11154)**
Burnt Circuit Inc ....G 215 913-6594
Ambler **(G-572)**
Castgrabber LLC ....F 412 362-6802
Pittsburgh **(G-14825)**
Cinemaplex Technologies Corp ....G 610 935-8366
Spring City **(G-17857)**
Clair Bros Audio Entps Inc ....D 717 626-4000
Manheim **(G-10377)**
East Hill Video Prod Co LLC ....F 215 855-4457
Lansdale **(G-9364)**
Jcm Audio Inc ....G 570 323-9014
Williamsport **(G-20028)**
Legrand Home Systems Inc ....E 717 702-2532
Middletown **(G-11061)**
Legrand Home Systems Inc ....D 717 702-2532
Middletown **(G-11060)**
Lord Corporation ....D 814 398-4641
Cambridge Springs **(G-2481)**
Lord Corporation ....A 877 275-5673
Erie **(G-5373)**

Phoenix Avs LLC...............................G 610 910-6251
Broomall **(G-2302)**
Siemens Industry Inc ....C 724 339-9500
New Kensington **(G-12375)**
Simply Automated Llc ....G 412 343-0348
Pittsburgh **(G-15539)**
Spectrum Microwave Inc ....D 215 464-0586
Philadelphia **(G-14333)**
Technicolor Usa Inc ....C 717 295-6100
Lancaster **(G-9214)**
Teledyne Defense Elec LLC ....D 814 238-3450
State College **(G-18036)**
Videon Central Inc ....D 814 235-1111
State College **(G-18041)**
Videotek Inc ....C 610 327-2292
Pottstown **(G-16068)**
World Video Sales Co Inc......................G 610 754-6800
Bechtelsville **(G-1038)**

AUDIO COMPONENTS

Aviom Inc ....D 610 738-9005
West Chester **(G-19505)**
Oswaldsmill Inc.................................G 610 298-3271
New Tripoli **(G-12459)**

AUDIO ELECTRONIC SYSTEMS

Media Rooms Inc ....G 610 719-8500
West Chester **(G-19600)**
Optima Plus International LLC ....G 717 207-9037
Lancaster **(G-9156)**
Rogue Audio Inc ....G 570 992-9901
Brodheadsville **(G-2238)**
Sigma Technology Systems LLC ....F 717 569-2926
Lancaster **(G-9197)**

AUDIO-VISUAL PROGRAM PRODUCTION SVCS

Corporate Arts Inc ....G 610 298-8374
New Tripoli **(G-12454)**
Creative Systems Usa LLC ....G 610 450-6580
Collegeville **(G-3373)**
Mohawk Industries Inc ....G 215 977-2871
Philadelphia **(G-14031)**

AUDIOLOGICAL EQPT: Electronic

Instrumental Associates ....G 610 992-3300
Phoenixville **(G-14554)**
Mg Development America Inc.................G 412 288-9959
Pittsburgh **(G-15282)**

AUDIOLOGISTS' OFFICES

Suburban Audiology Balance Ctr...........G 610 647-3710
Paoli **(G-13149)**

AUTO & HOME SUPPLY STORES: Auto & Truck Eqpt & Parts

Advance Stores Company Inc ....E 610 939-0120
Reading **(G-16311)**
Columbia Motor Parts Inc ....G 717 684-2501
Columbia **(G-3435)**

AUTO & HOME SUPPLY STORES: Auto Air Cond Eqpt, Sell/Install

Northeast Indus Batteries Inc ....E 215 788-8000
Bristol **(G-2172)**

AUTO & HOME SUPPLY STORES: Automotive Access

Darby Industries Inc ....G 570 388-6173
Falls **(G-5852)**
Homestead Automotive Supply ....G 412 462-4467
Homestead **(G-7686)**
Philip Cooke ....G 717 854-4081
York **(G-20627)**
Skyline Auto Supply LLC ....G 484 365-4040
Easton **(G-4752)**
Total Mobility Services Inc ....G 814 629-9935
Boswell **(G-1885)**

AUTO & HOME SUPPLY STORES: Automotive parts

B & R Speed Shop ....G 412 795-7022
Verona **(G-18748)**

Boyesen Inc ....E 610 756-6818
Lenhartsville *(G-9756)*
Bugstuff ....G 724 785-7000
Brownsville *(G-2310)*
East Penn Truck Eqp W Inc ....G 724 342-1800
Mercer *(G-10961)*
East Penn Truck Equipment Inc ....G 610 694-9234
Bethlehem *(G-1500)*
Genuine Parts Company ....G 215 968-4266
Newtown *(G-12504)*
Isaac Stephens & Assoc Inc ....G 215 576-5414
Oreland *(G-13024)*
J W Zaprazny Inc ....D 570 943-2860
New Ringgold *(G-12440)*
Keystone Spring Service Inc ....E 412 621-4800
Pittsburgh *(G-15176)*
Krimes Machine Shop Inc ....G 717 733-1271
Ephrata *(G-5116)*
Lebanon Parts Service Inc ....G 717 272-0181
Lebanon *(G-9602)*
Lehigh Services Inc ....G 610 966-2525
Macungie *(G-10152)*
Len Sabatine Automotive ....G 610 258-8020
Easton *(G-4714)*
Murdick Auto Parts & Racg Sups ....G 724 482-2177
Butler *(G-2425)*
Outlaw Performance Inc ....E 724 697-4876
Avonmore *(G-866)*
Rtr Manufacturing Co ....F 412 665-1500
East Liberty *(G-4580)*
Snyder County Automotive Inc ....G 570 374-2072
Selinsgrove *(G-17335)*
Somerset Welding & Steel Inc ....C 814 443-2671
Somerset *(G-17710)*

AUTO & HOME SUPPLY STORES: Batteries, Automotive & Truck

Energizer Battery Co ....G 215 572-0200
Jenkintown *(G-8286)*

AUTO & HOME SUPPLY STORES: Trailer Hitches, Automotive

Mustang Trailer Mfg ....F 724 628-1000
Connellsville *(G-3504)*

AUTO & HOME SUPPLY STORES: Truck Eqpt & Parts

Cheetah Chassis Corporation ....C 570 752-2708
Berwick *(G-1317)*
Dively Manufacture Co Inc ....F 814 239-5441
Claysburg *(G-3203)*
Overdrive Holdings Inc ....F 724 452-1500
Zelienople *(G-20813)*
Sabre Equipment Inc ....E 412 262-3080
Coraopolis *(G-3725)*
Terex Corporation ....E 717 840-0226
Mountville *(G-11803)*

AUTOCLAVES: Indl

Gyrotron Technology Inc ....G 215 244-4740
Bensalem *(G-1207)*
Moyers Service Co ....G 267 205-1105
Feasterville Trevose *(G-5920)*
Pb Heat LLC ....E 610 845-6100
Bally *(G-906)*

AUTOMATED TELLER MACHINE NETWORK

Atm Bancorp Inc ....G 610 279-9550
Norristown *(G-12636)*

AUTOMATED TELLER MACHINE OR ATM REPAIR SVCS

Atm Bancorp Inc ....G 610 279-9550
Norristown *(G-12636)*

AUTOMATIC REGULATING CNTRLS: Flame Safety, Furnaces & Boiler

MSA Advanced Detection LLC (.........G 724 776-8600
Cranberry Township *(G-3838)*

AUTOMATIC REGULATING CNTRLS: Steam Press, Residential/ Comm

P D Q Pest Control Inc ....G 814 774-8882
Girard *(G-6398)*

AUTOMATIC REGULATING CONTROL: Building Svcs Monitoring, Auto

Advanced Enviromation Inc ....G 610 422-3770
Fleetwood *(G-5967)*
First Quality Retail Svcs LLC ....C 610 265-5000
King of Prussia *(G-8619)*
Johnson Controls Inc ....E 717 531-5371
Hershey *(G-7619)*
Optimum Controls Corporation ....D 610 375-0990
Reading *(G-16459)*

AUTOMATIC REGULATING CONTROLS: AC & Refrigeration

Johnson Controls Inc ....D 610 276-3700
Horsham *(G-7828)*
Kustom Komponents ....G 484 671-3076
Leesport *(G-9667)*
Lundy Warehousing Inc ....G 570 327-4541
Williamsport *(G-20037)*
National Refrigerants Inc ....E 215 698-6620
Philadelphia *(G-14056)*
Resolve Trnchless Slutions Inc ....G 215 441-5544
Warminster *(G-18953)*
White Refrigeration Inc ....G 570 265-7335
Towanda *(G-18437)*

AUTOMATIC REGULATING CONTROLS: Hardware, Environmental Reg

Myexposome Inc ....G 610 668-0145
Philadelphia *(G-14049)*

AUTOMATIC REGULATING CONTROLS: Hydronic Pressure Or Temp

Advanced Technical Peddler Inc ....G 610 689-4017
Boyertown *(G-1893)*
Clean Power Resources Inc ....G 724 863-3768
Irwin *(G-8148)*

AUTOMATIC REGULATING CONTROLS: Incinerator, Residential/Comm

Hri Networks Inc ....F 267 515-5880
Philadelphia *(G-13838)*

AUTOMATIC REGULATING CONTROLS: Pneumatic Relays, Air-Cond

Janatics USA Inc ....G 610 443-2400
Whitehall *(G-19879)*

AUTOMATIC REGULATING CTRLS: Damper, Pneumatic Or Electric

Advanced Valve Design Inc ....F 610 435-8820
Whitehall *(G-19860)*
Keenan and Meier LLC ....G 215 766-3010
Plumsteadville *(G-15810)*
Lloyd Industries Inc ....E 215 367-5863
Montgomeryville *(G-11404)*

AUTOMATIC TELLER MACHINES

Atm Bancorp Inc ....G 610 279-9550
Norristown *(G-12636)*
Blessed Dough LLC ....F 717 368-4109
Easton *(G-4657)*
Matrix Atm ....G 215 661-2916
North Wales *(G-12813)*
Ukani Brothers Enterprise ....G 412 269-0499
Pittsburgh *(G-15667)*

AUTOMATIC VENDING MACHINES: Mechanisms & Parts

Tasty Fries Inc ....G 610 941-2109
Blue Bell *(G-1855)*
Teutech LLC ....E 814 486-1896
Emporium *(G-5077)*

AUTOMOTIVE & TRUCK GENERAL REPAIR SVC

Bowser Pontiac Inc ....C 412 469-2100
Pittsburgh *(G-14787)*
Cambria Springs Service Inc ....G 814 539-1629
Johnstown *(G-8362)*
Cumberland Valley Wldg & Repr ....G 717 249-1129
Carlisle *(G-2704)*
Hirt Powersports LLC ....G 717 834-9126
Duncannon *(G-4446)*
Ken Imler ....G 814 695-1310
East Freedom *(G-4564)*
Leonard Leibensperger ....G 610 926-7491
Mohrsville *(G-11277)*
Liberty Welding Co ....G 412 661-1776
Pittsburgh *(G-15228)*
Mardinly Enterprises LLC ....E 610 544-9490
Broomall *(G-2295)*
Myers Electrical Repairs ....G 717 334-8105
Gettysburg *(G-6309)*
New Harrisburg Truck Body Co ....E 717 766-7651
Mechanicsburg *(G-10873)*
S & W Race Cars Components Inc ....E 610 948-7303
Spring City *(G-17865)*
Saeilo Inc ....F 845 735-4500
Greeley *(G-6583)*
Vic Auto Tech Place ....G 215 969-2083
Philadelphia *(G-14445)*
Warren Installations Inc ....F 717 517-9321
Lancaster *(G-9235)*
Zambotti Collision & Wldg Ctr ....G 724 545-2305
Kittanning *(G-8804)*

AUTOMOTIVE BATTERIES WHOLESALERS

Exide Technologies ....G 724 239-2006
Charleroi *(G-3012)*
Exide Technologies ....E 610 921-4055
Reading *(G-16383)*
Steins Pasco Battery Starter ....G 215 969-6900
Philadelphia *(G-14343)*

AUTOMOTIVE BODY SHOP

Dangelos Custom Built Mfg LLC ....F 814 837-6053
Kane *(G-8462)*
Kovatch Corp ....D 570 669-5130
Nesquehoning *(G-12006)*
Physical Graffi-Tees ....G 610 439-3344
Allentown *(G-351)*

AUTOMOTIVE BODY, PAINT & INTERIOR REPAIR & MAINTENANCE SVC

Harners Auto Body Inc ....G 610 385-3825
Birdsboro *(G-1698)*
Statler Body Works Inc ....G 717 261-5936
Chambersburg *(G-2978)*

AUTOMOTIVE BRAKE REPAIR SHOPS

Brush Aftermarket N Amer Inc ....F 412 829-7500
Turtle Creek *(G-18560)*
Ultra Lite Brakes An C ....G 724 696-3743
Mount Pleasant *(G-11721)*

AUTOMOTIVE CUSTOMIZING SVCS, NONFACTORY BASIS

Laveings Mobility ....G 724 368-9417
Portersville *(G-15930)*
M & P Refinishing Co ....G 724 527-6360
Jeannette *(G-8262)*

AUTOMOTIVE EXTERIOR REPAIR SVCS

Narvon Construction LLC ....F 717 989-2026
Narvon *(G-11924)*

AUTOMOTIVE GLASS REPLACEMENT SHOPS

Micfralip Inc ....F 215 338-3293
Philadelphia *(G-14019)*

AUTOMOTIVE LETTERING SVCS

Driban Body Works Inc ....G 215 468-6900
Philadelphia *(G-13648)*
William F and Kathy A Yeager ....G 717 665-6964
Manheim *(G-10407)*

PRODUCT

AUTOMOTIVE PARTS, ACCESS & SPLYS

A-1 Racing Products Inc ....G....... 215 675-8442
Warminster (G-18816)

Alliance Remanufacturing Inc ....C....... 215 291-4640
Philadelphia (G-13368)

American Cycle Fabrication....................G....... 570 752-8715
Bloomsburg (G-1769)

Angel Colon ....G....... 215 455-4000
Philadelphia (G-13392)

Ansa Electric Vehicles LLC.....................G....... 610 955-5686
Narberth (G-11907)

Auto Accessories America Inc ....C....... 717 667-3004
Reedsville (G-16621)

Autocare Service Center Inc ....G....... 717 854-0242
York (G-20392)

Automated Unmanned Vehicle Sys........G....... 570 748-3844
Mill Hall (G-11171)

Autoneum North America Inc ....A....... 570 784-4100
Bloomsburg (G-1771)

Bigbee Steel and Tank Company ....C....... 814 893-5701
Manheim (G-10370)

Bugstuff ....G....... 724 785-7000
Brownsville (G-2310)

Cardone Industries Inc ....C....... 215 912-3000
Philadelphia (G-13503)

Cardone Industries Inc ....B....... 215 912-3000
Philadelphia (G-13505)

Cardone Industries Inc ....C....... 215 912-3000
Philadelphia (G-13506)

Cardone Industries Inc ....C....... 215 912-3000
Philadelphia (G-13507)

Cardone Industries Inc ....B....... 215 912-3000
Philadelphia (G-13504)

Clark Filter Inc ....G....... 717 285-5941
Lancaster (G-8979)

Conrad Enterprises Inc ....E....... 717 274-5151
Cornwall (G-3738)

Dana Auto Systems Group LLC ....B....... 610 323-4200
Pottstown (G-15978)

Darby Industries Inc ....G....... 570 388-6173
Falls (G-5852)

Dayton Parts LLC.....................................C....... 717 255-8500
Harrisburg (G-7116)

Diamondback Automotive ACC Inc.......E....... 800 935-4002
Philipsburg (G-14510)

Diverse Sales Company Inc ....G....... 215 317-1815
Perkasie (G-13274)

Dorman Products Inc ....C....... 215 997-1800
Colmar (G-3416)

Exotic Car Gear Inc ....G....... 215 371-2855
North Wales (G-12800)

Fenner ....C....... 717 665-2421
Manheim (G-10380)

FJ Performance Inc..................................G....... 724 681-7430
Export (G-5602)

Flextron Industries Inc ....F....... 610 459-4600
Aston (G-763)

George I Reitz & Sons Inc ....E....... 814 849-2308
Brookville (G-2261)

George I Reitz & Sons Inc ....G....... 412 824-9976
East Pittsburgh (G-4595)

Ground Force Marketing Co ....E....... 724 430-2068
Mount Braddock (G-11618)

HIG Capital LLC ....C....... 610 495-7011
Royersford (G-16851)

Johnson Controls Inc ....G....... 717 771-7890
York (G-20542)

Lear Corporation ....B....... 570 345-6725
Pine Grove (G-14597)

Lord Corporation ....B....... 814 868-0924
Erie (G-5371)

Lpw Racing Products Inc.........................G....... 717 394-7432
Lancaster (G-9115)

Lynn Parker Associates LLC ....G....... 561 406-6472
Rose Valley (G-16818)

M P N Inc..C....... 215 289-9480
Philadelphia (G-13981)

Mack Trucks Inc ....C....... 717 939-1338
Middletown (G-11064)

Maclean Saegertown LLC ....G....... 814 763-2655
Saegertown (G-16924)

Markel Corp ....C....... 610 272-8960
Plymouth Meeting (G-15855)

Matthewas Auto Supplies ....G....... 610 797-3729
Allentown (G-310)

Matthey Johnson Inc ....B....... 610 341-8300
Wayne (G-19352)

Metaldyne Snterforged Pdts LLC ....A....... 814 834-1222
Saint Marys (G-16993)

Modern Industries Inc.............................C....... 814 455-8061
Erie (G-5394)

Modern Industries Inc.............................F....... 814 885-8514
Kersey (G-8564)

Motorsport Green Engineer ....G....... 570 386-8600
New Ringgold (G-12442)

NC Industries Antiq Auto Parts ....G....... 570 888-6216
Sayre (G-17120)

O & N Arcft Modification Inc ....E....... 570 945-3769
Factoryville (G-5760)

Osram Sylvania Inc ....C....... 814 726-6600
Warren (G-19041)

Penntecq Inc...C....... 724 646-4250
Greenville (G-6765)

Precision Transmission Inc ....G....... 215 822-8300
Colmar (G-3418)

Quality Trailer Products LP ....F....... 717 354-7070
New Holland (G-12277)

R E M Automotive Parts Inc ....F....... 717 838-4242
Annville (G-657)

RB Distribution Inc ....B....... 215 997-1800
Colmar (G-3419)

RG Industries Inc ....E....... 717 849-0345
York (G-20658)

Robert Bosch LLC ....B....... 610 694-8200
Bethlehem (G-1612)

S & W Race Cars Components Inc..........E....... 610 948-7303
Spring City (G-17865)

Saegertown Manufacturing Corp ....C....... 814 763-2655
Saegertown (G-16932)

Spalding Automotive Inc ....E....... 215 638-3334
Bensalem (G-1255)

Spohn Performance Inc...........................G....... 717 866-6033
Myerstown (G-11898)

Strobic Air Corporation ....F....... 215 723-4700
Telford (G-18321)

Torcomp Usa LLC ....G....... 717 261-1530
Chambersburg (G-2987)

US Axle Inc ....D....... 610 323-3800
Pottstown (G-16063)

W W Engine and Supply Inc ....E....... 814 345-5693
Kylertown (G-8868)

Westport Axle ....B....... 610 366-2900
Breinigsville (G-2032)

World Motorsports Inc............................G....... 610 929-1982
Reading (G-16570)

AUTOMOTIVE PARTS: Plastic

Eznergy LLC ....G....... 215 361-7332
Lansdale (G-9366)

Maxima Tech & Systems Inc ....B....... 717 569-5713
Lancaster (G-9129)

Smooth Line Inc ....G....... 412 828-3599
Cheswick (G-3118)

AUTOMOTIVE RADIATOR REPAIR SHOPS

Condos Incorporated...............................E....... 570 748-9265
Mill Hall (G-11174)

Dukane Radiator Inc ....G....... 412 233-3300
Bethel Park (G-1413)

Marko Radiator Inc..................................F....... 570 462-2281
Shenandoah (G-17495)

R S Myers Welding ....G....... 717 532-4714
Shippensburg (G-17543)

AUTOMOTIVE REPAIR SHOPS: Alternators/Generator, Rebuild/Rpr

Brickhouse Services.................................G....... 570 869-1871
Laceyville (G-8870)

AUTOMOTIVE REPAIR SHOPS: Auto Brake Lining, Installation

Keystone Spring Service Inc ....E....... 412 621-4800
Pittsburgh (G-15176)

AUTOMOTIVE REPAIR SHOPS: Diesel Engine Repair

Brumbaugh Body Co Inc ....G....... 814 696-9552
Duncansville (G-4450)

AUTOMOTIVE REPAIR SHOPS: Electrical Svcs

Arm Camco LLC ....E....... 814 472-7980
Ebensburg (G-4779)

Auto Care..G....... 814 943-8155
Altoona (G-475)

Auto Diesel Electric Inc ....G....... 570 874-2100
Frackville (G-6102)

Excel-Pro ....G....... 610 845-9752
Barto (G-942)

United Commercial Supply LLC ....G....... 412 835-2690
South Park (G-17786)

AUTOMOTIVE REPAIR SHOPS: Engine Rebuilding

L & M Engines Inc ....G....... 215 675-8485
Hatboro (G-7291)

Ritter Precision Machining ....G....... 610 377-2011
Lehighton (G-9725)

S & L Motors Inc......................................G....... 570 342-9718
Scranton (G-17280)

AUTOMOTIVE REPAIR SHOPS: Engine Repair

Randall Lesso ....G....... 724 746-2100
Houston (G-7878)

SKF USA Inc ....C....... 717 637-8981
Hanover (G-6953)

AUTOMOTIVE REPAIR SHOPS: Frame & Front End Repair Svcs

Burkholder s Motor Repair......................G....... 717 866-9724
Myerstown (G-11878)

Cambria Springs Service Inc ....G....... 814 539-1629
Johnstown (G-8362)

AUTOMOTIVE REPAIR SHOPS: Machine Shop

Caldwell Corporation...............................E....... 814 486-3493
Emporium (G-5051)

P & R Engine Rebuilders ....G....... 724 837-7590
Greensburg (G-6698)

Peak Precision Inc ....G....... 215 799-1929
Hatfield (G-7378)

Ritter Precision Machining......................G....... 610 377-2011
Lehighton (G-9725)

SMS Group Inc ....C....... 412 231-1200
Pittsburgh (G-15552)

Wagner & Sons Machine Shop ....G....... 610 434-6640
Allentown (G-429)

AUTOMOTIVE REPAIR SHOPS: Sound System Svc & Installation

Jcm Audio Inc ....G....... 570 323-9014
Williamsport (G-20028)

Willow Grove Auto Top Inc......................G....... 215 659-3276
Willow Grove (G-20150)

AUTOMOTIVE REPAIR SHOPS: Springs, Rebuilding & Repair

Dayton Parts LLC......................................C....... 717 255-8500
Harrisburg (G-7116)

AUTOMOTIVE REPAIR SHOPS: Trailer Repair

Great Dane LLC..B....... 717 492-0057
Mount Joy (G-11659)

Mgs Inc...C....... 717 336-7528
Denver (G-4083)

Total Mobility Services Inc ....G....... 814 629-9935
Boswell (G-1885)

Triad Truck Equipment ....G....... 484 614-7349
Pottstown (G-16059)

Viking Vee Inc..G....... 724 789-9194
Renfrew (G-16643)

AUTOMOTIVE REPAIR SHOPS: Truck Engine Repair, Exc Indl

Zimm-O-Matic LLC ....G....... 717 445-6432
Denver (G-4098)

AUTOMOTIVE REPAIR SHOPS: Turbocharger & Blower Repair

Hill John M Machine Co Inc ....E....... 610 562-8690
Hamburg (G-6841)

AUTOMOTIVE REPAIR SVC

H & Z Auto LLC ....G...... 610 419-8012
Bethlehem *(G-1527)*

Hussey Performance LLC ....G...... 724 318-8292
Ambridge *(G-619)*

Jj Kennedy Inc ....E...... 724 452-6260
Fombell *(G-6033)*

Lblock Transportation Inc ....G...... 347 533-0943
York *(G-20563)*

Mshar Power Train Specialists ....G...... 717 231-3900
Harrisburg *(G-7181)*

AUTOMOTIVE REPAIR SVCS, MISCELLANEOUS

Corry Laser Technology Inc ....F...... 814 664-7212
Corry *(G-3751)*

AUTOMOTIVE SPLYS & PARTS, NEW, WHOLESALE: Engines/Eng Parts

Industrial Diesel Power Inc ....F 215 781-2378
Croydon *(G-3919)*

AUTOMOTIVE SPLYS & PARTS, NEW, WHOLESALE: Filters, Air & Oil

Myers Electrical Repairs ....G...... 717 334-8105
Gettysburg *(G-6309)*

AUTOMOTIVE SPLYS & PARTS, NEW, WHOLESALE: Pumps, Oil & Gas

Kada Energy Resources LLC ....G...... 215 839-9159
Philadelphia *(G-13919)*

AUTOMOTIVE SPLYS & PARTS, NEW, WHOLESALE: Splys

Car Cleen Systems Inc ....F 717 795-8995
Bethel Park *(G-1408)*

Colonial Auto Supply Co ....C...... 215 643-3699
Fort Washington *(G-6065)*

Poly Lite Windshield Repr Sups ....G...... 717 845-1596
York *(G-20631)*

AUTOMOTIVE SPLYS & PARTS, NEW, WHOLESALE: Trailer Parts

Great Dane LLC ....B...... 717 492-0057
Mount Joy *(G-11659)*

Overdrive Holdings Inc ....F...... 724 452-1500
Zelienople *(G-20813)*

AUTOMOTIVE SPLYS & PARTS, USED, WHOLESALE

Anderson Inc ....F...... 412 486-2211
Allison Park *(G-447)*

Dock Tool & Machine Inc ....G...... 215 338-8989
Philadelphia *(G-13638)*

AUTOMOTIVE SPLYS & PARTS, USED, WHOLESALE: Access, NEC

Keystone Truck Caps LLC ....G...... 570 836-4322
Tunkhannock *(G-18540)*

AUTOMOTIVE SPLYS & PARTS, USED, WHOLESALE: Engines

Holtrys LLC ....G...... 717 532-7261
Roxbury *(G-16838)*

AUTOMOTIVE SPLYS & PARTS, WHOLESALE, NEC

Auto Accessories America Inc ....C...... 717 667-3004
Reedsville *(G-16621)*

Bohlinger Inc ....G...... 610 825-0440
Conshohocken *(G-3524)*

Bugstuff ....G...... 724 785-7000
Brownsville *(G-2310)*

Dick Rughs Auto Parts Inc ....G...... 724 438-3425
Uniontown *(G-18623)*

Genuine Parts Company ....G...... 215 968-4266
Newtown *(G-12504)*

Hirschmann Electronics Inc ....F 717 217-2200
Chambersburg *(G-2940)*

Homestead Automotive Supply ....G...... 412 462-4467
Homestead *(G-7686)*

Isaac Stephens & Assoc Inc 215 576-5414
Oreland *(G-13024)*

Keystone Automotive Inds Inc ....D...... 610 866-0313
Bethlehem *(G-1550)*

Keystone Automotive Inds Inc ....F...... 717 843-8927
York *(G-20552)*

La France Corp ....C...... 610 361-4300
Concordville *(G-3457)*

Len Sabatine Automotive ....G...... 610 258-8020
Easton *(G-4714)*

Murdick Auto Parts & Racg Sups ....G...... 724 482-2177
Butler *(G-2425)*

S & W Race Cars Components Inc ....E...... 610 948-7303
Spring City *(G-17865)*

Snyder County Automotive Inc ....G...... 570 374-2072
Selinsgrove *(G-17335)*

Warren Installations Inc ....F...... 717 517-9321
Lancaster *(G-9235)*

AUTOMOTIVE SPLYS/PART, NEW, WHOL: Spring, Shock Absorb/Strut

Keystone Spring Service Inc ....E...... 412 621-4800
Pittsburgh *(G-15176)*

Triangle Sspension Systems Inc ....D...... 814 375-7211
Du Bois *(G-4425)*

AUTOMOTIVE SPLYS/PARTS, NEW, WHOL: Body Rpr/Paint Shop Splys

Keystone Automotive Inds Inc ....E...... 814 467-5531
Windber *(G-20184)*

Wendells Prfmce Trck Sp LLC ....G...... 717 458-8404
Mechanicsburg *(G-10906)*

AUTOMOTIVE SVCS, EXC REPAIR & CARWASHES: Insp & Diagnostic

Advance Stores Company Inc ....E...... 610 939-0120
Reading *(G-16311)*

AUTOMOTIVE SVCS, EXC REPAIR & CARWASHES: Lubrication

Lube Systems Company ....G...... 724 335-4050
Apollo *(G-682)*

AUTOMOTIVE SVCS, EXC REPAIR & CARWASHES: Maintenance

Rohrers Quarry Inc ....D...... 717 626-9760
Lititz *(G-10043)*

AUTOMOTIVE SVCS, EXC REPAIR & CARWASHES: Trailer Maintenance

Wherleys Trailer Inc ....G...... 717 624-2268
New Oxford *(G-12426)*

AUTOMOTIVE SVCS, EXC REPAIR: Carwash, Automatic

Elm Ave Car Wash ....G...... 717 637-7392
Hanover *(G-6881)*

AUTOMOTIVE SVCS, EXC REPAIR: Carwash, Self-Service

Mannis Wash Systems ....G...... 724 337-8255
New Kensington *(G-12354)*

AUTOMOTIVE SVCS, EXC REPAIR: Washing & Polishing

American Auto Wash Inc ....F...... 610 265-3222
King of Prussia *(G-8580)*

Hotwash ....F...... 610 351-2119
Allentown *(G-247)*

Murrysville Auto LLC ....F...... 724 387-1607
Murrysville *(G-11860)*

AUTOMOTIVE SVCS, EXC RPR/CARWASHES: High Perf Auto Rpr/Svc

H & Z Auto LLC ....G...... 610 419-8012
Bethlehem *(G-1527)*

AUTOMOTIVE TOWING SVCS

Smith Auto Service ....G...... 215 788-2401
Bristol *(G-2198)*

AUTOMOTIVE UPHOLSTERY SHOPS

Auto Seat Cover Company ....G...... 814 453-5897
Erie *(G-5196)*

AUTOMOTIVE WELDING SVCS

Corry Laser Technology Inc ....F...... 814 664-7212
Corry *(G-3751)*

Edward H Quay Welding Spc ....G...... 610 326-8050
Pottstown *(G-15985)*

Friesens Welding ....G...... 570 523-3580
Lewisburg *(G-9910)*

Kutzner Manufacturing Inds Inc ....E...... 215 721-1712
Telford *(G-18300)*

Liberty Welding Co ....G...... 412 661-1776
Pittsburgh *(G-15228)*

R S Myers Welding ....G...... 717 532-4714
Shippensburg *(G-17543)*

Sunnyburn Welding ....G...... 717 862-3878
Airville *(G-32)*

Swartfager Welding Inc ....G...... 814 797-0394
Knox *(G-8811)*

Vr Enterprises Llc ....G...... 215 932-1113
Lansdale *(G-9426)*

Yarmouth Construction ....G...... 267 592-1432
Philadelphia *(G-14498)*

Z Weldco ....G...... 610 689-8773
Oley *(G-12982)*

AUTOMOTIVE: Bodies

Harners Auto Body Inc ....G...... 610 385-3825
Birdsboro *(G-1698)*

Outlaw Performance Inc ....E...... 724 697-4876
Avonmore *(G-866)*

Philip Cooke ....G...... 717 854-4081
York *(G-20627)*

Rizworks ....G...... 570 226-7611
Hawley *(G-7437)*

Wolfington Body Company Inc ....C...... 610 458-8501
Exton *(G-5751)*

AUTOMOTIVE: Seating

Johnson Controls Inc ....D...... 717 765-2461
Waynesboro *(G-19414)*

Johnson Controls Inc ....G...... 800 877-9675
Audubon *(G-828)*

Johnson Controls Inc ....D...... 717 815-4200
York *(G-20544)*

Ussc LLC ....D...... 610 265-3610
Exton *(G-5744)*

AUTOTRANSFORMERS: Electric

Alstom Grid LLC ....D...... 412 967-0765
Pittsburgh *(G-14689)*

Alstom Power Conversion Inc ....C...... 412 967-0765
Cranberry Township *(G-3801)*

AWNING REPAIR SHOP

Lingenfelter Awning ....G...... 814 696-4353
Duncansville *(G-4455)*

Y T & A Inc ....F...... 717 854-3806
York *(G-20722)*

AWNINGS & CANOPIES

F Creative Impressions Inc ....G...... 215 743-7577
Lansdowne *(G-9432)*

G & S Metal Products Inc ....G...... 412 462-7000
Pittsburgh *(G-15039)*

G T Watts Inc ....G...... 717 732-1111
Enola *(G-5080)*

Jefco Manufacturing Inc ....F...... 215 334-3220
Wynnewood *(G-20270)*

R A Egan Sign & Awng Co Inc ....F...... 610 777-3795
Reading *(G-16482)*

Rabe Environmental Systems Inc ....D...... 814 456-5374
Erie *(G-5451)*

Southwest Vinyl Windows Inc ....F...... 610 626-8826
Lansdowne *(G-9444)*

Vh Service LLC ....G...... 267 808-9745
Feasterville Trevose *(G-5938)*

P R O D U C T

AWNINGS & CANOPIES: Awnings, Fabric, From Purchased Matls

549 Industrial Holdings Inc ....F 610 622-7211
Philadelphia *(G-13320)*

A Mamaux & Son Inc ....F 412 771-8432
Mc Kees Rocks *(G-10599)*

A Wbrown Awning ....G 610 372-2908
Reading *(G-16308)*

Aerial Signs & Awnings Inc ....F 610 494-1415
Chester *(G-3037)*

Als Awning Shop Inc ....G 814 456-6262
Erie *(G-5183)*

Canvas Awnings Inc ....G 215 423-1213
Philadelphia *(G-13498)*

Canvas Specialties Inc ....G 570 825-9282
Hanover Township *(G-6983)*

Creative Awnings Inc ....E 610 282-3305
Coopersburg *(G-3626)*

F Creative Impressions Inc ....G 215 743-7577
Philadelphia *(G-13690)*

Fehl Awning Company Inc ....G 717 776-3162
Walnut Bottom *(G-18789)*

G T Watts Inc ....G 717 732-1111
Enola *(G-5080)*

Grimms Inc ....G 724 346-4952
Sharon *(G-17435)*

HA Harper Sons Inc ....G 610 485-4776
Upper Chichester *(G-18663)*

Hamilton Awning Co ....F 724 774-7644
Beaver *(G-983)*

Hendersons Tarpaulin Covers ....G 717 944-5865
Middletown *(G-11056)*

Hibbs Awning Company Inc ....G 724 437-1494
Uniontown *(G-18630)*

Indutex Inc ....F 724 935-1482
McKeesport *(G-10673)*

Jefco Manufacturing Inc ....F 215 334-3220
Wynnewood *(G-20270)*

Kreiders Canvas Service Inc ....G 717 656-7387
Leola *(G-9791)*

Laurel Industrial Fabric Entps ....E 724 567-5689
Apollo *(G-681)*

McCloy Awning Company ....F 412 271-4044
Swissvale *(G-18192)*

McCullough Manufacturing Inc ....G 717 687-8784
Strasburg *(G-18092)*

Mid-State Awning Inc ....G 814 355-8979
Bellefonte *(G-1108)*

Mt Lebanon Awning & Tent Co ....E 412 221-2233
Presto *(G-16104)*

Nicewonger Awning Co ....G 724 837-5920
Greensburg *(G-6692)*

O K McCloyawnings Inc ....F 412 271-4044
Swissvale *(G-18193)*

Reeves Awning Inc ....F 570 876-0350
Jermyn *(G-8309)*

Reinhardt Awning Co ....G 610 965-2544
Emmaus *(G-5041)*

Rose A Rupp ....G 412 622-6827
Pittsburgh *(G-15496)*

Rothman Awning Co Inc ....F 412 589-9974
Pittsburgh *(G-15498)*

Tmu Inc ....F 717 392-0578
Lancaster *(G-9220)*

Todd Lengle & Co Inc ....E 610 777-0731
Reading *(G-16541)*

Undercoveralls Inc ....G 610 519-0858
Bryn Mawr *(G-2336)*

Y T & A Inc ....F 717 854-3806
York *(G-20722)*

AWNINGS: Fiberglass

Afca Company Inc ....E 215 425-2300
Philadelphia *(G-13351)*

Atlas Neon Sign Corp ....G 724 935-2171
Warrendale *(G-19068)*

AWNINGS: Metal

Afca Company Inc ....E 215 425-2300
Philadelphia *(G-13351)*

Age-Craft Manufacturing Inc ....F 724 838-5580
Greensburg *(G-6648)*

Charles F Woodill ....G 215 457-5858
Philadelphia *(G-13528)*

Craft-Bilt Manufacturing Co ....D 215 721-7700
Souderton *(G-17731)*

Diamond Awning Mfg Co ....G 610 656-1924
Folcroft *(G-6002)*

E R Schantz Inc ....G 610 272-3603
Norristown *(G-12652)*

F & M Designs Inc ....G 717 564-8120
Harrisburg *(G-7128)*

Grimms Inc ....G 724 346-4952
Sharon *(G-17435)*

Hibbs Awning Company Inc ....G 724 437-1494
Uniontown *(G-18630)*

Lingenfelter Awning ....G 814 696-4353
Duncansville *(G-4455)*

Pennsylvania Aluminum ....G 570 752-2666
Berwick *(G-1341)*

Rainbow Awnings Inc ....F 610 534-5380
Folcroft *(G-6014)*

Scatton Bros Mfg Co ....E 215 362-6830
Lansdale *(G-9409)*

Standard Awnings & Aluminum ....G 570 824-3535
Hanover Township *(G-7006)*

AWNINGS: Wood

Muldoon Window Door & Awning ....G 570 347-9453
Scranton *(G-17261)*

AXLES: Rolled Or Forged, Made In Steel Mills

Standard Forged Products LLC ....D 412 778-2020
Mc Kees Rocks *(G-10637)*

Ammunition Loading & Assembling Plant

Steel Valley Casting LLC ....G 724 777-4025
New Brighton *(G-12044)*

BACKHOES

C&C Backhoe Service LLC ....G 724 438-5283
Uniontown *(G-18619)*

James P Wolfley ....G 570 541-0414
Mc Clure *(G-10559)*

BADGES, WHOLESALE

Kevins Wholesale LLC ....D 570 344-9055
Scranton *(G-17250)*

Robert H Berenson ....G 610 642-9380
Haverford *(G-7414)*

BADGES: Identification & Insignia

B & N Trophies & Awards LLC ....G 814 723-8130
Warren *(G-19012)*

City Engraving & Awards LLC ....G 215 731-0200
Philadelphia *(G-13547)*

Philadelphia Regalia Co ....G 610 237-9757
Prospect Park *(G-16117)*

BAFFLES

Panel Solutions Inc ....E 570 459-3490
Hazleton *(G-7515)*

BAGS & CONTAINERS: Textile, Exc Sleeping

A Rifkin Co ....D 570 825-9551
Hanover Township *(G-6978)*

Wester Burlap Bag & Supply Co ....G 412 835-4314
Bethel Park *(G-1439)*

BAGS: Canvas

Covers All Canvas Products ....G 412 653-6010
Pittsburgh *(G-14881)*

BAGS: Cellophane

Chalmur Bag LLC ....F 215 455-1360
Philadelphia *(G-13522)*

BAGS: Duffle, Canvas, Made From Purchased Materials

Nicole Lynn Inc ....G 717 292-6130
Dover *(G-4197)*

BAGS: Food Storage & Frozen Food, Plastic

Mri Flexible Packaging Company ....F 215 860-7676
Newtown *(G-12525)*

Reynolds Presto Products Inc ....B 866 254-3310
Pittsburgh *(G-15483)*

BAGS: Laundry, Garment & Storage

Organic Climbing LLC ....G 651 245-1079
Philipsburg *(G-14523)*

BAGS: Paper

Dade Paper Co ....G 570 579-6780
Hazle Township *(G-7450)*

Knight Corporation ....E 610 853-2161
Havertown *(G-7423)*

Superior Packaging Inc ....F 570 824-3577
Plains *(G-15789)*

Uniflex Holdings Inc ....E 516 932-2000
Philadelphia *(G-14419)*

BAGS: Plastic

Bemis Company Inc ....C 570 501-1400
West Hazleton *(G-19706)*

Bomboy Inc ....F 610 266-1553
Allentown *(G-157)*

Cjc Contract Packaging Inc ....G 570 209-7836
Avoca *(G-842)*

Gateway Packaging Corp ....E 724 327-7400
Export *(G-5607)*

Innovative Plastics of PA LLC ....G 717 529-2699
Christiana *(G-3136)*

Retal Pa LLC ....F 724 705-3975
Donora *(G-4160)*

Sealed Air Corporation ....C 717 637-5905
Hanover *(G-6949)*

Transcontinental US LLC ....C 570 384-4674
Hazle Township *(G-7486)*

Viridor Global ....G 202 360-1617
Philadelphia *(G-14450)*

Wester Burlap Bag & Supply Co ....G 412 835-4314
Bethel Park *(G-1439)*

BAGS: Plastic & Pliofilm

CJ Packaging Inc ....G 570 209-7836
Avoca *(G-841)*

Consolidated Packaging LLC ....G 215 968-6260
Langhorne *(G-9286)*

Sealed Air Corporation ....G 610 926-7517
Reading *(G-16509)*

Uniflex Holdings Inc ....E 516 932-2000
Philadelphia *(G-14419)*

BAGS: Plastic, Made From Purchased Materials

Alpine Packaging Inc ....E 412 664-4000
North Versailles *(G-12771)*

Harmony LL Plastics Inc ....G 215 943-8888
Bristol *(G-2151)*

Hilex Poly Co LLC ....C 814 355-7410
Milesburg *(G-11151)*

Knf Flexpak Corporation ....D 570 386-3550
Tamaqua *(G-18214)*

Lancaster Extrusion Inc ....G 717 392-9622
Lancaster *(G-9093)*

North Coast Plastics Inc ....F 814 838-1343
Erie *(G-5407)*

Peace Products Co Inc ....E 610 296-4222
Malvern *(G-10294)*

Royco Packaging Inc ....G 215 322-8082
Huntingdon Valley *(G-8030)*

Sheth International Inc ....G 610 584-8670
Norristown *(G-12712)*

Sunshine Plastics Inc ....F 215 943-8888
Bristol *(G-2202)*

Superior Packaging Inc ....F 570 824-3577
Plains *(G-15789)*

Trinity Plastics Inc ....B 717 242-2355
Lewistown *(G-9950)*

West Pharmaceutical Svcs Inc ....B 610 594-2900
Exton *(G-5748)*

BAGS: Shopping, Made From Purchased Materials

Handelok Bag Company Inc ....E 215 362-3400
Lansdale *(G-9375)*

BAGS: Tea, Fabric, Made From Purchased Materials

Darling Blends LLC ....G 215 630-2802
Langhorne *(G-9288)*

Redco Foods Inc .... G 800 556-6674
   Bethlehem (G-1609)

BAGS: Textile

Cambria County Asso .... B 814 536-3531
   Johnstown (G-8360)
D C Humphrys Co .... D 215 307-3363
   Philadelphia (G-13599)
Equinox Ltd .... E 570 322-5900
   Williamsport (G-20011)
Hamilton Awning Co .... F 724 774-7644
   Beaver (G-983)
Jetnet Corporation .... D 412 741-0100
   Sewickley (G-17396)
Nyp Corp (frmr Ny-Pters Corp) .... G 717 656-0299
   Leola (G-9796)

BAGS: Wardrobe, Closet Access, Made From Purchased Materials

Closet Space .... G 610 359-0583
   Broomall (G-2283)

BAKERIES, COMMERCIAL: On Premises Baking Only

A Cupcake Wonderland LLC .... G 267 324-5579
   Philadelphia (G-13327)
Abes Bakery .... G 717 232-1330
   Harrisburg (G-7081)
Achenbachs Pastry Inc .... E 717 656-6671
   Leola (G-9765)
Acme Markets Inc .... C 215 725-9310
   Philadelphia (G-13341)
Addison Baking Company .... E 215 464-8055
   Philadelphia (G-13344)
Alfred Nickles Bakery Inc .... F 814 471-6913
   Ebensburg (G-4778)
Anthony Mieczkowski .... G 610 489-2523
   Collegeville (G-3369)
Arnold Foods Company Inc .... A 215 672-8010
   Horsham (G-7788)
ASA Baking Corp .... G 267 535-1618
   Philadelphia (G-13418)
Auntie Annes Inc .... D 717 435-1435
   Lancaster (G-8947)
Bakerly Barn LLC .... E 610 829-1500
   Easton (G-4647)
Bbu Inc .... C 215 347-5500
   Horsham (G-7795)
Best Bakery Inc .... G 215 855-3831
   Lansdale (G-9345)
Better Baked Foods LLC .... B 814 725-8778
   North East (G-12732)
Better Baked Foods LLC .... E 814 899-6128
   Erie (G-5210)
Bimbo Bakeries .... G 570 888-2289
   Sayre (G-17112)
Bimbo Bakeries Usa Inc .... C 717 764-9999
   York (G-20407)
Bimbo Bakeries Usa Inc .... G 610 478-9369
   Reading (G-16332)
Bimbo Bakeries Usa Inc .... E 814 456-2596
   Erie (G-5211)
Bimbo Bakeries Usa Inc .... F 570 455-7691
   West Hazleton (G-19707)
Bimbo Bakeries Usa Inc .... E 610 921-2715
   Reading (G-16333)
Bimbo Bakeries Usa Inc .... B 570 455-2066
   West Hazleton (G-19708)
Ccffg Inc .... D 570 270-3976
   Wilkes Barre (G-19911)
Chau Fresh Donuts .... G 215 474-1533
   Philadelphia (G-13535)
Community Services Group Inc .... E 570 286-0111
   Sunbury (G-18167)
Conshohocken Italian Bakery .... E 610 825-9334
   Conshohocken (G-3533)
Cora Lee Cupcakes .... G 724 681-5498
   New Kensington (G-12336)
Cordova .... G 570 578-7413
   Whitehall (G-19868)
Country Club Restaurant .... D 215 722-0500
   Philadelphia (G-13575)
Country Cupboard Cookies Lt .... G 724 325-3045
   Pittsburgh (G-14880)
Cramer Partnership .... G 215 378-6024
   Yardley (G-20301)
Crave Cupcakes By Tamara LLC .... G 610 417-4909
   Allentown (G-184)

Cupcake Momma .... G 724 516-5098
   Jeannette (G-8251)
DAmbrosio Bakery LLC .... E 610 560-4700
   King of Prussia (G-8604)
Dawn Food Products Inc .... C 717 840-0044
   York (G-20445)
Daye-Licious Baking .... G 570 965-2491
   Springville (G-17928)
Deangelis Bros Inc .... E 724 775-1641
   Rochester (G-16784)
Demestia Baking Company LLC .... G 215 896-2289
   Lansdale (G-9360)
Dianas Heavenly Cupcakes .... G 412 628-0642
   Jeannette (G-8252)
Don Saylors Markets Inc .... G 717 776-7551
   Newville (G-12600)
Dons Lykens Food Market Inc .... D 717 453-7042
   Lykens (G-10132)
Duritzas Enterprises Inc .... C 724 223-5494
   Washington (G-19165)
Early Morning Donuts Corp .... G 570 961-5150
   Scranton (G-17230)
Federal Pretzel Baking Co .... E 215 467-0505
   Philadelphia (G-13695)
Ferguson and Hassler Inc .... E 717 786-7301
   Quarryville (G-16269)
Fred Fairburn .... E 570 282-3364
   Carbondale (G-2675)
Frosted Fantasia Cupcakes LLC .... G 724 601-9440
   Oakdale (G-12899)
Gannons Gourmet .... F 610 439-8949
   Allentown (G-223)
Gerritys Super Market Inc .... D 570 961-9030
   Scranton (G-17239)
Giant Eagle .... C 724 772-1030
   Cranberry Township (G-3821)
Harrys Famous Pudding .... F 484 494-6400
   Glenolden (G-6475)
Heathers Cupcakes N Things LLC ..... G 717 329-2324
   Harrisburg (G-7147)
Howard Donuts Inc .... E 215 634-7750
   Philadelphia (G-13836)
Ising LLC .... G 610 216-2644
   Allentown (G-266)
Its Only Cupcakes LLC .... G 717 421-6646
   Wayne (G-19340)
James J Tuzzi Jr .... E 570 752-2704
   Berwick (G-1329)
Kellogg Company .... B 570 546-0200
   Muncy (G-11823)
Klosterman Baking Co .... G 412 564-1023
   Bridgeville (G-2076)
Kretchmar Bakery Inc .... E 724 774-2324
   Beaver (G-986)
Kurts Making Whoopie .... G 570 888-9102
   Sayre (G-17117)
Kyjs Bakery .... E 610 494-9400
   Chester (G-3054)
Larry Darling .... G 215 677-1452
   Philadelphia (G-13957)
Le Bus Bakery Inc .... E 610 337-1444
   King of Prussia (G-8639)
Luccis Bakery .... F 570 876-3830
   Archbald (G-692)
Macs Donut Shop Inc .... E 724 375-6776
   Aliquippa (G-82)
Maple Donuts Inc .... F 717 843-4276
   York (G-20579)
Michels Bakery Inc .... C 215 742-3900
   Philadelphia (G-14022)
Mighty Fine Inc .... D 814 455-6408
   Erie (G-5391)
Moms Wholesale Foods Inc .... G 724 856-3049
   New Castle (G-12122)
Mr ZS Food Mart .... G 570 421-7070
   Stroudsburg (G-18132)
National Bakery Inc .... E 570 343-1609
   Scranton (G-17264)
Native Foods LLC .... E 717 298-6157
   Hershey (G-7622)
New Lycoming Bakery Inc .... E 570 326-9426
   Williamsport (G-20046)
Odellick Baking LLC .... E 814 515-1337
   Altoona (G-533)
OH Little Town Cupcakes LLC .... G 484 353-9709
   Bethlehem (G-1586)
Paddycake Bakery .... E 412 621-4477
   Pittsburgh (G-15367)
Philadelphia Soft Pretzels .... E 215 324-4315
   Philadelphia (G-14155)

Prantls of Shadyside LLC .... F 412 621-2092
   Pittsburgh (G-15428)
Redners Markets Inc .... G 610 678-2900
   Reading (G-16494)
Redners Markets Inc .... D 610 776-2726
   Allentown (G-372)
Robert Bath .... G 610 588-0423
   Roseto (G-16822)
S Don Food Market Inc .... E 717 453-7470
   Lykens (G-10135)
Safran Brothers Inc .... C 724 266-9758
   Ambridge (G-633)
Schiel Inc .... C 570 970-4460
   Wilkes Barre (G-19962)
Schwebel Baking Co of PA Inc .... C 412 751-4080
   McKeesport (G-10680)
Schwebel Baking Company .... E 412 257-6067
   Bridgeville (G-2088)
Scratch Cupcakes .... G 717 271-2466
   Ephrata (G-5139)
Shivkanta Corporation .... G 610 376-3515
   Reading (G-16517)
Simple Treat Bakery .... F 412 681-0303
   Pittsburgh (G-15538)
Smucker Management Corporation ..... G 717 768-1501
   Bird In Hand (G-1681)
Soumaya & Sons Bakery LLC .... G 610 432-0405
   Whitehall (G-19889)
Spin-A-Latte Tm .... G 215 285-1567
   Lansdale (G-9412)
Stagnos Bakery Inc .... G 412 361-2093
   Pittsburgh (G-15574)
Sunnyway Foods Inc .... D 717 264-6001
   Chambersburg (G-2980)
Sunnyway Foods Inc .... D 717 597-7121
   Greencastle (G-6637)
Tasty Baking Company .... G 570 961-8211
   Dunmore (G-4485)
Terranettis Italian Bakery .... E 717 697-5434
   Mechanicsburg (G-10896)
Tops Markets LLC .... C 570 882-9188
   Sayre (G-17123)
Travaglini Enterprises Inc .... E 814 898-1212
   Erie (G-5515)
Travaglini Enterprises Inc .... E 724 342-3334
   Hermitage (G-7596)
Trofi Idoni Specialty Baking .... G 484 892-0876
   Bethlehem (G-1643)
Village Farm Market .... G 717 733-5340
   Ephrata (G-5154)
Wakefern Food Corp .... D 215 744-9500
   Philadelphia (G-14457)
Weis Markets Inc .... C 570 724-6364
   Wellsboro (G-19474)
Zynnie Bakes .... G 610 905-6283
   Philadelphia (G-14506)

BAKERIES: On Premises Baking & Consumption

Agostini Bakery Inc .... E 570 457-2021
   Old Forge (G-12962)
Best Bakery Inc .... G 215 855-3831
   Lansdale (G-9345)
Bimbo Bakeries Usa Inc .... E 800 222-7495
   York (G-20406)
Bimbo Bakeries USA Inc .... B 610 258-7131
   Easton (G-4656)
Conshohocken Italian Bakery .... E 610 825-9334
   Conshohocken (G-3533)
Country Club Restaurant .... D 215 722-0500
   Philadelphia (G-13575)
Dalos Bakery Inc .... E 570 752-4519
   Berwick (G-1322)
Egypt Star Inc .... E 610 434-8516
   Allentown (G-204)
Ford City National Bakery .... G 724 763-7684
   Ford City (G-6046)
James J Tuzzi Jr .... E 570 752-2704
   Berwick (G-1329)
Kesser Baking Co .... F 215 878-8080
   Philadelphia (G-13928)
Kyjs Bakery .... E 610 494-9400
   Chester (G-3054)
Le Bus Bakery Inc .... E 610 337-1444
   King of Prussia (G-8639)
Maple Donuts Inc .... C 717 757-7826
   York (G-20578)
Maple Donuts Inc .... D 814 774-3131
   Lake City (G-8905)

Employee Codes: A=Over 500 employees, B=251-500
C=101-250, D=51-100, E=20-50, F=10-19, G=3-9

2019 Harris Pennsylvania
Manufacturers Directory

PRODUCT

1305

National Bakery Inc...............E....... 570 343-1609
Scranton (G-17264)

Robert Bath...............G....... 610 588-0423
Roseto (G-16822)

Senapes Bakery Inc...............E....... 570 454-0839
Hazleton (G-7526)

Smucker Management Corporation ......G....... 717 768-1501
Bird In Hand (G-1681)

Soumaya & Sons Bakery LLC...............G....... 610 432-0405
Whitehall (G-19889)

Stagnos Bakery Inc...............G....... 412 361-2093
Pittsburgh (G-15574)

Tops Markets LLC...............C....... 570 882-9188
Sayre (G-17123)

William Aupperle...............G....... 724 583-8310
Masontown (G-10538)

BAKERY FOR HOME SVC DELIVERY

Mama DS Buns Inc...............G....... 724 752-1700
Ellwood City (G-4944)

BAKERY MACHINERY

American Waffle Company LLC...............E....... 717 632-6000
Hanover (G-6860)

Eastern Bakery Equipment Co ....F....... 717 938-8278
York Haven (G-20758)

Gemini Bakery Equipment Co ....D....... 215 673-3520
Philadelphia (G-13747)

KB Systems Inc...............D....... 610 588-7788
Bangor (G-919)

Oshikiri Corporation America...............F....... 215 637-6005
Philadelphia (G-14103)

Pittsburgh Bakery Equipment Co...............G....... 724 533-2158
Volant (G-18776)

BAKERY PRDTS: Bagels, Fresh Or Frozen

Bimbo Bakeries Usa Inc...............F....... 570 494-1191
Williamsport (G-19993)

Northwest Bagel Corporation...............G....... 610 237-0586
Downingtown (G-4245)

T & P Bagels Inc...............G....... 610 867-8695
Bethlehem (G-1637)

BAKERY PRDTS: Bakery Prdts, Partially Cooked, Exc frozen

Egypt Star Inc...............E....... 610 434-8516
Allentown (G-204)

Hartings Bakery Inc...............E....... 717 445-5644
Bowmansville (G-1887)

BAKERY PRDTS: Biscuits, Baked, Baking Powder & Raised

La Gourmandine LLC...............G....... 412 291-8146
Hazelwood (G-7446)

BAKERY PRDTS: Biscuits, Dry

Amco Biscuit Distributors Inc ....F....... 215 467-8775
Philadelphia (G-13376)

Mondelez Global LLC...............E....... 215 673-4800
Philadelphia (G-14034)

BAKERY PRDTS: Bread, All Types, Fresh Or Frozen

A T V Bakery Inc...............E....... 610 374-5577
Reading (G-16307)

Bimbo Bakeries Usa Inc...............B....... 610 825-1140
Conshohocken (G-3522)

Bimbo Bakeries Usa Inc...............D....... 570 654-4668
Pittston (G-15743)

Bimbo Bakeries Usa Inc...............E....... 800 635-1685
Aston (G-752)

Bimbo Bakeries USA Inc...............B....... 610 258-7131
Easton (G-4656)

Gonnella Frozen Products LLC ....F....... 570 455-3194
Hazle Township (G-7459)

International Bakery...............E....... 814 452-3435
Erie (G-5329)

Kaplans New Model Baking Co ....E....... 215 627-5288
Philadelphia (G-13921)

Lee High Valley Bakers LLC...............F....... 610 868-2392
Bethlehem (G-1556)

Royal Bake Shop...............G....... 570 654-2011
Exeter (G-5584)

BAKERY PRDTS: Buns, Bread Type, Fresh Or Frozen

Northeast Foods Inc...............C....... 215 638-2400
Bensalem (G-1231)

BAKERY PRDTS: Cakes, Bakery, Exc Frozen

Crofchick Inc...............G....... 570 287-3940
Swoyersville (G-18197)

Fresh Foods Manufacturing...............E....... 724 683-3639
Freedom (G-6190)

Jtm Foods LLC...............D....... 814 899-0886
Erie (G-5340)

Nawalany-Franciotti LLC...............F....... 215 342-3005
Philadelphia (G-14059)

Philly Originals...............G....... 724 728-3011
Beaver (G-989)

Sophisticakes Inc...............G....... 610 626-9991
Drexel Hill (G-4371)

BAKERY PRDTS: Cakes, Bakery, Frozen

Dawn Food Products Inc...............C....... 717 840-0044
York (G-20445)

Dices Creative Cakes...............G....... 610 367-0107
Boyertown (G-1906)

Luscious Layers...............G....... 724 967-2357
Grove City (G-6796)

BAKERY PRDTS: Cones, Ice Cream

Als Conezone...............G....... 412 405-9601
Clairton (G-3147)

Bucks Creamery LLC...............E....... 732 387-3535
Feasterville Trevose (G-5895)

Claudes Creamery...............G....... 610 826-2663
Palmerton (G-13103)

Cone Guys Ltd...............F....... 215 781-6996
Bristol (G-2128)

Joy Cone Co...............B....... 724 962-5747
Hermitage (G-7589)

Rjj Mobile LLC...............F....... 215 796-1935
Philadelphia (G-14253)

Rjj Wayne LLC...............G....... 215 796-1935
Lafayette Hill (G-8884)

Scooperman Water Ice Inc...............G....... 267 623-8494
Philadelphia (G-14285)

BAKERY PRDTS: Cookies

Bainbridge Group Inc...............F....... 215 922-3274
Philadelphia (G-13442)

Charlies Specialties Inc...............D....... 724 346-2350
Hermitage (G-7577)

Cookie Grams...............G....... 814 942-4220
Altoona (G-494)

Country Fresh Batter Inc...............D....... 610 272-5751
King of Prussia (G-8600)

D F Stauffer Biscuit Co Inc...............B....... 717 815-4600
York (G-20441)

Davis Cookie Company...............D....... 814 473-3125
Rimersburg (G-16749)

Keebler Company...............F....... 717 790-9886
Mechanicsburg (G-10862)

Keebler Company...............E....... 215 752-4010
Horsham (G-7830)

Kelloggs Snacks...............G....... 412 787-1183
Pittsburgh (G-15165)

Pati Petite Butter Cookies Inc...............E....... 412 221-4033
Bridgeville (G-2085)

Pepperidge Farm Incorporated...............G....... 610 356-0553
Broomall (G-2301)

Pepperidge Farm Incorporated...............G....... 717 336-8500
Denver (G-4087)

Shirleys Cookie Company Inc...............D....... 814 239-2208
Claysburg (G-3208)

Snyders-Lance Inc...............B....... 724 929-6270
Rostraver Township (G-16830)

Sophisticakes Inc...............G....... 610 626-9991
Drexel Hill (G-4371)

Sweetzels Foods LLC...............G....... 610 278-8700
Blue Bell (G-1854)

Unique Desserts Inc...............G....... 610 372-7879
Reading (G-16552)

BAKERY PRDTS: Cookies & crackers

Amarriage Entertainment LLC...............F....... 267 973-5288
Upper Darby (G-18678)

Cramer Partnership...............G....... 215 378-6024
Yardley (G-20301)

Cupoladua Oven LLC...............G....... 412 592-5378
Mars (G-10493)

Dalos Bakery Inc...............E....... 570 752-4519
Berwick (G-1322)

Egypt Star Inc...............E....... 610 434-8516
Allentown (G-204)

Flowers Baking Co Oxford Inc...............E....... 610 932-2147
Oxford (G-13079)

Kretchmar Bakery Inc...............E....... 724 774-2324
Beaver (G-986)

M Cibrone & Sons Bakery Inc...............E....... 412 885-6200
Pittsburgh (G-15244)

Nabisco Brands Inc...............G....... 570 820-1669
Wilkes Barre (G-19948)

Nuts & Such Ltd...............G....... 215 708-8500
Philadelphia (G-14089)

Paddycake Bakery...............E....... 412 621-4477
Pittsburgh (G-15367)

Shearers Fods Canonsburg Plant...............G....... 724 746-1162
Canonsburg (G-2635)

BAKERY PRDTS: Croissants, Exc Frozen

Au Fournil Inc...............G....... 610 664-0235
Narberth (G-11908)

BAKERY PRDTS: Doughnuts, Exc Frozen

Brinic Donuts Inc...............E....... 814 944-5242
Altoona (G-484)

Dharini LLC...............F....... 215 595-3915
Yardley (G-20306)

Donut Connection...............F....... 724 282-6214
Butler (G-2395)

Donut Shack...............G....... 412 793-4222
Pittsburgh (G-14931)

Dough Nuts For Doughnuts LLC...........F....... 610 642-6186
Haverford (G-7409)

Dunkin Donuts...............G....... 610 992-0111
King of Prussia (G-8613)

Fresh Donuts...............G....... 717 273-8886
Lebanon (G-9572)

Ganesh Donuts Inc...............G....... 215 351-9370
Philadelphia (G-13743)

J F M Philadelphia Donut Inc...............G....... 215 676-0700
Philadelphia (G-13883)

Jo Suzy Donuts...............G....... 610 279-1350
Bridgeport (G-2038)

Krispy Kreme Doughnuts...............G....... 724 228-1800
Washington (G-19194)

Maple Donuts Inc...............C....... 717 757-7826
York (G-20578)

Maple Donuts Inc...............D....... 814 774-3131
Lake City (G-8905)

Shree Swami Narayan Corp...............E....... 610 272-8404
Norristown (G-12713)

Yum Yum Bake Shops Inc...............G....... 215 675-9874
Warminster (G-19005)

Yum-Yum Colmar Inc...............E....... 215 822-9468
Colmar (G-3426)

BAKERY PRDTS: Dry

Better Batter Gluten Free Flur...............G....... 814 946-0958
Altoona (G-476)

Tasty Baking Company...............E....... 215 221-8500
Philadelphia (G-14374)

Tasty Baking Company...............A....... 215 221-8500
Philadelphia (G-14375)

BAKERY PRDTS: Frozen

Happy Baking Co...............G....... 412 621-4020
Pittsburgh (G-15081)

Icy Bites Inc...............G....... 570 558-5558
Scranton (G-17242)

Pepperidge Farm Incorporated...............G....... 610 356-0553
Broomall (G-2301)

Pepperidge Farm Incorporated...............G....... 717 336-8500
Denver (G-4087)

Pretzelworks Inc...............D....... 215 288-4002
Philadelphia (G-14199)

Sunbeam Morrisville Inc...............G....... 215 736-9991
Morrisville (G-11583)

BAKERY PRDTS: Pies, Exc Frozen

Leibys Ichr LLC...............G....... 570 778-0108
Tamaqua (G-18217)

McClures Pie and Salad Inc...............F....... 717 442-4461
Gap (G-6253)

Specialty Bakers LLC...............D....... 717 626-8002
Marysville (G-10533)

Teris Deli & Bakery LLC ....G...... 570 785-7007
Forest City (G-6055)

Wixons Bakery Inc ....F...... 610 777-6056
Reading (G-16568)

BAKERY PRDTS: Pretzels

A Taste of Philly ....G...... 215 639-3997
Feasterville Trevose (G-5882)

Auntie Annes Soft Pretzels ....G...... 724 349-2825
Indiana (G-8084)

Bakers Best Snack Foods Inc...............E...... 215 822-3511
Hatfield (G-7320)

Bickels Snack Foods Inc ....E...... 800 233-1933
York (G-20403)

Center City Pretzel Co ....F...... 215 463-5664
Philadelphia (G-13519)

Condor Corporation ....C...... 717 560-1882
Lititz (G-10001)

Dutch Cntry Soft Pretzels LLC ....G...... 717 354-4493
New Holland (G-12244)

Epex Soft Petals ....F...... 717 848-8488
York (G-20469)

Gotcha Covered Pretzels LLC ....G...... 215 253-3176
Warrington (G-19118)

Hammond Pretzel Bakery Inc ....E...... 717 392-7532
Lancaster (G-9038)

Intercourse Pretzel Factory...................E...... 717 768-3432
Intercourse (G-8137)

Jims Soft Pretzel Bakery LLC ....G...... 215 431-1045
Ivyland (G-8213)

Kings Potato Chip Company ....E...... 717 445-4521
Mohnton (G-11268)

Leclerc Foods Usa Inc..........................D...... 570 547-6295
Montgomery (G-11375)

Martins Pretzel Bakery ....E...... 717 859-1272
Akron (G-36)

Philadelphia Soft Pretzels ....E...... 215 324-4315
Philadelphia (G-14155)

Philly Pretzel Factory ....E...... 215 962-5593
Philadelphia (G-14169)

Pretzel Lady ....G...... 717 632-7046
Hanover (G-6937)

Pretzel Shop ....F...... 412 431-2574
Pittsburgh (G-15437)

Pretzels Plus ....G...... 724 228-9785
Washington (G-19218)

Revonah Pretzel LLC ....G...... 717 632-4477
Hanover (G-6943)

S-L Snacks Real Estate Inc ....A...... 717 632-4477
Hanover (G-6948)

Sansom Street Soft Pretzel Fac ....G...... 215 569-3988
Philadelphia (G-14279)

Savor Street Foods Inc ....E...... 610 320-7800
Wyomissing (G-20288)

Snyders Hanover Mfg Inc ....G...... 800 233-7125
Hanover (G-6954)

Snyders-Lance Inc ....D...... 717 632-4477
Hanover (G-6955)

Star Brands North America Inc..............G...... 610 775-4100
Mohnton (G-11270)

Suzie BS Pretzeltown Inc ....E...... 814 868-8443
Erie (G-5498)

Tasty Twisters Inc ....G...... 215 487-7828
Philadelphia (G-14376)

Todds Snax Inc.....................................C...... 717 637-5931
Hanover (G-6961)

Tom Sturgis Pretzels Inc ....E...... 610 775-0335
Reading (G-16544)

Troyer Inc..E...... 724 746-1162
Canonsburg (G-2648)

Tshudy Snacks Inc................................F...... 717 626-4354
Lititz (G-10055)

Uncle Henrys Pretzel Bakery ....E...... 717 445-4698
Bowmansville (G-1888)

Unique Pretzel Bakery Inc.....................E...... 610 929-3172
Reading (G-16553)

Utz Quality Foods Inc ....C...... 717 637-5666
Hanover (G-6966)

Utz Quality Foods LLC ....A...... 800 367-7629
Hanover (G-6967)

Village Pretzels ....F...... 215 674-5070
Hatboro (G-7309)

Wege Pretzel Co Inc ....D...... 717 843-0738
Hanover (G-6973)

BAKERY PRDTS: Rolls, Bread Type, Fresh Or Frozen

Martins Fmous Pstry Shoppe Inc ....C...... 717 263-9580
Chambersburg (G-2957)

Martins Fmous Pstry Shoppe Inc...........C...... 717 263-9580
Chambersburg (G-2958)

BAKERY PRDTS: Wholesalers

Addison Baking Company ....E...... 215 464-8055
Philadelphia (G-13344)

Au Fournil Inc..G...... 610 664-0235
Narberth (G-11908)

Byrnes and Kiefer Company ....E...... 724 538-5200
Callery (G-2467)

Conshohocken Italian Bakery ....E...... 610 825-9334
Conshohocken (G-3533)

Dalos Bakery Inc ....E...... 570 752-4519
Berwick (G-1322)

James J Tuzzi Jr ....E...... 570 752-2704
Berwick (G-1329)

Le Bus Bakery Inc.................................E...... 610 337-1444
King of Prussia (G-8639)

Macs Donut Shop Inc ....E...... 724 375-6776
Aliquippa (G-82)

Mighty Fine Inc......................................D...... 814 455-6408
Erie (G-5391)

Schwebel Baking Co of PA Inc ....C...... 412 751-4080
McKeesport (G-10680)

Soumaya & Sons Bakery LLC ....G...... 610 432-0405
Whitehall (G-19889)

Teris Deli & Bakery LLC ....G...... 570 785-7007
Forest City (G-6055)

Terranettis Italian Bakery ....E...... 717 697-5434
Mechanicsburg (G-10896)

BAKERY: Wholesale Or Wholesale & Retail Combined

5 Generation Bakers LLC......................E...... 412 444-8200
Mc Kees Rocks (G-10597)

Amega Holdings LLC..............................G...... 718 775-7188
Jamison (G-8242)

Backdoor Bakershop ....G...... 610 625-0987
Bethlehem (G-1456)

Bakkavor Foods Usa Inc ....F...... 570 383-9800
Jessup (G-8327)

Bimbo Bakeries Usa Inc ....F...... 814 941-1102
Altoona (G-477)

Bimbo Bakeries Usa Inc ....F...... 800 222-7495
York (G-20406)

Bimbo Bakeries Usa Inc ....E...... 724 251-0971
Leetsdale (G-9684)

Bimbo Bakeries Usa Inc ....F...... 412 443-3499
Leetsdale (G-9685)

Bimbo Bakeries Usa Inc ....A...... 814 456-4575
Erie (G-5212)

Bimbo Bakeries Usa Inc ....D...... 610 391-7490
Breinigsville (G-2010)

Bimbo Bakeries Usa Inc ....F...... 610 865-7402
Bethlehem (G-1466)

Bimbo Bakeries Usa Inc ....B...... 215 347-5500
Horsham (G-7796)

Bimbo Bakeries Usa Inc ....F...... 724 733-2332
Pittsburgh (G-14766)

Bimbo Hungria Company ....F...... 866 506-6807
Horsham (G-7797)

Cakeworks LLC ....G...... 917 744-1375
Henryville (G-7565)

Carlisle Foods Inc ....C...... 717 218-9880
Carlisle (G-2696)

Dalos Bakery Inc ....E...... 570 752-4519
Berwick (G-1322)

Dia Doce ....G...... 610 476-5684
Glenmoore (G-6465)

Earthgrains Distribution LLC ....F...... 215 672-8010
Horsham (G-7813)

Enrico Biscotti Company ....G...... 412 281-2602
Pittsburgh (G-14977)

Flowers Baking Co Oxford Inc................E...... 610 932-2147
Oxford (G-13079)

Flowers Foods Inc ....E...... 717 528-4108
York Springs (G-20765)

Ford City National Bakery ....G...... 724 763-7684
Ford City (G-6046)

G Weston Bakeries ....G...... 570 455-2066
West Hazleton (G-19710)

Grand Finale Desserts ....G...... 610 864-3824
Paoli (G-13141)

Half Plus Half Inc Enterprise..................D...... 800 252-4545
Philadelphia (G-13796)

Hallelujah Ink ....G...... 215 510-1152
Philadelphia (G-13798)

Hoyt Inc...F...... 570 326-9426
South Williamsport (G-17792)

Imperial Bakery ....G...... 570 343-4537
Scranton (G-17243)

Kesser Baking Co ....F...... 215 878-8080
Philadelphia (G-13928)

La Gourmandine LLC ....G...... 412 682-2210
Pittsburgh (G-15210)

La Gourmandine LLC ....G...... 412 200-7969
Pittsburgh (G-15211)

Lizzie BS Bakery ....G...... 717 817-1791
Glenville (G-6545)

Longos Bakery Inc ....F...... 570 233-0558
Hazleton (G-7508)

M Cibrone & Sons Bakery Inc ....E...... 412 885-6200
Pittsburgh (G-15244)

Mama Nardone Baking Co Inc ....G...... 570 825-3421
Hazleton (G-7509)

Megan Sweet Baking Company ....G...... 267 288-5080
Holland (G-7641)

Morabito Baking Co Inc ....D...... 610 275-5419
Norristown (G-12688)

Petruzzis Manufacturing Inc ....G...... 570 459-5957
Hazleton (G-7518)

Pittston Baking Co Inc ....G...... 570 343-2102
Scranton (G-17272)

Potomac Bakery Inc ....E...... 412 531-5066
Pittsburgh (G-15421)

Queen of Hearts Inc ....E...... 610 889-0477
Malvern (G-10305)

Red Mill Farms LLC ....F...... 570 457-2400
Moosic (G-11513)

Rosciolis Bakery ....G...... 570 961-1151
Scranton (G-17279)

Schwebel Baking Company ....G...... 814 333-2498
Meadville (G-10789)

Senapes Bakery Inc ....G...... 570 454-0839
Hazleton (G-7526)

Soft Pretzels Franchise System ....G...... 215 338-4606
Bensalem (G-1254)

Stagnos Bakery Inc ....E...... 412 441-3485
East Liberty (G-4581)

Tasty Baking Company ....G...... 717 295-2530
Lancaster (G-9212)

Termini Brothers Inc ....E...... 215 334-1816
Philadelphia (G-14381)

Unique Desserts Inc ....G...... 610 372-7879
Reading (G-16552)

Vallos Bakery LLC ....E...... 610 866-1012
Bethlehem (G-1650)

Warrington Pastry Shop ....F...... 215 343-1946
Warrington (G-19139)

Weinrich Bakery ....E...... 215 659-7062
Willow Grove (G-20148)

William Aupperle ....G...... 724 583-8310
Masontown (G-10538)

Zakes Cakes ....G...... 215 654-7600
Fort Washington (G-6097)

BALANCES EXC LABORATORY WHOLESALERS

Industrial Instrs & Sups Inc ....F...... 215 396-0822
Wycombe (G-20260)

BALANCING SVC

Integrated Power Services LLC ....F...... 724 225-2900
Washington (G-19186)

BALERS

American Baling Products Inc.................G...... 724 758-5566
Ellwood City (G-4925)

MDC Romani Inc ....F...... 724 349-5533
Indiana (G-8113)

BALLOONS: Hot Air

Air Ventures Balloon Rides....................G...... 610 827-2138
Chester Springs (G-3070)

BALLOONS: Novelty & Toy

Shenango Operating Inc ....E...... 724 657-3650
New Castle (G-12151)

BALLOONS: Toy & Advertising, Rubber

Fast Shelter Inc ....G...... 610 415-0225
Phoenixville (G-14549)

Port Richman Holdings LLC ....G...... 212 777-1178
Philadelphia (G-14189)

PRODUCT

BALLS: Rubber, Exc Athletic

Business Applications Ltd ....G....... 814 677-7056
Reno (G-16645)

BANDS: Copper & Copper Alloy

Philadelphia Pipe Bending Co ....E....... 215 225-8955
Philadelphia (G-14149)

BANDS: Plastic

New Concept Manufacturing LLC ....C....... 717 741-0840
Emigsville (G-4994)
New Concept Technology Inc ....E....... 717 741-0840
Emigsville (G-4995)
Pac Strapping Products Inc ....E....... 610 363-8805
Exton (G-5721)

BANISTERS: Metal Pipe

American Railing Systems Inc..............E....... 814 899-7677
Erie (G-5188)

BANK & TURN INDICATORS & COMPONENTS

Remcal Products Corporation ....F....... 215 343-5500
Warrington (G-19130)

BANNERS: Fabric

Graphcom Inc....................................C....... 800 699-1664
Gettysburg (G-6295)

BANQUET HALL FACILITIES

Mayberry Hospitality LLC....................G....... 570 275-9292
Northumberland (G-12871)
Stoudt Brewing Company ....E....... 717 484-4386
Adamstown (G-24)
Wilbos Inc ....G....... 267 490-5168
Quakertown (G-16259)

BAR

Beckers Cafe ....G....... 412 331-1373
Mc Kees Rocks (G-10604)
Mudhook Brewing Company LLC ....F....... 717 747-3605
York (G-20606)
Schnoch Corporation ....E....... 570 326-4700
Williamsport (G-20070)
Wilbos Inc ....G....... 267 490-5168
Quakertown (G-16259)

BAR FIXTURES: Wood

Ruby Custom Woodcraft Inc.................G....... 570 698-7741
Lake Ariel (G-8891)

BAR JOISTS & CONCRETE REINFORCING BARS: Fabricated

Harris Rebar Atlantic Inc ....D....... 610 882-1401
Bethlehem (G-1529)

BARBECUE EQPT

Appalachain Grills ....G....... 717 762-3321
Waynesboro (G-19397)
Ellco Products Inc...............................G....... 724 758-3526
Ellwood City (G-4930)

BARGES BUILDING & REPAIR

C & C Marine Maintenance Co ....C....... 724 746-9550
Houston (G-7868)
Heartland Fabrication LLC ....C....... 724 785-2575
Brownsville (G-2312)
NCM Barge Maintence ....F....... 724 469-0083
Rostraver Township (G-16828)

BARRELS: Shipping, Metal

Lancaster Container Inc ....E....... 717 285-3312
Columbia (G-3442)

BARRICADES: Metal

F R Industries Inc................................F....... 412 242-5903
Pittsburgh (G-14999)
Pro Barrier Engineering LLC ....G....... 717 944-6056
Hummelstown (G-7922)
Roadsafe Traffic Systems Inc ....D....... 412 559-1396
Gibsonia (G-6350)

Tamis Corporation ....F....... 412 241-7161
Pittsburgh (G-15595)
Trinity Highway Rentals Inc ....G....... 570 380-2856
Bloomsburg (G-1804)

BARS, COLD FINISHED: Steel, From Purchased Hot-Rolled

Precision Industries Inc ....D....... 724 222-2100
Washington (G-19217)

BARS, PIPES, PLATES & SHAPES: Lead/Lead Alloy Bars, Pipe

Atomic Industries Inc ....F....... 610 754-6400
Frederick (G-6171)

BARS: Concrete Reinforcing, Fabricated Steel

Cmw Technologies Inc ....F....... 215 721-5824
Telford (G-18274)
Contrast Metalworks LLC......................G....... 484 624-5542
Pottstown (G-15975)
Custom Mfg & Indus Svcs LLC...............G....... 412 621-2982
Pittsburgh (G-14894)
Diversified Fabrications Inc ....G....... 814 344-8434
Carrolltown (G-2807)
Extreme Manufacturing Inc...................F....... 717 369-0044
Saint Thomas (G-17039)
Florig R & J Industrial Co Inc................E....... 610 825-6655
Conshohocken (G-3548)
Gerdau Ameristeel US Inc ....D....... 717 846-7865
York (G-20498)
Ivy Steel & Wire Inc ....D....... 570 450-2090
Hazle Township (G-7465)
Jasper Steel Fabrication Inc ....G....... 570 329-3330
Williamsport (G-20027)
Keamco Industries Inc ....G....... 215 938-6050
Feasterville Trevose (G-5916)
Lee Michael Industries Inc ....E....... 724 656-0890
New Castle (G-12115)
Lineman & Sons ....Mc...... 814 677-7215
Oil City (G-12951)
Little Wash Fabricators Inc ....F....... 717 768-7356
Christiana (G-3141)
Men of Steel Enterprises LLC ....E....... 609 871-2000
Bensalem (G-1226)
Penn Fabrication LLC...........................F....... 610 292-1980
Norristown (G-12702)
Simpson Reinforcing Inc.......................F....... 412 362-6200
New Kensington (G-12376)
Sippel Co Inc ....D....... 724 266-9800
Ambridge (G-634)
Structural Services Inc ....G....... 610 282-5810
Coopersburg (G-3636)
Tye Bar LLC ....F....... 412 896-1376
Glassport (G-6422)
Ward Fabricating Inc............................G....... 814 345-6707
Morrisdale (G-11549)

BARS: Iron, Made In Steel Mills

Ipsco Koppel Tubulars Llc ....B....... 724 266-8830
Ambridge (G-620)

BASEMENT WINDOW AREAWAYS: Concrete

Jamison Bsmnt Wterproofing Inc ....G....... 215 885-2424
Oreland (G-13025)

BASES, BEVERAGE

Cameron Supply Corporation................F....... 610 866-9632
Bethlehem (G-1478)
Kauffmantreatscom LLC ....G....... 717 715-6409
Ronks (G-16809)
Pitts Doggn It LLC................................G....... 412 687-1440
Pittsburgh (G-15385)

BASKETS, GIFT, WHOLESALE

Basket Works Inc ....G....... 516 367-9200
Tannersville (G-18234)

BASKETS, WHOLESALE

Sutherland Baskets ....G....... 610 438-8233
Easton (G-4759)

BATCHING PLANTS: Aggregate Concrete & Bulk Cement

K & B Aqua Express Co LLC ....G....... 215 343-2247
Chalfont (G-2879)

BATCHING PLANTS: Bituminous

Mayer Brothers Construction Co ....F....... 814 452-3748
Erie (G-5383)

BATH SALTS

Westlab Distribution Inc.......................G....... 800 699-0301
Montoursville (G-11456)

BATHING SUIT STORES

Transfer Junction................................G....... 814 942-4434
Williamsburg (G-19982)

BATHMATS: Rubber

Innocor Foam Tech - Acp Inc ....G....... 570 876-4544
Archbald (G-687)

BATHROOM FIXTURES: Plastic

Hunter Kitchen & Bath LLC..................G....... 570 926-0777
Exton (G-5693)
Space Age Plastics Inc ....F....... 570 630-6060
Jefferson Township (G-8279)
Top Notch Products Inc........................G....... 724 475-2341
Fredonia (G-6187)

BATTERIES, EXC AUTOMOTIVE: Wholesalers

Energizer Battery Co ....G....... 215 572-0200
Jenkintown (G-8286)

BATTERIES: Dry

E I T Corporation Phoenix....................F....... 570 286-7744
Sunbury (G-18168)

BATTERIES: Lead Acid, Storage

C&D Technologies Inc ....C....... 215 619-2700
Blue Bell (G-1820)
East Penn Manufacturing Co ....F....... 412 793-0283
Pittsburgh (G-14956)
East Penn Manufacturing Co ....E....... 610 682-6361
Kutztown (G-8840)
Enersys..D....... 724 223-4255
Washington (G-19169)
Enersys..F....... 215 420-1000
Warminster (G-18873)
Enersys..C....... 610 208-1991
Reading (G-16375)
Enersys Capital Inc.............................F....... 610 208-1991
Reading (G-16376)
Enersys Delaware Inc ....B....... 214 324-8990
Reading (G-16377)
Enersys Delaware Inc ....G....... 484 244-4150
Allentown (G-206)
Exide Technologies ....C....... 717 464-2721
Lampeter (G-8917)
Exide Technologies ....G....... 304 345-5616
Rostraver Township (G-16826)
New Castle Battery Mfg Co ....C....... 724 658-5501
New Castle (G-12127)

BATTERIES: Rechargeable

Battery Tech LLC ....G....... 570 253-6908
Honesdale (G-7702)
Battery Zone ....F....... 800 371-5033
Bethlehem (G-1458)
Cell-Con Inc ....D....... 800 771-7139
Exton (G-5660)
Exide Corporation Smelter....................F....... 610 921-4003
Reading (G-16382)
Maxpower Inc ....F....... 215 256-4575
Harleysville (G-7047)

BATTERIES: Storage

Aquion Energy Inc ....C....... 412 904-6400
Pittsburgh (G-14715)
Avex Electronics Corp..........................E....... 215 245-4848
Bensalem (G-1152)
CD Technologies Inc............................E....... 215 619-2700
Horsham (G-7801)

Cell-Con Inc ....E 814 623-7057
Bedford *(G-1046)*

East Penn Manufacturing Co ....F 610 682-6361
Topton *(G-18411)*

Exide Technologies ....G 610 269-0429
Downingtown *(G-4226)*

Juline-Titans LLC 412 352-4744
Pittsburgh *(G-15158)*

Lithium Technology Corporation ....G 888 776-0942
Plymouth Meeting *(G-15854)*

Northeast Indus Batteries Inc ....E 215 788-8000
Bristol *(G-2172)*

Philadelphia Scientific LLC ....E 215 616-0390
Montgomeryville *(G-11414)*

Rm Battery Doctors LLC ....G 570 441-9184
Millville *(G-11227)*

BATTERIES: Wet

Axion Power Battery Mfg Inc ....E 724 654-9300
New Castle *(G-12061)*

Battery Builders Inc ....G 717 751-2705
Red Lion *(G-16590)*

Battery Zone ....F 800 371-5033
Bethlehem *(G-1458)*

C&D Technologies Inc ....C 215 619-2700
Blue Bell *(G-1820)*

CD Technologies Inc ....E 215 619-2700
Horsham *(G-7801)*

Energizer Battery Co ....G 215 572-0200
Jenkintown *(G-8286)*

Enersys Advanced Systems Inc ....D 215 674-3800
Horsham *(G-7816)*

Yuasa Battery Inc ....B 610 929-5781
Reading *(G-16571)*

BATTERY CASES: Plastic Or Plastics Combination

Greiner Packaging Corp ....F 570 602-3900
Pittston *(G-15754)*

BATTERY CHARGERS

C&D Intrntnal Inv Holdings Inc ....G 215 619-2700
Blue Bell *(G-1819)*

Exide Technologies ....C 717 464-2721
Lampeter *(G-8917)*

Exide Technologies ....G 610 269-0429
Downingtown *(G-4226)*

Exide Technologies ....G 724 239-2006
Charleroi *(G-3012)*

Exide Technologies ....E 610 921-4055
Reading *(G-16383)*

Exide Technologies ....G 304 345-5616
Rostraver Township *(G-16826)*

Northeast Indus Batteries Inc ....E 215 788-8000
Bristol *(G-2172)*

Power Products Inc ....G 610 532-3880
Sharon Hill *(G-17459)*

BATTERY REPAIR & SVCS

Computer Pwr Solutions PA Inc ....F 724 898-2223
Mars *(G-10491)*

BATTS & BATTING: Cotton

Milliken Nonwovens LLC ....G 610 544-7117
Broomall *(G-2298)*

BAUXITE MINING

Alcoa USA Corp 212 518-5400
Pittsburgh *(G-14666)*

Alcoa World Alumina LLC ....E 412 315-2900
Pittsburgh *(G-14670)*

Boke Investment Company ....A 412 321-4252
Pittsburgh *(G-14780)*

Compagnie Des Bxites De Guinee ......A 412 235-0279
Pittsburgh *(G-14870)*

Halco (mining) Inc ....A 412 235-0265
Pittsburgh *(G-15074)*

BEADS, WHOLESALE

James Jesse & Co Inc ....E 610 419-9880
Bethlehem *(G-1544)*

BEADS: Unassembled

James Jesse & Co Inc ....E 610 419-9880
Bethlehem *(G-1544)*

BEARINGS

Elliott Company ....D 724 379-5440
Donora *(G-4155)*

BEARINGS & PARTS Ball

Bearing Service Company PA ....D 412 963-7710
Pittsburgh *(G-14758)*

Cbh of Lancaster Company ....D 717 569-0485
Manheim *(G-10375)*

Hollow Ball Group LLC ....G 215 822-3380
Hatfield *(G-7351)*

Kingsbury Inc ....E 215 824-4000
Philadelphia *(G-13939)*

Metalkraft Industries Inc ....E 570 724-6800
Wellsboro *(G-19469)*

Precision Metal Pdts Co Inc ....F 724 758-5555
Ellwood City *(G-4947)*

Scheerer Bearing Corporation ....E 215 443-5252
Willow Grove *(G-20140)*

Scheerer Bearing Corporation ....E 215 443-5252
Horsham *(G-7848)*

Tribology Systems ....G 610 466-7547
Warminster *(G-18985)*

BEARINGS: Ball & Roller

Keystone North Inc ....E 570 662-3882
Mansfield *(G-10420)*

Proform Powdered Metals Inc ....E 814 938-7411
Punxsutawney *(G-16154)*

Royersford Fndry & Mch Co Inc ....E 610 935-7200
Phoenixville *(G-14576)*

SKF Motion Technologies LLC ....E 267 436-6000
Lansdale *(G-9411)*

Timken Company ....E 215 654-7606
Malvern *(G-10331)*

BEARINGS: Plastic

Allegheny Plastics Inc ....E 412 741-4416
Leetsdale *(G-9680)*

Enpro Industries Inc ....G 215 946-0845
Bristol *(G-2141)*

BEAUTY & BARBER SHOP EQPT

Adams Mfg Corp ....G 724 758-2125
Ellwood City *(G-4924)*

Arbco Industries LLC ....E 724 327-6300
Export *(G-5590)*

Bedford Manufacturing LP ....G 717 419-2680
Everett *(G-5566)*

Bg Industries LLC ....G 267 374-8565
Pennsburg *(G-13244)*

Bonland Industries Inc ....D 215 949-3720
Fairless Hills *(G-5774)*

Browning-Ferris Industries Inc ....G 814 453-6608
Erie *(G-5216)*

Construction Specialties Inc ....D 570 546-5941
Muncy *(G-11814)*

Danita Container Inc ....G 570 448-3606
Honesdale *(G-7709)*

Ft Pitt Acquisition Corp ....E 412 269-2950
Coraopolis *(G-3691)*

Galomb Inc ....G 610 434-3283
Allentown *(G-222)*

Hawke Aerospace Holdings LLC ....F 610 372-5141
Reading *(G-16399)*

Hawke Aerospace Holdings LLC ....G 610 372-5191
Morgantown *(G-11523)*

Horning Manufacturing LLC ....F 717 354-5040
New Holland *(G-12253)*

Idlewood Industries Inc ....G 724 624-1499
Beaver *(G-984)*

Innovative Manufacturing Svcs ....G 610 583-4883
Folcroft *(G-6006)*

Johnson Machine & Prod Inc ....G 570 724-2042
Wellsboro *(G-19467)*

Krem Cars/Racing Inc ....G 814 336-6619
Meadville *(G-10745)*

Millcraft Industries Inc ....C 412 281-7675
Pittsburgh *(G-15288)*

Mineral Manufacturing Corp ....E 814 643-0410
Huntingdon *(G-7951)*

Mt Chemical Company LLC ....G 570 474-2200
Mountain Top *(G-11767)*

Panache Plus ....G 717 812-8999
York *(G-20618)*

Philly Fades Inc ....G 678 672-9727
Phoenixville *(G-14567)*

Radio Parts Company ....E 412 963-6202
Pittsburgh *(G-15465)*

Tait Towers Manufacturing LLC ....G 717 626-9571
Lititz *(G-10052)*

Transtar Industries Inc ....G 412 441-7353
Pittsburgh *(G-15640)*

Veeco Precision Surfc Proc LLC ....D 215 328-0700
Horsham *(G-7863)*

BEAUTY SALONS

Marilyn Strawser Beauty Salon ....G 717 463-2804
Thompsontown *(G-18349)*

BEDDING, BEDSPREAD, BLANKET/SHEET: Pillowcase, Purchd Mtrl

American Textile Company Inc ....C 412 948-1020
Duquesne *(G-4494)*

BEDS & ACCESS STORES

Duckloe Frederick and Bros ....F 570 897-6172
Portland *(G-15939)*

BEDSPREADS & BED SETS, FROM PURCHASED MATERIALS

Lincoln Textile Pdts Co Inc ....D 484 281-3999
Bath *(G-965)*

Samuel Gerber Inc ....G 717 761-0250
Harrisburg *(G-7212)*

BEDSPREADS, FROM SILK OR MANMADE FIBER

Fabtex Inc ....D 910 739-0019
Danville *(G-4001)*

BEEKEEPERS' SPLYS

Keystone Industries ....F 717 866-7571
Myerstown *(G-11890)*

BEEKEEPERS' SPLYS: Bee Smokers

Pointer Hill Pets Inc ....G 610 754-7830
Bechtelsville *(G-1035)*

BEEKEEPERS' SPLYS: Honeycomb Foundations

Bee Positive Foundation ....G 484 302-8234
Phoenixville *(G-14530)*

BEER & ALE WHOLESALERS

Buddy Boy Winery ....G 814 772-3751
Ridgway *(G-16698)*

Gablers Beverage Distributors ....G 717 532-2241
Shippensburg *(G-17528)*

Northern Tier Beverage Inc ....G 570 662-2523
Mansfield *(G-10423)*

Raceway Beverage Center ....G 724 695-3130
Imperial *(G-8075)*

BEER & ALE, WHOLESALE: Beer & Other Fermented Malt Liquors

Brewers Outlet ....G 717 848-5250
York *(G-20413)*

City Btlg Co of New Kensington ....F 724 335-3350
New Kensington *(G-12334)*

Duquesne Distributing Co ....G 724 465-6141
Indiana *(G-8092)*

Kutztown Bottling Works Inc ....G 610 683-7377
Kutztown *(G-8847)*

Muller Inc ....C 215 676-7575
Philadelphia *(G-14044)*

Posties Beverages Inc ....G 570 929-2464
McAdoo *(G-10656)*

Stoudt Brewing Company ....E 717 484-4386
Adamstown *(G-24)*

BEER, WINE & LIQUOR STORES

Buddy Boy Winery ....G 814 772-3751
Ridgway *(G-16698)*

Gablers Beverage Distributors ....G 717 532-2241
Shippensburg *(G-17528)*

PRODUCT

BEER, WINE & LIQUOR STORES: Beer, Packaged

A&A Beverages Warehouse ....F 570 344-0024
Scranton (G-17204)
Alfreds Village Beverage Inc..............G....... 215 676-2537
Philadelphia (G-13363)
Cassidys Brew Zoo...............................G....... 814 946-2739
Altoona (G-487)
Duquesne Distributing Co.....................G....... 724 465-6141
Indiana (G-8092)
Kutztown Bottling Works Inc ....G....... 610 683-7377
Kutztown (G-8847)
Liberty Bell Bottling Co Inc ....G....... 610 820-6020
Allentown (G-294)
Pavlish Beverage Co Inc ....G....... 610 866-7722
Bethlehem (G-1592)
Potter Distributing Co...........................G....... 724 495-3189
Monaca (G-11294)
SMK & Son Inc ....G....... 215 455-7867
Philadelphia (G-14317)
Stoudt Brewing Company ....E 717 484-4386
Adamstown (G-24)
Superior Value Beverage Co ....G....... 610 935-3111
Phoenixville (G-14581)
Wheeland Inc ....F 570 323-3237
Williamsport (G-20091)
Wychocks Mountaintop Beverage ....G....... 570 474-5577
Mountain Top (G-11782)

BEER, WINE & LIQUOR STORES: Wine

Benignas Creek Vineyard & Wine ....G....... 570 546-0744
Muncy (G-11809)
Chaddsford Winery Ltd ....E 610 388-6221
Chadds Ford (G-2849)
First Class Specialties.........................F 724 446-1000
Herminie (G-7570)
Hawstone Hollow Winery LLC ....G....... 717 953-9613
Lewistown (G-9935)
Heritage Wine Cellars Inc ....F 814 725-8015
North East (G-12748)
Hunter Valley Winery ....G....... 717 444-7211
Liverpool (G-10078)
Liquor Control Board PA ....G....... 570 383-5248
Scranton (G-17255)
Nordberg John ....G....... 814 371-2217
Falls Creek (G-5856)
Oak Spring Winery Incorporated ....G....... 814 946-3799
Altoona (G-532)
Sand Castle Winery ....F 610 294-9181
Erwinna (G-5539)

BELLOWS

Aviva Technology Inc ....G....... 610 228-4689
Broomall (G-2279)
Gardan Manufacturing Company ....G....... 724 652-8171
New Wilmington (G-12466)
V2r2 LLC ....G....... 215 277-2181
Harleysville (G-7063)

BELTING: Rubber

Fenner Inc...D....... 717 665-2421
Manheim (G-10381)
Fenner Inc...G....... 717 665-2421
Manheim (G-10382)
Gates Corporation ....C....... 717 267-7000
Chambersburg (G-2935)

BELTING: Transmission, Rubber

Shingle Belting Inc..............................E 610 825-5500
King of Prussia (G-8674)

BELTS & BELT PRDTS

Fenner Inc...D....... 717 665-2421
Manheim (G-10381)
Fenner Inc...G....... 717 665-2421
Manheim (G-10382)
Fenner Dunlop Americas LLC ....C....... 412 249-0692
Pittsburgh (G-15012)

BELTS: Conveyor, Made From Purchased Wire

Apple Belting Company ....G....... 717 293-8903
Lancaster (G-8936)
Apx-Seetech Systems Inc ....G....... 717 751-6445
York (G-20383)

Fenner Dunlop Americas LLC ....C....... 412 249-0700
Pittsburgh (G-15013)
International Conveyor Rbr LLC ....G....... 724 343-4225
Blairsville (G-1726)
Victor-Balata Belting Company ....E 610 258-2010
Easton (G-4772)

BELTS: Money

Skyline Technology Inc ....G....... 610 296-7501
Malvern (G-10319)

BENTONITE MINING

American Colloid Company ....E 717 845-3077
York (G-20371)

BERYLLIUM

Materion Brush Inc ....C....... 610 562-2211
Shoemakersville (G-17572)

BEVERAGE BASES & SYRUPS

Byrnes and Kiefer Company ....E 724 538-5200
Callery (G-2467)
Imperial Beverage Systems Inc ....F 717 238-6870
Harrisburg (G-7154)
Multi-Flow Industries LLC ....C....... 215 322-1800
Huntingdon Valley (G-8015)
Quaker Oats Company ....C....... 570 474-3800
Mountain Top (G-11774)
Upinya Beverages LLC ....G....... 717 398-7309
Fairfield (G-5769)

BEVERAGE POWDERS

Mondelez Global LLC ....A....... 570 820-1200
Wilkes Barre (G-19945)

BEVERAGE PRDTS: Brewers' Grain

Something Wicked Brewing LLC...........G....... 717 316-5488
Hanover (G-6956)

BEVERAGE PRDTS: Malt Syrup

Kreiders Mulch ....G....... 717 871-9177
Washington Boro (G-19250)

BEVERAGE STORES

A&A Beverages Warehouse ....F 570 344-0024
Scranton (G-17204)

BEVERAGE, NONALCOHOLIC: Iced Tea/Fruit Drink, Bottled/Canned

Clover Farms Dairy Company...............B........ 610 921-9111
Reading (G-16346)
Schneiders Dairy Inc ....C....... 412 881-3525
Pittsburgh (G-15516)

BEVERAGES, ALCOHOLIC: Ale

Here and Now Brewing Co LLC ....G....... 570 647-6085
Honesdale (G-7713)
Lost Tavern Brewing LLC....................F 484 851-3980
Hellertown (G-7558)

BEVERAGES, ALCOHOLIC: Beer

2124 Brewing Company LLC ....G....... 724 260-8737
Pittsburgh (G-14624)
American Beer Beverage Ltd.................G....... 610 352-2211
Upper Darby (G-18679)
American Craft Brewery LLC ....B....... 610 391-4700
Breinigsville (G-2007)
Appalachian Brewing Co Inc ....D....... 717 221-1080
Harrisburg (G-7087)
B & B Beverage ....G....... 570 742-7782
Milton (G-11233)
B & S Beverage L L C ....G....... 814 674-2223
Patton (G-13187)
Bayfront Brewing Co ....G....... 814 333-8641
Meadville (G-10705)
Beer 4 Less ....G....... 724 452-7860
Zelienople (G-20791)
Beer Brothers ....G....... 610 438-3900
Easton (G-4652)
Beer To Go Inc ....G....... 610 253-2954
Easton (G-4653)
Benny Brewing Company LLC ....G....... 570 235-6995
Hanover Township (G-6980)

Bernies Beer & Beverage Inc...............G....... 215 744-1946
Philadelphia (G-13457)
Berrys Beverage Inc ....G....... 724 867-9480
Emlenton (G-5006)
Better World Spirits Inc ....G....... 717 758-9346
York (G-20402)
Bonn Place Brewing Inc ....G....... 845 325-6748
Bethlehem (G-1469)
Brewskees of Shiloh.............................G....... 717 764-2994
York (G-20414)
Bucks Cnty Brewing Distlg LLC ....G....... 215 766-7711
Pipersville (G-14612)
City Brewing ....F 724 532-5454
Latrobe (G-9466)
Clarion River Brewing Co ....G....... 814 297-8399
Clarion (G-3174)
Costar Brewing Inc ....G....... 412 401-8433
Pittsburgh (G-14877)
Cranberry Beverage Corp ....G....... 814 437-7998
Franklin (G-6123)
D G Yuengling and Son Inc ....E 570 622-4141
Pottsville (G-16075)
D G Yuengling and Son Inc ....E 570 622-0153
Pottsville (G-16076)
Desi S Interstate Beer ....G....... 814 528-5914
Erie (G-5246)
East Falls Beverage LLC......................G....... 215 844-5600
Philadelphia (G-13656)
Easton Beer ....G....... 215 884-1252
Glenside (G-6514)
Frankensteins..G....... 814 938-2571
Punxsutawney (G-16140)
Highway Manor Brewing ....G....... 717 743-0613
Camp Hill (G-2501)
Icb Acquisitions LLC ....F 412 682-7400
Pittsburgh (G-15112)
Jones Brewing Company Inc ....G....... 724 872-2337
Smithton (G-17661)
Kennedy Beverage LLC........................G....... 724 302-0123
Aliquippa (G-78)
Lackawanna Distributor Corp................G....... 570 342-8245
Dunmore (G-4476)
Lancaster Brewing Company ....E 717 391-6258
Lancaster (G-9090)
Lion Brewery Inc...................................C....... 570 823-8801
Wilkes Barre (G-19936)
Mary Ann Pensiero Inc ....G....... 717 545-8289
Harrisburg (G-7173)
Marzonies..D....... 814 695-2931
Duncansville (G-4456)
Miscreation Brewing ....G....... 717 698-3666
Hanover (G-6922)
Muller Inc ....C....... 215 676-7575
Philadelphia (G-14044)
Pennsylvania Brewing Company ....E 412 237-9400
Pittsburgh (G-15375)
Petes Beverage ....G....... 814 563-7374
Youngsville (G-20774)
Pittsburgh Brewing Company ....B....... 412 682-7400
Pittsburgh (G-15388)
Reclamation Brewing Company ....F 724 282-0831
Butler (G-2437)
SMK & Son Inc ....G....... 215 455-7867
Philadelphia (G-14317)
Stoudt Brewing Company ....E 717 484-4386
Adamstown (G-24)
Terry Baker ....G....... 717 263-5942
Chambersburg (G-2985)
Tk Beer Inc..G....... 610 446-2337
Upper Darby (G-18693)
Tower Hill Berery...................................G....... 267 308-8992
Chalfont (G-2893)
West End Beer Mart ....G....... 814 536-1846
Johnstown (G-8443)
Weyerbacher Brewing Co ....G....... 610 559-5561
Easton (G-4775)
Wilbos Inc ....G....... 267 490-5168
Quakertown (G-16259)
Ybc Holdings Inc...................................F 215 634-2600
Philadelphia (G-14499)

BEVERAGES, ALCOHOLIC: Beer & Ale

AR Tart LLC ....G....... 267 408-6507
Philadelphia (G-13404)
Battlefield Brew Works..........................G....... 717 398-2907
Gettysburg (G-6284)
Boneshire Brew Works..........................G....... 717 469-5007
Harrisburg (G-7098)
Boston Beer Company Inc ....C....... 610 395-1885
Breinigsville (G-2011)

(G-0000) Company's Geographic Section entry number

Brewers Outlet .... G 717 848-5250
   York (G-20413)
Broker Brewing Company LLC .... G 610 304-0822
   Creamery (G-3873)
Buddys Brews .... G 724 970-2739
   Lemont Furnace (G-9733)
Chesapeake Del Brewing Co LLC .... C 610 627-9000
   Media (G-10918)
Cnc Malting Company .... G 570 954-4500
   Fenelton (G-5944)
East End Brewing Company Inc .... F 412 361-2848
   Pittsburgh (G-14955)
Firewlkers Small Btch Dist LLC .... G 610 737-7900
   Coplay (G-3643)
Guys Round Brewing Company .... F 215 368-2640
   Lansdale (G-9374)
Linda K Woodward Inc .... G 610 791-3694
   Allentown (G-296)
McLaughlin Distillery .... G 315 486-1372
   Sewickley (G-17400)
ME 5 Cents LLC .... F 570 574-4701
   Hanover Township (G-6994)
Mindful Brewing Company LLC .... G 412 965-8428
   Pittsburgh (G-15290)
Mudhook Brewing Company LLC .... F 717 747-3605
   York (G-20606)
New Liberty Distillery .... G 800 996-0595
   Philadelphia (G-14067)
One Brew At A Time .... G 267 797-5437
   Morrisville (G-11575)
Philadelphia Beer Works Inc .... C 215 482-8220
   Philadelphia (G-14142)
Schnoch Corporation .... E 570 326-4700
   Williamsport (G-20070)
Sole Artisan Ales Llc .... F 570 977-0053
   Easton (G-4753)
South Hills Brewing Supply .... G 412 937-0773
   Monroeville (G-11356)
St Benjamins Brewing Co .... F 215 232-4305
   Philadelphia (G-14338)
Stickman Brews .... G 484 938-5900
   Royersford (G-16866)
Stickman Brews .... G 856 912-4372
   Wayne (G-19373)
Sunrise Naturals LLC .... G 717 350-6169
   Millersburg (G-11201)
Symphony Brewing Systems LLC .... G 215 493-0430
   Yardley (G-20342)
Victory Brewing Company LLC .... E 610 873-0881
   Downingtown (G-4261)
Victory Parkesburg .... G 610 574-4000
   Parkesburg (G-13183)
Vink & Beri LLC .... F 215 654-5252
   Montgomeryville (G-11426)

BEVERAGES, ALCOHOLIC: Brandy & Brandy Spirits

Galer Estates Vinyrd & Winery .... G 484 899-8013
   Kennett Square (G-8511)

BEVERAGES, ALCOHOLIC: Cordials

Chambord Et Cie Sarl .... E 215 425-9300
   Philadelphia (G-13523)
Charles Jacquin Et Cie Inc .... D 215 425-9300
   Philadelphia (G-13529)

BEVERAGES, ALCOHOLIC: Cordials & Premixed Cocktails

Hidden Still Inc .... G 717 270-1753
   Lebanon (G-9581)

BEVERAGES, ALCOHOLIC: Distilled Liquors

Allegheny Distilling LLC .... G 412 709-6480
   Pittsburgh (G-14677)
Bald Hills Distillery .... G 717 858-2152
   Dover (G-4184)
Blue Ridge Distillery LLC .... G 610 895-4205
   Saylorsburg (G-17103)
Blue Steel Distillery .... G 610 820-7116
   Allentown (G-155)
Bluebird Distilling LLC .... F 610 933-7827
   Phoenixville (G-14535)
Brandywine Branch Distillers .... G 610 326-8151
   Pottstown (G-15945)
Brandywine Branch Distlrs LLC .... G 610 901-3668
   Elverson (G-4962)

Central Penn Distilling .... G 717 808-7695
   Gettysburg (G-6285)
Custom Blends Inc .... G 215 934-7080
   Philadelphia (G-13592)
Dead Lightning Distillery .... G 717 695-0927
   New Cumberland (G-12185)
Dead Lightning Distillery LLC .... G 717 798-2021
   Lemoyne (G-9743)
Eight Oaks Craft Distillery Co .... G 484 387-5287
   New Tripoli (G-12455)
Five STS Dstlg Intl Sprits LLC .... G 610 279-5364
   Norristown (G-12659)
Hazards Distillery Inc .... G 717 994-4860
   Mifflintown (G-11121)
Kilimanjaro Distillery .... G 484 661-2488
   Allentown (G-282)
Manatawny Still Works .... G 484 624-8271
   Pottstown (G-16014)
Mason-Dixon Distillery .... G 717 314-2070
   Gettysburg (G-6306)
Midnight Madness Distlg LLC .... G 215 268-6071
   Trumbauersville (G-18532)
Mingo Creek Craft Distillers .... G 724 503-4014
   Washington (G-19207)
Moonshine Mine Distillery Inc .... G 814 749-3038
   Nanty Glo (G-11906)
Pennsylvania Pure Dstllries LLC .... F 412 486-8666
   Glenshaw (G-6496)
Pittsburgh Distilling Co LLC .... C 412 224-2827
   Pittsburgh (G-15394)
Pollyodd .... G 215 271-1161
   Philadelphia (G-14186)
Ponfeigh Distillery Inc .... G 919 606-0526
   Meyersdale (G-11018)
Port Pittsburgh Distillery LLC .... G 412 294-8071
   Pittsburgh (G-15420)
Social Still LLC .... E 610 625-4585
   Bethlehem (G-1621)
Tall Pines Distillery LLC .... G 814 442-2245
   Salisbury (G-17046)
This Life Forever Inc .... G 707 733-0383
   Lansford (G-9450)

BEVERAGES, ALCOHOLIC: Liquors, Malt

Big Valley Beverage Inc .... G 717 667-1414
   Reedsville (G-16622)
Jskc LLC .... G 724 933-5575
   Wexford (G-19809)
Southside Brew-Thru LLC .... G 814 254-4828
   Johnstown (G-8437)

BEVERAGES, ALCOHOLIC: Near Beer

Molly Pitcher Brewing Company .... G 717 609-0969
   Carlisle (G-2727)
Wissahickon Brewing Company .... G 267 239-6596
   Philadelphia (G-14480)

BEVERAGES, ALCOHOLIC: Neutral Spirits, Exc Fruit

Brave Spirits LLC .... G 610 453-3917
   Narberth (G-11909)

BEVERAGES, ALCOHOLIC: Vodka

Olifant USA Inc .... G 916 996-6207
   Camp Hill (G-2507)
Vodka Brands Corp .... G 412 681-7777
   Pittsburgh (G-15704)

BEVERAGES, ALCOHOLIC: Wines

A & R Nissley Inc .... E 717 426-3514
   Bainbridge (G-871)
A & R Nissley Inc .... G 717 541-1004
   Harrisburg (G-7078)
Adams Vintner LLC .... G 717 685-1336
   Annville (G-641)
Amore Vineyards and Winery .... G 610 837-1683
   Nazareth (G-11954)
Antler Ridge Winery .... G 570 247-7222
   Ulster (G-18597)
Arrowhead Wine Cellars Inc .... F 814 725-5509
   North East (G-12729)
Benignas Creek Vineyard & Wine .... G 570 546-0744
   Muncy (G-11809)
Benignas Creek Vineyard Wine .... G 570 374-4750
   Selinsgrove (G-17321)
Benignas Creek Vnyrd Wnery Inc .... G 570 523-4997
   Klingerstown (G-8805)

Big Creek Vineyard .... G 570 325-8138
   Jim Thorpe (G-8337)
Big Hill Winery .... G 717 226-8702
   Gardners (G-6259)
Black Walnut Winery .... G 610 857-5566
   Sadsburyville (G-16904)
Blair Vineyards .... G 610 682-0075
   Mertztown (G-11001)
Blue Mtn Vineyards & Cellars .... F 610 298-3068
   New Tripoli (G-12453)
Broad Mountain Vineyard LLC .... G 717 362-8044
   Elizabethville (G-4892)
Buddy Boy Winery & Vineyard .... F 717 834-5606
   Duncannon (G-4444)
Capra Collina Vineyard Inc .... G 570 489-0489
   Blakely (G-1746)
Chaddsford Winery Ltd .... E 610 388-6221
   Chadds Ford (G-2849)
Charles Jacquin Et Cie Inc .... D 215 425-9300
   Philadelphia (G-13529)
Christian W Klay Winery Inc .... F 724 439-3424
   Chalk Hill (G-2895)
Clover Hill Enterprises Inc .... E 610 395-2468
   Breinigsville (G-2012)
Country Creek Winery .... G 215 723-6516
   Telford (G-18278)
Courtyard Wineries LLC .... G 814 725-0236
   North East (G-12736)
Crossing Vineyards and Winery .... E 215 493-6500
   Washington Crossing (G-19255)
Cullari Vineyards & Winery Inc .... F 717 571-2376
   Hershey (G-7607)
Deer Creek Winery LLC .... D 814 354-7392
   Shippenville (G-17560)
Direnzo Inc .... G 215 740-6166
   Warrington (G-19115)
Eagle Rock Winery .... G 570 567-7715
   Williamsport (G-20009)
El Serrano Inc .... G 717 397-6191
   York (G-20465)
Fero Vineyards and Winery LLC .... F 570 568-0846
   Lewisburg (G-9907)
Foxburg Wine Cellars Inc .... G 724 659-0021
   Foxburg (G-6101)
Franklin Hill Vineyards Inc .... G 610 332-9463
   Bethlehem (G-1519)
Franklin Hill Vineyards Inc .... G 610 588-8708
   Bangor (G-914)
Franklin Hill Vineyards Inc .... G 610 559-8966
   Easton (G-4686)
Germantown Winery LLC .... G 814 241-8458
   Portage (G-15917)
Glades Pike Winery Inc .... F 814 445-3753
   Somerset (G-17689)
Glendale Valley Winery .... G 814 687-3438
   Flinton (G-5983)
Grace Winery LLC .... G 610 459-4711
   Glen Mills (G-6437)
Greenhouse Winery .... G 412 892-9017
   Pittsburgh (G-15063)
Grovedale Winery & Vinyard .... G 570 746-1400
   Wyalusing (G-20253)
Happy Vly Vinyrd & Winery LLC .... G 814 308-8756
   State College (G-17973)
Hauser Estate Winery .... D 717 334-4888
   Biglerville (G-1663)
Hawstone Hollow Winery LLC .... G 717 953-9613
   Lewistown (G-9935)
Heritage Wine Cellars .... G 724 748-5070
   Grove City (G-6790)
Hiwassee Acres LLC .... G 717 334-1381
   Gettysburg (G-6301)
James Kirkpatrick .... D 610 869-4412
   West Grove (G-19701)
Lacasa Narcisi Winery .... F 724 444-4744
   Gibsonia (G-6342)
Liquor Control Board PA .... G 570 383-5248
   Scranton (G-17255)
Maiolatesi Wine Cellar .... G 570 254-9977
   Scott Township (G-17185)
Marilake Winery LLC .... G 570 536-6575
   Childs (G-3131)
Mazza Chautauqua Cellars LLC .... G 814 725-8695
   North East (G-12751)
Mazza Vineyards Inc .... E 717 665-7021
   Manheim (G-10394)
Mobilia Fruit Farm Inc .... F 814 725-4077
   North East (G-12752)
Moon Dancer Vineyards & Winery .... G 717 252-9463
   Wrightsville (G-20242)

PRODUCT

Mountain Lake Winery LLC ....G..... 267 664-6343
   Towanda (G-18433)
Novosel LLC ....G..... 724 230-6686
   New Wilmington (G-12468)
Oak Spring Winery Incorporated ....G..... 814 946-3799
   Altoona (G-532)
Oliveros Vineyard LLC ....G..... 717 856-4566
   Mc Alisterville (G-10551)
Paradocx Vineyard LLC ....G..... 610 255-5684
   Landenberg (G-9252)
Pickering Winery ....G..... 570 247-7269
   Wysox (G-20290)
Pinnacle Ridge Winery ....G..... 610 756-4481
   Kutztown (G-8855)
Pittsburgh Winery ....G..... 412 566-1000
   Pittsburgh (G-15412)
Purple Cow Winery ....G..... 570 854-6969
   Bloomsburg (G-1797)
Radical Wine Company ....G..... 610 365-7969
   Lehighton (G-9723)
Ridgewood Winery ....G..... 484 509-0100
   Birdsboro (G-1705)
Robert Mazza Inc ....F...... 814 725-8695
   North East (G-12759)
Royal Welsh Winery ....G..... 724 396-7560
   Ligonier (G-9964)
Rushland Rdge Vineyards Winery ....G..... 215 598-0251
   Jamison (G-8246)
Sand Castle Winery ....G..... 484 924-9530
   Phoenixville (G-14578)
Shade Mountain Winery Inc ....G..... 570 837-3644
   Middleburg (G-11040)
Shawn Paul Zimmerman Kevin Joh .....G..... 814 594-1371
   Weedville (G-19459)
Sorrenti Orchards Inc ....G..... 570 992-2255
   Saylorsburg (G-17108)
Spitzenburg Cider House LLC ....G..... 484 357-2058
   Kempton (G-8494)
Spring Gate Vineyard ....F...... 717 599-5574
   Harrisburg (G-7218)
Starr Financial Group Inc ....G..... 814 236-0910
   Curwensville (G-3955)
Thistlethwaite Vineyards ....G..... 724 883-3372
   Jefferson (G-8271)
Thorn Hill Vineyards ....G..... 717 517-7839
   Lancaster (G-9218)
Tolino Vineyards LLC ....G..... 610 588-9463
   Bangor (G-931)
Totem Pole Ranch and Winery ....G..... 717 448-8370
   Carlisle (G-2742)
Twisted Vine Winery ....G..... 814 512-4330
   Kane (G-8479)
Unami Ridge Winery ....G..... 215 804-5445
   Quakertown (G-16253)
Vinoski Winery LLC ....G..... 724 872-3333
   Rostraver Township (G-16832)
Vivino Selections Inc ....G..... 412 920-1336
   Pittsburgh (G-15700)
Volant Enterprises Ltd ....G..... 724 533-2500
   Volant (G-18778)
Vynecrest LLC ....G..... 610 398-7525
   Breinigsville (G-2031)
Weathered Vineyards LLC ....G..... 484 560-1528
   New Tripoli (G-12462)
West Hanover Winery Inc ....G..... 717 652-3711
   Harrisburg (G-7246)
Whispering Oaks Vineyard ....G..... 570 495-4054
   Sunbury (G-18176)
Wilhelm Winery Inc ....G..... 724 253-3700
   Hadley (G-6823)
Windgate Vineyards Inc ....E...... 814 257-8797
   Smicksburg (G-17640)
Winery At Wilcox Inc ....G..... 412 490-9590
   Pittsburgh (G-15720)
Winery At Wilcox Inc ....E...... 814 929-5598
   Wilcox (G-19901)
Winery of Wilcox ....G..... 814 375-4501
   Du Bois (G-4428)
Winfield Winery LLC ....G..... 724 352-9589
   Cabot (G-2462)
Wooden Door Winery LLC ....G..... 724 889-7244
   New Kensington (G-12390)

BEVERAGES, MALT

Purblu Beverages Inc ....G..... 412 281-9808
   Pittsburgh (G-15456)

BEVERAGES, NONALCOHOLIC: Bottled & canned soft drinks

A&A Beverages Warehouse ....F...... 570 344-0024
   Scranton (G-17204)
Alfreds Village Beverage Inc ....G..... 215 676-2537
   Philadelphia (G-13363)
B&B Sales Consulting Corp Inc ....G..... 215 225-3200
   Philadelphia (G-13439)
Bottling Group LLC ....G..... 215 676-6400
   Philadelphia (G-13474)
Cassidys Brew Zoo ....G..... 814 946-2739
   Altoona (G-487)
Cbc Latrobe Acquisition LLC ....C...... 724 532-5444
   Latrobe (G-9462)
Coca Cola Refreshments US ....G..... 814 357-8628
   Howard (G-7887)
Coca-Cola Btlg Co of NY Inc ....C...... 718 326-3334
   Philadelphia (G-13556)
Coca-Cola Btlg Co Pottsville ....E...... 570 622-6991
   Reading (G-16349)
Coca-Cola Refreshments USA Inc ....E...... 570 839-6706
   Mount Pocono (G-11734)
Dahill Bottling Company Inc ....G..... 215 699-6432
   Blue Bell (G-1825)
Djquesne Bottling Company ....G..... 412 831-2779
   Pittsburgh (G-14927)
Duquesne Distributing Co ....G..... 724 465-6141
   Indiana (G-8092)
Gablers Beverage Distributors ....G..... 717 532-2241
   Shippensburg (G-17528)
Happy Valley Com ....G..... 814 238-8066
   State College (G-17972)
Jordan Draft Service ....G..... 412 382-4299
   Clairton (G-3152)
Liberty Bell Beverages ....G..... 610 799-6600
   Schnecksville (G-17141)
Mr TS Sixpack ....G..... 814 226-8890
   Clarion (G-3184)
Nestle Waters ....E...... 484 221-0876
   Breinigsville (G-2021)
Northern Tier Beverage Inc ....G..... 570 662-2523
   Mansfield (G-10423)
Pavlish Beverage Co Inc ....G..... 610 866-7722
   Bethlehem (G-1592)
Pbg Johnstown ....G..... 814 262-1125
   Johnstown (G-8420)
Pepsi-Cola Metro Btlg Co Inc ....E...... 814 834-5700
   Saint Marys (G-17005)
Potter Distributing Co ....G..... 724 495-3189
   Monaca (G-11294)
Quaker Oats Company ....C...... 570 474-3800
   Mountain Top (G-11774)
Reading Draft Birch Co ....G..... 610 372-2565
   Reading (G-16487)
Refresco Beverages US Inc ....F...... 484 840-4800
   Glen Mills (G-6441)
Roaring Spring Blank Book Co ....E...... 717 334-8080
   Gettysburg (G-6313)
Rochester Coca Cola Bottling ....D...... 717 730-2100
   Lemoyne (G-9752)
Rochester Coca Cola Bottling ....D...... 717 209-4411
   Lancaster (G-9190)
Rochester Coca Cola Bottling ....D...... 610 916-3996
   Reading (G-16502)
Rochester Coca Cola Bottling ....D...... 814 833-0101
   Erie (G-5465)
Rochester Coca Cola Bottling ....D...... 412 787-3610
   Houston (G-7879)
Shs Drinks Us LLC ....G..... 412 854-9012
   Pittsburgh (G-15535)
Six Pak Shack ....G..... 724 593-2401
   Jones Mills (G-8448)
Superior Value Beverage Co ....G..... 610 935-3111
   Phoenixville (G-14581)
Take Six ....G..... 814 237-4350
   State College (G-18035)
Victory Brewing Company LLC ....E...... 610 873-0881
   Downingtown (G-4261)
Wychocks Mountaintop Beverage ....G..... 570 474-5577
   Mountain Top (G-11782)
Zeiglers Beverages LLC ....E...... 215 855-5161
   Lansdale (G-9428)

BEVERAGES, NONALCOHOLIC: Carbonated

Pbg Philadelphia 2120 ....E...... 215 676-6401
   Philadelphia (G-14127)
Pepsi Co Inc ....G..... 717 792-2935
   York (G-20623)

Pepsi-Cola Metro Btlg Co Inc ....E...... 412 331-6775
   Mc Kees Rocks (G-10625)
Pepsi-Cola Metro Btlg Co Inc ....D...... 570 326-9086
   Williamsport (G-20056)
Pepsico Inc ....B...... 814 266-6005
   Johnstown (G-8423)
Terry Baker ....G..... 717 263-5942
   Chambersburg (G-2985)

BEVERAGES, NONALCOHOLIC: Carbonated, Canned & Bottled, Etc

Fentimans North America Inc ....F...... 877 326-3248
   Wilkes Barre (G-19921)
Hanks Beverage Company ....G..... 215 396-2809
   Southampton (G-17815)
Kutztown Bottling Works Inc ....G..... 610 683-7377
   Kutztown (G-8847)
Liberty Coca-Cola Bevs LLC ....F...... 215 427-4500
   Philadelphia (G-13969)
Pepsi-Cola Metro Btlg Co Inc ....D...... 570 344-1159
   Pittston (G-15775)
Reading Soda Works & Carbonic ....G..... 610 372-2565
   Reading (G-16491)
Shared Financial Services ....E...... 412 968-1178
   Pittsburgh (G-15528)

BEVERAGES, NONALCOHOLIC: Cider

Country Acres Cider & Prod Inc ....G..... 717 263-9349
   Waynesboro (G-19406)
Kime Cider Mill ....F...... 717 677-7539
   Bendersville (G-1139)

BEVERAGES, NONALCOHOLIC: Flavoring extracts & syrups, nec

Carbonator Rental Service Inc ....E...... 215 726-9100
   Philadelphia (G-13500)
David Michael & Co Inc ....F...... 909 887-3800
   Philadelphia (G-13608)
David Michael & Co Inc ....D...... 215 632-3100
   Philadelphia (G-13607)
Emericks Maple Products ....G..... 814 324-4536
   Hyndman (G-8049)
Knouse Foods Cooperative Inc ....C...... 717 677-9115
   Biglerville (G-1666)
Richards and Danielson LLC ....F...... 610 435-4300
   Allentown (G-375)
Ungerer Industries Inc ....D...... 610 868-7266
   Bethlehem (G-1647)
Welch Foods Inc A Cooperative ....B...... 814 725-4577
   North East (G-12766)
World Flavors Inc ....D...... 215 672-4400
   Warminster (G-19003)

BEVERAGES, NONALCOHOLIC: Fruit Drnks, Under 100% Juice, Can

Coca-Cola Company ....C...... 610 530-3900
   Allentown (G-172)
Everfresh Juice Co Pgh ....G..... 412 777-9660
   Mc Kees Rocks (G-10608)

BEVERAGES, NONALCOHOLIC: Soft Drinks, Canned & Bottled, Etc

Abarta Inc ....G..... 610 807-5319
   Bethlehem (G-1441)
American Bottling Company ....E...... 724 776-6111
   Cranberry Township (G-3802)
Biagio Schiano Di Cola Debora ....E...... 724 224-9906
   Natrona Heights (G-11935)
C S M Bottling Inc ....G..... 570 489-6071
   Jessup (G-8328)
City Btlg Co of New Kensington ....F...... 724 335-3350
   New Kensington (G-12334)
Coatesvlle Coca Cola Btlg Wrks ....E...... 610 384-4343
   Downingtown (G-4221)
Coca- Cola ....G..... 412 726-1482
   Pittsburgh (G-14864)
Coca-Cola Btlg of Lehigh Vly ....C...... 610 866-8020
   Bethlehem (G-1486)
Cola International LLC ....G..... 267 977-6700
   Bensalem (G-1170)
Cott Beverages Wyomissing Inc ....C...... 484 840-4800
   Concordville (G-3456)
Days Beverage Inc ....D...... 215 990-0983
   Newtown Square (G-12572)
Dr Pepper Snapple Group ....G..... 724 776-6111
   Cranberry Township (G-3816)

Glen Carbonic Gas Co ....F 570 779-1226
Plymouth **(G-15819)**

Keurig Dr Pepper Inc ....C 610 264-5151
Bethlehem **(G-1549)**

Keurig Dr Pepper Inc ....D 570 547-0777
Montgomery **(G-11372)**

Keurig Dr Pepper Inc ....D 717 677-7121
Aspers **(G-741)**

Lion Brewery Inc ....C 570 823-8801
Wilkes Barre **(G-19936)**

Natrona Bottling Works Inc ....G 724 224-9224
Natrona Heights **(G-11947)**

New Bern Pbg Pepsi ....G 570 320-3324
Williamsport **(G-20045)**

Pepsi Beverages Company ....E 412 778-4552
Mc Kees Rocks **(G-10624)**

Pepsi-Cola Btlg Co of Scranton ....D 570 344-1159
Pittston **(G-15774)**

Pepsi-Cola Metro Btlg Co Inc ....C 814 266-9556
Johnstown **(G-8422)**

Pepsi-Cola Metro Btlg Co Inc ....F 215 937-6102
Philadelphia **(G-14135)**

Posties Beverages Inc ....G 570 929-2464
McAdoo **(G-10656)**

Rochester Coca Cola Bottling ....E 570 655-2874
Pittston **(G-15782)**

Rochester Coca Cola Bottling ....E 724 834-2700
Greensburg **(G-6712)**

Rochester Coca Cola Bottling ....D 814 472-6113
Ebensburg **(G-4795)**

BEVERAGES, NONALCOHOLIC: Tea, Iced, Bottled & Canned, Etc

Galliker Dairy Company ....C 814 266-8702
Johnstown **(G-8374)**

Renewal Kombucha LLC ....G 484 525-3575
Lititz **(G-10040)**

Shangri-La Beverage LLC ....G 724 222-2222
Washington **(G-19225)**

BEVERAGES, WINE & DISTILLED ALCOHOLIC, WHOLESALE: Wine

Heritage Wine Cellars Inc ....F 814 725-8015
North East **(G-12748)**

Southern Glazer s Wine and Sp ....C 610 265-6800
King of Prussia **(G-8678)**

BEVERAGES, WINE/DISTILLED ALCOHOLIC, WHOL: Bttlg Wine/Liquor

Newman Wine & Spirits Gp LLC ....G 610 476-3964
Bryn Mawr **(G-2331)**

Vivino Selections Inc ....G 412 920-1336
Pittsburgh **(G-15700)**

BICYCLE SHOPS

Champion Choice Sports ....G 814 236-2930
Curwensville **(G-3948)**

BICYCLES, PARTS & ACCESS

Cycling Sports Group Inc ....D 203 749-7000
Bedford **(G-1048)**

Freeze Thaw Cycles ....G 814 272-0178
State College **(G-17966)**

BILLETS: Steel

AMG Resources Corporation ....E 412 777-7300
Pittsburgh **(G-14710)**

Larimer & Norton Inc ....G 814 435-2202
Galeton **(G-6240)**

BILLING & BOOKKEEPING SVCS

Monitor Data Corp ....F 215 887-8343
Glenside **(G-6530)**

Verizon Communications Inc ....C 570 387-3840
Bloomsburg **(G-1806)**

Verizon Pennsylvania Inc ....D 215 879-7898
Philadelphia **(G-14441)**

BINDING SVC: Books & Manuals

69th St Commercial Printers ....G 610 539-8412
Norristown **(G-12627)**

A J Printing ....F 610 337-7468
King of Prussia **(G-8575)**

Alcom Printing Group Inc ....C 215 513-1600
Harleysville **(G-7015)**

Apple Press Ltd ....E 610 363-1776
Exton **(G-5644)**

Benkalu Group Lmtd Ta Jaguar ....G 215 646-5896
Huntingdon Valley **(G-7965)**

Bestway Printing ....G 215 368-4140
Lansdale **(G-9346)**

Bonnie Kaiser ....G 215 331-6555
Philadelphia **(G-13471)**

Book Bindery Co Inc ....G 717 244-4343
Dallastown **(G-3972)**

Bridget Morris ....G 215 828-9261
Philadelphia **(G-13480)**

Brodart Co ....D 570 326-2461
Williamsport **(G-19995)**

Brookshire Printing Inc ....E 717 392-1321
Lancaster **(G-8961)**

Castor Printing Company Inc ....F 215 535-1471
Philadelphia **(G-13512)**

Champ Printing Company Inc ....E 412 269-0197
Coraopolis **(G-3675)**

Chernay Printing Inc ....D 610 282-3774
Coopersburg **(G-3625)**

Chrisber Corporation ....E 800 872-7436
West Chester **(G-19525)**

Christmas City Printing Co Inc ....E 610 868-5844
Bethlehem **(G-1483)**

Clinton Press Inc ....G 814 455-9089
Erie **(G-5227)**

Complete Hand Assembly Finshg ....E 215 634-7490
Philadelphia **(G-13563)**

Copy Management Inc ....E 610 993-8686
Malvern **(G-10217)**

Copy Management Inc ....F 215 269-5000
Huntingdon Valley **(G-7972)**

D & Sr Inc ....D 717 569-3264
Lancaster **(G-8989)**

Davco Advertising Inc ....E 717 442-4155
Kinzers **(G-8736)**

Digital-Ink Inc ....D 717 731-8890
Dillsburg **(G-4126)**

Dilullo Graphics Inc ....E 610 775-4360
Mohnton **(G-11262)**

Donald Blyler Offset Inc ....D 717 949-6831
Lebanon **(G-9561)**

Fedex Office & Print Svcs Inc ....E 412 856-8016
Monroeville **(G-11337)**

Fedex Office & Print Svcs Inc ....G 215 386-5679
Philadelphia **(G-13696)**

Fedex Office & Print Svcs Inc ....F 412 788-0552
Pittsburgh **(G-15009)**

Fedex Office & Print Svcs Inc ....F 412 366-9750
Pittsburgh **(G-15011)**

Fox Group Inc ....E 215 538-5380
Lansdale **(G-9370)**

Grafika Commercial Prtg Inc ....B 610 678-8630
Reading **(G-16396)**

Griffiths Printing Co ....F 610 623-3822
Lansdowne **(G-9433)**

Guy Coder ....G 814 265-0519
Brockway **(G-2227)**

Guy Hrezik ....G 610 779-7609
Reading **(G-16397)**

Hapsco Design and Prtg Svcs ....G 717 564-2323
Harrisburg **(G-7139)**

Harmony Press Inc ....G 610 559-9800
Easton **(G-4695)**

Harper Printing Service ....G 412 884-2666
Pittsburgh **(G-15082)**

Indiana Printing and Pubg Co ....C 724 349-3434
Indiana **(G-8106)**

Indus Graphics Inc ....G 215 443-7773
Warminster **(G-18896)**

Jim Mannello ....G 610 681-6467
Gilbert **(G-6362)**

John Galt Bndery Publ Svcs Inc ....E 724 733-1439
Export **(G-5611)**

Joseph Lagrua ....G 814 274-7163
Coudersport **(G-3783)**

K B Offset Printing Inc ....E 814 238-8445
State College **(G-17982)**

Kappa Graphics L P ....G 570 655-9681
Hughestown **(G-7893)**

Killeen Printing Co ....G 412 381-4090
Pittsburgh **(G-15177)**

Kisel Printing Service Inc ....E 570 489-7666
Dickson City **(G-4121)**

Labels By Pulizzi Inc ....E 570 326-1244
Williamsport **(G-20034)**

Lancaster General Svcs Bus Tr ....F 717 544-5474
Lancaster **(G-9095)**

Leon Spangler ....F 570 837-7903
Middleburg **(G-11028)**

Lesko Enterprises Inc ....C 814 756-4030
Albion **(G-46)**

Lsc Communications Us LLC ....A 717 392-4074
Lancaster **(G-9116)**

M & M Manufacturing Co ....E 724 274-0767
Cheswick **(G-3111)**

Maple Press Company ....C 717 764-5911
York **(G-20580)**

McCarty Printing Corp ....D 814 454-4561
Erie **(G-5385)**

McGivern Bindery Inc ....F 610 770-9611
Allentown **(G-312)**

Mdg Associates ....E 215 969-6623
Philadelphia **(G-14000)**

Mifflinburg Telegraph Inc ....G 570 966-2255
Mifflinburg **(G-11099)**

Minuteman Press ....G 412 621-7456
Pittsburgh **(G-15294)**

Minuteman Press ....G 724 846-9740
Beaver Falls **(G-1005)**

Movad LLC ....F 215 638-2679
Plymouth Meeting **(G-15858)**

National Publishing Company ....B 215 676-1863
Philadelphia **(G-14055)**

National Ticket Company ....C 570 672-2900
Paxinos **(G-13190)**

Npc Inc ....B 814 239-8787
Claysburg **(G-3207)**

Pace Resources Inc ....E 717 852-1300
York **(G-20616)**

Partners Press Inc ....F 610 666-7960
Oaks **(G-12935)**

Payne Printery Inc ....D 570 675-1147
Dallas **(G-3965)**

Pikewood Inc ....F 610 974-8000
Bethlehem **(G-1597)**

Pleasant Luck Corp ....G 215 968-2080
Newtown **(G-12537)**

Print Works On Demand Inc ....G 717 545-5215
Harrisburg **(G-7202)**

Print-O-Stat Inc ....E 717 812-9476
York **(G-20640)**

R R Donnelley & Sons Company ....C 215 671-9500
Philadelphia **(G-14225)**

Raff Printing Inc ....D 412 431-4044
Pittsburgh **(G-15466)**

Reed & Witting Company ....E 412 682-1000
Pittsburgh **(G-15476)**

Ricks Quick Printing Inc ....E 412 571-0333
Pittsburgh **(G-15485)**

Ridgways Inc ....E 215 735-8055
Philadelphia **(G-14250)**

Rowland Printing Inc ....E 610 933-7400
Phoenixville **(G-14575)**

S G Business Services Inc ....F 215 567-7107
Philadelphia **(G-14271)**

Sir James Prtg & Bus Forms Inc ....G 724 339-2122
New Kensington **(G-12377)**

Slavia Printing Co Inc ....G 412 343-4444
Pittsburgh **(G-15545)**

Specialty Group Printing Inc ....F 814 425-3061
Cochranton **(G-3351)**

Stauffer Acquisition Corp ....E 717 569-3200
East Petersburg **(G-4591)**

Sun Litho Print Inc ....F 570 421-3250
East Stroudsburg **(G-4636)**

Third Dimension Spc LLC ....G 570 969-0623
Scranton **(G-17301)**

Typecraft Press Inc ....E 412 488-1600
Pittsburgh **(G-15663)**

Unity Printing Company Inc ....E 724 537-5800
Latrobe **(G-9527)**

University Copy Service Inc ....G 215 898-5574
Philadelphia **(G-14429)**

Venango Training & Dev Ctr Inc ....D 814 676-5755
Seneca **(G-17371)**

Vocam Corp ....G 215 348-7115
Doylestown **(G-4344)**

Webb Communications Inc ....E 570 326-7634
Plymouth **(G-15824)**

BINDING SVC: Pamphlets

Parkland Bindery Inc ....G 610 433-6153
Allentown **(G-344)**

PRODUCT

BINDING SVC: Trade

Direct Mail Service Inc...............................D....... 412 471-6300
Pittsburgh (G-14925)

BINS: Prefabricated, Sheet Metal

Coopers...G....... 610 369-8992
Boyertown (G-1905)

BIOLOGICAL PRDTS: Bacterial Vaccines

Renaptys Vaccines LLC ....G....... 917 620-2256
Philadelphia (G-14240)

BIOLOGICAL PRDTS: Blood Derivatives

Cocalico Biologicals Inc.........................E....... 717 336-1990
Reamstown (G-16575)
Csl Behring LLC ....B....... 610 878-4000
King of Prussia (G-8601)
Immunotek Bio Centers LLC...................E....... 570 300-7940
Pittston (G-15756)
Immunotek Bio Centers LLC...................E....... 484 408-6376
Allentown (G-254)
Immunotek Bio Centers LLC...................E....... 814 283-6421
Altoona (G-516)

BIOLOGICAL PRDTS: Exc Diagnostic

Avax Technologies Inc ....E....... 215 241-9760
Philadelphia (G-13426)
Bioscience Management Inc....................F....... 484 245-5232
Allentown (G-152)
Biospectra Inc....................................E....... 610 599-3400
Bangor (G-908)
Biospectra Inc....................................D....... 610 599-3400
Stroudsburg (G-18108)
Eusa Pharma (usa) Inc ....E....... 215 867-4900
Langhorne (G-9295)
Fibrocell Science Inc ....D....... 484 713-6000
Exton (G-5678)
Fibrocell Technologies Inc.....................F....... 484 713-6000
Exton (G-5679)
Genomind LLC ....E....... 877 895-8658
Chalfont (G-2876)
Idera Pharmaceuticals Inc.....................D....... 484 348-1600
Exton (G-5695)
Integrated Tech Svcs Intl LLC ....F....... 814 262-7332
Johnstown (G-8382)
Krystal Biotech Inc ....E....... 412 586-5830
Pittsburgh (G-15202)
Merck Sharp & Dohme Corp ....C....... 215 631-5000
West Point (G-19762)
Novavax Execoffice ....G....... 484 913-1200
Malvern (G-10288)
Quotient Biodiagnostics Inc ....F....... 215 497-8820
Newtown (G-12541)
Rapid Pathogen Screening Inc ....E....... 718 288-4318
Montoursville (G-11449)
Renmatix Inc.......................................D....... 484 681-9246
King of Prussia (G-8669)
Safc Biosciences Inc ....G....... 610 750-8801
Reading (G-16507)
Sanofi Pasteur Inc ....A....... 570 839-7187
Swiftwater (G-18190)
Sanofi Pasteur Inc ....F....... 570 957-7187
Taylor (G-18261)
Sigma Biologics Inc ....G....... 215 741-1523
Yardley (G-20339)
Spark Therapeutics Inc ....C....... 888 772-7560
Philadelphia (G-14327)
Spectragenetics Inc ....G....... 412 488-9350
Pittsburgh (G-15570)
Sylvan Bio Inc ....G....... 724 543-3900
Kittanning (G-8798)
Tulip Biolabs Inc ....G....... 610 584-2706
Lansdale (G-9419)
Windtree Therapeutics Inc ....D....... 215 488-9300
Warrington (G-19140)
Wuxi Apptec Inc ....D....... 215 218-5500
Philadelphia (G-14492)

BIOLOGICAL PRDTS: Extracts

Herbal Extracts Plus ....G....... 215 245-5055
Bensalem (G-1209)

BIOLOGICAL PRDTS: Vaccines

Immunotope Inc ....G....... 215 489-4945
Doylestown (G-4307)

McM Vaccine Co ....G....... 570 957-7187
Swiftwater (G-18188)
Medimmune LLC ....B....... 215 501-1300
Bensalem (G-1225)

BIOLOGICAL PRDTS: Vaccines & Immunizing

Janus Biogenics LLC ....G....... 814 215-3013
Clarion (G-3180)
Richard J McMenamin Inc ....G....... 215 673-1200
Philadelphia (G-14246)

BIOLOGICAL PRDTS: Venoms

Lehigh Valley Venom Basbal CLB ....G....... 610 262-1750
Whitehall (G-19882)
River City Venom ....G....... 724 316-5886
Butler (G-2439)
Spider Venom Racing Pdts LLC ....G....... 484 547-1400
East Texas (G-4639)
Venom Power Sports ....G....... 717 467-5190
Dover (G-4206)

BIOLOGICAL PRDTS: Veterinary

Hersehy Veterinary Hospital ....F....... 717 534-2244
Hershey (G-7612)
Rockland Immunochemicals Inc ....D....... 484 791-3823
Pottstown (G-16041)

BIRTH CONTROL DEVICES: Rubber

Gothic Inc ....G....... 610 923-9180
Easton (G-4692)

BITUMINOUS & LIGNITE COAL LOADING & PREPARATION

Schuylkill Coal Processing ....G....... 570 875-3123
Ashland (G-736)

BITUMINOUS LIMESTONE QUARRYING SVCS

Martin Limestone Inc ....B....... 717 354-1370
East Earl (G-4549)
New Enterprise Stone Lime Inc ....F....... 717 442-4148
Gap (G-6254)

BLACKBOARDS & CHALKBOARDS

American Atelier Inc ....C....... 610 439-4040
Allentown (G-133)

BLACKBOARDS: Slate

Aywon Chalkboard Corkboard Inc ....E....... 570 459-3490
Hazleton (G-7491)
Berkheimer Realty Company Inc ....G....... 610 588-0965
Pen Argyl (G-13211)
Dally Slate Company Inc ....D....... 610 863-4172
Pen Argyl (G-13213)
Wirthmore Pdts & Svc Co Inc ....G....... 610 430-0300
West Chester (G-19680)

BLADES: Knife

Easy Use Air Tools Inc...........................G....... 412 486-2270
Allison Park (G-450)
Guardian Tactical Inc............................G....... 814 558-6761
Emporium (G-5062)

BLADES: Saw, Hand Or Power

York Saw & Knife Company Inc................E....... 717 767-6402
Emigsville (G-5003)

BLANKBOOKS & LOOSELEAF BINDERS

M & M Manufacturing Co ....E....... 724 274-0767
Cheswick (G-3111)
Wise Business Forms Inc ....D....... 724 789-0010
Butler (G-2449)

BLANKBOOKS: Albums

Crg Holding Inc ....G....... 215 569-9900
Philadelphia (G-13581)

BLANKBOOKS: Albums, Record

Get Hip Inc ....G....... 412 231-4766
Pittsburgh (G-15048)

HW Marston & Co..................................G....... 610 328-6669
West Chester (G-19565)

BLANKBOOKS: Passbooks, Bank, Etc

Kunz Business Products Inc ....C....... 814 643-4320
Huntingdon (G-7949)

BLANKBOOKS: Scrapbooks

Scrapbook Station ....G....... 724 287-4311
Butler (G-2440)

BLANKETS & BLANKETING, COTTON

East Cast Erosion Blankets LLC ....F....... 610 488-8496
Bernville (G-1298)

BLANKETS: Horse

Hillside Horse Sew-It ....G....... 717 548-2293
Peach Bottom (G-13199)

BLAST FURNACE & RELATED PRDTS

ATI Flat Rlled Pdts Hldngs LLC ....G....... 800 323-1240
Natrona Heights (G-11933)
Millcraft Industries Inc ....F....... 724 229-8800
Washington (G-19205)
Millcraft SMS Services LLC.....................C....... 724 222-5000
Washington (G-19206)

BLASTING SVC: Sand, Metal Parts

American Hard Chrome LLC ....G....... 412 951-9051
New Castle (G-12057)
Blastco ....G....... 215 529-7100
Quakertown (G-16173)
M & A Coatings LLC...............................F....... 724 267-2868
Washington (G-19196)

BLINDS & SHADES: Porch, Wood Slat

Columbia Porch Shade Co ....G....... 570 639-1223
Dallas (G-3961)

BLINDS & SHADES: Vertical

Age-Craft Manufacturing Inc...................F....... 724 838-5580
Greensburg (G-6648)
OEM Shades Inc ....E....... 724 763-3600
Sarver (G-17077)
Springs Window Fashions LLC ....E....... 570 547-6671
Montgomery (G-11378)
Vertical Access Solutions LLC ....G....... 412 787-9102
Pittsburgh (G-15693)
Vertical Access Solutions LLC ....F....... 412 787-9102
Lancaster (G-9234)

BLINDS : Window

Jerry Lister Custom Upholsteri ....G....... 215 639-3880
Bensalem (G-1213)
Jerry Lister Custom Upholsteri ....F....... 215 639-3882
Huntingdon Valley (G-8004)
New Home Window Shade Co Inc ....E....... 570 346-2047
Clarks Green (G-3189)
Nicholas Meyokovich ....G....... 724 439-0955
Uniontown (G-18638)
Penn Blind Manufacturing Inc ....F....... 610 770-1700
Allentown (G-347)
Worldwide Fabricating Ltd ....D....... 215 455-2266
Philadelphia (G-14489)

BLINDS, WOOD

Philadelphia Shutter Company ....G....... 610 685-2344
Temple (G-18335)

BLOCKS & BRICKS: Concrete

A Duchini Inc ....E....... 814 456-7027
Erie (G-5165)
Burrell Group Inc ....F....... 724 337-3557
New Kensington (G-12328)
Burrell Mining Products Inc ....F....... 724 966-5183
Waynesburg (G-19435)
CTS Bulk Terminals ....G....... 610 759-8330
Bethlehem (G-1491)
EP Henry Corporation ....E....... 610 495-8533
Parker Ford (G-13168)
Fizzano Bros Concrete Pdts Inc...............E....... 610 363-6290
Malvern (G-10235)
Fizzano Bros Concrete Pdts Inc...............G....... 215 355-6160
Langhorne (G-9298)

Hanover Brick and Block Co .... F 717 637-0500
  Hanover (G-6892)
Hanover Prest-Paving Company .... E 717 637-0500
  Hanover (G-6900)
Juniata Concrete Co .... G 717 567-3183
  Newport (G-12491)
Martin Limestone Inc .... D 717 354-1200
  New Holland (G-12258)
New Enterprise Stone Lime Inc .... E 814 443-6494
  Somerset (G-17698)
Oesterlings Concrete Co Inc .... G 724 282-8556
  Butler (G-2428)
Vcw Enterprises Inc .... D 610 847-5112
  Ottsville (G-13068)
Wendell H Stone Company Inc .... E 724 483-6571
  Charleroi (G-3025)
York Building Products Co Inc .... E 717 845-5333
  York (G-20727)
York Building Products Co Inc .... F 717 792-4700
  Thomasville (G-18345)
York Building Products Co Inc .... F 717 792-1200
  York (G-20730)
Young and Brothers Constuction ..... G 215 852-5398
  Philadelphia (G-14502)

BLOCKS: Glazed Face, Concrete

Trenwyth Industries Inc .... D 717 767-6868
  Emigsville (G-5002)

BLOCKS: Hat

View Works Inc .... G 724 226-9773
  Springdale (G-17905)

BLOCKS: Landscape Or Retaining Wall, Concrete

B V Landscape Supplies Inc .... G 610 316-1099
  Malvern (G-10191)
Colussy Enterprises Inc .... G 412 221-4750
  Bridgeville (G-2057)
Distinctive Outdoor Spaces LLC ...... F 484 718-5050
  Parkesburg (G-13173)
Green Scenes Landscape Inc .... G 610 566-3154
  Media (G-10930)
Hopper Lawn & Ldscp MGT LLC .... G 610 692-3879
  West Chester (G-19563)
Mountain-Valley Services LLC .... G 814 594-3167
  Ridgway (G-16718)
Refined Outoor Lvng Envirnmnts ..... G 412 635-8440
  Pittsburgh (G-15477)
Sweetwater Natural Pdts LLC .... G 610 321-1900
  Chester Springs (G-3086)

BLOCKS: Paving

Jason A Kreinbrook .... G 724 493-6202
  Natrona Heights (G-11944)

BLOCKS: Paving, Concrete

Cenprepavandcon .... G 215 778-6103
  Willow Grove (G-20111)
Techo-Bloc Corp .... C 610 863-2300
  Pen Argyl (G-13220)

BLOCKS: Paving, Cut Stone

EP Henry Corporation .... E 610 495-8533
  Parker Ford (G-13168)
William J Judge .... F 610 348-8070
  Collegeville (G-3400)

BLOCKS: Pillow, With Plain Bearings

Royersford Fndry & Mch Co Inc .... E 610 935-7200
  Phoenixville (G-14576)

BLOCKS: Plinth, Precast Terrazzo

Hawk Construction Products .... G 610 873-8658
  Downingtown (G-4233)

BLOCKS: Radiation-Proof, Concrete

Ray-Guard International Ltd .... G 215 543-3849
  Pottstown (G-16038)

BLOCKS: Standard, Concrete Or Cinder

A A Robbins Inc .... F 814 398-4607
  Cambridge Springs (G-2473)

Bauer Company Inc .... G 724 548-8101
  Kittanning (G-8756)
Beavertown Block Co Inc .... E 814 359-2771
  Bellefonte (G-1093)
Beavertown Block Co Inc .... F 814 695-4448
  East Freedom (G-4559)
Burrell Mining Products Inc .... F 724 339-2511
  New Kensington (G-12329)
C Strunk Inc .... G 610 678-1960
  Reading (G-16339)
Calcium Chloride Sales Inc .... G 724 458-5778
  Grove City (G-6781)
Castle Builders Supply Inc .... E 724 981-4212
  Hermitage (G-7573)
Castle Builders Supply Inc .... E 724 658-5656
  New Castle (G-12070)
Craigjill Inc .... E 570 803-0234
  Ashley (G-739)
Crete NYCE Co Inc .... E 215 855-4628
  Lansdale (G-9354)
Eastern Industries Inc .... E 570 265-9191
  Towanda (G-18425)
Fizzano Bros Inc .... D 610 833-1100
  Crum Lynne (G-3937)
Fizzano Bros Inc .... E 215 355-6160
  Feasterville Trevose (G-5910)
Fleetwood Building Block Inc .... F 610 944-8385
  Fleetwood (G-5973)
H&K Group Inc .... E 610 250-7703
  Easton (G-4694)
J A Kohlhepp Sons Inc .... E 814 371-5200
  Du Bois (G-4398)
Jdn Block Inc .... E 215 723-5506
  Souderton (G-17745)
Jokers Coal & Building Sups .... G 570 724-4912
  Wellsboro (G-19468)
Keystone Con Block Sup Co Inc .... E 570 346-7701
  Scranton (G-17251)
Klondike Block Masnry Sups Inc ...... G 724 439-3888
  Smithfield (G-17652)
Lane Holdings LLC .... E 412 279-1234
  Carnegie (G-2775)
Leonard Block Company Inc .... G 570 398-3376
  Jersey Shore (G-8317)
Lucisano Bros Inc .... E 215 945-2700
  Bristol (G-2162)
Martin Limestone Inc .... E 717 335-4500
  East Earl (G-4548)
Montgomery Block Works Inc .... F 724 735-2931
  Harrisville (G-7253)
Nitterhouse Masonry Pdts LLC .... D 717 268-4137
  Chambersburg (G-2963)
Oldcastle Apg Northeast Inc .... F 484 240-2176
  Allentown (G-338)
R I Lampus Company .... C 412 362-3800
  Springdale (G-17900)
R W Sidley Inc .... E 724 794-4451
  Slippery Rock (G-17625)
Riverview Block Inc .... G 570 752-7191
  Berwick (G-1342)
Santarelli Vibrated Block LLC .... F 570 693-2200
  Wyoming (G-20284)
Seymore Bros Inc .... E 814 944-2074
  Altoona (G-548)
Shaffer Block and Con Pdts Inc .... E 814 445-4414
  Somerset (G-17705)
Standard Concrete Products Co .... E 717 843-8074
  York (G-20679)
Swisher Concrete Products Inc .... E 814 765-9502
  Clearfield (G-3231)
Wool Concrete Block .... G 570 322-1943
  Williamsport (G-20099)
York Building Products Co Inc .... E 717 848-2831
  York (G-20726)
York Building Products Co Inc .... F 717 944-1488
  Middletown (G-11086)
York Building Products Co Inc .... F 717 324-2379
  York (G-20728)

BLOOD RELATED HEALTH SVCS

Custom Ultrasonics Inc .... D 215 364-1477
  Ivyland (G-8208)

BLOWERS & FANS

Advanced Design and Ctrl Corp .... F 215 723-7200
  Souderton (G-17720)
Air/Tak Inc .... F 724 297-3416
  Worthington (G-20226)
Beach Filter Products Inc .... G 717 235-1136
  Hanover (G-6862)

Bradford Allegheny Corporation .... D 814 362-2593
  Lewis Run (G-9874)
Brentwood Industries Inc .... D 717 274-1827
  Lebanon (G-9548)
Centria Inc .... C 412 299-8000
  Moon Township (G-11483)
Clarcor Air Filtration Pdts .... D 570 602-6274
  Pittston (G-15745)
Coil Specialty Co Inc .... E 814 234-7044
  State College (G-17952)
Diamond Power Intl Inc .... D 484 875-1600
  Exton (G-5667)
Eastern Manufacturing LLC .... G 215 702-3600
  Langhorne (G-9292)
Excelsior Blower Systems Inc .... F 610 921-9558
  Blandon (G-1753)
Flsmidth Inc .... A 610 264-6101
  Bethlehem (G-1513)
Galaxy Global Products LLC .... G 610 692-7400
  West Chester (G-19557)
Gardner Denver Holdings Inc .... F 814 742-9600
  Altoona (G-509)
Hauck Manufacturing Company .... D 717 272-3051
  Cleona (G-3244)
Hydra-Matic Packing Co Inc .... E 215 676-2992
  Huntingdon Valley (G-7995)
Kottcamp Sheet Metal .... E 717 845-7616
  York (G-20558)
Laminar Flow Inc .... D 215 672-0232
  Warminster (G-18909)
Lasko Products LLC .... G 610 692-7400
  West Chester (G-19588)
Loranger International Corp .... D 814 723-2250
  Warren (G-19038)
Marg Inc .... F 724 703-3020
  Oakdale (G-12906)
Matthey Johnson Inc .... B 610 341-8300
  Wayne (G-19352)
Met-Pro Technologies LLC .... E 215 822-1963
  Telford (G-18303)
Micro-Coax Inc .... C 610 495-4438
  Pottstown (G-16019)
Respironics Inc .... B 724 387-4270
  Monroeville (G-11354)
Respironics Inc .... C 724 334-3100
  New Kensington (G-12370)
Respironics Inc .... D 724 387-5200
  Murrysville (G-11865)
Skc Inc .... D 724 260-0741
  Eighty Four (G-4849)
Sp Environmental Inc .... E 724 935-1300
  Sewickley (G-17412)
Spectrum Control Inc .... C 814 835-4000
  Fairview (G-5844)
Tm Industrial Supply Inc .... E 814 453-5014
  Erie (G-5510)
Tps LLC .... C 570 538-7200
  New Columbia (G-12177)
USA Coil & Air Inc .... E 610 296-9668
  Malvern (G-10336)
Wayne Products Inc .... F 800 255-5665
  Broomall (G-2305)

BLOWERS & FANS

Jadco Manufacturing Inc .... E 724 452-5252
  Harmony (G-7070)
Jaybird Manufacturing Inc .... E 814 364-1800
  Centre Hall (G-2842)
RM Benney Technical Sls Inc .... G 724 935-0150
  Wexford (G-19828)
Robinson Fans Inc .... B 863 646-5270
  Zelienople (G-20817)
Robinson Fans Holdings Inc .... G 724 452-6121
  Zelienople (G-20818)
Strobic Air Corporation .... F 215 723-4700
  Telford (G-18321)

BLUEPRINTING SVCS

Fotorecord Print Center Inc .... G 724 837-0530
  Greensburg (G-6667)
Print-O-Stat Inc .... F 717 795-9255
  Mechanicsburg (G-10882)
Print-O-Stat Inc .... F 724 742-9811
  Cranberry Township (G-3845)
Print-O-Stat Inc .... G 610 265-5470
  King of Prussia (G-8664)
Procopy Inc .... F 814 231-1256
  State College (G-18010)
Semler Enterprises Inc .... G 717 242-0322
  Burnham (G-2361)

Tri-State Reprographics Inc ....F 412 281-3538
Pittsburgh (G-15647)
Wick Copy Center ....G 814 942-8040
Altoona (G-558)

BLUESTONE: Dimension

Balducci Stoneyard LLC ....G 410 627-0594
New Freedom (G-12201)
CK Stone LLC ....G 570 903-5868
Tunkhannock (G-18534)
Compton Quarry ....G 570 222-9489
Greenfield Township (G-6643)
J & E Flagstone ....F 570 869-2718
Laceyville (G-8871)
Mid-Life Stone Works LLC ....G 570 928-8802
Dushore (G-4509)
Rock Lake Inc ....F 570 465-2986
New Milford (G-12399)
Stoney Lonesome Quarry Inc ....G 570 434-2509
Kingsley (G-8709)

BOARDS: Stove, Sheet Metal

Alaska Stoker Stove Inc ....G 570 387-0260
Bloomsburg (G-1767)

BOAT BUILDING & REPAIR

Blackbird Industries Inc ....F 724 283-2537
West Sunbury (G-19769)
C & C Marine Maintenance Co ....C 724 746-9550
Houston (G-7868)
Coletech ....G 814 474-3370
Fairview (G-5816)
Daves Boat Repair LLC ....G 215 453-6904
Sellersville (G-17343)
Indian Lake Marina Inc ....G 814 754-4774
Central City (G-2839)
Rock Proof Boats ....G 717 957-3282
Marysville (G-10532)
Stoltzfus Trailer Sales Inc ....D 610 399-0628
West Chester (G-19645)

BOAT BUILDING & REPAIRING: Fiberglass

24-7 Innovations LLC ....G 570 676-8888
Greentown (G-6732)
George Kranich ....G 610 295-2039
Marcus Hook (G-10442)

BOAT BUILDING & REPAIRING: Houseboats

Mellinger Manufacturing Co Inc ....F 717 464-3318
Willow Street (G-20154)

BOAT BUILDING & REPAIRING: Jet Skis

Hydrosource ....F 570 676-8500
Canadensis (G-2530)

BOAT BUILDING & REPAIRING: Kayaks

P S Composites Inc ....G 724 329-4413
Markleysburg (G-10483)

BOAT DEALERS

Stoltzfus Trailer Sales Inc ....D 610 399-0628
West Chester (G-19645)

BOAT DEALERS: Marine Splys & Eqpt

Marine Acquisition US Inc ....E 610 495-7011
Limerick (G-9970)

BOAT DEALERS: Motor

Indian Lake Marina Inc ....G 814 754-4774
Central City (G-2839)

BOAT YARD: Boat yards, storage & incidental repair

Indian Lake Marina Inc ....G 814 754-4774
Central City (G-2839)
Leco Corporation ....E 814 355-7903
Bellefonte (G-1107)

BODIES: Truck & Bus

East Penn Truck Eqp W Inc ....G 724 342-1800
Mercer (G-10961)
East Penn Truck Equipment Inc ....G 610 694-9234
Bethlehem (G-1500)

Harners Auto Body Inc ....G 610 385-3825
Birdsboro (G-1698)
J Thomas Ltd ....E 717 397-3483
Lancaster (G-9069)
Jones Performance Products Inc ....D 724 528-3569
West Middlesex (G-19727)
Metalsa SA De CV ....C 610 371-7000
Reading (G-16441)
New Harrisburg Truck Body Co ....E 717 766-7651
Mechanicsburg (G-10873)
Riggs Industries Inc ....F 814 629-5621
Stoystown (G-18085)
Rizworks ....G 570 226-7611
Hawley (G-7437)
Statler Body Works Inc ....G 717 261-5936
Chambersburg (G-2978)
Strick Corporation ....F 215 949-3600
Fairless Hills (G-5799)

BODY PARTS: Automobile, Stamped Metal

Cardone Industries Inc ....B 215 912-3000
Philadelphia (G-13504)
Century Motors Inc ....G 215 724-8845
Philadelphia (G-13521)
Colours Inc ....G 814 542-4215
Mount Union (G-11740)
Eugene Zapsky ....G 814 378-6157
Madera (G-10163)
Finish Technology Inc ....E 570 421-4110
Stroudsburg (G-18120)
Metro Manufacturing & Supply ....G 610 891-1899
Media (G-10939)
Mikey Gs ....G 717 820-4053
Jonestown (G-8450)
Osterwalder Inc ....G 570 325-2500
Northampton (G-12858)
Sikkens Inc ....G 610 337-8710
King of Prussia (G-8675)
Sjm Manufacturing Inc ....G 724 478-5580
Apollo (G-685)
Waupaca Foundry Inc ....C 570 724-5191
Tioga (G-18367)
Waupaca Foundry Inc ....B 570 827-3245
Tioga (G-18368)

BOILER & HEATING REPAIR SVCS

Temperature Ctrl Professionals ....G 215 295-1616
Fairless Hills (G-5803)
V P L Inc ....G 814 652-6767
Everett (G-5579)

BOILER GAGE COCKS

Quadax Valves Inc ....F 713 429-5458
Bristol (G-2191)

BOILER REPAIR SHOP

Cannon Boiler Works Inc ....D 724 335-8541
New Kensington (G-12332)
Crees Wldg & Fabrication Inc ....G 717 795-8711
Mechanicsburg (G-10832)
Mobile Welding & Boiler Repair ....F 610 253-9688
Easton (G-4725)

BOILERS & BOILER SHOP WORK

Advanced Thermal Hydronics ....F 610 473-1036
Boyertown (G-1894)
Munroe Incorporated ....D 412 231-0600
Pittsburgh (G-15311)
Penn Separator Corp ....E 814 849-7328
Brookville (G-2269)
Pressure-Tech Inc ....F 717 597-1868
Greencastle (G-6628)
Richardson Coolg Packages LLC ....E 724 698-2302
New Castle (G-12142)

BOILERS: Low-Pressure Heating, Steam Or Hot Water

Axeman-Anderson Company ....E 570 326-9114
Williamsport (G-19991)
Boyertown Foundry Company ....C 610 473-1000
Boyertown (G-1899)
Burnham Holdings Inc ....E 717 390-7800
Lancaster (G-8964)
Columbia Boiler Company ....E 610 323-9200
Pottstown (G-15972)
Crown Boiler Co ....E 215 535-8900
Philadelphia (G-13586)

BOLTS: Metal

B&G Manufacturing Co Inc ....C 215 822-1925
Hatfield (G-7319)
Baden Steelbar & Bolt Corp ....F 724 266-3003
Sewickley (G-17383)
East Coast Metals Inc ....E 215 256-9550
Harleysville (G-7031)
Erie Bolt Corporation ....D 814 456-4287
Blairsville (G-1720)
J B Booth and Co ....F 724 452-8400
Zelienople (G-20805)
J B Booth and Co ....G 724 452-1313
Zelienople (G-20806)
Jennmar Corp of West Virginia ....E 412 963-9071
Pittsburgh (G-15149)
Pittsburgh Bolt Company LLC ....G 724 935-6844
Wexford (G-19820)
Rocwel Industries Inc ....G 610 459-5490
Concordville (G-3458)
S & S Fasteners Inc ....G 724 251-9288
Ambridge (G-632)
Watson Metal Products Corp ....D 908 276-2202
Lancaster (G-9236)

BOLTS: Wooden, Hewn

Koppers Utility Indus Pdts Inc ....D 412 620-6238
Pittsburgh (G-15193)

BONDERIZING: Bonderizing, Metal Or Metal Prdts

Ems Engnred Mtls Solutions LLC ....D 610 562-3841
Hamburg (G-6838)

BOOK STORES

Brodart Co ....D 570 326-2461
Williamsport (G-19995)
Dorrance Publishing Co Inc ....E 800 788-7654
Pittsburgh (G-14934)
Fab Universal Corp ....F 412 621-0902
Pittsburgh (G-15002)
Lemar Mast ....G 610 286-0258
Morgantown (G-11524)
Mechling Associates Inc ....F 724 287-2120
Butler (G-2422)
Zur Ltd ....E 717 761-7044
Camp Hill (G-2528)

BOOK STORES: Religious

Bible Lighthouse Inc ....G 570 888-6615
Sayre (G-17111)
Grace Press Inc ....F 717 354-0475
Ephrata (G-5107)

BOOKS, WHOLESALE

Brodart Co ....D 570 326-2461
Williamsport (G-19995)
Paul Withers ....G 717 896-3173
Halifax (G-6827)
Stan Clark Military Books ....G 717 337-1728
Gettysburg (G-6315)
Taylor & Francis Inc ....D 215 625-8900
Philadelphia (G-14378)
Thomas ....G 717 642-6600
Gettysburg (G-6318)
Whitaker Corporation ....C 724 334-7000
New Kensington (G-12389)

BOOTHS: Spray, Sheet Metal, Prefabricated

WD Services Inc ....G 610 970-7946
Pottstown (G-16071)

BOOTS: Men's

Abilene Boot Co Inc ....E 814 445-6545
Somerset (G-17672)
C & J Clark America Inc ....D 717 632-2444
Hanover (G-6864)
Vf Outdoor LLC ....G 610 265-2193
King of Prussia (G-8696)

BOOTS: Women's

Abilene Boot Co Inc ....E 814 445-6545
Somerset (G-17672)

BOTTLE CAPS & RESEALERS: Plastic

Aspire Technologies ....G...... 610 491-8162
King of Prussia (G-8586)
Berry Global Inc ....B...... 570 759-6240
Berwick (G-1309)
Berry Global Inc ....E...... 717 299-6511
Lancaster (G-8952)

BOTTLED GAS DEALERS: Propane

Demarchi John ....G...... 724 547-6440
Mount Pleasant (G-11696)
Lancaster Propane Gas Inc ....F...... 717 898-0800
Lancaster (G-9104)
Potter Distributing Co ....G...... 724 495-3189
Monaca (G-11294)

BOTTLED WATER DELIVERY

Superior Value Beverage Co ....G...... 610 935-3111
Phoenixville (G-14581)
Trilli Holdings Inc ....G...... 724 736-8000
Star Junction (G-17938)

BOTTLES: Plastic

Alpha Packaging North East Inc ....D...... 610 974-9001
Bethlehem (G-1448)
Alpla Inc ....E...... 770 914-1407
Bethlehem (G-1449)
Consolidated Container Co LLC ....D...... 724 658-4578
New Castle (G-12075)
Consolidated Container Co LLC ....D...... 412 828-1111
Verona (G-18754)
Consolidated Container Co LLC ....C...... 570 759-0823
Berwick (G-1319)
Diamond Drinks Inc ....D...... 570 326-2003
Williamsport (G-20005)
Drug Plastics and Glass Inc ....D...... 724 548-5654
Kittanning (G-8767)
Drug Plastics and Glass Co Inc ....D...... 570 672-3215
Elysburg (G-4975)
Graham Packaging Company LP ....E...... 717 849-8700
York (G-20509)
Graham Packaging Company LP ....E...... 717 849-8500
York (G-20511)
Mohawk Inc ....G...... 717 243-9231
Carlisle (G-2726)
Novapak Corporation ....F...... 717 266-6687
Manchester (G-10359)
Pvc Container Corporation ....G...... 570 384-3930
Hazle Township (G-7476)
Pvc Container Corporation ....D...... 717 266-9100
Manchester (G-10363)
Sean S Zuniga ....G...... 215 757-2676
Langhorne (G-9324)
Silgan Plastics LLC ....D...... 215 727-2676
Langhorne (G-9325)
Springdale Specialty Plas Inc ....E...... 724 274-4144
Springdale (G-17901)
Staychilled Usa LLC ....G...... 215 284-6018
Plymouth Meeting (G-15874)
Suscon Inc ....D...... 570 326-2003
Williamsport (G-20078)
West Pharmaceutical Svcs Inc ....E...... 610 594-2900
Exton (G-5748)

BOULDER: Crushed & Broken

Allan Myers Inc ....E...... 717 442-4191
Paradise (G-13152)
Blue Mountain Buildng Stone Co ....G...... 717 671-8711
Harrisburg (G-7096)

BOUTIQUE STORES

A Tru Diva LLC ....G...... 888 400-1034
Brookhaven (G-2241)
Imposters LLC ....G...... 412 781-3443
Pittsburgh (G-15115)
Roberta Weissburg Leathers ....G...... 412 681-8188
Pittsburgh (G-15494)

BOWLING EQPT & SPLY STORES

Terre Trophy Co ....G...... 610 777-2050
Reading (G-16536)

BOWLING EQPT & SPLYS

T & J Bowling Products Corp ....F...... 717 428-0100
Jacobus (G-8231)

BOX & CARTON MANUFACTURING EQPT

Sig Combibloc Inc ....E...... 610 546-4200
Chester (G-3062)

BOXES & CRATES: Rectangular, Wood

Howe Wood Products Inc ....F...... 717 266-9855
York (G-20529)
JB Mill & Fabricating Inc ....E...... 724 202-6814
New Castle (G-12108)
Newshams Woodshop Inc ....E...... 610 622-5800
Clifton Heights (G-3256)
Treen Box & Pallet Corp ....E...... 717 535-5800
Mifflintown (G-11136)
Ufp Gordon LLC ....E...... 570 875-2811
Gordon (G-6547)

BOXES & SHOOK: Nailed Wood

Achieva ....D...... 412 221-6609
Bridgeville (G-2052)
Achieva ....D...... 412 995-5000
Pittsburgh (G-14640)
JB Mill & Fabricating Inc ....E...... 724 202-6814
New Castle (G-12108)
Molded Fiber Glass Companies ....C...... 814 683-4500
Linesville (G-9984)
Overend & Krill Lumber Inc ....G...... 724 348-7511
Finleyville (G-5962)
Sheffield Container Corp ....E...... 814 968-3287
Sheffield (G-17483)
Treen Box & Pallet Corp ....E...... 717 535-5800
Mifflintown (G-11136)
Wayne Lawson ....G...... 814 757-8424
Russell (G-16882)

BOXES: Corrugated

Acme Corrugated Box Co Inc ....C...... 215 444-8000
Hatboro (G-7264)
Alden Industries Inc ....G...... 267 460-8904
North Wales (G-12787)
Alpha Packaging Corporation ....F...... 610 926-5100
Mohrsville (G-11273)
Beacon Container Corporation ....C...... 610 582-2222
Birdsboro (G-1688)
Beacon Container Corporation ....E...... 570 433-3800
Montoursville (G-11433)
Brown Jr Merritt ....G...... 610 253-0425
Easton (G-4658)
Buckeye Corrugated Inc ....E...... 717 684-6921
Columbia (G-3432)
Cas Pack Corporation ....E...... 215 254-7225
Bensalem (G-1165)
Century Packaging Co Inc ....E...... 610 262-8860
Whitehall (G-19864)
Cor-Rite Corrugated Inc ....F...... 570 287-1718
Kingston (G-8714)
David Weber Co Inc ....C...... 215 426-3500
Philadelphia (G-13610)
Dee Paper Company Inc ....D...... 610 876-9285
Chester (G-3046)
Duerr Packaging Company Inc ....E...... 724 695-2226
Imperial (G-8064)
Edwin Bell Cooperage Company ....E...... 412 221-1830
Cuddy (G-3942)
Fitzpatrick Container Company ....E...... 215 699-3515
Allentown (G-214)
Freedom Corrugated LLC ....E...... 570 384-7500
Hazle Township (G-7458)
Gateway Packaging Corp ....E...... 724 327-7400
Export (G-5607)
Georgia-Pacific LLC ....B...... 610 250-1400
Easton (G-4690)
Georgia-Pacific LLC ....C...... 717 266-3621
Mount Wolf (G-11747)
Georgia-Pacific LLC ....C...... 814 368-8700
Bradford (G-1969)
H P Cadwallader Inc ....E...... 215 256-6651
Harleysville (G-7036)
International Paper Company ....D...... 717 677-8121
Biglerville (G-1664)
International Paper Company ....C...... 570 339-1611
Mount Carmel (G-11625)
International Paper Company ....E...... 610 268-5456
Toughkenamon (G-18419)
Interstate Cont Brunswick LLC ....E...... 610 208-9300
Reading (G-16408)
M & G Packaging Corp ....F...... 610 363-7455
Exton (G-5707)

Menasha Packaging Company LLC .....G...... 570 243-5512
Tobyhanna (G-18407)
Menasha Packaging Company LLC .....C...... 630 236-4925
Bethlehem (G-1567)
Menasha Packaging Company LLC .....E...... 717 776-2900
Newville (G-12607)
Menasha Packaging Company LLC .....D...... 800 477-8746
York (G-20587)
Menasha Packaging Company LLC .....E...... 800 477-8746
York (G-20588)
Menasha Packaging Company LLC .....C...... 215 426-7110
Philadelphia (G-14008)
Montco Packaging Co Inc ....G...... 610 935-9545
Phoenixville (G-14562)
Montgomery Products Ltd ....E...... 610 933-2500
Phoenixville (G-14563)
Multicell North Inc ....F...... 610 683-9000
Kutztown (G-8850)
Packaging Corp O ....G...... 717 293-2877
Lancaster (G-9158)
Packaging Corporation America ....E...... 301 497-9090
Hanover (G-6929)
Packaging Corporation America ....G...... 610 366-6501
Allentown (G-342)
Packaging Corporation America ....G...... 610 366-6500
Allentown (G-343)
Packaging Corporation America ....E...... 610 916-3200
Reading (G-16462)
Packaging Corporation America ....D...... 724 275-3700
Cheswick (G-3114)
Packaging Corporation America ....C...... 717 397-3591
Lancaster (G-9159)
Packaging Corporation America ....E...... 717 637-3758
Hanover (G-6931)
Packaging Corporation America ....F...... 717 653-0420
Manheim (G-10398)
Paperworks Industries Inc ....C...... 215 984-7000
Bala Cynwyd (G-888)
PCA Corrugated and Display LLC ....G...... 800 572-6061
Hanover (G-6932)
PCA Corrugated and Display LLC ....G...... 800 572-6061
Hanover (G-6933)
PCA Corrugated and Display LLC ....G...... 800 572-6061
Hanover (G-6934)
PCA Corrugated and Display LLC ....D...... 717 624-2122
New Oxford (G-12421)
PCA Corrugated and Display LLC ....G...... 610 489-8740
Collegeville (G-3386)
Perkasie Container Corporation ....F...... 215 257-3683
Perkasie (G-13287)
Pratt Industries USA Inc ....D...... 610 967-6027
Emmaus (G-5040)
Pro Pac Inc ....G...... 717 646-9555
Hanover (G-6938)
PSI Container Inc ....D...... 570 929-1600
McAdoo (G-10658)
PSI Packaging Services Inc ....E...... 724 626-0100
Connellsville (G-3506)
Reliance Packaging & Supply Co ....G...... 724 468-8849
Export (G-5624)
Roaring Spring Blank Book Co ....B...... 814 224-2306
Roaring Spring (G-16768)
S & G Corrugated Packaging Inc ....C...... 570 287-1718
Swoyersville (G-18198)
Schrage Box & Design Inc ....F...... 215 604-0800
Bensalem (G-1252)
Service Die Cutng & Packg Corp ....F...... 215 739-8809
Philadelphia (G-14294)
Sonoco Display & Packaging LLC ....C...... 717 757-2683
York (G-20672)
Southern Container Corp ....C...... 717 393-0436
Lancaster (G-9203)
St Marys Box Company ....E...... 814 834-3819
Saint Marys (G-17015)
Strine Corrugated Products ....G...... 717 764-4800
Emigsville (G-5000)
Tri-State Container Corp ....E...... 215 638-1311
Bensalem (G-1263)
Tyoga Container Company Inc ....E...... 570 835-5295
Tioga (G-18366)
US Corrugated Inc ....E...... 724 345-2050
Washington (G-19237)
Westrock Cp LLC ....G...... 610 485-8700
Aston (G-798)
Westrock Rkt LLC ....G...... 717 393-0436
Lancaster (G-9239)
Westrock Usc Inc ....G...... 724 938-3020
Coal Center (G-3278)
York Container Company ....C...... 717 757-7611
York (G-20733)

PRODUCT

BOXES: Filing, Paperboard Made From Purchased Materials

Albright Paper & Box Corp ....G....... 484 524-8424
Boyertown *(G-1895)*

Concept Products Corporation ....G....... 610 722-0830
Mertztown *(G-11002)*

Pittsburgh File & Box Co....................G....... 412 431-5465
Pittsburgh *(G-15396)*

BOXES: Junction, Electric

Cott Manufacturing Company..............F 412 675-0101
Glassport *(G-6410)*

Cott Manufacturing Company..............E 724 625-3730
Glassport *(G-6411)*

Penn Panel & Box Company ....E 610 586-2700
Collingdale *(G-3409)*

BOXES: Mail Or Post Office, Collection/Storage, Sheet Metal

North American Mfg Co........................E 570 348-1163
Scranton *(G-17266)*

BOXES: Outlet, Electric Wiring Device

Electrical Design Developm.................G....... 412 747-4970
Pittsburgh *(G-14962)*

BOXES: Packing & Shipping, Metal

Daniel C Tanney Inc ....D...... 215 639-3131
Bensalem *(G-1179)*

Moore Push Pin Company ....D...... 215 233-5700
Glenside *(G-6531)*

BOXES: Paperboard, Folding

Beistle Company...................................B 717 532-2131
Shippensburg *(G-17517)*

Corrugated Specialties ....F 814 337-5705
Meadville *(G-10715)*

Corrugated Specialties ....F 814 337-5705
Meadville *(G-10714)*

Duerr Packaging Company Inc ....E 724 695-2226
Imperial *(G-8064)*

Graphic Packaging Intl LLC ....C...... 610 935-4000
Phoenixville *(G-14551)*

K & L Operating Co ....G....... 215 646-0760
Ambler *(G-584)*

Menasha Packaging Company LLC .....E 800 477-8746
York *(G-20588)*

Midvale Paper Box Company.................G....... 610 649-6992
Haverford *(G-7413)*

Midvale Paper Box Company.................F 570 824-3577
Plains *(G-15786)*

Northeastern PA Carton Co Inc ....E 570 457-7711
Moosic *(G-11510)*

Opi Holdings Inc ....E 610 857-2000
Old Forge *(G-12973)*

Prestige Gift Box Systems ....F 610 865-6768
Bethlehem *(G-1605)*

Service Die Cutng & Packg Corp...........F 215 739-8809
Philadelphia *(G-14294)*

Southern Container Corp ....C...... 717 393-0436
Lancaster *(G-9203)*

Superior Packaging Inc ....F 570 824-3577
Plains *(G-15789)*

Tapestration...G....... 215 536-0977
Quakertown *(G-16248)*

Tavo Packaging Inc ....D...... 215 428-0900
Fairless Hills *(G-5802)*

Union Packaging LLC ....D...... 610 572-7265
Yeadon *(G-20356)*

Unipak Inc ....E 610 436-6600
West Chester *(G-19670)*

Vogel Carton LLC ....E 215 957-0612
Warminster *(G-18997)*

Xomox Corporation ....G....... 570 824-3577
Wilkes Barre *(G-19980)*

BOXES: Paperboard, Set-Up

Achieva..F 412 391-4660
Pittsburgh *(G-14641)*

Duerr Packaging Company Inc..............E 724 695-2226
Imperial *(G-8064)*

Friendly City Box Co Inc ....F 814 266-6287
Johnstown *(G-8373)*

Gateway Packaging Corp ....E 724 327-7400
Export *(G-5607)*

Hanover Paper Box Company Inc ....G....... 215 432-5033
Allentown *(G-242)*

McLean Packaging Corporation ....C...... 610 759-3550
Nazareth *(G-11981)*

Michael J Doyle ....G....... 215 587-1000
Philadelphia *(G-14021)*

Northeastern PA Carton Co Inc ....E 570 457-7711
Moosic *(G-11510)*

Opi Holdings Inc ....E 610 857-2000
Old Forge *(G-12973)*

PCA Corrugated and Display LLC ....G....... 610 489-8740
Collegeville *(G-3386)*

Reliance Paragon Paper Box ....G....... 215 743-1231
Philadelphia *(G-14239)*

Simkins Corporation ....E 215 739-4033
Jenkintown *(G-8301)*

Simplex Paper Box Corp ....E 717 757-3611
Hellam *(G-7552)*

Superior Packaging Inc ....F 570 824-3577
Plains *(G-15789)*

Unipak Inc ....E 610 436-6600
West Chester *(G-19670)*

Westrock Rkt LLC ....C...... 717 393-0436
Lancaster *(G-9239)*

BOXES: Plastic

Hidensee Inc..G....... 614 465-3375
Wallingford *(G-18784)*

BOXES: Solid Fiber

Carton Edge International Inc.................F 215 699-8755
North Wales *(G-12794)*

Interstate Cont Reading LLC ....C...... 800 822-2002
Reading *(G-16409)*

Jmg Inc ....G....... 215 659-4087
Willow Grove *(G-20121)*

Pittsburgh File & Box Co........................G....... 412 431-5465
Pittsburgh *(G-15396)*

BOXES: Wirebound, Wood

Bishop Wood Products Inc ....F 215 723-6644
Souderton *(G-17726)*

BOXES: Wooden

C & S Wood Products Inc.......................E 570 489-8633
Olyphant *(G-12985)*

Export Boxing & Crating Inc ....F 412 675-1000
Glassport *(G-6412)*

Heritage Box Co ....G....... 724 728-0200
Aliquippa *(G-76)*

Honeybrook Woods ....G....... 610 380-7108
Coatesville *(G-3308)*

Millennium Packaging Svc Inc...............E 570 282-2990
Carbondale *(G-2683)*

Nelson Company Inc ....G....... 717 593-0600
Greencastle *(G-6624)*

Reading Box Company Inc ....F 610 374-2080
Reading *(G-16485)*

Ron Anthony Wood Products Inc...........F 724 459-7620
Blairsville *(G-1740)*

Ted Venesky Co Inc ....G....... 724 224-7992
Tarentum *(G-18248)*

Woodruff Corporation ....G....... 570 675-0890
Shavertown *(G-17481)*

BRAKE LININGS

Ferotec Friction Inc...............................F 717 492-9600
Manheim *(G-10384)*

BRAKES & BRAKE PARTS

Continental Corporation.........................G....... 610 289-0488
Allentown *(G-178)*

Haldex Brake Products Corp ....F 717 939-5928
Middletown *(G-11055)*

Industrial Brake Company Inc ....G....... 724 625-0010
Mars *(G-10500)*

Quick Clamp 2 ....G....... 724 336-5719
Enon Valley *(G-5087)*

Red Devil Brakes Inc ....F 724 696-3744
Mount Pleasant *(G-11712)*

Ultra Lite Brakes An C ....G....... 724 696-3743
Mount Pleasant *(G-11721)*

BRAKES: Metal Forming

Auto Care ....G....... 814 943-8155
Altoona *(G-475)*

BRASS & BRONZE PRDTS: Die-casted

J Clem Kline & Son Inc.........................G....... 610 258-6071
Easton *(G-4708)*

K Castings Inc ....G....... 724 539-9753
Latrobe *(G-9485)*

West Phila Bronze Co Inc ....E 610 874-1454
Chester *(G-3067)*

BRASS FOUNDRY, NEC

Lincoln Foundry Inc..............................E 814 833-1514
Erie *(G-5366)*

Miller J Walter Company Inc ....E 717 392-7428
Lancaster *(G-9136)*

Smoyer L M Brass Products Inc.............G....... 610 867-5011
Bethlehem *(G-1620)*

Williamsport Foundry Co Inc ....E 570 323-6216
Williamsport *(G-20093)*

BRASS GOODS, WHOLESALE

Perma Cast LLC ....E 724 325-1662
Export *(G-5620)*

BRAZING SVCS

D & M Welding Co Inc ....E 717 767-9353
York *(G-20440)*

Pelets Welding Inc ....E 610 384-5048
Coatesville *(G-3323)*

BRAZING: Metal

Acme Heat Treating Co..........................F 215 743-8500
Philadelphia *(G-13340)*

Bennett Heat Trting Brzing Inc ....F 215 674-8120
Warminster *(G-18836)*

Kinton Carbide Inc ....F 724 327-3141
Export *(G-5613)*

Penna Flame Industries Inc ....E 724 452-8750
Zelienople *(G-20815)*

Peters Heat Treating Inc ....E 814 333-1782
Meadville *(G-10779)*

R H Carbide & Epoxy Inc ....G....... 724 356-2277
Hickory *(G-7630)*

Vacu-Braze Inc ....F 215 453-0414
Quakertown *(G-16254)*

BREECHINGS

Hydroflex Systems Inc ....F 717 480-4200
Lewisberry *(G-9887)*

BRICK & SHAPES: Dolomite Or Dolomite, Magnesite

Lwb Holding Company ....C...... 717 792-3611
York *(G-20569)*

Lwb Holding Company ....G....... 717 792-3611
York *(G-20570)*

Magnesita Refractories Company ....B 717 792-3611
York *(G-20572)*

Magnesita Refractories Company ....B 717 792-4216
York *(G-20573)*

Magnesita Refractories Company ....C...... 717 792-3611
York *(G-20574)*

BRICK, STONE & RELATED PRDTS WHOLESALERS

Armina Stone Inc ....G....... 412 406-8442
Cheswick *(G-3101)*

Belden Brick Sales & Svc Inc ....F 215 639-6561
Trevose *(G-18487)*

Interstate Building Mtls Inc ....E 570 655-2811
Pittston *(G-15758)*

Krehling Industries Inc ....D...... 717 232-7936
Harrisburg *(G-7165)*

Nitterhouse Masonry Pdts LLC ....D...... 717 268-4137
Chambersburg *(G-2963)*

Specialty Minerals Inc ....C...... 212 878-1800
Bethlehem *(G-1626)*

Stone & Wood Inc ....G....... 814 857-7621
Woodland *(G-20214)*

Thermolite Inc ....E 570 969-1957
Scranton *(G-17300)*

W R Meadows Inc ....E 717 792-2627
York *(G-20701)*

BRICKS : Paving, Clay

McAvoy Brick Company ....G...... 610 933-2932
   Phoenixville *(G-14560)*

BRICKS: Clay

Glen-Gery Corporation ....E 610 374-4011
   Reading *(G-16393)*
Glen-Gery Corporation ....D 610 374-4011
   Shoemakersville *(G-17570)*
Glen-Gery Corporation ....D 717 854-8802
   York *(G-20503)*
Glen-Gery Corporation ....D 717 848-2589
   York *(G-20504)*
Glen-Gery Corporation ....D 814 857-7688
   Bigler *(G-1660)*
Midwest Material Inds Inc ....G...... 610 882-5000
   Bethlehem *(G-1573)*

BRICKS: Concrete

MBR Inc ....G...... 570 386-8820
   Reading *(G-16440)*
Nortons Building Supply Inc ....G...... 814 697-6351
   Shinglehouse *(G-17510)*

BRIDAL SHOPS

Amc Inc ....G...... 412 531-3160
   Pittsburgh *(G-14698)*
Davids Bridal Inc ....E 610 943-6210
   Conshohocken *(G-3536)*

BRIDGE COMPONENTS: Bridge sections, prefabricated, highway

R PS Machinery Sales Inc ....E 570 398-7456
   Jersey Shore *(G-8322)*

BROADCASTING & COMMS EQPT: Antennas, Transmitting/Comms

General Dynmics Stcom Tech Inc ....C 814 238-2700
   State College *(G-17969)*
Kreco Antennas ....G...... 570 595-2212
   Cresco *(G-3894)*

BROADCASTING & COMMS EQPT: Rcvr-Transmitter Unt, Transceiver

Contrail Systems Inc ....F 724 353-1127
   Sarver *(G-17067)*

BROADCASTING & COMMUNICATION EQPT: Transmit-Receiver, Radio

Hilltop Tower Leasing Inc ....E 814 942-1888
   Altoona *(G-514)*

BROADCASTING & COMMUNICATIONS EQPT: Transmitting, Radio/TV

Arris Technology Inc ....F 215 323-2590
   Horsham *(G-7790)*

BROKERS & DEALERS: Securities

Mds Securities LLC ....G...... 724 548-2501
   Kittanning *(G-8783)*

BROKERS' SVCS

Jerry James Trdng As Mnls BSC ....G...... 425 255-0199
   Lafayette Hill *(G-8882)*

BROKERS: Commodity Contracts

Universal Pioneers LLC.........................G...... 570 239-3950
   Plymouth *(G-15822)*

BROKERS: Contract Basis

Innovtive Print Mdia Group Inc ....D 610 489-4800
   Phoenixville *(G-14553)*
Kaufer Associates Inc ....G...... 814 756-4997
   Girard *(G-6394)*

BROKERS: Food

Rebecca Wilson Ltd Lblty Co ....G...... 973 670-7089
   York *(G-20654)*

Stone County Specialties Inc................G...... 570 467-2850
   Tamaqua *(G-18228)*
Van Bennett Food Co Inc ....E 610 374-8348
   Mohnton *(G-11272)*

BROKERS: Mortgage, Arranging For Loans

Inspire Closing Services LLC ....G...... 412 348-8367
   Moon Township *(G-11494)*

BROKERS: Printing

Digital-Ink Inc ....D 717 731-8890
   Dillsburg *(G-4126)*
Integra Graphix Inc ....G...... 717 626-7895
   Lititz *(G-10019)*

BROKERS: Security

Exco Resources LLC ....D 724 720-2500
   Kittanning *(G-8768)*

BRONZE FOUNDRY, NEC

Franklin Bronze & Alloy Co Inc ....F 814 437-6891
   Franklin *(G-6126)*
Franklin Bronze Precision Comp ....D 814 437-6891
   Franklin *(G-6127)*
Matthews International Corp..................E 412 442-8200
   Pittsburgh *(G-15264)*
Matthews International Corp..................E 412 571-5500
   Pittsburgh *(G-15266)*
Paul W Zimmerman Foundries Co ....F 717 285-5253
   Columbia *(G-3446)*
Phoenix Bronze Resources LLC ....G...... 724 857-2225
   Aliquippa *(G-88)*

BROOMS & BRUSHES

Anderson Products Incorporated..........D 570 595-7495
   Cresco *(G-3890)*
Blind and Vision Rehab ....D 412 368-4400
   Pittsburgh *(G-14771)*
Blind and Vision Rehab ....F 412 325-7504
   Homestead *(G-7683)*
J Penner Corporation ....E 215 340-9700
   Doylestown *(G-4308)*
Maugus Manufacturing Inc ....F 717 299-5681
   Lancaster *(G-9126)*
Maugus Manufacturing Inc ....D 717 481-4823
   Lancaster *(G-9127)*

BROOMS & BRUSHES: Household Or Indl

Alvord-Polk Inc.................................D 605 847-4823
   Millersburg *(G-11188)*
Cocker-Weber Brush Co ....F 215 723-3880
   Telford *(G-18275)*
Nation Ruskin Holdings Inc ....F 267 654-4000
   Montgomeryville *(G-11409)*
R S Quality Products Inc ....G...... 610 266-1916
   Allentown *(G-367)*
Silber Brush Manufacturing Co ....G...... 215 634-4063
   Philadelphia *(G-14306)*
Weiler Corporation ....B 570 595-7495
   Cresco *(G-3896)*

BROOMS & BRUSHES: Street Sweeping, Hand Or Machine

Valley Broom Inc ....G...... 717 349-2614
   East Waterford *(G-4642)*

BRUCITE MINING

Refractory Machining Services ....F 724 285-7674
   Butler *(G-2438)*

BRUSH BLOCKS: Carbon Or Molded Graphite

St Marys Carbon Co Inc ....D 814 781-7333
   Saint Marys *(G-17018)*

BRUSHES & BRUSH STOCK CONTACTS: Electric

Galaxy Mfg Company Inc ....F 570 457-5199
   Avoca *(G-843)*
St Marys Carbon Co Inc ....C 814 781-7333
   Saint Marys *(G-17016)*

BUCKETS: Plastic

Nation Ruskin Holdings Inc ....F 267 654-4000
   Montgomeryville *(G-11409)*

BUFFET

Hibachi Grill Supreme Buffet.................F 215 728-7222
   Philadelphia *(G-13822)*

BUILDING & OFFICE CLEANING SVCS

Shamaseen Hamzah ....G...... 484 557-5051
   Center Valley *(G-2830)*

BUILDING & STRUCTURAL WOOD MBRS: Timbers, Struct, Lam Lumber

Musselman Lumber - US Lbm LLC ......D 717 354-4321
   New Holland *(G-12264)*

BUILDING & STRUCTURAL WOOD MEMBERS

84 Lumber Company ....B 724 228-8820
   Eighty Four *(G-4830)*
Brownlee Lumber Inc ....E 814 328-2991
   Brookville *(G-2255)*
F DEFrank& Son Custom Cabinets ......G...... 724 430-1812
   Smock *(G-17665)*
Keystone Casework Inc ....E 814 941-7250
   Altoona *(G-520)*
Oakes & McClelland Co ....F 724 588-6400
   Greenville *(G-6761)*
Salem Millwork Inc ....E 724 468-5701
   Delmont *(G-4056)*
United Panel Inc ....E 610 588-6871
   Mount Bethel *(G-11615)*
Your Building Centers Inc ....E 570 962-2129
   Beech Creek *(G-1084)*

BUILDING BOARD & WALLBOARD, EXC GYPSUM, NEC

Wirthmore Pdts & Svc Co Inc ....G...... 610 430-0300
   West Chester *(G-19680)*

BUILDING CLEANING & MAINTENANCE SVCS

Barc Developmental Services................E 215 794-0800
   Holicong *(G-7638)*
Under Pressure Connections LLC ....G 570 326-1117
   South Williamsport *(G-17793)*
Universal Services Assoc Inc ....E 610 461-0300
   Folcroft *(G-6018)*

BUILDING COMPONENTS: Structural Steel

Australtek LLC ....G...... 412 257-2377
   Bridgeville *(G-2054)*
Azek Building Products Inc ....F 877 275-2935
   Scranton *(G-17210)*
B D & D Spclty Fabrication Mch ....E 814 236-3810
   Curwensville *(G-3946)*
Cid Associates Inc ....E 724 353-0300
   Sarver *(G-17066)*
David J Hohenshilt Welding LLC...........E 610 349-2937
   Neffs *(G-11998)*
Delvania Indus Fabrication Inc ....G...... 732 417-0333
   Pine Forge *(G-14587)*
Fabbco Steel Inc ....E 717 792-4904
   York *(G-20474)*
Helcrist LLC ....F 215 727-2050
   Philadelphia *(G-13811)*
JGM Fabricators & Constrs LLC ....D 484 698-6201
   Coatesville *(G-3309)*
Job-Fab Inc ....G...... 724 225-8225
   Washington *(G-19190)*
Kutz Fabricating Inc............................F 412 771-4161
   Pittsburgh *(G-15204)*
L & M Fabrication and Mch Inc ....D 610 837-1848
   Bath *(G-963)*
Moore & Morford Inc..........................E 724 834-1100
   Greensburg *(G-6689)*
MRS and Son LLC...............................G...... 215 750-7828
   Morrisville *(G-11572)*
Penn Steel Fabrication Inc ....E 267 878-0705
   Bristol *(G-2180)*
Pleasant Mount Welding Inc ....D 570 282-6164
   Carbondale *(G-2684)*

Employee Codes: A=Over 500 employees, B=251-500
C=101-250, D=51-100, E=20-50, F=10-19, G=3-9   2019 Harris Pennsylvania
Manufacturers Directory   1319

PRODUCT

R&N Manufacturing LLC ....E 412 778-4103
Pittsburgh *(G-15464)*

Reynolds Manufacturing Co Inc ....F 724 697-4522
Avonmore *(G-867)*

Ritner Steel Inc.................................E 717 249-1449
Carlisle *(G-2736)*

Russell Rolls Inc.................................G 412 321-6623
Pittsburgh *(G-15503)*

Sippel Co Inc ....E 724 266-9800
Ambridge *(G-635)*

Specialty Retail Fabricators ....F 215 477-5977
Philadelphia *(G-14332)*

Staar Distributing Llc.........................D 814 612-2115
Reynoldsville *(G-16666)*

Stewart-Amos Steel Inc ....E 717 564-3931
Harrisburg *(G-7221)*

Strait Steel Inc ....D 717 597-3125
Greencastle *(G-6636)*

Szoke Iron Works Inc.........................F 610 760-9565
Walnutport *(G-18794)*

T Bruce Campbell Cnstr Co Inc ....C 724 528-9944
West Middlesex *(G-19730)*

Tri-Vet Design Fabrication LLC............F 570 462-4941
Shenandoah *(G-17497)*

Tri-Way Metalworkers Inc ....E 570 462-4941
Shenandoah *(G-17498)*

Vmf Inc ....E 570 575-0997
Scranton *(G-17310)*

Wegco Welding Inc ....G 412 833-7020
Bethel Park *(G-1438)*

Woolf Steel Inc ....E 717 944-1423
Middletown *(G-11085)*

BUILDING EXTERIOR CLEANING SVCS

Mobile Wash Power Wash Inc...............G 814 327-3820
Bedford *(G-1065)*

BUILDING ITEM REPAIR SVCS, MISCELLANEOUS

Thyssnkrupp Indus Slutions USA.........D 412 257-8277
Bridgeville *(G-2095)*

BUILDING MAINTENANCE SVCS, EXC REPAIRS

Northeast Fabricators Inc ....G 570 883-0936
Pittston *(G-15771)*

BUILDING PRDTS & MATERIALS DEALERS

84 Lumber Company ....B 724 228-8820
Eighty Four *(G-4830)*

A A Robbins Inc..................................F 814 398-4607
Cambridge Springs *(G-2473)*

American Tank & Concrete Svc............F 724 837-4410
Greensburg *(G-6650)*

Bailey Wood Products Inc....................G 610 756-6827
Kempton *(G-8490)*

BMC East LLC ....E 717 866-2167
Myerstown *(G-11877)*

Calvert Lumber Company Inc ....F 724 346-5553
Sharon *(G-17430)*

Cedar Forest Products Company ....F 815 946-3994
Media *(G-10917)*

Cessna Bros Lumber ....F 814 767-9518
Clearville *(G-3239)*

Colonial Craft Kitchens Inc ....G 717 867-1145
Annville *(G-645)*

E B Endres Inc...................................E 814 643-1860
Huntingdon *(G-7942)*

Fizzano Bros Concrete Pdts Inc ....E 610 363-6290
Malvern *(G-10235)*

Flint Road Welding ....G 717 535-5282
Mifflintown *(G-11118)*

Forcey Lumber Co Inc ....E 814 857-5002
Woodland *(G-20211)*

George Nkashima Woodworker S A......F 215 862-2272
New Hope *(G-12302)*

Historic York Inc................................G 717 843-0320
York *(G-20523)*

J A Kohlhepp Sons Inc........................D 814 371-5200
Du Bois *(G-4398)*

J C Snavely & Sons Inc ....C 717 898-2241
Landisville *(G-9262)*

J/M Fence & Deck Company ....G 610 488-7382
Mohrsville *(G-11276)*

JC Vinyl Fence Rail & Deck..................G 570 282-2222
Carbondale *(G-2680)*

L & R Lumber Inc................................G 717 463-3411
Mc Alisterville *(G-10550)*

Lucisano Bros Inc...............................E 215 945-2700
Bristol *(G-2162)*

Marion Center Supply Inc....................G 724 354-2143
Shelocta *(G-17487)*

Martin Limestone Inc ....E 717 335-4500
East Earl *(G-4548)*

Moxham Lumber Co ....E 814 536-5186
Johnstown *(G-8411)*

Newtown-Slocomb Mfg Inc ....E 570 825-3675
Hanover Township *(G-7000)*

Nortons Building Supply Inc.................G 814 697-6351
Shinglehouse *(G-17510)*

Perry Pallet Inc ....E 717 589-3345
Millerstown *(G-11207)*

Plain n Fancy Kitchens Inc ....C 717 949-6571
Schaefferstown *(G-17129)*

R L Kingsley Lumber Company.............F 570 596-3575
Milan *(G-11148)*

Riverside Builders Supply ....E 412 264-8835
Coraopolis *(G-3721)*

Saner Architecture Millwork ....G 717 786-2014
Quarryville *(G-16279)*

Shelly Enterprises -US Lbm LLC ....F 610 933-1116
Kimberton *(G-8574)*

Slate Road Supply LLC ....G 717 445-5222
Ephrata *(G-5141)*

Somerset Door and Column Co.............E 814 445-9608
Somerset *(G-17708)*

Standard Concrete Products Co ....E 717 843-8074
York *(G-20679)*

Thruways Door Systems Inc.................F 412 781-4030
Pittsburgh *(G-15622)*

Vcw Enterprises Inc ....D 610 847-5112
Ottsville *(G-13068)*

Vista Custom Millwork Inc ....F 724 376-4093
Sandy Lake *(G-17063)*

Walter and Jackson Inc ....D 610 593-5195
Christiana *(G-3144)*

Wattsburg Lumber Co LLC ....G 814 739-2770
Wattsburg *(G-19284)*

Wendell H Stone Company Inc ....E 724 836-1400
Greensburg *(G-6729)*

BUILDING PRDTS: Concrete

Building Specialties............................G 814 454-4345
Erie *(G-5217)*

Cfb LLC ....G 717 769-0857
Elizabethtown *(G-4868)*

Cpg International LLC ....G 570 558-8000
Scranton *(G-17224)*

Doren Inc Parkway..............................G 724 375-6637
Aliquippa *(G-74)*

Edge Building Products Inc ....E 717 567-2311
Newport *(G-12489)*

Interstate Safety Service Inc ....E 570 563-1161
Clarks Summit *(G-3194)*

Mountain Side Supply LLC ....E 814 201-2525
Altoona *(G-529)*

Slate Road Supply LLC ....G 717 445-5222
Ephrata *(G-5141)*

BUILDING PRDTS: Stone

AAA Hellenic Marble Inc......................E 610 344-7700
West Chester *(G-19493)*

Czar Imports Inc................................D 800 577-2927
Huntingdon Valley *(G-7973)*

Hanson Aggregates PA LLC ....F 570 324-2514
Blossburg *(G-1807)*

Majesty Marble and Granite Inc ....E 610 859-8181
Aston *(G-774)*

Prada Company Inc ....F 412 751-4900
McKeesport *(G-10678)*

Rolling Rock Bldg Stone Inc.................D 610 987-6226
Boyertown *(G-1926)*

Whitley East LLC................................D 717 656-2081
Leola *(G-9808)*

BUILDING STONE, ARTIFICIAL: Concrete

Masons Mark Stone Veneer Corp ....G 724 635-0082
New Stanton *(G-12449)*

Tervo Masonry Llc ....E 724 944-6179
New Wilmington *(G-12471)*

BUILDINGS & COMPONENTS: Prefabricated Metal

1998 Equipment Leasing Corp ....G 412 771-2944
Mc Kees Rocks *(G-10596)*

American Conservatory Co Inc ....F 724 465-1800
Indiana *(G-8079)*

Bluescope Buildings N Amer Inc ....D 717 867-4651
Annville *(G-643)*

Bracalente Global Ltd ....C 215 536-3077
Trumbauersville *(G-18530)*

Century Buildings ....G 814 336-1446
Saegertown *(G-16910)*

Corle Building Systems Inc ....B 814 276-9611
Imler *(G-8054)*

Custom Container Solutions LLC ....F 570 524-7835
Lewisburg *(G-9902)*

Dura-Bilt Products Inc ....D 570 596-2000
Gillett *(G-6380)*

Epic Metals Corporation......................D 412 351-3913
Rankin *(G-16305)*

Farmer Boy Ag Inc ....D 717 866-7565
Myerstown *(G-11885)*

Flexospan Steel Buildings Inc ....D 724 376-7221
Sandy Lake *(G-17060)*

G & D Erectors Inc ....E 724 587-0590
Avella *(G-836)*

Gichner Systems Intl Inc ....G 717 244-7611
Dallastown *(G-3978)*

Great Day Improvements LLC ....E 412 304-0089
Pittsburgh *(G-15060)*

Heintz Storage Center ....G 412 931-3444
Pittsburgh *(G-15087)*

Keystone Metal Structures LLC............G 717 816-3631
Chambersburg *(G-2947)*

Metal Sales Manufacturing Corp ....E 570 366-2020
Orwigsburg *(G-13049)*

Modern Precast Concrete Inc ....E 484 548-6200
Easton *(G-4726)*

Morton Buildings Inc ....F 814 364-9500
Centre Hall *(G-2843)*

Morton Buildings Inc ....F 724 542-7930
Mount Pleasant *(G-11707)*

Oldcastle Precast Inc..........................C 215 257-8081
Telford *(G-18306)*

Scenic Ridge Company ....D 717 768-7522
Gordonville *(G-6564)*

Sukup Steel Structures LLC ....C 724 266-6484
Ambridge *(G-636)*

Uh Structures Inc...............................F 724 628-6100
Connellsville *(G-3509)*

BUILDINGS: Farm & Utility

JE Lyons Construction Inc ....G 724 686-3967
Latrobe *(G-9483)*

Johnathan Stoltzfus ....G 717 768-7922
Ronks *(G-16808)*

Morton Buildings Inc ....E 717 624-8000
Gettysburg *(G-6308)*

BUILDINGS: Farm, Prefabricated Or Portable, Wood

Reynolds Building Systems Inc ....G 724 646-0771
Greenville *(G-6769)*

Strat-O-Span Buildings Inc ....G 717 334-4606
Gettysburg *(G-6316)*

Timberhaven Log Homes LLC ....F 570 568-1422
Lewisburg *(G-9922)*

Tuscarora Structures Inc.....................G 717 436-5591
Mifflin *(G-11091)*

BUILDINGS: Portable

American Manufactured Struc...............G 703 403-4656
Hellertown *(G-7553)*

Central States Mfg Inc ....E 814 239-2764
Claysburg *(G-3202)*

Gichner Systems Group LLC.................B 717 244-7611
Dallastown *(G-3977)*

Jadco Manufacturing Inc......................E 724 452-5252
Harmony *(G-7070)*

Keystone Structures Inc......................E 610 444-9525
Kennett Square *(G-8521)*

Mobile Mini Inc ....E 484 540-9072
Allentown *(G-318)*

Mobile Mini Inc ....E 412 220-4477
Bridgeville *(G-2079)*

Mobile Mini Inc ....F 484 540-9073
Essington *(G-5544)*

Penn State Cnstr J&D LLC.................G......717 953-9200
Lewistown *(G-9943)*

Shelter Structures Inc.................G......267 239-5906
Philadelphia *(G-14301)*

Signature Structures LLC.................G......610 882-9030
Bethlehem *(G-1618)*

Timber Mill Woodcraft LLC.................G......717 597-7433
Greencastle *(G-6640)*

BUILDINGS: Prefabricated, Metal

Starflite Systems Inc.................E......724 789-9200
Connoquenessing *(G-3513)*

Steel Factory Corp.................F......412 771-2944
Mc Kees Rocks *(G-10638)*

BUILDINGS: Prefabricated, Wood

Black Bear Structures Inc.................G......717 225-0377
York *(G-20410)*

Cedar Forest Products Company.................F......815 946-3994
Media *(G-10917)*

Cove Stake & Wood Products GP.................G......814 793-3257
Martinsburg *(G-10522)*

David S Stoltzsus.................G......717 556-0462
Bird In Hand *(G-1673)*

Elvin B Zimmerman.................G......717 656-9327
Leola *(G-9780)*

Farmer Boy Ag Inc.................D......717 866-7565
Myerstown *(G-11885)*

Innovative Building Systems, L.................F......717 458-1400
Mechanicsburg *(G-10859)*

Jacob B Kauffman.................G......717 529-6522
Christiana *(G-3139)*

Modern Precast Concrete Inc.................E......484 548-6200
Easton *(G-4726)*

Morton Buildings Inc.................E......717 624-8000
Gettysburg *(G-6308)*

Myerstown Sheds.................G......717 866-7644
Lebanon *(G-9613)*

Myerstown Sheds and Fencing.................G......717 866-7015
Myerstown *(G-11894)*

Noble Road Woodworks LLC.................G......610 593-5122
Christiana *(G-3143)*

North Mountain Structures LLC.................G......717 369-3400
Chambersburg *(G-2964)*

Pear Tree Mfg.................G......610 273-9281
Honey Brook *(G-7755)*

Professional Bldg Systems Inc.................C......570 837-1424
Middleburg *(G-11036)*

Sarik Corporation.................G......215 538-2269
Quakertown *(G-16243)*

Shawnee Structures.................G......814 623-8212
Bedford *(G-1076)*

Sheds Unlimited Inc.................F......717 442-3281
Morgantown *(G-11534)*

Sunset Valley Structures.................G......570 758-2840
Dalmatia *(G-3986)*

Wargo Interior Systems Inc.................D......215 723-6200
Telford *(G-18325)*

BUILDINGS: Prefabricated, Wood

B & B Structures.................G......717 656-0783
Bird In Hand *(G-1669)*

Barn Yard LLC.................G......717 314-9667
Paradise *(G-13153)*

Black Bear Structures Inc.................E......717 824-0983
Peach Bottom *(G-13196)*

Dalton Pavillions Inc.................G......215 721-1492
Telford *(G-18279)*

Fisher Structures.................G......717 789-4569
Loysville *(G-10114)*

Foxs Country Sheds.................F......717 626-9560
Lititz *(G-10010)*

Haven Homes Inc.................C......410 694-0091
King of Prussia *(G-8628)*

Lanco Sheds Inc.................F......717 351-7100
New Holland *(G-12256)*

Lantz Structures LLC.................G......717 656-9418
Leola *(G-9792)*

Martins Buildings.................G......717 733-6689
Ephrata *(G-5125)*

Millcreek Structures.................F......717 656-2797
Leola *(G-9794)*

New Enterprise Stone Lime Inc.................D......610 374-5131
Kutztown *(G-8851)*

Pequea Storage Sheds LLC.................F......717 768-8980
Kinzers *(G-8740)*

Pittsburgh Shed Company Inc.................G......724 745-4422
Canonsburg *(G-2619)*

Riehl Quality Stor Barns LLC.................F......717 442-8655
Kinzers *(G-8741)*

Stoltzfus Ephram.................G......717 656-0513
Bird In Hand *(G-1682)*

Stoltzfus Structures.................F......610 593-7700
Atglen *(G-808)*

T-Town Sheds & Supply.................G......570 836-5686
Tunkhannock *(G-18550)*

Waterloo Structures.................G......610 857-2170
Parkesburg *(G-13184)*

Woodhouse Post & Beam.................E......570 549-6232
Mansfield *(G-10428)*

BULLETIN BOARDS: Cork

Aywon Chalkboard Corkboard Inc.................E......570 459-3490
Hazleton *(G-7491)*

Engine Cycle Inc.................G......717 214-4177
Highspire *(G-7632)*

BULLETPROOF VESTS

Arma Co LLC.................E......717 295-6805
Lancaster *(G-8939)*

T G Faust Inc.................F......610 375-8549
Reading *(G-16533)*

BUMPERS: Motor Vehicle

Keystone Automotive Inds Inc.................F......717 843-8927
York *(G-20552)*

BUOYS: Metal

Proweld.................G......724 836-0207
Greensburg *(G-6706)*

BUOYS: Plastic

Moog Inc.................C......610 328-4000
Springfield *(G-17919)*

BURGLAR ALARM MAINTENANCE & MONITORING SVCS

Abe Alarm Service.................G......484 664-7304
Allentown *(G-113)*

BURIAL VAULTS: Concrete Or Precast Terrazzo

Alternative Burial Corporation.................G......814 533-5832
Johnstown *(G-8353)*

Annuity Vault.................G......215 830-8666
Willow Grove *(G-20107)*

Blairsville Wilbert Burial Vlt.................E......724 459-9677
Blairsville *(G-1717)*

Blairsville Wilbert Burial Vlt.................G......724 324-2010
Mount Morris *(G-11679)*

Blairsville Wilbert Burial Vlt.................E......724 547-2865
Mount Pleasant *(G-11689)*

Blairsville Wilbert Burial Vlt.................F......814 495-5921
South Fork *(G-17772)*

Carlisle Vault LLC.................G......717 382-8588
Carlisle *(G-2699)*

Central PA Wilbert Vault.................G......717 248-3777
Burnham *(G-2359)*

CMS East Inc.................D......724 527-6700
Jeannette *(G-8250)*

Colonial Concrete Industries.................F......610 279-2102
King of Prussia *(G-8593)*

Cooper Wilbert Vault Co Inc.................G......610 842-7782
Berwyn *(G-1357)*

Deihl Vault & Precast Inc.................F......570 458-6466
Orangeville *(G-13005)*

Esterly Concrete Co Inc.................F......610 376-2791
West Reading *(G-19764)*

Evans Eagle Burial Vaults Inc.................F......717 656-2213
Leola *(G-9781)*

Fi-Hoff Concrete Products Inc.................F......814 266-5834
Johnstown *(G-8372)*

Forsht Concrete Pdts Co Inc.................G......814 944-1617
Altoona *(G-507)*

Gamers Vault.................G......609 781-0938
Montgomeryville *(G-11398)*

H Troxel Cemetery Service Inc.................G......610 489-4426
Norristown *(G-12663)*

Harvil Inc.................G......412 682-1500
Pittsburgh *(G-15083)*

Hg Smith Wilbert Vault Company.................G......570 420-9599
Stroudsburg *(G-18123)*

Ink Vault.................G......724 355-8616
Butler *(G-2410)*

Jefferson Memorial Park Inc.................E......412 655-4500
Pittsburgh *(G-15147)*

Kemosabe Inc.................G......412 961-0190
Glenshaw *(G-6494)*

Kimenski Burial Vaults.................G......724 223-0364
Washington *(G-19191)*

Klocek Burial Vault Co.................G......724 547-2865
Mount Pleasant *(G-11704)*

Lycoming Burial Vault Co Inc.................F......570 368-8642
Montoursville *(G-11446)*

Michael P Hoover Company Inc.................G......717 757-7842
York *(G-20593)*

Miller Burial Vault Co.................G......570 386-5479
New Ringgold *(G-12441)*

Milroy Enterprises Inc.................E......610 678-4537
Reading *(G-16444)*

New Bethlehem Burial Service.................F......814 275-3333
New Bethlehem *(G-12028)*

Parnell Enterprises Inc.................G......724 258-3320
Monongahela *(G-11312)*

Piles Concrete Products Co Inc.................F......814 445-6619
Friedens *(G-6225)*

Pioneer Burial Vault Co Inc.................F......215 766-2943
Doylestown *(G-4325)*

Ray Burial Vault Company Inc.................F......814 684-0104
Tyrone *(G-18591)*

Richard Rhodes.................F......814 535-3633
Johnstown *(G-8430)*

Ron Mulkerrin.................G......724 693-8920
Oakdale *(G-12910)*

Scranton Wilbert Vault Inc.................F......570 489-5065
Jessup *(G-8336)*

Silbaugh Vault and Burial Svc.................G......724 437-3002
Uniontown *(G-18642)*

Smiths Wilbert Vault Company.................E......610 588-5259
Bangor *(G-928)*

Vault Clothing Store.................G......570 871-4135
Scranton *(G-17309)*

Vault Clothing Store Inc.................G......570 780-8240
S Abingtn Twp *(G-16902)*

Vault My Keys LLC.................G......267 575-0506
Glenside *(G-6542)*

Vault Services.................G......814 282-8143
Saegertown *(G-16935)*

Wilbert Vault Co.................G......724 459-8400
Blairsville *(G-1745)*

Wilkes Barre Burial Vault.................F......570 824-8268
Hanover Township *(G-7007)*

Willard Burial Service Inc.................G......724 528-9965
West Middlesex *(G-19732)*

BURNERS: Oil, Domestic Or Indl

Division of Thermo Dynamics.................C......570 385-0731
Schuylkill Haven *(G-17154)*

Hauck Manufacturing Company.................D......717 272-3051
Cleona *(G-3244)*

BURNT WOOD ARTICLES

Coinco Inc.................E......814 425-7476
Cochranton *(G-3338)*

BUS BARS: Electrical

Micro Facture LLC.................E......717 285-9700
Mountville *(G-11799)*

BUSHINGS & BEARINGS

Precision Bushing Inc.................F......717 264-6461
Chambersburg *(G-2970)*

Roser Technologies Inc.................D......814 589-7031
Titusville *(G-18394)*

BUSHINGS: Cast Steel, Exc Investment

Wescott Steel Inc.................E......215 364-3636
Langhorne *(G-9335)*

BUSINESS ACTIVITIES: Non-Commercial Site

A & L Iron Works LLC.................G......717 768-0705
Narvon *(G-11915)*

A Better Power LLC.................G......412 498-6537
Ligonier *(G-9956)*

AAR Plastic & Glass Llc.................G......410 200-6369
Gettysburg *(G-6281)*

Above Rim International LLC.................G......215 789-7893
Philadelphia *(G-13336)*

PRODUCT

Alert Enterprises Ltd Lblty Co ....G....... 570 373-2821
  Kulpmont *(G-8821)*

Altamira Ltd ....G....... 800 343-1066
  Pittsburgh *(G-14692)*

Altus Refractories LLC ....G....... 412 430-0138
  Pittsburgh *(G-14693)*

AMD Group Inc ....G....... 610 972-4491
  Riegelsville *(G-16743)*

American Engineers Group LLC ....G....... 484 920-8010
  Phoenixville *(G-14527)*

Bacon Jams LLC ....G....... 856 720-0255
  West Chester *(G-19507)*

Becker Fashion Tech LLC ....G....... 215 776-2589
  Philadelphia *(G-13450)*

Blue Toro Technologies LLC ....G....... 610 428-0891
  Bethlehem *(G-1468)*

Brop Tech LLC ....F....... 323 229-7390
  Upper Darby *(G-18683)*

C&G Arms LLC ....G....... 724 858-2856
  Natrona Heights *(G-11937)*

Cawley Environmental Svcs Inc ....F....... 610 594-0101
  Downingtown *(G-4219)*

Chestnut Vly Ctrl Systems LLC ....G....... 717 330-2356
  Manheim *(G-10376)*

Cogan Wind LLC ....G....... 570 998-9554
  Trout Run *(G-18513)*

Converging Sciences Tech Inc ....G....... 215 626-5705
  Warminster *(G-18847)*

Creative Kink LLC ....G....... 610 506-9809
  Royersford *(G-16848)*

Critical Systems LLC ....G....... 570 643-6903
  Tannersville *(G-18235)*

Dharini LLC ....F....... 215 595-3915
  Yardley *(G-20306)*

Dooner Ventures LLC ....G....... 610 420-1100
  Bryn Mawr *(G-2320)*

Elements Direct LLC ....G....... 903 343-5441
  New Brighton *(G-12035)*

Elk Systems LLC ....G....... 717 884-9355
  Lewisberry *(G-9885)*

Eznergy LLC ....G....... 215 361-7332
  Lansdale *(G-9366)*

Feast Mag LLC ....F....... 484 343-5483
  Wynnewood *(G-20267)*

Fiftyone K LLC ....G....... 908 222-8780
  Pittsburgh *(G-15017)*

Foambeak LLC ....G....... 814 452-3626
  Erie *(G-5299)*

Forallsecure Inc ....F....... 412 256-8809
  Pittsburgh *(G-15024)*

Fry International LLC ....G....... 215 847-6359
  Elkins Park *(G-4903)*

Glw Global Inc ....G....... 412 664-7946
  McKeesport *(G-10668)*

Goodstate Inc ....G....... 215 366-2030
  Glenside *(G-6523)*

Grammaton Research LLC ....G....... 410 703-9237
  York *(G-20513)*

Grandshare LLC ....G....... 919 308-5115
  Philadelphia *(G-13781)*

Great Meadows Sawmill Frm Inc ....G....... 724 329-7771
  Farmington *(G-5862)*

Ground 34 LLC ....G....... 914 299-7212
  Pittsburgh *(G-15066)*

H & M Lumber ....G....... 717 535-5080
  Mifflintown *(G-11120)*

Hallelujah Ink ....G....... 215 510-1152
  Philadelphia *(G-13798)*

Hamiltonian Systems Inc ....F....... 412 327-7204
  Coraopolis *(G-3697)*

HB Trading LLC ....G....... 610 212-4565
  Wayne *(G-19336)*

Healthy Pet Foods Inc ....G....... 610 918-4702
  West Chester *(G-19560)*

High Tech Aquatics Inc ....G....... 570 546-3557
  Muncy *(G-11819)*

Hillside Equity Inc ....G....... 484 707-9012
  Bethlehem *(G-1531)*

Hipps Tool & Design ....G....... 814 236-3600
  Curwensville *(G-3953)*

HLS Therapeutics (usa) Inc ....F....... 844 457-8900
  Bryn Mawr *(G-2324)*

Hootboard LLC ....G....... 610 844-2423
  Yardley *(G-20320)*

Hopper Lawn & Ldscp MGT LLC ....G....... 610 692-3879
  West Chester *(G-19563)*

Hydrogen Electrics LLC ....G....... 267 334-3155
  Jenkintown *(G-8290)*

I H Rissler Mfg LLC ....G....... 717 484-0551
  Mohnton *(G-11265)*

Imf Printing LLC ....G....... 844 463-2726
  Allentown *(G-253)*

J Rybnick Mech Contr Inc ....G....... 570 222-2544
  Nicholson *(G-12616)*

James Confer ....G....... 814 945-7013
  Ludlow *(G-10118)*

Joe Bento Construction Co Inc ....G....... 215 969-1505
  Philadelphia *(G-13901)*

Johnson Quarries Inc ....E....... 570 744-1284
  Stevensville *(G-18059)*

Johnsons Frog & Rail Wldg Inc ....G....... 724 475-2305
  Greenville *(G-6752)*

Johnstown Foundry Castings Inc ....G....... 814 539-8840
  Johnstown *(G-8389)*

K-R-K Paving LLC ....G....... 267 602-7715
  Philadelphia *(G-13918)*

Karp Excavating Ltd ....G....... 570 840-9026
  Factoryville *(G-5757)*

Kimberly A Spickler ....G....... 814 627-2316
  Hesston *(G-7627)*

Lettuce Turnip The Beet ....G....... 412 334-8631
  South Park *(G-17784)*

Light Tool and Machine Inc ....F....... 814 684-2755
  Tyrone *(G-18586)*

Long Drop Games LLC ....G....... 814 460-7961
  Erie *(G-5370)*

Lunchera LLC ....E....... 787 607-8914
  Pittsburgh *(G-15240)*

Luxury Electronics LLC ....G....... 215 847-0937
  Yardley *(G-20324)*

Marshall Flp LP ....G....... 570 465-3817
  New Milford *(G-12398)*

Me Ken + Jen Crative Svcs LLC ....G....... 215 997-2355
  Chalfont *(G-2883)*

Michael Z Gehman ....G....... 814 483-0488
  Friedens *(G-6221)*

Modzori LLC ....G....... 215 833-3618
  Newtown *(G-12522)*

Neuroflow Inc ....G....... 347 881-6306
  Philadelphia *(G-14064)*

Neurologix Technologies Inc ....F....... 512 914-7941
  Cherry Tree *(G-3033)*

Nine 2 Five Ceo ....G....... 919 729-2536
  Philadelphia *(G-14075)*

Oc Canvas Studio LLC ....G....... 717 510-4847
  Harrisburg *(G-7187)*

Onlyboth Inc ....G....... 412 303-8798
  Pittsburgh *(G-15360)*

Oswaldsmill Inc ....G....... 610 298-3271
  New Tripoli *(G-12459)*

Pennergy Solutions LLC ....G....... 484 393-1539
  Royersford *(G-16859)*

Penngear LLC ....G....... 215 968-2403
  Yardley *(G-20331)*

Personlytics LLC ....G....... 484 929-0853
  West Chester *(G-19616)*

Probee Safety LLC ....G....... 302 893-0258
  Telford *(G-18310)*

Reilly Plating Company Inc ....D....... 570 735-7777
  Nanticoke *(G-11902)*

Renerva LLC ....G....... 412 841-7966
  Pittsburgh *(G-15478)*

Rgl Distributors LLC ....G....... 610 207-9000
  Ardmore *(G-715)*

Road Ready LLC ....G....... 717 647-7902
  Williamstown *(G-20103)*

Savemypixcom LLC ....G....... 800 535-6299
  Thornton *(G-18355)*

Select Veal Feeds Inc ....F....... 215 721-7131
  Souderton *(G-17762)*

Shade Mountain Countertops ....F....... 717 463-2729
  Mc Alisterville *(G-10552)*

Shamaseen Hamzah ....G....... 484 557-5051
  Center Valley *(G-2830)*

Skyroc LLC ....G....... 215 840-5466
  Philadelphia *(G-14315)*

Smart Potato LLC ....G....... 215 380-5050
  Oreland *(G-13029)*

Smokey Mountain Woodworking ....G....... 717 445-5120
  Ephrata *(G-5143)*

Snakable Inc ....G....... 347 449-3378
  Prospect Park *(G-16120)*

Solarian US ....G....... 610 550-6350
  Ardmore *(G-717)*

Sonic Energy Services USA Inc ....G....... 724 782-0560
  Venetia *(G-18744)*

Special T Electronic LLC ....G....... 412 635-4997
  Pittsburgh *(G-15568)*

Specialty Tstg & Dev Co Inc ....G....... 717 428-0186
  Seven Valleys *(G-17380)*

Starfire Corporation ....G....... 814 948-5164
  Carrolltown *(G-2810)*

Strasburg Lawn Structures LLC ....G....... 717 687-8210
  Strasburg *(G-18093)*

Sugar Valley Collar Shop Inc ....G....... 570 725-3499
  Loganton *(G-10099)*

Taty Bug Inc ....G....... 814 856-3323
  Mayport *(G-10547)*

Terry D Miles ....G....... 814 686-1997
  Tyrone *(G-18596)*

Titan Robotics Inc ....G....... 724 986-6737
  Pittsburgh *(G-15625)*

Tremco Incorporated ....D....... 717 944-9702
  Middletown *(G-11083)*

TRM Emergency Vehicles LLC ....G....... 610 689-0702
  Boyertown *(G-1932)*

Ue Lifesciences Inc ....G....... 631 980-8340
  Philadelphia *(G-14416)*

Unek Designs EMB & Sew Sp LLC .....G....... 610 563-6676
  Coatesville *(G-3327)*

Vermiculite Association Inc ....G....... 717 238-9902
  Harrisburg *(G-7242)*

Virtic Industries LLC ....G....... 610 246-9428
  Wayne *(G-19388)*

Waltco Inc ....E....... 724 625-3110
  Mars *(G-10512)*

Weston Commercial Group Inc ....G....... 215 717-9675
  Philadelphia *(G-14467)*

Winfield Winery LLC ....G....... 724 352-9589
  Cabot *(G-2462)*

Wintercorp LLC ....G....... 717 848-3425
  York *(G-20712)*

Xiii Touches Printing ....F....... 484 754-6504
  King of Prussia *(G-8700)*

Ziel Technologies LLC ....G....... 717 951-7485
  Lancaster *(G-9245)*

BUSINESS FORMS WHOLESALERS

Action Printing and Bus Forms ....F....... 814 453-5977
  Erie *(G-5173)*

American Printing Co & Pdts ....G....... 412 422-3488
  Pittsburgh *(G-14704)*

American Printing Group Inc ....G....... 215 442-0500
  Horsham *(G-7783)*

Effective Software Products ....G....... 717 267-2054
  Chambersburg *(G-2929)*

Five Thousand Forms Inc ....F....... 610 395-0900
  Fogelsville *(G-5994)*

Jerry James Trdng As Mnls BSC ....G....... 425 255-0199
  Lafayette Hill *(G-8882)*

Jka Inc ....F....... 412 741-9288
  Sewickley *(G-17397)*

Magagna Associates Inc ....F....... 610 213-2335
  Souderton *(G-17751)*

Paragon Print Systems Inc ....F....... 814 456-8331
  Erie *(G-5413)*

Printforce Inc ....G....... 610 797-6455
  Allentown *(G-360)*

Professional Graphic Co ....E....... 724 318-8530
  Sewickley *(G-17405)*

Riggans Advg Specialty Co ....F....... 724 654-5741
  New Castle *(G-12143)*

Safeguard Business Systems Inc ....C....... 215 631-7500
  Lansdale *(G-9408)*

Steve Schwartz Associates Inc ....E....... 412 765-3400
  Pittsburgh *(G-15583)*

Synergy Business Forms Inc ....G....... 814 833-3344
  Erie *(G-5502)*

Wheeler Enterprises Inc ....G....... 610 975-9230
  Wayne *(G-19392)*

BUSINESS FORMS: Printed, Continuous

Interform Corporation ....C....... 412 221-7321
  Bridgeville *(G-2070)*

Phoenix Data Inc ....D....... 570 547-1665
  Montgomery *(G-11377)*

BUSINESS FORMS: Printed, Manifold

Campbell Business Forms Inc ....G....... 610 356-0626
  Newtown Square *(G-12568)*

Federal Business Products Inc ....D....... 570 454-2451
  West Hazleton *(G-19709)*

Graphcom Inc ....C....... 800 699-1664
  Gettysburg *(G-6295)*

RPM Nittany Printing ....G....... 814 941-7775
  Altoona *(G-545)*

RR Donnelley & Sons Company ....E....... 610 391-8825
  Allentown *(G-380)*

Safeguard Business Systems Inc .... C 215 631-7500
  Lansdale (G-9408)
Steele Print Inc .... G 724 758-6178
  Ellwood City (G-4952)
Steve Schwartz Associates Inc .... E 412 765-3400
  Pittsburgh (G-15583)
Taylor Communications Inc .... G 610 688-9090
  Wayne (G-19378)
Techni-Forms Inc .... E 215 345-0333
  Doylestown (G-4341)
The Reynolds and Reynolds Co .... E 717 767-5264
  Emigsville (G-5001)
Tor Industries Inc .... G 570 622-7370
  Pottsville (G-16099)
Victor Printing Inc .... D 724 342-2106
  Sharon (G-17444)
Wise Business Forms Inc .... D 724 789-0010
  Butler (G-2449)

BUSINESS MACHINE REPAIR, ELECTRIC

Beaver Valley Cash Register Co .... G 724 728-0800
  New Brighton (G-12031)
Ellis Machine .... G 724 657-4519
  Pulaski (G-16123)
Mark Grim .... G 724 758-2270
  Ellwood City (G-4945)
Neopost USA Inc .... E 717 939-2700
  Middletown (G-11066)
Neopost USA Inc .... G 717 939-2700
  King of Prussia (G-8654)
R T R Business Products Inc .... E 724 733-7373
  Export (G-5622)
Xerox Corporation .... C 412 506-4000
  Pittsburgh (G-15726)

BUSINESS SUPPORT SVCS

Aapryl LLC .... G 215 567-1100
  Philadelphia (G-13332)
Dita Exchange Inc .... E 267 327-4889
  Radnor (G-16293)
Evergreen Oilfld Solutions LLC .... F 570 485-9998
  Wyalusing (G-20251)
Pequea Storage Sheds LLC .... F 717 768-8980
  Kinzers (G-8740)
Pump Station Ridgway .... G 814 772-3251
  Ridgway (G-16725)
Smart Systems Enterprises Inc .... G 412 323-2128
  Pittsburgh (G-15547)

BUSINESS TRAINING SVCS

Action Centered Training Inc .... G 610 630-3325
  Norristown (G-12630)

CABINETS & CASES: Show, Display & Storage, Exc Wood

Bishop Metals Incorporated .... F 412 481-5501
  Pittsburgh (G-14768)
Bornmann Mfg Co Inc .... G 215 228-5826
  Philadelphia (G-13473)
Custom Craft Cabinets .... G 215 886-6105
  Abington (G-10)
Kardex Systems Inc .... G 610 296-9730
  Paoli (G-13142)
Mastercraft Woodworking Co Inc .... E 610 926-1500
  Shoemakersville (G-17571)
Metro International Corp .... E 570 825-2741
  Wilkes Barre (G-19943)
Otto Design Casefixture Inc .... G 412 824-3580
  Greenock (G-6645)

CABINETS: Bathroom Vanities, Wood

Art Craft Cabinets Inc .... G 717 397-7817
  Lancaster (G-8943)
Asels Cabinet Company .... G 814 677-3063
  Rouseville (G-16835)
Dennis Downing .... G 724 598-0043
  New Castle (G-12081)
Dodson Bros Inc .... G 412 793-0600
  Verona (G-18755)
GP Cabinets LLC .... G 814 933-8902
  Snow Shoe (G-17669)
Hampton Cabinet Shop .... G 717 898-7806
  Manheim (G-10387)
Harrison Custom Cabinets .... G 215 548-2450
  Philadelphia (G-13804)
Jemson Cabinetry Inc .... G 717 733-0540
  Ephrata (G-5112)

Lancaster Maid Cabinets Inc .... F 717 336-0111
  Reinholds (G-16635)
Mar-Van Industries Inc .... G 215 249-3336
  Dublin (G-4435)
Melvin Stoltzfus .... F 717 656-3520
  Talmage (G-18207)
North Country Woodworking Inc .... G 570 549-8105
  Mansfield (G-10422)
Rj Custom Products Llc .... F 717 246-2693
  Dallastown (G-3980)
Shawn Harr .... G 215 258-5434
  Perkasie (G-13292)
Superior Woodcraft Inc .... E 215 348-9942
  Doylestown (G-4340)
Sykes-Scholtz-Collins Lbr Inc .... E 610 494-2700
  Chester (G-3066)
Wayneco Inc .... D 717 225-4413
  York (G-20704)
Wood-Mode Incorporated .... A 570 374-2711
  Kreamer (G-8819)
Ye Olde Village Workshop .... Ye 570 595-2593
  Mountainhome (G-11788)

CABINETS: Entertainment

Ames Construction Inc .... E 717 299-1395
  Lancaster (G-8932)
Effort Woodcraft Inc .... E 570 629-1160
  Effort (G-4825)
Richard Riberich .... G 412 271-8427
  Pittsburgh (G-15484)
Sam King .... G 610 273-7979
  Honey Brook (G-7760)
Schubert Custom Cabinetry Inc .... G 610 372-5559
  Reading (G-16508)

CABINETS: Entertainment Units, Household, Wood

Bostock Company Inc .... E 215 343-7040
  Warrington (G-19110)
Conestoga Valley Cstm Kitchens .... E 717 445-5415
  Narvon (G-11919)

CABINETS: Factory

Acorn Manufacturing Inc .... E 717 964-1111
  Denver (G-4065)
Kaufer Associates Inc .... G 814 756-4997
  Girard (G-6394)
ONeils Custom Cab & Design .... F 412 422-4723
  Pittsburgh (G-15359)
Quakermaid Cabinets Inc .... E 570 207-4432
  Scranton (G-17277)
Riverwoods Cabinetry LLC .... G 724 807-1045
  Harrisville (G-7255)

CABINETS: Filing, Wood

Conestoga Valley Cstm Kitchens .... E 717 445-5415
  Narvon (G-11919)

CABINETS: Kitchen, Metal

Earl West Industries .... G 717 656-6600
  Leola (G-9779)
George J Bush Kitchen Center .... G 724 694-9533
  Derry (G-4101)
Harold M Horst Inc .... G 717 354-5815
  New Holland (G-12251)

CABINETS: Kitchen, Wood

75 Cabinets LLC .... G 215 343-7500
  Warrington (G-19104)
A Kuhns Cabinets .... G 717 263-4306
  Chambersburg (G-2896)
Adelphi Kitchens Inc .... C 610 693-3101
  Robesonia (G-16772)
Aiellos International Inc .... F 717 451-3910
  New Oxford (G-12403)
Alan Pepper Designs .... G 412 244-9299
  Pittsburgh (G-14659)
Alvin Reiff Woodworking .... G 570 966-1149
  Mifflinburg (G-11092)
American Mllwk & Cabinetry Inc .... E 610 965-0040
  Emmaus (G-5019)
Ames Construction Inc .... E 717 299-1395
  Lancaster (G-8932)
Antones At The Mark Inc .... G 610 798-9218
  Allentown (G-138)
Appalachian Mill Inc .... E 717 328-2805
  Greencastle (G-6598)

Beilers Woodworking .... G 717 656-8956
  Talmage (G-18206)
Bentley & Collins Company .... F 570 546-3250
  Muncy (G-11810)
Bhagyas Kitchen .... G 215 233-1587
  Glenside (G-6508)
Birchcraft Kitchens Inc .... E 610 375-4391
  Reading (G-16334)
Bittner Distributors Company .... G 412 261-8000
  Pittsburgh (G-14770)
Blue Mountain Woodworking .... E 610 746-2588
  Bath (G-952)
Braders Woodcraft Inc .... F 610 262-3452
  Laurys Station (G-9532)
Brightbill Industries Inc .... E 717 233-4121
  Harrisburg (G-7099)
Brubaker Kitchens Inc .... E 717 394-5622
  Lancaster (G-8963)
Cabinet Connections .... G 215 429-9431
  Feasterville Trevose (G-5899)
Cabinet Store .... G 814 677-5522
  Seneca (G-17365)
Cameo Kitchens Inc .... E 717 436-9598
  Mifflintown (G-11111)
Canaan Cabinetry Inc .... G 215 348-0551
  Doylestown (G-4286)
Cbc Cabinetry & Home Services .... F 717 564-2521
  Harrisburg (G-7103)
Centerville Cabinet Shop .... G 717 351-0708
  Gordonville (G-6551)
Chadds Ford Cabinet Inc .... G 610 388-6005
  Kennett Square (G-8503)
Churchtowne Cabinetry .... G 717 354-6682
  Narvon (G-11918)
Closet City Ltd .... F 215 855-4400
  Harleysville (G-7028)
Cold Spring Cabinetry Inc .... G 215 348-8001
  Doylestown (G-4293)
Colonial Craft Kitchens Inc .... G 717 867-1145
  Annville (G-645)
Conestoga Valley Cstm Kitchens .... E 717 445-5415
  Narvon (G-11919)
Conestoga Wood Spc Corp .... A 717 445-6701
  East Earl (G-4540)
Contemprary Artisans Cabinetry .... E 215 723-8803
  Telford (G-18276)
Craft-Maid Kitchen Inc .... E 610 376-8686
  Reading (G-16352)
Crawford Dzignes Inc .... G 724 872-4644
  West Newton (G-19750)
Creekhill Cabinetry .... G 717 656-7438
  Paradise (G-13155)
Crownwood LLC .... G 717 463-2942
  Mc Alisterville (G-10548)
Crystal Custom Kitchens Inc .... G 610 683-8187
  Kutztown (G-8839)
Custom Cabinetry Unlimited LLC .... G 717 656-9170
  Leola (G-9776)
Custom Designs & Mfg Co .... E 570 207-4432
  Scranton (G-17226)
Custom Woodworking .... E 610 273-2907
  Honey Brook (G-7743)
Daniel W Benedict .... G 717 709-0149
  Waynesboro (G-19408)
David Jonathan Wdwkg & Mfg Co .... G 724 499-5225
  Rogersville (G-16795)
Db & S Cabinets .... G 814 437-2529
  Franklin (G-6124)
Deely Custom Cabinetry .... G 267 566-5704
  North Wales (G-12798)
Del-Wood Kitchens Inc .... E 717 637-9320
  Hanover (G-6876)
Dinneen & Son Inc .... G 412 241-2727
  Pittsburgh (G-14924)
Donatucci Kitchens & Appls .... E 215 545-5755
  Philadelphia (G-13639)
Dutch Wood LLC .... G 717 933-5133
  Myerstown (G-11882)
E Beiler Cabinetry .... E 717 354-5515
  New Holland (G-12245)
Eagle Displays LLC .... F 724 335-8900
  North Apollo (G-12726)
EDM Co .... E 717 626-2186
  Lititz (G-10005)
Effort Woodcraft Inc .... E 570 629-1160
  Effort (G-4825)
Ehst Custom Kitchens Inc .... F 610 367-2074
  Boyertown (G-1910)
Elegant Marble Products Inc .... F 717 939-0373
  Middletown (G-11052)

PRODUCT

Elite Cabinetry Inc .....G..... 717 993-5269	Lancaster Cabinet Company LLC ....G..... 717 556-8420	Richard Riberich .....G..... 412 271-8427
New Park (G-12429)	Bird In Hand (G-1678)	Pittsburgh (G-15484)
Elkay Wood Products Company .....B..... 570 966-1076	Larkin C Cabinets Inc .....G..... 610 696-9096	Rissler Custom Kitchens .....G..... 717 656-6101
Mifflinburg (G-11094)	West Chester (G-19586)	Leola (G-9800)
Empire Building Products Inc .....F..... 610 926-0500	Leo Taur Technology Group Inc .....F..... 610 966-3484	Riverwoods Cabinetry .....G..... 724 991-0097
Leesport (G-9662)	Macungie (G-10153)	Grove City (G-6803)
Ethan Horwitz Cabinet Mak .....G..... 610 948-4889	Lewistown Cabinet Center Inc .....D..... 717 667-2121	Rocher Incorporated .....G..... 717 637-9320
Pottstown (G-15987)	Milroy (G-11231)	Hanover (G-6945)
F DEFrank& Son Custom Cabinets .....F..... 724 430-1812	Lyndan Cabinets Inc .....G..... 724 626-9630	Rosewood Kitchens Inc .....E..... 717 436-9878
Smock (G-17665)	Connellsville (G-3502)	Mifflintown (G-11134)
Fedor Fabrication Inc .....F..... 610 431-7150	Lyndan Designs Inc .....G..... 724 626-9630	Rossi Brothers Cabinet Makers .....F..... 215 426-9960
West Chester (G-19554)	Connellsville (G-3503)	Philadelphia (G-14260)
Fine Line Cabinets Inc .....F..... 814 695-8133	Macson Company .....G..... 610 264-7733	Rynone Manufacturing Corp .....C..... 570 888-5272
Hollidaysburg (G-7647)	Allentown (G-305)	Sayre (G-17121)
Fiorella Woodworking Inc .....G..... 215 843-5870	Mario Dinardo Jr Custom WD Wkg .....E..... 610 495-7010	Salix Cabinetry Inc .....G..... 814 266-4181
Philadelphia (G-13702)	Pottstown (G-16015)	Salix (G-17048)
Foxcraft Cabinets .....G..... 717 859-3261	Martins Wood Products LLC .....E..... 717 933-5115	Schubert Custom Cabinetry Inc .....G..... 610 372-5559
Ephrata (G-5105)	Myerstown (G-11893)	Reading (G-16508)
Frank Griffith .....G..... 570 524-7175	Master Woodcraft Corporation .....E..... 724 225-5530	Schutte Woodworking & Mfg Co .....G..... 814 453-5110
Lewisburg (G-9909)	Washington (G-19201)	Erie (G-5470)
Freelands Fine Wood Finishings .....G..... 814 922-7101	Masterbrand Cabinets Inc .....A..... 717 359-4131	Shady Grove Cabinet Shop Inc .....G..... 717 597-0825
West Springfield (G-19768)	Carlisle (G-2725)	Greencastle (G-6632)
Glicks Woodcraft LLC .....G..... 717 536-3670	Mc Norton Cabinet Co .....G..... 724 538-5680	Sherman & Gosweiler Inc .....G..... 610 270-0825
Loysville (G-10115)	Cranberry Township (G-3834)	Bridgeport (G-2046)
Goebel Cabinetry .....G..... 610 363-8970	Meridian Products Inc .....D..... 717 355-7700	Signature Custom Cabinetry Inc .....C..... 717 738-4884
Exton (G-5690)	New Holland (G-12263)	Ephrata (G-5140)
Goebelwood Industries Inc .....F..... 610 532-4644	Millwork Solutions Inc .....E..... 814 446-4009	Smith Lawton Millwork .....G..... 570 934-2544
Folsom (G-6024)	Seward (G-17382)	Montrose (G-11477)
Harmony Plus Woodworks Inc .....G..... 717 432-0372	Mountain City Cabinets Inc .....G..... 814 652-3977	Snitz Creek Cabinet Shop LLC .....F..... 717 273-9861
Dillsburg (G-4131)	Everett (G-5575)	Lebanon (G-9632)
Haugh Woodworking .....G..... 724 894-2205	Mountainside Wood Products .....F..... 717 935-5753	Solid Wood Cabinet Company LLC .....C..... 267 288-1200
West Sunbury (G-19770)	Belleville (G-1133)	Levittown (G-9864)
Heirloom Cabinetry PA Inc .....F..... 717 436-8091	Myers Cabinet Co .....G..... 724 887-4070	St Martin America Inc .....E..... 570 593-8596
Mifflintown (G-11122)	Scottdale (G-17196)	Cressona (G-3908)
Hess C & Sons Cabinets Inc .....G..... 717 597-3295	Nailed It Ii LLC .....G..... 215 803-2060	Stansons Kitchens & Vanities .....G..... 570 648-4660
Greencastle (G-6618)	Langhorne (G-9312)	Coal Township (G-3282)
Hilltop Woodshop Inc .....G..... 724 697-4506	National Forest Products Ltd .....G..... 814 927-5622	Stasik Custom Cabinetry .....G..... 215 357-7277
Avonmore (G-865)	Marienville (G-10458)	Feasterville Trevose (G-5931)
Hoff Enterprises Inc .....E..... 814 535-8371	Natures Blend Wood Pdts Inc .....D..... 724 763-7057	Stauffer Wood Products .....G..... 717 647-4372
Johnstown (G-8381)	Ford City (G-6050)	Tower City (G-18441)
Homestead Custom Cabinetry .....E..... 717 859-8788	Noah F Boyle Cabinets .....G..... 717 944-1007	Steigrwalds Kitchens Baths Inc .....F..... 724 458-0280
Akron (G-35)	Elizabethtown (G-4880)	Grove City (G-6804)
Honey Brook Cstm Cabinets Inc .....E..... 610 273-2436	Northeast Cabinet Center Inc .....G..... 570 226-5005	Superior Cabinet Co .....G..... 724 569-9581
Honey Brook (G-7749)	Hawley (G-7434)	Smithfield (G-17655)
Infinite Quest Cabinetry Corp .....G..... 301 222-3592	Oak Park Cabinetry Inc .....F..... 717 561-4216	Superior Cabinet Company .....G..... 215 536-5228
Red Lion (G-16601)	Harrisburg (G-7186)	Quakertown (G-16247)
Innovative Custom Cabinetry .....G..... 724 624-0164	Olde Mill Cabinet Co .....G..... 717 866-6504	Susquhnna Vly Woodcrafters Inc .....E..... 717 898-7564
Rochester (G-16786)	Myerstown (G-11895)	Salunga (G-17057)
Irving K Doremus Jr .....G..... 215 679-6653	Otto Design Casefixture Inc .....G..... 412 378-6460	Taylormaid Custom Cabinetry .....G..... 717 865-6598
Pennsburg (G-13249)	Irwin (G-8187)	Annville (G-660)
Jay Zimmerman .....G..... 717 445-7246	Oxford Cabinetry LLC .....G..... 610 932-3793	Tedd Wood LLC .....D..... 717 463-3615
East Earl (G-4546)	Nottingham (G-12884)	Thompsontown (G-18352)
Jeffrey R Knudsen .....G..... 717 529-4011	Pannebaker Holdings Inc .....D..... 717 463-3615	Trim Tech Inc .....F..... 215 321-0841
Kirkwood (G-8749)	Thompsontown (G-18350)	Newtown (G-12556)
Jerry D Watson Jr .....G..... 814 355-7104	Patrick Aiello Cabinetry LLC .....G..... 610 681-7167	Trinity Sup & Installation LLC .....F..... 412 331-3044
Milesburg (G-11152)	Kunkletown (G-8834)	Pittsburgh (G-15650)
JI Cabinet Company .....G..... 412 931-8580	Paul H Nolt Woodworking .....G..... 717 445-4972	Valley Custom Cabinetry .....G..... 717 957-2819
Pittsburgh (G-15154)	East Earl (G-4552)	Marysville (G-10534)
John Kegges Jr .....G..... 412 821-5535	Paul Scalese .....G..... 814 743-5121	Viking Woodworking Llc .....G..... 412 381-5171
Pittsburgh (G-15155)	Cherry Tree (G-3034)	Pittsburgh (G-15698)
Joseph Mikstas .....G..... 215 271-2419	Paulus & Son Cabinet Co .....G..... 717 896-3610	Village Hndcrfted Cbinetry Inc .....G..... 215 393-3040
Philadelphia (G-13911)	Halifax (G-6828)	Lansdale (G-9424)
K & H Cabinet Company Inc .....F..... 717 949-6551	Penncraft Cabinet Co .....G..... 724 379-7040	Wagner Masters Custom Wdwkg .....G..... 570 748-9424
Newmanstown (G-12478)	Monongahela (G-11313)	Lock Haven (G-10093)
Kabinet Koncepts Inc .....G..... 724 327-7737	Philip J Stofanak Inc .....E..... 610 759-9311	Walnut Burl Woodmill .....G..... 717 259-8479
Murrysville (G-11854)	Bethlehem (G-1595)	Thomasville (G-18343)
Kahles Kitchens Inc .....D..... 814 744-9388	Phoenix Cabinetry Inc .....G..... 484 831-5741	Walter S Custom Cabinetry .....G..... 570 420-9800
Leeper (G-9656)	Phoenixville (G-14568)	Stroudsburg (G-18142)
Kares Krafted Kitchen Inc .....G..... 610 694-0180	Plain n Fancy Kitchens Inc .....C..... 717 949-6571	Waterloo Woodcraft .....G..... 724 221-0438
Freemansburg (G-6197)	Schaefferstown (G-17129)	Blairsville (G-1744)
Kelly Custom Furn & Cabinetry .....G..... 412 781-3997	Precision Countertops Mllwk Inc .....G..... 215 598-7161	Weir Kitchens .....F..... 717 292-6829
Pittsburgh (G-15166)	Hatboro (G-7298)	Dover (G-4207)
Kitchen Express Inc .....F..... 570 693-0285	Precision Dimension Inc .....F..... 814 684-4150	Wellborn Holdings Inc .....C..... 717 351-1700
Wyoming (G-20281)	Tyrone (G-18590)	New Holland (G-12293)
Kitchen Express of Wyoming .....G..... 570 693-0285	Precision Wood Works .....G..... 814 793-9900	Whole House Cabinetry .....G..... 610 286-2901
Wyoming (G-20282)	Martinsburg (G-10528)	Elverson (G-4969)
Kitchen Gallery Inc .....G..... 724 838-0911	Quaker Valley Specialties .....G..... 717 694-3999	Wood Creations LLC .....G..... 717 445-7007
Greensburg (G-6682)	Richfield (G-16681)	Terre Hill (G-18340)
Kitchens By Meade Inc .....F..... 814 453-4888	Quality Custom Cabinetry Inc .....C..... 717 656-2721	Wood Ya Like Cabinets .....G..... 570 725-2523
Erie (G-5345)	New Holland (G-12275)	Loganton (G-10100)
Kitchenview Custom Cabinets .....G..... 717 687-6740	Quality Custom Cabinetry Inc .....F..... 717 661-6565	Wood-Mode Incorporated .....E..... 570 374-1176
Paradise (G-13161)	Leola (G-9798)	Selinsgrove (G-17338)
Kountry Kraft Kitchens Inc .....C..... 610 589-4575	Ram-Wood Custom Cabinetry LLC .....G..... 717 242-6357	Woodcraft Industries .....G..... 570 323-4458
Newmanstown (G-12479)	Lewistown (G-9945)	Williamsport (G-20098)
Kountry Kustom Kitchens .....G..... 717 768-3091	Red Rose Cabinetry .....G..... 717 625-4456	Woodcraft Industries Inc .....E..... 724 638-4044
Bird In Hand (G-1677)	Lititz (G-10038)	Greenville (G-6777)
Kross Cabinets .....G..... 724 375-7504	Renningers Cabinetree Inc .....E..... 570 726-6494	Woodmasters Cabinetry Inc .....E..... 717 949-3937
Aliquippa (G-79)	Mill Hall (G-11181)	Newmanstown (G-12485)
L & D Cabinetry .....G..... 717 484-1272	Richard Hurst .....G..... 717 866-2343	Woodshop LLC .....G..... 610 647-4190
Denver (G-4080)	Myerstown (G-11897)	Malvern (G-10348)

2019 Harris Pennsylvania
Manufacturers Directory

(G-0000) Company's Geographic Section entry number

Y&Q Home Plus LLC ....G..... 412 642-6708
Pittsburgh (G-15728)

CABINETS: Office, Metal

Gichner Systems Group LLC ....B...... 717 244-7611
Dallastown (G-3977)
Superior Cabinet Company ....G...... 215 536-5228
Quakertown (G-16247)
Vicjah Corporation ....G...... 610 826-7475
Palmerton (G-13114)

CABINETS: Office, Wood

Contemprary Artisans Cabinetry..........E...... 215 723-8803
Telford (G-18276)
David Jonathan Wdwkg & Mfg Co ....G...... 724 499-5225
Rogersville (G-16795)
French Creek Woodworking Inc ....G...... 610 286-9295
Elverson (G-4963)
Primrose Consulting Inc ....G...... 724 816-5769
Mars (G-10510)
Robisons Cabinet Studio ....G...... 717 677-9828
Aspers (G-745)

CABINETS: Show, Display, Etc, Wood, Exc Refrigerated

A & V Woodwork Co ....F...... 215 727-8832
Philadelphia (G-13322)
Big Valley Cabinets............................G...... 717 935-2788
Belleville (G-1127)
Caseworks Inc....................................F...... 724 522-5068
Jeannette (G-8249)
Cedars Wdwkg & Renovations LLC ......G...... 717 392-1736
Lancaster (G-8972)
Custom Wood Crafters Inc...................G...... 215 357-6677
Warminster (G-18853)
Holly Woodcrafters Inc ....E...... 717 486-5862
Mount Holly Springs (G-11634)
Kol Industries Inc ....F...... 717 630-0600
Hanover (G-6911)
Macson Company ....G...... 610 264-7733
Allentown (G-305)
Millers Fabricating ....G...... 717 733-9311
Ephrata (G-5129)
Odhner and Odhner Fine Wdwkg ....G...... 610 258-9300
Easton (G-4734)
Rynone Manufacturing Corp.................C...... 570 888-5272
Sayre (G-17121)
T L King Cabinetmaker ....G...... 610 869-4220
Cochranville (G-3356)
William Cottage ....G...... 724 266-2961
Ambridge (G-639)
Wood-Mode Incorporated ....E...... 570 374-1176
Selinsgrove (G-17338)

CABINETS: Stereo, Wood

Identity Group ....G...... 610 767-4700
Slatington (G-17607)

CABLE TELEVISION

Central Penn Wire and Cable...............G...... 717 945-5540
Lancaster (G-8974)
Pagnotti Enterprises Inc ....E...... 570 825-8700
Wilkes Barre (G-19954)
Pencor Services Inc ....E...... 610 826-2115
Palmerton (G-13110)

CABLE TELEVISION PRDTS

Cheetah Technologies LP ....G...... 412 928-7707
Pittsburgh (G-14842)
Professional Electronic Compon ....G...... 215 245-1550
Philadelphia (G-14205)

CABLE WIRING SETS: Battery, Internal Combustion Engines

East Penn Manufacturing Co ....G...... 610 929-4920
Reading (G-16368)
East Penn Manufacturing Co ....E...... 610 682-6361
Kutztown (G-8840)

CABLE: Coaxial

Berk-Tek LLC ....G...... 717 354-6200
New Holland (G-12230)
Mueller Industries Inc ....D...... 215 699-5801
North Wales (G-12820)

Nexans USA Inc ....B...... 717 354-6200
New Holland (G-12271)
Prysmian Cbles Systems USA LLC ....D...... 570 385-4381
Schuylkill Haven (G-17164)

CABLE: Fiber

Network Products & Services................G...... 724 229-0332
Washington (G-19210)
Squid Wire LLC ....G...... 484 235-5155
Conshohocken (G-3606)
TVC Communications LLC....................E...... 717 838-3790
Annville (G-661)

CABLE: Fiber Optic

Cable Associates Inc ....E...... 570 876-4565
Archbald (G-686)
Fiberopticscom Inc ....E...... 610 973-6000
Breinigsville (G-2016)
Ruckus Wireless Inc ....E...... 814 231-3710
State College (G-18018)

CABLE: Nonferrous, Shipboard

Naval Company Inc.............................G...... 215 348-8982
Doylestown (G-4318)

CABLE: Noninsulated

Bridon-American Corporation ....C...... 570 822-3349
Exeter (G-5581)
Tri-Com Inc ....E...... 610 259-7400
Clifton Heights (G-3259)

CABLE: Ropes & Fiber

Lift-Tech Inc ....G...... 717 898-6615
Landisville (G-9263)

CABLE: Steel, Insulated Or Armored

Avant-Garde Technology Inc ....G...... 215 345-8228
Doylestown (G-4273)
Drs Laurel Technologies ....B...... 814 534-8900
Johnstown (G-8370)

CABS: Indl Trucks & Tractors

Beco Truck Cap Outlet ....F...... 717 336-3141
Denver (G-4067)

CAFES

Crumbs ....F...... 717 609-1120
Mount Holly Springs (G-11633)

CAGES: Wire

Pointer Hill Pets Inc ....G...... 610 754-7830
Bechtelsville (G-1035)
Precision Wire Products Inc ....E...... 724 459-5601
Blairsville (G-1737)
Safeguard Products Inc.......................E...... 717 354-4586
New Holland (G-12280)
Woodstream Corporation.....................E...... 717 626-2125
Lititz (G-10060)

CALCULATING & ACCOUNTING EQPT

Remcal Products Corporation ....F...... 215 343-5500
Warrington (G-19130)

CALENDARS: Framed

Coinco Inc..E...... 814 425-7407
Cochranton (G-3337)

CALIBRATING SVCS, NEC

Gamma Irradiator Service LLC ....G...... 570 925-5681
Benton (G-1280)
Jrt Calibration Services Inc..................G...... 610 327-9610
Pottstown (G-16006)

CALIPERS & DIVIDERS

Cianflone Scientific LLC......................G...... 412 787-3600
Pittsburgh (G-14851)

CALLIGRAPHER

Giving Tree Inc ....G...... 215 968-2487
New Hope (G-12303)

CAMERA & PHOTOGRAPHIC SPLYS STORES

Creative Stitches By Dina Inc ....G....... 724 863-4104
Irwin (G-8152)
Rockafellow John ....G....... 717 359-4276
Littlestown (G-10076)

CAMERA & PHOTOGRAPHIC SPLYS STORES: Cameras

All Tech-D Out LLC ....F....... 610 814-0888
Allentown (G-124)

CAMERA & PHOTOGRAPHIC SPLYS STORES: Photographic Splys

Lowlander Corporation ....G....... 412 221-1240
Monaca (G-11291)

CAMERAS & RELATED EQPT: Photographic

Allison Park Group Inc ....G....... 412 487-8211
Allison Park (G-446)
George T Faraghan Studios ....G....... 215 928-0499
Philadelphia (G-13756)
Mosaic Engineering Inc.......................G....... 406 544-7902
State College (G-17995)

CANDLE SHOPS

Colonial Candlecrafters........................G....... 570 524-4556
Lewisburg (G-9900)
Early American Pittsburgh Inc..............D....... 412 486-6757
Mount Pleasant (G-11698)
Howanitz Associates Inc ....E....... 570 629-3388
Bartonsville (G-946)
Pocono Candle Works Inc ....F....... 570 421-1832
East Stroudsburg (G-4627)
Terra Essential Scents Sy ....G....... 412 213-3600
Allison Park (G-464)

CANDLES

Barrick Design Inc ....G....... 717 295-4800
Lancaster (G-8948)
Binder Industries-Candlewic ....F....... 215 230-3601
Doylestown (G-4275)
Byrne Candle Co Inc...........................E....... 570 346-4070
Scranton (G-17213)
Candlerock ....G....... 724 503-2231
New Kensington (G-12331)
Candles In Cove ....G....... 518 368-3381
Roaring Spring (G-16762)
Candlewic Company ....G....... 215 230-3601
Doylestown (G-4287)
Candlsetcetera Candles ACC LLC ....G....... 610 507-7830
Reinholds (G-16630)
Carla Bella Ent LLC ....G....... 570 704-0077
Wilkes Barre (G-19910)
Colonial Candlecrafters........................G....... 570 524-4556
Lewisburg (G-9900)
Dine-Glow Dblo Fd Svc Fels LLC ....E....... 800 526-7583
Phoenixville (G-14545)
Early American Pittsburgh Inc..............D....... 412 486-6757
Mount Pleasant (G-11698)
Eastern Oil Corporation ....G....... 412 221-2911
Bridgeville (G-2060)
Edinboro Creations ....G....... 412 462-0370
Homestead (G-7685)
Everclear Valley Inc ....G....... 724 676-4703
New Florence (G-12196)
F & H Wax Works Ltd ....E....... 610 336-0308
Macungie (G-10145)
Good Scents Candle Co Inc ....G....... 814 349-5848
Millheim (G-11218)
Hayloft Candles..................................G....... 717 656-9463
Leola (G-9786)
House of Candles................................F....... 570 629-1953
Henryville (G-7567)
Howanitz Associates Inc ....E....... 570 629-3388
Bartonsville (G-946)
Jarcandlestorecom..............................G....... 412 758-8855
Pittsburgh (G-15144)
Old Candle Barn Inc ....E....... 717 768-3231
Intercourse (G-8138)
Pocono Candle Works Inc ....F....... 570 421-1832
East Stroudsburg (G-4627)
Sugar Creek Candles LLC ....G....... 724 261-1927
Irwin (G-8202)
Terra Essential Scents Sy ....G....... 412 213-3600
Allison Park (G-464)

PRODUCT

Thompsons Candle Co ....E 814 641-7490
Huntingdon *(G-7957)*

TMC Candies LLC ....G 814 623-1545
Bedford *(G-1078)*

CANDLES: Wholesalers

Colonial Candlecrafters ....G 570 524-4556
Lewisburg *(G-9900)*

Edinboro Creations ....G 412 462-0370
Homestead *(G-7685)*

F & H Wax Works Ltd ....E 610 336-0308
Macungie *(G-10145)*

Good Scents Candle Co Inc ....G 814 349-5848
Millheim *(G-11218)*

Sugar Creek Candles LLC ....G 724 261-1927
Irwin *(G-8202)*

Thompsons Candle Co ....E 814 641-7490
Huntingdon *(G-7957)*

CANDY & CONFECTIONS: Candy Bars, Including Chocolate Covered

Boyer Candy Company Inc ....D 814 944-9401
Altoona *(G-483)*

Hershey Company ....B 570 384-3271
Hazle Township *(G-7463)*

CANDY & CONFECTIONS: Chocolate Candy, Exc Solid Chocolate

4sis LLC ....E 814 459-2451
Erie *(G-5162)*

Barchemy LLC ....E 724 379-4405
Donora *(G-4147)*

Catoris Candies Inc ....F 724 335-4371
New Kensington *(G-12333)*

Clark Candies Inc ....G 724 226-0866
Tarentum *(G-18239)*

Dan Smith Candies Inc ....F 814 849-8221
Brookville *(G-2259)*

Evans Candy LLC ....G 717 295-7510
Lancaster *(G-9012)*

James A Marquette ....G 570 523-3873
Lewisburg *(G-9913)*

John L Stopay LLC ....G 570 562-6541
Taylor *(G-18259)*

Miesse Candies Corp ....G 717 299-5427
Lancaster *(G-9135)*

Nuts About Granola LLC ....G 717 814-9648
York *(G-20613)*

R M Palmer Company ....E 610 582-5551
Reading *(G-16483)*

R M Palmer Company ....C 610 374-5224
Wyomissing *(G-20287)*

Romolo Chocolates Inc ....E 814 452-1933
Erie *(G-5466)*

Rosalind Candy Castle Inc ....F 724 843-1144
New Brighton *(G-12041)*

Shannons Kandy Kitchen ....G 724 662-5211
Mercer *(G-10975)*

Zitner Candy Corp ....E 215 229-4990
Philadelphia *(G-14505)*

CANDY & CONFECTIONS: Chocolate Covered Dates

Wilson Candy Co Inc ....F 724 523-3151
Jeannette *(G-8268)*

CANDY & CONFECTIONS: Fudge

Copper Kettle Fudge Factory ....F 412 824-1233
North Versailles *(G-12773)*

Groffs Candies ....G 717 872-2845
Lancaster *(G-9033)*

Halls Candies LLC ....G 570 596-2267
Gillett *(G-6381)*

CANDY & CONFECTIONS: Licorice

Hershey Company ....A 717 509-9795
Lancaster *(G-9045)*

CANDY & CONFECTIONS: Nuts, Candy Covered

Naylor Candies Inc ....F 717 266-2706
Mount Wolf *(G-11748)*

Nuts & Such Ltd ....G 215 708-8500
Philadelphia *(G-14089)*

Plantation Candies Inc ....F 215 723-6810
Telford *(G-18309)*

CANDY & CONFECTIONS: Popcorn Balls/Other Trtd Popcorn Prdts

Mostollers Mfg & Distrg ....F 814 445-7281
Friedens *(G-6223)*

Popcorn Alley Inc ....F 877 292-5611
Dover *(G-4199)*

Specialty Snacks Inc ....G 215 721-0414
Telford *(G-18317)*

CANDY, NUT & CONFECTIONERY STORES: Candy

Andersons Candies Inc ....E 724 869-3018
Baden *(G-869)*

B & E Candy ....G 724 327-8898
Jeannette *(G-8247)*

Bevans Candies Inc ....F 610 566-0581
Media *(G-10915)*

Catoris Candies Inc ....F 724 335-4371
New Kensington *(G-12333)*

Edwards Sherm Candies Inc ....E 412 372-4331
Trafford *(G-18454)*

Esthers Sweet Shop Inc ....G 412 884-4224
Pittsburgh *(G-14986)*

Evans Candy LLC ....G 717 295-7510
Lancaster *(G-9012)*

Fitzkees Candies Inc ....F 717 741-1031
York *(G-20482)*

Halls Candies LLC ....G 570 596-2267
Gillett *(G-6381)*

J S Zimmerman Co ....G 717 232-6842
Harrisburg *(G-7157)*

John L Stopay LLC ....G 570 562-6541
Taylor *(G-18259)*

Josh Early Candies Inc ....F 610 395-4321
Allentown *(G-271)*

Michael Mootz Candies Inc ....F 570 823-8272
Hanover Township *(G-6997)*

Penn Gold Hughes ....G 724 735-2121
Harrisville *(G-7254)*

Purity Candy Co ....F 570 538-9502
Allenwood *(G-442)*

Repperts Candy ....F 610 689-9200
Oley *(G-12980)*

Robert W Gastel Jr ....E 412 678-2723
White Oak *(G-19858)*

Rosalind Candy Castle Inc ....F 724 843-1144
New Brighton *(G-12041)*

Stutz Candy Company ....E 215 675-2630
Hatboro *(G-7307)*

Thomson Candies ....G 610 268-8337
Avondale *(G-861)*

TMC Candies LLC ....G 814 623-1545
Bedford *(G-1078)*

Warners Candies ....G 215 639-1615
Bensalem *(G-1269)*

Wfc & C Inc ....F 215 627-3233
Philadelphia *(G-14471)*

Wilson Candy Co Inc ....F 724 523-3151
Jeannette *(G-8268)*

CANDY, NUT & CONFECTIONERY STORES: Confectionery

Blaine Boring Chocolates ....G 814 539-6244
Johnstown *(G-8358)*

Daffins Inc ....E 724 342-2892
Sharon *(G-17432)*

Valos House of Candy ....G 724 339-2669
New Kensington *(G-12385)*

CANDY, NUT & CONFECTIONERY STORES: Nuts

Bal Nut Inc ....G 570 675-2712
Dallas *(G-3958)*

CANDY, NUT & CONFECTIONERY STORES: Produced For Direct Sale

Callies Candy Kitchens Inc ....F 570 595-2280
Mountainhome *(G-11786)*

Miesse Candies Corp ....G 717 299-5427
Lancaster *(G-9135)*

OSheas Candies ....F 814 536-4800
Johnstown *(G-8414)*

Victorias Candies Inc ....G 570 455-6341
Hazleton *(G-7534)*

CANDY: Chocolate From Cacao Beans

Basket Works Inc ....G 516 367-9200
Tannersville *(G-18234)*

Chester A Asher Inc ....C 215 721-3000
Souderton *(G-17729)*

My Aunties Candies ....G 610 269-0919
Downingtown *(G-4243)*

Premise Maid Candies Inc ....E 610 395-3221
Breinigsville *(G-2024)*

R M Palmer Company ....E 610 582-5551
Reading *(G-16483)*

R M Palmer Company ....C 610 374-5224
Wyomissing *(G-20287)*

Romolo Chocolates Inc ....E 814 452-1933
Erie *(G-5466)*

Sarris Candies Inc ....B 724 745-4042
Canonsburg *(G-2632)*

Warrell Corporation ....B 717 761-5440
Camp Hill *(G-2523)*

CANDY: Hard

Hiddie Kitchen Inc ....F 717 566-2211
Hummelstown *(G-7913)*

Lollipop HM Hlthcare Svcs LLC ....G 570 286-9460
Sunbury *(G-18171)*

My Aunties Candies ....G 610 269-0919
Downingtown *(G-4243)*

Pharmaloz Manufacturing Inc ....E 717 274-9800
Lebanon *(G-9621)*

Topps Company Inc ....D 570 346-5874
Scranton *(G-17305)*

CANDY: Soft

Marshmallowmba ....G 703 340-7157
Red Lion *(G-16607)*

CANNED SPECIALTIES

AFP Advanced Food Products LLC ......E 717 354-6560
New Holland *(G-12228)*

Ask Foods Inc ....E 717 838-6356
Palmyra *(G-13118)*

Hanover Foods Corporation ....A 717 632-6000
Hanover *(G-6894)*

Kraft Heinz Foods Company ....E 412 237-5868
Gibsonia *(G-6341)*

Kraft Heinz Foods Company ....E 412 237-5715
Carnegie *(G-2774)*

Nestle Usa Inc ....C 818 549-6000
King of Prussia *(G-8655)*

Winter Gardens Qulty Foods Inc ....C 717 624-4911
New Oxford *(G-12427)*

CANOE BUILDING & REPAIR

Altra Marine ....G 814 786-8346
Jackson Center *(G-8225)*

CANS & TUBES: Ammunition, Board Laminated With Metal Foil

United Ammunition Container ....G 610 658-0888
Wynnewood *(G-20273)*

CANS: Aluminum

CCL Container (hermitage) Inc ....G 724 981-4420
Hermitage *(G-7574)*

CCL Container Corporation ....C 724 981-4420
Hermitage *(G-7575)*

Reynolds Metals Company LLC ....F 412 343-5020
Pittsburgh *(G-15482)*

CANS: Beer, Metal

American Keg Company LLC ....E 484 524-8251
Pottstown *(G-15963)*

CANS: Composite Foil-Fiber, Made From Purchased Materials

Proline Composites Corp ....G 814 536-8491
South Fork *(G-17776)*

Stealth Composites Inc ....G 215 919-7584
Pottstown *(G-16051)*

CANS: Garbage, Stamped Or Pressed Metal

Paulsonbilt Ltd ....F 610 384-6112
Coatesville (G-3322)

CANS: Metal

Ardagh Metal Packaging USA Inc ....C 570 389-5563
Bloomsburg (G-1770)
Ball Arosol Specialty Cont Inc ....C 215 442-5462
Horsham (G-7794)
Can Corporation America Inc ....C 610 926-3044
Blandon (G-1752)
Can Corporation America Inc ....E 610 921-3460
Reading (G-16342)
Crown Americas LLC ....E 215 698-5100
Philadelphia (G-13584)
Crown Beverage Packaging LLC ....B 215 698-5100
Philadelphia (G-13585)
Crown Cork & Seal Usa Inc ....C 215 322-5507
Feasterville Trevose (G-5901)
Crown Cork & Seal Usa Inc ....C 724 626-0121
Connellsville (G-3493)
Crown Cork & Seal Usa Inc ....D 717 633-1163
Hanover (G-6871)
Crown Cork Seal ....G 610 687-2616
Wayne (G-19315)
Crown Holdings Inc ....C 215 698-5100
Yardley (G-20304)
Crown Intl Holdings Inc ....B 215 698-5100
Yardley (G-20305)
Deist Industries Inc ....E 800 233-0867
Hadley (G-6819)
JL Clark LLC ....C 717 392-4125
Lancaster (G-9073)
Lanco Industries ....G 717 949-3435
Lebanon (G-9597)
Michelman Steel Entps LLC ....F 610 395-3472
Allentown (G-315)
Nationwide Recyclers Inc ....G 215 698-5100
Philadelphia (G-14057)
Nestle Purina Petcare Company ....D 610 398-4667
Allentown (G-328)
Silgan Containers Corporation ....G 484 223-3189
Breinigsville (G-2027)
Silgan Containers Mfg Corp ....D 610 337-2203
King of Prussia (G-8676)
Silgan White Cap Corporation ....C 570 455-7781
Hazle Township (G-7480)
Universal Protective Packg Inc ....D 717 766-1578
Mechanicsburg (G-10903)

CANS: Tin

Crown Cork & Seal Company Inc ....A 215 698-5100
Yardley (G-20302)
Crown Cork & Seal Usa Inc ....G 215 698-5100
Philadelphia (G-13587)
Crown Cork & Seal Usa Inc ....B 215 698-5100
Yardley (G-20303)
Crown Holdings Inc ....E 215 322-3533
Feasterville Trevose (G-5902)

CANVAS PRDTS

Craft-Bilt Manufacturing Co ....D 215 721-7700
Souderton (G-17731)
Creative Logistics Ltd ....E 724 458-6560
Grove City (G-6782)
E R Schantz Inc ....G 610 272-3603
Norristown (G-12652)
Grid Electric Inc ....E 610 466-7030
Coatesville (G-3306)
Leathersmith Inc ....G 717 933-8084
Myerstown (G-11891)
Lightweight Manufacturing Inc ....F 610 435-4720
Whitehall (G-19883)
Mamaux Supply Co ....F 412 782-3456
Pittsburgh (G-15249)
Monarch Global Brands Inc ....D 215 482-6100
Philadelphia (G-14033)
Organic Climbing LLC ....G 651 245-1079
Philipsburg (G-14523)
Quality Canvas ....G 724 329-1571
Confluence (G-3468)
Quality Canvas ....G 814 695-8343
Duncansville (G-4461)
Robertson Manufacturing Inc ....E 610 869-9600
West Grove (G-19705)
Wondering Canvas Tattoos ....G 717 244-8260
Dallastown (G-3983)

CANVAS PRDTS: Convertible Tops, Car/Boat, Fm Purchased Mtrl

Auto Seat Cover Company ....G 814 453-5897
Erie (G-5196)

CAPACITORS & CONDENSERS

High Energy Corp ....E 610 593-2800
Parkesburg (G-13175)

CAPACITORS: Fixed Or Variable

Cmsjlp LLC ....F 814 834-2817
Ridgway (G-16700)

CAPACITORS: NEC

Dean Technology Inc ....E 724 479-3533
Lucernemines (G-10117)
Evaporated Coatings Inc ....E 215 659-3080
Willow Grove (G-20116)
High Energy Corp ....E 610 593-2800
Parkesburg (G-13175)
Kemet Investment Ltd Partnr ....G 215 822-1550
Chalfont (G-2880)
Kemet Investments Inc ....G 215 822-1550
Chalfont (G-2881)
Optixtal Inc ....G 215 254-5225
Philadelphia (G-14099)
Spectrum Control Inc ....C 814 474-1571
Fairview (G-5843)
Spectrum Control Inc ....C 814 835-4000
Fairview (G-5844)
Vishay Intertechnology Inc ....B 610 644-1300
Malvern (G-10341)

CAPS & TOPS: Bottle, Stamped Metal

Crown Holdings Inc ....C 215 698-5100
Yardley (G-20304)

CAPS: Plastic

Drug Plastics and Glass Co ....G 610 367-5000
Boyertown (G-1907)
Drug Plastics Closures Inc ....D 610 367-5000
Boyertown (G-1908)
Polymer Molding Inc ....E 800 344-7584
Erie (G-5429)
Protective Industries Inc ....C 814 868-3671
Erie (G-5441)
Supreme Corq LLC ....G 610 408-0500
Newtown Square (G-12594)

CAR LOADING SVCS

Coal Loaders Inc ....F 724 238-6601
Ligonier (G-9958)

CAR WASH EQPT

American Auto Wash Inc ....F 610 265-3222
King of Prussia (G-8580)
Elm Ave Car Wash ....G 717 637-7392
Hanover (G-6881)
Hotwash ....F 610 351-2119
Allentown (G-247)
Innovative Control Systems Inc ....E 610 881-8061
Easton (G-4706)
Innovative Control Systems Inc ....C 610 881-8000
Wind Gap (G-20169)
Landons Car Wash and Laundry ....G 570 673-4188
Canton (G-2665)
Mannis Wash Systems ....G 724 337-8255
New Kensington (G-12354)
N/S Corporation ....G 610 436-5552
West Chester (G-19605)
Pump-Warehouse Co Inc ....E 215 536-0500
Quakertown (G-16236)
USA All Pro Auto Salon Inc ....G 267 230-7442
Warminster (G-18992)

CAR WASH EQPT & SPLYS WHOLESALERS

Landons Car Wash and Laundry ....G 570 673-4188
Canton (G-2665)

CAR WASHES

Bonehead Performance Inc ....F 215 674-8206
Warminster (G-18839)
Harris Graphics & Detailing ....G 610 532-0209
Norwood (G-12880)

Rizworks ....G 570 226-7611
Hawley (G-7437)

CARBIDES

Advanced Carbide Grinding Inc ....E 724 537-3393
Derry (G-4099)
Basic Carbide Corporation ....D 412 751-3774
Buena Vista (G-2340)
D K P -Hardy Inc ....G 215 441-0383
Warminster (G-18854)
Deangelis Carbide Tooling Inc ....G 724 224-7280
Brackenridge (G-1938)
Hydro Carbide Inc ....G 724 539-9701
Latrobe (G-9480)
Phoenix Cfb Inc ....G 215 957-0500
Warminster (G-18941)
Siem Tool Company Inc ....E 724 520-1904
Latrobe (G-9520)

CARBON & GRAPHITE PRDTS, NEC

Aluminum & Carbon Plus Inc ....G 724 368-9200
Portersville (G-15924)
Anthracite Industries Inc ....E 570 286-2176
Sunbury (G-18163)
Asbury Carbons Inc ....G 570 286-9721
Sunbury (G-18164)
Asbury Graphite Mills Inc ....D 724 543-1343
Kittanning (G-8755)
Ges Graphite ....G 205 838-0820
Emlenton (G-5009)
Graftech Usa LLC ....C 814 781-2478
Saint Marys (G-16979)
Graphite Machining Inc ....E 610 682-0080
Topton (G-18413)
Graphtek LLC ....F 724 564-9211
Smithfield (G-17651)
Mersen USA Bn Corp ....C 814 781-1234
Saint Marys (G-16988)
Mersen USA St Marys-PA Corp ....D 814 781-1234
Saint Marys (G-16989)
Mersen USA St Marys-PA Corp ....C 814 781-1234
Saint Marys (G-16990)
Micron Research Corporation ....E 814 486-2444
Emporium (G-5069)
Morgan Advanced Mtls Tech Inc ....D 814 274-6132
Coudersport (G-3785)
Morgan Advanced Mtls Tech Inc ....G 570 421-9921
East Stroudsburg (G-4623)
Morgan Advanced Mtls Tech Inc ....C 814 781-1573
Saint Marys (G-16998)
Nac Carbon Products Inc ....E 814 938-7450
Punxsutawney (G-16148)
Nac Joint Venture Pipeline ....D 814 938-7450
Punxsutawney (G-16149)
National Elec Carbn Pdts Inc ....D 570 476-9004
East Stroudsburg (G-4624)
Sgl LLC ....E 610 670-4040
Reading (G-16514)
Shamokin Filler Co Inc ....G 570 644-0437
Coal Township (G-3281)
Smith Group Inc ....E 215 957-7800
Warminster (G-18966)
Stein Seal Company ....C 215 256-0201
Kulpsville (G-8831)
Tyk America Inc ....E 412 384-4259
Clairton (G-3158)
Weaver Industries Inc ....D 717 336-7507
Denver (G-4097)

CARBON BLACK

Koppers Holdings Inc ....C 412 227-2001
Pittsburgh (G-15187)
Rockwood Pigments Na Inc ....F 610 279-6450
King of Prussia (G-8670)

CARBON PAPER & INKED RIBBONS

Aserdiv Inc ....E 800 966-7770
Springfield (G-17907)
Dnp Imagingcomm America Corp ....D 724 696-7500
Mount Pleasant (G-11697)

CARBON SPECIALTIES Electrical Use

Samuel Son & Co (usa) Inc ....E 412 865-4444
Pittsburgh (G-15510)

PRODUCT

CARBONS: Electric

E-Carbon America LLC ....F 814 834-7777
Saint Marys (G-16965)

CARDIOVASCULAR SYSTEM DRUGS, EXC DIAGNOSTIC

Hercon Laboratories Inc ....D 717 764-1191
Emigsville (G-4990)

CARDS: Greeting

CSS Industries Inc ....C 610 729-3959
Plymouth Meeting (G-15840)
CSS Industries Inc ....G 570 275-5241
Danville (G-3999)
Jennifers Cards & Gifts ....G 412 462-8505
Homestead (G-1671)
Paper Magic Group Inc ....C 570 961-3863
Moosic (G-11511)
Paper Magic Group Inc ....B 570 644-0842
Elysburg (G-4978)
Rekord Printing Co ....G 570 648-3231
Elysburg (G-4980)
S E Hagarman Designs LLC ....G 717 633-5336
Hanover (G-6947)

CARDS: Identification

Dual Core LLC ....D 800 233-0298
Manheim (G-10379)

CARPET & RUG CLEANING & REPAIRING PLANTS

Certified Carpet Service Inc ....D 717 393-3012
Lancaster (G-8976)
Custom Carpet & Bedding Inc ....G 570 344-7533
Dunmore (G-4472)

CARPET & UPHOLSTERY CLEANING SVCS

Steam Mad Carpet Cleaners Inc ....G 215 283-9833
Horsham (G-7853)

CARPETS, RUGS & FLOOR COVERING

All Floor Supplies Inc ....F 412 793-6421
Monroeville (G-11323)
Carpenter Co ....C 814 944-8612
Altoona (G-486)
Flextron Industries Inc ....F 610 459-4600
Aston (G-763)
Great Northern Foam ....E 610 791-3356
Allentown (G-237)
Hurlock Bros Co Inc ....F 610 659-8153
Drexel Hill (G-4366)
Jordans Bear Den ....G 814 938-4081
Northpoint (G-12864)
Oxford Market Place Inc ....G 610 998-9080
Oxford (G-13086)
Prosource of Lancaster ....G 717 299-5680
Lancaster (G-9176)
Shaw Industries Group Inc ....E 724 266-0315
Leetsdale (G-9705)
Steam Mad Carpet Cleaners Inc ....G 215 283-9833
Horsham (G-7853)

CARPETS: Hand & Machine Made

Bloomsburg Carpet Inds Inc ....C 800 233-8773
Bloomsburg (G-1775)

CARPETS: Wilton

Langhorne Carpet Company Inc ....E 215 757-5155
Penndel (G-13239)

CARPORTS: Prefabricated Metal

American Steel Carports Inc ....F 570 825-8260
Wilkes Barre (G-19905)
Pennsylvania Aluminum ....G 570 752-2666
Berwick (G-1341)

CARRIAGES: Horse Drawn

Carriage Machine Shop LLC ....F 717 397-4079
Bird In Hand (G-1674)
Vicksburg Buggy Shop ....G 570 966-3658
Mifflinburg (G-11104)
Weaver Carriage Shop ....G 717 445-7191
East Earl (G-4557)

Weavertown Coach Shop ....G 717 768-3299
Bird In Hand (G-1685)

CARRIERS: Infant, Textile

C&H7 LLC ....G 215 887-7411
Exton (G-5658)

CARTONS: Egg, Molded Pulp, Made From Purchased Materials

Tekni-Plex Inc ....E 484 690-1520
Wayne (G-19381)
Trident Tpi Holdings Inc ....A 484 690-1520
Wayne (G-19384)

CARTS: Grocery

Blair Fixtures & Millwork Inc ....E 814 940-1913
Altoona (G-482)

CASEMENTS: Aluminum

Northeast Building Pdts Corp ....F 215 331-2400
Philadelphia (G-14080)

CASES, WOOD

Bomboy Inc ....F 610 266-1553
Allentown (G-157)

CASES: Attache'

American Accessories Inc ....E 215 639-8000
Bensalem (G-1148)

CASES: Carrying

Case Design Corporation ....D 215 703-0130
Telford (G-18270)
Case Design Corporation ....G 800 847-4176
Telford (G-18271)
Codi Inc ....F 717 540-1337
Harrisburg (G-7108)
Tre-Ray Cases Inc ....F 215 551-6811
Philadelphia (G-14404)

CASES: Carrying, Clothing & Apparel

Discovery Direct Inc ....G 610 252-3809
Easton (G-4670)
Shine Moon L P ....F 570 539-8602
Mount Pleasant Mills (G-11732)
Silver Charm Clothing Company ....G 484 274-6796
Allentown (G-393)

CASES: Nonrefrigerated, Exc Wood

CNT Fixture Company Inc ....E 412 443-6260
Glenshaw (G-6484)

CASES: Packing, Nailed Or Lock Corner, Wood

Industrial Shipping Pdts Isp ....G 724 423-6533
Latrobe (G-9481)
Timber Pallet & Lumber Co Inc ....G 610 562-8442
Hamburg (G-6853)

CASES: Plastic

Miller Plastic Products Inc ....F 724 947-5000
Burgettstown (G-2350)

CASES: Shipping, Nailed Or Lock Corner, Wood

Ishman Plastic & Wood Cutting ....G 814 849-9961
Brookville (G-2262)
James C Richards ....G 724 758-9032
Ellwood City (G-4941)
Limpach Industries Inc ....F 724 646-4011
Sharpsville (G-17473)
OMalley Wood Products Inc ....E 717 677-6550
Gardners (G-6261)

CASH REGISTER REPAIR SVCS

Excellent Tool Inc ....G 814 337-7705
Meadville (G-10704)
Integrated Myers Systems LLC ....G 814 937-3958
Gallitzin (G-6246)
Rearden Steel Fabrication Inc ....F 717 503-1989
Lemoyne (G-9750)

CASINGS: Storage, Missile & Missile Components

General Dynamics Ots PA Inc ....C 570 342-7801
Scranton (G-17238)

CASKETS & ACCESS

Casket Shells Incorporated ....G 570 876-2642
Eynon (G-5754)
Matthews International Corp ....E 412 442-8200
Pittsburgh (G-15264)
McKennas Woodworking ....G 570 836-3652
Tunkhannock (G-18542)
Miller Casket Company Inc ....D 570 876-3872
Jermyn (G-8308)
Reynoldsville Casket Company ....G 814 653-9666
Reynoldsville (G-16663)
Smiths Wilbert Vault Company ....E 610 588-5259
Bangor (G-928)
Werzalit of America Inc ....D 814 362-3881
Bradford (G-1995)
York Casket Company ....B 717 854-9566
York (G-20731)

CASKETS WHOLESALERS

Smiths Wilbert Vault Company ....E 610 588-5259
Bangor (G-928)

CAST STONE: Concrete

Coalisland Cast Stone Inc ....F 610 476-1683
Collegeville (G-3372)
Igneous Rock Gallery ....G 717 774-4074
Mechanicsburg (G-10857)
Joseph Riepole Construction ....G 412 833-6611
Library (G-9955)
Sun Precast Company ....E 570 658-8000
Beaver Springs (G-1024)

CASTERS

Barkby Group Inc ....G 717 292-4148
Dover (G-4185)
Penn A Caster Loft Offices ....G 412 471-3285
Pittsburgh (G-15373)

CASTINGS GRINDING: For The Trade

A C Grinding & Supply Co Inc ....G 215 946-3760
Levittown (G-9811)
Carlsons Industrial Grinding ....G 814 864-8640
Erie (G-5221)
Daily Grind Quarryville ....G 717 786-0615
Quarryville (G-16268)
Fluid Energy Proc & Eqp Co ....E 215 721-8990
Telford (G-18289)
Fluid Energy Proc & Eqp Co ....D 215 368-2510
Hatfield (G-7343)
Holt Le Grinding Service ....F 724 864-6865
Rillton (G-16747)
Industrial Machine Works Inc ....E 412 782-5055
Pittsburgh (G-15119)
J & S Grinding Co Inc ....F 814 776-1113
Ridgway (G-16713)
K & K Precision Grinding Co ....G 215 333-1276
Philadelphia (G-13917)
Ruch Carbide Burs Inc ....E 215 657-3660
Willow Grove (G-20139)
Shasta Holdings Company ....C 724 378-8280
Aliquippa (G-95)
Spring Tool & Die Co Inc ....G 814 224-5173
Roaring Spring (G-16771)
Thorsens Precision Grinding ....G 717 765-9090
Waynesboro (G-19427)
Wash n Grind LLC ....G 814 383-4707
Bellefonte (G-1124)

CASTINGS: Aerospace Investment, Ferrous

Precision Castparts Corp ....B 570 474-6371
Mountain Top (G-11771)

CASTINGS: Aerospace, Aluminum

Cera-Met LLC ....C 610 266-0270
Bethlehem (G-1481)

CASTINGS: Aerospace, Nonferrous, Exc Aluminum

Haas Group ....A 484 564-4500
West Chester (G-19559)
Master Replicas Group Inc....................G 610 652-2265
Zieglerville (G-20833)

CASTINGS: Aluminum

Active Brass Foundry Inc.....................F 215 257-6519
Telford (G-18266)
Boose Aluminum Foundry Co Inc ....C 717 336-5581
Reamstown (G-16574)
Bridesburg Foundry Company ....D 610 266-0900
Whitehall (G-19863)
Buckeye Aluminum Foundry Inc ....E 814 683-4011
Linesville (G-9978)
Carroll Manufacturing Co LLC..............G 724 266-0400
Leetsdale (G-9688)
Carson Industries Inc ....G 724 295-5147
Kittanning (G-8760)
Carson Industries Inc ....E 724 295-5147
Freeport (G-6201)
Cast-Rite Metal Company.......................G 610 582-1300
Birdsboro (G-1691)
Hopewell Non-Ferrous Foundry ....G 610 385-6747
Douglassville (G-4178)
Jacob Pattern Works Inc ....F 610 326-1100
Pottstown (G-16004)
K & S Castings Inc ....E 717 272-9775
Lebanon (G-9585)
Laminators Incorporated ....D 215 723-5285
Hatfield (G-7362)
Latrobe Foundry Mch & Sup Co ....F 724 537-3341
Latrobe (G-9489)
Lenape Tooling Inc ....F 215 257-0431
Perkasie (G-13283)
New Hegedus Aluminum Co Inc...........E 814 676-5635
Oil City (G-12953)
New Jersey Shell Casting Corp............E 717 426-1835
Marietta (G-10465)
Pennex Aluminum Company LLC ....E 724 373-8471
Greenville (G-6764)
Perfect Stride Ltd ....G 412 221-1722
Pittsburgh (G-15378)
Quality Aluminum Casting Co ....F 717 484-4545
Denver (G-4090)
Royer Quality Castings Inc ....G 610 367-1390
Boyertown (G-1927)
Schmitt Aluminum Foundry Inc............F 717 299-5651
Smoketown (G-17668)
Trega Corporation ....F 610 562-5558
Hamburg (G-6854)
United Bronze of Pittsburgh ....G 724 226-8500
Tarentum (G-18252)
WER Corporation ....C 610 678-8023
Reading (G-16564)
Williamsport Foundry Co Inc ....E 570 323-6216
Williamsport (G-20093)

CASTINGS: Brass, Bronze & Copper

Goldsborough & Vansant Inc.................G 724 782-0393
Finleyville (G-5959)

CASTINGS: Brass, NEC, Exc Die

A Cubed Corporation.............................C 724 538-4000
Mars (G-10485)
Active Brass Foundry Inc.....................F 215 257-6519
Telford (G-18266)
Bridesburg Foundry Company ....D 610 266-0900
Whitehall (G-19863)
Concast Metal Products Company........C 724 538-4000
Mars (G-10492)
Flury Foundry Company ....F 717 397-9080
Lancaster (G-9023)
New Jersey Shell Casting Corp............E 717 426-1835
Marietta (G-10465)
United Brass Works Inc ....E 814 456-4296
Erie (G-5524)

CASTINGS: Bronze, NEC, Exc Die

ART Research Enterprises.....................E 717 290-1303
Lancaster (G-8944)
Clearfield Energy Inc............................G 610 293-0410
Conshohocken (G-3529)
Considine Studios Inc ....G 215 362-8922
Lansdale (G-9353)

Erie Bronze & Aluminum Company ......E 814 838-8602
Erie (G-5263)
United Bronze of Pittsburgh ....G 724 226-8500
Tarentum (G-18252)

CASTINGS: Commercial Investment, Ferrous

Nova Precision Casting Corp ....E 570 366-2679
Auburn (G-819)
Post Precision Castings Inc ....C 610 488-1011
Strausstown (G-18099)

CASTINGS: Copper & Copper-Base Alloy, NEC, Exc Die

Perma Cast LLC ....E 724 325-1662
Export (G-5620)

CASTINGS: Die, Aluminum

Accuride Erie LP ....B 814 480-6400
Erie (G-5170)
Alcast Metals Inc..................................E 215 368-5865
Montgomeryville (G-11382)
Alcoa Corporation ....G 412 553-4001
Pittsburgh (G-14661)
Alcoa Corporation ....G 412 315-2900
Pittsburgh (G-14662)
Bardane Mfg Co ....D 570 876-4844
Jermyn (G-8305)
C Palmer Manufacturing Inc ....F 724 872-8200
West Newton (G-19748)
E A Quirin Machine Shop Inc ....E 570 429-0590
Saint Clair (G-16937)
Howmet Castings & Services Inc ....F 973 361-2310
Pittsburgh (G-15102)
J Clem Kline & Son Inc........................G 610 258-6071
Easton (G-4708)
K Castings Inc ....G 724 539-9753
Latrobe (G-9485)
Pace Industries LLC ....B 724 539-4527
Loyalhanna (G-10112)
Parker White Metal Company ....A 814 474-5511
Fairview (G-5835)
Phb Inc ....A 814 474-5511
Fairview (G-5837)
Phb Inc ....D 814 474-2683
Fairview (G-5838)
Scicast International Inc ....E 610 369-3060
Bechtelsville (G-1036)
Sensus USA Inc ....C 800 375-8875
Du Bois (G-4419)
Sensus USA Inc ....C 724 430-3956
Pittsburgh (G-15524)
T Helbling LLC.......................................G 724 601-9819
Beaver (G-992)
Tilden Manufacturing Inc ....G 610 562-4682
Hamburg (G-6852)
West Phila Bronze Co Inc......................E 610 874-1454
Chester (G-3067)

CASTINGS: Die, Copper & Copper Alloy

Metallurgical Products Company ....E 610 696-6770
West Chester (G-19601)

CASTINGS: Die, Nonferrous

Franklin Bronze Precision Comp ....D 814 437-6891
Franklin (G-6127)

CASTINGS: Die, Zinc

Bardane Mfg Co ....D 570 876-4844
Jermyn (G-8305)
La France Corp.....................................C 610 361-4300
Concordville (G-3457)
Parker White Metal Company ....A 814 474-5511
Fairview (G-5835)
Phb Inc ....A 814 474-5511
Fairview (G-5837)
Scicast International Inc ....E 610 369-3060
Bechtelsville (G-1036)

CASTINGS: Ductile

Metso Minerals Industries Inc..............B 717 843-8671
York (G-20590)
Victaulic Company ....A 610 559-3300
Easton (G-4770)
Waupaca Foundry Inc...........................C 570 724-5191
Tioga (G-18367)

Waupaca Foundry Inc...........................B 570 827-3245
Tioga (G-18368)

CASTINGS: Gray Iron

B & B Foundry Inc.................................E 215 333-7100
Philadelphia (G-13435)
Benton Foundry Inc ....C 570 925-6711
Benton (G-1277)
Charter Dura-Bar Inc ....F 717 779-0807
York (G-20424)
Clearfield Machine Company ....F 814 765-6544
Clearfield (G-3214)
Donsco Inc..C 717 653-1851
Mount Joy (G-11653)
Donsco Inc..C 717 252-1561
Belleville (G-1131)
Donsco Inc..B 717 252-1561
Wrightsville (G-20236)
General Foundry LLC ....G 610 997-8660
Bethlehem (G-1525)
H and H Foundry Machine Co ....G 724 863-3251
Manor (G-10411)
Hamburg Manufacturing Inc ....E 610 562-2203
Hamburg (G-6840)
Hodge Foundry Inc ....C 724 588-4100
Greenville (G-6746)
Jdh Pacific Inc ....E 562 926-8088
Reading (G-16413)
Kulp Foundry Inc ....D 610 881-8093
Wind Gap (G-20170)
McLanahan Corporation ....B 814 695-9807
Hollidaysburg (G-7651)
Penn Mar Castings Inc ....D 717 632-4165
Hanover (G-6935)
R H Sheppard Co Inc ....A 717 637-3751
Hanover (G-6941)
S & B Foundry Co ....E 570 784-2047
Bloomsburg (G-1800)
Somerset Consolidated Inds Inc ....E 814 445-7927
Somerset (G-17706)
Unicast Company..................................D 610 366-8836
Boyertown (G-1934)
Unicast Company..................................G 610 366-8836
Allentown (G-417)
Weatherly Casting and Mch Co ....D 570 427-8611
Weatherly (G-19455)
Wellsville Foundry Inc ....G 330 532-2995
Meadville (G-10812)
West Salisbury Fndry Mch Inc...............E 814 662-2809
West Salisbury (G-19765)
Williamsport Foundry Co Inc ....E 570 323-6216
Williamsport (G-20093)

CASTINGS: Machinery, Aluminum

Aqua Enterprises ....F 215 257-2231
Perkasie (G-13266)
Gupta Permold Corporation..................C 412 793-3511
Pittsburgh (G-15067)
Kebeico Inc ....E 610 241-8163
Chadds Ford (G-2852)

CASTINGS: Machinery, Brass

United Foundry Company Inc................E 814 539-8840
Johnstown (G-8440)

CASTINGS: Machinery, Nonferrous, Exc Die or Aluminum Copper

Elecast Inc ....F 570 587-5105
S Abingtn Twp (G-16895)

CASTINGS: Precision

A M Industries Inc ....G 215 362-2525
Lansdale (G-9339)
D & M Precision Mfg Inc ....G 724 727-3039
Apollo (G-674)
De Technologies Inc ....E 610 337-2800
King of Prussia (G-8605)
Latrobe Specialty Mtls Co LLC ....A 724 537-7711
Latrobe (G-9494)
Piad Precision Casting Corp ....C 724 838-5500
Greensburg (G-6700)
Prl Industries Inc..................................E 717 273-6787
Cornwall (G-3740)
Seybert Castings Inc ....F 215 364-7115
Huntingdon Valley (G-8038)

PRODUCT

CASTINGS: Steel

Beaver Valley Alloy Foundry Co ....E 724 775-1987
Monaca (G-11283)
Brighton Steel Inc ....E 724 846-7377
Beaver Falls (G-997)
Dickson Investment Hdwr Inc ....E 610 272-0764
King of Prussia (G-8609)
Duraloy Technologies Inc ....C 724 887-5100
Scottdale (G-17190)
Export USA LLC ....G 215 949-3380
Levittown (G-9835)
Hazleton Casting Company ....E 570 453-0199
Hazleton (G-7500)
Rochester Alloy Casting Co ....E 724 452-5659
Zelienople (G-20819)
Whemco - Steel Castings Inc ....F 724 643-7001
Midland (G-11089)
Whemco - Steel Castings Inc ....D 412 390-2700
Pittsburgh (G-15714)
Whemco Inc ....E 412 390-2700
Pittsburgh (G-15715)

CASTINGS: Titanium

Oregon Metallurgical LLC ....F 541 967-9000
Pittsburgh (G-15363)

CASTINGS: Zinc

Hopewell Non-Ferrous Foundry ....G 610 385-6747
Douglassville (G-4178)
Schmitt Aluminum Foundry Inc ....F 717 299-5651
Smoketown (G-17668)

CATALOG & MAIL-ORDER HOUSES

Brodart Co ....C 570 769-3265
Mc Elhattan (G-10586)
Brynavon Group Inc ....G 610 525-2102
Villanova (G-18765)
Captek Inc ....G 610 296-2111
Berwyn (G-1355)
Critical Path Project Inc ....G 215 545-2212
Philadelphia (G-13583)
Go Tell It Inc ....G 212 769-3220
Robesonia (G-16774)
Herb Penn Co Ltd ....E 215 632-6100
Philadelphia (G-13816)
Lexicon International Corp ....E 215 639-8220
Bensalem (G-1220)
Mason Jars Company ....F 877 490-5565
Erie (G-5381)
Matangos Candies Inc ....G 717 234-0882
Harrisburg (G-7174)
Merck Sharp & Dohme Corp ....C 215 631-5000
West Point (G-19762)
Sculptz Inc ....E 215 494-2900
Trevose (G-18503)
Veritas Press Inc ....F 717 519-1974
Lancaster (G-9233)
Wendell August Forge Inc ....D 724 748-9500
Mercer (G-10979)
WM Enterprises Inc ....E 717 238-5751
Harrisburg (G-7248)

CATALOG SALES

Industrial Instrs & Sups Inc ....F 215 396-0822
Wycombe (G-20260)

CATALOG SHOWROOMS

Susquehanna Glass Co ....E 717 684-2155
Columbia (G-3451)

CATALYSTS: Chemical

PQ Group Holdings Inc ....F 610 651-4400
Malvern (G-10301)

CATERERS

Carrollsisters ....E 215 969-4688
Philadelphia (G-13509)
Davenmark Inc ....F 484 461-8683
Upper Darby (G-18684)
Franks Ice Service LLC ....G 215 741-2026
Bensalem (G-1198)
Queen of Hearts Inc ....E 610 889-0477
Malvern (G-10305)
Woods Wings ....G 610 417-5684
Kintnersville (G-8730)

CATTLE WHOLESALERS

Nicholas Meat Packing Co ....C 570 725-3511
Loganton (G-10097)

CAULKING COMPOUNDS

United Gilsonite Laboratories ....D 570 344-1202
Scranton (G-17308)

CEILING SYSTEMS: Luminous, Commercial

Armstrong World Industries Inc ....A 717 397-0611
Lancaster (G-8942)

CEMENT & CONCRETE RELATED PRDTS & EQPT: Bituminous

Aces Inc ....G 215 458-7143
Morrisville (G-11551)
Admixtures Inc ....F 610 775-0371
Wernersville (G-19483)
Highway Materials Inc ....E 215 234-4522
Perkiomenville (G-13301)
L & M Construction ....G 610 326-9970
Pottstown (G-15951)

CEMENT ROCK: Crushed & Broken

International Mill Service ....A 215 956-5500
Horsham (G-7824)
Mill Services Corp ....F 412 678-6141
Glassport (G-6413)
Quarry Management LLC ....F 646 599-5893
Lackawaxen (G-8876)
Tms International LLC ....F 814 535-5081
Johnstown (G-8439)
Tms International LLC ....D 215 956-5500
Horsham (G-7859)

CEMENT, EXC LINOLEUM & TILE

Atlas Minerals & Chemicals Inc ....E 800 523-8269
Mertztown (G-11000)

CEMENT: High Temperature, Refractory, Nonclay

Krosaki Mgnsita Rfrctories LLC ....E 717 793-5536
York (G-20560)
M J Stranko Inc ....G 610 929-8080
Reading (G-16436)
Mssi Refractory LLC ....E 412 771-5533
Mc Kees Rocks (G-10621)
Resco Group Inc ....F 412 494-4491
Pittsburgh (G-15479)
Sauereisen Inc ....E 412 963-0303
Pittsburgh (G-15514)

CEMENT: Hydraulic

Antonio Colella Cement Work ....G 215 745-2951
Philadelphia (G-13396)
Ardex L P ....C 724 203-5000
Aliquippa (G-66)
Cemex Cnstr Mtls ATL LLC ....C 724 535-4311
Wampum (G-18798)
Erie Strayer Company ....C 814 456-7001
Erie (G-5275)
Essroc Cement ....G 610 882-2498
Bethlehem (G-1504)
Federal White Cement ....G 814 946-8950
Altoona (G-506)
Harsco Corporation ....C 570 421-7500
East Stroudsburg (G-4617)
Keystone Cement Co ....G 610 837-1881
Exton (G-5705)
Lafarge North America Inc ....E 412 461-1163
Pittsburgh (G-15216)
Lehigh Cement Company LLC ....D 717 843-0811
York (G-20565)
Quikrete Companies LLC ....E 724 539-6600
Latrobe (G-9513)
R & D Packaging PA Inc ....G 570 235-2310
Wilkes Barre (G-19960)
SAI Hydraulics Inc ....E 610 497-0190
Linwood (G-9991)

CEMENT: Masonry

Buzzi Unicem USA Inc ....E 610 746-6222
Stockertown (G-18064)

Essroc Corp ....F 610 759-4211
Nazareth (G-11963)
Essroc Corp ....G 610 837-6725
Nazareth (G-11964)

CEMENT: Natural

Eastern Architectural Pdts LLC ....G 724 513-1630
Zelienople (G-20797)
G M C Inc ....E 215 638-4400
Bensalem (G-1201)
Happy Valley Blended Pdts LLC ....F 814 548-7090
Pleasant Gap (G-15793)

CEMENT: Portland

Armstrong Cement & Supply Corp ....D 724 352-9401
Cabot (G-2452)
Buzzi Unicem USA Inc ....E 610 882-5000
Bethlehem (G-1476)
Hercules Cement Company LP ....C 610 759-6300
Stockertown (G-18065)
Holcim (us) Inc ....G 724 226-1449
Tarentum (G-18245)
Keystone Cement Company ....C 610 837-1881
Bath (G-962)
Lafarge North America Inc ....D 610 262-7831
Whitehall (G-19880)
Lehigh Cement Company LLC ....C 610 926-1024
Fleetwood (G-5976)
Lehigh Cement Company LLC ....G 610 562-3000
Hamburg (G-6844)
Midwest Material Inds Inc ....G 610 882-5000
Bethlehem (G-1573)
RC Lonestar Inc ....D 610 882-5000
Bethlehem (G-1608)

CEMETERIES: Real Estate Operation

Jefferson Memorial Park Inc ....E 412 655-4500
Pittsburgh (G-15147)

CEMETERY ASSOCIATION

Catholic Scl Svcs of Scranton ....D 570 207-2283
Scranton (G-17216)
Catholic Scl Svcs of Scranton ....G 570 454-6693
Hazleton (G-7494)

CEMETERY MEMORIAL DEALERS

Gingrich Memorials Inc ....F 717 272-0901
Lebanon (G-9574)
Howell Craft Inc ....G 412 751-6861
Elizabeth (G-4860)
Jones Stone & Marble Inc ....G 724 838-7625
Greensburg (G-6681)
Oliver T Korb & Sons Inc ....G 814 371-4545
Du Bois (G-4408)

CERAMIC FIBER

Custom Sintered Specialties ....G 814 834-5154
Saint Marys (G-16959)

CERAMIC FLOOR & WALL TILE WHOLESALERS

Dal-Tile Corporation ....C 717 334-1181
Gettysburg (G-6287)

CERAMIC SCHOOLS

Aud-A-Bud Ceramics ....G 717 898-7537
Landisville (G-9258)

CHAIN: Tire, Made From Purchased Wire

South Fork Hardware Company ....G 814 248-3375
Johnstown (G-8436)

CHAIN: Wire

Safety Sling Company Inc ....F 412 231-6684
Pittsburgh (G-15506)

CHALK MINING: Crushed & Broken

Edward M Arnold Jr ....F 610 689-5636
Douglassville (G-4175)

CHANDELIERS: Commercial

Camman Industries Inc ....E 724 539-7670
Derry (G-4100)

Carey Schuster LLC.............................G....... 610 431-2512
West Chester (G-19519)

CHANGE MAKING MACHINES

Crane Payment Innovations Inc ....B....... 610 430-2700
Malvern (G-10218)

CHARCOAL

Milazzo Industries Inc............................E....... 570 722-0522
Pittston (G-15767)

CHARCOAL: Activated

Blind and Vision Rehab ....F....... 412 325-7504
Homestead (G-7683)
Calgon Carbon Corporation....................C....... 412 787-6700
Moon Township (G-11482)
Calgon Carbon Corporation....................G....... 610 873-3071
Downingtown (G-4218)
Calgon Carbon Corporation....................B....... 412 787-6700
Pittsburgh (G-14803)
Envirotrol Inc ....E....... 412 741-2030
Rochester (G-16785)
Evoqua Water Technologies LLC ....E....... 724 827-8181
Darlington (G-4028)
Haycarb Usa Inc ....G....... 281 292-8678
Oakdale (G-12900)
Indocarb AC LLC ....G....... 412 928-4970
Pittsburgh (G-15117)
Oxbow Activated Carbon LLC ....F....... 724 791-2411
Emlenton (G-5013)

CHART & GRAPH DESIGN SVCS

Daedal Group Inc ....G....... 215 745-8718
Philadelphia (G-13603)
Informing Design Inc ....G....... 412 465-0047
Pittsburgh (G-15124)

CHASSIS: Automobile Trailer

Anderson Inc ....F....... 412 486-2211
Allison Park (G-447)

CHASSIS: Motor Vehicle

Carriers Wreckers By Kimes.................G....... 724 342-2930
Mercer (G-10960)
Cheetah Chassis Corporation ....C....... 570 752-2708
Berwick (G-1317)
Gregory Racing Fabrications.................G....... 610 759-8217
Nazareth (G-11970)
Kovatch Mobile Equipment Corp ....A....... 570 669-9461
Nesquehoning (G-12007)
Wood Racing Products LLC ....G....... 717 454-7003
Pine Grove (G-14608)

CHASSIS: Travel Trailer

Conrad Enterprises Inc ....E....... 717 274-5151
Cornwall (G-3738)
Warrington Equipment Mfg Co ....E....... 215 343-1714
Warrington (G-19138)

CHECK CASHING SVCS

Express Money Services Inc.................G....... 717 235-5993
New Freedom (G-12208)
Tobacco Plus Cash Checking................G....... 267 585-3802
Levittown (G-9868)

CHEESE WHOLESALERS

Grammeco Inc ....C....... 610 352-4400
Upper Darby (G-18686)
Ken Weaver Meats Inc ....E....... 717 502-0118
Wellsville (G-19479)
Murazzi Provision Co............................F....... 570 344-2285
Scranton (G-17262)
Savencia Cheese USA LLC ....D....... 717 355-8500
New Holland (G-12281)

CHEESECLOTH

Armstrong/Kover Kwick Inc ....E....... 412 771-2200
Mc Kees Rocks (G-10603)

CHEMICAL CLEANING SVCS

Active Chemical Corporation................F....... 215 322-0377
Langhorne (G-9272)
Projectile Tube Cleaning Inc ....E....... 724 763-7633
Ford City (G-6051)

Recirculation Technologies LLC ....F....... 215 682-7099
Fort Washington (G-6090)

CHEMICAL ELEMENTS

4 Elements of Life LLC ....G....... 215 668-1643
Philadelphia (G-13318)
Allegheny Alloys ....G....... 412 833-9733
Pittsburgh (G-14676)
Doctor Bart Ayurveda ....G....... 717 524-4208
Hanover (G-6878)
Element 1 LLC ....G....... 570 593-8177
Schuylkill Haven (G-17156)
Element Granite & Quartz ....G....... 215 437-9368
Philadelphia (G-13666)
Element Roofing LLC ....G....... 610 737-0641
Bethlehem (G-1502)
Elements Home Accents LLC ....G....... 412 521-0724
Pittsburgh (G-14963)
Elements of Love ....G....... 267 262-9796
Philadelphia (G-13668)
Elements Skin Care LLC ....G....... 814 254-4227
Johnstown (G-8371)
Grotto ....G....... 610 570-9060
Allentown (G-238)
Synergy Core Elements.........................G....... 267 885-5832
New Hope (G-12316)

CHEMICAL PROCESSING MACHINERY & EQPT

Allied Foam Tech Corp ....G....... 215 540-2666
Montgomeryville (G-11384)
Chemcut Corporation ....B....... 814 272-2800
State College (G-17950)
Chemcut Holdings LLC ....D....... 814 272-2800
State College (G-17951)
Global Chem Feed Solutions LLC ....E....... 215 675-2777
Warminster (G-18888)
Orchem Pumps Inc ....G....... 215 743-6352
Philadelphia (G-14101)
Rusmar Incorporated............................F....... 610 436-4314
West Chester (G-19632)
Sergood Corp ....G....... 724 772-5600
Cranberry Township (G-3849)

CHEMICAL SPLYS FOR FOUNDRIES

Callery LLC ....G....... 724 538-1200
Evans City (G-5556)
Euclid Chemical Company ....G....... 610 438-2409
Easton (G-4681)
K2 Concepts Inc ....F....... 717 207-0820
Lancaster (G-9077)
Rowa Corporation.................................G....... 609 567-8600
Croydon (G-3927)

CHEMICALS & ALLIED PRDTS WHOLESALERS, NEC

Alpha Aromatics Inc ....D....... 412 252-1012
Pittsburgh (G-14686)
Archer Instruments LLC ....G....... 215 589-0356
Catasauqua (G-2814)
Baker Petrolite LLC ....F....... 610 876-2200
Crum Lynne (G-3935)
Chemex Inc..G....... 610 398-6200
Allentown (G-168)
Chemical Equipment Labs VA Inc ....E....... 610 497-9390
Newtown Square (G-12570)
CRC Industries Inc ....G....... 215 441-4380
Warminster (G-18851)
Cummings Group Ltd ....F....... 814 774-8238
Girard (G-6385)
Di Chem Concentrate Inc ....F....... 717 938-8391
Lewisberry (G-9883)
Dreumex USA Inc ....E....... 717 767-6881
York (G-20457)
Fisher Scientific Company LLC ....B....... 724 517-1500
Pittsburgh (G-15019)
Illinois Tool Works Inc ....D....... 215 855-8450
Montgomeryville (G-11399)
Interstate Chemical Co Inc ....E....... 724 813-2576
Erie (G-5331)
Mary Hail Rubber Co Inc ....F....... 215 343-1955
Warrington (G-19124)
McAdoo & Allen Inc ....E....... 215 536-3520
Quakertown (G-16214)
Peroxychem LLC...................................E....... 267 422-2400
Philadelphia (G-14138)

Praxair Distribution Inc ....F....... 215 736-8005
Morrisville (G-11579)
Rockwood Pigments Na Inc ....F....... 610 279-6450
King of Prussia (G-8670)
Sartomer Company Divison Total ....E....... 610 692-8401
West Chester (G-19637)
Specialty Chemical Systems Inc ....F....... 610 323-2716
Pottstown (G-16050)
Taylor Chemical Inc ....F....... 570 562-7771
Taylor (G-18262)
United Oil Company Corp ....F....... 412 231-1269
Pittsburgh (G-15674)
Varsal LLC ....C....... 215 957-5880
Warminster (G-18993)
Zep Inc ....C....... 610 295-1360
Breinigsville (G-2033)

CHEMICALS & ALLIED PRDTS, WHOL: Chemical, Organic, Synthetic

Houghton Chemical Corporation ....G....... 800 777-2466
Scranton (G-17241)

CHEMICALS & ALLIED PRDTS, WHOL: Noncorrosive Prdts/Matls

Valley Wholesale & Supply ....E....... 724 783-6531
Kittanning (G-8801)

CHEMICALS & ALLIED PRDTS, WHOLESALE: Adhesives

Alacer Corp...C....... 717 258-2000
Carlisle (G-2688)

CHEMICALS & ALLIED PRDTS, WHOLESALE: Aerosols

Perfectdata Corporation........................G....... 800 973-7332
Plymouth Meeting (G-15863)

CHEMICALS & ALLIED PRDTS, WHOLESALE: Alcohols

Lancaster Brewing Company ....E....... 717 391-6258
Lancaster (G-9090)

CHEMICALS & ALLIED PRDTS, WHOLESALE: Alkalines & Chlorine

Mt Chemical Company LLC ....G....... 570 474-2200
Mountain Top (G-11767)

CHEMICALS & ALLIED PRDTS, WHOLESALE: Anti-Corrosion Prdts

Wendells Prfmce Trck Sp LLC...............G....... 717 458-8404
Mechanicsburg (G-10906)

CHEMICALS & ALLIED PRDTS, WHOLESALE: Aromatic

Turtle Moon Gardens ....G....... 814 639-0287
Port Matilda (G-15907)

CHEMICALS & ALLIED PRDTS, WHOLESALE: Calcium Chloride

Calcium Chloride Sales Inc ....G....... 724 458-5778
Grove City (G-6781)
Eco Solution Distributing LLC...............F....... 724 941-4140
Pittsburgh (G-14959)

CHEMICALS & ALLIED PRDTS, WHOLESALE: Carbon Black

Rwe Holding Company ....F....... 724 752-9082
New Castle (G-12146)

CHEMICALS & ALLIED PRDTS, WHOLESALE: Chemical Additives

Nanohorizons Inc ....E....... 814 355-4700
Bellefonte (G-1109)

CHEMICALS & ALLIED PRDTS, WHOLESALE: Chemicals, Indl

Barbers Chemicals Inc ....F....... 724 962-7886
Sharpsville (G-17469)

P
R
O
D
U
C
T

E E Zimmerman Company ....F 412 963-0949
Pittsburgh *(G-14950)*

Interstate Chemical Co Inc..................C 724 981-3771
Hermitage *(G-7588)*

Interstate Chemical Co Inc..................G 724 774-1669
Beaver *(G-985)*

Kleen Line Service Co Inc ....C 412 466-6277
Dravosburg *(G-4351)*

Univar USA Inc ....D 717 944-7471
Middletown *(G-11084)*

Wacker Chemical Corporation...............D 610 336-2700
Allentown *(G-428)*

CHEMICALS & ALLIED PRDTS, WHOLESALE: Chemicals, Indl & Heavy

FBC Chemical Corporation ....G 724 625-3116
Mars *(G-10497)*

CHEMICALS & ALLIED PRDTS, WHOLESALE: Concrete Additives

Cellular Concrete LLC ....F 610 398-7833
Allentown *(G-166)*

Frank Casilio and Sons Inc....................G 610 253-3558
Easton *(G-4685)*

Surtreat Holding LLC..............................G 412 281-1202
Pittsburgh *(G-15592)*

Vci Coatings LLC ....G 412 281-1202
Pittsburgh *(G-15689)*

CHEMICALS & ALLIED PRDTS, WHOLESALE: Indl Gases

American Welding & Gas Inc ....F 570 323-8400
Williamsport *(G-19985)*

Specgas Inc ....G 215 355-2405
Warminster *(G-18971)*

CHEMICALS & ALLIED PRDTS, WHOLESALE: Plastics Film

Packaging Science Inc ....F 610 992-9991
King of Prussia *(G-8658)*

Robert Mrvel Plastic Mulch LLC ....F 717 838-0976
Annville *(G-658)*

CHEMICALS & ALLIED PRDTS, WHOLESALE: Plastics Materials, NEC

Chemex Inc...G 610 398-6200
Allentown *(G-168)*

Graham Packaging Company Inc..........C 717 849-8500
Lancaster *(G-9031)*

Hpi Processes Inc ....G 215 799-0450
Telford *(G-18294)*

CHEMICALS & ALLIED PRDTS, WHOLESALE: Plastics Prdts, NEC

Essentra Plastics LLC ....C 814 899-7671
Erie *(G-5282)*

General Technical Plastics......................E 610 363-5480
Exton *(G-5687)*

J Benson Corp ....G 610 678-2692
Reading *(G-16411)*

Laminated Materials Corp......................E 215 425-4100
Bensalem *(G-1218)*

Plastic Profiles LLC ....G 717 593-9200
Greencastle *(G-6626)*

Robert H Berenson ....G 610 642-9380
Haverford *(G-7414)*

Smart Systems Inc ....G 412 323-2128
Pittsburgh *(G-15546)*

Trident Plastics Inc ....E 215 443-7147
Warminster *(G-18986)*

CHEMICALS & ALLIED PRDTS, WHOLESALE: Plastics Sheets & Rods

Central Distribution Co Inc ....G 717 393-4851
Lancaster *(G-8973)*

Total Plastics Inc...................................G 877 677-8872
Philadelphia *(G-14399)*

Total Plastics Resources LLC...............E 215 637-2221
Bensalem *(G-1261)*

CHEMICALS & ALLIED PRDTS, WHOLESALE: Plastics, Basic Shapes

Alpha Aromatics Inc ....D 412 252-1012
Pittsburgh *(G-14686)*

CHEMICALS & ALLIED PRDTS, WHOLESALE: Polyurethane Prdts

Smith Group Inc ....E 215 957-7800
Warminster *(G-18966)*

CHEMICALS & ALLIED PRDTS, WHOLESALE: Resins

Advansix Inc..C 215 533-3000
Philadelphia *(G-13349)*

CHEMICALS & ALLIED PRDTS, WHOLESALE: Resins, Plastics

Galomb Inc ....G 610 434-3283
Allentown *(G-222)*

CHEMICALS & ALLIED PRDTS, WHOLESALE: Spec Clean/Sanitation

Mspi Enterprises LLC ....G 814 258-7500
Knoxville *(G-8812)*

CHEMICALS & ALLIED PRDTS, WHOLESALE: Syn Resin, Rub/Plastic

Versico Incorporated ....E 717 960-4024
Carlisle *(G-2747)*

CHEMICALS & ALLIED PRDTS, WHOLESALE: Waxes, Exc Petroleum

International Group Inc ....E 814 827-4900
Titusville *(G-18385)*

CHEMICALS & OTHER PRDTS DERIVED FROM COKING

Arcelormittal Holdings LLC ....C 724 684-1000
Monessen *(G-11297)*

Millcraft Corporation..............................G 724 743-3400
Washington *(G-19204)*

CHEMICALS, AGRICULTURE: Wholesalers

Helena Agri-Enterprises LLC ....G 814 632-5177
Warriors Mark *(G-19142)*

Kirby Agri Inc ....E 717 299-2541
Lancaster *(G-9087)*

Upl NA Inc ....E 610 491-2800
King of Prussia *(G-8694)*

Webbs Super-Gro Products Inc.............E 570 726-4525
Mill Hall *(G-11184)*

CHEMICALS: Agricultural

All Star Pest Servcies LLC ....G 215 828-9099
Philadelphia *(G-13365)*

Chem Service Inc ....E 610 692-3026
West Chester *(G-19523)*

FMC Corporation...................................B 215 299-6000
Philadelphia *(G-13709)*

FMC Corporation...................................B 800 526-3649
Philadelphia *(G-13711)*

Gallimed Sciences Inc ....G 814 777-2973
State College *(G-17967)*

Miller Chemical & Fert Corp ....G 717 632-8921
Hanover *(G-6920)*

Nutrient Control Systems Inc ....G 717 261-5711
Chambersburg *(G-2965)*

Upl NA Inc ....E 610 491-2800
King of Prussia *(G-8694)*

CHEMICALS: Alkali Metals, Lithium, Cesium, Francium/Rubidium

Solvay USA Inc......................................C 609 860-4000
Pittsburgh *(G-15555)*

CHEMICALS: Aluminum Oxide

Metal Exchange Corporation ....G 724 373-8471
Greenville *(G-6755)*

CHEMICALS: Aluminum Sulfate

Chemtrade Chemicals Corp...................G 814 965-4118
Johnsonburg *(G-8344)*

Geo Specialty Chemicals Inc.................E 215 773-9280
Horsham *(G-7821)*

Neo-Solutions Inc ....E 724 728-7360
Beaver *(G-988)*

CHEMICALS: Bauxite, Refined

Alcoa Corporation..................................G 412 553-4001
Pittsburgh *(G-14661)*

Alcoa Corporation..................................E 412 315-2900
Pittsburgh *(G-14662)*

CHEMICALS: Bleaching Powder, Lime Bleaching Compounds

Cantol USA Inc ....F 905 475-6141
Sharon Hill *(G-17455)*

CHEMICALS: Brine

Tetra Technologies Inc ....E 610 853-1679
Havertown *(G-7430)*

Tetra Technologies Inc ....E 570 659-5357
Mansfield *(G-10426)*

CHEMICALS: Calcium & Calcium Compounds

Omya PCC USA Inc...............................E 814 965-3400
Johnsonburg *(G-8348)*

CHEMICALS: Calcium Chloride

Milazzo Industries Inc...........................E 570 722-0522
Pittston *(G-15767)*

CHEMICALS: Chromates & Bichromates

Macherey-Nagel Inc ....F 484 821-0984
Bethlehem *(G-1564)*

CHEMICALS: Cyanides

Cyanide Vs Xaneria................................G 570 968-4522
Orwigsburg *(G-13041)*

CHEMICALS: Fire Retardant

National Foam Inc ....G 610 363-1400
West Chester *(G-19607)*

CHEMICALS: Fuel Tank Or Engine Cleaning

Vtg Tanktainer North Amer Inc ....F 610 429-5440
West Chester *(G-19675)*

CHEMICALS: High Purity Grade, Organic

Creative Chemical Co ....G 724 443-5010
Allison Park *(G-448)*

Innaventure LLC....................................G 570 371-9390
Wilkes Barre *(G-19928)*

Interphase Materials Inc ....G 814 282-8119
Pittsburgh *(G-15133)*

CHEMICALS: High Purity, Refined From Technical Grade

Afab Industrial Services Inc...................E 215 245-1280
Bensalem *(G-1145)*

Avantor Performance Mtls LLC ....C 610 573-2600
Radnor *(G-16287)*

Helena Agri-Enterprises LLC ....G 814 632-5177
Warriors Mark *(G-19142)*

Helena Chemical Company ....G 724 538-3304
Evans City *(G-5559)*

Lockhart Chemical Company ....E 724 444-1900
Gibsonia *(G-6344)*

Lockhart Company ....E 724 444-1900
Gibsonia *(G-6345)*

Lockhart Holdings Inc ....E 724 444-1900
Gibsonia *(G-6346)*

Powsus Inc ....F 610 296-2237
Chesterbrook *(G-3095)*

Rohm and Haas Company ....A 989 636-1000
Collegeville *(G-3392)*

Ultra Chem LLC.....................................G 215 778-5967
Warminster *(G-18990)*

CHEMICALS: Hydrogen Peroxide

Peroxychem LLC ....E 267 422-2400
Philadelphia *(G-14138)*

CHEMICALS: Inorganic, NEC

Active Chemical Corporation ....F 215 322-0377
Langhorne *(G-9272)*

Albemarle Corporation ....C 814 684-4310
Tyrone *(G-18575)*

Almatis Inc ....D 412 630-2800
Leetsdale *(G-9681)*

Alpont II Inc ....E 814 456-7561
Erie *(G-5182)*

Altuglas International ....G 610 878-6423
King of Prussia *(G-8578)*

Angstrom Sciences Inc ....E 412 469-8466
Duquesne *(G-4495)*

Arkema Delaware Inc ....A 610 205-7000
King of Prussia *(G-8582)*

Arkema Inc ....C 610 363-4100
Exton *(G-5646)*

Arkema Inc ....C 215 826-2600
Bristol *(G-2109)*

Avantor Inc ....F 610 386-1700
Radnor *(G-16286)*

Avantor Prfmce Mtls Hldngs LLC ....G 610 573-2600
Radnor *(G-16288)*

Barbers Chemicals Inc ....F 724 962-7886
Sharpsville *(G-17469)*

Bayer Corporation ....A 412 777-2000
Pittsburgh *(G-14750)*

Bimax Inc ....E 717 235-3136
Glen Rock *(G-6453)*

Calgon Carbon Corporation ....F 724 218-7001
Coraopolis *(G-3668)*

Calgon Carbon Corporation ....D 412 771-4050
Pittsburgh *(G-14801)*

Calgon Carbon Corporation ....F 412 269-4188
Pittsburgh *(G-14802)*

Calgon Carbon Investments Inc ....E 412 787-6700
Coraopolis *(G-3669)*

Carbon Sales Inc ....E 570 823-7664
Wilkes Barre *(G-19909)*

Ceramic Color and Chem Mfg Co ....E 724 846-4000
New Brighton *(G-12032)*

Chem Service Inc ....E 610 692-3026
West Chester *(G-19523)*

Chemalloy Company LLC ....E 610 527-3700
Conshohocken *(G-3527)*

Compound Technology Inc ....G 717 845-8646
York *(G-20430)*

Craft Products Co Inc ....G 412 821-8102
Pittsburgh *(G-14885)*

Dischem Inc ....G 814 772-6603
Ridgway *(G-16704)*

Dow Chemical Co ....G 610 244-7101
Lansdale *(G-9363)*

Dow Chemical Company ....D 215 641-7000
Collegeville *(G-3375)*

Dow Chemical Company ....C 610 775-6640
Reading *(G-16365)*

Dow Chemical Company 215 592-3000
Philadelphia *(G-13641)*

Dow Chemical Company ....D 215 785-7000
Bristol *(G-2133)*

Dupont Specialty Pdts USA LLC ....E 570 265-6141
Towanda *(G-18424)*

Dyno Nobel Inc ....E 724 379-8100
Donora *(G-4152)*

E I Du Pont De Nemours & Co ....G 302 996-7165
Avondale *(G-850)*

Edt ....G 724 217-4008
Greensburg *(G-6663)*

Elements For Motion LLC ....G 215 768-1641
Kulpsville *(G-8826)*

EMD Performance Materials Corp ....G 888 367-3275
Philadelphia *(G-13672)*

Esm Group Inc ....E 724 538-8974
Mars *(G-10496)*

Evonik Corporation ....G 610 990-8100
Chester *(G-3050)*

Fedchem LLC ....E 610 837-1808
Bethlehem *(G-1507)*

Fedchem LLC ....G 610 837-1808
Bethlehem *(G-1508)*

Filmtronics Inc ....E 724 352-3790
Butler *(G-2401)*

Fine Grinding Corporation ....E 610 828-7250
Conshohocken *(G-3547)*

Fisher Scientific Company LLC ....B 724 517-1500
Pittsburgh *(G-15019)*

Gb Biosciences Corporation ....G 713 453-7281
Willow Grove *(G-20118)*

Gelest Inc ....E 215 547-1015
Morrisville *(G-11561)*

Gelest Realty Inc ....G 215 547-1015
Morrisville *(G-11562)*

Gelest Technologies Inc ....G 215 547-1015
Morrisville *(G-11563)*

General Carbide Corporation ....C 724 836-3000
Greensburg *(G-6668)*

Geo Specialty Chemicals Inc ....D 610 433-6331
Allentown *(G-229)*

Gharda Chemicals Limited ....G 215 968-9474
Newtown *(G-12505)*

Gilberton Energy Corporation ....E 570 874-1602
Gilberton *(G-6368)*

Indspec Chemical Corporation ....E 412 826-3666
Pittsburgh *(G-15118)*

International Raw Mtls Ltd ....E 215 928-1010
Philadelphia *(G-13867)*

Interstate Chemical Co Inc ....C 724 981-3771
Hermitage *(G-7588)*

Interstate Chemical Co Inc ....E 724 813-2576
Erie *(G-5331)*

Interstate Chemical Co Inc ....G 724 774-1669
Beaver *(G-985)*

J & B Blending & Technologies ....G 412 331-2850
Mc Kees Rocks *(G-10615)*

Kimre Inc ....G 305 233-4249
Bensalem *(G-1215)*

L R M Inc ....G 215 721-4840
Souderton *(G-17747)*

Lamberti Usa Incorporated ....G 610 862-1400
Conshohocken *(G-3571)*

Lanxess Corporation ....A 800 526-9377
Pittsburgh *(G-15219)*

Laurel Products LLC ....C 610 286-2534
Elverson *(G-4964)*

Lonza Inc ....C 570 321-3900
Williamsport *(G-20035)*

Metallurgical Products Company ....E 610 696-6770
West Chester *(G-19601)*

Monomer-Polymer and Dajac Labs ....G 215 364-1155
Ambler *(G-592)*

Multisorb Tech Intl LLC ....G 412 521-3685
Pittsburgh *(G-15309)*

Murlin Chemical Inc ....F 610 825-1165
Conshohocken *(G-3579)*

Occidental Chemical Corp ....F 610 327-4145
Pottstown *(G-16022)*

Penn United Technologies Inc ....A 724 352-1507
Cabot *(G-2460)*

PPG Architectural Finishes Inc ....D 610 380-6200
Downingtown *(G-4250)*

PQ Corporation ....E 610 447-3900
Chester *(G-3059)*

PQ Corporation ....B 610 651-4600
Conshohocken *(G-3591)*

PQ Export Company ....G 610 651-4200
Malvern *(G-10300)*

Ridgway Industries Inc ....F 610 259-5534
Lansdowne *(G-9442)*

Royal Chemical Company Ltd ....F 570 421-7850
East Stroudsburg *(G-4634)*

Russell Standard Corporation ....G 724 748-3700
Mercer *(G-10973)*

Saint-Gobain Ceramics Plas Inc ....A 508 795-5000
Valley Forge *(G-18711)*

Silberline Mfg Co Inc ....C 570 668-6050
Tamaqua *(G-18225)*

Silberline Mfg Co Inc ....D 570 668-6050
Lansford *(G-9449)*

Solvay USA Inc ....E 570 748-4450
Castanea *(G-2811)*

Solvay USA Inc ....D 215 781-6001
Bristol *(G-2199)*

Specialty Chemical Systems Inc ....F 610 323-2716
Pottstown *(G-16050)*

Specialty Minerals Inc ....B 860 824-5435
Bethlehem *(G-1624)*

Specialty Minerals Inc ....B 610 861-3400
Bethlehem *(G-1625)*

Specialty Minerals Inc ....C 212 878-1800
Bethlehem *(G-1626)*

Tetra Technologies Inc ....E 717 545-3580
Harrisburg *(G-7230)*

Thermo Shandon Inc ....G 412 788-1133
Pittsburgh *(G-15615)*

Uct Inc ....E 215 781-9255
Bristol *(G-2213)*

Univar USA Inc ....D 717 944-7471
Middletown *(G-11084)*

Valtech Corporation ....E 610 705-5900
Pottstown *(G-16064)*

Van Air Inc 814 774-2631
Lake City *(G-8909)*

Vexcon Chemicals Inc ....E 215 332-7709
Philadelphia *(G-14443)*

Vision Technology UHS LLC ....G 717 465-0694
Hanover *(G-6969)*

Westinghouse Electric Co LLC ....A 412 374-2020
Cranberry Township *(G-3865)*

Westinghouse Electric Co LLC ....D 412 256-1085
Pittsburgh *(G-15710)*

Zeolyst International ....E 610 651-4200
Malvern *(G-10352)*

CHEMICALS: Lithium Compounds, Inorganic

Livent Corporation ....A 215 299-6000
Philadelphia *(G-13973)*

CHEMICALS: Magnesium Compounds Or Salts, Inorganic

Agsalt Processing ....G 717 632-9144
Gettysburg *(G-6283)*

Luxfer Magtech Inc ....E 570 668-0001
Tamaqua *(G-18219)*

Magnesium Elektron ....F 570 668-0001
Tamaqua *(G-18220)*

CHEMICALS: Medicinal

Frontida Biopharm Inc ....E 215 288-6500
Philadelphia *(G-13728)*

Frontida Biopharm Inc ....G 610 232-0112
Philadelphia *(G-13729)*

Sani-Brands Inc ....G 610 841-1599
Allentown *(G-382)*

CHEMICALS: Medicinal, Organic, Uncompounded, Bulk

Prwt Services Inc ....D 570 275-2220
Riverside *(G-16758)*

CHEMICALS: Mercury, Redistilled

Bethlehem Apparatus Co Inc ....F 610 838-7034
Hellertown *(G-7554)*

Bethlehem Apparatus Co Inc ....G 610 882-2611
Bethlehem *(G-1460)*

Bethlehem Apparatus Co Inc ....E 610 838-7034
Bethlehem *(G-1461)*

CHEMICALS: NEC

Acrymax Technologies Inc ....F 610 566-7470
Media *(G-10913)*

Advanced Lubrication Spc Inc ....E 215 244-2114
Bensalem *(G-1144)*

Advanced Powder Products Inc ....F 814 342-5898
Philipsburg *(G-14507)*

Air Products and Chemicals Inc ....B 570 467-2981
Tamaqua *(G-18208)*

American Colloid Company ....E 717 845-3077
York *(G-20371)*

American Inks & Coatings Corp ....D 610 933-5848
Phoenixville *(G-14528)*

American Solder & Flux Co Inc ....G 610 647-3575
Paoli *(G-13135)*

Astatech Inc ....E 215 785-3197
Bristol *(G-2110)*

Atotech Usa LLC ....E 814 238-0514
State College *(G-17943)*

Axiall LLC ....A 412 515-8149
Pittsburgh *(G-14744)*

Baker Petrolite LLC ....E 610 876-2200
Crum Lynne *(G-3935)*

Bulk Chemicals Inc ....F 610 926-4128
Mohrsville *(G-11275)*

Carlisle Construction Mtls LLC ....B 717 245-7000
Carlisle *(G-2695)*

Charkit Chemical Company LLC ....G 267 573-4062
Yardley *(G-20300)*

Chase Corporation ....E 412 828-1500
Pittsburgh *(G-14840)*

Chemalloy Company LLC ....E 610 527-3700
Conshohocken *(G-3527)*

Employee Codes: A=Over 500 employees, B=251-500
C=101-250, D=51-100, E=20-50, F=10-19, G=3-9

2019 Harris Pennsylvania
Manufacturers Directory

1333

PRODUCT

Cheminova Inc ....G....... 919 474-6600
  Philadelphia *(G-13538)*

Clean World Industries Inc.................G....... 724 962-0720
  Hermitage *(G-7578)*

Coates Electrographics Inc.................E....... 570 675-1131
  Dallas *(G-3960)*

Coopers Creek Chemical Corp ....E....... 610 828-0375
  Conshohocken *(G-3534)*

CRC Industries Inc ....G....... 800 556-5074
  Warminster *(G-18850)*

CRC Industries Inc ....C....... 215 674-4300
  Horsham *(G-7806)*

Creative Chemical Co ....G....... 724 443-5010
  Allison Park *(G-448)*

Croda Inc ....E....... 570 893-7650
  Mill Hall *(G-11175)*

Crystal Inc - PMC ....D....... 215 368-1661
  Lansdale *(G-9355)*

Dyneon LLC ....D....... 610 497-8899
  Aston *(G-759)*

E E Zimmerman Company ....F....... 412 963-0949
  Pittsburgh *(G-14950)*

Elizabeth Milling Company LLC ....F....... 724 872-9404
  Smithton *(G-17660)*

Elkem Materials Inc ....G....... 412 299-7200
  Moon Township *(G-11486)*

Esf Enterprise LLC ....G....... 610 334-2615
  Reading *(G-16380)*

Fragrance Manufacturing Inc ....E....... 610 266-7580
  Allentown *(G-218)*

Fuchs Lubricants Co ....E....... 724 867-5000
  Emlenton *(G-5008)*

Honeywell Resins & Chem LLC ....C....... 215 533-3000
  Philadelphia *(G-13833)*

Hydrol Chemical Company Inc ....F....... 610 622-3603
  Yeadon *(G-20354)*

Ifs Industries Inc ....C....... 610 378-1381
  Reading *(G-16406)*

Industrial Terminal Systems ....E....... 724 335-9837
  New Kensington *(G-12346)*

International Raw Mtls Ltd ....E....... 215 928-1010
  Philadelphia *(G-13867)*

Justi Group Inc ....E....... 484 318-7158
  Berwyn *(G-1367)*

Koppers Holdings Inc ....C....... 412 227-2001
  Pittsburgh *(G-15187)*

Labchem Inc ....E....... 412 826-5230
  Zelienople *(G-20809)*

Lamberti Usa Incorporated ....G....... 610 862-1400
  Conshohocken *(G-3571)*

Lockhart Chemical Company ....E....... 724 444-1900
  Gibsonia *(G-6344)*

Lonza Inc ....C....... 570 321-3900
  Williamsport *(G-20035)*

Lord Corporation ....C....... 814 763-2345
  Saegertown *(G-16923)*

Lyondell Chemical Company ....D....... 610 359-2360
  Newtown Square *(G-12583)*

McGee Industries Inc ....E....... 610 459-1890
  Aston *(G-775)*

Milazzo Industries Inc ....E....... 570 722-0522
  Pittston *(G-15767)*

Mimco Products LLC ....G....... 724 258-8208
  Monongahela *(G-11311)*

Montgomery Chemicals LLC ....E....... 610 567-0877
  Conshohocken *(G-3577)*

National Chemical Labs PA Inc..........C....... 215 922-1200
  Philadelphia *(G-14053)*

Norquay Technology Inc ....E....... 610 874-4330
  Chester *(G-3058)*

Paradigm Labs Inc ....F....... 570 345-2600
  Pine Grove *(G-14601)*

Performance Coatings Corp ....F....... 610 525-1190
  Levittown *(G-9854)*

Pitt Penn Oil Co LLC ....D....... 813 968-9635
  Creighton *(G-3883)*

Polysciences Inc ....C....... 215 343-6484
  Warrington *(G-19128)*

Polysciences Inc ....G....... 215 520-9358
  Warrington *(G-19129)*

Preservation Technologies LP............D....... 724 779-2111
  Cranberry Township *(G-3844)*

Pressure Chemical Co ....E....... 412 682-5882
  Pittsburgh *(G-15435)*

Prwt Services Inc ....D....... 570 275-2220
  Riverside *(G-16758)*

Rohm and Haas Chemicals LLC ....G....... 215 592-3696
  Philadelphia *(G-14257)*

Rohm and Haas Chemicals LLC..........C....... 989 636-1000
  Collegeville *(G-3391)*

Sauereisen Inc ....E....... 412 963-0303
  Pittsburgh *(G-15514)*

SOS Products Company Inc ....E....... 215 679-6262
  East Greenville *(G-4576)*

Spray Products Corporation ....D....... 610 277-1010
  Plymouth Meeting *(G-15872)*

Total Ptrchemicals Ref USA Inc..........B....... 877 871-2729
  Exton *(G-5737)*

Total Ptrchemicals Ref USA Inc..........D....... 610 692-8401
  West Chester *(G-19667)*

Total Systems Technology Inc ....F....... 412 653-7690
  Pittsburgh *(G-15633)*

W R Meadows Inc ....E....... 717 792-2627
  York *(G-20701)*

Water Treatment Services Inc ....F....... 800 817-5116
  Monroeville *(G-11363)*

White Engrg Surfaces Corp ....C....... 215 968-5021
  Newtown *(G-12563)*

Whitford Corporation ....D....... 610 286-3500
  Elverson *(G-4967)*

Wilson Pdts Compressed Gas Co ....E....... 610 253-9608
  Easton *(G-4777)*

CHEMICALS: Nonmetallic Compounds

Pressure Chemical Co ....E..... 412 682-5882
  Pittsburgh *(G-15435)*

CHEMICALS: Organic, NEC

Agrofresh Solutions Inc ....G....... 267 317-9139
  Philadelphia *(G-13356)*

Akzo Nobel Inc ....G....... 312 544-7000
  Reading *(G-16315)*

Albemarle Corporation ....C....... 814 684-4310
  Tyrone *(G-18575)*

Alex Color Company Inc ....G....... 570 875-3300
  Ashland *(G-725)*

Alex Color Company Inc ....G....... 570 875-3300
  Ashland *(G-726)*

Arkema Delaware Inc ....A....... 610 205-7000
  King of Prussia *(G-8582)*

Arkema Inc ....C....... 215 826-2600
  Bristol *(G-2109)*

B Asf Corp ....G....... 814 453-7186
  Erie *(G-5201)*

BASF Catalysts LLC ....C....... 814 870-3900
  Erie *(G-5204)*

BASF Corporation ....C....... 724 728-6900
  Monaca *(G-11281)*

Borchers Americas Inc ....E....... 814 432-2125
  Franklin *(G-6117)*

Carpenter Co ....D....... 610 366-5110
  Fogelsville *(G-5993)*

Carpenter Co ....C....... 814 944-8612
  Altoona *(G-486)*

Chem Service Inc ....E....... 610 692-3026
  West Chester *(G-19523)*

CMA Refinishing Solutions Inc...........G....... 215 427-1141
  Philadelphia *(G-13552)*

Craft Products Co Inc ....G....... 412 821-8102
  Pittsburgh *(G-14885)*

Ddp Specialty Electronic MA ....G....... 610 244-6000
  Collegeville *(G-3374)*

Dl1 Processing LLC ....G....... 215 582-3263
  Chester *(G-3048)*

Dow Chemical Company ....F....... 215 785-8000
  Croydon *(G-3916)*

Dr G H Michel Restor-Skin Co ....G....... 724 526-5551
  East Brady *(G-4529)*

Esstech Inc ....F....... 610 521-3800
  Essington *(G-5543)*

Evonik Oil Additives Usa Inc ....D....... 215 706-5800
  Horsham *(G-7817)*

Evoqua Water Technologies LLC ....E....... 724 827-8181
  Darlington *(G-4028)*

Fenner Precision Inc ....C....... 800 327-2288
  Manheim *(G-10383)*

Filmtronics Inc ....E....... 724 352-3790
  Butler *(G-2401)*

Fine Grinding Corporation ....E....... 610 828-7250
  Conshohocken *(G-3547)*

Five Star Group Inc ....G....... 814 237-0241
  State College *(G-17965)*

Fluorous Technologies Inc ....F....... 267 225-5384
  Pittsburgh *(G-15022)*

FMC Corporation ....B....... 215 299-6000
  Philadelphia *(G-13709)*

FMC Overseas Ltd ....G....... 215 299-6000
  Philadelphia *(G-13712)*

Geo Specialty Chemicals Inc ....E....... 215 773-9280
  Ambler *(G-579)*

Greenerways LLC ....F....... 215 280-7658
  Yardley *(G-20313)*

Henkel Corp ....G....... 267 424-5645
  Sellersville *(G-17349)*

Hercon Laboratories Corp ....E....... 717 764-1191
  Emigsville *(G-4989)*

Inolex Group Inc ....D....... 215 271-0800
  Philadelphia *(G-13859)*

J & B Blending & Technologies............G....... 412 331-2850
  Mc Kees Rocks *(G-10615)*

Lamberti Usa Incorporated ....G....... 610 862-1400
  Conshohocken *(G-3571)*

Lanxess Corporation ....E....... 412 809-4735
  Burgettstown *(G-2348)*

Lyco I LLC ....G....... 570 784-0903
  Bloomsburg *(G-1788)*

Merisol Antioxidants LLC ....E....... 814 677-2028
  Oil City *(G-12952)*

Neo-Solutions Inc ....E....... 724 728-7360
  Beaver *(G-988)*

Nonlethal Technologies Inc ....E....... 724 479-5100
  Homer City *(G-7679)*

Norquay Technology Inc ....E....... 610 874-4330
  Chester *(G-3058)*

Nurture Inc ....G....... 610 989-0945
  Devon *(G-4114)*

Occidental Chemical Corp ....F....... 610 327-4145
  Pottstown *(G-16022)*

Polonier Corporation ....G....... 267 994-1698
  Fairless Hills *(G-5792)*

Polymeric Systems Inc ....D....... 610 286-2500
  Elverson *(G-4965)*

Quanta Technologies Inc ....G....... 610 644-7101
  Lancaster *(G-9180)*

Royal Chemical Company Ltd ....F....... 570 421-7850
  East Stroudsburg *(G-4634)*

Sanda Corporation ....G....... 502 510-8782
  Media *(G-10947)*

Sbn Holding LLC ....G....... 724 756-2210
  Petrolia *(G-13307)*

Sonneborn LLC ....C....... 724 756-9337
  Petrolia *(G-13308)*

Sunoco Inc ....D....... 215 977-3000
  Newtown Square *(G-12591)*

Synthex Organics LLC ....G....... 814 941-8375
  Altoona *(G-550)*

Thermo Shandon Inc ....G....... 412 788-1133
  Pittsburgh *(G-15615)*

Uct Inc ....E....... 215 781-9255
  Bristol *(G-2213)*

Ungerer Industries Inc ....D....... 610 868-7266
  Bethlehem *(G-1647)*

Vision Technology UHS LLC ....G....... 717 465-0694
  Hanover *(G-6969)*

VWR Corporation ....C....... 610 386-1700
  Radnor *(G-16304)*

CHEMICALS: Phenol

Sunoco Inc ....D....... 215 977-3000
  Newtown Square *(G-12591)*

CHEMICALS: Phosphates, Defluorinated/Ammoniated, Exc Fertlr

Bulk Chemicals Inc ....E....... 610 926-4128
  Reading *(G-16337)*

Bulk Chemicals Inc ....F....... 610 926-4128
  Mohrsville *(G-11275)*

FMC Asia-Pacific Inc.........................G..... 215 299-6000
  Philadelphia *(G-13708)*

CHEMICALS: Reagent Grade, Refined From Technical Grade

Curtiss Laboratories Inc....................G....... 215 245-8833
  Bensalem *(G-1177)*

VWR Corporation ....C....... 610 386-1700
  Radnor *(G-16304)*

CHEMICALS: Silica Compounds

Elkem Materials Inc..........................G....... 412 299-7200
  Moon Township *(G-11486)*

CHEMICALS: Soda Ash

FMC Asia-Pacific Inc.........................G....... 215 299-6000
  Philadelphia *(G-13708)*

FMC Corporation ....B....... 215 299-6000
  Philadelphia *(G-13709)*

FMC Corporation..................G........215 717-7500
Philadelphia *(G-13710)*
Genesis Alkali Wyoming LP..........E....215 299-6904
Philadelphia *(G-13751)*
Genesis Alkali Wyoming LP..........D....215 845-4500
Philadelphia *(G-13752)*

CHEMICALS: Sodium Bicarbonate

Genesis Specialty Alkali LLC........D....215 845-4550
Philadelphia *(G-13753)*

CHEMICALS: Sodium Silicate

PQ Corporation..................C........610 651-4200
Malvern *(G-10299)*
PQ Holding Inc..................F........610 651-4400
Malvern *(G-10302)*

CHEMICALS: Sodium/Potassium Cmpnds,Exc Bleach,Alkalies/Alum

Indspec Chemical Corporation........B....724 756-2370
Petrolia *(G-13305)*
Niagara Holdings Inc..............A....610 651-4200
Malvern *(G-10286)*

CHEMICALS: Sulfur, Incl Rcvrd/Refined, Fm Sour Natural Gas

Akzo Nobel Chemicals Inc..........D....724 258-6200
Monongahela *(G-11303)*

CHEMICALS: Tin, Stannic/Stannous, Compounds/Salts, Inorganic

Reaxis Inc......................E........412 517-6070
Mc Donald *(G-10580)*

CHEMICALS: Water Treatment

Armstrongs.....................G........717 543-5488
Mc Clure *(G-10557)*
Blue Boy Products Inc.............G....610 284-1055
Downingtown *(G-4215)*
Chemical Equipment Labs VA Inc.....E....610 497-9390
Newtown Square *(G-12570)*
Chemstream Inc..................F........814 629-7118
Homer City *(G-7672)*
Custom Blends Inc................G....215 934-7080
Philadelphia *(G-13592)*
Eastern Technologies Inc..........F....610 286-2010
Morgantown *(G-11522)*
Enchlor Inc.....................G........215 453-2533
Silverdale *(G-17591)*
GE Betz International Inc..........E....215 957-2200
Langhorne *(G-9300)*
GE Infrastructure Sensing.........F....617 926-1749
Feasterville Trevose *(G-5912)*
Klenzoid Inc....................F........610 825-9494
Conshohocken *(G-3570)*
Phoenix Laboratories Inc..........F....215 295-5222
Levittown *(G-9855)*
Prochemtech International Inc.......E....814 265-0959
Brockway *(G-2231)*
Service Rite....................G........814 774-8716
Cranesville *(G-3871)*
Suez Wts Systems Usa Inc..........B....781 359-7000
Trevose *(G-18505)*
Suez Wts Usa Inc................A....215 355-3300
Trevose *(G-18506)*
Tricorn Inc.....................G........610 777-6823
Reading *(G-16550)*
Wilkinsburg Penn Joint Wtr........D....412 243-6254
Verona *(G-18764)*

CHESTS: Bank, Metal

Fabco Inc.......................G........814 944-1631
Altoona *(G-504)*

CHICKEN SLAUGHTERING & PROCESSING

David Elliot Poultry Farm Inc......C....570 344-6348
Scranton *(G-17228)*
Tyson Foods Inc.................A....717 354-4211
New Holland *(G-12289)*

CHILD DAY CARE SVCS

Respironics Inc.................B....724 387-4270
Monroeville *(G-11354)*

Respironics Inc.................C....724 334-3100
New Kensington *(G-12370)*
Respironics Inc.................D....724 387-5200
Murrysville *(G-11865)*

CHINA & GLASS REPAIR SVCS

Healy Glass Artistry LLC..........G....484 241-0989
Bethlehem *(G-1530)*

CHINA & GLASS: Decalcomania Work

Americana Art China Co Inc........F....330 938-6133
Mercer *(G-10959)*
Sdi Custom Decow................G....570 685-7278
Hawley *(G-7438)*

CHINA: Fired & Decorated

Bryan China Company.............D....724 658-3098
New Castle *(G-12068)*

CHINAWARE STORES

Ceramic Art Company Inc..........A....952 944-5600
Bristol *(G-2124)*
Lenox Corporation...............F....267 525-7800
Bristol *(G-2159)*

CHINAWARE WHOLESALERS

Sdi Custom Decow................G....570 685-7278
Hawley *(G-7438)*

CHIROPRACTORS' OFFICES

Holistic Horse Inc...............G....215 249-1965
Perkasie *(G-13279)*
Koren Publications Inc............G....267 498-0071
Hatfield *(G-7360)*

CHLORINE

Arkema Delaware Inc..............A....610 205-7000
King of Prussia *(G-8582)*
Arkema Inc......................C........215 826-2600
Bristol *(G-2109)*

CHOCOLATE, EXC CANDY FROM BEANS: Chips, Powder, Block, Syrup

4sis LLC.......................E........814 459-2451
Erie *(G-5162)*
Andersons Candies Inc............E....724 869-3018
Baden *(G-869)*
Artisan Confections Company.......G....717 534-4200
Hershey *(G-7604)*
Barry Callebaut USA LLC..........E....610 872-4528
Eddystone *(G-4798)*
Barry Callebaut USA LLC..........G....312 496-7305
Bethlehem *(G-1457)*
Barry Callebaut USA LLC..........G....570 342-7556
Dunmore *(G-4470)*
Beckers Cafe....................G........412 331-1373
Mc Kees Rocks *(G-10604)*
Bevans Candies Inc...............F....610 566-0581
Media *(G-10915)*
Blaine Boring Chocolates..........G....814 539-6244
Johnstown *(G-8358)*
Blommer Chocolate Company........C....215 679-4472
East Greenville *(G-4566)*
Chocodiem......................G........908 200-7044
Easton *(G-4661)*
Chocolate Creations.............G....724 774-7675
Monaca *(G-11288)*
Colebrook Chocolate Co LLC........G....724 628-8383
Connellsville *(G-3492)*
Daffins Inc.....................E........724 983-8336
Farrell *(G-5867)*
Edwards Sherm Candies Inc.........E....412 372-4331
Trafford *(G-18454)*
Event Horizon LLC...............G....717 557-1427
Hershey *(G-7610)*
Frankford Candy LLC.............C....215 735-5200
Philadelphia *(G-13720)*
Gertrude Hawk Chocolates Inc......B....570 342-7556
Dunmore *(G-4473)*
Hershey Company................B....717 534-4200
Hershey *(G-7613)*
Hershey Company................B....717 534-4100
Hershey *(G-7614)*
Hershey Company................B....570 384-3271
Hazle Township *(G-7463)*

Hershey Digital.................G........717 431-9602
Willow Street *(G-20151)*
Mars Chocolate North Amer LLC......B....717 367-1500
Elizabethtown *(G-4878)*
Matangos Candies Inc.............G....717 234-0882
Harrisburg *(G-7174)*
OSheas Candies..................F....814 536-4800
Johnstown *(G-8414)*
Painted Truffle.................G....215 996-0606
North Wales *(G-12823)*
Purity Candy Co.................F....570 538-9502
Allenwood *(G-442)*
Robert W Gastel Jr..............E....412 678-2723
White Oak *(G-19858)*
Stutz Candy Company.............E....215 675-2630
Hatboro *(G-7307)*
Sweet Jubilee Gourmet...........G....717 691-9782
Mechanicsburg *(G-10893)*
Victorias Candies Inc...........G....570 455-6341
Hazleton *(G-7534)*
Wfc & C Inc.....................F....215 627-3233
Philadelphia *(G-14471)*

CHOCOLATE, EXC CANDY FROM PURCH CHOC: Chips, Powder, Block

926 Partners Inc................F....814 452-4026
Erie *(G-5163)*
Candy Cottage Co Inc.............G....215 322-6618
Huntingdon Valley *(G-7967)*
Cargill Cocoa & Chocolate Inc......B....717 653-1471
Mount Joy *(G-11647)*
Cargill Cocoa & Chocolate Inc......B....570 453-6825
Hazle Township *(G-7448)*
Cherrydale Fundraising LLC........G....610 366-1606
Allentown *(G-169)*
Chocolate Creations.............G....570 383-9931
Peckville *(G-13207)*
Confiseurs Inc..................E....610 932-2706
Oxford *(G-13076)*
Godiva Chocolatier Inc...........B....610 779-3797
Reading *(G-16394)*
Suzannes Choclat & Confections.....G....570 753-8545
Avis *(G-838)*
Sweet Salvation Truffle..........G....610 220-4157
Haverford *(G-7415)*
Trufood Mfg Inc.................B....412 963-6600
Pittsburgh *(G-15655)*
Trufood Mfg Inc.................B....412 963-2330
Pittsburgh *(G-15656)*

CHRISTMAS NOVELTIES, WHOLESALE

F C Young & Co Inc..............C....215 788-9226
Bristol *(G-2143)*
J Kinderman & Sons Inc...........E....215 271-7600
Philadelphia *(G-13884)*

CHRISTMAS TREE LIGHTING SETS: Electric

Design Decorators...............E....215 634-8300
Philadelphia *(G-13620)*
Fiber Optic Designs Inc..........G....215 321-9750
Yardley *(G-20311)*

CHRISTMAS TREES WHOLESALERS

Sheerlund Products LLC...........F....484 248-2650
Reading *(G-16516)*

CHROMATOGRAPHY EQPT

Teledyne Instruments Inc..........D....814 234-7311
State College *(G-18037)*
Thermo Hypersil-Keystone LLC......E....814 353-2300
Bellefonte *(G-1121)*
Waters Corporation..............G....484 344-5404
Plymouth Meeting *(G-15879)*

CHRONOGRAPHS, SPRING WOUND

Rgm Watch Company..............F....717 653-9799
Mount Joy *(G-11670)*

CHUTES & TROUGHS

General Fabricating Svcs LLC......F....412 262-1131
Coraopolis *(G-3692)*

CHUTES: Coal, Sheet Metal, Prefabricated

Coilplus Inc....................D....215 331-5200
Philadelphia *(G-13559)*

CIGARETTE & CIGAR PRDTS & ACCESS

A Class Corp ....G....... 717 695-0597
Harrisburg *(G-7079)*

Cigar N More ....G....... 717 541-1341
Harrisburg *(G-7105)*

Cloud Chemistry LLC ....F....... 570 851-1680
East Stroudsburg *(G-4609)*

D&D Cigar & Cigarette Emporium ....G....... 570 722-4665
Albrightsville *(G-48)*

Sinking Ship Premium Juice LLC........G....... 570 855-2316
Glen Lyon *(G-6427)*

Smoke Town LLC ....G....... 570 383-7833
Olyphant *(G-13000)*

Smokers Stop.................................G....... 717 232-5206
Harrisburg *(G-7216)*

CIGARETTE LIGHTERS

Zipcorp Inc....................................B....... 814 368-2700
Bradford *(G-1997)*

CIGARETTE STORES

Quik Piks & Paks Inc ....G....... 570 459-3099
Hazle Township *(G-7477)*

CIRCUIT BOARDS, PRINTED: Television & Radio

Compunetics Inc ....D....... 412 373-8110
Monroeville *(G-11328)*

Electronic Service & Design ....G....... 717 243-7743
Hummelstown *(G-7909)*

Fineline Circuits Inc........................E....... 215 364-3311
Feasterville Trevose *(G-5909)*

Mid-Atlantic Circuit Inc....................F....... 215 672-8480
Warminster *(G-18922)*

Positran Manufacturing Inc................D....... 610 277-0500
Norristown *(G-12704)*

R&D Sockets Inc ....G....... 610 443-2299
Allentown *(G-369)*

Secure Components LLC...................F....... 610 551-3475
Norristown *(G-12711)*

Smg-Global Circuits Inc ....E....... 724 229-3200
Washington *(G-19226)*

Strategic Mfg Tech LLC ....E....... 610 269-0054
Downingtown *(G-4257)*

CIRCUIT BOARDS: Wiring

Rfcircuits Inc ....F....... 215 364-2450
Huntingdon Valley *(G-8029)*

World Elec Sls & Svc Inc ....C....... 610 939-9800
Reading *(G-16569)*

CIRCUIT BREAKERS

Mitsubishi Elc Pwr Pdts Inc ....C....... 724 772-2555
Freedom *(G-6191)*

Mitsubishi Elc Pwr Pdts Inc ....C....... 724 772-2555
Warrendale *(G-19088)*

Mitsubishi Elc Pwr Pdts Inc ....G....... 724 778-5112
Warrendale *(G-19089)*

CIRCUIT BREAKERS: Air

Spectrum Microwave Inc...................D....... 215 464-0586
Philadelphia *(G-14333)*

CIRCUITS: Electronic

Ability Systems Corporation...............G....... 215 657-4338
Abington *(G-9)*

American Precision Inds Inc...............C....... 610 235-5499
West Chester *(G-19498)*

American Products Inc......................D....... 717 767-6510
York *(G-20375)*

B and N Electronics ....G....... 724 484-0164
West Alexander *(G-19490)*

C M R Usa LLC ....F....... 724 452-2200
Leetsdale *(G-9687)*

Caron Enterprises Inc........................B....... 814 774-5658
Lake City *(G-8898)*

CMR USA Inc ....F....... 724 452-2200
Leetsdale *(G-9689)*

Coax Incorporated ....F....... 717 227-0045
Glen Rock *(G-6454)*

Component Intrtechnologies Inc..........E....... 724 253-3161
Hadley *(G-6816)*

Controls Service & Repair..................G....... 412 487-7310
Glenshaw *(G-6486)*

D L Electronics Inc...........................F....... 215 742-2666
Philadelphia *(G-13600)*

Danco Precision Inc..........................E....... 610 933-1090
Phoenixville *(G-14543)*

Danco Precision Inc..........................F....... 610 933-8981
Phoenixville *(G-14542)*

E-Nanomedsys LLC ....G....... 917 734-1462
State College *(G-17958)*

Effective Shielding Company ....F....... 610 429-9449
West Chester *(G-19547)*

Electronic Assembly Co Inc................E....... 215 799-0600
Souderton *(G-17732)*

Electronic Prototype Dev Inc..............E....... 412 767-4111
Natrona Heights *(G-11941)*

Erie Specialty Products Inc................E....... 814 453-5611
Erie *(G-5274)*

FCG Inc ....C....... 215 343-4617
Warrington *(G-19117)*

Genesys Controls Corporation............F....... 717 291-1116
Landisville *(G-9261)*

Gorden Inc ....G....... 610 644-4476
Reading *(G-16395)*

Homeland Mfg Svcs Inc.....................F....... 814 862-9103
State College *(G-17976)*

Hound Dog Corp ....G....... 215 355-6424
Huntingdon Valley *(G-7994)*

Industrial Enterprises Inc..................D....... 215 355-7080
Southampton *(G-17819)*

Industrial Enterprises Inc..................D....... 215 355-7080
Warminster *(G-18897)*

Integrated Power Designs Inc.............D....... 570 824-4666
Hanover Township *(G-6990)*

Integrted Assembly Systems Inc........E....... 724 746-6532
Canonsburg *(G-2597)*

Iqe Rf LLC ....D....... 732 271-5990
Bethlehem *(G-1541)*

Iqe Usa Inc ....D....... 610 861-6930
Bethlehem *(G-1542)*

Juergensen Defense Corporation ....G....... 814 395-9509
Addison *(G-27)*

Keystone Test Solutions Inc ....G....... 814 733-4490
Schellsburg *(G-17133)*

Kitron Holding USA Inc ....G....... 814 467-9060
Windber *(G-20186)*

L3 Electron Devices Inc.....................C....... 570 326-3561
Williamsport *(G-20033)*

Laboratory Control Systems Inc ....G....... 570 487-2490
Scott Township *(G-17184)*

Lynn Electronics Corp........................E....... 215 826-9600
Bristol *(G-2163)*

Majr Products Corporation ....F....... 814 763-3211
Saegertown *(G-16925)*

Maro Electronics Inc.........................E....... 215 788-7919
Bristol *(G-2164)*

Mbpj Corporation ....G....... 814 461-9120
Erie *(G-5384)*

Mdbel Inc ....G....... 215 738-3383
Southampton *(G-17825)*

Micromechatronics Inc......................G....... 814 861-5688
State College *(G-17990)*

Nichols Electronics Inc......................G....... 724 668-2526
Greensburg *(G-6693)*

Nicomatic LP ....E....... 215 444-9580
Horsham *(G-7836)*

Nth Solutions LLC............................G....... 610 594-2191
Exton *(G-5715)*

Oneida Instant Log ....E....... 814 336-2125
Meadville *(G-10770)*

Piezo Kinetics Inc ....E....... 814 355-1593
Bellefonte *(G-1112)*

Qualastat Electronics Inc...................E....... 717 253-9301
Gettysburg *(G-6311)*

R F Circuits & Cad Services................G....... 215 368-6483
Harleysville *(G-7053)*

Rcd Technology Inc..........................F....... 215 529-9440
Newtown *(G-12542)*

Sendec Corp...................................C....... 585 425-3390
Windber *(G-20192)*

Sense Technology Inc........................G....... 724 733-2277
Halifax *(G-6831)*

Sensor Corporation ....G....... 724 887-4080
Scottdale *(G-17200)*

Servedio A Elc Mtr Svc Inc.................F....... 724 658-8041
New Castle *(G-12148)*

Smt Manufacturing Group LLC............E....... 717 767-4900
York *(G-20670)*

Te Connectivity Corporation ....C....... 717 492-2000
Manheim *(G-10405)*

Te Connectivity Corporation ....C....... 717 898-4302
Landisville *(G-9267)*

Te Connectivity Corporation ....D....... 717 691-5842
Mechanicsburg *(G-10895)*

Telan Corporation ....E....... 215 822-1234
Hatfield *(G-7400)*

Thin Film Industries Inc.....................G....... 267 316-9999
Morrisville *(G-11585)*

Tq Electronics Inc ....G....... 570 320-1760
Williamsport *(G-20084)*

Tsrubnus Liquidation Inc ....D....... 814 461-9120
Erie *(G-5520)*

Vizinex LLC ....G....... 215 529-9440
Bethlehem *(G-1652)*

Weld Tooling Corporation ....E....... 412 331-1776
Canonsburg *(G-2658)*

CIRCULAR KNIT FABRICS DYEING & FINISHING

Chloe Textiles Incorporated................D....... 717 848-2800
York *(G-20425)*

CIVIL SVCS TRAINING SCHOOL

Interntnal Def Systems USA LLC ....G....... 610 973-2228
Orefield *(G-13012)*

CLAIMS ADJUSTING SVCS

D L Dravis & Associates Inc................G....... 814 943-6155
Altoona *(G-496)*

D L Dravis & Associates Inc................G....... 814 944-5880
Altoona *(G-497)*

CLAMPS & COUPLINGS: Hose

Ctc Pressure Products LLC.................G....... 814 315-6427
Erie *(G-5235)*

Norma Pennsylvania Inc ....B....... 724 639-3571
Saltsburg *(G-17052)*

CLAMPS: Metal

Grate Clip Company Inc ....G....... 215 230-8015
Doylestown *(G-4304)*

Rollock Company..............................E....... 814 893-6421
Stoystown *(G-18086)*

CLAY MINING, COMMON

Fink & Stackhouse Inc.......................G....... 570 323-3475
Williamsport *(G-20013)*

CLEANERS: Boiler Tube

Projectile Tube Cleaning Inc ....E....... 724 763-7633
Ford City *(G-6051)*

CLEANERS: Paintbrush

Bonnit Brush LLC ....G....... 215 355-4115
Bensalem *(G-1159)*

CLEANING & DESCALING SVC: Metal Prdts

Evergreen Synergies LLC ....E....... 610 239-9425
King of Prussia *(G-8617)*

M J M Industries..............................G....... 724 368-8400
Portersville *(G-15931)*

Ore Enterprises Inc..........................G....... 814 898-3933
Erie *(G-5410)*

Shammy Solutions...........................G....... 412 871-0939
Pittsburgh *(G-15527)*

Tiger Enterprises Inc ....G....... 717 786-5441
Strasburg *(G-18095)*

Tri State Metal Cleaning Inc ....G....... 814 898-3933
Erie *(G-5516)*

CLEANING & DYEING PLANTS, EXC RUGS

Undercoveralls Inc............................F....... 610 519-0858
Bryn Mawr *(G-2336)*

CLEANING COMPOUNDS: Rifle Bore

Mark Gingerella...............................G....... 570 213-5603
Susquehanna *(G-18181)*

CLEANING EQPT: Blast, Dustless

Chant Engineering Co Inc...................E....... 215 230-4260
New Britain *(G-12046)*

Metalworking Machinery Co Inc...........F....... 724 625-3181
New Kensington *(G-12355)*

Titan Abrasive Systems LLC...............G....... 215 310-5055
Ivyland *(G-8223)*

CLEANING EQPT: Commercial

Alfa Laval Inc ....G 610 594-1830
Exton **(G-5638)**

EMC Global Technologies Inc ....F 267 347-5100
Telford **(G-18287)**

Full-On Filters ....G 610 970-4701
Pottstown **(G-15989)**

Gamajet Cleaning Systems Inc ....F 610 408-9940
Exton **(G-5684)**

Ial Assoc LLC ....E 215 887-5114
Elkins Park **(G-4906)**

Metro Building Services ....G 412 221-1284
Pittsburgh **(G-15281)**

Mid-Atlntic Bldg Solutions LLC ....G 484 532-7269
Blue Bell **(G-1848)**

Morantz Inc ....G 215 969-0266
Philadelphia **(G-14038)**

R & R Briggs Inc ....G 215 357-3413
Southampton **(G-17833)**

S Morantz Inc ....D 215 969-0266
Philadelphia **(G-14273)**

Spec Sciences Inc ....G 607 972-3159
Sharon **(G-17443)**

Turf Teq LLC ....E 484 798-6300
Honey Brook **(G-7767)**

CLEANING EQPT: Floor Washing & Polishing, Commercial

Aztec Products Inc ....F 215 393-4700
Montgomeryville **(G-11387)**

Emsco Inc ....E 814 774-3137
Girard **(G-6387)**

CLEANING EQPT: High Pressure

Collins Deck Sealing ....G 717 789-3322
Landisburg **(G-9256)**

Ctc Pressure Products LLC ....G 814 315-6427
Erie **(G-5235)**

DW Services LLC ....G 484 241-8915
Allentown **(G-198)**

Jenny Products Inc ....E 814 445-3400
Somerset **(G-17693)**

Mendit Chemical Inc ....F 610 239-5120
Bridgeport **(G-2039)**

Mobile Wash Power Wash Inc ....G 814 327-3820
Bedford **(G-1065)**

Pure Power ....G 412 673-5285
White Oak **(G-19857)**

Sponge-Jet Inc ....G 570 278-4563
Montrose **(G-11478)**

CLEANING OR POLISHING PREPARATIONS, NEC

Afco C&S LLC ....G 717 264-9147
Chambersburg **(G-2898)**

Alex C Fergusson LLC ....D 717 264-9147
Chambersburg **(G-2899)**

Apter Industries Inc ....F 412 672-9628
White Oak **(G-19853)**

Carbon Clean Industries Inc ....E 570 288-1155
Kingston **(G-8713)**

CPA Operations LLC ....G 215 743-6860
Philadelphia **(G-13576)**

Diversey Inc ....D 570 421-7850
East Stroudsburg **(G-4613)**

Dreumex USA Inc ....E 717 767-6881
York **(G-20457)**

International Chemical Company ....F 215 739-2313
Philadelphia **(G-13865)**

Island Fragrances Inc ....E 570 793-1680
Pittston **(G-15759)**

N B Garber Inc ....G 267 387-6225
Warminster **(G-18927)**

National Chemical Labs PA Inc ....C 215 922-1200
Philadelphia **(G-14053)**

Stoner Incorporated ....F 717 786-7355
Quarryville **(G-16282)**

Svt Inc ....G 215 245-5055
Bensalem **(G-1258)**

CLEANING PRDTS: Ammonia, Household

Air Products and Chemicals Inc ....A 610 481-4911
Allentown **(G-119)**

Air Products and Chemicals Inc ....E 724 266-1563
Leetsdale **(G-9677)**

Versum Materials Us LLC ....G 570 467-2981
Tamaqua **(G-18231)**

CLEANING PRDTS: Degreasing Solvent

Alkali Beaver Products ....G 724 709-7857
Rochester **(G-16781)**

Environmental Chem & Lubr Co ....G 610 923-6492
Easton **(G-4680)**

Ultronix Inc ....F 215 822-8206
Hatfield **(G-7404)**

Valley Wholesale & Supply ....E 724 783-6531
Kittanning **(G-8801)**

Zep Inc ....C 610 295-1360
Breinigsville **(G-2033)**

CLEANING PRDTS: Deodorants, Nonpersonal

Air-Scent International ....D 412 252-2000
Pittsburgh **(G-14658)**

Associated Products LLC ....E 412 486-2255
Glenshaw **(G-6482)**

Dyvex Industries Inc ....F 570 281-7141
Carbondale **(G-2674)**

Ogi Inc ....G 610 623-6747
Drexel Hill **(G-4370)**

CLEANING PRDTS: Dusting Cloths, Chemically Treated

Viking LLC ....F 570 645-3633
Nesquehoning **(G-12010)**

CLEANING PRDTS: Floor Waxes

Misco Products Corporation ....D 610 926-4106
Reading **(G-16445)**

Vision Technology UHS LLC ....G 717 465-0694
Hanover **(G-6969)**

CLEANING PRDTS: Laundry Preparations

D&B Tailors Inc ....E 610 356-9279
Newtown Square **(G-12571)**

Titusville Laundry Center ....G 814 827-9127
Titusville **(G-18401)**

CLEANING PRDTS: Paint & Wallpaper

Big Oaks Ltd Partnership II ....F 724 444-0055
Gibsonia **(G-6326)**

CLEANING PRDTS: Polishing Preparations & Related Prdts

Lincoln Industrial Chemical Co ....F 610 375-4596
Reading **(G-16430)**

CLEANING PRDTS: Sanitation Preparations

Bio Sun Systems Inc ....G 570 537-2200
Millerton **(G-11214)**

Clarkson Chemical Company Inc ....G 570 323-3631
Williamsport **(G-20000)**

CLEANING PRDTS: Sanitation Preps, Disinfectants/Deodorants

Mspi Enterprises LLC ....G 814 258-7500
Knoxville **(G-8812)**

On Track Enterprises Inc ....F 610 277-4995
Norristown **(G-12699)**

Veltek Associates Inc ....E 610 644-8335
Malvern **(G-10338)**

CLEANING PRDTS: Shoe Polish Or Cleaner

Cei-Douglassville Inc ....D 610 385-9500
Douglassville **(G-4172)**

CLEANING PRDTS: Specialty

A Better Power LLC ....G 412 498-6537
Ligonier **(G-9956)**

Better Air Management LLC ....G 215 362-5677
Lansdale **(G-9347)**

Big 3 Packaging LLC ....F 215 743-4201
Philadelphia **(G-13459)**

Church & Dwight Co Inc ....D 717 781-8800
York **(G-20426)**

Decon Laboratories Inc ....E 610 755-0800
King of Prussia **(G-8606)**

Dixie S Young Cleaning ....G 814 623-3015
Bedford **(G-1049)**

Penn Kleen Ex-Its Inc ....G 717 792-3608
York **(G-20620)**

Perfectdata Corporation ....G 800 973-7332
Plymouth Meeting **(G-15863)**

Quantum Global Tech LLC ....C 215 892-9300
Quakertown **(G-16239)**

Randall Inds Ltd Liablility Co ....F 814 743-6630
Cherry Tree **(G-3035)**

Recirculation Technologies LLC ....F 215 682-7099
Fort Washington **(G-6090)**

Richardsapex Inc ....E 215 487-1100
Philadelphia **(G-14247)**

Shore Corporation ....F 412 471-3330
Pittsburgh **(G-15534)**

Versum Materials Us LLC ....F 610 481-3946
Allentown **(G-423)**

CLEANING PRDTS: Window Cleaning Preparations

DW Services LLC ....G 484 241-8915
Allentown **(G-198)**

Milazzo Industries Inc ....E 570 722-0522
Pittston **(G-15767)**

CLEANING SVCS

Caldwell Corporation ....E 814 486-3493
Emporium **(G-5051)**

Morantz Inc ....G 215 969-0266
Philadelphia **(G-14038)**

CLEANING SVCS: Industrial Or Commercial

Crg Resources LLC ....E 814 571-7190
Curwensville **(G-3950)**

Lesher Inc ....F 717 944-4431
Middletown **(G-11062)**

Quality Millwork Inc ....G 412 831-3500
Finleyville **(G-5964)**

Sun Valley Film Wash Inc ....G 610 497-1743
Aston **(G-794)**

CLIPS & FASTENERS, MADE FROM PURCHASED WIRE

Acme Stamping Wire Forming Co ....E 412 771-5720
Pittsburgh **(G-14644)**

CLOSURES: Closures, Stamped Metal

Dayton Superior Corporation ....D 570 695-3163
Tremont **(G-18480)**

Keystone Cap Co Inc ....G 717 684-3716
Columbia **(G-3440)**

West Pharmaceutical Svcs Inc ....B 610 594-2900
Exton **(G-5748)**

CLOSURES: Plastic

Bprex Plastic Packaging Inc ....C 814 849-4240
Brookville **(G-2251)**

Kerr Group LLC ....E 812 424-2904
Lancaster **(G-9082)**

Scaffs Enterprises Inc ....G 570 725-3497
Loganton **(G-10098)**

Silgan Ipec Corporation ....D 724 658-3004
New Castle **(G-12152)**

Silgan Ipec Corporation ....D 724 658-3004
New Castle **(G-12153)**

Tef - Cap Industries Inc ....G 610 692-2576
West Chester **(G-19657)**

CLOTHING & ACCESS, WOMEN, CHILD & INFANT, WHOL: Scarves

Kevin OBrien Studio Inc ....G 215 923-6378
Philadelphia **(G-13929)**

CLOTHING & ACCESS, WOMEN, CHILD & INFANT, WHSLE: Sportswear

Marcus J Wholesalers Inc ....F 412 261-3315
Pittsburgh **(G-15252)**

CLOTHING & ACCESS, WOMEN, CHILDREN & INFANT, WHOL: Handbags

Fleuri LLC ....G 724 539-7566
Latrobe **(G-9476)**

Employee Codes: A=Over 500 employees, B=251-500
C=101-250, D=51-100, E=20-50, F=10-19, G=3-9

2019 Harris Pennsylvania
Manufacturers Directory

1337

PRODUCT

CLOTHING & ACCESS, WOMEN, CHILDREN & INFANT, WHOL: Sweaters

Dualsun International Inc ....G....... 412 421-7934
Pittsburgh (G-14939)

CLOTHING & ACCESS, WOMEN, CHILDREN & INFANT, WHOL: Uniforms

Pinnacle Textile Inds LLC......................E....... 800 901-4784
King of Prussia (G-8663)

CLOTHING & ACCESS, WOMEN, CHILDREN/INFANT, WHOL: Outerwear

Alex and Ani LLC ....G....... 412 367-1362
Pittsburgh (G-14672)

CLOTHING & ACCESS, WOMEN, CHILDREN/INFANT, WHOL: Underwear

Wundies ....G....... 570 322-7245
Williamsport (G-20102)

CLOTHING & ACCESS: Costumes, Masquerade

Williamson Costume Company ....F 215 925-7121
Philadelphia (G-14476)

CLOTHING & ACCESS: Costumes, Theatrical

Character Translation Inc......................G....... 610 279-3970
Norristown (G-12644)
James May Costume Co..........................G....... 610 532-3430
Folsom (G-6026)

CLOTHING & ACCESS: Handicapped

C K Sportwear Inc ....E....... 717 733-4786
Ephrata (G-5094)
Meredith Banzhoff LLC...........................G....... 717 919-5074
Mechanicsburg (G-10868)
Sugartown Worldwide LLC ....F 610 265-7607
King of Prussia (G-8681)

CLOTHING & ACCESS: Men's Miscellaneous Access

Aeo Management Co ....G....... 724 776-4857
Warrendale (G-19067)
Aeo Management Co ....F 412 432-3300
Pittsburgh (G-14654)
Alex and Ani LLC ....G....... 412 367-1362
Pittsburgh (G-14672)
Breet Incorporated.................................G....... 610 558-4006
Glen Mills (G-6432)
Eros Hosiery Co Del Vly Inc..................G....... 215 342-2121
Huntingdon Valley (G-7978)
Gift Is In You Llc ....G....... 267 974-3376
Philadelphia (G-13761)
Imposters LLC.......................................G....... 412 781-3443
Pittsburgh (G-15115)
Premier Brnds Group Hldngs LLC ....E....... 212 835-3672
Bristol (G-2186)
Roeberg Enterprises Inc ....E....... 800 523-8197
Reading (G-16503)
Steve Goldberg Company ....G....... 215 322-0615
Southampton (G-17837)
Supreme Trading Ltd ....E....... 215 739-2237
Philadelphia (G-14361)
Vivid Products LLC.................................G....... 215 394-0235
Warminster (G-18996)

CLOTHING & ACCESS: Regalia

American Legion Post 548 ....D....... 724 443-0047
Gibsonia (G-6324)

CLOTHING & APPAREL STORES: Custom

C & G Wilcox Engrv & Images ....G....... 570 265-3621
Towanda (G-18422)
Rob Kei Inc ....G....... 717 293-8991
Lancaster (G-9189)
Tiadaghton Embroidery...........................G....... 570 398-4477
Jersey Shore (G-8323)
Todd Weikel ....G....... 610 779-5508
Reading (G-16542)

CLOTHING & FURNISHINGS, MEN'S & BOYS', WHOLESALE: Caps

Bollman Industries Inc ....C....... 717 484-4361
Adamstown (G-20)

CLOTHING & FURNISHINGS, MEN'S & BOYS', WHOLESALE: Coats

Jacob Siegel LP ....G....... 610 828-8400
Conshohocken (G-3567)

CLOTHING & FURNISHINGS, MEN'S & BOYS', WHOLESALE: Gloves

Brookville Glove Mfg Co Inc ....E....... 814 849-7324
Brookville (G-2253)

CLOTHING & FURNISHINGS, MEN'S & BOYS', WHOLESALE: Hats

Bollman Hat Company.............................B....... 717 484-4361
Adamstown (G-19)

CLOTHING & FURNISHINGS, MEN'S & BOYS', WHOLESALE: Shirts

Eric and Christopher LLC ....F 215 257-2400
Perkasie (G-13276)
Peerless Printery....................................G....... 610 258-5226
Easton (G-4741)

CLOTHING & FURNISHINGS, MEN'S & BOYS', WHOLESALE: Sweaters

Dualsun International Inc ....G....... 412 421-7934
Pittsburgh (G-14939)

CLOTHING & FURNISHINGS, MEN'S & BOYS', WHOLESALE: Uniforms

Imagewear International Inc...................G....... 724 335-2425
Murrysville (G-11853)
Pinnacle Textile Inds LLC......................E....... 800 901-4784
King of Prussia (G-8663)

CLOTHING & FURNISHINGS, MENS & BOYS, WHOL: Sportswear/Work

Marcus J Wholesalers Inc ....F 412 261-3315
Pittsburgh (G-15252)

CLOTHING & FURNISHINGS, MENS & BOYS, WHOLESALE: Lined

Sickafus Sheepskins ....E....... 610 488-1782
Strausstown (G-18100)

CLOTHING STORES, NEC

Coloratura Inc...G....... 717 867-1144
Lebanon (G-9555)

CLOTHING STORES: Caps & Gowns

Bentley Robe Factory Inc......................G....... 215 531-3862
Philadelphia (G-13455)

CLOTHING STORES: Designer Apparel

DOC Printing LLC ....G....... 267 702-6196
Philadelphia (G-13637)
Ibis Tek Apparel LLC..............................E....... 724 586-2179
Butler (G-2408)

CLOTHING STORES: Dresses, Knit, Made To Order

Gloray If LLC ....F 610 921-3300
Bernville (G-1299)

CLOTHING STORES: Formal Wear

Amc Inc...G....... 412 531-3160
Pittsburgh (G-14698)

CLOTHING STORES: Leather

Ambassador Bags & Spats Mfg Co.......G....... 610 532-7840
Folcroft (G-5998)
Roberta Weissburg Leathers ....G....... 412 681-8188
Pittsburgh (G-15494)

Sickafus Sheepskins ....E....... 610 488-1782
Strausstown (G-18100)

CLOTHING STORES: Shirts, Custom Made

Effective Plan Inc ....G....... 717 428-6190
Seven Valleys (G-17378)

CLOTHING STORES: T-Shirts, Printed, Custom

Corporate Print Solutions Inc ....G 215 774-1119
Glenolden (G-6472)
Lawrence R Gilman LLC.......................G....... 215 432-2733
Philadelphia (G-13960)
Smith Prints Inc......................................G....... 215 997-8077
Chalfont (G-2888)
T Shirt Loft ....G....... 724 452-4380
Zelienople (G-20823)
Wet Paint T Shirts Inc ....G....... 570 822-2221
Wilkes Barre (G-19973)

CLOTHING STORES: Uniforms & Work

Aramark Unf Creer AP Group Inc ....A....... 215 238-3000
Philadelphia (G-13406)
Maroco Ltd..B....... 610 746-6800
Easton (G-4719)

CLOTHING STORES: Unisex

Samuelson Leather LLC.........................G....... 610 719-7391
West Chester (G-19636)
Samuelson Leather LLC.........................G....... 484 328-3273
Malvern (G-10314)
Shine Moon L P ....F 570 539-8602
Mount Pleasant Mills (G-11732)

CLOTHING: Access

Futernal Order Police Lodge..................G....... 610 655-6116
Reading (G-16386)

CLOTHING: Access, Women's & Misses'

Aeo Management Co ....G....... 724 776-4857
Warrendale (G-19067)
Aeo Management Co ....F 412 432-3300
Pittsburgh (G-14654)
Cute Loops ....G....... 484 318-7175
Chesterbrook (G-3091)
Lavender Badge LLC.............................G....... 610 994-9476
King of Prussia (G-8638)
Lindas Stuff Inc ....F 215 956-9190
Hatboro (G-7292)
Little Earth Productions Inc ....E....... 412 471-0909
Pittsburgh (G-15237)
Mifflinburg Farmers Exchange ....G....... 570 966-4030
Mifflinburg (G-11098)
Premier Brnds Group Hldngs LLC ....E....... 212 835-3672
Bristol (G-2186)

CLOTHING: Aprons, Harness

Ambassador Bags & Spats Mfg Co.......G....... 610 532-7840
Folcroft (G-5998)

CLOTHING: Aprons, Work, Exc Rubberized & Plastic, Men's

Davy Manufacturing Inc ....F 610 583-8240
Havertown (G-7420)

CLOTHING: Athletic & Sportswear, Men's & Boys'

Alpha Mills Corporation ....D....... 570 385-1791
Schuylkill Haven (G-17145)
Aramark Services Inc ....F 800 999-8989
Philadelphia (G-13405)
Bitars Sportswear ....G....... 610 435-4923
Allentown (G-153)
Boathouse Row Sports Ltd...................C....... 215 425-4300
Philadelphia (G-13469)
C K Sportwear Inc ....E....... 717 733-4786
Ephrata (G-5094)
Camber Sportswear Inc........................E....... 610 239-9910
Norristown (G-12643)
Coopersburg Products LLC....................G....... 610 282-1360
Center Valley (G-2826)
Cycling Sports Group Inc.....................D....... 203 749-7000
Bedford (G-1048)

D & S Clothing Inc..............................G...... 856 383-3794
Philadelphia *(G-13598)*

Gregg Shirtmakers Inc.......................G...... 215 329-7700
Philadelphia *(G-13787)*

HB Sportswear Inc............................G...... 717 354-2306
New Holland *(G-12252)*

La Salle Products Inc........................F...... 412 488-1585
Pittsburgh *(G-15213)*

Majestic Athletic Intl Ltd...................G...... 610 746-7494
Easton *(G-4718)*

Maroco Ltd.....................................B...... 610 746-6800
Easton *(G-4719)*

Meke Corp.......................................F...... 717 354-6353
East Earl *(G-4550)*

Nautica of Lancaster........................F...... 717 396-9414
Lancaster *(G-9143)*

P & S Sportswear Inc........................G...... 215 455-7133
Philadelphia *(G-14110)*

Performance Sports Apparel Inc........E...... 508 384-8036
Reading *(G-16468)*

PS & QS Inc....................................G...... 215 592-0888
Philadelphia *(G-14213)*

CLOTHING: Athletic & Sportswear, Women's & Girls'

Anthony Hauze.................................G...... 610 432-3533
Allentown *(G-137)*

C K Sportwear Inc............................E...... 717 733-4786
Ephrata *(G-5094)*

Eco Product Group LLC.....................G...... 412 364-1792
Pittsburgh *(G-14958)*

Gear Racewear Inc...........................F...... 724 458-6336
Grove City *(G-6786)*

HB Sportswear Inc............................G...... 717 354-2306
New Holland *(G-12252)*

T A E Ltd...G...... 215 925-7860
Philadelphia *(G-14364)*

Vf Imagewear Inc..............................G...... 610 746-6800
Easton *(G-4768)*

Windridge Design Inc........................F...... 610 692-1919
West Chester *(G-19678)*

CLOTHING: Blouses, Women's & Girls'

Designer Fashions Plus......................G...... 215 416-5062
Philadelphia *(G-13621)*

Gloninger Brothers Inc.......................G...... 215 456-5100
Philadelphia *(G-13774)*

Jarmens Fashion...............................G...... 215 441-5242
Warminster *(G-18901)*

Lifewear Inc.....................................E...... 610 327-2884
Pottstown *(G-16011)*

Mona Lisa Fashions..........................G...... 610 770-0806
Allentown *(G-319)*

R & M Apparel Inc............................C...... 814 886-9272
Gallitzin *(G-6247)*

CLOTHING: Blouses, Womens & Juniors, From Purchased Mtrls

Meredith Banzhoff LLC......................G...... 717 919-5074
Mechanicsburg *(G-10868)*

Notations Inc...................................C...... 215 259-2000
Warminster *(G-18930)*

Sarah Lynn Sportswear Inc................E...... 610 770-1702
Allentown *(G-384)*

CLOTHING: Brassieres

Farel Corp.......................................E...... 814 495-4625
South Fork *(G-17774)*

CLOTHING: Bridal Gowns

Davids Bridal Inc..............................E...... 610 943-6210
Conshohocken *(G-3536)*

Johnny Appleseeds Inc......................G...... 800 546-4554
Warren *(G-19034)*

CLOTHING: Burial

Gardinier Associates Inc....................E...... 570 385-2721
Schuylkill Haven *(G-17157)*

CLOTHING: Capes & Jackets, Women's & Misses'

Donora Sportswear Company Inc........G...... 724 929-2387
Donora *(G-4151)*

Greco International Inc.......................F...... 215 628-2557
Ambler *(G-580)*

CLOTHING: Children & Infants'

Baby Sparkles.................................G...... 267 304-8787
Philadelphia *(G-13440)*

Emma One Sock Inc.........................G...... 215 542-1082
Dresher *(G-4354)*

Sugartown Worldwide LLC..................C...... 610 878-5550
King of Prussia *(G-8682)*

CLOTHING: Children's, Girls'

Alpha Mills Corporation......................D...... 570 385-1791
Schuylkill Haven *(G-17145)*

Alpha Mills Corporation......................E...... 570 385-1791
Schuylkill Haven *(G-17146)*

Alpha Mills Corporation......................D...... 570 385-2400
Pottsville *(G-16072)*

C&H7 LLC.......................................G...... 215 887-7411
Exton *(G-5658)*

Delta Galil USA Inc...........................B...... 570 326-2451
Williamsport *(G-20004)*

Good Lad Co....................................B...... 215 739-0200
Philadelphia *(G-13777)*

Kahn-Lucas-Lancaster Inc.................E...... 717 537-4140
Mountville *(G-11797)*

Meke Corp.......................................F...... 717 354-6353
East Earl *(G-4550)*

R & M Apparel Inc............................C...... 814 886-9272
Gallitzin *(G-6247)*

CLOTHING: Coats & Jackets, Leather & Sheep-Lined

Torgeman Gabi.................................G...... 215 563-0882
Philadelphia *(G-14397)*

Vf Outdoor LLC.................................G...... 610 265-2193
King of Prussia *(G-8696)*

CLOTHING: Coats & Suits, Men's & Boys'

Bodine Business Products..................G...... 610 827-0138
Malvern *(G-10194)*

F&T Apparel LLC..............................D...... 610 828-8400
Plymouth Meeting *(G-15844)*

Jacob Siegel LP...............................G...... 610 828-8400
Conshohocken *(G-3567)*

Northside Manufacturing Inc...............E...... 814 342-4638
Philipsburg *(G-14521)*

Tlr Redwood Inc................................G...... 215 322-1005
Southampton *(G-17841)*

CLOTHING: Coats, Hunting & Vests, Men's

Innovative Designs Inc.......................G...... 412 799-0350
Pittsburgh *(G-15127)*

Iwom Outerwear LLC.........................G...... 814 272-5400
State College *(G-17979)*

Prosco Inc.......................................E...... 814 375-0484
Du Bois *(G-4414)*

CLOTHING: Coats, Leatherette, Oiled Fabric, Etc, Mens & Boys

Vf Outdoor LLC.................................G...... 610 265-2193
King of Prussia *(G-8696)*

CLOTHING: Coats, Tailored, Mens/Boys, From Purchased Mtls

Woolrich Inc.....................................C...... 570 769-6464
Woolrich *(G-20220)*

CLOTHING: Costumes

Angelie Original................................G...... 814 798-3312
Hooversville *(G-7770)*

B & D Advertising Inc.........................D...... 717 852-6950
York *(G-20394)*

Cicci Dance Supply Inc......................E...... 724 348-7359
Finleyville *(G-5953)*

CSS Industries Inc............................C...... 610 729-3959
Plymouth Meeting *(G-15840)*

David Moscinski...............................G...... 215 271-6193
Philadelphia *(G-13609)*

Perform Group LLC...........................B...... 717 852-6950
York *(G-20624)*

Perform Group LLC...........................C...... 717 252-1578
York *(G-20625)*

T J Corporation................................E...... 724 929-7300
Verona *(G-18763)*

CLOTHING: Disposable

Lakeland Industries Inc......................G...... 610 775-0505
Reading *(G-16426)*

Valumax International Inc....................F...... 610 336-0101
Allentown *(G-421)*

CLOTHING: Dresses

Center Fashions Inc..........................D...... 570 655-2861
Dupont *(G-4489)*

CFM Designs Inc..............................G...... 610 520-7777
Bryn Mawr *(G-2318)*

Donna Karan Company LLC................C...... 610 625-4410
Bethlehem *(G-1498)*

Donna Karan Company LLC................C...... 717 299-1706
Lancaster *(G-9001)*

Joel Mfg Co Inc................................G...... 570 822-1182
Wilkes Barre *(G-19934)*

R & M Apparel Inc............................C...... 814 886-9272
Gallitzin *(G-6247)*

Runway Liquidation LLC.....................G...... 401 351-4994
Philadelphia *(G-14264)*

CLOTHING: Foundation Garments, Women's

Glamorise Foundations Inc.................C...... 570 322-7806
Williamsport *(G-20018)*

Lontex Corporation............................E...... 610 272-5040
Norristown *(G-12678)*

CLOTHING: Garments, Indl, Men's & Boys

Innovative Designs Inc.......................G...... 412 799-0350
Pittsburgh *(G-15127)*

CLOTHING: Gloves & Mittens, Knit

Dbi Inc..D...... 814 653-7625
Fairmount City *(G-5808)*

CLOTHING: Gowns & Dresses, Wedding

Alfred Angelo - The Brdes Std............F...... 813 872-1881
Fort Washington *(G-6061)*

Amc Inc...G...... 412 531-3160
Pittsburgh *(G-14698)*

Icbridal LLC.....................................G...... 570 409-6333
Milford *(G-11161)*

Priscilla of Boston Inc.......................D...... 610 943-5000
Conshohocken *(G-3592)*

Sweethearts Bridal Formalwear..........G...... 610 750-5087
Reading *(G-16532)*

CLOTHING: Hats & Caps, NEC

Bollman Hat Company........................D...... 717 336-0545
Denver *(G-4069)*

Hatcrafters Inc.................................G...... 610 623-2620
Clifton Heights *(G-3253)*

Lids Corporation...............................G...... 814 868-1944
Erie *(G-5364)*

Outback Trading Company Ltd.............E...... 610 932-5314
Oxford *(G-13084)*

P & L Sportswear Inc.........................G...... 717 359-9000
Littlestown *(G-10074)*

Weisman Novelty Co Inc....................F...... 215 635-0147
Elkins Park *(G-4914)*

CLOTHING: Hats & Caps, Uniform

Keystone Uniform Cap LP...................E...... 215 821-3434
Philadelphia *(G-13933)*

CLOTHING: Hats, Harvest, Straw

Bollman Industries Inc.......................C...... 717 484-4361
Adamstown *(G-20)*

CLOTHING: Hosiery, Pantyhose & Knee Length, Sheer

Sculptz Inc......................................E...... 215 494-2900
Trevose *(G-18503)*

U S Textile Corp...............................E...... 803 283-6800
Feasterville Trevose *(G-5935)*

CLOTHING: Hospital, Men's

Combined Tactical Systems Inc...........C...... 724 932-2177
Jamestown *(G-8236)*

Enterprise Fashions...........................G...... 570 489-1863
Olyphant *(G-12989)*

PRODUCT

Pinnacle Textile Inds LLC..........E 800 901-4784
King of Prussia (G-8663)

CLOTHING: Jackets, Field, Military

Scottys Fashion of Lehighton ....G 610 377-3032
Pen Argyl (G-13216)
Transfer Junction ....G 814 942-4434
Williamsburg (G-19982)

CLOTHING: Jogging & Warm-Up Suits, Knit

Continental Apparel Corp ....G 814 495-4625
South Fork (G-17773)

CLOTHING: Knit Underwear & Nightwear

American Sports Apparel Inc..........D 570 357-8155
Avoca (G-839)

CLOTHING: Leather

Fusion Five USA LLC ....G 267 507-6127
Philadelphia (G-13735)
Hal-Jo Corp..........F 215 885-4747
Jenkintown (G-8289)
Pocono Mountain Leather Co ....G 570 814-6672
Hanover Township (G-7004)
Samuelson Leather LLC..........G 484 328-3273
Malvern (G-10314)

CLOTHING: Maternity

Matthew Cole Inc..........G 215 425-6606
Philadelphia (G-13995)

CLOTHING: Men's & boy's underwear & nightwear

Wundies ....G 570 322-7245
Williamsport (G-20102)

CLOTHING: Neckwear

Tom James Company ....D 717 264-5768
Chambersburg (G-2986)

CLOTHING: Outerwear, Knit

Alpha Mills Corporation ....D 570 385-1791
Schuylkill Haven (G-17145)
Alpha Mills Corporation ....D 570 385-2400
Pottsville (G-16072)
Alpha Mills Corporation ....E 570 385-1791
Schuylkill Haven (G-17146)
Gloray If LLC ....F 610 921-3300
Bernville (G-1299)
Merry Maid Novelties ....F 610 599-4104
Bangor (G-922)
Warrior Fashions Inc ....G 215 925-7905
Philadelphia (G-14460)

CLOTHING: Outerwear, Lthr, Wool/Down-Filled, Men, Youth/Boy

American Trench LLC..........G 215 360-3493
Ardmore (G-700)
Outback Trading Company Ltd..........E 610 932-5314
Oxford (G-13084)
Vf Outdoor LLC ....G 610 323-6575
Pottstown (G-16066)

CLOTHING: Outerwear, Women's & Misses' NEC

A & H Sportswear Co Inc..........C 610 759-9550
Stockertown (G-18063)
Alpha Mills Corporation ....D 570 385-1791
Schuylkill Haven (G-17145)
Alpha Mills Corporation ....D 570 385-2400
Pottsville (G-16072)
Cheryl Nash Apparel LLC..........G 610 692-1919
Kennett Square (G-8504)
Danskin ....F 717 747-3051
York (G-20444)
Farnsworth Gowns and Fnrl Sups ....G 412 881-4696
Pittsburgh (G-15004)
Frox ....G 215 822-9011
Perkasie (G-13277)
Henson Company Inc ....D 800 486-2788
Reading (G-16400)
Hey Girl Inc ....G 610 945-6138
Newtown Square (G-12575)

Jade Fashion Corporation ....G 215 922-3953
Philadelphia (G-13888)
Meke Corp..........F 717 354-6353
East Earl (G-4550)
Merry Maid Inc..........E 800 360-3836
Bangor (G-921)
Milco Industries Inc ....C 570 784-0400
Bloomsburg (G-1790)
Nightlife & Clothing Co..........G 718 415-6391
Philadelphia (G-14074)
Notations Inc ....C 215 259-2000
Warminster (G-18930)
P & L Sportswear Inc ....G 717 359-9000
Littlestown (G-10074)
P & S Sportswear Inc..........E 215 455-7133
Philadelphia (G-14110)
Perform Group LLC ....C 717 252-1578
York (G-20625)
R & M Apparel Inc ....C 814 886-9272
Gallitzin (G-6247)
Red Lion Manufacturing Inc..........C 717 767-6511
York (G-20656)

CLOTHING: Overcoats & Topcoats, Men/Boy, Purchased Materials

Donora Sportswear Company Inc ....G 724 929-2387
Donora (G-4151)

CLOTHING: Pants, Work, Men's, Youths' & Boys'

Elbeco Incorporated ....D 610 921-0651
Reading (G-16370)

CLOTHING: Raincoats, Exc Vulcanized Rubber, Purchased Matls

Keystone Niteware Co Inc..........E 717 336-7534
Reinholds (G-16634)

CLOTHING: Robes & Dressing Gowns

Bentley Robe Factory Inc..........G 215 531-3862
Philadelphia (G-13455)
Milco Industries Inc ....C 570 784-0400
Bloomsburg (G-1790)

CLOTHING: Rubber, Vulcanized Or Rubberized Fabric

Harris Manufacturing Company ....G 609 393-3717
Southampton (G-17816)

CLOTHING: Sheep-Lined

Sickafus Sheepskins ....E 610 488-1782
Strausstown (G-18100)

CLOTHING: Shirts

Hancock Company..........G 570 875-3100
Ashland (G-731)
Lifewear Inc ....E 610 327-2884
Pottstown (G-16011)
Tom James Company ....D 717 264-5768
Chambersburg (G-2986)
Vf Outdoor LLC ....G 610 265-2193
King of Prussia (G-8696)

CLOTHING: Shirts & T-Shirts, Knit

City Shirt Co ....G 570 874-4251
Frackville (G-6104)

CLOTHING: Shirts, Dress, Men's & Boys'

Taraco Sportswear Inc..........G 570 669-9004
Nesquehoning (G-12009)

CLOTHING: Shirts, Sports & Polo, Men & Boy, Purchased Mtrl

Kaylin Mfg Co ....F 610 820-6224
Allentown (G-280)

CLOTHING: Shirts, Sports & Polo, Men's & Boys'

F&T Apparel LLC..........D 646 839-7000
Plymouth Meeting (G-15843)

Trau & Loevner Inc..........D 412 361-7700
Braddock (G-1949)
Vf Imagewear Inc..........G 610 746-6800
Easton (G-4768)

CLOTHING: Shirts, Uniform, From Purchased Materials

Elbeco Incorporated ....D 610 921-0651
Reading (G-16370)
Trademark Specialties ....G 412 353-3752
Cheswick (G-3119)

CLOTHING: Shirts, Women's & Juniors', From Purchased Mtrls

Taraco Sportswear Inc..........G 570 669-9004
Nesquehoning (G-12009)
Woolrich Inc ....C 570 769-6464
Woolrich (G-20220)

CLOTHING: Skirts

D D J Manufacturing Inc..........D 814 378-7625
Madera (G-10162)
Tama Mfg Co Inc ....B 610 231-3100
Allentown (G-407)
Tan Clothing Co Inc ....E 215 625-2536
Philadelphia (G-14370)

CLOTHING: Slacks & Shorts, Dress, Men's, Youths' & Boys'

F&T Apparel LLC..........D 646 839-7000
Plymouth Meeting (G-15843)

CLOTHING: Socks

CM Industries Inc ....C 717 336-4545
Lancaster (G-8980)
Comfort Sportswear Inc ....G 215 781-0300
Croydon (G-3914)
Eric L Socks ....G 717 762-7488
Waynesboro (G-19409)
Frog Creek Socks ....G 215 997-6104
Chalfont (G-2875)
Inspyr Apparel Co LLC ....G 267 784-3036
Oreland (G-13022)
Top Circle Hosiery Mills Co..........E 610 379-0470
Weissport (G-19461)

CLOTHING: Sportswear, Women's

Bitars Sportswear ....G 610 435-4923
Allentown (G-153)
G H Lainez Manufacturing Inc ....F 610 776-0778
Allentown (G-221)
Rich Reenie Inc ....F 610 439-7962
Allentown (G-374)
Roeberg Enterprises Inc ....E 800 523-8197
Reading (G-16503)
Roseys Creations Inc ....G 610 704-8591
Allentown (G-379)
Sugartown Worldwide LLC ....C 610 878-5550
King of Prussia (G-8682)
Tukes Tearoff ....G 570 695-3171
Tremont (G-18483)

CLOTHING: Suits, Men's & Boys', From Purchased Materials

Dream World International Inc..........G 215 320-0200
Philadelphia (G-13644)
F&T Apparel LLC..........D 646 839-7000
Plymouth Meeting (G-15843)
Majer Brand Company Inc..........F 717 632-1320
Hanover (G-6916)
Tom James Company ....E 570 875-3100
Ashland (G-737)
Tom James Company ....F 412 642-2797
Pittsburgh (G-15631)
Tom James Company ....D 717 264-5768
Chambersburg (G-2986)

CLOTHING: Sweaters & Sweater Coats, Knit

El-Ana Collection Inc..........F 215 953-8820
Huntingdon Valley (G-7977)

CLOTHING: Sweaters, Men's & Boys'

Woolrich Inc ....C 570 769-6464
Woolrich (G-20220)

CLOTHING: Sweatshirts & T-Shirts, Men's & Boys'

E-Nanomedsys LLC ....G 917 734-1462
State College (G-17958)
Ocello Inc ....C 717 866-5778
Richland (G-16688)
Windjammer Corporation Inc.............E 610 588-0626
Bangor (G-935)
Windjammer Corporation Inc.............G 610 588-2137
Bangor (G-936)
Woolrich Inc ....C 570 769-6464
Woolrich (G-20220)

CLOTHING: Swimwear, Men's & Boys'

Urban Outfitters Wholesale Inc ....G 215 454-5500
Philadelphia (G-14431)

CLOTHING: Swimwear, Women's & Misses'

A & H Sportswear Co Inc ....D 610 746-0922
Nazareth (G-11951)
A & H Sportswear Co Inc ....D 484 373-3600
Easton (G-4643)
Longevity Brands LLC ....E 484 373-3600
Easton (G-4715)
Mainstream Swimsuits Inc ....G 484 373-3600
Easton (G-4717)

CLOTHING: T-Shirts & Tops, Knit

Apex Apparel Inc ....D 610 432-8007
Allentown (G-140)
C & L Enterprises LLC.........................G 215 589-4553
Doylestown (G-4284)
Effective Plan Inc ....G 717 428-6190
Seven Valleys (G-17378)
Ems Clothing & Novelty Inc ....G 570 752-2896
Berwick (G-1324)
Hanesbrands Inc ....G 610 970-5767
Pottstown (G-15996)
Lawrence R Gilman LLC ....G 215 432-2733
Philadelphia (G-13960)
Lifewear Inc ....E 610 327-2884
Pottstown (G-16011)
Lifewear Inc ....G 610 327-9938
Pottstown (G-15953)
Wet Paint T Shirts Inc ....G 570 822-2221
Wilkes Barre (G-19973)

CLOTHING: T-Shirts & Tops, Women's & Girls'

Dallco Industries Inc ....E 717 854-7875
York (G-20443)
E-Nanomedsys LLC ....G 917 734-1462
State College (G-17958)
Trau & Loevner Inc..............................D 412 361-7700
Braddock (G-1949)

CLOTHING: Tailored Dress/Sport Coats, Mens & Boys

Ikor Industries Inc ....D 302 456-0280
Kennett Square (G-8514)
Union Apparel Inc ....A 724 423-4900
Norvelt (G-12879)

CLOTHING: Tailored Suits & Formal Jackets

Ideal Products America LP ....F 484 320-6194
Malvern (G-10250)

CLOTHING: Ties, Neck & Bow, Men's & Boys'

Joyce Inc..G 206 937-4633
Pittsburgh (G-15156)

CLOTHING: Trousers & Slacks, Men's & Boys'

D D J Manufacturing Inc......................D 814 378-7625
Madera (G-10162)
Freespiritjeanscom Inc ....G 302 319-9313
Philadelphia (G-13723)

Majer Brand Company Inc...................F 717 632-1320
Hanover (G-6916)
Tan Clothing Co Inc ....E 215 625-2536
Philadelphia (G-14370)
Tom James Company ....D 717 264-5768
Chambersburg (G-2986)
Vf Outdoor LLC ....G 610 265-2193
King of Prussia (G-8696)

CLOTHING: Tuxedos, From Purchased Materials

Jack OReilly Tuxedos ....G 610 929-9409
Reading (G-16412)

CLOTHING: Underwear, Knit

Alpha Mills Corporation ....D 570 385-1791
Schuylkill Haven (G-17145)
Alpha Mills Corporation ....D 570 385-2400
Pottsville (G-16072)
Alpha Mills Corporation ....E 570 385-1791
Schuylkill Haven (G-17146)
Lake Erie Regional Center For.............G 814 725-4601
North East (G-12749)

CLOTHING: Underwear, Women's & Children's

Alpha Mills Corporation ....D 570 385-2400
Pottsville (G-16072)
Alpha Mills Corporation ....D 570 385-1791
Schuylkill Haven (G-17145)
Artworks Silk Screen Printers ....G 717 238-5087
Harrisburg (G-7092)
Charles Komar & Sons Inc ....C 570 326-3741
Williamsport (G-19997)
Glamorise Foundations Inc ....G 570 322-7806
Williamsport (G-20018)
Sculptz Inc ....E 215 494-2900
Trevose (G-18503)
Wundies ....G 570 322-7245
Williamsport (G-20102)

CLOTHING: Uniforms & Vestments

Imagewear International Inc.................G 724 335-2425
Murrysville (G-11853)

CLOTHING: Uniforms, Ex Athletic, Women's, Misses' & Juniors'

Amrit Works LLC...................................G 267 475-7129
Morton (G-11589)
Aramark Unf Creer AP Group Inc ....A 215 238-3000
Philadelphia (G-13406)
Cintas Corporation No 2 ....D 724 696-5640
Mount Pleasant (G-11692)
Executive Apparel Inc ....F 215 464-5400
Philadelphia (G-13686)
Flagstaff Industries Corp ....C 215 638-9662
Bensalem (G-1195)
Flynn & OHara Uniforms Inc ....D 800 441-4122
Philadelphia (G-13707)

CLOTHING: Uniforms, Men's & Boys'

Aramark Unf Creer AP Group Inc ....A 215 238-3000
Philadelphia (G-13406)
Cintas Corporation No 2 ....D 440 352-4003
Erie (G-5224)
D & S Clothing Inc ....G 856 383-3794
Philadelphia (G-13598)
Dynamic Team Sports Inc ....D 610 518-3300
Exton (G-5670)
Flagstaff Industries Corp ....C 215 638-9662
Bensalem (G-1195)
Flynn & OHara Uniforms Inc ....D 800 441-4122
Philadelphia (G-13707)

CLOTHING: Uniforms, Policemen's, From Purchased Materials

Hope Uniform Co Inc ....E 908 496-4899
Bangor (G-916)

CLOTHING: Uniforms, Team Athletic

Footers Inc ....G 610 437-2233
Allentown (G-217)
Henson Company Inc ....D 800 486-2788
Reading (G-16400)

CLOTHING: Uniforms, Work

Cintas Corporation No 2 ....D 724 696-5640
Mount Pleasant (G-11692)
Executive Apparel Inc ....F 215 464-5400
Philadelphia (G-13686)
Roeberg Enterprises Inc ....E 800 523-8197
Reading (G-16503)
Unek Designs EMB & Sew Sp LLC.......G 610 563-6676
Coatesville (G-3327)

CLOTHING: Vests

Stonemak Enterprises Inc ....G 570 752-3209
Berwick (G-1345)

CLOTHING: WarmUp, Jogging & Sweat Suits, Girls' & Children's

HB Sportswear Inc ....G 717 354-2306
New Holland (G-12252)

CLOTHING: Waterproof Outerwear

Harris Manufacturing Company ....G 609 393-3717
Southampton (G-17816)
Red Lion Manufacturing Inc.................C 717 767-6511
York (G-20656)

CLOTHING: Work Apparel, Exc Uniforms

Majestic Fire Apparel Inc......................E 610 377-6273
Lehighton (G-9719)

CLOTHING: Work, Men's

AC Fashion LLC ....G 570 291-5982
Moosic (G-11501)
Amrit Works LLC...................................G 267 475-7129
Morton (G-11589)
Bashlin Industries Inc...........................D 724 458-8340
Grove City (G-6780)
Blind and Vision Rehab ....F 412 325-7504
Homestead (G-7683)
Blind and Vision Rehab ....D 412 368-4400
Pittsburgh (G-14771)
C K Sportwear Inc ....E 717 733-4786
Ephrata (G-5094)
D & S Clothing Inc ....G 856 383-3794
Philadelphia (G-13598)
G H Lainez Manufacturing Inc ....F 610 776-0778
Allentown (G-221)
Hatcrafters Inc ....G 610 623-2620
Clifton Heights (G-3253)
Hings Lai Fashion ....G 215 530-0348
Philadelphia (G-13827)
Hope Uniform Co Inc ....E 908 496-4899
Bangor (G-916)
Mifflin Valley Inc ....E 610 775-0505
Reading (G-16443)
Suns Manufacturing Inc ....E 610 837-0798
Bath (G-971)
Threshold Rhbltation Svcs Inc ....B 610 777-7691
Reading (G-16538)

CLOTHS: Dish, Textile, Nonwoven, From Purchased Materials

General Medical Mfg LLC ....G 610 599-0961
Bangor (G-915)

CLOTHS: Dust, Made From Purchased Materials

Factory Linens Inc ....E 610 825-2790
Conshohocken (G-3545)
Shen Manufacturing Company Inc........G 570 278-3707
Montrose (G-11476)

COAL & OTHER MINERALS & ORES WHOLESALERS

Angstrom Sciences Inc ....E 412 469-8466
Duquesne (G-4495)
Gale Mining Co ....G 570 622-2524
Pottsville (G-16079)
Wilson Creek Energy LLC.....................E 724 754-0028
Canonsburg (G-2660)
Wilson Creek Energy LLC.....................E 814 443-4668
Friedens (G-6228)

P
R
O
D
U
C
T

COAL LIQUEFACTION

Lehigh Anthracite LP ....G..... 570 668-9060
Tamaqua (G-18215)

COAL MINING EXPLORATION & TEST BORING SVC

PA Mining Professional ....G..... 717 761-4646
Camp Hill (G-2509)

Reading Fracture Inc ....G..... 570 628-2308
Pottsville (G-16094)

COAL MINING EXPLORATION SVCS: Bituminous Or Lignite

Snyder Exploration Co ....G..... 724 548-8101
Kittanning (G-8796)

COAL MINING SERVICES

Amfire Mining Co ....G..... 724 254-9554
Clymer (G-3269)

Amfire Mining Company LLC ....F..... 724 532-4307
Latrobe (G-9455)

B & B Coal Company ....G..... 570 695-3188
Tremont (G-18479)

Bellaire Corporation ....G..... 814 446-5631
Armagh (G-723)

Britt Resources Inc ....G..... 724 465-9333
Spring Church (G-17855)

Buckley Associates Inc ....G..... 412 963-7070
Pittsburgh (G-14796)

C & K Coal Company ....D..... 814 226-6911
Clarion (G-3172)

C L I Corporation ....G..... 724 348-4800
Finleyville (G-5952)

Christopher Resources Inc ....G..... 724 430-9610
Uniontown (G-18620)

Coal Innovations LLC ....G..... 814 893-5790
Friedens (G-6219)

D L Enterprise Inc ....G..... 814 948-6060
Barnesboro (G-939)

Duquesne Mine Supply Company ....G..... 412 821-2100
Pittsburgh (G-14944)

E P Bender Coal Company ....E..... 814 344-8063
Carrolltown (G-2808)

F & D Coal Sales Co Inc ....G..... 570 455-4745
Hazle Township (G-7456)

Freys Farm Dairy LLC ....G..... 717 860-8015
Chambersburg (G-2934)

Gale Mining Co ....G..... 570 622-2524
Pottsville (G-16079)

Gary Gioia Coal Co ....G..... 412 754-0994
Elizabeth (G-4859)

George Skebeck ....G..... 814 674-8169
Patton (G-13188)

Girard Estate Fee ....E..... 570 276-1404
Girardville (G-6405)

Joliett Coal Co ....G..... 717 647-9628
Tower City (G-18438)

Kimmels Coal and Packaging Inc ....E..... 717 453-7151
Wiconisco (G-19895)

Kovalchick Corporation ....E..... 724 349-3300
Indiana (G-8110)

Laurel Energy LP ....G..... 724 537-5731
Latrobe (G-9496)

Longwall Mining Services Inc ....G..... 724 816-7871
Allison Park (G-456)

McKee Drilling ....G..... 814 427-2444
Rossiter (G-16823)

Mulligan Mining Inc ....G..... 412 831-1787
Bethel Park (G-1427)

Northern Son Inc ....E..... 724 548-1137
Du Bois (G-4407)

Orchard Coal Company ....G..... 570 695-2301
Tremont (G-18482)

Parkwood Resources Inc ....E..... 724 479-4090
Kittanning (G-8787)

Penn Crossing Limited ....G..... 724 744-7725
Harrison City (G-7250)

R G Johnson Company Inc ....D..... 724 225-4969
Washington (G-19221)

RES Coal LLC ....E..... 814 765-7525
Clearfield (G-3230)

RES Coal LLC ....D..... 814 765-0352
West Decatur (G-19690)

RNS Services Inc ....E..... 814 472-5202
Ebensburg (G-4794)

Rosebud Coal Sales Inc ....G..... 724 545-6222
Kittanning (G-8789)

Rosebud Mining Co ....D..... 814 948-6390
Heilwood (G-7548)

Rosebud Mining Company ....E..... 724 459-4970
Clarksburg (G-3199)

Rosini Coal Inc ....E..... 570 874-2879
Frackville (G-6107)

Sebastian Management LLC ....D..... 412 203-1273
Pittsburgh (G-15519)

Sherpa Mining Contractors Inc ....E..... 814 754-5560
Hooversville (G-7771)

Solar Fuel Co Inc ....G..... 814 443-2646
Friedens (G-6227)

South Penn Resources LLC ....F..... 724 880-5882
Mc Clellandtown (G-10556)

Summit Packaging LLC ....G..... 570 622-5150
Pottsville (G-16098)

Uae Coalcorp Associates ....G..... 570 339-4090
Mount Carmel (G-11630)

Waste Management & Processors ....E..... 570 874-2003
Frackville (G-6109)

Wilson Creek Energy LLC ....G..... 814 619-4600
Johnstown (G-8445)

WJM Coal Co Inc ....F..... 724 354-2922
Shelocta (G-17491)

Xylem Wtr Sltons Zlienople LLC ....G..... 570 538-2260
Watsontown (G-19281)

COAL MINING SVCS: Bituminous, Contract Basis

Mirada Energy Inc ....E..... 717 730-9412
Camp Hill (G-2505)

COAL MINING: Anthracite

Anthracite Industries Inc ....E..... 570 286-2176
Sunbury (G-18163)

B D Mining Co Inc ....E..... 570 874-1602
Gilberton (G-6365)

Dennis Snyder ....F..... 570 682-9698
Hegins (G-7540)

Hecla Machinery & Equipment Co ....F..... 570 385-4783
Schuylkill Haven (G-17158)

Hudson Anthracite Inc ....G..... 570 823-0531
Plains (G-15785)

Hudson Anthracite Inc ....F..... 570 655-4151
Avoca (G-844)

Keystone Anthracite Co Inc ....E..... 570 276-6480
Girardville (G-6406)

Mountaintop Anthracite Inc ....F..... 570 474-1222
Mountain Top (G-11766)

Postupack Russell Culm Corp ....G..... 570 929-1699
McAdoo (G-10657)

Sherman Coal Company Inc ....G..... 570 695-2690
Elysburg (G-4981)

West Point Mining Corp ....E..... 570 339-5259
Stoystown (G-18089)

COAL MINING: Anthracite, Strip

Carol Fetterolf ....G..... 570 875-2026
Ashland (G-728)

Coal Contractors (1991) Inc ....D..... 570 450-5086
Hazle Township (G-7449)

Denis Bell Inc ....E..... 570 450-5086
Hazle Township (G-7451)

E O J Incorporated ....G..... 570 943-2860
New Ringgold (G-12438)

Jeddo-Highland Coal Company ....G..... 570 825-8700
Wilkes Barre (G-19933)

Joe Kuperavage ....F..... 570 622-8080
Port Carbon (G-15897)

K & K Coal Company ....G..... 570 622-0220
Port Carbon (G-15898)

Mallard Contracting Co Inc ....E..... 570 339-2930
Mount Carmel (G-11626)

Mammoth Materials ....G..... 570 385-4232
Schuylkill Haven (G-17162)

Northeast Energy Co Inc ....G..... 570 823-1719
Wilkes Barre (G-19951)

Pagnotti Enterprises Inc ....E..... 570 825-8700
Wilkes Barre (G-19954)

Reading Anthracite Company ....E..... 570 622-5150
Pottsville (G-16093)

Rossi Excavating Company ....G..... 570 455-9607
Beaver Meadows (G-1018)

COAL MINING: Anthracite, Underground

Silverbrook Anthracite Inc ....F..... 570 654-3560
Wilkes Barre (G-19963)

COAL MINING: Bituminous & Lignite Surface

Buchanan Mining Company LLC ....F..... 724 485-4000
Canonsburg (G-2553)

Central Ohio Coal Company ....C..... 740 338-3100
Canonsburg (G-2558)

Consolidation Coal Company ....G..... 740 338-3100
Canonsburg (G-2572)

Enercorp Inc ....G..... 814 345-6225
Morrisdale (G-11548)

Gre Ventures Inc ....G..... 814 226-6911
Clarion (G-3179)

Junior Coal Contracting Inc ....E..... 814 342-2012
Philipsburg (G-14516)

Keystone Coal Mining Corp ....B..... 740 338-3100
Canonsburg (G-2598)

Lost Creek Mining ....G..... 724 335-8780
New Kensington (G-12353)

McElroy Coal Company ....F..... 724 485-4000
Canonsburg (G-2602)

Montour Creek Mining Co ....G..... 717 582-7526
Elliottsburg (G-4921)

New Enterprise Stone Lime Inc ....E..... 570 823-0531
Plains (G-15787)

COAL MINING: Bituminous Coal & Lignite- Surface Mining

Alpha Coal Sales Co ....G..... 304 256-1015
Clearfield (G-3210)

Bullskin Tipple Company ....G..... 724 628-7807
Perryopolis (G-13303)

Charles L Swenglish Sons Coal ....G..... 724 437-3541
Smithfield (G-17646)

Coalview Recovery Group LLC ....G..... 814 443-6454
Somerset (G-17681)

Consol Energy Inc ....C..... 724 785-6242
East Millsboro (G-4583)

Consol Energy Inc ....E..... 412 854-6600
Canonsburg (G-2569)

Consol Energy Inc ....F..... 724 485-3300
Canonsburg (G-2568)

Consol Mining Company LLC ....F..... 724 485-4000
Canonsburg (G-2570)

Corsa Coal Corp ....G..... 724 754-0028
Canonsburg (G-2574)

Fairview Coal Co Inc ....G..... 814 776-1158
Ridgway (G-16708)

Gre Mining Company ....G..... 814 226-6911
Clarion (G-3178)

Greenley Engery Holdings of PA ....G..... 724 238-8177
Central City (G-2838)

Hanson Aggregates Bmc Inc ....F..... 724 626-0080
Connellsville (G-3498)

Philip Reese Coal Co Inc ....G..... 814 263-4231
Karthaus (G-8483)

Quality Aggregates Inc ....E..... 724 924-2198
Portersville (G-15935)

Quality Aggregates Inc ....F..... 412 777-6704
Pittsburgh (G-15459)

Rausch Creek Land LP ....E..... 570 682-4600
Valley View (G-18717)

Reclamation Inc ....F..... 814 265-2564
Brockway (G-2233)

River Hill Coal Co Inc ....G..... 814 263-4506
Karthaus (G-8484)

River Hill Coal Co Inc ....F..... 814 263-4341
Karthaus (G-8486)

Rjc Kohl Inc ....F..... 814 948-5903
Nicktown (G-12621)

Rosebud Mining Company ....E..... 724 354-4050
Shelocta (G-17488)

Valier Coal Yard ....F..... 814 938-5171
Valier (G-18706)

Victor LLC ....G..... 814 765-5681
Clearfield (G-3233)

Warren C Hartman Contracting ....G..... 814 765-8842
Clearfield (G-3237)

COAL MINING: Bituminous Underground

Black Hawk Mining Inc ....E..... 724 783-6433
Rural Valley (G-16876)

Chemstream Holdings Inc ....G..... 724 545-6222
Kittanning (G-8761)

Consol Coal Resources LP ....A..... 724 485-3300
Canonsburg (G-2567)

Consol Energy Inc ....F..... 724 485-3300
Canonsburg (G-2568)

Consol PA Coal Co LLC ....A..... 724 485-4000
Canonsburg (G-2571)

Cumberland Coal Resources LP ....E 724 852-5845
Waynesburg *(G-19436)*
Cumberland Coal Resources LP ....A 724 627-7500
Waynesburg *(G-19437)*
Cumberland Contura LLC ....G 724 627-7500
Waynesburg *(G-19438)*
Eighty-Four Mining Company ....G 740 338-3100
Canonsburg *(G-2581)*
F/K Industries Inc ....G 412 655-4982
Pittsburgh *(G-15001)*
GM&s Coal Corp ....G 814 629-5661
Stoystown *(G-18079)*
Hanson Aggregates Bmc Inc ....F 724 626-0080
Connellsville *(G-3498)*
Honey-Creek Stone Co ....F 724 654-5538
Edinburg *(G-4822)*
Laurel Run Mining Company LLC ....D 412 831-4000
Canonsburg *(G-2599)*
Marquise Mining Corp ....F 724 459-5775
Johnstown *(G-8406)*
Rosebud Mining Company ....E 724 354-4050
Shelocta *(G-17488)*
Rosebud Mining Company ....E 724 545-6222
Kittanning *(G-8790)*
Roxcoal Inc ....D 814 443-4668
Friedens *(G-6226)*
Snyder Assod Companies Inc ....E 724 548-8101
Kittanning *(G-8793)*
Snyder Enterprises Inc ....G 724 548-8101
Kittanning *(G-8795)*
Southern Ohio Coal Company ....G 740 338-3100
Canonsburg *(G-2638)*
Swisher Contracting Inc ....F 814 765-6006
Clearfield *(G-3232)*
Waroquier Coal Inc ....E 814 765-5681
Clearfield *(G-3236)*
Wilson Creek Energy LLC ....E 724 754-0028
Canonsburg *(G-2660)*
Wilson Creek Energy LLC ....E 814 443-4668
Friedens *(G-6228)*

COAL MINING: Bituminous, Auger

Black Hawk Mining Inc ....E 724 783-6433
Rural Valley *(G-16876)*
Ckl Augering Inc ....G 724 479-0213
Homer City *(G-7673)*
Consol Amonate Mining Co LLC ....G 724 485-4000
Canonsburg *(G-2566)*
E E S Augering Company ....G 724 397-8821
Home *(G-7668)*

COAL MINING: Bituminous, Strip

Amerikohl Mining Inc ....D 724 282-2339
Butler *(G-2374)*
Amerikohl Mining Inc ....E 724 282-2339
Stahlstown *(G-17935)*
Beth Mining Co ....G 814 845-7390
Glen Campbell *(G-6423)*
Bognar and Company Inc ....G 412 344-9900
Pittsburgh *(G-14779)*
C & M Aggregate Company Inc ....E 724 796-3821
Bulger *(G-2342)*
Carlson Mining ....F 724 924-2188
New Castle *(G-12069)*
Chemstream Holdings Inc ....G 724 545-6222
Kittanning *(G-8761)*
Cookport Coal Co Inc ....G 814 938-4253
Kittanning *(G-8762)*
Durant Excavating ....G 724 583-9800
Masontown *(G-10535)*
Fieg Brothers Coal ....F 814 893-5270
Stoystown *(G-18077)*
Freno Jr A J Mining ....G 814 845-2286
Glen Campbell *(G-6424)*
Greenwood Enterprises ....E 412 429-6800
Carnegie *(G-2770)*
Kerry Coal Company Inc ....F 724 535-1311
Wampum *(G-18801)*
King Coal Sales Inc ....E 814 342-6610
Philipsburg *(G-14517)*
L and J Equipment Co Inc ....G 724 437-5405
Uniontown *(G-18633)*
Larry D Baumgardner Coal Co ....F 814 345-6404
Lanse *(G-9446)*
Larson Enterprises Inc ....F 814 345-5101
Kylertown *(G-8866)*
Mincorp Inc ....F 814 443-4668
Friedens *(G-6222)*
Original Fuels Inc ....E 814 938-5171
Coolspring *(G-3622)*

P & N Coal Co Inc ....E 814 938-7660
Punxsutawney *(G-16152)*
Pbs Coals Inc ....E 814 443-4668
Canonsburg *(G-2617)*
Piccolomini Contractors Inc ....G 724 437-7946
Waltersburg *(G-18795)*
R S Carlin Inc ....E 814 387-4190
Snow Shoe *(G-17670)*
River Hill Coal Co Inc ....E 814 345-5642
Kylertown *(G-8867)*
River Hill Coal Co Inc ....E 814 263-4506
Karthaus *(G-8485)*
Rosebud Mining Company ....E 724 545-6222
Kittanning *(G-8790)*
Seven Sisters Mining Company ....G 724 468-8232
Delmont *(G-4058)*
Sky Haven Coal Inc ....C 814 765-1665
Penfield *(G-13223)*
State Industries Inc ....G 724 548-8101
Kittanning *(G-8797)*
Usnr LLC ....F 724 929-8405
Belle Vernon *(G-1089)*
Waroquier Coal Inc ....E 814 765-5681
Clearfield *(G-3235)*
Xecol Corporation ....G 412 262-5222
Coraopolis *(G-3736)*
Zubek Inc ....G 814 443-4441
Berlin *(G-1294)*

COAL MINING: Bituminous, Surface, NEC

E P Bender Coal Company ....E 814 344-8063
Carrolltown *(G-2808)*
Finch Flagstone ....G 570 965-0982
Springville *(G-17929)*
G L R Mining Inc ....G 724 254-4043
Clymer *(G-3272)*
Godin Bros Inc ....F 814 629-5117
Friedens *(G-6220)*
Hepburnia Coal Company ....G 814 236-0473
Grampian *(G-6571)*
Strishock Coal Co ....E 814 375-1245
Du Bois *(G-4422)*
Twin Brook Coal Co ....G 724 254-4030
Clymer *(G-3274)*

COAL MINING: Lignite, Strip

Hal Ben Mining Co ....G 724 748-4528
Grove City *(G-6789)*

COAL MINING: Underground, Subbituminous

Emerald Coal Resources LP ....A 724 627-7500
Waynesburg *(G-19440)*

COAL PREPARATION PLANT: Bituminous or Lignite

Bentley Development Co Inc ....F 724 459-5775
Blairsville *(G-1715)*
Coal Loaders Inc ....F 724 238-6601
Ligonier *(G-9958)*
GM&s Coal Corp ....D 814 629-5661
Stoystown *(G-18079)*
Homer City Coal Proc Corp ....E 724 348-4800
Finleyville *(G-5960)*
Lehigh Anthracite Coal LLC ....G 814 446-6700
Armagh *(G-724)*
Senate Coal Mines ....G 724 537-2062
Latrobe *(G-9519)*
WJM Coal Co Inc ....F 724 354-2922
Shelocta *(G-17491)*

COAL TAR PRDTS

Coppers Inc ....E 412 233-2137
Pittsburgh *(G-14875)*

COAL, MINERALS & ORES, WHOLESALE: Coal

Amerikohl Mining Inc ....D 724 282-2339
Butler *(G-2374)*
Amerikohl Mining Inc ....E 724 282-2339
Stahlstown *(G-17935)*
Enercorp Inc ....G 814 345-6225
Morrisdale *(G-11548)*
Kimmels Coal and Packaging Inc ....E 717 453-7151
Wiconisco *(G-19895)*
King Coal Sales Inc ....E 814 342-6610
Philipsburg *(G-14517)*

Naughton Energy Corporation ....F 570 646-0422
Pocono Pines *(G-15882)*
North Star Leasing Inc ....G 814 629-6999
Friedens *(G-6224)*
Sherman Coal Company Inc ....G 570 695-2690
Elysburg *(G-4981)*
Waroquier Coal Inc ....G 814 765-5681
Clearfield *(G-3235)*

COAL, MINERALS & ORES, WHOLESALE: Coal & Coke

Sunoco Inc ....D 215 977-3000
Newtown Square *(G-12591)*

COATED OR PLATED PRDTS

Electrospray Incorporated ....F 215 322-5255
Feasterville Trevose *(G-5904)*
Electrospray Incorporated ....G 215 322-5255
Feasterville Trevose *(G-5905)*

COATING COMPOUNDS: Tar

Gateway Paint & Chemical Co ....E 412 261-6642
Pittsburgh *(G-15042)*
Mountain Brook Industrial Coat ....G 717 369-4040
Saint Thomas *(G-17040)*

COATING OR WRAPPING SVC: Steel Pipe

Dura-Bond Coating Inc ....E 412 436-2411
Duquesne *(G-4496)*
Dura-Bond Coating Inc ....C 717 939-1079
Steelton *(G-18046)*
Lane Enterprises Inc ....G 610 272-4531
King of Prussia *(G-8637)*
Shawcor Pipe Protection LLC ....E 215 736-1111
Morrisville *(G-11581)*

COATING SVC

Metal Litho and Laminating LLC ....E 724 646-1222
Greenville *(G-6756)*

COATING SVC: Aluminum, Metal Prdts

Amanita Technologies LLC ....G 215 353-1984
Dublin *(G-4430)*
Hadco Aluminum & Metal Corp PA ....D 215 695-2705
Philadelphia *(G-13795)*
Punxsutawney Finshg Works ....C 814 938-9164
Punxsutawney *(G-16155)*

COATING SVC: Hot Dip, Metals Or Formed Prdts

East Coast Atv Inc ....F 267 733-7364
Coopersburg *(G-3627)*
Korns Galvanizing Company Inc ....E 814 535-3293
Johnstown *(G-8401)*
Reh Holdings Inc ....G 717 843-0021
York *(G-20657)*

COATING SVC: Metals & Formed Prdts

Absolute Powder Coating LLC ....G 814 781-1160
Saint Marys *(G-16944)*
Advanced Metal Coatings Inc ....E 570 538-1249
Watsontown *(G-19273)*
Advanced Polymer Coatings Inc ....G 215 943-1466
Levittown *(G-9812)*
American Precision Powder ....G 724 788-1691
Aliquippa *(G-65)*
American Safety Technologies ....G 215 855-8450
Montgomeryville *(G-11386)*
Antietam Iron Works LLC ....G 717 485-5557
Mc Connellsburg *(G-10562)*
Apply Powder & Coating ....G 610 361-1889
Middletown *(G-11048)*
Apx Industrial Coatings Inc ....G 717 369-0037
Saint Thomas *(G-17037)*
Armolco Co of Philadelphia ....G 215 788-0841
Croydon *(G-3910)*
Armoloy Western Pennsylvania ....F 412 823-1030
Turtle Creek *(G-18558)*
Bbm Technologies Inc ....G 412 269-4546
Coraopolis *(G-3662)*
Bonehead Performance Inc ....F 215 674-8206
Warminster *(G-18839)*
Cardolite Corporation ....E 609 436-0902
Bristol *(G-2123)*

PRODUCT

Carma Industrial Coatings Inc ....G...... 717 624-6239
New Oxford (G-12405)

Celf Services LLC ....G...... 717 643-0039
Greencastle (G-6602)

Coating Concepts LLC ....G...... 717 240-0010
Carlisle (G-2701)

Cronimet Spcialty Mtls USA Inc ....E...... 724 347-2208
Wheatland (G-19835)

Cummings Group Ltd ....F...... 814 774-8238
Girard (G-6385)

Custom Polishing and Finishing ....G...... 215 331-0960
Philadelphia (G-13595)

Delp Family Powder Coatings ....G...... 724 287-3200
Butler (G-2394)

Diamond Manufacturing Company ......C...... 570 693-0300
Wyoming (G-20275)

Diamond Manufacturing Company ......F...... 570 693-0300
Wyoming (G-20276)

Diversified Coatings Inc ....C...... 814 772-3850
Ridgway (G-16705)

Dm Coatings Inc ....F...... 717 561-1175
Harrisburg (G-7121)

FAD Corporation ....G...... 610 872-3844
Eddystone (G-4802)

FMR Industries Inc ....E...... 215 536-2222
Quakertown (G-16194)

G V D Inc ....G...... 724 537-5586
Latrobe (G-9477)

Ganoe Paving Inc ....E...... 717 597-2567
Greencastle (G-6613)

Gill Powder Coating Inc ....E...... 215 639-5486
Bensalem (G-1204)

Hoffman Powder Coating ....G...... 610 845-1422
Macungie (G-10147)

Hofmann Industries Inc ....B...... 610 678-8051
Reading (G-16403)

ICP Industries LLC ....E...... 888 672-2123
Birdsboro (G-1700)

Inghams Regrooving Service Inc ....E...... 717 336-8473
Denver (G-4076)

Innovative Finishers Inc ....G...... 215 536-2222
Telford (G-18296)

Keener Coatings Inc ....E...... 717 764-9412
York (G-20549)

Keystone Koating LLC ....E...... 717 738-2148
Lititz (G-10021)

King Coatings LLC ....G...... 610 435-1212
Allentown (G-283)

Lane Enterprises Inc ....F...... 717 761-8175
Camp Hill (G-2503)

Longevity Coatings ....G...... 610 871-1427
Saylorsburg (G-17105)

M J M Industries ....G...... 724 368-8400
Portersville (G-15931)

Mshar Power Train Specialists ....G...... 717 231-3900
Harrisburg (G-7181)

NC Industries Inc ....F...... 248 528-5200
Reynoldsville (G-16658)

North American Compounding ....E...... 814 899-0621
Erie (G-5406)

Patriot Metal Products Inc ....E...... 570 759-3634
Berwick (G-1339)

Penn Protective Coatings Corp ....F...... 215 355-0708
Huntingdon Valley (G-8022)

Powder Coating ....G...... 570 837-3325
Middleburg (G-11035)

Precision Coating Tech Mfg Inc ....E...... 717 336-5030
Denver (G-4088)

Premier Applied Coatings Inc ....F...... 610 367-2635
Boyertown (G-1924)

Purtech Inc ....F...... 570 424-1669
East Stroudsburg (G-4632)

Quality Metal Coatings Inc ....G...... 814 781-6161
Saint Marys (G-17012)

Richter Precision Inc ....D...... 717 560-9990
East Petersburg (G-4589)

Schake Industries Inc ....E...... 814 677-9333
Seneca (G-17369)

Surtech Industries Inc ....E...... 717 767-6808
York (G-20682)

Tms International LLC ....G...... 412 257-1083
Bridgeville (G-2096)

Turri Associates Incorporated ....F...... 717 795-9936
Mechanicsburg (G-10900)

Vorteq Coil Finishers LLC ....D...... 610 797-5200
Allentown (G-426)

Vorteq Coil Finishers LLC ....F...... 724 898-1511
Valencia (G-18704)

Wismarq Valencia LLC ....F...... 724 898-1511
Valencia (G-18705)

COATING SVC: Metals, With Plastic Or Resins

Advanced Finishing Usa Inc ....E...... 814 474-5200
Fairview (G-5810)

Coating Technology Inc ....G...... 610 296-7722
Malvern (G-10213)

F3 Metalworx Inc ....E...... 814 725-8637
North East (G-12743)

First Line Coatings Inc ....G...... 814 452-0046
Erie (G-5291)

Fusion Coatings Inc ....E...... 610 693-5886
Robesonia (G-16773)

Mxl Industries Inc ....D...... 717 569-8711
Lancaster (G-9141)

Nittany Coatings Inc ....G...... 724 588-1898
Greenville (G-6759)

Plastic Dip Moldings Inc ....E...... 215 766-2020
Quakertown (G-16229)

Powder Coating Co ....G...... 610 273-9007
Honey Brook (G-7756)

Spec Industries Inc ....G...... 610 497-4220
Chester (G-3063)

Total Systems Technology Inc ....F...... 412 653-7690
Pittsburgh (G-15633)

COATING SVC: Rust Preventative

J & M Custom Powdr Coating LLC ....G...... 717 445-4869
Denver (G-4077)

COATINGS: Epoxy

B & T Contractors Inc ....C...... 814 368-7199
Bradford (G-1956)

Corban Corporation ....D...... 610 837-9700
Bath (G-956)

COATINGS: Polyurethane

Axalta Coating Systems LLC ....C...... 215 255-4347
Philadelphia (G-13431)

Axalta Coating Systems LLC ....E...... 610 358-2228
Glen Mills (G-6430)

COCKTAIL LOUNGE

Angelos Inc ....E...... 724 350-8715
Washington (G-19150)

COFFEE SVCS

Mvc Industries Inc ....D...... 610 650-0500
Norristown (G-12690)

Roaring Spring Blank Book Co ....B...... 814 224-2306
Roaring Spring (G-16768)

COILS & TRANSFORMERS

Danco Precision Inc ....F...... 610 933-8981
Phoenixville (G-14542)

Halsit Holdings LLC ....E...... 814 724-6440
Meadville (G-10733)

Lrt Sensors Inc ....G...... 877 299-8595
Huntingdon Valley (G-8009)

Micro-Coax Inc ....C...... 610 495-4438
Pottstown (G-16019)

Pennsylvania Trans Tech Inc ....B...... 724 873-2100
Canonsburg (G-2618)

Precisian Inc ....G...... 610 861-0844
Tannersville (G-18236)

Raycom Electronics Inc ....D...... 717 292-3641
Dover (G-4203)

Stimple and Ward Company ....E...... 412 364-5200
Pittsburgh (G-15584)

Tinicum Magnetics Inc ....F...... 717 530-2424
Shippensburg (G-17551)

Vishay Intertechnology Inc ....B...... 610 644-1300
Malvern (G-10341)

COILS: Electric Motors Or Generators

Capital Coil & Air LLC ....G...... 484 498-6880
West Chester (G-19518)

Stimple and Ward Company ....G...... 724 772-0049
Cranberry Township (G-3851)

COILS: Pipe

Flexsteel Pipeline Tech Inc ....G...... 570 505-3491
Montoursville (G-11439)

Greenbank Group Inc ....G...... 724 229-1180
Washington (G-19180)

Philadelphia Pipe Bending Co ....E...... 215 225-8955
Philadelphia (G-14149)

COIN COUNTERS

Garda CL Technical Svcs Inc ....D...... 610 926-7400
Reading (G-16389)

COIN OPERATED LAUNDRIES & DRYCLEANERS

Landons Car Wash and Laundry ....G...... 570 673-4188
Canton (G-2665)

COIN-OPERATED LAUNDRY

Forest City News Inc ....G...... 570 785-3800
Forest City (G-6053)

COKE: Petroleum

Bognar and Company Inc ....E...... 724 336-5000
New Galilee (G-12220)

COKE: Produced In Chemical Recovery Coke Ovens

Koppers Holdings Inc ....C...... 412 227-2001
Pittsburgh (G-15187)

Koppers Inc ....C...... 412 227-2001
Pittsburgh (G-15188)

Shenango Group Inc ....C...... 412 771-4400
Pittsburgh (G-15530)

Shenango Incorporated ....C...... 412 771-4400
Pittsburgh (G-15531)

COLD REMEDIES

Prophase Labs Inc ....E...... 215 345-0919
Doylestown (G-4329)

COLLATING MACHINES:Printing Or Bindery

Consolidated Printing Inc ....E...... 215 879-1400
Philadelphia (G-13571)

COLOR LAKES OR TONERS

Itc Supplies LLC ....G...... 610 430-1300
West Chester (G-19574)

Sanyo Chemical & Resins LLC ....G...... 412 384-5700
West Elizabeth (G-19697)

Toner Holdings LLC ....E...... 570 675-1131
Dallas (G-3969)

COLOR PIGMENTS

Ferro Corporation ....C...... 724 207-2152
Washington (G-19176)

Impact Colors Inc ....E...... 302 224-8310
Conshohocken (G-3561)

Penn Color Inc ....E...... 215 345-6550
Doylestown (G-4322)

Rebus Inc ....E...... 610 459-1597
West Chester (G-19628)

COLORING & FINISHING SVC: Aluminum Or Formed Prdts

Quality Dispersions Inc ....F...... 814 781-7927
Kersey (G-8567)

COLORS: Pigments, Inorganic

Amdex Metallizing Inc ....G...... 724 887-4977
Scottdale (G-17189)

Ceramic Color and Chem Mfg Co ....E...... 724 846-4000
New Brighton (G-12032)

Ferro Corporation ....E...... 412 331-3550
Pittsburgh (G-15015)

Lanxess Corporation ....A...... 800 526-9377
Pittsburgh (G-15219)

Lanxess Corporation ....E...... 412 809-4735
Burgettstown (G-2348)

Lord Corporation ....A...... 877 275-5673
Erie (G-5373)

McAdoo & Allen Inc ....E...... 215 536-3520
Quakertown (G-16214)

Penn Color Inc ....C...... 215 997-2221
Hatfield (G-7380)

Silberline Mfg Co Inc ....D...... 570 668-6050
Lansford (G-9449)

Whitford Corporation..................................D..... 610 286-3500
  Elverson (G-4967)

COLORS: Pigments, Organic

Alex Color Company Inc ....G..... 570 875-3300
  Ashland (G-725)
Blue Mountain Pigment ....G..... 610 261-4963
  Northampton (G-12846)
Heucotech Ltd A NJ Ltd Partnr..............D..... 215 736-0712
  Fairless Hills (G-5785)
Penn Color Inc...E..... 215 345-6550
  Doylestown (G-4322)
Penn Color Inc...C..... 215 997-9206
  Hatfield (G-7379)
United Color Manufacturing Inc ....F..... 215 423-2527
  Philadelphia (G-14420)

COLUMNS, FRACTIONING: Metal Plate

Hanover Iron Works Inc..........................E..... 717 632-5624
  Hanover (G-6896)

COMB MOUNTINGS

American Lady US Male Hair Sln...........G..... 570 286-7759
  Sunbury (G-18162)

COMBINATION UTILITIES, NEC

First Class Energy LLC ....E..... 724 548-2501
  Kittanning (G-8770)
Tuscarora Usa Inc ....G..... 717 491-2861
  Chambersburg (G-2991)

COMBS, EXC HARD RUBBER

Antonios Manufacturing Inc ....F..... 814 886-8171
  Cresson (G-3897)

COMFORTERS & QUILTS, FROM MANMADE FIBER OR SILK

Fisher S Hand Made Quilts ....G..... 717 392-5440
  Bird In Hand (G-1674)

COMMERCIAL & INDL SHELVING WHOLESALERS

Northeast Indus Batteries Inc.................E..... 215 788-8000
  Bristol (G-2172)

COMMERCIAL & LITERARY WRITINGS

Paeonia Arts & Literature LLC...............G..... 267 520-4572
  Philadelphia (G-14114)

COMMERCIAL & OFFICE BUILDINGS RENOVATION & REPAIR

Advanced Building Products.................G..... 717 661-7520
  Leola (G-9766)
Rizzo & Sons Industrial Svc Co.............E..... 814 948-5381
  Pittsburgh (G-15489)

COMMERCIAL ART & GRAPHIC DESIGN SVCS

Advision Signs Inc ....F..... 412 788-8440
  Pittsburgh (G-14653)
Altris Incorporated..................................G..... 724 259-8338
  Greensburg (G-6649)
Atlantic Cmmncations Group Inc ....E..... 215 836-4683
  Flourtown (G-5984)
Bourne Graphics Inc...............................G..... 610 584-6120
  Worcester (G-20224)
Bunting Graphics Inc..............................C..... 412 481-0445
  Verona (G-18751)
Color Scan LLC ....G..... 814 949-2032
  Altoona (G-493)
Creative Characters ....G..... 215 923-2679
  Philadelphia (G-13578)
Digital Color Graphics Inc ....E..... 215 942-7500
  Southampton (G-17808)
Direct Line Productions Inc ....G..... 610 633-7082
  Glen Mills (G-6435)
Elmark Sign & Graphics Inc...................F..... 610 692-0525
  West Chester (G-19549)
Five Thousand Forms Inc ....F..... 610 395-0900
  Fogelsville (G-5994)
Hollinger Tchncal Pblctons Inc..............G..... 717 755-8800
  York (G-20524)

Hopewell Manufacturing Inc ....G..... 717 593-9400
  Waynesboro (G-19412)
Hunts Promotions ....G..... 814 623-2751
  Bedford (G-1054)
Innovative Designs & Pubg.....................E..... 610 923-8000
  Palmer (G-13098)
Jem Graphics LLC ....G..... 412 220-0290
  Bridgeville (G-2074)
Magnus Group Inc ....E..... 717 764-5908
  York (G-20575)
Maiden Formats Inc ....G..... 412 884-4716
  Pittsburgh (G-15248)
Modern Reproductions Inc ....F..... 412 488-7700
  Pittsburgh (G-15298)
Morris Print Management........................G..... 610 408-8922
  Berwyn (G-1369)
Munro Prtg Graphic Design LLC ....G..... 610 485-1966
  Marcus Hook (G-10451)
Noel Interactive Group LLC ....G..... 732 991-1484
  Easton (G-4732)
Parkside Graphics Inc ....G..... 215 453-1123
  Sellersville (G-17356)
Plymouth Graphics Inc............................G..... 570 779-9645
  Plymouth (G-15820)
Tamarack Packaging Ltd ....E..... 814 724-2860
  Meadville (G-10798)
Xiii Touches Printing ....F..... 484 754-6504
  King of Prussia (G-8700)
Ygs Group Inc ....G..... 425 251-5005
  York (G-20724)
Ygs Group Inc ....D..... 717 505-9701
  York (G-20723)

COMMERCIAL ART & ILLUSTRATION SVCS

Artworks Silk Screen Printers ....G..... 717 238-5087
  Harrisburg (G-7092)
Image 360..G..... 717 317-9147
  Harrisburg (G-7153)
North Penn Art Inc ....F..... 215 362-2494
  Lansdale (G-9393)

COMMERCIAL CONTAINERS WHOLESALERS

Alphasource Inc ....F..... 215 844-6470
  Philadelphia (G-13372)

COMMERCIAL EQPT & SPLYS, WHOLESALE: Hotel

Yes Towels Inc..G..... 215 538-5230
  Quakertown (G-16261)

COMMERCIAL EQPT WHOLESALERS, NEC

Bonehead Performance Inc ....F..... 215 674-8206
  Warminster (G-18839)
Cummins - Allison Corp ....F..... 610 355-1400
  Broomall (G-2284)
Cummins-Wagner Company Inc...........E..... 717 367-8294
  Elizabethtown (G-4870)
Motts LLP ....B..... 717 677-7121
  Aspers (G-743)
S F U LLC ....G..... 610 473-0730
  Gilbertsville (G-6377)

COMMERCIAL EQPT, WHOLESALE: Bakery Eqpt & Splys

Premier Pan Company Inc ....D..... 724 457-4220
  Crescent (G-3887)
Topos Mondial Corp ....E..... 610 970-2270
  Pottstown (G-16055)

COMMERCIAL EQPT, WHOLESALE: Comm Cooking & Food Svc Eqpt

Commercial Stainless Inc ....E..... 570 387-8980
  Bloomsburg (G-1776)

COMMERCIAL EQPT, WHOLESALE: Parking Meters

Dein-Verbit Associates Inc.....................F..... 610 649-9674
  Ardmore (G-707)

COMMERCIAL EQPT, WHOLESALE: Restaurant, NEC

Agri Welding Service Inc ....F..... 570 437-3330
  Danville (G-3996)
C & J Metals...F..... 562 634-3101
  Avella (G-834)
Deffibaugh Butcher Supply.....................G..... 814 944-1297
  Altoona (G-498)
Michalski Refrigeration Inc ....G..... 724 352-1666
  Butler (G-2423)

COMMERCIAL EQPT, WHOLESALE: Scales, Exc Laboratory

Cambridge Scale Works Inc....................F..... 610 273-7040
  Honey Brook (G-7740)
Kanawha Scales & Systems Inc ....F..... 724 258-6650
  Monongahela (G-11309)

COMMERCIAL EQPT, WHOLESALE: Store Fixtures & Display Eqpt

Vitra Retail Inc..G..... 610 366-1658
  Allentown (G-425)

COMMERCIAL PHOTOGRAPHIC STUDIO

George T Faraghan Studios ....G..... 215 928-0499
  Philadelphia (G-13756)
Image 360..G..... 717 317-9147
  Harrisburg (G-7153)
Michael Furman Photography ....G..... 215 925-4233
  Philadelphia (G-14020)

COMMERCIAL PRINTING & NEWSPAPER PUBLISHING COMBINED

Berks-Mont Newspapers Inc...................F..... 610 683-7343
  Pottstown (G-15966)
Bucks County Herald...............................E..... 215 794-1096
  Buckingham (G-2339)
Bucks County Herald Corp ....G..... 215 794-2601
  Doylestown (G-4282)
Calkins Media Incorporated ....C..... 215 949-4000
  Levittown (G-9822)
Cameron County Echo Inc ....G..... 814 486-3711
  Emporium (G-5053)
Citizens Voice ....B..... 570 821-2000
  Wilkes Barre (G-19912)
City Suburban News ....G..... 610 667-6623
  Penn Valley (G-13234)
Corporate Distribution Ltd ....E..... 717 697-6900
  Harrisburg (G-7109)
Courier Times Inc....................................A..... 215 949-4011
  Levittown (G-9828)
Daily American ....E..... 814 444-5900
  Somerset (G-17683)
Derrick Publishing Company ....E..... 814 676-7444
  Oil City (G-12944)
Elizabethtown Advocate..........................G..... 717 361-0340
  Elizabethtown (G-4873)
Frediani Printing Company ....G..... 412 281-8533
  Pittsburgh (G-15035)
Fulton County News ....F..... 717 485-4513
  Mc Connellsburg (G-10565)
Gateway Publications ....G..... 412 856-7400
  Mckees Rocks (G-10660)
Green Tree Times ....G..... 412 481-7830
  Pittsburgh (G-15062)
Indiana Printing and Pubg Co.................C..... 724 465-5555
  Indiana (G-8105)
Islamic Communication Network ....G..... 215 227-0640
  Philadelphia (G-13877)
JS&d Graphics Inc ....G..... 717 397-3440
  Lancaster (G-9075)
Latrobe Printing and Pubg Co ....G..... 724 537-3351
  Latrobe (G-9493)
Lebanon Daily News ....F..... 717 272-5615
  Lebanon (G-9599)
Lee Enterprises Inc Sentinel...................C..... 717 240-7135
  Carlisle (G-2721)
Medianews Group Inc.............................C..... 717 637-3736
  Hanover (G-6919)
News of Delaware County ....G..... 610 583-4432
  Swarthmore (G-18185)
Newspaper Holding Inc ....D..... 814 532-5102
  Johnstown (G-8412)
Newtown Gazette ....G..... 215 702-3405
  Langhorne (G-9314)

PRODUCT

Nittany Printing and Pubg Co ....D 814 238-5000
State College (G-18000)

Northampton Herald ....G...... 215 702-3405
Langhorne (G-9316)

Our Town ....F 814 269-9704
Johnstown (G-8418)

Peerless Publications Inc....................C 610 323-3000
Pottstown (G-16027)

Pg Publishing Company.......................A 412 263-1100
Clinton (G-3265)

Phildelphia-Newspapers-Llc ....A 215 854-2000
Philadelphia (G-14167)

Pottsville Republican Inc ....E 570 622-3456
Pottsville (G-16092)

Press-Enterprise Inc ....F 610 807-9619
Bethlehem (G-1604)

Press-Enterprise Inc............................C 570 784-2121
Bloomsburg (G-1795)

Reading Eagle Company ....E 610 371-5000
Reading (G-16488)

Record Herald Publishing Co ....E 717 762-2151
Waynesboro (G-19422)

Sullivan Review...................................G 570 928-8403
Dushore (G-4511)

Sun-Gazette Company..........................C 570 326-1551
Williamsport (G-20076)

The M & A Journal Inc ....G 215 238-0506
Philadelphia (G-14386)

Times-Shamrock ....D 570 501-0278
Hazleton (G-7531)

Tioga Publishing Company....................A 814 371-4200
Du Bois (G-4424)

Tioga Publishing Company.....................F 814 274-8044
Coudersport (G-3789)

Tioga Publishing Company.....................E 570 724-2287
Wellsboro (G-19473)

Titusville Herald Inc ....E 814 827-3634
Titusville (G-18400)

Towanda Printing Co Inc ....C 570 265-2151
Towanda (G-18436)

Trib Total Media LLC ....D 412 871-2301
Tarentum (G-18250)

Uniontown Newspapers Inc ....C 724 439-7500
Uniontown (G-18644)

Webb Communications Inc ....E 570 326-7634
Plymouth (G-15823)

Windsor-Press Inc ....E 610 562-3624
Hamburg (G-6857)

COMMODITY INVESTORS

Millcraft Corporation............................G 724 743-3400
Washington (G-19204)

COMMON SAND MINING

Alliance Sand Co Inc ....F 610 826-2248
Palmerton (G-13099)

Bill Barry Excavating Inc.......................G 570 595-2269
Cresco (G-3891)

EJ Bognar Incorporated ....G 412 344-9900
Pittsburgh (G-14960)

Hanson Aggregates PA LLC ....D 610 269-1710
Downingtown (G-4232)

Hanson Aggregates PA LLC ....F 570 368-2481
Jersey Shore (G-8314)

Hanson Aggregates PA LLC ....F 570 584-2153
Muncy (G-11818)

Hanson Aggregates PA LLC ....F 570 437-4068
Milton (G-11240)

Hanson Aggregates PA LLC ....F 814 466-5101
Boalsburg (G-1867)

Hanson Aggregates PA LLC ....E 610 366-4626
Allentown (G-243)

Middleport Materials Inc ....F 570 277-0335
Middleport (G-11046)

Pocono Industries Inc ....G 570 421-3889
Stroudsburg (G-18134)

COMMUNICATION HEADGEAR: Telephone

Fetterolf Group Inc..............................G 814 443-4688
Somerset (G-17688)

Rajant Corporation ....D 484 595-0233
Malvern (G-10307)

COMMUNICATIONS CARRIER: Wired

Audio Video Automation SEC Inc..........G 814 313-1108
Warren (G-19011)

COMMUNICATIONS EQPT & SYSTEMS, NEC

Kykayke Inc ....G...... 610 522-0106
Holmes (G-7663)

COMMUNICATIONS EQPT REPAIR & MAINTENANCE

Mol Communications & Elec..................G...... 570 383-3658
Dickson City (G-4122)

Warren Installations Inc ....F 717 517-9321
Lancaster (G-9235)

COMMUNICATIONS EQPT WHOLESALERS

Acra Control Inc ....G...... 714 382-1863
Newtown (G-12494)

Advanced Network Products Inc...........E 215 572-0111
Glenside (G-6503)

Belden Inc..E 717 263-7655
Chambersburg (G-2910)

Fortmex Corporation ....G...... 215 990-9688
Merion Station (G-10997)

Omnispread Communications Inc..........G...... 215 654-9900
North Wales (G-12821)

Telamon Corporation ....E 800 945-8800
Levittown (G-9867)

COMMUNICATIONS EQPT: Microwave

CPI Locus Microwave Inc......................E 814 466-6275
Boalsburg (G-1866)

Wave Central LLC ....F 717 503-7157
Carlisle (G-2750)

COMMUNICATIONS SVCS

Bosha Design Inc..................................G...... 610 622-4422
Drexel Hill (G-4361)

David Jefferys LLC ....G...... 215 977-9900
Wallingford (G-18783)

COMMUNICATIONS SVCS: Cellular

Cricket Communications LLC................G...... 267 687-5949
Philadelphia (G-13582)

Verizon Communications Inc.................C 570 387-3840
Bloomsburg (G-1806)

COMMUNICATIONS SVCS: Data

East Hill Video Prod Co LLC ....F 215 855-4457
Lansdale (G-9364)

Ncn Data Networks LLC ....G...... 570 213-8300
Stroudsburg (G-18133)

COMMUNICATIONS SVCS: Facsimile Transmission

Copy Corner Inc ....G...... 570 992-4769
Saylorsburg (G-17104)

Fedex Office & Print Svcs Inc ....G...... 215 576-1687
Jenkintown (G-8287)

Fedex Office & Print Svcs Inc ....F 412 366-9750
Pittsburgh (G-15011)

COMMUNICATIONS SVCS: Internet Connectivity Svcs

Ats-Needham LLC.................................F 617 375-7500
Philadelphia (G-13424)

Nzinganet Inc.......................................G...... 877 709-6459
Fort Washington (G-6087)

COMMUNICATIONS SVCS: Internet Host Svcs

Centre of Web Inc ....G...... 814 235-9592
State College (G-17949)

Digital Media Solutions LLC ....G...... 610 234-3834
Conshohocken (G-3538)

COMMUNICATIONS SVCS: Online Svc Providers

Advanced Network Products Inc...........E 215 572-0111
Glenside (G-6503)

Iota Communications Inc ....G...... 855 743-6478
New Hope (G-12306)

Ldp Inc ....D 570 455-8511
West Hazleton (G-19713)

Westcom Wireless Inc ....G...... 412 228-5507
McKeesport (G-10686)

COMMUNICATIONS SVCS: Signal Enhancement Network Svcs

McNs Technologies LLC ....G...... 610 269-2891
Chadds Ford (G-2855)

COMMUNICATIONS SVCS: Telephone, Data

Ncn Data Networks LLC ....G...... 570 213-8300
Stroudsburg (G-18133)

Verizon Communications Inc.................C 570 387-3840
Bloomsburg (G-1806)

COMMUNICATIONS SVCS: Telephone, Local

Verizon Pennsylvania Inc......................D 215 879-7898
Philadelphia (G-14441)

COMMUNICATIONS SVCS: Telephone, Local & Long Distance

Pencor Services Inc.............................E 610 826-2115
Palmerton (G-13110)

COMMUNITY CENTERS: Adult

Catholic Golden Age Inc ....F 570 586-1091
Scott Township (G-17183)

COMMUNITY CENTERS: Youth

Catholic Scl Svcs of Scranton ....D 570 207-2283
Scranton (G-17216)

Catholic Scl Svcs of Scranton ....G...... 570 454-6693
Hazleton (G-7494)

COMMUNITY DEVELOPMENT GROUPS

Bee Positive Foundation.......................G...... 484 302-8234
Phoenixville (G-14530)

It Takes A Village To Feed ....G...... 888 702-9610
Ridley Park (G-16739)

COMMUTATORS: Electronic

Cougar Metals Inc................................G...... 724 251-9030
Leetsdale (G-9690)

COMPACT DISCS OR CD'S, WHOLESALE

Fab Universal Corp ....F 412 621-0902
Pittsburgh (G-15002)

COMPACT LASER DISCS: Prerecorded

Disc Hounds LLC..................................G...... 610 696-8668
West Chester (G-19542)

Gilead Enterprises Inc ....G...... 717 733-2003
Ephrata (G-5106)

Private Zone Productions Corp ....G...... 267 592-5447
Philadelphia (G-14204)

COMPACTORS: Trash & Garbage, Residential

Molek Brothers.....................................G...... 717 248-8032
Yeagertown (G-20357)

COMPOST

A & M Compost ....F 215 256-1900
Norristown (G-12629)

Barnside Mulch and Compost ....G...... 610 287-8880
Schwenksville (G-17174)

Bennett Compost ....G...... 215 520-2406
Philadelphia (G-13453)

Compost Films Inc................................G...... 215 668-3001
Wallingford (G-18782)

Earth Friendly Compost Inc ....G...... 570 760-4510
Harveys Lake (G-7256)

First Regional Compost Auth ....G...... 610 262-1000
Northampton (G-12850)

Green n Grow Compost LLC..................G...... 717 284-5710
Holtwood (G-7667)

Laurel Valley Soils ....G...... 610 268-5555
Avondale (G-854)

Mulch Works Recycling Inc ....F 888 214-4628
Aston (G-779)

Natural Soil Products Company ....D 570 695-2211
Tremont (G-18481)

Ontelaunee Farms Inc ....E 610 929-5753
Temple (G-18334)
Penn Jersey Farms Inc ....G 610 488-7003
Bethel (G-1397)
Spring Valley Mulch Brian 717 292-7945
Dover (G-4205)

COMPRESSORS, AIR CONDITIONING: Wholesalers

Neac Compressor Svcs USA Inc ....G 814 437-3711
Franklin (G-6150)

COMPRESSORS: Air & Gas

Aerzen USA Corp ....D 610 380-0244
Coatesville (G-3285)
Atlas Copco Compressors LLC ....E 610 916-4002
Reading (G-16325)
Blue Mtn A Comprsr Svcs LLC ....G 717 423-5262
Shippensburg (G-17519)
C H Reed Inc ....E 717 632-4261
Hanover (G-6865)
C H Reed Inc ....G 412 380-1334
Monroeville (G-11326)
Cameron Compression Systems ....G 610 265-2410
King of Prussia (G-8590)
Cersell Company LLC ....E 484 753-2655
Exton (G-5661)
CFM Air Inc ....G 814 539-6922
Johnstown (G-8365)
Cmpressed A Zeks Solutions LLC ....C 610 692-9100
West Chester (G-19526)
Columbia Industries Inc ....E 570 520-4048
Berwick (G-1318)
Compressed Air Systems Inc ....G 215 340-1307
Pipersville (G-14613)
Dresser-Rand Company ....E 215 441-0400
Horsham (G-7810)
Dynaflo Inc ....G 610 200-8017
Reading (G-16367)
Earl E Knox Company ....E 814 459-2754
Erie (G-5255)
Elliott Company ....A 724 527-2811
Jeannette (G-8254)
Elliott Company ....D 724 379-5440
Donora (G-4155)
Fs-North America Inc ....G 724 387-3200
Export (G-5605)
Gas & Air Systems Inc ....F 610 838-9625
Hellertown (G-7556)
Howden Compressors Inc ....F 610 313-9800
Plymouth Meeting (G-15849)
Hydro-Pac Inc ....E 814 474-1511
Fairview (G-5829)
Ingersoll-Rand Company ....E 410 238-0542
Shrewsbury (G-17584)
Jenny Products Inc ....E 814 445-3400
Somerset (G-17693)
Kingsly Compression Inc ....E 724 524-1840
Saxonburg (G-17091)
Knox-Western Inc ....G 814 459-2754
Erie (G-5348)
Maxpro Technologies Inc ....F 814 474-9191
Fairview (G-5833)
Neac Compressor Svcs USA Inc ....G 814 437-3711
Franklin (G-6150)
PDC Machines Inc ....D 215 443-9442
Warminster (G-18937)
Smuckers Sales & Services LLC ....G 717 354-4158
New Holland (G-12285)
Spray-Tek Inc ....E 610 814-2922
Bethlehem (G-1627)
Stauffer Compressor N Machine ....G 717 733-4128
Ephrata (G-5146)
Van Air Inc ....E 814 774-2631
Lake City (G-8909)
Ventwell Inc ....G 717 683-1477
York (G-20697)

COMPRESSORS: Air & Gas, Including Vacuum Pumps

Air Products Corporation ....D 800 345-8207
Exton (G-5637)
Applied Equipment Co ....G 610 258-7941
Easton (G-4646)
Barts Pneumatics Corp ....G 717 392-1568
Lancaster (G-8949)
Diversified Air Systems Inc ....G 724 873-0884
Washington (G-19164)

Earl E Knox Company ....F 814 459-2754
Erie (G-5254)
Flsmidth Inc ....C 717 665-2224
Manheim (G-10385)
Fs-Elliott Co LLC ....B 724 387-3200
Export (G-5604)
Gardner Denver Nash LLC ....G 203 459-3923
Charleroi (G-3015)
General Air Products Inc ....E 610 524-8950
Exton (G-5685)
Myers Vacuum Repair Svcs Inc ....F 724 545-8331
Kittanning (G-8785)

COMPRESSORS: Refrigeration & Air Conditioning Eqpt

Hermetics Inc ....G 215 848-9522
Philadelphia (G-13818)
U R I Compressors Inc ....G 484 223-3265
Allentown (G-416)

COMPRESSORS: Repairing

East West Drilling Inc ....E 570 966-7312
Mifflinburg (G-11093)
Elliott Company ....D 724 379-5440
Donora (G-4155)
G Beswick Enterprises Inc ....G 412 829-3068
North Versailles (G-12775)

COMPRESSORS: Wholesalers

Air Products Corporation ....D 800 345-8207
Exton (G-5637)
Applied Equipment Co ....F 610 258-7941
Easton (G-4646)
Barts Pneumatics Corp ....G 717 392-1568
Lancaster (G-8949)
Gardner Denver Nash LLC ....G 203 459-3923
Charleroi (G-3015)
Kingsly Compression Inc ....E 724 524-1840
Saxonburg (G-17091)
North End Electric Service Inc ....E 570 342-6740
Scranton (G-17267)
Stauffer Compressor N Machine ....G 717 733-4128
Ephrata (G-5146)
Titus Company ....E 610 913-9100
Morgantown (G-11540)

COMPUTER & COMPUTER SOFTWARE STORES

Lasertek Tner Crtrdge Rchrging ....G 412 244-9505
Pittsburgh (G-15220)
R Fritz Enterprises Inc ....G 814 267-4204
Berlin (G-1292)
Sterling Computer Sales LLC ....G 610 255-0198
Landenberg (G-9253)
Validity LLC ....G 610 768-8042
Malvern (G-10337)

COMPUTER & COMPUTER SOFTWARE STORES: Peripheral Eqpt

Estari Inc ....F 717 233-1518
Harrisburg (G-7127)
Tech Equipment Sales Inc ....E 610 279-0370
Norristown (G-12716)

COMPUTER & COMPUTER SOFTWARE STORES: Personal Computers

Integrated Software Services ....G 717 534-1480
Hershey (G-7618)
McNs Technologies LLC ....G 610 269-2891
Chadds Ford (G-2855)
Pcxpert Company Inc ....G 717 792-0005
York (G-20619)
Software Engineering Assoc ....F 570 803-0535
Archbald (G-695)

COMPUTER & COMPUTER SOFTWARE STORES: Printers & Plotters

Printers Parts Store Inc ....F 610 279-6660
Bridgeport (G-2044)

COMPUTER & COMPUTER SOFTWARE STORES: Software & Access

Accustar Inc ....G 610 459-0123
Garnet Valley (G-6264)
Advanced Software Inc ....F 215 369-7800
Yardley (G-20293)
Effective Software Products ....G 717 267-2054
Chambersburg (G-2929)

COMPUTER & COMPUTER SOFTWARE STORES: Software, Bus/Non-Game

Paulhus and Associates Inc ....F 717 274-5621
Lebanon (G-9616)

COMPUTER & COMPUTER SOFTWARE STORES: Software, Computer Game

Undernet Gaming Incorporated ....G 484 544-8943
Harrisburg (G-7240)

COMPUTER & DATA PROCESSING EQPT REPAIR & MAINTENANCE

All Tech-D Out LLC ....F 610 814-0888
Allentown (G-124)
Support McRcomputers Assoc Inc ......F 215 496-0303
Philadelphia (G-14359)

COMPUTER & OFFICE MACHINE MAINTENANCE & REPAIR

Allegheny Fabg & Sups Inc ....G 412 828-3320
Pittsburgh (G-14678)
Binary Research Inc ....E 215 233-3200
Ambler (G-570)
Cartridge Specialist ....G 412 741-4442
Sewickley (G-17384)
Effective Software Products ....G 717 267-2054
Chambersburg (G-2929)
Fis Avantgard LLC ....E 800 468-7483
Wayne (G-19329)
Integrated Software Services ....G 717 534-1480
Hershey (G-7618)
International Bus Mchs Corp ....A 610 578-2017
Wayne (G-19339)
Laser Lab Inc ....F 717 738-3333
Ephrata (G-5120)
Lasertek Tner Crtrdge Rchrging 412 244-9505
Pittsburgh (G-15220)
Mergtech Inc ....G 570 584-3388
Hughesville (G-7896)
Mpm Holdings Inc ....E 610 678-8131
Reading (G-16450)
Print Happy LLC ....G 717 699-4465
York (G-20639)
Progressive Computer Svcs Inc ....E 215 226-2220
Philadelphia (G-14207)
R Fritz Enterprises Inc ....G 814 267-4204
Berlin (G-1292)
Teeco Associates Inc ....E 610 539-4708
Schwenksville (G-17179)

COMPUTER & SFTWR STORE: Modem, Monitor, Terminal/Disk Drive

Copitech Associates ....G 570 963-1391
Scranton (G-17219)
Digital Plaza LLC ....F 267 515-8000
Ambler (G-575)

COMPUTER FACILITIES MANAGEMENT SVCS

PC Network Inc ....D 267 236-0015
Philadelphia (G-14128)

COMPUTER FORMS

Borough of Slippery Rock ....G 724 794-3823
Slippery Rock (G-17618)
Star Continuous Card Systems ....G 800 458-1413
Glenmoore (G-6470)

COMPUTER GRAPHICS SVCS

Bondata Inc ....G 717 566-5550
Hummelstown (G-7903)
Byrd Alley LLC ....F 215 669-0068
Philadelphia (G-13489)

Computer Dev Systems LLC.................G........ 717 591-0995
Mechanicsburg *(G-10830)*

Eko Solutions Plus Inc ....G...... 215 856-9517
Elkins Park *(G-4902)*

Expert Pr-Press Consulting Ltd...........G...... 484 401-9821
Downingtown *(G-4227)*

Innovtive Print Mdia Group Inc ....D...... 610 489-4800
Phoenixville *(G-14553)*

Noel Interactive Group LLC ....G...... 732 991-1484
Easton *(G-4732)*

St Clair Graphics Inc ....F....... 570 253-6692
Honesdale *(G-7726)*

WM Enterprises Inc.............................E....... 717 238-5751
Harrisburg *(G-7248)*

COMPUTER INTERFACE EQPT: Indl Process

H M W Enterprises Inc.........................F....... 717 765-4690
Waynesboro *(G-19410)*

Kenai Associates Inc ....G...... 412 655-2079
Pittsburgh *(G-15168)*

Process Control Spc Inc ....G...... 570 753-5799
Jersey Shore *(G-8321)*

COMPUTER PAPER TAPE EQPT: Punches, Readers, Etc

Whiteman Tower Inc ....G....... 800 748-3891
Wilkes Barre *(G-19974)*

COMPUTER PAPER WHOLESALERS

Lasting Expressions ....G....... 724 776-3953
Cranberry Township *(G-3831)*

COMPUTER PERIPHERAL EQPT REPAIR & MAINTENANCE

Xerox Corporation ....C....... 412 506-4000
Pittsburgh *(G-15726)*

COMPUTER PERIPHERAL EQPT, NEC

ACS Investors LLC ....G...... 724 746-5500
Lawrence *(G-9533)*

Advanced Network Products Inc...........E...... 215 572-0111
Glenside *(G-6503)*

Birdbrain Technologies LLC ....G...... 412 216-5833
Pittsburgh *(G-14767)*

Black Box Corporation ....G...... 724 746-5500
Lawrence *(G-9535)*

Black Box Corporation ....G...... 215 274-1044
Blue Bell *(G-1816)*

Black Box Services Company ....G...... 724 746-5500
Lawrence *(G-9536)*

Brocade Cmmnctions Systems Inc.......G...... 610 648-3915
Malvern *(G-10195)*

Capsen Robotics Inc ....G...... 203 218-0204
Pittsburgh *(G-14806)*

Cisco Systems Inc ....A...... 610 336-8500
Allentown *(G-170)*

Claypoole Hex Signs ....G...... 610 562-8911
Lenhartsville *(G-9757)*

Comdoc Inc ....D...... 800 321-1009
Pittsburgh *(G-14868)*

Daisy Data Displays Inc ....E....... 717 932-9999
York Haven *(G-20756)*

Dawar Technologies Inc ....E....... 412 322-9900
Pittsburgh *(G-14909)*

Decora Industries Inc ....D...... 215 698-2600
Philadelphia *(G-13614)*

Deltronic Labs Inc.................................E....... 215 997-8616
Chalfont *(G-2872)*

Effective CD Llc....................................G...... 607 351-5949
Lawrenceville *(G-9541)*

Gda Corp ....F....... 814 237-4060
State College *(G-17968)*

General Metal Company Inc ....E....... 215 638-3242
Bensalem *(G-1203)*

Griffith Inc ....C....... 215 322-8100
Huntingdon Valley *(G-7992)*

H M W Enterprises Inc..........................F....... 717 765-4690
Waynesboro *(G-19410)*

Intel Corporation ....G...... 908 894-6035
Allentown *(G-263)*

Intel Network Systems Inc ....F....... 610 973-5566
Allentown *(G-264)*

J Penner Corporation ....E....... 215 340-9700
Doylestown *(G-4308)*

Lee Rj Group Inc ....C....... 800 860-1775
Monroeville *(G-11342)*

Legrand Home Systems Inc..................E....... 717 702-2532
Middletown *(G-11061)*

Legrand Home Systems Inc..................D...... 717 702-2532
Middletown *(G-11060)*

Lexicon International Corp ....E....... 215 639-8220
Bensalem *(G-1220)*

Library Video Company ....D...... 610 645-4000
Conshohocken *(G-3572)*

Loranger International Corp ....D...... 814 723-2250
Warren *(G-19038)*

Matthews International Corp..................D...... 412 665-2500
Pittsburgh *(G-15265)*

Mergtech Inc ....G...... 570 584-3388
Hughesville *(G-7896)*

Moog Inc ....C....... 610 328-4000
Springfield *(G-17919)*

Next Rev Distribution Inc ....G...... 717 576-9050
Hershey *(G-7623)*

Oberon Inc ....F....... 814 867-2312
State College *(G-18003)*

Omega Piezo Technologies Inc ....F....... 814 861-4160
State College *(G-18004)*

Online Data Systems Inc ....E....... 610 967-5821
Emmaus *(G-5037)*

Pixel Innovations Inc ....G...... 724 935-8366
Wexford *(G-19821)*

Riverbed Technology Inc ....G...... 610 648-3819
Malvern *(G-10310)*

RTD Embedded Technologies Inc.........E....... 814 234-8087
State College *(G-18017)*

Videotek Inc ....C....... 610 327-2292
Pottstown *(G-16068)*

Vocollect Healthcare Systems ....E....... 412 829-8145
Pittsburgh *(G-15703)*

Watch My Net Inc ....G...... 267 625-6000
Glenside *(G-6543)*

World Video Sales Co Inc......................G...... 610 754-6800
Bechtelsville *(G-1038)*

Xerox Corporation ....C....... 412 506-4000
Pittsburgh *(G-15726)*

Zemco Tool & Die Inc...........................D...... 717 647-7151
Williamstown *(G-20104)*

COMPUTER PERIPHERAL EQPT, WHOLESALE

Black Box Corporation ....G...... 724 746-5500
Lawrence *(G-9535)*

Microlite Corporation............................G...... 724 375-6711
Aliquippa *(G-85)*

Oberon Inc ....F....... 814 867-2312
State College *(G-18003)*

Tech Equipment Sales Inc....................E....... 610 279-0370
Norristown *(G-12716)*

Weidenhammer Systems Corp ....D...... 610 378-1149
Reading *(G-16562)*

COMPUTER PERIPHERAL EQPT: Decoders

Datapath North America Inc..................G...... 484 679-1553
Norristown *(G-12650)*

COMPUTER PERIPHERAL EQPT: Encoders

Vocollect Inc ....C....... 412 829-8145
Pittsburgh *(G-15702)*

COMPUTER PERIPHERAL EQPT: Graphic Displays, Exc Terminals

Butler Technologies Inc ....D...... 724 283-6656
Butler *(G-2386)*

Carpenter Connection Inc ....E....... 412 881-3900
Pittsburgh *(G-14821)*

Goodway Graphics Inc ....B...... 215 887-5700
Jenkintown *(G-8288)*

COMPUTER PERIPHERAL EQPT: Input Or Output

Application Consultants Inc ....F....... 610 521-1529
Ridley Park *(G-16733)*

Tsitouch Inc ....E....... 802 874-0123
Uniontown *(G-18643)*

COMPUTER PERIPHERAL EQPT: Output To Microfilm Units

W Graphics Digital Services ....G...... 610 252-3565
Easton *(G-4773)*

COMPUTER PHOTOGRAPHY OR PORTRAIT SVC

Dave Zerbe Studio ....G...... 610 376-0379
Reading *(G-16360)*

COMPUTER PLOTTERS

Commerce Drive Enterprises LLC.........D...... 215 362-2766
Montgomeryville *(G-11389)*

COMPUTER PROCESSING SVCS

Scribe Inc..G...... 215 336-5094
Philadelphia *(G-14289)*

COMPUTER PROGRAMMING SVCS

Audio Video Automation SEC Inc..........G...... 814 313-1108
Warren *(G-19011)*

Automatic Forecasting Systems ....F....... 215 675-0652
Warminster *(G-18832)*

Best Medical International Inc ....D...... 412 312-6700
Pittsburgh *(G-14764)*

Businessone Technologies Inc ....G...... 215 953-6660
Feasterville Trevose *(G-5896)*

Computer Dev Systems LLC.................G...... 717 591-0995
Mechanicsburg *(G-10830)*

Dqe Communications LLC ....G...... 412 393-1033
Pittsburgh *(G-14936)*

Eastern Systems Management...............G...... 717 391-9700
Lancaster *(G-9006)*

Education MGT Solutions LLC ....D...... 610 701-7002
Exton *(G-5671)*

Environmental Systems Research ....E....... 909 793-2853
Chesterbrook *(G-3092)*

FEC Technologies Inc...........................E....... 717 764-5959
York *(G-20477)*

Flexible Informatics LLC ....G...... 215 253-8765
Lafayette Hill *(G-8880)*

Franklin Potter Associates....................G...... 215 345-0844
Doylestown *(G-4300)*

Fry International LLC ....G...... 215 847-6359
Elkins Park *(G-4903)*

Ggs Information Services Inc ....C....... 717 764-2222
York *(G-20499)*

Graphcom Inc..C....... 800 699-1664
Gettysburg *(G-6295)*

Intelligent Micro Systems Ltd ....G...... 610 664-1207
Haverford *(G-7412)*

Keystone Nap LLC ....G...... 215 280-6614
Fairless Hills *(G-5786)*

Mobius Acquisition LLC ....G...... 412 281-7000
Pittsburgh *(G-15297)*

Mtekka LLC ....G...... 610 619-3555
Kennett Square *(G-8532)*

Policymap Inc ....G...... 866 923-6277
Philadelphia *(G-14185)*

Premier Semiconductor Svcs LLC.........D...... 267 954-0130
Hatfield *(G-7384)*

Ram Technologies Inc ....E....... 215 654-8810
Fort Washington *(G-6089)*

Raytheon Company ....B...... 814 278-2256
State College *(G-18012)*

Reed Micro Automation Inc ....G...... 814 941-0225
Altoona *(G-543)*

Servant PC Resources Inc ....F....... 570 748-2800
Lock Haven *(G-10092)*

Staneco Corporation ....E....... 215 672-6500
Horsham *(G-7852)*

Tactile Design Group LLC ....F....... 215 732-2311
Philadelphia *(G-14367)*

Titan Technologies Inc ....G...... 888 671-6649
Pittsburgh *(G-15626)*

Ygs Group Inc ....D...... 717 505-9701
York *(G-20723)*

COMPUTER PROGRAMMING SVCS: Custom

Ascentive LLC.......................................D...... 215 395-8559
Philadelphia *(G-13419)*

Impac Technology Inc ....E....... 610 430-1400
West Chester *(G-19569)*

Pencor Services Inc..............................E....... 610 826-2115
Palmerton *(G-13110)*

Prosoft Technologies Inc ....F....... 412 835-6217
Bethel Park *(G-1429)*

Tal Technologies Inc.............................E....... 215 496-0222
Philadelphia *(G-14369)*

COMPUTER RELATED MAINTENANCE SVCS

21st Century Software Tech Inc..............E...... 610 341-9017
Wayne *(G-19290)*

Cyrus-Xp Inc...................................E...... 610 986-8408
Ardmore *(G-706)*

Education MGT Solutions LLC............D...... 610 701-7002
Exton *(G-5671)*

Environmental Systems Research........E...... 909 793-2853
Chesterbrook *(G-3092)*

Global Data Consultants LLC..............E...... 717 697-7500
Mechanicsburg *(G-10849)*

Saxon Office Technology Inc..............F...... 215 736-2620
Fairless Hills *(G-5795)*

Virtix Consulting LLC.........................G...... 412 440-4835
Wexford *(G-19832)*

COMPUTER SERVICE BUREAU

Bucks County Type & Design Inc..........F...... 215 579-4200
Newtown *(G-12499)*

COMPUTER SOFTWARE DEVELOPMENT

21st Century Software Tech Inc............E...... 610 341-9017
Wayne *(G-19290)*

Advanced Acoustic Concepts LLC.......D...... 724 434-5100
Lemont Furnace *(G-9732)*

Application Consultants Inc.................F...... 610 521-1529
Ridley Park *(G-16733)*

Communication Automation Corp........E...... 610 692-9526
West Chester *(G-19527)*

Componentone Enterprises LLC..........D...... 412 681-4343
Pittsburgh *(G-14871)*

Compututor Inc.................................G...... 610 260-0300
Conshohocken *(G-3531)*

Datatech Software Inc........................F...... 717 652-4344
Harrisburg *(G-7113)*

Deadsolid Simulations Inc.................F...... 570 655-6500
Pittston *(G-15748)*

Eko Solutions Plus Inc.......................G...... 215 856-9517
Elkins Park *(G-4902)*

Evolve Guest Controls LLC.................F...... 855 750-9090
West Chester *(G-19553)*

Faro Laser Division LLC......................G...... 610 444-2300
Kennett Square *(G-8510)*

GL Trade Capitl Mkts Solutions..........D...... 484 530-4400
Wayne *(G-19332)*

Health Market Science Inc...................C...... 610 940-4002
King of Prussia *(G-8629)*

Horeb Inc..G...... 610 285-1917
West Chester *(G-19564)*

Ker Communications..........................G...... 412 310-1973
Pittsburgh *(G-15172)*

Lantica Software LLC.........................G...... 215 598-8419
Newtown *(G-12517)*

Mumps Audiofax Inc..........................E...... 610 293-2160
Wayne *(G-19358)*

Neat Company Inc.............................C...... 215 382-4283
Philadelphia *(G-14060)*

Netbeez Inc......................................G...... 412 465-0638
Pittsburgh *(G-15328)*

Progressive Computer Svcs Inc..........E...... 215 226-2220
Philadelphia *(G-14207)*

Questar Corporation..........................E...... 215 862-5277
New Hope *(G-12312)*

Tenex Systems Inc.............................F...... 610 239-9988
King of Prussia *(G-8685)*

Ursoft Inc...F...... 724 452-2150
Zelienople *(G-20827)*

Vega Applications Development...........G...... 610 892-1812
Media *(G-10956)*

COMPUTER SOFTWARE DEVELOPMENT & APPLICATIONS

Aaxios Technologies LLC.....................G...... 267 545-7400
Warrington *(G-19106)*

Accustar Inc.....................................G...... 610 459-0123
Garnet Valley *(G-6264)*

Adenine Solutions Inc........................G...... 267 684-6013
Southampton *(G-17796)*

API Cryptek Inc.................................F...... 908 546-3900
State College *(G-17941)*

Appligent Inc....................................E...... 610 284-4006
Lansdowne *(G-9429)*

Elemental 3 LLC...............................G...... 267 217-3592
Philadelphia *(G-13667)*

Fairmount Automation Inc...................F...... 610 356-9840
Conshohocken *(G-3546)*

Galeron Consulting LLC......................E...... 267 293-9221
Bensalem *(G-1202)*

Grandshare LLC................................G...... 919 308-5115
Philadelphia *(G-13781)*

Impilo LLC..G...... 610 662-2867
Wynnewood *(G-20269)*

Innovtive Slutions Support Inc............D...... 610 646-9800
Exton *(G-5699)*

Legal Sifter Inc.................................G...... 724 221-7438
Pittsburgh *(G-15223)*

Magnus Group Inc.............................E...... 717 764-5908
York *(G-20575)*

Medchive LLC...................................G...... 215 688-7475
Philadelphia *(G-14004)*

Method Automation Services Inc..........G...... 724 337-9064
New Kensington *(G-12356)*

Oakwood Controls Corporation............F...... 717 801-1515
Glen Rock *(G-6458)*

Prism Engineering LLC.......................E...... 215 784-0800
Horsham *(G-7842)*

Pulsemetrics LLC..............................G...... 412 656-5776
Allison Park *(G-460)*

Simplr Technologies LLC.....................G...... 814 883-6463
State College *(G-18025)*

Solo Soundz LLC...............................G...... 610 931-8448
Philadelphia *(G-14323)*

Technology Dynamics Inc....................G...... 888 988-3243
Wayne *(G-19380)*

Undernet Gaming Incorporated............G...... 484 544-8943
Harrisburg *(G-7240)*

COMPUTER SOFTWARE SYSTEMS ANALYSIS & DESIGN: Custom

Aapryl LLC.......................................G...... 215 567-1100
Philadelphia *(G-13332)*

Ability Systems Corporation................G...... 215 657-4338
Abington *(G-9)*

Acutedge Inc....................................G...... 484 846-6275
King of Prussia *(G-8577)*

Ark Ideaz Inc....................................G...... 610 246-9106
Pottstown *(G-15943)*

Byrd Alley LLC..................................F...... 215 669-0068
Philadelphia *(G-13489)*

Corestar International Corp..................E...... 724 744-4094
Irwin *(G-8151)*

Datumrite Corporation........................F...... 215 407-4447
North Wales *(G-12797)*

Efficient Ip Inc..................................F...... 888 228-4655
West Chester *(G-19548)*

First Supply Chain LLC.......................G...... 215 527-2264
Hummelstown *(G-7910)*

Forallsecure Inc................................F...... 412 256-8809
Pittsburgh *(G-15024)*

Garth Groft......................................G...... 717 819-9479
York *(G-20491)*

Kos & Associates Inc..........................F...... 412 367-7444
Pittsburgh *(G-15195)*

Leanfm Technologies Inc.....................E...... 412 818-5167
Pittsburgh *(G-15222)*

Managing Editor Inc...........................E...... 215 517-5116
Jenkintown *(G-8295)*

Mousley Consulting Inc.......................G...... 610 539-0150
Norristown *(G-12689)*

Net Reach Technologies LLC................F...... 215 283-2300
Ambler *(G-593)*

Noblesoft Solutions Inc.......................F...... 713 480-7510
Langhorne *(G-9315)*

Orkist LLC..G...... 412 346-8316
Pittsburgh *(G-15364)*

PC Network Inc..................................D...... 267 236-0015
Philadelphia *(G-14128)*

Quality Systems Integrators................G...... 610 458-0539
Chester Springs *(G-3085)*

Software Engineering Assoc................F...... 570 803-0535
Archbald *(G-695)*

COMPUTER SOFTWARE WRITERS

Arcweb Technologies LLC....................G...... 800 846-7980
Philadelphia *(G-13409)*

Scribe Inc..G...... 215 336-5094
Philadelphia *(G-14289)*

COMPUTER SOFTWARE WRITERS: Freelance

Pat Landgraf....................................G...... 412 221-0347
Bridgeville *(G-2084)*

COMPUTER STORAGE DEVICES, NEC

Ecm Energy Services Inc....................E...... 888 659-2413
Williamsport *(G-20010)*

EMC Corporation...............................C...... 484 322-1000
Norristown *(G-12654)*

EMC Corporation...............................B...... 610 834-0471
Conshohocken *(G-3542)*

EMC Fintech.....................................G...... 814 230-9157
Warren *(G-19024)*

EMC Metals Inc.................................G...... 412 299-7200
Coraopolis *(G-3689)*

Griffith Inc..C...... 215 322-8100
Huntingdon Valley *(G-7992)*

Integration Tech Systems Inc..............E...... 724 696-3000
Mount Pleasant *(G-11701)*

International Bus Mchs Corp................A...... 610 578-2017
Wayne *(G-19339)*

Mtekka LLC......................................G...... 610 619-3555
Kennett Square *(G-8532)*

North Central Sight Svcs Inc...............D...... 570 323-9401
Williamsport *(G-20050)*

Quantum Connection.........................G...... 814 333-9398
Meadville *(G-10786)*

Quantum One....................................F...... 412 432-5234
Pittsburgh *(G-15461)*

Quantum Qube Inc.............................G...... 412 767-0506
Sewickley *(G-17406)*

Quantum Restoration LLC....................E...... 215 259-3402
Conshohocken *(G-3596)*

Quantum Vortex Inc...........................G...... 814 325-0148
State College *(G-18011)*

COMPUTER STORAGE UNITS: Auxiliary

High Avlblty Stor Systems Inc..............E...... 610 254-5090
Audubon *(G-827)*

COMPUTER SYSTEM SELLING SVCS

Mack Information Systems Inc..............F...... 215 884-8123
Wyncote *(G-20264)*

COMPUTER SYSTEMS ANALYSIS & DESIGN

Achieva...D...... 412 995-5000
Pittsburgh *(G-14640)*

M Squared Electronics Inc...................F...... 215 945-6658
Levittown *(G-9848)*

COMPUTER TERMINALS

Accustar Inc.....................................G...... 610 459-0123
Garnet Valley *(G-6264)*

Capsen Robotics Inc..........................G...... 203 218-0204
Pittsburgh *(G-14806)*

Datacap Systems Inc..........................E...... 215 997-8989
Chalfont *(G-2871)*

Go Main Domains LLC........................G...... 480 624-2500
Darby *(G-4018)*

H M W Enterprises Inc........................F...... 717 765-4690
Waynesboro *(G-19410)*

Marco Manufacturing Co Inc...............E...... 215 463-2332
Philadelphia *(G-13992)*

Two Technologies Inc.........................E...... 215 441-5305
Horsham *(G-7861)*

COMPUTER-AIDED DESIGN SYSTEMS SVCS

RC & Design Company........................G...... 484 626-1216
Lehighton *(G-9724)*

COMPUTER-AIDED MANUFACTURING SYSTEMS SVCS

Hills Micro Weld Inc...........................G...... 814 336-4511
Meadville *(G-10735)*

Responselogix Inc..............................E...... 215 256-1700
Harleysville *(G-7055)*

COMPUTERS, NEC

Audio Video Automation SEC Inc..........G...... 814 313-1108
Warren *(G-19011)*

Cobalt Computers Inc.........................F...... 610 395-3771
Schnecksville *(G-17137)*

Consyst Inc.......................................G...... 610 398-0752
Orefield *(G-13010)*

Daisy Data Displays Inc......................E...... 717 932-9999
York Haven *(G-20756)*

Devon International Group Inc...............D...... 866 312-3373
King of Prussia *(G-8607)*

PRODUCT

Devon It Inc ....E 610 757-4220
King of Prussia *(G-8608)*

Dynamic Manufacturing LLC ....D ... 724 295-4200
Freeport *(G-6203)*

Eagle Mfg & Design Corp ....E ... 717 848-9767
York *(G-20459)*

Element 27 Inc ....G....... 610 502-2727
Schnecksville *(G-17139)*

Elk Systems Inc ....G ... 717 884-9355
Lewisberry *(G-9885)*

Flight Systems Inc ....E ... 717 590-7330
Mechanicsburg *(G-10844)*

General Dynamics Mission ....E ... 412 488-8605
Pittsburgh *(G-15045)*

H M W Enterprises Inc ....F ... 717 765-4690
Waynesboro *(G-19410)*

International Bus Mchs Corp ....A ... 610 578-2017
Wayne *(G-19339)*

J J Cacchio Enterprises ....G ... 610 399-9750
West Chester *(G-19575)*

Jli Electronics Inc ....G ... 215 256-3200
Harleysville *(G-7042)*

Lexicon International Corp ....E ... 215 639-8220
Bensalem *(G-1220)*

Library Video Company ....D ... 610 645-4000
Conshohocken *(G-3572)*

Matric Group LLC ....B ... 814 677-0716
Seneca *(G-17366)*

Medcomp Technologies Inc ....G ... 814 504-3328
East Springfield *(G-4600)*

National Hybrid Inc ....D ... 814 467-9060
Windber *(G-20190)*

Not For Radio LLC ....G ... 484 437-9962
Manheim *(G-10397)*

Progeny Systems Corporation ....F ... 724 239-3939
Charleroi *(G-3019)*

Real Automotive Pc Inc ....G ... 609 876-7450
Paoli *(G-13148)*

Reclamere Inc ....E ... 814 684-5505
Tyrone *(G-18592)*

Right Reason Technologies LLC ....F ... 570 234-0324
Tobyhanna *(G-18408)*

RMS Systems Inc ....G ... 724 458-7580
Mercer *(G-10972)*

Sparton Aydin LLC ....D ... 610 404-7400
Birdsboro *(G-1706)*

T-R Associates Inc ....E ... 570 876-4067
Archbald *(G-696)*

Time Man Jr Corporation ....D ... 856 244-1485
Philadelphia *(G-14389)*

Two Technologies Inc ....E ... 215 441-5305
Horsham *(G-7861)*

Venture 3 Systems LLC ....F ... 267 954-0100
Hatfield *(G-7405)*

VIP Tech LLC ....G ... 267 582-1554
Philadelphia *(G-14448)*

Viper Network Systems LLC ....G ... 855 758-4737
West View *(G-19774)*

Voci Technologies Incorporated...........F ... 412 621-9310
Pittsburgh *(G-15701)*

Vocollect Inc ....C ... 412 829-8145
Pittsburgh *(G-15702)*

White Box Systems LLC...................G....... 717 612-9911
Lemoyne *(G-9755)*

COMPUTERS, NEC, WHOLESALE

Advanced Software Inc ....F 215 369-7800
Yardley *(G-20293)*

Copiers Inc ....G....... 610 837-7400
Bath *(G-955)*

Fox IV Technologies Inc ....E ... 724 387-3500
Export *(G-5603)*

Progressive Computer Svcs Inc ....E ... 215 226-2220
Philadelphia *(G-14207)*

Symbol Technologies LLC ....F ... 610 834-8900
Plymouth Meeting *(G-15875)*

COMPUTERS, PERIPH & SOFTWARE, WHLSE: Personal & Home Entrtn

Eastern Systems Management..............G ... 717 391-9700
Lancaster *(G-9006)*

COMPUTERS, PERIPHERALS & SOFTWARE, WHOLESALE: Printers

Supra Office Solutions Inc...................G....... 267 275-8888
Philadelphia *(G-14360)*

COMPUTERS, PERIPHERALS & SOFTWARE, WHOLESALE: Software

Aserdiv Inc...................E 800 966-7770
Springfield *(G-17907)*

Binary Research Inc ....E ... 215 233-3200
Ambler *(G-570)*

Business Intelligence Intl Inc...................E ... 484 688-8300
Wayne *(G-19311)*

Compudata Inc ....E ... 215 969-1000
Philadelphia *(G-13566)*

Datatech Software Inc ....F ... 717 652-4344
Harrisburg *(G-7113)*

Environmental Systems Research ....E ... 909 793-2853
Chesterbrook *(G-3092)*

Horeb Inc ....G....... 610 285-1917
West Chester *(G-19564)*

Mpm Holdings Inc ....E ... 610 678-8131
Reading *(G-16450)*

Paulhus and Associates Inc ....F ... 717 274-5621
Lebanon *(G-9616)*

Prism Engineering LLC ....E ... 215 784-0800
Horsham *(G-7842)*

COMPUTERS, PERIPHERALS & SOFTWARE, WHOLESALE: Terminals

Sicom Systems Inc ....D....... 215 489-2500
Lansdale *(G-9410)*

COMPUTERS: Indl, Process, Gas Flow

Texan Corporation ....E ... 215 441-8967
Warminster *(G-18979)*

COMPUTERS: Mainframe

Blue Toro Technologies LLC ....G....... 610 428-0891
Bethlehem *(G-1468)*

Horeb Inc ....G....... 610 285-1917
West Chester *(G-19564)*

COMPUTERS: Personal

ABS and Apples ....G....... 646 847-8262
Tobyhanna *(G-18406)*

Apple Alley Associates-Ii LP...................G....... 215 817-2828
Langhorne *(G-9276)*

Apple Fox...................G....... 484 388-0011
Bernville *(G-1296)*

Effective Software Products ....G....... 717 267-2054
Chambersburg *(G-2929)*

Egg To Apples LLC...................G....... 610 822-3670
Haverford *(G-7410)*

Evergreen Group Inc ....G....... 610 799-2263
Schnecksville *(G-17140)*

HP Inc ....F ... 412 928-4978
Pittsburgh *(G-15103)*

Sterling Computer Sales LLC ....G....... 610 255-0198
Landenberg *(G-9253)*

CONCENTRATES, DRINK

Coca-Cola Company ....C ... 610 530-3900
Allentown *(G-172)*

CONCRETE BUILDING PRDTS WHOLESALERS

43rd St Inc...................E ... 412 682-4090
Pittsburgh *(G-14626)*

Concrete Texturing LLC ....G ... 570 489-6025
Throop *(G-18357)*

Pipe & Precast Cnstr Pdts Inc ....F ... 610 644-7338
Devault *(G-4112)*

Wendell H Stone Company Inc ....E ... 724 483-6571
Charleroi *(G-3025)*

CONCRETE CURING & HARDENING COMPOUNDS

BASF Construction Chem LLC...............G ... 215 945-3900
Levittown *(G-9818)*

BASF Construction Chem LLC...............G ... 610 391-0633
Allentown *(G-146)*

Poly Sat Inc...................E ... 215 332-7700
Philadelphia *(G-14187)*

Sealmaster Pennsylvania Inc...................F ... 724 667-0444
Hillsville *(G-7636)*

Wicktek Inc ....G....... 513 474-4518
Farmington *(G-5864)*

CONCRETE MIXERS

Bramley Machinery Corporation ....F ... 610 326-2500
Pottstown *(G-15968)*

Zimmerman Industries Inc ....E ... 717 733-6166
Ephrata *(G-5158)*

CONCRETE PLANTS

Erie Strayer Company ....C ... 814 456-7001
Erie *(G-5275)*

Masters RMC Inc ....E ... 570 278-3258
Montrose *(G-11470)*

CONCRETE PRDTS

Advanced Drainage Systems Inc ....E ... 570 546-7686
Muncy *(G-11805)*

Altomare Precast Inc ....F ... 215 225-8800
Philadelphia *(G-13373)*

Architectural Polymers Inc ....E ... 610 824-3322
Palmerton *(G-13102)*

Atlantic Precast Concrete ....D ... 215 945-5600
Bristol *(G-2112)*

Bauer Company Inc ....E ... 724 297-3200
Worthington *(G-20228)*

Bonsal American Inc ....E ... 724 475-2511
Fredonia *(G-6179)*

Bonsal American Inc ....F ... 215 785-1290
Bristol *(G-2120)*

Brentano Concrete Connection............G ... 412 731-8485
Pittsburgh *(G-14791)*

Cellular Concrete LLC ....F ... 610 398-7833
Allentown *(G-166)*

Cgm Incorporated...................E ... 215 638-4400
Bensalem *(G-1167)*

Colonial Concrete Industries ....G ... 610 279-2102
King of Prussia *(G-8594)*

Commercial Precast ....G ... 724 873-0708
Canonsburg *(G-2564)*

Concrete Simplicity Cons ....G ... 814 857-7500
Dover *(G-4191)*

Concrete Texturing LLC ....G ... 570 489-6025
Throop *(G-18357)*

Dayton Superior Corporation ....D ... 570 695-3163
Tremont *(G-18480)*

Dogs In Cast Stone ....G ... 717 291-9696
Lancaster *(G-9000)*

Doren Inc ....F ... 724 535-4397
Wampum *(G-18799)*

Essroc Corp...................F ... 610 759-4211
Nazareth *(G-11963)*

Furnley H Frisch...................F ... 717 957-3261
Duncannon *(G-4445)*

H&K Group Inc ....E ... 610 250-7703
Easton *(G-4694)*

Hanover Prest-Paving Company ....E ... 717 637-0500
Hanover *(G-6900)*

Henry S Esh ....G....... 717 627-2585
Lititz *(G-10015)*

Hessian Co Ltd...................G ... 610 683-5464
Kutztown *(G-8844)*

High Steel Structures LLC ....G ... 717 299-5211
Lancaster *(G-9049)*

Hpkd Inc...................E ... 412 922-7600
Pittsburgh *(G-15104)*

Jna Materials LLC ....G ... 215 233-0121
Ambler *(G-583)*

L B Foster Company ....E ... 814 623-6101
Bedford *(G-1060)*

Lebanon Valley Enterprises...................G ... 717 866-2030
Newmanstown *(G-12480)*

New Enterprise Stone Lime Inc ....C ... 814 224-2121
Roaring Spring *(G-16766)*

Oldcastle Precast Inc...................D ... 888 965-3227
Croydon *(G-3923)*

Oldcastle Precast Inc...................D ... 215 736-9576
Morrisville *(G-11574)*

Omega Transworld Ltd ....F ... 724 966-5183
Waynesburg *(G-19450)*

Perma-Column East...................G ... 610 562-7161
Lenhartsville *(G-9760)*

Peter Mamienski...................G ... 215 822-3293
Hatfield *(G-7381)*

Pittsburgh Mobile Concrete Inc...........F ... 412 486-0186
Pittsburgh *(G-15402)*

Pre Cast Systems LLC...................F ... 717 369-3773
Greencastle *(G-6627)*

Pre-Blend Products Inc ....E ... 215 295-6004
Fairless Hills *(G-5793)*

Quikrete Companies LLC ....E ... 724 539-6600
Latrobe *(G-9513)*

R A S Industries Inc ....E 215 541-4627
Pennsburg (G-13254)

R I Lampus Company ....C 412 362-3800
Springdale (G-17900)

R W Sidley Inc ....E 724 794-4451
Slippery Rock (G-17625)

Silvi Concrete Products Inc ....C 215 295-0777
Fairless Hills (G-5797)

Solution People Inc ....G 215 750-2694
Newtown (G-12551)

Standard Concrete Products Co ....E 717 843-8074
York (G-20679)

Techo-Bloc (ne) Corp ....G 610 863-2300
Pen Argyl (G-13219)

Techo-Bloc Corp ....G 610 326-3677
Douglassville (G-4181)

Terre Hill Concrete ....F 717 738-9164
Ephrata (G-5152)

Toma Inc ....F 717 597-7194
Harrisburg (G-7232)

Unistress Corp ....G 610 395-5930
Macungie (G-10160)

W R Meadows Inc ....E 717 792-2627
York (G-20701)

Waterford Precast & Sales Inc .....G 814 864-4956
Erie (G-5527)

Wendell H Stone Company Inc ....E 724 836-1400
Greensburg (G-6729)

York Building Products Co Inc ....E 717 764-5996
York (G-20729)

CONCRETE PRDTS, PRECAST, NEC

A & A Concrete Products Inc ......F 724 538-1114
Evans City (G-5555)

A C Miller Concrete Pdts Inc ......C 610 948-4600
Spring City (G-17856)

A C Miller Concrete Pdts Inc ......D 724 459-5950
Blairsville (G-1712)

Advanced Cast Stone Inc Inc ......G 817 572-0018
Girard (G-6383)

Appleridge Stone Intl Inc ....E 724 459-9511
Blairsville (G-1713)

Architctral Prcast Innovations ....D 570 837-1774
Middleburg (G-11023)

Atlantic Concrete Products Inc ....E 215 945-5600
Bristol (G-2111)

Beavertown Block Co Inc ....E 814 359-2771
Bellefonte (G-1093)

Bethlehem Pre-Cast Inc ....G 610 967-5531
Macungie (G-10143)

Bethlehem Pre-Cast Inc ....G 610 691-1336
Bethlehem (G-1462)

Bodon Industries Inc ....F 610 323-0700
Douglassville (G-4170)

Castek Inc ....F 570 759-3540
Berwick (G-1316)

Concrete Safety Systems LLC .....E 717 933-4107
Bethel (G-1394)

Continental Concrete Pdts Inc .....E 610 327-3700
Pottstown (G-15974)

Coudersport Precast Inc ....F 814 274-9634
Coudersport (G-3780)

Dutchland Inc ....C 717 442-8282
Gap (G-6249)

EP Henry Corporation ....E 610 495-8533
Parker Ford (G-13168)

Fizzano Bros Concrete Pdts Inc ....G 215 355-6160
Langhorne (G-9298)

Great Lakes Cast Stone Inc ....F 814 402-1055
Girard (G-6390)

Guyers Superior Walls ....C 814 725-8575
North East (G-12745)

J & R Slaw Inc ....D 610 852-2020
Lehighton (G-9717)

Juniata Concrete Co ....E 717 436-2176
Mifflintown (G-11125)

Kennedy Concrete Inc ....F 570 875-2780
Ashland (G-733)

Keystone Precast Inc ....G 570 837-1864
Middleburg (G-11026)

Lockcrete Bauer ....G 800 419-9255
Worthington (G-20230)

Macinnis Group LLC ....D 814 695-2016
Roaring Spring (G-16765)

Marion Center Supply Inc ....F 724 397-5505
Marion Center (G-10473)

Martin Limestone Inc ....D 717 354-1200
New Holland (G-12258)

Merchants Metals LLC ....D 570 384-3063
Hazle Township (G-7469)

Northeast Prestressed Pdts LLC ....C 570 385-2352
Cressona (G-3906)

Oldcastle Precast Inc ....D 484 548-6200
Easton (G-4735)

Oldcastle Precast Inc ....C 215 257-8081
Telford (G-18306)

Paxton Precast LLC ....G 717 692-5686
Dalmatia (G-3985)

Precast Systems LLC ....E 717 267-4500
Chambersburg (G-2969)

Quality Concrete Inc ....G 412 922-0200
Pittsburgh (G-15460)

Reading Precast Inc ....E 610 926-5000
Leesport (G-9673)

Rotondo Weirich Entps Inc ....D 215 256-7940
Lansdale (G-9407)

Say-Core Inc ....D 814 736-8018
Portage (G-15920)

St Clair Precast Concrete Inc ......E 412 221-2577
Bridgeville (G-2091)

Stacy Lloyd ....G 724 265-3445
Tarentum (G-18247)

Terre Hill Silo Company Inc ....E 717 445-3100
Terre Hill (G-18339)

Universal Concrete Pdts Corp ......F 610 323-0700
Stowe (G-18073)

Windy Hill Concrete Inc ....E 717 464-3889
Lancaster (G-9243)

CONCRETE REINFORCING MATERIAL

Tri-Boro Construction Sups Inc ....D 717 246-3095
Dallastown (G-3982)

CONCRETE: Asphaltic, Not From Refineries

Treyco Manufacturing Inc ....E 717 273-6504
Lebanon (G-9636)

CONCRETE: Bituminous

Bituminous Pav Mtls York Inc ......G 717 843-4573
York (G-20408)

Hanson Aggregates PA LLC ....E 610 366-4626
Allentown (G-243)

New Enterprise Stone Lime Inc ....E 814 443-6494
Somerset (G-17698)

New Enterprise Stone Lime Inc ....E 814 224-2121
Roaring Spring (G-16766)

Russell Standard Corporation ......F 412 449-0700
Pittsburgh (G-15504)

York Building Products Co Inc ....E 717 848-2831
York (G-20726)

CONCRETE: Dry Mixture

Quikrete Companies Inc ....E 570 672-1063
Paxinos (G-13192)

CONCRETE: Ready-Mixed

43rd St Inc ....E 412 682-4090
Pittsburgh (G-14626)

A Anthony & Sons Inc ....E 814 454-2883
Erie (G-5164)

A D Swartzlander & Sons ....G 724 282-2706
Butler (G-2370)

Advance Transit Mix Inc ....F 610 461-2182
Glenolden (G-6471)

Allied Concrete & Supply Corp ....E 215 646-8484
Dresher (G-4352)

Baycrete Inc ....F 814 454-5001
Erie (G-5205)

Beaver Concrete & Supply Inc ....F 724 774-5100
Monaca (G-11282)

Big Valley Concrete ....E 717 483-6538
Belleville (G-1128)

Blank Concrete and Supply ....F 724 758-7596
Ellwood City (G-4928)

Castle Builders Supply Inc ....F 724 658-5656
New Castle (G-12070)

Castle Builders Supply Inc ....E 724 981-4212
Hermitage (G-7573)

CE Ready Mix ....E 724 727-3331
Apollo (G-667)

Central Builders Supply Co ....G 570 524-9147
Lewisburg (G-9899)

Central Concrete Co Inc ....E 215 953-9736
Southampton (G-17801)

Central Concrete Supply Coinc ....G 215 927-4686
Philadelphia (G-13520)

Centre Concrete Company ....F 570 748-7747
Lock Haven (G-10085)

Centre Concrete Company ....E 570 433-3186
Montoursville (G-11435)

Concrete Services Corporation ....E 814 774-8807
Fairview (G-5817)

Conewago Ready Mix ....G 717 633-5022
Hanover (G-6869)

Construction Dynamics Inc ....D 215 295-0777
Fairless Hills (G-5775)

Coon Industries Inc ....G 570 735-6852
Nanticoke (G-11899)

Coon Industries Inc ....G 570 341-8033
Dunmore (G-4471)

County Line Quarry Inc ....E 717 252-1584
Wrightsville (G-20235)

Crete NYCE Co Inc ....E 215 855-4628
Lansdale (G-9354)

De Paul Concrete ....G 610 832-8000
Flourtown (G-5986)

Delaware Valley Con Co Inc ....D 215 675-8900
Hatboro (G-7278)

Delco Mini Mix LLC ....G 610 809-0316
Chester (G-3047)

Dinardo Brothers Material Inc ......G 215 535-4645
Philadelphia (G-13633)

Donaldson Supply & Eqp Co ....F 724 745-5250
Canonsburg (G-2579)

Drd Inc ....G 215 879-1055
Philadelphia (G-13643)

Dubrook Inc ....G 814 371-3113
Du Bois (G-4389)

Dubrook Inc ....G 724 538-3111
Evans City (G-5558)

Dubrook Inc ....E 724 283-3111
Butler (G-2396)

Dubrook Inc ....E 814 371-3111
Du Bois (G-4390)

Dubrook Inc ....F 814 834-3111
Saint Marys (G-16964)

E M Brown Incorporated ....E 814 765-7519
Clearfield (G-3218)

East Side Concrete Supply Co ......F 814 944-8175
Altoona (G-499)

Eastern Industries Inc ....B 610 866-0932
Whitehall (G-19873)

Eastern Industries Inc ....E 717 362-3388
Elizabethville (G-4893)

Eastern Industries Inc ....E 570 265-9191
Towanda (G-18425)

Edwards Concrete ....F 570 842-8438
Elmhurst Township (G-4957)

Eles Bros Inc ....E 412 824-6161
Monroeville (G-11335)

Emporium Contractors Inc ....E 814 562-0631
Emporium (G-5056)

Essroc Corp ....G 610 837-6725
Nazareth (G-11964)

Eureka Stone Quarry Inc ....F 570 842-7694
Moscow (G-11596)

Eureka Stone Quarry Inc ....G 215 723-9801
Telford (G-18288)

Family Ready Labor Inc ....G 717 615-4900
Lancaster (G-9014)

Fi-Hoff Concrete Products Inc ......F 814 266-5834
Johnstown (G-8372)

Fly Mix Entertainment ....G 215 722-6287
Philadelphia (G-13706)

Four Winds Concrete Inc ....E 610 865-1788
Bethlehem (G-1517)

Four Winds Concrete Inc ....E 610 865-1788
Center Valley (G-2827)

Frank Bryan Inc ....G 412 331-1630
Mc Kees Rocks (G-10609)

Frank Bryan Inc ....F 412 431-2700
Pittsburgh (G-15031)

Frank Casilio and Sons Inc ....G 610 253-3558
Easton (G-4685)

Frank Casilio and Sons Inc ....F 610 867-5886
Bethlehem (G-1518)

Frankenstein Builders Supply ....G 724 333-5260
Zelienople (G-20802)

G F Edwards Inc ....G 570 842-8438
Elmhurst Township (G-4958)

Gettysburg Concrete Co Inc ....G 717 334-1494
Gettysburg (G-6291)

GF Edwards Inc ....G 570 842-8438
Elmhurst Township (G-4959)

GF Edwards Inc ....E 570 676-3200
South Sterling (G-17787)

Giovanni Demarco ....G 724 898-7239
Valencia (G-18697)

Glenside Ready Mix Concrete Co..........G....... 215 659-1500
Erie *(G-5304)*
Glossners Concrete Inc..........F....... 570 962-2564
Beech Creek *(G-1082)*
H & L Concrete..........F....... 610 562-8273
Virginville *(G-18770)*
H Y K Construction Co Inc..........D....... 610 489-2646
Collegeville *(G-3381)*
H Y K Construction Co Inc..........E....... 610 282-2300
Coopersburg *(G-3628)*
Hanover Concrete Co..........E....... 717 637-2288
Hanover *(G-6893)*
Hanson Aggregates Bmc Inc..........G....... 610 847-5211
Ottsville *(G-13062)*
Hanson Aggregates Bmc Inc..........F....... 724 229-5840
Eighty Four *(G-4842)*
Hanson Lehigh Inc..........G....... 610 366-4600
Allentown *(G-244)*
Hanson Ready Mix Inc..........F....... 814 238-1781
State College *(G-17971)*
Hanson Ready Mix Inc..........F....... 814 269-9600
Johnstown *(G-8379)*
Hanson Ready Mix Inc..........E....... 412 431-6001
Pittsburgh *(G-15080)*
Hanson Ready Mix Inc..........G....... 610 837-6725
Nazareth *(G-11971)*
Hempt Bros Inc..........D....... 717 774-2911
Camp Hill *(G-2500)*
Hess Ready Mix Inc..........F....... 570 385-0300
Schuylkill Haven *(G-17159)*
Hopper T and J Building Sups..........F....... 724 443-2222
Gibsonia *(G-6340)*
Hosmer Supply Company Inc..........F....... 412 892-2525
Pittsburgh *(G-15101)*
Hoys Construction Company Inc..........F....... 724 852-1112
Waynesburg *(G-19445)*
Hunlock Sand & Gravel Company..........F....... 570 256-3036
Bath *(G-960)*
Irwin Concrete Co..........F....... 724 863-1848
Apollo *(G-677)*
J & H Concrete Co..........E....... 570 824-3565
Wilkes Barre *(G-19931)*
J A & W A Hess Inc..........E....... 570 454-3731
Hazleton *(G-7504)*
J A & W A Hess Inc..........F....... 570 271-0227
Danville *(G-4007)*
J A & W A Hess Inc..........F....... 570 385-0300
Schuylkill Haven *(G-17160)*
James D Morrissey Inc..........G....... 267 554-7946
Bristol *(G-2156)*
James W Quandel & Sons Inc..........E....... 570 544-2261
Minersville *(G-11255)*
JDM Materials..........E....... 215 357-5505
Huntingdon Valley *(G-8003)*
Jfi Redi-Mix LLC..........F....... 215 428-3560
Morrisville *(G-11564)*
Jj Kennedy Inc..........E....... 724 452-6260
Fombell *(G-6033)*
Jj Kennedy Inc..........F....... 724 783-6081
Kittanning *(G-8776)*
Jj Kennedy Inc..........G....... 814 226-6320
Shippenville *(G-17562)*
Jj Kennedy Inc..........G....... 724 357-9696
Penn Run *(G-13228)*
Jj Kennedy Inc..........G....... 724 368-8660
Portersville *(G-15928)*
John Stephen Golob..........G....... 717 469-7931
Harrisburg *(G-7158)*
John W Thrower Inc..........G....... 724 352-9421
Saxonburg *(G-17090)*
Juniata Concrete Co..........E....... 717 436-2176
Mifflintown *(G-11125)*
Juniata Concrete Co..........G....... 717 567-3183
Newport *(G-12491)*
Juniata Concrete Co..........G....... 717 248-9677
Lewistown *(G-9937)*
Kibbes Concrete..........G....... 814 334-5537
Mills *(G-11222)*
Kiefer Coal and Supply Co..........G....... 412 835-7900
Bethel Park *(G-1422)*
Kinsley Construction Inc..........E....... 717 846-6711
York *(G-20554)*
Koller Concrete Inc..........E....... 610 865-5034
Bethlehem *(G-1553)*
Kraft Concrete Products Inc..........E....... 814 677-3019
Oil City *(G-12950)*
Lane Holdings LLC..........E....... 412 279-1234
Carnegie *(G-2775)*
Lehigh Cement Company LLC..........G....... 610 366-4600
Allentown *(G-292)*
Lehigh Cement Company LLC..........G....... 610 837-6725
Nazareth *(G-11976)*
Lehigh Cement Company LLC..........G....... 610 759-2222
Nazareth *(G-11977)*
Lehigh Cement Company LLC..........G....... 724 378-2232
Aliquippa *(G-80)*
Lehigh Cement Company LLC..........G....... 610 366-0500
Macungie *(G-10149)*
Lehigh Cement Company LLC..........C....... 610 926-1024
Fleetwood *(G-5976)*
Lehigh Hanson Ecc Inc..........D....... 610 837-6725
Nazareth *(G-11978)*
Lehigh Hanson Ecc Inc..........D....... 610 837-3312
Nazareth *(G-11979)*
Lehigh Hanson Ecc Inc..........D....... 610 759-2222
Nazareth *(G-11980)*
Ligonier Stone & Lime Company..........E....... 724 537-6023
Latrobe *(G-9500)*
Limestone Mobile Concrete..........G....... 570 437-2640
Milton *(G-11247)*
Limestone Products & Supply Co..........G....... 412 221-5120
Bridgeville *(G-2077)*
Lisa Little Inc..........G....... 814 697-7500
Shinglehouse *(G-17509)*
Main Line Concrete & Sup Inc..........F....... 610 269-5556
Downingtown *(G-4238)*
Marion Center Supply Inc..........F....... 724 397-5505
Marion Center *(G-10473)*
Marion Center Supply Inc..........G....... 724 354-2143
Shelocta *(G-17487)*
Marstellar Concrete Inc..........G....... 717 834-6200
Duncannon *(G-4448)*
Martin Limestone Inc..........E....... 717 335-4500
East Earl *(G-4548)*
Martin Limestone Inc..........D....... 717 354-1200
New Holland *(G-12258)*
Martin Limestone Inc..........E....... 717 335-4523
Denver *(G-4082)*
Martin Limestone Inc..........G....... 814 224-6837
West Chester *(G-19597)*
Martin Limestone Inc..........D....... 717 354-1298
New Holland *(G-12259)*
Masters Concrete..........E....... 570 798-2680
Lakewood *(G-8915)*
Meadville Redi-Mix Concrete..........G....... 814 734-1644
Edinboro *(G-4816)*
Middleburg Pre Cast LLC..........F....... 570 837-1463
Middleburg *(G-11029)*
Midwest Material Inds Inc..........G....... 610 882-5000
Bethlehem *(G-1573)*
Mix Earl..........G....... 610 444-3245
Kennett Square *(G-8530)*
Mon River Supply LLC..........G....... 412 382-7178
West Elizabeth *(G-19695)*
Montgomery Block Works Inc..........F....... 724 735-2931
Harrisville *(G-7253)*
Naceville Materials JV..........F....... 215 453-8933
Sellersville *(G-17354)*
New Enterprise Stone Lime Inc..........E....... 814 472-4717
Ebensburg *(G-4790)*
New Enterprise Stone Lime Inc..........E....... 610 374-5131
Allentown *(G-330)*
New Enterprise Stone Lime Inc..........G....... 717 349-2412
Dry Run *(G-4384)*
New Enterprise Stone Lime Inc..........D....... 814 652-5121
Everett *(G-5576)*
New Enterprise Stone Lime Inc..........E....... 814 443-6494
Somerset *(G-17698)*
New Enterprise Stone Lime Inc..........B....... 610 374-5131
Leesport *(G-9668)*
New Enterprise Stone Lime Inc..........C....... 814 224-2121
Roaring Spring *(G-16766)*
Oldcastle Materials Inc..........G....... 717 898-2278
Annville *(G-655)*
Parmer Metered Concrete Inc..........G....... 717 533-3344
Hershey *(G-7624)*
Pennsy Supply Inc..........G....... 570 833-4497
Montrose *(G-11474)*
Pennsy Supply Inc..........G....... 717 569-2623
Manheim *(G-10400)*
Pennsy Supply Inc..........G....... 717 397-0391
Lancaster *(G-9165)*
Pennsy Supply Inc..........G....... 570 471-7358
Avoca *(G-847)*
Pennsy Supply Inc..........D....... 717 792-2631
Thomasville *(G-18342)*
Pennsy Supply Inc..........E....... 570 868-6936
Wapwallopen *(G-18808)*
Pennsy Supply Inc..........F....... 570 654-3462
Pittston *(G-15773)*
Pennsy Supply Inc..........E....... 717 566-0222
Hummelstown *(G-7921)*
Pennsy Supply Inc..........E....... 717 766-7676
Mechanicsburg *(G-10879)*
Pennsy Supply Inc..........D....... 717 274-3661
Lebanon *(G-9619)*
Pennsylvania Supply Inc..........G....... 717 567-3197
Harrisburg *(G-7196)*
Pike County Concrete Inc..........F....... 570 775-7880
Hawley *(G-7435)*
Pocono Transcrete Incorporated..........E....... 570 646-2662
Blakeslee *(G-1749)*
Pocono Transcrete Incorporated..........G....... 570 655-9166
Pittston *(G-15777)*
Prospect Concrete Inc..........F....... 717 898-2277
Landisville *(G-9265)*
Quality Concrete Inc..........G....... 412 922-0200
Pittsburgh *(G-15460)*
R W Sidley Inc..........E....... 724 794-4451
Slippery Rock *(G-17625)*
R W Sidley Incorporated..........F....... 724 755-0205
Youngwood *(G-20783)*
R W Sidley Incorporated..........G....... 724 794-4451
Slippery Rock *(G-17626)*
Rahns Construction Material Co..........G....... 610 584-8500
Collegeville *(G-3390)*
RC Concrete Inc..........G....... 724 947-9005
Burgettstown *(G-2353)*
Ready Set Live Inc..........G....... 215 953-1509
Feasterville Trevose *(G-5928)*
Ready Training Inc..........G....... 717 366-4253
Elizabethtown *(G-4883)*
Redmonds Ready Mix Inc..........G....... 814 776-1437
Ridgway *(G-16726)*
Reeser Bros..........G....... 717 266-6644
York Haven *(G-20761)*
Riverside Builders Supply..........E....... 412 264-8835
Coraopolis *(G-3721)*
Robert J Quinn Jr..........G....... 570 622-4420
Pottsville *(G-16095)*
Rock Hill Materials Company..........E....... 610 264-5586
Catasauqua *(G-2817)*
Rock Hill Materials Company..........G....... 610 852-2314
Parryville *(G-13186)*
Rohrers Quarry Inc..........D....... 717 626-9760
Lititz *(G-10043)*
Rohrers Quarry Inc..........G....... 717 626-9756
Lititz *(G-10044)*
Rose Wild Inc..........G....... 570 835-4329
Tioga *(G-18364)*
S J A Construction Inc..........E....... 856 985-3400
Philadelphia *(G-14272)*
Santarelli Vibrated Block LLC..........F....... 570 693-2200
Wyoming *(G-20284)*
Scott R Mix..........G....... 570 220-5887
Bellefonte *(G-1117)*
Scranton Craftsmen Excvtg Inc..........D....... 800 775-1479
Throop *(G-18360)*
Scranton Craftsmen Inc..........D....... 570 347-5125
Throop *(G-18361)*
Sebastian Brothers..........F....... 717 930-8797
Middletown *(G-11075)*
Shaffer Block and Con Pdts Inc..........E....... 814 445-4414
Somerset *(G-17705)*
Shamrock Metered Concrete Inc..........G....... 570 672-3223
Paxinos *(G-13193)*
Shawnee Ready Mix Con & Asp Co..........E....... 570 779-9586
Plymouth *(G-15821)*
Sikorsky Concrete Product LLC..........G....... 610 826-3676
Palmerton *(G-13111)*
Sil Kemp Concrete Inc..........G....... 215 295-0777
Fairless Hills *(G-5796)*
Silhol Builders Supply Co Inc..........E....... 412 221-7400
Bridgeville *(G-2089)*
Skrapits Concrete Company..........G....... 610 262-8830
Northampton *(G-12861)*
Skrapits Concrete Company..........F....... 610 442-5355
Coplay *(G-3649)*
Stacy Lloyd..........G....... 724 265-3445
Tarentum *(G-18247)*
T C Redi Mix Youngstown Inc..........G....... 724 652-7878
New Castle *(G-12158)*
Tafisco Inc..........G....... 215 493-3167
Philadelphia *(G-14368)*
Tarrs Concrete & Supplies..........G....... 724 438-4114
Washington *(G-19231)*
Toma Inc..........G....... 717 597-7194
Greencastle *(G-6641)*
Trenton Group Inc..........E....... 717 637-2288
Hanover *(G-6962)*

Trenton Group Inc ....G....... 717 235-3807
  Shrewsbury (G-17589)
Tresco Concrete Products Inc ....F....... 724 468-4640
  Export (G-5629)
Tri-Boro Construction Sups Inc ....E....... 717 249-6448
  Carlisle (G-2743)
Union Quarries Inc ....E....... 717 249-5012
  Carlisle (G-2745)
Universal Ready Mix & Supply ....F....... 724 529-2950
  Dawson (G-4033)
US Concrete Inc ....E....... 610 532-6290
  Sharon Hill (G-17465)
Valley Quarries Inc ....F....... 717 267-2244
  Chambersburg (G-2994)
Valley Quarries Inc ....F....... 717 532-4161
  Shippensburg (G-17552)
Valley Quarries Inc ....F....... 717 264-4178
  Chambersburg (G-2995)
Vincent Lohuvey ....G....... 724 527-2994
  Greensburg (G-6727)
Wayne Concrete Inc ....F....... 814 697-7500
  Shinglehouse (G-17514)
Wayne County Ready Mix Inc ....F....... 570 253-4341
  Honesdale (G-7733)
Wendell H Stone and Company ....G....... 412 331-1944
  Mc Kees Rocks (G-10641)
Wendell H Stone Company Inc ....F....... 724 836-1400
  Connellsville (G-3510)
Wendell H Stone Company Inc ....E....... 724 224-7688
  Connellsville (G-3511)
Wendell H Stone Company Inc ....E....... 724 836-1400
  Greensburg (G-6729)
Wendell H Stone Company Inc ....E....... 412 373-6235
  Monroeville (G-11364)
Wendell H Stone Company Inc ....E....... 724 483-6571
  Charleroi (G-3025)
Westmoreland Advanced Mtls Inc ....G....... 724 684-5902
  Charleroi (G-3026)
Wine Concrete Products Inc ....E....... 724 266-9500
  Sewickley (G-17415)
Wolyniec Construction Inc ....E....... 570 322-8634
  Williamsport (G-20097)
Wysox S&G Inc ....F....... 570 265-6760
  Wysox (G-20291)
York Concrete Company ....F....... 717 843-8746
  York (G-20732)

CONDENSERS & CONDENSING UNITS: Air Conditioner

Building Inspectors Contrs Inc ....G....... 215 481-0606
  Glenside (G-6509)
Everything Ice Inc ....E....... 814 244-5477
  Salix (G-17047)

CONDENSERS: Heat Transfer Eqpt, Evaporative

Harsco Corporation ....E....... 570 421-7500
  East Stroudsburg (G-4618)
Imprintables Warehouse LLC ....G....... 724 966-8599
  Carmichaels (G-2758)
Narsa ....F....... 724 799-8415
  Wexford (G-19814)

CONDENSERS: Steam

SPX Heat Transfer LLC ....E....... 610 250-1146
  Bethlehem (G-1628)

CONDUITS & FITTINGS: Electric

Conestoga USA Inc ....G....... 610 327-2882
  Pottstown (G-15973)
Gibson Stainless Specialty Inc ....F....... 724 838-8320
  Greensburg (G-6669)
Specialty Conduit & Mfg LLC ....F....... 724 439-9371
  Mount Braddock (G-11621)
Wheatland Tube LLC ....D....... 724 981-5200
  Sharon (G-17445)

CONFECTIONERY PRDTS WHOLESALERS

Gold Medal Products Co ....G....... 412 787-1030
  Pittsburgh (G-15056)
Victorias Candies Inc ....G....... 570 455-6341
  Hazleton (G-7534)

CONFECTIONS & CANDY

Andersons Candies Inc ....E....... 724 869-3018
  Baden (G-869)

Anstines Candy Box ....G....... 717 854-9269
  York (G-20379)
B & E Candy ....G....... 724 327-8898
  Jeannette (G-8247)
Bazzini Holdings LLC ....C....... 610 366-1606
  Allentown (G-147)
Bevans Candies Inc ....F....... 610 566-0581
  Media (G-10915)
Blaine Boring Chocolates ....G....... 814 539-6244
  Johnstown (G-8358)
Byrnes and Kiefer Company ....G....... 724 538-5200
  Callery (G-2467)
Callies Candy Kitchens Inc ....E....... 570 595-3257
  Cresco (G-3892)
Callies Candy Kitchens Inc ....F....... 570 595-2280
  Mountainhome (G-11786)
Char-Val Candies ....G....... 814 275-1602
  New Bethlehem (G-12025)
Chester A Asher Inc ....G....... 717 248-8613
  Lewistown (G-9925)
Chester A Asher Inc ....C....... 215 721-3000
  Souderton (G-17729)
Chris Candies Inc ....E....... 412 322-9400
  Pittsburgh (G-14849)
Daffins Inc ....E....... 724 342-2892
  Sharon (G-17432)
Daffins Inc ....E....... 724 983-8336
  Farrell (G-5867)
Edwards Sherm Candies Inc ....E....... 412 372-4331
  Trafford (G-18454)
Elite Sweets Inc ....F....... 610 391-1719
  Trexlertown (G-18510)
Esthers Sweet Shop Inc ....G....... 412 884-4224
  Pittsburgh (G-14986)
Fitzkees Candies Inc ....F....... 717 741-1031
  York (G-20482)
Fox Run Usa LLC ....D....... 215 675-7700
  Ivyland (G-8211)
Gertrude Hawk Chocolates Inc ....B....... 570 342-7556
  Dunmore (G-4473)
Godiva Chocolatier Inc ....B....... 610 779-3797
  Reading (G-16394)
Hershey Company ....B....... 717 534-4100
  Hershey (G-7614)
Hershey Company ....B....... 717 534-4200
  Hershey (G-7615)
Hershey Company ....B....... 717 534-4200
  Hershey (G-7613)
Hershey Foods Corporation - MA.......F....... 717 534-6799
  Hershey (G-7616)
Jamesons Candy Inc ....F....... 724 658-7441
  New Castle (G-12107)
Josh Early Candies Inc ....F....... 610 395-4321
  Allentown (G-271)
Just Born Inc ....B....... 610 867-7568
  Bethlehem (G-1548)
Just Born Inc ....D....... 215 335-4500
  Philadelphia (G-13915)
Lerro Candy Co ....F....... 610 461-8886
  Darby (G-4021)
Lukas Confections Inc ....E....... 717 843-0921
  Ebensburg (G-4787)
Marc Edward Brands Inc ....D....... 412 380-0888
  Pittsburgh (G-15250)
Mars Incorporated ....E....... 717 367-1500
  Elizabethtown (G-4877)
Mars Chocolate North Amer LLC ....B....... 717 367-1500
  Elizabethtown (G-4878)
Matangos Candies Inc ....G....... 717 234-0882
  Harrisburg (G-7174)
Michael Mootz Candies Inc ....F....... 570 823-8272
  Hanover Township (G-6997)
Moyer Specialty Foods LLC ....F....... 215 703-0100
  Souderton (G-17754)
Nestle Usa Inc ....C....... 818 549-6000
  King of Prussia (G-8655)
Oak Spring Enterprises Inc ....F....... 570 622-2001
  Pottsville (G-16090)
OH Ryans Irish Potatoes ....F....... 610 494-7123
  Marcus Hook (G-10452)
OSheas Candies ....F....... 814 536-4800
  Johnstown (G-8414)
OSheas Candies ....G....... 814 266-7041
  Johnstown (G-8415)
Popcorn Buddha Inc ....F....... 570 476-5676
  East Stroudsburg (G-4629)
Purity Candy Co ....F....... 570 538-9502
  Allenwood (G-442)
Remarkable Designs Inc ....G....... 412 512-6564
  Glenshaw (G-6499)

Repperts Candy ....F....... 610 689-9200
  Oley (G-12980)
Resource Dynamics Incorporated ......G....... 412 369-7760
  Pittsburgh (G-15480)
Sarris Candies Inc ....B....... 724 745-4042
  Canonsburg (G-2632)
Shane Candy Co ....F....... 215 922-1048
  Philadelphia (G-14296)
Stutz Candy Company ....E....... 215 675-2630
  Hatboro (G-7307)
Suzannes Choclat & Confections ....G....... 570 753-8545
  Avis (G-838)
Thomson Candies ....G....... 610 268-8337
  Avondale (G-861)
Three Rivers Confections LLC ....D....... 412 402-0388
  Pittsburgh (G-15618)
Toad-Ally Snax Inc ....E....... 215 788-7500
  Bristol (G-2208)
Tootsie Roll Industries Inc ....G....... 570 455-2975
  Hazle Township (G-7485)
Topps Company Inc ....G....... 570 471-7649
  Old Forge (G-12975)
Trufood Mfg Inc ....C....... 412 963-2330
  Pittsburgh (G-15656)
Valos House of Candy ....G....... 724 339-2669
  New Kensington (G-12385)
Victorias Candies Inc ....G....... 570 455-6341
  Hazleton (G-7534)
Victorias Candies Inc ....G....... 570 455-6345
  West Hazleton (G-19718)
Warners Candies ....G....... 215 639-1615
  Bensalem (G-1269)
Warrell Corporation ....B....... 717 761-5440
  Camp Hill (G-2523)
Werther Partners LLC ....G....... 215 677-5200
  Philadelphia (G-14465)
Wfc & C Inc ....F....... 215 627-3233
  Philadelphia (G-14471)
Wolfgang Operations LLC ....D....... 717 843-5536
  York (G-20718)
Wolfgang Operations LLC ....E....... 717 843-5536
  York (G-20719)

CONNECTORS & TERMINALS: Electrical Device Uses

Ava Electronics Corp ....E....... 610 284-2500
  Drexel Hill (G-4360)
Fci USA LLC ....B....... 717 938-7200
  Etters (G-5548)
Halsit Holdings LLC ....E....... 814 724-6440
  Meadville (G-10733)
Ilsco Extrusions Inc ....G....... 724 589-5888
  Greenville (G-6748)
Lynn Electronics Corp ....D....... 215 355-8200
  Ivyland (G-8216)
Lynn Electronics Corp ....F....... 954 977-3800
  Warminster (G-18915)
N T M Inc ....E....... 717 567-9374
  Newport (G-12492)
Penn-Union Corp ....D....... 814 734-1631
  Edinboro (G-4820)
Te Connectivity Corporation ....C....... 717 986-3028
  Middletown (G-11079)
Te Connectivity Corporation ....B....... 717 227-4400
  Shrewsbury (G-17588)
Z-Axis Connector Company ....F....... 267 803-9000
  Warminster (G-19006)

CONNECTORS: Cord, Electric

King Associates Ltd ....D....... 717 556-5673
  Lancaster (G-9086)
Warners Innvtive Solutions Inc ....F....... 814 201-2429
  Altoona (G-557)

CONNECTORS: Electrical

EBY Group LLC ....E....... 215 537-4700
  Philadelphia (G-13657)
Te Connectivity Corporation ....B....... 717 653-8151
  Mount Joy (G-11672)
Tilsit Corporation ....F....... 610 681-5951
  Gilbert (G-6364)

CONNECTORS: Electronic

Avant-Garde Technology Inc ....G....... 215 345-8228
  Doylestown (G-4273)
Bel Connector Inc ....D....... 717 235-7512
  Glen Rock (G-6452)

PRODUCT

Belden Inc..............................E.......717 263-7655
Chambersburg (G-2910)

Component Enterprises Co Inc ....E.......610 272-7900
Norristown (G-12646)

Continental-Wirt Elec Corp ....C......215 355-7080
Southampton (G-17805)

Cooper Interconnect Inc......................E.......630 248-4007
King of Prussia (G-8597)

Eagle Design Group............................E.......610 321-2488
Chester Springs (G-3076)

Eagle Design Innovation LLC ....F......610 321-2488
Chester Springs (G-3077)

EBY Group LLC...................................E.......215 537-4700
Philadelphia (G-13657)

Electroline Corp..................................E.......215 766-2229
Pipersville (G-14614)

Fci USA LLC..B......717 938-7200
Etters (G-5548)

Halsit Holdings LLC...........................E.......814 724-6440
Meadville (G-10733)

Hirschmann Electronics Inc................F......717 217-2200
Chambersburg (G-2940)

Industrial Enterprises Inc..................D......215 355-7080
Southampton (G-17819)

Keystone Controls Company..............G......215 355-7080
Southampton (G-17820)

Koaxis Inc...E.......610 222-0154
Schwenksville (G-17178)

Loranger International Corp ....D......814 723-2250
Warren (G-19038)

Megaphase LLC..................................E.......570 424-8400
Stroudsburg (G-18130)

Optima Technology Assoc Inc...........D......717 932-5877
Lewisberry (G-9889)

Ospcom LLC..G......267 356-7124
Doylestown (G-4321)

Osram Sylvania Inc............................C......814 726-6600
Warren (G-19041)

Pei/Genesis Inc..................................G......215 638-1645
Bensalem (G-1238)

Pei/Genesis Inc..................................C......215 464-1410
Philadelphia (G-14129)

Pennatronics Corporation..................D......724 938-1800
California (G-2464)

Phoenix Contact Dev & Mfg Inc..........B......717 944-1300
Middletown (G-11068)

Precise Plastics Inc............................D......814 474-5504
Fairview (G-5840)

Rocal Corporation..............................E.......215 343-2400
Warrington (G-19132)

Rosenberger N Amer Akron LLC...........C......717 859-8900
Akron (G-38)

Sentinel Connector Systems Inc..........E.......717 843-4240
York (G-20664)

Sentinel Holding Inc...........................E.......717 843-4240
York (G-20665)

Te Connectivity Corporation..............C......610 893-9800
Berwyn (G-1376)

Te Connectivity Corporation..............C......717 564-0100
Middletown (G-11078)

Te Connectivity Corporation..............D......717 564-0100
Harrisburg (G-7228)

Te Connectivity Corporation..............B......717 861-5000
Jonestown (G-8452)

Te Connectivity Corporation..............F......717 492-1000
Mount Joy (G-11671)

Te Connectivity Corporation..............A......866 743-6440
Middletown (G-11080)

Te Connectivity Corporation..............B......717 986-3743
Middletown (G-11081)

Te Connectivity Corporation..............B......717 653-8151
Mount Joy (G-11672)

Te Connectivity Corporation..............B......717 564-0100
Middletown (G-11082)

Te Connectivity Corporation..............B......717 564-0100
Harrisburg (G-7229)

Te Connectivity Corporation..............C......717 762-9186
Waynesboro (G-19426)

Valley Precision TI & Tech Inc ....E.......717 647-7550
Tower City (G-18443)

Video Display Corporation..................F......770 938-2080
Howard (G-7892)

CONSTRUCTION & MINING MACHINERY WHOLESALERS

Great Lakes Power Products Inc..........G......724 266-4000
Leetsdale (G-9691)

Mpi Supply Incorporated....................G......412 664-9320
Glassport (G-6414)

CONSTRUCTION EQPT REPAIR SVCS

Atlantic Crane Inc ....F......610 366-1540
Fogelsville (G-5991)

Facchiano Ironworks Inc.....................G......610 865-1503
Bethlehem (G-1506)

Ribarchik John ....G......215 547-8901
Levittown (G-9861)

CONSTRUCTION EQPT: Airport

Blazing Technologies Inc ....G......484 722-4800
Mohnton (G-11260)

CONSTRUCTION EQPT: Attachments

Kennametal Inc ....A......412 248-8000
Pittsburgh (G-15169)

Rockland Inc.......................................B......814 623-1115
Bedford (G-1075)

Woodings Doweling Tech Inc ....G......724 625-3131
Mars (G-10514)

CONSTRUCTION EQPT: Attachments, Snow Plow

Dant Enterprises ....G......570 379-3121
Nescopeck (G-12000)

Valk Manufacturing Company..............D......717 766-0711
New Kingstown (G-12394)

Valley Broom Inc.................................G......717 349-2614
East Waterford (G-4642)

CONSTRUCTION EQPT: Backhoes, Tractors, Cranes & Similar Eqpt

Concept Engineering Group ....G......412 826-8800
Verona (G-18753)

Doyle Equipment Company ....G......724 837-4500
Delmont (G-4050)

Groff Tractor & Equipment LLC............F......814 353-8400
Bellefonte (G-1100)

CONSTRUCTION EQPT: Blade, Grader, Scraper, Dozer/Snow Plow

Disston Precision Inc ....G......215 338-1200
Philadelphia (G-13635)

Wagman Metal Products Inc ....E.......717 854-2120
York (G-20702)

CONSTRUCTION EQPT: Buckets, Excavating, Clamshell, Etc

Artman Equipment Company Inc ....F......724 337-3700
Apollo (G-662)

T & N Excavating LLC..........................G......717 801-5525
Etters (G-5553)

CONSTRUCTION EQPT: Crane Carriers

Gantrex Crane Rail I Installat...............G......412 655-1400
Canonsburg (G-2592)

CONSTRUCTION EQPT: Cranes

Grove Investors Inc ....A......717 597-8121
Greencastle (G-6616)

Grove US LLc ....D......717 597-8121
Shady Grove (G-17420)

Jlg Industries Inc ....C......814 623-0045
Bedford (G-1056)

National Crane Corporation ....G......717 597-8121
Shady Grove (G-17422)

William Sport Crane & Rigging..............G......570 433-3300
Montoursville (G-11457)

CONSTRUCTION EQPT: Hammer Mills, Port, Incl Rock/Ore Crush

Pulva Corporation...............................E.......724 898-3000
Valencia (G-18700)

CONSTRUCTION EQPT: Rakes, Land Clearing, Mechanical

Lanco Manufacturing Company ....G......717 556-4143
Bird In Hand (G-1679)

CONSTRUCTION EQPT: Roofing Eqpt

L A Welte Inc......................................G......412 341-9400
Pittsburgh (G-15206)

Mongoose Products Inc.......................G......215 887-6600
Glenside (G-6529)

Rooftop Equipment Inc ....G......724 946-9999
New Wilmington (G-12470)

CONSTRUCTION EQPT: SCRAPERS, GRADERS, ROLLERS & SIMILAR EQPT

Sunnyburn Welding ....G......717 862-3878
Airville (G-32)

CONSTRUCTION EQPT: Spreaders, Aggregates

Buffalo Limestone Inc ....G......724 545-7478
Ford City (G-6044)

M C E Development Inc ....G......412 952-0918
Irwin (G-8181)

CONSTRUCTION EQPT: Tractors

Craneco LLC.......................................G......610 948-1400
Royersford (G-16847)

CONSTRUCTION EQPT: Trucks, Off-Highway

August Transport Inc..........................E.......724 462-1445
Leetsdale (G-9683)

CONSTRUCTION EQPT: Wrecker Hoists, Automobile

Star Surplus One................................G......215 654-9237
Ambler (G-603)

Top of Line Auto Svc II LLC ....G......215 727-6958
Philadelphia (G-14395)

CONSTRUCTION MATERIALS, WHOL: Concrete/Cinder Bldg Prdts

Frankenstein Builders Supply ....G......724 333-5260
Zelienople (G-20802)

Kiefer Coal and Supply Co..................G......412 835-7900
Bethel Park (G-1422)

Marstellar Concrete Inc ....G......717 834-6200
Duncannon (G-4448)

CONSTRUCTION MATERIALS, WHOLESALE: Aggregate

Buffalo Limestone Inc ....G......724 545-7478
Ford City (G-6044)

Dubrook Inc..G......814 371-3113
Du Bois (G-4389)

McClure Enterprises Inc......................G......570 562-1180
Old Forge (G-12970)

CONSTRUCTION MATERIALS, WHOLESALE: Architectural Metalwork

Fisher & Ludlow Inc............................F......859 282-7767
Wexford (G-19801)

McM Architectural Products LLC ....G......240 416-2809
Indiana (G-8112)

R M Metals Inc ....G......717 656-8737
Lancaster (G-9182)

CONSTRUCTION MATERIALS, WHOLESALE: Asphalt Felts & coating

Lane Enterprises Inc...........................E.......610 272-4531
King of Prussia (G-8637)

CONSTRUCTION MATERIALS, WHOLESALE: Awnings

Covers All Canvas Products.................G......412 653-6010
Pittsburgh (G-14881)

Diamond Awning Mfg Co......................G......610 656-1924
Folcroft (G-6002)

Muldoon Window Door & Awning ....G......570 347-9453
Scranton (G-17261)

Universal Awnings & Signs Inc ....G......215 634-7150
Philadelphia (G-14425)

CONSTRUCTION MATERIALS, WHOLESALE: Block, Concrete & Cinder

Fizzano Bros Inc ....E 215 355-6160
Feasterville Trevose **(G-5910)**
Kraft Concrete Products Inc ....E 814 677-3019
Oil City **(G-12950)**

CONSTRUCTION MATERIALS, WHOLESALE: Blocks, Building, NEC

Hopper T and J Building Sups..............F 724 443-2222
Gibsonia **(G-6340)**

CONSTRUCTION MATERIALS, WHOLESALE: Brick, Exc Refractory

Lock 3 Company ....F 724 258-7773
Monongahela **(G-11310)**

CONSTRUCTION MATERIALS, WHOLESALE: Building Stone

Dente Pittsburgh Inc............................G 412 828-1772
Oakmont **(G-12916)**
Mid-Life Stone Works LLC ....G 570 928-8802
Dushore **(G-4509)**

CONSTRUCTION MATERIALS, WHOLESALE: Building Stone, Granite

Custom Kitchens Inc ....G 814 833-5338
Erie **(G-5238)**
Porto Exim Usa LLC ....G 412 406-8442
Cheswick **(G-3115)**
Princeton Trade Consulting Gro...........E 610 683-9348
Kutztown **(G-8856)**

CONSTRUCTION MATERIALS, WHOLESALE: Building Stone, Marble

AAA Hellenic Marble Inc.......................E 610 344-7700
West Chester **(G-19493)**
Dal-Tile Corporation ....F 484 530-9066
Plymouth Meeting **(G-15841)**
Jones Stone & Marble Inc ....G 724 838-7625
Greensburg **(G-6681)**
Keystone Granite Tile Inc ....F 717 394-4972
Lancaster **(G-9084)**
Majesty Marble and Granite Inc ....E 610 859-8181
Aston **(G-774)**
Unity Marble and Granite Inc ....G 412 793-4220
Pittsburgh **(G-15681)**

CONSTRUCTION MATERIALS, WHOLESALE: Building, Exterior

Al Lorenzi Lumber Co Inc ....D 724 222-6100
Canonsburg **(G-2534)**
Best Group Holdings Inc ....E 814 536-1422
Johnstown **(G-8357)**
Carlisle Construction Mtls LLC ....B 717 245-7000
Carlisle **(G-2695)**
Glen Mills Sand & Gravel Inc ....E 610 459-4988
Media **(G-10929)**
Newtown-Slocomb Mfg Inc ....G 570 825-3675
Hanover Township **(G-7001)**
Slate Road Supply LLC ....G 717 445-5222
Ephrata **(G-5141)**

CONSTRUCTION MATERIALS, WHOLESALE: Building, Interior

Doellken- Woodtape Inc ....G 610 929-1910
Temple **(G-18328)**
Vangura Kitchen Tops Inc ....D 412 824-0772
Irwin **(G-8204)**

CONSTRUCTION MATERIALS, WHOLESALE: Cement

CTS Bulk Terminals ....G 610 759-8330
Bethlehem **(G-1491)**
Essroc Corp..G 610 837-6725
Nazareth **(G-11964)**

CONSTRUCTION MATERIALS, WHOLESALE: Concrete Mixtures

Admixtures Inc ....F 610 775-0371
Wernersville **(G-19483)**
Blank Concrete and Supply ....F 724 758-7596
Ellwood City **(G-4928)**
Oesterlings Concrete Co Inc.................G 724 282-8556
Butler **(G-2428)**
US Concrete Inc ....E 610 532-6290
Sharon Hill **(G-17465)**

CONSTRUCTION MATERIALS, WHOLESALE: Door Frames

Roma Aluminum Co Inc ....F 215 545-5700
Philadelphia **(G-14259)**

CONSTRUCTION MATERIALS, WHOLESALE: Fiberglass Building Mat

Hydra-Matic Packing Co Inc..................E 215 676-2992
Huntingdon Valley **(G-7995)**

CONSTRUCTION MATERIALS, WHOLESALE: Glass

Bent Glass Design Inc ....E 215 441-9101
Hatboro **(G-7273)**
Consolidated GL Holdings Inc...............G 866 412-6977
East Butler **(G-4531)**
Interstate Building Mtls Inc ....E 570 655-2811
Pittston **(G-15758)**

CONSTRUCTION MATERIALS, WHOLESALE: Guardrails, Metal

Lane Enterprises Inc.............................D 717 249-8342
Carlisle **(G-2720)**

CONSTRUCTION MATERIALS, WHOLESALE: Hardboard

Foster-Kmetz Woodworking ....G 570 325-8222
Jim Thorpe **(G-8340)**

CONSTRUCTION MATERIALS, WHOLESALE: Limestone

Hal Ben Mining Co ....G 724 748-4528
Grove City **(G-6789)**
New Enterprise Stone Lime Inc ....E 814 684-4905
Tyrone **(G-18587)**

CONSTRUCTION MATERIALS, WHOLESALE: Metal Buildings

Strat-O-Span Buildings Inc ....G 717 334-4606
Gettysburg **(G-6316)**

CONSTRUCTION MATERIALS, WHOLESALE: Millwork

American Mllwk & Cabinetry Inc ....E 610 965-0040
Emmaus **(G-5019)**
Craig A Scholedice Inc ....F 610 683-8910
Kutztown **(G-8838)**
Harsco Corporation ....E 724 287-4791
Butler **(G-2405)**
Heister House Millworks Inc ....D 570 539-2611
Mount Pleasant Mills **(G-11725)**
M4I Inc..F 717 566-1610
Hummelstown **(G-7916)**
Reinert & Sons Inc ....F 215 781-8311
Bristol **(G-2194)**
Specialty Millworks Inc.........................G 610 682-6334
Topton **(G-18416)**
Wilson & Mc Cracken Inc ....G 412 784-1772
Pittsburgh **(G-15718)**

CONSTRUCTION MATERIALS, WHOLESALE: Pallets, Wood

Sutherland Lumber Co ....E 724 947-3388
Burgettstown **(G-2355)**

CONSTRUCTION MATERIALS, WHOLESALE: Paneling, Wood

Wood Fabricators Inc ....F 717 284-4849
Quarryville **(G-16284)**

CONSTRUCTION MATERIALS, WHOLESALE: Paving Materials

Asphalt Press Industries.......................G 610 489-7283
Arcola **(G-697)**
Eastern Industries Inc ....E 717 667-2015
Milroy **(G-11230)**
Eastern Industries Inc ....E 610 683-7400
Kutztown **(G-8842)**
Erie Asphalt Paving Co ....D 814 898-4151
Erie **(G-5262)**
Glasgow Inc ....E 610 251-0760
Malvern **(G-10240)**
H&K Group Inc ....C 610 705-0500
Pottstown **(G-15947)**
Highway Materials Inc ....G 610 647-5902
Malvern **(G-10245)**
Highway Materials Inc ....G 717 252-3636
Wrightsville **(G-20237)**
Highway Materials Inc ....E 610 828-4300
Plymouth Meeting **(G-15846)**

CONSTRUCTION MATERIALS, WHOLESALE: Paving Mixtures

Eastern Industries Inc ....B 610 866-0932
Whitehall **(G-19873)**
Eastern Industries Inc ....E 570 524-2251
Winfield **(G-20199)**
Eastern Industries Inc ....E 717 362-3388
Elizabethville **(G-4893)**
Stabler Companies Inc...........................F 717 236-9307
Harrisburg **(G-7219)**

CONSTRUCTION MATERIALS, WHOLESALE: Plastering Materials

R A S Industries Inc ....E 215 541-4627
Pennsburg **(G-13254)**

CONSTRUCTION MATERIALS, WHOLESALE: Prefabricated Structures

Honeybrook Woodworks.........................F 610 593-6884
Christiana **(G-3135)**
Morton Buildings Inc ....F 717 624-8000
Gettysburg **(G-6308)**
Sweetwater Natural Pdts LLC ....G 610 321-1900
Chester Springs **(G-3086)**

CONSTRUCTION MATERIALS, WHOLESALE: Roof, Asphalt/Sheet Metal

Hinkel-Hofmann Supply Co Inc ....E 412 231-3131
Pittsburgh **(G-15095)**
Histand Brothers Inc..............................F 215 348-4121
Ambler **(G-581)**
J & L Building Materials Inc ....C 610 644-6311
Malvern **(G-10257)**

CONSTRUCTION MATERIALS, WHOLESALE: Roofing & Siding Material

Slate and Copper Sales Co ....F 814 455-7430
Erie **(G-5481)**

CONSTRUCTION MATERIALS, WHOLESALE: Sand

Donaldson Supply & Eqp Co ....F 724 745-5250
Canonsburg **(G-2579)**
East Loop Sand Company Inc ....F 814 695-3082
Hollidaysburg **(G-7646)**
Eureka Stone Quarry Inc ....E 215 822-0593
Chalfont **(G-2874)**
Glen Mills Sand & Gravel Inc ....E 610 459-4988
Media **(G-10929)**
J A & W A Hess Inc ....E 570 454-3731
Hazleton **(G-7504)**
Limestone Products & Supply Co.........G 412 221-5120
Bridgeville **(G-2077)**
Martin Marietta Materials Inc................F 724 573-9518
Georgetown **(G-6277)**

PRODUCT

Meadville Redi-Mix Concrete ....G....... 814 734-1644
Edinboro (G-4816)
R W Sidley Inc ....E....... 724 794-4451
Slippery Rock (G-17625)
Waterford Sand & Gravel Co...............E....... 814 796-6250
Union City (G-18613)

CONSTRUCTION MATERIALS, WHOLESALE: Septic Tanks

American Tank & Concrete Svc.............F....... 724 837-4410
Greensburg (G-6650)
Blank Concrete and Supply ....F....... 724 758-7596
Ellwood City (G-4928)
Lisa Little Inc ....G....... 814 697-7500
Shinglehouse (G-17509)
Lycoming Burial Vault Co Inc ....F....... 570 368-8642
Montoursville (G-11446)
Pipe & Precast Cnstr Pdts Inc ....F....... 610 644-7338
Devault (G-4112)
William Elston Incorporated ....F....... 570 689-2203
Jefferson Township (G-8280)

CONSTRUCTION MATERIALS, WHOLESALE: Siding, Exc Wood

Muldoon Window Door & Awning ....G....... 570 347-9453
Scranton (G-17261)

CONSTRUCTION MATERIALS, WHOLESALE: Stone, Crushed Or Broken

Coolspring Stone Supply Inc.................G....... 724 437-5200
Uniontown (G-18622)
Dyer Quarry Inc ....E....... 610 582-6010
Birdsboro (G-1693)
Eureka Stone Quarry Inc ....E....... 570 992-4210
Stroudsburg (G-18116)
Eureka Stone Quarry Inc ....G....... 570 689-2901
Sterling (G-18049)
Glasgow Inc ....E....... 610 279-6840
King of Prussia (G-8620)
Glenn O Hawbaker Inc ....E....... 814 359-3411
Pleasant Gap (G-15792)
Highway Materials Inc ....F....... 610 832-8000
Flourtown (G-5987)
Highway Materials Inc ....E....... 215 234-4522
Perkiomenville (G-13301)
Kimmels Coal and Packaging Inc.........E....... 717 453-7151
Wiconisco (G-19895)
New Enterprise Stone Lime Inc ....G....... 610 683-3302
East Earl (G-4551)
Tms International LLC ....F....... 724 929-4515
Belle Vernon (G-1088)
Tms International LLC ....F....... 814 535-5081
Johnstown (G-8439)
Valley Quarries Inc ....G....... 814 766-2211
Fayetteville (G-5879)
Williams & Sons Slate & Tile.................E....... 610 863-4161
Wind Gap (G-20175)

CONSTRUCTION MATERIALS, WHOLESALE: Stucco

Essroc Cement.................................G....... 610 882-2498
Bethlehem (G-1504)

CONSTRUCTION MATERIALS, WHOLESALE: Tile & Clay Prdts

Robin Morris....................................G....... 814 395-9555
Confluence (G-3469)

CONSTRUCTION MATERIALS, WHOLESALE: Tile, Clay/Other Ceramic

Brian Giniewski LLC ....G....... 610 858-2821
Philadelphia (G-13479)
Ross Mould LLC................................C....... 724 222-7006
Washington (G-19222)

CONSTRUCTION MATERIALS, WHOLESALE: Trim, Sheet Metal

Raytec LLC ....E....... 717 445-0510
Ephrata (G-5138)

CONSTRUCTION MATERIALS, WHOLESALE: Veneer

David R Webb Company Inc ....C....... 570 322-7186
Williamsport (G-20003)
Interforest Corp ....D....... 724 827-8366
Darlington (G-4029)

CONSTRUCTION MATERIALS, WHOLESALE: Windows

J & L Building Materials Inc ....C....... 610 644-6311
Malvern (G-10257)

CONSTRUCTION MATLS, WHOL: Composite Board Prdts, Woodboard

Interntional Timber Veneer LLC...........C....... 724 662-0880
Jackson Center (G-8228)

CONSTRUCTION MATLS, WHOL: Lumber, Rough, Dressed/Finished

Bailey Wood Products Inc.....................G....... 610 756-6827
Kempton (G-8490)
Bingaman & Son Lumber Inc.................E....... 814 723-2612
Clarendon (G-3167)
Cameron Lumber LLP ....E....... 814 749-9635
Homer City (G-7671)
Collins Pine Company ....D....... 814 837-6941
Kane (G-8461)
Deer Park Lumber Inc.........................D....... 570 836-1133
Tunkhannock (G-18538)
Diamond Road Resawing LLC...............G....... 717 738-3741
Ephrata (G-5100)
Dwight Lewis Lumber Co Inc................E....... 570 924-3507
Hillsgrove (G-7635)
Highland Forest Resources Inc ....E....... 814 837-6760
Kane (G-8466)
Holt and Bugbee Company ....E....... 724 277-8510
Mount Braddock (G-11619)
Hoover Treated Wood Pdts Inc.............G....... 800 220-6046
Oxford (G-13081)
Itl Corp ....D....... 814 463-7701
Endeavor (G-5079)
Keslar Lumber Co ....E....... 724 455-3210
White (G-19845)
L & R Lumber Inc ....G....... 717 463-3411
Mc Alisterville (G-10550)
Leonard Forest Products ....F....... 724 329-4703
Markleysburg (G-10481)
Mount Hope Lumber ....G....... 814 789-4953
Guys Mills (G-6811)
Moxham Lumber Co ....E....... 814 536-5186
Johnstown (G-8411)
New Enterprise Stone Lime Inc ....B....... 610 374-5131
Leesport (G-9668)
Noll Pallet Inc ....E....... 610 926-2500
Leesport (G-9671)
Penn-Sylvan International Inc................F....... 814 654-7111
Spartansburg (G-17853)
Price C L Lumber LLC ....F....... 814 349-5505
Aaronsburg (G-2)
R & R Wood Products Inc ....E....... 215 723-3470
Mainland (G-10175)
Robert P Williams ....G....... 814 563-7660
Youngsville (G-20775)
Silhol Builders Supply Co Inc...............E....... 412 221-7400
Bridgeville (G-2089)
Z Wood Products Co Inc ....E....... 215 423-9891
Philadelphia (G-14503)

CONSTRUCTION MATLS, WHOLESALE: Soil Erosion Cntrl Fabrics

Johnston-Morehouse-Dickey Co...........E....... 412 833-7100
Bethel Park (G-1421)
Johnston-Morehouse-Dickey Co...........G....... 814 684-0916
Tyrone (G-18584)

CONSTRUCTION MATLS, WHOLESALE: Struct Assy, Prefab, NonWood

Choice Granite and Marble LLC ....G....... 412 821-3900
Pittsburgh (G-14848)

CONSTRUCTION MTRLS, WHOL: Exterior Flat Glass, Plate/Window

Trulite GL Alum Solutions LLC..............D....... 570 282-6711
Carbondale (G-2687)

CONSTRUCTION MTRLS, WHOL: Interior Flat Glass, Plate/Window

Warner-Crivellaro Stained Glas ....F....... 610 264-1100
Whitehall (G-19893)

CONSTRUCTION SAND MINING

C & M Aggregate Company Inc ....E....... 724 796-3821
Bulger (G-2342)
Earl F Dean Inc.................................G....... 814 435-6581
Galeton (G-6239)
Eastern Industries Inc ....E....... 570 265-9191
Towanda (G-18425)
H & H Materials Inc ....E....... 724 376-2834
Stoneboro (G-18069)
Hempt Bros Inc ....G....... 717 486-5111
Gardners (G-6260)
Hempt Bros Inc ....D....... 717 774-2911
Camp Hill (G-2500)
Lakeland Sand & Gravel Inc.................E....... 724 588-7020
Conneaut Lake (G-3475)
Pennsy Supply Inc............................F....... 717 486-5414
Mount Holly Springs (G-11638)
York Building Products Co Inc ....E....... 717 848-2831
York (G-20726)

CONSTRUCTION SITE PREPARATION SVCS

Charlies Tree Service..........................G....... 814 943-1131
Altoona (G-491)
New Growth Resources Inc ....G....... 814 837-2206
Kane (G-8473)
Thomas Timberland Enterprises.........G....... 814 359-2890
Bellefonte (G-1122)
W D Zwicky & Son Inc ....E....... 484 248-5300
Fleetwood (G-5982)

CONSTRUCTION: Agricultural Building

Sky Point Crane LLC ....G....... 724 471-5710
Indiana (G-8129)

CONSTRUCTION: Athletic & Recreation Facilities

Everything Ice Inc ....E....... 814 244-5477
Salix (G-17047)

CONSTRUCTION: Athletic & Recreation Facilities

Blue Sky International Inc ....G....... 610 306-1234
Phoenixville (G-14534)

CONSTRUCTION: Bridge

Glenn O Hawbaker Inc ....D....... 814 237-1444
State College (G-17970)
IA Construction Corporation ....E....... 814 432-3184
Franklin (G-6136)
Interlocking Deck Systems Inte............D....... 412 682-3041
Sewickley (G-17395)
Wolyniec Construction Inc....................E....... 570 322-8634
Williamsport (G-20097)

CONSTRUCTION: Commercial & Institutional Building

Century Buildings..............................G....... 814 336-1446
Saegertown (G-16910)
Farmer Boy Ag Inc ....D....... 717 866-7565
Myerstown (G-11885)
George Skebeck................................G....... 814 674-8169
Patton (G-13188)
High Steel Structures LLC ....G....... 717 299-5211
Lancaster (G-9049)
Maple Mountain Industries Inc ....E....... 724 676-4703
New Florence (G-12198)
Service Construction Co Inc.................F....... 610 377-2111
Lehighton (G-9727)
Zooks Woodworking............................G....... 570 758-3579
Dornsife (G-4165)

CONSTRUCTION: Commercial & Office Building, New

Ames Construction Inc........................E...... 717 299-1395
Lancaster *(G-8932)*

Aurora Electrical & Data Svcs ....G...... 412 255-4060
Pittsburgh *(G-14739)*

Dectile Harkus Construction..............E...... 724 789-7125
Butler *(G-2393)* .

Elvin B Zimmerman ....G...... 717 656-9327
Leola *(G-9780)*

Giffin Interior & Fixture Inc ....C...... 412 221-1166
Bridgeville *(G-2066)*

Kapanick Construction Inc ....F...... 814 763-3681
Meadville *(G-10742)*

Specialty Retail Fabricators................F...... 215 477-5977
Philadelphia *(G-14332)*

CONSTRUCTION: Dams, Waterways, Docks & Other Marine

S & G Water Conditioning Inc ....G...... 215 672-2030
Warminster *(G-18957)*

CONSTRUCTION: Drainage System

R PS Machinery Sales Inc ....E...... 570 398-7456
Jersey Shore *(G-8322)*

CONSTRUCTION: Electric Power Line

Kozik Bros Inc....................................E...... 724 443-2230
Cranberry Township *(G-3829)*

CONSTRUCTION: Farm Building

Allensville Planing Mill Inc ....F...... 717 543-4954
Huntingdon *(G-7938)*

CONSTRUCTION: Foundation & Retaining Wall

Mountain-Valley Services LLC...............G...... 814 594-3167
Ridgway *(G-16718)*

Redstone International Inc....................D...... 724 439-1500
Scenery Hill *(G-17125)*

Superior Walls of Colorado..................F...... 412 664-7788
Glassport *(G-6417)*

CONSTRUCTION: Guardrails, Highway

Reh Holdings Inc................................G...... 717 843-0021
York *(G-20657)*

CONSTRUCTION: Heavy Highway & Street

Dean Construction LLC.........................G...... 814 887-8750
Smethport *(G-17634)*

Eastern Industries Inc ....E...... 570 524-2251
Winfield *(G-20199)*

Ganoe Paving Inc................................E...... 717 597-2567
Greencastle *(G-6613)*

Glenn O Hawbaker Inc..........................E...... 814 359-3411
Pleasant Gap *(G-15792)*

Keystone Lime Company ....E...... 814 662-2025
Springs *(G-17925)*

New Enterprise Stone Lime Inc ....E...... 610 678-1913
Reading *(G-16454)*

New Enterprise Stone Lime Inc ....G...... 610 678-1913
Leesport *(G-9669)*

Structural Services Inc........................G...... 610 282-5810
Coopersburg *(G-3636)*

Valley Quarries Inc.............................F...... 717 267-2244
Chambersburg *(G-2994)*

CONSTRUCTION: Indl Building & Warehouse

Atc Technology Corporation..................E...... 412 820-3700
Cranberry Township *(G-3806)*

High Steel Structures LLC ....G...... 717 299-5211
Lancaster *(G-9049)*

JGM Welding & Fabg Svcs Inc ....D...... 610 873-0081
Coatesville *(G-3310)*

Noise Solutions (usa) Inc.....................E...... 724 308-6901
Sharon *(G-17441)*

CONSTRUCTION: Indl Building, Prefabricated

Poly-Growers Inc ....F...... 570 546-3216
Muncy *(G-11831)*

Reynolds Sales Co Inc ....G...... 412 461-7877
Homestead *(G-7692)*

CONSTRUCTION: Indl Buildings, New, NEC

General Civil Company Inc ....F...... 484 571-1998
Aston *(G-767)*

JGM Fabricators & Constrs LLC ....D...... 484 698-6201
Coatesville *(G-3309)*

Oxford Construction PA Inc ....D...... 215 809-2245
Philadelphia *(G-14106)*

Rtb Products Inc ....F...... 724 861-2080
Irwin *(G-8198)*

T Bruce Campbell Cnstr Co Inc.............C...... 724 528-9944
West Middlesex *(G-19730)*

CONSTRUCTION: Indl Plant

C L I Corporation...............................G...... 724 348-4800
Finleyville *(G-5952)*

CONSTRUCTION: Irrigation System

Thermigate LLC...................................G...... 610 931-1023
Lansdowne *(G-9445)*

CONSTRUCTION: Land Preparation

Accurate Logging LLC..........................G...... 724 354-3094
Creekside *(G-3874)*

Dean Construction LLC.........................G...... 814 887-8750
Smethport *(G-17634)*

CONSTRUCTION: Manhole

Altomare Precast Inc ....F...... 215 225-8800
Philadelphia *(G-13373)*

CONSTRUCTION: Marine

Blank River Services Inc ....E...... 412 384-2489
Elizabeth *(G-4857)*

CONSTRUCTION: Mausoleum

Earl Wenz Inc.....................................F...... 610 395-2331
Breinigsville *(G-2014)*

Matthews International Corp..................E...... 412 442-8200
Pittsburgh *(G-15264)*

CONSTRUCTION: Natural Gas Compressor Station

Appellation Cnstr Svcs LLC..................D...... 570 601-4765
Montoursville *(G-11431)*

Bethlehem Hydrogen Inc........................G...... 610 762-1706
Northampton *(G-12845)*

CONSTRUCTION: Nonresidential Buildings, Custom

Greentree Lumber................................F...... 814 257-9878
Smicksburg *(G-17638)*

Somerset Enterprises Inc......................F...... 724 734-9497
Farrell *(G-5874)*

CONSTRUCTION: Oil & Gas Pipeline Construction

Clipper Pipe & Service Inc ....G...... 610 872-9067
Eddystone *(G-4799)*

Rettew Field Services Inc ....E...... 717 697-3551
Lancaster *(G-9187)*

CONSTRUCTION: Parking Lot

Hri Inc..D...... 570 322-6737
Muncy *(G-11821)*

New Enterprise Stone Lime Inc ....G...... 610 678-1913
Leesport *(G-9669)*

CONSTRUCTION: Pipeline, NEC

Elite Midstream Services Inc ....E...... 412 220-3082
Cuddy *(G-3943)*

Flexsteel Pipeline Tech Inc ....G...... 570 505-3491
Montoursville *(G-11439)*

Michels Corporation ....G...... 724 249-2065
Washington *(G-19202)*

CONSTRUCTION: Power & Communication Transmission Tower

Oxford Construction PA Inc ....D...... 215 809-2245
Philadelphia *(G-14106)*

CONSTRUCTION: Railroad & Subway

Tangent Rail Corporation ....G...... 412 325-0202
Pittsburgh *(G-15596)*

CONSTRUCTION: Refineries

Michels Corporation ....G...... 724 249-2065
Washington *(G-19202)*

CONSTRUCTION: Residential, Nec

Gardner S Construction........................G...... 610 395-6614
Macungie *(G-10146)*

George Skebeck..................................G...... 814 674-8169
Patton *(G-13188)*

Stephens Excavating Svc LLC ....G...... 484 888-1010
Kennett Square *(G-8545)*

CONSTRUCTION: Roads, Gravel or Dirt

Streamline Energy Services LLC...........F...... 610 415-1220
Valley Forge *(G-18715)*

CONSTRUCTION: School Building

Schalow Visual Concepts Inc ....G...... 570 336-2714
Benton *(G-1282)*

CONSTRUCTION: Sewer Line

Ursa Mjor Drctnal Crssings LLC...........F...... 866 410-9719
Greentown *(G-6735)*

Wolyniec Construction Inc.....................E...... 570 322-8634
Williamsport *(G-20097)*

CONSTRUCTION: Single-Family Housing

Allensville Planing Mill Inc ....F...... 717 248-9688
Lewistown *(G-9924)*

Custom Stair Builders Inc ....G...... 717 261-0551
Chambersburg *(G-2922)*

Guyers Superior Walls ....C...... 814 725-8575
North East *(G-12745)*

JE Lyons Construction Inc ....G...... 724 686-3967
Latrobe *(G-9483)*

Milton Home Systems Inc ....D...... 800 533-4402
Milton *(G-11249)*

Penn State Cnstr J&D LLC ....G...... 717 953-9200
Lewistown *(G-9943)*

Peyty Construction ....G...... 570 764-5995
Bloomsburg *(G-1793)*

Professional Bldg Systems Inc ....C...... 570 837-1424
Middleburg *(G-11036)*

Sky Point Crane LLC.............................G...... 724 471-5710
Indiana *(G-8129)*

CONSTRUCTION: Single-family Housing, New

Cedar Forest Products Company...........F...... 815 946-3994
Media *(G-10917)*

Elc Manufacturing...............................G...... 570 655-3060
West Pittston *(G-19755)*

G and H Contracting Inc........................G...... 610 826-7542
Palmerton *(G-13106)*

Greg Kline...G...... 610 367-4060
Boyertown *(G-1914)*

Kapanick Construction Inc ....F...... 814 763-3681
Meadville *(G-10742)*

Maple Mountain Industries Inc ....E...... 724 676-4703
New Florence *(G-12198)*

Morey General Contracting ....G...... 570 759-2021
Berwick *(G-1336)*

Priest Enterprises ....G...... 724 658-7692
Grove City *(G-6802)*

Service Construction Co Inc..................F...... 610 377-2111
Lehighton *(G-9727)*

CONSTRUCTION: Stadium

Robo Construction LLC ....E...... 570 494-1028
Williamsport *(G-20069)*

CONSTRUCTION: Steel Buildings

Rizzo & Sons Industrial Svc Co............E...... 814 948-5381
Pittsburgh *(G-15489)*

Robo Construction LLC ....E....... 570 494-1028
Williamsport (G-20069)

Scenic Ridge Company ....D....... 717 768-7522
Gordonville (G-6564)

CONSTRUCTION: Street Surfacing & Paving

Bituminous Pav Mtls York Inc................G....... 717 632-8919
Hanover (G-6863)

Glen Blooming Contractors Inc............C....... 717 566-3711
Hummelstown (G-7912)

H&K Group Inc ....G....... 610 584-8500
Skippack (G-17597)

Mukies/Mccarty Seal Coating C..........G....... 717 684-2799
Columbia (G-3444)

Russell Standard Corporation ....E....... 724 625-1505
Valencia (G-18701)

Tresco Paving Corporation ....G....... 412 793-0651
Pittsburgh (G-15643)

CONSTRUCTION: Svc Station

Richard J Clickett Inc ....E....... 814 827-7548
Titusville (G-18391)

CONSTRUCTION: Transmitting Tower, Telecommunication

Lee Antenna & Line Service Inc ....F....... 610 346-7999
Springtown (G-17927)

CONSTRUCTION: Truck & Automobile Assembly Plant

Carriers Wreckers By Kimes.................G....... 724 342-2930
Mercer (G-10960)

CONSTRUCTION: Utility Line

A D M Welding & Fabrication ....G....... 814 723-7227
Warren (G-19007)

Protechs LLC ....G....... 717 768-0800
New Holland (G-12273)

S & S Sbsrface Invstgtions Inc ....G....... 610 738-8762
West Chester (G-19634)

Sunbelt Drilling Services Inc ....F....... 215 764-9544
Blue Bell (G-1853)

CONSTRUCTION: Waste Disposal Plant

Tms International Corp..........................E....... 215 956-5500
Horsham (G-7860)

CONSTRUCTION: Water & Sewer Line

Resolve Trnchless Slutions Inc............G....... 215 441-5544
Warminster (G-18953)

CONSTRUCTION: Water Main

IA Construction Corporation ....E....... 814 432-3184
Franklin (G-6136)

CONSULTING SVC: Business, NEC

25 Fathoms International Inc ....G....... 610 558-1101
Glen Mills (G-6428)

9dots Management Corp LLC ....E....... 610 825-2027
Conshohocken (G-3514)

A Tru Diva LLC ....G....... 888 400-1034
Brookhaven (G-2241)

Aberdeen Road Company ....D....... 717 764-1192
Emigsville (G-4983)

Aradiant Corporation............................G....... 717 838-7220
Palmyra (G-13116)

Design Space Inpharmatics LLC ....G....... 215 272-4275
Green Lane (G-6587)

First Quality Products Inc ....B....... 610 265-5000
King of Prussia (G-8618)

Healing Environments Intl Inc ....G....... 215 758-2107
Philadelphia (G-13808)

Icon Marketing LLC.............................G....... 610 356-4050
Broomall (G-2289)

Industrial Controls Inc.........................G....... 717 697-7555
Mechanicsburg (G-10858)

Inframark LLC.......................................E....... 215 646-9201
Horsham (G-7823)

Innovate Software Inc ....G....... 724 935-1790
Bradfordwoods (G-1998)

J G Press Inc ....G....... 610 967-4135
Emmaus (G-5029)

Joseph Nedorezov ....G....... 215 661-0600
North Wales (G-12808)

Joseph Nedorezov ....G....... 610 278-9325
Blue Bell (G-1837)

Media Management Services Inc..........E....... 800 523-5948
Newtown (G-12521)

Mesta Electronics Inc ....F....... 412 754-3000
Irwin (G-8182)

Morantz Inc ....G....... 215 969-0266
Philadelphia (G-14038)

Multimedia Training Systems ....G....... 412 341-2185
Pittsburgh (G-15308)

Process Sltions Consulting Inc ....G....... 610 248-2002
New Tripoli (G-12460)

Ron Lee Inc ....F....... 570 784-6020
Bloomsburg (G-1799)

Spyware ....F....... 215 444-0405
Warminster (G-18973)

Staneco Corporation ....E....... 215 672-6500
Horsham (G-7852)

Synergy Health Systems Inc ....E....... 570 473-7506
Northumberland (G-12877)

Tip Top Resources LLC ....G....... 407 818-6937
Reedsville (G-16628)

Trillion Source Inc................................F....... 631 949-2304
Emmaus (G-5045)

Wolters Kluwer Health Inc...................C....... 215 521-8300
Philadelphia (G-14482)

CONSULTING SVC: Chemical

PRI International Inc ....G....... 610 436-8292
West Chester (G-19619)

CONSULTING SVC: Computer

Advanced Technical Peddler Inc ....G....... 610 689-4017
Boyertown (G-1893)

Aserdiv Inc..E....... 800 966-7770
Springfield (G-17907)

Automatic Forecasting Systems ....F....... 215 675-0652
Warminster (G-18832)

Business Planning Inc..........................G....... 610 649-0550
Ardmore (G-703)

Compudata Inc ....E....... 215 969-1000
Philadelphia (G-13566)

Computertalk Associates Inc...............G....... 610 825-7686
Blue Bell (G-1823)

Fis Avantgard LLC ....E....... 800 468-7483
Wayne (G-19329)

Fry International LLC............................G....... 215 847-6359
Elkins Park (G-4903)

Grammaton Research LLC.....................G....... 410 703-9237
York (G-20513)

Kenexa Learning Inc.............................E....... 610 971-9171
Wayne (G-19346)

Keystone Sftwr Solutions Inc ....G....... 610 685-2111
Reading (G-16421)

Mtekka LLC...G....... 610 619-3555
Kennett Square (G-8532)

Proportal LLC ....G....... 215 923-7100
Philadelphia (G-14210)

Ram Technologies Inc ....E....... 215 654-8810
Fort Washington (G-6089)

Reclamere Inc.......................................E....... 814 684-5505
Tyrone (G-18592)

Runwell Solutions Inc ....F....... 610 376-7773
Reading (G-16506)

Sicom Systems Inc ....D....... 215 489-2500
Lansdale (G-9410)

Titan Technologies Inc ....G....... 888 671-6649
Pittsburgh (G-15626)

Valira LLC ....G....... 973 216-5803
Conshohocken (G-3615)

Veeva Systems Inc...............................G....... 215 422-3356
Fort Washington (G-6095)

CONSULTING SVC: Educational

Organization Design & Dev Inc.............E....... 610 279-2202
West Chester (G-19612)

CONSULTING SVC: Engineering

Advanced Integration Group Inc ....E....... 412 722-0065
Mc Kees Rocks (G-10602)

Advent Design Corporation ....C....... 215 781-0500
Bristol (G-2104)

American Engineers Group LLC ....G....... 484 920-8010
Phoenixville (G-14527)

Beaumont Development LLC..................F....... 814 899-6390
Erie (G-5207)

Carpenter Engineering Inc....................G....... 717 274-8808
Lebanon (G-9553)

Consyst Inc...G....... 610 398-0752
Orefield (G-13010)

D & B Services Inc ....F....... 610 381-2848
Kunkletown (G-8832)

De Technologies Inc ....E....... 610 337-2800
King of Prussia (G-8605)

Dyna East Corporation ....E....... 610 270-9900
King of Prussia (G-8614)

Erie Technical Systems Inc ....G....... 814 899-2103
Erie (G-5276)

Gesco Inc..F....... 724 846-8700
Beaver Falls (G-999)

Kcf Technologies Inc.............................F....... 814 867-4097
State College (G-17983)

Kyron Naval Architecture ....G....... 516 304-1769
Bensalem (G-1217)

Laessig Associates...............................G....... 610 353-3543
Newtown Square (G-12581)

Lawrie Technology Inc ....G....... 814 402-1208
Girard (G-6396)

LSI Controls Inc ....G....... 717 762-2191
Waynesboro (G-19415)

Metvac Inc..G....... 215 541-4495
Hereford (G-7568)

Nacah Tech LLC ....G....... 412 833-0687
Pittsburgh (G-15316)

Northeimer Manufacturing ....E....... 610 926-1136
Leesport (G-9672)

Nuwave Technologies Inc ....G....... 610 584-8428
Norristown (G-12695)

Optima Technology Assoc Inc..............D....... 717 932-5877
Lewisberry (G-9889)

Polymer Instrumentation & C ....E....... 814 357-5860
State College (G-18007)

Rail Transit Products Inc......................G....... 724 527-2386
Penn (G-13227)

Technical Process & Engrg Inc ....E....... 570 386-4777
Lehighton (G-9730)

Texan Corporation ....E....... 215 441-8967
Warminster (G-18979)

Tritech Applied Sciences Inc ....G....... 215 362-6890
Lansdale (G-9417)

Volian Enterprises Inc ....F....... 724 335-3744
New Kensington (G-12388)

CONSULTING SVC: Executive Placement & Search

Graphic Search Associates ....G....... 610 344-0644
Glen Mills (G-6438)

Molloy Associates Inc ....E....... 610 293-1300
Bryn Mawr (G-2330)

CONSULTING SVC: Financial Management

Galeron Consulting LLC........................E....... 267 293-9230
Bensalem (G-1202)

CONSULTING SVC: Management

Ajax Electric Company ....E....... 215 947-8500
Huntingdon Valley (G-7962)

Chemical Equipment Labs VA Inc ....E....... 610 497-9390
Newtown Square (G-12570)

Corrugated Services Corp ....D....... 215 639-9540
Fort Washington (G-6067)

Electronic Tech Systems Inc ....D....... 724 295-6000
Natrona Heights (G-11942)

Great Oak Energy Inc ....G....... 412 828-2900
Oakmont (G-12918)

Hds Marketing Inc.................................E....... 412 279-1600
Pittsburgh (G-15084)

Jerry James Trdng As Mnls BSC...........G....... 425 255-0199
Lafayette Hill (G-8882)

Kuper Technologies LLC........................G....... 610 358-5120
Garnet Valley (G-6266)

Markowski International Pubg ....G....... 717 566-0468
Hummelstown (G-7917)

Media Management Services Inc...........E....... 800 523-5948
Newtown (G-12521)

Noel Interactive Group LLC ....G....... 732 991-1484
Easton (G-4732)

Redstone Corporation ....G....... 321 213-2135
Johnstown (G-8429)

Sid Global Solutions LLC ....G....... 484 218-0021
Exton (G-5733)

Smartops Corporation...........................E....... 412 231-0115
Pittsburgh (G-15548)

Steel Consulting Services LLC..............G....... 412 727-6645
Pittsburgh (G-15580)

Synchrgnix Info Strategies Inc ....G....... 302 892-4800
Malvern (G-10325)

Trinity Partners LLC ....F 610 233-1210
East Norriton (G-4585)
Virtix Consulting LLC ....G...... 412 440-4835
Wexford (G-19832)
Ygs Group Inc ....D...... 717 505-9701
York (G-20723)

CONSULTING SVC: Marketing Management

Alpha Advertising & Mktg LLC ....G...... 717 445-4200
Bowmansville (G-1886)
Altris Incorporated ....G...... 724 259-8338
Greensburg (G-6649)
Artskills Inc ....E...... 610 253-6663
Bethlehem (G-1453)
Atlantic Alliance Pubg Co ....G...... 267 319-1659
Philadelphia (G-13421)
Berm Studios Incorporated ....D...... 610 622-2100
Garnet Valley (G-6265)
Chelsea Partners Inc ....E...... 215 603-7300
Philadelphia (G-13537)
Creative Characters ....G...... 215 923-2679
Philadelphia (G-13578)
Creative Labworks Inc ....G...... 724 667-4093
Bessemer (G-1390)
Electronic Imaging Svcs Inc ....G...... 215 785-2284
Bristol (G-2139)
Ernie Saxton ....G...... 215 752-7797
Langhorne (G-9294)
Gibson Graphics Group Inc ....G...... 717 755-7192
Hellam (G-7550)
Ker Communications ....G...... 412 310-1973
Pittsburgh (G-15172)
Me Ken + Jen Crative Svcs LLC ....G...... 215 997-2355
Chalfont (G-2883)
Nth Solutions LLC ....G...... 610 594-2191
Exton (G-5715)
Premier Graphics LLC ....F...... 814 894-2467
Sykesville (G-18202)
Printing Consulting Inc ....G...... 610 933-9311
Phoenixville (G-14571)
Quigley Nutraceuticals LLC ....F...... 646 499-5100
Exton (G-5725)
Union Packaging LLC ....D...... 610 572-7265
Yeadon (G-20356)
Victory Media Inc ....G...... 412 269-1663
Coraopolis (G-3731)

CONSULTING SVC: Online Technology

Forallsecure Inc ....F...... 412 256-8809
Pittsburgh (G-15024)
Ker Communications ....G...... 412 310-1973
Pittsburgh (G-15172)
Lunacor Inc ....G...... 610 328-6150
Springfield (G-17917)
Medshifts Inc ....G...... 856 834-0074
Philadelphia (G-14006)
Nzinganet Inc ....G...... 877 709-6459
Fort Washington (G-6087)
TApp Technology LLC ....G...... 800 288-3184
Ardmore (G-721)
Web Age Solutions Inc ....E...... 215 517-6540
Jenkintown (G-8304)
Weidenhammer Systems Corp ....E...... 610 687-0037
Blue Bell (G-1857)

CONSULTING SVC: Sales Management

Handling Products Inc ....G...... 724 443-1100
Gibsonia (G-6339)
Icon Marketing LLC ....G...... 610 356-4050
Broomall (G-2289)
Wm Industries Inc ....G...... 215 822-2525
Colmar (G-3423)

CONSULTING SVC: Telecommunications

Electronic Concepts Inc ....G...... 717 235-9450
New Freedom (G-12207)
Fusion Five USA LLC ....G...... 267 507-6127
Philadelphia (G-13735)
Mashan Inc ....G...... 724 397-4008
Home (G-7669)
Wirecard North America Inc ....D...... 610 234-4410
Conshohocken (G-3617)

CONSULTING SVCS, BUSINESS: Environmental

Akj Industries Inc ....G...... 412 233-7222
Clairton (G-3146)

American Engineers Group LLC ....G...... 484 920-8010
Phoenixville (G-14527)
Busch Company...........................F...... 724 940-2326
Wexford (G-19832)
Cardinal Resources Inc ....G...... 412 374-0989
Pittsburgh (G-14809)
Gaadt Perspectives LLC ....G...... 610 388-7641
Chadds Ford (G-2851)
Hazardous Materials Mgt Team ....G...... 215 968-4044
Newtown (G-12507)

CONSULTING SVCS, BUSINESS: Indl Development Planning

Kyron Naval Architecture ....G...... 516 304-1769
Bensalem (G-1217)

CONSULTING SVCS, BUSINESS: Lighting

Lumenoptix LLC........................E...... 215 671-2029
Montgomeryville (G-11405)

CONSULTING SVCS, BUSINESS: Publishing

Bucks County Type & Design Inc ....F...... 215 579-4200
Newtown (G-12499)
D Dietrich Associates Inc ....G...... 215 258-1071
Sellersville (G-17342)
Direct Marketing Publishers ....G...... 215 321-3068
Yardley (G-20308)
Galeron Consulting LLC................E...... 267 293-9230
Bensalem (G-1202)
On Line Publishers Inc ....G...... 717 285-1350
Columbia (G-3445)

CONSULTING SVCS, BUSINESS: Safety Training Svcs

Alpha Safety USA......................G...... 814 236-3344
Clearfield (G-3211)
ARC Rmediation Specialists Inc...........F...... 386 405-6760
Bristol (G-2108)
Ashland Industrial Svcs LLC ....G...... 717 347-5616
Shrewsbury (G-17581)
Interntnal Def Systems USA LLC ....G...... 610 973-2228
Orefield (G-13012)
Tripwire Operations Group LLC ....G...... 717 648-2792
Gettysburg (G-6319)

CONSULTING SVCS, BUSINESS: Sys Engnrg, Exc Computer/Prof

Chant Engineering Co Inc ....E...... 215 230-4260
New Britain (G-12045)
Habsco Inc............................G...... 724 337-9498
New Kensington (G-12345)
Robar Industries Inc ....G...... 484 688-0300
Plymouth Meeting (G-15868)
Virtix Consulting LLC ....G...... 412 440-4835
Wexford (G-19832)

CONSULTING SVCS, BUSINESS: Systems Analysis & Engineering

Evans Commercial Services LLC ....F...... 412 573-9442
Bridgeville (G-2061)
Medchive LLC..........................G...... 215 688-7475
Philadelphia (G-14004)
Moberg Research Inc ....F...... 215 283-0860
Ambler (G-591)
Valira LLC ....G...... 973 216-5803
Conshohocken (G-3615)

CONSULTING SVCS, BUSINESS: Systems Analysis Or Design

ADS LLC ....G...... 717 554-7552
Lemoyne (G-9740)

CONSULTING SVCS, BUSINESS: Testing, Educational Or Personnel

It Takes A Village To Feed ....G...... 888 702-9610
Ridley Park (G-16739)

CONSULTING SVCS, BUSINESS: Traffic

Clark Traffic Control Inc ....F...... 724 388-4023
Homer City (G-7674)

CONSULTING SVCS: Geological

Geosonics Inc ....F...... 724 934-2900
Warrendale (G-19076)

CONSULTING SVCS: Nuclear

Custom Nuclear Fabrication LLC ....G...... 724 271-3006
Canonsburg (G-2575)

CONSULTING SVCS: Oil

Alma Gas Inc ....G...... 814 225-3480
Eldred (G-4852)
Henderson Resource Group LLC ....G...... 814 203-3226
Hazel Hurst (G-7445)
Roach & Associates Inc ....G...... 412 344-9310
Pittsburgh (G-15491)
Subterranean Tech Inc ....G...... 610 517-0995
West Chester (G-19647)
Willow Terrace ....G...... 215 951-8500
Philadelphia (G-14478)

CONSULTING SVCS: Scientific

Integrated Tech Svcs Intl LLC...........F...... 814 262-7332
Johnstown (G-8382)

CONSUMER ELECTRONICS STORE: Video & Disc Recorder/Player

Venus Video............................G...... 215 937-1545
Philadelphia (G-14440)

CONTACT LENSES

Lancaster Contact Lens Inc ....G...... 717 569-7386
Lancaster (G-9092)
Leechburg Contact Lens Lab ....G...... 724 845-7777
Leechburg (G-9648)

CONTACTS: Electrical

Checon Powder Met Contacts LLC ....G...... 814 753-4466
Kersey (G-8554)
Contact Technologies Inc ....C...... 814 834-9000
Saint Marys (G-16957)
Metalor Electronics USA Corp ....C...... 724 733-8332
Export (G-5618)
Precision Fbrction Contrls Inc...........E...... 814 368-7320
Bradford (G-1987)

CONTAINERS, GLASS: Food

Mason Jars Company...................F...... 877 490-5565
Erie (G-5381)

CONTAINERS, GLASS: Medicine Bottles

Homeopathic Natural Healing...........G...... 412 646-4151
Monroeville (G-11340)
Ompi of America Inc ....G...... 267 757-8747
Newtown (G-12531)

CONTAINERS, GLASS: Packers' Ware

Owens-Brockway Glass Cont Inc...........C...... 814 226-0500
Clarion (G-3185)

CONTAINERS, GLASS: Water Bottles

Kelman Holdings Llc ....G...... 412 486-9100
Glenshaw (G-6493)

CONTAINERS: Air Cargo, Metal

F & R Cargo Express LLC ....G...... 610 351-9200
Allentown (G-211)

CONTAINERS: Cargo, Wood

Sheffield Container Corp...............E...... 814 968-3287
Sheffield (G-17483)

CONTAINERS: Corrugated

Achieva................................F...... 412 391-4660
Pittsburgh (G-14641)
Achieva................................D...... 412 995-5000
Pittsburgh (G-14640)
Cor-Rite Inc ....F...... 570 287-1718
Swoyersville (G-18196)
Corrugated Specialties ....F...... 814 337-5705
Meadville (G-10715)

PRODUCT

Cummings Custom Saw Milling ....G...... 570 586-3277
Clarks Summit (G-3190)

Fca LLC...E...... 309 792-3444
Corry (G-3760)

Flextron Industries Inc......................F...... 610 459-4600
Aston (G-763)

Georgia-Pacific Bldg Pdts LLC...........F...... 814 778-6000
Kane (G-8464)

Global Packaging Solutions Inc ....G...... 717 653-2345
Mount Joy (G-11658)

Lemac Packaging Inc ....G...... 814 453-7652
Erie (G-5361)

Menasha Packaging Company LLC ......C...... 800 245-2486
Ruffs Dale (G-16874)

Menasha Packaging Company LLC ......G...... 215 426-7110
Philadelphia (G-14009)

Menasha Packaging Company LLC ......D...... 800 783-4563
Latrobe (G-9504)

Packaging Corporation America ....G...... 717 624-2122
New Oxford (G-12418)

Packaging Corporation America ....G...... 717 632-4800
Hanover (G-6930)

PCA Corrugated and Display LLC ....G...... 717 624-3500
New Oxford (G-12420)

Righters Associat Ferry ....G...... 610 667-6767
Bala Cynwyd (G-891)

Roaring Spring Blank Book Co ....E...... 814 224-2222
Roaring Spring (G-16769)

Sheffield Container Corp......................E...... 814 968-3287
Sheffield (G-17483)

Sonoco Products Company..................E...... 610 323-9221
Pottstown (G-16049)

Sparks Exhibits Holding Corp ....G...... 215 676-1100
Philadelphia (G-14330)

Supplyone Holdings Company Inc.......D...... 484 582-5005
Newtown Square (G-12593)

CONTAINERS: Foil, Bakery Goods & Frozen Foods

Original Little Pepis Inc ....F....... 215 822-9650
Hatfield (G-7376)

CONTAINERS: Food & Beverage

Lilys LLC...G...... 814 938-9419
Punxsutawney (G-16147)

CONTAINERS: Food, Folding, Made From Purchased Materials

Sterling Paper Company ....D...... 215 744-5350
Philadelphia (G-14347)

CONTAINERS: Glass

Certainteed Corporation......................B...... 610 893-5000
Malvern (G-10204)

Certainteed Corporation......................G...... 610 651-8706
Malvern (G-10205)

Owens-Brockway Glass Cont Inc.........C...... 814 461-5100
Erie (G-5412)

Owens-Brockway Glass Cont Inc.........G...... 814 849-4265
Brookville (G-2267)

Owens-Brockway Glass Cont Inc.........C...... 814 261-6284
Brockway (G-2229)

Owens-Illinois Inc ....B...... 814 261-5200
Brockport (G-2222)

Saint-Gobain Delaware Corp ....G...... 610 341-7000
Valley Forge (G-18712)

Sonoco Products Company..................E...... 610 323-9221
Pottstown (G-16049)

Verallia..G...... 814 642-2521
Port Allegany (G-15896)

CONTAINERS: Laminated Phenolic & Vulcanized Fiber

Sonoco Products Company..................C...... 717 637-2103
Hanover (G-6957)

CONTAINERS: Liquid Tight Fiber, From Purchased Materials

Bushnell Alvah Company.....................E...... 215 842-9520
Philadelphia (G-13488)

Sheen Kleen Inc ....G...... 610 337-3969
King of Prussia (G-8673)

CONTAINERS: Metal

Altrax..G...... 814 379-3706
Summerville (G-18156)

Berenfield Cntrs Northeast Inc ....C...... 610 258-2700
Easton (G-4654)

Cleveland Steel Container Corp ....E...... 215 536-4477
Quakertown (G-16180)

Container Research Corporation ....C...... 610 459-2160
Aston (G-757)

Georgia-Pacific LLC............................C...... 814 368-8700
Bradford (G-1969)

Italian Mutual Benefit Society ....G...... 412 221-0751
Bridgeville (G-2071)

Northeast Industrial Mfg Inc ....E...... 724 588-7711
Greenville (G-6760)

Sonoco Display & Packaging LLC ....C...... 717 757-2683
York (G-20672)

Talk Express.......................................G...... 412 977-1786
Natrona Heights (G-11950)

Williamsport Steel Cont Corp ....E...... 570 323-9473
Williamsport (G-20095)

CONTAINERS: Plastic

Agd Products Inc ....G...... 215 682-9643
Warminster (G-18824)

Allentown Plastics Inc.........................E...... 610 391-8383
Breinigsville (G-2006)

Amcor Rigid Plastics Usa LLC ....C...... 610 871-9035
Allentown (G-131)

Analytic Plastic Inc ....E...... 215 638-7505
Philadelphia (G-13389)

Anholt Technologies Inc......................F...... 610 268-2758
Avondale (G-848)

Associated Packaging Entps Inc...........B...... 484 785-1120
Chadds Ford (G-2848)

Berry Global Inc ....G...... 814 455-9051
Erie (G-5209)

Berry Global Inc ....G...... 717 393-3498
Lancaster (G-8951)

Berry Global Inc ....E...... 814 849-4234
Brookville (G-2248)

Chem-Tainer Industries Inc ....F...... 717 469-7316
Hummelstown (G-7906)

Consolidated Cont Holdings LLC...........D...... 717 854-3454
York (G-20437)

Consolidated Container Co LLC............G...... 724 658-4570
New Castle (G-12074)

Consolidated Container Co LLC............D...... 724 658-4578
New Castle (G-12075)

Consolidated Container Co LLC............G...... 724 658-0549
New Castle (G-12076)

Consolidated Container Co LLC............F...... 717 267-3533
Chambersburg (G-2920)

Consolidated Container Co LP ....E...... 814 676-5671
Oil City (G-12943)

Crncte LLC...F...... 610 648-0419
Malvern (G-10219)

Drug Plastics and Glass Co Inc............D...... 570 672-3215
Elysburg (G-4974)

Dyneon LLC..D...... 610 497-8899
Aston (G-759)

Glass Molders Pottry Plstc ....D...... 814 756-4042
Albion (G-44)

Graham Packaging Co Europe LLC ......E...... 209 572-5187
York (G-20508)

Graham Packaging Company LP ....D...... 814 362-3861
Bradford (G-1970)

Graham Packaging Company LP ....E...... 717 849-8700
York (G-20509)

Graham Packaging Company LP ....E...... 717 849-8500
York (G-20511)

Graham Packaging Company LP ....E...... 570 454-8261
Hazle Township (G-7460)

Graham Packaging Company Inc..........C...... 717 849-8500
Lancaster (G-9031)

Havpack...G...... 814 452-4989
Erie (G-5312)

Jarden Corporation.............................C...... 717 667-2131
Reedsville (G-16624)

Keltrol Enterprises Inc.........................G...... 717 764-5940
York (G-20550)

Kerr Group LLC..................................C...... 812 424-2904
Lancaster (G-9083)

Keystone Containers Inc......................D...... 603 888-1315
Reading (G-16420)

L & L Industrial Chemical Inc ....G...... 215 368-7813
North Wales (G-12811)

Laminations Inc..................................C...... 570 876-8199
Archbald (G-690)

Letica Corporation..............................D...... 570 654-2451
Pittston (G-15763)

Meadville New Products Inc ....F...... 814 336-2174
Meadville (G-10759)

Multicolor Corp...................................G...... 610 262-8420
Coplay (G-3646)

Munot Plastics Inc ....E...... 814 838-7721
Erie (G-5399)

Novelty Concepts Inc ....G...... 215 245-5570
Bensalem (G-1233)

Nylacast LLC......................................G...... 717 270-5600
Harrisburg (G-7185)

Pactiv LLC..C...... 610 269-1776
Downingtown (G-4247)

Panthera Products Inc.........................G...... 724 532-3362
Latrobe (G-9509)

Plastic Solutions Inc...........................G...... 215 968-3242
Newtown (G-12536)

Plastics Services Network ....G...... 814 898-6317
Erie (G-5426)

Polar Tech Industries Inc ....E...... 800 423-2749
Elysburg (G-4979)

Premium Plastics Solutions LLC...........D...... 724 424-7000
Latrobe (G-9511)

Pretium Packaging LLC........................C...... 717 266-6687
Manchester (G-10362)

Ptr Tool & Plastics LLC.......................E...... 814 724-6979
Meadville (G-10783)

Rubbermaid Commercial Pdts LLC.......F...... 570 622-7715
Pottsville (G-16096)

Sharp Coatings...................................F...... 215 324-8500
Philadelphia (G-14298)

Silgan Plastics LLC.............................D...... 215 727-2676
Langhorne (G-9325)

Tmf Corporation..................................G...... 610 853-3080
Havertown (G-7431)

Trident Plastics Inc ....G...... 215 946-3999
Bristol (G-2210)

Universal Protective Packg Inc..............D...... 717 766-1578
Mechanicsburg (G-10903)

Vanguard Manufacturing Inc................F...... 610 481-0655
Allentown (G-422)

West Pharmaceutical Svcs Inc ....B...... 610 594-2900
Exton (G-5748)

Whirley Industries Inc..........................C...... 814 723-7600
Warren (G-19064)

Whirley Industries Inc..........................G...... 814 723-7600
Warren (G-19065)

CONTAINERS: Plywood & Veneer, Wood

Van Mar Manufacturing ....G...... 717 733-8948
Ephrata (G-5153)

CONTAINERS: Sanitary, Food

Consolidated Container Co LLC............C...... 570 759-0823
Berwick (G-1319)

Ecopax LLC..D...... 484 546-0700
Easton (G-4676)

Georgia-Pacific LLC............................B...... 610 250-1400
Easton (G-4690)

Northstar Sales ....G...... 215 364-5540
Southampton (G-17828)

CONTAINERS: Shipping & Mailing, Fiber

American Paper Products of PHI...........G...... 215 739-5718
Philadelphia (G-13387)

CONTAINERS: Shipping, Bombs, Metal Plate

Charleston Marine Cntrs Inc ....D...... 843 745-0022
Dallastown (G-3973)

CONTAINERS: Shipping, Wood

Zeiglers Packing and Crating ....G...... 814 238-4021
Port Matilda (G-15908)

CONTAINERS: Wood

A+ Packaging ....G...... 610 864-1758
Narvon (G-11916)

Fulton Forest Products ....E...... 814 782-3448
Shippenville (G-17561)

Greenfield Basket Factory Inc ....E...... 814 725-3419
North East (G-12744)

Little Johns Woodshop ....G...... 724 924-9029
New Castle (G-12116)

PA Packing Products & Svcs Inc...........G...... 717 486-8100
Carlisle (G-2728)

Strasburg Pallet Co Inc ....E 717 687-8131
Strasburg (G-18094)
Walker Wood Products Inc ....F 717 436-2105
Mifflintown (G-11141)

CONTRACT FOOD SVCS

Nutrition Inc ....E 724 978-2100
Irwin (G-8185)
Nutrition Inc ....E 814 382-3656
Irwin (G-8186)
Preferred Meal Systems Inc ....C 570 457-8311
Moosic (G-11512)

CONTRACTOR: Framing

Pocopson Industries Inc ....F 610 793-0344
West Chester (G-19618)

CONTRACTOR: Rigging & Scaffolding

Hayes Industries Inc ....G 484 624-5314
Pottstown (G-15998)
Mill Professional Services ....F 724 335-4625
New Kensington (G-12357)
Rhoads Industries Inc ....D 267 728-6300
Philadelphia (G-14244)
Steffan Industries Inc ....G 412 751-4484
McKeesport (G-10683)
Winola Industrial Inc ....F 570 378-3808
Factoryville (G-5763)

CONTRACTORS: Acoustical & Ceiling Work

Wargo Interior Systems Inc ....D 215 723-6200
Telford (G-18325)

CONTRACTORS: Acoustical & Insulation Work

Interntonal Mar Outfitting LLC ....G 215 875-9911
Philadelphia (G-13871)

CONTRACTORS: Airwave Shielding Installation, Computer Rooms

Tritech Applied Sciences Inc ....G 215 362-6890
Lansdale (G-9417)

CONTRACTORS: Artificial Turf Installation

Specialty Surfaces Intl Inc ....C 877 686-8873
King of Prussia (G-8679)

CONTRACTORS: Asbestos Removal & Encapsulation

Baxter Group Inc ....F 717 263-7341
Chambersburg (G-2909)

CONTRACTORS: Asphalt

Allen P Sutton ....G 717 957-2047
Marysville (G-10531)
Derry Construction Co Inc ....F 724 539-7600
Latrobe (G-9471)
Ganoe Paving Inc ....E 717 597-2567
Greencastle (G-6613)
Glenn O Hawbaker Inc ....E 814 359-3411
Pleasant Gap (G-15792)
Hanson Aggregates Bmc Inc ....F 724 626-0080
Connellsville (G-3498)
Hri Inc ....G 570 437-4315
Milton (G-11242)
Meckleys Limestone Pdts Inc ....D 570 758-3011
Herndon (G-7601)
Meckleys Limestone Pdts Inc ....G 570 837-5228
Beavertown (G-1027)
Wiest Asphalt Products and Pav ....F 724 282-6913
Butler (G-2448)
Wilson Paving Inc ....E 717 249-3227
Carlisle (G-2751)

CONTRACTORS: Awning Installation

E R Schantz Inc ....G 610 272-3603
Norristown (G-12652)
Lingenfelter Awning ....G 814 696-4353
Duncansville (G-4455)
Mid-State Awning Inc ....G 814 355-8979
Bellefonte (G-1108)
Mt Lebanon Awning & Tent Co ....E 412 221-2233
Presto (G-16104)

Rothman Awning Co Inc ....F 412 589-9974
Pittsburgh (G-15498)

CONTRACTORS: Blasting, Exc Building Demolition

Silver Vly Drlg & Blastg Inc ....G 570 992-1125
Saylorsburg (G-17107)

CONTRACTORS: Boiler & Furnace

Historic York Inc ....G 717 843-0320
York (G-20523)

CONTRACTORS: Boiler Maintenance Contractor

Park Corporation ....G 412 472-0500
Coraopolis (G-3711)

CONTRACTORS: Boring, Building Construction

Aaron Enterprises Inc ....D 717 854-2641
York (G-20362)
Pennsylvania Drilling Company ....E 412 771-2110
Imperial (G-8074)

CONTRACTORS: Bowling Alley Installation & Svc

S H Sharpless & Son Inc ....E 570 454-6685
Hazleton (G-7524)

CONTRACTORS: Building Eqpt & Machinery Installation

Boiler Erection and Repair Co ....E 215 721-7900
Souderton (G-17727)
James A Schultz ....F 814 763-5561
Saegertown (G-16919)
McDal Corporation ....F 800 626-2325
King of Prussia (G-8649)
Radius Systems LLC ....E 610 388-9940
Chadds Ford (G-2859)
Thyssenkrupp Elevator Corp ....E 610 366-0161
Allentown (G-409)

CONTRACTORS: Building Fireproofing

Marcon & Boyer Inc ....D 610 866-5959
Allentown (G-307)

CONTRACTORS: Building Sign Installation & Mntnce

Crest Advertising Co ....F 724 774-4413
Monaca (G-11289)
Custom Signs Inc ....F 814 786-7232
Grove City (G-6783)
East Coast Sign Advg Co Inc ....C 888 724-0380
Bristol (G-2136)
Grid Electric Inc ....E 610 466-7030
Coatesville (G-3306)
Kgc Enterprises Inc ....E 610 497-0111
Aston (G-771)
Nation-Wide Sign Service Inc ....G 888 234-5300
Drexel Hill (G-4369)
Pike Graphics Inc ....F 215 836-9120
Flourtown (G-5990)
Rhoads Sign Systems ....G 717 776-7309
Newville (G-12609)
Sign Creators Inc ....G 412 461-3567
West Homestead (G-19720)
Sign Here Sign Co Inc ....G 845 858-6366
Matamoras (G-10540)
Sign Medix Inc ....F 717 396-9749
Lancaster (G-9198)
Signage Unlimited Inc ....F 610 647-6962
Malvern (G-10316)
Signstat ....F 724 527-7475
Jeannette (G-8264)
Vh Service LLC ....G 267 808-9745
Feasterville Trevose (G-5938)
Wiley Electric Sign Service ....G 610 759-8167
Nazareth (G-11994)

CONTRACTORS: Building Site Preparation

General Civil Company Inc ....F 484 571-1998
Aston (G-767)

CONTRACTORS: Cable Laying

Glasgow Inc ....D 215 884-8800
Glenside (G-6521)

CONTRACTORS: Caisson Drilling

Tophole Drilling LLC ....F 724 272-1932
Saxonburg (G-17098)

CONTRACTORS: Carpentry Work

Gap Ridge Contractors LLC ....F 717 442-4386
Kinzers (G-8738)
Kitchens By Meade Inc ....F 814 453-4888
Erie (G-5345)
Martin Custom Cabinets LLC ....G 717 721-1859
East Earl (G-4547)
Misko Inc ....F 610 524-1881
Exton (G-5712)
S D L Custom Cabinetry Inc ....G 215 355-8188
Langhorne (G-9323)
Stoltzfus Sylvan Lee ....G 570 682-9755
Hegins (G-7544)

CONTRACTORS: Carpentry, Cabinet & Finish Work

Erector Sets Inc ....G 215 289-1505
Philadelphia (G-13677)
Master Woodcraft Corporation ....E 724 225-5530
Washington (G-19201)
Otto Design Casefixture Inc ....G 412 378-6460
Irwin (G-8187)
Richard Riberich ....G 412 271-8427
Pittsburgh (G-15484)
Signature Gallery ....G 610 792-5399
Royersford (G-16864)
Staurowsky Woodworking ....G 610 489-0770
Collegeville (G-3394)
Unique Wood Creation LLC ....G 717 687-8843
Paradise (G-13163)
Unique Wood Creation LLC ....G 717 687-7900
Paradise (G-13164)
Van Etten James ....G 215 453-8228
Perkasie (G-13297)
Van Heyneker Fine Woodworking ....G 610 388-1772
West Chester (G-19671)

CONTRACTORS: Carpentry, Cabinet Building & Installation

Closet Works Inc ....E 215 675-6430
Montgomeryville (G-11388)
Ehst Custom Kitchens Inc ....F 610 367-2074
Boyertown (G-1910)
Elc Manufacturing ....G 570 655-3060
West Pittston (G-19755)
Kol Industries Inc ....F 717 630-0600
Hanover (G-6911)
ONeils Custom Cab & Design ....F 412 422-4723
Pittsburgh (G-15359)
Precision Millwork & Cabinetry ....E 814 445-9669
Somerset (G-17700)
Renningers Cabinetree Inc ....E 570 726-6494
Mill Hall (G-11181)
Round River Woodworking ....G 717 776-5876
Newville (G-12610)

CONTRACTORS: Carpentry, Finish & Trim Work

Daniel W Benedict ....G 717 709-0149
Waynesboro (G-19408)
P & H Lumber Millwork Co Inc ....E 215 699-9365
North Wales (G-12822)

CONTRACTORS: Carpet Laying

Commercial Flrg Professionals ....G 717 576-7847
Mechanicsburg (G-10829)
Ferrante Uphlstrng & Crptng ....F 724 535-8866
Wampum (G-18800)
R & R Briggs Inc ....G 215 357-3413
Southampton (G-17833)

CONTRACTORS: Central Vacuum Cleaning System Installation

Better Living Center LLC ....G 724 266-3750
Ambridge (G-611)

CONTRACTORS: Closet Organizers, Installation & Design

Closet Works Inc ....E 215 675-6430
Montgomeryville (G-11388)

CONTRACTORS: Coating, Caulking & Weather, Water & Fire

Electrospray Incorporated ....F 215 322-5255
Feasterville Trevose (G-5904)
Electrospray Incorporated ....G 215 322-5255
Feasterville Trevose (G-5905)
Specialty Fabrication and Powd...........D 814 432-6406
Franklin (G-6161)
Yarmouth Construction ....G 267 592-1432
Philadelphia (G-14498)

CONTRACTORS: Commercial & Office Building

Absolute Pallet Inc ....G 215 331-4510
Bensalem (G-1142)
Cedar Forest Products Company ....F 815 946-3994
Media (G-10917)
Epic Industries Inc ....G 570 586-0253
Clarks Summit (G-3192)
JGM Welding & Fabg Svcs Inc ....D 610 873-0081
Coatesville (G-3310)
Mesko Glass and Mirror Co Inc ....D 570 457-1700
Avoca (G-845)
New Hudson Facades LLC ....C 610 494-8100
Upper Chichester (G-18668)
Penn State Cnstr J&D LLC ....G 717 953-9200
Lewistown (G-9943)
Sfk Ventures Inc ....D 610 825-5151
King of Prussia (G-8672)

CONTRACTORS: Communications Svcs

Bpl Global LLC ....F 724 933-7700
Canonsburg (G-2550)

CONTRACTORS: Computerized Controls Installation

Radius Systems LLC ....E 610 388-9940
Chadds Ford (G-2859)

CONTRACTORS: Concrete

A Anthony & Sons Inc ....E 814 454-2883
Erie (G-5164)
Emporium Contractors Inc......................E 814 562-0631
Emporium (G-5056)
Esterly Concrete Co Inc ....F 610 376-2791
West Reading (G-19764)
Gruber Con Specialists Inc ....F 610 760-0925
New Tripoli (G-12456)
IA Construction Corporation ....E 724 368-2140
Franklin (G-6137)
Joseph Riepole Construction ....G 412 833-6611
Library (G-9955)
Kinsley Construction Inc........................E 717 846-6711
York (G-20554)
Mayer Brothers Construction Co ....F 814 452-3748
Erie (G-5383)
Miller and Son Paving Inc ....F 215 598-7801
Rushland (G-16879)
Monroe Scale Company Inc ....G 412 793-8134
Pittsburgh (G-15300)
Pcm Contracting Inc ....G 215 675-8846
Hatboro (G-7296)
Solid Steel Buildings Inc ....F 800 377-6543
Pittsburgh (G-15553)
Surtreat Holding LLC.............................G 412 281-1202
Pittsburgh (G-15592)
Vci Coatings LLC ....G 412 281-1202
Pittsburgh (G-15689)
Wolyniec Construction Inc.....................E 570 322-8634
Williamsport (G-20097)

CONTRACTORS: Concrete Block Masonry Laying

General Civil Company Inc ....F 484 571-1998
Aston (G-767)
Ray-Guard International Ltd ....G 215 543-3849
Pottstown (G-16038)

CONTRACTORS: Concrete Breaking, Street & Highway

Arcman Corporation ....G 570 489-6402
Dunmore (G-4467)

CONTRACTORS: Concrete Pumping

T Helbling LLC.......................................G 724 601-9819
Beaver (G-992)

CONTRACTORS: Concrete Reinforcement Placing

Harris Rebar Atlantic Inc ....D 610 882-1401
Bethlehem (G-1529)

CONTRACTORS: Concrete Repair

Staar Distributing Llc.............................D 814 612-2115
Reynoldsville (G-16666)

CONTRACTORS: Concrete Structure Coating, Plastic

Durex Coverings Inc ....E 717 626-8566
Brownstown (G-2307)

CONTRACTORS: Corrosion Control Installation

Cott Manufacturing Company.................E 724 625-3730
Glassport (G-6411)

CONTRACTORS: Countertop Installation

Desavino & Sons Inc ....E 570 383-3988
Olyphant (G-12988)
Eastern Surfaces Inc ....D 610 266-3121
Allentown (G-201)
Excel Glass and Granite ....E 724 523-6190
Jeannette (G-8255)
Robertsons Inc.......................................G 814 838-2313
Erie (G-5464)
Top Notch Products Inc..........................G 724 475-2341
Fredonia (G-6187)
Unity Marble and Granite Inc ....G 412 793-4220
Pittsburgh (G-15681)
Wagner Masters Custom Wdwkg ....G 570 748-9424
Lock Haven (G-10093)

CONTRACTORS: Demolition, Building & Other Structures

Cheri-Lee Inc ....G 570 339-4195
Kulpmont (G-8822)
Select Dismantling Corp ....F 724 861-6004
Wendel (G-19482)

CONTRACTORS: Directional Oil & Gas Well Drilling Svc

Chevron Ae Resources LLC ....E 724 662-0300
Jackson Center (G-8226)
Collins Drilling LLC................................F 814 489-3297
Sugar Grove (G-18144)
Dallas - Morris Drilling Inc....................D 814 362-6493
Bradford (G-1964)
Dallas - Morris Drilling Inc....................E 814 362-6493
Bradford (G-1965)
Donald W Deitz ....G 814 745-2857
Clarion (G-3177)
Eagle Line Corporation ....F 814 589-7724
Pleasantville (G-15801)
Frederick Drilling Co & Sons ....G 814 744-8581
Tylersburg (G-18573)
Minard Run Oil Company ....D 814 362-3531
Bradford (G-1982)
Northeast Energy MGT Inc ....C 724 465-7958
Indiana (G-8115)
Patriot Exploration ....F 724 593-4427
Stahlstown (G-17936)
Patriot Exploration Corp ....G 724 282-2339
Butler (G-2432)
Target Drilling Inc..................................E 724 633-3927
Smithton (G-17663)

CONTRACTORS: Drapery Track Installation

De Lucas Draperys ....G 610 284-2464
Clifton Heights (G-3251)

CONTRACTORS: Driveway

G & K Watterson Company ....G 724 827-2800
New Brighton (G-12037)
Mukies/Mccarty Seal Coating C ....G 717 684-2799
Columbia (G-3444)
Sebastian Brothers ....F 717 930-8797
Middletown (G-11075)

CONTRACTORS: Drywall

Advanced Cnstr Estimating LLC............F 724 747-7032
Mc Murray (G-10643)
Marcon & Boyer Inc ....D 610 866-5959
Allentown (G-307)

CONTRACTORS: Earthmoving

Bentley Development Co Inc ....F 724 459-5775
Blairsville (G-1715)

CONTRACTORS: Electric Power Systems

Rizzo & Sons Industrial Svc Co.............E 814 948-5381
Pittsburgh (G-15489)

CONTRACTORS: Electrical

Berrena Jseph T McHanicals Inc...........E 814 643-2645
Huntingdon (G-7939)
Better Living Center LLC ....G 724 266-3750
Ambridge (G-611)
Cellco Partnership ....D 610 431-5800
West Chester (G-19520)
East Hill Video Prod Co LLC ....F 215 855-4457
Lansdale (G-9364)
Electric City Yoga..................................G 570 558-9642
Scranton (G-17233)
Electric Pepper Company LLC ....G 812 340-4321
Russell (G-16880)
Goodhart Sons Inc ....C 717 656-2404
Lancaster (G-9030)
Harlan Electric ....G 717 243-4600
Harrisburg (G-7140)
Jeffrey Shepler......................................G 724 537-7411
Latrobe (G-9484)
John Bachman Hvac..............................G 610 266-3877
Catasauqua (G-2815)
Lengyel Electric ....G 724 475-2045
Fredonia (G-6186)
M & R Electric Inc..................................E 412 831-6101
Bethel Park (G-1423)
Northeast Fence & Ir Works Inc.............E 215 335-1681
Philadelphia (G-14082)
Oxford Construction PA Inc ....D 215 809-2245
Philadelphia (G-14106)
Tarpon Energy Services LLC ....D 570 547-0442
Bridgeville (G-2093)
West End Electric Inc ....F 570 682-9292
Hegins (G-7547)

CONTRACTORS: Electronic Controls Installation

B & C Controls Inc ....F 610 738-9204
West Chester (G-19506)
Dew Electric Inc ....G 724 628-9711
Connellsville (G-3494)
Industrial Systems & Controls...............G 412 638-4977
Pittsburgh (G-15121)
J J Cacchio Enterprises ....G 610 399-9750
West Chester (G-19575)
Summit Contracting Svcs Inc ....G 570 943-2232
Orwigsburg (G-13053)

CONTRACTORS: Excavating

Bill Barry Excavating Inc.......................G 570 595-2269
Cresco (G-3891)
Charles L Swenglish Sons Coal ....G 724 437-3541
Smithfield (G-17646)
Concrete Services Corporation ....E 814 774-8807
Fairview (G-5817)
D E Hyde Contracting ....G 814 228-3685
Genesee (G-6271)
Durant Excavating ....G 724 583-9800
Masontown (G-10535)
Fenton Welding LLC ....E 570 746-9018
Wyalusing (G-20252)
Force Inc ....E 724 465-9394
Indiana (G-8100)
Gaberseck Bros ....G 814 274-0763
Coudersport (G-3781)

Glen Blooming Contractors Inc ....C 717 566-3711
  Hummelstown *(G-7912)*
Glenn O Hawbaker Inc ....D 814 237-1444
  State College *(G-17970)*
H&K Group Inc ....C 610 584-8500
  Skippack *(G-17597)*
Hg Smith Wilbert Vault Company ....G 570 420-9599
  Stroudsburg *(G-18123)*
Michels Corporation ....G 724 249-2065
  Washington *(G-19202)*
Northeast Energy Co Inc ....G 570 823-1719
  Wilkes Barre *(G-19951)*
Postupack Russell Culm Corp ....G 570 929-1699
  McAdoo *(G-10657)*
Richard E Krall Inc ....G 717 432-4179
  Rossville *(G-16824)*
Rossi Excavating Company ....G 570 455-9607
  Beaver Meadows *(G-1018)*
Sam Beachy & Sons ....G 814 662-2220
  Salisbury *(G-17045)*
Shallenberger Construction Inc ....D 724 628-8408
  Connellsville *(G-3508)*
Solid Steel Buildings Inc ....F 800 377-6543
  Pittsburgh *(G-15553)*
Stauffer Con Pdts & Excvtg Inc ....G 570 629-1977
  Kunkletown *(G-8835)*
Thompson Logging and Trckg Inc ....E 570 923-2590
  North Bend *(G-12727)*
Waterford Sand & Gravel Co ....E 814 796-6250
  Union City *(G-18613)*
William J Judge ....F 610 348-8070
  Collegeville *(G-3400)*

CONTRACTORS: Excavating Slush Pits & Cellars Svcs

Jackie L Trout Septic ....G 717 244-6640
  Felton *(G-5940)*
Joseph F Mariani Contrs Inc ....F 610 358-9746
  Aston *(G-770)*
Karp Excavating Ltd ....G 570 840-9026
  Factoryville *(G-5757)*
Klapec Excavating Inc ....G 814 678-3478
  Oil City *(G-12949)*
Michael R Skrip Excavating ....G 610 965-5331
  Emmaus *(G-5034)*
Penn Quaker Site Contrs Inc ....G 610 614-0401
  Nazareth *(G-11985)*
RB Farms Inc ....G 570 842-7246
  Moscow *(G-11602)*
Shearer Elbie ....G 814 266-7548
  Johnstown *(G-8434)*

CONTRACTORS: Exterior Concrete Stucco

Yarmouth Construction ....G 267 592-1432
  Philadelphia *(G-14498)*

CONTRACTORS: Fence Construction

All Type Fence Co Inc ....G 610 718-1151
  Douglassville *(G-4166)*
American Fence Inc ....F 610 437-1944
  Whitehall *(G-19861)*
County Line Fence Co ....F 215 343-5085
  Warrington *(G-19112)*
Curtis Leljedal Trading Loggn ....G 570 924-3938
  Forksville *(G-6056)*
Genie Electronics Co Inc ....D 717 244-1099
  Red Lion *(G-16598)*
Genie Electronics Co Inc ....C 717 244-1099
  Red Lion *(G-16599)*
Helm Fencing Inc ....E 215 822-5595
  Hatfield *(G-7348)*
Heritage Fence & Deck LLC ....G 610 476-0003
  Skippack *(G-17598)*
J/M Fence & Deck Company ....G 610 488-7382
  Mohrsville *(G-11276)*
Manley Fence Co ....G 610 842-8833
  Coatesville *(G-3316)*
Marietta Fence Experts LLC ....G 724 925-6100
  Hunker *(G-7929)*
North American Fencing Corp ....F 412 362-3900
  Cheswick *(G-3113)*
Northeast Fence & Ir Works Inc ....E 215 335-1681
  Philadelphia *(G-14082)*
Pittsburgh Fence Co Inc ....G 724 775-6550
  Carnegie *(G-2780)*
Premier Fence & Iron Works Inc ....G 267 567-2078
  Philadelphia *(G-14197)*
The Adirondack Group Inc ....E 610 431-4343
  West Chester *(G-19660)*

CONTRACTORS: Fiber Optic Cable Installation

Fibertel Inc ....F 570 714-7189
  Plymouth *(G-15817)*
JAS Precision Inc ....G 215 239-7299
  Yardley *(G-20322)*

CONTRACTORS: Fiberglass Work

Riggeals Performance Fibrgls ....G 717 677-4167
  Gettysburg *(G-6312)*

CONTRACTORS: Fire Sprinkler System Installation Svcs

Bnb Fire Protection Inc ....G 610 944-0594
  Fleetwood *(G-5968)*
Hope Good Animal Clinic ....G 717 766-5535
  Mechanicsburg *(G-10854)*
Rowe Sprinkler Systems Inc ....E 570 837-7647
  Middletown *(G-11039)*
Sentry Fire Protection Inc ....F 717 843-4973
  York *(G-20666)*

CONTRACTORS: Floor Laying & Other Floor Work

Industrial Floor Corporation ....F 215 886-1800
  Jenkintown *(G-8291)*
Robertsons Inc ....G 814 838-2313
  Erie *(G-5464)*

CONTRACTORS: Flooring

Durex Coverings Inc ....E 717 626-8566
  Brownstown *(G-2307)*

CONTRACTORS: Food Svcs Eqpt Installation

Greiner Industries Inc ....B 717 653-8111
  Mount Joy *(G-11660)*
Watermark Usa LLC ....F 610 983-0500
  Gladwyne *(G-6409)*

CONTRACTORS: Foundation Building

McKinney Drilling Company LLC ....E 724 468-4139
  Delmont *(G-4051)*

CONTRACTORS: Garage Doors

Bbk Industries LLC ....G 215 676-1500
  Langhorne *(G-9280)*
Door Stop Ltd ....G 610 353-8707
  Wayne *(G-19318)*
Overhead Door Corporation ....B 717 248-0131
  Lewistown *(G-9942)*
Stoltzfus Ephram ....G 717 656-0513
  Bird In Hand *(G-1682)*

CONTRACTORS: Gas Detection & Analysis Svcs

T C S Industries Inc ....G 717 657-7032
  Harrisburg *(G-7225)*
Timothy A Musser & Co Inc ....G 610 433-6380
  Allentown *(G-410)*

CONTRACTORS: Gas Field Svcs, NEC

Appalachian Drilling Svcs Inc ....F 570 907-0136
  Beech Creek *(G-1081)*
AR Trucking ....E 814 723-1245
  Warren *(G-19010)*
Clearfield Ohio Holdings Inc ....G 610 293-0410
  Radnor *(G-16291)*
Crg Resources LLC ....G 814 571-7190
  Curwensville *(G-3950)*
Dg Services LLC ....G 724 845-7300
  Leechburg *(G-9644)*
Em1 Services LLC ....F 570 560-2561
  Unityville *(G-18650)*
Energy Field Services LLC ....G 717 791-1018
  Dillsburg *(G-4128)*
Exterran Energy Solutions LP ....D 724 935-7660
  Wexford *(G-19799)*
Fawnwood Energy Inc ....G 724 753-2416
  Bruin *(G-2314)*
Gas & Oil Management Assoc ....G 814 563-4601
  Youngsville *(G-20771)*

Gas Analytical Services Inc ....G 724 349-8133
  Indiana *(G-8102)*
Marshall Flp LP ....G 570 465-3817
  New Milford *(G-12398)*
Nortech Energy Solutions LLC ....G 570 323-3060
  Williamsport *(G-20049)*
Northern Tier Inc ....G 814 465-2299
  Rew *(G-16654)*
Superior Energy Resources LLC ....G 814 265-1080
  Brockway *(G-2235)*
Superior Energy Resources LLC ....E 814 265-1080
  Brockway *(G-2236)*
UGI Newco LLC ....C 610 337-7000
  King of Prussia *(G-8693)*
Washita Valley Enterprises Inc ....F 724 437-1593
  Hopwood *(G-7777)*
Wolverine Enterprise LLC ....G 570 463-4103
  Mansfield *(G-10427)*

CONTRACTORS: General Electric

Amy Semler ....G 717 593-9243
  Greencastle *(G-6596)*
Appellation Cnstr Svcs LLC ....D 570 601-4765
  Montoursville *(G-11431)*
Edwin L Heim Co ....E 717 233-8711
  Harrisburg *(G-7125)*
Greiner Industries Inc ....B 717 653-8111
  Mount Joy *(G-11660)*
Jeffers & Leek Electric Inc ....G 724 384-0315
  New Brighton *(G-12038)*
K&L Services ....G 610 349-1358
  Allentown *(G-277)*
Miller Electric Service & Sup ....F 814 942-9943
  Altoona *(G-527)*
R & D Machine Controls Inc ....G 267 205-5976
  Bristol *(G-2192)*
R L Snelbecker Inc ....G 717 292-4971
  Dover *(G-4202)*
Schrantz Indus Electricians ....G 610 435-8255
  Allentown *(G-386)*

CONTRACTORS: Geothermal Drilling

Bucks Cnty Artesian Well Drlg ....F 215 493-1867
  Washington Crossing *(G-19253)*
Eznergy LLC ....G 215 361-7332
  Lansdale *(G-9366)*

CONTRACTORS: Glass Tinting, Architectural & Automotive

Sunsational Signs Win Tinting ....G 610 277-4344
  Norristown *(G-12715)*

CONTRACTORS: Glass, Glazing & Tinting

Cathedral Stained GL Studios ....G 215 379-5360
  Cheltenham *(G-3027)*
Chango Inc ....G 215 634-0400
  Philadelphia *(G-13525)*
Consolidated GL Holdings Inc ....G 866 412-6977
  East Butler *(G-4531)*
Hc Hoodco Inc ....F 814 355-4003
  Bellefonte *(G-1104)*
Kasmark & Marshall Inc ....G 570 287-3663
  Hunlock Creek *(G-7932)*
Latrobe Glass & Mirror Inc ....G 724 539-2431
  Latrobe *(G-9490)*
Mesko Glass and Mirror Co Inc ....D 570 457-1700
  Avoca *(G-845)*
Neidighs Inc ....F 814 237-3985
  State College *(G-17996)*
Pittsburgh Stained GL Studio ....F 412 921-2500
  Pittsburgh *(G-15409)*
Renaissance Glassworks Inc ....G 724 969-9009
  Canonsburg *(G-2626)*
Robert L Baker ....F 443 617-0164
  Chambersburg *(G-2973)*
Studio 8 ....G 610 372-7065
  Reading *(G-16527)*

CONTRACTORS: Grave Excavation

H Troxel Cemetery Service Inc ....G 610 489-4426
  Norristown *(G-12663)*

CONTRACTORS: Gutters & Downspouts

Lehigh Gap Seamless Gutter LLC ....G 610 824-4888
  Palmerton *(G-13108)*
Rdy Gutters Plus LLC ....G 610 488-5666
  Bernville *(G-1304)*

P
R
O
D
U
C
T

Sensenigs Spouting ....F 717 627-6886
Lititz (G-10049)

William J Koshinskie ....G 570 742-4969
Milton (G-11251)

CONTRACTORS: Heating & Air Conditioning

Building Inspectors Contrs Inc ....G 215 481-0606
Glenside (G-6509)

E F Laudenslager Inc ....F 610 395-1582
Orefield (G-13011)

Sky Point Crane LLC ....G 724 471-5710
Indiana (G-8129)

Walter B Staller Inc ....G 570 385-5386
Schuylkill Haven (G-17171)

CONTRACTORS: Heating Systems Repair & Maintenance Svc

Marilyn Strawser Beauty Salon ....G 717 463-2804
Thompsontown (G-18349)

McCleary Heating & Cooling LLC ....F 717 263-3833
Chambersburg (G-2959)

Penn-MO Fire Brick Co Inc ....G 717 234-4504
Harrisburg (G-7193)

Zampell Refractories Inc ....E 215 788-3000
Croydon (G-3934)

CONTRACTORS: Highway & Street Construction, General

E M Brown Incorporated ....E 814 765-7519
Clearfield (G-3218)

Glasgow Inc ....D 215 884-8800
Glenside (G-6521)

Hempt Bros Inc ....D 717 774-2911
Camp Hill (G-2500)

Hri Inc ....D 570 322-6737
Muncy (G-11821)

IA Construction Corporation ....E 814 432-3184
Franklin (G-6136)

Lee Michael Industries Inc ....E 724 656-0890
New Castle (G-12115)

Lehigh Asphalt Pav & Cnstr Co ....F 570 668-2040
Tamaqua (G-18216)

New Enterprise Stone Lime Inc ....C 814 224-2121
Roaring Spring (G-16766)

Sssi Inc ....B 724 743-5815
Washington (G-19228)

Synergy Contracting Svcs LLC ....G 724 349-0855
Indiana (G-8132)

CONTRACTORS: Highway & Street Paving

American Asphalt Paving Co ....C 570 696-1181
Shavertown (G-17478)

Eastern Industries Inc ....B 610 866-0932
Whitehall (G-19873)

Glenn O Hawbaker Inc ....D 814 237-1444
State College (G-17970)

Golden Eagle Construction Co ....E 724 437-6495
Uniontown (G-18628)

H&K Group Inc ....C 610 705-0500
Pottstown (G-15947)

Heilman Pavement Specialties ....G 724 353-2700
Sarver (G-17073)

Joseph McCormick Cnstr Co Inc ....E 814 899-3111
Erie (G-5339)

Landfried Paving Inc ....F 724 646-2505
Greenville (G-6753)

Lane Construction Corporation ....D 412 838-0251
Pittsburgh (G-15218)

Martin Limestone Inc ....D 717 354-1340
Ephrata (G-5123)

Martin Limestone Inc ....E 717 335-4500
East Earl (G-4548)

Mayer Brothers Construction Co ....F 814 452-3748
Erie (G-5383)

New Enterprise Stone Lime Inc ....D 814 224-6883
New Enterprise (G-12194)

Pottstown Trap Rock Quarries ....F 610 326-4843
Pottstown (G-16034)

Quaker Sales Corporation ....F 814 536-7541
Johnstown (G-8426)

Russell Standard Corporation ....F 412 449-0700
Pittsburgh (G-15504)

Stabler Companies Inc ....F 717 236-9307
Harrisburg (G-7219)

Stopper Construction Co Inc ....E 570 322-5947
Williamsport (G-20075)

Suit-Kote Corporation ....D 814 337-1171
Meadville (G-10796)

CONTRACTORS: Home & Office Intrs Finish, Furnish/Remodel

Trim P A C LLC ....G 717 375-2366
Chambersburg (G-2989)

Wescho Company Inc ....E 610 436-5866
West Chester (G-19676)

CONTRACTORS: Hot Shot Svcs

Northern Hot Shot Services LLC ....G 724 664-5477
Kittanning (G-8786)

CONTRACTORS: Hotel, Motel/Multi-Famly Home Renovtn/Remodel

M L Scott & Sons ....G 610 847-5671
Revere (G-16653)

CONTRACTORS: Hydraulic Eqpt Installation & Svcs

Florig R & J Industrial Co Inc ....E 610 825-6655
Conshohocken (G-3548)

CONTRACTORS: Hydraulic Well Fracturing Svcs

Curtis Well Service Company ....F 814 489-7858
Sugargrove (G-18151)

Reliance Well Services LLC ....E 814 454-1644
Erie (G-5461)

Rettew Field Services Inc ....E 717 697-3551
Lancaster (G-9187)

Universal Well Services Inc ....E 814 337-1983
Meadville (G-10807)

Universal Well Services Inc ....E 814 333-2656
Meadville (G-10808)

Universal Well Services Inc ....E 814 938-2051
Punxsutawney (G-16166)

CONTRACTORS: Indl Building Renovation, Remodeling & Repair

Hc Hoodco Inc ....F 814 355-4003
Bellefonte (G-1104)

CONTRACTORS: Insulation Installation, Building

Baxter Group Inc ....F 717 263-7341
Chambersburg (G-2909)

Mito Insulation Company ....E 724 335-8551
New Kensington (G-12359)

CONTRACTORS: Kitchen & Bathroom Remodeling

Lexmarusa Inc ....G 412 896-9266
McKeesport (G-10675)

Luicana Industries Inc ....G 570 325-9699
Jim Thorpe (G-8341)

Porto Exim Usa LLC ....G 412 406-8442
Cheswick (G-3115)

Superior Flrcvgs Kitchens LLC ....G 717 264-9096
Chambersburg (G-2981)

Ye Olde Village Workshop ....G 570 595-2593
Mountainhome (G-11788)

CONTRACTORS: Kitchen Cabinet Installation

Asels Cabinet Company ....G 814 677-3063
Rouseville (G-16835)

Dennis Downing ....G 724 598-0043
New Castle (G-12081)

Henry H Ross & Son Inc ....E 717 626-6268
Lititz (G-10014)

CONTRACTORS: Lighting Syst

Vh Service LLC ....G 267 808-9745
Feasterville Trevose (G-5938)

CONTRACTORS: Lightweight Steel Framing Installation

Advanced Cnstr Estimating LLC ....F 724 747-7032
Mc Murray (G-10643)

CONTRACTORS: Machine Rigging & Moving

Advanced Industrial Svcs Inc ....C 717 764-9811
York (G-20368)

Hayes Industries Inc ....G 484 624-5314
Pottstown (G-15998)

Herr Industrial Inc ....E 717 569-6619
Lititz (G-10016)

CONTRACTORS: Machinery Dismantling

Culpepper Corporation ....E 215 425-6532
Philadelphia (G-13590)

CONTRACTORS: Machinery Installation

Hanel Storage Systems ....E 412 788-0509
Pittsburgh (G-15079)

John R Wald Company Inc ....E 814 643-3908
Huntingdon (G-7947)

CONTRACTORS: Maintenance, Parking Facility Eqpt

Hub Parking Technology USA Inc ....E 724 772-2400
Warrendale (G-19082)

CONTRACTORS: Mantel Work

Howell Craft Inc ....G 412 751-6861
Elizabeth (G-4860)

CONTRACTORS: Marble Installation, Interior

AAA Hellenic Marble Inc ....E 610 344-7700
West Chester (G-19493)

Lesher Inc ....F 717 944-4431
Middletown (G-11062)

CONTRACTORS: Masonry & Stonework

G and H Contracting Inc ....G 610 826-7542
Palmerton (G-13106)

New Hudson Facades LLC ....C 610 494-8100
Upper Chichester (G-18668)

CONTRACTORS: Mechanical

Blanski Energy Management Inc ....E 610 373-5273
Reading (G-16335)

Brodys Welding and Mech Contrs ....G 215 941-7914
Philadelphia (G-13486)

Condos Incorporated ....E 570 748-9265
Mill Hall (G-11174)

Dasco Inc ....G 412 771-4140
Pittsburgh (G-14906)

Deshlers Machine Inc ....G 610 588-5622
Bangor (G-912)

GSM Industrial Inc ....C 717 207-8985
Lancaster (G-9034)

Hranec Sheet Metal Inc ....C 724 437-2211
Uniontown (G-18631)

J Rybnick Mech Contr Inc ....G 570 222-2544
Nicholson (G-12616)

James Craft & Son Inc ....C 717 266-6629
York Haven (G-20759)

Krimes Industrial and Mech Inc ....G 717 628-1301
Ephrata (G-5115)

Power Mechanical Corp ....E 570 823-8824
Wilkes Barre (G-19958)

Rado Enterprises Inc ....E 570 759-0303
Benton (G-1281)

Robbie Holland ....G 610 495-5441
Royersford (G-16862)

Wm T Spaeder Co Inc ....D 814 456-7014
Erie (G-5532)

Yorkaire Inc ....E 717 755-2836
York (G-20755)

CONTRACTORS: Millwrights

Bortnick Construction Inc ....G 814 587-6023
Springboro (G-17894)

J Rybnick Mech Contr Inc ....G 570 222-2544
Nicholson (G-12616)

S F Spector Inc ....G 717 236-0805
Harrisburg (G-7211)

Starflite Systems Inc ....E 724 789-9200
Connoquenessing (G-3513)

CONTRACTORS: Office Furniture Installation

Stanley Storage Systems Inc ....G 610 797-6600
Allentown (G-401)

CONTRACTORS: Oil & Gas Aerial Geophysical Exploration Svcs

Bop Land Services LP ....F 724 747-1594
Pittsburgh (G-14785)

Civic Mapper LLC ....G 315 729-7869
Pittsburgh (G-14856)

Eye-Bot Aerial Solutions LLC ....G 724 904-7706
New Kensington (G-12340)

Terraviz Geospatial Inc ....G 717 938-3591
Conshohocken (G-3612)

Terraviz Geospatial Inc ....G 717 512-9658
Etters (G-5554)

CONTRACTORS: Oil & Gas Building, Repairing & Dismantling Svc

Baron Crest Energy Company ....G 724 478-1121
Apollo (G-663)

Dan-Beck Well Services Inc ....E 724 538-1001
Evans City (G-5557)

Developed Resources Inc ....G 724 274-6956
Cheswick (G-3106)

Evergreen Oilfld Solutions LLC ....F 570 485-9998
Wyalusing (G-20251)

General Civil Company Inc ....F 484 571-1998
Aston (G-767)

Pennsylvania Production Svcs ....E 724 463-0729
Indiana (G-8118)

Sentry Wellhead Systems LLC ....E 724 422-8108
Canonsburg (G-2634)

Springhill Well Service Inc ....E 724 447-2449
New Freeport (G-12218)

Streamline Energy Services LLC ....F 610 415-1220
Valley Forge (G-18715)

Tetra Technologies Inc ....E 570 659-5357
Mansfield (G-10426)

Winn-Marion Barber LLC ....G 412 319-7392
Bridgeville (G-2099)

CONTRACTORS: Oil & Gas Field Fire Fighting Svcs

Wild Well Control Inc ....G 724 873-5083
Canonsburg (G-2659)

CONTRACTORS: Oil & Gas Field Geological Exploration Svcs

American Petroleum Partners ....G 844 835-5277
Canonsburg (G-2539)

Daleco Resources Corporation ....G 570 795-4347
West Chester (G-19531)

Eclipse Resources Oper LLC ....G 814 308-9731
State College (G-17961)

Pardee Resources Company ....F 215 405-1260
Philadelphia (G-14122)

CONTRACTORS: Oil & Gas Field Geophysical Exploration Svcs

Schlumberger Technology Corp ....C 814 220-1900
Brookville (G-2271)

CONTRACTORS: Oil & Gas Field Salt Water Impound/Storing Svc

Franklin Brine Treatment Corp ....G 814 437-3593
Franklin (G-6125)

Seahorse Oilfield Services LLC ....G 724 597-2039
Canonsburg (G-2633)

CONTRACTORS: Oil & Gas Field Tools Fishing Svcs

Klx Energy Services LLC ....G 570 835-0149
Tioga (G-18363)

CONTRACTORS: Oil & Gas Well Casing Cement Svcs

Kada Energy Resources LLC ....G 215 839-9159
Philadelphia (G-13919)

Kimzey Casing Service LLC ....G 724 225-0529
Washington (G-19192)

Mds Securities LLC ....G 724 548-2501
Kittanning (G-8783)

Power Ign Cntrls Applachia LLC ....G 724 746-3700
Lawrence (G-9539)

Ursa Mjor Drctnal Crssings LLC ....F 866 410-9719
Greentown (G-6735)

Welltec Inc ....G 724 553-5922
Cranberry Township (G-3864)

CONTRACTORS: Oil & Gas Well Drilling Svc

AEC Services Company LLC ....G 610 246-6470
Plymouth Meeting (G-15828)

AES Drilling Fluids LLC ....E 724 743-2934
Canonsburg (G-2533)

Alternative Petroleum Svcs LLC ....G 570 807-1797
Milford (G-11155)

Appalachian Drillers LLC ....G 724 548-2501
Kittanning (G-8754)

Ardent Resources Inc ....G 412 854-1193
Pittsburgh (G-14720)

Arsenal Resources LLC ....E 724 940-1100
Wexford (G-19791)

Atlas America Public 10 Ltd ....G 412 262-2830
Coraopolis (G-3659)

Atlas Energy Operating Co LLC ....B 412 262-2830
Coraopolis (G-3660)

Baron Crest Energy Company ....G 724 478-1121
Apollo (G-663)

Bittinger Drilling Co ....G 724 727-3822
Apollo (G-664)

Black Viper Energy Services ....D 432 561-8801
Cuddy (G-3940)

Brown Brothers Drilling Inc ....G 717 548-2500
Nottingham (G-12881)

Calder Transport ....G 724 787-8390
Greensburg (G-6654)

Catalyst Energy Inc ....E 412 325-4350
Pittsburgh (G-14828)

Commonwealth Drilling Company ....G 610 940-4015
Plymouth Meeting (G-15839)

Curtis and Son Oil Inc ....G 814 489-7858
Sugargrove (G-18150)

D K Gas Inc ....G 814 365-5621
Hawthorn (G-7443)

Deepwell Energy Services LLC ....E 412 316-5243
Eighty Four (G-4837)

Eastern Environmental Inds LLC ....E 814 371-2221
Brockway (G-2224)

Edgemarc Energy Holdings LLC ....E 724 749-8466
Canonsburg (G-2580)

Empire Energy E&P LLC ....E 724 483-2070
Canonsburg (G-2584)

Exco Resources LLC ....D 724 720-2500
Kittanning (G-8768)

First Class Energy LLC ....E 724 548-2501
Kittanning (G-8771)

First Class Energy LLC ....E 724 548-2501
Kittanning (G-8770)

Gas & Oil Management Assoc ....G 814 563-4601
Youngsville (G-20771)

Gill Rock Drill Company Inc ....E 717 272-3861
Lebanon (G-9573)

Great Plains Oilfld Rentl LLC ....G 570 882-7700
Sayre (G-17115)

Helmerich & Payne Intl Drlg Co ....C 814 353-3450
Howard (G-7891)

Hemlock Oil & Gas Co Inc ....G 814 368-6261
Bradford (G-1972)

Howard Drilling Inc ....G 814 778-5820
Mount Jewett (G-11642)

J H R Inc ....G 412 221-1617
Bridgeville (G-2072)

JM Enterprise LLC ....G 814 758-5998
Tionesta (G-18373)

Keane Frac LP ....E 570 302-4050
Mansfield (G-10417)

Keane Frac Tx LLC ....G 570 302-4050
Mansfield (G-10418)

Key Energy Services Inc ....E 878 302-3333
New Kensington (G-12351)

Kriebel Gas Inc ....D 814 226-4160
Clarion (G-3181)

Kriebel Gas Inc ....G 814 938-2010
Punxsutawney (G-16146)

Michels Corporation ....G 724 249-2065
Washington (G-19202)

Mine Drilling Services LL ....F 814 765-1075
Clearfield (G-3225)

Nabors Drilling Tech USA ....G 814 768-4640
Clearfield (G-3226)

Northstern Cnsld Enrgy Prtners ....G 412 491-6660
Wexford (G-19816)

Northwest Synergy Corp ....G 814 726-0543
Warren (G-19040)

Papco Inc ....F 814 726-2130
Warren (G-19042)

Penn Production Group LLC ....G 724 349-6690
Indiana (G-8117)

Penneco Oil Company ....F 724 468-8232
Delmont (G-4052)

Phillips Drilling Company ....F 724 479-1135
Warrendale (G-19091)

Phillips Drilling Company ....G 724 479-1135
Indiana (G-8120)

Pioneer Drilling Services Ltd ....G 724 592-6707
Rices Landing (G-16671)

Precision Drilling Oilfld Svcs ....G 570 329-5100
Williamsport (G-20062)

Ristau Drilling Co ....G 814 723-4858
Warren (G-19046)

Rock Run Enterprises LLC ....G 814 938-8778
Punxsutawney (G-16159)

Silver Vly Drlg & Blastg Inc ....G 570 992-1125
Saylorsburg (G-17107)

Simon of Bolivar Enterprises ....G 814 697-7891
Shinglehouse (G-17513)

Sonic Energy Services USA Inc ....G 724 782-0560
Venetia (G-18744)

Southwell Oil Co ....G 814 723-5178
Warren (G-19047)

Texas Keystone Inc ....E 412 435-6555
Oakmont (G-12926)

Universal Pressure Pumping Inc ....G 814 373-3226
Meadville (G-10806)

Universal Well Services Inc ....G 814 938-5327
Punxsutawney (G-16165)

US Crossings Unlimited LLC ....G 888 359-1115
Cranberry Township (G-3861)

US Energy Expl Corp ....G 724 783-7624
Rural Valley (G-16878)

Vertical Resources Inc ....F 814 489-3931
Sugar Grove (G-18148)

Victory Energy Corporation ....E 724 349-6366
Indiana (G-8133)

Vista Resources Inc ....G 412 833-8884
Pittsburgh (G-15699)

Wgm Gas Company Inc ....E 724 397-9600
Creekside (G-3878)

Yost Drilling LLC ....D 724 324-2253
Mount Morris (G-11684)

CONTRACTORS: Oil & Gas Well Foundation Grading Svcs

Dean Construction LLC ....G 814 887-8750
Smethport (G-17634)

Kozik Bros Inc ....E 724 443-2230
Cranberry Township (G-3829)

CONTRACTORS: Oil & Gas Well On-Site Foundation Building Svcs

Shallenberger Construction Inc ....D 724 628-8408
Connellsville (G-3508)

Staar Distributing Llc ....D 814 612-2115
Reynoldsville (G-16666)

Sunbelt Drilling Services Inc ....F 215 764-9544
Blue Bell (G-1853)

CONTRACTORS: Oil & Gas Well Plugging & Abandoning Svcs

Minard Run Oil Company ....D 814 362-3531
Bradford (G-1982)

Phillips & Dart Oil Field Svc ....G 814 465-2292
Gifford (G-6360)

Randy Larkin ....G 814 358-2508
Callensburg (G-2465)

Silver Creek Services Inc ....E 724 710-0440
Canonsburg (G-2637)

CONTRACTORS: Oil & Gas Well reworking

Greene County Gas & Oil Co ....G 724 627-3393
Waynesburg (G-19444)

CONTRACTORS: Oil & Gas Wells Pumping Svcs

G B Well Service ....G 412 221-3102
Bridgeville (G-2065)

Oakes Gas Co Inc ....G 814 837-7972
Kane (G-8475)

P
R
O
D
U
C
T

CONTRACTORS: Oil & Gas Wells Svcs

Capstone Energy Services LLC...........C...... 724 326-0190
  Allenport **(G-104)**
Greene County Drilling Co Inc...........G...... 724 627-3393
  Waynesburg **(G-19443)**
Key Energy Services Inc ....E...... 878 302-3333
  New Kensington **(G-12351)**
Puraglobe Florida LLC ....G...... 813 247-1754
  Wayne **(G-19366)**
Texas Ces Inc ....B...... 412 490-9200
  Pittsburgh **(G-15606)**
Uav Aviation Services.......................G...... 717 691-8882
  Mechanicsburg **(G-10901)**

CONTRACTORS: Oil Field Haulage Svcs

Geyer & Son Inc ....F...... 412 431-5231
  Pittsburgh **(G-15049)**

CONTRACTORS: Oil Field Mud Drilling Svcs

Susquehanna Services LLC.................G...... 570 288-5269
  Swoyersville **(G-18200)**

CONTRACTORS: Oil/Gas Well Construction, Rpr/Dismantling Svcs

Arrowwood Construction.....................G...... 610 799-6040
  Coplay **(G-3639)**
Avc Solutions LLC ....G...... 412 737-8945
  Pittsburgh **(G-14743)**
B & C Meter Inc ....G...... 814 257-8464
  Dayton **(G-4036)**
City of Pittsburgh...........................E...... 412 255-2883
  Pittsburgh **(G-14854)**
Complete Fluid Control Inc ....E...... 570 382-3376
  S Abingtn Twp **(G-16893)**
Completion Snubbing Servi................G...... 940 668-5109
  Smithton **(G-17659)**
Donawald Enterprises LLC ....F...... 215 962-3635
  Doylestown **(G-4295)**
Glasgow Hauling Inc........................D...... 215 884-8800
  Glenside **(G-6522)**
Homescapers ....G...... 814 353-0507
  Bellefonte **(G-1105)**
Homestead Inspection Service.............G...... 717 691-1586
  Mechanicsburg **(G-10853)**
Howard Drilling Inc ....G...... 814 778-5820
  Mount Jewett **(G-11642)**
In A Week Guaranteed Inc ....G...... 610 965-7700
  Emmaus **(G-5028)**
J C K Services ....G...... 814 755-7772
  Tionesta **(G-18372)**
Newpark Mats Intgrted Svcs LLC ....F...... 570 323-4970
  Williamsport **(G-20047)**
Oxford Construction PA Inc ....D...... 215 809-2245
  Philadelphia **(G-14106)**
R P Neese & Sons LLC ....G...... 724 465-5718
  Marion Center **(G-10476)**
Select Dismantling Corp ....F...... 724 861-6004
  Wendel **(G-19482)**
Tarpon Energy Services LLC ....D...... 570 547-0442
  Bridgeville **(G-2093)**
Timothy R Brennan Jr ....G...... 570 281-9504
  Carbondale **(G-2686)**
U S Weatherford L P ....E...... 724 745-7050
  Canonsburg **(G-2649)**

CONTRACTORS: On-Site Welding

Agar Welding Service & Stl Sup ....E...... 717 532-1000
  Walnut Bottom **(G-18788)**
Bill Hards ....F...... 814 677-2460
  Seneca **(G-17364)**
Brodys Welding and Mech Contrs ....G...... 215 941-7914
  Philadelphia **(G-13486)**
Cambria Welding & Fabg Inc ....G...... 814 948-5072
  Saint Benedict **(G-16936)**
Claylick Enterprises LLC....................F...... 717 328-9876
  Mercersburg **(G-10983)**
Craig Sidleck ....F...... 610 261-9580
  Whitehall **(G-19869)**
D & R Steel Construction Inc ....F...... 570 265-6216
  Milan **(G-11147)**
D & S Fabricating & Welding ....G...... 412 653-9185
  Clairton **(G-3148)**
D A D Fabrication and Welding............G...... 814 781-1886
  Saint Marys **(G-16960)**
Dolans Wldg Stl Fbrication Inc ....E...... 814 749-8639
  Johnstown **(G-8369)**

Fab-Rick Industries Inc ....E...... 717 859-5633
  Lancaster **(G-9013)**
Gambone Steel Company Inc ....E...... 610 539-6505
  Norristown **(G-12660)**
Hart McHncl-Lctrcal Contrs Inc ....E...... 215 257-1666
  Perkasie **(G-13278)**
Hines Industries Inc ....G...... 610 264-1656
  Whitehall **(G-19875)**
J Rybnick Mech Contr Inc ....G...... 570 222-2544
  Nicholson **(G-12616)**
Klk Welding Inc ....F...... 717 637-0080
  Hanover **(G-6910)**
Lehigh Services Inc ....G...... 610 966-2525
  Macungie **(G-10152)**
Martys Muffler & Weld Shop ....G...... 412 673-4141
  North Versailles **(G-12781)**
Maxwell Welding and Mch Inc ....E...... 724 729-3160
  Burgettstown **(G-2349)**
Mdl Manufacturing Inds Inc ....E...... 814 623-0888
  Bedford **(G-1064)**
Morocco Welding LLC ....F...... 814 444-9353
  Somerset **(G-17697)**
Murslack Welding Inc ....G...... 412 364-5554
  Pittsburgh **(G-15312)**
Nestors Welding Co ....G...... 570 668-3401
  Tamaqua **(G-18221)**
Precision Metal Crafters Ltd ....E...... 724 837-2511
  Greensburg **(G-6704)**
Raphael A Ingaglio ....G...... 570 289-5000
  Hop Bottom **(G-7775)**
Sanitary Process Systems Inc..............E...... 717 627-6630
  Lititz **(G-10045)**
Skias Chuck Wldg & Fabricators..........G...... 610 375-0912
  Reading **(G-16519)**
Snyder Welding LLC ....G...... 610 657-4916
  Slatington **(G-17614)**
Tool City Welding LLC.......................G...... 814 333-9353
  Meadville **(G-10802)**
Trico Welding Company ....F...... 724 722-1300
  Yukon **(G-20785)**
W & W Welding Inc ....G...... 717 336-4314
  Reinholds **(G-6637)**
Westmrland Stl Fabrication Inc ....E...... 724 446-0555
  Madison **(G-10167)**

CONTRACTORS: Ornamental Metal Work

Anderson Welding & Sons LLC...........G...... 215 886-1726
  Oreland **(G-13017)**
Antietam Iron Works LLC ....G...... 717 485-5557
  Mc Connellsburg **(G-10562)**
Armin Ironworks Inc ....G...... 412 322-1622
  Pittsburgh **(G-14725)**
Custom Iron Works Welding ....F...... 814 444-1315
  Somerset **(G-17682)**
Frank Bellace Welding ....G...... 856 488-8099
  Danville **(G-4002)**
Matthews International Corp ....B...... 412 571-5500
  Pittsburgh **(G-15266)**
Pencoyd Iron Works Inc ....E...... 610 522-5000
  Folcroft **(G-6012)**
Scranton Craftsmen Inc ....D...... 570 347-5125
  Throop **(G-18361)**
Veyko Design Inc ....G...... 215 928-1349
  Philadelphia **(G-14444)**

CONTRACTORS: Painting & Wall Covering

Capital Coating Inc ....F...... 717 442-0979
  Kinzers **(G-8735)**
Coopers ....G...... 610 369-8992
  Boyertown **(G-1905)**
Reese Daryl C Wallpapering ....G...... 717 597-2532
  Greencastle **(G-6629)**

CONTRACTORS: Painting, Commercial

Flinchbaugh Company Inc ....E...... 717 266-2202
  Manchester **(G-10356)**
Oesterlings Sndblst & Pntg Inc ....E...... 724 282-1391
  Butler **(G-2429)**

CONTRACTORS: Painting, Commercial, Interior

Fedco Manufacturing Inc ....F...... 724 863-2252
  Larimer **(G-9451)**

CONTRACTORS: Painting, Indl

Blastco...G...... 215 529-7100
  Quakertown **(G-16173)**

Conway-Phillips Holding LLC...............E...... 412 315-7963
  Braddock **(G-1943)**
M & A Coatings LLC.........................F...... 724 267-2868
  Washington **(G-19196)**

CONTRACTORS: Painting, Residential

Lepko J D Finishing..........................G...... 215 538-9717
  Quakertown **(G-16210)**
R M Frantz Inc ....G...... 570 421-3020
  Stroudsburg **(G-18137)**

CONTRACTORS: Parking Lot Maintenance

D E Gemill Inc.................................E...... 717 755-9794
  Red Lion **(G-16593)**

CONTRACTORS: Patio & Deck Construction & Repair

American Fence Inc ....F...... 610 437-1944
  Whitehall **(G-19861)**
Black Bear Structures Inc ....G...... 717 225-0377
  York **(G-20410)**
Mid-State Awning Inc ....G...... 814 355-8979
  Bellefonte **(G-1108)**
Superior Window Mfg Inc ....F...... 412 793-3500
  Pittsburgh **(G-15589)**

CONTRACTORS: Pavement Marking

Allen P Sutton ....G...... 717 957-2047
  Marysville **(G-10531)**
Alpha Space Control Co Inc.................G...... 717 263-0182
  Chambersburg **(G-2900)**

CONTRACTORS: Pipe & Boiler Insulating

A & B Steelworks LLC ....F...... 717 823-8599
  Myerstown **(G-11872)**

CONTRACTORS: Pipe Laying

Pennsylvania Drilling Company ....E...... 412 771-2110
  Imperial **(G-8074)**
Specialty Tank & Wldg Co Inc..............E...... 215 949-2939
  Bristol **(G-2201)**

CONTRACTORS: Plastering, Plain or Ornamental

Callahan David E Pool Plst Inc ....E...... 610 429-4496
  West Chester **(G-19517)**

CONTRACTORS: Plumbing

Clapper Leon Plbg Htg Wtr Cond ....F...... 570 629-2833
  Stroudsburg **(G-18110)**
Frey Lutz Corp ....C...... 717 394-4635
  Lancaster **(G-9025)**
JM Daugherty Industries LLC..............G...... 412 835-2135
  Bethel Park **(G-1419)**
Resolve Trnchless Slutions Inc ....G...... 215 441-5544
  Warminster **(G-18953)**
Wierman Diller Inc............................G...... 717 637-3871
  Hanover **(G-6975)**

CONTRACTORS: Pole Cutting

Smith Lumber Co ....F...... 570 923-0188
  Renovo **(G-16650)**

CONTRACTORS: Pollution Control Eqpt Installation

Goodhart Sons Inc............................C...... 717 656-2404
  Lancaster **(G-9030)**

CONTRACTORS: Power Generating Eqpt Installation

American Hydro Corporation................C...... 717 755-5300
  York **(G-20374)**

CONTRACTORS: Precast Concrete Struct Framing & Panel Placing

High Concrete Group LLC...................B...... 717 336-9300
  Denver **(G-4075)**
Kca Enterprises...............................G...... 724 880-2534
  Connellsville **(G-3501)**

CONTRACTORS: Prefabricated Window & Door Installation

Emerald Windows Inc ....F 215 236-6767
Philadelphia (G-13673)
Hc Hoodco Inc ....F 814 355-4003
Bellefonte (G-1104)
Korsak Glass & Aluminum Inc ....G 610 987-9888
Boyertown (G-1923)
Micfralip Inc ....F 215 338-3293
Philadelphia (G-14019)
Thermo-Twin Industries Inc ....C 412 826-1000
Oakmont (G-12927)
Tyger Construction ....G 814 467-9342
Windber (G-20193)

CONTRACTORS: Refractory or Acid Brick Masonry

Grc Holding Inc ....G 610 667-6640
Bala Cynwyd (G-879)
Reading Refractories Company ....F 610 375-4422
Bala Cynwyd (G-890)

CONTRACTORS: Refrigeration

Michalski Refrigeration Inc ....G 724 352-1666
Butler (G-2423)
Summers & Zims Inc ....E 610 593-2420
Atglen (G-809)
Thd Contracting Service LLC ....G 215 626-1548
Philadelphia (G-14385)
White Refrigeration Inc ....G 570 265-7335
Towanda (G-18437)

CONTRACTORS: Roofing

Donald B Smith Incorporated ....E 717 632-2100
Hanover (G-6879)
Histand Brothers Inc ....F 215 348-4121
Ambler (G-581)
L A Welte Inc ....G 412 341-9400
Pittsburgh (G-15206)
L Richard Sensenig Co ....D 717 733-0364
Ephrata (G-5117)
M&B Enterprises Inc ....G 814 454-4461
Erie (G-5377)
Union Roofing and Shtmtl Co ....E 814 946-0824
Altoona (G-553)
Voegele Company Inc ....E 412 781-0940
Pittsburgh (G-15705)
Walter B Staller Inc ....G 570 385-5386
Schuylkill Haven (G-17171)

CONTRACTORS: Roustabout Svcs

All Climate Servicing ....G 570 686-4629
Milford (G-11153)
Default Servicing Inc ....G 502 968-1400
Pittsburgh (G-14915)
Youth Services Agency ....F 215 752-7050
Penndel (G-13242)

CONTRACTORS: Safety & Security Eqpt

Alert Enterprises Ltd Lblty Co ....G 570 373-2821
Kulpmont (G-8821)
Aqua Enterprises ....F 215 257-2231
Perkasie (G-13266)
Martin Communications Inc ....F 412 498-0157
Mc Kees Rocks (G-10619)

CONTRACTORS: Sandblasting Svc, Building Exteriors

APS Advance Products & Svcs ....G 610 863-0570
Wind Gap (G-20165)
Arcman Corporation ....G 570 489-6402
Dunmore (G-4467)
Inghams Regrooving Service Inc ....E 717 336-8473
Denver (G-4076)
Oesterlings Sndblst & Pntg Inc ....E 724 282-1391
Butler (G-2429)

CONTRACTORS: Seismograph Survey Svcs

Welltech Products Inc ....G 610 417-8928
Macungie (G-10161)

CONTRACTORS: Septic System

Forsht Concrete Pdts Co Inc ....G 814 944-1617
Altoona (G-507)

Reeser Bros ....G 717 266-6644
York Haven (G-20761)
Rosenberry Septic Tank Service ....G 717 532-4026
Shippensburg (G-17545)
Scranton Craftsmen Inc ....D 570 347-5125
Throop (G-18361)

CONTRACTORS: Sheet Metal Work, NEC

A M Sheet Metal Inc ....F 570 322-5417
South Williamsport (G-17789)
Aviva Technology Inc ....G 610 228-4689
Broomall (G-2279)
Bevilacqua Sheet Metal Inc ....G 570 558-0397
Scranton (G-17211)
Blanski Energy Management Inc ....E 610 373-5273
Reading (G-16335)
Coraopolis Light Metal Inc ....G 412 264-2252
Coraopolis (G-3680)
Edward J Deseta Co Inc ....G 302 691-2040
Harleysville (G-7032)
Frey Lutz Corp ....C 717 394-4635
Lancaster (G-9025)
Harold M Horst Inc ....G 717 354-5815
New Holland (G-12251)
Herb Sheet Metal Inc ....F 717 273-8001
Lebanon (G-9579)
J & S Fabrication Inc ....G 717 469-1409
Grantville (G-6574)
Ken F Smith Custom Shtmtl LLC ....G 717 624-4214
New Oxford (G-12415)
Laminar Flow Inc ....D 215 672-0232
Warminster (G-18909)
Martin Metal Works Inc ....F 717 292-5691
East Berlin (G-4523)
Mc Mahon Welding Inc ....G 215 794-0260
Mechanicsville (G-10912)
Pennmark Technologies Corp ....E 570 255-5000
Dallas (G-3966)
Quality Perforating Inc ....D 570 267-2092
Carbondale (G-2685)
Rhoads Industries Inc ....D 267 728-6300
Philadelphia (G-14244)
Schatzie Ltd ....G 610 834-1240
Conshohocken (G-3604)
Superior Metalworks Inc ....F 717 245-2446
Carlisle (G-2740)
Tuckey Metal Fabricators Inc ....E 717 249-8111
Carlisle (G-2744)

CONTRACTORS: Sheet metal Work, Architectural

Double D Sheet Metal Inc ....G 610 987-3733
Oley (G-12978)
Fabri-Weld LLC ....G 814 490-7324
Erie (G-5287)
River Supply Inc ....E 717 927-1555
Brogue (G-2240)

CONTRACTORS: Ship Joinery

Interntonal Mar Outfitting LLC ....G 215 875-9911
Philadelphia (G-13871)

CONTRACTORS: Shoring & Underpinning

Trench Shoring Services ....G 412 331-8118
Pittsburgh (G-15642)

CONTRACTORS: Siding

Superior Window Mfg Inc ....F 412 793-3500
Pittsburgh (G-15589)
Tyger Construction ....G 814 467-9342
Windber (G-20193)

CONTRACTORS: Single-family Home General Remodeling

CMI Systems ....F 215 596-0306
Philadelphia (G-13553)
Dun Rite Window and Door ....G 412 781-8200
Pittsburgh (G-14942)
Frank Griffith ....G 570 524-7175
Lewisburg (G-9909)
Great Additions Inc ....F 570 675-0852
Luzerne (G-10124)
Martin Fabricating Inc ....E 610 435-5700
Allentown (G-309)
Mc Norton Cabinet Co ....G 724 538-5680
Cranberry Township (G-3834)

William Cottage ....G 724 266-2961
Ambridge (G-639)
Yesco Handyman Services ....G 724 206-9541
Washington (G-19249)

CONTRACTORS: Solar Energy Eqpt

Beneficial Enrgy Solutions LLC ....G 844 237-7697
Jonestown (G-8449)
Eznergy LLC ....G 215 361-7332
Lansdale (G-9366)

CONTRACTORS: Sound Eqpt Installation

Audio Video Automation SEC Inc ....G 814 313-1108
Warren (G-19011)

CONTRACTORS: Special Trades, NEC

E D I Enviro-Drill Inc ....F 412 788-1046
Pittsburgh (G-14949)
Omega Fence Co ....G 215 729-7474
Philadelphia (G-14094)

CONTRACTORS: Stone Masonry

Tervo Masonry Llc ....E 724 944-6179
New Wilmington (G-12471)

CONTRACTORS: Storage Tank Erection, Metal

Conway-Phillips Holding LLC ....E 412 315-7963
Braddock (G-1943)
Evergreen Tank Solutions Inc ....G 484 268-5168
Philadelphia (G-13684)
Fisher Tank Company ....E 610 494-7200
Chester (G-3051)
Schake Industries Inc ....E 814 677-9333
Seneca (G-17369)

CONTRACTORS: Structural Iron Work, Structural

Anvil Iron Works Inc ....G 215 468-8300
Philadelphia (G-13397)
Dedicated Customs Inc ....G 724 678-6609
Burgettstown (G-2345)
F F Frickanisce Iron Works ....G 724 568-2001
Vandergrift (G-18726)
Hines Industries Inc ....G 610 264-1656
Whitehall (G-19875)
Raphael A Ingaglio ....G 570 289-5000
Hop Bottom (G-7775)

CONTRACTORS: Structural Steel Erection

A & R Iron Works Inc ....F 610 497-8770
Trainer (G-18462)
Anderson Welding & Sons LLC ....G 215 886-1726
Oreland (G-13017)
Chowns Fabrication Rigging Inc ....D 610 584-0240
Skippack (G-17595)
D & R Steel Construction Inc ....F 570 265-6216
Milan (G-11147)
DH Steel Products LLC ....E 814 459-2715
Erie (G-5247)
G & D Erectors Inc ....E 724 587-0590
Avella (G-836)
High Industries Inc ....B 717 293-4444
Lancaster (G-9046)
High Steel Structures LLC ....G 717 299-5211
Lancaster (G-9049)
Ira G Steffy and Son Inc ....D 717 626-6500
Ephrata (G-5111)
Kelly Iron Works Inc ....G 610 872-5436
Hazleton (G-7505)
Nichols Welding Service Inc ....G 412 362-8855
Pittsburgh (G-15338)

CONTRACTORS: Svc Station Eqpt Installation, Maint & Repair

Millennium Machining Spc ....G 570 501-2002
Hazleton (G-7510)

CONTRACTORS: Svc Well Drilling Svcs

A & S Production Inc ....G 814 463-9310
Endeavor (G-5078)
Bucks Cnty Artesian Well Drlg ....F 215 493-1867
Washington Crossing (G-19253)

PRODUCT

Drillmasters LLC ....G...... 717 319-8657
Telford (G-18285)

S & S Sbsrface Invstgtions Inc ....G...... 610 738-8762
West Chester (G-19634)

S & T Supply Co ....F 814 589-7025
Pleasantville (G-15803)

Sallack Well Services Inc ....G...... 814 938-8179
Punxsutawney (G-16160)

Tophole Drilling LLC ....F 724 272-1932
Saxonburg (G-17098)

CONTRACTORS: Tile Installation, Ceramic

Callahan David E Pool Plst Inc ....E 610 429-4496
West Chester (G-19517)

Marcon & Boyer Inc ....D...... 610 866-5959
Allentown (G-307)

Unity Marble and Granite Inc ....G...... 412 793-4220
Pittsburgh (G-15681)

CONTRACTORS: Tuck Pointing & Restoration

Shamrock Building Services Inc ....E 412 279-2800
Carnegie (G-2792)

CONTRACTORS: Underground Utilities

Linde Corporation ....C...... 570 299-5700
Pittston (G-15765)

CONTRACTORS: Ventilation & Duct Work

K & I Sheet Metal Inc........................E 412 781-8111
Pittsburgh (G-15159)

Sheet Metal Specialists LLC ....E 717 910-7000
Harrisburg (G-7215)

Walsh Sheet Metal Inc ....G...... 570 344-3495
Scranton (G-17311)

William J Koshinskie ....G...... 570 742-4969
Milton (G-11251)

CONTRACTORS: Warm Air Heating & Air Conditioning

College Town Inc................................G...... 717 532-7354
Shippensburg (G-17523)

College Town Inc................................G...... 717 532-3034
Shippensburg (G-17524)

James E Roth Inc ....D...... 724 776-1910
Cranberry Township (G-3826)

Marc-Service Inc ....E 814 467-8611
Windber (G-20189)

Mounts Equipment Co Inc..................G...... 724 225-0460
Washington (G-19208)

New Enterprise Stone Lime Inc ....B 610 374-5131
Leesport (G-9668)

Robert G Dent Heating & AC ....F 570 784-6721
Bloomsburg (G-1798)

Russo Heating & Cooling Inc..............F 814 454-6263
Erie (G-5468)

Schatzie Ltd.....................................G...... 610 834-1240
Conshohocken (G-3604)

Scranton Sheet Metal Inc ....E 570 342-2904
Scranton (G-17288)

Sunoco Inc.......................................E 717 564-1440
Harrisburg (G-7222)

United Coolair Corporation ....C...... 717 845-8685
York (G-20694)

CONTRACTORS: Water Intake Well Drilling Svc

Andrew E Trautner & Sons Inc ....G....... 570 494-0191
Cogan Station (G-3358)

CONTRACTORS: Water Well Drilling

C S Garber & Sons Inc......................E 610 367-2861
Boyertown (G-1902)

Funks Drilling Incorporated ....F 717 423-6688
Newville (G-12601)

McKay & Gould Drilling Inc ....E 724 436-6823
Darlington (G-4030)

McKinney Drilling Company LLC ....E 724 468-4139
Delmont (G-4051)

Middleburg Pre Cast LLC ....F 570 837-1463
Middleburg (G-11029)

Phillips Drilling Company ....G...... 724 479-1135
Indiana (G-8120)

CONTRACTORS: Water Well Servicing

Altoona Soft Water Company ....F 814 943-2768
Altoona (G-473)

Frederick Drilling Co & Sons ....G...... 814 744-8581
Tylersburg (G-18573)

CONTRACTORS: Waterproofing

Grant Belcher ....F 814 853-9640
Greenville (G-6741)

CONTRACTORS: Well Bailing, Cleaning, Swabbing & Treating Svc

Oil States Energy Services LLC ....D....... 570 538-1623
Watsontown (G-19278)

CONTRACTORS: Well Casings Perforating Svcs

Beckley Perforating Corp....................G...... 570 267-2092
Carbondale (G-2669)

CDK Perforating LLC ....E 570 358-3250
Ulster (G-18598)

Titan Wireline Service Inc ....F 724 354-2629
Shelocta (G-17489)

CONTRACTORS: Well Logging Svcs

Cellar Tech LLC...............................E 724 519-2139
Murrysville (G-11849)

Gas Well Services 24-7 LLC...............G...... 570 398-7879
Jersey Shore (G-8313)

Schlumberger Technology Corp ....C....... 814 220-1900
Brookville (G-2271)

CONTRACTORS: Well Surveying Svcs

C&J Well Services Inc ....E 724 746-2467
Canonsburg (G-2555)

CONTRACTORS: Window Treatment Installation

Bon Air Products Inc ....G...... 412 793-8600
Verona (G-18749)

R and R Glass Inc ....G...... 215 443-7010
Warminster (G-18950)

CONTRACTORS: Windows & Doors

Pittsburgh Aluminum Co LLC...............F 724 452-5900
Pittsburgh (G-15386)

CONTRACTORS: Wood Floor Installation & Refinishing

Allegheny Strl Components Inc............G....... 724 867-1100
Emlenton (G-5005)

CONTRACTORS: Wrecking & Demolition

Joseph McCormick Cnstr Co Inc........E 814 899-3111
Erie (G-5339)

Thompson Logging and Trckg Inc ....E 570 923-2590
North Bend (G-12727)

CONTROL CIRCUIT DEVICES

Corby Industries Inc ....G...... 610 433-1412
Allentown (G-180)

M Squared Electronics Inc.................F 215 945-6658
Levittown (G-9848)

CONTROL EQPT: Electric

Aaim Controls Inc ....F 717 765-9100
Waynesboro (G-19393)

American Sensors Corporation............F 412 242-5903
Pittsburgh (G-14706)

Amtek Inc...F 814 734-3327
Edinboro (G-4808)

Bender Electronics Inc ....D...... 610 383-9200
Exton (G-5652)

Carnegie Robotics LLC ....D...... 412 251-0321
Pittsburgh (G-14819)

Chestnut Vly Ctrl Systems LLC ....G...... 717 330-2356
Manheim (G-10376)

Industrial Controls Inc.......................G...... 717 697-7555
Mechanicsburg (G-10858)

ITT Corporation ....B 717 509-2200
Lancaster (G-9065)

ITT LLC...D...... 215 218-7400
Philadelphia (G-13878)

J & Ak Inc..D...... 412 787-9750
Pittsburgh (G-15139)

Lutron Electronics Co Inc ....D...... 610 282-6617
Alburtis (G-56)

Lutron Electronics Co Inc ....F 610 282-6268
Allentown (G-302)

Metso Automation USA Inc ....G...... 215 393-3900
Lansdale (G-9387)

Metso Automation USA Inc ....E 215 393-3947
Lansdale (G-9388)

Morningstar Corporation.....................F 267 685-0500
Newtown (G-12523)

Novatech LLC ....C...... 484 812-6000
Quakertown (G-16224)

RSR Industries Inc ....G...... 215 543-3350
Warminster (G-18956)

Siemens Industry Inc........................C...... 724 339-9500
New Kensington (G-12375)

Siemens Industry Inc........................E 724 733-2569
Murrysville (G-11866)

Siemens Industry Inc........................D...... 724 743-5913
Canonsburg (G-2636)

Urania Engineering Co Inc ....E 570 455-0776
Hazleton (G-7532)

WAsnyder An Son LLC ....G...... 724 260-0695
Canonsburg (G-2655)

Wells Technology Inc ....G...... 215 672-7000
Warminster (G-18999)

CONTROL EQPT: Noise

Brd Noise & Vibration Ctrl Inc ....G...... 610 863-6300
Wind Gap (G-20167)

J A Brown Company ....G...... 610 832-0400
Conshohocken (G-3566)

Mason East Inc.................................G...... 631 254-2240
Feasterville Trevose (G-5917)

Noise Solutions (usa) Inc ....E 724 308-6901
Sharon (G-17441)

CONTROL PANELS: Electrical

Accurate Control & Design Co ....G...... 412 884-3723
Pittsburgh (G-14638)

Ai Control Systems Inc......................F 610 921-9670
Reading (G-16313)

Ajax Electric Company ....E 215 947-8500
Huntingdon Valley (G-7962)

American Mfg & Integration LLC ....F 724 861-2080
North Huntingdon (G-12767)

ARc Technologies Corporation ....F 724 722-7066
Yukon (G-20784)

B & C Controls Inc ....F 610 738-9204
West Chester (G-19506)

Basic Power Inc ....G...... 570 872-9666
East Stroudsburg (G-4608)

Carpenter Engineering Inc ....G...... 717 274-8808
Lebanon (G-9553)

Central Panel Inc ....G...... 215 947-8500
Huntingdon Valley (G-7968)

Clinton Controls Inc..........................G...... 570 748-4042
Lock Haven (G-10086)

Control Design Inc ....E 412 788-2280
Pittsburgh (G-14873)

Control Design Inc ....F 814 833-4663
Erie (G-5232)

Del Electronic Co ....G...... 412 787-1177
Pittsburgh (G-14916)

Dr Controls Inc.................................G...... 570 622-7109
Pottsville (G-16077)

Edwin L Heim Co...............................E 717 233-8711
Harrisburg (G-7125)

Erickson Corporation ....E 814 371-4350
Du Bois (G-4391)

FEC Technologies Inc........................E 717 764-5959
York (G-20477)

Genesys Controls Corporation ....G...... 717 291-1116
Landisville (G-9260)

Genesys Controls Corporation............F 717 291-1116
Landisville (G-9261)

Industrial Ctrl Concepts Inc ....G...... 412 464-1905
Homestead (G-7687)

Industrial Ctrl Concepts Inc ....G...... 412 464-1905
Homestead (G-7688)

Industrial Systems & Controls.............G...... 412 638-4977
Pittsburgh (G-15121)

Kauffman Elec Contrls & Contg ....E 717 252-3667
Wrightsville (G-20240)

Lighthouse Electric Contrls Co ....F 814 835-2348
Erie (G-5365)

Marvin Dale Slaymaker.................G...... 717 684-5050
  Washington Boro (G-19251)
Mauell Corporation ....E...... 717 432-8686
  Dillsburg (G-4137)
Oak Hill Controls LLC....................F...... 610 758-9500
  Bethlehem (G-1585)
Schrantz Indus Electricians ....G...... 610 435-8255
  Allentown (G-386)
Staneco Corporation ....E...... 215 672-6500
  Horsham (G-7852)
U B R LLC ....G...... 717 432-3490
  Dillsburg (G-4141)

CONTROLS & ACCESS: Indl, Electric

Advanced Controls Inc...................G...... 724 776-0224
  Cranberry Township (G-3799)
Automted Lgic Corp Kennesaw GA ......G...... 717 909-7000
  Harrisburg (G-7093)
Egr Ventures Inc.............................E...... 610 358-0500
  Aston (G-761)
Electronic Instrument Res Ltd ....G...... 724 744-7028
  Irwin (G-8158)
Hillside Equity Inc ....G...... 484 707-9012
  Bethlehem (G-1531)
Onexia Inc ....G...... 610 431-7271
  Exton (G-5720)
Rockwell Automation Inc ....F...... 717 747-8240
  York (G-20659)
Trio Motion Technology LLC............G...... 724 472-4100
  Freeport (G-6215)
Westinghouse Industry Products..........G...... 412 374-2020
  Cranberry Township (G-3866)

CONTROLS & ACCESS: Motor

Homewood Products Corporation ....E...... 412 665-2700
  Pittsburgh (G-15099)
Seastar Solutions ....G...... 610 495-7011
  Limerick (G-9971)
Solcon USA LLC ....F...... 724 728-2100
  Monroeville (G-11355)
Steel City Controls Inc....................G...... 412 851-8566
  Bethel Park (G-1434)

CONTROLS: Access, Motor

Intellidrives Inc.............................F...... 215 728-6804
  Philadelphia (G-13862)
Rockwell Automation Inc ....E...... 610 650-6840
  Norristown (G-12706)

CONTROLS: Automatic Temperature

Eccotrol LLC...................................G...... 877 322-6876
  Huntingdon Valley (G-7974)
Julabo Usa Inc................................E...... 610 231-0250
  Allentown (G-272)
Oven Industries Inc........................E...... 717 766-0721
  Camp Hill (G-2508)
Psg Controls Inc ....D...... 215 257-3621
  Philadelphia (G-14214)
Radius Systems LLC ....E...... 610 388-9940
  Chadds Ford (G-2859)
Thermo Electric Company Inc ....D...... 610 692-7990
  West Chester (G-19661)

CONTROLS: Crane & Hoist, Including Metal Mill

Karma Industrial Services LLC............G...... 717 814-7101
  York (G-20547)
Thackray Inc ....G...... 800 245-4387
  Philadelphia (G-14383)

CONTROLS: Electric Motor

Benshaw Inc ....G...... 412 487-8235
  Glenshaw (G-6483)
Centroid Corporation......................E...... 814 353-9290
  Howard (G-7886)

CONTROLS: Environmental

Absolute Acstic Noise Ctrl LLC............F...... 304 670-0095
  Oakdale (G-12887)
Arbutus Electronics Inc..................F...... 717 764-3565
  York (G-20384)
Automatic Control Elec Co ....F...... 210 661-4111
  Harleysville (G-7021)
Boss Controls LLC ....G...... 724 396-8131
  Pittsburgh (G-14786)

C S Fuller Inc ....G...... 610 941-9225
  Plymouth Meeting (G-15837)
Control Tech USA Ltd ....D...... 570 529-6011
  Troy (G-18519)
Controlsoft Inc ....E...... 724 733-2000
  Export (G-5595)
Evolve Guest Controls LLC ....F...... 855 750-9090
  West Chester (G-19553)
Healthy Home Resources.................F...... 412 431-4449
  Pittsburgh (G-15086)
Institute Prof Envmtl Practice ....E...... 412 396-1703
  Pittsburgh (G-15130)
Jordan Acquisition Group LLC............D...... 724 733-2000
  Export (G-5612)
Kanawha Scales & Systems Inc............F...... 724 258-6650
  Monongahela (G-11309)
Laminar Flow Inc............................D...... 215 672-0232
  Warminster (G-18909)
Mainline Environmental LLC............G...... 215 651-6635
  Trevose (G-18501)
Novatech LLC..................................C...... 484 812-6000
  Quakertown (G-16224)
Phonetics Inc..................................E...... 610 558-2700
  Aston (G-787)
Precision Technology Assoc Inc............G...... 412 881-8006
  Pittsburgh (G-15433)
Probes Unlimited Inc ....E...... 267 263-0400
  Lansdale (G-9401)
Process Instruments Inc ....E...... 412 431-4600
  Pittsburgh (G-15451)
Siemens Industry Inc......................D...... 215 654-8040
  Blue Bell (G-1852)
Strobic Air Corporation ....F...... 215 723-4700
  Telford (G-18321)
Strubles Fire and Safety ....G...... 814 594-0840
  Kersey (G-8571)
Therm-Omega-Tech Inc ....D...... 877 379-8258
  Warminster (G-18980)
Warren Controls Inc........................D...... 610 317-0800
  Bethlehem (G-1653)

CONTROLS: Fan, Temperature Responsive

Hvl LLC ....E...... 412 494-9600
  Pittsburgh (G-15107)

CONTROLS: Hydronic

Integritas Inc.................................G...... 814 941-7006
  Altoona (G-517)

CONTROLS: Marine & Navy, Auxiliary

HIG Capital LLC..............................C...... 610 495-7011
  Royersford (G-16851)

CONTROLS: Nuclear Reactor

Apantec LLC....................................F...... 267 436-3991
  Lansdale (G-9342)
Tsb Nclear Enrgy USA Group Inc ....G...... 412 374-4111
  Cranberry Township (G-3859)

CONTROLS: Positioning, Electric

Domenic Stangherlin.......................G...... 610 434-5624
  Allentown (G-195)
East Coast Control Systems.................G...... 814 857-5420
  Bigler (G-1658)

CONTROLS: Relay & Ind

3si Security Systems Holdg Inc............G...... 610 280-2000
  Malvern (G-10177)
Advanced Systems Technologies..........G...... 610 682-0610
  Topton (G-18410)
Ametek Inc.....................................D...... 215 256-6601
  Harleysville (G-7020)
Arbutus Electronics Inc..................F...... 717 764-3565
  York (G-20384)
Auma Actuators Inc........................C...... 724 743-2862
  Canonsburg (G-2545)
Automatic Control Elec Co ....F...... 210 661-4111
  Harleysville (G-7021)
Belden Inc......................................E...... 717 263-7655
  Chambersburg (G-2910)
Brentek International Inc.................G...... 814 259-3333
  York (G-20412)
Cmu Robotics..................................G...... 412 681-6900
  Pittsburgh (G-14863)
Columbia Research Labs Inc............E...... 610 872-3900
  Woodlyn (G-20218)

Control Chief Corporation................E...... 814 362-6811
  Bradford (G-1962)
Control Chief Holdings Inc..............D...... 814 362-6811
  Bradford (G-1963)
Control Design Inc..........................E...... 412 788-2280
  Pittsburgh (G-14873)
Control Dynamics Corporation............G...... 215 956-0700
  Warminster (G-18846)
Cse Corporation ....E...... 724 733-2247
  Pittsburgh (G-14891)
Deltronic Labs Inc ....E...... 215 997-8616
  Chalfont (G-2872)
Dew Electric Inc ....G...... 724 628-9711
  Connellsville (G-3494)
Eaton Corporation ....B...... 412 893-3300
  Coraopolis (G-3685)
Eaton Corporation ....B...... 724 773-1231
  Beaver (G-980)
Eaton Corporation ....E...... 412 893-3300
  Moon Township (G-11484)
Eaton Electrical Inc.........................E...... 412 893-3300
  Moon Township (G-11485)
Ellison Industrial Contrls LLC ....G...... 724 483-0251
  Belle Vernon (G-1086)
Ernst Timing Screw Company ....G...... 215 639-1438
  Bensalem (G-1191)
Ges Automation Technology ....E...... 717 236-8733
  Harrisburg (G-7133)
Hartronics....................................... G...... 717 597-3931
  Greencastle (G-6617)
Industrial Systems & Controls..........G...... 412 638-4977
  Pittsburgh (G-15121)
Infinite Control Systems Inc ....G...... 610 696-8600
  West Chester (G-19570)
Jls Automation LLC.........................E...... 717 505-3800
  York (G-20541)
Jordan Acquisition Group LLC............D...... 724 733-2000
  Export (G-5612)
Malvern Scale Data Systems ....G...... 610 296-9642
  Malvern (G-10274)
Mass Industrial Control ....G...... 610 678-8228
  Reading (G-16439)
Optimum Controls Corporation............D...... 610 375-0990
  Reading (G-16459)
Oven Industries Inc........................E...... 717 766-0721
  Camp Hill (G-2508)
Parker-Hannifin Corporation............C...... 215 723-4000
  Hatfield (G-7377)
Parker-Hannifin Corporation............C...... 724 861-8200
  Irwin (G-8188)
Powerex Inc....................................E...... 724 925-7272
  Youngwood (G-20781)
Process Instruments Inc ....E...... 412 431-4600
  Pittsburgh (G-15451)
R L Snelbecker Inc...........................G...... 717 292-4971
  Dover (G-4202)
Ralph A Hiller Company ....E...... 724 325-1200
  Export (G-5623)
Rdp Technologies Inc.......................F...... 610 650-9900
  Conshohocken (G-3599)
Rockwell Automation Inc ....D...... 724 741-4000
  Coraopolis (G-3722)
Rockwell Automation Inc ....G...... 412 375-4700
  Coraopolis (G-3723)
RPM Industries LLC.........................E...... 724 228-5130
  Washington (G-19224)
Sauer Industries Inc........................G...... 412 687-4100
  Pittsburgh (G-15513)
Sensor Corporation ....G...... 724 887-4080
  Scottdale (G-17200)
Sigma Controls Inc ....F...... 215 257-3412
  Perkasie (G-13293)
Spang & Company ....G...... 724 376-7515
  Sandy Lake (G-17062)
Synergistic Systems Inc...................G...... 814 796-4217
  Waterford (G-19272)
Technical Applications Inc ....G...... 610 353-0722
  Broomall (G-2303)
Teleflex Incorporated......................C...... 610 495-7011
  Royersford (G-16867)
Vektron Corporation ....G...... 215 354-0300
  Southampton (G-17845)

CONTROLS: Thermostats

Astrometrics Inc.............................E...... 610 280-0869
  Downingtown (G-4212)

CONTROLS: Thermostats, Exc Built-in

Philadelphia Instrs & Contrls............F...... 215 329-8828
  Philadelphia (G-14146)

PRODUCT

CONTROLS: Truck, Indl Battery

Nickel Cobalt Battery LLC ....G....... 412 567-6828
Pittsburgh *(G-15341)*

CONTROLS: Voice

Richard J Clickett Inc ....E 814 827-7548
Titusville *(G-18391)*

Ultravoice Ltd ....G....... 610 356-6443
Newtown Square *(G-12595)*

CONVENIENCE STORES

Ayrshire Dairy ....F 814 781-1978
Saint Marys *(G-16950)*

United Refining Inc ....D....... 814 723-1500
Warren *(G-19054)*

CONVENTION & TRADE SHOW SVCS

Motorama Assoc ....G....... 717 359-4310
Hanover *(G-6924)*

CONVERTERS: Data

Alfred Troilo ....G 610 544-0115
Springfield *(G-17906)*

Aurora Electrical & Data Svcs ....G....... 412 255-4060
Pittsburgh *(G-14739)*

Bxvideo Solutions LLC ....G....... 724 940-4190
Wexford *(G-19793)*

Cisco Systems Inc ....A 814 789-2990
Guys Mills *(G-6809)*

Cisco Systems Inc ....D....... 610 695-6000
Malvern *(G-10210)*

Digital Media Solutions LLC ....G....... 610 234-3834
Conshohocken *(G-3538)*

CONVERTERS: Frequency

Advanced Mobile Power Systems.........G....... 610 440-0195
Coplay *(G-3638)*

Milan Energy LLC ....G....... 724 933-0140
Pittsburgh *(G-15287)*

CONVERTERS: Power, AC to DC

Afterglo Lighting Co Inc ....G....... 215 355-7942
Warminster *(G-18822)*

GE Enrgy Pwr Cnversion USA Inc........C 412 967-0765
Cranberry Township *(G-3820)*

K H Controls Inc...............................D....... 724 459-7474
Blairsville *(G-1728)*

Power One Inc ....G....... 267 429-0374
Perkasie *(G-13290)*

Schneider Electric It Corp ....B 717 948-1200
Middletown *(G-11074)*

CONVEYOR SYSTEMS

Daniel B Proffitt Jr ....F 717 529-2194
Kirkwood *(G-8747)*

Industrial Composites Inc ....G....... 412 221-2662
Bridgeville *(G-2069)*

New Castle Company Inc ....G....... 724 658-4516
New Castle *(G-12128)*

Paragon Technologies Inc ....E 610 252-7321
Easton *(G-4740)*

CONVEYOR SYSTEMS: Belt, General Indl Use

Advantage Puck Technologies ....G....... 814 664-4810
Corry *(G-3742)*

C C B B Inc ....F 215 364-5377
Feasterville Trevose *(G-5898)*

Eta Industries Inc ....G....... 724 453-1722
New Brighton *(G-12036)*

Homer City Automation Inc...............G....... 724 479-4503
New Alexandria *(G-12019)*

Hosch Company LP ....E 724 695-3002
Oakdale *(G-12903)*

Industrial Svc Instllation Inc ....D....... 717 767-1129
Emigsville *(G-4992)*

Ipeg Inc ....C 814 437-6861
Franklin *(G-6138)*

Lumsden Corporation ....C 717 394-6871
Lancaster *(G-9117)*

Rtj Inc A Close Corporation ....F 215 943-9220
Levittown *(G-9862)*

Steel Systems Installation Inc ....E 717 786-1264
Quarryville *(G-16280)*

CONVEYOR SYSTEMS: Bucket Type

Joy Global Underground Min LLC........C 724 873-4200
Houston *(G-7872)*

Joy Global Underground Min LLC........D....... 724 915-2200
Homer City *(G-7677)*

Joy Global Underground Min LLC........G....... 724 873-4200
Houston *(G-7873)*

Sapient Automation LLC ....E 877 451-4044
Hatfield *(G-7394)*

CONVEYOR SYSTEMS: Bulk Handling

Aggregates Equipment Inc ....E 717 656-2131
Leola *(G-9767)*

Unimove LLC ....G....... 610 826-7855
Palmerton *(G-13112)*

CONVEYOR SYSTEMS: Pneumatic Tube

Fluidtechnik USA ....G....... 610 321-2407
Glenmoore *(G-6466)*

ITOH Denki USA Inc ....E 570 820-8811
Wilkes Barre *(G-19930)*

CONVEYOR SYSTEMS: Robotic

Jam Works LLC ....G....... 570 972-1562
Mayfield *(G-10541)*

Platypus LLC ....G....... 412 979-4629
Pittsburgh *(G-15416)*

Proconveyor LLC ....G....... 717 887-5897
York *(G-20643)*

Production Systems Automtn LLC........F 610 358-0500
Aston *(G-788)*

Production Systems Automtn LLC........E 570 602-4200
Duryea *(G-4506)*

Ropro Design Inc ....G....... 724 630-1976
Beaver *(G-991)*

CONVEYORS & CONVEYING EQPT

Advanced Bulk & Conveying Inc...........F 724 588-9327
Greenville *(G-6736)*

Advanced Bulk & Conveying Inc...........G....... 724 588-9327
Greenville *(G-6737)*

Asgco ....G....... 610 821-0216
Allentown *(G-144)*

Augers Unlimited Inc ....E 610 380-1660
Coatesville *(G-3292)*

Automted Conveying Systems Inc........G....... 215 368-0500
Harleysville *(G-7022)*

Capway Systems Inc ....E 717 843-0003
York *(G-20417)*

Cbf Systems ....F 717 793-2941
York *(G-20422)*

Dairy Conveyor Corp ....G....... 717 431-3121
Lancaster *(G-8990)*

Delta/Ducon Conveying Techlgy ....E 610 695-9700
Malvern *(G-10222)*

Demco Enterprises Inc ....F 888 419-3343
Quakertown *(G-16184)*

Dyco Inc ....D....... 800 545-3926
Bloomsburg *(G-1779)*

Erie Technical Systems Inc.................G....... 814 899-2103
Erie *(G-5276)*

Esco Windber ....G....... 814 509-8927
Windber *(G-20181)*

Fenner Inc ....C 717 665-2421
Manheim *(G-10380)*

Ferag Inc ....D....... 215 788-0892
Bristol *(G-2144)*

Fessler Machine Company ....E 724 346-0878
Sharon *(G-17433)*

Flexicon Corporation ....C 610 814-2400
Bethlehem *(G-1510)*

Flexlink Systems Inc ....D....... 610 973-8200
Allentown *(G-216)*

Flexmove Americas LLC ....G....... 267 203-8351
Souderton *(G-17734)*

FLS US Holdings Inc ....F 610 264-6011
Bethlehem *(G-1512)*

Flsmidth Inc ....C 717 665-2224
Manheim *(G-10385)*

Hamilton High Heat Inc ....G....... 814 635-4131
Saxton *(G-17101)*

Hammertek Corporation ....E 717 898-7665
Bethlehem *(G-1528)*

Handling Products Inc ....G....... 724 443-1100
Gibsonia *(G-6339)*

Hoover Cnvyor Fabrication Corp ....E 814 634-5431
Meyersdale *(G-11011)*

CONVEYORS: Overhead

B & C Material Handling Inc...............G....... 724 814-7910
Cranberry Township *(G-3808)*

Irwin Car & Equipment Inc ....F 724 864-5170
Irwin *(G-8173)*

Irwin Car & Equipment Inc ....E 724 864-8900
Irwin *(G-8174)*

J & L Professional Sales Inc ....G....... 412 788-4927
Mc Kees Rocks *(G-10616)*

J A Emilius Sons Inc ....F 215 379-6162
Cheltenham *(G-3030)*

J W Steel Fabricating Co ....E 724 625-1355
Mars *(G-10503)*

James Eagen Sons Company ....E 570 693-2100
Wyoming *(G-20280)*

Jlg Industries Inc ....C 717 485-5161
Mc Connellsburg *(G-10569)*

Jmg Inc ....G....... 215 659-4087
Willow Grove *(G-20121)*

Joy Global Underground Min LLC........C 724 779-4500
Warrendale *(G-19083)*

K & K Mine Products Inc ....E 724 463-5000
Indiana *(G-8109)*

Master Solutions Inc ....E 717 243-6849
Carlisle *(G-2724)*

Muller Martini Mailroom....................C 610 266-7000
Allentown *(G-323)*

N C Stauffer & Sons Inc....................D....... 570 945-3047
Factoryville *(G-5758)*

Ncc Automated Systems Inc..............E 215 721-1900
Souderton *(G-17756)*

Pennram Diversified Mfg Corp ....E 570 327-2802
Williamsport *(G-20055)*

Precision Feedscrews Inc ....E 724 654-9676
New Castle *(G-12139)*

Rage Bulk Systems Ltd ....E 215 489-5373
Doylestown *(G-4333)*

Rissler Conveyors ....G....... 717 336-2244
Stevens *(G-18055)*

Rissler E Manufacturing LLC...............G....... 814 766-2246
New Enterprise *(G-12195)*

Schake Industries Inc ....E 814 677-9333
Seneca *(G-17369)*

Sensible Components LLC ....F 855 548-7587
Oakdale *(G-12911)*

Shingle Belting Inc ....E 610 825-5500
King of Prussia *(G-8674)*

Shumars Welding & Mch Svc Inc ....D....... 724 246-8095
Grindstone *(G-6779)*

SKF USA Inc ....F 610 954-7000
Allentown *(G-395)*

Sparks Belting Company Inc ....G....... 717 767-1490
York *(G-20675)*

Thomas & Muller Systems Ltd............G....... 215 541-1961
Red Hill *(G-16585)*

Vibro Industries Inc ....G....... 717 527-2094
Fogelsville *(G-5997)*

Walsh Tool Company Inc....................G....... 570 823-1375
Wilkes Barre *(G-19969)*

Weldon Machine Tool Inc ....E 717 846-4000
York *(G-20706)*

Westfalia Technologies Inc ....D....... 717 764-1115
York *(G-20708)*

CONVEYORS: Overhead

B & C Material Handling Inc...............G....... 724 814-7910
Cranberry Township *(G-3808)*

COOKING & FOOD WARMING EQPT: Commercial

BSC Technologies Inc ....G....... 570 825-9196
Dallas *(G-3959)*

Crown Food Carts Incorporated...........G....... 610 628-9612
Allentown *(G-187)*

Custom Fab Co Inc ....F 570 784-0874
Bloomsburg *(G-1777)*

East West Component Inc...................G....... 215 616-4414
North Wales *(G-12799)*

EMC Global Technologies Inc ....G....... 215 340-0650
Doylestown *(G-4298)*

Filter Technology Inc ....G....... 866 992-9490
Gladwyne *(G-6407)*

Sawcom Tech Inc ....G....... 610 433-7900
Whitehall *(G-19888)*

TSS Industries Inc.............................G....... 717 821-6570
Pine Grove *(G-14606)*

COOKING & FOODWARMING EQPT: Coffee Brewing

Espresso Analysts ....G....... 724 541-2151
Indiana *(G-8097)*

Espresso Solutions ....G....... 412 326-0170
West Mifflin (G-19737)
Fresh Roasted Coffee LLC..................F....... 570 743-9228
Sunbury (G-18169)

COOKING EQPT, HOUSEHOLD: Ranges, Electric

Alaska Company Inc.................F....... 570 387-0260
Bloomsburg (G-1766)

COOKWARE, STONEWARE: Coarse Earthenware & Pottery

Pots By Deperrot.................G....... 717 627-6789
Lititz (G-10034)

COOLING TOWERS: Metal

Ice Qube Inc.................D....... 724 837-7600
Greensburg (G-6676)
SPX Corporation.................C....... 724 746-4240
Washington (G-19227)

COPINGS: Concrete

Callahan David E Pool Plst Inc ....E....... 610 429-4496
West Chester (G-19517)
Custom Pool Coping Inc ....G....... 215 822-9098
Hatfield (G-7330)

COPPER PRDTS: Refined, Primary

Edward C Rinck Associates Inc ....G....... 610 397-1727
Lafayette Hill (G-8879)

COPPER: Bars, Primary

WMS Metals - Welding Alloys ....G....... 412 231-3811
Pittsburgh (G-15722)

COPPER: Rolling & Drawing

Cerro Fabricated Products LLC.............G....... 724 451-8202
Brave (G-2002)
Garretts Fabricating.................G....... 724 528-8193
West Middlesex (G-19725)
Gesco Inc.................F....... 724 846-8700
Beaver Falls (G-999)
Libertas Copper LLC.................A....... 724 251-4200
Leetsdale (G-9697)
Southwire Company LLC ....F....... 717 266-2004
York (G-20674)

CORD & TWINE

American Manufacturing & Engrg.........F....... 215 362-9694
Montgomeryville (G-11385)
Plum Manufacturing Co Inc ....G....... 215 520-2236
North Wales (G-12825)
Troyer Rope Co ....G....... 814 587-3879
Conneautville (G-3488)

CORES: Magnetic

Spang & Company.................C....... 412 963-9363
Pittsburgh (G-15567)
SPS Technologies LLC.................A....... 215 572-3000
Jenkintown (G-8302)

CORK & CORK PRDTS

Ecore International Inc ....C....... 717 295-3400
Lancaster (G-9007)

CORRECTION FLUID

Skm Industries Inc.................F....... 570 383-3062
Olyphant (G-12999)

CORRECTIONAL INSTITUTIONS

Federal Prison Industries.................E....... 570 544-7343
Minersville (G-11254)

CORRECTIONAL INSTITUTIONS, GOVERNMENT: Federal

Federal Prison Industries.................B....... 570 524-0096
Lewisburg (G-9906)

CORRUGATED PRDTS: Boxes, Partition, Display Items, Sheet/Pad

Acco Gbc.................G....... 267 880-6797
Doylestown (G-4267)
Npc Acquisition Inc ....C....... 215 946-2000
Bristol (G-2176)

COSMETIC PREPARATIONS

Bed Bath & Beyond Inc ....G....... 717 397-0206
Lancaster (G-8950)
Conrex Pharmaceutical Corp..................F....... 610 355-2454
West Chester (G-19529)
Copperhead Chemical Co Inc ....E....... 570 386-6123
Tamaqua (G-18209)
Davidson Supply Co Inc ....G....... 412 635-2671
Pittsburgh (G-14908)
Function Inc.................G....... 570 317-0737
Catawissa (G-2818)
Hayward Laboratories Inc ....C....... 570 424-9512
East Stroudsburg (G-4619)
Makes Scents LLC ....G....... 717 824-3094
Lancaster (G-9124)
Marula Oil Holdings LLC ....G....... 310 559-8600
Ardmore (G-712)
National Dermalogy Image Corp ....G....... 610 756-0065
Kempton (G-8493)
Northtec LLC.................F....... 215 781-2731
Bristol (G-2173)
Northtec LLC.................E....... 215 781-1600
Bristol (G-2174)
Phytogenx Inc ....E....... 610 286-0111
Morgantown (G-11530)
Process Tech & Packg LLC.................C....... 570 587-8326
Scott Township (G-17188)
Renu Labs Inc ....G....... 215 675-5227
Warminster (G-18952)
Revelations Perfume Cosmt Inc ....G....... 215 396-7286
Hatboro (G-7300)
Rice Aesthetics LLC ....G....... 814 503-8540
Du Bois (G-4416)
Sun Laboratories Inc ....E....... 215 659-1111
Willow Grove (G-20144)

COSMETICS & TOILETRIES

Alpha Aromatics Inc ....D....... 412 252-1012
Pittsburgh (G-14686)
Art of Shaving - Fl LLC ....G....... 610 962-1000
King of Prussia (G-8585)
Bodybuilders Bodywash LLC ....G....... 954 682-8191
Quakertown (G-16174)
Designer Michael Todd LLC ....F....... 215 376-0145
Jenkintown (G-8283)
Estee Lauder Companies Inc..................A....... 215 826-4247
Bristol (G-2142)
Honest Industries LLC ....E....... 724 588-1540
Greenville (G-6747)
Melinessence LLC.................G....... 717 668-3730
York (G-20586)
Padc 1 ....C....... 215 781-1600
Bristol (G-2179)
Padc 1 ....E....... 215 322-3300
Feasterville Trevose (G-5925)
Paper Magic Group Inc.................C....... 570 961-3863
Moosic (G-11511)
Power Line Packaging Inc.................E....... 610 239-7088
Conshohocken (G-3590)
Retrohair Inc.................G....... 412 278-2383
Carnegie (G-2787)
Rgl Distributors LLC ....E....... 610 207-9000
Ardmore (G-715)
Sharp & Wily LLC.................G....... 717 893-2970
York (G-20667)
T&T Buttas LLC.................G....... 833 251-1357
Philadelphia (G-14365)
Una Biologicals LLC ....G....... 412 889-9746
Pittsburgh (G-15668)
Ungerer Industries Inc.................D....... 610 868-7266
Bethlehem (G-1647)
Unilever ....F....... 717 776-2180
Newville (G-12611)
Unipack Inc ....G....... 724 733-7381
Pittsburgh (G-15673)
Williams Fresh Scents LLC ....G....... 484 838-0147
Nazareth (G-11995)

COSMETOLOGY & BEAUTY SCHOOLS

National Dermalogy Image Corp ....G....... 610 756-0065
Kempton (G-8493)

COSTUME JEWELRY & NOVELTIES: Apparel, Exc Precious Metals

Lema Novelty Co Inc.................G....... 610 754-7242
Glenside (G-6526)

COSTUME JEWELRY & NOVELTIES: Exc Semi & Precious

Laura J Designs ....G....... 610 213-1082
Lansdowne (G-9437)

COSTUME JEWELRY & NOVELTIES: Rosaries & Sm Religious Items

Treasures Inc.................G....... 412 920-5421
Pittsburgh (G-15641)
Wallace Brothers Mfg Co ....F....... 570 822-3808
Wilkes Barre (G-19968)

COSTUME JEWELRY STORES

Swarovski North America Ltd.................G....... 412 833-3708
Pittsburgh (G-15593)

COUGH MEDICINES

Glaxosmithkline LLC.................E....... 610 270-4800
King of Prussia (G-8624)

COUNTER & SINK TOPS

Allegheny Solid Surfc Tech LLC.................E....... 717 630-1251
Mc Sherrystown (G-10649)
API Americas Inc.................F....... 785 842-7674
Levittown (G-9817)
Countertek Inc.................E....... 717 336-2371
Ephrata (G-5097)
Custom Kitchens Inc ....G....... 814 833-5338
Erie (G-5238)
Dutka Inc.................G....... 717 285-5880
Mountville (G-11794)
Henry H Ross & Son Inc.................E....... 717 626-6268
Lititz (G-10014)
M & M Creative Laminates Inc ....G....... 412 781-4700
Aspinwall (G-746)
McGrory Inc.................D....... 610 444-1512
Kennett Square (G-8526)
REA Jobber Inc ....G....... 814 226-9552
Clarion (G-3186)
Shade Mountain Countertops.................F....... 717 463-2729
Mc Alisterville (G-10552)
Sunworks Etc LLC.................G....... 717 473-3743
Annville (G-659)

COUNTERS & COUNTING DEVICES

Emw Inc.................F....... 717 626-0248
Lititz (G-10006)
Mol Communications & Elec.................G....... 570 383-3658
Dickson City (G-4122)

COUNTERS OR COUNTER DISPLAY CASES, WOOD

Broc Supply Co Inc.................E....... 610 433-4646
Emmaus (G-5022)

COUNTING DEVICES: Controls, Revolution & Timing

Schlumberger Technology Corp ....C....... 814 220-1900
Brookville (G-2271)
Techsource Engineering Inc ....G....... 814 459-2150
Erie (G-5505)

COUNTING DEVICES: Electromechanical

Monitor Data Corp.................F....... 215 887-8343
Glenside (G-6530)

COUNTING DEVICES: Registers

Integrated Myers Systems LLC ....G....... 814 937-3958
Gallitzin (G-6246)

COUNTING DEVICES: Tachometer, Centrifugal

Maxima Tech & Systems LLC ....C....... 717 581-1000
Lancaster (G-9130)

PRODUCT

COUNTING DEVICES: Vehicle Instruments

Ametek Inc.................................D...... 610 647-2121
Berwyn (G-1351)

COUPLINGS, EXC PRESSURE & SOIL PIPE

Parker-Hannifin Corporation.................A...... 814 866-4100
Erie (G-5414)

Victaulic Company..............................A...... 610 559-3300
Easton (G-4770)

COUPLINGS: Hose & Tube, Hydraulic Or Pneumatic

Genuine Parts Company.....................G...... 215 968-4266
Newtown (G-12504)

I D Technologies Inc..........................G...... 610 652-2418
Gilbertsville (G-6374)

COUPLINGS: Pipe

Kennedy Tubular Products Inc............F...... 724 658-5508
New Castle (G-12113)

Maclean Saegertown LLC...................G...... 814 763-2655
Saegertown (G-16924)

Saegertown Manufacturing Corp.........C...... 814 763-2655
Saegertown (G-16932)

COUPLINGS: Shaft

Ameridrives International LLC..............D...... 814 480-5000
Erie (G-5192)

Morris Coupling Company.....................D...... 814 459-1741
Erie (G-5396)

COURIER SVCS: Air

Birdsboro Extrusions LLC....................G...... 610 582-0400
Birdsboro (G-1689)

Garda CL Technical Svcs Inc..............D...... 610 926-7400
Reading (G-16389)

COVERS: Automobile Seat

N F C Industries Inc...........................E...... 215 766-8890
Plumsteadville (G-15812)

Willow Grove Auto Top Inc...................G...... 215 659-3276
Willow Grove (G-20150)

COVERS: Automotive, Exc Seat & Tire

Sheep Thrills...................................G...... 724 465-2617
Indiana (G-8127)

COVERS: Canvas

Ehmke Manufacturing Co Inc..............D...... 215 324-4200
Philadelphia (G-13664)

Waugaman Awnings...........................G...... 724 837-1239
Greensburg (G-6728)

COVERS: Metal Plate

Petrex Inc..E...... 814 723-2050
Warren (G-19044)

CRADLES: Aircraft Engine

Oppenheimer Precision Pdts Inc...........D...... 215 674-9100
Horsham (G-7837)

CRADLES: Drum

Sterling-Fleischman Inc.......................F...... 610 647-1717
Media (G-10951)

CRANE & AERIAL LIFT SVCS

American Crane & Eqp Corp.................F...... 484 945-0420
Douglassville (G-4167)

American Crane & Eqp Corp.................F...... 610 521-9000
Essington (G-5541)

American Crane & Eqp Corp.................C...... 610 385-6061
Douglassville (G-4168)

Custom Signs Inc..............................F...... 814 786-7232
Grove City (G-6783)

Lafayette Welding Inc.........................G...... 610 489-3529
Royersford (G-16857)

William Sport Crane & Rigging.............G...... 570 433-3300
Montoursville (G-11457)

CRANES & MONORAIL SYSTEMS

KKR & Co LP.....................................C...... 717 741-4863
York (G-20555)

CRANES: Indl Plant

B E Wallace Products Corp..................F...... 610 647-1400
Malvern (G-10190)

Gantrex Inc......................................F...... 412 347-0300
Canonsburg (G-2591)

Konecranes Inc.................................F...... 814 237-2663
Philipsburg (G-14518)

Konecranes Inc.................................E...... 610 321-2900
Pottstown (G-16008)

CRANES: Overhead

Altec Industries Inc...........................C...... 570 822-3104
Wilkes Barre (G-19904)

American Crane & Eqp Corp.................C...... 610 385-6061
Douglassville (G-4168)

Atlantic Crane Inc.............................F...... 610 366-1540
Fogelsville (G-5991)

D & S Industrial Contg Inc..................E...... 412 490-3215
Coraopolis (G-3683)

Kone Cranes Inc...............................F...... 814 878-8070
Erie (G-5351)

Transol Corporation...........................G...... 610 527-0234
Morgantown (G-11542)

CRANKSHAFTS & CAMSHAFTS: Machining

Advanced Welding Tech Inc.................E...... 814 899-3584
Erie (G-5176)

Ellwood Crankshaft and Mch Co...........C...... 724 347-0250
Hermitage (G-7581)

Ellwood Nat Crankshaft Svcs...............G...... 724 342-4965
Hermitage (G-7583)

Great Lakes Automtn Svcs Inc.............F...... 814 774-3144
Lake City (G-8901)

Kutzner Manufacturing Inds Inc............E...... 215 721-1712
Telford (G-18300)

CRATES: Fruit, Wood Wirebound

Saylors Farm & Wood Products............F...... 814 745-2306
Sligo (G-17616)

CRAYONS

Crayola LLC......................................A...... 610 253-6272
Easton (G-4663)

CREDIT CARD SVCS

Shift4 Payments LLC..........................D...... 800 201-0461
Allentown (G-389)

CREDIT INST, SHORT-TERM BUSINESS: Financing Dealers

Torcomp Usa LLC..............................G...... 717 261-1530
Chambersburg (G-2987)

CREMATORIES

Silbaugh Vault and Burial Svc..............G...... 724 437-3002
Uniontown (G-18642)

Wilkes Barre Burial Vault.....................F...... 570 824-8268
Hanover Township (G-7007)

CROWNS & CLOSURES

Crown Beverage Packaging LLC...........B...... 215 698-5100
Philadelphia (G-13585)

Crown Cork & Seal Usa Inc..................B...... 215 698-5100
Yardley (G-20303)

Crown Holdings Inc............................E...... 215 322-3533
Feasterville Trevose (G-5902)

Guida Inc...E...... 215 727-2222
Marcus Hook (G-10444)

Maugus Manufacturing Inc..................F...... 717 299-5681
Lancaster (G-9126)

CRUCIBLES

Osram Sylvania Inc...........................B...... 570 724-8200
Wellsboro (G-19471)

CRUDE PETROLEUM & NATURAL GAS PRODUCTION

Arg Resources Inc.............................E...... 814 837-7477
Kane (G-8459)

Arg Resources Inc.............................E...... 610 940-4420
West Conshohocken (G-19685)

Center Independent Oil Company..........G...... 724 437-6607
Lemont Furnace (G-9734)

Imod Oil Production LLC......................G...... 814 589-7539
Pleasantville (G-15802)

Kriebel Minerals Inc...........................E...... 814 226-4160
Clarion (G-3182)

Mds Energy Development LLC..............E...... 724 548-2501
Kittanning (G-8781)

Mds Energy Partners Gp LLC...............G...... 724 548-2501
Kittanning (G-8782)

Minard Run Oil Company......................G...... 814 368-4931
Bradford (G-1983)

Mmscc-2 LLC....................................F...... 610 266-8990
Allentown (G-317)

New Century Energy Inc......................G...... 724 693-9266
Oakdale (G-12908)

Open Flow Gas Supply Corp.................F...... 814 371-2228
Du Bois (G-4409)

R C Southwell..................................G...... 814 723-7182
Warren (G-19045)

Targa Pipeline Oper Partnr LP..............G...... 412 489-0006
Philadelphia (G-14371)

Targa Pipeline Partners GP LLC............D...... 215 546-5005
Philadelphia (G-14372)

Trans Energy Inc...............................F...... 304 684-7053
Pittsburgh (G-15638)

Xto Energy Inc..................................G...... 570 368-8920
Montoursville (G-11458)

CRUDE PETROLEUM & NATURAL GAS PRODUCTION

Afco Energy Production Co Inc.............G...... 724 463-3350
Barnesboro (G-937)

Apex Energy LLC...............................E...... 724 719-2611
Wexford (G-19788)

Atlas America Pub 11-2002 Ltd.............G...... 412 262-2830
Moon Township (G-11480)

Atlas Resources LLC..........................F...... 800 251-0171
Pittsburgh (G-14734)

Atlas Rsrces Pub 18-2009 B LP............G...... 330 896-8510
Coraopolis (G-3661)

Atlas Rsrces Series 28-2010 LP............G...... 412 489-0006
Pittsburgh (G-14735)

Bakwell LLC......................................G...... 570 724-7067
Wellsboro (G-19462)

BDH Oil Inc......................................G...... 814 362-5447
Bradford (G-1957)

Brymone Inc.....................................G...... 724 746-4004
Canonsburg (G-2552)

Campbell Oil LLC...............................G...... 814 749-0002
Nanty Glo (G-11905)

Carpenter Co....................................D...... 610 366-5110
Fogelsville (G-5993)

Carpenter Co....................................C...... 814 944-8612
Altoona (G-486)

Carrizo (marcellus) LLC......................G...... 570 278-7450
Montrose (G-11460)

Carrizo Oil & Gas Inc.........................G...... 570 278-7009
Montrose (G-11461)

Cnx Land LLC....................................C...... 724 485-4000
Canonsburg (G-2561)

Dominion Energy Transm Inc................G...... 724 354-3433
Shelocta (G-17485)

Eclipse Resources Holdings LP.............C...... 814 308-9754
State College (G-17959)

Eqt Re LLC.......................................G...... 274 271-7200
Canonsburg (G-2587)

Exco Resources LLC..........................D...... 724 720-2500
Kittanning (G-8768)

Jj Bucher Producing Corp....................G...... 814 697-6593
Shinglehouse (G-17508)

John Wallace....................................G...... 814 374-4619
Cooperstown (G-3637)

KCS Energy Inc.................................G...... 814 723-4672
Warren (G-19035)

Lock 3 Company................................F...... 724 258-7773
Monongahela (G-11310)

Mds Well Holdings LLC........................G...... 724 548-2501
Kittanning (G-8784)

Midnight Oil Express...........................G...... 215 933-9690
Quakertown (G-16217)

Montauk Energy Holdings LLC..............D...... 412 747-8700
Pittsburgh (G-15301)

N A Petroleum Corp ....G...... 610 438-5463
Easton (G-4728)
Northwestern Energy Corp ....G...... 814 277-9935
Mahaffey (G-10172)
Regency Energy Partners LP ....G...... 610 687-8900
Wayne (G-19369)
Rex Energy Corporation......................D...... 814 278-7267
State College (G-18014)
Rice Olympus Midstream LLC ....D...... 724 746-6720
Canonsburg (G-2629)
Rice Poseidon Midstream LLC ....C...... 724 746-6720
Canonsburg (G-2630)
Rustys Oil and Propane Inc ....G...... 814 497-4423
Houtzdale (G-7884)
Tall Oak Energy Inc ....G...... 724 636-0621
Boyers (G-1891)
Targa Energy LP ....F...... 412 489-0006
Pittsburgh (G-15598)
Triangle Petroleum Inc ....G...... 908 380-2685
Warren (G-19052)
Zavillas Oil Co ....G...... 724 445-3702
Chicora (G-3130)

CRUDE PETROLEUM PRODUCTION

Anadarko Petroleum Corp ....F...... 570 323-4157
Williamsport (G-19987)
Anadarko Petroleum Corporation ....G...... 570 323-4157
Williamsport (G-19988)
B & B Oil & Gas Production Co ....G...... 814 257-8760
Dayton (G-4035)
Baron Development Company...............G...... 814 676-8703
Oil City (G-12940)
Belden & Blake Corporation ....F...... 814 589-7091
Pleasantville (G-15797)
Bucher Jj Producing Corp ....G...... 814 697-6593
Shinglehouse (G-17504)
Chevron Ae Resources LLC ....E...... 724 662-0300
Jackson Center (G-8226)
Cline Oil Inc ....G...... 814 368-5395
Bradford (G-1961)
Cumberland Farms Inc ....G...... 412 331-4419
Pittsburgh (G-14892)
Devon Energy Corporation ....F...... 412 366-7474
Pittsburgh (G-14920)
Eagle Line Corporation ....F...... 814 589-7724
Pleasantville (G-15801)
Eastern American Energy Corp ....G...... 724 463-8400
Indiana (G-8093)
Eclipse Resources I LP ....F...... 814 308-9754
State College (G-17960)
Eog Resources Inc..............................E...... 724 745-9063
Canonsburg (G-2586)
Eqt Corporation..................................C...... 412 553-5700
Pittsburgh (G-14981)
Frederick Drilling Co & Sons ....G...... 814 744-8581
Tylersburg (G-18573)
Laurel Mountain Production LLC ....G...... 412 595-8700
Pittsburgh (G-15221)
Pennsylvania Gen Enrgy Corp ....D...... 814 723-3230
Warren (G-19043)
Pennzoil-Quaker State Company ....B...... 724 756-0110
Karns City (G-8482)
Royal Oil & Gas Corporation ....E...... 724 463-0246
Indiana (G-8124)
Royal Production Company Inc.............E...... 724 463-0246
Indiana (G-8125)
Van Hampton Gas & Oil Inc.................F...... 814 589-7061
Pleasantville (G-15805)
Vineyard Oil & Gas Company ....F...... 814 725-8742
North East (G-12764)
Wilmoth Interests Inc..........................G...... 724 397-5558
Marion Center (G-10478)
Xto Energy Inc ....D...... 540 772-3220
Renfrew (G-16644)
Xto Energy Inc ....D...... 724 772-3500
Warrendale (G-19103)
Zama Petroleum Inc............................G...... 360 321-6160
Pittsburgh (G-15732)

CRUDES: Cyclic, Organic

Palmer International Inc ....E...... 610 584-4241
Skippack (G-17602)

CRYOGENIC COOLING DEVICES: Infrared Detectors, Masers

Cryostar USA ....G...... 484 281-3261
Bethlehem (G-1490)

CRYSTALS

Saint-Gobain Ceramics Plas Inc..........A...... 508 795-5000
Valley Forge (G-18711)
Te Connectivity Foundation ....E...... 717 810-2987
Berwyn (G-1377)

CRYSTALS & CRYSTAL ASSEMBLIES: Radio

Keystone Crystal Corporation ....G...... 724 282-1506
Butler (G-2416)

CRYSTALS: Piezoelectric

Kinetic Ceramics LLC ....F...... 510 264-2140
Philadelphia (G-13937)

CULVERTS: Sheet Metal

Culverts Inc ....G...... 412 262-3111
Coraopolis (G-3682)
Lane Enterprises Inc...........................E...... 814 623-1191
Bedford (G-1061)

CUPS & PLATES: Foamed Plastics

Dart Container Corp PA.......................G...... 717 656-2236
Leola (G-9777)
Dart Container Corp PA.......................A...... 717 397-1032
Lancaster (G-8992)

CUPS: Paper, Made From Purchased Materials

Letica Corporation ....C...... 570 883-0299
Pittston (G-15764)

CUPS: Plastic Exc Polystyrene Foam

Georgia-Pacific LLC............................B...... 610 250-1400
Easton (G-4690)
Smartshake...F...... 724 396-7947
Pittsburgh (G-15549)

CURBING: Granite Or Stone

Dente Pittsburgh Inc...........................G...... 412 828-1772
Oakmont (G-12916)

CURTAIN & DRAPERY FIXTURES: Poles, Rods & Rollers

Acacia Corp ....F...... 412 771-6144
Mc Kees Rocks (G-10600)
Bishops Inc...G...... 412 821-3333
Mars (G-10488)
Blind Doctors ....G...... 412 822-8580
Pittsburgh (G-14772)
Caldwells Windoware Inc ....E...... 412 922-1132
Pittsburgh (G-14800)
Carol Vinck Window Creation ....G...... 717 730-0303
Camp Hill (G-2494)
Hamilton Awning Co ....F...... 724 774-7644
Beaver (G-983)
Indoor Sky LLC ....G...... 570 220-1903
Williamsport (G-20024)
Lafayette Venetian Blind Inc ....E...... 717 652-3750
Harrisburg (G-7167)
Plymouth Interiors LP..........................F...... 412 771-8569
Mc Kees Rocks (G-10627)
S Morantz Inc.....................................D...... 215 969-0266
Philadelphia (G-14273)
Shaffer Desouza Brown Inc ....F...... 610 449-6400
Havertown (G-7427)
TMW Associates Inc ....G...... 215 624-3940
Philadelphia (G-14393)

CURTAIN WALLS: Building, Steel

New Hudson Facades LLC....................C...... 610 494-8100
Upper Chichester (G-18668)

CURTAINS: Shower

Kartri Sales Company Inc ....E...... 570 785-3365
Forest City (G-6054)

CURTAINS: Window, From Purchased Materials

Lincoln Textile Pdts Co Inc ....D...... 484 281-3999
Bath (G-965)

CUSHIONS & PILLOWS

Dallco Industries Inc............................E...... 717 854-7875
York (G-20443)
Natures Pillows Inc ....G...... 215 633-9801
Feasterville Trevose (G-5921)
Precision Rehab Manufacturing............G...... 814 899-8731
Erie (G-5432)

CUSHIONS & PILLOWS: Bed, From Purchased Materials

Hollander Sleep Products LLC ....C...... 570 874-2114
Frackville (G-6105)
Neuropedic LLC ....F...... 570 501-7713
West Hazleton (G-19714)
Paradise Pillow Inc ....E...... 215 225-8700
Philadelphia (G-14120)
Salmon Pillowmakers...........................G...... 717 767-4978
York (G-20663)

CUSHIONS: Carpet & Rug, Foamed Plastics

Foamex International Inc......................C...... 610 744-2300
Media (G-10924)
Foamex LP ....D...... 610 565-2374
Media (G-10925)
Fxi Inc..C...... 610 744-2300
Media (G-10926)
Fxi Holdings Inc..................................C...... 610 744-2300
Media (G-10928)

CUSTOM COMPOUNDING OF RUBBER MATERIALS

Presti Group Inc ....F....... 215 340-2870
Doylestown (G-4327)
Q-Cast Inc ....E........ 724 728-7440
Rochester (G-16789)
Techline Technologies Inc ....E........ 215 657-1909
Willow Grove (G-20146)

CUT STONE & STONE PRODUCTS

Armina Stone Inc ....G...... 412 406-8442
Cheswick (G-3101)
BS Quarries Inc ....C...... 570 278-4901
Montrose (G-11459)
Butler Stonecraft Inc...........................G...... 724 352-3520
Cabot (G-2453)
Cava Intl MBL & Gran Inc ....E...... 215 732-7800
Philadelphia (G-13516)
Custom Stone Interiors Inc ....G...... 814 548-0120
Bellefonte (G-1096)
Designs In Stone Inc...........................G...... 800 878-6631
Hatboro (G-7279)
Diaz Stone and Pallet Inc ....F...... 570 289-8760
Kingsley (G-8703)
Diaz Stone and Pallet Inc ....E...... 570 289-8760
Kingsley (G-8704)
Dingmans Ferry Stone Inc ....G...... 570 828-2617
Dingmans Ferry (G-4142)
Dyer Quarry Inc ....E...... 610 582-6010
Birdsboro (G-1693)
Eureka Stone Quarry Inc ....E...... 570 296-6632
Milford (G-11160)
G Wb European Treasures ....G...... 610 275-4395
Bridgeport (G-2037)
Gill Quarries Incorporated ....G...... 610 584-6061
East Norriton (G-4584)
H B Mellott Estate Inc ....F...... 301 678-2050
Warfordsburg (G-18812)
Indoor City Granite & MBL Inc.............F...... 717 393-3931
Lancaster (G-9056)
Jet Stream Manufacturing Inc..............G...... 610 532-6632
Darby (G-4020)
L & D Stoneworks Inc ....E...... 570 553-1670
Montrose (G-11469)
L&S Stone LLC ....F...... 717 264-3559
Chambersburg (G-2950)
Lexmarusa Inc....................................G...... 412 896-9266
McKeesport (G-10675)
Macson Company ....G...... 610 264-7733
Allentown (G-305)
Matthews International Corp.................B...... 412 571-5500
Pittsburgh (G-15266)
McAvoy Brick Company ....G...... 610 933-2932
Phoenixville (G-14560)
Media Quarry Co Inc ....E...... 610 566-6667
Media (G-10938)
Monticello Granite Ltd ....F...... 215 677-1000
Collegeville (G-3383)

Employee Codes: A=Over 500 employees, B=251-500
C=101-250, D=51-100, E=20-50, F=10-19, G=3-9   2019 Harris Pennsylvania
Manufacturers Directory   1373

PRODUCT

Natstone LLC ....E 570 278-1611
Montrose (G-11472)

Patrick G Stinely ....G 814 528-3832
Erie (G-5417)

Porto Exim Usa LLC ....G 412 406-8442
Cheswick (G-3115)

Princeton Trade Consulting Gro ....E 610 683-9348
Kutztown (G-8856)

Suburban Marble LLC ....G 215 734-9100
Warminster (G-18974)

Wilder Diamond Blades Inc ....G 570 222-9590
Kingsley (G-8710)

CUTLERY

Backus Company ....E 814 887-5705
Smethport (G-17632)

Jet Plastica Industries Inc ....B 800 220-5381
Hatfield (G-7356)

CUTTING SVC: Paper, Exc Die-Cut

Tinicum Research Company ....F 215 766-7277
Plumsteadville (G-15814)

CUTTING SVC: Paperboard

Acme Specialties Inc ....G 215 822-5900
Hatfield (G-7314)

CYCLE CONDENSATE PRODUCTION

UGI Europe Inc ....G 610 337-1000
King of Prussia (G-8692)

CYCLIC CRUDES & INTERMEDIATES

Braskem America Inc ....E 412 208-8100
Pittsburgh (G-14790)

Braskem America Inc ....C 610 497-8378
Marcus Hook (G-10438)

Braskem America Inc ....C 215 841-3100
Philadelphia (G-13478)

Chem Service Inc ....E 610 692-3026
West Chester (G-19523)

Dura-Bond Coating Inc ....E 412 436-2411
Duquesne (G-4496)

Honeywell Resins & Chem LLC ....C 215 533-3000
Philadelphia (G-13833)

Lockhart Chemical Company ....E 724 444-1900
Gibsonia (G-6344)

Lyondell Chemical Company ....D 610 359-2360
Newtown Square (G-12583)

Paper Magic Group Inc ....C 570 961-3863
Moosic (G-11511)

Presto Dyechem Co Inc ....E 215 627-1863
Philadelphia (G-14198)

Tangent Rail Corporation ....G 412 325-0202
Pittsburgh (G-15596)

Verichem Inc ....E 412 331-2616
Pittsburgh (G-15692)

Youghiogheny Opalescent GL Inc ....E 724 628-3000
Connellsville (G-3512)

CYCLO RUBBERS: Natural

Norstone Incorporated ....G 484 684-6986
Bridgeport (G-2041)

CYLINDER & ACTUATORS: Fluid Power

Alliance Remanufacturing Inc ....C 215 291-4640
Philadelphia (G-13368)

Auma Actuators Inc ....G 714 247-1250
Canonsburg (G-2546)

Basic - Psa Inc ....E 814 266-8646
Johnstown (G-8356)

Ecobee Advanced Tech LLC ....G 609 474-0010
Warminster (G-18869)

Hydac Corp ....E 610 266-0100
Bethlehem (G-1533)

Kerry Company Inc ....F 412 486-3388
Allison Park (G-455)

Moog Inc ....C 610 328-4000
Springfield (G-17919)

Parker-Hannifin Corporation ....E 814 866-4100
Erie (G-5416)

PBM Inc ....D 724 863-0550
Irwin (G-8189)

Ralph A Hiller Company ....E 724 325-1200
Export (G-5623)

RG Industries Inc ....E 717 849-0345
York (G-20658)

Tri-State Hydraulics Inc ....E 724 483-1790
Charleroi (G-3022)

Wellm Dyna Mach and Asse Inc ....E 717 764-8855
York (G-20707)

CYLINDERS: Pressure

Woodings Industrial Corp ....C 724 625-3131
Mars (G-10515)

CYLINDERS: Pump

Airgas Safety Inc ....C 215 826-9000
Levittown (G-9814)

Fessler Machine Company ....G 412 367-3663
Sharon (G-17434)

Gardner Denver Nash LLC ....E 724 239-1522
Charleroi (G-3014)

DAIRY EQPT

CK Manufacturing LLC ....E 717 442-8912
Lancaster (G-8978)

Middlecreek Welding & Mfg ....G 315 853-3936
Newmanstown (G-12481)

Pbz LLC ....E 800 578-1121
Lititz (G-10029)

Sturdy Built Manufacturing LLC ....E 717 484-2233
Denver (G-4095)

DAIRY PRDTS STORE: Cheese

Calandra Cheese ....G 610 759-2299
Nazareth (G-11958)

Caputo Brothers Creamery LLC ....G 717 739-1087
Spring Grove (G-17876)

Dibruno Bros Inc ....G 215 665-9220
Philadelphia (G-13630)

Ken Weaver Meats Inc ....E 717 502-0118
Wellsville (G-19479)

DAIRY PRDTS STORE: Ice Cream, Packaged

Allen McKinney Inc ....G 717 428-2321
Loganville (G-10101)

Gibbys Ice Cream Inc ....F 215 547-7253
Levittown (G-9840)

Halls Ice Cream Inc ....F 717 589-3290
Millerstown (G-11204)

JAS Wholesale & Supply Co Inc ....E 610 967-0663
Emmaus (G-5031)

Mazzolis Ice Cream ....G 717 533-2252
Hershey (G-7620)

DAIRY PRDTS STORES

Blue Ribbon Farm Dairy ....G 570 763-5570
Swoyersville (G-18195)

Conjelko Dairy & Ice Service ....G 814 467-9997
Windber (G-20179)

Turner Dairy Farms Inc ....D 412 372-7155
Pittsburgh (G-15661)

DAIRY PRDTS WHOLESALERS: Fresh

Clair D Thompson & Sons Inc ....E 570 398-1880
Jersey Shore (G-8311)

O Land Lakes ....F 717 845-8076
York (G-20614)

DAIRY PRDTS: Butter

Calkins Creamery LLC ....F 570 729-8103
Honesdale (G-7704)

Campus Creamery LLC ....G 570 351-1738
S Abingtn Twp (G-16890)

Cathys Creamery ....G 570 916-3386
Milton (G-11235)

Creamery On Main ....G 610 928-1500
Emmaus (G-5024)

Dairy Farmers America Inc ....E 724 946-8729
West Middlesex (G-19722)

Dietrichs Milk Products LLC ....D 570 376-2001
Middlebury Center (G-11044)

Fresh Made Inc ....G 215 725-9013
Philadelphia (G-13724)

Half Pint Creamery LLC ....G 717 634-5459
Hanover (G-6890)

Half Pint Creamery LLC ....G 717 420-2110
Gettysburg (G-6297)

High View Inc ....E 814 886-7171
Loretto (G-10104)

Honey Butter Products Co Inc ....G 717 665-9323
Manheim (G-10389)

Ironstone Creamery ....G 610 952-2748
Pottstown (G-15949)

Kellers Creamery LLC ....D 215 256-8871
Harleysville (G-7043)

Land OLakes Inc ....C 717 486-7000
Carlisle (G-2719)

Liberty View Creamery LLC ....G 717 359-8206
Littlestown (G-10070)

Paula Keswick ....G 574 298-2022
Reynoldsville (G-16660)

Pocono Mountain Creamery LLC ....G 570 443-9868
White Haven (G-19850)

Strasburg Creamery LLC ....G 717 456-7497
Delta (G-4064)

Turner Dairy Farms Inc ....D 412 372-7155
Pittsburgh (G-15661)

DAIRY PRDTS: Buttermilk, Cultured

Galliker Dairy Company ....C 814 266-8702
Johnstown (G-8374)

Galliker Dairy Company ....G 814 623-8597
Bedford (G-1051)

Galliker Dairy Company ....G 717 258-6199
Carlisle (G-2716)

DAIRY PRDTS: Cheese

Caputo Brothers Creamery LLC ....G 717 739-1087
Spring Grove (G-17876)

Castle Cheese Inc ....E 724 368-3022
Pittsburgh (G-14826)

Dibruno Bros Inc ....G 215 665-9220
Philadelphia (G-13630)

Gods Country Creamery ....G 814 848-7262
Ulysses (G-18602)

HP Hood LLC ....C 215 637-2507
Philadelphia (G-13837)

Ncc Wholesome Foods Inc ....F 724 652-3440
New Castle (G-12124)

Oak Shade Cheese LLC ....G 717 529-6049
Kirkwood (G-8752)

Savencia Cheese USA LLC ....D 717 355-8500
New Holland (G-12281)

Villanova Cheese Shop Inc ....F 610 495-8343
Pottstown (G-16069)

Whitehall Specialties ....G 724 368-3959
Slippery Rock (G-17629)

DAIRY PRDTS: Condensed Milk

Dairy Farmers America Inc ....E 724 946-8729
West Middlesex (G-19722)

DAIRY PRDTS: Custard, Frozen

Turkey Hill LP ....B 717 872-5461
Conestoga (G-3462)

DAIRY PRDTS: Dairy Based Desserts, Frozen

Brook Meadow Dairy Company ....C 814 899-3191
Erie (G-5215)

Six Pack Creamery LLC ....G 267 261-2727
Hatboro (G-7305)

DAIRY PRDTS: Dietary Supplements, Dairy & Non-Dairy Based

Exclusive Supplements Inc ....F 412 787-2770
Oakdale (G-12898)

General Nutrition Centers Inc ....B 412 288-4600
Pittsburgh (G-15046)

GNC Corporation ....G 412 288-4600
Pittsburgh (G-15054)

GNC Parent LLC ....G 412 288-4600
Pittsburgh (G-15055)

Hi-Tech Nutraceuticals LLC ....E 717 667-2142
Reedsville (G-16623)

Hpf LLC ....G 215 321-8170
Yardley (G-20321)

Powder City LLC ....F 717 745-4795
York (G-20634)

Proper Nutrition Inc ....G 610 692-2060
West Chester (G-19621)

Trugen3 LLC ....G 412 668-3831
Pittsburgh (G-15657)

Vinomis Laboratories LLC ....G 877 484-6664
Aliquippa (G-101)

DAIRY PRDTS: Dips & Spreads, Cheese Based

AFP Advanced Food Products LLC ......C 717 355-8667
New Holland (G-12227)
Cowz Leap Creamery LLC ....G 717 653-1532
Mount Joy (G-11651)
Dairiconcepts LP...............................E 717 566-4500
Hummelstown (G-7908)
Fleur De Lait East LLC........................G 717 355-8580
New Holland (G-12249)
Key Ingredient Market LLC ....G 484 281-3900
Bath (G-961)
Kraft Heinz Foods Company ....C 412 456-5700
Pittsburgh (G-15197)
Shenks Foods Inc ....G 717 393-4240
Lancaster (G-9195)

DAIRY PRDTS: Dips & Spreads, Sour Cream Based

Schneiders Dairy Holdings Inc ....B 412 881-3525
Pittsburgh (G-15517)

DAIRY PRDTS: Dried Nonfat Milk

Dietrichs Milk Products LLC ....D 610 929-5736
Reading (G-16361)

DAIRY PRDTS: Evaporated Milk

Nestle Usa Inc ....C 610 391-7900
Breinigsville (G-2020)
Nestle Usa Inc ....C 818 549-6000
King of Prussia (G-8655)

DAIRY PRDTS: Farmers' Cheese

Topsmal Dairy LLC ....G 814 880-3724
Bellefonte (G-1123)

DAIRY PRDTS: Fermented & Cultured Milk Prdts

Tuscan/Lehigh Dairies Inc ....F 610 434-9666
Allentown (G-415)
Upstate Niagara Coop Inc ....D 570 326-2021
Williamsport (G-20087)
Villanova Cheese Shop Inc ....F 610 495-8343
Pottstown (G-16069)

DAIRY PRDTS: Frozen Desserts & Novelties

Arties Unlimited LLC ....G 267 516-2575
Philadelphia (G-13413)
Awesome Ice Inc ....F 717 519-2423
East Petersburg (G-4586)
Bill Macks Ice Cream ....E 717 292-1931
Dover (G-4188)
Blue Ribbon Farm Dairy ....G 570 763-5570
Swoyersville (G-18195)
Bobs Diner Enterprises Inc ....F 412 221-7474
Pittsburgh (G-14778)
Brusters Old Fashioned Ice Cre ....G 724 772-9999
Seven Fields (G-17374)
Buffs Ice Cream ....G 814 849-8335
Brookville (G-2257)
Chill Frozen Desserts ....G 724 695-8855
Imperial (G-8060)
Creperie Bechamel LLC ....G 610 964-9700
Radnor (G-16292)
Deer Creek Winery LLC ....D 814 354-7392
Shippenville (G-17560)
Dudley Enterprises Inc ....E 724 523-5522
Jeannette (G-8253)
Fox Meadows Creamery Inc ....E 717 721-6455
Ephrata (G-5104)
Frogurt LLC ....F 724 263-4299
Monroeville (G-11338)
Gelateria...G 484 466-4228
Primos (G-16108)
High View Inc.....................................E 814 886-7171
Loretto (G-10104)
Jackson Farms Dairy ....E 724 246-7010
New Salem (G-12445)
JAS Wholesale & Supply Co Inc ....E 610 967-0663
Emmaus (G-5031)
Joshi Bharkatkumar ....F 610 861-7733
Bethlehem (G-1547)
Kelley ....G 412 833-4559
Pittsburgh (G-15163)

Leibys Ichr LLC ....G 570 778-0108
Tamaqua (G-18217)
Manning Farm Dairy ....G 570 563-2016
Dalton (G-3987)
Marcies Homemade Ice Cream ....G 814 336-1749
Meadville (G-10756)
MJM Ices LLC ....G 412 401-4610
North Huntingdon (G-12770)
Nelsons Creamery LLC ....E 610 948-3000
Plymouth Meeting (G-15859)
Ritcheys Dairy Inc ....E 814 793-2157
Martinsburg (G-10529)
Steffees ....F 814 827-4332
Titusville (G-18397)
Sugar Magnolia Inc ....G 610 649-9462
Ardmore (G-719)
Sweetdreams Brusters LLC ....G 717 261-1484
Chambersburg (G-2982)
Titusville Dairy Products Co ....E 814 827-1833
Titusville (G-18399)
Topit Toppings LLC ....G 267 263-2590
Harleysville (G-7062)
Trickling Springs Creamery LLC ....E 717 709-0711
Chambersburg (G-2988)
Turner Dairy Farms Inc ....D 412 372-7155
Pittsburgh (G-15661)

DAIRY PRDTS: Ice Cream & Ice Milk

Dairy Farmers America Inc ....E 724 946-8729
West Middlesex (G-19722)
Donna Stanton ....G 412 561-2661
South Park (G-17781)
Galliker Dairy Company ....G 814 266-8702
Johnstown (G-8374)
Mazzolis Ice Cream ....G 717 533-2252
Hershey (G-7620)
Premise Maid Candies Inc ....E 610 395-3221
Breinigsville (G-2024)

DAIRY PRDTS: Ice Cream, Bulk

Back Mountain Creamery.....................G 570 855-3487
Shavertown (G-17479)
Berkey Creamery ....G 814 865-7535
University Park (G-18651)
Fritz Tastee Creme ....G 570 925-2404
Benton (G-1279)
Gibbys Ice Cream Inc ....F 215 547-7253
Levittown (G-9840)
Goodie Bar Ice-Cream Co Inc ....G 412 828-2840
Oakmont (G-12917)
Goose Bros Inc ....G 717 477-0010
Shippensburg (G-17530)
Hayloft Candles ....G 717 656-9463
Leola (G-9786)
Hershey Creamery Company ....C 717 238-8134
Harrisburg (G-7149)
Mercurios Mulberry Creamery ....F 412 621-6220
Pittsburgh (G-15278)
Mr Moo Cow LLC ....G 570 235-1061
Wilkes Barre (G-19947)
Paul Erivan ....G 215 887-2009
Oreland (G-13026)
Penn Gold Hughes ....G 724 735-2121
Harrisville (G-7254)
Purple Cow Creamery Ltd ....G 610 252-5544
Easton (G-4745)
Robert Gerenser ....F 215 646-1853
New Hope (G-12314)
Shake and Twist Chartiers Ave ....G 412 331-9606
Mc Kees Rocks (G-10634)
Sinfully Sweet.....................................G 412 523-1887
Pittsburgh (G-15541)
Snack Shack ....G 570 270-2929
Wilkes Barre (G-19964)
Sterns Soft Serve LLC ....G 724 349-4118
Creekside (G-3877)
Sunset Ice Cream ....E 570 326-3902
Williamsport (G-20077)

DAIRY PRDTS: Ice Cream, Packaged, Molded, On Sticks, Etc.

Allen McKinney Inc ....G 717 428-2321
Loganville (G-10101)
Fikes Dairy Inc ....C 724 437-7931
Uniontown (G-18627)
Halls Ice Cream Inc ....F 717 589-3290
Millerstown (G-11204)
Parkside Creamery LLC ....G 412 372-1110
Trafford (G-18460)

DAIRY PRDTS: Ice milk, Bulk

J&J Snack Foods Corp/Mia..................E 570 457-7431
Moosic (G-11509)

DAIRY PRDTS: Milk, Chocolate

Barchemy LLC ....E 724 379-4405
Donora (G-4147)

DAIRY PRDTS: Milk, Condensed & Evaporated

HB Trading LLC ....G 610 212-4565
Wayne (G-19336)
Kellers Creamery LLC ....D 215 256-8871
Harleysville (G-7043)

DAIRY PRDTS: Milk, Fluid

AFP Advanced Food Products LLC ......C 717 355-8667
New Holland (G-12227)
Clover Farms Transportation Co ....G 610 921-9111
Reading (G-16347)
Dairy Farmers America Inc ....E 717 691-4141
Mechanicsburg (G-10836)
Dean Foods Company ....G 717 522-5653
Mountville (G-11793)
Dean Foods Company ....G 215 855-8205
Lansdale (G-9358)
Dean Transporation Inc ....G 570 385-1884
Schuylkill Haven (G-17153)
Dell Perry Farms ....E 717 741-3485
York (G-20447)
Dietrichs Milk Products LLC ....D 610 929-5736
Reading (G-16361)
Family Farm Creamery ....G 412 418-2596
Washington (G-19174)
Galliker Dairy Company ....F 814 944-8193
Altoona (G-508)
High View Inc......................................E 814 886-7171
Loretto (G-10104)
Jackson Farms Dairy ....E 724 246-7010
New Salem (G-12445)
Land OLakes Inc ....C 717 486-7000
Carlisle (G-2719)
Pittsburgh Special-T Dairy LLC ....E 412 881-1409
Pittsburgh (G-15407)
Ritcheys Dairy Inc ....E 814 793-2157
Martinsburg (G-10529)
Schneiders Dairy Inc ....C 412 881-3525
Pittsburgh (G-15516)
Three Rivers Mothers Milk Bank ....F 412 281-4400
Pittsburgh (G-15619)
Trickling Springs Creamery LLC ....E 717 709-0711
Chambersburg (G-2988)

DAIRY PRDTS: Milk, Processed, Pasteurized, Homogenized/Btld

Ayrshire Dairy ....F 814 781-1978
Saint Marys (G-16950)
Brook Meadow Dairy Company ....C 814 899-3191
Erie (G-5215)
Clover Farms Dairy Company...............B 610 921-9111
Reading (G-16346)
Dairy Farmers America Inc ....D 724 946-8729
New Wilmington (G-12465)
Dairy Farmers America Inc ....E 724 946-8729
West Middlesex (G-19722)
Dean Dairy Products Company ....B 724 962-7801
Sharpsville (G-17471)
Dean Foods Company ....D 724 962-7801
Sharpsville (G-17472)
Dean Foods Company ....C 717 228-0445
Lebanon (G-9560)
Fikes Dairy Inc ....C 724 437-7931
Uniontown (G-18627)
Harrisburg Dairies Inc ....C 717 233-8701
Harrisburg (G-7142)
HP Hood LLC ....B 215 855-9074
Allentown (G-248)
Longacres Modern Dairy Inc ....E 610 845-7551
Barto (G-945)
Montdale Farm Dairy ....G 570 254-6511
Scott Township (G-17186)
Rutter Bros Dairy Inc ....C 717 848-9827
York (G-20661)
Rutter Bros Dairy Inc ....F 717 388-1665
Middletown (G-11073)
Turner Dairy Farms Inc ....D 412 372-7155
Pittsburgh (G-15661)

PRODUCT

Tuscan/Lehigh Dairies Inc..........F.......215 855-8205
Lansdale (G-9420)
Wwf Operating Company ....C.......814 590-8511
Du Bois (G-4429)

DAIRY PRDTS: Natural Cheese

Calandra Cheese.........................G.......610 759-2299
Nazareth (G-11958)
Dairy Farmers America Inc ....E.......724 946-8729
West Middlesex (G-19722)
Ingretec Ltd ....F.......717 273-0711
Lebanon (G-9582)
John Koller and Son Inc ....F.......724 475-4154
Fredonia (G-6185)
Leprino Foods Company ....C.......570 888-9658
Sayre (G-17118)
Mrckl Closeco Inc ....E.......412 828-6112
Verona (G-18758)
Penn Cheese Corporation.............F.......570 524-7700
Winfield (G-20202)
Penn Dairy LLC ....G.......570 524-7700
Winfield (G-20203)
Sun-RE Cheese Corp ....E.......570 286-1511
Sunbury (G-18173)
Three Belle Cheese ....G.......570 713-8722
Mifflinburg (G-11103)
Vetch LLC ....F.......570 524-7700
Winfield (G-20204)
Zausner Foods Corp ....B.......717 355-8505
New Holland (G-12296)

DAIRY PRDTS: Powdered Milk

Dietrichs Milk Products LLC ....D.......570 376-2001
Middlebury Center (G-11044)

DAIRY PRDTS: Processed Cheese

Euclid Technologies Inc ....G.......610 515-1842
Easton (G-4682)
John F Kraft ....G.......570 516-1092
Auburn (G-817)
Kraft and Jute Incorporated.........G.......814 969-8121
Cambridge Springs (G-2480)
Kraft Home Solutions LLC ....G.......717 819-2690
York (G-20559)
KS Krafts ....G.......717 764-7033
York (G-20561)
Mondelez Global LLC ....A.......570 820-1200
Wilkes Barre (G-19945)
Scents Krafts & Stitches ....G.......610 770-0204
Allentown (G-385)
Turner Dairy Farms Inc ....D.......412 372-7155
Pittsburgh (G-15661)
Wakefield Dairy LLC ....G.......717 548-2179
Peach Bottom (G-13203)

DAIRY PRDTS: Spreads, Cheese

Schreiber Foods Inc ....C.......717 530-5000
Shippensburg (G-17546)

DAIRY PRDTS: Whey Butter

L D Kallman Inc ....F.......610 384-1200
Coatesville (G-3312)

DAIRY PRDTS: Whey, Powdered

Land OLakes Inc ....C.......717 486-7000
Carlisle (G-2719)

DAIRY PRDTS: Whipped Topping, Exc Frozen Or Dry Mix

HP Hood LLC..............................C.......215 637-2507
Philadelphia (G-13837)
Ready Food Products Inc..............C.......215 824-2800
Philadelphia (G-14231)

DAIRY PRDTS: Yogurt, Exc Frozen

Country Food LLC ....G.......717 506-0393
Mechanicsburg (G-10831)
Fresh Made Inc...........................G.......215 725-9013
Philadelphia (G-13724)
Hyproca Nutrition USA Inc ....F.......416 565-4364
Pittsburgh (G-15108)
Loco Yoco ....G.......570 331-4529
Kingston (G-8722)
Paul Erivan ....G.......215 887-2009
Oreland (G-13026)

Polar Peach LLC ....G.......717 517-9497
Lancaster (G-9172)
Razzy Fresh Frz Yogurt Forbes ....G.......412 586-5270
Pittsburgh (G-15470)
Whirled Peace Inc ....G.......484 318-7735
Paoli (G-13151)
Yogo Factories ....G.......215 230-9646
Doylestown (G-4347)

DAIRY PRDTS: Yogurt, Frozen

Georgeos Water Ice Inc ....F.......610 494-4975
Marcus Hook (G-10443)
Justfroyo Inc ....G.......215 355-7555
Feasterville Trevose (G-5914)
Union Square Frog LLC ....G.......717 561-0623
Harrisburg (G-7241)

DAMAGED MERCHANDISE SALVAGING, SVCS ONLY

Slates Salvage...........................G.......814 448-3218
Three Springs (G-18356)

DATA ENTRY SVCS

Threshold Rhblitation Svcs Inc .....B.......610 777-7691
Reading (G-16538)

DATA PROCESSING & PREPARATION SVCS

Associated Prtg Graphics Svcs.....G.......215 322-6762
Feasterville Trevose (G-5887)
Education MGT Solutions LLC ....D.......610 701-7002
Exton (G-5671)
Fis Sg LLC ....C.......484 582-5400
Wayne (G-19330)
PC Network Inc...........................D.......267 236-0015
Philadelphia (G-14128)
Policymap Inc ....G.......866 923-6277
Philadelphia (G-14185)
Solution Systems Inc...................F.......610 668-4620
Narberth (G-11912)
Sungard Capital Corp II ....F.......484 582-2000
Wayne (G-19375)
Sungard Holdco LLC ....A.......484 582-2000
Wayne (G-19376)
Sungard Holding Corp ....G.......888 332-2564
Wayne (G-19377)
Teledyne Defense Elec LLC ....D.......814 238-3450
State College (G-18036)

DATA PROCESSING SVCS

East Associates Inc ....G.......610 667-3980
Bala Cynwyd (G-878)
Fis Data Systems Inc ....E.......484 582-2000
Collegeville (G-3377)
Keystone Nap LLC ....G.......215 280-6614
Fairless Hills (G-5786)
Ldp Inc ....G.......717 657-8500
Harrisburg (G-7171)
Pemcor Printing Company LLC......D.......717 898-1555
Lancaster (G-9162)
Source Hlthcare Analytics LLC .....D.......602 381-9500
Conshohocken (G-3605)
Sungard Asset MGT Systems Inc...C.......610 251-6500
Collegeville (G-3396)

DATABASE INFORMATION RETRIEVAL SVCS

Business Planning Inc..................G.......610 649-0550
Ardmore (G-703)
Farm Journal Inc ....E.......215 557-8900
Philadelphia (G-13694)
Intelligent Direct Inc...................E.......570 724-7355
Wellsboro (G-19466)

DECORATIVE WOOD & WOODWORK

A/S Custom Furniture Company .....E.......215 491-3100
Warrington (G-19105)
Aunt Barbies..............................G.......717 445-6386
East Earl (G-4537)
Baut Studios Inc.........................E.......570 288-1431
Swoyersville (G-18194)
Beck & Ness Woodworking LLC .....G.......717 764-3984
Emigsville (G-4984)
Bemenn Wood Products Inc ....G.......717 738-3530
Ephrata (G-5093)
Byerstown Woodwork Shop ....G.......717 442-8586
Kinzers (G-8734)

Cedar Craft ....G.......610 273-9224
Honey Brook (G-7741)
Country Cupola Ltd ....G.......717 866-8801
Myerstown (G-11881)
Country Lane Woodworking LLC ....E.......717 351-9250
New Holland (G-12238)
Countryside Woodcrafts Inc ....F.......717 627-5641
Lititz (G-10004)
Creative Kink LLC ....G.......610 506-9809
Royersford (G-16848)
David R Webb Company Inc ....C.......570 322-7186
Williamsport (G-20003)
Erector Sets Inc.........................G.......215 289-1505
Philadelphia (G-13677)
Glenshaw Distributors Inc ....E.......412 753-0231
Allison Park (G-451)
Kings Kountry Korner LLC ....G.......717 768-3425
Gordonville (G-6560)
Kings Woodwork Shop ....G.......717 768-7721
Kinzers (G-8739)
Lanchester Woodworking ....G.......717 355-2184
Narvon (G-11923)
M & R Woodworks Inc ....G.......724 378-7677
Aliquippa (G-81)
Martin Custom Cabinets LLC ....G.......717 721-1859
East Earl (G-4547)
Mike Steck ....G.......610 287-3518
Harleysville (G-7048)
Miller Country Craft ....G.......717 336-1318
Denver (G-4084)
Newshams Woodshop Inc ....G.......610 622-5800
Clifton Heights (G-3256)
Precision Woodworking & C ....G.......215 317-3533
Warminster (G-18943)
Ridge Woodworking ....G.......814 839-0151
Schellsburg (G-17135)
Robert Wirth ....G.......724 947-3615
Burgettstown (G-2354)
Round River Woodworking ....G.......717 776-5876
Newville (G-12610)
Sensenigs Wood Shavings ....G.......717 336-2047
Denver (G-4093)
South Penn Restoration Shop ....G.......717 264-2602
Chambersburg (G-2977)
Spring Mill Woodworking ....G.......610 286-7051
Morgantown (G-11536)
Staurowsky Woodworking ....G.......610 489-0770
Collegeville (G-3394)
Summitville Woodworking ....G.......717 355-5337
New Holland (G-12287)
Van Heyneker Fine Woodworking ...G.......610 388-1772
West Chester (G-19671)
Waltersdorf Manufacturing Co ....G.......717 630-0036
Hanover (G-6971)
William Cottage ....G.......724 266-2961
Ambridge (G-639)
Wilson & Mc Cracken Inc ....G.......412 784-1772
Pittsburgh (G-15718)
Worthington Stowe Fine Woodwor ...F.......215 504-5500
Newtown (G-12564)
Wyatt Incorporated ....E.......724 684-7060
Monessen (G-11302)
Zell Manufacturing Co Inc.............G.......724 327-4771
Export (G-5632)

DEFENSE SYSTEMS & EQPT

Bayhill Defense LLC ....G.......412 877-9372
Pittsburgh (G-14757)
Clear Align LLC ....D.......484 956-0510
Eagleville (G-4512)
Coastal Defense ....G.......570 858-1139
Lock Haven (G-10087)
Damsel In Defense ....G.......215 262-3643
Morrisville (G-11557)
Defense Training Solutions LLC.....G.......484 240-1188
Nazareth (G-11961)
Geissele Automatics LLC ....F.......610 272-2060
North Wales (G-12803)
Gray Space Defense ....G.......814 475-2749
Berlin (G-1288)
Heilig Defense LLC ....G.......717 490-6833
Lancaster (G-9041)
Oto Melara North America Inc ....G.......314 707-4223
Johnstown (G-8417)
Point Blank Defense LLC ....G.......717 801-2632
York (G-20630)
Strategic Defense Unit LLC...........G.......267 591-0725
Philadelphia (G-14351)
Suburban Deer Defense Llc ....G.......717 632-8844
Hanover (G-6959)

Then Defense Group.................................G...... 717 465-0584
  Gettysburg (G-6317)
Tiger PC Defense ....G...... 888 531-1530
  Whitehall (G-19891)

DEGREASING MACHINES

Federal-Mogul Motorparts LLC.............G...... 717 430-5021
  York (G-20479)
Vmf Inc ....E...... 570 575-0997
  Scranton (G-17310)

DEHYDRATION EQPT

JD Product Solutions LLC ....G...... 570 234-9421
  Bartonsville (G-947)

DEICING OR DEFROSTING FLUID

Seneca Mineral Company ....G...... 814 476-0076
  Erie (G-5475)

DELIVERY SVCS, BY VEHICLE

P G Recycling Incorporated....................F...... 814 696-6000
  Tyrone (G-18588)

DENTAL EQPT

Bti of America LLC..................................G...... 215 646-4067
  Blue Bell (G-1818)
Dental Imaging Tech Corp.......................D...... 215 997-5666
  Hatfield (G-7333)
Dentalez Inc ....E...... 610 725-8004
  Malvern (G-10223)
Dentalez Inc ....C...... 717 291-1161
  Lancaster (G-8993)
Spring Health Products Inc ....F...... 610 630-8024
  Norristown (G-12714)

DENTAL EQPT & SPLYS

5p Corporation ....G...... 215 997-5666
  Hatfield (G-7312)
Benjamin Industries and Mfg.................G...... 724 523-9615
  Jeannette (G-8248)
Burmans Medical Supplies Inc..............F...... 610 876-6068
  Upper Chichester (G-18657)
Conicella-Fessler Dental Lab................G...... 610 622-3298
  Drexel Hill (G-4362)
Dent-Chew Brush LLC.............................G...... 610 520-9941
  Haverford (G-7408)
Dentsply International Inc.......................D...... 717 767-8500
  York (G-20449)
Dentsply International Inc......................D...... 717 487-0100
  York (G-20450)
Dentsply LLC..D...... 800 323-0970
  York (G-20451)
Dentsply North America LLC ....G...... 717 849-4229
  York (G-20452)
Dentsply Sirona Inc ....C...... 717 849-7747
  Lancaster (G-8994)
Dentsply Sirona Inc ....E...... 717 699-4100
  York (G-20453)
Gudebrod Inc...C...... 610 327-4050
  Pottstown (G-15993)
Holmes Dental Company........................G...... 215 675-2877
  Hatboro (G-7287)
J R Ramos Dental Lab Inc.......................G...... 717 272-5821
  Lebanon (G-9584)
Jasinski Dental Lab Inc ....G...... 215 699-8861
  Lansdale (G-9379)
Osspray Inc ....G...... 866 238-9902
  Abbottstown (G-6)
Premier Dental Products Co ....E...... 610 239-6000
  Plymouth Meeting (G-15865)
Print A Tooth Inc ....G...... 610 647-6990
  Malvern (G-10303)
Quanotech Inc ....G...... 610 658-0116
  Wynnewood (G-20271)
Radius Corporation ....E...... 484 646-9122
  Kutztown (G-8858)
Sentage Corporation ....D...... 412 431-3353
  Pittsburgh (G-15525)
Siemens Med Solutions USA Inc ....B...... 888 826-9702
  Malvern (G-10315)
Sodium Systems LLC..............................F...... 800 821-8962
  York (G-20671)
Stan Bender ....G...... 610 759-4021
  Nazareth (G-11989)
Urgent Denture Repair LLC....................G...... 412 714-8157
  Pittsburgh (G-15685)

West Hills Specialty Supply Co ....G...... 412 279-6766
  Carnegie (G-2806)

DENTAL EQPT & SPLYS WHOLESALERS

Dentsply Sirona Inc ....F...... 717 845-7511
  York (G-20455)
Premier Dental Products Co ....E...... 610 239-6000
  Plymouth Meeting (G-15865)
Sodium Systems LLC..............................F...... 800 821-8962
  York (G-20671)

DENTAL EQPT & SPLYS: Dental Hand Instruments, NEC

Frank J May Co Inc ....G...... 215 923-3165
  Philadelphia (G-13719)

DENTAL EQPT & SPLYS: Dental Materials

American Dental Supply Inc ....F...... 484 223-3940
  Allentown (G-134)
Orahealth International...........................G...... 610 971-9600
  Wayne (G-19361)

DENTAL EQPT & SPLYS: Enamels

David C Weigle ....G...... 610 327-1616
  Pottstown (G-15980)
Everest Dental LLC.................................G...... 215 671-0188
  Philadelphia (G-13683)
Flenniken & Flenniken PC ....G...... 717 249-7777
  Carlisle (G-2713)
Mobility and Access Inc ....G...... 724 695-1590
  Oakdale (G-12907)
Taylor Made Smiles................................G...... 724 212-3167
  New Kensington (G-12381)

DENTAL EQPT & SPLYS: Hand Pieces & Parts

MTI Precision Products LLC ....F...... 610 679-5280
  Coatesville (G-3318)

DENTAL EQPT & SPLYS: Impression Materials

Dentsply Holding Company ....E...... 717 845-7511
  York (G-20448)
Dentsply Sirona Inc ....A...... 717 845-7511
  York (G-20454)

DENTAL EQPT & SPLYS: Laboratory

Dental Corp of America ....F...... 610 344-7488
  West Chester (G-19535)
Margraf Dental Mfg Inc ....G...... 215 884-0369
  Jenkintown (G-8296)

DENTAL EQPT & SPLYS: Metal

Prosthetic Arts Inc ....G...... 570 842-2929
  Moscow (G-11601)

DENTAL EQPT & SPLYS: Orthodontic Appliances

American Cnsld Mfg Co Inc ....E...... 610 825-2630
  Conshohocken (G-3519)
B E V O L ....G...... 570 962-3644
  Howard (G-7885)
Harbor Orthodontic Services.................G...... 724 654-3599
  New Castle (G-12099)
Northeast Dental Laboratories ....G...... 215 725-0950
  Elkins Park (G-4909)
Orthopli Corp..E...... 215 671-1000
  Philadelphia (G-14102)
RED Orthodontic Lab ....G...... 610 237-1100
  Kennett Square (G-8539)

DENTAL EQPT & SPLYS: Teeth, Artificial, Exc In Dental Labs

Dentsply Sirona Inc ....F...... 717 845-7511
  York (G-20455)

DENTAL EQPT & SPLYS: Tools, NEC

Premier Dental Products Co Inc............E...... 215 676-9090
  Philadelphia (G-14196)

DENTAL INSTRUMENT REPAIR SVCS

Frank J May Co Inc ....G...... 215 923-3165
  Philadelphia (G-13719)

DENTISTS' OFFICES & CLINICS

David R Englehart...................................G...... 814 238-6734
  State College (G-17957)

DEODORANTS: Personal

Procter & Gamble Company ....C...... 570 833-5141
  Tunkhannock (G-18547)

DEPARTMENT STORES: Country General

Ferguson and Hassler Inc ....C...... 717 786-7301
  Quarryville (G-16269)

DERMATOLOGICALS

Aclaris Therapeutics Inc ....D...... 484 324-7933
  Wayne (G-19293)
Almirall LLC..D...... 610 644-7000
  Exton (G-5641)
Main Line Center For Skin Surg ....G...... 610 664-1414
  Bala Cynwyd (G-884)
Microgenics ....G...... 412 490-8365
  Pittsburgh (G-15285)
Summers Laboratories Inc.....................F...... 610 454-1471
  Collegeville (G-3395)
Verrica Pharmaceuticals Inc ....F...... 484 453-3300
  West Chester (G-19674)

DERRICKS

Altec Industries Inc................................C...... 570 822-3104
  Wilkes Barre (G-19904)

DESIGN SVCS, NEC

Advent Design Corporation ....C...... 215 781-0500
  Bristol (G-2104)
Allimage Graphics LLC ....G...... 814 728-8650
  Warren (G-19009)
Allison Park Group Inc ....F...... 412 487-8211
  Allison Park (G-446)
Banc Technic Inc....................................F...... 610 756-4440
  Kutztown (G-8836)
Bayter Technologies Inc.........................G...... 610 948-7447
  Phoenixville (G-14529)
Danaken Designs Inc ....F...... 570 445-9797
  Scranton (G-17227)
Frontier LLC..F...... 570 265-2500
  Towanda (G-18426)
Greater Pttsbrgh Spcialty Advg ....E...... 412 821-5976
  Millvale (G-11223)
Keeney Printing Group Inc ....G...... 215 855-6116
  Lansdale (G-9383)
La France Corp.......................................C...... 610 361-4300
  Concordville (G-3457)
Laura J Designs ....G...... 610 213-1082
  Lansdowne (G-9437)
ONeils Custom Cab & Design.................F...... 412 422-4723
  Pittsburgh (G-15359)
Printfresh Studio LLC.............................E...... 215 426-1661
  Philadelphia (G-14203)
Srm Entertainment Group LLC ....F...... 610 825-1039
  Doylestown (G-4338)
Training Resource Corporation ....F...... 717 652-3100
  Harrisburg (G-7234)
Vicious Cycle Works Llc ....G...... 724 662-0581
  Mercer (G-10977)
VIP Tech LLC ....G...... 267 582-1554
  Philadelphia (G-14448)
XA Fishing Inc ....G...... 610 356-0340
  Broomall (G-2306)

DESIGN SVCS: Commercial & Indl

Andritz Inc ....C...... 724 597-7801
  Canonsburg (G-2540)
Conn & Company LLC..............................G...... 814 723-7980
  Warren (G-19018)
Keims Machine & Tool Co Inc ....G...... 570 758-2605
  Herndon (G-7600)
Kfw Automation Inc ....G...... 610 266-5731
  Allentown (G-281)
M E Inc ....E...... 610 820-5250
  Whitehall (G-19884)
Magee Plastics Company ....D...... 724 776-2220
  Warrendale (G-19087)

PRODUCT

Ruck Engineering Inc ....G....... 412 835-2408
  Bethel Park (G-1431)

DESIGN SVCS: Computer Integrated Systems

Advanced McRo Cmpt Specialists.......G....... 215 773-9700
  Plymouth Meeting (G-15827)
API Cryptek Inc ....F....... 908 546-3900
  State College (G-17941)
Bentley Systems Incorporated ....B....... 610 458-5000
  Exton (G-5654)
Education MGT Solutions LLC ....D....... 610 701-7002
  Exton (G-5671)
Elk Systems Inc...................................G....... 717 884-9355
  Lewisberry (G-9885)
Environmental Systems Research ....E....... 909 793-2853
  Chesterbrook (G-3092)
Impac Technology Inc ....E....... 610 430-1400
  West Chester (G-19569)
Intelligent Micro Systems Ltd...............G....... 610 664-1207
  Haverford (G-7412)
Koryak Consulting Inc ....E....... 412 364-6600
  Pittsburgh (G-15194)
Merkin Body and Hoist Company........G....... 610 258-6179
  Easton (G-4721)
Onexia Inc..E....... 610 431-7271
  Exton (G-5720)
Pulsemetrics LLC..................................G....... 412 656-5776
  Allison Park (G-460)
RTD Embedded Technologies Inc ....E....... 814 234-8087
  State College (G-18017)
Verizon Communications Inc ....C....... 570 387-3840
  Bloomsburg (G-1806)
Virtix Consulting LLC ....G....... 412 440-4835
  Wexford (G-19832)

DESIGN SVCS: Hand Tools

CP Precision Inc....................................G....... 267 364-0870
  Warminster (G-18849)

DESIGNS SVCS: Scenery, Theatrical

Fay Studios..G....... 215 672-2599
  Hatboro (G-7285)

DETECTION APPARATUS: Electronic/Magnetic Field, Light/Heat

Laser-View Technologies Inc...............F....... 610 497-8910
  Chester Springs (G-3082)

DETECTION EQPT: Aeronautical Electronic Field

Raytheon Company ....B....... 814 278-2256
  State College (G-18012)

DETECTION EQPT: Magnetic Field

Applied Magnetics Lab Inc....................G....... 717 430-2774
  York (G-20381)
Gerome Manufacturing Co Inc..............D....... 724 438-8544
  Smithfield (G-17650)
Velocity Magnetics Inc.........................G....... 724 657-8290
  New Castle (G-12163)

DETECTORS: Water Leak

American Leak Detection ....G....... 412 859-6000
  Coraopolis (G-3657)
Watermark Usa LLC..............................F....... 610 983-0500
  Gladwyne (G-6409)

DETINNING: Cans & Scrap

AMG Resources Corporation.................E....... 412 777-7300
  Pittsburgh (G-14710)

DIAGNOSTIC SUBSTANCES

Abbott Laboratories..............................G....... 610 444-9818
  Kennett Square (G-8500)
Aquaphoenix Scientific Inc ....D....... 717 632-1291
  Hanover (G-6861)
Bio/Data Corporation............................E....... 215 441-4000
  Horsham (G-7798)
Celsense Inc ....G....... 412 263-2870
  Pittsburgh (G-14834)
Cernostics Inc ....G....... 412 315-7359
  Pittsburgh (G-14835)

East York Diagnostic Center...............G....... 717 851-1850
  York (G-20460)
Esoterix Genetic Labs LLC ....E....... 215 351-2331
  Philadelphia (G-13679)
Excela Health Holding Co Inc ....G....... 724 832-4450
  Greensburg (G-6665)
Orasure Technologies Inc ....E....... 610 882-1820
  Bethlehem (G-1589)
Orasure Technologies Inc ....E....... 610 882-1820
  Bethlehem (G-1590)
Rapid Pathogen Screening Inc ....E....... 718 288-4318
  Montoursville (G-11449)
Saint Lukes Hosp Bethlehem PA..........G....... 610 954-3531
  Bethlehem (G-1614)

DIAGNOSTIC SUBSTANCES OR AGENTS: Blood Derivative

Avid Radiopharmaceuticals Inc............F....... 215 298-0700
  Philadelphia (G-13427)
Bramante Bioscience LLC ....G....... 860 634-0015
  Philadelphia (G-13476)
Lifescan Inc ....A....... 800 227-8862
  Chesterbrook (G-3093)

DIAGNOSTIC SUBSTANCES OR AGENTS: Enzyme & Isoenzyme

N-Zyme Scientifics LLC.........................G....... 267 218-1098
  Doylestown (G-4317)

DIAGNOSTIC SUBSTANCES OR AGENTS: In Vitro

Biodetego LLC ....G....... 856 701-2453
  Philadelphia (G-13464)
Biomagnetic Solutions LLC....................G....... 814 689-1801
  State College (G-17945)
Janssen Biotech Inc ....G....... 610 407-0194
  Malvern (G-10259)
Janssen Biotech Inc ....B....... 610 651-6000
  Horsham (G-7827)
Janssen Biotech Inc ....G....... 610 651-6000
  Malvern (G-10262)
Lia Diagnostics Inc ....G....... 267 362-9670
  Philadelphia (G-13967)
Orasure Technologies Inc ....B....... 610 882-1820
  Bethlehem (G-1588)
Saladax Biomedical Inc ....E....... 610 419-6731
  Bethlehem (G-1615)
Salimetrics LLC ....E....... 814 234-7748
  State College (G-18019)
SMC Direct LLC ....E....... 800 521-1635
  Evans City (G-5563)

DIAGNOSTIC SUBSTANCES OR AGENTS: In Vivo

Avidtox Inc...G....... 610 738-7938
  West Chester (G-19504)
Jt-Mesh Diagnostics LLC.......................G....... 610 299-7482
  Kennett Square (G-8517)

DIAGNOSTIC SUBSTANCES OR AGENTS: Microbiology & Virology

Biorealize Inc.......................................G....... 610 216-5554
  Philadelphia (G-13466)
Interntnal Soc of Nurovirology ....G....... 215 707-9788
  Philadelphia (G-13870)
Limitless Longevity LLC ....F....... 215 279-8376
  Philadelphia (G-13971)
Microbiology Lab Co ....G....... 570 800-5795
  Scranton (G-17259)

DIAGNOSTIC SUBSTANCES OR AGENTS: Radioactive

Bio-Nucleonics Inc................................F....... 305 576-0996
  Philadelphia (G-13461)
Petnet Solutions Inc ....G....... 865 218-2000
  North Wales (G-12824)

DIAMONDS, GEMS, WHOLESALE

Wallace Brothers Mfg Co ....F....... 570 822-3808
  Wilkes Barre (G-19968)

DIAPERS: Disposable

First Quality Baby Pdts LLC ....A....... 717 247-3516
  Lewistown (G-9928)
First Quality Enterprises Inc ....C....... 570 384-1600
  Hazleton (G-7498)
First Quality Products Inc ....B....... 610 265-5000
  King of Prussia (G-8618)

DIATOMACEOUS EARTH MINING SVCS

Grc Holding Inc ....G....... 610 667-6640
  Bala Cynwyd (G-879)

DIE CUTTING SVC: Paper

CCT Manufacturing & Fulfillmen ....F....... 724 652-0818
  New Castle (G-12072)

DIE SETS: Presses, Metal Stamping

Bra-Vor Tool & Die Co Inc ....E....... 814 724-1557
  Meadville (G-10708)
Cir-Cut Corporation ....G....... 215 324-1000
  Philadelphia (G-13545)
Composidie Inc ....D....... 717 764-2233
  York (G-20429)
Composidie Inc ....C....... 724 845-8602
  Apollo (G-673)
D&M Tool Inc ....F....... 814 724-6743
  Meadville (G-10716)
Elizabeth Carbide Die Co Inc ....E....... 412 751-3000
  McKeesport (G-10667)
Hytech Tool & Design Co ....F....... 814 734-6000
  Edinboro (G-4815)
Indiana Tool & Die LLC ....G....... 724 463-0386
  Indiana (G-8107)
Mac Tool & Die Inc ....G....... 814 337-9105
  Meadville (G-10752)
Pace Precisions Products Inc ....E....... 814 371-6201
  Du Bois (G-4411)
Samuel Stamping Tech LLC..................E....... 724 981-5042
  Hermitage (G-7594)
Tottser Tool and Die Shop Inc ....D....... 215 357-7600
  Southampton (G-17842)

DIES & TOOLS: Special

Abbottstown Industries Inc..................E....... 717 259-8715
  Abbottstown (G-3)
Accudie Inc..G....... 724 222-8447
  Meadow Lands (G-10689)
Actco Tool & Mfg Co............................E....... 814 336-4235
  Meadville (G-10694)
Allegheny Tool & Mfg Co......................F....... 814 337-2795
  Meadville (G-10700)
Allegheny Tool Mold & Mfg Inc.............F....... 814 726-0200
  Clarendon (G-3166)
Alpha Carb Enterprises Inc..................E....... 724 845-2500
  Leechburg (G-9641)
Angermeier Tool & Die Inc ....G....... 814 445-2285
  Somerset (G-17673)
Area Tool & Manufacturing Inc ....F....... 814 724-3166
  Meadville (G-10703)
Arkay Tool & Die Inc ....F....... 215 322-2039
  Langhorne (G-9279)
Arrow Tool Die & Machine Co ....F....... 215 676-1300
  Hatboro (G-7270)
Arthur R Warner Company.....................F....... 724 539-9229
  Latrobe (G-9458)
B-TEC Solutions Inc ....D....... 215 785-2400
  Croydon (G-3911)
Backus Company ....E....... 814 887-5705
  Smethport (G-17632)
Beck Tool Inc.......................................E....... 814 734-8513
  Edinboro (G-4809)
Bloom Machine Works Inc ....G....... 814 789-4234
  Guys Mills (G-6808)
Boyle Incorporated ....G....... 724 295-2420
  Freeport (G-6200)
Brandt Tool & Die Co Inc ....G....... 717 359-5995
  Littlestown (G-10064)
C & C Tooling Inc ....F....... 724 845-0939
  Leechburg (G-9642)
C Palmer Manufacturing Inc ....F....... 724 872-8200
  West Newton (G-19748)
Canto Tool Corporation ....F....... 814 724-2865
  Meadville (G-10710)
Carbigrind Inc......................................G....... 724 722-3536
  Ruffs Dale (G-16871)
Char-Mark Inc ....G....... 570 754-7310
  Auburn (G-815)

Choice Tool..G........ 814 474-4656
   Fairview (G-5815)
Christiansbrunn Die Fmlies Der.........G........ 570 425-2548
   Pitman (G-14621)
CK Tool & Die Inc...........................G........ 814 836-9600
   Erie (G-5225)
Cumberland Tool & Die Inc...............E........ 717 691-1125
   Mechanicsburg (G-10835)
Custom Die Services Inc.................F........ 717 867-5400
   Annville (G-646)
Custom Tool and Die Inc.................F........ 717 522-1440
   Mountville (G-11792)
Danco Precision Inc......................E........ 610 933-1090
   Phoenixville (G-14543)
Danco Precision Inc......................E........ 610 933-8981
   Phoenixville (G-14544)
Danco Precision Inc......................F........ 610 933-8981
   Phoenixville (G-14542)
De Vore Tool Co Inc......................G........ 814 425-2566
   Cochranton (G-3341)
Deasey Machine Tl & Die Works........G........ 814 847-2728
   Everett (G-5570)
Detwiler Tool Co............................G........ 215 257-5770
   Sellersville (G-17344)
Die Botschaft................................G........ 717 433-4417
   Millersburg (G-11193)
Die Urglaawisch Sippschaft............G........ 215 499-1323
   Bristol (G-2131)
Dietech Tool & Die Inc...................F........ 814 834-2779
   Saint Marys (G-16962)
Dixon Tool & Die Inc......................F........ 814 684-0266
   Tyrone (G-18581)
Do-Co Inc.....................................F........ 814 382-8339
   Conneaut Lake (G-3471)
Double H Manufacturing Corp..........D........ 215 674-4100
   Warminster (G-18860)
Double H Manufacturing Corp..........G........ 215 674-4100
   Warminster (G-18861)
Doutt Tool Inc...............................E........ 814 398-2989
   Venango (G-18740)
Drumm & Oharah Tl & Design Inc.....G........ 814 476-1349
   Erie (G-5251)
Dunay Tool & Die Co.....................G........ 724 335-7972
   Tarentum (G-18241)
Eagle Tool & Die Co Inc.................G........ 610 264-6011
   Malvern (G-10226)
Electronic Tool & Die Works............G........ 215 639-0730
   Bensalem (G-1187)
Engdahl Manufacturing Inc.............G........ 717 854-7114
   York (G-20468)
Evansburg Tool Corporation............G........ 610 489-7580
   Collegeville (G-3376)
Excellent Tool Inc.........................G........ 814 337-7705
   Meadville (G-10724)
Florio Tooling Inc..........................G........ 814 781-3973
   Saint Marys (G-16974)
Frew Mill Die Crafts Inc.................F........ 724 658-9026
   New Castle (G-12095)
General Carbide Corporation...........C........ 724 836-3000
   Greensburg (G-6668)
George J Anderton........................G........ 814 382-9201
   Conneaut Lake (G-3473)
Gma Manufacturing Inc..................F........ 215 355-3105
   Huntingdon Valley (G-7990)
Gma Tooling Company....................E........ 215 355-3107
   Huntingdon Valley (G-7991)
Graham Tech Inc...........................G........ 814 807-1778
   Meadville (G-10729)
Greenbriar Indus Systems Inc.........D........ 814 474-1400
   Fairview (G-5824)
H and H Tool................................G........ 814 333-4677
   Meadville (G-10732)
H and K Tool and Mch Co Inc..........E........ 215 322-0380
   Huntingdon Valley (G-7993)
Hill Precision Manufacturing............G........ 814 827-4333
   Titusville (G-18380)
Hodge Tool Co Inc.........................E........ 717 393-5543
   Lancaster (G-9051)
Holt Precision Tool Co....................G........ 814 342-3595
   West Decatur (G-19688)
Innovative Carbide Inc...................D........ 412 751-6900
   Irwin (G-8171)
J K Tool Inc..................................E........ 724 727-2490
   Apollo (G-678)
J K Tool Die Co.............................G........ 724 339-1858
   New Kensington (G-12347)
Jay-Ell Industries Inc.....................F........ 610 326-0921
   Pottstown (G-16005)
Jepson Precision Tool Inc...............F........ 814 756-4806
   Cranesville (G-3867)

JV Manufacturing Co Inc.................D........ 724 224-1704
   Natrona Heights (G-11945)
K V Inc...F........ 215 322-4044
   Huntingdon Valley (G-8006)
K-Fab Inc......................................D........ 570 759-8411
   Berwick (G-1331)
Karadon Corporation......................F........ 724 676-5790
   Blairsville (G-1729)
Kdc Engineering............................G........ 267 203-8487
   Telford (G-18298)
Kersey Tool and Die Co Inc............G........ 814 885-8045
   Kersey (G-8562)
Kroesen Tool Co Inc......................F........ 717 653-1392
   Mount Joy (G-11665)
Kuhn Tool & Die Co.......................E........ 814 336-2123
   Meadville (G-10747)
Lake Tool Inc................................G........ 814 374-4401
   Franklin (G-6146)
Lakeland Precision Inc...................G........ 814 382-6811
   Conneaut Lake (G-3474)
Laser Tool Inc...............................E........ 814 763-2032
   Saegertown (G-16921)
Laureldale Tool Co Inc...................G........ 610 929-5406
   Reading (G-16427)
Leefson Tool & Die Company...........E........ 610 461-7772
   Folcroft (G-6008)
Lehr Design & Manufacturing..........G........ 717 428-1828
   Jacobus (G-8230)
Leiss Tool & Die............................G........ 814 444-1444
   Somerset (G-17695)
Lionheart Industrial Group LLC........G........ 215 283-8400
   Newtown (G-12520)
M & M Tool & Die Inc.....................E........ 717 359-7178
   Littlestown (G-10071)
M C Tool & Die Inc.........................E........ 814 944-8654
   Altoona (G-523)
Mal-Ber Manufacturing Company......E........ 215 672-6440
   Huntingdon Valley (G-8010)
Maloney Tool & Mold Inc................E........ 814 337-8407
   Meadville (G-10754)
Marlan Tool Inc.............................E........ 814 382-2744
   Meadville (G-10757)
McNulty Tool Die...........................G........ 215 957-9900
   Warminster (G-18919)
Mears Tool & Die Inc.....................F........ 814 425-8304
   Cochranton (G-3344)
Medl Tool & Die Inc.......................G........ 215 443-5457
   Warminster (G-18921)
Minco Tool & Mold Inc...................G........ 814 724-1376
   Meadville (G-10764)
Mxl Industries Inc.........................D........ 717 569-8711
   Lancaster (G-9141)
Nemco...E........ 215 355-2100
   Feasterville Trevose (G-5922)
Nordic Tool & Die Co......................G........ 570 889-5650
   Ringtown (G-16755)
North American Tooling Inc.............G........ 814 486-3700
   Emporium (G-5070)
Northwest Tool & Die Inc................F........ 814 763-5087
   Saegertown (G-16926)
Ofcg Inc.......................................G........ 570 655-0804
   Dupont (G-4493)
Paul E Seymour Tool & Die LLC.......F........ 814 725-5170
   North East (G-12754)
Penn United Technologies Inc.........E........ 724 431-2482
   Sarver (G-17078)
Penn United Technologies Inc.........C........ 724 352-5151
   Saxonburg (G-17092)
Penn United Technologies Inc.........A........ 724 352-1507
   Cabot (G-2460)
Pennco Tool & Die Inc...................E........ 814 336-5035
   Meadville (G-10776)
Phaztech Inc................................E........ 814 834-3262
   Saint Marys (G-17006)
Philadelphia Carbide Co Inc............G........ 215 885-0770
   Oreland (G-13027)
Port Richmond Tool & Die Inc..........F........ 215 426-2287
   Philadelphia (G-14191)
Precise Tool & Die Inc...................E........ 724 845-1285
   Leechburg (G-9650)
Precision Carbide Inc....................G........ 215 355-4220
   Feasterville Trevose (G-5927)
Prism Technologies Inc..................G........ 412 751-3090
   Elizabeth (G-4863)
Quality Metal Products Inc.............E........ 570 333-4248
   Dallas (G-3967)
Ram Tool Co Inc...........................F........ 814 382-1842
   Conneaut Lake (G-3478)
Rapid Mold Solutions Inc...............G........ 814 833-2721
   Erie (G-5456)

Reubes Machine & Tool Co Inc........G........ 215 368-0200
   Lansdale (G-9404)
Rhkg Holdings Inc.........................E........ 814 337-8407
   Meadville (G-10787)
Ronal Tool Company Inc.................F........ 717 741-0880
   York (G-20660)
Saint-Gobain Ceramics Plas Inc......A........ 508 795-5000
   Valley Forge (G-18711)
Sansom Tool & Die Inc...................G........ 814 967-4985
   Centerville (G-2835)
Scientific Tool Inc.........................E........ 724 446-9311
   New Stanton (G-12450)
Signal Machine Co.........................G........ 717 354-9994
   New Holland (G-12284)
Spark Technologies Inc..................F........ 724 295-3860
   Schenley (G-17136)
Spring Tool & Die Co Inc................G........ 814 224-5173
   Roaring Spring (G-16771)
St Marys Tool & Die Co Inc.............E........ 814 834-7420
   Saint Marys (G-17021)
Standard Precision Mfg Inc.............E........ 814 724-1202
   Meadville (G-10792)
Stanko Products Inc.......................F........ 724 834-8080
   Greensburg (G-6717)
Starn Tool & Manufacturing Co........D........ 814 724-1057
   Meadville (G-10794)
Steadman Tool & Die Inc................G........ 814 967-4333
   Townville (G-18447)
Steer Machine Tool & Die Corp........F........ 570 253-5152
   Honesdale (G-7727)
Suburban Precison Mold Company....F........ 814 337-3413
   Meadville (G-10795)
Suburban Tool & Die Co Inc............E........ 814 833-4882
   Erie (G-5495)
Superior Tool and Die Co................F........ 215 638-1904
   Bensalem (G-1257)
Talbar Inc.....................................E........ 814 337-8400
   Meadville (G-10797)
Taylor Tool Inc..............................G........ 814 967-4642
   Townville (G-18448)
Technical Precision Inc..................E........ 724 253-2800
   Hadley (G-6821)
Tohickon Tool & Die Co..................G........ 215 766-8285
   Doylestown (G-4343)
Tool & Die Productions..................G........ 814 838-3304
   Erie (G-5511)
Tottser Tool and Die Shop Inc.........D........ 215 357-7600
   Southampton (G-17843)
Turner Tool & Die Inc.....................F........ 570 378-3233
   Lake Winola (G-8912)
Ultra Precision Incorporated...........E........ 724 295-5161
   Freeport (G-6216)
Unique Machine Co........................E........ 215 368-8550
   Montgomeryville (G-11425)
Viant Westfield LLC.......................D........ 215 675-4653
   Warminster (G-18994)
Viking Tool & Gage Inc...................C........ 814 382-8691
   Conneaut Lake (G-3482)
Whitehead Tool & Design Inc...........F........ 814 967-3064
   Guys Mills (G-6814)
Wilmington Die Inc.........................G........ 724 946-8020
   New Wilmington (G-12473)
Wolfe Tool & Machine Company........F........ 717 848-6375
   York (G-20717)
Wycon Mold & Tool Inc...................G........ 215 675-2945
   Warminster (G-19004)

DIES: Cutting, Exc Metal

Paramount Die Corporation.............F........ 814 734-6999
   Edinboro (G-4819)

DIES: Extrusion

Bower Wire Cloth Tl & Die Inc.........G........ 570 398-4488
   Jersey Shore (G-8310)
Quality Die Makers Inc...................E........ 724 325-1264
   Turtle Creek (G-18568)

DIES: Plastic Forming

Custom Tool & Design Inc...............E........ 814 838-9777
   Erie (G-5241)
Proto-Cast LLC.............................E........ 610 326-1723
   Douglassville (G-4180)
Shaw Industries Inc.......................E........ 814 432-0954
   Franklin (G-6159)

DIES: Steel Rule

Coinco Inc....................................E........ 814 425-7407
   Cochranton (G-3337)

P R O D U C T

Coinco Inc.......................................E...... 814 425-7476
Cochranton (G-3338)
Compacting Tooling Inc ....E...... 412 751-3535
McKeesport (G-10664)
Donlee Tool Corp ....F...... 814 398-8215
Cambridge Springs (G-2477)
Dynamic Dies Inc...............................E...... 724 325-1514
Pittsburgh (G-14947)
New Castle Company Inc ....G...... 724 658-4516
New Castle (G-12128)
P D Q Tooling Inc...............................G...... 412 751-2214
Mckeesport (G-10677)
Paramount Die Corporation ....F...... 814 734-6999
Edinboro (G-4819)
Pittsburgh Carbide Die Co LLC ....F...... 412 384-5785
Elizabeth (G-4862)
Willamsport Dies & Cuts Inc ....G...... 570 323-8351
Williamsport (G-20092)
York Steel Rule Dies Inc ....E...... 717 846-6002
York (G-20750)

DIFFERENTIAL ASSEMBLIES & PARTS

Greensburg Mch & Driveline LLC..........G...... 724 837-8233
Greensburg (G-6670)

DIODES: Light Emitting

Aron Lighting LLC ....G...... 484 681-5687
King of Prussia (G-8584)

DIODES: Solid State, Germanium, Silicon, Etc

Dean Technology Inc ....E...... 724 479-3533
Lucernemines (G-10117)

DIORITE: Crushed & Broken

Keystone Granite Tile Inc ....F...... 717 394-4972
Lancaster (G-9084)
Penn Run Quarry Spruce Mine ....F...... 724 465-0272
Penn Run (G-13231)

DIRECT SELLING ESTABLISHMENTS, NEC

Mergtech Inc......................................G...... 570 584-3388
Hughesville (G-7896)

DIRECT SELLING ESTABLISHMENTS: Cosmetic, House-To-House

T&T Buttas LLC....................................G...... 833 251-1357
Philadelphia (G-14365)

DIRECT SELLING ESTABLISHMENTS: Food Svcs

Lancaster Fine Foods Inc......................E...... 717 397-9578
Lancaster (G-9094)

DIRECT SELLING ESTABLISHMENTS: Lunch Wagon

Apontes Latin Flavor Inc ....G...... 727 247-2001
Glenshaw (G-6481)

DISCS & TAPE: Optical, Blank

Optium Corporation..............................D...... 215 675-3105
Horsham (G-7838)

DISHWASHING EQPT: Commercial

Hobart Sales and Service Inc................G...... 301 733-6560
Harrisburg (G-7150)
Insinger Machine Company ....D...... 215 624-4800
Philadelphia (G-13860)
Somat Company...................................E...... 717 397-5100
Lancaster (G-9202)

DISK & DISKETTE CONVERSION SVCS

Griffith Inc...C...... 215 322-8100
Huntingdon Valley (G-7992)

DISK DRIVES: Computer

Seagate Technology LLC ....C...... 412 918-7000
Pittsburgh (G-15518)

DISKS & DRUMS Magnetic

James Jesse & Co Inc ....E...... 610 419-9880
Bethlehem (G-1544)

DISPENSERS: Soap

Weston Commercial Group Inc ....G...... 215 717-9675
Philadelphia (G-14467)

DISPENSING EQPT & PARTS, BEVERAGE: Beer

Tuna Enterprises..................................G...... 724 205-6535
Greensburg (G-6722)

DISPENSING EQPT & PARTS, BEVERAGE: Cold, Exc Coin-Operated

Beverage-Air Corporation ....C...... 814 849-7336
Brookville (G-2250)

DISPENSING EQPT & PARTS, BEVERAGE: Coolers, Milk/Water, Elec

Trilli Holdings Inc ....G...... 724 736-8000
Star Junction (G-17938)

DISPENSING EQPT & PARTS, BEVERAGE: Fountain/Other Beverage

Liberty Bell Bottling Co Inc...................G...... 610 820-6020
Allentown (G-294)

DISPENSING EQPT & PARTS, BEVERAGE: Fountains, Parts/Access

Apex Fountain Sales Inc ....G...... 215 627-4526
Philadelphia (G-13398)
Multi-Flow Dispensers LP ....D...... 215 322-1800
Huntingdon Valley (G-8014)

DISPLAY CASES, REFRIGERATED: Wholesalers

Gem Refrigerator Co.............................F...... 877 436-7374
Philadelphia (G-13746)

DISPLAY FIXTURES: Wood

3-D Creative Services Inc ....F...... 570 329-1111
Williamsport (G-19983)
Gh Silver Asset Corp ....G...... 404 432-3707
Philadelphia (G-13760)
Interior Creations Inc...........................E...... 215 425-9390
Philadelphia (G-13864)
Keystone Casework Inc........................E...... 814 941-7250
Altoona (G-520)
RLB Ventures Inc ....E...... 717 964-1111
Denver (G-4091)
S F U LLC...G...... 610 473-0730
Gilbertsville (G-6377)
Versatek Enterprises LLC ....D...... 717 626-6390
Lititz (G-10057)
Visual Merchandising LLC ....G...... 610 353-7550
Newtown Square (G-12597)

DISPLAY ITEMS: Corrugated, Made From Purchased Materials

Creative Management Svcs LLC ....E...... 610 863-1900
Pen Argyl (G-13212)
Graphex Inc ....G...... 610 524-9525
Exton (G-5691)
Packaging Corporation America ....D...... 717 632-4727
New Oxford (G-12419)

DISPLAY ITEMS: Solid Fiber, Made From Purchased Materials

Keystone Displays Corporation ....G...... 717 612-0340
Lemoyne (G-9746)
Pratt Rock Solid Displays LLC ....E...... 610 929-4800
Reading (G-16474)
Shenango Operating Inc ....E...... 724 657-3650
New Castle (G-12151)

DISPLAY LETTERING SVCS

Athletic Lettering Inc ....F...... 717 840-6373
York (G-20389)

DISPLAY STANDS: Merchandise, Exc Wood

School Gate Guardian Inc......................F...... 800 805-3808
State College (G-18020)

DISTANCE MEASURING EQPT OR DME: Aeronautical

Arin Technologies Inc...........................G...... 412 877-2877
Pittsburgh (G-14722)

DOCKS: Prefabricated Metal

United Fence Supply Company ....G...... 570 307-0782
Olyphant (G-13002)

DOCUMENT DESTRUCTION SVC

Rapid Recycling Inc.............................D...... 610 650-0737
Oaks (G-12936)

DOCUMENTATION CENTER

Ois LLC...G...... 717 447-0265
Mount Union (G-11746)

DOLLIES: Industrial

Deval Life Cycle Support LLC...............E...... 865 786-8675
Philadelphia (G-13624)
Metro International Corp ....E...... 570 825-2741
Wilkes Barre (G-19943)
Penn Manufacturing ....G...... 717 626-8879
Lititz (G-10030)

DOLOMITE: Crushed & Broken

Lwb Holding Company ....G...... 717 792-3611
York (G-20570)
Magnesita Refractories Company ....B...... 717 792-3611
York (G-20572)
Magnesita Refractories Company ....B...... 717 792-4216
York (G-20573)

DOOR & WINDOW REPAIR SVCS

Hordis Doors Inc ....G...... 215 957-9585
Warminster (G-18895)

DOOR FRAMES: Wood

Frp Door Concepts Inc ....G...... 215 604-1545
Bensalem (G-1200)

DOOR OPERATING SYSTEMS: Electric

Fclz Holdings Inc ....F...... 412 788-4991
Pittsburgh (G-15007)
Overhead Door Corporation ....D...... 215 368-8700
Lansdale (G-9396)
Stanley Access Tech LLC......................G...... 570 368-1435
Montgomery (G-11380)
Stanley Vidmar ....E...... 610 797-6600
Allentown (G-402)

DOORS & WINDOWS WHOLESALERS: All Materials

Eden Inc...E...... 814 797-1160
Knox (G-8809)
Jefco Manufacturing Inc.......................F...... 215 334-3220
Wynnewood (G-20270)
Rdy Gutters Plus LLC...........................G...... 610 488-5666
Bernville (G-1304)
Tell Manufacturing Inc ....E...... 717 625-2990
Lititz (G-10054)
Thermolite Inc ....E...... 570 969-1957
Scranton (G-17300)
Trinity Sup & Installation LLC................F...... 412 331-3044
Pittsburgh (G-15650)

DOORS & WINDOWS: Screen & Storm

Armaclad Inc ....E...... 717 749-3141
Waynesboro (G-19398)
G & S Metal Products Inc ....G...... 412 462-7000
Pittsburgh (G-15039)
Graham Architectural Pdts Corp ....B...... 717 849-8100
York (G-20506)

Kenbern Storm Doors........................G...... 412 678-7210
McKeesport (G-10674)

Thermolite Inc ....E...... 570 969-1957
Scranton (G-17300)

DOORS & WINDOWS: Storm, Metal

Custom Entryways & Millwork...............G...... 814 798-2500
Stoystown (G-18074)

Dailey Manufacturing Co...................F...... 215 659-0477
Willow Grove (G-20113)

Dun Rite Window and Door.................G...... 412 781-8200
Pittsburgh (G-14942)

Emerald Windows Inc ....F...... 215 236-6767
Philadelphia (G-13673)

Graham Thermal Products LLC...........E...... 724 658-0500
New Castle (G-12098)

Kane Innovations Inc ....D...... 814 838-7731
Erie (G-5342)

Millcreek Metals Inc ....G...... 814 764-3708
Strattanville (G-18098)

Muldoon Window Door & Awning ....G...... 570 347-9453
Scranton (G-17261)

Nortek Global Hvac LLC ....B...... 814 938-1408
Punxsutawney (G-16151)

Northeast Building Pdts Corp ....C...... 215 535-7110
Philadelphia (G-14079)

Northeast Glass Co..........................G...... 267 991-0054
Philadelphia (G-14083)

Roma Aluminum Co Inc ....F...... 215 545-5700
Philadelphia (G-14259)

Scatton Bros Mfg Co ....G...... 215 362-6830
Lansdale (G-9409)

Seaway Manufacturing Corp..............D...... 814 898-2255
Erie (G-5472)

Thermo-Twin Industries Inc ....C...... 412 826-1000
Oakmont (G-12927)

Traco Delaware Inc ....F...... 724 776-7000
Cranberry Township (G-3856)

Tri City Aluminum Company ....A...... 724 799-8917
Cranberry Township (G-3857)

Victor Sun Ctrl of Phladelphia ....E...... 215 743-0800
Philadelphia (G-14446)

Weather Shield Mfg Inc ....B...... 717 761-7131
Camp Hill (G-2524)

Zurn Aluminum Products Co ....G...... 814 774-2681
Girard (G-6404)

DOORS: Combination Screen & Storm, Wood

Hordis Doors Inc ....G...... 215 957-9585
Warminster (G-18895)

DOORS: Fiberglass

Best Group Holdings Inc ....E...... 814 536-1422
Johnstown (G-8357)

DOORS: Garage, Overhead, Metal

Alto Garage Door Manufacturing ....G...... 717 546-0056
Middletown (G-11047)

Ezy Products Co Inc ....G...... 570 822-9600
Wilkes Barre (G-19919)

Howell Manufacturing Company ....F...... 814 652-5143
Everett (G-5573)

McBrothers Inc.................................F...... 215 675-3003
Warminster (G-18918)

Overhead Door Corporation ....D...... 215 368-8700
Lansdale (G-9396)

Overhead Door Corporation ....C...... 570 326-7325
Williamsport (G-20053)

DOORS: Garage, Overhead, Wood

Eidemiller Door Co...........................G...... 724 668-8294
New Alexandria (G-12018)

Global Custom ....G...... 844 782-2653
Folsom (G-6023)

Howell Manufacturing Company ....F...... 814 652-5143
Everett (G-5573)

Pittsburgh Shed Company Inc.............G...... 724 745-4422
Canonsburg (G-2619)

DOORS: Glass

Park & Park Norristown Inc................G...... 267 346-0932
Norristown (G-12700)

DOORS: Rolling, Indl Building Or Warehouse, Metal

Action Materials Inc ....G...... 610 377-3037
Lehighton (G-9709)

Bristol Rolling Door Inc.....................G...... 215 949-9090
Levittown (G-9821)

Ciw Enterprises Inc..........................E...... 800 233-8366
Mountain Top (G-11755)

Cornellcookson LLC.........................B...... 800 294-4358
Mountain Top (G-11756)

Cornellcookson Inc...........................C...... 570 474-6773
Mountain Top (G-11757)

Termac Corp ....G...... 610 863-5356
Wind Gap (G-20174)

Thruways Door Systems Inc ....F...... 412 781-4030
Pittsburgh (G-15622)

DOORS: Screen, Metal

Mid Atlantic Retractable ....G...... 610 496-8062
Malvern (G-10279)

DOORS: Wooden

Allegheny Wood Works Inc.................E...... 814 774-7338
Lake City (G-8897)

B & L Manufacturing Corp ....F...... 412 784-9400
Pittsburgh (G-14745)

Conestoga Wood Spc Corp ....A...... 717 445-6701
East Earl (G-4540)

Fine Line Homes ....F...... 717 561-2040
Harrisburg (G-7129)

Ivan C Dutterer Inc ....D...... 717 637-8977
Hanover (G-6904)

Jeld-Wen Inc ....A...... 570 628-5317
Pottsville (G-16084)

Keystone Wood Specialties Inc...........G...... 717 299-6288
Lancaster (G-9085)

Marshall Woodworks Ltd ....F...... 412 321-1685
Pittsburgh (G-15257)

Masco Cabinetry LLC ....G...... 570 882-8565
Athens (G-812)

Masonite Corporation ....C...... 570 473-3557
Northumberland (G-12870)

Overhead Door Corporation ....C...... 570 326-7325
Williamsport (G-20053)

Overhead Door Corporation ....B...... 717 248-0131
Lewistown (G-9942)

Overhead Door Corporation ....D...... 215 368-8700
Lansdale (G-9396)

Signature Door Inc...........................D...... 814 949-2770
Altoona (G-549)

Somerset Door & Column Company.....F...... 814 444-9427
Somerset (G-17707)

DOWELS & DOWEL RODS

Thompson Maple Products Inc............E...... 814 664-7717
Corry (G-3775)

DOWNSPOUTS: Sheet Metal

Raytec LLC ....E...... 717 445-0510
Ephrata (G-5138)

DRAFTING SPLYS WHOLESALERS

Pace Resources Inc ....E...... 717 852-1300
York (G-20616)

Print-O-Stat Inc................................E...... 717 812-9476
York (G-20640)

Print-O-Stat Inc................................G...... 610 265-5470
King of Prussia (G-8664)

DRAFTING SVCS

Lord Corporation ....B...... 814 868-0924
Erie (G-5371)

Tudor Design ....G...... 215 638-3366
Bensalem (G-1266)

DRAPERIES & CURTAINS

Bishops Inc ....G...... 412 821-3333
Mars (G-10488)

Brookline Fabrics Co Inc...................E...... 412 665-4925
Pittsburgh (G-14794)

Caldwells Windoware Inc ....E...... 412 922-1132
Pittsburgh (G-14800)

De Lucas Draperys ....G...... 610 284-2464
Clifton Heights (G-3251)

Fabtex Inc ....D...... 910 739-0019
Danville (G-4001)

Fabtex Inc ....C...... 570 275-7500
Danville (G-4000)

Fay Studios......................................G...... 215 672-2599
Hatboro (G-7285)

Ferrante Uphlstrng & Crptng ....F...... 724 535-8866
Wampum (G-18800)

Hamilton Awning Co ....F...... 724 774-7644
Beaver (G-983)

Kartri Sales Company Inc ....E...... 570 785-3365
Forest City (G-6054)

Martins Draperies & Interiors..............G...... 717 239-0501
Lancaster (G-9125)

Merrill Y Landis Ltd ....D...... 215 723-8177
Telford (G-18302)

Plymouth Blind Co Inc ....E...... 412 771-8569
Mc Kees Rocks (G-10626)

Plymouth Interiors LP ....F...... 412 771-8569
Mc Kees Rocks (G-10627)

S Morantz Inc..................................D...... 215 969-0266
Philadelphia (G-14273)

DRAPERIES & DRAPERY FABRICS, COTTON

Bachman Drapery Studio Inc..............G...... 215 257-8810
Tylersport (G-18574)

Dwell America LLC ....G...... 717 272-4666
Lebanon (G-9562)

Lachina Drapery Company Inc ....E...... 412 665-4900
Pittsburgh (G-15215)

DRAPERIES: Plastic & Textile, From Purchased Materials

Decopro Inc.....................................G...... 215 939-7983
Philadelphia (G-13613)

L A Draperies Inc.............................G...... 610 375-2224
Reading (G-16425)

Lafayette Venetian Blind Inc ....E...... 717 652-3750
Harrisburg (G-7167)

Lewrene Interiors ....G...... 717 263-8300
Chambersburg (G-2953)

Morantz Inc.....................................G...... 215 969-0266
Philadelphia (G-14038)

Samuel Gerber Inc ....G...... 717 761-0250
Harrisburg (G-7212)

Westerbrook Custom Made Drap ....G...... 717 737-8185
Camp Hill (G-2525)

DRAPERY & UPHOLSTERY STORES: Draperies

Burton Springcrest Interiors ....G...... 724 468-3000
Delmont (G-4049)

L A Draperies Inc.............................G...... 610 375-2224
Reading (G-16425)

Nicholas Meyokovich ....G...... 724 439-0955
Uniontown (G-18638)

DRAPES & DRAPERY FABRICS, FROM MANMADE FIBER

Bachman Drapery Studio Inc..............G...... 215 257-8810
Tylersport (G-18574)

Fabtex Inc ....C...... 570 275-7500
Danville (G-4000)

Todd Lengle & Co Inc ....E...... 610 777-0731
Reading (G-16541)

DRESSES WHOLESALERS

Amc Inc...G...... 412 531-3160
Pittsburgh (G-14698)

DRIED FRUITS WHOLESALERS

A L Bazzini Co Inc ....E...... 610 366-1606
Allentown (G-111)

Ames Enterprises Inc ....G...... 814 474-2700
Fairview (G-5813)

DRILL BITS

Drebo America Inc ....D...... 724 938-0690
Coal Center (G-3275)

DRILLING MACHINERY & EQPT: Oil & Gas

Cactus Wellhead LLC ....G...... 814 308-0344
Reynoldsville (G-16656)

PRODUCT

Superior Energy Resources LLC.........E 814 265-1080
Brockway (G-2236)
Superior Energy Resources LLC.........G 814 265-1080
Brockway (G-2235)

DRILLING MACHINERY & EQPT: Water Well

Schramm Inc ....C...... 610 696-2500
West Chester (G-19638)

DRILLS & DRILLING EQPT: Mining

Center Rock Inc.........................G 814 267-7100
Berlin (G-1287)
Gill Rock Drill Company Inc..............E 717 272-3861
Lebanon (G-9573)
Pennsylvania Drilling Company ....E 412 771-2110
Mc Kees Rocks (G-10623)
Reichdrill LLC..........................D 814 342-5500
Philipsburg (G-14525)
Watts Brothers Tool Works Inc..........F 412 823-7877
Wilmerding (G-20162)

DRILLS: Core

Acker Drill Co Inc......................E 570 586-2061
S Abingtn Twp (G-16888)
Angelo Nieto Inc.......................F 570 489-6761
Jessup (G-8326)
Pennsylvania Drilling Company ....E 412 771-2110
Imperial (G-8074)
Sandvik Mining and Cnstr ....G 215 245-0280
Bensalem (G-1250)

DRILLS: Rock, Portable

Blue Mountain Lawn Service ....G 610 759-6979
Wind Gap (G-20166)

DRINKING FOUNTAINS: Mechanically Refrigerated

Rich Industrial Services Inc ....F 610 534-0195
Holmes (G-7664)

DRINKING PLACES: Alcoholic Beverages

Boardroom Spirits LLC ....G 215 815-5351
Lansdale (G-9348)
Chesapeake Del Brewing Co LLC ....C 610 627-9000
Media (G-10918)
Weyerbacher Brewing Co ....G 610 559-5561
Easton (G-4775)

DRINKING PLACES: Beer Garden

Reclamation Brewing Company ....F 724 282-0831
Butler (G-2437)

DRINKING PLACES: Tavern

Cooke Tavern Ltd......................G 814 422-7687
Spring Mills (G-17887)
Pennsylvania Brewing Company ....E 412 237-9400
Pittsburgh (G-15375)

DRINKING WATER COOLERS WHOLESALERS: Mechanical

Roaring Spring Water ....G 814 942-9844
Roaring Spring (G-16770)

DRIVE SHAFTS

Point Spring Company ....F 724 658-9076
New Castle (G-12138)
Westmoreland Machine & Elc Co ....G 412 784-1991
Pittsburgh (G-15712)

DRUG STORES

Mrlrx LLC ....F 610 485-7750
Marcus Hook (G-10450)
Spectragenetics Inc ....G 412 488-9350
Pittsburgh (G-15570)

DRUG TESTING KITS: Blood & Urine

Allsorce Scrning Solutions LLC ....E 724 515-2637
Irwin (G-8143)
Gerson Associates PC ....E 215 637-6800
Philadelphia (G-13759)
Recovery Environment Inc................G 717 625-0040
Lititz (G-10037)

Toxicity Asssors Globl PA LLC............G 215 921-6972
Philadelphia (G-14401)

DRUGS & DRUG PROPRIETARIES, WHOLESALE

Thg/Paradigm Health Intl Inc ....G 610 998-1080
Oxford (G-13093)

DRUGS & DRUG PROPRIETARIES, WHOLESALE: Druggists' Sundries

SMC Direct LLC ....E 800 521-1635
Evans City (G-5563)

DRUGS & DRUG PROPRIETARIES, WHOLESALE: Medicinals/Botanicals

Goodstate Inc ....G 215 366-2030
Glenside (G-6523)

DRUGS & DRUG PROPRIETARIES, WHOLESALE: Pharmaceuticals

Agri Welding Service Inc.................F 570 437-3330
Danville (G-3996)
Allergan Inc ....D 610 691-2880
Center Valley (G-2824)
AR Scientific Inc.......................G 215 288-6500
Philadelphia (G-13402)
Central Admxture Phrm Svcs Inc ....E 215 706-4001
Horsham (G-7803)
Cognition Therapeutics Inc ....G 412 481-2210
Pittsburgh (G-14865)
Genoa Healthcare LLC ....G 215 426-1007
Philadelphia (G-13754)
Glaxosmithkline LLC ....G 215 751-4000
Philadelphia (G-13766)
Laron Pharma Inc.......................F 267 575-1470
Fort Washington (G-6082)
Medarbor LLC ....G 732 887-6111
Bristol (G-2165)
Mrlrx LLC ....F 610 485-7750
Marcus Hook (G-10450)
Myers Drugstore Inc ....F 610 233-3300
Norristown (G-12691)
Nabriva Therapeutics Us Inc ....F 610 816-6640
King of Prussia (G-8653)
Pfizer Inc..............................B 717 932-3701
Lewisberry (G-9890)
Qol Meds ....G 724 602-0532
Butler (G-2436)
Teva Pharmaceuticals Usa Inc...........B 215 591-3000
North Wales (G-12834)
Thresher Pharmaceuticals ....G 215 826-0227
Bristol (G-2206)
Url Pharma Inc.........................E 215 288-6500
Philadelphia (G-14433)
US Specialty Formulations LLC ....F 610 849-5030
Bethlehem (G-1648)
Williams Richard H Pharmacist..........G 717 393-6708
Lancaster (G-9242)

DRUGS & DRUG PROPRIETARIES, WHOLESALE: Vitamins & Minerals

Douglas Laboratories ....E 412 494-0122
Pittsburgh (G-14935)
Muscle Gauge Nutrition LLC.............F 484 840-8006
West Chester (G-19602)
Trugen3 LLC ....G 412 668-3831
Pittsburgh (G-15657)

DRUGS ACTING ON THE CENTRAL NERVOUS SYSTEM & SENSE ORGANS

Allergan Inc ....G 610 262-4844
Northampton (G-12842)
Allergan Inc ....F 610 352-4992
Upper Darby (G-18677)
Allergan Inc ....D 610 691-2880
Center Valley (G-2824)
Braeburn Pharmaceuticals Inc ....D 609 751-5375
Plymouth Meeting (G-15835)
Cephalon Inc ....A 610 344-0200
Malvern (G-10203)
Merck Sharp & Dohme Corp ....C 215 631-5000
West Point (G-19762)
Neurokine Therapeutics LLC ....G 609 937-0409
Philadelphia (G-14065)

Nupathe Inc ....F 610 232-0800
Malvern (G-10289)
Piramal Critical Care Inc.................E 800 414-1901
Bethlehem (G-1598)

DRUGS AFFECTING NEOPLASMS & ENDOCRINE SYSTEMS

Madrigal Pharmaceuticals Inc ....G 484 380-9263
Conshohocken (G-3573)

DRUGS: Parasitic & Infective Disease Affecting

Zavante Therapeutics Inc................G 610 816-6640
King of Prussia (G-8701)

DRUMS: Fiber

Greif Inc ....D 610 485-8148
Upper Chichester (G-18662)
Mauser Usa LLC........................E 610 258-2700
Easton (G-4720)

DRUMS: Magnetic

Magnetizer Industrial Tech ....G 215 766-9150
Hatfield (G-7367)

DRYCLEANING & LAUNDRY SVCS: Commercial & Family

Thomas Nay LLC.......................F 215 613-8367
Philadelphia (G-14388)

DRYCLEANING PLANTS

First Class Specialties...................F 724 446-1000
Herminie (G-7570)

DRYCLEANING SVC: Collecting & Distributing Agency

Titusville Laundry Center.................G 814 827-9127
Titusville (G-18401)

DRYERS & REDRYERS: Indl

A Stucki Company ....E 724 746-4240
Canonsburg (G-2531)
Aztec Machinery Company ....E 215 672-2600
Warminster (G-18833)

DUCTING: Metal Plate

Mounts Equipment Co Inc................G 724 225-0460
Washington (G-19208)

DUCTS: Sheet Metal

Aella Industries Corporation..............G 610 399-9086
Aston (G-749)
American Air Duct Inc ....E 724 483-8057
Charleroi (G-3006)
Ductmate Industries Inc ....G 724 258-0500
Monongahela (G-11307)
Ductmate Industries Inc ....E 800 990-8459
Charleroi (G-3011)
Environmental Air Inc ....E 412 922-8988
Pittsburgh (G-14979)
Hennemuth Metal Fabricators ....G 724 693-9605
Oakdale (G-12901)
Hennemuth Metal Fabricators ....G 724 693-9605
Oakdale (G-12902)
Hranec Sheet Metal Inc..................C 724 437-2211
Uniontown (G-18631)
J A Smith Inc ....G 724 295-1133
Freeport (G-6206)
K & I Sheet Metal Inc....................E 412 781-8111
Pittsburgh (G-15159)
Kutzner Manufacturing Inds Inc ....E 215 721-1712
Telford (G-18300)
Little Sheet Metal Inc ....F 215 946-9970
Bristol (G-2161)
Moltec Heating and AC ....F 215 755-2169
Philadelphia (G-14032)
Noftz Sheet Metal Inc ....E 412 471-1983
Pittsburgh (G-15343)
R E Wildes Sheet Metal Inc ....G 570 501-3828
Hazle Township (G-7478)
Rado Enterprises Inc ....E 570 759-0303
Benton (G-1281)

Schatzie Ltd................................G...... 610 834-1240
Conshohocken (G-3604)

T D Landis Air Flow Design ....G...... 215 679-4395
Pennsburg (G-13257)

Wierman Diller Inc.........................G...... 717 637-3871
Hanover (G-6975)

William J Koshinskie ....G...... 570 742-4969
Milton (G-11251)

DUMBWAITERS

Buddy Butlers Inc ....G...... 570 759-0550
Berwick (G-1315)

DUMPSTERS: Garbage

Careys Dumpster Services ....G...... 717 258-1400
Carlisle (G-2692)

Creekside Welding LLC.....................G...... 717 355-2008
New Holland (G-12241)

Custom Container Vly Can LLC...........F...... 724 253-2038
Lewisburg (G-9903)

De Marco Waste Dumpster Svc ....G...... 412 904-4260
Pittsburgh (G-14912)

Deist Industries Inc........................E...... 800 233-0867
Hadley (G-6819)

Glens Dumpster Service LLC ....G...... 202 521-1493
Pottstown (G-15991)

H & C Giamo Inc ....G...... 610 941-0909
Conshohocken (G-3552)

National Dumpster Service LLC ....G...... 484 949-1060
Coatesville (G-3319)

Northeast Industrial Mfg...................G...... 724 253-3110
Hadley (G-6820)

Pts Industries Corp........................F...... 814 345-5200
Drifting (G-4375)

Stoltzfus Steel Manufacturing ....G...... 570 524-7835
Lewisburg (G-9919)

Thrifty Dumpster Inc.......................G...... 215 688-1774
Eagleville (G-4518)

Valley Can Inc...............................F...... 724 253-2038
Hadley (G-6822)

Valley Enterprise Cont Inc..................F...... 570 962-2194
Blanchard (G-1750)

Valley Enterprise Cont LLC ....F...... 570 962-2194
Blanchard (G-1751)

DURABLE GOODS WHOLESALERS, NEC

Davidson Supply Co Inc ....G...... 412 635-2671
Pittsburgh (G-14908)

Pittsburgh Mobile Concrete Inc............F...... 412 486-0186
Pittsburgh (G-15402)

DUST OR FUME COLLECTING EQPT: Indl

Imperial Systems Inc ....E...... 724 662-2801
Mercer (G-10964)

Johnson March Systems Inc ....E...... 215 364-2500
Warminster (G-18903)

M & M Sheet Metal Inc ....F...... 570 326-4655
Williamsport (G-20039)

Schutte Koerting Acquisition ....E...... 215 639-0900
Trevose (G-18502)

DYEING & FINISHING: Wool Or Similar Fibers

Chloe Textiles Incorporated ....D...... 717 848-2800
York (G-20425)

Dualsun International Inc ....G...... 412 421-7934
Pittsburgh (G-14939)

G J Littlewood & Son Inc....................E...... 215 483-3970
Philadelphia (G-13739)

DYES & PIGMENTS: Organic

CSS Industries Inc ....C...... 610 729-3959
Plymouth Meeting (G-15840)

Hamburger Color Company Inc............F...... 610 279-6450
King of Prussia (G-8627)

Penn Color Inc..............................C...... 215 997-2221
Hatfield (G-7380)

United Color Manufacturing Inc ....F...... 215 860-2165
Newtown (G-12557)

DYES OR COLORS: Food, Synthetic

Byrnes and Kiefer Company................E...... 724 538-5200
Callery (G-2467)

DYES: Acid, Synthetic

Abbey Color Incorporated...................E...... 215 739-9960
Philadelphia (G-13334)

EARTH SCIENCE SVCS

American Slar Envmtl Technolog.........G...... 570 279-0338
Lewisburg (G-9897)

ARC Rmediation Specialists Inc............F...... 386 405-6760
Bristol (G-2108)

EATING PLACES

Appalachian Brewing Co Inc ....D...... 717 221-1080
Harrisburg (G-7087)

Aramark Unf Creer AP Group Inc ....A...... 215 238-3000
Philadelphia (G-13406)

Belletieri Sauces Inc ....G...... 610 433-4334
Allentown (G-149)

Empire Kosher Poultry Inc ....A...... 717 436-5921
Mifflintown (G-11114)

Ethnic Gourmet Foods Inc ....E...... 610 692-2209
West Chester (G-19552)

Fresh Donuts ....G...... 717 273-8886
Lebanon (G-9572)

Gerritys Super Market Inc ....D...... 570 961-9030
Scranton (G-17239)

Lionette Enterprises ....G...... 814 274-9401
Coudersport (G-3784)

Mindful Brewing Company LLC ....G...... 412 965-8428
Pittsburgh (G-15290)

Nardone Brothers Baking Co ....C...... 570 823-0141
Hanover Township (G-6999)

S Don Food Market Inc ....E...... 717 453-7470
Lykens (G-10135)

Safran Brothers Inc ....E...... 724 266-9758
Ambridge (G-633)

Schiel Inc ....C...... 570 970-4460
Wilkes Barre (G-19962)

Schnoch Corporation ....E...... 570 326-4700
Williamsport (G-20070)

Shree Swami Narayan Corp ....E...... 610 272-8404
Norristown (G-12713)

Sunnyway Foods Inc ....E...... 717 597-7121
Greencastle (G-6637)

Victory Brewing Company LLC ....E...... 610 873-0881
Downingtown (G-4261)

Wilbos Inc ....G...... 267 490-5168
Quakertown (G-16259)

EDITORIAL SVCS

Highlights For Children Inc.................E...... 570 253-1080
Honesdale (G-7714)

EDUCATIONAL PROGRAMS ADMINISTRATION SVCS

Charlene Crawford..........................G...... 215 432-7542
Elkins Park (G-4901)

Millersville University PA ....E...... 717 871-4636
Millersville (G-11213)

EDUCATIONAL SVCS

Marcom Group Ltd..........................F...... 610 859-8989
Upper Chichester (G-18667)

Rapid Learning Institute.....................F...... 877 792-2172
Wayne (G-19368)

Society of Clinical ....F...... 215 822-8644
Chalfont (G-2889)

Web Age Solutions Inc ....E...... 215 517-6540
Jenkintown (G-8304)

EDUCATIONAL SVCS, NONDEGREE GRANTING: Continuing Education

Ganesco Incorporated......................G...... 931 284-9033
Pittsburgh (G-15040)

Toastmasters International ....E...... 215 355-4838
Warminster (G-18983)

EGG WHOLESALERS

Wenger Feeds LLC ....G...... 717 367-1195
Muncy (G-11841)

Wenger Feeds LLC ....B...... 717 367-1195
Lancaster (G-9238)

ELASTOMERS

Arlanxeo USA Holdings Corp ....G...... 412 809-1000
Pittsburgh (G-14723)

Arlanxeo USA LLC ....B...... 412 809-1000
Pittsburgh (G-14724)

ELECTRIC FENCE CHARGERS

Zareba Systems Inc ....D...... 763 551-1125
Lititz (G-10061)

ELECTRIC MOTOR & GENERATOR AUXILIARY PARTS

Lemm Liquidating Company LLC.........D...... 724 325-7140
Export (G-5615)

ELECTRIC MOTOR REPAIR SVCS

A J Smith Electric Motor Svc ....G...... 570 424-8743
East Stroudsburg (G-4601)

Ace Viking Electric Mtr Co Inc ....G...... 814 897-9445
Erie (G-5171)

Albarell Electric Inc.........................G...... 610 691-7030
Bethlehem (G-1447)

Ampere Electric Co ....G...... 215 426-5356
Broomall (G-2278)

Breons Inc A Close Corporation............G...... 814 359-3182
Pleasant Gap (G-15791)

Burkholder s Motor Repair ....G...... 717 866-9724
Myerstown (G-11878)

Charles W Romano Co ....G...... 215 535-3800
Philadelphia (G-13532)

Coleman & Schmidt Inc ....G...... 610 275-0796
Norristown (G-12645)

Curio Electrical Motor Repr Sp ....G...... 610 432-9923
Allentown (G-189)

D-Electric Inc ....F...... 215 529-6020
Quakertown (G-16182)

Daniels Electric Service ....G...... 412 821-2594
Pittsburgh (G-14905)

Deckman Electric Inc ....G...... 610 272-6944
Bridgeport (G-2034)

Delaware Electric Inc ....G...... 610 252-7803
Easton (G-4668)

Dorwards Electric Corp ....G...... 610 767-8148
Slatington (G-17605)

Edwin L Heim Co ....E...... 717 233-8711
Harrisburg (G-7125)

Electric Motor & Supply Inc ....E...... 814 946-0401
Altoona (G-501)

Electric Motor Service Inc ....G...... 724 348-6858
Finleyville (G-5958)

Electric Rewind Co Inc ....G...... 215 675-6912
Hatboro (G-7284)

Gerald Boughner............................G...... 814 432-3519
Franklin (G-6132)

Globe Electric Company Inc ....E...... 412 781-2671
Pittsburgh (G-15053)

Hodge Electric Motors Inc..................G...... 724 834-8420
Greensburg (G-6674)

Huntingdon Elc Mtr Svc Inc ....G...... 814 643-3921
Huntingdon (G-7944)

Integrated Power Services LLC ....E...... 215 365-1500
Philadelphia (G-13861)

Irvin G Tyson & Son Inc.....................G...... 610 754-0930
Perkiomenville (G-13302)

Jeffrey Shepler ....G...... 724 537-7411
Latrobe (G-9484)

Johnstone Supply ....G...... 610 967-9900
Alburtis (G-53)

Keener Electric Motors Inc..................G...... 717 272-7686
Lebanon (G-9589)

Kufen Electric Motors Inc...................G...... 215 672-5250
Warminster (G-18907)

Kufen Motor and Pump Tech ....G...... 215 672-5250
Warminster (G-18908)

Leboeuf Industries Inc ....F...... 814 796-9000
Waterford (G-19265)

Ligus Electric Mtr & Pump Svc ....G...... 570 287-1272
Luzerne (G-10126)

Lyons Electric Motor Service................G...... 814 456-7127
Erie (G-5376)

M & R Electric Inc...........................E...... 412 831-6101
Bethel Park (G-1423)

Mikron Valve & Mfr Inc......................G...... 814 453-2337
Erie (G-5392)

Miller Electric Service & Sup ....F...... 814 942-9943
Altoona (G-527)

Motor Technology Inc ....D...... 717 266-4045
York (G-20605)

Myers Electrical Repairs ....G...... 717 334-8105
Gettysburg (G-6309)

North End Electric Service Inc..............E...... 570 342-6740
Scranton (G-17267)

Pittsburgh Elc Mtr Repr Inc.................G...... 724 443-2333
Allison Park (G-458)

PRODUCT

R Scheinert & Son Inc ....E...... 215 673-9800
Philadelphia *(G-14227)*

Ram Industrial Services LLC ....E...... 717 232-4414
Camp Hill *(G-2514)*

Rice Electric Company ....E...... 724 225-4180
Eighty Four *(G-4846)*

S & S Electric Motors Inc ....G...... 717 263-1919
Chambersburg *(G-2975)*

Special Electric Motor Company ....G...... 724 378-4200
Aliquippa *(G-97)*

Tims Electric Motor Repair Co..........G...... 814 445-5078
Somerset *(G-17714)*

Warren Electric Motor Service ....G...... 814 723-2045
Warren *(G-19057)*

Weber Electmotor Service ....G...... 717 436-8120
Mifflintown *(G-11143)*

West End Electric Inc ....F...... 570 682-9292
Hegins *(G-7547)*

Willier Elc Mtr Repr Co Inc ....G...... 215 426-9920
Philadelphia *(G-14477)*

ELECTRIC SERVICES

Alcoa World Alumina LLC ....E...... 412 315-2900
Pittsburgh *(G-14670)*

Colonial Electric Supply Inc...........G...... 610 935-2493
Phoenixville *(G-14540)*

Jeffers & Leek Electric Inc ....G...... 724 384-0315
New Brighton *(G-12038)*

Ocean Thermal Energy Corp ....F...... 717 299-1344
Lancaster *(G-9150)*

Xpress Energy ....F...... 610 935-9200
Phoenixville *(G-14584)*

ELECTRIC SVCS, NEC Power Broker

American Powernet MGT LP.................G...... 610 372-8500
Wyomissing *(G-20286)*

United Enrgy Plus Trminals LLC ....E...... 610 774-5151
Allentown *(G-418)*

ELECTRIC SVCS, NEC: Power Generation

Ohio Valley Indus Svcs Inc ....G...... 412 269-0020
Moon Township *(G-11498)*

ELECTRICAL APPARATUS & EQPT WHOLESALERS

Ademco Inc ....G...... 215 244-6377
Bensalem *(G-1143)*

American Data Link Inc ....G...... 724 503-4290
Washington *(G-19146)*

Associated Specialty Co ....F...... 610 395-9172
Orefield *(G-13008)*

Black Box Corporation ....G...... 724 746-5500
Lawrence *(G-9535)*

Cell-Con Inc ....D...... 800 771-7139
Exton *(G-5660)*

CMI America Inc ....F...... 814 897-7000
Erie *(G-5228)*

Dein-Verbit Associates Inc ....F...... 610 649-9674
Ardmore *(G-707)*

E-Finity Dstrbted Gnration LLC ....G...... 610 688-6212
Wayne *(G-19321)*

Eaton Corporation ....E...... 610 497-6100
Boothwyn *(G-1877)*

Eaton Corporation ....E...... 412 893-3300
Moon Township *(G-11484)*

Eaton Electrical Inc ....E...... 412 893-3300
Moon Township *(G-11485)*

Enersys ....C...... 610 208-1991
Reading *(G-16375)*

Enersys Delaware Inc ....G...... 484 244-4150
Allentown *(G-206)*

Enersys Delaware Inc ....B...... 214 324-8990
Reading *(G-16377)*

Exide Technologies ....G...... 304 345-5616
Rostraver Township *(G-16826)*

Interlectric Corporation ....C...... 814 723-6061
Warren *(G-19033)*

Lake City Power Systems LLC ....G...... 814 774-2034
Lake City *(G-8902)*

Neo Lights Holdings Inc ....G...... 215 831-7700
Philadelphia *(G-14062)*

Pennsylvania Trans Tech Inc ....B...... 724 873-2100
Canonsburg *(G-2618)*

Phoenix Contact Dev & Mfg Inc ....B...... 717 944-1300
Middletown *(G-11068)*

Rebecca Wilson Ltd Lblty Co ....G...... 973 670-7089
York *(G-20654)*

Sales Marketing Group Inc..................G...... 412 928-0422
Pittsburgh *(G-15507)*

Simkar LLC ....C...... 215 831-7700
Philadelphia *(G-14307)*

Staneco Corporation ....E...... 215 672-6500
Horsham *(G-7852)*

Witmer Motor Service ....G...... 717 336-2949
Stevens *(G-18058)*

ELECTRICAL APPLIANCES, TELEVISIONS & RADIOS WHOLESALERS

Conair Corporation ....D...... 717 485-4871
Mc Connellsburg *(G-10563)*

Galaxy Global Products LLC ....G...... 610 692-7400
West Chester *(G-19557)*

Petrillos Appliance..................G...... 215 491-9400
Warrington *(G-19127)*

ELECTRICAL CURRENT CARRYING WIRING DEVICES

3si Security Systems Holdg Inc...........G...... 610 280-2000
Malvern *(G-10177)*

A E Pakos Inc ....G...... 724 539-1790
Latrobe *(G-9452)*

Achieva ....D...... 412 995-5000
Pittsburgh *(G-14640)*

Burndy LLC ....G...... 717 938-7258
Etters *(G-5547)*

Cjc Contract Packaging Inc ....G...... 570 209-7836
Avoca *(G-842)*

Cooper Interconnect Inc ....E...... 630 248-4007
King of Prussia *(G-8597)*

Corey Associates Inc..................E...... 570 676-4800
Greentown *(G-6733)*

Custom Systems Technology Inc..........G...... 215 822-2525
Colmar *(G-3415)*

Datacap Systems Inc ....E...... 215 997-8989
Chalfont *(G-2871)*

Dean Technology Inc ....E...... 724 479-3533
Lucernemines *(G-10117)*

E F E Laboratories Inc ....E...... 215 672-2400
Horsham *(G-7812)*

Eaton Corporation ....B...... 724 773-1231
Beaver *(G-980)*

Eaton Corporation ....E...... 412 893-3300
Moon Township *(G-11484)*

Eaton Electrical Inc ....E...... 412 893-3300
Moon Township *(G-11485)*

Elec Const Jt ....G...... 610 777-3150
Reading *(G-16371)*

Electro Soft Inc ....E...... 215 654-0701
Montgomeryville *(G-11394)*

F Tinker and Sons Company ....E...... 412 781-3553
Pittsburgh *(G-15000)*

Greenbriar Indus Systems Inc ....D...... 814 474-1400
Fairview *(G-5824)*

Industrial Enterprises Inc..................D...... 215 355-7080
Southampton *(G-17819)*

Lynn Electronics Corp ....E...... 215 826-9600
Bristol *(G-2163)*

Marco Manufacturing Co Inc.................E...... 215 463-2332
Philadelphia *(G-13992)*

Metallurgical Products Company ....E...... 610 696-6770
West Chester *(G-19601)*

Nexans USA Inc ....B...... 717 354-6200
New Holland *(G-12271)*

Orion Systems Inc ....E...... 215 346-8200
Huntingdon Valley *(G-8019)*

Osram Sylvania Inc..................B...... 570 724-8200
Wellsboro *(G-19471)*

Osram Sylvania Inc..................D...... 412 856-2111
Monroeville *(G-11347)*

Paxson Lightning Rods Inc..................G...... 610 696-8290
West Chester *(G-19615)*

PC Systems Inc ....E...... 814 772-6359
Ridgway *(G-16724)*

Phoenix Contact Dev & Mfg Inc...........B...... 717 944-1300
Middletown *(G-11068)*

Powersafe Inc..................G...... 717 436-5380
Mifflintown *(G-11132)*

Precise Plastics Inc ....D...... 814 474-5504
Fairview *(G-5840)*

Precision Assembly Inc..................E...... 215 784-0861
Willow Grove *(G-20136)*

Prysmian Cbles Systems USA LLC.......D...... 570 385-4381
Schuylkill Haven *(G-17164)*

Qualastat Electronics Inc.................E...... 717 253-9301
Gettysburg *(G-6311)*

Reiner Associates Inc..................G...... 717 647-7454
Tower City *(G-18440)*

Sensor Corporation ....G...... 724 887-4080
Scottdale *(G-17200)*

Silicon Power Corporation..................D...... 610 407-4700
Malvern *(G-10317)*

Souriau Usa Inc ....F...... 717 718-8810
York *(G-20673)*

Spectrum Control Inc ....C...... 814 835-4000
Fairview *(G-5844)*

Spectrum Microwave Inc ....D...... 215 464-0586
Philadelphia *(G-14333)*

St Marys Carbon Co Inc ....E...... 814 781-7333
Saint Marys *(G-17016)*

Te Connectivity Corporation ....C...... 610 893-9800
Berwyn *(G-1376)*

Te Connectivity Corporation ....E...... 717 564-0100
Middletown *(G-11078)*

Te Connectivity Corporation ....B...... 717 861-5000
Jonestown *(G-8452)*

Torpedo Specialty Wire Inc ....E...... 814 563-7505
Pittsfield *(G-15739)*

Tyco Elec Latin Amer Holdg LLC...........G...... 610 893-9800
Berwyn *(G-1389)*

Universal Electric Corporation ....B...... 724 597-7800
Canonsburg *(G-2652)*

ELECTRICAL DISCHARGE MACHINING, EDM

Microcut Inc..................G...... 717 848-4150
York *(G-20594)*

Stellar Prcsion Components Ltd ....D...... 724 523-5559
Jeannette *(G-8265)*

Turning Solutions Inc ....F...... 814 723-1134
Warren *(G-19053)*

Wilsey Tool Company Inc..................D...... 215 538-0800
Quakertown *(G-16260)*

ELECTRICAL EQPT & SPLYS

3si Security Systems Holdg Inc...........G...... 610 280-2000
Malvern *(G-10177)*

Advanced Integration Group Inc ....E...... 412 722-0065
Mc Kees Rocks *(G-10602)*

Advanced PDT Design & Mfg Inc ....E...... 610 380-9140
Coatesville *(G-3284)*

Aerotech Inc ....B...... 412 963-7470
Pittsburgh *(G-14655)*

Air-Scent International ....D...... 412 252-2000
Pittsburgh *(G-14658)*

Ajm Electric Inc ....G...... 610 494-5735
Chester Township *(G-3088)*

Allentown Auto Electric LLC ....G...... 610 432-2888
Allentown *(G-127)*

Alpine Electric ....G...... 412 257-4827
Bridgeville *(G-2053)*

Arm Camco LLC ....E...... 814 472-7980
Ebensburg *(G-4779)*

Bsg Corporation..................G...... 267 230-0514
Huntingdon Valley *(G-7966)*

Colonial Electric Supply Inc..................G...... 610 935-2493
Phoenixville *(G-14540)*

Corey Associates Inc..................E...... 570 676-4800
Greentown *(G-6733)*

Delta Information Systems Inc ....E...... 215 657-5270
Horsham *(G-7809)*

Demco Enterprises Inc..................F...... 888 419-3343
Quakertown *(G-16184)*

Dvm Manufacturing LLC ....F...... 215 839-3425
Warminster *(G-18864)*

E F E Laboratories Inc ....E...... 215 672-2400
Horsham *(G-7812)*

Electric City Baseball & Soft..................G...... 570 955-0471
Scranton *(G-17232)*

Electric City Yoga..................G...... 570 558-9642
Scranton *(G-17233)*

Enersys ....C...... 610 208-1991
Reading *(G-16375)*

Evaporated Coatings Inc ....E...... 215 659-3080
Willow Grove *(G-20116)*

Everson Tesla Inc..................D...... 610 746-1520
Nazareth *(G-11965)*

Fargo Assembly of Pa Inc ....C...... 717 866-5800
Richland *(G-16687)*

FEC Technologies Inc..................E...... 717 764-5959
York *(G-20477)*

Fromm Elc Sup Corp Rding Penna ....G...... 570 387-9711
Bloomsburg *(G-1783)*

Gamlet Inc..................D...... 717 852-9200
York *(G-20489)*

Gerome Manufacturing Co Inc.................D...... 724 438-8544
Smithfield *(G-17650)*

Gexpro ....G...... 570 265-2420
 Towanda *(G-18428)*

Glen L Myers Inc ....G...... 717 352-0035
 Fayetteville *(G-5877)*

Grid Elc & Solar Solutions LLC ....G...... 717 885-5249
 York *(G-20514)*

Gupta Permold Corporation ....G...... 412 793-3511
 Pittsburgh *(G-15067)*

Harlan Electric ....G...... 717 243-4600
 Harrisburg *(G-7140)*

Homewood Energy Services Corp ....G...... 256 882-2796
 Pittsburgh *(G-15098)*

Horizon Electric Lighting LLC ....G...... 267 288-5353
 Richboro *(G-16675)*

Ifco Enterprises Inc. ....G...... 610 651-0999
 Malvern *(G-10251)*

Jeffers & Leek Electric Inc ....G...... 724 384-0315
 New Brighton *(G-12038)*

Jod Contracting Inc ....G...... 724 323-2124
 Fayette City *(G-5875)*

John A Romeo & Associates Inc ....F...... 724 586-6961
 Butler *(G-2413)*

Kirkwood Electric ....G...... 814 467-7171
 Windber *(G-20185)*

Lengyel Electric ....G...... 724 475-2045
 Fredonia *(G-6186)*

Maro Electronics Inc ....E...... 215 788-7919
 Bristol *(G-2164)*

Miller Edge Inc ....D...... 610 869-4422
 West Grove *(G-19702)*

Northeimer Manufacturing ....E...... 610 926-1136
 Leesport *(G-9672)*

Novasentis Inc. ....F...... 814 238-7400
 State College *(G-18002)*

Nuwave Technologies Inc ....G...... 610 584-8428
 Norristown *(G-12695)*

Qortek Inc ....G...... 570 322-2700
 Williamsport *(G-20066)*

Raco International LP ....F...... 412 835-5744
 Bethel Park *(G-1430)*

Response Electric Inc ....G...... 215 799-2400
 Green Lane *(G-6592)*

Rfcircuits Inc ....F...... 215 364-2450
 Huntingdon Valley *(G-8029)*

Rockwell Collins Inc ....F...... 610 925-5844
 Kennett Square *(G-8540)*

Sales Marketing Group Inc ....G...... 412 928-0422
 Pittsburgh *(G-15507)*

Schneder Elc Bldngs Amrcas Inc.........E...... 215 441-4389
 Horsham *(G-7849)*

Semilab USA LLC ....F...... 610 377-5990
 Lehighton *(G-9726)*

Shepherd Good Work Services ....G...... 610 776-8353
 Allentown *(G-388)*

Sinacom North America Inc ....E...... 610 337-2250
 King of Prussia *(G-8677)*

Slater Electric & Sons...................G...... 724 306-1060
 Prospect *(G-16112)*

Spang & Company ....E...... 724 376-7515
 Sandy Lake *(G-17062)*

SPD Electrical Systems Inc ....B...... 215 698-6426
 Philadelphia *(G-14331)*

Synergy Contracting Svcs LLC ....E...... 724 349-0855
 Indiana *(G-8132)*

Synergy Electrical Sales Inc ....F...... 215 428-1130
 Fairless Hills *(G-5801)*

T T M Contacts Corporation ....G...... 215 497-1078
 Newtown *(G-12554)*

Titanium Metals Corporation ....E...... 702 564-2544
 Morgantown *(G-11539)*

Tri-Rivers Electric Inc ....G...... 412 290-6525
 Pittsburgh *(G-15646)*

Tridex Technology Ltd ....F...... 484 388-5000
 Philadelphia *(G-14410)*

Two M Electric Inc ....F...... 215 530-9964
 Warminster *(G-18988)*

Universal Electric Corporation ....B...... 724 597-7800
 Canonsburg *(G-2652)*

Wesco Distribution Inc ....F...... 724 772-5000
 Warrendale *(G-19101)*

Windurance LLC ....B...... 412 424-8900
 Coraopolis *(G-3733)*

Wistex II LLC ....G...... 215 328-9100
 Warminster *(G-19002)*

Wm Industries Inc ....G...... 215 822-2525
 Colmar *(G-3423)*

ELECTRICAL EQPT FOR ENGINES

Allied Tube & Conduit Corp ....B...... 215 676-6464
 Philadelphia *(G-13369)*

Atc Technology Corporation.............E...... 412 820-3700
 Cranberry Township *(G-3806)*

Auto Diesel Electric Inc ....G...... 570 874-2100
 Frackville *(G-6102)*

Creative Engnred Solutions Inc ....G...... 570 655-3399
 Pittston *(G-15747)*

Industrial Harness Company Inc ....D...... 717 477-0100
 Shippensburg *(G-17532)*

Kalas Mfg Inc ....D...... 717 336-5575
 Lancaster *(G-9078)*

Keystone Automatic Tech Inc ....E...... 814 486-0513
 Emporium *(G-5066)*

Moore Performance Pwr Pdts LLC ....G...... 610 507-2344
 Reading *(G-16448)*

Northeimer Manufacturing ....E...... 610 926-1136
 Leesport *(G-9672)*

Pittsburgh Electric Engs Inc ....F...... 724 547-9170
 Mount Pleasant *(G-11711)*

Plan B Consultants LLC ....G...... 215 638-0767
 Huntingdon Valley *(G-8026)*

Reading Electric Motor Svc Inc ....D...... 610 929-5777
 Reading *(G-16490)*

ELECTRICAL EQPT REPAIR & MAINTENANCE

Advanced Mobile Power Systems.........G...... 610 440-0195
 Coplay *(G-3638)*

Altoona Neon Sign Service ....G...... 814 942-7488
 Altoona *(G-472)*

Avo Multi-AMP Corporation ....G...... 610 676-8501
 Norristown *(G-12638)*

Burkholder s Motor Repair ....G...... 717 866-9724
 Myerstown *(G-11878)*

Caterpillar Globl Min Amer LLC...........C...... 724 743-1200
 Houston *(G-7869)*

City Sign Service Inc ....E...... 800 523-4452
 Horsham *(G-7804)*

D L Electronics Inc. ....F...... 215 742-2666
 Philadelphia *(G-13600)*

Emp Industries Inc ....G...... 215 357-5333
 Warminster *(G-18871)*

Femco Machine Company LLC............C...... 814 938-9763
 Punxsutawney *(G-16139)*

General Electric Company ....E...... 215 289-0400
 Philadelphia *(G-13749)*

H & R Neon Service Inc ....G...... 724 222-6115
 Washington *(G-19183)*

Hetrick Mfg Inc ....G...... 724 335-0455
 Lower Burrell *(G-10106)*

Integrated Power Services LLC ....F...... 724 225-2900
 Washington *(G-19186)*

J G Mundy Machine LLC ....G...... 610 583-1200
 Collingdale *(G-3405)*

Kykayke Inc ....G...... 610 522-0106
 Holmes *(G-7663)*

Lehigh Valley Sign & Service ....G...... 610 760-8590
 Germansville *(G-6280)*

Medart Inc ....E...... 724 752-3555
 Ellwood City *(G-4946)*

Micro-Trap Corporation ....G...... 215 295-8208
 Morrisville *(G-11571)*

Pcxpert Company Inc ....G...... 717 792-0005
 York *(G-20619)*

Randy Brensinger ....G...... 610 562-2184
 Hamburg *(G-6851)*

Total Scope Inc ....E...... 484 490-2100
 Upper Chichester *(G-18674)*

Wiley Electric Sign Service ....G...... 610 759-8167
 Nazareth *(G-11994)*

Wolfe Tool & Machine Company ....F...... 717 848-6375
 York *(G-20717)*

ELECTRICAL EQPT REPAIR SVCS

Sign Medix Inc ....F...... 717 396-9749
 Lancaster *(G-9198)*

Wistex II LLC ....G...... 215 328-9100
 Warminster *(G-19002)*

ELECTRICAL EQPT REPAIR SVCS: High Voltage

Arm Camco LLC........................E...... 814 472-7980
 Ebensburg *(G-4779)*

General Electric Company ....D...... 412 469-6080
 West Mifflin *(G-19739)*

ELECTRICAL EQPT: Automotive, NEC

Fci USA LLC ....B...... 717 938-7200
 Etters *(G-5548)*

Flight Systems Auto Group LLC ....C...... 717 932-7000
 Lewisberry *(G-9886)*

Kuhn Auto Electric ....G...... 717 632-4197
 Hanover *(G-6912)*

Martins Starter Service ....G...... 814 398-2496
 Cambridge Springs *(G-2482)*

R T Grim Co ....E...... 717 761-4113
 Camp Hill *(G-2513)*

ELECTRICAL GOODS, WHOLESALE: Alarms & Signaling Eqpt

Abe Alarm Service ....G...... 484 664-7304
 Allentown *(G-113)*

ELECTRICAL GOODS, WHOLESALE: Batteries, Dry Cell

Laurel Holdings Inc......................G...... 814 533-5777
 Johnstown *(G-8402)*

ELECTRICAL GOODS, WHOLESALE: Batteries, Storage, Indl

Battery Zone ....F...... 800 371-5033
 Bethlehem *(G-1458)*

ELECTRICAL GOODS, WHOLESALE: Boxes & Fittings

Aurora Electrical & Data Svcs ....G...... 412 255-4060
 Pittsburgh *(G-14739)*

ELECTRICAL GOODS, WHOLESALE: Burglar Alarm Systems

Stanley Security Solutions Inc ....F...... 888 265-0412
 Monroeville *(G-11358)*

ELECTRICAL GOODS, WHOLESALE: Connectors

Component Enterprises Co Inc ....E...... 610 272-7900
 Norristown *(G-12646)*

Hirschmann Electronics Inc...............F...... 717 217-2200
 Chambersburg *(G-2940)*

ELECTRICAL GOODS, WHOLESALE: Electrical Appliances, Major

Leslie S Geissel..........................G...... 215 884-1050
 Jenkintown *(G-8294)*

ELECTRICAL GOODS, WHOLESALE: Electronic Parts

Harmonic Rays Mfg Group Inc ....G...... 267 761-9558
 Philadelphia *(G-13803)*

Motor Technology Inc..................D...... 717 266-4045
 York *(G-20605)*

Radio Parts Company ....E...... 412 963-6202
 Pittsburgh *(G-15465)*

Techsource Engineering Inc ....G...... 814 459-2150
 Erie *(G-5505)*

Tri-Com Inc ....E...... 610 259-7400
 Clifton Heights *(G-3259)*

W H Cooke & Co Inc ....G...... 717 630-2222
 Hanover *(G-6970)*

ELECTRICAL GOODS, WHOLESALE: Facsimile Or Fax Eqpt

Print-O-Stat Inc........................G...... 610 265-5470
 King of Prussia *(G-8664)*

ELECTRICAL GOODS, WHOLESALE: Fire Alarm Systems

Salmen Tech Co Inc ....G...... 412 854-1822
 Bethel Park *(G-1432)*

ELECTRICAL GOODS, WHOLESALE: Fittings & Construction Mat

Conestoga USA Inc ....G...... 610 327-2882
 Pottstown *(G-15973)*

Employee Codes: A=Over 500 employees, B=251-500
C=101-250, D=51-100, E=20-50, F=10-19, G=3-9

2019 Harris Pennsylvania
Manufacturers Directory

PRODUCT

1385

Marino Indus Systems Svcs Inc ....E 610 872-3630
  Chester (G-3057)

ELECTRICAL GOODS, WHOLESALE: Garbage Disposals

Pts Industries Corp ....F 814 345-5200
  Drifting (G-4375)

ELECTRICAL GOODS, WHOLESALE: Generators

Dyna-Tech Industries Ltd ....F 717 274-3099
  Lebanon (G-9564)
Emerson Process Management ....A 412 963-4000
  Pittsburgh (G-14971)
Nearhoof Machine Inc ....G 814 339-6621
  Osceola Mills (G-13056)
R Scheinert & Son Inc ....E 215 673-9800
  Philadelphia (G-14227)

ELECTRICAL GOODS, WHOLESALE: Household Appliances, NEC

Mayer Electric Supply Co Inc ....G 814 765-7531
  Clearfield (G-3224)

ELECTRICAL GOODS, WHOLESALE: Insulators

Lectromat Inc ....F 724 625-3502
  Mars (G-10505)

ELECTRICAL GOODS, WHOLESALE: Light Bulbs & Related Splys

Led Tube USA ....G 724 650-0691
  Ambridge (G-625)

ELECTRICAL GOODS, WHOLESALE: Lighting Fixtures, Comm & Indl

Elk Lighting Inc ....F 800 613-3261
  Summit Hill (G-18160)
Just Normlicht Inc ....G 267 852-2200
  Langhorne (G-9305)
Pittsburgh Stage Inc ....E 412 534-4500
  Sewickley (G-17403)
Trans-Tech Technologies Inc ....G 724 327-6600
  Pittsburgh (G-15639)

ELECTRICAL GOODS, WHOLESALE: Lighting Fixtures, Residential

American Period Lighting Inc ....G 717 392-5649
  Lancaster (G-8931)

ELECTRICAL GOODS, WHOLESALE: Modems, Computer

Black Box Corporation ....G 724 746-5500
  Lawrence (G-9535)

ELECTRICAL GOODS, WHOLESALE: Motor Ctrls, Starters & Relays

Benshaw Inc ....G 412 487-8235
  Glenshaw (G-6483)
Electric Motor & Supply Inc ....E 814 946-0401
  Altoona (G-501)
G I Electric Company ....G 570 323-6147
  Williamsport (G-20015)
Steins Pasco Battery Starter ....G 215 969-6900
  Philadelphia (G-14343)

ELECTRICAL GOODS, WHOLESALE: Motors

A J Smith Electric Motor Svc ....G 570 424-8743
  East Stroudsburg (G-4601)
Ace Viking Electric Mtr Co Inc ....G 814 897-9445
  Erie (G-5171)
Ampere Electric Co ....G 215 426-5356
  Broomall (G-2278)
Charles W Romano Co ....G 215 535-3800
  Philadelphia (G-13532)
Deckman Electric Inc ....G 610 272-6944
  Bridgeport (G-2034)
Delaware Electric Inc ....G 610 252-7803
  Easton (G-4668)

Globe Electric Company Inc ....E 412 781-2671
  Pittsburgh (G-15053)
Irvin G Tyson & Son Inc ....G 610 754-0930
  Perkiomenville (G-13302)
Keener Electric Motors Inc ....G 717 272-7686
  Lebanon (G-9589)
Ligus Electric Mtr & Pump Svc ....G 570 287-1272
  Luzerne (G-10126)
Motor Technology Inc ....D 717 266-4045
  York (G-20605)
Ramsay Machine Development ....F 610 395-4764
  Allentown (G-370)
Rice Electric Company ....E 724 225-4180
  Eighty Four (G-4846)
Servedio A Elc Mtr Svc Inc ....F 724 658-8041
  New Castle (G-12148)
United Industrial Group Inc ....F 724 746-4700
  Washington (G-19234)
Warren Electric Motor Service ....G 814 723-2045
  Warren (G-19057)
Wells Technology Inc ....G 215 672-7000
  Warminster (G-18999)
Willier Elc Mtr Repr Co Inc ....G 215 426-9920
  Philadelphia (G-14477)

ELECTRICAL GOODS, WHOLESALE: Paging & Signaling Eqpt

Blockcom ....G 215 794-9575
  Doylestown (G-4277)

ELECTRICAL GOODS, WHOLESALE: Security Control Eqpt & Systems

Alert Enterprises Ltd Lblty Co ....G 570 373-2821
  Kulpmont (G-8821)
Martin Communications Inc ....F 412 498-0157
  Mc Kees Rocks (G-10619)
Zareba Systems Inc ....D 763 551-1125
  Lititz (G-10061)

ELECTRICAL GOODS, WHOLESALE: Semiconductor Devices

Component Intrtechnologies Inc ....E 724 253-3161
  Hadley (G-6816)
Crystalplex Corporation ....G 412 787-1525
  Pittsburgh (G-14889)

ELECTRICAL GOODS, WHOLESALE: Signaling, Eqpt

Diversified Traffic Pdts Inc ....C 717 428-0222
  Seven Valleys (G-17377)

ELECTRICAL GOODS, WHOLESALE: Sound Eqpt

Identity Group ....G 610 767-4700
  Slatington (G-17607)
Lehigh Electric Products Co ....E 610 395-3386
  Allentown (G-293)

ELECTRICAL GOODS, WHOLESALE: Switches, Exc Electronic, NEC

Wise Electronic Systems Inc ....G 717 244-0111
  Windsor (G-20197)

ELECTRICAL GOODS, WHOLESALE: Telephone & Telegraphic Eqpt

Element Id Inc ....F 610 419-8822
  Bethlehem (G-1501)

ELECTRICAL GOODS, WHOLESALE: Transformer & Transmission Eqpt

Philadelphia Electrical Eqp Co ....F 484 840-0860
  Aston (G-786)

ELECTRICAL GOODS, WHOLESALE: Video Eqpt

Education MGT Solutions LLC ....D 610 701-7002
  Exton (G-5671)

ELECTRICAL GOODS, WHOLESALE: Wire & Cable

Galaxy Wire and Cable Inc ....F 215 957-8714
  Horsham (G-7820)
Keystone Scrw Corp ....D 215 657-7100
  Willow Grove (G-20123)
Silvine Inc ....E 215 657-2345
  Willow Grove (G-20142)

ELECTRICAL GOODS, WHOLESALE: Wire & Cable, Electronic

Cobra Wire & Cable Inc ....E 215 674-8773
  Huntingdon Valley (G-7970)
EBY Group LLC ....E 215 537-4700
  Philadelphia (G-13657)
Eis Inc ....E 215 674-8773
  Huntingdon Valley (G-7976)

ELECTRICAL GOODS, WHOLESALE: Wire & Cable, Power

Direct Wire & Cable Inc ....D 717 336-2842
  Denver (G-4070)
Global Trade Links LLC ....E 888 777-1577
  Chester Springs (G-3079)

ELECTRICAL MEASURING INSTRUMENT REPAIR & CALIBRATION SVCS

CM Technologies Corporation ....F 412 262-0734
  Coraopolis (G-3678)
Pruftechnik Inc ....E 844 242-6296
  Philadelphia (G-14211)

ELECTRICAL SPLYS

Fromm Elc Sup Corp Rding Penna ....G 570 387-9711
  Bloomsburg (G-1783)
Hodge Electric Motors Inc ....G 724 834-8420
  Greensburg (G-6674)
Johnstone Supply ....G 610 967-9900
  Alburtis (G-53)
Miller Electric Service & Sup ....F 814 942-9943
  Altoona (G-527)
Pioneer Electric Supply Co Inc ....G 814 437-1342
  Franklin (G-6152)
Powerex Inc ....E 724 925-7272
  Youngwood (G-20781)
Wesco Distribution Inc ....F 724 772-5000
  Warrendale (G-19101)
Wistex II LLC ....G 215 328-9100
  Warminster (G-19002)
Yesco New Castle Elec Sup ....G 724 656-0911
  New Castle (G-12171)

ELECTRICAL SUPPLIES: Porcelain

Alumina Ceramic Components Inc ....F 724 532-1900
  Latrobe (G-9454)
Carson Industries Inc ....E 724 295-5147
  Freeport (G-6201)
Du-Co Ceramics Company ....C 724 352-1511
  Saxonburg (G-17085)
Electro-Glass Products Inc ....E 724 423-5000
  Norvelt (G-12878)
Insaco Incorporated ....D 215 536-3500
  Quakertown (G-16202)
Kadco Ceramics LLC ....F 610 252-5424
  Easton (G-4710)
Leco Corporation ....E 814 355-7903
  Bellefonte (G-1107)
Mersen USA St Marys-PA Corp ....C 814 781-1234
  Saint Marys (G-16990)
Morgan Advanced Mtls Tech Inc ....C 814 781-1573
  Saint Marys (G-16998)
Spectrum Control Inc ....C 814 835-4000
  Fairview (G-5844)
Vesuvius U S A Corporation ....F 412 429-1800
  Pittsburgh (G-15697)

ELECTRODES: Thermal & Electrolytic

Ameri-Surce Specialty Pdts Inc ....E 412 831-9400
  Bethel Park (G-1402)

ELECTROMEDICAL EQPT

Alung Technologies Inc ....E 412 697-3370
  Pittsburgh (G-14697)

Biotelemetry Inc ....D 610 729-7000
  Malvern (G-10193)
Boehringer Laboratories Inc ....E 610 278-0900
  Phoenixville (G-14536)
Bond With Me LLC ....G 267 334-1233
  Doylestown (G-4278)
Devilbiss Healthcare LLC ....B 814 443-4881
  Somerset (G-17684)
Eveos Corporation ....G 412 366-0159
  Sewickley (G-17388)
Forest Devices Inc ....G 724 612-1504
  Pittsburgh (G-15025)
Medtronic Monitoring Inc ....G 610 257-3640
  Bala Cynwyd (G-885)
Moberg Research Inc ....F 215 283-0860
  Ambler (G-591)
Mobile Medical Innovations ....G 724 646-2200
  Mercer (G-10969)
Perseon Corporation ....G 201 486-5924
  Newtown Square (G-12589)
Philips Ultrasound Inc ....E 717 667-5000
  Reedsville (G-16626)
Photosonix Medical Inc ....G 215 641-4909
  Ambler (G-598)
Pro-Sltons For Chropractic Inc ....G 724 942-4284
  Canonsburg (G-2621)
Radiancy Inc ....F 845 398-1647
  Willow Grove (G-20138)
Renal Solutions Inc ....G 724 772-6900
  Warrendale (G-19095)
Respironics Inc ....C 724 387-5200
  Mount Pleasant (G-11714)
Rtm Vital Signs LLC ....G 215 643-1286
  Fort Washington (G-6091)
Surgical Laser Tech Inc ....G 215 619-3600
  Montgomeryville (G-11420)
Technical Vision Inc ....F 215 205-6084
  Pipersville (G-14620)
Total Scope Inc ....E 484 490-2100
  Upper Chichester (G-18674)
Ursus Medical LLC ....G 412 779-4016
  Pittsburgh (G-15686)
Xgen LLC 877 450-9436
  Horsham (G-7865)
Zoll ....G 717 761-1842
  Camp Hill (G-2527)
Zoll Manufacturing Corporation ....D 412 968-3333
  Pittsburgh (G-15734)
Zoll Manufacturing Corporation ....D 412 968-3333
  Cheswick (G-3123)
Zoll Medical Corporation ....G 412 968-3333
  Cheswick (G-3124)

ELECTROMEDICAL EQPT WHOLESALERS

Cardiac Telecom Corporation ....F 800 355-2594
  Greensburg (G-6656)
Spectrasonics Inc ....G 610 964-9637
  Wayne (G-19372)
Sylvan Corporation ....G 724 864-9350
  Irwin (G-8203)

ELECTROMETALLURGICAL PRDTS

Aviva Technology Inc ....G 610 228-4689
  Broomall (G-2279)
G O Carlson Inc ....E 814 678-4100
  Oil City (G-12945)
Ironmaster LLC ....G 412 554-6705
  Export (G-5609)
Kennametal Inc ....A 412 248-8000
  Pittsburgh (G-15169)
Neh Inc ....B 412 299-7200
  Coraopolis (G-3706)

ELECTRON TUBES

Eag Electronics Corp ....C 814 836-8080
  Fairview (G-5820)
Vectron International Inc ....E 603 598-0070
  Mount Holly Springs (G-11640)

ELECTRONIC COMPONENTS

Ametek Europe LLC ....G 610 647-2121
  Berwyn (G-1353)
Current Circuits Inc ....G 215 444-9295
  Warminster (G-18852)
Diverse Tchnical Solutions LLC ....G 717 630-8522
  Hanover (G-6877)
Equate Space-Time Tech LLC ....G 814 838-3571
  Erie (G-5261)

ELECTRONIC DETECTION SYSTEMS: Aeronautical

Photonis Defense Inc ....D 717 295-6000
  Lancaster (G-9170)
Wm Robots, LLC ....F 215 822-2525
  Colmar (G-3424)

ELECTRONIC DEVICES: Solid State, NEC

Kontron America Incorporated ....F 412 921-3322
  Pittsburgh (G-15182)
Mesta Electronics Inc ....F 412 754-3000
  Irwin (G-8182)
Novatech Industries Inc ....G 610 584-8996
  Skippack (G-17601)

ELECTRONIC EQPT REPAIR SVCS

Controls Service & Repair ....G 412 487-7310
  Glenshaw (G-6486)
Optimum Controls Corporation ....D 610 375-0990
  Reading (G-16459)
Strainsense Enterprises Inc ....G 412 751-3055
  McKeesport (G-10684)
Valley Instrument Co Inc ....F 610 363-2650
  Exton (G-5746)

ELECTRONIC LOADS & POWER SPLYS

Advanced Electronics Systems ....G 717 263-5681
  Chambersburg (G-2897)
Eaglerise E&E Inc ....F 215 675-5953
  Warminster (G-18867)
Everson Tesla Inc ....D 610 746-1520
  Nazareth (G-11965)
Malvern Scale Data Systems ....G 610 296-9642
  Malvern (G-10274)
Phlexglobal Inc ....D 484 324-7921
  Malvern (G-10296)
Solar Transformers Inc ....F 267 384-5231
  Telford (G-18316)

ELECTRONIC PARTS & EQPT WHOLESALERS

American Innovations Inc ....G 215 249-1840
  Dublin (G-4431)
Avox Inc ....G 267 404-2676
  Perkasie (G-13267)
Canterbery Industries LLC ....G 724 697-4231
  Avonmore (G-863)
Coil Specialty Co Inc ....E 814 234-7044
  State College (G-17952)
D L Electronics Inc. ....G 215 742-2666
  Philadelphia (G-13600)
D-Electric Inc ....F 215 529-6020
  Quakertown (G-16182)
Foerster Instruments Inc ....F 412 788-8976
  Pittsburgh (G-15023)
Genie Electronics Co Inc ....D 717 244-1099
  Red Lion (G-16598)
Genie Electronics Co Inc ....C 717 244-1099
  Red Lion (G-16599)
K&S Interconnect Inc. ....D 267 256-1725
  Fort Washington (G-6078)
L R M Inc ....G 215 721-4840
  Souderton (G-17747)
Micro Oscillator Inc ....G 610 617-8682
  Bala Cynwyd (G-886)
Onexia Inc. ....G 610 431-7271
  Exton (G-5720)
P J Electronics Inc ....G 412 793-3912
  Pittsburgh (G-15366)
Sawcom Tech Inc ....G 610 433-7900
  Whitehall (G-19888)
Spang & Company ....C 412 963-9363
  Pittsburgh (G-15567)
Te Connectivity Corporation ....D 717 691-5842
  Mechanicsburg (G-10895)
Video Visions Inc ....F 215 942-6642
  Trevose (G-18508)

ELECTRONIC SHOPPING

My Biblical Perception LLC ....G 267 450-9655
  Perkasie (G-13285)
Trbz Ink LLC ....G 267 918-2242
  Philadelphia (G-14403)

ELECTRONIC TRAINING DEVICES

Five Star Associates Inc ....F 610 588-7426
  Bangor (G-913)

ELECTROPLATING & PLATING SVC

JMJ Finishing ....G 814 838-4050
  Erie (G-5337)
Met-Fin Co Inc ....F 215 699-3505
  North Wales (G-12818)
Simms Abrasives ....G 610 327-1877
  Pottstown (G-16046)
Wade Technology Incorporated ....G 215 765-2478
  Philadelphia (G-14456)

ELEMENTARY & SECONDARY PRIVATE DENOMINATIONAL SCHOOLS

Catholic Scl Svcs of Scranton ....G 570 454-6693
  Hazleton (G-7494)

ELEVATORS & EQPT

Benton Elevator ....G 215 795-0650
  Ottsville (G-13059)
Door Guard Inc ....G 724 695-8936
  Pittsburgh (G-14932)
International Union-Elevator ....G 570 842-5430
  Sprng Brk Twp (G-17932)
Stiltz Inc ....G 610 443-2282
  Bethlehem (G-1629)

ELEVATORS WHOLESALERS

Ashland Industrial Svcs LLC ....G 717 347-5616
  Shrewsbury (G-17581)
Otis Elevator Company ....G 814 452-2703
  Erie (G-5411)
Stiltz Inc ....G 610 443-2282
  Bethlehem (G-1629)
Thyssenkrupp Elevator Corp ....E 610 366-0161
  Allentown (G-409)

ELEVATORS: Installation & Conversion

Bostock Company Inc ....E 215 343-7040
  Warrington (G-19110)
Manns Sickroom Service Inc ....E 412 672-5680
  White Oak (G-19856)
Thyssenkrupp Elevator Corp ....E 412 364-2624
  Pittsburgh (G-15623)

EMBALMING FLUID

Hydrol Chemical Company Inc ....F 610 622-3603
  Yeadon (G-20354)

EMBLEMS: Embroidered

Embroidery Factory Inc ....G 570 654-7640
  Pittston (G-15749)
Ibis Tek Apparel LLC ....E 724 586-2179
  Butler (G-2408)
In Stitches Embroidery ....G 570 368-5525
  Montoursville (G-11441)
Kevins Wholesale LLC ....D 570 344-9055
  Scranton (G-17250)
Moritz Embroidery Works Inc ....E 570 839-9600
  Mount Pocono (G-11736)
Penn Emblem Company ....D 215 632-7800
  Feasterville Trevose (G-5926)

EMBOSSING SVC: Paper

Dynamic Graphic Finishing Inc ....E 215 441-8880
  Horsham (G-7811)
Gregory Troyer ....G 717 393-0233
  Bird In Hand (G-1676)
Hot Off Press Inc ....F 610 473-5700
  Boyertown (G-1916)

EMBROIDERING & ART NEEDLEWORK FOR THE TRADE

4 Life Promotions LLC ....G 215 919-4985
  Philadelphia (G-13319)
A R Groff Transport Inc ....G 717 859-4661
  Leola (G-9764)
Air Conway Inc ....F 610 534-0500
  Collingdale (G-3402)
Art Tech Designs ....G 412 754-0391
  Elizabeth (G-4855)

PRODUCT

Awards & More ....G....... 724 444-1040
  Gibsonia (G-6325)

Blue Mountain Sports AP Inc ....G..... 717 263-4124
  Chambersburg (G-2912)

Bsg Custom Designs LLC ....G..... 610 867-7361
  Bethlehem (G-1475)

Busy Bee Embroidery & More ....G..... 717 540-1955
  Harrisburg (G-7102)

Caffrey Michael & Sons ....G.... 610 252-1299
  Easton (G-4659)

Callery Sr John ....G.... 412 344-9010
  Pittsburgh (G-14805)

Creative Embroidery Designs ....G.... 412 793-1923
  Douglassville (G-4173)

Creative Stitches By Dina Inc ....G.... 724 863-4104
  Irwin (G-8152)

Custom Corner Sportswear ....G.... 724 588-1667
  Greenville (G-6740)

Cutting Edge Embroidery Inc ....G.... 412 732-9990
  Pittsburgh (G-14897)

Danowski ....G.... 717 328-5057
  Mercersburg (G-10985)

Embroider Smith ....G.... 570 961-8781
  Scranton (G-17234)

Embroidery Concepts ....G.... 724 225-3644
  Washington (G-19168)

Greater Pttsbrgh Spcialty Advg ....E.... 412 821-5976
  Millvale (G-11223)

Keystone Uniform Cap LP ....E.... 215 821-3434
  Philadelphia (G-13933)

La Perla LLC ....G.... 717 561-1257
  Harrisburg (G-7166)

Larry D Mays ....F.... 814 833-7988
  Erie (G-5360)

Lee Regional Health System Inc ....G.... 814 254-4716
  Johnstown (G-8403)

Log Cabin Embroidery Inc ....G.... 724 327-5929
  Murrysville (G-11855)

Marathon Embroidery ....G.... 215 627-8848
  Philadelphia (G-13990)

Mister Bobbin Embroidery Inc ....F.... 717 838-5841
  Annville (G-654)

Nittany EMB & Digitizing ....F.... 814 359-0905
  State College (G-17998)

Physical Graffi-Tees ....G.... 610 439-3344
  Allentown (G-351)

Preferred Sportswear Inc ....G.... 484 494-3067
  Darby (G-4024)

Ravine Inc ....F.... 814 946-5006
  Altoona (G-541)

Rowe Screen Print Inc ....F.... 717 774-8920
  New Cumberland (G-12190)

Royalty Promotions Inc ....G.... 215 794-2707
  Furlong (G-6233)

Samfam Inc ....G.... 814 941-1915
  Altoona (G-546)

Sew Special ....G.... 724 438-1765
  Uniontown (G-18641)

Sez Sew Stitching Inc ....F.... 814 339-6734
  Osceola Mills (G-13057)

Smith Prints Inc ....G.... 215 997-8077
  Chalfont (G-2888)

Stitch Crazy ....G.... 610 526-0154
  Conshohocken (G-3607)

Summer Valley EMB ....F.... 570 386-3711
  New Ringgold (G-12443)

W S Lee & Sons LP ....G.... 814 317-5010
  Altoona (G-556)

EMBROIDERING SVC

A & D Fashions Inc ....G.... 610 967-1440
  Emmaus (G-5017)

All Pro Embroidery Inc ....F.... 412 942-0735
  Pittsburgh (G-14675)

Anything Sews ....G.... 412 486-1055
  Glenshaw (G-6480)

Art Stitch Inc ....G.... 717 652-8992
  Harrisburg (G-7091)

Artistagraphics Inc ....F.... 412 271-3252
  Pittsburgh (G-14727)

Arty Embroidery & Design Inc ....F.... 215 423-8114
  Philadelphia (G-13417)

Atlantic Embroidery Company ....G.... 215 514-2154
  Glenside (G-6507)

Bluestar Marketing Inc ....G.... 215 886-4002
  Elkins Park (G-4900)

C & S Sports & Promotions ....G.... 724 775-1655
  Monaca (G-11287)

Charles F May Co ....G.... 215 634-7257
  Philadelphia (G-13527)

Cross Works Embroidery Sp Inc ....G.... 610 261-1690
  Coplay (G-3642)

Designs Unlimited ....G.... 717 367-4405
  Elizabethtown (G-4872)

Eberharts Cstm Embroidery Inc ....G.... 215 639-9530
  Bensalem (G-14968)

Embroidery Etc Inc ....G.... 412 381-6884
  Pittsburgh (G-14968)

Fawn Embroidery Punching Svcs ....G.... 717 382-4855
  New Park (G-12430)

Fawn Industries Inc ....D.... 717 382-4855
  New Park (G-12431)

Great Lakes Custom Graphics ....G.... 814 723-0110
  Warren (G-19029)

Griffith Pottery House Inc ....G.... 215 887-2222
  Oreland (G-13021)

Hess Embroidery & Uniforms LLC ....G.... 610 816-5234
  Reading (G-16401)

Hollys Embroidery ....G.... 717 599-5975
  Harrisburg (G-7151)

Home Town Sports Inc ....G.... 412 672-2242
  McKeesport (G-10671)

Imagewear Ltd ....G.... 704 999-9979
  Easton (G-4704)

Kampus Klothes Inc ....E.... 215 357-0892
  Warminster (G-18904)

Kartri Sales Company Inc ....E.... 570 785-3365
  Forest City (G-6054)

Mark Im Com ....G.... 724 282-0997
  Butler (G-2421)

N J K Lettering ....G.... 724 356-2583
  Avella (G-837)

National Embroidery ....G.... 610 323-4400
  Pottstown (G-16020)

New Look Uniform & Embroidery ....F.... 814 944-5515
  Altoona (G-530)

Nice Threads International ....G.... 610 259-0788
  Clifton Heights (G-3257)

Nicholas Wohlfarth ....F.... 412 373-6811
  Pittsburgh (G-15337)

Ray Derstine ....G.... 215 723-6573
  Telford (G-18311)

Reid S Tannery ....G.... 610 929-4403
  Reading (G-16495)

Rockland Embroidery Inc ....E.... 610 682-5042
  Topton (G-18415)

S B I Inc ....G.... 610 595-3300
  Prospect Park (G-16119)

Sharper Embroidery Inc ....G.... 570 714-3617
  Swoyersville (G-18199)

Shields Embroidery By Design ....F.... 412 531-2321
  Pittsburgh (G-15533)

Snowberger Embroidery ....G.... 814 696-6499
  Duncansville (G-4464)

Stitch Art Custom Embroidery ....G.... 814 382-2702
  Conneaut Lake (G-3479)

Stitch U S A Inc ....F.... 215 699-0123
  North Wales (G-12828)

Stitch Wizards Inc ....G.... 412 264-9973
  Coraopolis (G-3726)

Tiadaghton Embroidery ....G.... 570 398-4477
  Jersey Shore (G-8323)

Tom Russell ....G.... 724 746-5029
  Houston (G-7882)

Trautman Associates Inc ....F.... 570 743-0430
  Shamokin Dam (G-17429)

USA Embroidery & Silkscre ....G.... 570 837-7700
  Beavertown (G-1029)

Vitabru Embroidery ....G.... 610 296-0181
  Malvern (G-10345)

Waterfront Embroidery ....G.... 412 337-9269
  Homestead (G-7697)

X-Deco LLC ....F.... 412 257-9755
  Pittsburgh (G-15725)

York Towne Embroidery Works ....G.... 717 854-0006
  York (G-20753)

EMBROIDERING SVC: Schiffli Machine

Moritz Embroidery Works Inc ....E.... 570 839-9600
  Mount Pocono (G-11736)

EMBROIDERY ADVERTISING SVCS

Busy Bee Embroidery & More ....G.... 717 540-1955
  Harrisburg (G-7102)

Donora Sportswear Company Inc ....G.... 724 929-2387
  Donora (G-4151)

Lykens Corporation ....F.... 814 375-9961
  Du Bois (G-4403)

Ras Sports Inc ....E.... 814 833-9111
  Erie (G-5457)

Teamwork Graphic Inc ....G.... 570 368-2360
  Montoursville (G-11452)

Upper Perk Sportswear Inc ....G.... 215 541-3211
  Pennsburg (G-13261)

EMERGENCY ALARMS

Ademco Inc ....G.... 215 244-6377
  Bensalem (G-1143)

Alertone Services Inc ....F.... 570 321-5433
  Williamsport (G-19984)

Digital Care Sysytems Inc ....F.... 215 946-7700
  Levittown (G-9831)

Hri Networks Inc ....F.... 267 515-5880
  Philadelphia (G-13838)

Hubbell Incorporated Delaware ....B.... 574 234-7151
  Mohnton (G-11264)

Johnson Controls ....D.... 717 610-8100
  New Cumberland (G-12187)

Johnson Controls ....D.... 610 398-7260
  Allentown (G-270)

Mashan Inc ....G.... 724 397-4008
  Home (G-7669)

Medical Alarm Concepts LLC ....G.... 877 639-2929
  King of Prussia (G-8650)

Mercury Systems Inc ....G.... 215 245-0546
  Bensalem (G-1227)

Micro-Trap Corporation ....G.... 215 295-8208
  Morrisville (G-11571)

Ncn Data Networks LLC ....G.... 570 213-8300
  Stroudsburg (G-18133)

Unique Systems Inc ....G.... 610 499-1463
  Wallingford (G-18787)

Wearable Health Solutions Inc ....F.... 877 639-2929
  King of Prussia (G-8698)

EMPLOYMENT AGENCY SVCS

First Quality Enterprises Inc ....C.... 570 384-1600
  Hazleton (G-7498)

National Assn Cllges Employers ....E.... 610 868-1421
  Bethlehem (G-1577)

Threshold Rhblitation Svcs Inc ....B.... 610 777-7691
  Reading (G-16538)

Tomayko Group LLC ....F.... 412 481-0600
  Pittsburgh (G-15632)

Voicestars Inc ....G.... 305 902-9666
  Emmaus (G-5046)

ENAMELING SVC: Metal Prdts, Including Porcelain

Amdex Metallizing Inc ....G.... 724 887-4977
  Scottdale (G-17189)

Andrew W Nissly Inc ....G.... 717 393-3841
  Lancaster (G-8934)

ENCLOSURES: Electronic

Ice Qube Inc ....D.... 724 837-7600
  Greensburg (G-6676)

ENCLOSURES: Screen

Scatton Bros Mfg Co ....E.... 215 362-6830
  Lansdale (G-9409)

ENCODERS: Digital

Digital Card Inc ....F.... 215 275-7100
  Langhorne (G-9290)

Payloadz Inc ....G.... 609 510-3074
  Newtown Square (G-12587)

ENCRYPTION EQPT & DEVICES

Validity LLC ....G.... 610 768-8042
  Malvern (G-10337)

ENERGY MEASUREMENT EQPT

Basic Power Inc ....G.... 570 872-9666
  East Stroudsburg (G-4608)

ENGINE PARTS & ACCESS: Internal Combustion

Efi Connection LLC ....G.... 814 566-0946
  Erie (G-5257)

Precision Castparts Corp ....B.... 570 474-6371
  Mountain Top (G-11771)

ENGINE REBUILDING: Diesel

Hassinger Diesel Service LLC ....G 570 837-3412
Middleburg (G-11025)

ENGINE REBUILDING: Gas

Aztec Products Inc ....F 215 393-4700
Montgomeryville (G-11387)
Ritter Precision Machining ....G 610 377-2011
Lehighton (G-9725)

ENGINEERING SVCS

A J Drgon Associates Inc ....G 412 771-5160
Mc Kees Rocks (G-10598)
Abec Inc ....C 610 882-1541
Bethlehem (G-1442)
Advanced Design and Ctrl Corp ....F 215 723-7200
Souderton (G-17720)
Aegis Software Corporation ....G 724 325-5595
Murrysville (G-11845)
Anholt Technologies Inc ....F 610 268-2758
Avondale (G-848)
Astrobotic Technology Inc ....F 412 682-3282
Pittsburgh (G-14729)
Bae Systems Land Armaments LP ....D 717 225-8000
York (G-20397)
Bti-Coopermatics Inc ....G 610 262-7700
Northampton (G-12847)
Cardinal Resources Inc ....G 412 374-0989
Pittsburgh (G-14809)
Cardinal Resources LLC ....G 412 374-0989
Pittsburgh (G-14810)
Carroll Manufacturing Co LLC ....G 724 266-0400
Leetsdale (G-9688)
Compunetics Inc ....D 412 373-8110
Monroeville (G-11328)
Cory Reservior Testing Inc ....G 814 438-2006
Union City (G-18606)
Demco Enterprises Inc ....F 888 419-3343
Quakertown (G-16184)
East Coast Control Systems ....G 814 857-5420
Bigler (G-1658)
Erie Protective Coatings Inc ....G 814 833-0095
Erie (G-5273)
Fineline Circuits Inc ....E 215 364-3311
Feasterville Trevose (G-5909)
Five Star Associates Inc ....F 610 588-7426
Bangor (G-913)
Flir Government Systems Pittsb ....D 724 295-2880
Freeport (G-6204)
Flsmidth Inc ....A 610 264-6101
Bethlehem (G-1513)
Gardner Denver Nash LLC ....G 203 459-3923
Charleroi (G-3015)
Ggs Information Services Inc ....C 717 764-2222
York (G-20499)
Global Utility Structures LLC ....G 570 788-0826
Sugarloaf (G-18153)
Hapeman Electronics Inc ....G 724 475-2033
Mercer (G-10962)
Industrial Harness Company Inc ....D 717 477-0100
Shippensburg (G-17532)
J A Brown Company ....G 610 832-0400
Conshohocken (G-3566)
JGM Welding & Fabg Svcs Inc ....D 610 873-0081
Coatesville (G-3310)
Jls Automation LLC ....E 717 505-3800
York (G-20541)
Keane Frac Tx LLC ....G 570 302-4050
Mansfield (G-10418)
Kena Corporation ....F 717 292-7097
Dover (G-4193)
Kongsberg Integrated Tactical ....E 814 269-5700
Johnstown (G-8399)
M E Inc ....E 610 820-5250
Whitehall (G-19884)
M Squared Electronics Inc ....F 215 945-6658
Levittown (G-9848)
Matthey Johnson Inc ....C 610 648-8000
West Chester (G-19598)
Metco Manufacturing Co Inc ....E 215 518-7400
Huntingdon Valley (G-8013)
Mosaic Engineering Inc ....G 406 544-7902
State College (G-17995)
Msf Management LLC ....E 724 371-3059
Beaver (G-987)
National Center For Def ....E 724 539-8811
Blairsville (G-1735)
Onexia Inc ....E 610 431-7271
Exton (G-5720)

Paradigm Corporation ....F 215 675-9488
Hatboro (G-7295)
Pennergy Solutions LLC ....G 484 393-1539
Royersford (G-16859)
Powercast Corporation ....G 412 455-5800
Pittsburgh (G-15422)
Product Design and Development ....E 717 741-4844
York (G-20644)
R & E International Inc ....F 610 664-5637
Merion Station (G-10998)
Re2 Inc ....E 412 681-6382
Pittsburgh (G-15472)
Redstone Corporation ....G 321 213-2135
Johnstown (G-8429)
Rfcircuits Inc ....G 215 364-2450
Huntingdon Valley (G-8029)
Riise Inc ....G 724 528-3305
West Middlesex (G-19729)
RLC Electronic Systems Inc ....E 610 898-4902
Reading (G-16500)
Sabold Design Inc ....G 610 401-4086
Bernville (G-1305)
Sawcom Tech Inc ....G 610 433-7900
Whitehall (G-19888)
Sense Technology Inc ....G 724 733-2277
Halifax (G-6831)
Sensortex Inc ....G 302 444-2383
Kennett Square (G-8542)
Sp Environmental Inc ....E 724 935-1300
Sewickley (G-17412)
Specialty Support Systems Inc ....F 215 945-1033
Levittown (G-9865)
Techniserv Inc ....D 570 759-2315
Berwick (G-1346)
Telefactor Robotics LLC ....G 610 940-6040
Conshohocken (G-3611)
Temtek Solutions Inc ....G 724 980-4270
Canonsburg (G-2647)
Trijay Systems Inc...............................F 215 997-5833
Line Lexington (G-9977)
Trilion Quality Systems LLC ....E 215 710-3000
King of Prussia (G-8690)
Trs Technologies Inc ....E 814 238-7485
State College (G-18040)
U B R LLC ....G 717 432-3490
Dillsburg (G-4141)
Urania Engineering Co Inc ....D 570 455-0776
Hazleton (G-7532)
Valira LLC ....F 973 216-5803
Conshohocken (G-3615)
Vortx United Inc ....G 570 742-7859
Milton (G-11250)
Wise Machine Co Inc ....E 724 287-2705
Butler (G-2450)
Wm Robots, LLC ....F 215 822-2525
Colmar (G-3424)

ENGINEERING SVCS: Acoustical

Kada Energy Resources LLC ....G 215 839-9159
Philadelphia (G-13919)

ENGINEERING SVCS: Building Construction

Haberle Upholstery ....G 215 679-8195
Zionsville (G-20835)
Taylored Building Solutions ....G 570 898-5361
Taylor (G-18263)

ENGINEERING SVCS: Civil

Elk Lake Services LLC ....F 724 463-7303
Indiana (G-8094)

ENGINEERING SVCS: Construction & Civil

Sunbelt Drilling Services Inc ....F 215 764-9544
Blue Bell (G-1853)

ENGINEERING SVCS: Electrical Or Electronic

Aaim Controls Inc ....F 717 765-9100
Waynesboro (G-19393)
Alstom Grid LLC ....D 412 967-0765
Pittsburgh (G-14689)
Australtek LLC ....F 412 257-2377
Bridgeville (G-2054)
Egr Ventures Inc ....E 610 358-0500
Aston (G-761)
Electronic Prototype Dev Inc ....E 412 767-4111
Natrona Heights (G-11941)

FEC Technologies Inc ....E 717 764-5959
York (G-20477)
Fluid Intelligence LLC ....G 610 405-2698
Berwyn (G-1362)
Islip Transformer and Metal Co ....F 814 272-2700
State College (G-17978)
Qortek Inc ....G 570 322-2700
Williamsport (G-20066)
Quick Assembly Inc ....F 215 361-4100
Hatfield (G-7388)
Staneco Corporation ....E 215 672-6500
Horsham (G-7852)
Westinghouse Electric Co LLC ....A 412 374-2020
Cranberry Township (G-3865)
Westinghouse Electric Co LLC ....D 412 256-1085
Pittsburgh (G-15710)

ENGINEERING SVCS: Energy conservation

Everpower Wind Holdings Inc ....E 412 253-9400
Pittsburgh (G-14989)

ENGINEERING SVCS: Heating & Ventilation

Jarex Enterprises ....G 215 855-2149
Lansdale (G-9378)

ENGINEERING SVCS: Industrial

Andritz Inc ....C 724 597-7801
Canonsburg (G-2540)
Andritz Inc ....B 570 546-8211
Muncy (G-11807)
Penn Engineering & Mfg Corp ....B 215 766-8853
Danboro (G-3991)
Unison Engine Components Inc ....C 570 825-4544
Wilkes Barre (G-19967)

ENGINEERING SVCS: Machine Tool Design

Karadon Corporation ....F 724 676-5790
Blairsville (G-1729)
New Oxford Tool & Die Inc ....G 717 624-8441
New Oxford (G-12417)
Phoenix Combustion Inc ....F 610 495-5800
Pottstown (G-16031)
Summit Contracting Svcs Inc ....G 570 943-2232
Orwigsburg (G-13053)
Winston & Duke Inc ....E 814 456-0582
Erie (G-5530)

ENGINEERING SVCS: Mechanical

Advanced Solutions Network LLC ....F 814 464-0791
Erie (G-5175)
Advanced VSR Technology ....G 215 366-3315
Philadelphia (G-13348)
Carleton Inc ....E 215 230-8900
Doylestown (G-4289)
Concept Engineering Group ....G 412 826-8800
Verona (G-18753)
Frontier LLC ....F 570 265-2500
Towanda (G-18426)
Hiltz Propane Systems Inc ....E 717 799-4322
Marietta (G-10464)
Marando Industries Inc ....G 610 621-2536
Reading (G-16437)
RC & Design Company ....G 484 626-1216
Lehighton (G-9724)
Universal Mch Co Pottstown Inc ....D 610 323-1810
Pottstown (G-16062)
Vanzel Inc ....G 215 223-1000
Philadelphia (G-14438)

ENGINEERING SVCS: Pollution Control

Advanced Industrial Tech Corp ....F 201 483-7235
Langhorne (G-9273)

ENGINEERING SVCS: Professional

Conway-Phillips Holding LLC ....E 412 315-7963
Braddock (G-1943)

ENGINEERING SVCS: Structural

Oswald & Associates Inc ....G 814 627-0300
Huntingdon (G-7954)
VSI Sales LLC ....F 724 625-4060
Hazleton (G-7536)

PRODUCT

ENGINES & ENGINE PARTS: Guided Missile

Reaction Chemicals..................G...... 610 838-5496
  Hellertown (G-7561)

ENGINES & ENGINE PARTS: Guided Missile, Research & Develpt

Kyron Naval Architecture.................G...... 516 304-1769
  Bensalem (G-1217)

ENGINES: Diesel & Semi-Diesel Or Duel Fuel

Enpro Industries Inc ....G...... 215 946-0845
  Bristol (G-2141)
Fyda Frghtliner Pittsburgh Inc..........D...... 724 514-2055
  Canonsburg (G-2590)
G2 Diesel Products Inc ....F...... 717 525-8709
  Harrisburg (G-7132)

ENGINES: Internal Combustion, NEC

Ash/Tec Inc ....E...... 570 682-0933
  Hegins (G-7539)
Boyesen Inc.................E...... 610 756-6818
  Lenhartsville (G-9756)
Cummins - Allison Corp ....F...... 610 355-1400
  Broomall (G-2284)
Cummins - Allison Corp ....G...... 215 245-8436
  Bensalem (G-1176)
Cummins Inc ....G...... 724 798-4511
  Belle Vernon (G-1085)
Cummins Inc ....E...... 412 820-0330
  Pittsburgh (G-14893)
Cummins Inc ....D...... 717 564-1344
  Harrisburg (G-7110)
Cummins Inc ....G...... 570 333-0360
  Tunkhannock (G-18535)
Cummins Inc ....G...... 215 785-6005
  Bristol (G-2129)
Cummins-Wagner Company Inc ....E...... 717 367-8294
  Elizabethtown (G-4870)
General Electric Company ....B...... 724 450-1887
  Grove City (G-6787)
L & M Engines Inc ....G...... 215 675-8485
  Hatboro (G-7291)
Mack Trucks Inc ....C...... 717 939-1338
  Middletown (G-11064)
Navistar Inc.................B...... 610 375-4230
  Reading (G-16452)
Optimus Technologies Inc ....F...... 412 727-8228
  Pittsburgh (G-15362)
Penn Power Group LLC.................E...... 570 208-1192
  Hanover Township (G-7003)
Rutts Machine Inc ....F...... 717 367-3011
  Elizabethtown (G-4885)
W W Engine and Supply Inc.................E...... 814 345-5693
  Kylertown (G-8868)

ENGINES: Marine

HIG Capital LLC.................C...... 610 495-7011
  Royersford (G-16851)
Ransome Idealease LLC.................E...... 215 639-4300
  Bensalem (G-1248)

ENGRAVING SVC, NEC

Etched In Time.................G...... 717 334-3600
  Gettysburg (G-6290)
Lee Engraving Services Inc ....G...... 412 788-4224
  Oakdale (G-12905)
Richman Industries Inc ....G...... 717 561-1766
  Harrisburg (G-7206)
Spencer Industries Inc ....F...... 215 634-2700
  Philadelphia (G-14334)
Stationary Engravers Inc.................F...... 215 739-3538
  Philadelphia (G-14342)

ENGRAVING SVC: Jewelry & Personal Goods

A A A Engraving.................G...... 412 281-7756
  Pittsburgh (G-14628)
Addies Inc.................G...... 570 748-2966
  Lock Haven (G-10081)
H & H Wholesale Inc ....G...... 724 733-8338
  Pittsburgh (G-15069)
Lee Engraving Services Inc ....G...... 412 788-4224
  Oakdale (G-12905)
R & H Jewelers.................G...... 215 928-1240
  Philadelphia (G-14222)

ENGRAVING SVCS

A A A Engraving.................G...... 412 281-7756
  Pittsburgh (G-14628)
Awards & More.................G...... 724 444-1040
  Gibsonia (G-6325)
Blasi Printing Inc.................F...... 570 824-3557
  Hanover Township (G-6981)
Bux Mont Awards.................G...... 215 855-5052
  Lansdale (G-9349)
Bux Mont Awards.................G...... 215 257-5432
  Sellersville (G-17341)
C & G Wilcox Engrv & Images ....G...... 570 265-3621
  Towanda (G-18422)
Crownwood LLC.................G...... 717 463-2942
  Mc Alisterville (G-10548)
Jmc Engraving Inc.................G...... 610 759-0140
  Nazareth (G-11974)
Keystone Printing Services ....G...... 215 675-6464
  Hatboro (G-7289)
Lasermation Inc.................E...... 215 228-7900
  Philadelphia (G-13959)
Micheners Engraving Inc ....G...... 717 738-9630
  Ephrata (G-5127)
Precision Grit Etching & Engrv ....G...... 412 828-5790
  Oakmont (G-12924)
Richland Plastics & Engraving ....G...... 814 266-3002
  Johnstown (G-8431)

ENGRAVING SVCS: Tombstone

Mulch Works Recycling Inc ....F...... 888 214-4628
  Aston (G-779)

ENGRAVING: Currency

American Bank Note Company ....E...... 215 396-8707
  Trevose (G-18486)
HB Trading LLC.................G...... 610 212-4565
  Wayne (G-19336)

ENGRAVINGS: Plastic

Jbr Associates Inc ....G...... 215 362-1318
  Lansdale (G-9380)
Jmc Engraving Inc.................G...... 610 759-0140
  Nazareth (G-11974)
Tpl Plastic Engraving ....G...... 412 771-3773
  Coraopolis (G-3728)

ENVELOPES

Cenveo Worldwide Limited ....F...... 717 285-9095
  Lancaster (G-8975)
Direct Line Productions Inc ....G...... 610 633-7082
  Glen Mills (G-6435)
Great Northern Press of Wilkes.............E...... 570 822-3147
  Wilkes Barre (G-19922)
National Imprint Corporation ....E...... 814 239-8141
  Claysburg (G-3205)
National Imprint Corporation ....E...... 814 239-5116
  Claysburg (G-3206)
National Mail Graphics Corp.................D...... 610 524-1600
  Exton (G-5713)
North Amrcn Communications Inc........A...... 814 696-3553
  Duncansville (G-4458)
Northeastern Envelope Company ....D...... 800 233-4285
  Old Forge (G-12971)
Suplee Envelope Co Inc ....E...... 610 352-2900
  Garnet Valley (G-6269)
Tension Envelope Corporation.............E...... 570 429-1444
  Saint Clair (G-16942)
Tri-State Envelope Corporation ....B...... 570 875-0433
  Ashland (G-738)

ENVELOPES WHOLESALERS

Northeastern Envelope Company ....D...... 800 233-4285
  Old Forge (G-12971)
Suplee Envelope Co Inc ....E...... 610 352-2900
  Garnet Valley (G-6269)

EPOXY RESINS

Smooth-On Inc ....C...... 610 252-5800
  Macungie (G-10159)

EQUIPMENT & VEHICLE FINANCE LEASING COMPANIES

Xerox Corporation ....C...... 412 506-4000
  Pittsburgh (G-15726)

EQUIPMENT: Pedestrian Traffic Control

Alpha Space Control Co Inc.................G...... 717 263-0182
  Chambersburg (G-2900)

EQUIPMENT: Rental & Leasing, NEC

A & P Support Inc.................D...... 570 265-9157
  Pittsburgh (G-14627)
Altair Equipment Company Inc.................E...... 215 672-9000
  Warminster (G-18826)
Bolttech Mannings Inc.................D...... 724 872-4873
  North Versailles (G-12772)
Cameron Supply Corporation.................F...... 610 866-9632
  Bethlehem (G-1478)
Carbonator Rental Service Inc.................E...... 215 726-9100
  Philadelphia (G-13500)
J A Kohlhepp Sons Inc ....D...... 814 371-5200
  Du Bois (G-4398)
Kingsly Compression Inc.................E...... 724 524-1840
  Saxonburg (G-17091)
Multi-Flow Dispensers LP ....D...... 215 322-1800
  Huntingdon Valley (G-8014)
Roadsafe Traffic Systems Inc ....F...... 904 350-0080
  Lemoyne (G-9751)
Rock Hill Materials Company ....E...... 610 264-5586
  Catasauqua (G-2817)
Spring Lock Scaffolding Eqp Co.................G...... 215 426-5727
  Plymouth Meeting (G-15873)
SPX Flow Us LLC.................G...... 814 476-5800
  Mc Kean (G-10594)
Tms International LLC.................D...... 412 678-6141
  Glassport (G-6419)
Tms International Corp.................C...... 412 678-6141
  Glassport (G-6420)
Tms International Corporation ....E...... 412 675-8251
  Glassport (G-6421)
Wave Central LLC.................F...... 717 503-7157
  Carlisle (G-2750)

ESCALATORS: Passenger & Freight

Otis Elevator Company ....G...... 814 452-2703
  Erie (G-5411)

ETCHING & ENGRAVING SVC

Centria Inc.................F...... 724 251-2300
  Ambridge (G-612)
Chase Corporation.................F...... 412 963-6285
  Pittsburgh (G-14837)
City Engraving & Awards LLC ....G...... 215 731-0200
  Philadelphia (G-13547)
Eclat Industries Inc ....G...... 215 547-2684
  Levittown (G-9834)
Freys Research Inc.................G...... 724 586-5659
  Renfrew (G-16639)
H & W Global Industries Inc.................E...... 724 459-5316
  Blairsville (G-1721)
Hd Laser Engrv & Etching LLC.................G...... 724 924-9241
  New Castle (G-12101)
Healy Glass Artistry LLC ....G...... 484 241-0989
  Bethlehem (G-1530)
Helfran Glass.................G...... 570 287-8105
  Kingston (G-8719)
Johnstown Wldg Fabrication Inc..........C...... 800 225-9353
  Johnstown (G-8394)
K Matkem of Morrisville LP ....G...... 215 428-3664
  Allentown (G-276)
K Matkem of Morrisville LP ....G...... 215 295-4158
  Morrisville (G-11566)
Keystone Koating LLC ....D...... 717 436-2056
  Mifflintown (G-11127)
Mystic Assembly & Dctg Co ....E...... 215 957-0280
  Warminster (G-18926)
Performance Coatings Corp ....F...... 610 525-1190
  Levittown (G-9854)
Precision Grit Etching & Engrv ....G...... 412 828-5790
  Oakmont (G-12924)
Robert H Berenson.................G...... 610 642-9380
  Haverford (G-7414)
Velocity Powder Coating LLC.................G...... 704 287-1024
  New Castle (G-12164)
Voigt & Schweitzer LLC.................E...... 717 861-7777
  Jonestown (G-8454)
Xser Coatings Llc.................G...... 732 754-9887
  Philadelphia (G-14495)

ETCHING SVC: Metal

Composidie Inc ....C...... 724 845-8602
  Apollo (G-673)

Custom Etch Inc ....E 724 652-7117
New Castle *(G-12079)*

Tech Met Inc ....E 412 678-8277
Glassport *(G-6418)*

ETHANOLAMINES

Pennsylvania Grains Proc LLC ....E 877 871-0774
Clearfield *(G-3228)*

ETHYLENE

Westlake Chemical Partners LP ....G 484 253-4545
Wayne *(G-19391)*

EXCAVATING EQPT

Caterpillar Inc ....B 717 751-5123
York *(G-20421)*

EXCAVATING MACHINERY & EQPT WHOLESALERS

Artman Equipment Company Inc ....F 724 337-3700
Apollo *(G-662)*

EXHAUST SYSTEMS: Eqpt & Parts

Matthey Johnson Holdings Inc ....E 610 971-3000
Wayne *(G-19350)*

Matthey Johnson Inc ....F 724 564-7200
Smithfield *(G-17653)*

Matthey Johnson Inc ....E 610 971-3000
Wayne *(G-19351)*

N F C Industries Inc ....E 215 766-8890
Plumsteadville *(G-15812)*

Smith Auto Service ....G 215 788-2401
Bristol *(G-2198)*

EXPLORATION, METAL MINING

Leber Mining Company Inc ....G 717 367-1453
Elizabethtown *(G-4876)*

EXPLOSIVES

Action Manufacturing Company ....B 267 540-4041
Bristol *(G-2103)*

Action Manufacturing Company ....D 610 593-1800
Atglen *(G-799)*

Cheri-Lee Inc ....G 570 339-4195
Kulpmont *(G-8822)*

Douglas Explosives Inc ....E 814 342-0782
Philipsburg *(G-14511)*

Dyno Nobel Inc ....E 814 938-2035
Punxsutawney *(G-16135)*

Nonlethal Technologies Inc ....G 724 479-5100
Homer City *(G-7679)*

Tripwire Operations Group LLC ....G 717 648-2792
Gettysburg *(G-6319)*

Wampum Hardware Co ....G 724 336-4501
New Galilee *(G-12223)*

EXPLOSIVES, EXC AMMO & FIREWORKS WHOLESALERS

B W E Ltd ....E 724 246-0470
Republic *(G-16652)*

Douglas Explosives Inc ....E 814 342-0782
Philipsburg *(G-14511)*

EXPLOSIVES, FUSES & DETONATORS: Primary explosives

Copperhead Chemical Co Inc ....E 570 386-6123
Tamaqua *(G-18209)*

EXPLOSIVES: Cartridges For Concussion Forming Of Metal

Blasting Products Inc ....E 412 221-5722
Cuddy *(G-3941)*

EXPLOSIVES: Emulsions

Ametek Inc ....D 215 256-6601
Harleysville *(G-7020)*

EXTENSION CORDS

Direct Wire & Cable Inc ....D 717 336-2842
Denver *(G-4070)*

Electri-Cord Manufacturing Co ....C 814 367-2265
Westfield *(G-19777)*

EXTRACTS, FLAVORING

Byrnes and Kiefer Company ....E 724 538-5200
Callery *(G-2468)*

Henry H Ottens Mfg Co Inc ....D 215 365-7800
Philadelphia *(G-13814)*

Sensoryeffects Inc ....G 610 582-2170
Reading *(G-16512)*

EXTRUDED SHAPES, NEC: Copper & Copper Alloy

Electric Materials Company ....C 814 725-9621
North East *(G-12739)*

EYEGLASS CASES

Korsak Glass & Aluminum Inc ....G 610 987-9888
Boyertown *(G-1923)*

EYEGLASSES

B & G Optics Inc ....E 215 289-2480
Philadelphia *(G-13437)*

Beitler-Mckee Optical Company ....G 412 381-7953
Pittsburgh *(G-14759)*

Bruce N Pelsh Inc ....G 724 346-2020
Hermitage *(G-7572)*

Geryville Eye Associates PC ....F 215 679-3500
Pennsburg *(G-13248)*

Novotny Micheal ....F 724 785-2160
Brownsville *(G-2313)*

Point of View LLC ....G 215 340-1725
Doylestown *(G-4326)*

Rss Optometry LLC ....G 610 933-2177
Phoenixville *(G-14577)*

Walman Optical Company ....E 717 767-5193
York *(G-20703)*

EYEGLASSES: Sunglasses

Chambersburg Optical Service ....G 717 263-4898
Chambersburg *(G-2917)*

Prairie Products Inc ....G 717 292-0421
Dover *(G-4200)*

EYES: Artificial

Bartolotta Vision Care LLC ....G 814 472-8010
Ebensburg *(G-4781)*

John J Kelley Associates Ltd ....G 215 545-0939
Philadelphia *(G-13903)*

Le Grand Assoc of Pittsburgh ....G 215 496-1307
Philadelphia *(G-13962)*

Tohickon Corp ....G 267 450-5020
Sellersville *(G-17360)*

Ethylene Glycols

Glycol Technologies Inc ....G 724 776-3554
Warrendale *(G-19077)*

Sunoco (R&m) LLC ....D 215 977-3000
Newtown Square *(G-12592)*

FABRIC STORES

Belmont Fabrics LLC ....F 717 768-0077
Paradise *(G-13154)*

Canvas Specialties Inc ....G 570 825-9282
Hanover Township *(G-6983)*

Samuel Gerber Inc ....G 717 761-0250
Harrisburg *(G-7212)*

FABRICATED METAL PRODUCTS, NEC

C L Ward Family ....F 724 743-5903
Canonsburg *(G-2554)*

Chelate Incorporated ....G 717 203-0415
Lititz *(G-9997)*

Crouse Run Ventures Inc ....G 412 491-5738
Sewickley *(G-17385)*

GP Metal Fabrication ....G 570 494-1002
Williamsport *(G-20019)*

Reiff Metal Fabrications ....G 717 445-7050
East Earl *(G-4554)*

FABRICS & CLOTH: Quilted

Mayport Cottons & Quilt Shop ....G 814 365-2212
Mayport *(G-10546)*

Milliken Nonwovens LLC ....G 610 544-7117
Broomall *(G-2298)*

FABRICS: Alpacas, Cotton

Cloverleaf Alpacas ....G 717 492-0504
Mount Joy *(G-11650)*

FABRICS: Alpacas, Mohair, Woven

Bucks County Alpacas LLC ....G 215 795-2453
Perkasie *(G-13269)*

Dark Star Alpacas LLC ....G 610 235-6638
Schwenksville *(G-17175)*

Little Bear Creek Alpacas ....G 814 788-0971
Kane *(G-8471)*

Nobility Alpacas ....G 484 332-1499
Wernersville *(G-19486)*

Rejniaks Alpaca ....G 724 265-4062
Gibsonia *(G-6349)*

FABRICS: Apparel & Outerwear, Broadwoven

C J Apparel Inc ....E 610 432-8265
Allentown *(G-159)*

Immersion Research Inc ....F 814 395-9191
Confluence *(G-3466)*

FABRICS: Apparel & Outerwear, Cotton

American Trench LLC ....G 215 360-3493
Ardmore *(G-700)*

Hanesbrands Inc ....G 336 519-8080
Philadelphia *(G-13800)*

FABRICS: Bags & Bagging, Cotton

O S A Global LLC ....G 724 698-7042
New Castle *(G-12135)*

FABRICS: Broad Woven, Goods, Cotton

American Silk Mills LLC ....G 215 561-4901
Jenkintown *(G-8281)*

Craftex Mills Inc Pennsylvania ....E 610 941-1212
Blue Bell *(G-1824)*

FABRICS: Broadwoven, Cotton

Casner Fabrics ....G 215 946-3334
Levittown *(G-9823)*

Ems Surgical LP ....F 570 374-0569
Selinsgrove *(G-17325)*

Juniata Fabrics Inc ....F 814 944-9381
Altoona *(G-519)*

Lmt Corp of Pennsylvania ....E 610 921-3926
Reading *(G-16432)*

Monarch Global Brands Inc ....D 215 482-6100
Philadelphia *(G-14033)*

Oscar Daniels & Company Inc ....F 610 678-8144
Reading *(G-16460)*

Romar Textile Co Inc ....C 724 535-7787
Wampum *(G-18804)*

FABRICS: Broadwoven, Synthetic Manmade Fiber & Silk

American Silk Mills LLC ....G 215 561-4901
Jenkintown *(G-8281)*

Atlantex Manufacturing Corp ....F 610 518-6601
Downingtown *(G-4213)*

Cambria County Asso ....B 814 536-3531
Johnstown *(G-8360)*

Chapel Hill Mfg Co ....F 215 884-3614
Oreland *(G-13020)*

Greenbriar Indus Systems Inc ....D 814 474-1400
Fairview *(G-5824)*

Honeywell International Inc ....B 570 621-6000
Pottsville *(G-16080)*

Jetnet Corporation ....D 412 741-0100
Sewickley *(G-17396)*

Juniata Fabrics Inc ....F 814 944-9381
Altoona *(G-519)*

Mutual Industries North Inc ....E 215 927-6000
Philadelphia *(G-14046)*

New York Wire Company ....C 717 637-3795
Hanover *(G-6926)*

Ono Industries Inc ....E 717 865-6619
Ono *(G-13004)*

Thomaston Manufacturing LLC ....G 215 576-6352
Wyncote *(G-20266)*

PRODUCT

FABRICS: Broadwoven, Wool

Finishing Associates LLC ....F 517 371-2460
  Warminster *(G-18880)*

Mamaux Supply Co ....F 412 782-3456
  Pittsburgh *(G-15249)*

FABRICS: Canvas

A Olek & Son Inc ....F 215 638-4550
  Bensalem *(G-1141)*

Oc Canvas Studio LLC ....G 717 510-4847
  Harrisburg *(G-7187)*

FABRICS: Coated Or Treated

Converters Inc ....E 215 355-5400
  Huntingdon Valley *(G-7971)*

D C Humphrys Co ....D 215 307-3363
  Philadelphia *(G-13599)*

Fabricated Products ....G 570 588-1794
  Bushkill *(G-2365)*

Fortune Fabrics Inc ....E 570 288-3666
  Kingston *(G-8717)*

Gentex Corporation ....B 570 282-3550
  Simpson *(G-17593)*

Henderson Construction Fabrics ....G 724 368-1145
  Harmony *(G-7069)*

Hill Crest Laminating LLC ....G 570 437-3357
  Danville *(G-4005)*

Lite Fibers LLC ....G 724 758-0123
  Ellwood City *(G-4943)*

Penlin Fabricators LLC ....G 610 837-6667
  Bath *(G-968)*

Phb Inc ....C 814 474-1552
  Fairview *(G-5839)*

FABRICS: Coutil, Cotton

Cressona Textile Waste Inc ....G 570 385-4556
  Cressona *(G-3903)*

FABRICS: Decorative Trim & Specialty, Including Twist Weave

Phoenix Trim Works Inc ....E 570 320-0322
  Williamsport *(G-20057)*

Tmu Inc ....F 717 392-0578
  Lancaster *(G-9220)*

FABRICS: Denims

Denim Inc Division ....F 215 627-1400
  Philadelphia *(G-13619)*

FABRICS: Dishcloths

Factory Linens Inc ....E 610 825-2790
  Conshohocken *(G-3545)*

FABRICS: Fiberglass, Broadwoven

Amatex Corporation ....D 610 277-6100
  Norristown *(G-12632)*

Huntingdon Fiberglass Pdts LLC ....E 814 641-8129
  Huntingdon *(G-7945)*

FABRICS: Furniture Denim

Johnnys Discount Furniture ....G 717 564-1898
  Harrisburg *(G-7159)*

FABRICS: Jacquard Woven, From Manmade Fiber Or Silk

Dwell America LLC ....G 717 272-4666
  Lebanon *(G-9562)*

FABRICS: Lace & Decorative Trim, Narrow

Yarrington Mills Corporation ....E 215 674-5125
  Hatboro *(G-7311)*

FABRICS: Lacings, Textile

Lear Corporation ....G 570 345-2611
  Pine Grove *(G-14598)*

FABRICS: Laminated

Aberdeen Road Company ....D 717 764-1192
  Emigsville *(G-4983)*

Akas Tex LLC ....F 215 244-2589
  Bensalem *(G-1146)*

Clarion Boards LLC ....C 814 226-0851
  Shippenville *(G-17557)*

Clarion Laminates LLC ....D 814 226-8032
  Shippenville *(G-17559)*

FABRICS: Manmade Fiber, Narrow

Bally Ribbon Mills ....C 610 845-2211
  Bally *(G-900)*

Bally Ribbon Mills ....E 610 845-2211
  Bally *(G-902)*

Textemp LLC ....F 215 322-9670
  Quakertown *(G-16249)*

FABRICS: Marquisettes, From Manmade Fiber

Dwell America Holdings Inc ....E 717 272-4665
  Lebanon *(G-9563)*

FABRICS: Metallized

Bruce Banning ....G 724 226-0818
  Natrona Heights *(G-11936)*

Nye Technical Sales ....G 610 639-9985
  Downingtown *(G-4246)*

FABRICS: Nonwoven

Armstrong/Kover Kwick Inc ....E 412 771-2200
  Mc Kees Rocks *(G-10603)*

Chicopee Inc ....G 800 835-2442
  Smithfield *(G-17647)*

First Quality Enterprises Inc ....C 570 384-1600
  Hazleton *(G-7498)*

Horizon House Inc ....G 610 532-7423
  Darby *(G-4019)*

Microsilver Wear LLC ....G 215 917-7203
  Yardley *(G-20325)*

Monadnock Non-Wovens LLC ....E 570 839-9210
  Mount Pocono *(G-11735)*

Sellars Nonwovens ....E 610 593-5145
  Atglen *(G-807)*

United States Hardmetal ....G 724 834-8381
  Greensburg *(G-6725)*

FABRICS: Nylon, Broadwoven

Craftex Mills Inc Pennsylvania ....E 610 941-1212
  Blue Bell *(G-1824)*

FABRICS: Oilcloth

Freckled Sage ....G 610 888-2037
  Philadelphia *(G-13722)*

FABRICS: Press Cloth

Ed Cini Enterprises Inc ....G 215 432-3855
  Plumsteadville *(G-15809)*

FABRICS: Rayon, Narrow

American Ribbon Manufacturers ....E 570 421-7470
  Stroudsburg *(G-18102)*

FABRICS: Resin Or Plastic Coated

Curbell Inc ....G 724 772-6800
  Cranberry Township *(G-3813)*

Fielco LLC ....G 215 674-8700
  Huntingdon Valley *(G-7981)*

Ltl Color Compounders LLC ....D 215 736-1126
  Morrisville *(G-11570)*

Performnce Ctngs Intl Labs LLC ....F 610 588-7900
  Bangor *(G-924)*

Poward Plastics Incorporated ....G 484 660-3690
  Hamburg *(G-6849)*

FABRICS: Rubberized

Lebanon Gasket and Seal Inc ....G 717 274-3684
  Lebanon *(G-9600)*

FABRICS: Shirting, Cotton

Norfab Corporation ....E 610 275-7270
  Norristown *(G-12694)*

FABRICS: Specialty Including Twisted Weaves, Broadwoven

Fabric Development Inc ....C 215 536-1420
  Quakertown *(G-16192)*

Material Tech & Logistics Inc ....D 570 487-6162
  Jessup *(G-8332)*

Sauquoit Industries LLC ....D 570 348-2751
  Scranton *(G-17283)*

FABRICS: Spunbonded

Pfnonwovens LLC ....B 570 384-1600
  Hazle Township *(G-7472)*

FABRICS: Table Cover, Cotton

Bright Banners ....G 570 326-3524
  Williamsport *(G-19994)*

FABRICS: Tricot

Milco Industries Inc ....C 570 784-0400
  Bloomsburg *(G-1790)*

FABRICS: Trimmings

A & W Screen Printing Inc ....F 717 738-2726
  Ephrata *(G-5089)*

Ad-Art Sign Co ....G 412 373-0960
  Pittsburgh *(G-14649)*

Al Tedeschi ....G 724 746-3755
  Canonsburg *(G-2535)*

American Ribbon Manufacturers ....E 570 421-7470
  Stroudsburg *(G-18103)*

B L Tees Inc ....F 724 325-1882
  Export *(G-5591)*

Berwick Offray LLC ....B 570 752-5934
  Berwick *(G-1311)*

Berwick Offray LLC ....A 570 752-5934
  Berwick *(G-1312)*

Coinco Inc ....E 814 425-7476
  Cochranton *(G-3338)*

Craig Hollern ....E 814 539-2974
  Johnstown *(G-8366)*

Dispatch Printing Inc ....F 814 870-9600
  Erie *(G-5248)*

Excl Inc ....E 412 856-7616
  Trafford *(G-18456)*

Grafika Commercial Prtg Inc ....B 610 678-8630
  Reading *(G-16396)*

Industrial Nameplate Inc ....E 215 322-1111
  Warminster *(G-18898)*

Joseph Lagrua ....G 814 274-7163
  Coudersport *(G-3783)*

Lawrence Schiff Silk Mills Inc ....D 717 776-4073
  Newville *(G-12605)*

Lesko Enterprises Inc ....C 814 756-4030
  Albion *(G-46)*

M & M Manufacturing Co ....E 724 274-0767
  Cheswick *(G-3111)*

Marco Manufacturing Co Inc ....E 215 463-2332
  Philadelphia *(G-13992)*

Mt Lebanon Awning & Tent Co ....E 412 221-2233
  Presto *(G-16104)*

Mystic Assembly & Dctg Co ....E 215 957-0280
  Warminster *(G-18926)*

Nittany Printing and Pubg Co ....D 814 238-5000
  State College *(G-18000)*

Peerless Printery ....G 610 258-5226
  Easton *(G-4741)*

Quick Print Center PA ....G 717 637-2838
  Hanover *(G-6939)*

Ras Sports Inc ....E 814 833-9111
  Erie *(G-5457)*

Rowland Printing Inc ....E 610 933-7400
  Phoenixville *(G-14575)*

Schuylkill Vly Spt Trappe Ctr ....F 877 711-8100
  Pottstown *(G-16044)*

Scream Graphix Inc ....G 215 638-3900
  Philadelphia *(G-14288)*

Screening Room Inc ....G 610 363-5405
  Exton *(G-5729)*

Shenk Athletic Equipment Co ....F 717 766-6600
  Mechanicsburg *(G-10888)*

Stineman Management Corp ....E 814 495-4686
  South Fork *(G-17778)*

T Shirt Loft ....G 724 452-4380
  Zelienople *(G-20823)*

T Shirt Printer ....G 717 367-1167
  Elizabethtown *(G-4889)*

Thomas A Laskowski ....F 215 957-1544
  Warminster *(G-18981)*

Tukes Tearoff ....G 570 695-3171
  Tremont *(G-18483)*

Vocam Corp ....G 215 348-7115
  Doylestown *(G-4344)*

Warrior Wiper Wraps LLC ....G....... 720 577-9499
Philadelphia *(G-14461)*

FABRICS: Trimmings, Textile

Fine Trim Line LLC.............................G....... 717 642-9032
Fairfield *(G-5767)*
Horn Textile Inc ....E....... 814 827-3606
Titusville *(G-18384)*

FABRICS: Tubing, Seamless, Cotton

York Textile Products Inc ....G....... 717 764-2528
York *(G-20751)*

FABRICS: Tubing, Textile, Varnished

Chapel Hill Mfg Co ....F....... 215 884-3614
Oreland *(G-13020)*

FABRICS: Upholstery, Cotton

Akas Tex LLC ....F....... 215 244-2589
Bensalem *(G-1146)*

FABRICS: Wall Covering, From Manmade Fiber Or Silk

MBA Design & Display Pdts Corp ....G....... 610 524-7590
Exton *(G-5709)*
Shaffer Desouza Brown Inc ....F....... 610 449-6400
Havertown *(G-7427)*

FABRICS: Weft Or Circular Knit

Chapel Hill Mfg Co ....F....... 215 884-3614
Oreland *(G-13020)*
Jetnet Corporation ....D....... 412 741-0100
Sewickley *(G-17396)*
Robert W Turner................................G....... 610 372-8863
Reading *(G-16501)*

FABRICS: Wool, Broadwoven

Craftex Mills Inc Pennsylvania ....E....... 610 941-1212
Blue Bell *(G-1824)*
Woolrich Inc ....C....... 570 769-6464
Woolrich *(G-20220)*

FABRICS: Woven Wire, Made From Purchased Wire

Nick-Of-Time Textiles Ltd ....G....... 610 395-4641
Allentown *(G-332)*

FABRICS: Woven, Narrow Cotton, Wool, Silk

Bally Ribbon Mills ....E....... 610 845-2211
Bally *(G-901)*
Chase Corporation............................E....... 412 828-1500
Pittsburgh *(G-14840)*
Juniata Fabrics Inc ....F....... 814 944-9381
Altoona *(G-519)*
Plum Manufacturing Co Inc ....G....... 215 520-2236
North Wales *(G-12825)*
Russell Ribbon & Trim Co ....G....... 215 938-8550
Huntingdon Valley *(G-8031)*
Tapestration.....................................G....... 215 536-0977
Quakertown *(G-16248)*
Wayne Mills Company Inc ....D....... 215 842-2134
Philadelphia *(G-14463)*
William J Dixon Company ....E....... 610 524-1131
Exton *(G-5750)*

FABRICS: Yarn-Dyed, Cotton

Aura Tiedye ....G....... 888 474-2872
Equinunk *(G-5159)*
Globe Dye Works ....E....... 215 288-4554
Philadelphia *(G-13772)*

FACILITIES SUPPORT SVCS

Metalsa SA De CV ....C....... 610 371-7000
Reading *(G-16441)*

FACSIMILE COMMUNICATION EQPT

Advanced Laser Printer S ....G....... 717 764-3272
York *(G-20369)*
Copitech Associates...........................G....... 570 963-1391
Scranton *(G-17219)*

FAMILY CLOTHING STORES

Greco International Inc.......................F....... 215 628-2557
Ambler *(G-580)*
Nittany EMB & Digitizing ....F....... 814 359-0905
State College *(G-17998)*

FANS, BLOWING: Indl Or Commercial

General Air Products Inc ....E....... 610 524-8950
Exton *(G-5685)*
Mas Engineering LLC ....F....... 724 652-1367
New Castle *(G-12120)*
Tri Bms LLC ....E....... 610 495-9700
Spring City *(G-17870)*

FANS, EXHAUST: Indl Or Commercial

Exhaust Track Inc ....G....... 215 675-1021
Warminster *(G-18875)*
ODonnell Metal Fabricators ....F....... 610 279-8810
Norristown *(G-12697)*

FANS, VENTILATING: Indl Or Commercial

Tuscarora Electric Mfg Co....................G....... 570 836-2101
Tunkhannock *(G-18551)*

FANS: Ceiling

Lasko Group Inc................................D....... 610 692-7400
West Chester *(G-19587)*

FARM & GARDEN MACHINERY WHOLESALERS

Farm-Bilt Machine LLC......................F....... 717 442-5020
Gap *(G-6251)*
Farmer Boy Ag Inc ....D....... 717 866-7565
Myerstown *(G-11885)*
Somerset Welding & Steel Inc ....E....... 814 444-7000
Somerset *(G-17711)*
Somerset Welding & Steel Inc ....C....... 814 443-2671
Somerset *(G-17710)*

FARM BUREAUS

Bedford Farm Bureau Coop Assn ....F....... 814 793-2721
Curryville *(G-3945)*

FARM MACHINERY REPAIR SVCS

DC Welding ....G....... 717 361-9400
Elizabethtown *(G-4871)*
Holtrys LLC ....F....... 717 532-7261
Roxbury *(G-16838)*
I & J Manufacturing LLC....................G....... 717 442-9451
Gordonville *(G-6558)*
Maple Mountain Industries Inc ....E....... 724 676-4703
New Florence *(G-12198)*
Pequea Planter LLC ....F....... 717 442-4406
Gap *(G-6255)*
S W Machine ....G....... 717 336-2699
Stevens *(G-18056)*
Z Weldco ....G....... 610 689-8773
Oley *(G-12982)*

FARM PRDTS, RAW MATERIAL, WHOLESALE: Tobacco & Tobacco Prdts

Lancaster Leaf Tob Co PA Inc..............E....... 717 394-2676
Lancaster *(G-9097)*
Lancaster Leaf Tob Co PA Inc..............G....... 717 393-1526
Lancaster *(G-9099)*

FARM PRDTS, RAW MATERIALS, WHOLESALE: Fibers, Vegetable

Haycarb Usa Inc ....G....... 281 292-8678
Oakdale *(G-12900)*

FARM PRDTS, RAW MATERIALS, WHOLESALE: Sugar

CSC Sugar LLC ....F....... 215 428-3670
Fairless Hills *(G-5777)*

FARM SPLY STORES

Davis Feed of Bucks County ....G....... 215 257-2966
Perkasie *(G-13272)*
Knittle & Frey AG-Center Inc ....G....... 570 323-7554
Williamsport *(G-20032)*

Mc Crackens Feed Mill Inc ....F....... 717 665-2186
Manheim *(G-10395)*
Organic Unlimited Inc........................G....... 610 593-2995
Atglen *(G-802)*
Rockwells Feed Farm & Pet Sup ....G....... 877 797-4575
Wellsboro *(G-19472)*

FARM SPLYS WHOLESALERS

Bedford Farm Bureau Coop Assn ....F....... 814 623-6194
Bedford *(G-1040)*
Cochecton Mills Inc ....E....... 570 224-4144
Honesdale *(G-7707)*
Groffdale Machine Co Inc....................G....... 717 656-3249
Leola *(G-9785)*
Laneys Feed Mill Inc ....F....... 814 643-3211
Huntingdon *(G-7950)*
Natural Soil Products Company ....D....... 570 695-2211
Tremont *(G-18481)*

FARM SPLYS, WHOLESALE: Equestrian Eqpt

Dr Davies Products Inc......................G....... 570 321-5423
Williamsport *(G-20007)*
Smuckers Harness Shop Inc ....F....... 717 445-5956
Narvon *(G-11927)*

FARM SPLYS, WHOLESALE: Feed

Agricultural Commodities Inc................D....... 717 624-6858
Gettysburg *(G-6282)*
Albrights Mill LLC ....E....... 610 756-6022
Kempton *(G-8489)*
Best Feeds & Farm Supplies Inc ....C....... 724 693-9417
Oakdale *(G-12894)*
Cargill Incorporated..........................E....... 814 793-2137
Martinsburg *(G-10521)*
F M Browns Sons Incorporated............E....... 610 582-2741
Birdsboro *(G-1695)*
F M Browns Sons Incorporated............D....... 800 334-8816
Reading *(G-16384)*
Leroy M Sensenig Inc ....E....... 717 354-4756
New Holland *(G-12257)*
Meiserville Milling Co ....G....... 570 539-8855
Mount Pleasant Mills *(G-11727)*
Waynesburg Milling Co ....G....... 724 627-6137
Waynesburg *(G-19452)*

FARM SPLYS, WHOLESALE: Fertilizers & Agricultural Chemicals

Chemgro Fertilizer Co Inc ....F....... 717 935-2185
Belleville *(G-1129)*
Frontier Wood Products Inc.................E....... 215 538-2330
Quakertown *(G-16195)*
Helena Chemical Company ....G....... 724 538-3304
Evans City *(G-5559)*
Pine Valley Supply Corporation............G....... 215 676-8100
Philadelphia *(G-14178)*

FARM SPLYS, WHOLESALE: Greenhouse Eqpt & Splys

Edward Hecht Importers Inc ....G....... 215 925-5520
Philadelphia *(G-13661)*
Jaybird Manufacturing Inc ....G....... 814 364-1800
Centre Hall *(G-2842)*

FARM SPLYS, WHOLESALE: Harness Eqpt

Beilers Manufacturing & Supply............G....... 717 768-0174
Ronks *(G-16804)*
Beilers Manufacturing & Supply............F....... 717 656-2179
Leola *(G-9772)*
E Z Sensenig & Son ....G....... 717 445-5580
New Holland *(G-12246)*

FASTENERS WHOLESALERS

Associated Fasteners Inc....................F....... 610 837-9200
Bath *(G-951)*
Fabtex Inc ....C....... 570 275-7500
Danville *(G-4000)*
General Manufacturing Co ....F....... 412 833-4300
Bethel Park *(G-1415)*
Jnb Industrial Supply Inc ....G....... 412 455-5170
Blawnox *(G-1764)*

PRODUCT

FASTENERS: Brads, Alum, Brass/Other Nonferrous Metal/Wire

Cmg Process Inc ....E 724 962-8717
Clark (G-3188)

FASTENERS: Metal

Back Bay Industries Inc ....G 724 941-5825
Venetia (G-18741)

Cordray Corporation ....F 610 644-6200
King of Prussia (G-8598)

Griffin Sealing LLC ....G 267 328-6600
Kulpsville (G-8828)

Robvon Backing Ring Co Inc ....F 570 945-3800
Factoryville (G-5761)

World Resources Company ....E 570 622-4747
Pottsville (G-16103)

FASTENERS: Metal

Aviva Technology Inc ....G 610 228-4689
Broomall (G-2279)

B G M Fastener Co Inc ....E 570 253-5046
Honesdale (G-7701)

Peerless Hardware Mfg Co ....F 717 684-2889
Columbia (G-3447)

Penn Engineering & Mfg Corp ....B 215 766-8853
Danboro (G-3991)

San-Fab Co Inc ....G 570 385-2551
Schuylkill Haven (G-17166)

Standard Steel Specialty Co ....D 724 846-7600
Beaver Falls (G-1014)

V2r2 LLC ....G 215 277-2181
Harleysville (G-7063)

Yardley Products LLC ....E 215 493-2700
Yardley (G-20346)

FASTENERS: Notions, NEC

American Fastener Tech Corp ....F 724 444-6940
Gibsonia (G-6323)

Bolt Works Inc ....F 724 776-7273
Warrendale (G-19069)

Dorman Products Inc ....C 215 997-1800
Colmar (G-3416)

Ideal Building Fasteners Inc ....F 412 299-6199
Coraopolis (G-3699)

Innovation Plus Llc ....G 610 272-2600
King of Prussia (G-8634)

Inofast Manufacturing Inc ....G 215 996-9963
Hatfield (G-7354)

Maclean Saegertown LLC ....G 814 763-2655
Saegertown (G-16924)

Southco Inc ....A 610 459-4000
Concordville (G-3459)

FATTY ACID ESTERS & AMINOS

N3 Oceanic Inc ....E 215 541-1073
Pennsburg (G-13251)

FEATHERS & FEATHER PRODUCTS

American Plume Fancy Feather ....F 570 586-8400
S Abingtn Twp (G-16889)

FELT PARTS

Aetna Felt Corp ....D 610 791-0900
Allentown (G-117)

FELTS: Saturated

Lectromat Inc ....F 724 625-3502
Mars (G-10505)

FENCE POSTS: Iron & Steel

Franklin Industries Inc ....B 814 437-3726
Franklin (G-6129)

Premier Fence & Iron Works Inc ....G 267 567-2078
Philadelphia (G-14197)

FENCES & FENCING MATERIALS

Leahmarlin Corp ....G 610 692-7378
West Chester (G-19589)

Myerstown Sheds ....G 717 866-7644
Lebanon (G-9613)

FENCES OR POSTS: Ornamental Iron Or Steel

American Ornamental Iron Corp ....F 724 639-8684
Saltsburg (G-17050)

Heritage Fence Company ....F 610 584-6710
Skippack (G-17599)

Heritage Industries Inc ....G 412 435-0091
Pittsburgh (G-15091)

International Gate Devices ....G 610 461-0811
Folsom (G-6025)

Jerith Manufacturing LLC ....D 215 676-4068
Philadelphia (G-13893)

Mountain Metal Studio Inc ....G 724 329-0238
Markleysburg (G-10482)

FENCING DEALERS

All Type Fence Co Inc ....G 610 718-1151
Douglassville (G-4166)

American Fence Inc ....F 610 437-1944
Whitehall (G-19861)

Helm Fencing Inc ....E 215 822-5595
Hatfield (G-7348)

Heritage Fence Company ....F 610 584-6710
Skippack (G-17599)

Machining Center ....G 724 530-7212
Slippery Rock (G-17621)

Prestige Fence Co Inc ....D 215 362-8200
Hatfield (G-7385)

Rusticraft Fence Co ....G 610 644-6770
Malvern (G-10311)

Sonco Worldwide Inc ....F 215 337-9651
Bristol (G-2200)

The Adirondack Group Inc ....E 610 431-4343
West Chester (G-19660)

FENCING MADE IN WIREDRAWING PLANTS

County Line Fence Co ....F 215 343-5085
Warrington (G-19112)

Omega Fence Co ....G 215 729-7474
Philadelphia (G-14094)

FENCING MATERIALS: Docks & Other Outdoor Prdts, Wood

Calvert Lumber Company Inc ....F 724 346-5553
Sharon (G-17430)

Honeybrook Woodworks ....F 610 593-6884
Christiana (G-3135)

Northeast Products & Svcs Inc ....G 610 899-0286
Topton (G-18414)

FENCING MATERIALS: Plastic

Heritage Fence & Deck LLC ....G 610 476-0003
Skippack (G-17598)

John Wall Inc ....F 724 966-9255
Carmichaels (G-2759)

K D Home & Garden Inc ....F 610 929-5794
Temple (G-18331)

LLC Snyder Gates ....G 877 621-0195
Millerstown (G-11205)

Marietta Fence Experts LLC ....G 724 925-6100
Hunker (G-7929)

Proplastix International Inc ....C 717 692-4733
Millersburg (G-11198)

Quality Fencing & Supply ....E 717 355-7112
New Holland (G-12276)

Superior Plastic Products Inc ....E 717 355-7100
New Holland (G-12288)

Superior Plastic Products LLC ....G 717 556-3240
Leola (G-9806)

United Fence Supply Company ....G 570 307-0782
Olyphant (G-13002)

FENCING MATERIALS: Wood

All Type Fence Co Inc ....G 610 718-1151
Douglassville (G-4166)

Helm Fencing Inc ....E 215 822-5595
Hatfield (G-7348)

J/M Fence & Deck Company ....G 610 488-7382
Mohrsville (G-11276)

Leahmarlin Corp ....G 610 692-7378
West Chester (G-19589)

Manley Fence Co ....G 610 842-8833
Coatesville (G-3316)

New Holland Fence LLC ....F 717 355-2204
New Holland (G-12265)

Prestige Fence Co Inc ....D 215 362-8200
Hatfield (G-7385)

Rusticraft Fence Co ....G 610 644-6770
Malvern (G-10311)

The Adirondack Group Inc ....E 610 431-4343
West Chester (G-19660)

FERRALLOY ORES, EXC VANADIUM

Langeloth Metallurgical Co LLC ....C 724 947-2201
Langeloth (G-9270)

FERRITES

National Magnetics Group Inc ....E 610 867-7600
Bethlehem (G-1578)

National Magnetics Group Inc ....E 610 867-7600
Bethlehem (G-1580)

National Magnetics Group Inc ....E 610 867-7600
Bethlehem (G-1581)

FERROALLOYS

Elkem Holding Inc ....B 412 299-7200
Coraopolis (G-3687)

Elkem Materials Inc ....G 412 299-7200
Coraopolis (G-3688)

Reading Alloys Inc ....C 610 693-5822
Robesonia (G-16777)

FERROALLOYS: Produced In Blast Furnaces

Ellwood Group Inc ....E 724 658-3685
New Castle (G-12084)

FERROMOLYBDENUM

BMC Liquidation Company ....E 724 431-2800
Butler (G-2382)

Evergreen Metallurgical LLC ....G 724 431-2800
Butler (G-2400)

FERROUS METALS: Reclaimed From Clay

Northeastern Hydro-Seeding Inc ....G 570 668-1108
Tamaqua (G-18222)

FERTILIZER MINERAL MINING

Corry Peat Products Co Inc ....G 814 665-7101
Corry (G-3756)

FERTILIZER, AGRICULTURAL: Wholesalers

Timac Agro Usa Inc ....E 610 375-7272
Reading (G-16539)

FERTILIZERS: NEC

Bedford Farm Bureau Coop Assn ....F 814 623-6194
Bedford (G-1040)

Bedford Farm Bureau Coop Assn ....F 814 793-2721
Curryville (G-3945)

Cornell Bros Inc ....F 570 376-2471
Middlebury Center (G-11043)

Dyno Nobel Inc ....E 724 379-8100
Donora (G-4152)

Growmark Fs LLC ....G 814 359-2725
Bellefonte (G-1102)

Growmark Fs LLC ....E 724 543-1101
Adrian (G-30)

International Raw Mtls Ltd ....E 215 928-1010
Philadelphia (G-13867)

J R Peters Inc ....E 610 395-7104
Allentown (G-267)

Joe Grow Inc ....F 814 355-2878
Bellefonte (G-1106)

Kirby Agri Inc ....E 717 299-2541
Lancaster (G-9087)

Klingler Incorporated ....G 717 535-5151
Thompsontown (G-18347)

Laurel Valley Farms Inc ....E 610 268-2074
Landenberg (G-9251)

Magnesita Refractories Company ....C 717 792-3611
York (G-20574)

Mainville AG Services Inc ....G 570 784-6922
Bloomsburg (G-1789)

Moyer & Son Inc ....C 215 799-2000
Souderton (G-17753)

Pine Valley Supply Corporation ....G 215 676-8100
Philadelphia (G-14178)

Scotts Company LLC ....E 610 268-3006
Avondale (G-860)

Synatek LP ....D...... 888 408-5433
  Souderton (G-17767)
Webbs Super-Gro Products Inc ....E 570 726-4525
  Mill Hall (G-11184)

FERTILIZERS: Nitrogen Solutions

Growmark Fs LLC ....E 724 543-1101
  Adrian (G-30)

FERTILIZERS: Nitrogenous

Agrium Advanced Tech US Inc ....G 724 865-9180
  Butler (G-2372)
Chemgro Fertilizer Co Inc ....F 717 935-2185
  Belleville (G-1129)
Cumberland Valley Coop Assn ....E 717 532-2197
  Shippensburg (G-17525)
Dyno Nobel Inc ....E 724 379-8100
  Donora (G-4152)
Growmark Fs LLC ....E 814 359-2725
  Bellefonte (G-1102)
International Raw Mtls Ltd ....E 215 928-1010
  Philadelphia (G-13867)
Laurel Valley Farms Inc ....E 610 268-2074
  Landenberg (G-9251)
Smart Fertilizer LLC ....E 814 880-8873
  State College (G-18026)
Timac Agro Usa Inc ....E 610 375-7272
  Reading (G-16539)

FERTILIZERS: Phosphatic

Agricultural Commodities Inc ....D...... 717 624-6858
  Gettysburg (G-6282)
Growmark Fs LLC ....E 724 543-1101
  Adrian (G-30)
Growmark Fs LLC ....E 610 926-6339
  Leesport (G-9664)
Growmark Fs LLC ....F 717 854-3818
  York (G-20515)
Growmark Fs LLC ....E 814 359-2725
  Bellefonte (G-1102)
International Raw Mtls Ltd ....E 215 928-1010
  Philadelphia (G-13867)
Occidental Chemical Corp ....F 610 327-4145
  Pottstown (G-16022)
Willard Agri-Service Inc ....F 717 375-2229
  Marion (G-10471)

FIBER & FIBER PRDTS: Cigarette Tow Cellulosic

Quik Piks & Paks Inc ....G...... 570 459-3099
  Hazle Township (G-7477)

FIBER & FIBER PRDTS: Elastomeric

Arlanxeo USA Holdings Corp ....G 412 809-1000
  Pittsburgh (G-14723)
Arlanxeo USA LLC ....B 412 809-1000
  Pittsburgh (G-14724)
SRC Elastomerics Inc ....D 215 335-2049
  Philadelphia (G-14336)

FIBER & FIBER PRDTS: Organic, Noncellulose

Abtrex Industries Inc ....E 724 266-5425
  Leetsdale (G-9676)
Gudebrod Inc ....C 610 327-4050
  Pottstown (G-15993)
Solutia Inc ....C 724 258-6200
  Monongahela (G-11316)

FIBER & FIBER PRDTS: Synthetic Cellulosic

Atwater Inc ....D 570 779-9568
  Plymouth (G-15815)
C P Converters Inc ....D 717 764-1193
  York (G-20415)
Carpenter Co ....C 814 944-8612
  Altoona (G-486)
Forta Corporation ....E 724 458-5221
  Grove City (G-6785)
FP Woll & Company ....E 215 934-5966
  Philadelphia (G-13717)
Ne Fibers LLC ....E 610 366-8600
  Allentown (G-326)

FIBER OPTICS

Dqe Communications LLC ....G....... 412 393-1033
  Pittsburgh (G-14936)
Fibertel Inc ....F 570 714-7189
  Plymouth (G-15817)
Martra LLC ....G 610 444-9469
  Kennett Square (G-8525)
Qualastat Electronics Inc ....E 717 253-9301
  Gettysburg (G-6311)

FIBER PRDTS: Pressed, Wood Pulp, From Purchased Materials

Erie Energy Products Inc ....F 814 454-2828
  Erie (G-5266)

FIBERS: Carbon & Graphite

Caldwell Corporation ....E 814 486-3493
  Emporium (G-5051)
Lancer Systems LP ....E 610 973-2600
  Quakertown (G-16208)

FILE FOLDERS

Alfred Envelope Company Inc ....F 215 739-1500
  Philadelphia (G-13362)
Tele-Media Sfp LLC ....E 570 271-0810
  Danville (G-4014)

FILLING SVCS: Pressure Containers

Encotech Inc ....E 724 222-3334
  Eighty Four (G-4839)

FILM & SHEET: Unsuppported Plastic

Abtrex Industries Inc ....E 724 266-5425
  Leetsdale (G-9676)
Acton Technologies Inc ....D...... 570 654-0612
  Pittston (G-15741)
Berry Global Inc ....B 570 759-6240
  Berwick (G-1309)
Berry Global Inc ....E 814 849-4234
  Brookville (G-2248)
Cpg International LLC ....F 570 348-0997
  Scranton (G-17223)
CPI Scranton Inc ....B 570 558-8000
  Scranton (G-17225)
Delstar Technologies Inc ....G 717 866-7472
  Richland (G-16685)
Dunmore Corporation ....D 215 781-8895
  Bristol (G-2134)
Dunmore International Corp ....G 215 781-8895
  Bristol (G-2135)
Easter Unlimited Inc ....E 814 542-8661
  Mount Union (G-11744)
Ensinger Penn Fibre Inc ....D...... 215 702-9551
  Bensalem (G-1190)
Gateway Packaging Corp ....E 724 327-7400
  Export (G-5607)
Honeywell International Inc ....B 570 621-6000
  Pottsville (G-16080)
J Benson Corp ....G 610 678-2692
  Reading (G-16411)
Meadville New Products Inc ....F 814 336-2174
  Meadville (G-10759)
Omnova Solutions Inc ....B 570 366-1051
  Auburn (G-820)
Penn Fibre & Specialty Co ....G....... 215 702-9551
  Bensalem (G-1242)
PPG Architectural Finishes Inc ....D...... 610 380-6200
  Downingtown (G-4250)
Protostar Technologies ....G....... 484 988-0964
  Lincoln University (G-9974)
Robert Mrvel Plastic Mulch LLC ....F 717 838-0976
  Annville (G-658)
Simona America Inc ....D 570 579-1300
  Archbald (G-694)
Specialty Extrusion Inc ....G 610 792-3800
  Royersford (G-16865)
Tech Packaging Inc ....E 570 759-7717
  Hazle Township (G-7483)
Tredegar Corporation ....C 570 544-7600
  Pottsville (G-16100)
United Laminations Inc ....F 570 876-1360
  Mayfield (G-10544)
Westlake Plastics Company ....C 610 459-1000
  Lenni (G-9763)
Westlake United Corporation ....F 570 876-0222
  Mayfield (G-10545)

FILM: Motion Picture

Creative Thought Media LLC ....G 267 270-5147
  Philadelphia (G-13579)
Lions World Media LLC ....F 917 645-7590
  Bushkill (G-2366)
Lunacor Inc ....G 610 328-6150
  Springfield (G-17917)

FILTER ELEMENTS: Fluid & Hydraulic Line

A-1 Babbitt Co Inc ....F 724 379-6588
  Donora (G-4144)
Diversatech Industrial LLC ....G 724 887-4199
  Connellsville (G-3495)

FILTERING MEDIA: Pottery

Chem-Clay Corporation ....E 412 276-6333
  Carnegie (G-2765)

FILTERS

Advanced Machine Technologies ....G....... 717 871-9724
  Millersville (G-11209)
Ameri-Surce Specialty Pdts Inc ....E 412 831-9400
  Bethel Park (G-1402)
American Tool Mfg LLC ....G 610 837-8573
  Bath (G-950)
Ddp Specialty Electronic MA ....G 610 244-6000
  Collegeville (G-3374)
Ecco/Gregory Inc ....E 610 840-0390
  West Chester (G-19545)
Eisenhower Tool Inc ....F 215 538-9381
  Quakertown (G-16187)
Enhanced Systems & Products ....G 215 794-6942
  Doylestown (G-4299)
Filpro Corporation ....F 215 699-4510
  North Wales (G-12801)
Filter Shine Inc ....G 866 977-4463
  Reinholds (G-16631)
Filter Technology Inc ....G 866 992-9490
  Gladwyne (G-6407)
Filtrtion of Wstn Pnnsylvania ....G 412 855-7372
  Cranberry Township (G-3818)
Fluid Conditioning Pdts Inc ....E 717 627-1550
  Lititz (G-10008)
Full-On Filters ....G 610 970-4701
  Pottstown (G-15989)
Grace Filter Company Inc ....G 610 664-5790
  Philadelphia (G-13778)
Green Filter Usa Inc ....E 724 430-2050
  Mount Braddock (G-11617)
Knight Corporation ....E 610 853-2161
  Havertown (G-7423)
Mar Cor Purification Inc ....C 800 633-3080
  Skippack (G-17600)
Met-Pro Technologies LLC ....E 215 822-1963
  Telford (G-18303)
Next Generation Filtration ....G 412 548-1659
  Pittsburgh (G-15335)
Pall Corporation ....D 610 458-9500
  Exton (G-5722)
Penn-Central Industries Inc ....G 814 371-3211
  Du Bois (G-4413)
Schroeder Industries LLC ....D 724 318-1100
  Leetsdale (G-9704)
Skc Gulf Coast Inc ....G 724 677-0340
  Smock (G-17667)
Spectrum Microwave Inc ....E 814 272-2700
  State College (G-18033)
Synergy Applications Inc ....F 814 454-8803
  Erie (G-5501)
Tri-Dim Filter Corporation ....F 610 481-9926
  Allentown (G-414)
Wayne Products Inc ....F 800 255-5665
  Broomall (G-2305)

FILTERS & SOFTENERS: Water, Household

Aqua Treatment Services Inc ....E 717 697-4998
  Mechanicsburg (G-10820)
C-B Tool Co ....E 717 397-3521
  Lancaster (G-8967)
Lester Water Inc ....E 610 444-4660
  Kennett Square (G-8522)
Pure Flow Water Co ....G 215 723-0237
  Souderton (G-17761)
Trilli Holdings Inc ....G 724 736-8000
  Star Junction (G-17938)
Zero Technologies LLC ....F 215 244-0823
  Trevose (G-18509)

P
R
O
D
U
C
T

FILTERS & STRAINERS: Pipeline

Erie Metal Basket Inc ....F 814 833-1745
Erie (G-5270)
Filterfab Manufacturing Corp ....G 724 643-4000
Industry (G-8136)

FILTERS: Air

Air Dynmics Indus Systems Corp ....F 717 854-4050
York (G-20370)
Air Turbine Propeller Company ....E 724 452-9540
Zelienople (G-20787)
Ceco Filters Inc ....F 215 723-8155
Telford (G-18272)
Clark Filter Inc ....G 717 285-5941
Lancaster (G-8979)
Filter Service & Installation ....G 724 274-5220
Cheswick (G-3109)
Full-On Filters ....G 610 970-4701
Pottstown (G-15989)
G-O-Metric Incorporated ....G 814 376-6940
Philipsburg (G-14514)
Historic York Inc ....G 717 843-0320
York (G-20523)
McCleary Heating & Cooling LLC ....F 717 263-3833
Chambersburg (G-2959)
Precision Filtration Pdts Inc ....E 215 679-6645
Pennsburg (G-13252)
RAF Industries Inc ....F 215 572-0738
Jenkintown (G-8299)
Tri State Filter Mfg Co ....G 412 621-8491
Pittsburgh (G-15644)

FILTERS: Air Intake, Internal Combustion Engine, Exc Auto

Kaf-Tech Industries Inc ....G 724 523-2343
Jeannette (G-8259)

FILTERS: General Line, Indl

A Stucki Company ....E 412 424-0560
Coraopolis (G-3653)
Air Liquid Systems Inc ....G 724 834-8090
Forbes Road (G-6040)
Matthew McKeon ....G 215 234-8505
Green Lane (G-6589)
Oil Process Systems Inc ....E 610 437-4618
Allentown (G-337)
Separation Technologies Inc ....G 724 325-4546
Export (G-5626)
Service Filtration Corp ....E 717 656-2161
Lancaster (G-9194)

FILTRATION DEVICES: Electronic

Chemrock Corporation ....F 610 667-6640
Bala Cynwyd (G-875)
Customized Envmtl Systems ....G 412 380-2311
Pittsburgh (G-14896)
Ikor Industries Inc ....D 302 456-0280
Kennett Square (G-8514)
Mar Cor Purification Inc ....C 800 633-3080
Skippack (G-17600)
Schneider Electric It Corp ....B 717 948-1200
Middletown (G-11074)
Spectrum Control Inc ....B 814 474-2207
Fairview (G-5842)
Spectrum Control Inc ....C 814 272-2700
State College (G-18031)
Spectrum Control Inc ....C 814 474-1571
Fairview (G-5843)
Spectrum Control Inc ....C 814 835-4000
Fairview (G-5844)
Spectrum Control Inc ....E 814 272-2700
State College (G-18032)
Spectrum Control Inc ....G 814 474-4315
Fairview (G-5845)
Unifilt Corporation ....G 717 823-0313
Wilkes Barre (G-19966)

FINANCIAL SVCS

Lang Speciality Trailers LLC ....G 724 972-6590
Latrobe (G-9487)
Mg Financial Services Inc ....E 215 364-7555
Fort Washington (G-6086)

FINDINGS & TRIMMINGS Shoulder Straps, Women's Undergarments

Annville Shoulder Strap Co ....E 717 867-4831
Annville (G-642)

FINDINGS & TRIMMINGS: Apparel

Yarrington Mills Corporation ....E 215 674-5125
Hatboro (G-7311)

FINDINGS & TRIMMINGS: Fabric

Auto Accessories America Inc ....C 717 667-3004
Reedsville (G-16621)
Grip-Flex Corp ....E 215 743-7492
Philadelphia (G-13789)

FINISHING AGENTS: Textile

Leatex Chemical Co ....E 215 739-2000
Philadelphia (G-13964)

FIRE ARMS, SMALL: Guns Or Gun Parts, 30 mm & Below

American Built Arms Company ....G 443 807-3022
Glen Rock (G-6450)
Anthony Burney ....G 412 606-7336
Monongahela (G-11304)
Combat Arms LLC ....G 412 245-0824
Carlisle (G-2702)
Ford City Gun Workd ....G 724 994-9501
Ford City (G-6045)
Gunsmiths Stainless Clg Rods ....G 215 256-9208
Harleysville (G-7035)
Iwi Us Inc ....E 717 695-2081
Middletown (G-11058)
Lesleh Precision Inc ....E 724 823-0901
Rostraver Township (G-16827)
Micro Facture LLC ....E 717 285-9700
Mountville (G-11799)
Penn Arms Inc ....E 814 938-5279
Jamestown (G-8238)
S & K Scope Mounts ....G 814 489-3091
Sugar Grove (G-18146)
Tar Hunt Custom Rifles Inc ....G 570 784-6368
Bloomsburg (G-1803)

FIRE ARMS, SMALL: Pellet & BB guns

Gog Paintball USA ....G 724 520-8690
Loyalhanna (G-10111)

FIRE ARMS, SMALL: Pistols Or Pistol Parts, 30 mm & below

Saeilo Inc ....F 845 735-4500
Greeley (G-6583)

FIRE ARMS, SMALL: Rifles Or Rifle Parts, 30 mm & below

E R Shaw Inc ....E 412 212-4343
Bridgeville (G-2059)
Garrett & Co Inc ....G 800 748-4608
New Kensington (G-12341)
Keystone Sporting Arms Llc ....D 570 742-2066
Milton (G-11246)
Lancer Systems LP ....E 610 973-2600
Quakertown (G-16208)

FIRE ARMS, SMALL: Shotguns Or Shotgun Parts, 30 mm & Below

Wyss-Gallifent Corporation ....G 215 343-3974
Warrington (G-19141)

FIRE CLAY MINING

EJ Bognar Incorporated ....G 412 344-9900
Pittsburgh (G-14960)

FIRE DETECTION SYSTEMS

Kidde Fire Protection Inc ....E 610 363-1400
West Chester (G-19581)

FIRE ESCAPES

Armin Ironworks Inc ....G 412 322-1622
Pittsburgh (G-14725)

C & B Iron Inc ....G 215 536-7162
Quakertown (G-16176)

FIRE EXTINGUISHER SVC

Softboss Corp ....G 215 563-7488
Philadelphia (G-14321)

FIRE EXTINGUISHERS: Portable

Danchcks Extinguishers Svc Inc ....G 570 589-1610
Edwardsville (G-4823)
Fire 1st Defense Inc ....G 610 296-7576
Berwyn (G-1361)
Kidde Fire Protection Inc ....E 610 363-1400
West Chester (G-19581)

FIRE OR BURGLARY RESISTIVE PRDTS

B Wise Trailers ....F 717 261-0922
Chambersburg (G-2908)
Bassett Industries Inc ....E 610 327-1200
Pottstown (G-15965)
D & M Welding Co Inc ....E 717 767-9353
York (G-20440)
Great Lakes Case & Cab Co Inc ....G 814 663-6015
Corry (G-3763)
Great Lakes Case & Cab Co Inc ....C 814 734-7303
Edinboro (G-4812)
Hart McHncl-Lctrcal Contrs Inc ....E 215 257-1666
Perkasie (G-13278)
Horizon Technology Inc ....E 814 834-4004
Saint Marys (G-16980)
Louisville Ladder Inc ....G 215 638-8904
Bensalem (G-1222)
Zachary R Marella ....G 724 557-1671
Smithfield (G-17656)

FIRE PROTECTION EQPT

Chief Technologies LLC ....F 484 693-0750
Downingtown (G-4220)
D & A Emergency Equipment Inc ....G 610 691-6847
Bethlehem (G-1495)
Duncan Associates Inc ....G 717 299-6940
Lancaster (G-9003)
Gecco Inc ....G 570 945-3568
Fleetville (G-5966)
Jomarr Safety Systems Inc ....D 570 346-5330
Dunmore (G-4475)
Keystone Fire Apparatus Inc ....G 412 771-7722
Mc Kees Rocks (G-10618)
Municipal Fire Equipment Inc ....G 412 366-8180
Pittsburgh (G-15310)
National Foam Inc ....G 610 363-1400
West Chester (G-19607)
National Foam Inc ....D 610 363-1400
West Chester (G-19606)
Raceresq Inc ....G 724 891-3473
Beaver Falls (G-1010)
Trident Emergency Products LLC ....G 215 293-0700
Hatboro (G-7308)
Ziamatic Corp ....E 215 493-2777
Yardley (G-20347)

FIREARMS & AMMUNITION, EXC SPORTING, WHOLESALE

International Cartridge Corp ....F 814 938-6820
Reynoldsville (G-16657)

FIREARMS: Large, Greater Than 30mm

Evolution Gun Works Inc ....F 215 538-1012
Quakertown (G-16191)

FIREARMS: Small, 30mm or Less

Geissele Automatics LLC ....F 610 272-2060
North Wales (G-12803)
Gwynedd Manufacturing Inc ....E 610 272-2060
North Wales (G-12805)
Nonlethal Technologies Inc ....E 724 479-5100
Homer City (G-7679)
North American Arms Inc ....G 610 940-1668
Plymouth Meeting (G-15860)
Pneu-Dart Inc ....D 570 323-2710
Williamsport (G-20061)

FIREBRICK: Clay

Grc Holding Inc ....G 610 667-6640
Bala Cynwyd (G-879)

FIREFIGHTING APPARATUS

Salmen Tech Co Inc ....G....... 412 854-1822
Bethel Park *(G-1432)*

Smeal Ltc LLC ....E....... 717 918-1806
Ephrata *(G-5142)*

FIREPLACE & CHIMNEY MATERIAL: Concrete

Reecon North America LLC ....G....... 412 850-8001
Pittsburgh *(G-15475)*

FIREPLACE EQPT & ACCESS

Gregg Lane LLC ....G....... 215 269-9900
Fairless Hills *(G-5781)*

Hearth & Home Technologies LLC ....G....... 717 362-9080
Halifax *(G-6826)*

FIREPLACE LOGS: Electric

Reecon North America LLC ....G....... 412 850-8001
Pittsburgh *(G-15475)*

FIREWOOD, WHOLESALE

Gish Logging Inc ....E....... 717 369-2783
Fort Loudon *(G-6059)*

FIREWORKS

Keystone Frewrks Specialty Sls...........G....... 724 277-4294
Dunbar *(G-4442)*

Schaefer Pyrotechnics Inc ....G....... 717 687-0647
Ronks *(G-16814)*

Spectacular Fire Works USA ....G....... 570 465-2100
New Milford *(G-12400)*

Starfire Corporation.........................G....... 814 948-5164
Carrolltown *(G-2810)*

Starfire Corporation.........................G....... 814 948-5164
Northern Cambria *(G-12863)*

Zambelli Fireworks Mfg Co ....G....... 724 652-1156
New Castle *(G-12172)*

FIREWORKS DISPLAY SVCS

Starfire Corporation.........................G....... 814 948-5164
Carrolltown *(G-2810)*

FIREWORKS SHOPS

Keystone Frewrks Specialty Sls...........G....... 724 277-4294
Dunbar *(G-4442)*

FIREWORKS: Wholesalers

Schaefer Pyrotechnics Inc ....G....... 717 687-0647
Ronks *(G-16814)*

FISH & SEAFOOD MARKETS

Herkys Food Products Inc ....E....... 412 683-8511
Pittsburgh *(G-15092)*

FISH & SEAFOOD PROCESSORS: Canned Or Cured

Bar Bq Town Inc ....G....... 215 549-9666
Philadelphia *(G-13444)*

Starkist Co ....D....... 412 323-7400
Pittsburgh *(G-15578)*

FISH & SEAFOOD PROCESSORS: Fresh Or Frozen

Hills Qulty Seafood Mkts Inc ....F....... 610 359-1888
Newtown Square *(G-12576)*

Ocean King Enterprises Inc ....C....... 215 365-2500
Philadelphia *(G-14092)*

Stone Silo Foods Inc ....G....... 570 676-0809
South Sterling *(G-17788)*

FISH & SEAFOOD WHOLESALERS

Clair D Thompson & Sons Inc ....E....... 570 398-1880
Jersey Shore *(G-8311)*

Stone Silo Foods Inc ....G....... 570 676-0809
South Sterling *(G-17788)*

FISH FOOD

Dietrich Bros Dream Catchr Fly............G....... 717 267-0515
Chambersburg *(G-2925)*

FISHING EQPT: Lures

Clelan Industries Inc ....G....... 717 248-5061
Lewistown *(G-9926)*

Gaines Company ....G....... 814 435-2332
Gaines *(G-6236)*

Hi-TEC Custom Painting Inc ....F....... 724 932-2631
Jamestown *(G-8237)*

Hoyes Outdoor Products ....G....... 570 275-2953
Danville *(G-4006)*

Thomas Spinning Lures Inc ....G....... 570 226-4011
Hawley *(G-7439)*

FISHING EQPT: Nets & Seines

Gudebrod Inc ....C....... 610 327-4050
Pottstown *(G-15993)*

FITTINGS & ASSEMBLIES: Hose & Tube, Hydraulic Or Pneumatic

Applied Indus Tech — PA LLC ....G....... 724 696-3099
Mount Pleasant *(G-11686)*

Cypher Company Inc ....F....... 412 661-4913
Monroeville *(G-11331)*

Delri Industrial Supplies Inc................G....... 610 833-2070
Crum Lynne *(G-3936)*

Dispersion Tech Systems LLC ....G....... 610 832-2040
Conshohocken *(G-3539)*

Flotran Exton Inc ....G....... 610 640-4141
Malvern *(G-10236)*

Ghx Industrial LLC ....G....... 410 687-7900
Greencastle *(G-6615)*

Global Passive Safety Systems ....G....... 267 297-2340
Springfield *(G-17916)*

J & K Industrial Sales ....G....... 724 458-7670
Grove City *(G-6791)*

National Hydraulic Systems LLC...........G....... 724 628-4010
Connellsville *(G-3505)*

Penndel Hydraulic Sls & Svc Co ....G....... 215 757-2000
Langhorne *(G-9317)*

Powertrack International LLC ....G....... 412 787-4444
Pittsburgh *(G-15424)*

Superior Energy Resources LLC..........G....... 814 265-1080
Brockway *(G-2235)*

Superior Energy Resources LLC..........E....... 814 265-1080
Brockway *(G-2236)*

FITTINGS & SPECIALTIES: Steam

Ogontz Corporation ....F....... 215 657-4770
Willow Grove *(G-20131)*

Sfc Valve Corporation ....D....... 814 445-9671
Somerset *(G-17704)*

FITTINGS: Pipe

Advanced Welding Tech Inc ....E....... 814 899-3584
Erie *(G-5176)*

Bitrekpasub Inc ....D....... 717 762-9141
Waynesboro *(G-19401)*

Campbell Fittings Inc ....E....... 610 367-6916
Boyertown *(G-1903)*

Campbell Manufacturing Inc ....D....... 610 367-2107
Bechtelsville *(G-1030)*

Expansion Seal Technologies ....G....... 215 513-4300
Harleysville *(G-7033)*

Ezeflow Usa Inc ....G....... 724 658-3711
New Castle *(G-12090)*

Hailiang America Corporation ....F....... 877 515-4522
Leesport *(G-9665)*

Hy-Tech Machine Inc ....D....... 724 776-2400
Cranberry Township *(G-3824)*

Merit Manufacturing Corp ....D....... 610 327-4000
Pottstown *(G-16018)*

Pittsburgh Plug and Pdts Corp...........E....... 724 538-4022
Evans City *(G-5561)*

Popit Inc ....G....... 215 945-5201
Levittown *(G-9859)*

Victaulic Holding Company LLC ....G....... 610 559-3300
Easton *(G-4771)*

FITTINGS: Pipe, Fabricated

Boiler Erection and Repair Co ....E....... 215 721-7900
Souderton *(G-17727)*

D & R Steel Construction Inc...............F....... 570 265-6216
Milan *(G-11147)*

D L George & Sons Mfg Inc................D....... 717 765-4700
Waynesboro *(G-19407)*

Markovitz Enterprises Inc ....D....... 724 452-4500
Zelienople *(G-20810)*

Pennsylvania Machine Works Inc ....C....... 610 497-3300
Upper Chichester *(G-18669)*

FIXTURES & EQPT: Kitchen, Metal, Exc Cast Aluminum

Archetype Design Studio LLC ....G....... 412 369-2900
West View *(G-19773)*

C & J Metals ....F....... 562 634-3101
Avella *(G-834)*

Eagle Displays LLC ....F....... 724 335-8900
North Apollo *(G-12726)*

Frank Custom Stainless Inc ....G....... 412 784-0300
Pittsburgh *(G-15033)*

IKEA Indirect Mtl & Svcs LLC ....G....... 610 834-0150
Conshohocken *(G-3559)*

PMI Stainless ....E....... 412 461-1463
Homestead *(G-7691)*

FIXTURES & EQPT: Kitchen, Porcelain Enameled

Hunter Kitchen & Bath LLC ....G....... 570 926-0777
Exton *(G-5693)*

FLAGPOLES

Genie Electronics Co Inc....................D....... 717 244-1099
Red Lion *(G-16598)*

Genie Electronics Co Inc....................C....... 717 244-1099
Red Lion *(G-16599)*

FLAGS: Fabric

Agas Mfg Inc ....E....... 212 777-1178
Philadelphia *(G-13354)*

Baker Ballistics LLC ....F....... 717 625-2016
Lititz *(G-9994)*

Flags For All Seasons Inc ....G....... 610 688-4235
Wayne *(G-19331)*

Flagzone LLC ....C....... 610 367-9900
Gilbertsville *(G-6372)*

John W Keplinger & Son ....G....... 610 666-6191
Norristown *(G-12674)*

FLAGSTONE: Dimension

Chilewski Flagstone ....F....... 570 756-3096
Susquehanna *(G-18179)*

Glenwood Stone Co Inc ....E....... 570 942-6420
Nicholson *(G-12614)*

Johnson Quarries Inc ....E....... 570 744-1284
Stevensville *(G-18059)*

P & P Stone LLC ....G....... 570 967-2279
Hallstead *(G-6835)*

Powers Stone Inc ....E....... 570 553-4276
Montrose *(G-11475)*

FLAGSTONES

Bob Johnson Flagstone Inc ....G....... 570 746-0907
Wyalusing *(G-20246)*

Carl J Kaetzel ....G....... 570 434-2391
Kingsley *(G-8702)*

Compton Flagstone Quarry ....G....... 570 942-6359
Hop Bottom *(G-7773)*

David R Kipar ....E....... 570 833-4068
Meshoppen *(G-11006)*

Flagstone Small Bus Vltons LLC..........G....... 484 515-2621
Bethlehem *(G-1509)*

GK Flagstone Inc ....G....... 570 942-4393
Nicholson *(G-12613)*

Harford Stone Company ....F....... 570 434-9141
Kingsley *(G-8705)*

Harmony Flagstone LLC ....G....... 570 727-2077
Susquehanna *(G-18180)*

Herb Kilmer & Sons Flagstone ....E....... 570 434-2060
Kingsley *(G-8706)*

Kenneth E Decker ....G....... 570 677-3710
Hop Bottom *(G-7774)*

Matt Kilmer Flagstone LLC ....G....... 570 756-2591
South Gibson *(G-17779)*

Meshoppen Stone Incorporated ....C....... 570 833-2767
Meshoppen *(G-11007)*

New Way Homes ....G....... 570 967-2187
Hallstead *(G-6834)*

Powers Stone Inc ....E....... 570 553-4276
Montrose *(G-11475)*

Premier Bluestone Inc ....E....... 570 465-7200
Susquehanna *(G-18182)*

Tony Bennett Flagstone ....G....... 570 746-6015
Wyalusing *(G-20259)*

PRODUCT

FLAKES: Metal

Industrial Services ....F 610 437-1453
Whitehall **(G-19877)**

FLAT GLASS: Cathedral

Youghiogheny Opalescent GL Inc ....E 724 628-3000
Connellsville **(G-3512)**

FLAT GLASS: Construction

Universal Glass Cnstr Inc ....G 570 390-4900
Lake Ariel **(G-8895)**

FLAT GLASS: Float

Vitro Flat Glass LLC ....B 717 486-3366
Carlisle **(G-2748)**

FLAT GLASS: Laminated

Northeast Laminated Glass Corp ....G 570 489-6421
Jessup **(G-8334)**

FLAT GLASS: Optical, Transparent, Exc Lenses

Spectrocell Inc ....F 215 572-7605
Oreland **(G-13030)**

FLAT GLASS: Picture

Lot Made Gallery LLC ....G 717 458-8716
Mechanicsburg **(G-10866)**

FLAT GLASS: Skylight

Cascade Architectural Products ....G 412 824-9313
Turtle Creek **(G-18561)**
Traco Delaware Inc ....F 724 776-7000
Cranberry Township **(G-3856)**

FLAT GLASS: Strengthened Or Reinforced

Kane Innovations Inc ....D 814 838-7731
Erie **(G-5342)**

FLAT GLASS: Tempered

AGC Flat Glass North Amer Inc ....E 215 538-9424
Quakertown **(G-16167)**
Chango Inc ....G 215 634-0400
Philadelphia **(G-13525)**
Trulite GL Alum Solutions LLC ....D 570 282-6711
Carbondale **(G-2687)**

FLAT GLASS: Window, Clear & Colored

Associated Windows ....G 814 445-9744
Somerset **(G-17674)**
Bryn Mawr Shower Door Inc ....G 610 647-0357
Berwyn **(G-1354)**
Greenheat LP ....F 724 545-6540
Cowansville **(G-3796)**

FLAVORS OR FLAVORING MATERIALS: Synthetic

Interntnal Flvors Frgrnces Inc ....G 215 365-7800
Philadelphia **(G-13869)**
Vigon International Inc ....D 877 844-6639
East Stroudsburg **(G-4638)**

FLOOR CLEANING & MAINTENANCE EQPT: Household

Vistappliances ....G 215 600-1232
Morrisville **(G-11587)**

FLOOR COVERING STORES

Robertsons Inc ....G 814 838-2313
Erie **(G-5464)**

FLOOR COVERING STORES: Carpets

Carpet and Furniture Depot Inc ....G 814 239-5865
Claysburg **(G-3201)**
Certified Carpet Service Inc ....D 717 393-3012
Lancaster **(G-8976)**
Custom Carpet & Bedding Inc ....G 570 344-7533
Dunmore **(G-4472)**
Czar Imports Inc ....D 800 577-2927
Huntingdon Valley **(G-7973)**

Ferrante Uphlstrng & Crptng ....F 724 535-8866
Wampum **(G-18800)**
Superior Flrcvgs Kitchens LLC ....G 717 264-9096
Chambersburg **(G-2981)**

FLOOR COVERING STORES: Floor Tile

Lachina Drapery Company Inc ....E 412 665-4900
Pittsburgh **(G-15215)**

FLOOR COVERING STORES: Linoleum

Harvey Bell ....G 215 634-4900
Philadelphia **(G-13806)**

FLOOR COVERING STORES: Vinyl Covering

F&M Surfaces Inc ....G 717 267-3799
Chambersburg **(G-2931)**

FLOOR COVERING: Plastic

Entrance Inc ....F 610 926-0126
Leesport **(G-9663)**
Industrial Floor Corporation ....F 215 886-1800
Jenkintown **(G-8291)**

FLOOR COVERINGS WHOLESALERS

Hinkel-Hofmann Supply Co Inc ....E 412 231-3131
Pittsburgh **(G-15095)**

FLOOR COVERINGS: Rubber

Global Rubber LLC ....G 610 878-9200
Wayne **(G-19333)**
Mondo Usa Inc ....G 610 834-3835
Conshohocken **(G-3576)**
Regupol America LLC ....E 717 675-2198
Lebanon **(G-9626)**

FLOOR COVERINGS: Twisted Paper, Grass, Reed, Coir, Etc

Durex Coverings Inc ....E 717 626-8566
Brownstown **(G-2307)**

FLOORING & GRATINGS: Open, Construction Applications

Ciw Enterprises Inc ....E 800 233-8366
Mountain Top **(G-11755)**
Cornellcookson Inc ....C 570 474-6773
Mountain Top **(G-11757)**
Goldsborough & Vansant Inc ....G 724 782-0393
Finleyville **(G-5959)**
Oldcastle Precast Inc ....D 484 548-6200
Easton **(G-4735)**

FLOORING & SIDING: Metal

Centria Inc ....C 412 299-8000
Moon Township **(G-11483)**

FLOORING: Baseboards, Wood

Nature Flooring Industries Inc ....E 610 280-9800
Malvern **(G-10283)**
Quehanna Millwork ....G 814 263-4145
Frenchville **(G-6218)**

FLOORING: Cellular Steel

Epic Metals Corporation ....D 412 351-3913
Rankin **(G-16305)**

FLOORING: Hard Surface

Ahf Holding Inc ....G 800 233-3823
Lancaster **(G-8922)**
Armstrong Flooring Inc ....A 717 672-9611
Lancaster **(G-8940)**
Armstrong World Industries Inc ....F 717 426-4171
Marietta **(G-10460)**
Commercial Flrg Professionals ....G 717 576-7847
Mechanicsburg **(G-10829)**
Congoleum Corporation ....B 609 584-3000
Marcus Hook **(G-10439)**

FLOORING: Hardwood

Ahf Products LLC ....A 800 233-3823
Lancaster **(G-8923)**
Armstrong Hardwood Flooring Co ....A 717 672-9611
Lancaster **(G-8941)**

Bennett Flooring LLC ....E 724 586-9350
Butler **(G-2378)**
Centria Inc ....E 724 251-2208
Coraopolis **(G-3674)**
Homerwood Hardwood Flooring Co .....D 814 827-3855
Titusville **(G-18382)**
Lewis Lumber Products Inc ....D 570 584-6167
Picture Rocks **(G-14585)**
Strick Corporation ....F 215 949-3600
Fairless Hills **(G-5799)**
Thomas Gross Woodworking ....G 724 593-7044
Ligonier **(G-9967)**
Woodside Glueing ....G 814 349-5646
Rebersburg **(G-16579)**

FLOORING: Parquet, Hardwood

Czar Imports Inc ....D 800 577-2927
Huntingdon Valley **(G-7973)**
Tindall Virgin Timbers Clnl WD ....G 717 548-2435
Peach Bottom **(G-13202)**

FLOORING: Rubber

Abacus Surfaces Inc ....F 717 560-8050
Lancaster **(G-8920)**
Capri Cork LLC ....F 717 627-5701
Lititz **(G-9995)**

FLOORING: Tile

Harvey Bell ....G 215 634-4900
Philadelphia **(G-13806)**

FLORIST: Plants, Potted

Plantscape Inc ....D 412 281-6352
Pittsburgh **(G-15415)**

FLORISTS

Duritzas Enterprises Inc ....C 724 223-5494
Washington **(G-19165)**
Mr ZS Food Mart ....G 570 421-7070
Stroudsburg **(G-18132)**
Seasons Specialties Inc ....F 570 928-9522
Dushore **(G-4510)**
Tops Markets LLC ....C 570 882-9188
Sayre **(G-17123)**

FLOWER ARRANGEMENTS: Artificial

Lasting Expressions ....G 724 776-3953
Cranberry Township **(G-3831)**

FLOWERS & FLORISTS' SPLYS WHOLESALERS

H & H General Excavating Co ....D 717 225-4669
Spring Grove **(G-17877)**
Red Bandana Co ....F 215 744-3144
Philadelphia **(G-14236)**

FLOWERS & NURSERY STOCK, WHOLESALE

Sauders Nursery ....F 717 354-9851
East Earl **(G-4555)**

FLOWERS: Artificial & Preserved

London Wreath Co Inc ....G 215 739-6440
Philadelphia **(G-13974)**
Red Bandana Co ....F 215 744-3144
Philadelphia **(G-14236)**

FLUE LINING: Clay

Mill Hall Clay Products Inc ....E 570 726-6752
Mill Hall **(G-11179)**

FLUID METERS & COUNTING DEVICES

FMC Technologies Inc ....F 814 898-5000
Erie **(G-5296)**
Maguire Products Inc ....G 610 494-6566
Media **(G-10937)**
Matheson Tri-Gas Inc ....D 215 641-2700
Montgomeryville **(G-11406)**
Parker-Hannifin Corporation ....C 215 723-4000
Hatfield **(G-7377)**
Prominent Fluid Controls Inc ....E 412 787-2484
Pittsburgh **(G-15453)**

Strube Inc ....F 717 426-1906
Marietta (G-10468)
Utilities & Industries Inc ....D 814 653-8269
Reynoldsville (G-16667)
Veeder-Root Company ....E 814 695-4476
Duncansville (G-4465)
World Wide Plastics Inc ....E 215 357-0893
Langhorne (G-9336)

FLUID POWER PUMPS & MOTORS

Bosch Rexroth Corporation ....A 610 694-8300
Bethlehem (G-1470)
Eastern Industrial Pdts Inc ....E 610 459-1212
Aston (G-760)
Eaton Aerospace LLC ....D 610 522-4000
Glenolden (G-6473)
Eaton Corporation ....E 412 893-3300
Moon Township (G-11484)
Eaton Electrical Inc ....E 412 893-3300
Moon Township (G-11485)
Global Trade Links LLC ....E 888 777-1577
Chester Springs (G-3079)
Hydac Corp ....E 610 266-0100
Bethlehem (G-1533)
Hydromotion Inc ....D 610 948-4150
Spring City (G-17860)
ITT Corporation ....G 717 262-2945
Chambersburg (G-2944)
Lionheart Holdings LLC ....D 215 283-8400
Newtown (G-12519)
Manchester Hydraulics Inc ....G 717 764-5226
Manchester (G-10357)
N-Jay Machines ....G 724 232-0110
Karns City (G-8481)
National Hydraulics Inc ....D 724 547-9222
Mount Pleasant (G-11708)
Nick Charles Kravitch ....G 412 882-6262
Pittsburgh (G-15340)
Parker-Hannifin Corporation ....D 814 438-3821
Union City (G-18612)
Ralph A Hiller Company ....E 724 325-1200
Export (G-5623)
Siemens Industry Inc ....C 724 339-9500
New Kensington (G-12375)
Weir Hazleton Inc ....D 570 455-7711
Hazleton (G-7537)
Wojanis Supply Company ....E 724 695-1415
Coraopolis (G-3734)

FLUID POWER VALVES & HOSE FITTINGS

Al Xander Co Inc ....E 814 665-8268
Corry (G-3743)
Appalachian Tank Car Svcs Inc ....D 412 741-1500
Leetsdale (G-9682)
Autoclave Engineers ....G 814 860-5700
Erie (G-5197)
Custom Hydraulics Inc ....F 724 729-3170
Burgettstown (G-2344)
Fessler Machine Company ....E 724 346-0878
Sharon (G-17433)
Hydac Technology Corp ....C 205 520-1220
Bethlehem (G-1534)
Innovative Pressure Tech LLC ....D 814 833-5200
Erie (G-5326)
Maxpro Technologies Inc ....F 814 474-9191
Fairview (G-5833)
National Hydraulics Inc ....D 724 547-9222
Mount Pleasant (G-11708)
Nick Charles Kravitch ....G 412 882-6262
Pittsburgh (G-15340)
Powertrack International LLC ....E 412 787-4444
Pittsburgh (G-15423)
Q-E Manufacturing Company ....E 570 966-1017
New Berlin (G-12023)
R/W Connection Inc ....F 717 767-3660
Emigsville (G-4998)
R/W Connection Inc ....E 717 898-5257
Landisville (G-9266)
Universal Fluids Inc ....G 267 639-2238
Philadelphia (G-14426)

FLUMES: Sheet Metal

Colmetal Incorporated ....G 215 225-1060
Philadelphia (G-13560)

FLUXES

American Solder & Flux Co Inc ....F 610 647-2375
Paoli (G-13134)

Force Industries Inc ....F 610 647-3575
Paoli (G-13140)
Morgan Advanced Ceramics Inc ....D 724 537-7791
Latrobe (G-9505)

FOAM CHARGE MIXTURES

Allied Foam Tech Corp ....G 215 540-2666
Montgomeryville (G-11384)
Foam Fabricators Inc ....E 570 752-7110
Bloomsburg (G-1782)
National Foam Inc ....D 610 363-1400
West Chester (G-19606)
Rusmar Incorporated ....F 610 436-4314
West Chester (G-19632)

FOAM RUBBER

Chestnut Ridge Foam Inc ....C 724 537-9000
Latrobe (G-9464)
Fxi Building Products Corp ....D 610 744-2230
Media (G-10927)
Gordon Seaver ....G 724 356-2313
Hickory (G-7628)
M B Bedding Co ....G 570 822-2491
Wilkes Barre (G-19939)
Penn Foam Corporation ....D 610 797-7500
Allentown (G-348)
Reilly Foam Corp ....D 610 834-1900
King of Prussia (G-8668)

FOAM RUBBER, WHOLESALE

Reilly Foam Corp ....D 610 834-1900
King of Prussia (G-8668)

FOIL & LEAF: Metal

JW Aluminum Company ....C 570 323-4430
Williamsport (G-20030)
Kurz-Hastings Inc ....G 215 632-2300
Philadelphia (G-13946)
Performance Coatings Corp ....F 610 525-1190
Levittown (G-9854)
South Pole Magnetics ....G 412 537-5625
Pittsburgh (G-15563)

FOIL: Magnesium & Magnesium-Base Alloy

Custom Processing Services Inc ....E 610 779-7001
Reading (G-16359)

FOOD CASINGS: Plastic

Consolidated Container Co LLC ....E 610 869-4021
York (G-20438)
Guenther & Sons Enterprises ....G 570 676-0585
Gouldsboro (G-6568)

FOOD COLORINGS

Interntnal Flvors Frgrnces Inc ....C 215 365-7800
Philadelphia (G-13868)

FOOD PRDTS, BREAKFAST: Cereal, Rice: Cereal Breakfast Food

General Mills Inc ....E 717 838-7600
Palmyra (G-13124)

FOOD PRDTS, CANNED OR FRESH PACK: Fruit Juices

Brook Meadow Dairy Company ....C 814 899-3191
Erie (G-5215)
HP Hood LLC ....B 215 855-9074
Allentown (G-248)
Welch Foods Inc A Cooperative ....B 814 725-4577
North East (G-12766)

FOOD PRDTS, CANNED, NEC

Valdez Foods Inc ....F 215 634-6106
Philadelphia (G-14436)

FOOD PRDTS, CANNED: Applesauce

Charles & Alice Inc ....E 717 537-4700
Lancaster (G-8977)

FOOD PRDTS, CANNED: Baby Food

Baby Matters LLC ....G 919 724-7087
Wayne (G-19304)

Kraft Heinz Company ....B 412 456-5700
Pittsburgh (G-15196)
Kraft Heinz Foods Company ....C 412 456-5700
Pittsburgh (G-15197)
Riverbend Foods LLC ....B 412 442-6989
Pittsburgh (G-15488)

FOOD PRDTS, CANNED: Barbecue Sauce

House of Wings Foods LLC ....G 570 627-6116
Sayre (G-17116)
Roadside Products Inc ....F 412 220-9694
Bridgeville (G-2087)

FOOD PRDTS, CANNED: Catsup

Kraft Heinz Foods Company ....B 724 778-5700
Warrendale (G-19085)

FOOD PRDTS, CANNED: Chili Sauce, Tomato

Electric Pepper Company LLC ....G 812 340-4321
Russell (G-16880)

FOOD PRDTS, CANNED: Ethnic

Anitas Vegan Kitchen ....G 786 512-1428
Philadelphia (G-13393)
Hazel and Ash Organics LLC ....G 717 521-9593
Coatesville (G-3307)

FOOD PRDTS, CANNED: Fruit Butters

Bauman Family ....F 610 754-7251
Sassamansville (G-17080)
Sam Beachy & Sons ....G 814 662-2220
Salisbury (G-17045)

FOOD PRDTS, CANNED: Fruit Juices, Fresh

Cliffstar LLC ....E 814 725-3801
North East (G-12735)
Coca-Cola Company ....C 610 530-3900
Allentown (G-172)
Good Crop Inc ....F 585 944-7982
Malvern (G-10241)
Knouse Foods Cooperative Inc ....B 717 263-9177
Chambersburg (G-2949)

FOOD PRDTS, CANNED: Fruits

Appeeling Fruit Inc ....F 610 926-6601
Dauberville (G-4032)
Knouse Foods Cooperative Inc ....B 717 677-8181
Peach Glen (G-13205)
Knouse Foods Cooperative Inc ....C 717 642-8291
Orrtanna (G-13036)
Knouse Foods Cooperative Inc ....C 717 677-9115
Biglerville (G-1666)
Nestle Usa Inc ....C 818 549-6000
King of Prussia (G-8655)

FOOD PRDTS, CANNED: Fruits

Bel Aire Foods Inc ....E 412 364-7277
Pittsburgh (G-14760)
Clover Farms Dairy Company ....B 610 921-9111
Reading (G-16346)
Del Monte Foods Inc ....C 412 222-2200
Pittsburgh (G-14917)
Dell Sunny Foods LLC ....D 610 932-5164
Oxford (G-13078)
Florida Key West ....G 717 208-3084
Lancaster (G-9022)
Hanover Foods Corporation ....C 814 364-1482
Centre Hall (G-2841)
High View Inc ....E 814 886-7171
Loretto (G-10104)
Hot Sauce Spot LLC ....G 717 341-7573
Lititz (G-10018)
J M Smucker Company ....F 724 228-6633
Washington (G-19187)
Knouse Foods Cooperative Inc ....G 717 328-3065
Mercersburg (G-10989)
Kraft Heinz Foods Company ....E 412 237-5757
Pittsburgh (G-15198)
Kraft Heinz Foods Company ....F 412 456-5773
Pittsburgh (G-15199)
Modern Mushroom Farms Inc ....B 610 268-3535
Toughkenamon (G-18420)
Motts LLP ....B 717 677-7121
Aspers (G-743)
Ocean Spray Cranberries Inc ....B 609 298-0905
Breinigsville (G-2022)

PRODUCT

River Run Foods Inc ....E ... 570 701-1192
Northumberland *(G-12875)*
Spring Glen Fresh Foods Inc ....D ... 717 733-2201
Ephrata *(G-5145)*
Sunsweet Growers Inc ....C ... 610 944-1005
Fleetwood *(G-5980)*
Zentis North America LLC ....D ... 215 676-3900
Philadelphia *(G-14504)*

FOOD PRDTS, CANNED: Fruits & Fruit Prdts

American Beverage Corporation ....C ... 412 828-9020
Verona *(G-18747)*
American Beverage Corporation ....G ... 412 828-9020
Pittsburgh *(G-14701)*

FOOD PRDTS, CANNED: Italian

Barbato Foods Inc ....F ... 814 899-3721
Erie *(G-5202)*
Farmers From Italy Foods LLC ....G ... 484 480-3836
Upper Chichester *(G-18661)*
Taif Inc ....F ... 610 534-0669
Ridley Park *(G-16742)*
Taif Inc ....E ... 610 522-0122
Folcroft *(G-6017)*

FOOD PRDTS, CANNED: Jams, Jellies & Preserves

Bacon Jams ....G ... 484 681-5674
Norristown *(G-12640)*
Hot Jams Dj Service ....G ... 814 246-8144
Punxsutawney *(G-16144)*
Shenks Foods Inc ....G ... 717 393-4240
Lancaster *(G-9195)*

FOOD PRDTS, CANNED: Macaroni

Fourth Street Barbecue Inc ....C ... 724 483-2000
Charleroi *(G-3013)*

FOOD PRDTS, CANNED: Marmalade

Eat This ....G ... 215 391-5807
Erwinna *(G-5538)*

FOOD PRDTS, CANNED: Mexican, NEC

Taste of Puebla ....G ... 484 467-8597
Kennett Square *(G-8548)*

FOOD PRDTS, CANNED: Mushrooms

California Mushroom Farm Inc ....B ... 805 642-3253
Toughkenamon *(G-18417)*
Digiorgio Mushroom Corp ....B ... 610 926-2139
Reading *(G-16362)*
Giorgio Foods Inc ....C ... 610 926-2139
Reading *(G-16391)*
Myers Canning Co ....C ... 610 929-8644
Reading *(G-16451)*
Snowtop LLC ....F ... 724 297-5491
Worthington *(G-20233)*

FOOD PRDTS, CANNED: Puddings, Exc Meat

AFP Advanced Food Products LLC ......C ... 717 355-8667
New Holland *(G-12227)*
Down Home Rice Pudding ....G ... 570 945-5744
Madison Township *(G-10168)*
Zausner Foods Corp ....B ... 717 355-8505
New Holland *(G-12296)*

FOOD PRDTS, CANNED: Spaghetti & Other Pasta Sauce

Delgrosso Foods Inc ....D ... 814 684-5880
Tipton *(G-18374)*

FOOD PRDTS, CANNED: Tomato Sauce.

Kraft Heinz Company ....B ... 412 456-5700
Pittsburgh *(G-15196)*
Kraft Heinz Foods Company ....B ... 412 456-2482
Moon Township *(G-11496)*
Kraft Heinz Foods Company ....C ... 412 456-5700
Pittsburgh *(G-15197)*

FOOD PRDTS, CANNED: Tomatoes

Hanover Foods Corporation ....F ... 717 843-0738
York *(G-20522)*

PCA Group Inc ....G ... 610 558-2802
Garnet Valley *(G-6267)*

FOOD PRDTS, CANNED: Vegetables

Furman Foods Inc ....C ... 570 473-3516
Northumberland *(G-12867)*
Greenline Foods Inc ....G ... 717 630-9200
Hanover *(G-6889)*
Grouse Hunt Farms Inc ....F ... 570 573-2868
Tamaqua *(G-18211)*
Hanover Foods Corporation ....A ... 717 632-6000
Hanover *(G-6894)*

FOOD PRDTS, CANNED: Vegetables

Hazel and Ash Organics LLC ....G ... 717 521-9593
Coatesville *(G-3307)*

FOOD PRDTS, CONFECTIONERY, WHOLESALE: Candy

4sis LLC ....E ... 814 459-2451
Erie *(G-5162)*
Esthers Sweet Shop Inc ....G ... 412 884-4224
Pittsburgh *(G-14986)*
James A Marquette ....G ... 570 523-3873
Lewisburg *(G-9913)*
Miesse Candies Corp ....G ... 717 299-5427
Lancaster *(G-9135)*
Tastysnack Quality Foods Inc ....E ... 717 259-6961
Abbottstown *(G-7)*

FOOD PRDTS, CONFECTIONERY, WHOLESALE: Corn Chips

Kings Potato Chip Company ....E ... 717 445-4521
Mohnton *(G-11268)*

FOOD PRDTS, CONFECTIONERY, WHOLESALE: Nuts, Salted/Roasted

A L Bazzini Co Inc ....E ... 610 366-1606
Allentown *(G-111)*
Bal Nut Inc ....G ... 570 675-2712
Dallas *(G-3958)*
J S Zimmerman Co ....G ... 717 232-6842
Harrisburg *(G-7157)*

FOOD PRDTS, CONFECTIONERY, WHOLESALE: Potato Chips

Herr Foods Incorporated ....E ... 610 395-6200
Allentown *(G-245)*
Troyer Inc ....E ... 724 746-1162
Canonsburg *(G-2648)*

FOOD PRDTS, CONFECTIONERY, WHOLESALE: Pretzels

Dutch Cntry Soft Pretzels LLC ....G ... 717 354-4493
New Holland *(G-12244)*
Federal Pretzel Baking Co ....E ... 215 467-0505
Philadelphia *(G-13695)*
Martins Potato Chips Inc ....C ... 717 792-3065
Thomasville *(G-18341)*
Tasty Twisters Inc ....G ... 215 487-7828
Philadelphia *(G-14376)*
Unique Pretzel Bakery Inc ....E ... 610 929-3172
Reading *(G-16553)*

FOOD PRDTS, CONFECTIONERY, WHOLESALE: Snack Foods

G & S Foods Inc ....E ... 717 259-5323
Abbottstown *(G-4)*
Pepperidge Farm Incorporated ....G ... 610 356-0553
Broomall *(G-2301)*
Pepperidge Farm Incorporated ....G ... 717 336-8500
Denver *(G-4087)*
Revonah Pretzel LLC ....E ... 717 632-4477
Hanover *(G-6943)*
Sb Global Foods Inc ....G ... 215 361-9500
Hatboro *(G-7303)*

FOOD PRDTS, DAIRY, WHOLESALE: Frozen Dairy Desserts

Brusters Old Fashioned Ice Cre ....G ... 724 772-9999
Seven Fields *(G-17374)*

Titusville Dairy Products Co ....E ... 814 827-1833
Titusville *(G-18399)*

FOOD PRDTS, DAIRY, WHOLESALE: Milk & Cream, Fluid

Pittsburgh Special-T Dairy LLC ....E ... 412 881-1409
Pittsburgh *(G-15407)*

FOOD PRDTS, FISH & SEAFOOD, WHOLESALE: Fresh

Grammeco Inc ....C ... 610 352-4400
Upper Darby *(G-18686)*

FOOD PRDTS, FISH & SEAFOOD, WHOLESALE: Seafood

Herkys Food Products Inc ....E ... 412 683-8511
Pittsburgh *(G-15092)*

FOOD PRDTS, FISH & SEAFOOD: Fish, Frozen, Prepared

H & G Diners Corp ....E ... 610 494-5107
Marcus Hook *(G-10445)*

FOOD PRDTS, FISH & SEAFOOD: Fresh, Prepared

Seafood Enterprises LP ....C ... 215 672-2211
Warminster *(G-18964)*

FOOD PRDTS, FISH & SEAFOOD: Fresh/Frozen Chowder, Soup/Stew

A C Kissling Company ....F ... 215 423-4700
Philadelphia *(G-13325)*
Charles Ernsts Sons LLC ....G ... 267 237-1271
Springfield *(G-17910)*

FOOD PRDTS, FISH & SEAFOOD: Prepared Cakes & Sticks

Herkys Food Products Inc ....E ... 412 683-8511
Pittsburgh *(G-15092)*
Rebecca Wilson Ltd Lblty Co ....G ... 973 670-7089
York *(G-20654)*

FOOD PRDTS, FISH & SEAFOOD: Seafood, Frozen, Prepared

Seaco Foods International ....F ... 844 579-1133
Newtown *(G-12547)*

FOOD PRDTS, FROZEN, WHOLESALE: Dinners

Ethnic Gourmet Foods Inc ....E ... 610 692-2209
West Chester *(G-19552)*

FOOD PRDTS, FROZEN, WHOLESALE: Vegetables & Fruit Prdts

Cambridge Farms Hanover LLC ....G ... 717 945-5178
Lancaster *(G-8969)*

FOOD PRDTS, FROZEN: Ethnic Foods, NEC

Almi Group Inc ....G ... 215 987-5768
Philadelphia *(G-13371)*
Ateeco Inc ....E ... 570 462-2745
Shenandoah *(G-17492)*
Davenmark Inc ....F ... 484 461-8683
Upper Darby *(G-18684)*
Icon Marketing LLC ....G ... 610 356-4050
Broomall *(G-2289)*
Lees Orntal Gourmet Foods Inc ....E ... 570 462-9505
Shenandoah *(G-17494)*
Rae Foods Inc ....G ... 716 326-7437
North East *(G-12755)*
Roccas Italian Foods Inc ....F ... 724 654-3344
New Castle *(G-12144)*
Rome At Home ....G ... 412 361-3782
East Liberty *(G-4579)*

FOOD PRDTS, FROZEN: Fruit Juice, Concentrates

Coca-Cola Company ....C 610 530-3900
Allentown (G-172)

Ocean Spray Cranberries Inc ....E 508 946-1000
Breinigsville (G-2023)

FOOD PRDTS, FROZEN: Fruits

Icy Feet Inc ....G 610 462-3887
Whitehall (G-19876)

Inventure Foods Inc ....B 623 932-6200
Hanover (G-6903)

Mgk Produce Co ....G 610 853-3678
Lansdowne (G-9438)

FOOD PRDTS, FROZEN: Fruits, Juices & Vegetables

Cambridge Farms Hanover LLC ....G 717 945-5178
Lancaster (G-8969)

H J Heinz Company Brands LLC ....G 412 456-5700
Pittsburgh (G-15072)

Hanover Foods Corporation ....A 717 632-6000
Hanover (G-6894)

Kreider Foods Inc ....F 717 898-3372
Lancaster (G-9088)

FOOD PRDTS, FROZEN: NEC

Atlantic Dev Corp of PA ....F 717 243-0212
Carlisle (G-2690)

Dawn Food Products Inc ....C 717 840-0044
York (G-20445)

Delicious Bite LLC ....F 610 701-4213
West Chester (G-19534)

Ethnic Gourmet Foods Inc ....E 610 692-2209
West Chester (G-19552)

Georgeos Water Ice Inc ....F 610 494-4975
Marcus Hook (G-10443)

Giorgio Foods Inc ....C 610 926-2139
Reading (G-16391)

H J Heinz Company LP ....C 412 237-5757
Pittsburgh (G-15071)

Hanover Foods Corporation ....A 717 632-6000
Hanover (G-6894)

Heinz Frozen Food Company ....A 412 237-5700
Pittsburgh (G-15088)

Kraft Heinz Company ....B 412 456-5700
Pittsburgh (G-15196)

Kraft Heinz Foods Company ....F 610 430-1536
West Chester (G-19584)

Kraft Heinz Foods Company ....C 412 456-5700
Pittsburgh (G-15197)

Leonetti Food Distributors Inc ....E 215 729-4200
Philadelphia (G-13966)

Moms Wholesale Foods Inc ....G 724 856-3049
New Castle (G-12122)

Murrys of Maryland Inc ....C 301 420-6400
Lebanon (G-9612)

Preferred Meal Systems Inc ....C 570 457-8311
Moosic (G-11512)

Real English Foods Inc ....G 610 863-9091
Pen Argyl (G-13215)

Sfc Global Supply Chain Inc ....B 610 327-5074
Pottstown (G-16045)

Van Bennett Food Co Inc ....E 610 374-8348
Mohnton (G-11272)

Wakins Food Corporation ....G 215 785-3420
Bristol (G-2216)

FOOD PRDTS, FROZEN: Pizza

B WS Pizza ....G 724 495-2898
Beaver (G-978)

Nardone Brothers Baking Co ....C 570 823-0141
Hanover Township (G-6999)

Ne Foods Inc ....A 814 725-4835
North East (G-12753)

Nestle Pizza Company Inc ....F 717 737-7268
Camp Hill (G-2506)

Petruzzi Pizza Mfg Inc ....E 570 454-5887
Hazleton (G-7517)

Poppi Als Inc ....G 717 652-6263
Harrisburg (G-7200)

FOOD PRDTS, FROZEN: Potato Prdts

Bel Aire Foods Inc ....E 412 364-7277
Pittsburgh (G-14760)

Heinz Frozen Food Company ....A 412 237-5700
Pittsburgh (G-15088)

FOOD PRDTS, FROZEN: Snack Items

Mybiani LLC ....G 267 253-1866
Willow Grove (G-20130)

Sb Global Foods Inc ....G 215 361-9500
Hatboro (G-7303)

FOOD PRDTS, FROZEN: Soups

Ask Foods Inc ....C 717 838-6356
Palmyra (G-13117)

Ask Foods Inc ....E 717 838-6356
Palmyra (G-13118)

Luccis ....G 903 600-5848
Hatboro (G-7293)

FOOD PRDTS, FROZEN: Vegetables, Exc Potato Prdts

Birds Eye Foods Inc ....C 814 267-4641
Berlin (G-1284)

Birds Eye Foods Inc ....F 814 942-6031
Altoona (G-478)

Digiorgio Mushroom Corp ....B 610 926-2139
Reading (G-16362)

Giorgio Foods Inc ....C 610 926-2139
Reading (G-16391)

FOOD PRDTS, FRUITS & VEGETABLES, FRESH, WHOLESALE: Vegetable

Dell Sunny Foods LLC ....D 610 932-5164
Oxford (G-13078)

Digiorgio Mushroom Corp ....B 610 926-2139
Reading (G-16362)

Giorgio Foods Inc ....C 610 926-2139
Reading (G-16391)

FOOD PRDTS, MEAT & MEAT PRDTS, WHOLESALE: Brokers

Alex Froehlich Packing Co ....F 814 535-7694
Johnstown (G-8349)

FOOD PRDTS, MEAT & MEAT PRDTS, WHOLESALE: Cured Or Smoked

Sechrist Bros Inc ....F 717 244-2975
Dallastown (G-3981)

FOOD PRDTS, MEAT & MEAT PRDTS, WHOLESALE: Fresh

Alderfer Inc ....D 215 256-8819
Harleysville (G-7016)

Clair D Thompson & Sons Inc ....E 570 398-1880
Jersey Shore (G-8311)

Emericks Meat & Packing Co ....E 814 842-6779
Hyndman (G-8050)

Ken Weaver Meats Inc ....E 717 502-0118
Wellsville (G-19479)

Korte & Co Inc ....F 610 253-9141
Easton (G-4712)

Leidys Inc ....D 215 723-4606
Souderton (G-17749)

OJacks Inc ....E 814 225-4755
Eldred (G-4854)

P & N Packing Inc ....E 570 746-1974
Wyalusing (G-20255)

Palumbos Meats Dubois Inc ....G 814 371-2150
Du Bois (G-4412)

Pudliners Packing ....F 814 539-5422
Johnstown (G-8425)

R & R Provision Co ....D 610 258-5366
Easton (G-4746)

S Schiff Restaurant Svc Inc ....C 570 343-1294
Scranton (G-17282)

FOOD PRDTS, MEAT & MEAT PRDTS, WHOLESALE: Lard

A La Henri Inc ....G 724 856-1374
New Castle (G-12052)

FOOD PRDTS, POULTRY, WHOLESALE: Live/Dressed/Frozen, Unpkgd

Mac Millan William Company ....F 215 627-3273
Philadelphia (G-13985)

FOOD PRDTS, POULTRY, WHOLESALE: Poultry Prdts, NEC

Clair D Thompson & Sons Inc ....E 570 398-1880
Jersey Shore (G-8311)

Joe Jurgielewicz & Son Ltd ....E 610 562-3825
Hamburg (G-6842)

Philadelphia Poultry Inc ....E 215 574-0343
Philadelphia (G-14150)

FOOD PRDTS, WHOLESALE: Beverages, Exc Coffee & Tea

B&B Sales Consulting Corp Inc ....G 215 225-3200
Philadelphia (G-13439)

Gablers Beverage Distributors ....G 717 532-2241
Shippensburg (G-17528)

FOOD PRDTS, WHOLESALE: Breakfast Cereals

General Mills Inc ....D 215 784-5100
Dresher (G-4355)

FOOD PRDTS, WHOLESALE: Chocolate

Colebrook Chocolate Co LLC ....G 724 628-8383
Connellsville (G-3492)

Confiseurs Inc ....E 610 932-2706
Oxford (G-13076)

FOOD PRDTS, WHOLESALE: Coffee & Tea

Fresh Roasted Coffee LLC ....F 570 743-9228
Sunbury (G-18169)

Noltpak LLC ....G 717 725-9862
Quarryville (G-16274)

FOOD PRDTS, WHOLESALE: Coffee, Green Or Roasted

Choccobutter Inc ....G 717 756-5590
New Cumberland (G-12184)

Union Chill Mat Co ....G 724 452-6400
Zelienople (G-20825)

FOOD PRDTS, WHOLESALE: Cooking Oils & Shortenings

Innofoods Usa Inc ....G 412 854-9012
Pittsburgh (G-15126)

FOOD PRDTS, WHOLESALE: Diet

Exclusive Supplements Inc ....F 412 787-2770
Oakdale (G-12898)

Gluten Free Food Group LLC ....E 570 689-9694
Moscow (G-11597)

FOOD PRDTS, WHOLESALE: Dog Food

Oscar & Banks LLC ....G 701 922-1005
Ligonier (G-9962)

FOOD PRDTS, WHOLESALE: Dried or Canned Foods

Ncc Wholesome Foods Inc ....F 724 652-3440
New Castle (G-12124)

FOOD PRDTS, WHOLESALE: Flavorings & Fragrances

Fragrance Manufacturing Inc ....E 610 266-7580
Allentown (G-218)

Vigon International Inc ....D 877 844-6639
East Stroudsburg (G-4638)

FOOD PRDTS, WHOLESALE: Flour

Roch Grande Gst Waffles LLC ....C 484 840-9179
Glen Mills (G-6442)

PRODUCT

FOOD PRDTS, WHOLESALE: Grain Elevators

International Union-Elevator...............G....... 570 842-5430
Sprng Brk Twp (G-17932)

FOOD PRDTS, WHOLESALE: Grains

Agricultural Commodities Inc..............D...... 717 624-6858
Gettysburg (G-6282)
Albrights Mill LLC...........................E...... 610 756-6022
Kempton (G-8489)
Boyd Station LLC.............................E...... 866 411-2693
Danville (G-3998)
F M Browns Sons Incorporated............E...... 610 582-2741
Birdsboro (G-1695)

FOOD PRDTS, WHOLESALE: Honey

Dutch Gold Honey Inc ....D...... 717 393-1716
Lancaster (G-9004)

FOOD PRDTS, WHOLESALE: Juices

Harrisburg Dairies Inc ....C...... 717 233-8701
Harrisburg (G-7142)

FOOD PRDTS, WHOLESALE: Molasses, Indl

M Simon Zook Co...............................C...... 610 273-3776
Honey Brook (G-7753)

FOOD PRDTS, WHOLESALE: Pasta & Rice

East Asia Noodle Inc ....F...... 215 923-6838
Philadelphia (G-13654)

FOOD PRDTS, WHOLESALE: Pizza Splys

Petruzzis Manufacturing Inc ....G...... 570 459-5957
Hazleton (G-7518)

FOOD PRDTS, WHOLESALE: Rice, Polished

Gokaaf International Inc ....G...... 267 343-3075
Philadelphia (G-13775)

FOOD PRDTS, WHOLESALE: Salt, Edible

Superior Value Beverage Co.................G...... 610 935-3111
Phoenixville (G-14581)

FOOD PRDTS, WHOLESALE: Sandwiches

Smuckers Salad ....G...... 267 757-0944
Newtown (G-12550)

FOOD PRDTS, WHOLESALE: Sauces

Woods Wings ....G...... 610 417-5684
Kintnersville (G-8730)

FOOD PRDTS, WHOLESALE: Shortening, Vegetable

Ventura Foods LLC ....C...... 717 263-6900
Chambersburg (G-2997)

FOOD PRDTS, WHOLESALE: Soybeans

Nature Soy LLC ....F...... 215 765-3289
Philadelphia (G-14058)

FOOD PRDTS, WHOLESALE: Specialty

Davis & Davis Gourmet Foods ....G...... 412 487-7770
Allison Park (G-449)
G & S Foods Inc ....E...... 717 259-5323
Abbottstown (G-4)
Murazzi Provision Co...........................F...... 570 344-2285
Scranton (G-17262)

FOOD PRDTS, WHOLESALE: Spices & Seasonings

Pittsburgh Spice Seasoning Co ....G...... 412 288-5036
Pittsburgh (G-15408)

FOOD PRDTS, WHOLESALE: Syrups, Exc Fountain Use

Sunrise Maple....................................F...... 814 628-3110
Westfield (G-19781)

FOOD PRDTS, WHOLESALE: Tea

Darling Blends LLC.............................G...... 215 630-2802
Langhorne (G-9288)
Gerhart Coffee Co ....G...... 717 397-8788
Lancaster (G-9028)

FOOD PRDTS, WHOLESALE: Water, Mineral Or Spring, Bottled

Roaring Spring Blank Book Co ....B...... 814 224-2306
Roaring Spring (G-16768)

FOOD PRDTS: Animal & marine fats & oils

A F Moyer Inc ....G...... 215 723-5555
Souderton (G-17719)
Griffin Industries LLC..........................E...... 610 273-7014
Honey Brook (G-7746)
Jbs Souderton Inc...............................A...... 215 723-5555
Souderton (G-17744)
Neatsfoot Oil Refineries Corp...............E...... 215 739-1291
Philadelphia (G-14061)
Vigon International Inc ....D...... 877 844-6639
East Stroudsburg (G-4638)

FOOD PRDTS: Baking Powder, Soda, Yeast & Leavenings

Hershey Company ....B...... 717 534-4200
Hershey (G-7613)

FOOD PRDTS: Bread Crumbs, Exc Made In Bakeries

F Ferrato Foods Company ....G...... 412 431-1479
Pittsburgh (G-14998)
Pepperidge Farm Incorporated.............G...... 610 356-0553
Broomall (G-2301)
Pepperidge Farm Incorporated.............G...... 717 336-8500
Denver (G-4087)

FOOD PRDTS: Breakfast Bars

WA Dehart Inc....................................D...... 570 568-1551
New Columbia (G-12179)

FOOD PRDTS: Cereals

Gluten Free Food Group LLC ....E...... 570 689-9694
Moscow (G-11597)
Homestat Farm Ltd ....F...... 717 939-0407
Highspire (G-7633)
Kellogg Company ....A...... 717 898-0161
Lancaster (G-9079)
Kellogg Company ....B...... 570 546-0200
Muncy (G-11823)
Mondelez Global LLC ....A...... 570 820-1200
Wilkes Barre (G-19945)
North American Packaging LLC ....D...... 570 296-4200
Milford (G-11165)
Treehouse Private Brands Inc ....G...... 610 589-4526
Womelsdorf (G-20209)

FOOD PRDTS: Cheese Curls & Puffs

Tastysnack Quality Foods Inc ....E...... 717 259-6961
Abbottstown (G-7)

FOOD PRDTS: Chicken, Processed, Cooked

Fourth Street Barbecue Inc..................C...... 724 483-2000
Charleroi (G-3013)

FOOD PRDTS: Chicken, Processed, Frozen

Lewistown Valley Entps Inc ....D...... 570 668-2089
Tamaqua (G-18218)
Philadelphia Poultry Inc ....E...... 215 574-0343
Philadelphia (G-14150)

FOOD PRDTS: Chicken, Processed, NEC

A La Henri Inc ....G...... 724 856-1374
New Castle (G-12052)
E K Holdings Inc ....G...... 717 436-5921
Mifflintown (G-11113)
Empire Kosher Poultry Inc....................E...... 570 374-0501
Selinsgrove (G-17324)
Empire Kosher Poultry Inc....................A...... 717 436-5921
Mifflintown (G-11114)
Mitchel Loading Crew..........................F...... 570 837-5907
Middleburg (G-11032)

FOOD PRDTS: Chicken, Slaughtered & Dressed

Farmers Pride Inc ....A...... 717 865-6626
Fredericksburg (G-6174)
Sechler Family Foods Inc.....................F...... 717 865-6626
Fredericksburg (G-6176)

FOOD PRDTS: Chocolate Bars, Solid

Lifestyle Evolution Inc ....F...... 412 828-4115
Oakmont (G-12920)
Pardoes Perky Peanuts Inc...................E...... 570 524-9595
Montandon (G-11366)

FOOD PRDTS: Chocolate Coatings & Syrup

Blommer Chocolate Company...............D...... 800 825-8181
East Greenville (G-4565)

FOOD PRDTS: Chocolate Liquor

Choccobutter Inc ....G...... 717 756-5590
New Cumberland (G-12184)

FOOD PRDTS: Chocolate, Baking

Casa Luker USA Inc............................... 412 854-9012
Pittsburgh (G-14824)

FOOD PRDTS: Coffee

Coffee and Tea Exchange Corp ....G...... 570 445-8778
Olyphant (G-12987)
East Indies Coffee & Tea ....F...... 717 228-2000
Lebanon (G-9566)
Flavorpros LLC ....F...... 610 435-4300
Allentown (G-215)
Fresh Roasted Coffee LLC....................F...... 570 743-9228
Sunbury (G-18169)
Gamut Enterprises Inc.........................G...... 717 627-5282
Lititz (G-10011)
Melitta Usa Inc...................................G...... 215 355-5581
Southampton (G-17826)
Thomas Miller & Co Inc ....F...... 215 822-3118
Colmar (G-3420)
Van Maanen Albert ....G...... 610 373-7292
Reading (G-16559)
Yum-Yum Colmar Inc ....E...... 215 822-9468
Colmar (G-3426)

FOOD PRDTS: Coffee Extracts

Fresh Start Vend & Cof Svc LLC ....G...... 215 322-8647
Southampton (G-17813)

FOOD PRDTS: Coffee Roasting, Exc Wholesale Grocers

Gerhart Coffee Co ....G...... 717 397-8788
Lancaster (G-9028)
La Prima Expresso Co..........................G...... 412 565-7070
Pittsburgh (G-15212)
Mondelez Global LLC ....A...... 570 820-1200
Wilkes Barre (G-19945)
Valerio Coffee Roasters Inc ....G...... 610 676-0034
Audubon (G-831)

FOOD PRDTS: Coffee, Ground, Mixed With Grain Or Chicory

Wilbur Enterprises Inc.........................G...... 724 625-8010
Gibsonia (G-6358)

FOOD PRDTS: Cole Slaw, Bulk

Chestnut Acres Specialty.....................G...... 717 949-2875
Myerstown (G-11879)

FOOD PRDTS: Cooking Oils, Refined Vegetable, Exc Corn

Good Food Inc....................................C...... 610 273-3776
Honey Brook (G-7745)

FOOD PRDTS: Corn Chips & Other Corn-Based Snacks

Svc Manufacturing Inc.........................G...... 623 907-1822
Mountain Top (G-11777)

FOOD PRDTS: Corn Oil, Refined

Cargill Incorporated................................F...... 717 273-1133
Lebanon (G-9552)

FOOD PRDTS: Corn Syrup, Dried Or Unmixed

Tate Lyle Ingrdnts Amricas LLC ....D 215 295-5011
Morrisville (G-11584)

FOOD PRDTS: Dessert Mixes & Fillings

Smuckers Salad ....G...... 267 757-0944
Newtown (G-12550)

FOOD PRDTS: Dips, Exc Cheese & Sour Cream Based

Easton Salsa Company LLC ....G...... 610 923-3692
Easton (G-4674)

FOOD PRDTS: Dough, Pizza, Prepared

Imperial Dough Company Inc ....G...... 724 695-3625
Oakdale (G-12904)
Rockfish Venture LLP............................F...... 215 968-5054
Newtown (G-12545)
Tomanetti Food Products Inc ....E...... 412 828-3040
Oakmont (G-12928)
Wpp Dough Company Inc ....F...... 814 539-7799
Johnstown (G-8446)

FOOD PRDTS: Doughs, Frozen Or Refrig From Purchased Flour

Plumpys Pierogies Inc ....G...... 570 489-5520
Jessup (G-8335)

FOOD PRDTS: Dressings, Salad, Raw & Cooked Exc Dry Mixes

Angelos Inc...E...... 724 350-8715
Washington (G-19150)
Best Dressed Associates Inc ....F...... 717 938-2222
Lewisberry (G-9881)
Conroy Foods Inc ....F...... 412 781-0977
Pittsburgh (G-14872)
Mondelez Global LLC ....A...... 570 820-1200
Wilkes Barre (G-19945)
Ventura Foods LLC ....G...... 215 223-8700
Philadelphia (G-14439)

FOOD PRDTS: Dried & Dehydrated Fruits, Vegetables & Soup Mix

A L Bazzini Co Inc ....E...... 610 366-1606
Allentown (G-111)
Hanover Foods Corporation ....B...... 800 888-4646
Hanover (G-6895)
Monterey Mushrooms Inc ....F...... 610 929-1961
Temple (G-18333)

FOOD PRDTS: Eggs, Processed

Browns Mill Farm LLC ....G...... 570 345-3153
Schuylkill Haven (G-17149)
Egglands Best Inc.................................E...... 610 265-6500
Malvern (G-10228)
Hillandale Farms of Pa Inc ....E...... 717 229-0601
Gettysburg (G-6299)

FOOD PRDTS: Eggs, Processed, Frozen

Crystal Frms Refrigerated Dist ....B...... 570 425-2910
Klingerstown (G-8807)

FOOD PRDTS: Emulsifiers

Johnnie Lustigs Hotdogs LLC...............G...... 484 661-8333
Bethlehem (G-1546)
S & K Vending ....G...... 570 675-5180
Hunlock Creek (G-7934)

FOOD PRDTS: Fish Oil

Marine Ingredients LLC ....E...... 570 260-6900
Mount Bethel (G-11613)

FOOD PRDTS: Flavored Ices, Frozen

Mia Products Company ....E...... 570 457-7431
Avoca (G-846)

Specialty Ice ....G...... 724 283-7000
Butler (G-2443)
SR Rosati Inc ....F...... 610 626-1818
Clifton Heights (G-3258)
Todd Curyto ....G...... 215 906-8097
Narberth (G-11913)
Via Veneto Italian Ice Inc ....G...... 610 630-3355
Norristown (G-12722)

FOOD PRDTS: Flour

Ardent Mills LLC ....F...... 972 660-9980
Treichlers (G-18476)
F M Browns Sons Incorporated.............D...... 800 334-8816
Reading (G-16384)

FOOD PRDTS: Flour & Other Grain Mill Products

Archer-Daniels-Midland Company ....E...... 717 761-5200
Camp Hill (G-2491)
Archer-Daniels-Midland Company ....E...... 215 547-8424
Langhorne (G-9278)
Ardent Mills LLC ....E...... 717 846-7773
York (G-20385)
Ardent Mills LLC ....E...... 570 839-8322
Pocono Summit (G-15885)
Bedford Farm Bureau Coop Assn ....F...... 814 793-2721
Curryville (G-3945)
Conagra Brands Inc ....F...... 717 846-7773
York (G-20431)
James F Sargent ....G...... 570 549-2168
Millerton (G-11215)
Jpmw Partners LLC ....G...... 484 888-8558
Parkesburg (G-13178)
Pillsbury Company LLC ....D...... 610 593-5133
Parkesburg (G-13182)
Roch Grande Gst Waffles LLC ....C...... 484 840-9179
Glen Mills (G-6442)
Ross Feeds Inc ....F...... 570 289-4388
Kingsley (G-8707)
White Oak Mills Inc ....E...... 717 367-1525
Elizabethtown (G-4891)

FOOD PRDTS: Flour Mixes & Doughs

Charlies Specialties Inc........................D...... 724 346-2350
Hermitage (G-7577)
Country Fresh Batter Inc ....D...... 610 272-5751
King of Prussia (G-8600)
Moms Wholesale Foods Inc ....G...... 724 856-3049
New Castle (G-12122)

FOOD PRDTS: Fruit Juices

Cliffstar LLC ....E...... 814 725-3801
North East (G-12735)
Juice Merchant ....G...... 215 483-8888
Philadelphia (G-13913)
Mr Smoothie ....G...... 412 630-9065
Pittsburgh (G-15306)

FOOD PRDTS: Fruits & Vegetables, Pickled

Epic Pickles LLC ....G...... 717 487-1323
Yoe (G-20360)
Spring Glen Fresh Foods Inc ....D...... 717 733-2201
Ephrata (G-5145)

FOOD PRDTS: Fruits, Dehydrated Or Dried

Moyer Specialty Foods LLC ....F...... 215 703-0100
Souderton (G-17754)

FOOD PRDTS: Fruits, Dried Or Dehydrated, Exc Freeze-Dried

Ames Enterprises Inc ....G...... 814 474-2700
Fairview (G-5813)
Sunsweet Growers Inc ....C...... 610 944-1005
Fleetwood (G-5980)

FOOD PRDTS: Granola & Energy Bars, Nonchocolate

Lifestyle Evolution Inc ....F...... 412 828-4115
Oakmont (G-12920)

FOOD PRDTS: Honey

Bee Positive Foundation ....G...... 484 302-8234
Phoenixville (G-14530)

Dutch Gold Honey Inc ....D...... 717 393-1716
Lancaster (G-9004)
Honey Sandts Co ....G...... 610 252-6511
Easton (G-4700)

FOOD PRDTS: Ice, Blocks

Americold Logistics LLC.......................C...... 215 721-0700
Hatfield (G-7316)
Lansdale Packaged Ice Inc ....F...... 215 256-8808
Harleysville (G-7044)
Rosenbergers Cold Storage ....B...... 215 721-0700
Hatfield (G-7392)
Sculpted Ice Works Inc ....F...... 570 226-6246
Lakeville (G-8913)
TLC Refreshments Inc ....F...... 610 429-4124
West Chester (G-19665)
Winola Ice Co ....F...... 570 378-2726
Dalton (G-3988)

FOOD PRDTS: Ice, Cubes

A E Falgiani Ice Co Inc ....G...... 412 344-7538
Pittsburgh (G-14629)
Good Time Ice ....G...... 717 234-1479
Harrisburg (G-7135)
Martin Associates Ephrata LLC.............F...... 717 733-7968
Ephrata (G-5122)
Nicholas Caputo ....G...... 570 454-8280
Hazleton (G-7513)

FOOD PRDTS: Instant Coffee

Noltpak LLC..G...... 717 725-9862
Quarryville (G-16274)

FOOD PRDTS: Lozenges, Non-Medicated

Adrenalation Inc ....F...... 215 324-3412
Philadelphia (G-13346)
Robert W Gastel Jr ....E...... 412 678-2723
White Oak (G-19858)

FOOD PRDTS: Macaroni, Noodles, Spaghetti, Pasta, Etc

Innofoods Usa Inc ....G...... 412 854-9012
Pittsburgh (G-15126)
Kraft Heinz Company.............................B...... 412 456-5700
Pittsburgh (G-15196)
Kraft Heinz Foods Company ....C...... 412 456-5700
Pittsburgh (G-15197)
P & S Ravioli Co ....G...... 215 339-9929
Philadelphia (G-14109)
P & S Ravioli Co ....F...... 215 465-8888
Philadelphia (G-14108)
Pasta Acquisition Corp ....G...... 559 485-8110
Harrisburg (G-7189)
PCA Group Inc ....G...... 610 558-2802
Garnet Valley (G-6267)
Philadelphia Macaroni Company...........E...... 215 441-5220
Warminster (G-18940)
Prince Company Inc ....G...... 717 526-2200
Harrisburg (G-7201)
Riviana Foods Inc ....C...... 717 526-2200
Harrisburg (G-7207)
Superior Pasta Company Inc ....G...... 215 627-3306
Philadelphia (G-14358)
Taif Inc ....G...... 610 522-0122
Folcroft (G-6017)

FOOD PRDTS: Malt

Deer Creek Malthouse LLC ....G...... 717 746-6258
Glen Mills (G-6433)
Deer Creek Malthouse LLC ....G...... 717 746-6258
Glen Mills (G-6434)
Philadelphia Beer Works Inc.................C...... 215 482-8220
Philadelphia (G-14142)

FOOD PRDTS: Margarine, Including Imitation

L D Kallman Inc ....F...... 610 384-1200
Coatesville (G-3312)

FOOD PRDTS: Mixes, Bread & Roll From Purchased Flour

Byrnes and Kiefer Company..................E...... 724 538-5200
Callery (G-2467)

PRODUCT

FOOD PRDTS: Mixes, Cake, From Purchased Flour

Better Bowls LLC ....G...... 717 298-1257
Hummelstown (G-7902)

FOOD PRDTS: Mixes, Flour

General Mills Inc ....E...... 717 838-7600
Palmyra (G-13124)

General Mills Inc ....D...... 215 784-5100
Dresher (G-4355)

FOOD PRDTS: Mixes, Pancake From Purchased Flour

Roch Grande Gst Waffles LLC ....C...... 484 840-9179
Glen Mills (G-6442)

FOOD PRDTS: Mixes, Sauces, Dry

Torchbearer Sauces LLC......................G...... 717 697-3568
Mechanicsburg (G-10898)

FOOD PRDTS: Molasses

Good Food Inc......................................C...... 610 273-3776
Honey Brook (G-7745)

FOOD PRDTS: Mustard, Prepared

Herlocher Foods Inc ....G...... 814 237-0134
State College (G-17975)

FOOD PRDTS: Noodles, Uncooked, Packaged W/Other Ingredients

East Asia Noodle Inc ....F...... 215 923-6838
Philadelphia (G-13654)

FOOD PRDTS: Nuts & Seeds

A L Bazzini Co Inc ....E...... 610 366-1606
Allentown (G-111)

Bal Nut Inc ....G...... 570 675-2712
Dallas (G-3958)

Bazzini Holdings LLC ....C...... 610 366-1606
Allentown (G-147)

Pardoes Perky Peanuts Inc ....E...... 570 524-9595
Montandon (G-11366)

Stutz Candy Company ....E...... 215 675-2630
Hatboro (G-7307)

FOOD PRDTS: Oil, Hydrogenated, Edible

Mallet and Company Inc.......................G...... 412 276-9000
Carnegie (G-2776)

FOOD PRDTS: Olive Oil

A & S Olive Oil Company Inc ....G...... 267 483-8379
Chalfont (G-2862)

Cape May Olive Oil Company ....G...... 610 256-3667
Morton (G-11590)

Cardenas Oil & Vinegar Taproom.........G...... 570 401-4718
Philadelphia (G-13501)

Kalamata Farms Llc ....F...... 570 972-1021
Allentown (G-279)

Kapothanasis Group Inc ....G...... 207 939-5680
Harrisburg (G-7160)

Maeva Usa Inc ....G...... 215 461-2453
Philadelphia (G-13986)

Olio Fresca Olive Oil Company ....G...... 585 820-8400
Ridgway (G-16722)

Olive Kastania Oil ....G...... 610 347-6736
Kennett Square (G-8533)

Olive Oakmont Oil Company ....G...... 412 435-6912
Oakmont (G-12921)

Olive Olio Oils and Balsamics ....G...... 717 627-0088
Lititz (G-10027)

PCA Group Inc ....G...... 610 558-2802
Garnet Valley (G-6267)

Two Rivers Olives Oil Company ....G...... 724 775-2748
Beaver (G-994)

FOOD PRDTS: Onions, Pickled

Gourmet Specialty Imports...................F...... 610 345-1113
Kelton (G-8488)

FOOD PRDTS: Oriental Noodles

Lung Hing Noodle Company Inc ....G...... 215 829-1988
Philadelphia (G-13976)

FOOD PRDTS: Pasta, Rice/Potatoes, Uncooked, Pkgd

Philadelphia Macaroni Company...........E...... 215 441-5220
Warminster (G-18940)

Quality Pasta Company LLC ....G...... 855 878-9630
Charleroi (G-3020)

Superior Pasta Company Inc ....G...... 215 627-3306
Philadelphia (G-14358)

T & L Pierogie Incorporated ....E...... 570 454-3198
Hazleton (G-7528)

U S Durum Products Limited ....F...... 717 293-8698
Lancaster (G-9226)

Zappone Bros Foods ....G...... 724 539-1430
Latrobe (G-9529)

FOOD PRDTS: Pasta, Uncooked, Packaged With Other Ingredients

Nestle Usa Inc ....C...... 818 549-6000
King of Prussia (G-8655)

PCA Group Inc ....G...... 610 558-2802
Garnet Valley (G-6267)

Positively Pasta ....G...... 484 945-1007
Pottstown (G-16032)

Springfield Pasta ....G...... 610 543-5687
Springfield (G-17923)

FOOD PRDTS: Peanut Butter

J M Smucker PA Inc ....E...... 814 275-1323
New Bethlehem (G-12026)

J S Zimmerman Co ....G...... 717 232-6842
Harrisburg (G-7157)

FOOD PRDTS: Pickles, Vinegar

Lionette Enterprises ....G...... 814 274-9401
Coudersport (G-3784)

William Kleinberger & Sons ....E...... 570 347-9331
Scranton (G-17314)

FOOD PRDTS: Pizza, Refrigerated

Mama Nardone Baking Co Inc ....E...... 570 825-3421
Hazleton (G-7509)

Petruzzi Pizza Mfg Inc..........................E...... 570 454-5887
Hazleton (G-7517)

FOOD PRDTS: Popcorn, Popped

Burkey Acquisition Inc ....D...... 717 292-5611
Dover (G-4189)

Utz Quality Foods Inc ....C...... 717 637-5666
Hanover (G-6966)

FOOD PRDTS: Popcorn, Unpopped

Reist Popcorn Company ....G...... 717 653-8078
Mount Joy (G-11669)

FOOD PRDTS: Pork Rinds

Keystone Food Products Inc ....C...... 610 258-2706
Easton (G-4711)

FOOD PRDTS: Potato & Corn Chips & Similar Prdts

Bickels Snack Foods Inc......................E...... 800 233-1933
York (G-20403)

Bickels Snack Foods Inc......................D...... 717 843-0738
York (G-20404)

Brothers Wood Company ....G...... 814 462-2422
Corry (G-3746)

Condor Snack Company ....C...... 303 333-6075
Hanover (G-6868)

Cuthbert & Son Inc ....E...... 717 657-1050
Harrisburg (G-7111)

Frito-Lay North America Inc ....E...... 570 323-6175
Williamsport (G-20014)

Frito-Lay North America Inc ....C...... 717 624-4206
New Oxford (G-12409)

Frito-Lay North America Inc ....B...... 717 792-2611
York (G-20488)

G & S Foods Inc ....E...... 717 259-5323
Abbottstown (G-4)

Good Health Natural Pdts Inc ....G...... 570 655-0823
Pittston (G-15753)

Herr Foods Incorporated......................E...... 610 395-6200
Allentown (G-245)

Herr Foods Incorporated......................E...... 215 934-7144
Philadelphia (G-13819)

Herr Foods Incorporated......................D...... 215 492-5990
Philadelphia (G-13820)

Innovative Advg Vend Svcs LLC ....G...... 814 528-7204
Erie (G-5325)

Inventure Foods Inc.............................B...... 623 932-6200
Hanover (G-6903)

Ira Middleswarth and Son Inc ....G...... 717 248-3093
Lewistown (G-9936)

Martins Potato Chips Inc......................G...... 610 777-3643
Reading (G-16438)

Middleswarth and Son Inc....................D...... 570 837-1431
Middleburg (G-11030)

Ralph Good Inc ....F...... 610 367-2253
Boyertown (G-1925)

Sensible Portions ....G...... 717 898-7131
Mountville (G-11802)

Wise Foods Inc ....A...... 888 759-4401
Berwick (G-1347)

Wise Foods Employees Chrtble E.........G...... 570 759-4095
Berwick (G-1348)

World Gourmet Acquisition LLC ....D...... 717 285-1884
Mountville (G-11804)

FOOD PRDTS: Potato Chips & Other Potato-Based Snacks

Birds Eye Foods Inc ....C...... 814 267-4641
Berlin (G-1284)

Birds Eye Foods Inc ....F...... 814 942-6031
Altoona (G-478)

Birds Eye Foods LLC ....B...... 814 267-4641
Berlin (G-1285)

Dieffenbachs Potato Chips Inc ....D...... 610 589-2385
Womelsdorf (G-20206)

Good Health Natural Pdts Inc ....F...... 336 285-0735
Hanover (G-6888)

Hanover Foods Corporation ....C...... 717 665-2002
York (G-20521)

Hartleys Potato Chip Mfg ....F...... 717 248-0526
Lewistown (G-9934)

Herr Foods Incorporated......................A...... 610 932-9330
Nottingham (G-12882)

Herr Foods Incorporated......................A...... 610 932-9330
Nottingham (G-12883)

Kings Potato Chip Company ....E...... 717 445-4521
Mohnton (G-11268)

Martins Potato Chips Inc......................C...... 717 792-3065
Thomasville (G-18341)

Ralph Good Inc ....E...... 717 484-4884
Adamstown (G-23)

S-L Snacks Real Estate Inc ....A...... 717 632-4477
Hanover (G-6948)

Savor Street Foods Inc.........................E...... 610 320-7800
Wyomissing (G-20288)

Utz Quality Foods Inc ....F...... 570 368-8050
Montoursville (G-11455)

Utz Quality Foods Inc ....D...... 717 637-6644
Hanover (G-6965)

Utz Quality Foods LLC ....A...... 800 367-7629
Hanover (G-6967)

Utz Quality Foods LLC ....B...... 717 698-4032
Hanover (G-6968)

FOOD PRDTS: Potatoes, Dried

Keystone Potato Products LLC.............D...... 570 695-0909
Hegins (G-7542)

FOOD PRDTS: Potatoes, Fresh Cut & Peeled

E&M Wholesale Foods ....F...... 610 367-2299
Boyertown (G-1909)

FOOD PRDTS: Poultry, Processed, Fresh

Mac Millan William Company................F...... 215 627-3273
Philadelphia (G-13985)

Sharon McGuigan Inc............................E...... 610 361-8100
Aston (G-793)

FOOD PRDTS: Poultry, Slaughtered & Dressed

Hain Pure Protein Corporation ....C...... 717 865-2136
Fredericksburg (G-6175)

FOOD PRDTS: Preparations

AFP Advanced Food Products LLC ......C...... 717 355-8667
New Holland (G-12227)

Angle Foods LLC ....G...... 724 900-0908
Pittsburgh (G-14711)

Arrow Supply Company Inc ....G...... 773 863-8655
Willow Grove (G-20108)
Bacon Jams LLC ....G...... 856 720-0255
West Chester (G-19507)
Bickels Snack Foods Inc ....D...... 717 843-0738
York (G-20404)
Brads Raw Chips LLC ....F...... 215 766-3739
Doylestown (G-4279)
Castle Cheese Inc ....E...... 724 368-3022
Pittsburgh (G-14826)
Charles Jacquin Et Cie Inc ....F...... 215 425-9300
Philadelphia (G-13530)
Choo R Choo Snacks Inc ....G...... 717 273-7499
Lebanon (G-9554)
Chucks Salsa ....G...... 724 513-5708
Baden (G-870)
Compass Group Usa Inc ....D...... 717 569-2671
Lancaster (G-8982)
Conagra Brands Inc ....A...... 570 742-7621
Milton (G-11236)
Conagra Brands Inc ....C...... 570 742-6607
Milton (G-11237)
Conagra Brands Inc ....E...... 570 742-8910
Milton (G-11238)
Cooke Tavern Ltd ....G...... 814 422-7687
Spring Mills (G-17887)
Country Fresh Pennsylvania LLC ....C...... 215 855-2408
Hatfield (G-7327)
Custom Particle Reduction Inc ....F...... 215 766-9791
Plumsteadville (G-15808)
Dalos Bakery Inc ....E...... 570 752-4519
Berwick (G-1322)
Davis & Davis Gourmet Foods ....G...... 412 487-7770
Allison Park (G-449)
Diabetic Pastry Chef Inc ....G...... 412 260-6468
Pittsburgh (G-14921)
East Indies Coffee & Tea ....F...... 717 228-2000
Lebanon (G-9566)
Ethnic Gourmet Foods Inc ....E...... 610 692-2209
West Chester (G-19552)
Federal Pretzel Baking Co ....E...... 215 467-0505
Philadelphia (G-13695)
Fresh Food Manufacturing Co ....A...... 412 963-6200
Pittsburgh (G-15037)
Frito-Lay North America Inc ....E...... 570 323-6175
Williamsport (G-20014)
Gmp Nutraceuticals Inc ....F...... 484 924-9042
King of Prussia (G-8625)
Goldfam Inc ....G...... 215 379-6433
Cheltenham (G-3028)
Gourmail Inc ....G...... 610 522-2650
Berwyn (G-1364)
Gruma Corporation ....B...... 570 474-6890
Mountain Top (G-11763)
Gtf Worldwide LLC ....D...... 610 873-3663
Downingtown (G-4231)
Hall Foods Inc ....G...... 412 257-9877
Bridgeville (G-2067)
Hanover Potato Products Inc ....G...... 717 632-0700
Hanover (G-6898)
Herb Penn Co Ltd ....E...... 215 632-6100
Philadelphia (G-13816)
Intercourse Pretzel Factory ....E...... 717 768-3432
Intercourse (G-8137)
International Bakery ....E...... 814 452-3435
Erie (G-5329)
Jackson Farms Dairy ....E...... 724 246-7010
New Salem (G-12445)
Jamaica Way Limited ....G...... 267 593-9724
Philadelphia (G-13889)
James J Tuzzi Jr ....E...... 570 752-2704
Berwick (G-1329)
Joo Young Inc ....G...... 267 298-0054
Willow Grove (G-20122)
Joy Cone Co ....B...... 724 962-5747
Hermitage (G-7589)
Knouse Foods Cooperative Inc ....C...... 717 677-9115
Biglerville (G-1666)
Leonetti Food Distributors Inc ....E...... 215 729-4200
Philadelphia (G-13966)
Lettuce Turnip The Beet ....G...... 412 334-8631
South Park (G-17784)
Mallet and Company Inc ....G...... 412 276-9000
Carnegie (G-2776)
Martins Potato Chips Inc ....C...... 717 792-3065
Thomasville (G-18341)
Masteros Homestyle Foods Inc ....G...... 215 551-2530
Philadelphia (G-13994)
Modern Mushroom Farms Inc ....B...... 610 268-3535
Toughkenamon (G-18420)

Moshes Foods LLC ....G...... 215 291-8333
Philadelphia (G-14041)
Nardone Brothers Baking Co ....C...... 570 823-0141
Hanover Township (G-6999)
Neillys Food LLC ....F...... 717 428-6431
York (G-20610)
Nissin Foods USA Company Inc ....C...... 717 291-5901
Lancaster (G-9146)
Nutrition Inc ....E...... 724 978-2100
Irwin (G-8185)
Nutrition Inc ....E...... 814 382-3656
Irwin (G-8186)
O Land Lakes ....F...... 717 845-8076
York (G-20614)
Palace Foods Inc ....F...... 610 939-0631
Wilkes Barre (G-19955)
Palace Foods Inc ....F...... 610 775-9947
Reading (G-16464)
Pizza Associates Incorporated ....C...... 570 822-6600
Wilkes Barre (G-19957)
Protica Inc ....E...... 610 832-2000
Whitehall (G-19887)
Purity Candy Co ....F...... 570 538-9502
Allenwood (G-442)
Qtg Qu Trop Gat9084 ....F...... 570 474-9995
Mountain Top (G-11773)
Revonah Pretzel LLC ....F...... 717 632-4477
Hanover (G-6943)
Rtcsnacks LLC ....G...... 570 234-7266
Effort (G-4828)
Saturnalian N Y A ....G...... 215 271-9181
Philadelphia (G-14282)
Savello USA Incorporated ....F...... 570 822-9743
Hanover Township (G-7005)
Savor Street Foods Inc ....E...... 610 320-7800
Wyomissing (G-20288)
Seneca Foods Corporation ....E...... 717 675-2074
Lebanon (G-9629)
Snap Kitchen 3 LLC ....G...... 215 845-0001
Philadelphia (G-14318)
Stone County Specialties Inc ....G...... 570 467-2850
Tamaqua (G-18228)
Sunsweet Growers Inc ....G...... 610 944-1005
Fleetwood (G-5980)
Todds Snax Inc ....C...... 717 637-5931
Hanover (G-6961)
Troyer Inc ....E...... 724 746-1162
Canonsburg (G-2648)
Tshudy Snacks Inc ....F...... 717 626-4354
Lititz (G-10055)
Uncle Henrys Pretzel Bakery ....E...... 717 445-4698
Bowmansville (G-1888)
Unique Pretzel Bakery Inc ....E...... 610 929-3172
Reading (G-16553)
Utz Quality Foods Inc ....D...... 717 637-6644
Hanover (G-6965)
Utz Quality Foods Inc ....C...... 717 637-5666
Hanover (G-6966)
Utz Quality Foods LLC ....A...... 800 367-7629
Hanover (G-6967)

FOOD PRDTS: Prepared Meat Sauces Exc Tomato & Dry

Sunrise Maple ....F...... 814 628-3110
Westfield (G-19781)
Woods Wings ....G...... 610 417-5684
Kintnersville (G-8730)

FOOD PRDTS: Prepared Sauces, Exc Tomato Based

Bay Valley Foods LLC ....C...... 814 725-9617
North East (G-12731)
Belletieri Sauces Inc ....G...... 610 433-4334
Allentown (G-149)
Golden Path LLC ....G...... 215 290-1582
Philadelphia (G-13776)
Lancaster Fine Foods Inc ....E...... 717 397-9578
Lancaster (G-9094)

FOOD PRDTS: Prepared Seafood Sauces Exc Tomato & Dry

Fresh Foods Manufacturing ....E...... 724 683-3639
Freedom (G-6190)

FOOD PRDTS: Relishes, Vinegar

Byler Relish House LLC ....G...... 814 763-6510
Saegertown (G-16908)

FOOD PRDTS: Salads

Aldon Food Corporation ....E...... 484 991-1000
Schwenksville (G-17172)
Andorra Salad Inc ....G...... 215 482-5750
Philadelphia (G-13390)
Ask Foods Inc ....C...... 717 838-6356
Palmyra (G-13117)
Ask Foods Inc ....E...... 717 838-6356
Palmyra (G-13118)
E S H Poultry ....F...... 717 517-9535
Lancaster (G-9005)
Fresh Express Mid-Atlantic LLC ....C...... 717 561-2900
Harrisburg (G-7131)
Hanover Foods Corporation ....A...... 717 632-6000
Hanover (G-6894)
Ooh Lala Salad ....G...... 215 769-1006
Philadelphia (G-14097)
Sadies Salads ....G...... 717 768-3774
Gordonville (G-6563)
Subway ....F...... 814 368-2576
Bradford (G-1993)
Van Bennett Food Co Inc ....E...... 610 374-8348
Mohnton (G-11272)
Verls Salads Inc ....F...... 717 865-2771
Fredericksburg (G-6177)
Winter Gardens Qulty Foods Inc ....C...... 717 624-4911
New Oxford (G-12427)

FOOD PRDTS: Sausage, Poultry

E S H Poultry ....F...... 717 517-9535
Lancaster (G-9005)

FOOD PRDTS: Seasonings & Spices

Con Yeager Company ....E...... 724 452-4120
Zelienople (G-20795)
Innofoods Usa Inc ....G...... 412 854-9012
Pittsburgh (G-15126)
Kestrel Growth Brands Inc ....G...... 484 932-8447
Phoenixville (G-14556)
Newly Weds Foods Inc ....C...... 610 758-9100
Bethlehem (G-1584)
Radiance ....G...... 717 290-1517
Lancaster (G-9185)
World Flavors Inc ....D...... 215 672-4400
Warminster (G-19003)

FOOD PRDTS: Soup Mixes

E S H Poultry ....F...... 717 517-9535
Lancaster (G-9005)

FOOD PRDTS: Soup Mixes, Dried

Ncc Wholesome Foods Inc ....F...... 724 652-3440
New Castle (G-12124)

FOOD PRDTS: Soups, Dehydrated

Cooke Tavern Ltd ....G...... 814 422-7687
Spring Mills (G-17887)

FOOD PRDTS: Soybean Flour & Grits

Nature Soy LLC ....F...... 215 765-3289
Philadelphia (G-14058)

FOOD PRDTS: Spices, Including Ground

Melt Enterprises LLC ....G...... 570 244-2970
Gouldsboro (G-6569)
Spices Inc ....E...... 570 509-2340
Elysburg (G-4982)
William Plange ....G...... 215 303-0069
Philadelphia (G-14475)

FOOD PRDTS: Spreads, Garlic

Ronald J Stidmon ....G...... 724 336-0501
Enon Valley (G-5088)

FOOD PRDTS: Sugar, Cane

Sugar Shack ....F...... 814 425-2220
Cochranton (G-3352)
Sugaright LLC ....F...... 215 295-4709
Fairless Hills (G-5800)

FOOD PRDTS: Sugar, Liquid Sugar Beet

CSC Sugar LLC ....F...... 215 428-3670
Fairless Hills (G-5777)

PRODUCT

FOOD PRDTS: Sugar, Maple, Indl

Paul Family Farms LLC ....G...... 570 772-2420
Galeton (G-6242)

Triple Creek ....G...... 814 756-4500
Cranesville (G-3872)

FOOD PRDTS: Sugar, Refined Cane, Purchased Raw Sugar/Syrup

CSC Sugar LLC ....F 215 428-3670
Fairless Hills (G-5777)

FOOD PRDTS: Syrup, Maple

Blue Mountain Farms LLC ....G...... 717 599-5110
Harrisburg (G-7097)

Brennemans Maple Syrup & Eqp ....G...... 814 941-8974
Salisbury (G-17044)

Citadelle ....G...... 610 777-8844
Shillington (G-17503)

Firth Maple Products Inc ....F 814 654-7265
Spartansburg (G-17850)

Hurry Hill Maple Syrup ....G...... 814 734-1358
Edinboro (G-4814)

Jacobsons Farm Syrup Co ....G...... 814 367-2880
Westfield (G-19778)

Lochs Maple Fiber Mill Inc ....G...... 570 965-2679
Springville (G-17931)

Speedwell Garage ....G...... 607 434-2376
Klingerstown (G-8808)

Sunrise Maple ....F 814 628-3110
Westfield (G-19781)

Wittmans Pure Maple Syrup LLC ....G...... 814 781-7523
Saint Marys (G-17030)

FOOD PRDTS: Tea

Darling Blends LLC ....G...... 215 630-2802
Langhorne (G-9288)

Flavorpros LLC ....F 610 435-4300
Allentown (G-215)

Harrowgate Fine Foods Inc ....G...... 717 823-6855
Lancaster (G-9039)

FOOD PRDTS: Tofu, Exc Frozen Desserts

Fresh Tofu Inc ....E 610 433-4711
Allentown (G-219)

Jadeite Foods LLC ....G...... 267 522-8193
Bensalem (G-1211)

Sun Kee Tofu Food Co ....G...... 215 625-3818
Philadelphia (G-14355)

FOOD PRDTS: Tortilla Chips

Gruma Corporation ....B 570 474-6890
Mountain Top (G-11763)

Reyna Foods Inc ....G...... 412 904-1242
Pittsburgh (G-15481)

FOOD PRDTS: Tortillas

El Milagro ....G...... 412 668-2627
Pittsburgh (G-14961)

Isabelles Kitchen Inc ....D 215 256-7987
Harleysville (G-7040)

FOOD PRDTS: Turkey, Processed, Cooked

Mrs Resslers Food Products Co ....D 215 744-4700
Philadelphia (G-14043)

FOOD PRDTS: Turkey, Processed, NEC

Jaindls Incorporated ....D 610 395-3333
Orefield (G-13013)

FOOD PRDTS: Vegetable Oil Mills, NEC

Boyd Station LLC ....E 866 411-2693
Danville (G-3998)

FOOD PRDTS: Vegetable Shortenings, Exc Corn Oil

Ventura Foods LLC ....C 717 263-6900
Chambersburg (G-2997)

FOOD PRDTS: Vinegar

Gourmet Vinegars By Linda Lu ....G...... 724 353-2026
Sarver (G-17070)

Oil & Vinegar ....G...... 724 840-9656
Chicora (G-3128)

Vinegar Hill Picture Works ....G...... 724 596-0023
Indiana (G-8134)

FOOD PRDTS: Wheat Flour

Snavelys Mill Inc ....G...... 717 626-6256
Lititz (G-10050)

Snavelys Mill Inc ....F 570 726-4747
Mill Hall (G-11182)

FOOD PRODUCTS MACHINERY

Abec Inc ....C 610 882-1541
Bethlehem (G-1442)

Beverage-Air Corporation ....C 814 849-7336
Brookville (G-2250)

Boy Machines Inc ....E 610 363-9121
Exton (G-5656)

Bradford Allegheny Corporation ....C 814 362-2590
Lewis Run (G-9871)

Bradford Allegheny Corporation ....D 814 362-2593
Lewis Run (G-9874)

Captain Chuckys Crab Cake Co I ....G...... 610 355-7525
Newtown Square (G-12569)

Conair Corporation ....D 717 485-4871
Mc Connellsburg (G-10563)

Craft Manufacturing Inc ....F 724 532-2702
Latrobe (G-9467)

Gold Medal Products Co ....G...... 412 787-1030
Pittsburgh (G-15056)

Graybill Machines Inc ....E 717 626-5221
Lititz (G-10013)

John Bean Technologies Corp ....C 215 822-4600
Chalfont (G-2877)

Lee Industries Inc ....C 814 342-0460
Philipsburg (G-14519)

Mallet and Company Inc ....G...... 412 276-9000
Carnegie (G-2776)

N C Stauffer & Sons Inc ....D 570 945-3047
Factoryville (G-5758)

ODonnell Metal Fabricators ....F 610 279-8810
Norristown (G-12697)

Packaging Progressions Inc ....E 610 489-9096
Souderton (G-17758)

Reading Bakery Systems Inc ....D 610 693-5816
Robesonia (G-16778)

Santucci Process Development ....G...... 412 787-0747
Mc Kees Rocks (G-10633)

Top Line Process Equipment ....D 814 362-4626
Bradford (G-1994)

Win-Holt Equipment Corp ....C 516 222-0335
Allentown (G-436)

FOOD STORES: Convenience, Chain

Atlantic Refining & Marketing ....C 215 977-3000
Philadelphia (G-13422)

Sunoco (R&m) LLC ....D 215 977-3000
Newtown Square (G-12592)

FOOD STORES: Convenience, Independent

Mimco Products LLC ....G...... 724 258-8208
Monongahela (G-11311)

FOOD STORES: Cooperative

Suzannes Choclat & Confections ....G...... 570 753-8545
Avis (G-838)

FOOD STORES: Delicatessen

McClures Pie and Salad Inc ....F 717 442-4461
Gap (G-6253)

New York Bagelry ....G...... 610 678-6420
Reading (G-16455)

FOOD STORES: Grocery, Independent

Ccffg Inc ....D 570 270-3976
Wilkes Barre (G-19911)

Darlings Locker Plant ....G...... 570 945-5716
La Plume (G-8869)

Don Saylors Markets Inc ....C 717 776-7551
Newville (G-12600)

Dons Lykens Food Market Inc ....D 717 453-7042
Lykens (G-10132)

Gerritys Super Market Inc ....D 570 961-9030
Scranton (G-17239)

Palumbos Meats Dubois Inc ....E 814 371-2150
Du Bois (G-4412)

Positively Pasta ....G...... 484 945-1007
Pottstown (G-16032)

Schiel Inc ....C 570 970-4460
Wilkes Barre (G-19962)

Spices Inc ....E 570 509-2340
Elysburg (G-4982)

Sunnyway Foods Inc ....D 717 264-6001
Chambersburg (G-2980)

Thoma Meat Market Inc ....E 724 352-2020
Saxonburg (G-17097)

William Aupperle ....G...... 724 583-8310
Masontown (G-10538)

FOOD STORES: Supermarkets

Duritzas Enterprises Inc ....C 724 223-5494
Washington (G-19165)

Ferguson and Hassler Inc ....C 717 786-7301
Quarryville (G-16269)

Gourmail Inc ....G...... 610 522-2650
Berwyn (G-1364)

Leclerc Foods Usa Inc ....D 570 547-6295
Montgomery (G-11375)

FOOD STORES: Supermarkets, Chain

Acme Markets Inc ....C 215 725-9310
Philadelphia (G-13341)

Giant Eagle ....C 724 772-1030
Cranberry Township (G-3821)

Redners Markets Inc ....C 610 678-2900
Reading (G-16494)

Redners Markets Inc ....D 610 776-2726
Allentown (G-372)

Tops Markets LLC ....D 570 882-9188
Sayre (G-17123)

Wakefern Food Corp ....D 215 744-9500
Philadelphia (G-14457)

Weis Markets Inc ....C 570 724-6364
Wellsboro (G-19474)

FOOD STORES: Supermarkets, Independent

Safran Brothers Inc ....E 724 266-9758
Ambridge (G-633)

Sunnyway Foods Inc ....D 717 597-7121
Greencastle (G-6637)

FOOTWEAR, WHOLESALE: Shoes

A Tru Diva LLC ....G...... 888 400-1034
Brookhaven (G-2241)

Modzori LLC ....G...... 215 833-3618
Newtown (G-12522)

Titan Group Ltd ....E 610 631-0831
Norristown (G-12719)

Up-Front Footwear Inc ....G...... 717 492-1875
Mount Joy (G-11674)

Urban Outfitters Wholesale Inc ....G...... 215 454-5500
Philadelphia (G-14431)

FOOTWEAR: Cut Stock

Keystone Leather Distrs LLC ....F 570 329-3780
Williamsport (G-20031)

Quality Crrctons Inspctons Inc ....D 814 696-3737
Duncansville (G-4462)

Stevens Clogging Supplies Inc ....G...... 724 662-0808
Mercer (G-10976)

FOOTWEAR: Except Rubber, NEC

Sunnys Fashions ....G...... 724 527-1800
Jeannette (G-8266)

Up-Front Footwear Inc ....G...... 717 492-1875
Mount Joy (G-11674)

FORESTRY EQPT WHOLESALERS

Horlacher & Sherwood ....G...... 570 836-6298
Tunkhannock (G-18539)

FORGES: Fan

Phoenix Forging Company Inc ....G...... 610 530-8249
Allentown (G-350)

FORGINGS

Accuride Akw LP ....G...... 814 459-7589
Erie (G-5168)

Adomis Industrial Mch Maint ....G...... 717 244-0716
Windsor (G-20195)

Allegheny Ludlum LLC ....F 724 567-2670
Vandergrift (G-18722)
American Hollow Boring Company ......E 800 673-2458
Erie (G-5187)
Architectural Iron Company ......E 570 296-7722
Milford (G-11156)
Arro Forge Inc ....F 814 724-4223
Meadville (G-10704)
ATI Operating Holdings LLC ......G 412 394-2800
Pittsburgh (G-14731)
Baldt Inc ....E 610 447-5200
Bryn Mawr (G-2315)
Brad Foote Gear Works Inc ......E 412 264-1428
Pittsburgh (G-14789)
Cobra Anchors Corp ....D 610 929-5764
Temple (G-18326)
Corry Forge Company ....E 814 664-9664
Corry (G-3749)
Corry Forge Company ....E 814 459-4495
Erie (G-5234)
Eaton Electric Holdings LLC ......D 717 755-2933
York (G-20462)
Ecm ....C 724 347-0250
Hermitage (G-7580)
Ellwood City Forge Company ......E 724 202-5008
New Castle (G-12083)
Ellwood Group Inc ....E 724 658-3685
New Castle (G-12084)
Ellwood Group Inc ....B 724 752-0055
Ellwood City (G-4931)
Ellwood Group Inc ....C 724 981-1012
Hermitage (G-7582)
Ellwood National Crankshaft Co ......C 814 563-7522
Irvine (G-8139)
Enginred Arrsting Systems Corp ......C 610 494-8000
Upper Chichester (G-18660)
Environmental Inc ....G 412 394-2800
Pittsburgh (G-14978)
Erie Bolt Corporation ....D 814 456-4287
Blairsville (G-1720)
Erie Forge and Steel Inc ....D 814 452-2300
Erie (G-5267)
Erie Tool and Forge Inc ....E 814 587-2841
Springboro (G-17895)
Federal-Mogul Motorparts LLC ......G 717 430-5021
York (G-20478)
Fessler Machine Company ....E 724 346-0878
Sharon (G-17433)
Fluid Gear Products LLC ....G 484 480-3923
Marcus Hook (G-10441)
General Dynamics Ots PA Inc ......C 570 342-7801
Scranton (G-17238)
General Electric Company ....D 412 469-6080
West Mifflin (G-19739)
Homewood Products Corporation ......E 412 665-2700
Pittsburgh (G-15099)
J B Booth and Co ....G 724 452-1313
Zelienople (G-20806)
J B Booth and Co ....F 724 452-8400
Zelienople (G-20805)
Kal-Cameron Manufacturing ......F 814 486-3394
Emporium (G-5065)
Keystone Forging Company ....C 570 473-3524
Northumberland (G-12868)
Klaric Forge & Machine Inc ......F 814 382-6290
Farrell (G-5868)
Lenape Forged Products Corp ......D 610 793-5090
West Chester (G-19592)
Markovitz Enterprises Inc ....D 724 452-4500
Zelienople (G-20810)
Markovitz Enterprises Inc ....E 724 658-6575
New Castle (G-12119)
Martin Sprocket & Gear Inc ......D 610 837-1841
Danielsville (G-3994)
Meadville Forging Company LP ......B 814 332-8200
Meadville (G-10758)
Meadville Forging Company LP ......D 814 398-2203
Cambridge Springs (G-2483)
Medico Industries Inc ....C 570 825-7711
Wilkes Barre (G-19942)
Medico Industries Inc ....E 570 825-7711
Hanover Township (G-6996)
Mercer Forge Corporation ....C 724 662-2750
Mercer (G-10968)
Metaltech Inc ....E 814 375-9399
Du Bois (G-4406)
North American Forgemasters Co ......E 724 656-6440
New Castle (G-12132)
Peerless Chain Company ....F 800 395-2445
Mount Pleasant (G-11710)

Penn Machine Company ....D 814 288-1547
Johnstown (G-8421)
Pennsylvania Machine Works Inc ......C 610 497-3300
Upper Chichester (G-18669)
Phoenix Forge Group LLC ....F 800 234-8665
Reading (G-16470)
Phoenix Forging Company Inc ......G 610 530-8249
Allentown (G-350)
Phoenix Forging Company Inc ......G 610 264-2861
Catasauqua (G-2816)
Prl Industries Inc ....E 717 273-6787
Cornwall (G-3740)
Process Science & Innovation ......G 717 428-3511
Glen Rock (G-6460)
Qdp Inc ....F 610 828-2324
Plymouth Meeting (G-15866)
Sac Industries Inc ....F 412 787-7500
Pittsburgh (G-15505)
Safari Tools Inc ....D 717 350-9869
Mercer (G-10974)
St Marys Pressed Metals Inc ......E 814 772-7455
Ridgway (G-16730)
T S K Partners Inc ....D 814 459-4495
Erie (G-5503)
Union Electric Steel Corp ....D 724 947-9595
Burgettstown (G-2358)
Unisteel LLC ....G 724 657-1160
New Castle (G-12161)
Whemco Inc ....E 412 390-2700
Pittsburgh (G-15715)

FORGINGS: Aircraft, Ferrous

Wyman-Gordon Pennsylvania LLC ......E 570 474-6371
Mountain Top (G-11783)

FORGINGS: Aluminum

Wendell August Forge Inc ....G 724 748-9500
Mercer (G-10979)

FORGINGS: Automotive & Internal Combustion Engine

Metaldyne Sintered Ridgway LLC ......D 814 776-1141
Ridgway (G-16717)
Mg Industries Inc ....G 724 694-8290
Derry (G-4105)

FORGINGS: Bearing & Bearing Race, Nonferrous

Symmco Inc ....C 814 894-2461
Sykesville (G-18203)

FORGINGS: Construction Or Mining Eqpt, Ferrous

Cleveland Brothers Eqp Co Inc ......F 717 564-2121
Harrisburg (G-7107)
S & S Slides Inc ....G 724 545-2001
Kittanning (G-8791)

FORGINGS: Gear & Chain

E-Tech Industrial ....G 570 297-1300
Troy (G-18522)
Timken Gears & Services Inc ......C 610 265-3000
King of Prussia (G-8689)

FORGINGS: Iron & Steel

Action Materials Inc ....G 610 377-3037
Lehighton (G-9709)
Ellwood National Forge Company ......C 814 563-7522
Irvine (G-8140)
Erie Forge and Steel Inc ....D 814 452-2300
Erie (G-5267)
Goldsborough & Vansant Inc ......E 724 287-5590
East Butler (G-4532)

FORGINGS: Machinery, Ferrous

Goldsborough & Vansant Inc ......G 724 782-0393
Finleyville (G-5959)
Winston & Duke Inc ....E 814 456-0582
Erie (G-5530)

FORGINGS: Machinery, Nonferrous

Winston & Duke Inc ....E 814 456-0582
Erie (G-5530)

FORGINGS: Metal , Ornamental, Ferrous

North Amrcn Hgnas Holdings Inc ......C 814 479-2551
Hollsopple (G-7659)

FORGINGS: Nonferrous

Electric Materials Company ....C 814 725-9621
North East (G-12739)
Eureka Electrical Products ....E 814 725-9638
North East (G-12742)
General Dynamics Ots PA Inc ......C 570 342-7801
Scranton (G-17238)
Hussey Marine Alloys Ltd ....E 724 251-4200
Leetsdale (G-9694)
Keystone Forging Company ....C 570 473-3524
Northumberland (G-12868)

FORGINGS: Nuclear Power Plant, Ferrous

Kepco Plant Service & Engrg Co ......G 412 374-3410
Cranberry Township (G-3828)

FORGINGS: Pump & Compressor, Ferrous

Tekni-Plex Inc ....E 484 690-1520
Wayne (G-19381)
Trident Tpi Holdings Inc ....A 484 690-1520
Wayne (G-19384)

FORMS: Concrete, Sheet Metal

CFC Manufacturing Co Inc ....G 570 281-9605
Carbondale (G-2671)
Concrete Form Consultants Inc ......F 570 281-9605
Carbondale (G-2672)
Form Tech Concrete Forms Inc ......F 412 331-4500
Gibsonia (G-6334)
George L Wilson & Co Inc A ....G 412 321-3217
Apollo (G-675)
Greg Kiser ....G 814 425-1678
Utica (G-18696)

FOUNDRIES: Aluminum

Advanced Metals Group LLC ....F 610 408-8006
Malvern (G-10180)
Ajax Xray Inc ....E 570 888-6605
Sayre (G-17109)
Altman Manufacturing Inc ....F 814 756-5254
Albion (G-40)
AMG Aluminum North America LLC ......F 610 293-2501
Wayne (G-19297)
Ashland Foundry & Mch Work LLC ......C 570 875-6100
Ashland (G-727)
Buck Company Inc ....G 717 284-4114
Quarryville (G-16266)
H & H Castings Inc ....D 717 751-0064
York (G-20518)
KB Alloys Holdings LLC ....F 484 582-3520
Wayne (G-19345)
Lincoln Foundry Inc ....E 814 833-1514
Erie (G-5366)
Paul W Zimmerman Foundries Co ......F 717 285-5253
Columbia (G-3446)
Performance Metals Inc ....D 610 369-3060
Bechtelsville (G-1034)
Poormans Wldg Fabrication Inc ......F 814 349-5893
Aaronsburg (G-1)
Q Aluminum LLC ....F 570 966-2800
New Berlin (G-12021)
Smoyer L M Brass Products Inc ......G 610 867-5011
Bethlehem (G-1620)
Viking Tool & Gage Inc ....C 814 382-8691
Conneaut Lake (G-3482)

FOUNDRIES: Brass, Bronze & Copper

Arrow Castings Co ....F 814 838-3561
Erie (G-5194)
Bowser Manufacturing Co ....F 570 368-5045
Montoursville (G-11434)
Buck Company Inc ....G 717 284-4114
Quarryville (G-16266)
Carbide Metals Inc ....F 724 459-6355
Blairsville (G-1718)
Eureka Electrical Products ....E 814 725-9638
North East (G-12742)
Fenner Inc ....C 717 665-2421
Manheim (G-10380)
GKN Sinter Metals - Dubois Inc ......D 814 375-0938
Du Bois (G-4393)

Heyco Metals Inc .... D 610 926-4131
  Reading (G-16402)
Hines Flask Div Bckeye Alnimum .... E 814 683-4420
  Linesville (G-9983)
Laran Bronze Inc .... G 610 874-4414
  Chester (G-3055)
Libertas Copper LLC .... A 724 251-4200
  Leetsdale (G-9697)
Matthews International Corp .... G 717 854-9566
  York (G-20584)
Metaltech Inc .... E 814 375-9399
  Du Bois (G-4406)
Piad Precision Casting Corp .... C 724 838-5500
  Greensburg (G-6700)
Proform Powdered Metals Inc .... E 814 938-7411
  Punxsutawney (G-16154)
St Marys Carbon Co Inc .... C 814 781-7333
  Saint Marys (G-17016)
Superior Bronze Corporation .... F 814 452-3474
  Erie (G-5496)
Temple Aluminum Foundry Inc .... E 610 926-2125
  Blandon (G-1761)
United States Dept of Navy .... C 215 897-3537
  Philadelphia (G-14423)
Vallorbs Jewel Company .... C 717 392-3978
  Bird In Hand (G-1684)

FOUNDRIES: Gray & Ductile Iron

Buck Company Inc .... G 717 284-4114
  Quarryville (G-16266)
Metso Minerals Industries Inc .... C 210 491-9521
  Greenville (G-6757)
Perfomance Castings LLC .... G 814 454-1243
  Fairview (G-5836)
Ross Sand Casting .... G 724 222-7006
  Washington (G-19223)

FOUNDRIES: Iron

Beaver Valley Alloy Foundry Co .... E 724 775-1987
  Monaca (G-11283)
Buck Company Inc .... G 717 284-4114
  Quarryville (G-16266)
Kulp Foundry Inc .... D 610 881-8093
  Wind Gap (G-20170)
Metso Minerals Industries Inc .... C 210 491-9521
  Greenville (G-6757)
Prime Metals Acquisition LLC .... D 724 479-4155
  Homer City (G-7680)
Ridge Tool Company .... D 814 454-2461
  Erie (G-5463)
Sinacom North America Inc .... E 610 337-2250
  King of Prussia (G-8677)
Ward Manufacturing LLC .... C 570 638-2131
  Blossburg (G-1810)

FOUNDRIES: Nonferrous

ATI Powder Metals LLC .... D 412 394-2800
  Pittsburgh (G-14732)
B & B Foundry Inc .... E 215 333-7100
  Philadelphia (G-13435)
Beaver Valley Alloy Foundry Co .... E 724 775-1987
  Monaca (G-11283)
Complexx Gases Inc .... G 610 969-6661
  East Stroudsburg (G-4611)
Donsco Inc .... C 717 653-1851
  Mount Joy (G-11653)
Duraloy Technologies Inc .... C 724 887-5100
  Scottdale (G-17190)
Eureka Electrical Products .... E 814 725-9638
  North East (G-12742)
G O Carlson Inc .... D 610 384-2800
  Downingtown (G-4228)
George J Anderton .... G 814 382-9201
  Conneaut Lake (G-3473)
Gupta Permold Corporation .... C 412 793-3511
  Pittsburgh (G-15067)
Hussey Marine Alloys Ltd .... E 724 251-4200
  Leetsdale (G-9694)
K & S Castings Inc .... E 717 272-9775
  Lebanon (G-9585)
M & M Industries Inc .... E 610 447-0663
  Chester (G-3056)
McC Holdings Company LLC .... D 724 745-0300
  Mc Donald (G-10576)
Miller J Walter Company Inc .... E 717 392-7428
  Lancaster (G-9136)
Nova Precision Casting Corp .... E 570 366-2679
  Auburn (G-819)

O-Z/Gedney Co Inc .... G 610 926-3645
  Shoemakersville (G-17573)
Phb Inc .... C 814 474-1552
  Fairview (G-5839)
Precision Castparts Corp .... B 570 474-6371
  Mountain Top (G-11771)
Regal Cast Inc .... F 717 270-1888
  Lebanon (G-9625)
Royer Quality Castings Inc .... G 610 367-1390
  Boyertown (G-1927)
Tdy Industries LLC .... D 412 394-2896
  Pittsburgh (G-15600)
Union City Non-Ferrous Inc .... E 937 968-5460
  Washington (G-19233)
US Bronze Foundry & Mch Inc .... D 814 337-4234
  Meadville (G-10810)
Weatherly Casting and Mch Co .... D 570 427-8611
  Weatherly (G-19455)
WER Corporation .... C 610 678-8023
  Reading (G-16564)
Whemco Inc .... E 412 390-2700
  Pittsburgh (G-15715)

FOUNDRIES: Steel

Akers National Roll Company .... C 724 697-4533
  Avonmore (G-862)
Amsi US LLC .... G 814 479-3380
  Hollsopple (G-7656)
Brighton Electric .... G 412 269-7000
  Coraopolis (G-3665)
Ccx Inc .... E 724 224-6900
  Lower Burrell (G-10105)
Effort Foundry Inc .... D 610 837-1837
  Bath (G-958)
Eureka Foundry Co .... G 412 963-7881
  Pittsburgh (G-14988)
Falvey Steel Castings .... G 484 678-2174
  Mohnton (G-11263)
Frog Switch and Mfg Co .... C 717 243-2454
  Carlisle (G-2715)
Lisa Thomas .... G 724 748-3600
  Mercer (G-10967)
Lzk Manufacturing Inc .... G 717 891-5792
  Shrewsbury (G-17585)
McConway & Torley LLC .... E 412 622-0494
  Pittsburgh (G-15269)
McConway & Torley LLC .... F 610 683-7351
  Kutztown (G-8849)
Raser Industries Inc .... F 610 320-5130
  Reading (G-16484)
Regal Cast Inc .... F 717 270-1888
  Lebanon (G-9625)
Tiger Brand Jack Post Co .... E 814 333-4302
  Meadville (G-10801)
United States Steel Corp .... A 412 433-1121
  Pittsburgh (G-15676)
Universal STAinless& Alloy .... D 814 827-9723
  Titusville (G-18402)
Victaulic Company of America .... G 610 614-1261
  Nazareth (G-11993)
Whemco-Steel Castings Inc .... G 724 643-7001
  Homestead (G-7698)

FOUNDRIES: Steel Investment

Bowser Manufacturing Co .... F 570 368-5045
  Montoursville (G-11434)
Esmark Inc .... F 412 259-8868
  Sewickley (G-17386)
Howmet Aluminum Casting Inc .... C 610 266-0270
  Bethlehem (G-1532)
Lee Industries Inc .... C 814 342-0460
  Philipsburg (G-14519)
Pennsylvannia Precision Cast P .... C 717 273-3338
  Lebanon (G-9620)
Wolf Technologies LLC .... E 610 385-6091
  Douglassville (G-4182)

FOUNDRY FACINGS: Ground Or Otherwise Treated

Latrobe Foundry Mch & Sup Co .... F 724 423-4210
  Whitney (G-19894)

FOUNDRY MACHINERY & EQPT

Castec Inc .... G 724 258-8700
  Monongahela (G-11306)
Clearfield Machine Company .... F 814 765-6544
  Clearfield (G-3214)

Economy Industrial Corporation .... G 724 266-5720
  Ambridge (G-616)
Wepco Inc .... E 570 368-8184
  Pittston (G-15784)
Wise Machine Co Inc .... E 724 287-2705
  Butler (G-2450)

FOUNDRY SAND MINING

G&U Sand Svcs .... G 717 246-6724
  Windsor (G-20196)

FRAMES & FRAMING WHOLESALE

L W Green Frames .... G 610 432-3726
  Westfield (G-19779)
Larson-Juhl US LLC .... G 215 638-5940
  Bensalem (G-1219)
Patton Picture Company .... C 717 796-1508
  Mechanicsburg (G-10877)

FRANCHISES, SELLING OR LICENSING

Auntie Annes Inc .... D 717 435-1435
  Lancaster (G-8947)
H&R Block Inc .... F 814 723-3001
  Warren (G-19030)
Philly Pretzel Factory .... E 215 962-5593
  Philadelphia (G-14169)
Zausner Foods Corp .... B 717 355-8505
  New Holland (G-12296)

FREIGHT TRANSPORTATION ARRANGEMENTS

Ballistic Applications .... F 724 282-0416
  East Butler (G-4530)
D E Errick Corporation .... F 814 642-2589
  Port Allegany (G-15893)
Jle Industries LLC .... E 724 603-2228
  Dunbar (G-4441)
Transporeon Group Americas Inc .... E 267 281-1555
  Fort Washington (G-6094)

FRICTION MATERIAL, MADE FROM POWDERED METAL

Ames Reese Inc .... E 717 393-1591
  Bird In Hand (G-1668)
Cardolite Corporation .... E 609 436-0902
  Bristol (G-2123)
Comtec Mfg Inc .... D 814 834-9300
  Saint Marys (G-16956)
Emporium Specialties Company .... E 814 647-8661
  Austin (G-833)
Innovative Sintered Metals Inc .... E 814 781-1033
  Saint Marys (G-16981)
Keystone Powdered Metal Co. .... E 814 781-1591
  Saint Marys (G-16984)
Lpw Technology Inc .... F 844 480-7663
  Imperial (G-8070)
Proform Powdered Metals Inc .... E 814 938-7411
  Punxsutawney (G-16154)

FRITS

Youghiogheny Opalescent GL Inc .... E 724 628-3000
  Connellsville (G-3512)

FRUIT STANDS OR MARKETS

Mobilia Fruit Farm Inc .... F 814 725-4077
  North East (G-12752)

FRUITS & VEGETABLES WHOLESALERS: Fresh

Appeeling Fruit Inc .... F 610 926-6601
  Dauberville (G-4032)

FUEL ADDITIVES

Rohmax Additives GMBH LLC .... E 215 706-5800
  Philadelphia (G-14258)

FUEL DEALERS, NEC

Sean Naughton .... G 570 646-0422
  Pocono Pines (G-15884)

FUEL DEALERS: Coal

Fi-Hoff Concrete Products Inc ....F 814 266-5834
Johnstown (G-8372)

Fogle Forest Products ....G 570 524-2580
Lewisburg (G-9908)

Jokers Coal & Building Sups ....G 570 724-4912
Wellsboro (G-19468)

Sherman Coal Company Inc ....G 570 695-2690
Elysburg (G-4981)

South Tamaqua Coal Pockets ....F 570 386-5445
Tamaqua (G-18226)

FUEL OIL DEALERS

Blank Concrete and Supply ....F 724 758-7596
Ellwood City (G-4928)

Fts International LLC ....G 724 873-1021
Canonsburg (G-2589)

Jj Kennedy Inc ....E 724 452-6260
Fombell (G-6033)

Lansdowne Ice & Coal Co Inc ....E 610 353-6500
Broomall (G-2293)

Moyer & Son Inc ....C 215 799-2000
Souderton (G-17753)

New Enterprise Stone Lime Inc ....B 610 374-5131
Leesport (G-9668)

Postupack Russell Culm Corp ....G 570 929-1699
McAdoo (G-10657)

R S Carlin Inc ....F 814 387-4190
Snow Shoe (G-17670)

Thomas E Ferro ....G 610 485-1356
Upper Chichester (G-18673)

Utility Service Group Inc ....E 717 737-6092
Camp Hill (G-2521)

FUEL TREATING

Thomas E Ferro ....G 610 485-1356
Upper Chichester (G-18673)

FUELS: Diesel

BP Oil Co Svc Stns Diesl Fuel ....G 412 264-6140
Coraopolis (G-3664)

C R Augenstein Inc ....G 724 206-0679
Eighty Four (G-4836)

Haller Energy Services LLC ....F 717 721-9560
Adamstown (G-22)

World Energy Harrisburg LLC ....F 717 412-0374
Camp Hill (G-2526)

FUELS: Ethanol

Affordable Home Fuel LLC ....G 610 847-0972
Ottsville (G-13058)

Ajay Fuel Inc ....G 570 223-1580
East Stroudsburg (G-4604)

Alco Fuel Inc ....G 215 638-4800
Bensalem (G-1147)

Alien Fuel Inc ....G 609 306-8592
Yardley (G-20294)

Ambition - The Fuel For Sccess ....G 215 668-9561
Philadelphia (G-13375)

American Fuels LLC ....G 610 222-3569
Skippack (G-17594)

Baker Outlaw Fuel Systems ....G 717 795-9383
Liverpool (G-10077)

Bam Fuel LLC ....G 814 255-1689
Johnstown (G-8355)

Barbary ....G 215 634-7400
Philadelphia (G-13445)

Biofuel Boiler Tech LLC ....G 717 436-9300
Mifflintown (G-11110)

Brandywine Fuel Inc ....G 610 455-0123
Chester (G-3041)

Brandywine Fuel Inc ....G 484 357-7683
Glen Mills (G-6431)

Brandywine Fuel Inc ....G 484 574-8274
Aston (G-753)

Bucks County Fuel LLC ....G 215 245-0807
Bensalem (G-1162)

C Ruffs Mini Mart Fuel ....G 484 619-6832
Coplay (G-3641)

Car Fuel 1 Inc ....G 215 545-2002
Philadelphia (G-13499)

Citi Fuel Convenience Inc ....F 215 724-2395
Philadelphia (G-13546)

CNG Mtor Fuels Clarion Cnty LP ....G 814 590-4498
Coolspring (G-3621)

Edmil Fuels Inc ....G 717 249-4901
Carlisle (G-2709)

Emil Rarick Fuel Delivery ....G 570 345-8584
Pine Grove (G-14592)

Friendly Fuel ....G 717 254-1932
Newburg (G-12475)

Fuel ....G 215 468-3835
Philadelphia (G-13730)

Fuel ....G 215 922-3835
Philadelphia (G-13731)

Fuel & Save Inc ....G 814 857-5356
Bigler (G-1659)

Fuel Cell Inc ....E 610 759-0143
Nazareth (G-11967)

Fuel Doctor Inc ....G 904 521-9889
Ronks (G-16807)

Fuel ME Green LLC ....G 267 825-7193
Philadelphia (G-13732)

Fuel On Whitehaven LLC ....G 570 443-8830
White Haven (G-19847)

Fuel One Gas Cnvnience Str LLC ....G 551 208-3490
Mountain Top (G-11761)

Fuel Recharge Yourself Inc 3 ....G 215 468-3835
Philadelphia (G-13733)

Fuel Treatment Solutions LLC ....G 215 914-1006
Huntingdon Valley (G-7986)

Fuel7 Inc ....G 267 980-7888
Langhorne (G-9299)

Fuelone Gas Cnvenience Str LLC ....G 570 443-8830
White Haven (G-19848)

Fuels & Lubes Technologies LLC ....G 724 282-8264
Fenelton (G-5945)

Gas N Go Washington ....G 724 228-2850
Washington (G-19178)

Geo Fuels LLC ....G 570 331-0800
Mountain Top (G-11762)

Gs Fuel Inc ....G 484 751-5414
Blue Bell (G-1831)

Gurpreet Fuel Company Llc ....G 215 493-6322
Philadelphia (G-13792)

Haller Energy Services LLC ....F 717 721-9560
Adamstown (G-22)

I Fuel ....G 570 524-6851
Lewisburg (G-9912)

Kelly Fuel Co Inc ....G 610 444-5055
Kennett Square (G-8518)

Keystone Fuels LLC ....G 724 357-1710
Blairsville (G-1730)

Kreiser Fuel Service Inc ....G 570 455-0418
Hazleton (G-7506)

Lake Erie Biofuels LLC ....E 814 528-9200
Erie (G-5353)

Lancaster Fuels ....G 717 687-5390
Strasburg (G-18090)

Louis Nardello Company ....G 215 467-1420
Newtown Square (G-12582)

Martino Fuel ....G 484 802-2183
Broomall (G-2296)

Maya Devi Inc ....G 717 420-7060
Gettysburg (G-6307)

Mobinol Fuel Company ....G 484 432-9007
Collegeville (G-3382)

Mtr Fuel LLC ....G 609 610-0783
Morrisville (G-11573)

National Fuel Gas Dist Corp ....G 814 837-9585
Kane (G-8472)

Nu-Chem Corp ....F 610 770-2000
Allentown (G-336)

On Fuel ....G 570 288-5805
Luzerne (G-10128)

On Fuel ....G 570 784-5320
Bloomsburg (G-1792)

On Fuel ....G 814 837-1017
Kane (G-8476)

On Fuel ....G 570 275-0170
Danville (G-4008)

Penn Fuel Gas Incorporated ....G 814 353-0404
Bellefonte (G-1111)

Pennsylvania Agri-Fuel Inc ....G 717 733-1050
Ephrata (G-5137)

Pottsville Fuel Stop Inc ....G 570 429-2970
Pottsville (G-16091)

PST Fuel Inc ....G 215 676-3545
Phila (G-13312)

Rawlee Fuels LLC ....G 724 349-3320
Indiana (G-8123)

REO & Sons Fuels LLC ....G 267 374-6400
Quakertown (G-16241)

Ritters Fuel Delivery LLC ....G 717 957-4477
Shermans Dale (G-17501)

Road Runner Race Fuels LLC ....G 717 587-1693
Mohnton (G-11269)

Sewickley Village Fuel and Svc ....G 412 741-9972
Sewickley (G-17410)

Shereen Fuel Inc ....G 215 632-2160
Philadelphia (G-14302)

Sign Fuel ....G 989 245-6284
Coplay (G-3648)

Sky Fuel Inc ....G 215 343-3825
Warrington (G-19134)

Sky Fuel Inc ....G 215 257-5392
Perkasie (G-13294)

Smart Fuels LLC ....G 717 645-8983
Mechanicsburg (G-10890)

Smarterfuel Inc ....E 570 972-4727
Wind Gap (G-20173)

Spring Vly Altrntive Fuels LLC ....G 814 587-3002
Conneautville (G-3487)

Total Ptrchemicals Ref USA Inc ....B 877 871-2729
Exton (G-5737)

Total Ptrchemicals Ref USA Inc ....D 610 692-8401
West Chester (G-19667)

Town & Country Fuel LLC ....F 717 252-2152
Conestoga (G-3461)

United Enrgy Plus Trminals LLC ....E 610 774-5151
Allentown (G-418)

Vista Fuels LLC ....G 570 385-7274
Schuylkill Haven (G-17170)

Watt Fuel Cell Corp ....E 724 547-9170
Mount Pleasant (G-11722)

Wayne Fueling Systems ....G 215 257-1046
Perkasie (G-13298)

FUELS: Jet

Aviation Technologies Inc ....G 570 457-4147
Avoca (G-840)

FUELS: Oil

American Natural Retail PA LLC ....G 212 359-4483
Wexford (G-19786)

Atls Production Company LLC ....C 412 489-0006
Pittsburgh (G-14736)

Equipment & Contrls Africa Inc ....C 412 489-3000
Pittsburgh (G-14983)

Innovalgae LLC ....G 412 996-2556
Wexford (G-19807)

Maxwell Canby Fuel Oil Co ....G 610 269-0288
Upper Darby (G-18688)

Sunoco Inc ....E 717 564-1440
Harrisburg (G-7222)

United Refining Company ....C 814 723-1500
Warren (G-19055)

FUNDRAISING SVCS

Choice Marketing Inc ....E 610 494-1270
Aston (G-755)

Copper Kettle Fudge Factory ....F 412 824-1233
North Versailles (G-12773)

FUNERAL HOMES & SVCS

Blairsville Wilbert Burial Vlt ....E 724 459-9677
Blairsville (G-1717)

Blairsville Wilbert Burial Vlt ....G 724 324-2010
Mount Morris (G-11679)

FUNGICIDES OR HERBICIDES

Bayer Cropscience LP ....D 412 777-2000
Pittsburgh (G-14752)

FUR APPAREL STORES: Made To Custom Order

Charles L Simpson Sr ....F 717 763-7023
New Cumberland (G-12182)

FUR STRIPPING

Bucks County Fur Products Inc ....G 215 536-6614
Quakertown (G-16175)

FUR: Apparel

Hal-Jo Corp ....F 215 885-4747
Jenkintown (G-8289)

FUR: Coats

Charles L Simpson Sr ....F 717 763-7023
New Cumberland (G-12182)

FURNACE CASINGS: Sheet Metal

American Roll Suppliers Inc ....G.... 610 857-2988
Parkesburg (G-13171)

FURNACES & OVENS: Indl

Abbott Furnace Company ....D.... 814 781-6355
Saint Marys (G-16943)

Air/Tak Inc ....F.... 724 297-3416
Worthington (G-20226)

Armstrong Engrg Assoc Inc ....G.... 610 436-6080
West Chester (G-19501)

C I Hayes Inc ....E.... 814 834-2200
Saint Marys (G-16951)

Ecco/Gregory Inc ....E.... 610 840-0390
West Chester (G-19545)

Frazier-Simplex Machine Co ....E.... 724 222-5700
Washington (G-19177)

Frontier LLC ....F.... 570 265-2500
Towanda (G-18426)

Gasbarre Products Inc ....E.... 814 834-2200
Saint Marys (G-16975)

Gasbarre Products Inc ....D.... 814 371-3015
Du Bois (G-4392)

Graftech Usa LLC ....E.... 814 781-2478
Saint Marys (G-16979)

Ipsen Inc ....G.... 215 723-8125
Souderton (G-17742)

J&R Cad Enterprise LLC ....G.... 724 695-4279
Imperial (G-8069)

Jmg Inc ....G.... 215 659-4087
Willow Grove (G-20121)

Jpw Design & Manufacturing Inc ....G.... 570 995-5025
Trout Run (G-18515)

L & L Special Furnace Co Inc ....F.... 610 459-9216
Aston (G-772)

Linde Engineering N Amer Inc ....E.... 610 834-0300
Blue Bell (G-1844)

Pinnacle Climate Tech Inc ....G.... 215 891-8460
Bristol (G-2182)

Riise Inc ....G.... 724 528-3305
West Middlesex (G-19729)

Signature Vacuum Systems Inc...........G.... 814 333-1110
Harmonsburg (G-7064)

SPX Flow Us LLC ....G.... 814 476-5800
Mc Kean (G-10594)

T Bruce Sales Inc ....D.... 724 528-9961
West Middlesex (G-19731)

Tate Jones Inc ....G.... 412 771-4200
Portersville (G-15937)

Tps LLC ....C.... 570 538-7200
New Columbia (G-12177)

Yorkaire Inc ....E.... 717 755-2836
York (G-20755)

FURNACES & OVENS: Vacuum

Metvac Inc ....G.... 215 541-4495
Hereford (G-7568)

Seco/Vacuum Technologies LLC ....G.... 814 332-8520
Meadville (G-10790)

Solar Atmospheres Mfg Inc ....E.... 267 384-5040
Souderton (G-17766)

V P L Inc ....G.... 814 652-6767
Everett (G-5579)

FURNACES: Indl, Electric

Ajax Electric Company ....E.... 215 947-8500
Huntingdon Valley (G-7962)

FURNACES: Indl, Fuel-Fired, Metal Melting

Boyertown Furnace Company ....E.... 610 369-1450
Boyertown (G-1900)

FURNISHINGS: Bridge Sets, Cloth/Napkin, From Purchased Matls

CMI Systems.............................F.... 215 596-0306
Philadelphia (G-13553)

FURNITURE & CABINET STORES: Cabinets, Custom Work

Alan Pepper Designs ....G.... 412 244-9299
Pittsburgh (G-14659)

Chadds Ford Cabinet Inc ....G.... 610 388-6005
Kennett Square (G-8503)

Keiths Cabinet Company ....E.... 814 793-2614
Martinsburg (G-10525)

Kitchens By Meade Inc...................F.... 814 453-4888
Erie (G-5345)

Ladmac Services ....G.... 724 679-8047
Butler (G-2418)

Modern Cabinet and Cnstr Co ....F.... 814 942-1000
Altoona (G-528)

Myers Cabinet Co ....G.... 724 887-4070
Scottdale (G-17196)

ONeils Custom Cab & Design.............F.... 412 422-4723
Pittsburgh (G-15359)

Philip J Stofanak Inc ....E.... 610 759-9311
Bethlehem (G-1595)

Shawn Harr ....G.... 215 258-5434
Perkasie (G-13292)

Staurowsky Woodworking ....G.... 610 489-0770
Collegeville (G-3394)

Woxall Woodcraft Inc ....G.... 215 234-8774
Green Lane (G-6594)

FURNITURE & CABINET STORES: Custom

Bostock Company Inc ....E.... 215 343-7040
Warrington (G-19110)

Creation Cabinetry & Sign Co...........G.... 717 246-3386
Red Lion (G-16591)

Infinite Quest Cabinetry Corp..........G.... 301 222-3592
Red Lion (G-16601)

Signature Gallery ....G.... 610 792-5399
Royersford (G-16864)

Superior Flrcvgs Kitchens LLC ....G.... 717 264-9096
Chambersburg (G-2981)

FURNITURE & FIXTURES Factory

Blair Fixtures & Millwork Inc...........E.... 814 940-1913
Altoona (G-482)

Brodart Co ....C.... 570 769-7412
Mc Elhattan (G-10585)

Econoco ....E.... 570 384-3000
Hazle Township (G-7453)

G Case Inc ....G.... 717 737-5000
Mechanicsburg (G-10847)

Gepharts Furniture ....G.... 814 276-3357
Alum Bank (G-561)

Laurence Ronald Entps Inc ....F.... 215 677-3801
Warminster (G-18910)

Markraft Company ....G.... 724 733-3654
Murrysville (G-11857)

Missing Piece ....G.... 610 759-4033
Nazareth (G-11982)

Top Shop ....G.... 610 622-6101
Philadelphia (G-14396)

FURNITURE PARTS: Metal

Stellar Machine Incorporated...........F.... 570 718-1733
Nanticoke (G-11903)

FURNITURE REFINISHING SVCS

Anthony Cocco Inc ....G.... 215 629-4100
Philadelphia (G-13394)

M & P Refinishing Co....................G.... 724 527-6360
Jeannette (G-8262)

FURNITURE STOCK & PARTS: Carvings, Wood

Infinite Quest Cabinetry Corp..........G.... 301 222-3592
Red Lion (G-16601)

Tellus Three Sixty ....E.... 717 628-1866
Palmyra (G-13133)

FURNITURE STOCK & PARTS: Chair Seats, Hardwood

Kgm Gaming LLC ....E.... 215 430-0388
Philadelphia (G-13934)

FURNITURE STOCK & PARTS: Dimension Stock, Hardwood

New Germany Wood Products Inc ....F.... 814 495-5923
Summerhill (G-18154)

FURNITURE STOCK & PARTS: Frames, Upholstered Furniture, Wood

A W Everett Furniture Frames ....F.... 610 377-0170
Lehighton (G-9708)

Gwynn-E-Co Inc ....G.... 215 423-6400
Philadelphia (G-13794)

John M Rohrbaugh Co Inc ....G.... 717 244-2895
Red Lion (G-16602)

Keiths Cabinet Company ....E.... 814 793-2614
Martinsburg (G-10525)

New Wave Custom Wdwkg Inc ....E.... 570 251-8218
Honesdale (G-7718)

Wood Specialty Company Inc ....F.... 610 539-6384
Norristown (G-12724)

Woodcraft Products Co Inc...............F.... 215 329-2793
Philadelphia (G-14485)

Woodcraft Products Co Inc...............F.... 215 426-6123
Philadelphia (G-14486)

FURNITURE STOCK & PARTS: Hardwood

Allegheny Mtn Hardwood Flrg ....F.... 724 867-9441
Emlenton (G-5004)

Bareville Woodcraft Co ....F.... 717 656-6261
Leola (G-9771)

Dsc2 Inc ....F.... 980 223-2270
York (G-20458)

Facio Concepts LLC ....G.... 717 945-8609
East Earl (G-4543)

Nelson Bridge Inc ....G.... 908 996-6646
New Hope (G-12309)

Walker Lumber Co Inc ....E.... 814 857-7642
Woodland (G-20215)

Werzalit of America Inc ....D.... 814 362-3881
Bradford (G-1995)

FURNITURE STOCK & PARTS: Squares, Hardwood

C A Elliot Lumber Co Inc ....E.... 814 544-7523
Roulette (G-16834)

FURNITURE STORES

Amanda Reiche ....G.... 570 424-0334
East Stroudsburg (G-4605)

Appalachian Mill Inc ....E.... 717 328-2805
Greencastle (G-6598)

B K Barrit Corp ....D.... 267 345-1200
Philadelphia (G-13438)

Beechdale Frames ....G.... 717 288-2723
Ronks (G-16803)

Carter Handcrafted Furniture ....G.... 610 847-2101
Ottsville (G-13061)

Collegiate Furnishings Inc ....E.... 814 234-1660
State College (G-17954)

Colonial Furniture Company..............D.... 570 374-6016
Freeburg (G-6188)

Countryside Woodcrafts Inc ....F.... 717 627-5641
Lititz (G-10004)

David Karr ....G.... 814 669-4406
Alexandria (G-63)

Easton Upholstery Furn Mfg Co ....G.... 610 252-3169
Easton (G-4675)

Elegant Furniture & Lighting ....G.... 888 388-3390
Philadelphia (G-13665)

George Nkashima Woodworker S A......F.... 215 862-2272
New Hope (G-12302)

Great Day Improvements LLC ....E.... 412 304-0089
Pittsburgh (G-15060)

Guildcraft Inc ....F.... 717 854-3888
York (G-20517)

IKEA Indirect Mtl & Svcs LLC ....G.... 610 834-0150
Conshohocken (G-3559)

Irvins Corp ....D.... 570 539-8200
Mount Pleasant Mills (G-11726)

Kings Kountry Korner LLC ....G.... 717 768-3425
Gordonville (G-6560)

Newburg Woodcrafts.....................G.... 717 530-8823
Shippensburg (G-17539)

Patterson Furniture Co ....G.... 412 771-0600
Mc Kees Rocks (G-10622)

Penn Foam Corporation ....D.... 610 797-7500
Allentown (G-348)

Roger S Wright Furniture Ltd ....G.... 215 257-5700
Blooming Glen (G-1765)

William Henry Orna Ir Works ....G.... 215 659-1887
Willow Grove (G-20149)

FURNITURE STORES: Cabinets, Kitchen, Exc Custom Made

W B Mason Co Inc.......................E.... 888 926-2766
Altoona (G-555)

Y&Q Home Plus LLC......................G.... 412 642-6708
Pittsburgh (G-15728)

FURNITURE STORES: Custom Made, Exc Cabinets

Martins Furniture LLC ....F 717 354-5657
  Ephrata (G-5126)
Turner John ....G 610 524-2050
  Exton (G-5740)

FURNITURE STORES: Office

Gc Enterprises LLC ....G 570 655-5543
  Pittston (G-15752)
Hanel Storage Systems ....E 412 788-0509
  Pittsburgh (G-15079)
Little Printing Co Inc ....F 724 437-4831
  Uniontown (G-18635)
Ogden Brothers Incorporated ....F 610 789-1258
  Havertown (G-7425)
Printing Plus+ Inc ....F 814 834-1000
  Saint Marys (G-17009)
Specialty Group Printing Inc ....F 814 425-3061
  Cochranton (G-3351)
W B Mason Co Inc ....D 888 926-2766
  Allentown (G-427)
Winterhouse Furniture Inc ....G 215 249-3410
  Dublin (G-4437)

FURNITURE STORES: Outdoor & Garden

A Mamaux & Son Inc ....F 412 771-8432
  Mc Kees Rocks (G-10599)
K D Home & Garden Inc ....F 610 929-5794
  Temple (G-18331)
Perennial Pleasures LLC ....G 484 318-8376
  Paoli (G-13147)

FURNITURE STORES: Unfinished

Recon Enterprises ....G 570 836-1179
  Tunkhannock (G-18548)

FURNITURE WHOLESALERS

Diamond Trpcl Hardwoods Intl ....G 215 257-2556
  Sellersville (G-17345)
Keystone Quality Products LLC ....E 717 354-2762
  Leola (G-9790)
Lee Sandusky Corporation ....E 717 359-4111
  Littlestown (G-10069)
National Furniture Assoc Inc ....G 814 342-2007
  Philipsburg (G-14520)
Plain n Fancy Kitchens Inc ....C 717 949-6571
  Schaefferstown (G-17129)

FURNITURE, HOUSEHOLD: Wholesalers

CMI Systems ....F 215 596-0306
  Philadelphia (G-13553)
Rio Brands LLC ....D 610 629-6200
  Conshohocken (G-3601)

FURNITURE, OFFICE: Wholesalers

Allegheny Fabg & Sups Inc ....G 412 828-3320
  Pittsburgh (G-14678)
Chapel Hill Mfg Co ....F 215 884-3614
  Oreland (G-13020)
Musumeci Santo ....G 215 467-2158
  Philadelphia (G-14045)
Supra Office Solutions Inc ....G 267 275-8888
  Philadelphia (G-14360)

FURNITURE, OUTDOOR & LAWN: Wholesalers

Charles Steckman ....G 724 789-7066
  Renfrew (G-16638)

FURNITURE, WHOLESALE: Beds

Golden Brothers Inc ....C 570 457-0867
  Old Forge (G-12965)

FURNITURE, WHOLESALE: Chairs

Neff Specialties LLC ....F 814 247-8887
  Hastings (G-7262)
New Stars LLC ....E 215 962-4239
  Philadelphia (G-14068)
PS Furniture Inc ....E 814 587-6313
  Conneautville (G-3486)

FURNITURE, WHOLESALE: Shelving

Witmer Public Safety Group Inc ....D 800 852-6088
  Coatesville (G-3331)

FURNITURE: Altars, Cut Stone

Britt Energies Inc ....G 724 465-9333
  Spring Church (G-17854)
Eastern Surfaces Inc ....D 610 266-3121
  Allentown (G-201)

FURNITURE: Bed Frames & Headboards, Wood

Big Boyz Industries Inc ....G 215 942-9971
  Warminster (G-18837)
Frame Up & Gallery ....G 724 627-0552
  Waynesburg (G-19441)
Hillside Enterprise ....G 724 479-3678
  Homer City (G-7675)

FURNITURE: Bedroom, Wood

Colonial Furniture Company ....D 570 374-6016
  Freeburg (G-6188)
Stony Hill Woodworks ....G 717 786-8358
  Quarryville (G-16283)

FURNITURE: Beds, Household, Incl Folding & Cabinet, Metal

Delweld Industries Corp ....F 814 535-2412
  Stoystown (G-18075)

FURNITURE: Bedsprings, Assembled

McMullens Furniture Store ....G 814 942-1202
  Altoona (G-526)

FURNITURE: Bookcases, Office, Wood

Bush Industries of PA ....C 814 868-2874
  Erie (G-5219)
Milder Office Inc ....G 215 717-7027
  Philadelphia (G-14023)

FURNITURE: Bookcases, Wood

Harmony Plus Woodworks Inc ....G 717 432-0372
  Dillsburg (G-4131)

FURNITURE: Bowling Establishment

Spare Time Bowling ....G 570 668-3210
  Tamaqua (G-18227)

FURNITURE: Box Springs, Assembled

Leggett & Platt Incorporated ....D 724 748-3057
  Mercer (G-10966)
Ohio Mat Lcnsing Cmpnnts Group ....D 570 715-7200
  Mountain Top (G-11768)
Z Wood Products Co Inc ....E 215 423-9891
  Philadelphia (G-14503)

FURNITURE: Cabinets & Filing Drawers, Office, Exc Wood

Charles Beseler Co Inc ....D 800 237-3537
  Stroudsburg (G-18109)
Precise Graphix LLC ....E 610 965-9400
  Allentown (G-357)
Primrose Consulting Inc ....G 724 816-5769
  Mars (G-10510)
Stanley Storage Systems Inc ....G 610 797-6600
  Allentown (G-401)

FURNITURE: Cabinets & Vanities, Medicine, Metal

Gk Inc ....F 215 223-7207
  Philadelphia (G-13764)
Robern Inc ....D 215 826-0280
  Bristol (G-2195)
Sett ....G 215 322-9301
  Huntingdon Valley (G-8037)

FURNITURE: Chair Beds

Manns Sickroom Service Inc ....E 412 672-5680
  White Oak (G-19856)

FURNITURE: Chairs, Folding

PS Furniture Inc ....E 814 587-6313
  Conneautville (G-3486)

FURNITURE: Chairs, Household Upholstered

American Atelier Inc ....C 610 439-4040
  Allentown (G-133)
Golden Brothers Inc ....E 570 714-5002
  Kingston (G-8718)
Golden Brothers Inc ....C 570 457-0867
  Old Forge (G-12965)
Golden Technologies Inc ....G 570 451-7477
  Old Forge (G-12966)
Lusch Frames LLC ....G 215 739-6264
  Philadelphia (G-13977)

FURNITURE: Chairs, Household Wood

Daniel G Berg ....G 610 856-7095
  Mohnton (G-11261)
Haltemans Hardwood Products ....G 814 745-2519
  Sligo (G-17615)
Saw Rocking Horse ....G 610 683-8075
  Kutztown (G-8860)
White Oak Woodcraft ....G 717 665-4738
  Manheim (G-10406)
Zimmerman Chair Shop ....E 717 273-2706
  Lebanon (G-9640)

FURNITURE: Chairs, Office Exc Wood

Emeco Industries Inc ....E 717 637-5951
  Hanover (G-6883)
Vitra Inc ....E 610 391-9780
  Allentown (G-424)

FURNITURE: Chests, Cedar

David Esh ....G 610 286-6225
  Morgantown (G-11521)

FURNITURE: Church

Bahrets Church Interiors ....G 717 540-1747
  Harrisburg (G-7094)

FURNITURE: Couches, Sofa/Davenport, Upholstered Wood Frames

Ferrante Uphlstrng & Crptng ....F 724 535-8866
  Wampum (G-18800)
Mega Motion LLC ....E 800 800-8586
  Exeter (G-5583)

FURNITURE: Cut Stone

G and H Contracting Inc ....G 610 826-7542
  Palmerton (G-13106)

FURNITURE: Desks & Tables, Office, Exc Wood

Ceraln Corp ....E 570 322-8400
  South Williamsport (G-17790)

FURNITURE: Desks & Tables, Office, Wood

ABF USA Ltd ....G 570 788-0888
  Drums (G-4380)
Ceraln Corp ....E 570 322-8400
  South Williamsport (G-17790)

FURNITURE: Desks, Household, Wood

Woxall Woodcraft Inc ....G 215 234-8774
  Green Lane (G-6594)

FURNITURE: Desks, Wood

Epic Industries Inc ....G 570 586-0253
  Clarks Summit (G-3192)

FURNITURE: Dining Room, Wood

Cramco Inc ....C 215 427-9500
  Philadelphia (G-13577)
George Nkashima Woodworker S A ......F 215 862-2272
  New Hope (G-12302)
Sensenig Chair Shop ....G 717 463-3480
  Thompsontown (G-18351)

FURNITURE: Foundations & Platforms

Jbs Woodwork Shop ....F 570 374-4883
Port Trevorton *(G-15914)*

FURNITURE: Garden, Metal

Schultz Richard Design & Mfg...............F 215 679-2222
East Greenville *(G-4574)*

FURNITURE: Garden, Wood

Schultz Richard Design & Mfg...............F 215 679-2222
East Greenville *(G-4574)*

Susquehanna Grdn Concepts LLC ....G 717 826-5144
Fleetwood *(G-5981)*

FURNITURE: Hospital

Caseworks Inc ....F 724 522-5068
Jeannette *(G-8249)*

FURNITURE: Household, Metal

Cramco Inc ....C 215 427-9500
Philadelphia *(G-13577)*

Federal Prison Industries ....B 570 524-0096
Lewisburg *(G-9906)*

Francis J Nowalk ....G 412 687-4017
Pittsburgh *(G-15030)*

Lee Sandusky Corporation ....E 717 359-4111
Littlestown *(G-10069)*

Sam Mannino Enterprises LLC ....E 814 692-4100
Pennsylvania Furnace *(G-13264)*

Village Craft Iron & Stone Inc ....E 814 353-1777
Julian *(G-8457)*

FURNITURE: Household, Upholstered On Metal Frames

Maple Mountain Industries Inc ....G 814 634-0674
Meyersdale *(G-11015)*

Racechairs LLC......................................G 267 632-5003
Perkasie *(G-13291)*

FURNITURE: Household, Upholstered, Exc Wood Or Metal

Edward Hennessy Co Inc ....G 215 426-4154
Philadelphia *(G-13662)*

Gene Sanes & Associates ....E 412 471-8224
Pittsburgh *(G-15043)*

Guildcraft Inc...F 717 854-3888
York *(G-20517)*

K T & Co ....G 610 520-0221
Bryn Mawr *(G-2328)*

FURNITURE: Household, Wood

2820 Associates Inc ....G 412 471-2525
Pittsburgh *(G-14625)*

4 Less Furniture and Rugs LLC...............F 610 650-4000
Oaks *(G-12930)*

Acorn Trail Woodcraft ....G 717 279-0261
Lebanon *(G-9545)*

Advantage Millwork Inc ....G 610 925-2785
Kennett Square *(G-8502)*

Alan Pepper Designs ....G 412 244-9299
Pittsburgh *(G-14659)*

Alvin Reiff Woodworking ....G 570 966-1149
Mifflinburg *(G-11092)*

Amanda Reiche ....G 570 424-0334
East Stroudsburg *(G-4605)*

American Atelier Inc ....C 610 439-4040
Allentown *(G-133)*

Ames Construction Inc ....E 717 299-1395
Lancaster *(G-8932)*

Ashley Furniture Inds Inc.......................A 610 926-0897
Leesport *(G-9657)*

B & S Woodcraft.....................................G 717 786-8154
Quarryville *(G-16262)*

Bareville Woodcraft Co ....F 717 656-6261
Leola *(G-9771)*

Bones and All LLC ....G 216 870-7177
Pittsburgh *(G-14783)*

Braders Woodcraft Inc ....F 610 262-3452
Laurys Station *(G-9532)*

Brodys Furniture Inc...............................G 724 745-4630
Canonsburg *(G-2551)*

Bush Industries of PA.............................C 814 868-2874
Erie *(G-5219)*

Carpet and Furniture Depot Inc.............G 814 239-5865
Claysburg *(G-3201)*

Carter Handcrafted Furniture.................G 610 847-2101
Ottsville *(G-13061)*

Cedar Ridge Furniture............................G 610 286-6225
Morgantown *(G-11519)*

Charles Ginty Associates Inc ....G 610 347-1101
Unionville *(G-18647)*

Chris S Sensenig...................................G 717 423-5311
Shippensburg *(G-17522)*

Classic Furniture...................................G 717 738-0088
Lititz *(G-9999)*

Clifton Custom Furn & Design................F 724 727-2045
Apollo *(G-670)*

Colonial Road Woodworks LLC ....E 717 354-8998
New Holland *(G-12237)*

Country Additions Inc ....G 610 404-2062
Birdsboro *(G-1692)*

Country Heirlooms Inc ....G 610 869-9550
West Grove *(G-19698)*

Country Value Woodworks LLC ....E 717 786-7949
Quarryville *(G-16267)*

David Karr ....G 814 669-4406
Alexandria *(G-63)*

David Lee Designs ....F 814 725-4289
North East *(G-12738)*

Delex Co ....G 724 938-2366
Brownsville *(G-2311)*

Destefanos Hardwood Lumber................G 724 483-6196
Charleroi *(G-3009)*

Ducklee Frederick and Bros ....F 570 897-6172
Portland *(G-15939)*

Edward Hennessy Co Inc ....G 215 426-4154
Philadelphia *(G-13662)*

Fab Dubrufaut Woodworking...................G 215 533-4853
Philadelphia *(G-13691)*

Federal Prison Industries ....B 570 524-0096
Lewisburg *(G-9906)*

Genesee River Trading Company...........G 724 533-5354
Volant *(G-18774)*

Giffin Interior & Fixture Inc ....C 412 221-1166
Bridgeville *(G-2066)*

Gleepet Inc...F 347 607-7850
Trevose *(G-18497)*

Godshall Woodcraft ....G 610 530-9386
Breinigsville *(G-2017)*

Hampton Cabinet Shop ....G 717 898-7806
Manheim *(G-10387)*

Henderson Bernard Furn Ardison ....G 215 930-0400
Philadelphia *(G-13813)*

Honey Brook Woodcrafts.........................G 610 273-2928
Honey Brook *(G-7750)*

Ingrain Construction LLC.......................G 717 205-1475
Columbia *(G-3439)*

Ingrain Construction LLC.......................F 717 205-1475
Lancaster *(G-9057)*

Interior Motives Inc ....G 814 672-3100
Coalport *(G-3283)*

J D Lohr Woodworking Inc ....G 610 287-7802
Schwenksville *(G-17177)*

Jacoby Transportation Inc ....E 717 677-7733
Gettysburg *(G-6302)*

KB Woodcraft Inc....................................G 502 533-2773
Phoenixville *(G-14555)*

Kitko Wood Products Inc ....C 814 672-3606
Glen Hope *(G-6426)*

Kosko Wood Products Inc ....G 814 427-2499
Stump Creek *(G-18143)*

Kountry Kraft Kitchens Inc ....C 610 589-4575
Newmanstown *(G-12479)*

Krehling Industries Inc ....D 717 232-7936
Harrisburg *(G-7165)*

Lehman Cabinetry..................................G 717 432-5014
Dillsburg *(G-4133)*

M & M Creative Laminates Inc ....G 412 781-4700
Aspinwall *(G-746)*

Maple Mountain Industries Inc ....E 724 676-4703
New Florence *(G-12198)*

Martins Furniture LLC ....F 717 354-5657
Ephrata *(G-5126)*

Martins Wood Products LLC...................E 717 933-5115
Myerstown *(G-11893)*

Missing Piece ....G 610 759-4033
Nazareth *(G-11982)*

New Wave Custom Wdwkg Inc ....E 570 251-8218
Honesdale *(G-7718)*

Newburg Woodcrafts...............................G 717 530-8823
Shippensburg *(G-17539)*

Newswanger Woods Specialties ....G 717 355-9274
New Holland *(G-12269)*

Patterson Furniture Co...........................G 412 771-0600
Mc Kees Rocks *(G-10622)*

Paul Dorazio Custom Furniture ....G 215 836-1057
Flourtown *(G-5989)*

PS Furniture Inc ....E 814 587-6313
Conneautville *(G-3486)*

Renningers Cabinetree Inc ....E 570 726-6494
Mill Hall *(G-11181)*

Ricks Custom Wood Design Inc.............F 717 627-2701
Akron *(G-37)*

Robert Trate Hogg Cbinetmakers..........G 717 529-2522
Oxford *(G-13088)*

Ruby Custom Woodcraft Inc ....G 570 698-7741
Lake Ariel *(G-8891)*

Rynone Manufacturing Corp...................C 570 888-5272
Sayre *(G-17121)*

S & R Woodworking..................................G 717 354-8628
Gordonville *(G-6562)*

S D L Custom Cabinetry Inc ....E 215 355-8188
Langhorne *(G-9323)*

S F Spector Inc ....G 717 236-0805
Harrisburg *(G-7211)*

Sam Beiler ....G 717 442-8990
Kinzers *(G-8742)*

Selectrim Corporation ....E 570 326-3662
Williamsport *(G-20071)*

Signature Gallery ....G 610 792-5399
Royersford *(G-16864)*

Smith Lawton Millwork ....G 570 934-2544
Montrose *(G-11477)*

Soltrace Inc..E 215 765-5700
Philadelphia *(G-14324)*

Spectra Inc ....G 814 238-6332
State College *(G-18030)*

Stauffer Wood Products...........................G 717 647-4372
Tower City *(G-18441)*

Stoltzfus John ....G 717 786-2481
Quarryville *(G-16281)*

T L King Cabinetmaker ....G 610 869-4220
Cochranville *(G-3356)*

Tiki Kevs ....E 267 718-4527
Chalfont *(G-2892)*

Top Shop ....G 610 622-6101
Philadelphia *(G-14396)*

Unique Wood Creation LLC ....G 717 687-7900
Paradise *(G-13164)*

Van Etten James ....G 215 453-8228
Perkasie *(G-13297)*

Varchettis Furniture ....G 814 733-4318
Berlin *(G-1293)*

Village Craft Iron & Stone Inc ....E 814 353-1777
Julian *(G-8457)*

Wallace Moving & Storage ....G 724 568-2411
Vandergrift *(G-18737)*

Wayneco Inc ....D 717 225-4413
York *(G-20704)*

Weaver Wood Specialties ....G 610 589-5889
Womelsdorf *(G-20210)*

Werzalit of America Inc..........................D 814 362-3881
Bradford *(G-1995)*

William Cottage ....G 724 266-2961
Ambridge *(G-639)*

Winterhouse Furniture Inc ....G 215 249-3410
Dublin *(G-4437)*

Woodpeckers Woodcraft Inc ....G 814 397-2282
Erie *(G-5533)*

FURNITURE: Institutional, Exc Wood

Ajjp Corporation.....................................C 215 968-6677
Newtown *(G-12495)*

Bird-In-Hand Woodworks Inc...................D 717 397-5686
Lancaster *(G-8954)*

Brodart Co ....C 570 769-7412
Mc Elhattan *(G-10585)*

Brodart Co ....D 570 326-2461
Williamsport *(G-19995)*

Cedar Ridge Furniture............................G 610 286-6225
Morgantown *(G-11519)*

Ceraln Corp ....E 570 322-8400
South Williamsport *(G-17790)*

Childcraft Education Corp ....C 717 653-7500
Mount Joy *(G-11649)*

Ducklee Frederick and Bros ....F 570 897-6172
Portland *(G-15939)*

Kettle Creek Corporation ....G 800 527-7848
Ottsville *(G-13064)*

Legnini RC Architectural Mllwk ....F 610 640-1227
Malvern *(G-10266)*

Missing Piece ....G 610 759-4033
Nazareth *(G-11982)*

Oakworks Inc..D 717 227-0516
New Freedom *(G-12213)*

Robert Trate Hogg Cbinetmakers..........G....... 717 529-2522
Oxford (G-13088)

FURNITURE: Juvenile, Metal

Little Partners Inc...............................G....... 318 220-7005
Reading (G-16431)

FURNITURE: Juvenile, Wood

Lightning Group Inc...........................G....... 717 834-3031
Duncannon (G-4447)

FURNITURE: Juvenile, Wood

Bird-In-Hand Woodworks Inc...............D....... 717 397-5686
Lancaster (G-8954)
Childcraft Education Corp....................C....... 717 653-7500
Mount Joy (G-11649)
Little Partners Inc...............................G....... 318 220-7005
Reading (G-16431)

FURNITURE: Kitchen & Dining Room

Brodart Co...E....... 570 326-2461
Montgomery (G-11368)
E H Woodworking................................G....... 717 445-6595
East Earl (G-4542)
Harrison Custom Cabinets....................E....... 215 548-2450
Philadelphia (G-13804)

FURNITURE: Kitchen & Dining Room, Metal

Tri State Kitchens and Baths ....F.....
Pottstown (G-16058)

FURNITURE: Laboratory

J H C Fabrications Inc ....G....... 570 277-6150
New Philadelphia (G-12432)
Reed Associates Inc ....F....... 215 256-9572
Hatfield (G-7389)

FURNITURE: Lawn & Garden, Except Wood & Metal

Gregg Lane LLC..................................G....... 215 269-9900
Fairless Hills (G-5781)

FURNITURE: Lawn & Garden, Metal

Casual Living Unlimited LLC ....G....... 717 351-7177
New Holland (G-12231)
Clear Creek Industries Inc....................F....... 814 834-9880
Saint Marys (G-16954)
Rio Brands LLC...................................D....... 610 629-6200
Conshohocken (G-3601)

FURNITURE: Lawn, Wood

Jonathans Woodcraft ....G....... 610 857-1359
Parkesburg (G-13177)
Lapp John ....G....... 717 442-8583
Gap (G-6252)
Pittsburgh Shed Company Inc..............G....... 724 745-4422
Canonsburg (G-2619)
Trim P A C LLC ....G....... 717 375-2366
Chambersburg (G-2989)
Wanner Road Woodcraft ....G....... 717 768-0207
Narvon (G-11931)
Wyomissing Structures LLC..................G....... 610 374-2370
New Providence (G-12436)

FURNITURE: Living Room, Upholstered On Wood Frames

Flexsteel Industries Inc ....C....... 717 392-4161
Lancaster (G-9019)

FURNITURE: Mattresses & Foundations

Bergad Inc ....E....... 724 763-2883
Kittanning (G-8757)
Custom Carpet & Bedding Inc...............G....... 570 344-7533
Dunmore (G-4472)
Elby Bedding Inc ....G....... 610 292-8700
Norristown (G-12653)
M B Bedding Co ....G....... 570 822-2491
Wilkes Barre (G-19939)
Neuropedic LLC...................................F....... 570 501-7713
West Hazleton (G-19714)
Park Place Pa LLC ....D....... 717 336-2846
Denver (G-4086)

FURNITURE: Mattresses, Box & Bedsprings

Chestnut Ridge Foam Inc.....................C....... 724 537-9000
Latrobe (G-9464)
Classic Bedding Mfg Co Inc..................G....... 800 810-0930
Conneaut Lake (G-3470)
Custom Bedframe Products ....F....... 570 539-8770
Port Trevorton (G-15911)
ES Kluft & Co East LLC ....E....... 570 384-2800
Denver (G-4072)
ES Kluft & Company Inc.......................D....... 570 384-2800
Hazle Township (G-7455)
Honey Brook Woodcrafts ....G....... 610 273-2928
Honey Brook (G-7750)
Leggett & Platt Incorporated................D....... 570 824-6622
Hanover Township (G-6992)
Leggett & Platt Incorporated................D....... 570 542-4171
Berwick (G-1332)
Stauffer Frames..................................E....... 570 374-7100
Port Trevorton (G-15915)
Tempur Production Usa LLC ....F....... 570 715-7200
Mountain Top (G-11778)

FURNITURE: Mattresses, Innerspring Or Box Spring

Eastern Sleep Products Company ....E....... 610 582-7228
Reading (G-16369)
Magic Sleeper Inc................................F....... 610 327-2322
Pottstown (G-16013)

FURNITURE: NEC

Hornings Woodcraft ....G....... 717 949-3524
Newmanstown (G-12477)

FURNITURE: Novelty, Wood

Coopersburg Associates Inc ....E....... 610 282-1360
Center Valley (G-2825)
Kinloch Woodworking Ltd ....G....... 610 347-2070
Unionville (G-18648)

FURNITURE: Office Panel Systems, Exc Wood

Flex-Y-Plan Industries Inc ....E....... 814 881-3436
Fairview (G-5822)
Transwall Office Systems Inc ....E....... 610 429-1400
West Chester (G-19669)

FURNITURE: Office Panel Systems, Wood

Conestoga Wood Spc Corp ....C....... 570 658-9663
Beavertown (G-1025)
Knoll Inc...E....... 215 988-1788
Philadelphia (G-13940)
Knoll Inc...D....... 484 224-3760
Allentown (G-285)
Knoll Inc...E....... 215 679-1218
East Greenville (G-4571)

FURNITURE: Office, Exc Wood

A/S Custom Furniture Company ....E....... 215 491-3100
Warrington (G-19105)
AAA Business Solutions LLC.................G....... 412 787-3333
Pittsburgh (G-14631)
Adelphia Steel Eqp Co Inc....................E....... 800 865-8211
Philadelphia (G-13345)
Ajjp Corporation..................................C....... 215 968-6677
Newtown (G-12495)
Datum Filing Systems Inc ....C....... 717 764-6350
Emigsville (G-4986)
Design Options Holdings LLC ....E....... 610 667-8180
Bala Cynwyd (G-877)
Ergogenic Technology Inc ....E....... 215 766-8545
Quakertown (G-16188)
Gk Inc...F....... 215 223-7207
Philadelphia (G-13764)
Innovative Office Products LLC ....C....... 610 559-6369
Easton (G-4707)
Interior Creations Inc...........................E....... 215 425-9390
Philadelphia (G-13864)
Knoll Inc...E....... 215 679-7991
East Greenville (G-4570)
Patterson Furniture Co.........................G....... 412 771-0600
Mc Kees Rocks (G-10622)
Perpetual Enterprises Inc.....................G....... 412 299-6356
Coraopolis (G-3712)
Perpetual Enterprises Inc.....................G....... 412 299-6356
Coraopolis (G-3713)

Perpetual Enterprises Inc.....................G....... 814 437-3705
Franklin (G-6151)
Pickell Enterprises Inc.........................E....... 215 244-7800
Bensalem (G-1243)
Racechairs LLC...................................G....... 267 632-5003
Perkasie (G-13291)
Robert Trate Hogg Cbinetmakers..........G....... 717 529-2522
Oxford (G-13088)
Spectra Inc...E....... 814 238-6332
State College (G-18030)
TC Millwork Inc...................................C....... 215 245-4210
Bensalem (G-1259)

FURNITURE: Office, Wood

A/S Custom Furniture Company ....E....... 215 491-3100
Warrington (G-19105)
Ajjp Corporation..................................C....... 215 968-6677
Newtown (G-12495)
American Atelier Inc ....C....... 610 439-4040
Allentown (G-133)
B K Barrit Corp....................................D....... 267 345-1200
Philadelphia (G-13438)
Biltwood Architectural Mllwk ....F....... 717 593-9400
Greencastle (G-6600)
Cedar Ridge Furniture.........................G....... 610 286-6225
Morgantown (G-11519)
Conestoga Wood Spc Corp ....A....... 717 445-6701
East Earl (G-4540)
Datum Filing Systems Inc ....C....... 717 764-6350
Emigsville (G-4986)
Dsc2 Inc...F....... 980 223-2270
York (G-20458)
Duckloe Frederick and Bros ....F....... 570 897-6172
Portland (G-15939)
Eye Design LLC...................................E....... 610 409-1900
Trappe (G-18468)
Federal Prison Industries.....................E....... 570 544-7343
Minersville (G-11254)
Gerald Maier ....G....... 215 744-9999
Philadelphia (G-13757)
Infinite Quest Cabinetry Corp ....G....... 301 222-3592
Red Lion (G-16601)
Joseph Mikstas ....G....... 215 271-2419
Philadelphia (G-13911)
Knoll Inc...D....... 215 679-7991
East Greenville (G-4570)
Krehling Industries Inc.........................D....... 717 232-7936
Harrisburg (G-7165)
Mahogany and More Inc ....F....... 610 666-6500
Oaks (G-12934)
Martins Furniture LLC ....F....... 717 354-5657
Ephrata (G-5126)
Millwork Solutions Inc..........................E....... 814 446-4009
Seward (G-17382)
Missing Piece ....G....... 610 759-4033
Nazareth (G-11982)
Odhner and Odhner Fine Wdwkg ....E....... 610 258-9300
Easton (G-4734)
Paul Downs Cabinet Makers Inc............F....... 610 239-0142
Bridgeport (G-2043)
Richard Riberich ....G....... 412 271-8427
Pittsburgh (G-15484)
Robert Trate Hogg Cbinetmakers..........G....... 717 529-2522
Oxford (G-13088)
Selinsgrove Instnl Csework LLC ....E....... 570 374-1176
Selinsgrove (G-17333)
Spectra Inc...E....... 814 238-6332
State College (G-18030)
Tha Inc...E....... 215 804-0220
Quakertown (G-16250)
Vitra Inc...E....... 610 391-9780
Allentown (G-424)
William Cottage ....G....... 724 266-2961
Ambridge (G-639)
Winterhouse Furniture Inc ....G....... 215 249-3410
Dublin (G-4437)
Wood-Mode Incorporated ....E....... 570 374-1176
Selinsgrove (G-17338)

FURNITURE: Outdoor, Wood

Benchsmith LLC..................................G....... 215 491-1711
Warrington (G-19109)
Diamond Trpcl Hardwoods Intl ....G....... 215 257-2556
Sellersville (G-17345)
Elmwood ....F....... 570 524-9663
Lewisburg (G-9905)
Lime Rock Gazebos LLC.......................G....... 717 625-4066
Lititz (G-10022)

PRODUCT

FURNITURE: Pews, Church

Schutte Woodworking & Mfg Co ....G....... 814 453-5110
Erie *(G-5470)*

FURNITURE: Picnic Tables Or Benches, Park

Carrier Class Green Infras ....G....... 267 419-8496
Willow Grove *(G-20110)*
County of Montgomery.........................E....... 215 234-4528
Green Lane *(G-6586)*
Keystone Ridge Designs Inc.............E....... 724 284-1213
Butler *(G-2417)*

FURNITURE: Restaurant

Ajjp Corporation...................................C....... 215 968-6677
Newtown *(G-12495)*
Hawk Industries Inc ....F....... 717 359-4138
Littlestown *(G-10066)*
Officelogic Inc ....G....... 215 752-3069
Bensalem *(G-1235)*
Siu King ....F....... 215 769-9863
Philadelphia *(G-14313)*

FURNITURE: School

Schalow Visual Concepts Inc ....G....... 570 336-2714
Benton *(G-1282)*

FURNITURE: Stools, Household, Wood

Lamens Furniture................................G....... 814 733-4537
Schellsburg *(G-17134)*

FURNITURE: Storage Chests, Household, Wood

Country Barns of Pittsburgh.................G....... 412 221-1630
Pittsburgh *(G-14879)*
Creekside Structures LLC...................G....... 717 627-5267
Leola *(G-9775)*
Interstate Self Storage.......................G....... 724 662-1186
Mercer *(G-10965)*
Pine Creek Construction LLC ....G....... 717 362-6974
Elizabethville *(G-4896)*

FURNITURE: Table Tops, Marble

J A Kohlepp and Sons Stone ....F....... 814 371-5200
Du Bois *(G-4397)*
Rynone Manufacturing Corp.................C....... 570 888-5272
Sayre *(G-17121)*
Tri City Marble Inc ....E....... 610 481-0177
Allentown *(G-412)*
Tri-City Marble LLC ....F....... 610 481-0177
Allentown *(G-413)*

FURNITURE: Tables & Table Tops, Wood

Leisters Furniture Inc ....D....... 717 632-8177
Hanover *(G-6914)*
RAD Mfg LLC ....D....... 570 752-4514
Nescopeck *(G-12001)*
Schutte Woodworking & Mfg Co ....G....... 814 453-5110
Erie *(G-5470)*

FURNITURE: Television, Wood

Touchstone Home Products Inc ....G....... 510 782-1282
Exton *(G-5738)*

FURNITURE: Unfinished, Wood

Closet Works Inc ....E....... 215 675-6430
Montgomeryville *(G-11388)*
Collegiate Furnishings Inc...................E....... 814 234-1660
State College *(G-17954)*

FURNITURE: Upholstered

Anthony Cocco Inc ....G....... 215 629-4100
Philadelphia *(G-13394)*
Ashley Furniture Inds Inc.....................A....... 610 926-0897
Leesport *(G-9657)*
B K Barrit Corp ....D....... 267 345-1200
Philadelphia *(G-13438)*
Chair Shoppe ....G....... 570 353-2735
Morris *(G-11544)*
Dronetti Upholstery Inc ....G....... 610 435-2957
Allentown *(G-196)*
Dsc2 Inc ....F....... 980 223-2270
York *(G-20458)*

Easton Upholstery Furn Mfg Co............G....... 610 252-3169
Easton *(G-4675)*
Ed RE Invent ....G....... 814 590-0771
Luthersburg *(G-10123)*
Everclear Valley Inc ....G....... 724 676-4703
New Florence *(G-12196)*
Fabtex Inc ....C....... 570 275-7500
Danville *(G-4000)*
Guildcraft Inc ....F....... 717 854-3888
York *(G-20517)*
Haberle Upholstery ....G....... 215 679-8195
Zionsville *(G-20835)*
Jerry Lister Custom Upholsteri.............G....... 215 639-3880
Bensalem *(G-1213)*
Jerry Lister Custom Upholsteri.............F....... 215 639-3882
Huntingdon Valley *(G-8004)*
Kauffmans Upholstery Inc....................G....... 610 262-8298
Northampton *(G-12852)*
Keystone Quality Products LLC ....E....... 717 354-2762
Leola *(G-9790)*
Maple Mountain Industries Inc ....F....... 724 439-1234
Uniontown *(G-18637)*
Maple Mountain Industries Inc ....E....... 570 662-3200
Mansfield *(G-10421)*
Maple Mountain Industries Inc ....G....... 724 676-4703
New Florence *(G-12198)*
Maple Mountain Industries Inc ....G....... 814 634-0674
Meyersdale *(G-11015)*
Noor Furniture Inc...............................G....... 215 533-0703
Philadelphia *(G-14077)*
Patterson Furniture Co ....G....... 412 771-0600
Mc Kees Rocks *(G-10622)*
Russell Upholstery Co Inc....................G....... 814 455-9021
Erie *(G-5467)*
S DRocco Upholstery ....G....... 215 745-2869
Philadelphia *(G-14270)*
Schuibbeo Holdings Inc ....G....... 610 268-2825
Avondale *(G-859)*
Tiffany Tiffany Designers Inc ....G....... 215 297-0550
Point Pleasant *(G-15888)*

FURNITURE: Vehicle

Racechairs LLC ....G....... 267 632-5003
Perkasie *(G-13291)*

FURRIERS

Hal-Jo Corp...F....... 215 885-4747
Jenkintown *(G-8289)*

FUSES: Electric

Cooper Bussmann LLC ....B....... 724 553-5449
Cranberry Township *(G-3812)*

Furs

Westmoreland Contract Fur..................G....... 724 838-7748
Greensburg *(G-6731)*

GAME MACHINES, COIN-OPERATED, WHOLESALE

Kgm Gaming LLC..................................E....... 215 430-0388
Philadelphia *(G-13934)*

GAMES & TOYS: Bingo Boards

Kelly Line Inc.......................................F....... 570 527-6822
Pottsville *(G-16085)*
Loyal Gaming Rewards LLC ....G....... 814 822-2008
Altoona *(G-522)*

GAMES & TOYS: Board Games, Children's & Adults'

Action Centered Training Inc ....G....... 610 630-3325
Norristown *(G-12630)*

GAMES & TOYS: Craft & Hobby Kits & Sets

Accent Shop ....G....... 724 695-7580
Imperial *(G-8056)*
Artskills Inc...E....... 610 253-6663
Bethlehem *(G-1453)*
Cook Forest Saw Mill Center ....F....... 814 927-6655
Cooksburg *(G-3620)*
Country Accents ....G....... 570 478-4127
Williamsport *(G-20001)*
Dimensions ....G....... 610 939-9900
Reading *(G-16363)*

Dodie Sable ....G....... 610 756-3836
Lenhartsville *(G-9758)*
Higley Enterprises ....G....... 610 693-4039
Levittown *(G-9843)*
Old Bedford Village Inc ....G....... 814 623-1156
Bedford *(G-1068)*
Senior Craftsmens Shop ....G....... 570 344-7089
Scranton *(G-17290)*
Wood Hollow Crafts LLC ....G....... 215 428-0870
Yardley *(G-20345)*

GAMES & TOYS: Darts & Dart Games

Apex Manufacturing Co........................G....... 610 272-0659
Norristown *(G-12635)*
Verus Sports Inc ....F....... 215 283-0153
Fort Washington *(G-6096)*

GAMES & TOYS: Doll Clothing

Lily Kay Doll Clothes LLC ....G....... 724 814-2210
Cranberry Township *(G-3832)*

GAMES & TOYS: Dollhouses & Furniture

Jake Stoltzfus.....................................F....... 717 529-4082
Christiana *(G-3140)*

GAMES & TOYS: Dolls, Exc Stuffed Toy Animals

Ladie & Friends Inc..............................G....... 215 453-8200
Sellersville *(G-17353)*
Little Souls Inc ....E....... 610 278-0500
Devon *(G-4113)*
Madame Alexander Doll Co LLC...........E....... 717 537-4140
Mountville *(G-11798)*

GAMES & TOYS: Electronic

Jumpbutton Studio LLC ....E....... 267 407-7535
Philadelphia *(G-13914)*

GAMES & TOYS: Engines, Miniature

Nelsons Competition Engines...............G....... 724 538-5282
Zelienople *(G-20812)*

GAMES & TOYS: Miniature Dolls, Collectors'

Country Traditions ....G....... 570 386-3621
New Ringgold *(G-12437)*

GAMES & TOYS: Models, Airplane, Toy & Hobby

Brodak Manufacturing & Distrg.............G....... 724 966-2726
Carmichaels *(G-2754)*

GAMES & TOYS: Models, Railroad, Toy & Hobby

Bowser Manufacturing Co ....F....... 570 368-5045
Montoursville *(G-11434)*
Jensen Manufacturing Co Inc ....G....... 800 525-5245
Jeannette *(G-8258)*

GAMES & TOYS: Trains & Eqpt, Electric & Mechanical

Christopher Gans.................................G....... 610 353-8585
Broomall *(G-2282)*
Specialty Products Company ....G....... 570 729-7192
Honesdale *(G-7724)*

GARAGES: Portable, Prefabricated Metal

Fork Creek Cabins LLC ....F....... 717 442-1902
Paradise *(G-13159)*

GARBAGE CONTAINERS: Plastic

Staggert Disposal ....G....... 570 547-6150
Montgomery *(G-11379)*
TNT Disposal ....G....... 570 297-0101
Troy *(G-18527)*
Yonish Disposal Company.....................G....... 814 839-4797
Alum Bank *(G-563)*

GARBAGE DISPOSERS & COMPACTORS: Commercial

Philadlphia Tramrail Entps Inc..............C....... 215 743-4359
Philadelphia (G-14165)
Ptr Baler and Compactor Co..............C....... 215 533-5100
Philadelphia (G-14215)

GARNET MINING SVCS

Gma Garnet (usa) Corp ....E....... 215 736-1868
Fairless Hills (G-5780)

GAS & OIL FIELD EXPLORATION SVCS

639 E Congress Realty Corp.................F....... 610 434-5195
Allentown (G-110)
Abarta Oil & Gas Co Inc....................E....... 412 963-6226
Pittsburgh (G-14632)
AEG Holdings Inc............................E....... 412 262-2830
Coraopolis (G-3654)
Alpha Safety USA...........................G....... 814 236-3344
Clearfield (G-3211)
American Oil & Gas LLC.....................G....... 724 852-2222
Mount Morris (G-11677)
Anadarko Petroleum.........................G....... 570 326-1535
Williamsport (G-19986)
Anderson Family Farm Inc...................F....... 814 463-0202
Tionesta (G-18369)
Apex Energy LLC.............................F....... 724 719-2611
Wexford (G-19787)
Ard Operating LLC...........................D....... 570 979-1240
Williamsport (G-19989)
Atlas Energy Company LLC...................E....... 877 280-2857
Philadelphia (G-13423)
Atlas Growth Partners LP ....C....... 412 489-0006
Pittsburgh (G-14733)
Atls Production Company LLC................C....... 412 489-0006
Pittsburgh (G-14736)
Beckman Production Svcs Inc................G....... 814 425-1066
Cochranton (G-3336)
Belden & Blake Corporation ....F....... 814 589-7091
Pleasantville (G-15797)
Blackhawk Specialty Tools LLC ....G....... 570 323-7100
Muncy (G-11811)
Brighton Resources Inc.....................G....... 412 661-1025
Pittsburgh (G-14792)
Cameron Technologies Us Inc................D....... 724 695-3798
Coraopolis (G-3671)
Campbell Oil & Gas Inc.....................G....... 724 465-9199
Indiana (G-8085)
Cody Well Service...........................G....... 814 726-3542
Clarendon (G-3168)
Core Laboratories LP ....F....... 412 884-9250
Pittsburgh (G-14876)
Dale Property Services Penn LP ....G....... 724 705-0444
Canonsburg (G-2576)
Dean Construction LLC......................G....... 814 887-8750
Smethport (G-17634)
Direct Energy Products Inc.................F....... 216 255-7777
Tionesta (G-18370)
Discovery Oil Gas LLC ....G....... 724 746-4004
Canonsburg (G-2578)
Dominion Exploration and Prod ....G....... 724 349-4450
Indiana (G-8091)
Doran & Associates Inc.....................G....... 412 344-5200
Pittsburgh (G-14933)
Dorso LLC....................................G....... 724 934-7710
Wexford (G-19798)
Duncan Land & Energy Inc...................G....... 412 922-0135
Pittsburgh (G-14943)
Eastern American Energy Corp...............F....... 814 938-9000
Punxsutawney (G-16136)
Eclipse Resources I LP ....F....... 814 308-9754
State College (G-17960)
Eclipse Resources-Pa LP ....F....... 814 409-7006
State College (G-17962)
Edward Oil Company..........................G....... 814 726-9576
Youngsville (G-20770)
Energy Corporation of America..............G....... 724 966-9000
Carmichaels (G-2756)
Eog Resources Inc...........................F....... 724 349-7620
Indiana (G-8095)
Esmark Inc...................................F....... 412 259-8868
Sewickley (G-17386)
Evolution Energy Services LLC..............D....... 412 946-1371
Mc Murray (G-10644)
Exco Resources LLC..........................D....... 724 720-2500
Kittanning (G-8768)
Explorations Inc............................G....... 814 365-2105
Punxsutawney (G-16137)

Fault Line Oil Corporation................G....... 814 368-5901
Bradford (G-1968)
Fossil Rock LLC.............................G....... 724 355-3747
Harmony (G-7067)
Fts International LLC.......................G....... 724 873-1021
Canonsburg (G-2589)
Haddad and Brooks Inc......................G....... 724 228-8811
Washington (G-19184)
Hep Pennsylvania Gathering LLC ....E....... 210 298-2229
Towanda (G-18430)
Hg Energy LLC...............................G....... 724 935-8952
Sewickley (G-17391)
Huntley & Huntley Inc......................F....... 412 380-2355
Monroeville (G-11341)
Keystone Wireline Inc......................G....... 814 362-0230
Bradford (G-1977)
Little Pine Resources ....E....... 814 765-6300
Clearfield (G-3223)
Natural Oil & Gas Corp.....................G....... 814 362-6890
Bradford (G-1985)
Oil & Gas Management Inc...................G....... 724 925-1568
Hunker (G-7930)
Oleum Exploration LLC......................F....... 855 912-6200
Brodheadsville (G-2237)
Paul G Benedum Jr..........................G....... 412 288-0280
Pittsburgh (G-15371)
Pennico Oil Co Inc.........................E....... 724 468-8232
Delmont (G-4053)
Per Midstream LLC..........................E....... 412 275-3200
Pittsburgh (G-15377)
Phoenix Energy Productions ....G....... 724 295-9220
Freeport (G-6213)
Plants and Goodwin Inc.....................E....... 814 697-6330
Shinglehouse (G-17511)
Preferred Proppants LLC ....F....... 610 834-1969
Radnor (G-16297)
Range Resources ....G....... 570 858-1200
Bradford (G-1989)
Range Rsources - Appalachia LLC ....F....... 724 887-5715
Scottdale (G-17198)
Range Rsources - Appalachia LLC ....E....... 724 783-7144
Yatesboro (G-20348)
Range Rsources - Appalachia LLC ....D....... 724 743-6700
Canonsburg (G-2624)
Range Rsources - Appalachia LLC ....D....... 817 870-2601
Carlton (G-2753)
RE Gas Development LLC ....E....... 814 278-7267
State College (G-18013)
Rex Energy Corporation.....................F....... 724 814-3230
Cranberry Township (G-3846)
Rex Energy IV LLC...........................E....... 814 278-7267
State College (G-18015)
Rex Energy Operating Corp..................E....... 814 278-7267
State College (G-18016)
Rice Drilling B LLC.........................E....... 274 281-7200
Canonsburg (G-2627)
Rice Drilling D LLC.........................D....... 274 281-7200
Canonsburg (G-2628)
Rjb Well Services Inc......................F....... 814 368-9570
Bradford (G-1990)
Royal Oil & Gas Corporation................E....... 724 463-0246
Indiana (G-8124)
Seneca Resources Company LLC...............D....... 412 548-2500
Pittsburgh (G-15523)
Snyder Brothers Inc.........................E....... 724 548-8101
Kittanning (G-8794)
Star Energy Inc.............................G....... 814 257-8485
Dayton (G-4040)
Straub Industries Inc......................G....... 814 364-9789
Centre Hall (G-2844)
Sun Energy Services LLC....................C....... 724 473-0687
Zelienople (G-20820)
Sun Energy Services LLC....................G....... 724 473-0687
Zelienople (G-20821)
Superior Applchian Ppeline LLC ....G....... 724 746-6744
Canonsburg (G-2643)
Trans Energy Inc............................F....... 304 684-7053
Pittsburgh (G-15638)
Universal Well Services Inc................F....... 570 321-5302
Williamsport (G-20086)
Universal Well Services Inc................G....... 814 337-1983
Meadville (G-10807)
US Energy Expl Corp.........................G....... 724 783-7624
Rural Valley (G-16878)
Vantage Energy LLC..........................D....... 724 746-6720
Canonsburg (G-2653)
Vineyard Oil & Gas Company ....F....... 814 725-8742
North East (G-12764)
Weaver Glen A & Son LLC ....G....... 814 432-3013
Franklin (G-6168)

White Oak Farms Inc ....G....... 814 257-8485
Dayton (G-4041)

GAS & OIL FIELD SVCS, NEC

Eden Green Energy Inc ....G....... 267 255-9462
Philadelphia (G-13659)
I L Geer and Sons ....G....... 814 723-7569
Clarendon (G-3169)
Kenic Gas & Oil Company....................G....... 724 445-7701
Fenelton (G-5946)
Magee and Magee Inc.........................F....... 814 966-3623
Rixford (G-16759)
Williams Field Services ....G....... 570 965-7643
Tunkhannock (G-18552)

GAS FIELD MACHINERY & EQPT

Gt Services LLC.............................E....... 215 256-9521
Kulpsville (G-8829)
Specialized Desanders USA Inc ....G....... 412 535-3396
Pittsburgh (G-15569)
Tru-Gas Inc.................................G....... 814 723-9260
Clarendon (G-3171)

GAS PRODUCTION & DISTRIBUTION

Hearth & Home Technologies LLC ....G....... 717 362-9080
Halifax (G-6826)
Praxair Dist Mid-Atlantic LLC ....A....... 610 398-2211
Allentown (G-355)
Praxair Distribution Inc...................A....... 610 398-2211
Allentown (G-356)
Williams Field Services ....G....... 570 965-7643
Tunkhannock (G-18552)

GAS PRODUCTION & DISTRIBUTION: Coke Oven

Sssi Inc....................................B....... 724 743-5815
Washington (G-19228)

GAS STATIONS

American Auto Wash Inc......................F....... 610 265-3222
King of Prussia (G-8580)
Atlantic Refining & Marketing..............C....... 215 977-3000
Philadelphia (G-13422)
Don Saylors Markets Inc ....C....... 717 776-7551
Newville (G-12600)
Fuel Cell Inc...............................E....... 610 759-0143
Nazareth (G-11967)
United Refining Inc.........................D....... 814 723-1500
Warren (G-19054)
United Refining Company ....C....... 814 723-1500
Warren (G-19055)

GASES & LIQUIFIED PETROLEUM GASES

Pricetown Ephrata Gas &F....................G....... 610 939-1701
Fleetwood (G-5978)

GASES: Carbon Dioxide

Glen Carbonic Gas Co ....F....... 570 779-1226
Plymouth (G-15819)
Praxair Distribution Inc ....F....... 412 781-6273
Pittsburgh (G-15429)

GASES: Hydrogen

Bethlehem Hydrogen Inc......................G....... 610 762-1706
Northampton (G-12845)
Hyrdogen Corp...............................G....... 412 405-1000
McKeesport (G-10672)
United Hydrogen Group Inc..................F....... 866 942-7763
Canonsburg (G-2651)

GASES: Indl

Air Liquide Electronics US LP ....F....... 215 428-4600
Morrisville (G-11553)
Air Liquide Electronics US LP ....G....... 570 897-2000
Mount Bethel (G-11606)
Air Liquide Electronics US LP ....E....... 215 736-2796
Morrisville (G-11554)
Air Products and Chemicals Inc..............E....... 610 317-8706
Bethlehem (G-1445)
Air Products and Chemicals Inc..............D....... 724 226-4434
Creighton (G-3879)
Air Products and Chemicals Inc..............B....... 570 467-2981
Tamaqua (G-18208)
Air Products and Chemicals Inc..............E....... 610 395-2101
Allentown (G-120)

PRODUCT

Air Products and Chemicals Inc ....G...... 610 481-2057
  Allentown (G-121)
Air Products and Chemicals Inc ....D...... 610 481-3706
  Allentown (G-122)
Air Products LLC ....C...... 610 481-4911
  Allentown (G-123)
Airgas Usa LLC ....G...... 814 437-2431
  Franklin (G-6113)
Airgas Usa LLC ....G...... 215 766-8860
  Plumsteadville (G-15806)
American Welding & Gas Inc ....F...... 570 323-8400
  Williamsport (G-19985)
Carbon Capture Scientific LLC ....G...... 412 854-6713
  Bethel Park (G-1409)
Keiper Tech LLC ....G...... 717 938-1674
  Etters (G-5551)
Marcellus Shale Coalition ....F...... 412 706-5160
  Pittsburgh (G-15251)
Messer Gt & S ....G...... 717 232-3173
  Harrisburg (G-7177)
Praxair Inc ....C...... 610 691-2474
  Bethlehem (G-1603)
Praxair Inc ....D...... 610 759-3923
  Stockertown (G-18066)
Praxair Inc ....E...... 610 530-3885
  Allentown (G-354)
Praxair Distribution Inc ....G...... 717 393-3681
  Lancaster (G-9174)
Praxair Distribution Inc ....E...... 610 921-9230
  Reading (G-16475)
Specgas Inc ....G...... 215 355-2405
  Warminster (G-18971)
Spray Products Corporation ....D...... 610 277-1010
  Plymouth Meeting (G-15872)
Ucg Georgia LLC ....G...... 610 515-8589
  Bethlehem (G-1646)
Wilson Pdts Compressed Gas Co ....E...... 610 253-9608
  Easton (G-4777)

GASES: Neon

Debbie Dengler ....G...... 717 755-5226
  York (G-20446)
Neon Moon ....G...... 814 332-0302
  Meadville (G-10767)
R K Neon Company ....G...... 724 539-9605
  Latrobe (G-9515)

GASES: Nitrogen

Air Products and Chemicals Inc ....D...... 717 291-1617
  Lancaster (G-8925)
Linde Gas North America LLC ....F...... 610 539-6510
  Norristown (G-12675)
Linde Gas North America LLC ....F...... 412 741-6613
  Sewickley (G-17399)
Matheson Tri-Gas Inc ....F...... 724 379-4104
  Donora (G-4156)
Matheson Tri-Gas Inc ....F...... 814 781-6990
  Saint Marys (G-16987)
Messer LLC ....F...... 412 351-4580
  Braddock (G-1947)
Nitrogen ....G...... 440 208-7474
  Yardley (G-20329)
Nitrogen (was Dorland ....G...... 215 928-2727
  Philadelphia (G-14076)

GASES: Oxygen

Air Liquide America LP ....E...... 610 383-5500
  Coatesville (G-3286)
Air Products and Chemicals Inc ....E...... 610 317-8715
  Bethlehem (G-1446)
Air Products and Chemicals Inc ....A...... 610 481-4911
  Allentown (G-119)
Air Products and Chemicals Inc ....E...... 724 266-1563
  Leetsdale (G-9677)
Alig LLC ....G...... 570 544-2540
  Minersville (G-11253)
Messer LLC ....G...... 610 317-8500
  Bethlehem (G-1569)
Praxair Distribution Inc ....G...... 570 655-3721
  Pittston (G-15778)
Praxair Distribution Inc ....F...... 215 736-8005
  Morrisville (G-11579)

GASKET MATERIALS

Argosy Capital Group LLC ....F...... 610 971-9685
  Wayne (G-19299)
Argosy Inv Partners IV LP ....F...... 610 971-9685
  Wayne (G-19300)

Fabritech Inc ....G...... 610 430-0027
  Chester Springs (G-3078)
Fibreflex Packing & Mfg Co ....E...... 215 482-1490
  Philadelphia (G-13700)
Lydall Performance Mtls US Inc ....C...... 717 207-6000
  Lancaster (G-9119)
Lydall Performance Mtls US Inc ....C...... 717 207-6025
  Lancaster (G-9120)
Lydall Performance Mtls US Inc ....E...... 717 390-1886
  Lancaster (G-9121)
R/W Connection Inc ....E...... 717 898-5257
  Landisville (G-9266)
R/W Connection Inc ....G...... 717 767-3660
  Emigsville (G-4998)
Susquehanna Capitl Acquisition ....A...... 800 942-7538
  Lancaster (G-9210)

GASKETS

Accutrex Products Inc ....C...... 724 746-4300
  Canonsburg (G-2532)
C E Conover & Co Inc ....E...... 215 639-6666
  Bensalem (G-1164)
D A R Industrial Pdts Inc ....G...... 610 825-4900
  Conshohocken (G-3535)
Dudlik Industries Inc ....E...... 215 674-4383
  Hatboro (G-7282)
Ensinger Penn Fibre Inc ....D...... 215 702-9551
  Bensalem (G-1190)
Gasket Resources Inc ....E...... 610 363-5800
  Downingtown (G-4229)
Has-Mor Industries Inc ....F...... 570 383-0185
  Olyphant (G-12992)
Hussey Performance LLC ....G...... 724 318-8292
  Ambridge (G-619)
Igs Industries Inc ....C...... 724 222-5800
  Meadow Lands (G-10690)
Lehigh Gasket Inc ....F...... 610 837-1818
  Bath (G-964)
Manufactured Rubber Pdts Co ....F...... 215 533-3600
  Philadelphia (G-13989)
Melrath Gasket Inc ....D...... 215 223-6000
  Philadelphia (G-14007)
R Way Gasket & Supply Company ....F...... 215 743-1650
  Philadelphia (G-14229)
Seal Science Inc ....F...... 610 868-2800
  Bethlehem (G-1616)
Staver Hydraulics Co Inc ....G...... 610 837-1818
  Bath (G-970)

GASKETS & SEALING DEVICES

American High Prfmce Seals Inc ....F...... 412 788-8815
  Oakdale (G-12889)
Corona Corporation ....F...... 215 679-9538
  Red Hill (G-16580)
Dooley Gasket and Seal Inc ....E...... 610 328-2720
  Broomall (G-2286)
Enpro Industries Inc ....E...... 800 618-4701
  Hatfield (G-7340)
Enpro Industries Inc ....G...... 215 946-0845
  Bristol (G-2141)
Eraseal Technologies LLC ....G...... 215 350-3633
  Hatfield (G-7342)
Garlock Sealing Tech LLC ....D...... 570 323-9409
  Williamsport (G-20016)
Greene Tweed & Co Inc ....A...... 215 256-9521
  Kulpsville (G-8827)
Hunter Sales Corporation ....F...... 412 341-2444
  Bethel Park (G-1416)
Inter Tech Supplies Inc ....F...... 610 435-1333
  Allentown (G-265)
Poly-TEC Products Inc ....F...... 215 547-3366
  Bristol (G-2185)
Scott H Payne ....G...... 215 723-0510
  Telford (G-18313)
Stein Seal Company ....E...... 215 256-0201
  Kulpsville (G-8831)
Toss Machine Components Inc ....F...... 610 759-8883
  Nazareth (G-11992)

GASOLINE BLENDING PLANT

Chevron USA Inc ....E...... 412 262-2830
  Coraopolis (G-3677)
Lyondell Chemical Company ....D...... 610 359-2360
  Newtown Square (G-12583)

GASOLINE FILLING STATIONS

Ayrshire Dairy ....F...... 814 781-1978
  Saint Marys (G-16950)

Black Lick Stake Plant ....G...... 724 459-7670
  Blairsville (G-1716)
Chevron USA Inc ....E...... 412 262-2830
  Coraopolis (G-3677)
Cumberland Farms Inc ....G...... 412 331-4419
  Pittsburgh (G-14892)
Sunoco Inc ....D...... 215 977-3000
  Newtown Square (G-12591)
Sunoco (R&m) LLC ....D...... 215 977-3000
  Newtown Square (G-12592)

GATES: Ornamental Metal

Filippi Bros Inc ....G...... 215 247-5973
  Philadelphia (G-13701)
Pencoyd Iron Works Inc ....E...... 610 522-5000
  Folcroft (G-6012)
Trailgate Tailgate Systems ....G...... 724 321-6558
  Rostraver Township (G-16831)

GAUGES

Intra Corporation ....G...... 215 672-7003
  Horsham (G-7825)
Layke Tool & Manufacturing Co ....E...... 814 333-1169
  Meadville (G-10748)

GAUGES: Pressure

Allen Gauge & Tool Company ....E...... 412 241-6410
  Pittsburgh (G-14684)
Astra Corporation ....G...... 215 674-3539
  Warminster (G-18830)
Dansway Incorporated ....G...... 570 672-1550
  Elysburg (G-4973)

GEARS

A & A Gear Inc ....G...... 215 364-3952
  Huntingdon Valley (G-7959)
Thompson Gear & Machine Co ....G...... 724 468-5625
  Delmont (G-4060)

GEARS: Power Transmission, Exc Auto

Alcast Metals Inc ....E...... 215 368-5865
  Montgomeryville (G-11382)
Atch-Mont Gear Co Inc ....F...... 215 355-5146
  Ivyland (G-8205)
B & F Tool & Gear Inc ....G...... 717 632-8977
  Spring Grove (G-17875)
Brad Foote Gear Works Inc ....E...... 412 264-1428
  Pittsburgh (G-14789)
Martin Sprocket & Gear Inc ....D...... 610 837-1841
  Danielsville (G-3994)
Strube Inc ....F...... 717 426-1906
  Marietta (G-10468)
Thunder Basin Corporation ....F...... 610 962-3770
  King of Prussia (G-8688)
Zia-Tech Gear Mfg Inc ....G...... 412 321-0770
  Pittsburgh (G-15733)

GENERATING APPARATUS & PARTS: Electrical

Berrena Jseph T McHanicals Inc ....E...... 814 643-2645
  Huntingdon (G-7939)
Lesleh Precision Inc ....E...... 724 823-0901
  Rostraver Township (G-16827)
LLC Armstrong Power ....F...... 724 354-5300
  Shelocta (G-17486)

GENERATION EQPT: Electronic

Advanced Electronics Systems ....G...... 717 263-5681
  Chambersburg (G-2897)
Alencon Acquisition Co LLC ....G...... 484 436-0035
  Hatboro (G-7266)
CM Technologies Corporation ....F...... 412 262-0734
  Coraopolis (G-3678)
Electrostatics Inc ....F...... 215 513-0850
  Hatfield (G-7337)
Illinois Tool Works Inc ....D...... 215 822-2171
  Hatfield (G-7352)
K&L Services ....G...... 610 349-1358
  Allentown (G-277)
Mayer Electric Supply Co Inc ....G...... 814 765-7531
  Clearfield (G-3224)
Strainsense Enterprises Inc ....G...... 412 751-3055
  McKeesport (G-10684)
Wirecard North America Inc ....D...... 610 234-4410
  Conshohocken (G-3617)

GENERATOR REPAIR SVCS

Dyna-Tech Industries Ltd ....F 717 274-3099
Lebanon (G-9564)
R Scheinert & Son Inc ....E 215 673-9800
Philadelphia (G-14227)

GENERATORS: Storage Battery Chargers

Computer Pwr Solutions PA Inc ....F 724 898-2223
Mars (G-10491)

GENERATORS: Ultrasonic

Sensor Networks Inc ....E 814 466-7207
Boalsburg (G-1869)

GIFT SHOP

Alpine Wurst & Meathouse Inc ....E 570 253-5899
Honesdale (G-7700)
Bakers Lawn Ornaments ....F 814 445-7028
Somerset (G-17678)
C Leslie Smith Inc ....E 610 439-8833
Allentown (G-160)
Etched In Glass ....G 724 444-0808
Gibsonia (G-6333)
Fired Up ....G 724 941-0302
Canonsburg (G-2588)
Fisher S Hand Made Quilts ....G 717 392-5440
Bird In Hand (G-1674)
Gift Is In You Llc ....G 267 974-3376
Philadelphia (G-13761)
Giving Tree Inc ....G 215 968-2487
New Hope (G-12303)
Good Scents Candle Co Inc ....G 814 349-5848
Millheim (G-11218)
Grace Press Inc ....F 717 354-0475
Ephrata (G-5107)
Hayloft Candles ....G 717 656-9463
Leola (G-9786)
House of Candles ....F 570 629-1953
Henryville (G-7567)
Howanitz Associates Inc ....E 570 629-3388
Bartonsville (G-946)
Hutton Metalcrafts Inc ....G 570 646-7778
Pocono Pines (G-15881)
Irvins Corp ....D 570 539-8200
Mount Pleasant Mills (G-11726)
Jacoby Transportation Inc ....E 717 677-7733
Gettysburg (G-6302)
Josh Early Candies Inc ....F 610 395-4321
Allentown (G-271)
Mifflinburg Farmers Exchange ....G 570 966-4030
Mifflinburg (G-11098)
Nittany EMB & Digitizing ....F 814 359-0905
State College (G-17998)
Old Candle Barn Inc ....E 717 768-3231
Intercourse (G-8138)
Pocono Candle Works Inc ....F 570 421-1832
East Stroudsburg (G-4627)
Robert Trate Hogg Cbinetmakers ....G 717 529-2522
Oxford (G-13088)
Sewickley Creek Greenhouse ....G 724 935-8500
Sewickley (G-17408)
Shannons Kandy Kitchen ....G 724 662-5211
Mercer (G-10975)
Southwind Studios Ltd ....G 610 664-4110
Lower Merion (G-10109)
Wendell August Forge Inc ....D 724 748-9500
Mercer (G-10979)

GIFT, NOVELTY & SOUVENIR STORES: Artcraft & carvings

Crystal Imagery Inc ....G 888 440-6073
York Springs (G-20764)

GIFT, NOVELTY & SOUVENIR STORES: Gift Baskets

Basket Works Inc ....G 516 367-9200
Tannersville (G-18234)
Chocolate Creations ....G 724 774-7675
Monaca (G-11288)

GIFT, NOVELTY & SOUVENIR STORES: Gifts & Novelties

Creative Impressions Advg LLC ....G 215 357-1228
Langhorne (G-9287)

GIFTS & NOVELTIES: Wholesalers

Becky Kens Duck & Geese Creat ....G 717 684-0252
Columbia (G-3431)
Gail Dagowitz ....G 610 642-7634
Gladwyne (G-6408)
Keystone Quality Products LLC ....E 717 354-2762
Leola (G-9790)
L & L K Incorporated ....E 215 732-2614
Philadelphia (G-13948)

GIFTWARE: Brass

Edward Hecht Importers Inc ....E 215 925-5520
Philadelphia (G-13661)
New View Gifts & ACC Ltd ....E 610 627-0190
Media (G-10940)

GIFTWARE: Copper

Hutton Metalcrafts Inc ....G 570 646-7778
Pocono Pines (G-15881)
Irvins Corp ....D 570 539-8200
Mount Pleasant Mills (G-11726)

GLASS & GLASS CERAMIC PRDTS, PRESSED OR BLOWN: Tableware

Brian Giniewski LLC ....G 610 858-2821
Philadelphia (G-13479)
Ceramic Art Company Inc ....A 952 944-5600
Bristol (G-2124)
Ghp II LLC ....A 724 775-0010
Monaca (G-11290)
Lenox Corporation ....G 610 954-7590
Bethlehem (G-1560)
Lenox Corporation ....F 267 525-7800
Bristol (G-2159)
Port Augustus Glass Co LLC ....F 412 486-9100
Glenshaw (G-6498)
Specialty Seal Group Inc ....E 724 539-1626
Latrobe (G-9522)

GLASS FABRICATORS

A J Blosenski Inc ....D 610 942-2707
Honey Brook (G-7734)
Amera Glass Inc ....G 814 696-0944
Duncansville (G-4449)
Americana Art China Co Inc ....F 330 938-6133
Mercer (G-10959)
Ardagh Glass Inc ....E 814 642-2521
Port Allegany (G-15891)
Art Glass Sgo Inc ....G 215 884-8543
Spring House (G-17881)
Cardinal Ig Company ....G 570 474-9204
Mountain Top (G-11753)
Cardinal Lg Company ....G 570 489-6421
Jessup (G-8329)
City Sign Service Inc ....E 800 523-4452
Horsham (G-7804)
Consolidated Glass Corporation ....E 724 658-4541
New Castle (G-12077)
Davis Trophies & Sports Wear ....G 610 455-0640
West Chester (G-19533)
Drummond Scientific Company ....D 610 353-0200
Broomall (G-2287)
Electro-Glass Products Inc ....E 724 423-5000
Norvelt (G-12878)
Emerald Art Glass Inc ....F 412 381-2274
Pittsburgh (G-14970)
Fredericks Company Inc ....E 215 947-2500
Huntingdon Valley (G-7985)
Greenstar Allentown LLC ....E 610 262-6988
Northampton (G-12851)
Illadelph Glass Inc ....G 215 483-1801
Philadelphia (G-13849)
Jeannette Shade and Novelty Co ....D 724 523-5567
Jeannette (G-8257)
Kmz Enterprises LLC ....E 215 659-8400
Willow Grove (G-20126)
Lifetime Bathtub Enclosures ....F 215 228-2500
Philadelphia (G-13970)
Martell Sales & Service Inc ....E 814 765-6557
Hyde (G-8047)
Mesko Glass and Mirror Co Inc ....D 570 457-1700
Avoca (G-845)
Neidighs Inc ....F 814 237-3985
State College (G-17996)
Niagara Holdings Inc ....A 610 651-4200
Malvern (G-10286)

Potters Industries LLC ....G 610 651-4600
Conshohocken (G-3589)
PQ Corporation ....C 610 651-4200
Malvern (G-10299)
Precision Glass Products Co ....F 215 885-0145
Oreland (G-13028)
Roma Aluminum Co Inc ....F 215 545-5700
Philadelphia (G-14259)
Signature Door Inc ....D 814 949-2770
Altoona (G-549)
Superior Autoglass LLC ....G 724 452-9870
Zelienople (G-20822)
Thermo-Twin Industries Inc ....C 412 826-1000
Oakmont (G-12927)
Tohickon Corp ....G 267 450-5020
Sellersville (G-17360)
World Wide Plastics Inc ....E 215 357-0893
Langhorne (G-9336)
Yorkshire Lead Glass Company ....F 215 694-2727
Bristol (G-2219)
Youghiogheny Opalescent GL Inc ....F 724 628-3000
Connellsville (G-3512)
Young Windows Inc ....D 610 828-5036
Conshohocken (G-3618)

GLASS PRDTS, FROM PURCHASED GLASS: Art

Mitchco Inc ....E 717 843-3345
York (G-20599)

GLASS PRDTS, FROM PURCHASED GLASS: Enameled

Ferro Color & Glass Corp ....B 724 223-5900
Washington (G-19175)

GLASS PRDTS, FROM PURCHASED GLASS: Glass Beads, Reflecting

Mark-A-Hydrant LLC ....G 888 399-5532
Allentown (G-308)
Potters Holdings II LP ....G 610 651-4200
Malvern (G-10297)
Potters Industries LLC ....G 610 651-4700
Malvern (G-10298)

GLASS PRDTS, FROM PURCHASED GLASS: Glassware

Archetype Frameless Glass Co ....G 717 244-5240
Yoe (G-20358)
Behrenberg Glass Company Inc ....F 724 468-4181
Delmont (G-4048)
Crystal Imagery Inc ....G 888 440-6073
York Springs (G-20764)
Culver Industries Inc ....F 724 857-5770
Aliquippa (G-72)
Moderne Glass Company Inc ....C 724 857-5700
Aliquippa (G-86)

GLASS PRDTS, FROM PURCHASED GLASS: Insulating

Northeast Glass Co ....G 267 991-0054
Philadelphia (G-14083)
Sarik Corporation ....G 215 538-2269
Quakertown (G-16243)

GLASS PRDTS, FROM PURCHASED GLASS: Mirrored

Clearview Mirror and Glass ....G 412 672-4122
McKeesport (G-10663)

GLASS PRDTS, FROM PURCHASED GLASS: Sheet, Bent

Standard Bent Glass LLC ....D 724 287-3747
East Butler (G-4536)

GLASS PRDTS, FROM PURCHASED GLASS: Silvered

Hunt Stained Glass Studios ....G 412 391-1796
Pittsburgh (G-15105)

PRODUCT

GLASS PRDTS, FROM PURCHD GLASS: Strengthened Or Reinforced

PPG Industries Inc ....A 412 434-3131
Pittsburgh *(G-15425)*

GLASS PRDTS, PRESSED OR BLOWN: Blocks & Bricks

Jeannette Shade and Novelty Co ....D 724 523-5567
Jeannette *(G-8257)*

GLASS PRDTS, PRESSED OR BLOWN: Furnishings & Access

Optical Filters USA LLC ....E 814 333-2222
Meadville *(G-10771)*

GLASS PRDTS, PRESSED OR BLOWN: Glassware, Art Or Decorative

A A A Engraving ....G 412 281-7756
Pittsburgh *(G-14628)*
Etched In Glass ....G 724 444-0808
Gibsonia *(G-6333)*
Kelman Bottles LLC ....F 412 486-9100
Glenshaw *(G-6492)*
Puchalski Inc ....G 570 842-0361
Covington Township *(G-3793)*
Rfsj Inc ....G 724 547-4457
Mount Pleasant *(G-11716)*

GLASS PRDTS, PRESSED OR BLOWN: Glassware, Novelty

Rob Kei Inc ....G 717 293-8991
Lancaster *(G-9189)*

GLASS PRDTS, PRESSED OR BLOWN: Lighting Eqpt Parts

Cpd Lighting LLC ....G 215 361-6100
Colmar *(G-3412)*

GLASS PRDTS, PRESSED OR BLOWN: Optical

Ctp Carrera Inc ....C 724 539-6995
Latrobe *(G-9468)*
Ii-VI Incorporated ....B 724 352-4455
Saxonburg *(G-17088)*
USA Optical Inc ....F 717 757-5632
York *(G-20695)*

GLASS PRDTS, PRESSED OR BLOWN: Scientific Glassware

Corning Incorporated ....D 570 883-9005
Pittston *(G-15746)*
E Victor Pesce ....G 610 444-5903
Kennett Square *(G-8508)*

GLASS PRDTS, PRESSED OR BLOWN: Vases

Taylor-Backes Inc ....G 610 367-4600
Boyertown *(G-1931)*

GLASS PRDTS, PRESSED/BLOWN: Glassware, Art, Decor/Novelty

Sentinel Process Systems Inc ....F 215 675-5700
Hatboro *(G-7304)*

GLASS PRDTS, PRESSED/BLOWN: Lenses, Lantern, Flshlght, Etc

Cellmylight Inc ....G 800 575-5913
Thorndale *(G-18354)*

GLASS PRDTS, PURCHASED GLASS: Glassware, Scientific/Tech

Francis L Freas Glass Works ....E 610 828-0430
Conshohocken *(G-3549)*
TFC LLC ....G 412 979-1670
Brackenridge *(G-1941)*

GLASS PRDTS, PURCHSD GLASS: Ornamental, Cut, Engraved/Décor

Bakers Lawn Ornaments ....F 814 445-7028
Somerset *(G-17678)*
Etched In Glass ....G 724 444-0808
Gibsonia *(G-6333)*

GLASS STORE: Leaded Or Stained

Cathedral Stained GL Studios ....G 215 379-5360
Cheltenham *(G-3027)*
John Beirs Studio ....G 215 627-1410
Philadelphia *(G-13902)*
Kasmark & Marshall Inc ....G 570 287-3663
Hunlock Creek *(G-7932)*
Stained Glass Creations ....G 570 629-5070
Tannersville *(G-18237)*
Warner-Crivellaro Stained Glas ....F 610 264-1100
Whitehall *(G-19893)*

GLASS STORES

Emerald Art Glass Inc ....F 412 381-2274
Pittsburgh *(G-14970)*
Neidighs Inc ....F 814 237-3985
State College *(G-17996)*
Park & Park Norristown Inc ....G 267 346-0932
Norristown *(G-12700)*

GLASS, AUTOMOTIVE: Wholesalers

Pittsburgh Glass Works LLC ....D 412 995-6500
Pittsburgh *(G-15398)*

GLASS: Fiber

Blair Composites LLC ....E 423 638-5847
Altoona *(G-481)*
Dielectric Sales LLC ....G 724 543-2333
Kittanning *(G-8766)*
JB Services of Indiana LLC ....G 215 862-2515
New Hope *(G-12307)*
PPG Industries Inc ....A 412 434-3131
Pittsburgh *(G-15425)*

GLASS: Flat

Baut Studios Inc ....E 570 288-1431
Swoyersville *(G-18194)*
Consolidated GL Holdings Inc ....G 866 412-6977
East Butler *(G-4531)*
Emerald Art Glass Inc ....F 412 381-2274
Pittsburgh *(G-14970)*
Glass Machinery Works LLC ....G 724 473-0666
Ellwood City *(G-4933)*
Global Custom Decorating Inc ....E 814 236-2110
Curwensville *(G-3952)*
Guardian Industries LLC ....D 717 242-2571
Lewistown *(G-9933)*
Hutts Glass Co Inc ....G 610 369-1028
Gilbertsville *(G-6373)*
Mesko Glass and Mirror Co Inc ....D 570 457-1700
Avoca *(G-845)*
Pennsylvania Insulating Glass ....F 717 247-0560
Lewistown *(G-9944)*
Pittsburgh Glass Works LLC ....D 412 995-6500
Pittsburgh *(G-15398)*
PPG Industries Inc ....A 412 434-3131
Pittsburgh *(G-15425)*
PPG Industries Inc ....C 412 820-8500
Cheswick *(G-3116)*
Schott North America Inc ....G 570 457-7485
Duryea *(G-4507)*
Standard Bent Glass LLC ....D 724 287-3747
East Butler *(G-4536)*
Thermo-Twin Industries Inc ....C 412 826-1000
Oakmont *(G-12927)*
Three Rivers Optical Company ....D 412 928-2020
Pittsburgh *(G-15620)*
Vitro Flat Glass LLC ....C 412 820-8500
Cheswick *(G-3122)*

GLASS: Indl Prdts

Bent Glass Design Inc ....E 215 441-9101
Hatboro *(G-7273)*
Bethlehem Apparatus Co Inc ....F 610 838-7034
Hellertown *(G-7554)*
Dielectric Solutions LLC ....E 724 543-2333
Pittsburgh *(G-14923)*
Greenstar Allentown LLC ....E 610 262-6988
Northampton *(G-12851)*

GLASS: Insulating

Pittsburgh Aluminum Co LLC ....F 724 452-5900
Pittsburgh *(G-15386)*
Poma GL Specialty Windows Inc ....D 215 538-9424
Quakertown *(G-16230)*
R and R Glass Inc ....G 215 443-7010
Warminster *(G-18950)*
Thermolite Inc ....E 570 969-1957
Scranton *(G-17300)*

GLASS: Leaded

Studio 8 ....G 610 372-7065
Reading *(G-16527)*

GLASS: Pressed & Blown, NEC

Dally Slate Company Inc ....D 610 863-4172
Pen Argyl *(G-13213)*
Dlubak Glass Company ....F 724 226-1991
Natrona Heights *(G-11939)*
Dlubak Glass Company ....F 724 224-5887
Natrona Heights *(G-11940)*
Drummond Scientific Company ....D 610 353-0200
Broomall *(G-2287)*
Eyeland Optical Corp ....D 215 368-1600
Philadelphia *(G-13688)*
K & N Enterprises Inc ....G 724 334-0698
New Kensington *(G-12350)*
Novotny Micheal ....F 724 785-2160
Brownsville *(G-2313)*
Osram Sylvania Inc ....B 570 724-8200
Wellsboro *(G-19471)*
Pittsburgh Corning LLC ....B 724 327-6100
Pittsburgh *(G-15392)*
Punxsutawney Tile & Glass Inc ....F 814 938-4200
Punxsutawney *(G-16156)*
Three Rivers Optical Company ....D 412 928-2020
Pittsburgh *(G-15620)*
West Penn Optical Inc ....E 814 833-1194
Erie *(G-5528)*

GLASS: Safety

AGC Flat Glass North Amer Inc ....E 215 538-9424
Quakertown *(G-16167)*

GLASS: Stained

Bahrets Church Interiors ....G 717 540-1747
Harrisburg *(G-7094)*
Baut Studios Inc ....E 570 288-1431
Swoyersville *(G-18194)*
Cathedral Stained GL Studios ....G 215 379-5360
Cheltenham *(G-3027)*
John Beirs Studio ....G 215 627-1410
Philadelphia *(G-13902)*
Kasmark & Marshall Inc ....G 570 287-3663
Hunlock Creek *(G-7932)*
Pittsburgh Stained GL Studio ....F 412 921-2500
Pittsburgh *(G-15409)*
Rainbow Vision Stained GL Ctr ....G 717 657-9737
Harrisburg *(G-7204)*
Renaissance Glassworks Inc ....G 724 969-9009
Canonsburg *(G-2626)*
Stained Glass Creations ....G 570 629-5070
Tannersville *(G-18237)*
Stellar Images Imges Dcrtv GLS ....G 717 367-6500
Elizabethtown *(G-4888)*

GLASS: Tempered

Santelli Tempered Glass Inc ....E 724 684-4144
Monessen *(G-11301)*

GLASSWARE STORES

E R Kinley & Sons ....G 570 323-6740
Williamsport *(G-20008)*
Helfran Glass ....G 570 287-8105
Kingston *(G-8719)*
Rob Kei Inc ....G 717 293-8991
Lancaster *(G-9189)*
Susquehanna Glass Co ....E 717 684-2155
Columbia *(G-3451)*

GLASSWARE WHOLESALERS

Culver Industries Inc ....F 724 857-5770
Aliquippa *(G-72)*
Emerald Art Glass Inc ....F 412 381-2274
Pittsburgh *(G-14970)*

Ghp II LLC .... A 724 775-0010
Monaca (G-11290)
Northeast Laminated Glass Corp .... G 570 489-6421
Jessup (G-8334)

GLASSWARE, NOVELTY, WHOLESALE

Americana Art China Co Inc .... F 330 938-6133
Mercer (G-10959)

GLASSWARE: Cut & Engraved

Atlantic Glass Etching Inc .... G 717 244-7045
Red Lion (G-16589)
Latrobe Glass & Mirror Inc .... G 724 539-2431
Latrobe (G-9490)
Susquehanna Glass Co .... E 717 684-2155
Columbia (G-3451)

GLASSWARE: Indl

Chromaglass Inc .... F 724 325-1437
Export (G-5594)

GLASSWARE: Laboratory

Hausser Scientific Company .... G 215 675-7769
Horsham (G-7822)

GLASSWARE: Laboratory & Medical

National Scientific Company .... G 215 536-2577
Quakertown (G-16222)
Pediatrix Medical Group PA PC .... F 717 782-3127
Harrisburg (G-7192)

GLOBAL POSITIONING SYSTEMS & EQPT

Global Monitoring LLC .... G 610 604-0760
Springfield (G-17915)
Spyware .... F 215 444-0405
Warminster (G-18973)

GLOVES: Fabric

Ladyfingers Sewing Studio .... G 610 689-0068
Oley (G-12979)
Red Lion Manufacturing Inc .... C 717 767-6511
York (G-20656)
Stone Breaker LLC .... G 312 203-5632
Ardmore (G-718)

GLOVES: Leather

Red Lion Manufacturing Inc .... C 717 767-6511
York (G-20656)
Stingfree Technologies Company .... G 610 444-2806
West Chester (G-19644)

GLOVES: Work

Brookville Glove Mfg Co Inc .... E 814 849-7324
Brookville (G-2253)
G N F Produts Inc .... G 215 781-6222
Croydon (G-3917)

GLUE

Clarance J Venne Inc .... G 215 547-7110
Levittown (G-9825)
S-Bond Technologies LLC .... G 215 631-7114
Hatfield (G-7393)

GOLF CARTS: Wholesalers

Hilltown Services .... G 215 249-3694
Dublin (G-4434)

GOLF COURSES: Public

Traco Delaware Inc .... F 724 776-7000
Cranberry Township (G-3856)
Tri City Aluminum Company .... A 724 799-8917
Cranberry Township (G-3857)
White Oak Farms Inc .... G 814 257-8485
Dayton (G-4041)

GOLF EQPT

Bailey & Izett Inc .... G 610 642-1887
Ardmore (G-702)
Mini-Golf Inc .... E 570 489-8623
Jessup (G-8333)

GOLF GOODS & EQPT

Bailey & Izett Inc .... G 610 642-1887
Ardmore (G-702)
Tee-To-Green .... G 570 275-8335
Danville (G-4013)

GOURMET FOOD STORES

P & S Ravioli Co .... F 215 465-8888
Philadelphia (G-14108)

GOVERNMENT, EXECUTIVE OFFICES: City & Town Managers' Offices

Borough of Slippery Rock .... G 724 794-3823
Slippery Rock (G-17618)
Greenwood Township .... G 570 458-0212
Millville (G-11225)

GOVERNMENT, EXECUTIVE OFFICES: Mayors'

Borough of Tyrone .... G 814 684-5396
Tyrone (G-18577)
City of New Castle .... G 724 654-1627
New Castle (G-12073)

GOVERNMENT, GENERAL: Administration

City of Pittsburgh .... E 412 255-2883
Pittsburgh (G-14854)
Publishing Office US Gvernment .... G 215 364-6465
Southampton (G-17832)

GOVERNORS: Diesel Engine, Pump

James E Krack .... G 724 864-4150
Irwin (G-8176)

GRAIN & FIELD BEANS WHOLESALERS

Cargill Incorporated .... F 717 273-1133
Lebanon (G-9552)

GRANITE: Crushed & Broken

Grannas Bros Stone Asp Co Inc .... D 814 695-5021
Hollidaysburg (G-7649)
Pennsylvanin Flagstone Inc .... F 814 544-7575
Coudersport (G-3787)
Signline LLC .... G 610 973-3600
Allentown (G-391)

GRANITE: Cut & Shaped

Charles Steckman .... G 724 789-7066
Renfrew (G-16638)
Choice Granite and Marble LLC .... G 412 821-3900
Pittsburgh (G-14848)
Environmental Stoneworks LLC .... E 570 366-6460
Orwigsburg (G-13043)
Excel Glass and Granite .... E 724 523-6190
Jeannette (G-8255)
Franks Marble & Granite LLC .... G 717 244-2685
Red Lion (G-16595)
Granite Gllria Fabrication Inc .... G 215 283-0341
Fort Washington (G-6073)
Jones Stone & Marble Inc .... G 724 838-7625
Greensburg (G-6681)
Lesher Inc .... F 717 944-4431
Middletown (G-11062)

GRANITE: Dimension

API Americas Inc .... F 785 842-7674
Levittown (G-9817)
Marble Crafters Inc .... D 610 497-6000
Marcus Hook (G-10448)

GRANITE: Dimension

Hepco Quarries Inc .... G 484 844-5024
West Chester (G-19561)
Miller and Roebuck Inc .... G 724 398-3054
Vanderbilt (G-18720)

GRAPHIC ARTS & RELATED DESIGN SVCS

Adams Graphics Inc .... G 215 751-1114
Philadelphia (G-13343)
Adcomm Inc .... F 610 820-8565
Allentown (G-115)

ADM Publications Inc .... G 610 565-8895
Media (G-10914)
Allimage Graphics LLC .... G 814 728-8650
Warren (G-19009)
Alpha Screen Graphics Inc .... G 412 431-9000
Pittsburgh (G-14687)
Altus Group Inc .... F 215 977-9900
Philadelphia (G-13374)
Art Communication Systems Inc .... E 717 232-0144
Harrisburg (G-7090)
Artistagraphics Inc .... F 412 271-3252
Pittsburgh (G-14727)
Atlantic Prtg Grphic Cmmnctons .... G 610 584-2060
Schwenksville (G-17173)
Bentley Grphic Cmmncations Inc .... E 610 933-7400
Phoenixville (G-14531)
Bosha Design Inc .... G 610 622-4422
Drexel Hill (G-4361)
Corporate Arts Inc .... G 610 298-8374
New Tripoli (G-12454)
Creative Graphics Inc .... E 610 973-8300
Allentown (G-185)
Goodway Graphics Inc .... B 215 887-5700
Jenkintown (G-8288)
Graphcom Inc .... C 800 699-1664
Gettysburg (G-6295)
Greg Speece .... G 717 838-8365
Palmyra (G-13125)
Homer Reproductions Inc .... F 610 539-8400
Norristown (G-12667)
Keystone Displays Corporation .... G 717 612-0340
Lemoyne (G-9746)
Malone & Blunt Inc .... G 215 563-1368
Philadelphia (G-13988)
Marathon Printing Inc .... F 215 238-1100
Philadelphia (G-13991)
Me Ken + Jen Crative Svcs LLC .... G 215 997-2355
Chalfont (G-2883)
Okumus Enterprises Ltd .... E 215 295-3340
Fairless Hills (G-5790)
Payne Printery Inc .... D 570 675-1147
Dallas (G-3965)
Phoenix Design & Print Inc .... F 412 264-4895
Coraopolis (G-3715)
Pollock Advertising .... G 724 794-6857
Slippery Rock (G-17624)
Popultion Hlth Innovations LLC .... G 717 735-8105
Lancaster (G-9173)
Precise Graphix LLC .... E 610 965-9400
Allentown (G-357)
Purpose 1 LLC .... G 717 232-9077
Lemoyne (G-9749)
Spencer Graphics Inc .... G 610 793-2348
West Chester (G-19643)

GRATINGS: Open Steel Flooring

Fisher & Ludlow Inc .... G 814 763-5914
Saegertown (G-16914)
Fisher & Ludlow Inc .... D 724 934-5320
Wexford (G-19803)
Northern Iron Works Inc .... F 215 947-1867
Huntingdon Valley (G-8018)
Nucor Grating .... G 724 934-5320
Wexford (G-19817)

GRATINGS: Tread, Fabricated Metal

Fairwinds Manufacturing Inc .... G 724 662-5210
Jackson Center (G-8227)
Neville Grating LLC .... G 412 771-6973
Pittsburgh (G-15332)

GRAVEL MINING

Brokenstraw Gravel Co Inc .... G 814 563-7911
Pittsfield (G-15738)
Hanson Aggregates PA LLC .... D 570 992-4951
Stroudsburg (G-18122)
Hanson Aggregates PA LLC .... F 570 324-2514
Blossburg (G-1807)
Hanson Aggregates PA LLC .... F 570 726-4511
Salona (G-17049)
Hanson Aggregates PA LLC .... F 570 784-1640
Bloomsburg (G-1784)
Hanson Aggregates PA LLC .... E 570 784-2888
Bloomsburg (G-1785)
Mayer Brothers Construction Co .... F 814 452-3748
Erie (G-5383)

PRODUCT

GREASE TRAPS: Concrete

Kuss Enterprises LLC ....G....... 412 583-0206
Pittsburgh *(G-15203)*

GREASES & INEDIBLE FATS, RENDERED

Darling Ingredients Inc ....F....... 724 695-1212
Imperial *(G-8063)*

GREENHOUSES: Prefabricated Metal

Integrated Metal Products Inc...............G....... 717 824-4052
Lancaster *(G-9058)*
Poly-Growers Inc ....F....... 570 546-3216
Muncy *(G-11831)*
Sewickley Creek Greenhouse ....G....... 724 935-8500
Sewickley *(G-17408)*
Solar Innovations Inc ....C....... 570 915-1500
Pine Grove *(G-14605)*
Traco Delaware Inc ....F....... 724 776-7000
Cranberry Township *(G-3856)*

GREETING CARD SHOPS

Daffins Inc...................E....... 724 342-2892
Sharon *(G-17432)*
OSheas Candies...................F....... 814 536-4800
Johnstown *(G-8414)*
Papyrus Inc...................F....... 610 354-9480
King of Prussia *(G-8659)*

GRILLES & REGISTERS: Ornamental Metal Work

Above Rim International LLC...................G....... 215 789-7893
Philadelphia *(G-13336)*
Facchiano Ironworks Inc...................G....... 610 865-1503
Bethlehem *(G-1506)*
Samuel Yellin Metalworkers Co ....G....... 610 527-2334
Bryn Mawr *(G-2333)*

GRILLS & GRILLWORK: Woven Wire, Made From Purchased Wire

Blue Ridge Mtn Cookery Inc ....E....... 717 762-1211
Waynesboro *(G-19402)*

GRINDING SAND MINING

American Hard Chrome LLC...................G....... 412 951-9051
New Castle *(G-12057)*

GRINDING SVC: Precision, Commercial Or Indl

Amat Inc...................G....... 717 235-8003
New Freedom *(G-12200)*
Carlsons Industrial Grinding ....G....... 814 864-8640
Erie *(G-5221)*
Char-Mark Inc...................G....... 570 754-7310
Auburn *(G-815)*
Ernest Hill Machine Co Inc...................F....... 215 467-7750
Philadelphia *(G-13678)*
Flinchbaugh Company Inc ....E....... 717 266-2202
Manchester *(G-10356)*
Gesco Inc...................F....... 724 846-8700
Beaver Falls *(G-999)*
Indian Head TI Cutter Grinding...............G....... 814 796-4954
Waterford *(G-19263)*
Precision Roll Grinders Inc...................D....... 610 395-6966
Allentown *(G-358)*
Reubes Machine & Tool Co Inc...................G....... 215 368-0200
Lansdale *(G-9404)*

GRINDING SVCS: Ophthalmic Lens, Exc Prescription

A-Boss Opticians...................G....... 412 271-4424
Braddock *(G-1942)*
Allentown Optical Corp ....E....... 610 433-5269
Allentown *(G-129)*
Dalmo Optical Corporation ....G....... 412 521-2100
Pittsburgh *(G-14903)*
Dalmo Optical Corporation ....G....... 412 937-1112
Pittsburgh *(G-14904)*
Gary N Snyder ....G....... 215 735-5656
Philadelphia *(G-13764)*
Kutztown Optical Corp ....G....... 610 683-5544
Kutztown *(G-8848)*
Sosniak Opticians...................G....... 412 281-9199
Pittsburgh *(G-15561)*

GRIPS OR HANDLES: Rubber

Stingfree Technologies Company ....G....... 610 444-2806
West Chester *(G-19644)*

GRITS: Crushed & Broken

Dyer Quarry Inc ....E....... 610 582-6010
Birdsboro *(G-1693)*
Edison Quarry Inc ....G....... 215 348-4382
Doylestown *(G-4297)*
Hanson Aggregates PA LLC ....E....... 610 366-4626
Allentown *(G-243)*
Hanson Aggrgates Southeast Inc ....G....... 570 784-2888
Bloomsburg *(G-1786)*

GROCERIES WHOLESALERS, NEC

Arnold Foods Company Inc ....A....... 215 672-8010
Horsham *(G-7788)*
Bakkavor Foods Usa Inc ....F....... 570 383-9800
Jessup *(G-8327)*
Bimbo Bakeries Usa Inc ....D....... 610 865-7402
Bethlehem *(G-1466)*
Bimbo Bakeries Usa Inc ....E....... 800 635-1685
Aston *(G-752)*
Captain Chuckys Crab Cake Co I ....G....... 610 355-7525
Newtown Square *(G-12569)*
Charlies Specialties Inc...................D....... 724 346-2350
Hermitage *(G-7577)*
DAmbrosio Bakery LLC...................E....... 610 560-4700
King of Prussia *(G-8604)*
McClures Pie and Salad Inc ....F....... 717 442-4461
Gap *(G-6253)*
National Bakery Inc...................E....... 570 343-1609
Scranton *(G-17264)*
Pepsi-Cola Metro Btlg Co Inc...................F....... 215 937-6102
Philadelphia *(G-14135)*
Philadelphia Soft Pretzels ....E....... 215 324-4315
Philadelphia *(G-14155)*
Stello Foods Inc ....E....... 814 938-8764
Punxsutawney *(G-16164)*
Troyer Inc...................E....... 724 746-1162
Canonsburg *(G-2648)*

GROCERIES, GENERAL LINE WHOLESALERS

Positively Pasta...................G....... 484 945-1007
Pottstown *(G-16032)*
R & R Provision Co...................D....... 610 258-5366
Easton *(G-4746)*
S Schiff Restaurant Svc Inc ....C....... 570 343-1294
Scranton *(G-17282)*
Savello USA Incorporated ....F....... 570 822-9743
Hanover Township *(G-7005)*
Theodore Fazen ....E....... 215 672-1122
Horsham *(G-7858)*
William Aupperle ....G....... 724 583-8310
Masontown *(G-10538)*

GUARD SVCS

Alert Enterprises Ltd Lblty Co ....G....... 570 373-2821
Kulpmont *(G-8821)*

GUARDRAILS

Herwin Inc...................G....... 724 446-2000
Rillton *(G-16746)*
Reh Holdings Inc...................G....... 717 843-0021
York *(G-20657)*

GUARDS: Machine, Sheet Metal

Pinnacle Systems ....G....... 412 262-3950
Coraopolis *(G-3716)*

GUARDS: Metal Pipe

N C Stauffer & Sons Inc...................D....... 570 945-3047
Factoryville *(G-5758)*

GUIDED MISSILES & SPACE VEHICLES

Lockheed Martin Corporation...................A....... 610 382-3200
King of Prussia *(G-8641)*
Lockheed Martin Corporation...................A....... 610 531-7400
King of Prussia *(G-8643)*
Lockheed Martin Corporation...................B....... 570 876-2132
Archbald *(G-691)*

GUIDED MISSILES & SPACE VEHICLES: Research & Development

Astrobotic Technology Inc...................F....... 412 682-3282
Pittsburgh *(G-14729)*
Kyron Naval Architecture ....G....... 516 304-1769
Bensalem *(G-1217)*

GUIDED MISSILES/SPACE VEHICLE PARTS/AUX EQPT: Research/Devel

Stellar Prcsion Components Ltd ....D....... 724 523-5559
Jeannette *(G-8265)*

GUM & WOOD CHEMICALS

Coopers Creek Chemical Corp ....E....... 610 828-0375
Conshohocken *(G-3534)*

GUN PARTS MADE TO INDIVIDUAL ORDER

Tiberi Gun Shop...................G....... 724 245-6151
Fairbank *(G-5764)*

GUN SVCS

A & S Firearm Supplies Inc ....G....... 724 925-1212
Youngwood *(G-20776)*
Evolution Gun Works Inc ....F....... 215 538-1012
Quakertown *(G-16191)*

GUNNING MIXES: Nonclay

Universal Refractories Inc...................E....... 724 535-4374
Wampum *(G-18806)*

GUNSMITHS

Craig Colabaugh Gunsmith Inc ....G....... 570 992-4499
Stroudsburg *(G-18111)*
Wyss-Gallifent Corporation ....G....... 215 343-3974
Warrington *(G-19141)*

GUTTERS: Sheet Metal

Lehigh Gap Seamless Gutter LLC.........G....... 610 824-4888
Palmerton *(G-13108)*
Raytec Fabricating LLC ....E....... 717 355-5333
New Holland *(G-12278)*
Rdy Gutters Plus LLC...................G....... 610 488-5666
Bernville *(G-1304)*

GYPSUM & CALCITE MINING SVCS

RC Cement Co Inc...................G....... 610 866-4400
Bethlehem *(G-1607)*

GYPSUM BOARD

New Ngc Inc ....D....... 724 643-3440
Shippingport *(G-17567)*

GYPSUM PRDTS

Agri Marketing Inc...................G....... 717 335-0379
Denver *(G-4066)*
Certainteed Gypsum Inc...................D....... 610 893-6000
Malvern *(G-10206)*
Certainteed Gypsum Mfg Inc ....E....... 813 286-3900
Wayne *(G-19312)*
Dentsply Holding Company ....E....... 717 845-7511
York *(G-20448)*
New Ngc Inc...................D....... 570 538-2531
New Columbia *(G-12174)*
Patrick Industries Inc...................E....... 717 653-2086
Mount Joy *(G-11668)*
Saint-Gobain Corporation ....A....... 610 893-6000
Malvern *(G-10313)*
Tate Access Floors Inc ....C....... 717 244-4071
Red Lion *(G-16617)*
United States Gypsum Company ....D....... 724 857-4300
Aliquippa *(G-98)*

HAIR & HAIR BASED PRDTS

Ryan Foster Inc...................G....... 215 769-0118
Philadelphia *(G-14268)*

HAIR CARE PRDTS: Hair Coloring Preparations

Jean Alexander Cosmetics Inc ....G....... 412 331-6069
Mc Kees Rocks *(G-10617)*

Jpms Manufacturing LLC ....E 610 373-1007
   Reading *(G-16416)*

HAMPERS: Shipping, Vulcanized Fiber, From Purchased Matls

Nem-Pak Llc ....G 215 785-6430
   Croydon *(G-3921)*

HAMPERS: Solid Fiber, Made From Purchased Materials

RTS Packaging LLC ....C 724 489-4495
   Charleroi *(G-3021)*

Westrock Rkt Company ....G 717 520-7600
   Hershey *(G-7626)*

HAND TOOLS, NEC: Wholesalers

Kal-Cameron Manufacturing ....F 814 486-3394
   Emporium *(G-5065)*

United Commercial Supply LLC ....G 412 835-2690
   South Park *(G-17786)*

HANDBAGS

Marcus J Wholesalers Inc ....F 412 261-3315
   Pittsburgh *(G-15252)*

Softkog Inc ....G 717 490-1091
   Harleysville *(G-7059)*

HANDBAGS: Women's

A Tru Diva LLC ....G 888 400-1034
   Brookhaven *(G-2241)*

Coach Inc ....F 215 659-6158
   Willow Grove *(G-20112)*

Eternity Fashion Inc ....E 215 567-5571
   Philadelphia *(G-13681)*

Fleuri LLC ....G 724 539-7566
   Latrobe *(G-9476)*

HANDCUFFS & LEG IRONS

Hiatt Thompson Corporation ....G 708 496-8585
   Greenville *(G-6745)*

HANDLES: Brush Or Tool, Plastic

Ram Precision Inc ....G 215 674-0663
   Horsham *(G-7843)*

HANGERS: Garment, Home & Store, Wooden

Visconti Garment Hangers Inc ....G 570 366-7745
   Orwigsburg *(G-13054)*

HANGERS: Garment, Plastic

Berry Global Inc ....B 570 889-3131
   Ringtown *(G-16752)*

HARD RUBBER PRDTS, NEC

General Rubber Corporation ....F 412 424-0270
   Coraopolis *(G-3693)*

Interntional Track Systems Inc ....G 724 658-5970
   New Castle *(G-12105)*

Mary Hail Rubber Co Inc ....F 215 343-1955
   Warrington *(G-19124)*

HARDWARE

A G Mauro Company ....E 717 938-4671
   Lewisberry *(G-9879)*

Austin Hardware ....E 610 921-2723
   Reading *(G-16326)*

Backus Company ....E 814 887-5705
   Smethport *(G-17632)*

Baileys Steel & Supply LLC ....G 724 267-4648
   Waynesburg *(G-19433)*

Ball & Ball LLP ....E 610 363-7330
   Exton *(G-5651)*

Barco Industries Inc ....E 610 374-3117
   Reading *(G-16328)*

Bergen Pipe Supports Inc ....D 724 379-5212
   Donora *(G-4148)*

Campbell Manufacturing Inc ....D 610 367-2107
   Bechtelsville *(G-1030)*

Chick Wrkholding Solutions Inc ......D 724 772-1644
   Warrendale *(G-19070)*

Chief Fire ....G 484 356-5316
   West Chester *(G-19524)*

Cir-Cut Corporation ....G 215 324-1000
   Philadelphia *(G-13545)*

Cobra Anchors Corp ....D 610 929-5764
   Temple *(G-18326)*

Emka-Incorporated ....E 717 986-1111
   Middletown *(G-11053)*

G G Greene Enterprises Inc ....E 814 723-5700
   Warren *(G-19027)*

H & B Enterprises Inc ....G 814 345-6416
   Kylertown *(G-8865)*

HIG Capital LLC ....E 610 495-7011
   Royersford *(G-16851)*

Loranger International Corp ....D 814 723-2250
   Warren *(G-19038)*

Martin Sprocket & Gear Inc ....D 610 837-1841
   Danielsville *(G-3994)*

Michael N Sullenberger ....G 724 725-5285
   Point Marion *(G-15886)*

Millheim Small Engine Inc ....G 814 349-5007
   Spring Mills *(G-17889)*

New Home Window Shade Co Inc ....E 570 346-2047
   Clarks Green *(G-3189)*

Penn Big Bed Slate Co Inc ....D 610 767-4601
   Slatington *(G-17611)*

Penn Engineering & Mfg Corp ....F 215 766-8853
   Danboro *(G-3992)*

Powertrack International LLC ....E 412 787-4444
   Pittsburgh *(G-15423)*

Staver Hydraulics Co Inc ....G 610 837-1818
   Bath *(G-970)*

Summers Acquisition Corp ....G 724 652-4673
   New Castle *(G-12156)*

Tell Manufacturing Inc ....E 717 625-2990
   Lititz *(G-10054)*

Top Notch Distributors Inc ....F 800 233-4210
   Honesdale *(G-7729)*

United Commercial Supply LLC ....G 412 835-2690
   South Park *(G-17786)*

Upson-Walton Company ....G 570 649-5188
   Turbotville *(G-18557)*

Vanguard Identification ....E 610 719-0700
   West Chester *(G-19672)*

HARDWARE & BUILDING PRDTS: Plastic

Adams Mfg Corp ....E 800 237-8287
   Portersville *(G-15923)*

Berger Building Products Inc ....G 215 355-1200
   Feastervlle Trevose *(G-5889)*

Certainteed Corporation ....B 610 893-5000
   Malvern *(G-10204)*

Certainteed Corporation ....E 610 651-8706
   Malvern *(G-10205)*

Cpg International LLC ....G 570 558-8000
   Scranton *(G-17224)*

Edon Corporation ....E 215 672-8050
   Horsham *(G-7814)*

Fiberglass Technologies Inc ....E 215 943-4567
   Levittown *(G-9836)*

Franconia Plastics Corp ....G 215 723-8926
   Souderton *(G-17735)*

H & F Manufacturing Corp ....F 215 355-0250
   Ivyland *(G-8212)*

Johnston-Morehouse-Dickey Co .....E 412 833-7100
   Bethel Park *(G-1421)*

Johnston-Morehouse-Dickey Co .....G 814 684-0916
   Tyrone *(G-18584)*

Nds Holdings LP ....A 610 408-0500
   Newtown Square *(G-12586)*

Newtown Mfg & Bldg Sup Corp ....D 570 825-3675
   Wilkes Barre *(G-19950)*

Newtown-Slocomb Mfg Inc ....G 570 825-3675
   Hanover Township *(G-7000)*

P E H Inc ....G 610 845-9111
   Bally *(G-905)*

Pexco LLC ....E 215 736-2553
   Morrisville *(G-11577)*

Polyfab Corporation ....E 610 926-3245
   Reading *(G-16472)*

Quality Perforating Inc ....D 570 267-2092
   Carbondale *(G-2685)*

Regenex Corporation ....D 724 528-5900
   West Middlesex *(G-19728)*

Structural Fiberglass Inc ....F 814 623-0458
   Bedford *(G-1077)*

T K Plastics Inc ....F 724 443-6760
   Gibsonia *(G-6355)*

Versatex Building Products LLC ......D 724 857-1111
   Aliquippa *(G-100)*

Wentzel Fabrication Inc ....F 610 987-6909
   Oley *(G-12981)*

Westlake United Corporation ....F 570 876-0222
   Mayfield *(G-10545)*

HARDWARE & EQPT: Stage, Exc Lighting

Pittsburgh Stage Inc ....E 412 534-4500
   Sewickley *(G-17403)*

HARDWARE CLOTH: Woven Wire, Made From Purchased Wire

Ferguson Perforating Company ....E 724 657-8703
   New Castle *(G-12092)*

HARDWARE STORES

A Duchini Inc ....E 814 456-7027
   Erie *(G-5165)*

Al Lorenzi Lumber Co Inc ....D 724 222-6100
   Canonsburg *(G-2534)*

American Data Link Inc ....G 724 503-4290
   Washington *(G-19146)*

Brickhouse Services ....G 570 869-1871
   Laceyville *(G-8870)*

Cornell Bros Inc ....F 570 376-2471
   Middlebury Center *(G-11043)*

Dennis Lumber and Concrete ....E 724 329-5542
   Marklesburg *(G-10480)*

Donald Beiswenger Inc ....G 814 886-8341
   Gallitzin *(G-6245)*

Fame Manufacturing Inc ....F 814 763-5645
   Saegertown *(G-16913)*

Farmers Union Coop Assn ....F 717 597-3191
   Greencastle *(G-6612)*

J A Kohlhepp Sons Inc ....D 814 371-5200
   Du Bois *(G-4398)*

Jacob Schmidt & Son Inc ....F 215 234-4641
   Harleysville *(G-7041)*

Johnstone Supply Inc ....E 484 765-1160
   Breinigsville *(G-2019)*

Ligonier Outfitters Newsstands ....G 724 238-4900
   Ligonier *(G-9961)*

MOr Saw Service Center Inc ....G 215 333-0441
   Philadelphia *(G-14037)*

Olde Mill Cabinet Co ....G 717 866-6504
   Myerstown *(G-11895)*

Ross Feeds Inc ....F 570 289-4388
   Kingsley *(G-8707)*

S & H Hardware & Supply Co ....G 267 288-5950
   Huntingdon Valley *(G-8033)*

Shade Gap Farm Supplies ....G 814 259-3258
   Shade Gap *(G-17416)*

Shaffer Block and Con Pdts Inc ......G 814 445-4414
   Somerset *(G-17705)*

Standard Concrete Products Co ......E 717 843-8074
   York *(G-20679)*

Walter and Jackson Inc ....D 610 593-5195
   Christiana *(G-3144)*

White Horse Machine LLC ....F 717 768-8313
   Gap *(G-6257)*

HARDWARE STORES: Builders'

Davies & Sons LLC ....G 814 723-7430
   Warren *(G-19020)*

Scranton Grinder & Hardware ....E 570 344-2520
   Scranton *(G-17285)*

HARDWARE STORES: Tools

Gerg Tool & Die Inc ....E 814 834-3888
   Saint Marys *(G-16977)*

S & H Hardware & Supply Co ....F 215 745-9375
   Philadelphia *(G-14269)*

HARDWARE STORES: Tools, Hand

Tri-Boro Construction Sups Inc ....D 717 246-3095
   Dallastown *(G-3982)*

Tri-Boro Construction Sups Inc ....E 717 249-6448
   Carlisle *(G-2743)*

HARDWARE WHOLESALERS

Al Lorenzi Lumber Co Inc ....D 724 222-6100
   Canonsburg *(G-2534)*

American Tack & Hdwr Co Inc ....E 610 336-1330
   Breinigsville *(G-2008)*

Barnes Group Inc ....G 215 785-4466
   Bristol *(G-2116)*

Bashlin Industries Inc ....D 724 458-8340
   Grove City *(G-6780)*

Employee Codes: A=Over 500 employees, B=251-500
C=101-250, D=51-100, E=20-50, F=10-19, G=3-9   2019 Harris Pennsylvania
Manufacturers Directory   1421

PRODUCT

Concrete Texturing LLC ....G...... 570 489-6025
Throop *(G-18357)*

Grate Clip Company Inc ....G...... 215 230-8015
Doylestown *(G-4304)*

J & L Building Materials Inc ....C...... 610 644-6311
Malvern *(G-10257)*

Jacob Schmidt & Son Inc ....F...... 215 234-4641
Harleysville *(G-7041)*

Military and Coml Fas Corp ....D...... 717 767-6856
York *(G-20598)*

S & H Hardware & Supply Co...........G...... 267 288-5950
Huntingdon Valley *(G-8033)*

S & H Hardware & Supply Co ....F...... 215 745-9375
Philadelphia *(G-14269)*

Safety Sling Company Inc ....F...... 412 231-6684
Pittsburgh *(G-15506)*

Sealmaster Pennsylvania Inc............F...... 724 667-0444
Hillsville *(G-7636)*

Somerset Welding & Steel Inc ....E...... 814 444-7000
Somerset *(G-17709)*

Somerset Welding & Steel Inc ....E...... 814 444-7000
Somerset *(G-17711)*

United States Hardware Mfg Inc ....G...... 724 222-5110
Washington *(G-19235)*

HARDWARE, WHOLESALE: Bolts

Baden Steelbar & Bolt Corp..............F...... 724 266-3003
Sewickley *(G-17383)*

Rocwel Industries Inc ....G...... 610 459-5490
Concordville *(G-3458)*

Specialty Support Systems Inc ....F...... 215 945-1033
Levittown *(G-9865)*

HARDWARE, WHOLESALE: Builders', NEC

A G Mauro Company ....E...... 717 938-4671
Lewisberry *(G-9879)*

Hc Hoodco Inc ....F...... 814 355-4003
Bellefonte *(G-1104)*

Heritage Fence Company ....F...... 610 584-6710
Skippack *(G-17599)*

Presta Contractor Supply Inc ....E...... 814 833-0655
Erie *(G-5436)*

HARDWARE, WHOLESALE: Garden Tools, Hand

G & F Products Inc......................F...... 215 781-6222
Philadelphia *(G-13737)*

HARDWARE, WHOLESALE: Padlocks

Garlits Industries Inc ....F...... 215 736-2121
Morrisville *(G-11559)*

HARDWARE, WHOLESALE: Power Tools & Access

Bolttech Mannings Inc......................D...... 724 872-4873
North Versailles *(G-12772)*

HARDWARE, WHOLESALE: Screws

Duco Holdings LLC........................G...... 215 942-6274
Ivyland *(G-8209)*

Keystone Scrw Corp......................D...... 215 657-7100
Willow Grove *(G-20123)*

HARDWARE, WHOLESALE: Security Devices, Locks

Stanley Security Solutions Inc ....F...... 888 265-0412
Monroeville *(G-11358)*

HARDWARE: Builders'

Baldwin Hardware Corporation ....B...... 610 777-7811
Leesport *(G-9659)*

Dayton Superior Corporation ....F...... 610 366-3890
Allentown *(G-193)*

Dormakaba USA Inc......................C...... 717 336-3881
Reamstown *(G-16576)*

Rockwood Manufacturing Company.....C...... 814 926-2026
Rockwood *(G-16792)*

Stanley Black & Decker Inc...............C...... 215 710-9300
Langhorne *(G-9326)*

HARDWARE: Cabinet

Clark Deco Moldings Inc ....G...... 412 363-9602
Pittsburgh *(G-14857)*

Draper Dbs Inc ....E...... 215 257-3833
Perkasie *(G-13275)*

Eastern Millwork Ltd ....G...... 570 344-7128
Scranton *(G-17231)*

Elite Cabinetry Inc.....................G...... 717 993-5269
New Park *(G-12429)*

JP Betz Inc ....G...... 610 458-8787
Glenmoore *(G-6468)*

HARDWARE: Furniture

Jacob Holtz Company LLC ....D...... 215 423-2800
Philadelphia *(G-13316)*

Onexia Brass Inc.......................G...... 610 431-3271
West Chester *(G-19611)*

Simpson Manufacturing Inc..................G...... 724 694-2708
Derry *(G-4107)*

The Keystone Friction Hinge Co ....G...... 570 321-0693
Williamsport *(G-20082)*

HARDWARE: Furniture, Builders' & Other Household

Ingersoll-Rand Company ....E...... 410 238-0542
Shrewsbury *(G-17584)*

Roger S Wright Furniture Ltd ....G...... 215 257-5700
Blooming Glen *(G-1765)*

HARDWARE: Harness

Rfcircuits Inc ....F...... 215 364-2450
Huntingdon Valley *(G-8029)*

HARDWARE: Luggage

Globe Metal Manufacturing Co ....F...... 215 763-1024
Philadelphia *(G-13773)*

HARDWARE: Plastic

Ammeraal Beltech Modular Inc ....E...... 610 372-1800
Reading *(G-16321)*

Blanchard Mfg & Engrg ....G...... 814 454-8995
Erie *(G-5213)*

Cpk Manufacturing LLC ....G...... 814 839-4186
Alum Bank *(G-559)*

Grate Clip Company Inc ....G...... 215 230-8015
Doylestown *(G-4304)*

Schlotter Precision Pdts Inc ....E...... 215 354-3280
Warminster *(G-18963)*

HARDWARE: Rubber

Overtime Tool Inc.......................F...... 814 734-0848
Edinboro *(G-4818)*

Starrhock Silicones Inc ....F...... 610 837-4883
Bath *(G-969)*

HARNESS ASSEMBLIES: Cable & Wire

American Cable Company ....D...... 215 456-0700
Philadelphia *(G-13380)*

American Mfg & Integration LLC ....F...... 724 861-2080
North Huntingdon *(G-12767)*

American Military Technologies ....G...... 215 550-7970
Huntingdon Valley *(G-7964)*

Avex Electronics Corp ....E...... 215 245-4848
Bensalem *(G-1152)*

Currency Inc ....E...... 814 509-6157
Windber *(G-20180)*

Custom Systems Technology Inc...........G...... 215 822-2525
Colmar *(G-3415)*

Diversified Traffic Pdts Inc ....C...... 717 428-0222
Seven Valleys *(G-17377)*

EBY Group LLC ....E...... 215 537-4700
Philadelphia *(G-13657)*

Electro Soft Inc........................E...... 215 654-0701
Montgomeryville *(G-11394)*

Energy Products & Technologies...........G...... 717 485-3137
Mc Connellsburg *(G-10564)*

Excel-Pro ....G...... 610 845-9752
Barto *(G-942)*

Fargo Assemblies ....G...... 610 272-5726
Norristown *(G-12656)*

Fargo Assembly of Pa Inc ....C...... 717 866-5800
Richland *(G-16687)*

Fargo Assembly of Pa Inc ....C...... 610 272-6850
Norristown *(G-12657)*

Ford City Gun Workd ....G...... 724 994-9501
Ford City *(G-6045)*

Galaxy Wire and Cable Inc ....F...... 215 957-8714
Horsham *(G-7820)*

Genie Electronics Co Inc................E...... 717 840-6999
York *(G-20496)*

Halsit Holdings LLC....................E...... 814 724-6440
Meadville *(G-10733)*

Keystone Electronics Inc ....E...... 717 747-5900
York *(G-20553)*

Liberty Electronics ....B...... 814 676-0600
Reno *(G-16646)*

Liberty Electronics Inc ....B...... 814 432-7505
Franklin *(G-6148)*

Lynn Electronics Corp ....D...... 215 355-8200
Ivyland *(G-8216)*

Lynn Electronics Corp...................G...... 954 977-3800
Warminster *(G-18915)*

Northeimer Manufacturing ....E...... 610 926-1136
Leesport *(G-9672)*

Powell Electro Systems LLC ....F...... 610 869-8393
West Grove *(G-19704)*

Smiths Group North America Inc ....F...... 772 286-9300
Malvern *(G-10322)*

Souders Industries Inc ....E...... 717 271-4975
Waynesboro *(G-19424)*

Souders Industries Inc ....D...... 717 749-3900
Mont Alto *(G-11365)*

Wire Works Enterprises Inc ....F...... 610 485-1981
Chester *(G-3069)*

Wmi Group Inc ....F...... 215 822-2525
Colmar *(G-3425)*

HARNESS REPAIR SHOP

Smuckers Harness Shop Inc ....F...... 717 445-5956
Narvon *(G-11927)*

HARNESSES, HALTERS, SADDLERY & STRAPS

Mac Inc................................G...... 717 560-0612
East Petersburg *(G-4588)*

Smuckers Harness Shop Inc ....F...... 717 445-5956
Narvon *(G-11927)*

HATS: Paper, Novelty, Made From Purchased Paper

Jacobson Hat Co Inc ....D...... 570 342-7887
Scranton *(G-17246)*

HEADPHONES: Radio

Acousticsheep LLC ....F...... 814 380-9296
Erie *(G-5172)*

Com Pros Inc...........................G...... 717 264-2769
Chambersburg *(G-2919)*

HEALTH AIDS: Exercise Eqpt

Abcore Fitness Inc......................G...... 570 424-1006
East Stroudsburg *(G-4602)*

Bike USA Inc...........................G...... 610 868-7652
Bethlehem *(G-1465)*

Fit Engineering ....G...... 717 432-2626
Dillsburg *(G-4129)*

Gratz Industries LLC...................E...... 215 739-7373
Philadelphia *(G-13783)*

Specialty Fitness Systems LLC...........G...... 814 432-6406
Franklin *(G-6162)*

HEALTH FOOD & SUPPLEMENT STORES

General Nutrition Centers Inc...............B...... 412 288-4600
Pittsburgh *(G-15046)*

HEALTH SYSTEMS AGENCY

Three Rivers Mothers Milk Bank ....F...... 412 281-4400
Pittsburgh *(G-15619)*

HEARING AID REPAIR SVCS

Audiology & Hearing Aid Center ....G...... 570 822-6122
Wilkes Barre *(G-19906)*

Professional Hearing Aid Svc ....G...... 724 548-4801
Kittanning *(G-8788)*

HEARING AIDS

America Hears Inc......................F...... 215 785-5437
Bristol *(G-2105)*

Authorized Earmold Labs ....D...... 215 788-0330
Bristol *(G-2114)*

Beltone Corporation ....G...... 717 300-7163
Shippensburg *(G-17518)*

(G-0000) Company's Geographic Section entry number

Beltone Corporation ....G...... 717 386-5640
Carlisle (G-2691)
Beltone Corporation ....G...... 412 490-4902
Pittsburgh (G-14761)
Genesis Hearing Systems ....G...... 610 759-0459
Nazareth (G-11969)
Hearing Lab Technology LLC ....A...... 215 785-5437
Bristol (G-2152)
Michels Hearing Aid Center ....G...... 570 622-9151
Pottsville (G-16088)
Ototech Inc ....G...... 215 781-7987
Bristol (G-2177)
Professional Hearing Aid Svc ....G...... 724 548-4801
Kittanning (G-8788)
Scott Gordon ....G...... 717 652-2828
Harrisburg (G-7213)
Suburban Audiology Balance Ctr ....G...... 610 647-3710
Paoli (G-13149)
West Penn Ear Nose and Throat ....G...... 412 621-2656
Pittsburgh (G-15709)

HEAT EXCHANGERS

Armstrong Engrg Assoc Inc ....D...... 610 436-6080
Coatesville (G-3291)
Armstrong Engrg Assoc Inc ....G...... 610 436-6080
West Chester (G-19501)
Gooch Thermal Mfg Inc ....F...... 610 285-2496
Whitehall (G-19874)

HEAT EXCHANGERS: After Or Inter Coolers Or Condensers, Etc

Ax Heat Transfer Inc ....F...... 724 654-7747
New Castle (G-12060)
Doyle & Roth Mfg Co Inc ....E...... 570 282-5010
Simpson (G-17592)
Energy Conversion Technology ....G...... 412 835-0191
Pittsburgh (G-14975)
Harsco Corporation ....C...... 570 421-7500
East Stroudsburg (G-4617)
Select Industries Inc ....G...... 724 654-7747
New Castle (G-12147)

HEAT TREATING: Metal

Bluewater Thermal Services ....G...... 814 772-8474
Ridgway (G-16697)
Bodycote Thermal Proc Inc ....E...... 717 767-6757
Emigsville (G-4985)
Bvht Inc ....G...... 724 728-4328
Monaca (G-11286)
Cooperheat Mqs Proj ....G...... 412 787-8690
Pittsburgh (G-14874)
DMC Global Inc ....E...... 724 277-9710
Mount Braddock (G-11616)
Donsco Inc ....B...... 717 252-1561
Wrightsville (G-20236)
Elk County Heat Treaters Inc ....F...... 814 834-0056
Saint Marys (G-16968)
Evans Heat Treating Company ....F...... 215 938-8791
Huntingdon Valley (G-7979)
F Tinker and Sons Company ....E...... 412 781-3553
Pittsburgh (G-15000)
Fenton Heat Treating Inc ....G...... 412 466-3960
West Mifflin (G-19738)
Goc Property Holdings LLC ....G...... 814 678-4193
Rouseville (G-16836)
Irwin Automation Inc ....E...... 724 834-7160
Greensburg (G-6679)
Irwin Car & Equipment Inc ....F...... 724 864-5170
Irwin (G-8173)
Irwin Car & Equipment Inc ....E...... 724 864-8900
Irwin (G-8174)
Jarex Enterprises ....G...... 215 855-2149
Lansdale (G-9378)
L B Toney Co ....F...... 814 375-9974
Du Bois (G-4401)
Machinery & Industrial Eqp Co ....G...... 412 781-8053
Pittsburgh (G-15245)
Madison Inds Holdings LLC ....C...... 717 762-3151
Waynesboro (G-19416)
Mannings USA Inc ....D...... 412 816-1264
North Versailles (G-12779)
Mannings USA ....G...... 863 619-8099
North Versailles (G-12780)
Metal Menders LLC ....G...... 412 580-8625
Trafford (G-18458)
Mexico Heat Treating ....G...... 717 535-5034
Mifflintown (G-11130)
Modern Industries Inc ....F...... 814 885-8514
Kersey (G-8564)

Modern Industries Inc ....C...... 814 455-8061
Erie (G-5394)
Orbel Corporation ....E...... 610 829-5000
Easton (G-4736)
Piht LLC ....D...... 814 781-6262
Saint Marys (G-17007)
Pittsburgh Metal Processing Co ....F...... 412 781-8053
Pittsburgh (G-15401)
Podcon Inc ....E...... 215 233-2600
Glenside (G-6533)
Precision Finishing Inc ....E...... 215 257-6862
Quakertown (G-16232)
Pressure Technology Inc ....F...... 215 674-8844
Warminster (G-18946)
R & R Heat Treating Inc ....G...... 570 424-8750
East Stroudsburg (G-4633)
Reading Coml Heat Treating Co ....G...... 610 376-3994
Reading (G-16486)
Rex Heat Treat -Lansdale Inc ....D...... 215 855-1131
Lansdale (G-9405)
Rex Heat Treat -Lansdale Inc ....E...... 814 623-1701
Bedford (G-1074)
Richter Precision Inc ....D...... 717 560-9990
East Petersburg (G-4589)
Robert Wooler Company ....E...... 215 542-7600
Dresher (G-4357)
Ronal Tool Company Inc ....F...... 717 741-0880
York (G-20660)
Solar Atmospheres Inc ....D...... 215 721-1502
Souderton (G-17765)
Solar Atmospheres Wstn PA Inc ....D...... 742 982-0660
Hermitage (G-7595)
Specialty Alloy Proc Co Inc ....G...... 724 339-0464
New Kensington (G-12379)
Specialty Bar Products Company ....C...... 724 459-0544
Blairsville (G-1742)
Ultramet Heat Treating Inc ....G...... 814 781-7215
Saint Marys (G-17025)
Union Electric Steel Corp ....D...... 412 429-7655
Carnegie (G-2800)

HEATER RADIANTS: Clay

Psnergy LLC ....G...... 724 581-3845
Erie (G-5443)

HEATERS: Space, Exc Electric

ABB Installation Products Inc ....B...... 724 662-4400
Mercer (G-10958)

HEATERS: Swimming Pool, Electric

Drake Refrigeration Inc ....F...... 215 638-5515
Bensalem (G-1183)

HEATERS: Swimming Pool, Oil Or Gas

Yeagers Field ....G...... 610 434-1516
Allentown (G-439)

HEATING & AIR CONDITIONING EQPT & SPLYS WHOLESALERS

A M Parts Inc ....G...... 412 367-8040
Pittsburgh (G-14630)
C S Fuller Inc ....G...... 610 941-9225
Plymouth Meeting (G-15837)
Crown Boiler Co ....E...... 215 535-8900
Philadelphia (G-13586)
Industrial Controls Inc ....G...... 717 697-7555
Mechanicsburg (G-10858)
Johnstone Supply ....G...... 610 967-9900
Alburtis (G-53)
Mounts Equipment Co Inc ....G...... 724 225-0460
Washington (G-19208)
National Rfrgn & AC Pdts Inc ....E...... 215 244-1400
Bensalem (G-1228)
Vanadium Enterprises Corp ....E...... 412 206-2990
Bridgeville (G-2098)

HEATING & AIR CONDITIONING UNITS, COMBINATION

A M Parts Inc ....G...... 412 367-8040
Pittsburgh (G-14630)
Coil Company LLC ....E...... 610 408-8361
Malvern (G-10214)
E-Finity Dstrbted Gnration LLC ....G...... 610 688-6212
Wayne (G-19321)
Nevco Service Co LLC ....G...... 717 626-1479
Lititz (G-10025)

Nortek Global Hvac LLC ....B...... 814 938-1408
Punxsutawney (G-16151)
Parts To Your Door LP ....G...... 610 916-5380
Reading (G-16466)
Pinnacle Products Intl Inc ....F...... 215 302-1417
Bristol (G-2183)
Poolpak International Inc ....E...... 717 757-2648
York (G-20633)
Tek-Temp Instruments Inc ....E...... 215 788-5528
Croydon (G-3930)
Trane US Inc ....E...... 717 561-5400
Harrisburg (G-7235)
Union Chill Mat Co ....G...... 724 452-6400
Zelienople (G-20825)

HEATING EQPT & SPLYS

A W Mercer Inc ....C...... 610 367-8460
Boyertown (G-1892)
Advanced Cooling Tech Inc ....D...... 717 208-2612
Lancaster (G-8921)
Alaska Company Inc ....F...... 570 387-0260
Bloomsburg (G-1766)
Alfa Laval Inc ....D...... 717 453-7143
Lykens (G-10129)
Applied Test Systems LLC ....E...... 724 283-1212
Butler (G-2375)
Boyertown Furnace Company ....E...... 610 369-1450
Boyertown (G-1900)
Bradford White Corporation ....D...... 215 641-9400
Ambler (G-571)
Combustion Service & Eqp Co ....D...... 412 821-8900
Pittsburgh (G-14867)
Ds Machine LLC ....E...... 717 768-3853
Gordonville (G-6552)
Fives N Amercn Combustn Inc ....E...... 717 228-0714
Lebanon (G-9570)
Fives N Amercn Combustn Inc ....E...... 610 996-8005
West Chester (G-19555)
Havaco Technologies Inc ....G...... 814 878-5509
Erie (G-5311)
Industrial Systems & Controls ....G...... 412 638-4977
Pittsburgh (G-15121)
Kottcamp Sheet Metal ....E...... 717 845-7616
York (G-20558)
Kt-Grant Inc ....E...... 724 468-4700
Export (G-5614)
Lionheart Holdings LLC ....D...... 215 283-8400
Newtown (G-12519)
McCleary Heating & Cooling LLC ....F...... 717 263-3833
Chambersburg (G-2959)
New Berry Inc ....F...... 724 452-8040
Harmony (G-7074)
S P Kinney Engineers Inc ....E...... 412 276-4600
Carnegie (G-2789)
Sil-Base Company Inc ....E...... 412 751-2314
McKeesport (G-10681)
Tdc Manufacturing Inc ....F...... 570 385-0731
Schuylkill Haven (G-17167)
USA Coil & Air Inc ....E...... 610 296-9668
Malvern (G-10336)
Van Air Inc ....E...... 814 774-2631
Lake City (G-8909)
Vari Corporation ....G...... 570 385-0731
Schuylkill Haven (G-17169)

HEATING EQPT: Complete

Bti-Coopermatics Inc ....G...... 610 262-7700
Northampton (G-12847)
Goodwest Industries LLC ....E...... 215 340-3100
Douglassville (G-4177)
Johnstone Supply Inc ....E...... 484 765-1160
Breinigsville (G-2019)
K C Stoves & Fireplaces Inc ....G...... 610 966-3556
Alburtis (G-54)
Keller Enterprises Inc ....G...... 866 359-6828
Northampton (G-12853)
Reliable Products Intl LLC ....G...... 717 261-1291
Mercersburg (G-10995)
Reznor LLC ....A...... 724 662-4400
Mercer (G-10971)
US Boiler ....G...... 215 535-8900
Philadelphia (G-14434)

HEATING EQPT: Induction

Seco/Warwick Corporation ....D...... 814 332-8400
Meadville (G-10791)

HEATING PADS: Nonelectric

Aavid Thermacore Inc ....C 717 569-6551
Lancaster (G-8919)

HEATING SYSTEMS: Radiant, Indl Process

Clean Energy Htg Systems LLC ....F 888 519-2347
Honey Brook (G-7742)

HEATING UNITS & DEVICES: Indl, Electric

Chromalox Inc ....D 412 967-3800
Pittsburgh (G-14850)
CMI America Inc ....F 814 897-7000
Erie (G-5228)
Creative Energy Distributors ....G 717 354-6090
New Holland (G-12240)
Dayco Inc ....G 610 326-4500
Pottstown (G-15981)
Fce LLC ....G 215 947-7333
Huntingdon Valley (G-7980)
Gyrotron Technology Inc ....G 215 244-4740
Bensalem (G-1207)
Lucifer Furnaces Inc ....F 215 343-0411
Warrington (G-19123)
Quartz Tubing Inc ....F 215 638-0909
Bensalem (G-1246)
Trent Inc ....F 215 482-5000
Philadelphia (G-14406)
World Marketing of America ....E 814 643-6500
Mill Creek (G-11169)

HEATING UNITS: Gas, Infrared

Spinworks International Corp ....E 814 725-1188
North East (G-12762)

HELICOPTERS

Agustwstland Philadelphia Corp ....D 215 281-1400
Philadelphia (G-13358)
Boeing Company ....G 610 591-2121
Ridley Park (G-16735)
Boeing Company ....B 610 591-2121
Ridley Park (G-16736)

HELMETS: Athletic

Stingfree Technologies Company ....G 610 444-2806
West Chester (G-19644)
Unequal Technologies Company ....G 610 444-5900
Glen Mills (G-6447)

HELMETS: Steel

Arai Helmet Americas Inc ....G 610 366-7220
Allentown (G-142)
Blind and Vision Rehab ....F 412 325-7504
Homestead (G-7683)
Witmer Public Safety Group Inc ....D 800 852-6088
Coatesville (G-3331)

HIGH ENERGY PARTICLE PHYSICS EQPT

Abe Alarm Service ....G 484 664-7304
Allentown (G-113)
Lighthouse Enrgy Solutions LLC ....G 610 269-0113
Morgantown (G-11525)
Navitek Group Inc ....G 814 474-2312
Fairview (G-5834)
Precision Cstm Components LLC ....B 717 848-1126
York (G-20638)

HOBBY & CRAFT SPLY STORES

Roberts Manufacturing LLC ....F 855 763-7450
Allentown (G-376)

HOBBY GOODS, WHOLESALE

Bowser Manufacturing Co ....F 570 368-5045
Montoursville (G-11434)

HOBBY SUPPLIES, WHOLESALE

H & H Wholesale LLC ....G 724 733-8338
Pittsburgh (G-15069)

HOBBY, TOY & GAME STORES: Arts & Crafts & Splys

Bg Jewelry ....G 610 691-0687
Bethlehem (G-1464)

Casner Fabrics ....G 215 946-3334
Levittown (G-9823)
Old Bedford Village Inc ....G 814 623-1156
Bedford (G-1068)

HOBBY, TOY & GAME STORES: Ceramics Splys

Aud-A-Bud Ceramics ....G 717 898-7537
Landisville (G-9258)

HOBBY, TOY & GAME STORES: Dolls & Access

Ladie & Friends Inc ....G 215 453-8200
Sellersville (G-17353)

HOBBY, TOY & GAME STORES: Toys & Games

Brickhouse Services ....G 570 869-1871
Laceyville (G-8870)
Compleat Strategist Inc ....G 610 265-8562
King of Prussia (G-8596)

HOISTING SLINGS

Liftex Corporation ....D 800 478-4651
Ivyland (G-8215)

HOISTS

American Crane & Eqp Corp ....F 484 945-0420
Douglassville (G-4167)
American Crane & Eqp Corp ....F 610 521-9000
Essington (G-5541)
Funks Drilling Incorporated ....F 717 423-6688
Newville (G-12601)
Lug-All Co Inc ....E 610 286-9884
Morgantown (G-11526)

HOLDING COMPANIES: Investment, Exc Banks

Ahf Holding Inc ....G 800 233-3823
Lancaster (G-8922)
B Braun of America Inc ....G 610 691-5400
Bethlehem (G-1455)
Consolidated GL Holdings Inc ....G 866 412-6977
East Butler (G-4531)
Ecotech Inc ....D 610 954-8480
Allentown (G-202)
Femco Holdings LLC ....E 906 576-0418
Punxsutawney (G-16138)
Fort Washington Pharma LLC ....G 800 279-7434
Fort Washington (G-6069)
GNC Corporation ....G 412 288-4600
Pittsburgh (G-15054)
GNC Parent LLC ....G 412 288-4600
Pittsburgh (G-15055)
Goc Property Holdings LLC ....F 814 678-4127
Oil City (G-12946)
Ibis Tek Holdings Inc ....G 724 431-3000
Butler (G-2409)
Ictv Holdings Inc ....F 484 598-2300
Wayne (G-19337)
Janatics USA Inc ....G 610 443-2400
Whitehall (G-19879)
M&Q Holdings LLC ....F 570 385-4991
Schuylkill Haven (G-17161)
Mds Associated Companies Inc ....D 724 548-2501
Kittanning (G-8780)
Neh Inc ....B 412 299-7200
Coraopolis (G-3706)
Original Philly Holdings Inc ....C 215 423-3333
Southampton (G-17829)
Siemens Gamesa Renewable ....G 215 710-3100
Feasterville Trevose (G-5930)
Soleo Health Holdings Inc ....G 888 244-2340
Sharon Hill (G-17460)
Susquehanna Capitl Acquisition ....A 800 942-7538
Lancaster (G-9210)
Synthes Inc ....G 610 647-9700
West Chester (G-19650)
Virtus Phrmctcals Holdings LLC ....C 267 938-4850
Langhorne (G-9332)

HOLDING COMPANIES: Personal, Exc Banks

Cpg International I Inc ....G 570 346-8797
Scranton (G-17222)

Integrated Cnstr Systems Inc ....F 724 528-9310
West Middlesex (G-19726)
Kapothanasis Group Inc ....G 207 939-5680
Harrisburg (G-7160)
O & P Benchmark Holdings Inc ....G 610 644-7824
Exton (G-5716)
Piramal Healthcare Inc ....G 610 974-9760
Bethlehem (G-1600)

HOLDING COMPANIES: Public Utility

Greenbank Group Inc ....G 724 229-1180
Washington (G-19180)

HOLLOWARE, SILVER

Rothrocks Silversmiths Inc ....G 570 253-1990
Honesdale (G-7722)

HOME CENTER STORES

Al Lorenzi Lumber Co Inc ....D 724 222-6100
Canonsburg (G-2534)
Allensville Planing Mill Inc ....F 717 543-4954
Huntingdon (G-7938)
Oakes & McClelland Co ....F 724 588-6400
Greenville (G-6761)
Whipple Bros Inc ....G 570 836-6262
Mountain Top (G-11780)

HOME ENTERTAINMENT EQPT: Electronic, NEC

Better Living Center LLC ....G 724 266-3750
Ambridge (G-611)
Electronic Concepts Inc ....G 717 235-9450
New Freedom (G-12207)
Global Home Automation LLC ....G 484 686-7374
Fort Washington (G-6072)
Luzerne Trading Company Inc ....F 866 954-4440
Wilkes Barre (G-19938)

HOME FURNISHINGS WHOLESALERS

Bachman Drapery Studio Inc ....G 215 257-8810
Tylersport (G-18574)
Beechdale Frames ....G 717 288-2723
Ronks (G-16803)
Golden Brothers Inc ....C 570 457-0867
Old Forge (G-12965)
Kartri Sales Company Inc ....E 570 785-3365
Forest City (G-6054)
L & L K Incorporated ....E 215 732-2614
Philadelphia (G-13948)
Marcus J Wholesalers Inc ....F 412 261-3315
Pittsburgh (G-15252)

HOME HEALTH CARE SVCS

Horizon House Inc ....G 610 532-7423
Darby (G-4019)
Keyscripts LLC ....G 866 446-2848
Mechanicsburg (G-10863)
Medihill Inc ....G 215 464-7016
Bensalem (G-1224)
Pentec Health Inc ....E 610 494-8700
Upper Chichester (G-18671)
Pentec Health Inc ....C 610 494-8700
Glen Mills (G-6440)

HOMEFURNISHING STORE: Bedding, Sheet, Blanket, Spread/Pillow

American Textile Company Inc ....C 412 948-1020
Duquesne (G-4494)
Heritage Gallery of Lace & Int ....G 717 359-4121
Littlestown (G-10067)

HOMEFURNISHING STORES: Beddings & Linens

Bed Bath & Beyond Inc ....G 717 397-0206
Lancaster (G-8950)

HOMEFURNISHING STORES: Closet organizers & shelving units

Closet-Tier ....G 412 421-7838
Pittsburgh (G-14862)

HOMEFURNISHING STORES: Lighting Fixtures

American Period Lighting Inc ....G....... 717 392-5649
Lancaster (G-8931)
Francis J Nowalk ....G....... 412 687-4017
Pittsburgh (G-15030)
Glasslight Inc ....G....... 610 469-9066
Saint Peters (G-17034)

HOMEFURNISHING STORES: Pictures, Wall

Southwind Studios Ltd ....G....... 610 664-4110
Lower Merion (G-10109)

HOMEFURNISHING STORES: Pottery

Brian Giniewski LLC ....G....... 610 858-2821
Philadelphia (G-13479)
Crow Valley Pottery ....G....... 360 376-4260
Jim Thorpe (G-8339)
Grandville Hollow Pottery Inc ....G....... 814 355-7928
Julian (G-8455)
Mill Hall Clay Products Inc ....E....... 570 726-6752
Mill Hall (G-11179)
Penn-MO Fire Brick Co Inc ....G....... 717 234-4504
Harrisburg (G-7193)
Robin Morris ....G....... 814 395-9555
Confluence (G-3469)

HOMEFURNISHING STORES: Wicker, Rattan, Or Reed

K T & Co ....G....... 610 520-0221
Bryn Mawr (G-2328)

HOMEFURNISHING STORES: Window Furnishings

Nicholas Meyokovich ....G....... 724 439-0955
Uniontown (G-18638)
Shutter Tech Inc ....G....... 610 696-9322
West Chester (G-19639)

HOMEFURNISHING STORES: Window Shades, NEC

HA Harper Sons Inc ....G....... 610 485-4776
Upper Chichester (G-18663)

HOMEFURNISHINGS & SPLYS, WHOLESALE: Decorative

Edward Hecht Importers Inc ....G....... 215 925-5520
Philadelphia (G-13661)
Primitives By Kathy Inc ....D....... 717 394-4220
Lancaster (G-9175)

HOMEFURNISHINGS, WHOLESALE: Blinds, Venetian

Penn Blind Manufacturing Inc ....F....... 610 770-1700
Allentown (G-347)

HOMEFURNISHINGS, WHOLESALE: Blinds, Vertical

Westerbrook Custom Made Drap ....G....... 717 737-8185
Camp Hill (G-2525)

HOMEFURNISHINGS, WHOLESALE: Carpets

Prosource of Lancaster ....G....... 717 299-5680
Lancaster (G-9176)
R & R Briggs Inc ....G....... 215 357-3413
Southampton (G-17833)
REA Jobber Inc ....G....... 814 226-9552
Clarion (G-3186)
William F Kempf & Son Inc ....G....... 610 532-2000
Folcroft (G-6020)

HOMEFURNISHINGS, WHOLESALE: Draperies

Brookline Fabrics Co Inc ....E....... 412 665-4925
Pittsburgh (G-14794)
Fabtex Inc ....D....... 910 739-0019
Danville (G-4001)
Fabtex Inc ....C....... 570 275-7500
Danville (G-4000)

Lewrene Interiors ....G....... 717 263-8300
Chambersburg (G-2953)
Skotz Manufacturing Inc ....G....... 610 286-0710
Elverson (G-4966)

HOMEFURNISHINGS, WHOLESALE: Kitchenware

Fox Run Holdings Inc ....G....... 215 675-7700
Warminster (G-18882)
Fox Run Usa LLC ....D....... 215 675-7700
Ivyland (G-8211)
M & M Creative Laminates Inc ....G....... 412 781-4700
Aspinwall (G-746)
Rwb Special Services Corp ....F....... 215 766-4800
Pipersville (G-14619)
Top Notch Products Inc ....G....... 724 475-2341
Fredonia (G-6187)
Wrapmaster Usa LLC ....G....... 215 782-2285
Elkins Park (G-4915)

HOMEFURNISHINGS, WHOLESALE: Pillowcases

Eric and Christopher LLC ....F....... 215 257-2400
Perkasie (G-13276)

HOMEFURNISHINGS, WHOLESALE: Towels

Monarch Global Brands Inc ....D....... 215 482-6100
Philadelphia (G-14033)

HOMEFURNISHINGS, WHOLESALE: Window Covering Parts & Access

TMW Associates Inc ....G....... 215 624-3940
Philadelphia (G-14393)

HOMEFURNISHINGS, WHOLESALE: Window Shades

Nortek Global Hvac LLC ....B....... 814 938-1408
Punxsutawney (G-16151)
Thermal Industries Inc ....G....... 814 944-4534
Altoona (G-551)

HOMES, MODULAR: Wooden

All American Homes Colo LLC ....E....... 970 587-0544
Mechanicsburg (G-10818)
Apex Homes Inc ....C....... 570 837-2333
Middleburg (G-11021)
Apex Homes of Pa LLC ....C....... 570 837-2333
Middleburg (G-11022)
Appalachian Woodcrafts LLC ....C....... 570 726-7149
Mill Hall (G-11170)
Buchanan Trail Industries Inc ....C....... 717 597-7166
Greencastle (G-6601)
Cappelli Enterprises Inc ....C....... 845 856-9033
Mechanicsburg (G-10826)
Cozy Cabins LLC ....C....... 717 354-3278
New Holland (G-12239)
Gardner S Construction ....G....... 610 395-6614
Macungie (G-10146)
Icon Lgacy Cstm Mdlar Hmes LLC ....E....... 570 374-3280
Selinsgrove (G-17326)
Lake Cy Manufactured Hsing Inc ....E....... 814 774-2033
Lake City (G-8903)
Milton Home Systems Inc ....D....... 800 533-4402
Milton (G-11249)
Muncy Homes ....B....... 570 546-2261
Muncy (G-11827)
Pleasant Valley Homes Inc ....C....... 570 345-2011
Pine Grove (G-14603)
Ridgeview Mdlar Hsing Group LP ....D....... 570 837-2333
Middleburg (G-11038)
Signature Building Systems Inc ....E....... 570 774-1000
Moosic (G-11515)
Signature Building Systems Inc ....D....... 570 774-1000
Moosic (G-11516)
Tcc Pennwest LLC ....C....... 724 867-0047
Emlenton (G-5015)

HOMES: Log Cabins

Crockett Log Homes of PA Inc ....G....... 717 697-6198
Mechanicsburg (G-10834)
Greg Kline ....G....... 610 367-4060
Boyertown (G-1914)
K S M Enterprises Inc ....G....... 717 463-2383
Mifflintown (G-11126)

Lancaster Log Cabins LLC ....G....... 717 445-5522
Denver (G-4081)
Morey General Contracting ....G....... 570 759-2021
Berwick (G-1336)
Mountainside Log Homes ....G....... 570 745-2388
Williamsport (G-20044)
Mr Luck Inc ....G....... 570 766-8734
Greentown (G-6734)
Peak Industries Inc ....E....... 717 306-4490
Lebanon (G-9617)
Peak Ventures Inc ....E....... 717 306-4490
Lebanon (G-9618)
Service Construction Co Inc ....F....... 610 377-2111
Lehighton (G-9727)

HONEYCOMB CORE & BOARD: Made From Purchased Materials

Signode Industrial Group LLC ....E....... 570 450-0123
Hazle Township (G-7479)

HOODS: Range, Sheet Metal

Superior Metalworks Inc ....F....... 717 245-2446
Carlisle (G-2740)

HOPPERS: End Dump

Steel Systems Installation Inc ....E....... 717 786-1264
Quarryville (G-16280)

HORMONE PREPARATIONS

Auxilium Pharmaceuticals LLC ....C....... 484 321-5900
Malvern (G-10189)
Physician Transformations LLC ....G....... 484 420-4407
Newtown Square (G-12590)

HORSE & PET ACCESSORIES: Textile

Kabar Tack and Feed ....G....... 717 416-0069
New Oxford (G-12414)
Total Equestrian Inc ....G....... 215 721-1247
Souderton (G-17768)

HORSE ACCESS: Harnesses & Riding Crops, Etc, Exc Leather

Beilers Manufacturing & Supply ....G....... 717 768-0174
Ronks (G-16804)
Beilers Manufacturing & Supply ....F....... 717 656-2179
Leola (G-9772)

HORSE DRAWN VEHICLE REPAIR SVCS

Vicksburg Buggy Shop ....G....... 570 966-3658
Mifflinburg (G-11104)
Weavertown Coach Shop ....G....... 717 768-3299
Bird In Hand (G-1685)

HORSESHOES

Soundhorse Technologies LLC ....G....... 610 347-0453
Unionville (G-18649)

HOSE: Air Line Or Air Brake, Rubber Or Rubberized Fabric

Polymeric Extruded Products ....G....... 215 943-1288
Levittown (G-9858)
R/W Connection Inc ....E....... 717 898-5257
Landisville (G-9266)
R/W Connection Inc ....G....... 717 767-3660
Emigsville (G-4998)

HOSE: Fire, Rubber

National Foam Inc ....D....... 610 363-1400
West Chester (G-19606)

HOSE: Flexible Metal

Clark Industrial Supply Inc ....F....... 610 705-3333
Pottstown (G-15970)
Omega Flex Inc ....C....... 610 524-7272
Exton (G-5719)
Paragon America LLC ....F....... 412 408-3447
Sharpsburg (G-17467)
Rhoads Industries Inc ....D....... 267 728-6300
Philadelphia (G-14244)

PRODUCT

HOSE: Garden, Plastic

Tekni-Plex Inc ....E 484 690-1520
Wayne (G-19381)
Trident Tpi Holdings Inc ....A 484 690-1520
Wayne (G-19384)
Zena Associates Llc ....E 215 730-9000
Folcroft (G-6021)

HOSE: Plastic

Powell Electro Systems LLC ....F 610 869-8393
West Grove (G-19704)
Quadrant Holding Inc ....C 724 468-7062
Delmont (G-4054)

HOSE: Pneumatic, Rubber Or Rubberized Fabric, NEC

Parker-Hannifin Corporation ....A 814 866-4100
Erie (G-5414)

HOSE: Rubber

Mason East Inc ....G 631 254-2240
Feasterville Trevose (G-5917)

HOSES & BELTING: Rubber & Plastic

All-American Holdings LLc ....C 814 438-7616
Union City (G-18605)
All-American Hose LLC ....E 814 438-7616
Erie (G-5180)
All-American Hose LLC ....E 814 838-3381
Erie (G-5181)
Allied Rubber & Rigging Sup Co ......G 724 535-7380
Wampum (G-18796)
American Metal & Rubber Inc ....F 215 225-3700
Philadelphia (G-13386)
Corry Rubber Corporation ....E 814 664-2313
Corry (G-3757)
Fenner Inc ....C 717 665-2421
Manheim (G-10380)
Iron Hose Company LLC ....G 877 277-9035
Corry (G-3765)
Jnb Industrial Supply Inc ....G 412 455-5170
Blawnox (G-1764)
Newage Industries Inc ....C 215 526-2151
Southampton (G-17827)
Paragon America LLC ....F 412 408-3447
Sharpsburg (G-17467)
Powertrack International LLC ....E 412 787-4444
Pittsburgh (G-15423)
Raymond Dunn ....G 412 734-2135
Pittsburgh (G-15469)

HOSPITALS: Medical & Surgical

Excela Health Holding Co Inc ....G 724 832-4450
Greensburg (G-6665)
Surgical Institute Reading LP ....G 610 378-8800
Reading (G-16530)

HOT TUBS

Plastic Development Company PA ......E 800 451-1420
Williamsport (G-20058)
Strong Industries Inc ....C 570 275-2700
Northumberland (G-12876)
Wexco Incorporated ....G 717 764-8585
York (G-20710)

HOUSEHOLD APPLIANCE STORES

Bevilacqua Sheet Metal Inc ....G 570 558-0397
Scranton (G-17211)
Donatucci Kitchens & Appls ....E 215 545-5755
Philadelphia (G-13639)
Lancaster Propane Gas Inc ....F 717 898-0800
Lancaster (G-9104)
Slate Road Supply LLC ....G 717 445-5222
Ephrata (G-5141)

HOUSEHOLD APPLIANCE STORES: Air Cond Rm Units, Self-Contnd

Johnstone Supply ....G 610 967-9900
Alburtis (G-53)
US Boiler ....G 215 535-8900
Philadelphia (G-14434)

HOUSEHOLD APPLIANCE STORES: Electric Household, Major

Ehst Custom Kitchens Inc ....F 610 367-2074
Boyertown (G-1910)
Johnstone Supply Inc ....E 484 765-1160
Breinigsville (G-2019)

HOUSEHOLD ARTICLES, EXC FURNITURE: Cut Stone

Elegant Marble Products Inc ....F 717 939-0373
Middletown (G-11052)

HOUSEHOLD ARTICLES: Metal

Celf Services LLC ....G 717 643-0039
Greencastle (G-6602)
Custom Built Products Inc ....F 215 946-9555
Bristol (G-2130)
Edwards Co ....G 215 343-2133
Warrington (G-19116)
Fox Run Holdings Inc ....G 215 675-7700
Warminster (G-18882)
James Derr ....G 724 475-2094
Greenville (G-6750)
Veyko Design Inc ....G 215 928-1349
Philadelphia (G-14444)

HOUSEHOLD FURNISHINGS, NEC

Armstrong/Kover Kwick Inc ....E 412 771-2200
Mc Kees Rocks (G-10603)
Brookline Fabrics Co Inc ....E 412 665-4925
Pittsburgh (G-14794)
Bryan Mfg Co ....E 724 245-8200
Eighty Four (G-4835)
Carpenter Co ....C 814 944-8612
Altoona (G-486)
Chestnut Ridge Foam Inc ....C 724 537-9000
Latrobe (G-9464)
Dame Design LLC ....G 610 458-3290
Phoenixville (G-14541)
Fabtex Inc ....D 910 739-0019
Danville (G-4001)
Fabtex Inc ....C 570 275-7500
Danville (G-4000)
Fibematics Inc ....E 215 226-2672
Philadelphia (G-13698)
Harmonic Rays Mfg Group Inc ....G 267 761-9558
Philadelphia (G-13803)
Home Grown Inc ....G 610 642-3601
Haverford (G-7411)
Monarch Global Brands Inc ....D 215 482-6100
Philadelphia (G-14033)
National Furniture Assoc Inc ....G 814 342-2007
Philipsburg (G-14520)
Sonoco Products Company ....E 610 323-9221
Pottstown (G-16049)
Trillion Source Inc ....F 631 949-2304
Emmaus (G-5045)
William H Kies Jr ....G 610 252-6261
Easton (G-4776)

HOUSEKEEPING & MAID SVCS

Merry Maid Inc ....E 800 360-3836
Bangor (G-921)

HOUSEWARES, ELECTRIC: Blenders

Harsco Corporation ....C 570 421-7500
East Stroudsburg (G-4617)

HOUSEWARES, ELECTRIC: Cooking Appliances

Edgecraft Corporation ....C 610 268-0500
Avondale (G-851)

HOUSEWARES, ELECTRIC: Fans, Exhaust & Ventilating

Hvl LLC ....E 412 494-9600
Pittsburgh (G-15107)

HOUSEWARES, ELECTRIC: Heaters, Space

Mosebach Manufacturing Company ...D 412 220-0200
Pittsburgh (G-15303)

HOUSEWARES, ELECTRIC: Heating Units, Electric Appliances

Heatron Inc ....E 814 868-8554
Erie (G-5314)
Schmitt Walter H and Assoc ....E 724 872-5007
West Newton (G-19751)

HOUSEWARES, ELECTRIC: Lighters, Cigar

Rebel Indian Smoke Shop ....G 610 499-1711
Brookhaven (G-2247)

HOUSEWARES, ELECTRIC: Massage Machines, Exc Beauty/Barber

Steel Fitness Premier LLC ....E 610 973-1500
Allentown (G-403)

HOUSEWARES: Dishes, Earthenware

Bryan China Company ....D 724 658-3098
New Castle (G-12068)
China Lenox Incorporated ....A 267 525-7800
Bristol (G-2125)

HOUSEWARES: Dishes, Plastic

Drinkworks Corporation ....E 800 825-5575
Warren (G-19021)
Halsey Inc ....F 570 278-3610
Montrose (G-11466)
Jan-Stix LLC ....G 267 918-9561
Huntingdon Valley (G-8002)
Mason Jars Company ....F 877 490-5565
Erie (G-5381)
Molded Fiber Glass Companies ....C 814 683-4500
Linesville (G-9984)
Quadrant Holding Inc ....C 570 558-6000
Scranton (G-17276)
Urban Outfitters Wholesale Inc ....G 215 454-5500
Philadelphia (G-14431)

HUMIDIFIERS & DEHUMIDIFIERS

Carel Usa Inc ....G 410 497-5128
Manheim (G-10374)

HYDRAULIC EQPT REPAIR SVC

ALe Hydraulic McHy Co LLC ....F 215 547-3351
Levittown (G-9815)
American Hydraulic Mfg ....G 610 264-8542
Allentown (G-135)
Crile Consolidated Inds Inc ....F 724 228-0880
Washington (G-19159)
Delri Industrial Supplies Inc ....G 610 833-2070
Crum Lynne (G-3936)
Dispersion Tech Systems LLC ....G 610 832-2040
Conshohocken (G-3539)
East End Welding ....G 570 726-7925
Mill Hall (G-11176)
Eastern Machine & Convyrs Inc ......F 724 379-4701
Donora (G-4154)
George Taylor Forklift Repair ....G 412 221-7206
Morgan (G-11517)
Hydra Service Inc ....G 724 852-2423
Waynesburg (G-19446)
Mac Machine LLC ....F 610 583-3055
Brookhaven (G-2246)
National Hydraulic Systems LLC ......G 724 628-4010
Connellsville (G-3505)
National Hydraulics Inc ....D 724 547-9222
Mount Pleasant (G-11708)
National Hydraulics Inc ....G 724 887-3850
Scottdale (G-17197)
Penndel Hydraulic Sls & Svc Co ......G 215 757-2000
Langhorne (G-9317)
Royal Hydraulic Svc & Mfg Inc ....E 724 945-6800
Cokeburg (G-3364)
Specialty Machine & Hydraulic ....G 814 589-7381
Pleasantville (G-15804)
Voith Hydro Inc ....B 717 792-7000
York (G-20699)
York Precision ....F 717 764-8855
York (G-20749)

HYDRAULIC FLUIDS: Synthetic Based

Gh Holdings Inc ....G 610 666-4000
Valley Forge (G-18707)
Hii Holding Corporation ....G 610 666-0219
Norristown (G-12666)

Houghton International Inc ....C 888 459-9844
Norristown (G-12668)
Hydac Technology Corp.....................G 610 266-3143
Bethlehem (G-1535)
Naughton Energy Corporation ....F 570 646-0422
Pocono Pines (G-15882)
Quaker Chemical Corporation ....A 610 832-4000
Conshohocken (G-3595)

HYDROPONIC EQPT

Pocono Hydrponic Solutions LLC........G 570 730-4544
Bartonsville (G-948)

Hard Rubber & Molded Rubber Prdts

Ecore International Inc ....C 717 295-3400
Lancaster (G-9007)
Lord Corporation ....D 814 398-4641
Cambridge Springs (G-2481)
Mason East Inc ....G 631 254-2240
Feasterville Trevose (G-5917)
Recycling Tech Intl LLC ....E 717 633-9008
York (G-20655)

ICE

Arctic Glacier Texas Inc ....G 610 494-8200
Upper Chichester (G-18656)
Carl R Harry ....G 610 865-7104
Bethlehem (G-1480)
Conjelko Dairy & Ice Service ....G 814 467-9997
Windber (G-20179)
Gaia Enterprises Inc ....F 800 783-7841
Huntingdon Valley (G-7988)
Hanover Ice Co Inc.........................G 717 637-9137
Spring Grove (G-17878)
Ice Butler...................................G 610 644-3243
Malvern (G-10249)
Kelly Dry Ice ....G 412 766-1555
Pittsburgh (G-15167)
Lansdowne Ice & Coal Co Inc ....E 610 353-6500
Broomall (G-2293)
Mastro Ice Inc ....G 412 681-4423
Pittsburgh (G-15261)
Michalski Refrigeration Inc ....G 724 352-1666
Butler (G-2423)
Refrigeration Care Inc ....F 724 746-1525
Canonsburg (G-2625)
Sugar Magnolia Inc ....G 610 649-9462
Ardmore (G-719)
Vision Warehousing and Dist ....G 717 762-5912
Waynesboro (G-19429)
Wheeland Inc ....F 570 323-3237
Williamsport (G-20091)
White Oak Ice Company LLC ....G 717 354-5322
New Holland (G-12294)
York Ice Co Inc ....E 717 848-2639
York (G-20739)
Zero Ice Corporation......................G 717 264-7912
Chambersburg (G-3002)

ICE BOXES: Indl

Follett LLC ....B 610 252-7301
Easton (G-4684)
Follett LLC ....G 800 523-9361
Bethlehem (G-1515)

ICE CREAM & ICES WHOLESALERS

Bill Macks Ice Cream ....E 717 292-1931
Dover (G-4188)
JAS Wholesale & Supply Co Inc..........E 610 967-0663
Emmaus (G-5031)
Joshi Bharkatkumar ....F 610 861-7733
Bethlehem (G-1547)
Mazzolis Ice Cream ....G 717 533-2252
Hershey (G-7620)
Sugar Magnolia Inc ....G 610 649-9462
Ardmore (G-719)

IDENTIFICATION PLATES

Ivy Graphics Inc ....F 215 396-9446
Warminster (G-18900)

IDENTIFICATION TAGS, EXC PAPER

Armark Authentication Tech LLC ....G 717 767-4651
York (G-20386)

IGNEOUS ROCK: Crushed & Broken

H&K Group Inc ....G 570 347-1800
Dunmore (G-4474)
Mammoth Materials ....G 570 385-4232
Schuylkill Haven (G-17162)
McClure Enterprises Inc ....G 570 562-1180
Old Forge (G-12970)

IGNITION APPARATUS & DISTRIBUTORS

Alcolock PA Inc ....G 800 452-1759
Mechanicsburg (G-10817)
Ecobee Advanced Tech LLC ....G 609 474-0010
Warminster (G-18869)

IGNITION SYSTEMS: Internal Combustion Engine

Remote Remotes............................G 215 420-7934
Horsham (G-7846)

INCENSE

African Cultural Art Forum LLC............G 215 476-0680
Philadelphia (G-13353)

INCINERATORS

Concept Products Corporation ....G 610 722-0830
Mertztown (G-11002)
Nass Inc ....G 717 846-3685
York (G-20609)
Pennram Diversified Mfg Corp ....E 570 327-2802
Williamsport (G-20055)

INDL & PERSONAL SVC PAPER WHOLESALERS

Argus Printing ....G 610 687-0411
Wayne (G-19301)
D-K Trading Corporation Inc..............G 570 586-9662
Clarks Summit (G-3191)
Frank Ferris Industries Inc.................G 724 352-9477
Cabot (G-2457)
Gold Medal Products Co ....G 412 787-1030
Pittsburgh (G-15056)
Griff and Associates LP ....D 215 428-1075
Levittown (G-9842)
Industrial Packaging Supplies.............G 724 459-8299
Blairsville (G-1725)
Supplyone Holdings Company Inc........D 484 582-5005
Newtown Square (G-12593)
Tinicum Research Company ....G 610 294-9390
Erwinna (G-5540)
Veritiv Operating Company ....E 724 776-3122
Cranberry Township (G-3863)

INDL & PERSONAL SVC PAPER, WHOL: Bags, Paper/Disp Plastic

Penn State Paper & Box Co Inc ....E 610 433-7468
Allentown (G-349)

INDL & PERSONAL SVC PAPER, WHOL: Boxes, Corrugtd/Solid Fiber

Beacon Container Corporation.............E 570 433-3800
Montoursville (G-11433)
Georgia-Pacific LLC.........................C 814 368-8700
Bradford (G-1969)

INDL & PERSONAL SVC PAPER, WHOL: Boxes, Paperbrd/Plastic

Midvale Paper Box Company.................F 570 824-3577
Plains (G-15786)

INDL & PERSONAL SVC PAPER, WHOL: Cups, Disp, Plastic/Paper

Smartshake.................................F 724 396-7947
Pittsburgh (G-15549)

INDL & PERSONAL SVC PAPER, WHOLESALE: Boxes & Containers

Albright Paper & Box Corp ....G 484 524-8424
Boyertown (G-1895)
Interstate Cont Reading LLC ....C 800 822-2002
Reading (G-16409)

INDL & PERSONAL SVC PAPER, WHOLESALE: Disposable

WA Dehart Inc...............................D 570 568-1551
New Columbia (G-12179)

INDL & PERSONAL SVC PAPER, WHOLESALE: Shipping Splys

Ekopak Inc ....F 412 264-9800
Coraopolis (G-3686)

INDL CONTRACTORS: Exhibit Construction

Promotion Centre Inc ....E 717 843-1582
York (G-20645)
Universal Services Assoc Inc ....E 610 461-0300
Folcroft (G-6018)

INDL EQPT CLEANING SVCS

Colmetal Incorporated......................G 215 225-1060
Philadelphia (G-13560)

INDL EQPT SVCS

Acf Group LLC ....E 724 364-7027
Allison (G-444)
Calgon Carbon Corporation...............C 412 787-6700
Moon Township (G-11482)
Calgon Carbon Corporation...............B 412 787-6700
Pittsburgh (G-14803)
D W Machine Co Inc........................G 215 672-3340
Hatboro (G-7277)
D-Electric Inc ....F 215 529-6020
Quakertown (G-16182)
Electronic Tech Systems Inc ....D 724 295-6000
Natrona Heights (G-11942)
Erie Weld Products Inc....................F 814 899-6320
Erie (G-5278)
Goshorn Industries LLC....................G 717 369-3654
Chambersburg (G-2936)
Industrial Controls & Eqp Inc ....E 724 746-3705
Lawrence (G-9537)
Loveshaw Corporation......................C 570 937-4921
South Canaan (G-17769)
Machine Specialties ....G 717 264-0061
Chambersburg (G-2955)
Mechanical Service Company ....F 570 654-2445
Pittston (G-15766)
Mervine Corp ....F 215 257-0431
Perkasie (G-13284)
Millcraft Industries Inc.....................F 724 229-8800
Washington (G-19205)
Millcraft SMS Services LLC ....C 724 222-5000
Washington (G-19206)
Pro Cel Inc ....G 215 322-9883
Warminster (G-18948)
Psb Industries Inc ....D 814 453-3651
Erie (G-5442)
S K P Company ....G 570 344-0561
Scranton (G-17281)
Signode Industrial Group LLC ....C 570 937-4921
South Canaan (G-17770)
SPX Flow Us LLC ....G 814 476-5800
Mc Kean (G-10594)
Sumitomo Shi Crygnics Amer Inc ....D 610 791-6700
Allentown (G-404)
Utilities & Industries Inc ....D 814 653-8269
Reynoldsville (G-16667)
Wise Machine Co Inc ....E 724 287-2705
Butler (G-2450)

INDL GASES WHOLESALERS

Air Products and Chemicals Inc............D 724 226-4434
Creighton (G-3879)
Wilson Pdts Compressed Gas Co ....E 610 253-9608
Easton (G-4777)

INDL MACHINERY & EQPT WHOLESALERS

A Stucki Company ....E 724 746-4240
Canonsburg (G-2531)
Air Dynmics Indus Systems Corp ....F 717 854-4050
York (G-20370)
Apex Hydraulic & Machine Inc.............F 814 342-1010
Philipsburg (G-14508)
Avure Autoclave Systems Inc............G 814 833-4331
Erie (G-5200)
Bionix Safety Technologies ....G 610 408-0555
Wayne (G-19307)

PRODUCT

Burlington Instr Sls Assoc ....G...... 215 322-8750
  Trevose *(G-18488)*
C and M Sales Co ....F...... 814 437-3095
  Franklin *(G-6118)*
CK Construction & Indus Inc ....G...... 570 286-4128
  Pitman *(G-14622)*
Dbi Inc ....D...... 814 653-7625
  Fairmount City *(G-5808)*
Digital Press Inc ....G...... 610 758-9680
  Bethlehem *(G-1497)*
Envirodyne Systems Inc ....E...... 717 763-0500
  Camp Hill *(G-2496)*
Filterfab Manufacturing Corp ....G...... 724 643-4000
  Industry *(G-8136)*
Fives N Amercn Combustn Inc ....G...... 412 655-0101
  Pittsburgh *(G-15020)*
General Air Products Inc ....E...... 610 524-8950
  Exton *(G-5685)*
Habsco Inc ....G...... 724 337-9498
  New Kensington *(G-12345)*
Hannon Company ....G...... 724 266-2712
  Ambridge *(G-618)*
Harold Beck & Sons Inc ....C...... 215 968-4600
  Newtown *(G-12506)*
Icreate Automation Inc ....F...... 610 443-1758
  Allentown *(G-251)*
ID Technology LLC ....E...... 717 848-3875
  York *(G-20533)*
Illinois Tool Works Inc ....D...... 215 822-2171
  Hatfield *(G-7352)*
Indeck Keystone Energy LLC ....E...... 814 452-6421
  Erie *(G-5322)*
Industrial Controls Inc ....G...... 717 697-7555
  Mechanicsburg *(G-10858)*
Inserta Products Inc ....E...... 215 643-0192
  Blue Bell *(G-1835)*
J & K Industrial Sales ....G...... 724 458-7670
  Grove City *(G-6791)*
Jaeco Fluid Solutions Inc ....G...... 610 407-7207
  Malvern *(G-10258)*
John A Manning Jr ....G...... 215 233-0976
  Glenside *(G-6524)*
John Eppler Machine Works ....E...... 215 624-3400
  Orwigsburg *(G-13046)*
Kerry Company Inc ....F...... 412 486-3388
  Allison Park *(G-455)*
Kinsley Incorporated ....G...... 215 348-7723
  Doylestown *(G-4311)*
Kras Corporation ....E...... 610 566-0271
  Media *(G-10935)*
Maxwell Truck & Equipment LLC ....G...... 814 359-2672
  Pleasant Gap *(G-15794)*
Megator Corporation ....G...... 412 963-9200
  Pittsburgh *(G-15275)*
Ncri Inc ....E...... 724 654-7711
  New Castle *(G-12125)*
Norstone Incorporated ....G...... 484 684-6986
  Bridgeport *(G-2041)*
Northeast Indus Batteries Inc ....E...... 215 788-8000
  Bristol *(G-2172)*
Paco Winders Mfg LLC ....E...... 215 673-6265
  Philadelphia *(G-14113)*
Park Corporation ....G...... 412 472-0500
  Coraopolis *(G-3711)*
Parker-Hannifin Corporation ....C...... 724 861-8200
  Irwin *(G-8188)*
Rtj Inc A Close Corporation ....F...... 215 943-9220
  Levittown *(G-9862)*
S & G Water Conditioning Inc ....G...... 215 672-2030
  Warminster *(G-18957)*
S H Sharpless & Son Inc ....G...... 570 454-6685
  Hazleton *(G-7524)*
Sigma Controls Inc ....F...... 215 257-3412
  Perkasie *(G-13293)*
Specialty Measurements Inc ....F...... 908 534-1500
  Bethlehem *(G-1623)*
Starlite Group Inc ....G...... 814 333-1377
  Meadville *(G-10793)*
Tallman Supply Company ....G...... 717 647-2123
  Tower City *(G-18442)*
Torcup Inc ....F...... 610 250-5800
  Easton *(G-4763)*
Ultra Pure Products Inc ....E...... 717 589-7001
  Mifflintown *(G-11139)*
Valley Broom Inc ....G...... 717 349-2614
  East Waterford *(G-4642)*
Van Tongeren America LLC ....G...... 717 450-3835
  Lebanon *(G-9637)*
Vanzel Inc ....G...... 215 223-1000
  Philadelphia *(G-14438)*

Vortx United Inc ....G...... 570 742-7859
  Milton *(G-11250)*
Washington Rotating Control ....F...... 724 228-8889
  Washington *(G-19243)*
Winterthur Wendt Usa Inc ....C...... 610 495-2850
  Royersford *(G-16869)*

INDL MACHINERY REPAIR & MAINTENANCE

Allegheny Mfg & Elec Svc Inc ....E...... 814 288-1597
  Johnstown *(G-8350)*
Boyer Machine ....G...... 570 473-1212
  Northumberland *(G-12865)*
Eastern Industrial Pdts Inc ....E...... 610 459-1212
  Aston *(G-760)*
G-S Hydraulics Inc ....F...... 814 938-2862
  Punxsutawney *(G-16141)*
Gampe Machine & Tool Co Inc ....E...... 814 696-6206
  Hollidaysburg *(G-7648)*
General Electric Company ....D...... 215 289-0400
  Philadelphia *(G-13749)*
Gill Rock Drill Company Inc ....E...... 717 272-3861
  Lebanon *(G-9573)*
Hanel Storage Systems ....E...... 412 788-0509
  Pittsburgh *(G-15079)*
Hawk Industrial Services LLC ....F...... 717 658-4332
  Chambersburg *(G-2939)*
J W Hoist and Crane LLC ....G...... 814 696-0350
  Duncansville *(G-4453)*
Kercher Industries Inc ....E...... 717 273-2111
  Lebanon *(G-9592)*
Kinetics Hydro Inc ....G...... 717 532-6016
  Shippensburg *(G-17535)*
Konecranes Inc ....E...... 610 321-2900
  Pottstown *(G-16008)*
Machine Rebuilders ....G...... 724 694-3190
  New Derry *(G-12191)*
Marando Industries Inc ....G...... 610 621-2536
  Reading *(G-16437)*
Martin Truck Bodies Inc ....E...... 814 793-3353
  Martinsburg *(G-10526)*
Myers Vacuum Repair Svcs Inc ....F...... 724 545-8331
  Kittanning *(G-8785)*
Nearhoof Machine Inc ....G...... 814 339-6621
  Osceola Mills *(G-13056)*
Penn Equipment Corporation ....E...... 570 622-9933
  Port Carbon *(G-15899)*
Pruftechnik Inc ....E...... 844 242-6296
  Philadelphia *(G-14211)*
Pruftechnik Service Inc ....E...... 856 401-3095
  Philadelphia *(G-14212)*
Raceresq Inc ....G...... 724 891-3473
  Beaver Falls *(G-1010)*
Robinson Fans Inc ....B...... 863 646-5270
  Zelienople *(G-20817)*
Ruch Carbide Burs Inc ....E...... 215 657-3660
  Willow Grove *(G-20139)*
S P Industries Inc ....D...... 215 672-7800
  Warminster *(G-18959)*
Scheerer Bearing Corporation ....E...... 215 443-5252
  Willow Grove *(G-20140)*
Scheerer Bearing Corporation ....E...... 215 443-5252
  Horsham *(G-7848)*
Swartfager Welding Inc ....D...... 814 797-0394
  Knox *(G-8811)*
Technical Process & Engrg Inc ....E...... 570 386-4777
  Lehighton *(G-9730)*
Wel-Mac Inc ....G...... 717 637-6921
  Hanover *(G-6974)*
Winn-Marion Barber LLC ....G...... 412 319-7392
  Bridgeville *(G-2099)*

INDL PATTERNS: Foundry Cores

Kore Mart Ltd ....E...... 610 562-5900
  Hamburg *(G-6843)*
Swope & Bartholomew Inc ....F...... 610 264-2672
  Whitehall *(G-19890)*

INDL PATTERNS: Foundry Patternmaking

Armstrong Patterns & Mfg ....G...... 724 845-1452
  Ford City *(G-6042)*
Latrobe Pattern Co ....E...... 724 539-9753
  Latrobe *(G-9492)*
Standard Pattern Works Inc ....G...... 814 455-5145
  Erie *(G-5490)*

INDL PROCESS INSTRUMENTS: Analyzers

Sensitron Associates Inc ....G...... 610 779-0939
  Reading *(G-16511)*

INDL PROCESS INSTRUMENTS: *Chromatographs*

Marg Inc ....F...... 724 703-3020
  Oakdale *(G-12906)*

INDL PROCESS INSTRUMENTS: *Control*

Cameron Technologies Us Inc ....F...... 724 273-9300
  Coraopolis *(G-3673)*
Industrial Control & Elec Inc ....G...... 610 859-9272
  Upper Chichester *(G-18665)*
Mine Safety Appliances Co LLC ....B...... 724 776-8600
  Cranberry Township *(G-3836)*
MSA Safety Incorporated ....B...... 724 776-8600
  Cranberry Township *(G-3839)*
MSA Safety Sales LLC ....G...... 724 776-8600
  Cranberry Township *(G-3841)*
Serv-I-Quip Inc ....E...... 610 873-7010
  Downingtown *(G-4256)*
Wortman Controls Inc ....G...... 814 834-1299
  Saint Marys *(G-17031)*
Wyman-Gordon Pennsylvania LLC ....F...... 570 474-3059
  Wilkes Barre *(G-19978)*

INDL PROCESS INSTRUMENTS: *Controllers, Process Variables*

Eaton Aerospace LLC ....D...... 610 522-4000
  Glenolden *(G-6473)*
Eaton Corporation ....C...... 610 522-4059
  Glenolden *(G-6474)*
Kontrol Automation Inc ....G...... 610 284-4106
  Secane *(G-17317)*
National Airoil Burner Co Inc ....G...... 215 743-5300
  Philadelphia *(G-14052)*
Responselogix Inc ....E...... 215 256-1700
  Harleysville *(G-7055)*
Wise Electronic Systems Inc ....G...... 717 244-0111
  Windsor *(G-20197)*
Wistex II LLC ....G...... 215 328-9100
  Warminster *(G-19002)*

INDL PROCESS INSTRUMENTS: *Digital Display, Process Variables*

Backe Digital Brand Marketing ....F...... 610 947-6922
  Radnor *(G-16289)*
Direct Digital Master Inc ....G...... 215 634-2235
  Philadelphia *(G-13634)*
United Partners Ltd ....G...... 570 283-0995
  Taylor *(G-18265)*

INDL PROCESS INSTRUMENTS: *Fluidic Devices, Circuit & Systems*

Stel Life Inc ....G...... 610 724-3688
  Philadelphia *(G-14344)*

INDL PROCESS INSTRUMENTS: *Indl Flow & Measuring*

Cameron Technologies Us Inc ....D...... 724 273-9300
  Coraopolis *(G-3672)*
Cannon Instrument Company ....D...... 814 353-8000
  State College *(G-17948)*
Global Trade Links LLC ....E...... 888 777-1577
  Chester Springs *(G-3079)*
Lin Kay Associates Inc ....G...... 610 469-6833
  Pottstown *(G-15954)*
Veeder-Root Company ....E...... 814 695-4476
  Duncansville *(G-4465)*

INDL PROCESS INSTRUMENTS: *Level & Bulk Measuring*

Rieker Electronics Inc ....E...... 610 500-2000
  Aston *(G-790)*

INDL PROCESS INSTRUMENTS: *Manometers*

Rosemount Inc ....F...... 412 788-1160
  Pittsburgh *(G-15497)*
Rosemount Inc ....F...... 724 746-3400
  Lawrence *(G-9540)*

INDL PROCESS INSTRUMENTS: *Moisture Meters*

GE Infrastructure Sensing Inc ....B...... 814 834-5506
  Saint Marys *(G-16976)*

Meeco Inc ....E 215 343-6600
Warrington (G-19125)

INDL PROCESS INSTRUMENTS: Temperature

Burlington Instr Sls Assoc ....G 215 322-8750
Trevose (G-18488)

Julabo Usa Inc ....E 610 231-0250
Allentown (G-272)

Kidde Fire Protection Inc ....E 610 363-1400
West Chester (G-19581)

Scritchfield Controls LLC ....G 717 887-5992
Wrightsville (G-20243)

Sensing Devices Inc ....E 717 295-4735
Lancaster (G-9193)

Siemens Industry Inc ....D 215 646-7400
Spring House (G-17883)

INDL PROCESS INSTRUMENTS: Thermistors

Amphenol Thermometrics Inc ....C 814 834-9140
Saint Marys (G-16948)

Keystone Powdered Metal Co ....C 814 834-9140
Saint Marys (G-16985)

INDL PROCESS INSTRUMENTS: Water Quality Monitoring/Cntrl Sys

ADS LLC ....G 717 554-7552
Lemoyne (G-9740)

Analytical Technology Inc ....F 610 917-0991
Collegeville (G-3368)

Bethlehem Waste Water ....E 610 865-7169
Bethlehem (G-1463)

Campbell Manufacturing Inc ....D 610 367-2107
Bechtelsville (G-1030)

Evoqua Water Technologies LLC ....E 215 638-7700
Bensalem (G-1192)

GE Infrastructure Sensing ....F 617 926-1749
Feasterville Trevose (G-5912)

Hydro Instruments Inc ....E 215 799-0980
Telford (G-18295)

Jeffery Faust ....G 610 759-1951
Nazareth (G-11973)

Siemens Industry Inc ....E 215 712-0280
Chalfont (G-2887)

Suburban Water Technology Inc ....F 610 696-1495
West Chester (G-19648)

Suez Wts Systems Usa Inc ....B 781 359-7000
Trevose (G-18505)

Xylem Wtr Sltons Zlienople LLC ....F 724 452-6300
Zelienople (G-20829)

INDL SPLYS WHOLESALERS

A C Grinding & Supply Co Inc ....G 215 946-3760
Levittown (G-9811)

All America Threaded Pdts Inc ....D 317 921-3000
Lancaster (G-8928)

Allegheny Fabg & Sups Inc ....G 412 828-3320
Pittsburgh (G-14678)

Allegheny Tool & Supply Inc ....F 814 437-7062
Franklin (G-6114)

Alvord-Polk Inc ....F 717 692-2128
Millersburg (G-11189)

Amat Inc ....G 717 235-8003
New Freedom (G-12200)

Apparel Machinery & Supply Co ....E 215 634-2626
Philadelphia (G-13400)

C H Reed Inc ....E 717 632-4261
Hanover (G-6865)

Cir-Cut Corporation ....G 215 324-1000
Philadelphia (G-13545)

Clark Industrial Supply Inc ....F 610 705-3333
Pottstown (G-15970)

Cornwell Quality Tools Company ....G 814 756-5484
Albion (G-41)

Delri Industrial Supplies Inc ....G 610 833-2070
Crum Lynne (G-3936)

E-Tech Industrial ....G 570 297-1300
Troy (G-18522)

Electronic Tech Systems Inc ....D 724 295-6000
Natrona Heights (G-11942)

Eneflux Armtek Magnetics Inc ....G 215 443-5303
Warminster (G-18872)

Fca LLC ....E 309 792-3444
Corry (G-3760)

Glassautomatic Inc ....E 724 547-7500
Mount Pleasant (G-11700)

Hunter Sales Corporation ....F 412 341-2444
Bethel Park (G-1416)

Hy-Tech Machine Inc ....D 724 776-6800
Cranberry Township (G-3823)

Intersource Inc ....F 724 940-2220
Mars (G-10501)

Irwin Car & Equipment Inc ....F 724 864-5170
Irwin (G-8173)

Irwin Car & Equipment Inc ....E 724 864-8900
Irwin (G-8174)

Louis Berkman Company ....E 740 283-3722
Pittsburgh (G-15238)

Lycoming Screen Printing Co ....G 570 326-3301
Williamsport (G-20038)

Mason East Inc ....G 631 254-2240
Feasterville Trevose (G-5917)

Met-Pro Technologies LLC ....E 215 822-1963
Telford (G-18303)

Mssi Refractory LLC ....E 412 771-5533
Mc Kees Rocks (G-10621)

Ohio Valley Indus Svcs Inc ....G 412 269-0020
Moon Township (G-11498)

P M Supply Co Inc ....E 814 472-4430
Ebensburg (G-4791)

PBM Inc ....D 724 863-0550
Irwin (G-8189)

Penn Fasteners Inc ....E 215 674-2772
Hatboro (G-7297)

Penn-MO Fire Brick Co Inc ....G 717 234-4504
Harrisburg (G-7193)

Pennsylvania Machine Works Inc ....C 610 497-3300
Upper Chichester (G-18669)

Pinnacle Systems ....G 412 262-3950
Coraopolis (G-3716)

Purtech Inc ....F 570 424-1669
East Stroudsburg (G-4632)

R & G Gorr Enterprises Inc ....G 610 356-8500
Phoenixville (G-14573)

R/W Connection Inc ....G 717 767-3660
Emigsville (G-4998)

Ralph A Hiller Company ....E 724 325-1200
Export (G-5623)

Sanders Saws & Blades Inc ....E 610 273-3733
Honey Brook (G-7761)

Sentinel Process Systems Inc ....F 215 675-5700
Hatboro (G-7304)

Specialty Support Systems Inc ....F 215 945-1033
Levittown (G-9865)

Starlite Industries Inc ....E 610 527-1300
Bryn Mawr (G-2334)

Swisher Concrete Products Inc ....G 814 765-9502
Clearfield (G-3231)

Ted Venesky Co Inc ....G 724 224-7992
Tarentum (G-18248)

Teflex Inc ....F 570 945-9185
Factoryville (G-5762)

Upson-Walton Company ....G 570 649-5188
Turbotville (G-18557)

US Municipal Supply Inc ....E 610 292-9450
Huntingdon (G-7958)

Valves Inc ....F 724 378-0600
Aliquippa (G-99)

Wesco Distribution Inc ....E 724 772-5000
Warrendale (G-19101)

West Hills Specialty Supply Co ....G 412 279-6766
Carnegie (G-2806)

INDL SPLYS, WHOL: Fasteners, Incl Nuts, Bolts, Screws, Etc

B G M Fastener Co Inc ....E 570 253-5046
Honesdale (G-7701)

B&G Manufacturing Co Inc ....C 215 822-1925
Hatfield (G-7319)

Emka-Incorporated ....E 717 986-1111
Middletown (G-11053)

Ideal Building Fasteners Inc ....F 412 299-6199
Coraopolis (G-3699)

Military and Coml Fas Corp ....D 717 767-6856
York (G-20598)

Molecular Finishing Systems ....G 724 695-0554
Imperial (G-8073)

S & S Fasteners Inc ....G 724 251-9288
Ambridge (G-632)

INDL SPLYS, WHOLESALE: Abrasives

Ameri-Surce Specialty Pdts Inc ....E 412 831-9400
Bethel Park (G-1402)

Keystone Abrasives Co ....F 610 939-1060
Reading (G-16419)

Simms Abrasives ....G 610 327-1877
Pottstown (G-16046)

Sponge-Jet Inc ....G 570 278-4563
Montrose (G-11478)

INDL SPLYS, WHOLESALE: Adhesives, Tape & Plasters

Addev Walco Inc ....E 412 486-4400
Glenshaw (G-6479)

Xode Inc ....E 610 683-8777
Kutztown (G-8864)

INDL SPLYS, WHOLESALE: Bearings

A-1 Babbitt Co Inc ....F 724 379-6588
Donora (G-4144)

Applied Indus Tech — PA LLC ....G 724 696-3099
Mount Pleasant (G-11686)

Bearing Service Company PA ....D 412 963-7710
Pittsburgh (G-14758)

J S H Industries LLC ....G 717 267-3566
Chambersburg (G-2945)

INDL SPLYS, WHOLESALE: Brushes, Indl

R S Quality Products Inc ....G 610 266-1916
Allentown (G-367)

INDL SPLYS, WHOLESALE: Electric Tools

Global Trade Links LLC ....E 888 777-1577
Chester Springs (G-3079)

INDL SPLYS, WHOLESALE: Fasteners & Fastening Eqpt

Division Seven Inc ....G 724 449-8400
Gibsonia (G-6332)

INDL SPLYS, WHOLESALE: Filters, Indl

Filpro Corporation ....F 215 699-4510
North Wales (G-12801)

Filterfab Manufacturing Corp ....G 724 643-4000
Industry (G-8136)

Full-On Filters ....G 610 970-4701
Pottstown (G-15989)

Knight Corporation ....E 610 853-2161
Havertown (G-7423)

Ohio Valley Indus Svcs Inc ....F 412 335-5237
Coraopolis (G-3708)

Precision Filtration Pdts Inc ....E 215 679-6645
Pennsburg (G-13252)

Separation Technologies Inc ....G 724 325-4546
Export (G-5626)

INDL SPLYS, WHOLESALE: Gaskets

Dooley Gasket and Seal Inc ....E 610 328-2720
Broomall (G-2286)

Mary Hail Rubber Co Inc ....F 215 343-1955
Warrington (G-19124)

INDL SPLYS, WHOLESALE: Gaskets & Seals

Scott H Payne ....G 215 723-0510
Telford (G-18313)

INDL SPLYS, WHOLESALE: Hydraulic & Pneumatic Pistons/Valves

Fluidtechnik USA ....G 610 321-2407
Glenmoore (G-6466)

INDL SPLYS, WHOLESALE: Knives, Indl

Deffibaugh Butcher Supply ....G 814 944-1297
Altoona (G-498)

Dull Knife Terminator Inc ....G 717 512-8596
Mechanicsburg (G-10839)

INDL SPLYS, WHOLESALE: Mill Splys

L M Stevenson Company Inc ....G 724 458-7510
Hermitage (G-7590)

Schermerhorn Bros Co ....G 610 284-7402
Lansdowne (G-9443)

INDL SPLYS, WHOLESALE: Pipeline Wrappings, Anti-Corrosive

Allegheny-York Co ....E 717 266-6617
Manchester (G-10354)

INDL SPLYS, WHOLESALE: Power Transmission, Eqpt & Apparatus

Haverstick Bros Inc ....F 717 392-5722
Lancaster (G-9040)

INDL SPLYS, WHOLESALE: Rope, Exc Wire

Nelson Wire Rope Corporation..............F 215 721-9449
Hatfield (G-7373)
Safety Sling Company Inc ....F 412 231-6684
Pittsburgh (G-15506)

INDL SPLYS, WHOLESALE: Rubber Goods, Mechanical

Irp Group Inc ....D 412 276-6400
Pittsburgh (G-15138)
Lambert-Jones Rubber Co ....G 412 781-8100
Pittsburgh (G-15217)
Lord Corporation ....B 814 868-3180
Erie (G-5372)
Manufactured Rubber Pdts Co ....F 215 533-3600
Philadelphia (G-13989)
Summers Acquisition Corp ....G 724 652-4673
New Castle (G-12156)

INDL SPLYS, WHOLESALE: Seals

Hoffman-Kane Distributors Inc.............F 412 653-6886
Pittsburgh (G-15097)

INDL SPLYS, WHOLESALE: Springs

Union Spring & Mfg Corp ....E 814 967-2545
Townville (G-18449)

INDL SPLYS, WHOLESALE: Tanks, Pressurized

Guardian CSC Corporation ....F 717 848-2540
Hellam (G-7551)
Lancaster Propane Gas Inc ....F 717 898-0800
Lancaster (G-9104)

INDL SPLYS, WHOLESALE: Textile Printers' Splys

Sportin My Stuff ....G 724 457-7005
Crescent (G-3889)

INDL SPLYS, WHOLESALE: Tools

Dinosaw Inc ....F 570 374-5531
Selinsgrove (G-17323)

INDL SPLYS, WHOLESALE: Tools, NEC

Duane Grant ....G 412 856-1357
Monroeville (G-11333)
Form Tool Technology Inc ....E 717 792-3626
York (G-20484)
Imperial Newbould Inc.....................F 814 337-8155
Meadville (G-10737)
John Stortz and Son Inc...................G 215 627-3855
Philadelphia (G-13906)
Keystone Precision Inc ....G 814 336-2187
Meadville (G-10743)
Victaulic Company ....A 610 559-3300
Easton (G-4770)

INDL SPLYS, WHOLESALE: Valves & Fittings

A/C Service and Repair Inc ....E 717 792-3492
York (G-20361)
Accu-Fire Fabrication Inc.................E 800 641-0005
Morrisville (G-11550)
American Cone Valve Inc ....F 717 792-3492
York (G-20372)
Clipper Pipe & Service Inc ....G 610 872-9067
Eddystone (G-4799)
Dansway Incorporated ....G 570 672-1550
Elysburg (G-4973)
Kobold Instruments Inc....................E 412 490-4806
Pittsburgh (G-15180)

Tyco Fire Products LP ....C 215 362-0700
Lansdale (G-9421)

INDL TOOL GRINDING SVCS

American Hard Chrome LLC..................G 412 951-9051
New Castle (G-12057)
Meadville Tool Grinding Inc ....F 814 382-1201
Conneaut Lake (G-3477)

INDL TRUCK REPAIR SVCS

Brumbaugh Body Co Inc.....................G 814 696-9552
Duncansville (G-4450)
Ken-Co Company Inc........................E 724 887-7070
Scottdale (G-17194)

INDUSTRIAL & COMMERCIAL EQPT INSPECTION SVCS

Faro Laser Division LLC...................G 610 444-2300
Kennett Square (G-8510)
Irwin Car & Equipment Inc ....F 724 864-5170
Irwin (G-8173)
Irwin Car & Equipment Inc ....E 724 864-8900
Irwin (G-8174)

INFANTS' WEAR STORES

A & H Sportswear Co Inc...................C 610 759-9550
Stockertown (G-18063)

INFORMATION RETRIEVAL SERVICES

Morningstar Credit Ratings LLC............E 800 299-1665
Horsham (G-7833)
PC Network Inc............................D 267 236-0015
Philadelphia (G-14128)

INGOT, EXTRUSION: Extrusion ingot, aluminum: rolling mills

New Werner Holding Co Inc ....G 724 588-2000
Greenville (G-6758)
Werner Co ....C 724 588-2000
Greenville (G-6775)
Werner Holding Co Inc ....A 888 523-3371
Greenville (G-6776)

INGOT: Aluminum

Prime Metals Acquisition LLC ....D 724 479-4155
Homer City (G-7680)

INK OR WRITING FLUIDS

Bms Inc ....G 609 883-5155
Yardley (G-20297)
Custom Mil & Consulting Inc ....E 610 926-0984
Fleetwood (G-5969)
Flint Group US LLC ....G 717 285-5454
Lancaster (G-9020)
Inksewn USA ....F 570 534-5199
Philadelphia (G-13856)
Premier Ink Systems Inc ....G 570 459-2300
West Hazleton (G-19715)
Raven Industries Inc......................D 724 539-8230
Latrobe (G-9516)
Watson Industries Inc.....................E 724 275-1000
Harwick (G-7257)

INK: Duplicating

Sanyo Chemical & Resins LLC...............G 412 384-5700
West Elizabeth (G-19697)

INK: Gravure

American Inks & Coatings Corp.............D 610 933-5848
Phoenixville (G-14528)

INK: Letterpress Or Offset

Dynamic Printing Inc ....G 215 793-9453
Ambler (G-577)

INK: Lithographic

Ink RE Phill ....G 717 840-0835
York (G-20537)

INK: Printing

Bell-Mark Sales Co Inc ....E 717 292-5641
Dover (G-4186)

Bell-Mark Technologies Corp ....E 717 292-5641
Dover (G-4187)
Cabrun Ink Products Corp ....E 215 533-2990
Philadelphia (G-13493)
Constaflow Pump Company LLC ....G 610 515-1753
Easton (G-4662)
Flint Group US LLC ....G 717 392-1953
Lancaster (G-9021)
Ink Division LLC..........................G 412 381-1104
Braddock (G-1945)
Keystone Printing Ink Co ....F 215 228-8100
Philadelphia (G-13932)
Liquid X Printed Metals Inc ....G 412 426-3521
Pittsburgh (G-15236)
N H Laboratories Inc......................F 717 545-3221
Harrisburg (G-7183)
Penn Color Inc............................E 215 997-2221
Hatfield (G-7380)
Print Happy LLC ....G 717 699-4465
York (G-20639)
Printed Ink LLC ....G 215 355-1683
Huntingdon Valley (G-8027)
Quality Dispersions Inc ....F 814 781-7927
Kersey (G-8567)
Raven Industries Inc......................D 724 539-8230
Latrobe (G-9516)
Siegwerk USA Inc ....G 570 708-0267
Drums (G-4383)
Standard Ink & Color Corp.................G 570 424-5214
East Stroudsburg (G-4635)
Sun Chemical Corporation..................D 215 223-8220
Philadelphia (G-14353)
Sun Chemical Corporation..................D 215 223-8220
Philadelphia (G-14354)
Tek Products & Services Inc ....F 610 376-0690
Reading (G-16354)
Two Cousins Holdings LLC ....G 717 637-1311
Hanover (G-6963)
Wampum Hardware Co........................F 814 893-5470
Stoystown (G-18088)
Wikoff Color Corporation ....G 484 681-4065
King of Prussia (G-8699)

INNER TUBES: Indl

Johnstown Tube Laser LLC ....E 814 532-4121
Johnstown (G-8392)

INSECTICIDES & PESTICIDES

Boos Bug Stoppers LLC ....G 724 601-3223
Fombell (G-6030)
Liquid Fence Co Inc.......................E 570 722-8165
Blakeslee (G-1748)
Senoret Chemical Company ....E 717 626-2125
Lititz (G-10047)

INSPECTION & TESTING SVCS

Arete Qis LLC ....D 814 781-1194
Ridgway (G-16696)
Ashland Industrial Svcs LLC ....G 717 347-5616
Shrewsbury (G-17581)
Sensor Corporation ....G 724 887-4080
Scottdale (G-17200)

INSTRUMENTS & ACCESSORIES: Surveying

Teletrix Corp ....G 412 798-3636
Pittsburgh (G-15605)

INSTRUMENTS & METERS: Measuring, Electric

Avex Electronics Corp.....................E 215 245-4848
Bensalem (G-1152)
Electric Metering Corp USA ....D 215 949-1900
Bristol (G-2138)
Schlumberger Technology Corp ....C 814 220-1900
Brookville (G-2271)

INSTRUMENTS, LAB: Spectroscopic/Optical Properties Measuring

Milton Roy LLC............................C 215 441-0800
Ivyland (G-8218)
Milton Roy LLC............................G 215 293-0401
Ivyland (G-8219)

INSTRUMENTS, LABORATORY: Analyzers, Thermal

Cdprintexpress LLC .... G 610 450-6176
Phoenixville (G-14539)

Conair Group Inc .... E 814 437-6861
Franklin (G-6122)

INSTRUMENTS, LABORATORY: Blood Testing

Abbott Laboratories .... G 610 444-9818
Kennett Square (G-8500)

Sanguis LLC .... G 267 228-7502
Philadelphia (G-14277)

INSTRUMENTS, LABORATORY: Infrared Analytical

Flir Systems Inc .... C 412 423-2100
Pittsburgh (G-15021)

INSTRUMENTS, LABORATORY: Mass Spectrometers

Extrel Cms LLC .... E 412 963-7530
Pittsburgh (G-14996)

INSTRUMENTS, LABORATORY: Spectrographs

Cianflone Scientific LLC .... G 412 787-3600
Pittsburgh (G-14851)

INSTRUMENTS, LABORATORY: Spectrometers

Applied RES & Photonics Inc .... G 717 220-1003
Harrisburg (G-7089)

Moa Instrumentation Inc .... F 609 352-9329
Levittown (G-9849)

INSTRUMENTS, LABORATORY: Titrimeters

Sanda Corporation .... G 502 510-8782
Media (G-10947)

INSTRUMENTS, MEASURING & CNTRG: Plotting, Drafting/Map Rdg

Bondata Inc .... G 717 566-5550
Hummelstown (G-7903)

INSTRUMENTS, MEASURING & CNTRL: Gauges, Auto, Computer

Clickcadence LLC .... G 412 434-4911
Pittsburgh (G-14860)

INSTRUMENTS, MEASURING & CNTRL: Radiation & Testing, Nuclear

Apantec LLC .... F 267 436-3991
Lansdale (G-9342)

Cdl Nuclear Technologies Inc .... E 724 933-5570
Wexford (G-19794)

Lakeshore Isotopes LLC .... F 814 836-0207
Erie (G-5357)

INSTRUMENTS, MEASURING & CNTRL: Tester, Acft Hydc Ctrl Test

Summit Control Panels .... G 814 431-4402
Waterford (G-19270)

INSTRUMENTS, MEASURING & CNTRL: Testing, Abrasion, Etc

AGR International Inc .... E 724 482-2164
Butler (G-2371)

Audiology & Hearing Aid Center .... G 570 822-6122
Wilkes Barre (G-19906)

M Squared Electronics Inc .... F 215 945-6658
Levittown (G-9848)

P J Electronics Inc .... G 412 793-3912
Pittsburgh (G-15366)

Technology Development Corp .... F 610 631-5043
Norristown (G-12717)

INSTRUMENTS, MEASURING & CNTRLG: Aircraft & Motor Vehicle

Hawk Grips .... G 484 351-8050
Conshohocken (G-3554)

Ideal Aerosmith Inc .... E 412 963-1495
Pittsburgh (G-15113)

Rieker Instrument Company Inc .... E 610 500-2000
Aston (G-791)

INSTRUMENTS, MEASURING & CNTRLG: Fatigue Test, Indl, Mech

B & Q Technical Service Inc .... G 610 872-8428
Wallingford (G-18781)

INSTRUMENTS, MEASURING & CNTRLG: Tensile Strength Testing

Forney Holdings Inc .... E 724 346-7400
Hermitage (G-7584)

OP Schuman & Sons Inc .... D 215 343-1530
Warminster (G-18932)

INSTRUMENTS, MEASURING & CNTRLG: Thermometers/Temp Sensors

Embedded Energy Technology LLC ..... G 412 254-3381
Pittsburgh (G-14967)

Julabo West Inc .... F 610 231-0250
Allentown (G-273)

Probes Unlimited Inc .... E 267 263-0400
Lansdale (G-9401)

Thermo Electric Company Inc .... D 610 692-7990
West Chester (G-19661)

Thermo Electric Pa Inc .... D 610 692-7990
West Chester (G-19662)

Thermocouple Technology LLC .... E 215 529-9394
Quakertown (G-16252)

INSTRUMENTS, MEASURING & CONTROLLING: Breathalyzers

Guth Laboratories Inc .... F 717 564-5470
Harrisburg (G-7137)

INSTRUMENTS, MEASURING & CONTROLLING: Coal Testing Apparatus

Greenbank Energy Solutions Inc .... G 724 229-4454
Washington (G-19179)

Greenbank Group Inc .... G 724 229-1180
Washington (G-19180)

INSTRUMENTS, MEASURING & CONTROLLING: Gas Detectors

Analytical Technology Inc .... F 610 917-0991
Collegeville (G-3368)

Grace Industries Inc .... E 724 962-9231
Fredonia (G-6180)

Industrial Scientific Corp .... B 412 788-4353
Pittsburgh (G-15120)

Jomarr Safety Systems Inc .... D 570 346-5330
Dunmore (G-4475)

Mine Safety Appliances Co LLC .... B 724 776-8600
Cranberry Township (G-3836)

MSA Safety Incorporated .... B 724 776-8600
Cranberry Township (G-3839)

MSA Safety Sales LLC .... G 724 776-8600
Cranberry Township (G-3841)

Rel-Tek Corporation .... F 412 373-4417
Monroeville (G-11353)

INSTRUMENTS, MEASURING & CONTROLLING: Leak Detection, Liquid

American Leak Detection .... G 412 859-6000
Coraopolis (G-3657)

Watermark Usa LLC .... F 610 983-0500
Gladwyne (G-6409)

INSTRUMENTS, MEASURING & CONTROLLING: Polygraph

Aaron J Michael .... G 724 745-0656
Cecil (G-2821)

Assured Polygraph Services Inc .... G 412 492-9980
Pittsburgh (G-14728)

INSTRUMENTS, MEASURING & CONTROLLING: Torsion Testing

Chant Engineering Co Inc .... E 215 230-4260
New Britain (G-12045)

INSTRUMENTS, MEASURING & CONTROLLING: Transits, Surveyors'

Tri County Transit Service Inc .... D 610 495-5640
Pottstown (G-16057)

INSTRUMENTS, MEASURING & CONTROLLING: Ultrasonic Testing

Sensor Networks Inc .... E 814 466-7207
Boalsburg (G-1869)

Sensor Networks Inc .... G 814 441-2476
Boalsburg (G-1870)

INSTRUMENTS, MEASURING & CONTROLLING: Weather Tracking

Boschung America LLC .... F 724 658-3300
New Castle (G-12065)

INSTRUMENTS, MEASURING/CNTRL: Gauging, Ultrasonic Thickness

Cianflone Scientific LLC .... G 412 787-3600
Pittsburgh (G-14851)

INSTRUMENTS, MEASURING/CNTRL: Testing/Measuring, Kinematic

Kinetics Hydro Inc .... G 717 532-6016
Shippensburg (G-17535)

Pruftechnik Inc .... E 844 242-6296
Philadelphia (G-14211)

Pruftechnik Service Inc .... E 856 401-3095
Philadelphia (G-14212)

Reliefband Technologies LLC .... F 877 735-2263
Horsham (G-7845)

INSTRUMENTS, MEASURING/CNTRLNG: Med Diagnostic Sys, Nuclear

Circa Healthcare LLC .... G 610 954-2340
Malvern (G-10209)

Encompass Health Corporation .... F 610 478-8797
Reading (G-16374)

Heart Masters Diagnsostics LLC .... G 267 503-3803
Philadelphia (G-13809)

Special T Electronic LLC .... G 412 635-4997
Pittsburgh (G-15568)

X-Bar Diagnostics Systems Inc .... G 610 388-2071
Kennett Square (G-8551)

INSTRUMENTS, OPTICAL: Cinetheodolites

L3 Technologies Inc .... C 412 967-7700
Pittsburgh (G-15209)

INSTRUMENTS, OPTICAL: Elements & Assemblies, Exc Ophthalmic

American Polarizers Inc .... E 610 373-5177
Reading (G-16320)

Ii-VI Incorporated .... B 724 352-4455
Saxonburg (G-17088)

Insaco Incorporated .... D 215 536-3500
Quakertown (G-16202)

Metaphase Technologies Inc .... E 215 639-8699
Bristol (G-2167)

Shadowfax Inc .... E 610 373-5177
Reading (G-16515)

View Thru Technologies Inc .... F 215 703-0950
Quakertown (G-16258)

INSTRUMENTS, OPTICAL: Lenses, All Types Exc Ophthalmic

American Precision Glass Corp .... G 570 457-9664
Duryea (G-4503)

Martin Rawdin Od .... G 610 323-8007
Pottstown (G-16016)

Telefactor Robotics LLC .... G 610 940-6040
Conshohocken (G-3611)

Three Rivers Optical Company .... D 412 928-2020
Pittsburgh (G-15620)

PRODUCT

INSTRUMENTS, OPTICAL: Magnifying, NEC

Captek Inc ....G 610 296-2111
Berwyn (G-1355)

INSTRUMENTS, OPTICAL: Metallographs

Sarclad (north America) LP ....F 412 466-2000
Duquesne (G-4499)

INSTRUMENTS, OPTICAL: Mirrors

Onyx Optical ....G 570 951-7750
Wilkes Barre (G-19953)

INSTRUMENTS, OPTICAL: Reflectors

Ctp Carrera Inc ....C 724 539-6995
Latrobe (G-9468)

INSTRUMENTS, OPTICAL: Sighting & Fire Control

Lost Creek Shoe Shop Inc ....G 717 463-3117
Mifflintown (G-11129)

INSTRUMENTS, OPTICAL: Test & Inspection

Ncrx Optical Solutions Inc ....G 724 745-1011
Lawrence (G-9538)

INSTRUMENTS, SURGICAL & MED: Cleaning Eqpt, Ultrasonic Med

Sonic Systems Inc ....E 267 803-1964
Warminster (G-18967)

INSTRUMENTS, SURGICAL & MEDI: Knife Blades/Handles, Surgical

Duane Grant ....G 412 856-1357
Monroeville (G-11333)
Unique Technologies Inc ....F 610 775-9191
Mohnton (G-11271)

INSTRUMENTS, SURGICAL & MEDICAL: Blood & Bone Work

Baxano Surgical Inc ....E 919 800-0020
Blue Bell (G-1815)
Bayter Technologies Inc ....G 610 948-7447
Phoenixville (G-14529)
Dgh Koi Inc ....G 717 582-7749
Shermans Dale (G-17500)
Haemonetics Corporation ....C 412 741-7399
Leetsdale (G-9692)
Hunter Russell Group ....G 724 445-7228
Chicora (G-3127)
Kc-13 LLC ....G 484 887-8900
West Chester (G-19578)
Lifescan Inc ....A 800 227-8862
Chesterbrook (G-3093)
Lifescan Global Corporation ....F 800 227-8862
Chesterbrook (G-3094)
Medisurg Ltd ....G 610 277-3937
Norristown (G-12682)
Onsite Sterilization LLC ....G 484 624-8566
Pottstown (G-16023)
Orthovita Inc ....B 610 640-1775
Malvern (G-10291)
Permegear Inc ....G 484 851-3688
Hellertown (G-7560)
Rex Medical Inc ....E 610 940-0665
Conshohocken (G-3600)
Siemens Med Solutions USA Inc ....E 610 834-1220
Plymouth Meeting (G-15870)
Sigma Instruments Inc ....F 724 776-9500
Cranberry Township (G-3850)
Sterilzer Rfurbishing Svcs Inc ....G 814 882-4116
Erie (G-5491)

INSTRUMENTS, SURGICAL & MEDICAL: Blood Pressure

Chrono-Log Corp ....E 610 853-1130
Havertown (G-7418)

INSTRUMENTS, SURGICAL & MEDICAL: Cannulae

Ultraoptics Inc ....G 724 838-7155
Greensburg (G-6723)

INSTRUMENTS, SURGICAL & MEDICAL: Catheters

Arrow International Inc ....A 610 225-6800
Wayne (G-19303)
Arrow International Inc ....C 610 655-8522
Reading (G-16323)
Arrow International Inc ....C 610 378-0131
Reading (G-16324)
B Braun Medical Inc ....A 610 336-9595
Breinigsville (G-2009)
Cook Vandergrift Inc ....C 724 845-8621
Vandergrift (G-18724)
Recathco LLC ....F 412 487-1482
Allison Park (G-461)

INSTRUMENTS, SURGICAL & MEDICAL: IV Transfusion

Icu Medical Sales Inc ....G 610 265-9100
King of Prussia (G-8633)

INSTRUMENTS, SURGICAL & MEDICAL: Inhalation Therapy

Instrumentation Industries Inc ....E 412 854-1133
Bethel Park (G-1418)

INSTRUMENTS, SURGICAL & MEDICAL: Knives

C L Sturkey Inc ....G 717 274-9441
Lebanon (G-9551)
Dghkoi Inc ....G 610 594-9100
Exton (G-5666)
Surgical Specialties Corp ....F 610 404-1000
Wyomissing (G-20289)

INSTRUMENTS, SURGICAL & MEDICAL: Lasers, Surgical

Snake Creek Lasers LLC ....F 570 553-1120
Friendsville (G-6230)

INSTRUMENTS, SURGICAL & MEDICAL: Muscle Exercise, Ophthalmic

Hill Laboratories Co ....E 610 644-2867
Malvern (G-10246)

INSTRUMENTS, SURGICAL & MEDICAL: Ophthalmic

Alcon Research Ltd ....B 610 670-3500
Reading (G-16317)
Dgh Technology Inc ....F 610 594-9100
Exton (G-5665)
Gulden Ophthalmics Inc ....F 215 884-8105
Elkins Park (G-4904)
Peregrine Surgical Ltd ....E 215 348-0456
Doylestown (G-4323)
Varitronics Inc ....F 610 356-3995
Broomall (G-2304)

INSTRUMENTS, SURGICAL & MEDICAL: Plates & Screws, Bone

Altus Partners LLC ....E 610 355-4156
West Chester (G-19497)

INSTRUMENTS, SURGICAL & MEDICAL: Rifles, Hypodermic, Animal

Tar Hunt Custom Rifles Inc ....G 570 784-6368
Bloomsburg (G-1803)

INSTRUMENTS: Analytical

Altamira Instruments Inc ....F 412 963-6385
Pittsburgh (G-14691)
Applied Separations Inc ....E 610 770-0900
Allentown (G-141)
Applied Test Systems LLC ....E 724 283-1212
Butler (G-2375)
Ardara Technologies LP ....F 724 863-0418
Ardara (G-698)
Avo Multi-AMP Corporation ....C 610 676-8501
Norristown (G-12638)
Bio-RAD Laboratories Inc ....B 267 322-6931
Philadelphia (G-13462)

Bio-RAD Laboratories Inc ....E 267 322-6945
Philadelphia (G-13463)
Bio/Data Corporation ....E 215 441-4000
Horsham (G-7798)
Biomeme Inc ....F 267 519-9066
Philadelphia (G-13465)
Bionix Safety Technologies ....G 610 408-0555
Wayne (G-19307)
Bioscience Management Inc ....F 484 245-5232
Allentown (G-152)
Boekel Industries Inc ....E 215 396-8200
Feasterville Trevose (G-5892)
Chem Image Bio Threat LLC ....E 412 241-7335
Pittsburgh (G-14843)
Chemimage Corporation ....E 412 241-7335
Pittsburgh (G-14845)
Chemimage Filter Tech LLC ....E 412 241-7335
Pittsburgh (G-14846)
Conspec Controls Inc ....F 724 489-8450
Charleroi (G-3008)
EA Fischione Instruments ....E 724 325-5444
Export (G-5600)
Ems Acquisition Corp ....E 215 412-8400
Hatfield (G-7339)
Fisher Scientific Company LLC ....B 724 517-1500
Pittsburgh (G-15019)
Foerster Instruments Inc ....E 412 788-8976
Pittsburgh (G-15023)
Gow-Mac Instrument Co ....E 610 954-9000
Bethlehem (G-1526)
Ideal Aerosmith Inc ....E 412 963-1495
Pittsburgh (G-15113)
Instech Laboratories Inc ....E 610 941-0132
Plymouth Meeting (G-15852)
Inteprod LLC ....F 610 650-9002
Norristown (G-12670)
Leco Corporation ....E 814 355-7903
Bellefonte (G-1107)
Lee Rj Group Inc ....C 800 860-1775
Monroeville (G-11342)
Magritek Inc ....G 855 667-6835
Malvern (G-10272)
Microtrac Inc ....E 215 619-9920
Montgomeryville (G-11408)
Microtrac Inc ....F 717 843-4433
York (G-20595)
Microtrac Inc ....F 717 843-4433
York (G-20596)
Molecular Devices LLC ....E 610 873-5610
Downingtown (G-4242)
Perkinelmer Inc ....D 215 368-6900
Montgomeryville (G-11413)
Phenomenex ....G 484 680-0678
Avondale (G-857)
Princeton Security Tech LLC ....G 609 915-9700
Croydon (G-3924)
Scs Inc ....G 866 727-4436
Harleysville (G-7057)
Solar Light Company Inc ....D 215 517-8700
Glenside (G-6538)
Specac Inc ....G 215 793-4044
Fort Washington (G-6092)
Thermo Fisher Scientific Inc ....F 610 837-5091
Nazareth (G-11991)
Thermo Fisher Scientific Inc ....B 561 688-8725
Stahlstown (G-17937)
Thermo Fisher Scientific Inc ....G 412 490-8000
Pittsburgh (G-15611)
Thermo Fisher Scientific Inc ....E 814 353-2300
Bellefonte (G-1120)
Thermo Fisher Scientific Inc ....C 215 964-6020
Philadelphia (G-14387)
Thermo Fisher Scientific Inc ....B 412 770-2326
Pittsburgh (G-15612)
Thermo Fisher Scientific Inc ....A 412 490-8300
Pittsburgh (G-15613)
Thermo Fisher Scientific Inc ....D 412 490-8000
Pittsburgh (G-15614)
Thermo Shandon Inc ....G 412 788-1133
Pittsburgh (G-15615)
Thermo-Electric Co ....G 724 695-2774
Imperial (G-8077)
Tiger Optics LLC ....F 215 343-6600
Warrington (G-19135)
Uct Inc ....G 215 781-9255
Bristol (G-2212)
Waters Corporation ....F 412 967-5665
Pittsburgh (G-15707)

INSTRUMENTS: Colonoscopes, Electromedical

Neurohabilitation Corporation .... G 215 809-2018
Newtown (G-12527)

INSTRUMENTS: Combustion Control, Indl

2000 F Process Htg & Contrls .... G 724 224-2800
Tarentum (G-18238)

Fives N Amercn Combustn Inc .... G 412 655-0101
Pittsburgh (G-15020)

General Regulator Corp .... E 717 848-5960
York (G-20495)

Nao Inc .... E 215 743-5300
Philadelphia (G-14051)

Phoenix Combustion Inc .... F 610 495-5800
Pottstown (G-16031)

Ridge Tool Company .... D 814 454-2461
Erie (G-5463)

INSTRUMENTS: Differential Pressure, Indl

Erie Technical Systems Inc .... G 814 899-2103
Erie (G-5277)

INSTRUMENTS: Elec Lab Stds, Resist, Inductance/Capacitance

Process Instruments Inc .... E 412 431-4600
Pittsburgh (G-15451)

INSTRUMENTS: Electrocardiographs

Lifewatch Services Inc .... B 847 720-2100
Malvern (G-10269)

Rijuven Corp .... G 412 404-6292
Wexford (G-19827)

Samir Corp .... G 412 647-6000
Pittsburgh (G-15509)

Triomi Inc .... G 215 756-2771
Philadelphia (G-14411)

INSTRUMENTS: Electrolytic Conductivity, Laboratory

Nikon Precision Inc .... G 610 439-6203
Allentown (G-334)

INSTRUMENTS: Electron Test Tube

E F E Laboratories Inc .... E 215 672-2400
Horsham (G-7812)

INSTRUMENTS: Electronic, Analog-Digital Converters

Asr Instruments Inc .... F 412 833-7577
Bethel Park (G-1405)

Islip Transformer and Metal Co .... F 814 272-2700
State College (G-17978)

INSTRUMENTS: Endoscopic Eqpt, Electromedical

Endoscopic Laser Technologies .... G 443 205-9340
Stewartstown (G-18061)

INSTRUMENTS: Eye Examination

Eyenavision Inc .... F 412 456-2736
Pittsburgh (G-14997)

INSTRUMENTS: Flow, Indl Process

Parker-Hannifin Corporation .... C 215 723-4000
Hatfield (G-7377)

Thermal Instrument Co Inc .... F 215 355-8400
Trevose (G-18507)

World Wide Plastics Inc .... E 215 357-0893
Langhorne (G-9336)

INSTRUMENTS: Frequency Meters, Electrical, Mech & Electronic

Ic Mechanics Inc .... F 412 682-5560
Pittsburgh (G-15111)

INSTRUMENTS: Galvanometers

Aerotech Inc .... B 412 963-7470
Pittsburgh (G-14655)

INSTRUMENTS: Humidity, Indl Process

Industrial Instrs & Sups Inc .... F 215 396-0822
Wycombe (G-20260)

INSTRUMENTS: Indl Process Control

ABB Inc .... D 724 295-6000
Oakmont (G-12913)

Ace Controls & Instrumentation .... G 610 876-2000
Brookhaven (G-2242)

Action Manufacturing Company .... D 610 593-1800
Atglen (G-799)

Ajax Electric Company .... E 215 947-8500
Huntingdon Valley (G-7962)

Alstom Power Conversion Inc .... C 412 967-0765
Cranberry Township (G-3801)

Ametek Inc .... D 610 647-2121
Berwyn (G-1351)

Ametek Inc .... D 215 355-6900
Horsham (G-7784)

Athena Controls Inc .... D 610 828-2490
Plymouth Meeting (G-15832)

Automatic Control Elec Co .... F 210 661-4111
Harleysville (G-7021)

Bacharach Inc .... C 724 334-5000
New Kensington (G-12326)

Bombardier Transportation .... A 412 655-5700
Pittsburgh (G-14782)

Bronkhorst USA Inc .... G 610 866-6750
Bethlehem (G-1474)

Columbia Research Labs Inc .... E 610 872-3900
Woodlyn (G-20218)

Conspec Controls Inc .... F 724 489-8450
Charleroi (G-3008)

Control Design Inc .... E 412 788-2280
Pittsburgh (G-14873)

Control Electronics Inc .... G 610 942-3190
Brandamore (G-2001)

Cryoguard Corporation .... G 215 712-9018
Colmar (G-3413)

Cyberscan Technologies Inc .... G 215 321-0447
Washington Crossing (G-19256)

Delta Information Systems Inc .... E 215 657-5270
Horsham (G-7809)

E F E Laboratories Inc .... E 215 672-2400
Horsham (G-7812)

Eaton Corporation .... B 724 773-1231
Beaver (G-980)

Electronic Tech Systems Inc .... D 724 295-6000
Natrona Heights (G-11942)

Ellison Industrial Contrls LLC .... G 724 483-0251
Belle Vernon (G-1086)

Emerson Electric Co .... E 610 569-4023
Royersford (G-16849)

Emerson Electric Co .... G 215 638-8904
Bensalem (G-1189)

Emerson Process Management .... A 412 963-4000
Pittsburgh (G-14971)

Endress + Hauser Inc .... G 317 535-7138
Chalfont (G-2873)

Environmental Tectonics Corp .... C 215 355-9100
Southampton (G-17809)

Erie Strayer Company .... C 814 456-7001
Erie (G-5275)

ESAB Group Inc .... B 717 637-8911
Hanover (G-6884)

Fairmount Automation Inc .... F 610 356-9840
Conshohocken (G-3546)

FEC Technologies Inc .... E 717 764-5959
York (G-20477)

Flow Measurement Technologies .... G 610 377-6050
Lehighton (G-9714)

Flw of Pa Inc .... G 610 251-9700
Malvern (G-10237)

FMC Technologies Measurement S ...... C 281 591-4000
Erie (G-5297)

Freas Glass Works Inc .... F 610 825-0430
Bridgeport (G-2036)

Fredericks Company Inc .... E 215 947-2500
Huntingdon Valley (G-7985)

General Nuclear Corp .... D 724 925-3565
Hunker (G-7928)

George J Anderton .... G 814 382-9201
Conneaut Lake (G-3473)

Gow-Mac Instrument Co .... E 610 954-9000
Bethlehem (G-1526)

Graftech Usa LLC .... C 814 781-2478
Saint Marys (G-16979)

H B Instrument Co .... E 610 489-5500
Trappe (G-18469)

Heraeus Sensor Tech USA LLC .... G 732 940-4400
Yardley (G-20319)

Homewood Products Corporation .... E 412 665-2700
Pittsburgh (G-15099)

Horiba Instruments Inc .... D 724 457-2424
Coraopolis (G-3698)

Industrial Learning Systems .... G 412 512-8257
Allison Park (G-453)

Instrument & Valve Services Co .... E 724 205-3348
Irwin (G-8172)

Johnson Controls Inc .... D 610 276-3700
Horsham (G-7828)

Johnson March Systems Inc .... E 215 364-2500
Warminster (G-18903)

Lawson Labs Inc .... G 610 725-8800
Malvern (G-10265)

Leco Corporation .... E 814 355-7903
Bellefonte (G-1107)

Lee Rj Group Inc .... C 800 860-1775
Monroeville (G-11342)

Lionheart Holdings LLC .... D 215 283-8400
Newtown (G-12519)

Liquid Meter Company Inc .... G 814 756-5602
Cranesville (G-3868)

Lord Corporation .... A 877 275-5673
Erie (G-5373)

LSI Controls Inc .... G 717 762-2191
Waynesboro (G-19415)

Maguire Products Inc .... E 610 459-4300
Aston (G-773)

Mansco Products Inc .... G 215 674-4395
Warminster (G-18917)

Master-Lee Engineered Products .... G 724 537-6002
Latrobe (G-9502)

Maxima Tech & Systems LLC .... C 717 581-1000
Lancaster (G-9130)

MSA Safety Incorporated .... B 724 733-9100
Murrysville (G-11858)

Nac Carbon Products Inc .... E 814 938-7450
Punxsutawney (G-16148)

Nu-Chem Corp .... F 610 770-2000
Allentown (G-336)

Parker-Hannifin Corporation .... C 724 861-8200
Irwin (G-8188)

RTD Embedded Technologies Inc .... E 814 234-8087
State College (G-18017)

S & G Water Conditioning Inc .... G 215 672-2030
Warminster (G-18957)

Sensing Devices LLC .... F 717 295-4735
Lancaster (G-9192)

Sensor Corporation .... G 724 887-4080
Scottdale (G-17200)

Seventy-Three Mfg Co Inc .... E 610 845-7823
Bechtelsville (G-1037)

Spectrodyne Inc .... F 215 804-1044
Quakertown (G-16246)

Staneco Corporation .... E 215 672-6500
Horsham (G-7852)

Suez Wts Usa Inc .... A 215 355-3300
Trevose (G-18506)

Thar Process Inc .... G 412 968-9180
Pittsburgh (G-15610)

Thermocouple Technologies Inc .... E 215 529-9394
Quakertown (G-16251)

Valley Instrument Co Inc .... F 610 363-2650
Exton (G-5746)

Westinghouse Electric Co LLC .... A 412 374-2020
Cranberry Township (G-3865)

Westinghouse Electric Co LLC .... D 412 256-1085
Pittsburgh (G-15710)

World Video Sales Co Inc .... G 610 754-6800
Bechtelsville (G-1038)

INSTRUMENTS: Laser, Scientific & Engineering

Advent Design Corporation .... C 215 781-0500
Bristol (G-2104)

Holo Image Technology Inc .... G 215 946-2190
Bristol (G-2153)

US Web Converting McHy Corp .... F 570 644-1401
Paxinos (G-13194)

INSTRUMENTS: Liquid Level, Indl Process

Mikron Valve & Mfr Inc .... G 814 453-2337
Erie (G-5392)

INSTRUMENTS: Measurement, Indl Process

Arcadia Controls .... G 724 538-8931
Cranberry Township (G-3804)

PRODUCT

Bafco Inc ....E 215 674-1700
Warminster (G-18834)
Brooks Instrument LLC ....C 215 362-3500
Hatfield (G-7322)
Delaware County Pennsylvania ....G 610 891-4865
Media (G-10920)
Delta Usa Inc ....G 412 429-3574
Carnegie (G-2766)
Garrett Precision LLC ....G 717 779-1384
York (G-20490)
Matthey Johnson Inc ....E 610 232-1900
West Chester (G-19599)
Wgs Equipment & Controls ....F 610 459-8800
Garnet Valley (G-6270)

INSTRUMENTS: Measuring & Controlling

Advanced Controls Inc ....F 412 322-0991
Pittsburgh (G-14651)
American Stress Tech Inc ....F 412 784-8400
Pittsburgh (G-14707)
Ametek Inc ....D 215 355-6900
Horsham (G-7784)
Amphenol Corporation ....G 814 834-9140
Saint Marys (G-16947)
Applied Controls Inc ....E 717 854-2889
York (G-20380)
Applied Separations Inc ....E 610 770-0900
Allentown (G-141)
Applied Test Systems LLC ....E 724 283-1212
Butler (G-2375)
Associated Ceramics & Tech ....D 724 353-1585
Sarver (G-17065)
Audiology & Hearing Aid Center ....G 570 383-0500
Peckville (G-13206)
Avo Multi-AMP Corporation ....C 610 676-8501
Norristown (G-12638)
Batterytest Equipment Co ....G 610 746-9449
Nazareth (G-11956)
Biocoat Incorporated ....E 215 734-0888
Horsham (G-7799)
Bionix Safety Technologies ....G 610 408-0555
Wayne (G-19307)
Blatek Industries Inc ....D 814 231-2085
State College (G-17946)
Bon Tool Company ....D 724 443-7080
Gibsonia (G-6328)
Bvs Inc ....G 610 273-2842
Honey Brook (G-7739)
Chemdaq Inc ....F 412 787-0202
Pittsburgh (G-14844)
Coinco Inc ....E 814 425-7476
Cochranton (G-3338)
Columbia Research Labs Inc ....E 610 872-3900
Woodlyn (G-20218)
Cornerstone Automation LLC ....G 215 513-4111
Telford (G-18277)
Delta Information Systems Inc ....E 215 657-5270
Horsham (G-7809)
Dynamic Control Systems Inc ....G 484 674-1408
King of Prussia (G-8616)
Eaton Aerospace LLC ....E 610 522-4000
Glenolden (G-6473)
Enginred Arrsting Systems Corp ....C 610 494-8000
Upper Chichester (G-18660)
Ev Products Inc ....E 724 352-5288
Zelienople (G-20799)
Evans John Sons Incorporated ....D 215 368-7700
Lansdale (G-9365)
Everight Position Tech Corp ....G 856 727-9500
Narberth (G-11910)
Faro Technologies Inc ....E 407 333-9911
Exton (G-5675)
FMC Technologies Measurement S ....C 281 591-4000
Erie (G-5297)
Foerster Instruments Inc ....E 412 788-8976
Pittsburgh (G-15023)
Forney LP ....E 724 346-7400
Zelienople (G-20801)
Francis L Freas Glass Works ....E 610 828-0430
Conshohocken (G-3549)
Gamry Instruments Inc ....E 215 682-9330
Warminster (G-18885)
Garment Dimensions Inc ....G 610 838-0484
Bethlehem (G-1524)
General Nuclear Corp ....D 724 925-3565
Hunker (G-7928)
Gerhart Systems & Contrls Corp ....F 610 264-2800
Allentown (G-231)
Hy-Tech Machine Inc ....D 724 776-2400
Cranberry Township (G-3824)

Imac Systems Inc ....E 215 946-2200
Bristol (G-2155)
Invensys Energy Metering Corp ....B 814 371-3011
Du Bois (G-4396)
Johnson Controls Inc ....E 717 531-5371
Hershey (G-7619)
King Tester Corporation ....F 610 279-6010
Phoenixville (G-14558)
Lasersense Inc ....G 856 207-5701
Media (G-10936)
Lenox Instrument Co Inc ....E 215 322-9990
Trevose (G-18500)
Long Island Pllution Strippers ....G 215 752-2709
Yardley (G-20323)
Lord Corporation ....D 814 398-4641
Cambridge Springs (G-2481)
Marvel Manufacturing Company ....G 570 421-6221
Stroudsburg (G-18128)
Marvel Manufacturing Company ....F 570 421-6221
Stroudsburg (G-18129)
Matt Machine & Mfg Inc ....E 412 793-6020
Pittsburgh (G-15263)
Measurement Specialties Inc ....G 610 971-9893
Wayne (G-19354)
Mistras Group Inc ....E 610 497-0400
Trainer (G-18463)
Mp Machinery and Testing LLC ....G 814 234-8860
Port Matilda (G-15902)
Optotech Optical Machinery Inc ....F 215 679-2091
Palm (G-13096)
Optotherm Inc ....G 724 940-7600
Sewickley (G-17401)
Pace Environmental ....G 610 262-3818
Whitehall (G-19885)
PH Tool LLC ....E 267 203-1600
Pipersville (G-14618)
Photonis Digital Imaging LLC ....G 972 987-1460
Lancaster (G-9171)
Precision Laser and Instr Inc ....E 724 266-1600
Ambridge (G-631)
Precision Medical Inc ....C 610 262-6090
Northampton (G-12860)
Proceq USA Inc ....G 724 512-0330
Aliquippa (G-90)
Process Instruments Inc ....E 412 431-4600
Pittsburgh (G-15451)
R L Holliday Company Inc ....G 412 561-7620
Pittsburgh (G-15463)
Sanavita Medical LLC ....E 267 517-3220
Telford (G-18312)
Scanmaster ....G 215 208-4732
Warminster (G-18962)
Sensing Devices Inc ....E 717 295-4735
Lancaster (G-9193)
Sensor Networks Corporation ....G 717 466-7207
Boalsburg (G-1871)
Skantra Diagnostics Inc ....G 215 990-0381
Radnor (G-16302)
Skc Inc ....D 724 260-0741
Eighty Four (G-4849)
Solar Light Company Inc ....D 215 517-8700
Glenside (G-6538)
Stretch Devices Inc ....E 215 739-3000
Philadelphia (G-14352)
Teeco Associates Inc ....E 610 539-4708
Schwenksville (G-17179)
Valco ....E 610 691-3205
Bethlehem (G-1649)
Videotek Inc ....C 610 327-2292
Pottstown (G-16068)
Westinghouse Electric Co LLC ....A 412 374-2020
Cranberry Township (G-3865)
Westinghouse Electric Co LLC ....A 412 374-4252
Warrendale (G-19102)
Westinghouse Electric Co LLC ....D 412 256-1085
Pittsburgh (G-15710)
Westinghouse Electric Company ....E 866 442-7873
Pittsburgh (G-15711)
World Video Sales Co Inc ....G 610 754-6800
Bechtelsville (G-1038)
Xensor Corporation ....E 610 284-2508
Drexel Hill (G-4373)

INSTRUMENTS: Measuring Electricity

Abl Engineering ....G 814 364-1333
Boalsburg (G-1863)
Advanced McRo Cmpt Specialists ....G 215 773-9700
Plymouth Meeting (G-15827)
Advent Design Corporation ....C 215 781-0500
Bristol (G-2104)

Ametek Inc ....D 267 933-2121
Harleysville (G-7018)
Ametek Inc ....E 267 933-2121
Harleysville (G-7019)
Applied Test Systems LLC ....E 724 283-1212
Butler (G-2375)
Avo International Inc ....G 610 676-8500
Norristown (G-12637)
Avo Multi-AMP Corporation ....C 610 676-8501
Norristown (G-12638)
Avox Inc ....G 267 404-2676
Perkasie (G-13267)
Core Technology Group Inc ....E 215 822-0120
Chalfont (G-2869)
FMC Technologies Measurement S ....C 281 591-4000
Erie (G-5297)
Foerster Instruments Inc ....E 412 788-8976
Pittsburgh (G-15023)
Francis L Freas Glass Works ....E 610 828-0430
Conshohocken (G-3549)
Geosonics Inc ....F 724 934-2900
Warrendale (G-19076)
Hirschmann Electronics Inc ....F 717 217-2200
Chambersburg (G-2940)
Leco Corporation ....E 814 355-7903
Bellefonte (G-1107)
Lee Rj Group Inc ....C 800 860-1775
Monroeville (G-11342)
Loranger International Corp ....D 814 723-2250
Warren (G-19038)
Mack Information Systems Inc ....E 215 884-8123
Wyncote (G-20264)
MMS Technologies LLC ....G 814 238-2323
State College (G-17993)
Morehouse Instrument Company ....F 717 843-0081
York (G-20603)
OHM- Labs Inc ....F 412 431-0640
Pittsburgh (G-15358)
Orbit Advanced Tech Inc ....E 215 674-5100
Warminster (G-18933)
Orbit/Fr Inc ....E 215 674-5100
Warminster (G-18934)
Pasadena Scientific Inc ....G 717 227-1220
Glen Rock (G-6459)
Semilab USA LLC ....F 610 377-5990
Lehighton (G-9726)
Sensor Corporation ....G 724 887-4080
Scottdale (G-17200)
Spectrum Microwave Inc ....D 215 464-0586
Philadelphia (G-14333)
Strainsert Company ....E 610 825-3310
Conshohocken (G-3608)
Thermo Shandon Inc ....G 412 788-1133
Pittsburgh (G-15615)
World Wide Plastics Inc ....E 215 357-0893
Langhorne (G-9336)

INSTRUMENTS: Measuring, Electrical Power

Bitronics LLC ....E 610 997-5100
Bethlehem (G-1467)

INSTRUMENTS: Measuring, Electrical Quantities

Electro-Tech Systems Inc ....E 215 887-2196
Glenside (G-6515)

INSTRUMENTS: Medical & Surgical

Accellent ....F 610 489-0300
Trappe (G-18466)
Accutome Inc ....E 800 979-2020
Malvern (G-10179)
Actuated Medical Inc ....F 814 355-0003
Bellefonte (G-1091)
Aesculap Biologics LLC ....E 610 984-9000
Breinigsville (G-2004)
Aesculap Implant Systems LLC ....G 610 984-9404
Breinigsville (G-2005)
Aesculap Implant Systems LLC ....G 610 984-9000
Center Valley (G-2823)
Airgas Safety Inc ....C 215 826-9000
Levittown (G-9814)
Airos Medical Inc ....G 866 991-6956
Audubon (G-822)
Alcon Manufacturing Ltd ....A 610 670-3500
Reading (G-16316)
Alliqua Biomedical Inc ....D 215 702-8550
Langhorne (G-9275)
American Contract Systems ....G 952 926-3515
Zelienople (G-20789)

American Proven Products LLC............G....... 215 876-5274
Philadelphia *(G-13388)*
Ardiem Medical Inc.............................F....... 724 349-0855
Indiana *(G-8082)*
Aspire Bariatrics Inc............................E....... 610 590-1577
Exton *(G-5647)*
B Braun Medical Inc...............................A....... 610 691-5400
Bethlehem *(G-1454)*
B Braun of America Inc..........................G....... 610 691-5400
Bethlehem *(G-1455)*
Bacharach Instruments Ltd..................F....... 724 334-5000
Pittsburgh *(G-14747)*
Barc Developmental Services................E....... 215 794-0800
Holicong *(G-7638)*
Baxter Healthcare Corporation.............B....... 717 232-1901
Harrisburg *(G-7095)*
Bayer Corporation....................................A....... 412 777-2000
Pittsburgh *(G-14750)*
Bayer Medical Care Inc..........................A....... 724 940-6800
Indianola *(G-8135)*
Bayer Medical Care Inc..........................D....... 724 360-7600
Saxonburg *(G-17081)*
Bayer Medical Care Inc..........................D....... 412 767-2400
Pittsburgh *(G-14756)*
Berkley Medical Resources Inc.............D....... 724 438-3000
Uniontown *(G-18617)*
Berkley Medical Resources Inc.............C....... 724 564-5002
Smithfield *(G-17642)*
Best Medical International Inc..............D....... 412 312-6700
Pittsburgh *(G-14764)*
Bio Med Sciences Inc..............................F....... 610 530-3193
Allentown *(G-151)*
Biochem Technology Inc........................G....... 484 674-7003
King of Prussia *(G-8588)*
Bioplast Manufacturing LLC..................E....... 609 807-3070
Bristol *(G-2118)*
Boehringer Laboratories Inc..................E....... 610 278-0900
Phoenixville *(G-14536)*
Boehringer Laboratories LLC................E....... 610 278-0900
Phoenixville *(G-14537)*
Boehringer Wound Systems LLC...........E....... 610 278-0900
Phoenixville *(G-14538)*
Branch Medical Group LLC....................D....... 877 992-7262
Norristown *(G-12642)*
Cardiac Telecom Corporation................F....... 800 355-2594
Greensburg *(G-6656)*
Clinton Industries Inc.............................E....... 717 848-2391
York *(G-20427)*
Coordinated Health Systems.................C....... 610 861-8080
Bethlehem *(G-1487)*
Cybersonics Inc.......................................G....... 814 898-4734
Erie *(G-5243)*
Depuy Synthes Inc..................................B....... 610 647-9700
Paoli *(G-13138)*
Depuy Synthes Products Inc.................G....... 610 719-5000
West Chester *(G-19539)*
Depuy Synthes Sales Inc.......................G....... 610 719-5000
West Chester *(G-19540)*
Depuy Synthes Sales Inc.......................F....... 610 738-4600
West Chester *(G-19541)*
Doctor In The House Inc.........................G....... 610 277-1998
Blue Bell *(G-1827)*
Drt Medical LLC......................................E....... 215 997-2900
Hatfield *(G-7336)*
DSM Biomedical Inc................................G....... 484 713-2100
Exton *(G-5668)*
Eastern Rail Systems Inc........................G....... 215 826-9980
Bristol *(G-2137)*
Easy Walking Inc......................................G....... 215 654-1626
Maple Glen *(G-10429)*
Endologix Inc..G....... 412 661-5877
Pittsburgh *(G-14973)*
Environmental Tectonics Corp..............C....... 215 355-9100
Southampton *(G-17809)*
Escalon Medical Corp..............................E....... 610 688-6830
Wayne *(G-19325)*
Essential Medical Inc...............................G....... 610 557-1009
Exton *(G-5673)*
Fluortek Inc...D....... 610 438-1800
Easton *(G-4683)*
Foranne Manufacturing Inc....................E....... 215 357-4650
Warminster *(G-18881)*
Foundation Surgery Center....................E....... 215 628-4300
Fort Washington *(G-6070)*
General Anesthetic Services..................F....... 412 851-4390
South Park *(G-17783)*
Globus Medical Inc..................................G....... 610 930-1800
Norristown *(G-12661)*
Globus Medical Inc..................................B....... 610 930-1800
Audubon *(G-826)*
Health-Chem Corporation.......................D....... 717 764-1191
Emigsville *(G-4988)*
Implant Research Center.......................G....... 215 571-4345
Philadelphia *(G-13851)*
Ingmar Medical Ltd.................................G....... 412 441-8228
Pittsburgh *(G-15125)*
Intact Vascular Inc..................................E....... 484 253-1048
Wayne *(G-19338)*
Intelomed Inc..F....... 412 536-7661
Wexford *(G-19808)*
Invibio Inc..E....... 484 342-6004
Conshohocken *(G-3565)*
Jade Prcsion Med Cmponents LLC.......G....... 215 947-5762
Huntingdon Valley *(G-8001)*
Keeler Instruments Inc............................E....... 610 353-4359
Malvern *(G-10264)*
Lake Region Medical Inc.........................C....... 610 489-0300
Trappe *(G-18471)*
Legend Spine LLC.....................................G....... 267 566-3273
Pottstown *(G-16010)*
Maculogix Inc...F....... 717 982-6751
Harrisburg *(G-7172)*
Mangar Medical Inc..................................C....... 215 230-0300
New Britain *(G-12048)*
Matt Machine & Mfg Inc...........................E....... 412 793-6020
Pittsburgh *(G-15263)*
Medcontrol Technologies LLC..............G....... 508 479-8109
Pittsburgh *(G-15272)*
Medical Creative Technologies.............G....... 267 347-4436
Quakertown *(G-16215)*
Medicapture Inc..F....... 610 238-0700
Plymouth Meeting *(G-15856)*
Medplast Engineered Pdts Inc..............D....... 814 367-2246
Westfield *(G-19780)*
Medrad Incorporated Ohara...................G....... 412 967-9700
Pittsburgh *(G-15273)*
Medtronic Usa Inc.....................................G....... 724 933-8100
Wexford *(G-19811)*
Medtronic Usa Inc.....................................G....... 717 657-6140
Harrisburg *(G-7176)*
Merit Medical..G....... 610 651-5000
Malvern *(G-10277)*
Micro Facture LLC....................................E....... 717 285-9700
Mountville *(G-11799)*
Micromed LLC..G....... 480 236-4705
Ambler *(G-590)*
Micronic..G....... 484 480-3372
Aston *(G-776)*
Molecular Devices LLC............................E....... 610 873-5610
Downingtown *(G-4242)*
Mytamed Inc..G....... 877 444-6982
Malvern *(G-10282)*
N E D LLC..G....... 610 442-1017
Slatington *(G-17609)*
N T M Inc..E....... 717 567-9374
Newport *(G-12492)*
Neurodx Development LLC......................G....... 609 865-4426
Yardley *(G-20328)*
Neuronetics Inc..C....... 610 640-4202
Malvern *(G-10285)*
Neurontrvntnal Thrapeutics Inc..............G....... 412 726-3111
Pittsburgh *(G-15330)*
Oakworks Inc..D....... 717 227-0516
New Freedom *(G-12213)*
Operating Room Safety LLC...................G....... 866 498-6882
Conshohocken *(G-3580)*
Orasure Technologies Inc.......................B....... 610 882-1820
Bethlehem *(G-1588)*
Ot Medical LLC...G....... 484 588-2063
Collegeville *(G-3385)*
Parker-Hannifin Corporation...................C....... 215 723-4000
Hatfield *(G-7377)*
Penn-Century Inc.......................................G....... 215 843-6540
Philadelphia *(G-14131)*
Perryman Company....................................D....... 724 745-7272
Houston *(G-7875)*
Pilling Company..F....... 215 643-2600
Fort Washington *(G-6088)*
Piramal Critical Care Inc..........................E....... 800 414-1901
Bethlehem *(G-1598)*
Porter Instrument..F....... 215 723-4000
Hatfield *(G-7383)*
Ppk Animal Healthcare LLC.....................G....... 718 288-4318
Montoursville *(G-11448)*
Precise Medical...E....... 215 345-6729
Furlong *(G-6232)*
Precision Medical Devices Inc...............G....... 717 795-9480
Mechanicsburg *(G-10881)*
Premier Dental Products Co....................E....... 610 239-6000
Plymouth Meeting *(G-15865)*
Premier Dental Products Co Inc............E....... 215 676-9090
Philadelphia *(G-14196)*
Pulse Technologies Inc............................C....... 267 733-0200
Quakertown *(G-16235)*
Qbc Diagnostics LLC................................C....... 814 342-6210
Port Matilda *(G-15905)*
Renerva LLC...G....... 412 841-7966
Pittsburgh *(G-15478)*
Respironics Inc...B....... 724 387-4270
Monroeville *(G-11354)*
Respironics Inc...C....... 724 334-3100
New Kensington *(G-12370)*
Respironics Inc...D....... 724 387-5200
Murrysville *(G-11865)*
Roechling Med Lancaster LLC................C....... 717 335-3700
Denver *(G-4092)*
Safe-TEC Clinical Products LLC............G....... 215 364-5582
Warminster *(G-18960)*
Seitz Tech LLC..G....... 610 268-2228
Oxford *(G-13090)*
Sleep Specialists LLC................................G....... 610 304-6408
Bala Cynwyd *(G-892)*
Somni Scientific LLC..................................F....... 412 851-4390
South Park *(G-17785)*
Spectrasonics Inc...G....... 610 964-9637
Wayne *(G-19372)*
Spinal Acoustics LLC..................................G....... 724 846-3600
Beaver Falls *(G-1013)*
Strata Skin Sciences Inc.............................D....... 215 619-3200
Horsham *(G-7854)*
Stryker Orthobiologics.................................G....... 610 407-5259
Malvern *(G-10324)*
Superior Surgical Ltd Lblty Co..................G....... 877 669-7646
Pottstown *(G-16053)*
Synthes Inc...G....... 610 647-9700
West Chester *(G-19650)*
Synthes Spine Inc...E....... 610 695-2424
West Chester *(G-19651)*
Synthes USA Products LLC.......................G....... 610 719-5000
West Chester *(G-19653)*
Talexmedical LLC..G....... 888 327-2221
Malvern *(G-10327)*
Tecomet Inc..F....... 215 826-8250
Bristol *(G-2204)*
Teleflex Incorporated...................................B....... 610 225-6800
Wayne *(G-19382)*
Thermo-Electric Co...G....... 724 695-2774
Imperial *(G-8077)*
Tyber Medical LLC..F....... 303 717-5060
Bethlehem *(G-1644)*
Ue Lifesciences Inc..G....... 631 980-8340
Philadelphia *(G-14416)*
Vcp Mobility Inc..B....... 814 443-4881
Somerset *(G-17715)*
Viant Westfield LLC..D....... 215 675-4653
Warminster *(G-18994)*
Wilmand Labglass..G....... 215 672-7800
Warminster *(G-19000)*
World Video Sales Co Inc................................G....... 610 754-6800
Bechtelsville *(G-1038)*
Wright Linear Pump Inc...................................G....... 724 695-0800
Oakdale *(G-12912)*
Xodus Medical Inc..G....... 724 337-5500
New Kensington *(G-12391)*
Xodus Medical Inc..E....... 724 337-5500
New Kensington *(G-12392)*
York Integra PA Inc..G....... 717 840-3438
York *(G-20743)*
Zynitech Medical Inc..G....... 610 592-0755
Exton *(G-5753)*

INSTRUMENTS: Meteorological

Warren Industries Incorporated...............G....... 215 464-9300
Philadelphia *(G-14458)*
Warren Industries Incorporated...............F....... 215 969-5011
Philadelphia *(G-14459)*

INSTRUMENTS: Microwave Test

Rfcircuits Inc..F....... 215 364-2450
Huntingdon Valley *(G-8029)*

INSTRUMENTS: Optical, Analytical

Cds Analytical LLC..G....... 610 932-3636
Oxford *(G-13074)*
Gatan Inc..D....... 724 779-2572
Warrendale *(G-19075)*
Structure Probe Inc..E....... 610 436-5400
West Chester *(G-19646)*

Vere Inc ....F 724 335-5530
New Kensington (G-12386)

INSTRUMENTS: Particle Size Analyzers

Delta Analytical Instruments ....G 412 372-0739
Trafford (G-18453)

INSTRUMENTS: Pressure Measurement, Indl

Avure Autoclave Systems Inc ....G 814 833-4331
Erie (G-5200)
Conflow Inc ....F 724 746-0200
Washington (G-19157)
Pdir Inc ....F 215 794-5011
Norristown (G-12701)
Vishay Precision Group Inc ....D 484 321-5300
Malvern (G-10343)

INSTRUMENTS: Radio Frequency Measuring

Inteligistics Inc ....G 412 826-0379
Pittsburgh (G-15132)
Vizinex LLC ....G 215 529-9440
Bethlehem (G-1652)

INSTRUMENTS: Seismographs

Geosonics Inc ....F 724 934-2900
Warrendale (G-19076)

INSTRUMENTS: Temperature Measurement, Indl

Freshtemp LLC ....G 844 370-1782
Pittsburgh (G-15038)
Heraeus Incorporated ....G 215 944-9981
Yardley (G-20314)
Process Instruments Inc ....E 412 431-4600
Pittsburgh (G-15451)
Psg Controls Inc ....D 215 257-3621
Philadelphia (G-14214)
Thermocouple Technology LLC ....E 215 529-9394
Quakertown (G-16252)
Tru Temp Sensors Inc ....G 215 396-1550
Southampton (G-17844)

INSTRUMENTS: Test, Digital, Electronic & Electrical Circuits

Hapeman Electronics Inc ....G 724 475-2033
Mercer (G-10962)
Industrial Instrs & Sups Inc ....F 215 396-0822
Wycombe (G-20260)
Oakwood Controls Corporation ....F 717 801-1515
Glen Rock (G-6458)
Optimum Controls Corporation ....D 610 375-0990
Reading (G-16459)

INSTRUMENTS: Test, Electrical, Engine

Ametek Inc ....D 610 647-2121
Berwyn (G-1351)

INSTRUMENTS: Test, Electronic & Electric Measurement

Bionix Safety Technologies ....G 610 408-0555
Wayne (G-19307)
Cygnus Technology Inc ....G 570 424-5701
Delaware Water Gap (G-4042)
Lehman Scientific LLC ....G 717 244-7540
Wrightsville (G-20241)
Link Group Inc ....E 215 957-6061
Warminster (G-18912)
Square Wheel Inc ....G 610 921-8561
Temple (G-18337)

INSTRUMENTS: Test, Electronic & Electrical Circuits

Advanced Avionics Inc ....F 215 441-0449
Warminster (G-18821)
Brynavon Group Inc ....G 610 525-2102
Villanova (G-18765)
Donart Electronics Inc ....G 724 796-3011
Mc Donald (G-10572)
Hannon Company ....G 724 266-2712
Ambridge (G-618)
K&S Interconnect Inc ....D 267 256-1725
Fort Washington (G-6078)

Testlink Corp ....G 267 743-2956
New Hope (G-12317)

INSTRUMENTS: Thermal Conductive, Indl

Westinghouse Plasma Corp ....F 724 722-7053
Mount Pleasant (G-11723)

INSTRUMENTS: Thermal Property Measurement

Climatic Testing Systems Inc ....E 215 773-9322
Hatfield (G-7326)
Reading Thermal Systems Inc ....G 610 678-5890
Reading (G-16492)
S P Industries Inc ....D 215 672-7800
Warminster (G-18959)

INSTRUMENTS: Transducers, Volts, Amperes, Watts, VARs & Freq

Columbia Research Labs Inc ....E 610 872-3900
Woodlyn (G-20218)
Sentech Inc ....F 215 887-8665
Glenside (G-6535)

INSULATING BOARD, CELLULAR FIBER

Erie Energy Products Inc ....F 814 454-2828
Erie (G-5266)

INSULATING BOARD, HARD PRESSED

Ipi Co Inc ....F 412 487-3995
Glenshaw (G-6491)

INSULATING COMPOUNDS

Paper and Ink of Pa LLC ....E 717 709-0533
Chambersburg (G-2967)

INSULATION & CUSHIONING FOAM: Polystyrene

Arctic Blast Covers ....E 724 213-8460
Indiana (G-8081)
Atlas Roofing Corporation ....E 717 760-5460
Camp Hill (G-2492)
Brd Noise & Vibration Ctrl Inc ....G 610 863-6300
Wind Gap (G-20167)
Carlisle Construction Mtls LLC ....E 724 564-5440
Smithfield (G-17645)
Carpenter Co ....G 610 366-5110
Allentown (G-163)
Carpenter Co ....G 610 366-8349
Allentown (G-164)
Carpenter Co ....D 610 366-5110
Fogelsville (G-5993)
Carpenter Co ....C 814 944-8612
Altoona (G-486)
Energy Innovation Ctr Inst Inc ....G 412 894-9800
Pittsburgh (G-14976)
G I S Inc ....F 412 771-8860
Mc Kees Rocks (G-10610)
Insul-Board Inc ....E 814 833-7400
Erie (G-5327)
Insulation Corporation America ....E 610 791-4200
Allentown (G-262)
Northeastern Foam and Fiber ....G 570 488-6859
Waymart (G-19288)
Sonoco Prtective Solutions Inc ....G 800 377-2692
Pittsburgh (G-15557)

INSULATION & ROOFING MATERIALS: Wood, Reconstituted

Applegate Insul Systems Inc ....E 717 709-0533
Chambersburg (G-2905)
New Heights LLC ....G 717 768-0070
Leola (G-9795)
Saint-Gobain Corporation ....A 610 893-6000
Malvern (G-10313)

INSULATION MATERIALS WHOLESALERS

G I S Inc ....F 412 771-8860
Mc Kees Rocks (G-10610)
Ipi Co Inc ....F 412 487-3995
Glenshaw (G-6491)
Lamtec Corporation ....C 570 897-8200
Mount Bethel (G-11611)

SMC Industries Inc ....G 610 647-5687
Malvern (G-10321)

INSULATION: Fiberglass

Certainteed Corporation ....B 570 474-6731
Mountain Top (G-11754)
Ica Inc ....F 610 377-6100
Lehighton (G-9716)
Mito Insulation Company ....E 724 335-8551
New Kensington (G-12359)
Molded Acstcal Pdts Easton Inc ....F 610 250-6738
Easton (G-4727)
Ohio Valley Indus Svcs Inc ....G 412 269-0020
Moon Township (G-11498)
Ohio Valley Indus Svcs Inc ....F 412 335-5237
Coraopolis (G-3708)
Owens Corning Sales LLC ....E 570 339-3374
Mount Carmel (G-11628)
Quanta Technologies Inc ....G 610 644-7101
Lancaster (G-9181)
Quiet Core Inc ....F 610 694-9190
Bethlehem (G-1606)
Saint-Gobain Delaware Corp ....G 610 341-7000
Valley Forge (G-18712)
Trinity Fibrgls Composites LLC ....G 412 855-3398
Carnegie (G-2798)

INSULATORS & INSULATION MATERIALS: Electrical

Bedford Materials Co Inc ....D 800 773-4276
Manns Choice (G-10408)
Carroll Manufacturing Co LLC ....G 724 266-0400
Leetsdale (G-9688)
Chase Corporation ....F 800 245-3209
Blawnox (G-1763)
Chase Corporation ....F 412 828-1500
Pittsburgh (G-14839)
Rochling Machined Plastics ....E 724 696-5200
Mount Pleasant (G-11717)
Specialty Products & Insul Co ....G 717 569-3900
East Petersburg (G-4590)

INSULATORS, GLASS MADE IN GLASS PLANTS: Electrical

Electro-Glass Products Inc ....E 724 423-5000
Norvelt (G-12878)

INSULATORS, PORCELAIN: Electrical

Associated Ceramics & Tech ....D 724 353-1585
Sarver (G-17065)
Dynamic Ceramics Inc ....E 724 353-9527
Sarver (G-17068)

INSURANCE AGENTS, NEC

Burrell Group Inc ....F 724 337-3557
New Kensington (G-12328)

INSURANCE BROKERS, NEC

Kajevi Services LLC ....G 215 722-0711
Philadelphia (G-13920)

INSURANCE CARRIERS: Life

Kyles Auto Tags & Insurance ....G 610 429-1447
West Chester (G-19585)

INSURANCE CARRIERS: Property & Casualty

Fetterolf Group Inc ....G 814 443-4688
Somerset (G-17688)
Woodbine Properties ....C 814 443-4688
Somerset (G-17718)

INSURANCE: Agents, Brokers & Service

Altus Group Inc ....F 215 977-9900
Philadelphia (G-13374)
Pagnotti Enterprises Inc ....E 570 825-8700
Wilkes Barre (G-19954)
Snyder County Times ....G 570 837-6065
Middleburg (G-11041)

INTEGRATED CIRCUITS, SEMICONDUCTOR NETWORKS, ETC

H & M Net Works ....F 484 344-2161
Blue Bell (G-1832)
Microsemi Stor Solutions Inc ....E 610 289-5200
Allentown (G-316)
R & E International Inc.........................F 610 664-5637
Merion Station (G-10998)
Rose Network Solutions.......................G 610 563-1958
Honey Brook (G-7759)

INTERCOMMUNICATIONS SYSTEMS: Electric

Acra Control Inc ....G 714 382-1863
Newtown (G-12494)
Ballistic Applications..........................F 724 282-0416
East Butler (G-4530)
Business Cmmunications Systems ......G 610 827-7061
Chester Springs (G-3073)
Comtrol International...........................E 724 864-3800
Irwin (G-8149)
Ecomm Life Safety Systems LLC........G 215 953-5858
Ivyland (G-8210)
Infinera Corporation ....G 408 572-5200
Allentown (G-259)
Orion Systems Inc ....E 215 346-8200
Huntingdon Valley (G-8019)
Orlotronics Corporation ....E 610 239-8200
Bridgeport (G-2042)

INTERIOR DECORATING SVCS

2820 Associates Inc ....G 412 471-2525
Pittsburgh (G-14625)

INTERIOR DESIGN SVCS, NEC

Charles Ginty Associates Inc ....G 610 347-1101
Unionville (G-18647)
Crawford Dzignes Inc ....G 724 872-4644
West Newton (G-19750)
Parabo Press LLC ....G 484 843-1230
Philadelphia (G-14118)

INTERIOR DESIGNING SVCS

Bahdeebahdu ....G 215 627-5002
Philadelphia (G-13441)
Eye Design LLC.................................E 610 409-1900
Trappe (G-18468)
G Case Inc ....G 717 737-5000
Mechanicsburg (G-10847)
Helene Batoff Interiors ....G 215 879-7727
Philadelphia (G-13812)
Martins Draperies & Interiors...............G 717 239-0501
Lancaster (G-9125)
Michael Dahma Associates..................G 412 607-1151
Irwin (G-8183)
Richard J Summons Sculpture..............G 610 223-9013
Reading (G-16497)

INTERIOR REPAIR SVCS

Baxter Group Inc...............................F 717 263-7341
Chambersburg (G-2909)
Warren Installations Inc ....F 717 517-9321
Lancaster (G-9235)
Willow Grove Auto Top Inc...................G 215 659-3276
Willow Grove (G-20150)

INVENTOR

Warners Innvtive Solutions Inc ....F 814 201-2429
Altoona (G-557)

INVERTERS: Nonrotating Electrical

Alencon Systems LLC.........................G 610 825-7094
Plymouth Meeting (G-15829)
Myers Power Products Inc ....D 610 868-3500
Bethlehem (G-1576)

INVERTERS: Rotating Electrical

Go2power LLC ....E 215 244-4202
Feasterville Trevose (G-5913)
Solaris Select ....G 267 987-2082
Morrisville (G-11582)

INVESTMENT FUNDS, NEC

Alpha Sintered Metals LLC ....C 814 773-3191
Ridgway (G-16694)

INVESTMENT FUNDS: Open-Ended

Morningstar Credit Ratings LLC............E 800 299-1665
Horsham (G-7833)

INVESTMENT RESEARCH SVCS

Robindale Export LLC ....B 724 879-4264
Latrobe (G-9517)

INVESTORS: Real Estate, Exc Property Operators

Galeron Consulting LLC.......................E 267 293-9230
Bensalem (G-1202)
Millcraft Industries Inc.........................F 724 229-8800
Washington (G-19205)

IRON & STEEL PRDTS: Hot-Rolled

Morgardshammar Inc ....G 724 778-5400
Cranberry Township (G-3837)
Olympic Steel Inc ....E 717 709-1515
Chambersburg (G-2966)
Rolled Steel Products Corp PA..............G 610 647-6264
Berwyn (G-1374)
Standard Iron Works...........................G 570 347-2058
Scranton (G-17293)

IRON ORE BENEFICIATING

Mountaineer Mining Corporation ....G 814 445-5806
Berlin (G-1291)

IRON ORE MINING

Thyssnkrupp Indus Slutions USA ....D 412 257-8277
Bridgeville (G-2095)

IRON ORES

Horlacher & Sherwood ....G 570 836-6298
Tunkhannock (G-18539)
Norton Oglebay Company.....................F 412 995-5500
Pittsburgh (G-15347)

IRON OXIDES

Bailey Oxides LLC ....G 724 745-9500
Canonsburg (G-2548)
PVS Steel Services Inc ....C 412 929-0177
Pittsburgh (G-15458)

IRRADIATION EQPT: Gamma Ray

American Access Care Holdings...........G 717 235-0181
Malvern (G-10183)
American Access Care Intermedi..........G 717 235-0181
Malvern (G-10184)
Gamma Irradiator Service LLC ....G 570 925-5681
Benton (G-1280)

JACKETS: Indl, Metal Plate

F R Industries Inc...............................F 412 242-5903
Pittsburgh (G-14999)

JACKS: Hydraulic

Airtek Inc..E 412 351-3837
Irwin (G-8141)
D L Martin Co.....................................C 717 328-2141
Mercersburg (G-10984)

JANITORIAL & CUSTODIAL SVCS

B & T Contractors Inc ....C 814 368-7199
Bradford (G-1956)
Laurel Holdings Inc.............................G 814 533-5777
Johnstown (G-8402)

JANITORIAL EQPT & SPLYS WHOLESALERS

Clarkson Chemical Company Inc..........G 570 323-3631
Williamsport (G-20000)
Lap Distributors Inc ....G 215 744-4000
Philadelphia (G-13955)

JARS: Plastic

Qtd Plastics Inc ....E 814 724-1641
Meadville (G-10784)

JEWELERS' FINDINGS & MATERIALS: Bearings, Synthetic

Aurele M Gatti Inc ....G 215 428-4500
Fairless Hills (G-5772)

JEWELERS' FINDINGS/MTRLS: Gem Prep, Settings, Real/Imitation

E R Kinley & Sons..............................G 570 323-6740
Williamsport (G-20008)
Metal Crafters Inc..............................G 215 491-9925
Warrington (G-19126)

JEWELRY & PRECIOUS STONES WHOLESALERS

Dein-Verbit Associates Inc ....F 610 649-9674
Ardmore (G-707)
Dernier Cree Inc ....G 917 287-7452
Shavertown (G-17480)

JEWELRY APPAREL

A Jacoby & Company ....G 610 828-0500
Conshohocken (G-3515)
Alex and Ani LLC ....G 412 367-1362
Pittsburgh (G-14672)
Norman Kivitz Co Inc...........................E 215 922-3038
Philadelphia (G-14078)

JEWELRY FINDINGS & LAPIDARY WORK

David I Helfer Inc................................G 412 281-6734
Pittsburgh (G-14907)
Keystone Findings Inc.........................D 215 723-4600
Telford (G-18299)
Meighen Jinjou ....G 717 846-5600
York (G-20585)
White Light Productions ....F 610 518-0644
Downingtown (G-4264)

JEWELRY REPAIR SVCS

David I Helfer Inc................................G 412 281-6734
Pittsburgh (G-14907)
Dutcher Brothers Inc ....G 215 922-4555
Philadelphia (G-13652)
J & D Jewelers Inc ....F 215 592-8956
Philadelphia (G-13880)
Janette Jewelers ....G 717 632-9478
Hanover (G-6908)
Jo-An Inc...G 610 664-8777
Bala Cynwyd (G-883)
Marc Williams Goldsmith Inc ....G 570 322-4248
Williamsport (G-20040)
Stonebraker John ....G 724 238-6466
Ligonier (G-9966)

JEWELRY STORES

Addies Inc...G 570 748-2966
Lock Haven (G-10081)
C & G Wilcox Engrv & Images ....G 570 265-3621
Towanda (G-18422)
G C Wyant Ltd ....G 724 357-8000
Indiana (G-8101)
Goldcrafters Corner ....G 717 412-4616
Harrisburg (G-7134)
Marshall Woodworks Ltd ....F 412 321-1685
Pittsburgh (G-15257)
Meighen Jinjou ....G 717 846-5600
York (G-20585)
Newell Brands Inc ....G 814 278-6771
State College (G-17997)
Robert H Berenson ....G 610 642-9380
Haverford (G-7414)
Simons Bros Company ....F 215 426-9901
Philadelphia (G-14308)
Stonebraker John ....G 724 238-6466
Ligonier (G-9966)

JEWELRY STORES: Precious Stones & Precious Metals

Bella Turka Inc...................................G 215 560-8733
Philadelphia (G-13452)

PRODUCT

C Leslie Smith Inc .... E 610 439-8833
Allentown (G-160)

David Craig Jewelers Ltd .... G 215 968-8900
Langhorne (G-9289)

E R Kinley & Sons .... G 570 323-6740
Williamsport (G-20008)

Fensemaker John .... G 215 572-1444
Glenside (G-6517)

Hope Paige Designs LLC .... E 610 234-0093
Conshohocken (G-3558)

J & D Jewelers Inc .... F 215 592-8956
Philadelphia (G-13880)

Jan & Dans Jewelry .... G 814 452-3336
Erie (G-5334)

Janette Jewelers .... G 717 632-9478
Hanover (G-6908)

Jo-An Inc .... G 610 664-8777
Bala Cynwyd (G-883)

Marc Williams Goldsmith Inc .... G 570 322-4248
Williamsport (G-20040)

My Jewel Shop Inc .... G 215 887-3881
Jenkintown (G-8297)

N Barsky & Sons .... F 215 925-8639
Philadelphia (G-14050)

T Foster & Co Inc .... G 215 493-1044
Yardley (G-20343)

Uniquely Diamonds .... G 610 356-5025
Newtown Square (G-12596)

JEWELRY STORES: Silverware

Rothrocks Silversmiths Inc .... G 570 253-1990
Honesdale (G-7722)

JEWELRY, PRECIOUS METAL: Bracelets

N Barsky & Sons .... F 215 925-8639
Philadelphia (G-14050)

JEWELRY, PRECIOUS METAL: Cigar & Cigarette Access

Roll Your Own .... G 215 420-7441
Hatboro (G-7302)

JEWELRY, PRECIOUS METAL: Mountings & Trimmings

Colucci and Co .... G 717 243-5562
Boiling Springs (G-1873)

JEWELRY, PRECIOUS METAL: Pearl, Natural Or Cultured

Helm & Hahn Co Inc .... G 412 854-4367
Pittsburgh (G-15089)

Jo-An Inc .... G 610 664-8777
Bala Cynwyd (G-883)

Paul F Rothstein Inc .... F 215 884-4720
Glenside (G-6532)

JEWELRY, PRECIOUS METAL: Pins

Casting Headquarters Inc .... G 215 922-2278
Philadelphia (G-13511)

Dexter Rosettes Inc .... G 215 542-0118
Gwynedd Valley (G-6815)

JEWELRY, PRECIOUS METAL: Rings, Finger

Herff Jones LLC .... F 215 638-2490
Bensalem (G-1210)

Herff Jones LLC .... G 717 697-0649
Mechanicsburg (G-10852)

Jostens Inc .... B 814 237-5771
State College (G-17981)

Superfit Inc .... F 215 391-4380
Philadelphia (G-14357)

JEWELRY, PRECIOUS METAL: Settings & Mountings

J & D Jewelers Inc .... F 215 592-8956
Philadelphia (G-13880)

Lagos Inc .... D 215 925-1693
Philadelphia (G-13950)

T Foster & Co Inc .... G 215 493-1044
Yardley (G-20343)

JEWELRY, WHOLESALE

Hope Paige Designs LLC .... E 610 234-0093
Conshohocken (G-3558)

Jan & Dans Jewelry .... G 814 452-3336
Erie (G-5334)

Katz Imports Inc .... G 215 238-0197
Philadelphia (G-13923)

Meighen Jinjou .... G 717 846-5600
York (G-20585)

Robert H Berenson .... G 610 642-9380
Haverford (G-7414)

T Foster & Co Inc .... G 215 493-1044
Yardley (G-20343)

JEWELRY: Decorative, Fashion & Costume

Becker Fashion Tech LLC .... G 215 776-2589
Philadelphia (G-13450)

Bg Jewelry .... G 610 691-0687
Bethlehem (G-1464)

Pardees Jewelry & Accessories ...... G 814 282-1172
Meadville (G-10774)

Sandys Fashion Jewelry LLC .... G 814 938-4356
Punxsutawney (G-16161)

Sorrelli Inc .... F 610 894-9857
Kutztown (G-8861)

Swarovski North America Ltd .... G 412 833-3708
Pittsburgh (G-15593)

Swarovski North America Ltd .... G 215 752-3198
Langhorne (G-9327)

Swarovski Retail Ventures Ltd .... G 215 659-3649
Willow Grove (G-20145)

Swarovski US Holding Limited .... G 610 992-9661
King of Prussia (G-8683)

JEWELRY: Precious Metal

Al May Manufacturing Jewelers ...... G 412 391-8736
Bethel Park (G-1401)

Alex and Ani LLC .... G 412 742-4968
Pittsburgh (G-14671)

Armadani Inc .... G 215 627-2601
Philadelphia (G-13412)

Bella Turka Inc .... G 215 560-8733
Philadelphia (G-13452)

Body Gems .... G 215 357-9552
Feasterville Trevose (G-5891)

Brown Industries Inc .... E 610 544-8888
Media (G-10916)

Byard F Brogan Inc .... F 215 885-3550
Glenside (G-6510)

C Leslie Smith Inc .... E 610 439-8833
Allentown (G-160)

Courtney Metal Design .... G 610 932-6065
Lincoln University (G-9973)

David Craig Jewelers Ltd .... G 215 968-8900
Langhorne (G-9289)

Dutcher Brothers Inc .... G 215 922-4555
Philadelphia (G-13652)

E R Kinley & Sons .... G 570 323-6740
Williamsport (G-20008)

Fensemaker John .... G 215 572-1444
Glenside (G-6517)

G C Wyant Ltd .... G 724 357-8000
Indiana (G-8101)

G D C Manufacturing Inc .... G 724 864-5000
Irwin (G-8163)

Goldcrafters Corner .... G 717 412-4616
Harrisburg (G-7134)

Golden Specialties Ltd .... G 717 273-9731
Lebanon (G-9575)

Herff Jones LLC .... F 717 526-4373
Harrisburg (G-7148)

Hersh Imports Inc .... G 215 627-1128
Philadelphia (G-13821)

International Mfg Corp .... F 215 925-7558
Philadelphia (G-13866)

Jan & Dans Jewelry .... G 814 452-3336
Erie (G-5334)

Janette Jewelers .... G 717 632-9478
Hanover (G-6908)

Katz Imports Inc .... G 215 238-0197
Philadelphia (G-13923)

Larry Paul Casting Co Inc .... G 215 928-1644
Philadelphia (G-13958)

Leon Miller & Company Ltd .... F 412 281-8498
Pittsburgh (G-15224)

Levine Design Incorporated .... G 412 288-0220
Pittsburgh (G-15226)

M B Mumma Inc .... G 610 372-6962
Reading (G-16435)

Majestic Creations Inc .... G 215 968-5411
Southampton (G-17824)

Marc Williams Goldsmith Inc .... G 570 322-4248
Williamsport (G-20040)

Marilyn Cohen Designs .... G 610 664-6219
Penn Valley (G-13237)

Maximal Art Inc .... G 484 840-0600
Philadelphia (G-13997)

Meighen Jinjou .... G 717 846-5600
York (G-20585)

My Jewel Shop Inc .... G 215 887-3881
Jenkintown (G-8297)

Nexus Inc .... G 412 391-2444
Pittsburgh (G-15336)

O C Tanner Company .... G 610 458-1245
Chester Springs (G-3083)

Paul Morelli Design Inc .... F 215 922-7392
Philadelphia (G-14125)

RBS Impex Inc .... G 412 566-2488
Pittsburgh (G-15471)

Rubertones Casting Division .... G 215 922-1314
Philadelphia (G-14262)

Ruud Kahle Master Goldsmith .... F 215 947-5050
Huntingdon Valley (G-8032)

Semi-Mounts Inc .... G 412 422-7988
Pittsburgh (G-15522)

Simons Bros Company .... F 215 426-9901
Philadelphia (G-14308)

Stonebraker John .... G 724 238-6466
Ligonier (G-9966)

Uniquely Diamonds .... G 610 356-5025
Newtown Square (G-12596)

JIGS & FIXTURES

Alvord-Polk Inc .... F 717 692-2128
Millersburg (G-11189)

Mitchell Apx Machine Shop Inc ...... G 717 597-2157
Greencastle (G-6623)

JIGS: Welding Positioners

General Welding & Machine Co .... G 570 889-3776
Ringtown (G-16753)

JOB PRINTING & NEWSPAPER PUBLISHING COMBINED

Advance Publications .... F 717 582-4305
New Bloomfield (G-12029)

Advance Publications .... F 717 436-8206
Mifflintown (G-11108)

Franklin Penn Publishing Co .... F 724 327-3471
Murrysville (G-11851)

Johnsonburg Press Inc .... G 814 965-2503
Johnsonburg (G-8347)

McLean Publishing Co .... F 814 275-3131
New Bethlehem (G-12027)

Morrisons Cove Herald Inc .... G 814 793-2144
Martinsburg (G-10527)

Wysocki-Cole Enterprises Inc .... E 724 567-5656
Vandergrift (G-18738)

JOB TRAINING & VOCATIONAL REHABILITATION SVCS

Achieva .... D 412 221-6609
Bridgeville (G-2052)

Blind and Vision Rehab .... D 412 368-4400
Pittsburgh (G-14771)

Cambria County Asso .... B 814 536-3531
Johnstown (G-8360)

Cambria County Asso .... C 814 472-5077
Ebensburg (G-4782)

Parc Productions .... G 724 283-3300
Butler (G-2431)

Tripwire Operations Group LLC ...... G 717 648-2792
Gettysburg (G-6319)

JOB TRAINING SVCS

Achieva .... F 412 391-4660
Pittsburgh (G-14641)

JOINTS & COUPLINGS

Certainteed Gypsum Mfg Inc .... E 813 286-3900
Wayne (G-19312)

JOINTS: Expansion

Cherry Steel Corp ....F...... 215 340-2239
Doylestown (G-4291)
Dynamic Surfc Applications Ltd ....E...... 570 546-6041
Pennsdale (G-13262)
Eagle Far East Inc ....E...... 215 957-9333
Warminster (G-18866)
J B Booth and Co ....F...... 724 452-8400
Zelienople (G-20805)

JOINTS: Expansion, Pipe

Flexible Compensators Inc ....F...... 610 837-3812
Bath (G-959)

JOISTS: Long-Span Series, Open Web Steel

Allegheny Strl Components Inc ....G...... 724 867-1100
Emlenton (G-5005)
C M C Steel Fabricators Inc ....C...... 570 568-6761
New Columbia (G-12173)
Energy Control Systems Inc ....E...... 412 781-8500
Pittsburgh (G-14974)

KAOLIN & BALL CLAY MINING

Resco Group Inc ....F...... 412 494-4491
Pittsburgh (G-15479)
Stephens Excavating Svc LLC ....G...... 484 888-1010
Kennett Square (G-8545)

KEYBOARDS: Computer Or Office Machine

Gc Enterprises LLC ....G...... 570 655-5543
Pittston (G-15752)
Northern Winding Inc ....G...... 724 776-4983
Mars (G-10509)

KEYS, KEY BLANKS

Keys Wholesale Distributors ....G...... 610 626-4787
Broomall (G-2291)

KEYS: Machine

Standard Horse Nail Corp ....F...... 724 846-4660
New Brighton (G-12043)

KILNS & FURNACES: Ceramic

Ceramic Services Inc ....G...... 215 245-4040
Bensalem (G-1166)

KILNS: Calcining

Thermtrend Inc ....G...... 215 752-0711
Bensalem (G-1260)

KITCHEN & COOKING ARTICLES: Pottery

Metalzed Ceramics For Elec Inc ....F...... 724 287-5752
East Butler (G-4535)
R A S Industries Inc ....E...... 215 541-4627
Pennsburg (G-13254)
Robin Morris ....G...... 814 395-9555
Confluence (G-3469)

KITCHEN CABINET STORES, EXC CUSTOM

Casework Cabinetry Cnstr ....G...... 814 236-7601
Curwensville (G-3947)
Joseph Mikstas ....G...... 215 271-2419
Philadelphia (G-13911)
Kabinet Koncepts Inc ....G...... 724 327-7737
Murrysville (G-11854)
Kitchen Express Inc ....F...... 570 693-0285
Wyoming (G-20281)
Lancaster Maid Cabinets Inc ....F...... 717 336-0111
Reinholds (G-16635)
North Country Woodworking Inc ....G...... 570 549-8105
Mansfield (G-10422)
Steigrwalds Kitchens Baths Inc ....F...... 724 458-0280
Grove City (G-6804)

KITCHEN CABINETS WHOLESALERS

Bhagyas Kitchen ....G...... 215 233-1587
Glenside (G-6508)
Big Valley Cabinets ....G...... 717 935-2788
Belleville (G-1127)
Desavino & Sons Inc ....E...... 570 383-3988
Olyphant (G-12988)
Desmond Wholesale Distrs Inc ....F...... 215 225-0300
Philadelphia (G-13623)

Fine Line Homes ....F...... 717 561-2040
Harrisburg (G-7129)
Infinite Quest Cabinetry Corp ....G...... 301 222-3592
Red Lion (G-16601)
Kitchens By Meade Inc ....F...... 814 453-4888
Erie (G-5345)
Mario Dinardo Jr Custom WD Wkg ....G...... 610 495-7010
Pottstown (G-16015)
REA Jobber Inc ....G...... 814 226-9552
Clarion (G-3186)
Signature Custom Cabinetry Inc ....C...... 717 738-4884
Ephrata (G-5140)
Sykes-Scholtz-Collins Lbr Inc ....E...... 610 494-2700
Chester (G-3066)
William Cottage ....G...... 724 266-2961
Ambridge (G-639)

KITCHEN UTENSILS: Wooden

Chef Specialties Inc ....E...... 814 887-5652
Smethport (G-17633)
Infinite Quest Cabinetry Corp ....G...... 301 222-3592
Red Lion (G-16601)
Spectra Inc ....E...... 814 238-6332
State College (G-18030)
Spoonwood Inc ....G...... 610 756-6464
Kempton (G-8495)
Thomas Pennise Jr ....G...... 215 822-1832
Colmar (G-3421)

KITCHENWARE STORES

Pfaltzgraff Factory Stores Inc ....B...... 717 848-5500
York (G-20626)
Terrain Merchandising LLC ....F...... 310 709-8784
Philadelphia (G-14382)
Vistappliances ....G...... 215 600-1232
Morrisville (G-11587)

KITCHENWARE: Plastic

Newmetro Design LLC ....G...... 814 696-2550
Duncansville (G-4457)
Rwb Special Services Corp ....F...... 215 766-4800
Pipersville (G-14619)

KNIT GOODS, WHOLESALE

El-Ana Collection Inc ....F...... 215 953-8820
Huntingdon Valley (G-7977)

KNIVES: Agricultural Or indl

Cutting Edge Knives Inc ....E...... 412 279-9350
Pittsburgh (G-14898)
Diatome U S Joint Venture ....G...... 215 646-1478
Hatfield (G-7334)
Lion Industrial Knife Co Inc ....G...... 717 244-8195
Red Lion (G-16605)
York Saw & Knife Company Inc ....E...... 717 767-6402
Emigsville (G-5003)

LABELS: Cotton, Printed

Holly Label Company Inc ....E...... 570 222-9000
Nicholson (G-12615)

LABELS: Paper, Made From Purchased Materials

East-West Label Co Inc ....E...... 610 825-0410
Conshohocken (G-3540)
Fox IV Technologies Inc ....E...... 724 387-3500
Export (G-5603)
Industrial Nameplate Inc ....E...... 215 322-1111
Warminster (G-18898)
Keebar Enterprises Inc ....G...... 610 873-0150
West Chester (G-19579)
Labelcom ....G...... 814 362-3252
Bradford (G-1978)
Lemac Packaging Inc ....G...... 814 453-7652
Erie (G-5361)
McCourt Label Cabinet Company ....D...... 800 458-2390
Lewis Run (G-9877)
Mri Flexible Packaging Company ....F...... 215 860-7676
Newtown (G-12525)
National Imprint Corporation ....E...... 814 239-8141
Claysburg (G-3205)
Peerless Paper Specialty Inc ....G...... 215 657-3460
Willow Grove (G-20133)
Taba Labels Company ....G...... 215 455-9977
Philadelphia (G-14366)

Tagline Inc ....G...... 610 594-9300
Exton (G-5735)
Tech Tag & Label Inc ....F...... 215 822-2400
Hatfield (G-7398)
Trautman Associates Inc ....F...... 570 743-0430
Shamokin Dam (G-17429)

LABOR UNION

Sheet Metal Wkrs Local Un 19 ....G...... 215 952-1999
Philadelphia (G-14299)

LABORATORIES, TESTING: Forensic

Gerson Associates PC ....E...... 215 637-6800
Philadelphia (G-13759)

LABORATORIES, TESTING: Metallurgical

Laboratory Testing Inc ....C...... 215 997-9080
Hatfield (G-7361)
Modern Industries Inc ....F...... 814 885-8514
Kersey (G-8564)
Modern Industries Inc ....C...... 814 455-8061
Erie (G-5394)
North American Hoganas Company ....B...... 814 479-3500
Hollsopple (G-7658)

LABORATORIES, TESTING: Pollution

Myexposome Inc ....G...... 610 668-0145
Philadelphia (G-14049)

LABORATORIES, TESTING: Product Testing

Techsource Engineering Inc ....G...... 814 459-2150
Erie (G-5505)

LABORATORIES, TESTING: Product Testing, Safety/Performance

Advanced Solutions Network LLC ....F...... 814 464-0791
Erie (G-5175)
B G M Fastener Co Inc ....E...... 570 253-5046
Honesdale (G-7701)
Dyna East Corporation ....E...... 610 270-9900
King of Prussia (G-8614)

LABORATORIES: Biological Research

Biorealize Inc ....G...... 610 216-5554
Philadelphia (G-13466)
Frontage Laboratories Inc ....C...... 610 232-0100
Exton (G-5682)
Nabriva Therapeutics Us Inc ....F...... 610 816-6640
King of Prussia (G-8653)
Venatorx Pharmaceuticals Inc ....G...... 610 644-8935
Malvern (G-10339)

LABORATORIES: Biotechnology

Aevi Genomic Medicine Inc ....F...... 610 254-4201
Wayne (G-19294)
Immunotope Inc ....G...... 215 489-4945
Doylestown (G-4307)
Integrated Tech Svcs Intl LLC ....F...... 814 262-7332
Johnstown (G-8382)
Nurture Inc ....G...... 610 989-0945
Devon (G-4114)
Steq America LLC ....G...... 267 644-5477
Doylestown (G-4339)

LABORATORIES: Dental

Northeast Dental Laboratories ....G...... 215 725-0950
Elkins Park (G-4909)
Sentage Corporation ....D...... 412 431-3353
Pittsburgh (G-15525)

LABORATORIES: Dental & Medical X-Ray

Sodium Systems LLC ....F...... 800 821-8962
York (G-20671)

LABORATORIES: Dental Orthodontic Appliance Production

Harbor Orthodontic Services ....G...... 724 654-3599
New Castle (G-12099)
RED Orthodontic Lab ....G...... 610 237-1100
Kennett Square (G-8539)

PRODUCT

LABORATORIES: Dental, Artificial Teeth Production

Conicella-Fessler Dental Lab..................G...... 610 622-3298
Drexel Hill *(G-4362)*

LABORATORIES: Dental, Denture Production

J R Ramos Dental Lab Inc..................G...... 717 272-5821
Lebanon *(G-9584)*

Jasinski Dental Lab Inc ....E...... 215 699-8861
Lansdale *(G-9379)*

LABORATORIES: Electronic Research

Advanced Technology Labs Inc ....B...... 215 355-8111
Richboro *(G-16673)*

Combat Arms LLC ....G...... 412 245-0824
Carlisle *(G-2702)*

Electronic Prototype Dev Inc ....E...... 412 767-4111
Natrona Heights *(G-11941)*

Tecnomasium Inc....................................F...... 412 264-7364
Coraopolis *(G-3727)*

LABORATORIES: Medical

Chiltern International Inc.......................E...... 484 679-2400
King of Prussia *(G-8592)*

Hamot Imaging Facility...........................F...... 814 877-5381
Erie *(G-5309)*

LABORATORIES: Medical Bacteriological

Biorealize Inc..G...... 610 216-5554
Philadelphia *(G-13466)*

LABORATORIES: Noncommercial Research

Pulsemetrics LLC....................................G...... 412 656-5776
Allison Park *(G-460)*

LABORATORIES: Physical Research, Commercial

Advanced Cooling Tech Inc ....D...... 717 208-2612
Lancaster *(G-8921)*

Aural Harmonics ....F...... 610 488-0232
Bernville *(G-1297)*

Biomagnetic Solutions LLC ....G...... 814 689-1801
State College *(G-17945)*

Converging Sciences Tech Inc ....G...... 215 626-5705
Warminster *(G-18847)*

Cyberscan Technologies Inc ....G...... 215 321-0447
Washington Crossing *(G-19256)*

Envirodyne Systems Inc ....E...... 717 763-0500
Camp Hill *(G-2496)*

Frontida Biopharm Inc............................E...... 215 288-6500
Philadelphia *(G-13728)*

Health-Chem Corporation ....D...... 717 764-1191
Emigsville *(G-4988)*

Led Living Technologies Inc ....E...... 215 633-1558
Bristol *(G-2158)*

Lockhart Chemical Company ....E...... 724 444-1900
Gibsonia *(G-6344)*

Lyondell Chemical Company ....D...... 610 359-2360
Newtown Square *(G-12583)*

Onconova Therapeutics Inc ....F...... 267 759-3680
Newtown *(G-12532)*

Opertech Bio Inc ....G...... 215 456-8765
Philadelphia *(G-14098)*

PPG Industries Inc ....E...... 412 487-4500
Allison Park *(G-459)*

PQ Corporation ....D...... 610 651-4600
Conshohocken *(G-3591)*

Re2 Inc ....E...... 412 681-6382
Pittsburgh *(G-15472)*

Rex Medical Inc ....E...... 610 940-0665
Conshohocken *(G-3600)*

Synchrgnix Info Strategies Inc ....G...... 302 892-4800
Malvern *(G-10325)*

Technicolor Usa Inc ....C...... 717 295-6100
Lancaster *(G-9214)*

Telefactor Robotics LLC.........................G...... 610 940-6040
Conshohocken *(G-3611)*

LABORATORIES: Testing

Almac Central Management LLC...........C...... 215 660-8500
Souderton *(G-17721)*

Lifewatch Services Inc ....B...... 847 720-2100
Malvern *(G-10269)*

Toxicity Asssssors Globl PA LLC...........G...... 215 921-6972
Philadelphia *(G-14401)*

LABORATORIES: Testing

Advanced Welding Tech Inc ....E...... 814 899-3584
Erie *(G-5176)*

Alliance Contract Pharma LLC ....F...... 215 256-5920
Harleysville *(G-7017)*

American Engineers Group LLC ....G...... 484 920-8010
Phoenixville *(G-14527)*

Cima Labs Inc ....D...... 763 488-4700
North Wales *(G-12795)*

Electro-Tech Systems Inc ....E...... 215 887-2196
Glenside *(G-6515)*

Ideal Aerosmith Inc................................E...... 412 963-1495
Pittsburgh *(G-15113)*

J R Peters Inc ....E...... 610 395-7104
Allentown *(G-267)*

Koppers Industries Inc ....E...... 412 826-3970
Pittsburgh *(G-15190)*

Lawrie Technology Inc ....G...... 814 402-1208
Girard *(G-6396)*

Prl Industries Inc ....E...... 717 273-6787
Cornwall *(G-3740)*

Salimetrics LLC ....E...... 814 234-7748
State College *(G-18019)*

Spectrodyne Inc ....F...... 215 804-1044
Quakertown *(G-16246)*

Srm-Avant Inc...G...... 724 537-0300
Greensburg *(G-6716)*

Watermark Usa LLC...............................F...... 610 983-0500
Gladwyne *(G-6409)*

LABORATORY APPARATUS & FURNITURE

Ajikabe Inc..G...... 484 424-9415
Holland *(G-7639)*

Applied Magnetics Lab Inc.....................G...... 717 430-2774
York *(G-20381)*

Applied Separations Inc ....E...... 610 770-0900
Allentown *(G-141)*

Applied Test Systems LLC ....E...... 724 283-1212
Butler *(G-2375)*

Boekel Industries Inc.............................E...... 215 396-8200
Feasterville Trevose *(G-5892)*

Brady Instruments ....G...... 717 453-7171
Lykens *(G-10130)*

Diversified Modular Casework...............G...... 484 442-8007
Media *(G-10922)*

Euthanex Corporation ....F...... 610 559-0159
Bethlehem *(G-1505)*

Eye Design LLC ....E...... 610 409-1900
Trappe *(G-18468)*

Hamilton L Fisher L C ....G...... 412 490-8300
Pittsburgh *(G-15075)*

HB Instrment Div Bel-Art Produ ....G...... 610 489-5500
Trappe *(G-18470)*

S P Industries Inc ....E...... 215 396-2200
Warminster *(G-18958)*

S P Industries Inc ....D...... 215 672-7800
Warminster *(G-18959)*

T B W Industries Inc ....F...... 215 794-8070
Furlong *(G-6234)*

Tech Equipment Sales Inc......................E...... 610 279-0370
Norristown *(G-12716)*

Thermo Hypersil-Keystone LLC ....E...... 814 353-2300
Bellefonte *(G-1121)*

Thoren Industries Inc ....F...... 570 454-3514
Hazleton *(G-7530)*

Towerview Health Inc.............................G...... 715 771-9831
Philadelphia *(G-14400)*

VWR Corporation ....C...... 610 386-1700
Radnor *(G-16304)*

VWR Scientific Inc ....G...... 412 487-1983
Allison Park *(G-466)*

LABORATORY APPARATUS & FURNITURE: Worktables

Vere Inc ....F...... 724 335-5530
New Kensington *(G-12386)*

LABORATORY APPARATUS, EXC HEATING & MEASURING

Burrell Scientific LLC ....F...... 412 747-2111
Pittsburgh *(G-14797)*

Leco Corporation ....E...... 814 355-7903
Bellefonte *(G-1107)*

Tbj Incorporated....................................F...... 717 261-9700
Chambersburg *(G-2984)*

Verder Scientific Inc..............................F...... 267 757-0351
Newtown *(G-12559)*

LABORATORY APPARATUS: Calibration Tapes, Phy Testing Mach

Jrt Calibration Services Inc...................G...... 610 327-9610
Pottstown *(G-16006)*

LABORATORY APPARATUS: Dryers

American Lyophilizer Inc ....F...... 610 999-4151
Yardley *(G-20295)*

LABORATORY APPARATUS: Particle Size Reduction

Powdersize LLC ....E...... 215 536-5605
Quakertown *(G-16231)*

LABORATORY APPARATUS: Physics, NEC

Base Lab Tools Inc ....G...... 570 371-5710
Stroudsburg *(G-18107)*

Blue Spin LLC ....G...... 814 863-4630
Boalsburg *(G-1864)*

LABORATORY APPARATUS: Sample Preparation Apparatus

Mdi Membrane Technologies Inc..........G...... 717 412-0943
Harrisburg *(G-7175)*

LABORATORY APPARATUS: Time Interval Measuring, Electric

Oakwood Controls Corporation ....F...... 717 801-1515
Glen Rock *(G-6458)*

LABORATORY CHEMICALS: Organic

3 Prime LLC..G...... 610 459-3468
Aston *(G-747)*

Astatech Inc..E...... 215 785-3197
Bristol *(G-2110)*

Connective Tssue Gene Tsts LLC ....F...... 484 244-2900
Allentown *(G-176)*

Elf Atochem ....G...... 215 826-2600
Bristol *(G-2140)*

Fisher Scientific Company LLC..............B...... 724 517-1500
Pittsburgh *(G-15019)*

Liquid Ion Solutions LLC ....G...... 412 275-0919
Pittsburgh *(G-15235)*

Uct LLC ....E...... 215 781-9255
Bristol *(G-2214)*

Vertellus DWG LLC ....B...... 800 344-3426
Delaware Water Gap *(G-4044)*

LABORATORY EQPT, EXC MEDICAL: Wholesalers

Fisher Scientific Company LLC..............B...... 724 517-1500
Pittsburgh *(G-15019)*

Lehman Scientific LLC ....G...... 717 244-7540
Wrightsville *(G-20241)*

Spectra Hardware Inc ....G...... 724 863-7527
Westmoreland City *(G-19785)*

Thermo Shandon Inc ....G...... 412 788-1133
Pittsburgh *(G-15615)*

LABORATORY EQPT: Centrifuges

Drucker Company LLC ....D...... 814 692-7661
Philipsburg *(G-14513)*

LABORATORY EQPT: Chemical

Archer Instruments LLC ....G...... 215 589-0356
Catasauqua *(G-2814)*

LABORATORY EQPT: Clinical Instruments Exc Medical

Biorealize Inc..G...... 610 216-5554
Philadelphia *(G-13466)*

David R Englehart ....G...... 814 238-6734
State College *(G-17957)*

Market Service Corp ....G...... 610 644-6211
Malvern *(G-10275)*

Prosoft Software Inc ....F...... 484 580-8162
Wayne *(G-19365)*

LABORATORY EQPT: Distilling

Finish Thompson Inc..................E...... 814 455-4478
Erie *(G-5290)*

LABORATORY EQPT: Incubators

Omnia LLC..................G...... 717 259-1633
Abbottstown *(G-5)*

LABORATORY EQPT: Measuring

Chatillon Scales Tester Co..................G...... 215 745-3304
Philadelphia *(G-13534)*

LABORATORY EQPT: Sterilizers

Aqua Treatment Services Inc..................E...... 717 697-4998
Mechanicsburg *(G-10820)*
Fedegari Technologies Inc..................F...... 215 453-0400
Sellersville *(G-17346)*
Fedegari Technologies Inc..................F...... 215 453-2180
Sellersville *(G-17347)*
Matachana USA Corp..................G...... 484 873-2763
Exton *(G-5708)*

LABORATORY INSTRUMENT REPAIR SVCS

E Victor Pesce..................G...... 610 444-5903
Kennett Square *(G-8508)*
Spectra Hardware Inc..................G...... 724 863-7527
Westmoreland City *(G-19785)*

LABORATORY SVCS: Motion Picture

Dynalene Inc..................F...... 610 262-9686
Whitehall *(G-19871)*

LACQUERING SVC: Metal Prdts

Pbz LLC..................E...... 800 578-1121
Lititz *(G-10029)*

LADDERS: Permanent Installation, Metal

Omni Fab Inc..................F...... 724 334-8851
New Kensington *(G-12364)*

LADDERS: Portable, Metal

Ballymore Holdings Inc..................E...... 610 593-5062
Coatesville *(G-3293)*
New Werner Holding Co Inc..................G...... 724 588-2000
Greenville *(G-6758)*
Old Ladder Co..................A...... 888 523-3371
Greenville *(G-6762)*
Sandlex Corporation..................G...... 570 820-8568
Wilkes Barre *(G-19961)*
Significant Developments LLC..................G...... 724 348-5277
Moon Township *(G-11500)*
TJ Cope Inc..................D...... 215 961-2570
Philadelphia *(G-14392)*
Werner Co..................C...... 724 588-2000
Greenville *(G-6775)*
Werner Holding Co Inc..................A...... 888 523-3371
Greenville *(G-6776)*

LAMINATED PLASTICS: Plate, Sheet, Rod & Tubes

Acrylics Unlimited..................G...... 215 443-2365
Horsham *(G-7778)*
Advanced Coil Industries..................F...... 724 225-1885
Washington *(G-19145)*
Adventek Corporation..................E...... 215 736-0961
Levittown *(G-9813)*
American Made LLC..................C...... 724 776-4044
Cranberry Township *(G-3803)*
Anholt Technologies Inc..................F...... 610 268-2758
Avondale *(G-848)*
Baw Plastics Inc..................C...... 412 384-3100
Jefferson Hills *(G-8273)*
C-Thru Products Inc..................E...... 610 586-1130
Ridley Park *(G-16738)*
CCL Tube Inc..................D...... 570 824-8485
Hanover Township *(G-6984)*
Ensinger Penn Fibre Inc..................D...... 215 702-9551
Bensalem *(G-1190)*
Fluortek Inc..................D...... 610 438-1800
Easton *(G-4683)*
Gateway Packaging Corp..................E...... 724 327-7400
Export *(G-5607)*
Hoff Enterprises Inc..................E...... 814 535-8371
Johnstown *(G-8381)*

J Benson Corp..................G...... 610 678-2692
Reading *(G-16411)*
Krehling Industries Inc..................D...... 717 232-7936
Harrisburg *(G-7165)*
Lambert-Jones Rubber Co..................G...... 412 781-8100
Pittsburgh *(G-15217)*
Lehigh Valley Plastics Inc..................D...... 484 893-5500
Bethlehem *(G-1558)*
M-B Companies Inc..................E...... 570 547-1621
Muncy *(G-11825)*
Markel Corp..................C...... 610 272-8960
Plymouth Meeting *(G-15855)*
Martech Medical Products Inc..................E...... 215 256-8833
Harleysville *(G-7046)*
Meadville New Products Inc..................F...... 814 336-2174
Meadville *(G-10759)*
Metplas Inc..................D...... 724 295-5200
Natrona Heights *(G-11946)*
Milner Enterprises Inc..................F...... 610 252-0700
Easton *(G-4722)*
Northway Industries Inc..................C...... 570 837-1564
Middleburg *(G-11034)*
Old Epp Inc..................G...... 570 430-9089
Tunkhannock *(G-18546)*
Panel Technologies Inc..................G...... 215 538-7055
Quakertown *(G-16226)*
Patrick Industries Inc..................E...... 717 653-2086
Mount Joy *(G-11668)*
Precise Plastics Inc..................D...... 814 474-5504
Fairview *(G-5840)*
Rochling Machined Plastics..................E...... 724 696-5200
Mount Pleasant *(G-11717)*
Washington Penn Mexico Holding..................G...... 724 228-1260
Washington *(G-19239)*
Washington Penn Plastic Co Inc..................G...... 724 228-1260
Washington *(G-19240)*
Washington Penn Plastic Co Inc..................E...... 724 228-3709
Eighty Four *(G-4851)*

LAMINATING SVCS

Alpha Screen Graphics Inc..................G...... 412 431-9000
Pittsburgh *(G-14687)*
Bell Graphics..................G...... 814 385-6222
Kennerdell *(G-8497)*
C P Converters Inc..................D...... 717 764-1193
York *(G-20415)*
Chroma Graphics..................G...... 724 693-9050
Oakdale *(G-12896)*
Heimer Enterprises Inc..................G...... 814 234-7446
State College *(G-17974)*

LAMP & LIGHT BULBS & TUBES

Adapt Technologies LLC..................G...... 610 896-7274
Conshohocken *(G-3516)*
Arcman Corporation..................G...... 570 489-6402
Dunmore *(G-4467)*
Davis Lamp & Shade Inc..................E...... 215 426-2777
Philadelphia *(G-13611)*
Ecotech Inc..................D...... 610 954-8480
Allentown *(G-202)*
K-B Lighting Manufacturing Co..................E...... 215 953-6663
Feasterville Trevose *(G-5915)*
Lightbox Inc..................E...... 610 954-8480
Bethlehem *(G-1561)*
Luxtech LLC..................F...... 888 340-4266
Philadelphia *(G-13978)*
Osram Sylvania Inc..................C...... 814 726-6600
Warren *(G-19041)*
Osram Sylvania Inc..................B...... 717 854-3499
Saint Marys *(G-17000)*
Osram Sylvania Inc..................B...... 814 269-1418
Johnstown *(G-8416)*
Osram Sylvania Inc..................B...... 570 724-8200
Wellsboro *(G-19471)*
Osram Sylvania Inc..................D...... 412 856-2111
Monroeville *(G-11347)*
Pureland Supply LLC..................F...... 610 444-0590
Kennett Square *(G-8537)*
Retrolite Corporation America..................G...... 215 443-9370
Warminster *(G-18954)*
Superior Quartz Products Inc..................D...... 610 317-3450
Bethlehem *(G-1634)*
Westinghouse Lighting Corp..................D...... 215 671-2000
Philadelphia *(G-14466)*

LAMP BULBS & TUBES, ELECTRIC: Electric Light

Led Tube USA..................G...... 724 650-0691
Ambridge *(G-625)*

LAMP BULBS & TUBES, ELECTRIC: Health, Infrared/Ultraviolet

Strategic Medicine Inc..................G...... 814 659-5450
Kennett Square *(G-8546)*

LAMP BULBS & TUBES, ELECTRIC: Light, Complete

Minleon Intl USA Ltd LLC..................G...... 717 991-1432
Mechanicsburg *(G-10870)*
Respironics Inc..................G...... 724 771-7837
Mount Pleasant *(G-11715)*
Respironics Inc..................D...... 724 387-5200
Murrysville *(G-11865)*
Trojan Inc..................E...... 814 336-4468
Meadville *(G-10804)*

LAMP BULBS & TUBES/PARTS, ELECTRIC: Generalized Applications

Fangio Enterprises Inc..................G...... 570 383-1030
Dickson City *(G-4120)*
Fangio Enterprises Inc..................E...... 570 383-1030
Olyphant *(G-12990)*
H H Fluorescent Parts Inc..................D...... 215 379-2750
Cheltenham *(G-3029)*

LAMP FRAMES: Wire

Frames & More..................G...... 724 933-5557
Wexford *(G-19804)*
J & R Wire Inc..................F...... 570 342-3193
Scranton *(G-17245)*
TG Marcis Wire Designs LLC..................G...... 412 391-5532
Pittsburgh *(G-15607)*

LAMP SHADES: Metal

American Period Lighting Inc..................G...... 717 392-5649
Lancaster *(G-8931)*

LAMP SHADES: Plastic

Shades of Country..................G...... 570 297-3327
Troy *(G-18526)*

LAMPS: Fluorescent

Interlectric Corporation..................C...... 814 723-6061
Warren *(G-19033)*

LAMPS: Incandescent, Filament

Koehler-Bright Star LLC..................E...... 570 825-1900
Hanover Township *(G-6991)*
Osram Sylvania Inc..................C...... 814 834-1800
Saint Marys *(G-16999)*

LAMPS: Table, Residential

Dine-Glow Dblo Fd Svc Fels LLC..................E...... 800 526-7583
Phoenixville *(G-14545)*
Rjf Enterprises Inc..................F...... 570 383-1030
Olyphant *(G-12997)*

LAND SUBDIVIDERS & DEVELOPERS: Residential

Amrep Corporation..................F...... 609 487-0905
Plymouth Meeting *(G-15831)*

LAND SUBDIVISION & DEVELOPMENT

De Limited Family Partnership..................F...... 814 938-0800
Punxsutawney *(G-16133)*
McClure Enterprises Inc..................G...... 570 562-1180
Old Forge *(G-12970)*
Penneco Oil Company..................F...... 724 468-8232
Delmont *(G-4052)*

LASER SYSTEMS & EQPT

Faro Laser Division LLC..................G...... 610 444-2300
Kennett Square *(G-8510)*
Faro Technologies Inc..................G...... 412 559-7737
Pittsburgh *(G-15005)*
Gsi..................G...... 610 667-4271
Penn Valley *(G-13236)*
Ictv Holdings Inc..................F...... 484 598-2300
Wayne *(G-19337)*
Precision Technical Sales LLC..................G...... 610 282-4541
Coopersburg *(G-3634)*

PRODUCT

LASERS: Welding, Drilling & Cutting Eqpt

Trexler Industries Inc...................E....... 610 974-9800
Bethlehem **(G-1641)**

D L George & Sons Mfg Inc.................D....... 717 765-4700
Waynesboro **(G-19407)**

Ii-VI Incorporated ....B....... 724 352-4455
Saxonburg **(G-17088)**

Laserfab Inc.................................F....... 717 272-0060
Lebanon **(G-9598)**

LATH: Expanded Metal

Neville Grating LLC.......................G....... 412 771-6973
Pittsburgh **(G-15332)**

LAUNDRY & GARMENT SVCS, NEC: Fur Cleaning, Repairing/Storage

Charles L Simpson Sr.....................F....... 717 763-7023
New Cumberland **(G-12182)**

Hal-Jo Corp.................................F....... 215 885-4747
Jenkintown **(G-8289)**

LAUNDRY & GARMENT SVCS, NEC: Garment Making, Alter & Repair

Anything Sews ....G....... 412 486-1055
Glenshaw **(G-6480)**

LAUNDRY & GARMENT SVCS, NEC: Reweaving, Textiles

Waugaman Awnings.....................G....... 724 837-1239
Greensburg **(G-6728)**

LAUNDRY & GARMENT SVCS, NEC: Seamstress

Rob Kei Inc................................G....... 717 293-8991
Lancaster **(G-9189)**

LAUNDRY EQPT: Commercial

Apparel Machinery & Supply Co ....E....... 215 634-2626
Philadelphia **(G-13400)**

Hang Xing Fa Inc.........................G....... 646 250-7175
Allentown **(G-241)**

LAUNDRY SVC: Safety Glove Sply

G & F Products Inc........................F....... 215 781-6222
Philadelphia **(G-13737)**

LAW LIBRARY

Wilkes Barre Law & Lib Assn..............G....... 570 822-6712
Wilkes Barre **(G-19975)**

LAWN & GARDEN EQPT

Ames Companies Inc.....................C....... 717 258-3001
Carlisle **(G-2689)**

Ames Companies Inc.....................B....... 717 737-1500
Camp Hill **(G-2488)**

Antonio Centeno Lawnkeeping ....G....... 267 580-0443
Levittown **(G-9816)**

Betts Equipment Inc ....G....... 215 598-7501
New Hope **(G-12298)**

Brickhouse Services......................G....... 570 869-1871
Laceyville **(G-8870)**

Bullgater Limited ....G....... 717 606-5414
Bird In Hand **(G-1670)**

Calgon Carbon Corporation.................F....... 412 269-4000
Pittsburgh **(G-14804)**

Edward T Regina ....G....... 570 223-8358
East Stroudsburg **(G-4614)**

Good Ideas Inc............................E....... 814 774-8231
Lake City **(G-8900)**

Lane Cherry Manufacturing ....G....... 717 687-9059
Ronks **(G-16810)**

Mackissic Inc..............................E....... 610 495-7181
Parker Ford **(G-13169)**

Pride Group Inc............................E....... 484 540-8059
Ridley Park **(G-16740)**

Pride Group Inc............................F....... 484 540-8059
Ridley Park **(G-16741)**

Schiller Grounds Care Inc................E....... 215 355-9700
Southampton **(G-17836)**

Schiller Grounds Care Inc................D....... 215 322-4970
Huntingdon Valley **(G-8035)**

Terrain Merchandising LLC.................F....... 310 709-8784
Philadelphia **(G-14382)**

LAWN & GARDEN EQPT STORES

Davies & Sons LLC.......................G....... 814 723-7430
Warren **(G-19020)**

K D Home & Garden Inc.................F....... 610 929-5794
Temple **(G-18331)**

M E Kmachine ....G....... 570 636-0710
Freeland **(G-6195)**

Sam Beachy & Sons ....G....... 814 662-2220
Salisbury **(G-17045)**

Triple W Enterprises Inc ....G....... 610 865-0071
Bethlehem **(G-1642)**

LAWN & GARDEN EQPT: Cultivators

Custom Turf Inc...........................G....... 412 384-4111
Finleyville **(G-5954)**

LAWN & GARDEN EQPT: Grass Catchers, Lawn Mower

Sunnys Sweeping Service Inc ....G....... 570 785-5564
Prompton **(G-16110)**

LAWN & GARDEN EQPT: Lawnmowers, Residential, Hand Or Power

Ephraim L King ....G....... 570 837-9470
Winfield **(G-20200)**

Stines Equipment & Maintenance ....G....... 717 432-4374
Dillsburg **(G-4140)**

LAWN & GARDEN EQPT: Loaders

Buchanan Hauling ....G....... 412 373-6760
Trafford **(G-18452)**

Walnut Industries Inc.....................E....... 215 638-7847
Bensalem **(G-1268)**

LAWN & GARDEN EQPT: Tractors & Eqpt

Hirt Powersports LLC ....G....... 717 834-9126
Duncannon **(G-4446)**

LAWN MOWER REPAIR SHOP

Scranton Grinder & Hardware ....E....... 570 344-2520
Scranton **(G-17285)**

LEAD & ZINC

Horsehead Corporation....................E....... 610 826-2111
Palmerton **(G-13107)**

LEAD PENCILS & ART GOODS

Colorfin LLC................................G....... 484 646-9900
Kutztown **(G-8837)**

Crayola LLC...............................B....... 610 253-6271
Fredericksburg **(G-6173)**

Crayola LLC...............................B....... 610 814-7681
Bethlehem **(G-1489)**

Crayola LLC...............................F....... 610 253-6272
Easton **(G-4664)**

Crayola LLC...............................B....... 610 515-8000
Easton **(G-4665)**

Graphic Display Systems ....F....... 717 274-3954
Lebanon **(G-9576)**

Pidilite Usa Inc............................G....... 800 424-3596
Hazleton **(G-7519)**

LEASING & RENTAL SVCS: Cranes & Aerial Lift Eqpt

Bright Sign and Maint Co Inc..............E....... 610 916-5100
Leesport **(G-9660)**

Bryce Saylor & Sons Inc ....F....... 814 942-2288
Altoona **(G-485)**

Greiner Industries Inc.....................B....... 717 653-8111
Mount Joy **(G-11660)**

Steffan Industries Inc ....G....... 412 751-4484
McKeesport **(G-10683)**

LEASING & RENTAL SVCS: Earth Moving Eqpt

Kt-Grant Inc...............................D....... 724 468-4700
Export **(G-5614)**

LEASING & RENTAL SVCS: Oil Well Drilling

Universal Well Services Inc ....E....... 814 368-6175
Meadville **(G-10809)**

LEASING & RENTAL: Computers & Eqpt

Pat Landgraf...............................G....... 412 221-0347
Bridgeville **(G-2084)**

LEASING & RENTAL: Construction & Mining Eqpt

Bentley Development Co Inc ....F....... 724 459-5775
Blairsville **(G-1715)**

Gill Rock Drill Company Inc................E....... 717 272-3861
Lebanon **(G-9573)**

Jlg Industries Inc ....C....... 717 485-5161
Mc Connellsburg **(G-10569)**

L and J Equipment Co Inc.................G....... 724 437-5405
Uniontown **(G-18633)**

Lincoln Contg & Eqp Co Inc...............D....... 814 629-6641
Stoystown **(G-18082)**

LEASING & RENTAL: Medical Machinery & Eqpt

101 Cameo Appearances LLC ....G....... 412 787-7981
Pittsburgh **(G-14623)**

Altamira Ltd ....G....... 800 343-1066
Pittsburgh **(G-14692)**

Clearcount Med Solutions Inc ....F....... 412 931-7233
Pittsburgh **(G-14859)**

LEASING & RENTAL: Office Machines & Eqpt

Gc Enterprises LLC ....G....... 570 655-5543
Pittston **(G-15752)**

LEASING & RENTAL: Other Real Estate Property

Imperial Eagle Products Inc...............F....... 717 252-1573
Wrightsville **(G-20238)**

LEASING & RENTAL: Trucks, Without Drivers

Arthur K Miller ....G....... 724 588-1118
Greenville **(G-6738)**

Davies & Sons LLC.......................G....... 814 723-7430
Warren **(G-19020)**

Interstate Self Storage.....................G....... 724 662-1186
Mercer **(G-10965)**

Murdick Auto Parts & Racg Sups ....G....... 724 482-2177
Butler **(G-2425)**

LEASING & RENTAL: Utility Trailers & RV's

Weldship Industries Inc....................F....... 610 861-7330
Bethlehem **(G-1655)**

LEASING: Residential Buildings

Kingsly Compression Inc...................E....... 724 524-1840
Saxonburg **(G-17091)**

LEATHER GOODS, EXC FOOTWEAR, GLOVES, LUGGAGE/BELTING, WHOL

Ambassador Bags & Spats Mfg Co.......G....... 610 532-7840
Folcroft **(G-5998)**

LEATHER GOODS: Checkbook Covers

American Accessories Inc ....E....... 215 639-8000
Bensalem **(G-1148)**

LEATHER GOODS: Desk Sets

Helene Batoff Interiors ....G....... 215 879-7727
Philadelphia **(G-13812)**

Polar Manufacturing Co Inc ....F....... 215 535-6940
Philadelphia **(G-14184)**

LEATHER GOODS: Garments

Roberta Weissburg Leathers ....G....... 412 681-8188
Pittsburgh **(G-15494)**

Samuelson Leather LLC...................G....... 610 719-7391
West Chester **(G-19636)**

Samuelson Leather LLC...................G....... 484 328-3273
Malvern **(G-10314)**

LEATHER GOODS: Harnesses Or Harness Parts

E Z Sensenig & Son ....G....... 717 445-5580
New Holland (G-12246)

LEATHER GOODS: Holsters

C&G Arms LLC ....G....... 724 858-2856
Natrona Heights (G-11937)

LEATHER GOODS: Key Cases

Dmi Locksmith Inc ....G....... 412 232-3000
Pittsburgh (G-14928)

LEATHER GOODS: Money Holders

Buffalo Billfold ....G....... 814 422-8955
Spring Mills (G-17885)

LEATHER GOODS: NEC

McCabes Custom Leather.......................G....... 814 414-1442
Altoona (G-525)

LEATHER GOODS: Personal

Bashlin Industries Inc............................D....... 724 458-8340
Grove City (G-6780)
Dr Davies Products Inc...........................G....... 570 321-5423
Williamsport (G-20007)
Leathersmith Inc ....G....... 717 933-8084
Myerstown (G-11891)

LEATHER GOODS: Saddles Or Parts

Shady Acres Saddlery Inc ....G....... 412 963-9454
Pittsburgh (G-15526)

LEATHER GOODS: Safety Belts

Bashlin Industries Inc............................D....... 724 458-8340
Grove City (G-6780)
Frenchcreek Production Inc ....E....... 814 437-1808
Franklin (G-6131)
Sperian Fall Protection Inc....................C....... 814 432-2118
Franklin (G-6163)

LEATHER GOODS: Spats

Ambassador Bags & Spats Mfg Co.......G....... 610 532-7840
Folcroft (G-5998)

LEATHER, LEATHER GOODS & FURS, WHOLESALE

Interntnal Lthers of Phldlphia.................G....... 610 793-1140
West Chester (G-19572)

LEATHER: Accessory Prdts

Clemintines..G....... 717 626-1378
Lititz (G-10000)
Thermo Electric Company Inc ....D....... 610 692-7990
West Chester (G-19661)

LEATHER: Artificial

Carlisle Construction Mtls Inc ....E....... 717 245-7142
Carlisle (G-2693)

LEATHER: Bag

New Gear Brands LLC ....G....... 407 674-6850
Milford (G-11163)

LEATHER: Collar

Daniel D Esh ....G....... 814 383-4579
Howard (G-7889)
Sugar Valley Collar Shop Inc ....G....... 570 725-3499
Loganton (G-10099)

LEATHER: Cut

Columbia Organ Works Inc ....G....... 717 684-3573
Columbia (G-3436)

LEATHER: Glove

Empire Glove Inc....................................G....... 570 824-4400
Wilkes Barre (G-19918)
G & F Products Inc ....F....... 215 781-6222
Philadelphia (G-13737)

LEATHER: Processed

Interntnal Lthers of Phldlphia...............G....... 610 793-1140
West Chester (G-19572)

LEATHER: Shoe

Titan Group Ltd ....E....... 610 631-0831
Norristown (G-12719)

LECTURE BUREAU

Foreign Policy Research Inst.................E....... 215 732-3774
Philadelphia (G-13714)

LEGAL AID SVCS

Community Resource Svcs Inc ....G....... 717 338-9100
Gettysburg (G-6286)

LEGAL OFFICES & SVCS

Lrp Publications Inc..............................F....... 215 784-0941
Horsham (G-7832)
The M & A Journal Inc ....G....... 215 238-0506
Philadelphia (G-14386)

LEGAL SVCS: Administrative & Government Law

Decilog Inc..G....... 215 657-0817
Willow Grove (G-20114)

LEGAL SVCS: General Practice Law Office

Horty Springer & Mattern ....E....... 412 687-7677
Pittsburgh (G-15100)

LEGAL SVCS: Specialized Law Offices, Attorney

American Law Institute..........................D....... 215 243-1600
Philadelphia (G-13385)

LENS COATING: Ophthalmic

Morgantown Eye Care Center................G....... 610 286-0206
Morgantown (G-11528)

LICENSE TAGS: Automobile, Stamped Metal

Ardsley Auto Tags.................................G....... 215 572-1409
Glenside (G-6506)
Bridge Auto Tags ....G....... 215 946-8026
Levittown (G-9819)
Kajevi Services LLC...............................G....... 215 722-0711
Philadelphia (G-13920)
Kyles Auto Tags & Insurance.................G....... 610 429-1447
West Chester (G-19585)
Transportation PA Dept ....E....... 717 787-2304
Harrisburg (G-7236)
Venango County Notary ....G....... 814 677-2216
Seneca (G-17370)
Vic Auto Tech Place ....G....... 215 969-2083
Philadelphia (G-14445)
Wm C Haldeman......................................G....... 215 324-2400
Philadelphia (G-14481)

LIGHT OR HEAT EMISSION OPERATING APPARATUS

Environmental Solut World Inc.............E....... 215 699-0730
Montgomeryville (G-11396)
Matthey Johnson Inc ....C....... 610 341-8300
Wayne (G-19353)

LIGHTING EQPT: Flashlights

Koehler-Bright Star LLC ....E....... 570 825-1900
Hanover Township (G-6991)
Nitebrite Ltd ....G....... 215 493-9361
Washington Crossing (G-19257)
Streamlight Inc ....B....... 610 631-0600
Eagleville (G-4517)

LIGHTING EQPT: Locomotive & Railroad Car Lights

Railpower LLC ....C....... 814 835-2212
Erie (G-5453)

LIGHTING EQPT: Miners' Lamps

MSA Safety Incorporated ....B....... 724 733-9100
Murrysville (G-11858)

LIGHTING EQPT: Motor Vehicle

TRM Emergency Vehicles LLC ....G....... 610 689-0702
Boyertown (G-1932)
Truck-Lite Co LLC..................................D....... 814 274-5400
Coudersport (G-3790)

LIGHTING EQPT: Motor Vehicle, Headlights

Osram Sylvania Inc...............................B....... 570 724-8200
Wellsboro (G-19471)

LIGHTING EQPT: Outdoor

Bluestem Industries Pa LLC ....G....... 412 585-6220
Moon Township (G-11481)
Challenger Manufacturing Ltd ....C....... 215 968-6004
Southampton (G-17802)
Litescaping LLC ....G....... 814 833-6200
Erie (G-5368)
Spring City Electrical Mfg Co ....C....... 610 948-4000
Spring City (G-17867)
Spring City Electrical Mfg Co ....D....... 610 948-4000
Spring City (G-17868)

LIGHTING EQPT: Searchlights

Peak Beam Systems Inc........................E....... 610 353-8505
Newtown Square (G-12588)

LIGHTING EQPT: Spotlights

Comcast Spotlight ....G....... 610 784-2560
Conshohocken (G-3530)

LIGHTING FIXTURES WHOLESALERS

Brontech Industries Inc.........................G....... 717 672-0240
Lancaster (G-8960)
Candela Corporation ....G....... 610 861-8772
Bethlehem (G-1479)
Elk Lighting Inc ....G....... 610 767-0511
Walnutport (G-18791)
Gexpro ....G....... 570 265-2420
Towanda (G-18428)
Led Living Technologies Inc..................E....... 215 633-1558
Bristol (G-2158)
Litescaping LLC ....G....... 814 833-6200
Erie (G-5368)
Retrolite Corporation America................G....... 215 443-9370
Warminster (G-18954)
Stellar Industries Inc.............................G....... 724 335-5525
New Kensington (G-12380)
Truck-Lite Co LLC..................................D....... 814 274-5400
Coudersport (G-3790)
United Electric Supply Co Inc................G....... 717 632-7640
Hanover (G-6964)
Westinghouse Lighting Corp..................D....... 215 671-2000
Philadelphia (G-14466)

LIGHTING FIXTURES, NEC

Anaconda Enterprises LLC.....................G....... 908 910-7150
Nazareth (G-11955)
Black Bear Associates LLC ....G....... 610 470-6477
Lancaster (G-8956)
Doner Design Inc ....G....... 717 786-4172
New Providence (G-12433)
Evenlite Inc ....E....... 215 244-4201
Feasterville Trevose (G-5906)
Feng Shui Lighting Inc ....G....... 215 393-5500
Lansdale (G-9367)
Jcr Sales & Mfg LLC ....G....... 814 897-8870
Erie (G-5335)
Just Normlicht Inc.................................G....... 267 852-2200
Langhorne (G-9305)
Lighting Accents Inc.............................G....... 412 761-5000
Pittsburgh (G-15230)
Lighting By Led LLC ....F....... 412 600-3132
Pittsburgh (G-15231)
Lloyd Jones ....G....... 610 395-3386
Allentown (G-298)
Lumi Trak Inc ....F....... 717 235-2863
New Freedom (G-12212)
Mdl Lighting LLC ....E....... 267 968-3611
Philadelphia (G-14001)
Mine Safety Appliances Co LLC ....B....... 724 776-8600
Cranberry Township (G-3836)

PRODUCT

MSA Safety Incorporated ....B 724 776-8600
Cranberry Township **(G-3839)**

MSA Safety Sales LLC ....G 724 776-8600
Cranberry Township **(G-3841)**

Orlotronics Corporation ....E 610 239-8200
Bridgeport **(G-2042)**

Solar Light Company Inc ....D 215 517-8700
Glenside **(G-6538)**

Special-Lite Products LLC ....F 724 537-4711
Loyalhanna **(G-10113)**

Stabler Companies Inc ....F 717 236-9307
Harrisburg **(G-7219)**

Sylvan Corporation ....G 724 864-9350
Irwin **(G-8203)**

Tait Towers Inc ....D 717 626-9571
Lititz **(G-10051)**

Theotek Corporation ....F 610 336-9191
Orefield **(G-13015)**

We-Ef Lighting USA LLC ....G 724 742-0027
Warrendale **(G-19100)**

LIGHTING FIXTURES: Decorative Area

American Tack & Hdwr Co Inc ....E 610 336-1330
Breinigsville **(G-2008)**

RC & Design Company ....G 484 626-1216
Lehighton **(G-9724)**

LIGHTING FIXTURES: Fluorescent, Commercial

Emw Inc ....F 717 626-0248
Lititz **(G-10006)**

Forum Inc ....D 412 781-5970
Pittsburgh **(G-15028)**

Led Tube USA ....G 724 650-0691
Ambridge **(G-625)**

Metal Light Manufacturing ....F 215 430-7200
Philadelphia **(G-14013)**

Neo Lights Holdings Inc ....G 215 831-7700
Philadelphia **(G-14062)**

Perkasie Industries Corp ....D 215 257-6581
Perkasie **(G-13288)**

Simkar LLC ....C 215 831-7700
Philadelphia **(G-14307)**

Tristar Lighting Company ....E 215 245-3400
Bensalem **(G-1264)**

LIGHTING FIXTURES: Fluorescent, Residential

K-B Lighting Manufacturing Co ....E 215 953-6663
Feasterville Trevose **(G-5915)**

LIGHTING FIXTURES: Gas

American Gas Lamp Works LLC ....G 724 274-7131
Springdale **(G-17897)**

American Gas Lamp Works LLC ....F 724 274-7131
Springdale **(G-17898)**

LIGHTING FIXTURES: Indl & Commercial

8 12 Illumination LLC ....G 717 285-9700
Mountville **(G-11789)**

Andromeda Led Lighting LLC ....G 610 336-7474
Macungie **(G-10140)**

Appalachian Ltg Systems Inc ....E 724 752-0326
Ellwood City **(G-4927)**

Bluestem Industries Pa LLC ....G 412 585-6220
Moon Township **(G-11481)**

CNT Fixture Company Inc ....G 412 443-6260
Glenshaw **(G-6484)**

Custom Manufactured Products ....E 215 228-3830
Philadelphia **(G-13594)**

Donohoe Corporation ....F 724 850-2433
Greensburg **(G-6660)**

Eaton Electric Holdings LLC ....G 724 228-7333
Washington **(G-19167)**

Ecotech Inc ....D 610 954-8480
Allentown **(G-202)**

Elegant Furniture & Lighting ....G 888 388-3390
Philadelphia **(G-13665)**

Elk Group International LLC ....G 800 613-3261
Easton **(G-4679)**

Elk Lighting Inc ....F 800 613-3261
Summit Hill **(G-18160)**

Envoy Lighting Inc ....G 215 512-7000
Trevose **(G-18493)**

Exit Store LLC ....G 310 305-4646
Wayne **(G-19326)**

Global Indus Ltg Solutions LLC ....E 215 671-2029
Philadelphia **(G-13768)**

Innogreen USA LLC ....G 814 880-4493
State College **(G-17977)**

Le Jo Enterprises Incorporated ....E 484 921-9000
Phoenixville **(G-14559)**

Led Saving Solutions LLC ....G 484 588-5401
Wayne **(G-19347)**

Lighting Accents Inc ....E 412 761-5000
Pittsburgh **(G-15230)**

Lumenoptix LLC ....G 215 671-2029
Montgomeryville **(G-11405)**

Modular International Inc ....E 412 734-9000
Pittsburgh **(G-15299)**

Nu Tech Inc ....E 215 297-8889
Doylestown **(G-4319)**

Osram Sylvania Inc ....B 570 724-8200
Wellsboro **(G-19471)**

Osram Sylvania Inc ....D 412 856-2111
Monroeville **(G-11347)**

Pendants Systems Mfg Co ....F 215 638-8552
Bensalem **(G-1240)**

Pieri Creations LLC ....E 215 634-4000
Philadelphia **(G-14176)**

Plant Growers Workshop Inc ....G 724 473-1079
Callery **(G-2470)**

Practicom ....G 267 979-5446
Philadelphia **(G-14194)**

Pureoptix Led LLC ....G 610 301-9767
Macungie **(G-10157)**

RC & Design Company ....G 484 626-1216
Lehighton **(G-9724)**

Rogerson & Associates ....G 724 943-3934
Dilliner **(G-4125)**

Self-Powered Lighting Inc ....E 484 595-9130
Berwyn **(G-1375)**

Stellar Industries Inc ....G 724 335-5525
New Kensington **(G-12380)**

Terra-Glo Lighting Corporation ....E 267 430-1259
Ivyland **(G-8222)**

Trans-Tech Technologies Inc ....G 724 327-6600
Pittsburgh **(G-15639)**

LIGHTING FIXTURES: Marine

Ziamatic Corp ....E 215 493-2777
Yardley **(G-20347)**

LIGHTING FIXTURES: Motor Vehicle

Betts Industries Inc ....C 814 723-1250
Warren **(G-19013)**

Liberty Vhcl Ltg & Safety Sup ....G 610 356-5320
Prospect Park **(G-16116)**

Osram Sylvania Inc ....D 412 856-2111
Monroeville **(G-11347)**

Truck Lite Co Inc ....G 716 664-3519
Beech Creek **(G-1083)**

Truck-Lite Co LLC ....D 570 769-7231
Mc Elhattan **(G-10590)**

LIGHTING FIXTURES: Ornamental, Commercial

American Period Lighting Inc ....G 717 392-5649
Lancaster **(G-8931)**

Olde Mill Lighting Limited ....G 717 299-7240
Lancaster **(G-9151)**

Reece Lighting & Prod LLC ....G 215 460-8560
Bristol **(G-2193)**

Retrolite Corporation America ....G 215 443-9370
Warminster **(G-18954)**

LIGHTING FIXTURES: Residential

Andromeda Led Lighting LLC ....G 610 336-7474
Macungie **(G-10140)**

Appalachian Ltg Systems Inc ....E 724 752-0326
Ellwood City **(G-4927)**

Bahdeebahdu ....G 215 627-5002
Philadelphia **(G-13441)**

Brightline LP ....F 412 206-0106
Bridgeville **(G-2056)**

Brontech Industries Inc ....G 717 672-0240
Lancaster **(G-8960)**

Candela Corporation ....G 610 861-8772
Bethlehem **(G-1479)**

Craft Lite Inc ....G 717 359-7131
Littlestown **(G-10065)**

Decora Industries Inc ....D 215 698-2600
Philadelphia **(G-13614)**

Elk Group International LLC ....G 800 613-3261
Easton **(G-4679)**

Elk Lighting Inc ....G 610 767-0511
Walnutport **(G-18791)**

Elk Lighting Inc ....F 800 613-3261
Summit Hill **(G-18160)**

Francis J Nowalk ....G 412 687-4017
Pittsburgh **(G-15030)**

Gexpro ....G 570 265-2420
Towanda **(G-18428)**

Glasslight Inc ....G 610 469-9066
Saint Peters **(G-17034)**

Hartman Design Inc ....G 610 670-2517
Wernersville **(G-19484)**

Hutton Metalcrafts Inc ....G 570 646-7778
Pocono Pines **(G-15881)**

Led Living Technologies Inc ....E 215 633-1558
Bristol **(G-2158)**

Lighting Accents Inc ....E 412 761-5000
Pittsburgh **(G-15230)**

Makefield Collection Inc ....F 610 496-4649
Coopersburg **(G-3631)**

Oaklawn Metal Craft Shop Inc ....G 215 794-7387
Lahaska **(G-8885)**

Penn Shadecrafters Inc ....E 570 342-3193
Scranton **(G-17271)**

Philips-Hadco ....F 717 359-7131
Littlestown **(G-10075)**

RC & Design Company ....G 484 626-1216
Lehighton **(G-9724)**

Retrolite Corporation America ....G 215 443-9370
Warminster **(G-18954)**

Richard Scofield Hstorc Lghtng ....F 860 767-7032
Downingtown **(G-4254)**

Silvine Inc ....E 215 657-2345
Willow Grove **(G-20142)**

Sitka Enterprises Inc ....G 610 393-6708
Macungie **(G-10158)**

Soltech Solutions LLC ....G 484 821-1001
Bethlehem **(G-1622)**

Stellar Industries Inc ....G 724 335-5525
New Kensington **(G-12380)**

United Electric Supply Co Inc ....G 717 632-7640
Hanover **(G-6964)**

Victorian Lighting Works Inc ....G 814 364-9577
Centre Hall **(G-2845)**

Westinghouse Lighting Corp ....D 215 671-2000
Philadelphia **(G-14466)**

LIGHTING FIXTURES: Street

H B Instrument Co ....E 610 489-5500
Trappe **(G-18469)**

LIME

Allegheny Mineral Corporation ....E 724 735-2088
Harrisville **(G-7252)**

Bullskin Stone & Lime LLC ....F 724 537-7505
Laughlintown **(G-9531)**

Carmeuse Lime Inc ....D 412 995-5500
Pittsburgh **(G-14814)**

Carmeuse Lime Inc ....G 717 867-4441
Annville **(G-644)**

Glasgow Inc ....E 610 251-0760
Malvern **(G-10240)**

Highway Materials Inc ....E 610 828-4300
Plymouth Meeting **(G-15846)**

Luxfer Magtech Inc ....E 570 668-0001
Tamaqua **(G-18219)**

Magnesita Refractories Company ....B 717 792-3611
York **(G-20572)**

Magnesita Refractories Company ....B 717 792-4216
York **(G-20573)**

Magnesita Refractories Company ....C 717 792-3611
York **(G-20574)**

Martin Limestone Inc ....B 717 354-1370
East Earl **(G-4549)**

LIME ROCK: Ground

Graymont Inc ....F 814 357-4500
Bellefonte **(G-1099)**

H&K Group Inc ....C 570 646-3324
Pocono Lake **(G-15880)**

New Hope Crushed Stone Lime Co ......E 215 862-5295
New Hope **(G-12310)**

LIME: Agricultural

Allegheny Mineral Corporation ....G 724 548-8101
Kittanning **(G-8753)**

Graymont Inc ....D...... 814 353-4613
Bellefonte (G-1097)
Keystone Lime Company ....E...... 814 662-2025
Springs (G-17925)
Rohrers Quarry Inc ....D...... 717 626-9760
Lititz (G-10043)

LIME: Building

Lancaster Lime Works ....F 717 207-7014
Lancaster (G-9100)
Mercer Lime Company ....G...... 412 220-0316
Bridgeville (G-2078)

LIMESTONE & MARBLE: Dimension

Allegheny Mineral Corporation ....E 724 794-6911
Slippery Rock (G-17617)
Allegheny Urn Company ....G...... 814 437-3208
Franklin (G-6115)
Graymont Inc ....F 814 359-2313
Bellefonte (G-1098)

LIMESTONE: Crushed & Broken

Allan Myers Inc ....E 717 442-4191
Paradise (G-13152)
C & M Aggregate Company Inc ....E 724 796-3821
Bulger (G-2342)
Carmeuse Lime Inc ....D...... 412 995-5500
Pittsburgh (G-14814)
Carmeuse Lime Inc ....G...... 717 867-4441
Annville (G-644)
Carmeuse Lime & Stone Inc ....F 412 777-0724
Pittsburgh (G-14815)
Carmeuse Lime & Stone Inc ....C 412 995-5500
Pittsburgh (G-14816)
Cemex Cnstr Mtls ATL LLC ....C 724 535-4311
Wampum (G-18798)
County Line Quarry Inc ....E 717 252-1584
Wrightsville (G-20235)
Eastern Industries Inc ....E 717 667-2015
Milroy (G-11230)
Erie Sand & Gravel Co Inc ....E 412 995-5500
Pittsburgh (G-14984)
Eureka Stone Quarry Inc ....E 570 992-4210
Stroudsburg (G-18116)
Glasgow Inc ....G...... 610 251-0760
Malvern (G-10240)
Glenn O Hawbaker Inc ....D...... 814 237-1444
State College (G-17970)
Greystone Materials BT ....G...... 814 748-7652
Colver (G-3454)
Greystone Materials BT ....G...... 570 244-2082
Herndon (G-7598)
Greystone Quarries Inc ....G...... 610 987-8055
Boyertown (G-1915)
H&K Group Inc ....F 610 250-7700
Easton (G-4693)
Hanson Aggregates Bmc Inc ....F 724 626-0080
Connellsville (G-3498)
Hanson Aggregates PA LLC ....F 570 368-2481
Jersey Shore (G-8314)
Hanson Aggregates PA LLC ....F 814 466-5101
Boalsburg (G-1867)
Hepco Quarries Incorporated ....G...... 570 955-8545
New Milford (G-12396)
Honey-Creek Stone Co ....F 724 654-5538
Edinburg (G-4822)
Hoovers Stone Quarry LLC ....F 724 639-9813
Saltsburg (G-17051)
Iddings Quarry Inc ....G...... 570 966-1551
Mifflinburg (G-11096)
Keystone Lime Company ....E 814 662-2025
Springs (G-17925)
Kimmels Coal and Packaging Inc ....E 717 453-7151
Wiconisco (G-19895)
Kowalewski Quarries ....G...... 570 465-7025
New Milford (G-12397)
Laurel Aggregates Inc ....E 724 564-5099
Uniontown (G-18634)
Legacy Vulcan LLC ....G...... 717 792-6996
York (G-20564)
Legacy Vulcan LLC ....D...... 717 637-7121
Hanover (G-6913)
M & M Lime Co Inc ....E 724 297-3958
Worthington (G-20231)
Martin Limestone Inc ....B 717 354-1370
East Earl (G-4549)
Martin Limestone Inc ....E 717 335-4500
East Earl (G-4548)

Miller and Son Paving Inc ....F 215 598-7801
Rushland (G-16879)
New Enterprise Stone Lime Inc ....D...... 814 224-6883
New Enterprise (G-12194)
New Enterprise Stone Lime Inc ....G...... 610 683-3302
East Earl (G-4551)
New Enterprise Stone Lime Inc ....E 814 342-7096
West Decatur (G-19689)
New Enterprise Stone Lime Inc ....E 814 796-1413
Cambridge Springs (G-2484)
New Enterprise Stone Lime Inc ....E 814 754-4921
Cairnbrook (G-2463)
New Enterprise Stone Lime Inc ....E 814 684-4905
Tyrone (G-18587)
New Enterprise Stone Lime Inc ....E 814 443-6494
Somerset (G-17698)
Norton Oglebay Company ....F 412 995-5500
Pittsburgh (G-15347)
Norton Oglebay Specialty Mnrl ....D...... 412 995-5500
Pittsburgh (G-15348)
O-N Minerals Chemstone Company ......C 412 995-5500
Pittsburgh (G-15352)
O-N Minerals Company (ohio) ....G...... 412 995-5500
Pittsburgh (G-15353)
O-N Minerals Luttrell Company ....F 412 995-5500
Pittsburgh (G-15354)
O-N Minerals Michigan Company ....G...... 412 995-5500
Pittsburgh (G-15355)
O-N Minerals Portage Co LLC ....D...... 412 995-5500
Pittsburgh (G-15356)
P Stone Inc ....G...... 570 745-7166
Jersey Shore (G-8319)
Pennsy Supply Inc ....F 717 486-5414
Mount Holly Springs (G-11638)
Pickett Quarries Inc ....G...... 570 869-1817
Laceyville (G-8873)
Rock Star Quarries LLC ....G...... 570 721-1426
Wyalusing (G-20257)
Rohrers Quarry Inc ....D...... 717 626-9760
Lititz (G-10043)
Rohrers Quarry Inc ....G...... 717 626-9756
Lititz (G-10044)
Stabler Companies Inc ....G...... 610 799-2421
Coplay (G-3650)
Thomas E Siegel ....G...... 814 226-7421
Shippenville (G-17564)
Union Quarries Inc ....E 717 249-5012
Carlisle (G-2745)
Valley Quarries Inc ....E 717 334-3281
Gettysburg (G-6320)
Valley Quarries Inc ....E 717 263-9186
Chambersburg (G-2993)
Valley Quarries Inc ....G...... 717 264-5811
Chambersburg (G-2996)
Valley Quarries Inc ....E 717 642-8535
Fairfield (G-5770)
Valley Quarries Inc ....F 717 267-2244
Chambersburg (G-2994)
Valley Quarries Inc ....E 717 264-4178
Chambersburg (G-2995)
Winfield Lime & Stone Co Inc ....F 724 352-3596
Cabot (G-2461)
York Building Products Co Inc ....E 717 848-2831
York (G-20726)

LIMESTONE: Cut & Shaped

Allegheny Mineral Corporation ....G...... 724 548-8101
Kittanning (G-8753)
Devido Ranier Stone Co ....E 724 658-8518
New Castle (G-12082)
Snyder Assod Companies Inc ....E 724 548-8101
Kittanning (G-8793)
York Building Products Co Inc ....E 717 848-2831
York (G-20726)

LIMESTONE: Dimension

Bluegrass Materials Co LLC ....G...... 410 683-1250
Warfordsburg (G-18811)
Coolspring Stone Supply Inc ....G...... 724 437-5200
Uniontown (G-18622)
H&K Group Inc ....F 717 548-2147
Peach Bottom (G-13198)
South Bend Limestone Company ....G...... 724 468-8232
Delmont (G-4059)

LIMESTONE: Ground

Allan Myers Management Inc ....D...... 717 656-2411
Leola (G-9768)

Allan Myers Management Inc ....F 717 548-2191
Peach Bottom (G-13195)
Black Knight Quarries Inc ....G...... 570 265-8991
Towanda (G-18421)
Bradys Bend Corporation ....G...... 724 526-3353
East Brady (G-4527)
Bradys Bend Corporation ....E 724 526-3353
East Brady (G-4528)
Graymont Inc ....D...... 814 353-4613
Bellefonte (G-1097)
H&K Group Inc ....C 610 584-8500
Skippack (G-17597)
Hanson Aggregates PA LLC ....E 610 366-4626
Allentown (G-243)
Hanson Aggregates PA LLC ....F 570 584-2153
Muncy (G-11818)
Hanson Aggregates PA LLC ....E 814 355-4226
Bellefonte (G-1103)
Meckleys Limestone Pdts Inc ....D...... 570 758-3011
Herndon (G-7601)
Meckleys Limestone Pdts Inc ....G...... 570 837-5228
Beavertown (G-1027)
National Limestone Quarry ....E 570 837-1635
Middleburg (G-11033)
New Enterprise Stone Lime Inc ....G...... 717 349-2412
Dry Run (G-4384)
New Enterprise Stone Lime Inc ....D...... 814 652-5121
Everett (G-5576)
Pennsy Supply Inc ....D...... 717 274-3661
Lebanon (G-9619)
Valley Quarries Inc ....F 717 532-4456
Shippensburg (G-17553)
York Building Products Co Inc ....F 717 792-9922
Thomasville (G-18344)

LINEN SPLY SVC: Uniform

Cintas Corporation No 2 ....D...... 724 696-5640
Mount Pleasant (G-11692)

LINENS & TOWELS WHOLESALERS

Pinnacle Textile Inds LLC ....E 800 901-4784
King of Prussia (G-8663)

LINENS: Table & Dresser Scarves, From Purchased Materials

Bess Manufacturing Company ....G...... 215 447-1032
Bensalem (G-1157)

LINERS & COVERS: Fabric

Garrett Liners Inc ....E 215 295-0200
Levittown (G-9838)

LINERS & LINING

American Made Systems Inc ....G...... 412 771-3300
Pittsburgh (G-14703)

LINERS: Indl, Metal Plate

Scott Metals Inc ....E 412 279-7021
Carnegie (G-2790)

LININGS: Shoe, Knit

Yarrington Mills Corporation ....E 215 674-5125
Hatboro (G-7311)

LININGS: Vulcanizable Rubber

JM Industries Inc ....G...... 724 452-6060
Harmony (G-7071)
Tech-Seal Products Inc ....G...... 847 805-6400
Wayne (G-19379)

LINTELS

Hessian Co Ltd ....G...... 610 683-0067
Kutztown (G-8845)
Hessian Co Ltd ....E 610 269-4685
Honey Brook (G-7747)
Hessian Co Ltd ....G...... 610 683-0067
Kutztown (G-8846)
Hessian Co Ltd ....E 724 658-6638
New Castle (G-12104)

LIQUEFIED PETROLEUM GAS DEALERS

Praxair Distribution Inc ....G...... 570 655-3721
Pittston (G-15778)

PRODUCT

Praxair Distribution Inc ....F 814 238-5092
State College (G-18009)

Praxair Distribution Inc ....F 215 736-8005
Morrisville (G-11579)

Sky Oxygen Inc ....E 412 278-3001
Carnegie (G-2793)

LIQUEFIED PETROLEUM GAS WHOLESALERS

Handygas Corporation ....G 717 428-2506
Seven Valleys (G-17379)

LIQUID CRYSTAL DISPLAYS

Thin Labs Inc ....G 215 269-3322
Fairless Hills (G-5804)

LITHOGRAPHIC PLATES

Color House Company Ltd ....F 215 322-4310
Warminster (G-18845)

Select Industries Inc ....G 724 654-7747
New Castle (G-12147)

LOCKS

Idn Global Inc ....G 215 698-8155
Philadelphia (G-13846)

Philadelphia Security Pdts Inc.....G 610 521-4400
Essington (G-5546)

Stanley Security Solutions Inc .....F 877 476-4968
Monroeville (G-11357)

Stanley Security Solutions Inc .....F 888 265-0412
Monroeville (G-11358)

LOCKS & LOCK SETS, WHOLESALE

Stanley Security Solutions Inc .....F 877 476-4968
Monroeville (G-11357)

Stanley Security Solutions Inc .....F 888 265-0412
Monroeville (G-11358)

LOCKS: Safe & Vault, Metal

Banc Technic Inc ....F 610 756-4440
Kutztown (G-8836)

LOCOMOTIVES & PARTS

Brookville Equipment Corp ....C 814 849-2000
Brookville (G-2252)

McHugh Railroad Maint Eqp ....F 215 949-0430
Fairless Hills (G-5788)

Rail Transit Products Inc ....G 724 527-2386
Penn (G-13227)

LOG SPLITTERS

Beaver Concrete & Supply Inc......F 724 774-5100
Monaca (G-11282)

LOGGING

Awf Logging ....G 814 577-5070
Penfield (G-13221)

Berdines Custom Hardwoods.......G 724 447-2535
Holbrook (G-7637)

Black Logging ....G 717 263-6446
Chambersburg (G-2911)

Brian Kingsley ....G 570 888-8668
Athens (G-810)

Byers Logging LLC ....G 717 530-5995
Shippensburg (G-17520)

Cable Hardwoods Inc ....F 724 452-5927
Portersville (G-15926)

Canfield Logging LLC ....G 570 224-4507
Damascus (G-3990)

Charlies Tree Service ....G 814 943-1131
Altoona (G-491)

CL Logging Inc ....G 814 842-3725
Hyndman (G-8048)

CLB Logging ....G 814 784-3301
Clearville (G-3240)

Coastal Treated Products Co.......E 610 932-5100
Oxford (G-13075)

Colonial Logging ....F 814 583-5901
Luthersburg (G-10122)

Crown Hardwood West Inc ....G 717 436-9677
Mifflintown (G-11112)

D Luther Trucking ....G 814 952-2136
Punxsutawney (G-16132)

Dean W Brouse & Sons ....G 570 374-7695
Kreamer (G-8817)

Diiulio Logging ....G 814 965-3183
Johnsonburg (G-8345)

Diversified Logging ....G 724 228-4143
Eighty Four (G-4838)

Edmund Burke Inc ....F 724 932-5200
Adamsville (G-25)

Edsell & Edsell Logging ....G 570 746-3203
Wyalusing (G-20250)

Elk River Logging Inc ....G 814 787-4327
Weedville (G-19458)

Emanuel K Fisher ....G 570 547-2599
Allenwood (G-441)

Energex Inc ....G 717 436-2400
Mifflintown (G-11115)

Eschrich and Son Logging ....G 814 362-1371
Lewis Run (G-9875)

Eugene Flynn Logging ....G 814 772-1219
Kersey (G-8558)

Full Strut Logging LLC ....G 814 323-5292
Corry (G-3761)

Fulton Forest Products ....E 814 782-3448
Shippenville (G-17561)

Gaberseck Bros ....G 814 274-0763
Coudersport (G-3781)

Gary Fike Logging ....G 724 329-7175
Farmington (G-5861)

Gary T Rossman ....G 814 837-7017
Kane (G-8463)

Gillens Logging Inc ....G 814 236-3999
Curwensville (G-3951)

Guy Sexton Timber Mgmt ....G 717 548-3422
Peach Bottom (G-13197)

Harold Graves Trucking ....G 814 654-7836
Spartansburg (G-17851)

Hopkins Logging ....G 814 827-1681
Titusville (G-18383)

Horlacher & Sherwood ....G 570 836-6298
Tunkhannock (G-18539)

Horsepower Logging ....G 814 274-2236
Coudersport (G-3782)

J&B Tree Service ....G 570 282-1193
Carbondale (G-2678)

James K Reisinger ....G 717 275-2124
Loysville (G-10116)

James Sluga ....G 814 778-5100
Mount Jewett (G-11643)

Jersey Shore Steel Company ....C 570 368-2601
Montoursville (G-11443)

John Carvell Logging ....G 717 354-8136
New Holland (G-12254)

John F Biel ....G 814 945-6306
Ludlow (G-10119)

John Hunt Logging ....G 814 967-4464
Townville (G-18445)

John R Holt ....G 814 837-8687
Kane (G-8468)

John W Burdge ....G 814 259-3901
Blairs Mills (G-1711)

Johnson Sawmill Logging ....G 717 532-7784
Orrstown (G-13033)

Justin L Zehr ....G 717 582-6436
Ickesburg (G-8052)

Koppers Industries Inc ....E 412 227-2001
Pittsburgh (G-15189)

Kovalick Lumber Co ....F 814 263-4928
Frenchville (G-6217)

Krause C W & Son Lumber ....G 814 378-8919
Houtzdale (G-7883)

Kt Zimmerman Lumber & Logging......G 570 345-2542
Pine Grove (G-14595)

Lapps Logging ....G 814 642-7949
Port Allegany (G-15894)

Lefever Logging ....G 717 587-7889
Bethel (G-1396)

Malsom Logging ....G 570 840-1044
Moscow (G-11598)

Mark A Kulka ....G 814 726-7331
Warren (G-19039)

Mason Hill Logging ....G 814 546-2478
Driftwood (G-4377)

Matteson Logging Inc ....G 814 848-9863
Genesee (G-6273)

Nicole M Reasner ....G 814 259-3827
Neelyton (G-11997)

Northwest Logging LLC ....G 814 598-1350
Kane (G-8474)

Oak Ridge Logging LLC ....G 717 687-8168
Quarryville (G-16275)

Patrick Donovan ....G 724 238-9038
Ligonier (G-9963)

Paul Danfelt ....G 814 448-2592
Mapleton Depot (G-10431)

Pendu Manufacturing Inc ....E 717 354-4348
New Holland (G-12272)

Penn West Trading Co Inc ....G 814 664-7649
Corry (G-3771)

R and C Logging ....G 814 590-4422
Reynoldsville (G-16661)

R E B Bloxham Inc ....G 570 222-4693
Clifford Township (G-3249)

R J & Sons Hoffman ....E 570 539-2428
Mount Pleasant Mills (G-11730)

Ricky E Shaffer ....G 814 328-2318
Brookville (G-2270)

Robert A Crooks ....G 724 541-2746
Marion Center (G-10477)

Roderick Duvall ....G 814 735-4969
Crystal Spring (G-3938)

Ron Andrus Logging ....G 814 435-6484
Gaines (G-6237)

S & S Loggs Inc ....G 814 339-7375
West Decatur (G-19691)

Scalpy Hollow Timber Service.......G 717 284-2862
Drumore (G-4379)

Sewell Logging ....G 814 837-7136
Harrisburg (G-7214)

Shaffer Logging ....G 814 827-1729
Titusville (G-18395)

Shetler Lumber Company Inc ....E 814 796-0303
Waterford (G-19269)

Shields Logging LLC ....G 814 778-6183
Kane (G-8478)

Smith Logging ....G 814 371-2698
Reynoldsville (G-16665)

Snyder & Sons Tree Surgeons ....G 610 932-2966
Lincoln University (G-9975)

Spigelmyer Wood Products Inc......F 717 248-6555
Lewistown (G-9948)

Stella-Jones Corporation ....E 814 371-7331
Du Bois (G-4421)

Stout Lumber Company ....G 814 443-9920
Somerset (G-17712)

T & B Logging Inc ....G 570 561-4847
Tunkhannock (G-18549)

Taylor Logging ....G 814 642-2788
Port Allegany (G-15895)

Thoman Logging ....G 570 265-4993
Le Raysville (G-9543)

Todd A Forsythe ....G 814 512-1457
Weedville (G-19460)

Twisted Tmber Deadwood Log Inc......G 215 541-4140
Pennsburg (G-13258)

Wenturine Bros Lumber Inc ....D 814 948-6050
Nicktown (G-12622)

LOGGING CAMPS & CONTRACTORS

A M Logging LLC ....F 814 349-8089
Spring Mills (G-17884)

Accurate Logging LLC ....G 724 354-3094
Creekside (G-3874)

Albert Miller Logging Inc ....G 570 295-4040
Lock Haven (G-10084)

Appalachian Timber Products ....F 724 329-1990
Markleysburg (G-10479)

Basinger Logging ....G 724 455-1067
Connellsville (G-3491)

Beavers Logging Inc ....G 570 842-4034
Gouldsboro (G-6567)

Brown & Lounsberry Inc ....G 610 847-2242
Ottsville (G-13060)

Cameron Lumber LLP ....E 814 749-9635
Homer City (G-7671)

CB Excavating & Logging LLC ....G 570 756-2749
Susquehanna (G-18178)

Coulter Logging ....G 814 236-2855
Curwensville (G-3949)

Curtis Leljedal Trading Loggn ....G 570 924-3938
Forksville (G-6056)

D & K Logging Inc ....G 814 663-0210
Spartansburg (G-17849)

D E Hyde Contracting ....G 814 228-3685
Genesee (G-6271)

D&R Logging ....G 570 345-4632
Pine Grove (G-14591)

Deems Logging ....G 724 657-7384
Volant (G-18772)

Donnelley Jr Joseph ....G 570 998-2541
Cogan Station (G-3359)

Double A Logging LLC ....G 814 885-6844
Kersey (G-8556)

Dunns Sawmill LLP..............................G....... 570 253-5217
  Honesdale (G-7710)
E & E Logging & Sons ....G....... 814 886-4440
  Loretto (G-10102)
Elick Logging Inc ....G....... 814 743-5546
  Cherry Tree (G-3032)
Elite Timber Harvesting LLC ....G....... 570 836-2453
  Factoryville (G-5756)
Fowlers Logging ....G....... 814 684-9883
  Tyrone (G-18583)
Fritz Logging ....G....... 814 623-6011
  Bedford (G-1050)
Gates Logging LLC ....G....... 814 353-1238
  Howard (G-7890)
Gessner Logging & Sawmill Inc ....F....... 717 365-3883
  Lykens (G-10133)
Gilbert Logging and Supply ....G....... 717 528-4919
  York Springs (G-20766)
Gosnell Logging ....G....... 814 776-2038
  Ridgway (G-16710)
J & L Logging ....G....... 717 687-8096
  Lancaster (G-9067)
Je Logging ....G....... 724 455-5723
  Normalville (G-12623)
JOB Logging Inc ....G....... 814 772-0513
  Ridgway (G-16714)
John L Luchs Logging ....G....... 814 772-5767
  Ridgway (G-16715)
Joni Britton Logging ....G....... 814 887-9920
  Smethport (G-17635)
K J Shaffer Milled Products ....F....... 570 698-8650
  Lake Ariel (G-8889)
Kio Logging LLC ....G....... 570 584-0283
  Hughesville (G-7895)
Klingler Family Sawmill........................G....... 717 677-4957
  Biglerville (G-1665)
Lipinski Logging and Lbr Inc ....G....... 814 385-4101
  Kennerdell (G-8498)
Mark Case Logging..............................G....... 570 729-8856
  Beach Lake (G-975)
Mark R Stairs ....G....... 814 634-0871
  Meyersdale (G-11016)
McVeys Logging & Lumbe ....G....... 814 542-2776
  Mount Union (G-11745)
Mitcheltree Bros ....G....... 814 665-4019
  Corry (G-3768)
Mitcheltree Bros Logging & Lbr ....G....... 724 598-7885
  Pulaski (G-16125)
Noga Logging ....G....... 724 224-6369
  New Kensington (G-12363)
Omega Logging Inc ....F....... 724 342-5430
  Wheatland (G-19839)
Pequignot Logging ....G....... 570 659-5251
  Covington (G-3792)
Perry S Swanson Logging ....G....... 814 837-7020
  Kane (G-8477)
R & J Logging Inc ....G....... 717 933-5646
  Bethel (G-1398)
R & K Wettlaufer Logging Inc ....G....... 570 924-4752
  New Albany (G-12015)
Rhoades Logging ....G....... 814 757-4711
  Sugar Grove (G-18145)
Robbins Logging & Lumber...................F....... 814 236-3384
  Olanta (G-12961)
Rockwell Lumber Co Inc ....G....... 717 597-7428
  Greencastle (G-6631)
S & H Logging LLC ....S....... 570 966-8958
  Mifflinburg (G-11102)
Scott Zimmerman Logging Inc ....G....... 814 965-5070
  Wilcox (G-19900)
Smoker Logging Inc ....G....... 814 486-2570
  Emporium (G-5075)
Stalnaker Lumber ....G....... 724 447-2248
  New Freeport (G-12219)
T&G Logging ....G....... 814 589-1731
  Grand Valley (G-6573)
Thomas Timberland Enterprises ....G....... 814 359-2890
  Bellefonte (G-1122)
Timinski Logging Co ....G....... 570 457-2641
  Sprng Brk Twp (G-17934)
Todd Smith Logging Inc ....G....... 814 887-2183
  Smethport (G-17637)
Wodrig Logging Corporation.................G....... 570 435-0783
  Muncy (G-11842)
Ye Logging Veneer...............................G....... 814 387-6503
  Moshannon (G-11604)

LOGGING: Peeler Logs

Blue Ox Timber Resources Inc.............F....... 814 437-2019
  Franklin (G-6116)

LOGGING: Skidding Logs

Ronnas Ruff Bark Trucking Inc ....G....... 814 221-4410
  Shippenville (G-17563)

LOGGING: Stumping For Turpentine Or Powder Manufacturing

Out of Site Stump Removal LLC............G....... 610 692-9907
  West Chester (G-19614)

LOGGING: Timber, Cut At Logging Camp

C Clark & Sons ....G....... 814 652-5370
  Everett (G-5568)
James Confer ....G....... 814 945-7013
  Ludlow (G-10118)
Ruffcutt Timber LLC ....G....... 724 626-7306
  Connellsville (G-3507)
Trumco Inc ....E....... 814 382-7767
  Atlantic (G-814)

LOGGING: Wood Chips, Produced In The Field

New Growth Resources Inc ....G....... 814 837-2206
  Kane (G-8473)
W D Zwicky & Son Inc ....E....... 484 248-5300
  Fleetwood (G-5982)

LOGGING: Wooden Logs

Justick & Justick Inc ....G....... 570 840-0187
  Sprng Brk Twp (G-17933)

LOGS: Gas, Fireplace

Log Hard Premium Pellets Inc ....G....... 814 654-2100
  Spartansburg (G-17852)

LOOSELEAF BINDERS

Sperry Graphic Inc..............................E....... 610 534-8585
  Folcroft (G-6016)
Tamarack Packaging Ltd ....E....... 814 724-2860
  Meadville (G-10798)

LOOSELEAF BINDERS: Library

Brodart Co ....D....... 570 326-2461
  Williamsport (G-19995)

LOTIONS OR CREAMS: Face

Advanced Skin Technologies Inc ....G....... 610 488-7643
  Bernville (G-1295)
Aucourant LLC ....F....... 800 682-1623
  East Stroudsburg (G-4606)
Decon Laboratories Inc ....E....... 610 755-0800
  King of Prussia (G-8606)
Donald Trammell ....G....... 484 238-5467
  Coatesville (G-3301)
Hawkeye-Jensen Inc ....E....... 610 488-8500
  Bernville (G-1300)
Sensible Organics Inc ....E....... 724 891-4560
  Beaver Falls (G-1011)
Strong Body Care Products Inc............G....... 717 786-8947
  New Providence (G-12435)

LOUDSPEAKERS

Community Light & Sound Inc ....D....... 610 876-3400
  Chester (G-3043)
Dnh Speakers Inc ....G....... 484 494-5790
  Sharon Hill (G-17457)

LOUVERS: Ventilating

North East Louvers Inc........................F....... 717 436-5300
  Mifflintown (G-11131)

LUBRICANTS: Corrosion Preventive

Castrol Industrial N Amer Inc ....D....... 877 641-1600
  Levittown (G-9824)
Harsco Corporation ....C....... 570 421-7500
  East Stroudsburg (G-4617)
Hollyfrontier Corporation ....G....... 800 395-2786
  Plymouth Meeting (G-15848)
Quaker Chemical Corporation ....A....... 610 832-4000
  Conshohocken (G-3595)
Staar Distributing Llc...........................E....... 814 371-3500
  Du Bois (G-4420)

LUBRICATING EQPT: Indl

C and M Sales Co.................................F....... 814 437-3095
  Franklin (G-6118)
Jnb Industrial Supply Inc ....G....... 412 455-5170
  Blawnox (G-1764)

LUBRICATING OIL & GREASE WHOLESALERS

Advanced Lubrication Spc Inc ....E....... 215 244-2114
  Bensalem (G-1144)
American Refining Group Inc ....B....... 814 368-1378
  Bradford (G-1955)
Fuchs Lubricants Co ....E....... 724 867-5000
  Emlenton (G-5008)
Naughton Energy Corporation ....F....... 570 646-0422
  Pocono Pines (G-15882)
Trac Products Inc.................................G....... 610 789-7853
  Havertown (G-7432)

LUBRICATION SYSTEMS & EQPT

Lube Systems Company ....G....... 724 335-4050
  Apollo (G-682)

LUGGAGE & BRIEFCASES

Ceramic Art Company Inc ....A....... 952 944-5600
  Bristol (G-2124)
Lenox Corporation ....F....... 267 525-7800
  Bristol (G-2159)
M & M Manufacturing Co......................E....... 724 274-0767
  Cheswick (G-3111)
Tom James Company ....D....... 717 264-5768
  Chambersburg (G-2986)

LUGGAGE & LEATHER GOODS STORES

Ceramic Art Company Inc ....A....... 952 944-5600
  Bristol (G-2124)
Lenox Corporation ....F....... 267 525-7800
  Bristol (G-2159)

LUGGAGE & LEATHER GOODS STORES: Leather, Exc Luggage & Shoes

Columbia Organ Works Inc...................G....... 717 684-3573
  Columbia (G-3436)

LUGGAGE & LEATHER GOODS STORES: Luggage, Exc Footlckr/Trunk

Richard Zerbe Ltd ....G....... 717 564-2024
  Harrisburg (G-7205)

LUMBER & BLDG MATLS DEALER, RET: Electric Constructn Matls

Medico Industries Inc ....C....... 570 825-7711
  Wilkes Barre (G-19942)
Medico Industries Inc ....E....... 570 825-7711
  Hanover Township (G-6996)
Pioneer Electric Supply Co Inc.............G....... 814 437-1342
  Franklin (G-6152)

LUMBER & BLDG MATLS DEALER, RET: Wallboard, Compositn/Panel

Wood Fabricators Inc ....F....... 717 284-4849
  Quarryville (G-16284)

LUMBER & BLDG MATLS DEALERS, RET: Energy Conservation Prdts

Xto Energy Inc.....................................G....... 570 368-8920
  Montoursville (G-11458)

LUMBER & BLDG MATRLS DEALERS, RET: Bath Fixtures, Eqpt/Sply

Archetype Design Studio LLC ....G....... 412 369-2900
  West View (G-19773)
Luicana Industries Inc ....G....... 570 325-9699
  Jim Thorpe (G-8341)
Thebathoutlet LLC ....F....... 877 256-1645
  Lansdale (G-9414)

PRODUCT

LUMBER & BLDG MTRLS DEALERS, RET: Closets, Interiors/Access

P A Office and Closet Systems ....F 610 944-1333
Fleetwood *(G-5977)*

LUMBER & BLDG MTRLS DEALERS, RET: Doors, Storm, Wood/Metal

Burke & Sons Inc ....E 814 938-7303
Punxsutawney *(G-16129)*
Dailey Manufacturing Co ....F 215 659-0477
Willow Grove *(G-20113)*
Standard Awnings & Aluminum ....G 570 824-3535
Hanover Township *(G-7006)*
Tri-State Door and Hardware ....G 215 455-2100
Philadelphia *(G-14408)*
Trinity Glass Intl Inc ....D 610 395-2030
Breinigsville *(G-2028)*

LUMBER & BLDG MTRLS DEALERS, RET: Planing Mill Prdts/Lumber

Aldenville Log and Lumberinc ....G 570 785-3141
Prompton *(G-16109)*
Andreas Lumber Inc ....G 570 379-3644
Wapwallopen *(G-18807)*
Eutsey Lumber Co Inc ....F 724 887-8404
Scottdale *(G-17191)*
Gift Lumber Co Inc ....G 610 689-9483
Douglassville *(G-4176)*
Goshorn Industries LLC ....G 717 369-3654
Chambersburg *(G-2936)*
Horner Lumber Company ....G 814 629-5861
Boswell *(G-1883)*
John M Fink Lumber ....G 570 435-0362
Montoursville *(G-11444)*
Krause C W & Son Lumber ....G 814 378-8919
Houtzdale *(G-7883)*
Ralph Stuck Lumber Company ....G 570 539-8666
Mount Pleasant Mills *(G-11731)*
Shaffer Brothers Lumber Co ....G 814 842-3996
Hyndman *(G-8051)*
Silhol Builders Supply Co Inc ....E 412 221-7400
Bridgeville *(G-2089)*
Tony L Stec Lumber Company ....F 814 563-9002
Garland *(G-6263)*

LUMBER & BUILDING MATERIAL DEALERS, RETAIL: Roofing Material

Johns Manville Corporation ....D 570 455-5340
Hazle Township *(G-7467)*
Joseph Jenkins Inc ....G 814 786-9085
Grove City *(G-6792)*
New Heights LLC ....G 717 768-0070
Leola *(G-9795)*

LUMBER & BUILDING MATERIALS DEALER, RET: Door & Window Prdts

Biltwood Architectural Mllwk ....F 717 593-9400
Greencastle *(G-6600)*
Superior Window Mfg Inc ....F 412 793-3500
Pittsburgh *(G-15589)*
Thermal Industries Inc ....G 814 944-4534
Altoona *(G-551)*
Thermolite Inc ....E 570 969-1957
Scranton *(G-17300)*
Zurn Aluminum Products Co ....G 814 774-2681
Girard *(G-6404)*

LUMBER & BUILDING MATERIALS DEALER, RET: Masonry Matls/Splys

A & A Concrete Products Inc ....F 724 538-1114
Evans City *(G-5555)*
A C Miller Concrete Pdts Inc ....D 724 459-5950
Blairsville *(G-1712)*
Balducci Stoneyard LLC ....G 410 627-0594
New Freedom *(G-12201)*
Castek Inc ....F 570 759-3540
Berwick *(G-1316)*
Colonial Concrete Industries ....G 610 279-2102
King of Prussia *(G-8594)*
Commonwealth Precast Inc ....F 215 721-6005
Souderton *(G-17730)*
EP Henry Corporation ....E 610 495-8533
Parker Ford *(G-13168)*

Forsht Concrete Pdts Co Inc ....G 814 944-1617
Altoona *(G-507)*
Laurel Aggregates Inc ....E 724 564-5099
Uniontown *(G-18634)*
Limestone Mobile Concrete ....G 570 437-2640
Milton *(G-11247)*
McAvoy Brick Company ....G 610 933-2932
Phoenixville *(G-14560)*
Pipe & Precast Cnstr Pdts Inc ....F 610 644-7338
Devault *(G-4112)*
Sakala Stone Products ....G 724 339-2224
New Kensington *(G-12374)*
Scranton Craftsmen Inc ....D 570 347-5125
Throop *(G-18361)*

LUMBER & BUILDING MATERIALS DEALERS, RET: Solar Heating Eqpt

Ecolution Energy LLC ....G 908 707-1400
Lehighton *(G-9713)*

LUMBER & BUILDING MATERIALS DEALERS, RETAIL: Brick

Beavertown Block Co Inc ....E 814 359-2771
Bellefonte *(G-1093)*
Redland Brick Inc ....E 412 828-8046
Cheswick *(G-3117)*
Wendell H Stone Company Inc ....F 412 373-6235
Monroeville *(G-11364)*

LUMBER & BUILDING MATERIALS DEALERS, RETAIL: Cement

East Side Concrete Supply Co ....F 814 944-8175
Altoona *(G-499)*
Marstellar Concrete Inc ....G 717 834-6200
Duncannon *(G-4448)*
Pocono Transcrete Incorporated ....G 570 655-9166
Pittston *(G-15777)*

LUMBER & BUILDING MATERIALS DEALERS, RETAIL: Countertops

Custom Stone Interiors Inc ....G 814 548-0120
Bellefonte *(G-1096)*
Robertsons Inc ....G 814 838-2313
Erie *(G-5464)*

LUMBER & BUILDING MATERIALS DEALERS, RETAIL: Lime & Plaster

Valley Quarries Inc ....G 814 766-2211
Fayetteville *(G-5879)*

LUMBER & BUILDING MATERIALS DEALERS, RETAIL: Modular Homes

A & B Homes Inc ....G 570 253-3888
Honesdale *(G-7699)*
Signature Building Systems Inc ....E 570 774-1000
Moosic *(G-11515)*

LUMBER & BUILDING MATERIALS DEALERS, RETAIL: Paving Stones

Marble Crafters Inc ....D 610 497-6000
Marcus Hook *(G-10448)*

LUMBER & BUILDING MATERIALS DEALERS, RETAIL: Sand & Gravel

Fiesler Sand & Gravel LLC ....G 814 899-6161
Erie *(G-5289)*
Four Winds Concrete Inc ....E 610 865-1788
Bethlehem *(G-1517)*
Four Winds Concrete Inc ....E 610 865-1788
Center Valley *(G-2827)*
Frank Casilio and Sons Inc ....F 610 867-5886
Bethlehem *(G-1518)*
GF Edwards Inc ....G 570 842-8438
Elmhurst Township *(G-4959)*
GF Edwards Inc ....E 570 676-3200
South Sterling *(G-17787)*
Jdn Block Inc ....E 215 723-5506
Souderton *(G-17745)*
Jokers Coal & Building Sups ....G 570 724-4912
Wellsboro *(G-19468)*

LUMBER & BUILDING MATERIALS DEALERS, RETAIL: Siding

Rdy Gutters Plus LLC ....G 610 488-5666
Bernville *(G-1304)*

LUMBER & BUILDING MATERIALS RET DEALERS: Millwork & Lumber

Allensville Planing Mill Inc ....C 717 483-6386
Allensville *(G-106)*
Allensville Planing Mill Inc ....F 717 248-9688
Lewistown *(G-9924)*
Berdines Custom Hardwoods ....G 724 447-2535
Holbrook *(G-7637)*
Bingaman & Son Lumber Inc ....E 570 726-7795
Mill Hall *(G-11173)*
Bishop Wood Products Inc ....F 215 723-6644
Souderton *(G-17726)*
Bowser Lumber Co Inc ....F 814 277-9956
Mahaffey *(G-10170)*
Foster-Kmetz Woodworking ....G 570 325-8222
Jim Thorpe *(G-8340)*
M & R Woodworks Inc ....G 724 378-7677
Aliquippa *(G-81)*
New Enterprise Stone Lime Inc ....D 610 374-5131
Kutztown *(G-8851)*
Seals of Blossburg ....G 570 638-2161
Blossburg *(G-1809)*
Seaquay Archtctural Mllwk Corp ....F 610 279-1201
Bridgeport *(G-2045)*
Shady Grove Cabinet Shop Inc ....G 717 597-0825
Greencastle *(G-6632)*
Specialty Millworks Inc ....G 610 682-6334
Topton *(G-18416)*
Staurowsky Woodworking ....G 610 489-0770
Collegeville *(G-3394)*
Thomas Gross Woodworking ....G 724 593-7044
Ligonier *(G-9967)*

LUMBER & BUILDING MATLS DEALERS, RET: Concrete/Cinder Block

De Paul Concrete ....G 610 832-8000
Flourtown *(G-5986)*
Fizzano Bros Inc ....D 610 833-1100
Crum Lynne *(G-3937)*
Fizzano Bros Inc ....E 215 355-6160
Feasterville Trevose *(G-5910)*
Main Line Concrete & Sup Inc ....F 610 269-5556
Downingtown *(G-4238)*
Tri-City Marble LLC ....F 610 481-0177
Allentown *(G-413)*

LUMBER: Cants, Resawn

Price C L Lumber LLC ....F 814 349-5505
Aaronsburg *(G-2)*

LUMBER: Dimension, Hardwood

Hope Good Hardwoods Inc ....G 610 350-1556
Landenberg *(G-9250)*
Weaber Inc ....C 717 867-2212
Lebanon *(G-9638)*
Wilson Global Inc ....D 724 883-4952
Jefferson *(G-8272)*

LUMBER: Fuelwood, From Mill Waste

PA Pellets LLC ....F 814 848-9970
Ulysses *(G-18604)*
Pellheat Inc ....G 724 850-8169
Greensburg *(G-6699)*

LUMBER: Furniture Dimension Stock, Softwood

Price Lumber Company ....G 814 231-0260
Port Matilda *(G-15904)*

LUMBER: Hardboard

Jeld-Wen Inc ....C 570 265-9121
Towanda *(G-18431)*

LUMBER: Hardwood Dimension

Babcock Lumber Company ....G 814 239-2281
Pittsburgh *(G-14746)*
Brownlee Lumber Inc ....E 814 328-2991
Brookville *(G-2255)*

(G-0000) Company's Geographic Section entry number

Colonial Hardwoods & Logging ....F 814 583-5901
Luthersburg (G-10121)
Culver Hardwoods ....G 814 827-3202
Titusville (G-18377)
Gutchess Lumber Co Inc ....D 724 537-6447
Latrobe (G-9479)
Horstcraft Millworks LLC ....G 717 694-9222
Richfield (G-16680)
J M Wood Products ....F 717 483-6700
Allensville (G-108)
Lew-Hoc Wood Products Inc ....E 814 486-0359
Emporium (G-5067)
M & C Lumber Co Inc ....G 717 573-2200
Warfordsburg (G-18813)
Mick Brothers Lumber Inc ....E 814 664-8700
Corry (G-3767)
Musselman Lumber - US Lbm LLC ......D 717 354-4321
New Holland (G-12264)
Structural Glulam LLC ....E 717 355-9813
New Holland (G-12286)

LUMBER: Hardwood Dimension & Flooring Mills

Allegheny Wood Products Inc ....D 814 354-7304
Marble (G-10434)
Appalachian Wood Products Inc ....B 814 765-2003
Clearfield (G-3212)
Armstrong Flooring Inc ....A 717 672-9611
Lancaster (G-8940)
Bingaman & Son Lumber Inc ....E 570 726-7795
Mill Hall (G-11173)
Boswell Lumber Company ....E 814 629-5625
Boswell (G-1881)
Brian O Keffe ....G 570 477-3962
Sweet Valley (G-18187)
Brodart Co ....E 570 326-2461
Montgomery (G-11368)
Brown Timber and Land Co Inc ....F 724 547-7777
Acme (G-15)
Carol Zuzek ....G 814 837-7090
Kane (G-8460)
Center Hardwood LLC ....F 814 684-3600
Tyrone (G-18579)
Clymer Quality Hardwood ....G 724 463-1827
Clymer (G-3271)
Collins Pine Company ....D 814 837-6941
Kane (G-8461)
Conestoga Wood Spc Corp ....C 570 658-9663
Beavertown (G-1025)
Danzer Lumber North Amer Inc ....C 814 368-3701
Bradford (G-1966)
Deer Park Lumber Inc ....D 570 836-1133
Tunkhannock (G-18538)
Ed Nicholson & Sons Lumber Co ....F 724 628-4440
Connellsville (G-3496)
Frank D Suppa Lumber Inc ....F 814 723-7360
Warren (G-19026)
Fulton Forest Products ....E 814 782-3448
Shippenville (G-17561)
Heritage Wood Products LLC ....G 814 629-9265
Boswell (G-1882)
Highland Forest Resources Inc ....E 814 837-6760
Kane (G-8466)
Hyma Devore Lumber Mill Inc ....E 814 563-4646
Youngsville (G-20772)
Itl Corp ....D 814 463-7701
Endeavor (G-5079)
John L Luchs Logging ....G 814 772-5767
Ridgway (G-16715)
Kovalick Lumber Co ....F 814 263-4928
Frenchville (G-6217)
Lewis & Hockenberry Inc ....E 814 486-0359
Emporium (G-5068)
Mitcheltree Bros Logging & Lbr ....G 724 598-7885
Pulaski (G-16125)
Modern Cabinet and Cnstr Co ....F 814 942-1000
Altoona (G-528)
Noah Shirk Sawmill ....G 717 354-0192
Ephrata (G-5132)
Oakes & McClelland Co ....F 724 588-6400
Greenville (G-6761)
Ordie Price Sawmill Inc ....F 570 222-3986
South Gibson (G-17780)
Patterson Lumber Co Inc ....E 814 435-2210
Galeton (G-6241)
Pendu Manufacturing Inc ....E 717 354-4348
New Holland (G-12272)
Penn Wood Products Inc ....D 717 259-9551
East Berlin (G-4524)

RAD Mfg LLC ....D 570 752-4514
Nescopeck (G-12001)
RAD Mfg LLC ....E 570 752-4514
Nescopeck (G-12002)
Ram Forest Products Inc ....D 814 697-7185
Shinglehouse (G-17512)
Rgm Hardwoods Inc ....E 570 842-4533
Moscow (G-11603)
Richard K Mohn ....G 717 762-7646
Waynesboro (G-19423)
Robbins Logging & Lumber ....F 814 236-3384
Olanta (G-12961)
Seneca Hardwood Lumber Co Inc ....E 814 498-2241
Cranberry (G-3797)
Shetler Lumber Company Inc ....E 814 796-0303
Waterford (G-19269)
Specialty Surfaces Intl Inc ....C 877 686-8873
King of Prussia (G-8679)
Thomas Timberland Enterprises ....G 814 359-2890
Bellefonte (G-1122)
Thompson Maple Products Inc ....E 814 664-7717
Corry (G-3775)
Walter and Jackson Inc ....D 610 593-5195
Christiana (G-3144)
Weaber Inc ....E 814 827-4621
Titusville (G-18403)
Wenturine Bros Lumber Inc ....D 814 948-6050
Nicktown (G-12622)
Weyerhaeuser Company ....C 814 827-4621
Titusville (G-18404)
Wheeland Lumber Co Inc ....D 570 324-6042
Liberty (G-9952)
Wt Hardwoods Group Inc ....F 717 867-2212
Lebanon (G-9639)

LUMBER: Kiln Dried

Forcey Lumber Co Inc ....E 814 857-5002
Woodland (G-20211)
Ordie Price Sawmill Inc ....F 570 222-3986
South Gibson (G-17780)
Ralph Stuck Lumber Company ....G 570 539-8666
Mount Pleasant Mills (G-11731)
Walker Lumber Co Inc ....E 814 857-7642
Woodland (G-20215)

LUMBER: Mine Props, Treated

Arrison H B West Virginia Inc ....G 724 324-2106
Mount Morris (G-11678)
Rockwell Venture Capital ....G 412 281-4620
Pittsburgh (G-15495)

LUMBER: Piles, Foundation & Marine Construction, Treated

Redstone International Inc ....D 724 439-1500
Scenery Hill (G-17125)
Sewsations LLC ....G 484 842-1024
Garnet Valley (G-6268)

LUMBER: Plywood, Hardwood

Collins Pine Company ....D 814 837-6941
Kane (G-8461)
Cummings Veneer Products Inc ....G 570 995-1892
Troy (G-18520)
Dally Slate Company Inc ....D 610 863-4172
Pen Argyl (G-13213)
Danzer Veneer Americas Inc ....D 570 322-4400
Williamsport (G-20002)
Danzer Veneer Americas Inc ....D 724 827-8366
Darlington (G-4026)
Graham Paining Co ....D 215 447-8552
Bensalem (G-1206)
Heirloom Engraving LLC ....G 717 336-8451
Stevens (G-18052)
Interforest Corp ....D 724 827-8366
Darlington (G-4029)
J C Snavely & Sons Inc ....C 717 898-2241
Landisville (G-9262)
Mars Lumber Inc ....G 724 625-2224
Mars (G-10506)
Ram Forest Products Inc ....D 814 697-7185
Shinglehouse (G-17512)
Somerset Door and Column Co ....E 814 445-9608
Somerset (G-17708)
United Panel Inc ....E 610 588-6871
Mount Bethel (G-11615)

LUMBER: Plywood, Hardwood or Hardwood Faced

Mike Woodshop ....G 724 272-0259
Mars (G-10507)

LUMBER: Plywood, Prefinished, Hardwood

Wehrungs Specialty Woods ....D 610 847-6002
Ottsville (G-13069)

LUMBER: Plywood, Softwood

Howe Wood Products Inc ....F 717 266-9855
York (G-20529)

LUMBER: Plywood, Softwood

Ufp Gordon LLC ....E 570 875-2811
Gordon (G-6547)
Ufp Stockertown LLC ....G 610 759-8536
Stockertown (G-18067)

LUMBER: Rails, Fence, Round Or Split

Dimec Rail Service ....E 844 362-9221
Pottstown (G-15983)
Heritage Fence & Deck LLC ....G 610 476-0003
Skippack (G-17598)
Marietta Fence Experts LLC ....G 724 925-6100
Hunker (G-7929)

LUMBER: Resawn, Small Dimension

Diamond Road Resawing LLC ....G 717 738-3741
Ephrata (G-5100)
Fairmans Wood Processing Inc ....G 724 349-6778
Creekside (G-3876)

LUMBER: Siding, Dressed

Guyon Industries Inc ....G 717 528-0154
York Springs (G-20767)

LUMBER: Treated

Champion Lumber Company Inc ....F 724 455-3401
Champion (G-3003)
Great Lakes Framing LLC ....G 724 399-0220
Parker (G-13165)
Koppers Industries Inc ....E 412 826-3970
Pittsburgh (G-15190)
Koppers Industries Inc ....G 724 684-1000
Monessen (G-11299)
Mellott Wood Preserving Inc ....E 717 573-2519
Needmore (G-11996)
Property Preservers ....G 267 975-3990
Philadelphia (G-14209)
Stella-Jones Corporation ....G 717 721-3113
Ephrata (G-5148)
Stella-Jones US Holding Corp ....E 304 372-2211
Pittsburgh (G-15582)
Tangent Rail Corporation ....G 412 325-0202
Pittsburgh (G-15596)
Tangent Rail Products Inc ....F 412 325-0202
Pittsburgh (G-15597)
TSO of Ohio Inc ....G 724 452-6161
Fombell (G-6035)

LUMBER: Veneer, Hardwood

Edgemate Inc ....C 814 224-5717
Roaring Spring (G-16764)
Interntional Timber Veneer LLC ....C 724 662-0880
Jackson Center (G-8228)
Oak Hill Veneer Inc ....D 570 297-4137
Troy (G-18524)
Sieling and Jones Inc ....D 717 235-7931
New Freedom (G-12215)
Signature Stone Inc ....G 717 397-2364
Lancaster (G-9200)

LUMBER: Veneer, Softwood

Wilson Global Inc ....D 724 883-4952
Jefferson (G-8272)

LUMINOUS PRDTS, EXC ELECTRIC, WHOLESALE:

Jalite Inc ....G 570 491-2205
Matamoras (G-10539)

PRODUCT

MACHINE PARTS: Stamped Or Pressed Metal

Acme Stamping Wire Forming Co ....E 412 771-5720
Pittsburgh *(G-14644)*

Advanced Feedscrews Inc ....E 724 924-9877
New Castle *(G-12054)*

Aeroparts Fabg & Machining Inc ....E 814 948-6015
Nicktown *(G-12618)*

Aetna Machine Company ....F 814 425-3881
Cochranton *(G-3334)*

American Machine Co ....G 717 533-5678
Palmyra *(G-13115)*

Axiom Inc ....F 570 385-1944
Schuylkill Haven *(G-17148)*

C G S Enterprises Inc ....F 610 758-9263
Bethlehem *(G-1477)*

Camco Manufacturing Inc ....E 570 731-4109
Sayre *(G-17113)*

Century Propeller Corporation ....F 814 677-7100
Franklin *(G-6119)*

Chase Manufacturing ....E 814 664-9069
Corry *(G-3747)*

Cumberland Tool & Die Inc ....E 717 691-1125
Mechanicsburg *(G-10835)*

Dallas Machine Inc ....E 610 799-2800
Schnecksville *(G-17138)*

Evans Machining Service Inc ....G 412 233-3556
Clairton *(G-3150)*

Federal Metal Products Inc ....G 610 847-2077
Ferndale *(G-5950)*

Gemel Precision Tool Inc ....E 215 355-2174
Warminster *(G-18886)*

Heraeus Incorporated ....G 215 944-9981
Yardley *(G-20314)*

Heritage Maintenance Pdts LLC ....G 610 277-5070
Harleysville *(G-7038)*

Hillcrest Tool & Die Inc ....F 814 827-1296
Titusville *(G-18381)*

Hpt Pharma LLC ....F 215 792-0020
Warrington *(G-19121)*

Igb Tool & Machine Inc ....G 215 338-1420
Philadelphia *(G-13847)*

Independent Tool & Mfg ....G 814 336-5168
Meadville *(G-10738)*

Jackson & Sons Machine Co ....G 724 744-2116
Harrison City *(G-7249)*

Kreckel Enterprises Inc ....F 814 834-1874
Saint Marys *(G-16986)*

Metal Powder Products LLC ....D 814 834-2886
Saint Marys *(G-16991)*

Metalkraft Industries Inc ....E 570 724-6800
Wellsboro *(G-19469)*

Perry C Ritter ....G 215 699-7079
Lansdale *(G-9398)*

Stellar Machine Incorporated ....F 570 718-1733
Nanticoke *(G-11903)*

Tecklane Manufacturing Inc ....F 724 274-9464
Springdale *(G-17903)*

Vertech International Inc ....E 215 529-0300
Quakertown *(G-16257)*

Windle Mech Solutions Inc ....G 215 624-8600
Philadelphia *(G-14479)*

Winston & Duke Inc ....E 814 456-0582
Erie *(G-5530)*

MACHINE SHOPS

Agape Precision Mfg LLC ....E 484 704-2601
Pottstown *(G-15961)*

Alessi Manufacturing Corp ....E 610 586-4200
Collingdale *(G-3403)*

Alpha Omega Machine Shop ....G 570 573-4610
Pine Grove *(G-14589)*

American Prcsion Machining LLC ....G 484 632-9449
Portland *(G-15938)*

Automated Concepts Tooling Inc ....F 814 796-6302
Waterford *(G-19259)*

Bolt Works Inc ....F 724 776-7273
Warrendale *(G-19069)*

Bolttech Mannings Inc ....D 724 872-4873
North Versailles *(G-12772)*

Brandywine Machine Co Inc ....F 610 269-1221
Downingtown *(G-4216)*

Brent D Beistel ....G 724 823-0099
Donora *(G-4149)*

Central Hydraulics Inc ....E 814 224-0375
East Freedom *(G-4562)*

Conn & Company LLC ....G 814 723-7980
Warren *(G-19018)*

CRC Manufacturing Inc ....G 703 408-0645
Everett *(G-5569)*

D L George & Sons Mfg Inc ....D 717 765-4700
Waynesboro *(G-19407)*

Dean Barrett ....G 814 427-2586
Punxsutawney *(G-16134)*

Dedicated Customs Inc ....G 724 678-6609
Burgettstown *(G-2345)*

Digital Press Inc ....G 610 758-9680
Bethlehem *(G-1497)*

DMC Global Inc ....E 724 277-9710
Mount Braddock *(G-11616)*

East Bank Machine Inc ....G 412 384-4721
Finleyville *(G-5956)*

Ellwood National Forge Company ....C 814 563-7522
Irvine *(G-8140)*

Excellent Tool Inc ....G 814 337-7705
Meadville *(G-10724)*

Fairfield Manufacturing Co Inc ....F 570 368-8624
Montoursville *(G-11438)*

Ford City Gun Workd ....G 724 994-9501
Ford City *(G-6045)*

Giesler Engineering Inc ....G 800 428-8616
Aston *(G-768)*

Greenetech Mfg Co Inc ....E 724 228-2400
Washington *(G-19181)*

Hillside Custom Mac Wel & Fab ....F 610 942-3093
Honey Brook *(G-7748)*

Hoffman-Kane Distributors Inc ....F 412 653-6886
Pittsburgh *(G-15097)*

Image Components Inc ....G 215 739-3599
Philadelphia *(G-13850)*

Industrial Consortium Inc ....F 610 777-1653
Mohnton *(G-11267)*

J I T Tool & Die Inc ....E 814 265-0257
Brockport *(G-2221)*

Jade Equipment Corporation ....C 215 947-3333
Huntingdon Valley *(G-7999)*

Jbm Metalcraft Corp ....G 814 241-0448
Johnstown *(G-8384)*

Jeglinski Group Inc ....E 814 807-0681
Meadville *(G-10739)*

Kelly Precision Machining Co ....G 717 396-8622
Lancaster *(G-9080)*

Kercher Enterprises Inc ....E 717 273-2111
Lebanon *(G-9591)*

Lewis Welding & Xcavating ....G 570 353-7301
Morris *(G-11545)*

Lwe Inc ....G 814 336-3553
Meadville *(G-10751)*

M and P Custom Design Inc ....F 610 444-0244
Kennett Square *(G-8524)*

M I P Inc ....G 724 643-5114
Midland *(G-11087)*

Mdc Machine Incorporated ....F 814 372-2345
Du Bois *(G-4405)*

Meck Manufacturing ....G 610 756-6284
Lenhartsville *(G-9759)*

Metal Integrity Inc ....E 814 234-7399
State College *(G-17989)*

Micro Precision Corporation ....D 717 393-4100
Lancaster *(G-9133)*

Minnotte Manufacturing Corp ....D 412 373-5270
Trafford *(G-18459)*

Morocco Welding LLC ....F 814 444-9353
Somerset *(G-17697)*

Muncy Machine & Tool Co Inc ....E 570 649-5188
Turbotville *(G-18555)*

Orr Screw Machine Products ....E 724 668-2256
Greensburg *(G-6695)*

Pb Holdings Inc ....G 215 947-3333
Huntingdon Valley *(G-8021)*

R&R Machine Inc ....G 724 286-9507
Rochester Mills *(G-16790)*

Reilly Plating Company Inc ....D 570 735-7777
Nanticoke *(G-11902)*

Reuss Industries Inc ....E 724 722-3300
Madison *(G-10166)*

Saeilo Inc ....F 845 735-4500
Greeley *(G-6583)*

Sinacom North America Inc ....E 610 337-2250
King of Prussia *(G-8677)*

SMI IL Inc ....E 847 228-0090
Greeley *(G-6585)*

T H E M Services Inc ....G 610 559-9341
Easton *(G-4761)*

Tooling Specialists Inc ....G 724 837-0433
Latrobe *(G-9525)*

Tory Tool Inc ....E 814 772-5439
Saint Marys *(G-17023)*

Tory Tool Inc ....E 814 772-5439
Ridgway *(G-16732)*

Under Pressure Connections LLC ....G 570 326-1117
South Williamsport *(G-17793)*

Universal Mch Co Pottstown Inc ....D 610 323-1810
Pottstown *(G-16062)*

Wagner Industries Inc ....F 570 874-4400
Frackville *(G-6108)*

Winston & Duke Inc ....E 814 456-0582
Erie *(G-5530)*

York Precision ....F 717 764-8855
York *(G-20749)*

Z-Axis Connector Company ....F 267 803-9000
Warminster *(G-19006)*

MACHINE TOOL ACCESS: Balancing Machines

Dynamic Balancing Co Inc ....G 610 337-2757
King of Prussia *(G-8615)*

Southco Inc ....E 215 957-9260
Warminster *(G-18969)*

MACHINE TOOL ACCESS: Cutting

A & H Industries Inc ....E 717 866-7591
Myerstown *(G-11873)*

A and M Tool LLC ....G 215 513-0968
Harleysville *(G-7011)*

Advanced Carbide Tool Company ....F 267 960-1222
Southampton *(G-17797)*

Allegheny Tool & Supply Inc ....F 814 437-7062
Franklin *(G-6114)*

Amat Inc ....G 717 235-8003
New Freedom *(G-12200)*

Dauphin Precision Tool LLC ....C 800 522-8665
Millersburg *(G-11192)*

Deane Carbide Products Inc ....F 215 639-3333
Trevose *(G-18492)*

Dynacut Inc ....G 610 346-7386
Springtown *(G-17926)*

Eastcoast Cutter Inc ....G 717 933-5566
Myerstown *(G-11883)*

Form Tool Technology Inc ....E 717 792-3626
York *(G-20484)*

Greenleaf Corporation ....B 814 763-2915
Saegertown *(G-16915)*

Hamilton Tool Co Inc ....G 814 382-3419
Meadville *(G-10734)*

Harpoint Holdings Inc ....G 717 692-2113
Millersburg *(G-11194)*

J & J Carbide Tool Co Inc ....G 570 538-9283
Watsontown *(G-19276)*

K-Tool Inc ....F 717 632-3015
Gettysburg *(G-6303)*

Kennametal Inc ....C 814 623-2711
Bedford *(G-1057)*

Kennametal Inc ....A 412 539-5000
Latrobe *(G-9486)*

Kennametal Inc ....C 724 864-5900
Irwin *(G-8178)*

Kennametal Inc ....F 724 657-1967
New Castle *(G-12112)*

Kennametal Inc ....A 412 248-8000
Pittsburgh *(G-15169)*

Kermitool Liquidation Company ....F 717 846-8665
York *(G-20551)*

Magnum Carbide LLC ....G 717 762-7181
Waynesboro *(G-19417)*

NC Industries Inc ....F 248 528-5200
Reynoldsville *(G-16658)*

Niagara Cutter PA Inc ....E 814 653-8211
Reynoldsville *(G-16659)*

Precision Carbide Tooling Inc ....G 717 244-4771
Red Lion *(G-16611)*

Preform Specialties Inc ....E 724 459-0808
Blairsville *(G-1738)*

Reed Tool & Die Inc ....E 724 547-3500
Mount Pleasant *(G-11713)*

Richter Precision Inc ....D 717 560-9990
East Petersburg *(G-4589)*

Talbot Holdings LLC ....C 717 692-2113
Millersburg *(G-11202)*

MACHINE TOOL ACCESS: Diamond Cutting, For Turning, Etc

A Landau Diamond Co ....G 215 675-2700
Warminster *(G-18815)*

ARC Diamond Tooling ....G 724 593-5814
Ligonier *(G-9957)*

Ernst Hoffmann Inc ....G 610 593-2280
Atglen *(G-800)*

Imex Pa LLC ....G....... 607 343-3160
Hallstead *(G-6833)*
Stone Supply Inc ....G....... 570 434-2076
Kingsley *(G-8708)*

MACHINE TOOL ACCESS: Dresser, Abrasive Wheel Or Other

Calder Industries Inc ....F....... 814 422-8026
Spring Mills *(G-17886)*

MACHINE TOOL ACCESS: Drills

Ashcombe Products Company Inc ....G....... 717 848-1271
York *(G-20387)*
Construction Tool Service Inc ....G....... 814 231-3090
State College *(G-17955)*
Washington Rotating Control ....F....... 724 228-8889
Washington *(G-19243)*

MACHINE TOOL ACCESS: Knives, Metalworking

Leverwood Machine Works Inc ....F....... 717 246-4105
Red Lion *(G-16604)*

MACHINE TOOL ACCESS: Knives, Shear

F Tinker and Sons Company ....E....... 412 781-3553
Pittsburgh *(G-15000)*
Gesco Inc ....F....... 724 846-8700
Beaver Falls *(G-999)*

MACHINE TOOL ACCESS: Machine Attachments & Access, Drilling

Acker Drill Co Inc ....E....... 570 586-2061
S Abingtn Twp *(G-16888)*
Wheeler Tool Co ....G....... 570 888-2275
Athens *(G-813)*

MACHINE TOOL ACCESS: Shaping Tools

Hewlett Manufacturing Co ....G....... 814 683-4762
Linesville *(G-9981)*

MACHINE TOOL ACCESS: Tool Holders

Clifford Cnc Tling Surgeon LLC ....G....... 717 528-4264
New Oxford *(G-12406)*

MACHINE TOOL ACCESS: Tools & Access

Clarks Expert Sales & Service ....G....... 570 321-8206
Williamsport *(G-19999)*
Dock Tool & Machine Inc ....G....... 215 338-8989
Philadelphia *(G-13638)*
Eysters Machine Shop Inc ....E....... 717 227-8400
Shrewsbury *(G-17583)*
Frew Mill Die Crafts Inc ....F....... 724 658-9026
New Castle *(G-12095)*
Parker Machine and Fabrication...........G....... 570 673-4160
Canton *(G-2666)*
Phb Inc ....A....... 814 474-5511
Fairview *(G-5837)*
Robert Boone Company ....G....... 215 362-2577
Lansdale *(G-9406)*
Steven Laucks ....G....... 717 244-6310
Red Lion *(G-16615)*
Sureflow Corporation ....F....... 412 828-5900
Pittsburgh *(G-15591)*
Velocity Eqp Solutions LLC ....F....... 800 521-1368
New Castle *(G-12162)*

MACHINE TOOL ACCESS: Wheel Turning Eqpt, Diamond Point, Etc

Starlite Industries Inc ....E....... 610 527-1300
Bryn Mawr *(G-2334)*

MACHINE TOOL ATTACHMENTS & ACCESS

Accurate Tool Co Inc ....E....... 610 436-4500
West Chester *(G-19494)*
Bock Workholding Inc ....G....... 724 763-1776
Ford City *(G-6043)*
Hy-Tech Machine Inc ....D....... 724 776-6800
Cranberry Township *(G-3823)*
Oberg Industries Inc ....C....... 724 353-9700
Sarver *(G-17076)*
Pioneer Tool & Forge Inc ....F....... 724 337-4700
New Kensington *(G-12366)*

Quality Tool & Die Inc ....F....... 814 336-6364
Meadville *(G-10785)*
Titan Tool Company ....F....... 814 474-1583
Fairview *(G-5848)*
Venus Machines & Tool ....G....... 570 421-4564
Stroudsburg *(G-18141)*
Vista Metals Inc ....C....... 412 751-4600
McKeesport *(G-10685)*

MACHINE TOOLS & ACCESS

Al Xander Co Inc ....E....... 814 665-8268
Corry *(G-3743)*
Allegheny Technologies Inc ....D....... 412 394-2800
Pittsburgh *(G-14682)*
Allen Gauge & Tool Company ....E....... 412 241-6410
Pittsburgh *(G-14684)*
American Hollow Boring Company ....E....... 800 673-2458
Erie *(G-5187)*
Bolttech Mannings Inc ....D....... 724 872-4873
North Versailles *(G-12772)*
Bon Tool Company ....D....... 724 443-7080
Gibsonia *(G-6328)*
Brubaker Tool Corporation ....B....... 717 692-2113
Millersburg *(G-11191)*
Carbide Metals Inc ....F....... 724 459-6355
Blairsville *(G-1718)*
Cenco Grinding Corporation ....G....... 610 434-5740
Allentown *(G-167)*
Custom Tool & Grinding Inc ....F....... 724 223-1555
Washington *(G-19161)*
Dacval LLC ....F....... 215 331-9600
Philadelphia *(G-13601)*
Decherts Machine Shop Inc ....E....... 717 838-1326
Palmyra *(G-13121)*
Deetag USA Inc ....G....... 828 465-2644
Chambersburg *(G-2924)*
Electroline Corp ....E....... 215 766-2229
Pipersville *(G-14614)*
Elizabeth Carbide Components............E....... 724 539-3574
Latrobe *(G-9474)*
Exim Steel & Shipbroking Inc ....G....... 215 369-9746
Yardley *(G-20310)*
Fabricating Technology Inc ....F....... 814 774-4403
Girard *(G-6388)*
Frazier-Simplex Machine Co ....G....... 724 222-5700
Washington *(G-19177)*
Gasbarre Products Inc ....E....... 814 236-3108
Olanta *(G-12960)*
Gemel Precision Tool Inc ....E....... 215 355-2174
Warminster *(G-18886)*
General Carbide Corporation...............C....... 724 836-3000
Greensburg *(G-6668)*
General Dynamics Ots PA Inc ....C....... 570 342-7801
Scranton *(G-17238)*
Hosch Company LP ....E....... 724 695-3002
Oakdale *(G-12903)*
Ideal Aerosmith Inc ....E....... 412 963-1495
Pittsburgh *(G-15113)*
J K J Tool Co ....G....... 570 322-1411
Williamsport *(G-20026)*
Jade Equipment Corporation...............C....... 215 947-3333
Huntingdon Valley *(G-7999)*
Jepson Precision Tool Inc ....F....... 814 756-4806
Cranesville *(G-3867)*
John R Bromiley Company Inc ....E....... 215 822-7723
Chalfont *(G-2878)*
Kdc Engineering ....G....... 267 203-8487
Telford *(G-18298)*
Kennametal Inc ....E....... 814 624-2406
Bedford *(G-1058)*
Kennametal Inc ....C....... 276 646-0080
Bedford *(G-1059)*
Kurtzs Machining LLC ....G....... 717 899-6125
Mc Veytown *(G-10653)*
Loudon Industries Inc ....E....... 717 328-9808
Mercersburg *(G-10991)*
Madison Inds Holdings LLC..................C....... 717 762-3151
Waynesboro *(G-19416)*
Oberg Carbide Punch & Die ....G....... 724 295-2118
Freeport *(G-6208)*
Ofcg Inc ....G....... 570 655-0804
Dupont *(G-4493)*
Paco Winders Mfg LLC ....E....... 215 673-6265
Philadelphia *(G-14113)*
Parker-Hannifin Corporation ....C....... 724 861-8200
Irwin *(G-8188)*
Pb Holdings Inc ....G....... 215 947-3333
Huntingdon Valley *(G-8021)*
Penn Scientific Products Co ....F....... 888 238-6710
Abington *(G-13)*

Penn United Technologies Inc ....E....... 724 431-2482
Sarver *(G-17078)*
Pressure Innovators LLC ....G....... 215 431-6520
Warminster *(G-18945)*
Price Tool Inc ....F....... 814 763-4410
Saegertown *(G-16927)*
Product Design and Development ....E....... 717 741-4844
York *(G-20644)*
Q Company LLC ....E....... 570 966-1017
New Berlin *(G-12022)*
Ronal Tool Company Inc ....F....... 717 741-0880
York *(G-20660)*
Ruch Carbide Burs Inc ....E....... 215 657-3660
Willow Grove *(G-20139)*
Saegertown Manufacturing Corp ....C....... 814 763-2655
Saegertown *(G-16932)*
Starn Tool & Manufacturing Co ....D....... 814 724-1057
Meadville *(G-10794)*
Swissaero Inc ....F....... 814 796-4166
Waterford *(G-19271)*
T-Bird McHning Fabrication LLC ....F....... 717 384-8362
York *(G-20683)*
TI Oregon Inc ....G....... 412 394-2800
Pittsburgh *(G-15624)*
Uhl Technologies LLC ....G....... 814 437-6346
Franklin *(G-6166)*
Vista Metals Inc ....G....... 724 545-7750
Kittanning *(G-8803)*
Winterthur Wendt Usa Inc ....C....... 610 495-2850
Royersford *(G-16869)*

MACHINE TOOLS, METAL CUTTING: Drilling

Composidie Inc ....C....... 724 845-8602
Apollo *(G-673)*
Heisey Machine Co Inc ....G....... 717 293-1373
Lancaster *(G-9042)*
Woodings Industrial Corp ....C....... 724 625-3131
Mars *(G-10515)*

MACHINE TOOLS, METAL CUTTING: Drilling & Boring

Aaron Enterprises Inc ....D....... 717 854-2641
York *(G-20362)*
Clln Directional Drilling Inc ....G....... 814 460-0248
Centerville *(G-2833)*
Stone & Wood Inc ....G....... 814 857-7621
Woodland *(G-20214)*
US Energy ....G....... 724 783-7532
Rural Valley *(G-16877)*

MACHINE TOOLS, METAL CUTTING: Exotic, Including Explosive

Madison Inds Holdings LLC..................C....... 717 762-3151
Waynesboro *(G-19416)*
Plasma Automation Incorporated ....F....... 814 333-2181
Meadville *(G-10780)*
Quality Metal Products Inc ....E....... 570 333-4248
Dallas *(G-3967)*

MACHINE TOOLS, METAL CUTTING: Numerically Controlled

Forest Scientific Corporation ....G....... 814 463-5006
Tionesta *(G-18371)*
Mazak Corporation ....G....... 610 481-0850
Allentown *(G-311)*
Orr Screw Machine Products................E....... 724 668-2256
Greensburg *(G-6695)*

MACHINE TOOLS, METAL CUTTING: Pipe Cutting & Threading

Reed Manufacturing Company ....D....... 814 452-3691
Erie *(G-5459)*

MACHINE TOOLS, METAL CUTTING: Pointing & Burring

Abe Custom Metal Products ....G....... 412 298-0200
Bethel Park *(G-1399)*

MACHINE TOOLS, METAL CUTTING: Reboring, Cylinder

Hone Alone Inc ....G....... 610 495-5832
Spring City *(G-17859)*

PRODUCT

MACHINE TOOLS, METAL CUTTING: Regrinding, Crankshaft

Ellwood Crankshaft and Mch Co ....C 724 347-0250
Hermitage *(G-7581)*

MACHINE TOOLS, METAL CUTTING: Tool Replacement & Rpr Parts

D & D Machine ....G 412 821-3725
Pittsburgh *(G-14900)*

Ettco Tool & Machine Co Inc ....F 717 792-1417
York *(G-20471)*

Exact Machine Service Inc ....G 717 848-2121
York *(G-20473)*

HMS Industries Inc ....E 724 459-5090
Blairsville *(G-1724)*

Innovative Design Inc ....E 717 202-1306
Lebanon *(G-9583)*

Machine Tl Rebuild Specialists ....G 717 423-6073
Shippensburg *(G-17538)*

Price Machine Tool Repair ....G 215 631-9440
Lansdale *(G-9399)*

Ressler Enterprises Inc ....E 717 933-5611
Mount Aetna *(G-11605)*

Tms Precision Machining Inc ....G 215 547-6070
Bristol *(G-2207)*

USA Spares Inc ....E 717 241-9222
Carlisle *(G-2746)*

MACHINE TOOLS, METAL CUTTING: Vertical Turning & Boring

South Morgan Technologies LLC ....G 814 774-2000
Girard *(G-6402)*

MACHINE TOOLS, METAL FORMING: Electroforming

Max Levy Autograph Inc ....G 215 842-3675
Philadelphia *(G-13996)*

MACHINE TOOLS, METAL FORMING: Marking

Automated Indus Systems Inc ....E 814 838-2270
Erie *(G-5198)*

Bell-Mark Sales Co Inc ....E 717 292-5641
Dover *(G-4186)*

Pannier Corporation ....F 412 323-4900
Pittsburgh *(G-15368)*

MACHINE TOOLS, METAL FORMING: Mechanical, Pneumatic Or Hyd

Clearfield Metal Tech Inc ....F 814 765-7860
Clearfield *(G-3215)*

CPM Wolverine Proctor LLC ....D 215 443-5200
Horsham *(G-7805)*

MACHINE TOOLS, METAL FORMING: Presses, Hyd & Pneumatic

Erie M & P Company Inc ....E 814 454-1581
Erie *(G-5269)*

MACHINE TOOLS, METAL FORMING: Pressing

Daugherty Tool and Die Inc ....D 412 754-0200
Buena Vista *(G-2341)*

PTX - Pentronix Inc ....G 734 667-2897
Du Bois *(G-4415)*

MACHINE TOOLS, METAL FORMING: Rebuilt

Machine Tl Rebuild Specialists ....G 717 423-6073
Shippensburg *(G-17538)*

MACHINE TOOLS, METAL FORMING: Spinning, Spline Rollg/Windg

Dreistern Inc ....G 215 799-0220
Telford *(G-18284)*

Showmark LLC ....G 610 458-0304
Exton *(G-5732)*

MACHINE TOOLS: Metal Cutting

Adams County Laser LLC ....G 717 359-4030
Littlestown *(G-10062)*

Andritz Herr-Voss Stamco Inc ....E 724 251-8745
Ambridge *(G-609)*

Arthur R Warner Company ....F 724 539-9229
Latrobe *(G-9458)*

Branson Ultrasonics Corp ....E 610 251-9776
Paoli *(G-13136)*

Brighton Machine Company Inc ....F 724 378-0960
Aliquippa *(G-70)*

Brubaker Tool Corporation ....B 717 692-2113
Millersburg *(G-11191)*

CAM Industries Inc ....E 717 637-5988
Hanover *(G-6866)*

Carton Edge International Inc ....F 215 699-8755
North Wales *(G-12794)*

Center Machine Company ....G 724 379-4066
Webster *(G-19456)*

Cherryhill Manufacturing Corp ....F 724 254-2185
Clymer *(G-3270)*

CNT Motion Systems Inc ....G 412 244-5770
Glenshaw *(G-6485)*

Conicity Technologies LLC ....G 412 601-1874
Turtle Creek *(G-18563)*

Coretech International Inc ....F 908 454-7999
Allentown *(G-181)*

Custom Engineering Co ....C 814 898-1390
Erie *(G-5237)*

Emporium Specialties Company ....E 814 647-8661
Austin *(G-833)*

F Tinker and Sons Company ....E 412 781-3553
Pittsburgh *(G-15000)*

Fabworks Inc ....F 570 814-1515
Dallas *(G-3962)*

Faivre Mch & Fabrication Inc ....G 814 724-7160
Meadville *(G-10725)*

Frazier Machine Company Inc ....G 717 632-1101
Hanover *(G-6887)*

Freedom Components Inc ....G 717 242-0101
Lewistown *(G-9930)*

G F Goodman & Son Inc ....F 215 672-8810
Warminster *(G-18884)*

Gardner Associate Enterprises ....G 717 624-2003
New Oxford *(G-12410)*

Genesis Worldwide II Inc ....B 724 538-3180
Callery *(G-2469)*

Golis Machine Inc ....F 570 278-1963
Montrose *(G-11465)*

Greenleaf Corporation ....B 814 763-2915
Saegertown *(G-16915)*

Hetrick Mfg Inc ....F 724 335-0455
Lower Burrell *(G-10106)*

Highland Carbide Tool Co ....F 724 863-7151
Irwin *(G-8167)*

I T C Industrial Tube Cleaning ....F 724 752-3100
Ellwood City *(G-4937)*

John R Bromiley Company Inc ....E 215 822-7723
Chalfont *(G-2878)*

K Tool Inc ....G 717 624-3866
New Oxford *(G-12413)*

Kaast Machine Tools Inc ....G 224 216-8886
Ardmore *(G-710)*

Kauffman Elec Contrls & Contg ....E 717 252-3667
Wrightsville *(G-20240)*

Kinetigear LLC ....G 412 810-0049
Pittsburgh *(G-15178)*

Lehigh Machine Tools Inc ....G 215 493-6446
Morrisville *(G-11569)*

Medco Process Inc ....G 717 453-7298
Wiconisco *(G-19896)*

Mk Precision ....G 215 675-4590
Warminster *(G-18924)*

Mpe Machine Tool Inc ....E 814 664-4822
Corry *(G-3769)*

Penn United Technologies Inc ....E 724 431-2482
Sarver *(G-17078)*

PR Hoffman Machine Pdts Inc ....E 717 243-9900
Carlisle *(G-2732)*

Ruch Carbide Burs Inc ....E 215 657-3660
Willow Grove *(G-20139)*

S Morantz Inc ....D 215 969-0266
Philadelphia *(G-14273)*

Scientific Tool Inc ....E 724 446-9311
New Stanton *(G-12450)*

Srd Design Corp ....G 717 699-0005
York *(G-20678)*

Talbot Holdings LLC ....C 717 692-2113
Millersburg *(G-11202)*

Td & Company ....G 610 637-6100
Morgantown *(G-11538)*

Time Machine Inc ....D 814 432-5281
Polk *(G-15889)*

Top Notch Cnc Machining Inc ....F 570 658-3725
Beavertown *(G-1028)*

Trident Plastics Inc ....E 215 443-7147
Warminster *(G-18986)*

Vallorbs Jewel Company ....C 717 392-3978
Bird In Hand *(G-1684)*

Vanalstine Manufacturing Co ....G 610 489-7670
Trappe *(G-18475)*

Vollmer of America Corp ....F 412 278-0655
Carnegie *(G-2804)*

Yardley Products LLC ....E 215 493-2700
Yardley *(G-20346)*

MACHINE TOOLS: Metal Forming

Anvil Forge & Hammer Ir Works ....G 610 837-9951
Allentown *(G-139)*

C I Hayes Inc ....E 814 834-2200
Saint Marys *(G-16951)*

Chant Engineering Co Inc ....E 215 230-4260
New Britain *(G-12046)*

Custom Engineering Co ....C 814 898-1390
Erie *(G-5237)*

Efco Inc ....E 814 455-3941
Erie *(G-5256)*

Elizabeth Carbide Die Co Inc ....C 412 751-3000
McKeesport *(G-10667)*

Elizabeth Carbide Die Co Inc ....E 412 829-7700
Irwin *(G-8160)*

Engineered Devices Corporation ....F 570 455-4897
Hazleton *(G-7497)*

Gasbarre Products Inc ....D 814 371-3015
Du Bois *(G-4392)*

Gasbarre Products Inc ....E 814 834-2200
Saint Marys *(G-16975)*

Kaast Machine Tools Inc ....G 224 216-8886
Ardmore *(G-710)*

Machine Rebuilders ....G 724 694-3190
New Derry *(G-12191)*

Morlin Inc ....G 814 454-5559
Erie *(G-5395)*

Oakwood Bindery ....E 717 396-9559
Lancaster *(G-9149)*

PR Hoffman Machine Pdts Inc ....E 717 243-9900
Carlisle *(G-2732)*

Pro Tech Machining Inc ....E 814 587-3200
Conneautville *(G-3484)*

Schwenk Custom Machining Inc ....G 610 367-1777
Boyertown *(G-1928)*

Talbot Holdings LLC ....C 717 692-2113
Millersburg *(G-11202)*

Wesel Manufacturing Company ....E 570 586-8978
S Abingtn Twp *(G-16903)*

MACHINERY & EQPT FINANCE LEASING

Global Capital Corp ....G 610 857-1900
Coatesville *(G-3305)*

MACHINERY & EQPT, AGRICULTURAL, WHOLESALE: Dairy

Dairy Farmers America Inc ....E 724 946-8729
West Middlesex *(G-19722)*

MACHINERY & EQPT, AGRICULTURAL, WHOLESALE: Lawn

Lwe Inc ....G 814 336-3553
Meadville *(G-10751)*

MACHINERY & EQPT, AGRICULTURAL, WHOLESALE: Lawn & Garden

Best Feeds & Farm Supplies Inc ....C 724 693-9417
Oakdale *(G-12894)*

MACHINERY & EQPT, AGRICULTURAL, WHOLESALE: Tractors

Holtrys LLC ....G 717 532-7261
Roxbury *(G-16838)*

MACHINERY & EQPT, INDL, WHOL: Controlling Instruments/Access

Contrail Systems Inc ....F 724 353-1127
Sarver *(G-17067)*

Precision Controls LLC ....G 267 337-9812
Levittown *(G-9860)*

MACHINERY & EQPT, INDL, WHOLESALE: Alcoholic Beverage Mfrg

American Keg Company LLC ....E 484 524-8251
Pottstown (G-15963)

MACHINERY & EQPT, INDL, WHOLESALE: Chemical Process

Bethlehem Hydrogen Inc ....G 610 762-1706
Northampton (G-12845)
Cummings Group Ltd ....F 814 774-8238
Girard (G-6385)

MACHINERY & EQPT, INDL, WHOLESALE: Conveyor Systems

Apx-Seetech Systems Inc ....G 717 751-6445
York (G-20383)
C C B B Inc ....F 215 364-5377
Feasterville Trevose (G-5898)
Eastern Machine & Convyrs Inc ....F 724 379-4701
Donora (G-4154)
Industrial Composites Inc ....G 412 221-2662
Bridgeville (G-2069)
L M Robbins Co ....F 610 760-8301
Slatington (G-17608)

MACHINERY & EQPT, INDL, WHOLESALE: Cranes

Bridon-American Corporation ....B 570 822-3349
Hanover Township (G-6982)
Edmiston Signs ....G 814 742-8930
Bellwood (G-1137)
Pittsburgh Design Services Inc ....F 412 276-3000
Carnegie (G-2779)

MACHINERY & EQPT, INDL, WHOLESALE: Crushing

Aggregates Equipment Inc ....E 717 656-2131
Leola (G-9767)

MACHINERY & EQPT, INDL, WHOLESALE: Dairy Prdts Manufacturing

D Cooper Works LLC ....G 717 733-4220
Ephrata (G-5099)

MACHINERY & EQPT, INDL, WHOLESALE: Drilling, Exc Bits

Acker Drill Co Inc ....E 570 586-2061
S Abingtn Twp (G-16888)
Wearforce North America LLC ....F 215 996-1770
Chalfont (G-2894)

MACHINERY & EQPT, INDL, WHOLESALE: Engines & Parts, Diesel

Cummins Inc ....D 717 564-1344
Harrisburg (G-7110)
Cummins Inc ....G 570 333-0360
Tunkhannock (G-18535)
Holtrys LLC ....G 717 532-7261
Roxbury (G-16838)
Raco International LP ....F 412 835-5744
Bethel Park (G-1430)
Smuckers Sales & Services LLC ....G 717 354-4158
New Holland (G-12285)

MACHINERY & EQPT, INDL, WHOLESALE: Engines, Gasoline

CDI Lawn Equipment & Grdn Sup ....E 610 489-3474
Collegeville (G-3371)
Cummins Inc ....G 215 785-6005
Bristol (G-2129)
Marilyn Strawser Beauty Salon ....G 717 463-2804
Thompsontown (G-18349)

MACHINERY & EQPT, INDL, WHOLESALE: Engs & Parts, Air-Cooled

W W Engine and Supply Inc ....E 814 345-5693
Kylertown (G-8868)

MACHINERY & EQPT, INDL, WHOLESALE: Fans

RM Benney Technical Sls Inc ....G 724 935-0150
Wexford (G-19828)

MACHINERY & EQPT, INDL, WHOLESALE: Food Manufacturing

Delmar Enterprises Inc ....F 215 674-4534
Warminster (G-18856)

MACHINERY & EQPT, INDL, WHOLESALE: Fuel Injection Systems

Continental Auto Systems Inc ....E 610 289-1390
Allentown (G-177)

MACHINERY & EQPT, INDL, WHOLESALE: Hydraulic Systems

ALe Hydraulic McHy Co LLC ....F 215 547-3351
Levittown (G-9815)
Amacoil Inc ....G 610 485-8300
Aston (G-750)
Delri Industrial Supplies Inc ....G 610 833-2070
Crum Lynne (G-3936)
Dispersion Tech Systems LLC ....G 610 832-2040
Conshohocken (G-3539)
Flotran Exton Inc ....G 610 640-4141
Malvern (G-10236)
Force America Inc ....G 610 495-4590
Pottstown (G-15988)
G-S Hydraulics Inc ....G 814 938-2862
Punxsutawney (G-16141)
Haverstick Bros Inc ....F 717 392-5722
Lancaster (G-9040)
National Hydraulic Systems LLC ....G 724 628-4010
Connellsville (G-3505)
Nick Charles Kravitch ....G 412 341-7265
Pittsburgh (G-15339)
Ralph A Hiller Company ....G 724 325-1200
Export (G-5623)
Wojanis Supply Company ....E 724 695-1415
Coraopolis (G-3734)

MACHINERY & EQPT, INDL, WHOLESALE: Indl Machine Parts

Applied Indus Tech — PA LLC ....G 724 696-3099
Mount Pleasant (G-11686)

MACHINERY & EQPT, INDL, WHOLESALE: Instruments & Cntrl Eqpt

David Kovalcik ....G 724 539-3181
Loyalhanna (G-10110)
Imac Systems Inc ....E 215 946-2200
Bristol (G-2155)
Pro-Mic Corp ....G 610 783-7901
King of Prussia (G-8665)
Radius Systems LLC ....E 610 388-9940
Chadds Ford (G-2859)
Sarclad (north America) LP ....F 412 466-2000
Duquesne (G-4499)
Wgs Equipment & Controls ....F 610 459-8800
Garnet Valley (G-6270)

MACHINERY & EQPT, INDL, WHOLESALE: Machine Tools & Access

Fsm Tools ....G 717 867-5359
Annville (G-648)
NC Industries Inc ....F 248 528-5200
Reynoldsville (G-16658)

MACHINERY & EQPT, INDL, WHOLESALE: Machine Tools & Metalwork

Cambridge-Lee Holdings Inc ....F 610 926-4141
Reading (G-16340)
Cummins - Allison Corp ....G 215 245-8436
Bensalem (G-1176)
Esmark Industrial Group LLC ....F 412 259-8868
Sewickley (G-17387)
Hoffman Diamond Products Inc ....E 814 938-7600
Punxsutawney (G-16143)
Wesel Manufacturing Company ....E 570 586-8978
S Abingtn Twp (G-16903)

MACHINERY & EQPT, INDL, WHOLESALE: Measure/Test, Electric

Morlin Inc ....G 814 454-5559
Erie (G-5395)
Valco ....E 610 691-3205
Bethlehem (G-1649)

MACHINERY & EQPT, INDL, WHOLESALE: Packaging

Eam-Mosca Corp ....C 570 459-3426
Hazle Township (G-7452)
Fres-Co Systems Usa Inc ....B 215 721-4600
Telford (G-18290)
Loveshaw Corporation ....C 570 937-4921
South Canaan (G-17769)
Millwood Inc ....F 724 266-7030
Leetsdale (G-9699)
Millwood Inc ....F 717 790-9118
Mechanicsburg (G-10869)
Millwood Inc ....F 570 836-9280
Tunkhannock (G-18543)
Packaging Coordinators Inc ....F 215 613-3600
Philadelphia (G-14111)
Peters Equipment Corp ....E 215 364-9147
Huntingdon Valley (G-8024)
Signode Industrial Group LLC ....C 570 937-4921
South Canaan (G-17770)
Signode Industrial Group LLC ....G 570 937-4921
South Canaan (G-17771)

MACHINERY & EQPT, INDL, WHOLESALE: Petroleum Industry

Dressel Welding Supply Inc ....G 570 505-1994
Cogan Station (G-3360)
National Oilwell Varco Inc ....D 814 427-2555
Punxsutawney (G-16150)

MACHINERY & EQPT, INDL, WHOLESALE: Plastic Prdts Machinery

General Plastics Inc ....G 215 423-8200
Philadelphia (G-13750)

MACHINERY & EQPT, INDL, WHOLESALE: Pneumatic Tools

Airtek Inc ....E 412 351-3837
Irwin (G-8141)
Al Xander Co Inc ....E 814 665-8268
Corry (G-3743)
Tri-State Hydraulics Inc ....E 724 483-1790
Charleroi (G-3022)

MACHINERY & EQPT, INDL, WHOLESALE: Processing & Packaging

Doyle Equipment Company ....G 724 837-4500
Delmont (G-4050)
Horix Manufacturing Company ....E 412 771-1111
Mc Kees Rocks (G-10614)
Riise Inc ....G 724 528-3305
West Middlesex (G-19729)

MACHINERY & EQPT, INDL, WHOLESALE: Propane Conversion

Aztec Products Inc ....F 215 393-4700
Montgomeryville (G-11387)

MACHINERY & EQPT, INDL, WHOLESALE: Safety Eqpt

Airgas Safety Inc ....C 215 826-9000
Levittown (G-9814)
Chapel Hill Mfg Co ....F 215 884-3614
Oreland (G-13020)
Compressed Air Systems Inc ....G 215 340-1307
Pipersville (G-14613)
MSA Safety Incorporated ....A 724 733-9100
Murrysville (G-11859)
National Towelette Company ....E 215 245-7300
Bensalem (G-1229)

PRODUCT

MACHINERY & EQPT, INDL, WHOLESALE: Sawmill

American Carbide Saw Co ....F 215 672-1466
Hatboro *(G-7267)*

MACHINERY & EQPT, INDL, WHOLESALE: Sewing

North American Mfg Co ....E 570 348-1163
Scranton *(G-17266)*

MACHINERY & EQPT, INDL, WHOLESALE: Tanks, Storage

Evergreen Tank Solutions Inc ....G 484 268-5168
Philadelphia *(G-13684)*

MACHINERY & EQPT, INDL, WHOLESALE: Tapping Attachments

Brubaker Tool Corporation ....B 717 692-2113
Millersburg *(G-11191)*

MACHINERY & EQPT, INDL, WHOLESALE: Textile

Apparel Machinery & Supply Co ....E 215 634-2626
Philadelphia *(G-13400)*
Bond Products Inc ....F 215 842-0200
Philadelphia *(G-13470)*
Versitex of America Ltd ....F 610 948-4442
Spring City *(G-17872)*

MACHINERY & EQPT, INDL, WHOLESALE: Trailers, Indl

Smouse Trucks & Vans Inc ....G 724 887-7777
Mount Pleasant *(G-11718)*

MACHINERY & EQPT, INDL, WHOLESALE: Water Pumps

Equisol LLC ....F 866 629-7646
Conshohocken *(G-3544)*
Jnb Industrial Supply Inc ....G 412 455-5170
Blawnox *(G-1764)*
Masterflo Pump Inc ....G 724 443-1122
Gibsonia *(G-6347)*

MACHINERY & EQPT, INDL, WHOLESALE: Woodworking

Herndon Reload Company ....E 570 758-2597
Herndon *(G-7599)*
John M Sensenig ....G 717 445-4669
New Holland *(G-12255)*

MACHINERY & EQPT, WHOLESALE: Concrete Processing

Global Polishing Solutions LLC ....F 619 295-0893
Folcroft *(G-6003)*

MACHINERY & EQPT, WHOLESALE: Construction, Cranes

Kone Cranes Inc ....F 814 878-8070
Erie *(G-5351)*

MACHINERY & EQPT, WHOLESALE: Construction, General

Andrew E Reken ....G 724 783-7878
Dayton *(G-4034)*
Concrete Service Materials Co ....G 610 825-1554
Conshohocken *(G-3532)*
Doyle Equipment Company ....G 724 837-4500
Delmont *(G-4050)*
George L Wilson & Co Inc A ....G 412 321-3217
Apollo *(G-675)*
Groff Tractor & Equipment LLC ....F 814 353-8400
Bellefonte *(G-1100)*
Trench Shoring Services ....G 412 331-8118
Pittsburgh *(G-15642)*

MACHINERY & EQPT, WHOLESALE: Crushing, Pulverizng & Screeng

Klinger Machinery Co Inc ....G 717 362-8656
Elizabethville *(G-4894)*

MACHINERY & EQPT, WHOLESALE: Masonry

Tri-Boro Construction Sups Inc ....D 717 246-3095
Dallastown *(G-3982)*
Tri-Boro Construction Sups Inc ....E 717 249-6448
Carlisle *(G-2743)*

MACHINERY & EQPT, WHOLESALE: Oil Field Eqpt

Belden & Blake Corporation ....F 814 589-7091
Pleasantville *(G-15797)*
Oil States Energy Services LLC ....G 724 746-1168
Canonsburg *(G-2615)*

MACHINERY & EQPT: Electroplating

Frontier LLC ....F 570 265-2500
Towanda *(G-18426)*
Jet Plate Inc ....F 610 373-6600
Reading *(G-16414)*

MACHINERY & EQPT: Farm

Allegheny-Wagner Inds Inc ....E 724 468-4300
Delmont *(G-4047)*
Barebo Inc ....E 610 965-6018
Emmaus *(G-5020)*
Bhs Energy LLC ....G 570 696-3754
Wyoming *(G-20274)*
Case Mondern Work ....G 717 785-1232
Fairfield *(G-5765)*
Closet Cases ....G 570 262-9092
Jim Thorpe *(G-8338)*
Cnh Inc ....G 717 355-1121
New Holland *(G-12233)*
Cnh Industrial America LLC ....B 262 636-6011
Lancaster *(G-8981)*
Cnh Industrial America LLC ....E 800 501-5711
New Holland *(G-12234)*
Cnh Industrial America LLC ....C 717 355-1121
New Holland *(G-12235)*
Cnh Industrial America LLC ....C 717 355-1902
New Holland *(G-12236)*
Cold Case Beverage LLC ....G 570 388-2297
Harding *(G-7010)*
Conestoga Mfg LLC ....G 717 529-0199
Kirkwood *(G-8745)*
Demuth Steel Products Inc ....F 717 653-2239
Mount Joy *(G-11652)*
Earth & Turf Products LLC ....G 717 355-2276
New Holland *(G-12247)*
Farm-Bilt Machine LLC ....F 717 442-5020
Gap *(G-6251)*
Farmer Boy Ag Inc ....D 717 866-7565
Myerstown *(G-11885)*
Groffdale Machine Co Inc ....G 717 656-3249
Leola *(G-9785)*
I & J Manufacturing LLC ....G 717 442-9451
Gordonville *(G-6558)*
John H Bricker Welding ....F 717 263-5588
Chambersburg *(G-2946)*
Kneppco Equipment LLC ....G 814 483-0108
Berlin *(G-1289)*
Lancaster Parts & Eqp Inc ....F 717 299-3721
Lancaster *(G-9103)*
Mc Dowell Implement Company ....G 814 786-7955
Grove City *(G-6797)*
McLanahan Corporation ....B 814 695-9807
Hollidaysburg *(G-7651)*
New Holland North America ....B 717 354-4514
New Holland *(G-12266)*
New Holland North America ....A 717 355-1121
New Holland *(G-12267)*
New Holland North America ....B 717 355-1121
New Holland *(G-12268)*
Quality Fencing & Supply ....E 717 355-7112
New Holland *(G-12276)*
Scenic Road Manufacturing ....G 717 768-7300
Gordonville *(G-6565)*
Stengels Welding Shop Inc ....G 610 444-4110
Kennett Square *(G-8544)*
Stoltz Mfg LLC ....E 610 286-5146
Morgantown *(G-11537)*
Stoltzfus Manufacturing Inc ....G 610 273-3603
Honey Brook *(G-7764)*

Tj Manufacturing LLC ....G 717 575-0675
Narvon *(G-11930)*
Val Products Inc ....F 717 354-4586
New Holland *(G-12291)*
Val Products Inc ....D 717 392-3978
Bird In Hand *(G-1683)*
Weaverline LLC ....F 717 445-6724
Narvon *(G-11932)*

MACHINERY & EQPT: Gas Producers, Generators/Other Rltd Eqpt

Air Products and Chemicals Inc ....A 610 481-4911
Allentown *(G-119)*
Air Products and Chemicals Inc ....E 724 266-1563
Leetsdale *(G-9677)*
Barebo Inc ....E 610 965-6018
Emmaus *(G-5020)*
Empire Energy E&P LLC ....F 814 365-5621
Hawthorn *(G-7444)*
Matheson Tri-Gas Inc ....D 215 641-2700
Montgomeryville *(G-11406)*
Psb Industries Inc ....D 814 453-3651
Erie *(G-5442)*
Versum Materials Us LLC ....F 610 481-3946
Allentown *(G-423)*
Versum Materials Us LLC ....G 570 467-2981
Tamaqua *(G-18231)*

MACHINERY & EQPT: Liquid Automation

Apss Inc ....F 724 368-3001
Portersville *(G-15925)*
JM Automation Services ....G 215 675-0125
Warminster *(G-18902)*
Pkt Technologies ....E 412 494-5600
Pittsburgh *(G-15414)*
S P Kinney Engineers Inc ....E 412 276-4600
Carnegie *(G-2789)*

MACHINERY & EQPT: Metal Finishing, Plating Etc

Andritz Herr-Voss Stamco Inc ....C 724 538-3180
Callery *(G-2466)*
Carlson Erie Corporation ....F 814 455-2768
Erie *(G-5220)*
Pds Paint Inc ....F 717 393-5838
Lancaster *(G-9161)*
Powder Coating Specialists LLC ....G 717 968-1479
York *(G-20635)*

MACHINERY & EQPT: Petroleum Refinery

Sunoco (R&m) LLC ....E 215 339-2000
Philadelphia *(G-14356)*

MACHINERY BASES

Adams County Laser LLC ....G 717 359-4030
Littlestown *(G-10062)*
Crumbs ....F 717 609-1120
Mount Holly Springs *(G-11633)*
M D Cline Metal Fabg Inc ....G 724 459-8968
Blairsville *(G-1733)*
Trinity Mining Services Inc ....G 412 605-0612
Pittsburgh *(G-15649)*
Win-Holt Equipment Corp ....C 516 222-0335
Allentown *(G-436)*

MACHINERY CLEANING SVCS

Holdrens Precision Machining ....F 570 358-3377
Ulster *(G-18599)*

MACHINERY, COMM LAUNDRY: Rug Cleaning, Drying Or Napping

Shamaseen Hamzah ....G 484 557-5051
Center Valley *(G-2830)*

MACHINERY, COMMERCIAL LAUNDRY & Drycleaning: Pressing

Schreiber & Goldberg Ltd ....E 570 344-4000
Dunmore *(G-4483)*

MACHINERY, EQPT & SUPPLIES: Parking Facility

Hub Parking Technology USA Inc ....E 724 772-2400
Warrendale *(G-19082)*

MACHINERY, FLOOR SANDING: Commercial

A I Floor Products..............................G...... 215 355-2798
   Feasterville Trevose **(G-5881)**
R M Frantz Inc.................................... 570 421-3020
   Stroudsburg **(G-18137)**
S H Sharpless & Son Inc ....G...... 570 454-6685
   Hazleton **(G-7524)**

MACHINERY, FOOD PRDTS: Chocolate Processing

Woody Associates Inc ....F...... 717 843-3975
   York **(G-20720)**

MACHINERY, FOOD PRDTS: Confectionery

Fairfield Confectionery......................G...... 724 654-3888
   New Castle **(G-12091)**
Purcell Company................................E...... 717 838-5611
   Palmyra **(G-13130)**

MACHINERY, FOOD PRDTS: Dairy, Pasteurizing

Krishna Protects Cows Inc ....G...... 717 527-4101
   Port Royal **(G-15910)**

MACHINERY, FOOD PRDTS: Distillery

Boardroom Spirits LLC ....G...... 215 815-5351
   Lansdale **(G-9348)**
Christmas City Spirits LLC ....G...... 484 893-0590
   Bethlehem **(G-1484)**

MACHINERY, FOOD PRDTS: Food Processing, Smokers

B & J Sheet Metal Inc ....F...... 215 538-9543
   Trumbauersville **(G-18529)**
Smokers Outlet ....G...... 814 827-1104
   Titusville **(G-18396)**

MACHINERY, FOOD PRDTS: Grinders, Commercial

Chop - Rite Two Inc.............................F...... 215 256-4620
   Harleysville **(G-7027)**

MACHINERY, FOOD PRDTS: Mixers, Commercial

Victoria Orchard LLC ....G...... 610 873-2848
   Downingtown **(G-4260)**

MACHINERY, FOOD PRDTS: Ovens, Bakery

New York Bagelry ....G...... 610 678-6420
   Reading **(G-16455)**

MACHINERY, FOOD PRDTS: Pasta

Arcobaleno LLC ....F...... 717 394-1402
   Lancaster **(G-8937)**

MACHINERY, FOOD PRDTS: Potato Peelers, Electric

Insinger Machine Company ....D...... 215 624-4800
   Philadelphia **(G-13860)**

MACHINERY, FOOD PRDTS: Processing, Poultry

D Cooper Works LLC ....G...... 717 733-4220
   Ephrata **(G-5099)**
Mgs Inc...C...... 717 336-7528
   Denver **(G-4083)**

MACHINERY, FOOD PRDTS: Roasting, Coffee, Peanut, Etc.

Schnupps Grain Roasting LLC.............F........ 717 865-6611
   Lebanon **(G-9627)**

MACHINERY, FOOD PRDTS: Sausage Stuffers

Allen Gauge & Tool Company...............E...... 412 241-6410
   Pittsburgh **(G-14684)**

MACHINERY, FOOD PRDTS: Slicers, Commercial

Le Jo Enterprises Incorporated.............E........ 484 921-9000
   Phoenixville **(G-14559)**

MACHINERY, FOOD PRDTS: Sugar Plant

Idreco USA Ltd ....F...... 610 701-9944
   West Chester **(G-19566)**

MACHINERY, LUBRICATION: Automatic

Marando Industries Inc........................G...... 610 621-2536
   Reading **(G-16437)**

MACHINERY, MAILING: Mailing

Pitney Bowes Inc ....E........ 412 689-6639
   Pittsburgh **(G-15383)**

MACHINERY, MAILING: Postage Meters

Mg Financial Services Inc ....E........ 215 364-7555
   Fort Washington **(G-6086)**
Neopost USA Inc..................................E........ 717 939-2700
   Middletown **(G-11066)**
Neopost USA Inc..................................G...... 717 939-2700
   King of Prussia **(G-8654)**
Pitney Bowes Inc ....E........ 717 884-1882
   Harrisburg **(G-7199)**
Pitney Bowes Inc ....E........ 215 751-9800
   Philadelphia **(G-14180)**
Pitney Bowes Inc ....E........ 215 946-2863
   Levittown **(G-9856)**

MACHINERY, METALWORKING: Assembly, Including Robotic

Astro Automation Inc ....G...... 724 864-2500
   Irwin **(G-8145)**
Automated Concepts Tooling Inc.........F........ 814 796-6302
   Waterford **(G-19259)**
Automation Products Inc ....F........ 814 453-5841
   Erie **(G-5199)**
Omnitech Automation Inc ....E........ 610 965-3279
   Emmaus **(G-5036)**
Schake Industries Inc ....E........ 814 677-9333
   Seneca **(G-17369)**
Seegrid Corporation ....D...... 412 379-4500
   Pittsburgh **(G-15520)**
Steimer and Co Inc ....F........ 610 933-7450
   Phoenixville **(G-14579)**
Weld Tooling Corporation ....D...... 412 331-1776
   Canonsburg **(G-2657)**

MACHINERY, METALWORKING: Coilers, Metalworking

Grattons Fabricating & Mfg....................G...... 724 527-5681
   Adamsburg **(G-18)**

MACHINERY, METALWORKING: Cutting & Slitting

Keystone Diamond Blades Inc ....G...... 570 942-4526
   Nicholson **(G-12617)**

MACHINERY, METALWORKING: Draw Benches

Micro Miniature Manufacturing.............G...... 724 481-1033
   Butler **(G-2424)**

MACHINERY, OFFICE: Embossing, Store Or Office

Roovers Inc ....G...... 570 455-7548
   Hazleton **(G-7523)**

MACHINERY, OFFICE: Perforators

Packaging Progressions Inc.................E........ 610 489-9096
   Souderton **(G-17758)**

MACHINERY, OFFICE: Time Clocks &Time Recording Devices

Dein-Verbit Associates Inc....................F........ 610 649-9674
   Ardmore **(G-707)**
Sapling Inc...E........ 215 322-6063
   Warminster **(G-18961)**

MACHINERY, PACKAGING: Packing & Wrapping

Emp Industries Inc ....G...... 215 357-5333
   Warminster **(G-18871)**
Nelson Wrap Dispenser Inc ....G...... 814 623-1317
   Bedford **(G-1066)**

MACHINERY, PACKAGING: Wrapping

Pack Pro Technologies LLC.................G...... 717 517-9065
   Lititz **(G-10028)**

MACHINERY, PAPER INDUSTRY: Converting, Die Cutting & Stampng

Accurate Die Wrks of Phldlphia.............F........ 610 667-9200
   Penn Valley **(G-13233)**
Elsner Engineering Works Inc ....D...... 717 637-5991
   Hanover **(G-6882)**

MACHINERY, PAPER INDUSTRY: Paper Mill, Plating, Etc

A & F Holdings LLC ....E........ 215 289-8300
   Feasterville Trevose **(G-5880)**

MACHINERY, PAPER INDUSTRY: Pulp Mill

Andritz Inc ....C...... 724 597-7801
   Canonsburg **(G-2540)**
Andritz Inc ....B...... 570 546-1253
   Muncy **(G-11806)**
Andritz Inc ....B...... 570 546-8211
   Muncy **(G-11807)**
Norton Pulpstones Incorporated..........F........ 610 964-0544
   Villanova **(G-18767)**

MACHINERY, PRINTING TRADES: Bronzing Or Dusting

Susquehanna Glass Co ....E........ 717 684-2155
   Columbia **(G-3451)**

MACHINERY, PRINTING TRADES: Copy Holders

Copy Rite ....G...... 814 644-0360
   Huntingdon **(G-7941)**
Marcus Uppe Inc ....E........ 412 261-4233
   Pittsburgh **(G-15253)**

MACHINERY, PRINTING TRADES: Galleys Or Chases

Lycoming Screen Printing Co...............G...... 570 326-3301
   Williamsport **(G-20038)**

MACHINERY, PRINTING TRADES: Plates

Custom Platecrafters Inc......................F........ 215 997-1990
   Colmar **(G-3414)**
Expert Pr-Press Consulting Ltd.............G...... 484 401-9821
   Downingtown **(G-4227)**
Sh Quints Sons Company ....F........ 215 533-1988
   Philadelphia **(G-14295)**
Southern Graphic Systems LLC...........C...... 215 843-2243
   Philadelphia **(G-14325)**

MACHINERY, SERVICING: Coin-Operated, Exc Dry Clean & Laundry

Solar Laundry & Dry Cleaning ....G...... 610 323-2121
   Pottstown **(G-16048)**

MACHINERY, SEWING: Sewing & Hat & Zipper Making

Hunter Engineering Company ....D...... 610 330-9024
   Easton **(G-4702)**

MACHINERY, TEXTILE: Braiding

Westerly Incorporated ....E........ 610 693-8866
   Robesonia **(G-16780)**

MACHINERY, TEXTILE: Embroidery

Caldwells of Bucks County...................G...... 215 345-1348
   Doylestown **(G-4285)**

PRODUCT

MACHINERY, TEXTILE: Frames, Double & Twisting

Stretch Devices Inc ....E 215 739-3000
Philadelphia (G-14352)

MACHINERY, TEXTILE: Printing

Bell-Mark Technologies Corp ....E 717 292-5641
Dover (G-4187)
Frontier LLC ....F 570 265-2500
Towanda (G-18426)
No Fear Inc ....F 484 527-8000
Malvern (G-10287)

MACHINERY, TEXTILE: Shearing

Sheerlund Products LLC ....F 484 248-2650
Reading (G-16516)

MACHINERY, TEXTILE: Silk Screens

Andrew W Nissly Inc ....G 717 393-3841
Lancaster (G-8934)
Finetex Rotary Engraving Inc ....G 717 273-6841
Lebanon (G-9567)
Miller Screen & Design Inc ....F 724 625-1870
Mars (G-10508)
Strutz Fabricators Inc ....E 724 625-1501
Valencia (G-18702)
T Shirt Printer ....G 717 367-1167
Elizabethtown (G-4889)

MACHINERY, WOODWORKING: Cabinet Makers'

Casework Cabinetry Cnstr ....G 814 236-7601
Curwensville (G-3947)
Steves Refacing ....G 724 274-4740
Springdale (G-17902)

MACHINERY, WOODWORKING: Furniture Makers

KB Woodcraft Inc ....G 502 533-2773
Phoenixville (G-14555)

MACHINERY/EQPT, INDL, WHOL: Cleaning, High Press, Sand/Steam

Valley Wholesale & Supply ....E 724 783-6531
Kittanning (G-8801)

MACHINERY: Ammunition & Explosives Loading

Eriez Manufacturing Co ....G 814 520-8540
Erie (G-5281)
Wiggins Shredding Inc ....G 610 692-8327
West Chester (G-19677)

MACHINERY: Assembly, Exc Metalworking

Automation Devices Inc ....E 814 474-5561
Fairview (G-5814)
Dynamic Manufacturing LLC ....D 724 295-4200
Freeport (G-6203)
Equipment Technology Inc ....G 570 489-8651
Peckville (G-13208)
Gaydos Equipment LLC ....E 724 272-6951
Gibsonia (G-6336)
Hennecke Inc ....D 724 271-3686
Bridgeville (G-2068)
Matric Group LLC ....B 814 677-0716
Seneca (G-17366)
McFadden Machine & Mfg Co ....E 724 459-9278
Blairsville (G-1734)
Newco Industries ....F 717 566-9560
Hummelstown (G-7919)
Precision Assembly Inc ....E 215 784-0861
Willow Grove (G-20136)
Projectile Tube Cleaning Inc ....E 724 763-7633
Ford City (G-6051)
SMS Group Inc ....C 412 231-1200
Pittsburgh (G-15552)
Swanson Systems Inc ....D 814 453-5841
Erie (G-5499)
Swanson-Erie Corporation ....D 814 453-5841
Erie (G-5500)
Tool O Matic Inc ....G 724 776-3232
Cranberry Township (G-3855)

W O Hickok Manufacturing Co ....E 717 234-8041
Harrisburg (G-7243)
Xcell Automation Inc ....D 717 755-6800
York (G-20721)

MACHINERY: Automobile Garage, Frame Straighteners

Garl Machine & Fabrication Inc ....G 610 929-7886
Temple (G-18330)
Specialty Automation Inc ....G 215 453-0817
Perkasie (G-13295)

MACHINERY: Automotive Maintenance

Churchville Mech Assoc LLC ....G 267 231-5968
Southampton (G-17803)
City of Pittsburgh ....E 412 255-2330
Pittsburgh (G-14855)
Isaac Stephens & Assoc Inc ....G 215 576-5414
Oreland (G-13024)
J-Mar Metal Fabricating Co ....G 215 785-6521
Croydon (G-3920)
Kleen Line Service Co Inc ....G 412 466-6277
Dravosburg (G-4351)
Mega Enterprises Inc ....G 610 380-0255
Parkesburg (G-13179)
Shenango Auto Mall LLC ....C 724 698-7304
New Castle (G-12150)

MACHINERY: Automotive Related

Alexanderwerk Inc ....G 215 442-0270
Montgomeryville (G-11383)
Hn Automotive Inc ....D 570 724-5191
Wellsboro (G-19465)
International Marketing Inc ....F 717 264-5819
Chambersburg (G-2942)
Production Systems Automtn LLC ....E 570 602-4200
Duryea (G-4506)
Rbna Fluid Exchange Inc ....E 717 840-0678
York (G-20651)
Waupaca Foundry Inc ....C 570 724-5191
Tioga (G-18367)
Waupaca Foundry Inc ....B 570 827-3245
Tioga (G-18368)

MACHINERY: Banking

Talaris Inc ....G 215 674-2882
Horsham (G-7855)

MACHINERY: Blasting, Electrical

E I T Corporation Phoenix ....F 570 286-7744
Sunbury (G-18168)

MACHINERY: Bottling & Canning

Enchanted Acres Farm Group LLC ....G 877 707-3833
Reading (G-16373)
Gideon B Stoltzfus ....G 717 656-4903
Bird In Hand (G-1675)
Veeco Precision Surfc Proc LLC ....D 215 328-0700
Horsham (G-7863)

MACHINERY: Brewery & Malting

Bog Turtle Brewery LLC ....G 484 758-0416
Oxford (G-13072)

MACHINERY: Brick Making

Kercher Industries Inc ....E 717 273-2111
Lebanon (G-9592)

MACHINERY: Bridge Or Gate, Hydraulic

Apex Hydraulic & Machine Inc ....F 814 342-1010
Philipsburg (G-14508)

MACHINERY: Cement Making

FLS US Holdings Inc ....F 610 264-6011
Bethlehem (G-1512)

MACHINERY: Centrifugal

Aml Industries Inc ....D 215 674-2424
Hatboro (G-7269)
Coal Centrifuge Service ....G 724 478-4205
Apollo (G-672)
Drucker Company Intl Inc ....E 814 342-6210
Philipsburg (G-14512)

Hydrogen Electrics LLC ....G 267 334-3155
Jenkintown (G-8290)

MACHINERY: Coin Wrapping

Allegheny-Wagner Inds Inc ....E 724 468-4300
Delmont (G-4047)

MACHINERY: Concrete Prdts

Hanover Prest-Paving Company ....E 717 637-0500
Hanover (G-6900)

MACHINERY: Construction

A Crane Rental LLC ....E 412 469-1776
Dravosburg (G-4350)
Advanced Cnstr Robotics Inc ....G 412 756-3360
Allison Park (G-445)
Altrax ....G 814 379-3706
Summerville (G-18156)
Bon Tool Company ....D 724 443-7080
Gibsonia (G-6328)
Brookville Locomotive Inc ....C 814 849-2000
Brookville (G-2254)
Caterpillar Inc ....B 724 743-0566
Houston (G-7870)
Caterpillar URS Storeroom ....F 610 293-5576
Radnor (G-16290)
Cellular Concrete LLC ....F 610 398-7833
Allentown (G-166)
Cnh Industrial America LLC ....C 717 355-1902
New Holland (G-12236)
Conrad Enterprises Inc ....E 717 274-5151
Cornwall (G-3738)
Dayton Superior Corporation ....D 570 695-3163
Tremont (G-18480)
Dieci United States LLC ....G 724 215-7081
Wyalusing (G-20249)
Future-All Inc ....E 412 279-2670
Carnegie (G-2768)
Hobart Corporation ....E 717 397-5100
Lancaster (G-9050)
J R Young ....G 717 935-2919
Belleville (G-1132)
Jlg Industries Inc ....C 717 485-5161
Mc Connellsburg (G-10569)
Jlg Industries Inc ....F 814 623-2156
Bedford (G-1055)
Kenco Construction Pdts Inc ....F 724 238-3387
Ligonier (G-9960)
Kennametal Inc ....C 276 646-0080
Bedford (G-1059)
Lee Industries Inc ....C 814 342-0460
Philipsburg (G-14519)
Lemco Tool Corporation ....E 570 494-0620
Cogan Station (G-3361)
Ls Steel Inc ....G 717 669-4581
Coatesville (G-3314)
M-B Companies Inc ....E 570 547-1621
Muncy (G-11825)
Maguire Products Inc ....E 610 459-4300
Aston (G-773)
McNeilus Truck and Mfg Inc ....E 610 286-0400
Morgantown (G-11527)
MIC Industries Inc ....D 814 266-8226
Elton (G-4960)
Mzp Kiln Services Inc ....G 412 825-5100
Pittsburgh (G-15313)
Promachining and Technology ....F 814 796-3254
Waterford (G-19268)
Ratchet Rake LLC ....G 717 249-1228
Carlisle (G-2734)
Richard E Krall Inc ....E 717 432-4179
Rossville (G-16824)
Roadsafe Traffic Systems Inc ....F 904 350-0080
Lemoyne (G-9751)
Russ Industrial Solutions LLC ....G 724 736-2580
Perryopolis (G-13304)
Saba Holding Company Inc ....G 717 737-3431
Camp Hill (G-2517)
Screen Service Tech Inc ....G 610 497-3555
Marcus Hook (G-10454)
Speciality Precast Company ....G 724 865-9255
Prospect (G-16113)
Tamco Inc ....E 724 258-6622
Monongahela (G-11317)
Try Tek Machine Works Inc ....E 717 428-1477
Jacobus (G-8232)
Tybot LLC ....G 412 756-3360
Allison Park (G-465)

Umoja Erectors LLC ....G...... 215 235-7662
Philadelphia **(G-14417)**

Vollmer Tar & Chip Inc ....G...... 814 834-1332
Saint Marys **(G-17027)**

Weir Hazleton Inc ....D...... 570 455-7711
Hazleton **(G-7537)**

MACHINERY: Cryogenic, Industrial

Acme Cryogenics Inc ....E...... 610 966-4488
Alburtis **(G-49)**

Acme Cryogenics Inc ....D...... 610 966-4488
Allentown **(G-114)**

Bethlehem Hydrogen Inc ....G...... 610 762-1706
Northampton **(G-12845)**

Cryogenic Gas Technologies Inc ....E...... 610 530-7288
Allentown **(G-188)**

Sumitomo Shi Crygnics Amer Inc ....D...... 610 791-6700
Allentown **(G-404)**

MACHINERY: Custom

Adept Corporation ....D...... 800 451-2254
York **(G-20366)**

Advanced VSR Technology ....G...... 215 366-3315
Philadelphia **(G-13348)**

ALe Hydraulic McHy Co LLC ....F...... 215 547-3351
Levittown **(G-9815)**

Amacoil Inc ....E...... 610 485-8300
Aston **(G-750)**

Ay Machine Co ....F...... 717 733-0335
Ephrata **(G-5091)**

B & J Sheet Metal Inc ....F...... 215 538-9543
Trumbauersville **(G-18529)**

Berks Engineering Company ....E...... 610 926-4146
Reading **(G-16330)**

Boekeloo Inc ....F...... 814 723-5950
Warren **(G-19014)**

CAM Industries Inc ....E...... 717 637-5988
Hanover **(G-6866)**

CAM Innovation Inc ....E...... 717 637-5988
Hanover **(G-6867)**

CNG One Source Inc ....F...... 814 673-4980
Franklin **(G-6120)**

Custom Hydraulics Inc ....F...... 724 729-3170
Burgettstown **(G-2344)**

Custom Mfg & Indus Svcs LLC ....G...... 412 621-2982
Pittsburgh **(G-14894)**

Cygnus Manufacturing Co LLC ....C...... 724 352-8000
Saxonburg **(G-17082)**

David Kovalcik ....G...... 724 539-3181
Loyalhanna **(G-10110)**

Demco Enterprises Inc ....F...... 888 419-3343
Quakertown **(G-16184)**

Diversified Design & Mfg Inc ....G...... 610 337-1969
King of Prussia **(G-8611)**

Eagle Microsystems ....E...... 610 323-2250
Pottstown **(G-15984)**

Elizabeth Carbide Die Co Inc ....E...... 412 829-7700
Irwin **(G-8160)**

Flinchbaugh Company Inc ....E...... 717 266-2202
Manchester **(G-10356)**

G C Carl Klemmer Inc ....G...... 215 329-4100
Philadelphia **(G-13738)**

Gosiger Inc ....F...... 724 778-3220
Warrendale **(G-19078)**

Guardian Tactical Inc ....G...... 814 558-6761
Emporium **(G-5062)**

Hanel Storage Systems ....E...... 412 788-0509
Pittsburgh **(G-15079)**

Hardy Machine Inc ....E...... 215 822-9359
Hatfield **(G-7345)**

Hood & Son Inc ....G...... 215 822-5750
Line Lexington **(G-9976)**

Hoover Design & Manufacturing ....G...... 717 767-9555
York **(G-20528)**

Hydra Service Inc ....G...... 724 852-2423
Waynesburg **(G-19446)**

Jade Holdings Inc ....C...... 215 947-3333
Huntingdon Valley **(G-8000)**

Johnstown McHning Fbrction Inc ....E...... 814 539-2209
Johnstown **(G-8390)**

Kfw Automation Inc ....G...... 610 266-5731
Allentown **(G-281)**

Kinsley Incorporated ....G...... 215 348-7723
Doylestown **(G-4311)**

Lamjen Inc ....E...... 814 459-5277
Erie **(G-5359)**

M D Cline Metal Fabg Inc ....G...... 724 459-8968
Blairsville **(G-1733)**

Mac Machine LLC ....F...... 610 583-3055
Brookhaven **(G-2246)**

Marando Industries Inc ....G...... 610 621-2536
Reading **(G-16437)**

Martin Truck Bodies Inc ....E...... 814 793-3353
Martinsburg **(G-10526)**

Ofcg Inc ....G...... 570 655-0804
Dupont **(G-4493)**

Onexia Inc ....E...... 610 431-7271
Exton **(G-5720)**

Precision TI & Die Mfg Co Inc ....F...... 814 676-1864
Oil City **(G-12955)**

Purcell Company ....E...... 717 838-5611
Palmyra **(G-13130)**

Racoh Products Inc ....E...... 814 486-3288
Emporium **(G-5073)**

Ramsay Machine Development ....F...... 610 395-4764
Allentown **(G-370)**

Rightnour Manufacturing Co Inc ....E...... 800 326-9113
Mingoville **(G-11257)**

Rod Quellette ....G...... 814 274-8812
Coudersport **(G-3788)**

Rsj Technologies LLC ....E...... 570 673-4173
Canton **(G-2668)**

Ruck Engineering Inc ....G...... 412 835-2408
Bethel Park **(G-1431)**

Skylon Inc ....F...... 814 489-3622
Sugar Grove **(G-18147)**

Stellar Machine Incorporated ....F...... 570 718-1733
Nanticoke **(G-11903)**

Trimach LLC ....G...... 610 252-8983
Easton **(G-4764)**

United Theatrical Services ....G...... 215 242-2134
Philadelphia **(G-14424)**

Vanzel Inc ....E...... 215 223-1000
Philadelphia **(G-14438)**

Vortx United Inc ....G...... 570 742-7859
Milton **(G-11250)**

W & H Machine Shop Inc ....F...... 814 834-6258
Saint Marys **(G-17029)**

Wel-Mac Inc ....G...... 717 637-6921
Hanover **(G-6974)**

Westrock Packaging Inc ....D...... 215 785-3350
Croydon **(G-3933)**

Z & Z Machine Inc ....G...... 717 428-0354
Jacobus **(G-8233)**

Zero Error Racing Inc ....G...... 724 588-5898
Greenville **(G-6778)**

MACHINERY: Desalination Eqpt

GE Infrastructure Sensing ....F...... 617 926-1749
Feasterville Trevose **(G-5912)**

Suez Wts Systems Usa Inc ....B...... 781 359-7000
Trevose **(G-18505)**

MACHINERY: Die Casting

Die-Quip Corporation ....F...... 412 833-1662
Bethel Park **(G-1411)**

MACHINERY: Drill Presses

Keane Group Holdings LLC ....E...... 570 302-4050
Mansfield **(G-10419)**

MACHINERY: Electrical Discharge Erosion

Universal Pioneers LLC ....G...... 570 239-3950
Plymouth **(G-15822)**

MACHINERY: Electronic Component Making

Allegheny Fabg & Sups Inc ....G...... 412 828-3320
Pittsburgh **(G-14678)**

Ccr Electronics ....G...... 317 469-4855
Pittsburgh **(G-14832)**

Ddm Novastar Inc ....E...... 610 337-3050
Warminster **(G-18855)**

Iheadbones Inc ....G...... 888 866-0807
Newtown **(G-12512)**

Kras Corporation ....E...... 610 566-0271
Media **(G-10935)**

MACHINERY: Electronic Teaching Aids

Oakwood Controls Corporation ....F...... 717 801-1515
Glen Rock **(G-6458)**

Right Reason Technologies LLC ....G...... 484 898-1967
Bethlehem **(G-1611)**

MACHINERY: Extruding

Composidie Inc ....C...... 724 845-8602
Apollo **(G-673)**

SMS Group Inc ....C...... 412 231-1200
Pittsburgh **(G-15552)**

MACHINERY: Gear Cutting & Finishing

Ellwood Group Inc ....C...... 724 981-1012
Hermitage **(G-7582)**

MACHINERY: Glassmaking

Bethlehem Apparatus Co Inc ....G...... 610 882-2611
Bethlehem **(G-1460)**

Bethlehem Apparatus Co Inc ....E...... 610 838-7034
Bethlehem **(G-1461)**

Billco Manufacturing Inc ....C...... 724 452-7390
Zelienople **(G-20792)**

Brockport Glass Components LLC ....G...... 814 265-1479
Brockport **(G-2220)**

Carl Strutz & Company Inc ....E...... 724 625-1501
Mars **(G-10489)**

Carl Strutz & Company Inc ....D...... 724 625-1501
Mars **(G-10490)**

Quantum Engineered Pdts Inc ....E...... 724 352-5100
Saxonburg **(G-17093)**

MACHINERY: Grinding

Commercial Metal Polishing ....F...... 610 837-0267
Bath **(G-954)**

Herkules USA Corporation ....C...... 724 763-2066
Ford City **(G-6047)**

Herkules USA Corporation ....D...... 724 763-2066
Ford City **(G-6048)**

Imperial Newbould Inc ....F...... 814 337-8155
Meadville **(G-10737)**

M & S Centerless Grinding Inc ....F...... 215 675-4144
Hatboro **(G-7294)**

Waldrich GMBH Inc ....G...... 724 763-3889
Ford City **(G-6052)**

Weldon Machine Tool Inc ....E...... 717 846-4000
York **(G-20706)**

MACHINERY: Ice Making

Kold Draft International LLC ....E...... 814 453-6761
Erie **(G-5350)**

MACHINERY: Industrial, NEC

Alberts Jennings ....G...... 215 766-2852
Pipersville **(G-14610)**

Bell Manufacturing ....G...... 717 529-2600
Christiana **(G-3133)**

Cewa Technologies Inc ....G...... 484 695-5489
Bethlehem **(G-1482)**

Hotronix LLC ....G...... 800 727-8520
Carmichaels **(G-2757)**

Wintercorp LLC ....G...... 717 848-3425
York **(G-20712)**

Yoh Industrial LLC ....E...... 215 656-2650
Philadelphia **(G-14501)**

MACHINERY: Kilns

Chestnut Rd Lumber & Dry Kiln ....G...... 717 423-5941
Newburg **(G-12474)**

Lime Kiln AG LLC ....G...... 610 589-4302
Womelsdorf **(G-20207)**

Mzp Kiln Services Inc ....G...... 724 318-8653
Ambridge **(G-629)**

MACHINERY: Kilns, Cement

Thyssnkrupp Indus Slutions USA ....D...... 412 257-8277
Bridgeville **(G-2095)**

MACHINERY: Kilns, Lumber

Riethmiller Lumber Mfg Corp ....G...... 724 946-8608
New Wilmington **(G-12469)**

MACHINERY: Knitting

Bearing Products Company ....F...... 215 659-4768
Philadelphia **(G-13449)**

MACHINERY: Labeling

Fox IV Technologies Inc ....E...... 724 387-3500
Export **(G-5603)**

I D Tek Inc ....E...... 215 699-8888
North Wales **(G-12806)**

ID Technology LLC ....E...... 717 235-8345
New Freedom **(G-12209)**

PRODUCT

ID Technology LLC ....E.... 717 848-3875
York (G-20533)
Labelpack Automation Inc ....E.... 814 362-1528
Bradford (G-1979)
Tek ID ....F.... 215 699-8888
North Wales (G-12831)

MACHINERY: Marking, Metalworking

Mecco Partners LLC ....F.... 724 779-9555
Cranberry Township (G-3835)

MACHINERY: Metalworking

All-Fill Corporation ....D.... 866 255-3455
Exton (G-5639)
Ay Machine Co ....F.... 717 733-0335
Ephrata (G-5091)
Bella Machine Inc ....G.... 570 826-9127
Wilkes Barre (G-19908)
C I Hayes Inc ....E.... 814 834-2200
Saint Marys (G-16951)
CAM Industries Inc ....E.... 717 637-5988
Hanover (G-6866)
Charles Smith ....G.... 724 727-3455
Apollo (G-668)
Cnc Technology Inc ....G.... 610 444-4437
Coatesville (G-3298)
Coinco Inc ....E.... 814 425-7407
Cochranton (G-3337)
Daltech Inc ....E.... 570 823-9911
Hanover Township (G-6987)
Emp Industries Inc ....G.... 215 357-5333
Warminster (G-18871)
Exim Steel & Shipbroking Inc ....G.... 215 369-9746
Yardley (G-20310)
FLS US Holdings Inc ....F.... 610 264-6011
Bethlehem (G-1512)
Frazier-Simplex Machine Co ....E.... 724 222-5700
Washington (G-19177)
Gasbarre Products Inc ....E.... 814 834-2200
Saint Marys (G-16975)
Geissele Automatics LLC ....F.... 610 272-2060
North Wales (G-12803)
Holdrens Precision Machining ....F.... 570 358-3377
Ulster (G-18599)
Industrial Machine Designs Inc ....G.... 724 981-2707
Wheatland (G-19838)
J & S Machining Corp ....F.... 717 653-6358
Manheim (G-10391)
John A Manning Jr ....G.... 215 233-0976
Glenside (G-6524)
Joseph Machine Company Inc ....E.... 717 432-3442
Dillsburg (G-4132)
K & N Machine Shop LLC ....G.... 717 624-3403
New Oxford (G-12412)
LAY Machine and Tool Inc ....G.... 610 469-0928
Pottstown (G-15952)
Leefson Tool & Die Company ....E.... 610 461-7772
Folcroft (G-6008)
Mae-Eitel Inc ....D.... 570 366-0585
Orwigsburg (G-13048)
Matthews International Corp ....D.... 412 665-2500
Pittsburgh (G-15265)
McC International Inc ....D.... 724 745-0300
Mc Donald (G-10577)
MIC Industries Inc ....D.... 814 266-8226
Elton (G-4960)
Pannier Corporation ....F.... 412 323-4900
Pittsburgh (G-15368)
Penn Engineering & Mfg Corp ....B.... 215 766-8853
Danboro (G-3991)
Precision Tool & Mfg Corp ....G.... 717 767-6454
Emigsville (G-4997)
Precision Tool and Machine Co ....F.... 570 868-3920
Mountain Top (G-11772)
Readco Kurimoto LLC ....E.... 717 848-2801
York (G-20652)
Ribarchik John ....G.... 215 547-8901
Levittown (G-9861)
Scheirer Machine Company Inc ....E.... 412 833-6500
Bethel Park (G-1433)
Specialty Design & Mfg Co Inc ....E.... 610 779-1357
Reading (G-16520)
Specialty Holdings Corp ....E.... 610 779-1357
Reading (G-16521)
Tool Tec Inc ....F.... 610 688-9086
Wayne (G-19383)
Universal Mch Co Pottstown Inc ....D.... 610 323-1810
Pottstown (G-16062)
Wesel Manufacturing Company ....E.... 570 586-8978
S Abingtn Twp (G-16903)

Westerly Incorporated ....E.... 610 693-8866
Robesonia (G-16780)
X Material Processing Company ....G.... 717 968-8765
State College (G-18042)
Xact Metal Inc ....G.... 814 777-7727
State College (G-18043)

MACHINERY: Milling

Asm Products Inc ....G.... 724 861-8026
North Huntingdon (G-12768)
Custom Mil & Consulting Inc ....E.... 610 926-0984
Fleetwood (G-5969)
Extrude Hone LLC ....D.... 724 863-5900
Irwin (G-8162)

MACHINERY: Mining

Becker/Wholesale Mine Sup LLC ....E.... 724 515-4993
Greensburg (G-6653)
Bridon-American Corporation ....B.... 570 822-3349
Hanover Township (G-6982)
Brookville Locomotive Inc ....C.... 814 849-2000
Brookville (G-2254)
Burch Supplies Company Inc ....G.... 610 640-4877
Malvern (G-10197)
Caterpillar Globl Min Amer LLC ....C.... 724 743-1200
Houston (G-7869)
Eastern Machine & Convyrs Inc ....F.... 724 379-4701
Donora (G-4154)
Eickhoff Corporation ....F.... 724 218-1856
Georgetown (G-6275)
Gcl Inc ....G.... 724 933-7260
Wexford (G-19805)
Irwin Car & Equipment Inc ....F.... 724 864-5170
Irwin (G-8173)
Irwin Car & Equipment Inc ....E.... 724 864-8900
Irwin (G-8174)
Jennmar Corporation ....D.... 814 886-4121
Cresson (G-3899)
Jennmar of Kentucky Inc ....E.... 412 963-9071
Pittsburgh (G-15150)
Jennmar of Pennsylvania LLC ....E.... 412 963-9071
Pittsburgh (G-15151)
Joy Global Inc ....C.... 814 432-1202
Franklin (G-6142)
Joy Global Underground Min LLC ....D.... 814 676-8531
Franklin (G-6143)
Joy Global Underground Min LLC ....D.... 814 432-1647
Franklin (G-6144)
Joy Global Underground Min LLC ....C.... 814 437-5731
Franklin (G-6145)
K & K Mine Products Inc ....E.... 724 463-5000
Indiana (G-8109)
Kennametal Inc ....A.... 412 248-8000
Pittsburgh (G-15169)
Kennametal Inc ....C.... 276 646-0080
Bedford (G-1059)
Leman Machine Company ....E.... 814 736-9696
Portage (G-15918)
Master Machine Co Inc ....F.... 814 495-4900
South Fork (G-17775)
Mining Clamps Fasteners & More ....G.... 724 324-2430
Mount Morris (G-11681)
Mpi Supply Incorporated ....G.... 412 664-9320
Glassport (G-6414)
Penn Machine Company ....D.... 814 288-1547
Johnstown (G-8421)
Sandvik Inc ....E.... 724 246-2901
Brier Hill (G-2101)
Steel Systems Installation Inc ....E.... 717 786-1264
Quarryville (G-16280)
Strata Products Worldwide LLC ....G.... 724 745-5030
Canonsburg (G-2641)
Tallman Supply Company ....G.... 717 647-2123
Tower City (G-18442)
Terrasource Global Corporation ....E.... 610 544-7200
Media (G-10953)
Testa Machine Company Inc ....E.... 724 947-9397
Slovan (G-17631)
Titan Metal & Machine Co Inc ....G.... 724 747-9528
Washington (G-19232)

MACHINERY: Nuclear Reactor Control Rod & Drive Mechanism

Tsb Nclear Enrgy USA Group Inc ....G.... 412 374-4111
Cranberry Township (G-3859)

MACHINERY: Optical Lens

Electro-Optical Systems Inc ....F.... 610 935-5838
Phoenixville (G-14547)
Nestor Systems International ....G.... 610 767-5000
Treichlers (G-18477)

MACHINERY: Packaging

Advanced Machine Systems Inc ....F.... 610 837-8677
Bath (G-949)
All-Fill Corporation ....D.... 866 255-3455
Exton (G-5639)
All-Fill Inc ....G.... 610 524-7350
Exton (G-5640)
Ameripak ....E.... 215 343-1530
Warrington (G-19107)
AMS Liquidating Co Inc ....D.... 610 942-4200
Honey Brook (G-7736)
Ardagh Metal Packaging USA Inc ....E.... 412 923-1080
Carnegie (G-2764)
Beta Industries Inc ....G.... 610 363-6555
Exton (G-5655)
Carleton Inc ....E.... 215 230-8900
Doylestown (G-4289)
Charles Beseler Co Inc ....D.... 800 237-3537
Stroudsburg (G-18109)
CSS International Corporation ....F.... 215 533-6110
Philadelphia (G-13589)
Dyco Inc ....D.... 800 545-3926
Bloomsburg (G-1779)
E S S Packaging Machinery ....G.... 610 588-8579
Roseto (G-16820)
Ergonomic Mfg Group Inc ....G.... 800 223-6430
Quakertown (G-16189)
Erie Technical Systems Inc ....G.... 814 899-2103
Erie (G-5276)
Farason Corporation ....E.... 610 383-6224
Coatesville (G-3303)
Fres-Co Systems Usa Inc ....B.... 215 721-4600
Telford (G-18290)
Gottscho Printing Systems Inc ....G.... 267 387-3005
Warminster (G-18890)
Harro Hofliger Packg Systems ....E.... 215 345-4256
Doylestown (G-4305)
Hostvedt Pavoni Inc ....F.... 215 489-7300
Doylestown (G-4306)
Jls Automation LLC ....E.... 717 505-3800
York (G-20541)
Libra Three Inc ....G.... 610 217-9992
Palmerton (G-13109)
Loveshaw Corporation ....C.... 570 937-4921
South Canaan (G-17769)
McNeilus Truck and Mfg Inc ....E.... 610 286-0400
Morgantown (G-11527)
Millwood Inc ....C.... 610 421-6230
Alburtis (G-57)
Millwood Inc ....F.... 724 266-7030
Leetsdale (G-9699)
Millwood Inc ....F.... 717 790-9118
Mechanicsburg (G-10869)
Millwood Inc ....F.... 570 836-9280
Tunkhannock (G-18543)
New Way Packaging Machinery ....G.... 717 637-2133
Hanover (G-6925)
Omega Design Corporation ....D.... 610 363-6555
Exton (G-5718)
OP Schuman & Sons Inc ....D.... 215 343-1530
Warminster (G-18932)
Packaging Progressions Inc ....E.... 610 489-9096
Souderton (G-17758)
Pak-Rapid Inc ....G.... 610 828-3511
Conshohocken (G-3585)
Palace Packaging Machines Inc ....E.... 610 873-7252
Downingtown (G-4249)
Paragon Print Systems Inc ....F.... 814 456-8331
Erie (G-5413)
Peters Equipment Corp ....G.... 215 364-9147
Huntingdon Valley (G-8024)
R R Pankratz Inc ....G.... 610 696-1043
West Chester (G-19627)
RE Pack Inc ....G.... 215 699-9252
Lansdale (G-9403)
Signode Industrial Group LLC ....C.... 570 937-4921
South Canaan (G-17770)
Signode Industrial Group LLC ....G.... 570 937-4921
South Canaan (G-17771)
Smit Corporation ....E.... 215 396-2200
Warminster (G-18965)
Telstar North America Inc ....A.... 215 826-0770
Bristol (G-2205)

Urania Engineering Co Inc .... E 570 455-0776
Hazleton (G-7532)

Wayne Automation Corporation .... D 610 630-8900
Norristown (G-12723)

MACHINERY: Paint Making

Herr Industrial Inc .... E 717 569-6619
Lititz (G-10016)

MACHINERY: Paper Industry Miscellaneous

Ferag Inc .... D 215 788-0892
Bristol (G-2144)

FLS US Holdings Inc .... F 610 264-6011
Bethlehem (G-1512)

H M Spencer Wire .... G 570 726-7495
Mill Hall (G-11177)

Hobart Corporation .... E 717 397-5100
Lancaster (G-9050)

John Eppler Machine Works .... E 215 624-3400
Orwigsburg (G-13046)

Marquip Ward United .... G 570 742-7859
Milton (G-11248)

Paco Winders Mfg LLC .... E 215 673-6265
Philadelphia (G-14113)

Paper Converting Machine Co .... C 814 695-5521
Duncansville (G-4459)

Pcmc .... C 814 934-3262
Duncansville (G-4460)

MACHINERY: Pharmaciutical

Abps, Inc. .... E 800 552-9980
Exton (G-5635)

Bradford Allegheny Corporation .... C 814 362-2590
Lewis Run (G-9871)

Gil Prebelli .... F 215 281-0300
Philadelphia (G-13762)

Jay-Ell Industries Inc .... F 610 326-0921
Pottstown (G-16005)

Ladisch Corporation Inc .... G 267 313-4189
Alburtis (G-55)

LB Bohle LLC .... F 215 957-1240
Warminster (G-18911)

Lee Industries Inc .... C 814 342-0460
Philipsburg (G-14519)

R-V Industries Inc .... E 800 552-9980
Exton (G-5726)

Simkins Corporation .... E 215 739-4033
Jenkintown (G-8301)

Specialty Measurements Inc .... F 908 534-1500
Bethlehem (G-1623)

Steq America LLC .... G 267 644-5477
Doylestown (G-4339)

West Pharmaceutical Services D .... E 610 594-2900
Exton (G-5747)

MACHINERY: Plastic Working

Allegheny Plastics Inc .... C 412 741-4416
Leetsdale (G-9679)

Berner Industries Inc .... F 724 924-9240
New Castle (G-12062)

Cannon U S A Inc .... E 724 772-5600
Cranberry Township (G-3810)

Cannon U S A Inc .... G 724 452-5358
Zelienople (G-20794)

Chant Engineering Co Inc .... E 215 230-4260
New Britain (G-12046)

Conair Group Inc .... E 724 584-5500
Cranberry Township (G-3811)

Graham Engineering Corporation .... G 717 848-3755
York (G-20507)

Ipeg Inc .... E 814 437-6861
Franklin (G-6140)

Molded Fiber Glass Companies .... C 814 683-4500
Linesville (G-9984)

Technical Process & Engrg Inc .... E 570 386-4777
Lehighton (G-9730)

United Plastics Machinery Inc .... E 610 363-0990
Exton (G-5742)

MACHINERY: Printing Presses

Kennett Advance Printing House .... G 610 444-5840
Kennett Square (G-8519)

MACHINERY: Recycling

Allegheny-Wagner Inds Inc .... E 724 468-4300
Delmont (G-4047)

Blue Valley Industries Inc .... G 717 436-8266
Port Royal (G-15909)

Camden Iron & Metal Inc .... G 215 952-1500
Philadelphia (G-13495)

Collegecart Innovations Inc .... G 215 813-3900
Holland (G-7640)

Rapid Granulator Inc .... F 724 584-5220
Leetsdale (G-9702)

Rapid Granulator Inc .... F 814 437-6861
Franklin (G-6154)

Stanko Products Inc .... F 724 834-8080
Greensburg (G-6717)

MACHINERY: Riveting

Baltec Corporation .... E 724 873-5757
Canonsburg (G-2549)

Chicago Rivet & Machine Co .... D 814 684-2430
Tyrone (G-18580)

MACHINERY: Road Construction & Maintenance

City of Washington .... G 724 225-4883
Washington (G-19156)

Greenwood Township .... G 570 458-0212
Millville (G-11225)

Stabler Companies Inc .... F 717 236-9307
Harrisburg (G-7219)

Trench Shoring Services .... G 412 331-8118
Pittsburgh (G-15642)

MACHINERY: Robots, Molding & Forming Plastics

Astro Automation Inc .... G 724 864-2500
Irwin (G-8145)

Ilsemann Corp .... G 610 323-4143
Pottstown (G-16000)

New Precision Technology Inc .... G 412 596-5948
Pittsburgh (G-15334)

MACHINERY: Rubber Working

Dartonya Manufacturing Inc .... G 814 849-3240
Brookville (G-2260)

MACHINERY: Semiconductor Manufacturing

Angstrom Sciences Inc .... E 412 469-8466
Duquesne (G-4495)

Crystalplex Corporation .... G 412 787-1525
Pittsburgh (G-14889)

Emp Industries Inc .... G 215 357-5333
Warminster (G-18871)

Global Machine and Maint LLC .... G 215 356-3077
Rydal (G-16885)

Kuper Technologies LLC .... G 610 358-5120
Garnet Valley (G-6266)

Kurt J Lesker Company .... G 412 387-9200
Jefferson Hills (G-8277)

Microprocess Technolgies LLC .... G 570 778-0925
Palm (G-13095)

Mivatek Global LLC .... F 610 358-5120
Chadds Ford (G-2856)

Naura Akrion Inc .... D 610 391-9200
Allentown (G-325)

Primaxx Inc .... F 610 336-0314
Allentown (G-359)

Veeco Precision Surfc Proc LLC .... D 215 328-0700
Horsham (G-7863)

MACHINERY: Separation Eqpt, Magnetic

Eriez Manufacturing Co .... B 814 835-6000
Erie (G-5280)

MACHINERY: Separators, Mineral

Mineral Processing Spc Inc .... G 724 339-8630
New Kensington (G-12358)

MACHINERY: Service Industry, NEC

CCL Restoration LLC .... G 412 926-6156
Pittsburgh (G-14830)

Double D Service Center LLC .... F 717 201-2800
Columbia (G-3437)

Fermentec Inc .... G 203 809-8078
Philadelphia (G-13697)

Lancaster Pump .... E 717 397-3521
Lancaster (G-9105)

Protechs LLC .... G 717 768-0800
New Holland (G-12273)

MACHINERY: Sheet Metal Working

Wemco Inc .... F 570 869-9660
Laceyville (G-8875)

MACHINERY: Specialty

Cryocal .... G 714 568-0201
Imperial (G-8061)

Montgmrys Atomtn Parts Sls Svc .... G 724 368-3001
Portersville (G-15933)

MACHINERY: Stone Working

Fluid Energy Proc & Eqp Co .... G 215 721-8990
Telford (G-18289)

Fluid Energy Proc & Eqp Co .... D 215 368-2510
Hatfield (G-7343)

Rocksolid Installation Inc .... G 717 548-8700
Peach Bottom (G-13201)

MACHINERY: Textile

Automated Components Intl .... E 570 344-4000
Dunmore (G-4469)

Aztec Machinery Company .... E 215 672-2600
Warminster (G-18833)

Ken-Tex Corp .... E 570 374-4476
Selinsgrove (G-17328)

OP Schuman & Sons Inc .... D 215 343-1530
Warminster (G-18932)

Pennsylvania Sewing Res Co .... F 570 344-4000
Dunmore (G-4480)

S Morantz Inc .... D 215 969-0266
Philadelphia (G-14273)

Stahls Special Projects Inc .... E 724 583-1176
Masontown (G-10537)

Textured Yarn Co Inc .... G 610 444-5400
Kennett Square (G-8549)

Tsg Finishing .... F 828 850-4381
North Wales (G-12838)

MACHINERY: Tire Shredding

Approved Info Destruction Inc .... G 412 722-8124
Bethel Park (G-1403)

Shredstation Express of Montgo .... G 215 723-1694
Franconia (G-6110)

MACHINERY: Wire Drawing

Shaffers Fabricating Inc .... G 724 583-2833
Masontown (G-10536)

MACHINERY: Woodworking

CNE Machinery Ltd .... G 814 723-1685
Warren (G-19017)

Dan Dulls Specialty Wdwkg .... G 724 843-6223
New Brighton (G-12033)

E & E Building Group LP .... F 215 453-5124
Ambler (G-578)

Econotool Inc .... G 215 947-2404
Huntingdon Valley (G-7975)

Hermance Machine Company .... E 570 326-9156
Williamsport (G-20021)

John M Sensenig .... G 717 445-4669
New Holland (G-12255)

Unique Wood Creation LLC .... G 717 687-8843
Paradise (G-13163)

Unique Wood Creation LLC .... G 717 687-7900
Paradise (G-13164)

Wood Machinery Mfrs Amer .... G 215 564-3484
Philadelphia (G-14483)

MACHINES: Forming, Sheet Metal

Mellinger Manufacturing Co Inc .... F 717 464-3318
Willow Street (G-20154)

Sonic Systems Inc .... E 267 803-1964
Warminster (G-18967)

MACHINISTS' TOOLS: Measuring, Precision

Chemcut Corporation .... B 814 272-2800
State College (G-17950)

Elbach & Johnson Inc .... G 724 457-6180
Glenwillard (G-6546)

JB Anderson & Son Inc .... G 724 523-9610
Irwin (G-8177)

PRODUCT

JV Manufacturing Co Inc.................D..... 724 224-1704
　Natrona Heights (G-11945)
Oppenheimer Precision Pdts Inc..........D..... 215 674-9100
　Horsham (G-7837)
Siemens Industry Inc.....................D..... 215 646-7400
　Spring House (G-17883)
Trilion Quality Systems LLC.............E..... 215 710-3000
　King of Prussia (G-8690)

MACHINISTS' TOOLS: Precision

Dj Machining LLC........................G..... 724 938-0812
　Greensburg (G-6659)
Foust Machine & Tool....................G..... 717 766-7841
　Mechanicsburg (G-10845)
Jade Holdings Inc.......................C..... 215 947-3333
　Huntingdon Valley (G-8000)
Molinaro Tool & Die Inc.................F..... 724 654-5141
　New Castle (G-12121)
Oberg Industries Inc....................A..... 724 295-2121
　Freeport (G-6209)
Quality Machine Tools LLC...............G..... 412 787-2876
　Coraopolis (G-3720)
Rjc Manufacturing Services LLC..........G..... 724 836-3636
　Irwin (G-8197)
Unison Engine Components Inc............C..... 570 825-4544
　Wilkes Barre (G-19967)
William Lammers........................G..... 610 894-9502
　Kutztown (G-8863)

MACHINISTS' TOOLS: Scales, Measuring, Precision

PDC Machines Inc........................D..... 215 443-9442
　Warminster (G-18937)

MAGAZINE STAND

Fab Universal Corp......................F..... 412 621-0902
　Pittsburgh (G-15002)

MAGAZINES, WHOLESALE

Roman Press Inc.........................G..... 215 997-9650
　Chalfont (G-2886)

MAGNESITE MINING

Harbisnwlker Intl Holdings Inc..........G..... 412 375-6600
　Moon Township (G-11488)
Harbisonwalker Intl Inc.................C..... 412 375-6600
　Moon Township (G-11490)

MAGNETIC INK & OPTICAL SCANNING EQPT

Craddock & Lerro Associates.............G..... 610 543-0200
　Drexel Hill (G-4363)
Fox IV Technologies Inc.................E..... 724 387-3500
　Export (G-5603)
Symbol Technologies LLC.................F..... 610 834-8900
　Plymouth Meeting (G-15875)

MAGNETIC INK RECOGNITION DEVICES

Solvay.................................D..... 412 423-2030
　Pittsburgh (G-15554)

MAGNETIC RESONANCE IMAGING DEVICES: Nonmedical

Extremity Imaging Partners..............G..... 610 432-1055
　Allentown (G-210)
Hamot Imaging Facility..................F..... 814 877-5381
　Erie (G-5309)
N Pgh Imaging Specialists...............F..... 724 935-6200
　Wexford (G-19813)
Nanomagnetics Instrs USA LLC............G..... 610 417-3857
　Easton (G-4730)

MAGNETIC SHIELDS, METAL

Gaven Industries Inc....................E..... 724 352-8100
　Saxonburg (G-17087)
Tritech Applied Sciences Inc............G..... 215 362-6890
　Lansdale (G-9417)

MAGNETIC TAPE, AUDIO: Prerecorded

Atr Magnetics LLC.......................G..... 717 718-8008
　York (G-20391)

MAGNETS: Ceramic

Eneflux Armtek Magnetics Inc............G..... 215 443-5303
　Warminster (G-18872)
SPS Technologies LLC....................A..... 215 572-3000
　Jenkintown (G-8302)

MAGNETS: Permanent

Electron Energy Corporation.............E..... 717 898-2294
　Landisville (G-9259)
Hi-TEC Magnetics Inc....................G..... 484 681-4265
　King of Prussia (G-8631)
K & J Magnetics Inc.....................E..... 215 766-8055
　Pipersville (G-14617)
Musumeci Santo.........................G..... 215 467-2158
　Philadelphia (G-14045)
SPS Technologies LLC....................A..... 215 572-3000
　Jenkintown (G-8302)

MAIL-ORDER HOUSE, NEC

Ceramic Art Company Inc.................A..... 952 944-5600
　Bristol (G-2124)
E R Shaw Inc............................E..... 412 212-4343
　Bridgeville (G-2059)
Oakwood Bindery........................E..... 717 396-9559
　Lancaster (G-9149)
Quaker Boy Inc.........................F..... 814 362-7073
　Bradford (G-1988)
W C Wolff Company......................F..... 610 359-9600
　Newtown Square (G-12598)

MAIL-ORDER HOUSES: Automotive Splys & Eqpt

Auto Weld Chassis & Components..........G..... 570 275-1411
　Danville (G-3997)

MAIL-ORDER HOUSES: Book & Record Clubs

Organ Historical Society................G..... 804 353-9226
　Villanova (G-18768)

MAIL-ORDER HOUSES: Clothing, Exc Women's

AC Fashion LLC.........................G..... 570 291-5982
　Moosic (G-11501)
Aramark Unf Creer AP Group Inc..........A..... 215 238-3000
　Philadelphia (G-13406)

MAIL-ORDER HOUSES: Computer Software

Datatech Software Inc...................F..... 717 652-4344
　Harrisburg (G-7113)

MAIL-ORDER HOUSES: Food

Cooke Tavern Ltd.......................G..... 814 422-7687
　Spring Mills (G-17887)
Termini Brothers Inc....................E..... 215 334-1816
　Philadelphia (G-14381)

MAIL-ORDER HOUSES: General Merchandise

Twenty61 LLC...........................G..... 215 370-7076
　Philadelphia (G-14415)

MAIL-ORDER HOUSES: Magazines

Roxanne Toser Non-Sport Entps..........G..... 717 238-1936
　Harrisburg (G-7209)

MAIL-ORDER HOUSES: Women's Apparel

Ems Clothing & Novelty Inc..............G..... 570 752-2896
　Berwick (G-1324)

MAILBOX RENTAL & RELATED SVCS

FB Shoemaker LLC.......................G..... 717 852-8029
　York (G-20476)
Laurel Parcel Services Inc..............G..... 724 850-6245
　Greensburg (G-6683)
Minton Holdings LLC....................G..... 412 787-5912
　Pittsburgh (G-15293)
UPS Store Inc..........................G..... 724 934-1088
　Wexford (G-19831)
UPS Store 6410.........................G..... 484 816-0252
　Aston (G-795)

MAILING & MESSENGER SVCS

Everything Postal Inc...................G..... 610 367-7444
　Bechtelsville (G-1032)
Fotorecord Print Center Inc.............G..... 724 837-0530
　Greensburg (G-6667)

MAILING LIST: Brokers

Jay Weiss Corporation...................G..... 610 834-8585
　Lafayette Hill (G-8881)

MAILING MACHINES WHOLESALERS

Sinacom North America Inc...............E..... 610 337-2250
　King of Prussia (G-8677)

MAILING SVCS, NEC

Bonnie Kaiser..........................G..... 215 331-6555
　Philadelphia (G-13471)
Clinton Press Inc......................G..... 814 455-9089
　Erie (G-5227)
CMI Printgraphix Inc....................G..... 717 697-4567
　Mechanicsburg (G-10827)
Direct Mail Service & Press.............F..... 610 432-4538
　Allentown (G-194)
Kennedy Printing Co Inc.................F..... 215 474-5150
　Philadelphia (G-13926)
Marathon Printing Inc...................F..... 215 238-1100
　Philadelphia (G-13991)
Pemcor Printing Company LLC.............D..... 717 898-1555
　Lancaster (G-9162)
Print City Graphics Inc.................G..... 610 495-5524
　Phoenixville (G-14570)
Professional Graphic Co.................E..... 724 318-8530
　Sewickley (G-17405)
UPS Store Inc..........................G..... 724 934-1088
　Wexford (G-19831)

MANAGEMENT CONSULTING SVCS: Automation & Robotics

Icreate Automation Inc..................F..... 610 443-1758
　Allentown (G-251)

MANAGEMENT CONSULTING SVCS: Business

Ballistic Applications..................F..... 724 282-0416
　East Butler (G-4530)
C and M Sales Co.......................F..... 814 437-3095
　Franklin (G-6118)
Cyrus-Xp Inc...........................E..... 610 986-8408
　Ardmore (G-706)
Hiatt Thompson Corporation..............G..... 708 496-8585
　Greenville (G-6745)

MANAGEMENT CONSULTING SVCS: Business Planning & Organizing

Sustrana LLC...........................G..... 610 651-2870
　Devon (G-4116)

MANAGEMENT CONSULTING SVCS: Construction Project

Avc Solutions LLC......................G..... 412 737-8945
　Pittsburgh (G-14743)

MANAGEMENT CONSULTING SVCS: Distribution Channels

Azar International Inc...................G..... 570 288-0786
　Kingston (G-8712)
Mobile Video Devices Inc................G..... 610 921-5720
　Reading (G-16447)
RAF Industries Inc......................F..... 215 572-0738
　Jenkintown (G-8299)

MANAGEMENT CONSULTING SVCS: Hospital & Health

Campbell 3.............................G..... 724 322-1043
　New Stanton (G-12447)

MANAGEMENT CONSULTING SVCS: Industrial

Industrial Consortium Inc...............F..... 610 777-1653
　Mohnton (G-11267)

Shasta Inc ....E 724 378-8280
Aliquippa (G-94)

Shasta Holdings Company ....C 724 378-8280
Aliquippa (G-95)

MANAGEMENT CONSULTING SVCS:
Industrial & Labor

Mxstrategies LLC ....G 610 241-2099
West Chester (G-19604)

MANAGEMENT CONSULTING SVCS:
Industry Specialist

RMS Systems Inc ....G 724 458-7580
Mercer (G-10972)

MANAGEMENT CONSULTING SVCS:
Information Systems

Acutedge Inc ....G 484 846-6275
King of Prussia (G-8577)

Koryak Consulting Inc ....E 412 364-6600
Pittsburgh (G-15194)

Neurologix Technologies Inc ....F 512 914-7941
Cherry Tree (G-3033)

Spm Global Services Inc ....D 610 340-2828
Chester (G-3065)

MANAGEMENT CONSULTING SVCS:
Manufacturing

Plastic Solutions Inc ....G 215 968-3242
Newtown (G-12536)

Quality Millwork Inc ....G 412 831-3500
Finleyville (G-5964)

MANAGEMENT CONSULTING SVCS:
Planning

Lettuce Turnip The Beet ....G 412 334-8631
South Park (G-17784)

MANAGEMENT CONSULTING SVCS: Public
Utilities

International Mill Service ....A 215 956-5500
Horsham (G-7824)

Mill Services Corp ....F 412 678-6141
Glassport (G-6413)

Tms International LLC ....D 215 956-5500
Horsham (G-7859)

MANAGEMENT CONSULTING SVCS:
Restaurant & Food

Carrollsisters ....E 215 969-4688
Philadelphia (G-13509)

MANAGEMENT CONSULTING SVCS: Retail
Trade Consultant

Seder Gaming Inc ....G 814 736-3611
Ebensburg (G-4796)

MANAGEMENT CONSULTING SVCS:
Training & Development

Action Centered Training Inc ....G 610 630-3325
Norristown (G-12630)

Energize Inc ....G 215 438-8342
Philadelphia (G-13674)

Organization Design & Dev Inc ......E 610 279-2202
West Chester (G-19612)

Team Approach Inc ....G 847 259-0005
Lancaster (G-9213)

MANAGEMENT SERVICES

C L I Corporation ....G 724 348-4800
Finleyville (G-5952)

Central Penn Distilling ....G 717 808-7695
Gettysburg (G-6285)

Efco Inc ....E 814 455-3941
Erie (G-5256)

Exco Resources LLC ....D 724 720-2500
Kittanning (G-8768)

Genie Electronics Co Inc ....D 717 244-1099
Red Lion (G-16598)

Genie Electronics Co Inc ....C 717 244-1099
Red Lion (G-16599)

Heinz Frozen Food Company ....A 412 237-5700
Pittsburgh (G-15088)

Kartri Sales Company Inc ....E 570 785-3365
Forest City (G-6054)

P R L Inc ....E 717 273-2470
Cornwall (G-3739)

Sinacom North America Inc ....E 610 337-2250
King of Prussia (G-8677)

Tomayko Group LLC ....F 412 481-0600
Pittsburgh (G-15632)

Tsi Associates Inc ....F 610 375-4371
Reading (G-16551)

Union Packaging LLC ....D 610 572-7265
Yeadon (G-20356)

MANAGEMENT SVCS, FACILITIES SUPPORT:
Environ Remediation

ARC Rmediation Specialists Inc .....F 386 405-6760
Bristol (G-2108)

Better Air Management LLC ....G 215 362-5677
Lansdale (G-9347)

General Civil Company Inc ....F 484 571-1998
Aston (G-767)

MANAGEMENT SVCS: Business

Haas Group ....A 484 564-4500
West Chester (G-19559)

Martin Limestone Inc ....E 717 335-4500
East Earl (G-4548)

Pardee Resources Company ....F 215 405-1260
Philadelphia (G-14122)

Veeco Precision Surfc Proc LLC .....D 215 328-0700
Horsham (G-7863)

MANAGEMENT SVCS: Construction

Jod Contracting Inc ....G 724 323-2124
Fayette City (G-5875)

K M B Inc ....G 215 643-7999
Ambler (G-585)

MANAGEMENT SVCS: Restaurant

Davenmark Inc ....F 484 461-8683
Upper Darby (G-18684)

MANHOLES & COVERS: Metal

Betts Industries Inc ....C 814 723-1250
Warren (G-19013)

Craigg Manufacturing Corp ....G 610 678-8200
Reading (G-16353)

Ej Usa Inc ....F 412 795-6000
Monroeville (G-11334)

Man Pan LLC ....G 724 942-9500
Mc Murray (G-10645)

MANHOLES COVERS: Concrete

Wm S Long Inc ....G 724 538-3775
Callery (G-2471)

MANICURE PREPARATIONS

AAA Nail ....G 814 362-2863
Bradford (G-1953)

Nail Central ....G 717 664-5051
Manheim (G-10396)

New Stars LLC ....E 215 962-4239
Philadelphia (G-14068)

Sandys Nail ....G 215 848-0299
Philadelphia (G-14276)

Skyline Beauty Supply Inc ....G 215 468-1888
Philadelphia (G-14314)

Venus Nail & Spa ....G 610 660-6180
Narberth (G-11914)

MANUFACTURING INDUSTRIES, NEC

7th Soul LLC ....G 917 880-8423
Stroudsburg (G-18101)

8 12 Innovations Inc ....G 717 413-7656
Mount Joy (G-11644)

A & D Manufacturing ....G 717 768-7330
Gordonville (G-6548)

Aaxis Distributors ....G 717 762-2947
Waynesboro (G-19394)

Abililife Inc ....G 443 326-6395
Pittsburgh (G-14635)

Accurate Components ....G 215 442-1023
Warminster (G-18819)

Albrighten Industries Inc ....F 724 222-2959
Eighty Four (G-4832)

Alpha Advertising & Mktg LLC ....G 717 445-4200
Bowmansville (G-1886)

Apex Manufacturing Company ....G 215 345-4400
Doylestown (G-4270)

Arch Mfg LLC ....G 724 438-5170
Uniontown (G-18616)

Armstrong Precision Mfg LLC ....G 412 449-0160
Pittsburgh (G-14726)

Blue Flame Heater Mfg ....G 717 768-0301
Gordonville (G-6550)

Boxwood Manufacturing Corp ....G 717 751-2712
York (G-20411)

Breeze Dryer ....G 215 794-2421
Doylestown (G-4280)

Bristol Industries Pennsylv ....G 215 493-7230
Langhorne (G-9281)

Broderick Industries LLC ....G 215 409-5771
Philadelphia (G-13485)

Cappelli Industries Inc ....G 724 745-6766
Canonsburg (G-2557)

Cessna Industries ....G 610 636-9282
Harleysville (G-7025)

Cincinnatus Group ....G 724 600-0221
Greensburg (G-6658)

Circle Manufacturing Company ....G 570 585-2139
S Abingtn Twp (G-16892)

Cla Industries Inc ....G 724 858-7112
Oakdale (G-12897)

Costa Industries LLC ....F 412 384-8170
Elizabeth (G-4858)

Creek View Manufacturing LLC ....G 717 445-4922
East Earl (G-4541)

Crespo & Diaz Industries LLC ....G 484 895-7139
Allentown (G-186)

Custom Metal Innovations Inc ....G 724 965-3929
Wheatland (G-19836)

Drindustries ....G 412 704-5840
Pittsburgh (G-14937)

East West Manufacturing A ....F 412 207-7385
Pittsburgh (G-14957)

Ecco Industries Inc ....G 570 288-1226
Kingston (G-8716)

Echo Delta Charlie Inc ....G 267 278-7598
Mechanicsburg (G-10841)

Edge Rubber LLC ....E 717 660-2353
Chambersburg (G-2927)

Endeavour Sky Inc ....G 610 872-5694
Brookhaven (G-2244)

Factory Unlocked LLC ....G 724 882-9940
Pittsburgh (G-15003)

Felchar Manufacturing Corp ....G 607 723-4076
Williamsport (G-20012)

Fig Industries LLC ....G 803 414-3950
Lancaster (G-9016)

First Rspnse Ltg Solutions LLC ....G 412 585-6220
Pittsburgh (G-15018)

FSI Industries Inc ....G 215 295-0552
Levittown (G-9837)

Full Throttle Industries LLC ....G 724 926-2140
Mc Donald (G-10574)

Gardencraft Mfg ....G 717 354-3430
Gordonville (G-6555)

Glow Mfg ....G 814 798-2215
Stoystown (G-18078)

Gordon Industries ....G 516 354-8888
Indiana (G-8103)

Grundy Industries LLC ....G 570 609-5487
Wyoming (G-20278)

Hatfield Manufacturing Inc ....G 215 368-9574
Hatfield (G-7346)

Heathen Mfg ....G 724 887-0337
White (G-19844)

Hoehl Assoc ....G 412 741-4170
Sewickley (G-17392)

Hoff Industries LLC ....G 215 516-9849
Souderton (G-17740)

Homestead Valve Mfg Co ....G 610 770-1100
Allentown (G-246)

Hooke Mfg LLC ....G 570 876-6787
Eynon (G-5755)

Ideal Manufacturing LLC ....G 717 629-3751
Gordonville (G-6559)

Ikan Industries Inc ....G 412 670-6026
Pittsburgh (G-15114)

Industrial Vision Systems Inc ....G 215 393-5300
Bryn Mawr (G-2326)

PRODUCT

Intents Mfg .... G 215 527-6441
East Greenville (G-4569)
Jacob Gerger & Sons Inc .... G 215 491-4659
Warrington (G-19122)
JRKN Industries LLC .... G 717 324-3996
York (G-20545)
Ke Custom PC Mfg .... G 215 228-6437
Philadelphia (G-13925)
Kern Industries Inc .... G 814 691-4211
Dover (G-4194)
Kerr Light Manufacturing LLC .... G 724 309-6598
Apollo (G-680)
Kessler Industries LLC .... G 570 590-2333
Frackville (G-6106)
King Coils Manufacturing Inc .... G 484 645-4054
Boyertown (G-1922)
Kykayke Inc .... G 610 522-0106
Holmes (G-7663)
Lock and Mane .... G 215 221-2131
New Hope (G-12308)
Lombardo Industries .... G 412 264-4588
Coraopolis (G-3702)
M & T Industries LLC .... G 724 216-5256
Greensburg (G-6686)
M G Industries .... F 814 238-5092
State College (G-17987)
Manchester Industries Inc .... F 717 764-1161
York (G-20576)
Martin Amr LLC .... G 908 313-2459
Altoona (G-524)
Meeco Manufacturing Targe .... G 412 653-1323
Pittsburgh (G-15274)
Mognet Industries LLC .... G 814 418-0864
Mineral Point (G-11252)
Montco Industries .... G 610 233-1081
King of Prussia (G-8652)
Msh Industries .... G 814 866-0777
Erie (G-5397)
Msk Industries LLC .... G 570 485-4908
Rome (G-16800)
Musser Manufacturing .... G 717 271-2321
Denver (G-4085)
Natawill Industries LLC .... G 610 574-8226
Phoenixville (G-14564)
New Hope Industries LLC .... G 570 994-6391
Bushkill (G-2367)
Nutricia Mfg USA Inc .... G 412 288-4600
Pittsburgh (G-15351)
Oak Crest Industries Inc .... G 610 246-9177
Wallingford (G-18786)
On The Edge Mfg Inc .... F 724 285-6802
Butler (G-2430)
OSI Industries .... G 412 741-3630
Sewickley (G-17402)
Palace Industries .... G 215 442-5508
Warminster (G-18936)
Perfect Precision .... G 610 461-3625
Darby (G-4023)
Polkabla Industries LLC .... G 724 322-7740
Smock (G-17666)
Prb Mfg Representatives .... G 814 466-2161
Boalsburg (G-1868)
Quietflex Manufacturing .... F 570 883-9019
Pittston (G-15780)
Rakoczy Industries Inc .... G 412 389-3123
Canonsburg (G-2622)
Randall Industries LLC .... G 412 281-6901
Pittsburgh (G-15467)
Raster Manufacturing LLC .... G 724 837-7354
Greensburg (G-6710)
Ronco Machine Inc .... F 570 319-1832
S Abingtn Twp (G-16898)
Roppa Industries LLC .... G 412 749-9250
Leetsdale (G-9703)
Sabold Design Inc .... G 610 401-4086
Bernville (G-1305)
Shiloh Industries .... G 717 779-7654
Dover (G-4204)
Silberine Manufacturing .... G 570 668-8361
Allentown (G-392)
Sky Point Crane LLC .... G 724 471-5710
Indiana (G-8129)
Smart Systems Enterprises Inc .... G 412 323-2128
Pittsburgh (G-15547)
Stampede Industries LLC .... G 724 239-2104
Eighty Four (G-4850)
Stx Industries .... G 412 513-6689
Pittsburgh (G-15586)
Suprawater .... G 717 528-9949
York Springs (G-20768)

Supreme Zipper Industries .... G 570 226-9501
Lakeville (G-8914)
Sylray Manufacturing LLC .... G 570 640-0689
Allentown (G-406)
Temco Industries Inc .... G 412 831-5620
Burgettstown (G-2356)
Tkd Mfg Inc .... F 717 266-3156
York (G-20689)
Tompkins Manufacturing Co .... G 724 287-4927
Butler (G-2446)
Trotter Industries .... F 610 369-9473
Boyertown (G-1933)
Uhuru Mfg LLC .... G 717 345-3366
New Holland (G-12290)
W S Display .... G 717 460-3485
Carlisle (G-2749)
Wave Swimmer Inc .... G 215 367-3778
Ardmore (G-722)
Weahterford Manufacturing .... G 724 239-1404
Charleroi (G-3024)
West Penn Mfg Tech LLC .... F 814 886-4100
Cresson (G-3901)
Wkw Associates LLC .... F 215 348-1257
Doylestown (G-4346)
Zerbe Manufacturing .... G 570 640-1528
Pine Grove (G-14609)

MAPMAKING SVCS

Infomat Associates Inc .... G 610 668-8306
Narberth (G-11911)

MARBLE, BUILDING: Cut & Shaped

Allegheny Cut Stone Co .... G 814 943-4157
Altoona (G-469)
Concure Inc .... G 610 497-0198
Chester (G-3044)
Gingrich Memorials Inc .... F 717 272-0901
Lebanon (G-9574)
Howell Craft Inc .... G 412 751-6861
Elizabeth (G-4860)
Kerrico Corporation .... E 570 374-9831
Selinsgrove (G-17329)
Luicana Industries Inc .... G 570 325-9699
Jim Thorpe (G-8341)
Marble Source Inc .... G 610 847-5694
Ottsville (G-13067)
Unity Marble and Granite Inc .... G 412 793-4220
Pittsburgh (G-15681)

MARINE CARGO HANDLING SVCS

Clairton Slag Inc .... F 412 384-8420
West Elizabeth (G-19693)

MARINE HARDWARE

Baldt Inc .... E 610 447-5200
Bryn Mawr (G-2315)
Calgon Carbon Uv Tech LLC .... G 724 218-7001
Coraopolis (G-3670)
G G Schmitt & Sons Inc .... F 717 394-3701
Lancaster (G-9026)
Schmitt Mar Stering Wheels Inc ...... G 717 431-2316
Lancaster (G-9191)
W W Patterson Company .... E 412 322-2012
Pittsburgh (G-15706)

MARINE RELATED EQPT

Caulfield Associates Inc .... E 215 480-1940
Doylestown (G-4290)
Ironshore Marine LLC .... G 484 941-3914
Spring City (G-17861)
Marine Acquisition US Inc .... E 610 495-7011
Limerick (G-9970)

MARINE RELATED EQPT: Cranes, Ship

Atlantic Track & Turnout Co .... G 610 916-2840
Leesport (G-9658)

MARKERS

Clarence J Venne LLC .... D 215 547-7110
Bristol (G-2126)
Skm Industries Inc .... F 570 383-3062
Olyphant (G-12999)

MARKETS: Meat & fish

Alpine Wurst & Meathouse Inc .... E 570 253-5899
Honesdale (G-7700)

Mr ZS Food Mart .... G 570 421-7070
Stroudsburg (G-18132)
Tops Markets LLC .... C 570 882-9188
Sayre (G-17123)

MARKING DEVICES

Ad-Art Sign Co .... G 412 373-0960
Pittsburgh (G-14649)
Advance Sign Company LLC .... E 412 481-6990
Pittsburgh (G-14650)
Automated Indus Systems Inc .... E 814 838-2270
Erie (G-5198)
Bunting Inc .... C 412 820-2200
Verona (G-18750)
Bunting Stamp Company .... C 412 820-2200
Verona (G-18752)
Gvm Inc .... D 717 677-6197
Biglerville (G-1662)
Harrisburg Stamp & Stencil Co .... G 717 236-9000
Harrisburg (G-7144)
ID Technology LLC .... E 717 848-3875
York (G-20533)
Krengel Quaker City Corp .... E 215 969-9800
Philadelphia (G-13944)
Lasermation Inc .... E 215 228-7900
Philadelphia (G-13959)
Liberty Craftsmen Inc .... G 717 871-0125
Millersville (G-11211)
Marking Device Mfg Co Inc .... E 215 632-9583
Fairless Hills (G-5787)
Matthews International Corp .... D 412 665-2500
Pittsburgh (G-15265)
Matthews International Corp .... D 412 665-2500
Pittsburgh (G-15267)
Matthews International Corp .... B 412 571-5500
Pittsburgh (G-15266)
Matthews International Corp .... E 412 442-8200
Pittsburgh (G-15264)
Mecco Partners LLC .... F 724 779-9555
Cranberry Township (G-3835)
Notaries Equipment Co .... F 215 563-8190
Philadelphia (G-14085)
Pannier Corporation .... E 724 265-4900
Gibsonia (G-6348)
Pannier Corporation .... E 412 492-1400
Glenshaw (G-6495)
Sic Marking Usa Inc .... G 412 487-1165
Pittsburgh (G-15536)
Srm-Avant Inc .... G 724 537-0300
Greensburg (G-6716)
Steele Print Inc .... G 724 758-6178
Ellwood City (G-4952)
Unity Printing Company Inc .... E 724 537-5800
Latrobe (G-9527)

MARKING DEVICES: Canceling Stamps, Hand, Rubber Or Metal

Causco .... G 814 452-2004
Erie (G-5223)

MARKING DEVICES: Date Stamps, Hand, Rubber Or Metal

Richland Plastics & Engraving .... G 814 266-3002
Johnstown (G-8431)

MARKING DEVICES: Embossing Seals & Hand Stamps

Allegheny Rubber Stamp Inc .... G 412 826-8662
Blawnox (G-1762)
Atlas Rubber Stamp & Printing .... G 717 755-3882
York (G-20390)
Marvel Marking Products .... F 412 381-0700
Pittsburgh (G-15260)
Opsec Security Inc .... D 717 293-4110
Lancaster (G-9155)
Wakefoose Office Supply & Prtg .... G 814 623-5742
Bedford (G-1079)

MARKING DEVICES: Figures, Metal

Viking Electronic Services .... E 610 992-0400
King of Prussia (G-8697)

MARKING DEVICES: Irons, Marking Or Branding

Bosha Design Inc ....G 610 622-4422
Drexel Hill (G-4361)

MARKING DEVICES: Printing Dies, Marking Mach, Rubber/Plastic

Accurate Marking Products Inc ....F 724 337-8390
New Kensington (G-12321)

Pannier Corporation ....F 412 323-4900
Pittsburgh (G-15368)

MARKING DEVICES: Seal Presses, Notary & Hand

Minton Holdings LLC ....G 412 787-5912
Pittsburgh (G-15293)

MASKS: Gas

Circadiance LLC ....F 724 858-2837
Turtle Creek (G-18562)

MASQUERADE OR THEATRICAL COSTUMES STORES

Williamson Costume Company ....F 215 925-7121
Philadelphia (G-14476)

MASTS: Cast Aluminum

Erie Bronze & Aluminum Company ......E 814 838-8602
Erie (G-5263)

MATERIAL GRINDING & PULVERIZING SVCS NEC

CSS International Corporation ....F 215 533-6110
Philadelphia (G-13589)

Global Ceramic Services Inc...............F 724 545-7224
Kittanning (G-8774)

Hv2 Enterprises Inc ....F 610 330-9300
Easton (G-4703)

L E Holt Grinding Service Inc ....G 724 446-0977
Rillton (G-16748)

Marios Tree Service Inc ....G 610 637-1405
King of Prussia (G-8648)

Spadre Investments Inc......................E 724 452-8440
Evans City (G-5564)

Wilder Diamond Blades Inc................G 570 222-9590
Kingsley (G-8710)

MATERIALS HANDLING EQPT WHOLESALERS

Airgas Usa LLC ....G 215 766-8860
Plumsteadville (G-15806)

Charles Bond Company ....F 610 593-5171
Christiana (G-3134)

D-K Trading Corporation Inc ....G 570 586-9662
Clarks Summit (G-3191)

H & K Equipment Inc ....D 412 490-5300
Coraopolis (G-3696)

Hanel Storage Systems ....E 412 788-0509
Pittsburgh (G-15079)

Ncc Automated Systems Inc ....E 215 721-1900
Souderton (G-17756)

Peerless Chain Company ....F 800 395-2445
Mount Pleasant (G-11710)

Pro Dyne Corporation ....G 610 789-0606
Phoenixville (G-14572)

Wepco Inc ....E 570 368-8184
Pittston (G-15784)

MATS OR MATTING, NEC: Rubber

Certified Carpet Service Inc ....D 717 393-3012
Lancaster (G-8976)

William F Kempf & Son Inc ....G 610 532-2000
Folcroft (G-6020)

MATS, MATTING & PADS: Door, Paper, Grass, Reed, Coir, Etc

Municipal Publications ....G 724 397-9812
Marion Center (G-10474)

MATS, MATTING & PADS: Nonwoven

Office Mats Inc ....G 717 359-9571
Littlestown (G-10073)

MATTRESS RENOVATING & REPAIR SHOP

Custom Carpet & Bedding Inc ....G 570 344-7533
Dunmore (G-4472)

MATTRESS STORES

Custom Carpet & Bedding Inc ....G 570 344-7533
Dunmore (G-4472)

Johnnys Discount Furniture ....G 717 564-1898
Harrisburg (G-7159)

McMullens Furniture Store ....G 814 942-1202
Altoona (G-526)

MEAT & MEAT PRDTS WHOLESALERS

Alpine Wurst & Meathouse Inc ....E 570 253-5899
Honesdale (G-7700)

CP Food Stores Inc ....F 412 831-7777
Pittsburgh (G-14884)

Grammeco Inc ....C 610 352-4400
Upper Darby (G-18686)

Liberty Bell Steak Co ....E 215 537-4797
Philadelphia (G-13968)

Thoma Meat Market Inc ....E 724 352-2020
Saxonburg (G-17097)

MEAT CUTTING & PACKING

Al Marwa LLC ....G 215 536-6050
Quakertown (G-16168)

Alex Froehlich Packing Co ....F 814 535-7694
Johnstown (G-8349)

Alpine Wurst & Meathouse Inc ....E 570 253-5899
Honesdale (G-7700)

American Foods Inc ....F 724 223-0820
Washington (G-19147)

Astra Foods Inc ....D 610 352-4400
Upper Darby (G-18681)

Bingman Packing Co ....G 814 267-3413
Berlin (G-1283)

Cargill Incorporated ....G 717 273-1133
Lebanon (G-9552)

Cargill Meat Solutions Corp ....A 570 384-8350
Hazleton (G-7493)

Cck Inc ....C 814 684-2270
Tyrone (G-18578)

Clemens Family Corporation ....A 800 523-5291
Hatfield (G-7324)

Clemens Food Group LLC ....D 215 368-2500
Emmaus (G-5023)

Country Butcher Shop ....F 717 249-4691
Carlisle (G-2703)

CTI King of Prussia LLC ....G 610 879-2868
King of Prussia (G-8603)

Darlings Locker Plant ....G 570 945-5716
La Plume (G-8869)

Devault Packing Company Inc............C 610 644-2536
Devault (G-4111)

Doug Pfers Deer Ctng Smoke Hse .....G 724 758-7965
Ellwood City (G-4929)

Drexel Foods Inc ....D 215 425-9900
Philadelphia (G-13646)

Emericks Meat & Packing Co..............E 814 842-6779
Hyndman (G-8050)

Farrs Meat Processing ....G 570 827-2241
Lawrenceville (G-9542)

Ferncliff Meat Processing ....G 724 592-6042
Rices Landing (G-16669)

Grammeco Inc ....C 610 352-4400
Upper Darby (G-18686)

Herfurth Brothers Inc ....E 610 681-4515
Gilbert (G-6361)

Howard & Son Meatpacking.................F 724 662-3700
Mercer (G-10963)

Johnston Meat Processing ....G 814 225-3495
Eldred (G-4853)

K Heeps Inc ....C 610 434-4312
Allentown (G-275)

Korte & Co Inc ....F 610 253-9141
Easton (G-4712)

Kunzler & Company Inc ....B 717 299-6301
Lancaster (G-9089)

Laudermilch Meats Inc ....D 717 867-1251
Annville (G-652)

Leidys Inc ....D 215 723-4606
Souderton (G-17749)

MEAT MARKETS

Leona Meat Plant Inc ....F 570 297-3574
Troy (G-18523)

Louis G Sredy ....G 814 445-7229
Somerset (G-17696)

M Robzen Inc ....E 570 283-1226
Kingston (G-8723)

Mc Kruit Meat Packing ....G 724 352-2988
Cabot (G-2459)

Mikes Packing Company ....F 724 222-5476
Washington (G-19203)

Mountain Man Deer Processing ....G 717 532-7295
Orrstown (G-13034)

Mrg Food LLC ....F 412 482-7430
McKeesport (G-10676)

Murrys of Maryland Inc ....C 301 420-6400
Lebanon (G-9612)

National Beef Packing Co LLC ....C 570 743-4420
Hummels Wharf (G-7900)

Nema Usa Inc ....E 412 678-9541
Pittsburgh (G-15325)

October 6 2011 ....G 814 422-8810
Spring Mills (G-17891)

OJacks Inc ....E 814 225-4755
Eldred (G-4854)

P & N Packing Inc ....E 570 746-1974
Wyalusing (G-20255)

Painter Meat Processing ....G 814 258-7283
Elkland (G-4917)

Palmyra Bologna Company ....G 717 273-9581
Lebanon (G-9614)

Phillys Best Steak Company Inc ....F 610 259-6000
Lansdowne (G-9441)

Polarized Meat Co Inc ....B 570 347-3396
Dunmore (G-4481)

Pudliners Packing ....F 814 539-5422
Johnstown (G-8425)

R & R Provision Co ....D 610 258-5366
Easton (G-4746)

R C Silivis & Sons ....G 814 257-8401
Dayton (G-4039)

R L Sipes Locker Plant ....G 814 652-2714
Everett (G-5578)

Rendulic Packing Company ....E 412 678-9541
McKeesport (G-10679)

Rosss Custom Butchering...................F 570 634-3571
Trout Run (G-18516)

S Schiff Restaurant Svc Inc ....C 570 343-1294
Scranton (G-17282)

Sechrist Bros Inc ....F 717 244-2975
Dallastown (G-3981)

Sharon McGuigan Inc ....E 610 361-8100
Aston (G-793)

Silver Springs Farm Inc ....E 215 256-4321
Harleysville (G-7058)

Smithfield Foods Inc ....A 215 752-1090
Middletown (G-11077)

Smithfield Packaged Meats Corp ....B 724 335-5800
New Kensington (G-12378)

Tags Processing ....G 724 345-8279
Washington (G-19230)

Thoma Meat Market Inc ....E 724 352-2020
Saxonburg (G-17097)

Tyson...G 717 755-4782
Red Lion (G-16618)

Tyson Foods Inc ....E 717 653-8326
Mount Joy (G-11673)

Tyson Foods Inc ....B 412 257-3224
Pittsburgh (G-15664)

USA Pork Packers Inc ....E 570 501-7675
Hazleton (G-7533)

Wright Meat Packing Co Inc................G 724 368-8571
Fombell (G-6039)

MEAT MARKETS

Alex Froehlich Packing Co ....F 814 535-7694
Johnstown (G-8349)

Country Butcher Shop ....F 717 249-4691
Carlisle (G-2703)

Emericks Meat & Packing Co..............E 814 842-6779
Hyndman (G-8050)

George Farms ....F 570 275-0239
Danville (G-4003)

Ken Weaver Meats Inc ....E 717 502-0118
Wellsville (G-19479)

Laudermilch Meats Inc ....D 717 867-1251
Annville (G-652)

Leona Meat Plant Inc ....F 570 297-3574
Troy (G-18523)

Mikes Packing Company ....F 724 222-5476
Washington (G-19203)

PRODUCT

P & N Packing Inc ....E 570 746-1974
Wyalusing **(G-20255)**

Pudliners Packing ....F 814 539-5422
Johnstown **(G-8425)**

Richard Baringer ....G 610 346-7661
Richlandtown **(G-16690)**

Sechrist Bros Inc ....F 717 244-2975
Dallastown **(G-3981)**

Thoma Meat Market Inc ....E 724 352-2020
Saxonburg **(G-17097)**

Wright Meat Packing Co Inc......G 724 368-8571
Fombell **(G-6039)**

MEAT PRDTS: Bacon, Side & Sliced, From Purchased Meat

John F Martin & Sons LLC ....C 717 336-2804
Stevens **(G-18054)**

MEAT PRDTS: Bacon, Slab & Sliced, From Slaughtered Meat

1732 Meats LLC ....G 267 879-7214
Yeadon **(G-20350)**

Dibruno Bros Inc ....G 215 665-9220
Philadelphia **(G-13630)**

MEAT PRDTS: Beef Stew, From Purchased Meat

Philadlphia Pr-Coked Steak Inc ....E .. 215 426-4949
Philadelphia **(G-14164)**

MEAT PRDTS: Bologna, From Purchased Meat

Palmyra Bologna Company ....E 717 838-6336
Palmyra **(G-13128)**

Palumbos Meats Dubois Inc ......E 814 371-2150
Du Bois **(G-4412)**

MEAT PRDTS: Boneless Meat, From Purchased Meat

Devault Packing Company Inc.......C 610 644-2536
Devault **(G-4111)**

MEAT PRDTS: Boxed Beef, From Slaughtered Meat

Dave Fine Meat Packer Inc.........G 724 352-1537
Saxonburg **(G-17083)**

J R Kline Butchery LLC ....G 570 220-4229
New Albany **(G-12012)**

J R Kline Butchery LLC ....G 570 220-4229
New Albany **(G-12013)**

Nicholas Meat LLC ....D 570 725-3511
Loganton **(G-10096)**

MEAT PRDTS: Corned Beef, From Purchased Meat

Mrs Resslers Food Products Co ....D 215 744-4700
Philadelphia **(G-14043)**

Sheinman Provision Co Inc ....E 305 592-0300
Philadelphia **(G-14300)**

MEAT PRDTS: Cured Meats, From Purchased Meat

Alderfer Inc ....D 215 256-8819
Harleysville **(G-7016)**

MEAT PRDTS: Dried Beef, From Purchased Meat

Knauss Inc ....D 215 536-4220
Quakertown **(G-16206)**

MEAT PRDTS: Frozen

M Robzen Inc ....E 570 283-1226
Kingston **(G-8723)**

Maid-Rite Specialty Foods LLC ....F .. 570 346-3572
Scranton **(G-17258)**

Polarized Meat Co Inc ....B 570 347-3396
Dunmore **(G-4481)**

Quaker Maid Meats Inc ....C 610 376-1500
Reading **(G-16478)**

Quaker Maid Meats Inc ....E 610 376-1500
Reading **(G-16479)**

Tri-Our Brands ....G 570 655-1512
Pittston **(G-15783)**

MEAT PRDTS: Hams & Picnics, From Slaughtered Meat

Silver Star Meats Inc ....D 412 771-5539
Mc Kees Rocks **(G-10635)**

MEAT PRDTS: Head Cheese, From Purchased Meat

Topsmal Dairy LLC ....G 814 880-3724
Bellefonte **(G-1123)**

MEAT PRDTS: Lamb, From Slaughtered Meat

Locker Plant LLC ....G 814 652-2714
Everett **(G-5574)**

MEAT PRDTS: Luncheon Meat, From Purchased Meat

Euro Foods Inc ....C 570 636-3171
Freeland **(G-6194)**

MEAT PRDTS: Meat By-Prdts, From Slaughtered Meat

George Farms ....F 570 275-0239
Danville **(G-4003)**

Richard Baringer ....G 610 346-7661
Richlandtown **(G-16690)**

MEAT PRDTS: Pork, From Slaughtered Meat

Clemens Food Group LLC ....A 215 368-2500
Hatfield **(G-7325)**

MEAT PRDTS: Prepared Beef Prdts From Purchased Beef

CFC Leola Properties Inc ....F 717 390-1978
Middletown **(G-11050)**

Jbs Packerland Inc ....F 215 723-5559
Souderton **(G-17743)**

Silver Springs Farm Inc ....E 215 256-4321
Harleysville **(G-7058)**

Vantage Foods PA LP ....E 717 691-4728
Camp Hill **(G-2522)**

MEAT PRDTS: Roast Beef, From Purchased Meat

Vincent Giordano Corp...............D 215 467-6629
Philadelphia **(G-14447)**

MEAT PRDTS: Sausage Casings, Natural

Pittsburgh Spice Seasoning Co ....G .. 412 288-5036
Pittsburgh **(G-15408)**

MEAT PRDTS: Sausages & Related Prdts, From Purchased Meat

Clair D Thompson & Sons Inc ....E .. 570 398-1880
Jersey Shore **(G-8311)**

MEAT PRDTS: Sausages, From Purchased Meat

Alpine Wurst & Meathouse Inc ....E .. 570 253-5899
Honesdale **(G-7700)**

Daniel Weaver Company Inc.......E 717 274-6100
Lebanon **(G-9558)**

Ernest Ricci ....G 412 490-9531
Mc Kees Rocks **(G-10607)**

European & American Sausage Co ....G .. 215 232-1716
Philadelphia **(G-13682)**

Ken Weaver Meats Inc ....E 717 502-0118
Wellsville **(G-19479)**

Labriola Sausage Co ....G 412 281-5966
Pittsburgh **(G-15214)**

Maglio Bros Inc ....D 215 465-3902
Philadelphia **(G-13987)**

Olde Recipe Foods Inc ....G 724 654-5779
Portersville **(G-15934)**

Parma Sausage Products Inc ....F .. 412 261-2532
Pittsburgh **(G-15370)**

Uncle Charleys Sausage Co LLC ....E .. 724 845-3302
Vandergrift **(G-18736)**

MEAT PRDTS: Smoked

Kunzler & Company Inc...............B 717 299-6301
Lancaster **(G-9089)**

Philadelphia Provision Co...........G 215 423-1707
Philadelphia **(G-14151)**

MEAT PRDTS: Snack Sticks, Incl Jerky, From Purchased Meat

Protos Foods Inc ....G 724 836-1802
Greensburg **(G-6705)**

S M E Foods LLC ....G 717 852-8515
York **(G-20662)**

MEAT PRDTS: Veal, From Slaughtered Meat

Atlantic Veal and Lamb Inc ....E 570 489-4781
Olyphant **(G-12984)**

Marcho Farms Inc ....C 215 721-7131
Harleysville **(G-7045)**

MEAT PROCESSED FROM PURCHASED CARCASSES

Alex Froehlich Packing Co...........F 814 535-7694
Johnstown **(G-8349)**

Ask Foods Inc ....E 717 838-6356
Palmyra **(G-13118)**

Bethlehem Sausage Works Inc............G 800 478-2302
Easton **(G-4655)**

Brother and Sister Fd Svc Inc...........G .. 717 558-0108
Camp Hill **(G-2493)**

Cargill Meat Solutions Corp.........A 570 746-3000
Wyalusing **(G-20248)**

Cck Inc ....C 814 684-2270
Tyrone **(G-18578)**

Charles Ritter Incorporated ....C 215 320-5000
Philadelphia **(G-13531)**

Clemens Food Group LLC ....A 215 368-2500
Hatfield **(G-7325)**

CP Food Stores Inc ....F 412 831-7777
Pittsburgh **(G-14884)**

Dietz & Watson Inc....................A 800 333-1974
Philadelphia **(G-13631)**

Drexel Foods Inc ....E 215 425-9900
Philadelphia **(G-13646)**

Family Food Products Inc ....D 215 633-1515
Bensalem **(G-1193)**

Gillo Brothers ....G 724 254-4845
Clymer **(G-3273)**

Hazle Park Packing Co ....E 570 455-7571
Hazle Township **(G-7461)**

Hillshire Brands Company ....F 724 772-3440
Cranberry Township **(G-3822)**

Jbs Souderton Inc.....................A 215 723-5555
Souderton **(G-17744)**

Laudermilch Meats Inc ....D 717 867-1251
Annville **(G-652)**

Leona Meat Plant Inc ....F 570 297-3574
Troy **(G-18523)**

Liberty Bell Steak Co ....E 215 537-4797
Philadelphia **(G-13968)**

Louis G Sredy..........................G 814 445-7229
Somerset **(G-17696)**

Mikes Packing Company ....F 724 222-5476
Washington **(G-19203)**

Moms Wholesale Foods Inc........G 724 856-3049
New Castle **(G-12122)**

Mondelez Global LLC ....A 570 820-1200
Wilkes Barre **(G-19945)**

Murazzi Provision Co..................F 570 344-2285
Scranton **(G-17262)**

Murrys of Maryland Inc...............C 301 420-6400
Lebanon **(G-9612)**

Nicholas Meat Packing Co ....C 570 725-3511
Loganton **(G-10097)**

OJacks Inc ....E 814 225-4755
Eldred **(G-4854)**

Original Philly Holdings Inc ....C 215 423-3333
Southampton **(G-17829)**

Perfection Foods Company Inc...........D .. 215 455-5400
Philadelphia **(G-14137)**

S Schiff Restaurant Svc Inc ....C 570 343-1294
Scranton **(G-17282)**

Silver Star Meats Inc..................D 412 771-5539
Mc Kees Rocks **(G-10635)**

Smith Provision Co Inc.................E 814 459-4974
Erie (G-5482)
Smith Provision Co Inc.................G....... 814 459-4974
Erie (G-5483)
Theodore Fazen ....E 215 672-1122
Horsham (G-7858)

MEATS, PACKAGED FROZEN: Wholesalers

Original Philly Holdings Inc ....C 215 423-3333
Southampton (G-17829)

MEDIA: Magnetic & Optical Recording

Spang & Company ....E 724 376-7515
Sandy Lake (G-17062)

MEDICAL & HOSPITAL EQPT WHOLESALERS

101 Cameo Appearances LLC ....G 412 787-7981
Pittsburgh (G-14623)
Caseworks Inc ....F 724 522-5068
Jeannette (G-8249)
Dentalez Inc ....C 717 291-1161
Lancaster (G-8993)
Diamond Trpcl Hardwoods Intl ....G 215 257-2556
Sellersville (G-17345)
E S Specialty Manufacturing..............G 215 635-0973
Wyncote (G-20262)
F M P Healthcare Products ....G 800 611-7776
Bridgeville (G-2063)
Malek Ham ....G 610 691-7600
Bethlehem (G-1565)
Rapid Pathogen Screening Inc ....E 718 288-4318
Montoursville (G-11449)
Scott Gordon ....G 717 652-2828
Harrisburg (G-7213)
SMC Direct LLC ....E 800 521-1635
Evans City (G-5563)
Susquehanna Valley Prosthetics..........F 570 743-1414
Selinsgrove (G-17337)
Wakeem Inc ....F 610 258-2311
Easton (G-4774)

MEDICAL & HOSPITAL SPLYS: Radiation Shielding Garments

Bar-Ray Products Inc ....D 717 359-9100
Littlestown (G-10063)

MEDICAL & SURGICAL SPLYS: Abdominal Support, Braces/Trusses

Activaided Orthotics LLC...................G 412 901-2658
West Mifflin (G-19734)
Olde Town Grove City.......................G 724 458-0301
Grove City (G-6799)
Phufar...G...... 215 483-0487
Philadelphia (G-14174)

MEDICAL & SURGICAL SPLYS: Autoclaves

Surgical Institute Reading LP ....G...... 610 378-8800
Reading (G-16530)

MEDICAL & SURGICAL SPLYS: Bandages & Dressings

Aquamed Technologies Inc ....F 215 702-8550
Langhorne (G-9277)

MEDICAL & SURGICAL SPLYS: Braces, Orthopedic

C-Fab-1 Inc ....G 215 331-2797
Trevose (G-18489)
Ellwood Safety Appliance Co ....F 724 758-7538
Ellwood City (G-4932)
Kinetic..G 814 603-1131
Du Bois (G-4400)
PA Artificial Limb & Brace Co ....G 724 588-6860
Greenville (G-6763)
Presque Isle Orthpd Lab Inc ....F 814 838-0002
Erie (G-5435)

MEDICAL & SURGICAL SPLYS: Canes, Orthopedic

Snapper Cane LLC..........................G 516 770-3569
West Chester (G-19641)

MEDICAL & SURGICAL SPLYS: Clothing, Fire Resistant & Protect

911 Safety Equipment LLC................F 610 279-6808
Norristown (G-12628)
Choice Cleangear LLC.....................G....... 610 497-9756
Aston (G-754)
Lite Tech Inc ....E 610 650-8690
Norristown (G-12676)
Mifflin Valley Inc ....E 610 775-0505
Reading (G-16443)
Quaker Safety Products Corp ....E 215 536-2991
Quakertown (G-16238)
Ricochet Manufacturing Corp...............E 888 462-1999
Philadelphia (G-14249)

MEDICAL & SURGICAL SPLYS: Cosmetic Restorations

Factor Medical LLC.........................G 215 862-5345
New Hope (G-12301)
Groman Restoration Inc ....G...... 724 235-5000
New Florence (G-12197)

MEDICAL & SURGICAL SPLYS: Dressings, Surgical

McKesson Ptent Care Sltons Inc..........D 814 860-8160
Erie (G-5386)

MEDICAL & SURGICAL SPLYS: Extension Shoes, Orthopedic

Jumpers Shoe Service ....G 717 766-3422
Mechanicsburg (G-10860)

MEDICAL & SURGICAL SPLYS: Hosiery, Support

Garnes Park E Jr............................G 757 502-3381
Newville (G-12602)

MEDICAL & SURGICAL SPLYS: Iron Lungs

Iron Lung LLC ....G 412 291-8928
Pittsburgh (G-15136)

MEDICAL & SURGICAL SPLYS: Limbs, Artificial

Allentown Limb & Brace Inc ....G 610 437-2254
Allentown (G-128)
Cape Prosthetics-Orthotics ....G 610 644-7824
Exton (G-5659)
Center For Orthtic and Prsthtc ....F 570 382-8208
Dickson Cty (G-4123)
Colburn Orthopedics Inc...................G 814 432-5252
Franklin (G-6121)
Green Prosthetics & Orthotics ....F...... 814 833-2311
Erie (G-5307)
Green Prosthetics & Orthotics ....G...... 814 833-2311
Erie (G-5308)
Green Prosthetics & Orthotics ....G...... 814 337-1159
Meadville (G-10730)
Hanger Prsthetcs & Ortho Inc.............E 714 774-0637
West Bridgewater (G-19491)
Hanger Prsthetcs & Ortho Inc.............G 814 368-3702
Bradford (G-1971)
Hanger Prsthetcs & Ortho Inc.............G 724 836-4949
Greensburg (G-6672)
Hanger Prsthetcs & Ortho Inc.............G 717 264-7117
Chambersburg (G-2938)
Hanger Prsthetcs & Ortho Inc.............G 724 438-4582
Uniontown (G-18629)
Harry J Lawall & Son Inc ....G 215 338-6611
Philadelphia (G-13805)
Limb Technologies Inc ....F 215 781-8454
Bristol (G-2160)
National Artificial Limb Co ....G 412 608-9910
Pittsburgh (G-15321)
O & P Benchmark Holdings Inc ....G 610 644-7824
Exton (G-5716)
Out On A Limb Creations ....G 570 287-3778
Forty Fort (G-6098)
Riverview Orthotics ....G 570 270-6231
Plains (G-15788)
Riverview Orthtics Prosthetics............G 570 743-1414
Selinsgrove (G-17332)
Riverview Orthtics Prosthetics............F 570 284-4291
Danville (G-4010)

Union Orthotics Prosthetics Co ....G...... 724 836-6656
Greensburg (G-6724)
Union Orthotics Prosthetics Co ....G...... 412 943-1950
Pittsburgh (G-15670)
Union Orthotics Prosthetics Co ....E 412 621-2698
Pittsburgh (G-15671)
Wyoming Vly Prsthtic Orthotics ....G 570 283-3835
Wilkes Barre (G-19979)

MEDICAL & SURGICAL SPLYS: Orthopedic Appliances

Ability Prsthtics Orthtics Inc..................G 717 337-2277
Exton (G-5634)
American Artisan Orthotics ....G...... 724 776-6030
Hermitage (G-7571)
Avanta Orthopaedics Inc ....G...... 215 428-1792
Morrisville (G-11555)
Benchmark Orthot & Prosth Inc ....G...... 724 825-4200
Washington (G-19154)
Biowerk USA Inc ....G...... 717 697-3310
Mechanicsburg (G-10825)
Central Orthotic Prosthetic Co ....F 814 535-8221
Johnstown (G-8364)
CMS Orthotic Lab LLC ....G...... 717 329-9301
Carlisle (G-2700)
Cocco Bros ....E 215 334-3816
Philadelphia (G-13557)
Core Essence Orthopedics Inc ....F 215 660-5014
King of Prussia (G-8599)
Curvebeam LLC ....E 267 483-8081
Hatfield (G-7329)
Def Medical Technologies LLC ....G...... 802 299-8457
Philadelphia (G-13615)
Global Medical Solutions Inc ....G...... 215 440-7701
Philadelphia (G-13770)
Hanger Prsthetcs & Ortho Inc..............G 215 365-1532
Philadelphia (G-13801)
Hanger Prsthetcs & Ortho Inc..............G 570 421-8221
East Stroudsburg (G-4615)
Hanger Prsthetcs & Ortho Inc..............G 717 767-6667
York (G-20520)
Keystone Surgical Systems Inc............G 717 412-4383
Harrisburg (G-7162)
Pride Mobility Products Corp ....E 570 655-5574
Pittston (G-15779)
Reaction Orthotics...........................G...... 717 609-2361
Carlisle (G-2735)
Restorative Care America Inc ....G...... 215 592-8880
Philadelphia (G-14241)
Siemens Med Solutions USA Inc...........B 888 826-9702
Malvern (G-10315)
Stelkast Inc ....E 888 273-1583
Mc Murray (G-10646)
Susquehanna Valley Prosthetics..........F 570 743-1414
Selinsgrove (G-17337)
Three Rivers Orthotics Prsthti..............G 412 371-2318
Pittsburgh (G-15621)
Ultraflex Systems Inc........................E 610 906-1410
Pottstown (G-16061)
Williamsport Orthopedic ....G...... 570 322-5277
Williamsport (G-20094)

MEDICAL & SURGICAL SPLYS: Personal Safety Eqpt

ARC Rmediation Specialists Inc............F 386 405-6760
Bristol (G-2108)
Decon Laboratories Inc.....................E 610 755-0800
King of Prussia (G-8606)
Lakeland Industries Inc ....G...... 610 775-0505
Reading (G-16426)
Life Support International ....E 215 785-2870
Langhorne (G-9308)
Mechanical Safety Equipment ....E 215 676-7828
Philadelphia (G-14003)
Mine Safety Appliances Co LLC............B 724 776-8600
Cranberry Township (G-3836)
Mio Mechanical Corporation...............F 215 613-8189
Philadelphia (G-14026)
MSA Pittsburgh Dist Ctr ....G 724 742-8090
New Galilee (G-12221)
MSA Safety Incorporated ....B 724 733-9100
Murrysville (G-11858)
MSA Safety Incorporated ....D 724 776-7700
Cranberry Township (G-3840)
MSA Safety Incorporated ....B 724 776-8600
Cranberry Township (G-3839)
MSA Safety Sales LLC......................G 724 776-8600
Cranberry Township (G-3841)

PRODUCT

Mutual Industries North Inc ....E 215 927-6000
Philadelphia (G-14046)
Safeware Inc ....G...... 215 354-1401
Huntingdon Valley (G-8034)

MEDICAL & SURGICAL SPLYS: Prosthetic Appliances

Boas Surgical Inc.................................E 484 895-3451
Allentown (G-156)
Freedom Management Svcs LLC ....G 215 328-9111
Horsham (G-7819)
Gerber Chair Mates Inc.......................G...... 814 266-6588
Johnstown (G-8377)
Hanger Inc ....E 724 836-4949
Greensburg (G-6671)
Hanger Prsthetcs & Ortho Inc...........G...... 724 285-1284
Butler (G-2404)
Hanger Prsthetcs & Ortho Inc...........G...... 717 564-4521
Harrisburg (G-7138)
Hanger Prsthetcs & Ortho Inc...........G...... 724 981-5775
Hermitage (G-7587)
J G McGinness Prosthetics ....F 610 278-1866
Norristown (G-12671)
Jeffrey L Roberts ....G...... 724 627-4600
Waynesburg (G-19447)
McGinness Group LLC ....G...... 610 278-1866
Norristown (G-12681)
O and P Svetz Inc................................F 724 834-1448
Greensburg (G-6694)
Occuped Orthotics...............................G...... 717 949-2377
Newmanstown (G-12482)
Precision Castparts Corp....................B 570 474-6371
Mountain Top (G-11771)
Profile Shop Inc...................................F 215 633-3461
Bensalem (G-1244)
Prosthetic Artworks LLC ....G...... 570 828-6177
Dingmans Ferry (G-4143)
Prosthetic Cad-CAM Tech Inc.............G...... 814 763-1151
Saegertown (G-16929)
Robert John Enterprises Inc..............F 814 944-0187
Altoona (G-544)
Smith & Nephew Inc ....E 412 914-1190
Bridgeville (G-2090)
State of Art Prosthetics ....G...... 215 914-1222
Huntingdon Valley (G-8040)
Svpo Inc ....F 570 743-1414
Shamokin Dam (G-17428)

MEDICAL & SURGICAL SPLYS: Respiratory Protect Eqpt, Personal

Health Solutions Inc ....G...... 610 379-0300
Lehighton (G-9715)
Respironics Inc ....B 724 387-4270
Monroeville (G-11354)
Respironics Inc ....C...... 724 334-3100
New Kensington (G-12370)
Seal Glove Mfg Inc ....F 717 692-4837
Millersburg (G-11200)
Super Can Industries Inc.....................G...... 215 945-1075
Levittown (G-9866)

MEDICAL & SURGICAL SPLYS: Socks, Stump

Comfort Stump Sock Mfg Co ....F 215 781-0300
Croydon (G-3915)

MEDICAL & SURGICAL SPLYS: Space Helmets

Gentex Corporation ....B 570 282-3550
Simpson (G-17593)

MEDICAL & SURGICAL SPLYS: Sponges

Clearcount Med Solutions Inc ....F 412 931-7233
Pittsburgh (G-14859)

MEDICAL & SURGICAL SPLYS: Stretchers

Oakworks Inc...D 717 227-0516
New Freedom (G-12213)

MEDICAL & SURGICAL SPLYS: Supports, Abdominal, Ankle, Etc

Applied Technology Intl Ltd.................F 610 363-1077
Exton (G-5645)

Specialty Millworks Inc.......................G...... 610 682-6334
Topton (G-18416)

MEDICAL & SURGICAL SPLYS: Sutures, Non & Absorbable

Surgical Specialties Corp....................F 610 404-1000
Wyomissing (G-20289)

MEDICAL & SURGICAL SPLYS: Swabs, Sanitary Cotton

Reynolds Presto Products Inc..............B 866 254-3310
Pittsburgh (G-15483)

MEDICAL & SURGICAL SPLYS: Technical Aids, Handicapped

American Innovations Inc ....G...... 215 249-1840
Dublin (G-4431)

MEDICAL & SURGICAL SPLYS: Trusses, Orthopedic & Surgical

Implant Research Center......................G...... 215 571-4345
Philadelphia (G-13851)

MEDICAL & SURGICAL SPLYS: Walkers

J Walker & Associates LLC..................G....... 717 755-7142
York (G-20539)

MEDICAL & SURGICAL SPLYS: Welders' Hoods

Micro-Fusion LLC ....G....... 717 244-4648
Red Lion (G-16609)

MEDICAL CENTERS

Main Line Center For Skin Surg ....G....... 610 664-1414
Bala Cynwyd (G-884)
Ophthalmic Associates PC ....E 215 368-1646
Lansdale (G-9395)

MEDICAL EQPT REPAIR SVCS, NON-ELECTRIC

Total Scope Inc....................................E 484 490-2100
Upper Chichester (G-18674)

MEDICAL EQPT: CAT Scanner Or Computerized Axial Tomography

Cygnus Manufacturing Co LLC ....C 724 352-8000
Saxonburg (G-17082)
Extremity Imaging Partners ....F 724 493-7452
Wexford (G-19800)

MEDICAL EQPT: Defibrillators

Gregory W Moyer Defibrillato ....G....... 570 421-9993
Stroudsburg (G-18121)
Zoll Medical Corporation......................F 800 543-3267
Pittsburgh (G-15735)

MEDICAL EQPT: Diagnostic

Abbott Laboratories..............................G....... 610 444-9818
Kennett Square (G-8500)
Amax Solutions Inc...............................G....... 717 798-8070
Lemoyne (G-9742)
Bayer Medical Care Inc.........................D....... 724 337-8176
New Kensington (G-12327)
Biomeme Inc...F 267 519-9066
Philadelphia (G-13465)
Glutalor Medical Inc..............................F 610 492-5710
Exton (G-5689)
Hyq Research Solutions LLC.................G....... 717 439-9320
Hummelstown (G-7914)
Infrascan Inc..G....... 215 387-6784
Philadelphia (G-13855)
Keyscripts LLC.......................................G....... 866 446-2848
Mechanicsburg (G-10863)
Lampire Biological Labs Inc ....E 215 795-2838
Ottsville (G-13065)
Lifesensors Inc......................................F 610 644-8845
Malvern (G-10268)
Neuro Kinetics Inc ....F 412 963-6649
Pittsburgh (G-15329)
Neurologix Technologies Inc ....F 512 914-7941
Cherry Tree (G-3033)

Peca Labs Inc ....G...... 412 589-9847
Pittsburgh (G-15372)
Qualtek Molecular Laboratories ....G...... 215 504-7402
Newtown (G-12540)
Safeguard Scientifics Inc ....E 610 293-0600
Radnor (G-16301)
Sekisui Diagnostics LLC ....G...... 610 594-8590
Exton (G-5730)
Timm Medical Technologies Inc ....E 484 321-5900
Fort Washington (G-6093)
Vicor Technologies Inc ....F 570 897-5797
Bangor (G-933)

MEDICAL EQPT: Electromedical Apparatus

C W E Inc ....G...... 610 642-7719
Ardmore (G-704)
Helius Medical Tech Inc........................F 215 944-6100
Newtown (G-12510)
Nian-Crae Inc ....G...... 732 545-5881
Philadelphia (G-14072)
Sense Technology Inc...........................G...... 724 733-2277
Halifax (G-6831)
Siemens Med Solutions USA Inc ....B 888 826-9702
Malvern (G-10315)

MEDICAL EQPT: Electrotherapeutic Apparatus

Reccare Incorporated............................E 215 886-0880
Philadelphia (G-14232)
Reha Technology Usa Inc ....G...... 267 419-8690
Plymouth Meeting (G-15867)
Spectrum Healthcare Inc......................E 888 210-5576
Eagleville (G-4516)

MEDICAL EQPT: Heart & Lung

Perfusion Management Group...............F 717 392-4112
Lancaster (G-9169)

MEDICAL EQPT: Heart-Lung Machines, Exc Iron Lungs

Heartsine Technologies LLC.................E 215 860-8100
Newtown (G-12508)
Valira LLC ....G...... 973 216-5803
Conshohocken (G-3615)

MEDICAL EQPT: Laser Systems

Atoptix LLC..G...... 814 808-7056
State College (G-17942)
Composiflex Inc ....D...... 814 866-8616
Erie (G-5229)
Gianna Skin & Laser Ltd ....G...... 610 356-7870
Newtown Square (G-12574)
Ictv Holdings Inc...................................F 484 598-2300
Wayne (G-19337)
Laser Center of Central PA ....G...... 814 867-1852
State College (G-17986)
Laser Hair Enhancemen ....G...... 724 591-5670
Harmony (G-7072)
Laser Vginal Rejuvenation Inst.............G...... 610 584-0584
Lansdale (G-9384)
Nu-U Laser Center ....G...... 717 718-7880
York (G-20612)
Snake Creek Lasers LLC ....F 570 553-1120
Friendsville (G-6230)

MEDICAL EQPT: MRI/Magnetic Resonance Imaging Devs, Nuclear

Acryl8 LLC ....G...... 484 695-6209
Coopersburg (G-3623)

MEDICAL EQPT: Pacemakers

Cardionet Inc ....G...... 888 312-2328
Malvern (G-10199)

MEDICAL EQPT: Patient Monitoring

Dbmtion Inc ....G...... 412 605-1952
Pittsburgh (G-14911)
Medihill Inc ....G...... 215 464-7016
Bensalem (G-1224)
Respironics Inc ....B 724 387-4270
Monroeville (G-11354)
Respironics Inc ....C...... 724 334-3100
New Kensington (G-12370)

Respironics Inc ....D....... 724 387-5200
Murrysville (G-11865)

MEDICAL EQPT: Sterilizers

Environmental Tectonics Corp ....C....... 215 355-9100
Southampton (G-17809)
Sterilzer Rfurbishing Svcs Inc ....F....... 814 456-2616
Erie (G-5492)

MEDICAL EQPT: Ultrasonic Scanning Devices

Applied RES & Photonics Inc ....G....... 717 220-1003
Harrisburg (G-7089)
Pittsburgh Medical Device ....F....... 724 325-1869
Murrysville (G-11861)
Pyxidis ....G....... 267 614-8348
Doylestown (G-4330)
Zoll Services LLC ....A....... 412 968-3333
Pittsburgh (G-15736)

MEDICAL EQPT: Ultrasonic, Exc Cleaning

Dymax Corporation ....E....... 800 296-4146
Warrendale (G-19072)
Market Service Corp ....G....... 610 696-1884
West Chester (G-19596)

MEDICAL EQPT: X-Ray Apparatus & Tubes, Therapeutic

Arrow International Inc ....A....... 610 225-6800
Wayne (G-19303)

MEDICAL FIELD ASSOCIATION

American Law Institute ....D....... 215 243-1600
Philadelphia (G-13385)
Association Test Publishers ....G....... 717 755-9747
York (G-20388)
Health Care Council Western PA ....F....... 724 776-6400
Warrendale (G-19080)

MEDICAL HELP SVCS

McKesson Ptent Care Sltons Inc ....D....... 814 860-8160
Erie (G-5386)

MEDICAL INSURANCE CLAIM PROCESSING: Contract Or Fee Basis

Merck Sharp & Dohme Corp ....C....... 215 631-5000
West Point (G-19762)

MEDICAL TRAINING SERVICES

Healing Environments Intl Inc ....G....... 215 758-2107
Philadelphia (G-13808)

MEDICAL X-RAY MACHINES & TUBES WHOLESALERS

Dental Imaging Tech Corp ....D....... 215 997-5666
Hatfield (G-7333)

MEDICAL, DENTAL & HOSPITAL EQPT, WHOL: Dentists' Prof Splys

Dental Corp of America ....F....... 610 344-7488
West Chester (G-19535)

MEDICAL, DENTAL & HOSPITAL EQPT, WHOL: Hospital Eqpt & Splys

Burmans Medical Supplies Inc ....F....... 610 876-6068
Upper Chichester (G-18657)
JD Product Solutions LLC ....G....... 570 234-9421
Bartonsville (G-947)

MEDICAL, DENTAL & HOSPITAL EQPT, WHOL: Hosptl Eqpt/Furniture

McKnight Surgical Inc ....G....... 412 821-9000
Pittsburgh (G-15270)

MEDICAL, DENTAL & HOSPITAL EQPT, WHOL: Surgical Eqpt & Splys

Haemonetics Corporation ....C....... 412 741-7399
Leetsdale (G-9692)

MEDICAL, DENTAL & HOSPITAL EQPT, WHOLESALE: Hearing Aids

America Hears Inc.............................F....... 215 785-5437
Bristol (G-2105)

MEDICAL, DENTAL & HOSPITAL EQPT, WHOLESALE: Med Eqpt & Splys

Allegheny Fabg & Sups Inc....................G....... 412 828-3320
Pittsburgh (G-14678)
Altamira Ltd ....G....... 800 343-1066
Pittsburgh (G-14692)
Burrell Scientific LLC ....F....... 412 747-2111
Pittsburgh (G-14797)
Choice Therapeutics Inc ....G....... 508 384-0425
Langhorne (G-9284)
Fox Pool Lancaster Inc.......................D....... 717 718-1977
York (G-20487)
Ikor Industries Inc ....D....... 302 456-0280
Kennett Square (G-8514)
Jod Contracting Inc ....G....... 724 323-2124
Fayette City (G-5875)
Keyscripts LLC ....G....... 866 446-2848
Mechanicsburg (G-10863)
Life Support International ....E....... 215 785-2870
Langhorne (G-9308)
Medihill Inc ....G....... 215 464-7016
Bensalem (G-1224)
Mrlrx LLC ....F....... 610 485-7750
Marcus Hook (G-10450)
Permegear Inc ....G....... 484 851-3688
Hellertown (G-7560)
Siemens Med Solutions USA Inc ....B....... 888 826-9702
Malvern (G-10315)
Ultraflex Systems Inc..........................G....... 610 906-1410
Pottstown (G-16061)

MEDICAL, DENTAL & HOSPITAL EQPT, WHOLESALE: Medical Lab

VWR Corporation ....C....... 610 386-1700
Radnor (G-16304)

MEDICAL, DENTAL & HOSPITAL EQPT, WHOLESALE: Orthopedic

Howmedica Osteonics Corp ....F....... 610 760-7007
Neffs (G-11999)

MEDICAL, DENTAL & HOSPITAL EQPT, WHOLESALE: Safety

Circadiance LLC.................................F....... 724 858-2837
Turtle Creek (G-18562)

MEDICAL, DENTAL & HOSPITAL EQPT, WHOLESALE: Therapy

Mgs04 Corporation ....G....... 267 249-2372
Philadelphia (G-14018)

MEDICAL, DENTAL/HOSPITAL EQPT, WHOL: Veterinarian Eqpt/Sply

Penn Veterinary Supply Inc...................D....... 717 656-4121
Lancaster (G-9163)

MEMBERSHIP ORGANIZATIONS, NEC: Charitable

For Lenfest Institute ....G....... 215 854-5600
Philadelphia (G-13713)
Hapsco Design and Prtg Svcs ....G....... 717 564-2323
Harrisburg (G-7139)
Philadelphia Photo Arts Center ....G....... 215 232-5678
Philadelphia (G-14148)
Postal History Society Inc ....F....... 717 624-5941
New Oxford (G-12422)
Society of Good Shepherd....................G....... 717 349-7033
Amberson (G-565)

MEMBERSHIP ORGANIZATIONS, NEC: Historical Club

Organ Historical Society ....G....... 804 353-9226
Villanova (G-18768)

MEMBERSHIP ORGANIZATIONS, PROF: Education/Teacher Assoc

National Assn Cllges Employers ....E....... 610 868-1421
Bethlehem (G-1577)
Society For Industrial & Appli................D....... 215 382-9800
Philadelphia (G-14320)

MEMBERSHIP ORGANIZATIONS, PROFESSIONAL: Accounting Assoc

Pennsylvania Institute of CPA ....E....... 215 496-9272
Philadelphia (G-14132)

MEMBERSHIP ORGANIZATIONS, PROFESSIONAL: Health Association

American Association For Cance...........D....... 215 440-9300
Philadelphia (G-13378)
American Cllege Physicians Inc............B....... 215 351-2400
Philadelphia (G-13384)

MEMBERSHIP ORGANIZATIONS, REL: Churches, Temples & Shrines

Assemblies of Yahweh ....F....... 717 933-4518
Bethel (G-1392)
Watchword Worldwide...........................G....... 814 366-2770
Ambridge (G-638)

MEMBERSHIP ORGANIZATIONS, RELIGIOUS: Baptist Church

American Baptst HM Mission Soc.........D....... 610 768-2465
King of Prussia (G-8581)

MEMBERSHIP ORGANIZATIONS, RELIGIOUS: Catholic Church

Catholic Scl Svcs of Scranton ....D....... 570 207-2283
Scranton (G-17216)
Catholic Scl Svcs of Scranton ....G....... 570 454-6693
Hazleton (G-7494)

MEMBERSHIP ORGANIZATIONS, RELIGIOUS: Lutheran Church

Society of Good Shepherd....................G....... 717 349-7033
Amberson (G-565)

MEMBERSHIP ORGANIZATIONS, RELIGIOUS: Religious Instruction

Transport For Christ Inc ....G....... 717 426-9977
Marietta (G-10469)

MEMORIALS, MONUMENTS & MARKERS

Craig Walters.....................................G....... 570 645-3415
Summit Hill (G-18159)
Richard Freeman.................................G....... 717 597-4580
Greencastle (G-6630)

MEN'S & BOYS' CLOTHING ACCESS STORES

J & P Incorporated ....G....... 610 759-2378
Nazareth (G-11972)
Youre Putting ME On Inc ....E....... 412 655-9666
Pittsburgh (G-15731)

MEN'S & BOYS' CLOTHING STORES

Tom James Company ....D....... 717 264-5768
Chambersburg (G-2986)

MEN'S & BOYS' CLOTHING WHOLESALERS, NEC

Charles F May Co...............................G....... 215 634-7257
Philadelphia (G-13527)
Dream World International Inc................G....... 215 320-0200
Philadelphia (G-13644)
Keystone Nitewear Co Inc ....F....... 717 336-7534
Reinholds (G-16634)
Lifewear Inc ....E....... 610 327-2884
Pottstown (G-16011)
P & S Sportswear Inc ....E....... 215 455-7133
Philadelphia (G-14110)
Sez Sew Stitching Inc ....F....... 814 339-6734
Osceola Mills (G-13057)

P R O D U C T

MEN'S & BOYS' HATS STORES

Rob Kei Inc ....G...... 717 293-8991
Lancaster **(G-9189)**

MEN'S & BOYS' HOSIERY WHOLESALERS

Discovery Direct Inc ....G...... 610 252-3809
Easton **(G-4670)**

MEN'S & BOYS' SPORTSWEAR CLOTHING STORES

C & S Sports & Promotions ....G...... 724 775-1655
Monaca **(G-11287)**
Maroco Ltd ....B...... 610 746-6800
Easton **(G-4719)**
Sugartown Worldwide LLC ....C...... 610 878-5550
King of Prussia **(G-8682)**

MEN'S & BOYS' SPORTSWEAR WHOLESALERS

Excl Inc ....E...... 412 856-7616
Trafford **(G-18456)**
La Salle Products Inc ....F...... 412 488-1585
Pittsburgh **(G-15213)**
Robanco ....G...... 412 795-7444
Pittsburgh **(G-15493)**
Sugartown Worldwide LLC ....C...... 610 878-5550
King of Prussia **(G-8682)**
Windjammer Corporation Inc ....G...... 610 588-0626
Bangor **(G-935)**
Windjammer Corporation Inc ....G...... 610 588-2137
Bangor **(G-936)**

MEN'S & BOYS' UNDERWEAR WHOLESALERS

Wundies ....G...... 570 322-7245
Williamsport **(G-20102)**

MEN'S SUITS STORES

D&B Tailors Inc ....E...... 610 356-9279
Newtown Square **(G-12571)**

MERCHANDISING MACHINE OPERATORS: Vending

Rochester Coca Cola Bottling ....E...... 570 655-2874
Pittston **(G-15782)**

MESH, REINFORCING: Plastic

Bedford Reinforced Plas Inc ....D...... 814 623-8125
Bedford **(G-1044)**
Composite Pnels Innvations LLC ....G...... 814 317-5023
Hollidaysburg **(G-7644)**

METAL & STEEL PRDTS: Abrasive

Cady Enterprises ....G...... 814 848-7408
Ulysses **(G-18600)**
Phoenixx Intl Resources Inc ....G...... 412 782-7060
Pittsburgh **(G-15380)**
Power & Industrial Svcs Corp ....E...... 800 676-7116
Donora **(G-4158)**

METAL COMPONENTS: Prefabricated

Cid Associates Inc ....E...... 724 353-0300
Sarver **(G-17066)**
Nucor Corporation ....G...... 717 735-7766
Lancaster **(G-9148)**
Speed Partz LLC ....G...... 513 874-2034
Fayetteville **(G-5878)**

METAL CUTTING SVCS

Conicity Technologies LLC ....G...... 412 601-1874
Turtle Creek **(G-18563)**
Fluid Conditioning Pdts Inc ....E...... 717 627-1550
Lititz **(G-10008)**
Progress Rail Services Corp ....E...... 610 779-2039
Reading **(G-16476)**

METAL DETECTORS

Metabloc Inc ....G...... 717 764-4937
York **(G-20589)**

METAL FABRICATORS: Architechtural

A & R Iron Works Inc ....F...... 610 497-8770
Trainer **(G-18462)**
A B N A Inc ....E...... 724 527-2866
Penn **(G-13226)**
All Metal Fabricating Co Inc ....G...... 724 925-3537
Youngwood **(G-20777)**
Alumax LLC ....C...... 412 553-4545
Pittsburgh **(G-14695)**
Anvil Iron Works Inc ....G...... 215 468-8300
Philadelphia **(G-13397)**
Architectural Woodsmiths Inc ......D...... 717 532-7700
Shippensburg **(G-17515)**
Artline Ornamental Iron Works ......G...... 215 727-2923
Philadelphia **(G-13416)**
Baut Studios Inc ....E...... 570 288-1431
Swoyersville **(G-18194)**
Bedford Reinforced Plas Inc ....D...... 814 623-8125
Bedford **(G-1044)**
Bethlehem Aluminum Inc ....F...... 610 432-4541
Allentown **(G-150)**
Bon Tool Company ....D...... 724 443-7080
Gibsonia **(G-6328)**
Carl E Reichert Corp ....G...... 215 723-9525
Telford **(G-18269)**
Cid Associates Inc ....E...... 724 353-0300
Sarver **(G-17066)**
Country Accents ....G...... 570 478-4127
Williamsport **(G-20001)**
Creative Architectural Metals ....E...... 215 638-1650
Bensalem **(G-1175)**
Del Ren Assoc Inc ....G...... 215 467-7000
Philadelphia **(G-13616)**
Exeter Architectural Products ....F...... 570 693-4220
Wyoming **(G-20277)**
F F Frickanisce Iron Works ....G...... 724 568-2001
Vandergrift **(G-18726)**
Fairway Building Products LLC ......D...... 717 653-6777
Mount Joy **(G-11657)**
Fisher & Ludlow Inc ....D...... 217 324-6106
Wexford **(G-19802)**
Forms and Surfaces Inc ....A...... 412 781-9003
Pittsburgh **(G-15026)**
Frey Lutz Corp ....C...... 717 394-4635
Lancaster **(G-9025)**
Gratz Industries LLC ....E...... 215 739-7373
Philadelphia **(G-13783)**
Groll Ornamental Ir Works LLC ......G...... 412 431-4444
Pittsburgh **(G-15065)**
Guida Inc ....E...... 215 727-2222
Marcus Hook **(G-10444)**
Hendricks Welding Service Inc ....G...... 215 757-5369
Langhorne **(G-9301)**
Heritage Metalworks Ltd ....G...... 610 518-3999
Downingtown **(G-4234)**
Herman Iron Works Inc ....G...... 215 727-1127
Philadelphia **(G-13817)**
Janzer Corporation ....G...... 215 757-1168
Bensalem **(G-1212)**
John Jost Jr Inc ....G...... 610 395-5461
Allentown **(G-269)**
Kane Innovations Inc ....D...... 814 838-7731
Erie **(G-5342)**
Kauffmans Welding Iron Wo ....G...... 717 361-9844
Manheim **(G-10392)**
Kawneer Company Inc ....B...... 570 784-8000
Bloomsburg **(G-1787)**
Kawneer Company Inc ....D...... 570 784-8000
Pittsburgh **(G-15162)**
Kebb Inc ....G...... 610 859-0907
Upper Chichester **(G-18666)**
L B Foster Company ....E...... 814 623-6101
Bedford **(G-1060)**
Laminators Incorporated ....D...... 215 723-5285
Hatfield **(G-7362)**
Manley Fence Co ....G...... 610 842-8833
Coatesville **(G-3316)**
McGregor Industries Inc ....E...... 570 343-2436
Dunmore **(G-4478)**
McM Architectural Products LLC ....G...... 240 416-2809
Indiana **(G-8112)**
McShane Welding Company Inc .....E...... 814 459-3797
Erie **(G-5387)**
Mendel Steel & Orna Ir Co ....F...... 412 341-7778
Bethel Park **(G-1425)**
Overly Manufacturing Company .....E...... 724 834-7300
Greensburg **(G-6697)**
Pleasant Mount Welding Inc ....D...... 570 282-6164
Carbondale **(G-2684)**

Randy Brensinger ....G...... 610 562-2184
Hamburg **(G-6851)**
Reynolds Iron Works Inc ....F...... 570 323-4663
Williamsport **(G-20068)**
Robert L Baker ....F...... 443 617-0164
Chambersburg **(G-2973)**
Scranton Craftsmen Excvtg Inc .....D...... 800 775-1479
Throop **(G-18360)**
Standard & Custom LLC ....G...... 412 345-7901
Pittsburgh **(G-15575)**
Standard Iron Works ....E...... 570 347-2058
Scranton **(G-17293)**
Standard Tool & Machine Co ....E...... 724 758-5522
Ellwood City **(G-4951)**
Structural Fiberglass Inc ....F...... 814 623-0458
Bedford **(G-1077)**
Technique Architectural Pdts ....G...... 412 241-1644
Wilkinsburg **(G-19981)**
Vangura Iron Inc ....F...... 412 461-7825
Clairton **(G-3159)**
Vanquish Fencing Incorporated .....F...... 215 295-2863
Morrisville **(G-11586)**
William Henry Orna Ir Works ....G...... 215 659-1887
Willow Grove **(G-20149)**
Zottola Fab A PA Bus Tr ....G...... 412 221-4488
Cuddy **(G-3944)**

METAL FABRICATORS: Plate

A & R Iron Works Inc ....F...... 610 497-8770
Trainer **(G-18462)**
Aaron King ....G...... 610 273-1365
Honey Brook **(G-7735)**
ABT LLC ....E...... 412 826-8002
Pittsburgh **(G-14636)**
Advanced Welding Tech Inc ....E...... 814 899-3584
Erie **(G-5176)**
Alfa Laval Inc ....D...... 717 453-7143
Lykens **(G-10129)**
All Metal Fabricating Co Inc ....G...... 724 925-3537
Youngwood **(G-20777)**
All-Steel Fabricators Co Inc ....E...... 610 687-2267
Wayne **(G-19296)**
Allegheny Plastics Inc ....C...... 412 741-4416
Leetsdale **(G-9679)**
Allentown Steel Fabg Co Inc ....F...... 610 264-2815
Catasauqua **(G-2813)**
Alloy Fabrication Inc ....G...... 610 921-9212
Reading **(G-16318)**
Alternate Heating Systems LLC .....E...... 717 261-0922
Chambersburg **(G-2901)**
Altrax ....A...... 814 379-3706
Summerville **(G-18156)**
American Hollow Boring Company ..E...... 800 673-2458
Erie **(G-5187)**
Anderson Tube Company Inc ....G...... 215 855-0118
Hatfield **(G-7317)**
Axeman-Anderson Company ....E...... 570 326-9114
Williamsport **(G-19991)**
Babcock Wlcox Ebnsburg Pwr Inc ..G...... 814 472-1140
Ebensburg **(G-4780)**
Biofab Products Inc ....E...... 724 283-4801
Butler **(G-2379)**
Blank River Services Inc ....E...... 412 384-2489
Elizabeth **(G-4857)**
Bradford Allegheny Corporation .....D...... 814 362-2593
Lewis Run **(G-9874)**
Brandywine Machine Co Inc ....F...... 610 269-1221
Downingtown **(G-4216)**
Brandywine Valley Fabricators ....F...... 610 384-7440
Coatesville **(G-3295)**
Brentwood Industries Inc ....D...... 717 274-1827
Lebanon **(G-9548)**
Charles R Kelley ....G...... 717 840-0181
York **(G-20423)**
Clipper Pipe & Service Inc ....G...... 610 872-9067
Eddystone **(G-4799)**
Combustion Service & Eqp Co ....D...... 412 821-8900
Pittsburgh **(G-14867)**
Containment Solutions Inc ....C...... 814 542-8621
Mount Union **(G-11741)**
Contech Engnered Solutions LLC ....E...... 717 597-2148
Greencastle **(G-6604)**
Crown Boiler Co ....E...... 215 535-8900
Philadelphia **(G-13586)**
D L George & Sons Mfg Inc ....D...... 717 765-4700
Waynesboro **(G-19407)**
Delta Mechanical Inc ....F...... 570 752-5511
Berwick **(G-1323)**
DHL Machine Co Inc ....E...... 215 536-3591
Quakertown **(G-16186)**

DMC Global Inc ....E 724 277-9710
　Mount Braddock (G-11616)
Dolans Wldg Stl Fbrication Inc ....E 814 749-8639
　Johnstown (G-8369)
Doucette Industries Inc ....E 717 845-8746
　York (G-20456)
Drv Metal Fab LLC ....F 717 968-9028
　East Waterford (G-4640)
Edlon Inc ....D 610 268-3101
　Avondale (G-852)
Electronics Instrs & Optics ....E 215 245-6300
　Bensalem (G-1188)
F F Frickanisce Iron Works ....G 724 568-2001
　Vandergrift (G-18726)
Fab-TEC Industries Inc ....E 412 262-1144
　Coraopolis (G-3690)
Faull Fabricating Inc ....G 724 458-7662
　Grove City (G-6784)
Gardner Cryogenics Inc ....C 610 264-4523
　Bethlehem (G-1523)
General Weldments Inc ....F 724 744-2105
　Irwin (G-8164)
Gerome Manufacturing Co Inc ....D 724 438-8544
　Smithfield (G-17650)
Goodhart Sons Inc ....C 717 656-2404
　Lancaster (G-9030)
Gouldey Welding & Fabrications ....E 215 721-9522
　Souderton (G-17737)
Greenetech Mfg Co Inc ....C 724 228-2400
　Washington (G-19181)
Harbor Steel Inc ....F 724 658-7748
　New Castle (G-12100)
Hydac Corp ....E 610 266-0100
　Bethlehem (G-1533)
Ik Stotzfus Service Corp ....E 717 397-3503
　Manheim (G-10390)
J Thomas Ltd ....E 717 397-3483
　Lancaster (G-9069)
Lancaster Metal Mfg Inc ....D 717 293-4480
　Lancaster (G-9101)
Larry J Epps Inc ....G 724 712-1156
　Butler (G-2419)
Lee Industries Inc ....C 814 342-0460
　Philipsburg (G-14519)
Liberty Welding Co ....G 412 661-1776
　Pittsburgh (G-15228)
Longwood Manufacturing Corp ....F 610 444-4200
　Kennett Square (G-8523)
M & D Industries Inc ....F 814 723-2381
　Clarendon (G-3170)
Maguire Products Inc ....E 610 459-4300
　Aston (G-773)
McShane Welding Company Inc ....E 814 459-3797
　Erie (G-5387)
Metplas Inc ....D 724 295-5200
　Natrona Heights (G-11946)
Modern Precast Concrete Inc ....E 484 548-6200
　Easton (G-4726)
MSA Safety Incorporated ....A 724 733-9100
　Murrysville (G-11859)
Multitherm Heat Transfer ....G 610 408-8361
　Malvern (G-10281)
Munroe Incorporated ....G 412 231-0600
　Ambridge (G-628)
New Castle Industries Inc ....G 724 656-5600
　New Castle (G-12129)
Olmsted Inc ....F 412 384-2161
　West Elizabeth (G-19696)
ORourke & Sons Inc ....E 610 436-0932
　West Chester (G-19613)
Pennmark Technologies Corp ....C 570 255-5000
　Dallas (G-3966)
Precision Components Group LLC ....C 717 848-1126
　York (G-20637)
Precision Cstm Components LLC ....B 717 848-1126
　York (G-20638)
Precision Tool & Mfg Corp ....G 717 767-6454
　Emigsville (G-4997)
R-V Industries Inc ....E 610 273-2457
　Honey Brook (G-7758)
Reynolds Sales Co Inc ....G 412 461-7877
　Homestead (G-7692)
Reynolds Services Inc ....D 724 646-2600
　Greenville (G-6770)
RG Industries Inc ....E 717 849-0345
　York (G-20658)
Scranton Craftsmen Excvtg Inc ....D 800 775-1479
　Throop (G-18360)
Sheet Metal Specialists LLC ....E 717 910-7000
　Harrisburg (G-7215)

Sidehill Copper Works Inc ....G 814 451-0400
　Erie (G-5477)
Somerset Door and Column Co............E 814 445-9608
　Somerset (G-17708)
SPX Cooling Technologies Inc ....E 717 845-4830
　York (G-20677)
Standard Tool & Machine Co ....E 724 758-5522
　Ellwood City (G-4951)
Superior Metalworks Inc ....F 717 245-2446
　Carlisle (G-2740)
Therma-Fab Inc ....E 814 664-9429
　Corry (G-3774)
Therma-Fab Inc ....E 814 827-9455
　Titusville (G-18398)
Thermacore International Inc ....B 717 569-6551
　Lancaster (G-9216)
Vari Corporation ....G 570 385-0731
　Schuylkill Haven (G-17169)
Vcw Enterprises Inc ....D 610 847-5112
　Ottsville (G-13068)
Walter Long Mfg Co Inc ....E 724 348-6631
　Finleyville (G-5965)
Warren Industries Inc ....E 814 723-2050
　Warren (G-19059)
Waste Gas Fabricating Co Inc ....E 215 736-9240
　Fairless Hills (G-5807)
Wcr Inc ....G 215 447-8152
　Bensalem (G-1270)
Wedj/Three CS Inc ....D 717 845-8685
　York (G-20705)
Western PA Stl Fabg Inc ....E 724 658-8575
　New Castle (G-12169)
Wheaton & Sons Inc ....F 412 351-0405
　McKeesport (G-10687)
Wolfe Metal Fab Inc ....G 724 339-7790
　Lower Burrell (G-10108)
X-Mark/Cdt Inc ....E 724 228-7373
　Washington (G-19248)

METAL FABRICATORS: Sheet

486 Associates Inc ....E 717 691-7077
　Mechanicsburg (G-10815)
A C Gentry Inc ....F 215 927-9948
　Philadelphia (G-13324)
A W Mercer Inc ....C 610 367-8460
　Boyertown (G-1892)
ABT LLC ....E 412 826-8002
　Pittsburgh (G-14636)
Acacia Corp ....F 412 771-6144
　Mc Kees Rocks (G-10600)
Accrotool Inc ....C 724 339-3560
　New Kensington (G-12320)
Accu Machining Center Inc ....E 610 252-6855
　Easton (G-4644)
Ace Metal Inc ....E 610 623-2204
　Clifton Heights (G-3250)
Acf Group LLC ....E 724 364-7027
　Allison (G-444)
Acurlite Strl Skylights Inc ....E 570 759-6882
　Berwick (G-1307)
ADG Fabrication LLC ....G 724 658-3000
　New Castle (G-12053)
Advanced Drainage Systems Inc ....E 570 546-7686
　Muncy (G-11805)
Aeroparts Fabg & Machining Inc ....E 814 948-6015
　Nicktown (G-12618)
Agape Precision Mfg LLC ....E 484 704-2601
　Pottstown (G-15961)
Airsources Inc ....G 610 983-0102
　Malvern (G-10181)
Alberts Custom Shtmtl & Wldg............E 814 454-4461
　Erie (G-5179)
Allentech Inc ....D 484 664-7887
　Allentown (G-126)
Alumax LLC ....E 570 784-7481
　Bloomsburg (G-1768)
American Alloy Fabricators ....E 610 635-0205
　Norristown (G-12633)
American Metals & Mfg Co..................G 724 934-8866
　Sarver (G-17064)
American Metals Company ....E 724 625-8666
　Mars (G-10486)
Amity Industries Inc ....D 610 385-6075
　Douglassville (G-4169)
Apx York Sheet Metal Inc ....E 717 767-2704
　York (G-20382)
Arconic Inc ....C 717 393-9641
　Lancaster (G-8938)
ATI Corporation ....E 717 354-8721
　New Holland (G-12229)

Atkinson Industries Inc ....G 570 366-2114
　Orwigsburg (G-13039)
Auger Fabrication Inc ....E 610 524-3350
　Exton (G-5648)
Bcl Manufacturing Inc ....E 814 467-8225
　Windber (G-20178)
Bellwether Corp ....F 610 534-5382
　Folcroft (G-5999)
Bensalem Metal Inc ....G 215 526-3355
　Bensalem (G-1156)
Berger Building Products Inc ....G 215 355-1200
　Feasterville Trevose (G-5889)
Biofab Products Inc ....E 724 283-4801
　Butler (G-2379)
Blank River Services Inc ....E 412 384-2489
　Elizabeth (G-4857)
Blanski Energy Management Inc ....E 610 373-5273
　Reading (G-16335)
Bork Inc ....G 215 324-1155
　Philadelphia (G-13472)
Boyertown Shtmtl Fbrcators Inc ....E 610 689-0991
　Douglassville (G-4171)
Bradford Allegheny Corporation ....D 814 362-2593
　Lewis Run (G-9874)
Brandywine Machine Co Inc ....F 610 269-1221
　Downingtown (G-4216)
Brandywine Valley Fabricators ....F 610 384-7440
　Coatesville (G-3295)
Brd Noise & Vibration Ctrl Inc ....G 610 863-6300
　Wind Gap (G-20167)
Brown Machine Co Inc ....G 610 932-3359
　Oxford (G-13073)
C A Spalding Company ....E 267 550-9000
　Bensalem (G-1163)
Cardinal Systems Inc ....G 570 385-4733
　Schuylkill Haven (G-17151)
Carlisle Systems LLC ....G 610 821-4222
　Fogelsville (G-5992)
Charles Cracciolo Stl Met Yard ....E 814 944-4051
　Altoona (G-490)
Charles Machine Inc ....E 814 379-3706
　Summerville (G-18157)
Cid Associates Inc ....E 724 353-0300
　Sarver (G-17066)
Clarion Bathware Inc ....D 814 782-3016
　Marble (G-10436)
Computer Components Corp.................D 215 676-7600
　Philadelphia (G-13567)
Coraopolis Light Metal Inc ....G 412 264-2252
　Coraopolis (G-3680)
Coren Metal Inc ....E 215 244-4260
　Bensalem (G-1173)
Craft Metal Products Inc ....G 570 829-2441
　Sugar Notch (G-18149)
Craftweld Fabrication Co Inc ....E 267 492-1100
　Montgomeryville (G-11391)
Creston E Lockbaum Inc ....E 717 414-6885
　Chambersburg (G-2921)
Cronan Sheet Metal Inc ....G 610 375-9230
　Reading (G-16354)
Curbs Plus Inc ....E 888 639-2872
　Mount Union (G-11743)
Custom Manufacturing Corp ....E 215 638-3888
　Bensalem (G-1178)
D L George & Sons Mfg Inc ....D 717 765-4700
　Waynesboro (G-19407)
Daniel C Tanney Inc ....D 215 639-3131
　Bensalem (G-1179)
David Seidel ....F 610 921-8310
　Temple (G-18327)
Dedicated Customs Inc ....G 724 678-6609
　Burgettstown (G-2345)
Designer Cabinets and Hdwr Co ....E 610 622-4455
　Clifton Heights (G-3252)
Diversified Metal Products Co..............G 215 423-8877
　Philadelphia (G-13636)
Division Seven Inc ....G 724 449-8400
　Gibsonia (G-6332)
DMC Global Inc ....E 724 277-9710
　Mount Braddock (G-11616)
Donald B Smith Incorporated ....E 717 632-2100
　Hanover (G-6879)
Donald Campbell ....D 412 793-6067
　Pittsburgh (G-14930)
Double D Sheet Metal Inc ....G 610 987-3733
　Oley (G-12978)
Duct Shop USA Inc ....G 412 231-2330
　Pittsburgh (G-14940)
Ductworks Inc ....G 412 231-2330
　Pittsburgh (G-14941)

PRODUCT

Dudlik Industries Inc ....E 215 674-4383
Hatboro (G-7282)

Dukane Radiator Inc ....G 412 233-3300
Bethel Park (G-1413)

Dunbar Machine Co Inc ....G 724 277-8711
Dunbar (G-4439)

Edward J Deseta Co Inc ....C 302 691-2040
Harleysville (G-7032)

Ehc Industries Inc ....E 724 696-1212
Mount Pleasant (G-11699)

Electronics Instrs & Optics ....E 215 245-6300
Bensalem (G-1188)

Emp Industries Inc ....G 215 357-5333
Warminster (G-18871)

Enclosure Direct Corp ....E 724 697-5191
Avonmore (G-864)

Erie Metal Basket Inc ....F 814 833-1745
Erie (G-5270)

F F Frickanisce Iron Works ....G 724 568-2001
Vandergrift (G-18726)

Fabricated Products ....G 570 588-1794
Bushkill (G-2365)

Fabricon Inc ....E 610 921-0203
Temple (G-18329)

Fairmans Roof Trusses Inc ....G 724 349-6778
Creekside (G-3875)

FEC Technologies Inc ....E 717 764-5959
York (G-20477)

Fedco Manufacturing Inc ....F 724 863-2252
Larimer (G-9451)

Fetchen Sheet Metal Inc ....E 570 457-3560
Old Forge (G-12964)

First State Sheet Metal Inc ....G 215 766-9510
Bedminster (G-1080)

First State Sheet Metal Inc ....G 302 521-1609
Pipersville (G-14615)

Fisher Iron Works ....G 717 687-7595
Gordonville (G-6554)

Fountain Fabricating Co ....G 570 682-9018
Hegins (G-7541)

Francis J Nowalk ....G 412 687-4017
Pittsburgh (G-15030)

Freedom Components Inc ....G 717 242-0101
Lewistown (G-9930)

Frey Lutz Corp ....C 717 394-4635
Lancaster (G-9025)

General Weldments Inc ....F 724 744-2105
Irwin (G-8164)

George I Reitz & Sons Inc ....E 814 849-2308
Brookville (G-2261)

George I Reitz & Sons Inc ....G 412 824-9976
East Pittsburgh (G-4595)

Graham Thermal Products LLC ....E 724 658-0500
New Castle (G-12098)

Grid Electric Inc ....E 610 466-7030
Coatesville (G-3306)

GSM Industrial Inc ....C 717 207-8985
Lancaster (G-9034)

Hamill Manufacturing Company ....D 724 744-2131
Trafford (G-18457)

Havaco Technologies Inc ....G 814 878-5509
Erie (G-5311)

Hawkins Metal ....G 215 538-9668
Quakertown (G-16199)

Hendrick Manufacturing Company ......G 570 282-1010
Carbondale (G-2677)

Herb Sheet Metal Inc ....F 717 273-8001
Lebanon (G-9579)

Hillside Custom Mac Wel & Fab ....F 610 942-3093
Honey Brook (G-7748)

Hoover Cnvyor Fabrication Corp ......E 814 634-5431
Meyersdale (G-11011)

Hutchinson & Gunter Inc ....F 724 837-3200
Greensburg (G-6675)

Ira G Steffy and Son Inc ....D 717 626-6500
Ephrata (G-5111)

Ironridge Inc ....G 800 227-9523
Fort Washington (G-6077)

J & S Fabrication Inc ....F 717 469-1409
Grantville (G-6574)

J M S Fabricated Systems Inc ....E 724 832-3640
Latrobe (G-9482)

J W Steel Fabricating Co ....E 724 625-1355
Mars (G-10503)

J-Mar Metal Fabricating Co ....G 215 785-6521
Croydon (G-3920)

James Craft & Son Inc ....C 717 266-6629
York Haven (G-20759)

James McAtee ....G 724 789-9078
Renfrew (G-16640)

JL Clark LLC ....C 717 392-4125
Lancaster (G-9073)

John R Novak & Son Inc ....G 724 285-6802
Butler (G-2414)

Kampel Enterprises Inc ....E 717 432-9688
Wellsville (G-19478)

Kendred F Hunt ....G 610 327-4131
Pottstown (G-16007)

Keystone Flashing Co ....G 215 329-8500
Philadelphia (G-13930)

Keystone Truck & Trailer LLC ....G 570 903-1902
Madison Township (G-10169)

Kline Bros ....F 717 469-0699
Grantville (G-6575)

Kloeckner Metals Corporation ....D 717 755-1923
York (G-20557)

Kottcamp Sheet Metal ....E 717 845-7616
York (G-20558)

L & M Fabrication and Mch Inc ....D 610 837-1848
Bath (G-963)

L B Foster Company ....E 814 623-6101
Bedford (G-1060)

Lane Enterprises Inc ....E 724 652-7747
Pulaski (G-16124)

Leedom Welding & Fabricating ....G 215 757-8787
Newtown (G-12518)

Lehigh Services Inc ....G 610 966-2525
Macungie (G-10152)

Leiss Tool & Die ....C 814 444-1444
Somerset (G-17695)

Leman Machine Company ....E 814 736-9696
Portage (G-15918)

Lighthouse Electric Contrls Co ....F 814 835-2348
Erie (G-5365)

Lockheed Martin Aeroparts ....C 814 262-3000
Johnstown (G-8404)

Logue Industries Inc ....E 570 368-2639
Montoursville (G-11445)

Lukjan Supply & Manufacturing ....F 814 838-1328
Erie (G-5374)

Marc-Service Inc ....E 814 467-8611
Windber (G-20189)

Martin Metal Works Inc ....F 717 292-5691
East Berlin (G-4523)

Martys Muffler & Weld Shop ....G 412 673-4141
North Versailles (G-12781)

Matthey Johnson Inc ....C 610 648-8000
West Chester (G-19598)

Mc Mahon Welding Inc ....G 215 794-0260
Mechanicsville (G-10912)

McShane Welding Company Inc ....E 814 459-3797
Erie (G-5387)

Mdl Manufacturing Inds Inc ....E 814 623-0888
Bedford (G-1064)

Mestek Inc ....C 570 746-1888
Wyalusing (G-20254)

Metal Finishing Systems Inc ....E 610 524-9336
Exton (G-5710)

Metal Integrity LLC ....F 570 281-2303
Carbondale (G-2682)

Metalwerks Inc ....E 724 378-9020
Aliquippa (G-84)

Mi-Kee-Tro Metal Mfg Inc ....D 717 764-9090
York (G-20592)

Miller Welding and Machine Co ....C 814 849-3061
Brookville (G-2265)

Munroe Incorporated ....D 412 231-0600
Pittsburgh (G-15311)

N C Stauffer & Sons Inc ....D 570 945-3047
Factoryville (G-5758)

National Material LP ....E 724 337-6551
New Kensington (G-12362)

Northstern Precision Pdts Corp ....E 215 245-6300
Bensalem (G-1232)

ODonnell Metal Fabricators ....F 610 279-8810
Norristown (G-12697)

Old Ladder Co ....A 888 523-3371
Greenville (G-6762)

Omnimax International Inc ....C 215 355-1200
Feasterville Trevose (G-5924)

Omnimax International Inc ....E 717 299-3711
Lancaster (G-9152)

Omnimax International Inc ....B 717 397-2741
Lancaster (G-9153)

Palermo Metal Products Inc ....E 610 253-6230
Easton (G-4737)

Palladino Mtal Fabrication Inc ....G 610 323-9439
Pottstown (G-16025)

Panel Technologies Inc ....G 215 538-7055
Quakertown (G-16226)

Pbz LLC ....E 800 578-1121
Lititz (G-10029)

Pennmark Technologies Corp ....C 570 255-5000
Dallas (G-3966)

Petrex Inc ....E 814 723-2050
Warren (G-19044)

Pfa Inc ....G 717 664-4216
Manheim (G-10401)

Philadelphia Pipe Bending Co ....E 215 225-8955
Philadelphia (G-14149)

Pioneer Electric Supply Co Inc ....G 814 437-1342
Franklin (G-6152)

Pittsburgh Design Services Inc ....F 412 276-3000
Carnegie (G-2779)

Pittsburgh Fence Co Inc ....E 724 775-6550
Carnegie (G-2780)

PMF Industries Inc ....D 570 323-9944
Williamsport (G-20059)

Power Mechanical Corp ....E 570 823-8824
Wilkes Barre (G-19958)

Precision Sheet Metal LLC ....G 570 254-6670
Scott Township (G-17187)

Preferred Sheet Metal Inc ....E 717 732-7100
Enola (G-5084)

Presco Sheet Metal Fabricators ....G 215 672-7200
Warminster (G-18944)

Pressure-Tech Inc ....F 717 597-1868
Greencastle (G-6628)

Prizer-Painter Stove Works Inc ....E 610 376-7479
Blandon (G-1757)

Prl Industries Inc ....E 717 273-6787
Cornwall (G-3740)

Proshort Stamping Services Inc ....G 814 371-9633
Brockway (G-2232)

Randy Brensinger ....G 610 562-2184
Hamburg (G-6851)

Robert G Dent Heating & AC ....F 570 784-6721
Bloomsburg (G-1798)

Roll Former Corporation ....E 215 997-2511
Chalfont (G-2885)

Russo Heating & Cooling Inc ....F 814 454-6263
Erie (G-5468)

S & N Industries LLC ....G 724 406-0322
Slippery Rock (G-17627)

Saeger Machine Inc ....F 215 256-8754
Harleysville (G-7056)

Sanitary Process Systems Inc ....E 717 627-6630
Lititz (G-10045)

Schiller Grounds Care Inc ....D 215 322-4970
Huntingdon Valley (G-8035)

Scranton Sheet Metal Inc ....E 570 342-2904
Scranton (G-17288)

Sheet Metal Wkrs Local Un 19 ....G 215 952-1999
Philadelphia (G-14299)

Sk Sales Company Inc ....F 570 474-5600
Mountain Top (G-11775)

Somerset Welding & Steel Inc ....E 814 444-7000
Somerset (G-17709)

Somerset Welding & Steel Inc ....E 814 444-7000
Somerset (G-17711)

Ssm Industries Inc ....D 215 288-7777
Philadelphia (G-14337)

Stambaugh Metal Inc ....E 717 632-5957
Hanover (G-6958)

Standard Tool & Machine Co ....E 724 758-5522
Ellwood City (G-4951)

Stewart Welding & Fabg Inc ....D 717 252-3948
Wrightsville (G-20244)

Stewarts Fabrication Inc ....G 610 921-1600
Temple (G-18338)

Subcon Tl/Cctool Mch Group Inc ....E 814 456-7797
Erie (G-5494)

Suez Wts Systems Usa Inc ....C 724 743-0270
Canonsburg (G-2642)

Summers & Zims Inc ....E 610 593-2420
Atglen (G-809)

Superior Metal Products Co ....E 610 326-0607
Pottstown (G-16052)

Supply Technologies LLC ....E 724 745-8877
Carnegie (G-2797)

Tate Access Floors Inc ....C 717 244-4071
Red Lion (G-16617)

Tech Sheet Metal Company Inc ....F 724 539-3763
Bradenville (G-1952)

Titan Metal & Machine Co Inc ....G 724 747-9528
Washington (G-19232)

Union Roofing and Shtmtl Co ....E 814 946-0824
Altoona (G-553)

United States Steel Corp ....C 412 675-7459
West Mifflin (G-19746)

Vari Corporation ....G...... 570 385-0731
Schuylkill Haven (G-17169)
Versa-Fab Inc ....E...... 724 889-0137
New Kensington (G-12387)
Walter B Staller Inc ....G...... 570 385-5386
Schuylkill Haven (G-17171)
Walter Long Mfg Co Inc ....E...... 724 348-6631
Finleyville (G-5965)
Waste Gas Fabricating Co Inc ....E...... 215 736-9240
Fairless Hills (G-5807)
Watt Enterprises Inc ....G...... 570 698-8081
Lake Ariel (G-8896)
Weaver Metal Fab LLC ....F...... 717 466-6601
Ephrata (G-5155)
Wintercorp LLC ....G...... 717 848-3425
York (G-20712)
X-Mark/Cdt Inc ....G...... 724 228-7373
Washington (G-19248)
Zambotti Collision & Wldg Ctr ....G...... 724 545-2305
Kittanning (G-8804)

METAL FABRICATORS: Structural, Ship

Minnotte Manufacturing Corp ....D...... 412 373-5270
Trafford (G-18459)

METAL FABRICATORS: Structural, Ship

American Bridge Mfg Co ....E...... 412 631-3000
Coraopolis (G-3655)
American Bridge Mfg Co ....G...... 541 271-1100
Coraopolis (G-3656)
Bridges & Towers Inc ....F...... 724 654-6672
New Castle (G-12066)
Hayes Metal Fabrication LLC ....G...... 724 694-5280
Derry (G-4103)
Interlocking Deck Systems Inte ....D...... 412 682-3041
Sewickley (G-17395)
Jasper Steel Fabrication Inc ....G...... 570 329-3330
Williamsport (G-20027)
Robo Construction LLC ....E...... 570 494-1028
Williamsport (G-20069)

METAL FINISHING SVCS

Accu-Grind Inc ....D...... 814 965-5475
Johnsonburg (G-8343)
Allegheny Metal Finishing ....G...... 724 695-3233
Imperial (G-8057)
Allegheny Technologies Inc ....F...... 724 775-1554
Monaca (G-11279)
ATI Precision Finishing LLC ....G...... 724 775-1664
Rochester (G-16782)
ATI Precision Finishing LLC ....E...... 724 452-1726
Zelienople (G-20790)
Benco Technology LLC ....F...... 610 273-3364
Honey Brook (G-7738)
Blue Mountain Metal Finishing ....G...... 717 933-1643
Bethel (G-1393)
Bradford Allegheny Corporation ....F...... 814 368-4465
Lewis Run (G-9873)
Centria Inc ....F...... 724 251-2300
Ambridge (G-612)
Clark Metal Products Co ....C...... 724 459-7550
Blairsville (G-1719)
Dgm Custom Plsg Finsg C ....G...... 215 331-0960
Philadelphia (G-13627)
G Beswick Enterprises Inc ....G...... 412 829-3068
North Versailles (G-12775)
J P Cerini Technologies Inc ....G...... 215 457-7337
Philadelphia (G-13886)
James K Wallick ....G...... 717 471-8152
Lancaster (G-9070)
John R Armstrong ....G...... 717 464-3239
Willow Street (G-20152)
Lepko J D Finishing ....G...... 215 538-9717
Quakertown (G-16210)
Main Steel LLC ....D...... 724 453-3000
Harmony (G-7073)
Metal Finishing Industries ....G...... 724 836-1003
Greensburg (G-6688)
Molecular Finishing Systems ....G...... 724 695-0554
Imperial (G-8073)
Precision Finishing Inc ....E...... 215 257-6862
Quakertown (G-16232)
Surtech Industries Inc ....E...... 717 767-6808
York (G-20682)

METAL MINING SVCS

Alcoa World Alumina LLC ....E...... 412 315-2900
Pittsburgh (G-14670)

Cru Group ....G...... 724 940-7100
Wexford (G-19797)
Duquesne Mine Supply Company ....G...... 412 821-2100
Pittsburgh (G-14944)
E D I Enviro-Drill Inc ....F...... 412 788-1046
Pittsburgh (G-14949)
Latona Mining LLC ....F...... 570 654-3525
Pittston (G-15761)
McKay & Gould Drilling Inc ....E...... 724 436-6823
Darlington (G-4030)
McKinney Drilling Company LLC ....E...... 724 468-4139
Delmont (G-4051)
Metallurg Inc ....G...... 610 293-2501
Wayne (G-19355)
Metallurg Holdings Inc ....F...... 610 293-2501
Wayne (G-19356)
Mine Vision Systems Inc ....G...... 412 626-7461
Pittsburgh (G-15292)
Nexgen Industrial Services Inc ....E...... 724 592-5133
Rices Landing (G-16670)
Prco America Inc ....F...... 412 837-2798
Pittsburgh (G-15431)
Robindale Export LLC ....B...... 724 879-4264
Latrobe (G-9517)
Sheridan Supply Company Inc ....G...... 610 589-4361
Newmanstown (G-12484)
Surface Mining Reclamation Off ....G...... 717 782-4036
Harrisburg (G-7224)
Takraf Usa Inc ....F...... 215 822-4485
Lansdale (G-9413)

METAL ORES, NEC

Westmoreland Iron and Met LLC ....G...... 724 523-8151
Jeannette (G-8267)

METAL RESHAPING & REPLATING SVCS

Hollowell Aluminum ....G...... 717 597-0826
Waynesboro (G-19411)
Northwestern Welding & Mch Co ....G...... 814 774-2866
Lake City (G-8907)

METAL SERVICE CENTERS & OFFICES

Accent Metals Inc ....G...... 717 699-5676
York (G-20364)
Accent Metals Inc ....F...... 717 699-5676
York (G-20363)
Allegheny-Wagner Inds Inc ....E...... 724 468-4300
Delmont (G-4047)
Angstrom Sciences Inc ....E...... 412 469-8466
Duquesne (G-4495)
ATI Flat Rlled Pdts Hldngs LLC ....G...... 800 323-1240
Natrona Heights (G-11933)
ATI Precision Finishing LLC ....E...... 724 452-1726
Zelienople (G-20790)
Blair Strip Steel Company ....D...... 724 658-2611
New Castle (G-12064)
Cronimet Spcialty Mtls USA Inc ....E...... 724 347-2208
Wheatland (G-19835)
Dura-Bond Pipe LLC ....F...... 412 672-0764
McKeesport (G-10666)
EPI of Cleveland Inc ....D...... 330 468-2872
Pittsburgh (G-14980)
Federal Metal Products Inc ....G...... 610 847-2077
Ferndale (G-5950)
Handy & Harman Tube Co Inc ....B...... 610 539-3900
Norristown (G-12664)
High Steel Structures LLC ....G...... 717 299-5211
Lancaster (G-9049)
Keystone Flashing Co ....G...... 215 329-8500
Philadelphia (G-13930)
Kms Fab LLC ....E...... 570 338-0200
Luzerne (G-10125)
Metals Usa Inc ....F...... 215 540-8004
Fort Washington (G-6084)
ODonnell Metal Fabricators ....F...... 610 279-8810
Norristown (G-12697)
Specialty Steel Supply Co Inc ....F...... 215 949-8800
Fairless Hills (G-5798)
Speedwell Garage ....G...... 607 434-2376
Klingerstown (G-8808)
Techspec Inc ....E...... 724 694-2716
Derry (G-4108)
United States Steel Corp ....D...... 412 273-7000
Braddock (G-1950)
United States Steel Corp ....D...... 215 736-4000
Fairless Hills (G-5805)
Valley Quarries Inc ....G...... 814 766-2211
Fayetteville (G-5879)

METAL SPINNING FOR THE TRADE

Charles Schillinger Co Inc ....E...... 215 638-7200
Bensalem (G-1168)
E H Schwab Company ....E...... 412 823-5003
Turtle Creek (G-18564)
Langhorne Metal Spinning Inc ....G...... 215 497-8876
Langhorne (G-9307)

METAL STAMPING, FOR THE TRADE

A V Weber Co Inc ....G...... 215 699-3527
North Wales (G-12784)
Accutrex Products Inc ....C...... 724 746-4300
Canonsburg (G-2532)
Action Materials Inc ....G...... 610 377-3037
Lehighton (G-9709)
American Metal Finishers Inc ....F...... 610 323-1394
Pottstown (G-15964)
B-TEC Solutions Inc ....D...... 215 785-2400
Croydon (G-3911)
Backus Company ....E...... 814 887-5705
Smethport (G-17632)
Bhm Metal Products & Inds LLC ....G...... 570 785-2032
Crescent (G-3886)
C T E Inc ....E...... 717 767-6636
York (G-20416)
Coinco Inc ....E...... 814 425-7407
Cochranton (G-3337)
Corona Corporation ....F...... 215 679-9538
Red Hill (G-16580)
F B F Inc ....E...... 215 322-7110
Southampton (G-17811)
F B F Industries Inc ....D...... 215 322-7110
Southampton (G-17812)
Falls Mfg Co ....D...... 215 736-2557
Fairless Hills (G-5778)
G G Greene Enterprises Inc ....E...... 814 723-5700
Warren (G-19027)
Gcl Inc ....F...... 724 282-2221
Butler (G-2403)
Glenfield Supply Company Inc ....G...... 412 781-8188
Pittsburgh (G-15051)
HMS Industries Inc ....E...... 724 459-5090
Blairsville (G-1724)
Igs Industries Inc ....C...... 724 222-5800
Meadow Lands (G-10690)
J & R Metal Products LLC ....G...... 717 656-6241
Leola (G-9788)
Jade Holdings Inc ....C...... 215 947-3333
Huntingdon Valley (G-8000)
Kimjohn Industries Inc ....F...... 610 436-8600
West Chester (G-19582)
Leefson Tool & Die Company ....E...... 610 461-7772
Folcroft (G-6008)
Lewistown Manufacturing Inc ....F...... 717 242-1468
Lewistown (G-9938)
New Standard Corporation ....D...... 717 757-9450
York (G-20611)
Norwood Manufacture Co LLC ....G...... 724 652-0698
New Castle (G-12134)
Oberg Industries Inc ....A...... 724 295-2121
Freeport (G-6209)
Oberg Industries Inc ....C...... 724 353-9700
Sarver (G-17074)
Oberg Industries Inc ....C...... 724 353-9700
Sarver (G-17075)
Penn Metal Stamping Inc ....E...... 814 834-7171
Kersey (G-8565)
Pilot-Run Stamping Company ....E...... 440 255-8821
Corry (G-3772)
Specialty Products Inc ....C...... 814 455-6978
Erie (G-5486)
Tate Access Floors Inc ....C...... 717 244-4071
Red Lion (G-16616)
The Keystone Friction Hinge Co ....C...... 570 321-0693
Williamsport (G-20082)
Tonnard Manufacturing Corp ....D...... 814 664-7794
Corry (G-3776)
Tooling Dynamics LLC ....C...... 717 764-8873
York (G-20690)
Tottser Tool and Die Shop Inc ....D...... 215 357-7600
Southampton (G-17842)
Tucker Industries Incorporated ....D...... 215 638-1900
Bensalem (G-1265)
United Fabricating Inc ....F...... 724 663-5891
Claysville (G-3209)

METAL STAMPINGS: Perforated

Diamond Manufacturing Company ....C...... 570 693-0300
Wyoming (G-20275)

PRODUCT

Diamond Manufacturing Company ....F 570 693-0300
Wyoming (G-20276)
Ferguson Perforating Company ....E 724 657-8703
New Castle (G-12092)
Hendrick Manufacturing Company ......G 570 282-1010
Carbondale (G-2677)
Orbel Corporation ....E 610 829-5000
Easton (G-4736)
Quality Perforating Inc ....D 570 267-2092
Carbondale (G-2685)

METAL TREATING COMPOUNDS

Arkema Delaware Inc ....A 610 205-7000
King of Prussia (G-8582)
Arkema Inc ....C 215 826-2600
Bristol (G-2109)
Engineered Pressed Materials ....G 814 772-6127
Ridgway (G-16707)
Haas Chem Managmt of Mexico ....F 610 656-7454
West Chester (G-19558)
Mg Industrial Products Inc ....G 814 255-2471
Johnstown (G-8408)

METAL TREATING: Cryogenic

Advanced Research Systems Inc ....E 610 967-2120
Macungie (G-10138)
Cryo Tempering Tech of Ne PA ....G 570 287-7443
Kingston (G-8715)

METAL, TITANIUM: Sponge & Granules

Oregon Metallurgical LLC ....F 541 967-9000
Pittsburgh (G-15363)
Titanium Metals Corporation ....E 702 564-2544
Morgantown (G-11539)

METAL: Battery

Vargo Outdoors Incorporated ....G 570 437-0990
Lewisburg (G-9923)

METALS SVC CENTERS & WHOL: Structural Shapes, Iron Or Steel

Baileys Steel & Supply LLC ....G 724 267-4648
Waynesburg (G-19433)

METALS SVC CENTERS & WHOLESALERS: Bars, Metal

Clipper Pipe & Service Inc ....G 610 872-9067
Eddystone (G-4799)
East Coast Metals Inc ....E 215 256-9550
Harleysville (G-7031)
Farm-Bilt Machine LLC ....F 717 442-5020
Gap (G-6251)

METALS SVC CENTERS & WHOLESALERS: Cable, Wire

Squid Wire LLC ....G 484 235-5155
Conshohocken (G-3606)

METALS SVC CENTERS & WHOLESALERS: Copper Prdts

Eastern Tool Steel Service Inc ....G 814 834-7224
Saint Marys (G-16967)
Stimple and Ward Company ....E 412 364-5200
Pittsburgh (G-15584)

METALS SVC CENTERS & WHOLESALERS: Forgings, Ferrous

Erie Forge and Steel Inc ....D 814 452-2300
Erie (G-5267)
Goldsborough & Vansant Inc ....G 724 782-0393
Finleyville (G-5959)
Stainless Distributors Inc ....G 215 369-9746
Yardley (G-20341)

METALS SVC CENTERS & WHOLESALERS: Iron & Steel Prdt, Ferrous

Cronimet Corporation ....D 724 375-5004
Aliquippa (G-71)
Dreistern Inc ....G 215 799-0220
Telford (G-18284)
J B Booth and Co ....F 724 452-8400
Zelienople (G-20805)

Rose Corporation ....D 610 376-5004
Reading (G-16504)
Worthington Armstrong Intl LLC ....G 610 722-1200
Malvern (G-10350)
Worthington Armstrong Venture ....C 610 722-1200
Malvern (G-10351)

METALS SVC CENTERS & WHOLESALERS: Lead

Hammond Group Inc ....E 610 327-1400
Pottstown (G-15995)

METALS SVC CENTERS & WHOLESALERS: Misc Nonferrous Prdts

Liberty Electronics Inc ....B 814 432-7505
Franklin (G-6148)

METALS SVC CENTERS & WHOLESALERS: Nonferrous Sheets, Etc

Brock Associates LLC ....F 412 919-0690
Pittsburgh (G-14793)

METALS SVC CENTERS & WHOLESALERS: Piling, Iron & Steel

Iusa Wire Inc ....G 610 926-4141
Reading (G-16410)

METALS SVC CENTERS & WHOLESALERS: Pipe & Tubing, Steel

Advanced Drainage Systems Inc ....E 570 546-7686
Muncy (G-11805)
Forsht Concrete Pdts Co Inc ....G 814 944-1617
Altoona (G-507)
J-M Manufacturing Company Inc ....D 814 337-7675
Cochranton (G-3343)
Lane Enterprises Inc ....E 610 272-4531
King of Prussia (G-8637)
Pipe & Precast Cnstr Pdts Inc ....F 610 644-7338
Devault (G-4112)
Trojan Tube Sls & Fabrications ....F 570 546-8860
Muncy (G-11836)

METALS SVC CENTERS & WHOLESALERS: Rails & Access

United Fence Supply Company ....G 570 307-0782
Olyphant (G-13002)
Vossloh Track Material Inc ....D 610 926-5400
Reading (G-16560)

METALS SVC CENTERS & WHOLESALERS: Rope, Wire, Exc Insulated

American Lifting Products Inc ....E 610 384-1300
Coatesville (G-3287)
Nelson Wire Rope Corporation ....F 215 721-9449
Hatfield (G-7373)

METALS SVC CENTERS & WHOLESALERS: Sheets, Metal

Diamond Manufacturing Company ....F 570 693-0300
Wyoming (G-20276)
M D Cline Metal Fabg Inc ....G 724 459-8968
Blairsville (G-1733)
T Bruce Sales Inc ....D 724 528-9961
West Middlesex (G-19731)

METALS SVC CENTERS & WHOLESALERS: Steel

A C Grinding & Supply Co Inc ....G 215 946-3760
Levittown (G-9811)
Agar Welding Service & Stl Sup ....E 717 532-1000
Walnut Bottom (G-18788)
Bassett Industries Inc ....E 610 327-1200
Pottstown (G-15965)
Brandywine Machine Co Inc ....F 610 269-1221
Downingtown (G-4216)
Cambridge-Lee Holdings Inc ....F 610 926-4141
Reading (G-16340)
Cambridge-Lee Industries LLC ....C 610 926-4141
Reading (G-16341)
Charter Dura-Bar Inc ....F 717 779-0807
York (G-20424)

Coilplus Inc ....D 215 331-5200
Philadelphia (G-13559)
Colonial Metal Products Inc ....E 724 346-5550
Hermitage (G-7579)
Ellwood Specialty Steel Co ....D 724 657-1160
New Castle (G-12088)
Exim Steel & Shipbroking Inc ....G 215 369-9746
Yardley (G-20310)
High Industries Inc ....B 717 293-4444
Lancaster (G-9046)
Jadco Manufacturing Inc ....E 724 452-5252
Harmony (G-7070)
Joseph T Ryerson & Son Inc ....F 215 736-8970
Morrisville (G-11565)
Kloeckner Metals Corporation ....D 717 755-1923
York (G-20557)
Ls Steel Inc ....G 717 669-4581
Coatesville (G-3314)
M Glosser & Sons Inc ....E 412 751-4700
Mc Keesport (G-10642)
Martins Steel LLC ....G 570 966-3775
Mifflinburg (G-11097)
National Material LP ....E 724 337-6551
New Kensington (G-12362)
Olympic Steel Inc ....E 717 709-1515
Chambersburg (G-2966)
ORourke & Sons Inc ....E 610 436-0932
West Chester (G-19613)
R G Steel Corp ....D 724 656-1722
Pulaski (G-16126)
Rearden Steel Fabrication Inc ....F 717 503-1989
Lemoyne (G-9750)
Riise Inc ....G 724 528-3305
West Middlesex (G-19729)
Rolled Steel Products Corp PA ....G 610 647-6264
Berwyn (G-1374)
Sb Specialty Metals LLC ....G 814 337-8804
Meadville (G-10788)
Scranton Craftsmen Inc ....D 570 347-5125
Throop (G-18361)
Triumph Group Operations Inc ....F 610 251-1000
Berwyn (G-1386)

METALS SVC CENTERS & WHOLESALERS: Steel Decking

DSI-Lang Geotech LLC ....G 610 268-2221
Toughkenamon (G-18418)
Juniata Concrete Co ....E 717 436-2176
Mifflintown (G-11125)

METALS SVC CENTERS & WHOLESALERS: Tubing, Metal

Keystone Powdered Metal Co ....B 814 781-1591
Saint Marys (G-16984)
Superior Group Inc ....E 610 397-2040
Conshohocken (G-3610)

METALS SVC CENTERS/WHOL: Forms, Steel Concrete Construction

Greg Kiser ....G 814 425-1678
Utica (G-18696)

METALS SVC CNTRS & WHOL: Metal Wires, Ties, Cables/Screening

Quality Wire Forming ....G 717 656-4478
Leola (G-9799)
Yarde Metals Inc ....G 610 495-7545
Limerick (G-9972)

METALS SVC CTRS & WHOLESALERS: Aluminum Bars, Rods, Etc

Bethlehem Aluminum Inc ....F 610 432-4541
Allentown (G-150)
Hadco Aluminum & Metal Corp PA ....D 215 695-2705
Philadelphia (G-13795)
Korsak Glass & Aluminum Inc ....G 610 987-9888
Boyertown (G-1923)

METALS: Antifriction Bearing, Lead-Base

New Way Machine Components Inc ......E 610 494-6700
Aston (G-781)

METALS: Precious NEC

A Plus Precious Metals ....G...... 215 821-3751
Philadelphia *(G-13328)*
Crown Precious Metals ....G...... 267 923-5263
Pennsburg *(G-13247)*
Dallice Precious Metals ....G...... 570 501-0850
Hazleton *(G-7496)*
Geneva Roth International LLC ....G...... 724 887-8771
Scottdale *(G-17192)*
Gold Bug Exchange.........................G...... 724 770-9008
Beaver *(G-982)*
Heraeus Incorporated ....G...... 215 944-9981
Yardley *(G-20314)*
Heraeus Kulzer LLC ....G...... 215 944-9968
Langhorne *(G-9302)*
Hipps Sons Coins Precious Mtls..........G...... 215 550-6854
Newtown *(G-12511)*
Pyropure Inc ....E...... 610 497-1743
Aston *(G-789)*

METALS: Precious, Secondary

Profiners Inc ....G...... 215 997-1060
Hatfield *(G-7387)*

METALS: Primary Nonferrous, NEC

Allegheny Technologies Inc................D...... 412 394-2800
Pittsburgh *(G-14682)*
Alpha Assembly Solutions Inc ....C...... 814 946-1611
Altoona *(G-470)*
AMG Aluminum North America LLC ....F....... 610 293-2501
Wayne *(G-19297)*
ATI Powder Metals LLC ....D...... 412 394-2800
Pittsburgh *(G-14732)*
Global Advanced Metals USA Inc.........D...... 610 367-2181
Boyertown *(G-1912)*
Hammond Group Inc ....E...... 610 327-1400
Pottstown *(G-15995)*
Heraeus Incorporated ....B...... 480 961-9200
Yardley *(G-20315)*
KB Alloys Holdings LLC ....F....... 484 582-3520
Wayne *(G-19345)*
Luxfer Magtech Inc ....E...... 570 668-0001
Tamaqua *(G-18219)*
Matthey Johnson Inc ....C...... 610 648-8000
West Chester *(G-19598)*
Reichdrill LLC ....D...... 814 342-5500
Philipsburg *(G-14525)*
Tdy Industries LLC ....D...... 412 394-2896
Pittsburgh *(G-15600)*
Thermoclad Company ....F....... 814 456-1243
Erie *(G-5507)*
TI Oregon Inc ....G...... 412 394-2800
Pittsburgh *(G-15624)*

METALWORK: Miscellaneous

A & L Iron Works LLC ....G...... 717 768-0705
Narvon *(G-11915)*
Acco Mtl Hdlg Solutions Inc ....D...... 800 967-7333
York *(G-20365)*
Alumax LLC ....C...... 412 553-4545
Pittsburgh *(G-14695)*
Baileys Steel & Supply LLC ....G...... 724 267-4648
Waynesburg *(G-19433)*
Brandywine Valley Fabricators...........F....... 610 384-7440
Coatesville *(G-3295)*
C & C Welding and Fabg Inc ....G...... 814 387-6556
Clarence *(G-3161)*
Centria Inc ....C...... 412 299-8000
Moon Township *(G-11483)*
Craft-Bilt Manufacturing Co ....D...... 215 721-7700
Souderton *(G-17731)*
Dek Machine Co Inc ....G...... 215 794-5791
Mechanicsville *(G-10911)*
DMS Shredding Inc ....F....... 570 819-3339
Hanover Township *(G-6988)*
Doerschner Machine.........................G...... 724 625-1350
Mars *(G-10494)*
Dura-Bilt Products Inc ....D...... 570 596-2000
Gillett *(G-6380)*
Enhanced Sintered Products Inc..........G...... 814 834-2470
Saint Marys *(G-16973)*
Guida Inc ....E...... 215 727-2222
Marcus Hook *(G-10444)*
Hunter Highway Inc ....F....... 570 454-8161
Lattimer Mines *(G-9530)*
Industrial Polsg & Grinding ....D...... 717 854-9001
York *(G-20536)*

Kreico LLC......................................G...... 717 228-7312
Lebanon *(G-9595)*
Laneko Roll Form Inc ....E...... 215 822-1930
Hatfield *(G-7363)*
Martellis Mtal Fabrication Inc..............E...... 215 957-9700
Ivyland *(G-8217)*
Morgan Brothers Company.................F....... 724 843-7485
Beaver Falls *(G-1006)*
Mpc Industries LLC ....E...... 717 393-4100
Lancaster *(G-9138)*
Omni Fab Inc ....F....... 724 334-8851
New Kensington *(G-12364)*
P G A Machine Co Inc ....G...... 610 874-1335
Eddystone *(G-4806)*
Pennsylvania Insert Corp ....F....... 610 474-0112
Royersford *(G-16860)*
Rapid Reaction Inc ....G...... 814 432-9832
Franklin *(G-6155)*
Roll Forming Corp - Sharon ....E...... 724 982-0400
Farrell *(G-5873)*
Standard Metal Industries LLC ....G...... 610 377-5400
Lehighton *(G-9728)*
Standard Tool & Machine Co ....E...... 724 758-5522
Ellwood City *(G-4951)*
Van Varick Inc ....G...... 610 588-9997
Bangor *(G-932)*
Walter Long Mfg Co Inc ....E...... 724 348-6631
Finleyville *(G-5965)*
Welding Technologies Inc ....F....... 814 432-0954
Franklin *(G-6169)*
Zenzel III Michael ....G...... 570 752-2666
Berwick *(G-1350)*

METALWORK: Ornamental

Hampton Concrete Products Inc ....F....... 724 443-7205
Valencia *(G-18698)*
Joseph Lee & Son Inc........................G...... 610 825-1944
Lafayette Hill *(G-8883)*
Louis Emmel Co ....G...... 412 859-6781
Boyers *(G-1889)*
Lux Ornamental Iron Works Inc............G...... 412 481-5677
Pittsburgh *(G-15243)*
Peter Mamienski...............................G...... 215 822-3293
Hatfield *(G-7381)*
Redstar Ironworks LLC ....G...... 412 821-3630
Pittsburgh *(G-15474)*
Shedaker Metal Arts Inc ....E...... 215 788-3383
Croydon *(G-3928)*
Swick Ornamental Iron ....G...... 412 487-5755
Gibsonia *(G-6354)*
Termaco USA Inc ....E...... 610 916-2600
Reading *(G-16535)*
Wilmington Metalcraft ....G...... 717 442-9834
Gap *(G-6258)*

METALWORKING MACHINERY WHOLESALERS

Engineered Pressed Materials ....G...... 814 834-3189
Saint Marys *(G-16972)*
Industrial Consortium Inc....................F....... 610 777-1653
Mohnton *(G-11267)*
Marando Industries Inc.......................G...... 610 621-2536
Reading *(G-16437)*
Weaver Sheet Metal LLC ....F....... 717 733-4763
Ephrata *(G-5156)*

METERING DEVICES: Gas Meters, Domestic & Large Cap, Indl

Invensys Energy Metering Corp............B...... 814 371-3011
Du Bois *(G-4396)*
Sensus USA Inc ....G...... 800 375-8875
Du Bois *(G-4419)*
Sensus USA Inc ....C...... 724 430-3956
Pittsburgh *(G-15524)*

METERING DEVICES: Integrating & Totalizing, Gas & Liquids

Elster American Meter Co LLC ....G...... 412 833-2550
Pittsburgh *(G-14965)*
Maguire Products Inc ....E...... 610 459-4300
Aston *(G-773)*

METERING DEVICES: Positive Displacement Meters

FMC Technologies Measurement S......C...... 281 591-4000
Erie *(G-5297)*

METERING DEVICES: Rotary Type

Seventy-Three Mfg Co Inc ....E...... 610 845-7823
Bechtelsville *(G-1037)*

METERING DEVICES: Water Quality Monitoring & Control Systems

Sensus Metering Systems-North.........A...... 724 439-7700
Uniontown *(G-18639)*
Sensus USA Inc ....C...... 814 375-8354
Du Bois *(G-4418)*
Sensus USA Inc ....B...... 724 439-7700
Uniontown *(G-18640)*
Wellspring Wireless Inc......................F....... 215 788-8485
Bensalem *(G-1271)*

METERS: Elasped Time

Maxima Tech & Systems LLC ....C...... 717 581-1000
Lancaster *(G-9130)*

METERS: Hydrometers, Indl Process

Francis L Freas Glass Works................E...... 610 828-0430
Conshohocken *(G-3549)*
G & W Instruments Inc ....G...... 570 282-7352
Carbondale *(G-2676)*

METERS: Magnetic Flow, Indl Process

Lawco Inc ....G...... 717 691-6965
Enola *(G-5082)*

MGMT CONSULTING SVCS: Matls, Incl Purch, Handle & Invntry

D-K Trading Corporation Inc................G...... 570 586-9662
Clarks Summit *(G-3191)*

MGT SVCS, FACIL SUPPT: Base Maint Or Provide Personnel

Hawk Industrial Services LLC..............F....... 717 658-4332
Chambersburg *(G-2939)*

MICROCIRCUITS, INTEGRATED: Semiconductor

Agere Systems Inc...........................A...... 610 712-1000
Allentown *(G-118)*
Applied Micro Circuits Corp ....E...... 267 757-8722
Newtown *(G-12496)*
National Hybrid Inc ....D...... 814 467-9060
Windber *(G-20190)*
Quad Tron Inc..................................G...... 215 441-9303
Warminster *(G-18949)*

MICROFILM EQPT

Mobile Video Corporation ....F....... 215 863-1072
Broomall *(G-2299)*

MICROFILM SVCS

Craddock & Lerro Associates...............G...... 610 543-0200
Drexel Hill *(G-4363)*
Griffith Inc......................................C...... 215 322-8100
Huntingdon Valley *(G-7992)*
Threshold Rhblitation Svcs Inc ....B...... 610 777-7691
Reading *(G-16538)*

MICROPROCESSORS

Intel Homes Ltd Liability Co.................G...... 570 872-9559
East Stroudsburg *(G-4620)*
Intervideo Inc..................................G...... 717 435-9433
Lancaster *(G-9061)*
Sentinel Power Inc ....G...... 724 925-8181
New Stanton *(G-12451)*

MICROSCOPES

Bioptechs Inc..................................F....... 724 282-7145
Butler *(G-2380)*

MICROSCOPES: Electron & Proton

Wel Instrument Co ....G...... 724 625-9041
Mars *(G-10513)*

PRODUCT

MICROWAVE COMPONENTS

Clear Microwave Inc ....F 610 844-6421
  Malvern (G-10211)
Corry Micronics Inc ....F 814 664-7728
  Corry (G-3754)
Dbwave Technologies LLC ....G 412 345-8081
  Cranberry Township (G-3815)
Epoxtal LLC ....G 908 376-9825
  Philadelphia (G-13676)
Herley Industries Inc ....G 717 397-2779
  Lancaster (G-9044)
Herley Industries Inc ....B 717 397-2777
  Lancaster (G-9043)
L3 Technologies Inc ....C 267 545-7000
  Bristol (G-2157)
Micro-Coax Inc ....C 610 495-4438
  Pottstown (G-16019)
Microsphere Inc ....G 610 444-3450
  Kennett Square (G-8528)
National Magnetics Group Inc ....D 610 867-6003
  Bethlehem (G-1582)
Spectrum Microwave Inc ....D 814 474-4300
  Fairview (G-5847)
Spectrum Microwave Inc ....D 215 464-0586
  Philadelphia (G-14333)
Spectrum Microwave Inc ....E 814 272-2700
  State College (G-18033)
Trak Ceramics Inc ....E 610 867-7600
  Bethlehem (G-1640)

MILITARY GOODS & REGALIA STORES

Chestnut Group Inc ....G 610 688-3300
  Wayne (G-19313)

MILITARY INSIGNIA

Gohn Mfg ....G 717 426-3875
  Marietta (G-10463)
Malatesta Enterprises ....F 570 752-2516
  Berwick (G-1334)

MILITARY INSIGNIA, TEXTILE

Otte Gear LLC ....G 917 923-6230
  New Hope (G-12311)

MILL PRDTS: Structural & Rail

Arcelormittal Steelton LLC ....A 717 986-2000
  Steelton (G-18044)
Progress Rail Services Corp ....E 610 779-2039
  Reading (G-16476)

MILLINERY SUPPLIES: Veils & Veiling, Bridal, Funeral, Etc

Priscilla of Boston Inc ....D 610 943-5000
  Conshohocken (G-3592)

MILLING: Cereal Flour, Exc Rice

Curry Flour Mills Inc ....F 717 838-2421
  Palmyra (G-13119)
F M Browns Sons Incorporated ....E 610 944-7654
  Fleetwood (G-5972)

MILLING: Chemical

Lancaster Metals Science Corp ....E 717 299-9709
  Lancaster (G-9102)

MILLING: Grains, Exc Rice

ADM Milling Co ....E 717 737-0529
  Camp Hill (G-2485)
Cornell Bros Inc ....F 570 376-2471
  Middlebury Center (G-11043)

MILLS: Bar

Titan Metal & Machine Co Inc ....G 724 747-9528
  Washington (G-19232)

MILLS: Ferrous & Nonferrous

S S Salvage Recycling Inc ....F 717 444-0008
  Liverpool (G-10079)

MILLWORK

84 Lumber Company ....B 724 228-8820
  Eighty Four (G-4830)

A & V Woodwork Co ....F 215 727-8832
  Philadelphia (G-13322)
Abel Millwork LLC ....G 412 296-2254
  Finleyville (G-5951)
Ajjp Corporation ....C 215 968-6677
  Newtown (G-12495)
Al Lorenzi Lumber Co Inc ....D 724 222-6100
  Canonsburg (G-2534)
Allegheny Millwork Pbt ....C 724 873-8700
  Lawrence (G-9534)
Allensville Planing Mill Inc ....F 717 248-9688
  Lewistown (G-9924)
AMD Group Inc ....G 610 972-4491
  Riegelsville (G-16743)
American Mllwk & Cabinetry Inc ....E 610 965-0040
  Emmaus (G-5019)
American Wood Design Inc ....F 302 792-2100
  Chester (G-3039)
Appalachian Millwork ....G 724 539-1944
  Latrobe (G-9456)
Appalachian Wood Products Inc ....B 814 765-2003
  Clearfield (G-3212)
Architectural Millwork Assoc ....G 215 699-0346
  North Wales (G-12789)
Asels Cabinet Company ....G 814 677-3063
  Rouseville (G-16835)
B & L Woodworking ....G 717 354-5430
  Kinzers (G-8732)
Barmah Co ....G 724 539-8477
  Latrobe (G-9459)
Beam S Custom Woodworking ....F 610 286-9040
  Morgantown (G-11518)
Beaver Dam Woodworks LLC ....G 610 273-7656
  Honey Brook (G-7737)
Bentley & Collins Company ....F 570 546-3250
  Muncy (G-11810)
Biltwood Architectural Mllwk ....F 717 593-9400
  Greencastle (G-6600)
BMC East LLC ....E 717 866-2167
  Myerstown (G-11877)
Boswell Lumber Company ....E 814 629-5625
  Boswell (G-1881)
Bounds Wood Products Ltd ....G 215 646-2122
  North Wales (G-12793)
Brampton Entp & Design LLC ....G 484 678-4855
  Thorndale (G-18353)
Brandywine Woodworks LLC ....G 610 793-7979
  West Chester (G-19514)
Breezecraft LLC ....G 717 397-8584
  Lancaster (G-8958)
Bristol Millwork Co Inc ....F 215 533-1921
  Philadelphia (G-13484)
Brookside Woodworks ....G 717 768-0241
  Narvon (G-11917)
Campbells Custom Woodworks LLC .....G 484 300-4175
  Pottstown (G-15969)
Cantwell Woodworking LLC ....E 215 710-3030
  Fort Washington (G-6064)
Carpenter Shop Inc ....F 814 848-7448
  Ulysses (G-18601)
Cedars Wdwkg & Renovations LLC ......F 717 392-1736
  Lancaster (G-8972)
Center Hardwood LLC ....F 814 684-3600
  Tyrone (G-18579)
Cider Press Woodworks LLC ....G 215 804-1100
  Quakertown (G-16178)
Ciw Enterprises Inc ....E 800 233-8366
  Mountain Top (G-11755)
Clear Visions Inc ....G 717 236-4526
  Harrisburg (G-7106)
Closet-Tier ....G 412 421-7838
  Pittsburgh (G-14862)
Conoco Woodworking ....G 717 536-3948
  Blain (G-1710)
Contemprary Artisans Cabinetry ....E 215 723-8803
  Telford (G-18276)
Cornellcookson Inc ....C 570 474-6773
  Mountain Top (G-11757)
Cornerstone Woodworks LLC ....G 717 866-0230
  Myerstown (G-11880)
Craig A Scholedice Inc ....F 610 683-8910
  Kutztown (G-8838)
Custom Doorcraft LLC ....F 717 768-7613
  Bird In Hand (G-1672)
Custom Stair Builders Inc ....G 717 261-0551
  Chambersburg (G-2922)
D and S Artistic Wdwkg LLC ....G 973 495-7008
  Henryville (G-7566)
D and S Artistic Wdwkg LLC ....G 973 495-7008
  Stroudsburg (G-18113)

D G Woodworks LLC ....G 215 368-8001
  Lansdale (G-9356)
Dennis Downing ....G 724 598-0043
  New Castle (G-12081)
Dimpter Woodworking ....G 215 855-2335
  Lansdale (G-9361)
Dmm Woodworking ....G 717 390-2828
  Lancaster (G-8999)
Donald Beiswenger Inc ....G 814 886-8341
  Gallitzin (G-6245)
Dp Millwork Inc ....G 215 996-1179
  Hatfield (G-7335)
E B Endres Inc ....E 814 643-1860
  Huntingdon (G-7942)
Eagle Woodworking LLC ....G 484 764-7275
  Northampton (G-12849)
Ed Nicholson & Sons Lumber Co ....F 724 628-4440
  Connellsville (G-3496)
Eden Inc ....E 814 797-1160
  Knox (G-8809)
Eisenhardt Mills Inc ....E 610 253-2791
  Easton (G-4677)
Elc Manufacturing ....G 570 655-3060
  West Pittston (G-19755)
Eli K Lapp Jr ....G 717 768-0258
  Gordonville (G-6553)
Everite Door Company ....F 814 652-5143
  Everett (G-5571)
Fishers Woodworking ....G 570 725-2310
  Loganton (G-10095)
Forest Hill Woodworking ....G 717 806-0193
  Paradise (G-13157)
Forest Ridge Woodworking ....G 717 442-3191
  Paradise (G-13158)
Foster-Kmetz Woodworking ....G 570 325-8222
  Jim Thorpe (G-8340)
Frank Daddario Wdwrkng ....G 610 476-3414
  Audubon (G-825)
Freedom Millwork Corp ....G 215 642-2213
  Pipersville (G-14616)
Fulton Forest Products ....E 814 782-3448
  Shippenville (G-17561)
Gene Forrey Millwork ....F 717 285-4046
  Mountville (G-11795)
Glenn A Hissim Woodworking LLC ....G 610 847-8961
  Kintnersville (G-8727)
Glicks Woodworking ....G 717 768-8958
  Gordonville (G-6556)
Goebelwood Industries Inc ....F 610 532-4644
  Folsom (G-6024)
Greenville Wood Products Inc ....G 724 646-1193
  Greenville (G-6743)
Grothouse Lumber Company ....F 610 767-6515
  Germansville (G-6278)
Haas Architectural Mllwk Inc ....E 717 840-4227
  York (G-20519)
Hampton Cabinet Shop ....G 717 898-7806
  Manheim (G-10387)
Hand Crafted Furniture Co Inc ....G 717 630-0036
  Hanover (G-6891)
Hardwoods Millworking ....G 814 395-5474
  Confluence (G-3465)
Harris Woodworking ....G 610 932-2646
  Oxford (G-13080)
Harvest Moon Woodworking ....G 717 521-4204
  Mc Sherrystown (G-10651)
Highpoint Woodworks LLC ....G 610 346-7739
  Coopersburg (G-3629)
Hoff Enterprises Inc ....E 814 535-8371
  Johnstown (G-8381)
Hoff Woodworking ....G 717 259-6040
  East Berlin (G-4522)
Horstcraft Millworks LLC ....G 717 694-9222
  Richfield (G-16680)
Innovative Displays ....G 570 386-8121
  New Ringgold (G-12439)
J C Snavely & Sons Inc ....E 717 291-8989
  Lancaster (G-9068)
J D R Fixtures Inc ....E 610 323-6599
  Pottstown (G-16003)
James Richard Woodworking ....F 717 397-4790
  Lancaster (G-9071)
Jay Zimmerman ....G 717 445-7246
  East Earl (G-4546)
JC Woodworking Inc ....G 215 651-2049
  Quakertown (G-16203)
JC Woodworking Inc ....F 215 651-2049
  Sellersville (G-17351)
Jeffrey R Knudsen ....G 717 529-4011
  Kirkwood (G-8749)

John J Peachey ....F 717 667-9373
Reedsville (G-16625)

Jonathan Fallos Cabinetmaker ....G 610 253-4063
Easton (G-4709)

Joseph Mikstas ....G 215 271-2419
Philadelphia (G-13911)

K & L Woodworking Inc ....E 610 372-0738
Reading (G-16417)

Keystone Wood Turning ....G 717 354-2435
Ephrata (G-5114)

Kilbane Wood Creations ....G 814 664-0563
Union City (G-18608)

Knock On Woodwork ....G 717 579-8179
Mechanicsburg (G-10865)

Koch S Custom Woodworking ....G 610 261-2607
Northampton (G-12854)

Larkin C Company Inc ....G 610 696-9096
West Chester (G-19586)

Lb Woodworking LLC ....G 570 729-0000
Beach Lake (G-974)

Legacy Restoration LLC ....G 716 239-0695
Philadelphia (G-13965)

Leidys Custom Woodworking ....G 717 328-9323
Mercersburg (G-10990)

Lexyline Millwork ....E 267 895-1733
Doylestown (G-4312)

Lignitech Inc ....F 814 474-9590
Fairview (G-5832)

Locust Ridge Woodworks LLC ....G 610 350-6029
Kirkwood (G-8750)

M & M Cabinets LLC ....G 412 220-9663
Cecil (G-2822)

M & R Woodworks Inc ....G 724 378-7677
Aliquippa (G-81)

Mario Dinardo Jr Custom WD Wkg ......E 610 495-7010
Pottstown (G-16015)

Master Woodcraft Corporation ....E 724 225-5530
Washington (G-19201)

Merrigan Corporation ....F 610 317-6300
Bethlehem (G-1568)

MI Windows and Doors Inc ....C 570 682-1206
Hegins (G-7543)

Millwork Solutions Inc ....E 814 446-4009
Seward (G-17382)

Millwork Specialties ....G 610 261-2878
Northampton (G-12855)

Morris Millwork LLC ....G 215 667-1889
Philadelphia (G-14039)

Morris Millwork LLC ....G 215 736-0708
Yardley (G-20327)

Mountain Mouldings ....F 814 535-8563
Johnstown (G-8410)

Moxham Lumber Co ....E 814 536-5186
Johnstown (G-8411)

National Woodworks LLC ....G 412 431-7071
Pittsburgh (G-15322)

Neshaminy Valley Millwork ....F 215 604-0251
Bensalem (G-1230)

Northern Millwork Inc ....F 215 393-7242
Lansdale (G-9394)

Oakes & McClelland Co ....F 724 588-6400
Greenville (G-6761)

Old Town Woodworking Inc ....G 570 562-2117
Old Forge (G-12972)

Oskis Woodworks ....G 215 444-0523
Warminster (G-18935)

P & H Lumber Millwork Co Inc ....E 215 699-9365
North Wales (G-12822)

Pappajohn Woodworking Inc ....G 215 289-8625
Philadelphia (G-14117)

Peyty Construction ....G 570 764-5995
Bloomsburg (G-1793)

Philadelphia Woodworks LLC ....G 267 331-5880
Philadelphia (G-14160)

Phoenix Woodworking Inc ....F 610 209-9030
East Earl (G-4553)

Pioneer Woodcrafts LLC ....F 717 656-0776
Leola (G-9797)

Pittston Lumber & Mfg Co ....E 570 654-3328
Pittston (G-15776)

Port Richmond Millwork ....G 215 423-4803
Philadelphia (G-14190)

Precision Millwork & Cabinetry ....E 814 445-9669
Somerset (G-17700)

Presta Contractor Supply Inc ....E 814 833-0655
Erie (G-5436)

Quality Millwork Inc ....G 412 831-3500
Finleyville (G-5964)

R & C Foltz LLC ....F 717 927-9771
Brogue (G-2239)

RAD Mfg LLC ....E 570 752-4514
Nescopeck (G-12002)

Ralston Shop Inc ....F 610 268-3829
Avondale (G-858)

Randy George Wdwkg Cstm Signs ......G 724 514-7201
Canonsburg (G-2623)

Recon Enterprises ....G 570 836-1179
Tunkhannock (G-18548)

Rehmeyer Precision Mllwk Inc ....F 717 235-0607
Shrewsbury (G-17587)

Ridgeview Forest Products LLC ....E 717 423-6465
Shippensburg (G-17544)

Roderick Duvall ....G 814 735-4969
Crystal Spring (G-3938)

Rolands Special Millwork Inc ....G 215 885-5588
Glenside (G-6534)

Rosenberry Bros Lumber Co ....F 717 349-7196
Fannettsburg (G-5858)

Roth Woodworking LLC ....G 717 476-8609
New Oxford (G-12423)

S F Spector Inc ....G 717 236-0805
Harrisburg (G-7211)

Salem Millwork Inc ....E 724 468-5701
Delmont (G-4056)

Saner Architecture Millwork ....G 717 786-2014
Quarryville (G-16279)

Seay Custom Woodworking ....G 814 422-8986
Spring Mills (G-17892)

Selectrim Corporation ....E 570 326-3662
Williamsport (G-20071)

Seneca Hardwood Lumber Co Inc ....E 814 498-2241
Cranberry (G-3797)

Seven Trees Woodworking LLC ....F 717 351-6300
New Holland (G-12282)

Shady Grove Woodworking ....G 610 273-7038
Narvon (G-11925)

Shelly Enterprises -US Lbm LLC ....D 215 723-5108
Telford (G-18315)

Shelly Enterprises -US Lbm LLC ....E 610 432-4511
Bethlehem (G-1617)

Shelly Enterprises -US Lbm LLC ....F 610 933-1116
Kimberton (G-8574)

Shuler Woodworking ....G 724 679-5222
Fenelton (G-5948)

Smokey Mountain Woodworking ....G 717 445-5120
Ephrata (G-5143)

Spectrim Building Products LLC ....F 267 223-1030
Bensalem (G-1256)

Spring Hill Woodworks ....G 724 762-0111
Cherry Tree (G-3036)

Spring Mill Woodworks ....G 267 408-9469
Glenside (G-6540)

Stairworks Inc ....E 215 703-0823
Telford (G-18320)

Starke Millwork Inc ....F 610 759-1753
Nazareth (G-11990)

Steigrwalds Kitchens Baths Inc ....F 724 458-0280
Grove City (G-6804)

Stevens Woodworks ....G 412 487-4408
Allison Park (G-463)

Stoltzfus Woodturning ....G 717 687-8237
Ronks (G-16816)

Stoltzfus Woodworking ....G 717 656-4823
Lancaster (G-9207)

Sweet Water Woodworks LLC ....G 610 273-1270
Narvon (G-11929)

TC Millwork Inc ....C 215 245-4210
Bensalem (G-1259)

Thermo-Twin Industries Inc ....C 412 826-1000
Oakmont (G-12927)

Thomas Gross Woodworking ....G 724 593-7044
Ligonier (G-9967)

Tilo Industries ....E 570 524-9990
Lewisburg (G-9921)

Top Shop ....G 610 622-6101
Philadelphia (G-14396)

Vangura Kitchen Tops Inc ....D 412 824-0772
Irwin (G-8204)

Weyerhaeuser Company ....E 814 827-4621
Titusville (G-18404)

Whispering Pine Woodworking ....G 570 922-4530
Mifflinburg (G-11105)

White Deer Woodworking ....G 570 547-1664
Allenwood (G-443)

Wilson & Mc Cracken Inc ....G 412 784-1772
Pittsburgh (G-15718)

Wolf Lumber and Millwork Inc ....G 814 317-5111
Duncansville (G-4466)

Woodshop LLC ....G 610 647-4190
Malvern (G-10348)

Wyatt Incorporated ....E 724 684-7060
Monessen (G-11302)

Wyatt Woodworking ....G 717 246-8740
Felton (G-5943)

Zaveta Millwork Spc Inc ....G 215 489-4065
Doylestown (G-4348)

MIMEOGRAPHING SVCS

Benkalu Group Lmtd Ta Jaguar ....G 215 646-5896
Huntingdon Valley (G-7965)

Copy Right Printing & Graphics ....G 814 838-6255
Erie (G-5233)

MINE & QUARRY SVCS: Nonmetallic Minerals

C S Garber & Sons Inc ....E 610 367-2861
Boyertown (G-1902)

Envirnmntal Protection PA Dept ....F 570 621-3139
Pottsville (G-16078)

Sheridan Construction Group ....G 717 948-0507
Middletown (G-11076)

Te Stone Products LLC ....G 570 335-4921
Mayfield (G-10543)

MINE PREPARATION SVCS

C & J Welding & Cnstr LLC ....C 724 564-7120
Mc Clellandtown (G-10555)

Donald Greathouse ....G 814 242-7624
Stoystown (G-18076)

Drill Management Inc ....G 717 227-8189
Glen Rock (G-6456)

Kentucky Berwind Land Company ....G 215 563-2800
Philadelphia (G-13927)

Lincoln Contg & Eqp Co Inc ....D 814 629-6641
Stoystown (G-18082)

MINE PUMPING OR DRAINING SVCS: Nonmetallic Minerals

Nolt Services LLC ....G 717 738-1066
Lititz (G-10026)

MINE SHAFT OR TUNNEL PREPARATION SVCS: Anthracite

Frank Calandra Inc ....E 412 963-9071
Pittsburgh (G-15032)

MINE SHAFT OR TUNNEL PREPARATION SVCS: Bituminous Or Lignite

R G Johnson Company Inc ....F 724 222-6810
Washington (G-19220)

MINE SHAFT SINKING SVCS: Nonmetallic Minerals

Hazleton Shaft Corporation ....E 570 450-0900
Hazleton (G-7503)

North American Drillers LLC ....C 304 291-0175
Mount Morris (G-11683)

MINERAL MINING: Nonmetallic

Black Diamond Mining Inc ....G 570 672-9917
Elysburg (G-4972)

Jigging Tech LLC DBA Atoll ....G 814 619-5187
Johnstown (G-8385)

Premier Chemicals LLC ....G 610 420-7500
Kennett Square (G-8536)

MINERAL WOOL

Alpha Assembly Solutions Inc ....C 814 946-1611
Altoona (G-470)

Bloom Engineering Company Inc ....F 412 653-3500
Pittsburgh (G-14773)

Brd Noise & Vibration Ctrl Inc ....G 610 863-6300
Wind Gap (G-20167)

Epic Metals Corporation ....D 412 351-3913
Rankin (G-16305)

Ranbar Electrical Mtls LLC ....E 724 864-8200
Harrison City (G-7251)

Therm-O-Rock East Inc ....D 724 258-3670
New Eagle (G-12193)

Employee Codes: A=Over 500 employees, B=251-500
C=101-250, D=51-100, E=20-50, F=10-19, G=3-9

2019 Harris Pennsylvania
Manufacturers Directory

1475

PRODUCT

MINERALS: Ground Or Otherwise Treated

Keystone Filler & Mfg Co ....E 570 546-3148
Muncy (G-11824)

MINERALS: Ground or Treated

Allegheny Mineral Corporation.............G...... 724 548-8101
Kittanning (G-8753)

Anthracite Industries Inc ....E 570 286-2176
Sunbury (G-18163)

Bpi Inc ....F....... 412 771-8176
Mc Kees Rocks (G-10605)

C-E Minerals Inc ....G...... 610 768-8800
King of Prussia (G-8589)

Chemalloy Company LLC ....E 610 527-3700
Conshohocken (G-3527)

East Loop Sand Company Inc ....F 814 695-3082
Hollidaysburg (G-7646)

Fluid Energy Proc & Eqp Co ....G...... 215 721-8990
Telford (G-18289)

Fluid Energy Proc & Eqp Co ....D...... 215 368-2510
Hatfield (G-7343)

Harsco Corporation ....E 724 287-4791
Butler (G-2405)

Harsco Minerals PA LLC......................G...... 717 506-7157
Fairless Hills (G-5784)

Jobomax Global Ltd ....G...... 215 253-3691
Philadelphia (G-13900)

Nittany Extraction Tech LLC ....G...... 814 571-4776
State College (G-17999)

Penn Mag Incorporated ....F 724 545-2300
Adrian (G-31)

Pennsylvania Perlite Corp York............G...... 610 868-0992
Bethlehem (G-1594)

Premier Magnesia LLC.......................E 610 828-6929
Wayne (G-19364)

Premier Magnesia LLC.......................F....... 717 677-7313
Aspers (G-744)

Reed Minerals.....................................G...... 215 295-8675
Fairless Hills (G-5794)

Specialty Minerals Inc ....F 610 250-3000
Easton (G-4755)

MINIATURE GOLF COURSES

Lionette Enterprises ....G...... 814 274-9401
Coudersport (G-3784)

Tee-To-Green ....G...... 570 275-8335
Danville (G-4013)

MINIATURES

Barkby Group Inc................................G...... 717 292-4148
Dover (G-4185)

Byers Choice Ltd ....C...... 215 822-6700
Chalfont (G-2864)

MINING EXPLORATION & DEVELOPMENT SVCS

Cbmm North America Inc ....G...... 412 221-7008
Pittsburgh (G-14829)

Daleco Resources Corporation ....G...... 570 795-4347
West Chester (G-19531)

Preferred Rocks LLC ....F....... 484 684-1221
Wayne (G-19363)

MINING MACHINERY & EQPT WHOLESALERS

Conflow Inc...F 724 746-0200
Washington (G-19157)

Eastern Machine & Convyrs Inc ....F 724 379-4701
Donora (G-4154)

Eickhoff Corporation ....F 724 218-1856
Georgetown (G-6275)

Irwin Car & Equipment Inc ....F 724 864-5170
Irwin (G-8173)

Irwin Car & Equipment Inc ....G...... 724 864-8900
Irwin (G-8174)

Norstone Incorporated ....G...... 484 684-6986
Bridgeport (G-2041)

Tallman Supply Company ....G...... 717 647-2123
Tower City (G-18442)

MINING MACHINES & EQPT: Augers

Longwall Services Inc ....G...... 724 228-9898
Meadow Lands (G-10691)

MINING MACHINES & EQPT: Bits, Rock, Exc Oil/Gas Field Tools

Hoffman Diamond Products Inc ....E 814 938-7600
Punxsutawney (G-16143)

Maclean Saegertown LLC....................G...... 814 763-2655
Saegertown (G-16924)

Saegertown Manufacturing Corp ....C...... 814 763-2655
Saegertown (G-16932)

MINING MACHINES & EQPT: Cleaning, Mineral

J & L Professional Sales Inc ....G...... 412 788-4927
Mc Kees Rocks (G-10616)

MINING MACHINES & EQPT: Crushers, Stationary

McLanahan Corporation........................B...... 814 695-9807
Hollidaysburg (G-7651)

MINING MACHINES & EQPT: Flotation

Scheirer Machine Company Inc...........E 412 833-6500
Bethel Park (G-1433)

MINING MACHINES & EQPT: Grinders, Stone, Stationary

Ottinger Machine Co Inc ....G...... 610 933-2101
Phoenixville (G-14565)

MINING MACHINES & EQPT: Mineral Beneficiation

Advanced Processes Inc.....................F 724 266-7274
Ambridge (G-606)

MINING MACHINES & EQPT: Pellet Mills

Barefoot Pellet Company ....G...... 570 297-4771
York (G-20400)

MINING MACHINES & EQPT: Pulverizers, Stone, Stationary

Bradley Pulverizer Company ....F 610 432-2101
Allentown (G-158)

MINING MACHINES & EQPT: Rock Crushing, Stationary

Klinger Machinery Co Inc.....................G...... 717 362-8656
Elizabethville (G-4894)

MINING MACHINES & EQPT: Shuttle Cars, Underground

Daves Airport Shuttle LLC ....G...... 215 288-1000
Philadelphia (G-13606)

MINING MACHINES/EQPT: Mine Car, Plow, Loader, Feeder/Eqpt

Balco Inc...F 724 459-6814
Blairsville (G-1714)

MINING SVCS, NEC: Anthracite

Alpha Safety USA.................................G...... 814 236-3344
Clearfield (G-3211)

B & B Anthracite Coal ....G...... 570 695-3707
Tremont (G-18478)

Burrell Mining Services Inc..................G...... 724 339-2220
New Kensington (G-12330)

Superior Coal Prep Coop LLC ....F 570 682-3246
Hegins (G-7545)

MINING SVCS, NEC: Lignite

Amerihohl Mining.................................G...... 724 455-4450
Mill Run (G-11185)

MINING: Sand & Shale Oil

Minichi Energy LLC ....G...... 570 654-8332
Dupont (G-4492)

MIRRORS: Motor Vehicle

Dorman Products Inc...........................C...... 215 997-1800
Colmar (G-3416)

Flabeg Automotive US Corp ....E 724 224-1800
Brackenridge (G-1939)

Micfralip Inc ....F 215 338-3293
Philadelphia (G-14019)

Pittsburgh Glass Works LLC ....B...... 814 684-2300
Tyrone (G-18589)

RB Distribution Inc ....B...... 215 997-1800
Colmar (G-3419)

MISCELLANEOUS FINANCIAL INVEST ACT: Oil/Gas Lease Brokers

Rosebud Mining Co ....E 814 749-5208
Twin Rocks (G-18572)

MIXING EQPT

Abbottstown Stamping Co Inc...............F 717 632-0588
Hanover (G-6859)

Acumix Inc...G...... 717 540-9738
Harrisburg (G-7082)

MIXTURES & BLOCKS: Asphalt Paving

Advanced Asphalt LLC.........................G...... 717 965-2406
New Oxford (G-12402)

Allan Myers Materials Inc ....G...... 610 442-4191
Devault (G-4110)

Atlas Minerals & Chemicals Inc ....E 800 523-8269
Mertztown (G-11000)

Beaver Valley Slag Inc ....G...... 724 375-8173
Monaca (G-11285)

Becks Paving ....G...... 814 692-7797
Port Matilda (G-15901)

Coopers Creek Chemical Corp ....E 610 828-0375
Conshohocken (G-3534)

Derry Construction Co Inc...................F 724 539-7600
Latrobe (G-9471)

Dunbar Asphalt Products Inc ....G...... 724 346-3594
Wheatland (G-19837)

Dunbar Asphalt Products Inc ....G...... 724 528-9310
West Middlesex (G-19723)

Eastern Industries Inc ....E 570 524-2251
Winfield (G-20199)

Eastern Industries Inc ....E 717 362-3388
Elizabethville (G-4893)

Ergon Asphalt & Emulsions Inc ....G...... 484 471-3999
Springfield (G-17912)

Erie Asphalt Paving Co ....D...... 814 898-4151
Erie (G-5262)

Getz Paving ....G...... 570 629-3007
Kunkletown (G-8833)

Glen Blooming Contractors Inc.............C...... 717 566-3711
Hummelstown (G-7912)

Glenn O Hawbaker Inc.........................E 814 359-3411
Pleasant Gap (G-15792)

Grannas Bros Stone Asp Co Inc ....D...... 814 695-5021
Hollidaysburg (G-7649)

H&K Group Inc ....G...... 717 867-0701
Annville (G-650)

H&K Group Inc ....C...... 610 584-8500
Skippack (G-17597)

Hammaker East ....G...... 717 263-0434
Chambersburg (G-2937)

Hammaker East Emulsions LLC...........E 412 449-0700
Pittsburgh (G-15077)

Hanover Prest-Paving Company ....E 717 637-0500
Hanover (G-6900)

Hanson Aggregates PA LLC ....D...... 570 992-4951
Stroudsburg (G-18122)

HEI-Way Inc ....F 724 353-2700
Sarver (G-17072)

Heilman Pavement Specialties ....G...... 724 353-2700
Sarver (G-17073)

Henry Company LLC ....B...... 610 933-8888
Kimberton (G-8573)

Highway Materials Inc.........................G...... 610 828-9525
Conshohocken (G-3557)

Highway Materials Inc.........................E 215 234-4522
Perkiomenville (G-13301)

Hri Inc ....G...... 570 437-4315
Milton (G-11242)

Hri Inc ....D...... 570 322-6737
Muncy (G-11821)

Integrated Cnstr Systems Inc ....F 724 528-9310
West Middlesex (G-19726)

Jem Industries LLC.............................G...... 412 818-2606
Pittsburgh (G-15148)

K-R-K Paving LLC..................................G...... 267 602-7715
  Philadelphia (G-13918)
Martin Limestone Inc...........................D...... 717 354-1340
  Ephrata (G-5123)
Mayer Brothers Construction Co ....F 814 452-3748
  Erie (G-5383)
Mukies/Mccarty Seal Coating C............G...... 717 684-2799
  Columbia (G-3444)
New Enterprise Stone Lime Inc ....D...... 814 652-5121
  Everett (G-5576)
Pcm Contracting Inc..............................G...... 215 675-8846
  Hatboro (G-7296)
Pennsy Supply Inc..................................D...... 717 274-3661
  Lebanon (G-9619)
Petrunak & Company Inc ....E 814 467-7860
  Windber (G-20191)
Pignuts Inc..G...... 610 530-8788
  Allentown (G-352)
Quaker Sales Corporation ....G...... 814 539-1376
  Johnstown (G-8427)
Redland Brick Inc...................................E 412 828-8046
  Cheswick (G-3117)
Rs Asphalt Maintenance Inc ....G...... 717 367-4914
  Elizabethtown (G-4884)
Sealmaster Pennsylvania Inc..................F 724 667-0444
  Hillsville (G-7636)
Specialty Emulsions Inc ....G...... 717 849-5020
  York (G-20676)
St Thomas Development Inc...................G...... 717 369-3030
  Saint Thomas (G-17041)
Stouffers Asphalt Construction..............G...... 724 527-0917
  Mount Pleasant (G-11719)
Sunoco (R&m) LLC................................E 215 339-2000
  Philadelphia (G-14356)
Tangent Rail Corporation ....G...... 412 325-0202
  Pittsburgh (G-15596)
Valley Quarries Inc.................................E 717 264-4178
  Chambersburg (G-2995)
Walter R Erle - Mrrisville LLC.................G...... 215 736-1708
  Morrisville (G-11588)
Windsor Service Trucking Corp ....C...... 610 929-0716
  Reading (G-16567)

MOBILE COMMUNICATIONS EQPT

Activeblu Corporation ....G...... 412 490-1929
  Pittsburgh (G-14646)
E-Nanomedsys LLC.................................G...... 917 734-1462
  State College (G-17958)

MOBILE HOME & TRAILER REPAIR

Vr Enterprises Llc ....G 215 932-1113
  Lansdale (G-9426)

MOBILE HOME DEALERS: Mobile Home Parts & Access

R S W Enterprises Inc.............................G...... 570 888-2184
  Milan (G-11149)

MOBILE HOME FRAMES

Garretts Fabricating...............................G...... 724 528-8193
  West Middlesex (G-19725)

MOBILE HOMES

Commodore Corporation ....C...... 814 226-9210
  Clarion (G-3175)
Mobile Concepts By Scotty Inc ....E 724 542-7640
  Mount Pleasant (G-11706)
R S W Enterprises Inc.............................G...... 570 888-2184
  Milan (G-11149)
Simplex Industries Inc............................C...... 570 346-5113
  Scranton (G-17291)
Skyline Champion Corporation ....E 717 656-2071
  Leola (G-9803)
Stoltzfoos Layers ....G...... 717 826-0371
  Kinzers (G-8743)
Taylored Building Solutions ....G...... 570 898-5361
  Taylor (G-18263)
United States Hardware Mfg Inc............G...... 724 222-5110
  Washington (G-19235)
Village At Overlook LLC..........................G...... 570 538-9167
  New Columbia (G-12178)
Wireless Experience of PA Inc................G...... 215 340-1382
  Doylestown (G-4345)

MOBILE HOMES, EXC RECREATIONAL

Liberty Homes Inc...................................C...... 717 656-2381
  Leola (G-9793)

Pine Grove Mnfctured Homes Inc ....D...... 570 345-2011
  Pine Grove (G-14602)
Pleasant Valley Homes Inc......................C...... 570 345-2011
  Pine Grove (G-14603)

MODELS

Core House...G...... 717 566-3810
  Hummelstown (G-7907)

MODELS: General, Exc Toy

Magnum Model Concepts Inc ....G...... 717 529-0912
  Kirkwood (G-8751)

MOLDED RUBBER PRDTS

Associated Rubber Inc ....E 215 536-2800
  Quakertown (G-16169)
Hilmarr Rubber Co Inc............................G...... 215 426-3628
  Philadelphia (G-13826)
Lake Erie Rubber Works Inc ....F 814 835-0170
  Erie (G-5355)
Mason Rubber Co Inc ....E 215 355-3440
  Feasterville Trevose (G-5918)
Scully Enterprises Inc.............................G...... 814 835-0173
  Erie (G-5471)
Surco Inc..F 215 855-9551
  Hatfield (G-7397)

MOLDING COMPOUNDS

Advanced Solutions Network LLC ....F 814 464-0791
  Erie (G-5175)
Asm Industries Inc..................................E 717 656-2166
  Leola (G-9769)
Bellisimo LLC..G...... 215 781-1700
  Croydon (G-3912)
Eastman Chemical Resins Inc ....E 412 384-2520
  Jefferson Hills (G-8276)
Execumold Inc...E 814 864-2535
  Waterford (G-19262)
ICO Polymers North America Inc ....C...... 610 398-5900
  Allentown (G-250)
Imperial Tool Co ....G...... 215 947-7650
  Huntingdon Valley (G-7996)
Pak Innovations Inc................................G...... 215 723-0498
  Souderton (G-17759)
Piccolo Group Inc...................................G...... 610 738-7733
  West Chester (G-19617)
Plastic Profiles LLC................................G...... 717 593-9200
  Greencastle (G-6626)

MOLDING SAND MINING

Custom Entryways & Millwork................G...... 814 798-2500
  Stoystown (G-18074)

MOLDINGS & TRIM: Metal, Exc Automobile

Hagerty Precision Tool ....G...... 814 734-8668
  Edinboro (G-4813)

MOLDINGS & TRIM: Wood

Architectural Woodsmiths Inc ....D...... 717 532-7700
  Shippensburg (G-17515)
Brahma Building Products LLC...............F 717 567-2571
  Newport (G-12487)
Flagship City Hardwoods ....G...... 814 835-1178
  Erie (G-5292)
Lewis Lumber Products Inc ....D...... 570 584-6167
  Picture Rocks (G-14585)
Longs Hardwoods Inc ....F 814 472-4740
  Ebensburg (G-4786)
Markraft Company ....G...... 724 733-3654
  Murrysville (G-11857)

MOLDINGS: Picture Frame

Christopher Co Ltd ....G...... 215 331-8290
  Philadelphia (G-13543)
L W Green Frames ....G...... 610 432-3726
  Westfield (G-19779)
Larson-Juhl US LLC ....G...... 215 638-5940
  Bensalem (G-1219)
Steve A Vitelli ....G...... 570 937-4546
  Lake Ariel (G-8893)

MOLDS: Indl

Accudyn Products Inc ....G...... 814 835-5088
  Fairview (G-5809)

Augustine Die & Mold Inc......................F 814 443-2390
  Somerset (G-17676)
Castle Mold & Tool Co Inc ....G...... 724 652-4737
  New Castle (G-12071)
Central Penna Tool & Mfg Inc ....G...... 717 932-1294
  New Cumberland (G-12181)
Culver Tool & Die Inc.............................G...... 717 932-2000
  Lewisberry (G-9882)
D & F Tool Inc...G...... 814 899-6364
  Erie (G-5244)
Executool ....G...... 814 836-1141
  Erie (G-5284)
Fiber Productions II Inc..........................G...... 267 546-7025
  Bristol (G-2145)
J L W Ventures Incorporated ....F 814 765-9648
  Clearfield (G-3221)
Jatco Machine & Tool Co Inc ....E 412 761-4344
  Pittsburgh (G-15145)
Johnson Pattern & Machine Shop.........G...... 724 697-4079
  Salina (G-17043)
Lemm Liquidating Company LLC...........D...... 724 325-7140
  Export (G-5615)
M S & M Manufacturing Co Inc ....G...... 215 743-3930
  Philadelphia (G-13982)
Master Tool and Mold Inc ....F 717 757-3671
  York (G-20582)
Mervine Corp ....F 215 257-0431
  Perkasie (G-13284)
Mold 911 LLC..G...... 267 312-1432
  Blue Bell (G-1849)
Mold-Base Industries Inc ....D...... 717 564-7960
  Harrisburg (G-7180)
Moldex Tool & Design Corp ....D...... 814 337-3190
  Meadville (G-10766)
Mountain Vly Mold Solution LLC ....G...... 570 460-6592
  Stroudsburg (G-18131)
Neu Dynamics Corp ....F 215 355-2460
  Warminster (G-18929)
Omco Cast Metals Inc............................G...... 724 222-7006
  Washington (G-19213)
Phoenix Mold and Machine LLC............G...... 215 355-1985
  Warminster (G-18942)
Pickar Brothers Inc................................E 610 582-0967
  Birdsboro (G-1703)
Pro Cel Inc..G...... 215 322-9883
  Warminster (G-18948)
Ptc-In-Liquidation Inc............................E 814 763-2000
  Saegertown (G-16930)
Quality Mold Inc ....E 814 866-2255
  Erie (G-5445)
Reddog Industries Inc ....D...... 814 898-4321
  Erie (G-5458)
Roser Technologies Inc ....D...... 814 827-7717
  Titusville (G-18393)
Ross Mould LLC......................................C...... 724 222-7006
  Washington (G-19222)
Sutley Tool Co ....G...... 814 789-4332
  Guys Mills (G-6813)
Theodore W Styborski.............................G...... 814 337-8535
  Meadville (G-10800)
Tool-All Inc..D...... 814 898-3917
  Erie (G-5512)
Triangle Tool Company Inc ....E 814 878-4603
  Erie (G-5519)
Trimetric Enterprises Inc.........................G...... 610 670-2099
  Wernersville (G-19487)
United Tool & Die Inc..............................F 814 763-1133
  Meadville (G-10805)

MOLDS: Plastic Working & Foundry

Advanced Plastix Injection Mol ....F 215 453-7808
  Perkasie (G-13265)
Dennis Sanders ....G...... 814 833-5497
  Erie (G-5245)
Eagle Precision Tooling Inc ....F 814 838-3515
  Erie (G-5253)
F & S Tool Inc ....E 814 838-7991
  Erie (G-5286)
Franconia Plastics Corp..........................G...... 215 723-8926
  Souderton (G-17735)
Imperial Tool Co ....G...... 215 947-7650
  Huntingdon Valley (G-7996)
Johnstown Foundry Castings Inc ....G...... 814 539-8840
  Johnstown (G-8389)
K & A Tool Co ....G...... 814 835-1405
  Erie (G-5341)
Ken-Tex Corp ....E 570 374-4476
  Selinsgrove (G-17328)
Kw Inc ....E 610 582-8735
  Birdsboro (G-1702)

Ram Precision Inc ....G...... 215 674-0663
Horsham (G-7843)
Reliable Equipment Mfg Co ....E...... 215 357-7015
Warminster (G-18951)
Triangle Tool Company Inc ....E...... 814 878-4400
Erie (G-5518)
Ultimate Tool Inc ....F...... 814 835-2291
Erie (G-5522)
Vanicek Precision Machining Co..........G...... 814 774-9012
Lake City (G-8910)
Xaloy Superior Holdings Inc ....G...... 724 656-5600
New Castle (G-12170)

MONORAIL SYSTEMS

Interstate Equipment Corp ....G...... 412 563-5556
Pittsburgh (G-15134)

MONUMENTS & GRAVE MARKERS, EXC TERRAZZO

Craig Walters ....G...... 570 645-3415
Summit Hill (G-18159)
F & G Monument Lettering LLC ....G...... 814 247-5032
Hastings (G-7260)
Monumental Express ....G...... 570 501-1009
Hazleton (G-7511)
Monumental Touch ....G...... 484 226-7277
Walnutport (G-18792)

MONUMENTS: Concrete

Edward T Christiansen & Sons.............G...... 215 368-1001
Montgomeryville (G-11393)
Shetler Memorials Inc ....G...... 814 288-1087
Johnstown (G-8435)

MONUMENTS: Cut Stone, Exc Finishing Or Lettering Only

Carlini Brothers Co ....G...... 412 421-9301
Pittsburgh (G-14813)
Gary Foster.....................................G...... 717 248-5322
Lewistown (G-9932)
Oliver T Korb & Sons Inc...................G...... 814 371-4545
Du Bois (G-4408)
Owens Monumental Company..............G...... 610 588-3370
Bangor (G-923)
Pennsylvania Monument Co ....F...... 570 454-2621
Hazleton (G-7516)
Wenz Co Inc....................................G...... 610 434-6157
Allentown (G-431)

MOPS: Floor & Dust

Norshel Industries Inc ....E...... 215 788-2200
Croydon (G-3922)

MOTION PICTURE & VIDEO PRODUCTION SVCS

Beye LLC ....G...... 484 581-1840
Wayne (G-19305)
Jayco Grafix Inc ....D...... 610 678-2640
Reinholds (G-16633)
Mirage Advertising Inc ....G...... 412 372-4181
Monroeville (G-11345)
Noel Interactive Group LLC ....G...... 732 991-1484
Easton (G-4732)

MOTION PICTURE & VIDEO PRODUCTION SVCS: Indl

Debenham Media Group.....................F...... 412 264-2526
Coraopolis (G-3684)

MOTION PICTURE & VIDEO PRODUCTION SVCS: Training

In-Tec Inc ....G...... 570 342-8464
Waverly (G-19285)

MOTOR & GENERATOR PARTS: Electric

A B M Motors Inc..............................G...... 215 781-9400
Croydon (G-3909)
Allegheny Mfg & Elec Svc Inc.............E...... 814 288-1597
Johnstown (G-8350)
Alstom Signaling Operation LLC..........A...... 814 486-0235
Emporium (G-5048)
Dyna-Tech Industries Ltd ....F...... 717 274-3099
Lebanon (G-9564)

Generator and Mtr Svcs PA LLC...........D...... 412 829-7500
Turtle Creek (G-18565)
Marvin Dale Slaymaker.....................G...... 717 684-5050
Washington Boro (G-19251)

MOTOR HOMES

GM Home Inc ....G...... 888 352-3442
Southampton (G-17814)

MOTOR REBUILDING SVCS, EXC AUTOMOTIVE

C & S Repair Center Inc....................G...... 610 524-9724
Downingtown (G-4217)
G I Electric Company.........................G...... 570 323-6147
Williamsport (G-20015)
Habsco Inc.......................................G...... 724 337-9498
New Kensington (G-12345)
Topos Mondial Corp ....E...... 610 970-2270
Pottstown (G-16055)
United Industrial Group Inc ....F...... 724 746-4700
Washington (G-19234)

MOTOR REPAIR SVCS

Action Cycle & Atv LLC ....G...... 814 765-2578
West Decatur (G-19687)
Associated Machine Service................G...... 215 335-1940
Bensalem (G-1149)
H & Z Auto LLC ....G...... 610 419-8012
Bethlehem (G-1527)
Industrial Pump & Mtr Repr Inc ....F...... 412 369-5060
Glenshaw (G-6490)
Nearhoof Machine Inc.......................G...... 814 339-6621
Osceola Mills (G-13056)
Servedio A Elc Mtr Svc Inc.................F...... 724 658-8041
New Castle (G-12148)

MOTOR VEHICLE ASSEMBLY, COMPLETE: Autos, Incl Specialty

Aircooled Racing and Parts ....G...... 717 432-4116
Wellsville (G-19476)
Ben Cook Racing Ltd.........................G...... 570 788-4223
Sugarloaf (G-18152)
Hot Rod Fabrications LLP ....G...... 717 774-6302
New Cumberland (G-12186)
Martz Chassis Inc.............................G...... 814 623-9501
Bedford (G-1063)
S & W Race Cars Components Inc........E...... 610 948-7303
Spring City (G-17865)
Skyline Auto Supply LLC ....G...... 484 365-4040
Easton (G-4752)
Versalift East LLC ....C...... 610 866-1400
Bethlehem (G-1651)

MOTOR VEHICLE ASSEMBLY, COMPLETE: Bus/Large Spclty Vehicles

Industrial Food Truck LLC ....F...... 215 596-0010
Philadelphia (G-13854)
Lge Coachworks Inc..........................G...... 814 434-0856
North East (G-12750)
Specialty Vhcl Solutions LLC ....E...... 609 882-1900
Warminster (G-18972)

MOTOR VEHICLE ASSEMBLY, COMPLETE: Buses, All Types

Rockland Coach Works LLC ....G...... 610 682-2830
Mertztown (G-11003)

MOTOR VEHICLE ASSEMBLY, COMPLETE: Cars, Armored

Blockcom ....G...... 215 794-9575
Doylestown (G-4277)

MOTOR VEHICLE ASSEMBLY, COMPLETE: Fire Department Vehicles

Kovatch Corp ....D...... 570 669-5130
Nesquehoning (G-12006)
Smeal Ltc LLC ....E...... 717 918-1806
Ephrata (G-5142)
Spartan Motors Usa Inc.....................F...... 605 582-4000
Ephrata (G-5144)
Upper Milford Western Dst Fire ....G...... 610 966-3541
Zionsville (G-20837)

MOTOR VEHICLE ASSEMBLY, COMPLETE: Military Motor Vehicle

Ibis Tek Inc.....................................D...... 724 431-3000
Butler (G-2407)

MOTOR VEHICLE ASSEMBLY, COMPLETE: Mobile Lounges

Filly Fabricating Inc ....G...... 412 896-6452
North Versailles (G-12774)

MOTOR VEHICLE ASSEMBLY, COMPLETE: Motor Homes, Self Contain

Steelway Cellar Doors LLC ....F...... 610 277-9988
King of Prussia (G-8680)

MOTOR VEHICLE ASSEMBLY, COMPLETE: Reconnaissance Cars

Dan Donahue....................................G...... 814 336-3262
Meadville (G-10718)

MOTOR VEHICLE ASSEMBLY, COMPLETE: Snow Plows

Louis Berkman Company.....................E...... 740 283-3722
Pittsburgh (G-15238)

MOTOR VEHICLE ASSEMBLY, COMPLETE: Truck & Tractor Trucks

Diamond Hvy Vhcl Solutions LLC.........G...... 717 695-9378
Harrisburg (G-7119)
Navistar Inc.....................................D...... 717 767-3800
Manchester (G-10358)
Paccar Inc.......................................E...... 717 397-4111
Lancaster (G-9157)

MOTOR VEHICLE ASSEMBLY, COMPLETE: Truck Tractors, Highway

Mack Trucks Inc...............................C...... 717 939-1338
Middletown (G-11064)
Mack Trucks Inc ....A...... 610 966-8800
Macungie (G-10154)

MOTOR VEHICLE ASSEMBLY, COMPLETE: Universal Carriers, Mil

Interntnal Def Systems USA LLC ....G...... 610 973-2228
Orefield (G-13012)

MOTOR VEHICLE ASSEMBLY, COMPLETE: Wreckers, Tow Truck

B & C Auto Wreckers Inc....................G...... 570 547-1040
Montgomery (G-11367)
Dangelos Custom Built Mfg LLC ....F...... 814 837-6053
Kane (G-8462)
Roadside PA LLC ....G...... 412 464-1452
Pittsburgh (G-15492)

MOTOR VEHICLE DEALERS: Automobiles, New & Used

Bowser Pontiac Inc...........................C...... 412 469-2100
Pittsburgh (G-14787)
Chevron USA Inc...............................E...... 412 262-2830
Coraopolis (G-3677)
East Penn Truck Eqp W Inc.................G...... 724 342-1800
Mercer (G-10961)
East Penn Truck Equipment Inc ....G...... 610 694-9234
Bethlehem (G-1500)
Krem Cars/Racing Inc........................G...... 814 336-6619
Meadville (G-10745)
W W Engine and Supply Inc.................E...... 814 345-5693
Kylertown (G-8868)

MOTOR VEHICLE DEALERS: Cars, Used Only

Barnharts Honda Suzuki ....F...... 724 627-5819
Prosperity (G-16122)

MOTOR VEHICLE PARTS & ACCESS: Acceleration Eqpt

Wheeler Bros Inc...................................G....... 814 443-3269
Somerset (G-17716)
Wheeler Bros Inc...................................D....... 814 443-7000
Somerset (G-17717)

MOTOR VEHICLE PARTS & ACCESS: Bearings

J S H Industries LLC.............................G....... 717 267-3566
Chambersburg (G-2945)
Metal Powder Products LLC ....C....... 814 834-7261
Saint Marys (G-16992)
N C B Technologies Inc ....G....... 724 658-5544
New Castle (G-12123)

MOTOR VEHICLE PARTS & ACCESS: Body Components & Frames

G Adasavage LLC..................................E....... 215 355-3105
Huntingdon Valley (G-7987)
Ladmac Services...................................G....... 724 679-8047
Butler (G-2418)
Mancor-Pa Inc.......................................D....... 610 398-2300
Allentown (G-306)

MOTOR VEHICLE PARTS & ACCESS: Booster Cables, Jump-Start

American Cable Systems LLC ....G....... 215 456-0700
Philadelphia (G-13381)

MOTOR VEHICLE PARTS & ACCESS: Clutches

Boninfante Friction Inc..........................E....... 610 626-2194
Lansdowne (G-9431)
Emporium Specialties Company ....E....... 814 647-8661
Austin (G-833)
H R Sales Inc ....G....... 215 639-7150
Bensalem (G-1208)

MOTOR VEHICLE PARTS & ACCESS: Cylinder Heads

Slawko Racing Heads Inc......................G....... 610 286-1822
Morgantown (G-11535)

MOTOR VEHICLE PARTS & ACCESS: Engines & Parts

Boyesen Inc...E....... 610 756-6818
Lenhartsville (G-9756)
Corry Manufacturing Company ....C....... 814 664-9611
Corry (G-3752)
General Electric Company ....B....... 724 450-1887
Grove City (G-6787)
Jones Machine Racing Products............G....... 610 847-2028
Ottsville (G-13063)
Krem Speed Equipment Inc ....G....... 814 724-4806
Meadville (G-10746)
RPM Industries LLC...............................E....... 724 228-5130
Washington (G-19224)
Rtr Manufacturing Co ....F....... 412 665-1500
East Liberty (G-4580)

MOTOR VEHICLE PARTS & ACCESS: Fuel Pumps

Continental Auto Systems Inc ....E....... 610 289-1390
Allentown (G-177)
Diesel Pro Inc ....G....... 717 235-4996
Glen Rock (G-6455)

MOTOR VEHICLE PARTS & ACCESS: Gears

R H Sheppard Co Inc ....A....... 717 637-3751
Hanover (G-6941)
R H Sheppard Co Inc ....F....... 717 633-4106
Hanover (G-6942)

MOTOR VEHICLE PARTS & ACCESS: Hoods

Jones Performance Products Inc...........D....... 724 528-3569
West Middlesex (G-19727)

MOTOR VEHICLE PARTS & ACCESS: Instrument Board Assemblies

L & P Machine Shop Inc ....G....... 610 262-7356
Coplay (G-3645)

MOTOR VEHICLE PARTS & ACCESS: Lubrication Systems & Parts

Graco Inc ....A....... 412 771-5774
Mc Kees Rocks (G-10613)
Steel Shield Technologies Inc ....G....... 412 479-0024
Bethel Park (G-1435)

MOTOR VEHICLE PARTS & ACCESS: Mufflers, Exhaust

Innotech Industries Inc.........................E....... 215 533-6400
Philadelphia (G-13858)
Technology Fabricators Inc ....E....... 215 699-0731
Montgomeryville (G-11421)

MOTOR VEHICLE PARTS & ACCESS: Pickup Truck Bed Liners

Stk LLC ....F....... 724 430-2477
Lemont Furnace (G-9738)

MOTOR VEHICLE PARTS & ACCESS: Propane Conversion Eqpt

Bluhms Gas Sales Inc ....F....... 570 746-2440
Wyalusing (G-20245)
Hoffman Bros Speed ....G....... 610 760-6274
New Tripoli (G-12458)

MOTOR VEHICLE PARTS & ACCESS: Tops

Auto Tops Inc ....F....... 215 785-3310
Bristol (G-2115)
Pillings FRP ....F....... 570 538-9202
New Columbia (G-12175)

MOTOR VEHICLE PARTS & ACCESS: Transmission Housings Or Parts

Neapco Components LLC ....E....... 610 323-6000
Pottstown (G-16021)

MOTOR VEHICLE PARTS & ACCESS: Transmissions

Great Lakes Power Products Inc............G....... 724 266-4000
Leetsdale (G-9691)
Great Valley Automotive.........................G....... 412 829-8904
North Versailles (G-12776)
Gregory Racing Fabrications..................G....... 610 759-8217
Nazareth (G-11970)
Overdrive Holdings Inc..........................F....... 724 452-1500
Zelienople (G-20813)
Park Place Transmission Inc ....G....... 717 859-2998
Ephrata (G-5136)
Winters Performance Pdts Inc................E....... 717 764-9844
York (G-20713)

MOTOR VEHICLE PARTS & ACCESS: Universal Joints

Dana Driveshaft Products LLC ....B....... 610 323-4200
Pottstown (G-15979)

MOTOR VEHICLE PARTS & ACCESS: Windshield Frames

Young Windows Inc ....D....... 610 828-5036
Conshohocken (G-3618)

MOTOR VEHICLE PARTS & ACCESS: Wipers, Windshield

Advance Stores Company Inc ....E....... 610 939-0120
Reading (G-16311)

MOTOR VEHICLE PARTS & ACCESS: Wiring Harness Sets

Centech Inc..G....... 610 754-0720
Perkiomenville (G-13300)
EBY Group LLC.....................................E....... 215 537-4700
Philadelphia (G-13657)

Efi Connection LLC................................G....... 814 566-0946
Erie (G-5257)
Industrial Harness Company Inc ....D....... 717 477-0100
Shippensburg (G-17532)

MOTOR VEHICLE RACING & DRIVER SVCS

Design Dynamics Inc.............................F....... 724 266-4826
Ambridge (G-615)
Krem Cars/Racing Inc............................G....... 814 336-6619
Meadville (G-10745)

MOTOR VEHICLE SPLYS & PARTS WHOLESALERS: New

Boyesen Inc...E....... 610 756-6818
Lenhartsville (G-9756)
Exide Technologies ....G....... 304 345-5616
Rostraver Township (G-16826)
James E Krack ....G....... 724 864-4150
Irwin (G-8176)
Metro Manufacturing & Supply..............G....... 610 891-1899
Media (G-10939)
Mg Industries Inc ....G....... 724 694-8290
Derry (G-4105)
R J Machine Co Inc ....G....... 610 494-8107
Upper Chichester (G-18672)
Wheeler Bros Inc...................................D....... 814 443-7000
Somerset (G-17717)

MOTOR VEHICLE SPLYS & PARTS WHOLESALERS: Used

B & C Auto Wreckers Inc ....G....... 570 547-1040
Montgomery (G-11367)

MOTOR VEHICLE: Hardware

Winner International Inc ....D....... 724 981-1152
Sharon (G-17448)

MOTOR VEHICLE: Radiators

Dukane Radiator Inc ....G....... 412 233-3300
Bethel Park (G-1413)
Marko Radiator Inc...............................F....... 570 462-2281
Shenandoah (G-17495)
Mr Rebuildables Inc ....G....... 610 767-2100
Walnutport (G-18793)
Nrf US Inc...G....... 814 947-1378
Plymouth Meeting (G-15861)
Universal Carnegie Mfg ....G....... 800 867-9554
Carnegie (G-2802)

MOTOR VEHICLE: Wheels

Accuride Corporation ....B....... 814 480-6400
Erie (G-5169)
Keystone Automotive Inds Inc ....D....... 610 866-0313
Bethlehem (G-1550)
Penn Machine Company ....D....... 814 288-1547
Johnstown (G-8421)

MOTOR VEHICLES & CAR BODIES

American Classic Motors Inc................F....... 610 754-8500
Zieglerville (G-20831)
Bowser Pontiac Inc................................C....... 412 469-2100
Pittsburgh (G-14787)
Bugstuff ....G....... 724 785-7000
Brownsville (G-2310)
East Coast Partners LLC ....D....... 215 207-9360
Philadelphia (G-13655)
Edward H Quay Welding Spc ....G....... 610 326-8050
Pottstown (G-15985)
Garnon Truck Equipment Inc.................F....... 814 833-6000
Erie (G-5300)
Ibis Tek Holdings Inc ....G....... 724 431-3000
Butler (G-2409)
Mack Defense LLC ....E....... 484 387-5911
Allentown (G-304)
Murrysville Auto LLC.............................F....... 724 387-1607
Murrysville (G-11860)
Riggeals Performance Fibrgls................G....... 717 677-4167
Gettysburg (G-6312)
Superior Custom Designs Inc.................G....... 412 744-0110
Glassport (G-6416)
Tesla Inc ....F....... 484 235-5858
King of Prussia (G-8686)
Wayne Abel Repairs ....G....... 610 857-1708
Parkesburg (G-13185)

PRODUCT

William T Jenkins ....G....... 610 644-7052
Malvern (G-10346)

MOTOR VEHICLES, WHOLESALE: Commercial

Garnon Truck Equipment Inc ....F....... 814 833-6000
Erie (G-5300)

Wolfington Body Company Inc ....C....... 610 458-8501
Exton (G-5751)

MOTOR VEHICLES, WHOLESALE: Fire Trucks

National Foam Inc ....D....... 610 363-1400
West Chester (G-19606)

MOTOR VEHICLES, WHOLESALE: Trailers for passenger vehicles

Smouse Trucks & Vans Inc ....G....... 724 887-7777
Mount Pleasant (G-11718)

MOTOR VEHICLES, WHOLESALE: Trailers, Truck, New & Used

Great Dane LLC ....B....... 717 492-0057
Mount Joy (G-11659)

M H EBY Inc ....C....... 800 292-4752
Blue Ball (G-1811)

MOTOR VEHICLES, WHOLESALE: Truck bodies

D K Hostetler Inc ....F....... 717 667-3921
Milroy (G-11229)

Feedmobile Inc ....F....... 717 626-8318
Lititz (G-10007)

New Harrisburg Truck Body Co ....E....... 717 766-7651
Mechanicsburg (G-10873)

Sabre Equipment Inc ....E....... 412 262-3080
Coraopolis (G-3725)

MOTOR VEHICLES, WHOLESALE: Truck tractors

Pfa Inc ....G....... 717 664-4216
Manheim (G-10401)

MOTOR VEHICLES, WHOLESALE: Trucks, Noncommercial

Mack Defense LLC ....E....... 484 387-5911
Allentown (G-304)

W W Engine and Supply Inc ....E....... 814 345-5693
Kylertown (G-8868)

MOTOR VEHICLES, WHOLESALE: Trucks, commercial

Fyda Frghtliner Pittsburgh Inc ....D....... 724 514-2055
Canonsburg (G-2590)

Robert P Williams ....G....... 814 563-7660
Youngsville (G-20775)

Robinson Vacuum Tanks Inc ....G....... 814 355-4474
Bellefonte (G-1116)

MOTORCYCLE & BICYCLE PARTS: Frames

Bikes & Trikes For ....G....... 267 304-1534
Philadelphia (G-13460)

MOTORCYCLE ACCESS

Road Ready LLC ....G....... 717 647-7902
Williamstown (G-20103)

MOTORCYCLE DEALERS

American Classic Motors Inc ....F....... 610 754-8500
Zieglerville (G-20831)

World of Wheels Inc ....F....... 814 676-5721
Seneca (G-17373)

MOTORCYCLE DEALERS

Arthur K Miller ....G....... 724 588-1118
Greenville (G-6738)

Giesler Engineering Inc ....G....... 800 428-8616
Aston (G-768)

Hirt Powersports LLC ....G....... 717 834-9126
Duncannon (G-4446)

MOTORCYCLE PARTS & ACCESS DEALERS

Action Cycle & Atv LLC ....G....... 814 765-2578
West Decatur (G-19687)

Pro Action Inc ....F....... 724 846-9055
Beaver Falls (G-1007)

MOTORCYCLE PARTS: Wholesalers

Fast By Ferracci Inc ....F....... 215 657-1276
Abington (G-12)

MOTORCYCLE RACING

RC & Design Company ....G....... 484 626-1216
Lehighton (G-9724)

MOTORCYCLE REPAIR SHOPS

American Cycle Fabrication ....G....... 570 752-8715
Bloomsburg (G-1769)

Arthur K Miller ....G....... 724 588-1118
Greenville (G-6738)

CCS Machining Inc ....G....... 724 668-7706
Greensburg (G-6657)

East Coast Atv Inc ....F....... 267 733-7364
Coopersburg (G-3627)

Freeze Thaw Cycles ....G....... 814 272-0178
State College (G-17966)

Hirt Powersports LLC ....G....... 717 834-9126
Duncannon (G-4446)

Pro Action Inc ....F....... 724 846-9055
Beaver Falls (G-1007)

Tech Cycle Performance Pdts ....G....... 215 702-8324
Langhorne (G-9328)

MOTORCYCLES & RELATED PARTS

Barnharts Honda Suzuki ....F....... 724 627-5819
Prosperity (G-16122)

Christini Technologies Inc ....G....... 215 351-9895
Philadelphia (G-13542)

Fast By Ferracci Inc ....F....... 215 657-1276
Abington (G-12)

Integrated Machine Company ....G....... 814 835-4949
Erie (G-5328)

P K Choppers Mobile ....G....... 570 458-6983
Millville (G-11226)

Price Chopper Oper Co of PA ....G....... 570 223-2410
East Stroudsburg (G-4631)

Pro Action Inc ....F....... 724 846-9055
Beaver Falls (G-1007)

Tech Cycle Performance Pdts ....G....... 215 702-8324
Langhorne (G-9328)

Vicious Cycle Works Llc ....G....... 724 662-0581
Mercer (G-10977)

MOTORS: Electric

Ametek Inc ....D....... 215 256-6601
Harleysville (G-7020)

Ametek Inc ....D....... 610 647-2121
Berwyn (G-1351)

Bohlinger Inc ....G....... 610 825-0440
Conshohocken (G-3524)

Danaher Corporation ....D....... 610 692-2700
West Chester (G-19532)

Duryea Technologies Inc ....G....... 610 939-0480
Reading (G-16366)

Hannon Company ....G....... 724 266-2712
Ambridge (G-618)

Marino Indus Systems Svcs Inc ....E....... 610 872-3630
Chester (G-3057)

Rockwell Automation Inc ....G....... 412 375-4700
Coraopolis (G-3723)

RR Enterprises Inc ....G....... 610 266-9600
Allentown (G-381)

Siemens Industry Inc ....D....... 724 743-5913
Canonsburg (G-2636)

W M S Phase Converters ....G....... 717 336-6566
Stevens (G-18057)

MOTORS: Generators

Ametek Inc ....D....... 215 355-6900
Horsham (G-7784)

Ametek Inc ....D....... 570 645-2191
Nesquehoning (G-12003)

Ametek Inc ....D....... 717 569-7061
Lancaster (G-8933)

Ametek Emg Holdings Inc ....G....... 610 647-2121
Berwyn (G-1352)

Ametek Inc ....D....... 724 225-8400
Eighty Four (G-4833)

Brodrick Hughes Energy LLC ....G....... 570 662-2464
Covington (G-3791)

Brush Aftermarket N Amer Inc ....F....... 412 829-7500
Turtle Creek (G-18560)

California Linear Devices Inc ....F....... 610 328-4000
Springfield (G-17909)

Coil Specialty Co Inc ....E....... 814 234-7044
State College (G-17952)

Converter Accessory Corp ....F....... 610 863-6008
Wind Gap (G-20168)

Critical Systems LLC ....G....... 570 643-6903
Tannersville (G-18235)

Crystal Engineering Corp ....G....... 610 647-2121
Berwyn (G-1358)

Curtiss-Wright Electro- ....A....... 724 275-5000
Cheswick (G-3105)

Danco Precision Inc ....F....... 610 933-8981
Phoenixville (G-14542)

Everson Tesla Inc ....D....... 610 746-1520
Nazareth (G-11965)

Gettysburg Transformer Corp ....E....... 717 334-2191
Gettysburg (G-6293)

Grays Automotive Speed Eqp ....G....... 717 436-8777
Mifflintown (G-11119)

Gupta Permold Corporation ....C....... 412 793-3511
Pittsburgh (G-15067)

Homewood Products Corporation ....E....... 412 665-2700
Pittsburgh (G-15099)

Hydromotion Inc ....D....... 610 948-4150
Spring City (G-17860)

Integrated Power Services LLC ....F....... 724 225-2900
Washington (G-19186)

Lake City Power Systems LLC ....G....... 814 774-2034
Lake City (G-8902)

Mechanical Service Company ....F....... 570 654-2445
Pittston (G-15766)

Mgs Inc ....C....... 717 336-7528
Denver (G-4083)

Nearhoof Machine Inc ....G....... 814 339-6621
Osceola Mills (G-13056)

NRG Texas Power LLC ....G....... 412 655-4134
West Mifflin (G-19743)

Patriot Sensors & Contrls Corp ....C....... 336 449-3400
Horsham (G-7840)

S & L Motors Inc ....G....... 570 342-9718
Scranton (G-17280)

Toshiba International Corp ....G....... 215 830-3340
Dresher (G-4359)

Videotek Inc ....C....... 610 327-2292
Pottstown (G-16068)

World of Wheels Inc ....F....... 814 676-5721
Seneca (G-17373)

MOUTHWASHES

Gentell Inc ....D....... 215 788-2700
Bristol (G-2147)

MOWERS & ACCESSORIES

Robert J Brown ....E....... 814 486-1768
Emporium (G-5074)

Saylor Industries Inc ....G....... 814 479-4964
Johnstown (G-8432)

MULTI-SVCS CENTER

Catalyst Crossroads LLC ....G....... 412 969-2733
Pittsburgh (G-14827)

MUSEUMS & ART GALLERIES

Historical Documents Co ....G....... 215 533-4500
Philadelphia (G-13830)

MUSIC BROADCASTING SVCS

Business Cmmunications Systems ....G....... 610 827-7061
Chester Springs (G-3073)

MUSIC SCHOOLS

Bucks Musical Instrument Pdts ....G....... 215 345-9442
Doylestown (G-4283)

MUSICAL INSTRUMENT PARTS & ACCESS, WHOLESALE

Gorden Inc ....G....... 610 644-4476
Reading (G-16395)

MUSICAL INSTRUMENT REPAIR

Bucks Musical Instrument Pdts............G...... 215 345-9442
  Doylestown (G-4283)
Elderhorst Bells Inc ....G...... 215 679-3264
  Palm (G-13094)

MUSICAL INSTRUMENTS & ACCESS: Carrying Cases

Susan Reabuck ....G...... 610 797-7014
  Allentown (G-405)

MUSICAL INSTRUMENTS & ACCESS: NEC

Blocki Flute Method LLC ....G...... 866 463-5883
  Gibsonia (G-6327)
Carson Industries Inc ....E...... 724 295-5147
  Freeport (G-6201)
Catania Folk Instruments Inc ....G...... 570 922-4487
  Millmont (G-11219)
Smuckers Harness Shop Inc ....F 717 445-5956
  Narvon (G-11927)
Summer Music Festival ....G...... 570 343-7271
  Dunmore (G-4484)

MUSICAL INSTRUMENTS & ACCESS: Pipe Organs

Fritzsche Organ Co Inc ....G...... 610 797-2510
  Allentown (G-220)
Hunter Mudler Inc ....F 215 229-5470
  Philadelphia (G-13843)
Lawless Assoc Pipe Organ Inc ....G...... 717 593-0398
  Greencastle (G-6621)
R J Brunner & Company ....G...... 717 285-3534
  Silver Spring (G-17590)

MUSICAL INSTRUMENTS & PARTS: String

C F Martin & Co Inc ....A 610 759-2837
  Nazareth (G-11957)
DAddario & Company Inc ....D...... 856 217-4954
  Philadelphia (G-13602)

MUSICAL INSTRUMENTS & SPLYS STORES

B X S Bass Inc ....G...... 724 378-8697
  Aliquippa (G-67)
Bucks Musical Instrument Pdts............G...... 215 345-9442
  Doylestown (G-4283)
Chimneys Violin Shop ....G...... 717 258-3203
  Boiling Springs (G-1872)

MUSICAL INSTRUMENTS & SPLYS STORES: Keyboards

Qrs Music Inc ....G...... 239 597-5888
  Seneca (G-17367)
Qrs Music Technologies Inc ....G...... 814 676-6683
  Seneca (G-17368)

MUSICAL INSTRUMENTS: Bells

Malmark Incorporated ....E...... 215 766-7200
  Plumsteadville (G-15811)

MUSICAL INSTRUMENTS: Carillon Bells

Elderhorst Bells Inc ....G...... 215 679-3264
  Palm (G-13094)
Schulmerich Bells LLC ....F 215 257-2771
  Hatfield (G-7395)

MUSICAL INSTRUMENTS: Electric & Electronic

B X S Bass Inc ....G...... 724 378-8697
  Aliquippa (G-67)

MUSICAL INSTRUMENTS: Guitars & Parts, Electric & Acoustic

Breezy Ridge Instruments Ltd ....G...... 610 691-3302
  Bethlehem (G-1473)
Bucks Musical Instrument Pdts............G...... 215 345-9442
  Doylestown (G-4283)

MUSICAL INSTRUMENTS: Harpsichords

Bedside Harp LLC ....F 215 752-7599
  Bensalem (G-1155)

MUSICAL INSTRUMENTS: Mouthpieces

David R Houser ....G...... 610 505-5924
  Norristown (G-12651)

MUSICAL INSTRUMENTS: Music Rolls, Perforated

Qrs Music Inc ....G...... 239 597-5888
  Seneca (G-17367)
Qrs Music Technologies Inc ....G...... 814 676-6683
  Seneca (G-17368)

MUSICAL INSTRUMENTS: Organs

Columbia Organ Works Inc ....G...... 717 684-3573
  Columbia (G-3436)

MUSICAL INSTRUMENTS: Synthesizers, Music

Lyrrus Inc ....E 215 922-0880
  Philadelphia (G-13979)

MUSICAL INSTRUMENTS: Violins & Parts

Chimneys Violin Shop ....G...... 717 258-3203
  Boiling Springs (G-1872)

NAME PLATES: Engraved Or Etched

Cedar Hollow Sales Inc ....G...... 610 644-2660
  Malvern (G-10201)
Industrial Nameplate Inc ....E...... 215 322-1111
  Warminster (G-18898)
Ivy Graphics Inc ....F 215 396-9446
  Warminster (G-18900)

NAMEPLATES

Gerding Corp ....G...... 215 441-0900
  Warminster (G-18887)
Ivy Graphics Inc ....F 215 396-9446
  Warminster (G-18900)
La France Corp ....C 610 361-4300
  Concordville (G-3457)
Promark Industries Inc ....G...... 724 356-4060
  Mc Donald (G-10579)

NATIONAL SECURITY FORCES

Dla Document Services ....F 717 605-3777
  Mechanicsburg (G-10837)
Interntnal Def Systems USA LLC ....G...... 610 973-2228
  Orefield (G-13012)

NATURAL GAS COMPRESSING SVC, On-Site

Archrock Inc ....E...... 724 464-2291
  Indiana (G-8080)
Archrock Services LP ....G...... 724 935-7660
  Wexford (G-19789)
Archrock Services LP ....G...... 570 567-7162
  Canton (G-2662)
Markwest Liberty Midstream ....D...... 724 514-4401
  Washington (G-19199)
Thyssnkrupp Indus Slutions USA ....D...... 412 257-8277
  Bridgeville (G-2095)

NATURAL GAS DISTRIBUTION TO CONSUMERS

Carlson Technologies Inc ....F 814 371-5500
  Du Bois (G-4386)
Chevron Ae Resources LLC ....E...... 724 662-0300
  Jackson Center (G-8226)
Cnx Resources Corporation ....B...... 724 485-4000
  Canonsburg (G-2562)
Direct Energy Products Inc ....F 216 255-7777
  Tionesta (G-18370)
Em Energy Employer LLC ....E...... 412 564-1300
  Canonsburg (G-2582)
Em Energy Pennsylvania LLC ....E...... 412 564-1300
  Canonsburg (G-2583)
Kriebel Minerals Inc ....G...... 814 226-4160
  Clarion (G-3182)
Markwest Hydrocarbon Inc ....E...... 724 514-4398
  Washington (G-19198)
Range Resources ....G...... 570 858-1200
  Bradford (G-1989)
United Enrgy Plus Trminals LLC ....E...... 610 774-5151
  Allentown (G-418)

Williams Companies Inc ....D....... 717 490-6857
  Lancaster (G-9241)

NATURAL GAS LIQUID FRACTIONATING SVC

Markwest Hydrocarbon Inc ....E....... 724 514-4398
  Washington (G-19198)
Markwest Liberty Midstream................D....... 724 514-4401
  Washington (G-19199)

NATURAL GAS LIQUIDS PRODUCTION

American Petroleum Partners ....G...... 844 835-5277
  Canonsburg (G-2539)
Finnegan Gas Corp ....G...... 724 428-3688
  Wind Ridge (G-20176)

NATURAL GAS LIQUIDS PRODUCTION

Arsenal Resources Energy LLC ....F....... 724 940-1100
  Wexford (G-19790)
Eqt Corporation ....G...... 412 395-2080
  Pittsburgh (G-14982)
Four Three Energy Services LLC ....G...... 814 797-0021
  Knox (G-8810)
Kriebel Wells ....G...... 814 226-4160
  Clarion (G-3183)
M W Gary and Associates ....G...... 724 206-0071
  Washington (G-19197)
Praxair Inc ....G...... 215 721-9099
  Souderton (G-17760)
Trans Energy Inc ....F....... 304 684-7053
  Pittsburgh (G-15638)
Williams Companies Inc ....D...... 717 490-6857
  Lancaster (G-9241)

NATURAL GAS PRODUCTION

Ardent Resources Inc ....G...... 412 854-1193
  Pittsburgh (G-14720)
Baker Gas Inc ....F....... 724 297-3456
  Worthington (G-20227)
Blx Inc ....G...... 724 543-5743
  Kittanning (G-8758)
Carlson Technologies Inc ....F....... 814 371-5500
  Du Bois (G-4386)
CE Ready Mix ....E....... 724 727-3331
  Apollo (G-667)
Cnx Gas Company LLC ....G...... 724 485-4000
  Canonsburg (G-2559)
Cnx Gas Corporation ....D...... 724 485-4000
  Canonsburg (G-2560)
Cnx Resources Corporation ....B...... 724 485-4000
  Canonsburg (G-2562)
Consol PA Coal Co LLC ....A...... 724 485-4000
  Canonsburg (G-2571)
Dannic Energy Corporation ....G...... 724 465-6663
  Indiana (G-8089)
Davies & Sons LLC ....G...... 814 723-7430
  Warren (G-19020)
De Limited Family Partnership ....F....... 814 938-0800
  Punxsutawney (G-16133)
Devonian Resources Inc ....E....... 814 589-7061
  Pleasantville (G-15800)
Dominion Exploration and Prod ....G...... 724 349-4450
  Indiana (G-8091)
Elkhorn Operating Company ....G...... 814 723-4390
  Warren (G-19023)
Em Energy Employer LLC ....E....... 412 564-1300
  Canonsburg (G-2582)
Em Energy Pennsylvania LLC ....E....... 412 564-1300
  Canonsburg (G-2583)
Grayco Controls LLC ....G...... 724 545-2300
  Adrian (G-29)
Inflection Energy 303 531-2343
  Williamsport (G-20025)
J R Resources L P ....G...... 814 365-5821
  Ringgold (G-16751)
Kriebel Gas Inc ....D...... 814 226-4160
  Clarion (G-3181)
Kriebel Gas Inc ....G...... 814 938-2010
  Punxsutawney (G-16146)
Maple Grove Enterprises Inc ....G...... 814 473-6272
  Rimersburg (G-16750)
Mountain Energy Inc ....F....... 724 428-5200
  Aleppo (G-61)
Papco Inc ....F....... 814 726-2130
  Warren (G-19042)
Petronorth Ltd ....G...... 814 368-6992
  Smethport (G-17636)

PRODUCT

NATURAL GAS PRODUCTION (cont.)

Phillips Exploration LLC ....D..... 724 772-3500
Warrendale (G-19092)
Questa Petroleum Co ....G..... 724 832-7297
Greensburg (G-6708)
Questa Petroleum Company ....G..... 412 220-9210
Pittsburgh (G-15462)
Repsol Oil & Gas Usa LLC ....G..... 724 814-5300
Warrendale (G-19096)
Williams Companies Inc ....D..... 717 490-6857
Lancaster (G-9241)

NATURAL GAS TRANSMISSION

Atlas Energy Company LLC ....E..... 877 280-2857
Philadelphia (G-13423)
Belden & Blake Corporation ....F..... 814 589-7091
Pleasantville (G-15797)
Dominion Energy Transm Inc ....G..... 724 354-3433
Shelocta (G-17485)
Praxair Inc ....G..... 215 721-9099
Souderton (G-17760)
Targa Energy LP ....F..... 412 489-0006
Pittsburgh (G-15598)

NATURAL GASOLINE PRODUCTION

De Limited Family Partnership ....F..... 814 938-0800
Punxsutawney (G-16133)
M/D Gas Inc ....G..... 724 548-2501
Kittanning (G-8778)
Mds Associated Companies Inc ....D..... 724 548-2501
Kittanning (G-8780)

NATURAL PROPANE PRODUCTION

E F Laudenslager Inc ....F..... 610 395-1582
Orefield (G-13011)
Falcon Propane LLC ....G..... 570 207-1711
Blakely (G-1747)
Lancaster Propane Gas Inc ....F..... 717 898-0800
Lancaster (G-9104)
Plains Lpg Services ....G..... 717 376-0830
Lebanon (G-9262)
Streamline Propane Llc ....G..... 215 919-4500
Green Lane (G-6593)

NAVIGATIONAL SYSTEMS & INSTRUMENTS

Pennsylvania State University ....E..... 215 682-4000
Warminster (G-18939)
Warren Machine Co Inc ....F..... 215 491-5500
Warrington (G-19136)

NETS: Laundry

Shen Manufacturing Company Inc ....G..... 570 278-3707
Montrose (G-11476)

NETTING: Elastic, Meat

Jetnet Corporation ....D..... 412 741-0100
Sewickley (G-17396)
York Textile Products Inc ....G..... 717 764-2528
York (G-20751)

NEWS DEALERS & NEWSSTANDS

Carreon Publishing LLC ....G..... 570 673-5151
Canton (G-2663)
Ligonier Outfitters Newsstands ....G..... 724 238-4900
Ligonier (G-9961)
Venus Video ....G..... 215 937-1545
Philadelphia (G-14440)

NEWSPAPER COLUMN WRITING SVCS

Icon/Information Concepts Inc ....G..... 215 545-6700
Langhorne (G-9303)

NEWSSTAND

Ledger Newspapers ....G..... 610 444-6590
West Chester (G-19590)

NICKEL ALLOY

Basically Nickel ....G..... 717 292-7232
East Berlin (G-4519)
Double Nickel Delivery LLC ....G..... 412 721-0550
Irwin (G-8157)
Nichols4nickels ....G..... 215 317-6717
Philadelphia (G-14073)
Wooden Nickels LLC ....G..... 484 408-4901
Pottstown (G-15958)

NONCURRENT CARRYING WIRING DEVICES

A W Mercer Inc ....C..... 610 367-8460
Boyertown (G-1892)
Robroy Industries Inc ....F..... 412 828-2100
Verona (G-18761)
Silvine Inc ....E..... 215 657-2345
Willow Grove (G-20142)

NONFERROUS: Rolling & Drawing, NEC

Hammond Group Inc ....E..... 610 327-1400
Pottstown (G-15995)
Hygrade Acquisition Corp ....D..... 610 866-2441
Bethlehem (G-1536)
Hygrade Mtal Moulding Mfg Corp ....E..... 610 866-2441
Bethlehem (G-1538)
Inweld Corporation ....F..... 610 261-1900
Coplay (G-3644)
Milner Enterprises Inc ....F..... 610 252-0700
Easton (G-4722)
Nlmk Pennsylvania LLC ....B..... 724 983-6464
Farrell (G-5869)
Perryman Company ....F..... 724 746-9390
Coal Center (G-3276)
Salem Tube Inc ....C..... 724 646-4301
Greenville (G-6772)
Selectrode Industries Inc ....E..... 724 378-6351
Aliquippa (G-93)
Techspec Inc ....E..... 724 694-2716
Derry (G-4108)
Torpedo Specialty Wire Inc ....E..... 814 563-7505
Pittsfield (G-15739)
Vsmpo-Tirus US Inc ....G..... 724 251-9400
Leetsdale (G-9706)
Watson Metal Products Corp ....D..... 908 276-2202
Lancaster (G-9236)

NONMETALLIC MINERALS: Support Activities, Exc Fuels

Covia Holdings Corporation ....G..... 412 431-4777
Pittsburgh (G-14883)
Preptech Inc ....G..... 724 727-3439
Apollo (G-684)
Rosebud Mining Co ....E..... 814 749-5208
Twin Rocks (G-18572)
Seneca Mineral Co Inc ....G..... 814 476-0076
Erie (G-5474)

NOTARIES PUBLIC

First Class Specialties ....F..... 724 446-1000
Herminie (G-7570)
Notaries Equipment Co ....F..... 215 563-8190
Philadelphia (G-14085)

NOTIONS: Pins & Needles

Chima Inc ....E..... 610 372-6508
Reading (G-16345)
Moore Push Pin Company ....D..... 215 233-5700
Glenside (G-6531)

NOVELTIES

Fun-Time International Inc ....C..... 215 925-1450
Philadelphia (G-13734)
Gail Dagowitz ....G..... 610 642-7634
Gladwyne (G-6408)
Paul William Boyle ....G..... 412 828-0883
Oakmont (G-12923)

NOVELTIES & SPECIALTIES: Metal

Primitives By Kathy Inc ....D..... 717 394-4220
Lancaster (G-9175)

NOVELTIES, PAPER, WHOLESALE

Butts Ticket Company Inc ....F..... 610 869-7450
Cochranville (G-3355)
Devra Party Corp ....G..... 718 522-7421
Philadelphia (G-13626)
Kelly Line Inc ....F..... 570 527-6822
Pottsville (G-16085)

NOVELTIES: Leather

Dull Knife Terminator Inc ....G..... 717 512-8596
Mechanicsburg (G-10839)
Spiders Den Inc ....G..... 724 445-7450
Chicora (G-3129)

Todd Weikel ....G..... 610 779-5508
Reading (G-16542)

NOVELTIES: Paper, Made From Purchased Materials

Beistle Company ....B..... 717 532-2131
Shippensburg (G-17517)
Devra Party Corp ....G..... 718 522-7421
Philadelphia (G-13626)
Paper Magic Group Inc ....C..... 570 961-3863
Moosic (G-11511)
Party Time Manufacturing Co ....G..... 800 346-3847
Hughestown (G-7894)
Pocket Cross Inc ....G..... 724 745-1140
Houston (G-7877)
Todd Weikel ....G..... 610 779-5508
Reading (G-16542)

NOVELTIES: Plastic

Em-Bed-It & Co Inc ....F..... 412 781-8585
Pittsburgh (G-14966)
Helix Scientific Inc ....G..... 215 953-2072
Southampton (G-17817)
Kindle Creations Inc ....E..... 215 997-6878
Chalfont (G-2882)
Todd Weikel ....G..... 610 779-5508
Reading (G-16542)

NOVELTY SHOPS

Becky Kens Duck & Geese Creat ....G..... 717 684-0252
Columbia (G-3431)
Paul William Boyle ....G..... 412 828-0883
Oakmont (G-12923)
Stanhope Microworks ....G..... 717 796-9000
Mechanicsburg (G-10891)
Telepole Manufacturing Inc ....G..... 570 546-3699
Muncy (G-11835)

NOZZLES & SPRINKLERS Lawn Hose

Green Garden Inc ....E..... 814 623-2735
Bedford (G-1053)
Rowe Sprinkler Systems Inc ....E..... 570 837-7647
Middleburg (G-11039)

NURSERIES & LAWN & GARDEN SPLY STORE, RET: Lawn/Garden Splys

Diamond Milling Company Inc ....G..... 724 846-0920
New Brighton (G-12034)
Hampsons Farm & Garden Inc ....G..... 570 724-3012
Wellsboro (G-19464)
Spring Valley Mulch Brian ....G..... 717 292-7945
Dover (G-4205)

NURSERIES & LAWN & GARDEN SPLY STORES, RETAIL

Sauders Nursery ....F..... 717 354-9851
East Earl (G-4555)
Village Farm Market ....G..... 717 733-5340
Ephrata (G-5154)

NURSERIES & LAWN & GARDEN SPLY STORES, RETAIL: Fertilizer

Joe Grow Inc ....F..... 814 355-2878
Bellefonte (G-1106)
Knittle & Frey AG-Center Inc ....G..... 570 323-7554
Williamsport (G-20032)
Lawn & Garden ....G..... 724 458-6141
Grove City (G-6794)

NURSERIES & LAWN & GARDEN SPLY STORES, RETAIL: Lawn Ornament

Campania International Inc ....D..... 215 541-4627
Pennsburg (G-13246)

NURSERIES & LAWN/GARDEN SPLY STORE, RET: Lawnmowers/Tractors

Betts Equipment Inc ....G..... 215 598-7501
New Hope (G-12298)
Ephraim L King ....G..... 570 837-9470
Winfield (G-20200)
Scranton Grinder & Hardware ....E..... 570 344-2520
Scranton (G-17285)

NURSERIES & LAWN/GARDEN SPLY STORES, RET: Garden Splys/Tools

Mifflinburg Farmers Exchange ....G....... 570 966-4030
Mifflinburg (G-11098)

NURSERIES/LAWN/GARDEN SPLY STORES, RET: Hydroponic Eqpt/Sply

National Hydraulics Inc ....G....... 724 887-3850
Scottdale (G-17197)

NURSERY & GARDEN CENTERS

Dingmans Ferry Stone Inc ....G....... 570 828-2617
Dingmans Ferry (G-4142)
Edward T Regina ....G....... 570 223-8358
East Stroudsburg (G-4614)

NUTRITION SVCS

Nutrition Inc ....E....... 724 978-2100
Irwin (G-8185)
Rae Foods Inc ....G....... 716 326-7437
North East (G-12755)
Steel Fitness Premier LLC ....E....... 610 973-1500
Allentown (G-403)

NUTS: Metal

American Fastener Tech Corp ....F....... 724 444-6940
Gibsonia (G-6323)
Superbolt Inc ....D....... 412 279-1149
Carnegie (G-2795)
Touchpoint Inc ....A....... 610 459-4000
Concordville (G-3460)

NYLON FIBERS

Honeywell International Inc ....A....... 215 533-3000
Philadelphia (G-13832)
James R Hanlon Inc ....E....... 610 631-9999
Eagleville (G-4514)
Quadrant Holding Inc ....C....... 724 468-7062
Delmont (G-4054)

NYLON RESINS

Knf Corporation ....E....... 570 386-3550
Tamaqua (G-18213)
Quadrant Holding Inc ....C....... 724 468-7062
Delmont (G-4054)

OAKUM

Oaks Industrial Supply Inc ....G....... 610 539-7008
Norristown (G-12696)

OFFICE EQPT WHOLESALERS

Armstrong Supply Co ....G....... 215 643-0310
Ambler (G-567)
Automated Indus Systems Inc.............E....... 814 838-2270
Erie (G-5198)
Comdoc Inc ....D....... 800 321-1009
Pittsburgh (G-14868)
Ois LLC ....G....... 717 447-0265
Mount Union (G-11746)
William A Fraser Inc ....G....... 570 622-7347
Pottsville (G-16102)

OFFICE EQPT, WHOLESALE: Blueprinting

Print-O-Stat Inc................................F....... 724 742-9811
Cranberry Township (G-3845)
Print-O-Stat Inc................................G....... 610 265-5470
King of Prussia (G-8664)

OFFICE EQPT, WHOLESALE: Micrographic

Craddock & Lerro Associates...............G....... 610 543-0200
Drexel Hill (G-4363)

OFFICE EQPT, WHOLESALE: Photocopy Machines

Minton Holdings LLC.........................G....... 412 787-5912
Pittsburgh (G-15293)

OFFICE SPLY & STATIONERY STORES: Office Forms & Splys

Arkwood Products Inc........................G....... 412 835-8730
Bethel Park (G-1404)

Byrne Enterprises Inc ....G....... 610 670-0767
Reading (G-16338)
Commercial Prtg & Off Suppy ....G....... 814 765-4731
Clearfield (G-3217)
Fox IV Technologies Inc ....E....... 724 387-3500
Export (G-5603)
Gc Enterprises LLC ....G....... 570 655-5543
Pittston (G-15752)
Globe Print Shop...............................G....... 570 454-8031
Hazleton (G-7499)
Interform Corporation ....F....... 610 566-1515
Media (G-10934)
Little Printing Co Inc ....F....... 724 437-4831
Uniontown (G-18635)
Mark Grim ....G....... 724 758-2270
Ellwood City (G-4945)
Morrisons Cove Herald Inc ....G....... 814 793-2144
Martinsburg (G-10527)
Northeastern Envelope Company ....D....... 800 233-4285
Old Forge (G-12971)
Ogden Brothers Incorporated.............F....... 610 789-1258
Havertown (G-7425)
R T R Business Products Inc ....E....... 724 733-7373
Export (G-5622)
Specialty Group Printing Inc...............E....... 814 425-3061
Cochranton (G-3351)
Thorndale Press Inc..........................G....... 610 384-3363
Downingtown (G-4258)
W B Mason Co Inc.............................D....... 888 926-2766
Allentown (G-427)
Wakefoose Office Supply & Prtg ....G....... 814 623-5742
Bedford (G-1079)

OFFICE SPLY & STATIONERY STORES: Writing Splys

Auskin Inc ....G....... 610 696-0234
West Chester (G-19503)
W B Mason Co Inc ....E....... 888 926-2766
Altoona (G-555)

OFFICE SPLYS, NEC, WHOLESALE

Free Energy Systems Inc ....E....... 610 583-2640
Collingdale (G-3404)
R T R Business Products Inc................E....... 724 733-7373
Export (G-5622)

OFFICES & CLINICS OF DENTISTS: Dental Clinic

Everest Dental LLC ....G....... 215 671-0188
Philadelphia (G-13683)
Urgent Denture Repair LLC.................G....... 412 714-8157
Pittsburgh (G-15685)

OFFICES & CLINICS OF DOCTORS OF MEDICINE: Surgeon

PA & Implant Surgery LLC ....G....... 814 375-0500
Du Bois (G-4410)

OFFICES & CLINICS OF DRS OF MEDICINE: Physician, Orthopedic

Coordinated Health Systems................C....... 610 861-8080
Bethlehem (G-1487)
Hanger Prsthetcs & Ortho Inc.............G....... 724 438-4582
Uniontown (G-18629)

OFFICES & CLINICS OF HEALTH PRACTITIONERS: Nutrition

Catalyst Crossroads LLC ....G....... 412 969-2733
Pittsburgh (G-14827)

OFFICES & CLINICS OF OPTOMETRISTS: Specialist, Optometrists

Karen Wrigley Dr..............................G....... 215 563-8440
Philadelphia (G-13922)
Rss Optometry LLC ....G....... 610 933-2177
Phoenixville (G-14577)

OIL & GAS FIELD MACHINERY

Baker Hghes Olfld Oprtions Inc............G....... 724 266-4725
Ambridge (G-610)
Blowout Tools Inc ....F....... 724 627-0208
Waynesburg (G-19434)

Bridon-American Corporation ....B....... 570 822-3349
Hanover Township (G-6982)
Central Penn Rig Service ....G....... 814 342-4800
Morrisdale (G-11547)
Funks Drilling Incorporated ....F....... 717 423-6688
Newville (G-12601)
General Electric Company ....G....... 610 876-2200
Eddystone (G-4803)
Gill Rock Drill Company Inc ....E....... 717 272-3861
Lebanon (G-9573)
Heisey Machine Co Inc ....G....... 717 293-1373
Lancaster (G-9042)
Matheson Tri-Gas Inc........................D....... 215 641-2700
Montgomeryville (G-11406)
National Oilwell Varco Inc ....F....... 724 745-6005
Canonsburg (G-2611)
National Oilwell Varco Inc ....G....... 724 947-4581
Burgettstown (G-2352)
National Oilwell Varco Inc ....E....... 318 243-5910
Washington (G-19209)
Oil Process Systems Inc ....E....... 610 437-4618
Allentown (G-337)
Robroy Industries Inc ....F....... 412 828-2100
Verona (G-18761)
Technipfmc US Holdings Inc ....G....... 303 217-2030
Erie (G-5504)
Technipfmc US Holdings Inc ....F....... 724 459-7350
Blairsville (G-1743)
Technipfmc US Holdings Inc ....E....... 570 546-2380
Muncy (G-11834)
Technipfmc US Holdings Inc ....E....... 724 820-5023
Canonsburg (G-2646)
Vetco Gray Inc ....G....... 570 435-8027
Muncy (G-11837)
Wc Welding Services ....G....... 570 798-2300
Lakewood (G-8916)
Weatherford International LLC ....E....... 570 326-2754
Muncy (G-11839)
Weatherford International LLC ....D....... 570 546-0745
Muncy (G-11840)

OIL BURNER REPAIR SVCS

Building Inspectors Contrs Inc.............G....... 215 481-0606
Glenside (G-6509)

OIL FIELD MACHINERY & EQPT

Electrichp USA Corp...........................E....... 724 678-5084
Venetia (G-18742)
FMC Technologies Inc ....E....... 570 546-2441
Muncy (G-11816)
FMC Technologies Inc ....F....... 215 822-4485
Lansdale (G-9368)
National Oilwell Varco Inc ....D....... 814 427-2555
Punxsutawney (G-16150)
National Oilwell Varco LP ....E....... 570 862-2548
Leetsdale (G-9700)
Oil States Energy Services LLC ....G....... 724 746-1168
Canonsburg (G-2615)
Pcs Ferguson Inc ....G....... 412 264-6000
Brookville (G-2268)
Stream-Flo USA LLC...........................G....... 724 349-6090
Indiana (G-8131)
Wise Intervention Svcs USA Inc ....D....... 724 405-6660
Smithton (G-17664)

OIL FIELD SVCS, NEC

A & P Support Inc..............................D....... 570 265-9157
Pittsburgh (G-14627)
Alderdice Inc ....D....... 570 996-1609
Meshoppen (G-11005)
American Exploration Company ....D....... 610 940-4015
Plymouth Meeting (G-15830)
American Well Service LLC ....D....... 724 206-9372
Washington (G-19149)
B B Oilfield Equipment ....F....... 724 668-2509
New Alexandria (G-12017)
Baker Hghes Olfld Oprtions LLC...........G....... 724 695-2266
Imperial (G-8059)
Baker Hughes A GE Company LLC.......D....... 724 696-3059
Mount Pleasant (G-11687)
Belden & Blake Corporation ....F....... 814 589-7091
Pleasantville (G-15797)
C&J Energy Services Inc.....................D....... 724 354-5225
Shelocta (G-17484)
Calfrac Well Services Corp ....G....... 724 564-5350
Smithfield (G-17643)
Cameron Technologies Us Inc.............D....... 724 695-3798
Coraopolis (G-3671)

Canary LLC ....F 724 483-2224
Charleroi *(G-3007)*
CDK Perforating LLC ....G 724 222-8900
Washington *(G-19155)*
Cimarron Energy ....G 724 801-8517
Indiana *(G-8086)*
Cogan Wind LLC ....G 570 998-9554
Trout Run *(G-18513)*
Costys Energy Services ....G 570 662-2752
Mansfield *(G-10413)*
Cs Trucking LLC ....G 814 224-0395
East Freedom *(G-4563)*
Cudd Pressure Control Inc ....E 570 250-9043
Lemont Furnace *(G-9735)*
Dmand Energy ....F 970 201-4976
Cabot *(G-2455)*
Elements Direct LLC ....G 903 343-5441
New Brighton *(G-12035)*
Elite Oil Field Services Inc ....G 724 627-6060
Uniontown *(G-18624)*
Energy Worx Inc ....G 321 610-4676
Mansfield *(G-10414)*
Franks International LLC ....G 724 943-3243
Greensboro *(G-6646)*
Gas Field Specialists Inc ....D 814 698-2122
Shinglehouse *(G-17507)*
Great Lakes Wellhead Inc ....G 570 723-8995
Wellsboro *(G-19463)*
Great Oak Energy Inc ....G 412 828-2900
Oakmont *(G-12918)*
Halliburton Company ....C 570 547-5800
Montgomery *(G-11370)*
Horizontal Wireline Svcs LLC ....E 724 382-5012
Irwin *(G-8169)*
Infinity Oilfield Services LLC ....G 570 327-8114
Montoursville *(G-11442)*
J C& Well Services Inc ....E 724 475-4881
Fredonia *(G-6184)*
Jcs Oilfield Services LLC ....F 814 665-4008
Corry *(G-3766)*
Jklm Energy LLC ....G 561 826-3620
Sewickley *(G-17398)*
Kapanick Construction Inc ....F 814 763-3681
Meadville *(G-10742)*
Linde Corporation ....C 570 299-5700
Pittston *(G-15765)*
MI Swaco ....G 724 820-3306
Canonsburg *(G-2603)*
Mountain Resources Inc ....G 814 734-1496
Edinboro *(G-4817)*
Msl Oil & Gas Corp ....E 814 362-6891
Lewis Run *(G-9878)*
Oil States Energy Services LLC .....G 814 290-6755
Clearfield *(G-3227)*
Pacific Process Systems Inc ....C 724 993-4445
Washington *(G-19214)*
Petroleum Service Partners ....G 724 349-1536
Indiana *(G-8119)*
Petta Enterprises ....G 607 857-5915
Mansfield *(G-10425)*
Quality Process Services ....G 724 455-1687
Normalville *(G-12625)*
Rjb Well Services Inc ....F 814 368-9570
Bradford *(G-1990)*
ROC Service Company Ltd ....G 724 745-3319
Canonsburg *(G-2631)*
Rpc Inc ....E 570 673-5965
Canton *(G-2667)*
Scott Neilly ....G 814 362-4443
Bradford *(G-1991)*
Select Energy Services LLC ....D 724 239-2056
Eighty Four *(G-4848)*
Sooner Pipe LLC ....G 570 368-4590
Montoursville *(G-11450)*
SPM Flow Control Inc ....C 570 546-1005
Muncy *(G-11833)*
Stallion Littlefield Services ....G 724 966-2272
Carmichaels *(G-2761)*
Stallion Oilfield Services Ltd ....E 724 743-4801
Canonsburg *(G-2639)*
Stallion Oilfield Services Ltd ....G 570 494-0760
Cogan Station *(G-3362)*
Stallion Oilfield Services Ltd ....E 724 222-9059
Washington *(G-19229)*
Steven E Tachoir ....G 814 726-1572
Marienville *(G-10459)*
Team Oil Tools LP ....G 724 301-2659
Grove City *(G-6806)*
Thru Tubing Solutions Inc ....G 412 787-8060
Imperial *(G-8078)*

Thru Tubing Solutions Inc ....G 570 546-0323
Montoursville *(G-11453)*
Universal Well Services Inc ....C 724 430-6201
Lemont Furnace *(G-9739)*
Universal Well Services Inc ....E 814 368-6175
Meadville *(G-10809)*
Vulcan Oilfield Services LLC ....G 724 698-1008
New Castle *(G-12165)*
Warrior Energy Services Corp ....F 814 637-5191
Penfield *(G-13225)*
Weatherford International LLC ....F 724 745-7050
Canonsburg *(G-2656)*
West Penn Energy Services LLC ....C 724 354-4118
Shelocta *(G-17490)*
Wood Group Usa Inc ....G 724 514-1600
Canonsburg *(G-2661)*
Wyoming Casing Service Inc ....E 570 363-2883
New Albany *(G-12016)*

OILS & ESSENTIAL OILS

Koppers Inc ....C 412 227-2001
Pittsburgh *(G-15188)*

OILS & GREASES: Blended & Compounded

Allegheny Petroleum Pdts Co ....D 412 829-1990
Wilmerding *(G-20158)*
BP Lubricants USA Inc ....E 215 674-5301
Warminster *(G-18841)*
GTS Enterprises Inc ....E 610 798-9922
Allentown *(G-239)*
Richardsapex Inc ....E 215 487-1100
Philadelphia *(G-14247)*
Stevenson-Cooper Inc ....G 215 223-2600
Philadelphia *(G-14348)*

OILS & GREASES: Lubricating

Advanced Lubrication Spc Inc ....E 215 244-2114
Bensalem *(G-1144)*
Afco C&S LLC ....G 717 264-9147
Chambersburg *(G-2898)*
Alex C Fergusson LLC ....D 717 264-9147
Chambersburg *(G-2899)*
Allegheny Petroleum Pdts Co ....G 724 266-3247
Ambridge *(G-608)*
Applied Creativity Inc ....G 724 327-0054
Export *(G-5589)*
Arkema Delaware Inc ....A 610 205-7000
King of Prussia *(G-8582)*
Arkema Inc ....C 215 826-2600
Bristol *(G-2109)*
Castrol Industrial N Amer Inc ....D 877 641-1600
Levittown *(G-9824)*
CRC Industries Inc ....G 800 556-5074
Warminster *(G-18850)*
CRC Industries Inc ....C 215 674-4300
Horsham *(G-7806)*
Eni USA R & M Co Inc ....E 724 352-4451
Cabot *(G-2456)*
Fuchs Lubricants Co ....E 724 867-5000
Emlenton *(G-5008)*
General Polymeric Corporation ....D 610 374-5171
Reading *(G-16390)*
Gh Holdings Inc ....G 610 666-4000
Valley Forge *(G-18707)*
Graham Packaging Company LP .....E 717 849-8500
York *(G-20511)*
Houghton International Inc ....C 888 459-9844
Norristown *(G-12668)*
Kenum Distribution LLC ....G 814 383-2626
Mingoville *(G-11256)*
Levroil LLC ....G 412 722-9849
Pittsburgh *(G-15227)*
Lubedealercom ....G 814 521-9625
Berlin *(G-1290)*
McMillan Music Co LLC ....G 215 441-0212
New Britain *(G-12049)*
Noco Distribution LLC ....G 866 946-3927
Ridgway *(G-16719)*
Pennzoil-Quaker State Company ......B 724 756-0110
Karns City *(G-8482)*
PPG Architectural Finishes Inc ....D 610 380-6200
Downingtown *(G-4250)*
Sean Naughton ....G 570 646-0422
Pocono Pines *(G-15884)*
Sensible Components LLC ....F 855 548-7587
Oakdale *(G-12911)*
Stoner Incorporated ....F 800 227-5538
Lancaster *(G-9208)*

Whitmore Manufacturing Company ...G 724 225-4151
Washington *(G-19245)*
Whitmore Manufacturing Company ...F 724 225-8008
Washington *(G-19246)*

OILS: Acid

Fisher-Klosterman Inc ....F 717 274-7280
Lebanon *(G-9568)*

OILS: Core Or Binders

Interstate Foundry Products ....F 814 456-4202
Erie *(G-5332)*

OILS: Cutting

Twin Specialties Corporation ....G 610 834-7900
Conshohocken *(G-3614)*

OILS: Essential

Revoltnary Elctrnic Design LLC ......G 814 977-9546
Bedford *(G-1073)*
Ungerer Industries Inc ....D 610 868-7266
Bethlehem *(G-1647)*

OILS: Lubricating

International Group Inc ....E 814 827-4900
Titusville *(G-18385)*

OILS: Lubricating

BP Lubricants USA Inc ....D 215 443-5220
Warminster *(G-18840)*
Byrne Energy Corp ....G 570 895-4333
Mount Pocono *(G-11733)*
CRC Industries Inc ....C 215 441-4380
Warminster *(G-18851)*
Gordon Terminal Service Co PA ......C 412 331-9410
Mckees Rocks *(G-10661)*
Lube Center ....G 717 848-4885
York *(G-20567)*
Pennstar LLC ....F 484 275-7990
Northampton *(G-12859)*
Pitt Oil Service Inc ....G 412 771-6950
Pittsburgh *(G-15384)*
Quaker Chemical Corporation ....A 610 832-4000
Conshohocken *(G-3595)*
United Oil Company Corp ....F 412 231-1269
Pittsburgh *(G-15674)*

OINTMENTS

Gentell Inc ....D 215 788-2700
Bristol *(G-2147)*
Medarbor LLC ....G 732 887-6111
Bristol *(G-2165)*

OLEFINS

Lyondell Chemical Company ....D 610 359-2360
Newtown Square *(G-12583)*

ON-LINE DATABASE INFORMATION RETRIEVAL SVCS

Cricket Communications LLC ....G 267 687-5949
Philadelphia *(G-13582)*
Reclamere Inc ....E 814 684-5505
Tyrone *(G-18592)*
Search Live Today LLC ....G 610 805-7734
Norristown *(G-12710)*

ONYX MARBLE: Dimension

Newport Aggregate Inc ....G 570 736-6612
Nanticoke *(G-11900)*

OPERATIVE BUILDERS: Condominiums

Baron Development Company ....G 814 676-8703
Oil City *(G-12940)*

OPERATOR: Apartment Buildings

J H R Inc ....G 412 221-1617
Bridgeville *(G-2072)*
James May Costume Co ....G 610 532-3430
Folsom *(G-6026)*
Kingsly Compression Inc ....E 724 524-1840
Saxonburg *(G-17091)*
Lomma Investments ....E 570 346-5555
Scranton *(G-17256)*

Mdg Associates.........................E........ 215 969-6623
Philadelphia (G-14000)

OPERATOR: Nonresidential Buildings

Burrell Group Inc ....F........ 724 337-3557
New Kensington (G-12328)
College Town Inc.........................G........ 717 532-7354
Shippensburg (G-17523)
College Town Inc.........................G........ 717 532-3034
Shippensburg (G-17524)
Lancaster General Svcs Bus Tr.....F........ 717 544-5474
Lancaster (G-9095)
Lightning Group Inc.....................G........ 717 834-3031
Duncannon (G-4447)
New Werner Holding Co Inc.........G........ 724 588-2000
Greenville (G-6758)
Woodbine Properties....................C........ 814 443-4688
Somerset (G-17718)

OPHTHALMIC GOODS

Cima Technology Inc ....F........ 724 733-2627
Pittsburgh (G-14852)
Curry Spectacle Shop Inc ....G........ 814 899-6833
Erie (G-5236)
Fashion Optical Inc.....................G........ 724 339-4595
Sarver (G-17069)
Homer Optical Company Inc........F........ 717 843-1822
York (G-20525)
Karen Wrigley Dr.........................G........ 215 563-8440
Philadelphia (G-13922)
Lens Contact Center ....G........ 724 543-2702
Kittanning (G-8777)
Luxottica of America Inc ....E........ 412 373-2200
Monroeville (G-11344)
Luxottica of America Inc ....E........ 610 543-8622
Springfield (G-17918)
Luxottica of America Inc ....E........ 610 962-5945
King of Prussia (G-8647)
Luxottica of America Inc ....E........ 814 868-7502
Erie (G-5375)
Luxottica of America Inc ....E........ 717 295-3001
Lancaster (G-9118)
Mxl Industries Inc.......................D........ 717 569-8711
Lancaster (G-9141)
New Vision Lens Lab LLC ....G........ 610 351-7376
Allentown (G-331)
Peppers Performance Eyeware .....E........ 412 688-8555
Pittsburgh (G-15376)
PNC Equity Partners LP ....F........ 412 914-0175
Pittsburgh (G-15417)
Schneck Art Optical Co ....F........ 610 965-4066
Emmaus (G-5042)
Three Rivers Optical Company.......D........ 412 928-2020
Pittsburgh (G-15620)
Usv Optical Inc ....G........ 412 655-8311
West Mifflin (G-19747)
Xray Eyewear..............................G........ 215 545-3361
Philadelphia (G-14494)

OPHTHALMIC GOODS WHOLESALERS

Allentown Optical Corp ....E........ 610 433-5269
Allentown (G-129)
Beitler-Mckee Optical Company .....G........ 412 381-7953
Pittsburgh (G-14759)
Ross Mc Donnell Optical..............G........ 570 348-0464
Dunmore (G-4482)

OPHTHALMIC GOODS, NEC, WHOLESALE: Frames

Ultraoptics Inc ....G........ 724 838-7155
Greensburg (G-6723)

OPHTHALMIC GOODS, NEC, WHOLESALE: Lenses

Ophthalmic Associates PC ....E........ 215 368-1646
Lansdale (G-9395)

OPHTHALMIC GOODS: Frames & Parts, Eyeglass & Spectacle

R & R Eyewear Imports Inc ....E........ 215 393-5895
Willow Grove (G-20137)
Scott Smith G ....G........ 724 378-2880
Aliquippa (G-92)

OPHTHALMIC GOODS: Lenses, Ophthalmic

Nix Optical Co Inc ....G........ 724 483-6527
Charleroi (G-3018)
Ross Mc Donnell Optical..............G........ 570 348-0464
Dunmore (G-4482)
West Penn Optical Inc ....E........ 814 833-1194
Erie (G-5528)

OPHTHALMIC GOODS: Mountings, Eyeglass & Spectacle

Chadwick Optical Inc...................G........ 267 203-8665
Harleysville (G-7026)

OPHTHALMIC GOODS: Protectors, Eye

Chromagen Vision LLC ....G........ 610 628-2941
Kennett Square (G-8505)

OPTICAL GOODS STORES

Karen Wrigley Dr.........................G........ 215 563-8440
Philadelphia (G-13922)
Kutztown Optical Corp ....G........ 610 683-5544
Kutztown (G-8848)
Luxottica of America Inc ....E........ 610 962-5945
King of Prussia (G-8647)
Morgantown Eye Care Center........G........ 610 286-0206
Morgantown (G-11528)

OPTICAL GOODS STORES: Contact Lenses, Prescription

Dalmo Optical Corporation ....G........ 412 521-2100
Pittsburgh (G-14903)
Dalmo Optical Corporation ....G........ 412 937-1112
Pittsburgh (G-14904)
Rss Optometry LLC ....G........ 610 933-2177
Phoenixville (G-14577)

OPTICAL GOODS STORES: Eyeglasses, Prescription

A-Boss Opticians ....G........ 412 271-4424
Braddock (G-1942)
Curry Spectacle Shop Inc ....G........ 814 899-6833
Erie (G-5236)
Gary N Snyder ....G........ 215 735-5656
Philadelphia (G-13744)
Lancaster Contact Lens Inc ....G........ 717 569-7386
Lancaster (G-9092)
Luxottica of America Inc ....E........ 412 373-2200
Monroeville (G-11344)
Luxottica of America Inc ....E........ 610 543-8622
Springfield (G-17918)
Luxottica of America Inc ....E........ 814 868-7502
Erie (G-5375)
Luxottica of America Inc ....E........ 717 295-3001
Lancaster (G-9118)
Nix Optical Co Inc ....G........ 724 483-6527
Charleroi (G-3018)
Usv Optical Inc ....G........ 412 655-8311
West Mifflin (G-19747)
West Penn Optical Inc ....E........ 814 833-1194
Erie (G-5528)

OPTICAL GOODS STORES: Opticians

Eyeland Optical ....G........ 888 603-3937
Mount Joy (G-11656)
Eyeland Optical Corp ....D........ 215 368-1600
Philadelphia (G-13688)
Fashion Optical Inc.....................G........ 724 339-4595
Sarver (G-17069)
Sosniak Opticians ....G........ 412 281-9199
Pittsburgh (G-15561)

OPTICAL INSTRUMENT REPAIR SVCS

Atlas Instrument Co Inc...............G........ 717 267-1250
Chambersburg (G-2907)

OPTICAL INSTRUMENTS & APPARATUS

Atlas Instrument Co Inc...............G........ 717 267-1250
Chambersburg (G-2907)
Avo Photonics Inc........................F........ 215 441-0107
Horsham (G-7793)
Ii-VI Optical Systems Inc ....E........ 215 842-3675
Philadelphia (G-13848)
James B Carty Jr MD ....G........ 610 527-0897
Bryn Mawr (G-2327)

JAS Precision Inc.........................G........ 215 239-7299
Yardley (G-20322)
Leica Microsystems Inc................G........ 610 321-0434
Exton (G-5706)
Optical Crosslinks Inc ....G........ 610 444-9469
Kennett Square (G-8534)
Precision Glass Technologies.........G........ 610 323-2825
Sanatoga (G-17058)
Questar Corporation ....E........ 215 862-5277
New Hope (G-12312)
Republic Lens Co Inc ....F........ 610 588-7867
Bangor (G-926)

OPTICAL INSTRUMENTS & LENSES

A&J Optical Inc ....G........ 215 338-7645
Philadelphia (G-13330)
Accutome Inc ....E........ 800 979-2020
Malvern (G-10179)
Allentown Optical Corp ....E........ 610 433-5269
Allentown (G-129)
Broadband Networks Inc..............D........ 814 237-4073
State College (G-17947)
CJ Optical Holdings LLC ....F........ 610 264-8537
Whitehall (G-19866)
Co Optics Inc ....G........ 610 478-1884
Reading (G-16348)
Cybel LLC ....G........ 610 691-7012
Bethlehem (G-1494)
Cyoptics Inc................................B........ 484 397-2000
Breinigsville (G-2013)
Davro Optical Systems Inc ....G........ 215 362-3870
Lansdale (G-9357)
E O S Group Inc ....G........ 412 781-6023
Pittsburgh (G-14951)
Evaporated Coatings Inc ....E........ 215 659-3080
Willow Grove (G-20116)
Eyeland Optical ....G........ 888 603-3937
Mount Joy (G-11656)
Flir Government Systems Pittsb .....D........ 724 295-2880
Freeport (G-6204)
Gatan Inc ....D........ 724 779-2572
Warrendale (G-19075)
Hampton Controls Inc ....F........ 724 861-0150
Wendel (G-19481)
I Optical City ....G........ 412 881-3090
Pittsburgh (G-15109)
Infinera Corporation ....G........ 408 572-5200
Allentown (G-259)
Leonard Anderson ....G........ 724 463-3615
Indiana (G-8111)
Luzerne Optical Laboratories.........G........ 570 822-3183
Wilkes Barre (G-19937)
N Vision Group Inc......................G........ 610 278-1900
Morton (G-11592)
Nexans USA Inc ....B........ 717 354-6200
New Holland (G-12271)
Omnitech Partners Inc.................G........ 724 295-2880
Freeport (G-6211)
Ophthalmic Associates PC ....E........ 215 368-1646
Lansdale (G-9395)
Optical Systems Technology ....E........ 724 295-2880
Freeport (G-6212)
Opticscampcom ....G........ 888 978-5330
Williamsport (G-20052)
P D Plastics ....G........ 724 941-3930
Canonsburg (G-2616)
Parker-Hannifin Corporation ....C........ 724 861-8200
Irwin (G-8188)
Proteus Optics LLC ....G........ 215 204-5241
Media (G-10945)
Solar Light Company Inc..............D........ 215 517-8700
Glenside (G-6538)
Spitz Inc ....D........ 610 459-5200
Chadds Ford (G-2860)
Te Connectivity Corporation ....B........ 717 986-3743
Middletown (G-11081)
Vision Optics ....G........ 267 639-5773
Philadelphia (G-14452)
Vista Optical ....G........ 724 458-0333
Grove City (G-6807)

OPTOMETRIC EQPT & SPLYS WHOLESALERS

Eyeland Optical ....G........ 888 603-3937
Mount Joy (G-11656)
Walman Optical Company ....E........ 717 767-5193
York (G-20703)

PRODUCT

OPTOMETRISTS' OFFICES

CJ Optical Holdings LLC ....F 610 264-8537
Whitehall **(G-19866)**

Geryville Eye Associates PC ....F 215 679-3500
Pennsburg **(G-13248)**

Leechburg Contact Lens Lab ....G 724 845-7777
Leechburg **(G-9648)**

Lens Contact Center.........................G 724 543-2702
Kittanning **(G-8777)**

Martin Rawdin Od ....G 610 323-8007
Pottstown **(G-16016)**

Morgantown Eye Care Center............G 610 286-0206
Morgantown **(G-11528)**

ORAL PREPARATIONS

Profresh International Corp ....F 800 610-5110
Philadelphia **(G-14206)**

ORDNANCE

Action Manufacturing Company..........B 267 540-4041
Bristol **(G-2103)**

Action Manufacturing Company..........D 610 593-1800
Atglen **(G-799)**

Alloy Surfaces Company Inc ....C 610 497-7979
Chester **(G-3038)**

Alloy Surfaces Company Inc ....E 610 558-7100
Boothwyn **(G-1875)**

Avant-Garde Technology Inc ....G 215 345-8228
Doylestown **(G-4273)**

E W Yost Co ....F 215 699-4868
Blue Bell **(G-1828)**

G G Greene Enterprises Inc ....E 814 723-5700
Warren **(G-19027)**

General Dynamics Corporation ....F 570 340-1136
Scranton **(G-17237)**

Kongsberg Protech Systems...............D 814 269-5700
Johnstown **(G-8400)**

Lockheed Martin Corporation ....B 570 876-2132
Archbald **(G-691)**

Orlotronics Corporation ....E 610 239-8200
Bridgeport **(G-2042)**

ORGAN TUNING & REPAIR SVCS

Columbia Organ Works Inc ....G 717 684-3573
Columbia **(G-3436)**

Hunter Mudler Inc ....F 215 229-5470
Philadelphia **(G-13843)**

ORGANIZATIONS: Civic & Social

American Soc For Deaf Children ....G 717 909-5577
Camp Hill **(G-2486)**

Ccn America LP ....G 412 349-6300
Pittsburgh **(G-14831)**

Summer Music Festival ....G 570 343-7271
Dunmore **(G-4484)**

ORGANIZATIONS: Educational Research Agency

Printing Inds Amer Foundation ....F 412 741-6860
Warrendale **(G-19094)**

Rodale Institute ....E 610 683-6009
Kutztown **(G-8859)**

ORGANIZATIONS: Medical Research

Aquamed Technologies Inc ....F 215 702-8550
Langhorne **(G-9277)**

Complexa Inc...................................G 412 727-8727
Berwyn **(G-1356)**

Douglas Pharma Us Inc.....................F 267 317-2010
Warminster **(G-18862)**

Noblemedical LLC.............................G 917 750-9605
Bryn Mawr **(G-2332)**

ORGANIZATIONS: Professional

Global Institute For Strgc Inv.............G 215 300-0907
Philadelphia **(G-13769)**

ORGANIZATIONS: Religious

American Bible Society ....C 212 408-1200
Philadelphia **(G-13379)**

Beverly Hall Co.................................E 215 536-7048
Quakertown **(G-16172)**

Bible Visuals International ....G 717 859-1131
Akron **(G-34)**

Catholic Golden Age Inc ....F 570 586-1091
Scott Township **(G-17183)**

Catholic Register..............................G 814 695-7563
Hollidaysburg **(G-7643)**

Clarence Larkin Estate ....G 215 576-5590
Glenside **(G-6512)**

Clemens Family Corporation ....A 800 523-5291
Hatfield **(G-7324)**

Pittsburgh Catholic Pubg Assoc ....F 412 471-1252
Pittsburgh **(G-15390)**

Pittsburgh Jewish Publication.............F 412 687-1000
Pittsburgh **(G-15399)**

Scripture Union ....F 610 935-2807
Valley Forge **(G-18714)**

Selah Publshng Co Inc ....F 412 886-1020
Pittsburgh **(G-15521)**

Swedenborg Foundation Inc................G 610 430-3222
West Chester **(G-19649)**

ORGANIZATIONS: Research Institute

Alcon Research Ltd ....B 610 670-3500
Reading **(G-16317)**

Foreign Policy Research Inst...............E 215 732-3774
Philadelphia **(G-13714)**

Moberg Research Inc.........................F 215 283-0860
Ambler **(G-591)**

Pennsylvania State University.............E 215 682-4000
Warminster **(G-18939)**

ORGANIZATIONS: Scientific Research Agency

Energy Conversion Technology ....G 412 835-0191
Pittsburgh **(G-14975)**

ORGANIZERS, CLOSET & DRAWER Plastic

Good Neighbors Inc...........................F 610 444-1860
Kennett Square **(G-8513)**

R & G Products Inc ....F 717 633-0011
Hanover **(G-6940)**

ORNAMENTS: Lawn

Concrete Jungle................................G 717 528-8851
York Springs **(G-20763)**

Free Energy Systems Inc ....E 610 583-2640
Collingdale **(G-3404)**

OSCILLATORS

Anderson Electronics LLC..................E 814 695-4428
Hollidaysburg **(G-7642)**

Greenray Industries Inc......................E 717 766-0223
Mechanicsburg **(G-10850)**

Micro Oscillator Inc...........................G 610 617-8682
Bala Cynwyd **(G-886)**

Olympus Advanced Tech LLC ....G 814 838-3571
Erie **(G-5408)**

OSICIZERS: Inorganic

Bpi Inc ....F 412 371-8554
Pittsburgh **(G-14788)**

Bpi Inc ....F 412 771-8176
Mc Kees Rocks **(G-10605)**

OUTLETS: Electric, Convenience

Gettysburg Village Factory Str ....F 717 334-2332
Gettysburg **(G-6294)**

H H Fluorescent Parts Inc ....D 215 379-2750
Cheltenham **(G-3029)**

Hartstrings LLC.................................G 610 326-8221
Pottstown **(G-15997)**

Leggs Hanes Bali Factory Otlt............G 717 392-2511
Lancaster **(G-9109)**

Woolrich Inc ....G 570 769-7401
Woolrich **(G-20221)**

OVENS: Cremating

Matthews International Corp................E 412 442-8200
Pittsburgh **(G-15264)**

OVENS: Laboratory

Tps LLC..C 570 538-7200
New Columbia **(G-12177)**

OVERBURDEN REMOVAL, METAL MINING

Joe Bento Construction Co Inc ....G 215 969-1505
Philadelphia **(G-13901)**

PACKAGE DESIGN SVCS

Amatech Inc......................................E 814 452-0010
Erie **(G-5185)**

Corrugated Specialties ....F 814 337-5705
Meadville **(G-10715)**

Rpw Group Inc ....E 215 493-7456
Yardley **(G-20337)**

Triangle Printing Company Inc ....E 717 854-1521
York **(G-20692)**

PACKAGED FROZEN FOODS WHOLESALERS, NEC

Charlies Specialties Inc ....D 724 346-2350
Hermitage **(G-7577)**

Crystal Frms Refrigerated Dist ....B 570 425-2910
Klingerstown **(G-8807)**

E&M Wholesale Foods ....F 610 367-2299
Boyertown **(G-1909)**

P & S Ravioli Co ....F 215 465-8888
Philadelphia **(G-14108)**

Pretzelworks Inc................................D 215 288-4002
Philadelphia **(G-14199)**

PACKAGING & LABELING SVCS

Beidel Printing House Inc ....E 717 532-5063
Shippensburg **(G-17516)**

Cardinal Health 407 Inc ....A 215 501-1210
Philadelphia **(G-13502)**

Cast Pac Inc......................................E 610 264-8131
Allentown **(G-165)**

CCT Manufacturing & Fulfillmen ....F 724 652-0818
New Castle **(G-12072)**

Dispatch Printing Inc..........................F 814 870-9600
Erie **(G-5248)**

G & S Foods Inc ....E 717 259-5323
Abbottstown **(G-4)**

Harbor Bay Group Inc.........................G 610 566-5290
Prospect Park **(G-16115)**

Hendersons Printing Inc ....E 814 944-0855
Altoona **(G-512)**

In Speck Corporation.........................E 610 272-9500
Norristown **(G-12669)**

Industrial Terminal Systems ....E 724 335-9837
New Kensington **(G-12346)**

J Penner Corporation ....E 215 340-9700
Doylestown **(G-4308)**

Keystone Printed Spc Co LLC ....C 570 457-8334
Old Forge **(G-12967)**

Mystic Assembly & Dctg Co ....E 215 957-0280
Warminster **(G-18926)**

Overend & Krill Lumber Inc ....G 724 348-7511
Finleyville **(G-5962)**

Schaefer Paint Company.....................F 717 687-7017
Ronks **(G-16813)**

Select Medical Systems Inc ....F 215 207-9003
Philadelphia **(G-14293)**

Simkins Corporation...........................E 215 739-4033
Jenkintown **(G-8301)**

Superior Group Inc ....E 610 397-2040
Conshohocken **(G-3610)**

Urania Engineering Co Inc ....E 570 455-0776
Hazleton **(G-7532)**

PACKAGING MATERIALS, INDL: Wholesalers

Has-Mor Industries Inc ....F 570 383-0185
Olyphant **(G-12992)**

Industrial Packaging Supplies..............G 724 459-8299
Blairsville **(G-1725)**

Lemac Packaging Inc ....G 814 453-7652
Erie **(G-5361)**

Wester Burlap Bag & Supply Co ....G 412 835-4314
Bethel Park **(G-1439)**

PACKAGING MATERIALS, WHOLESALE

Graham Packaging Company Inc..........C 717 849-8500
Lancaster **(G-9031)**

Guildcraft Inc....................................F 717 854-3888
York **(G-20517)**

Harbor Bay Group Inc.........................G 610 566-5290
Prospect Park **(G-16115)**

Ideal Sleeves Intl LLC........................F 570 823-8456
Wilkes Barre **(G-19926)**

Packaging Progressions Inc ....E 610 489-9096
Souderton (G-17758)

R W Pefferle Inc............................G...... 724 265-2764
Oakmont (G-12925)

Smith Group Inc ....E 215 957-7800
Warminster (G-18966)

Ty-Pak Inc ....E 570 835-5269
Tioga (G-18365)

Urania Engineering Co Inc ....E 570 455-0776
Hazleton (G-7532)

PACKAGING MATERIALS: Paper

Acro Labels Inc ....E 215 657-5366
Willow Grove (G-20105)

Bestway Printing ....G...... 215 368-4140
Lansdale (G-9346)

Cas Pack Corporation ....E 215 254-7225
Bensalem (G-1165)

Century Packaging Co Inc ....E 610 262-8860
Whitehall (G-19864)

Coating & Converting Tech Corp ....E 215 271-0610
Philadelphia (G-13554)

Donald B Remmey Inc ....G...... 570 386-5379
Lehighton (G-9711)

Easter Unlimited Inc ....E 814 542-8661
Mount Union (G-11744)

FP Woll & Company ....E 215 934-5966
Philadelphia (G-13717)

Great Northern Corporation ....E 610 706-0910
Allentown (G-236)

Guildcraft Inc ....F 717 854-3888
York (G-20517)

Harte Hanks Inc ....C 570 826-0414
Hanover Township (G-6989)

Holly Label Company Inc ....E 570 222-9000
Nicholson (G-12615)

Ideal Sleeves Intl LLC ....F 570 823-8456
Wilkes Barre (G-19926)

Interstate Paper Supply Co Inc ....D 724 938-2218
Roscoe (G-16817)

Labelcom ....G...... 814 362-3252
Bradford (G-1978)

Lbp Manufacturing LLC ....E 570 291-5463
Jessup (G-8330)

Mangar Industries Inc ....C 215 230-0300
New Britain (G-12047)

Mangar Medical Inc ....C 215 230-0300
New Britain (G-12048)

McCourt Label Cabinet Company ....D 800 458-2390
Lewis Run (G-9877)

News Chronicle Co Inc ....E 717 532-4101
Shippensburg (G-17540)

Okumus Enterprises Ltd ....E 215 295-3340
Fairless Hills (G-5790)

Oliver-Tlas Hlthcare Packg Inc ....C 215 322-7900
Feasterville Trevose (G-5923)

Opsec Security Inc ....D 717 293-4110
Lancaster (G-9155)

Presto Packaging Inc ....E 215 646-7514
Ambler (G-599)

Prime Packaging LLC ....D 215 499-0446
Yardley (G-20333)

R & G Gorr Enterprises Inc ....G...... 610 356-8500
Phoenixville (G-14573)

Sealed Air Corporation ....G...... 610 926-7517
Reading (G-16509)

Signode Industrial Group LLC ....E 570 450-0123
Hazle Township (G-7479)

Steele Print Inc ....G...... 724 758-6178
Ellwood City (G-4952)

Taba Labels Company ....G...... 215 455-9977
Philadelphia (G-14366)

U S Textile Corp ....E 803 283-6800
Feasterville Trevose (G-5935)

Universal Protective Packg Inc ....D 717 766-1578
Mechanicsburg (G-10903)

Vanguard Identification ....E 610 719-0700
West Chester (G-19672)

Westrock Packaging Inc ....D 215 785-3350
Croydon (G-3933)

PACKAGING MATERIALS: Paper, Coated Or Laminated

Bemis Company Inc ....C 570 501-1400
West Hazleton (G-19706)

PACKAGING MATERIALS: Paper, Thermoplastic Coated

Emball Iso Inc..............................G....... 267 687-8570
Montgomeryville (G-11395)

PACKAGING MATERIALS: Plastic Film, Coated Or Laminated

Amatech Inc................................E 814 452-0010
Erie (G-5185)

B W E Ltd ....E 724 246-0470
Republic (G-16652)

Bemis Packaging Inc ....E 717 279-5000
Lebanon (G-9547)

Central Distribution Co Inc ....G....... 717 393-4851
Lancaster (G-8973)

Cjc Contract Packaging Inc ....G....... 570 209-7836
Avoca (G-842)

Constantia Colmar LLC ....D 215 997-6222
Colmar (G-3411)

Cw Thomas LLC ....E 215 335-0200
Philadelphia (G-13596)

Greiner Packaging Corp ....F 570 602-3900
Pittston (G-15754)

Harbor Bay Group Inc ....G....... 610 566-5290
Prospect Park (G-16115)

Nanopack Inc...............................G....... 484 367-7015
Wayne (G-19359)

Print Solutions Ltd ....G....... 484 538-3938
Coopersburg (G-3635)

Reynolds Presto Products Inc............B 866 254-3310
Pittsburgh (G-15483)

Tredegar Corporation ....C 570 544-7600
Pottsville (G-16100)

PACKAGING MATERIALS: Polystyrene Foam

Amatech Inc................................E 814 452-0010
Erie (G-5185)

Bryn Hill Industries Inc...................E 610 623-4005
Yeadon (G-20351)

Cardinal Health 407 Inc ....A 215 501-1210
Philadelphia (G-13502)

Clarke Container Inc ....F 814 452-4848
Erie (G-5226)

Cryovac Inc.................................C 610 926-7500
Reading (G-16356)

Cryovac Inc.................................F 610 929-9190
Reading (G-16357)

Duerr Packaging Company Inc..........D 724 947-1234
Burgettstown (G-2346)

Duerr Packaging Company Inc..........E 724 695-2226
Imperial (G-8064)

Ekopak Inc ....F 412 264-9800
Coraopolis (G-3686)

Epe Industries Usa Inc ....G....... 800 315-0336
Carlisle (G-2710)

Essity North America Inc ....C 610 499-3700
Philadelphia (G-13680)

Flextron Industries Inc ....F 610 459-4600
Aston (G-763)

Foam Fair Industries Inc ....E 610 622-4665
Aldan (G-59)

Future Foam Inc ....D 215 736-8611
Fairless Hills (G-5779)

Fxi Inc.......................................C 814 664-7771
Corry (G-3762)

Greiner Packaging Corp ....F 570 602-3900
Pittston (G-15754)

Laurel Parcel Services Inc ....G....... 724 850-6245
Greensburg (G-6683)

Polar Tech Industries Inc ....E 800 423-2749
Elysburg (G-4979)

Presto Packaging Inc.....................G....... 215 822-9598
Hatfield (G-7386)

Presto Packaging Inc.....................E 215 646-7514
Ambler (G-599)

Protective Packaging Corp ....G....... 610 398-2229
Allentown (G-362)

R W Pefferle Inc............................G....... 724 265-2764
Oakmont (G-12925)

Rogers Foam Corporation ....D 215 295-8720
Morrisville (G-11580)

Rpw Group Inc ....E 215 493-7456
Yardley (G-20337)

Sealed Air Corporation ....E 610 384-2650
Modena (G-11259)

Sealed Air Corporation ....E 610 375-4281
Reading (G-16510)

Sonoco Prtective Solutions Inc ....E 412 415-1462
Pittsburgh (G-15558)

Sonoco Prtective Solutions Inc ....E 412 415-3784
Pittsburgh (G-15559)

Stephen Gould Corporation ....G....... 724 933-1400
Wexford (G-19829)

Temperatsure LLC ....G....... 775 358-1999
Hatfield (G-7401)

Ty-Pak Inc ....E 570 835-5269
Tioga (G-18365)

PACKAGING: Blister Or Bubble Formed, Plastic

Cjc Contract Packaging Inc ....G....... 570 209-7836
Avoca (G-842)

CSP Technologies Inc ....G....... 610 635-1202
Audubon (G-824)

Plastic Components Inc ....F 215 235-5550
Philadelphia (G-14182)

PACKING & CRATING SVC

Amcor Group GMBH........................G....... 570 474-9739
Mountain Top (G-11750)

PACKING & CRATING SVCS: Containerized Goods For Shipping

CCT Manufacturing & Fulfillmen ....F 724 652-0818
New Castle (G-12072)

PACKING MATERIALS: Mechanical

Prime Contract Pkg Svcs Corp ....E 570 876-2300
Olyphant (G-12996)

Process Technologies Inc ....G....... 412 771-8555
Mc Kees Rocks (G-10628)

PACKING SVCS: Shipping

Jankensteph Inc ....G....... 412 446-2777
Bridgeville (G-2073)

Pikewood Inc ....F 610 974-8000
Bethlehem (G-1597)

PACKING: Metallic

Aviva Technology Inc ....G....... 610 228-4689
Broomall (G-2279)

PACKING: Rubber

Flextron Industries Inc ....F 610 459-4600
Aston (G-763)

PADDING: Foamed Plastics

Bergad Inc ....E 724 763-2883
Kittanning (G-8757)

Novipax LLC ....E 570 644-0314
Paxinos (G-13191)

PADS: Mattress

Hotlineglass-Usa LLC ....G....... 800 634-9252
Butler (G-2406)

Peter Sheims Cow Mattress ....G....... 717 786-2918
Quarryville (G-16276)

PAGING SVCS

Mol Communications & Elec...............G....... 570 383-3658
Dickson City (G-4122)

PAINT STORE

A & L Paint Co Llc ....G....... 814 349-8064
Rebersburg (G-16577)

Haley Paint Company ....D 717 299-6771
Lancaster (G-9037)

Pandalai Coatings Company Inc ....G....... 724 224-5600
Brackenridge (G-1940)

Sherwin-Williams Company...............G....... 610 975-0126
Wayne (G-19371)

PAINTING SVC: Metal Prdts

American Metal Finishers Inc ....F 610 323-1394
Pottstown (G-15964)

Blastmaster Surface Restoratio ....G....... 724 282-7669
Butler (G-2381)

Commercial Metal Polishing ....F 610 837-0267
Bath (G-954)

P
R
O
D
U
C
T

Laurel Highlands Finishing.............G...... 724 537-9850
Latrobe (G-9497)
Luna Collison Ltd...........................F...... 412 466-8866
Duquesne (G-4497)

PAINTS & ADDITIVES

Berkley Products Company.............F...... 717 859-1104
Akron (G-33)
Bradley Coatings Group Inc ....F...... 724 444-4400
Gibsonia (G-6329)
Brunner Industrial Group Inc ....F...... 717 233-8781
Harrisburg (G-7100)
Chemcoat Inc ....E...... 570 368-8631
Montoursville (G-11436)
Consolidated Coatings Inc.............G...... 215 949-1474
Levittown (G-9826)
Gateway Paint & Chemical Co.........E...... 412 261-6642
Pittsburgh (G-15042)
J & M Industrial Coatings Inc..........G...... 570 547-1825
Montgomery (G-11371)
James G Bohn................................G...... 717 597-1901
Greencastle (G-6619)
Lockhart Company..........................E...... 724 444-1900
Gibsonia (G-6345)
Pro Guard Coatings Inc ....F...... 717 336-7900
Denver (G-4089)
R & D Coatings Inc.........................F...... 412 771-8110
Mc Kees Rocks (G-10630)
Rohm and Haas Company ....A...... 989 636-1000
Collegeville (G-3392)
Walton Paint Company Inc...............G...... 724 932-3101
Jamestown (G-8241)

PAINTS & ALLIED PRODUCTS

A & L Paint Co Llc..........................G...... 814 349-8064
Rebersburg (G-16577)
Advanced Finishing Usa Inc ....E...... 814 474-5200
Fairview (G-5810)
Amdex Metallizing Inc ....G...... 724 887-4977
Scottdale (G-17189)
American Inks & Coatings Corp.........D...... 610 933-5848
Phoenixville (G-14528)
APT Advanced Polymer Tech Corp......D...... 724 452-1330
Harmony (G-7066)
Axalta Coating Systems Ip LLC ....G...... 855 547-1461
Philadelphia (G-13432)
Axalta Coating Systems Ltd ....B...... 855 547-1461
Philadelphia (G-13433)
Behr Process Corporation ....C...... 610 391-1085
Allentown (G-148)
Belden Inc.....................................C...... 724 222-7060
Washington (G-19153)
Biocoat Incorporated......................E...... 215 734-0888
Horsham (G-7799)
Bulk Chemicals Inc.........................F...... 610 926-4128
Mohrsville (G-11275)
Capital Coating Inc ....F...... 717 442-0979
Kinzers (G-8735)
Cardinal Industrial Finishes.............G...... 814 723-0721
Warren (G-19015)
Chase Corporation..........................E...... 412 828-1500
Pittsburgh (G-14840)
Clearkin Chemical Corp ....G...... 215 426-7230
Philadelphia (G-13549)
Coopers Creek Chemical Corp..........E...... 610 828-0375
Conshohocken (G-3534)
Custom Mil & Consulting Inc.............E...... 610 926-0984
Fleetwood (G-5969)
Dajr Enterprises Inc........................F...... 215 949-0800
Levittown (G-9830)
Donaldson Company Inc..................G...... 215 396-8349
Warminster (G-18859)
Dow Chemical Company...................C...... 215 785-8000
Bristol (G-2132)
Dura-Bond Coating Inc....................E...... 412 436-2411
Duquesne (G-4496)
Dura-Bond Coating Inc....................E...... 724 327-0782
Export (G-5598)
E E Zimmerman Company................F...... 412 963-0949
Pittsburgh (G-14950)
Evaporated Coatings Inc..................E...... 215 659-3080
Willow Grove (G-20116)
Evonik Corporation..........................G...... 800 345-3148
Allentown (G-208)
Fuchs Lubricants Co ....E...... 724 867-5000
Emlenton (G-5008)
Gryphin Elements LLC.....................G...... 215 694-7727
Philadelphia (G-13790)
Harsco Corporation.........................C...... 570 421-7500
East Stroudsburg (G-4617)

Henry Company LLC........................B...... 610 933-8888
Kimberton (G-8573)
IC&s Distributing Co........................E...... 717 391-6250
Lancaster (G-9053)
International Marketing Inc ....F...... 717 264-5819
Chambersburg (G-2942)
Kop-Coat Inc..................................E...... 412 826-3387
Pittsburgh (G-15184)
Lafarge Rd Marking Inc....................G...... 570 547-1621
Montgomery (G-11374)
Lord Corporation.............................C...... 814 763-2345
Saegertown (G-16923)
Lord Corporation.............................A...... 877 275-5673
Erie (G-5373)
M-B Companies Inc.........................E...... 570 547-1621
Muncy (G-11825)
Mark Gingerella..............................G...... 570 213-5603
Susquehanna (G-18181)
McAdoo & Allen Inc.........................E...... 215 536-3520
Quakertown (G-16214)
Minusnine Technologies Inc..............G...... 215 704-9396
Philadelphia (G-14025)
Mxl Industries Inc............................D...... 717 569-8711
Lancaster (G-9141)
Norstone Incorporated.....................G...... 484 684-6986
Bridgeport (G-2041)
One Day Baths Inc...........................G...... 570 402-2337
Effort (G-4827)
Pelmor Laboratories Inc...................E...... 215 968-3334
Newtown (G-12533)
Performance Coatings Corp..............F...... 610 525-1190
Levittown (G-9854)
Pittsburgh Glass Works LLC.............B...... 419 683-2400
Creighton (G-3884)
Pittsburgh Glass Works LLC.............B...... 814 336-4411
Cochranton (G-3347)
Pittsburgh Powder Coat L.................G...... 724 348-8434
Bridgeville (G-2086)
Polymeric Systems Inc.....................D...... 610 286-2500
Elverson (G-4965)
PPG Industries Inc...........................A...... 412 434-3131
Pittsburgh (G-15425)
PPG Industries Inc...........................E...... 724 274-7900
Springdale (G-17899)
PPG Industries Inc...........................G...... 215 873-8940
Philadelphia (G-14193)
PPG Industries Inc...........................G...... 717 218-5400
Carlisle (G-2730)
PPG Industries Inc...........................E...... 724 224-6500
Creighton (G-3885)
PPG Industries Inc...........................G...... 717 763-1030
Lemoyne (G-9748)
PPG Industries Inc...........................G...... 610 544-1925
Springfield (G-17920)
PPG Industries Inc...........................G...... 888 774-1010
Reading (G-16473)
PPG Industries Inc...........................F...... 412 820-8116
Carlisle (G-2731)
PPG Industries Inc...........................C...... 412 820-8500
Cheswick (G-3116)
PPG Industries Inc...........................G...... 412 276-1922
Carnegie (G-2781)
PPG Industries Inc...........................F...... 412 434-4463
Pittsburgh (G-15426)
PPG Industries Inc...........................G...... 724 772-0005
Cranberry Township (G-3843)
PPG Industries Inc...........................G...... 724 863-4473
Irwin (G-8192)
PPG Industries Inc...........................E...... 412 487-4500
Allison Park (G-459)
PPG Industries Inc...........................E...... 724 327-3000
Monroeville (G-11350)
PPG Industries Foundation................G...... 412 434-3131
Pittsburgh (G-15427)
Protech Powder Coatings ....G...... 814 456-1243
Erie (G-5440)
Protech Powder Coatings Inc............E...... 717 767-6996
York (G-20646)
Qovalent.......................................G...... 610 269-3075
Downingtown (G-4253)
Richardson Paint Co Inc...................F...... 215 535-4500
Philadelphia (G-14248)
Richter Precision Inc........................D...... 717 560-9990
East Petersburg (G-4589)
Sargent Realty Inc...........................D...... 570 454-3596
Hazleton (G-7525)
Sarver Hardware Co Inc....................G...... 724 295-5131
Sarver (G-17079)
Sauereisen Inc................................E...... 412 963-0303
Pittsburgh (G-15514)

Schaefer Paint Company...................F...... 717 687-7017
Ronks (G-16813)
Sherwin-Williams Company ....G...... 610 975-0126
Wayne (G-19371)
Specialty Paints Coatings Inc............G...... 717 249-5523
Carlisle (G-2739)
Spectra-Kote Corporation ....E...... 717 334-3177
Gettysburg (G-6314)
Spray Products Corporation..............D...... 610 277-1010
Plymouth Meeting (G-15872)
Thermoclad Company ....F...... 814 456-1243
Erie (G-5507)
Thermoclad Company ....E...... 814 899-7628
Erie (G-5508)
Total Systems Technology Inc............F...... 412 653-7690
Pittsburgh (G-15633)
Vexcon Chemicals Inc ....E...... 215 332-7709
Philadelphia (G-14443)

PAINTS & VARNISHES: Plastics Based

Chem-Clay Corporation.....................E...... 412 276-6333
Carnegie (G-2765)

PAINTS, VARNISHES & SPLYS, WHOLESALE: Colors & Pigments

Heucotech Ltd A NJ Ltd Partnr............D...... 215 736-0712
Fairless Hills (G-5785)

PAINTS, VARNISHES & SPLYS, WHOLESALE: Paints

Akzo Nobel Coatings Inc...................E...... 610 372-3600
Reading (G-16314)
Behr Process Corporation ....C...... 610 391-1085
Allentown (G-148)
Sherwin-Williams Company ....G...... 610 975-0126
Wayne (G-19371)
Valley Wholesale & Supply ....E...... 724 783-6531
Kittanning (G-8801)

PAINTS: Asphalt Or Bituminous

Watson Industries Inc.......................E...... 724 275-1000
Harwick (G-7257)
Watson Standard Company ....D...... 724 275-1000
Harwick (G-7259)

PAINTS: Marine

Kop-Coat Inc..................................F...... 412 227-2426
Pittsburgh (G-15183)

PAINTS: Oil Or Alkyd Vehicle Or Water Thinned

Akzo Nobel Coatings Inc...................E...... 610 372-3600
Reading (G-16314)
Chroma Acrylics Inc.........................E...... 717 626-8866
Lititz (G-9998)
Haley Paint Company.......................D...... 717 299-6771
Lancaster (G-9037)
Pandalai Coatings Company Inc.........G...... 724 224-5600
Brackenridge (G-1940)
Walton Paint Company Inc.................F...... 814 774-3042
Girard (G-6403)

PAINTS: Waterproof

Sealmark Manufacturing Corp............G...... 724 379-4442
Donora (G-4161)

PALLET REPAIR SVCS

J & J Pallet Co Inc...........................E...... 570 489-7705
Throop (G-18359)
Nazareth Pallet Co Inc......................E...... 610 262-9799
Northampton (G-12856)

PALLETS

Absolute Pallet Inc...........................G...... 215 331-4510
Bensalem (G-1142)
Aj Pallet LLC..................................E...... 717 597-3545
Waynesboro (G-19395)
B V Pallets....................................F...... 717 935-5740
Belleville (G-1125)
Brian M Pallet................................G...... 484 720-8052
Landenberg (G-9247)
Carpenter Pallets ....G...... 570 465-2573
New Milford (G-12395)

Cedar Lane Pallets ....G...... 717 365-4014
  Lykens (G-10131)
Centre Pallets LLC ....F...... 814 349-8693
  Rebersburg (G-16578)
Custom Bins Pallet Mfg ....G...... 570 539-4158
  Port Trevorton (G-15912)
D&J Pallet Services Inc ....G...... 717 275-1064
  Landisburg (G-9257)
Delco Pallets LLC ....G...... 267 438-1227
  Morton (G-11591)
Diaz Stone and Pallet Inc ....E...... 570 289-8760
  Kingsley (G-8704)
Hornings Pallet Forks ....G...... 570 966-1025
  Mifflinburg (G-11095)
M & M Salt & Pallet ....G...... 717 845-4039
  Dallastown (G-3979)
Pallet Connection ....G...... 570 963-1432
  Scranton (G-17269)
Pallets Unlimited Inc ....G...... 717 755-3691
  York (G-20617)
Pro Pallet Partners ....G...... 717 741-2418
  York (G-20642)
R&F Pallet Co ....G...... 717 463-3560
  Mifflintown (G-11133)
Recycled Pallets ....G...... 717 754-3114
  Schuylkill Haven (G-17165)
Rick Degeorge ....G...... 717 684-4555
  Columbia (G-3449)
S&K Pallet LLC ....G...... 717 667-0001
  Reedsville (G-16627)
Superior Pallet LLC ....G...... 717 789-9525
  Ickesburg (G-8053)
Weaver Pallet Company ....F...... 717 463-3037
  Mifflintown (G-11142)
Zooks Pallets LLC ....G...... 717 899-5212
  Mc Veytown (G-10654)

PALLETS & SKIDS: Wood

Achieva ....D...... 412 221-6609
  Bridgeville (G-2052)
Achieva ....D...... 412 995-5000
  Pittsburgh (G-14640)
All Pallet Inc ....C...... 610 614-1905
  Wind Gap (G-20164)
Beenah Enterprises LLC ....G...... 570 546-9388
  Muncy (G-11808)
Bio-Diversity LLC ....F...... 570 884-3057
  Selinsgrove (G-17322)
Dick Warner Sales & Contg ....G...... 814 683-4606
  Linesville (G-9980)
Donovan Schoonover Lumber Co ....G...... 814 697-7266
  Shinglehouse (G-17506)
EMC Global Technologies Inc ....F...... 267 347-5100
  Telford (G-18287)
Gerald S Stillman ....G...... 610 377-7650
  Allentown (G-230)
Gupta Permold Corporation ....C...... 412 793-3511
  Pittsburgh (G-15067)
Harvey Leon ....G...... 570 337-2665
  South Williamsport (G-17791)
JB Mill & Fabricating Inc ....E...... 724 202-6814
  New Castle (G-12108)
Jos Pallets ....G...... 570 278-8935
  Montrose (G-11468)
Lignetics New England Inc ....G...... 814 563-4358
  Youngsville (G-20773)
Mhp Industries Inc ....E...... 717 450-4753
  Lebanon (G-9609)
Midlantic Pallet LLC ....F...... 717 266-0300
  York (G-20597)
Noll Pallet Inc ....E...... 610 926-2500
  Leesport (G-9671)
Nova Global Inc ....F...... 619 822-2465
  Philadelphia (G-14086)
Overend & Krill Lumber Inc ....G...... 724 348-7511
  Finleyville (G-5962)
Paser Inc ....G...... 814 623-7221
  Bedford (G-1070)
Pieces By Pallets LLC ....G...... 717 872-7238
  Quarryville (G-16277)
Robert D Rennick ....G...... 570 429-0784
  Saint Clair (G-16940)
Rosewood Company A Partnership ....G...... 717 349-2289
  Fort Loudon (G-6060)
Ted Venesky Co Inc ....G...... 724 224-7992
  Tarentum (G-18248)
Ufp Gordon LLC ....E...... 570 875-2811
  Gordon (G-6547)
Vepar LLC ....G...... 610 462-4545
  Spring City (G-17871)

W W McFarland Inc ....G...... 724 946-9663
  New Wilmington (G-12472)
Weaver Sawmill ....F...... 570 539-8420
  Liverpool (G-10080)

PALLETS: Corrugated

Jem Pallets ....G...... 717 532-5304
  Orrstown (G-13032)

PALLETS: Metal

Devaltronix Inc ....F...... 215 331-9600
  Philadelphia (G-13625)
Sha Co Welding & Fabrication ....G...... 724 588-0993
  Greenville (G-6773)

PALLETS: Plastic

Consolidated Container Co LLC ....D...... 412 828-1111
  Verona (G-18754)
Rehrig Pacific Company ....D...... 814 455-8023
  Erie (G-5460)

PALLETS: Solid Fiber, Made From Purchased Materials

Laurel Ridge Resawing ....G...... 814 629-5026
  Boswell (G-1884)

PALLETS: Wood & Metal Combination

Remington Pallets & Crates ....G...... 814 749-7557
  Vintondale (G-18769)

PALLETS: Wooden

A & L Wood Inc ....E...... 570 539-8922
  Mount Pleasant Mills (G-11724)
Albert Gray ....F...... 717 436-8585
  Mifflintown (G-11109)
American Fibertech Corporation ....E...... 717 597-5708
  Greencastle (G-6595)
Annalee Wood Products Inc ....F...... 610 436-0142
  Coatesville (G-3288)
Annalee Wood Products Inc ....G...... 610 436-0142
  West Chester (G-19499)
Barville Lumber ....G...... 717 667-9600
  Belleville (G-1126)
Bass Pallets LLC ....E...... 717 731-1091
  Shiremanstown (G-17568)
Bedford Pallets ....F...... 814 623-1521
  Bedford (G-1043)
Better Built Products ....G...... 724 423-5268
  Mount Pleasant (G-11688)
Bishop Wood Products Inc ....F...... 215 723-6644
  Souderton (G-17726)
C & G Pallet Company Inc ....G...... 610 759-5625
  Bath (G-953)
C & S Wood Products Inc ....E...... 570 489-8633
  Olyphant (G-12985)
C Knaub & Sons ....G...... 717 292-3908
  Dover (G-4190)
Chep (usa) Inc ....D...... 717 778-4279
  Biglerville (G-1661)
Clark H Ream Lumber ....G...... 814 445-8185
  Somerset (G-17680)
Clinton Pallet Company Inc ....F...... 570 753-3010
  Jersey Shore (G-8312)
Colebrook Supply ....G...... 717 684-6287
  Columbia (G-3433)
Columbia Wood Industries Inc ....F...... 570 458-4311
  Millville (G-11224)
Cove Stake & Wood Products GP ....G...... 814 793-3257
  Martinsburg (G-10522)
Crouses Pallet Service ....G...... 717 577-9012
  Red Lion (G-16592)
Custom Pallet Recycler ....G...... 724 658-6086
  New Castle (G-12080)
Dach Dime Manufacture ....G...... 814 336-2376
  Meadville (G-10717)
Davco Pallet ....G...... 570 837-5910
  Middleburg (G-11024)
Donald B Remmey Inc ....G...... 570 386-5379
  Lehighton (G-9711)
Donald B Remmey Inc ....E...... 570 386-5379
  Lehighton (G-9712)
Erie Wood Products LLC ....F...... 814 452-4961
  Erie (G-5279)
Esten Lumber Products Inc ....G...... 215 536-4976
  Quakertown (G-16190)
Evergreen Pallet Company ....G...... 717 463-3217
  Mc Alisterville (G-10549)

Frank Ferris Industries Inc ....G...... 724 352-9477
  Cabot (G-2457)
Gilliland Pallet Company Inc ....G...... 724 946-2222
  New Wilmington (G-12467)
H & M Lumber ....G...... 717 535-5080
  Mifflintown (G-11120)
Hannahoes Pallets & Skids ....F...... 610 926-4699
  Reading (G-16398)
Hess Wood Recycling Inc ....F...... 610 614-9070
  Easton (G-4698)
House Wood Products Co ....G...... 570 662-3868
  Mansfield (G-10416)
J & J Pallet Co Inc ....E...... 570 489-7705
  Throop (G-18359)
J & M Pallet LLC ....G...... 717 463-9205
  Mifflintown (G-11124)
J F Rohrbaugh & Co ....D...... 800 800-4353
  Hanover (G-6906)
Jacob E Leisenring Lumber ....G...... 570 672-9793
  Elysburg (G-4977)
James C Richards ....G...... 724 758-9032
  Ellwood City (G-4941)
Jo MI Pallet Co Inc ....G...... 570 875-3540
  Ashland (G-732)
John Dibble Tree Service ....G...... 814 825-4543
  Erie (G-5338)
John Rock Inc ....D...... 610 857-8080
  Coatesville (G-3311)
Jrm Pallets Inc ....G...... 717 926-6812
  Myerstown (G-11888)
Keystone Pallet and Recycl LLC ....F...... 570 279-7236
  Milton (G-11245)
Kiefer Pallet ....G...... 610 599-0971
  Bangor (G-920)
Kopenitz Lumber Co ....G...... 570 544-2131
  Pottsville (G-16087)
Kuhns Bros Lumber Co Inc ....E...... 570 568-1412
  Lewisburg (G-9914)
Lapps Pallet Repair LLC ....F...... 717 806-5348
  Quarryville (G-16273)
Latrobe Pallet Inc ....G...... 724 537-9636
  Latrobe (G-9491)
Laurel Run Pallet Company LLC ....F...... 717 436-5428
  Mifflintown (G-11128)
Limpach Industries Inc ....F...... 724 646-4011
  Sharpsville (G-17473)
Little Johns Woodshop ....G...... 724 924-9029
  New Castle (G-12116)
Locust Run Pallet LLC ....F...... 717 535-5883
  Thompsontown (G-18348)
Lumber and Things Inc ....G...... 717 848-1622
  York (G-20568)
M & M Wood Products Inc ....F...... 570 638-2234
  Morris Run (G-11546)
M and M Pallet LLC ....F...... 717 845-4039
  York (G-20571)
Mark Rioux Pallets ....G...... 610 562-7030
  Hamburg (G-6845)
Michael Meyer Pallets ....G...... 814 781-1107
  Saint Marys (G-16995)
Middlecreek Pallet ....G...... 570 658-7667
  Beaver Springs (G-1019)
Nazareth Pallet Co Inc ....E...... 610 262-9799
  Northampton (G-12856)
Nelson Company ....G...... 724 652-6681
  New Castle (G-12126)
Nelson Company Inc ....G...... 717 593-0600
  Greencastle (G-6624)
Noll Pallet & Lumber Co ....E...... 610 926-3502
  Leesport (G-9670)
Northern Pallet Inc ....F...... 570 945-3920
  Factoryville (G-5759)
OMalley Wood Products Inc ....E...... 717 677-6550
  Gardners (G-6261)
P & S Pallet Inc ....G...... 570 655-4628
  Pittston (G-15772)
P G Recycling Incorporated ....F...... 814 696-6000
  Tyrone (G-18588)
Palcon LLC ....G...... 570 546-9032
  Muncy (G-11828)
Palcon LLC ....G...... 570 546-9032
  Muncy (G-11829)
Pallet Express Inc ....D...... 610 258-8846
  Easton (G-4738)
Peachey-Yoder LP ....F...... 570 658-8371
  Beaver Springs (G-1020)
Penn Pallet Inc ....G...... 814 857-2988
  Woodland (G-20213)
Penn Pallet Inc ....D...... 814 834-1700
  Saint Marys (G-17002)

PRODUCT

Perry Pallet Inc ....E 717 589-3345
Millerstown (G-11207)
Precision Pallets & Lumber Inc ......F 814 395-5351
Addison (G-28)
Pro Pallet LLC ....C 717 292-5510
Dover (G-4201)
Quality Penn Products Inc ....G 215 430-0117
Philadelphia (G-14220)
R & D Pallett Co. ....G 610 944-9484
Blandon (G-1758)
R & R Wood Products Inc ....E 215 723-3470
Mainland (G-10175)
Recycled Pallets Inc ....G 724 657-6978
New Castle (G-12141)
Refined Pallet ....G 570 238-9455
Middleburg (G-11037)
Remmey Pallet Co ....E 570 658-7575
Beaver Springs (G-1021)
Robert Aguglia ....F 412 487-6511
Glenshaw (G-6500)
Rockwell Lumber Co Inc ....G 717 597-7428
Greencastle (G-6631)
S Frey Pallets ....G 717 284-9937
Quarryville (G-16278)
Shade Lumber Company Inc ....E 570 658-2425
Beaver Springs (G-1023)
Shank Pallet Recyclers Inc ....G 717 597-3545
Greencastle (G-6634)
Shank Pallet Recyclers Inc ....G 717 597-3545
Greencastle (G-6635)
Sheltons Pallet Company ....E 610 932-3182
Oxford (G-13091)
Sovereign Services Inc ....E 412 331-6704
Pittsburgh (G-15565)
Strasburg Pallet Co Inc ....E 717 687-8131
Strasburg (G-18094)
Sutherland Lumber Co ....E 724 947-3388
Burgettstown (G-2355)
T/A Reborn Pallets ....G 484 841-3085
Bath (G-972)
Top Box Inc ....F 724 258-8966
Monongahela (G-11318)
Treen Box & Pallet Corp ....E 717 535-5800
Mifflintown (G-11136)
Troyer Pallet Company ....G 717 535-4499
Mifflintown (G-11137)
W W Pallet Co ....F 717 362-9388
Elizabethville (G-4899)
Wayne Lawson ....G 814 757-8424
Russell (G-16882)
Weaver Pallet Company LLC ....G 717 463-2770
Mc Alisterville (G-10553)
Wengerd Pallet Company ....E 717 463-3274
Mifflintown (G-11144)
West Side Wood Products Inc ....F 610 562-8166
Hamburg (G-6856)
Woodruff Corporation ....G 570 675-0890
Shavertown (G-17481)
Wyoming Valley Pallets Inc ....G 570 655-3640
Exeter (G-5586)
Zooks Pallets Inc ....G 717 935-5030
Belleville (G-1135)
Zooks Pallets LLC ....F 717 667-9077
Belleville (G-1136)

PANEL & DISTRIBUTION BOARDS & OTHER RELATED APPARATUS

C&D Technologies Inc ....C 215 619-2700
Blue Bell (G-1820)
Caruso Inc ....G 717 738-0248
Ephrata (G-5095)

PANEL & DISTRIBUTION BOARDS: Electric

Essex Engineering Corp ....G 215 322-5880
Warminster (G-18874)
Ges Automation Technology ....E 717 236-8733
Harrisburg (G-7133)
R & D Machine Controls Inc ....G 267 205-5976
Bristol (G-2192)
Scott Metals Inc ....E 412 279-7021
Carnegie (G-2790)
Spang & Company ....C 412 963-9363
Pittsburgh (G-15566)

PANELS & SECTIONS: Prefabricated, Concrete

Concrete Concepts Inc ....F 412 331-1500
Mc Kees Rocks (G-10606)

Fabcon East LLC ....D 610 530-4470
Mahanoy City (G-10173)
Taktl LLC ....C 412 486-1600
Turtle Creek (G-18569)

PANELS, FLAT: Plastic

Mtl Holdings Inc ....C 570 343-7921
Archbald (G-693)

PANELS: Building, Metal

Brock Associates LLC ....F 412 919-0690
Pittsburgh (G-14793)
Marcon & Boyer Inc ....D 610 866-5959
Allentown (G-307)

PANELS: Building, Plastic, NEC

Eks Vinyl Structures ....G 570 725-3439
Loganton (G-10094)
Panel Technologies Inc ....G 215 538-7055
Quakertown (G-16226)

PANELS: Building, Wood

Eastern Exterior Wall ....D 610 868-5522
Allentown (G-200)
J C Snavely & Sons Inc ....C 717 898-2241
Landisville (G-9262)
Whipple Bros Inc ....G 570 836-6262
Mountain Top (G-11780)

PANELS: Cardboard, Die-Cut, Made From Purchased Materials

Folded Structures Company LLC ....G 908 237-1955
Newtown (G-12502)

PANELS: Wood

Northeast Products & Svcs Inc ....G 610 899-0286
Topton (G-18414)

PAPER & BOARD: Die-cut

Beistle Company ....B 717 532-2131
Shippensburg (G-17517)
Complete Hand Assembly Finshg ....E 215 634-7490
Philadelphia (G-13563)
Converters Inc ....E 215 355-5400
Huntingdon Valley (G-7971)
Delaware Valley Shipping & Pac ....E 215 638-8900
Bensalem (G-1182)
Harrier Mfg Corp ....G 814 838-9957
Erie (G-5310)
Hot Off Press Inc ....F 610 473-5700
Boyertown (G-1916)
Kisel Printing Service Inc ....E 570 489-7666
Dickson City (G-4121)
Lemac Packaging Inc ....G 814 453-7652
Erie (G-5361)
Nupak Printing LLC ....D 717 244-4041
Red Lion (G-16610)
Paper Magic Group Inc ....B 570 644-0842
Elysburg (G-4978)
Penn State Paper & Box Co Inc ....E 610 433-7468
Allentown (G-349)
Phillips Graphic Finishing LLC ....D 717 653-4565
Manheim (G-10402)
Raymond Sherman Co Inc ....G 610 272-4640
Conshohocken (G-3597)
Superior Packaging Inc ....F 570 824-3577
Plains (G-15789)

PAPER & PAPER PRDTS: Crepe, Made From Purchased Materials

American Crepe Corporation ....G 570 433-3319
Montoursville (G-11430)

PAPER CONVERTING

Amercareroyal LLC ....E 610 384-3400
Exton (G-5642)
Bengal Converting Services Inc ....E 610 787-0900
Linfield (G-9987)
Fibematics Inc ....E 215 226-2672
Philadelphia (G-13698)
Hpi Plastics Incorporated ....F 610 273-7113
Honey Brook (G-7751)
Interstate Paper Supply Co Inc ....D 724 938-2218
Roscoe (G-16817)

Lap Distributors Inc ....G 215 744-4000
Philadelphia (G-13955)
Max Intrntional Converters Inc ....E 717 898-0147
Lancaster (G-9128)
Neenah Northeast LLC ....C 215 536-4600
Quakertown (G-16223)
Northwoods Ppr Converting Inc ....D 570 424-8786
East Stroudsburg (G-4625)
Paper Exchange Inc ....F 412 325-7075
Allison Park (G-457)
Progressive Converting Inc ....D 570 384-2979
Hazle Township (G-7475)
Sappi North America Inc ....D 610 398-8400
Allentown (G-383)
Specialty Industries Inc ....C 717 246-1661
Red Lion (G-16613)
Tele-Media Sfp LLC ....E 570 271-0810
Danville (G-4014)
Treco Incorporated ....F 215 226-0908
Philadelphia (G-14405)
Weyerhaeuser Company ....D 814 371-0630
Du Bois (G-4427)

PAPER MANUFACTURERS: Exc Newsprint

American Crepe Corporation ....G 570 433-3319
Montoursville (G-11430)
Avery Dennison Corporation ....D 215 536-9000
Quakertown (G-16170)
Beistle Company ....B 717 532-2131
Shippensburg (G-17517)
Cascades Tissue Group - PA Inc ....C 570 388-4307
Pittston (G-15744)
Case Paper Co Inc ....C 215 430-6400
Philadelphia (G-13510)
Devra Party Corp. ....G 718 522-7421
Philadelphia (G-13626)
Domtar Paper Company LLC ....A 814 965-2521
Johnsonburg (G-8346)
Domtar Paper Company LLC ....E 814 371-0630
Du Bois (G-4387)
Essity North America Inc ....G 610 499-3700
Eddystone (G-4801)
Fortney Packages Inc ....G 717 243-1826
Carlisle (G-2714)
Georgia-Pacific LLC ....E 215 538-7549
Quakertown (G-16196)
Georgia-Pacific LLC ....E 610 250-7402
Easton (G-4691)
Glatfelter Holdings LLC ....G 717 225-2772
York (G-20500)
Hampden Papers Inc ....G 610 255-4166
Landenberg (G-9249)
International Paper Company ....C 570 384-3251
Hazle Township (G-7464)
International Paper Company ....F 724 745-2288
Eighty Four (G-4843)
International Paper Company ....C 717 391-3400
Lancaster (G-9060)
International Paper Company ....C 814 454-9001
Erie (G-5330)
Metso Minerals Industries Inc ....C 717 843-8671
York (G-20591)
Nittany Paper Mills Inc ....D 888 288-7907
Lewistown (G-9940)
R C Paper Company ....G 610 821-9610
Allentown (G-366)
S E Hagarman Designs LLC ....G 717 633-5336
Hanover (G-6947)
Sealed Air Corporation ....E 610 384-2650
Modena (G-11259)
Sealed Air Corporation ....E 610 375-4281
Reading (G-16510)
Select Tissue Pennsylvania LLC ....E 570 785-2000
Vandling (G-18739)
Weyerhaeuser Company ....D 814 371-0630
Du Bois (G-4427)

PAPER PRDTS

Hampshire Paper Company ....G 570 759-7245
Berwick (G-1328)
Vetpack Enterprises LLC ....G 215 680-8637
Merion Station (G-10999)

PAPER PRDTS: Book Covers

Brodart Co ....C 570 769-3265
Mc Elhattan (G-10586)

PAPER PRDTS: Cleansing Tissues, Made From Purchased Material

F M P Healthcare Products ....G....... 800 611-7776
Bridgeville **(G-2063)**

PAPER PRDTS: Feminine Hygiene Prdts

First Quality Hygienic Inc ....G..... 570 769-6900
Mc Elhattan **(G-10587)**

PAPER PRDTS: Infant & Baby Prdts

Kimberly-Clark Corporation ....D..... 610 874-4331
Chester **(G-3053)**

PAPER PRDTS: Molded Pulp Prdts

Doellken- Woodtape Inc ....G..... 610 929-1910
Temple **(G-18328)**

PAPER PRDTS: Sanitary

Bellemarque LLC ....E....... 855 262-7783
Hazle Township **(G-7447)**
Cellucap Manufacturing Co ....E....... 800 523-3814
Philadelphia **(G-13518)**
Essity North America Inc ....C....... 610 499-3700
Philadelphia **(G-13680)**
Nutek Disposables Inc ....D....... 570 769-6900
Mc Elhattan **(G-10589)**

PAPER PRDTS: Sanitary Tissue Paper

Cascades Tissue Group - PA Inc ....F 570 388-6161
Ransom **(G-16306)**
Kimberly-Clark Corporation ....D..... 610 874-4331
Chester **(G-3053)**

PAPER PRDTS: Toilet Paper, Made From Purchased Materials

Lake Paper Products Inc ....E..... 570 836-8815
Tunkhannock **(G-18541)**

PAPER PRDTS: Toweling Tissue

First Quality Products Inc ....B..... 570 769-6900
Mc Elhattan **(G-10588)**

PAPER PRDTS: Towels, Napkins/Tissue Paper, From Purchd Mtrls

First Quality Products Inc ....B..... 570 769-6900
Mc Elhattan **(G-10588)**

PAPER PRDTS: Wrappers, Blank, Made From Purchased Materials

N F String & Son Inc ....D..... 717 234-2441
Harrisburg **(G-7182)**

PAPER, WHOLESALE: Fine

Xerox Corporation ....C 412 506-4000
Pittsburgh **(G-15726)**

PAPER, WHOLESALE: Printing

Case Paper Co Inc ....C..... 215 430-6400
Philadelphia **(G-13510)**
Kappa Media Group Inc ....C..... 215 643-5800
Fort Washington **(G-6080)**

PAPER: Adhesive

Avery Dennison Corporation ....D..... 215 536-9000
Quakertown **(G-16170)**
Butler Technologies Inc ....D..... 724 283-6656
Butler **(G-2386)**
Mgi Seagull Inc ....E....... 610 380-6470
Downingtown **(G-4241)**
Topflight Corporation ....C..... 717 227-5400
Glen Rock **(G-6461)**

PAPER: Art

Atlantic Enterprise Inc ....G....... 800 367-8547
Ivyland **(G-8206)**
Chiyoda America Inc ....D..... 610 286-3100
Morgantown **(G-11520)**

PAPER: Bank Note

Viking Importing Co ....G....... 610 690-2900
Springfield **(G-17924)**

PAPER: Book

P H Glatfelter Company ....A 717 225-4711
York **(G-20615)**

PAPER: Bristols

Hibachi Grill Supreme Buffet ....F 215 728-7222
Philadelphia **(G-13822)**

PAPER: Building, Insulation

Ne Fibers LLC ....E....... 570 445-2086
Wilkes Barre **(G-19949)**

PAPER: Business Form

Appvion Operations Inc ....B..... 814 224-2131
Roaring Spring **(G-16761)**
Digital-Ink Inc ....D..... 717 731-8890
Dillsburg **(G-4126)**
Jerry James Trdng As Mnls BSC ....G..... 425 255-0199
Lafayette Hill **(G-8882)**

PAPER: Card

Access Credential Systems LLC ....G..... 724 820-1160
Eighty Four **(G-4831)**

PAPER: Cardboard

Danaken Designs Inc ....F 570 445-9797
Scranton **(G-17227)**

PAPER: Cloth, Lined, Made From Purchased Materials

Tekni-Plex Inc ....E....... 484 690-1520
Wayne **(G-19381)**
Trident Tpi Holdings Inc ....A..... 484 690-1520
Wayne **(G-19384)**

PAPER: Coated & Laminated, NEC

Appvion Operations Inc ....B..... 814 224-2131
Roaring Spring **(G-16761)**
Bestway Printing ....G....... 215 368-4140
Lansdale **(G-9346)**
Cas Pack Corporation ....E....... 215 254-7225
Bensalem **(G-1165)**
Chiyoda America Inc ....D..... 610 286-3100
Morgantown **(G-11520)**
Fedex Office & Print Svcs Inc ....E..... 412 835-4005
Pittsburgh **(G-15010)**
Fedex Office & Print Svcs Inc ....F..... 412 788-0552
Pittsburgh **(G-15009)**
Grafika Commercial Prtg Inc ....B..... 610 678-8630
Reading **(G-16396)**
Great Northern Corporation ....E..... 610 706-0910
Allentown **(G-236)**
Guy Coder ....G....... 814 265-0519
Brockway **(G-2227)**
Jon Swan Inc ....E....... 412 264-9000
Coraopolis **(G-3700)**
Lemac Packaging Inc ....G....... 814 453-7652
Erie **(G-5361)**
Mito Insulation Company ....G....... 724 335-8551
New Kensington **(G-12359)**
Modern Reproductions Inc ....F..... 412 488-7700
Pittsburgh **(G-15298)**
Moore Push Pin Company ....D..... 215 233-5700
Glenside **(G-6531)**
Neenah Northeast LLC ....C..... 215 536-4600
Quakertown **(G-16223)**
Neenah Northeast LLC ....E..... 610 926-1996
Reading **(G-16453)**
Reed & Witting Company ....E..... 412 682-1000
Pittsburgh **(G-15476)**
Shepherd Good Work Services ....G..... 610 776-8353
Allentown **(G-388)**
Tele-Media Sfp LLC ....E....... 570 271-0810
Danville **(G-4014)**
Tinicum Research Company ....G..... 610 294-9390
Erwinna **(G-5540)**
Uniflex Holdings Inc ....E....... 516 932-2000
Philadelphia **(G-14419)**

PAPER: Coated, Exc Photographic, Carbon Or Abrasive

Avery Dennison Corporation ....D..... 570 888-6641
Sayre **(G-17110)**
Avery Dennison Corporation ....D..... 570 748-7701
Mill Hall **(G-11172)**
Spectra-Kote Corporation ....E..... 717 334-3177
Gettysburg **(G-6314)**

PAPER: Envelope

Suplee Envelope Co Inc ....E....... 610 352-2900
Garnet Valley **(G-6269)**

PAPER: Fine

Factor X Graffics ....G....... 717 590-7402
Mechanicsburg **(G-10842)**
Harmony Paper Company LLC ....G 724 991-1110
Harmony **(G-7068)**

PAPER: Gift Wrap

CSS Industries Inc ....C..... 610 729-3959
Plymouth Meeting **(G-15840)**
CSS Industries Inc ....G....... 570 275-5241
Danville **(G-3999)**
Harmony Designs Inc ....G....... 610 869-4234
West Grove **(G-19700)**
Thomas Catanese & Co ....G....... 610 277-6230
Plymouth Meeting **(G-15876)**

PAPER: Insulation Siding

Penn Pro Manufacturing Inc ....F 724 222-6450
Washington **(G-19215)**

PAPER: Offset

Supra Office Solutions Inc ....G..... 267 275-8888
Philadelphia **(G-14360)**

PAPER: Packaging

Flextron Industries Inc ....F 610 459-4600
Aston **(G-763)**
Kmn Packaging Inc ....G....... 610 376-3606
Reading **(G-16422)**
Pratt Industries USA Inc ....D..... 610 967-6027
Emmaus **(G-5040)**
Roddy Products ....G....... 610 623-7040
Aldan **(G-60)**

PAPER: Parchment

Historical Documents Co ....G....... 215 533-4500
Philadelphia **(G-13830)**

PAPER: Poster & Art

Statement Walls LLC ....G....... 267 266-0869
Philadelphia **(G-14341)**

PAPER: Printer

Everything Postal Inc ....G....... 610 367-7444
Bechtelsville **(G-1032)**
Maiden Formats Inc ....G....... 412 884-4716
Pittsburgh **(G-15248)**
Minton Holdings LLC ....G....... 412 787-5912
Pittsburgh **(G-15293)**
Mri Flexible Packaging Company ....F 215 860-7676
Newtown **(G-12525)**
UPS Store Inc ....G....... 724 934-1088
Wexford **(G-19831)**

PAPER: Specialty

Mt Holly Sprng Specialty Ppr ....F 717 486-8500
Mount Holly Springs **(G-11637)**

PAPER: Specialty Or Chemically Treated

Ahlstrom Mount Holly Sprng LLC ....E 717 486-3438
Mount Holly Springs **(G-11631)**
Ahlstrom Mount Holly Sprng LLC ....C..... 717 486-3438
Mount Holly Springs **(G-11632)**
Hawk Mountain Editions Ltd ....C..... 484 220-0524
Leesport **(G-9666)**
Pixelle Spcialty Solutions LLC ....G....... 717 225-4711
Spring Grove **(G-17880)**

PRODUCT

PAPER: Tablet

Kurtz Bros.....................................D 814 765-6561
Clearfield *(G-3222)*

PAPER: Tissue

CSS Industries Inc........................C 610 729-3959
Plymouth Meeting *(G-15840)*
First Quality Tissue LLC.................B 570 748-1200
Lock Haven *(G-10089)*

PAPER: Uncoated

Team Ten LLC...............................B 814 684-1610
Tyrone *(G-18595)*

PAPER: Wallpaper

465 Devon Park Drive Inc...............G 610 293-1330
Wayne *(G-19292)*
Anderson Prints LLC.....................F 610 293-1330
Wayne *(G-19298)*
Gty Inc...D 717 764-8969
York *(G-20516)*
New Ngc Inc.................................D 570 538-2531
New Columbia *(G-12174)*
Vornhold Wallpapers Inc...............G 215 757-6641
Langhorne *(G-9334)*

PAPER: Wrapping & Packaging

R & D Americas Best Packaging ....G 610 435-4300
Allentown *(G-364)*
Warren Products Inc......................G 570 655-4596
West Pittston *(G-19757)*

PAPERBOARD

American Paper Products of PHI.....E 508 879-1141
Lansdale *(G-9341)*
Beistle Company...........................B 717 532-2131
Shippensburg *(G-17517)*
Brandywine Industrial Paper ....G 610 212-9949
Coatesville *(G-3294)*
Caraustar Industries Inc................G 717 534-2206
Hershey *(G-7605)*
Case Paper Co Inc........................C 215 430-6400
Philadelphia *(G-13510)*
Century Packaging Co Inc..............E 610 262-8860
Whitehall *(G-19864)*
General Partition Company Inc........E 215 785-1000
Croydon *(G-3918)*
Georgia-Pacific LLC.......................B 610 250-1400
Easton *(G-4690)*
Graphic Packaging Intl LLC ....B 610 725-9840
Phoenixville *(G-14552)*
Great Northern Corporation............E 610 706-0910
Allentown *(G-236)*
Hurlock Bros Co Inc......................F 610 659-8153
Drexel Hill *(G-4366)*
Industrial Packaging Supplies.........G 724 459-8299
Blairsville *(G-1725)*
New Ngc Inc.................................D 570 538-2531
New Columbia *(G-12174)*
Newman & Company Inc.................C 215 333-8700
Philadelphia *(G-14070)*
Ox Paperboard LLC.......................C 304 725-2076
Hanover *(G-6928)*
Rixie Paper Products Inc................F 610 323-9220
Pottstown *(G-16040)*
Signode Industrial Group LLC.........E 570 450-0123
Hazle Township *(G-7479)*
Somerset Enterprises Inc...............F 724 734-9497
Farrell *(G-5874)*
St Marys Box Company...................E 814 834-3819
Saint Marys *(G-17015)*
Sterling Paper Company.................D 215 744-5350
Philadelphia *(G-14347)*
Westrock Company.........................G 215 826-2497
Croydon *(G-3932)*
Westrock Cp LLC...........................C 215 984-7000
Philadelphia *(G-14468)*
Westrock Rkt LLC..........................D 570 476-0120
Delaware Water Gap *(G-4045)*
Westrock Rkt LLC..........................D 570 454-0433
Hazleton *(G-7538)*
Westrock Rkt LLC..........................C 717 393-0436
Lancaster *(G-9239)*

PAPERBOARD CONVERTING

Bengal Direct LLC.........................F 610 245-5901
Linfield *(G-9988)*
Beverage Coasters Inc...................G 610 916-4864
Centerport *(G-2832)*

PAPERBOARD PRDTS: Building Insulating & Packaging

Sonoco Prtective Solutions Inc.......E 412 415-3784
Pittsburgh *(G-15559)*

PAPERBOARD PRDTS: Container Board

Brazilian Paper Corporation ....G 215 369-7000
New Hope *(G-12299)*

PAPERBOARD PRDTS: Folding Boxboard

Northeastern PA Carton Co Inc ....E 570 457-7711
Moosic *(G-11510)*
Vogel Carton LLC..........................E 215 957-0612
Warminster *(G-18997)*
Westrock Cp LLC...........................F 215 699-4444
North Wales *(G-12840)*

PAPERBOARD PRDTS: Pressboard

Neenah Northeast LLC...................C 215 536-4600
Quakertown *(G-16223)*
Neenah Northeast LLC...................E 610 926-1996
Reading *(G-16453)*

PAPERBOARD PRDTS: Setup Boxboard

McLean Packaging Corporation........C 610 759-3550
Nazareth *(G-11981)*

PAPERBOARD: Boxboard

Superior Packaging Inc...................F 570 824-3577
Plains *(G-15789)*

PAPERBOARD: Corrugated

Sheffield Container Corp.................E 814 968-3287
Sheffield *(G-17483)*
United Corrstack LLC......................D 610 374-3000
Reading *(G-16554)*
Westrock Cp LLC...........................C 904 751-6400
York *(G-20709)*

PARACHUTES

Life Support International ....E 215 785-2870
Langhorne *(G-9308)*
Skydive Store Inc..........................G 856 629-4600
Bushkill *(G-2369)*

PARTICLEBOARD

Georgia-Pacific LLC.......................C 814 778-6000
Kane *(G-8465)*

PARTICLEBOARD: Laminated, Plastic

Rynone Manufacturing Corp.............C 570 888-5272
Sayre *(G-17121)*

PARTITIONS & FIXTURES: Except Wood

A W Mercer Inc.............................C 610 367-8460
Boyertown *(G-1892)*
Adelphia Steel Eqp Co Inc..............E 800 865-8211
Philadelphia *(G-13445)*
Architectural Woodsmiths Inc..........D 717 532-7700
Shippensburg *(G-17515)*
Bentech Inc...................................E 215 223-9420
Philadelphia *(G-13454)*
Cpg International LLC ....F 570 348-0997
Scranton *(G-17223)*
Crawford Dzignes Inc.....................G 724 872-4644
West Newton *(G-19750)*
Duckloe Frederick and Bros ....F 570 897-6172
Portland *(G-15939)*
Federal Prison Industries...............B 570 524-0096
Lewisburg *(G-9906)*
General Metal Company Inc.............E 215 638-3242
Bensalem *(G-1203)*
Graphic Display Systems................F 717 274-3954
Lebanon *(G-9576)*
Interior Creations Inc.....................E 215 425-9390
Philadelphia *(G-13864)*

Intermetro Industries Corp..............B 570 825-2741
Wilkes Barre *(G-19929)*
Moore Push Pin Company...............D 215 233-5700
Glenside *(G-6531)*
Northway Industries Inc ....C 570 837-1564
Middleburg *(G-11034)*
ODonnell Metal Fabricators.............F 610 279-8810
Norristown *(G-12697)*
P A Office and Closet Systems.........F 610 944-1333
Fleetwood *(G-5977)*
Promotion Centre Inc.....................E 717 843-1582
York *(G-20645)*
Resun Modspace Inc......................F 610 232-1200
Berwyn *(G-1373)*
Ridg-U-Rak Inc..............................G 814 725-8751
North East *(G-12757)*
Scranton Products Inc....................C 570 558-8000
Scranton *(G-17287)*
Superior Cabinet Co.......................G 724 569-9581
Smithfield *(G-17655)*
Superior Cabinet Company..............E 215 536-5228
Quakertown *(G-16247)*
T C B Displays Inc.........................E 610 983-0500
Phoenixville *(G-14582)*

PARTITIONS WHOLESALERS

Neff Specialties LLC......................F 814 247-8887
Hastings *(G-7262)*

PARTITIONS: Nonwood, Floor Attached

Customfold Inc..............................F 724 376-8565
Stoneboro *(G-18068)*
General Partitions Mfg Corp............E 814 833-1154
Erie *(G-5302)*
Transwall Corp..............................D 610 429-1400
West Chester *(G-19668)*

PARTITIONS: Solid Fiber, Made From Purchased Materials

Westrock Rkt Company...................G 717 790-1596
Mechanicsburg *(G-10909)*

PARTITIONS: Wood & Fixtures

Ajjp Corporation.............................C 215 968-6677
Newtown *(G-12495)*
Ames Construction Inc....................E 717 299-1395
Lancaster *(G-8932)*
Architectural Woodsmiths Inc..........D 717 532-7700
Shippensburg *(G-17515)*
Atlantic Shelving Systems LLC........G 215 245-1310
Bensalem *(G-1151)*
Bendersville Wood Crafts................G 717 677-6458
Bendersville *(G-1138)*
Boyce Products Ltd.........................F 570 224-6570
Damascus *(G-3989)*
Charles Steckman.........................G 724 789-7066
Renfrew *(G-16638)*
CNT Fixture Company Inc...............E 412 443-6260
Glenshaw *(G-6484)*
Craft-Maid Kitchen Inc...................E 610 376-8686
Reading *(G-16352)*
Custom Designs & Mfg Co..............E 570 207-4432
Scranton *(G-17226)*
Dally Slate Company Inc.................D 610 863-4172
Pen Argyl *(G-13213)*
Dennis Downing............................G 724 598-0043
New Castle *(G-12081)*
Desmond Wholesale Distrs Inc ....F 215 225-0300
Philadelphia *(G-13623)*
Donatucci Kitchens & Appls............E 215 545-5755
Philadelphia *(G-13639)*
EDM Co..E 717 626-2186
Lititz *(G-10005)*
Hoff Enterprises Inc.......................E 814 535-8371
Johnstown *(G-8381)*
Kitchens By Meade Inc...................F 814 453-4888
Erie *(G-5345)*
Kountry Kraft Kitchens Inc ....C 610 589-4575
Newmanstown *(G-12479)*
Krehling Industries Inc....................D 717 232-7936
Harrisburg *(G-7165)*
M & M Manufacturing Co.................E 724 274-0767
Cheswick *(G-3111)*
Melvin Stoltzfus............................F 717 656-3520
Talmage *(G-18207)*
Millwork Solutions Inc....................E 814 446-4009
Seward *(G-17382)*

Northway Industries Inc ....C...... 570 837-1564
  Middleburg (G-11034)
Quality Custom Cabinetry Inc.............C...... 717 656-2721
  New Holland (G-12275)
Ralston Shop Inc...................................F...... 610 268-3829
  Avondale (G-858)
Schubert Custom Cabinetry Inc ....G...... 610 372-5559
  Reading (G-16508)
Staurowsky Woodworking ....G...... 610 489-0770
  Collegeville (G-3394)
Top Shop..G...... 610 622-6101
  Philadelphia (G-14396)

PARTS: Metal

Integrated Fabrication Mch Inc............E...... 724 962-3526
  Greenville (G-6749)
M and P Custom Design Inc..................F...... 610 444-0244
  Kennett Square (G-8524)
Mgk Technologies Inc..........................E...... 814 849-3061
  Homer City (G-7678)
Philadlphia Mtal Rsrce Rcovery ....E...... 215 423-4800
  Philadelphia (G-14163)
River Supply Inc..................................E...... 717 927-1555
  Brogue (G-2240)

PARTY & SPECIAL EVENT PLANNING SVCS

Merry Maid Inc....................................E...... 800 360-3836
  Bangor (G-921)

PASTES: Metal

Heraeus Incorporated..........................G...... 215 944-9981
  Yardley (G-20314)

PATENT OWNERS & LESSORS

Brown Brothers LLP.............................G...... 570 689-9688
  Sterling (G-18048)
Nocopi Technologies Inc......................G...... 610 834-9600
  King of Prussia (G-8657)

PATIENT MONITORING EQPT WHOLESALERS

Lifewatch Services Inc ....B...... 847 720-2100
  Malvern (G-10269)

PATTERNS: Indl

A B Patterns Models ....G...... 215 322-8226
  Huntingdon Valley (G-7960)
Able Pattern Company ....F...... 724 327-1401
  Export (G-5587)
Bassler Wllmsport Pttern Works ....G...... 570 368-2471
  Montoursville (G-11432)
Baum & Hersh Inc ....G...... 717 229-2255
  Codorus (G-3357)
Blatts Pattern Shop ....F...... 717 933-5633
  Fredericksburg (G-6172)
Castek Innovations Inc.........................E...... 717 267-2748
  Chambersburg (G-2915)
Effort Enterprises Inc ....G...... 610 837-7003
  Bath (G-957)
Frederick Wohlgemuth Inc....................E...... 215 638-9672
  Bensalem (G-1199)
Hains Pattern Shop Inc.........................F...... 717 273-6351
  Lebanon (G-9578)
Independent Pattern Shop ....E...... 814 459-2591
  Erie (G-5323)
J Clem Kline & Son Inc.........................G...... 610 258-6071
  Easton (G-4708)
Jacob Pattern Works Inc.......................F...... 610 326-1100
  Pottstown (G-16004)
Johnson Pattern & Machine Shop.........G...... 724 697-4079
  Salina (G-17043)
Lebanon Pattern Shop Inc ....G...... 717 273-8159
  Lebanon (G-9603)
Patterson Plastics & Mfg.......................G...... 215 736-3020
  Levittown (G-9853)
Pennsylvania Patterns..........................G...... 717 533-4188
  Hershey (G-7625)
Precision Pattern & Wdwkg ....G...... 724 588-2224
  Greenville (G-6766)
Spring Ford Castings Inc ....G...... 610 489-2600
  Trappe (G-18473)
Steffys Pattern Shop ....G...... 717 656-6032
  Leola (G-9805)
Tammy Williams ....G...... 814 654-7127
  Conneaut Lake (G-3481)
Threeway Pattern Enterprises ....G...... 610 929-2889
  Reading (G-16537)

Weatherly Casting and Mch Co ....D...... 570 427-8611
  Weatherly (G-19455)

PAVERS

Force Inc ....E...... 724 465-9399
  Indiana (G-8100)

PAVING MATERIALS: Prefabricated, Concrete

Hanover Prest Paving Company ....E...... 717 637-0500
  Hanover (G-6899)

PAVING MIXTURES

Allegheny Asphalt Services LLC...........G...... 724 732-6637
  Ambridge (G-607)
Golden Eagle Construction Co...............E...... 724 437-6495
  Uniontown (G-18628)
Hempt Bros Inc ....D...... 717 774-2911
  Camp Hill (G-2500)

PEARLS, WHOLESALE

Impact Colors Inc ....E...... 302 224-8310
  Conshohocken (G-3561)

PENCILS & PENS WHOLESALERS

Universal Pen & Pencil Co Inc ....G...... 610 670-4720
  Reading (G-16555)

PENHOLDERS & PARTS

Pen Pal LLC..G...... 917 882-1441
  Allentown (G-345)

PENNANTS

Standard Pennant Company Inc............E...... 814 427-2066
  Big Run (G-1657)

PENS & PARTS: Ball Point

Hanover Pen Corp.................................E...... 717 637-3729
  Hanover (G-6897)
Universal Pen & Pencil Co Inc ....G...... 610 670-4720
  Reading (G-16555)

PENS & PARTS: Cartridges, Refill, Ball Point

Cartridge World York ....G...... 717 699-4465
  York (G-20419)

PERFUMES

Revoltnary Elctrnic Design LLC ....G...... 814 977-9546
  Bedford (G-1073)

PERISCOPES

Lenox Instrument Co Inc ....E...... 215 322-9990
  Trevose (G-18500)

PERLITE MINING SVCS

Norton Oglebay Company......................F...... 412 995-5500
  Pittsburgh (G-15347)

PERLITE: Processed

Chemrock Corporation..........................F...... 610 667-6640
  Bala Cynwyd (G-875)
Metal Services LLC..............................E...... 610 347-0444
  Kennett Square (G-8527)
Therm-O-Rock East Inc ....D...... 724 258-3670
  New Eagle (G-12193)
Therm-O-Rock East Inc ....E...... 724 379-8604
  Donora (G-4163)

PERSONAL & HOUSEHOLD GOODS REPAIR, NEC

Nicewonger Awning Co.........................G...... 724 837-5920
  Greensburg (G-6692)

PERSONAL CARE FACILITY

Impact Colors Inc ....E...... 302 224-8310
  Conshohocken (G-3561)

PEST CONTROL SVCS

Boos Bug Stoppers LLC ....G...... 724 601-3223
  Fombell (G-6030)

P D Q Pest Control Inc.........................G...... 814 774-8882
  Girard (G-6398)

PESTICIDES

Bayer Corporation ....A...... 412 777-2000
  Pittsburgh (G-14750)
Chemgro Fertilizer Co Inc ....F...... 717 935-2185
  Belleville (G-1129)
FMC Asia-Pacific Inc............................G...... 215 299-6000
  Philadelphia (G-13708)
Specilized Svcs Promotions Inc...........G...... 814 864-4984
  Erie (G-5487)
Weiser Group LLC ....F...... 724 452-6535
  Evans City (G-5565)
Zep Inc ....C...... 610 295-1360
  Breinigsville (G-2033)

PESTICIDES WHOLESALERS

Growmark Fs LLC ....E...... 610 926-6339
  Leesport (G-9664)
Growmark Fs LLC ....E...... 724 543-1101
  Adrian (G-30)
Growmark Fs LLC ....G...... 814 359-2725
  Bellefonte (G-1102)
Liquid Fence Co Inc.............................E...... 570 722-8165
  Blakeslee (G-1748)

PET & PET SPLYS STORES

Diamond Milling Company Inc...............G...... 724 846-0920
  New Brighton (G-12034)
Wild Birds Unlimited ....G...... 610 366-1725
  Allentown (G-434)

PET COLLARS, LEASHES, MUZZLES & HARNESSES: Leather

Graham International Inc........................F...... 203 838-3355
  Philadelphia (G-13779)
Kimberly A Spickler ....G...... 814 627-2316
  Hesston (G-7627)
Lb Full Circle Canine Fitness................G...... 267 825-7375
  Philadelphia (G-13961)

PET FOOD WHOLESALERS

Agri-Dynamics Inc ....G...... 610 250-9280
  Martins Creek (G-10517)
Pets United LLC ....G...... 570 384-5555
  Hazle Township (G-7471)

PET SPLYS

201 Distributing Inc ....G...... 724 529-2320
  Vanderbilt (G-18719)
Agri-Dynamics Inc ....G...... 610 250-9280
  Martins Creek (G-10517)
Beaver Creek Aviary ....G...... 717 369-9983
  Saint Thomas (G-17038)
Cummings Group Inc ....G...... 714 237-1140
  Bethlehem (G-1492)
Five Points Pet Supply LLC ....G...... 724 857-6000
  Aliquippa (G-75)
Golden Bone Pet Resort Inc ....E...... 412 661-7001
  Pittsburgh (G-15057)
Healthy Pet Foods Inc ....G...... 610 918-4702
  West Chester (G-19560)
Hope Good Animal Clinic ....G...... 717 766-5535
  Mechanicsburg (G-10854)
Nestle Purina Petcare Company...........D...... 610 398-4667
  Allentown (G-328)
Petnovations Inc ....E...... 610 994-2103
  Phoenixville (G-14566)
Pets United LLC ....G...... 570 384-5555
  Hazle Township (G-7471)
Premium Pet Division ....G...... 215 364-0211
  Langhorne (G-9321)
Sageking Inc ....G...... 717 540-0525
  Irwin (G-8199)
Targeted Pet Treats LLC ....C...... 814 406-7351
  Warren (G-19051)
Tlb Industries Inc ....G...... 570 729-7192
  Honesdale (G-7728)
Towerstar Pets LLC ....G...... 610 296-4970
  Malvern (G-10334)

PET SPLYS WHOLESALERS

Pets United LLC ....G...... 570 384-5555
  Hazle Township (G-7471)

PRODUCT

PETROLATUMS: Nonmedicinal

Lanxess Solutions US Inc ....C 724 756-2210
  Petrolia *(G-13306)*

PETROLEUM & PETROLEUM PRDTS, WHOLESALE Engine Fuels & Oils

Kapothanasis Group Inc ....G 207 939-5680
  Harrisburg *(G-7160)*

PETROLEUM & PETROLEUM PRDTS, WHOLESALE Fuel Oil

New Enterprise Stone Lime Inc ....B 610 374-5131
  Leesport *(G-9668)*

PETROLEUM & PETROLEUM PRDTS, WHOLESALE Petroleum Terminals

Atlantic Refining & Marketing ....C 215 977-3000
  Philadelphia *(G-13422)*
Sunoco Inc ....D 215 977-3000
  Newtown Square *(G-12591)*

PETROLEUM & PETROLEUM PRDTS, WHOLESALE: Bulk Stations

Chevron USA Inc ....E 412 262-2830
  Coraopolis *(G-3677)*
Hiltz Propane Systems Inc ....E 717 799-4322
  Marietta *(G-10464)*
Sunoco Inc ....E 717 564-1440
  Harrisburg *(G-7222)*

PETROLEUM BULK STATIONS & TERMINALS

American Refining Group Inc ....B 814 368-1378
  Bradford *(G-1955)*

PETROLEUM PRDTS WHOLESALERS

American Petroleum Partners ....G 844 835-5277
  Canonsburg *(G-2539)*
Anadarko Petroleum ....G 570 326-1535
  Williamsport *(G-19986)*
Eni USA R & M Co Inc ....E 724 352-4451
  Cabot *(G-2456)*
Morgan Brothers Company ....F 724 843-7485
  Beaver Falls *(G-1006)*
Noco Distribution LLC ....G 866 946-3927
  Ridgway *(G-16719)*
Petroleum Products Corp ....G 412 264-8242
  Coraopolis *(G-3714)*
Zipcorp Inc ....B 814 368-2700
  Bradford *(G-1997)*

PEWTER WARE

Coventry Pewter Inc ....G 610 328-1557
  Springfield *(G-17911)*
Old Glory Corp ....F 724 423-3580
  Mount Pleasant *(G-11709)*
Wendell August Forge Inc ....D 724 748-9500
  Mercer *(G-10979)*

PHARMACEUTICAL PREPARATIONS: Adrenal

Med-Fast Pharmacy LP ....G 866 979-7378
  Aliquippa *(G-83)*
Techniserv Inc ....D 570 759-2315
  Berwick *(G-1346)*

PHARMACEUTICAL PREPARATIONS: Druggists' Preparations

Abbott Laboratories ....D 717 545-8159
  Harrisburg *(G-7080)*
Abbott Laboratories ....G 610 444-9818
  Kennett Square *(G-8500)*
Alcobra Inc ....G 610 940-1630
  Conshohocken *(G-3517)*
Almac Pharma Services LLC ....C 610 666-9500
  Audubon *(G-823)*
Biomed Healthcare Inc ....G 888 244-2340
  Sharon Hill *(G-17453)*
Cognition Therapeutics Inc ....G 412 481-2210
  Pittsburgh *(G-14865)*

Douglas Pharma Us Inc ....F 267 317-2010
  Warminster *(G-18862)*
Janssen Research & Dev LLC ....C 215 628-5000
  Spring House *(G-17882)*
McNeil Consmr Pharmaceuticals ....C 215 273-7700
  Fort Washington *(G-6083)*
Merck & Co Inc ....D 215 652-5000
  North Wales *(G-12814)*
Mrlrx LLC ....F 610 485-7750
  Marcus Hook *(G-10450)*
Mylan Inc ....G 724 514-1800
  Canonsburg *(G-2607)*
Packaging Coordinators Inc ....F 215 613-3600
  Philadelphia *(G-14111)*
Pentec Health Inc ....C 610 494-8700
  Glen Mills *(G-6440)*
Pentec Health Inc ....E 610 494-8700
  Upper Chichester *(G-18671)*
Soleo Health Holdings Inc ....G 888 244-2340
  Sharon Hill *(G-17460)*
Soleo Health Inc ....D 888 244-2340
  Sharon Hill *(G-17461)*
Synchrony Medical LLC ....E 484 947-5003
  Kennett Square *(G-8547)*
Torresdale Pharmacy ....G 215 612-5400
  Philadelphia *(G-14398)*
Viral Genomix Inc ....F 267 440-4200
  Blue Bell *(G-1856)*
Wakeem Inc ....F 610 258-2311
  Easton *(G-4774)*

PHARMACEUTICAL PREPARATIONS: Emulsions

Patwell Phrm Solutions LLC ....G 610 380-7101
  Coatesville *(G-3321)*

PHARMACEUTICAL PREPARATIONS: Medicines, Capsule Or Ampule

Drugdev Inc ....F 888 650-1860
  Wayne *(G-19320)*
Genomind LLC ....E 877 895-8658
  Chalfont *(G-2876)*
Renee Awad ND ....G 717 875-3056
  Columbia *(G-3448)*
Strategic Medicine Inc ....G 814 659-5450
  Kennett Square *(G-8546)*
University Pittsburgh Med Ctr ....F 412 647-8762
  Pittsburgh *(G-15684)*
Workcenter ....E 570 320-7444
  Williamsport *(G-20100)*

PHARMACEUTICAL PREPARATIONS: Penicillin

Othera Pharmaceuticals Inc ....G 484 879-2800
  Conshohocken *(G-3584)*
Teva Branded Phrm Pdts R&D Inc ....D 215 591-3000
  West Chester *(G-19659)*
Teva Branded Phrm Pdts R&D Inc ....G 215 591-3000
  Malvern *(G-10329)*
Teva Pharmaceuticals Usa Inc ....B 215 591-3000
  North Wales *(G-12834)*

PHARMACEUTICAL PREPARATIONS: Pills

Alliance Contract Pharma LLC ....F 215 256-5920
  Harleysville *(G-7017)*
Arx LLC ....E 717 253-7979
  Glen Rock *(G-6451)*
Coeptis Pharmaceuticals Inc ....G 724 290-1183
  Wexford *(G-19795)*
Duchesnay Usa Inc ....G 484 380-2641
  Bryn Mawr *(G-2321)*
Locus Pharmaceuticals Inc ....D 215 358-2000
  Blue Bell *(G-1845)*
Quality Health and Life Inc ....G 866 547-8447
  Philadelphia *(G-14219)*

PHARMACEUTICAL PREPARATIONS: Pituitary Gland

Harmony Biosciences LLC ....E 847 715-0500
  Plymouth Meeting *(G-15845)*

PHARMACEUTICAL PREPARATIONS: Powders

Matthey Johnson Holdings Inc ....E 610 971-3000
  Wayne *(G-19350)*

Matthey Johnson Inc ....E 610 971-3000
  Wayne *(G-19351)*
Matthey Johnson Inc ....C 610 341-8300
  Wayne *(G-19353)*
Shire US Manufacturing Inc ....E 484 595-8800
  Chesterbrook *(G-3098)*
Unipack Inc ....G 724 733-7381
  Pittsburgh *(G-15673)*

PHARMACEUTICAL PREPARATIONS: Proprietary Drug PRDTS

Barr Laboratories Inc ....C 215 591-3000
  North Wales *(G-12790)*
Copperhead Chemical Co Inc ....E 570 386-6123
  Tamaqua *(G-18209)*
HLS Therapeutics (usa) Inc ....F 844 457-8900
  Bryn Mawr *(G-2324)*
Iroko Pharmaceuticals Inc ....G 267 546-3003
  Philadelphia *(G-13875)*
Renaissance Ssa LLC ....F 267 685-0340
  Newtown *(G-12544)*

PHARMACEUTICAL PREPARATIONS: Solutions

Btg International Inc ....D 610 943-6000
  West Conshohocken *(G-19686)*
Ccn America LP ....G 412 349-6300
  Pittsburgh *(G-14831)*
Complete Intrvnous Access Svcs ....F 724 226-2618
  Creighton *(G-3881)*
Tarsa Therapeutics Inc ....F 267 273-7940
  Philadelphia *(G-14373)*
Tasman Pharma Inc ....G 267 317-2010
  Warminster *(G-18975)*

PHARMACEUTICAL PREPARATIONS: Tablets

Clinical Supplies MGT LLC ....F 215 596-4356
  Malvern *(G-10212)*
Double DS Roadhouse LLc ....G 814 395-3535
  Confluence *(G-3464)*
Medunik Usa Inc ....F 484 380-2641
  Bryn Mawr *(G-2329)*
Sigmapharm Laboratories LLC ....C 215 352-6655
  Bensalem *(G-1253)*

PHARMACEUTICAL PREPARATIONS: Tranquilizers Or Mental Drug

Mlre LLC ....G 724 514-1800
  Canonsburg *(G-2604)*

PHARMACEUTICALS

A & C Pharmtech Inc ....G 215 968-5605
  Newtown *(G-12493)*
Abbott Laboratories ....E 610 265-9100
  King of Prussia *(G-8576)*
Abbott Laboratories ....G 570 347-0319
  Scranton *(G-17205)*
Actavis Pharma Inc ....F 847 377-5508
  North Wales *(G-12785)*
Actavis Pharma Inc ....C 847 855-0812
  North Wales *(G-12786)*
Adapt Pharma Inc ....F 844 232-7811
  Radnor *(G-16285)*
Aevi Genomic Medicine Inc ....F 610 254-4201
  Wayne *(G-19294)*
Akamara Therapeutics Inc ....G 617 888-9191
  Philadelphia *(G-13360)*
Alliqua Biomedical Inc ....D 215 702-8550
  Langhorne *(G-9275)*
Allpure Technologies Inc ....G 717 624-3241
  New Oxford *(G-12404)*
Almac Central Management LLC ....C 215 660-8500
  Souderton *(G-17721)*
Almac Clinical Services LLC ....F 610 666-9500
  Souderton *(G-17722)*
Almac Group Incorporated ....A 215 660-8500
  Souderton *(G-17723)*
Amchemteq Inc ....G 814 234-0123
  State College *(G-17940)*
Amedra Pharmaceuticals LLC ....F 215 259-3601
  Fort Washington *(G-6062)*
American Medical Systems Inc ....F 512 808-4974
  Malvern *(G-10187)*
American Pharmaceutical ....G 610 366-9000
  Allentown *(G-136)*

American Regent Inc ....E 610 650-4200
Norristown *(G-12634)*

Angiotech Pharmaceuticals Inc ....G... 610 404-1000
Reading *(G-16322)*

Applied Clinical Concepts Inc ....G... 215 660-8500
Souderton *(G-17725)*

Aquacap Pharmaceutical Inc ....F ... 610 361-2800
Chadds Ford *(G-2847)*

Aquamed Technologies Inc ....G... 215 970-7194
Yardley *(G-20296)*

AR Scientific Inc ....G... 215 288-6500
Philadelphia *(G-13402)*

AR Scientific Inc ....G... 215 807-1312
Philadelphia *(G-13403)*

Aralez Pharmaceuticals MGT Inc ....G... 609 917-9330
Royersford *(G-16843)*

Aralez Pharmaceuticals R&D Inc ....G... 609 917-9330
Royersford *(G-16844)*

Aralez Pharmaceuticals US Inc ....F ... 609 917-9330
Royersford *(G-16845)*

Arbutus Biopharma Corporation ....F ... 267 469-0914
Warminster *(G-18828)*

Arbutus Biopharma Inc ....G... 215 675-5921
Warminster *(G-18829)*

Astrazeneca Pharmaceuticals LP ....G... 215 501-1739
Bensalem *(G-1150)*

Aumapharma LLC ....G... 215 345-4150
Doylestown *(G-4272)*

Azur Pharma Inc ....G... 215 832-3750
Philadelphia *(G-13434)*

Barr Laboratories Inc ....C ... 845 362-1100
North Wales *(G-12791)*

Bayer Corporation ....A ... 717 866-2141
Myerstown *(G-11875)*

Bayer Corporation ....A ... 412 777-2000
Pittsburgh *(G-14750)*

Bayer Data Center Pittsburgh ....G... 412 920-2950
Pittsburgh *(G-14753)*

Bayer Healthcare LLC ....B ... 717 866-2141
Myerstown *(G-11876)*

Bayer Healthcare LLC ....C ... 412 777-2000
Pittsburgh *(G-14754)*

Bayer Hlthcare Phrmcticals Inc ....C ... 717 713-7173
Mechanicsburg *(G-10823)*

Becton Dickinson and Company ....G... 610 948-3492
Royersford *(G-16846)*

Bilcare Inc ....C ... 610 935-4300
Phoenixville *(G-14532)*

Bioleap Inc ....G... 609 575-8645
Doylestown *(G-4276)*

Biotest Pharmaceuticals Corp ....G... 570 383-5341
Dickson City *(G-4119)*

Boiron Inc ....E ... 610 325-7464
Newtown Square *(G-12567)*

Brandywine Pharmaceuticals Inc ....F ... 800 647-0172
West Chester *(G-19513)*

Bristol-Myers Squibb Company ....D ... 609 818-5513
Southampton *(G-17800)*

Bvi C/O Genco ....G... 712 228-3338
Lebanon *(G-9550)*

Caliber Therapeutics Inc ....F ... 215 862-5797
New Hope *(G-12300)*

Canticle Pharmaceuticals Inc ....G... 404 380-9263
Conshohocken *(G-3526)*

Capnostics LLC ....G... 610 442-1363
Doylestown *(G-4288)*

Catalent Cts Inc ....C ... 816 767-6013
Philadelphia *(G-13513)*

Catalent Pharma Solutions Inc ....E ... 215 637-3565
Philadelphia *(G-13514)*

Catalent Pharma Solutions Inc ....E ... 215 613-3001
Philadelphia *(G-13515)*

Centocor Inc ....G... 215 325-2297
Horsham *(G-7802)*

Central Admxture Phrm Svcs Inc ....E ... 215 706-4001
Horsham *(G-7803)*

Cephalon Inc ....B ... 610 738-6410
West Chester *(G-19521)*

Cephalon Clinical Partners LP ....G... 610 883-5260
West Chester *(G-19522)*

Ch James G Thornton ....G... 412 207-2153
Pittsburgh *(G-14836)*

Chemgenex Pharmaceuticals Inc ....F ... 650 804-7660
Malvern *(G-10207)*

Cherokee Pharmaceuticals LLC ....B ... 570 271-4195
Riverside *(G-16757)*

Chiltern International Inc ....E ... 484 679-2400
King of Prussia *(G-8592)*

Choice Therapeutics Inc ....G... 508 384-0425
Langhorne *(G-9284)*

Chromatan Corporation ....F ... 617 529-0784
Ambler *(G-573)*

Cima Labs Inc ....E ... 763 315-4178
North Wales *(G-12796)*

Cima Labs Inc ....D ... 763 488-4700
North Wales *(G-12795)*

Colorcon Inc ....F ... 215 256-7700
Harleysville *(G-7029)*

Colorcon Inc ....B ... 215 699-7733
West Point *(G-19758)*

Colorcon Inc ....F ... 267 695-7700
Chalfont *(G-2867)*

Complexa Inc ....G... 412 727-8727
Berwyn *(G-1356)*

Connie Fogarty ....G... 610 647-3172
Malvern *(G-10216)*

Cool Bio Inc ....G... 973 452-8309
Wayne *(G-19314)*

Correvio LLC ....F ... 610 833-6050
Chadds Ford *(G-2850)*

Corry Opothecary ....G... 814 452-4220
Corry *(G-3755)*

Cortendo AB Inc ....G... 610 254-9200
Trevose *(G-18490)*

Cslb Holdings Inc ....G... 610 878-4000
King of Prussia *(G-8602)*

Curtis Pharmaceutical Service ....F ... 724 223-1114
Washington *(G-19160)*

Cutanea Life Sciences Inc ....E ... 484 568-0100
Chesterbrook *(G-3090)*

Cutix Inc ....G... 610 246-7518
Wayne *(G-19316)*

Danmir Therapeutics LLC ....G... 610 896-8826
Haverford *(G-7407)*

Dercher Enterprises Inc ....E ... 610 734-2011
Upper Darby *(G-18685)*

Dermavance Pharmaceuticals Inc ....F ... 610 727-3935
Berwyn *(G-1360)*

Design Space Inpharmatics LLC ....G... 215 272-4275
Green Lane *(G-6587)*

Digestive Care Inc ....E ... 610 882-5950
Bethlehem *(G-1496)*

Dolphin Group ....G... 610 640-7513
Paoli *(G-13139)*

Egalet Corporation ....E ... 610 833-4200
Wayne *(G-19322)*

Egalet Ltd ....F ... 484 875-3095
Wayne *(G-19323)*

Egalet US Inc ....F ... 610 833-4200
Wayne *(G-19324)*

Endo Finance Co ....G... 484 216-0000
Malvern *(G-10231)*

Endo Pharmaceutical Inc ....G... 484 216-2759
Horsham *(G-7815)*

Endo Pharmaceuticals Inc ....G... 484 216-0000
Malvern *(G-10233)*

Endo Phrmcticals Solutions Inc ....E ... 484 216-0000
Malvern *(G-10234)*

Epharmasolutions ....G... 610 832-2100
Conshohocken *(G-3543)*

Escalon Medical Corp ....E ... 610 688-6830
Wayne *(G-19325)*

Eurand Pharmaceuticals Inc ....E ... 937 898-9669
Yardley *(G-20309)*

Eusa Pharma (usa) Inc ....E ... 215 867-4900
Langhorne *(G-9295)*

Fallien Cosmeceuticals Ltd ....F ... 610 630-6800
Norristown *(G-12655)*

Femmephrma Cnsmr Hlthcare LLC ....G... 610 995-0801
Wayne *(G-19328)*

Fiberopticscom ....G... 215 499-8959
Quakertown *(G-16193)*

Fibrocell Science Inc ....D ... 484 713-6000
Exton *(G-5678)*

Formula Pharmaceuticals Inc ....G... 610 727-4172
Berwyn *(G-1363)*

Fresenius Kabi Usa Inc ....G... 724 772-6900
Warrendale *(G-19073)*

Frontage Laboratories Inc ....C ... 610 232-0100
Exton *(G-5682)*

Frontage Laboratories Inc ....G... 610 232-0100
Exton *(G-5683)*

Frontida Biopharm Inc ....E ... 215 288-6500
Philadelphia *(G-13728)*

G&W PA Laboratories LLC ....G... 215 799-5333
Sellersville *(G-17348)*

Gendx Products Inc ....G... 443 543-5254
Downingtown *(G-4230)*

Genentech ....G... 717 572-8001
Lititz *(G-10012)*

Generics International US Inc ....G... 256 859-2575
Malvern *(G-10239)*

Genoa Healthcare LLC ....G... 215 426-1007
Philadelphia *(G-13754)*

Genus Lifesciences Inc ....C ... 610 782-9780
Allentown *(G-227)*

Genzyme Corporation ....F ... 610 594-8590
Exton *(G-5688)*

Gjv Pharma LLC ....G... 267 880-6375
Doylestown *(G-4302)*

Glaxosmithkline ....E ... 717 426-6644
Marietta *(G-10462)*

Glaxosmithkline Consumer ....D ... 717 268-0110
York *(G-20501)*

Glaxosmithkline LLC ....G... 215 751-4000
Philadelphia *(G-13766)*

Glaxosmithkline LLC ....E ... 610 223-9089
Blandon *(G-1754)*

Glaxosmithkline LLC ....E ... 610 917-4085
Royersford *(G-16850)*

Glaxosmithkline LLC ....E ... 610 270-5836
Harleysville *(G-7034)*

Glaxosmithkline LLC ....E ... 610 962-7548
Willow Grove *(G-20119)*

Glaxosmithkline LLC ....E ... 814 243-0366
Johnstown *(G-8378)*

Glaxosmithkline LLC ....E ... 412 860-5475
Export *(G-5608)*

Glaxosmithkline LLC ....E ... 412 726-6041
Imperial *(G-8066)*

Glaxosmithkline LLC ....G... 717 268-0319
York *(G-20502)*

Glaxosmithkline LLC ....E ... 412 398-2600
Pittsburgh *(G-15050)*

Glaxosmithkline LLC ....D ... 610 270-7125
King of Prussia *(G-8621)*

Glaxosmithkline LLC ....E ... 610 270-4692
King of Prussia *(G-8622)*

Glaxosmithkline LLC ....E ... 610 917-4941
Collegeville *(G-3379)*

Glaxosmithkline LLC ....F ... 610 768-3150
King of Prussia *(G-8623)*

Glaxosmithkline LLC ....E ... 610 779-4774
Reading *(G-16392)*

Glaxosmithkline LLC ....E ... 610 270-4800
Conshohocken *(G-3551)*

Glaxosmithkline LLC ....E ... 814 935-5693
Newville *(G-12603)*

Glaxosmithkline LLC ....F ... 610 917-3493
Collegeville *(G-3380)*

Glaxosmithkline PLC ....E ... 215 336-0824
Philadelphia *(G-13767)*

Gnosis USA Inc ....G... 215 340-7960
Doylestown *(G-4303)*

Heraeus Precious Metals Nor ....C ... 610 825-6050
Conshohocken *(G-3556)*

Hercon Pharmaceuticals LLC ....E ... 717 764-1191
Emigsville *(G-4991)*

Horse Systems Inc ....G... 724 544-9686
Fombell *(G-6032)*

Hr Pharmaceuticals Inc ....E ... 877 302-1110
York *(G-20530)*

Iceutica Inc ....G... 267 546-1400
King of Prussia *(G-8632)*

Ictv Holdings Inc ....F ... 484 598-2300
Wayne *(G-19337)*

Idera Pharmaceuticals Inc ....D ... 484 348-1600
Exton *(G-5695)*

Immunocore ....G... 484 534-5261
Conshohocken *(G-3560)*

Immunome Inc ....G... 610 716-3599
Exton *(G-5696)*

Impax Laboratories Inc ....D ... 215 289-2220
Fort Washington *(G-6075)*

Impax Laboratories LLC ....D ... 215 558-4300
Fort Washington *(G-6076)*

Incyte Corporation ....D ... 302 498-6700
Broomall *(G-2290)*

Infacare Pharmaceutical Corp ....G... 267 515-5850
Trevose *(G-18499)*

Innochem Inc ....G... 610 323-0730
Pottstown *(G-16002)*

Innocoll Inc ....F ... 484 406-5200
Newtown Square *(G-12577)*

Iroko Intermediate Holdings ....G... 267 546-3003
Philadelphia *(G-13874)*

Iroko Pharmaceuticals LLC ....G... 267 546-3003
Philadelphia *(G-13876)*

Itf Pharma Inc ....G... 484 328-4964
Berwyn *(G-1366)*

Employee Codes: A=Over 500 employees, B=251-500
C=101-250, D=51-100, E=20-50, F=10-19, G=3-9

2019 Harris Pennsylvania
Manufacturers Directory

1495

PRODUCT

Ivax Pharmaceuticals LLC	G	215 591-3000	North Wales (G-12807)
Ivd LLC	G	949 664-5500	Philadelphia (G-13879)
Janssen Biotech Inc	G	610 407-0194	Malvern (G-10259)
Janssen Biotech Inc	D	610 651-6000	Malvern (G-10260)
Janssen Biotech Inc	D	610 651-7200	Royersford (G-16853)
Janssen Biotech Inc	B	610 651-6000	Horsham (G-7827)
Janssen Biotech Inc	G	215 325-4250	Malvern (G-10261)
Janssen Biotech Inc	G	610 651-6000	Malvern (G-10262)
Janssen Research & Dev LLC	C	610 458-2192	Exton (G-5701)
Jazz Pharmaceuticals	F	215 832-3750	Philadelphia (G-13892)
Jazz Pharmaceuticals	E	215 867-4900	Langhorne (G-9304)
Jdp Therapeutics Inc	G	215 661-8557	Lansdale (G-9381)
Johnson & Johnson Consumer Inc	C	717 207-3500	Lancaster (G-9074)
Johnsons Pharmaceuticals	F	412 655-2151	West Mifflin (G-19741)
K & H Pharma LLC	G	267 893-6578	Doylestown (G-4310)
Kadmon Pharmaceuticals LLC	D	724 778-6100	Warrendale (G-19084)
Kdl Pharmaceutical Co Ltd	G	215 259-3024	Hatfield (G-7357)
Kremers Urban Pharmaceuticals	G	609 936-5940	Philadelphia (G-13942)
Kremers Urban Phrmcuticals Inc	F	609 936-5940	Philadelphia (G-13943)
Krystal Biotech Inc	E	412 586-5830	Pittsburgh (G-15202)
Kvk-Tech Inc	E	215 579-1842	Newtown (G-12515)
Kvk-Tech Inc	B	215 579-1842	Newtown (G-12516)
Lannett Company Inc	B	215 333-9000	Philadelphia (G-13952)
Lannett Company Inc	D	215 333-9000	Philadelphia (G-13953)
Laron Pharma Inc	F	267 575-1470	Fort Washington (G-6082)
Life Tree Pharmacy Svcs LLC	G	610 522-2010	Sharon Hill (G-17458)
Lipella Pharmaceuticals Inc	F	412 901-0315	Pittsburgh (G-15234)
Lomed Inc	G	800 477-0239	Ottsville (G-13066)
Louston International Inc	G	610 859-9860	Marcus Hook (G-10447)
M D Pharma Connection LLC	G	814 371-7726	Du Bois (G-4404)
Mainline Biosciences LLC	G	610 643-4881	Malvern (G-10273)
Mallinckrodt LLC	F	570 824-8980	Wilkes Barre (G-19940)
Marinus Pharmaceuticals Inc	F	267 440-4200	Radnor (G-16295)
McCahans Pharmacy Inc	G	814 635-2911	Saxton (G-17102)
Medical Products Labs Inc	C	215 677-2700	Philadelphia (G-14005)
Medimmune	G	240 751-5625	Royersford (G-16858)
Merck and Company Inc	F	215 993-1616	North Wales (G-12815)
Merck Sharp & Dohme Corp	F	215 652-6777	West Point (G-19760)
Merck Sharp & Dohme Corp	C	215 652-5000	North Wales (G-12816)
Merck Sharp & Dohme Corp	E	215 652-8368	West Point (G-19761)
Merck Sharp & Dohme Corp	B	484 344-2493	Blue Bell (G-1847)
Merck Sharp & Dohme Corp	C	267 305-5000	North Wales (G-12817)
Merck Sharp & Dohme Corp	G	215 397-2541	Hatfield (G-7368)
Merck Sharp & Dohme Corp	B	215 652-5000	West Point (G-19763)
Merck Sharp Dhme Argentina Inc	F	215 996-3806	Lansdale (G-9386)
Metcure Inc	G	813 601-3533	Newtown Square (G-12585)
Mirador Global LP	G	302 983-3430	Kennett Square (G-8529)
Mito Biopharm	G	215 767-9700	Radnor (G-16296)
Montgomery Laboratories Inc	F	570 752-7712	Berwick (G-1335)
MSP Distribution Svcs C LLC	C	215 652-6160	North Wales (G-12819)
Mutual Pharmaceutical Co Inc	C	215 288-6500	Philadelphia (G-14047)
Mutual Pharmaceutical Co Inc	G	215 807-1312	Philadelphia (G-14048)
Myers Drugstore Inc	F	610 233-3300	Norristown (G-12691)
Mylan Pharmaceuticals Inc	E	724 514-1800	Canonsburg (G-2608)
Nanoscan Imaging LLC	G	215 699-1703	Lansdale (G-9390)
National Generic Distributors	G	215 788-3113	Levittown (G-9852)
Norcom Systems Inc	F	610 592-0167	Norristown (G-12693)
Norquay Technology Inc	E	610 874-4330	Chester (G-3058)
Novartis Corporation	D	215 255-4200	Philadelphia (G-14087)
Novartis Pharmaceuticals Corp	G	717 901-1916	Mechanicsburg (G-10874)
Oncoceutics Inc	G	678 897-0563	Philadelphia (G-14095)
Onconova Therapeutics Inc	F	267 759-3680	Newtown (G-12532)
Oncore Biopharma Inc	F	215 589-6378	Doylestown (G-4320)
Opertech Bio Inc	G	215 456-8765	Philadelphia (G-14098)
Optinose Inc	C	267 364-3500	Yardley (G-20330)
Optofluidics Inc	F	215 253-5777	Philadelphia (G-14100)
Par Pharmaceutical 2 Inc	D	484 216-7741	Malvern (G-10293)
Paratek Pharmaceuticals Inc	G	484 751-4920	King of Prussia (G-8660)
Particle Sciences Inc	E	610 861-4701	Bethlehem (G-1591)
Patriot Pharmaceuticals LLC	G	215 325-7676	Horsham (G-7839)
Pentec Health Inc	C	800 223-4376	Upper Chichester (G-18670)
Pfizer Inc	G	484 865-5000	Collegeville (G-3387)
Pfizer Inc	A	717 627-2211	Lititz (G-10032)
Pfizer Inc	G	484 865-0288	Collegeville (G-3388)
Pfizer Inc	F	717 932-3701	Lewisberry (G-9891)
Pfizer Inc	B	717 932-3701	Lewisberry (G-9890)
Pharma Acumen LLC	G	215 885-1029	Rydal (G-16886)
Pharma Innvtion Srcing Ctr LLC	G	203 314-8095	Newtown (G-12535)
Pharma Rep Training	G	215 369-1719	Washington Crossing (G-19258)
Pharma Tech Pro LLC	G	570 412-4008	Danville (G-4009)
Pharmaceutical Procurement	F	610 680-7708	Coatesville (G-3324)
Pharmceutical Mfg RES Svcs Inc	E	267 960-3300	Horsham (G-7841)
Pharmctcal Stffing Sltons Inc	G	215 322-5392	Richboro (G-16677)
Phasebio Pharmaceuticals Inc	F	610 981-6500	Malvern (G-10295)
Phibro Animal Health Corp	F	201 329-7300	State College (G-18005)
Philarx Pharmacy Inc	G	267 324-5231	Philadelphia (G-14166)
Photomedex Inc	G	215 619-3286	Willow Grove (G-20134)
Photomedex Inc	F	215 619-3235	Willow Grove (G-20135)
Piramal Healthcare Inc	G	610 974-9760	Bethlehem (G-1600)
Plurogen Therapeutics LLC	G	610 539-3670	Norristown (G-12703)
Pompa Trssler Chiropractic LLC	G	724 327-5665	Monroeville (G-11349)
Protarga Inc	G	610 260-4000	King of Prussia (G-8666)
Protherics Inc	C	615 327-1027	Conshohocken (G-3593)
Provell Pharmaceuticals LLC	G	610 942-8970	Honey Brook (G-7757)
PSI Pharma Support America Inc	C	267 464-2500	King of Prussia (G-8667)
Qilu Pharma Inc	D	484 443-2935	Malvern (G-10304)
Qol Meds	G	724 602-0532	Butler (G-2436)
Qualitox Laboratories LLC	G	412 458-5431	Mc Kees Rocks (G-10629)
Quinnova Pharmaceuticals Inc	G	215 860-6263	Jamison (G-8245)
Quotient Sciences - Phila	C	610 485-4270	Boothwyn (G-1880)
Recro Pharma Inc	D	484 395-2470	Malvern (G-10309)
Reliable Products Inc	G	215 860-2011	Newtown (G-12543)
Rhotau Pharma Services LLC	G	484 437-2654	West Chester (G-19629)
Ribonova Inc	G	610 801-2541	Wynnewood (G-20272)
Rochester Pharmaceuticals	G	215 345-4880	Doylestown (G-4335)
Sfa Therapeutics LLC	G	267 584-1080	Jenkintown (G-8300)
Shire Holdings US AG	F	484 595-8800	Chesterbrook (G-3096)
Shire Pharmaceuticals LLC	C	484 595-8800	Chesterbrook (G-3097)
Shire Viropharma Incorporated	E	610 644-9929	Exton (G-5731)
Silarx Pharmaceuticals Inc	G	845 225-1500	Philadelphia (G-14305)
Sirtris Pharmaceuticals Inc	D	585 275-5774	Collegeville (G-3393)
Slate Pharmaceuticals Inc	D	484 321-5900	Malvern (G-10320)
Smithkline Beecham Corporation	G	215 751-4000	Philadelphia (G-14316)
Specialty Phrm Pdts LLC	F	215 321-5836	Yardley (G-20340)
STI Pharma LLC	G	215 710-3270	Newtown (G-12553)
Storeflex LLC	G	856 498-0079	New Hope (G-12315)
Strongbridge Biopharma PLC	E	610 254-9200	Trevose (G-18504)
Sunshine Biologies Inc	E	484 494-0818	Sharon Hill (G-17463)
Svm2 Pharma Inc	G	717 369-4636	Saint Thomas (G-17042)
Synergy Health Systems Inc	E	570 473-7506	Northumberland (G-12877)
Telesis Therapeutics LLC	G	215 848-4773	Philadelphia (G-14380)
Tetralgic Pharmaceuticals Corp	F	610 889-9900	Malvern (G-10328)
Teva Bopharmaceuticals USA Inc	D	240 821-9000	West Chester (G-19658)
Teva Neuroscience	G	215 591-6309	Horsham (G-7856)
Teva Pharmaceutical Fin Co LLC	G	215 591-3000	North Wales (G-12832)
Teva Pharmaceutical Fin IV LLC	F	215 591-3000	North Wales (G-12833)
Teva Pharmaceuticals Usa Inc	D	215 591-3000	North Wales (G-12835)
Teva Pharmaceuticals Usa Inc	G	240 821-9000	North Wales (G-12836)
Teva Pharmaceuticals Usa Inc	C	215 591-3000	Sellersville (G-17359)
Teva Pharmaceuticals Usa Inc	D	215 591-3000	Horsham (G-7857)
Teva Pharmaceuticals Usa Inc	D	215 591-3000	Chalfont (G-2891)
Teva Respiratory LLC	D	610 344-0200	Malvern (G-10330)
Thar Pharmaceuticals Inc	E	412 963-6800	Pittsburgh (G-15609)
Thresher Pharmaceuticals	G	215 826-0227	Bristol (G-2206)
Tmw Products LLC	G	215 997-9687	Perkasie (G-13296)

2019 Harris Pennsylvania Manufacturers Directory

(G-0000) Company's Geographic Section entry number

Tomayko Group LLC ....F 412 481-0600
Pittsburgh *(G-15632)*

Torrent Pharma Inc ....D 215 949-3711
Levittown *(G-9869)*

Transcelerate Biopharma ....G 484 539-1236
Conshohocken *(G-3613)*

Trevena Inc ....D 610 354-8840
Chesterbrook *(G-3099)*

Tri- Med Laboratories Inc ....E 732 249-6363
York *(G-20691)*

Triad Isotopes Inc 717 558-8640
Harrisburg *(G-7237)*

Trinity Partners LLC ....F 610 233-1210
East Norriton *(G-4585)*

Troy Manufacturing Co Inc ....G 570 453-5252
Hazle Township *(G-7488)*

United Research Labs Inc ....E 215 535-7460
Philadelphia *(G-14422)*

Upreach Inc ....G 215 536-8758
Easton *(G-4766)*

Url Pharma Inc ....E 215 288-6500
Philadelphia *(G-14433)*

US Specialty Formulations LLC ....F 610 849-5030
Bethlehem *(G-1648)*

V L H Inc ....B 800 245-4440
Pittsburgh *(G-15688)*

Varinel Inc ....G 610 256-3119
West Chester *(G-19673)*

Velicept Therapeutics Inc 484 318-2988
Wayne *(G-19387)*

Vgx Pharmaceuticals LLC ....E 215 542-5912
Plymouth Meeting *(G-15878)*

Virtus Pharmaceuticals LLC ....E 267 938-4850
Bristol *(G-2215)*

Virtus Pharmaceuticals LLC ....E 267 938-4850
Langhorne *(G-9331)*

Virtus Pharmaceuticals LLC 813 283-1344
Newtown *(G-12561)*

Virtus Phrmctcals Holdings LLC ....G 267 938-4850
Langhorne *(G-9332)*

Virtus Phrmcticals Opco II LLC ....G 267 938-4850
Langhorne *(G-9333)*

Wallace Pharmaceuticals Inc ....C 732 564-2700
Canonsburg *(G-2654)*

Watson Laboratories Inc ....G 951 493-5300
North Wales *(G-12839)*

West Pharmaceutical Svcs Inc ....C 570 398-5411
Jersey Shore *(G-8325)*

West Pharmaceutical Svcs Inc ....E 717 560-8460
Lititz *(G-10059)*

West Pharmaceutical Svcs Inc ....F 610 853-3200
Upper Darby *(G-18694)*

Williams Richard H Pharmacist ....G 717 393-6708
Lancaster *(G-9242)*

Wuxi Apptec Inc ....G 215 334-1380
Philadelphia *(G-14491)*

Wyeth LLC 610 696-3100
West Chester *(G-19682)*

Zeomedix Inc ....G 610 517-7818
Malvern *(G-10353)*

Zoetis Inc ....F 908 901-1116
Exton *(G-5752)*

Zoetis LLC 717 932-3702
Lewisberry *(G-9895)*

Zynerba Pharmaceuticals Inc ....F 484 581-7505
Devon *(G-4117)*

PHARMACEUTICALS: Medicinal & Botanical Prdts

Croda Inc ....E 570 893-7650
Mill Hall *(G-11175)*

Di Chem Concentrate Inc ....E 717 938-8391
Lewisberry *(G-9883)*

Herb Penn Co Ltd ....E 215 632-6100
Philadelphia *(G-13816)*

Longevity Prmier Ntraceuticals 877 529-1118
Philadelphia *(G-13975)*

Nabi Genmed LLC ....G 610 258-5627
Easton *(G-4729)*

Niramaya Inc ....G 267 799-2120
Wallingford *(G-18785)*

Reaction Nutrition LLC ....F 412 276-7800
Carnegie *(G-2784)*

SDC Nutrition Inc ....F 412 276-7800
Carnegie *(G-2791)*

Specialty Measurements Inc ....F 908 534-1500
Bethlehem *(G-1623)*

Teva Pharmaceuticals Usa Inc ....B 215 591-3000
North Wales *(G-12834)*

PHARMACIES & DRUG STORES

Biomed Healthcare Inc ....G 888 244-2340
Sharon Hill *(G-17453)*

Genoa Healthcare LLC ....G 215 426-1007
Philadelphia *(G-13754)*

Giant Eagle ....C 724 772-1030
Cranberry Township *(G-3821)*

Qol Meds ....G 724 602-0532
Butler *(G-2436)*

Soleo Health Holdings Inc. ....G 888 244-2340
Sharon Hill *(G-17460)*

Soleo Health Inc ....D 888 244-2340
Sharon Hill *(G-17461)*

Wakefern Food Corp ....D 215 744-9500
Philadelphia *(G-14457)*

Weis Markets Inc ....C 570 724-6364
Wellsboro *(G-19474)*

Williams Richard H Pharmacist ....G 717 393-6708
Lancaster *(G-9242)*

PHONOGRAPH RECORDS WHOLESALERS

Get Hip Inc 412 231-4766
Pittsburgh *(G-15048)*

PHONOGRAPH RECORDS: Prerecorded

Warner Music Inc ....D 570 383-3291
Olyphant *(G-13003)*

PHOTOCOPY MACHINES

Copitech Associates ....G 570 963-1391
Scranton *(G-17219)*

Xerox Corporation ....C 412 506-4000
Pittsburgh *(G-15726)*

PHOTOCOPYING & DUPLICATING SVCS

3d Printing and Copy Ctr Inc ....F 215 968-7900
Bensalem *(G-1140)*

A J Printing ....F 610 337-7468
King of Prussia *(G-8575)*

A Stuart Morton Inc ....F 610 692-1190
West Chester *(G-19492)*

Aeroprint Graphics Inc ....G 215 752-1089
Langhorne *(G-9274)*

Allegra Print Imaging ....G 610 882-2229
Allentown *(G-125)*

AlphaGraphics 717 731-8444
Mechanicsburg *(G-10819)*

Athens Reproduction ....G 610 649-5761
Ardmore *(G-701)*

B O H I C A Inc ....G 610 489-4540
Trappe *(G-18467)*

Bodrie Inc ....G 724 836-3666
Smithton *(G-17658)*

Byrne Enterprises Inc ....G 610 670-0767
Reading *(G-16338)*

C3 Media LLC ....E 610 832-8077
Philadelphia *(G-13492)*

Campus Copy Center ....F 215 386-6410
Philadelphia *(G-13496)*

Copiers Inc ....G 610 837-7400
Bath *(G-955)*

Copy Corner Inc ....G 570 992-4769
Saylorsburg *(G-17104)*

Copy Shop ....G 724 654-6515
New Castle *(G-12078)*

Copy Stop Inc ....G 412 271-4444
Swissvale *(G-18191)*

Copy Systems Group Inc ....G 215 355-2223
Southampton *(G-17806)*

Cs-B2 Investments Inc ....E 412 261-1300
Pittsburgh *(G-14890)*

Curry Printing & Copy ....G 610 373-2890
Reading *(G-16358)*

D L Dravis & Associates Inc ....G 814 943-6155
Altoona *(G-496)*

D L Dravis & Associates Inc ....G 814 944-5880
Altoona *(G-497)*

Degadan Corp ....G 610 940-1282
Conshohocken *(G-3537)*

Elizabeth C Baker ....F 610 566-0691
Media *(G-10923)*

Emerald Printing & Imaging ....G 814 899-6959
Erie *(G-5258)*

Fedex Office & Print Svcs Inc ....E 412 856-8016
Monroeville *(G-11337)*

Fedex Office & Print Svcs Inc 215 386-5679
Philadelphia *(G-13696)*

Fedex Office & Print Svcs Inc ....F 412 788-0552
Pittsburgh *(G-15009)*

Fedex Office & Print Svcs Inc ....E 412 835-4005
Pittsburgh *(G-15010)*

Fedex Office & Print Svcs Inc ....F 412 366-9750
Pittsburgh *(G-15011)*

Fedex Office & Print Svcs Inc ....G 215 576-1687
Jenkintown *(G-8287)*

H & H Graphics Inc ....E 717 393-3941
Lancaster *(G-9036)*

Hodgsons Quick Printing ....G 215 362-1356
Kulpsville *(G-8830)*

Huepenbecker Enterprises Inc ....F 717 393-3941
Lancaster *(G-9052)*

Ink Spot Printing & Copy Ctr ....G 610 647-0776
Malvern *(G-10255)*

J D Printing Inc ....G 724 327-0006
Pittsburgh *(G-15141)*

Jayco Grafix Inc ....D 610 678-2640
Reinholds *(G-16633)*

Jem Graphics LLC 412 220-0290
Bridgeville *(G-2074)*

Kalnin Graphics Inc ....E 215 887-3203
Jenkintown *(G-8292)*

Keeney Printing Group Inc ....G 215 855-6116
Lansdale *(G-9383)*

Kimkopy Printing Inc ....G 814 454-6635
Erie *(G-5343)*

Kirkland Printing Inc. ....G 215 706-2399
Willow Grove *(G-20124)*

Kwikticketscom Inc ....F 724 438-7712
Uniontown *(G-18632)*

Magna Graphics Inc ....G 412 687-0500
Pittsburgh *(G-15247)*

Movad LLC ....F 215 638-2679
Plymouth Meeting *(G-15858)*

Multiscope Incorporated ....E 724 743-1083
Canonsburg *(G-2606)*

New Centuries LLC ....G 724 347-3030
Hermitage *(G-7593)*

Pace Resources Inc ....E 717 852-1300
York *(G-20616)*

Pikewood Inc ....F 610 974-8000
Bethlehem *(G-1597)*

Pjr Printing Inc ....G 724 283-2666
Butler *(G-2434)*

Portico Group LLC ....G 610 566-8499
Media *(G-10943)*

Print Tech Western PA ....E 412 963-1500
Pittsburgh *(G-15440)*

Print-O-Stat Inc ....E 717 812-9476
York *(G-20640)*

Printers Printer Inc ....F 610 454-0102
Collegeville *(G-3389)*

Printforce Inc ....G 610 797-6455
Allentown *(G-360)*

Ricks Quick Printing Inc. ....E 412 571-0333
Pittsburgh *(G-15485)*

Ridgways Inc ....E 215 735-8055
Philadelphia *(G-14250)*

Rittenhouse Instant Press ....G 215 854-0505
Philadelphia *(G-14251)*

Rowe Printing Shop ....F 717 249-5485
Carlisle *(G-2737)*

S G Business Services Inc ....G 215 567-7107
Philadelphia *(G-14271)*

Sir Speedy 7108 Inc ....F 412 787-9898
Pittsburgh *(G-15542)*

State Street Copy and Press ....G 717 232-6684
Harrisburg *(G-7220)*

University Copy Service Inc ....G 215 898-5574
Philadelphia *(G-14429)*

Wolf Printing ....G 717 755-1560
York *(G-20716)*

PHOTOELECTRIC DEVICES: Magnetic

Electromagnetic Liberation ....G 724 568-2869
Vandergrift *(G-18725)*

PHOTOENGRAVING SVC

Aeco Service Inc ....G 610 372-0561
Pottstown *(G-15941)*

PHOTOFINISHING LABORATORIES

Filmet Color Lab Inc ....D 724 275-1700
Cheswick *(G-3108)*

Lustra-Line Inc ....E 412 766-5757
Pittsburgh *(G-15242)*

PRODUCT

PHOTOFINISHING LABORATORIES

Rich-Art Sign Co Inc.............................G....... 215 922-1539
Philadelphia *(G-14245)*

PHOTOGRAMMATIC MAPPING SVCS

Civic Mapper LLC................................G....... 315 729-7869
Pittsburgh *(G-14856)*

PHOTOGRAPHIC EQPT & SPLY: Sound Recordg/Reprod Eqpt, Motion

Corporate Arts Inc..............................G...... 610 298-8374
New Tripoli *(G-12454)*

PHOTOGRAPHIC EQPT & SPLYS

Aserdiv Inc...E....... 800 966-7770
Springfield *(G-17907)*
Bms Inc..G....... 609 883-5155
Yardley *(G-20297)*
Charles Beseler Co Inc........................D....... 800 237-3537
Stroudsburg *(G-18109)*
Coates Electrographics Inc..................E....... 570 675-1131
Dallas *(G-3960)*
Dual Core LLC.....................................D....... 800 233-0298
Manheim *(G-10379)*
Evaporated Coatings Inc.....................E....... 215 659-3080
Willow Grove *(G-20116)*
Griffith Inc..C....... 215 322-8100
Huntingdon Valley *(G-7992)*
Stanhope Microworks..........................G....... 717 796-9000
Mechanicsburg *(G-10891)*
Steel City Optronics LLC......................E....... 412 501-3849
Gibsonia *(G-6352)*
UTC Fire SEC Americas Corp Inc.........C....... 717 569-5797
Lititz *(G-10056)*

PHOTOGRAPHIC EQPT & SPLYS WHOLESALERS

Charles Beseler Co Inc.........................D....... 800 237-3537
Stroudsburg *(G-18109)*

PHOTOGRAPHIC EQPT & SPLYS, WHOLESALE: Project, Motion/Slide

Global Home Automation LLC...............G....... 484 686-7374
Fort Washington *(G-6072)*

PHOTOGRAPHIC EQPT & SPLYS: Cameras, Aerial

Pixcontroller Inc..................................G....... 724 733-0970
Export *(G-5621)*

PHOTOGRAPHIC EQPT & SPLYS: Cameras, Still & Motion Pictures

Creative Systems Usa LLC ....G....... 610 450-6580
Collegeville *(G-3373)*
Debenham Media Group........................F....... 412 264-2526
Coraopolis *(G-3684)*

PHOTOGRAPHIC EQPT & SPLYS: Developers, Not Chemical Plants

Red Associates ....G....... 215 722-4895
Philadelphia *(G-14235)*
Vertex Image Products Inc ....G....... 724 722-3400
Yukon *(G-20786)*

PHOTOGRAPHIC EQPT & SPLYS: Graphic Arts Plates, Sensitized

FCG Inc...C....... 215 343-4617
Warrington *(G-19117)*

PHOTOGRAPHIC EQPT & SPLYS: Printing Eqpt

Clover Technologies Group LLC ....F....... 818 407-7500
Exton *(G-5662)*
Mvp Prnting Prmtional Pdts LLC...........G....... 814 520-8392
Erie *(G-5400)*

PHOTOGRAPHIC EQPT & SPLYS: Printing Frames

Pocono Screen Supply LLC...................G....... 570 253-6375
Scranton *(G-17273)*

PHOTOGRAPHIC EQPT & SPLYS: Processing Eqpt

Glunz & Jensen Inc.............................E....... 574 272-9950
Quakertown *(G-16197)*

PHOTOGRAPHIC EQPT & SPLYS: Toners, Prprd, Not Chem Plnts

Itc Supplies LLC.................................G....... 610 430-1300
West Chester *(G-19574)*
Lasertek Tner Crtrdge Rchrging............G....... 412 244-9505
Pittsburgh *(G-15220)*
Raven Industries Inc...........................D....... 724 539-8230
Latrobe *(G-9516)*

PHOTOGRAPHIC EQPT & SPLYS: Washers, Print & Film

Sun Valley Film Wash Inc.....................G....... 610 497-1743
Aston *(G-794)*

PHOTOGRAPHIC EQPT/SPLYS, WHOL: Cameras/Projectors/Eqpt/Splys

Digital Plaza LLC.................................F....... 267 515-8000
Ambler *(G-575)*

PHOTOGRAPHY SVCS: Commercial

Bell Graphics......................................G....... 814 385-6222
Kennerdell *(G-8497)*
Brown Brothers LLP.............................G....... 570 689-9688
Sterling *(G-18048)*
Dave Zerbe Studio ....G....... 610 376-0379
Reading *(G-16360)*
Me Ken + Jen Crative Svcs LLC ....G....... 215 997-2355
Chalfont *(G-2883)*
Simone Associates Inc........................G....... 717 274-3621
Lebanon *(G-9631)*
Wenning Entertainment LLC.................F....... 412 292-8776
East Mc Keesport *(G-4582)*

PHOTOGRAPHY SVCS: Passport

Minton Holdings LLC............................G....... 412 787-5912
Pittsburgh *(G-15293)*

PHOTOGRAPHY SVCS: Portrait Studios

Creative Thought Media LLC ....G....... 267 270-5147
Philadelphia *(G-13579)*
East Hill Video Prod Co LLC ....F....... 215 855-4457
Lansdale *(G-9364)*

PHOTOGRAPHY SVCS: School

Philadelphia Photo Arts Center ....G....... 215 232-5678
Philadelphia *(G-14148)*

PHOTOGRAPHY SVCS: Still Or Video

Dave Zerbe Studio ....G....... 610 376-0379
Reading *(G-16360)*

PHOTOGRAPHY: Aerial

Eye-Bot Aerial Solutions LLC ....G....... 724 904-7706
New Kensington *(G-12340)*

PHOTOTYPESETTING SVC

American Directory Systems Co ....F....... 610 640-1774
Malvern *(G-10185)*
Ggs Information Services Inc ....C....... 717 764-2222
York *(G-20499)*
Malone & Blunt Inc..............................G....... 215 563-1368
Philadelphia *(G-13988)*
Maple Press Company..........................C....... 717 764-5911
York *(G-20580)*

PHOTOVOLTAIC Solid State

Bfhj Enrgy Solutions Ltd Lblty ....G....... 717 458-0927
Mechanicsburg *(G-10824)*
Griff and Associates LP ....D....... 215 428-1075
Levittown *(G-9842)*

Thermigate LLC...................................G....... 610 931-1023
Lansdowne *(G-9445)*

PHYSICAL EXAMINATION & TESTING SVCS

Gerson Associates PC ....E....... 215 637-6800
Philadelphia *(G-13759)*

PHYSICAL EXAMINATION SVCS, INSURANCE

Lifewatch Services Inc ....B....... 847 720-2100
Malvern *(G-10269)*

PHYSICAL FITNESS CENTERS

Bodyx LLC...G....... 610 519-9999
Bryn Mawr *(G-2316)*

PHYSICIANS' OFFICES & CLINICS: Medical doctors

Protarga Inc..G....... 610 260-4000
King of Prussia *(G-8666)*
Source Halthcare Analytics LLC ....D....... 602 381-9500
Conshohocken *(G-3605)*

PICTURE FRAMES: Metal

David B Lytle Products Inc ....G....... 724 352-3322
Cabot *(G-2454)*

PICTURE FRAMES: Wood

Frame Outlet Inc..................................G....... 412 351-7283
Pittsburgh *(G-15029)*
North Penn Art Inc...............................F....... 215 362-2494
Lansdale *(G-9393)*
Patton Picture Company ....C....... 717 796-1508
Mechanicsburg *(G-10877)*
Perakis Frames Inc..............................G....... 215 627-7700
Philadelphia *(G-14136)*

PICTURE FRAMING SVCS, CUSTOM

Dave Zerbe Studio ....G....... 610 376-0379
Reading *(G-16360)*
North Penn Art Inc...............................F....... 215 362-2494
Lansdale *(G-9393)*

PICTURE PROJECTION EQPT

Spitz Inc...D....... 610 459-5200
Chadds Ford *(G-2860)*

PIECE GOODS & NOTIONS WHOLESALERS

Bond Products Inc...............................F....... 215 842-0200
Philadelphia *(G-13470)*

PIECE GOODS, NOTIONS & DRY GOODS, WHOL: Textiles, Woven

Ambassador Bags & Spats Mfg Co.......G....... 610 532-7840
Folcroft *(G-5998)*
Covers All Canvas Products.................G....... 412 653-6010
Pittsburgh *(G-14881)*
Great American Weaving Corp ....F....... 610 845-9200
Bally *(G-903)*
Natural Textiles Solutions LLC ....G....... 484 660-4085
Macungie *(G-10155)*

PIECE GOODS, NOTIONS & DRY GOODS, WHOLESALE: Fabrics, Knit

Nick-Of-Time Textiles Ltd ....G....... 610 395-4641
Allentown *(G-332)*
York Textile Products Inc ....G....... 717 764-2528
York *(G-20751)*

PIECE GOODS, NOTIONS & OTHER DRY GOODS, WHOL: Flags/Banners

Bright Banners.....................................G....... 570 326-3524
Williamsport *(G-19994)*
Majestic Windsocks.............................G....... 717 264-3113
Chambersburg *(G-2956)*

PIECE GOODS, NOTIONS & OTHER DRY GOODS, WHOLESALE: Buttons

James Jesse & Co Inc..........................E....... 610 419-9880
Bethlehem *(G-1544)*

PIECE GOODS, NOTIONS & OTHER DRY GOODS, WHOLESALE: Fabrics

B L Tees Inc ....F 724 325-1882
Export **(G-5591)**

Belmont Fabrics LLC ....F 717 768-0077
Paradise **(G-13154)**

Mutual Industries North Inc ....D ... 215 679-7682
Red Hill **(G-16583)**

Robert W Turner ....G ... 610 372-8863
Reading **(G-16501)**

Shaffer Desouza Brown Inc ....F ... 610 449-6400
Havertown **(G-7427)**

PIECE GOODS, NOTIONS & OTHER DRY GOODS, WHOLESALE: Ribbons

American Ribbon Manufacturers ....E 570 421-7470
Stroudsburg **(G-18102)**

American Ribbon Manufacturers ....E 570 421-7470
Stroudsburg **(G-18103)**

Lawrence Schiff Silk Mills Inc ....D ... 717 776-4073
Newville **(G-12605)**

PIECE GOODS, NOTIONS & OTHER DRY GOODS, WHOLESALE: Zippers

Supreme Zipper Industries ....G ... 570 226-9501
Lakeville **(G-8914)**

PIECE GOODS, NOTIONS/DRY GOODS, WHOL: Drapery Mtrl, Woven

Lachina Drapery Company Inc ....E ... 412 665-4900
Pittsburgh **(G-15215)**

PIGMENTS, INORGANIC: Metallic & Mineral, NEC

Edgmont Metallic Pigment Inc ....F ... 610 429-1345
West Chester **(G-19546)**

Silberline Holding Co ....F ... 570 668-6050
Tamaqua **(G-18224)**

Silberline Mfg Co Inc ....C ... 570 668-6050
Tamaqua **(G-18225)**

Sussex Wire Inc ....D ... 610 250-7750
Easton **(G-4758)**

PIGMENTS, INORGANIC: Zinc Oxide, Zinc Sulfide

Rockwood Pigments Na Inc ....F ... 610 279-6450
King of Prussia **(G-8670)**

Venator Americas LLC ....C ... 610 279-6450
King of Prussia **(G-8695)**

PINS

American Patch and Pin ....G ... 814 935-4289
Altoona **(G-474)**

Angel Pins and More ....G ... 717 692-5086
Millersburg **(G-11190)**

Clothes-Pin ....G ... 215 888-5784
Philadelphia **(G-13550)**

Kingpin Production Vans Inc ....G ... 305 772-0687
Germansville **(G-6279)**

Needle and Pin ....G ... 412 207-9724
Pittsburgh **(G-15323)**

Pin Hsun Kuo ....G ... 717 795-7297
Mechanicsburg **(G-10880)**

PINS: Cotter

Amsteel Inc ....F ... 724 758-5566
Ellwood City **(G-4926)**

PINS: Spring

Connex Inc ....F ... 814 474-4550
Fairview **(G-5818)**

PIPE & FITTING: Fabrication

A M Sheet Metal Inc ....F ... 570 322-5417
South Williamsport **(G-17789)**

ABT LLC ....E ... 412 826-8002
Pittsburgh **(G-14636)**

Abtrex Industries Inc ....E ... 724 266-5425
Leetsdale **(G-9676)**

Accumetrics Limited ....E ... 610 948-0181
Royersford **(G-16840)**

Admiral Valve LLC ....E 215 386-6508
Kennett Square **(G-8501)**

Al Xander Co Inc ....E ... 814 665-8268
Corry **(G-3743)**

American Air Duct Inc ....G ... 724 483-8057
Charleroi **(G-3006)**

Anvil International LLC ....G ... 717 684-4400
Columbia **(G-3427)**

Anvil International LLC ....C ... 256 238-0579
Columbia **(G-3429)**

Anvil International LLC ....G ... 717 762-9141
Waynesboro **(G-19396)**

Appellation Cnstr Svcs LLC ....D ... 570 601-4765
Montoursville **(G-11431)**

Beck Manufacturing Company ....F ... 717 593-0197
Greencastle **(G-6599)**

Beck Manufacturing Company ....E ... 717 762-9141
Waynesboro **(G-19399)**

Bergen Pipe Supports Inc ....D ... 724 379-5212
Donora **(G-4148)**

Bitrekpasub Inc ....D ... 717 762-9141
Waynesboro **(G-19401)**

BJ REO Inc ....E ... 412 384-2161
West Elizabeth **(G-19692)**

Bonney Forge Corporation ....B ... 814 542-2545
Mount Union **(G-11739)**

Brandywine Valley Fabricators ....F ... 610 384-7440
Coatesville **(G-3295)**

Browns Welding Inc ....G ... 717 762-6467
Waynesboro **(G-19403)**

Campbell Manufacturing Inc ....G ... 610 367-2107
Bechtelsville **(G-1030)**

Clipper Pipe & Service Inc ....G ... 610 872-9067
Eddystone **(G-4799)**

Coil Company LLC ....E ... 610 408-8361
Malvern **(G-10214)**

Colonial Machine Company Inc ....E ... 814 589-7033
Pleasantville **(G-15798)**

Cooney Manufacturing Co LLC ....G ... 610 272-2100
Pottstown **(G-15976)**

Crees Wldg & Fabrication Inc ....G ... 717 795-8711
Mechanicsburg **(G-10832)**

Cvip Inc ....D ... 610 967-1525
Emmaus **(G-5025)**

Dedicated Customs Inc ....G ... 724 678-6609
Burgettstown **(G-2345)**

Dresser LLC ....C ... 814 362-9200
Bradford **(G-1967)**

East Coast Constructors Inc ....F ... 610 532-3650
Holmes **(G-7661)**

Eastern Manufacturing LLC ....D ... 215 702-3600
Langhorne **(G-9293)**

General Fabricating Svcs LLC ....F ... 412 262-1131
Coraopolis **(G-3692)**

Hastings Machine Company Inc ....E ... 814 247-6562
Hastings **(G-7261)**

High Pressure Equipment Co Inc ....D ... 800 289-7447
Erie **(G-5318)**

Hofmann Industries Inc ....B ... 610 678-8051
Reading **(G-16403)**

Industrial Eqp Fabricators Inc ....F ... 724 752-8819
Ellwood City **(G-4938)**

Ipsco Tubulars Inc ....G ... 724 251-2539
Ambridge **(G-621)**

J Rybnick Mech Contr Inc ....G ... 570 222-2544
Nicholson **(G-12616)**

L S Martin LLC ....G ... 717 859-3073
Ephrata **(G-5118)**

Madison Inds Holdings LLC ....C ... 717 762-3151
Waynesboro **(G-19416)**

McCarls Inc ....F ... 724 581-5409
Muncy **(G-11826)**

Michels Corporation ....G ... 724 249-2065
Washington **(G-19202)**

Mueller Industries Inc ....D ... 215 699-5801
North Wales **(G-12820)**

Propipe ....G ... 610 518-6320
Downingtown **(G-4252)**

RG Industries Inc ....E ... 717 849-0345
York **(G-20658)**

Sentry Fire Protection Inc ....F ... 717 843-4973
York **(G-20666)**

Ward Manufacturing LLC ....C ... 570 638-2131
Blossburg **(G-1810)**

Watson McDaniel Company ....E ... 610 495-5131
Pottstown **(G-16070)**

Wm T Spaeder Co Inc ....D ... 814 456-7014
Erie **(G-5532)**

PIPE & FITTINGS: Cast Iron

Advanced Metals Group LLC ....F ... 610 408-8006
Malvern **(G-10180)**

Fry & 146 Cast Division ....G ... 570 546-2109
Muncy **(G-11817)**

Ward Manufacturing LLC ....C ... 570 638-2131
Blossburg **(G-1810)**

PIPE & TUBES: Aluminum

Hygrade Acquisition Corp ....D ... 610 866-2441
Bethlehem **(G-1536)**

Hygrade Mtal Moulding Mfg Corp ....E ... 610 866-2441
Bethlehem **(G-1538)**

PIPE & TUBES: Copper & Copper Alloy

Ampco-Pittsburgh Corporation ....D ... 412 456-4400
Carnegie **(G-2763)**

Ptubes Inc ....F ... 201 560-7127
Honesdale **(G-7721)**

PIPE FITTINGS: Plastic

Kerotest Industries Inc ....E ... 412 521-4200
Pittsburgh **(G-15173)**

Kerotest Manufacturing Corp ....E ... 412 521-4200
Pittsburgh **(G-15174)**

Normandy Industries Inc ....G ... 412 826-1825
Pittsburgh **(G-15344)**

Normandy Products Company ....G ... 412 826-1825
Pittsburgh **(G-15345)**

Popit Inc ....G ... 215 752-8410
Langhorne **(G-9320)**

Poux Plastics Inc ....G ... 814 425-2100
Cochranton **(G-3348)**

PIPE SECTIONS, FABRICATED FROM PURCHASED PIPE

P & R United Welding and Fabg ....F ... 610 375-9928
Reading **(G-16461)**

Scott Metals Inc ....E ... 412 279-7021
Carnegie **(G-2790)**

Trojan Tube Sls & Fabrications ....F ... 570 546-8860
Muncy **(G-11836)**

PIPE, SEWER: Concrete

Concrete Pipe & Precast LLC ....E ... 717 597-5000
Greencastle **(G-6603)**

PIPE: Plastic

Advanced Drainage Systems Inc ....E ... 570 546-7686
Muncy **(G-11805)**

Certainteed Corporation ....B ... 610 893-5000
Malvern **(G-10204)**

Certainteed Corporation ....G ... 610 651-8706
Malvern **(G-10205)**

Charlotte Pipe and Foundry Co ....E ... 570 546-7666
Muncy **(G-11812)**

Chemex Inc ....G ... 610 398-6200
Allentown **(G-168)**

Cresline Plastic Pipe Co Inc ....D ... 717 766-9262
Mechanicsburg **(G-10833)**

D A R A Inc ....F ... 717 274-1800
Lebanon **(G-9557)**

Georg Fischer Harvel LLC ....C ... 610 252-7355
Easton **(G-4688)**

Georg Fischer Harvel LLC ....E ... 610 252-7355
Easton **(G-4689)**

Harvel Plastics Inc ....G ... 610 252-7355
Easton **(G-4696)**

J-M Manufacturing Company Inc ....C ... 814 432-2166
Franklin **(G-6141)**

J-M Manufacturing Company Inc ....D ... 814 337-7675
Cochranton **(G-3343)**

Miller Plastic Products Inc ....F ... 724 947-5000
Burgettstown **(G-2350)**

Ocp Inc ....E ... 814 827-3661
Titusville **(G-18389)**

Ono Industries Inc ....E ... 717 865-6619
Ono **(G-13004)**

Premier Conduit Inc ....E ... 814 451-0898
Erie **(G-5433)**

Premier Conduit Inc ....G ... 814 451-0898
Erie **(G-5434)**

Saint-Gobain Delaware Corp ....E ... 610 341-7000
Valley Forge **(G-18712)**

Spears Manufacturing Co ....E ... 717 938-8844
Lewisberry **(G-9893)**

PRODUCT

PIPE: Plate Fabricated, Large Diameter

James F Kemp Inc ....G...... 412 233-8166
Clairton (G-3151)

PIPE: Seamless Steel

Dura-Bond Steel Corp ....C...... 724 327-0280
Export (G-5599)
Wheatland Tube LLC ....D...... 724 981-5200
Sharon (G-17445)
Wheatland Tube LLC ....C...... 724 342-6851
Sharon (G-17446)
Zekelman Industries Inc ....D...... 610 889-3337
Newtown Square (G-12599)
Zekelman Industries Inc ....C...... 724 342-6851
Sharon (G-17450)

PIPE: Sheet Metal

Lane Enterprises Inc ....E...... 717 532-5959
Shippensburg (G-17537)
Lane Enterprises Inc ....F...... 717 761-8175
Camp Hill (G-2503)
Shoemaker Mfg Solutions Inc ....E...... 215 723-5567
Souderton (G-17764)
TW Metals LLC ....D...... 610 458-1300
Exton (G-5741)

PIPE: Water, Cast Iron

Louis P Canuso Inc ....F...... 610 366-7914
Allentown (G-301)
Tyco Fire Products LP ....C...... 215 362-0700
Lansdale (G-9421)

PIPELINE & POWER LINE INSPECTION SVCS

Uav Aviation Services ....G...... 717 691-8882
Mechanicsburg (G-10901)

PIPELINE TERMINAL FACILITIES: Independent

Gordon Terminal Service Co PA ....C...... 412 331-9410
Mckees Rocks (G-10661)
Oto Melara North America Inc .....G...... 314 707-4223
Johnstown (G-8417)
Vepar LLC ....G...... 610 462-4545
Spring City (G-17871)

PIPELINES: Crude Petroleum

United Refining Inc ....D...... 814 723-1500
Warren (G-19054)

PIPELINES: Natural Gas

Markwest Liberty Midstream ....D...... 724 514-4401
Washington (G-19199)
Williams Companies Inc ....D...... 717 490-6857
Lancaster (G-9241)

PIPELINES: Refined Petroleum

Gordon Terminal Service Co PA ....C...... 412 331-9410
Mckees Rocks (G-10661)

PIPES & FITTINGS: Fiber, Made From Purchased Materials

Aegis Technologies Inc ....F...... 610 676-0300
Oaks (G-12931)
Four Stars Pipe & Supply Inc .....G...... 724 746-2029
Eighty Four (G-4841)

PIPES & TUBES

Ellis Machine ....G...... 724 657-4519
Pulaski (G-16123)
Flowline ....F...... 724 658-3711
New Castle (G-12094)
Ipsco Koppel Tubulars LLC ....B...... 724 847-6389
Koppel (G-8814)

PIPES & TUBES: Steel

A F Necastro Inc ....G...... 724 981-3239
Farrell (G-5865)
ABT LLC ....E...... 412 826-8002
Pittsburgh (G-14636)
Abtrex Industries Inc ....E...... 724 266-5425
Leetsdale (G-9676)

Allied Tube & Conduit Corp ....B...... 215 676-6464
Philadelphia (G-13369)
American Tube Company Inc ....D...... 610 759-8700
Nazareth (G-11953)
Baileys Steel & Supply LLC ....G...... 724 267-4648
Waynesburg (G-19433)
Bradford Allegheny Corporation ...C...... 814 362-2590
Lewis Run (G-9871)
Bradford Allegheny Corporation ...D...... 814 362-2593
Lewis Run (G-9874)
Custom Fab Inc ....G...... 717 721-5008
Ephrata (G-5098)
Dura-Bond Coating Inc ....E...... 724 327-0782
Export (G-5598)
Dura-Bond Pipe LLC ....D...... 717 986-1100
Steelton (G-18047)
Ipsco Koppel Tubulars Llc ....B...... 724 266-8830
Ambridge (G-620)
Kloeckner Metals Corporation .....A...... 215 245-3300
Bensalem (G-1216)
L B Foster Company ....D...... 412 928-3400
Pittsburgh (G-15207)
Pennsylvania Steel Company ......E...... 610 432-4541
Whitehall (G-19886)
Phoenix Tube Co Inc ....C...... 610 865-5337
Bethlehem (G-1596)
Ptc Holdings I Corp ....G...... 412 299-7900
Wexford (G-19825)
Salem Tube Inc ....C...... 724 646-4301
Greenville (G-6772)
Sinnott Industries Inc ....G...... 215 677-7793
Philadelphia (G-14309)
Steel Consulting Services LLC ....G...... 412 727-6645
Pittsburgh (G-15580)
Summit Steel & Mfg Inc ....D...... 610 921-1119
Reading (G-16528)
T Helbling LLC ....G...... 724 601-9819
Beaver (G-992)
Tapco Tube Company ....E...... 814 336-2201
Meadville (G-10799)
United States Steel Corp ....C...... 215 736-4600
Fairless Hills (G-5806)
United States Steel Corp ....C...... 412 433-7215
Homestead (G-7695)
United States Steel Corp ....B...... 412 433-1121
Pittsburgh (G-15677)
US Steel Holdings Inc ....G...... 412 433-1121
Pittsburgh (G-15687)
Valmont Newmark Inc ....C...... 570 454-8730
West Hazleton (G-19717)
Victaulic Company of America .....C...... 610 966-3966
Alburtis (G-58)
Webco Industries Inc ....C...... 814 678-1325
Oil City (G-12959)
Zekelman Industries Inc ....D...... 724 342-6851
Sharon (G-17451)

PIPES & TUBES: Welded

Avidon Welding Inc ....G...... 570 421-2307
East Stroudsburg (G-4607)
Marcegaglia Usa Inc ....C...... 412 462-2185
Munhall (G-11844)
Summerill Tube Corporation ....D...... 724 887-9700
Scottdale (G-17202)

PIPES OR FITTINGS: Sewer, Clay

JM Daugherty Industries LLC .....G...... 412 835-2135
Bethel Park (G-1419)

PIPES: Tobacco

R J Reynolds Tobacco Company ...G...... 570 654-0770
Pittston (G-15781)

PISTONS & PISTON RINGS

Niagara Piston Ring Works Inc .....F...... 716 782-2307
Corry (G-3770)

PLANING MILL, NEC

Donald Beiswenger Inc ....G...... 814 886-8341
Gallitzin (G-6245)
Gutchess Lumber Co Inc ....D...... 724 537-6447
Latrobe (G-9479)
Moxham Lumber Co ....E...... 814 536-5186
Johnstown (G-8411)

PLANING MILLS: Millwork

Alan Pepper Designs ....G...... 412 244-9299
Pittsburgh (G-14659)
EDM Co ....E...... 717 626-2186
Lititz (G-10005)
Industrial Shipping Pdts Isp ....G...... 724 423-6533
Latrobe (G-9481)
Marsh Planing Inc ....G...... 814 827-9947
Titusville (G-18388)
Solidays Millwork ....G...... 717 274-2841
Lebanon (G-9633)

PLANTS, POTTED, WHOLESALE

Buzzy Inc ....F...... 570 621-2883
Pottsville (G-16074)

PLANTS: Artificial & Preserved

Buzzy Inc ....F...... 570 621-2883
Pottsville (G-16074)
Plantarium Living Envirom ....G...... 215 338-2008
Philadelphia (G-14181)

PLAQUES: Picture, Laminated

Barhill Manufacturing Corp ....E...... 570 655-2005
Pittston (G-15742)
Bry Mar Trophy Inc ....G...... 215 295-4053
Yardley (G-20298)
Gerding Corp ....G...... 215 441-0900
Warminster (G-18887)
Nippon Panel Inc ....G...... 570 326-4258
Williamsport (G-20048)

PLASMAS

AA Plasma LLC ....G...... 312 371-7947
Warminster (G-18817)
Advanced Plasma Solutions Inc ...F...... 484 568-4942
Richboro (G-16672)
Csl Plasma Inc ....G...... 717 767-2348
York (G-20439)
Plasma Source ....G...... 215 942-6370
Southampton (G-17830)

PLASTER WORK: Ornamental & Architectural

G R G Technologies LLC ....F...... 610 325-6701
Newtown Square (G-12573)

PLASTIC COLORING & FINISHING

Ipeg Inc ....F...... 814 437-6861
Franklin (G-6139)
J Meyer & Sons Inc ....F...... 215 324-4440
Philadelphia (G-13885)
Olde Slate Mtn Color Co Inc ....G...... 570 421-8910
East Stroudsburg (G-4626)

PLASTIC PRDTS

Amcor Group GMBH ....G...... 570 474-9739
Mountain Top (G-11750)
Chautauqua Mfg Corp ....G...... 513 423-8840
Sharpsville (G-17470)
Focus Noise Ltd Liability Co ....G...... 484 886-7242
Exton (G-5680)
Infinity Marketing Inc ....G...... 610 296-0653
Malvern (G-10253)
Jenard Corporation ....G...... 610 622-3600
Lansdowne (G-9436)
Misterplexi ....G...... 724 759-7500
Wexford (G-19812)
Northern Engrg Plas Corp PR ......G...... 724 658-9019
New Castle (G-12133)
Obh Enterprises LLC ....G...... 610 436-0796
West Chester (G-19609)
PMI Inc ....G...... 814 455-8085
Erie (G-5428)
Polycube Company LLC ....F...... 215 946-2823
Levittown (G-9857)
Suntuf 2000 Inc ....G...... 610 285-6968
Kutztown (G-8862)
Zehrco-Giancola Composites Inc ...G...... 814 406-7033
Warren (G-19066)

PLASTIC PRDTS REPAIR SVCS

Blair Tool & Plastic Co Inc ....E...... 814 695-2726
East Freedom (G-4560)

PLASTIC WOOD

Plastic Lumber Yard LLC ....G....... 610 277-3900
Plymouth Meeting (G-15864)

PLASTICIZERS, ORGANIC: Cyclic & Acyclic

Duco Holdings LLC...............................G....... 215 942-6274
Ivyland (G-8209)

PLASTICS FILM & SHEET

Cjc Contract Packaging Inc ....G....... 570 209-7836
Avoca (G-842)

Compression Polymers ....G....... 570 558-8000
Scranton (G-17217)

Coupler Enterprises Inc ....G....... 267 487-8982
Warrington (G-19113)

Cpg International Holdings LP ....A....... 570 558-8000
Scranton (G-17221)

Laminations Inc.....................................C....... 570 876-8199
Archbald (G-690)

Omnova Solutions Inc ....B....... 724 523-5441
Jeannette (G-8263)

Palram Panels Inc ....G....... 610 285-9918
Kutztown (G-8854)

Precision Polymer Processors ....F....... 570 344-9916
Scranton (G-17274)

Tarp America Inc ....G....... 724 339-4771
Murrysville (G-11869)

Transparent Protection Syst ....E....... 215 638-0800
Bensalem (G-1262)

PLASTICS FILM & SHEET: Polyethylene

Berry Global Films LLC ....C....... 570 474-9700
Mountain Top (G-11752)

Centric Plastics LLC ....G....... 215 309-1999
Hatfield (G-7323)

CJ Packaging Inc ....G....... 570 209-7836
Avoca (G-841)

Crosstex International Inc ....E....... 724 347-0400
Sharon (G-17431)

Filmtech Corp...D....... 610 709-9999
Allentown (G-213)

Nova Chemicals Inc ....B....... 724 770-5542
Monaca (G-11293)

PLASTICS FILM & SHEET: Polypropylene

Berwick Offray LLC.................................B....... 570 752-5934
Berwick (G-1311)

Berwick Offray LLC.................................A....... 570 752-5934
Berwick (G-1312)

Kw Plastics ....E....... 334 566-1563
Allentown (G-288)

Lion Ribbon Company LLC.....................G....... 570 752-5934
Berwick (G-1333)

PLASTICS FILM & SHEET: Polyvinyl

Azek Building Products Inc ....E....... 877 275-2935
Scranton (G-17210)

Cpg International I Inc ....G....... 570 346-8797
Scranton (G-17222)

Crestwood Membranes Inc ....D....... 570 474-6741
Mountain Top (G-11758)

PLASTICS FILM & SHEET: Vinyl

International Vectors Ltd ....E....... 717 767-4008
Emigsville (G-4993)

Proplastix International Inc ....C....... 717 692-4733
Millersburg (G-11198)

Vinyl Window Wells LLC ....E....... 717 768-0618
Gordonville (G-6566)

Wexco Incorporated ....G....... 717 764-8585
York (G-20710)

PLASTICS FINISHED PRDTS: Laminated

Adams Manufacturing Corp....................G....... 724 758-2125
Ellwood City (G-4923)

Adept Corporation ....D....... 800 451-2254
York (G-20366)

Duco Holdings LLC................................G....... 215 942-6274
Ivyland (G-8209)

Finish Tech Corp....................................F....... 215 396-8800
Warminster (G-18878)

Finish Tech Corp....................................E....... 215 396-8800
Warminster (G-18879)

Grims Plastics ....G....... 717 526-7980
Harrisburg (G-7136)

Isola Services Inc..................................G....... 724 547-5142
Mount Pleasant (G-11702)

Magee Plastics Company ....D....... 724 776-2220
Warrendale (G-19087)

McClarin Plastics Llc ....C....... 717 637-2241
Hanover (G-6918)

Mohawk Inc..G....... 717 243-9231
Carlisle (G-2726)

Perkasie Industries Corp ....D....... 215 257-6581
Perkasie (G-13288)

William Deleeuw Co ....G....... 570 296-2694
Milford (G-11168)

PLASTICS FOAM, WHOLESALE

R & M Targets Inc ....G....... 814 774-0160
Girard (G-6400)

PLASTICS MATERIAL & RESINS

3M Company...F....... 610 497-7032
Aston (G-748)

7106 Dow Chemical ....F....... 610 244-6000
Collegeville (G-3365)

A Schulman Inc ....G....... 610 398-5900
Allentown (G-112)

Advansix Inc...C....... 215 533-3000
Philadelphia (G-13349)

Afab Industrial Services Inc...................E....... 215 245-1280
Bensalem (G-1145)

AGC Chemicals Americas Inc ....E....... 610 380-6200
Downingtown (G-4209)

Akzo Nobel Coatings Inc ....E....... 610 372-3600
Reading (G-16314)

Anholt Technologies Inc ....F....... 610 268-2758
Avondale (G-848)

Apexco-Ppsi LLC ....G....... 937 935-0164
Horsham (G-7787)

Atochem Intl Inc/Polymers Div ....G....... 610 582-1551
Birdsboro (G-1687)

Atrp Solutions Inc ....E....... 412 735-4799
Pittsburgh (G-14737)

Berry Global Films LLC ....C....... 570 474-9700
Mountain Top (G-11752)

Biocoat Incorporated ....E....... 215 734-0888
Horsham (G-7799)

Blair Tool and Plastics Co LLC..............G....... 814 695-2726
East Freedom (G-4561)

C E N Inc ....G....... 412 749-0442
Leetsdale (G-9686)

C P Converters Inc ....D....... 717 764-1193
York (G-20415)

C Purolite Corporation ....A....... 610 668-9090
Bala Cynwyd (G-874)

Cambria Plastics LLC ....G....... 814 472-6189
Ebensburg (G-4783)

Cashel LLC ....G....... 610 853-8227
Havertown (G-7417)

Chase Corporation ....E....... 412 828-1500
Pittsburgh (G-14840)

Chestnut Ridge Foam Inc ....C....... 724 537-9000
Latrobe (G-9464)

Cott Manufacturing Company ....E....... 724 625-3730
Glassport (G-6411)

Creative Pultrusions Inc........................C....... 814 839-4186
Alum Bank (G-560)

Ddp Specialty Electronic MA ....G....... 610 244-6000
Collegeville (G-3374)

Desavino & Sons Inc ....E....... 570 383-3988
Olyphant (G-12988)

Dow Chemical Company ....C....... 610 775-6640
Reading (G-16365)

Dow Chemical Company ....G....... 215 592-3000
Philadelphia (G-13641)

Dow Chemical Company ....D....... 215 785-7000
Bristol (G-2133)

Eagle Spinco Inc ....G....... 412 434-3131
Pittsburgh (G-14952)

Eastman Chemical Company ....E....... 412 384-2520
Jefferson Hills (G-8274)

Eastman Chemical Company ....A....... 423 229-2000
Jefferson Hills (G-8275)

Efs Plastics US Inc................................G....... 570 455-0925
Hazle Township (G-7454)

Em-Bed-It & Co Inc ....F....... 412 781-8585
Pittsburgh (G-14966)

Esschem Inc ....D....... 610 497-9000
Linwood (G-9989)

Fenner Precision Inc..............................C....... 800 327-2288
Manheim (G-10383)

FP Woll & Company ....E....... 215 934-5966
Philadelphia (G-13717)

G Scudese Consultants Inc ....F....... 610 250-7800
Nazareth (G-11968)

Gampe Machine & Tool Co Inc ....E....... 814 696-6206
Hollidaysburg (G-7648)

Gellner Industrial LLC ....E....... 570 668-8800
Tamaqua (G-18210)

General Polymeric Corporation ....D....... 610 374-5171
Reading (G-16390)

Geo Specialty Chemicals Inc ....E....... 215 773-9280
Ambler (G-579)

Graham Recycling Company LP ....D....... 717 852-7744
York (G-20512)

Haysite Reinforced Plas LLC ....D....... 814 868-3691
Erie (G-5313)

Hydra-Matic Packing Co Inc...................E....... 215 676-2992
Huntingdon Valley (G-7995)

Idemia America Corp ....C....... 610 524-2410
Exton (G-5694)

Illinois Tool Works Inc ....D....... 215 855-8450
Montgomeryville (G-11399)

Kozmer Technologies Ltd ....G....... 610 358-4099
Newtown Square (G-12580)

Lanxess Corporation ....A....... 800 526-9377
Pittsburgh (G-15219)

Lanxess Corporation ....E....... 412 809-4735
Burgettstown (G-2348)

Lehigh Valley Plastics Inc ....D....... 484 893-5500
Bethlehem (G-1558)

Lord Corporation ....B....... 814 868-0924
Erie (G-5371)

Mitsubishi Chemical Advncd Mtr ....G....... 610 320-6600
Reading (G-16446)

Multi-Plastics Extrusions Inc ....C....... 570 455-2021
Hazleton (G-7512)

National Plas Acquisition LLC ....G....... 610 250-7800
Easton (G-4731)

National Plastics ....G....... 610 252-6172
Bethlehem (G-1583)

North Amrcn Specialty Pdts LLC ....D....... 484 253-4545
Wayne (G-19360)

Nova Chemicals Inc ....B....... 724 770-5542
Monaca (G-11293)

Occidental Chemical Corp ....F....... 610 327-4145
Pottstown (G-16022)

Ocp Inc..E....... 814 827-3661
Titusville (G-18389)

Old Glory Corp.......................................F....... 724 423-3580
Mount Pleasant (G-11709)

Ono Industries Inc ....E....... 717 865-6619
Ono (G-13004)

Otoole Plastic Surgery Dr ....G....... 412 345-1615
Pittsburgh (G-15365)

Palram Americas Inc..............................D....... 610 285-9918
Kutztown (G-8853)

Penn Foam Corporation ....D....... 610 797-7500
Allentown (G-348)

Pepperell Braiding Company Inc............D....... 814 368-4454
Bradford (G-1986)

Performance Additives LLC ....F....... 215 321-4388
Yardley (G-20332)

Pleiger Plastics Company ....D....... 724 228-2244
Washington (G-19216)

Poly Lite Windshield Repr Sups.............G....... 717 845-1596
York (G-20631)

Polymer Instrumentation & C ....E....... 814 357-5860
State College (G-18007)

Polymeric Systems Inc...........................D....... 610 286-2500
Elverson (G-4965)

Polyone Corporation ....F....... 610 317-3300
Bethlehem (G-1602)

Polytek Development Corp ....E....... 610 559-8620
Easton (G-4743)

Polyvisions Holdings Inc ....F....... 717 266-3031
Manchester (G-10361)

PPG Architectural Finishes Inc ....D....... 610 380-6200
Downingtown (G-4250)

PPG Industries Inc ....A....... 412 434-3131
Pittsburgh (G-15425)

Prestige Institute For Plastic ....G....... 215 275-1011
Doylestown (G-4328)

Purolite Corporation ....C....... 610 668-9090
Bala Cynwyd (G-889)

Purolite Corporation ....C....... 610 668-9090
Philadelphia (G-14218)

Ravago Americas LLC.............................G....... 215 591-9641
Ambler (G-601)

Riverdale Global LLC..............................G....... 610 358-2900
Aston (G-792)

Sabic Innovative Plas US LLC ....C....... 610 383-8900
Exton (G-5728)

PRODUCT

Sekisui Polymr Innovations LLC ....B 570 387-6997
Bloomsburg (G-1801)
T P Schwartz Inc ....G 724 266-7045
Pittsburgh (G-15594)
Technetics ....G 215 855-9916
Hatfield (G-7399)
Teflex Inc ....F 570 945-9185
Factoryville (G-5762)
Trinseo LLC ....C 610 240-3200
Berwyn (G-1378)
Trinseo Materials Finance Inc ....C 610 240-3200
Berwyn (G-1379)
Trinseo S A ....E 610 240-3200
Berwyn (G-1380)
True Form Plastics LLC ....G 717 875-4521
Strasburg (G-18096)
Ultra-Poly Corporation ....G 570 784-1586
Bloomsburg (G-1805)
Washington Penn Plastic Co Inc ....E 724 206-2120
Washington (G-19242)

PLASTICS MATERIALS, BASIC FORMS & SHAPES WHOLESALERS

Centric Plastics LLC ....G 215 309-1999
Hatfield (G-7323)
Duco Holdings LLC ....G 215 942-6274
Ivyland (G-8209)
Opco Inc ....E 724 537-9300
Latrobe (G-9507)
Plastic Lumber Yard LLC ....G 610 277-3900
Plymouth Meeting (G-15864)
Spears Manufacturing Co ....E 717 938-8844
Lewisberry (G-9893)

PLASTICS PROCESSING

Allegheny Plastics Inc ....C 412 741-4416
Leetsdale (G-9679)
Atlas Minerals & Chemicals Inc ....E 800 523-8269
Mertztown (G-11000)
B-TEC Solutions Inc ....D 215 785-2400
Croydon (G-3911)
Back 2 Earth Recycling LLC ....G 717 389-6591
Myerstown (G-11874)
Baw Plastics Inc ....D 215 333-6508
Philadelphia (G-13447)
Cellcon Plastics Inc ....F 814 763-2195
Saegertown (G-16909)
D&W Fine Pack LLC ....B 215 362-1501
Hatfield (G-7331)
Diamond Manufacturing Company ......C 570 693-0300
Wyoming (G-20275)
Diamond Manufacturing Company ......F 570 693-0300
Wyoming (G-20276)
Engineered Plastics LLC ....D 814 452-6632
Erie (G-5259)
F R P Fabricators Inc ....G 814 643-2525
Huntingdon (G-7943)
Faivre Mch & Fabrication Inc ....G 814 724-7160
Meadville (G-10725)
General Technical Plastics ....E 610 363-5480
Exton (G-5687)
Haemer/Wright Tool & Die Inc ....E 814 763-6076
Saegertown (G-16916)
Hanes Erie Inc ....C 814 474-1999
Fairview (G-5826)
Hunsinger Plastics ....G 610 845-9111
Bally (G-904)
Industrial Plas Fabrication ....G 610 524-7090
Exton (G-5697)
Lancer Systems LP ....E 610 973-2600
Quakertown (G-16208)
Lawrie Technology Inc ....G 814 402-1208
Girard (G-6396)
M&Q Holdings LLC ....F 570 385-4991
Schuylkill Haven (G-17161)
Matamatic Inc ....G 724 696-5678
Mount Pleasant (G-11705)
Microsonic Inc ....E 724 266-2031
Ambridge (G-627)
Nethercraft Incorporated ....G 248 224-1963
Bridgeville (G-2081)
Nytef Plastics Ltd ....G 215 244-6950
Bensalem (G-1234)
Orange Products Inc ....D 610 791-9711
Allentown (G-341)
Penn Fibre Inc ....G 800 662-7366
Bensalem (G-1241)
R J Evercrest Polymers Inc ....G 610 647-1555
West Chester (G-19626)

Richman Industries Inc ....G 717 561-1766
Harrisburg (G-7206)
Rj Evercrests Inc ....G 610 431-4200
West Chester (G-19630)
Sealed Air Corporation ....G 610 926-7517
Reading (G-16509)
Smart Systems Inc ....G 412 323-2128
Pittsburgh (G-15546)
Space Age Plastics Inc ....F 570 630-6060
Jefferson Township (G-8279)
Tamarack Packaging Ltd ....E 814 724-2860
Meadville (G-10798)
Theodore W Styborski ....G 814 337-8535
Meadville (G-10800)
Trans Western Polymers Inc ....E 570 668-5690
Tamaqua (G-18230)
Trio Plastics Inc ....F 814 724-1640
Meadville (G-10803)
U S Plastic Coatings Corp ....E 215 257-5300
Sellersville (G-17361)

PLASTICS SHEET: Packing Materials

Computer Designs Inc ....D 610 261-2100
Whitehall (G-19867)
FP Woll & Company ....E 215 934-5966
Philadelphia (G-13717)
General Plastics Inc ....G 215 423-8200
Philadelphia (G-13750)
Packaging Science Inc ....F 610 992-9991
King of Prussia (G-8658)
Rose Plastic Usa Lllp ....D 724 938-8530
Coal Center (G-3277)
S & S Packaging Products Inc ....E 800 633-0272
Cranesville (G-3870)

PLASTICS: Blow Molded

Amcor Rigid Plastics Usa Inc ....E 610 871-9000
Allentown (G-130)
Dove Plastics Inc ....E 610 562-2600
Hamburg (G-6837)
Falcon Plastics Inc ....D 724 222-2620
Washington (G-19172)
Gpc Capital Corp II ....A 717 849-8500
York (G-20505)
Graham Packaging Company LP ....E 717 849-1800
York (G-20510)
M & Q Plastic Products Co ....F 484 369-8906
Limerick (G-9969)
Plastic System Packaging Mille ....F 717 277-7404
Lebanon (G-9623)
SLC Sales and Service Inc ....G 724 238-7692
Ligonier (G-9965)
Velocity Eqp Solutions LLC ....F 800 521-1368
New Castle (G-12162)

PLASTICS: Cast

Seybert Castings Inc ....F 215 364-7115
Huntingdon Valley (G-8038)
Superior Transparent Noise ....G 610 715-1969
Ardmore (G-720)

PLASTICS: Extruded

Berwick Offray LLC ....B 570 752-5934
Berwick (G-1311)
Berwick Offray LLC ....A 570 752-5934
Berwick (G-1312)
Berwick Offray LLC ....G 570 752-5934
Berwick (G-1313)
Coretec Plastics Inc ....F 717 866-7472
Richland (G-16684)
Formtech Enterprises Inc ....E 814 474-1940
Fairview (G-5823)
Honeywell International Inc ....B 570 621-6000
Pottsville (G-16080)
Medical Precision Plastics Inc ....F 215 441-4800
Warminster (G-18920)
Meridian Precision Inc ....E 570 345-6600
Pine Grove (G-14599)
Ono Industries Inc ....E 717 865-6619
Ono (G-13004)
Palmer Plastics Inc ....F 610 330-9900
Easton (G-4739)
Plasticoncentrates Inc ....G 215 243-4143
Philadelphia (G-14183)
Valley Extrusions LLC ....E 610 266-8550
Allentown (G-420)
Valtech Corporation ....E 610 705-5900
Pottstown (G-16064)

Veka Holdings Inc ....E 724 452-1000
Fombell (G-6036)
Veka Inc ....B 800 654-5589
Fombell (G-6037)
Veka West Inc ....G 724 452-1000
Fombell (G-6038)
Wexco Incorporated ....G 717 764-8585
York (G-20710)

PLASTICS: Finished Injection Molded

Apex Urethane Millworks LLC ....E 717 246-1948
Red Lion (G-16587)
Custom Extruders Inc ....G 570 345-6600
Pine Grove (G-14590)
E-Slinger LLC ....G 412 848-1742
Meadville (G-10720)
Fluortek Inc ....D 610 438-1800
Easton (G-4683)
Independent Tool & Mfg ....G 814 336-5168
Meadville (G-10738)
Kena Corporation ....F 717 292-7097
Dover (G-4193)
Knf Corporation ....E 570 386-3550
Tamaqua (G-18213)
La France Corp ....C 610 361-4300
Concordville (G-3457)
Laminated Materials Corp ....E 215 425-4100
Bensalem (G-1218)
Metamora Products Corp Elkland ....C 814 258-7122
Elkland (G-4916)
P & C Tool Inc ....F 814 425-7050
Meadville (G-10773)
Parker Industries Inc ....E 412 561-6902
Pittsburgh (G-15369)
Precise Plastics Inc ....D 814 474-5504
Fairview (G-5840)
Rapid Mold Solutions Inc ....G 814 833-2721
Erie (G-5456)
Scully Enterprises Inc ....G 814 835-0173
Erie (G-5471)
Shop Vac Corporation ....B 570 673-5145
Williamsport (G-20072)
Spears Manufacturing Co ....G 570 384-4832
Hazle Township (G-7482)
Standard Industries Inc ....F 570 568-7230
New Columbia (G-12176)
Steinmetz Inc ....E 570 842-6161
Roaring Brook Twp (G-16760)
T M Fitzgerald & Assoc Inc ....G 610 853-2008
Havertown (G-7429)
Vision Custom Tooling Inc ....F 610 582-1640
Birdsboro (G-1708)

PLASTICS: Injection Molded

100 Thompson Street LLC ....G 866 654-2676
Pittston (G-15740)
Abtec Incorporated ....D 215 788-0950
Bristol (G-2102)
Accu-Mold & Tool Company Inc ....E 717 896-3937
Halifax (G-6824)
Accudyn Products Inc ....D 814 833-7615
Erie (G-5167)
Advanced Solutions Network LLC ....F 814 464-0791
Erie (G-5175)
Advantage Precision Plastics ....E 814 337-8535
Meadville (G-10696)
Adventek Corporation ....E 215 736-0961
Levittown (G-9813)
AIN Plastics ....G 717 291-9300
Lancaster (G-8924)
Airlite Plastics Co ....D 610 759-0280
Nazareth (G-11952)
Aline Components Inc ....E 215 368-0300
Kulpsville (G-8823)
Allegheny Performance Plas LLC ....E 412 741-4416
Leetsdale (G-9678)
Alltrista Plastics Corporation ....E 717 667-2131
Reedsville (G-16620)
Almega Plastics Inc ....E 724 652-6411
New Castle (G-12056)
American Molding and Tech Inc ....E 814 836-0202
Fairview (G-5811)
Ames Industries Inc ....E 877 296-9977
Hershey (G-7603)
Anderson Plastics Inc ....F 814 774-0076
Girard (G-6384)
Atalanti Polymer Inc ....G 412 321-7411
Pittsburgh (G-14730)
Augustine Plastics Inc ....E 814 443-7428
Somerset (G-17677)

Bardot Plastics Inc....................C...... 610 252-5900
  Easton **(G-4650)**
Beaumont Advanced Proc LLC ....F...... 814 899-6390
  Erie **(G-5206)**
Bidwell Machining Inc..................G...... 570 222-5575
  Clifford Township **(G-3247)**
Blair Tool & Plastic Co Inc ....E...... 814 695-2726
  East Freedom **(G-4560)**
Boyer Machine ....G...... 570 473-1212
  Northumberland **(G-12865)**
C & E Plastic East ....F...... 724 457-0594
  Coraopolis **(G-3666)**
C & E Plastics Inc ....E...... 724 947-4949
  Georgetown **(G-6274)**
C & J Industries Inc ....B...... 814 724-4950
  Meadville **(G-10709)**
C & M Mold & Tool Inc ....G...... 215 741-2081
  Feasterville Trevose **(G-5897)**
C Sharkey Keyboard Covers Inc ....F...... 215 969-8783
  Philadelphia **(G-13491)**
C-K Composites Co LLC ....G...... 724 547-4581
  Mount Pleasant **(G-11690)**
Ci Medical Technologies Inc ....E...... 724 537-9600
  Latrobe **(G-9465)**
Comor Inc ....C...... 814 425-3943
  Cochranton **(G-3339)**
Controlled Molding Inc ....E...... 724 253-3550
  Hadley **(G-6817)**
Cook & Frey Inc ....E...... 717 336-1200
  Lititz **(G-10002)**
Crescent Industries Inc ....C...... 717 235-3844
  New Freedom **(G-12203)**
Crescent Industries Inc ....D...... 717 235-3844
  New Freedom **(G-12204)**
Ctp Carrera Inc ....D...... 724 733-2994
  Export **(G-5596)**
Ctp Carrera Inc ....E...... 724 539-6995
  Latrobe **(G-9468)**
Custom Molds Plastic ....G...... 717 417-5639
  Yoe **(G-20359)**
Delstar Technologies Inc ....E...... 717 866-7472
  Richland **(G-16686)**
Diamond Tech Group Inc ....F...... 814 445-8953
  Somerset **(G-17685)**
Electroline Corp ....E...... 215 766-2229
  Pipersville **(G-14614)**
Eljobo Inc ....D...... 215 822-5544
  Hatfield **(G-7338)**
Emsco Inc ....C...... 814 774-3137
  Girard **(G-6386)**
Engineered Plastics LLC ....D...... 814 774-2970
  Lake City **(G-8899)**
Ensinger Industries Inc ....D...... 724 746-6050
  Washington **(G-19171)**
Entech Plastics Inc ....E...... 814 664-7205
  Corry **(G-3759)**
Epc Inc ....E...... 215 464-1440
  Philadelphia **(G-13675)**
Erie OEM Inc ....B...... 814 459-8024
  Erie **(G-5271)**
Essentra Plastics LLC ....C...... 814 899-7671
  Erie **(G-5282)**
Essentra Porous Tech Corp ....E...... 814 898-3238
  Erie **(G-5283)**
Evolution Mlding Solutions Inc ....G...... 814 807-1982
  Meadville **(G-10722)**
Executool Prcision Tooling Inc........E...... 814 836-1141
  Erie **(G-5285)**
Flontech USA LLC ....E...... 866 654-2676
  Pittston **(G-15751)**
Galomb Inc ....G...... 610 434-3283
  Allentown **(G-222)**
Gemini Plastics Inc ....E...... 215 736-1313
  Levittown **(G-9839)**
George-Ko Industries Inc ....E...... 814 838-6992
  Erie **(G-5303)**
Greenbriar Indus Systems Inc ....D...... 814 474-1400
  Fairview **(G-5824)**
Grimm Industries Inc ....C...... 814 474-2648
  Fairview **(G-5825)**
Harry Rhoades ....F...... 814 474-1099
  Fairview **(G-5827)**
Havis Inc ....E...... 215 354-3280
  Warminster **(G-18893)**
Holbrook Tool & Molding Inc ....E...... 814 336-4113
  Meadville **(G-10736)**
Jet Plastica Industries Inc ....B...... 800 220-5381
  Hatfield **(G-7356)**
Jml Industries Inc ....F...... 570 453-1201
  Hazle Township **(G-7466)**

K & H Die and Mold Inc ....G...... 814 445-9584
  Somerset **(G-17694)**
Kenson Plastics Inc ....E...... 724 776-6820
  Beaver Falls **(G-1003)**
Ker Custom Molders Inc ....E...... 610 582-0967
  Birdsboro **(G-1701)**
King Precision Solutions LLC ....F...... 877 312-3858
  Erie **(G-5344)**
Latrobe Associates Inc ....E...... 724 539-1612
  Latrobe **(G-9488)**
Lesko Enterprises Inc ....C...... 814 756-4030
  Albion **(G-46)**
Maloney Plastics Inc ....E...... 814 337-8417
  Meadville **(G-10753)**
Micor Inc ....E...... 412 487-1113
  Bethlehem **(G-1571)**
Micro Dimensional Products ....D...... 610 239-7940
  Norristown **(G-12683)**
Micro Mold Co Inc ....E...... 814 838-3404
  Erie **(G-5389)**
Micro Plastics Inc ....G...... 814 337-0781
  Meadville **(G-10763)**
Midgard Inc ....D...... 215 536-3174
  Green Lane **(G-6590)**
Millet Plastics Inc ....E...... 717 277-7404
  Lebanon **(G-9611)**
Moldamatic LLC ....G...... 215 785-2356
  Levittown **(G-9851)**
Mxl Industries Inc ....D...... 717 569-8711
  Lancaster **(G-9141)**
Namsco Plastics Inds Inc ....D...... 724 339-3591
  New Kensington **(G-12360)**
Namsco Plastics Industries ....E...... 724 339-3100
  New Kensington **(G-12361)**
Nazareth Industrial Corp ....F...... 610 759-9776
  Nazareth **(G-11983)**
New Thermo-Serv Ltd ....D...... 215 646-7667
  Ambler **(G-594)**
Niagara Plastics ....G...... 814 464-8169
  Erie **(G-5404)**
Novares US LLC ....D...... 717 244-0151
  Felton **(G-5941)**
Novares US LLC ....B...... 717 244-4581
  Felton **(G-5942)**
Nzk Plastics LLC ....G...... 412 823-8630
  Turtle Creek **(G-18566)**
Omega Plastics LLC ....F...... 814 452-4989
  Erie **(G-5409)**
Parker Precision Molding Inc ....E...... 724 930-8099
  Rostraver Township **(G-16829)**
Pickar Brothers Inc ....E...... 610 582-0967
  Birdsboro **(G-1703)**
Pittsburgh Technologies Inc ....E...... 724 339-0900
  New Kensington **(G-12367)**
Plastek Industries Inc ....D...... 814 878-4400
  Erie **(G-5420)**
Plastek Industries Inc ....E...... 814 878-4741
  Erie **(G-5421)**
Plastek Industries Inc ....E...... 814 878-4719
  Erie **(G-5422)**
Plastek Industries Inc ....E...... 814 878-4601
  Erie **(G-5423)**
Plastek Industries Inc ....B...... 814 878-4466
  Erie **(G-5424)**
Plastek Industries Inc ....A...... 814 878-4515
  Erie **(G-5425)**
Plastikos Inc ....E...... 814 868-1656
  Erie **(G-5427)**
Polyflo Inc ....E...... 570 429-2340
  Saint Clair **(G-16938)**
Polymer Div of Wyomissing Spc ....G...... 610 488-0981
  Bernville **(G-1303)**
Polymer Instrumentation & C ....E...... 814 357-5860
  State College **(G-18007)**
Port Erie Plastics Inc ....E...... 814 899-7602
  Harborcreek **(G-7009)**
Precision Polymer Products Inc ....C...... 610 326-0921
  Pottstown **(G-16035)**
Precision Polymers Inc ....F...... 814 838-9288
  Erie **(G-5431)**
Prime Plastics Inc ....E...... 724 250-7172
  Washington **(G-19219)**
Proto-Cast LLC ....E...... 610 326-1723
  Douglassville **(G-4180)**
Quality Mold Inc ....G...... 814 459-1084
  Erie **(G-5444)**
R-G-T Plastics Company ....E...... 814 683-2161
  Linesville **(G-9986)**
Reading Plastic Products Inc ....G...... 610 779-3128
  Reading Station **(G-16573)**

Relianology International Ltd ....G...... 412 607-1503
  Export **(G-5625)**
Reliant Molding Inc ....G...... 814 756-5522
  Cranesville **(G-3869)**
Reubes Plastics Co Inc ....E...... 215 368-3010
  Hatfield **(G-7390)**
Rhkg Holdings Inc ....G...... 814 337-8407
  Meadville **(G-10787)**
Rick Leasure..............................G...... 814 739-9521
  Wattsburg **(G-19282)**
Rodon Group ....D...... 215 822-5544
  Hatfield **(G-7391)**
S E Moulding Inc ....G...... 717 385-4119
  Carlisle **(G-2738)**
Say Plastics Inc ....G...... 717 624-3222
  New Oxford **(G-12424)**
Schubert Plastics Inc ....F...... 610 358-4920
  Lenni **(G-9762)**
Sein Organizing Solutions ....G...... 215 932-8837
  East Greenville **(G-4575)**
Selmax Corp ....E...... 570 374-2833
  Selinsgrove **(G-17334)**
Shape TEC Ltd ....G...... 610 689-8940
  Limekiln **(G-9968)**
Sterling Technologies Inc ....C...... 814 774-2500
  Lake City **(G-8908)**
Sun Star Inc ....E...... 724 537-5990
  Latrobe **(G-9523)**
Target Precision ....F...... 814 382-3000
  Harmonsburg **(G-7065)**
Tech Group North America Inc ....C...... 570 326-7673
  Williamsport **(G-20080)**
Tech Group North America Inc ....G...... 480 281-4500
  Exton **(G-5736)**
Techna-Plastic Services Inc ....E...... 570 386-2732
  Lehighton **(G-9729)**
Tetra Tool Company ....F...... 814 833-6127
  Erie **(G-5506)**
Tool-Rite Inc ....E...... 814 587-3151
  Springboro **(G-17896)**
Top Gun Tool Inc ....G...... 814 454-4849
  Erie **(G-5513)**
Tri-Tech Injection Molding Inc ....E...... 814 476-7748
  Mc Kean **(G-10595)**
Triangle Tool Company Inc ....C...... 814 878-4400
  Erie **(G-5517)**
True Precision Plastics LLC ....E...... 717 358-9251
  Lancaster **(G-9223)**
Two Togethers Inc ....G...... 814 838-1234
  Erie **(G-5521)**
Venture Precision Tool Inc ....F...... 717 566-6496
  Hummelstown **(G-7927)**
Viant Westfield LLC ....D...... 215 675-4653
  Warminster **(G-18994)**
VPI Acquisition LLC ....C...... 814 664-8671
  Corry **(G-3779)**
Warren Plastics Mfg.....................G...... 814 726-9511
  Warren **(G-19060)**
Wise Plastics ....G...... 847 697-2840
  Harrisburg **(G-7247)**
Wolverine Plastics Inc ....E...... 724 856-5610
  Ellwood City **(G-4955)**
X-Act Technology Incorporated........G...... 814 824-6811
  Erie **(G-5534)**
York Imperial Plastics Inc ....E...... 717 428-3939
  York **(G-20740)**
Zemco Tool & Die Inc ....D...... 717 647-7151
  Williamstown **(G-20104)**
Zircon Corp ....G...... 215 757-7156
  Langhorne **(G-9337)**

PLASTICS: *Molded*

Advanced Alloy Dvsion/Nmc Corp........F...... 724 266-8770
  Ambridge **(G-605)**
Advanced Composite Pdts Inc ....E...... 717 232-8237
  Harrisburg **(G-7083)**
Advanced Mold Technologies ....F...... 814 899-1233
  Erie **(G-5174)**
Advanced Pultrusions LLC ....D...... 412 466-8611
  West Mifflin **(G-19735)**
American Molding Incorporated..........G...... 215 822-5544
  Hatfield **(G-7315)**
Atlas Molding LLC ....F...... 717 556-8193
  Leola **(G-9770)**
Automating Molding Tech LLC ....G...... 610 497-7162
  Marcus Hook **(G-10437)**
Beaumont Development LLC ....E...... 814 899-6390
  Erie **(G-5207)**
Belco Tool & Mfg Inc ....F...... 814 337-3403
  Meadville **(G-10706)**

P
R
O
D
U
C
T

Brentwood Industries Inc ....C 610 374-5109
Reading *(G-16336)*

Brentwood Industries Inc ....D ... 717 274-1827
Lebanon *(G-9548)*

Chelsea Building Products ....C 412 826-8077
Oakmont *(G-12914)*

Covington Plastic Molding ....G ... 717 624-1111
New Oxford *(G-12408)*

Crown Molding ....G ... 412 779-9209
Pittsburgh *(G-14888)*

Emporeum Plastics Corporation ....G ... 610 698-6347
Birdsboro *(G-1694)*

Fluoro-Plastics Inc ....F ... 215 425-5500
Philadelphia *(G-13705)*

Insert Molding Tech Inc ....E ... 814 406-7033
Warren *(G-19032)*

Ishman Plastic & Wood Cutting ....G ... 814 849-9961
Brookville *(G-2262)*

Klimek Molding Corp ....G ... 814 774-4051
Girard *(G-6395)*

Kw Plastics ....E ... 334 566-1563
Allentown *(G-288)*

Molded Fiber Glass Companies ....C ... 814 438-3841
Union City *(G-18610)*

Plastic Dip Moldings Inc ....E ... 215 766-2020
Quakertown *(G-16229)*

Pleiger Plastics Company ....D ... 724 228-2244
Washington *(G-19216)*

Port Erie Plastics Inc ....C ... 814 899-7602
Harborcreek *(G-7008)*

Premium Molding Inc ....G ... 724 424-7000
Derry *(G-4106)*

Prism Plastics Inc ....C ... 814 724-8222
Meadville *(G-10781)*

Q-Cast Inc ....E ... 724 728-7440
Rochester *(G-16789)*

Remcon Plastics Inc ....D ... 610 376-2666
Reading *(G-16496)*

Shorts Tool & Mfg Inc ....E ... 814 763-2401
Saegertown *(G-16933)*

Sonoco Prtective Solutions Inc ....E ... 412 415-1462
Pittsburgh *(G-15558)*

Strauss Engineering Company ....D ... 215 947-1083
Huntingdon Valley *(G-8041)*

Torytown Sculpture ....E ... 215 458-8092
Bristol *(G-2209)*

Trojan Inc ....E ... 814 336-4468
Meadville *(G-10804)*

Tubro Company Inc ....E ... 800 673-7887
Warminster *(G-18987)*

Ultra-Mold Corporation ....G ... 215 493-9840
Yardley *(G-20344)*

Unipar Inc ....E ... 717 667-3354
Reedsville *(G-16629)*

Walters Mlding Fabrication LLC ....G ... 724 662-4836
Mercer *(G-10978)*

WFC Company Inc ....D ... 215 953-1260
Southampton *(G-17846)*

X-Cell Molding Inc ....G ... 814 836-0202
Erie *(G-5535)*

PLASTICS: Polystyrene Foam

A C F Ltd ....G ... 610 459-5397
Glen Mills *(G-6429)*

Alberts Spray Solutions LLC ....G ... 570 368-6653
Montoursville *(G-11429)*

Azek Building Products Inc ....E ... 877 275-2935
Scranton *(G-17210)*

B H B Industries ....G ... 814 398-8011
Cambridge Springs *(G-2474)*

Carlisle Construction Mtls LLC ....C ... 724 564-5440
Smithfield *(G-17644)*

Carpenter Co ....F ... 717 627-1878
Lititz *(G-9996)*

Corrugated Specialties ....F ... 814 337-5705
Meadville *(G-10715)*

Corrugated Specialties ....E ... 814 337-5705
Meadville *(G-10714)*

Cpg International I Inc ....G ... 570 346-8797
Scranton *(G-17222)*

Custom Pack Inc ....F ... 610 363-1900
Exton *(G-5663)*

Ddp Specialty Electronic MA ....G ... 610 244-6000
Collegeville *(G-3374)*

Downing Enterprises Inc ....E ... 610 873-0070
Downingtown *(G-4224)*

Foam Fabricators Inc ....F ... 814 838-4538
Erie *(G-5298)*

Foam Fabricators Inc ....E ... 570 752-7110
Bloomsburg *(G-1782)*

FP Woll & Company ....E ... 215 934-5966
Philadelphia *(G-13717)*

Fxi Inc ....C ... 610 245-2800
Aston *(G-766)*

Great Northern Foam ....E ... 610 791-3356
Allentown *(G-237)*

Highwood Usa LLC ....E ... 570 668-6113
Tamaqua *(G-18212)*

Ica Inc ....F ... 610 377-6100
Lehighton *(G-9716)*

Innocor Foam Tech - Acp Inc ....G ... 570 876-4544
Archbald *(G-688)*

Interstate Paper Supply Co Inc ....D ... 724 938-2218
Roscoe *(G-16817)*

Johns Manville Corporation ....D ... 570 455-5340
Hazle Township *(G-7467)*

Sealed Air Corporation ....G ... 610 926-7517
Reading *(G-16509)*

Sterling Paper Company ....D ... 215 744-5350
Philadelphia *(G-14347)*

PLASTICS: Thermoformed

Accurate Marking Products Inc ....F ... 724 337-8390
New Kensington *(G-12321)*

Cardinal Health 407 Inc ....A ... 215 501-1210
Philadelphia *(G-13502)*

Carlisle Tpo Inc ....G ... 717 245-7000
Carlisle *(G-2698)*

Crighton Plastics Inc ....E ... 724 457-0594
Coraopolis *(G-3681)*

Custom Pack Inc ....F ... 610 363-1900
Exton *(G-5663)*

Cw Thomas LLC ....E ... 215 335-0200
Philadelphia *(G-13596)*

Fabri-Kal Corporation ....B ... 570 501-2018
Hazle Township *(G-7457)*

Fabri-Kal Corporation ....C ... 570 454-6672
Mountain Top *(G-11759)*

Jetnet Corporation ....D ... 412 741-0100
Sewickley *(G-17396)*

Munot Plastics Inc ....E ... 814 838-7721
Erie *(G-5398)*

National Molding LLC ....E ... 724 266-8770
Ambridge *(G-630)*

Opi Holdings Inc ....E ... 610 857-2000
Old Forge *(G-12973)*

Pennsylvania Insert Corp ....F ... 610 474-0112
Royersford *(G-16860)*

Plastic Fabricators Inc ....F ... 717 843-4222
York *(G-20628)*

Rocal Corporation ....E ... 215 343-2400
Warrington *(G-19132)*

Say Plastics Inc ....E ... 717 633-6333
Mc Sherrystown *(G-10652)*

Tri-State Plastics Inc ....F ... 724 457-2847
Coraopolis *(G-3729)*

Valley Plastics Inc ....G ... 570 287-7964
Forty Fort *(G-6099)*

Veritiv Operating Company ....E ... 724 776-3122
Cranberry Township *(G-3863)*

PLATE WORK: For Nuclear Industry

Carpenter Technology Corp ....B ... 610 208-2000
Philadelphia *(G-13508)*

Ray-Guard International Ltd ....G ... 215 543-3849
Pottstown *(G-16038)*

Spomin Metals Inc ....F ... 724 924-9718
New Castle *(G-12155)*

PLATE WORK: Metalworking Trade

M Glosser & Sons Inc ....E ... 412 751-4700
Mc Keesport *(G-10642)*

TW Metals LLC ....D ... 610 458-1300
Exton *(G-5741)*

PLATEMAKING SVC: Color Separations, For The Printing Trade

Color Scan LLC ....G ... 814 949-2032
Altoona *(G-493)*

Colortech Inc ....E ... 717 450-5416
Lebanon *(G-9556)*

Ggs Information Services Inc ....C ... 717 764-2222
York *(G-20499)*

PLATENS, EXC PRINTERS': Rubber, Solid Or Covered

Specialty Roller and Mch Inc ....F ... 570 759-1278
Berwick *(G-1344)*

PLATES

American Bank Note Holographic ....E ... 215 357-5300
Huntingdon Valley *(G-7963)*

Dynamic Dies Inc ....E ... 724 325-1514
Pittsburgh *(G-14947)*

Holly Label Company Inc ....E ... 570 222-9000
Nicholson *(G-12615)*

I P Graphics Inc ....E ... 215 673-2600
Philadelphia *(G-13845)*

Matthews International Corp ....E ... 412 442-8200
Pittsburgh *(G-15264)*

McCarty Printing Corp ....D ... 814 454-4561
Erie *(G-5385)*

Movad LLC ....F ... 215 638-2679
Plymouth Meeting *(G-15858)*

Navitor Inc ....B ... 717 765-3121
Waynesboro *(G-19419)*

Payne Printery Inc ....D ... 570 675-1147
Dallas *(G-3965)*

Professional Graphic Co ....E ... 724 318-8530
Sewickley *(G-17405)*

R R Donnelley & Sons Company ....C ... 215 671-9500
Philadelphia *(G-14225)*

Trophy Works ....G ... 412 279-0111
Carnegie *(G-2799)*

W Graphics Digital Services ....G ... 610 252-3565
Easton *(G-4773)*

PLATES: Plastic Exc Polystyrene Foam

Apexco-Ppsi LLC ....G ... 937 935-0164
Horsham *(G-7787)*

PLATES: Steel

Acrelormittal Us LLC ....D ... 724 222-7769
Washington *(G-19144)*

Arcelormittal Plate LLC ....A ... 610 383-2000
Coatesville *(G-3289)*

Lukens Inc ....D ... 610 383-2000
Coatesville *(G-3315)*

Nexarc Inc ....G ... 570 458-6990
Bloomsburg *(G-1791)*

United States Steel Corp ....C ... 412 433-1121
Pittsburgh *(G-15678)*

United States Steel Corp ....C ... 215 736-4600
Fairless Hills *(G-5806)*

United States Steel Corp ....C ... 412 433-7215
Homestead *(G-7695)*

US Steel Holdings Inc ....G ... 412 433-1121
Pittsburgh *(G-15687)*

Woodward Inc ....E ... 724 538-3110
Mars *(G-10516)*

PLATFORMS: Cargo

Grove US LLc ....D ... 717 597-8121
Shady Grove *(G-17420)*

Hoover Cnvyor Fabrication Corp ....E ... 814 634-5431
Meyersdale *(G-11011)*

PLATING & POLISHING SVC

Advanced Finishing Usa Inc ....E ... 814 474-5200
Fairview *(G-5810)*

All-Clad Metalcrafters LLC ....G ... 724 745-8300
Canonsburg *(G-2538)*

Allegheny Ludlum LLC ....C ... 724 567-2001
Vandergrift *(G-18721)*

American Nickeloid Company ....G ... 610 767-3842
Walnutport *(G-18790)*

B & G Finishing LLC ....G ... 267 229-2569
Philadelphia *(G-13436)*

Classic Metal ....G ... 724 991-2659
Prospect *(G-16111)*

Cnc Specialties Mfg Inc ....E ... 724 727-5680
Apollo *(G-671)*

Composidie Inc ....C ... 724 845-8602
Apollo *(G-673)*

CRC Industries Inc ....C ... 215 674-4300
Horsham *(G-7806)*

Elsie A Mundkowsky ....G ... 814 922-3072
West Springfield *(G-19767)*

G O Carlson Inc ....D ... 610 384-2800
Downingtown *(G-4228)*

Hall Industries Incorporated ....E 724 752-2000
Ellwood City (G-4934)
Hofmann Industries Inc ....B 610 678-8051
Reading (G-16403)
Imp Inc ....G 610 458-1533
West Chester (G-19568)
Industrial Polsg & Grinding ....D 717 854-9001
York (G-20536)
Insaco Incorporated ....D 215 536-3500
Quakertown (G-16202)
James Abbott ....F 215 426-8070
Philadelphia (G-13890)
Keystone Coating LLC ....G 717 440-5922
Boiling Springs (G-1874)
Lasermation Inc ....E 215 228-7900
Philadelphia (G-13959)
Leading Technologies Inc ....E 724 842-3400
Leechburg (G-9647)
Leonhardt Manufacturing Co Inc ......D 717 632-4150
Hanover (G-6915)
Librandi Machine Shop Inc ....D 717 944-9442
Middletown (G-11063)
Multiple Metal Processing Inc ....G 570 620-7254
Effort (G-4826)
Nak International Corp ....E 724 774-9200
Monaca (G-11292)
New Castle Industries Inc ....G 724 656-5600
New Castle (G-12129)
Oesterlings Sndblst & Pntg Inc ....E 724 282-1391
Butler (G-2429)
Orbel Corporation ....E 610 829-5000
Easton (G-4736)
Prism Powder Coating Services ....G 724 457-2836
Crescent (G-3888)
Quality Metal Coatings Inc ....G 814 781-6161
Saint Marys (G-17012)
Revel Capewell Inc ....G 610 272-8075
Norristown (G-12705)
Schake Industries Inc ....E 814 677-9333
Seneca (G-17369)
Stambaugh Metal Inc ....E 717 632-5957
Hanover (G-6958)
Torpedo Specialty Wire Inc ....E 814 563-7505
Pittsfield (G-15739)
Tumbling With Jojo ....G 267 574-5074
King of Prussia (G-8691)
Vallorbs Jewel Company ....C 717 392-3978
Bird In Hand (G-1684)

PLATING SVC: Chromium, Metals Or Formed Prdts

Erie Hard Chrome Inc ....E 814 459-5114
Erie (G-5268)
HI Tech Plating Co Inc ....F 814 455-4231
Erie (G-5317)
Industrial Machine Works Inc ....E 412 782-5055
Pittsburgh (G-15119)
Jersey Chrome Plating Co ....F 412 681-7044
Pittsburgh (G-15152)
Meadville Plating Company Inc ....F 814 724-1084
Meadville (G-10760)
Pauls Chrome Plating Inc ....E 724 538-3367
Evans City (G-5560)
Steel City Chromium Plating Co ....G 610 838-8441
Hellertown (G-7563)

PLATING SVC: Electro

Advanced Metal Coatings Inc ....E 570 538-1249
Watsontown (G-19273)
Aeco Inc ....G 215 335-2974
Philadelphia (G-13350)
American Tinning Galvanizing ....D 814 456-7053
Erie (G-5189)
Amz Manufacturing Corporation ......E 717 751-2714
York (G-20376)
Amz Manufacturing Corporation ......F 717 848-2565
York (G-20377)
Apollo Metals Ltd ....E 610 867-5826
Bethlehem (G-1450)
B&B Metal Finishing Inc ....E 717 764-8941
Manchester (G-10355)
Bfg Manufacturing Services Inc ....D 814 938-9164
Punxsutawney (G-16128)
Canalley Painting ....G 215 443-9505
Hatboro (G-7276)
Custom Industrial Processing ....F 814 834-1883
Saint Marys (G-16958)
East Liberty Elcpltg Inc ....E 412 487-4080
Glenshaw (G-6487)

Easton Pltg & Met Finshg Inc ....E 610 252-9007
Easton (G-4672)
Electro-Platers of York Inc ....F 717 751-2712
York (G-20466)
Epy Industries Inc ....F 717 751-2712
York (G-20470)
Erie Plating Company ....D 814 453-7531
Erie (G-5272)
Frank Mance Plating Service ....G 412 281-5748
Pittsburgh (G-15034)
Great Lakes Metal Finishing ....E 814 452-1886
Erie (G-5306)
Keystone Rustproofing Inc ....E 724 339-7588
New Kensington (G-12352)
Metalife Industries Inc ....E 814 676-5661
Reno (G-16647)
Millcreek Metal Finishing Inc ....G 814 833-9045
Erie (G-5393)
Multiflex Plating Company Inc ....E 610 461-7700
Collingdale (G-3408)
P R Finishing Inc ....G 610 565-0378
Folcroft (G-6011)
Philadelphia Chrome ....G 267 988-5834
Philadelphia (G-14143)
Philadelphia Rust Proof Co ....F 215 425-3000
Philadelphia (G-14153)
Pottsgrove Metal Finishers ....F 610 323-7004
Pottstown (G-16033)
Precious Metal Plating Co Inc ....G 610 586-1500
Glenolden (G-6476)
Progress For Industry Inc ....F 814 763-3707
Saegertown (G-16928)
Punxsutawney Finshg Works Inc ......C 814 938-9164
Punxsutawney (G-16155)
Select-Tron Industries Inc ....F 814 459-0847
Erie (G-5473)
Sharretts Plating Co Inc ....D 717 767-6702
Emigsville (G-4999)
St Marys Metal Finishing Inc ....G 814 834-6500
Saint Marys (G-17019)
Titanium Finishing Co ....F 215 679-4181
East Greenville (G-4577)

PLATING SVC: NEC

24k Gold Plating ....G 610 255-4676
Landenberg (G-9246)
Crile Consolidated Inds Inc ....F 724 228-0880
Washington (G-19159)
Frankford Plating Inc ....G 215 288-4518
Philadelphia (G-13721)
Harvey M Stern & Co ....G 610 649-1728
Wynnewood (G-20268)
Hkp Metals Inc ....G 412 751-0500
McKeesport (G-10670)
Ion Technologies Inc ....F 814 772-0440
Ridgway (G-16712)
K&L Plating Company Inc ....F 717 397-9819
Lancaster (G-9076)
Keystone Automotive Inds Inc ....E 814 467-5531
Windber (G-20184)
M & P Refinishing Co ....G 724 527-6360
Jeannette (G-8262)
Mance Plating Co ....G 724 695-0550
Imperial (G-8071)
Micro Plating Inc ....G 814 866-0073
Erie (G-5390)
North Penn Polishing and Pltg ....E 215 257-4945
Sellersville (G-17355)
Plating Unlimited LLC ....G 814 952-3135
Punxsutawney (G-16153)
Precision Plating Co Inc ....G 724 652-2393
New Castle (G-12140)
Products Finishing Inc ....F 814 452-4887
Erie (G-5439)
Quantum Plating Inc ....G 814 835-9213
Erie (G-5446)
Reilly Plating Company Inc ....D 570 735-7777
Nanticoke (G-11902)
Rick Radvansky & Sons ....G 724 335-7411
New Kensington (G-12371)
Vibroplating Inc ....G 215 638-4413
Bensalem (G-1267)

PLAYGROUND EQPT

Adventure Systems Inc ....F 717 351-7177
New Holland (G-12226)
Bellview Lawn Furniture ....G 717 786-1286
Quarryville (G-16265)
Casual Living Unlimited LLC ....G 717 351-7177
New Holland (G-12231)

Designed For Fun Inc ....G 215 675-4718
Warminster (G-18857)
Foxs Country Sheds ....F 717 626-9560
Lititz (G-10010)
Huna Designs Ltd ....G 570 522-9800
Lewisburg (G-9911)
Lilliput Play Homes Inc ....G 724 348-7071
Finleyville (G-5961)
Nest ....G 215 545-6378
Philadelphia (G-14063)
Playpower Inc ....B 570 522-9800
Lewisburg (G-9916)
Playworld Systems Incorporated ......E 570 522-5435
Lewisburg (G-9917)
Recreation Resource Usa LLC ....G 610 444-4402
Kennett Square (G-8538)
Stoltzfus Sylvan Lee ....G 570 682-9755
Hegins (G-7544)
Strasburg Lawn Structures LLC ....G 717 687-8210
Strasburg (G-18093)
Swing Kingdom LLC ....F 717 656-4449
Leola (G-9807)

PLEATING & STITCHING FOR THE TRADE: Decorative & Novelty

Perennial Pleasures LLC ....G 484 318-8376
Paoli (G-13147)

PLEATING & STITCHING SVC

Craig Hollern ....E 814 539-2974
Johnstown (G-8366)
Donora Sportswear Company Inc ......G 724 929-2387
Donora (G-4151)
Iehle Enterprises Inc ....E 717 859-1113
Lancaster (G-9055)
Ras Sports Inc ....E 814 833-9111
Erie (G-5457)
Schuylkill Vly Spt Trappe Ctr ....F 877 711-8100
Pottstown (G-16044)
Shenk Athletic Equipment Co ....F 717 766-6600
Mechanicsburg (G-10888)
T Shirt Printer ....G 717 367-1167
Elizabethtown (G-4889)
Thomas A Laskowski ....F 215 957-1544
Warminster (G-18981)
Tukes Tearoff ....G 570 695-3171
Tremont (G-18483)

PLUMBING & HEATING EQPT & SPLY, WHOL: Htg Eqpt/Panels, Solar

Dayco Inc ....G 610 326-4500
Pottstown (G-15981)
Quartz Tubing Inc ....F 215 638-0909
Bensalem (G-1246)
Ritter Group Usa Inc ....G 570 517-5380
Stroudsburg (G-18140)
Xcell Automation Inc ....D 717 755-6800
York (G-20721)

PLUMBING & HEATING EQPT & SPLY, WHOLESALE: Hydronic Htg Eqpt

486 Associates Inc ....E 717 691-7077
Mechanicsburg (G-10815)
Columbia Boiler Company ....E 610 323-9200
Pottstown (G-15972)
Combustion Service & Eqp Co ....D 412 821-8900
Pittsburgh (G-14867)
Lukjan Supply & Manufacturing ....F 814 838-1328
Erie (G-5374)
SPX Flow Us LLC ....G 814 476-5800
Mc Kean (G-10594)
World Marketing of America ....E 814 643-6500
Mill Creek (G-11169)

PLUMBING & HEATING EQPT & SPLYS WHOLESALERS

Hajoca Corporation ....G 215 657-0700
Willow Grove (G-20120)
Hannmann Machinery Systems Inc ....E 610 583-6900
Folcroft (G-6005)
Lebanon Parts Service Inc ....G 717 272-0181
Lebanon (G-9602)
Maxpro Technologies Inc ....F 814 474-9191
Fairview (G-5833)
Schmitt Walter H and Assoc ....E 724 872-5007
West Newton (G-19751)

PRODUCT

Ultra Pure Products Inc....................E......717 589-7001
Mifflintown (G-11139)
Vcw Enterprises Inc.....................D......610 847-5112
Ottsville (G-13068)

PLUMBING & HEATING EQPT & SPLYS, WHOL: Pipe/Fitting, Plastic

J & Ak Inc...................................D......412 787-9750
Pittsburgh (G-15139)
James F Geibel..........................G......724 287-1964
Butler (G-2412)
Piles Concrete Products Co Inc..........F......814 445-6619
Friedens (G-6225)
Pipe & Precast Cnstr Pdts Inc............F......610 644-7338
Devault (G-4112)

PLUMBING & HEATING EQPT & SPLYS, WHOL: Plumbing Fitting/Sply

Apr Supply Co..............................G......215 592-1935
Philadelphia (G-13401)
Atlantis Technologies LLC...............G......724 695-2900
Oakdale (G-12893)
G O Carlson Inc...........................D......610 384-2800
Downingtown (G-4228)
Moen Incorporated......................F......570 345-8021
Pine Grove (G-14600)
Pennypack Supply Company.............G......215 338-2200
Philadelphia (G-14133)
Pipe Dreams Plumbing Sup Inc........G......215 741-0889
Langhorne (G-9319)
Triumph Sales Inc.......................G......412 781-0950
Pittsburgh (G-15654)
United Commercial Supply LLC.........G......412 835-2690
South Park (G-17786)
Zurn Industries LLC.....................G......814 455-0921
Erie (G-5537)

PLUMBING & HEATING EQPT & SPLYS, WHOL: Plumbng/Heatng Valves

Cimberio Valve Co Inc...................G......610 560-0802
Malvern (G-10208)

PLUMBING & HEATING EQPT & SPLYS, WHOL: Water Purif Eqpt

Active Chemical Corporation............F......215 322-0377
Langhorne (G-9272)
Blue Boy Products Inc....................G......610 284-1055
Downingtown (G-4215)
Ds Services of America Inc..............F......717 901-4620
Harrisburg (G-7122)
Nalco Wtr Prtrtment Sltons LLC.........E......610 358-0717
Aston (G-780)

PLUMBING & HEATING EQPT & SPLYS, WHOLESALE: Boilers, Steam

Faber Burner Company..................E......570 748-4009
Lock Haven (G-10088)
Guardian CSC Corporation..............F......717 848-2540
Hellam (G-7551)

PLUMBING & HEATING EQPT & SPLYS, WHOLESALE: Pwr Indl Boiler

Advanced Thermal Hydronics...........F......610 473-1036
Boyertown (G-1894)
Industrial Controls Inc...................G......717 697-7555
Mechanicsburg (G-10858)

PLUMBING & HEATING EQPT, WHOLESALE: Water Heaters/Purif

Unifilt Corporation.......................G......717 823-0313
Wilkes Barre (G-19966)

PLUMBING & HEATING EQPT/SPLYS, WHOL: Boilers, Hot Water Htg

York Corrugating Company..............D......717 845-3512
York (G-20734)

PLUMBING FIXTURES

Apr Supply Co..............................G......215 592-1935
Philadelphia (G-13401)
Cimberio Valve Co Inc...................G......610 560-0802
Malvern (G-10208)

Corry Rubber Corporation...............E......814 664-2313
Corry (G-3757)
E S Specialty Manufacturing............G......215 635-0973
Wyncote (G-20262)
Four Guys Stnless Tank Eqp Inc........D......814 634-8373
Meyersdale (G-11010)
Greenfield Mfg Co Inc...................F......215 535-4141
Philadelphia (G-13785)
Hajoca Corporation.....................G......215 657-0700
Willow Grove (G-20120)
Innovative Pressure Tech LLC..........D......814 833-5200
Erie (G-5326)
Moen Incorporated......................F......570 345-8021
Pine Grove (G-14600)
Pipe Dreams Plumbing Sup Inc........G......215 741-0889
Langhorne (G-9319)
Rayco Process Services Inc.............G......717 464-2572
Willow Street (G-20155)
Space Age Plastics Inc...................F......570 630-6060
Jefferson Township (G-8279)
Speakman Company......................C......302 764-7100
Glen Mills (G-6444)
Triumph Sales Inc.......................G......412 781-0950
Pittsburgh (G-15654)

PLUMBING FIXTURES: Plastic

Abtrex Industries Inc...................E......724 266-5425
Leetsdale (G-9676)
Containment Solutions Inc..............C......814 542-8621
Mount Union (G-11741)
Elegant Marble Products Inc............F......717 939-0373
Middletown (G-11052)
Grape Fiberglass Inc.....................F......814 938-8118
Punxsutawney (G-16142)
Legacy Polymer Products Inc...........G......570 344-5019
Dunmore (G-4477)
Macson Company.........................G......610 264-7733
Allentown (G-305)
Plastic Development Company PA.......E......800 451-1420
Williamsport (G-20058)
Yarmouth Construction...................G......267 592-1432
Philadelphia (G-14498)

POINT OF SALE DEVICES

Data Tech Pos Inc.......................G......215 925-8888
Philadelphia (G-13605)
Datacap Systems Inc....................E......215 997-8989
Chalfont (G-2871)
Menasha Packaging Company LLC....G......717 520-5990
Hershey (G-7621)
Sicom Systems Inc.......................D......215 489-2500
Lansdale (G-9410)

POLE LINE HARDWARE

Winola Industrial Inc....................F......570 378-3808
Factoryville (G-5763)

POLES & POSTS: Concrete

Bradley E Miller..........................G......717 566-6243
Hummelstown (G-7904)
Valmont Newmark Inc...................C......570 454-8730
West Hazleton (G-19717)

POLISHING SVC: Metals Or Formed Prdts

Accent Metals Inc........................F......717 699-5676
York (G-20363)
Accent Metals Inc........................G......717 699-5676
York (G-20364)
American Metal Finishers Inc............F......610 323-1394
Pottstown (G-15964)
Benders Buffing & Polishing............G......717 226-1850
Elizabethtown (G-4866)
Commercial Metal Polishing............F......610 837-0267
Bath (G-954)
Custom Polishing and Finishing.........G......215 331-0960
Philadelphia (G-13595)
Francis J Nowalk.........................G......412 687-4017
Pittsburgh (G-15030)
J M Caldwell Co Inc......................G......610 436-9997
West Chester (G-19576)
Jamarco....................................G......814 833-3159
Erie (G-5333)
Polish This Inc............................G......484 269-9450
Royersford (G-16861)
Precision Roll Grinders Inc.............D......610 395-6966
Allentown (G-358)
Reisingers Precision Polsg LLC.........G......814 763-2226
Saegertown (G-16931)

Scoopermarket Inc........................G......215 925-1132
Philadelphia (G-14286)
Shalmet Corporation....................C......570 366-1414
Orwigsburg (G-13052)
Stainless Steel Services Inc............F......215 831-1471
Philadelphia (G-14340)
Sunshine Polishing Systems............G......610 828-6197
Conshohocken (G-3609)
Williams Metalfinishing Inc.............D......610 670-1077
Reading (G-16566)

POLITICAL ACTION COMMITTEES

Kane Republican.........................G......814 837-6000
Kane (G-8470)

POLYCARBONATE RESINS

Highline Polycarbonate LLC.............G......267 847-0056
Philadelphia (G-13824)
Palram 2000 Inc..........................E......610 285-9918
Kutztown (G-8852)
Sunnyside Supply Inc....................G......724 947-9966
Slovan (G-17630)
Usnr LLC...................................G......724 929-8405
Belle Vernon (G-1090)

POLYESTERS

Ashland LLC................................E......215 446-7900
Philadelphia (G-13420)
Inolex Group Inc..........................D......215 271-0800
Philadelphia (G-13859)
Ranbar Electrical Mtls LLC..............E......724 864-8200
Harrison City (G-7251)
Sealguard Inc.............................G......724 625-4550
Gibsonia (G-6351)

POLYETHYLENE RESINS

Honeywell International Inc.............A......215 533-3000
Philadelphia (G-13832)
Nova Chemicals Inc......................C......412 490-4000
Moon Township (G-11497)
Ultra-Poly Corporation...................E......570 897-7500
Portland (G-15940)

POLYMETHYL METHACRYLATE RESINS: Plexiglas

Sartomer Company Divison Total.......E......610 692-8401
West Chester (G-19637)
Taylor Chemical Inc......................F......570 562-7771
Taylor (G-18262)

POLYPROPYLENE RESINS

Audia International Inc...................F......724 228-1260
Washington (G-19151)
Bayer Corporation.......................A......412 777-2000
Pittsburgh (G-14750)
Bayer Cropscience Holding Inc.........G......412 777-2000
Pittsburgh (G-14751)
Bayer Intl Trade Svcs Corp.............G......412 777-2000
Pittsburgh (G-14755)
Braskem America Inc....................E......412 208-8100
Pittsburgh (G-14790)
Braskem America Inc....................C......610 497-8378
Marcus Hook (G-10438)
Braskem America Inc....................C......215 841-3100
Philadelphia (G-13478)
Forta Corporation........................E......724 458-5221
Grove City (G-6785)
Jsp International Group Ltd..............G......610 651-8600
Wayne (G-19342)
Jsp International LLC.....................F......610 651-8600
Wayne (G-19343)
Jsp International LLC.....................C......724 477-5100
Butler (G-2415)
Jsp Resins LLC............................F......610 651-8600
Wayne (G-19344)

POLYSTYRENE RESINS

Northern Lehigh Erectors Corp.........E......610 791-4200
Allentown (G-335)
Opco Inc...................................E......724 537-9300
Latrobe (G-9507)
Soroka Sales Inc..........................E......412 381-7700
Pittsburgh (G-15560)

POLYSULFIDES

Morton International LLC ....C...... 989 636-1000
  Collegeville (G-3384)
Smooth-On Inc ....C...... 610 252-5800
  Macungie (G-10159)

POLYTETRAFLUOROETHYLENE RESINS

Edlon Inc ....D...... 610 268-3101
  Avondale (G-852)
Total Systems Technology Inc.............F..... 412 653-7690
  Pittsburgh (G-15633)
W L Gore & Associates Inc ....A....... 610 268-1864
  Landenberg (G-9255)

POLYURETHANE RESINS

Covestro LLC ....A....... 412 413-2000
  Pittsburgh (G-14882)
Foam Fabricators Inc......................F...... 814 838-4538
  Erie (G-5298)
Steinmetz Inc ....E...... 570 842-6161
  Roaring Brook Twp (G-16760)

POLYVINYL CHLORIDE RESINS

Cpg International I Inc ....G...... 570 346-8797
  Scranton (G-17222)
Extruded Plastic Solutions ....G...... 610 756-6602
  Kempton (G-8491)
J-M Manufacturing Company Inc ....C...... 814 432-2166
  Franklin (G-6141)
J-M Manufacturing Company Inc ....D...... 814 337-7675
  Cochranton (G-3343)
Plasti-Coat Corp ....E...... 475 235-2761
  Sellersville (G-17357)
Plastic Dip Moldings Inc ....E...... 215 766-2020
  Quakertown (G-16229)
TMI International LLC ....D...... 412 787-9750
  Pittsburgh (G-15628)

PORCELAIN ENAMELED PRDTS & UTENSILS

American Trim LLC ....C...... 814 833-7758
  Erie (G-5190)
Prizer-Painter Stove Works Inc............E...... 610 376-7479
  Blandon (G-1757)
Steril-Sil Co LLC ....G...... 617 739-2970
  Denver (G-4094)

POSTERS

Design Dynamics Inc ....F...... 724 266-4826
  Ambridge (G-615)
Heraclitean Corporation ....F 215 862-5518
  New Hope (G-12305)

POTTERY

Creative Ceramics.........................G...... 724 504-4318
  Butler (G-2391)
Jens Flowers & More ....G...... 570 898-3176
  Shamokin (G-17424)
Steve Day...................................G...... 610 916-1317
  Blandon (G-1760)

POTTERY: Laboratory & Indl

Saint-Gobain Corporation ....A...... 610 893-6000
  Malvern (G-10313)
Saint-Gobain Delaware Corp ....G...... 610 341-7000
  Valley Forge (G-18712)

POTTING SOILS

Mastermix Inc ....G...... 610 346-8723
  Quakertown (G-16213)
Organic Mechanics Soil Co LLC...........G...... 484 557-2961
  Modena (G-11258)

POULTRY & POULTRY PRDTS WHOLESALERS

Oaks Poultry Co Inc.......................F...... 814 798-3631
  Stoystown (G-18083)

POULTRY & SMALL GAME SLAUGHTERING & PROCESSING

Birdsboro Kosher Farms Corp ....C...... 610 404-0001
  Birdsboro (G-1690)

Cargill Incorporated.......................F...... 717 273-1133
  Lebanon (G-9552)
Drexel Foods Inc ....E...... 215 425-9900
  Philadelphia (G-13646)
EG Emils and Son Inc.....................G...... 800 228-3645
  Philadelphia (G-13663)
Hain Pure Protein Corporation ....D...... 717 624-2191
  New Oxford (G-12411)
Hillandale-Gettysburg LP ....C...... 717 334-1973
  Gettysburg (G-6300)
Jim Neidermyer Poultry...................G...... 717 738-1036
  Denver (G-4078)
Joe Jurgielewicz & Son Ltd ....E...... 610 562-3825
  Hamburg (G-6842)
Murrys of Maryland Inc ....C...... 301 420-6400
  Lebanon (G-9612)
Perdue Farms Inc..........................B...... 717 426-1961
  Marietta (G-10466)
Perdue Farms Inc..........................C...... 610 388-1385
  Chadds Ford (G-2858)
Tran Hoang ....G...... 215 833-0923
  Philadelphia (G-14402)
Tri-Our Brands ....G...... 570 655-1512
  Pittston (G-15783)

POULTRY SLAUGHTERING & PROCESSING

Oaks Poultry Co Inc.......................F...... 814 798-3631
  Stoystown (G-18083)

POWDER: Aluminum Atomized

Ampal Inc ....E...... 610 826-7020
  Palmerton (G-13101)
Engineered Pressed Materials..............G...... 814 772-6127
  Ridgway (G-16707)
Metal Powder Products LLC ....D...... 814 834-2886
  Saint Marys (G-16991)

POWDER: Iron

Formfast Powder Mtl Tech LLC ....G...... 814 201-5292
  Ridgway (G-16709)
Hoeganaes Corporation ....E...... 570 538-3587
  Watsontown (G-19275)
Ssw International Inc ....E...... 412 922-9100
  Pittsburgh (G-15572)
Tms International LLC ....D...... 412 678-6141
  Glassport (G-6419)
Tms International Corp.....................C...... 412 678-6141
  Glassport (G-6420)
Tms International Corporation ....E...... 412 675-8251
  Glassport (G-6421)

POWDER: Metal

Accu-Grind Inc ....D...... 814 965-5475
  Johnsonburg (G-8343)
Advantage Metal Powders Inc ....F...... 814 772-5363
  Ridgway (G-16691)
Alpha Precision Group LLC ....G...... 814 773-3191
  Ridgway (G-16693)
Alpha Sintered Metals LLC ....C...... 814 773-3191
  Ridgway (G-16694)
Ampal Inc ....G...... 610 826-7020
  Palmerton (G-13100)
APS Advance Products & Svcs ....G...... 610 863-0570
  Wind Gap (G-20165)
ARC Metals Corporation ....G...... 814 776-2116
  Ridgway (G-16695)
B & B Tool and Die Inc ....F...... 814 486-5355
  Emporium (G-5050)
Biltwood Powder Coating LLC ....G...... 717 655-5664
  Waynesboro (G-19400)
Brockway Sintered Technology............G...... 814 265-8090
  Brockway (G-2223)
Cameron Diversified Pdts Inc ....E...... 814 929-5834
  Wilcox (G-19897)
Carbon City Products Inc..................D...... 814 834-2886
  Saint Marys (G-16952)
Catalus Corporation ....F...... 814 781-7004
  Saint Marys (G-16953)
Catalus Corporation ....D...... 814 435-6541
  Galeton (G-6238)
Chemalloy Company LLC ....E...... 610 527-3700
  Conshohocken (G-3527)
Clarion Sintered Metals Inc ....B...... 814 773-3124
  Ridgway (G-16699)
Continuous Metal Tech Inc ....E...... 814 772-9274
  Ridgway (G-16701)
Eastern Sintered Alloys Inc ....B....... 814 834-1216
  Saint Marys (G-16966)

Elcam Tool & Die Inc ....E...... 814 929-5831
  Wilcox (G-19898)
Elco Sintered Alloys Co Inc ....E...... 814 885-8031
  Kersey (G-8557)
Elk Metals Inc ....F...... 814 834-4959
  Saint Marys (G-16971)
Embassy Powdered Metals Inc............E...... 814 486-1011
  Emporium (G-5055)
Emporium Powdered Metal Inc............F...... 814 486-0136
  Emporium (G-5058)
Emporium Secondaries Inc ....E...... 814 486-1881
  Emporium (G-5059)
Engineered Pressed Materials ....G...... 814 834-3189
  Saint Marys (G-16972)
EPC Powder Manufacturing Inc ....E...... 814 725-2012
  North East (G-12740)
Falls Creek Powdered Metals ....F...... 814 265-8771
  Brockway (G-2225)
GKN Sinter Metals LLC ....A...... 814 486-9234
  Emporium (G-5061)
GKN Sinter Metals LLC ....D...... 814 885-8053
  Kersey (G-8559)
GKN Sinter Metals LLC ....C...... 814 781-6500
  Kersey (G-8560)
GKN Sinter Metals - Dubois Inc ....D...... 814 375-0938
  Du Bois (G-4393)
Global Metal Products Inc ....G...... 814 834-2214
  Saint Marys (G-16978)
Hawk Precision Components ....G...... 814 371-0184
  Falls Creek (G-5854)
Intech P/M Stainless Inc ....E...... 814 776-6150
  Ridgway (G-16711)
Jet Metals Inc ....E...... 814 781-7399
  Saint Marys (G-16982)
Liberty Pressed Metals LLC ....F...... 814 885-6277
  Kersey (G-8563)
Metal Powder Products LLC ....G...... 814 834-7261
  Saint Marys (G-16992)
Metal Powder Products LLC ....C...... 814 776-2141
  Ridgway (G-16716)
Metaldyne Sintered Ridgway LLC ....D...... 814 776-1141
  Ridgway (G-16717)
Metaltech Inc ....E...... 814 375-9399
  Du Bois (G-4406)
Metco Industries Inc ....D...... 814 781-3630
  Saint Marys (G-16994)
Netshape Technologies LLC ....G...... 814 371-0184
  Falls Creek (G-5855)
North Amer Hoganas High Alloys ....D...... 814 361-6800
  Johnstown (G-8413)
O Alpine Pressed Metals Inc ....D...... 814 776-2141
  Ridgway (G-16721)
P/M National Inc ....E...... 814 781-1960
  Saint Marys (G-17001)
Pennsylvania Powdered Mtls Inc ....E...... 814 834-9565
  Saint Marys (G-17004)
Pennsylvania Sintered Mtls Inc ....E...... 814 486-1768
  Emporium (G-5071)
Phoenix Sintered Metals LLC ....E...... 814 268-3455
  Brockway (G-2230)
Powder Metal Products Inc ....C...... 814 834-7261
  Saint Marys (G-17008)
Precision Cmpcted Cmpnents LLC.......D...... 814 929-5805
  Wilcox (G-19899)
Quality Compacted Metals Inc.............F...... 814 486-1500
  Emporium (G-5072)
Quality Metal Coatings Inc ....G...... 814 781-6161
  Saint Marys (G-17012)
Rebco Inc ....C...... 814 885-8035
  Kersey (G-8568)
Ridgway Powdered Metals Inc.............E...... 814 772-5551
  Ridgway (G-16727)
Rolling Ridge Metals LLC...................G...... 724 588-2375
  Greenville (G-6771)
Silcotek Corp ....E...... 814 353-1778
  Bellefonte (G-1118)
Specilty Mtallurgical Pdts Inc ....F...... 717 246-0385
  Red Lion (G-16614)
Spinworks LLC ....G...... 814 725-1188
  North East (G-12761)
St Marys Carbon Co Inc ....D...... 814 781-7333
  Saint Marys (G-17018)
St Marys Pressed Metals Inc...............E...... 814 772-7455
  Ridgway (G-16730)
Superior Powder Coating Inc...............G...... 412 221-8250
  Mc Donald (G-10583)
Symmco Group Inc ....D...... 814 894-2461
  Sykesville (G-18204)
United Sttes Metal Powders Inc...........F...... 908 782-5454
  Palmerton (G-13113)

PRODUCT

POWDER: Silver

HRP Metals Inc ....G...... 412 741-6781
Sewickley *(G-17393)*

POWDERS, FLAVORING, EXC DRINK

Creative Flavor Concepts Inc ....G...... 949 705-6584
Lancaster *(G-8988)*

Pardoes Perky Peanuts Inc ....E...... 570 524-9595
Montandon *(G-11366)*

POWER DISTRIBUTION BOARDS: Electric

Io Solutions & Controls ....F...... 215 635-4480
Elkins Park *(G-4907)*

POWER GENERATORS

Colonial EP LLC ....E...... 844 376-9374
King of Prussia *(G-8595)*

Ecolution Energy LLC ....G...... 908 707-1400
Lehighton *(G-9713)*

Evans Commercial Services LLC ....F...... 412 573-9442
Bridgeville *(G-2061)*

Klinge Corporation ....D...... 717 840-4500
York *(G-20556)*

Powerhouse Generator Inc ....G...... 717 759-8535
New Freedom *(G-12214)*

Wg Products Pittsburgh LLC ....G...... 412 795-7177
Pittsburgh *(G-15713)*

POWER SUPPLIES: All Types, Static

APC International Ltd ....E...... 570 726-6961
Mackeyville *(G-10137)*

Corey Associates Inc ....E...... 570 676-4800
Greentown *(G-6733)*

Martek Power Laser Drive LLC ....D...... 805 383-5548
Pittsburgh *(G-15259)*

Simco Industrial Static Cntrl ....D...... 215 822-2171
Hatfield *(G-7396)*

Trs Technologies Inc ....E...... 814 238-7485
State College *(G-18040)*

POWER SUPPLIES: Transformer, Electronic Type

Digital Plaza LLC ....F...... 267 515-8000
Ambler *(G-575)*

Gkld Corp ....G...... 215 643-6950
Blue Bell *(G-1830)*

Pei/Genesis Inc ....G...... 215 638-1645
Bensalem *(G-1238)*

Pei/Genesis Inc ....C...... 215 464-1410
Philadelphia *(G-14129)*

Solid State Ceramics Inc ....G...... 570 322-2700
State College *(G-18028)*

Wist Enterprises Inc ....F...... 724 283-7230
Butler *(G-2451)*

POWER TOOL REPAIR SVCS

Black & Decker (us) Inc ....F...... 215 271-0402
Philadelphia *(G-13467)*

Brian O Keffe ....G...... 570 477-3962
Sweet Valley *(G-18187)*

POWER TOOLS, HAND: Drills & Drilling Tools

Tamco Inc ....E...... 724 258-6622
Monongahela *(G-11317)*

POWER TRANSMISSION EQPT WHOLESALERS

Applied Indus Tech — PA LLC ....G...... 724 696-3099
Mount Pleasant *(G-11686)*

POWER TRANSMISSION EQPT: Mechanical

Altra Industrial Motion ....G...... 781 917-0600
Chambersburg *(G-2902)*

Altra Industrial Motion Corp ....G...... 717 261-2550
Chambersburg *(G-2903)*

American Hollow Boring Company ....E...... 800 673-2458
Erie *(G-5187)*

Cbh of Lancaster Company ....D...... 717 569-0485
Manheim *(G-10375)*

Converter Accessory Corp ....F...... 610 863-6008
Wind Gap *(G-20168)*

Dana Driveshaft Products LLC ....B...... 610 323-4200
Pottstown *(G-15979)*

Edlon Inc ....D...... 610 268-3101
Avondale *(G-852)*

Fenner Inc ....G...... 717 665-2421
Lancaster *(G-9015)*

Fenner Inc ....D...... 717 665-2421
Manheim *(G-10381)*

Fenner Inc ....G...... 717 665-2421
Manheim *(G-10382)*

Fenner Inc ....G...... 717 665-2421
Manheim *(G-10380)*

General Carbide Corporation ....C...... 724 836-3000
Greensburg *(G-6668)*

General Dynamics Ots PA Inc ....C...... 570 342-7801
Scranton *(G-17238)*

GKN Sinter Metals - Dubois Inc ....D...... 814 375-0938
Du Bois *(G-4393)*

Keystone Powdered Metal Co ....D...... 814 368-5320
Lewis Run *(G-9876)*

Kingsbury Inc ....E...... 215 824-4000
Philadelphia *(G-13939)*

Kingsbury Inc ....F...... 215 824-4000
Hatboro *(G-7290)*

Lord Corporation ....B...... 814 868-3180
Erie *(G-5372)*

Lord Corporation ....D...... 814 398-4641
Cambridge Springs *(G-2481)*

Lord Corporation ....B...... 814 868-0924
Erie *(G-5371)*

Medart Inc ....E...... 724 752-3555
Ellwood City *(G-4946)*

Metal Powder Products LLC ....C...... 814 834-7261
Saint Marys *(G-16992)*

Metaltech Inc ....E...... 814 375-9399
Du Bois *(G-4406)*

Morgan Advanced Mtls Tech Inc ....C...... 814 781-1573
Saint Marys *(G-16998)*

N C B Technologies Inc ....G...... 724 658-5544
New Castle *(G-12123)*

Neapco Components LLC ....E...... 610 323-6000
Pottstown *(G-16021)*

Nick Charles Kravitch ....G...... 412 882-6262
Pittsburgh *(G-15340)*

Orville Bronze and Alum LLC ....G...... 330 948-1231
Meadville *(G-10772)*

Oswald & Associates Inc ....G...... 814 627-0300
Huntingdon *(G-7954)*

Pittsbrgh Tubular Shafting Inc ....E...... 724 774-7212
Rochester *(G-16787)*

Proform Powdered Metals Inc ....E...... 814 938-7411
Punxsutawney *(G-16154)*

Scheerer Bearing Corporation ....E...... 215 443-5252
Willow Grove *(G-20140)*

Scheerer Bearing Corporation ....E...... 215 443-5252
Horsham *(G-7848)*

Schneider Electric It Corp ....G...... 215 230-7270
Doylestown *(G-4336)*

St Marys Pressed Metals Inc ....E...... 814 772-7455
Ridgway *(G-16730)*

Stapf Energy Services ....G...... 610 831-1500
Trappe *(G-18474)*

Tb Woods Incorporated ....C...... 717 264-7161
Chambersburg *(G-2983)*

Triple W Enterprises Inc ....G...... 610 865-0071
Bethlehem *(G-1642)*

Vallorbs Jewel Company ....C...... 717 392-3978
Bird In Hand *(G-1684)*

Wise Machine Co Inc ....E...... 724 287-2705
Butler *(G-2450)*

PRECAST TERRAZZO OR CONCRETE PRDTS

Big Bear Concrete Works ....G...... 570 584-0107
Lairdsville *(G-8886)*

Commonwealth Precast Inc ....F...... 215 721-6005
Souderton *(G-17730)*

Gcl Inc ....G...... 724 933-7260
Wexford *(G-19805)*

Lehigh Fabrication LLC ....E...... 908 791-4800
Whitehall *(G-19881)*

Northwest PA Burial Service ....G...... 814 425-2436
Cochranton *(G-3346)*

Oldcastle Precast Inc ....E...... 215 257-2255
Telford *(G-18307)*

Omni Precast Products Inc ....G...... 724 316-1582
Wampum *(G-18803)*

Pipe & Precast Cnstr Pdts Inc ....F...... 610 644-7338
Devault *(G-4112)*

Precast Services Inc ....D...... 330 425-2880
Morgantown *(G-11531)*

Wine Concrete Products Inc ....E...... 724 266-9500
Sewickley *(G-17415)*

PRECIOUS METALS

Matthey Johnson Holdings Inc ....E...... 610 971-3000
Wayne *(G-19350)*

Matthey Johnson Inc ....E...... 610 971-3000
Wayne *(G-19351)*

Matthey Johnson Inc ....C...... 610 341-8300
Wayne *(G-19353)*

PRECIOUS METALS WHOLESALERS

Gold Bug Exchange ....G...... 724 770-9008
Beaver *(G-982)*

PRECIOUS STONES WHOLESALERS

RBS Impex Inc ....G...... 412 566-2488
Pittsburgh *(G-15471)*

PREFABRICATED BUILDING DEALERS

Honeybrook Woodworks ....F...... 610 593-6884
Christiana *(G-3135)*

Myerstown Sheds ....G...... 717 866-7644
Lebanon *(G-9613)*

T-Town Sheds & Supply ....G...... 570 836-5686
Tunkhannock *(G-18550)*

PREPARING SHAFTS OR TUNNELS, METAL MINING

Minichi Inc ....D...... 570 654-8332
Dupont *(G-4491)*

US Crossings Unlimited LLC ....G...... 888 359-1115
Cranberry Township *(G-3861)*

PRERECORDED TAPE, COMPACT DISC & RECORD STORES: Compact Disc

Fab Universal Corp ....F...... 412 621-0902
Pittsburgh *(G-15002)*

PRESCHOOL CENTERS

It Takes A Village To Feed ....G...... 888 702-9610
Ridley Park *(G-16739)*

PRESSED FIBER & MOLDED PULP PRDTS, EXC FOOD PRDTS

Keystone Converting Inc ....F...... 215 661-9004
Montgomeryville *(G-11400)*

Manchester Industries Inc VA ....E...... 570 822-9308
Hanover Township *(G-6993)*

PRESSES

Gasbarre Products Inc ....E...... 814 236-3108
Olanta *(G-12960)*

Loomis Products Company ....F...... 215 547-2121
Levittown *(G-9847)*

Samuel Stamping Tech LLC ....E...... 724 981-5042
Hermitage *(G-7594)*

Schmidt Technology Corporation ....F...... 724 772-4600
Cranberry Township *(G-3848)*

PRESTRESSED CONCRETE PRDTS

H Y K Construction Co Inc ....D...... 610 489-2646
Collegeville *(G-3381)*

High Concrete Group LLC ....B...... 717 336-9300
Denver *(G-4075)*

High Industries Inc ....B...... 717 293-4444
Lancaster *(G-9046)*

Nitterhouse Concrete Pdts Inc ....C...... 717 207-7837
Chambersburg *(G-2962)*

Rahns Construction Material Co ....G...... 610 584-8500
Collegeville *(G-3390)*

PRIMARY METAL PRODUCTS

B B Express ....G...... 717 573-2686
Warfordsburg *(G-18810)*

Dominion Powdered Metals ....G...... 814 598-4684
Saint Marys *(G-16963)*

Metal Group ....G...... 215 438-6156
Philadelphia *(G-14012)*

Technitrol Inc ....G....... 215 355-2900
Feasterville Trevose *(G-5932)*

PRIMARY ROLLING MILL EQPT

Rotation Dynamics Corporation ....E....... 717 656-4252
Leola *(G-9802)*

PRINT CARTRIDGES: Laser & Other Computer Printers

Cartridge Specialist ....G....... 412 741-4442
Sewickley *(G-17384)*
D B Products Inc ....E....... 215 628-0416
Montgomeryville *(G-11392)*
Itc Supplies LLC ....G....... 610 430-1300
West Chester *(G-19574)*
Laser Lab Inc ....F....... 717 738-3333
Ephrata *(G-5120)*
Mark Grim ....G....... 724 758-2270
Ellwood City *(G-4945)*
West Point Acquisition LLC ....C....... 724 222-2354
Washington *(G-19244)*

PRINTED CIRCUIT BOARDS

4front Solutions LLC ....C....... 814 464-2000
Erie *(G-5161)*
Aci Technologies Inc ....E....... 610 362-1200
Philadelphia *(G-13313)*
Advanced Electrocircuits Corp ....E....... 412 278-5200
Pittsburgh *(G-14652)*
Advanced Mfg Tech Inc ....D....... 724 327-3001
Export *(G-5588)*
Advanced Technology Labs Inc ....B....... 215 355-8111
Richboro *(G-16673)*
Allen Integrated Assemblies ....G....... 610 966-2200
Macungie *(G-10139)*
Alstom Power Conversion Inc ....C....... 412 967-0765
Cranberry Township *(G-3801)*
Alstom Signaling Operation LLC ....B....... 800 825-3178
Erie *(G-5184)*
Amptech Inc ....E....... 724 843-7605
Wampum *(G-18797)*
Ansen Corporation ....G....... 315 393-3573
Pittsburgh *(G-14712)*
AOC Acquisition Inc ....B....... 610 966-2200
Macungie *(G-10141)*
Bayter Technologies Inc ....G....... 610 948-7447
Phoenixville *(G-14529)*
Circuit Foil Trading Inc ....G....... 215 887-7255
Glenside *(G-6511)*
Communication Automation Corp ....E....... 610 692-9526
West Chester *(G-19527)*
Compunetics Inc ....E....... 724 519-4773
Murrysville *(G-11850)*
Compunetix Inc ....D....... 412 373-8110
Monroeville *(G-11329)*
Currency Inc ....E....... 814 509-6157
Windber *(G-20180)*
Ddm Novastar Inc ....E....... 610 337-3050
Warminster *(G-18855)*
Diamond Mt Inc ....E....... 814 535-3505
Johnstown *(G-8368)*
Drs Laurel Technologies ....B....... 814 534-8900
Johnstown *(G-8370)*
Dynamic Manufacturing LLC ....D....... 724 295-4200
Freeport *(G-6203)*
Electro Soft Inc ....E....... 215 654-0701
Montgomeryville *(G-11394)*
Electronic Integration Inc ....F....... 215 364-3390
Feasterville Trevose *(G-5903)*
Electronic Mfg Svcs Group Inc ....D....... 717 764-0002
York *(G-20467)*
Electronic Prototype Dev Inc ....E....... 412 767-4111
Natrona Heights *(G-11941)*
Electronic Test Eqp Mfg Co ....E....... 717 393-9653
Lancaster *(G-9008)*
Flex Rig Inc ....F....... 215 638-5743
Bensalem *(G-1196)*
Ford City Gun Workd ....G....... 724 994-9501
Ford City *(G-6045)*
Genie Electronics Co Inc ....F....... 717 840-6999
York *(G-20496)*
Genie Electronics Co Inc ....D....... 717 244-1099
Red Lion *(G-16598)*
Genie Electronics Co Inc ....C....... 717 244-1099
Red Lion *(G-16599)*
In Speck Corporation ....E....... 610 272-9500
Norristown *(G-12669)*
Keystone Electronics Inc ....E....... 717 747-5900
York *(G-20553)*

Kitron Technologies Inc ....C....... 814 474-4300
Windber *(G-20187)*
Loranger International Corp ....D....... 814 723-2250
Warren *(G-19038)*
Manncorp Inc ....F....... 215 830-1200
Huntingdon Valley *(G-8011)*
Matric Group LLC ....B....... 814 677-0716
Seneca *(G-17366)*
Millennium Circuits Limited ....F....... 717 558-5975
Harrisburg *(G-7178)*
Monach Associates Inc ....G....... 888 849-0149
Bristol *(G-2169)*
National Hybrid Inc ....D....... 814 467-9060
Windber *(G-20190)*
Niche Electronics Tech Inc ....E....... 717 532-6620
Shippensburg *(G-17541)*
Nupak Printing LLC ....D....... 717 244-4041
Red Lion *(G-16610)*
Pennatronics Corporation ....D....... 724 938-1800
California *(G-2464)*
Pergamon Corp ....F....... 610 239-0721
King of Prussia *(G-8661)*
Pine Electronics Inc ....D....... 724 458-6391
Grove City *(G-6800)*
Pine Instrument Company ....D....... 724 458-6391
Grove City *(G-6801)*
Primus Technologies Corp ....B....... 570 326-6591
Williamsport *(G-20063)*
Reed Micro Automation Inc ....D....... 814 941-0225
Altoona *(G-543)*
Sen Dec Corp ....F....... 585 425-3390
Fairview *(G-5841)*
Spang & Company ....C....... 412 963-9363
Pittsburgh *(G-15566)*
Technical Fabrication Inc ....E....... 717 227-0909
New Freedom *(G-12216)*
Ted J Tedesco ....G....... 215 316-8303
Media *(G-10952)*
Telan Corporation ....E....... 215 822-1234
Hatfield *(G-7400)*
Tudor Design ....G....... 215 638-3366
Bensalem *(G-1266)*
Wintronics Inc ....E....... 724 981-5770
Sharon *(G-17449)*
Woodward McCoach Inc ....F....... 610 692-9526
West Chester *(G-19681)*
Youngtron Inc ....G....... 215 822-7866
Hatfield *(G-7406)*
Ziel Technologies LLC ....G....... 717 951-7485
Lancaster *(G-9245)*

PRINTERS & PLOTTERS

Decal Specialties Inc ....G....... 610 644-9200
Paoli *(G-13137)*
G&R Designs LLC ....G....... 717 697-4538
Mechanicsburg *(G-10848)*
Menu For Less ....G....... 215 240-1582
Feasterville Trevose *(G-5919)*
Support McRcomputers Assoc Inc ....F....... 215 496-0303
Philadelphia *(G-14359)*

PRINTERS' SVCS: Folding, Collating, Etc

A Link Prtg & Promotions LLC ....G....... 412 220-0290
Bridgeville *(G-2049)*
Degadan Corp ....G....... 610 940-1282
Conshohocken *(G-3537)*
Larry Myers ....G....... 717 564-8300
Harrisburg *(G-7169)*
Triangle Press Inc ....E....... 717 541-9315
Harrisburg *(G-7238)*

PRINTERS: Computer

Copiers Inc ....G....... 610 837-7400
Bath *(G-955)*
Cybertech Inc ....F....... 215 957-6220
Horsham *(G-7807)*
Intermec Technologies Corp ....F....... 724 218-1444
Imperial *(G-8068)*
Lexmark International Inc ....F....... 610 966-8283
Coopersburg *(G-3630)*
Loveshaw Corporation ....C....... 570 937-4921
South Canaan *(G-17769)*
Monroeville Ink Refills Inc ....G....... 412 374-1700
Monroeville *(G-11346)*
Phxco LLC ....D....... 608 203-1500
Middletown *(G-11069)*
R T R Business Products Inc ....E....... 724 733-7373
Export *(G-5622)*

Saxon Office Technology Inc ....F....... 215 736-2620
Fairless Hills *(G-5795)*

PRINTERS: Magnetic Ink, Bar Code

Advanced Mobile Group LLC ....F....... 215 489-2538
Doylestown *(G-4268)*
Mecco ....G....... 412 548-3549
Pittsburgh *(G-15271)*
Pannier Corporation ....F....... 412 323-4900
Pittsburgh *(G-15368)*
RMS Omega Tech Grouping ....G....... 610 917-0472
Phoenixville *(G-14574)*
Vanguard Identification ....E....... 610 719-0700
West Chester *(G-19672)*
Whiskey Dicks ....G....... 570 342-9824
Scranton *(G-17312)*

PRINTING & BINDING: Books

Bela Printing & Packaging Corp ....G....... 215 664-7090
Lansdale *(G-9344)*
Hf Group LLC ....E....... 215 855-2293
Hatfield *(G-7350)*
Lisa Leleu Studios Inc ....G....... 215 345-1233
Doylestown *(G-4313)*
Maple Press Company ....C....... 717 764-5911
York *(G-20580)*
National Publishing Company ....B....... 215 676-1863
Philadelphia *(G-14055)*
Sheridan Group LLC ....D....... 717 632-3535
Hanover *(G-6950)*
Squibb Alvah M Company Inc ....F....... 412 751-2301
McKeesport *(G-10682)*

PRINTING & BINDING: Pamphlets

Valley Business Services Inc ....F....... 610 366-1970
Trexlertown *(G-18511)*

PRINTING & BINDING: Textbooks

Great American Printer Inc ....G....... 570 752-7341
Berwick *(G-1326)*

PRINTING & EMBOSSING: Plastic Fabric Articles

Advantech US Inc ....E....... 412 706-5400
Beaver *(G-977)*
Allegheny Plastics Inc ....D....... 724 776-0100
Cranberry Township *(G-3800)*
Ravine Inc ....F....... 814 946-5006
Altoona *(G-541)*
Ron Lee Inc ....F....... 570 784-6020
Bloomsburg *(G-1799)*

PRINTING & ENGRAVING: Card, Exc Greeting

Arkwood Products Inc ....G....... 412 835-8730
Bethel Park *(G-1404)*
Choice Marketing Inc ....E....... 610 494-1270
Aston *(G-755)*
City Engraving & Awards LLC ....G....... 215 731-0200
Philadelphia *(G-13547)*
Two Paperdolls LLC ....F....... 610 293-4933
Wayne *(G-19386)*

PRINTING & ENGRAVING: Financial Notes & Certificates

Scullin Group Inc ....G....... 215 640-3330
Philadelphia *(G-14290)*

PRINTING & ENGRAVING: Invitation & Stationery

A A A Engraving ....G....... 412 281-7756
Pittsburgh *(G-14628)*
Art Printing Co of Lancaster ....G....... 717 397-6029
Columbia *(G-3430)*
Artistagraphics Inc ....F....... 412 271-3252
Pittsburgh *(G-14727)*
Chocolatecovers Ltd Inc ....G....... 717 534-1992
Hershey *(G-7606)*
Copy Shop ....G....... 724 654-6515
New Castle *(G-12078)*
Giving Tree Inc ....G....... 215 968-2487
New Hope *(G-12303)*
Paperia ....G....... 215 247-8521
Philadelphia *(G-14116)*

P
R
O
D
U
C
T

Papyrus Inc...............................F 610 354-9480
King of Prussia (G-8659)

PRINTING & ENGRAVING: Poster & Decal

Commercial Color Inc...................G...... 610 391-7444
Allentown (G-173)

Rockpetz Ventures LLC....................G...... 610 608-2788
Philadelphia (G-14256)

PRINTING & ENGRAVING: Rolls, Textile Printing

Lebanon Valley Engraving Inc ....F 717 273-7913
Lebanon (G-9605)

Luminite Products Corporation............D...... 814 817-1420
Bradford (G-1980)

PRINTING & STAMPING: Fabric Articles

Printdropper Inc..........................F 412 657-6170
Pittsburgh (G-15443)

Statement Walls LLC....................G...... 267 266-0869
Philadelphia (G-14341)

Wallquest Inc............................D...... 610 293-1330
Wayne (G-19389)

Xiii Touches Printing ....F 484 754-6504
King of Prussia (G-8700)

PRINTING & WRITING PAPER WHOLESALERS

Veritiv Operating Company ....E 724 776-3122
Cranberry Township (G-3863)

PRINTING INKS WHOLESALERS

Itc Supplies LLC..........................G...... 610 430-1300
West Chester (G-19574)

Weldship Industries Inc...................F 610 861-7330
Bethlehem (G-1655)

PRINTING MACHINERY

Advance Graphics Eqp of York ....E 717 292-9183
Dover (G-4183)

Apex North America LLC ....E 866 273-9872
Donora (G-4145)

Aradiant Corporation ....E 717 838-7220
Palmyra (G-13116)

Baldwin Technology Company Inc.......G...... 610 829-4240
Easton (G-4648)

Bell-Mark Sales Co Inc ....E 717 292-5641
Dover (G-4186)

Chant Engineering Co Inc ....E 215 230-4260
New Britain (G-12046)

David K Hart Co...........................G...... 610 527-0388
Bryn Mawr (G-2319)

Exone Company...........................E 724 863-9663
North Huntingdon (G-12769)

Ferag Inc...................................D...... 215 788-0892
Bristol (G-2144)

Global Inserting Systems LLC ....E 610 217-3019
Emmaus (G-5027)

Glunz & Jensen K&F Inc ....C...... 267 227-3493
Quakertown (G-16198)

H D Sampey Inc...........................G...... 215 723-3471
Telford (G-18293)

J & J Specialties of PA ....F 717 838-7220
Palmyra (G-13126)

Jls Automation LLC ....E 717 505-3800
York (G-20541)

Kba North America Inc ....C...... 717 505-1150
York (G-20548)

Keystone Printing Services ....G...... 215 675-6464
Hatboro (G-7289)

Manugraph Americas Inc ....E 717 362-3243
Millersburg (G-11195)

Matthews International Corp...............D...... 412 665-2500
Pittsburgh (G-15265)

Muller Martini Mailroom...................C...... 610 266-7000
Allentown (G-323)

R W Hartnett Company....................E 215 969-9190
Philadelphia (G-14228)

Recognition Engraving.....................G...... 717 242-1166
Lewistown (G-9946)

Rotation Dynamics Corporation...........F 717 464-2724
Willow Street (G-20156)

S Morantz Inc..............................D...... 215 969-0266
Philadelphia (G-14273)

W O Hickok Manufacturing Co ....E 717 234-8041
Harrisburg (G-7243)

Wood Specialty Company Inc................F 610 539-6384
Norristown (G-12724)

PRINTING MACHINERY, EQPT & SPLYS: Wholesalers

Cabrun Ink Products Corp ....E 215 533-2990
Philadelphia (G-13493)

Sportin My Stuff..........................G...... 724 457-7005
Crescent (G-3889)

PRINTING TRADES MACHINERY & EQPT REPAIR SVCS

Deckman Electric Inc.....................G...... 610 272-6944
Bridgeport (G-2034)

Manugraph Americas Inc ....E 717 362-3243
Millersburg (G-11195)

Teeco Associates Inc.....................E 610 539-4708
Schwenksville (G-17179)

PRINTING, COMMERCIAL Newspapers, NEC

Carrollsisters ....E 215 969-4688
Philadelphia (G-13509)

Courier Times Inc.........................C...... 215 949-4219
Fairless Hills (G-5776)

Indiana Printing and Pubg Co.............C...... 724 349-3434
Indiana (G-8106)

Miller Printing & Publishing ....E 814 425-7272
Cochranton (G-3345)

PRINTING, COMMERCIAL: Announcements, NEC

Cenveo Worldwide Limited ....C....... 724 887-5400
Mount Pleasant (G-11691)

PRINTING, COMMERCIAL: Bags, Plastic, NEC

Mri Flexible Packaging Company.........E 215 860-7676
Bristol (G-2171)

National Film Converting Inc ....F 800 422-6651
Berwick (G-1338)

PRINTING, COMMERCIAL: Business Forms, NEC

Forms Graphics LLC ....F 215 639-3504
Bensalem (G-1197)

Parabo Press LLC.........................G...... 484 843-1230
Philadelphia (G-14118)

Perry Printing Company....................G...... 717 582-2838
New Bloomfield (G-12030)

Thorn Hill Printing Inc ....E 724 774-4700
Freedom (G-6192)

PRINTING, COMMERCIAL: Calendars, NEC

Focus One Promotions Inc ....G....... 610 459-7781
Aston (G-764)

Paper Magic Group Inc....................B...... 570 644-0842
Elysburg (G-4978)

PRINTING, COMMERCIAL: Catalogs, NEC

Hilsher Graphics Flp.......................F 570 326-9159
Williamsport (G-20023)

House of Printing..........................G...... 814 723-3701
Warren (G-19031)

PRINTING, COMMERCIAL: Decals, NEC

Accu-Decal Inc ....G...... 215 535-0320
Philadelphia (G-13338)

Clarion Safety Systems LLC ....E 570 296-5686
Milford (G-11157)

Decalcraft Corp ....G...... 215 822-0517
Hatfield (G-7332)

E P M Corporation........................F 814 825-6650
Erie (G-5252)

Fleet Decal & Graphics Inc...............F 570 779-4343
Plymouth (G-15818)

National Decal Craft Corp ....G...... 215 822-0517
Hatfield (G-7371)

Nu-Art Graphics Inc ....F 610 436-4336
West Chester (G-19608)

Screening Room Inc ....G...... 610 363-5405
Exton (G-5729)

PRINTING, COMMERCIAL: Directories, Exc Telephone, NEC

Kunz Business Products Inc ....C...... 814 643-4320
Huntingdon (G-7949)

PRINTING, COMMERCIAL: Envelopes, NEC

Brandywine Envelope Corp ....G...... 800 887-9399
Cochranville (G-3354)

Dupli Graphics Corporation...............E 610 644-4188
Malvern (G-10225)

Kelly Line Inc..............................F 570 527-6822
Pottsville (G-16085)

Motto Graphics Inc ....G...... 570 639-5555
Dallas (G-3963)

Rite Envelope and Graphics Inc ....F 610 518-1601
Downingtown (G-4255)

PRINTING, COMMERCIAL: Invitations, NEC

Invitations Plus ....G...... 412 421-7778
Pittsburgh (G-15135)

Navitor Inc.................................B...... 717 765-3121
Waynesboro (G-19419)

Superior Printing & Engraving ....G...... 610 352-1966
Upper Darby (G-18692)

PRINTING, COMMERCIAL: Labels & Seals, NEC

Ap-O-Gee Industries Inc..................F 610 719-8010
West Chester (G-19500)

General Graphics ....G...... 724 337-1470
New Kensington (G-12342)

Graphic Communications Inc ....F 215 441-5335
Warminster (G-18891)

Valley Forge Tape Label Co Inc ....D...... 610 524-8900
Exton (G-5745)

PRINTING, COMMERCIAL: Letterpress & Screen

Call Newspapers Inc......................F 570 385-3120
Schuylkill Haven (G-17150)

Chrisber Corporation......................E 800 872-7436
West Chester (G-19525)

Cross Works Embroidery Sp Inc ....G...... 610 261-1690
Coplay (G-3642)

Custom Printing Unlimited.................F 724 339-3000
New Kensington (G-12338)

Ivy Graphics Inc ....F 215 396-9446
Warminster (G-18900)

Letterpress Shop ....G...... 412 231-2282
Pittsburgh (G-15225)

PRINTING, COMMERCIAL: Literature, Advertising, NEC

Corporate Distribution Ltd ....E 717 697-6900
Harrisburg (G-7109)

Mirage Advertising Inc ....G...... 412 372-4181
Monroeville (G-11345)

Pro Active Sports Inc......................G...... 814 943-4651
Altoona (G-539)

RMH Image Group LLC...................G...... 610 731-0050
Conshohocken (G-3602)

Sea Group Graphics Inc ....G...... 215 805-0290
Huntingdon Valley (G-8036)

PRINTING, COMMERCIAL: Magazines, NEC

Kappa Graphics L P......................C...... 570 655-9681
Hughestown (G-7893)

PRINTING, COMMERCIAL: Menus, NEC

Jaren Enterprises Inc ....G...... 717 394-2671
Lancaster (G-9072)

PRINTING, COMMERCIAL: Periodicals, NEC

Pennsylvania Legislative Svcs ....G...... 717 236-6984
Harrisburg (G-7194)

PRINTING, COMMERCIAL: Promotional

American Printing Co & Pdts...............G...... 412 422-3488
Pittsburgh (G-14704)

Clayton Kendall Inc........................C...... 412 798-7120
Monroeville (G-11327)

Creative Impressions Advg LLC ... G ... 215 357-1228
Langhorne *(G-9287)*
Crogan Inc ... G ... 814 944-3057
Altoona *(G-495)*
Easton Photoworks Inc ... G ... 610 559-1998
Easton *(G-4671)*
Forsythe Marketing ... G ... 717 764-9863
York *(G-20486)*
Hope Paige Designs LLC ... E ... 610 234-0093
Conshohocken *(G-3558)*
Interform Corporation ... F ... 610 566-1515
Media *(G-10934)*
Michael Dahma Associates ... G ... 412 607-1151
Irwin *(G-8183)*
N H Morgan Inc ... G ... 412 561-1046
Pittsburgh *(G-15314)*
Print City Graphics Inc ... G ... 610 495-5524
Phoenixville *(G-14570)*
R A Palmer Products Company ... F ... 412 823-5971
Monroeville *(G-11351)*
Reed Drabick Inc ... G ... 215 794-2068
Doylestown *(G-4334)*
Valley Business Services Inc ... F ... 610 366-1970
Trexlertown *(G-18511)*

PRINTING, COMMERCIAL: Publications

Abardia Media ... G ... 215 893-5100
Philadelphia *(G-13333)*
American Future Systems Inc ... E ... 814 724-2035
Meadville *(G-10702)*
Baltimore Corp ... E ... 215 957-6200
Warminster *(G-18835)*
Cyberink LLC ... G ... 814 870-1600
Erie *(G-5242)*
Kappa Publishing Group Inc ... D ... 215 643-6385
Blue Bell *(G-1842)*
Marine Information Tech LLC ... G ... 610 429-5180
West Chester *(G-19595)*
National Cthlic Bthics Ctr Inc ... F ... 215 877-2660
Philadelphia *(G-14054)*
Newell Brands Inc ... G ... 814 278-6771
State College *(G-17997)*
Pathfnder Eqine Pblcations LLC ... G ... 610 488-1282
Mohrsville *(G-11278)*
Trans Atlantic Publications ... G ... 215 925-2762
Schwenksville *(G-17180)*

PRINTING, COMMERCIAL: Schedules, Transportation, NEC

Aviation Technologies Inc ... G ... 570 457-4147
Avoca *(G-840)*

PRINTING, COMMERCIAL: Screen

Ad-Art Sign Co ... G ... 412 373-0960
Pittsburgh *(G-14649)*
Al Tedeschi ... G ... 724 746-3755
Canonsburg *(G-2535)*
Alpha Screen Graphics Inc ... G ... 412 431-9000
Pittsburgh *(G-14687)*
Apex Screen Printing & EMB ... G ... 814 634-5992
Meyersdale *(G-11008)*
Art & Ink ... G ... 814 486-0606
Emporium *(G-5049)*
Artistic Image ... G ... 717 567-7070
Newport *(G-12486)*
Atiyeh Printing Inc ... G ... 610 439-8978
Allentown *(G-145)*
Awards & More ... G ... 724 444-1040
Gibsonia *(G-6325)*
Axelrad LLC ... G ... 570 714-3278
Wilkes Barre *(G-19907)*
B & E Sportswear LP ... F ... 610 328-9266
Broomall *(G-2280)*
B L Tees Inc ... F ... 724 325-1882
Export *(G-5591)*
Bangtees LLC ... G ... 484 767-2382
Easton *(G-4649)*
Blue Mountain Sports AP Inc ... G ... 717 263-4124
Chambersburg *(G-2912)*
Bluegill Graphix ... G ... 814 827-7003
Titusville *(G-18376)*
Boulevard Sports ... G ... 724 378-9191
Aliquippa *(G-69)*
Bourne Graphics Inc ... G ... 610 584-6120
Worcester *(G-20224)*
Bsg Custom Designs LLC ... G ... 610 867-7361
Bethlehem *(G-1475)*
Bubco Enterprise Inc ... G ... 724 274-4930
Cheswick *(G-3102)*
Caffrey Michael & Sons ... G ... 610 252-1299
Easton *(G-4659)*
Champion Choice Sports ... G ... 814 236-2930
Curwensville *(G-3948)*
Charles R Eckert Signs Inc ... G ... 717 733-4601
Ephrata *(G-5096)*
Chroma Graphics ... G ... 724 693-9050
Oakdale *(G-12896)*
Classic Ink USA LLC ... G ... 724 482-1727
Butler *(G-2389)*
Clockwise Tees ... G ... 412 727-1602
Pittsburgh *(G-14861)*
Composing Room Inc ... G ... 215 310-5559
Philadelphia *(G-13565)*
Corporate Images Company ... G ... 610 439-7961
Allentown *(G-182)*
Cotton Bureau ... F ... 412 573-9041
Pittsburgh *(G-14878)*
Country Tees & Grafx LLC ... G ... 570 568-0973
Lewisburg *(G-9901)*
County Line Screenprinting ... G ... 570 758-5397
Dalmatia *(G-3984)*
Custom Design ... G ... 570 462-0041
Shenandoah *(G-17493)*
Danowski ... G ... 717 328-5057
Mercersburg *(G-10985)*
Darra Group Inc ... G ... 724 684-6040
Monessen *(G-11298)*
Del Martin Screen Prtg & EMB ... F ... 717 597-5751
Greencastle *(G-6606)*
Duff Al Bag Screenprinting Co ... G ... 717 249-8686
Carlisle *(G-2708)*
Dynamic Creations Screen Prtg ... G ... 724 229-1157
Washington *(G-19166)*
Eagle Printery Inc ... F ... 724 287-0754
Butler *(G-2397)*
Ed Cini Enterprises Inc ... G ... 215 432-3855
Plumsteadville *(G-15809)*
Elliott Printing Services LLC ... F ... 610 614-1500
Bethlehem *(G-1503)*
Embroidery Concepts ... G ... 724 225-3644
Washington *(G-19168)*
Eps Printing Services Inc ... G ... 610 701-6403
West Chester *(G-19551)*
Eric and Christopher LLC ... F ... 215 257-2400
Perkasie *(G-13276)*
Excel Sportswear Inc ... D ... 412 856-7616
Trafford *(G-18455)*
Expression Tees ... G ... 631 523-5673
Exton *(G-5674)*
EZ Garment Printing Inc ... G ... 570 703-0961
Scranton *(G-17236)*
Fast Ink Apparel ... G ... 717 328-5057
Mercersburg *(G-10986)*
Fast Time Screen Printing ... F ... 724 463-9007
Indiana *(G-8099)*
G&R Designs LLC ... G ... 717 697-4538
Mechanicsburg *(G-10848)*
Galaxy Products ... G ... 215 426-8640
Philadelphia *(G-13740)*
Gambal Printing & Design ... G ... 570 265-8968
Towanda *(G-18427)*
Gary James Designs ... G ... 814 623-2477
Bedford *(G-1052)*
Good ... G ... 717 271-2917
Stevens *(G-18051)*
Grafika Commercial Prtg Inc ... B ... 610 678-8630
Reading *(G-16396)*
Gran Enterprises ... G ... 215 634-2883
Philadelphia *(G-13780)*
Graphic Connections ... G ... 814 948-5810
Cresson *(G-3898)*
Graphic Garage ... G ... 724 274-4930
Cheswick *(G-3110)*
Greg Speece ... G ... 717 838-8365
Palmyra *(G-13125)*
Griffith Pottery House Inc ... G ... 215 887-2222
Oreland *(G-13021)*
H B Fowler Co Inc ... G ... 610 688-0567
Wayne *(G-19334)*
Head To Toe Sportswear ... G ... 814 371-5119
Du Bois *(G-4395)*
Heritage Screen Printing Inc ... G ... 215 672-2382
Warrington *(G-19120)*
Howetts Custom Screen Printing ... G ... 610 932-3697
Oxford *(G-13082)*
Huntingdon Offset Printing Co ... G ... 814 641-7310
Huntingdon *(G-7946)*
Icon Screenprinting Inc ... G ... 814 454-0086
Erie *(G-5321)*
Imprinted Promotions ... G ... 215 342-7226
Philadelphia *(G-13852)*
Imprints Unlimited ... G ... 215 879-9484
Philadelphia *(G-13853)*
In Stitches Embroidery ... G ... 570 368-5525
Montoursville *(G-11441)*
Inkster Prints ... G ... 267 886-0021
Philadelphia *(G-13857)*
Izzo Embroidery & Screen Prtg ... F ... 724 843-2334
Beaver Falls *(G-1001)*
J Carlton Jones & Associates ... G ... 267 538-5009
Philadelphia *(G-13881)*
J L Screen Printing ... G ... 724 696-5630
Ruffs Dale *(G-16873)*
Jbr Associates Inc ... G ... 215 362-1318
Lansdale *(G-9380)*
Jerome W Sinclair ... G ... 215 477-3996
Philadelphia *(G-13894)*
Lehigh Valley Printing LLC ... G ... 610 905-5686
Bethlehem *(G-1559)*
Leisure Graphics Inc ... G ... 610 692-9872
West Chester *(G-19591)*
Lem Products Inc ... E ... 800 220-2400
Montgomeryville *(G-11403)*
Lighthouse Studios Inc ... G ... 717 394-1300
Lancaster *(G-9111)*
Lime Sportswear ... F ... 484 461-7000
Secane *(G-17318)*
Logo Depot Inc ... G ... 610 543-3890
Broomall *(G-2294)*
Lycoming Screen Printing Co ... G ... 570 326-3301
Williamsport *(G-20038)*
Lykens Corporation ... F ... 814 375-9961
Du Bois *(G-4403)*
Major League Screen Prtg & EMB ... F ... 717 270-9511
Lebanon *(G-9607)*
Montco Advertising Spc Inc ... E ... 610 270-9800
Norristown *(G-12687)*
Montco Scientific Inc ... G ... 215 699-8057
Lansdale *(G-9389)*
Moonlight Graphics Studio ... G ... 570 322-6570
Williamsport *(G-20042)*
Motson Graphics Inc ... F ... 215 233-0500
Flourtown *(G-5988)*
Mountain Side Scrn Prnt/Desgn ... G ... 570 539-2400
Mount Pleasant Mills *(G-11728)*
Mystic Assembly & Dctg Co ... E ... 215 957-0280
Warminster *(G-18926)*
Mystic Screen Printing and EMB ... F ... 570 628-3520
Pottsville *(G-16089)*
Nash Printing LLC ... F ... 215 855-4267
Lansdale *(G-9391)*
Nicholas Wohlfarth ... F ... 412 373-6811
Pittsburgh *(G-15337)*
Nittany EMB & Digitizing ... F ... 814 359-0905
State College *(G-17998)*
Northeast Discount Printing ... G ... 215 742-3111
Philadelphia *(G-14081)*
Oldskool Produxions Inc ... G ... 215 638-4804
Bensalem *(G-1236)*
Parrot Graphics ... G ... 570 746-1745
New Albany *(G-12014)*
Patrick Mc Cool ... F ... 814 359-2447
Bellefonte *(G-1110)*
Pedco-Hill Inc ... F ... 215 942-5193
Warminster *(G-18938)*
Penn Print & Graphics ... G ... 724 239-5849
Bentleyville *(G-1273)*
Photo Process Screen Mfg Co ... F ... 215 426-5473
Philadelphia *(G-14172)*
Plymouth Graphics Inc ... G ... 570 779-9645
Plymouth *(G-15820)*
Premier Screen Printing Inc ... G ... 717 560-9088
Lititz *(G-10036)*
Print and Sew Inc ... G ... 215 281-3909
Philadelphia *(G-14201)*
Print Factory ... G ... 570 961-2111
Scranton *(G-17275)*
Print Shop Inc ... G ... 570 784-4020
Bloomsburg *(G-1796)*
Printfly Corporation ... E ... 800 620-1233
Philadelphia *(G-14202)*
Printmark Industries Inc ... E ... 570 501-0547
Hazleton *(G-7521)*
Promo Gear ... G ... 570 775-4078
Hawley *(G-7436)*
Pure Screenprinting Inc ... G ... 412 246-2048
Pittsburgh *(G-15457)*
R C Print Specialist ... G ... 814 942-1204
Altoona *(G-540)*

R R Donnelley & Sons Company ....G 814 266-6031
Johnstown (G-8428)

R R Donnelley & Sons Company ....E 215 564-3220
Philadelphia (G-14226)

R&S Ventures LLC ....G 610 532-2950
Prospect Park (G-16118)

Ras Sports Inc ....E 814 833-9111
Erie (G-5457)

Ravine Inc ....F 814 946-5006
Altoona (G-541)

Ream Printing Co Inc ....E 717 764-5663
York (G-20653)

Red Rose Screen Prtg Awrds Inc ....G 717 625-1581
Lititz (G-10039)

Rmb Specialtees LLC ....G 570 578-8258
Beaver Meadows (G-1017)

Robanco ....G 412 795-7444
Pittsburgh (G-15493)

Rock It Printwear ....G 717 697-3983
Mechanicsburg (G-10885)

Roo Tees Inc ....G 412 279-9889
Carnegie (G-2788)

Rush Order Tees ....G 215 677-9200
Philadelphia (G-14266)

Santees Love ....G 215 821-9679
Philadelphia (G-14280)

School Colors Inc ....G 570 561-2632
Scranton (G-17284)

Schuylkill Valley Sports Inc ....D 717 627-0417
Lititz (G-10046)

Screen Images Inc ....G 610 926-3061
Shoemakersville (G-17575)

Screenprinted Grafix Inc ....G 717 564-7464
Halifax (G-6830)

Shirt Gallery Inc ....G 215 364-1212
Feasterville Trevose (G-5929)

Sign Creators Inc ....G 412 461-3567
West Homestead (G-19720)

Silk Screen Printers ....G 717 761-1121
Camp Hill (G-2518)

Slavic Group Inc ....G 724 437-6756
Lemont Furnace (G-9737)

Specialty Group Printing Inc ....F 814 425-3061
Cochranton (G-3351)

Sportin My Stuff ....G 724 457-7005
Crescent (G-3889)

Standard Pennant Company Inc ....E 814 427-2066
Big Run (G-1657)

Sunflower Graphics ....G 412 369-7769
Pittsburgh (G-15587)

Sunsational Signs Win Tinting ....G 610 277-4344
Norristown (G-12715)

Susan Becker ....G 610 378-7844
Reading (G-16531)

SYN Apparel LLC ....G 484 821-3664
Bethlehem (G-1636)

Synergy Print Design LLC ....G 610 532-2950
Prospect Park (G-16121)

T N T Manufacturing ....G 724 745-6242
Canonsburg (G-2644)

T Shirt Loft ....G 724 452-4380
Zelienople (G-20823)

Teamwork Graphic Inc ....G 570 368-2360
Montoursville (G-11452)

Teeship LLC ....G 717 497-2970
Hummelstown (G-7926)

Tex Styles LLC ....G 610 562-4939
Shoemakersville (G-17576)

Tex Visions LLC ....D 717 240-0213
Carlisle (G-2741)

Thomas A Laskowski ....F 215 957-1544
Warminster (G-18981)

Timber Skate Shop ....G 570 492-6063
Sunbury (G-18175)

TN TS ....G 717 248-2278
Lewistown (G-9949)

Tom Russell ....G 724 746-5029
Houston (G-7882)

Tookan Screening & Design Inc ....G 724 846-2264
Beaver Falls (G-1015)

Trautman Associates Inc ....F 570 743-0430
Shamokin Dam (G-17429)

Upper Perk Sportswear Inc ....G 215 541-3211
Pennsburg (G-13261)

Upper Room Inc ....F 724 437-5815
Uniontown (G-18646)

Urban Tees Inc DBA Soho G ....G 646 295-8923
Philadelphia (G-14432)

Vertees ....G 570 630-0678
Hawley (G-7441)

Victory Athletics ....G 814 886-4866
Cresson (G-3900)

Weaver Screen Printing Inc ....G 717 632-9158
Hanover (G-6972)

Williamsigns ....G 610 530-0300
Allentown (G-435)

X-Deco LLC ....F 412 257-9755
Pittsburgh (G-15725)

PRINTING, COMMERCIAL: Stationery, NEC

Novelli Inc ....F 215 739-3538
Philadelphia (G-14088)

PRINTING, COMMERCIAL: Tickets, NEC

Paramount Games Inc ....D 800 282-5766
Wheatland (G-19840)

PRINTING, LITHOGRAPHIC: Advertising Posters

Pecks Graphics LLC ....G 717 963-7588
Harrisburg (G-7191)

PRINTING, LITHOGRAPHIC: Billheads

Dynamic Printing Inc ....G 215 793-9453
Ambler (G-577)

PRINTING, LITHOGRAPHIC: Calendars

Homer Reproductions Inc ....F 610 539-8400
Norristown (G-12667)

PRINTING, LITHOGRAPHIC: Catalogs

Catalogs By Design ....E 610 337-9133
King of Prussia (G-8591)

PRINTING, LITHOGRAPHIC: Circulars

Great American Printer Inc ....G 570 752-7341
Berwick (G-1326)

PRINTING, LITHOGRAPHIC: Color

Butler Color Press Inc ....C 724 283-9132
Butler (G-2385)

Dynamic Systems ....F 412 835-6100
Library (G-9954)

HI-Tech Color Inc ....F 724 463-8522
Indiana (G-8104)

Jka Inc ....F 412 741-9288
Sewickley (G-17397)

Services Unlimited Mstr Prtg ....G 610 891-7877
Media (G-10949)

York Newspaper Company ....B 717 767-6397
York (G-20746)

PRINTING, LITHOGRAPHIC: Coupons

Northern Hardwoods Inc ....G 814 274-8060
Coudersport (G-3786)

PRINTING, LITHOGRAPHIC: Decals

Promark Industries Inc ....G 724 356-4060
Mc Donald (G-10579)

Reidler Decal Corporation ....E 800 628-7770
Saint Clair (G-16939)

Uticom Systems Inc ....E 610 857-2655
Coatesville (G-3328)

PRINTING, LITHOGRAPHIC: Fashion Plates

N H Morgan Inc ....G 412 561-1046
Pittsburgh (G-15314)

PRINTING, LITHOGRAPHIC: Forms & Cards, Business

Conant Corporation ....F 215 557-7466
Philadelphia (G-13569)

Consolidated Printing Inc ....E 215 879-1400
Philadelphia (G-13571)

Dispatch Printing Inc ....F 814 870-9600
Erie (G-5248)

Webb-Mason Inc ....E 724 935-1770
Wexford (G-19833)

PRINTING, LITHOGRAPHIC: Forms, Business

Campbell Business Forms Inc ....G 610 356-0626
Newtown Square (G-12568)

D & A Associates ....G 610 534-4840
Darby (G-4017)

D & H Inc ....G 800 340-1001
Harrisburg (G-7112)

Dennis Albertson LLC ....G 570 784-1677
Bloomsburg (G-1778)

Steffy Printing Inc ....G 717 859-5040
Brownstown (G-2309)

Tsi Associates Inc ....F 610 375-4371
Reading (G-16551)

PRINTING, LITHOGRAPHIC: Letters, Circular Or Form

Huston National Printing Co ....G 412 431-5335
Pittsburgh (G-15106)

Snellbaker Printing Inc ....G 215 885-0674
Glenside (G-6536)

PRINTING, LITHOGRAPHIC: Offset & photolithographic printing

Jem Graphics LLC ....G 412 220-0290
Bridgeville (G-2074)

Oberthur Card Systems Inc ....B 610 280-2707
Exton (G-5717)

Ridgways Inc ....E 215 735-8055
Philadelphia (G-14250)

Triune Color Corporation ....D 856 829-5600
Huntingdon Valley (G-8045)

PRINTING, LITHOGRAPHIC: On Metal

Acorn Company ....F 215 743-6100
Philadelphia (G-13342)

Andrew H Lawson Co ....G 215 235-1609
Philadelphia (G-13391)

Banes and Mayer Inc ....G 215 641-1750
Blue Bell (G-1814)

Campus Copy Center ....F 215 386-6410
Philadelphia (G-13496)

Dixon-Saunders Enterprises ....G 215 335-2150
Lafayette Hill (G-8878)

Gary Murelle ....G 570 888-7006
Sayre (G-17114)

Goodway Graphics Inc ....B 215 887-5700
Jenkintown (G-8288)

Joseph Lagrua ....G 814 274-7163
Coudersport (G-3783)

Leon Spangler ....F 570 837-7903
Middleburg (G-11028)

Valley Instant Printing ....G 610 439-4122
Orefield (G-13016)

PRINTING, LITHOGRAPHIC: Post Cards, Picture

Morlatton Post Card Club ....E 717 263-1638
Chambersburg (G-2961)

PRINTING, LITHOGRAPHIC: Posters & Decals

Cerra Signs Inc ....G 570 282-6283
Carbondale (G-2670)

White Castle Services LLC ....G 484 560-5961
New Tripoli (G-12463)

PRINTING, LITHOGRAPHIC: Promotional

Badzik Printing Service Inc ....G 724 379-4299
Donora (G-4146)

Kurtz Bros ....D 814 765-6561
Clearfield (G-3222)

National Center For Def ....E 724 539-8811
Blairsville (G-1735)

PRINTING, LITHOGRAPHIC: Publications

York Newspapers Inc ....D 717 767-6397
York (G-20747)

PRINTING, LITHOGRAPHIC: Tickets

Globe Data Systems Inc ....D 215 443-7960
Warminster (G-18889)

National Ticket Company ....C 570 672-2900
Paxinos (G-13190)
Pap Technologies Inc ....E 717 399-3333
Lancaster (G-9160)
Seneca Enterprises Inc ....G 814 432-7890
Franklin (G-6156)

PRINTING, LITHOGRAPHIC: Transfers, Decalcomania Or Dry

Mdg Associates ....E 215 969-6623
Philadelphia (G-14000)
Universal Transfers Inc ....E 215 744-6227
Philadelphia (G-14427)

PRINTING: Books

Community Resource Svcs Inc ....G 717 338-9100
Gettysburg (G-6286)
Kappa Graphics L P ....F 215 542-2800
Blue Bell (G-1840)
Murrelle Printing Co Inc ....F 570 888-2244
Sayre (G-17119)
Triangle Press Inc ....E 717 541-9315
Harrisburg (G-7238)

PRINTING: Books

Armstrong Supply Co ....G 215 643-0310
Ambler (G-567)
Beidel Printing House Inc ....E 717 532-5063
Shippensburg (G-17516)
Corporate Print Solutions Inc ....G 215 774-1119
Glenolden (G-6472)
P A Hutchison Company ....C 570 876-4560
Mayfield (G-10542)

PRINTING: Checkbooks

Deluxe Corporation ....C 215 631-7500
Lansdale (G-9359)

PRINTING: Commercial, NEC

69th St Commercial Printers ....G 610 539-8412
Norristown (G-12627)
A Funky Little Sign Shop ....G 215 489-2880
Doylestown (G-4266)
A J Printing ....F 610 337-7468
King of Prussia (G-8575)
Acro Labels Inc ....E 215 657-5366
Willow Grove (G-20105)
Ad-Rax Productions LLC ....G 610 264-8405
Catasauqua (G-2812)
ADM Publications Inc ....G 610 565-8895
Media (G-10914)
Advance Central Services PA ....G 717 255-8400
Mechanicsburg (G-10816)
Alpha Advertising & Mktg LLC ....G 717 445-4200
Bowmansville (G-1886)
Alpha Printing ....G 814 536-8721
Johnstown (G-8352)
Altris Incorporated ....G 724 259-8338
Greensburg (G-6649)
Altus Group Inc ....F 215 977-9900
Philadelphia (G-13374)
American Additive Mfg LLC ....F 215 559-1200
Horsham (G-7782)
American Brchure Catalogue Inc ....G 215 259-1600
Warminster (G-18827)
American Calendar Inc ....F 215 743-3834
Philadelphia (G-13382)
Anstadt Printing Corporation ....E 717 767-6891
York (G-20378)
Apple Press Ltd ....E 610 363-1776
Exton (G-5644)
Argus Printing & Copy ....G 610 687-0411
Wayne (G-19302)
Ask IV Screen Printing ....G 412 200-5610
Imperial (G-8058)
Associated Prtg Graphics Svcs ....G 215 322-6762
Feasterville Trevose (G-5887)
Bonnie Kaiser ....G 215 331-6555
Philadelphia (G-13471)
Bradco Printers Inc ....G 570 297-3024
Troy (G-18517)
Cannon Graphics Inc ....G 215 676-5114
Philadelphia (G-13497)
Castor Printing Company Inc ....F 215 535-1471
Philadelphia (G-13512)
Champ Printing Company Inc ....E 412 269-0197
Coraopolis (G-3675)

Christmas City Printing Co Inc ....E 610 868-5844
Bethlehem (G-1483)
CMI Printgraphix Inc ....G 717 697-4567
Mechanicsburg (G-10827)
Cobb & Dabaldo Printing Co ....G 724 942-0544
Canonsburg (G-2563)
Comporto LLC ....G 215 595-6224
Philadelphia (G-13564)
Constantia Colmar LLC ....D 215 997-6222
Colmar (G-3411)
Copy Corner Inc ....G 570 992-4769
Saylorsburg (G-17104)
Copy Stop Inc ....G 412 271-4444
Swissvale (G-18191)
Cornerstone Printing Services ....G 717 626-7895
Lititz (G-10003)
Corporate Print Solutions Inc ....G 215 774-1119
Glenolden (G-6472)
D & Sr Inc ....D 717 569-3264
Lancaster (G-8989)
Daisy Mae Prtg & Design LLC ....G 610 467-1989
Oxford (G-13077)
David Bream ....E 717 334-1513
Gettysburg (G-6288)
Diamond Graphics Inc ....E 610 269-7335
Downingtown (G-4223)
Digital Color Graphics Inc ....E 215 942-7500
Southampton (G-17808)
Digital Direct Tm Inc ....G 215 491-1725
Warrington (G-19114)
Dilullo Graphics Inc ....E 610 775-4360
Mohnton (G-11262)
Direct Mail Service Inc ....D 412 471-6300
Pittsburgh (G-14925)
Dispatch Printing Inc ....F 814 870-9600
Erie (G-5248)
Dynamic Systems ....F 412 835-6100
Library (G-9954)
Electronic Imaging Svcs Inc ....G 215 785-2284
Bristol (G-2139)
Emerald Printing & Imaging ....G 814 899-6959
Erie (G-5258)
Emp Sales Associates Inc ....E 412 731-9899
Pittsburgh (G-14972)
Express Business Center Inc ....G 610 366-1970
Allentown (G-209)
Fedex Office & Print Svcs Inc ....E 215 576-1687
Jenkintown (G-8287)
Fedex Office & Print Svcs Inc ....F 412 788-0552
Pittsburgh (G-15009)
Fedex Office & Print Svcs Inc ....F 412 366-9750
Pittsburgh (G-15011)
Filmet Color Lab Inc ....D 724 275-1700
Cheswick (G-3108)
First Class Specialties ....F 724 446-1000
Herminie (G-7570)
Frontline Graphics Inc ....G 610 941-2750
Conshohocken (G-3550)
Gary Murelle ....G 570 888-7006
Sayre (G-17114)
Gate 7 LLC ....F 717 593-0204
Greencastle (G-6614)
General Press Corporation ....E 724 224-3500
Natrona Heights (G-11943)
Grandshare LLC ....G 919 308-5115
Philadelphia (G-13781)
Graphic Products Inc ....G 724 935-6600
Warrendale (G-19079)
Graphic Search Associates ....G 610 344-0644
Glen Mills (G-6438)
Harmony Labels Inc ....G 570 664-6700
East Stroudsburg (G-4616)
Harte Hanks Inc ....C 570 826-0414
Hanover Township (G-6989)
Hds Marketing Inc ....E 412 279-1600
Pittsburgh (G-15084)
Heatha Henrys LLC ....G 215 968-2080
Newtown (G-12509)
Heritage Screen Printing Inc ....G 215 672-2382
Warminster (G-18894)
Hesford Keystone Printing Co ....G 814 942-2911
Altoona (G-513)
High Printing & Graphics Inc ....G 610 693-5399
Robesonia (G-16776)
Himalayan Intl Ins of Yoga Ins ....G 570 634-5168
Honesdale (G-7716)
Holly Label Company Inc ....E 570 222-9000
Nicholson (G-12615)
Homer Reproductions Inc ....F 610 539-8400
Norristown (G-12667)

Hullihens Printery ....G 570 288-6804
Wilkes Barre (G-19925)
ID Technology LLC ....E 717 848-3875
York (G-20533)
Impressions Printing & Pubg ....G 717 436-2034
Mifflintown (G-11123)
Industrial Nameplate Inc ....E 215 322-1111
Warminster (G-18898)
Instant Print ....G 724 261-5153
Greensburg (G-6677)
Integra Graphix Inc ....E 717 626-7895
Lititz (G-10019)
Interform Corporation ....C 412 221-7321
Bridgeville (G-2070)
J B Kreider Co Inc ....F 412 246-0343
Pittsburgh (G-15140)
J Davis Printing LLC ....G 215 483-1006
Philadelphia (G-13882)
Jankensteph Inc ....G 412 446-2777
Bridgeville (G-2073)
Jayco Grafix Inc ....D 610 678-2640
Reinholds (G-16633)
Jerry James Trdng As Mnls BSC ....G 425 255-0199
Lafayette Hill (G-8882)
John Schmidt Printing Co ....E 215 624-2945
Philadelphia (G-13905)
Joseph Lagrua ....G 814 274-7163
Coudersport (G-3783)
Kalil Printing Inc ....E 610 948-9330
Royersford (G-16854)
Karen Holbrook ....G 724 628-3858
Connellsville (G-3500)
Kemko Industries Inc ....G 267 613-8651
Upper Gwynedd (G-18695)
Keystone Expressions Ltd ....E 570 648-5785
Coal Township (G-3279)
Keystone Printed Spc Co LLC ....C 570 457-8334
Old Forge (G-12967)
Kim Kraft Inc ....F 814 870-9600
Fairview (G-5830)
Kimkopy Printing Inc ....G 814 454-6635
Erie (G-5343)
Kisel Printing Service Inc ....E 570 489-7666
Dickson City (G-4121)
Labels By Pulizzi Inc ....E 570 326-1244
Williamsport (G-20034)
Lemac Packaging Inc ....E 814 866-7469
Erie (G-5362)
Lemar Mast ....G 610 286-0258
Morgantown (G-11524)
Lowlander Corporation ....G 412 221-1240
Monaca (G-11291)
Lsc Communications Us LLC ....A 717 392-4074
Lancaster (G-9116)
Luposello Enterprises ....F 570 994-2500
Milford (G-11162)
Marcus Uppe Inc ....G 412 391-1218
Pittsburgh (G-15254)
Marquee Graphx LLC ....G 215 538-2992
Quakertown (G-16212)
Martin Design Group LLC ....G 717 633-9214
Hanover (G-6917)
Mary J Backaroo ....E 570 819-4809
Wilkes Barre (G-19941)
Mbr2 Graphic Services LLC ....G 610 490-8996
Norristown (G-12680)
McCarty Printing Corp ....D 814 454-4561
Erie (G-5385)
McCourt Label Cabinet Company ....D 800 458-2390
Lewis Run (G-9877)
Medianews Group Inc ....C 717 637-3736
Hanover (G-6919)
Memory Makers Ltd ....E 215 679-3636
Pennsburg (G-13250)
Menu World Inc ....G 267 784-8515
Willow Grove (G-20127)
Merrill Corporation ....F 215 405-8443
Philadelphia (G-14010)
Mifflinburg Telegraph Inc ....G 570 966-2255
Mifflinburg (G-11099)
Miller Process Coatingmiller ....G 724 274-5880
Pittsburgh (G-15289)
Modern Reproductions Inc ....F 412 488-7700
Pittsburgh (G-15298)
Morris Print Management ....G 610 408-8922
Berwyn (G-1369)
Movad LLC ....F 215 638-2679
Plymouth Meeting (G-15858)
Mri Flexible Packaging Company ....E 800 448-8183
Bristol (G-2170)

P
R
O
D
U
C
T

Multiscope Dcment Slutions Inc............E 724 743-1083
Bridgeville (G-2080)
National Imprint Corporation.............E 814 239-5116
Claysburg (G-3206)
National Ticket Company ....C 570 672-2900
Paxinos (G-13190)
Nefra Communication Center ....E 717 509-1430
Lancaster (G-9144)
Newtown Printing Corp ....G 215 968-6876
Newtown (G-12528)
Nittany Printing and Pubg Co ....D 814 238-5000
State College (G-18000)
Nk Graphics Inc..............................G 717 838-8324
Palmyra (G-13127)
NMB Signs Inc.................................F 412 344-5700
Pittsburgh (G-15342)
Npc Inc...B 814 239-8787
Claysburg (G-3207)
Omnipress Inc.................................G 610 631-2171
Norristown (G-12698)
On Demand Printing ....G 610 696-2258
West Chester (G-19610)
Parc Productions ....G 724 283-3300
Butler (G-2431)
Park Press Inc ....G 724 465-5812
Indiana (G-8116)
PDQ Print Center.............................G 570 283-0995
Kingston (G-8724)
PDQ Printing Services ....G 717 691-4777
Mechanicsburg (G-10878)
Pemcor Printing Company LLC ....D 717 898-1555
Lancaster (G-9162)
Penn Graphics Equipment Inc...........E 610 488-7414
Hamburg (G-6848)
Penn Jersey Advance Inc..................B 610 258-7171
Easton (G-4742)
Perkiomen Valley Printing Inc...........G 215 679-4000
East Greenville (G-4573)
Phila Legnds of Jazz Orchestra..........F 215 763-2819
Philadelphia (G-14140)
Phoenix Printers Inc ....G 610 427-3069
Phoenixville (G-14569)
Pittsburgh Prtg Solutions LLC ....G 412 977-2026
Pittsburgh (G-15406)
Preferred Sportswear Inc ....G 484 494-3067
Darby (G-4024)
Premier Graphics LLC ....F 814 894-2467
Sykesville (G-18202)
Premier Printing Services Inc ....G 724 588-5577
Greenville (G-6767)
Press Box Printing ....G 814 944-3057
Altoona (G-538)
Print Tech Western PA ....F 412 963-1500
Pittsburgh (G-15441)
Print Works On Demand Inc ....G 717 545-5215
Harrisburg (G-7202)
Prints & More By Holly ....G 814 453-5548
Erie (G-5438)
Printworx Inc ....G 412 939-6004
Pittsburgh (G-15446)
Prism Graphics Inc ....G 215 782-1600
Elkins Park (G-4910)
Pro Printing & Office LLC...................G 814 834-3006
Saint Marys (G-17010)
Professional Graphic Co ....E 724 318-8530
Sewickley (G-17405)
Promote ME Printing ....G 412 486-2504
Pittsburgh (G-15454)
Prosit LLC.......................................G 610 430-1470
West Chester (G-19622)
Quality Brand Printing Inc.................G 724 864-1731
Irwin (G-8194)
Quick Print Center PA.......................G 717 637-2838
Hanover (G-6939)
R Graphics Inc.................................G 610 918-0373
West Chester (G-19625)
R R Donnelley & Sons Company ....G 610 688-9090
Wayne (G-19367)
R R Donnelley & Sons Company ....A 717 295-4002
Lancaster (G-9183)
R R Donnelley & Sons Company ....C 610 391-0203
Breinigsville (G-2026)
R R Donnelley & Sons Company ....C 215 671-9500
Philadelphia (G-14225)
Rainbow Graphics Inc ....G 724 228-3007
Bentleyville (G-1275)
RB Concepts LLC.............................G 484 351-8211
Conshohocken (G-3598)
Reed & Witting Company ....E 412 682-1000
Pittsburgh (G-15476)

Ricks Quick Printing Inc....................E 412 571-0333
Pittsburgh (G-15485)
Ridgways Inc...................................E 215 735-8055
Philadelphia (G-14250)
Riggans Advg Specialty Co ....F 724 654-5741
New Castle (G-12143)
RR Donnelley & Sons Company...........C 412 241-8200
Pittsburgh (G-15500)
Scream Graphix Inc..........................G 215 638-3900
Philadelphia (G-14288)
Serigraph Factory ....G 570 647-0644
Honesdale (G-7723)
Serve Inc...G 570 265-3119
Monroeton (G-11320)
Services Unlimited Mstr Prtg ....G 610 891-7877
Media (G-10949)
Skylon Inc..F 814 489-3622
Sugar Grove (G-18147)
Slavia Printing Co Inc.......................G 412 343-4444
Pittsburgh (G-15545)
Smith Prints Inc...............................G 215 997-8077
Chalfont (G-2888)
Snyder Printing & Promotional...........G 215 358-3178
Ambler (G-602)
Sports Factory Promotions Inc ....G 724 847-2684
New Brighton (G-12042)
Steele Print Inc................................G 724 758-6178
Ellwood City (G-4952)
Straz ....G 570 344-1513
Scranton (G-17294)
Taylor Communications Inc ....G 412 594-2800
Pittsburgh (G-15599)
Taylor Communications Inc ....D 717 755-1051
York (G-20684)
Technosystems Service Corp ....F 412 288-2525
Pittsburgh (G-15602)
Tokarick Printing Services ....F 570 385-4639
Schuylkill Haven (G-17168)
Tri-State Reprographics Inc ....F 412 281-3538
Pittsburgh (G-15647)
Triangle Poster and Prtg Co...............F 412 371-0774
Pittsburgh (G-15648)
Triple Play Sports.............................F 215 923-5466
Philadelphia (G-14412)
Two Letters Ink ....E 717 393-8989
Lancaster (G-9225)
Typecraft Press Inc ....E 412 488-1600
Pittsburgh (G-15663)
United Envelope LLC ....B 570 839-1600
Mount Pocono (G-11738)
UPS Store 6410 ....G 484 816-0252
Aston (G-795)
Urban Enterprises T & M LLC ....G 215 485-5209
Feasterville Trevose (G-5936)
Uticom Systems Inc..........................E 610 857-2655
Coatesville (G-3328)
Vernon Printing Inc...........................F 724 283-9242
Butler (G-2447)
Vintage Color Graphics Inc ....G 215 646-6589
Ambler (G-604)
Visual Resources LLC ....G 484 351-8100
Conshohocken (G-3616)
Vocam Corp ....G 215 348-7115
Doylestown (G-4344)
Wakefoose Office Supply & Prtg ....G 814 623-5742
Bedford (G-1079)
Werzalit of America Inc.....................D 814 362-3881
Bradford (G-1995)
Wick Copy Center ....G 814 942-8040
Altoona (G-558)
Wise Business Forms Inc ....D 724 789-0010
Butler (G-2449)
World Chronicle Inc ....G 724 745-3808
Mc Donald (G-10584)
Wright Appellate Services LLC ....G 215 733-9870
Philadelphia (G-14490)
York Graphic Services Co ....C 717 505-9701
York (G-20738)
Yurchak Printing Inc ....E 717 399-0209
Landisville (G-9269)

PRINTING: Engraving & Plate

Van Eerden Coatings Company............G 484 368-3073
Plymouth Meeting (G-15877)

PRINTING: Flexographic

Butts Ticket Company Inc...................F 610 869-7450
Cochranville (G-3355)
C P Converters Inc ....D 717 764-1193
York (G-20415)

Interstate Cont New Castle LLC ....E 724 657-3650
New Castle (G-12106)
Prime Packaging LLC ....D 215 499-0446
Yardley (G-20333)
Superpac Inc ....C 215 322-1010
Southampton (G-17838)

PRINTING: Gravure, Business Form & Card

Chelsea Partners Inc ....E 215 603-7300
Philadelphia (G-13537)
Dynamic Business Systems ....G 800 782-2946
South Park (G-17782)
Kustom Cards International ....G 215 233-1678
Glenside (G-6525)
Samson Paper Co Inc........................E 610 630-9090
Norristown (G-12708)

PRINTING: Gravure, Calendar & Card, Exc Business

Kim Kraft Inc....................................F 814 870-9600
Fairview (G-5830)

PRINTING: Gravure, Certificates, Security

Nocopi Technologies Inc....................G 610 834-9600
King of Prussia (G-8657)

PRINTING: Gravure, Coupons

Clipper Magazine LLC ....B 717 569-5100
Mountville (G-11791)

PRINTING: Gravure, Envelopes

Dupli Graphics Corporation................E 610 644-4188
Malvern (G-10225)

PRINTING: Gravure, Forms, Business

Magagna Associates Inc ....F 610 213-2335
Souderton (G-17751)

PRINTING: Gravure, Invitations

Paravano Company Inc ....G 215 659-4600
Willow Grove (G-20132)

PRINTING: Gravure, Labels

Alpine Packaging Inc.........................E 412 664-4000
North Versailles (G-12771)
Jon Swan Inc....................................E 412 264-9000
Coraopolis (G-3700)
Keystone Converting Inc....................F 215 661-9004
Montgomeryville (G-11400)

PRINTING: Gravure, Promotional

Griffith Pottery House Inc ....G 215 887-2222
Oreland (G-13021)

PRINTING: Gravure, Publications

Ygs Group Inc ....D 717 505-9701
York (G-20723)

PRINTING: Gravure, Rotogravure

Allimage Graphics LLC ....G 814 728-8650
Warren (G-19009)
Alm Media LLC.................................E 215 557-2300
Philadelphia (G-13370)
Chroma Graphics...............................G 724 693-9050
Oakdale (G-12896)
Colorworks Graphic Svcs Inc ....E 610 367-7599
Gilbertsville (G-6371)
Innovtive Print Mdia Group Inc............D 610 489-4800
Phoenixville (G-14553)
Qg LLC...C 414 208-2700
Atglen (G-803)
Quad/Graphics Inc ....B 215 541-2729
Pennsburg (G-13253)
R R Donnelley & Sons Company..........D 610 391-3900
Breinigsville (G-2025)
Ygs Group Inc ....G 425 251-5005
York (G-20724)

PRINTING: Gravure, Seals

Westrock Packaging Inc.....................D 215 785-3350
Croydon (G-3933)

PRINTING: Laser

Concepts ....G...... 717 600-2964
  York (G-20432)
Great Northern Press of Wilkes ....E...... 570 822-3147
  Wilkes Barre (G-19922)
Laser Imaging Systems Inc ....E...... 717 266-1700
  Lancaster (G-9108)
Mercersburg Printing Inc ....E...... 717 328-3902
  Mercersburg (G-10993)
Quality Laser Alternatives ....G...... 610 373-0788
  Reading (G-16480)
Spring Hill Laser Services ....E...... 570 689-0970
  Lake Ariel (G-8892)

PRINTING: Letterpress

Action Printing and Bus Forms ......F...... 814 453-5977
  Erie (G-5173)
Argus Printing ....G...... 610 687-0411
  Wayne (G-19301)
Auskin Inc ....G...... 610 696-0234
  West Chester (G-19503)
Berks-Mont Newspapers Inc ....F...... 610 683-7343
  Pottstown (G-15966)
Birds Printing ....G...... 570 784-8136
  Bloomsburg (G-1774)
Brindle Printing Co Inc ....G...... 724 658-8549
  New Castle (G-12067)
Buhl Bros Printing Inc ....F...... 724 335-0970
  Creighton (G-3880)
Charles A Henderson Prtg Svc ....G...... 724 775-2623
  Rochester (G-16783)
Citizen Publishing Company ....G...... 570 454-5911
  Hazleton (G-7495)
Conrad Printing Co Inc ....G...... 717 637-5414
  Hanover (G-6870)
Creative Printing Co ....G...... 570 875-1811
  Ashland (G-729)
Creighton Printing Inc ....G...... 724 224-0444
  Creighton (G-3882)
Gillespie Printing Inc ....F...... 610 264-1863
  Allentown (G-232)
Globe Print Shop ....G...... 570 454-8031
  Hazleton (G-7499)
Griffiths Printing Co. ....F...... 610 623-3822
  Lansdowne (G-9433)
Guyasuta Printing Co ....G...... 412 782-0112
  Pittsburgh (G-15068)
Haines Printing Co ....G...... 814 725-1955
  North East (G-12746)
Houck Printing Company Inc ....F...... 717 233-5205
  Harrisburg (G-7152)
Ink Spot Printing ....G...... 570 743-7979
  Selinsgrove (G-17327)
J D Printing Inc ....G...... 724 327-0006
  Pittsburgh (G-15141)
Joseph H Tees & Son Inc ....G...... 215 638-3368
  Bensalem (G-1214)
Keystone Prtg & Graphics Inc ....G...... 570 648-5785
  Coal Township (G-3280)
Killeen Printing Co ....G...... 412 381-4090
  Pittsburgh (G-15177)
Kistler Printing Co Inc ....F...... 570 421-2050
  East Stroudsburg (G-4622)
Labelcraft Press Inc ....G...... 215 257-6368
  Perkasie (G-13282)
Levittown Printing Inc ....G...... 215 945-8156
  Levittown (G-9845)
Liberty Craftsmen Inc ....G...... 717 871-0125
  Millersville (G-11211)
Marlin A Inch ....G...... 570 374-1106
  Selinsgrove (G-17330)
Mercersburg Printing Inc ....G...... 717 762-8204
  Waynesboro (G-19418)
Mifflin Press Inc ....G...... 717 684-2253
  Columbia (G-3443)
Milan Printing ....G...... 570 325-2649
  Jim Thorpe (G-8342)
Miller Printing Inc ....G...... 717 626-5800
  Ephrata (G-5128)
Munro Prtg Graphic Design LLC ....G...... 610 485-1966
  Marcus Hook (G-10451)
Okumus Enterprises Ltd ....E...... 215 295-3340
  Fairless Hills (G-5790)
Olenicks Prtg & Photography Sp ......G...... 814 342-2853
  Philipsburg (G-14522)
Paravano Company Inc ....G...... 215 659-4600
  Willow Grove (G-20132)
Parkland Bindery Inc ....G...... 610 433-6153
  Allentown (G-344)

Payne Printery Inc ....D...... 570 675-1147
  Dallas (G-3965)
Penn Valley Printing Company ....G...... 215 295-5755
  Morrisville (G-11576)
Press Craft Printers Inc ....G...... 412 761-8200
  Pittsburgh (G-15434)
Prince Printing ....G...... 412 233-3555
  Clairton (G-3156)
Quality Print Shop Inc ....G...... 570 473-1122
  Northumberland (G-12874)
Randall A Reese ....G...... 570 748-6528
  Lock Haven (G-10091)
Riecks Letter Service Inc ....F...... 610 375-8581
  Reading (G-16498)
Rowe Printing Shop ....F...... 717 249-5485
  Carlisle (G-2737)
Royalton Press Inc ....G...... 610 929-4040
  Camp Hill (G-2516)
Sandt Printing Co Inc ....G...... 610 258-7445
  Easton (G-4751)
Schank Printing Inc ....F...... 610 828-1623
  Conshohocken (G-3603)
Seiders Printing Co Inc ....G...... 570 622-0570
  Pottsville (G-16097)
Smales Printery Inc ....G...... 610 323-7775
  Pottstown (G-16047)
Star Printing Company ....G...... 717 456-5692
  Delta (G-4063)
Sun Litho Print Inc ....F...... 570 421-3250
  East Stroudsburg (G-4636)
Tor Industries Inc ....G...... 570 622-7370
  Pottsville (G-16099)
Valley Litho Inc ....G...... 610 437-5122
  Whitehall (G-19892)
Valley Printing and Design Co ....G...... 814 536-5990
  Johnstown (G-8442)
W L Fegley & Son Inc ....G...... 610 779-0277
  Reading (G-16561)
Williams Business Forms Ltd ....F...... 724 444-6771
  Gibsonia (G-6359)
Wise Printing Co Inc ....G...... 717 741-2751
  York (G-20715)

PRINTING: Lithographic

21st Century Media Newsppr LLC .....E...... 814 238-3071
  State College (G-17939)
21st N College ....G...... 814 502-1542
  Martinsburg (G-10518)
3d Printing Service LLC ....G...... 215 426-1510
  Philadelphia (G-13317)
A J Printing ....F...... 610 337-7468
  King of Prussia (G-8575)
A Stuart Morton Inc ....F...... 610 692-1190
  West Chester (G-19492)
Abboud Samar ....G...... 412 343-6899
  Pittsburgh (G-14634)
Action Screen Printing Inc ....F...... 610 359-1777
  Broomall (G-2277)
Allegheny Plastics Inc ....D...... 724 776-0100
  Cranberry Township (G-3800)
American Bank Note Holographic ......E...... 215 357-5300
  Huntingdon Valley (G-7963)
American Bank Printers ....G...... 412 566-6737
  Pittsburgh (G-14700)
American Calendar Inc ....F...... 215 743-3834
  Philadelphia (G-13491)
American Printing Group Inc ....G...... 215 442-0500
  Horsham (G-7783)
Arch Parent Inc ....A...... 570 534-6026
  Stroudsburg (G-18104)
Atlantic Prtg Grphic Cmmnctons ......G...... 610 584-2060
  Schwenksville (G-17173)
Awesome Dudes Printingg LLC ....G...... 267 886-8492
  Philadelphia (G-13429)
Bai Printing ....G...... 412 400-5555
  Pittsburgh (G-14749)
Bedford Gazette LLC ....E...... 814 623-1151
  Bedford (G-1042)
Bela Printing & Packaging Corp ....G...... 215 664-7090
  Lansdale (G-9344)
Benkalu Group Lmtd Ta Jaguar ....G...... 215 646-5896
  Huntingdon Valley (G-7965)
Bentley Grphic Cmmncations Inc ......E...... 610 933-7400
  Phoenixville (G-14531)
Bill Straley Printing ....G...... 717 328-5404
  Lemasters (G-9731)
Blatts Printing Co ....G...... 610 926-2289
  Mohrsville (G-11274)
Blue Dog Printing & Design ....G...... 610 430-7992
  West Chester (G-19511)

Boltz Printing Company LLC ....G...... 724 772-4911
  Cranberry Township (G-3809)
Bonnie Kaiser ....G...... 215 331-6555
  Philadelphia (G-13471)
Brilliant Inc ....G...... 215 271-5041
  Philadelphia (G-13482)
Brodart Co ....D...... 570 326-2461
  Williamsport (G-19995)
Buck County Print ....G...... 215 741-3250
  Langhorne (G-9283)
Call Newspapers Inc ....F...... 570 385-3120
  Schuylkill Haven (G-17150)
Cameron County Echo Inc ....G...... 814 486-3711
  Emporium (G-5053)
Card Prsnlzation Solutions LLC ....D...... 610 231-1860
  Allentown (G-161)
Carol Fanelli ....G...... 717 945-7418
  Lancaster (G-8971)
Chambersburg Screen Print EMB ......G...... 717 262-2111
  Chambersburg (G-2918)
Child Evngelism Fellowship Inc ....E...... 215 837-6324
  Philadelphia (G-13541)
Child Evngelism Fellowship Inc ....E...... 724 463-1600
  Somerset (G-17679)
Child Evngelism Fellowship Inc ....E...... 724 339-4825
  Apollo (G-669)
Chrisber Corporation ....E...... 800 872-7436
  West Chester (G-19525)
Chroma Graphics ....G...... 724 693-9050
  Oakdale (G-12896)
Clarion Printing - Litho ....G...... 814 226-9453
  Clarion (G-3173)
Colonial Press LLC ....G...... 814 466-3380
  Boalsburg (G-1865)
Color House Company Ltd ....F...... 215 322-4310
  Warminster (G-18845)
Colorworks Graphic Svcs Inc ....E...... 610 367-7599
  Gilbertsville (G-6371)
Con-Wald Corp ....E...... 215 879-1400
  Philadelphia (G-13568)
Conestoga Dpi LLC ....G...... 717 665-0298
  Manheim (G-10378)
Corcoran Printing Inc ....F...... 570 822-1991
  Wilkes Barre (G-19914)
Corporate Graphics Inc ....G...... 570 424-0475
  East Stroudsburg (G-4612)
Courtside Document Svcs Inc ....G...... 570 969-2991
  Scranton (G-17220)
D L Dravis & Associates Inc ....G...... 814 943-6155
  Altoona (G-496)
D L Dravis & Associates Inc ....G...... 814 944-5880
  Altoona (G-497)
Democratic Print Shop ....E...... 717 787-3307
  Harrisburg (G-7118)
Digital Color Graphics Inc ....E...... 215 942-7500
  Southampton (G-17808)
Digital-Ink Inc ....D...... 717 731-8890
  Dillsburg (G-4126)
Direct Mail Service & Press ....F...... 610 432-4538
  Allentown (G-194)
Direct Mail Service Inc ....D...... 412 471-6300
  Pittsburgh (G-14925)
Djf Print Xpress ....G...... 215 964-1258
  Levittown (G-9833)
Dla Document Services ....F...... 717 605-3777
  Mechanicsburg (G-10837)
Drexel Bindery Inc ....F...... 215 232-3808
  Philadelphia (G-13645)
Eagle Graphics Inc ....D...... 717 867-5576
  Annville (G-647)
Eagle Printery Inc ....F...... 724 287-0754
  Butler (G-2397)
Eagle Printing Company ....D...... 724 282-8000
  Butler (G-2398)
Edwin Ringer ....G...... 724 746-3374
  Westland (G-19782)
Evolution Printing Systems ....G...... 814 724-5831
  Meadville (G-10723)
Express Prtg & Graphics Inc ....G...... 724 274-7700
  Cheswick (G-3107)
Express Screenprinting ....G...... 215 579-8819
  Langhorne (G-9296)
Fantasy Printing Supplies LLC ....G...... 215 569-3744
  Philadelphia (G-13693)
FB Shoemaker LLC ....G...... 717 852-8029
  York (G-20476)
Federal Business Products Inc ....D...... 570 454-2451
  West Hazleton (G-19709)
Fedex Corporation ....G...... 412 441-2379
  Pittsburgh (G-15008)

PRODUCT

Fencor Graphics Inc ....E 215 745-2266
Bensalem *(G-1194)*

Filmet Color Lab Inc ....D 724 275-1700
Cheswick *(G-3108)*

Five Thousand Forms Inc ....F 610 395-0900
Fogelsville *(G-5994)*

Formex Business Printing ....G 717 737-3430
Lemoyne *(G-9744)*

Fort Dearborn Company.................G 814 686-7656
Tyrone *(G-18582)*

Fry Communications Inc ....A 717 766-0211
Mechanicsburg *(G-10846)*

Gable Printing ....G 724 443-3444
Gibsonia *(G-6335)*

Gallop Printing ....G 215 542-0887
Fort Washington *(G-6071)*

Gesualdi Printing ....G 215 785-3960
Bristol *(G-2148)*

Gibson Graphics Group Inc ....G 717 755-7192
Hellam *(G-7550)*

Gilbert Printing Services ....G 215 483-7772
Philadelphia *(G-13763)*

Gillespie Printing Inc ....F 610 264-1863
Allentown *(G-232)*

Great Northern Press of Wilkes ......E 570 822-3147
Wilkes Barre *(G-19922)*

Groffs Printing Company ....G 717 786-1511
Quarryville *(G-16272)*

Guy Hrezik ....G 610 779-7609
Reading *(G-16397)*

H & H Graphics Inc ....E 717 393-3941
Lancaster *(G-9035)*

Hammond Press Inc ....E 412 821-4100
Pittsburgh *(G-15078)*

Hapsco Design and Prtg Svcs ....G 717 564-2323
Harrisburg *(G-7139)*

Healthcare Information Corp ....F 724 776-9411
Warrendale *(G-19081)*

Heatha Henrys LLC ....G 215 968-2080
Newtown *(G-12509)*

Heirloom Engraving LLC ....G 717 336-8451
Stevens *(G-18052)*

Hesford Keystone Printing Co ....G 814 942-2911
Altoona *(G-513)*

Hessinger Group Inc ....G 814 480-8912
Erie *(G-5316)*

Hot Frog Print Media LLC ....E 717 697-2204
Mechanicsburg *(G-10855)*

House of Printing ....G 814 723-3701
Warren *(G-19031)*

Hullihens Printery ....G 570 288-6804
Wilkes Barre *(G-19925)*

Imaging Fx Inc ....G 484 223-3311
Allentown *(G-252)*

Imf Printing LLC...........................G 844 463-2726
Allentown *(G-253)*

Impact Printing and Embroidery .....G 814 857-7246
Woodland *(G-20212)*

Indiana Printing and Pubg Co ....C 724 465-5555
Indiana *(G-8105)*

Indiana Printing and Pubg Co ....C 724 349-3434
Indiana *(G-8106)*

Instant Response Inc ....G 215 322-1271
Huntingdon Valley *(G-7997)*

Interform Corporation ....C 412 221-7321
Bridgeville *(G-2070)*

J D Enterprise-Mp LLC ....G 215 855-4003
Lansdale *(G-9377)*

Jack Pressman ....G 610 668-8847
Bala Cynwyd *(G-882)*

James Irwin ....G 724 867-6083
Emlenton *(G-5012)*

Jerden Industries Inc ....F 814 375-7822
Du Bois *(G-4399)*

Jim Mannello ....G 610 681-6467
Gilbert *(G-6362)*

Jma Group ....G 724 444-0004
Allison Park *(G-454)*

Jnb Screen Printing Inc ....G 610 845-7680
Alburtis *(G-52)*

Joan Vadyak Printing Inc ....G 570 645-5507
Lansford *(G-9448)*

Jpa Printing ....G 610 270-8855
Blue Bell *(G-1838)*

Kappa Graphics L P ....C 570 655-9681
Hughestown *(G-7893)*

Kappa Media LLC ....C 215 643-5800
Fort Washington *(G-6079)*

Karen Holbrook ....G 724 628-3858
Connellsville *(G-3500)*

Kendalls Kreations ....G 814 427-2517
Big Run *(G-1656)*

Keystone Printed Spc Co LLC ....C 570 457-8334
Old Forge *(G-12967)*

Keystone Printing Co ....F 570 622-4377
Pottsville *(G-16086)*

Kingdom Exposure Ltd ....G 215 621-8291
Drexel Hill *(G-4368)*

Kreider Digital Communications .....G 412 446-2784
Pittsburgh *(G-15200)*

Krohmalys Printing Co ....G 412 271-4234
Pittsburgh *(G-15201)*

Kwikticketscom Inc ....F 724 438-7712
Uniontown *(G-18632)*

Lancaster General Svcs Bus Tr ....F 717 544-5474
Lancaster *(G-9095)*

Lee Enterprises Inc Sentinel ....C 717 240-7135
Carlisle *(G-2721)*

Legacy Printing and Pubg Co ....G 724 567-5657
Vandergrift *(G-18732)*

Lem Products Inc ....E 800 220-2400
Montgomeryville *(G-11403)*

Lesko Enterprises Inc ....C 814 756-4030
Albion *(G-46)*

Liberty Products Group Inc ....G 215 631-1700
Hatfield *(G-7364)*

Magna Graphics Inc......................G 412 687-0500
Pittsburgh *(G-15247)*

Mandelbroks ....G 814 813-5555
Meadville *(G-10755)*

Maple Press Company ....C 717 764-5911
York *(G-20580)*

Marcan Advertising Inc ....G 717 270-6929
Cleona *(G-3245)*

Marlo Enterprises Inc ....F 412 678-3800
Duquesne *(G-4498)*

McCarty Printing Corp ....D 814 454-4561
Erie *(G-5385)*

McCourt Label Cabinet Company .....D 800 458-2390
Lewis Run *(G-9877)*

McLean Publishing Co ....F 814 275-3131
New Bethlehem *(G-12027)*

Medianews Group Inc ....C 717 637-3736
Hanover *(G-6919)*

Meinert Holdings Inc ....F 412 835-2727
Bethel Park *(G-1424)*

Michael S Cwalina ....G 412 341-1606
Pittsburgh *(G-15284)*

Milan Printing ....G 570 325-2649
Jim Thorpe *(G-8342)*

Minuteman Press ....G 610 272-6220
Norristown *(G-12685)*

Minuteman Press ....G 724 236-0261
Leechburg *(G-9649)*

Minuteman Press Inc ....G 610 923-9266
Easton *(G-4724)*

Minuteman Press International ....G 610 539-6707
Norristown *(G-12686)*

Minuteman Press of Glenside ....G 267 626-2706
Glenside *(G-6528)*

Minuteman Press of Hanover ....G 717 632-5400
Hanover *(G-6921)*

Morning Call LLC ....A 610 820-6500
Allentown *(G-322)*

Mr Printer Inc ....G 215 354-5533
Richboro *(G-16676)*

Mulligan Printing Corporation ....E 570 278-3271
Tunkhannock *(G-18544)*

Multi-Color Corporation ....D 717 266-9675
York *(G-20607)*

Murrelle Printing Co Inc ....F 570 888-2244
Sayre *(G-17119)*

My Instant Benefits ....G 724 465-6075
Indiana *(G-8114)*

National Dermalogy Image Corp ......G 610 756-0065
Kempton *(G-8493)*

National Imprint Corporation ....E 814 239-5116
Claysburg *(G-3206)*

Navitor Inc ....B 717 765-3121
Waynesboro *(G-19419)*

Nazareth Key Youngs Press ....G 610 759-5000
Nazareth *(G-11984)*

News Eagle ....E 570 226-4547
Honesdale *(G-7719)*

Newspaper Holding Inc ....D 814 724-6370
Meadville *(G-10769)*

Newspaper Holding Inc ....D 724 654-6651
New Castle *(G-12131)*

Nittany Printing and Pubg Co ....D 814 238-5000
State College *(G-18000)*

North Amrcn Communications Inc......A 814 696-3553
Duncansville *(G-4458)*

Nosco Inc ....G 215 788-1105
Bristol *(G-2175)*

Okumus Enterprises Ltd ....E 215 295-3340
Fairless Hills *(G-5790)*

Outlook Printing Solutions Inc ....G 215 680-4014
Harleysville *(G-7050)*

Pacemaker Press PP&s Inc ....E 301 696-9629
Waynesboro *(G-19421)*

Parc Productions ....G 724 283-3300
Butler *(G-2431)*

Parks Design & Ink ....G 814 643-1120
Huntingdon *(G-7955)*

Parkside Graphics Inc ....G 215 453-1123
Sellersville *(G-17356)*

Parkway Printing ....G 610 928-3433
Emmaus *(G-5039)*

Pemcor Printing Company LLC ....D 717 898-1555
Lancaster *(G-9162)*

Pencor Services Inc ....C 570 386-2660
Lehighton *(G-9721)*

Perfect Impression.......................G 610 444-9493
Kennett Square *(G-8535)*

Perry Printing ....G 215 256-8074
Harleysville *(G-7052)*

Perry Printing Company ....G 717 582-2838
New Bloomfield *(G-12030)*

Philadelphia Photo Arts Center ....G 215 232-5678
Philadelphia *(G-14148)*

Philly Banner Express LLC ....G 267 385-5451
Philadelphia *(G-14168)*

Phoenix Data Inc ....D 570 547-1665
Montgomery *(G-11377)*

Phresh Prints Ink LLC ....G 267 687-7483
Philadelphia *(G-14173)*

Pic Mobile Advertising LLC ....G 570 208-1459
Wilkes Barre *(G-19956)*

Pleasant Luck Corp ....G 215 968-2080
Newtown *(G-12537)*

Pomco Graphics Inc ....F 215 455-9500
Philadelphia *(G-14188)*

Precise Graphic Products Inc ....G 412 481-0952
Coraopolis *(G-3717)*

Print Box Inc ....G 212 741-1381
Downingtown *(G-4251)*

Print Charming Design ....G 412 519-5226
Clairton *(G-3157)*

Print Escape LLC ....G 888 524-8690
Pittsburgh *(G-15439)*

Printbiz LLC ....G 412 881-3318
Pittsburgh *(G-15442)*

Printcompass LLC ....G 610 541-6763
Springfield *(G-17921)*

Printers Edge ....G 570 454-4803
Hazleton *(G-7520)*

Printing Craftsmen Inc ....F 570 646-2121
Pocono Pines *(G-15883)*

Printing Mas ....G 570 326-9222
Williamsport *(G-20065)*

Printing Works ....G 215 357-5609
Southampton *(G-17831)*

Printwearonline ....G 267 987-6118
Yardley *(G-20335)*

Procopy Inc ....F 814 231-1256
State College *(G-18010)*

Professional Graphic Co ....E 724 318-8530
Sewickley *(G-17405)*

Proforma Graphic Impressions ....G 610 759-2430
Nazareth *(G-11986)*

Public Image Printing Inc ....G 215 677-4088
Philadelphia *(G-14216)*

Q D F Inc ....G 610 670-2090
Reading *(G-16477)*

Qg Llc ....C 414 208-2700
Atglen *(G-803)*

Quiet Valley Printing LLC ....G 908 400-3689
Mount Bethel *(G-11614)*

R Graphics Inc ....G 610 918-0373
West Chester *(G-19625)*

R M S Graphics Inc ....G 215 322-6000
Huntingdon Valley *(G-8028)*

R R Donnelley & Sons Company ....C 570 524-2224
Lewisburg *(G-9918)*

R R Donnelley & Sons Company ....C 717 209-7700
Lancaster *(G-9184)*

Rancatore & Lavender Inc ....G 412 829-7456
North Versailles *(G-12782)*

Ream Printing Co Inc ....E 717 764-5663
York *(G-20653)*

Record Herald Publishing Co ... E ... 717 762-2151 Waynesboro *(G-19422)*
Red Gravel Partners LLC ... G ... 570 445-3553 Scranton *(G-17278)*
Rekord Printing Co ... G ... 570 648-3231 Elysburg *(G-4980)*
Ricks Quick Printing Inc ... E ... 412 571-0333 Pittsburgh *(G-15485)*
Rogers & Deturck Printing Inc ... G ... 412 828-8868 Verona *(G-18762)*
RR Donnelley & Sons Company ... D ... 412 281-7401 Pittsburgh *(G-15501)*
S G Business Services Inc ... G ... 215 567-7107 Philadelphia *(G-14271)*
Safeguard Business Systems Inc ... C ... 215 631-7500 Lansdale *(G-9408)*
Salem Printing Inc ... F ... 724 468-8604 Delmont *(G-4057)*
Scantron Corporation ... C ... 717 684-4600 Columbia *(G-3450)*
Serve Inc ... G ... 570 265-3119 Monroeton *(G-11320)*
Silverline Screen Printing ... G ... 570 275-8866 Danville *(G-4011)*
Simply Business LLC ... G ... 814 241-7113 Summerhill *(G-18155)*
Sir Speedy Inc ... F ... 215 877-8888 Philadelphia *(G-14311)*
Sir Speedy 7108 Inc ... F ... 412 787-9898 Pittsburgh *(G-15542)*
Smart Print Technologies Inc ... G ... 412 771-8307 Mc Kees Rocks *(G-10636)*
Specialty Group Printing Inc ... F ... 814 425-3061 Cochranton *(G-3351)*
Spencer Graphics Inc ... G ... 610 793-2348 West Chester *(G-19643)*
Sunshine Screen Print ... G ... 610 678-9034 Reading *(G-16529)*
Sycamore Partners MGT LP ... G ... 724 748-0052 Grove City *(G-6805)*
Synergy Business Forms Inc ... G ... 814 833-3344 Erie *(G-5502)*
T & T Prtg T & Symbol T Printi ... G ... 724 938-9495 Allenport *(G-105)*
Tammy M Tibbens ... G ... 717 979-3063 Harrisburg *(G-7226)*
Tcg Document Solutions LLC ... F ... 215 957-0600 Huntingdon Valley *(G-8043)*
Tcg Document Solutions LLC ... E ... 610 356-4700 Paoli *(G-13150)*
Telepole Manufacturing Inc ... G ... 570 546-3699 Muncy *(G-11835)*
Theprinterscom Inc ... G ... 814 238-8445 State College *(G-18038)*
Tiger Printing Group LLC ... E ... 215 799-0500 Telford *(G-18323)*
Times Publishing Company ... D ... 814 453-4691 Erie *(G-5509)*
Tioga Publishing Company ... A ... 814 371-4200 Du Bois *(G-4424)*
Toppan Interamerica Inc ... E ... 610 286-3100 Morgantown *(G-11541)*
Total Document Resource Inc ... G ... 717 648-6234 Lancaster *(G-9221)*
Towanda Printing Co Inc ... C ... 570 265-2151 Towanda *(G-18436)*
TP (old) LLC ... E ... 412 488-1600 Pittsburgh *(G-15634)*
Triangle Printing Company Inc ... E ... 717 854-1521 York *(G-20692)*
Type Set Print ... G ... 570 542-5910 Hunlock Creek *(G-7935)*
Unipak Inc ... E ... 610 436-6600 West Chester *(G-19670)*
Universal Network Technologies ... G ... 412 490-0990 Monroeville *(G-11362)*
Victor Printing Inc ... D ... 724 342-2106 Sharon *(G-17444)*
Village Publishing Operations ... G ... 215 794-0202 Furlong *(G-6235)*
VIP Advertising & Printing ... G ... 570 251-7897 Honesdale *(G-7731)*
Virgo Investment LLC ... F ... 215 339-1596 Philadelphia *(G-14449)*
W B Mason Co Inc ... D ... 888 926-2766 Allentown *(G-427)*
W B Mason Co Inc ... E ... 888 926-2766 Altoona *(G-555)*
Webb Communications Inc ... E ... 570 326-7634 Plymouth *(G-15824)*
Webb Communications Inc ... E ... 570 326-7634 Plymouth *(G-15823)*
Webb Communications Inc ... D ... 570 326-7634 Williamsport *(G-20089)*
Wheeler Enterprises Inc ... G ... 610 975-9230 Wayne *(G-19392)*
Yurchak Printing Inc ... E ... 717 399-0209 Landisville *(G-9269)*

PRINTING: Manmade Fiber & Silk, Broadwoven Fabric

Bell Graphics ... G ... 814 385-6222 Kennerdell *(G-8497)*
Tee Printing Inc ... G ... 717 394-2978 Lancaster *(G-9215)*

PRINTING: Offset

3d Printing and Copy Ctr Inc ... F ... 215 968-7900 Bensalem *(G-1140)*
69th St Commercial Printers ... G ... 610 539-8412 Norristown *(G-12627)*
A Archery and Printing Place ... G ... 717 274-1811 Lebanon *(G-9544)*
A Link Prtg & Promotions LLC ... G ... 412 220-0290 Bridgeville *(G-2049)*
A+ Printing Inc ... G ... 814 942-4257 Altoona *(G-468)*
AAA Color Card Company ... G ... 814 793-2342 Martinsburg *(G-10519)*
Abbi Print LLC ... G ... 215 471-8801 Philadelphia *(G-13335)*
Acumark Inc ... G ... 570 883-1800 West Pittston *(G-19753)*
Ad Forms LLC ... G ... 724 379-6022 Charleroi *(G-3004)*
Ad Post Graphics Inc ... F ... 412 405-9163 Library *(G-9953)*
Ad-Net Services Incorporated ... F ... 610 374-4200 Reading *(G-16310)*
Adcomm Inc ... F ... 610 820-8565 Allentown *(G-115)*
Advanced Color Graphics ... E ... 814 235-1200 Huntingdon *(G-7937)*
Aeroprint Graphics Inc ... G ... 215 752-1089 Langhorne *(G-9274)*
Air Conway Inc ... F ... 610 534-0500 Collingdale *(G-3402)*
Alcom Printing Group Inc ... C ... 215 513-1600 Harleysville *(G-7015)*
Alfred Envelope Company Inc ... F ... 215 739-1500 Philadelphia *(G-13362)*
Allegra Mktg Print Mail 408 ... G ... 717 839-6390 Harrisburg *(G-7085)*
Allegra Print & Imaging ... F ... 412 922-0422 Pittsburgh *(G-14683)*
Allegra Print & Imaging ... E ... 717 397-3440 Lancaster *(G-8929)*
Allegra Print Imaging ... G ... 610 882-2229 Allentown *(G-125)*
AlphaGraphics ... G ... 717 731-8444 Mechanicsburg *(G-10819)*
AMD Graphics Inc ... G ... 215 728-8600 Philadelphia *(G-13377)*
American Bank Note Company ... E ... 215 396-8707 Trevose *(G-18486)*
American Brchure Catalogue Inc ... E ... 215 259-1600 Warminster *(G-18827)*
Amherst Corporation ... F ... 610 589-1090 Womelsdorf *(G-20205)*
Anstadt Printing Corporation ... E ... 717 767-6891 York *(G-20378)*
Apparel Print Promotionals ... G ... 717 233-4277 Harrisburg *(G-7088)*
Apple Press Ltd ... E ... 610 363-1776 Exton *(G-5644)*
ARA Corporation ... G ... 724 843-5378 Koppel *(G-8813)*
Arbil Enterprises Inc ... G ... 215 969-0500 Philadelphia *(G-13407)*
Archway Press Inc ... F ... 610 583-4004 Sharon Hill *(G-17452)*
Arcs Design & Printing Inc ... G ... 215 238-1831 Philadelphia *(G-13408)*
Art Communication Systems Inc ... E ... 717 232-0144 Harrisburg *(G-7090)*
Art Printing Co of Lancaster ... G ... 717 397-6029 Columbia *(G-3430)*
Artcraft Printers Inc ... G ... 724 537-5231 Latrobe *(G-9457)*
ASAP Printing & Copying Inc ... F ... 215 357-5033 Southampton *(G-17798)*
Astro Printing Services Inc ... F ... 215 441-4444 Warminster *(G-18831)*
Athens Reproduction ... G ... 610 649-5761 Ardmore *(G-701)*
Atlas Printing Company ... G ... 814 445-2516 Somerset *(G-17675)*
Atlas Rubber Stamp & Printing ... G ... 717 755-3882 York *(G-20390)*
Auch Printing Inc ... G ... 215 886-9133 Dresher *(G-4353)*
Auxiliary Business Services ... G ... 215 836-4833 Fort Washington *(G-6063)*
B O H I C A Inc ... G ... 610 489-4540 Trappe *(G-18467)*
B P S Communications Inc ... F ... 215 830-8467 Willow Grove *(G-20109)*
Balfour Sales Company ... G ... 215 542-9745 Ambler *(G-569)*
Becotte Design Inc ... G ... 215 641-1257 Philadelphia *(G-13451)*
Bedwick and Jones Printing Inc ... F ... 570 829-1951 Hanover Township *(G-6979)*
Bee Offset Printing ... G ... 610 253-0926 Easton *(G-4651)*
Beggs Brothers Printing Co ... G ... 814 395-3241 Confluence *(G-3463)*
Beidel Printing House Inc ... E ... 717 532-5063 Shippensburg *(G-17516)*
Beiler Printing LLC ... G ... 717 336-1148 Denver *(G-4068)*
Berks Digital Inc ... G ... 610 929-1200 Reading *(G-16329)*
Bestway Printing ... G ... 215 368-4140 Lansdale *(G-9346)*
Birds Printing ... G ... 570 784-8136 Bloomsburg *(G-1774)*
Birrbatt Printing Inc ... G ... 412 373-9047 Trafford *(G-18451)*
Blasi Printing Inc ... F ... 570 824-3557 Hanover Township *(G-6981)*
Blose Printing ... G ... 717 838-9129 Campbelltown *(G-2529)*
Blue Bell Print Solutions ... G ... 215 591-3903 Blue Bell *(G-1817)*
Bodrie Inc ... G ... 724 836-3666 Smithton *(G-17658)*
Boggs Printing Inc ... G ... 215 675-1203 Hatboro *(G-7274)*
Bondi Printing Co Inc ... F ... 724 327-6022 Murrysville *(G-11848)*
Bradco Printers Inc ... G ... 570 297-3024 Troy *(G-18517)*
Bradley Graphic Solutions Inc ... E ... 215 638-8771 Bensalem *(G-1160)*
Brendan G Stover Printing ... G ... 610 459-2851 Boothwyn *(G-1876)*
Brenneman Printing Inc ... E ... 717 299-2847 Lancaster *(G-8959)*
Brilliant Studio Inc ... G ... 610 458-7977 Exton *(G-5657)*
Brindle Printing Co Inc ... G ... 724 658-8549 New Castle *(G-12067)*
Brodak Printing Company ... G ... 724 966-5178 Carmichaels *(G-2755)*
Brookshire Printing Inc ... E ... 717 392-1321 Lancaster *(G-8961)*
Bucks County Off Svcs & Prtg ... G ... 215 295-7060 Bristol *(G-2121)*
Bucks Ship & Print ... G ... 215 493-8100 Yardley *(G-20299)*
Buhl Bros Printing Inc ... F ... 724 335-0970 Creighton *(G-3880)*
Butter Milk Falls Inc ... G ... 724 548-7388 Kittanning *(G-8759)*
Butts Ticket Company Inc ... F ... 610 869-7450 Cochranville *(G-3355)*
Byrne Enterprises Inc ... G ... 610 670-0767 Reading *(G-16338)*
C P Commercial Printing Inc ... G ... 215 675-7605 Warminster *(G-18843)*
C3 Media LLC ... E ... 610 832-8077 Philadelphia *(G-13492)*
Cab Technologies & Printing So ... G ... 724 457-8880 Coraopolis *(G-3667)*
Carnegie Printing Company ... G ... 412 788-4399 Oakdale *(G-12895)*
Caskey Printing Inc ... E ... 717 764-4500 York *(G-20420)*

Employee Codes: A=Over 500 employees, B=251-500 C=101-250, D=51-100, E=20-50, F=10-19, G=3-9
2019 Harris Pennsylvania Manufacturers Directory
1517

Castor Printing Company Inc ....F 215 535-1471
Philadelphia (G-13512)

CDI Printing Services Inc ....F 724 444-6160
Gibsonia (G-6330)

Champ Printing Company Inc...........E 412 269-0197
Coraopolis (G-3675)

Charles A Henderson Prtg Svc ....G 724 775-2623
Rochester (G-16783)

Chaucer Press Inc.............................D 570 825-2005
Hanover Township (G-6986)

Chernay Printing Inc.........................D 610 282-3774
Coopersburg (G-3625)

Chester Multi Copy Inc.....................G 610 876-1285
Brookhaven (G-2243)

Christmas City Printing Co Inc ....E 610 868-5844
Bethlehem (G-1483)

Citizen Publishing Company ....G 570 454-5911
Hazleton (G-7495)

Clever Inc...G 717 762-7508
Waynesboro (G-19404)

Clinton Press Inc...............................G 814 455-9089
Erie (G-5227)

Clore Enterprise ....G 724 745-0673
Houston (G-7871)

College Town Inc...............................G 717 532-7354
Shippensburg (G-17523)

College Town Inc...............................G 717 532-3034
Shippensburg (G-17524)

Color Impressions Inc ....G 717 872-2666
Millersville (G-11210)

Colortech Inc ....E 717 450-5416
Lebanon (G-9556)

Commercial Job Printing Inc ....G 814 765-1925
Clearfield (G-3216)

Commercial Prtg & Off Suppy ....G 814 765-4731
Clearfield (G-3217)

Communication Graphics Inc ....F 215 646-2225
Blue Bell (G-1821)

Communication Svcs & Support ....G 215 540-5888
Blue Bell (G-1822)

Computer Print Inc.............................G 717 397-9174
Lancaster (G-8983)

Conner Printing Inc...........................G 610 494-2222
Aston (G-756)

Conrad Printing Co Inc ....G 717 637-5414
Hanover (G-6870)

Continental Press Inc ....C 717 367-1836
Elizabethtown (G-4869)

Cooper Printing Inc............................G 717 871-8856
Lancaster (G-8986)

Copy Center Plus...............................G 724 547-5850
Mount Pleasant (G-11694)

Copy Management Inc........................G 610 993-8686
Malvern (G-10217)

Copy Management Inc........................F 215 269-5000
Huntingdon Valley (G-7972)

Copy Right Printing & Graphics ....G 814 838-6255
Erie (G-5233)

Corles Printing ....G 814 276-3775
Imler (G-8055)

Corporate Arts Inc ....G 610 298-8374
New Tripoli (G-12454)

Corporate Graphics Intl Inc...............F 800 247-2751
Waynesboro (G-19405)

Corporate Print Solutions Inc ....G 215 774-1119
Glenolden (G-6472)

Cortineo Creative LLC.......................F 215 348-1100
Doylestown (G-4294)

Country Press Inc ....F 610 565-8808
Media (G-10919)

Creative Characters ....G 215 923-2679
Philadelphia (G-13578)

Creative Printing & Graphics ....G 724 222-8304
Washington (G-19158)

Creative Printing Co ....G 570 875-1811
Ashland (G-729)

Creighton Printing Inc ....G 724 224-0444
Creighton (G-3882)

Creps United Publications Inc ....D 724 463-9722
Indiana (G-8088)

Cs-B2 Investments Inc......................E 412 261-1300
Pittsburgh (G-14890)

Curry Printing & Copy ....G 610 373-2890
Reading (G-16358)

D & S Business Services Inc ....G 724 545-3143
Kittanning (G-8765)

D & Sr Inc..D 717 569-3264
Lancaster (G-8989)

D & Z Printers ....G 724 539-8922
Latrobe (G-9470)

D G A Inc..G 717 249-8542
Carlisle (G-2706)

D R M Services Corporation ....G 610 789-2685
Havertown (G-7419)

Daedal Group Inc ....G 215 745-8718
Philadelphia (G-13603)

Damin Printing Co LLC......................G 814 472-9530
Ebensburg (G-4784)

Data Print ....G 484 329-7553
Malvern (G-10221)

Davco Advertising Inc ....E 717 442-4155
Kinzers (G-8736)

David A Smith Printing Inc ....E 717 564-3719
Harrisburg (G-7114)

David Bream ....G 717 334-1513
Gettysburg (G-6288)

Davinci Graphics Inc ....G 215 441-8180
Horsham (G-7808)

Degadan Corp ....G 610 940-1282
Conshohocken (G-3537)

Delco Trade Services Inc...................G 610 659-9978
Wayne (G-19317)

Digital Impact LLC ....G 610 623-1269
Yeadon (G-20353)

Digital Print & Design Inc ....G 570 347-6001
Old Forge (G-12963)

Dilullo Graphics Inc ....E 610 775-4360
Mohnton (G-11262)

Dn Printer Solutions ....G 717 606-6233
Ephrata (G-5101)

Donald Blyler Offset Inc ....D 717 949-6831
Lebanon (G-9561)

Donnelley Financial LLC ....F 717 293-3725
Glen Mills (G-6436)

Doodad Printing LLC.........................D 800 383-6973
Lancaster (G-9002)

Drs Printing Services Inc ....G 717 502-1117
Dillsburg (G-4127)

Dubose Printing & Bus Svcs ....G 215 877-9071
Philadelphia (G-13649)

Dupli Craft Printing Inc.....................G 570 344-8980
Scranton (G-17229)

Durham Press Inc ....G 610 346-6133
Durham (G-4502)

East Associates Inc ....G 610 667-3980
Bala Cynwyd (G-878)

Eastern Die Cutting & Finshg ....F 610 917-9765
Phoenixville (G-14546)

Elizabeth C Baker..............................F 610 566-0691
Media (G-10923)

Engle Printing & Pubg Co Inc ....F 717 892-6800
Lancaster (G-9010)

Engle Printing & Pubg Co Inc ....F 717 653-1833
Mount Joy (G-11654)

Engle Printing & Pubg Co Inc ....C 717 653-1833
Lancaster (G-9009)

Ensinger Printing Service ....G 717 484-4451
Adamstown (G-21)

Epic Litho..E 610 933-7400
Phoenixville (G-14548)

Executive Print Solutions LLC............G 570 421-1437
Stroudsburg (G-18117)

Executive Printing Company Inc ....F 717 664-3636
Elm (G-4956)

Express Press Inc ....G 412 824-1000
Pittsburgh (G-14994)

Express Printing ....G 215 357-7033
Southampton (G-17810)

Expressway Printing Inc ....G 215 244-0233
Warminster (G-18876)

Fine Print Commercial Printers ....G 814 337-7468
Meadville (G-10726)

First Shelburne Corporation ....G 610 544-8660
Springfield (G-17914)

Fortney Printing ....F 717 939-6422
Harrisburg (G-7130)

Fotorecord Print Center Inc ....G 724 837-0530
Greensburg (G-6667)

Foundation Print Solutions................G 717 330-0544
Lititz (G-10009)

French Creek Offset Inc ....G 610 582-3241
Birdsboro (G-1696)

G R Graphics ....G 814 774-9592
Girard (G-6389)

Gallagher Printing Inc.......................G 717 838-1527
Palmyra (G-13123)

Garlits Industries Inc ....F 215 736-2121
Morrisville (G-11559)

General Press Corporation ....E 724 224-3500
Natrona Heights (G-11943)

Globe Print Shop................................G 570 454-8031
Hazleton (G-7499)

Gloroy Inc ....G 610 435-7800
Allentown (G-235)

Godfreys Custom Printing ....G 717 530-8818
Shippensburg (G-17529)

Grace Press Inc ....F 717 354-0475
Ephrata (G-5107)

Grafika Commercial Prtg Inc..............B 610 678-8630
Reading (G-16396)

Gran Enterprises................................G 215 634-2883
Philadelphia (G-13780)

Graphcom Inc.....................................C 800 699-1664
Gettysburg (G-6295)

Graphic Arts Incorporated ....E 215 382-5500
Philadelphia (G-13782)

Graphic Impressions of America...........G 610 296-3939
Malvern (G-10243)

Graphic Print Solutions L...................G 610 845-0280
Barto (G-943)

Great Atlantic Graphics Inc...............D 610 296-8711
Lansdale (G-9373)

Greentree Printing Inc ....F 412 921-5570
Pittsburgh (G-15064)

Greenwood Business Printing............G 610 337-8887
King of Prussia (G-8626)

Griffiths Printing Co ....F 610 623-3822
Lansdowne (G-9433)

Grit Commercial Printing Inc ....E 570 368-8021
Montoursville (G-11440)

Grove Printing Inc ....G 814 355-2197
Bellefonte (G-1101)

Guy Coder ....G 814 265-0519
Brockway (G-2227)

Guyasuta Printing Co ....G 412 782-0112
Pittsburgh (G-15068)

H & H Graphics Inc ....E 717 393-3941
Lancaster (G-9036)

H B South Printing ....F 412 751-1300
McKeesport (G-10669)

Haas Printing Co Inc ....E 717 761-0277
Lemoyne (G-9745)

Harman Beach Corporation ....F 717 652-0556
Harrisburg (G-7141)

Harmony Press Inc ....E 610 559-9800
Easton (G-4695)

Harper Printing Service ....G 412 884-2666
Pittsburgh (G-15082)

Hayden Printing Co ....F 610 642-2105
Ardmore (G-708)

Heeter Printing Company Inc ....D 724 746-8900
Canonsburg (G-2595)

Hendersons Printing Inc ....E 814 944-0855
Altoona (G-512)

Herrmann Printing & Litho Inc...........E 412 243-4100
Pittsburgh (G-15093)

Hess Commercial Printing Inc ....E 724 652-6802
New Castle (G-12103)

Hocking Printing Co Inc ....D 717 738-1151
Ephrata (G-5109)

Hodgsons Quick Printing ....G 215 362-1356
Kulpsville (G-8830)

Hoffman Enterprises Inc ....G 610 944-8481
Fleetwood (G-5974)

Horton Printing..................................G 717 938-2777
Etters (G-5549)

Houck Printing Company Inc ....F 717 233-5205
Harrisburg (G-7152)

Huckstein Printing ....G 724 452-5777
Zelienople (G-20803)

Huepenbecker Enterprises Inc ....F 717 393-3941
Lancaster (G-9052)

Ideal Prtg Co Lancaster Inc...............G 717 299-2643
Lancaster (G-9054)

Independent Graphics Inc..................E 570 609-5267
Wyoming (G-20279)

Independent-Observer........................E 724 887-7400
Scottdale (G-17193)

Indian Valley Printing Co Inc.............E 215 723-7884
Souderton (G-17741)

Indus Graphics Inc............................G 215 443-7773
Warminster (G-18896)

Ink Spot Printing ....G 570 743-7979
Selinsgrove (G-17327)

Ink Spot Printing & Copy Ctr ....G 610 647-0776
Malvern (G-10255)

Instant Web Inc ....G 952 474-0961
Warminster (G-18899)

Intercon Printer & Consultants...........G 724 837-5428
Greensburg (G-6678)

Itp of Usa Inc	D	717 367-3670
Elizabethtown (G-4875)		
J & B Printing	G	570 587-4427
Clarks Summit (G-3195)		
J & R Beck Inc	F	724 981-5220
Sharon (G-17437)		
J A Mitch Printing & Copy Ctr	G	724 847-2940
Beaver Falls (G-1002)		
J D Printing Inc	G	724 327-0006
Pittsburgh (G-15141)		
J R B Printing	G	570 689-9114
Jefferson Township (G-8278)		
J R Finio & Sons Inc	F	610 623-5800
Lansdowne (G-9435)		
Jaak Holdings LLC	G	267 462-4092
Ambler (G-582)		
James Saks	G	570 343-8150
Scranton (G-17247)		
Jaren Enterprises Inc	G	717 394-2671
Lancaster (G-9072)		
Jayco Grafix Inc	D	610 678-2640
Reinholds (G-16633)		
Jaz Forms	G	610 272-0770
Norristown (G-12673)		
JC Printing	G	570 282-1187
Carbondale (G-2679)		
Jiffy Printing Inc	G	814 452-2067
Erie (G-5336)		
Joseph H Tees & Son Inc	G	215 638-3368
Bensalem (G-1214)		
JS Little Publication	G	412 343-5288
Pittsburgh (G-15157)		
K B Offset Printing Inc	E	814 238-8445
State College (G-17982)		
Kalil Printing Inc	E	610 948-9330
Royersford (G-16854)		
Kalnin Graphics Inc	E	215 887-3203
Jenkintown (G-8292)		
Keeney Printing Group Inc	G	215 855-6116
Lansdale (G-9383)		
Kelly Line Inc	F	570 527-6822
Pottsville (G-16085)		
Kennedy Printing Co Inc	F	215 474-5150
Philadelphia (G-13926)		
Kestone Digital Press	E	484 318-7017
Paoli (G-13143)		
Keystone Printing Services	G	215 675-6464
Hatboro (G-7288)		
Keystone Prtg & Graphics Inc	G	570 648-5785
Coal Township (G-3280)		
Killeen Printing Co	G	412 381-4090
Pittsburgh (G-15177)		
King Printing and Pubg Inc	G	814 238-2536
State College (G-17985)		
Kirkland Printing Inc	G	215 706-2399
Willow Grove (G-20124)		
Kisel Printing Service Inc	E	570 489-7666
Dickson City (G-4121)		
Kistler & Dinapoli Inc	G	215 428-4740
Morrisville (G-11567)		
Kistler Printing Co Inc	F	570 421-2050
East Stroudsburg (G-4622)		
Knepper Press Corporation	C	724 899-4200
Clinton (G-3263)		
Konhaus Farms Inc	G	717 731-9456
Camp Hill (G-2502)		
Kutztown Publishing Company	F	610 683-7341
Allentown (G-287)		
Kwik Quality Press Inc	G	717 273-0005
Lebanon (G-9596)		
L D H Printing Ltd Inc	F	609 924-4664
Morrisville (G-11568)		
L G Graphics Inc	F	412 421-6330
Pittsburgh (G-15208)		
Labelcraft Press Inc	G	215 257-6368
Perkasie (G-13282)		
Labels By Pulizzi Inc	F	570 326-1244
Williamsport (G-20034)		
Labue Printing Inc	G	814 371-5059
Du Bois (G-4402)		
Lackawanna Printing Co	G	570 342-0528
Scranton (G-17253)		
Lancaster General Svcs Bus Tr	F	800 341-2121
Lancaster (G-9096)		
Lapsley Printing Inc	G	215 332-7451
Philadelphia (G-13956)		
Laurel Printing	G	724 459-7554
Blairsville (G-1731)		
Laurel Valley Graphics Inc	F	724 539-4545
Latrobe (G-9498)		

Lawrence Printing Service	G	215 799-2332
Souderton (G-17748)		
Lehigh Print & Data LLC	G	610 421-8891
Macungie (G-10151)		
Levittown Printing Inc	G	215 945-8156
Levittown (G-9845)		
Liberty Craftsmen Inc	G	717 871-0125
Millersville (G-11211)		
Little Mountain Printing	F	717 933-8091
Myerstown (G-11892)		
Little Printing Co Inc	G	724 437-4831
Uniontown (G-18635)		
Lls Graphics	G	610 435-9055
Allentown (G-299)		
Lock Haven Express	E	570 748-6791
Lock Haven (G-10090)		
Lsc Communications Us LLC	A	717 392-4074
Lancaster (G-9116)		
M3 Media LLC	F	215 463-6348
Philadelphia (G-13983)		
Main Line Print Shop Inc	G	610 688-7782
Wayne (G-19349)		
Main St Prtg & Copy Ctr Inc	G	570 424-0800
Stroudsburg (G-18126)		
Marathon Printing Inc	F	215 238-1100
Philadelphia (G-13991)		
Marlin A Inch	G	570 374-1106
Selinsgrove (G-17330)		
Masters Ink Corporation	G	724 745-1122
Canonsburg (G-2601)		
Maximum Graphics Corporation	F	215 639-6700
Bensalem (G-1223)		
Mercersburg Printing Inc	E	717 328-3902
Mercersburg (G-10993)		
Mercersburg Printing Inc	G	717 762-8204
Waynesboro (G-19418)		
Metal Photo Service Inc	G	412 829-2992
Wall (G-18779)		
Michael Anthony Salvatori	G	570 326-9222
Williamsport (G-20041)		
Mifflin Press Inc	G	717 684-2253
Columbia (G-3443)		
Mifflinburg Telegraph Inc	G	570 966-2255
Mifflinburg (G-11099)		
Migu Press Inc	E	215 957-9763
Warminster (G-18923)		
Miller Printing Inc	G	717 626-5800
Ephrata (G-5128)		
Minit Rubber Stamps	G	610 352-8600
Upper Darby (G-18690)		
Minnich Limited	G	717 697-2204
Mechanicsburg (G-10871)		
Minuteman Press	G	412 621-7456
Pittsburgh (G-15294)		
Minuteman Press	G	724 346-1105
Hermitage (G-7592)		
Minuteman Press	G	724 846-9740
Beaver Falls (G-1005)		
Minuteman Press	G	215 538-2200
Quakertown (G-16221)		
Minuteman Press Intl Inc	G	610 902-0203
Wayne (G-19357)		
Minuteman Press South Hills	G	412 531-0809
Pittsburgh (G-15295)		
Mjjm Enterprises Inc	E	717 392-1711
Lancaster (G-9137)		
Modern Reproductions Inc	F	412 488-7700
Pittsburgh (G-15298)		
Mondlak Printery	G	570 654-9871
Pittston (G-15768)		
Morgan Printing Company	G	215 784-0966
Willow Grove (G-20129)		
Morris Printing Company	G	412 881-8626
Pittsburgh (G-15302)		
Motto Graphics Inc	G	570 639-5555
Dallas (G-3963)		
Movad LLC	F	215 638-2679
Plymouth Meeting (G-15858)		
Multiscope Incorporated	E	724 743-1083
Canonsburg (G-2606)		
Munro Prtg Graphic Design LLC	G	610 485-1966
Marcus Hook (G-10451)		
Murphy Printing Free Press	E	724 927-2222
Linesville (G-9985)		
Nacci Printing Inc	E	610 434-1224
Allentown (G-324)		
Nash Printing LLC	F	215 855-4267
Lansdale (G-9391)		
National Mail Graphics Corp	D	610 524-1600
Exton (G-5713)		

New Centuries LLC	G	724 347-3030
Hermitage (G-7593)		
News Chronicle Co Inc	E	717 532-4101
Shippensburg (G-17540)		
Newtown Business Forms Corp	F	215 364-3898
Huntingdon Valley (G-8017)		
Newville Print Shop	G	717 776-7673
Newville (G-12608)		
Norcorp Inc	G	814 445-2523
Somerset (G-17699)		
Northeastern Envelope Company	D	800 233-4285
Old Forge (G-12971)		
Northern Liberty Press LLC	G	215 634-3000
Philadelphia (G-14084)		
Npc Inc	B	814 239-8787
Claysburg (G-3207)		
Nuss Printing Inc	F	610 853-3005
Havertown (G-7424)		
Offset Paperback Mfrs Inc	A	570 675-5261
Dallas (G-3964)		
Ogden Brothers Incorporated	F	610 789-1258
Havertown (G-7425)		
Old York Road Printing LLC	E	215 957-6200
Warminster (G-18931)		
Olenicks Prtg & Photography Sp	G	814 342-2853
Philipsburg (G-14522)		
P A Hutchison Company	C	570 876-4560
Mayfield (G-10542)		
P/S Printing & Copy Services	G	814 623-7033
Bedford (G-1069)		
Pace Resources Inc	E	717 852-1300
York (G-20616)		
Paoli Print & Copy Inc	G	610 644-7471
Paoli (G-13145)		
Paravano Company Inc	G	215 659-4600
Willow Grove (G-20132)		
Park Press Inc	G	724 465-5812
Indiana (G-8116)		
Parkland Bindery Inc	G	610 433-6153
Allentown (G-344)		
Partners Press Inc	F	610 666-7960
Oaks (G-12935)		
Partridge Wirth Company Inc	F	570 344-8514
Scranton (G-17270)		
Patrick Mc Cool	F	814 359-2447
Bellefonte (G-1110)		
Payne Printery Inc	D	570 675-1147
Dallas (G-3965)		
Peacock Printing	D	814 336-5009
Erie (G-5418)		
Pegasus Print & Copy Centers	G	610 356-8787
Broomall (G-2300)		
Penn Print & Graphics	G	724 239-5849
Bentleyville (G-1273)		
Penn Valley Printing Company	G	215 295-5755
Morrisville (G-11576)		
Penny Mansfield Saver Inc	G	570 662-3277
Mansfield (G-10424)		
Penny Press of York Inc	G	717 843-4078
York (G-20622)		
Phoenix Design & Print Inc	F	412 264-4895
Coraopolis (G-3715)		
Phoenix Lithographing Corp	D	215 969-4600
Philadelphia (G-14170)		
Phoenix Lithographing Corp	C	215 698-9000
Philadelphia (G-14171)		
Pik-A-Boo Photos LLC	G	267 334-6379
Philadelphia (G-14177)		
Pikewood Inc	F	610 974-8000
Bethlehem (G-1597)		
Pjr Printing Inc	G	724 283-2666
Butler (G-2434)		
Placemat Printers Inc	F	610 285-2255
Fogelsville (G-5996)		
Portico Group LLC	G	610 566-8499
Media (G-10943)		
Portico Printing LLC	G	215 717-5151
Philadelphia (G-14192)		
Premier Printing Solutions LLC	G	570 426-1570
East Stroudsburg (G-4630)		
Press and Journal	E	717 944-4628
Middletown (G-11071)		
Press Box Printing	G	814 944-3057
Altoona (G-538)		
Press Craft Printers Inc	G	412 761-8200
Pittsburgh (G-15434)		
Prince Printing	G	412 233-3555
Clairton (G-3156)		
Print & Copy Center Inc	F	412 828-2205
Verona (G-18760)		

PRODUCT

Print and Graphics Scholrship ....G...... 412 741-6860
Warrendale *(G-19093)*

Print Shop ....G...... 215 788-1883
Croydon *(G-3925)*

Print Shop ....G...... 570 327-9005
Williamsport *(G-20064)*

Print Shop Inc ....G...... 610 692-1810
West Chester *(G-19620)*

Print Tech Western PA ....E...... 412 963-1500
Pittsburgh *(G-15440)*

Print Works On Demand Inc ....G...... 717 545-5215
Harrisburg *(G-7202)*

Print-O-Stat Inc ....F...... 724 742-9811
Cranberry Township *(G-3845)*

Print-O-Stat Inc ....E...... 717 812-9476
York *(G-20640)*

Print-O-Stat Inc ....G...... 610 265-5470
King of Prussia *(G-8664)*

Print-O-Stat Inc ....F...... 717 795-9255
Mechanicsburg *(G-10882)*

Print2finish LLC ....G...... 215 369-5494
Yardley *(G-20334)*

Printaway Inc ....G...... 717 263-1839
Chambersburg *(G-2971)*

Printers Parts Store Inc ....F...... 610 279-6660
Bridgeport *(G-2044)*

Printforce Inc ....G...... 610 797-6455
Allentown *(G-360)*

Printing 4u ....G...... 610 377-0111
Lehighton *(G-9722)*

Printing Concepts Inc ....E...... 814 833-8080
Erie *(G-5437)*

Printing Express Inc ....G...... 717 600-1111
York *(G-20641)*

Printing Plus+ Inc ....F...... 814 834-1000
Saint Marys *(G-17009)*

Printing Post LLC ....G...... 412 367-7468
Pittsburgh *(G-15445)*

Printing Press ....G...... 412 264-3355
Coraopolis *(G-3718)*

Printworks & Company Inc ....E...... 215 721-8500
Lansdale *(G-9400)*

Process Reproductions Inc ....E...... 412 321-3120
Pittsburgh *(G-15452)*

Professional Duplicating Inc ....E...... 610 891-7979
Media *(G-10944)*

Promotional Printing Assoc ....G...... 215 639-1662
Bensalem *(G-1245)*

Prova Inc ....G...... 412 278-3010
Carnegie *(G-2783)*

Qg Printing II Corp ....A...... 610 593-1445
Atglen *(G-804)*

Qg Printing II Corp ....B...... 717 642-5871
Fairfield *(G-5768)*

Quad/Graphics Inc ....B...... 215 541-2729
Pennsburg *(G-13253)*

Quad/Graphics Inc ....B...... 570 459-5700
Hazleton *(G-7522)*

Quality Print Shop Inc ....G...... 570 473-1122
Northumberland *(G-12874)*

Quick Print Center PA ....G...... 717 637-2838
Hanover *(G-6939)*

R R Donnelley & Sons Company ....C...... 215 671-9500
Philadelphia *(G-14225)*

Raff Printing Inc ....D...... 412 431-4044
Pittsburgh *(G-15466)*

Rainbow Graphics Inc ....G...... 724 228-3007
Bentleyville *(G-1275)*

Reading Eagle Company ....E...... 610 371-5000
Reading *(G-16488)*

Reed & Witting Company ....E...... 412 682-1000
Pittsburgh *(G-15476)*

Rhodes & Hammers Printing ....G...... 724 852-1457
Waynesburg *(G-19451)*

Riecks Letter Service Inc ....F...... 610 375-8581
Reading *(G-16498)*

Rittenhouse Instant Press ....G...... 215 854-0505
Philadelphia *(G-14251)*

Rocket-Courier Newspaper ....F...... 570 746-1217
Wyalusing *(G-20258)*

Roller Printing Company Inc ....G...... 717 632-1433
Hanover *(G-6946)*

Rowe Printing Shop ....F...... 717 249-5485
Carlisle *(G-2737)*

Rowland Printing Inc ....E...... 610 933-7400
Phoenixville *(G-14575)*

Royalton Press Inc ....G...... 610 929-4040
Camp Hill *(G-2516)*

Rozema Printing LLC ....G...... 717 564-4143
Harrisburg *(G-7210)*

S P Printing ....G...... 610 562-8551
Shoemakersville *(G-17574)*

Samuel C Rizzo Jr ....G...... 814 725-3047
North East *(G-12760)*

Sandt Printing Co Inc ....G...... 610 258-7445
Easton *(G-4751)*

Schank Printing Inc ....F...... 610 828-1623
Conshohocken *(G-3603)*

Seiders Printing Co Inc ....G...... 570 622-0570
Pottsville *(G-16097)*

Semler Enterprises Inc ....G...... 717 242-0322
Burnham *(G-2361)*

Seneca Printing & Label Inc ....D...... 814 437-5364
Franklin *(G-6157)*

Seneca Printing Express Inc ....G...... 814 437-5364
Franklin *(G-6158)*

Shemco Corp ....F...... 412 831-6022
Pittsburgh *(G-15529)*

Sheridan Group Inc ....D...... 717 632-3535
Hanover *(G-6950)*

Sheridan Press Inc ....G...... 717 632-3535
Hanover *(G-6951)*

Sir James Prtg & Bus Forms Inc ....G...... 724 339-2122
New Kensington *(G-12377)*

Sir Speedy Printing Center ....G...... 412 687-0500
Pittsburgh *(G-15543)*

Slate Belt Printers Inc ....G...... 610 863-6752
Pen Argyl *(G-13217)*

Slate Lick Printing Inc ....G...... 724 295-2053
Freeport *(G-6214)*

Slates Enterprises Inc ....G...... 814 695-2851
Duncansville *(G-4463)*

Slavia Printing Co Inc ....G...... 412 343-4444
Pittsburgh *(G-15545)*

Smales Printery Inc ....G...... 610 323-7775
Pottstown *(G-16047)*

South Greensburg Printing Co ....F...... 724 834-0295
Greensburg *(G-6715)*

Spahr-Evans Printers ....G...... 215 886-4057
Glenside *(G-6539)*

Spencer Printing Inc ....G...... 570 253-2001
Honesdale *(G-7725)*

Sprint Print Inc ....G...... 570 586-5947
Chinchilla *(G-3132)*

St Clair Graphics Inc ....F...... 570 253-6692
Honesdale *(G-7726)*

Standard Offset Prtg Co Inc ....D...... 610 375-6174
Reading *(G-16524)*

Star Printing Company ....G...... 717 456-5692
Delta *(G-4063)*

Starprint Publications Inc ....G...... 814 736-9666
Portage *(G-15922)*

State Street Copy and Press ....G...... 717 232-6684
Harrisburg *(G-7220)*

Stauffer Acquisition Corp ....E...... 717 569-3200
East Petersburg *(G-4591)*

Steckel Printing Inc ....D...... 717 898-1555
Lancaster *(G-9205)*

Steel City Graphics Inc ....G...... 724 942-5699
Canonsburg *(G-2640)*

Steele Print Inc ....G...... 724 758-6178
Ellwood City *(G-4952)*

Stefanos Printing Inc ....G...... 724 277-8374
Dunbar *(G-4443)*

Strassheim Printing Co Inc ....G...... 610 446-3637
Havertown *(G-7428)*

Sullivan Review ....G...... 570 928-8403
Dushore *(G-4511)*

Sun Litho Print Inc ....F...... 570 421-3250
East Stroudsburg *(G-4636)*

Taggart Printing Corporation ....F...... 610 431-2500
West Chester *(G-19655)*

Tech Support Screen P ....E...... 412 697-0171
Pittsburgh *(G-15601)*

Third Dimension Spc LLC ....G...... 570 969-0623
Scranton *(G-17301)*

Thorndale Press Inc ....G...... 610 384-3363
Downingtown *(G-4258)*

Tioga Publishing Company ....E...... 570 724-2287
Wellsboro *(G-19473)*

Todays Graphics Inc ....D...... 215 634-6200
Philadelphia *(G-14394)*

Tor Industries Inc ....G...... 570 622-7370
Pottsville *(G-16099)*

Tre Graphics Etc Inc ....G...... 610 821-8508
Allentown *(G-411)*

Tri-Ad Litho Inc ....F...... 412 795-3110
Pittsburgh *(G-15645)*

Tricounty Printers Ltd ....G...... 215 886-3737
Oreland *(G-13031)*

Tristate Blue Printing Inc ....E...... 412 281-3538
Pittsburgh *(G-15653)*

Trust Franklin Press Co ....F...... 412 481-6442
Pittsburgh *(G-15658)*

Type & Print Inc ....E...... 412 241-6070
Clinton *(G-3267)*

Typecraft Press Inc ....E...... 412 488-1600
Pittsburgh *(G-15663)*

TYT LLC ....E...... 800 511-2009
Bethlehem *(G-1645)*

Unigraphics Communications ....G...... 717 697-8132
Mechanicsburg *(G-10902)*

United Offset ....G...... 215 721-2251
Franconia *(G-6111)*

United Partners Ltd ....F...... 570 288-7603
Taylor *(G-18264)*

United Partners Ltd ....G...... 570 283-0995
Taylor *(G-18265)*

Unity Printing Company Inc ....E...... 724 537-5800
Latrobe *(G-9527)*

Universal Printing Company LLC ....D...... 570 342-1243
Dunmore *(G-4487)*

University Copy Service Inc ....G...... 215 898-5574
Philadelphia *(G-14429)*

Valley Business Services Inc ....F...... 610 366-1970
Trexlertown *(G-18511)*

Valley Litho Inc ....G...... 610 437-5122
Whitehall *(G-19892)*

Valley Press Inc ....E...... 610 664-7770
Bala Cynwyd *(G-895)*

Velocity Color Inc ....G...... 717 431-2591
Lancaster *(G-9232)*

Vernon Printing Inc ....F...... 724 283-9242
Butler *(G-2447)*

Vocam Corp ....G...... 215 348-7115
Doylestown *(G-4344)*

W L Fegley & Son Inc ....G...... 610 779-0277
Reading *(G-16561)*

W M Abene Co ....G...... 570 457-8334
Old Forge *(G-12977)*

Wakefoose Office Supply & Prtg ....G...... 814 623-5742
Bedford *(G-1079)*

Waveline Direct Llc ....E...... 717 795-8830
Mechanicsburg *(G-10905)*

Webb Communications Inc ....F...... 570 779-9543
Plymouth *(G-15825)*

West Penn Printing ....G...... 724 546-2020
New Castle *(G-12168)*

West Shore Prtg & Dist Corp ....E...... 717 691-8282
Mechanicsburg *(G-10908)*

White Oak Group Inc ....E...... 717 291-2222
Lancaster *(G-9240)*

Whitehead Eagle Corporation ....G...... 724 346-4280
Sharon *(G-17447)*

William A Fraser Inc ....G...... 570 622-7347
Pottsville *(G-16102)*

William Penn Printing Company ....G...... 412 322-3660
Pittsburgh *(G-15717)*

Wise Printing Co Inc ....G...... 717 741-2751
York *(G-20715)*

WM Enterprises Inc ....E...... 717 238-5751
Harrisburg *(G-7248)*

Wolf Printing ....G...... 717 755-1560
York *(G-20716)*

Ygs West LLC ....E...... 425 251-5005
York *(G-20725)*

Yurchak Printing Inc ....G...... 717 399-9551
Lancaster *(G-9244)*

Zodiac Printing Corporation ....E...... 570 474-9220
Mountain Top *(G-11784)*

PRINTING: Pamphlets

Amrep Corporation ....F...... 609 487-0905
Plymouth Meeting *(G-15831)*

Parker-Hannifin Corporation ....G...... 814 860-5700
Erie *(G-5415)*

PRINTING: Photo-Offset

Dave Zerbe Studio ....G...... 610 376-0379
Reading *(G-16360)*

Liberty Press LLC ....G...... 215 943-3788
Levittown *(G-9846)*

PRINTING: Screen, Broadwoven Fabrics, Cotton

Academy Sports Center Inc ....G...... 570 339-3399
Mount Carmel *(G-11622)*

All ADS Up ....G...... 412 881-4114
Pittsburgh *(G-14673)*

C Jthomas Screening Inc .... F 412 384-4279
Monongahela *(G-11305)*

Craig Hollern .... E 814 539-2974
Johnstown *(G-8366)*

Dante Defranco Printing .... E 610 588-7300
Roseto *(G-16819)*

Edwin Ringer .... G 724 746-3374
Westland *(G-19782)*

Greater Pitts Speciality .... G 412 821-5976
Pittsburgh *(G-15061)*

J P Tees Inc .... G 215 634-2348
Philadelphia *(G-13887)*

Larry D Mays .... F 814 833-7988
Erie *(G-5360)*

Lerko Products .... F 570 473-3501
Northumberland *(G-12869)*

Milford Sportswear Inc .... G 215 529-9316
Quakertown *(G-16219)*

Mountainview Graphics .... G 610 939-1471
Reading *(G-16449)*

Royalty Promotions Inc .... G 215 794-2707
Furlong *(G-6233)*

Shenk Athletic Equipment Co .... F 717 766-6600
Mechanicsburg *(G-10888)*

Southern Alleghenies Advg Inc ...... G 814 472-8593
Ebensburg *(G-4797)*

Trbz Ink LLC .... G 267 918-2242
Philadelphia *(G-14403)*

Village Idiot Designs .... G 724 545-7477
Kittanning *(G-8802)*

Youre Putting ME On Inc .... E 412 655-9666
Pittsburgh *(G-15731)*

PRINTING: Screen, Fabric

4 Life Promotions LLC .... G 215 919-4985
Philadelphia *(G-13319)*

Action Sportswear Inc .... F 610 623-1820
Primos *(G-16106)*

American Process Lettering Inc ...... C 610 623-9000
Primos *(G-16107)*

C & S Sports & Promotions .... G 724 775-1655
Monaca *(G-11287)*

Custom Corner Sportswear .... G 724 588-1667
Greenville *(G-6740)*

Custom Printed Graphics Inc .... E 412 881-8208
Pittsburgh *(G-14895)*

Daves Pro Shop Inc .... F 814 834-6116
Saint Marys *(G-16961)*

Epic Apparel LLC .... G 412 350-9543
West Mifflin *(G-19736)*

Heritage Screen Printing Inc .... G 215 672-2382
Warminster *(G-18894)*

Hunts Promotions .... G 814 623-2751
Bedford *(G-1054)*

Kampus Klothes Inc .... E 215 357-0892
Warminster *(G-18904)*

Karl Dodson .... G 717 938-6132
New Cumberland *(G-12188)*

Kinteco Inc .... G 610 921-1494
Temple *(G-18332)*

Log Cabin Embroidery Inc .... G 724 327-5929
Murrysville *(G-11855)*

Magnum Screening .... G 570 489-2902
Olyphant *(G-12993)*

Nittany EMB & Digitizing .... F 814 359-0905
State College *(G-17998)*

Nk Graphics Inc .... G 717 838-8324
Palmyra *(G-13127)*

Ohiopyle Prints Inc .... C 724 329-4652
Ohiopyle *(G-12939)*

Print Shop Inc .... G 570 784-4020
Bloomsburg *(G-1796)*

Printex LLC .... G 412 371-6667
Pittsburgh *(G-15444)*

Rowe Screen Print Inc .... F 717 774-8920
New Cumberland *(G-12190)*

Sez Sew Stitching Inc .... F 814 339-6734
Osceola Mills *(G-13057)*

Sunset Tees .... G 717 737-9919
Camp Hill *(G-2519)*

Three Soles Corp .... F 717 762-1945
Waynesboro *(G-19428)*

Todd Lengle & Co Inc .... G 610 777-0731
Reading *(G-16541)*

Todd Weikel .... G 610 779-5508
Reading *(G-16542)*

Trbz Ink LLC .... G 267 918-2242
Philadelphia *(G-14403)*

Triple D Screen Printing .... E 215 788-4877
Bristol *(G-2211)*

PRINTING: Screen, Manmade Fiber & Silk, Broadwoven Fabric

A & W Screen Printing Inc .... F 717 738-2726
Ephrata *(G-5089)*

Academy Sports Center Inc .... G 570 339-3399
Mount Carmel *(G-11622)*

Blue Heron Sportswear Inc .... G 570 742-3228
Milton *(G-11234)*

DOC Printing LLC .... G 267 702-6196
Philadelphia *(G-13637)*

Double M Productions LLC .... F 570 476-8000
Stroudsburg *(G-18114)*

Finish Line Screen Prtg Inc .... G 814 238-0122
State College *(G-17964)*

Go Tell It Inc .... G 212 769-3220
Robesonia *(G-16774)*

Newtown Printing Corp .... G 215 968-6876
Newtown *(G-12528)*

Pennsylvania Promotions Inc .... F 800 360-2800
Exton *(G-5724)*

Prince Printing .... G 412 233-3555
Clairton *(G-3156)*

Valley Silk Screening Inc .... G 724 962-5255
Sharpsville *(G-17477)*

PRINTING: Thermography

Hilden Enterprises Inc .... E 412 257-8459
Pittsburgh *(G-15094)*

Printers Printer Inc .... F 610 454-0102
Collegeville *(G-3389)*

Third Dimension Spc LLC .... G 570 969-0623
Scranton *(G-17301)*

PROFESSIONAL EQPT & SPLYS, WHOLESALE: Analytical Instruments

Microtrac Inc .... E 215 619-9920
Montgomeryville *(G-11408)*

PROFESSIONAL EQPT & SPLYS, WHOLESALE: Engineers', NEC

Print-O-Stat Inc .... F 724 742-9811
Cranberry Township *(G-3845)*

Ridgways Inc .... E 215 735-8055
Philadelphia *(G-14250)*

Ussc Group Inc .... D 610 265-3610
Exton *(G-5743)*

PROFESSIONAL EQPT & SPLYS, WHOLESALE: Optical Goods

Davro Optical Systems Inc .... G 215 362-3870
Lansdale *(G-9357)*

Vere Inc .... F 724 335-5530
New Kensington *(G-12386)*

PROFESSIONAL INSTRUMENT REPAIR SVCS

ADS LLC .... G 717 554-7552
Lemoyne *(G-9740)*

Geosonics Inc .... F 724 934-2900
Warrendale *(G-19076)*

Millennium Machining Spc .... G 570 501-2002
Hazleton *(G-7510)*

Sterilzer Rfurbishing Svcs Inc .... F 814 456-2616
Erie *(G-5492)*

Valmet Inc .... D 570 587-5111
S Abingtn Twp *(G-16900)*

PROFILE SHAPES: Unsupported Plastics

Cambria Plastics LLC .... G 814 535-5467
Johnstown *(G-8361)*

Ensinger Penn Fibre Inc .... D 215 702-9551
Bensalem *(G-1190)*

Essentra Porous Tech Corp .... E 814 898-3238
Erie *(G-5283)*

Formtech Enterprises Inc .... E 814 474-1940
Fairview *(G-5823)*

Gateway Packaging Corp .... F 724 327-7400
Export *(G-5607)*

H R Edgar Machining & Fabg Inc .... D 724 339-6694
New Kensington *(G-12344)*

J Benson Corp .... G 610 678-2692
Reading *(G-16411)*

Meadville New Products Inc .... F 814 336-2174
Meadville *(G-10759)*

Oilfield LLC .... G 814 623-8125
Bedford *(G-1067)*

Ono Industries Inc .... E 717 865-6619
Ono *(G-13004)*

Quadrant Holding Inc .... C 724 468-7062
Delmont *(G-4054)*

Resdel Corporation .... G 215 343-2400
Warrington *(G-19131)*

PROGRAMMERS: Indl Process

Advanced Automated Controls Co .... F 570 842-5842
Lake Ariel *(G-8887)*

Edwin L Heim Co .... E 717 233-8711
Harrisburg *(G-7125)*

Ges Automation Technology .... E 717 236-8733
Harrisburg *(G-7133)*

Te Connectivity Corporation .... C 717 762-9186
Waynesboro *(G-19425)*

PROMOTION SVCS

Ernie Saxton .... G 215 752-7797
Langhorne *(G-9294)*

Goodway Graphics Inc .... B 215 887-5700
Jenkintown *(G-8288)*

PROPELLERS: Boat & Ship, Cast

Century Propeller Corporation .... F 814 677-7100
Franklin *(G-6119)*

Sensenich Propeller Company .... E 717 560-3711
Lititz *(G-10048)*

PROPRIETARY STORES, NON-PRESCRIPTION MEDICINE

Burmans Medical Supplies Inc .... F 610 876-6068
Upper Chichester *(G-18657)*

PROTECTION EQPT: Lightning

G&W Solutions Inc .... G 610 704-6959
Emmaus *(G-5026)*

PUBLISHERS: Art Copy

Image Makers Art Inc .... G 610 722-5807
Berwyn *(G-1365)*

PUBLISHERS: Art Copy & Poster

Artistworks Wholesale Inc .... G 610 622-9940
Lansdowne *(G-9430)*

Sports Images International .... G 412 851-1610
Pittsburgh *(G-15571)*

PUBLISHERS: Book

American Law Institute .... D 215 243-1600
Philadelphia *(G-13385)*

Ascension Publishing LLC .... G 610 696-7795
West Chester *(G-19502)*

Atlantic Alliance Pubg Co .... G 267 319-1659
Philadelphia *(G-13421)*

Beard Group Inc .... E 240 629-3300
Fairless Hills *(G-5773)*

Beidel Printing House Inc .... E 717 532-5063
Shippensburg *(G-17516)*

Benetvison .... G 814 459-9224
Erie *(G-5208)*

Brooks Group and Assoc Inc .... E 610 429-8990
West Chester *(G-19515)*

Brookshire Printing Inc .... E 717 392-1321
Lancaster *(G-8961)*

Center Edctn & Empymnt Law .... E 800 365-4900
Malvern *(G-10202)*

Charlesworth Group (usa) Inc .... G 215 922-1611
Philadelphia *(G-13533)*

Church Publishing Incorporated ...... E 212 592-4229
Harrisburg *(G-7104)*

Concentrated Knowledge Corp .... E 610 388-5020
Kennett Square *(G-8507)*

Coronet Books Inc .... G 215 925-2762
Philadelphia *(G-13574)*

Cottage Communications Inc .... G 610 678-7473
Reading *(G-16351)*

Destiny Image Inc .... E 717 532-3040
Shippensburg *(G-17526)*

Dooner Ventures LLC .... G 610 420-1100
Bryn Mawr *(G-2320)*

Dorrance Publishing Co Inc .... E 800 788-7654
Pittsburgh *(G-14934)*

PRODUCT

Duquesne Univ of Holy Spirit ....G...... 412 396-6610
Pittsburgh (G-14945)

Elsevier Inc ....G...... 215 239-3900
Philadelphia (G-13670)

From Heart ....G...... 570 278-6343
Montrose (G-11464)

Galeron Consulting LLC ....E...... 267 293-9230
Bensalem (G-1202)

Idea Group Inc ....E...... 717 533-3673
Hershey (G-7617)

Keyword Communications Inc ....G...... 717 481-2960
Harrisburg (G-7163)

Knittle & Frey AG-Center Inc ....G...... 570 323-7554
Williamsport (G-20032)

Lunacor Inc ....G...... 610 328-6150
Springfield (G-17917)

Meniscus Limited ....D...... 610 567-2725
Conshohocken (G-3575)

Michael Furman Photography ....G...... 215 925-4233
Philadelphia (G-14020)

Mid Mon Valley Pub ....E...... 724 314-0030
Monessen (G-11300)

Miroglyphics ....G...... 215 224-2486
Philadelphia (G-14027)

Morning Call Inc ....E...... 610 861-3600
Bethlehem (G-1575)

National Publishing Company ....B...... 215 676-1863
Philadelphia (G-14055)

Nori Medical Group ....G...... 717 532-3040
Shippensburg (G-17542)

Offset Paperback Mfrs Inc ....A...... 570 675-5261
Dallas (G-3964)

Oz World Media LLC ....E...... 202 470-6757
Devon (G-4115)

Pennsylvania Fireman Inc ....F...... 717 397-9174
Lititz (G-10031)

Pennsylvania State University ....G...... 814 863-3764
University Park (G-18653)

Pennsylvania State University ....E...... 814 865-1327
University Park (G-18654)

Police Shield Corp ....G...... 215 788-3489
Bristol (G-2184)

Printing Inds Amer Foundation ....F...... 412 741-6860
Warrendale (G-19094)

Private Zone Productions Corp ....G...... 267 592-5447
Philadelphia (G-14204)

PSC Publishing ....E...... 570 443-9749
White Haven (G-19851)

Robar Industries Inc ....G...... 484 688-0300
Plymouth Meeting (G-15868)

Scribe Inc ....F...... 215 336-5095
Allentown (G-387)

Scribe Inc ....G...... 215 336-5094
Philadelphia (G-14289)

Secrets of Big Dogs ....G...... 814 696-0469
Hollidaysburg (G-7653)

Society For Industrial & Appli ....D...... 215 382-9800
Philadelphia (G-14320)

Sunrise Publishing & Distrg ....G...... 724 946-9057
Sharpsville (G-17476)

Thespiderfriends Com LLC ....G...... 412 257-2346
Bridgeville (G-2094)

Waza Inc ....G...... 610 827-7800
Chester Springs (G-3087)

Whispering Leaf Inc ....E...... 267 437-2991
Philadelphia (G-14473)

Zur Ltd ....E...... 717 761-7044
Camp Hill (G-2528)

PUBLISHERS: Books, No Printing

American Baptst HM Mission Soc ....D...... 610 768-2465
King of Prussia (G-8581)

American Bible Society ....C...... 212 408-1200
Philadelphia (G-13379)

Atlantic Cmmncations Group Inc ....E...... 215 836-4683
Flowertown (G-5984)

Beverly Hall Co ....E...... 215 536-7048
Quakertown (G-16172)

Bible Visuals International ....G...... 717 859-1131
Akron (G-34)

Boyds Mills Press Inc ....F...... 570 253-1164
Honesdale (G-7703)

Breakthrough Publications Inc ....G...... 610 928-4061
Emmaus (G-5021)

Brick Wall Ministries ....G...... 717 592-1798
Middletown (G-11049)

Business 21 Publishing LLC ....D...... 484 479-2700
Springfield (G-17908)

Caribbean Elite Magazine Inc ....G...... 718 702-0161
Allentown (G-162)

Chandler-White Publishing Co ....G...... 312 907-3271
Philadelphia (G-13524)

Charlene Crawford ....G...... 215 432-7542
Elkins Park (G-4901)

Clarence Larkin Estate ....G...... 215 576-5590
Glenside (G-6512)

Clp Publications Inc ....G...... 215 567-5080
Philadelphia (G-13551)

Cmmunications U Krienr-Ptthoff ....G...... 484 547-5261
Macungie (G-10144)

Creative Nonfiction Foundation ....G...... 412 688-0304
Pittsburgh (G-14886)

Destech Publications Inc ....G...... 717 290-1660
Lancaster (G-8996)

Direct Marketing Publishers ....G...... 215 321-3068
Yardley (G-20308)

Dorchester Publishing Co Inc ....E...... 212 725-8811
Wayne (G-19319)

Fox Chapel Publishing Co Inc ....E...... 800 457-9112
East Petersburg (G-4587)

Gutenberg Inc ....G...... 570 488-9820
Waymart (G-19287)

Harpercollins Publishers LLC ....C...... 570 941-1500
Moosic (G-11507)

Harrison House Inc ....C...... 918 523-5700
Shippensburg (G-17531)

J S Paluch Co Inc ....E...... 724 772-8850
Cranberry Township (G-3825)

Jeremiah Junction Inc ....G...... 215 529-6430
Quakertown (G-16204)

Jessica Kingsley Publishers ....G...... 215 922-1161
Philadelphia (G-13895)

Jewish Publication Soc of Amer ....F...... 215 832-0600
Philadelphia (G-13897)

Job Training Systems Inc ....G...... 610 444-0868
Kennett Square (G-8515)

Kerygma Inc ....G...... 412 344-6062
Bradford (G-1976)

Knowledge In A Nut Shell Inc ....G...... 412 765-2020
Pittsburgh (G-15179)

Landes Bioscience Inc ....E...... 512 637-6050
Philadelphia (G-13951)

Larry Arnold ....G...... 717 236-0080
Harrisburg (G-7168)

Lippincott Williams & Wilkins ....G...... 215 521-8300
Philadelphia (G-13972)

Markowski International Pubg ....G...... 717 566-0468
Hummelstown (G-7917)

Organization Design & Dev Inc ....E...... 610 279-2202
West Chester (G-19612)

Paul Withers ....G...... 717 896-3173
Halifax (G-6827)

Proofreaders LLC ....G...... 215 295-9400
Penns Park (G-13243)

Quirk Productions Inc ....F...... 215 627-3581
Philadelphia (G-14221)

Reading Reading Books LLC ....G...... 757 329-4224
Morgantown (G-11532)

Renaissance Press Inc ....G...... 717 534-0708
Hummelstown (G-7924)

Rowman & Littlefield Publish ....B...... 717 794-3800
Blue Ridge Summit (G-1859)

S&P Global Inc ....C...... 215 430-6000
Philadelphia (G-14274)

Shepherd Press Inc ....G...... 570 379-2015
Wapwallopen (G-18809)

Southside Holdings Inc ....E...... 412 431-8300
Pittsburgh (G-15564)

Springer Adis Us LLC ....G...... 215 574-2201
Philadelphia (G-14335)

Stan Clark Military Books ....G...... 717 337-1728
Gettysburg (G-6315)

Swedenborg Foundation Inc ....G...... 610 430-3222
West Chester (G-19649)

Thomas ....G...... 717 642-6600
Gettysburg (G-6318)

University of Pittsburgh ....F...... 412 383-2456
Pittsburgh (G-15682)

Warner-Crivellaro Stained Glas ....F...... 610 264-1100
Whitehall (G-19893)

Wolters Kluwer Health Inc ....C...... 215 521-8300
Philadelphia (G-14482)

Zondervan Corporation LLC ....C...... 570 941-1366
Dunmore (G-4488)

PUBLISHERS: Catalogs

Barkleigh Productions Inc ....F...... 717 691-3388
Mechanicsburg (G-10822)

Ggs Information Services Inc ....C...... 717 764-2222
York (G-20499)

P H A Finance Inc ....E...... 610 272-4700
Plymouth Meeting (G-15862)

PUBLISHERS: Directories, NEC

Supermedia LLC ....D...... 814 833-2121
Erie (G-5497)

Womens Yellw Pages Gtr Phil ....G...... 610 446-4747
Havertown (G-7433)

PUBLISHERS: Directories, Telephone

Supermedia LLC ....B...... 610 317-5500
Bethlehem (G-1635)

Supermedia LLC ....B...... 717 540-6500
Harrisburg (G-7223)

Verizon Communications Inc ....C...... 570 387-3840
Bloomsburg (G-1806)

Verizon Pennsylvania Inc ....D...... 215 879-7898
Philadelphia (G-14441)

PUBLISHERS: Guides

Upper Perk Shoppers Guide Inc ....G...... 215 679-4133
Pennsburg (G-13260)

PUBLISHERS: Magazines, No Printing

American Law Institute ....D...... 215 243-1600
Philadelphia (G-13385)

American Soc For Deaf Children ....G...... 717 909-5577
Camp Hill (G-2486)

American Waste Digest Corp ....G...... 610 326-9480
Pottstown (G-15942)

Benchmark Group Media Inc ....G...... 610 691-8833
Bethlehem (G-1459)

Bradley Communications Corp ....E...... 484 477-4220
Broomall (G-2281)

Bryn Mawr Communications LLC ....F...... 610 687-0887
Wayne (G-19309)

Catholic Golden Age Inc ....F...... 570 586-1091
Scott Township (G-17183)

Computertalk Associates Inc ....G...... 610 825-7686
Blue Bell (G-1823)

Dirt Rag Magazine ....G...... 412 767-9910
Pittsburgh (G-14926)

Farm Journal Inc ....E...... 215 557-8900
Philadelphia (G-13694)

Ferdic Inc ....G...... 717 731-1426
Camp Hill (G-2497)

Fx Express Publications Inc ....G...... 267 364-5811
Yardley (G-20312)

Innovative Advertising & Mktg ....G...... 717 788-1385
Waynesboro (G-19413)

J A Mitch Printing & Copy Ctr ....G...... 724 847-2940
Beaver Falls (G-1002)

J G Press Inc ....G...... 610 967-4135
Emmaus (G-5029)

J P R Publications Inc ....F...... 570 587-3532
Clarks Summit (G-3196)

Jewish Exponent Inc ....E...... 215 832-0700
Philadelphia (G-13896)

Kappa Books Publishers LLC ....G...... 215 643-6385
Blue Bell (G-1839)

Kappa Media Group Inc ....C...... 215 643-5800
Fort Washington (G-6080)

Kappa Publishing Group Inc ....D...... 215 643-6385
Blue Bell (G-1842)

Kappa Publishing Group Inc ....E...... 215 643-6385
Blue Bell (G-1843)

Kappa Publishing Group Inc ....E...... 215 643-6385
Ambler (G-586)

Kappa Publishing Group Inc ....E...... 215 643-6385
Ambler (G-587)

Kappa Publishing Group Inc ....D...... 215 643-6385
Ambler (G-588)

Lrp Magazine Group ....B...... 215 784-0860
Dresher (G-4356)

Lrp Publications Inc ....F...... 215 784-0941
Horsham (G-7832)

Lutz and Associates ....G...... 724 776-9800
Cranberry Township (G-3833)

Morgan Signs Inc ....E...... 814 238-5051
State College (G-17994)

Motivos LLC ....G...... 267 283-1733
Philadelphia (G-14042)

Mount Lebanon Municipality ....G...... 412 343-3400
Pittsburgh (G-15305)

O & B Communications ....G...... 610 647-8585
Paoli (G-13144)

Pathfinders Travel Inc ....G...... 215 438-2140
Philadelphia (G-14123)

Pittsburgh Magazine.................................F...... 412 622-1360
Pittsburgh (G-15400)

Pittsburgh Professional Magazi ....G...... 412 221-2992
Pittsburgh (G-15405)

Pocono Land & Homes Magazine P......G...... 570 424-1000
Stroudsburg (G-18135)

Red Flag Media Inc ....G...... 215 625-9850
Philadelphia (G-14237)

Relx Inc ....E...... 610 964-4516
Radnor (G-16300)

Roman Press Inc....................................G...... 215 997-9650
Chalfont (G-2886)

Roxanne Toser Non-Sport Entps..........G...... 717 238-1936
Harrisburg (G-7209)

Sing-Out Corporation ....G...... 610 865-5366
Bethlehem (G-1619)

Southside Holdings Inc ....E...... 412 431-8300
Pittsburgh (G-15564)

Sovereign Media Company Inc ....E...... 570 322-7848
Williamsport (G-20073)

Susquehanna Fishing Mag LLC ....G...... 570 441-4606
Bloomsburg (G-1802)

Susquehanna Life Magazine ....G...... 570 522-0149
Lewisburg (G-9920)

Susquehanna Times & Magazine ....G...... 717 898-9207
Salunga (G-17056)

Synchrgnix Info Strategies Inc ....G...... 302 892-4800
Malvern (G-10325)

Technology Data Exchange Inc ....G...... 610 668-4717
Bala Cynwyd (G-894)

Three Bridges Media LLC ....G...... 717 695-2621
Harrisburg (G-7231)

Toastmasters International ....E...... 215 355-4838
Warminster (G-18983)

Tri State Golf Inc ....G...... 215 200-7000
Philadelphia (G-14407)

Ventasia Inc ....G...... 412 661-6600
Pittsburgh (G-15691)

Vert Markets Inc...................................G...... 215 675-1800
Horsham (G-7864)

Victory Media Inc ....G...... 412 269-1663
Coraopolis (G-3731)

Whirl Publishing ....F...... 412 431-7888
Pittsburgh (G-15716)

World Poetry Inc ....G...... 215 309-3722
Philadelphia (G-14488)

PUBLISHERS: Maps

Infomat Associates Inc ....G...... 610 668-8306
Narberth (G-11911)

Kappa Map Group LLC..........................G...... 215 643-5800
Blue Bell (G-1841)

PUBLISHERS: Miscellaneous

3p Ltd ....G...... 717 566-5643
Hummelstown (G-7901)

Acorn Press Inc ....G...... 717 569-3264
Lititz (G-9992)

AMD Pennsylvania LLC.........................F...... 610 485-4400
King of Prussia (G-8579)

American Culture Publs LLC ....G...... 267 608-9734
Chalfont (G-2863)

Amigo Express ....G...... 484 461-3135
Upper Darby (G-18680)

Asphalt Press Industries ....G...... 610 489-7283
Arcola (G-697)

Aspx LLC ....G...... 215 345-6782
Doylestown (G-4271)

Awwsum Internet Services ....G...... 215 543-9078
Philadelphia (G-13430)

Bacon Press ....G...... 484 328-3118
Malvern (G-10192)

Baldwin Publishing Inc.........................F...... 215 369-1369
Washington Crossing (G-19252)

Beye LLC ....G...... 484 581-1840
Wayne (G-19305)

Bill Straley Printing.............................G...... 717 328-5404
Lemasters (G-9731)

BNP Media Inc ....E...... 412 531-3370
Pittsburgh (G-14776)

Bookhaven Press LLC ....G...... 412 494-6926
Coraopolis (G-3663)

Bpes Barr Publicatio Co ....G...... 215 765-0383
Philadelphia (G-13475)

Bradley Communications Corp ....E...... 484 477-4220
Broomall (G-2281)

Bryn and Danes LLC.............................G...... 844 328-2823
Horsham (G-7800)

Business 21 Publishing LLC..................G...... 484 490-9205
Wayne (G-19310)

Buy Photo Stock Lowes Digita ....G...... 814 954-0273
Reynoldsville (G-16655)

Carnegie Learning Inc ....C...... 412 690-2442
Pittsburgh (G-14817)

Carson Publishing Inc ....G...... 412 548-3798
Pittsburgh (G-14822)

Cellco Partnership ....D...... 610 431-5800
West Chester (G-19520)

Chandler-White Publishing Co ....G...... 312 907-3271
Philadelphia (G-13524)

Cider Press Woodworks LLC..................G...... 215 804-0880
Quakertown (G-16179)

Clarivate Analytics (us) LLC ....A...... 215 386-0100
Philadelphia (G-13548)

Collins Harper Publishers ....G...... 570 941-1557
Moosic (G-11504)

Commonwealth Press LLC ....G...... 412 431-4207
Pittsburgh (G-14869)

Contempory Pubg Group E LLC ....G...... 215 953-8210
Feasterville Trevose (G-5900)

Creative Nonfiction Foundation ....G...... 412 688-0304
Pittsburgh (G-14886)

Culturenik Publishing Inc.....................G...... 570 424-9848
Stroudsburg (G-18112)

Cutts Group LLC ....F...... 610 366-9620
Allentown (G-190)

D & A Business Services Inc ....G...... 610 837-7748
Nazareth (G-11960)

David Jefferys LLC ....G...... 215 977-9900
Wallingford (G-18783)

Digital Grapes LLC ....E...... 866 458-4226
King of Prussia (G-8610)

Dorrance Publishing Co Inc ....E...... 800 788-7654
Pittsburgh (G-14934)

Dream Publishing ....G...... 610 945-2017
King of Prussia (G-8612)

Dreamspring Institute ....G...... 570 829-1378
Wilkes Barre (G-19916)

Drexler Associates Inc ....G...... 724 888-2042
Mars (G-10495)

Eber & Wein Inc ....F...... 717 759-8065
New Freedom (G-12205)

Eber & Wein Inc ....F...... 717 759-8065
Shrewsbury (G-17582)

Elsevier Inc ....E...... 215 239-3441
Philadelphia (G-13669)

Energize Inc ....G...... 215 438-8342
Philadelphia (G-13674)

Engle Printing & Pubg Co Inc ....C...... 717 653-1833
Lancaster (G-9009)

Express Money Services Inc..................G...... 717 235-5993
New Freedom (G-12208)

Ficore Incorporated ....E...... 717 735-9740
York (G-20480)

Franchise Bsness Opportunities...........G...... 412 831-2522
Bethel Park (G-1414)

Friends Publishing Corp ....F...... 215 563-8629
Philadelphia (G-13727)

Galeron Consulting LLC.........................E...... 267 293-9230
Bensalem (G-1202)

Gentle Revolution Press ....G...... 215 233-2050
Glenside (G-6519)

Great Valley Publishing Co ....E...... 610 948-7639
Spring City (G-17858)

Grelin Press ....G...... 724 334-8240
New Kensington (G-12343)

Harpercollins Publishers LLC................G...... 800 242-7737
Moosic (G-11508)

Harte Hanks Inc ....G...... 570 826-0414
Hanover Township (G-6989)

Head & The Hand Press LLC..................G...... 856 562-8545
Philadelphia (G-13807)

Herman Geer Communications Inc.......G...... 724 652-0511
New Castle (G-12102)

Infinity Publishing ....F...... 610 941-9999
Conshohocken (G-3562)

Informing Design Inc ....G...... 412 465-0047
Pittsburgh (G-15124)

International Watch Magazine ....F...... 484 417-2122
Ardmore (G-709)

J L Communications Inc ....G...... 215 675-9133
Horsham (G-7826)

Jayco Grafix Inc ....D...... 610 678-2640
Reinholds (G-16633)

Just Kidstuff Inc ....D...... 610 336-9200
Allentown (G-274)

Kapp Advertising Services Inc ....F...... 717 632-8303
Hanover (G-6909)

Kappa Media Group Inc ....C...... 215 643-5800
Fort Washington (G-6080)

Kappa Publishing Group Inc.................D...... 215 643-6385
Blue Bell (G-1842)

King Publications ....G...... 610 395-4074
Allentown (G-284)

Kutztown Publishing Co Inc ....G...... 610 683-7341
Allentown (G-286)

Lancaster General Svcs Bus Tr............F...... 717 544-5474
Lancaster (G-9095)

Library Video Company.........................D...... 610 645-4000
Conshohocken (G-3572)

Lionshare Media Services ....G...... 724 837-9700
Greensburg (G-6685)

Localedge Media Inc ....E...... 716 875-9100
Erie (G-5369)

Louise Grace Publishing ....G...... 610 781-6874
Reading (G-16434)

Marcan Advertising Inc ....G...... 717 270-6929
Cleona (G-3245)

Marcom Group Ltd ....F...... 610 859-8989
Upper Chichester (G-18667)

Media Management Services Inc ....E...... 800 523-5948
Newtown (G-12521)

Meniscus Limited ....D...... 610 567-2725
Conshohocken (G-3575)

Millenium Medical Educational ....E...... 215 230-1960
Doylestown (G-4316)

Mm USA Holdings LLC ....B...... 267 685-2300
Yardley (G-20326)

Monroe Press Inc ....G...... 215 778-7868
Philadelphia (G-14035)

Morgan Signs Inc ....E...... 814 238-5051
State College (G-17994)

Multiscope Incorporated ....E...... 724 743-1083
Canonsburg (G-2606)

National Assn Cllges Employers ....E...... 610 868-1421
Bethlehem (G-1577)

National Hot Rod Association ....D...... 717 584-1200
Lancaster (G-9142)

New Mainstream Press Inc....................G...... 610 617-8800
Bala Cynwyd (G-887)

Newsletters Ink Corp ....E...... 717 393-1000
Lancaster (G-9145)

Newsline Publishing Inc ....E...... 610 337-1050
King of Prussia (G-8656)

Noel Interactive Group LLC ....G...... 732 991-1484
Easton (G-4732)

Old City Publishing ....E...... 215 925-4390
Philadelphia (G-14093)

On Line Publishers Inc ....G...... 717 285-1350
Lancaster (G-9154)

Organ Historical Society ....G...... 804 353-9226
Villanova (G-18768)

P R X ....G...... 570 578-0136
Hanover Township (G-7002)

PA Outdoor Times ....G...... 814 946-7400
Altoona (G-536)

Paul Dry Books Inc ....G...... 215 231-9939
Philadelphia (G-14124)

Penns Valley Publishers ....G...... 215 855-4948
Lansdale (G-9397)

Pennsylvania Equestrian ....G...... 717 509-9800
Lancaster (G-9167)

Pennsylvania State University...............E...... 814 865-1327
University Park (G-18654)

Philadelphia Photo Review ....G...... 215 364-9185
Langhorne (G-9318)

Pittsburgh Business Times ....G...... 412 481-6397
Pittsburgh (G-15389)

Pittsburgh Technology Council ....E...... 412 687-2700
Pittsburgh (G-15410)

Police Shield Corp ....E...... 215 788-3489
Bristol (G-2184)

Press and Journal.................................E...... 717 944-4628
Middletown (G-11071)

Press Bistro ....G...... 814 254-4835
Johnstown (G-8424)

Press Start Games ....G...... 267 253-0595
East Berlin (G-4525)

Prisma Inc ....E...... 412 503-4006
Pittsburgh (G-15448)

Publication Connexion LLC....................F...... 215 944-9400
Newtown (G-12539)

Real Estate Book South Cent ....G...... 814 943-8110
Altoona (G-542)

Recon Publications ....G...... 215 843-4256
Philadelphia (G-14233)

Regency Typographic Svcs Inc ....F...... 215 425-8810
Philadelphia (G-14238)

Riecks Publishing ....G...... 610 685-1222
Reading (G-16499)

PRODUCT

Rwg Company ....G....... 215 552-9541
Malvern *(G-10312)*

Saj Publishing ....G....... 610 544-5484
Springfield *(G-17922)*

Sandvik Pubg Interactive Inc ....E....... 203 205-0188
Yardley *(G-20338)*

Sapling Press ....G....... 412 681-1003
Pittsburgh *(G-15511)*

Sb Distribution Center Inc ....G....... 215 717-2600
Philadelphia *(G-14283)*

Schiffer Publishing Ltd ....E....... 610 593-1777
Atglen *(G-806)*

Schultz Mktg & Communications ....G....... 814 455-4772
Erie *(G-5469)*

Scroll Publishing Co ....G....... 717 349-7033
Doylesburg *(G-4265)*

Second Century Media LLC ....E....... 610 948-9500
Spring City *(G-17866)*

Simplicity Creative Corp ....G....... 800 653-7301
Plymouth Meeting *(G-15871)*

Sire Press LLC ....G....... 267 909-9233
Philadelphia *(G-14312)*

Source Halthcare Analytics LLC ....D....... 602 381-9500
Conshohocken *(G-3605)*

Strassheim Grphic Dsign & Pres ....F....... 215 525-5134
Philadelphia *(G-14350)*

Sunbury Press ....G....... 717 254-7274
Mechanicsburg *(G-10892)*

Swanson Publishing Company Inc ....G....... 724 940-2444
Wexford *(G-19830)*

Taylor & Francis Group LLC ....G....... 215 625-8900
Philadelphia *(G-14377)*

Taylor & Francis Inc ....D....... 215 625-8900
Philadelphia *(G-14378)*

The Scranton Times L P ....D....... 570 348-9146
Scranton *(G-17297)*

Training Resource Corporation ....F....... 717 652-3100
Harrisburg *(G-7234)*

Vaughens Price Pubg Co Inc ....G....... 412 367-5100
Bradfordwoods *(G-2000)*

Veritas Press Inc ....F....... 717 519-1974
Lancaster *(G-9233)*

Vert Markets Inc ....D....... 814 897-9000
Erie *(G-5525)*

Vivid Publishing Inc ....G....... 570 567-7808
Williamsport *(G-20088)*

Washington Radio Reports Inc ....F....... 717 334-0668
Gettysburg *(G-6321)*

White Mane Publishing Co Inc ....F....... 717 532-2237
Shippensburg *(G-17555)*

Wild Cat Publishing LLC ....G....... 570 966-1120
Mifflinburg *(G-11106)*

Wolters Kluwer Health Inc ....C....... 215 521-8300
Philadelphia *(G-14482)*

Young Face ....G....... 412 928-2676
Pittsburgh *(G-15730)*

Zenescope Entertainment Inc ....F....... 215 442-9094
Horsham *(G-7866)*

PUBLISHERS: Music Book

Dawn Evening Inc ....G....... 610 272-0518
Blue Bell *(G-1826)*

Sing-Out Corporation ....G....... 610 865-5366
Bethlehem *(G-1619)*

PUBLISHERS: Music, Sheet

Theodore Presser Company ....E....... 610 592-1222
King of Prussia *(G-8687)*

PUBLISHERS: Newsletter

American Future Systems Inc ....D....... 610 695-8600
Malvern *(G-10186)*

American Future Systems Inc ....E....... 610 375-8012
Reading *(G-16319)*

Community Resource Svcs Inc ....G....... 717 338-9100
Gettysburg *(G-6286)*

Critical Path Project Inc ....G....... 215 545-2212
Philadelphia *(G-13583)*

Ernie Saxton ....G....... 215 752-7797
Langhorne *(G-9294)*

Farm Journal Inc ....E....... 215 557-8900
Philadelphia *(G-13694)*

R M G Enterprises Inc.....................G....... 814 866-2247
Erie *(G-5448)*

Sports Management News Inc ....G....... 610 459-4040
Glen Mills *(G-6445)*

PUBLISHERS: Newspaper

21st Century Newspapers Inc ....Sj....... 215 504-4200
Yardley *(G-20292)*

21st Cntury Mdia Nwspapers LLC ....G....... 610 622-4186
Secane *(G-17316)*

Advertsing Otsourcing Svcs LLC ....E....... 570 793-2000
Wilkes Barre *(G-19903)*

Alm Media LLC ....E....... 215 557-2300
Philadelphia *(G-13370)*

American Chief Company ....G....... 267 984-8852
Philadelphia *(G-13383)*

Atlantic Publishing Group Inc ....F....... 800 832-3747
Flourtown *(G-5985)*

Barrys Lobby Shop ....F....... 215 925-1998
Philadelphia *(G-13446)*

Broad St Cmnty Newspapers Inc ....G....... 215 354-3135
Berlin *(G-1286)*

Brookshire Printing Inc ....E....... 717 392-1321
Lancaster *(G-8961)*

Burrells Information Services ....G....... 717 671-3872
Harrisburg *(G-7101)*

Car Gazette Co ....G....... 412 951-5572
Pittsburgh *(G-14807)*

Carnegie Mellon University ....E....... 412 268-2111
Pittsburgh *(G-14818)*

Catholic Register ....G....... 814 695-7563
Hollidaysburg *(G-7643)*

Central Pennsylvania.......................G....... 814 946-7411
Altoona *(G-489)*

Citywide Exclusive Newsppr Inc ....G....... 215 467-8214
Phila *(G-13309)*

Construction Equipment Guide..........E....... 215 885-2900
Fort Washington *(G-6066)*

Digital First Media Inc ....G....... 215 504-4200
Yardley *(G-20307)*

Fairylogue Press ....G....... 717 713-5788
Mechanicsburg *(G-10843)*

Fresh Press LLC ....G....... 717 504-9223
Hummelstown *(G-7911)*

Gazette Two DOT O.........................G....... 412 458-1526
Mc Kees Rocks *(G-10611)*

Great Valley Publishing Co ....E....... 610 948-7639
Spring City *(G-17858)*

Hammond Press Inc ....E....... 412 821-4100
Pittsburgh *(G-15078)*

Hocking Printing Co Inc ....D....... 717 738-1151
Ephrata *(G-5109)*

Horsey Darden Enterprises LLC ....G....... 215 309-3139
Philadelphia *(G-13834)*

Humble Elephant LLC ....G....... 814 434-1743
Erie *(G-5320)*

Independent-Observer ....G....... 724 238-2111
Ligonier *(G-9959)*

Independent-Observer ....G....... 724 547-5722
Connellsville *(G-3499)*

Journal Register Company ....D....... 215 368-6976
Lansdale *(G-9382)*

Jyoti N Stand ....G....... 215 843-5354
Philadelphia *(G-13916)*

Knight Ridder Inc ....G....... 570 829-7100
Wilkes Barre *(G-19935)*

Korean Phila Time Inc ....F....... 215 663-2400
Rockledge *(G-16791)*

La Cronica Newspaper ....G....... 484 357-2903
Allentown *(G-290)*

Lehigh Valley Chronicle ....G....... 610 965-1636
Emmaus *(G-5032)*

Leon Spangler ....F....... 570 837-7903
Middleburg *(G-11028)*

Margaret Mary Music Publishing.......G....... 570 282-3503
Carbondale *(G-2681)*

McNear Charles & Associates ....G....... 215 514-9431
Philadelphia *(G-13999)*

Metal Bulletin Holdings LLC ....F....... 412 765-2580
Pittsburgh *(G-15279)*

Mgtf Paper Company LLC ....E....... 412 316-3342
Pittsburgh *(G-15283)*

Miller Printing & Publishing ....E....... 814 425-7272
Cochranton *(G-3345)*

Morning Call Inc ....E....... 610 861-3600
Bethlehem *(G-1575)*

Moving Out ....G....... 724 794-6831
Slippery Rock *(G-17623)*

Mpc Liquidation Inc ....G....... 814 849-6737
Brookville *(G-2266)*

Newspaper Networks Inc ....G....... 610 853-2121
Upper Darby *(G-18691)*

Observer Publishing Company ....E....... 724 941-7725
Canonsburg *(G-2614)*

Ogden Newspapers of PA ....D....... 717 248-6741
Lewistown *(G-9941)*

Page 1 Publishers Inc ....G....... 610 380-8264
Downingtown *(G-4248)*

Patriot-News Co ....G....... 717 243-1758
Carlisle *(G-2729)*

Payal News ....G....... 215 625-3699
Philadelphia *(G-14126)*

Penco Products Inc ....G....... 800 562-1000
Skippack *(G-17603)*

Penn Jersey Advance Inc ....B....... 610 258-7171
Easton *(G-4742)*

Penn Jersey Advance Inc ....G....... 610 258-7171
Bethlehem *(G-1593)*

Penny Power Ltd ....F....... 610 282-4808
Coopersburg *(G-3633)*

Philadelphia Public Record ....F....... 215 755-2000
Philadelphia *(G-14152)*

Philadlphia Media Holdings LLC ....F....... 215 854-2000
Philadelphia *(G-14162)*

Pittsburgh City Paper Inc ....E....... 412 316-3342
Pittsburgh *(G-15391)*

Pittsburgh Postgazette.....................G....... 412 858-1850
Monroeville *(G-11348)*

Post Gazette ....G....... 412 854-9722
Bethel Park *(G-1428)*

Post Gazette ....G....... 412 965-6738
Mc Donald *(G-10578)*

Priceless Times ....G....... 267 538-5723
Philadelphia *(G-14200)*

Publicsource ....G....... 412 315-0264
Pittsburgh *(G-15455)*

Quickel International Corp ....G....... 215 862-1313
New Hope *(G-12313)*

Scranton Times-Tribune ....F....... 570 348-9100
Scranton *(G-17289)*

Spirit Media Group Inc ....G....... 610 447-8484
Chester *(G-3064)*

Spirit Publishing Company ....E....... 814 938-8740
Punxsutawney *(G-16163)*

Stott Publications Inc ....G....... 814 632-6700
Tyrone *(G-18593)*

Suburban Advertiser ....G....... 610 363-2815
Exton *(G-5734)*

Suburban Newspaper of America ....G....... 215 513-4145
Harleysville *(G-7060)*

Texas-New Mxico Newspapers LLC ......D....... 717 767-3554
York *(G-20686)*

Thepaperframercom ....G....... 570 239-1444
Ashley *(G-740)*

Trustees of The Univ of PA ....G....... 215 898-5555
Philadelphia *(G-14413)*

University City Review Inc ....G....... 215 222-2846
Philadelphia *(G-14428)*

University of Pittsburgh ....C....... 412 648-7980
Pittsburgh *(G-15683)*

Valley Voice Inc ....G....... 610 838-2066
Hellertown *(G-7564)*

Webb Communications Inc ....D....... 570 326-7634
Williamsport *(G-20089)*

Weekly Piper Ltd ....G....... 717 341-3726
Lititz *(G-10058)*

Wilkes-Barre Publishing Co Inc.........G....... 570 829-7100
Wilkes Barre *(G-19977)*

Xpress Energy ....F....... 610 935-9200
Phoenixville *(G-14584)*

Y H Newspaper Inc ....G....... 215 546-0372
Philadelphia *(G-14497)*

PUBLISHERS: Newspapers, No Printing

21st Century Media Newsppr LLC ....D....... 610 692-3790
Exton *(G-5633)*

Alvin Engle Associates Inc ....E....... 717 653-1833
Mount Joy *(G-11645)*

Alvin Engle Associates Inc ....G....... 717 653-1833
Mount Joy *(G-11646)*

Cameron County Community Chest .....G....... 814 486-0612
Emporium *(G-5052)*

Carbondale News.............................G....... 570 282-3300
Honesdale *(G-7705)*

Carbondale News.............................G....... 570 282-3300
Honesdale *(G-7706)*

Catholic Scl Svcs of Scranton ....D....... 570 207-2283
Scranton *(G-17216)*

Catholic Scl Svcs of Scranton ....G....... 570 454-6693
Hazleton *(G-7494)*

Chestnut Hill Local ....E....... 215 248-8800
Philadelphia *(G-13539)*

Citizen ....F....... 412 766-6679
Pittsburgh *(G-14853)*

Collegian Inc ....E 814 865-2531
State College (G-17953)
Community Newspaper Group LLC ......G 570 275-3235
Sunbury (G-18166)
Corry Journal Inc ....F 814 665-8291
Corry (G-3750)
Country Impressions Inc ....F 570 477-5000
Hunlock Creek (G-7931)
Derrick Publishing Company ....E 412 364-8202
Pittsburgh (G-14918)
Elsol Latino Newspaper ....G 215 424-1200
Philadelphia (G-13671)
Family Business Publishing Co ....G 215 567-3200
Philadelphia (G-13692)
Forest City News Inc ....G 570 785-3800
Forest City (G-6053)
Franklin Shopper ....F 717 263-0359
Chambersburg (G-2933)
Gannett Stllite Info Ntwrk Inc ....G 215 679-9561
Red Hill (G-16581)
Gary Edward Soden ....G 215 723-5964
Telford (G-18291)
Gatehouse Media LLC ....E 570 742-9671
Milton (G-11239)
Gettysburg Times Pubg LLC ....E 717 253-9403
Gettysburg (G-6292)
Greenville Record Argus Inc ....E 724 588-5000
Greenville (G-6742)
Herald Newspapers Company Inc ....D 412 782-2121
Pittsburgh (G-15090)
Irish Edition ....G 215 836-4900
Oreland (G-13023)
Jewish Chronicle ....G 412 687-1000
Pittsburgh (G-15153)
Jewish Exponent Inc ....E 215 832-0700
Philadelphia (G-13896)
Johnson Communications Inc ....G 215 474-7411
Philadelphia (G-13910)
Journal Newspapers Inc ....G 570 443-9131
White Haven (G-19849)
Journal Register Company ....D 610 323-3000
Exton (G-5702)
Kane Republican ....G 814 837-6000
Kane (G-8470)
Kapp Advertising Services Inc ....F 717 632-8303
Hanover (G-6909)
Krieg Dieter ....G 717 656-8050
Brownstown (G-2308)
Lititz Record Express Inc ....G 717 626-2191
Lititz (G-10023)
Local Media Group Inc ....C 570 421-3000
Stroudsburg (G-18125)
Local Media Group Inc ....F 724 458-5010
Grove City (G-6795)
Local Media Group Inc ....G 570 524-2261
Lewisburg (G-9915)
Lock Haven Express ....E 570 748-6791
Lock Haven (G-10090)
Marie Chomicki ....G 717 432-3456
Dillsburg (G-4136)
Mifflinburg Telegraph Inc ....G 570 966-2255
Mifflinburg (G-11099)
Molloy Associates Inc ....E 610 293-1300
Bryn Mawr (G-2330)
Mountaintop Eagle Inc ....G 570 474-6397
Wilkes Barre (G-19946)
National Hot Rod Association ....D 717 584-1200
Lancaster (G-9142)
Nazareth Key Youngs Press ....G 610 759-5000
Nazareth (G-11984)
Neighborhood Publications Inc ....G 412 481-0266
Pittsburgh (G-15324)
New Pittsburgh Courier Pubg Co ....F 412 481-8302
Pittsburgh (G-15333)
News Eagle ....E 570 226-4547
Honesdale (G-7719)
Newspaper Holding Inc ....D 814 724-6370
Meadville (G-10769)
Ogden Newspapers Inc ....C 814 946-7411
Altoona (G-535)
Ogden Newspapers Inc ....F 570 584-2134
Hughesville (G-7898)
Patriot-News Co ....G 717 255-8100
Mechanicsburg (G-10876)
Paxton Herald ....F 717 545-9868
Harrisburg (G-7190)
Pencor Services Inc ....G 570 668-1250
Tamaqua (G-18223)
Pencor Services Inc ....E 610 826-2115
Palmerton (G-13110)

Pencor Services Inc ....C 570 386-2660
Lehighton (G-9721)
Penny Mansfield Saver Inc ....G 570 662-3277
Mansfield (G-10424)
Pittsburgh Business Times ....G 412 481-6397
Pittsburgh (G-15389)
Pittsburgh Catholic Pubg Assoc ....F 412 471-1252
Pittsburgh (G-15390)
Pollock Advertising ....G 724 794-6857
Slippery Rock (G-17624)
Press-Enterprise Inc ....G 570 752-3645
Bloomsburg (G-1794)
Progress News ....G 724 867-2435
Emlenton (G-5014)
Ridgway Record ....G 814 773-3161
Ridgway (G-16728)
Rocket-Courier Newspaper ....F 570 746-1217
Wyalusing (G-20258)
Sell-It ....G 215 453-8937
Sellersville (G-17358)
Society of Good Shepherd ....G 717 349-7033
Amberson (G-565)
Susquehanna Independent Wkndr ....G 570 278-6397
Montrose (G-11479)
Susquehanna Transcript Inc ....G 570 853-3134
Susquehanna (G-18183)
Tioga Publishing Company ....G 814 849-6737
Brookville (G-2273)
Trib Total Media Inc ....D 724 684-5200
Greensburg (G-6719)
Trib Total Media LLC ....B 412 321-6460
Greensburg (G-6720)
Trib Total Media LLC ....E 724 543-1303
Kittanning (G-8800)
Triboro Banner ....G 570 348-9185
Scranton (G-17306)
Valley Mirror ....G 412 462-0626
Homestead (G-7696)
Vetmed Communications Inc ....G 610 361-0555
Glen Mills (G-6448)
Webb Weekly ....F 570 326-9322
Williamsport (G-20090)
Weekender ....F 570 831-7320
Wilkes Barre (G-19971)
Weekly Bargain Bulletin Inc ....G 724 654-5529
New Castle (G-12166)
Western PA Newsppr Co ....F 814 226-7000
Clarion (G-3187)
Wilkes-Barre Publishing Co ....C 570 829-7100
Wilkes Barre (G-19976)
Wyoming County Press Inc ....G 570 348-9185
Tunkhannock (G-18553)

PUBLISHERS: Pamphlets, No Printing

Assemblies of Yahweh ....F 717 933-4518
Bethel (G-1392)
Consumer Network Inc ....G 215 235-2400
Philadelphia (G-13572)

PUBLISHERS: Periodical Statistical Reports, No Printing

Career Communications Inc ....G 215 256-3130
Harleysville (G-7024)
D Dietrich Associates Inc ....G 215 258-1071
Sellersville (G-17342)
Morningstar Credit Ratings LLC ....E 800 299-1665
Horsham (G-7833)

PUBLISHERS: Periodical, With Printing

Bible Lighthouse Inc ....G 570 888-6615
Sayre (G-17111)
Innovative Designs & Pubg ....G 610 923-8000
Palmer (G-13098)
Mountaineer Publishing ....G 724 880-3753
Waynesburg (G-19448)
Suza Inc ....F 817 877-0067
East Petersburg (G-4592)

PUBLISHERS: Periodicals, Magazines

Act Inc ....G 484 562-0063
Bala Cynwyd (G-872)
American Association For Cance ....D 215 440-9300
Philadelphia (G-13378)
American Future Systems Inc ....E 610 375-8012
Reading (G-16319)
Association Test Publishers ....G 717 755-9747
York (G-20388)

Bb Vintage Magazine ADS ....G 717 235-1109
New Freedom (G-12202)
Blue Star Basketball ....G 215 638-7060
Bensalem (G-1158)
Bradford County Sanitation Inc ....G 570 673-3128
Troy (G-18518)
Brookshire Printing Inc ....E 717 392-1321
Lancaster (G-8961)
Campbell 3 ....G 724 322-1043
New Stanton (G-12447)
Clipper Magazine LLC ....B 717 569-5100
Mountville (G-11791)
Cycle Source Magazine ....G 724 226-2867
Tarentum (G-18240)
Daily American ....E 814 444-5900
Somerset (G-17683)
Diamond Rock Productions ....G 215 564-3401
Philadelphia (G-13629)
Drexel University ....G 215 590-8863
Philadelphia (G-13647)
Edgell Communications ....G 570 296-8330
Milford (G-11159)
Friends Boarding Ho Buc Qua ME ....G 215 968-3346
Newtown (G-12503)
Gene Szczurek S Quarterly P R ....G 215 887-7377
Wyncote (G-20263)
Health Care Council Western PA ....F 724 776-6400
Warrendale (G-19080)
Healthcare Information Corp ....F 724 776-9411
Warrendale (G-19081)
Highlights For Children Inc ....E 570 253-1080
Honesdale (G-7714)
Holistic Horse Inc ....G 215 249-1965
Perkasie (G-13279)
Kappa Graphics L P ....C 570 655-9681
Hughestown (G-7893)
Koren Publications ....G 267 498-0071
Philadelphia (G-13941)
Morning Call Inc ....E 610 861-3600
Bethlehem (G-1575)
Motorama Assoc ....G 717 359-4310
Hanover (G-6924)
National Assn Cllges Employers ....E 610 868-1421
Bethlehem (G-1577)
News Chronicle Co Inc ....E 717 532-4101
Shippensburg (G-17540)
Newsline Publishing Inc ....E 610 337-1050
King of Prussia (G-8656)
On Line Publishers Inc ....G 717 285-1350
Columbia (G-3445)
Penn Medical Education LLC ....G 215 524-2785
Newtown (G-12534)
Pennsylvania Institute of CPA ....G 215 496-9272
Philadelphia (G-14132)
Pennsylvania Motor Truck Assn ....G 717 761-7122
Camp Hill (G-2510)
Pittsburgh Business Times ....G 412 481-6397
Pittsburgh (G-15389)
Pittsburgh Technology Council ....E 412 687-2700
Pittsburgh (G-15410)
Printing Consulting Inc ....G 610 933-9311
Phoenixville (G-14571)
Printing Inds Amer Foundation ....F 412 741-6860
Warrendale (G-19094)
Rjw Hired Hands Inc ....F 412 341-1477
Pittsburgh (G-15490)
Ronald D Jones Financial Svc ....G 724 352-5020
Saxonburg (G-17094)
RSC Worldwide (us) Inc ....G 215 966-6206
Philadelphia (G-14261)
Seak Inc ....G 215 288-7209
Philadelphia (G-14291)
Shojoberry Magazine ....G 814 736-3210
Portage (G-15921)
Society For Industrial & Appli ....D 215 382-9800
Philadelphia (G-14320)
Wmpm LLC ....E 303 662-5231
Pittsburgh (G-15721)
Ygs Group Inc ....D 717 505-9701
York (G-20723)

PUBLISHERS: Periodicals, No Printing

Advertising Specialty Inst Inc ....B 800 546-1350
Feasterville Trevose (G-5883)
American Baptst HM Mission Soc ....D 610 768-2465
King of Prussia (G-8581)
B P S Communications Inc ....F 215 830-8467
Willow Grove (G-20109)
Breakthrough Publications Inc ....G 610 928-4061
Emmaus (G-5021)

Employee Codes: A=Over 500 employees, B=251-500
C=101-250, D=51-100, E=20-50, F=10-19, G=3-9

2019 Harris Pennsylvania
Manufacturers Directory

1525

PRODUCT

Current History Inc ....G..... 610 772-5709
Philadelphia (G-13591)
Current Therapeutics Inc ....G..... 610 644-5995
Berwyn (G-1359)
Easton Publishing Company ....G..... 610 258-7171
Easton (G-4673)
Flagship Multimedia Inc ....G..... 814 314-9364
Erie (G-5293)
Horty Springer & Mattern ....E..... 412 687-7677
Pittsburgh (G-15100)
Idea Group Inc ....E..... 717 533-3673
Hershey (G-7617)
Industrial Data Exchange Inc ....B..... 717 653-1833
Mount Joy (G-11662)
JS Little Publication ....G..... 412 343-5288
Pittsburgh (G-15157)
Scripture Union ....F..... 610 935-2807
Valley Forge (G-18714)
Turner White Cmmunications Inc ....F..... 610 975-4541
Bryn Mawr (G-2335)
Washington Radio Reports Inc ....F..... 717 334-0668
Gettysburg (G-6321)
Washington Radio Reports Inc ....F..... 717 334-0668
Gettysburg (G-6322)
York Graphic Services Co ....C..... 717 505-9701
York (G-20738)

PUBLISHERS: Sheet Music

Selah Publshng Co Inc ....G..... 412 886-1020
Pittsburgh (G-15521)

PUBLISHERS: Shopping News

Ad Star Inc ....F..... 724 439-5519
Uniontown (G-18614)
Penny Mansfield Saver Inc...............G..... 570 662-3277
Mansfield (G-10424)

PUBLISHERS: Technical Manuals

Associates In Medical Mktg Co ....E..... 215 860-9600
Newtown (G-12497)
Hollinger Tchncal Pblctons Inc..............G..... 717 755-8800
York (G-20524)
Iop Publishing Incorporated ....F..... 215 627-0880
Philadelphia (G-13872)

PUBLISHERS: Technical Manuals & Papers

Publishing Office US Gvernment ....G..... 215 364-6465
Southampton (G-17832)
Robar Industries Inc ....G..... 484 688-0300
Plymouth Meeting (G-15868)

PUBLISHERS: Technical Papers

Jcpds International Centre..................E..... 610 325-9814
Newtown Square (G-12578)
PRI International Inc ....G..... 610 436-8292
West Chester (G-19619)

PUBLISHERS: Telephone & Other Directory

Dex Media Inc ....E..... 412 858-4800
White Oak (G-19854)
Easy To Use Big Books ....D..... 814 946-7442
Altoona (G-500)
Kgb Usa Inc ....D..... 610 997-1000
Bethlehem (G-1552)
Local Pages Publishing LLC...............F..... 610 579-3809
Norristown (G-12677)
Ogden Directories PA Inc ....C..... 814 946-7404
Altoona (G-534)
Omni Publlishing Eastern PA ....G..... 610 626-8819
Lansdowne (G-9440)
Yellow Pages Group LLC ....E..... 610 825-7720
Blue Bell (G-1858)

PUBLISHERS: Textbooks, No Printing

F A Davis Company ....D..... 215 568-2270
Philadelphia (G-13689)
George T Bisel Co Inc......................F..... 215 922-5760
Philadelphia (G-13755)
Neil M Davis ....G..... 215 442-7430
Warminster (G-18928)
Rowman & Littlefield Publs Inc ....F..... 717 794-3800
Blue Ridge Summit (G-1860)
Taylor & Francis Inc........................D..... 215 625-8900
Philadelphia (G-14378)

PUBLISHERS: Trade journals, No Printing

American Cllege Physicians Inc...........B..... 215 351-2400
Philadelphia (G-13384)
BNP Media Inc ....F..... 610 436-4220
West Chester (G-19512)
BNP Media Inc ....G..... 412 531-3370
Pittsburgh (G-14777)
Construction Equipment Guide ....E..... 215 885-2900
Fort Washington (G-6066)
Foreign Policy Research Inst..............E..... 215 732-3774
Philadelphia (G-13714)
Hmp Cmmunications Holdings LLC......G..... 610 560-0500
Malvern (G-10247)
Hmp Communications LLC ....E..... 610 560-0500
Malvern (G-10248)
Kane Communications Inc ....F..... 610 645-6940
Ardmore (G-711)
Koren Publications Inc ....G..... 267 498-0071
Hatfield (G-7360)
Religious Theological Abstract ....G..... 717 866-6734
Myerstown (G-11896)
Roland Lynagh Associates LLC ....G..... 570 467-2528
Barnesville (G-940)
Smith-Freeman & Associates ....F..... 610 929-5728
Temple (G-18336)
Springer Adis Us LLC ....G..... 215 574-2201
Philadelphia (G-14335)
Wolters Kluwer Health Inc ....C..... 215 521-8300
Philadelphia (G-14482)

PUBLISHING & BROADCASTING: Internet Only

Coffee Cup Publishing ....G..... 215 887-7365
Jenkintown (G-8282)
Ker Communications........................G..... 412 310-1973
Pittsburgh (G-15172)
My Biblical Perception LLC ....G..... 267 450-9655
Perkasie (G-13285)
Solo Soundz LLC ....G..... 610 931-8448
Philadelphia (G-14323)
Textbook LLC ....G..... 717 779-7101
York (G-20687)
Thats True Media LLC......................G..... 215 437-3292
Philadelphia (G-14384)
Wharton School Univ of PA ....C..... 215 746-7846
Philadelphia (G-14472)

PUBLISHING & PRINTING: Art Copy

Avantext Inc..................................E..... 610 796-2383
Philadelphia (G-13425)
Baip Inc ....G..... 412 913-9826
Export (G-5592)
Brown Brothers LLP ....G..... 570 689-9688
Sterling (G-18048)
Glory Fibers ....G..... 610 444-5646
Kennett Square (G-8512)
Newtown Business Forms Corp...........F..... 215 364-3898
Huntingdon Valley (G-8017)

PUBLISHING & PRINTING: Book Music

Mosaic Entertainment House................D..... 215 353-1729
Philadelphia (G-14040)

PUBLISHING & PRINTING: Books

Clement Communications Inc ....D..... 610 497-6800
Upper Chichester (G-18658)
Dubose Printing & Bus Svcs ....G..... 215 877-9071
Philadelphia (G-13649)
Himalayan International Instit...............E..... 570 253-5551
Honesdale (G-7715)
Korea Week Inc ....G..... 215 782-8883
Ambler (G-589)
Louis Neibauer Co Inc ....E..... 215 322-6200
Warminster (G-18913)
Mason Crest Publishers Inc................G..... 610 543-6200
Broomall (G-2297)
Puchalski Inc ....G..... 570 842-0361
Covington Township (G-3793)
Rodale Inc ....E..... 610 398-2255
Allentown (G-377)
Rodale Institute ....E..... 610 683-6009
Kutztown (G-8859)
Stackpole Inc ....E..... 717 796-0411
Blue Ridge Summit (G-1862)
Three Brothers Publishing LLC............G..... 412 656-3905
Norristown (G-12718)

Vanroden Inc ....E..... 717 509-2600
Lancaster (G-9230)
Whitaker Corporation ....C..... 724 334-7000
New Kensington (G-12389)

PUBLISHING & PRINTING: Catalogs

Dubose Printing & Bus Svcs ....G..... 215 877-9071
Philadelphia (G-13649)
Marietta Closson ....G..... 724 337-4482
Apollo (G-683)

PUBLISHING & PRINTING: Comic Books

Daniel Parent.................................G..... 914 850-5473
Milford (G-11158)

PUBLISHING & PRINTING: Directories, NEC

Dorland Healthcare Information ....G..... 800 784-2332
Philadelphia (G-13640)

PUBLISHING & PRINTING: Directories, Telephone

EZ To Use Directories Inc ....E..... 814 949-7100
Altoona (G-503)
Jay Weiss Corporation ....G..... 610 834-8585
Lafayette Hill (G-8881)

PUBLISHING & PRINTING: Guides

Kapp Advertising Services Inc ....E..... 610 670-2595
Reading (G-16418)
Towanda Printing Co Inc ....C..... 570 265-2151
Towanda (G-18436)

PUBLISHING & PRINTING: Magazines: publishing & printing

310 Publishing LLC.........................G..... 717 564-0161
Harrisburg (G-7077)
Bwhip Magazine LLC ....G..... 412 607-3963
Pittsburgh (G-14798)
Chitra Publications ....E..... 570 278-1984
Montrose (G-11462)
Cibo Media Group LLC ....G..... 215 732-6700
Philadelphia (G-13544)
Connections Magazine ....G..... 570 647-0085
Honesdale (G-7708)
Critic Publications Inc ....G..... 215 536-8884
Quakertown (G-16181)
Days Communication Inc ....G..... 215 538-1240
Quakertown (G-16183)
Engle Printing & Pubg Co Inc ....F..... 717 892-6800
Lancaster (G-9010)
Engle Printing & Pubg Co Inc ....F..... 717 653-1833
Mount Joy (G-11654)
Engle Printing & Pubg Co Inc ....C..... 717 653-1833
Lancaster (G-9009)
Ep World Inc ....G..... 814 361-3860
Indiana (G-8096)
Feast Mag LLC ....F..... 484 343-5483
Wynnewood (G-20267)
Garden Pond Promotions Inc ....G..... 814 695-4325
Duncansville (G-4452)
Great American Printer Inc ....G..... 570 752-7341
Berwick (G-1326)
Harrisburg Magazine Inc ....F..... 717 233-0109
Harrisburg (G-7143)
Hounds & Hunting Publishing ....G..... 812 820-1588
Bradford (G-1973)
Joseph Jenkins Inc..........................G..... 814 786-9085
Grove City (G-6792)
M Shanken Communications Inc..........G..... 610 967-1083
Emmaus (G-5033)
Manor House Publishing Co Inc...........F..... 215 259-1700
Warminster (G-18916)
Metro Corp ....D..... 215 564-7700
Philadelphia (G-14014)
Metro Corp ....G..... 215 564-7700
Philadelphia (G-14015)
Metro Corp Holdings Inc ....E..... 215 564-7700
Philadelphia (G-14016)
Mlr Holdings LLC ....F..... 215 567-3200
Philadelphia (G-14029)
New Visions Magazine.......................F..... 215 627-0102
Philadelphia (G-14069)
Paul Withers ....G..... 717 896-3173
Halifax (G-6827)
Pentavision LLC..............................E..... 215 628-6550
Ambler (G-597)

Philadelphia Style Mag LLC ....F 215 468-6670
Philadelphia *(G-14156)*
Printing Craftsmen Inc ....F 570 646-2121
Pocono Pines *(G-15883)*
Quad/Graphics Inc ....B 215 541-2729
Pennsburg *(G-13253)*
Rodale Inc ....E 610 398-2255
Allentown *(G-377)*
Rodale Institute ....E 610 683-6009
Kutztown *(G-8859)*
Seapoint Enterprises Inc ....G 215 230-6933
Doylestown *(G-4337)*
Sharedxpertise Media LLC ....F 215 606-9520
Philadelphia *(G-14297)*
Snb Publishing Inc ....G 215 464-2500
Philadelphia *(G-14319)*
Stott Publications Inc ....G 814 632-6700
Tyrone *(G-18593)*
Transport For Christ Inc ....G 717 426-9977
Marietta *(G-10469)*
Tri-State Events Magazine Inc ....G 215 947-8600
Huntingdon Valley *(G-8044)*
USA Media LLC ....F 215 571-9241
Folcroft *(G-6019)*
Z Publication LLC ....G 484 574-5321
Coatesville *(G-3332)*

PUBLISHING & PRINTING: Music, Book

Blazing Passion Publ ....G 215 247-2024
Philadelphia *(G-13468)*

PUBLISHING & PRINTING: Newsletters, Business Svc

Global Institute For Strgc Inv ....G 215 300-0907
Philadelphia *(G-13769)*
Hodgsons Quick Printing ....G 215 362-1356
Kulpsville *(G-8830)*
Icon/Information Concepts Inc ....G 215 545-6700
Langhorne *(G-9303)*
Macnificent Pages ....G 610 323-6253
Pottstown *(G-16012)*
Saj Publishing ....G 814 445-9695
Somerset *(G-17703)*

PUBLISHING & PRINTING: Newspapers

21st Century Media Newsppr LLC ....E 814 238-3071
State College *(G-17939)*
21st Cntury Mdia Newpapers LLC ....G 215 368-6973
Lansdale *(G-9338)*
A & T News Service ....G 610 454-7787
Collegeville *(G-3366)*
A T J Printing Inc ....F 814 641-9614
Huntingdon *(G-7936)*
Acme Newspapers Inc ....C 610 642-4300
Ardmore *(G-699)*
Al Dia Newspaper Inc ....F 215 569-4666
Philadelphia *(G-13361)*
Altoona Mirror ....D 814 946-7506
Altoona *(G-471)*
Anthony Ds Daily Numbers ....G 215 537-0618
Philadelphia *(G-13395)*
Area Shopper ....G 814 425-7272
Cochranton *(G-3335)*
Balloon Flights Daily ....G 610 469-0782
Saint Peters *(G-17033)*
Bcmi Ad Concepts Inc ....E 215 354-3000
Bensalem *(G-1154)*
Beaver Newspapers Inc ....B 724 775-3200
Beaver *(G-979)*
Bedford Gazette LLC ....E 814 623-1151
Bedford *(G-1042)*
Bill ONeill ....G 610 688-6135
Wayne *(G-19306)*
Bradford Journal Miner ....G 814 465-3468
Bradford *(G-1959)*
Bradford Publishing Company ....D 814 368-3173
Bradford *(G-1960)*
Broadtop Bulletin ....G 814 635-2851
Saxton *(G-17099)*
Bucks County Midweek ....G 215 355-1234
Feasterville Trevose *(G-5894)*
Butler Circulation Calls ....G 724 282-1859
Butler *(G-2384)*
Call Newspapers Inc ....F 570 385-3120
Schuylkill Haven *(G-17150)*
Career Lfstyle Enhncment Jurnl ....G 724 872-5344
West Newton *(G-19749)*
Carreon Publishing LLC ....G 570 673-5151
Canton *(G-2663)*

Catholic Light Publishing Co ....G 570 207-2229
Scranton *(G-17215)*
Centre County Womens Journal ....G 814 349-8202
Millheim *(G-11217)*
Civitas Media LLC ....G 570 829-7100
Wilkes Barre *(G-19913)*
Classified Advertising ....G 814 723-1400
Warren *(G-19016)*
Cnhi LLC ....E 814 781-1596
Saint Marys *(G-16955)*
Community Newspaper ....G 814 683-4841
Linesville *(G-9979)*
Commuters Express Inc ....G 570 476-0601
East Stroudsburg *(G-4610)*
Daily ....G 610 384-0372
Coatesville *(G-3300)*
Daily Dove Care LLC ....G 215 316-5888
Philadelphia *(G-13604)*
Daily Informer LLC ....G 717 634-9087
Hanover *(G-6872)*
Delaware County Legal Journal ....G 717 337-9812
Gettysburg *(G-6289)*
Derrick Publishing Company ....E 814 226-7000
Clarion *(G-3176)*
Drdavesbestbodies Inc ....G 610 926-5728
Fleetwood *(G-5970)*
Eagle Printing Company ....D 724 282-8000
Butler *(G-2398)*
Eagle Printing Company ....G 724 776-4270
Cranberry Township *(G-3817)*
Echo Pilot ....G 717 597-2164
Greencastle *(G-6609)*
El Torero Spanish Newspaper ....G 610 435-6608
Allentown *(G-205)*
Eric Nemeyer Corporation ....G 215 887-8880
Glenside *(G-6516)*
Family-Life Media-Com Inc ....F 724 543-6397
Kittanning *(G-8769)*
Fly Magazine ....G 717 293-9772
Lancaster *(G-9024)*
Fulton County Reporter ....G 717 325-0079
Mc Connellsburg *(G-10566)*
Gannett Co Inc ....D 724 778-3388
Warrendale *(G-19074)*
Gannett Stllite Info Ntwrk LLC ....G 703 854-6185
Dillsburg *(G-4130)*
Gant Media Llc ....G 814 765-5256
Clearfield *(G-3219)*
Gatehouse Media LLC ....E 570 253-3055
Honesdale *(G-7712)*
Gateway Newspapers ....G 412 856-7400
Pittsburgh *(G-15041)*
Gateway Publications ....C 412 856-7400
Monroeville *(G-11339)*
Gibson Journal ....G 717 656-2582
Leola *(G-9784)*
Goodson Holding Company ....C 215 370-6069
Bristol *(G-2149)*
Hamburg Area Item ....G 610 367-6041
Pottstown *(G-15994)*
Hanover Publishing Co ....G 717 637-3736
Hanover *(G-6901)*
Hari Jayanti News Inc ....G 215 546-1350
Philadelphia *(G-13802)*
Hellenic News of America Inc ....G 484 427-7446
Havertown *(G-7422)*
Herald Standard ....G 724 626-8345
Dunbar *(G-4440)*
Impressions Media ....G 570 829-7140
Wilkes Barre *(G-19927)*
Independent-Observer ....E 724 887-7400
Scottdale *(G-17193)*
Inquirer & Daily News Fed CU ....G 610 292-6762
Conshohocken *(G-3564)*
Irish Network Philadelphia ....G 215 690-1353
Upper Darby *(G-18687)*
J H Zerbey Newspapers Inc ....F 570 622-3456
Pottsville *(G-16082)*
Jimmi News ....G 215 988-9095
Philadelphia *(G-13899)*
Joseph F Biddle Publishing Co ....G 814 684-4000
Tyrone *(G-18585)*
Journal Register Company ....D 610 280-2295
Exton *(G-5703)*
Journal Register Company ....G 610 696-1775
Exton *(G-5704)*
Kapp Advertising Services Inc ....D 717 270-2742
Lebanon *(G-9587)*
Korea Daily News Inc ....G 215 277-1112
Elkins Park *(G-4908)*

Lancaster County Weeklies ....A 717 626-2191
Ephrata *(G-5119)*
Ledger Newspapers ....G 610 444-6590
West Chester *(G-19590)*
Lee Publication Inc ....G 717 240-7167
Carlisle *(G-2722)*
Lewistown Sentinel Inc ....F 717 248-6741
Lewistown *(G-9939)*
Lnp Media Group Inc ....D 717 733-6397
Ephrata *(G-5121)*
Mainline Newspapers ....E 814 472-4110
Ebensburg *(G-4789)*
Masco Communications Inc ....F 215 625-8501
Philadelphia *(G-13993)*
Mercersburg Journal ....G 717 485-3162
Mc Connellsburg *(G-10571)*
Mercersburg Journal ....G 717 328-3223
Mercersburg *(G-10992)*
Metro News Gifts ....G 610 734-2262
Upper Darby *(G-18689)*
Metroweek Corp ....D 215 735-8444
Philadelphia *(G-14017)*
Mid-Atlantic Tech Publications ....F 610 783-6100
Valley Forge *(G-18709)*
Millersville University PA ....E 717 871-4636
Millersville *(G-11213)*
Milton Daily Standard ....E 570 742-9077
Montgomery *(G-11376)*
Mon Valley Independent ....G 724 314-0030
Charleroi *(G-3016)*
Morning Call LLC ....F 610 379-3200
Lehighton *(G-9720)*
Morning Call LLC ....A 610 820-6500
Allentown *(G-322)*
MSP Corporation ....G 570 344-7670
Scranton *(G-17260)*
Mulligan Printing Corporation ....E 570 278-3271
Tunkhannock *(G-18544)*
Muncy Luminary ....G 570 584-0111
Hughesville *(G-7897)*
New Republic ....G 814 634-8321
Meyersdale *(G-11017)*
News Chronicle Co Inc ....E 717 532-4101
Shippensburg *(G-17540)*
News Eagle ....G 570 296-4547
Milford *(G-11164)*
News Item Cin 5 ....F 570 644-0891
Shamokin *(G-17426)*
Newspaper Guild of Philadelphi ....G 215 928-0118
Philadelphia *(G-14071)*
Newspaper Holding Inc ....D 724 981-6100
Sharon *(G-17440)*
Newspaper Holding Inc ....D 724 654-6651
New Castle *(G-12131)*
Observer Publishing Company ....B 724 222-2200
Washington *(G-19212)*
Observer Publishing Company ....G 724 852-2602
Waynesburg *(G-19449)*
Oxford Daily LLC ....G 215 533-5656
Philadelphia *(G-14107)*
P & N Holdings Inc ....C 570 455-3636
Hazleton *(G-7514)*
Paradies Pleasant News LL ....G 610 521-2936
Essington *(G-5545)*
Patriot Kutztown Area ....G 610 367-6041
Pottstown *(G-16026)*
Patriot-News Co ....B 717 255-8100
Mechanicsburg *(G-10875)*
Peerless Publications Inc ....F 610 970-3210
Pottstown *(G-16028)*
Pencor Services Inc ....E 610 740-0944
Allentown *(G-346)*
Pennsylvnia Soc Newsppr Editor ....G 717 703-3000
Harrisburg *(G-7197)*
Philadelphia Media Network Pbc ....F 610 292-6389
Conshohocken *(G-3586)*
Philadelphia Media Network Pbc ....D 215 854-2000
Philadelphia *(G-14147)*
Philadelphia Newspapers Inc ....F 610 292-6200
Conshohocken *(G-3587)*
Philadelphia Sun Group Inc ....F 215 848-7864
Philadelphia *(G-14157)*
Philadelphia Tribune Company ....D 215 893-5636
Philadelphia *(G-14158)*
Phildelphia-Newspapers-Llc ....A 610 292-6200
Conshohocken *(G-3588)*
Philipsburg Journal ....G 814 342-1320
Philipsburg *(G-14524)*
Pike County Dispatch Inc ....F 570 296-2611
Milford *(G-11166)*

PRODUCT

Pittsburgh Jewish Publication...............F 412 687-1000
  Pittsburgh *(G-15399)*
Pittsburgh Post Gazette ....G....... 724 266-2701
  Leetsdale *(G-9701)*
Pocono Times ....G....... 570 421-4800
  East Stroudsburg *(G-4628)*
Press and Journal.............................E 717 944-4628
  Middletown *(G-11071)*
Progressive Publishing Company........D 814 765-5051
  Clearfield *(G-3229)*
Reading Eagle Company ....E 610 371-5180
  Reading *(G-16489)*
Review Publishing Ltd Partnr ....D 215 563-7400
  Philadelphia *(G-14242)*
Sample News Group LLC................C....... 814 665-8291
  Corry *(G-3773)*
Sample News Group LLC................F 814 774-7073
  Girard *(G-6401)*
Sample News Group LLC................E 570 888-9643
  Sayre *(G-17122)*
Saucon Source LLC ....G....... 610 442-3370
  Fountain Hill *(G-6100)*
Sb New York Inc ....E 215 717-2600
  Philadelphia *(G-14284)*
Sewickley Herald ....G....... 412 324-1403
  Sewickley *(G-17409)*
Shoppers Guide ....G....... 724 349-0336
  Indiana *(G-8128)*
Sip Bulletin LLC ....G....... 267 235-3359
  Philadelphia *(G-14310)*
Snyder County Times ....G....... 570 837-6065
  Middleburg *(G-11041)*
South Fork News Agency..................G....... 814 495-9394
  South Fork *(G-17777)*
Sunday Review ....G....... 570 265-2151
  Towanda *(G-18434)*
Sunday Topic Korean News ....G 215 935-1111
  Elkins Park *(G-4912)*
Technically Media Inc ....G....... 215 821-8745
  Philadelphia *(G-14379)*
The Scranton Times L P ....D....... 570 348-9146
  Scranton *(G-17297)*
The Scranton Times L P ....C....... 570 348-9100
  Scranton *(G-17298)*
The Scranton Times L P ....D....... 570 644-6397
  Shamokin *(G-17427)*
The Scranton Times L P ....C....... 570 821-2095
  Wilkes Barre *(G-19965)*
The Scranton Times L P ....E 410 523-2300
  Scranton *(G-17299)*
The Scranton Times L P ....G....... 570 682-9081
  Valley View *(G-18718)*
The Scranton Times L P ....G....... 570 265-2151
  Towanda *(G-18435)*
Times Partner LLC ....G....... 570 348-9100
  Scranton *(G-17302)*
Times Pubg Newspapers Inc ....F 215 702-3405
  Langhorne *(G-9329)*
Times Publishing Company ....D....... 814 453-4691
  Erie *(G-5509)*
Times Shamrock Newspaper Group .....G....... 570 348-9100
  Scranton *(G-17303)*
Towanda Printing Co Inc ....G....... 570 297-4158
  Troy *(G-18528)*
Town Talk Newspapers Inc ....E 610 583-4432
  Holmes *(G-7666)*
Tri County Record............................G....... 610 970-3218
  Pottstown *(G-16056)*
Trib Total Media LLC ....C....... 724 834-1151
  Greensburg *(G-6721)*
Tribune-Review Publishing Co ....G....... 724 779-8742
  Tarentum *(G-18251)*
Twanda Printing ....G....... 570 421-4800
  Scranton *(G-17307)*
Union News ....G....... 570 343-4958
  Dunmore *(G-4486)*
Victorian Publishing Co Inc ....G....... 814 634-8321
  Meyersdale *(G-11020)*
Warren Times Observer ....E 814 723-8200
  Warren *(G-19063)*
Wced News Talk ....G....... 814 372-1420
  Du Bois *(G-4426)*
Weekly Shopper ....D....... 412 243-4215
  Tarentum *(G-18254)*
Wwb Holdings LLC ....E 267 519-4500
  Philadelphia *(G-14493)*
Wyoming Valley Times Jurnl Inc ....G....... 570 288-8362
  Kingston *(G-8726)*
York County Womens Journal ....G....... 717 634-1658
  York *(G-20735)*

York Daily Record Sunday News ....F 717 771-2000
  York *(G-20736)*
York Newspaper Company....................B 717 767-6397
  York *(G-20746)*

PUBLISHING & PRINTING: Pamphlets

Sea Group Graphics Inc ....G....... 215 805-0290
  Huntingdon Valley *(G-8036)*
Tims Printing Inc ....G....... 215 208-0699
  Philadelphia *(G-14390)*

PUBLISHING & PRINTING: Periodical Statistical Reports

Natural Marketing Inst Inc ....E 215 513-7300
  Harleysville *(G-7049)*
Strategic Reports Inc ....G....... 610 370-5640
  Reading *(G-16526)*
Williams Company Limited ....G....... 610 409-0520
  Collegeville *(G-3401)*

PUBLISHING & PRINTING: Shopping News

Amy Semler ....G....... 717 593-9243
  Greencastle *(G-6596)*
Creative Printing Co ....G....... 570 875-1811
  Ashland *(G-729)*
Hocking Printing Co Inc ....D....... 717 738-1151
  Ephrata *(G-5109)*
Leon Spangler ....F 570 837-7903
  Middleburg *(G-11028)*
Miller Printing & Publishing ....E 814 425-7272
  Cochranton *(G-3345)*

PUBLISHING & PRINTING: Television Schedules

TV Guide Distribution Inc ....B 610 293-8500
  Wayne *(G-19385)*
TV Guide Magazine LLC ....E 212 852-7500
  Radnor *(G-16303)*

PUBLISHING & PRINTING: Textbooks

Continental Press Inc ....C....... 717 367-1836
  Elizabethtown *(G-4869)*
In-Tec Inc ....G....... 570 342-8464
  Waverly *(G-19285)*
Moyer Music Test Inc ....G....... 717 566-8778
  Hummelstown *(G-7918)*
Nine 2 Five Ceo ....G....... 919 729-2536
  Philadelphia *(G-14075)*

PUBLISHING & PRINTING: Trade Journals

American Economic Association ....F 412 432-2300
  Pittsburgh *(G-14702)*
Jobson Medical Information LLC ....E 610 492-1000
  Newtown Square *(G-12579)*
Postal History Society Inc ....F 717 624-5941
  New Oxford *(G-12422)*
Wilkes Barre Law & Lib Assn................G....... 570 822-6712
  Wilkes Barre *(G-19975)*

PULP MILLS

A J Blosenski Inc ....D....... 610 942-2707
  Honey Brook *(G-7734)*
K Diamond Incorporated ....E 570 346-4684
  Scranton *(G-17249)*
Rapid Recycling Inc ....D....... 610 650-0737
  Oaks *(G-12936)*
Roderick Duvall ....G....... 814 735-4969
  Crystal Spring *(G-3938)*
Staiman Recycling Corporation ....D....... 717 646-0951
  Williamsport *(G-20074)*
Unipaper Recycling Company ....F 412 429-8522
  Carnegie *(G-2801)*
Westrock Rkt LLC ....D....... 570 476-0120
  Delaware Water Gap *(G-4045)*

PULP MILLS: Chemical & Semichemical Processing

Recycled Oil ....F 610 250-8747
  Easton *(G-4748)*

PULP MILLS: Mechanical & Recycling Processing

Tin Technology and Ref LLC ....G....... 610 430-2225
  West Chester *(G-19663)*

PULSE FORMING NETWORKS

Pulser LLC ....E 215 781-6400
  Bristol *(G-2189)*
Pulser LLC ....E 215 781-6400
  Bristol *(G-2190)*

PUMP JACKS & OTHER PUMPING EQPT: Indl

Hydra-Tech Pumps Inc ....F 570 645-3779
  Nesquehoning *(G-12005)*
Whittco Inc ....F 570 645-3779
  Nesquehoning *(G-12011)*

PUMPS

American Pipe and Supply LLC............G....... 724 228-6360
  Washington *(G-19148)*
Ampco-Pittsburgh Corporation ....D....... 412 456-4400
  Carnegie *(G-2763)*
Barebo Inc ....E 610 965-6018
  Emmaus *(G-5020)*
Campbell Manufacturing LLC ....E 610 367-2107
  Bechtelsville *(G-1031)*
Chant Engineering Co Inc ....E 215 230-4260
  New Britain *(G-12046)*
Chesterfield Special Cylinders ....E 832 252-1082
  Pittsburgh *(G-14847)*
Compressed Air Specialists Co............G....... 814 835-2420
  Erie *(G-5230)*
Curtiss-Wright Electro- ....A 724 275-5000
  Cheswick *(G-3105)*
Derbyshire Marine Products LLC ....G....... 267 222-8900
  Harleysville *(G-7030)*
Ds Fabrication ....G....... 717 529-2282
  Kirkwood *(G-8748)*
Dynaflo Inc ....G....... 610 200-8017
  Reading *(G-16367)*
Eastern Industrial Pdts Inc..................E 610 459-1212
  Aston *(G-760)*
Ecotech Inc ....D....... 610 954-8480
  Allentown *(G-202)*
Ecotech Marine LLC ....F 610 954-8480
  Allentown *(G-203)*
Finish Thompson Inc ....E 814 455-4478
  Erie *(G-5290)*
Flowserve Corporation ....F 908 859-7408
  Bethlehem *(G-1511)*
Four Guys Stnless Tank Eqp Inc ....D....... 814 634-8373
  Meyersdale *(G-11010)*
Gardner Denver Nash LLC ....G....... 203 459-3923
  Charleroi *(G-3015)*
Hydro-Pac Inc ....E 814 474-1511
  Fairview *(G-5829)*
Idac Corporation ....G....... 570 534-4400
  Sciota *(G-17181)*
Ingersoll-Rand Company ....D....... 717 532-9181
  Chambersburg *(G-2941)*
Ingersoll-Rand Company ....E 410 238-0542
  Shrewsbury *(G-17584)*
Instech Laboratories Inc ....E 610 941-0132
  Plymouth Meeting *(G-15852)*
Integrated Envmtl Tech Inc ....G....... 412 298-5845
  Washington *(G-19185)*
ITT Water & Wastewater USA Inc.........E 610 647-6620
  Malvern *(G-10256)*
Jaeco Fluid Solutions Inc....................G....... 610 407-7207
  Malvern *(G-10258)*
Johnson March Systems Inc ....E 215 364-2500
  Warminster *(G-18903)*
Kitco Tool Inc ....G....... 570 726-6190
  Mill Hall *(G-11178)*
Lionheart Holdings LLC ....D....... 215 283-8400
  Newtown *(G-12519)*
Lonergan Pump Systems Inc ....G....... 610 770-2050
  Allentown *(G-300)*
Maguire Products Inc ....E 610 459-4300
  Aston *(G-773)*
Manchester Township ....G....... 717 779-0297
  York *(G-20577)*
Met-Pro Technologies LLC...................D....... 215 723-4700
  Telford *(G-18304)*
Milton Roy LLC ....C....... 215 441-0800
  Ivyland *(G-8218)*
Milton Roy LLC ....G....... 215 293-0401
  Ivyland *(G-8219)*

Monarch Precast Concrete Corp ....E 610 435-6746
    Allentown (G-320)
Neac Compressor Svcs USA Inc ....G 814 437-3711
    Franklin (G-6150)
Neco Equipment Company ....G 215 721-2200
    Malvern (G-10284)
Netzsch Pumps North Amer LLC ....E 610 363-8010
    Exton (G-5714)
Orr Screw Machine Products ....E 724 668-2256
    Greensburg (G-6695)
PDC Machines Inc ....D 215 443-9442
    Warminster (G-18937)
Pump Shop Inc ....G 610 431-6570
    West Chester (G-19623)
Service Filtration Corp ....E 717 656-2161
    Lancaster (G-9194)
Shippensburg Pump Co Inc ....E 717 532-7321
    Shippensburg (G-17549)
Skc Inc ....D 724 260-0741
    Eighty Four (G-4849)
Spirax Sarco Inc ....G 610 807-3500
    Center Valley (G-2831)
Travaini Pumps USA Inc ....E 757 988-3930
    Norristown (G-12720)
Vacuum Works LLC ....G 570 202-8407
    East Stroudsburg (G-4637)
Watson McDaniel Company ....G 610 367-7191
    Boyertown (G-1935)
Weir Hazleton Inc ....G 570 455-7711
    Hazleton (G-7537)
Xylem Water Solutions USA Inc ....F 724 452-6300
    Zelienople (G-20828)

PUMPS & PARTS: Indl

Amt Pump Company ....E 610 948-3800
    Royersford (G-16842)
Asm Industries Inc ....G 717 656-2161
    Lancaster (G-8945)
Asm Industries Inc ....E 717 656-2166
    Leola (G-9769)
Asm Industries Inc ....E 717 656-2161
    Lancaster (G-8946)
C W S Inc ....G 800 800-7867
    North East (G-12734)
C-B Tool Co ....E 717 393-3953
    Lancaster (G-8968)
Curtiss-Wright Electro- ....D 610 997-6400
    Bethlehem (G-1493)
Flowserve Corporation ....D 570 451-2200
    S Abingtn Twp (G-16896)
Flowserve Corporation ....D 570 451-2325
    Moosic (G-11505)
Flowserve Corporation ....D 412 257-4600
    Bridgeville (G-2064)
Fresh Link Industrial Ltd ....G 724 779-6880
    Cranberry Township (G-3819)
Goulds Pumps LLC ....C 570 875-2660
    Ashland (G-730)
Hannmann Machinery Systems Inc ....E 610 583-6900
    Folcroft (G-6005)
Industrial Service Co Ltd ....F 484 373-0410
    Easton (G-4705)
Masterflo Pump Inc ....G 724 443-1122
    Gibsonia (G-6347)
Neptune Pump Manufacturing Co ....F 484 901-4100
    Pottstown (G-15955)
Orchem Pumps Inc ....G 215 743-6352
    Philadelphia (G-14101)
Springer Pumps LLC ....F 484 949-2900
    Telford (G-18319)

PUMPS & PUMPING EQPT REPAIR SVCS

Bucks Cnty Artesian Well Drlg ....F 215 493-1867
    Washington Crossing (G-19253)
C S Garber & Sons Inc ....E 610 367-2861
    Boyertown (G-1902)
Hannmann Machinery Systems Inc ....E 610 583-6900
    Folcroft (G-6005)
Industrial Pump & Mtr Repr Inc ....F 412 369-5060
    Glenshaw (G-6490)
Kufen Motor and Pump Tech ....G 215 672-5250
    Warminster (G-18908)
Leboeuf Industries Inc ....F 814 796-9000
    Waterford (G-19265)
Suburban Pump and Mch Co Inc ....G 412 221-2823
    Bridgeville (G-2092)

PUMPS & PUMPING EQPT WHOLESALERS

Eastern Industrial Pdts Inc ....E 610 459-1212
    Aston (G-760)
George I Reitz & Sons Inc ....E 814 849-2308
    Brookville (G-2261)
George I Reitz & Sons Inc ....G 412 824-9976
    East Pittsburgh (G-4595)
GSM Hold Co ....G 412 487-7140
    Allison Park (G-452)
Hyvac Products Inc ....F 484 901-4100
    Pottstown (G-15948)
ITT Water & Wastewater USA Inc ....E 610 647-6620
    Malvern (G-10256)
Ligus Electric Mtr & Pump Svc ....G 570 287-1272
    Luzerne (G-10126)
Mimco Equipment Inc ....F 610 494-7400
    Linwood (G-9990)
Pump Shop Inc ....G 610 431-6570
    West Chester (G-19623)
Ronald Hines ....G 570 256-3355
    Shickshinny (G-17502)
Shippensburg Pump Co Inc ....E 717 532-7321
    Shippensburg (G-17549)
Suez Wts Usa Inc ....A 215 355-3300
    Trevose (G-18506)
Sunnyside Supply Inc ....G 724 947-9966
    Slovan (G-17630)
Travaini Pumps USA Inc ....E 757 988-3930
    Norristown (G-12720)

PUMPS, HEAT: Electric

Memrs Inc ....G 724 589-5567
    Greenville (G-6754)
Poolpak Inc ....D 717 757-2648
    York (G-20632)
United States Thermoamp Inc ....E 724 537-3500
    Latrobe (G-9526)

PUMPS: Domestic, Water Or Sump

C-B Tool Co ....E 717 397-3521
    Lancaster (G-8967)
Campbell Manufacturing Inc ....D 610 367-2107
    Bechtelsville (G-1030)
Coleman Water Services ....G 814 382-8004
    Meadville (G-10713)
Greentree Machine Works ....G 717 786-4047
    Quarryville (G-16271)
Hoover Pump Works ....G 717 733-0630
    Ephrata (G-5110)
Pump Station Ridgway ....G 814 772-3251
    Ridgway (G-16725)

PUMPS: Fluid Power

Parker-Hannifin Corporation ....C 717 263-5099
    Chambersburg (G-2968)
Sencillo Systems Inc ....G 610 340-2848
    Warrington (G-19133)
York Industries Inc ....E 717 764-8855
    York (G-20742)

PUMPS: Hydraulic Power Transfer

American Hydraulic Mfg ....G 610 264-8542
    Allentown (G-135)
Bosch Rexroth Corporation ....A 610 694-8300
    Bethlehem (G-1471)
Conestoga USA Inc ....G 610 327-2882
    Pottstown (G-15973)
Penndel Hydraulic Sls & Svc Co ....G 215 757-2000
    Langhorne (G-9317)
R H Sheppard Co Inc ....A 717 637-3751
    Hanover (G-6941)
Seko Dosing Systems Corp ....G 215 945-0125
    Bristol (G-2197)

PUMPS: Measuring & Dispensing

Atlantis Technologies LLC ....G 724 695-2900
    Oakdale (G-12893)
Drummond Scientific Company ....D 610 353-0200
    Broomall (G-2287)
Fluid Dynamics Inc ....E 215 699-8700
    North Wales (G-12802)
Jaeco Fluid Solutions Inc ....G 610 407-7207
    Malvern (G-10258)
Maguire Products Inc ....E 610 459-4300
    Aston (G-773)
Mechanical Service Co Inc ....F 610 351-1655
    Allentown (G-313)

Milton Roy LLC ....C 215 441-0800
    Ivyland (G-8218)
Milton Roy LLC ....G 215 293-0401
    Ivyland (G-8219)
Seventy-Three Mfg Co Inc ....E 610 845-7823
    Bechtelsville (G-1037)

PUMPS: Oil Well & Field

Keystone Containment Contrs LP ....F 412 921-2070
    Pittsburgh (G-15175)
Megator Corporation ....G 412 963-9200
    Pittsburgh (G-15275)
Weatherford Artificia ....G 570 308-3400
    Muncy (G-11838)

PUMPS: Vacuum, Exc Laboratory

Chant Engineering Co Inc ....E 215 230-4260
    New Britain (G-12046)
Leybold USA Inc ....D 724 327-5700
    Export (G-5616)
Vacuum Works LLC ....G 570 202-8407
    East Stroudsburg (G-4637)

PUNCHES: Forming & Stamping

Jennison Corporation ....E 412 429-0500
    Carnegie (G-2771)
Oberg Carbide Punch & Die ....G 724 295-2118
    Freeport (G-6208)

PUPPETS & MARIONETTES

Rob Kei Inc ....G 717 293-8991
    Lancaster (G-9189)

PURIFICATION & DUST COLLECTION EQPT

Filter Technology Inc ....G 866 992-9490
    Gladwyne (G-6407)

PURIFIERS: Centrifugal

Matthey Johnson Inc ....E 610 232-1900
    West Chester (G-19599)

PUSHCARTS

Pushcart USA Inc ....G 570 622-2479
    Port Carbon (G-15900)

QUARTZ CRYSTALS: Electronic

Heraeus Quartz America LLC ....D 512 703-9000
    Yardley (G-20317)
Heraeus Quartz America LLC ....G 512 251-2027
    Yardley (G-20318)
Hoffman Materials Inc ....E 717 243-2011
    Carlisle (G-2718)
Infineon Tech Americas Corp ....C 610 712-7100
    Allentown (G-258)
J K Miller Corp ....E 412 922-5070
    Pittsburgh (G-15143)
National Scientific Company ....G 215 536-2577
    Quakertown (G-16222)
Precision Glass Products Co ....F 215 885-0145
    Oreland (G-13028)

QUILTING SVC & SPLYS, FOR THE TRADE

Heritage Gallery of Lace & Int ....G 717 359-4121
    Littlestown (G-10067)
Sansom Quilting & EMB Co ....F 215 627-6990
    Philadelphia (G-14278)

RACETRACKS

William T Jenkins ....G 610 644-7052
    Malvern (G-10346)

RACETRACKS: Auto

National Hot Rod Association ....D 717 584-1200
    Lancaster (G-9142)

RACEWAYS

Allegheny Mountain Raceway ....G 814 598-9077
    Kane (G-8458)
Dcm Slot Car Raceway ....G 215 805-6887
    Newtown (G-12501)
Penns Creek Raceway Park ....G 570 473-9599
    Northumberland (G-12873)

PRODUCT

Pikes Creek Raceway Park Inc ....G 570 477-2226
Hunlock Creek *(G-7933)*

R & D Raceway Inc ....G 724 258-8754
Bentleyville *(G-1274)*

Raceway Beverage Center ....G 724 695-3130
Imperial *(G-8075)*

Smithton Raceway LLC ....G 724 797-1822
Smithton *(G-17662)*

Speed Raceway ....F 215 672-6128
Horsham *(G-7851)*

Stuart Kranzel ....G 717 737-7223
Lemoyne *(G-9754)*

Tom Hester Hiesters Ho Raceway ....G 610 796-0490
Reading *(G-16543)*

RACKS: Display

Getaways On Display Inc ....F 717 653-8070
Manheim *(G-10386)*

Ridg-U-Rak Inc ....B 814 725-8751
North East *(G-12756)*

Ridg-U-Rak Inc ....E 814 725-8751
North East *(G-12758)*

Vertirack Manufacturing Co ....G 484 971-7341
Bernville *(G-1306)*

Vicjah Corporation ....G 610 826-7475
Palmerton *(G-13114)*

Vmf Inc ....E 570 575-0997
Scranton *(G-17310)*

Walco Fabricating Inc ....F 570 628-4523
Pottsville *(G-16101)*

RACKS: Garment, Exc Wood

Vitra Retail Inc ....G 610 366-1658
Allentown *(G-425)*

RACKS: Garment, Wood

Gwiz Products ....G 724 864-0200
Irwin *(G-8165)*

RACKS: Luggage, Car Top

Larry Paige ....G 570 374-5650
Middleburg *(G-11027)*

RACKS: Trash, Metal Rack

Stone Valley Welding LLC ....E 814 667-2046
Huntingdon *(G-7956)*

Trashcans Unlimited LLC ....G 800 279-3615
Honesdale *(G-7730)*

RADIO & TELEVISION COMMUNICATIONS EQUIPMENT

App-Techs Corporation ....F 717 735-0848
Lancaster *(G-8935)*

Belar Electronics Lab Inc ....E 610 687-5550
West Chester *(G-19509)*

Broadband Networks Inc ....D 814 237-4073
State College *(G-17947)*

Comtrol International ....E 724 864-3800
Irwin *(G-8149)*

Control Dynamics Corporation ....G 215 956-0700
Warminster *(G-18846)*

Cricket Communications LLC ....C 267 687-5949
Philadelphia *(G-13582)*

Delta Information Systems Inc ....E 215 657-5270
Horsham *(G-7809)*

Dynamic Manufacturing LLC ....D 724 295-4200
Freeport *(G-6203)*

Fidelity Technologies Corp ....C 610 929-3330
Reading *(G-16385)*

Gai-Tronics Corporation ....C 610 777-1374
Reading *(G-16388)*

Gaintenna ....G 724 654-9900
New Castle *(G-12096)*

Hirschmann Electronics Inc ....F 717 217-2200
Chambersburg *(G-2940)*

Idsi LLC ....G 717 227-9055
New Freedom *(G-12210)*

Idsi LLC ....E 717 235-5474
New Freedom *(G-12211)*

Kykayke Inc ....G 610 522-0106
Holmes *(G-7663)*

Library Video Company ....D 610 645-4000
Conshohocken *(G-3572)*

Matric Group LLC ....B 814 677-0716
Seneca *(G-17366)*

Micro-Coax Inc ....C 610 495-4438
Pottstown *(G-16019)*

Motorola Mobility LLC ....D 215 674-4800
Horsham *(G-7834)*

Motorola Mobility LLC ....G 610 238-0109
Plymouth Meeting *(G-15857)*

Ospcom LLC ....G 267 356-7124
Doylestown *(G-4321)*

Prime Image Delaware Inc ....G 215 822-1561
Chalfont *(G-2884)*

Ruckus Wireless Inc ....E 814 231-3710
State College *(G-18018)*

Star-H Corporation ....G 717 826-7587
Lancaster *(G-9204)*

Teledyne Defense Elec LLC ....D 814 238-3450
State College *(G-18036)*

Tm Systems Inc ....F 814 272-2700
State College *(G-18039)*

TVC Communications LLC ....E 717 838-3790
Annville *(G-661)*

Videotek Inc ....C 610 327-2292
Pottstown *(G-16068)*

Warren Installations Inc ....F 717 517-9321
Lancaster *(G-9235)*

World Video Sales Co Inc ....G 610 754-6800
Bechtelsville *(G-1038)*

RADIO BROADCASTING & COMMUNICATIONS EQPT

Alstom Signaling Operation LLC ....B 800 825-3178
Erie *(G-5184)*

Ameritech Network Corp ....E 215 441-8310
Hatboro *(G-7268)*

Ats-Needham LLC ....F 617 375-7500
Philadelphia *(G-13424)*

H & S Electronics ....G 717 354-2200
New Holland *(G-12250)*

L3 Electron Devices Inc ....C 570 326-3561
Williamsport *(G-20033)*

Metroplitan Communications Inc ....F 610 874-7100
Eddystone *(G-4805)*

Motorola Solutions Inc ....C 724 837-3030
Greensburg *(G-6690)*

Phasetek Inc ....G 215 536-6648
Quakertown *(G-16228)*

R F Specialties Pennsylvania ....G 814 472-2000
Ebensburg *(G-4793)*

Structured Mining Systems Inc ....E 724 741-9000
Warrendale *(G-19098)*

Symbol Technologies LLC ....F 610 834-8900
Plymouth Meeting *(G-15875)*

Westcom Wireless Inc ....G 412 228-5507
McKeesport *(G-10686)*

RADIO BROADCASTING STATIONS

Assemblies of Yahweh ....F 717 933-4518
Bethel *(G-1392)*

Family-Life Media-Com Inc ....F 724 543-6397
Kittanning *(G-8769)*

The Scranton Times L P ....D 570 348-9146
Scranton *(G-17297)*

The Scranton Times L P ....C 570 348-9100
Scranton *(G-17298)*

The Scranton Times L P ....E 410 523-2300
Scranton *(G-17299)*

RADIO COMMUNICATIONS: Airborne Eqpt

Raytheon Company ....B 814 278-2256
State College *(G-18012)*

RADIO PRODUCERS

Bible Lighthouse Inc ....G 570 888-6615
Sayre *(G-17111)*

RADIO RECEIVER NETWORKS

Katz Media Group Inc ....E 215 567-5166
Philadelphia *(G-13924)*

RADIO REPAIR SHOP, NEC

R T Grim Co ....E 717 761-4113
Camp Hill *(G-2513)*

RADIO, TELEVISION & CONSUMER ELECTRONICS STORES: Eqpt, NEC

H & S Electronics ....G 717 354-2200
New Holland *(G-12250)*

RADIO, TV & CONSUMER ELECTRONICS: VCR & Access

Big Brother Hd Ltd Lblty Co ....G 201 355-8166
Tamiment *(G-18232)*

RADIO, TV/CONSUMER ELEC STORES: Antennas, Satellite Dish

B and N Electronics ....G 724 484-0164
West Alexander *(G-19490)*

RAIL & STRUCTURAL SHAPES: Aluminum rail & structural shapes

H & M Diversified Entps Inc ....G 717 531-3490
Hershey *(G-7611)*

Kane Innovations Inc ....D 814 838-7731
Kane *(G-8469)*

RAILINGS: Prefabricated, Metal

Anvil Forge & Hammer Ir Works ....G 610 837-9951
Allentown *(G-139)*

C & C Manufacturing & Fabg ....G 570 454-0819
Hazleton *(G-7492)*

Concrete Step Units Inc ....E 570 343-2458
Scranton *(G-17218)*

Dura-Bilt Products Inc ....D 570 596-2000
Gillett *(G-6380)*

Hanover Iron Works Inc ....E 717 632-5624
Hanover *(G-6896)*

Heritage Fence & Deck LLC ....G 610 476-0003
Skippack *(G-17598)*

Robern Inc ....D 215 826-0280
Bristol *(G-2195)*

Safety Rail Source LLC ....G 610 539-9535
Norristown *(G-12707)*

Shetron Wldg & Fabrication Inc ....E 717 776-4344
Shippensburg *(G-17548)*

Skitco Manufacturing Inc ....G 570 929-2100
Hazle Township *(G-7481)*

RAILINGS: Wood

Advanced Stair Systems - Penns ....F 215 256-7981
Harleysville *(G-7013)*

Elite Vinyl Railings LLC ....G 717 354-0524
New Holland *(G-12248)*

Ufp Stockertown LLC ....G 610 759-8536
Stockertown *(G-18067)*

RAILROAD CAR CUSTOMIZING SVCS

Kasgro Rail Corp ....D 724 658-9061
New Castle *(G-12111)*

Transco Railway Products Inc ....E 570 322-3411
Williamsport *(G-20085)*

RAILROAD CAR REPAIR SVCS

Lasko Group Inc ....D 610 692-7400
West Chester *(G-19587)*

Renovo Rail Industries LLC ....G 570 923-2093
Renovo *(G-16649)*

Warren Railcar Service Inc ....F 814 723-2500
Warren *(G-19061)*

RAILROAD CARGO LOADING & UNLOADING SVCS

Ehb Logisitics Inc ....F 717 764-5800
York *(G-20464)*

Transporeon Group Americas Inc ....E 267 281-1555
Fort Washington *(G-6094)*

RAILROAD CROSSINGS: Steel Or Iron

L B Foster Company ....D 412 928-3400
Pittsburgh *(G-15207)*

RAILROAD EQPT

Amsted Rail Company Inc ....D 717 761-3690
Camp Hill *(G-2489)*

Brookville Locomotive Inc ....C 814 849-2000
Brookville *(G-2254)*

Buncher Company ....G 724 925-3919
Youngwood *(G-20780)*

Carly Railcar Components LLC ....G 724 864-8170
Irwin *(G-8147)*

Damian Hntz Locomotive Svc Inc ....G....... 814 748-7222
Colver **(G-3453)**
Donohue Railroad Equipment Inc ....E....... 724 827-8104
Darlington **(G-4027)**
G G Schmitt & Sons Inc ....F 717 394-3701
Lancaster **(G-9026)**
General Electric Company ....G....... 814 875-2234
Erie **(G-5301)**
Hyundai Rotem USA Corporation ....F 215 227-6836
Fort Washington **(G-6074)**
Ionx LLC ....G....... 484 653-2600
West Chester **(G-19573)**
Keystone Rail Recovery LLC ....G....... 865 567-2166
Jersey Shore **(G-8316)**
Keystone Spike ....G....... 717 270-2700
Lebanon **(G-9594)**
Magee Plastics Company ....D....... 724 776-2220
Warrendale **(G-19087)**
Neville Island RR Holdings Inc ....F 724 981-4100
Sharon **(G-17439)**
Norfolk Southern Corporation ....E....... 814 949-1551
Altoona **(G-531)**
Rail Car Service Co ....G....... 724 662-3660
Mercer **(G-10970)**
Sardello Inc ....D....... 724 375-4101
Aliquippa **(G-91)**
Toyo Denki Usa Inc ....E....... 724 774-1760
Freedom **(G-6193)**
Trac Products Inc ....G....... 610 789-7853
Havertown **(G-7432)**
Transco Railway Products Inc ....E....... 570 322-3411
Williamsport **(G-20085)**
Union Tank Car Company ....D....... 814 944-4523
Altoona **(G-554)**
Utcras Inc..........D....... 610 328-1100
Morton **(G-11594)**
Utcras LLC ....D....... 610 328-1100
Morton **(G-11595)**
Vossloh Track Material Inc ....D....... 610 926-5400
Reading **(G-16560)**
Wabtec Corporation ....B....... 412 825-1000
Wilmerding **(G-20160)**
Wabtec Investments Limited LLC ....G....... 412 825-1000
Wilmerding **(G-20161)**
Webtrans Limited LLC ....E....... 215 260-3313
Lansdale **(G-9427)**
Westinghouse A Brake Tech Corp.........E....... 724 838-1317
Greensburg **(G-6730)**

RAILROAD EQPT & SPLYS WHOLESALERS

A Stucki Company ....E....... 412 424-0560
Coraopolis **(G-3653)**
Alstom Signaling Operation LLC..........B....... 800 825-3178
Erie **(G-5184)**
Curry Rail Services Inc ....G....... 814 793-7245
Hollidaysburg **(G-7645)**
Kovalchick Corporation ....E....... 724 349-3300
Indiana **(G-8110)**
Powerrail Distribution Inc ....D....... 570 883-7005
Duryea **(G-4504)**
Powerrail Holdings Inc ....E....... 570 883-7005
Duryea **(G-4505)**
Sardello Inc ....D....... 724 375-4101
Aliquippa **(G-91)**
Transportation Eqp Sup Co ....E....... 814 866-1952
Erie **(G-5514)**
Unitrac Railroad Materials Inc ....G....... 570 923-1514
Renovo **(G-16651)**

RAILROAD EQPT, EXC LOCOMOTIVES

Acf Industries LLC..........D....... 570 742-7601
Milton **(G-11232)**
Nascent Energy Systems LLC ....G....... 203 722-1101
Pittsburgh **(G-15320)**

RAILROAD EQPT: Brakes, Air & Vacuum

Appalachian Tank Car Svcs Inc..........D....... 412 741-1500
Leetsdale **(G-9682)**
Westinghouse A Brake Tech Corp.........B....... 412 825-1000
Wilmerding **(G-20163)**

RAILROAD EQPT: Cars & Eqpt, Dining

A Stucki Company ....E....... 412 424-0560
Coraopolis **(G-3653)**
Curry Rail Services Inc ....G....... 814 793-7245
Hollidaysburg **(G-7645)**
Johnstown America Corporation ....D....... 877 739-2006
Johnstown **(G-8388)**

Standard Car Truck Company ....D....... 412 782-7300
Pittsburgh **(G-15576)**

RAILROAD EQPT: Cars & Eqpt, Interurban

Bombardier Transportation..........A....... 412 655-5700
Pittsburgh **(G-14782)**
Gupta Permold Corporation..........C....... 412 793-3511
Pittsburgh **(G-15067)**

RAILROAD EQPT: Cars & Eqpt, Rapid Transit

Synergy Industries LLC..........F 215 699-4045
North Wales **(G-12829)**

RAILROAD EQPT: Cars & Eqpt, Train, Freight Or Passenger

Edens Ticketing ....D....... 215 625-0314
Philadelphia **(G-13660)**
Kinkisharyo USA Inc..........G....... 724 778-0100
Seven Fields **(G-17375)**
Priest Enterprises ....G....... 724 658-7692
Grove City **(G-6802)**

RAILROAD EQPT: Cars, Maintenance

Kasgro Rail Corp..........D....... 724 658-9061
New Castle **(G-12111)**

RAILROAD EQPT: Cars, Rebuilt

Appalachian Tank Car Svcs Inc..........F 724 925-3919
Youngwood **(G-20779)**
Renovo Rail Industries LLC..........G....... 570 923-2093
Renovo **(G-16649)**
Warren Railcar Service Inc..........F 814 723-2500
Warren **(G-19061)**

RAILROAD EQPT: Cars, Tank Freight & Eqpt

Precision Runners LLC ....E....... 330 240-5988
Sharpsville **(G-17474)**

RAILROAD EQPT: Locomotives & Parts, Electric Or Nonelectric

Powerrail Distribution Inc ....D....... 570 883-7005
Duryea **(G-4504)**
Powerrail Holdings Inc ....E....... 570 883-7005
Duryea **(G-4505)**
Verail Technologies Inc ....G....... 513 454-8192
Lansdale **(G-9422)**

RAILROAD FREIGHT AGENCY

Tms International LLC ....D....... 412 678-6141
Glassport **(G-6419)**
Tms International Corp..........C....... 412 678-6141
Glassport **(G-6420)**
Tms International Corporation ....E....... 412 675-8251
Glassport **(G-6421)**

RAILROAD MAINTENANCE & REPAIR SVCS

Cwi Inc..........E....... 610 652-2211
Barto **(G-941)**
Diversified Mech Svcs Inc..........G....... 215 368-3084
Lansdale **(G-9362)**
Progress Rail Services Corp..........E....... 610 779-2039
Reading **(G-16476)**

RAILROAD RELATED EQPT

Cwi Inc..........E....... 610 652-2211
Barto **(G-941)**
General Electric Company ....G....... 814 875-2234
Erie **(G-5301)**
Pohl Railroad Mtls Corp LLC ....G....... 610 916-7645
Reading **(G-16471)**

RAILROAD RELATED EQPT: Ballast Distributors

Keystone Technologies LLC..........G....... 215 283-2600
North Wales **(G-12810)**

RAILROAD RELATED EQPT: Laying Eqpt, Rail

Waldrich GMBH Inc..........G....... 724 763-3889
Ford City **(G-6052)**

RAILROAD RELATED EQPT: Railway Track

Darkar Railway Equipment Inc ....G....... 610 296-5712
Malvern **(G-10220)**

RAILROAD TIES: Concrete

Koppers Industries Del Inc ....G....... 412 227-2001
Pittsburgh **(G-15191)**
L B Foster Company ....D....... 412 928-3400
Pittsburgh **(G-15207)**

RAILROAD TIES: Wood

Axion LLC ....G....... 484 243-6127
Blue Bell **(G-1813)**
Burke Parsons Bowlby Corp ....G....... 814 371-3042
Du Bois **(G-4385)**
Koppers Industries Del Inc ....G....... 412 227-2001
Pittsburgh **(G-15191)**
Mellott Wood Preserving Inc..........E....... 717 573-2519
Needmore **(G-11996)**

RAILROADS: Long Haul

Hli Rail & Rigging LLC..........F 215 277-5558
Elkins Park **(G-4905)**
Norfolk Southern Corporation ....E....... 814 949-1551
Altoona **(G-531)**

RAILS: Copper & Copper Alloy

Hcl Liquidation Ltd ....A....... 724 251-4200
Leetsdale **(G-9693)**

RAILS: Elevator, Guide

Fisher & Ludlow Inc ....F 859 282-7767
Wexford **(G-19801)**

RAILS: Rails, rolled & drawn, aluminum

Hampton Concrete Products Inc..........F 724 443-7205
Valencia **(G-18698)**

RAILS: Steel Or Iron

A & R Iron Works Inc ....F 610 497-8770
Trainer **(G-18462)**
Allomet Corporation ....F 724 864-4787
Irwin **(G-8142)**
Jersey Shore Steel Company ....B....... 570 753-3000
Jersey Shore **(G-8315)**
Jersey Shore Steel Company ....C....... 570 368-2601
Montoursville **(G-11443)**
JM Welding Company Inc ....G....... 610 872-2049
Chester **(G-3052)**

RAZORS, RAZOR BLADES

Art of Shaving - FI LLC ....G....... 610 962-1000
King of Prussia **(G-8585)**

REAL ESTATE AGENCIES & BROKERS

Altrax..........G....... 814 379-3706
Summerville **(G-18156)**
Dbi Inc ....D....... 814 653-7625
Fairmount City **(G-5808)**

REAL ESTATE AGENCIES: Residential

Private Zone Productions Corp ....G....... 267 592-5447
Philadelphia **(G-14204)**

REAL ESTATE AGENTS & MANAGERS

Avc Solutions LLC ....G....... 412 737-8945
Pittsburgh **(G-14743)**
Jem Industries LLC..........G....... 412 818-2606
Pittsburgh **(G-15148)**

REAL ESTATE INVESTMENT TRUSTS

Gokaaf International Inc..........G....... 267 343-3075
Philadelphia **(G-13775)**

REAL ESTATE OPERATORS, EXC DEVELOPERS: Commercial/Indl Bldg

Cava Intl MBL & Gran Inc ....E....... 215 732-7800
Philadelphia **(G-13516)**
Cramer Partnership ....G....... 215 378-6024
Yardley **(G-20301)**

PRODUCT

Digiorgio Mushroom Corp ....B 610 926-2139
Reading *(G-16362)*

J H R Inc...G........ 412 221-1617
Bridgeville *(G-2072)*

J R Resources L P ....G........ 814 365-5821
Ringgold *(G-16751)*

James May Costume Co........................G...... 610 532-3430
Folsom *(G-6026)*

Lomma Investments ....E 570 346-5555
Scranton *(G-17256)*

Merry Maid Novelties ....F 610 599-4104
Bangor *(G-922)*

Park Corporation................................G...... 412 472-0500
Coraopolis *(G-3711)*

Prizer-Painter Stove Works Inc.............E 610 376-7479
Blandon *(G-1757)*

Starlite Group Inc...............................G...... 814 333-1377
Meadville *(G-10793)*

Touchpoint Inc ....A 610 459-4000
Concordville *(G-3460)*

REAL ESTATE OPERATORS, EXC DEVELOPERS: Property, Retail

Elemental 3 LLC ....G...... 267 217-3592
Philadelphia *(G-13667)*

REAMERS

Alvord-Polk Inc...................................D...... 605 847-4823
Millersburg *(G-11188)*

REBABBITTING SVCS

A-1 Babbitt Co Inc...............................F 724 379-6588
Donora *(G-4144)*

RECLAIMED RUBBER: Reworked By Manufacturing Process

Aspol LLC...G...... 412 628-0078
New Kensington *(G-12325)*

Glw Global Inc ....G...... 412 664-7946
McKeesport *(G-10668)*

RECORD BLANKS: Phonographic

Cinram Manufacturing Inc....................A 570 383-3291
Olyphant *(G-12986)*

RECORDING & PLAYBACK HEADS: Magnetic

Brush Industries Inc ....D 570 286-5611
Sunbury *(G-18165)*

RECORDING HEADS: Speech & Musical Eqpt

Retrolinear Inc....................................G...... 215 699-8000
North Wales *(G-12827)*

Tobii Dynavox LLC ....C 412 381-4883
Pittsburgh *(G-15630)*

RECORDS & TAPES: Prerecorded

Digital Dynamics Audio Inc...................G...... 412 434-1630
Bethel Park *(G-1412)*

His Light Kingdom LLC ....G...... 267 777-3866
Philadelphia *(G-13828)*

Najafi Companies LLC..........................G...... 570 383-3291
Olyphant *(G-12994)*

Sony Music Holdings Inc ....E 724 794-8500
Boyers *(G-1890)*

Sour Junkie LLC ....G...... 412 612-6860
Pittsburgh *(G-15562)*

Technicolor HM Entrmt Svcs Inc...........F 570 383-3291
Olyphant *(G-13001)*

Tuscarora Usa Inc ....G...... 717 491-2861
Chambersburg *(G-2991)*

Whitaker Corporation ....C 724 334-7000
New Kensington *(G-12389)*

RECORDS OR TAPES: Masters

Brooke Production Inc ....G...... 610 296-9394
Malvern *(G-10196)*

RECOVERY SVC: Iron Ore, From Open Hearth Slag

Tms International Corp.........................E 215 956-5500
Horsham *(G-7860)*

RECOVERY SVCS: Anthracite, Culm Bank

Gilberton Coal Company.......................E 570 874-1602
Gilberton *(G-6367)*

RNS Services Inc ....G 570 638-3322
Blossburg *(G-1808)*

Waste Management & Processors ....E 570 874-2003
Frackville *(G-6109)*

RECOVERY SVCS: Metal

Kalumetals Inc.....................................F 724 694-2800
Derry *(G-4104)*

Telex Metals LLC.................................E 215 781-6335
Croydon *(G-3931)*

Tms International Corp.........................E 215 956-5500
Horsham *(G-7860)*

RECREATIONAL CAMPS

Organic Climbing LLC ....G...... 651 245-1079
Philipsburg *(G-14523)*

RECREATIONAL DEALERS: Campers/Pickup Coaches Truck Mounted

Fame Manufacturing Inc.......................F 814 763-5645
Saegertown *(G-16913)*

Keystone Truck Caps LLC ....G...... 570 836-4322
Tunkhannock *(G-18540)*

RECREATIONAL VEHICLE DEALERS

Stoltzfus Trailer Sales Inc ....D 610 399-0628
West Chester *(G-19645)*

RECREATIONAL VEHICLE PARKS & CAMPGROUNDS

Rock Run Recreation Area.....................G...... 814 674-6026
Patton *(G-13189)*

RECREATIONAL VEHICLE PARTS & ACCESS STORES

Total Mobility Services Inc ....G...... 814 629-9935
Boswell *(G-1885)*

RECREATIONAL VEHICLE REPAIRS

Total Mobility Services Inc ....G...... 814 629-9935
Boswell *(G-1885)*

RECTIFIERS: Electronic, Exc Semiconductor

Power Products Inc ....G...... 610 532-3880
Sharon Hill *(G-17459)*

Sanford Miller Inc................................G...... 724 479-5090
Homer City *(G-7681)*

RECTIFIERS: Mercury Arc, Electrical

American Zinc Recycling Corp...............E 724 774-1020
Pittsburgh *(G-14708)*

RECYCLABLE SCRAP & WASTE MATERIALS WHOLESALERS

A J Blosenski Inc ....D 610 942-2707
Honey Brook *(G-7734)*

Alphasource Inc ....F 215 844-6470
Philadelphia *(G-13372)*

DMS Shredding Inc ....F 570 819-3339
Hanover Township *(G-6988)*

Exim Steel & Shipbroking Inc...............G...... 215 369-9746
Yardley *(G-20310)*

Oscar Daniels & Company Inc ....F 610 678-8144
Reading *(G-16460)*

Thread International Pbc Inc.................G...... 814 876-9999
Pittsburgh *(G-15617)*

RECYCLING: Paper

Graybill Farms Inc...............................G...... 717 361-8455
Elizabethtown *(G-4874)*

Maslo Company Inc ....F 610 540-9000
Malvern *(G-10276)*

Newstech PA LP ....G...... 315 955-6710
Northampton *(G-12857)*

Paper Recovery Systems Inc................G...... 215 423-6624
Philadelphia *(G-14115)*

Take Away Refuse ....G...... 717 490-9258
Lancaster *(G-9211)*

REELS: Cable, Metal

Ametek Inc..G...... 215 355-6900
Horsham *(G-7785)*

REELS: Wood

Limpach Industries Inc ....F 724 646-4011
Sharpsville *(G-17473)*

REFINERS & SMELTERS: Copper

All-Clad Metalcrafters LLC ....D 724 745-8300
Canonsburg *(G-2537)*

Birdsboro Extrusions LLC ....G...... 610 582-0400
Birdsboro *(G-1689)*

Electric Materials Company ....C 814 725-9621
North East *(G-12739)*

Eric Herr ....G...... 717 464-1829
Lancaster *(G-9011)*

Heyco Metals Inc.................................D 610 926-4131
Reading *(G-16402)*

REFINERS & SMELTERS: Copper, Secondary

New Frontier Industries Inc...................G...... 814 337-4234
Meadville *(G-10768)*

US Bronze Foundry & Mch Inc ....D 814 337-4234
Meadville *(G-10810)*

REFINERS & SMELTERS: Nonferrous Metal

A Allan Industries Inc ....E 570 826-0123
Wilkes Barre *(G-19902)*

A J Blosenski Inc ....D 610 942-2707
Honey Brook *(G-7734)*

Allegheny Iron & Metal Co ....E 215 743-7759
Philadelphia *(G-13366)*

Alpha Assembly Solutions Inc ....C 814 946-1611
Altoona *(G-470)*

Bolton Metal Products Co Inc................G...... 814 355-6217
Bellefonte *(G-1094)*

Brandywine Valley Fabricators ....F 610 384-7440
Coatesville *(G-3295)*

Charles Casturo ....G...... 412 672-1407
McKeesport *(G-10662)*

Coatesville Scrap Ir Met Inc ....E 610 384-9230
Coatesville *(G-3299)*

Colonial Metals Co ....C 717 684-2311
Columbia *(G-3434)*

Consoldted Scrap Resources Inc...........F 717 843-0931
York *(G-20434)*

Consoldted Scrap Resources Inc...........G...... 717 843-0931
York *(G-20436)*

Culpepper Corporation.........................E 215 425-6532
Philadelphia *(G-13590)*

DMC Global Inc ....E 724 277-9710
Mount Braddock *(G-11616)*

E Schneider & Sons Inc.......................E 610 435-3527
Allentown *(G-199)*

Electric Materials Company ....C 814 725-9621
North East *(G-12739)*

Grant Mfg & Alloying Inc ....G...... 610 404-1380
Birdsboro *(G-1697)*

Greenstar Allentown LLC......................E 610 262-6988
Northampton *(G-12851)*

Harsco Minerals PA LLC........................G...... 724 352-0066
Sarver *(G-17071)*

Heraeus Incorporated..........................B 480 961-9200
Yardley *(G-20315)*

Heyco Metals Inc.................................D 610 926-4131
Reading *(G-16402)*

International Mill Service......................A 215 956-5500
Horsham *(G-7824)*

Interntnal Mtal Rclaiming Corp.............C 724 758-5515
Ellwood City *(G-4939)*

J W Zaprazny Inc.................................D 570 943-2860
New Ringgold *(G-12440)*

Keywell Metals LLC ....F 412 462-5555
West Mifflin *(G-19742)*

Kovalchick Corporation ....E 724 349-3300
Indiana *(G-8110)*

Lee Metals Inc ....G...... 412 331-8630
Coraopolis *(G-3701)*

Matthey Johnson Inc ....C 610 648-8000
West Chester *(G-19598)*

Metallurgical Products Company ....E 610 696-6770
West Chester *(G-19601)*

Mill Services Corp...............................F 412 678-6141
Glassport *(G-6413)*

Nak International Corp ....E 724 774-9200
Monaca *(G-11292)*

Penn Recycling Inc ....E 570 326-9041
Williamsport (G-20054)
Phoenix Metals of Pa Inc ....F 724 282-0679
Butler (G-2433)
Pittsburgh Flatroll Company ....G 412 237-2260
Pittsburgh (G-15397)
Reading Alloys Inc ....C 610 693-5822
Robesonia (G-16777)
Slates Salvage ....G 814 448-3218
Three Springs (G-18356)
Specilty Mtallurgical Pdts Inc ....F 717 246-0385
Red Lion (G-16614)
SPS Technologies LLC ....A 215 572-3000
Jenkintown (G-8302)
Staiman Recycling Corporation ....D 717 646-0951
Williamsport (G-20074)
Titanium Metals Corporation ....E 702 564-2544
Morgantown (G-11539)
Tms International LLC ....E 412 885-3600
Pittsburgh (G-15629)
Tms International LLC ....D 215 956-5500
Horsham (G-7859)
United Metal Traders Inc ....E 215 288-6555
Philadelphia (G-14421)

REFINERS & SMELTERS: Platinum Group Metal Refining, Primary

Matthey Johnson Holdings Inc ....E 610 971-3000
Wayne (G-19350)
Matthey Johnson Inc ....E 610 971-3000
Wayne (G-19351)
Matthey Johnson Inc ....C 484 320-2223
Audubon (G-830)
Matthey Johnson Inc ....C 610 341-8300
Wayne (G-19353)
T M P Refining Corporation ....G 484 318-8285
Malvern (G-10326)

REFINERS & SMELTERS: Platinum Group Metals, Secondary

Matthey Johnson Holdings Inc ....E 610 971-3000
Wayne (G-19350)
Matthey Johnson Inc ....E 610 971-3000
Wayne (G-19351)
Matthey Johnson Inc ....C 484 320-2223
Audubon (G-830)
Matthey Johnson Inc ....F 610 292-4300
Conshohocken (G-3574)
Matthey Johnson Inc ....E 610 873-3200
Downingtown (G-4240)
Matthey Johnson Inc ....C 610 341-8300
Wayne (G-19353)

REFINERS & SMELTERS: Tin, Primary

Tin Technology and Ref LLC ....G 610 430-2225
West Chester (G-19663)

REFINERS & SMELTERS: Zinc, Primary, Including Slabs & Dust

American Zinc Recycling LLC ....E 724 773-2203
Pittsburgh (G-14709)
Patriot Metal Products Inc ....E 570 759-3634
Berwick (G-1339)

REFINERS & SMELTERS: Zinc, Primary, Including Zinc Residue

American Zinc Recycling Corp ....E 724 774-1020
Pittsburgh (G-14708)

REFINING LUBRICATING OILS & GREASES, NEC

Akj Industries Inc ....G 412 233-7222
Clairton (G-3146)
Muscle Products Corporation ....F 814 786-0166
Jackson Center (G-8229)
Recoil Inc ....G 814 623-3921
Bedford (G-1072)

REFINING: Petroleum

Airgas Usa LLC ....G 215 766-8860
Plumsteadville (G-15806)
American Ref & Biochem Inc ....G 610 940-4420
Conshohocken (G-3520)

American Refining Group Inc ....B 814 368-1378
Bradford (G-1955)
American Refining Group Inc ....F 412 826-3014
Pittsburgh (G-14705)
Atlantic Refining & Marketing ....C 215 977-3000
Philadelphia (G-13422)
B&B Gas & Oil Shop ....G 814 257-8032
Dayton (G-4037)
BP Stop N Go ....G 412 823-4500
Turtle Creek (G-18559)
Calumet Karns City Ref LLC ....G 724 756-9212
Karns City (G-8480)
Coopers Creek Chemical Corp ....E 610 828-0375
Conshohocken (G-3534)
Coppers Inc ....E 412 233-2137
Pittsburgh (G-14875)
Eagle Bio Diesel Inc ....E 814 773-3133
Ridgway (G-16706)
Hollyfrontier Corporation ....G 800 456-4786
Plymouth Meeting (G-15847)
Industrial Systems & Process C ....G 412 279-4750
Pittsburgh (G-15122)
Jadden Inc ....G 724 212-3715
New Kensington (G-12349)
Lakeside Stop-N-Go LLC ....G 814 213-0202
Conneaut Lake (G-3476)
Main St Stop N Go ....G 570 424-5505
Stroudsburg (G-18127)
Mipc LLC ....B 610 364-8660
Marcus Hook (G-10449)
Monroe Energy LLC ....B 610 364-8000
Trainer (G-18464)
Pennzoil-Quaker State Company ....B 724 756-0110
Karns City (G-8482)
Petroleum Products Corp ....G 412 264-8242
Coraopolis (G-3714)
Philadelphia Energy Solutions ....C 267 238-4300
Philadelphia (G-14144)
Philadelphia Energy Solutions ....A 215 339-1200
Philadelphia (G-14145)
Philadlphia Enrgy Slutions LLC ....C 267 238-4300
Philadelphia (G-14161)
Sunoco Inc ....D 215 977-3000
Newtown Square (G-12591)
Sunoco Inc (R&m) ....A 610 859-1000
Marcus Hook (G-10455)
Sunoco (R&m) LLC ....D 215 977-3000
Newtown Square (G-12592)
Tangent Rail Corporation ....G 412 325-0202
Pittsburgh (G-15596)
Total Ptrchemicals Ref USA Inc ....B 877 871-2729
Exton (G-5737)
Total Ptrchemicals Ref USA Inc ....D 610 692-8401
West Chester (G-19667)
Tri-State Petroleum Corp ....D 724 226-0135
Tarentum (G-18249)
United Refining Inc ....D 814 723-1500
Warren (G-19054)
United Refining Company ....G 814 723-6511
Warren (G-19056)
Van Tongeren America LLC ....G 717 450-3835
Lebanon (G-9637)

REFRACTORIES: Alumina Fused

Alcoa Corporation ....G 412 553-4001
Pittsburgh (G-14661)
Alcoa Corporation ....E 412 315-2900
Pittsburgh (G-14662)
UNI-Ref United Refractories Co ....G 724 941-9390
Canonsburg (G-2650)

REFRACTORIES: Brick

Fuzion Technologies Inc ....F 724 545-2223
Kittanning (G-8772)
Mount Svage Spclty Rfractories ....F 814 236-8370
Curwensville (G-3954)
Worldwide Refractories Inc ....D 724 224-8800
Tarentum (G-18255)

REFRACTORIES: Castable, Clay

Altus Refractories LLC ....G 412 430-0138
Pittsburgh (G-14693)
Universal Refractories Inc ....E 724 535-4374
Wampum (G-18806)

REFRACTORIES: Cement

Lehigh Cement Company LLC ....D 717 843-0811
York (G-20565)

REFRACTORIES: Cement, nonclay

Universal Refractories Inc ....E 412 787-7220
Coraopolis (G-3730)

REFRACTORIES: Clay

Bloom Refractory Products LLC ....G 412 653-3500
Pittsburgh (G-14774)
Bnz Materials Inc ....D 724 452-8650
Zelienople (G-20793)
Carpenter Technology Corp ....B 610 208-2000
Philadelphia (G-13508)
Certech Inc ....C 570 823-7400
Hanover Township (G-6985)
Glen-Gery Corporation ....D 610 374-4011
Shoemakersville (G-17570)
Glen-Gery Corporation ....D 814 856-2171
Summerville (G-18158)
Glen-Gery Corporation ....D 717 848-2589
York (G-20504)
Glen-Gery Corporation ....D 814 857-7688
Bigler (G-1660)
Harbison Walker ....G 215 364-5555
Trevose (G-18498)
Harbisonwalker Intl Foundation ....C 412 375-6600
Moon Township (G-11489)
Harbisonwalker Intl Inc ....E 412 469-3880
West Mifflin (G-19740)
Harbisonwalker Intl Inc ....D 814 239-2111
Claysburg (G-3204)
HWI Intermediate 1 Inc ....G 412 375-6800
Moon Township (G-11491)
Lionheart Holdings LLC ....D 215 283-8400
Newtown (G-12519)
Lwb Holding Company ....C 717 792-3611
York (G-20569)
M S S I Inc ....E 412 771-5533
Canonsburg (G-2600)
Magnesita Refractories Company ....C 717 792-3611
York (G-20574)
Minteq International Inc ....E 724 794-3000
Slippery Rock (G-17622)
Mssi Refractory LLC ....E 412 771-5533
Mc Kees Rocks (G-10621)
Ncri Inc ....E 724 654-7711
New Castle (G-12125)
New Castle Refactories Co In ....D 724 654-7711
New Castle (G-12130)
Redland Brick Inc ....E 412 828-8046
Cheswick (G-3117)
Resco Group Inc ....F 412 494-4491
Pittsburgh (G-15479)
Selas Heat Technology Co LLC ....C 215 646-6600
Newtown (G-12549)
Shenango Advanced Ceramics LLC .....E 724 652-6668
New Castle (G-12149)
Snow Shoe Refractories LLC ....E 814 387-6811
Clarence (G-3165)
T Helbling LLC ....G 724 601-9819
Beaver (G-992)
Tyk America Inc ....E 412 384-4259
Clairton (G-3158)
Union Min Co of Allegheny Cnty ....G 412 344-9900
Pittsburgh (G-15669)
Universal Refractories Inc ....E 412 787-7220
Coraopolis (G-3730)
Worldwide Refractories Inc ....D 724 224-8800
Tarentum (G-18255)
Zampell Refractories Inc ....E 215 788-3000
Croydon (G-3934)

REFRACTORIES: Foundry, Clay

Ona Corporation ....C 610 378-1381
Reading (G-16458)

REFRACTORIES: Glasshouse

Bmi Refractory Services Inc ....G 412 429-1800
Pittsburgh (G-14775)

REFRACTORIES: Graphite, Carbon Or Ceramic Bond

Snow Shoe Refractories LLC ....E 814 387-6811
Clarence (G-3165)
Varsal LLC ....C 215 957-5880
Warminster (G-18993)
Vesuvius U S A Corporation ....C 412 276-1750
Pittsburgh (G-15694)

PRODUCT

Vesuvius U S A Corporation ....D 814 387-6811
Snow Shoe (G-17671)

REFRACTORIES: Nonclay

A P Green Services Inc..........................F 412 375-6600
Coraopolis (G-3652)
Envirosafe Services of Ohio ....F 717 354-1025
Narvon (G-11921)
Harbisnwlker Intl Holdings Inc ....G 412 375-6600
Moon Township (G-11488)
Harbisonwalker Intl Inc..........................C 412 375-6600
Moon Township (G-11490)
Intersource Inc ....F 724 940-2220
Mars (G-10501)
J M S Fabricated Systems Inc ....E 724 832-3640
Latrobe (G-9482)
M S S I Inc..E 412 771-5533
Canonsburg (G-2600)
Minteq International Inc..........................E 610 250-3000
Easton (G-4723)
Minteq International Inc..........................E 724 794-3000
Slippery Rock (G-17622)
Minteq International Inc..........................A 724 794-3000
Bethlehem (G-1574)
Ncri Inc ....E 724 654-7711
New Castle (G-12125)
Ona Corporation ....C 610 378-1381
Reading (G-16458)
Osram Sylvania Inc.................................D 412 856-2111
Monroeville (G-11347)
Penn-MO Fire Brick Co Inc ....G 717 234-4504
Harrisburg (G-7193)
Pennsylvania Perlite Corp York............G 610 868-0992
Bethlehem (G-1594)
Pennsylvania Perlite Corp York............G 717 755-6206
York (G-20621)
Pyrotek Incorporated..............................D 717 249-2075
Carlisle (G-2733)
Reading Refractories Company ....F 610 375-4422
Bala Cynwyd (G-890)
Saint-Gobain Ceramics Plas Inc............E 570 383-3261
Olyphant (G-12998)
Saint-Gobain Ceramics Plas Inc............D 724 539-6000
Latrobe (G-9518)
Saint-Gobain Ceramics Plas Inc............A 508 795-5000
Valley Forge (G-18711)
Tyk America Inc......................................E 412 384-4259
Clairton (G-3158)
Vesuvius U S A Corporation ....G 215 708-7404
Philadelphia (G-14442)
Vesuvius U S A Corporation ....E 419 986-5126
Pittsburgh (G-15695)
Vesuvius U S A Corporation ....D 412 788-4441
Pittsburgh (G-15696)

REFRACTORY CASTABLES

Sil-Base Company Inc ....E 412 751-2314
McKeesport (G-10681)

REFRACTORY MATERIALS WHOLESALERS

M S S I Inc..E 412 771-5533
Canonsburg (G-2600)
Mimco Products LLC..............................G 724 258-8208
Monongahela (G-11311)
Reading Refractories Company ....F 610 375-4422
Bala Cynwyd (G-890)
Union Min Co of Allegheny Cnty ....E 412 344-9900
Pittsburgh (G-15669)
Worldwide Refractories Inc.....................D 724 224-8800
Tarentum (G-18255)

REFRIGERATION & HEATING EQUIPMENT

Advanced Thermal Solutions LLC ....G 610 966-2500
Emmaus (G-5018)
Airgreen LLC..G 610 209-8067
West Chester (G-19495)
Beneficial Enrgy Solutions LLC ....G 844 237-7697
Jonestown (G-8449)
Beverage Air ....F 814 849-2022
Brookville (G-2249)
Chipblaster Inc..D 814 724-6278
Meadville (G-10712)
Crown Boiler Co ....E 215 535-8900
Philadelphia (G-13586)
Custom Chill Inc......................................G 215 676-7600
Philadelphia (G-13593)
Drake Refrigeration Inc ....F 215 638-5515
Bensalem (G-1183)

Enerflex Energy Systems Inc..................E 724 627-0751
Canonsburg (G-2585)
Evapco Alcoil Inc ....E 717 347-7500
York (G-20472)
Galaxy Global Products LLC ....G 610 692-7400
West Chester (G-19557)
Gap Ridge Contractors LLC....................F 717 442-4386
Kinzers (G-8738)
Gea Systems North America Llc ....C 717 767-6411
York (G-20493)
Industrial Systems & Controls...............G 412 638-4977
Pittsburgh (G-15121)
J&M Fluidics Inc......................................G 888 539-1731
Telford (G-18297)
John Bachman Hvac................................G 610 266-3877
Catasauqua (G-2815)
Johnson Controls Inc..............................D 717 771-7890
York (G-20543)
Koch Filter Corporation...........................F 215 679-3135
East Greenville (G-4572)
Kottcamp Sheet Metal ....E 717 845-7616
York (G-20558)
Lasko Products LLC................................C 610 692-7400
West Chester (G-19588)
Micro Matic Usa Inc................................F 610 625-4464
Center Valley (G-2828)
National Rfrgn & AC Pdts Inc ....F 215 638-8909
Langhorne (G-9313)
Ocean Thermal Energy Corp ....F 717 299-1344
Lancaster (G-9150)
Pennergy Solutions LLC ....G 484 393-1539
Royersford (G-16859)
RG Industries Inc ....E 717 849-0345
York (G-20658)
S P Industries Inc....................................D 215 672-7800
Warminster (G-18959)
Tekgard Inc ....D 717 854-0005
York (G-20685)
Texan Corporation ....E 215 441-8967
Warminster (G-18979)
Thd Contracting Service LLC ....G 215 626-1548
Philadelphia (G-14385)
Thermal Care Inc.....................................G 724 584-5500
Franklin (G-6164)
Trane US Inc ....D 412 747-3000
Pittsburgh (G-15635)
Trane US Inc ....F 412 394-9021
Pittsburgh (G-15636)
Trane US Inc ....E 412 963-9021
Pittsburgh (G-15637)
TS McCorry Heating and Cooling..........G 215 379-2800
Rydal (G-16887)
United Technologies Corp ....B 800 227-7437
Scottdale (G-17203)
Wayne Products Inc.................................F 800 255-5665
Broomall (G-2305)
Wedj/Three CS Inc ....D 717 845-8685
York (G-20705)
York International Corporation ....E 414 524-1200
Audubon (G-832)
York International Corporation ....C 717 815-4200
York (G-20744)
York International Corporation ....B 717 762-1440
Waynesboro (G-19431)

REFRIGERATION EQPT & SPLYS WHOLESALERS

Hajoca Corporation.................................G 215 657-0700
Willow Grove (G-20120)
M C E Development Inc ....G 412 952-0918
Irwin (G-8181)
National Refrigerants Inc ....E 215 698-6620
Philadelphia (G-14056)
National Rfrgn & AC Pdts Inc ....F 215 638-8909
Langhorne (G-9313)
S & G Water Conditioning Inc ....G 215 672-2030
Warminster (G-18957)
Smuckers Sales & Services LLC ....G 717 354-4158
New Holland (G-12285)

REFRIGERATION EQPT & SPLYS, WHOLESALE: Beverage Dispensers

Jordan Draft Service ....G 412 382-4299
Clairton (G-3152)

REFRIGERATION EQPT & SPLYS, WHOLESALE: Ice Making Machines

Historic York Inc......................................G 717 843-0320
York (G-20523)
Mastro Ice Inc ....G 412 681-4423
Pittsburgh (G-15261)

REFRIGERATION EQPT: Complete

Air/Tak Inc...F 724 297-3416
Worthington (G-20226)
Enerflex Energy Systems Inc..................D 570 726-0500
Muncy (G-11815)
F W Lang Co ....G 267 401-8293
Havertown (G-7421)
Gem Refrigerator Co................................F 877 436-7374
Philadelphia (G-13746)
HMC Enterprises LLC.............................E 215 464-6800
Philadelphia (G-13831)
Klinge Corporation..................................D 717 840-4500
York (G-20556)
National Rfrgn & AC Pdts Inc ....E 215 244-1400
Bensalem (G-1228)
York International Corporation ....B 717 762-2121
Waynesboro (G-19432)

REFRIGERATION REPAIR SVCS

Temperature Ctrl Professionals..............G 215 295-1616
Fairless Hills (G-5803)

REFRIGERATION SVC & REPAIR

Dyna-Tech Industries Ltd ....F 717 274-3099
Lebanon (G-9564)
Thd Contracting Service LLC ....G 215 626-1548
Philadelphia (G-14385)

REFUSE SYSTEMS

Allegheny Iron & Metal Co ....E 215 743-7759
Philadelphia (G-13366)
Finish Thompson Inc................................E 814 455-4478
Erie (G-5290)
Penn Jersey Farms Inc............................G 610 488-7003
Bethel (G-1397)
United Metal Traders Inc ....E 215 288-6555
Philadelphia (G-14421)

REGULATE, LICENSE & INSPECT, GOVT: Alcoholic Bev Control Bd

Liquor Control Board PA..........................G 570 383-5248
Scranton (G-17255)

REGULATORS: Generator Voltage

Myers Power Products Inc ....D 610 868-3500
Bethlehem (G-1576)

REGULATORS: Power

Rtb Products Inc ....F 724 861-2080
Irwin (G-8198)

REGULATORS: Transmission & Distribution Voltage

Central Penn Wire and Cable..................G 717 945-5540
Lancaster (G-8974)

REHABILITATION SVCS

Help Every Addict Live ....G 484 598-3285
Drexel Hill (G-4364)
McKesson Ptent Care Sltons Inc............D 814 860-8160
Erie (G-5386)
Threshold Rhblitation Svcs Inc ....B 610 777-7691
Reading (G-16538)

RELAYS & SWITCHES: Indl, Electric

Accelight Networks Inc ....D 412 220-2102
Bridgeville (G-2050)
Canterbery Industries LLC......................G 724 697-4231
Avonmore (G-863)
Servedio A Elc Mtr Svc Inc.....................F 724 658-8041
New Castle (G-12148)

RELAYS: Control Circuit, Ind

Automation Devices Inc ....E 814 474-5561
Fairview (G-5814)

Cieco Inc ......G...... 412 262-5581
Clinton **(G-3261)**
Crisp Control Inc ......D...... 724 864-6777
Irwin **(G-8153)**
Hampton Controls Inc ......F...... 724 861-0150
Wendel **(G-19481)**

RELAYS: Electronic Usage

Intervala LLC ......C...... 412 829-4800
East Pittsburgh **(G-4596)**

RELAYS: Vacuum

Hullvac Pump Corp ......G...... 215 355-3995
Southampton **(G-17818)**

RELIGIOUS SCHOOL

Assemblies of Yahweh ......F...... 717 933-4518
Bethel **(G-1392)**

REMOVERS & CLEANERS

Craig R Wickett ......G...... 610 599-6882
Bangor **(G-910)**
Steves Ventures ......G...... 717 808-2501
Ephrata **(G-5149)**

REMOVERS: Paint

Baxter Group Inc ......F...... 717 263-7341
Chambersburg **(G-2909)**
Dumond Chemicals Inc ......G...... 609 655-7700
West Chester **(G-19544)**

RENDERING PLANT

Mountain View Rendering Co ......E...... 215 723-5555
Souderton **(G-17752)**
Valley Proteins Inc ......D...... 717 436-0004
Mifflintown **(G-11140)**

RENTAL CENTERS: Furniture

Village Craft Iron & Stone Inc ......E...... 814 353-1777
Julian **(G-8457)**

RENTAL SVCS: Aircraft

Aviation Technologies Inc ......G...... 570 457-4147
Avoca **(G-840)**

RENTAL SVCS: Business Machine & Electronic Eqpt

C3 Media LLC ......E...... 610 832-8077
Philadelphia **(G-13492)**
Neopost USA Inc ......E...... 717 939-2700
Middletown **(G-11066)**
Neopost USA Inc ......G...... 717 939-2700
King of Prussia **(G-8654)**
Pitney Bowes Inc ......E...... 717 884-1882
Harrisburg **(G-7199)**
Pitney Bowes Inc ......C...... 215 751-9800
Philadelphia **(G-14180)**
Pitney Bowes Inc ......E...... 215 946-2863
Levittown **(G-9856)**

RENTAL SVCS: Floor Maintenance Eqpt

Prosource of Lancaster ......G...... 717 299-5680
Lancaster **(G-9176)**

RENTAL SVCS: Personal Items, Exc Recreation & Medical

Certified Carpet Service Inc ......D...... 717 393-3012
Lancaster **(G-8976)**

RENTAL SVCS: Propane Eqpt

Rpc Inc ......E...... 570 673-5965
Canton **(G-2667)**

RENTAL SVCS: Sign

Mobile Technology Graphics LLC ......G...... 610 838-8075
Hellertown **(G-7559)**

RENTAL SVCS: Sound & Lighting Eqpt

Clair Bros Audio Entps Inc ......D...... 717 626-4000
Manheim **(G-10377)**

RENTAL SVCS: Stores & Yards Eqpt

Arthur K Miller ......G...... 724 588-1118
Greenville **(G-6738)**

RENTAL SVCS: Tent & Tarpaulin

Grimms Inc ......G...... 724 346-4952
Sharon **(G-17435)**
Northwest PA Burial Service ......G...... 814 425-2436
Cochranton **(G-3346)**
Tmu Inc ......F...... 717 392-0578
Lancaster **(G-9220)**

RENTAL SVCS: Trailer

Arthur K Miller ......G...... 724 588-1118
Greenville **(G-6738)**

RENTAL SVCS: Tuxedo

Jack OReilly Tuxedos ......G...... 610 929-9409
Reading **(G-16412)**

RENTAL SVCS: Work Zone Traffic Eqpt, Flags, Cones, Etc

Interstate Safety Service Inc ......E...... 570 563-1161
Clarks Summit **(G-3194)**
Port Richman Holdings LLC ......G...... 212 777-1178
Philadelphia **(G-14189)**
Stabler Companies Inc ......F...... 717 236-9307
Harrisburg **(G-7219)**
Superior Respiratory Home Care ......G...... 717 560-7806
Lancaster **(G-9209)**

RENTAL: Portable Toilet

Piles Concrete Products Co Inc ......F...... 814 445-6619
Friedens **(G-6225)**

REPAIR SERVICES, NEC

Fts International LLC ......G...... 724 873-1021
Canonsburg **(G-2589)**

REPRODUCTION SVCS: Video Tape Or Disk

Debenham Media Group ......F...... 412 264-2526
Coraopolis **(G-3684)**
Mirage Advertising Inc ......G...... 412 372-4181
Monroeville **(G-11345)**

RESEARCH & DEVELOPMENT SVCS, COMMERCIAL: Engineering Lab

Electro-Optical Systems Inc ......F...... 610 935-5838
Phoenixville **(G-14547)**
Structure Probe Inc ......E...... 610 436-5400
West Chester **(G-19646)**

RESEARCH, DEV & TESTING SVCS, COMM: Chem Lab, Exc Testing

Applied Creativity Inc ......G...... 724 327-0054
Export **(G-5589)**
Myexposome Inc ......G...... 610 668-0145
Philadelphia **(G-14049)**

RESEARCH, DEVELOPMENT & TEST SVCS, COMM: Cmptr Hardware Dev

Communication Automation Corp ......E...... 610 692-9526
West Chester **(G-19527)**

RESEARCH, DEVELOPMENT & TEST SVCS, COMM: Research, Exc Lab

Delta Information Systems Inc ......E...... 215 657-5270
Horsham **(G-7809)**
Sports Management News Inc ......G...... 610 459-4040
Glen Mills **(G-6445)**

RESEARCH, DEVELOPMENT & TESTING SVCS, COMM: Agricultural

Orasure Technologies Inc ......E...... 610 882-1820
Bethlehem **(G-1589)**

RESEARCH, DEVELOPMENT & TESTING SVCS, COMM: Natural Resource

Civic Mapper LLC ......G...... 315 729-7869
Pittsburgh **(G-14856)**

RESEARCH, DEVELOPMENT & TESTING SVCS, COMM: Research Lab

Aurora Optics Inc ......G...... 215 646-0690
Ambler **(G-568)**

RESEARCH, DEVELOPMENT & TESTING SVCS, COMM: Sociological

Larry Arnold ......G...... 717 236-0080
Harrisburg **(G-7168)**

RESEARCH, DEVELOPMENT & TESTING SVCS, COMMERCIAL: Business

Career Communications Inc ......G...... 215 256-3130
Harleysville **(G-7024)**

RESEARCH, DEVELOPMENT & TESTING SVCS, COMMERCIAL: Education

Noblemedical LLC ......G...... 917 750-9605
Bryn Mawr **(G-2332)**
Questar Corporation ......E...... 215 862-5277
New Hope **(G-12312)**
Sing-Out Corporation ......G...... 610 865-5366
Bethlehem **(G-1619)**

RESEARCH, DEVELOPMENT & TESTING SVCS, COMMERCIAL: Energy

Eccotrol LLC ......G...... 877 322-6876
Huntingdon Valley **(G-7974)**
Maxpower Inc ......F...... 215 256-4575
Harleysville **(G-7047)**
Robindale Export LLC ......B...... 724 879-4264
Latrobe **(G-9517)**

RESEARCH, DEVELOPMENT & TESTING SVCS, COMMERCIAL: Medical

Actuated Medical Inc ......F...... 814 355-0003
Bellefonte **(G-1091)**
Bio Med Sciences Inc ......F...... 610 530-3193
Allentown **(G-151)**
Btg International Inc ......D...... 610 943-6000
West Conshohocken **(G-19686)**
Chiltern International Inc ......E...... 484 679-2400
King of Prussia **(G-8592)**
E-Nanomedsys Inc ......G...... 917 734-1462
State College **(G-17958)**
Global Home Automation LLC ......G...... 484 686-7374
Fort Washington **(G-6072)**
Hyq Research Solutions LLC ......G...... 717 439-9320
Hummelstown **(G-7914)**
Protherics Inc ......C...... 615 327-1027
Conshohocken **(G-3593)**
Strongbridge Biopharma PLC ......E...... 610 254-9200
Trevose **(G-18504)**

RESEARCH, DEVELOPMENT & TESTING SVCS, COMMERCIAL: Physical

Aavid Thermacore Inc ......C...... 717 569-6551
Lancaster **(G-8919)**
Arkema Inc ......B...... 610 878-6500
King of Prussia **(G-8583)**
Gentex Corporation ......B...... 570 282-3550
Simpson **(G-17593)**
Oxicool Inc ......G...... 215 462-2665
Malvern **(G-10292)**
Precision Medical Devices Inc ......G...... 717 795-9480
Mechanicsburg **(G-10881)**
Prophase Labs Inc ......E...... 215 345-0919
Doylestown **(G-4329)**
Strata Skin Sciences Inc ......D...... 215 619-3200
Horsham **(G-7854)**
Thermacore International Inc ......B...... 717 569-6551
Lancaster **(G-9216)**

PRODUCT

RESEARCH, DEVELOPMENT SVCS, COMMERCIAL: Indl Lab

Bailey Oxides LLC ....G...... 724 745-9500
Canonsburg (G-2548)
Lee Rj Group Inc ....C...... 800 860-1775
Monroeville (G-11342)
Tribology Systems ....G...... 610 466-7547
Warminster (G-18985)

RESEARCH, DVLPT & TEST SVCS, COMM: Mkt Analysis or Research

Mm USA Holdings LLC ....B...... 267 685-2300
Yardley (G-20326)

RESEARCH, DVLPT & TESTING SVCS, COMM: Mkt, Bus & Economic

Vetstreet Incorporated..............E...... 267 685-2400
Feasterville Trevose (G-5937)

RESIDENTIAL REMODELERS

Foster-Kmetz Woodworking ....G...... 570 325-8222
Jim Thorpe (G-8340)

RESINS: Custom Compound Purchased

Dyneon LLC.............................D...... 610 497-8899
Aston (G-759)
Fielco Industries Inc ....E...... 215 674-8700
Huntingdon Valley (G-7983)
Hayes-Ivy Mfg Inc.....................E...... 610 767-3865
New Tripoli (G-12457)
J Meyer & Sons Inc....................C...... 215 699-7003
West Point (G-19759)
Ltl Color Compounders LLC.......D...... 215 736-1126
Morrisville (G-11570)
Polytek Development Corp ....E...... 610 559-8620
Easton (G-4743)
Ranbar Electrical Mtls LLC ....E...... 724 864-8200
Harrison City (G-7251)
Sabic Innovative Plas US LLC ....D...... 610 363-4500
Exton (G-5727)
Sealed Air Corporation..............G...... 610 926-7517
Reading (G-16509)
Ultra-Poly Corporation ....E...... 570 897-7500
Portland (G-15940)
Washington Penn Plastic Co Inc .....G...... 724 228-1260
Washington (G-19241)
Washington Penn Plastic Co Inc .....E...... 724 228-3709
Eighty Four (G-4851)
Washington Penn Plastic Co Inc .....C...... 724 228-1260
Washington (G-19240)

RESISTORS

Dean Technology Inc ....E...... 724 479-3533
Lucernemines (G-10117)
Grued Corporation ....G...... 610 644-1300
Malvern (G-10244)
In Speck Corporation................E...... 610 272-9500
Norristown (G-12669)
State of Art Inc ....C...... 814 355-2714
State College (G-18034)
Triaxial Structures Inc ....G...... 215 248-0380
Philadelphia (G-14409)
US Resistor Inc ....G...... 814 834-9369
Saint Marys (G-17026)
Vishay Precision Foil Inc............A...... 484 321-5300
Malvern (G-10342)
Vishay Precision Group Inc ....D...... 484 321-5300
Malvern (G-10343)

RESISTORS: Networks

Vishay Intertechnology Inc ....B...... 610 644-1300
Malvern (G-10341)

RESORCINOL

Indspec Chemical Corporation....B...... 724 756-2370
Petrolia (G-13305)

RESPIRATORS

Vcp Mobility Inc.......................B...... 814 443-4881
Somerset (G-17715)

RESPIRATORY SYSTEM DRUGS

Best Medical International Inc ....D....... 412 312-6700
Pittsburgh (G-14764)
Windtree Therapeutics Inc ....D...... 215 488-9300
Warrington (G-19140)

RESTAURANT EQPT: Carts

Goodwest Industries LLC ....E...... 215 340-3100
Douglassville (G-4177)

RESTAURANT EQPT: Food Wagons

Apontes Latin Flavor Inc ....G...... 727 247-2001
Glenshaw (G-6481)
Double DS Roadhouse LLc....................G...... 814 395-3535
Confluence (G-3464)

RESTAURANT EQPT: Sheet Metal

Commercial Stainless Inc ....E...... 570 387-8980
Bloomsburg (G-1776)

RESTAURANTS:Full Svc, American

Bill Macks Ice Cream ....E...... 717 292-1931
Dover (G-4188)
Chesapeake Del Brewing Co LLC ....C...... 610 627-9000
Media (G-10918)
Frankensteins..................................G...... 814 938-2571
Punxsutawney (G-16140)
Marzonies ....D...... 814 695-2931
Duncansville (G-4456)
ME 5 Cents LLC ....F...... 570 574-4701
Hanover Township (G-6994)
Mudhook Brewing Company LLC ....F...... 717 747-3605
York (G-20606)
Philadelphia Beer Works Inc...............C...... 215 482-8220
Philadelphia (G-14142)
Social Still LLC ....E...... 610 625-4585
Bethlehem (G-1621)
Stoudt Brewing Company ....E...... 717 484-4386
Adamstown (G-24)
William Plange..................................G...... 215 303-0069
Philadelphia (G-14475)

RESTAURANTS:Full Svc, Diner

Bobs Diner Enterprises Inc..................F...... 412 221-7474
Pittsburgh (G-14778)

RESTAURANTS:Full Svc, Family

Bhagyas Kitchen...............................G...... 215 233-1587
Glenside (G-6508)
Mostollers Mfg & Distrg.......................F...... 814 445-7281
Friedens (G-6223)

RESTAURANTS:Full Svc, Family, Chain

Travaglini Enterprises Inc ....E...... 814 898-1212
Erie (G-5515)
Travaglini Enterprises Inc ....E...... 724 342-3334
Hermitage (G-7596)

RESTAURANTS:Full Svc, Family, Independent

Country Club Restaurant ....D...... 215 722-0500
Philadelphia (G-13575)
Leibys Ichr LLC................................G...... 570 778-0108
Tamaqua (G-18217)
Novotny Micheal ....F...... 724 785-2160
Brownsville (G-2313)

RESTAURANTS:Full Svc, German

Alpine Wurst & Meathouse Inc ....E...... 570 253-5899
Honesdale (G-7700)

RESTAURANTS:Full Svc, Indian-Pakistan

Pita Pita LLC....................................G...... 267 440-7482
Philadelphia (G-14179)

RESTAURANTS:Full Svc, Italian

Angelos Inc......................................E...... 724 350-8715
Washington (G-19150)
Folino Estate LLC ....G...... 484 256-5300
Kutztown (G-8843)
Sorrenti Orchards Inc ....G...... 570 992-2255
Saylorsburg (G-17108)

RESTAURANTS:Full Svc, Mexican

Taste of Puebla................................G...... 484 467-8597
Kennett Square (G-8548)

RESTAURANTS:Full Svc, Vietnamese

Noodle King......................................G...... 717 299-2799
Lancaster (G-9147)

RESTAURANTS:Limited Svc, Coffee Shop

Deer Creek Winery LLC ....D...... 814 354-7392
Shippenville (G-17560)
Fresh Roasted Coffee LLC....................F...... 570 743-9228
Sunbury (G-18169)
La Prima Expresso Co ....G...... 412 565-7070
Pittsburgh (G-15212)

RESTAURANTS:Limited Svc, Ice Cream Stands Or Dairy Bars

Brusters Old Fashioned Ice Cre ....G...... 724 772-9999
Seven Fields (G-17374)
Bucks Creamery LLC..........................E...... 732 387-3535
Feasterville Trevose (G-5895)
Buffs Ice Cream.................................G...... 814 849-8335
Brookville (G-2257)
Joshi Bharkatkumar ....F...... 610 861-7733
Bethlehem (G-1547)
Manning Farm Dairy ....G...... 570 563-2016
Dalton (G-3987)
Robert Gerenser ....E...... 215 646-1853
New Hope (G-12314)
Sarris Candies Inc.............................B...... 724 745-4042
Canonsburg (G-2632)
Sunset Ice Cream ....E...... 570 326-3902
Williamsport (G-20077)
Tasty Fries Inc ....G...... 610 941-2109
Blue Bell (G-1855)

RESTAURANTS:Limited Svc, Lunch Counter

Academy Sports Center Inc...................G...... 570 339-3399
Mount Carmel (G-11622)

RESTAURANTS:Limited Svc, Pizza

Robert Bath ....G...... 610 588-0423
Roseto (G-16822)

RESTAURANTS:Limited Svc, Pizzeria, Chain

Atlantic Dev Corp of PA.......................F...... 717 243-0212
Carlisle (G-2690)

RESTAURANTS:Limited Svc, Pizzeria, Independent

Pizza Associates Incorporated ....C...... 570 822-6600
Wilkes Barre (G-19957)

RESTAURANTS:Limited Svc, Sandwiches & Submarines Shop

Maid-Rite Specialty Foods LLC ....F...... 570 346-3572
Scranton (G-17258)
Smuckers Salad ....G...... 267 757-0944
Newtown (G-12550)
Subway ....F...... 814 368-2576
Bradford (G-1993)

RESTAURANTS:Limited Svc, Snow Cone Stand

Scooperman Water Ice Inc ....G...... 267 623-8494
Philadelphia (G-14285)

RETAIL BAKERY: Bagels

Northwest Bagel Corporation...............G...... 610 237-0586
Downingtown (G-4245)
T & P Bagels Inc................................G...... 610 867-8695
Bethlehem (G-1637)

RETAIL BAKERY: Bread

Addison Baking Company ....E...... 215 464-8055
Philadelphia (G-13344)
Alfred Nickles Bakery Inc....................F...... 814 471-6913
Ebensburg (G-4778)
International Bakery ....E...... 814 452-3435
Erie (G-5329)

New Lycoming Bakery Inc ....E 570 326-9426
Williamsport (G-20046)
Potomac Bakery Inc..........................E 412 531-5066
Pittsburgh (G-15421)
Schwebel Baking Co of PA Inc ....C 412 751-4080
McKeesport (G-10680)
Warrington Pastry Shop.....................F 215 343-1946
Warrington (G-19139)

RETAIL BAKERY: Cakes

Dices Creative Cakes.........................G 610 367-0107
Boyertown (G-1906)
Kretchmar Bakery Inc.........................E 724 774-2324
Beaver (G-986)
Paddycake Bakery..............................G 412 621-4477
Pittsburgh (G-15367)
Prantls of Shadyside LLC ....F 412 621-2092
Pittsburgh (G-15428)
Weinrich Bakery.................................E 215 659-7062
Willow Grove (G-20148)

RETAIL BAKERY: Cookies

Country Fresh Batter Inc ....D 610 272-5751
King of Prussia (G-8600)

RETAIL BAKERY: Doughnuts

Brinic Donuts Inc ....E 814 944-5242
Altoona (G-484)
Deangelis Bros Inc..............................E 724 775-1641
Rochester (G-16784)
Donut Connection..............................F 724 282-6214
Butler (G-2395)
Donut Shack......................................G 412 793-4222
Pittsburgh (G-14931)
Dunkin Donuts...................................G 610 992-0111
King of Prussia (G-8613)
Early Morning Donuts Corp ....G 570 961-5150
Scranton (G-17230)
Fred Fairburn....................................E 570 282-3364
Carbondale (G-2675)
Howard Donuts Inc ....E 215 634-7750
Philadelphia (G-13836)
J F M Philadelphia Donut Inc ....G 215 676-0700
Philadelphia (G-13883)
Krispy Kreme Doughnuts....................G 724 228-1800
Washington (G-19194)
Macs Donut Shop Inc ....G 724 375-6776
Aliquippa (G-82)
Mighty Fine Inc..................................D 814 455-6408
Erie (G-5391)
Shree Swami Narayan Corp ....E 610 272-8404
Norristown (G-12713)
Yum-Yum Colmar Inc ....E 215 822-9468
Colmar (G-3426)

RETAIL BAKERY: Pastries

Achenbachs Pastry Inc ....E 717 656-6671
Leola (G-9765)

RETAIL BAKERY: Pretzels

Auntie Annes Inc ....D 717 435-1435
Lancaster (G-8947)
Auntie Annes Soft Pretzels ....G 724 349-2825
Indiana (G-8084)
Dutch Cntry Soft Pretzels LLC............G 717 354-4493
New Holland (G-12244)
Martins Pretzel Bakery ....E 717 859-1272
Akron (G-36)
Philadelphia Soft Pretzels ....E 215 324-4315
Philadelphia (G-14155)
Philly Pretzel Factory.........................E 215 962-5593
Philadelphia (G-14169)
Pretzel Shop......................................F 412 431-2574
Pittsburgh (G-15437)
Pretzels Plus.....................................G 724 228-9785
Washington (G-19218)
Unique Pretzel Bakery Inc ....E 610 929-3172
Reading (G-16553)

RETAIL LUMBER YARDS

Allegheny Millwork Pbt.......................C 724 873-8700
Lawrence (G-9534)
C C Allis & Sons Inc ....E 570 744-2631
Wyalusing (G-20247)
Destefanos Hardwood Lumber............G 724 483-6196
Charleroi (G-3009)

Dunns Sawmill LLP............................G 570 253-5217
Honesdale (G-7710)
JF Mill and Lumber Co ....G 724 654-9542
New Castle (G-12109)
Mars Lumber Inc ....G 724 625-2224
Mars (G-10506)
Newtown-Slocomb Mfg Inc ....G 570 825-3675
Hanover Township (G-7001)
Pittston Lumber & Mfg Co ....E 570 654-3328
Pittston (G-15776)
Quehanna Millwork ....G 814 263-4145
Frenchville (G-6218)
Ram Forest Products Inc ....D 814 697-7185
Shinglehouse (G-17512)
Shelly Enterprises -US Lbm LLC..........D 215 723-5108
Telford (G-18315)
Shelly Enterprises -US Lbm LLC..........E 610 432-4511
Bethlehem (G-1617)
Weaber Inc..E 814 827-4621
Titusville (G-18403)

RETAIL STORES, NEC

Timber Skate Shop ....G 570 492-6063
Sunbury (G-18175)

RETAIL STORES: Artificial Limbs

Union Orthotics Prosthetics Co ....G 724 836-6656
Greensburg (G-6724)
Union Orthotics Prosthetics Co ....G 412 943-1950
Pittsburgh (G-15670)
Union Orthotics Prosthetics Co ....G 412 621-2698
Pittsburgh (G-15671)

RETAIL STORES: Audio-Visual Eqpt & Splys

Naamans Creek Co Inc ....G 610 268-3833
Avondale (G-855)
Phoenix Avs LLC................................G 610 910-6251
Broomall (G-2302)
R G B Business Tech Solutions ....G 215 745-3646
Philadelphia (G-14224)

RETAIL STORES: Awnings

Advance Sign Company LLC................E 412 481-6990
Pittsburgh (G-14650)
Charles F Woodill..............................G 215 457-5858
Philadelphia (G-13528)
Diamond Awning Mfg Co....................G 610 656-1924
Folcroft (G-6002)
Edmiston Signs..................................G 814 742-8930
Bellwood (G-1137)
Fehl Awning Company Inc ....G 717 776-3162
Walnut Bottom (G-18789)
Lingenfelter Awning...........................G 814 696-4353
Duncansville (G-4455)
Rainbow Awnings Inc ....F 610 534-5380
Folcroft (G-6014)
Rose A Rupp.....................................G 412 622-6827
Pittsburgh (G-15496)
Zurn Aluminum Products Co ....G 814 774-2681
Girard (G-6404)

RETAIL STORES: Banners

Bright Banners ....G 570 326-3524
Williamsport (G-19994)

RETAIL STORES: Business Machines & Eqpt

Accustar Inc ....G 610 459-0123
Garnet Valley (G-6264)
Beaver Valley Cash Register Co...........G 724 728-0800
New Brighton (G-12031)
Image Net Ventures LLC.....................E 610 240-0800
West Chester (G-19567)
John M Sensenig ....G 717 445-4669
New Holland (G-12255)
Portico Group LLC.............................G 610 566-8499
Media (G-10943)

RETAIL STORES: Canvas Prdts

Hamilton Awning Co ....F 724 774-7644
Beaver (G-983)

RETAIL STORES: Children's Furniture, NEC

Little Partners Inc ....G 318 220-7005
Reading (G-16431)

RETAIL STORES: Christmas Lights & Decorations

Design Decorators.............................E 215 634-8300
Philadelphia (G-13620)
J Kinderman & Sons Inc ....E 215 271-7600
Philadelphia (G-13884)

RETAIL STORES: Cleaning Eqpt & Splys

Monarch Global Brands Inc ....D 215 482-6100
Philadelphia (G-14033)

RETAIL STORES: Concrete Prdts, Precast

Atlantic Precast Industries..................C 215 945-5600
Bristol (G-2113)
Juniata Concrete Co ....G 717 248-9677
Lewistown (G-9937)
Nitterhouse Concrete Pdts Inc ....C 717 207-7837
Chambersburg (G-2962)

RETAIL STORES: Cosmetics

Bismoline Manufacturing Co ....G 717 394-8795
Lancaster (G-8955)
Turtle Moon Gardens ....G 814 639-0287
Port Matilda (G-15907)

RETAIL STORES: Drafting Eqpt & Splys

Fotorecord Print Center Inc ....G 724 837-0530
Greensburg (G-6667)
Print-O-Stat Inc.................................G 610 265-5470
King of Prussia (G-8664)
Print-O-Stat Inc.................................F 717 795-9255
Mechanicsburg (G-10882)

RETAIL STORES: Educational Aids & Electronic Training Mat

Carnegie Learning Inc ....C 412 690-2442
Pittsburgh (G-14817)
Inert Products LLC.............................F 570 341-3751
Scranton (G-17244)

RETAIL STORES: Electronic Parts & Eqpt

Kms Fab LLC......................................E 570 338-0200
Luzerne (G-10125)
Metroplitan Communications Inc ....F 610 874-7100
Eddystone (G-4805)
Signstat..F 724 527-7475
Jeannette (G-8264)

RETAIL STORES: Engine & Motor Eqpt & Splys

C & S Repair Center Inc......................G 610 524-9724
Downingtown (G-4217)
Marilyn Strawser Beauty Salon ....G 717 463-2804
Thompsontown (G-18349)
Witmer Motor Service.........................G 717 336-2949
Stevens (G-18058)

RETAIL STORES: Engines & Parts, Air-Cooled

Holtrys LLC.......................................G 717 532-7261
Roxbury (G-16838)

RETAIL STORES: Farm Eqpt & Splys

Kutz Farm Equipment Inc...................G 570 345-4882
Pine Grove (G-14596)

RETAIL STORES: Farm Machinery, NEC

Maple Mountain Industries Inc ....E 724 676-4703
New Florence (G-12198)

RETAIL STORES: Fire Extinguishers

911 Safety Equipment LLC..................F 610 279-6808
Norristown (G-12628)

RETAIL STORES: Flags

Flags For All Seasons Inc ....G 610 688-4235
Wayne (G-19331)
John W Keplinger & Son.....................G 610 666-6191
Norristown (G-12674)

P
R
O
D
U
C
T

RETAIL STORES: Hair Care Prdts

Art of Shaving - FI LLC ....G 610 962-1000
King of Prussia (G-8585)

RETAIL STORES: Hearing Aids

America Hears Inc ....F 215 785-5437
Bristol (G-2105)
Audiology & Hearing Aid Center ....G 570 822-6122
Wilkes Barre (G-19906)
Professional Hearing Aid Svc ....G 724 548-4801
Kittanning (G-8788)
Scott Gordon ....G 717 652-2828
Harrisburg (G-7213)
Suburban Audiology Balance Ctr ....G 610 647-3710
Paoli (G-13149)

RETAIL STORES: Hospital Eqpt & Splys

Manns Sickroom Service Inc ....E 412 672-5680
White Oak (G-19856)

RETAIL STORES: Ice

Mastro Ice Inc ....G 412 681-4423
Pittsburgh (G-15261)
Pavlish Beverage Co Inc ....G 610 866-7722
Bethlehem (G-1592)
Sculpted Ice Works Inc ....F 570 226-6246
Lakeville (G-8913)
Superior Value Beverage Co ....G 610 935-3111
Phoenixville (G-14581)

RETAIL STORES: Medical Apparatus & Splys

Archer Instruments LLC ....G 215 589-0356
Catasauqua (G-2814)
Global Medical Solutions Inc ....G 215 440-7701
Philadelphia (G-13770)
McKnight Surgical Inc ....G 412 821-9000
Pittsburgh (G-15270)
Spectrum Healthcare Inc ....E 888 210-5576
Eagleville (G-4516)
Sylvan Corporation ....G 724 864-9350
Irwin (G-8203)

RETAIL STORES: Monuments, Finished To Custom Order

Allegheny Cut Stone Co ....G 814 943-4157
Altoona (G-469)
Craig Walters ....G 570 645-3415
Summit Hill (G-18159)
Edward T Christiansen & Sons ....G 215 368-1001
Montgomeryville (G-11393)
Johnson Memorial Co ....G 814 634-0622
Meyersdale (G-11014)
Milroy Enterprises Inc ....E 610 678-4537
Reading (G-16444)
Pennsylvania Monument Co ....F 570 454-2621
Hazleton (G-7516)
Richard Freeman ....G 717 597-4580
Greencastle (G-6630)
Shetler Memorials Inc ....G 814 288-1087
Johnstown (G-8435)

RETAIL STORES: Motors, Electric

Breons Inc A Close Corporation ....G 814 359-3182
Pleasant Gap (G-15791)
Electric Motor Service Inc ....G 724 348-6858
Finleyville (G-5958)
Electric Rewind Co Inc ....G 215 675-6912
Hatboro (G-7284)
Integrated Power Services LLC ....F 724 225-2900
Washington (G-19186)
Keener Electric Motors Inc ....G 717 272-7686
Lebanon (G-9589)
Pittsburgh Elc Mtr Repr Inc ....G 724 443-2333
Allison Park (G-458)
S & S Electric Motors Inc ....G 717 263-1919
Chambersburg (G-2975)
Tims Electric Motor Repair Co ....G 814 445-5078
Somerset (G-17714)

RETAIL STORES: Orthopedic & Prosthesis Applications

Boas Surgical Inc ....E 484 895-3451
Allentown (G-156)
Central Orthotic Prosthetic Co ....F 814 535-8221
Johnstown (G-8364)

Colburn Orthopedics Inc ....G 814 432-5252
Franklin (G-6121)
Green Prosthetics & Orthotics ....G 814 337-1159
Meadville (G-10730)
J G McGinness Prosthetics ....F 610 278-1866
Norristown (G-12671)
McKesson Ptent Care Sltons Inc ....D 814 860-8160
Erie (G-5386)
Riverview Orthotics ....G 570 270-6231
Plains (G-15788)
Robert John Enterprises Inc ....F 814 944-0187
Altoona (G-544)

RETAIL STORES: Pet Splys

Golden Bone Pet Resort Inc ....E 412 661-7001
Pittsburgh (G-15057)
Premium Pet Division ....G 215 364-0211
Langhorne (G-9321)
Veterinary Tag Supply Co Inc ....G 610 649-1550
Bridgeport (G-2048)

RETAIL STORES: Photocopy Machines

Copitech Associates ....G 570 963-1391
Scranton (G-17219)

RETAIL STORES: Picture Frames, Ready Made

Frame Outlet Inc ....G 412 351-7283
Pittsburgh (G-15029)

RETAIL STORES: Plumbing & Heating Splys

Bevilacqua Sheet Metal Inc ....G 570 558-0397
Scranton (G-17211)
Davies & Sons LLC ....G 814 723-7430
Warren (G-19020)
Hajoca Corporation ....G 610 432-0551
Allentown (G-240)

RETAIL STORES: Police Splys

D & A Emergency Equipment Inc ....G 610 691-6847
Bethlehem (G-1495)

RETAIL STORES: Rubber Stamps

Allegheny Rubber Stamp Inc ....G 412 826-8662
Blawnox (G-1762)

RETAIL STORES: Sauna Eqpt & Splys

Penn Sauna Corp ....E 610 932-5700
Paoli (G-13146)
Penn Sauna Corp ....E 610 932-5700
Oxford (G-13087)

RETAIL STORES: Swimming Pools, Above Ground

Feedmobile Inc ....F 717 626-8318
Lititz (G-10007)
Oldco Ep Inc ....G 484 768-1000
Aston (G-782)
Oldco Ep Inc ....G 888 314-9356
Aston (G-783)

RETAIL STORES: Telephone & Communication Eqpt

Ultravoice Ltd ....G 610 356-6443
Newtown Square (G-12595)

RETAIL STORES: Telephone Eqpt & Systems

Big Brother Hd Ltd Lblty Co ....G 201 355-8166
Tamiment (G-18232)

RETAIL STORES: Toilet Preparations

T&T Buttas LLC ....G 833 251-1357
Philadelphia (G-14365)

RETAIL STORES: Water Purification Eqpt

C S Garber & Sons Inc ....E 610 367-2861
Boyertown (G-1902)
Filson Water Treatment Inc ....F 717 240-0763
Carlisle (G-2712)
Pure Flow Water Co ....G 215 723-0237
Souderton (G-17761)

Terra Group Corp ....E 610 821-7003
Allentown (G-408)

RETAIL STORES: Welding Splys

Demarchi John ....G 724 547-6440
Mount Pleasant (G-11696)
Dressel Welding Supply Inc ....G 570 505-1994
Cogan Station (G-3360)
Dyeco Inc ....G 717 545-1882
Harrisburg (G-7123)
Praxair Distribution Inc ....F 412 781-6273
Pittsburgh (G-15429)

RETREADING MATERIALS: Tire

Bastian Tire Sales Inc ....E 570 323-8651
Williamsport (G-19992)

REUPHOLSTERY SVCS

Auto Seat Cover Company ....G 814 453-5897
Erie (G-5196)
Dronetti Upholstery Inc ....G 610 435-2957
Allentown (G-196)
Easton Upholstery Furn Mfg Co ....G 610 252-3169
Easton (G-4675)
Gene Sanes & Associates ....E 412 471-8224
Pittsburgh (G-15043)
Haberle Upholstery ....G 215 679-8195
Zionsville (G-20835)
Jerry Lister Custom Upholsteri ....G 215 639-3880
Bensalem (G-1213)
Jerry Lister Custom Upholsteri ....F 215 639-3882
Huntingdon Valley (G-8004)
Kauffmans Upholstery Inc ....G 610 262-8298
Northampton (G-12852)
M B Bedding Co ....G 570 822-2491
Wilkes Barre (G-19939)
Russell Upholstery Co Inc ....G 814 455-9021
Erie (G-5467)
S DRocco Upholstery ....G 215 745-2869
Philadelphia (G-14270)
Tapestration ....G 215 536-0977
Quakertown (G-16248)

RIBBONS & BOWS

CSS Industries Inc ....C 610 729-3959
Plymouth Meeting (G-15840)

RIBBONS, NEC

American Ribbon Manufacturers ....E 570 421-7470
Stroudsburg (G-18103)
B & N Trophies & Awards LLC ....G 814 723-8130
Warren (G-19012)
Otex Specialty Narrow Fabrics ....F 570 538-5990
Watsontown (G-19279)
Trims ....F 215 541-1946
East Greenville (G-4578)

RIBBONS: Machine, Inked Or Carbon

Impression Technology Inc ....G 412 318-4437
Pittsburgh (G-15116)
N H Laboratories Inc ....F 717 545-3221
Harrisburg (G-7183)
Prime Ribbon Inc ....G 412 761-4470
Pittsburgh (G-15438)

RIFLES: Recoilless

Jim Borden ....G 570 965-2505
Springville (G-17930)

RIVETS: Metal

C & L Rivet Co Inc ....E 215 672-1113
Hatboro (G-7275)
Penn Engineering & Mfg Corp ....E 215 766-8853
Danboro (G-3993)
Speedbear Fasteners ....G 724 695-3696
Imperial (G-8076)
Tri-State Tubular Rivet Co ....F 610 644-6060
Malvern (G-10335)

ROAD CONSTRUCTION EQUIPMENT WHOLESALERS

US Municipal Supply Inc ....E 610 292-9450
Huntingdon (G-7958)

(G-0000) Company's Geographic Section entry number

ROAD MATERIALS: Bituminous, Not From Refineries

Glasgow Inc ....D 215 884-8800
Glenside (G-6521)
Highway Materials Inc ....F 610 832-8000
Flourtown (G-5987)
Highway Materials Inc ....G 610 647-5902
Malvern (G-10245)
Highway Materials Inc ....E 215 225-7020
Blue Bell (G-1834)
IA Construction Corporation ....E 814 432-3184
Franklin (G-6136)
Landfried Paving Inc ....F 724 646-2505
Greenville (G-6753)

ROBOTS: Assembly Line

Advent Design Corporation ....C 215 781-0500
Bristol (G-2104)
American Robot Corporation ....G 724 695-9000
Oakdale (G-12890)
Demco Enterprises Inc ....F 888 419-3343
Quakertown (G-16184)
Homeland Mfg Svcs Inc ....F 814 862-9103
State College (G-17976)
Iam Robotics LLC ....G 412 636-7425
Pittsburgh (G-15110)
Paletti Usa LLC ....E 267 289-0020
Montgomeryville (G-11410)

ROD & BAR: Aluminum

AMG Aluminum North America LLC .....F 610 293-2501
Wayne (G-19297)
KB Alloys Holdings LLC ....F 484 582-3520
Wayne (G-19345)

RODS: Extruded, Aluminum

Paletti Usa LLC ....E 267 289-0020
Montgomeryville (G-11410)

RODS: Plastic

Lehigh Valley Plastics Inc ....D 484 893-5500
Bethlehem (G-1558)
Quadrant Holding Inc ....C 570 558-6000
Scranton (G-17276)

RODS: Steel & Iron, Made In Steel Mills

Magnetic Lifting Tech US LLC ....F 724 202-7987
New Castle (G-12118)
Molek Brothers ....G 717 248-8032
Yeagertown (G-20357)

RODS: Welding

ESAB Group Inc ....C 843 673-7700
Hanover (G-6885)
Robinson Technical Pdts Corp ....E 610 261-1900
Coplay (G-3647)

ROLL COVERINGS: Rubber

Rubber Technology Inc ....G 724 838-2340
Greensburg (G-6713)

ROLL FORMED SHAPES: Custom

M & S Conversion Company Inc ....F 570 368-1991
Montoursville (G-11447)
Precision Roll Grinders Inc ....D 610 395-6966
Allentown (G-358)

ROLLED OR DRAWN SHAPES, NEC: Copper & Copper Alloy

Heyco Metals Inc ....D 610 926-4131
Reading (G-16402)

ROLLING MACHINERY: Steel

Alpine Metal Tech N Amer Inc ....E 412 787-2832
Pittsburgh (G-14688)
Custom Mfg & Indus Svcs LLC ....G 412 621-2982
Pittsburgh (G-14894)
Presto Packaging Inc ....G 215 822-9598
Hatfield (G-7386)

ROLLING MILL EQPT: Rod Mills

SMS Group Inc ....C 412 231-1200
Pittsburgh (G-15552)

ROLLING MILL MACHINERY

Bailey Engineers Inc ....E 724 745-6200
Canonsburg (G-2547)
Danieli Corporation ....D 724 778-5400
Cranberry Township (G-3814)
Ewald A Stellrecht Inc ....F 610 363-1141
Coatesville (G-3302)
Fessler Machine Company ....E 724 346-0878
Sharon (G-17433)
Karadon Corporation ....F 724 676-5790
Blairsville (G-1729)
Kocks Pittsburgh Corporation ....G 412 367-4174
Pittsburgh (G-15181)
Laneko Roll Form Inc ....E 215 822-1930
Hatfield (G-7363)
Leman Machine Company ....E 814 736-9696
Portage (G-15918)
Park Corporation ....E 412 472-0500
Coraopolis (G-3711)
Presto Packaging Inc ....G 215 646-7514
Ambler (G-599)
S P Kinney Engineers Inc ....E 412 276-4600
Carnegie (G-2789)
Sme Sales and Service Inc ....C 724 384-1159
Beaver Falls (G-1012)
T Bruce Sales Inc ....D 724 528-9961
West Middlesex (G-19731)
Testa Machine Company Inc ....E 724 947-9397
Slovan (G-17631)

ROLLING MILL ROLLS: Cast Iron

Penna Flame Industries Inc ....E 724 452-8750
Zelienople (G-20815)
Rolls Technology Inc ....B 724 697-4533
Avonmore (G-868)

ROLLING MILL ROLLS: Cast Steel

Gautier Steel Ltd ....D 814 535-9200
Johnstown (G-8376)
Grid Company LLC ....E 610 341-7307
Valley Forge (G-18708)
Montrose Machine Works Inc ....F 570 278-7655
Montrose (G-11471)
Union Electric Steel Corp ....D 412 429-7655
Carnegie (G-2800)
Union Electric Steel Corp ....D 724 947-9595
Burgettstown (G-2358)

ROLLS & BLANKETS, PRINTERS': Rubber Or Rubberized Fabric

Valmet Inc ....E 570 587-5111
S Abingtn Twp (G-16901)

ROLLS & ROLL COVERINGS: Rubber

Eagle Rubber Products Inc ....F 724 452-3200
Zelienople (G-20796)
Montrose Machine Works Inc ....F 570 278-7655
Montrose (G-11471)

ROLLS: Rubber, Solid Or Covered

Polymer Enterprises Inc ....G 724 838-2340
Greensburg (G-6703)
Rubber Rolls Inc ....E 412 276-6400
Pittsburgh (G-15502)
Rubber Rolls Inc ....E 724 225-9240
Meadow Lands (G-10692)
Valmet Inc ....D 570 587-5111
S Abingtn Twp (G-16900)

ROOF DECKS

A M E R Inc ....E 724 229-8020
Washington (G-19143)
Aaron S Myers ....G 717 339-9304
New Oxford (G-12401)
Curbs Plus Inc ....E 888 639-2872
Mount Union (G-11742)
Dura-Bilt Products Inc ....D 570 596-2000
Gillett (G-6380)
Interlock Industries Inc ....D 570 366-2020
Orwigsburg (G-13045)

Metal Sales Manufacturing Corp .....E 570 366-2020
Orwigsburg (G-13049)
R M Metals Inc ....G 717 656-8737
Lancaster (G-9182)

ROOFING GRANULES

Specialty Granules Inc ....C 717 794-2184
Blue Ridge Summit (G-1861)

ROOFING MATERIALS: Asphalt

Designer Cabinets and Hdwr Co .....E 610 622-4455
Clifton Heights (G-3252)
Domar Group Inc ....G 714 674-0391
Finleyville (G-5955)
Elk Premium Building Products ....G 717 866-8300
Myerstown (G-11884)
R F Fager Company ....F 717 564-1166
Harrisburg (G-7203)
Slate and Copper Sales Co ....F 814 455-7430
Erie (G-5481)
Tarco Inc ....E 717 597-1876
Greencastle (G-6638)
Warrior Roofing Mfg Inc ....E 717 709-0323
Chambersburg (G-2998)

ROOFING MATERIALS: Sheet Metal

American Architectural Metal M ....F 610 432-9787
Allentown (G-132)
Berger Building Products Corp ....D 215 355-1200
Feasterville Trevose (G-5890)
Freedom Metals Mfg Inc ....G 814 224-4438
Duncansville (G-4451)
Narvon Construction LLC ....F 717 989-2026
Narvon (G-11924)

ROOFING MEMBRANE: Rubber

Carlisle Construction Mtls Inc ....E 717 245-7142
Carlisle (G-2693)
Carlisle Construction Mtls LLC ....G 717 245-7000
Carlisle (G-2694)
Carlisle Construction Mtls LLC ....B 717 245-7000
Carlisle (G-2695)
Devcom Manufacturing LLC ....G 484 462-4907
Easton (G-4669)
Grant Belcher ....F 814 853-9640
Greenville (G-6741)

ROPE

Phillystran Inc ....E 215 368-6611
Montgomeryville (G-11415)
Thunder Basin Corporation ....F 610 962-3770
King of Prussia (G-8688)
Whitehill Mfg Corp ....E 610 494-2378
Chester (G-3068)

ROTORS: Motor

Agustawestland Tilt-Rotor LLC ....F 215 281-1400
Philadelphia (G-13357)
Ultra Lite Brakes An C ....G 724 696-3743
Mount Pleasant (G-11721)

RUBBER

APT Advanced Polymer Tech Corp ....D 724 452-1330
Harmony (G-7066)
Covestro LLC ....F 215 428-4400
Morrisville (G-11556)
Lanxess Corporation ....A 800 526-9377
Pittsburgh (G-15219)
Lanxess Corporation ....E 412 809-4735
Burgettstown (G-2348)
Lebanon Gasket and Seal Inc ....G 717 274-3684
Lebanon (G-9600)
Palmer International Inc ....E 610 584-4241
Skippack (G-17602)
Palmer International Inc ....E 610 584-3204
Worcester (G-20225)
Pelmor Laboratories Inc ....E 215 968-3334
Newtown (G-12533)
Polytek Development Corp ....E 610 559-8620
Easton (G-4743)

RUBBER BANDS

Dykema Rubber Band ....G 412 771-1955
Pittsburgh (G-14946)

PRODUCT

RUBBER PRDTS

Edge Rubber Recycling LLC................E......717 660-2353
Chambersburg (G-2928)

Lake Erie Rubber & Mfg LLC...............F......814 835-0170
Erie (G-5354)

RUBBER PRDTS: Appliance, Mechanical

Corry Rubber Corporation.....................E......814 664-2313
Corry (G-3757)

RUBBER PRDTS: Mechanical

C E Conover & Co Inc...........................E......215 639-6666
Bensalem (G-1164)

Eagle Rubber Products Inc...................F......724 452-3200
Zelienople (G-20796)

Fenner Precision Inc............................C......800 327-2288
Manheim (G-10383)

Greenbriar Indus Systems Inc..............D......814 474-1400
Fairview (G-5824)

Pelmor Laboratories Inc.......................E......215 968-3334
Newtown (G-12533)

Phb Inc...D......814 474-2683
Fairview (G-5838)

Ross Enterprises Inc............................D......215 968-3334
Newtown (G-12546)

Rubber Rolls Inc..................................E......724 225-9240
Meadow Lands (G-10692)

Spadone Machine Inc...........................F......215 396-8005
Willow Grove (G-20143)

Valmet Inc...D......570 587-5111
S Abingtn Twp (G-16900)

RUBBER PRDTS: Reclaimed

Flexsys America LP..............................D......724 258-6200
Monongahela (G-11308)

Lord Corporation.................................A......877 275-5673
Erie (G-5373)

RUBBER PRDTS: Sheeting

Lambert-Jones Rubber Co.....................G......412 781-8100
Pittsburgh (G-15217)

SRC Elastomerics Inc...........................D......215 335-2049
Philadelphia (G-14336)

RUBBER PRDTS: Silicone

SRC Elastomerics Inc...........................D......215 335-2049
Philadelphia (G-14336)

RUBBER PRDTS: Sponge

Nation Ruskin Holdings Inc...................F......267 654-4000
Montgomeryville (G-11409)

Scrub Daddy Inc..................................E......610 583-4883
Folcroft (G-6015)

RUBBER STAMP, WHOLESALE

Bunting Stamp Company.......................C......412 820-2200
Verona (G-18752)

Causco...G......814 452-2004
Erie (G-5223)

RUGS : Braided & Hooked

House of Price Inc.................................G......724 625-3415
Mars (G-10499)

Stone Mill Rug Co.................................G......215 744-2331
Philadelphia (G-14349)

RUST PROOFING SVC: Hot Dipping, Metals & Formed Prdts

American Tinning Galvanizing...............D......814 456-7053
Erie (G-5189)

RUST REMOVERS

Arete Qis LLC......................................D......814 781-1194
Ridgway (G-16696)

Singerman Laboratories........................G......412 798-0447
Murrysville (G-11868)

RUST RESISTING

Dacar Industries..................................G......412 921-3620
Pittsburgh (G-14902)

SADDLERY STORES

Lost Creek Shoe Shop Inc.....................G......717 463-3117
Mifflintown (G-11129)

Shady Acres Saddlery Inc.....................G......412 963-9454
Pittsburgh (G-15526)

Smuckers Harness Shop Inc..................F......717 445-5956
Narvon (G-11927)

SAFE DEPOSIT BOXES

Yarde Metals Inc..................................G......610 495-7545
Limerick (G-9972)

SAFES & VAULTS: Metal

Smiths Wilbert Vault Company..............F......610 588-5259
Bangor (G-929)

Talaris Inc...G......215 674-2882
Horsham (G-7855)

SAFETY EQPT & SPLYS WHOLESALERS

Municipal Fire Equipment Inc................G......412 366-8180
Pittsburgh (G-15310)

Tamis Corporation...............................F......412 241-7161
Pittsburgh (G-15595)

UNI-Pro Inc...F......610 668-9191
Philadelphia (G-14418)

Witmer Public Safety Group Inc............D......800 852-6088
Coatesville (G-3331)

SAFETY INSPECTION SVCS

Alpha Safety USA.................................G......814 236-3344
Clearfield (G-3211)

ARC Rmediation Specialists Inc............F......386 405-6760
Bristol (G-2108)

SAILS

American Cruising Sails Inc...................G......814 456-7245
Erie (G-5186)

David A Bierig.....................................G......814 459-8001
North East (G-12737)

SALES PROMOTION SVCS

Printmark Industries Inc.......................E......570 501-0547
Hazleton (G-7521)

SALT

East Loop Sand Company Inc................F......814 695-3082
Hollidaysburg (G-7646)

Morton International LLC.......................C......989 636-1000
Collegeville (G-3384)

Morton Salt Inc....................................F......215 428-2012
Fairless Hills (G-5789)

Pepper Italian Bistro............................G......717 392-3000
Lancaster (G-9168)

Pike Creek Salt Company......................F......570 585-8818
Clarks Summit (G-3198)

Rohm and Haas Company.....................A......989 636-1000
Collegeville (G-3392)

Sabrosa Salt Company LLC...................G......610 250-9002
Easton (G-4750)

Salt Fctry By Snow Ice MGT Inc...........D......412 321-7669
Pittsburgh (G-15508)

SALT & SULFUR MINING

Morton International LLC.......................C......989 636-1000
Collegeville (G-3384)

SAND & GRAVEL

A C A Sand & Gravel............................G......814 665-6087
Corry (G-3741)

Afton Trucking Inc...............................F......814 825-7449
Erie (G-5177)

Allegheny Mineral Corporation.............E......724 735-2088
Harrisville (G-7252)

American Asphalt Paving Co.................C......570 696-1181
Shavertown (G-17478)

Belvidere Sand Gravel..........................G......267 880-2422
Doylestown (G-4274)

Chad Cross...E......570 549-3234
Mansfield (G-10412)

Dalyrmple Gravel and Contracti...........G......570 297-0340
Troy (G-18521)

Dingmans Ferry Stone Inc....................G......570 828-2617
Dingmans Ferry (G-4142)

Erie Strayer Company...........................C......814 456-7001
Erie (G-5275)

Fairmount Minerals...............................G......724 873-9039
Eighty Four (G-4840)

Fiesler Sand & Gravel LLC....................G......814 899-6161
Erie (G-5289)

Georgetown Sand & Gravel Inc.............G......724 573-9518
Georgetown (G-6276)

Glen Mills Sand & Gravel Inc................E......610 459-4988
Media (G-10929)

Gravel...G......215 675-3960
Hatboro (G-7286)

Gravel Bar Inc.....................................G......724 568-3518
Vandergrift (G-18729)

J A & W A Hess Inc.............................E......570 454-3731
Hazleton (G-7504)

Lane Construction Corporation.............D......412 838-0251
Pittsburgh (G-15218)

Legacy Vulcan LLC..............................D......717 637-7121
Hanover (G-6913)

Linen Sand Supplies.............................G......610 399-8305
West Chester (G-19594)

Martin Marietta Materials Inc...............F......724 573-9518
Georgetown (G-6277)

New Enterprise Stone Lime Inc.............C......814 224-2121
Roaring Spring (G-16766)

North Star Aggregates Inc....................G......814 637-5599
Penfield (G-13222)

Pennsy Supply Inc...............................F......570 754-7508
Schuylkill Haven (G-17163)

Pennsy Supply Inc...............................D......717 274-3661
Lebanon (G-9619)

Summers Construction..........................G......724 924-1700
New Castle (G-12157)

Svonavec Inc.......................................G......814 926-2815
Rockwood (G-16793)

T-M-T Gravel and Contg Inc.................F......570 537-2647
Millerton (G-11216)

Tri-State River Products Inc..................F......724 775-2221
Beaver (G-993)

Valley Quarries Inc..............................F......717 267-2244
Chambersburg (G-2994)

Valley Quarries Inc..............................E......717 264-4178
Chambersburg (G-2995)

Waterford Sand & Gravel Co.................E......814 796-6250
Union City (G-18613)

Wendell H Stone Company Inc..............E......724 483-6571
Charleroi (G-3025)

Williams Garden Center Inc...................G......570 842-7277
Covington Township (G-3794)

Wysox S&G Inc....................................F......570 265-6760
Wysox (G-20291)

SAND LIME PRDTS

McDanel Advnced Crmic Tech LLC.......C......724 843-8300
Beaver Falls (G-1004)

SAND MINING

Eastern Industries Inc.........................E......610 683-7400
Kutztown (G-8842)

Glacial Sand & Gravel Co.....................G......724 548-8101
Kittanning (G-8773)

Hunlock Sand & Gravel Company..........F......570 256-3036
Bath (G-960)

McDonald Sand & Gravel Inc................G......814 774-8149
Girard (G-6397)

Preferred Sands LLC............................D......610 834-1969
Radnor (G-16298)

Shenango Valley Sand and Grav............G......724 932-5600
Jamestown (G-8240)

Slippery Rock Materials Inc..................E......724 530-7472
Volant (G-18777)

Snyder Assod Companies Inc................E......724 548-8101
Kittanning (G-8793)

SAND: Hygrade

Allegheny Metals & Minerals.................G......412 344-9900
Pittsburgh (G-14681)

Aztec Materials LLC.............................G......215 675-8900
Hatboro (G-14681)

U S Silica Company.............................D......814 542-2561
Mapleton Depot (G-10432)

SAND: Silica

Aztec Materials LLC.............................G......215 675-8900
Hatboro (G-7271)

Hanson Aggregates PA LLC...................G......570 726-4511
Salona (G-17049)

Norton Oglebay Company ....F 412 995-5500
Pittsburgh **(G-15347)**

SANDBLASTING EQPT

CK Construction & Indus Inc ....G 570 286-4128
Pitman **(G-14622)**

SANDSTONE: Crushed & Broken

Bear Gap Stone Inc ....G 570 337-9831
Elysburg **(G-4971)**

SANDSTONE: Dimension

E&J Construction ....F 570 924-4455
Canton **(G-2664)**

Godino West Mtn Stone Quar ....G 570 342-4340
Scranton **(G-17240)**

SANITARY SVCS: Dumps, Operation Of

August Transport Inc ....E 724 462-1445
Leetsdale **(G-9683)**

SANITARY SVCS: Environmental Cleanup

ARC Rmediation Specialists Inc...........F 386 405-6760
Bristol **(G-2108)**

Specialty Tank & Wldg Co Inc ....E 215 949-2939
Bristol **(G-2201)**

Tiger Enterprises Inc ....G 717 786-5441
Strasburg **(G-18095)**

SANITARY SVCS: Hazardous Waste, Collection & Disposal

Tms International Corp ....E 215 956-5500
Horsham **(G-7860)**

SANITARY SVCS: Refuse Collection & Disposal Svcs

A & M Compost ....F 215 256-1900
Norristown **(G-12629)**

H & C Giamo Inc ....G 610 941-0909
Conshohocken **(G-3552)**

SANITARY SVCS: Waste Materials, Recycling

Advanced Processes Inc ....F 724 266-7274
Ambridge **(G-606)**

Akj Industries Inc ....G 412 233-7222
Clairton **(G-3146)**

ARC Metals Corporation ....G 814 776-2116
Ridgway **(G-16695)**

Calgon Carbon Corporation ....F 412 269-4000
Pittsburgh **(G-14804)**

Chemex Inc ....G 610 398-6200
Allentown **(G-168)**

D-K Trading Corporation Inc ....G 570 586-9662
Clarks Summit **(G-3191)**

Foam Fabricators Inc ....E 570 752-7110
Bloomsburg **(G-1782)**

Graham Recycling Company LP ....D 717 852-7744
York **(G-20512)**

Greenstar Allentown LLC ....E 610 262-6988
Northampton **(G-12851)**

Interntnal Mtal Rclaiming Corp ....C 724 758-5515
Ellwood City **(G-4939)**

K Diamond Incorporated ....E 570 346-4684
Scranton **(G-17249)**

Mulch Works Recycling Inc ....F 888 214-4628
Aston **(G-779)**

Penn Recycling Inc ....E 570 326-9041
Williamsport **(G-20054)**

Plastic Options LLC ....G 724 730-5225
New Castle **(G-12137)**

PVS Steel Services Inc ....C 412 929-0177
Pittsburgh **(G-15458)**

Rapid Recycling Inc ....D 610 650-0737
Oaks **(G-12936)**

S S Salvage Recycling Inc ....F 717 444-0008
Liverpool **(G-10079)**

Unipaper Recycling Company ....F 412 429-8522
Carnegie **(G-2801)**

SANITATION CHEMICALS & CLEANING AGENTS

Aquachempacs LLC ....E 215 396-7200
Feasterville Trevose **(G-5885)**

Berkley Products Company ....F 717 859-1104
Akron **(G-33)**

Car Cleen Systems Inc ....F 717 795-8995
Bethel Park **(G-1408)**

CRC Industries Inc ....C 215 674-4300
Horsham **(G-7806)**

Crystal Inc - PMC ....D 215 368-1661
Lansdale **(G-9355)**

Curtis Glenchem Corp ....G 610 876-9906
Eddystone **(G-4800)**

Ddp Specialty Electronic MA ....G 610 244-6000
Collegeville **(G-3374)**

E E Zimmerman Company ....F 412 963-0949
Pittsburgh **(G-14950)**

Emsco Inc ....C 814 774-3137
Girard **(G-6386)**

Evoqua Water Technologies LLC ....E 724 827-8181
Darlington **(G-4028)**

Houghton Chemical Corporation ....G 800 777-2466
Scranton **(G-17241)**

Industrial Floor Corporation ....F 215 886-1800
Jenkintown **(G-8291)**

James Austin Company ....C 724 625-1535
Mars **(G-10504)**

Nu-Chem Corp ....F 610 770-2000
Allentown **(G-336)**

Oscar Daniels & Company Inc...............F 610 678-8144
Reading **(G-16460)**

Reckitt Benckiser LLC ....C 717 506-0165
Mechanicsburg **(G-10883)**

Rugani & Rugani LLC ....G 412 223-6472
Mc Kees Rocks **(G-10632)**

Schaffner Manufacturing Co ....D 412 761-9902
Pittsburgh **(G-15515)**

Senoret Chemical Company ....E 717 626-2125
Lititz **(G-10047)**

Univar USA Inc ....D 717 944-7471
Middletown **(G-11084)**

SASHES: Door Or Window, Metal

Best Group Holdings Inc ....E 814 536-1422
Johnstown **(G-8357)**

Colfab Industries LLC ....E 215 768-2135
Bensalem **(G-1171)**

Extech/Exterior Tech Inc ....E 412 781-0991
Pittsburgh **(G-14995)**

Hinkel-Hofmann Supply Co Inc ....E 412 231-3131
Pittsburgh **(G-15095)**

Voegele Company Inc ....E 412 781-0940
Pittsburgh **(G-15705)**

SATELLITE COMMUNICATIONS EQPT

Hughes Network Systems LLC..............E 717 792-2987
York **(G-20531)**

SATELLITES: Communications

Hughes Network Systems LLC..............E 610 363-1427
Exton **(G-5692)**

Liberty Uplink Inc ....G 215 964-5222
Malvern **(G-10267)**

Mechantech Inc ....F 570 389-1039
Catawissa **(G-2820)**

Ruckus Wireless Inc ....E 215 323-1000
Horsham **(G-7847)**

Satcom Digital Networks LLC ....G 724 824-1699
Cranberry Township **(G-3847)**

SAUNA ROOMS: Prefabricated

Penn Sauna Corp ....E 610 932-5700
Oxford **(G-13087)**

Penn Sauna Corp ....E 610 932-5700
Paoli **(G-13146)**

SAW BLADES

A Lindemann Inc ....G 412 487-7282
Glenshaw **(G-6477)**

American Carbide Saw Co ....F 215 672-1466
Hatboro **(G-7267)**

Dinosaw Inc ....F 570 374-5531
Selinsgrove **(G-17323)**

Hoffman Diamond Products Inc ....E 814 938-7600
Punxsutawney **(G-16143)**

MOr Saw Service Center Inc ....G 215 333-0441
Philadelphia **(G-14037)**

Penn Scientific Products Co ....F 888 238-6710
Abington **(G-13)**

Sanders Saws & Blades Inc ....E 610 273-3733
Honey Brook **(G-7761)**

Suffolk McHy & Pwr TI Corp ....G 631 289-7153
Brockway **(G-2234)**

Wilder Diamond Blades Inc...................G 570 222-9590
Kingsley **(G-8710)**

SAWDUST & SHAVINGS

Emily J High ....G 570 345-6268
Pine Grove **(G-14593)**

Sensenigs Wood Shavings ....G 717 336-2047
Denver **(G-4093)**

SAWING & PLANING MILLS

A W Sawmill ....G 717 535-5081
Mifflintown **(G-11107)**

Aldenville Log and Lumberinc ....G 570 785-3141
Prompton **(G-16109)**

Allegheny Wood Pdts Intl Inc ....E 814 354-7304
Marble **(G-10433)**

Andreas Lumber Inc ....G 570 379-3644
Wapwallopen **(G-18807)**

Baillie Lumber Co LP ....D 814 827-1877
Titusville **(G-18375)**

Baumerts Wood Shavings ....G 570 758-1744
Herndon **(G-7597)**

Beegle Saw Mill ....G 814 784-5697
Clearville **(G-3238)**

Beiler Sawmill ....G 717 284-5271
Quarryville **(G-16264)**

Big Valley Hardwood ....F 717 483-6440
Allensville **(G-107)**

Bingaman & Son Lumber Inc ....E 814 723-2612
Clarendon **(G-3167)**

Bingaman & Son Lumber Inc ....E 570 726-7795
Mill Hall **(G-11173)**

Blue Triangle Hardwoods LLC...............C 814 652-9111
Everett **(G-5567)**

Boswell Lumber Company ....E 814 629-5625
Boswell **(G-1881)**

Brown Timber and Land Co Inc ....F 724 547-7777
Acme **(G-15)**

Brumbaugh Lumber LLC ....G 814 542-8880
Shirleysburg **(G-17569)**

Bucks Valley Sawmill LLC ....G 717 567-9663
Newport **(G-12488)**

Buttonwood Lumber Company Inc ....G 570 324-3421
Liberty **(G-9951)**

Bylers Saw Mill ....G 724 964-8528
New Wilmington **(G-12464)**

C & S Lumber Company Inc...................G 814 544-7544
Roulette **(G-16833)**

C C Allis & Sons Inc ....E 570 744-2631
Wyalusing **(G-20247)**

Cadosia Valley Lumber Company ....G 570 676-3400
Newfoundland **(G-12476)**

Carol Zuzek ....G 814 837-7090
Kane **(G-8460)**

Center Hardwood LLC ....F 814 684-3600
Tyrone **(G-18579)**

Cessna Bros Lumber ....E 814 767-9518
Clearville **(G-3239)**

Clark F Burger Inc ....G 610 681-4762
Kresgeville **(G-8820)**

Clark H Ream Lumber ....G 814 445-8185
Somerset **(G-17680)**

Coastal Forest Resources Co ....G 814 654-7111
Spartansburg **(G-17848)**

Collins Pine Company ....D 814 837-6941
Kane **(G-8461)**

Collins Tool Corporation ....E 717 543-6070
Lewistown **(G-9927)**

Cover Lumber Co ....G 814 750-2006
Bedford **(G-1047)**

Curtis Baker Lumber Inc ....F 814 425-3020
Cochranton **(G-3340)**

Custeads Sawmill Inc ....G 814 425-3863
Guys Mills **(G-6810)**

D & D Wood Sales Inc ....E 814 948-8672
Nicktown **(G-12620)**

Danzer Services Inc ....E 724 827-3700
Darlington **(G-4025)**

Deer Park Lumber Inc ....D 570 836-1133
Tunkhannock **(G-18538)**

Donald EBY ....G 814 767-9406
Clearville **(G-3241)**

Dubel D H Mill & Lumber Co ....G 717 993-2566
Stewartstown **(G-18060)**

E H Beiler Sawmill LLC ....F 610 593-5989
Paradise **(G-13156)**

EDM Co ....E 717 626-2186
Lititz **(G-10005)**

PRODUCT

Edwin Johnson & Sons ....G 570 458-4488
  Bloomsburg (G-1780)
Efflands Sawmill Repair S ....G 717 369-2391
  Fort Loudon (G-6058)
Emporium Hardwoods Oper Co LLC ....C 814 486-3764
  Emporium (G-5057)
Estemerwalt Lumber Pdts LLC ....F 570 729-8572
  Honesdale (G-7711)
Frontier Wood Products Inc ....E 215 538-2330
  Quakertown (G-16195)
Frosty Hollow Hardwoods ....G 724 568-2406
  Vandergrift (G-18728)
Gerald King Lumber Co Inc ....F 724 887-3688
  Ruffs Dale (G-16872)
Gessner Logging & Sawmill Inc ....F 717 365-3883
  Lykens (G-10133)
Gift Lumber Co Inc ....G 610 689-9483
  Douglassville (G-4176)
Great Meadows Sawmill Frm Inc ....G 724 329-7771
  Farmington (G-5862)
Greenwood Products ....G 717 337-2050
  Gettysburg (G-6296)
H & H General Excavating Co ....D 717 225-4669
  Spring Grove (G-17877)
Harmony Hill Forestry ....G 570 247-2676
  Rome (G-16799)
Higgins Saw Mill ....G 717 235-4189
  Glen Rock (G-6457)
Highland Forest Resources Inc ....E 814 927-2226
  Marienville (G-10457)
Highland Forest Resources Inc ....E 814 837-6760
  Kane (G-8466)
Hitchcock E & R & Sons Lbr Inc ....G 814 229-9402
  Strattanville (G-18097)
Horner Lumber Company ....G 814 629-5861
  Boswell (G-1883)
Horsepower Wood Products ....G 814 447-5662
  Orbisonia (G-13006)
Hyma Devore Lumber Mill Inc ....E 814 563-4646
  Youngsville (G-20772)
J C Moore Industries Inc ....F 724 475-3185
  Fredonia (G-6181)
J F Rohrbaugh & Co ....D 800 800-4353
  Hanover (G-6906)
John L Luchs Logging ....G 814 772-5767
  Ridgway (G-16715)
Kerex Inc ....E 814 735-3838
  Breezewood (G-2003)
Keslar Lumber Co ....E 724 455-3210
  White (G-19845)
King Logging and Sawmill ....G 717 365-3341
  Spring Glen (G-17873)
Klingler Family Sawmill ....G 717 677-4957
  Biglerville (G-1665)
Kochs Portable Sawmill & Lbr ....G 717 776-7961
  Newville (G-12604)
Kovalick Lumber Co ....F 814 263-4928
  Frenchville (G-6217)
Larimer & Norton Inc ....F 814 757-4532
  Russell (G-16881)
Lindenmuth Saw Mill ....G 570 875-3546
  Ashland (G-734)
Marsh Planing Inc ....G 814 827-9947
  Titusville (G-18388)
Matson Industries Inc ....E 814 849-5334
  Brookville (G-2263)
Mayberry Supply Company Inc ....G 724 652-6008
  Volant (G-18775)
Mitchell Hardwood ....G 814 796-4925
  Waterford (G-19266)
Mount Hope Lumber ....G 814 789-4953
  Guys Mills (G-6811)
Noah Shirk Sawmill ....G 717 354-0192
  Ephrata (G-5132)
Noll Pallet Inc ....E 610 926-2500
  Leesport (G-9671)
Oakes & McClelland Co ....F 724 588-6400
  Greenville (G-6761)
Omega Logging Inc ....F 724 342-5430
  Wheatland (G-19839)
Peacheys Sawmill Inc ....F 717 483-6336
  Belleville (G-1134)
Pinch Road Sawmill ....G 717 665-1096
  Manheim (G-10403)
Pittman Bros Lumber ....G 814 652-6396
  Everett (G-5577)
Pittston Lumber & Mfg Co ....E 570 654-3328
  Pittston (G-15776)
Pleasant Valley Saw Mill ....G 814 767-9016
  Clearville (G-3243)

Porosky Lumber Company Inc ....F 570 798-2326
  Preston Park (G-16105)
Portzlines Pallets ....G 717 694-3951
  Mount Pleasant Mills (G-11729)
Quaker Hardwoods Company ....G 215 538-0401
  Quakertown (G-16237)
R J Junk ....G 717 734-3838
  Honey Grove (G-7768)
R L Kingsley Lumber Company ....F 570 596-3575
  Milan (G-11148)
R Vbridendolph & Sons Inc ....G 717 328-3650
  Mercersburg (G-10994)
Robbins Logging & Lumber ....F 814 236-3384
  Olanta (G-12961)
Robinson Sawmill Works ....G 570 559-7454
  Shohola (G-17579)
Rock Creek Lumber ....F 570 756-2909
  Thompson (G-18346)
Rockwell Lumber Co Inc ....G 717 597-7428
  Greencastle (G-6631)
Roderick Duvall ....G 814 735-4969
  Crystal Spring (G-3938)
Ronald Kauffman ....G 717 589-3789
  Millerstown (G-11208)
S & S Processing Inc ....E 724 535-3110
  West Pittsburg (G-19752)
S&S Custom Sawing ....G 717 694-3248
  Richfield (G-16682)
Scalpy Hollow Timber Service ....G 717 284-2862
  Drumore (G-4379)
Schetler Lumber - Sawmill ....G 814 590-9592
  Punxsutawney (G-16162)
Seneca Hardwood Lumber Co Inc ....E 814 498-2241
  Cranberry (G-3797)
Shady Elms Sawmill LLC ....G 724 356-2594
  Hickory (G-7631)
Shady Hill Hardwood Inc ....G 717 463-9475
  Mifflintown (G-11135)
Shaffer Brothers Lumber Co ....G 814 842-3996
  Hyndman (G-8051)
Shanks Portable Sawmills ....G 717 334-0352
  Orrtanna (G-13037)
Shedio Logging & Lumber ....G 724 794-1321
  Renfrew (G-16642)
Shetler Lumber Company Inc ....E 814 796-0303
  Waterford (G-19269)
Shirks Saw Mill ....G 717 776-7083
  Shippensburg (G-17550)
Snooks Rhine & Arnold ....G 570 658-3410
  Mc Clure (G-10561)
Solts Sawmill Inc ....E 610 682-6179
  Mertztown (G-11004)
Somerset Door and Column Co ....E 814 445-9608
  Somerset (G-17708)
Spigelmyer Wood Products Inc ....F 717 248-6555
  Lewistown (G-9948)
Stella-Jones Corporation ....E 814 371-7331
  Du Bois (G-4421)
Sterling Forest Products ....G 570 226-4233
  Tafton (G-18205)
Straightline Saw Mill Inc ....G 724 639-3090
  Saltsburg (G-17053)
Summit Forest Resources Inc ....E 724 329-3314
  Markleysburg (G-10484)
T Baird McIlvain Company ....G 717 630-0025
  Hanover (G-6960)
Thomas Timberland Enterprises ....G 814 359-2890
  Bellefonte (G-1122)
Timberstrong LLC ....G 484 357-8730
  Kempton (G-8496)
Tom Cesarino Lumber ....G 724 329-0467
  Farmington (G-5863)
Tony L Stec Lumber Company ....F 814 563-9002
  Garland (G-6263)
Trumco Inc ....E 814 382-7767
  Atlantic (G-814)
Ufp Parker LLC ....G 724 399-2992
  Parker (G-13167)
Wattsburg Lumber Co LLC ....G 814 739-2770
  Wattsburg (G-19284)
Wenturine Bros Lumber Inc ....D 814 948-6050
  Nicktown (G-12622)
Werzalit of America Inc ....D 814 362-3881
  Bradford (G-1995)
William Richter Lumber ....G 814 926-4608
  Rockwood (G-16794)
Wilmer R EBY ....G 717 597-1090
  Waynesboro (G-19430)
Winters Lumber Co ....G 570 435-2231
  Cogan Station (G-3363)

Wlh Enterprise ....G 814 498-2040
  Emlenton (G-5016)
Wood Mizer ....G 814 259-9976
  Shade Gap (G-17418)
Wood-Mizer Holdings Inc ....G 814 259-9976
  Shade Gap (G-17419)
Yoder Lumber Co Inc ....G 717 463-9253
  Mc Alisterville (G-10554)
Zooks Sawmill LLC ....G 610 593-1040
  Christiana (G-3145)

SAWING & PLANING MILLS: Custom

Herndon Reload Company ....E 570 758-2597
  Herndon (G-7599)
Imperial Eagle Products Inc ....F 717 252-1573
  Wrightsville (G-20238)
Moyers Sawmill Company ....G 610 488-1462
  Bernville (G-1302)
Ram Forest Products Inc ....D 814 697-7185
  Shinglehouse (G-17512)
Shaffer Products LLC ....F 717 597-2688
  Greencastle (G-6633)

SAWMILL MACHINES

G&M Bandsaw Inc ....F 570 547-2386
  Montgomery (G-11369)
Pendu Manufacturing Inc ....E 717 354-4348
  New Holland (G-12272)

SAWS & SAWING EQPT

CDI Lawn Equipment & Grdn Sup ....E 610 489-3474
  Collegeville (G-3371)
Marilyn Strawser Beauty Salon ....G 717 463-2804
  Thompsontown (G-18349)

SAWS: Hand, Metalworking Or Woodworking

Victor Metals ....G 570 925-2618
  Stillwater (G-18062)

SAWS: Portable

Sanders Saws & Blades Inc ....E 610 273-3733
  Honey Brook (G-7761)

SCAFFOLDS: Mobile Or Stationary, Metal

New Werner Holding Co Inc ....G 724 588-2000
  Greenville (G-6758)
Old Ladder Co ....A 888 523-3371
  Greenville (G-6762)
Spring Lock Scaffolding Eqp Co ....G 215 426-5727
  Plymouth Meeting (G-15873)
Universal Manufacturing Corp ....E 724 452-8300
  Zelienople (G-20826)
Werner Co ....G 724 588-2000
  Greenville (G-6775)
Werner Holding Co Inc ....A 888 523-3371
  Greenville (G-6776)

SCALE REPAIR SVCS

Cambridge Scale Works Inc ....F 610 273-7040
  Honey Brook (G-7740)
Kanawha Scales & Systems Inc ....F 724 258-6650
  Monongahela (G-11309)

SCALES & BALANCES, EXC LABORATORY

All-Fill Corporation ....D 866 255-3455
  Exton (G-5639)
Jiba LLC ....F 215 739-9644
  Philadelphia (G-13898)
Kanawha Scales & Systems Inc ....F 724 258-6650
  Monongahela (G-11309)
Malvern Scale Data Systems ....G 610 296-9642
  Malvern (G-10274)
Measurement Specialties Inc ....G 610 971-9893
  Wayne (G-19354)
Monroe Scale Company Inc ....G 412 793-8134
  Pittsburgh (G-15300)

SCALES: Counting

Tri State Scales LLC ....G 610 779-5361
  Reading (G-16548)

SCALES: Indl

A H Emery Company ....F 717 295-6935
  Lancaster (G-8918)

Cambridge Scale Works Inc .... F 610 273-7040
Honey Brook (G-7740)
Drafto Corporation .... D 814 425-7445
Cochranton (G-3342)
Scaletron Industries Ltd .... F 215 766-2670
Plumsteadville (G-15813)
Zurex Corporation .... E 814 425-7445
Cochranton (G-3353)

SCALP TREATMENT SVCS

Physician Transformations LLC .... G 484 420-4407
Newtown Square (G-12590)

SCANNING DEVICES: Optical

Datalogic Usa Inc .... B 215 723-0981
Telford (G-18280)
Integrted Productivity Systems .... G 215 646-1374
Blue Bell (G-1836)
Light My Fiber LLC .... G 888 428-4454
West Chester (G-19593)

SCHOOL BUS SVC

Jacoby Transportation Inc .... E 717 677-7733
Gettysburg (G-6302)

SCHOOL SPLYS, EXC BOOKS: Wholesalers

Schalow Visual Concepts Inc .... G 570 336-2714
Benton (G-1282)

SCHOOLS & EDUCATIONAL SVCS, NEC

Electric City Baseball & Soft .... G 570 955-0471
Scranton (G-17232)

SCHOOLS: Elementary & Secondary

School Gate Guardian Inc .... F 800 805-3808
State College (G-18020)

SCIENTIFIC EQPT REPAIR SVCS

Gamma Irradiator Service LLC .... G 570 925-5681
Benton (G-1280)

SCRAP & WASTE MATERIALS, WHOLESALE: Ferrous Metal

A Allan Industries Inc .... E 570 826-0123
Wilkes Barre (G-19902)
Allegheny Iron & Metal Co .... E 215 743-7759
Philadelphia (G-13366)
Charles Casturo .... G 412 672-1407
McKeesport (G-10662)
Charles Cracciolo Stl Met Yard .... E 814 944-4051
Altoona (G-490)
Coatesville Scrap Ir Met Inc .... E 610 384-9230
Coatesville (G-3299)
Consoldted Scrap Resources Inc .... E 717 843-0660
York (G-20435)
Cronimet Corporation .... D 724 375-5004
Aliquippa (G-71)
E Schneider & Sons Inc .... E 610 435-3527
Allentown (G-199)
J W Zaprazny Inc .... D 570 943-2860
New Ringgold (G-12440)
Keywell Metals LLC .... F 412 462-5555
West Mifflin (G-19742)
Staiman Recycling Corporation .... D 717 646-0951
Williamsport (G-20074)
United Metal Traders Inc .... E 215 288-6555
Philadelphia (G-14421)

SCRAP & WASTE MATERIALS, WHOLESALE: Junk & Scrap

Consoldted Scrap Resources Inc .... F 717 843-0931
York (G-20434)
Rhino Inc .... F 215 442-1504
Hatboro (G-7301)

SCRAP & WASTE MATERIALS, WHOLESALE: Metal

AMG Resources Corporation .... E 412 777-7300
Pittsburgh (G-14710)
Consoldted Scrap Resources Inc .... G 717 843-0931
York (G-20436)
Kovalchick Corporation .... E 724 349-3300
Indiana (G-8110)

Penn Recycling Inc .... E 570 326-9041
Williamsport (G-20054)
Philadlphia Mtal Rsrce Rcovery .... E 215 423-4800
Philadelphia (G-14163)
Rollock Company .... E 814 893-6421
Stoystown (G-18086)
S S Salvage Recycling Inc .... F 717 444-0008
Liverpool (G-10079)

SCRAP & WASTE MATERIALS, WHOLESALE: Nonferrous Metals Scrap

Colonial Metals Co .... C 717 684-2311
Columbia (G-3434)
Tms International LLC .... E 412 885-3600
Pittsburgh (G-15629)

SCRAP & WASTE MATERIALS, WHOLESALE: Plastics Scrap

James R Hanlon Inc .... E 610 631-9999
Eagleville (G-4514)
P G Recycling Incorporated .... F 814 696-6000
Tyrone (G-18588)

SCREENS: Door, Metal Covered Wood

Ritescreen Company LLC .... C 717 362-7483
Elizabethville (G-4897)

SCREENS: Projection

Nick Mulone & Son .... G 724 274-3221
Cheswick (G-3112)
Photo Process Screen Mfg Co .... F 215 426-5473
Philadelphia (G-14172)
Rockwell Collins Inc .... F 610 925-5844
Kennett Square (G-8540)

SCREENS: Window, Metal

MI Windows and Doors Inc .... B 717 362-8196
Elizabethville (G-4895)
MI Windows and Doors Inc .... C 717 365-3300
Gratz (G-6579)
MI Windows and Doors Inc .... G 717 365-3300
Gratz (G-6578)
Pittsburgh Aluminum Co LLC .... F 724 452-5900
Pittsburgh (G-15386)
Thermal Industries Inc .... G 814 944-4534
Altoona (G-551)

SCREENS: Window, Wood Framed

Harmony Products Inc .... E 717 767-2779
Emigsville (G-4987)

SCREENS: Woven Wire

Hendrick Manufacturing Company ...... G 570 282-1010
Carbondale (G-2677)
Lumsden Corporation .... C 717 394-6871
Lancaster (G-9117)
Quality Perforating Inc .... D 570 267-2092
Carbondale (G-2685)

SCREW MACHINE PRDTS

American Turned Products Inc .... C 814 824-7600
Erie (G-5191)
American Turned Products Inc .... D 814 474-4200
Fairview (G-5812)
Automatic Machining Mfg Co Inc .... E 717 767-4448
York (G-20393)
Bonney Forge Corporation .... B 814 542-2545
Mount Union (G-11739)
Bracalentes Mfg Co Inc .... C 215 536-3077
Trumbauersville (G-18531)
C E Holden Inc .... E 412 767-5050
Cheswick (G-3103)
Cbh of Lancaster Company .... D 717 569-0485
Manheim (G-10375)
Chestnut Group Inc .... G 610 688-3300
Wayne (G-19313)
Clifton Tube Cutting Inc .... E 724 588-3241
Greenville (G-6739)
Compu-Craft Fabricators Inc .... E 215 646-2381
Montgomeryville (G-11390)
Corry Metal Products Inc .... G 814 664-7087
Corry (G-3753)
CP Precision Inc .... G 267 364-0870
Warminster (G-18848)

Diane A Walters .... G 215 453-0890
Perkasie (G-13273)
Elge Precision Machining Inc .... F 610 376-5458
Reading (G-16372)
Erie Specialty Products Inc .... E 814 453-5611
Erie (G-5274)
Ernst Timing Screw Company .... E 215 639-1438
Bensalem (G-1191)
Fostermation Inc .... G 814 336-6211
Meadville (G-10727)
Fostermation Inc .... F 814 336-6211
Meadville (G-10728)
Freedom Components Inc .... G 717 242-0101
Lewistown (G-9930)
G H Forbes Screw Machine Pdts .... G 215 884-4343
Glenside (G-6518)
Giordano Incorporated .... F 215 632-3470
Bensalem (G-1205)
Hall Industries Incorporated .... E 724 752-2000
Ellwood City (G-4934)
Hall Industries Incorporated .... F 724 758-5522
Ellwood City (G-4935)
Hall Technical Services LLC .... G 724 752-2000
Ellwood City (G-4936)
Helix Inc .... F 215 679-7924
Red Hill (G-16582)
Imperial Specialty Inc .... F 610 323-4531
Pottstown (G-16001)
In Speck Corporation .... E 610 272-9500
Norristown (G-12669)
J & J Precision Tech LLC .... F 717 625-0130
Lititz (G-10020)
Jensen Machine Co Inc .... G 724 568-3787
Vandergrift (G-18730)
John R Bromiley Company Inc .... E 215 822-7723
Chalfont (G-2878)
Kdl Industries .... G 814 398-1555
Cambridge Springs (G-2479)
Kevro Precision Components Inc .... G 814 834-5387
Saint Marys (G-16983)
Keystone Machine Inc .... E 717 359-9256
Littlestown (G-10068)
Lakeview Forge Company .... F 814 454-4518
Erie (G-5358)
Lsc Acquistion Company Inc .... E 412 795-6400
Pittsburgh (G-15239)
Mac-It Corporation .... E 717 397-3535
Lancaster (G-9122)
Orr Screw Machine Products .... E 724 668-2256
Greensburg (G-6695)
P & M Precision Machining Inc .... G 215 357-3313
Huntingdon Valley (G-8020)
Parker Snap-Tite Qdv Assembly .... D 814 438-3821
Union City (G-18611)
Perry Screw Machine Co Inc .... E 814 452-3095
Erie (G-5419)
Pittsburgh Precision .... E 412 712-1111
Pittsburgh (G-15404)
Precision Feedscrews Inc .... E 724 654-9676
New Castle (G-12139)
Precisionform Incorporated .... D 717 560-7610
Lititz (G-10035)
Q-E Manufacturing Company .... E 570 966-1017
New Berlin (G-12023)
Richlyn Manufacturing Inc .... E 814 833-8925
Erie (G-5462)
Shoemaker Mfg Solutions Inc .... E 215 723-5567
Souderton (G-17764)
South Erie Production Co Inc .... E 814 864-0311
Erie (G-5485)
Spectrum Automated Inc .... G 610 433-7755
Allentown (G-398)
Thomas W Springer Inc .... E 610 274-8400
Landenberg (G-9254)
Turning Solutions Inc .... F 814 723-1134
Warren (G-19053)
Turnmatic .... G 717 898-3200
Lancaster (G-9224)
Ultimate Screw Machine Pdts .... G 610 565-1565
Media (G-10955)
V R Machine Co Inc .... E 717 846-9250
York (G-20696)
Vallorbs Jewel Company .... C 717 392-3978
Bird In Hand (G-1684)
Wagman Manufacturing Inc .... F 717 266-5616
Manchester (G-10365)
White Engrg Surfaces Corp .... C 215 968-5021
Newtown (G-12563)

PRODUCT

SCREW MACHINES

Kaleidas Machining Inc ....G....... 814 398-4337
Cambridge Springs **(G-2478)**

Risco Industries Inc ....G....... 412 767-0349
Pittsburgh **(G-15487)**

SCREWS: Metal

Duco Holdings LLC ....G....... 215 942-6274
Ivyland **(G-8209)**

Fhritp Holdings LLC ....F....... 215 675-4590
Warminster **(G-18877)**

Keystone Scrw Corp ....D....... 215 657-7100
Willow Grove **(G-20123)**

Mitchell Apx Machine Shop Inc ....G....... 717 597-2157
Greencastle **(G-6623)**

Peerless Hardware Mfg Co ....F....... 717 684-2889
Columbia **(G-3447)**

Sfs Group Usa Inc ....D....... 610 376-5751
Reading **(G-16513)**

SPS Technologies LLC ....A....... 215 572-3000
Jenkintown **(G-8303)**

SPS Technologies LLC ....A....... 215 572-3000
Jenkintown **(G-8302)**

SEALANTS

Pecora Corporation ....C....... 215 723-6051
Harleysville **(G-7051)**

Polymeric Systems Inc ....D....... 610 286-2500
Elverson **(G-4965)**

PRC - Desoto International Inc ....G....... 412 434-3131
Pittsburgh **(G-15430)**

Quaker Chemical Corporation ....A....... 610 832-4000
Conshohocken **(G-3595)**

Sensus USA Inc ....C....... 800 375-8875
Du Bois **(G-4419)**

Sensus USA Inc ....C....... 724 430-3956
Pittsburgh **(G-15524)**

Smooth-On Inc ....C....... 610 252-5800
Macungie **(G-10159)**

Tremco Incorporated ....D....... 717 944-9702
Middletown **(G-11083)**

Union Sealants LLC ....G....... 610 473-2892
Gilbertsville **(G-6379)**

Whitmore Manufacturing Company ......F....... 724 225-8008
Washington **(G-19246)**

SEALING COMPOUNDS: Sealing, synthetic rubber or plastic

Chrysler Encpsulated Seals Inc ....E....... 570 319-1694
S Abingtn Twp **(G-16891)**

Marsh Laboratories Inc ....F....... 412 271-3060
Pittsburgh **(G-15256)**

SEALS: Hermetic

Gby Corporation ....D....... 724 539-1626
Latrobe **(G-9478)**

SEARCH & DETECTION SYSTEMS, EXC RADAR

Argon St Inc ....E....... 724 564-4100
Smithfield **(G-17641)**

Dep Technologies LLC ....G....... 800 578-7929
Lancaster **(G-8995)**

R G B Business Tech Solutions ....G....... 215 745-3646
Philadelphia **(G-14224)**

SEARCH & NAVIGATION SYSTEMS

Ametek Inc ....D....... 267 933-2121
Harleysville **(G-7018)**

Ametek Inc ....E....... 267 933-2121
Harleysville **(G-7019)**

Bae Systems Land Armaments LP ....D....... 717 225-8000
York **(G-20397)**

Conspec Controls Inc ....F....... 724 489-8450
Charleroi **(G-3008)**

Eaton Corporation ....E....... 412 893-3300
Moon Township **(G-11484)**

Eaton Electrical Inc ....E....... 412 893-3300
Moon Township **(G-11485)**

Endless Mountains Specialties ....G....... 570 432-4018
Montrose **(G-11463)**

Engined Arrsting Systems Corp ....C....... 610 494-8000
Upper Chichester **(G-18660)**

Herley Industries Inc ....B....... 717 397-2777
Lancaster **(G-9043)**

I2r Electronics Inc ....E....... 610 928-1045
Macungie **(G-10148)**

Kitron Inc ....E....... 814 619-0523
Johnstown **(G-8398)**

L3 Technologies Inc ....C....... 412 967-7700
Pittsburgh **(G-15209)**

Lighthouse Electric Contrls Co ....F....... 814 835-2348
Erie **(G-5365)**

Lockheed Martin Corporation ....B....... 570 307-1590
Jessup **(G-8331)**

Lockheed Martin Corporation ....F....... 717 267-5796
Chambersburg **(G-2954)**

Lockheed Martin Corporation ....A....... 610 382-3200
King of Prussia **(G-8641)**

Lockheed Martin Corporation ....E....... 610 354-7782
Audubon **(G-829)**

Lockheed Martin Corporation ....A....... 610 354-3083
King of Prussia **(G-8642)**

Lockheed Martin Corporation ....A....... 610 531-7400
King of Prussia **(G-8643)**

Lockheed Martin Corporation ....B....... 610 962-4954
King of Prussia **(G-8644)**

Lockheed Martin Corporation ....C....... 610 531-7400
King of Prussia **(G-8645)**

Lockheed Martin Corporation ....G....... 610 962-2264
King of Prussia **(G-8646)**

Maxima Tech & Systems LLC ....C....... 717 581-1000
Lancaster **(G-9130)**

Miller Edge Inc ....D....... 610 869-4422
West Grove **(G-19702)**

Moog Inc ....C....... 610 328-4000
Springfield **(G-17919)**

MSI Acquisition Corp ....G....... 717 397-2777
Lancaster **(G-9139)**

Night Vision Devices Inc ....F....... 610 395-9743
Allentown **(G-333)**

Oppenheimer Precision Pdts Inc ....D....... 215 674-9100
Horsham **(G-7837)**

Re2 Inc ....E....... 412 681-6382
Pittsburgh **(G-15472)**

Sensing Devices Inc ....E....... 717 295-4735
Lancaster **(G-9193)**

Shock Solutions Inc ....G....... 610 767-7090
Danielsville **(G-3995)**

Smart Avionics Inc ....G....... 717 928-4360
Marietta **(G-10467)**

Track Trail Search Rescue Inc ....G....... 814 715-5608
Brookville **(G-2274)**

Tru Temp Sensors Inc ....G....... 215 396-1550
Southampton **(G-17844)**

Unison Engine Components Inc ....C....... 570 825-4544
Wilkes Barre **(G-19967)**

Validus Inc ....G....... 215 822-2525
Colmar **(G-3422)**

Xensor Corporation ....E....... 610 284-2508
Drexel Hill **(G-4373)**

SEATING: Stadium

Contour Seats Inc ....G....... 610 395-5144
Allentown **(G-179)**

Great Eastern Seating Co ....G....... 610 366-8132
Breiningsville **(G-2018)**

Stadium Solutions Inc ....F....... 724 287-5330
Butler **(G-2444)**

SEATING: Transportation

Custom Seats Inc ....D....... 570 602-7408
Wilkes Barre **(G-19915)**

Freedman Seating Company ....C....... 610 265-3610
Exton **(G-5681)**

Ussc Group Inc ....D....... 610 265-3610
Exton **(G-5743)**

SECURE STORAGE SVC: Document

Lancaster General Svcs Bus Tr ....F....... 717 544-5474
Lancaster **(G-9095)**

Matrix Publishing Services Inc ....F....... 717 764-9673
York **(G-20583)**

SECURITY CONTROL EQPT & SYSTEMS

3si Security Systems Inc ....D....... 800 523-1430
Malvern **(G-10176)**

Alert Enterprises Ltd Lblty Co ....G....... 570 373-2821
Kulpmont **(G-8821)**

Bosch Security Systems Inc ....B....... 717 735-6300
Lancaster **(G-8957)**

Covenant Group of China Inc ....D....... 610 660-7828
Bala Cynwyd **(G-876)**

D&D Security Solutions LLC ....G....... 484 614-7024
Landenberg **(G-9248)**

Digital Designs Inc ....F....... 215 781-2525
Levittown **(G-9832)**

Dual Core LLC ....D....... 800 233-0298
Manheim **(G-10379)**

Emergensee Inc ....E....... 610 804-9007
Malvern **(G-10230)**

Fluid Intelligence LLC ....G....... 610 405-2698
Berwyn **(G-1362)**

Millstat LLC ....F....... 610 783-0181
Phoenixville **(G-14561)**

Profi Vision Inc ....G....... 610 530-2025
Allentown **(G-361)**

Reliant Systems LLC ....G....... 412 496-2580
Irwin **(G-8196)**

Reynolds & Reynolds Elec Inc ....F....... 484 221-6381
Bethlehem **(G-1610)**

Tecnomasium Inc ....F....... 412 264-7364
Coraopolis **(G-3727)**

Titan Security Group LLC ....G....... 914 474-2221
Lancaster **(G-9219)**

SECURITY DEVICES

3 T Secuirty LLC ....G....... 717 653-0019
Manheim **(G-10366)**

API Cryptek Inc ....F....... 908 546-3900
State College **(G-17941)**

Black & Decker (us) Inc ....A....... 610 797-6600
Allentown **(G-154)**

Eagle Energy Systems Ltd ....E....... 610 444-3388
Kennett Square **(G-8509)**

Eko Solutions Plus Inc ....G....... 215 856-9517
Elkins Park **(G-4902)**

Fitz Security Co Inc ....G....... 717 272-5020
Lebanon **(G-9569)**

Integrated Securty & Communctn ....E....... 610 397-0988
Plymouth Meeting **(G-15853)**

Kykayke Inc ....G....... 610 522-0106
Holmes **(G-7663)**

Martin Communications Inc ....F....... 412 498-0157
Mc Kees Rocks **(G-10619)**

Mititech LLC ....G....... 410 309-9447
Chambersburg **(G-2960)**

Ross Security Systems LLC ....E....... 717 656-2200
Leola **(G-9801)**

Salus Security Devices LLC ....G....... 610 388-6387
West Chester **(G-19635)**

Stanley Industrial & Auto LLC ....C....... 800 523-9462
Allentown **(G-400)**

Tactical Technologies Inc ....E....... 610 522-0106
Holmes **(G-7665)**

Tgb I LLC ....C....... 724 431-3090
Saxonburg **(G-17096)**

SECURITY EQPT STORES

Gettysburg Village Factory Str ....F....... 717 334-2332
Gettysburg **(G-6294)**

Martin Communications Inc ....F....... 412 498-0157
Mc Kees Rocks **(G-10619)**

Michels Hearing Aid Center ....G....... 570 622-9151
Pottsville **(G-16088)**

SECURITY PROTECTIVE DEVICES MAINTENANCE & MONITORING SVCS

Pixcontroller Inc ....G....... 724 733-0970
Export **(G-5621)**

Seal Glove Mfg Inc ....F....... 717 692-4837
Millersburg **(G-11200)**

SECURITY SYSTEMS SERVICES

API Cryptek Inc ....F....... 908 546-3900
State College **(G-17941)**

App-Techs Corporation ....F....... 717 735-0848
Lancaster **(G-8935)**

Martin Communications Inc ....F....... 412 498-0157
Mc Kees Rocks **(G-10619)**

Mk Solutions Inc ....G....... 860 760-0438
York **(G-20601)**

Safety House Inc ....F....... 610 344-0637
Glen Mills **(G-6443)**

Siemens Industry Inc ....D....... 215 654-8040
Blue Bell **(G-1852)**

SEEDS: Coated Or Treated, From Purchased Seeds

Future Generation Ag LLC ....G....... 844 993-3311
Leola (G-9783)
Penn Pro Manufacturing Inc ....F....... 724 222-6450
Washington (G-19215)

SELF-DEFENSE & ATHLETIC INSTRUCTION SVCS

Interntnal Def Systems USA LLC ....G....... 610 973-2228
Orefield (G-13012)

SEMICONDUCTOR CIRCUIT NETWORKS

Filmtronics Inc ....E....... 724 352-3790
Butler (G-2401)
Microchip Technology Inc ....F....... 610 630-0556
Norristown (G-12684)
Powerex Inc ....E....... 724 925-7272
Youngwood (G-20781)
Powerex Inc ....C....... 724 925-7272
Youngwood (G-20782)
Texas Instrs Lehigh Vly Inc ....G....... 610 849-5100
Bethlehem (G-1638)
Texas Instruments Incorporated ....E....... 610 849-5100
Bethlehem (G-1639)

SEMICONDUCTOR DEVICES: Wafers

Hoffman Materials LLC ....F....... 717 243-2011
Carlisle (G-2717)
Iqe Inc ....D....... 610 861-6930
Bethlehem (G-1540)
Laurell Technologies Corp ....F....... 215 699-7278
North Wales (G-12812)

SEMICONDUCTORS & RELATED DEVICES

American Innovations Inc ....G....... 215 249-1840
Dublin (G-4431)
Applied Materials Inc ....G....... 610 409-9187
Collegeville (G-3370)
Aural Harmonics ....F....... 610 488-0232
Bernville (G-1297)
C&D Technologies Inc ....C....... 215 619-2700
Blue Bell (G-1820)
Cymatics Laboratories Corp ....G....... 412 578-0280
Pittsburgh (G-14899)
Dean Technology Inc ....E....... 724 349-9440
Indiana (G-8090)
Esilicon Corporation ....G....... 610 439-6800
Allentown (G-207)
Everson Tesla Inc ....D....... 610 746-1520
Nazareth (G-11965)
F S Convergent ....E....... 484 581-7065
Wayne (G-19327)
Fairchild Semiconductor Corp ....C....... 570 474-6761
Mountain Top (G-11760)
First Level Inc ....F....... 717 266-2450
York (G-20481)
Heraeus Precious Metals Nor ....C....... 610 825-6050
Conshohocken (G-3556)
Ii-VI Incorporated ....B....... 724 352-4455
Saxonburg (G-17088)
Ii-VI Laser Enterprise Inc ....E....... 724 352-4455
Saxonburg (G-17089)
Infineon Tech Americas Corp ....E....... 408 503-2655
Allentown (G-257)
Infinera Corporation ....G....... 484 866-4600
Allentown (G-260)
Invensys Energy Metering Corp ....B....... 814 371-3011
Du Bois (G-4396)
Keytronics Inc ....D....... 814 272-2700
State College (G-17984)
Kulicke and Soffa Inds Inc ....C....... 215 784-6000
Fort Washington (G-6081)
Linear Technology LLC ....F....... 215 638-9667
Bensalem (G-1221)
Microsemi Corp ....E....... 610 929-7142
Reading (G-16442)
Microsemi Corp - High ....D....... 717 486-3411
Mount Holly Springs (G-11636)
Microsemi Corp - Mntgmeryville ....E....... 215 631-9840
Montgomeryville (G-11407)
Micross Components Inc ....G....... 215 997-3200
Hatfield (G-7369)
Moglabs Usa LLC ....G....... 814 251-4363
Huntingdon (G-7953)
Montco Enterprises Ltd ....E....... 610 948-5316
Spring City (G-17863)

NORTH PENN TECHNOLOGY INC ....E....... 215 997-3200
Hatfield (G-7374)
OEM Group East Inc ....D....... 610 282-0105
Coopersburg (G-3632)
On Semiconductor ....G....... 570 475-6030
Mountain Top (G-11769)
On Semiconductor Corp ....E....... 602 244-6600
Ambler (G-595)
On Semiconductor Corporation ....E....... 215 654-9700
Ambler (G-596)
Phase Guard Co Inc ....G....... 412 276-3415
Carnegie (G-2778)
Power & Energy Inc ....F....... 215 942-4600
Ivyland (G-8221)
Premier Semiconductor Svcs LLC ....D....... 267 954-0130
Hatfield (G-7384)
Process Sltions Consulting Inc ....G....... 610 248-2002
New Tripoli (G-12460)
Quick Assembly Inc ....F....... 215 361-4100
Hatfield (G-7388)
R & D Assembly Inc ....G....... 610 770-0700
Allentown (G-365)
R&D Circuits Inc ....G....... 610 443-2299
Allentown (G-368)
Raytheon Company ....B....... 814 278-2256
State College (G-18012)
RTD Embedded Technologies Inc ....E....... 814 234-8087
State College (G-18017)
Scitech Assoc Holdings Inc ....G....... 201 218-3777
State College (G-18021)
Secure Components LLC ....F....... 610 551-3475
Norristown (G-12711)
Semicndctor Ozone Slutions LLC ....G....... 541 936-0844
Fleetwood (G-5979)
Semilab USA LLC ....F....... 610 377-5990
Lehighton (G-9726)
SES Inc ....G....... 484 767-3280
Nazareth (G-11987)
Spectrum Control Tech Inc ....F....... 814 474-2207
Fairview (G-5846)
Spectrum Devices Corporation ....G....... 215 997-7870
Telford (G-18318)
Universal Display Corporation ....G....... 609 671-0980
Newtown (G-12558)
Victor Associates Inc ....G....... 215 393-5437
Lansdale (G-9423)
Vishay Intertechnology Inc ....B....... 610 644-1300
Malvern (G-10341)
Vishay Siliconix LLC ....A....... 408 567-8177
Malvern (G-10344)
Xensor Corporation ....E....... 610 284-2508
Drexel Hill (G-4373)

SEMINARY

Catholic Scl Svcs of Scranton ....D....... 570 207-2283
Scranton (G-17216)

SENSORS: Infrared, Solid State

Moog Inc ....C....... 610 328-4000
Springfield (G-17919)

SENSORS: Radiation

Conductive Technologies Inc ....D....... 717 764-6931
York (G-20433)
Sensortex Inc ....G....... 302 444-2383
Kennett Square (G-8542)

SENSORS: Temperature, Exc Indl Process

Tasseron Sensors Inc ....G....... 570 601-1971
Montoursville (G-11451)

SEPTIC TANK CLEANING SVCS

Bradford County Sanitation Inc ....G....... 570 673-3128
Troy (G-18518)
Piles Concrete Products Co Inc ....F....... 814 445-6619
Friedens (G-6225)

SEPTIC TANKS: Concrete

American Tank & Concrete Svc ....F....... 724 837-4410
Greensburg (G-6650)
Bauer Company Inc ....G....... 724 548-8101
Kittanning (G-8756)
Centermoreland Concrete Pdts ....F....... 570 333-4944
Tunkhannock (G-18533)
Dennis Lumber and Concrete ....E....... 724 329-5542
Markleysburg (G-10480)

Dymonds Concrete Products ....G....... 717 352-2321
Fayetteville (G-5876)
Hilltop Tank & Supply ....G....... 814 658-3915
James Creek (G-8234)
James F Geibel ....G....... 724 287-1964
Butler (G-2412)
Lee Concrete Products ....G....... 814 467-4470
Windber (G-20188)
Middleburg Pre Cast LLC ....F....... 570 837-1463
Middleburg (G-11029)
Modern Precast Concrete Inc ....G....... 484 548-6200
Easton (G-4726)
Monarch Precast Concrete Corp ....E....... 610 435-6746
Allentown (G-320)
Ringtown Wilbert Vault Works ....F....... 570 889-3153
Ringtown (G-16756)
Rosenberry Septic Tank Service ....G....... 717 532-4026
Shippensburg (G-17545)
Stauffer Con Pdts & Excvtg Inc ....G....... 570 629-1977
Kunkletown (G-8835)
Vcw Enterprises Inc ....D....... 610 847-5112
Ottsville (G-13068)
William Elston Incorporated ....F....... 570 689-2203
Jefferson Township (G-8280)

SERVOMOTORS: Electric

Servo Repair International ....F....... 412 492-8116
Allison Park (G-462)

SEWAGE & WATER TREATMENT EQPT

American Water Technologies ....E....... 724 850-9000
Youngwood (G-20778)
Campbell Manufacturing Inc ....D....... 610 367-2107
Bechtelsville (G-1030)
Chippewa Twp Sewage Plant ....G....... 724 846-3820
Beaver Falls (G-998)
City of New Castle ....G....... 724 654-1627
New Castle (G-12073)
Cromaflow Inc ....F....... 570 546-3557
Montoursville (G-11437)
Ewt Holdings III Corp ....G....... 724 772-0044
Pittsburgh (G-14991)
Filson Water Treatment Inc ....F....... 717 240-0763
Carlisle (G-2712)
High Tech Aquatics Inc ....G....... 570 546-3557
Muncy (G-11819)
Hobart Corporation ....E....... 717 397-5100
Lancaster (G-9050)
Hydroflow Pennsylvania LLC ....G....... 814 643-7135
Pennsylvania Furnace (G-13263)
Marg Inc ....F....... 724 703-3020
Oakdale (G-12906)
Mfg Water Treat Prod ....G....... 814 438-3959
Union City (G-18609)
Orbisonia Rockhill Joint ....G....... 814 447-5414
Orbisonia (G-13007)
Rdp Technologies Inc ....F....... 610 650-9900
Conshohocken (G-3599)
Scale Watcher North Amer Inc ....G....... 610 932-6888
Oxford (G-13089)
Siemens Industry Inc ....E....... 724 772-0044
Warrendale (G-19097)
Trijay Systems Inc ....F....... 215 997-5833
Line Lexington (G-9977)

SEWAGE TREATMENT SYSTEMS & EQPT

Easy Liner LLC ....G....... 717 825-7962
York (G-20461)
Ronald Hines ....G....... 570 256-3355
Shickshinny (G-17502)

SEWER CLEANING & RODDING SVC

Lb Full Circle Canine Fitness ....G....... 267 825-7375
Philadelphia (G-13961)

SEWER CLEANING EQPT: Power

General Wire Spring Company ....C....... 412 771-6300
Mc Kees Rocks (G-10612)
Oxford Area Sewer Authority ....G....... 610 932-3493
Oxford (G-13085)

SEWING CONTRACTORS

Eric and Christopher LLC ....F....... 215 257-2400
Perkasie (G-13276)
Sew Special ....G....... 724 438-1765
Uniontown (G-18641)

SEWING MACHINE STORES

Ladyfingers Sewing Studio ....G....... 610 689-0068
Oley *(G-12979)*
Sew Special ....G....... 724 438-1765
Uniontown *(G-18641)*

SEWING MACHINES & PARTS: Indl

M A Hanna Color ....F....... 610 317-3300
Bethlehem *(G-1563)*

SEWING, NEEDLEWORK & PIECE GOODS STORE: Quilting Matls/Splys

Fisher S Hand Made Quilts ....G....... 717 392-5440
Bird In Hand *(G-1674)*

SEWING, NEEDLEWORK & PIECE GOODS STORES: Fabric, Remnants

Gene Sanes & Associates ....E....... 412 471-8224
Pittsburgh *(G-15043)*

SHADE PULLS, WINDOW

Apple Fasteners Inc ....E....... 717 761-8962
Camp Hill *(G-2490)*

SHADES: Lamp & Light, Residential

Davis Lamp & Shade Inc ....E....... 215 426-2777
Philadelphia *(G-13611)*
Horizon Lamps Inc ....F....... 610 829-4220
Easton *(G-4701)*
Pieri Creations LLC ....E....... 215 634-4000
Philadelphia *(G-14176)*
Remilux LLC ....G....... 717 737-7120
Camp Hill *(G-2515)*
Varsal LLC ....C....... 215 957-5880
Warminster *(G-18993)*

SHADES: Lamp Or Candle

J Harris & Sons Co ....E....... 412 391-5532
Pittsburgh *(G-15142)*
Penn Shadecrafters Inc ....E....... 570 342-3193
Scranton *(G-17271)*

SHALE MINING, COMMON

G & K Watterson Company ....G....... 724 827-2800
New Brighton *(G-12037)*

SHAPES & PILINGS, STRUCTURAL: Steel

Istil (usa) Milton Inc ....E....... 570 742-7420
Milton *(G-11243)*
Quality Steel Fabricators ....F....... 724 646-0500
Greenville *(G-6768)*
Samuel Grossi & Sons Inc ....D....... 215 638-4470
Bensalem *(G-1249)*

SHAPES: Extruded, Aluminum, NEC

Hopewell Manufacturing Inc ....G....... 717 593-9400
Waynesboro *(G-19412)*

SHAPES: Flat, Rolled, Aluminum, NEC

Alumax LLC ....E....... 570 784-7481
Bloomsburg *(G-1768)*

SHEET METAL SPECIALTIES, EXC STAMPED

A & E Manufacturing Co Inc ....C....... 215 943-9460
Levittown *(G-9810)*
Acme Roofing and Heating Inc ....G....... 412 921-8218
Pittsburgh *(G-14643)*
Albert C Phy & Sons Inc ....F....... 215 659-2125
Willow Grove *(G-20106)*
Albright Precision Inc ....E....... 570 457-5744
Moosic *(G-11502)*
Apx Enclosures Inc ....E....... 717 328-9399
Mercersburg *(G-10981)*
ARS Metal Fabricators LLC ....G....... 215 855-6000
Hatfield *(G-7318)*
Arvite Technologies Inc ....F....... 814 838-9444
Erie *(G-5195)*
Bevilacqua Sheet Metal Inc ....G....... 570 558-0397
Scranton *(G-17211)*
Byrne Chiarlone LP ....E....... 610 874-8436
Chester *(G-3042)*

Clark Metal Products Co ....C....... 724 459-7550
Blairsville *(G-1719)*
Compu-Craft Fabricators Inc ....E....... 215 646-2381
Montgomeryville *(G-11390)*
Coren Metalcrafts Company ....F....... 215 244-0532
Bensalem *(G-1174)*
Corry Contract Inc ....C....... 814 665-8221
Corry *(G-3748)*
Crusader Precision Shtmtl Co ....G....... 610 485-4321
Marcus Hook *(G-10440)*
Csi Industries Inc ....E....... 814 474-9353
Fairview *(G-5819)*
Custom Products ....G....... 814 453-6803
Erie *(G-5240)*
Daria Metal Fabricators Inc ....E....... 215 453-2110
Perkasie *(G-13271)*
Davidsons Fabricating Inc ....E....... 610 544-9750
Broomall *(G-2285)*
Dennis Filges Co Inc ....E....... 724 287-3735
Chicora *(G-3126)*
Electro-Space Fabricators Inc ....D....... 610 682-7181
Topton *(G-18412)*
Expert Process Systems LLC ....G....... 570 424-0581
Stroudsburg *(G-18118)*
F W Lang Co ....G....... 267 401-8293
Havertown *(G-7421)*
Fabricated Components Inc ....D....... 570 421-4110
Stroudsburg *(G-18119)*
General Metal Company Inc ....E....... 215 638-3242
Bensalem *(G-1203)*
Gerome Manufacturing Co Inc ....D....... 724 438-8544
Smithfield *(G-17650)*
Great Lakes Manufacturing Inc ....C....... 814 734-2436
Corry *(G-3764)*
Harbor Steel Inc ....F....... 724 658-7748
New Castle *(G-12100)*
Histand Brothers Inc ....E....... 215 348-4121
Ambler *(G-581)*
Hoffman Manufacturing Inc ....F....... 610 821-4222
Fogelsville *(G-5995)*
Holly Metals Inc ....F....... 610 692-4989
West Chester *(G-19562)*
Keystone Cstm Fabricators Inc ....E....... 412 384-9131
Elizabeth *(G-4861)*
Keystone Fabricating Inc ....E....... 610 868-0900
Bethlehem *(G-1551)*
Kms Fab LLC ....E....... 570 338-0200
Luzerne *(G-10125)*
Little Round Industries LLC ....G....... 215 361-1456
Hatfield *(G-7366)*
M & M Sheet Metal Inc ....F....... 570 326-4655
Williamsport *(G-20039)*
Marine Sheet Metal Works ....G....... 814 455-9700
Erie *(G-5380)*
Newport Fabricators Inc ....E....... 215 234-4400
Green Lane *(G-6591)*
Omni Fab Inc ....F....... 724 334-8851
New Kensington *(G-12364)*
Panagraphics Inc ....E....... 717 292-5606
Dover *(G-4198)*
Paul Groth & Sons Inc ....F....... 724 843-8086
New Brighton *(G-12039)*
Plum Corporation ....F....... 724 836-7261
Greensburg *(G-6702)*
Poff Sheet Metal Inc ....G....... 717 845-9622
York *(G-20629)*
Production Components Corp ....E....... 215 368-7416
Lansdale *(G-9402)*
PSMLV Inc ....F....... 610 395-8214
Allentown *(G-363)*
Radiant Steel Products Company ....F....... 570 322-7828
Williamsport *(G-20067)*
Tech Manufacturing Corporation ....E....... 610 586-0620
Sharon Hill *(G-17464)*
Trexler Industries Inc ....E....... 610 974-9800
Bethlehem *(G-1641)*
Tuckey Metal Fabricators Inc ....E....... 717 249-8111
Carlisle *(G-2744)*
United Metal Products Corp ....G....... 570 226-3084
Hawley *(G-7440)*
Vertech International Inc ....E....... 215 529-0300
Quakertown *(G-16257)*
Victor Group Inc ....D....... 814 899-1079
Erie *(G-5526)*
Walsh Sheet Metal Inc ....G....... 570 344-3495
Scranton *(G-17311)*
Weaver Sheet Metal LLC ....F....... 717 733-4763
Ephrata *(G-5156)*
Welded Shtmtl Specialty Co ....G....... 412 331-3534
Pittsburgh *(G-15708)*

Yeager Wire Works Inc ....G....... 570 752-2769
Berwick *(G-1349)*
York Haven Fabricators Inc ....E....... 717 932-4000
York Haven *(G-20762)*

SHEET MUSIC STORES

Theodore Presser Company ....E....... 610 592-1222
King of Prussia *(G-8687)*

SHEETING: Laminated Plastic

Laminations Inc ....C....... 570 876-8199
Archbald *(G-690)*
United Laminations Inc ....F....... 570 876-1360
Mayfield *(G-10544)*

SHEETING: Window, Plastic

AAR Plastic & Glass Llc ....G....... 410 200-6369
Gettysburg *(G-6281)*
Dilworth Manufacturing Co ....G....... 717 354-8956
Narvon *(G-11920)*

SHEETS & SHEETINGS, COTTON

Microsilver Wear LLC ....G....... 215 917-7203
Yardley *(G-20325)*

SHEETS & STRIPS: Aluminum

Alcoa USA Corp ....G....... 212 518-5400
Pittsburgh *(G-14666)*
Alumax Mill Products Inc ....E....... 717 393-9641
Lancaster *(G-8930)*
Arconic Inc ....C....... 717 393-9641
Lancaster *(G-8938)*

SHEETS: Copper & Copper Alloy

American Alloy Fabricators ....G....... 610 635-0205
Norristown *(G-12633)*

SHEETS: Fabric, From Purchased Materials

Belmont Fabrics LLC ....F....... 717 768-0077
Paradise *(G-13154)*

SHELLAC

A I Floor Products ....G....... 215 355-2798
Feasterville Trevose *(G-5881)*
Aurora International Coat ....F....... 412 782-2984
Pittsburgh *(G-14740)*
Coating Innovations LLC ....F....... 412 269-0100
Coraopolis *(G-3679)*
Innovative Finishers Inc ....G....... 215 536-2222
Quakertown *(G-16201)*
Randall Publications ....G....... 610 871-1427
Allentown *(G-371)*

SHELLS: Metal Plate

Dedicated Customs Inc ....G....... 724 678-6609
Burgettstown *(G-2345)*
Lancaster Composite ....G....... 717 872-8999
Lancaster *(G-9091)*

SHELTERED WORKSHOPS

Achieva ....D....... 412 995-5000
Pittsburgh *(G-14640)*
Lark Enterprises Inc ....E....... 724 657-2001
New Castle *(G-12114)*
Shepherd Good Work Services ....C....... 610 776-8353
Allentown *(G-388)*

SHELVING: Office & Store, Exc Wood

Charles Beseler Co Inc ....D....... 800 237-3537
Stroudsburg *(G-18109)*
Consolidated Stor Companies Inc ....C....... 610 253-2775
Tatamy *(G-18256)*
Consolidated Stor Companies Inc ....C....... 610 253-2775
Tatamy *(G-18257)*

SHIELDS OR ENCLOSURES: Radiator, Sheet Metal

Bornmann Mfg Co Inc ....G....... 215 228-5826
Philadelphia *(G-13473)*

SHIMS: Metal

Bolsan Company Inc ....F 724 225-0446
Eighty Four (G-4834)
Igs Industries Inc ....C 724 222-5800
Meadow Lands (G-10690)
Specialty Bar Products Company ....C 724 459-0544
Blairsville (G-1742)

SHIP BLDG & RPRG: Drilling & Production Platforms, Oil/Gas

Kennedy Fuels Inc ....G 412 721-7404
Pittsburgh (G-15171)
Lion Energy Co LLC ....G 724 444-7501
Gibsonia (G-6343)

SHIP BUILDING & REPAIRING: Cargo, Commercial

Interntonal Mar Outfitting LLC ....G 215 875-9911
Philadelphia (G-13871)

SHIP BUILDING & REPAIRING: Combat Vessels

General Dynamics Corporation ....E 412 432-2200
Pittsburgh (G-15044)

SHIP BUILDING & REPAIRING: Dredges

Supreme - DSC Dredge LLC ....G 724 376-4368
Stoneboro (G-18070)

SHIP BUILDING & REPAIRING: Rigging, Marine

HIG Capital LLC ....C 610 495-7011
Royersford (G-16851)
Hli Rail & Rigging LLC ....F 215 277-5558
Elkins Park (G-4905)

SHIP COMPONENTS: Metal, Prefabricated

Kt-Grant Inc ....D 724 468-4700
Export (G-5614)
Railway Specialties Corp ....E 215 788-9242
Croydon (G-3926)

SHIPBUILDING & REPAIR

Donjon Shipbuilding & Repr LLC ....F 814 455-6442
Erie (G-5250)
Erie Forge and Steel Inc ....D 814 452-2300
Erie (G-5267)
Kvaerner Philadelphia Shi ....G 215 875-2725
Philadelphia (G-13947)
Philadelphia Ship Repair LLC ......F 215 339-1026
Philadelphia (G-14154)
Rhoads Industries Inc ....E 267 728-6544
Philadelphia (G-14243)
Rhoads Industries Inc ....D 267 728-6300
Philadelphia (G-14244)
Whemco Inc ....E 412 390-2700
Pittsburgh (G-15715)

SHIPS WHOLESALERS

Loeffler Corporation ....F 215 757-2404
Langhorne (G-9309)

SHOCK ABSORBERS: Indl

Modern Industries Inc ....F 814 885-8514
Kersey (G-8564)
Modern Industries Inc ....C 814 455-8061
Erie (G-5394)

SHOE & BOOT ACCESS

Richard Zerbe Ltd ....G 717 564-2024
Harrisburg (G-7205)

SHOE MATERIALS: Counters

Ticket Counter ....G 717 536-3092
Mechanicsburg (G-10897)

SHOE MATERIALS: Inner Parts

Three Dimensions Systems Inc ......G 724 779-3890
Cranberry Township (G-3852)

SHOE MATERIALS: Inner Soles

Unequal Technologies Company ....E 610 444-5900
Glen Mills (G-6446)

SHOE MATERIALS: Quarters

Country Flair Quarter Horses ....G 724 822-8413
Worthington (G-20229)
Dotted Quarter Music ....G 724 541-4211
Mechanicsburg (G-10838)
Fighters Quarters ....G 334 657-4128
Allentown (G-212)
French Quaters ....G 724 845-7387
Leechburg (G-9645)

SHOE MATERIALS: Rands

Ingersoll Rand Co ....G 215 345-4470
Furlong (G-6231)
Ingersoll-Rand Co ....G 717 530-1160
Shippensburg (G-17533)
Ingersoll-Rand Co ....G 610 882-8800
Bethlehem (G-1539)
L Rand Incorporated ....G 215 490-8090
Philadelphia (G-13949)
Rand 2339 Haverford LP ....G 215 620-6993
Ardmore (G-714)
Rob Rand Enterprises Inc ....G 724 927-6844
Jamestown (G-8239)

SHOE MATERIALS: Rubber

Unicast Inc ....E 610 559-9998
Easton (G-4765)

SHOE MATERIALS: Uppers

Hbg-Upper Saucon Inc ....G 215 491-7736
Jamison (G-8244)
Lucks Upper Bucks Gym LLC ....G 610 847-2392
Upper Black Eddy (G-18655)
North Pittsburgh Upper Cervica .....G 724 553-8526
Cranberry Township (G-3842)
Upper Case Living ....G 724 229-8190
Washington (G-19236)
Upper Delaware Valley ID ....G 570 251-8040
Bethany (G-1391)
Upper Moreland ....G 215 773-9880
Horsham (G-7862)
Upper Perk Robotics ....G 215 541-1654
Pennsburg (G-13259)
Upper Providence Township ....F 610 933-8179
Oaks (G-12937)

SHOE REPAIR SHOP

Perry Ercolino Inc ....G 215 348-5885
Doylestown (G-4324)

SHOE REPAIR SVC

Quality Crrctons Inspctons Inc ......D 814 696-3737
Duncansville (G-4462)

SHOE STORES

Eros Hosiery Co Del Vly Inc ....G 215 342-2121
Huntingdon Valley (G-7978)
Jumpers Shoe Service ....G 717 766-3422
Mechanicsburg (G-10860)
Lost Creek Shoe Shop Inc ....G 717 463-3117
Mifflintown (G-11129)

SHOE STORES: Boots, Women's

Lavender Badge LLC ....G 610 994-9476
King of Prussia (G-8638)

SHOE STORES: Custom & Orthopedic

Unequal Technologies Company ....E 610 444-5900
Glen Mills (G-6446)

SHOE STORES: Men's

Aramark Unf Creer AP Group Inc ....A 215 238-3000
Philadelphia (G-13406)
Lids Corporation ....G 814 868-1944
Erie (G-5364)

SHOE STORES: Orthopedic

Best-Made Shoes ....G 412 621-9363
Pittsburgh (G-14765)

Three Soles Corp ....G 717 762-1945
Waynesboro (G-19428)

SHOE STORES: Women's

Eternity Fashion Inc ....G 215 567-5571
Philadelphia (G-13681)
Modzori LLC ....G 215 833-3618
Newtown (G-12522)

SHOES & BOOTS WHOLESALERS

C & J Clark America Inc ....D 717 632-2444
Hanover (G-6864)
Sunnys Fashions ....G 724 527-1800
Jeannette (G-8266)

SHOES: Athletic, Exc Rubber Or Plastic

Greenkeepers Inc ....G 215 464-7540
Philadelphia (G-13786)

SHOES: Canvas, Rubber Soled

Vans Inc ....F 215 632-2481
Philadelphia (G-14437)

SHOES: Infants' & Children's

Kepner-Scott Shoe Co ....E 570 366-0229
Orwigsburg (G-13047)

SHOES: Men's

HH Brown Shoe Company Inc ....D 814 793-3786
Martinsburg (G-10524)
Perry Ercolino Inc ....G 215 348-5885
Doylestown (G-4324)
Primitive Country Tole ....G 570 247-2719
Rome (G-16801)
Quality Crrctons Inspctons Inc ......D 814 696-3737
Duncansville (G-4462)
Relay Shoe Company LLC ....G 610 970-6450
Pottstown (G-16039)
Vf Outdoor LLC ....G 610 327-1734
Pottstown (G-16065)

SHOES: Men's, Work

HH Brown Shoe Company Inc ....E 814 793-3786
Martinsburg (G-10523)

SHOES: Orthopedic, Men's

Best-Made Shoes ....G 412 621-9363
Pittsburgh (G-14765)

SHOES: Plastic Or Rubber

HH Brown Shoe Company Inc ....D 814 793-3786
Martinsburg (G-10524)
Joneric Products Inc ....F 215 441-9669
Horsham (G-7829)
Nike Inc ....G 412 922-3660
Coraopolis (G-3707)
Paragon Development Corp ....F 724 254-1551
Penn Run (G-13230)
Vans Inc ....G 717 291-8936
Lancaster (G-9231)

SHOES: Women's

Gleen ....G 570 457-3858
Moosic (G-11506)
HH Brown Shoe Company Inc ....D 814 793-3786
Martinsburg (G-10524)
Quality Crrctons Inspctons Inc ......D 814 696-3737
Duncansville (G-4462)
Vf Outdoor LLC ....G 610 265-2193
King of Prussia (G-8696)

SHOES: Women's, Dress

Modzori LLC ....G 215 833-3618
Newtown (G-12522)

SHOWCASES & DISPLAY FIXTURES: Office & Store

L&D Millwork Inc ....G 570 285-3200
Kingston (G-8720)
M & M Manufacturing Co ....E 724 274-0767
Cheswick (G-3111)
Sparks Custom Retail LLC ....E 215 602-8100
Philadelphia (G-14328)

PRODUCT

Wescho Company Inc.............E...... 610 436-5866
  West Chester (G-19676)

SHOWER STALLS: Metal

Crystal Shower Doors.............G....... 717 642-9689
  Fairfield (G-5766)

SHOWER STALLS: Plastic & Fiberglass

Aquatic Co............................C....... 717 367-1100
  Elizabethtown (G-4865)
Frameless Shower Doors.............G....... 215 534-0021
  Jamison (G-8243)
Robert J Fleig Inc.............G....... 215 702-7676
  Langhorne (G-9322)

SHREDDERS: Indl & Commercial

Allegheny Paper Shredders Corp.........E...... 800 245-2497
  Delmont (G-4046)
Allegheny-Wagner Inds Inc.............E...... 724 468-4300
  Delmont (G-4047)
Concept Products Corporation ....G...... 610 722-0830
  Mertztown (G-11002)
Hsm of America LLC.............E...... 610 918-4894
  Downingtown (G-4235)

SHUTTERS, DOOR & WINDOW: Metal

Bucks County Shutters LLC ....F...... 215 957-3333
  Warminster (G-18842)
Glenn Shutter.............G....... 717 867-2589
  Annville (G-649)
Peters James & Son Inc ....G...... 215 739-9500
  Philadelphia (G-14139)

SHUTTERS, DOOR & WINDOW: Plastic

Shutter Tech Inc.............G....... 610 696-9322
  West Chester (G-19639)

SHUTTERS: Door, Wood

Kellner Millwork Co Inc ....G...... 412 784-1414
  Pittsburgh (G-15164)

SHUTTERS: Window, Wood

Timberlane Inc.............E...... 215 616-0600
  Montgomeryville (G-11424)

SIDING & STRUCTURAL MATERIALS: Wood

Belden Brick Sales & Svc Inc ....F...... 215 639-6561
  Trevose (G-18487)
J Mastrocola Hauling Inc.............G...... 610 631-1773
  Norristown (G-12672)
Laceyville Lumber Inc ....G...... 570 869-1212
  Laceyville (G-8872)
Lindner Wood Technology Inc.............F...... 610 820-8310
  Allentown (G-297)
Martin Fabricating Inc.............E...... 610 435-5700
  Allentown (G-309)
Red Square Corp.............G...... 412 422-8631
  Pittsburgh (G-15473)
Sfk Ventures Inc.............D...... 610 825-5151
  King of Prussia (G-8672)
Ufp Eastern Division Inc.............G...... 724 399-2992
  Parker (G-13166)

SIDING: Precast Stone

Steel Stone Manufacturing Co.............F...... 610 837-9966
  Lehigh Valley (G-9707)

SIDING: Sheet Metal

Flexospan Steel Buildings Inc.............D...... 724 376-7221
  Sandy Lake (G-17060)
Legacy Service USA LLC.............D....... 215 675-7770
  Southampton (G-17822)

SIGN LETTERING & PAINTING SVCS

Advance Sign Company LLC.............E...... 412 481-6990
  Pittsburgh (G-14650)
Cariks Custom Decor ....G...... 412 882-1511
  Pittsburgh (G-14812)
Fedex Office & Print Svcs Inc.............F...... 412 366-9750
  Pittsburgh (G-15011)
Freds Signs.............G....... 412 741-3153
  Pittsburgh (G-15036)
Kurt Lebo.............G...... 610 682-4071
  Fleetwood (G-5975)

NMB Signs Inc.............F...... 412 344-5700
  Pittsburgh (G-15342)
Precisions Signs and Awning.............G...... 412 278-0400
  Carnegie (G-2782)

SIGN PAINTING & LETTERING SHOP

Alpha Space Control Co Inc.............G...... 717 263-0182
  Chambersburg (G-2900)
Art Sign Company.............G...... 717 264-4211
  Chambersburg (G-2906)
Image 360.............G...... 717 317-9147
  Harrisburg (G-7153)
Leiphart Enterprises LLC.............G...... 717 938-4100
  Lewisberry (G-9888)
Upper Darby Sign Company ....D...... 610 518-5881
  Downingtown (G-4259)
William F and Kathy A Yeager ....G...... 717 665-6964
  Manheim (G-10407)
William Klein Signs Inc.............G...... 610 374-5371
  Reading (G-16565)

SIGNALING APPARATUS: Electric

L3 Technologies Inc.............C...... 267 545-7000
  Bristol (G-2157)
Probee Safety LLC.............G...... 302 893-0258
  Telford (G-18310)

SIGNALS: Railroad, Electric

Alstom Signaling Operation LLC.........B...... 800 825-3178
  Erie (G-5184)
Hitachi Rail STS Usa Inc.............B...... 412 688-2400
  Pittsburgh (G-15096)

SIGNALS: Traffic Control, Electric

Solar Technology Inc.............D...... 610 391-8600
  Allentown (G-396)

SIGNALS: Transportation

Atlas Flasher & Supply Co Inc.............E...... 610 469-2602
  Pottstown (G-15944)
Clark Traffic Control Inc ....F...... 724 388-4023
  Homer City (G-7674)
Hirschmann Electronics Inc.............F...... 717 217-2200
  Chambersburg (G-2940)
Mainstream Industries ....G...... 610 488-1148
  Bernville (G-1301)
Otx Logistics Inc.............G...... 412 567-8821
  Clinton (G-3264)
Traffic Control Eqp & Sups Co ....G...... 412 882-2012
  Bentleyville (G-1276)

SIGNS & ADVERTISING SPECIALTIES

13 Big Bears Inc.............G...... 610 437-6123
  Allentown (G-109)
Acorn Manufacturing Inc.............E...... 717 964-1111
  Denver (G-4065)
Ad-Art Sign Co.............G...... 412 373-0960
  Pittsburgh (G-14649)
Adams Outdoor Advg Ltd Partnr.............E...... 610 266-9461
  Bethlehem (G-1444)
Addies Awards & Printing LLC ....G...... 570 484-9060
  Lock Haven (G-10082)
Advance Sign Company LLC.............E...... 412 481-6990
  Pittsburgh (G-14650)
Al Tedeschi.............G...... 724 746-3755
  Canonsburg (G-2535)
All-Sign Graphics & Design ....G...... 814 467-9995
  Windber (G-20177)
Ameraquick Inc.............G...... 724 733-5906
  Murrysville (G-11846)
American Brchure Catalogue Inc ....E...... 215 259-1600
  Warminster (G-18827)
Americana Art China Co Inc ....F...... 330 938-6133
  Mercer (G-10959)
Andrew W Nissly Inc.............G...... 717 393-3841
  Lancaster (G-8934)
Art Sign Company.............G...... 717 264-4211
  Chambersburg (G-2906)
Athletic Lettering Inc ....F...... 717 840-6373
  York (G-20389)
Atlas Sign Group LLC.............G...... 724 935-2160
  Mars (G-10487)
Autograph Signs Inc.............G...... 412 371-2877
  Pittsburgh (G-14741)
B and B Signs and Graphics.............G...... 717 737-4467
  Mechanicsburg (G-10821)

Bedford Reinforced Plas Inc.............D...... 814 623-8125
  Bedford (G-1044)
Beistle Company.............B...... 717 532-2131
  Shippensburg (G-17517)
Blind and Vision Rehab.............F...... 412 325-7504
  Homestead (G-7683)
Blind and Vision Rehab.............D...... 412 368-4400
  Pittsburgh (G-14771)
Bonura Jr Cabinets By Bill.............G...... 412 793-6790
  Pittsburgh (G-14784)
Boyd Geyer Sign Corporation ....G...... 215 860-3008
  Newtown (G-12498)
Brands Imaging LLC.............G...... 215 279-7218
  Philadelphia (G-13477)
Brenneman Printing Inc ....E...... 717 299-2847
  Lancaster (G-8959)
Bright Sign and Maint Co Inc ....E...... 610 916-5100
  Leesport (G-9660)
Browns Graphic Solutions ....G...... 717 721-6160
  Lancaster (G-8962)
Bruners Sign Service Inc ....G...... 717 896-7699
  Halifax (G-6825)
Bunting Inc.............C...... 412 820-2200
  Verona (G-18750)
Bunting Stamp Company.............C...... 412 820-2200
  Verona (G-18752)
Bux Mont Awards.............G...... 215 855-5052
  Lansdale (G-9349)
Bux Mont Awards.............G...... 215 257-5432
  Sellersville (G-17341)
Cerra Signs Inc.............G...... 570 282-6283
  Carbondale (G-2670)
Character Translation Inc.............G...... 610 279-3970
  Norristown (G-12644)
Charles Steckman.............G...... 724 789-7066
  Renfrew (G-16638)
CHI Signs & Designs Inc ....G...... 412 517-8691
  Oakmont (G-12915)
Cima Network Inc.............D...... 267 308-0575
  Chalfont (G-2866)
Clarke System.............E...... 610 434-9889
  Allentown (G-171)
Cott Manufacturing Company.............E...... 724 625-3730
  Glassport (G-6411)
Crawford Dzignes Inc ....G...... 724 872-4644
  West Newton (G-19750)
Creative Management Svcs LLC ....E...... 610 863-1900
  Pen Argyl (G-13212)
Custom Finishing Inc ....F...... 215 269-7500
  Levittown (G-9829)
D & N Enterprise Inc ....G...... 215 238-9050
  Philadelphia (G-13597)
Dan Orner Signs.............G...... 610 876-6042
  Chester (G-3045)
David Weber Co Inc.............C...... 215 426-3500
  Philadelphia (G-13610)
Davis Trophies & Sports Wear.............G...... 610 455-0640
  West Chester (G-19533)
Dawson Performance Inc ....F...... 717 261-1414
  Chambersburg (G-2923)
Dayton Computer & Sign Inc ....G...... 814 257-8670
  Dayton (G-4038)
De Signs By Ben Pogue ....G...... 724 592-5013
  Jefferson (G-8270)
Deltronic Labs Inc.............E...... 215 997-8616
  Chalfont (G-2872)
Deversign.............G...... 610 583-2312
  Sharon Hill (G-17456)
Digital Sign Id Corporation ....G...... 800 407-9188
  Richboro (G-16674)
Direct Results Bsp Inc.............F...... 724 627-2040
  Waynesburg (G-19439)
Displays and Graphics Inc ....G...... 717 540-1481
  Harrisburg (G-7120)
Dobish Signs & Display Inc ....G...... 724 375-3943
  Aliquippa (G-73)
DS Services Group Corp ....F...... 724 350-6429
  Charleroi (G-3010)
Elevated Sign Solutions LLC ....G...... 267 374-4758
  Abington (G-11)
Elmark Sign & Graphics Inc.............F...... 610 692-0525
  West Chester (G-19550)
Elmark Sign & Graphics Inc.............F...... 610 692-0525
  West Chester (G-19549)
Excel Signworks.............G...... 412 337-2966
  Pittsburgh (G-14992)
Excl Inc.............E...... 412 856-7616
  Trafford (G-18456)
Exhibit G LLC.............G...... 215 302-2260
  Philadelphia (G-13687)

Express Sign Outlet Inc	G	610 336-9636	Wescosville *(G-19489)*
Eye Catcher Graphics Inc	G	814 946-4080	Altoona *(G-502)*
Eye Design LLC	E	610 409-1900	Trappe *(G-18468)*
EZ Signs LLC	G	866 349-5444	Phila *(G-13311)*
F and T LP	G	215 355-2060	Feasterville Trevose *(G-5907)*
F Creative Impressions Inc	G	215 743-7577	Philadelphia *(G-13690)*
Factor X Graffics LLC	F	717 458-8336	Carlisle *(G-2711)*
Fassinger Products & Engraving	G	412 563-6226	Pittsburgh *(G-15006)*
Fast Signs of Willow Grove	G	215 830-9960	Willow Grove *(G-20117)*
Fast Signs of Wynnewood	G	484 278-4839	Penn Valley *(G-13235)*
Fastsigns	G	570 824-7446	Wilkes Barre *(G-19920)*
Fastsigns	G	610 280-6100	Exton *(G-5676)*
Fastsigns	G	610 296-0400	Phoenixville *(G-14550)*
Fastsigns International Inc	G	717 840-6400	York *(G-20475)*
Fastsigns of Uniontown	G	724 430-7446	Uniontown *(G-18626)*
Fejes Signs	G	724 527-7446	Jeannette *(G-8256)*
Ferri Design	G	412 276-3700	Carnegie *(G-2767)*
Fine Sign Designs Inc	G	610 277-9860	Norristown *(G-12658)*
Fleet Decal & Graphics Inc	F	570 779-4343	Plymouth *(G-15818)*
Futura Identities Inc	G	215 333-3337	Philadelphia *(G-13736)*
G & L Designs	G	610 868-1381	Bethlehem *(G-1521)*
GEC Enterprises Inc	G	570 662-8898	Mansfield *(G-10415)*
Gesualdi Printing	G	215 785-3960	Bristol *(G-2148)*
Graber Letterin Inc	G	610 369-1112	Boyertown *(G-1913)*
Grid Electric Inc	E	610 466-7030	Coatesville *(G-3306)*
H & R Neon Service Inc	G	724 222-6115	Washington *(G-19183)*
Harris Graphics & Detailing	G	610 532-0209	Norwood *(G-12880)*
Hicks Signs	G	717 328-3300	Mercersburg *(G-10987)*
Horsts Handpainting	G	717 336-7098	Reinholds *(G-16632)*
Howard Industries Inc	E	814 833-7000	Fairview *(G-5828)*
Identification Systems Inc	E	814 774-9656	Girard *(G-6391)*
Imagineered Signs & Display	G	717 846-6114	York *(G-20534)*
Interstate Self Storage	G	724 662-1186	Mercer *(G-10965)*
J & P Incorporated	G	610 759-2378	Nazareth *(G-11972)*
J & S Signco Inc	G	717 657-3800	Harrisburg *(G-7156)*
J Margulis Inc	G	215 739-9100	Bala Cynwyd *(G-881)*
Jack Murray Design	G	610 845-9154	Barto *(G-944)*
Jalite Inc	G	570 491-2205	Matamoras *(G-10539)*
Jeff Enterprises Inc	F	610 434-7353	Allentown *(G-268)*
Keystone Signs	G	717 486-5381	Mount Holly Springs *(G-11635)*
Kgc Enterprises Inc	E	610 497-0111	Aston *(G-771)*
Klein Electric Advertising Inc	F	215 657-6984	Willow Grove *(G-20125)*
Kochmer Graphics	G	570 222-5713	Clifford *(G-3246)*
Koroteo Investments Inc	G	570 342-4422	Scranton *(G-17252)*
Krohmalys Printing Co	G	412 271-4234	Pittsburgh *(G-15201)*

Kruppko Inc	F	610 489-2334	Royersford *(G-16856)*
Kurt Lebo	G	610 682-4071	Fleetwood *(G-5975)*
Laminators Incorporated	D	215 723-5285	Hatfield *(G-7362)*
Lancaster Sign Source Inc	F	717 569-7606	Lancaster *(G-9106)*
Lane Display Inc	G	610 361-1110	Chadds Ford *(G-2854)*
Lark Enterprises Inc	E	724 657-2001	New Castle *(G-12114)*
Laurelind Corp	G	215 368-5800	Montgomeryville *(G-11401)*
Laurelind Corp	G	215 230-4737	Montgomeryville *(G-11402)*
Linbob LLC	G	610 375-7446	Reading *(G-16429)*
Lionette Enterprises	G	814 274-9401	Coudersport *(G-3784)*
Lucky Sign Shop Inc	G	610 459-5825	Glen Mills *(G-6439)*
M & M Displays Inc	F	800 874-7171	Philadelphia *(G-13980)*
Madera Cabinets	F	412 793-5850	Pittsburgh *(G-15246)*
Martino Signs Inc	F	610 622-7446	Yeadon *(G-20355)*
Martino Signs Inc	G	610 355-9269	Newtown Square *(G-12584)*
Matthews International Corp	B	412 571-5500	Pittsburgh *(G-15266)*
Media Advantage Inc	G	800 985-5596	Huntingdon Valley *(G-8012)*
Minahan Corporation	G	814 288-1561	Johnstown *(G-8409)*
Mobile Technology Graphics LLC	G	610 838-8075	Hellertown *(G-7559)*
Morgan Signs Inc	E	814 238-5051	State College *(G-17994)*
MRC Electric	G	267 988-4370	Warminster *(G-18925)*
Mt Displays LLC	F	201 636-4144	Hanover Township *(G-6998)*
Mundorf Sign Co	G	717 854-3071	York *(G-20608)*
Naamans Creek Co Inc	G	610 268-3833	Avondale *(G-855)*
Nation-Wide Sign Service Inc	G	888 234-5300	Drexel Hill *(G-4369)*
National Signs Inc	G	724 375-3083	Aliquippa *(G-87)*
North American Display	G	412 209-9988	Pittsburgh *(G-15346)*
One Sign Inc	G	412 478-6809	Natrona Heights *(G-11948)*
Pannier Corporation	E	724 265-4900	Gibsonia *(G-6348)*
Pannier Corporation	E	412 492-1400	Glenshaw *(G-6495)*
Peachtree City Foamcraft Inc	G	610 769-0661	Schnecksville *(G-17142)*
Pike Graphics Inc	F	215 836-9120	Flourtown *(G-5990)*
Pioneer Supply Company Inc	G	856 314-8299	Greensburg *(G-6701)*
Pls Signs LLC	G	215 269-1400	Fairless Hills *(G-5791)*
Pmdi Signs Inc	G	215 526-0898	Ivyland *(G-8220)*
Promotion Centre Inc	E	717 843-1582	York *(G-20645)*
Purpose 1 LLC	G	717 232-9077	Lemoyne *(G-9749)*
R A Egan Sign & Awng Co Inc	F	610 777-3795	Reading *(G-16482)*
Ras Sports Inc	E	814 833-9111	Erie *(G-5457)*
Raucmin Seven LLC	G	412 374-1420	Monroeville *(G-11352)*
Reidler Decal Corporation	E	800 628-7770	Saint Clair *(G-16939)*
Reliable Sign & Striping Inc	G	610 767-8090	Slatington *(G-17612)*
Rick Weyand Signs	G	814 893-5524	Stoystown *(G-18084)*
RMS Kunkle Inc	G	717 564-8829	Harrisburg *(G-7208)*
Ruck Engineering Inc	G	412 835-2408	Bethel Park *(G-1431)*

Ryder Graphics	G	717 697-0187	Mechanicsburg *(G-10886)*
S & H Hardware & Supply Co	F	215 745-9375	Philadelphia *(G-14269)*
S & H Hardware & Supply Co	G	267 288-5950	Huntingdon Valley *(G-8033)*
Saupp Signs Co LLC	G	814 342-2100	Philipsburg *(G-14526)*
Savemypixcom Inc	G	800 535-6299	Thornton *(G-18355)*
Shamrock Building Services Inc	E	412 279-2800	Carnegie *(G-2792)*
Sign Here Inc	F	814 453-6711	Erie *(G-5478)*
Sign Here Sign Co Inc	G	845 858-6366	Matamoras *(G-10540)*
Sign O Rama Inc	G	215 784-9494	Willow Grove *(G-20141)*
Sign Services Inc	G	412 996-0824	East Pittsburgh *(G-4598)*
Sign Shop of The Poconos Inc	G	347 972-1775	Wind Gap *(G-20172)*
Sign Spot	G	570 455-7775	Hazleton *(G-7527)*
Sign Stop	G	814 238-3338	State College *(G-18024)*
Signarama	F	717 397-3173	Lancaster *(G-9199)*
Signs By Design	G	717 626-6212	Lancaster *(G-9201)*
Signs By Renee	G	814 763-4206	Saegertown *(G-16934)*
Signs By Sam	G	724 752-3711	Ellwood City *(G-4949)*
Signs By Tomorrow	G	717 757-4909	York *(G-20668)*
Signs By Tomorrow	G	724 838-9060	Greensburg *(G-6714)*
Signs By Tomorrow	G	484 356-0707	West Chester *(G-19640)*
Signs By Tomorrow Inc	G	717 975-2456	Lemoyne *(G-9753)*
Signs By Tomorrow USA Inc	G	484 592-0404	Ardmore *(G-716)*
Signs Now	G	717 633-5864	Hanover *(G-6952)*
Signs Now	G	814 453-6564	Erie *(G-5479)*
Signstat	F	724 527-7475	Jeannette *(G-8264)*
Sir Speedy 7108 Inc	F	412 787-9898	Pittsburgh *(G-15542)*
Skuta Signs of All Kinds	G	724 863-6159	Irwin *(G-8201)*
Smart Systems Inc	G	412 323-2128	Pittsburgh *(G-15546)*
Solar Technology Inc	D	610 391-8600	Allentown *(G-396)*
Sskj Enterprises Inc	G	412 494-3308	Carnegie *(G-2794)*
Star Organization Inc	G	412 374-1420	Monroeville *(G-11359)*
Steel City Graphics Inc	G	724 942-5699	Canonsburg *(G-2640)*
Steele Print Inc	G	724 758-6178	Ellwood City *(G-4952)*
Steve Schwartz Associates Inc	E	412 765-3400	Pittsburgh *(G-15583)*
Stoner Graphix Inc	G	717 469-7716	Hummelstown *(G-7925)*
Sunsational Signs Win Tinting	G	610 277-4344	Norristown *(G-12715)*
Surf & Turf Enterprises	G	610 338-0274	Morton *(G-11593)*
T C B Displays Inc	E	610 983-0500	Phoenixville *(G-14582)*
Terre Trophy Co	G	610 777-2050	Reading *(G-16536)*
Thomas Henry Potoeski	G	570 922-3361	Millmont *(G-11220)*
Tjaws LLC	G	570 344-2117	Scranton *(G-17304)*
Tomdel Inc	G	724 519-2697	Monroeville *(G-11360)*
Triton Signs Incorporated	G	610 495-4747	Pottstown *(G-16060)*
Two Toys Inc	G	717 840-6400	York *(G-20693)*
Universal Awnings & Signs Inc	G	215 634-7150	Philadelphia *(G-14425)*

PRODUCT

Universal Services Assoc Inc ....E 610 461-0300
Folcroft **(G-6018)**
US Municipal Supply Inc ....E 610 292-9450
Huntingdon **(G-7958)**
Verners Paint Center Inc ....F 724 224-7445
Tarentum **(G-18253)**
Vh Service LLC.........................G...... 267 808-9745
Feasterville Trevose **(G-5938)**
Viking Signs Inc ....G...... 570 455-4369
Hazleton **(G-7535)**
Vinyl Dizzign..........................G...... 267 246-7725
Lansdale **(G-9425)**
Vinyl Graphics Unlimited ....G...... 814 226-7887
Shippenville **(G-17566)**
Visualize Digitized LLC................G...... 610 494-9504
Upper Chichester **(G-18676)**
Vpak Technology ....G...... 610 458-8600
Downingtown **(G-4262)**
Web Paint Inc ....F 570 208-2528
Wilkes Barre **(G-19970)**
Wenning Entertainment LLC ....F 412 292-8776
East Mc Keesport **(G-4582)**
West Signs Inc ....G...... 724 443-5588
Allison Park **(G-467)**
White Trophy Co Inc ....G...... 215 638-9134
Bensalem **(G-1272)**
William F and Kathy A Yeager...........G...... 717 665-6964
Manheim **(G-10407)**
William Klein Signs Inc................G...... 610 374-5371
Reading **(G-16565)**
Yesco Handyman Services ....G...... 724 206-9541
Washington **(G-19249)**
Yesco New Castle Elec Sup ....G...... 724 656-0911
New Castle **(G-12171)**

SIGNS & ADVERTISING SPECIALTIES:
Artwork, Advertising

Rich-Art Sign Co Inc ....G...... 215 922-1539
Philadelphia **(G-14245)**
Simone Associates Inc ....G...... 717 274-3621
Lebanon **(G-9631)**

SIGNS & ADVERTISING SPECIALTIES:
Letters For Signs, Metal

Cariks Custom Decor ....G...... 412 882-1511
Pittsburgh **(G-14812)**
City Engraving & Awards LLC............G...... 215 731-0200
Philadelphia **(G-13547)**
Letterco Inc..........................G...... 215 721-9010
Souderton **(G-17750)**
Simco Sign Studios Inc ....F 610 534-5550
Collingdale **(G-3410)**
Spencer Industries Inc ....F 215 634-2700
Philadelphia **(G-14334)**
Weekend Directional Services...........D...... 800 494-4954
Beaver **(G-995)**

SIGNS & ADVERTISING SPECIALTIES:
Novelties

Coinco Inc............................E 814 425-7476
Cochranton **(G-3338)**
Coinco Inc............................E 814 425-7407
Cochranton **(G-3337)**
Custom Plastic Specialties LLC ....C...... 814 838-6471
Erie **(G-5239)**
Glass U LLC...........................F 855 687-7423
Philadelphia **(G-13765)**
Hanover Pen Corp......................E 717 637-3729
Hanover **(G-6897)**
Richman Industries Inc ....G...... 717 561-1766
Harrisburg **(G-7206)**
Wlek Inc ....C...... 800 772-8247
Erie **(G-5531)**

SIGNS & ADVERTISING SPECIALTIES: Signs

39 Design Company Inc ....G...... 215 563-1320
Wayne **(G-19291)**
Abby Signs of PA......................G...... 570 494-0600
Montoursville **(G-11428)**
Adelphia Graphic Systems Inc ....D...... 610 363-8150
Exton **(G-5636)**
Advision Signs Inc....................F 412 788-8440
Pittsburgh **(G-14653)**
Aerial Signs & Awnings Inc.............F 610 494-1415
Chester **(G-3037)**
Allimage Graphics LLC ....G...... 814 728-8650
Warren **(G-19009)**

Alphabet Signs Inc....................G...... 800 582-6366
Gap **(G-6248)**
Ameraquick Sign Systems ....G...... 724 733-5906
Murrysville **(G-11847)**
Architectural Sign Associates ....F 412 563-5657
Pittsburgh **(G-14717)**
Bernard Sign Corporation ....E 215 425-1700
Philadelphia **(G-13456)**
Bright Sign Co Inc....................G...... 215 563-9480
Philadelphia **(G-13481)**
Bunting Graphics Inc..................C...... 412 481-0445
Verona **(G-18751)**
Butz Sign Co..........................G...... 717 397-8565
Lancaster **(G-8966)**
C & G Wilcox Engrv & Images ....G...... 570 265-3621
Towanda **(G-18422)**
Charles R Eckert Signs Inc ....G...... 717 733-4601
Ephrata **(G-5096)**
Compass Sign Co LLC ....E 215 639-6777
Bensalem **(G-1172)**
Connor Sign Group Ltd ....G...... 215 741-1299
Langhorne **(G-9285)**
Creation Cabinetry & Sign Co...........G...... 717 246-3386
Red Lion **(G-16591)**
Crest Advertising Co ....F 724 774-4413
Monaca **(G-11289)**
Custom Signs Inc......................F 814 786-7232
Grove City **(G-6783)**
Davis Sign Service LLC ....G...... 412 856-5535
Monroeville **(G-11332)**
Digital Dsgns Grphics Sgns LLC.........G...... 724 568-1626
Gibsonia **(G-6331)**
East Coast Sign Advg Co Inc............C...... 888 724-0380
Bristol **(G-2136)**
Endagraph Inc ....E 724 327-9384
Export **(G-5601)**
F Creative Impressions Inc ....G...... 215 743-7577
Lansdowne **(G-9432)**
Fm2 Inc ....G...... 814 874-0090
Erie **(G-5295)**
Freds Signs ....G...... 412 741-3153
Pittsburgh **(G-15036)**
G S P Signs & Banners Inc ....G...... 610 430-7000
West Chester **(G-19556)**
Gallo Design Group ....G...... 724 628-0198
Connellsville **(G-3497)**
Graphics 22 Signs Inc ....F 412 422-1125
Pittsburgh **(G-15058)**
H H Seiferth Associates Inc ....G...... 412 281-4983
Pittsburgh **(G-15070)**
Heimer Enterprises Inc.................G...... 814 234-7446
State College **(G-17974)**
Horst Signs ....F 717 866-8899
Myerstown **(G-11887)**
Impressive Signs Inc ....G...... 717 848-9305
York **(G-20535)**
J L Screen Printing ....G...... 724 696-5630
Ruffs Dale **(G-16873)**
JMB Signs LLC.........................G...... 814 933-9725
State College **(G-17980)**
Ken Leaman Signs......................G...... 717 295-4531
Lancaster **(G-9081)**
Keystone Sign Systems Inc ....G...... 717 319-2265
Mechanicsburg **(G-10864)**
Lake Shore Industries Inc ....F 814 456-4277
Erie **(G-5356)**
Leonard Dick ....G...... 717 334-8992
Gettysburg **(G-6304)**
Marsh Creek Signs Inc ....G...... 610 458-5503
Downingtown **(G-4239)**
Montgomery Signs Inc ....G...... 610 834-5400
Conshohocken **(G-3578)**
MWM Graphics ....F 610 692-0525
West Chester **(G-19603)**
Nite Lite Sign Co ....G...... 570 649-5825
Turbotville **(G-18556)**
NMB Signs Inc.........................F 412 344-5700
Pittsburgh **(G-15342)**
Pannier Corporation ....F 412 323-4900
Pittsburgh **(G-15368)**
Penn Sign Company ....G...... 717 732-8900
Enola **(G-5083)**
Precision Sign & Awning ....G...... 412 281-0330
Pittsburgh **(G-15432)**
Rehoboth Signs ....G...... 717 458-8520
Mechanicsburg **(G-10884)**
Richland Plastics & Engraving ....G...... 814 266-3002
Johnstown **(G-8431)**
Roe Fabricators Inc ....F 610 485-4990
Chester **(G-3061)**

Sign Concepts Inc.....................G...... 610 586-7070
Folsom **(G-6028)**
Sign Design Associates Inc ....G...... 610 791-9301
Allentown **(G-390)**
Sign Guy ....G...... 724 483-2200
Monongahela **(G-11315)**
Sign Maker Inc ....G...... 215 676-6711
Philadelphia **(G-14304)**
Signs of Excellence Inc ....G...... 724 325-7446
Murrysville **(G-11867)**
Stop N Go Signs.......................G...... 570 374-3939
Selinsgrove **(G-17336)**
Sun and Shade Inc.....................G...... 610 409-0366
Boyertown **(G-1930)**
Superior Respiratory Home Care ....G...... 717 560-7806
Lancaster **(G-9209)**
Trafcon Industries Inc.................E 717 691-8007
Mechanicsburg **(G-10899)**
Traffic & Safety Signs Inc ....G...... 610 925-1990
Kennett Square **(G-8550)**
Upper Room Inc ....F 724 437-5815
Uniontown **(G-18646)**
Wertner Signs ....G...... 717 597-4502
Greencastle **(G-6642)**

SIGNS & ADVERTSG SPECIALTIES:
Displays/Cutouts Window/Lobby

Berm Studios Incorporated..............D...... 610 622-2100
Garnet Valley **(G-6265)**
Derse Inc.............................D...... 724 772-4853
Warrendale **(G-19071)**
Leon L Berkowitz Co ....F 215 654-0800
Glenside **(G-6527)**
Merchandising Methods Inc..............E 215 262-4842
Doylestown **(G-4315)**
Pak-It Displays Inc ....E 215 638-7510
Bensalem **(G-1237)**
Rosuco Inc............................G...... 724 297-5610
Worthington **(G-20232)**
Southern Glazer s Wine and Sp..........C...... 610 265-6800
King of Prussia **(G-8678)**
Sperry Graphic Inc ....E 610 534-8585
Folcroft **(G-6016)**
Vision Products Inc ....D...... 724 274-0767
Cheswick **(G-3121)**
Visual Information Services ....G...... 800 777-3565
Denver **(G-4096)**

SIGNS, ELECTRICAL: Wholesalers

Diversified Traffic Pdts Inc...........C...... 717 428-0222
Seven Valleys **(G-17377)**
Signstat..............................F 724 527-7475
Jeannette **(G-8264)**

SIGNS, EXC ELECTRIC, WHOLESALE

A Funky Little Sign Shop ....G...... 215 489-2880
Doylestown **(G-4266)**
Boulevard Sports ....G...... 724 378-9191
Aliquippa **(G-69)**
Fedex Office & Print Svcs Inc ....G...... 215 576-1687
Jenkintown **(G-8287)**
Gregory Troyer ....G...... 717 393-0233
Bird In Hand **(G-1676)**
Lionette Enterprises ....G...... 814 274-9401
Coudersport **(G-3784)**
Robert H Berenson ....G...... 610 642-9380
Haverford **(G-7414)**
Skuta Signs of All Kinds ....G...... 724 863-6159
Irwin **(G-8201)**

SIGNS: Electrical

Accel Sign Group Inc..................F 412 781-7735
Pittsburgh **(G-14637)**
Addaren Holdings LLC..................G...... 267 387-6029
Horsham **(G-7779)**
Affordable Signs Co Inc ....F 215 671-0646
Philadelphia **(G-13352)**
Alpine Sign and Lighting Inc ....F 717 246-2376
Dallastown **(G-3970)**
Bartlett Signs........................G...... 814 392-7082
Erie **(G-5203)**
Blair Companies ....D...... 814 949-8280
Altoona **(G-479)**
Blair Companies ....C...... 814 949-8287
Altoona **(G-480)**
Brown Signs Inc.......................G...... 717 866-2669
Richland **(G-16683)**

Burkhart & Quinn Sign Co Inc ....F 717 367-1375
   Elizabethtown (G-4867)
Capitol Sign Company Inc ....D 215 822-0166
   Lansdale (G-9350)
Clapper Enterprises Inc ....E 570 368-3327
   Williamsport (G-19998)
Decora Industries Inc ....D 215 698-2600
   Philadelphia (G-13614)
Deforest Signs & Lighting Inc ....F 717 564-6102
   Harrisburg (G-7117)
Denron Sign Co Inc ....G 610 269-6622
   Downingtown (G-4222)
Devaltronix Inc ....F 215 331-9600
   Philadelphia (G-13625)
ELM Enterprises Inc ....E 724 452-8699
   Zelienople (G-20798)
Gray Sign Advertising ....G 724 224-5008
   Tarentum (G-18244)
Horizon Signs LLC ....F 215 538-2600
   Quakertown (G-16200)
Image 360 ....G 717 317-9147
   Harrisburg (G-7153)
L & H Signs Inc ....E 610 374-2748
   Reading (G-16424)
Lancaster Sign Co Inc ....F 717 284-3500
   New Providence (G-12434)
Lititz Sign Company ....G 717 626-7715
   Lititz (G-10024)
Mac Sign Systems Inc ....F 570 347-7446
   Scranton (G-17257)
Monument Sign Mfg LLC ....G 570 366-9505
   Orwigsburg (G-13050)
Permanent Sign & Display ....G 610 736-3222
   Reading (G-16469)
Precisions Signs and Awning ....G 412 278-0400
   Carnegie (G-2782)
R & K Neon Inc ....G 724 834-8570
   Greensburg (G-6709)
Reed Sign Company ....F 215 679-5066
   Pennsburg (G-13256)
Rhoads Sign Systems ....G 717 776-7309
   Newville (G-12609)
Sarro Signs Inc ....G 610 444-2020
   Kennett Square (G-8541)
Scepter Signs Inc ....G 610 326-7446
   Pottstown (G-16043)
Sekula Sign Corporation ....E 814 371-4650
   Du Bois (G-4417)
Sign Medix Inc ....F 717 396-9749
   Lancaster (G-9198)
Signage Unlimited Inc ....F 610 647-6962
   Malvern (G-10316)
Signs By Rick Inc ....G 724 287-3887
   Butler (G-2441)
Signs Service & Crane Inc ....G 724 515-5272
   Irwin (G-8200)
Stephanie McClain ....G 267 820-9273
   Philadelphia (G-14345)
Sturdevant Signs ....G 814 723-3361
   Warren (G-19048)
TApp Technology LLC ....G 800 288-3184
   Ardmore (G-721)
Upper Darby Sign Company ....D 610 518-5881
   Downingtown (G-4259)
Wiley Electric Sign Service ....G 610 759-8167
   Nazareth (G-11994)

SIGNS: Neon

A C Signs Inc ....G 215 465-0274
   Philadelphia (G-13326)
Altoona Neon Sign Service ....G 814 942-7488
   Altoona (G-472)
Atlas Neon Sign Corp ....G 724 935-2171
   Warrendale (G-19068)
Bartush Signs Inc ....E 570 366-2311
   Orwigsburg (G-13040)
City Sign Service Inc ....E 800 523-4452
   Horsham (G-7804)
Crichton Diversfd Ventures LLC ....G 814 288-1561
   Johnstown (G-8367)
Edmiston Signs ....G 814 742-8930
   Bellwood (G-1137)
Fieseler Neon Sign Co ....G 570 655-2976
   Pittston (G-15750)
Forman Sign Co ....E 215 827-6500
   Philadelphia (G-13715)
Graham Sign Company ....G 814 765-7199
   Clearfield (G-3220)
Image Signs Inc ....G 814 946-4663
   Altoona (G-515)

Landis Neon Sign Co Inc ....G 717 397-0588
   Lancaster (G-9107)
Laret Sign Co ....G 814 695-4455
   Hollidaysburg (G-7650)
Laucks and Spaulding Inc ....F 717 845-3312
   York (G-20562)
Lehigh Valley Sign & Service ....G 610 760-8590
   Germansville (G-6280)
Leiphart Enterprises LLC ....G 717 938-4100
   Lewisberry (G-9888)
Neon Doctor LLC ....G 412 885-7075
   Pittsburgh (G-15326)
Neon Trading ....G 610 530-2988
   Allentown (G-327)
Prism Fiber Optics Inc ....G 412 802-0750
   Pittsburgh (G-15447)
Sign ME Up LLC ....G 814 931-0933
   Hollidaysburg (G-7655)
Slavic Group Inc ....G 724 437-6756
   Lemont Furnace (G-9737)
W J Strickler Signs Inc ....E 717 624-8450
   New Oxford (G-12425)
Widmer Sign Company Inc ....G 570 343-0319
   Scranton (G-17313)

SILICON & CHROMIUM

R I Lampus Company ....C 412 362-3800
   Springdale (G-17900)

SILICON: Pure

Ae Polysilicon Corporation ....E 215 337-8183
   Fairless Hills (G-5771)
RSI Silicon Products LLC ....E 610 258-3100
   Easton (G-4749)

SILICONE RESINS

Insta-Mold Products Inc ....F 610 935-7270
   Oaks (G-12933)
Rebtech Corporation ....F 570 421-6616
   Stroudsburg (G-18138)

SILICONES

Gelest Inc ....G 215 547-1015
   Morrisville (G-11560)
Wacker Chemical Corporation ....D 610 336-2700
   Allentown (G-428)

SILK SCREEN DESIGN SVCS

Action Screen Printing Inc ....F 610 359-1777
   Broomall (G-2277)
Air Conway Inc ....F 610 534-0500
   Collingdale (G-3402)
Bee Offset Printing ....G 610 253-0926
   Easton (G-4651)
Bubco Enterprise Inc ....G 724 274-4930
   Cheswick (G-3102)
Designs Unlimited ....G 717 367-4405
   Elizabethtown (G-4872)
Footers Inc ....G 610 437-2233
   Allentown (G-217)
Kampus Klothes Inc ....G 215 357-0892
   Warminster (G-18904)
Kevin OBrien Studio Inc ....G 215 923-6378
   Philadelphia (G-13929)
La Perla LLC ....G 717 561-1257
   Harrisburg (G-7166)
New Look Uniform & Embroidery ....F 814 944-5515
   Altoona (G-530)
R & J Trophy ....G 570 345-2277
   Pine Grove (G-14604)
Rich-Art Sign Co Inc ....G 215 922-1539
   Philadelphia (G-14245)

SILOS: Meal

Eagle Industrial Solutions ....G 610 509-8275
   Nazareth (G-11962)
Sollenberger Silos LLC ....G 717 264-9588
   Chambersburg (G-2976)

SILVER BULLION PRODUCTION

Cleogeo Inc ....G 610 868-7200
   Bethlehem (G-1485)

SILVERSMITHS

Martina Guerra Goldsmith ....G 570 398-1833
   Jersey Shore (G-8318)

SILVERWARE & PLATED WARE

Carson Industries Inc ....E 724 295-5147
   Freeport (G-6201)
Daniel C Tanney Inc ....D 215 639-3131
   Bensalem (G-1179)
L & L K Incorporated ....E 215 732-2614
   Philadelphia (G-13948)
Meighen Jinjou ....G 717 846-5600
   York (G-20585)

SIMULATORS: Flight

Fidelity Flight Simulation Inc ....F 412 321-3280
   Pittsburgh (G-15016)
Royal Karina Air Service Inc ....G 215 321-3981
   Yardley (G-20336)
Simulation Live Fire Training ....G 412 787-2832
   Pittsburgh (G-15540)

SINK TOPS, PLASTIC LAMINATED

K S Manufacturing Co LP ....F 412 931-5365
   Pittsburgh (G-15160)

SKIDS

Frey Pallet Corporation ....F 724 564-1888
   Smithfield (G-17649)

SKIDS: Wood

Howe Wood Products Inc ....F 717 266-9855
   York (G-20529)
Rebs Pallet Co Inc ....G 570 386-5516
   Andreas (G-640)

SKILL TRAINING CENTER

Barc Developmental Services ....E 215 794-0800
   Holicong (G-7638)

SKIN CARE PRDTS: Suntan Lotions & Oils

Teeter Enterprises Inc ....G 717 732-5994
   Enola (G-5086)

SKYLIGHTS

Extech/Exterior Tech Inc ....E 412 781-0991
   Pittsburgh (G-14995)
Traco Delaware Inc ....F 724 776-7000
   Cranberry Township (G-3856)
Voegele Company Inc ....E 412 781-0940
   Pittsburgh (G-15705)

SLAB & TILE, ROOFING: Concrete

Dectile Harkus Construction ....E 724 789-7125
   Butler (G-2393)

SLAB & TILE: Precast Concrete, Floor

All Aspects ....G 610 292-1955
   Norristown (G-12631)

SLABS: Steel

Jadco Manufacturing Inc ....E 724 452-5252
   Harmony (G-7070)

SLAG PRDTS

Tms International Corp ....E 215 956-5500
   Horsham (G-7860)

SLAG: Crushed Or Ground

Beaver Valley Slag Inc ....F 724 378-8888
   Aliquippa (G-68)
Beaver Valley Slag Inc ....F 724 773-0444
   Monaca (G-11284)
International Mill Service ....A 215 956-5500
   Horsham (G-7824)
Mill Services Corp ....F 412 678-6141
   Glassport (G-6413)
Tms International LLC ....G 724 746-5377
   Houston (G-7881)
Tms International LLC ....D 215 956-5500
   Horsham (G-7859)
Tms International LLC ....F 724 929-4515
   Belle Vernon (G-1088)

PRODUCT

SLATE PRDTS

Penn Big Bed Slate Co Inc ....D...... 610 767-4601
Slatington **(G-17611)**
Williams & Sons Slate & Tile ....E...... 610 863-4161
Wind Gap **(G-20175)**

SLATE: Crushed & Broken

Capozzolo Brothers ....G...... 610 588-7702
Bangor **(G-909)**
Hanson Aggregates PA LLC ....E...... 814 355-4226
Bellefonte **(G-1103)**

SLAUGHTERING & MEAT PACKING

Cargill Meat Solutions Corp ....A...... 570 746-3000
Wyalusing **(G-20248)**
Dietz & Watson Inc ....A...... 800 333-1974
Philadelphia **(G-13631)**
Hazle Park Packing Co ....E...... 570 455-7571
Hazle Township **(G-7461)**
Heinnickel Farms Inc ....G...... 724 837-9254
Greensburg **(G-6673)**
Jbs Packerland Inc ....F...... 215 723-5559
Souderton **(G-17743)**
Jbs Souderton Inc ....A...... 215 723-5555
Souderton **(G-17744)**
Lone Star Western Beef Inc ....G...... 484 509-2093
Reading **(G-16433)**
Nicholas Meat Packing Co ....C...... 570 725-3511
Loganton **(G-10097)**
Zrile Brothers Packing Inc ....G...... 724 528-9246
West Middlesex **(G-19733)**

SLIDES & EXHIBITS: Prepared

Innovative Exhibit Productions ....G...... 610 770-9833
Allentown **(G-261)**

SLINGS: Lifting, Made From Purchased Wire

I & I Sling Inc ....E...... 800 874-3539
Aston **(G-769)**
Nelson Wire Rope Corporation ....F...... 215 721-9449
Hatfield **(G-7373)**

SLINGS: Rope

Safety Sling Company Inc ....F...... 412 231-6684
Pittsburgh **(G-15506)**

SMOKE DETECTORS

Van Air Inc ....E...... 814 774-2631
Lake City **(G-8909)**

SNOW REMOVAL EQPT: Residential

A Cut Above Lawn Care & Landsp ....G...... 484 239-6825
Northampton **(G-12841)**
Iceblox Inc ....G...... 717 697-1900
Mechanicsburg **(G-10856)**
Thomas Nay LLC ....F...... 215 613-8367
Philadelphia **(G-14388)**

SNOWMOBILE DEALERS

Smouse Trucks & Vans Inc ....G...... 724 887-7777
Mount Pleasant **(G-11718)**
T E Fletcher Snowmobiles ....G...... 724 253-3225
Conneaut Lake **(G-3480)**

SNOWMOBILES

J&B Outdoor Center ....G...... 814 848-3838
Ulysses **(G-18603)**
Polar Blox Inc ....G...... 814 629-7397
Hollsopple **(G-7660)**
T E Fletcher Snowmobiles ....G...... 724 253-3225
Conneaut Lake **(G-3480)**

SOAP DISHES: Vitreous China

Soap Alchemy LLC ....G...... 412 671-4278
New Galilee **(G-12222)**

SOAPS & DETERGENTS

Advanced Skin Technologies Inc ....G...... 610 488-7643
Bernville **(G-1295)**
Alex C Fergusson LLC ....D...... 717 264-9147
Chambersburg **(G-2899)**
Bulk Chemicals Inc ....F...... 610 926-4128
Mohrsville **(G-11275)**

Cei-Douglassville Inc ....D...... 610 385-9500
Douglassville **(G-4172)**
Diversey Inc ....D...... 570 421-7850
East Stroudsburg **(G-4613)**
Ecolab Inc ....E...... 610 521-1072
Philadelphia **(G-13314)**
Essence of Old Woods ....G...... 215 258-0852
Green Lane **(G-6588)**
Evergreen Synergies LLC ....E...... 610 239-9425
King of Prussia **(G-8617)**
Friendly Organic LLC ....G...... 609 709-2924
Philadelphia **(G-13726)**
Good Health Natural Pdts Inc ....G...... 570 655-0823
Pittston **(G-15753)**
National Chemical Labs PA Inc ....C...... 215 922-1200
Philadelphia **(G-14053)**
Precision Finishing Inc ....E...... 215 257-6862
Quakertown **(G-16232)**
Select Medical Systems Inc ....F...... 215 207-9003
Philadelphia **(G-14293)**
Sensible Organics Inc ....E...... 724 891-4560
Beaver Falls **(G-1011)**
Soap Plant Inc ....G...... 724 656-3601
New Castle **(G-12154)**
Soaphies ....G...... 814 861-7627
State College **(G-18027)**
Straight Arrow Products Inc ....G...... 610 882-9606
Bethlehem **(G-1633)**
T&T Buttas LLC ....G...... 833 251-1357
Philadelphia **(G-14365)**
Tip Top Resources LLC ....G...... 407 818-6937
Reedsville **(G-16628)**
United Refining Company ....G...... 724 274-0885
Springdale **(G-17904)**
Wound Care Concepts Inc ....E...... 215 788-2700
Bristol **(G-2218)**

SOAPS & DETERGENTS: Dishwashing Compounds

Clean Concepts Group LLC ....G...... 908 229-8812
Washington Crossing **(G-19254)**

SOAPS & DETERGENTS: Glycerin, Crude Or Refined, From Fats

Eco Solution Distributing LLC ....F...... 724 941-4140
Pittsburgh **(G-14959)**

SOAPS & DETERGENTS: Scouring Compounds

Zep Inc ....C...... 610 295-1360
Breinigsville **(G-2033)**

SOCIAL SVCS CENTER

Achieva ....D...... 412 221-6609
Bridgeville **(G-2052)**

SOCIAL SVCS: Individual & Family

Parc Productions ....G...... 724 283-3300
Butler **(G-2431)**

SOCKETS & RECEPTACLES: Lamp, Electric Wiring Devices

Rubbermaid Commercial Pdts LLC ....F....... 570 622-7715
Pottsville **(G-16096)**

SOFT DRINKS WHOLESALERS

Days Beverage Inc ....D...... 215 990-0983
Newtown Square **(G-12572)**
Pepsi-Cola Metro Btlg Co Inc ....D...... 570 344-1159
Pittston **(G-15775)**
Pepsi-Cola Metro Btlg Co Inc ....E...... 814 834-5700
Saint Marys **(G-17005)**

SOFTWARE PUBLISHERS: Application

Aegis Industrial Software Corp ....E...... 215 773-3571
Horsham **(G-7780)**
Algorhythm Diagnostics LLC ....G...... 312 813-2959
Philadelphia **(G-13364)**
Ally Home Care Ltd Lblty Co ....G...... 800 930-0587
West Chester **(G-19496)**
Alumties Inc ....G...... 720 570-6259
Havertown **(G-7416)**
Andrew Torba ....G...... 570 209-1622
Moosic **(G-11503)**

Ansys Inc ....C...... 884 462-6797
Canonsburg **(G-2541)**
Applied Software Inc ....G...... 215 297-9441
New Hope **(G-12297)**
Arcweb Technologies LLC ....G...... 800 846-7980
Philadelphia **(G-13409)**
Ark Ideaz Inc ....G...... 610 246-9106
Pottstown **(G-15943)**
Artisan Mobile Inc ....F...... 610 209-1959
Philadelphia **(G-13414)**
Bentley Systems Incorporated ....C...... 610 458-5000
Exton **(G-5653)**
Bentley Systems Incorporated ....B...... 610 458-5000
Exton **(G-5654)**
Blupanda LLC ....G...... 724 494-2077
Apollo **(G-666)**
Bodyx LLC ....G...... 610 519-9999
Bryn Mawr **(G-2316)**
Byrd Alley LLC ....F...... 215 669-0068
Philadelphia **(G-13489)**
Centify LLC ....G...... 215 421-8375
Oreland **(G-13019)**
Ciright Automation LLC ....G...... 855 247-4448
Conshohocken **(G-3528)**
Cleararmor Solutions Corp ....G...... 610 816-0101
Riegelsville **(G-16744)**
Cognitive Oprtonal Systems LLC ....G...... 908 672-4711
Philadelphia **(G-13558)**
Compututor Inc ....G...... 610 260-0300
Conshohocken **(G-3531)**
Connectedsign LLC ....G...... 717 490-6431
Lancaster **(G-8985)**
Connectify Inc ....F...... 215 854-8432
Philadelphia **(G-13570)**
Cyrus-Xp Inc ....E...... 610 986-8408
Ardmore **(G-706)**
Digital Concepts Inc ....F...... 724 745-4000
Canonsburg **(G-2577)**
Dimension Data North Amer Inc ....E...... 484 362-2563
Malvern **(G-10224)**
Dynavox Inc ....B...... 412 381-4883
Pittsburgh **(G-14948)**
E-Lynxx Corporation ....E...... 717 709-0990
Chambersburg **(G-2926)**
Enterprise Cloudworks Corp ....E...... 215 395-6311
Bryn Mawr **(G-2322)**
Eplans Inc ....G...... 717 534-1183
Hershey **(G-7609)**
Fiftyone K LLC ....G...... 908 222-8780
Pittsburgh **(G-15017)**
For Lenfest Institute ....G...... 215 854-5600
Philadelphia **(G-13713)**
Forallsecure Inc ....F...... 412 256-8809
Pittsburgh **(G-15024)**
Fry International LLC ....G...... 215 847-6359
Elkins Park **(G-4903)**
Genilogix LLC ....E...... 412 444-0554
Pittsburgh **(G-15047)**
Guiding Technologies Corp ....G...... 609 605-9273
Philadelphia **(G-13791)**
H&R Block Inc ....F...... 814 723-3001
Warren **(G-19030)**
Healthstratica LLC ....G...... 412 956-1000
Pittsburgh **(G-15085)**
Help Every Addict Live ....G...... 484 598-3285
Drexel Hill **(G-4364)**
Horsey Darden Enterprises LLC ....G...... 215 309-3139
Philadelphia **(G-13834)**
Impilo LLC ....G...... 610 662-2867
Wynnewood **(G-20269)**
Industry Weapon Inc ....E...... 877 344-8450
Pittsburgh **(G-15123)**
Inspro Technologies Corp ....F...... 484 654-2200
Eddystone **(G-4804)**
Intelligent Micro Systems Ltd ....G...... 610 664-1207
Haverford **(G-7412)**
Iron Compass Map Company ....G...... 717 295-1194
Lancaster **(G-9064)**
Jujama Inc ....E...... 570 209-7670
Scranton **(G-17248)**
K12systems Inc ....F...... 610 366-9540
Allentown **(G-278)**
Keffer Development Svcs LLC ....G...... 724 458-5289
Grove City **(G-6793)**
Kickup LLC ....G...... 610 256-1004
Philadelphia **(G-13935)**
Leanfm Technologies Inc ....G...... 412 818-5167
Pittsburgh **(G-15222)**
Legacy Mark LLC ....G...... 800 444-9260
Chambersburg **(G-2951)**

Legal Sifter Inc ....G 724 221-7438
Pittsburgh *(G-15223)*

Lifeguard Health Networks Inc ....F 484 584-4071
Wayne *(G-19348)*

Long Drop Games LLC ....G 814 460-7961
Erie *(G-5370)*

Luxury Electronics LLC ....G 215 847-0937
Yardley *(G-20324)*

Medchive LLC ....G 215 688-7475
Philadelphia *(G-14004)*

Media Highway ....F 610 647-2255
Berwyn *(G-1368)*

Medshifts Inc ....G 856 834-0074
Philadelphia *(G-14006)*

Microsoft Corporation ....E 412 323-6700
Pittsburgh *(G-15286)*

Microsoft Corporation ....C 610 240-7000
Malvern *(G-10278)*

Modevity LLC ....E 610 251-0700
Malvern *(G-10280)*

Morrison Consulting Inc ....E 717 268-8201
York *(G-20604)*

Mother Nature Corporation ....G 412 798-3911
Pittsburgh *(G-15304)*

Mumps Audiofax Inc ....E 610 293-2160
Wayne *(G-19358)*

Net Reach Technologies LLC ....F 215 283-2300
Ambler *(G-593)*

O S I Software ....G 215 606-0612
Philadelphia *(G-14090)*

Opinionmeter International Ltd ....E 888 676-3837
Bethlehem *(G-1587)*

Optimized Markets Inc ....G 412 654-5994
Pittsburgh *(G-15361)*

Osisoft LLC ....F 215 606-0700
Philadelphia *(G-14104)*

Pcxpert Company Inc ....G 717 792-0005
York *(G-20619)*

Penn Assurance Software LLC ....F 610 996-6124
Aston *(G-785)*

Physiic LLC ....G 424 653-6410
Irwin *(G-8191)*

Pima LLC ....G 412 770-8130
Glenshaw *(G-6497)*

Pita Pita LLC ....G 267 440-7482
Philadelphia *(G-14179)*

Printfresh Studio LLC ....E 215 426-1661
Philadelphia *(G-14203)*

Ptc Inc ....F 724 219-2600
Greensburg *(G-6707)*

Quintiq Inc ....D 610 964-8111
Radnor *(G-16299)*

Relyence Corporation ....F 724 433-1909
Greensburg *(G-6711)*

RTD Embedded Technologies Inc ....E 814 234-8087
State College *(G-18017)*

Scorecast Medical LLC ....G 877 475-1001
Philadelphia *(G-14287)*

Search Live Today LLC ....G 610 805-7734
Norristown *(G-12710)*

Searer Solutions Inc ....G 302 475-6944
Philadelphia *(G-14292)*

Simplr Technologies LLC ....G 814 883-6463
State College *(G-18025)*

Sinclair Technologies LLC ....G 610 296-8259
Media *(G-10950)*

Skaffl LLC ....G 484 809-9351
Allentown *(G-394)*

Smartops Corporation ....E 412 231-0115
Pittsburgh *(G-15548)*

Society of Clinical ....F 215 822-8644
Chalfont *(G-2889)*

Softstuf Inc ....G 215 627-8850
Philadelphia *(G-14322)*

Southside Holdings Inc ....E 412 431-8300
Pittsburgh *(G-15564)*

Tactile Design Group LLC ....F 215 732-2311
Philadelphia *(G-14367)*

Tal Technologies Inc ....E 215 496-0222
Philadelphia *(G-14369)*

Team Approach Inc ....G 847 259-0005
Lancaster *(G-9213)*

Thebathoutlet LLC ....F 877 256-1645
Lansdale *(G-9414)*

Transporeon Group Americas Inc ....E 267 281-1555
Fort Washington *(G-6094)*

Tunefly LLC ....G 570 392-9239
Nanticoke *(G-11904)*

Twenty61 LLC ....G 215 370-7076
Philadelphia *(G-14415)*

U Squared Interactive LLC ....G 214 770-7437
Pittsburgh *(G-15665)*

Uber Atc ....G 412 587-2986
Pittsburgh *(G-15666)*

Vocollect Inc ....C 412 829-8145
Pittsburgh *(G-15702)*

Voicestars Inc ....G 305 902-9666
Emmaus *(G-5046)*

Watchword Worldwide ....G 814 366-2770
Ambridge *(G-638)*

SOFTWARE PUBLISHERS: Business & Professional

2w Technologies LLC ....G 814 333-3117
Meadville *(G-10693)*

9dots Management Corp LLC ....E 610 825-2027
Conshohocken *(G-3514)*

Aapryl LLC ....G 215 567-1100
Philadelphia *(G-13332)*

Accion Labs Us Inc ....E 724 260-5139
Bridgeville *(G-2051)*

Accustar Inc ....G 610 459-0123
Garnet Valley *(G-6264)*

Acutedge Inc ....G 484 846-6275
King of Prussia *(G-8577)*

Advanced Education Service ....G 717 545-8633
Harrisburg *(G-7084)*

Advanced Software Inc ....F 215 369-7800
Yardley *(G-20293)*

Airclic Inc ....D 215 504-0560
Trevose *(G-18485)*

Apprise Software Inc ....E 610 991-3600
Bethlehem *(G-1451)*

Aptech Computer Systems Inc ....E 412 963-7440
Pittsburgh *(G-14714)*

Ariba Inc ....F 215 246-3493
Philadelphia *(G-13410)*

Ariba Inc ....D 412 644-0160
Pittsburgh *(G-14721)*

Automated Fincl Systems Inc ....B 484 875-1250
Exton *(G-5649)*

Automated Fincl Systems Inc ....B 610 594-1037
Exton *(G-5650)*

Autosoft Inc ....D 800 473-4630
West Middlesex *(G-19721)*

B6 Systems Inc ....G 724 861-8080
Manor *(G-10409)*

Bisil North America Inc ....G 610 747-0340
Bala Cynwyd *(G-873)*

Bloksberg Inc ....F 724 727-9925
Apollo *(G-665)*

Business & Decision North Amer ....C 610 230-2500
Malvern *(G-10198)*

Businessone Technologies Inc ....G 215 953-6660
Feasterville Trevose *(G-5896)*

Computer Software Inc ....E 215 822-9100
Chalfont *(G-2868)*

Conestoga Data Services Inc ....F 717 569-7728
Lancaster *(G-8984)*

Corrugated Services Corp ....D 215 639-9540
Fort Washington *(G-6067)*

Dbmotion Inc ....F 412 605-1952
Pittsburgh *(G-14910)*

Dita Exchange Inc ....E 267 327-4889
Radnor *(G-16293)*

Dqe Communications LLC ....G 412 393-1033
Pittsburgh *(G-14936)*

Ellucian Support Inc ....C 610 647-5930
Malvern *(G-10229)*

Epilogue Systems LLC ....G 281 249-5405
Villanova *(G-18766)*

Eq Technologic Inc ....F 215 891-9010
Fort Washington *(G-6068)*

Expensewatch Inc ....F 610 397-0532
Plymouth Meeting *(G-15842)*

Fis Avantgard LLC ....E 800 468-7483
Wayne *(G-19329)*

Fis Avantgard LLC ....E 215 413-4700
Philadelphia *(G-13703)*

Fis Data Systems Inc ....E 484 582-2000
Collegeville *(G-3377)*

Fis Sg LLC ....C 484 582-5400
Wayne *(G-19330)*

Fis Sg LLC ....G 215 627-3800
Philadelphia *(G-13704)*

Fis Systems International LLC ....D 484 582-2000
Collegeville *(G-3378)*

Flexible Informatics LLC ....G 215 253-8765
Lafayette Hill *(G-8880)*

Franklin Potter Associates ....G 215 345-0844
Doylestown *(G-4300)*

Freedom Cyber Marketing LLC ....G 717 654-2392
Dallastown *(G-3975)*

Ganesco Incorporated ....G 931 284-9033
Pittsburgh *(G-15040)*

Globalsubmit Inc ....F 215 253-7471
Philadelphia *(G-13771)*

Hamiltonian Systems Inc ....F 412 327-7204
Coraopolis *(G-3697)*

Heraeus Prcous Mtls N Amer LLC ....G 562 921-7464
Yardley *(G-20316)*

Hootboard LLC ....G 610 844-2423
Yardley *(G-20320)*

Image Net Ventures LLC ....E 610 240-0800
West Chester *(G-19567)*

Information Mktg Group Inc ....F 508 626-8682
Bethel Park *(G-1417)*

Inspire Closing Services LLC ....G 412 348-8367
Moon Township *(G-11494)*

Integritas Inc ....G 800 411-6281
Pittsburgh *(G-15131)*

Ip Lasso LLC ....G 484 352-2029
King of Prussia *(G-8635)*

Ironwood Learning LLC ....G 412 784-1384
Pittsburgh *(G-15137)*

Kcf Technologies Inc ....F 814 867-4097
State College *(G-17983)*

Kenexa Learning Inc ....E 610 971-9171
Wayne *(G-19346)*

Kinetic Buildings LLC ....G 203 858-0813
Philadelphia *(G-13936)*

Knowledge MGT & Tech Corp ....G 412 503-3657
Washington *(G-19193)*

Kos & Associates Inc ....F 412 367-7444
Pittsburgh *(G-15195)*

Kronos Incorporated ....E 724 772-2400
Warrendale *(G-19086)*

Kronos Incorporated ....G 724 742-3142
Cranberry Township *(G-3830)*

Kynectiv Inc ....F 484 899-0746
Chadds Ford *(G-2853)*

Lease More ....G 814 796-4047
Waterford *(G-19264)*

Liquent Inc ....C 215 957-6401
Horsham *(G-7831)*

Lunchera LLC ....E 787 607-8914
Pittsburgh *(G-15240)*

Matrix Solutions LLC ....E 412 697-3000
Pittsburgh *(G-15262)*

McNs Technologies LLC ....G 610 269-2891
Chadds Ford *(G-2855)*

Metavis Technologies Inc ....E 484 288-2990
Exton *(G-5711)*

Method Automation Services Inc ....G 724 337-9064
New Kensington *(G-12356)*

Mindmatrix Inc ....F 412 381-0230
Pittsburgh *(G-15291)*

Minitab LLC ....B 814 238-3280
State College *(G-17992)*

Moai Technologies Inc ....E 412 454-5550
Pittsburgh *(G-15296)*

Mpm Holdings Inc ....E 610 678-8131
Reading *(G-16450)*

Mxstrategies LLC ....G 610 241-2099
West Chester *(G-19604)*

Netbeez Inc ....G 412 465-0638
Pittsburgh *(G-15328)*

Neuxpower Inc ....G 267 238-3833
Philadelphia *(G-14066)*

Noblemedical LLC ....G 917 750-9605
Bryn Mawr *(G-2332)*

Nurelm Inc ....F 724 430-0490
Pittsburgh *(G-15350)*

Onlyboth Inc ....G 412 303-8798
Pittsburgh *(G-15360)*

Oracle Corporation ....C 717 234-5858
Harrisburg *(G-7188)*

Oracle Systems Corporation ....C 610 729-3600
Conshohocken *(G-3582)*

Pat Landgraf ....G 412 221-0347
Bridgeville *(G-2084)*

Paulhus and Associates Inc ....F 717 274-5621
Lebanon *(G-9616)*

Personlytics LLC ....G 484 929-0853
West Chester *(G-19616)*

Plan Management Corporation ....F 610 359-5870
Wayne *(G-19362)*

Plumriver LLC ....F 781 577-9575
State College *(G-18006)*

Purple Deck Media Inc..........G...... 717 884-9529
　Scotland (G-17182)
Rackware Inc..........G...... 408 430-5821
　Trappe (G-18472)
Recovery Networks Inc..........G...... 215 809-1300
　Philadelphia (G-14234)
Robotic Services Inc..........G...... 215 550-1823
　Philadelphia (G-14255)
Rocket Cloud Inc..........G...... 484 948-0327
　Bethlehem (G-1613)
Runwell Solutions Inc..........F...... 610 376-7773
　Reading (G-16506)
Shift4 Payments LLC..........D...... 800 201-0461
　Allentown (G-389)
Sid Global Solutions LLC..........G...... 484 218-0021
　Exton (G-5733)
Siemens Product Life Mgmt Sftw..........G...... 717 299-1846
　Lancaster (G-9196)
Siemens Product Life Mgmt Sftw..........G...... 814 861-1651
　State College (G-18023)
Smith Micro Software Inc..........C...... 412 837-5300
　Pittsburgh (G-15550)
Sungard AR Financing LLC..........G...... 484 582-2000
　Wayne (G-19374)
Sy-Con Systems Inc..........G...... 610 253-0900
　Easton (G-4760)
Titan Technologies Inc..........G...... 888 671-6649
　Pittsburgh (G-15626)
Touchtown Inc..........E...... 412 826-0460
　Oakmont (G-12929)
Traction Software Inc..........G...... 401 528-1145
　Harrisburg (G-7233)
Validity LLC..........G...... 610 768-8042
　Malvern (G-10337)
Viper Network Systems LLC..........G...... 855 758-4737
　West View (G-19774)
Vitaltrax LLC..........G...... 610 864-0211
　Philadelphia (G-14453)
Winfosoft Inc..........E...... 717 226-1299
　York (G-20711)
Wombat Security Tech Inc..........E...... 412 621-1484
　Pittsburgh (G-15723)

SOFTWARE PUBLISHERS: Computer Utilities

Microlite Corporation..........G...... 724 375-6711
　Aliquippa (G-85)
Proportal LLC..........G...... 215 923-7100
　Philadelphia (G-14210)
Turbo Software LLC..........G...... 215 490-6806
　Philadelphia (G-14414)
Volian Enterprises Inc..........F...... 724 335-3744
　New Kensington (G-12388)

SOFTWARE PUBLISHERS: Education

Advantage Learning Technology..........G...... 610 217-8022
　Coopersburg (G-3624)
Appitur Co..........G...... 215 720-1420
　Newtown Square (G-12565)
Business Intelligence Intl Inc..........E...... 484 688-8300
　Wayne (G-19311)
Carnegie Learning Inc..........C...... 412 690-2442
　Pittsburgh (G-14817)
Carnegie Speech LLC..........F...... 412 471-1234
　Pittsburgh (G-14820)
Catalyst Crossroads LLC..........G...... 412 969-2733
　Pittsburgh (G-14827)
Classroom Salon LLC..........G...... 412 621-6287
　Pittsburgh (G-14858)
Cody Computer Services Inc..........E...... 610 326-7476
　Pottstown (G-15971)
Continental Press Inc..........C...... 717 367-1836
　Elizabethtown (G-4869)
Dbaza Inc..........F...... 412 681-1180
　Philadelphia (G-13612)
Ed Jupiter Inc..........F...... 888 367-6175
　Philadelphia (G-13658)
Education MGT Solutions LLC..........D...... 610 701-7002
　Exton (G-5671)
Elemental 3 LLC..........G...... 267 217-3592
　Philadelphia (G-13667)
Enlightening Lrng Minds LLC..........F...... 412 880-9601
　Monroeville (G-11336)
Gokaaf International Inc..........G...... 267 343-3075
　Philadelphia (G-13775)
Multimedia Training Systems..........G...... 412 341-2185
　Pittsburgh (G-15308)
Oa Systems Llc..........G...... 888 347-7950
　Wexford (G-19818)

Orkist LLC..........G...... 412 346-8316
　Pittsburgh (G-15364)
Popultion Hlth Innovations LLC..........G...... 717 735-8105
　Lancaster (G-9173)
Project One Inc..........G...... 267 901-7906
　Philadelphia (G-14208)
Rapid Learning Institute..........F...... 877 792-2172
　Wayne (G-19368)
Skyroc LLC..........G...... 215 840-5466
　Philadelphia (G-14315)
Turnitin LLC..........G...... 724 272-7250
　Pittsburgh (G-15662)
Tutorgen Inc..........G...... 704 710-8445
　Mars (G-10511)
Unlocked Entertainment Tech..........G...... 267 507-6028
　Philadelphia (G-14430)
Vantage Learning Usa LLC..........D...... 800 230-2213
　New Hope (G-12318)
Vantage Learning Usa LLC..........E...... 800 230-2213
　Langhorne (G-9330)
Web Age Solutions Inc..........E...... 215 517-6540
　Jenkintown (G-8304)
Worktask Media Inc..........G...... 610 762-9014
　Bath (G-973)

SOFTWARE PUBLISHERS: Home Entertainment

Gamefreaks101 Inc..........G...... 215 587-9787
　Philadelphia (G-13741)
Inter Media Outdoors..........G...... 717 695-8171
　Harrisburg (G-7155)
Jumpbutton Studio LLC..........E...... 267 407-7535
　Philadelphia (G-13914)
Quality Systems Associates..........G...... 215 345-5575
　Doylestown (G-4331)
Undernet Gaming Incorporated..........G...... 484 544-8943
　Harrisburg (G-7240)

SOFTWARE PUBLISHERS: NEC

ACC Accounting Solutions Inc..........G...... 215 253-4738
　Philadelphia (G-13337)
Accountable Software Inc..........E...... 610 983-3100
　Royersford (G-16839)
Action Wireless Network..........G...... 412 292-1712
　Bethel Park (G-1400)
Activestrategy Inc..........E...... 484 690-0700
　Plymouth Meeting (G-15826)
Adenine Solutions Inc..........G...... 267 684-6013
　Southampton (G-17796)
Amcs Group Inc..........E...... 610 932-4006
　Oxford (G-13071)
Analytical Graphics Inc..........C...... 610 981-8000
　Exton (G-5643)
Anju Sylogent LLC..........F...... 215 504-7000
　Bristol (G-2107)
Ansoft LLC..........G...... 412 261-3200
　Pittsburgh (G-14713)
Appligent Inc..........E...... 610 284-4006
　Lansdowne (G-9429)
Ariba Inc..........F...... 610 661-8413
　Newtown Square (G-12566)
Ascentive LLC..........D...... 215 395-8559
　Philadelphia (G-13419)
Astea International Inc..........D...... 215 682-2500
　Horsham (G-7791)
Ats Fleet Trcking MGT Slutions..........F...... 570 445-8805
　Dunmore (G-4468)
Augmentir Inc..........G...... 949 432-6450
　Horsham (G-7792)
Automated Enterprise Intl..........G...... 610 458-5810
　Glenmoore (G-6463)
Automatic Forecasting Systems..........F...... 215 675-0652
　Warminster (G-18832)
Best Medical International Inc..........D...... 412 312-6700
　Pittsburgh (G-14764)
BMC Software Inc..........E...... 610 941-2750
　Conshohocken (G-3523)
Bpl Global LLC..........F...... 724 933-7700
　Canonsburg (G-2550)
Business Planning Inc..........G...... 610 649-0550
　Ardmore (G-703)
Centre of Web Inc..........G...... 814 235-9592
　State College (G-17949)
Cherokee Software Systems..........G...... 717 932-5008
　New Cumberland (G-12183)
Clarivate Analytics (us) LLC..........A...... 215 386-0100
　Philadelphia (G-13548)
Cognos Corporation..........G...... 412 490-9804
　Pittsburgh (G-14866)

Collective Intelligence Inc..........G...... 717 545-9234
　Mechanicsburg (G-10828)
Communimetrics Group LLC..........G...... 215 260-5382
　Malvern (G-10215)
Componentone Enterprises LLC..........D...... 412 681-4343
　Pittsburgh (G-14871)
Compudata Inc..........E...... 215 969-1000
　Philadelphia (G-13566)
Computer Boss..........G...... 215 444-9393
　Southampton (G-17804)
Computer Designs Inc..........D...... 610 261-2100
　Whitehall (G-19867)
Computer Dev Systems LLC..........G...... 717 591-0995
　Mechanicsburg (G-10830)
Connectwo LLC..........G...... 215 421-4225
　Lansdale (G-9352)
Corestar International Corp..........E...... 724 744-4094
　Irwin (G-8151)
Creative Mountain Software LLC..........G...... 814 383-2685
　Howard (G-7888)
Datatech Software Inc..........F...... 717 652-4344
　Harrisburg (G-7113)
Datumrite Corporation..........F...... 215 407-4447
　North Wales (G-12797)
Decilog Inc..........G...... 215 657-0817
　Willow Grove (G-20114)
Dorado Solutions Inc..........G...... 480 216-1056
　West Chester (G-19543)
Dreamlike Entertainment..........G...... 610 392-5614
　Slatington (G-17606)
E Z Net Solutions Inc..........G...... 215 887-7200
　Jenkintown (G-8284)
Earthware Corporation..........G...... 412 563-1920
　Pittsburgh (G-14954)
Eastern Systems Management..........G...... 717 391-9700
　Lancaster (G-9006)
Ebroker Software LLC..........G...... 717 540-3720
　Harrisburg (G-7124)
Edaptive Systems LLC..........G...... 717 718-1230
　York (G-20463)
Electronics Boutique Amer Inc..........G...... 610 518-5300
　Downingtown (G-4225)
Environmental Systems Research..........E...... 909 793-2853
　Chesterbrook (G-3092)
Estari Inc..........F...... 717 233-1518
　Harrisburg (G-7127)
Everest Software LP..........E...... 412 206-0005
　Bridgeville (G-2062)
Ez-Plant Software Inc..........G...... 814 421-6744
　Ebensburg (G-4785)
Fab Universal Corp..........F...... 412 621-0902
　Pittsburgh (G-15002)
Fiberlink Communications Corp..........C...... 215 664-1600
　Blue Bell (G-1829)
First Supply Chain LLC..........G...... 215 527-2264
　Hummelstown (G-7910)
Garth Groft..........G...... 717 819-9479
　York (G-20491)
GL Trade Capitl Mkts Solutions..........D...... 484 530-4400
　Wayne (G-19332)
Goji Systems Inc..........G...... 267 309-2000
　Norristown (G-12662)
Grammaton Research LLC..........G...... 410 703-9237
　York (G-20513)
Gray Bridge Software Inc..........G...... 412 401-1045
　Pittsburgh (G-15059)
Green Hills Software LLC..........G...... 215 862-9474
　New Hope (G-12304)
Ground 34 LLC..........G...... 914 299-7212
　Pittsburgh (G-15066)
Guru Technologies Inc..........F...... 610 572-2086
　Philadelphia (G-13793)
Health Market Science Inc..........C...... 610 940-4002
　King of Prussia (G-8629)
Horizon Software Solutions..........G...... 610 225-0989
　Reading (G-16404)
Ima North America Inc..........G...... 215 826-8500
　Bristol (G-2154)
Impac Technology Inc..........E...... 610 430-1400
　West Chester (G-19569)
Industrybuilt Software Ltd..........E...... 866 788-1086
　Allentown (G-256)
Infor (us) Inc..........E...... 678 319-8000
　Malvern (G-10254)
Ingenuware Ltd..........G...... 724 843-3140
　Beaver Falls (G-1000)
Innovate Software Inc..........G...... 724 935-1790
　Bradfordwoods (G-1998)
Integrated Software Services..........G...... 717 534-1480
　Hershey (G-7618)

Intelipc ....G...... 610 534-8268
Folcroft (G-6007)

International Bus Mchs Corp ....A...... 610 578-2017
Wayne (G-19339)

International Road Dynamics ....G...... 717 264-2077
Chambersburg (G-2943)

Internet Pipeline Inc ....D...... 484 348-6555
Exton (G-5700)

Iota Communications Inc ....G...... 855 743-6478
New Hope (G-12306)

Ividix Software Inc ....G...... 484 580-9601
Eagleville (G-4513)

J & J Consulting Corp ....G...... 610 678-6611
Wernersville (G-19485)

K-Systems Inc ....F...... 717 795-7711
Mechanicsburg (G-10861)

Kennebec Inc ....G...... 412 278-2040
Pittsburgh (G-15170)

Keystone Sftwr Solutions Inc ....G...... 610 685-2111
Reading (G-16421)

Kinesis Software LLC ....G...... 610 353-4150
Broomall (G-2292)

Koryak Consulting Inc ....E...... 412 364-6600
Pittsburgh (G-15194)

Kronos Incorporated ....E...... 610 567-2127
Royersford (G-16855)

Lantica Software LLC ....G...... 215 598-8419
Newtown (G-12517)

Ldp Inc ....D...... 570 455-8511
West Hazleton (G-19713)

Ldp Inc ....G...... 717 657-8500
Harrisburg (G-7171)

Lee Rj Group Inc ....C...... 800 860-1775
Monroeville (G-11342)

Link Software Corp ....G...... 717 399-3023
Lancaster (G-9113)

Makteam Software Ltd Co ....G...... 814 504-1283
Erie (G-5379)

Mam Software Inc ....D...... 610 336-9045
Blue Bell (G-1846)

Managing Editor Inc ....E...... 215 517-5116
Jenkintown (G-8295)

Meshnet Inc ....G...... 215 237-7712
Philadelphia (G-14011)

Microsoft Corporation ....G...... 484 754-7600
King of Prussia (G-8651)

Mobius Acquisition LLC ....G...... 412 281-7000
Pittsburgh (G-15297)

Mousley Consulting Inc ....G...... 610 539-0150
Norristown (G-12689)

Mpower Software Services LLC ....D...... 215 497-9730
Newtown (G-12524)

MSI Technologies LLC ....G...... 215 968-5068
Newtown (G-12526)

Neat Company Inc ....C...... 215 382-4283
Philadelphia (G-14060)

Neuroflow Inc ....G...... 347 881-6306
Philadelphia (G-14064)

Next Generation Software ....G...... 215 361-2754
Lansdale (G-9392)

Noblesoft Solutions Inc ....G...... 713 480-7510
Langhorne (G-9315)

Novatech LLC ....C...... 484 812-6000
Quakertown (G-16224)

Nzinganet Inc ....G...... 877 709-6459
Fort Washington (G-6087)

Ois LLC ....G...... 717 447-0265
Mount Union (G-11746)

Open Solution ....G...... 646 696-8686
Bushkill (G-2368)

Oracle America Inc ....E...... 412 859-6051
Coraopolis (G-3709)

Oracle America Inc ....G...... 610 647-8530
Malvern (G-10290)

Oracle America Inc ....G...... 717 730-5501
Lemoyne (G-9747)

Oracle Corporation ....D...... 610 667-8600
Conshohocken (G-3581)

Oracle Systems Corporation ....G...... 412 262-5200
Coraopolis (G-3710)

Oracle Systems Corporation ....D...... 610 260-9000
Conshohocken (G-3583)

Orbit Software Inc ....F...... 484 941-0820
Pottstown (G-16024)

Payserv Inc ....G...... 610 524-3251
Media (G-10942)

PC Network Inc ....D...... 267 236-0015
Philadelphia (G-14128)

Pensionpro Software LLC ....G...... 717 545-6060
Harrisburg (G-7198)

Peoplejoy Inc ....G...... 267 603-7726
Philadelphia (G-14134)

Phl Collective LLC ....G...... 610 496-7758
Havertown (G-7426)

Picwell Inc ....F...... 215 563-0976
Philadelphia (G-14175)

Pittsburgh Digital ....G...... 412 431-6008
Pittsburgh (G-15393)

Poiesis Informatics Inc ....G...... 412 327-8766
Pittsburgh (G-15418)

Policymap Inc ....G...... 866 923-6277
Philadelphia (G-14185)

Prairie Dog Tech LLC ....G...... 215 558-4975
Philadelphia (G-14195)

Prism Engineering LLC ....E...... 215 784-0800
Horsham (G-7842)

Prismatic Consulting LLC ....G...... 412 915-9072
Pittsburgh (G-15449)

Prosoft Technologies Inc ....F...... 412 835-6217
Bethel Park (G-1429)

Pulsemetrics LLC ....G...... 412 656-5776
Allison Park (G-460)

Q-Linx Inc ....G...... 610 941-2756
Conshohocken (G-3594)

Quality Systems Integrators ....G...... 610 458-0539
Chester Springs (G-3085)

Quantam Software Solutions ....G...... 610 373-4770
Reading (G-16481)

Qube Global Software Americas ....G...... 610 431-9080
West Chester (G-19624)

R Fritz Enterprises Inc ....G...... 814 267-4204
Berlin (G-1292)

Ragnasoft Inc ....F...... 866 471-2001
Lancaster (G-9186)

Ram Technologies Inc ....E...... 215 654-8810
Fort Washington (G-6089)

Rough Stone Software LLC ....G...... 412 444-5295
Pittsburgh (G-15499)

Rovi Corporation ....G...... 610 293-8561
Wayne (G-19370)

Safeguard Scientifics Inc ....E...... 610 293-0600
Radnor (G-16301)

Schneider Electric It Corp ....B...... 717 948-1200
Middletown (G-11074)

Servant PC Resources Inc ....F...... 570 748-2800
Lock Haven (G-10092)

Siemens Product Life Mgmt Sftw ....G...... 814 237-4999
State College (G-18022)

SIS Software LLC ....G...... 888 844-6599
Pittsburgh (G-15544)

Softboss Corp ....G...... 215 563-7488
Philadelphia (G-14321)

Software Engineering Assoc ....F...... 570 803-0535
Archbald (G-695)

Solution Systems Inc ....F...... 610 668-4620
Narberth (G-11912)

Spectrum Software Innovations ....G...... 610 779-6974
Reading (G-16522)

Spm Global Services Inc ....D...... 610 340-2828
Chester (G-3065)

Stone Edge Technologies Inc ....G...... 484 927-4804
Phoenixville (G-14580)

Sungard Asset MGT Systems Inc ....C...... 610 251-6500
Collegeville (G-3396)

Sungard Capital Corp II ....F...... 484 582-2000
Wayne (G-19375)

Sungard Holdco LLC ....A...... 484 582-2000
Wayne (G-19376)

Sungard Holding Corp ....G...... 888 332-2564
Wayne (G-19377)

Sustrana LLC ....G...... 610 651-2870
Devon (G-4116)

Sweet Roll Studio Llc ....G...... 209 559-8219
Philadelphia (G-14363)

Tata America Intl Corp ....D...... 717 737-4737
Camp Hill (G-2520)

Technology Dynamics Inc ....G...... 888 988-3243
Wayne (G-19380)

Telefactor Robotics LLC ....G...... 610 940-6040
Conshohocken (G-3611)

Tenex Systems Inc ....F...... 610 239-9988
King of Prussia (G-8685)

Thoroughcare Inc ....G...... 412 737-7332
Pittsburgh (G-15616)

Town Square Software LLC ....G...... 610 374-7900
Reading (G-16545)

Ursoft Inc ....F...... 724 452-2150
Zelienople (G-20827)

Vanadium Enterprises Corp ....E...... 412 206-2990
Bridgeville (G-2098)

Vantage Online Store LLC ....C...... 267 756-1155
New Hope (G-12319)

Veeva Systems Inc ....G...... 215 422-3356
Fort Washington (G-6095)

Vega Applications Development ....G...... 610 892-1812
Media (G-10956)

Venus Video ....G...... 215 937-1545
Philadelphia (G-14440)

Versatile Credit Inc ....E...... 800 851-1281
Mechanicsburg (G-10904)

Vetstreet Incorporated ....E...... 267 685-2400
Feasterville Trevose (G-5937)

Via Design & Technologies ....G...... 215 579-5730
Newtown (G-12560)

Virtix Consulting LLC ....G...... 412 440-4835
Wexford (G-19832)

Weidenhammer Systems Corp ....E...... 610 317-4000
Allentown (G-430)

Weidenhammer Systems Corp ....D...... 610 378-1149
Reading (G-16562)

Weidenhammer Systems Corp ....E...... 610 378-1149
Lancaster (G-9237)

Weidenhammer Systems Corp ....E...... 610 687-0037
Blue Bell (G-1857)

Wolters Kluwer Health Inc ....C...... 215 521-8300
Philadelphia (G-14482)

Workzone LLC ....F...... 610 275-9861
Norristown (G-12725)

Wov Inc ....D...... 412 261-3791
Pittsburgh (G-15724)

SOFTWARE PUBLISHERS: Operating Systems

Aaxios Technologies LLC ....G...... 267 545-7400
Warrington (G-19106)

DMS Computer Services Inc ....G...... 412 835-3570
Pittsburgh (G-14929)

Efficient Ip Inc ....F...... 888 228-4655
West Chester (G-19548)

Embroidery Systems Inc ....G...... 412 967-9271
Pittsburgh (G-14969)

Emerging Computer Technologies ....G...... 717 761-4027
Camp Hill (G-2495)

Information Builders Inc ....F...... 610 940-0790
Plymouth Meeting (G-15851)

SOFTWARE PUBLISHERS: Publisher's

21st Century Software Tech Inc ....E...... 610 341-9017
Wayne (G-19290)

Active Data Inc ....E...... 610 997-8100
Bethlehem (G-1443)

Advertising Specialty Inst Inc ....B...... 800 546-1350
Feasterville Trevose (G-5883)

Aegis Software Corporation ....G...... 724 325-5595
Murrysville (G-11845)

Avatar Data Pubg Solutions ....G...... 412 921-7747
Pittsburgh (G-14742)

Bagatrix Solutions Ltd ....G...... 610 574-9607
Gilbertsville (G-6370)

Bryn Mawr Equipment Fin Inc ....F...... 610 581-4996
Bryn Mawr (G-2317)

Energycap Inc ....E...... 814 237-3744
State College (G-17963)

Offset Paperback ....G...... 570 602-1316
Wilkes Barre (G-19952)

Profit Engine LLC ....G...... 412 848-8187
Wexford (G-19822)

Quire LLC ....G...... 267 935-9777
Doylestown (G-4332)

Software Consulting Svcs LLC ....E...... 610 746-7700
Nazareth (G-11988)

SOFTWARE TRAINING, COMPUTER

Compututor Inc ....G...... 610 260-0300
Conshohocken (G-3531)

Validity LLC ....G...... 610 768-8042
Malvern (G-10337)

SOIL CONDITIONERS

Nutra-Soils Inc ....E...... 610 869-7645
West Grove (G-19703)

SOLAR CELLS

Solar Power Solutions LLC ....G...... 724 379-2002
Belle Vernon (G-1087)

Sun Prime Energy LLC ....G...... 215 962-4196
Chalfont (G-2890)

PRODUCT

Yingli Green Enrgy Amricas Inc ....F 212 609-4909
Philadelphia (G-14500)

SOLAR HEATING EQPT

American Slar Envmtl Technolog..........G... 570 279-0338
Lewisburg (G-9897)
Flabeg Solar US Corporation.................E ... 724 899-4622
Clinton (G-3262)
Lccm Solar LLC.......................................G... 717 514-0751
Harrisburg (G-7170)
Oerlikon Management USA Inc..............F ... 412 967-7016
Pittsburgh (G-15357)
Ritter Group Usa Inc ....G... 570 517-5380
Stroudsburg (G-18140)
Solar Technology Solutions.................G... 610 916-0864
Leesport (G-9674)

SOLDERING EQPT: Electrical, Exc Handheld

Xcell Automation Inc ....D... 717 755-6800
York (G-20721)

SOLDERING EQPT: Electrical, Handheld

Reliable Equipment Mfg Co ....E 215 357-7015
Warminster (G-18951)

SOLDERS

Alpha Assembly Solutions Inc ....C ... 814 946-1611
Altoona (G-470)
Kapp Alloy & Wire Inc..........................F ... 814 676-0613
Oil City (G-12948)

SOLID CONTAINING UNITS: Concrete

Harbisnwlker Intl Holdings Inc ....G... 412 375-6600
Moon Township (G-11488)
Harbisonwalker Intl Inc........................C... 412 375-6600
Moon Township (G-11490)

SOLVENTS

Elroy Turpentine Company ....G... 412 963-0949
Pittsburgh (G-14964)

SONAR SYSTEMS & EQPT

Raytheon Company ....G... 717 267-4200
Chambersburg (G-2972)

SOUND EQPT: Electric

Asr Enterprises Inc ....G... 610 873-7484
Downingtown (G-4211)
Duryea Technologies Inc.......................G... 610 939-0480
Reading (G-16366)
Extorr Inc ....F ... 724 337-3000
New Kensington (G-12339)

SOUND EQPT: Underwater

Videoray LLC..E ... 610 458-3000
Pottstown (G-16067)

SOUND REPRODUCING EQPT

Shangri La Productions ....G... 610 838-5188
Hellertown (G-7562)

SPACE VEHICLE EQPT

Delaware Tool & Machine Co ....E ... 610 259-1810
Yeadon (G-20352)
L3 Technologies Inc...............................C... 267 545-7000
Bristol (G-2157)
York Industries Inc................................E ... 717 764-8855
York (G-20742)

SPACE VEHICLES

Converging Sciences Tech Inc ....G... 215 626-5705
Warminster (G-18847)
Lockheed Martin Corporation...............B... 610 531-5640
Malvern (G-10271)

SPEAKER SYSTEMS

Zylux America Inc ....G... 412 221-5530
Bethel Park (G-1440)

SPECIAL EVENTS DECORATION SVCS

Paul William Boyle.................................G... 412 828-0883
Oakmont (G-12923)

SPECIALTY FOOD STORES: Coffee

East Indies Coffee & Tea ....F ... 717 228-2000
Lebanon (G-9566)

SPECIALTY FOOD STORES: Dried Fruit

Shaffers Feed Service Inc ....F ... 570 265-3300
Monroeton (G-11321)

SPECIALTY FOOD STORES: Health & Dietetic Food

GNC Corporation ....G... 412 288-4600
Pittsburgh (G-15054)
GNC Parent LLC.....................................G... 412 288-4600
Pittsburgh (G-15055)

SPECIALTY FOOD STORES: Soft Drinks

Liberty Bell Bottling Co Inc...................G... 610 820-6020
Allentown (G-294)
Wheeland Inc..F ... 570 323-3237
Williamsport (G-20091)

SPECIALTY FOOD STORES: Tea

Darling Blends LLC.................................G... 215 630-2802
Langhorne (G-9288)

SPECIALTY OUTPATIENT CLINICS, NEC

Biotelemetry Inc ....D... 610 729-7000
Malvern (G-10193)

SPECIALTY SAWMILL PRDTS

Brett W Shope ....G... 814 643-2921
Huntingdon (G-7940)
David M Byler ....F ... 717 667-6157
Belleville (G-1130)
Fedinetz Sawmill....................................G... 724 796-9461
Mc Donald (G-10573)

SPECULATIVE BUILDERS: Single-Family Housing

Morey General Contracting...................G... 570 759-2021
Berwick (G-1336)

SPEED CHANGERS

Charles Bond Company ....F ... 610 593-5171
Christiana (G-3134)
Rockwell Automation Inc ....G... 412 375-4700
Coraopolis (G-3723)

SPICE & HERB STORES

Ilera Healthcare LLC ....G... 610 440-8443
Plymouth Meeting (G-15850)
Pittsburgh Spice Seasoning Co ....G... 412 288-5036
Pittsburgh (G-15408)

SPORTING & ATHLETIC GOODS: Arrows, Archery

Kinseys Archery Products Inc...............D... 717 653-9074
Mount Joy (G-11664)

SPORTING & ATHLETIC GOODS: Balls, Baseball, Football, Etc

Gerald Laub ....G... 570 658-2609
Mc Clure (G-10558)

SPORTING & ATHLETIC GOODS: Batons

Top Hats Drum and Baton Co ....G... 724 339-7861
New Kensington (G-12383)

SPORTING & ATHLETIC GOODS: Bowling Alleys & Access

Mystic Lanes LLC ....G... 724 898-2960
Valencia (G-18699)
Sue N Doug Inc ....G... 717 838-6341
Palmyra (G-13132)

SPORTING & ATHLETIC GOODS: Bows, Archery

60x Custom Strings ....G... 724 525-0507
Cowansville (G-3795)

SPORTING & ATHLETIC GOODS: Buckets, Fish & Bait

Fergies Bait & Tackle.............................G... 724 253-3655
Sandy Lake (G-17059)

SPORTING & ATHLETIC GOODS: Camping Eqpt & Splys

American Adventure Sports ....G... 724 205-6450
Pittsburgh (G-14699)

SPORTING & ATHLETIC GOODS: Carts, Caddy

Duracart Usa LLC....................................G... 888 743-9957
Philadelphia (G-13650)

SPORTING & ATHLETIC GOODS: Cases, Gun & Rod

Skunkwirkz LLC ....G... 814 602-8936
Erie (G-5480)

SPORTING & ATHLETIC GOODS: Crossbows

Kodabow Inc...G... 484 947-5471
West Chester (G-19583)

SPORTING & ATHLETIC GOODS: Dartboards & Access

Verus Sports Inc....................................F ... 215 283-0153
Fort Washington (G-6096)

SPORTING & ATHLETIC GOODS: Darts & Table Sports Eqpt & Splys

Mvp Sports & Games Co ....G... 302 250-4836
Lancaster (G-9140)

SPORTING & ATHLETIC GOODS: Driving Ranges, Golf, Electronic

Deadsolid Simulations Inc ....F ... 570 655-6500
Pittston (G-15748)

SPORTING & ATHLETIC GOODS: Fencing Eqpt

State Line Fencing..................................G... 610 932-9352
Nottingham (G-12885)

SPORTING & ATHLETIC GOODS: Fishing Eqpt

Black Knight Industries Inc...................G... 814 676-3474
Oil City (G-12942)
Sea Mar Tackle Co Inc ....G... 610 769-0755
Schnecksville (G-17143)

SPORTING & ATHLETIC GOODS: Fishing Tackle, General

Bradley Walter Myers ....G... 717 413-0197
East Earl (G-4538)
Donald Plants ....G... 412 384-5911
West Elizabeth (G-19694)
Pure Fishing America Inc ....G... 215 229-9415
Philadelphia (G-14217)
XA Fishing Inc ....G... 610 356-0340
Broomall (G-2306)

SPORTING & ATHLETIC GOODS: Game Calls

Foxpro Inc...E ... 717 248-2507
Lewistown (G-9929)
Quaker Boy Inc.......................................F ... 814 362-7073
Bradford (G-1988)
Talkin Stick Game Calls Inc ....G... 724 758-3869
Ellwood City (G-4953)

SPORTING & ATHLETIC GOODS: Gymnasium Eqpt

Mancino Manufacturing Co Inc .... F 800 338-6287
Lansdale (G-9385)
Neff Specialties LLC .... F 814 247-8887
Hastings (G-7262)
Pure Hospitality LLC .... G 724 935-1515
Wexford (G-19826)

SPORTING & ATHLETIC GOODS: Hockey Eqpt & Splys, NEC

Pond Hockey Brewing Co LLC .... G 814 429-9846
State College (G-18008)

SPORTING & ATHLETIC GOODS: Hunting Eqpt

American Built Arms Company .... G 443 807-3022
Glen Rock (G-6450)
Be The Tree Llc .... G 717 887-0780
Hellam (G-7549)
Brutis Enterprises Inc .... G 412 431-5440
Pittsburgh (G-14795)
Protektor Model .... G 814 435-2442
Galeton (G-6244)
Real Scent .... G 717 692-0527
Millersburg (G-11199)
Xtreme Hunting Products .... G 610 967-4588
Emmaus (G-5047)

SPORTING & ATHLETIC GOODS: Pools, Swimming, Exc Plastic

Henry Jack Water On Wheels .... G 724 925-1727
New Stanton (G-12448)
Oldco Ep Inc .... G 484 768-1000
Aston (G-782)
Oldco Ep Inc .... G 888 314-9356
Aston (G-783)
Swimtech Distributing Inc .... G 570 595-7680
Cresco (G-3895)

SPORTING & ATHLETIC GOODS: Pools, Swimming, Plastic

Emsco Distributor Company .... G 412 754-1236
Irwin (G-8161)
Fox Pool Lancaster Inc .... D 717 718-1977
York (G-20487)
Jedco Products Inc .... G 724 453-3490
Zelienople (G-20807)
Pocono Pool Products Inc .... E 570 839-9291
Swiftwater (G-18189)
Wexco Incorporated .... G 717 764-8585
York (G-20710)
Wilkes Pool Corp .... E 570 759-0317
Mifflinville (G-11145)

SPORTING & ATHLETIC GOODS: Protective Sporting Eqpt

Brain-Pad Incorporated .... G 610 397-0893
Conshohocken (G-3525)
Impact Innovative Products LLC .... F 724 864-8440
Irwin (G-8170)

SPORTING & ATHLETIC GOODS: Reels, Fishing

Penn Fishing Tackle Mfg Co .... C 215 227-1087
Philadelphia (G-14130)

SPORTING & ATHLETIC GOODS: Rods & Rod Parts, Fishing

Versitex of America Ltd .... F 610 948-4442
Spring City (G-17872)

SPORTING & ATHLETIC GOODS: Shafts, Golf Club

Highlands of Donegal LLC .... G 717 653-2048
Mount Joy (G-11661)
Ryan Kanaskie .... G 717 248-9822
Lewistown (G-9947)
Tee-To-Green .... G 570 275-8335
Danville (G-4013)

SPORTING & ATHLETIC GOODS: Shooting Eqpt & Splys, General

Charles Hardy .... G 610 366-9752
Orefield (G-13009)

SPORTING & ATHLETIC GOODS: Skateboards

Space 1026 .... G 215 574-7630
Philadelphia (G-14326)
Titan Boards Inc .... G 814 516-1899
Oil City (G-12958)

SPORTING & ATHLETIC GOODS: Skates & Parts, Roller

Pipes Skate Park .... G 724 327-4247
Pittsburgh (G-15381)

SPORTING & ATHLETIC GOODS: Soccer Eqpt & Splys

Kwik Goal Ltd .... D 800 531-4252
Quakertown (G-16207)

SPORTING & ATHLETIC GOODS: Striking Or Punching Bags

Virtic Industries LLC .... G 610 246-9428
Wayne (G-19388)

SPORTING & ATHLETIC GOODS: Targets, Archery & Rifle Shooting

A & S Firearm Supplies Inc .... G 724 925-1212
Youngwood (G-20776)
Accubar Engineering & Rorco .... G 814 669-9005
Alexandria (G-62)
Bigshot Archery LLC .... G 610 873-0147
Elverson (G-4961)
R & M Targets Inc .... G 814 774-0160
Girard (G-6400)
University Rifle Club Inc .... G 610 927-1810
Reading (G-16556)

SPORTING & ATHLETIC GOODS: Team Sports Eqpt

Upper Perk Sportswear Inc .... G 215 541-3211
Pennsburg (G-13261)

SPORTING & ATHLETIC GOODS: Tennis Eqpt & Splys

Ferrari Importing Company .... E 412 323-0335
Pittsburgh (G-15014)

SPORTING & ATHLETIC GOODS: Track & Field Athletic Eqpt

Aluminum Athletic Equipment Co .... E 610 825-6565
Royersford (G-16841)

SPORTING & ATHLETIC GOODS: Trap Racks, Clay Targets

Shydas Services Inc .... G 717 274-8676
Lebanon (G-9630)

SPORTING & ATHLETIC GOODS: Water Sports Eqpt

25 Fathoms International Inc .... G 610 558-1101
Glen Mills (G-6428)

SPORTING & ATHLETIC GOODS: Winter Sports

Gilson Boards LLC .... F 570 798-9102
Winfield (G-20201)
Louis Fliszar .... G 610 865-6494
Bethlehem (G-1562)
Serendib Imports Inc .... G 610 203-3070
Media (G-10948)

SPORTING & REC GOODS, WHOLESALE: Camping Eqpt & Splys

Equinox Ltd .... E 570 322-5900
Williamsport (G-20011)

SPORTING & RECREATIONAL GOODS & SPLYS WHOLESALERS

Bob Allen & Sons Inc .... G 610 874-4391
Chester (G-3040)
Ferrari Importing Company .... E 412 323-0335
Pittsburgh (G-15014)
Henson Company Inc .... D 800 486-2788
Reading (G-16400)
Kwik Goal Ltd .... D 800 531-4252
Quakertown (G-16207)
Marcus J Wholesalers Inc .... F 412 261-3315
Pittsburgh (G-15252)
Multicolor Corp .... G 610 262-8420
Coplay (G-3646)
Nicholas Shea Co Inc .... G 610 296-9036
Reading (G-16456)
Prosco Inc .... E 814 375-0484
Du Bois (G-4414)
Recreation Resource Usa LLC .... G 610 444-4402
Kennett Square (G-8538)
Schmitt Mar Stering Wheels Inc .... G 717 431-2316
Lancaster (G-9191)
Schuylkill Vly Spt Trappe Ctr .... F 877 711-8100
Pottstown (G-16044)
Sport Manufacturing Group Inc .... G 718 575-1801
Huntingdon Valley (G-8039)

SPORTING & RECREATIONAL GOODS, WHOLESALE: Archery

A & B Homes Inc .... G 570 253-3888
Honesdale (G-7699)
Dorothy M Nelson .... G 724 837-6210
Greensburg (G-6662)
Kinseys Archery Products Inc .... D 717 653-9074
Mount Joy (G-11664)

SPORTING & RECREATIONAL GOODS, WHOLESALE: Athletic Goods

Athletic Lettering Inc .... F 717 840-6373
York (G-20389)
Roller Derby Skate Corp .... E 610 593-6931
Atglen (G-805)

SPORTING & RECREATIONAL GOODS, WHOLESALE: Dartboard & Access

Verus Sports Inc .... F 215 283-0153
Fort Washington (G-6096)

SPORTING & RECREATIONAL GOODS, WHOLESALE: Fishing

Penn Fishing Tackle Mfg Co .... C 215 227-1087
Philadelphia (G-14130)
Versitex of America Ltd .... F 610 948-4442
Spring City (G-17872)

SPORTING & RECREATIONAL GOODS, WHOLESALE: Fishing Tackle

Sea Mar Tackle Co Inc .... G 610 769-0755
Schnecksville (G-17143)
XA Fishing Inc .... G 610 356-0340
Broomall (G-2306)

SPORTING & RECREATIONAL GOODS, WHOLESALE: Fitness

Penn Sauna Corp .... E 610 932-5700
Paoli (G-13146)
Penn Sauna Corp .... E 610 932-5700
Oxford (G-13087)

SPORTING & RECREATIONAL GOODS, WHOLESALE: Golf & Skiing

Deadsolid Simulations Inc .... F 570 655-6500
Pittston (G-15748)
Unequal Technologies Company .... G 610 444-5900
Glen Mills (G-6447)

SPORTING & RECREATIONAL GOODS, WHOLESALE: Hunting

W C Wolff Company..............................F........610 359-9600
Newtown Square **(G-12598)**

SPORTING & RECREATIONAL GOODS, WHOLESALE: Watersports

Wexco Incorporated ....G........717 764-8585
York **(G-20710)**

SPORTING FIREARMS WHOLESALERS

Choice Cleangear LLC.........................G........610 497-9756
Aston **(G-754)**

SPORTING GOODS

2 Sports Inc ....G........484 679-1225
Norristown **(G-12626)**
Ace Sports Inc.....................................D........610 833-5513
Woodlyn **(G-20216)**
Aluminum Athletic Equipment Co.........E........610 825-6565
West Conshohocken **(G-19684)**
APT Advanced Polymer Tech Corp.......D........724 452-1330
Harmony **(G-7066)**
Archer Double Ds Product....................G........610 838-1121
Bethlehem **(G-1452)**
Arctic Star Sleds ....G........814 684-3594
Tyrone **(G-18576)**
Aul Company Jack...............................G........412 882-1836
Pittsburgh **(G-14738)**
Blue Sky International Inc....................G........610 306-1234
Phoenixville **(G-14534)**
Broken Straw Outdoors........................G........814 563-2200
Youngsville **(G-20769)**
Buck Koola Inc ....G........814 849-9695
Brookville **(G-2256)**
Cardinal Systems Inc..........................E........570 385-4733
Schuylkill Haven **(G-17151)**
Chester County Sports Products ....G........610 327-4843
Pottstown **(G-15946)**
Combined Tactical Systems Inc ....C........724 932-2177
Jamestown **(G-8236)**
Diamond Wear......................................G........610 433-2680
Whitehall **(G-19870)**
Es & Son of Union I..............................G........724 439-5589
Uniontown **(G-18625)**
Family First Sports Park.......................E........814 866-5425
Erie **(G-5288)**
Garrett Liners Inc ....E........215 295-0200
Levittown **(G-9838)**
Hanford & Hockenbrock.......................G........610 275-5373
Norristown **(G-12665)**
Heated Hunts ....G........570 575-5080
S Abingtn Twp **(G-16897)**
Inferno Sports & Athletics LLC.............G........610 633-0919
Exton **(G-5698)**
Innovative Designs Inc ....G........412 799-0350
Pittsburgh **(G-15128)**
International Vectors Ltd.......................E........717 767-4008
Emigsville **(G-4993)**
Johns Custom Leather.........................G........724 459-6802
Blairsville **(G-1727)**
Lomma Investments.............................E........570 346-5555
Scranton **(G-17256)**
Macris Sports Inc.................................G........724 654-6065
New Castle **(G-12117)**
McKenzie Sports Products LLC............C........717 731-9920
Camp Hill **(G-2504)**
Mgs04 Corporation..............................G........267 249-2372
Philadelphia **(G-14018)**
Olympian Athletics...............................G........717 765-8615
Waynesboro **(G-19420)**
Patternmaster Chokes LLC..................G........877 388-2259
Hollidaysburg **(G-7652)**
Penn Big Bed Slate Co Inc ....D........610 767-4601
Slatington **(G-17611)**
Pennsbury Enterprises Inc ....F........215 741-5960
Penndel **(G-13240)**
Pennsylvania Avenue Sports................G........610 533-4133
Roseto **(G-16821)**
Pete Rickard Company.........................G........518 234-3758
Galeton **(G-6243)**
Pioneer Enterprises Inc ....G........717 938-9388
Lewisberry **(G-9892)**
Plastic Development Company PA.........E........800 451-1420
Williamsport **(G-20058)**
Prosco Inc ....E........814 375-0484
Du Bois **(G-4414)**

Shubandit LLC.....................................G........610 916-8313
Blandon **(G-1759)**
Smokers Sports Store..........................G........717 687-9445
Ronks **(G-16815)**
Sport Manufacturing Group Inc............G........718 575-1801
Huntingdon Valley **(G-8039)**
Sportsmansliquidationcom LLC...........G........717 263-6000
Harrisburg **(G-7217)**
Stateasy ....G........412 437-8287
Pittsburgh **(G-15579)**
Stonybrook Shooting Supplies ....G........717 757-1088
York **(G-20681)**
Tri County Sports Inc...........................G........717 394-9169
Lancaster **(G-9222)**
Wild Asaph Outfitters...........................G........570 724-5155
Wellsboro **(G-19475)**
Xpogo LLC...G........717 650-5232
Pittsburgh **(G-15727)**

SPORTING GOODS STORES, NEC

Academy Sports Center Inc.................G........570 339-3399
Mount Carmel **(G-11622)**
Blue Heron Sportswear Inc..................G........570 742-3228
Milton **(G-11234)**
Boulevard Sports ....G........724 378-9191
Aliquippa **(G-69)**
Daves Pro Shop Inc ....F........814 834-6116
Saint Marys **(G-16961)**
Dirt Rag Magazine...............................G........412 767-9910
Pittsburgh **(G-14926)**
Gear Racewear Inc..............................F........724 458-6336
Grove City **(G-6786)**
Jim Borden..G........570 965-2505
Springville **(G-17930)**
Johns Custom Leather.........................G........724 459-6802
Blairsville **(G-1727)**
PA Outdoor Times ....G........814 946-7400
Altoona **(G-536)**
Schuylkill Valley Sports Inc ....D........717 627-0417
Lititz **(G-10046)**
Schuylkill Vly Spt Trappe Ctr...............F........877 711-8100
Pottstown **(G-16044)**
Sports Factory Promotions Inc ....G........724 847-2684
New Brighton **(G-12042)**
Synergy Print Design LLC....................G........610 532-2950
Prospect Park **(G-16121)**
Ultimate Screw Machine Pdts ....G........610 565-1565
Media **(G-10955)**
Videoray LLC.......................................E........610 458-3000
Pottstown **(G-16067)**

SPORTING GOODS STORES: Archery Splys

A & B Homes Inc ....G........570 253-3888
Honesdale **(G-7699)**
A Archery and Printing Place................G........717 274-1811
Lebanon **(G-9544)**

SPORTING GOODS STORES: Firearms

A & S Firearm Supplies Inc ....G........724 925-1212
Youngwood **(G-20776)**
C&G Arms LLC....................................C........724 858-2856
Natrona Heights **(G-11937)**
Dbi Inc ....D........814 653-7625
Fairmount City **(G-5808)**
F P Engbert Discount Guns ....G........724 465-9756
Indiana **(G-8098)**
R Fritz Enterprises Inc ....G........814 267-4204
Berlin **(G-1292)**

SPORTING GOODS STORES: Fishing Eqpt

Donald Plants ....G........412 384-5911
West Elizabeth **(G-19694)**

SPORTING GOODS STORES: Hunting Eqpt

Be The Tree Llc ....G........717 887-0780
Hellam **(G-7649)**
Brutis Enterprises Inc..........................G........412 431-5440
Pittsburgh **(G-14795)**
Quaker Boy Inc....................................F........814 362-7073
Bradford **(G-1988)**
Real Scent...G........717 692-0527
Millersburg **(G-11199)**
Vergona Outdoors LLC.........................G........814 967-4844
Centerville **(G-2837)**

SPORTING GOODS STORES: Playground Eqpt

Foxs Country Sheds ....F........717 626-9560
Lititz **(G-10010)**
Lilliput Play Homes Inc........................G........724 348-7071
Finleyville **(G-5961)**

SPORTING GOODS STORES: Skiing Eqpt

Idlewild Ski Shop Inc ....F........570 222-4200
Clifford Township **(G-3248)**

SPORTING GOODS STORES: Soccer Splys

Transfer Junction................................G........814 942-4434
Williamsburg **(G-19982)**

SPORTING GOODS STORES: Specialty Sport Splys, NEC

Skydive Sports Inc ....G........856 629-4600
Bushkill **(G-2369)**

SPORTING GOODS STORES: Team sports Eqpt

Tri County Sports Inc...........................G........717 394-9169
Lancaster **(G-9222)**

SPORTING GOODS STORES: Water Sport Eqpt

25 Fathoms International Inc ....G........610 558-1101
Glen Mills **(G-6428)**

SPORTING GOODS: Archery

A & B Homes Inc ....G........570 253-3888
Honesdale **(G-7699)**
Dorothy M Nelson ....G........724 837-6210
Greensburg **(G-6662)**
J and D Custom Strings ....F........717 252-4078
Wrightsville **(G-20239)**
Jo Jan Sportsequip Co Inc...................G........724 225-5582
Washington **(G-19189)**
Rightnour Manufacturing Co Inc...........E........800 326-9113
Mingoville **(G-11257)**
Triple Trophy Products Inc....................G........412 781-8801
Pittsburgh **(G-15651)**
Vergona Outdoors LLC.........................G........814 967-4844
Centerville **(G-2837)**
Vision Quest Inc...................................G........570 448-2845
Honesdale **(G-7732)**

SPORTING GOODS: Hammocks & Other Net Prdts

Jetnet Corporation...............................D........412 741-0100
Sewickley **(G-17396)**

SPORTING GOODS: Sleeping Bags

Innovative Designs Inc ....G........412 799-0350
Pittsburgh **(G-15127)**

SPORTING/ATHLETIC GOODS: Gloves, Boxing, Handball, Etc

Carson Boxing LLC ....G........814 839-2768
Bedford **(G-1045)**

SPORTS APPAREL STORES

All American Sweats Inc ....F........412 922-8999
Pittsburgh **(G-14674)**
Blue Mountain Sports AP Inc................G........717 263-4124
Chambersburg **(G-2912)**
Choice Cleangear LLC.........................G........610 497-9756
Aston **(G-754)**

SPORTS PROMOTION SVCS

Cutts Group LLC..................................F........610 366-9620
Allentown **(G-190)**

SPORTS TEAMS & CLUBS: Basketball

Blue Star Basketball ....G........215 638-7060
Bensalem **(G-1158)**

SPOUTING: Plastic & Fiberglass Reinforced

Mr Spouting ....G....... 814 692-4880
Port Matilda (G-15903)

Premier Spouting Design LLC ....G....... 717 336-1205
Reinholds (G-16636)

Saint-Gobain Vetrotex Amer Inc ....F....... 610 893-6000
Valley Forge (G-18713)

SPOUTS: Sheet Metal

Sensenigs Spouting ....F....... 717 627-6886
Lititz (G-10049)

SPRAYING EQPT: Agricultural

5 Star Plus Inc ....G....... 610 470-9187
Oxford (G-13070)

Bishop Equipment Manufacturing ....G....... 215 368-5307
Hatfield (G-7321)

Custom Linings Spray On Bed ....G....... 570 779-4609
Plymouth (G-15816)

SPRINGS: Automobile

Cambria Springs Service Inc ....G....... 814 539-1629
Johnstown (G-8362)

Fulmer Company Inc ....G....... 724 325-7140
Export (G-5606)

SPRINGS: Gun, Precision

W C Wolff Company ....F....... 610 359-9600
Newtown Square (G-12598)

SPRINGS: Hot Formed

Union Spring & Mfg Corp ....C....... 412 843-5900
Monroeville (G-11361)

SPRINGS: Hot Wound, Exc Wire

Standard Steel Specialty Co ....D....... 724 846-7600
Beaver Falls (G-1014)

SPRINGS: Leaf, Automobile, Locomotive, Etc

Triangle Sspension Systems Inc ....D....... 814 375-7211
Du Bois (G-4425)

SPRINGS: Mechanical, Precision

Lesjofors Springs America Inc ....E....... 800 551-0298
Pittston (G-15762)

SPRINGS: Precision

Chestnut Group Inc ....G....... 610 688-3300
Wayne (G-19313)

SPRINGS: Steel

Ace Wire Spring & Form Co Inc ....E....... 412 331-3353
Mc Kees Rocks (G-10601)

Ametek Inc ....G....... 215 355-6900
Horsham (G-7785)

General Wire Spring Company ....C....... 412 771-6300
Mc Kees Rocks (G-10612)

Keystone Spring Service Inc ....E....... 412 621-4800
Pittsburgh (G-15176)

Lesjofors Springs America Inc ....E....... 800 551-0298
Pittston (G-15762)

Standard Car Truck Company ....D....... 412 782-7300
Pittsburgh (G-15576)

Tricor Industries Inc ....F....... 610 265-1111
Norristown (G-12721)

SPRINGS: Torsion Bar

Union Spring & Mfg Corp ....E....... 814 967-2545
Townville (G-18449)

SPRINGS: Wire

A V Weber Co Inc ....G....... 215 699-3527
North Wales (G-12784)

Ace Wire Spring & Form Co Inc ....E....... 412 331-3353
Mc Kees Rocks (G-10601)

Barnes Group Inc ....C....... 814 663-6082
Corry (G-3745)

Barnes Group Inc ....G....... 215 785-4466
Bristol (G-2116)

Diamond Wire Spring Company ....E....... 412 821-2703
Pittsburgh (G-14922)

Evans John Sons Incorporated ....D....... 215 368-7700
Lansdale (G-9365)

General Wire Spring Company ....C....... 412 771-6300
Mc Kees Rocks (G-10612)

Liberty Spring Company Inc ....F....... 484 652-1100
Collingdale (G-3406)

Liberty Spring Usa LLC ....E....... 484 652-1100
Darby (G-4022)

Mercer Spring & Wire LLC ....E....... 814 967-2545
Townville (G-18446)

Navarro Spring Company ....G....... 610 259-3177
Lansdowne (G-9439)

Nelmark Electric Inc ....G....... 724 290-0314
Renfrew (G-16641)

Northeast Spring Inc ....E....... 610 374-8508
Reading (G-16457)

Oak Hill Controls LLC ....G....... 610 967-3985
Emmaus (G-5035)

Oak Hill Controls LLC ....F....... 610 758-9500
Bethlehem (G-1585)

Penn Central Spring Corp ....G....... 717 564-6792
Middletown (G-11067)

Penn-Elkco Inc ....F....... 814 834-4304
Saint Marys (G-17003)

Royersford Spring Co ....F....... 610 948-4440
Royersford (G-16863)

St Marys Spring Co ....G....... 814 834-2460
Saint Marys (G-17020)

Union Spring & Mfg Corp ....E....... 814 967-2545
Townville (G-18449)

Vodvarka Springs ....G....... 724 695-3268
Clinton (G-3268)

Wilder Diamond Blades Inc ....G....... 570 222-9590
Kingsley (G-8710)

SPRINKLING SYSTEMS: Fire Control

A G F Manufacturing Co Inc ....E....... 610 240-4900
Malvern (G-10178)

Air Products Corporation ....D....... 800 345-8207
Exton (G-5637)

Bnb Fire Protection Inc ....G....... 610 944-0594
Fleetwood (G-5968)

Rowe Sprinkler Systems Inc ....E....... 570 837-7647
Middleburg (G-11039)

Tyco Fire Products LP ....E....... 215 362-0700
Lansdale (G-9421)

Tyco Fire Products LP ....E....... 256 238-0579
Columbia (G-3452)

SPROCKETS: Power Transmission

Martin Sprocket & Gear Inc ....D....... 610 837-1841
Danielsville (G-3994)

STAGE LIGHTING SYSTEMS

Lehigh Electric Products Co ....E....... 610 395-3386
Allentown (G-293)

STAINLESS STEEL

Aii Acquisition LLC ....G....... 412 394-2800
Pittsburgh (G-14657)

Aii Acquisition LLC ....G....... 724 226-5947
Brackenridge (G-1936)

AK Steel Corporation ....A....... 724 284-2854
Butler (G-2373)

Allegheny Ludlum LLC ....D....... 724 226-5000
Brackenridge (G-1937)

Allegheny Ludlum LLC ....B....... 412 394-2800
Pittsburgh (G-14679)

Allegheny Ludlum LLC ....D....... 724 773-2700
Pittsburgh (G-14680)

Allegheny Technologies Inc ....G....... 724 224-1000
Oakdale (G-12888)

Allegheny Technologies Inc ....G....... 724 452-1726
Zelienople (G-20788)

Allegheny Technologies Inc ....D....... 412 394-2800
Pittsburgh (G-14682)

ATI Powder Metals LLC ....D....... 412 923-2670
Oakdale (G-12892)

ATI Precision Finishing LLC ....F....... 724 775-2618
Monaca (G-11280)

Bosio Metal Specialties Inc ....F....... 215 699-4100
North Wales (G-12792)

Carpenter Technology Corp ....B....... 610 208-2000
Philadelphia (G-13508)

Carpenter Technology Corp ....B....... 610 208-2000
Reading (G-16343)

Ellwood Quality Steels Company ....C....... 724 658-6502
New Castle (G-12087)

Exim Steel & Shipbroking Inc ....G....... 215 369-9746
Yardley (G-20310)

Geemacher LLC ....G....... 484 524-8251
Pottstown (G-15990)

Goc Property Holdings LLC ....F....... 814 678-4127
Oil City (G-12946)

Halferty Metals Company Inc ....F....... 724 694-5280
Derry (G-4102)

Hoodco Inc ....F....... 215 236-0951
Drexel Hill (G-4365)

Jessop Steel LLC ....E....... 724 222-4000
Washington (G-19188)

Johnstown Specialty Castings ....B....... 814 535-9002
Johnstown (G-8391)

Kasunick Welding & Fabg Co Inc ....F....... 412 321-2722
Pittsburgh (G-15161)

Klk Welding Inc ....F....... 717 637-0080
Hanover (G-6910)

Laurel Valley Metals LLC ....G....... 724 990-8189
Blairsville (G-1732)

North Jckson Specialty Stl LLC ....E....... 412 257-7600
Bridgeville (G-2082)

Olympia Chimney Supply Inc ....D....... 570 496-8890
Scranton (G-17268)

Poormans Wldg Fabrication Inc ....F....... 814 349-5893
Aaronsburg (G-1)

Sterling-Fleischman Inc ....F....... 610 647-1717
Media (G-10951)

Susini Specialty Steels Inc ....F....... 724 295-6511
Natrona Heights (G-11949)

TI Oregon Inc ....G....... 412 394-2800
Pittsburgh (G-15624)

STAIR TREADS: Rubber

Ace Panels Company ....G....... 814 583-5015
Luthersburg (G-10120)

STAIRCASES & STAIRS, WOOD

Durawood Products Inc ....C....... 717 336-0220
Denver (G-4071)

HOP Millwork Inc ....G....... 724 934-3880
Wexford (G-19806)

Jack Burnley Son Stair Contrs ....E....... 610 948-4166
Spring City (G-17862)

Johns Cstm Stairways Mllwk Co ....G....... 215 463-1211
Philadelphia (G-13908)

Joyce Stair Corp ....G....... 570 345-8000
Pine Grove (G-14594)

Moorhouse Stair ....G....... 610 367-9275
Bechtelsville (G-1033)

Spring Valley Millwork Inc ....E....... 610 927-0144
Reading (G-16523)

STAMPED ART GOODS FOR EMBROIDERING

Stitches Embroidery Inc ....E....... 412 781-7046
Pittsburgh (G-15585)

STAMPING SVC: Book, Gold

Fox Bindery Inc ....C....... 215 538-5380
Lansdale (G-9369)

STAMPING: Fabric Articles

East Penn Container Dctg Inc ....E....... 610 944-3227
Fleetwood (G-5971)

STAMPINGS: Automotive

Addev Walco Inc ....E....... 412 486-4400
Glenshaw (G-6479)

Angel Colon ....G....... 215 455-4000
Philadelphia (G-13392)

G Adasavage LLC ....E....... 215 355-3105
Huntingdon Valley (G-7987)

Henshell Corp ....E....... 215 225-7755
Philadelphia (G-13815)

HMS Industries Inc ....E....... 724 459-5090
Blairsville (G-1724)

New Standard Corporation ....D....... 717 757-9450
York (G-20611)

Norplas Industries Inc ....G....... 724 705-7483
Washington (G-19211)

Quality Stamping ....G....... 724 459-5060
Blairsville (G-1739)

York Corrugating Company ....D....... 717 845-3512
York (G-20734)

PRODUCT

STAMPINGS: Metal

A & S Manufacturing Co ....F 888 651-6149
Philadelphia *(G-13321)*

A W Mercer Inc ....C 610 367-8460
Boyertown *(G-1892)*

Abbottstown Stamping Co Inc ....F 717 632-0588
Hanover *(G-6859)*

Accrotool Inc ....C 724 339-3560
New Kensington *(G-12320)*

Adept Corporation ....D 800 451-2254
York *(G-20366)*

Barco Industries Inc ....E 610 374-3117
Reading *(G-16328)*

Barnes Group Inc ....C 814 663-6082
Corry *(G-3745)*

Bra-Vor Tool & Die Co Inc ....E 814 724-1557
Meadville *(G-10708)*

Brd Noise & Vibration Ctrl Inc ....G 610 863-6300
Wind Gap *(G-20167)*

Chestnut Group Inc ....G 610 688-3300
Wayne *(G-19313)*

Clark Metal Products Co ....C 724 459-7550
Blairsville *(G-1719)*

Composidie Inc ....C 724 845-8602
Apollo *(G-673)*

Composidie Inc ....E 724 845-8602
Leechburg *(G-9643)*

Danco Precision Inc ....F 610 933-8981
Phoenixville *(G-14542)*

Danco Precision Inc ....E 610 933-1090
Phoenixville *(G-14543)*

Die-Tech Inc ....E 717 938-6771
York Haven *(G-20757)*

Dyna East Corporation ....E 610 270-9900
King of Prussia *(G-8614)*

E F E Laboratories Inc ....E 215 672-2400
Horsham *(G-7812)*

Electronic Tool & Die Works ....G 215 639-0730
Bensalem *(G-1187)*

Emporium Specialties Company ....E 814 647-8661
Austin *(G-833)*

Fox Welding Shop Inc ....G 215 225-3069
Philadelphia *(G-13716)*

Freedom Components Inc ....G 717 242-0101
Lewistown *(G-9930)*

G & M Co Inc ....F 610 779-7812
Reading *(G-16387)*

G Adasavage LLC ....E 215 355-3105
Huntingdon Valley *(G-7987)*

Gap Stamping LLC ....G 610 759-7820
Bethlehem *(G-1522)*

Gerome Manufacturing Co Inc ....D 724 438-8544
Smithfield *(G-17650)*

Globe Metal Manufacturing Co ....F 215 763-1024
Philadelphia *(G-13773)*

Gma Tooling Company ....E 215 355-3107
Huntingdon Valley *(G-7991)*

Harter Precision ....G 724 459-5060
Blairsville *(G-1723)*

Heraeus Incorporated ....B 480 961-9200
Yardley *(G-20315)*

Jacob Holtz Company LLC ....D 215 423-2800
Philadelphia *(G-13316)*

Jade Equipment Corporation ....C 215 947-3333
Huntingdon Valley *(G-7999)*

Keystone North Inc ....E 570 662-3882
Mansfield *(G-10420)*

L-One Inc ....E 717 938-6771
York Haven *(G-20760)*

Laminar Flow Inc ....D 215 672-0232
Warminster *(G-18909)*

Leiss Tool & Die ....C 814 444-1444
Somerset *(G-17695)*

Marco Manufacturing Co Inc ....E 215 463-2332
Philadelphia *(G-13992)*

Metal Fabricating Co ....G 717 442-4729
Parkesburg *(G-13180)*

Metal Peddler Inc ....G 724 476-1061
West Sunbury *(G-19772)*

Moore Push Pin Company ....D 215 233-5700
Glenside *(G-6531)*

N C B Technologies Inc ....G 724 658-5544
New Castle *(G-12123)*

New Standard Corporation ....G 717 757-9450
Mount Joy *(G-11667)*

New Standard Corporation ....B 717 764-2409
Emigsville *(G-4996)*

Northeast Industrial Mfg Inc ....E 724 588-7711
Greenville *(G-6760)*

Osram Sylvania Inc ....B 717 854-3499
Saint Marys *(G-17000)*

P G A Machine Co Inc ....G 610 874-1335
Eddystone *(G-4806)*

Pb Holdings Inc ....G 215 947-3333
Huntingdon Valley *(G-8021)*

Penn-Elkco Inc ....F 814 834-4304
Saint Marys *(G-17003)*

Premier Pan Company Inc ....D 724 457-4220
Crescent *(G-3887)*

Qdp Inc ....F 610 828-2324
Plymouth Meeting *(G-15866)*

Reading Truck Body LLC ....C 610 775-3301
Reading *(G-16493)*

Schaffner Manufacturing Co ....D 412 761-9902
Pittsburgh *(G-15515)*

Schiller Grounds Care Inc ....D 215 322-4970
Huntingdon Valley *(G-8035)*

Smoyer L M Brass Products Inc ....G 610 867-5011
Bethlehem *(G-1620)*

Superior Group Inc ....E 610 397-2040
Conshohocken *(G-3610)*

Tottser Tool and Die Shop Inc ....D 215 357-7600
Southampton *(G-17843)*

Veterinary Tag Supply Co Inc ....G 610 649-1550
Bridgeport *(G-2048)*

Waverly Partners Inc ....C 610 687-7867
Wayne *(G-19390)*

Westwood Precision LLC ....G 610 264-7020
Allentown *(G-433)*

Winston Industries Inc ....F 215 394-8178
Warminster *(G-19001)*

York Corrugating Company ....D 717 845-3512
York *(G-20734)*

STANDPIPES

Conway-Phillips Holding LLC ....E 412 315-7963
Braddock *(G-1943)*

STARTERS & CONTROLLERS: Motor, Electric

Benshaw Inc ....D 412 968-0100
Pittsburgh *(G-14762)*

Vacon LLC ....C 717 261-5000
Chambersburg *(G-2992)*

STARTERS: Motor

S T M Heavy Duty Electric Inc ....F 610 967-3810
Zionsville *(G-20836)*

STATIONARY & OFFICE SPLYS, WHOLESALE: Inked Ribbons

Bms Inc ....G 609 883-5155
Yardley *(G-20297)*

Max Intrntional Converters Inc ....E 717 898-0147
Lancaster *(G-9128)*

STATIONARY & OFFICE SPLYS, WHOLESALE: Laser Printer Splys

Saxon Office Technology Inc ....F 215 736-2620
Fairless Hills *(G-5795)*

STATIONARY & OFFICE SPLYS, WHOLESALE: Manifold Business Form

Interform Corporation ....C 412 221-7321
Bridgeville *(G-2070)*

STATIONARY & OFFICE SPLYS, WHOLESALE: Office Filing Splys

Print Happy LLC ....G 717 699-4465
York *(G-20639)*

STATIONARY & OFFICE SPLYS, WHOLESALE: Stationers, Commercial

Samson Paper Co Inc ....E 610 630-9090
Norristown *(G-12708)*

STATIONARY & OFFICE SPLYS, WHOLESALE: Stationery

Squibb Alvah M Company Inc ....F 412 751-2301
McKeesport *(G-10682)*

Thorndale Press Inc ....G 610 384-3363
Downingtown *(G-4258)*

STATIONERY & OFFICE SPLYS WHOLESALERS

Apparel Print Promotionals ....G 717 233-4277
Harrisburg *(G-7088)*

Bay Sales LLC ....G 215 331-6466
Bristol *(G-2117)*

Lap Distributors Inc ....G 215 744-4000
Philadelphia *(G-13955)*

Prime Ribbon Inc ....G 412 761-4470
Pittsburgh *(G-15438)*

Supra Office Solutions Inc ....G 267 275-8888
Philadelphia *(G-14360)*

STATIONERY ARTICLES: Pottery

Horn Linda Collectibles & Co ....G 570 998-8401
Trout Run *(G-18514)*

STATIONERY PRDTS

Bay Sales LLC ....G 215 331-6466
Bristol *(G-2117)*

Digibuddha Design LLC ....F 267 387-8165
Hatboro *(G-7280)*

Foto-Wear Inc ....G 570 307-3600
Lake Ariel *(G-8888)*

Progressive Converting Inc ....D 570 384-2979
Hazle Township *(G-7475)*

STATIONERY: Made From Purchased Materials

Mbm Industries Inc ....E 215 844-2490
Philadelphia *(G-13998)*

National Imprint Corporation ....E 814 239-8141
Claysburg *(G-3205)*

Paper Magic Group Inc ....C 570 961-3863
Moosic *(G-11511)*

Roaring Spring Blank Book Co ....C 814 793-3744
Martinsburg *(G-10530)*

STATORS REWINDING SVCS

Witmer Motor Service ....G 717 336-2949
Stevens *(G-18058)*

STATUARY GOODS, EXC RELIGIOUS: Wholesalers

Accent Shop ....G 724 695-7580
Imperial *(G-8056)*

STEEL & ALLOYS: Tool & Die

Carpenter Technology Corp ....E 610 208-2000
Reading *(G-16344)*

Classic Tool Inc ....G 814 763-4805
Saegertown *(G-16911)*

Eastern Tool Steel Service Inc ....G 814 834-7224
Saint Marys *(G-16967)*

Ge-Hitachi Nuclear Energy ....C 724 743-0270
Canonsburg *(G-2593)*

John W Czech ....E 814 763-4470
Saegertown *(G-16920)*

PM Kalco Inc ....E 724 347-2208
Wheatland *(G-19841)*

Sharp Tool and Die Inc ....G 814 763-1133
Guys Mills *(G-6812)*

Superior Tooling Tech Inc ....F 814 486-9498
Emporium *(G-5076)*

Weichert Machining Inc ....G 717 235-6761
Glen Rock *(G-6462)*

STEEL FABRICATORS

A & R Iron Works Inc ....F 610 497-8770
Trainer *(G-18462)*

A D M Welding & Fabrication ....G 814 723-7227
Warren *(G-19007)*

A M Sheet Metal Inc ....F 570 322-5417
South Williamsport *(G-17789)*

Aaron S Myers ....G 717 339-9304
New Oxford *(G-12401)*

Abex Industries ....G 717 246-2611
Red Lion *(G-16586)*

Accutrex Products Inc ....C 724 746-4300
Canonsburg *(G-2532)*

Ace Metal Inc ... E ... 610 623-2204
Clifton Heights *(G-3250)*
Acf Group LLC ... E ... 724 364-7027
Allison *(G-444)*
Acme Metals Co ... G ... 412 331-4301
Pittsburgh *(G-14642)*
Advanced Fabrication Svcs Inc ... E ... 717 763-0286
Lemoyne *(G-9741)*
Advanced Industrial Svcs Inc ... C ... 717 764-9811
York *(G-20368)*
Afco C&S LLC ... G ... 717 264-9147
Chambersburg *(G-2898)*
Agar Welding Service & Stl Sup ... E ... 717 532-1000
Walnut Bottom *(G-18788)*
Al Kaczmarczyk ... G ... 724 775-1366
Beaver Falls *(G-996)*
Alex C Fergusson LLC ... D ... 717 264-9147
Chambersburg *(G-2899)*
All Weld Steel Co Inc ... F ... 215 884-6985
Glenside *(G-6504)*
Allfab Manufacturing Inc ... G ... 724 924-2725
New Castle *(G-12055)*
Alloy Design Inc ... G ... 610 369-9265
Boyertown *(G-1896)*
Altrax ... G ... 814 379-3706
Summerville *(G-18156)*
American Roll Suppliers Inc ... G ... 610 857-2988
Parkesburg *(G-13171)*
Amthor Steel Inc ... G ... 814 452-4700
Erie *(G-5193)*
Anvil Craft Corp ... E ... 610 250-9600
Easton *(G-4645)*
Anvil Iron Works Inc ... G ... 215 468-8300
Philadelphia *(G-13397)*
Apex Fabrication & Design Inc ... E ... 610 689-5880
Boyertown *(G-1897)*
Apex Manufacturing Co Inc ... G ... 215 343-4850
Warrington *(G-19108)*
Architectural Stl & Assod Pdts ... F ... 215 368-8113
Lansdale *(G-9343)*
Armin Ironworks Inc ... G ... 412 322-1622
Pittsburgh *(G-14725)*
ASP Services Inc ... E ... 570 374-5333
Selinsgrove *(G-17320)*
Atlantic Metal Industries LLC ... G ... 908 445-4299
Stroudsburg *(G-18106)*
Auto Weld Chassis & Components ... G ... 570 275-1411
Danville *(G-3997)*
B & T Fabrication ... G ... 814 634-0638
Meyersdale *(G-11009)*
Baileys Steel & Supply LLC ... G ... 724 267-4648
Waynesburg *(G-19433)*
Baillie Fabricating & Wldg Inc ... G ... 610 701-5808
West Chester *(G-19508)*
Ballymore Holdings Inc ... E ... 610 593-5062
Coatesville *(G-3293)*
Baut Studios Inc ... E ... 570 288-1431
Swoyersville *(G-18194)*
Ben Swaney ... G ... 412 372-8109
Monroeville *(G-11325)*
Berlin Steel Construction Co ... F ... 610 240-8953
West Chester *(G-19510)*
Bethlehem Aluminum Inc ... F ... 610 432-4541
Allentown *(G-150)*
Big B Manufacturing Inc ... E ... 570 648-2084
Klingerstown *(G-8806)*
Biofab Products Inc ... E ... 724 283-4801
Butler *(G-2379)*
Black Rock Fabrication LLC ... G ... 610 212-3528
Phoenixville *(G-14533)*
Black Rock Repair LLC ... G ... 717 529-6553
Kirkwood *(G-8744)*
Blue Valley Industries Inc ... G ... 717 436-8266
Port Royal *(G-15909)*
Bortnick Construction Inc ... G ... 814 587-6023
Springboro *(G-17894)*
Brad Foote Gear Works Inc ... E ... 412 264-1428
Pittsburgh *(G-14789)*
Brandywine Valley Fabricators ... F ... 610 384-7440
Coatesville *(G-3295)*
Bryce Saylor & Sons Inc ... F ... 814 942-2288
Altoona *(G-485)*
Byrne Chiarlone LP ... E ... 610 874-8436
Chester *(G-3042)*
Carl E Reichert Corp ... G ... 215 723-9525
Telford *(G-18269)*
Carrara Steel Inc ... E ... 814 452-4600
Erie *(G-5222)*
Carriage Machine Shop LLC ... F ... 717 397-4079
Bird In Hand *(G-1671)*
Carroll Manufacturing Co LLC ... G ... 724 266-0400
Leetsdale *(G-9688)*
Cast Pac Inc ... E ... 610 264-8131
Allentown *(G-165)*
Cava Intl MBL & Gran Inc ... E ... 215 732-7800
Philadelphia *(G-13516)*
Challenger Fabrication ... G ... 570 788-7911
Drums *(G-4381)*
Charters Fabg Pwdr Coating LLC ... E ... 412 203-5421
Coraopolis *(G-3676)*
Chase Industries Inc ... F ... 412 449-0160
Pittsburgh *(G-14841)*
Chowns Fabrication Rigging Inc ... D ... 610 584-0240
Skippack *(G-17595)*
Clipper Pipe & Service Inc ... G ... 610 872-9067
Eddystone *(G-4799)*
Compu-Craft Fabricators Inc ... E ... 215 646-2381
Montgomeryville *(G-11390)*
Conrad Enterprises Inc ... E ... 717 274-5151
Cornwall *(G-3738)*
Conshohocken Steel Pdts Inc ... E ... 215 283-9222
Ambler *(G-574)*
Consolidated Steel Svcs Inc ... E ... 814 944-5890
Fallentimber *(G-5851)*
Container Research Corporation ... C ... 610 459-2160
Aston *(G-757)*
Converters Inc ... E ... 215 355-5400
Huntingdon Valley *(G-7971)*
Cooks Machine Work ... G ... 814 589-5141
Pleasantville *(G-15799)*
Craftweld Fabrication Co Inc ... E ... 267 492-1100
Montgomeryville *(G-11391)*
Craig Sidleck ... F ... 610 261-9580
Whitehall *(G-19869)*
Crowell Metal Fabrication ... G ... 814 486-2664
Emporium *(G-5054)*
Custom Mfg & Indus Svcs LLC ... G ... 412 621-2982
Pittsburgh *(G-14894)*
Custom Steel Products Inc ... G ... 412 215-9923
Bridgeville *(G-2058)*
Cutting Edge Countertops ... G ... 724 397-8605
Marion Center *(G-10472)*
D & S Fabricating & Welding ... G ... 412 653-9185
Clairton *(G-3148)*
D A D Fabrication and Welding ... G ... 814 781-1886
Saint Marys *(G-16960)*
D L George & Sons Mfg Inc ... D ... 717 765-4700
Waynesboro *(G-19407)*
D L Machine LLC ... F ... 724 627-7870
Jefferson *(G-8269)*
Daniel C Tanney Inc ... D ... 215 639-3131
Bensalem *(G-1179)*
Dasco Inc ... G ... 412 771-4140
Pittsburgh *(G-14906)*
David Seidel ... F ... 610 921-8310
Temple *(G-18327)*
Demarchi John ... G ... 724 547-6440
Mount Pleasant *(G-11696)*
DH Steel Products LLC ... E ... 814 459-2715
Erie *(G-5247)*
Diamond Fabrications Inc ... G ... 724 228-8422
Washington *(G-19163)*
Dinsmore Wldg Fabrication Inc ... G ... 814 885-6407
Kersey *(G-8555)*
Dolans Wldg Stl Fbrication Inc ... E ... 814 749-8639
Johnstown *(G-8369)*
Dunbar Machine Co Inc ... G ... 724 277-8711
Dunbar *(G-4439)*
Dura-Bond Coating Inc ... E ... 724 327-0782
Export *(G-5598)*
Dura-Bond Steel Corp ... C ... 724 327-0280
Export *(G-5599)*
Duraloy Technologies Inc ... C ... 724 887-5100
Scottdale *(G-17190)*
E & E Metal Fabrications Inc ... E ... 717 228-3727
Lebanon *(G-9565)*
Earlys Body Machine & Welding ... G ... 717 838-1663
Palmyra *(G-13122)*
Eastern Alloy Inc ... G ... 724 379-5776
Donora *(G-4153)*
Economy Metal Inc ... G ... 724 869-2887
Freedom *(G-6189)*
Edlon Inc ... D ... 610 268-3101
Avondale *(G-852)*
Edro Engineering Inc ... F ... 610 940-1993
Conshohocken *(G-3541)*
Enclosures Direct Corporation ... G ... 724 837-7600
Greensburg *(G-6664)*
Erie Weld Products Inc ... F ... 814 899-6320
Erie *(G-5278)*
Esmark Excalibur LLC ... E ... 724 371-3059
Beaver *(G-981)*
Esmark Excalibur LLC ... E ... 814 382-5696
Conneaut Lake *(G-3472)*
Esmark Industrial Group LLC ... F ... 412 259-8868
Sewickley *(G-17387)*
Evco Embouchure Visualizer Co ... G ... 724 224-4817
Tarentum *(G-18243)*
F F Frickanisce Iron Works ... G ... 724 568-2001
Vandergrift *(G-18726)*
Fab Tech Industries ... G ... 717 597-4919
Greencastle *(G-6610)*
Fab Tech V Industries Inc ... E ... 717 597-4919
Greencastle *(G-6611)*
Fab-Rick Industries Inc ... E ... 717 859-5633
Lancaster *(G-9013)*
Fab-TEC Industries Inc ... E ... 412 262-1144
Coraopolis *(G-3690)*
Fabco Inc ... F ... 814 944-1631
Altoona *(G-505)*
Fabricon Inc ... E ... 610 921-0203
Temple *(G-18329)*
Fisher & Ludlow Inc ... D ... 217 324-6106
Wexford *(G-19802)*
Flint Road Welding ... G ... 717 535-5282
Mifflintown *(G-11118)*
Flintwood Metals Inc ... E ... 717 274-9481
Lebanon *(G-9571)*
Formit Metal Fabricators LLC ... G ... 717 650-2895
York *(G-20485)*
Forrest Steel Corporation ... F ... 412 884-5533
Pittsburgh *(G-15027)*
Frazier-Simplex Machine Co ... E ... 724 222-5700
Washington *(G-19177)*
Freedom Components Inc ... G ... 717 242-0101
Lewistown *(G-9930)*
Frey Lutz Corp ... C ... 717 394-4635
Lancaster *(G-9025)*
Fronti Fabrications Inc ... G ... 610 900-6160
Palmerton *(G-13105)*
Gambone Steel Company Inc ... E ... 610 539-6505
Norristown *(G-12660)*
Gateco Inc ... F ... 610 433-2100
Allentown *(G-224)*
Gcl Inc ... G ... 724 933-7260
Wexford *(G-19805)*
General Weldments Inc ... F ... 724 744-2105
Irwin *(G-8164)*
George I Reitz & Sons Inc ... E ... 814 849-2308
Brookville *(G-2261)*
George I Reitz & Sons Inc ... G ... 412 824-9976
East Pittsburgh *(G-4595)*
Gfs LLC ... D ... 412 262-1131
Coraopolis *(G-3694)*
Global Fabrication Inc ... D ... 814 372-1500
Du Bois *(G-4394)*
Goldsborough & Vansant Inc ... G ... 724 782-0393
Finleyville *(G-5959)*
Goodhart Sons Inc ... C ... 717 656-2404
Lancaster *(G-9030)*
Grand Valley Manufacturing Co ... D ... 814 728-8760
Titusville *(G-18379)*
Gray Wldg Fabrication Svcs Inc ... E ... 412 271-6900
Braddock *(G-1944)*
Greiner Industries Inc ... B ... 717 653-8111
Mount Joy *(G-11660)*
Groffdale Machine Co Inc ... G ... 717 656-3249
Leola *(G-9785)*
H & P Manufacturing ... G ... 610 565-7344
Media *(G-10932)*
H R Edgar Machining & Fabg Inc ... D ... 724 339-6694
New Kensington *(G-12344)*
H W Nicholson Wldg & Mfg Inc ... E ... 724 727-3461
Apollo *(G-676)*
Haberle Steel Inc ... D ... 215 723-8848
Souderton *(G-17738)*
Harris Rebar Atlantic Inc ... D ... 610 882-1401
Bethlehem *(G-1529)*
Hazleton Custom Metal Pdts Inc ... G ... 570 455-0450
Hazle Township *(G-7462)*
Hazleton Custom Metal Products ... F ... 570 455-0450
Hazleton *(G-7501)*
Hazleton Iron Works Inc ... G ... 570 455-0445
Hazleton *(G-7502)*
Heslin-Steel Fab Inc ... G ... 724 745-8282
Canonsburg *(G-2596)*
Hetran-B Inc ... G ... 570 366-1411
Orwigsburg *(G-13044)*
High Industries Inc ... B ... 717 293-4444
Lancaster *(G-9046)*

High Steel Structures LLC ....F 717 390-4227
Lancaster **(G-9047)**

High Steel Structures LLC ....F 570 326-9051
Williamsport **(G-20022)**

High Steel Structures LLC ....B 717 299-5211
Lancaster **(G-9048)**

High Steel Structures LLC ....G 717 299-5211
Lancaster **(G-9049)**

Hipps Tool & Design ....G 814 236-3600
Curwensville **(G-3953)**

HMS Industries Inc ....E 724 459-5090
Blairsville **(G-1724)**

Hwp Fabrications ....G 814 487-5507
Windber **(G-20183)**

Industrial Welding and Fabg ....G 724 266-2887
Leetsdale **(G-9696)**

Interstate Equipment Corp ....G 412 563-5556
Pittsburgh **(G-15134)**

Ira G Steffy and Son Inc ....D 717 626-6500
Ephrata **(G-5111)**

J & R Emerick Inc ....G 724 752-1251
Ellwood City **(G-4940)**

J B Cooper and Cooper Co Inc ....F 724 573-9860
Hookstown **(G-7769)**

J M S Fabricated Systems Inc ....E 724 832-3640
Latrobe **(G-9482)**

J Thomas Ltd ....E 717 397-3483
Lancaster **(G-9069)**

J W Steel Fabricating Co ....G 724 625-1355
Mars **(G-10503)**

James E Roth Inc ....D 724 776-1910
Cranberry Township **(G-3826)**

Jeff Hills ....G 570 322-4536
Williamsport **(G-20029)**

Jet Industries LLC ....D 724 758-5601
Ellwood City **(G-4942)**

Jet Industries Inc ....E 724 452-5780
Zelienople **(G-20808)**

JGM Welding & Fabg Svcs Inc ....D 610 873-0081
Coatesville **(G-3310)**

JM Fabrications LLC ....G 267 354-1741
Sellersville **(G-17352)**

Joes Welding Repairs ....G 570 546-5223
Muncy **(G-11822)**

John H Bricker Welding ....F 717 263-5588
Chambersburg **(G-2946)**

John Jost Jr Inc ....G 610 395-5461
Allentown **(G-269)**

Johnstown Wldg Fabrication Inc ....C 800 225-9353
Johnstown **(G-8394)**

Kbm Industries Inc ....G 717 938-2870
Etters **(G-5550)**

Keiths Truck Service ....G 814 696-6008
Duncansville **(G-4454)**

Kelly Iron Works Inc ....G 610 872-5436
Hazleton **(G-7505)**

Ken F Smith Custom Shtmtl LLC ....G 717 624-4214
New Oxford **(G-12415)**

Ken-Fab & Weld Inc ....G 724 283-8815
East Butler **(G-4533)**

Ken-Fab & Weld Inc ....G 724 283-8815
East Butler **(G-4534)**

Kiczan Manufacturing Inc ....E 412 678-0980
North Versailles **(G-12777)**

Kincaid Manufacturing Inc ....G 412 795-9811
Verona **(G-18756)**

Kloeckner Metals Corporation ....D 717 755-1923
York **(G-20557)**

Kreitz Wldg & Fabrication Inc ....F 610 678-6010
Reading **(G-16423)**

Krimes Industrial and Mech Inc ....G 717 628-1301
Ephrata **(G-5115)**

L B Foster Company ....E 814 623-6101
Bedford **(G-1060)**

Lafayette Welding Inc ....G 610 489-3529
Royersford **(G-16857)**

Lebanon Machine & Mfg Co LLC ....G 717 274-3636
Lebanon **(G-9601)**

Leiss Tool & Die ....C 814 444-1444
Somerset **(G-17695)**

Leman Machine Company ....E 814 736-9696
Portage **(G-15918)**

Lincoln Contg & Eqp Co Inc ....D 814 629-6641
Stoystown **(G-18082)**

Lincoln Fabricating Co Inc ....E 412 361-2400
Pittsburgh **(G-15232)**

Lisa Mikolajczak ....G 814 898-4700
Erie **(G-5367)**

Longwood Manufacturing Corp ....F 610 444-4200
Kennett Square **(G-8523)**

Lyons Industries Inc ....E 814 472-9770
Ebensburg **(G-4788)**

M & D Industries Inc ....F 814 723-2381
Clarendon **(G-3170)**

M E Enterprise Services Inc ....E 570 457-5221
Old Forge **(G-12968)**

Mancinci Metal Specialty Inc ....G 215 529-5800
Quakertown **(G-16211)**

Mariani Metal Fabricators Usa ....G 717 432-9241
Dillsburg **(G-4135)**

Marlowes Metal Fabricating ....G 717 292-7360
Dover **(G-4195)**

Marstrand Industries Inc ....D 412 921-1511
Pittsburgh **(G-15258)**

Martin Rollison Inc ....E 570 253-4141
Honesdale **(G-7717)**

Mas-Fab Inc ....E 717 244-4561
Red Lion **(G-16608)**

Mass Machine & Fabricating Co ....F 724 225-1125
Washington **(G-19200)**

Master Machine Co Inc ....F 814 495-4900
South Fork **(G-17775)**

Maverick Steel Company LLC ....D 412 271-1620
Braddock **(G-1946)**

Maxwell Welding and Mch Inc ....E 724 729-3160
Burgettstown **(G-2349)**

Mc Grew Welding and Fabg Inc ....F 724 379-9303
Donora **(G-4157)**

Mc Iron Works Inc ....D 610 837-9444
Bath **(G-966)**

McKinley Blacksmith Limited ....G 610 459-2730
Boothwyn **(G-1879)**

McMillen Welding Inc ....G 724 745-4507
Houston **(G-7874)**

McShane Welding Company Inc ....E 814 459-3797
Erie **(G-5387)**

Mechancal Fbrication Group Inc ....G 717 351-0437
New Holland **(G-12262)**

Metal USA Plates and Shapes ....D 724 266-1283
Ambridge **(G-626)**

Metaldyne Sintered Ridgway LLC ....D 814 776-1141
Ridgway **(G-16717)**

Metals Usa Inc ....F 215 540-8004
Fort Washington **(G-6084)**

Metals Usa Inc ....F 215 540-8004
Fort Washington **(G-6085)**

Micale Fabricators Inc ....G 814 368-7133
Bradford **(G-1981)**

Michelmn-Cncllere Irnworks Inc ....C 610 837-9914
Bath **(G-967)**

Mid Atlntic Stl Fbrication LLC ....G 717 687-0292
Ronks **(G-16811)**

Miller Fabrication Inc ....G 717 359-4433
Greencastle **(G-6622)**

Miller Metalcraft Inc ....E 717 399-8100
Millersville **(G-11212)**

Mkt Metal Manufacturing ....C 717 764-9090
York **(G-20602)**

Mohney Fabricating & Mfg LLC ....G 724 349-6136
Penn Run **(G-13229)**

Mong Fabrication & Machine ....G 724 745-8370
Canonsburg **(G-2605)**

Monocacy Fabs Inc ....D 610 866-7311
Pen Argyl **(G-13214)**

Moore Design Inc ....G 215 627-3379
Philadelphia **(G-14036)**

Multifab & Machine Inc ....F 724 947-7700
Burgettstown **(G-2351)**

Myers Steel Works Inc ....E 717 502-0266
Dillsburg **(G-4138)**

N C Stauffer & Sons Inc ....D 570 945-3047
Factoryville **(G-5758)**

Nabco Inc ....G 724 746-9617
Canonsburg **(G-2609)**

Nadine Corporation ....E 412 795-5100
Verona **(G-18759)**

Nestors Welding Co ....G 570 668-3401
Tamaqua **(G-18221)**

Northeast Industrial Mfg Inc ....E 724 588-7711
Greenville **(G-6760)**

Northwestern Welding & Mch Co ....G 814 774-2866
Lake City **(G-8907)**

Nuweld Inc ....C 570 505-1500
Williamsport **(G-20051)**

Oldcastle Precast Inc ....C 215 257-8081
Telford **(G-18306)**

Outlaw Performance Inc ....E 724 697-4876
Avonmore **(G-866)**

Pabcor Inc ....G 724 652-1930
New Castle **(G-12136)**

Palladino Mtal Fabrication Inc ....G 610 323-9439
Pottstown **(G-16025)**

Pelets Welding Inc ....E 610 384-5048
Coatesville **(G-3323)**

Penn Weld Inc ....G 814 332-3682
Meadville **(G-10775)**

Penn-American Inc ....E 570 649-5173
Muncy **(G-11830)**

Pennheat LLC ....E 814 282-6774
Meadville **(G-10777)**

Performance Proc Ventures LLC ....G 724 704-8827
Farrell **(G-5870)**

Philadelphia Pipe Bending Co ....E 215 225-8955
Philadelphia **(G-14149)**

Pittsburgh Fabrication Mch Inc ....E 412 771-1400
Pittsburgh **(G-15395)**

Poormans Wldg Fabrication Inc ....F 814 349-5893
Aaronsburg **(G-1)**

Power Pipe Supports Inc ....C 724 379-5212
Donora **(G-4159)**

Precision Cut Industries Inc ....D 717 632-2550
Hanover **(G-6936)**

Precision Fabg Group LLC ....G 610 438-3156
Easton **(G-4744)**

Precision Steel Services Inc ....F 724 347-2770
Farrell **(G-5871)**

Preferred Sheet Metal Inc ....E 717 732-7100
Enola **(G-5084)**

Prodex Inc ....F 215 679-2405
Red Hill **(G-16584)**

Psb Industries Inc ....D 814 453-3651
Erie **(G-5442)**

Pti Machine Inc ....G 410 452-8855
Delta **(G-4062)**

Quality Metal Works Inc ....F 717 367-2120
Elizabethtown **(G-4882)**

R & M Ship Tech USA Inc ....F 352 403-8365
Philadelphia **(G-14223)**

R G Steel Corp ....E 724 656-1722
Pulaski **(G-16126)**

R H Benedix Contracting ....G 610 889-7472
Malvern **(G-10306)**

R&M American Marine Pdts Inc ....F 352 345-4866
Philadelphia **(G-14230)**

Rackem Mfg LLC ....G 570 226-6093
Hawley **(G-7442)**

Ray-Guard International Ltd ....G 215 543-3849
Pottstown **(G-16038)**

Replicant Metals ....G 717 626-1618
Lititz **(G-10041)**

Reuss Industries Inc ....E 724 722-3300
Madison **(G-10166)**

Reynolds Iron Works Inc ....F 570 323-4663
Williamsport **(G-20068)**

Reynolds Sales Co Inc ....G 412 461-7877
Homestead **(G-7692)**

Riggs Industries Inc ....F 814 629-5621
Stoystown **(G-18085)**

Rissler E Manufacturing LLC ....G 814 766-2246
New Enterprise **(G-12195)**

Ritter Industries Inc ....F 724 225-6563
Eighty Four **(G-4847)**

Rochester Machine Corporation ....E 724 843-7820
New Brighton **(G-12040)**

Rose Corporation ....D 610 376-5004
Reading **(G-16504)**

Sac Industries Inc ....F 412 787-7500
Pittsburgh **(G-15505)**

Safety Guard Steel Fabg Co ....F 412 821-1177
McKnight **(G-10688)**

Samuel Grossi & Sons Inc ....D 215 638-4470
Bensalem **(G-1249)**

Saylorsburg Stl Fbricators Inc ....G 610 381-4444
Saylorsburg **(G-17106)**

Scenic Ridge Company ....D 717 768-7522
Gordonville **(G-6564)**

Scranton Craftsmen Excvtg Inc ....D 800 775-1479
Throop **(G-18360)**

Sender Ornamental Iron Works ....E 814 536-5139
Johnstown **(G-8433)**

Shoemaker Mfg Solutions Inc ....E 215 723-5567
Souderton **(G-17764)**

Shrock Fabrication ....G 717 397-9500
Bird In Hand **(G-1680)**

Shumars Welding & Mch Svc Inc ....D 724 246-8095
Grindstone **(G-6779)**

Signal Machine Co ....G 717 354-9994
New Holland **(G-12284)**

Siu King ....F 215 769-9863
Philadelphia **(G-14313)**

Skias Chuck Wldg & Fabricators.........G....... 610 375-0912
Reading *(G-16519)*
Smg Fab Inc.........F....... 717 556-8263
Leola *(G-9804)*
Solid Steel Buildings Inc.........F....... 800 377-6543
Pittsburgh *(G-15553)*
Somerset Welding & Steel Inc.........E....... 814 444-7000
Somerset *(G-17709)*
Soul Customs Metal Works.........G....... 610 881-4300
Pen Argyl *(G-13218)*
Southern Stretch Forming &.........G....... 724 256-8474
Butler *(G-2442)*
Specialty Fabrication and Powd.........D....... 814 432-6406
Franklin *(G-6161)*
Specialty Steel Supply Co Inc.........F....... 215 949-8800
Fairless Hills *(G-5798)*
Specialty Support Systems Inc.........F....... 215 945-1033
Levittown *(G-9865)*
Stambaugh Metal Inc.........E....... 717 632-5957
Hanover *(G-6958)*
Standard Iron Works.........E....... 570 347-2058
Scranton *(G-17293)*
Standard Tool & Machine Co.........E....... 724 758-5522
Ellwood City *(G-4951)*
State of ARC Wldg & Fabg LLC.........G....... 610 216-6862
Bangor *(G-930)*
Steel Fab Enterprises LLC.........E....... 717 464-0330
Lancaster *(G-9206)*
Steel Fabricators LLC.........G....... 610 775-3532
Reading *(G-16525)*
Steel Plus Inc.........E....... 717 274-9481
Lebanon *(G-9634)*
Steffan Industries Inc.........G....... 412 751-4484
McKeesport *(G-10683)*
Stewart Welding & Fabg Inc.........D....... 717 252-3948
Wrightsville *(G-20244)*
Stoltzfus Enterprises Ltd.........G....... 610 273-9266
Honey Brook *(G-7763)*
Structural Fiberglass Inc.........F....... 814 623-0458
Bedford *(G-1077)*
Structure Manufacturing Work.........G....... 570 271-2880
Danville *(G-4012)*
Subcon Tl/Cctool Mch Group Inc.........E....... 814 456-7797
Erie *(G-5494)*
Summit Contracting Svcs Inc.........G....... 570 943-2232
Orwigsburg *(G-13053)*
Sunset Creations.........G....... 717 768-7663
Narvon *(G-11928)*
Supreme Manufacturing Inc.........E....... 724 376-4110
Stoneboro *(G-18071)*
T Bruce Sales Inc.........D....... 724 528-9961
West Middlesex *(G-19731)*
Tbj Incorporated.........F....... 717 261-9700
Chambersburg *(G-2984)*
Temtek Solutions Inc.........G....... 724 980-4270
Canonsburg *(G-2647)*
Thompson Machine Company Inc.........E....... 814 941-4982
Altoona *(G-552)*
Tna Doors.........G....... 570 484-5858
Effort *(G-4829)*
Tool City Welding LLC.........G....... 814 333-9353
Meadville *(G-10802)*
Tri-Form Inc.........F....... 724 334-0237
New Kensington *(G-12384)*
Tri-State Rebar Company.........F....... 412 824-4000
Mount Pleasant *(G-11720)*
Trico Welding Company.........F....... 724 722-1300
Yukon *(G-20785)*
UNI-Pro Inc.........F....... 610 668-9191
Philadelphia *(G-14418)*
Unique Fabrication LLC.........G....... 814 227-2627
Shippenville *(G-17565)*
United Fabricating Inc.........F....... 724 663-5891
Claysville *(G-3209)*
United Industrial Electro.........D....... 814 539-6115
Johnstown *(G-8441)*
United Wldg & Fabrication Inc.........G....... 814 266-3598
Windber *(G-20194)*
Valero Service Inc.........E....... 724 468-1010
Delmont *(G-4061)*
Vangura Iron Inc.........F....... 412 461-7825
Clairton *(G-3159)*
Vautid North America Inc.........G....... 412 429-3288
Carnegie *(G-2803)*
Venango Steel Inc.........E....... 814 437-9353
Franklin *(G-6167)*
VSI Sales LLC.........F....... 724 625-4060
Hazleton *(G-7536)*
Vulcan Industries Inc.........F....... 412 269-7655
Coraopolis *(G-3732)*
W & K Steel LLC.........E....... 412 271-0540
Braddock *(G-1951)*
Waggoner Fbrction Mllwrght LLC.........E....... 717 486-7533
Mount Holly Springs *(G-11641)*
Walker Fabricating.........G....... 724 847-5111
Beaver Falls *(G-1016)*
Waltco Inc.........E....... 724 625-3110
Mars *(G-10512)*
Walter Long Mfg Co Inc.........E....... 724 348-6631
Finleyville *(G-5965)*
Warren Sheet Metal Inc.........G....... 814 726-5777
Warren *(G-19062)*
Waste Gas Fabricating Co Inc.........E....... 215 736-9240
Fairless Hills *(G-5807)*
Wearforce North America LLC.........F....... 215 996-1770
Chalfont *(G-2894)*
Weaver Metal Fab LLC.........F....... 717 466-6601
Ephrata *(G-5155)*
Weir Welding Company Inc.........D....... 610 974-8140
Bethlehem *(G-1654)*
Westmrland Stl Fabrication Inc.........E....... 724 446-0555
Madison *(G-10167)*
Wesworld Fabrications Inc.........G....... 215 455-5015
Philadelphia *(G-14470)*
Wheaton & Sons Inc.........F....... 412 351-0405
McKeesport *(G-10687)*
Whemco Inc.........E....... 412 390-2700
Pittsburgh *(G-15715)*
William Henry Orna Ir Works.........G....... 215 659-1887
Willow Grove *(G-20149)*
Wing Dynamics.........G....... 570 275-5502
Danville *(G-4016)*
Woodings Industrial Corp.........C....... 724 625-3131
Mars *(G-10515)*
Youngstown Alloy & Chain Corp.........G....... 724 347-1920
Mercer *(G-10980)*
Zottola Fab A PA Bus Tr.........G....... 412 221-4488
Cuddy *(G-3944)*
Zottola Steel Corporation.........G....... 412 362-5577
Pittsburgh *(G-15737)*
Zurenko Welding & Fabricating.........G....... 724 254-1131
Commodore *(G-3455)*

STEEL MILLS

Allegheny Iron & Metal Co.........E....... 215 743-7759
Philadelphia *(G-13366)*
Allegheny Ludlum LLC.........F....... 724 537-5551
Latrobe *(G-9453)*
Alpha Assembly Solutions Inc.........C....... 814 946-1611
Altoona *(G-470)*
Ampco-Pittsburgh Corporation.........D....... 412 456-4400
Carnegie *(G-2763)*
Anthracite Industries Inc.........E....... 570 286-2176
Sunbury *(G-18163)*
Arcelormittal USA LLC.........D....... 610 383-2000
Coatesville *(G-3290)*
Arcelormittal USA LLC.........A....... 717 986-2887
Steelton *(G-18045)*
Arcelormittal USA LLC.........B....... 610 825-6020
Conshohocken *(G-3521)*
Ashland Foundry & Mch Work LLC.........C....... 570 875-6100
Ashland *(G-727)*
ATI Powder Metals.........F....... 412 923-2670
Oakdale *(G-12891)*
ATI Powder Metals LLC.........D....... 412 394-2800
Pittsburgh *(G-14732)*
Atlantic Track & Turnout Co.........E....... 570 429-1462
Pottsville *(G-16073)*
Baileys Steel & Supply LLC.........G....... 724 267-4648
Waynesburg *(G-19433)*
Bedford Reinforced Plas Inc.........D....... 814 623-8125
Bedford *(G-1044)*
Blair Strip Steel Company.........D....... 724 658-2611
New Castle *(G-12064)*
Bpi Inc.........F....... 412 771-8176
Mc Kees Rocks *(G-10605)*
Camden Iron & Metal Llc.........C....... 610 532-1080
Sharon Hill *(G-17454)*
Cronimet Corporation.........D....... 724 375-5004
Aliquippa *(G-71)*
D I Furnace LLC.........G....... 412 231-1200
Pittsburgh *(G-14901)*
Ds Machine LLC.........E....... 717 768-3853
Gordonville *(G-6552)*
Dyer Quarry Inc.........E....... 610 582-6010
Birdsboro *(G-1693)*
East Coast Metals Inc.........E....... 215 256-9550
Harleysville *(G-7031)*
Elliott Bros Steel Company.........E....... 724 658-5561
Volant *(G-18773)*
Ellwood Mill Products Company.........E....... 724 752-0055
New Castle *(G-12085)*
Erie Coke Corp.........F....... 814 454-0177
Erie *(G-5264)*
Erie Coke Corporation.........C....... 814 454-0177
Erie *(G-5265)*
Evraz Inc NA.........A....... 610 743-5970
Reading *(G-16381)*
Franklin Industries Co.........B....... 814 437-3726
Franklin *(G-6128)*
Franklin Investment Corp.........C....... 814 437-3726
Franklin *(G-6130)*
G O Carlson Inc.........D....... 610 384-2800
Downingtown *(G-4228)*
Gautier Steel Ltd.........D....... 814 535-9200
Johnstown *(G-8376)*
General Carbide Corporation.........C....... 724 836-3000
Greensburg *(G-6668)*
Gerdau Ameristeel US Inc.........C....... 717 751-6898
York *(G-20497)*
Gill Rock Drill Company Inc.........E....... 717 272-3861
Lebanon *(G-9573)*
GKN Sinter Metals LLC.........A....... 814 486-3314
Emporium *(G-5060)*
Harsco Corporation.........E....... 724 287-4791
Butler *(G-2405)*
Industrial Composites Inc.........G....... 412 221-2662
Bridgeville *(G-2069)*
Inweld Corporation.........F....... 610 261-1900
Coplay *(G-3644)*
Kca Enterprises.........G....... 724 880-2534
Connellsville *(G-3501)*
Keystone Spike.........G....... 717 270-2700
Lebanon *(G-9594)*
Kloeckner Metals Corporation.........A....... 215 245-3300
Bensalem *(G-1216)*
Latrobe Specialty Mtls Co LLC.........D....... 814 432-8575
Franklin *(G-6147)*
Lehigh Heavy Forge Corporation.........C....... 610 332-8100
Bethlehem *(G-1557)*
Lehigh Specialty Melting Inc.........D....... 724 537-7731
Latrobe *(G-9499)*
Luzerne Ironworks Inc.........G....... 570 288-1950
Luzerne *(G-10127)*
Manufctring Technical Svcs Inc.........G....... 610 857-3500
Sadsburyville *(G-16905)*
Markovitz Enterprises Inc.........C....... 412 381-2305
Pittsburgh *(G-15255)*
Markovitz Enterprises Inc.........E....... 724 658-6575
New Castle *(G-12119)*
Materion Brush Inc.........C....... 610 562-2211
Shoemakersville *(G-17572)*
Mercer Co.........E....... 724 347-4534
Sharon *(G-17438)*
Metal Service Company Inc.........F....... 724 567-6500
Vandergrift *(G-18733)*
Molyneux Industries Inc.........F....... 724 695-3406
Coraopolis *(G-3705)*
New York Wire Company.........G....... 717 266-5626
Mount Wolf *(G-11749)*
Nlmk Pennsylvania LLC.........B....... 724 983-6464
Farrell *(G-5869)*
Penna Flame Industries Inc.........E....... 724 452-8750
Zelienople *(G-20815)*
Philadelphia Pipe Bending Co.........E....... 215 225-8955
Philadelphia *(G-14149)*
Pittsburgh Flatroll Company.........G....... 412 237-2260
Pittsburgh *(G-15397)*
Precision Kidd Steel Co Inc.........E....... 724 695-2216
Aliquippa *(G-89)*
Precision Kidd Steel Co Inc.........E....... 724 695-2216
Clinton *(G-3266)*
Primetals Technologies USA LLC.........C....... 724 514-8500
Canonsburg *(G-2620)*
Rose Corporation.........D....... 610 376-5004
Reading *(G-16504)*
Sandvik Inc.........B....... 570 585-7500
S Abingtn Twp *(G-16899)*
Sb Specialty Metals LLC.........G....... 814 337-8804
Meadville *(G-10788)*
Sharon Coating LLC.........C....... 724 983-6464
Sharon *(G-17442)*
SMS Demag Inc.........G....... 412 231-1200
Pittsburgh *(G-15551)*
Spang & Company.........C....... 412 963-9363
Pittsburgh *(G-15566)*
Spomin Metals Inc.........F....... 724 924-9718
New Castle *(G-12155)*
Sssi Inc.........B....... 724 743-5815
Washington *(G-19228)*

PRODUCT

Tdy Industries LLC ....D...... 412 394-2896
Pittsburgh *(G-15600)*

Tms International LLC ....D...... 412 678-6141
Glassport *(G-6419)*

Tms International LLC ....G...... 724 658-2004
New Castle *(G-12159)*

Tms International LLC ....G...... 814 535-1911
Johnstown *(G-8438)*

Tms International LLC ....G...... 412 271-4430
Braddock *(G-1948)*

Tms International LLC ....G...... 610 208-3293
Reading *(G-16540)*

Tms International Corp ....C...... 412 678-6141
Glassport *(G-6420)*

Tms International Corporation ....E...... 412 675-8251
Glassport *(G-6421)*

Tonda Inc ....G...... 570 454-3323
Hazle Township *(G-7484)*

Union Electric Company ....G...... 814 452-0587
Erie *(G-5523)*

Union Electric Steel Corp ....D...... 724 947-9595
Burgettstown *(G-2358)*

Union Electric Steel Corp ....D...... 412 429-7655
Carnegie *(G-2800)*

United States Steel Corp ....C...... 412 675-7459
West Mifflin *(G-19746)*

United States Steel Corp ....B...... 412 433-1121
Pittsburgh *(G-15677)*

United States Steel Corp ....D...... 412 273-7000
Braddock *(G-1950)*

United States Steel Corp ....D...... 215 736-4000
Fairless Hills *(G-5805)*

United States Steel Corp ....E...... 412 810-0286
Homestead *(G-7694)*

United States Steel Corp ....E...... 724 439-1116
Uniontown *(G-18645)*

United States Steel Corp ....C...... 412 433-1419
Pittsburgh *(G-15679)*

Unitrac Railroad Materials Inc ....G...... 570 923-1514
Renovo *(G-16651)*

Universal Stainless & Alloy ....B...... 412 257-7600
Bridgeville *(G-2097)*

Universal STAinless& Alloy ....D...... 814 827-9723
Titusville *(G-18402)*

Vai Pomini Inc ....F...... 610 921-9101
Reading *(G-16558)*

Victaulic Company of America ....C...... 610 966-3966
Alburtis *(G-58)*

Wescott Steel Inc ....E...... 215 364-3636
Langhorne *(G-9335)*

Whemco Inc ....E...... 412 390-2700
Pittsburgh *(G-15715)*

STEEL SHEET: Cold-Rolled

All-Clad Metalcrafters LLC ....D...... 724 745-8300
Canonsburg *(G-2537)*

Allegheny Ludlum LLC ....C...... 724 567-2001
Vandergrift *(G-18721)*

STEEL WOOL

Laminators Incorporated........................D...... 215 723-5285
Hatfield *(G-7362)*

STEEL, COLD-ROLLED: Sheet Or Strip, From Own Hot-Rolled

Superior Forge & Steel Corp..................D...... 412 431-8250
Pittsburgh *(G-15588)*

Wheatland Steel Processing Co ....E...... 724 981-4242
Wheatland *(G-19843)*

STEEL, COLD-ROLLED: Strip NEC, From Purchased Hot-Rolled

Blair Strip Steel Company ....D...... 724 658-2611
New Castle *(G-12064)*

Elliott Bros Steel Company.....................E...... 724 658-5561
Volant *(G-18773)*

STEEL, COLD-ROLLED: Strip Or Wire

Jabtek LLC...G...... 724 796-5656
New Kensington *(G-12348)*

STEEL: Cold-Rolled

ATI Powder Metals LLC ....D...... 412 394-2800
Pittsburgh *(G-14732)*

Carpenter Technology Corp....................B...... 610 208-2000
Philadelphia *(G-13508)*

Colonial Metal Products Inc...................E...... 724 346-5550
Hermitage *(G-7579)*

Hygrade Acquisition Corp.......................D...... 610 866-2441
Bethlehem *(G-1536)*

Hygrade Mtal Moulding Mfg Corp...........E...... 610 866-2441
Bethlehem *(G-1538)*

Joseph T Ryerson & Son Inc ....F...... 215 736-8970
Morrisville *(G-11565)*

Kloeckner Metals Corporation...............A...... 215 245-3300
Bensalem *(G-1216)*

Kloeckner Metals Corporation...............D...... 717 755-1923
York *(G-20557)*

Laneko Roll Form Inc ....E...... 215 822-1930
Hatfield *(G-7363)*

Markovitz Enterprises Inc ....E...... 724 658-6575
New Castle *(G-12119)*

Nlmk Pennsylvania LLC..........................B...... 724 983-6464
Farrell *(G-5869)*

Penna Flame Industries Inc ....E...... 724 452-8750
Zelienople *(G-20815)*

Perryman Company ....F...... 724 746-9390
Coal Center *(G-3276)*

Pilot-Run Stamping Company ....E...... 440 255-8821
Corry *(G-3772)*

Precision Kidd Steel Co Inc ....E...... 724 695-2216
Aliquippa *(G-89)*

Precision Kidd Steel Co Inc ....E...... 724 695-2216
Clinton *(G-3266)*

Rose Corporation ....F...... 610 921-9647
Reading *(G-16505)*

Saegertown Manufacturing Corp ....C...... 814 763-2655
Saegertown *(G-16932)*

Shalmet Corporation ....C...... 570 366-1414
Orwigsburg *(G-13052)*

Superior Forge & Steel Corp..................D...... 412 431-8250
Pittsburgh *(G-15588)*

Tdy Industries LLC ....D...... 412 394-2896
Pittsburgh *(G-15600)*

STEEL: Galvanized

Marcegaglia Usa Inc ....C...... 412 462-2185
Munhall *(G-11844)*

STEEL: Laminated

Custom Laminating Corporation............F...... 570 897-8300
Mount Bethel *(G-11609)*

Djk Properties LLC.................................G...... 717 597-5965
Greencastle *(G-6607)*

Metkote Laminated Products Inc...........F 570 562-0107
Taylor *(G-18260)*

P R L Inc..E...... 717 273-2470
Cornwall *(G-3739)*

STENCILS

Sh Quints Sons Company ....F...... 215 533-1988
Philadelphia *(G-14295)*

STERILIZERS, BARBER & BEAUTY SHOP

Tangled Manes ....G...... 717 581-0600
East Petersburg *(G-4593)*

STITCHING SVCS: Custom

Embroidery Factory Inc..........................G...... 570 654-7640
Pittston *(G-15749)*

Triple Play Sports.................................F 215 923-5466
Philadelphia *(G-14412)*

Village Idiot Designs.............................G...... 724 545-7477
Kittanning *(G-8802)*

STOCK SHAPES: Plastic

AAR Plastic & Glass Llc ....G...... 410 200-6369
Gettysburg *(G-6281)*

D A R A Inc ....F...... 717 274-1800
Lebanon *(G-9557)*

Ensinger Inc ....G...... 724 746-6050
Washington *(G-19170)*

Stabler Companies Inc ....F...... 717 236-9307
Harrisburg *(G-7219)*

STONE: Cast Concrete

F&M Surfaces Inc..................................G...... 717 267-3799
Chambersburg *(G-2931)*

Glasgow Inc ....E...... 610 251-0760
Malvern *(G-10240)*

Sakala Stone Products ....G...... 724 339-2224
New Kensington *(G-12374)*

Wissahickon Stone Quarry LLC ....G...... 215 887-3330
Glenside *(G-6544)*

STONE: Crushed & Broken, NEC

Slatedale Aggregate Mtls Inc ....G...... 610 767-4601
Slatington *(G-17613)*

STONE: Dimension, NEC

Bluestone Inc ....F...... 215 364-1415
Southampton *(G-17799)*

Cava Intl MBL & Gran Inc ....E...... 215 732-7800
Philadelphia *(G-13516)*

Coolspring Stone Supply Inc ....E...... 724 437-8663
Uniontown *(G-18621)*

Glasgow Inc ....E...... 610 279-6840
King of Prussia *(G-8620)*

H&K Group Inc ....C...... 610 705-0500
Pottstown *(G-15947)*

Hanson Aggregates PA LLC ....D...... 610 269-1710
Downingtown *(G-4232)*

Highway Materials Inc ....E...... 610 828-4300
Plymouth Meeting *(G-15846)*

Johnson & Son Stone Works..................G...... 570 278-9385
Montrose *(G-11467)*

M&M Stone Co.......................................D...... 215 723-1177
Telford *(G-18301)*

Media Quarry Co Inc ....E...... 610 566-6667
Media *(G-10938)*

North Star Leasing Inc ....G...... 814 629-6999
Friedens *(G-6224)*

Pottstown Trap Rock Quarries ....F...... 610 326-4843
Pottstown *(G-16034)*

Princeton Trade Consulting Gro ....E...... 610 683-9348
Kutztown *(G-8856)*

Robert Johnson ....G...... 570 746-1287
Wyalusing *(G-20256)*

Valley Quarries Inc ....G...... 814 766-2211
Fayetteville *(G-5879)*

STONE: Quarrying & Processing, Own Stone Prdts

Bakers Quarry ....G...... 570 942-6005
Nicholson *(G-12612)*

Brandywine Quarry Inc...........................G...... 610 857-4200
Parkesburg *(G-13172)*

Derry Stone & Lime Co Inc ....F...... 724 459-3971
Latrobe *(G-9472)*

Environmental Materials LLC ....C...... 570 366-6460
Orwigsburg *(G-13042)*

Eureka Stone Quarry Inc ....G...... 570 689-2901
Sterling *(G-18049)*

Eureka Stone Quarry Inc ....G...... 570 992-4444
Stroudsburg *(G-18115)*

Glenn O Hawbaker Inc ....D...... 814 237-1444
State College *(G-17970)*

Hanson Aggregates LLC ....E...... 724 459-6031
Blairsville *(G-1722)*

Heritage Stone & Marble Inc ....G...... 610 222-0856
Lansdale *(G-9376)*

L and J Equipment Co Inc ....G...... 724 437-5405
Uniontown *(G-18633)*

Magnesita Refractories Company ....C...... 717 792-3611
York *(G-20574)*

Mid-Life Stone Works LLC ....G...... 570 928-8802
Dushore *(G-4509)*

Pottstown Trap Rock Quarries ....F 610 326-4843
Pottstown *(G-16034)*

Pottstown Trap Rock Quarries ....F 610 326-5921
Douglassville *(G-4179)*

Russell Stone Products Inc ....G...... 814 236-2449
Grampian *(G-6572)*

Scranton Materials LLC ....F...... 570 961-8586
Scranton *(G-17286)*

STONEWARE CLAY MINING

E J Bognar Inc ....F 814 443-6000
Somerset *(G-17686)*

STONEWARE PRDTS: Pottery

Campbell Studios Inc ....E...... 814 398-2148
Cambridge Springs *(G-2475)*

Grandville Hollow Pottery Inc................G...... 814 355-7928
Julian *(G-8455)*

Pfaltzgraff Factory Stores Inc ....B...... 717 848-5500
York *(G-20626)*

STORE FIXTURES, EXC REFRIGERATED: Wholesalers

Allegheny Store Fixtures Inc ....E 814 362-6805
Bradford (G-1954)
Lozier Corporation ....C 570 658-8111
Mc Clure (G-10560)

STORE FIXTURES: Wood

Berkman John A Display Sls Inc ....G 412 421-0201
Pittsburgh (G-14763)
Compass Ret Display Group Inc ....G 215 744-2787
Philadelphia (G-13562)
Frederick Wohlgemuth Inc ....E 215 638-9672
Bensalem (G-1199)
Hilltop Woodshop Inc ....G 724 697-4506
Avonmore (G-865)
J D R Fixtures Inc ....E 610 323-6599
Pottstown (G-16003)
Krg Enterprises Inc ....C 215 708-2811
Philadelphia (G-13945)
Lozier Corporation ....C 570 658-8111
Mc Clure (G-10560)
Milford Enterprises Inc ....D 215 538-2778
Quakertown (G-16218)
Northeast Fabricators Inc ....G 570 883-0936
Pittston (G-15771)

STORE FRONTS: Prefabricated, Metal

Alumax LLC ....C 412 553-4545
Pittsburgh (G-14695)
Saha Industries Inc ....G 610 383-5070
Coatesville (G-3325)

STORES: Auto & Home Supply

A-1 Racing Products Inc ....G 215 675-8442
Warminster (G-18816)
Advanced Lubrication Spc Inc ....E 215 244-2114
Bensalem (G-1144)
Aircooled Racing and Parts ....G 717 432-4116
Wellsville (G-19476)
Bonehead Performance Inc ....F 215 674-8206
Warminster (G-18839)
Caro Brothers Inc ....F 724 265-1538
Russellton (G-16883)
Grays Automotive Speed Eqp ....G 717 436-8777
Mifflintown (G-11119)
Vanalstine Manufacturing Co ....G 610 489-7670
Trappe (G-18475)

STORES: Drapery & Upholstery

Anything Sews ....G 412 486-1055
Glenshaw (G-6480)

STOVES: Wood & Coal Burning

Arthur L Baker Enterprises ....G 717 432-9788
Lewisberry (G-9880)
Penn Manufacturing ....G 717 626-8879
Lititz (G-10030)

STRAIGHTENERS

Medart Inc ....E 724 752-3555
Ellwood City (G-4946)

STRAINERS: Line, Piping Systems

Spirax Sarco Inc ....G 610 807-3500
Center Valley (G-2831)

STRAPPING

Germantown Tool Machine Sp Inc ....E 215 322-4970
Huntingdon Valley (G-7989)
Linett Co Inc ....C 412 826-8531
Pittsburgh (G-15233)

STRAPS: Bindings, Textile

Barbett Industries Inc ....F 610 372-2872
Reading (G-16327)
Huepenbecker Enterprises Inc ....F 717 393-3941
Lancaster (G-9052)

STRAPS: Cotton Webbing

Eam-Mosca Corp ....C 570 459-3426
Hazle Township (G-7452)

STRAPS: Elastic Webbing

Zip-Net Inc ....E 610 939-9762
Reading (G-16572)

STRAPS: Webbing, Woven

Western PA Weather LLC ....G 814 341-5086
Johnstown (G-8444)

STRIPS: Copper & Copper Alloy

Eagle Metals Inc ....E 610 926-4111
Leesport (G-9661)

STRUCTURAL SUPPORT & BUILDING MATERIAL: Concrete

Superior Walls of Colorado ....F 412 664-7788
Glassport (G-6417)
Utility Service Group Inc ....E 717 737-6092
Camp Hill (G-2521)

STUCCO

Stucco Code Inc ....G 610 348-3905
Drexel Hill (G-4372)

STUDIOS: Artist

Bourne Graphics Inc ....G 610 584-6120
Worcester (G-20224)

STUDIOS: Sculptor's

2820 Associates Inc ....G 412 471-2525
Pittsburgh (G-14625)

STUDS & JOISTS: Sheet Metal

Watson Metal Products Corp ....D 908 276-2202
Lancaster (G-9236)

STYLING SVCS: Wigs

Amekor Industries Inc ....D 610 825-6747
Conshohocken (G-3518)

SUBDIVIDERS & DEVELOPERS: Real Property, Cemetery Lots Only

CMS East Inc ....D 724 527-6700
Jeannette (G-8250)

SUBMARINE BUILDING & REPAIR

Loeffler Corporation ....F 215 757-2404
Langhorne (G-9309)

SUBSCRIPTION FULFILLMENT SVCS: Magazine, Newspaper, Etc

Amrep Corporation ....F 609 487-0905
Plymouth Meeting (G-15831)

SUNDRIES & RELATED PRDTS: Medical & Laboratory, Rubber

Advanced Scientifics Inc ....B 717 692-2104
Millersburg (G-11186)
Arkmedica LLC ....F 724 349-0856
Indiana (G-8083)
Fred Foust ....G 724 845-7028
Vandergrift (G-18727)
Healing Environments Intl Inc ....G 215 758-2107
Philadelphia (G-13808)
Herbert Cooper Company Inc ....E 814 228-3417
Genesee (G-6272)
Martech Medical Products Inc ....E 215 256-8833
Harleysville (G-7046)
Svt Inc ....F 215 245-5055
Bensalem (G-1258)
Thermo Fisher Scientific Inc ....B 717 692-2104
Millersburg (G-11203)
Washington Greene County Blind ....F 724 228-0770
Washington (G-19238)
West Pharmaceutical Svcs Inc ....B 610 594-2900
Exton (G-5748)
West Phrm Svcs Del Inc ....F 610 594-2900
Exton (G-5749)

SUNROOMS: Prefabricated Metal

Advanced Building Products ....G 717 661-7520
Leola (G-9766)
Great Additions Inc ....F 570 675-0852
Luzerne (G-10124)

SUPERMARKETS & OTHER GROCERY STORES

Conjelko Dairy & Ice Service ....G 814 467-9997
Windber (G-20179)
Fresh Foods Manufacturing ....E 724 683-3639
Freedom (G-6190)
O Land Lakes ....F 717 845-8076
York (G-20614)
R & D Americas Best Packaging ....G 610 435-4300
Allentown (G-364)
Reyna Foods Inc ....G 412 904-1242
Pittsburgh (G-15481)
S Don Food Market Inc ....G 717 453-7470
Lykens (G-10135)
United Refining Company ....C 814 723-1500
Warren (G-19055)

SURFACE ACTIVE AGENTS

Acton Technologies Inc ....D 570 654-0612
Pittston (G-15741)
Lonza Inc ....C 570 321-3900
Williamsport (G-20035)
Neo-Solutions Inc ....E 724 728-7360
Beaver (G-988)

SURFACE ACTIVE AGENTS: Processing Assistants

Independent Concepts Inc ....G 412 741-7903
Sewickley (G-17394)

SURFACERS: Concrete Grinding

Global Polishing Solutions LLC ....F 619 295-0893
Folcroft (G-6003)

SURGICAL & MEDICAL INSTRUMENTS WHOLESALERS

Titan Manufacturing Inc ....G 781 767-1963
Malvern (G-10333)

SURGICAL APPLIANCES & SPLYS

Depuy Synthes Inc ....B 610 701-7078
West Chester (G-19536)
Synthes Inc ....G 610 647-9700
West Chester (G-19650)
Synthes Usa LLC ....G 610 719-5000
West Chester (G-19652)
Teleflex Incorporated ....B 610 225-6800
Wayne (G-19382)

SURGICAL APPLIANCES & SPLYS

Alpha Scientific Instrument ....G 610 647-7000
Malvern (G-10182)
Altamira Ltd ....G 800 343-1066
Pittsburgh (G-14692)
Altus Partners LLC ....E 610 355-4156
West Chester (G-19497)
American Safety Clothing Inc ....E 215 257-7667
Sellersville (G-17339)
Anatomical Designs Inc ....F 724 430-1470
Uniontown (G-18615)
Animas LLC ....B 610 644-8990
Chesterbrook (G-3089)
Bashlin Industries Inc ....D 724 458-8340
Grove City (G-6780)
Boehringer Laboratories Inc ....E 610 278-0900
Phoenixville (G-14536)
Church Communities PA Inc ....G 724 329-8573
Farmington (G-5860)
Crew Systems Corporation ....G 570 281-9221
Carbondale (G-2673)
Depuy Synthes Inc ....B 610 647-9700
Paoli (G-13138)
Depuy Synthes Inc ....B 610 738-4600
West Chester (G-19537)
Depuy Synthes Inc ....B 610 719-5000
West Chester (G-19538)
DT Davis Enterprises Ltd ....G 610 694-9600
Allentown (G-197)

P R O D U C T

Duralife Inc ....E...... 570 323-9743
  Philadelphia *(G-13651)*
Fort Washington Pharma LLC ....G...... 800 279-7434
  Fort Washington *(G-6069)*
Hanger Inc ....F...... 877 442-6437
  Wilkes Barre *(G-19923)*
Hanger Prsthetcs & Ortho Inc...............G...... 717 731-8181
  Camp Hill *(G-2499)*
Haveco Div of Ace Mobility ....F...... 717 558-4301
  Harrisburg *(G-7145)*
Howmedica Osteonics Corp ....F...... 610 760-7007
  Neffs *(G-11999)*
Instrumentation Industries Inc ....E...... 412 854-1133
  Bethel Park *(G-1418)*
Johnson & Johnson ....A...... 215 273-7000
  Philadelphia *(G-13909)*
Kinetic Concepts Inc ....G...... 717 558-0985
  Harrisburg *(G-7164)*
M-B Companies Inc.........................E...... 570 547-1621
  Muncy *(G-11825)*
Martech Medical Products Inc ....E...... 215 256-8833
  Harleysville *(G-7046)*
Mechanical Service Co Inc ....F...... 610 351-1655
  Allentown *(G-313)*
Medeast Post-Op & Surgical Inc...........G...... 888 629-2030
  Bethlehem *(G-1566)*
Medical Device Bus Svcs Inc................G...... 724 933-0288
  Wexford *(G-19810)*
Moberg Research Inc.......................F...... 215 283-0860
  Ambler *(G-591)*
MSA Safety Incorporated ....A...... 724 733-9100
  Murrysville *(G-11859)*
O2s LLC ....E...... 215 299-8500
  Philadelphia *(G-14091)*
Ortho Depot LLC ....G...... 800 992-9999
  Salunga *(G-17055)*
Plum Enterprises Inc ....E...... 610 783-7377
  Valley Forge *(G-18710)*
Respironics Inc ....C...... 724 387-5200
  Mount Pleasant *(G-11714)*
Respironics Inc ....B...... 724 733-0200
  Murrysville *(G-11864)*
Respironics Inc ....C...... 724 733-5803
  Sewickley *(G-17407)*
River Street Pedorthics Inc ....G...... 570 299-5472
  Gouldsboro *(G-6570)*
Steris Barrier Pdts Solutions ....D...... 215 763-8200
  Sharon Hill *(G-17462)*
Steris Corporation ....G...... 215 763-8200
  Philadelphia *(G-14346)*
Thomas Fetterman Inc ....G...... 215 355-8849
  Southampton *(G-17840)*
Tps LLC...................................C...... 570 538-7200
  New Columbia *(G-12177)*
Trigon Holding Inc ....E...... 724 941-5540
  Mc Murray *(G-10647)*
Trigon Incorporated ....D...... 724 941-5540
  Mc Murray *(G-10648)*
West Penn Optical Inc ....E...... 814 833-1194
  Erie *(G-5528)*

SURGICAL EQPT: See Also Instruments

Berkley Surgical Corporation ....C...... 724 438-3000
  Uniontown *(G-18618)*
Cardiacassist Inc ....E...... 412 963-8883
  Pittsburgh *(G-14808)*
Dermamed Usa Inc.........................F...... 610 358-4447
  Lenni *(G-9761)*
Kmi Surgical Ltd ....G...... 610 518-7110
  Downingtown *(G-4237)*
Piramal Critical Care Inc ....D...... 610 974-9760
  Bethlehem *(G-1599)*
Smiths Group North America Inc ....F...... 772 286-9300
  Malvern *(G-10322)*
Surgeoneering LLC ....G...... 412 292-2816
  Gibsonia *(G-6353)*
Titan Manufacturing Inc ....G...... 610 935-8203
  Malvern *(G-10332)*
Titan Manufacturing Inc ....G...... 781 767-1963
  Malvern *(G-10333)*

SURGICAL IMPLANTS

Axial Medical ....F...... 267 961-2600
  Ivyland *(G-8207)*
Envision Products Inc ....E...... 215 428-1791
  Morrisville *(G-11558)*
PA & Implant Surgery LLC ....G...... 814 375-0500
  Du Bois *(G-4410)*
Tornier Inc................................G...... 610 585-2111
  West Chester *(G-19666)*

Troutman Machine Shop Inc ....G...... 610 363-5480
  Exton *(G-5739)*
Xerothera Inc.............................G...... 610 525-9916
  Bryn Mawr *(G-2337)*

SURGICAL INSTRUMENT REPAIR SVCS

C L Sturkey Inc...........................G...... 717 274-9441
  Lebanon *(G-9551)*

SURVEYING & MAPPING: Land Parcels

American Engineers Group LLC ....G...... 484 920-8010
  Phoenixville *(G-14527)*
Terraviz Geospatial Inc....................G...... 717 938-3591
  Conshohocken *(G-3612)*
Terraviz Geospatial Inc....................G...... 717 512-9658
  Etters *(G-5554)*

SURVEYING SVCS: Aerial Digital Imaging

Civic Mapper LLC.........................G...... 315 729-7869
  Pittsburgh *(G-14856)*
Eye-Bot Aerial Solutions LLC ....G...... 724 904-7706
  New Kensington *(G-12340)*
Uav Aviation Services......................G...... 717 691-8882
  Mechanicsburg *(G-10901)*

SUSPENSION SYSTEMS: Acoustical, Metal

Advanced Cnstr Estimating LLC ....F...... 724 747-7032
  Mc Murray *(G-10643)*
Worthington Armstrong Intl LLC ....G...... 610 722-1200
  Malvern *(G-10350)*
Worthington Armstrong Venture ....C...... 610 722-1200
  Malvern *(G-10351)*

SVC ESTABLISHMENT EQPT & SPLYS WHOLESALERS

Car Cleen Systems Inc ....F...... 717 795-8995
  Bethel Park *(G-1408)*
E P M Corporation.........................F...... 814 825-6650
  Erie *(G-5252)*
Willard Burial Service Inc...................G...... 724 528-9965
  West Middlesex *(G-19732)*

SVC ESTABLISHMENT EQPT, WHOL: Concrete Burial Vaults & Boxes

Blairsville Wilbert Burial Vlt.................E...... 724 547-2865
  Mount Pleasant *(G-11689)*
Colonial Concrete Industries ....G...... 610 279-2102
  King of Prussia *(G-8594)*
Forsht Concrete Pdts Co Inc ....G...... 814 944-1617
  Altoona *(G-507)*

SVC ESTABLISHMENT EQPT, WHOL: Funeral Director's Eqpt/Splys

Farnsworth Gowns and Fnrl Sups ....G...... 412 881-4696
  Pittsburgh *(G-15004)*

SVC ESTABLISHMENT EQPT, WHOLESALE: Beauty Parlor Eqpt & Sply

American Cnsld Mfg Co Inc ....E...... 610 825-2630
  Conshohocken *(G-3519)*

SVC ESTABLISHMENT EQPT, WHOLESALE: Carpet Installation Eqpt

All Floor Supplies Inc ....F...... 412 793-6421
  Monroeville *(G-11323)*

SVC ESTABLISHMENT EQPT, WHOLESALE: Engraving Eqpt & Splys

Antares Instruments Inc....................F...... 215 441-5250
  Horsham *(G-7786)*

SVC ESTABLISHMENT EQPT, WHOLESALE: Firefighting Eqpt

911 Safety Equipment LLC..................F...... 610 279-6808
  Norristown *(G-12628)*

SVC ESTABLISHMENT EQPT, WHOLESALE: Locksmith Eqpt & Splys

Idn Global Inc ....G...... 215 698-8155
  Philadelphia *(G-13846)*

SVC ESTABLISHMENT EQPT, WHOLESALE: Shredders, Indl & Comm

Allegheny Paper Shredders Corp..........E...... 800 245-2497
  Delmont *(G-4046)*

SVC ESTABLISHMENT EQPT, WHOLESALE: Sprinkler Systems

Bnb Fire Protection Inc ....G...... 610 944-0594
  Fleetwood *(G-5968)*

SVC ESTABLISHMENT EQPT, WHOLESALE: Vending Machines & Splys

Vendors 1st Choice Inc ....G...... 215 804-1011
  Quakertown *(G-16256)*

SWEEPING COMPOUNDS

Spilltech Environmental Inc.................G...... 814 247-8566
  Hastings *(G-7263)*
Sweeper City Inc ....G...... 724 283-0859
  Butler *(G-2445)*

SWIMMING POOL ACCESS: Leaf Skimmers Or Pool Rakes

Aquador ....G...... 724 942-1525
  Canonsburg *(G-2542)*

SWIMMING POOL EQPT: Filters & Water Conditioning Systems

Bti-Coopermatics Inc.......................G...... 610 262-7700
  Northampton *(G-12847)*
Cardinal Systems Inc.......................E...... 570 385-4733
  Schuylkill Haven *(G-17151)*
Clapper Leon Plbg Htg Wtr Cond.........F...... 570 629-2833
  Stroudsburg *(G-18110)*
Guardian Filtration Pdts LLC ....G...... 724 646-0450
  Greenville *(G-6744)*
Pocono Water Centers Inc ....G...... 570 839-8012
  Moscow *(G-11600)*
Process Masters Corporation................G...... 610 683-5674
  Kutztown *(G-8857)*

SWIMMING POOL SPLY STORES

Barbers Chemicals Inc ....F...... 724 962-7886
  Sharpsville *(G-17469)*

SWIMMING POOLS, EQPT & SPLYS: Wholesalers

Emsco Distributor Company ....G...... 412 754-1236
  Irwin *(G-8161)*
Fox Pool Lancaster Inc......................D...... 717 718-1977
  York *(G-20487)*
Pocono Pool Products Inc ....E...... 570 839-9291
  Swiftwater *(G-18189)*
Swimtech Distributing Inc....................G...... 570 595-7680
  Cresco *(G-3895)*

SWITCHBOARDS & PARTS: Power

Penn Panel & Box Company ....E...... 610 586-2700
  Collingdale *(G-3409)*

SWITCHES

Milli-Switch Manufacturing Co...............G...... 610 270-9222
  Bridgeport *(G-2040)*

SWITCHES: Electric Power, Exc Snap, Push Button, Etc

Butler Technologies Inc ....D...... 724 283-6656
  Butler *(G-2386)*
Detroit Switch Inc..........................E...... 412 322-9144
  Pittsburgh *(G-14919)*
Premier Automotive........................G...... 570 966-0363
  Mifflinburg *(G-11100)*

SWITCHES: Electronic

Ambit Switch ....G...... 610 705-9695
  Pottstown *(G-15962)*
Black Box Corporation ....G...... 724 746-5500
  Lawrence *(G-9535)*
Conductive Technologies Inc ....D...... 717 764-6931
  York *(G-20433)*

Continental-Wirt Elec Corp ....C...... 215 355-7080
 Southampton (G-17805)
Deltronic Labs Inc ....E...... 215 997-8616
 Chalfont (G-2872)
Dynamic Manufacturing LLC ....D...... 724 295-4200
 Freeport (G-6203)
Ifm Efector Inc ....D...... 610 524-2000
 Auburn (G-816)
Ifm Efector Inc ....C...... 800 441-8246
 Malvern (G-10252)
Matric Group LLC ....B...... 814 677-0716
 Seneca (G-17366)
Nolatron Inc ....G...... 717 564-3398
 Harrisburg (G-7184)
Silicon Power Corporation ....D...... 610 407-4700
 Malvern (G-10317)
Union Switch and Signal ....G...... 412 688-2400
 Pittsburgh (G-15672)

SWITCHES: Electronic Applications

Bwi Eagle Inc ....F...... 724 283-4681
 Butler (G-2387)
Spectrum Microwave Inc ....D...... 215 464-0586
 Philadelphia (G-14333)
Te Connectivity Corporation ....C...... 717 762-9186
 Waynesboro (G-19425)

SWITCHES: Silicon Control

Silicon Power Corporation ....D...... 610 407-4700
 Malvern (G-10317)

SWITCHES: Stepping

Keystone Controls Company ....G...... 215 355-7080
 Southampton (G-17820)

SWITCHGEAR & SWITCHBOARD APPARATUS

Action Manufacturing Company ....D...... 610 593-1800
 Atglen (G-799)
Alstom Grid LLC ....D...... 724 483-7308
 Charleroi (G-3005)
Clark Metal Products Co ....C...... 724 459-7550
 Blairsville (G-1719)
Crisp Control Inc ....D...... 724 864-6777
 Irwin (G-8153)
Deltronic Labs Inc ....E...... 215 997-8616
 Chalfont (G-2872)
Duquesne Mine Supply Company ....G...... 412 821-2100
 Pittsburgh (G-14944)
E F E Laboratories Inc ....E...... 215 672-2400
 Horsham (G-7812)
Eaton Corporation ....B...... 724 773-1231
 Beaver (G-980)
Eaton Corporation ....E...... 610 497-6100
 Boothwyn (G-1877)
Eaton Corporation ....E...... 412 893-3300
 Moon Township (G-11484)
Eaton Electrical Inc ....E...... 412 893-3300
 Moon Township (G-11485)
Electro Soft Inc ....E...... 215 654-0701
 Montgomeryville (G-11394)
Ellison Industrial Contrls LLC ....G...... 724 483-0251
 Belle Vernon (G-1086)
Fenner Inc ....C...... 717 665-2421
 Manheim (G-10380)
Gerome Manufacturing Co Inc ....D...... 724 438-8544
 Smithfield (G-17650)
Homewood Products Corporation ....E...... 412 665-2700
 Pittsburgh (G-15099)
Invensys Energy Metering Corp ......B...... 814 371-3011
 Du Bois (G-4396)
J C H Associates Inc ....G...... 610 367-5000
 Boyertown (G-1919)
Kennametal Inc ....C...... 276 646-0080
 Bedford (G-1059)
Maxima Tech & Systems LLC ....C...... 717 581-1000
 Lancaster (G-9130)
Miller Edge Inc ....D...... 610 869-4422
 West Grove (G-19702)
Prominent Fluid Controls Inc ....E...... 412 787-2484
 Pittsburgh (G-15453)
RTD Embedded Technologies Inc ....E...... 814 234-8087
 State College (G-18017)
Siemens Industry Inc ....F...... 610 921-3135
 Reading (G-16518)
SPD Electrical Systems Inc ....B...... 215 698-6426
 Philadelphia (G-14331)

Te Connectivity Corporation ....B...... 717 986-3743
 Middletown (G-11081)
Videotek Inc ....C...... 610 327-2292
 Pottstown (G-16068)
Vishay Intertechnology Inc ....B...... 610 644-1300
 Malvern (G-10341)
W T Storey Inc ....F...... 570 923-2400
 North Bend (G-12728)

SWITCHGEAR & SWITCHGEAR ACCESS, NEC

Electric Materials Company ....C...... 814 725-9621
 North East (G-12739)
Siemens Industry Inc ....D...... 724 743-5913
 Canonsburg (G-2636)

SYNTHETIC RESIN FINISHED PRDTS, NEC

Fenner Precision Inc ....C...... 800 327-2288
 Manheim (G-10383)
Medart Inc ....E...... 724 752-3555
 Ellwood City (G-4946)
New Werner Holding Co Inc ....G...... 724 588-2000
 Greenville (G-6758)
Old Ladder Co ....A...... 888 523-3371
 Greenville (G-6762)
Omnova Solutions Inc ....B...... 570 366-1051
 Auburn (G-820)
Werner Co ....C...... 724 588-2000
 Greenville (G-6775)
Werner Holding Co Inc ....A...... 888 523-3371
 Greenville (G-6776)

SYRUPS, DRINK

Liberty Coca-Cola Bevs LLC ....F...... 215 427-4500
 Philadelphia (G-13969)

SYRUPS: Pharmaceutical

Axcentria Pharmaceutical LLC ....F...... 215 453-5055
 Telford (G-18268)
Medicine Shoppe ....G...... 717 208-3415
 Lancaster (G-9131)

SYSTEMS ENGINEERING: Computer Related

Daisy Data Displays Inc ....E...... 717 932-9999
 York Haven (G-20756)
Montgomery Products Ltd ....E...... 610 933-2500
 Phoenixville (G-14563)

SYSTEMS INTEGRATION SVCS

Corestar International Corp ....E...... 724 744-4094
 Irwin (G-8151)
Dimension Data North Amer Inc ....E...... 484 362-2563
 Malvern (G-10224)
Eti Closeco ....G...... 412 822-8250
 Pittsburgh (G-14987)
Global Data Consultants LLC ....E...... 717 697-7500
 Mechanicsburg (G-10849)
Labelpack Automation Inc ....E...... 814 362-1528
 Bradford (G-1979)
Support McRcomputers Assoc Inc ......F...... 215 496-0303
 Philadelphia (G-14359)

SYSTEMS INTEGRATION SVCS: Local Area Network

Cleararmor Solutions Corp ....G...... 610 816-0101
 Riegelsville (G-16744)
Ldp Inc ....D...... 570 455-8511
 West Hazleton (G-19713)
PC Network Inc ....D...... 267 236-0015
 Philadelphia (G-14128)

SYSTEMS INTEGRATION SVCS: Office Computer Automation

Hapeman Electronics Inc ....G...... 724 475-2033
 Mercer (G-10962)
Lighthouse Electric Contrls Co ....F...... 814 835-2348
 Erie (G-5365)
McNs Technologies LLC ....G...... 610 269-2891
 Chadds Ford (G-2855)

SYSTEMS SOFTWARE DEVELOPMENT SVCS

Accustar Inc ....G...... 610 459-0123
 Garnet Valley (G-6264)
App-Techs Corporation ....F...... 717 735-0848
 Lancaster (G-8935)
Arcweb Technologies LLC ....G...... 800 846-7980
 Philadelphia (G-13409)
Demco Enterprises Inc ....F...... 888 419-3343
 Quakertown (G-16184)
Forallsecure Inc ....F...... 412 256-8809
 Pittsburgh (G-15024)
Liquent Inc ....C...... 215 957-6401
 Horsham (G-7831)
Medshifts Inc ....G...... 856 834-0074
 Philadelphia (G-14006)
Mobile Video Corporation ....F...... 215 863-1072
 Broomall (G-2299)
Noblemedical LLC ....G...... 917 750-9605
 Bryn Mawr (G-2332)
Ragnasoft Inc ....F...... 866 471-2001
 Lancaster (G-9186)
Technology Dynamics Inc ....G...... 888 988-3243
 Wayne (G-19380)

TABLE OR COUNTERTOPS, PLASTIC LAMINATED

David Walters ....G...... 610 435-5433
 Allentown (G-192)
Desavino & Sons Inc ....E...... 570 383-3988
 Olyphant (G-12988)
Earnest Industries Inc ....G...... 412 323-1911
 Pittsburgh (G-14953)
Harrison Custom Cabinets ....G...... 215 548-2450
 Philadelphia (G-13804)
Imperial Counter Top Company ....G...... 610 435-4803
 Allentown (G-255)
Morrow Bros Countertop LP ....F...... 724 327-8980
 Export (G-5619)
Robertsons Inc ....G...... 814 838-2313
 Erie (G-5464)
Superior Cabinet Company ....G...... 215 536-5228
 Quakertown (G-16247)
Superior Flrcvgs Kitchens LLC ....G...... 717 264-9096
 Chambersburg (G-2981)
Vangura Kitchen Tops Inc ....D...... 412 824-0772
 Irwin (G-8204)

TABLES: Lift, Hydraulic

Ballymore Holdings Inc ....E...... 610 593-5062
 Coatesville (G-3293)

TABLETS & PADS

Vanroden Inc ....E...... 717 509-2600
 Lancaster (G-9230)

TABLETS & PADS: Book & Writing, Made From Purchased Material

Roaring Spring Blank Book Co ....B...... 814 224-2306
 Roaring Spring (G-16768)

TABLETS & PADS: Newsprint, Made From Purchased Materials

D-K Trading Corporation Inc ....G...... 570 586-9662
 Clarks Summit (G-3191)
Ligonier Outfitters Newsstands ....G...... 724 238-4900
 Ligonier (G-9961)

TABLETS: Bronze Or Other Metal

Compression Components Svc LLC .....F...... 267 387-2000
 Warrington (G-19111)

TABLEWARE: Vitreous China

Ceramic Art Company Inc ....A...... 952 944-5600
 Bristol (G-2124)

TACKS: Steel, Wire Or Cut

Moore Push Pin Company ....D...... 215 233-5700
 Glenside (G-6531)

PRODUCT

TAGS & LABELS: Paper

Ivy Graphics Inc ....F 215 396-9446
Warminster (G-18900)
Leonards Auto Tag Service ....G...... 570 489-4777
Dickson City (G-4124)
Leonards Auto Tag Service ....G...... 570 693-0122
Scranton (G-17254)
Spring Mills Manufacturing Inc ....G...... 814 422-8892
Spring Mills (G-17893)

TAGS: Paper, Blank, Made From Purchased Paper

Alumagraphics Inc ....E 412 787-7594
Pittsburgh (G-14694)
J F Chobert Associates Inc ....G...... 610 431-2200
Wayne (G-19341)

TALLOW: Animal

Valley Proteins Inc ....D 717 445-6890
East Earl (G-4556)

TANK COMPONENTS: Military, Specialized

Gichner Systems Group Inc ....B 877 520-1773
Dallastown (G-3976)

TANK REPAIR SVCS

Four Guys Stnless Tank Eqp Inc ....D 814 634-8373
Meyersdale (G-11010)
M & M Welding & Fabricating ....G...... 724 794-2045
Slippery Rock (G-17620)

TANKS & OTHER TRACKED VEHICLE CMPNTS

Bae Systems Land Armaments LP ....D 717 225-8000
York (G-20397)
Bosch Rexroth Corporation ....A 610 694-8300
Bethlehem (G-1470)
Hiltz Propane Systems Inc ....E 717 799-4322
Marietta (G-10464)
Humanistic Robotics Inc ....G...... 215 922-7803
Philadelphia (G-13840)
Medico Industries Inc ....C 570 825-7711
Wilkes Barre (G-19942)
Medico Industries Inc ....E 570 825-7711
Hanover Township (G-6996)
Shale Tank Solutions LLC ....F 724 823-0953
Donora (G-4162)

TANKS: Cryogenic, Metal

Cryognic Inds Svc Cmpanies LLC ....G...... 724 695-1910
Imperial (G-8062)
Messer LLC ....F 484 281-3261
Bethlehem (G-1570)
Titan Co2 Inc ....G...... 814 669-4544
Alexandria (G-64)

TANKS: For Tank Trucks, Metal Plate

M & M Welding & Fabricating ....G...... 724 794-2045
Slippery Rock (G-17620)
Nabco Systems LLC ....E 724 746-9617
Canonsburg (G-2610)

TANKS: Fuel, Including Oil & Gas, Metal Plate

Bristol Tank & Welding Co Inc ....F 215 752-8727
Langhorne (G-9282)
Harsco Corporation ....F 717 506-2071
Mechanicsburg (G-10851)
Mgs Inc ....C 717 336-7528
Denver (G-4083)

TANKS: Lined, Metal

Amity Industries Inc ....D 610 385-6075
Douglassville (G-4169)
Cooney Manufacturing Co LLC ....G...... 610 272-2100
Pottstown (G-15976)
Hpi Processes Inc ....G...... 215 799-0450
Telford (G-18294)
Specialty Tank & Wldg Co Inc ....E 215 949-2939
Bristol (G-2201)

TANKS: Military, Including Factory Rebuilding

Humanistic Robotics Inc ....G...... 267 515-5880
Philadelphia (G-13841)

TANKS: Plastic & Fiberglass

Coreco Fiberglass Inc ....F 724 463-3726
Indiana (G-8087)
Polycycle Industrial Pdts Inc ....E 412 747-1101
Pittsburgh (G-15419)
Sharpsville Container Corp ....E 724 962-1100
Sharpsville (G-17475)

TANKS: Standard Or Custom Fabricated, Metal Plate

Abtrex Industries Inc ....E 724 266-5425
Leetsdale (G-9676)
Bigbee Steel and Tank Company ....C 814 893-5701
Manheim (G-10370)
Bigbee Steel and Tank Company ....D 717 664-0600
Manheim (G-10371)
Dura-Bond Steel Corp ....C 724 327-0280
Export (G-5599)
Fisher Tank Company ....E 610 494-7200
Chester (G-3051)
Four Guys Stnless Tank Eqp Inc ....D 814 634-8373
Meyersdale (G-11010)
George I Reitz & Sons Inc ....E 814 849-2308
Brookville (G-2261)
George I Reitz & Sons Inc ....G...... 412 824-9976
East Pittsburgh (G-4595)
Highland Tank and Mfg Co ....C 814 893-5701
Stoystown (G-18080)
Industrial Eqp Fabricators Inc ....F 724 752-8819
Ellwood City (G-4938)
J W Steel Fabricating Co ....E 724 625-1355
Mars (G-10503)
Liquid Tech Tank Systems Inc ....F 717 796-7056
Dillsburg (G-4134)
Penn Iron Works Inc ....E 610 777-7656
Reading (G-16467)
Pittsburgh Tank Corporation ....E 724 258-0200
Monongahela (G-11314)
Prodex Inc ....G...... 215 536-4078
Quakertown (G-16234)
Richard J Summons Sculpture ....G...... 610 223-9013
Reading (G-16497)
Sharpsville Container Corp ....E 724 962-1100
Sharpsville (G-17475)
Stoystown Tank & Steel Co ....E 814 893-5133
Stoystown (G-18087)
Witherup Fbrction Erection Inc ....E 814 385-6601
Kennerdell (G-8499)

TANKS: Water, Metal Plate

Cemline Corporation ....D 724 274-5430
Cheswick (G-3104)

TANKS: Wood

Hall-Woolford Wood Tank Co Inc ....G...... 215 329-9022
Philadelphia (G-13797)

TANNERIES: Leather

Wickett & Craig America Inc ....D 814 236-2220
Curwensville (G-3956)

TANNING SALONS

American Lady US Male Hair Sln ....G...... 570 286-7759
Sunbury (G-18162)
Craze For Rayz Tanning Center ....G...... 484 231-1164
Norristown (G-12648)
Tammy Williams ....G...... 814 654-7127
Conneaut Lake (G-3481)

TAPE DRIVES

Progressive Computer Svcs Inc ....E 215 226-2220
Philadelphia (G-14207)
Seiberts Computers ....G...... 717 349-7859
Fannettsburg (G-5859)

TAPE: Instrumentation Type, Blank

E Instruments Group LLC ....G...... 215 750-1212
Langhorne (G-9291)

TAPES: Insulating

Get It Right Tape Company Inc ....G...... 570 383-6960
Olyphant (G-12991)

TAPES: Pressure Sensitive

Converters Inc ....E 215 355-5400
Huntingdon Valley (G-7971)
Cortape Ne Inc ....F 610 997-7900
Bethlehem (G-1488)
Labels By Pulizzi Inc ....E 570 326-1244
Williamsport (G-20034)
M & C Specialties Co ....B 215 322-7441
Southampton (G-17823)
Penn Emblem Company ....D 215 632-7800
Feasterville Trevose (G-5926)

TAPES: Tie, Woven Or Braided

Mutual Industries North Inc ....D 215 679-7682
Red Hill (G-16583)

TAPS

Reiff & Nestor Company ....F 717 453-7113
Lykens (G-10134)

TAR

Tangent Rail Products Inc ....F 412 325-0202
Pittsburgh (G-15597)

TARPAULINS

Covers All Canvas Products ....G...... 412 653-6010
Pittsburgh (G-14881)
D C Humphrys Co ....D 215 307-3363
Philadelphia (G-13599)
Madhavan Inc ....G...... 610 534-2600
Folcroft (G-6009)
Merlot Trpulin Sidekit Mfg Inc ....E 412 828-7664
Verona (G-18757)
Tarp America Inc ....G...... 724 339-4771
Murrysville (G-11869)
Tumacs Corp ....E 412 653-1188
Pittsburgh (G-15660)
Wagner Tarps Inc ....G...... 814 849-3422
Brookville (G-2275)

TARPAULINS, WHOLESALE

Merlot Trpulin Sidekit Mfg Inc ....E 412 828-7664
Verona (G-18757)
Tarp America Inc ....G...... 724 339-4771
Murrysville (G-11869)

TAX RETURN PREPARATION SVCS

H&R Block Inc ....F 814 723-3001
Warren (G-19030)

TAXIDERMISTS

Jordans Bear Den ....G...... 814 938-4081
Northpoint (G-12864)

TECHNICAL WRITING SVCS

Valira LLC ....G...... 973 216-5803
Conshohocken (G-3615)

TELECOMMUNICATION EQPT REPAIR SVCS, EXC TELEPHONES

Verizon Pennsylvania Inc ....D 215 879-7898
Philadelphia (G-14441)

TELECOMMUNICATION SYSTEMS & EQPT

Alcatel-Lucent Tech Inc ....G...... 215 752-1847
Feasterville Trevose (G-5884)
Amtel Systems Corporation ....G...... 610 458-3320
Chester Springs (G-3071)
Arris Global Services Inc ....G...... 215 323-1000
Horsham (G-7789)
B N I Solutions LLC ....G...... 814 237-4073
State College (G-17944)
Bluephone ....G...... 412 337-1965
Bridgeville (G-2055)
Broadband Networks Inc ....D 814 237-4073
State College (G-17947)
Cott Manufacturing Company ....F 412 675-0101
Glassport (G-6410)

Cott Manufacturing Company..........E 724 625-3730
Glassport (G-6411)
Delktech Systems Inc ....G 267 341-8391
Philadelphia (G-13618)
Greg Norton ....E 724 625-3426
Mars (G-10498)
ITI Inmate Telephone Inc ....D 814 944-0405
Altoona (G-518)
Legrand Home Systems Inc ....D 717 702-2532
Middletown (G-11060)
Library Video Company ....D 610 645-4000
Conshohocken (G-3572)
Ospcom LLC ....G 267 356-7124
Doylestown (G-4321)
Ruckus Wireless Inc ....E 215 323-1000
Horsham (G-7847)
Ruckus Wireless Inc ....G 215 209-6160
Philadelphia (G-14263)
Ruckus Wireless Inc ....E 814 231-3710
State College (G-18018)
Thales Transport & SEC Inc ....E 412 366-8814
Pittsburgh (G-15608)

TELECOMMUNICATIONS CARRIERS & SVCS: Wireless

Cellco Partnership ....D 610 431-5800
West Chester (G-19520)

TELEMARKETING BUREAUS

Impac Technology Inc ....E 610 430-1400
West Chester (G-19569)

TELEMETERING EQPT

L3 Technologies Inc ....C 267 545-7000
Bristol (G-2157)

TELEPHONE CENTRAL OFFICE EQPT: Dial Or Manual

Tollgrade Communications Inc ....E 724 720-1400
Cranberry Township (G-3854)

TELEPHONE EQPT INSTALLATION

ITI Inmate Telephone Inc ....D 814 944-0405
Altoona (G-518)

TELEPHONE EQPT: Modems

Black Box Corporation ....G 724 746-5500
Lawrence (G-9535)
C Dcap Modem Line ....G 814 966-3954
Duke Center (G-4438)
Netgear Inc ....G 724 941-5748
Canonsburg (G-2613)
Tech Modem CB Comcast ....G 267 288-5661
Warminster (G-18976)

TELEPHONE EQPT: NEC

Compunetix Inc ....B 412 373-8110
Monroeville (G-11330)
D&E Communications LLC ....E 814 238-0000
State College (G-17956)
D&E Communications LLC ....G 570 524-2200
Lewisburg (G-9904)
Gai-Tronics Corporation ....C 610 777-1374
Reading (G-16388)
Lexicon International Corp ....E 215 639-8220
Bensalem (G-1220)
Mobile Outfitters LLC ....F 215 325-0747
Philadelphia (G-14030)
Siemens Industry Inc ....F 412 829-7511
East Pittsburgh (G-4597)
Telamon Corporation ....E 800 945-8800
Levittown (G-9867)
Woodbine Properties ....C 814 443-4688
Somerset (G-17718)

TELEPHONE EQPT: PBX, Manual & Automatic

All Tech-D Out LLC ....F 610 814-0888
Allentown (G-124)
Voicestar Inc ....F 267 514-0000
Philadelphia (G-14455)

TELEPHONE SWITCHING EQPT

Quintech Elec Cmmnications Inc ....D 724 349-1412
Indiana (G-8122)

TELEPHONE: Fiber Optic Systems

Accelbeam Photonics LLC ....G 215 715-4345
Huntingdon Valley (G-7961)
Aurora Optics Inc ....G 215 646-0690
Ambler (G-568)
Finisar Corporation ....C 267 803-3800
Horsham (G-7818)
Omnispread Communications Inc ....G 215 654-9900
North Wales (G-12821)
Pittsburgh Photon Studio LLC ....G 724 263-6502
Pittsburgh (G-15403)

TELEPHONE: Headsets

Cardo Systems Inc ....E 412 788-4533
Pittsburgh (G-14811)

TELESCOPES

Fraser Optics LLC ....E 215 443-5240
Trevose (G-18494)
Fraser-Volpe LLC ....E 215 443-5240
Feasterville Trevose (G-5911)
John E Stiles Jr ....G 215 947-5571
Huntingdon Valley (G-8005)

TELEVISION BROADCASTING & COMMUNICATIONS EQPT

Linear Acoustic Inc ....G 717 735-6142
Lancaster (G-9112)
Sierra Media Services Inc ....G 412 722-1701
Pittsburgh (G-15537)
Video Visions Inc ....F 215 942-6642
Trevose (G-18508)
Wireless Acquisition LLC ....G 602 315-9979
Mountain Top (G-11781)

TELEVISION BROADCASTING STATIONS

East Hill Video Prod Co LLC ....F 215 855-4457
Lansdale (G-9364)
Family-Life Media-Com Inc ....F 724 543-6397
Kittanning (G-8769)

TELEVISION FILM PRODUCTION SVCS

Creative Thought Media LLC ....G 267 270-5147
Philadelphia (G-13579)
Lions World Media LLC ....F 917 645-7590
Bushkill (G-2366)

TELEVISION: Closed Circuit Eqpt

Rockwell Automation Inc ....G 412 375-4700
Coraopolis (G-3723)

TEN PIN CENTERS

Alkali Beaver Products ....G 724 709-7857
Rochester (G-16781)

TENT REPAIR SHOP

Als Awning Shop Inc ....G 814 456-6262
Erie (G-5183)

TENTS: All Materials

Amish Country Gazebos Inc ....G 717 665-0365
Manheim (G-10367)
Sprung Instant Structures Inc ....G 610 391-9553
Allentown (G-399)

TERMINAL BOARDS

Marco Manufacturing Co Inc ....E 215 463-2332
Philadelphia (G-13992)

TEST BORING SVCS: Nonmetallic Minerals

Test Boring Services Inc ....F 724 267-4649
Scenery Hill (G-17126)

TESTERS: Battery

Advance Stores Company Inc ....E 610 939-0120
Reading (G-16311)

TESTERS: Environmental

Busch Company ....F 724 940-2326
Wexford (G-19792)
Environmental Tectonics Corp ....C 215 355-9100
Southampton (G-17809)
Greendesign LLC ....G 215 242-0700
Philadelphia (G-13784)
Hazardous Materials Mgt Team ....G 215 968-4044
Newtown (G-12507)
Humanistic Robotics Inc ....G 267 515-5880
Philadelphia (G-13842)
Lemos Labs LLC ....G 724 519-2936
Butler (G-2420)
Mine Safety Appliances Co LLC ....B 724 776-8600
Cranberry Township (G-3836)
MSA Safety Incorporated ....B 724 776-8600
Cranberry Township (G-3839)
MSA Safety Sales LLC ....G 724 776-8600
Cranberry Township (G-3841)
Sloan Equipment Sales Co Inc ....G 215 784-0771
Dresher (G-4358)
Tescor Inc ....E 215 957-6061
Warminster (G-18977)
Welltech Products Inc ....G 610 417-8928
Macungie (G-10161)

TESTERS: Gas, Exc Indl Process

First Choice Radon Testing Co ....G 215 947-1995
Huntingdon Valley (G-7984)

TESTERS: Hardness

Industrial Instrs & Sups Inc ....F 215 396-0822
Wycombe (G-20260)
King Tester Corporation ....F 610 279-6010
Phoenixville (G-14557)
Newage Testing Instruments ....E 215 355-6900
Horsham (G-7835)

TESTERS: Integrated Circuit

Lehighton Electronics Inc ....F 610 377-5990
Lehighton (G-9718)

TESTERS: Liquid, Exc Indl Process

EMD Millipore Corporation ....B 484 652-5600
Philadelphia (G-13315)

TESTERS: Physical Property

Custom Scientific Instruments ....G 610 923-6500
Easton (G-4667)
Genisphere LLC ....G 215 996-3002
Hatfield (G-7344)

TESTERS: Sewage

Industrial Instrs & Sups Inc ....F 215 396-0822
Wycombe (G-20260)

TESTERS: Water, Exc Indl Process

Suez Wts Usa Inc ....A 215 355-3300
Trevose (G-18506)

TESTING SVCS

Almac Central Management LLC ....C 215 660-8500
Souderton (G-17721)

TEXTILE & APPAREL SVCS

Finetex Rotary Engraving Inc ....G 717 273-6841
Lebanon (G-9567)

TEXTILE CONVERTERS: Knit Goods

Annville Shoulder Strap Co ....E 717 867-4831
Annville (G-642)

TEXTILE DESIGNERS

Carey Schuster LLC ....G 610 431-2512
West Chester (G-19519)

TEXTILE FABRICATORS

Del Val Flag Philadelphia Sp ....G 610 235-7179
Aston (G-758)
Msjc Inc ....G 717 930-0718
Middletown (G-11065)

PRODUCT

TEXTILE FINISHING: Bleaching, Broadwoven, Cotton

Mindy Inc ....F 215 739-0432
Philadelphia (G-14024)

TEXTILE FINISHING: Bleaching, Man Fiber & Silk, Broadwoven

Mindy Inc ....F 215 739-0432
Philadelphia (G-14024)

TEXTILE FINISHING: Cloth Mending, For The Trade

Supreme Trading Ltd ....E 215 739-2237
Philadelphia (G-14361)

TEXTILE FINISHING: Dyeing, Finishing & Printng, Linen Fabric

Sterling Finishing ....F 267 682-0844
Glenside (G-6541)
Sure Fold Co Inc ....F 215 634-7480
Philadelphia (G-14362)

TEXTILE FINISHING: Dyeing, Manmade Fiber & Silk, Broadwoven

Columbia Silk Dyeing Company ....E 215 739-2289
Philadelphia (G-13561)
G J Littlewood & Son Inc ....E 215 483-3970
Philadelphia (G-13739)

TEXTILE FINISHING: Preshrinking, Cotton

Country Keepsakes ....G 570 744-2246
Rome (G-16796)

TEXTILE PRDTS: Hand Woven & Crocheted

All American Sweats Inc ....F 412 922-8999
Pittsburgh (G-14674)
Jan Lew Textile Corp ....D 610 857-8050
Parkesburg (G-13176)

TEXTILE: Finishing, Cotton Broadwoven

Chloe Textiles Incorporated ....D 717 848-2800
York (G-20425)
Columbia Silk Dyeing Company ....E 215 739-2289
Philadelphia (G-13561)
G J Littlewood & Son Inc ....E 215 483-3970
Philadelphia (G-13739)
Hlc Industries Inc ....F 610 668-9112
Bala Cynwyd (G-880)
Lawrence Schiff Silk Mills Inc ....F 215 536-5460
Quakertown (G-16209)
Maroco Ltd ....B 610 746-6800
Easton (G-4719)
Quality Crrctons Inspctons Inc ....D 814 696-3737
Duncansville (G-4462)
Romar Textile Co Inc ....C 724 535-7787
Wampum (G-18804)
William J Dixon Company ....E 610 524-1131
Exton (G-5750)

TEXTILE: Finishing, Raw Stock NEC

Art Stitch Inc ....G 717 652-8992
Harrisburg (G-7091)
Charles F May Co ....G 215 634-7257
Philadelphia (G-13527)
G J Littlewood & Son Inc ....E 215 483-3970
Philadelphia (G-13739)
Lawrence Schiff Silk Mills Inc ....F 215 536-5460
Quakertown (G-16209)
Magiseal Services ....G 724 327-3068
Export (G-5617)
Tom Russell ....G 724 746-5029
Houston (G-7882)

TEXTILE: Goods, NEC

Executive Distributors Intl ....G 610 608-1664
Bryn Mawr (G-2323)
Tetratec Corp ....F 215 396-8349
Warminster (G-18978)

TEXTILES

Advanced Tex Composites Inc ....E 570 207-7000
Scranton (G-17206)
Akas Tex LLC ....F 215 244-2589
Bensalem (G-1146)

TEXTILES: Carbonized Rags

Armstrong/Kover Kwick Inc ....E 412 771-2200
Mc Kees Rocks (G-10603)

TEXTILES: Fibers, Textile, Rcvrd From Mill Waste/Rags

Oscar Daniels & Company Inc ....F 610 678-8144
Reading (G-16460)
Penn Pro Manufacturing Inc ....F 724 222-6450
Washington (G-19215)

TEXTILES: Linen Fabrics

Bed Bath & Beyond Inc ....G 717 397-0206
Lancaster (G-8950)
Pinnacle Textile Inds LLC ....E 800 901-4784
King of Prussia (G-8663)
Unitex Group Usa LLC ....E 864 846-8700
Warminster (G-18991)

TEXTILES: Linings, Carpet, Exc Felt

Bond Products Inc ....F 215 842-0200
Philadelphia (G-13470)

TEXTILES: Mill Waste & Remnant

Thread International Pbc Inc ....G 814 876-9999
Pittsburgh (G-15617)

TEXTILES: Scouring & Combing

Fiberland Inc ....E 215 744-5446
Philadelphia (G-13699)

THEATRICAL LIGHTING SVCS

Creative Systems Usa LLC ....G 610 450-6580
Collegeville (G-3373)

THEATRICAL PRODUCERS & SVCS

Fly Magazine ....G 717 293-9772
Lancaster (G-9024)

THEATRICAL SCENERY

Quinlan Scenic Studio Inc ....F 610 859-9130
Marcus Hook (G-10453)
Stagestep Inc ....F 267 672-2900
Philadelphia (G-14339)
Tait Towers Inc ....D 717 626-9571
Lititz (G-10051)

THERMISTORS, EXC TEMPERATURE SENSORS

Spectrum Control Inc ....B 814 474-2207
Fairview (G-5842)
Thermistors Unlimited Inc ....G 814 781-5920
Saint Marys (G-17022)

THERMOCOUPLES

Lpg Industries Inc ....E 610 622-2900
Clifton Heights (G-3254)
National Basic Sensor Corp ....F 215 322-4700
Huntingdon Valley (G-8016)

THERMOCOUPLES: Indl Process

I F H Industries Inc ....G 215 699-9344
Royersford (G-16852)
Pyco LLC ....G 215 757-3704
Penndel (G-13241)
W H Cooke & Co Inc ....G 717 630-2222
Hanover (G-6970)

THERMOELECTRIC DEVICES: Solid State

Advanced Plasma Solutions ....G 267 679-4077
Reading (G-16312)

THERMOMETERS: Indl

Philadelphia Instrs & Contrls ....F 215 329-8828
Philadelphia (G-14146)

THERMOPLASTIC MATERIALS

Air Products and Chemicals Inc ....E 724 266-1563
Leetsdale (G-9677)
Cellomics Inc ....G 412 770-2500
Pittsburgh (G-14833)
Evolution Mlding Solutions Inc ....G 814 807-1982
Meadville (G-10722)
Impact Guard LLC ....E 724 318-8800
Leetsdale (G-9695)
Simtech Industrial Pdts Inc ....F 215 547-0444
Levittown (G-9863)

THERMOPLASTICS

Apexco-Ppsi LLC ....G 937 935-0164
Horsham (G-7787)
Global Epp Inc ....G 412 580-4780
Pittsburgh (G-15052)
Gt Services LLC ....E 215 256-9521
Kulpsville (G-8829)
Rapid Tpc LLC ....F 412 450-0482
Pittsburgh (G-15468)
Romax Hose Inc ....F 570 869-0860
Laceyville (G-8874)
Superior Dual Laminates Inc ....G 610 965-9061
Emmaus (G-5043)
Tomark-Worthen LLC ....G 610 978-1889
Chadds Ford (G-2861)
Total Plastics Inc ....G 877 677-8872
Philadelphia (G-14399)
Total Plastics Resources LLC ....E 215 637-2221
Bensalem (G-1261)
U E C Inc ....D 724 772-5225
Cranberry Township (G-3860)

THERMOSETTING MATERIALS

Laminations Inc ....C 570 876-8199
Archbald (G-690)

THREAD, ELASTIC: Fabric Covered

Liberty Throwing Company ....D 570 287-1114
Kingston (G-8721)

THREAD: All Fibers

Liberty Throwing Company ....D 570 287-1114
Kingston (G-8721)
Middleburg Yarn Processing Co ....D 570 374-1284
Selinsgrove (G-17331)
Roselon Industries Inc ....D 215 536-3275
Quakertown (G-16242)

THREAD: Embroidery

Lets Get Personal ....G 412 829-0975
Monroeville (G-11343)
SYN Apparel LLC ....G 484 821-3664
Bethlehem (G-1636)

THREAD: Natural Fiber

Natural Textiles Solutions LLC ....G 484 660-4085
Macungie (G-10155)

THREAD: Sewing

Eddington Thread Mfg Co Inc ....E 215 639-8900
Bensalem (G-1186)

THREAD: Thread, From Manmade Fiber

Sauquoit Industries LLC ....D 570 348-2751
Scranton (G-17283)

TIES, FORM: Metal

Jacob Schmidt & Son Inc ....F 215 234-4641
Harleysville (G-7041)

TILE: Brick & Structural, Clay

Dectile Harkus Construction ....E 724 789-7125
Butler (G-2393)
Glen-Gery Corporation ....G 484 240-4000
Allentown (G-233)
Glen-Gery Corporation ....G 570 742-4721
Watsontown (G-19274)

Glen-Gery Corporation ....G....... 717 939-6061
Middletown (G-11054)
Gruber Con Specialists Inc ....F 610 760-0925
New Tripoli (G-12456)
Morgan Advanced Ceramics Inc ....E....... 610 366-7100
Allentown (G-321)
Mulch Barn ....G....... 215 703-0300
Souderton (G-17755)
Sil-Base Company Inc ....E....... 412 751-2314
McKeesport (G-10681)

TILE: Clay, Drain & Structural

Septic Surgeons LLC ....G....... 570 224-4822
Equinunk (G-5160)

TILE: Clay, Roof

Brinkmann Bros Inc ....G....... 215 739-4769
Philadelphia (G-13483)
Certainteed Corporation ....B....... 610 893-5000
Malvern (G-10204)
Certainteed Corporation ....G....... 610 651-8706
Malvern (G-10205)
Polyglass USA Inc ....E....... 570 384-1230
Hazle Township (G-7474)

TILE: Mosaic, Ceramic

Alumina Ceramic Components Inc ....F 724 532-1900
Latrobe (G-9454)

TILE: Partition, Clay

Cpg International LLC ....F 570 348-0997
Scranton (G-17223)

TILE: Quarry, Clay

Glenn O Hawbaker Inc ....E 814 359-3411
Pleasant Gap (G-15792)

TILE: Structural Clay

Glen-Gery Corporation ....D....... 814 856-2171
Summerville (G-18158)

TILE: Wall, Fiberboard

Soroka Sales Inc ....E....... 412 381-7700
Pittsburgh (G-15560)

TIMBER PRDTS WHOLESALERS

Sheth International Inc ....G....... 610 584-8670
Norristown (G-12712)
Timberhaven Log Homes LLC ....F 570 568-1422
Lewisburg (G-9922)

TIMING DEVICES: Electronic

Oakwood Controls Corporation ....F 717 801-1515
Glen Rock (G-6458)

TIN

Rin Tin Tim Inc ....G....... 412 403-5378
Pittsburgh (G-15486)
Tel Tin...G....... 717 259-9004
Abbottstown (G-8)
Tin Cup Inc ....G 570 322-1115
Williamsport (G-20083)
Tin Lizzy Inc................................G....... 724 836-0281
Greensburg (G-6718)
Tin Man Sweets ....G....... 724 432-3930
Zelienople (G-20824)
Tin Roof Enterprises LLC ....G....... 610 659-3989
Media (G-10954)
Tin Tinker ....G....... 215 230-9619
Doylestown (G-4342)
United States Steel Corp ....C....... 215 736-4600
Fairless Hills (G-5806)
United States Steel Corp ....C....... 412 433-7215
Homestead (G-7695)
United States Steel Corp ....B....... 412 433-1121
Pittsburgh (G-15677)
US Steel Holdings Inc ....G....... 412 433-1121
Pittsburgh (G-15687)

TINSEL

F C Young & Co Inc ....C....... 215 788-9226
Bristol (G-2143)
J Kinderman & Sons Inc ....E....... 215 271-7600
Philadelphia (G-13884)

TIRE & INNER TUBE MATERIALS & RELATED PRDTS

Polymer Tennessee Holdings ....G....... 724 838-2340
Indiana (G-8121)

TIRE CORD & FABRIC: Fuel Cells, Reinforcing

Dynacell Life Sciences LLC ....F 215 813-8775
Ambler (G-576)

TIRE DEALERS

Aaron Wenger ....G....... 717 656-9876
New Holland (G-12225)
Jack Williams Tire Co Inc ....F 610 437-4651
Whitehall (G-19878)
Steve Shannon Tire Company Inc........G....... 570 675-8473
Dallas (G-3968)

TIRE RECAPPING & RETREADING

Bastian Tire Sales Inc....................E....... 570 323-8651
Williamsport (G-19992)

TIRE SUNDRIES OR REPAIR MATERIALS: Rubber

Barnes P S P Inc ....G....... 724 287-6711
Butler (G-2376)
International Marketing Inc ....F 717 264-5819
Chambersburg (G-2942)

TIRES & INNER TUBES

BF Hiestand House ....G....... 717 426-8415
Marietta (G-10461)
Cooper Tire & Rubber Company ....E....... 610 967-0860
Alburtis (G-51)
Jack Williams Tire Co Inc ....F 610 437-4651
Whitehall (G-19878)
Michelin North America Inc...............B....... 301 641-0121
Seven Fields (G-17376)
Micronic Manufacturingusa LLC ....F 484 483-8075
Aston (G-778)
Polymer Enterprises Inc ....G....... 724 838-2340
Greensburg (G-6703)
Steve Shannon Tire Company Inc.......G....... 570 675-8473
Dallas (G-3968)
Superior Tire & Rubber Corp ....D....... 814 723-2370
Warren (G-19050)
Valley Retreading Inc ....F 724 489-4483
Charleroi (G-3023)

TIRES: Cushion Or Solid Rubber

Superior Tire & Rubber Corp ....C....... 814 723-2370
Warren (G-19049)

TIRES: Indl Vehicles

American Industrial Parts ....G....... 800 421-1180
Monroeville (G-11324)
Pomps Tire Service Inc ....F 814 623-6764
Bedford (G-1071)

TITANIUM MILL PRDTS

Nak International Corp ....E....... 724 774-9200
Monaca (G-11292)
Oregon Metallurgical LLC ....F 541 967-9000
Pittsburgh (G-15363)
Titanium 40 LLC ....G....... 610 338-0446
Swarthmore (G-18186)
Titanium Brkg Solutions LLC ....G....... 267 506-6642
Philadelphia (G-14391)
Titanium Foundation ....G....... 717 668-8423
New Freedom (G-12217)
Titanium Wealth Advisors LLC ....G....... 610 429-1700
West Chester (G-19664)
Uniti Titanium LLC ....G....... 412 424-0440
Pittsburgh (G-15680)

TOBACCO & PRDTS, WHOLESALE: Smoking

Tobacco Plus Cash Checking ....G....... 267 585-3802
Levittown (G-9868)

TOBACCO & TOBACCO PRDTS WHOLESALERS

Planet Ryo ....G....... 717 938-8860
Etters (G-5552)
WA Dehart Inc...............................D....... 570 568-1551
New Columbia (G-12179)

TOBACCO LEAF PROCESSING

Lancaster Leaf Tob Co PA Inc.............E....... 717 291-1528
Lancaster (G-9098)
Lancaster Leaf Tob Co PA Inc.............E....... 717 394-2676
Lancaster (G-9097)
Lancaster Leaf Tob Co PA Inc.............G....... 717 393-1526
Lancaster (G-9099)

TOBACCO STORES & STANDS

R J Reynolds Tobacco Company ....G....... 570 654-0770
Pittston (G-15781)
South Hills Brewing Supply ....G....... 412 937-0773
Monroeville (G-11356)

TOBACCO: Chewing & Snuff

Planet Ryo ....G....... 717 938-8860
Etters (G-5552)

TOBACCO: Cigarettes

Klafters Inc ....G....... 814 833-7444
Erie (G-5346)
R J Reynolds Tobacco Company ....G....... 215 244-9071
Bensalem (G-1247)
Rebel Indian Smoke Shop.................G....... 610 499-1711
Brookhaven (G-2247)
Tabacos USA Inc ....G....... 610 438-2005
Easton (G-4762)
Tobacco Plus Cash Checking ....G....... 267 585-3802
Levittown (G-9868)

TOBACCO: Cigars

Altadis USA Inc ....D....... 570 929-2220
McAdoo (G-10655)
F X Smiths Sons Co ....F 717 637-5232
Mc Sherrystown (G-10650)
John Middleton Co..........................F 804 274-2000
King of Prussia (G-8636)
Parodi Holdings LLC ....E....... 570 344-8566
Dunmore (G-4479)
Rebel Indian Smoke Shop.................G....... 610 499-1711
Brookhaven (G-2247)

TOILET PREPARATIONS

Surco Products Inc ....F 412 252-7000
Pittsburgh (G-15590)

TOILETRIES, COSMETICS & PERFUME STORES

Alpha Aromatics Inc ....D....... 412 252-1012
Pittsburgh (G-14686)
Brickhouse Services.......................G....... 570 869-1871
Laceyville (G-8870)

TOILETRIES, WHOLESALE: Razor Blades

Art of Shaving - Fl LLC ....G....... 610 962-1000
King of Prussia (G-8585)

TOMBSTONES: Cut Stone, Exc Finishing Or Lettering Only

Earl Wenz Inc...............................F 610 395-2331
Breinigsville (G-2014)
Wenzco Supplies ....F 610 434-6157
Allentown (G-432)

TOOL & DIE STEEL

Ashby Mfg Co Inc..........................F 724 776-5566
Cranberry Township (G-3805)
Bangor Steel Erectors Inc ....E....... 215 338-1200
Philadelphia (G-13443)
Brown Tool & Die Inc ....G....... 724 547-3366
Acme (G-16)
Capo and Kifer Pultrusions................G....... 412 751-3489
Greenock (G-6644)
Composidie Inc ....E....... 724 845-8602
Leechburg (G-9643)

P R O D U C T

Dyer Industries Inc..................F....... 724 258-3400
Bunola (G-2343)
Economy Tooling Corp PA..................G....... 724 266-4546
Ambridge (G-617)
Eden Tool Company..................G....... 717 235-7009
New Freedom (G-12206)
Ellwood Mill Products Company........E....... 724 658-9632
New Castle (G-12086)
Ellwood Specialty Steel Co..................D....... 724 657-1160
New Castle (G-12088)
Harter Precision..................G....... 724 459-5060
Blairsville (G-1723)
Himes Machine Inc..................F....... 724 927-6850
Linesville (G-9982)
James A & Paulette M Berry..................G....... 814 486-2323
Emporium (G-5064)
Latrobe Specialty Mtls Co LLC..................A....... 724 537-7711
Latrobe (G-9494)
Lloyd Industries Inc..................E....... 215 367-5863
Montgomeryville (G-11404)
Pickar Brothers Inc..................E....... 610 582-0967
Birdsboro (G-1703)
Rossi Precision Inc..................G....... 724 667-9334
New Castle (G-12145)
Te Connectivity Corporation..................C....... 717 762-9186
Waynesboro (G-19426)
X-Cell Tool and Mold Inc..................E....... 814 474-9100
Fairview (G-5850)

TOOL REPAIR SVCS

J K J Tool Co..................F....... 570 322-1411
Williamsport (G-20026)

TOOLS & EQPT: Used With Sporting Arms

Craig Colabaugh Gunsmith Inc..........G....... 570 992-4499
Stroudsburg (G-18111)

TOOLS: Carpenters', Including Levels & Chisels, Exc Saws

Ingrain Construction LLC..................F....... 717 205-1475
Lancaster (G-9057)

TOOLS: Hand

Auger Mfg Specialists Co..................E....... 610 647-4677
Malvern (G-10188)
Bolttech Mannings Inc..................D....... 724 872-4873
North Versailles (G-12772)
Bostock Inc..................G....... 610 650-9650
Norristown (G-12641)
Channellock Inc..................B....... 814 337-9200
Meadville (G-10711)
CP Precision Inc..................G....... 267 364-0870
Warminster (G-18849)
Electro-Glass Products Inc..................E....... 724 423-5000
Norvelt (G-12878)
Electroline Corp..................E....... 215 766-2229
Pipersville (G-14614)
Elge Precision Machining Inc..................F....... 610 376-5458
Reading (G-16372)
Emsco Inc..................C....... 814 774-3137
Girard (G-6386)
F Tinker and Sons Company..................E....... 412 781-3553
Pittsburgh (G-15000)
General Wire Spring Company..................C....... 412 771-6300
Mc Kees Rocks (G-10612)
Hewlett Manufacturing Co..................G....... 814 683-4762
Linesville (G-9981)
Jiba LLC..................F....... 215 739-9644
Philadelphia (G-13898)
John Stortz and Son Inc..................G....... 215 627-3855
Philadelphia (G-13906)
Kal-Cameron Manufacturing..................F....... 814 486-3394
Emporium (G-5065)
Pro Tool Industries Inc..................F....... 484 945-5001
Pottstown (G-16037)
Quality Tool & Die Enterprises..........G....... 814 834-2384
Saint Marys (G-17013)
Reed Manufacturing Company..................D....... 814 452-3691
Erie (G-5459)
Ronal Tool Company Inc..................F....... 717 741-0880
York (G-20660)
Ruch Carbide Burs Inc..................E....... 215 657-3660
Willow Grove (G-20139)
Sanders Saws & Blades Inc..................E....... 610 273-3733
Honey Brook (G-7761)
SPS Technologies LLC..................A....... 215 572-3000
Jenkintown (G-8302)

Three M Tool and Die Corp..................F....... 717 854-6379
York (G-20688)
Vollman Pershing H Inc..................G....... 215 956-1971
Warminster (G-18998)
Woodings Industrial Corp..................C....... 724 625-3131
Mars (G-10515)

TOOLS: Hand, Carpet Layers

Halex Corporation..................E....... 909 622-3537
Fairless Hills (G-5782)

TOOLS: Hand, Engravers'

Antares Instruments Inc..................F....... 215 441-5250
Horsham (G-7786)

TOOLS: Hand, Hammers

Barco Industries Inc..................E....... 610 374-3117
Reading (G-16328)

TOOLS: Hand, Masons'

Bon Tool Company..................D....... 724 443-7080
Gibsonia (G-6328)
W Rose Inc..................E....... 610 583-4125
Sharon Hill (G-17466)

TOOLS: Hand, Mechanics

Cornwell Quality Tools Company..........G....... 814 756-5484
Albion (G-41)
Transportation Eqp Sup Co..................E....... 814 866-1952
Erie (G-5514)

TOOLS: Hand, Power

Atsco Holdings Corp..................D....... 440 701-1021
Cranberry Township (G-3807)
Black & Decker (us) Inc..................F....... 215 271-0402
Philadelphia (G-13467)
Black & Decker (us) Inc..................G....... 717 755-3441
York (G-20409)
Bolttech Mannings Inc..................D....... 724 872-4873
North Versailles (G-12772)
Bon Tool Company..................D....... 724 443-7080
Gibsonia (G-6328)
Eaton Electric Holdings LLC..................D....... 717 755-2933
York (G-20462)
Fsm Tools..................G....... 717 867-5359
Annville (G-648)
JD Delta Company Inc..................G....... 484 320-7600
Malvern (G-10263)
Kdc Engineering..................G....... 267 203-8487
Telford (G-18298)
Keystone Machine Inc..................E....... 717 359-9256
Littlestown (G-10068)
Lemco Tool Corporation..................E....... 570 494-0620
Cogan Station (G-3361)
Modern Manufacturing Co Inc..................F....... 215 659-4820
Willow Grove (G-20128)
Novative Designs Inc..................G....... 215 794-3380
Blue Bell (G-1850)
R E Dupill & Associates Ltd..................G....... 724 845-7900
Leechburg (G-9651)
Torcup Inc..................F....... 610 250-5800
Easton (G-4763)
Transportation Eqp Sup Co..................E....... 814 866-1952
Erie (G-5514)
Velocity Robotics..................G....... 412 254-3011
Pittsburgh (G-15690)
Wheeler Tool Co..................G....... 570 888-2275
Athens (G-813)
Woodings Industrial Corp..................C....... 724 625-3131
Mars (G-10515)

TOOTHBRUSHES: Exc Electric

Radius Corporation..................E....... 484 646-9122
Kutztown (G-8858)

TOPS: Automobile, Stamped Metal

Cosma USA LLC..................G....... 412 551-0708
Wexford (G-19796)
Designs By Lawrence Inc..................E....... 215 698-4555
Philadelphia (G-13622)

TOURIST LODGINGS

Fork Creek Cabins LLC..................F....... 717 442-1902
Paradise (G-13159)

TOWELETTES: Premoistened

National Towelette Company..................E....... 215 245-7300
Bensalem (G-1229)

TOWELS: Indl

Yes Towels Inc..................G....... 215 538-5230
Quakertown (G-16261)

TOWELS: Linen & Linen & Cotton Mixtures

Arkwright LLC..................G....... 732 246-1506
Philadelphia (G-13411)

TOWELS: Paper

Berk International LLC..................D....... 610 369-0600
Boyertown (G-1898)
Procter & Gamble Paper Pdts Co..........B....... 570 833-5141
Mehoopany (G-10957)

TOWERS, SECTIONS: Transmission, Radio & Television

Global Utility Structures LLC..................G....... 570 788-0826
Sugarloaf (G-18153)
Lee Antenna & Line Service Inc..........F....... 610 346-7999
Springtown (G-17927)
Sabre Tblar Strctures - PA LLC..................D....... 724 201-9968
Ellwood City (G-4948)
Solarian US..................G....... 610 550-6350
Ardmore (G-717)

TOYS

Ack Displays Inc..................G....... 215 236-3000
Merion Station (G-10996)
Bleacher Creatures LLC..................G....... 484 534-2398
Plymouth Meeting (G-15834)
Church Communities PA Inc..................G....... 724 329-8573
Farmington (G-5860)
Compleat Strategist Inc..................G....... 610 265-8562
King of Prussia (G-8596)
Conestoga Co Inc..................G....... 610 866-0777
Allentown (G-174)
Creative Designs Intl Ltd..................D....... 215 953-2800
Trevose (G-18491)
Engineered Plastics LLC..................D....... 814 452-6632
Erie (G-5259)
Fisher Woodcraft..................G....... 610 273-2076
Honey Brook (G-7744)
Gemini Precision Products Ltd..........G....... 724 452-8700
Gibsonia (G-6337)
Goliath Development LLC..................G....... 310 748-6288
Jermyn (G-8306)
Holly Woodcrafters Inc..................E....... 717 486-5862
Mount Holly Springs (G-11634)
Jay Weller..................G....... 215 257-4859
Sellersville (G-17350)
Just Play..................E....... 215 953-1208
Newtown (G-12513)
KNex Industries Inc..................C....... 215 997-7722
Hatfield (G-7358)
KNex Ltd Partnership Group..................D....... 215 997-7722
Hatfield (G-7359)
Lisa Leleu Studios Inc..................G....... 215 345-1233
Doylestown (G-4313)
Martin Weaver R..................G....... 717 354-8970
New Holland (G-12260)
Nocopi Technologies Inc..................G....... 610 834-9600
King of Prussia (G-8657)
Old Time Games Inc..................G....... 215 538-5422
Quakertown (G-16225)
Orange Products Inc..................D....... 610 791-9711
Allentown (G-341)
Paper Magic Group Inc..................C....... 570 961-3863
Moosic (G-11511)
Second Play LLC..................G....... 267 229-8033
Newtown (G-12548)
Seder Gaming Inc..................G....... 814 736-3611
Ebensburg (G-4796)
Smart Potato LLC..................G....... 215 380-5050
Oreland (G-13029)
Sonic Tronics Inc..................G....... 215 635-6520
Elkins Park (G-4911)
Spang & Company..................C....... 412 963-9363
Pittsburgh (G-15566)
Srm Entertainment Group LLC..........F....... 610 825-1039
Doylestown (G-4338)
Susquehanna Games & Bingo Sups.....G....... 570 322-9941
Williamsport (G-20079)

Wicked Cool Toys Holdings LLC..........E....... 267 536-9186
Bristol (G-2217)

TOYS & HOBBY GOODS & SPLYS, WHOLESALE: Arts/Crafts Eqpt/Sply

Roberts Manufacturing LLC..................F....... 855 763-7450
Allentown (G-376)

TOYS & HOBBY GOODS & SPLYS, WHOLESALE: Toys, NEC

Double M Productions LLC....................F....... 570 476-8000
Stroudsburg (G-18114)
Marcus J Wholesalers Inc ....F....... 412 261-3315
Pittsburgh (G-15252)

TOYS: Dolls, Stuffed Animals & Parts

Aimee & Darias Doll Outlet ....G....... 717 687-8118
Ronks (G-16802)
Teddy Wears ....G....... 610 273-3234
Honey Brook (G-7766)

TOYS: Rubber

Crazy Aaron Enterprises Inc..................F....... 866 578-2845
Norristown (G-12649)

TRADE SHOW ARRANGEMENT SVCS

Mother Nature Corporation ....G....... 412 798-3911
Pittsburgh (G-15304)
Purpose 1 LLC......................................G....... 717 232-9077
Lemoyne (G-9749)
Sparks Exhbits Envrnments Corp.........D....... 215 676-1100
Philadelphia (G-14329)

TRADERS: Commodity, Contracts

International Raw Mtls Ltd ....E....... 215 928-1010
Philadelphia (G-13867)

TRAILER COACHES: Automobile

Bailey Leasing Inc................................D....... 717 718-0490
York (G-20398)

TRAILERS & CHASSIS: Camping

Columbia Northwest Inc.........................F....... 724 423-7440
Mount Pleasant (G-11693)

TRAILERS & PARTS: Truck & Semi's

3nt-3 Nieces Trucking Inc......................G....... 360 815-0938
Grassflat (G-6577)
Belmont Machine Co ....G....... 717 556-0040
Leola (G-9773)
Borco Equipment Inc ....E....... 814 535-1400
Johnstown (G-8359)
Bri-Mar Manufacturing LLC....................F....... 717 263-6116
Chambersburg (G-2913)
Comanche Manufacturing Inc.................G....... 724 530-7278
Volant (G-18771)
Delaware Valley Shippers Inc ....G....... 215 633-1535
Bensalem (G-1181)
Dively Manufacture Co Inc ....F....... 814 239-5441
Claysburg (G-3203)
Ehb Logisitics Inc ....F....... 717 764-5800
York (G-20464)
Great Dane LLC......................................B....... 717 492-0057
Mount Joy (G-11659)
Great Dane Trailers Inc ....G....... 570 221-6920
Elysburg (G-4976)
Lang Speciality Trailers LLC ....G....... 724 972-6590
Latrobe (G-9487)
Master Solutions Inc ....E....... 717 243-6849
Carlisle (G-2724)
Rt 66 Tractor Supply ....G....... 724 668-2000
New Alexandria (G-12020)
Shetron Manufacturing LLC....................G....... 717 532-4400
Shippensburg (G-17547)
Somerset Welding & Steel Inc ....C....... 814 443-2671
Somerset (G-17710)
Stanton Dynamics Inc ....F....... 814 849-6255
Brookville (G-2272)
Viking Vee Inc ....G....... 724 789-9194
Renfrew (G-16643)
Windview Truck & Trlr Repr LLC ....G....... 570 374-8077
Port Trevorton (G-15916)
Worthington Trailers LP ....F....... 570 567-7921
Williamsport (G-20101)

TRAILERS & TRAILER EQPT

101 Cameo Appearances LLC ....G....... 412 787-7981
Pittsburgh (G-14623)
Arthur L Baker Enterprises ....G....... 717 432-9788
Lewisberry (G-9880)
Bri-Mar Manufacturing LLC....................E....... 717 263-6116
Chambersburg (G-2913)
C & C Manufacturing & Fabg ....G....... 570 454-0819
Hazleton (G-7492)
Dutchie Manufacturing LLC ....G....... 717 656-2186
Leola (G-9778)
Fiba Technologies Inc ....F....... 215 679-7823
East Greenville (G-4568)
Gold Rush Inc...E....... 717 484-2424
Denver (G-4074)
Hilltown Services ....G....... 215 249-3694
Dublin (G-4434)
Kutz Farm Equipment Inc.......................G....... 570 345-4882
Pine Grove (G-14596)
Mgs Inc...C....... 717 336-7528
Denver (G-4083)
Miller Inds Towing Eqp Inc ....G....... 724 981-3328
Hermitage (G-7591)
Mustang Trailer Mfg ....F....... 724 628-1000
Connellsville (G-3504)
Rail Ryder LLC.......................................G....... 814 873-1623
Erie (G-5452)
Smouse Trucks & Vans Inc ....G....... 724 887-7777
Mount Pleasant (G-11718)
Stanton Dynamics Inc ....F....... 814 849-6255
Brookville (G-2272)
Stauffer Manufacturing LLC....................G....... 717 445-6122
Ephrata (G-5147)
Superior Custom Designs Inc.................E....... 412 744-0110
Glassport (G-6416)
Transport Custom Designs LLC.............G....... 570 368-1403
Montoursville (G-11454)
Worthington Trailers LP ....F....... 570 567-7921
Williamsport (G-20101)

TRAILERS OR VANS: Horse Transportation, Fifth-Wheel Type

Phoenix Coach Works Inc......................G....... 610 495-2266
Pottstown (G-16030)

TRAILERS: Bodies

Gregory Racing Fabrications.................G....... 610 759-8217
Nazareth (G-11970)
International Trailers Inc ....D....... 814 634-1922
Meyersdale (G-11012)
ITI Trailers & Trck Bodies Inc ....E....... 814 634-0080
Meyersdale (G-11013)
Pine Hill Manufacturing LLC ....F....... 717 288-2443
Gordonville (G-6561)
Reitnouer Inc ....E....... 610 929-4856
Birdsboro (G-1704)
Schnure Manufacturing Co Inc ....F....... 610 273-3352
Honey Brook (G-7762)
Strick Corporation ....F....... 215 949-3600
Fairless Hills (G-5799)
Summit Trailer Sales Inc ....E....... 570 754-3511
Summit Station (G-18161)
Transport Custom Designs LLC.............G....... 570 368-1403
Montoursville (G-11454)

TRAILERS: Demountable Cargo Containers

Custom Fab Trailers Inc ....G....... 724 548-5529
Kittanning (G-8764)
Great Dane LLC......................................B....... 570 437-3141
Danville (G-4004)
Universal Trlr Crgo Group Inc.................F....... 570 929-3761
McAdoo (G-10659)

TRAILERS: Semitrailers, Truck Tractors

Manac Trailers Inc.................................G....... 724 294-0007
Freeport (G-6207)
Spector Manufacturing Inc.....................E....... 570 429-2510
Saint Clair (G-16941)
Wherleys Trailer Inc ....G....... 717 624-2268
New Oxford (G-12426)

TRAILERS: Truck, Chassis

Daniel Leo Olesnevich...........................G....... 724 352-3160
Butler (G-2392)

TRANSDUCERS: Electrical Properties

Blatek Industries Inc..............................D....... 814 231-2085
State College (G-17946)
Sound Technology Inc ....C....... 814 234-4377
State College (G-18029)

TRANSDUCERS: Pressure

Strainsert Company................................E....... 610 825-3310
Conshohocken (G-3608)

TRANSFORMERS: Airport Lighting

Orlotronics Corporation ....E....... 610 239-8200
Bridgeport (G-2042)

TRANSFORMERS: Control

Innovative Control Systems Inc ....C....... 610 881-8000
Wind Gap (G-20169)

TRANSFORMERS: Distribution

ABB Inc..D....... 724 696-1300
Mount Pleasant (G-11685)
Evans Commercial Services LLC ....F....... 412 573-9442
Bridgeville (G-2061)
Fortune Electric Co Ltd ....F....... 724 346-2722
Hermitage (G-7585)
Kongsberg Integrated Tactical ....E....... 814 269-5700
Johnstown (G-8399)
Mimco Equipment Inc.............................F....... 610 494-7400
Linwood (G-9990)

TRANSFORMERS: Distribution, Electric

Pennsylvania Trans Tech Inc ....B....... 724 873-2100
Canonsburg (G-2618)
Yesco Pittsburgh Inc ....G....... 330 747-8593
Pittsburgh (G-15729)

TRANSFORMERS: Electric

American Powernet MGT LP ....G....... 610 372-8500
Wyomissing (G-20286)
Associated Specialty Co ....F....... 610 395-9172
Orefield (G-13008)
Cooper Power Systems LLC ....G....... 636 394-2877
Canonsburg (G-2573)
Magnetic Windings Company Inc............E....... 610 253-2751
Easton (G-4716)
RE Uptegraff Mfg Co LLC.......................D....... 724 887-7700
Scottdale (G-17199)
Siemens Industry Inc ....D....... 724 743-5913
Canonsburg (G-2636)
Spang & Company ....C....... 412 963-9363
Pittsburgh (G-15566)

TRANSFORMERS: Electronic

API Technologies Corp...........................G....... 215 464-4000
Philadelphia (G-13399)
Gettysburg Transformer Corp ....E....... 717 334-2191
Gettysburg (G-6293)
Spang & Company ....E....... 724 376-7515
Sandy Lake (G-17062)

TRANSFORMERS: Meters, Electronic

VSI Meter Services Inc...........................G....... 484 482-2480
Aston (G-796)

TRANSFORMERS: Power Related

ABB Inc..D....... 724 838-8622
Greensburg (G-6647)
ABB Inc..C....... 215 674-6000
Warminster (G-18818)
Acutran LP ....E....... 724 452-4130
Fombell (G-6029)
Agileswitch LLC......................................F....... 484 483-3256
Philadelphia (G-13355)
Coil Specialty Co Inc ....E....... 814 234-7044
State College (G-17952)
Eaton Corporation ....B....... 724 773-1231
Beaver (G-980)
Gentherm Incorporated ....G....... 215 362-9191
Lansdale (G-9372)
Gettysburg Transformer Corp ....E....... 717 334-2191
Gettysburg (G-6293)
High Voltage Solutions Sls Inc ....G....... 412 523-0238
Sharon (G-17436)

Employee Codes: A=Over 500 employees, B=251-500
C=101-250, D=51-100, E=20-50, F=10-19, G=3-9

2019 Harris Pennsylvania
Manufacturers Directory

1573

PRODUCT

Hindle Power Inc ....D 610 330-9000
  Easton (G-4699)
Hydro Partners LLC ....G 717 825-1332
  York (G-20532)
Ifco Enterprises Inc ....C 610 651-0999
  Malvern (G-10251)
Invensys Energy Metering Corp ....B 814 371-3011
  Du Bois (G-4396)
Micro-Coax Inc ....C 610 495-4438
  Pottstown (G-16019)
Parker-Hannifin Corporation ....C 215 723-4000
  Hatfield (G-7377)
Philadelphia Electrical Eqp Co ....F 484 840-0860
  Aston (G-786)
Power Systems Specialists Inc ....F 570 296-4573
  Milford (G-11167)
Progressive Power Tech LLC ....F 724 452-6064
  Harmony (G-7075)
Schneider Electric It Corp ....B 717 948-1200
  Middletown (G-11074)
Silicon Power Corporation ....D 610 407-4700
  Malvern (G-10317)
Spang & Company ....E 724 376-7515
  Sandy Lake (G-17062)
SPD Electrical Systems Inc ....B 215 698-6426
  Philadelphia (G-14331)
Spectrum Control Inc ....B 814 474-2207
  Fairview (G-5842)
Spectrum Control Inc ....G 814 474-4315
  Fairview (G-5845)
Tamini Transformers USA LLC ....G 412 534-4275
  Sewickley (G-17414)
Transicoil LLC ....C 484 902-1100
  Collegeville (G-3397)
Vishay Intertechnology Inc ....B 610 644-1300
  Malvern (G-10341)

TRANSFORMERS: Rectifier

C&D Technologies Inc ....C 215 619-2700
  Blue Bell (G-1820)

TRANSFORMERS: Specialty

Thomas Magnetix Inc ....E 570 879-4363
  Hallstead (G-6836)

TRANSISTORS

Infineon Tech Americas Corp ....C 610 712-7100
  Allentown (G-258)

TRANSLATION & INTERPRETATION SVCS

Multilingual Communications ....G 412 621-7450
  Pittsburgh (G-15307)

TRANSMISSIONS: Motor Vehicle

Quigley Motor Company Inc ....D 717 266-5631
  Manchester (G-10364)

TRANSPORTATION AGENTS & BROKERS

Americold Logistics LLC ....C 215 721-0700
  Hatfield (G-7316)
Rosenbergers Cold Storage ....B 215 721-0700
  Hatfield (G-7392)

TRANSPORTATION EPQT & SPLYS, WHOL: Aeronautical Eqpt & Splys

Agustwstland Philadelphia Corp ....D 215 281-1400
  Philadelphia (G-13358)

TRANSPORTATION EQPT & SPLYS WHOLESALERS, NEC

Avantext Inc ....E 610 796-2383
  Philadelphia (G-13425)
Bohlinger Inc ....G 610 825-0440
  Conshohocken (G-3524)
Raceresq Inc ....G 724 891-3473
  Beaver Falls (G-1010)
Schmitt Mar Stering Wheels Inc ....G 717 431-2316
  Lancaster (G-9191)

TRANSPORTATION EQUIPMENT, NEC

Allan A Myers ....G 610 584-6020
  Worcester (G-20223)
Lblock Transportation Inc ....G 347 533-0943
  York (G-20563)

TRANSPORTATION PROGRAM REGULATION & ADMIN GOVT: Local

City of Pittsburgh ....E 412 255-2330
  Pittsburgh (G-14855)

TRANSPORTATION SVCS: Airport

Bailey Leasing Inc ....D 717 718-0490
  York (G-20398)

TRANSPORTATION SVCS: Railroad Terminals

Herndon Reload Company ....E 570 758-2597
  Herndon (G-7599)
M Simon Zook Co ....C 610 273-3776
  Honey Brook (G-7753)

TRANSPORTATION SVCS: Railroads, Interurban

Pohl Railroad Mtls Corp LLC ....G 610 916-7645
  Reading (G-16471)

TRANSPORTATION: Air, Scheduled Passenger

Aviation Technologies Inc ....G 570 457-4147
  Avoca (G-840)

TRANSPORTATION: Great Lakes Domestic Freight

Norton Oglebay Company ....F 412 995-5500
  Pittsburgh (G-15347)

TRANSPORTATION: Transit Systems, NEC

Southeastern PA Trnsp Auth ....B 215 580-7800
  Malvern (G-10323)

TRAP ROCK: Crushed & Broken

Highway Materials Inc ....E 215 234-4522
  Perkiomenville (G-13301)
Pennsy Supply Inc ....F 570 754-7508
  Schuylkill Haven (G-17163)

TRAP ROCK: Dimension

H&K Group Inc ....E 717 445-0961
  Narvon (G-11922)

TRAPS: Crab, Steel

Pitcal Inc ....G 412 433-1121
  Pittsburgh (G-15382)

TRAPS: Stem

Spirax Sarco Inc ....G 610 807-3500
  Center Valley (G-2831)
Watson McDaniel Company ....E 610 495-5131
  Pottstown (G-16070)

TRAVEL AGENCIES

Laurel Holdings Inc ....G 814 533-5777
  Johnstown (G-8402)
Pathfinders Travel Inc ....G 215 438-2140
  Philadelphia (G-14123)

TRAVEL TRAILER DEALERS

Mgs Inc ....C 717 336-7528
  Denver (G-4083)
VT Hackney Inc ....D 570 547-1681
  Montgomery (G-11381)

TRAVEL TRAILERS & CAMPERS

Fame Manufacturing Inc ....F 814 763-5645
  Saegertown (G-16913)
Jeraco Enterprises Inc ....D 570 742-9688
  Milton (G-11244)
Mobile Concepts By Scotty Inc ....E 724 542-7640
  Mount Pleasant (G-11706)
Quantum Leap Engnered Pdts LLC ......G 814 289-1476
  Somerset (G-17702)
Reading Truck Body LLC ....C 610 775-3301
  Reading (G-16493)

Transport Custom Designs LLC ....G 570 368-1403
  Montoursville (G-11454)

TRAVELER ACCOMMODATIONS, NEC

BF Hiestand House ....G 717 426-8415
  Marietta (G-10461)

TRAYS: Greenhouse Flats, Wood

Carl Amore Greenhouses ....G 610 837-7038
  Nazareth (G-11959)
Carson Street Commons ....G 412 431-1183
  Pittsburgh (G-14823)
Integrated Metal Products Inc ....G 717 824-4052
  Lancaster (G-9058)

TRAYS: Plastic

Tray-Pak Corporation ....C 888 926-1777
  Reading (G-16546)

TRIM: Window, Wood

William H Hammonds & Bros ....G 610 489-7924
  Collegeville (G-3399)

TROPHIES, NEC

Award Products Inc ....E 215 324-0414
  Philadelphia (G-13428)
Bob Allen & Sons Inc ....G 610 874-4391
  Chester (G-3040)
Micheners Engraving Inc ....G 717 738-9630
  Ephrata (G-5127)
Pittsburgh Trophy Company Inc ....G 412 261-4376
  Pittsburgh (G-15411)
Superior Trophy & Engraving Co ....G 570 343-4087
  Scranton (G-17295)
Trophy Works ....G 412 279-0111
  Carnegie (G-2799)

TROPHIES, PEWTER

White Trophy Co Inc ....G 215 638-9134
  Bensalem (G-1272)

TROPHIES, PLATED, ALL METALS

Bry Mar Trophy Inc ....G 215 295-4053
  Yardley (G-20298)
Creative Embedments ....G 717 299-0385
  Lancaster (G-8987)
Kellys Trophies ....F 610 626-3300
  Drexel Hill (G-4367)
R & J Trophy ....G 570 345-2277
  Pine Grove (G-14604)
Richland Plastics & Engraving ....G 814 266-3002
  Johnstown (G-8431)

TROPHIES, WHOLESALE

Athletic Lettering Inc ....F 717 840-6373
  York (G-20389)
Kellys Trophies ....F 610 626-3300
  Drexel Hill (G-4367)

TROPHIES: Metal, Exc Silver

All - American Trophy Company ....G 570 342-2613
  Scranton (G-17207)
Stineman Management Corp ....E 814 495-4686
  South Fork (G-17778)

TROPHY & PLAQUE STORES

A A A Engraving ....G 412 281-7756
  Pittsburgh (G-14628)
All - American Trophy Company ....G 570 342-2613
  Scranton (G-17207)
Award Products Inc ....E 215 324-0414
  Philadelphia (G-13428)
Awards & More ....G 724 444-1040
  Gibsonia (G-6325)
Bry Mar Trophy Inc ....G 215 295-4053
  Yardley (G-20298)
Davis Trophies & Sports Wear ....G 610 455-0640
  West Chester (G-19533)
Etched In Glass ....G 724 444-0808
  Gibsonia (G-6333)
Hope Good Animal Clinic ....G 717 766-5535
  Mechanicsburg (G-10854)
Kellys Trophies ....F 610 626-3300
  Drexel Hill (G-4367)

Larry D Mays ....F 814 833-7988
Erie (G-5360)
Pittsburgh Trophy Company Inc ....G...... 412 261-4376
Pittsburgh (G-15411)
Recognition Engraving ....G 717 242-1166
Lewistown (G-9946)
Superior Trophy & Engraving Co ....G 570 343-4087
Scranton (G-17295)
Terre Trophy Co ....G 610 777-2050
Reading (G-16536)
Three Soles Corp ....G 717 762-1945
Waynesboro (G-19428)
Trautman Associates Inc ....F 570 743-0430
Shamokin Dam (G-17429)
Trophy Works ....G 412 279-0111
Carnegie (G-2799)
Upper Perk Sportswear Inc ....G 215 541-3211
Pennsburg (G-13261)

TRUCK & BUS BODIES: Automobile Wrecker Truck

Asco Enterprises Inc ....G...... 724 945-5525
Scenery Hill (G-17124)

TRUCK & BUS BODIES: Beverage Truck

VT Hackney Inc ....D 570 547-1681
Montgomery (G-11381)

TRUCK & BUS BODIES: Bus Bodies

Asone Technologies Inc ....E 570 443-5700
White Haven (G-19846)
Superior Custom Designs Inc ....G 412 744-0110
Glassport (G-6416)
Wolfington Body Company Inc ....C 610 458-8501
Exton (G-5751)

TRUCK & BUS BODIES: Car Carrier

Champion Carrier Corporation ....E 724 981-3328
Hermitage (G-7576)
Standard Iron Works ....E 570 347-2058
Scranton (G-17293)

TRUCK & BUS BODIES: Cement Mixer

McNeilus Truck and Mfg Inc ....E 610 286-0400
Morgantown (G-11527)

TRUCK & BUS BODIES: Dump Truck

D K Hostetler Inc ....F 717 667-3921
Milroy (G-11229)
Hill John M Machine Co Inc ....E 610 562-8690
Hamburg (G-6841)
Somerset Welding & Steel Inc ....C 814 443-2671
Somerset (G-17710)
Tamaqua Truck & Trailer Inc ....G 570 386-5994
Tamaqua (G-18229)
Triad Truck Equipment ....G 484 614-7349
Pottstown (G-16059)

TRUCK & BUS BODIES: Garbage Or Refuse Truck

Conrad Enterprises Inc ....E 717 274-5151
Cornwall (G-3738)

TRUCK & BUS BODIES: Motor Vehicle, Specialty

Ken-Co Company Inc ....E 724 887-7070
Scottdale (G-17194)
Sabre Equipment Inc ....E 412 262-3080
Coraopolis (G-3725)
Swab Wagon Company ....E 717 362-8151
Elizabethville (G-4898)

TRUCK & BUS BODIES: Stake Platform Truck

R E B Inc ....G 215 538-7875
Quakertown (G-16240)
Wade Holdings LLC ....G 717 375-2251
Marion (G-10470)

TRUCK & BUS BODIES: Truck Cabs, Motor Vehicles

Commonwealth Utility Eqp Inc ....E 724 283-8400
Butler (G-2390)

TRUCK & BUS BODIES: Truck Tops

Gra-Ter Industries Inc ....G....... 570 658-7652
Beavertown (G-1026)

TRUCK & BUS BODIES: Truck, Motor Vehicle

Altec Industries Inc ....C 570 822-3104
Wilkes Barre (G-19904)
Andrew Billets & Son Inc ....G 570 207-7253
Scranton (G-17208)
Columbia Industries Inc ....E 570 520-4048
Berwick (G-1318)
Darco Inc ....E 717 597-7139
Greencastle (G-6605)
Driban Body Works Inc ....G 215 468-6900
Philadelphia (G-13648)
Gsp Marketing Inc ....E 814 445-5866
Somerset (G-17692)
Hewey Welding ....G 717 867-5222
Lebanon (G-9580)
Imperial Truck Body & Eqp ....F 724 695-3165
Imperial (G-8067)
J C Moore Industries Inc ....F 724 475-3185
Fredonia (G-6181)
J C Moore Industries Sales ....G 724 475-3185
Fredonia (G-6182)
Jerrdan Corporation ....D 717 597-7111
Greencastle (G-6620)
M H EBY Inc ....C 800 292-4752
Blue Ball (G-1811)
Mid Atlantic Municipal LLC ....E 717 394-2647
Lancaster (G-9134)
Morgan Truck Body LLC ....C 717 733-8644
Ephrata (G-5130)
Samco Inc ....G 814 495-4632
Saint Michael (G-17032)
Supreme Mid-Atlantic Corp ....D 717 865-0031
Jonestown (G-8451)
Truckcraft Corporation ....E 717 375-2900
Chambersburg (G-2990)
Warrington Equipment Mfg Co ....E 215 343-1714
Warrington (G-19138)

TRUCK & BUS BODIES: Utility Truck

Envirnmntal Enrgy Slutions LLC ....G 814 446-5625
Seward (G-17381)
Reading Truck Body LLC ....C 610 775-3301
Reading (G-16493)

TRUCK BODIES: Body Parts

Dayton Parts LLC ....F 717 255-8548
Harrisburg (G-7115)
Heritage Truck Equipment LLC ....G 215 256-0951
Harleysville (G-7039)
J C Moore Sales Corp ....G 724 475-4605
Fredonia (G-6183)
Maxwell Truck & Equipment LLC ....G 814 359-2672
Pleasant Gap (G-15794)
Merlot Trpulin Sidekit Mfg Inc ....E 412 828-7664
Verona (G-18757)
Penn Fabrication LLC ....F 610 292-1980
Norristown (G-12702)
Reading Equipment & Dist LLC ....E 717 445-6746
Abington (G-14)
Sixth Wheel Inc ....G 610 647-0880
Malvern (G-10318)

TRUCK BODY SHOP

Tamaqua Truck & Trailer Inc ....G 570 386-5994
Tamaqua (G-18229)

TRUCK GENERAL REPAIR SVC

Andrew Billets & Son Inc ....G 570 207-7253
Scranton (G-17208)
Ben Swaney ....G 412 372-8109
Monroeville (G-11325)
Keiths Truck Service ....G 814 696-6008
Duncansville (G-4454)
Keystone Fire Apparatus Inc ....G 412 771-7722
Mc Kees Rocks (G-10618)
Kone Cranes Inc ....F 814 878-8070
Erie (G-5351)
Merlot Trpulin Sidekit Mfg Inc ....E 412 828-7664
Verona (G-18757)
Mueller Industries Inc ....D 215 699-5801
North Wales (G-12820)
Penn Public Truck & Equipment ....F 814 944-5314
Altoona (G-537)

Reading Equipment & Dist LLC ....E 717 445-6746
Abington (G-14)
Vr Enterprises Llc ....G 215 932-1113
Lansdale (G-9426)
Youngs Truck Repair LLC ....F 570 329-3571
South Williamsport (G-17794)

TRUCK PAINTING & LETTERING SVCS

A Funky Little Sign Shop ....G 215 489-2880
Doylestown (G-4266)
Brown Signs Inc ....G 717 866-2669
Richland (G-16683)
Charles R Eckert Signs Inc ....G 717 733-4601
Ephrata (G-5096)
Graber Letterin Inc ....G 610 369-1112
Boyertown (G-1913)
Graphics 22 Signs Inc ....F 412 422-1125
Pittsburgh (G-15058)
Gregory Troyer ....G 717 393-0233
Bird In Hand (G-1676)
Impressive Signs Inc ....G 717 848-9305
York (G-20535)

TRUCK PARTS & ACCESSORIES: Wholesalers

Diamond Hvy Vhcl Solutions LLC ....G 717 695-9378
Harrisburg (G-7119)
Mariano Welding Corp ....G 610 626-0975
Clifton Heights (G-3255)
N F C Industries Inc ....E 215 766-8890
Plumsteadville (G-15812)
Point Spring Company ....F 724 658-9076
New Castle (G-12138)
Reading Equipment & Dist LLC ....E 717 445-6746
Abington (G-14)
Robert P Williams ....G 814 563-7660
Youngsville (G-20775)
Triad Truck Equipment ....G 484 614-7349
Pottstown (G-16059)

TRUCKING & HAULING SVCS: Contract Basis

Buchanan Hauling ....G 412 373-6760
Trafford (G-18452)
Calcium Chloride Sales Inc ....G 724 458-5778
Grove City (G-6781)
Wallace Moving & Storage ....G 724 568-2411
Vandergrift (G-18737)
William H Kies Jr ....G 610 252-6261
Easton (G-4776)

TRUCKING & HAULING SVCS: Draying, Local, Without Storage

New Enterprise Stone Lime Inc ....E 570 823-0531
Plains (G-15787)

TRUCKING & HAULING SVCS: Heavy Machinery, Local

Advanced Industrial Svcs Inc ....C 717 764-9811
York (G-20368)

TRUCKING & HAULING SVCS: Heavy, NEC

Cs Trucking LLC ....G 814 224-0395
East Freedom (G-4563)
Fink & Stackhouse Inc ....G 570 323-3475
Williamsport (G-20013)
Hecla Machinery & Equipment Co ....F 570 385-4783
Schuylkill Haven (G-17158)
Ls Steel Inc ....G 717 669-4581
Coatesville (G-3314)

TRUCKING & HAULING SVCS: Lumber & Log, Local

Harold Graves Trucking ....G 814 654-7836
Spartansburg (G-17851)
Patrick Donovan ....G 724 238-9038
Ligonier (G-9963)

TRUCKING & HAULING SVCS: Steel, Local

Tms International Corp ....E 215 956-5500
Horsham (G-7860)

TRUCKING & HAULING SVCS: Timber, Local

Donnelley Jr Joseph ....G....... 570 998-2541
  Cogan Station *(G-3359)*

TRUCKING, AUTOMOBILE CARRIER

Lunchera LLC ....E....... 787 607-8914
  Pittsburgh *(G-15240)*

TRUCKING: Except Local

Afton Trucking Inc ....F....... 814 825-7449
  Erie *(G-5177)*
Brett W Shope ....G....... 814 643-2921
  Huntingdon *(G-7940)*
Casket Shells Incorporated............G....... 570 876-2642
  Eynon *(G-5754)*
Drebo America Inc ....D....... 724 938-0690
  Coal Center *(G-3275)*
M Simon Zook Co............................C....... 610 273-3776
  Honey Brook *(G-7753)*
Pennsylvanin Flagstone Inc............F....... 814 544-7575
  Coudersport *(G-3787)*
Pharmaceutical Procurement ....F....... 610 680-7708
  Coatesville *(G-3324)*
Thompson Logging and Trckg Inc ......E....... 570 923-2590
  North Bend *(G-12727)*
Tms International LLC......................D....... 412 678-6141
  Glassport *(G-6419)*
Tms International Corp....................C....... 412 678-6141
  Glassport *(G-6420)*
Tms International Corporation ....E....... 412 675-8251
  Glassport *(G-6421)*
Windsor Service Trucking Corp ....C....... 610 929-0716
  Reading *(G-16567)*

TRUCKING: Local, Without Storage

3nt-3 Nieces Trucking Inc...............G....... 360 815-0938
  Grassflat *(G-6577)*
A J Blosenski Inc............................D....... 610 942-2707
  Honey Brook *(G-7734)*
Afton Trucking Inc ....F....... 814 825-7449
  Erie *(G-5177)*
Allied Concrete & Supply Corp............E....... 215 646-8484
  Dresher *(G-4352)*
American Exploration Company ....D....... 610 940-4015
  Plymouth Meeting *(G-15830)*
Brett W Shope ....G....... 814 643-2921
  Huntingdon *(G-7940)*
Diamond Manufacturing Company ......F....... 570 693-0300
  Wyoming *(G-20276)*
Force Inc...E....... 724 465-9399
  Indiana *(G-8100)*
Jle Industries LLC..........................E....... 724 603-2228
  Dunbar *(G-4441)*
K Diamond Incorporated ....E....... 570 346-4684
  Scranton *(G-17249)*
Lindenmuth Saw Mill ....G....... 570 875-3546
  Ashland *(G-734)*
North Star Leasing Inc....................G....... 814 629-6999
  Friedens *(G-6224)*
Pitt Oil Service Inc ....G....... 412 771-6950
  Pittsburgh *(G-15384)*
Rock Hill Materials Company............E....... 610 264-5586
  Catasauqua *(G-2817)*
Roderick Duvall ....G....... 814 735-4969
  Crystal Spring *(G-3938)*
Vepar LLC ....G....... 610 462-4545
  Spring City *(G-17871)*
Wallace Moving & Storage ....G....... 724 568-2411
  Vandergrift *(G-18737)*
William H Kies Jr............................G....... 610 252-6261
  Easton *(G-4776)*
Winfield Lime & Stone Co Inc ....F....... 724 352-3596
  Cabot *(G-2461)*
York Daily Record Sunday News..........F....... 717 771-2000
  York *(G-20736)*

TRUCKS & TRACTORS: Industrial

Acco Mtl Hdlg Solutions Inc ....D....... 800 967-7333
  York *(G-20365)*
Altec Industries Inc........................C....... 570 822-3104
  Wilkes Barre *(G-19904)*
Brookville Locomotive Inc ....C....... 814 849-2000
  Brookville *(G-2254)*
Cheetah Chassis Corporation ....C....... 570 752-2708
  Berwick *(G-1317)*
Commonwealth Utility Eqp Inc ....E....... 724 283-8400
  Butler *(G-2390)*

Conrad Enterprises Inc ....E....... 717 274-5151
  Cornwall *(G-3738)*
Craneco LLC....................................G....... 610 948-1400
  Royersford *(G-16847)*
Daynight Transport LLC...................G....... 800 288-4996
  Carlisle *(G-2707)*
Ferag Inc..D....... 215 788-0892
  Bristol *(G-2144)*
Gold Rush Inc..................................E....... 717 484-2424
  Denver *(G-4074)*
Hosch Company LP ....E....... 724 695-3002
  Oakdale *(G-12903)*
Jlg Industries Inc............................F....... 814 623-2156
  Bedford *(G-1055)*
K & K Mine Products Inc ....E....... 724 463-5000
  Indiana *(G-8109)*
Mack Trucks Inc..............................A....... 610 966-8800
  Macungie *(G-10154)*
Martin Sprocket & Gear Inc ....D....... 610 837-1841
  Danielsville *(G-3994)*
Molded Fiber Glass Companies ....C....... 814 683-4500
  Linesville *(G-9984)*
Overhead Door Corporation ....D....... 215 368-8700
  Lansdale *(G-9396)*
Reitnouer Inc..................................E....... 610 929-4856
  Birdsboro *(G-1704)*
Robinson Vacuum Tanks Inc ....G....... 814 355-4474
  Bellefonte *(G-1116)*
Rock-Built Inc.................................E....... 878 302-3978
  New Kensington *(G-12372)*
Stanko Products Inc ....F....... 724 834-8080
  Greensburg *(G-6717)*
Strick Corporation ....F....... 215 949-3600
  Fairless Hills *(G-5799)*
T Bruce Sales Inc............................D....... 724 528-9961
  West Middlesex *(G-19731)*
T S Beh Trucking Services...............G....... 267 918-0493
  Bristol *(G-2203)*
Terex Corporation ....E....... 717 840-0226
  Mountville *(G-11803)*
Top-Notch Trucking Inc ....G....... 267 456-1744
  Elkins Park *(G-4913)*
Weldship Industries Inc....................F....... 610 861-7330
  Bethlehem *(G-1655)*
Win-Holt Equipment Corp ....C....... 516 222-0335
  Allentown *(G-436)*

TRUCKS, INDL: Wholesalers

Robinson Vacuum Tanks Inc ....G....... 814 355-4474
  Bellefonte *(G-1116)*

TRUCKS: Forklift

George Taylor Forklift Repair ....G....... 412 221-7206
  Morgan *(G-11517)*
Jkr Prolift ....G....... 724 547-5955
  Mount Pleasant *(G-11703)*

TRUCKS: Indl

Bornmann Mfg Co Inc......................G....... 215 228-5826
  Philadelphia *(G-13473)*
David J Klein Inc..............................F....... 610 385-4888
  Douglassville *(G-4174)*
Wolenski Enterprises Inc..................E....... 205 307-9862
  White Oak *(G-19859)*

TRUNKS

David Trunk ....G....... 570 247-2012
  Rome *(G-16798)*

TRUSSES: Wood, Floor

J C Snavely & Sons Inc ....C....... 717 898-2241
  Landisville *(G-9262)*
Rigidply Rafters Inc ....C....... 717 866-6581
  Richland *(G-16689)*
S R Sloan Inc..................................E....... 570 366-8934
  Orwigsburg *(G-13051)*
Shelly Enterprises -US Lbm LLC..........D....... 215 723-5108
  Telford *(G-18315)*
Shelly Enterprises -US Lbm LLC..........E....... 610 432-4511
  Bethlehem *(G-1617)*
York P-B Truss Inc ....E....... 717 779-0327
  York *(G-20748)*

TRUSSES: Wood, Roof

Allensville Planing Mill Inc...............C....... 717 483-6386
  Allensville *(G-106)*

Bell Wall & Truss LLC ....F....... 717 768-8338
  Gordonville *(G-6549)*
Cussewago Truss LLC ....E....... 814 763-3229
  Cambridge Springs *(G-2476)*
DI Truss LLC...................................G....... 717 355-9813
  New Holland *(G-12243)*
Fairmans Roof Trusses Inc ....E....... 724 349-6778
  Creekside *(G-3875)*
Maronda Systems Inc Florida ....G....... 724 695-1200
  Imperial *(G-8072)*
Montgomery Truss & Panel Inc ....D....... 724 458-7500
  Grove City *(G-6798)*
New Enterprise Stone Lime Inc ....D....... 610 374-5131
  Kutztown *(G-8851)*
New Enterprise Stone Lime Inc ....B....... 610 374-5131
  Leesport *(G-9668)*
Pocopson Industries Inc ....F....... 610 793-0344
  West Chester *(G-19618)*
Provance Truss LLC ....G....... 724 437-0585
  Lemont Furnace *(G-9736)*
R & R Components Inc ....E....... 717 792-4641
  York *(G-20649)*
Seals of Blossburg ....G....... 570 638-2161
  Blossburg *(G-1809)*
Seven D Truss LP ....E....... 814 317-4077
  Altoona *(G-547)*
Superior Trusses LLC......................E....... 717 721-2411
  Ephrata *(G-5151)*
Triple D Truss LLC ....E....... 570 726-7092
  Mill Hall *(G-11183)*
Truss-Tech Inc.................................E....... 717 436-9778
  Mifflintown *(G-11138)*
V Menghini & Sons Inc ....F....... 570 455-6315
  Hazle Township *(G-7489)*
Whipple Bros Inc.............................G....... 570 836-6262
  Mountain Top *(G-11780)*
Wood Fabricators Inc ....F....... 717 284-4849
  Quarryville *(G-16284)*

TUB CONTAINERS: Plastic

RPC Bramlage-Wiko-Usa Inc ....D....... 610 286-0805
  Morgantown *(G-11533)*
Tray-Pak Corporation ....C....... 484 509-0046
  Reading *(G-16547)*

TUBE & TUBING FABRICATORS

Accu-Fire Fabrication Inc.................E....... 800 641-0005
  Morrisville *(G-11550)*
Bentech Inc.....................................E....... 215 223-9420
  Philadelphia *(G-13454)*
Dlubak Fabrication Inc ....F....... 724 224-5887
  Natrona Heights *(G-11938)*
Dormont Manufacturing Company ......C....... 724 327-7909
  Export *(G-5597)*
JI Hartman Stainless LLC.................G....... 724 646-1150
  Greenville *(G-6751)*
Judson A Smith Company ....C....... 610 367-2021
  Boyertown *(G-1920)*
Leonhardt Manufacturing Co Inc..........D....... 717 632-4150
  Hanover *(G-6915)*
Morris Coupling Company.................D....... 814 459-1741
  Erie *(G-5396)*
Pittsbrgh Tubular Shafting Inc............E....... 724 774-7212
  Rochester *(G-16787)*
Pittsbrgh Tubular Shafting Inc............G....... 724 774-7212
  Rochester *(G-16788)*
Pro Tube Inc ....F....... 717 765-9400
  Zullinger *(G-20838)*
Quaker State Tube Mfg Corp............E....... 610 287-8841
  Zieglerville *(G-20834)*
TW Metals LLC ....D....... 610 458-1300
  Exton *(G-5741)*

TUBES: Boiler, Wrought

State Line Supply Company ....F....... 814 362-7433
  Bradford *(G-1992)*

TUBES: Electron, Indl

Triton Services Inc...........................G....... 484 851-3883
  Breinigsville *(G-2029)*

TUBES: Light Sensing & Emitting

Optilumen Inc..................................G....... 717 547-5417
  Pillow *(G-14586)*

TUBES: Mailing

Self-Seal Cont Corp Del Vly ....G........ 610 275-2300
  Boyertown (G-1929)

TUBES: Paper

American Paper Products of PHI..........E 215 855-3327
  Lansdale (G-9340)
Ox Paper Tube and Core Inc ....E 800 414-2476
  Hanover (G-6927)
Yazoo Mills Incorporated......................D........ 717 624-8993
  New Oxford (G-12428)

TUBES: Paper Or Fiber, Chemical Or Electrical Uses

Jst Corporation ....G 717 920-7700
  Middletown (G-11059)
Micronic America LLC ....G....... 484 483-8075
  Aston (G-777)

TUBES: Photomultiplier

Hamamatsu Corporation ....G....... 724 935-3600
  Sewickley (G-17390)

TUBES: Steel & Iron

Eastern Manufacturing LLC ....G....... 215 702-3600
  Langhorne (G-9292)
Summerill Tube Corporation..................G....... 724 887-9700
  Koppel (G-8816)

TUBES: Vacuum

Photonis Defense Inc ....D........ 717 295-6000
  Lancaster (G-9170)

TUBES: Welded, Aluminum

Mueller Industries Inc ....D........ 215 699-5801
  North Wales (G-12820)
Precision Tube Company Inc.................C........ 215 699-5801
  North Wales (G-12826)
Swampy Hollow Mfg LLC ....F 610 273-0157
  Honey Brook (G-7765)

TUBES: Wrought, Welded Or Lock Joint

Hofmann Industries Inc ....B........ 610 678-8051
  Reading (G-16403)

TUBING, COLD-DRAWN: Mech Or Hypodermic Sizes, Stainless

Accumetrics Limited...............................E 610 948-0181
  Royersford (G-16840)
Parade Strapping & Baling LLC...........G....... 215 537-9473
  Philadelphia (G-14119)
Ptc Alliance Corp ....D........ 412 299-7900
  Wexford (G-19823)
Ptc Alliance Corp ....D........ 724 847-7137
  Beaver Falls (G-1008)
Ptc Group Holdings Corp ....D........ 724 847-7137
  Beaver Falls (G-1009)
Ptc Group Holdings Corp ....E 412 299-7900
  Wexford (G-19824)
Superior Group Inc ....E 610 397-2040
  Conshohocken (G-3610)
Tech Tube Inc ....D........ 610 491-8000
  King of Prussia (G-8684)

TUBING: Copper

C F Moores Co Inc ....F 215 248-1250
  Philadelphia (G-13490)
Cambridge-Lee Holdings Inc ....F 610 926-4141
  Reading (G-16340)
Cambridge-Lee Industries LLC..............C........ 610 926-4141
  Reading (G-16341)
Iusa Wire Inc ....G....... 610 926-4141
  Reading (G-16410)
Precision Tube Company Inc.................C........ 215 699-5801
  North Wales (G-12826)

TUBING: Plastic

Iridium Industries Inc...........................C........ 570 476-8800
  East Stroudsburg (G-4621)
Markel Corp ....C........ 610 272-8960
  Plymouth Meeting (G-15855)
Westlake Plastics Company ....C........ 610 459-1000
  Lenni (G-9763)

Westrock Packaging Inc...................D........ 215 785-3350
  Croydon (G-3933)

TUBING: Rubber

Polymeric Extruded Products.............G........ 215 943-1288
  Levittown (G-9858)

TUBING: Seamless

A & L Tubular Specialties ....G....... 724 667-6101
  New Castle (G-12051)
Arcelrmttal Tblar Pdts USA LLC ....E 419 342-1200
  Pittsburgh (G-14716)
Crp Inc..G....... 610 970-7663
  Pottstown (G-15977)
Handy & Harman Tube Co Inc ....B........ 610 539-3900
  Norristown (G-12664)
Penn State Special Metals LLC ....E 724 847-4623
  Koppel (G-8815)
Tube Methods Inc................................C........ 610 279-7700
  Bridgeport (G-2047)

TUMBLERS: Plastic

Easygo Drinkware LLC.........................E 814 723-7600
  Warren (G-19022)

TUNGSTEN CARBIDE

GKN Sinter Metals LLC.........................C........ 814 781-6500
  Kersey (G-8561)
National Magnetics Group Inc ....G....... 610 867-7600
  Bethlehem (G-1579)
R H Carbide & Epoxy Inc......................G....... 724 356-2277
  Hickory (G-7630)

TUNGSTEN CARBIDE POWDER

Global Tungsten & Powders Corp........B........ 570 268-5000
  Towanda (G-18429)

TUNGSTEN MILL PRDTS

Leech Inc ....D........ 814 724-5454
  Meadville (G-10749)
Sintermet LLC ....D........ 724 548-7631
  Kittanning (G-8792)

TURBINE GENERATOR SET UNITS: Hydraulic, Complete

Genx Sustainable Solutions Inc ....G....... 484 244-7016
  Allentown (G-228)

TURBINES & TURBINE GENERATOR SET UNITS: Gas, Complete

Solar Turbines Incorporated ....D....... 724 759-7800
  Sewickley (G-17411)

TURBINES & TURBINE GENERATOR SETS

ABB Inc ....F 412 963-7530
  Pittsburgh (G-14633)
Adaconn...E 215 643-1900
  Blue Bell (G-1812)
Agripower Mfg & Svcs Inc....................G....... 814 781-1009
  Saint Marys (G-16946)
Alessi Manufacturing Corp ....E 610 586-4200
  Collingdale (G-3403)
Apache Turbines ....G....... 814 880-0053
  Bellefonte (G-1092)
Babcock & Wilcox Company ....G....... 724 479-3585
  Homer City (G-7670)
Curtiss-Wright Electro-.........................A 724 275-5000
  Cheswick (G-3105)
Dynamic Manufacturing LLC ....D........ 724 295-4200
  Freeport (G-6203)
E-Finity Dstrbted Gnration LLC ....G....... 610 688-6212
  Wayne (G-19321)
E-Harvest Systems ....G....... 908 832-0400
  Mechanicsburg (G-10840)
Eaton Aerospace LLC...........................D........ 610 522-4000
  Glenolden (G-6473)
Everpower Wind Holdings Inc ....E 412 253-9400
  Pittsburgh (G-14989)
Hydrocoil Power Inc ....G....... 610 745-1990
  Bryn Mawr (G-2325)
ITT Water & Wastewater USA Inc.........E 610 647-6620
  Malvern (G-10256)
Matric Group LLC.................................B........ 814 677-0716
  Seneca (G-17366)

Penn Wind Energy LLC ....G....... 814 288-8064
  Ebensburg (G-4792)
Windkits LLC ....E 610 530-5704
  Allentown (G-437)
Windstax Inc ....G....... 412 235-7907
  Pittsburgh (G-15719)
Windurance LLC ....B........ 412 424-8900
  Coraopolis (G-3733)
Worldwide Turbine LLC ....E 610 821-9500
  Allentown (G-438)

TURBINES & TURBINE GENERATOR SETS & PARTS

Erie Forge and Steel Inc ....D........ 814 452-2300
  Erie (G-5267)
Precision Castparts Corp......................B........ 570 474-6371
  Mountain Top (G-11771)
Trireme Energy Development LLC ....D........ 412 253-9400
  Pittsburgh (G-15652)

TURBINES: Gas, Mechanical Drive

E C T Inc..G....... 610 239-5120
  Bridgeport (G-2035)
Nickles Industries ....G....... 724 422-7211
  Marion Center (G-10475)

TURBINES: Hydraulic, Complete

American Hydro Corporation.................C........ 717 755-5300
  York (G-20374)
Voith Hydro Inc ....B........ 717 792-7000
  York (G-20699)

TURBINES: Steam

Elliott Company...................................A 724 527-2811
  Jeannette (G-8254)
Eznergy LLC ....G....... 215 361-7332
  Lansdale (G-9366)

TURKEY PROCESSING & SLAUGHTERING

E G Emils and Son Inc..........................E 215 763-3311
  Philadelphia (G-13653)

TURNKEY VENDORS: Computer Systems

Advanced Technology Labs Inc ....B........ 215 355-8111
  Richboro (G-16673)
VIP Tech LLC ....G....... 267 582-1554
  Philadelphia (G-14448)

TWINE

Schermerhorn Bros Co ....G....... 610 284-7402
  Lansdowne (G-9443)

TWINE PRDTS

Eddington Thread Mfg Co Inc...............E 215 639-8900
  Bensalem (G-1186)
Zippercord Llc ....F 610 797-6564
  Allentown (G-440)

TWINE: Binder & Baler

Hahn Universal ....G....... 724 941-6444
  Canonsburg (G-2594)

TYPE: Rubber

California Med Innovations LLC ....E 909 621-5871
  Easton (G-4660)

TYPESETTING SVC

Adcomm Inc ....F 610 820-8565
  Allentown (G-115)
Alcom Printing Group Inc ....C........ 215 513-1600
  Harleysville (G-7015)
AlphaGraphics ....G....... 717 731-8444
  Mechanicsburg (G-10819)
American Brchure Catalogue Inc ....E 215 259-1600
  Warminster (G-18827)
Athens Reproduction ....G....... 610 649-5761
  Ardmore (G-701)
Benkalu Group Lmtd Ta Jaguar...........G....... 215 646-5896
  Huntingdon Valley (G-7965)
Bentley Grphic Cmmncations Inc ....E 610 933-7400
  Phoenixville (G-14531)
Brindle Printing Co Inc ....G....... 724 658-8549
  New Castle (G-12067)

PRODUCT

Brookshire Printing Inc ....E 717 392-1321
Lancaster (G-8961)

Castor Printing Company Inc ....F 215 535-1471
Philadelphia (G-13512)

Champ Printing Company Inc ....E 412 269-0197
Coraopolis (G-3675)

Chandler-White Publishing Co ....G 312 907-3271
Philadelphia (G-13524)

Chernay Printing Inc ....D 610 282-3774
Coopersburg (G-3625)

Chrisber Corporation ....E 800 872-7436
West Chester (G-19525)

Christmas City Printing Co Inc ....E 610 868-5844
Bethlehem (G-1483)

Clinton Press Inc ....G 814 455-9089
Erie (G-5227)

Clp Publications Inc ....C 215 567-5080
Philadelphia (G-13551)

Colorworks Graphic Svcs Inc ....E 610 367-7599
Gilbertsville (G-6371)

Copy Corner Inc ....G 570 992-4769
Saylorsburg (G-17104)

Copy Management Inc ....G 610 993-8686
Malvern (G-10217)

Copy Management Inc ....F 215 269-5000
Huntingdon Valley (G-7972)

Copy Right Printing & Graphics ....G 814 838-6255
Erie (G-5233)

Copy Systems Group Inc ....G 215 355-2223
Southampton (G-17806)

Creative Graphics Inc ....E 610 973-8300
Allentown (G-185)

Davco Advertising Inc ....E 717 442-4155
Kinzers (G-8736)

David Bream ....G 717 334-1513
Gettysburg (G-6288)

Digital-Ink Inc ....D 717 731-8890
Dillsburg (G-4126)

Dilullo Graphics Inc ....E 610 775-4360
Mohnton (G-11262)

Dispatch Printing Inc ....F 814 870-9600
Erie (G-5248)

Donald Blyler Offset Inc ....D 717 949-6831
Lebanon (G-9561)

Engle Printing & Pubg Co Inc ....C 717 653-1833
Lancaster (G-9009)

Fedex Office & Print Svcs Inc ....E 412 856-8016
Monroeville (G-11337)

Fedex Office & Print Svcs Inc ....G 215 386-5679
Philadelphia (G-13696)

Fedex Office & Print Svcs Inc ....F 412 788-0552
Pittsburgh (G-15009)

Fedex Office & Print Svcs Inc ....E 412 835-4005
Pittsburgh (G-15010)

Fedex Office & Print Svcs Inc ....F 412 366-9750
Pittsburgh (G-15011)

Fidelity Graphics ....F 610 586-9300
Holmes (G-7662)

Gary Murelle ....G 570 888-7006
Sayre (G-17114)

Gillespie Printing Inc ....F 610 264-1863
Allentown (G-232)

Graphic Arts Camera Service ....G 610 647-6395
Malvern (G-10242)

Griffiths Printing Co ....F 610 623-3822
Lansdowne (G-9433)

Guy Coder ....G 814 265-0519
Brockway (G-2227)

Guy Hrezik ....G 610 779-7609
Reading (G-16397)

Harmony Press Inc ....E 610 559-9800
Easton (G-4695)

Harper Printing Service ....G 412 884-2666
Pittsburgh (G-15082)

Herrmann Printing & Litho Inc ....E 412 243-4100
Pittsburgh (G-15093)

I P Graphics Inc ....E 215 673-2600
Philadelphia (G-13845)

Indiana Printing and Pubg Co ....C 724 349-3434
Indiana (G-8106)

Indus Graphics Inc ....G 215 443-7773
Warminster (G-18896)

Interform Corporation ....C 412 221-7321
Bridgeville (G-2070)

James Saks ....G 570 343-8150
Scranton (G-17247)

Jim Mannello ....G 610 681-6467
Gilbert (G-6362)

Joseph Lagrua ....G 814 274-7163
Coudersport (G-3783)

K B Offset Printing Inc ....E 814 238-8445
State College (G-17982)

Keeney Printing Group Inc ....G 215 855-6116
Lansdale (G-9383)

Keystone Printed Spc Co LLC ....C 570 457-8334
Old Forge (G-12967)

Killeen Printing Co ....G 412 381-4090
Pittsburgh (G-15177)

Kisel Printing Service Inc ....E 570 489-7666
Dickson City (G-4121)

L D H Printing Ltd Inc ....F 609 924-4664
Morrisville (G-11568)

L G Graphics Inc ....F 412 421-6330
Pittsburgh (G-15208)

Labels By Pulizzi Inc ....E 570 326-1244
Williamsport (G-20034)

Matrix Publishing Services Inc ....F 717 764-9673
York (G-20583)

McCarty Printing Corp ....D 814 454-4561
Erie (G-5385)

Medianews Group Inc ....C 717 637-3736
Hanover (G-6919)

Mifflinburg Telegraph Inc ....G 570 966-2255
Mifflinburg (G-11099)

Minuteman Press ....G 724 846-9740
Beaver Falls (G-1005)

Movad LLC ....F 215 638-2679
Plymouth Meeting (G-15858)

Multilingual Communications ....G 412 621-7450
Pittsburgh (G-15307)

Murrelle Printing Co Inc ....F 570 888-2244
Sayre (G-17119)

Nartak Media Group ....F 412 276-4000
Pittsburgh (G-15319)

National Ticket Company ....C 570 672-2900
Paxinos (G-13190)

P A Hutchison Company ....C 570 876-4560
Mayfield (G-10542)

Partners Press Inc ....F 610 666-7960
Oaks (G-12935)

Payne Printery Inc ....D 570 675-1147
Dallas (G-3965)

Pikewood Inc ....F 610 974-8000
Bethlehem (G-1597)

Pindar Set Inc ....C 610 731-2921
King of Prussia (G-8662)

Pleasant Luck Corp ....G 215 968-2080
Newtown (G-12537)

Print Tech Western PA ....E 412 963-1500
Pittsburgh (G-15440)

Printworks & Company Inc ....E 215 721-8500
Lansdale (G-9400)

Professional Graphic Co ....E 724 318-8530
Sewickley (G-17405)

Public Image Printing Inc ....G 215 677-4088
Philadelphia (G-14216)

R Graphics Inc ....G 610 918-0373
West Chester (G-19625)

R R Donnelley & Sons Company ....C 215 671-9500
Philadelphia (G-14225)

Raff Printing Inc ....D 412 431-4044
Pittsburgh (G-15466)

Rainbow Graphics Inc ....G 724 228-3007
Bentleyville (G-1275)

Regency Typographic Svcs Inc ....F 215 425-8810
Philadelphia (G-14238)

Ricks Quick Printing Inc ....E 412 571-0333
Pittsburgh (G-15485)

Ridgways Inc ....E 215 735-8055
Philadelphia (G-14250)

Rowland Printing Inc ....E 610 933-7400
Phoenixville (G-14575)

RR Donnelley & Sons Company ....D 412 281-7401
Pittsburgh (G-15501)

S G Business Services Inc ....G 215 567-7107
Philadelphia (G-14271)

Serve Inc ....G 570 265-3119
Monroeton (G-11320)

Specialty Group Printing Inc ....F 814 425-3061
Cochranton (G-3351)

Stauffer Acquisition Corp ....E 717 569-3200
East Petersburg (G-4591)

Third Dimension Spc LLC ....G 570 969-0623
Scranton (G-17301)

Towanda Printing Co Inc ....C 570 265-2151
Towanda (G-18436)

Type & Print Inc ....E 412 241-6070
Clinton (G-3267)

Typecraft Press Inc ....E 412 488-1600
Pittsburgh (G-15663)

United Partners Ltd ....F 570 288-7603
Taylor (G-18264)

Unity Printing Company Inc ....E 724 537-5800
Latrobe (G-9527)

University Copy Service Inc ....G 215 898-5574
Philadelphia (G-14429)

Victorian Publishing Co Inc ....G 814 634-8321
Meyersdale (G-11020)

Vocam Corp ....G 215 348-7115
Doylestown (G-4344)

Wakefoose Office Supply & Prtg ....G 814 623-5742
Bedford (G-1079)

Webb Communications Inc ....E 570 326-7634
Plymouth (G-15824)

TYPESETTING SVC: Computer

A Stuart Morton Inc ....F 610 692-1190
West Chester (G-19492)

Borris Information Group Inc ....G 717 285-9141
Mountville (G-11790)

Magnus Group Inc ....E 717 764-5908
York (G-20575)

Me Ken + Jen Crative Svcs LLC ....G 215 997-2355
Chalfont (G-2883)

Reed Tech & Info Svcs Inc ....B 215 441-6400
Horsham (G-7844)

TYPOGRAPHY

Adams Graphics Inc ....E 215 751-1114
Philadelphia (G-13343)

Bucks County Type & Design Inc ......F 215 579-4200
Newtown (G-12499)

Infotechnologies Inc ....G 717 285-7105
Mountville (G-11796)

ULTRASONIC EQPT: Cleaning, Exc Med & Dental

Branson Ultrasonics Corp ....E 610 251-9776
Paoli (G-13136)

Custom Ultrasonics Inc ....D 215 364-1477
Ivyland (G-8208)

Sonic Systems Inc ....E 267 803-1964
Warminster (G-18967)

Spec Sciences Inc ....G 607 972-3159
Sharon (G-17443)

Wm Robots, LLC ....F 215 822-2525
Colmar (G-3424)

UNDERCOATINGS: Paint

Acrysystems Laboratories Inc ....G 610 273-1355
Reading (G-16309)

Wendells Prfmce Trck Sp LLC ....G 717 458-8404
Mechanicsburg (G-10906)

UNIFORM SPLY SVCS: Indl

Cintas Corporation No 2 ....D 724 696-5640
Mount Pleasant (G-11692)

UNIFORM STORES

Enterprise Fashions ....G 570 489-1863
Olyphant (G-12989)

Log Cabin Embroidery Inc ....G 724 327-5929
Murrysville (G-11855)

New Look Uniform & Embroidery ....F 814 944-5515
Altoona (G-530)

UNISEX HAIR SALONS

American Lady US Male Hair Sln ....G 570 286-7759
Sunbury (G-18162)

Ryan Foster Inc ....G 215 769-0118
Philadelphia (G-14268)

UNIVERSITY

Carnegie Mellon University ....E 412 268-2111
Pittsburgh (G-14818)

Drexel University ....G 215 590-8863
Philadelphia (G-13647)

Duquesne Univ of Holy Spirit ....G 412 396-6610
Pittsburgh (G-14945)

Millersville University PA ....E 717 871-4636
Millersville (G-11213)

Pennsylvania State University ....G 814 865-4963
University Park (G-18652)

Pennsylvania State University ....G 814 863-3764
University Park (G-18653)

UPHOLSTERERS' EQPT & SPLYS WHOLESALERS

Gordon Seaver ....G....... 724 356-2313
Hickory (G-7628)

UPHOLSTERY FILLING MATERIALS

Knoll Inc ....D....... 215 679-7991
East Greenville (G-4570)

UPHOLSTERY MATERIAL

Canvas Specialties Inc ....G....... 570 825-9282
Hanover Township (G-6983)

UPHOLSTERY MATERIALS, BROADWOVEN

Fortune Fabrics Inc...........................E....... 570 288-3666
Kingston (G-8717)

UPHOLSTERY WORK SVCS

Nicewonger Awning Co ....G....... 724 837-5920
Greensburg (G-6692)
Paul Dorazio Custom Furniture ....G....... 215 836-1057
Flourtown (G-5989)

URINALS: Vitreous China

Jdl Equipment Co ....G....... 215 489-0134
Doylestown (G-4309)

USED CAR DEALERS

Bowser Pontiac Inc...........................C....... 412 469-2100
Pittsburgh (G-14787)
Quigley Motor Company Inc ....D....... 717 266-5631
Manchester (G-10364)
Saeilo Inc ....F....... 845 735-4500
Greeley (G-6583)
Sell-It ....G....... 215 453-8937
Sellersville (G-17358)

UTENSILS: Household, Cooking & Kitchen, Metal

Dudlik Industries Inc.........................E....... 215 674-4383
Hatboro (G-7282)
Get-A-Grip Chafing Pans ....G....... 724 443-6037
Gibsonia (G-6338)
Orlotronics Corporation ....E....... 610 239-8200
Bridgeport (G-2042)
Wrapmaster Usa LLC ....G....... 215 782-2285
Elkins Park (G-4915)

UTENSILS: Household, Metal, Exc Cast

All-Clad Holdings Inc ....G....... 724 745-8300
Canonsburg (G-2536)
All-Clad Metalcrafters LLC ....G....... 724 745-8300
Canonsburg (G-2538)
All-Clad Metalcrafters LLC ....D....... 724 745-8300
Canonsburg (G-2537)

UTILITY TRAILER DEALERS

Mustang Trailer Mfg ....F....... 724 628-1000
Connellsville (G-3504)
Superior Custom Designs Inc.............G....... 412 744-0110
Glassport (G-6416)
Worthington Trailers LP ....F....... 570 567-7921
Williamsport (G-20101)

VACUUM CLEANER REPAIR SVCS

Sweeper City Inc ....G....... 724 283-0859
Butler (G-2445)

VACUUM CLEANER STORES

Myerstown Sheds and Fencing ....G....... 717 866-7015
Myerstown (G-11894)

VACUUM CLEANERS: Household

Nilfisk Inc ....D....... 800 645-3475
Morgantown (G-11529)

Supercleanscom Inc ....G....... 412 429-1640
Carnegie (G-2796)

VACUUM CLEANERS: Indl Type

MPW Industrial Services Inc ....G....... 412 233-4060
Clairton (G-3154)
Overhead Door Corporation ....D....... 215 368-8700
Lansdale (G-9396)

VACUUM PUMPS & EQPT: Laboratory

Applied Equipment Co ....G....... 610 258-7941
Easton (G-4646)
Hyvac Products Inc ....F....... 484 901-4100
Pottstown (G-15948)
Leybold USA Inc ....D....... 724 327-5700
Export (G-5616)

VACUUM SYSTEMS: Air Extraction, Indl

Gap Pollution & Envmtl Ctrl ....E....... 814 266-9469
Johnstown (G-8375)
Polvac Corp ....G....... 610 625-1505
Bethlehem (G-1601)
Travaini Pumps USA Inc ....E....... 757 988-3930
Norristown (G-12720)

VALUE-ADDED RESELLERS: Computer Systems

Digital Plaza LLC ....F....... 267 515-8000
Ambler (G-575)
K-Systems Inc ....F....... 717 795-7711
Mechanicsburg (G-10861)
Prism Engineering LLC ....E....... 215 784-0800
Horsham (G-7842)

VALVE REPAIR SVCS, INDL

A/C Service and Repair Inc ....E....... 717 792-3492
York (G-20361)
American Cone Valve Inc ....E....... 717 792-3492
York (G-20372)
Valves Inc ....F....... 724 378-0600
Aliquippa (G-99)

VALVES

Mercer Valve Co Inc ....G....... 412 859-0300
Pittsburgh (G-15277)
Mikron Valve & Mfr Inc ....G....... 814 453-2337
Erie (G-5392)
Philadelphia Valve Company Inc ....E....... 570 669-9461
Nesquehoning (G-12008)
Sloan Valve Company ....G....... 717 387-3959
Mechanicsburg (G-10889)
Tru Tech Valve LLC ....E....... 724 916-4805
New Castle (G-12160)

VALVES & PARTS: Gas, Indl

Gas Breaker Inc ....E....... 610 407-7200
Malvern (G-10238)
Taylor-Wharton Intl LLC ....G....... 717 763-5060
Mechanicsburg (G-10894)
Wyman-Gordon Pennsylvania LLC ......F....... 570 474-3059
Wilkes Barre (G-19978)

VALVES & PIPE FITTINGS

Acme Cryogenics Inc ....D....... 610 966-4488
Allentown (G-114)
Allegheny Valve & Coupling Inc ....E....... 814 723-8150
Warren (G-19008)
American Pipe and Supply LLC...........G....... 724 228-6360
Washington (G-19148)
Anthracite Industries Inc ....E....... 570 286-2176
Sunbury (G-18163)
Anvil International LLC ....C....... 717 684-4400
Columbia (G-3428)
Atsco Holdings Corp ....D....... 440 701-1021
Cranberry Township (G-3807)
Betts Industries Inc..........................E....... 814 723-1250
Warren (G-19013)
Bonney Forge Corporation ....B....... 814 542-2545
Mount Union (G-11739)
Bradford Allegheny Corporation ....C....... 814 362-2590
Lewis Run (G-9871)
Bradford Allegheny Corporation ....D....... 814 362-2593
Lewis Run (G-9874)
Carpenter & Paterson Inc ....F....... 724 379-8461
Donora (G-4150)

Ctc Pressure Products LLC ....G....... 814 315-6427
Erie (G-5235)
Derbyshire Marine Products LLC.........G....... 267 222-8900
Harleysville (G-7030)
Dresser LLC ....C....... 814 362-9200
Bradford (G-1967)
Exigo Manufacturing Inc ....F....... 484 285-0200
Nazareth (G-11966)
Fessler Machine Company.................E....... 724 346-0878
Sharon (G-17433)
Global Trade Links LLC ....E....... 888 777-1577
Chester Springs (G-3079)
Hajoca Corporation...........................G....... 610 432-0551
Allentown (G-240)
Hall Industries Incorporated ....E....... 724 752-2000
Ellwood City (G-4934)
Hy-Tech Machine Inc ....D....... 724 776-6800
Cranberry Township (G-3823)
Ideal Aerosmith Inc ....E....... 412 963-1495
Pittsburgh (G-15113)
Jet Tool Company Inc ....G....... 814 756-3169
Albion (G-45)
Kerotest Industries Inc ....E....... 412 521-4200
Pittsburgh (G-15173)
Kerotest Manufacturing Corp ....E....... 412 521-4200
Pittsburgh (G-15174)
Lasco Fittings Inc ....F....... 570 301-1170
Pittston (G-15760)
Lee Industries Inc ....C....... 814 342-0460
Philipsburg (G-14519)
Multiplex Manufacturing Co ....E....... 570 752-4524
Berwick (G-1337)
Nick Charles Kravitch ....G....... 412 882-6262
Pittsburgh (G-15340)
Norwin Mfg Inc ....G....... 724 515-7092
Irwin (G-8184)
Parker-Hannifin Corporation..............C....... 215 723-4000
Hatfield (G-7377)
PBM Inc ....D....... 724 863-0550
Irwin (G-8189)
Phoenix Forging Company Inc ....G....... 610 264-2861
Catasauqua (G-2816)
Pittsburgh Plug and Pdts Corp...........G....... 724 538-4022
Evans City (G-5562)
Plastinetics Inc................................G....... 570 384-4832
Hazle Township (G-7473)
Process Development & Ctrl LLC.........E....... 724 695-3440
Coraopolis (G-3719)
Process Technology of PA ....F....... 215 628-2222
Ambler (G-600)
Q-E Manufacturing Company ....G....... 570 966-1017
New Berlin (G-12023)
S P Kinney Engineers Inc...................E....... 412 276-4600
Carnegie (G-2789)
Spears Manufacturing Co ....G....... 570 384-4832
Hazle Township (G-7482)
SPX Flow Us LLC ....G....... 814 476-5842
Mc Kean (G-10593)
SPX Flow Us LLC ....G....... 814 476-5800
Mc Kean (G-10594)
Staver Hydraulics Co Inc ....G....... 610 837-1818
Bath (G-970)
Strahman Valves Inc ....D....... 877 787-2462
Bethlehem (G-1631)
Swagelok Company ....G....... 610 799-9001
Schnecksville (G-17144)
Therm-Omega-Tech Inc ....D....... 877 379-8258
Warminster (G-18980)
Titan Metal & Machine Co Inc ....G....... 724 747-9528
Washington (G-19232)
Turning Solutions Inc ....F....... 814 723-1134
Warren (G-19053)
Tyco Fire Products LP ....C....... 215 362-0700
Lansdale (G-9421)
Vag USA LLC ....G....... 978 544-2511
Cranberry Township (G-3862)
Valves Inc.......................................F....... 724 378-0600
Aliquippa (G-99)
Victaulic LLC ....G....... 610 559-3300
Easton (G-4769)
Watson McDaniel Company................E....... 610 495-5131
Pottstown (G-16070)
World Wide Plastics Inc ....E....... 215 357-0893
Langhorne (G-9336)
Wtk Holdings Inc..............................E....... 724 695-3440
Coraopolis (G-3735)

VALVES & REGULATORS: Pressure, Indl

Ecco/Gregory Inc ....E....... 610 840-0390
West Chester (G-19545)

Trustees of The Univ of PA ....G....... 215 898-5555
Philadelphia (G-14413)
University of Pittsburgh ....F....... 412 383-2456
Pittsburgh (G-15682)
University of Pittsburgh ....C....... 412 648-7980
Pittsburgh (G-15683)

Multiplex Manufacturing Co ....E 570 752-4524
  Berwick (G-1337)
Red Valve Company Inc ....D 412 279-0044
  Carnegie (G-2785)
Red Valve Company Inc ....E 412 279-0044
  Carnegie (G-2786)
Sunbury Controls Inc ....G 570 274-7847
  Sunbury (G-18174)
Zeyon Inc ....E 814 899-3311
  Erie (G-5536)

VALVES: Aerosol, Metal

Ashcombe Products Company Inc ......G 717 848-1271
  York (G-20387)
CDM Holdings Inc ....E 215 724-8640
  Philadelphia (G-13517)
Crown Holdings Inc ....C 215 698-5100
  Yardley (G-20304)
Fisher & Ludlow Inc.........................F 859 282-7767
  Wexford (G-19801)
Ideal Products America LP ....F 484 320-6194
  Malvern (G-10250)
Phoenix Corporation ....E 215 295-9510
  Morrisville (G-11578)
Vicjah Corporation ....G 610 826-7475
  Palmerton (G-13114)

VALVES: Control, Automatic

K- Flo Butterfly ....G 570 752-4524
  Berwick (G-1330)
Keims Machine & Tool Co Inc ....G 570 758-2605
  Herndon (G-7600)

VALVES: Electrohydraulic Servo, Metal

Independent Hose Co ....G 570 544-9528
  Pottsville (G-16081)

VALVES: Engine

Philapack LLC ....G 215 322-2122
  Huntingdon Valley (G-8025)
Precision Controls LLC ....G 267 337-9812
  Levittown (G-9860)

VALVES: Fire Hydrant

Sigelock Systems LLC ....G 814 673-2791
  Franklin (G-6160)

VALVES: Fluid Power, Control, Hydraulic & pneumatic

Admiral Valve LLC ....E 215 386-6508
  Kennett Square (G-8501)
Crane Co ....D 610 631-7700
  Norristown (G-12647)
Fluid Intelligence LLC.......................G 610 405-2698
  Berwyn (G-1362)
Kobold Instruments Inc ....E 412 490-4806
  Pittsburgh (G-15180)
Parker-Hannifin Corporation..............A 814 866-4100
  Erie (G-5414)
PBM Inc ....D 724 863-0550
  Irwin (G-8189)
Rle Systems LLC...............................G 610 518-3751
  West Chester (G-19631)
Seventy-Three Mfg Co Inc ....E 610 845-7823
  Bechtelsville (G-1037)
York Industries Inc...........................E 717 764-8855
  York (G-20742)

VALVES: Gas Cylinder, Compressed

American Cap Company LLC ....D 724 981-4461
  Wheatland (G-19834)
Mawa Inc ....G 610 539-5007
  Norristown (G-12679)

VALVES: Indl

A/C Service and Repair Inc ....E 717 792-3492
  York (G-20361)
Actaire Inc.......................................G 412 851-1040
  Pittsburgh (G-14645)
Advanced Valve Design Inc ....F 610 435-8820
  Whitehall (G-19860)
Al Xander Co Inc ....E 814 665-8268
  Corry (G-3743)
American Cone Valve Inc ....F 717 792-3492
  York (G-20372)

Co-Ax Valves Inc ....F 215 757-3725
  Bristol (G-2127)
Crispin Valve LLC.............................G 570 752-4524
  Berwick (G-1321)
Curtiss-Wright Corporation ....A 724 275-5277
  New Kensington (G-12337)
Curtiss-Wright Corporation ....F 215 721-1100
  Hatfield (G-7328)
Curtiss-Wright Flow Control ....G 724 295-6200
  Freeport (G-6202)
Elite Midstream Services Inc ....E 412 220-3082
  Cuddy (G-3943)
Eriks Na LLC....................................E 412 787-2400
  Pittsburgh (G-14985)
Fetterolf Corporation ....D 610 584-1500
  Skippack (G-17596)
Global Trade Links LLC ....E 888 777-1577
  Chester Springs (G-3079)
Graco High Pressure Eqp Inc ....G 800 289-7447
  Erie (G-5305)
Industrial Controls & Eqp Inc ....E 724 746-3705
  Lawrence (G-9537)
Innovative Pressure Tech LLC............D 814 833-5200
  Erie (G-5326)
ITT Engineered Valves LLC................F 717 509-2200
  Lancaster (G-9066)
Ogontz Corporation ....F 215 657-4770
  Willow Grove (G-20131)
Olson Technologies Inc.....................E 610 770-1100
  Allentown (G-339)
R Conrader Company ....G 814 898-2727
  Erie (G-5447)
S P Kinney Engineers Inc ....E 412 276-4600
  Carnegie (G-2789)
Schutte Koerting Acquisition ....E 215 639-0900
  Trevose (G-18502)
Sensus USA Inc ....C 800 375-8875
  Du Bois (G-4419)
Sensus USA Inc ....C 724 430-3956
  Pittsburgh (G-15524)
Solenoid Solutions Inc ....E 814 838-3190
  Erie (G-5484)
Sooner Pipe LLC...............................G 570 368-4590
  Montoursville (G-11450)
SPX Corporation ....F 814 476-5800
  Mc Kean (G-10592)
Strahman Industries Inc ....C 484 893-5080
  Bethlehem (G-1630)
Superior Group Inc ....E 610 397-2040
  Conshohocken (G-3610)
Tru-Tech Industries Inc.....................D 724 776-1020
  Cranberry Township (G-3858)
Turning Solutions Inc ....F 814 723-1134
  Warren (G-19053)
Victaulic Company............................A 610 559-3300
  Easton (G-4770)
Watson McDaniel Company ....G 610 367-7191
  Boyertown (G-1935)
World Wide Plastics Inc ....E 215 357-0893
  Langhorne (G-9336)

VALVES: Plumbing & Heating

Danzi Energy ....G 814 723-8640
  Warren (G-19019)

VALVES: Regulating & Control, Automatic

Air-Con Inc.......................................F 814 838-6373
  Erie (G-5178)
Nutech LLC.......................................F 215 361-0373
  Hatfield (G-7375)
Sherwood Valve LLC ....C 724 225-8000
  Pittsburgh (G-15532)
Therm-Omega-Tech Inc ....D 877 379-8258
  Warminster (G-18980)
Vmd Machine Co Inc..........................F 215 723-7782
  Telford (G-18324)
Warren Controls Inc..........................D 610 317-0800
  Bethlehem (G-1653)

VALVES: Regulating, Process Control

DFT Inc ....E 610 363-8903
  Exton (G-5664)

VALVES: Water Works

Penn Troy Manufacturing Inc..............E 570 297-2125
  Troy (G-18525)

VAN CONVERSIONS

Total Mobility Services Inc ....G 814 629-9935
  Boswell (G-1885)

VARNISHES, NEC

Parrish R Varnish ....G 814 242-1786
  Johnstown (G-8419)
United Gilsonite Laboratories..............D 570 344-1202
  Scranton (G-17308)

VASES: Pottery

Pennsylvania Dry Mix ....G 717 509-3520
  Lancaster (G-9166)

VAULTS & SAFES WHOLESALERS

Lycoming Burial Vault Co Inc ....F 570 368-8642
  Montoursville (G-11446)

VEGETABLES, FROZEN: Wholesaler

Clair D Thompson & Sons Inc ....E 570 398-1880
  Jersey Shore (G-8311)

VEHICLES: All Terrain

JB Racing Inc ....G 814 922-3523
  East Springfield (G-4599)
John L Mary D Shaffer ....G 814 427-2894
  Punxsutawney (G-16145)
Mission Critical Solutions LLC ....E 814 839-2078
  Alum Bank (G-562)
Rock Run Recreation Area..................G 814 674-6026
  Patton (G-13189)
World of Wheels Inc..........................F 814 676-5721
  Seneca (G-17373)

VEHICLES: Recreational

Four Wheeling For Less LLC ....G 724 287-7852
  Butler (G-2402)

VENDING MACHINE OPERATORS: Candy & Snack Food

Mvc Industries Inc............................D 610 650-0500
  Norristown (G-12690)

VENDING MACHINE OPERATORS: Sandwich & Hot Food

Compass Group Usa Inc ....D 717 569-2671
  Lancaster (G-8982)

VENDING MACHINES & PARTS

Compass Group USA Investments ......F 717 939-1200
  Middletown (G-11051)
Evive Station LLC ....G 724 972-6421
  Rostraver Township (G-16825)
Jennison Ice LLC ....G 412 596-5914
  Carnegie (G-2772)
Mk Solutions Inc ....G 860 760-0438
  York (G-20601)
Sapor Food Group LLC ....F 267 714-4382
  Philadelphia (G-14281)
Vend Natural of Western PA................G 724 518-6594
  Donora (G-4164)
Vendors 1st Choice Inc ....G 215 804-1011
  Quakertown (G-16256)
West Dairy Inc ....E 610 495-0100
  Parker Ford (G-13170)

VENETIAN BLINDS & SHADES

Plymouth Blind Co Inc.......................E 412 771-8569
  Mc Kees Rocks (G-10626)
Todd Lengle & Co Inc ....E 610 777-0731
  Reading (G-16541)

VENTILATING EQPT: Sheet Metal

Georgia Web Inc ....F 215 887-6600
  Glenside (G-6520)

VENTURE CAPITAL COMPANIES

Brynavon Group Inc ....G 610 525-2102
  Villanova (G-18765)
Safeguard Scientifics Inc ....E 610 293-0600
  Radnor (G-16301)

VERMICULITE MINING SVCS

Specialty Vermiculite Corp..................D...... 610 660-8840
Bala Cynwyd (G-893)
Vermiculite Association Inc ....G...... 717 238-9902
Harrisburg (G-7242)

VETERINARY PHARMACEUTICAL PREPARATIONS

Edward A Shelly Vmd ....G...... 610 826-2793
Palmerton (G-13104)
Philadelphia Animal Health LLC ....G...... 215 573-4503
Philadelphia (G-14141)

VETERINARY PRDTS: Instruments & Apparatus

Pneu-Dart Inc..D...... 570 323-2710
Williamsport (G-20061)

VIALS: Glass

Schott North America Inc ....C...... 717 228-4200
Lebanon (G-9628)

VIDEO & AUDIO EQPT, WHOLESALE

Media Rooms Inc ....G...... 610 719-8500
West Chester (G-19600)

VIDEO EQPT

Mobile Video Devices Inc ....G...... 610 921-5720
Reading (G-16447)

VIDEO TAPE PRODUCTION SVCS

East Hill Video Prod Co LLC ....F...... 215 855-4457
Lansdale (G-9364)
Marcom Group Ltd................................F...... 610 859-8989
Upper Chichester (G-18667)
Parker-Hannifin Corporation................G...... 814 860-5700
Erie (G-5415)

VIDEO TRIGGERS EXC REMOTE CONTROL TV DEVICES

Z-Band Technologies LLC....................G...... 717 249-2606
Carlisle (G-2752)

VINYL RESINS, NEC

Polyone Corporation ....F...... 570 474-7770
Mountain Top (G-11770)

VISES: Machine

Chick Wrkholding Solutions Inc...........D...... 724 772-1644
Warrendale (G-19070)

VISUAL COMMUNICATIONS SYSTEMS

Gaadt Perspectives LLC.......................G...... 610 388-7641
Chadds Ford (G-2851)
Intuidex Inc ....E...... 484 851-3423
Hellertown (G-7557)
Kongsberg Integrated Tactical ....E...... 814 269-5700
Johnstown (G-8399)
Ospcom LLC...G...... 267 356-7124
Doylestown (G-4321)
Pls Signs LLC.......................................G...... 215 269-1400
Fairless Hills (G-5791)
Two Toys Inc...G...... 717 840-6400
York (G-20693)

VITAMINS: Natural Or Synthetic, Uncompounded, Bulk

Douglas Laboratories...........................E...... 412 494-0122
Pittsburgh (G-14935)
Goodstate Inc ....G...... 215 366-2030
Glenside (G-6523)
Muscle Gauge Nutrition LLC................F...... 484 840-8006
West Chester (G-19602)
Natures Bounty Co ....F...... 570 384-2270
Hazle Township (G-7470)
Stemmetry ....G...... 678 770-6781
Sewickley (G-17413)
V L H Inc...B...... 800 245-4440
Pittsburgh (G-15688)

VITAMINS: Pharmaceutical Preparations

Accucorp Packaging Inc ....C...... 215 673-3375
Philadelphia (G-13339)
Alacer Corp...C...... 717 258-2000
Carlisle (G-2688)
Delavau LLC ....C...... 215 671-1400
Philadelphia (G-13617)

VOCATIONAL OR TECHNICAL SCHOOLS, PUBLIC

Blind and Vision Rehab.........................D...... 412 368-4400
Pittsburgh (G-14771)

VOCATIONAL REHABILITATION AGENCY

North Central Sight Svcs Inc ....D...... 570 323-9401
Williamsport (G-20050)
Serve Inc ....G...... 570 265-3119
Monroeton (G-11320)

VOCATIONAL TRAINING AGENCY

Venango Training & Dev Ctr Inc ....D...... 814 676-5755
Seneca (G-17371)

WALLBOARD: Decorated, Made From Purchased Materials

Cariks Custom Decor ....G...... 412 882-1511
Pittsburgh (G-14812)
Southwind Studios Ltd..........................G...... 610 664-4110
Lower Merion (G-10109)

WALLPAPER & WALL COVERINGS

Reese Daryl C Wallpapering ....G...... 717 597-2532
Greencastle (G-6629)
Wallquest Inc ....D...... 610 293-1330
Wayne (G-19389)

WALLPAPER: Made From Purchased Paper

York Wallcoverings Inc.........................C...... 717 846-4456
York (G-20754)

WAREHOUSING & STORAGE FACILITIES, NEC

Atlantic Track & Turnout Co..................E...... 570 429-1462
Pottsville (G-16073)
Essentra Porous Tech Corp ....E...... 814 898-3238
Erie (G-5283)
Foulk Equipment Leasing Inc...............G...... 610 838-2260
Bethlehem (G-1516)
Marilyn Strawser Beauty Salon ....G...... 717 463-2804
Thompsontown (G-18349)
Sony Music Holdings Inc ....E...... 724 794-8500
Boyers (G-1890)
Spilltech Environmental Inc ....G...... 814 247-8566
Hastings (G-7263)
Te Connectivity Corporation.................D...... 717 691-5842
Mechanicsburg (G-10895)

WAREHOUSING & STORAGE, REFRIGERATED: Cold Storage Or Refrig

Americold Logistics LLC.......................C...... 215 721-0700
Hatfield (G-7316)
Clemens Family Corporation ....A...... 800 523-5291
Hatfield (G-7324)
Rosenbergers Cold Storage ....B...... 215 721-0700
Hatfield (G-7392)
Vision Warehousing and Dist ....G...... 717 762-5912
Waynesboro (G-19429)

WAREHOUSING & STORAGE, REFRIGERATED: Frozen Or Refrig Goods

R L Sipes Locker Plant ....G...... 814 652-2714
Everett (G-5578)

WAREHOUSING & STORAGE: Bulk St & Termnls, Hire, Petro/Chem

Gordon Terminal Service Co PA ....C...... 412 331-9410
Mckees Rocks (G-10661)

WAREHOUSING & STORAGE: General

Allied Concrete & Supply Corp.............E...... 215 646-8484
Dresher (G-4352)
Allied Tube & Conduit Corp ....B...... 215 676-6464
Philadelphia (G-13369)
Archrock Inc ....E...... 724 464-2291
Indiana (G-8080)
Archrock Services LP...........................G...... 570 567-7162
Canton (G-2662)
Astro Apparel Inc ....E...... 570 346-1700
Scranton (G-17209)
Atlantic Track & Turnout Co..................E...... 570 429-1462
Pottsville (G-16073)
Baker Petrolite LLC...............................F...... 610 876-2200
Crum Lynne (G-3935)
Charles Komar & Sons Inc...................C...... 570 326-3741
Williamsport (G-19997)
Corrugated Specialties..........................F...... 814 337-5705
Meadville (G-10714)
Export Boxing & Crating Inc ....F...... 412 675-1000
Glassport (G-6412)
Imprintables Warehouse LLC ....G...... 724 966-8599
Carmichaels (G-2758)
Sheridan Supply Company Inc ....G...... 610 589-4361
Newmanstown (G-12484)
Tsi Associates Inc................................F...... 610 375-4371
Reading (G-16551)

WAREHOUSING & STORAGE: General

Atc Technology Corporation.................E...... 412 820-3700
Cranberry Township (G-3806)
Continental Auto Systems Inc ....E...... 610 289-1390
Allentown (G-177)
Harvey Bell ....G...... 215 634-4900
Philadelphia (G-13806)
Pepsi-Cola Metro Btlg Co Inc ....F...... 215 937-6102
Philadelphia (G-14135)
Royersford Spring Co...........................F...... 610 948-4440
Royersford (G-16863)
Sappi North America Inc ....D...... 610 398-8400
Allentown (G-383)
Trident Plastics Inc ....G...... 215 946-3999
Bristol (G-2210)
Union Packaging LLC............................D...... 610 572-7265
Yeadon (G-20356)

WAREHOUSING & STORAGE: Refrigerated

Zero Ice Corporation.............................G...... 717 264-7912
Chambersburg (G-3002)

WAREHOUSING & STORAGE: Self Storage

Interstate Self Storage..........................G...... 724 662-1186
Mercer (G-10965)

WARM AIR HEAT & AC EQPT & SPLYS, WHOLESALE Fan, Heat & Vent

New Busch Co Inc.................................G...... 724 940-2326
Wexford (G-19815)

WARM AIR HEATING & AC EQPT & SPLYS, WHOL: Dust Collecting

Donaldson Company Inc.......................G...... 215 396-8349
Warminster (G-18859)

WARM AIR HEATING & AC EQPT & SPLYS, WHOL: Elec Heating Eqpt

Penn-Central Industries Inc ....G...... 814 371-3211
Du Bois (G-4413)

WARM AIR HEATING & AC EQPT & SPLYS, WHOLESALE Heat Exchgrs

Thermal Transfer Corporation ....D...... 412 460-4004
Duquesne (G-4500)

WARM AIR HEATING/AC EQPT/SPLYS, WHOL Warm Air Htg Eqpt/Splys

Hennemuth Metal Fabricators ....G...... 724 693-9605
Oakdale (G-12902)
Johnstone Supply Inc...........................E...... 484 765-1160
Breinigsville (G-2019)
Rose Corporation..................................D...... 610 376-5004
Reading (G-16504)

PRODUCT

Union Chill Mat Co ....G....... 724 452-6400
Zelienople *(G-20825)*

US Boiler ....G....... 215 535-8900
Philadelphia *(G-14434)*

WASHERS

History Washer Inc ....G....... 717 275-3101
Elliottsburg *(G-4920)*

Jim Airgood Pressure Washer..............G....... 814 837-7626
Kane *(G-8467)*

Philadelphia Window Washers ....G....... 215 742-3875
Philadelphia *(G-14159)*

Pressure Water Systems of PA............G....... 412 668-0878
Pittsburgh *(G-15436)*

Westbrook Window Washers LLC ....G....... 610 873-0245
Downingtown *(G-4263)*

WASHERS: Spring, Metal

Belleville International LLC.................E....... 724 431-0444
Butler *(G-2377)*

WATCH REPAIR SVCS

E R Kinley & Sons ....G....... 570 323-6740
Williamsport *(G-20008)*

Rgm Watch Company ....F....... 717 653-9799
Mount Joy *(G-11670)*

WATCHES

Watch U Want Inc.......................G....... 954 961-1445
Bala Cynwyd *(G-896)*

WATCHES & PARTS, WHOLESALE

Dutcher Brothers Inc ....G....... 215 922-4555
Philadelphia *(G-13652)*

Watch U Want Inc.......................G....... 954 961-1445
Bala Cynwyd *(G-896)*

WATER HEATERS

Cemline Corporation ....D....... 724 274-5430
Cheswick *(G-3104)*

Harsco Corporation ....C....... 570 421-7500
East Stroudsburg *(G-4617)*

WATER PURIFICATION EQPT: Household

Blue Boy Products Inc...................G....... 610 284-1055
Downingtown *(G-4215)*

Ds Services of America Inc ....F....... 717 901-4620
Harrisburg *(G-7122)*

GE Infrastructure Sensing ....F....... 617 926-1749
Feasterville Trevose *(G-5912)*

General Ecology Inc ....E....... 610 363-7900
Exton *(G-5686)*

Master Water Conditioning Corp..........F....... 610 323-8358
Pottstown *(G-16017)*

Pennsylvania American Water -..........D....... 412 884-5113
Pittsburgh *(G-15374)*

Suez Wts Systems Usa Inc ....B....... 781 359-7000
Trevose *(G-18505)*

Water Gem Inc ....F....... 717 561-4440
Harrisburg *(G-7244)*

Water Master Inc ....G....... 717 561-4440
Harrisburg *(G-7245)*

Watermark Usa LLC ....F....... 610 983-0500
Gladwyne *(G-6409)*

WATER PURIFICATION PRDTS: Chlorination Tablets & Kits

Dbex Tek LLC ....G....... 267 566-0354
Bensalem *(G-1180)*

WATER SOFTENER SVCS

Altoona Soft Water Company ....F....... 814 943-2768
Altoona *(G-473)*

Bucks Cnty Artesian Well Drlg ....F....... 215 493-1867
Washington Crossing *(G-19253)*

Complete Fluid Control Inc ....E....... 570 382-3376
S Abingtn Twp *(G-16893)*

Lester Water Inc ....F....... 610 444-4660
Kennett Square *(G-8522)*

Watermark Usa LLC ....F....... 610 983-0500
Gladwyne *(G-6409)*

WATER SUPPLY

Ecotech Inc...............................D....... 610 954-8480
Allentown *(G-202)*

GE Infrastructure Sensing ....F....... 617 926-1749
Feasterville Trevose *(G-5912)*

Laurel Holdings Inc......................G....... 814 533-5777
Johnstown *(G-8402)*

Suez Wts Systems Usa Inc ....B....... 781 359-7000
Trevose *(G-18505)*

WATER TREATMENT EQPT: Indl

A3-Usa Inc ....G....... 724 871-7170
Westmoreland City *(G-19783)*

Agape Water Solutions Inc ....G....... 215 631-7035
Harleysville *(G-7014)*

Altair Equipment Company Inc............E....... 215 672-9000
Warminster *(G-18826)*

Aquatech International LLC ....G....... 724 746-5300
Canonsburg *(G-2543)*

Aquatech Intl Sls Corp ....G....... 724 746-5300
Canonsburg *(G-2544)*

Biss Nuss Inc ....G....... 412 221-1200
Pittsburgh *(G-14769)*

Borough of Tyrone ....G....... 814 684-5396
Tyrone *(G-18577)*

Calgon Carbon Corporation ....C....... 412 787-6700
Moon Township *(G-11482)*

Calgon Carbon Corporation ....B....... 412 787-6700
Pittsburgh *(G-14803)*

Cardinal Resources Inc ....G....... 412 374-0989
Pittsburgh *(G-14809)*

Cardinal Resources LLC ....G....... 412 374-0989
Pittsburgh *(G-14810)*

Cawley Environmental Svcs Inc ....F....... 610 594-0101
Downingtown *(G-4219)*

Chemical Equipment Labs VA Inc ....E....... 610 497-9390
Newtown Square *(G-12570)*

Comtech Industries Inc ....E....... 724 884-0101
Canonsburg *(G-2565)*

Corrosion Technology Inc................G....... 610 429-1450
West Chester *(G-19530)*

County of Somerset ....G....... 814 629-9460
Hollsopple *(G-7657)*

Craft Products Co Inc ....G....... 412 821-8102
Pittsburgh *(G-14885)*

Custom Blends Inc ....G....... 215 934-7080
Philadelphia *(G-13592)*

De Nora Water Technologies Inc ....G....... 412 494-4077
Pittsburgh *(G-14913)*

De Nora Water Technologies Inc ....E....... 412 788-8300
Pittsburgh *(G-14914)*

Electrocell Systems Inc ....G....... 610 438-2969
Easton *(G-4678)*

Encotech Inc.............................E....... 724 222-3334
Eighty Four *(G-4839)*

Enquip Co ....G....... 610 363-8275
Exton *(G-5672)*

Envirodyne Systems Inc ....E....... 717 763-0500
Camp Hill *(G-2496)*

Equisol LLC ....F....... 866 629-7646
Conshohocken *(G-3544)*

Essential Water Technologies............F....... 570 317-2583
Bloomsburg *(G-1781)*

Evoqua Water Technologies Corp.........D....... 724 772-0044
Pittsburgh *(G-14990)*

FB Leopold Company Inc.................F....... 724 452-6300
Zelienople *(G-20800)*

Filter & Water Technologies..............G....... 267 450-4900
Montgomeryville *(G-11397)*

Foxcroft Equipment & Svcs Co ....F....... 610 942-2888
Glenmoore *(G-6467)*

Global Environmental Tech...............G....... 610 821-4901
Allentown *(G-234)*

GSM Hold Co ....G....... 412 487-7140
Allison Park *(G-452)*

Guardian CSC Corporation ....F....... 717 848-2540
Hellam *(G-7551)*

Hess Machine International ....G....... 717 733-0005
Ephrata *(G-5108)*

Idreco USA Ltd ....F....... 610 701-9944
West Chester *(G-19566)*

Inframark LLC ....D....... 215 822-2258
Colmar *(G-3417)*

Inframark LLC ....E....... 215 646-9201
Horsham *(G-7823)*

Infrastructure H Environmental...........F....... 866 629-7646
Conshohocken *(G-3563)*

Kneppers Kleen Water ....G....... 717 264-9715
Chambersburg *(G-2948)*

Lang Filter Media LP ....F....... 570 459-7005
Hazleton *(G-7507)*

Lebanon Water Treatment Plant ....F....... 717 865-2191
Lebanon *(G-9606)*

Longs Water Technol ....G....... 610 398-3737
Orefield *(G-13014)*

Mount Plsnt Twnshp-Wshngtn CNT ......F....... 724 356-7974
Hickory *(G-7629)*

Nalco Company LLC ....E....... 412 278-8600
Pittsburgh *(G-15317)*

Nalco Wtr Prtrtment Sltons LLC ....E....... 610 358-0717
Aston *(G-780)*

Neptune-Benson Inc ....G....... 724 772-0044
Pittsburgh *(G-15327)*

Newterra Inc ....G....... 610 631-7700
Norristown *(G-12692)*

Otterbine Barebo Inc ....G....... 610 965-6018
Emmaus *(G-5038)*

Philadlphia Mxing Slutions Ltd............D....... 717 832-2800
Palmyra *(G-13129)*

PNC Equity Partners LP ....F....... 412 914-0175
Pittsburgh *(G-15417)*

Realm Therapeutics Inc..................D....... 484 321-2700
Malvern *(G-10308)*

Roberts Filter Holding Company..........G....... 610 583-3131
Media *(G-10946)*

S & G Water Conditioning Inc ....G....... 215 672-2030
Warminster *(G-18957)*

Sanatoga Water Cond Inc ....G....... 610 326-9803
Pottstown *(G-16042)*

Shenandoah Water Trtmnt Plant ....G....... 570 462-4918
Shenandoah *(G-17496)*

Suez Wts Systems Usa Inc ....C....... 724 743-0270
Canonsburg *(G-2642)*

Taylor Run ....G....... 610 436-1369
West Chester *(G-19656)*

Terra Group Corp ....E....... 610 821-7003
Allentown *(G-408)*

Ultra Pure Products Inc ....E....... 717 589-7001
Mifflintown *(G-11139)*

Water Treatment By Design LLC ....G....... 717 938-0670
Lewisberry *(G-9894)*

Wsg & Solutions Inc ....E....... 267 638-3000
Montgomeryville *(G-11427)*

Xylem Wtr Sltons Zlienople LLC..........C....... 724 452-6300
Zelienople *(G-20830)*

WATER: Mineral, Carbonated, Canned & Bottled, Etc

Crossroads Beverage Group LLC ....G....... 352 509-3127
Reading *(G-16355)*

Kamila Farm LLC ....G....... 570 427-8318
Weatherly *(G-19454)*

Mvc Industries Inc.......................D....... 610 650-0500
Norristown *(G-12690)*

Roaring Spring Water ....G....... 814 942-9844
Roaring Spring *(G-16770)*

WATER: Pasteurized & Mineral, Bottled & Canned

Altoona Soft Water Company ....F....... 814 943-2768
Altoona *(G-473)*

Natures Way Pure Water ....G....... 800 407-7873
Pittston *(G-15770)*

Pure Flow Water Co ....G....... 215 723-0237
Souderton *(G-17761)*

Safe Pac Pasteurization LLC ....F....... 267 324-5631
Philadelphia *(G-14275)*

WATER: Pasteurized, Canned & Bottled, Etc

Creekside Springs LLC ....E....... 724 266-9000
Ambridge *(G-613)*

Creekside Springs LLC ....E....... 724 266-9000
Ambridge *(G-614)*

GE Infrastructure Sensing ....F....... 617 926-1749
Feasterville Trevose *(G-5912)*

Ice River Springs Usa Inc.................E....... 828 391-6900
Allentown *(G-249)*

Natures Way Prwter Systems Inc ....D....... 570 655-7755
Pittston *(G-15769)*

Niagara Bottling LLC ....E....... 610 562-2176
Hamburg *(G-6847)*

Suez Wts Systems Usa Inc ....B....... 781 359-7000
Trevose *(G-18505)*

(G-0000) Company's Geographic Section entry number

WATERPROOFING COMPOUNDS

Concrete Service Materials Co ....G....... 610 825-1554
Conshohocken (G-3532)
IPA Systems Inc ....F....... 215 425-6607
Philadelphia (G-13873)
Wall Firma Inc ....F....... 724 258-6873
Monongahela (G-11319)

WAXES: Mineral, Natural

Matreya LLC ....F....... 814 355-1030
State College (G-17988)

WAXES: Petroleum, Not Produced In Petroleum Refineries

International Waxes Inc ....E....... 814 827-3609
Titusville (G-18386)
Stevenson-Cooper Inc ....G....... 215 223-2600
Philadelphia (G-14348)
Wall Firma Inc ....F....... 724 258-6873
Monongahela (G-11319)

WEAVING MILL, BROADWOVEN FABRICS: Wool Or Similar Fabric

Rockafellow John ....G....... 717 359-4276
Littlestown (G-10076)

WEIGHING MACHINERY & APPARATUS

Libra Scale ....G....... 412 782-0611
Pittsburgh (G-15229)
Raytec LLC ....E....... 717 445-0510
Ephrata (G-5138)

WELDING & CUTTING APPARATUS & ACCESS, NEC

New Berry Inc ....F....... 724 452-8040
Harmony (G-7074)
Omnitech Automation Inc ....E....... 610 965-3279
Emmaus (G-5036)
Praxair Distribution Inc ....F....... 814 238-5092
State College (G-18009)
Welding Alloys USA ....G....... 724 202-7497
New Castle (G-12167)
Weldsale Company LLC ....G....... 215 739-7474
Philadelphia (G-14464)

WELDING EQPT

Arcos Industries LLC ....D....... 570 339-5200
Mount Carmel (G-11623)
Bestweld Inc ....E....... 610 718-9700
Pottstown (G-15967)
Branson Ultrasonics Corp ....E....... 610 251-9776
Paoli (G-13136)
Direct Wire & Cable Inc ....D....... 717 336-2842
Denver (G-4070)
Electro-Glass Products Inc ....E....... 724 423-5000
Norvelt (G-12878)
ESAB Group Inc ....B....... 717 637-8911
Hanover (G-6884)
ESAB Group Inc ....C....... 843 673-7700
Hanover (G-6885)
Garretts Fabricating ....G....... 724 528-8193
West Middlesex (G-19725)
Joseph Nedorezov ....G....... 215 661-0600
North Wales (G-12808)
Joseph Nedorezov ....G....... 610 278-9325
Blue Bell (G-1837)
Matheson Tri-Gas Inc ....G....... 814 453-5637
Erie (G-5382)
Praxair Dist Mid-Atlantic LLC ....A....... 610 398-2211
Allentown (G-355)
Praxair Distribution Inc ....A....... 610 398-2211
Allentown (G-356)
Weld Tooling Corporation ....E....... 412 331-1776
Canonsburg (G-2658)

WELDING EQPT & SPLYS WHOLESALERS

Air Products and Chemicals Inc ....E....... 610 317-8706
Bethlehem (G-1445)
Airgas Usa LLC ....G....... 814 437-2431
Franklin (G-6113)
American Welding & Gas Inc ....F....... 570 323-8400
Williamsport (G-19985)
Goss Inc ....D....... 412 486-6100
Glenshaw (G-6489)

Industrial Welding and Fabg ....G....... 724 266-2887
Leetsdale (G-9696)
Lwe Inc ....G....... 814 336-3553
Meadville (G-10751)
Matheson Tri-Gas Inc ....F....... 724 379-4104
Donora (G-4156)
Matheson Tri-Gas Inc ....F....... 814 781-6990
Saint Marys (G-16987)
Praxair Distribution Inc ....F....... 412 781-6273
Pittsburgh (G-15429)
Robinson Technical Pdts Corp ....E....... 610 261-1900
Coplay (G-3647)

WELDING EQPT & SPLYS: Electrodes

Nexarc Inc ....G....... 570 458-6990
Bloomsburg (G-1791)
Oaks Welding LLC ....G....... 570 527-7328
Ashland (G-735)

WELDING EQPT & SPLYS: Gas

Goss Inc ....D....... 412 486-6100
Glenshaw (G-6489)
Systematics Inc ....D....... 610 696-9040
West Chester (G-19654)

WELDING EQPT & SPLYS: Resistance, Electric

Stored Energy Concepts Inc ....F....... 610 469-6543
Saint Peters (G-17035)

WELDING EQPT REPAIR SVCS

Bailey Machine Company ....E....... 724 628-4730
Connellsville (G-3490)
Blank River Services Inc ....E....... 412 384-2489
Elizabeth (G-4857)
C & J Welding & Cnstr LLC ....C....... 724 564-7120
Mc Clellandtown (G-10555)
Moritz Machine & Repairs LLC ....G....... 717 677-6838
Biglerville (G-1667)
Safety Guard Steel Fabg Co ....F....... 412 821-1177
McKnight (G-10688)

WELDING EQPT: Electric

ESAB Group Inc ....B....... 717 637-8911
Hanover (G-6886)

WELDING EQPT: Electrical

Steimer and Co Inc ....F....... 610 933-7450
Phoenixville (G-14579)

WELDING MACHINES & EQPT: Ultrasonic

Sonobond Ultrasonics Inc ....F....... 610 696-4710
West Chester (G-19642)
Tru-Lite International Inc ....G....... 724 443-6821
Gibsonia (G-6356)

WELDING REPAIR SVC

A A A Welding Service Inc ....E....... 215 426-2240
Philadelphia (G-13323)
A D M Welding & Fabrication ....G....... 814 723-7227
Warren (G-19007)
Aaron Wenger ....G....... 717 656-9876
New Holland (G-12225)
Abbottstown Industries Inc ....E....... 717 259-8715
Abbottstown (G-3)
Accu Machining Center Inc ....E....... 610 252-6855
Easton (G-4644)
Affil Distributors ....G....... 610 977-3100
Wayne (G-19295)
Agri Welding Service Inc ....F....... 570 437-3330
Danville (G-3996)
Altrax ....G....... 814 379-3706
Summerville (G-18156)
American Machine Co ....G....... 717 533-5678
Palmyra (G-13115)
Anderson Welding & Sons LLC ....G....... 215 886-1726
Oreland (G-13017)
Andrew E Reken ....G....... 724 783-7878
Dayton (G-4034)
Artman Equipment Company Inc ....F....... 724 337-3700
Apollo (G-662)
Auman Machine Company Inc ....E....... 717 273-4604
Lebanon (G-9546)
Auto Weld Chassis & Components ....G....... 570 275-1411
Danville (G-3997)

B & W Metal Works Inc ....G....... 717 848-1077
York (G-20396)
Bailey Machine Company ....E....... 724 628-4730
Connellsville (G-3490)
Barretts Custom Wrought Iron ....G....... 814 676-4575
Oil City (G-12941)
Bell-Mark Sales Co Inc ....E....... 717 292-5641
Dover (G-4186)
Bissinger and Stein Inc ....E....... 215 256-1122
Kulpsville (G-8824)
Blank River Services Inc ....E....... 412 384-2489
Elizabeth (G-4857)
Brighton Machine Company Inc ....F....... 724 378-0960
Aliquippa (G-70)
Brodys Welding and Mech Contrs ....G....... 215 941-7914
Philadelphia (G-13486)
Browns Welding Inc ....G....... 717 762-6467
Waynesboro (G-19403)
Budget Portable Welding Mch ....G....... 717 865-0473
Lebanon (G-9549)
Burnells Welding Corporation ....G....... 215 757-2896
Bristol (G-2122)
Butler Machine Inc ....G....... 814 355-5605
Bellefonte (G-1095)
C & C Welding and Fabg Inc ....G....... 814 387-6556
Clarence (G-3161)
C & T Machining Inc ....E....... 717 328-9572
Mercersburg (G-10982)
C A Spalding Company ....E....... 267 550-9000
Bensalem (G-1163)
C/C Welding/Fabrict Inc ....G....... 814 364-9460
Clarence (G-3162)
Caldwell Corporation ....E....... 814 486-3493
Emporium (G-5051)
Cambria Welding & Fabg Inc ....G....... 814 948-5072
Saint Benedict (G-16936)
Cannon Tool Company ....F....... 724 745-1070
Canonsburg (G-2556)
Claylick Enterprises LLC ....G....... 717 328-9876
Mercersburg (G-10983)
Comfab Inc ....G....... 724 339-1750
New Kensington (G-12335)
Compass Welding LLC ....G....... 570 928-7472
Dushore (G-4508)
Condos Incorporated ....E....... 570 748-9265
Mill Hall (G-11174)
Conshohocken Steel Pdts Inc ....E....... 215 283-9222
Ambler (G-574)
Construction On Site Welding ....G....... 610 367-1895
Boyertown (G-1904)
Creative Design & Machining ....E....... 570 587-3077
S Abingtn Twp (G-16894)
Cumberland Valley Wldg & Repr ....G....... 717 249-1129
Carlisle (G-2704)
Custom Iron Works Welding ....F....... 814 444-1315
Somerset (G-17682)
D & S Fabricating & Welding ....G....... 412 653-9185
Clairton (G-3148)
D R Gaumer Metal Fabricating ....G....... 610 395-5101
Wescosville (G-19488)
Dallas Machine Inc ....E....... 610 799-2800
Schnecksville (G-17138)
Daves Welding Shop ....G....... 814 796-6520
Waterford (G-19261)
DC Welding ....G....... 717 361-9400
Elizabethtown (G-4871)
Decherts Machine Shop Inc ....E....... 717 838-1326
Palmyra (G-13121)
Dennys Welding ....G....... 570 265-8015
Towanda (G-18423)
Dewitt Fab Welding Co ....G....... 215 538-9477
Quakertown (G-16185)
DHL Machine Co Inc ....E....... 215 536-3591
Quakertown (G-16186)
Diversified Mech Svcs Inc ....G....... 215 368-3084
Lansdale (G-9362)
Donald Campbell ....G....... 412 793-6068
Pittsburgh (G-14930)
Doug Herhold ....G....... 814 756-5141
Albion (G-43)
Dressel Welding Supply Inc ....G....... 570 505-1994
Cogan Station (G-3360)
Dunbar Machine Co Inc ....G....... 724 277-8711
Dunbar (G-4439)
Dyeco Inc ....G....... 717 545-1882
Harrisburg (G-7123)
E K L Machine Inc ....E....... 215 639-0150
Bensalem (G-1184)
E M United Wldg & Fabrication ....G....... 570 595-0695
Cresco (G-3893)

PRODUCT

East End Welding	G	570 726-7925	Mill Hall (G-11176)
East Penn Welding Inc	G	610 682-2290	Kutztown (G-8841)
Edgewood Welding & Fabrication	F	814 445-7746	Somerset (G-17687)
Edinboro Industries		814 734-1100	Edinboro (G-4811)
Elliott Machine Company	G	610 485-5345	Upper Chichester (G-18659)
Enrico J Fiore	G	570 489-8430	Throop (G-18358)
F F Frickanisce Iron Works	G	724 568-2001	Vandergrift (G-18726)
F W B & Sons Welding Inc	G	610 543-0348	Springfield (G-17913)
Fab Tech Industries	G	717 597-4919	Greencastle (G-6610)
Fab Tech V Industries Inc	E	717 597-4919	Greencastle (G-6611)
Fabri-Weld LLC		814 490-7324	Erie (G-5287)
Facchiano Ironworks Inc	G	610 865-1503	Bethlehem (G-1506)
Faull Fabricating Inc	G	724 458-7662	Grove City (G-6784)
Fenton Welding LLC	E	570 746-9018	Wyalusing (G-20252)
Ferguson Welding Inc	F	717 292-4179	Dover (G-4192)
Flinchbaugh Company Inc	E	717 266-2202	Manchester (G-10356)
Flint Road Welding	G	717 535-5282	Mifflintown (G-11118)
Flurer Machine and Tool	G	610 759-6114	Bethlehem (G-1514)
Fountain Fabricating Co	G	570 682-9018	Hegins (G-7541)
Fox Welding Shop Inc	G	215 225-3069	Philadelphia (G-13716)
Frank Bellace Welding	G	856 488-8099	Danville (G-4002)
Frazier-Simplex Machine Co	E	724 222-5700	Washington (G-19177)
Freedom Welding	G	717 437-0943	Burnham (G-2360)
G-S Hydraulics Inc	F	814 938-2862	Punxsutawney (G-16141)
General Welding & Machine Co	G	570 889-3776	Ringtown (G-16753)
General Weldments Inc	F	724 744-2105	Irwin (G-8164)
George I Reitz & Sons Inc	E	814 849-2308	Brookville (G-2261)
George I Reitz & Sons Inc	G	412 824-9976	East Pittsburgh (G-4595)
Germantown Welding Co	G	215 843-2643	Philadelphia (G-13758)
Gouldey Welding & Fabrications	E	215 721-9522	Souderton (G-17737)
Grahams Welding	G	724 627-6082	Waynesburg (G-19442)
Gregory Racing Fabrications	G	610 759-8217	Nazareth (G-11970)
Grimm Machine & Model	G	724 228-2133	Washington (G-19182)
Gross Bros Wldg Fbrication Inc	G	814 443-1130	Somerset (G-17691)
H & H Manufacturing Co Inc	D	610 532-1250	Folcroft (G-6004)
H and H Tool	G	814 333-4677	Meadville (G-10732)
Hamill Manufacturing Company	D	724 744-2131	Trafford (G-18457)
Haverstick Bros Inc	F	717 392-5722	Lancaster (G-9040)
Hawk Industrial Services LLC	F	717 658-4332	Chambersburg (G-2939)
Hazleton Custom Metal Products	F	570 455-0450	Hazleton (G-7501)
Healey Welding Co Inc	G	570 655-9437	Pittston (G-15755)
Hendricks Welding Service Inc	G	215 757-5369	Langhorne (G-9301)
Henrys Welding Inc	G	717 548-2460	Drumore (G-4378)
Herkules USA Corporation	C	724 763-2066	Ford City (G-6047)
Hetrick Mfg Inc	F	724 335-0455	Lower Burrell (G-10106)

Hill John M Machine Co Inc	E	610 562-8690	Hamburg (G-6841)
Hills Machine Shop	G	570 645-8787	Lansford (G-9447)
Hills Micro Weld Inc	G	814 336-4511	Meadville (G-10735)
Hillside Custom Mac Wel & Fab	F	610 942-3093	Honey Brook (G-7748)
Hines Industries Inc	G	610 264-1656	Whitehall (G-19875)
Hy-Tech Machine Inc	D	724 776-6800	Cranberry Township (G-3823)
Innovative Machining Tech Inc	E	610 473-5600	Boyertown (G-1918)
Integrated Power Services LLC	F	724 225-2900	Washington (G-19186)
Ira G Steffy and Son Inc	D	717 626-6500	Ephrata (G-5111)
J & S Machining Corp	F	717 653-6358	Manheim (G-10391)
J and B Precision Machine Co	G	215 822-1400	Hatfield (G-7355)
J C Moore Sales Corp	G	724 475-4605	Fredonia (G-6183)
J M T Machine Company	E	215 934-7600	Huntingdon Valley (G-7998)
J R Young	G	717 935-2919	Belleville (G-1132)
J Russel Tooling Co	G	724 423-2766	Calumet (G-2472)
Jack Garner & Sons Inc	G	717 367-8866	Mount Joy (G-11663)
James A Schultz	F	814 763-5561	Saegertown (G-16919)
Jeffery Faust	G	610 759-1951	Nazareth (G-11973)
Jfs Welding	G	717 687-6554	Paradise (G-13160)
Jobco Mfg & Stl Fabrication	G	724 266-3210	Ambridge (G-622)
Joel Freidhoff	G	814 536-6458	Johnstown (G-8387)
Joes Welding Repairs	G	570 546-5223	Muncy (G-11822)
John H Bricker Welding	F	717 263-5588	Chambersburg (G-2946)
John Jost Jr Inc	G	610 395-5461	Allentown (G-269)
Johns Welding Shop	G	814 643-4564	Huntingdon (G-7948)
Johnsons Frog & Rail Wldg Inc	G	724 475-2305	Greenville (G-6752)
Johnstown Wldg Fabrication Inc	C	800 225-9353	Johnstown (G-8394)
Keystone Foundation Service	G	215 968-2955	Newtown (G-12514)
Kiski Precision Industries LLC	E	724 845-2799	Leechburg (G-9646)
Kittatinny Manufacturing Svcs	F	717 530-1242	Shippensburg (G-17536)
Kottcamp Sheet Metal	E	717 845-7616	York (G-20558)
Kovacs Manufacturing Inc	F	215 355-1985	Southampton (G-17821)
L Richard Sensenig Co	D	717 733-0364	Ephrata (G-5117)
Leiss Tool & Die	C	814 444-1444	Somerset (G-17695)
Leonhardt Manufacturing Co Inc	D	717 632-4150	Hanover (G-6915)
Lesko Enterprises Inc	C	814 756-4030	Albion (G-46)
Lewis Welding Services Inc	G	814 838-1074	Erie (G-5363)
Lights Welding Inc	F	717 838-3931	Annville (G-653)
Logue Industries Inc	E	570 368-2639	Montoursville (G-11445)
Longwood Manufacturing Corp	F	610 444-4200	Kennett Square (G-8523)
M and P Custom Design Inc	F	610 444-0244	Kennett Square (G-8524)
M&B Enterprises Inc	G	814 454-4461	Erie (G-5377)
Machine Specialties	G	717 264-0061	Chambersburg (G-2955)
Machining Center	G	724 530-7212	Slippery Rock (G-17621)
Mariano Welding Corp	G	610 626-0975	Clifton Heights (G-3255)

Mark Tk Welding Inc	F	724 545-2001	Kittanning (G-8779)
Martindale Welding LLC	G	717 445-4666	Ephrata (G-5124)
Martins Steel LLC	G	570 966-3775	Mifflinburg (G-11097)
Martys Muffler & Weld Shop	G	412 673-4141	North Versailles (G-12781)
Maxwell Welding and Mch Inc	E	724 729-3160	Burgettstown (G-2349)
McKinley Blacksmith Limited	G	610 459-2730	Boothwyn (G-1879)
McShane Welding Company Inc	E	814 459-3797	Erie (G-5387)
Meadowcreek Welding LLC	G	717 354-7533	New Holland (G-12261)
Mill Professional Services	F	724 335-4625	New Kensington (G-12357)
Miller Welding and Machine Co	C	814 849-3061	Brookville (G-2265)
Miller Welding Service	G	814 238-2950	State College (G-17991)
Millers Welding & Repair	G	610 593-6112	Christiana (G-3142)
Mobile Welding & Boiler Repair	F	610 253-9688	Easton (G-4725)
Mohney Fabricating & Mfg LLC	G	724 349-6136	Penn Run (G-13229)
Moore Welding	G	814 328-2399	Brockway (G-2228)
Moreno Welding Service	G	717 646-0000	Hanover (G-6923)
Moritz Machine & Repairs LLC	G	717 677-6838	Biglerville (G-1667)
Mountain Top Welding & Repair	G	570 888-7174	Gillett (G-6382)
Mountaintop Welding	G	814 387-9353	Clarence (G-3164)
Murslack Welding Inc	G	412 364-5554	Pittsburgh (G-15312)
Mwi Service	G	717 578-2324	Spring Grove (G-17879)
Myers Wldg & Fabrication Inc	G	717 502-7473	Dillsburg (G-4139)
Napotnik Welding Inc	G	814 446-4500	New Florence (G-12199)
Nelson Stud Welding Inc	G	610 873-0012	Downingtown (G-4244)
Nestors Welding Co	G	570 668-3401	Tamaqua (G-18221)
Niagara Manufacturing Co	F	814 838-4511	Erie (G-5403)
Nichols Welding Service Inc	G	412 362-8855	Pittsburgh (G-15338)
Norman Hoover Welding LLC	G	717 445-5333	Ephrata (G-5134)
Novinger Welding Repair Inc	G	570 758-6592	Herndon (G-7602)
Nuweld Inc	C	570 505-1500	Williamsport (G-20051)
P & R United Welding and Fabg	F	610 375-9928	Reading (G-16461)
P K B Inc	G	215 826-1988	Bristol (G-2178)
Pannell Mfg Corp	G	610 268-2012	Avondale (G-856)
Paragon Welding Company Inc	G	215 634-7300	Philadelphia (G-14121)
Penn Fabrication LLC	F	610 292-1980	Norristown (G-12702)
Penn Weld Inc	G	814 332-3682	Meadville (G-10775)
Phil Skrzat	G	215 257-8583	Perkasie (G-13289)
Philadelphia Pipe Bending Co	E	215 225-8955	Philadelphia (G-14149)
Pocono Protech	G	610 681-3550	Gilbert (G-6363)
Precision Metal Crafters Ltd	E	724 837-2511	Greensburg (G-6704)
Production Plus Steel Inc	G	724 376-3634	Sandy Lake (G-17061)
Prompton Tool Inc	D	570 253-4141	Honesdale (G-7720)
Quality Metal Works Inc	F	717 367-2120	Elizabethtown (G-4882)
R G S Machine Inc	G	610 532-1850	Folsom (G-6027)
R H Benedix Contracting	G	610 889-7472	Malvern (G-10306)

Randy Brensinger ....G....... 610 562-2184
  Hamburg (G-6851)
Raphael A Ingaglio ....G....... 570 289-5000
  Hop Bottom (G-7775)
Raser Industries Inc ....F....... 610 320-5130
  Reading (G-16484)
Reading Equipment & Dist LLC ....E....... 717 445-6746
  Abington (G-14)
Red Bank Welding ....G....... 570 966-0695
  Mifflinburg (G-11101)
Revtur Welding Company LLC ....G....... 215 672-8233
  Warminster (G-18955)
Riley Welding and Fabg Inc ....F....... 717 637-6014
  Hanover (G-6944)
Rizzo & Sons Industrial Svc Co ....E....... 814 948-5381
  Pittsburgh (G-15489)
Robbie Holland ....G....... 610 495-5441
  Royersford (G-16862)
Robert Urda Jr ....G....... 724 775-9333
  Monaca (G-11295)
Rochester Machine Corporation ....E....... 724 843-7820
  New Brighton (G-12040)
Rod Quellette ....G....... 814 274-8812
  Coudersport (G-3788)
Ronald E Koller Welding ....G....... 412 859-6781
  Coraopolis (G-3724)
Rose Corporation ....D....... 610 376-5004
  Reading (G-16504)
Royal Hydraulic Svc & Mfg Inc ....E....... 724 945-6800
  Cokeburg (G-3364)
Ryders Welding LLC ....G....... 717 369-5198
  Chambersburg (G-2974)
S & D Welding Inc ....G....... 570 546-8772
  Muncy (G-11832)
Sac Industries Inc ....F....... 412 787-7500
  Pittsburgh (G-15505)
Saeger Machine Inc ....G....... 215 256-8754
  Harleysville (G-7056)
Sanfelice Wldg Fabrication LLC ....G....... 610 337-4125
  Norristown (G-12709)
Schnure Manufacturing Co Inc ....F....... 610 273-3352
  Honey Brook (G-7762)
Scranton Sheet Metal Inc ....E....... 570 342-2904
  Scranton (G-17288)
Servedio A Elc Mtr Svc Inc ....F....... 724 658-8041
  New Castle (G-12148)
Sha Co Welding & Fabrication.............G....... 724 588-0993
  Greenville (G-6773)
Shearers Welding Inc ....G....... 717 361-9196
  Elizabethtown (G-4887)
Skias Chuck Wldg & Fabricators..........G....... 610 375-0912
  Reading (G-16519)
Sky Oxygen Inc ....E....... 412 278-3001
  Carnegie (G-2793)
Smoker Manufacturing ....G....... 717 529-6915
  Oxford (G-13092)
Snyder Welding LLC ....G....... 610 657-4916
  Slatington (G-17614)
Soul Customs Metal Works ....G....... 610 881-4300
  Pen Argyl (G-13218)
Specialized Welding Inc ....G....... 724 733-7801
  Export (G-5627)
Speranza Specialty Machining ....G....... 724 733-8045
  Export (G-5628)
Spicer Wldg & Fabrication Inc ....G....... 814 355-7046
  Bellefonte (G-1119)
Spicer Wldg & Fabrication Inc ....G....... 814 355-7046
  Julian (G-8456)
State of ARC Wldg & Fabg LLC ....G....... 610 216-6862
  Bangor (G-930)
Stengels Welding Shop Inc ....G....... 610 444-4110
  Kennett Square (G-8544)
Stephen R Lechman ....G....... 570 636-3159
  Freeland (G-6196)
Stoltzfus Custom Welding ....G....... 717 477-8200
  Orrstown (G-13035)
Subcon Tl/Cctool Mch Group Inc ....E....... 814 456-7797
  Erie (G-5494)
Sullis Wldg & Pipe Fitting LLC ....G....... 814 445-9147
  Somerset (G-17713)
Superior Welding Co ....G....... 570 344-4212
  Scranton (G-17296)
T & L Welding ....F....... 724 354-3538
  Kittanning (G-8799)
T & T Machine & Welding Co ....G....... 814 845-9054
  Glen Campbell (G-6425)
Temperature Ctrl Professionals...........G....... 215 295-1616
  Fairless Hills (G-5803)
Terry L Handwerk ....G....... 610 262-0986
  Northampton (G-12862)

Three Rivers Gamma Service ....G....... 724 947-9020
  Burgettstown (G-2357)
Titan Metal & Machine Co Inc ....G....... 724 747-9528
  Washington (G-19232)
Tooling Specialists Inc ....D....... 724 539-2534
  Latrobe (G-9524)
Tri-State Welding Corp ....G....... 610 374-0321
  Reading (G-16549)
Trico Welding Company ....F....... 724 722-1300
  Yukon (G-20785)
Trs Welding & Fabrication Inc ....F....... 610 369-0897
  Gilbertsville (G-6378)
True Position Inc ....F....... 724 444-0300
  Gibsonia (G-6357)
Unity Fabrication Tech Inc ....F....... 724 423-7500
  Greensburg (G-6726)
Universal Mch Co Pottstown Inc ....D....... 610 323-1810
  Pottstown (G-16062)
Vegely Welding Inc ....F....... 412 469-9808
  Duquesne (G-4501)
Versatech Incorporated ....D....... 724 327-8324
  Export (G-5631)
W & W Welding Inc ....G....... 717 336-4314
  Reinholds (G-16637)
W C H Inc ....G....... 814 725-8431
  North East (G-12765)
W V Fabricating & Welding Inc ....G....... 724 266-3000
  Ambridge (G-637)
Wakefield Steel & Welding LLC ....E....... 717 548-2172
  Peach Bottom (G-13204)
Walsh Tool Company Inc ....G....... 570 823-1375
  Wilkes Barre (G-19969)
Walter McClelland Jr LLC ....G....... 814 378-7434
  Madera (G-10164)
Waste Gas Fabricating Co Inc ....E....... 215 736-9240
  Fairless Hills (G-5807)
Watts Welding Shop LLC ....G....... 570 398-1184
  Jersey Shore (G-8324)
Wegco Welding Inc ....G....... 412 833-7020
  Bethel Park (G-1438)
Wel-Mac Inc ....G....... 717 637-6921
  Hanover (G-6974)
Weld Tek Ltd ....G....... 717 367-0666
  Elizabethtown (G-4890)
Welding & Thermal Technologies ....G....... 610 678-4847
  Reading (G-16563)
Welding Alloys USA ....G....... 724 202-7497
  New Castle (G-12167)
Werner Welding LLC ....G....... 724 379-4240
  Elizabeth (G-4864)
Westmrland Stl Fabrication Inc ....E....... 724 446-0555
  Madison (G-10167)
Wolbert Welding Inc ....G....... 814 437-2870
  Franklin (G-6170)
X-Mark/Cdt Inc ....G....... 724 228-7373
  Washington (G-19248)
Y B Welding Inc ....G....... 717 267-0104
  Chambersburg (G-3001)
Youngs Truck Repair LLC ....F....... 570 329-3571
  South Williamsport (G-17794)
Zambotti Collision & Wldg Ctr ....G....... 724 545-2305
  Kittanning (G-8804)
Zimm-O-Matic LLC ....G....... 717 445-6432
  Denver (G-4098)

WELDING SPLYS, EXC GASES: Wholesalers

Airgas Safety Inc ....C....... 215 826-9000
  Levittown (G-9814)
Sky Oxygen Inc ....E....... 412 278-3001
  Carnegie (G-2793)
Wilson Pdts Compressed Gas Co ....E....... 610 253-9608
  Easton (G-4777)

WELDMENTS

Custom Engineering Co ....C....... 814 898-1390
  Erie (G-5237)
Harliss Specialties Corp ....E....... 724 863-0321
  Irwin (G-8166)
Shoemaker Mfg Solutions Inc ....E....... 215 723-5567
  Souderton (G-17764)
Van Industries Inc ....E....... 610 582-1118
  Birdsboro (G-1707)
Zeyon Inc ....E....... 814 899-3311
  Erie (G-5536)

WET CORN MILLING

Penford Carolina LLC ....E....... 570 218-4321
  Berwick (G-1340)

WHEEL & CASTER REPAIR SVCS

Advanced Machine Systems Inc ....F....... 610 837-8677
  Bath (G-949)

WHEELBARROWS

Ames Companies Inc ....B....... 717 737-1500
  Camp Hill (G-2488)

WHEELCHAIR LIFTS

Haveco Inc ....G....... 717 558-4301
  Harrisburg (G-7146)
Malek Ham ....G....... 610 691-7600
  Bethlehem (G-1565)
McKnight Surgical Inc ....G....... 412 821-9000
  Pittsburgh (G-15270)
Sure-Lok Inc ....E....... 610 814-0300
  Easton (G-4757)
Thyssenkrupp Elevator Corp ....E....... 412 364-2624
  Pittsburgh (G-15623)
Total Mobility Services Inc ....G....... 814 629-9935
  Boswell (G-1885)

WHEELCHAIRS

Golden Brothers Inc ....C....... 570 457-0867
  Old Forge (G-12965)
Laveings Mobility ....G....... 724 368-9417
  Portersville (G-15930)
Ms Wheelchair PA Program ....G....... 814 331-1722
  Bradford (G-1984)
Sr Jan Fisher ....G....... 724 841-0508
  Lyndora (G-10136)
Trac Fabrication Inc ....G....... 717 862-8722
  Slippery Rock (G-17628)
Uds Home Medical Equipment LLC ....G....... 717 665-1490
  Lancaster (G-9227)
Visco ....G....... 215 420-7437
  Warminster (G-18995)

WHEELS & BRAKE SHOES: Railroad, Cast Iron

Workmaster Inc ....G....... 866 476-9217
  Malvern (G-10349)

WHEELS & GRINDSTONES, EXC ARTIFICIAL: Abrasive

Jowitt & Rodgers Company ....E....... 215 824-0401
  Philadelphia (G-13912)
Red Hill Grinding Wheel Corp................E....... 215 679-7964
  Pennsburg (G-13255)
Wilder Diamond Blades Inc....................G....... 570 222-9590
  Kingsley (G-8710)

WHEELS & PARTS

Jack Williams Tire Co Inc ....F....... 610 437-4651
  Whitehall (G-19878)

WHEELS: Abrasive

Calder Industries Inc ....F....... 814 422-8026
  Spring Mills (G-17886)
Edmar Abrasive Company ....F....... 610 544-4900
  Broomall (G-2288)
Pacer Industries Inc ....F....... 610 383-4200
  Coatesville (G-3320)
Schaffner Manufacturing Co ....D....... 412 761-9902
  Pittsburgh (G-15515)

WHEELS: Disc, Wheelbarrow, Stroller, Etc, Stamped Metal

Bond Caster and Wheel Corp ....F....... 717 665-2275
  Manheim (G-10372)
Sosko Manufacturing Inc ....G....... 724 879-4117
  Latrobe (G-9521)

WHEELS: Iron & Steel, Locomotive & Car

Standard Steel LLC ....B....... 717 242-4615
  Burnham (G-2362)

WHEELS: Railroad Car, Cast Steel

Trinity Industries ....G....... 724 588-7000
  Greenville (G-6774)

PRODUCT

WHEELS: Rolled, Locomotive

N M A ....F 814 453-6787
Erie (G-5401)

WHIRLPOOL BATHS: Hydrotherapy

Baker Hydro Incorporated ....G...... 717 764-8581
York (G-20399)

Hydroworx International Inc ....E 717 902-1923
Middletown (G-11057)

Mgs04 Corporation ....G...... 267 249-2372
Philadelphia (G-14018)

WHISTLES

Whistle Pig Pumpkin Patch ....G...... 570 298-0962
Noxen (G-12886)

WHITING MINING: Crushed & Broken

Allan Myers Materials Inc ....C 610 560-7900
Worcester (G-20222)

WIGS & HAIRPIECES

Amekor Industries Inc ....D...... 610 825-6747
Conshohocken (G-3518)

Henry Margu Inc ....F 610 622-0515
Lansdowne (G-9434)

WIGS, WHOLESALE

Amekor Industries Inc ....D...... 610 825-6747
Conshohocken (G-3518)

WINCHES

General Machine Pdts Kt LLC ....D...... 215 357-5500
Trevose (G-18496)

United Theatrical Services ....G...... 215 242-2134
Philadelphia (G-14424)

WINDINGS: Coil, Electronic

Coil Specialty Co Inc ....E 814 234-7044
State College (G-17952)

Northern Winding Inc ....G...... 724 776-4983
Mars (G-10509)

WINDMILLS: Electric Power Generation

American Eagle Windmills LLC ....G...... 814 922-3180
West Springfield (G-19766)

Fiberblade LLC ....C...... 814 361-8730
Feasterville Trevose (G-5908)

Gamesa Energy Usa Inc ....F 215 665-9810
Trevose (G-18495)

Gamesa Wind Pa LLC ....F 215 665-9810
Philadelphia (G-13742)

Iberdrola Renewable ....F 610 254-9800
Radnor (G-16294)

Siemens Gamesa Renewable ....G...... 215 665-9810
Philadelphia (G-14303)

Siemens Gamesa Renewable ....G...... 215 710-3100
Feasterville Trevose (G-5930)

Windurance ....G...... 814 678-1318
Seneca (G-17372)

WINDOW & DOOR FRAMES

Caff Co ....G...... 412 787-1761
Pittsburgh (G-14799)

Household Metals Inc ....D...... 215 634-2800
Philadelphia (G-13835)

Kawneer Commercial Windows LLC ....D...... 724 776-7000
Cranberry Township (G-3827)

Kensington Hpp Inc ....E 866 318-6628
Vandergrift (G-18731)

Pella Corporation ....G...... 610 648-0922
Berwyn (G-1370)

Q C M Corporation ....F 610 586-4770
Folcroft (G-6013)

Solar Innovations Inc ....C 570 915-1500
Pine Grove (G-14605)

Trimline Windows Inc ....D...... 215 672-5233
Ivyland (G-8224)

WINDOW CLEANING SVCS

DW Services LLC ....G...... 484 241-8915
Allentown (G-198)

Shamrock Building Services Inc ....E 412 279-2800
Carnegie (G-2792)

WINDOW FRAMES & SASHES: Plastic

Grand Openings Inc ....G...... 724 325-2029
Murrysville (G-11852)

Interstate Building Mtls Inc ....D...... 570 655-8496
Pittston (G-15757)

Interstate Building Mtls Inc ....E 570 655-2811
Pittston (G-15758)

J & L Building Materials Inc ....C 610 644-6311
Malvern (G-10257)

MI Windows and Doors Inc ....G...... 717 365-3300
Gratz (G-6578)

Regency Plus Inc ....E 570 339-1390
Mount Carmel (G-11629)

WINDOW FRAMES, MOLDING & TRIM: Vinyl

JC Vinyl Fence Rail & Deck ....G...... 570 282-2222
Carbondale (G-2680)

Seaway Manufacturing Corp ....D...... 814 898-2255
Erie (G-5472)

Seven D Industries LP ....C 814 317-4077
Hollidaysburg (G-7654)

Southwest Vinyl Windows Inc ....F 610 626-8826
Lansdowne (G-9444)

Superior Window Mfg Inc ....F 412 793-3500
Pittsburgh (G-15589)

Ventana USA ....D...... 724 325-3400
Export (G-5630)

Viwinco Inc ....C 610 286-8884
Morgantown (G-11543)

WINDOW FURNISHINGS WHOLESALERS

Bishops Inc ....G...... 412 821-3333
Mars (G-10488)

New Home Window Shade Co Inc ....E 570 346-2047
Clarks Green (G-3189)

WINDOW SCREENING: Plastic

Nushield Inc ....G...... 215 500-6426
Newtown (G-12530)

WINDOWS: Frames, Wood

Allied Millwork of Pittsburgh ....G...... 412 471-9229
Pittsburgh (G-14685)

Burke & Sons Inc ....E 814 938-7303
Punxsutawney (G-16129)

Jeld-Wen Inc ....C 570 889-3173
Ringtown (G-16754)

JF Mill and Lumber Co ....G...... 724 654-9542
New Castle (G-12109)

Northeast Building Pdts Corp ....C 215 535-7110
Philadelphia (G-14079)

Weather Shield Mfg Inc ....B 717 761-7131
Camp Hill (G-2524)

WINDOWS: Wood

Detroit Switch Inc ....E 412 322-9144
Pittsburgh (G-14919)

Jwi Architectural Millwork Inc ....E 717 328-5880
Mercersburg (G-10988)

Pella Corporation ....G...... 610 648-0922
Berwyn (G-1370)

Pella Corporation ....B 610 648-0922
Berwyn (G-1371)

Pella Corporation ....B 610 648-0922
Berwyn (G-1372)

WINDSHIELD WIPER SYSTEMS

Raineater LLC ....G...... 814 806-3100
Erie (G-5454)

Thermalblade LLC ....G...... 570 995-1425
Muncy Valley (G-11843)

WINDSHIELDS: Plastic

L P Aero Plastics Inc ....E 724 744-4448
Jeannette (G-8260)

WINE & DISTILLED ALCOHOLIC BEVERAGES WHOLESALERS

Boardroom Spirits LLC ....G...... 215 815-5351
Lansdale (G-9348)

Gablers Beverage Distributors ....G...... 717 532-2241
Shippensburg (G-17528)

WINE CELLARS, BONDED: Wine, Blended

ADello Vineyard & Winery LLC ....G...... 610 754-0006
Perkiomenville (G-13299)

Bostwick Enterprises Inc ....F 814 725-8015
North East (G-12733)

Buckingham Valley Vineyards ....G...... 215 794-7188
Buckingham (G-2338)

Cassel Vineyards Hershey LLC ....G...... 717 533-2008
Hummelstown (G-7905)

Folino Estate LLC ....G...... 484 256-5300
Kutztown (G-8843)

Hauser Estate Inc ....G...... 717 334-4888
Gettysburg (G-6298)

Heritage Wine Cellars Inc ....F 814 725-8748
North East (G-12748)

Hunter Valley Winery ....G...... 717 444-7211
Liverpool (G-10078)

Penn Sauna Corp ....E 610 932-5700
Oxford (G-13087)

Penn Sauna Corp ....E 610 932-5700
Paoli (G-13146)

Sand Castle Winery ....F 610 294-9181
Erwinna (G-5539)

Vineyard At Grandview LLC ....G...... 717 653-4825
Mount Joy (G-11675)

Vynecrest LLC ....F 610 398-7525
Breinigsville (G-2030)

WIRE

Aristo-TEC Metal Forms Inc ....E 724 626-5900
Connellsville (G-3489)

Iwm International LLC ....G...... 800 323-5585
York (G-20538)

Legrand Home Systems Inc ....D...... 717 702-2532
Middletown (G-11060)

Lift-Tech Inc ....G...... 717 898-6615
Landisville (G-9263)

Mount Joy Wire Corporation ....C 717 653-1461
Mount Joy (G-11666)

Pennheat LLC ....E 814 282-6774
Meadville (G-10777)

Quality Wire Forming ....G...... 717 656-4478
Leola (G-9799)

Tatano Wire and Steel Inc ....E 724 746-3118
Canonsburg (G-2645)

Z & F USA ....G...... 412 257-8575
Bridgeville (G-2100)

WIRE & CABLE: Aluminum

Bower Wire Cloth TI & Die Inc ....G...... 570 398-4488
Jersey Shore (G-8310)

US Custom Wiring LLC ....G...... 856 905-0250
Philadelphia (G-14435)

WIRE & CABLE: Aluminum

Valley Precision TI & Tech Inc ....E 717 647-7550
Tower City (G-18443)

WIRE & CABLE: Nonferrous, Building

Genergy Power LLC ....G...... 717 584-0375
Lancaster (G-9027)

WIRE & WIRE PRDTS

A V Weber Co Inc ....G...... 215 699-3527
North Wales (G-12784)

Ace Wire Spring & Form Co Inc ....E 412 331-3353
Mc Kees Rocks (G-10601)

Aeroparts Fabg & Machining Inc ....E 814 948-6015
Nicktown (G-12618)

American Lifting Products Inc ....E 610 384-1300
Coatesville (G-3287)

Amsteel Inc ....F 724 758-5566
Ellwood City (G-4926)

Bedford Reinforced Plas Inc ....D...... 814 623-8125
Bedford (G-1044)

Cambria County Asso ....B 814 536-3531
Johnstown (G-8360)

Cambria County Asso ....C 814 472-5077
Ebensburg (G-4782)

Cobra Wire & Cable Inc ....E 215 674-8773
Huntingdon Valley (G-7970)

Daniel Gerard Worldwide Inc ....G...... 717 630-3787
Hanover (G-6874)

Daniel Gerard Worldwide Inc ....C 717 637-3250
Hanover (G-6875)

Display Source Alliance LLC ....G...... 717 534-0884
Hershey (G-7608)

Eis Inc ....E 215 674-8773
Huntingdon Valley (G-7976)

Erisco Industries Inc ....D 814 459-2720
North East (G-12741)

ESAB Group Inc ....B 717 637-8911
Hanover (G-6884)

ESAB Group Inc ....C 843 673-7700
Hanover (G-6885)

Eysters Machine Shop Inc ....E 717 227-8400
Shrewsbury (G-17583)

Federal-Mogul Powertrain LLC ....D 610 363-2600
Exton (G-5677)

Gemel Precision Tool Inc ....E 215 355-2174
Warminster (G-18886)

Gems Services Inc ....G 215 399-8932
Philadelphia (G-13748)

General Cable Corporation ....C 570 321-7750
Williamsport (G-20017)

Hanover Wire Cloth ....G 717 637-3795
Hanover (G-6902)

Heritage Fence Company ....F 610 584-6710
Skippack (G-17599)

Hohmann & Barnard Inc ....G 610 873-0070
Chester Springs (G-3080)

Ivy Steel & Wire Inc ....D 570 450-2090
Hazle Township (G-7465)

Iwm International LLC ....C 717 637-3795
Hanover (G-6905)

Jackburn Corporation ....E 814 774-3573
Girard (G-6392)

Jackburn Mfg Inc ....F 814 774-3573
Girard (G-6393)

Jerith Manufacturing LLC ....D 215 676-4068
Philadelphia (G-13893)

Kane Innovations Inc ....D 814 838-7731
Erie (G-5342)

Keystone Automatic Tech Inc ......E 814 486-0513
Emporium (G-5066)

Leonard Leibensperger ....G 610 926-7491
Mohrsville (G-11277)

M Dobron & Sons Inc ....G 215 297-5331
Point Pleasant (G-15887)

Manley Fence Co ....G 610 842-8833
Coatesville (G-3316)

Markel Corp ....C 610 272-8960
Plymouth Meeting (G-15855)

Metro International Corp ....E 570 825-2741
Wilkes Barre (G-19943)

Miller Edge Inc ....D 610 869-4422
West Grove (G-19702)

N C Stauffer & Sons Inc ....D 570 945-3047
Factoryville (G-5758)

North American Fencing Corp ......E 412 362-3900
Cheswick (G-3113)

North American Stl & Wire Inc .....E 724 431-0626
Butler (G-2426)

North American Wire LLC ....G 724 431-0626
Butler (G-2427)

Northeast Fence & Ir Works Inc ...E 215 335-1681
Philadelphia (G-14082)

Northeimer Manufacturing ....E 610 926-1136
Leesport (G-9672)

Peerless Chain Company ....F 800 395-2445
Mount Pleasant (G-11710)

Pendu Manufacturing Inc ....E 717 354-4348
New Holland (G-12272)

Penn-Elkco Inc ....F 814 834-4304
Saint Marys (G-17003)

Pennsylvania Sling Co ....G 717 657-7700
Harrisburg (G-7195)

Pittsburgh Fence Co Inc ....E 724 775-6550
Carnegie (G-2780)

Quality Fencing & Supply ....E 717 355-7112
New Holland (G-12276)

Rfcircuits Inc ....F 215 364-2450
Huntingdon Valley (G-8029)

Selectrode Industries Inc ....E 724 378-6351
Aliquippa (G-93)

Sheffield Container Corp ....E 814 968-3287
Sheffield (G-17483)

Stanton Dynamics Inc ....F 814 849-6255
Brookville (G-2272)

Tatano Wire and Steel Inc ....E 724 746-3118
Canonsburg (G-2645)

Tatano Wire and Steel Inc ....G 724 746-3118
Houston (G-7880)

Torpedo Specialty Wire Inc ....E 814 563-7505
Pittsfield (G-15739)

Tricor Industries Inc ....F 610 265-1111
Norristown (G-12721)

Vogan Mfg Inc ....G 717 354-9954
New Holland (G-12292)

Wire and Cable Specialties Inc ....D 610 466-6200
Coatesville (G-3330)

Wire and Cable Specialties Inc ....E 610 692-7551
West Chester (G-19679)

Wire Crafters ....D 610 296-2538
Malvern (G-10347)

Wire Mesh Products Inc ....E 717 848-3620
York (G-20714)

Wire Mesh Sales LLC ....E 724 245-9577
New Salem (G-12446)

Wirerope Works Inc ....B 570 327-4229
Williamsport (G-20096)

Yeager Wire Works Inc ....G 570 752-2769
Berwick (G-1349)

WIRE CLOTH & WOVEN WIRE PRDTS, MADE FROM PURCHASED WIRE

C C B B Inc ....F 215 364-5377
Feasterville Trevose (G-5898)

Melrath Gasket Inc ....D 215 223-6000
Philadelphia (G-14007)

WIRE CLOTH: Fourdrinier, Made From Purchased Wire

Voith Paper Fabric and Roll Sy .....C 717 792-7000
York (G-20700)

WIRE FABRIC: Welded Steel

A & B Steelworks LLC ....F 717 823-8599
Myerstown (G-11872)

Dellovade Fabricators Inc ....F 615 370-7000
Avella (G-835)

WIRE FENCING & ACCESS WHOLESALERS

American Fence Inc ....F 610 437-1944
Whitehall (G-19861)

County Line Fence Co ....F 215 343-5085
Warrington (G-19112)

Genie Electronics Co Inc ....D 717 244-1099
Red Lion (G-16598)

Genie Electronics Co Inc ....D 717 244-1099
Red Lion (G-16599)

Leahmarlin Corp ....G 610 692-7378
West Chester (G-19589)

Machining Center ....G 724 530-7212
Slippery Rock (G-17621)

Specialty Building Systems ....G 610 954-0595
Easton (G-4754)

United Fence Supply Company .....G 570 307-0782
Olyphant (G-13002)

WIRE MATERIALS: Aluminum

General Cable Corporation ....C 570 321-7750
Williamsport (G-20017)

WIRE MATERIALS: Copper

General Cable Corporation ....C 570 321-7750
Williamsport (G-20017)

WIRE MATERIALS: Steel

Ace Wire Spring & Form Co Inc ....E 412 331-3353
Mc Kees Rocks (G-10601)

All Steel Supply Inc ....E 215 672-0883
Horsham (G-7781)

American Wire Research Inc ....E 412 349-8431
Wilmerding (G-20159)

Belden Inc ....C 724 222-7060
Washington (G-19153)

Bombardier Transportation ....A 412 655-5700
Pittsburgh (G-14782)

Business Wire Inc ....G 610 617-9560
Plymouth Meeting (G-15836)

Carpenter Technology Corp ....B 610 208-2000
Philadelphia (G-13508)

DSI-Lang Geotech LLC ....G 610 268-2221
Toughkenamon (G-18418)

ESAB Group Inc ....B 717 637-8911
Hanover (G-6884)

ESAB Group Inc ....C 843 673-7700
Hanover (G-6885)

Esmark Excalibur LLC ....E 814 382-5696
Meadville (G-10721)

Glenfield Supply Company Inc .....G 412 781-8188
Pittsburgh (G-15051)

Grassroots Unwired Inc ....G 215 788-1210
Bristol (G-2150)

HIG Capital LLC ....C 610 495-7011
Royersford (G-16851)

Ism Enterprises Inc ....G 800 378-3430
Butler (G-2411)

Ivy Steel & Wire Inc ....D 570 450-2090
Hazle Township (G-7465)

Keystone Spike ....G 717 270-2700
Lebanon (G-9594)

Markel Corp ....C 610 272-8960
Plymouth Meeting (G-15855)

Mlp Steel LLC ....E 724 887-7720
Everson (G-5580)

Mlp Steel LLC ....E 724 887-8100
Scottdale (G-17195)

Nexans USA Inc ....B 717 354-6200
New Holland (G-12271)

North Jckson Specialty Stl LLC ....C 412 257-7600
Bridgeville (G-2083)

Northeast Fence & Ir Works Inc ...E 215 335-1681
Philadelphia (G-14082)

Perryman Company ....F 724 746-9390
Coal Center (G-3276)

Precision Kidd Steel Co Inc ....G 724 695-2216
Aliquippa (G-89)

Precision Kidd Steel Co Inc ....E 724 695-2216
Clinton (G-3266)

Rapid Tag & Wire Co ....G 724 452-7760
Fombell (G-6034)

Rocky Ridge Steel LLC ....G 717 626-0153
Lititz (G-10042)

Shirk Manufacturing ....G 717 445-9353
Narvon (G-11926)

Sonco Worldwide Inc ....F 215 337-9651
Bristol (G-2200)

Susquhnna Wire Rope Rgging Inc ....G 814 772-4766
Ridgway (G-16731)

Three M Tool and Die Corp ....F 717 854-6379
York (G-20688)

Wire and Cable Specialties Inc ....D 610 466-6200
Coatesville (G-3330)

WIRE PRDTS: Ferrous Or Iron, Made In Wiredrawing Plants

Erisco Industries Inc ....D 814 459-2720
North East (G-12741)

WIRE PRDTS: Steel & Iron

Affival Inc ....G 412 826-9430
Verona (G-18745)

Affival Inc ....E 412 826-9430
Verona (G-18746)

Tatano Wire and Steel Inc ....G 724 746-3118
Houston (G-7880)

WIRE ROPE CENTERS

I & I Sling Inc ....E 800 874-3539
Aston (G-769)

Muncy Industries LLC ....G 570 649-5188
Turbotville (G-18554)

Spencer Industries Inc ....G 570 969-9931
Scranton (G-17292)

Wirerope Works Inc ....B 570 327-4229
Williamsport (G-20096)

Wirerope Works Inc ....E 570 286-0115
Sunbury (G-18177)

WIRE WHOLESALERS

Coletech ....G 814 474-3370
Fairview (G-5816)

WIRE: Communication

Brop Tech LLC ....F 323 229-7390
Upper Darby (G-18683)

Fortmex Corporation ....G 215 990-9688
Merion Station (G-10997)

Lancer Systems LP ....E 610 973-2600
Quakertown (G-16208)

WIRE: Mesh

Penn Wire Products Corporation ....G 717 664-4411
Manheim (G-10399)

Penn Wire Products Corporation ....G 717 393-2352
Lancaster (G-9164)

PRODUCT

WIRE: Nonferrous

Alpha Assembly Solutions Inc ....C 814 946-1611
Altoona **(G-470)**

American Data Link Inc ....G....... 724 503-4290
Washington **(G-19146)**

Belden Inc..D....... 724 228-7373
Washington **(G-19152)**

Belden Inc..C....... 724 222-7060
Washington **(G-19153)**

Coleman Cable LLC ....E 717 845-5100
York **(G-20428)**

Diversified Traffic Pdts Inc.................C....... 717 428-0222
Seven Valleys **(G-17377)**

Fiber Optic Marketplace LLC ....F 610 973-6000
Breinigsville **(G-2015)**

General Cable Corporation ....C....... 570 321-7750
Williamsport **(G-20017)**

General Cable Industries Inc ....C....... 814 944-5002
Altoona **(G-510)**

Industrial Enterprises Inc..................D....... 215 355-7080
Southampton **(G-17819)**

Industrial Harness Company Inc ....D....... 717 477-0100
Shippensburg **(G-17532)**

Kalas Mfg Inc.....................................D....... 717 336-5575
Lancaster **(G-9078)**

Kalas Mfg Inc.....................................D....... 717 335-0193
Denver **(G-4079)**

Marine Tech Wire and Cable Inc ....E 717 854-1992
York **(G-20581)**

Markel Corp..C....... 610 272-8960
Plymouth Meeting **(G-15855)**

Micro-Coax Inc ....C....... 610 495-4438
Pottstown **(G-16019)**

Nexans Aerospace USA LLC ....C....... 252 236-4311
New Holland **(G-12270)**

Optium Corporation...........................D....... 215 675-3105
Horsham **(G-7838)**

Ospcom LLC.......................................G....... 267 356-7124
Doylestown **(G-4321)**

Point 2 Point Wireless Inc ....G....... 347 543-5227
Macungie **(G-10156)**

Professional Electronic Compon ....G....... 215 245-1550
Philadelphia **(G-14205)**

Superior Group Inc ....E 610 397-2040
Conshohocken **(G-3610)**

Torpedo Specialty Wire Inc ....E 814 563-7505
Pittsfield **(G-15739)**

Trojan Inc...E 814 336-4468
Meadville **(G-10804)**

Tru Temp Sensors Inc ....G....... 215 396-1550
Southampton **(G-17844)**

W L Gore & Associates Inc ....A 610 268-1864
Landenberg **(G-9255)**

WIRE: Nonferrous, Appliance Fixture

Direct Wire & Cable Inc ....D....... 717 336-2842
Denver **(G-4070)**

WIRE: Steel, Insulated Or Armored

Nelson Steel Products Inc...................E 215 721-9449
Hatfield **(G-7372)**

Wirerope Works Inc ....B 570 327-4229
Williamsport **(G-20096)**

WIRE: Wire, Ferrous Or Iron

Muncy Machine & Tool Co Inc ....E 570 649-5188
Turbotville **(G-18555)**

WIRING DEVICES WHOLESALERS

T-R Associates Inc ....E 570 876-4067
Archbald **(G-696)**

WOMEN'S & CHILDREN'S CLOTHING WHOLESALERS, NEC

Alex and Ani LLC ....G....... 412 742-4968
Pittsburgh **(G-14671)**

Lifewear Inc ....E 610 327-2884
Pottstown **(G-16011)**

Peerless Printery..............................G....... 610 258-5226
Easton **(G-4741)**

Sugartown Worldwide LLC ....F 610 265-7607
King of Prussia **(G-8681)**

WOMEN'S & GIRLS' SPORTSWEAR WHOLESALERS

Robanco...G....... 412 795-7444
Pittsburgh **(G-15493)**

T A E Ltd ....G....... 215 925-7860
Philadelphia **(G-14364)**

WOMEN'S CLOTHING STORES

Eternity Fashion Inc...........................G....... 215 567-5571
Philadelphia **(G-13681)**

Mifflinburg Farmers Exchange ....G....... 570 966-4030
Mifflinburg **(G-11098)**

Youre Putting ME On Inc ....E 412 655-9666
Pittsburgh **(G-15731)**

WOMEN'S CLOTHING STORES: Ready-To-Wear

Maroco Ltd ....B 610 746-6800
Easton **(G-4719)**

Nightlife & Clothing Co.......................G....... 718 415-6391
Philadelphia **(G-14074)**

WOMEN'S FULL & KNEE LENGTH HOSIERY DYEING & FINISHING

Highland Hosiery Mills Inc ....F 215 249-3934
Dublin **(G-4433)**

U S Textile Corp ....B 828 733-9244
Feasterville Trevose **(G-5934)**

WOMEN'S KNITWEAR STORES

Gloray If LLC ....F 610 921-3300
Bernville **(G-1299)**

WOMEN'S SPORTSWEAR STORES

A & H Sportswear Co Inc......................C....... 610 759-9550
Stockertown **(G-18063)**

WOOD CARVINGS, WHOLESALE

York P-B Truss Inc ....E 717 779-0327
York **(G-20748)**

WOOD CHIPS, PRODUCED AT THE MILL

Phillips Wood Products Inc ....F 570 726-3515
Mill Hall **(G-11180)**

WOOD FENCING WHOLESALERS

Prestige Fence Co Inc ....D....... 215 362-8200
Hatfield **(G-7385)**

The Adirondack Group Inc...................E 610 431-4343
West Chester **(G-19660)**

WOOD PRDTS

Aaron E Beiler...................................G....... 717 656-9596
New Holland **(G-12224)**

Trotwood Manor.................................G....... 724 635-3057
New Stanton **(G-12452)**

WOOD PRDTS: Applicators

Great Coasters Intl Inc........................F 570 286-9330
Sunbury **(G-18170)**

WOOD PRDTS: Barrel Heading, Sawn or split

Wilson Global Inc...............................D....... 724 883-4952
Jefferson **(G-8272)**

WOOD PRDTS: Barrels & Barrel Parts

Scenic Road Manufacturing.................G....... 717 768-7300
Gordonville **(G-6565)**

WOOD PRDTS: Baskets, Fruit & Veg, Round Stave, Till, Etc

Bkts Inc..G....... 814 724-1547
Meadville **(G-10707)**

Sutherland Baskets ....G....... 610 438-8233
Easton **(G-4759)**

WOOD PRDTS: Beekeeping Splys

Door Stop Ltd ....G....... 610 353-8707
Wayne **(G-19318)**

WOOD PRDTS: Engraved

A Word Concepts Inc...........................G....... 215 924-2226
Philadelphia **(G-13329)**

Identification Systems Inc...................E 814 774-9656
Girard **(G-6391)**

Jones Crafts Inc ....G....... 610 346-6247
Kintnersville **(G-8729)**

WOOD PRDTS: Handles, Tool

Riley Tool Incorporated ....F 814 425-4140
Cochranton **(G-3350)**

WOOD PRDTS: Laundry

Groman Restoration Inc.......................G....... 724 235-5000
New Florence **(G-12197)**

John M Rohrbaugh Co Inc ....G....... 717 244-2895
Red Lion **(G-16602)**

WOOD PRDTS: Logs Of Sawdust & Wood Particles, Pressed

Ironstone Mills Inc ....G....... 717 656-4539
Leola **(G-9787)**

WOOD PRDTS: Moldings, Unfinished & Prefinished

Custer Ave Woodworking LLC ....G....... 717 354-3999
New Holland **(G-12242)**

Fremer Moulding Inc...........................F 814 265-0671
Brockway **(G-2226)**

Frosty Hollow Hardwoods....................G....... 724 568-2406
Vandergrift **(G-18728)**

Heister House Millworks Inc ....D....... 570 539-2611
Mount Pleasant Mills **(G-11725)**

Kestner Wood Products Inc ....G....... 724 368-3605
Portersville **(G-15929)**

Mars Lumber Inc ....G....... 724 625-2224
Mars **(G-10506)**

Penn Wood Products Inc ....D....... 717 259-9551
East Berlin **(G-4524)**

Smith Lawton Millwork ....G....... 570 934-2544
Montrose **(G-11477)**

Souto Mould..G....... 570 596-3128
Milan **(G-11150)**

Wood Moulding and Millwork ....F 215 324-8400
Philadelphia **(G-14484)**

WOOD PRDTS: Mulch Or Sawdust

Applegate Insul Systems Inc ....E 717 709-0533
Chambersburg **(G-2905)**

Fogle Forest Products.........................G....... 570 524-2580
Lewisburg **(G-9908)**

Frey Group LLC...................................F 717 786-2146
Quarryville **(G-16270)**

Kennett Square Specialties LLC............D....... 610 444-8122
Kennett Square **(G-8520)**

S & S Processing Inc...........................E 724 535-3110
West Pittsburg **(G-19752)**

WOOD PRDTS: Mulch, Wood & Bark

B V Landscape Supplies Inc ....G....... 610 316-1099
Malvern **(G-10191)**

Blue Mountain Processors Inc ....F 717 438-3296
Elliottsburg **(G-4919)**

Gish Logging Inc.................................E 717 369-2783
Fort Loudon **(G-6059)**

J & J Pallet Co Inc...............................E 570 489-7705
Throop **(G-18359)**

Kaiser Mulch......................................G....... 610 588-8111
Bangor **(G-918)**

Kuhns Bros Lumber Co Inc ....E 570 568-1412
Lewisburg **(G-9914)**

Sauders Nursery ....F 717 354-9851
East Earl **(G-4555)**

Tuscarora Hardwoods Inc ....D....... 717 582-4122
Elliottsburg **(G-4922)**

Weaver Mulch LLC..............................E 610 383-6818
Coatesville **(G-3329)**

WOOD PRDTS: Novelties, Fiber

M K Crafts ....G....... 717 786-6080
Strasburg **(G-18091)**

WOOD PRDTS: Oars & Paddles

Norse Paddle Co ....G 814 422-8844
  Spring Mills (G-17890)

WOOD PRDTS: Outdoor, Structural

Nicholas Shea Co Inc ....G 610 296-9036
  Reading (G-16456)
Patiova LLC ....G 610 857-1359
  Parkesburg (G-13181)
Yardcraft Products LLC ....G 866 210-9273
  New Holland (G-12295)

WOOD PRDTS: Panel Work

Clarion Boards LLC ....C 814 226-0851
  Shippenville (G-17557)
Clarion Laminates LLC ....D 814 226-8032
  Shippenville (G-17559)
K & M Wood Products ....F 814 967-4613
  Centerville (G-2834)
Lew-Hoc Wood Products Inc ....E 814 486-0359
  Emporium (G-5067)
Mil-Del Corporation.........................G 215 788-9277
  Bristol (G-2168)

WOOD PRDTS: Porch Columns

Custom Entryways & Millwork.............G 814 798-2500
  Stoystown (G-18074)

WOOD PRDTS: Rulers & Yardsticks

Beechdale Frames ....G 717 288-2723
  Ronks (G-16803)

WOOD PRDTS: Shoe Trees

Elmwood.......................................F 570 524-9663
  Lewisburg (G-9905)

WOOD PRDTS: Signboards

D E Gemill Inc................................E 717 755-9794
  Red Lion (G-16593)

WOOD PRDTS: Spars

Woodline Productions Inc.................G 814 362-5397
  Bradford (G-1996)

WOOD PRDTS: Stepladders

New Werner Holding Co Inc.............G 724 588-2000
  Greenville (G-6758)
Werner Co.....................................C 724 588-2000
  Greenville (G-6775)
Werner Holding Co Inc ....A 888 523-3371
  Greenville (G-6776)

WOOD PRDTS: Survey Stakes

Black Lick Stake Plant.....................G 724 459-7670
  Blairsville (G-1716)

WOOD PRDTS: Trim

Doellken- Woodtape Inc ....G 610 929-1910
  Temple (G-18328)

WOOD PRDTS: Yard Sticks

Stauffers Mini Barns.......................G 724 479-0760
  Indiana (G-8130)

WOOD PRODUCTS: Reconstituted

Clarion Industries LLC ....E 814 226-0851
  Shippenville (G-17558)
Energex American Inc ....E 717 436-2400
  Mifflintown (G-11116)
Energex Corporation ....D 717 436-2400
  Mifflintown (G-11117)

WOOD TREATING: Bridges

Steve Eversoll ....G 717 768-3298
  Gap (G-6256)

WOOD TREATING: Creosoting

Koppers Performance Chem Inc ....G 412 227-2001
  Pittsburgh (G-15192)
Stella-Jones Corporation ....E 814 371-7331
  Du Bois (G-4421)

WOOD TREATING: Flooring, Block

Sutherland Lumber Co ....E 724 947-3388
  Burgettstown (G-2355)
Woods Company Inc ....E 717 263-6524
  Chambersburg (G-3000)

WOOD TREATING: Millwork

Effort Woodcraft Inc ....E 570 629-1160
  Effort (G-4825)
Gutchess Lumber Co Inc ....D 724 537-6447
  Latrobe (G-9479)
Perrotte Wood Finishing Co ....G 412 322-2592
  Pittsburgh (G-15379)

WOOD TREATING: Railroad Cross Bridges & Switch Ties

Stella-Jones Corporation ....E 412 325-0202
  Pittsburgh (G-15581)

WOOD TREATING: Structural Lumber & Timber

Hoover Treated Wood Pdts Inc ....G 800 220-6046
  Oxford (G-13081)
Patrick Donovan.............................G 724 238-9038
  Ligonier (G-9963)
Schroth Industries Inc ....G 724 465-5701
  Indiana (G-8126)
Somerset Enterprises Inc ....F 724 734-9497
  Farrell (G-5874)
Ufp Stockertown LLC ....G 610 759-8536
  Stockertown (G-18067)

WOOD TREATING: Wood Prdts, Creosoted

Beecher & Myers Company Inc ....F 717 292-3031
  York (G-20401)

WOODWORK & TRIM: Exterior & Ornamental

4 Daughters LLC ....D 570 283-5934
  Kingston (G-8711)

WOODWORK & TRIM: Interior & Ornamental

Historic Doors LLC ....G 610 756-6187
  Kempton (G-8492)
Ridge Craft...................................F 717 355-2254
  New Holland (G-12279)
Turner John ....G 610 524-2050
  Exton (G-5740)
William Bender Trimming..................G 570 922-4274
  Millmont (G-11221)

WOODWORK: Carved & Turned

A A A Engraving............................G 412 281-7756
  Pittsburgh (G-14628)
Cheryl Hewitt.................................G 814 943-7222
  Altoona (G-492)
Flexcut Tool Co Inc ....E 814 864-7855
  Erie (G-5294)
Turnings By Edric ....G 412 833-5127
  Bethel Park (G-1436)

WOODWORK: Interior & Ornamental, NEC

Cumberland Woodcraft Co Inc ....E 717 243-0063
  Carlisle (G-2705)
David M Oley.................................F 570 247-5599
  Rome (G-16797)
Doyle Design.................................G 215 456-9745
  Philadelphia (G-13642)
Giuntas Fine Woodworking ....G 610 287-1749
  Schwenksville (G-17176)
Goods From Woods........................G 215 699-6866
  North Wales (G-12804)
Halkett Woodworking Inc ....E 215 721-9331
  Souderton (G-17739)
Jerry G Martin ....G 814 395-5475
  Confluence (G-3467)
KB Woodcraft Inc ....G 502 533-2773
  Phoenixville (G-14555)
North Country Woodworking Inc..........G 570 549-8105
  Mansfield (G-10422)
Orwin Lathe & Dowel ....G 717 647-4397
  Tower City (G-18439)
Shirks Custom Wood Turning ....G 717 656-6295
  New Holland (G-12283)

Staurowsky Woodworking ....G 610 489-0770
  Collegeville (G-3394)
Zooks Woodworking ....G 570 758-3579
  Dornsife (G-4165)

WOODWORK: Ornamental, Cornices, Mantels, Etc.

Advanced Trim Specialties ....E 717 442-8098
  Kinzers (G-8731)
Allensville Planing Mill Inc ....F 717 543-4954
  Huntingdon (G-7938)
Alvin Reiff Woodworking ....G 570 966-1149
  Mifflinburg (G-11092)

WOOL PULLING SVC

Pittsburgh Wool Co Inc ....G 412 642-0606
  Pittsburgh (G-15413)

WOOLEN & WORSTED YARNS, WHOLESALES

Natural Textiles Solutions LLC ....G 484 660-4085
  Macungie (G-10155)

WOVEN WIRE PRDTS, NEC

Aristo-TEC Metal Forms Inc...............E 724 626-5900
  Connellsville (G-3489)
Daniel Gerard Worldwide Inc ....D 800 232-3332
  Hanover (G-6873)
Gehret Wire Works Inc ....G 215 236-3322
  Philadelphia (G-13745)
Wire Company Holdings Inc ....B 717 637-3795
  Hanover (G-6977)
Wireco Worldgroup Inc ....F 412 373-6122
  Trafford (G-18461)

WRENCHES

Emporium Specialties Company ....E 814 647-8661
  Austin (G-833)

WRITING FOR PUBLICATION SVCS

Synchrgnix Info Strategies Inc ....G 302 892-4800
  Malvern (G-10325)

X-RAY EQPT & TUBES

Anholt Technologies Inc ....F 610 268-2758
  Avondale (G-848)
Best Solutions Med Systems LLC........G 814 577-4184
  Philipsburg (G-14509)
Dentsply Holding Company ....E 717 845-7511
  York (G-20448)
Dentsply LLC.................................D 800 323-0970
  York (G-20451)
Endicott Interconnect Tech...............G 724 352-6315
  Saxonburg (G-17086)
Imaging Sciences Intl LLC ....E 215 997-5666
  Hatfield (G-7353)
Lustra-Line Inc ....E 412 766-5757
  Pittsburgh (G-15242)
Novus X-Ray LLC...........................F 215 962-3171
  Blue Bell (G-1851)

YARN & YARN SPINNING

Coren-Indik Inc..............................F 267 288-1200
  Levittown (G-9827)
Family Heir-Loom Weavers Inc............F 717 246-2431
  Red Lion (G-16594)
Globe Dye Works ....E 215 288-4554
  Philadelphia (G-13772)
Middleburg Yarn Processing Co..........D 570 374-1284
  Selinsgrove (G-17331)
Roselon Industries Inc ....D 215 536-3275
  Quakertown (G-16242)
Warp Processing Inc ....C 570 655-1275
  Exeter (G-5585)

YARN MILLS: Texturizing

Roselon Industries Inc ....D 215 536-3275
  Quakertown (G-16242)

YARN MILLS: Texturizing, Throwing & Twisting

BRB Technology Corporation.............G 215 364-4115
  Feasterville Trevose (G-5893)

Employee Codes: A=Over 500 employees, B=251-500
C=101-250, D=51-100, E=20-50, F=10-19, G=3-9

PRODUCT

YARN MILLS: Throwing

Middleburg Yarn Processing Co............D....... 570 374-1284
  Selinsgrove *(G-17331)*

YARN MILLS: Winding

Globe Dye Works ....E....... 215 288-4554
  Philadelphia *(G-13772)*
Warp Processing Inc ....C....... 570 655-1275
  Exeter *(G-5585)*

YARN: Knitting, Spun

Chima Inc...E....... 610 372-6508
  Reading *(G-16345)*

YARN: Manmade & Synthetic Fiber, Spun

Kraemer Textiles Inc.............................C....... 610 759-4030
  Nazareth *(G-11975)*

YARN: Specialty & Novelty

Huntingdon Yarn Mills Inc.................E....... 215 425-5656
  Philadelphia *(G-13844)*

YARN: Weaving, Spun

Elkay Weaving Co Inc..........................G....... 570 822-5371
  Wilkes Barre *(G-19917)*

YARNS & ROVING: Coir

Marionette Company Inc ....F....... 570 644-1936
  Shamokin *(G-17425)*

YARNS & ROVING: Flax

Natural Textiles Solutions LLC ....G....... 484 660-4085
  Macungie *(G-10155)*

ZIRCONIUM

ATI Powder Metals LLC ....D....... 412 394-2800
  Pittsburgh *(G-14732)*
Tdy Industries LLC ....D....... 412 394-2896
  Pittsburgh *(G-15600)*

2019 Harris Pennsylvania
Manufacturers Directory

(G-0000) Company's Geographic Section entry number